MW00448078

THE CIA WORLD FACTBOOK 2023–2024

CENTRAL INTELLIGENCE AGENCY

Skyhorse Publishing

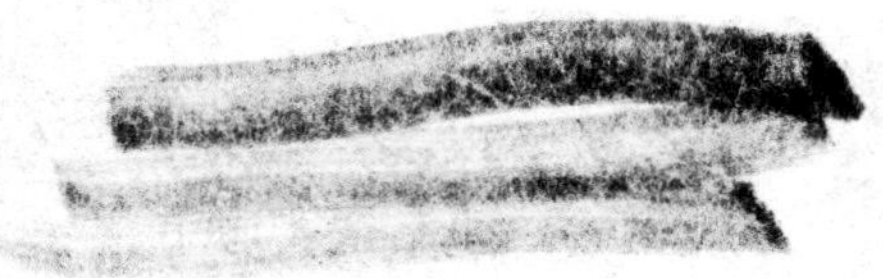

Copyright © 2023 by Skyhorse Publishing

All rights reserved. No part of this book may be reproduced in any manner without the express written consent of the publisher, except in the case of brief excerpts in critical reviews or articles. All inquiries should be addressed to Skyhorse Publishing, 306 West 37th Street, 11th Floor, New York, NY 10018.

Skyhorse Publishing books may be purchased in bulk at special discounts for sales promotion, corporate gifts, fundraising, or educational purposes. Special editions can also be created to specifications. For details, contact the Special Sales Department, Skyhorse Publishing, 307 West 36th Street, 11th Floor, New York, NY 10018 or info@skyhorsepublishing.com.

Skyhorse® and Skyhorse Publishing® are registered trademarks of Skyhorse Publishing, Inc.®, a Delaware corporation.

Visit our website at www.skyhorsepublishing.com.

10 9 8 7 6 5 4 3 2 1

Library of Congress Cataloging-in-Publication Data is available on file.

Cover design by Brian Peterson

Print ISBN: 978-1-5107-7592-3
Ebook ISBN: 978-1-5107-7593-0

Printed in the United States of America

CONTENTS

COUNTRY PROFILES

APPENDICES

REFERENCE MAPS

A BRIEF HISTORY OF BASIC INTELLIGENCE AND *THE WORLD FACTBOOK*

The Intelligence Cycle is the process by which information is acquired, converted into intelligence, and made available to policymakers. Information is raw data from any source, data that may be fragmentary, contradictory, unreliable, ambiguous, deceptive, or wrong. Intelligence is information that has been collected, integrated, evaluated, analyzed, and interpreted. Finished intelligence is the final product of the Intelligence Cycle ready to be delivered to the policymaker.

The three types of finished intelligence are: basic, current, and estimative. Basic intelligence provides the fundamental and factual reference material on a country or issue. Current intelligence reports on new developments. Estimative intelligence judges probable outcomes. The three are mutually supportive: basic intelligence is the foundation on which the other two are constructed; current intelligence continually updates the inventory of knowledge; and estimative intelligence revises overall interpretations of country and issue prospects for guidance of basic and current intelligence. *The World Factbook*, *The President's Daily Brief*, and the *National Intelligence Estimates* are examples of the three types of finished intelligence.

The United States has carried on foreign intelligence activities since the days of George Washington but only since World War II have they been coordinated on a government-wide basis. Three programs have highlighted the development of coordinated basic intelligence since that time: (1) *the Joint Army Navy Intelligence Studies* (JANIS), (2) *the National Intelligence Survey* (NIS), and (3) *The World Factbook*.

During World War II, intelligence consumers realized that the production of basic intelligence by different components of the US Government resulted in a great duplication of effort and conflicting information. The Japanese attack on Pearl Harbor in 1941 brought home to leaders in Congress and the executive branch the need for integrating departmental reports to national policymakers. Detailed and coordinated information was needed not only on such major powers as Germany and Japan, but also on places of little previous interest. In the Pacific Theater, for example, the Navy and Marines had to launch amphibious operations against many islands about which information was unconfirmed or nonexistent. Intelligence authorities resolved that the United States should never again be caught unprepared.

In 1943, Gen. George B. Strong (G-2), Adm. H. C. Train (Office of Naval Intelligence – ONI), and Gen. William J. Donovan (Director of the Office of Strategic Services – OSS) decided that a joint effort should be initiated. A steering committee was appointed on 27 April 1943 that recommended the formation of a Joint Intelligence Study Publishing Board to assemble, edit, coordinate, and publish the *Joint Army Navy Intelligence Studies* (JANIS). JANIS was the first interdepartmental basic intelligence program to fulfill the needs of the US Government for an authoritative and coordinated appraisal of strategic basic intelligence. Between April 1943 and July 1947, the board published 34 JANIS studies. JANIS performed well in the war effort, and numerous letters of commendation were received, including a statement from Adm. Forrest Sherman, Chief of Staff, Pacific Ocean Areas, which said, "JANIS has become the indispensable reference work for the shore-based planners."

The need for more comprehensive basic intelligence in the postwar world was well expressed in 1946 by George S. Pettee, a noted author on national security. He wrote in *The Future of American Secret Intelligence* (Infantry Journal Press, 1946, page 46) that world leadership in peace requires even more elaborate intelligence than in war. "The conduct of peace involves all countries, all human activities – not just the enemy and his war production."

The Central Intelligence Agency was established on 26 July 1947 and officially began operating on 18 September 1947. Effective 1 October 1947, the Director of Central Intelligence assumed operational responsibility for JANIS. On 13 January 1948, the National Security Council issued Intelligence Directive (NSCID) No. 3, which authorized the *National Intelligence Survey* (NIS) program as a peacetime replacement for the wartime JANIS program. Before adequate NIS country sections could be produced, government agencies had to develop more comprehensive gazetteers and better maps. The US Board on Geographic Names (BGN) compiled the names; the Department of the Interior produced the gazetteers; and CIA produced the maps.

The Hoover Commission's Clark Committee, set up in 1954 to study the structure and administration of the CIA, reported to Congress in 1955 that: "The National Intelligence Survey is an invaluable publication which provides the essential elements of basic intelligence on all areas of the world. There will always be a continuing requirement for keeping the Survey up-to-date." The *Factbook* was created as an annual summary and update to the encyclopedic NIS studies. The first classified *Factbook* was published in August 1962, and the first unclassified version was published in June 1971. The NIS program was terminated in 1973 except for the *Factbook*, map, and gazetteer components. The 1975 *Factbook* was the first to be made available to the public with sales through the US Government Printing Office (GPO). The *Factbook* was first made available on the Internet in June 1997. The year 2022 marks the 75th anniversary of the establishment of the Central Intelligence Agency and the 79th year of continuous basic intelligence support to the US Government by *The World Factbook* and its two predecessor programs.

THE EVOLUTION OF THE WORLD FACTBOOK

National Basic Intelligence Factbook produced semiannually until 1980. Country entries include sections on Land, Water, People, Government, Economy, Communications, and Defense Forces.

1981: Publication becomes an annual product and is renamed *The World Factbook*. A total of 165 nations are covered on 225 pages.

1983: Appendices (Conversion Factors, International Organizations) first introduced.

1984: Appendices expanded; now include: A. The United Nations, B. Selected United Nations Organizations, C. Selected International Organizations, D. Country Membership in Selected Organizations, E. Conversion Factors.

1987: A new Geography section replaces the former separate Land and Water sections. UN Organizations and Selected International Organizations appendices merged into a new International Organizations appendix. First multi-color-cover *Factbook*.

1988: More than 40 new geographic entities added to provide complete world coverage without overlap or omission. Among the new entities are Antarctica, oceans (Arctic, Atlantic, Indian, Pacific), and the World. The front-of-the-book explanatory introduction expanded and retitled to Notes, Definitions, and Abbreviations. Two new Appendices added: Weights and Measures (in place of Conversion Factors) and a Cross-Reference List of Geographic Names. *Factbook* size reaches 300 pages.

1989: Economy section completely revised and now includes an "Overview" briefly describing a country's economy. New entries added under People, Government, and Communications.

1990: The Government section revised and considerably expanded with new entries.

1991: A new International Organizations and Groups appendix added. *Factbook* size reaches 405 pages.

1992: Twenty new successor state entries replace those of the Soviet Union and Yugoslavia. New countries are respectively: Armenia, Azerbaijan, Belarus, Estonia, Georgia, Kazakhstan, Kyrgyzstan, Latvia, Lithuania, Moldova, Russia, Tajikistan, Turkmenistan, Ukraine, Uzbekistan; and Bosnia and Hercegovina, Croatia, Macedonia, Serbia and Montenegro, Slovenia. Number of nations in the *Factbook* rises to 188.

1993: Czechoslovakia's split necessitates new Czech Republic and Slovakia entries. New Eritrea entry added after it secedes from Ethiopia. Substantial enhancements made to Geography section.

1994: Two new appendices address Selected International Environmental Agreements. The gross domestic product (GDP) of most developing countries changed to a purchasing power parity (PPP) basis rather than an exchange rate basis. *Factbook* size up to 512 pages.

1995: The GDP of all countries now presented on a PPP basis. New appendix lists estimates of GDP on an exchange rate basis. Communications category split; "Railroads," "Highways," "Inland waterways," "Pipelines," "Merchant marine," and "Airports" entries now make up a new Transportation category. *The World Factbook* is first produced on CD-ROM.

1996: Maps accompanying each entry now present more detail. Flags also introduced for nearly all entities. Various new entries appear under Geography and Communications. *Factbook* abbreviations consolidated into a new Appendix A. Two new appendices present a Cross-Reference List of Country Data Codes and a Cross-Reference List of Hydrogeographic Data Codes. Geographic coordinates added to Appendix H, Cross-Reference List of Geographic Names. *Factbook* size expands by 95 pages in one year to reach 652.

1997: *The World Factbook* introduced onto the Internet. A special printed edition prepared for the CIA's 50th anniversary. A schema or Guide to Country Profiles introduced. New color maps and flags now accompany each country profile. Category headings distinguished by shaded backgrounds. Number of categories expanded to nine with the addition of an Introduction (for only a few countries) and Transnational Issues (which includes "Disputes-international" and "Illicit drugs").

1998: The Introduction category with two entries, "Current issues" and "Historical perspective," expanded to more countries. Last year for the production of CD-ROM versions of the *Factbook*.

1999: "Historical perspective" and "Current issues" entries in the Introduction category combined into a new "Background" statement. Several new Economy entries introduced. A new physical map of the world added to the back-of-the-book reference maps.

2000: A new "country profile" added on the Southern Ocean. The Background statements dramatically expanded to over 200 countries and possessions. A number of new Communications entries added.

2001: Background entries completed for all 267 entities in the *Factbook*. Several new HIV/AIDS entries introduced under the People category. Revision begun on individual country maps to include elevation extremes and a partial geographic grid. Weights and Measures appendix deleted.

2002: New entry on "Distribution of Family income – Gini index" added. Revision of individual country maps continued (process ongoing).

2003: In the Economy category, petroleum entries added for "oil production," "consumption," "exports," "imports," and "proved reserves," as well as "natural gas proved reserves."

2004: Bi-weekly updates launched on *The World Factbook* website. Additional petroleum entries included for "natural gas production," "consumption," "exports," and "imports." In the Transportation category, under "Merchant marine," subfields added for foreign-owned vessels and those registered in other countries. Descriptions of the many forms of government mentioned in the Factbook incorporated into the Definitions and Notes.

2005: In the People category, a "Major infectious diseases" field added for countries deemed to pose a higher risk for travelers. In the Economy category, entries included for "Current account balance," "Investment," "Public debt," and "Reserves of foreign exchange and gold." The Transnational issues category expanded to include "Refugees and internally displaced persons." Size of the printed *Factbook* reaches 702 pages.

2006: In the Economy category, national GDP figures now presented at Official Exchange Rates (OER) in addition to GDP at purchasing power parity (PPP). Entries in the Transportation section reordered; "Highways" changed to "Roadways," and "Ports and harbors" to "Ports and terminals."

2007: In the Government category, the "Capital" entry significantly expanded with up to four subfields, including new information having to do with time. The subfields consist of the name of the capital itself, its geographic coordinates, the time difference at the capital from coordinated universal time (UTC), and, if applicable, information on daylight saving time (DST). Where appropriate, a special note is added to highlight those countries with multiple time zones. A "Trafficking in persons" entry added to the Transnational issues category. A new appendix, Weights and Measures, (re)introduced to the online version of the *Factbook*.

2008: In the Geography category, two fields focus on the increasingly vital resource of water: "Total renewable water resources" and "Freshwater withdrawal." In the Economy category, three fields added for: "Stock of direct foreign investment – at home," "Stock of direct foreign investment – abroad," and "Market value of publicly traded shares." Concise descriptions of all major religions included in the Definitions and Notes. Responsibility for printing of *The World Factbook* turned over to the Government Printing Office.

2009: The online *Factbook* site completely redesigned with many new features. In the People category, two new fields provide information on education in terms of opportunity and resources: "School Life Expectancy" and "Education expenditures." Additionally, the "Urbanization" entry expanded to include all countries. In the Economy category, five fields added: "Central bank discount rate," "Commercial bank prime lending rate," "Stock of narrow money," "Stock of broad money," and "Stock of domestic credit."

2010: Weekly updates inaugurated on the *The World Factbook* website. The dissolution of the Netherlands Antilles results in two new listings: Curacao and Sint Maarten. In the Communications category, a "Broadcast media" field replaces the former "Radio broadcast stations" and "TV broadcast stations" entries. In the Geography section, under "Natural hazards," a Volcanism subfield added for countries with historically active volcanoes. In the Government category, a new "National anthems" field introduced. Concise descriptions of all major Legal systems incorporated into the Definitions and Notes. In order to facilitate comparisons over time, dozens of the entries in the Economy category expanded to include two (and in some cases three) years' worth of data.

2011: The People section expanded to People and Society, incorporating ten new fields. The Economy category added "Taxes and other revenues" and "Budget surplus (+) or deficit (-)," while the Government section introduced "International law organization participation" and "National symbols." A new African nation, South Sudan, brings the total number of countries in *The World Factbook* to 195.

2012: A new Energy category introduced with 23 energy-related fields. Several distinctive features added to *The World Factbook* website: 1) playable audio files in the Government section for the National Anthems entry, 2) online graphics in the form of a Population Pyramid feature in the People and Society category's Age Structure field, and 3) a Users Guide enabling visitors to navigate the *Factbook* more easily and efficiently. A new and distinctive Map of the World Oceans highlights an expanded array of regional and country maps. Size of the printed *Factbook*'s 50th anniversary edition reaches 847 pages.

2013: In the People and Society section five fields introduced: "Demographic profile," "Mother's mean age at first birth," "Contraceptive prevalence rate," "Dependency ratios," and "Child labor – children ages 5-14." In the Transnational Issues category, a new *stateless persons* subfield embedded under the "Refugees and internally displaced persons" entry. In the Economy section two fields added: "GDP – composition by end use" and "Gross national saving." In the Government category the "Judicial branch" entry revised and expanded to include three new subfields: *highest court(s), judge selection and term of office*, and *subordinate courts*.

2014: In the Transportation category, the "Ports and terminals" field substantially expanded with subfields for *major seaport(s), river port(s), lake port(s), oil/gas terminal(s), LNG terminal(s), dry bulk cargo port(s), container port(s)*, and *cruise/ferry port(s)*. In the Geography section, the "Land boundaries entry" revised for all countries, including the *total* country border length as well as the border lengths for all *neighboring countries*.

2015: In the Government category, the first part of the "Legislative branch" field thoroughly revised, expanded, and updated for all countries under a new description heading. This subentry includes the legislative structure, the formal name(s), the number of legislative seats, the types of voting constituencies and voting systems, and the member term of office. In the Geography category, the "Land use" entry expanded to include *agricultural land, forest land*, and *other* uses. Area Comparison Maps introduced online for about half of the world's countries. These graphics show the size of a country in relation to a part of the United States. (More maps to follow as they become available.)

2016: In the Government section for all countries, a new "Citizenship" field added to describe policies related to the acquisition of citizenship and to the recognition of dual citizenship. Also, under the "Country name" entry, *etymologies* (historical origins) added to explain how countries acquired their names. In the Energy section, an "Electricity access" field introduced with subfields summarizing *total* access to electricity within an country, as well as for *urban* and *rural* populations. In the Transportation category, an expansive "National air transport system" field presents info on the *number of registered air carriers, number of operating aircraft, annual passenger traffic*, and *annual freight traffic*.

2017: In the Government category, the "Constitution" entry revised and expanded with new subfields for *history* and *amendments*. Information on piracy moved from the Transportation category to a new "Maritime threats" field in the Military and Security category. In the Transportation section, the "Merchant marine" entry revised to not only include the *total* number of ships, but also the major *types*: bulk carrier, container ship, general cargo, oil tanker, and other. A new "Population distribution" field added to both the Geography and People and Society categories. The Government Printing Office discontinued printing *The Word Factbook*, but annual online editions may be downloaded from the *Factbook* site.

2018: One-Page Country Summaries introduced for selected countries in the *Factbook*; more to follow in the future. The Summaries highlight key information from lengthier *World Factbook* entries and are intended for use by teachers, students, travelers, researchers, news reporters, or anyone with an interest in geography. Dozens of additional area comparison maps added; about two-thirds of country entries now include these popular maps. In the Communications category, a "Broadband – fixed subscriptions" entry now included.

2019: The *Factbook*'s World entry acquires many new Top Ten listings including those for the largest forests, largest deserts, longest mountain ranges, and climate extremes (Top Ten driest, wettest, coldest, and hottest places on earth). Also in the World entry, seven new continent area comparison maps compare their size to that of the US. In each of the five ocean entries, under the Economy section, a "Maritime fisheries" field includes info on major fishing regions, total tonnage caught, and principal fish catches. A Travel Facts feature added to every country entry; this one-page summary compiles important facts to know before travelling to a country and it quickly becomes one of the most popular features on the website. A new Appendix H: Strategic Materials lists all of the compounds, metals, non-metals, and rare earth elements deemed to be of critical importance to US national security.

2020: Three new fields added to the Military and Security category for every country: "Military and security service personnel strengths," "Military equipment inventories and acquisitions," and "Military deployments." One-Page Summaries completed for all of the World's countries and more than two dozen territories and possessions. Capital city name etymologies entered for all national capitals. A new Terrorism category with a "Terrorist group(s)" entry added to more than 60 countries where the US State Department has these groups operating. A supplemental Appendix T: Terrorist Organizations provides details on each cited group's history, goals, leadership, organization, areas of operation, tactics, weapons, size, and sources of support. Completion of the multi-year effort to add area comparison maps for all countries.

2021: A new Environment category introduced with fields that include information on air pollution, water supplies, revenues from natural resources, food insecurity, and waste and recycling. Fields from other Factbook sections – climate, land use, urbanization, and major infectious diseases – also gathered into this new category. In the People and Society section, under "Languages," new *major-language sample(s)* and *audio sample(s)* added. The Travel Facts for all countries acquire additional entries on Tipping Guidelines, Tourist Attractions, and Major Sports.

DEFINITIONS AND NOTES

Abbreviations This information is included in Appendix A: Abbreviations, which includes all abbreviations and acronyms used in the *Factbook*, with their expansions.

Acronyms An acronym is an abbreviation coined from the initial letter of each successive word in a term or phrase. In general, an acronym made up solely from the first letter of the major words in the expanded form is rendered in all capital letters (NATO from North Atlantic Treaty Organization; an exception would be ASEAN for Association of Southeast Asian Nations). In general, an acronym made up of more than the first letter of the major words in the expanded form is rendered with only an initial capital letter (Comsat from Communications Satellite Corporation; an exception would be NAM from Nonaligned Movement). Hybrid forms are sometimes used to distinguish between initially identical terms (ICC for International Chamber of Commerce and ICCt for International Criminal Court).

Administrative divisions This entry generally gives the numbers, designatory terms, and first-order administrative divisions as approved by the US Board on Geographic Names (BGN). Changes that have been reported but not yet acted on by the BGN are noted. Geographic names conform to spellings approved by the BGN with the exception of the omission of diacritical marks and special characters.

Age structure This entry provides the distribution of the population according to age. Information is included by sex and age group as follows: *0-14 years (children), 15-24 years (early working age), 25-54 years (prime working age), 55-64 years (mature working age), 65 years and over (elderly)*. The age structure of a population affects a nation's key socioeconomic issues. Countries with young populations (high percentage under age 15) need to invest more in schools, while countries with older populations (high percentage ages 65 and over) need to invest more in the health sector. The age structure can also be used to help predict potential political issues. For example, the rapid growth of a young adult population unable to find employment can lead to unrest.

Agricultural products This entry provides a list of a country's most important agricultural products, listed by annual tonnage.

Air pollutants This entry refers to specified gases and particulates released by various sources of animals, plants, goods, and processes that can contribute to global warming, poor air quality, pollution, and climate change.

particulate matter emissions - This entry provides the modeled annual mean concentration of particulate matter of less than 2.5 microns in diameter ($PM_{2.5}$) measured in micrograms per cubic meter of air. Exposure to $PM_{2.5}$ pollutants should not exceed an annual mean concentration of 10 micrograms per cubic meter, according to World Health Organization guidelines. Particulate matter are inhalable and respirable particles composed of sulphate, nitrates, ammonia, sodium chloride, black carbon, mineral dust, and water. Fine particles less than 2.5 microns pose the greatest health risks because they can penetrate the lungs and enter the bloodstream. Sources include combustion engines, solid-fuel combustion, and other industrial activities. Exposure to high concentrations of particulate matter is associated with increased mortality and morbidity, although even low concentrations of particulate matter can impact health. By reducing air pollution levels, countries can decrease the burden of disease from stroke, heart disease, lung cancer, and both chronic and acute respiratory diseases, including asthma.

carbon dioxide emissions - This entry provides the annual quantity of carbon dioxide emissions for a country, as measured in megatons. Carbon dioxide is a greenhouse gas emitted through human-influenced and natural processes. Human-influenced sources include the burning of fossil fuels (including coal, natural gas, and oil), solid waste, trees, and other biological materials, as well as certain chemical processes, such as cement production. Natural sources include decomposition, ocean release, and respiration. Carbon dioxide is a major contributor to climate warming, air quality, global warming, and pollution.

methane emissions - This entry provides the annual quantity of methane emissions for a country, as measured in megatons. Methane is a greenhouse gas emitted from the breakdown of organic material from human-influenced and natural processes. Human-influenced sources include the production and transport of coal, natural gas, and oil; the decay of organic waste in landfills; agricultural activities; stationary and mobile combustion; waste water treatment; and certain industrial processes. Natural sources include the decay of plant material in wetlands, the seepage of gas from underground deposits, and the digestion of food by ruminants. Methane emissions cause poor air quality, health issues for animals and humans, and reduced crop yields, and are a contributor to climate change.

Airports This entry gives the total number of airports or airfields recognizable from the air. The runway(s) may be paved (concrete or asphalt surfaces) or unpaved (grass, earth, sand, or gravel surfaces) and may include closed or abandoned installations. Airports or airfields that are no longer recognizable (overgrown, no facilities, etc.) are not included. Note that not all airports have accommodations for refueling, maintenance, or air traffic control.

Airports - with paved runways This entry gives the *total* number of airports with paved runways (concrete or asphalt surfaces) by length. For airports with more than one runway, only the longest runway is included according to the following five groups - (1) *over 3,047 m* (over 10,000 ft), (2) *2,438 to 3,047 m* (8,000 to 10,000 ft), (3) *1,524 to 2,437 m* (5,000 to 8,000 ft), (4) *914 to 1,523 m* (3,000 to 5,000 ft), and (5) *under 914 m* (under 3,000 ft). Only airports with usable runways are included in this listing. Not all airports have facilities for refueling, maintenance, or air traffic control. The type of aircraft capable of operating from a runway of a given length is dependent upon a number of factors including elevation of the runway, runway gradient, average maximum daily temperature at the airport, engine types, flap settings, and take-off weight of the aircraft.

Airports - with unpaved runways This entry gives the *total* number of airports with unpaved runways (grass, dirt, sand, or gravel surfaces) by length. For airports with more than one runway, only the longest runway is included according to the following five groups - (1) *over 3,047 m* (over 10,000 ft), (2) *2,438 to 3,047 m* (8,000 to 10,000 ft), (3) *1,524 to 2,437 m* (5,000 to 8,000 ft), (4) *914 to 1,523 m* (3,000 to 5,000 ft), and (5) *under 914 m* (under 3,000 ft). Only airports with usable runways are included in this listing. Not all airports have facilities for refueling, maintenance, or air traffic control. The type of aircraft capable of operating from a runway of a given length is dependent upon a number of factors including elevation of the runway, runway gradient, average maximum daily temperature at the airport, engine types, flap settings, and take-off weight of the aircraft.

Alcohol consumption per capita This entry provides information on alcohol consumption per capita (APC), which is the recorded amount of alcohol consumed per capita by persons aged 15 years and over in a calendar year, measured in liters of pure alcohol. APC is broken down further into beer, wine, spirits, and other subfields. Beer includes malt beers, wine includes wine made from grapes, spirits include all distilled beverages, and other includes one or several other alcoholic beverages, such as fermented beverages made from sorghum, maize, millet, rice, or cider, fruit wine, and fortified wine. APC only takes into account the consumption that is recorded from production, import, export, and sales data, primarily derived from taxation.

Appendixes This section includes *Factbook*-related material by topic.

Area This entry includes three subfields. *Total area* is the sum of all land and water areas delimited by international boundaries and/or coastlines. *Land area* is the aggregate of all surfaces delimited by international boundaries and/or coastlines, excluding inland water bodies (lakes, reservoirs, rivers). *Water area* is the sum of the surfaces of all inland water bodies, such as lakes, reservoirs, or rivers, as delimited by international boundaries and/or coastlines.

Area - comparative This entry provides an area comparison based on total area equivalents. Most entities are compared with the entire US or one of the 50 states based on area measurements (1990 revised) provided by the US Bureau of the Census. The smaller entities are compared with Washington, DC (178 sq km, 69 sq mi) or The Mall in Washington, DC (0.59 sq km, 0.23 sq mi, 146 acres).

Area - rankings This entry, which appears only in the World, Geography category, provides rankings for the earth's largest (or smallest) continents, countries, oceans, islands, mountain ranges, or other physical features.

Background This entry usually highlights major historic events and current issues and may include a statement about one or two key future trends.

Birth rate This entry gives the average annual number of births during a year per 1,000 persons in the population at midyear; also known as crude birth rate. The birth rate is usually the dominant factor in determining the rate of population growth. It depends on both the level of fertility and the age structure of the population.

Broadband - fixed subscriptions This entry gives the total number of fixed-broadband subscriptions, as well as the number of subscriptions per 100 inhabitants. Fixed broadband is a physical wired connection to the Internet (e.g., coaxial cable, optical fiber) at speeds equal to or greater than 256 kilobits/second (256 kbit/s).

Broadcast media This entry provides information on the approximate number of public and private TV and radio stations in a country, as well as basic information on the availability of satellite and cable TV services.

Budget This entry includes *revenues* and *expenditures*. These figures are calculated on an exchange rate basis, i.e., not in purchasing power parity (PPP) terms.

Budget surplus (+) or deficit (-) This entry records the difference between national government revenues and expenditures, expressed as a percent of GDP. A positive (+) number indicates that revenues exceeded expenditures (a budget surplus), while a negative (-) number indicates the reverse (a budget deficit). Normalizing the data, by dividing the budget balance by GDP, enables easy comparisons across countries and indicates whether a national government saves or borrows money. Countries with high budget deficits (relative to their GDPs) generally have more difficulty raising funds to finance expenditures, than those with lower deficits.

Capital This entry gives the *name* of the seat of government, its *geographic coordinates*, the *time difference* relative to **Coordinated Universal Time (UTC)** and the time observed in Washington, DC, and, if applicable, information on *daylight saving time* **(DST)**. Where appropriate, a special *time zone note* has been added to highlight those countries that have multiple time zones. Finally, *etymology* explains how the capital acquired its name.

Carbon dioxide emissions This field refers to a country's amount of carbon dioxide released by burning coal, petroleum, and natural gas. Data are reported in metric tonnes of CO_2.

Child marriage This entry provides data on the prevalence of child marriage in a country. Data includes the percentage of women aged 20 to 24 years who were first married or in union before age 15, and before age 18; and men aged 20 to 24 years who were first married or in union before age 18. Most girls who marry early drop out of school and often have early, high-risk pregnancies. Child brides are also at risk of abuse, exploitation, and separation from relatives and friends.

Children under the age of 5 years underweight This entry gives the percent of children under five considered to be underweight. Underweight means weight-for-age is less than minus two standard deviations from the median of the World Health Organization Child Growth Standards among children under 5 years of age. This statistic is an indicator of the nutritional status of a community. Children who suffer from growth retardation as a result of poor diets and/or recurrent infections tend to have a greater risk of suffering illness and death.

Citizenship This entry provides information related to the acquisition and exercise of citizenship; it includes four subfields:

citizenship by birth describes the acquisition of citizenship based on place of birth, known as *Jus soli*, regardless of the citizenship of parents.

citizenship by descent only describes the acquisition of citizenship based on the principle of *Jus sanguinis*, or by descent, where at least one parent is a citizen of the state and being born within the territorial limits of the state is not required. The majority of countries adhere to this practice. In some cases, citizenship is conferred through the father or mother exclusively.

dual citizenship recognized indicates whether a state permits a citizen to simultaneously hold citizenship in another state. Many states do not permit dual citizenship and the voluntary acquisition of citizenship in another country is grounds for revocation of citizenship. Holding dual citizenship makes an individual legally obligated to more than one state and can negate the normal consular protections afforded to citizens outside their original country of citizenship.

residency requirement for naturalization lists the length of time an applicant is required to live in a state before applying for naturalization. In most countries citizenship can be acquired through the legal process of naturalization. The requirements for naturalization vary by state but generally include no criminal record, good health, economic wherewithal, and a period of authorized residency in the state. This time period can vary enormously among states and is often used to make the acquisition of citizenship difficult or impossible.

Civil aircraft registration country code prefix This entry provides the one- or two-character alphanumeric code indicating the nationality of civil aircraft. Article 20 of the Convention on International Civil Aviation (Chicago Convention), signed in 1944, requires that all aircraft engaged in international air navigation bear appropriate nationality marks. The aircraft registration number consists of two parts: a prefix consisting of a one- or two-character alphanumeric code indicating nationality and a registration suffix of one to five characters for the specific aircraft. The prefix codes are based upon radio call-signs allocated by the International Telecommunications Union (ITU) to each country. Since 1947, the International Civil Aviation Organization (ICAO) has managed code standards and their allocation.

Climate This entry includes a brief description of typical weather regimes throughout the year; in the World entry only, it includes four subfields that describe climate extremes:

ten driest places on earth (average annual precipitation) describes the annual average precipitation measured in both millimeters and inches for selected countries with climate extremes.

ten wettest places on earth (average annual precipitation) describes the annual average precipitation measured in both millimeters and inches for selected countries with climate extremes.

ten coldest places on earth (lowest average monthly temperature) describes temperature measured in both degrees Celsius and Fahrenheit as well as the month of the year for selected countries with climate extremes.

ten hottest places on earth (highest average monthly temperature) describes the temperature measured both in degrees Celsius and Fahrenheit as well the month of the year for selected countries with climate extremes.

Coal This field refers to a country's coal and metallurgical coke *production*, *consumption*, *exports*, *imports*, and *proven reserves*. These energy sources include anthracite, metallurgical, bituminous, subbituminous, and lignite coal and metallurgical coke. *Proven reserves* are those quantities of coal that have been analyzed as commercially recoverable in the future based on known reservoirs and assuming current economic conditions. Data are reported in metric tons, and one metric ton is 1,000 kilograms.

Coastline This entry gives the total length of the boundary between the land area (including islands) and the sea.

Communications This category deals with the means of exchanging information and includes entries on telephones (fixed and mobile), telecommunication systems, broadcast media, Internet users, and broadband subscriptions.

Communications - note This entry includes miscellaneous communications information of significance not included elsewhere.

Constitution This entry provides information on a country's constitution and includes two subfields. The history subfield includes the dates of previous constitutions and the main steps and dates in formulating and implementing the latest constitution. For countries with 1-3 previous constitutions, the years are listed; for those with 4-9 previous, the entry is listed as "several previous," and for those with 10 or more, the entry is "many previous." The amendments subfield summarizes the process of amending a country's constitution – from proposal through passage – and the dates of amendments, which are treated in the same manner as the constitution dates. Where appropriate, summaries are composed from English-language translations of non-English constitutions, which derive from official or non-official translations or machine translators.

The main steps in creating a constitution and amending it usually include the following steps: proposal, drafting, legislative and/or executive branch review and approval, public referendum, and entry into law. This process is lengthy in many countries. Terms commonly used to describe constitutional changes are "amended," "revised," or "reformed." In countries such as South Korea and Turkmenistan, sources differ as to whether changes are stated as new constitutions or are amendments/revisions to existing ones.

A few countries including Canada, Israel, and the UK, have no single constitution document, but have various written and unwritten acts, statutes, common laws, and practices that, when taken together, describe a body of fundamental principles or established precedents as to how their countries are governed. Some special regions (Hong Kong, Macau) and countries (Oman, Saudi Arabia) use the term "basic law" instead of constitution.

A number of self-governing dependencies and territories, such as the Cayman Islands, Bermuda, and Gibraltar (UK), Greenland and Faroe Islands (Denmark), Aruba, Curacao, and Sint Maarten (Netherlands), and Puerto Rico and the Virgin Islands (US), have their own constitutions.

Contraceptive prevalence rate This field gives the percent of women of reproductive age (15-49) who are married or in union and are using, or whose sexual partner is using, a method of contraception according to the date of the most recent available data. The contraceptive prevalence rate is an indicator of health services, development, and women's empowerment. It is also useful in understanding, past, present, and future fertility trends, especially in developing countries.

Coordinated Universal Time (UTC) UTC is the international atomic time scale that serves as the basis of timekeeping for most of the world. The hours, minutes, and seconds expressed by UTC represent the time of day at the Prime Meridian (0º longitude) located near Greenwich, England, UK as reckoned from midnight. UTC is calculated by the Bureau International des Poids et Measures (BIPM) in Sevres, France. The BIPM averages data collected from more than 200 atomic time and frequency standards located at about 50 laboratories worldwide. UTC is the basis for all civil time, with the world divided into time zones expressed as positive or negative differences from UTC. UTC is also referred to as "Zulu time." See the Standard Time Zones of the World map included with the **Reference Maps**.

Country data codes See **Data codes**.

Country map Most versions of the *Factbook* website provides a map in color for each country. The maps were produced from the best information available at the time of preparation. Names and/or boundaries may have changed subsequently.

Country name This entry includes all forms of the country's name approved by the US Board on Geographic Names (Italy is used as an example): *conventional long form* (Italian Republic), *conventional short form* (Italy), *local long form* (Repubblica Italiana), *local short form* (Italia), *former* (Kingdom of Italy), as well as the *abbreviation* (if applicable). Additionally, an *etymology* entry explains how the country acquired its name. Also see the **Terminology** note.

Credit ratings This entry provides the current bond ratings for a country or territory from each of the three major credit bureaus (Fitch, Moody's, and Standard & Poors). These ratings allow investors, including international finance institutions (e.g., the World Bank Group, the International Monetary Fund, etc.) to understand how likely a government's bond is to default. Rating factors include the following aspects: current account balance, debt payment history and timeliness, banking and financial operations, future economic outlook, and national economic strength. While in recent years other credit rating agencies have proliferated, these three credit agencies constitute more than 95% of the credit evaluation market globally and are the primary sovereign debt ratings considered by international and regional finance institutions.

Crude oil - exports This entry is the total amount of crude oil exported, in barrels per day (bbl/day).

Crude oil - imports This entry is the total amount of crude oil imported, in barrels per day (bbl/day).

Crude oil - production This entry is the total amount of crude oil produced, in barrels per day (bbl/day).

Crude oil - proved reserves This entry is the stock of proved reserves of crude oil, in barrels (bbl). Proved reserves are those quantities of petroleum which, by analysis of geological and engineering data, can be estimated with a high degree of confidence to be commercially recoverable from a given date forward, from known reservoirs and under current economic conditions.

Current account balance This entry records a country's net trade in goods and services, plus net earnings from rents, interest, profits, and dividends, and net transfer payments (such as pension funds and worker remittances) to and from the rest of the world during the period specified. These figures are calculated on an exchange rate basis, i.e., not in purchasing power parity (PPP) terms.

Current health expenditure Current health expenditure (CHE) describes the share of spending on health in each country relative to the size of its economy. It includes expenditures corresponding to the final consumption of health care goods and services and excludes investment, exports, and intermediate consumption. CHE shows the importance of the health sector in the economy and indicates the priority given to health in monetary terms. **Note:** Current health expenditure replaces the former Health Expenditures field and is calculated differently.

Date of information In general, information available as of January in a given year is used in the preparation of the printed edition.

Daylight Saving Time (DST) This entry is included for those entities that have adopted a policy of adjusting the official local time forward, usually one hour, from Standard Time during summer months. Such policies are most common in mid-latitude regions.

Death rate This entry gives the average annual number of deaths during a year per 1,000 persons at midyear; also known as crude death rate. The death rate, while only a rough indicator of the mortality situation in a country, accurately indicates the current mortality impact on population growth. This indicator is significantly affected by age distribution, and most countries will eventually show a rise in the overall death rate, in spite of continued decline in mortality at all ages, as declining fertility and increased lifespans result in an aging population.

Debt - external This entry gives the total public and private debt owed to nonresidents repayable in internationally accepted currencies, goods, or services. These figures are calculated on an exchange rate basis, i.e., not in purchasing power parity (PPP) terms.

Demographic profile This entry describes a country's key demographic features and trends and how they vary among regional, ethnic, and socioeconomic sub-populations. Some of the topics addressed are population age structure, fertility, health, mortality, poverty, education, and migration.

Dependency ratios Dependency ratios are a measure of the age structure of a population. They relate the number of individuals that are likely to be economically "dependent" on the support of others. Dependency ratios contrast the ratio of youths (ages 0-14) and the elderly (ages 65+) to the number of those in the working-age group (ages 15-64). Changes in the dependency ratio provide an indication of potential social support requirements resulting from changes in population age structures. As fertility levels decline, the dependency ratio initially falls because the proportion of youths decreases while the proportion of the population of working age increases. As fertility levels continue to decline, dependency ratios eventually increase because the proportion of the population of working age starts to decline and the proportion of elderly persons continues to increase.

total dependency ratio - The total dependency ratio is the ratio of combined youth population (ages 0-14) and elderly population (ages 65+) per 100 people of working age (ages 15-64). A high total dependency ratio indicates that the working-age population and the overall economy face a greater burden to support and provide social services for youth and elderly persons, who are often economically dependent.

youth dependency ratio - The youth dependency ratio is the ratio of the youth population (ages 0-14) per 100 people of working age (ages 15-64). A high youth dependency ratio indicates that a greater investment needs to be made in schooling and other services for children.

elderly dependency ratio - The elderly dependency ratio is the ratio of the elderly population (ages 65+) per 100 people of working age (ages 15-64). Increases in the elderly dependency ratio put added pressure on governments to fund pensions and healthcare.

potential support ratio - The potential support ratio is the number of working-age people (ages 15-64) per one elderly person (ages 65+). As a population ages, the potential support ratio tends to fall, meaning there are fewer potential workers to support the elderly.

Dependency status This entry describes the formal relationship between a particular nonindependent entity and an independent state.

Dependent areas This entry contains an alphabetical listing of all nonindependent entities associated in some way with a particular independent state.

Diplomatic representation The US Government has diplomatic relations with 190 independent states, including 188 of the 193 UN members (excluded UN members are Bhutan, Cuba, Iran, North Korea, and the US itself). In addition, the US has diplomatic relations with 2 independent states that are not in the UN, the Holy See and Kosovo, as well as with the EU.

Diplomatic representation from the US This entry includes the *chief of mission*, *embassy* address, *mailing address*, *telephone* number, *FAX* number, *email and website addresses*, *branch office* locations, *consulate general* locations, and *consulate* locations.

Diplomatic representation in the US This entry includes the *chief of mission*, *chancery address*, *telephone*, *FAX*, *email and website addresses*, *consulate general* locations, and *consulate* locations. The use of the annotated title Appointed Ambassador refers to a new ambassador who has presented his/her credentials to the secretary of state but not the US president. Such ambassadors fulfill all diplomatic functions except meeting with or appearing at functions attended by the president until such time as they formally present their credentials at a White House ceremony.

Disputes - international This entry includes a wide variety of situations that range from traditional bilateral boundary disputes to unilateral claims of one sort or another. Information regarding disputes over international terrestrial and maritime boundaries has been reviewed by the US Department of State. References to other situations involving borders or frontiers may also be included, such as resource disputes, geopolitical questions, or irredentist issues; however, inclusion does not necessarily constitute official acceptance or recognition by the US Government.

Drinking water source This entry provides information about access to improved or unimproved drinking water sources available to segments of the population of a country. *Improved* drinking water - use of any of the following sources: piped water into dwelling, yard, or plot; public tap or standpipe; tubewell or borehole; protected dug well; protected spring; or rainwater collection. *Unimproved* drinking water - use of any of the following sources: unprotected dug well; unprotected spring; cart with small tank or drum; tanker truck; surface water, which includes rivers, dams, lakes, ponds, streams, canals or irrigation channels; or bottled water.

Economic overview This entry briefly describes five economic components for a given country:

* *National Economy*, including a brief economic history;

* *Domestic Markets*, including labor and wage markets, as well as brief commentary on economic sector portfolios;

* *Financial Power and Public Finance*, including brief discussions of financial market strengths and security, lending/exchange rates (especially if abnormalities exist), and foreign direct investments;

* *Trade Power and Influence*, including brief commentary on chief imports and exports; and

* *Regional Strategy and Efforts*, including key partners, regional economic development efforts, and any underlying economic data integrity concerns.

Economy This category includes the entries dealing with the size, development, and management of productive resources, i.e., land, labor, and capital.

Economy of the area administered by Turkish Cypriots This entry, which appears only in the Cyprus, Economy category, provides economic information about the area administered by the Turkish Cypriots.

Education expenditures This entry provides the public expenditure on education as a percent of GDP.

Electricity This field refers to a country's installed generating capacities, consumption, exports, imports, and transmission/distribution losses.

installed generating capacity - the total capacity of a country's currently operational electric power generation, expressed in kilowatts (kW). A kilowatt produces one hour of continuously run electricity, referred to commonly in many appliances as a kilowatt hour (kWh).

consumption - a country's total electricity generated annually plus any imports and minus exports, expressed in kWh.

exports - a country's total amount of exported electricity in kWh.

imports - a country's total amount of imported electricity in kWh.

transmission/distribution losses - the combined difference between the amount of electricity generated and/or imported and the amount consumed and/or exported.

Electricity access This entry provides information on access to electricity. Electrification data – collected from industry reports, national surveys, and international sources – consists of four subfields. *Population without electricity* provides an estimate of the number of citizens that do not have access to electricity. *Electrification – total population* is the percent of a country's total population with access to electricity, *electrification – urban areas* is the percent of a country's urban population with access to electricity, while *electrification – rural areas* is the percent of a country's rural population with access to electricity. Due to differences in definitions and methodology from different sources, data quality may vary from country to country.

Electricity generation sources This field refers a country's energy portfolio of *fossil fuels*, *nuclear*, *solar*, *wind*, *hydroelectricity*, *tide and wave*, *geothermal*, and *biomass and waste*. Portfolios are expressed as a percentage share of a country's total generating capacity.

Elevation This entry includes the *mean elevation* and elevation extremes, *lowest point* and *highest point*.

Energy This category includes entries dealing with the production, consumption, import, and export of various forms of energy, including electricity, crude oil, refined petroleum products, and natural gas.

Energy consumption per capita This entry refers to a country's total energy consumption per capita, including the consumption of petroleum, dry natural gas, coal, net nuclear, hydroelectric, and non-hydroelectric renewable electricity. Data are reported in British thermal Units per person (Btu/person).

Entities Some of the independent states, dependencies, areas of special sovereignty, and governments included in this publication are not independent, and others are not officially recognized by the US Government. "Independent state" refers to a people politically organized into a sovereign state with a definite territory. "Dependencies" and "areas of special sovereignty" refer to a broad category of political entities that are associated in some way with an independent state. "Country" names used in the table of contents or for page headings are usually the short-form names as approved by the US Board on Geographic Names and may include independent states, dependencies, and areas of special sovereignty, or other geographic entities. There are a total of 266 separate geographic entities in *The World Factbook* that may be categorized as follows:

INDEPENDENT STATES

195 Afghanistan, Albania, Algeria, Andorra, Angola, Antigua and Barbuda, Argentina, Armenia, Australia, Austria, Azerbaijan, The Bahamas, Bahrain, Bangladesh, Barbados, Belarus, Belgium, Belize, Benin, Bhutan, Bolivia, Bosnia and Herzegovina, Botswana, Brazil, Brunei, Bulgaria, Burkina Faso, Burma, Burundi, Cambodia, Cameroon, Canada, Cape Verde, Central African Republic, Chad, Chile, China, Colombia, Comoros, Democratic Republic of the Congo, Republic of the Congo, Costa Rica, Cote d'Ivoire, Croatia, Cuba, Cyprus, Czechia, Denmark, Djibouti, Dominica, Dominican Republic, Ecuador, Egypt, El Salvador, Equatorial Guinea, Eritrea, Estonia, Ethiopia, Fiji, Finland, France, Gabon, The Gambia, Georgia, Germany, Ghana, Greece, Grenada, Guatemala, Guinea, Guinea-Bissau, Guyana, Haiti, Holy See, Honduras, Hungary, Iceland, India, Indonesia, Iran, Iraq, Ireland, Israel, Italy, Jamaica, Japan, Jordan, Kazakhstan, Kenya, Kiribati, North Korea, South Korea, Kosovo, Kuwait, Kyrgyzstan, Laos, Latvia, Lebanon, Lesotho, Liberia, Libya, Liechtenstein, Lithuania, Luxembourg, Macedonia, Madagascar, Malawi, Malaysia, Maldives, Mali, Malta, Marshall Islands, Mauritania, Mauritius, Mexico, Federated States of Micronesia, Moldova, Monaco, Mongolia, Montenegro, Morocco, Mozambique, Namibia, Nauru, Nepal, Netherlands, NZ, Nicaragua, Niger, Nigeria, Norway, Oman, Pakistan, Palau, Panama, Papua New Guinea, Paraguay, Peru, Philippines, Poland, Portugal, Qatar, Romania, Russia, Rwanda, Saint Kitts and Nevis, Saint Lucia, Saint Vincent and the Grenadines, Samoa, San Marino, Sao Tome and Principe, Saudi Arabia, Senegal, Serbia, Seychelles, Sierra Leone, Singapore, Slovakia, Slovenia, Solomon Islands, Somalia, South Africa, South Sudan, Spain, Sri Lanka, Sudan, Suriname, Swaziland, Sweden, Switzerland, Syria, Tajikistan, Tanzania, Thailand, Timor-Leste, Togo, Tonga, Trinidad and Tobago, Tunisia, Turkey, Turkmenistan, Tuvalu, Uganda, Ukraine, UAE, UK, US, Uruguay, Uzbekistan, Vanuatu, Venezuela, Vietnam, Yemen, Zambia, Zimbabwe

OTHER

2 Taiwan, European Union

DEPENDENCIES AND AREAS OF SPECIAL SOVEREIGNTY

6 Australia - Ashmore and Cartier Islands, Christmas Island, Cocos (Keeling) Islands, Coral Sea Islands, Heard Island and McDonald Islands, Norfolk Island
2 China - Hong Kong, Macau
2 Denmark - Faroe Islands, Greenland
8 France - Clipperton Island, French Polynesia, French Southern and Antarctic Lands, New Caledonia, Saint Barthelemy, Saint Martin, Saint Pierre and Miquelon, Wallis and Futuna
3 Netherlands - Aruba, Curacao, Sint Maarten
3 New Zealand - Cook Islands, Niue, Tokelau
3 Norway - Bouvet Island, Jan Mayen, Svalbard
17 UK - Akrotiri, Anguilla, Bermuda, British Indian Ocean Territory, British Virgin Islands, Cayman Islands, Dhekelia, Falkland Islands, Gibraltar, Guernsey, Jersey, Isle of Man, Montserrat, Pitcairn Islands, Saint Helena, South Georgia and the South Sandwich Islands, Turks and Caicos Islands
14 US - American Samoa, Baker Island*, Guam, Howland Island*, Jarvis Island*, Johnston Atoll*, Kingman Reef*, Midway Islands*, Navassa Island, Northern Mariana Islands, Palmyra Atoll*, Puerto Rico, Virgin Islands, Wake Island (* consolidated in United States Pacific Island Wildlife Refuges entry)

MISCELLANEOUS

5 Antarctica, Gaza Strip, Paracel Islands, Spratly Islands, West Bank

OTHER ENTITIES

5 oceans - Arctic Ocean, Atlantic Ocean, Indian Ocean, Pacific Ocean, Southern Ocean
1 World

266 total

Environment - current issues This entry lists the most pressing and important environmental problems. The following terms and abbreviations are used throughout the entry:

Acidification - the lowering of soil and water pH due to acid precipitation and deposition usually through precipitation; this process disrupts ecosystem nutrient flows and may kill freshwater fish and plants dependent on more neutral or alkaline conditions (see acid rain).

Acid rain - characterized as containing harmful levels of sulfur dioxide or nitrogen oxide; acid rain is damaging and potentially deadly to the earth's fragile ecosystems; acidity is measured using the pH scale where 7 is neutral, values greater than 7 are considered alkaline, and values below 5.6 are considered acid precipitation; note - a pH of 2.4 (the acidity of vinegar) has been measured in rainfall in New England.

Aerosol - a collection of airborne particles dispersed in a gas, smoke, or fog.

Afforestation - converting a bare or agricultural space by planting trees and plants; reforestation involves replanting trees on areas that have been cut or destroyed by fire.

Asbestos - a naturally occurring soft fibrous mineral commonly used in fireproofing materials and considered to be highly carcinogenic in particulate form.

Biodiversity - also biological diversity; the relative number of species, diverse in form and function, at the genetic, organism, community, and ecosystem level; loss of biodiversity reduces an ecosystem's ability to recover from natural or man-induced disruption.

Bio-indicators - a plant or animal species whose presence, abundance, and health reveal the general condition of its habitat.

Biomass - the total weight or volume of living matter in a given area or volume.

Carbon cycle - the term used to describe the exchange of carbon (in various forms, e.g., as carbon dioxide) between the atmosphere, ocean, terrestrial biosphere, and geological deposits.

Catchments - assemblages used to capture and retain rainwater and runoff; an important water management technique in areas with limited freshwater resources, such as Gibraltar.

DDT (dichloro-diphenyl-trichloro-ethane) - a colorless, odorless insecticide that has toxic effects on most animals; the use of DDT was banned in the US in 1972.

Defoliants - chemicals which cause plants to lose their leaves artificially; often used in agricultural practices for weed control, and may have detrimental impacts on human and ecosystem health.

Deforestation - the destruction of vast areas of forest (e.g., unsustainable forestry practices, agricultural and range land clearing, and the over exploitation of wood products for use as fuel) without planting new growth.

Desertification - the spread of desert-like conditions in arid or semi-arid areas, due to overgrazing, loss of agriculturally productive soils, or climate change.

Dredging - the practice of deepening an existing waterway; also, a technique used for collecting bottom-dwelling marine organisms (e.g., shellfish) or harvesting coral, often causing significant destruction of reef and ocean-floor ecosystems.
Drift-net fishing - done with a net, miles in extent, that is generally anchored to a boat and left to float with the tide; often results in an over harvesting and waste of large populations of non-commercial marine species (by-catch) by its effect of "sweeping the ocean clean."
Ecosystems - ecological units comprised of complex communities of organisms and their specific environments.
Effluents - waste materials, such as smoke, sewage, or industrial waste which are released into the environment, subsequently polluting it.
Endangered species - a species that is threatened with extinction either by direct hunting or habitat destruction.
Freshwater - water with very low soluble mineral content; sources include lakes, streams, rivers, glaciers, and underground aquifers.
Greenhouse gas - a gas that "traps" infrared radiation in the lower atmosphere causing surface warming; water vapor, carbon dioxide, nitrous oxide, methane, hydrofluorocarbons, and ozone are the primary greenhouse gases in the Earth's atmosphere.
Groundwater - water sources found below the surface of the earth often in naturally occurring reservoirs in permeable rock strata; the source for wells and natural springs.
Highlands Water Project - a series of dams constructed jointly by Lesotho and South Africa to redirect Lesotho's abundant water supply into a rapidly growing area in South Africa; while it is the largest infrastructure project in southern Africa, it is also the most costly and controversial; objections to the project include claims that it forces people from their homes, submerges farmlands, and squanders economic resources.
Inuit Circumpolar Conference (ICC) - represents the roughly 150,000 Inuits of Alaska, Canada, Greenland, and Russia in international environmental issues; a General Assembly convenes every three years to determine the focus of the ICC; the most current concerns are long-range transport of pollutants, sustainable development, and climate change.
Metallurgical plants - industries which specialize in the science, technology, and processing of metals; these plants produce highly concentrated and toxic wastes which can contribute to pollution of ground water and air when not properly disposed.
Noxious substances - injurious, very harmful to living beings.
Overgrazing - the grazing of animals on plant material faster than it can naturally regrow leading to the permanent loss of plant cover, a common effect of too many animals grazing limited range land.
Ozone shield - a layer of the atmosphere composed of ozone gas (O3) that resides approximately 25 miles above the Earth's surface and absorbs solar ultraviolet radiation that can be harmful to living organisms.
Poaching - the illegal killing of animals or fish, a great concern with respect to endangered or threatened species.
Pollution - the contamination of a healthy environment by man-made waste.
Potable water - water that is drinkable, safe to be consumed.
Salination - the process through which fresh (drinkable) water becomes salt (undrinkable) water; hence, desalination is the reverse process; also involves the accumulation of salts in topsoil caused by evaporation of excessive irrigation water, a process that can eventually render soil incapable of supporting crops.
Siltation - occurs when water channels and reservoirs become clotted with silt and mud, a side effect of deforestation and soil erosion.
Slash-and-burn agriculture - a rotating cultivation technique in which trees are cut down and burned in order to clear land for temporary agriculture; the land is used until its productivity declines at which point a new plot is selected and the process repeats; this practice is sustainable while population levels are low and time is permitted for regrowth of natural vegetation; conversely, where these conditions do not exist, the practice can have disastrous consequences for the environment.
Soil degradation - damage to the land's productive capacity because of poor agricultural practices such as the excessive use of pesticides or fertilizers, soil compaction from heavy equipment, or erosion of topsoil, eventually resulting in reduced ability to produce agricultural products.
Soil erosion - the removal of soil by the action of water or wind, compounded by poor agricultural practices, deforestation, overgrazing, and desertification.
Ultraviolet (UV) radiation - a portion of the electromagnetic energy emitted by the sun and naturally filtered in the upper atmosphere by the ozone layer; UV radiation can be harmful to living organisms and has been linked to increasing rates of skin cancer in humans.
Waterborne diseases - those in which bacteria survive in, and are transmitted through, water; always a serious threat in areas with an untreated water supply.

Environment - international agreements This entry separates country participation in international environmental agreements into two levels - *party to* and *signed, but not ratified*. Agreements are listed in alphabetical order by the abbreviated form of the full name.

Environmental agreements This information is presented in Appendix C: Selected International Environmental Agreements, which includes the name, abbreviation, date opened for signature, date entered into force, objective, and parties by category. Refer to an online edition of *The World Factbook* to access this appendix.

Ethnic groups This entry provides an ordered listing of ethnic groups starting with the largest and normally includes the percent of total population.

Exchange rates This entry provides the average annual price of a country's monetary unit for the time period specified, expressed in units of local currency per US dollar, as determined by international market forces or by official fiat. The International Organization for Standardization (ISO) 4217 alphabetic currency code for the national medium of exchange is presented in parenthesis. Closing daily exchange rates are not presented in *The World Factbook*, but are used to convert stock values - e.g., the market value of publicly traded shares - to US dollars as of the specified date.

Executive branch This entry includes five subentries: *chief of state; head of government; cabinet; elections/appointments; election results. Chief of state* includes the name, title, and beginning date in office of the titular leader of the country who represents the state at official and ceremonial functions but may not be involved with the day-to-day activities of the government. *Head of government* includes the name, title of the top executive designated to manage the executive branch of the government, and the beginning date in office. *Cabinet* includes the official name of the executive branch's high-ranking body and the method of member selection. *Elections/appointments* includes the process for accession to office, date of the last election, and date of the next election. *Election results* includes each candidate's political affiliation, percent of direct popular vote or indirect legislative/parliamentary percent vote or vote count in the last election.

The executive branches in approximately 80% of the world's countries have separate chiefs of state and heads of government; for the remainder, the chief of state is also the head of government, such as in Argentina, Kenya, the Philippines, the US, and Venezuela. Chiefs of state in just over 100 countries are directly elected, most by majority popular vote; those in another 55 are indirectly elected by their national legislatures, parliaments, or electoral colleges. Another 29 countries have a monarch as the chief of state. In dependencies, territories, and collectivities of sovereign countries - except those of the US - representatives are appointed to serve as chiefs of state.

Heads of government in the majority of countries are appointed either by the president or the monarch or selected by the majority party in the legislative body. Excluding countries where the chief of state is also head of government, in only a few countries is the head of government directly elected through popular vote.

Most of the world's countries have cabinets, the majority of which are appointed by the chief of state or prime minister, many in consultation with each other or with the legislature. Cabinets in only about a dozen countries are elected solely by their legislative bodies.

Exports This entry provides the total US dollar amount of merchandise exports on an f.o.b. (free on board) basis. These figures are calculated on an exchange rate basis, i.e., not in purchasing power parity (PPP) terms.

Exports - commodities This entry provides a listing of the highest-valued exported commodities.

Exports - partners This entry provides a rank ordering of trading partners starting with the most important; it sometimes includes the percent of total dollar value.

Fiscal year This entry identifies the beginning and ending months for a country's accounting period of 12 months, which often is the calendar year but which may begin in any month. All yearly references are for the calendar year (CY) unless indicated as a noncalendar fiscal year (FY).

Flag description This entry provides a written flag description produced from actual flags or the best information available at the time the entry was written. The flags of independent states are used by their dependencies unless there is an officially recognized local flag. Some disputed and other areas do not have flags.

Flag graphic Most versions of the *Factbook* include a color flag at the beginning of the country profile. The flag graphics were produced from actual flags or the best information available at the time of preparation. The flags of independent states are used by their dependencies unless there is an officially recognized local flag. Some disputed and other areas do not have flags.

Food insecurity Food crises are nearly always due to a combination of factors, but it is important to establish whether the nature of food crises is predominantly related to lack of food availability, limited access to food, or severe but localized problems. Countries in crisis requiring external assistance for food are expected to lack the resources to deal with reported critical problems of food insecurity. Three levels of crises are described in this field in descending severity: countries facing an exceptional shortfall in aggregate food production/supplies as a result of crop failure, natural disasters, interruption of imports, disruption of distribution, excessive post-harvest losses, or other supply bottlenecks; countries with widespread lack of access, where a majority of the population is considered to be unable to procure food from local markets, due to very low incomes, exceptionally high food prices, or the inability to circulate within the country; countries with severe localized food insecurity due to the influx of refugees, a concentration of internally displaced persons, or areas with combinations of crop failure and deep poverty.

GDP (official exchange rate) This entry gives the gross domestic product (GDP) or value of all final goods and services produced within a nation in a given year. A nation's GDP at official exchange rates (OER) is the home-currency-denominated annual GDP figure divided by the bilateral average US exchange rate with that country in that year. The measure is simple to compute and gives a precise measure of the value of output. Many economists prefer this measure when gauging the economic power an economy maintains vis-à-vis its neighbors, judging that an exchange rate captures the purchasing power a nation enjoys in the international marketplace. Official exchange rates, however, can be artificially fixed and/or subject to manipulation - resulting in claims of the country having an under- or over-valued currency - and are not necessarily the equivalent of a market-determined exchange rate. Moreover, even if the official exchange rate is market-determined, market exchange rates are frequently established by a relatively small set of goods and services (the ones the country trades) and may not capture the value of the larger set of goods the country produces. Furthermore, OER-converted GDP is not well suited to comparing domestic GDP over time, since appreciation/depreciation from one year to the next will make the OER GDP value rise/fall regardless of whether home-currency-denominated GDP changed.

GDP - composition, by end use This entry shows who does the spending in an economy: consumers, businesses, government, and foreigners. The distribution gives the percentage contribution to total GDP of *household consumption, government consumption, investment in fixed capital, investment in inventories, exports of goods and services, and imports of goods and services,* and will total 100 percent of GDP if the data are complete.

household consumption consists of expenditures by resident households, and by nonprofit institutions that serve households, on goods and services that are consumed by individuals. This includes consumption of both domestically produced and foreign goods and services.

government consumption consists of government expenditures on goods and services. These figures exclude government transfer payments, such as interest on debt, unemployment, and social security, since such payments are not made in exchange for goods and services supplied.

investment in fixed capital consists of total business spending on fixed assets, such as factories, machinery, equipment, dwellings, and inventories of raw materials, which provide the basis for future production. It is measured gross of the depreciation of the assets, i.e., it includes investment that merely replaces worn-out or scrapped capital. Earlier editions of *The World Factbook* referred to this concept as Investment (gross fixed) and that data now have been moved to this new field.

investment in inventories consists of net changes to the stock of outputs that are still held by the units that produce them, awaiting further sale to an end user, such as automobiles sitting on a dealer's lot or groceries on the store shelves. This figure may be positive or negative. If the stock of unsold output increases during the relevant time period, *investment in inventories* is positive, but, if the stock of unsold goods declines, it will be negative. *Investment in inventories* normally is an early indicator of the state of the economy. If the stock of unsold items increases unexpectedly – because people stop buying - the economy may be entering a recession; but if the stock of unsold items falls - and goods "go flying off the shelves" - businesses normally try to replace those stocks, and the economy is likely to accelerate.

exports of goods and services consist of sales, barter, gifts, or grants of goods and services from residents to nonresidents.

imports of goods and services consist of purchases, barter, or receipts of gifts, or grants of goods and services by residents from nonresidents. *Exports* are treated as a positive item, while imports are treated as a negative item. In a purely accounting sense, *imports* have no direct impact on GDP, which only measures output of the domestic economy. Imports are entered as a negative item to offset the fact that the expenditure figures for consumption, investment, government, and exports also include expenditures on imports. These imports contribute directly to foreign GDP but only indirectly to domestic GDP. Because of this negative offset for imports of goods and services, the sum of the other five items, excluding imports, will always total more than 100 percent of GDP. A surplus of exports of goods and services over imports indicates an economy is investing abroad, while a deficit indicates an economy is borrowing from abroad.

GDP - composition, by sector of origin This entry shows where production takes place in an economy. The distribution gives the percentage contribution of *agriculture, industry,* and *services* to total GDP, and will total 100 percent of GDP if the data are complete. Agriculture includes farming, fishing, and forestry. Industry includes mining, manufacturing, energy production, and construction. Services cover government activities, communications, transportation, finance, and all other private economic activities that do not produce material goods.

GDP methodology In the **Economy** category, GDP dollar estimates for countries are reported both on an official exchange rate

(OER) and a purchasing power parity (PPP) basis. Both measures contain information that is useful to the reader. The PPP method involves the use of standardized international dollar price weights, which are applied to the quantities of final goods and services produced in a given economy. The data derived from the PPP method probably provide the best available starting point for comparisons of economic strength and well-being between countries. In contrast, the currency exchange rate method involves a variety of international and domestic financial forces that may not capture the value of domestic output. Whereas PPP estimates for OECD countries are quite reliable, PPP estimates for developing countries are often rough approximations. In developing countries with weak currencies, the exchange rate estimate of GDP in dollars is typically one-fourth to one-half the PPP estimate. Most of the GDP estimates for developing countries are based on extrapolation of PPP numbers published by the UN International Comparison Program (UNICP) and by Professors Robert Summers and Alan Heston of the University of Pennsylvania and their colleagues. GDP derived using the OER method should be used for the purpose of calculating the share of items such as exports, imports, military expenditures, external debt, or the current account balance, because the dollar values presented in the *Factbook* for these items have been converted at official exchange rates, not at PPP. One should use the OER GDP figure to calculate the proportion of, say, Chinese defense expenditures in GDP, because that share will be the same as one calculated in local currency units. Comparison of OER GDP with PPP GDP may also indicate whether a currency is over- or under-valued. If OER GDP is smaller than PPP GDP, the official exchange rate may be undervalued, and vice versa. However, there is no strong historical evidence that market exchange rates move in the direction implied by the PPP rate, at least not in the short- or medium-term. Note: the numbers for GDP and other economic data should not be chained together from successive volumes of the *Factbook* because of changes in the US dollar measuring rod, revisions of data by statistical agencies, use of new or different sources of information, and changes in national statistical methods and practices.

Geographic coordinates This entry includes rounded latitude and longitude figures for the centroid or center point of a country expressed in degrees and minutes; it is based on the locations provided in the Geographic Names Server (GNS), maintained by the National Geospatial-Intelligence Agency on behalf of the US Board on Geographic Names.

Geographic names Spellings are normally, but not always, those approved by the US Board on Geographic Names (BGN). Alternate names and additional information are included in parentheses.

Geographic overview This entry, which appears only in the World, Geography category, provides basic geographic information about the earth's oceans and continents. The entry also lists all of the countries that compose each continent.

Geography This category includes the entries dealing with the natural environment and the effects of human activity.

Geography - note This entry includes miscellaneous geographic information of significance not included elsewhere.

Gini index See entry for Distribution of family income - Gini index

Gini Index coefficient - distribution of family income This entry measures the degree of inequality in the distribution of family income in a country. The index is calculated from the Lorenz curve, in which cumulative family income is plotted against the number of families arranged from the poorest to the richest. The index is the ratio of (a) the area between a country's Lorenz curve and the 45 degree helping line to (b) the entire triangular area under the 45 degree line. The more nearly equal a country's income distribution, the closer its Lorenz curve to the 45 degree line and the lower its Gini index, e.g., a Scandinavian country with an index of 25. The more unequal a country's income distribution, the farther its Lorenz curve from the 45 degree line and the higher its Gini index, e.g., a Sub-Saharan country with an index of 50. If income were distributed with perfect equality, the Lorenz curve would coincide with the 45 degree line and the index would be zero; if income were distributed with perfect inequality, the Lorenz curve would coincide with the horizontal axis and the right vertical axis and the index would be 100.

GNP Gross national product (GNP) is the value of all final goods and services produced within a nation in a given year, plus income earned by its citizens abroad, minus income earned by foreigners from domestic production. The *Factbook*, following current practice, uses GDP rather than GNP to measure national production. However, the user must realize that in certain countries net remittances from citizens working abroad may be important to national well-being.

Government This category includes the entries dealing with the system for the adoption and administration of public policy.

Government - note This entry includes miscellaneous government information of significance not included elsewhere.

Government type This entry gives the basic form of government. Definitions of the major governmental terms are as follows. (Note that for some countries more than one definition applies.):

Absolute monarchy - a form of government where the monarch rules unhindered, i.e., without any laws, constitution, or legally organized opposition.

Anarchy - a condition of lawlessness or political disorder brought about by the absence of governmental authority.

Authoritarian - a form of government in which state authority is imposed onto many aspects of citizens' lives.

Commonwealth - a nation, state, or other political entity founded on law and united by a compact of the people for the common good.

Communist - a system of government in which the state plans and controls the economy and a single - often authoritarian - party holds power; state controls are imposed with the elimination of private ownership of property or capital while claiming to make progress toward a higher social order in which all goods are equally shared by the people (i.e., a classless society).

Confederacy (Confederation) - a union by compact or treaty between states, provinces, or territories, that creates a central government with limited powers; the constituent entities retain supreme authority over all matters except those delegated to the central government.

Constitutional - a government by or operating under an authoritative document (constitution) that sets forth the system of fundamental laws and principles that determines the nature, functions, and limits of that government.

Constitutional democracy - a form of government in which the sovereign power of the people is spelled out in a governing constitution.

Constitutional monarchy - a system of government in which a monarch is guided by a constitution whereby his/her rights, duties, and responsibilities are spelled out in written law or by custom.

Democracy - a form of government in which the supreme power is retained by the people, but which is usually exercised indirectly through a system of representation and delegated authority periodically renewed.

Democratic republic - a state in which the supreme power rests in the body of citizens entitled to vote for officers and representatives responsible to them.

Dictatorship - a form of government in which a ruler or small clique wield absolute power (not restricted by a constitution or laws).

Ecclesiastical - a government administrated by a church.

Emirate - similar to a monarchy or sultanate, but a government in which the supreme power is in the hands of an emir (the ruler of a Muslim state); the emir may be an absolute overlord or a sovereign with constitutionally limited authority.

Federal (Federation) - a form of government in which sovereign power is formally divided - usually by means of a constitution - between a central authority and a number of constituent regions (states, colonies, or provinces) so that each region retains some management of its internal affairs; differs from a confederacy in that the central government exerts influence directly upon both individuals as well as upon the regional units.

Federal republic - a state in which the powers of the central government are restricted and in which the component parts (states, colonies, or provinces) retain a degree of self-government; ultimate sovereign power rests with the voters who chose their governmental representatives.

Islamic republic - a particular form of government adopted by some Muslim states; although such a state is, in theory, a theocracy, it remains a republic, but its laws are required to be compatible with the laws of Islam.

Maoism - the theory and practice of Marxism-Leninism developed in China by Mao Zedong (Mao Tse-tung), which states that a continuous revolution is necessary if the leaders of a communist state are to keep in touch with the people.

Marxism - the political, economic, and social principles espoused by 19th century economist Karl Marx; he viewed the struggle of workers as a progression of historical forces that would proceed from a class struggle of the proletariat (workers) exploited by capitalists (business owners), to a socialist"dictatorship of the proletariat," to, finally, a classless society - Communism.

Marxism-Leninism - an expanded form of communism developed by Lenin from doctrines of Karl Marx; Lenin saw imperialism as the final stage of capitalism and shifted the focus of workers' struggle from developed to underdeveloped countries.

Monarchy - a government in which the supreme power is lodged in the hands of a monarch who reigns over a state or territory, usually for life and by hereditary right; the monarch may be either a sole absolute ruler or a sovereign - such as a king, queen, or prince - with constitutionally limited authority.

Oligarchy - a government in which control is exercised by a small group of individuals whose authority generally is based on wealth or power.

Parliamentary democracy - a political system in which the legislature (parliament) selects the government - a prime minister, premier, or chancellor along with the cabinet ministers - according to party strength as expressed in elections; by this system, the government acquires a dual responsibility: to the people as well as to the parliament.

Parliamentary government (Cabinet-Parliamentary government) - a government in which members of an executive branch (the cabinet and its leader - a prime minister, premier, or chancellor) are nominated to their positions by a legislature or parliament, and are directly responsible to it; this type of government can be dissolved at will by the parliament (legislature) by means of a no confidence vote or the leader of the cabinet may dissolve the parliament if it can no longer function.

Parliamentary monarchy - a state headed by a monarch who is not actively involved in policy formation or implementation (i.e., the exercise of sovereign powers by a monarch in a ceremonial capacity); true governmental leadership is carried out by a cabinet and its head - a prime minister, premier, or chancellor - who are drawn from a legislature (parliament).

Presidential - a system of government where the executive branch exists separately from a legislature (to which it is generally not accountable).

Republic - a representative democracy in which the people's elected deputies (representatives), not the people themselves, vote on legislation.

Socialism - a government in which the means of planning, producing, and distributing goods is controlled by a central government that theoretically seeks a more just and equitable distribution of property and labor; in actuality, most socialist governments have ended up being no more than dictatorships over workers by a ruling elite.

Sultanate - similar to a monarchy, but a government in which the supreme power is in the hands of a sultan (the head of a Muslim state); the sultan may be an absolute ruler or a sovereign with constitutionally limited authority.

Theocracy - a form of government in which a Deity is recognized as the supreme civil ruler, but the Deity's laws are interpreted by ecclesiastical authorities (bishops, mullahs, etc.); a government subject to religious authority.

Totalitarian - a government that seeks to subordinate the individual to the state by controlling not only all political and economic matters, but also the attitudes, values, and beliefs of its population.

Greenwich Mean Time (GMT) The mean solar time at the Greenwich Meridian, Greenwich, England, with the hours and days, since 1925, reckoned from midnight. GMT is now a historical term having been replaced by UTC on 1 January 1972. See **Coordinated Universal Time**.

Gross domestic product See GDP

Gross national product See GNP

Gross world product See GWP

GWP This entry gives the gross world product (GWP) or aggregate value of all final goods and services produced worldwide in a given year.

Heliports This entry gives the total number of heliports with hard-surface runways, helipads, or landing areas that support routine sustained helicopter operations exclusively and have support facilities including one or more of the following facilities: lighting, fuel, passenger handling, or maintenance. It includes former airports used exclusively for helicopter operations but excludes heliports limited to day operations and natural clearings that could support helicopter landings and takeoffs.

HIV/AIDS - adult prevalence rate This entry gives an estimate of the percentage of adults (aged 15-49) living with HIV/AIDS. The adult prevalence rate is calculated by dividing the estimated number of adults living with HIV/AIDS at yearend by the total adult population at yearend.

HIV/AIDS - deaths This entry gives an estimate of the number of adults and children who died of AIDS during a given calendar year.

HIV/AIDS - people living with HIV/AIDS This entry gives an estimate of all people (adults and children) alive at yearend with HIV infection, whether or not they have developed symptoms of AIDS.

Hospital bed density This entry provides the number of hospital beds per 1,000 people; it serves as a general measure of inpatient service availability. Hospital beds include inpatient beds available in public, private, general, and specialized hospitals and rehabilitation centers. In most cases, beds for both acute and chronic care are included. Because the level of inpatient services required for individual countries depends on several factors - such as demographic issues and the burden of disease - there is no global target for the number of hospital beds per country. So, while 2 beds per 1,000 in one country may be sufficient, 2 beds per 1,000 in another may be woefully inadequate because of the number of people hospitalized by disease.

Household income or consumption by percentage share Data on household income or consumption come from household surveys, with the results adjusted for household size. Nations use different standards and procedures in collecting and adjusting the data. Surveys based on income will normally show a more unequal distribution than surveys based on consumption. The quality of surveys is improving with time, yet caution is still necessary in making inter-country comparisons.

Hydrographic data codes See Data codes

Illicit drugs This entry gives information on the five categories of illicit drugs - narcotics, stimulants, depressants (sedatives), hallucinogens, and cannabis. These categories include many drugs legally produced and prescribed by doctors as well as those illegally produced and sold outside of medical channels.

Cannabis (*Cannabis sativa*) is the common hemp plant, which provides hallucinogens with some sedative properties, and includes marijuana (pot, Acapulco gold, grass, reefer), tetrahydrocannabinol (THC, Marinol), hashish (hash), and hashish oil (hash oil).

Coca (mostly *Erythroxylum coca*) is a bush with leaves that contain the stimulant used to make cocaine. Coca is not to be confused with cocoa, which comes from cacao seeds and is used in making chocolate, cocoa, and cocoa butter.

Cocaine is a stimulant derived from the leaves of the coca bush.

Depressants (sedatives) are drugs that reduce tension and anxiety and include chloral hydrate, barbiturates (Amytal, Nembutal, Seconal, phenobarbital), benzodiazepines (Librium, Valium), methaqualone (Quaalude), glutethimide (Doriden), and others (Equanil, Placidyl, Valmid).

Drugs are any chemical substances that effect a physical, mental, emotional, or behavioral change in an individual.

Drug abuse is the excessive use of any licit or illicit chemical substance that results in physical, mental, emotional, or behavioral impairment in an individual.

Hallucinogens are drugs that affect sensation, thinking, self-awareness, and emotion. Hallucinogens include LSD (acid, microdot), mescaline and peyote (mexc, buttons, cactus), amphetamine variants (PMA, STP, DOB), phencyclidine (PCP, angel dust, hog), phencyclidine analogues (PCE, PCPy, TCP), and others (psilocybin, psilocyn).

Hashish is the resinous exudate of the cannabis or hemp plant (*Cannabis sativa*).

Heroin is a semisynthetic derivative of morphine.

Mandrax is a trade name for methaqualone, a pharmaceutical depressant.

Marijuana is the dried leaf of the cannabis or hemp plant (*Cannabis sativa*).

Methaqualone is a pharmaceutical depressant, referred to as mandrax in Southwest Asia and Africa.

Narcotics are drugs that relieve pain, often induce sleep, and refer to opium, opium derivatives, and synthetic substitutes. Natural narcotics include opium (paregoric, parepectolin), morphine (MS-Contin, Roxanol), codeine (Tylenol with codeine, Empirin with codeine, Robitussin AC), and thebaine. Semisynthetic narcotics include heroin (horse, smack), and hydromorphone (Dilaudid). Synthetic narcotics include meperidine or Pethidine (Demerol, Mepergan), methadone (Dolophine, Methadose), and others (Darvon, Lomotil).

Opium is the brown, gummy exudate of the incised, unripe seedpod of the opium poppy.

Opium poppy (*Papaver somniferum*) is the source for the natural and semisynthetic narcotics.

Poppy straw is the entire cut and dried opium poppy-plant material, other than the seeds. Opium is extracted from poppy straw in commercial operations that produce the drug for medical use.

Qat (kat, khat) is a stimulant from the buds or leaves of *Catha edulis* that is chewed or drunk as tea.

Quaaludes is the North American slang term for methaqualone, a pharmaceutical depressant.

Stimulants are drugs that relieve mild depression, increase energy and activity, and include cocaine (coke, snow, crack), amphetamines (Desoxyn, Dexedrine), ephedrine, ecstasy (clarity, essence, doctor, Adam), phenmetrazine (Preludin), methylphenidate (Ritalin), and others (Cylert, Sanorex, Tenuate).

Imports This entry provides the total US dollar amount of merchandise imports on a c.i.f. (cost, insurance, and freight) or f.o.b. (free on board) basis. These figures are calculated on an exchange rate basis, i.e., not in purchasing power parity (PPP) terms.

Imports - commodities This entry provides a listing of the highest-valued imported commodities.

Imports - partners This entry provides a rank ordering of trading partners starting with the most important; it sometimes includes the percent of total dollar value.

Independence For most countries, this entry gives the date that sovereignty was achieved and from which nation, empire, or trusteeship. For the other countries, the date given may not represent "independence" in the strict sense, but rather some significant nationhood event such as the traditional founding date or the date of unification, federation, confederation, establishment, fundamental change in the form of government, or state succession. For a number of countries, the establishment of statehood was a lengthy evolutionary process occurring over decades or even centuries. In such cases, several significant dates are cited. Dependent areas include the notation "none" followed by the nature of their dependency status. Also see the **Terminology** note.

Industrial production growth rate This entry gives the annual percentage increase in industrial production (includes manufacturing, mining, and construction).

Industries This entry provides a rank ordering of industries starting with the largest by value of annual output.

Infant mortality rate This entry gives the number of deaths of infants under one year old in a given year per 1,000 live births in the same year. This rate is often used as an indicator of the level of health in a country.

Inflation rate (consumer prices) This entry provides the annual inflation rate, as calculated by the percent change in current consumer prices from the previous year's consumer prices.

International disputes see **Disputes – international**.

International law organization participation This entry includes information on a country's acceptance of jurisdiction of the International Court of Justice (ICJ) and of the International Criminal Court (ICCt); 61 countries have accepted ICJ jurisdiction with reservations and 12 have accepted ICJ jurisdiction without reservations; 123 countries and the Palestine Liberation Organization have accepted ICCt jurisdiction. Appendix B: International Organizations and Groups explains the differing mandates of the ICJ and ICCt. Refer to an online edition of *The World Factbook* to access this appendix.

International organization participation This entry lists in alphabetical order by abbreviation those international organizations in which the subject country is a member or participates in some other way.

International organizations This information is presented in Appendix B: International Organizations and Groups which includes the name, abbreviation, date established, aim, members by category, and, when available, contact information (including address, phone, fax, email address, and website address). Refer to an online edition of *The World Factbook* to access this appendix.

Internet country code This entry includes the two-letter codes maintained by the International Organization for Standardization (ISO) in the ISO 3166 Alpha-2 list and used by the Internet Assigned Numbers Authority (IANA) to establish country-coded top-level domains (ccTLDs).

Internet users This entry gives the *total* number of individuals within a country who can access the Internet at home, via any device type (computer or mobile) and connection. The *percent of population* with Internet access (i.e., the penetration rate) helps gauge how widespread Internet use is within a country. Statistics vary from country to country and may include users who access the Internet at least several times a week to those who access it only once within a period of several months.

Introduction This category includes one entry, **Background**.

Investment (gross fixed) This entry records total business spending on fixed assets, such as factories, machinery, equipment, dwellings, and inventories of raw materials, which provide the basis for future production. It is the measured gross of the depreciation of the assets, i.e., it includes investment that merely replaces worn-out or scrapped capital.

Irrigated land This entry gives the number of square kilometers of land area that is artificially supplied with water.

Judicial branch This entry includes three subfields. The *highest court(s)* subfield includes the name(s) of a country's highest level court(s), the number and titles of the judges, and the types of cases heard by the court, which commonly are based on civil, criminal, administrative, and constitutional law. A number of countries have separate constitutional courts. The *judge selection and term of office* subfield includes the organizations and associated officials responsible for nominating and appointing judges, and a brief description of the process. The selection process can be indicative of the independence of a country's court system from other branches of its government. Also included in this subfield are judges' tenures, which can range from a few years, to a specified retirement age, to lifelong appointments. The *subordinate courts* subfield lists the courts lower in the hierarchy of a country's court system. A few countries with federal-style governments, such as Brazil, Canada, and the US, in addition to their federal court, have separate state- or province-level court systems, though generally the two systems interact.

Labor force This entry contains the total labor force figure.

Labor force - by occupation This entry lists the percentage distribution of the labor force by sector of occupation. *Agriculture* includes farming, fishing, and forestry. *Industry* includes mining, manufacturing, energy production, and construction. *Services* cover government activities, communications, transportation, finance, and all other economic activities that do not produce material goods. The distribution will total less than 100 percent if the data are incomplete and may range from 99-101 percent due to rounding.

Land boundaries This entry contains the *total* length of all land boundaries and the individual lengths for each of the contiguous *border countries*. When available, official lengths published by national statistical agencies are used. Because surveying methods may differ, country border lengths reported by contiguous countries may differ.

Land use This entry contains the percentage shares of total land area for three different types of land use: *agricultural land, forest, and other*; *agricultural land* is further divided into *arable land* - land cultivated for crops like wheat, maize, and rice that are replanted after each harvest, *permanent crops* - land cultivated for crops like citrus, coffee, and rubber that are not replanted after each harvest, and includes land under flowering shrubs, fruit trees, nut trees, and vines, and *permanent pastures* and meadows – land used for at least five years or more to grow herbaceous forage, either cultivated or growing naturally; *forest* area is land spanning more than 0.5 hectare with trees higher than five meters and a canopy cover of more than 10% to include windbreaks, shelterbelts, and corridors of trees greater than 0.5 hectare and at least 20 m wide; land classified as *other* includes built-up areas, roads and other transportation features, barren land, or wasteland.

Languages This entry provides a listing of languages spoken in each country and specifies any that are official national or regional languages. When data is available, the languages spoken in each country are broken down according to the percent of the total population speaking each language as a first language, unless otherwise noted. For those countries without available data, languages are listed in rank order based on prevalence, starting with the most-spoken language.

Legal system This entry provides the description of a country's legal system. A statement on judicial review of legislative acts is also included for a number of countries. The legal systems of nearly all countries are generally modeled upon elements of five main types: civil law (including French law, the Napoleonic Code, Roman law, Roman-Dutch law, and Spanish law); common law (including United State law); customary law; mixed or pluralistic law; and religious law (including Islamic law). An additional type of legal system - international law, which governs the conduct of independent nations in their relationships with one another - is also addressed below. The following list describes these legal systems, the countries or world regions where these systems are enforced, and a brief statement on the origins and major features of each.

Civil Law - The most widespread type of legal system in the world, applied in various forms in approximately 150 countries. Also referred to as European continental law, the civil law system is derived mainly from the Roman *Corpus Juris Civilus*, (Body of Civil Law), a collection of laws and legal interpretations compiled under the East Roman (Byzantine) Emperor Justinian I between A.D. 528 and 565. The major feature of civil law systems is that the laws are organized into systematic written codes. In civil law the sources recognized as authoritative are principally legislation - especially codifications in constitutions or statutes enacted by governments - and secondarily, custom. The civil law systems in some countries are based on more than one code.

Common Law - A type of legal system, often synonymous with "English common law," which is the system of England and Wales in the UK, and is also in force in approximately 80 countries formerly part of or influenced by the former British Empire. English common law reflects Biblical influences as well as remnants of law systems imposed by early conquerors including the Romans, Anglo-Saxons, and Normans. Some legal scholars attribute the formation of the English common law system to King Henry II (r.1154-1189). Until the time of his reign, laws customary among England's various manorial and ecclesiastical (church) jurisdictions were administered locally. Henry II established the king's court and designated that laws were "common" to the entire English realm. The foundation of English common law is "legal precedent" - referred to as *stare decisis*, meaning "to stand by things decided." In the English common law system, court judges are bound in their decisions in large part by the rules and other doctrines developed - and supplemented over time - by the judges of earlier English courts.

Customary Law - A type of legal system that serves as the basis of, or has influenced, the present-day laws in approximately 40 countries - mostly in Africa, but some in the Pacific islands, Europe, and the Near East. Customary law is also referred to as "primitive law," "unwritten law," "indigenous law," and "folk law." There is no single history of customary law such as that found in Roman civil law, English common law, Islamic law, or the Napoleonic Civil Code. The earliest systems of law in human society were customary, and usually developed in small agrarian and hunter-gatherer communities. As the term implies, customary law is based upon the customs of a community. Common attributes of customary legal systems are that they are seldom written down, they embody an organized set of rules regulating social relations, and they are agreed upon by members of the community. Although such law systems include sanctions for law infractions, resolution tends to be reconciliatory rather than punitive. A number of African states practiced customary law many centuries prior to colonial influences. Following colonization, such laws were written down and incorporated to varying extents into the legal systems imposed by their colonial powers.

European Union Law - A sub-discipline of international law known as "supranational law" in which the rights of sovereign nations are limited in relation to one another. Also referred to as the Law of the European Union or Community Law, it is the unique and complex legal system that operates in tandem with the laws of the 27 member states of the European Union (EU). Similar to federal states, the EU legal system ensures compliance from the member states because of the Union's decentralized political nature. The European Court of Justice (ECJ), established in 1952 by the Treaty of Paris, has been largely responsible for the development of EU law. Fundamental principles of European Union law include: *subsidiarity* - the notion that issues be handled by the smallest, lowest, or least centralized competent authority; *proportionality* - the EU may only act to the extent needed to achieve its objectives; *conferral* - the EU is a union of member states, and all its authorities are voluntarily granted by its members; *legal certainty* - requires that legal rules be clear and precise; and *precautionary principle* - a moral and political principle stating that if an action or policy might cause severe or irreversible harm to the public or to the environment, in the absence of a scientific consensus that harm would not ensue, the burden of proof falls on those who would advocate taking the action.

French Law - A type of civil law that is the legal system of France. The French system also serves as the basis for, or is mixed with, other legal systems in approximately 50 countries, notably in North Africa, the Near East, and the French territories and dependencies. French law is primarily codified or systematic written civil law. Prior to the French Revolution (1789-1799), France had no single national legal system. Laws in the northern areas of present-day France were mostly local customs based on privileges and exemptions granted by kings and feudal lords, while in the southern areas Roman law predominated. The introduction of the Napoleonic Civil Code during the reign of Napoleon I in the first decade of the 19th century brought major reforms to the French legal system, many of which remain part of France's current legal structure, though all have been extensively amended or redrafted to address a modern nation. French law distinguishes between"public law" and "private law." Public law relates to government, the French Constitution, public administration, and criminal law. Private law covers issues between private citizens or corporations. The most recent changes to the French legal system - introduced in the 1980s - were the decentralization laws, which transferred authority from centrally appointed government representatives to locally elected representatives of the people.

International Law - The law of the international community, or the body of customary rules and treaty rules accepted as legally binding by states in their relations with each other. International law differs from other legal systems in that it primarily concerns sovereign political entities. There are three separate disciplines of international law: public international law, which governs the relationship between provinces and international entities and includes treaty law, law of the sea, international criminal law, and international humanitarian law; private international law, which addresses legal jurisdiction; and supranational law - a legal framework wherein countries are bound by regional agreements in which the laws of the member countries are held inapplicable when in conflict with supranational laws. At present the European Union is the only entity under a supranational legal system. The term "international law" was coined by Jeremy Bentham in 1780 in his *Principles of Morals and Legislation*, though laws governing relations between states have been recognized from very early times (many centuries B.C.). Modern international law developed alongside the emergence and growth of the European nation-states beginning in the early 16th century. Other factors that influenced the development of international law included the revival of legal studies, the growth of international trade, and the practice of exchanging emissaries and establishing legations. The sources of International law are set out in Article 38-1 of the Statute of the International Court of Justice within the UN Charter.

Islamic Law - The most widespread type of religious law, it is the legal system enforced in over 30 countries, particularly in the Near East, but also in Central and South Asia, Africa, and Indonesia. In many countries Islamic law operates in tandem with a civil law system. Islamic law is embodied in the sharia, an Arabic word meaning"the right path." Sharia covers all aspects of public and private life and organizes them into five categories: obligatory, recommended, permitted, disliked, and forbidden. The primary sources of sharia law are the Qur'an, believed by Muslims to be the word of God revealed to the Prophet Muhammad by the angel Gabriel, and the Sunnah, the teachings of the Prophet and his works. In addition to these two primary sources, traditional Sunni Muslims recognize the consensus of Muhammad's companions and Islamic jurists on certain issues, called ijmas, and various forms of reasoning, including analogy by legal scholars, referred to as qiyas. Shia Muslims reject ijmas and qiyas as sources of sharia law.

Mixed Law - Also referred to as pluralistic law, mixed law consists of elements of some or all of the other main types of legal systems - civil, common, customary, and religious. The mixed legal systems of a number of countries came about when colonial powers overlaid their own legal systems upon colonized regions but retained elements of the colonies' existing legal systems.

Napoleonic Civil Code - A type of civil law, referred to as the Civil Code or *Code Civil des Francais*, forms part of the legal system of France, and underpins the legal systems of Bolivia, Egypt, Lebanon, Poland, and the US state of Louisiana. The Civil Code was established under Napoleon I, enacted in 1804, and officially designated the *Code Napoleon* in 1807. This legal system combined the Teutonic civil law tradition of the northern provinces of France with the Roman law tradition of the southern and eastern regions of the country. The Civil Code bears similarities in its arrangement to the Roman *Body of Civil Law* (see Civil Law above). As enacted in 1804, the Code addressed personal status, property, and the acquisition of property. Codes added over the following six years included civil procedures, commercial law, criminal law and procedures, and a penal code.

Religious Law - A legal system which stems from the sacred texts of religious traditions and in most cases professes to cover all aspects of life as a seamless part of devotional obligations to a transcendent, imminent, or deep philosophical reality. Implied as the basis of religious law is the concept of unalterability, because the word of God cannot be amended or legislated against by judges or governments. However, a detailed legal system generally requires human elaboration. The main types of religious law are sharia in Islam, halakha in Judaism, and canon law in some Christian groups. Sharia is the most widespread religious legal system (see Islamic Law), and is the sole system of law for countries including Iran, the Maldives, and Saudi Arabia. No country is fully governed by halakha, but Jewish people may decide to settle disputes through Jewish courts and be bound by their rulings. Canon law is not a divine law as such because it is not found in revelation. It is viewed instead as human law inspired by the word of God and applying the demands of that revelation to the actual situation of the church. Canon law regulates the internal ordering of the Roman Catholic Church, the Eastern Orthodox Church, and the Anglican Communion.

Roman Law - A type of civil law developed in ancient Rome and practiced from the time of the city's founding (traditionally 753 B.C.) until the fall of the Western Empire in the 5th century A.D. Roman law remained the legal system of the Byzantine (Eastern Empire) until the fall of Constantinople in 1453. Preserved fragments of the first legal text, known as the Law of the Twelve Tables, dating from the 5th century B.C., contained specific provisions designed to change the prevailing customary law. Early Roman law was drawn from custom and statutes; later, during the time of the empire, emperors asserted their authority as the ultimate source of law. The basis for Roman laws was the idea that the exact form - not the intention - of words or of actions produced legal consequences. It was only in the late 6th century A.D. that a comprehensive Roman code of laws was published (see Civil Law above). Roman law served as the basis of law systems developed in a number of continental European countries.

Roman-Dutch Law - A type of civil law based on Roman law as applied in the Netherlands. Roman-Dutch law serves as the basis for legal systems in seven African countries, as well as Guyana, Indonesia, and Sri Lanka. This law system, which originated in the province of Holland and expanded throughout the Netherlands (to be replaced by the French Civil Code in 1809), was instituted in a number of sub-Saharan African countries during the Dutch colonial period. The Dutch jurist/philosopher Hugo Grotius was the first to attempt to reduce Roman-Dutch civil law into a system in his *Jurisprudence of Holland* (written 1619-20, commentary published 1621). The Dutch historian/lawyer Simon van Leeuwen coined the term "Roman-Dutch law" in 1652.

Spanish Law - A type of civil law, often referred to as the Spanish Civil Code, it is the present legal system of Spain and is the basis of legal systems in 12 countries mostly in Central and South America, but also in southwestern Europe, northern and western Africa, and southeastern Asia. The Spanish Civil Code reflects a complex mixture of customary, Roman, Napoleonic, local, and modern codified law. The laws of the Visigoth invaders of Spain in the 5th to 7th centuries had the earliest major influence on Spanish legal system development. The Christian Reconquest of Spain in the 11th through 15th centuries witnessed the development of customary law, which combined canon (religious) and Roman law. During several centuries of Hapsburg and Bourbon rule, systematic recompilations of the existing national legal system were attempted, but these often conflicted with local and regional customary civil laws. Legal system development for most of the 19th century concentrated on formulating a national civil law system, which was finally enacted in 1889 as the Spanish Civil Code. Several sections of the code have been revised, the most recent of which are the penal code in 1989 and the judiciary code in 2001. The Spanish Civil Code separates public and private law. Public law includes constitutional law, administrative law, criminal law, process law, financial and tax law, and international public law. Private law includes civil law, commercial law, labor law, and international private law.

United States Law - A type of common law, which is the basis of the legal system of the United States and that of its island possessions in the Caribbean and the Pacific. This legal system has several layers, more possibly than in most other countries, and is due in part to the division between federal and state law. The United States was founded not as one nation but as a union of 13 colonies, each claiming independence from the British Crown. The US Constitution, implemented in 1789, began shifting power away from the states and toward the federal government, though the states today retain substantial legal authority. US law draws its authority from four sources: *constitutional law, statutory law, administrative regulations*, and *case law*. Constitutional law is based on the US Constitution and serves as the supreme federal law. Taken together with those of the state constitutions, these documents outline the general structure of the federal and state governments and provide the rules and limits of power. US statutory law is legislation enacted by the US Congress and is codified in the United States Code. The 50 state legislatures have similar authority to enact state statutes. Administrative law is the authority delegated to federal and state executive agencies. Case law, also referred to as common law, covers areas where constitutional or statutory law is lacking. Case law is a collection of judicial decisions, customs, and general principles that began in England centuries ago, that were adopted in America at the time of the Revolution, and that continue to develop today.

Legislative branch This entry has three subfields. The *description* subfield provides the legislative structure (unicameral – single house; bicameral – an upper and a lower house); formal name(s); number of member seats; types of constituencies or voting districts (single seat, multi-seat, nationwide); electoral voting system(s); and member term of office. The elections subfield includes the dates of the last election and next election. The *election results* subfield lists *percent of vote by party/coalition* and *number of seats by party/coalition* in the last election (in bicameral legislatures, upper house results are listed first). In general, parties with less than four seats and less than 4 percent of the vote are aggregated and listed as "other," and non-party-affiliated seats are listed as "independent." Also, the entries for some countries include two sets of *percent of vote by party* and *seats by party*; the former reflects results following a formal election announcement, and the latter – following a mid-term or byelection – reflects changes in a legislature's political party composition.

Of the approximately 240 countries with legislative bodies, approximately two-thirds are unicameral, and the remainder, bicameral. The selection of legislative members is typically governed by a country's constitution and/or its electoral laws. In general, members are either directly elected by a country's eligible voters using a defined electoral system; indirectly elected or selected by its province, state, or department legislatures; or appointed by the country's executive body. Legislative members in many countries are selected both directly and indirectly, and the electoral laws of some countries reserve seats for women and various ethnic and minority groups.

Worldwide, the two predominant direct voting systems are plurality/majority and proportional representation. The most common of the several plurality/majority systems is simple majority vote, or first-past-the-post, in which the candidate receiving the most votes is elected. Countries' legislatures such as Bangladesh's Parliament, Malaysia's House of Representatives, and the United Kingdom's House of Commons use this system. Another common plurality/majority system – absolute majority or two-round – requires that candidates win at least 50 percent of the votes to be elected. If none of the candidates meets that vote threshold in the initial election, a second poll or"runoff" is held soon after for the two top vote getters, and the candidate receiving a simple vote majority is declared the winner. Examples of the two-round system are Haiti's Chamber of Deputies, Mali's National Assembly, and Uzbekistan's Legislative Chamber. Other plurality/majority voting systems, referred to as preferential voting and generally used in multi-seat constituencies, are block vote and single non-transferable vote, in which voters cast their ballots by ranking their candidate preferences from highest to lowest.

Proportional representation electoral systems – in contrast to plurality/majority systems – generally award legislative seats to political parties in approximate proportion to the number of votes each receives. For example, in a 100-member legislature, if Party A receives 50 percent of the total vote, Party B, 30 percent, and Party C, 20 percent, then Party A would be awarded 50 seats, Party B 30 seats, and Party C 20 seats. There are various forms of proportional representation and the degree of reaching proportionality varies. Some forms of proportional representation are focused solely on achieving the proportional representation of different political parties and voters cast ballots only for political parties, whereas in other forms, voters cast ballots for individual candidates within a political party.

Many countries - both unicameral and bicameral - use a mix of electoral methods, in which a portion of legislative seats are awarded using one system, such as plurality/majority, while the remaining seats are awarded by another system, such as proportional representation. Many countries with bicameral legislatures use different voting systems for the two chambers.

Life expectancy at birth This entry contains the average number of years to be lived by a group of people born in the same year, if mortality at each age remains constant in the future. Life expectancy at birth is also a measure of overall quality of life in a country and summarizes the mortality at all ages. It can also be thought of as indicating the potential return on investment in human capital and is necessary for the calculation of various actuarial measures.

Literacy This entry includes a *definition* of literacy and UNESCO's percentage estimates for populations aged 15 years and over, including *total population, males*, and *females*. There are no universal definitions and standards of literacy. Unless otherwise specified, all rates are based on the most common definition - the ability to read and write at a specified age. Detailing the standards that individual countries use to assess the ability to read and write is beyond the scope of the *Factbook*. Information on literacy, while not a perfect measure of educational results, is probably the most easily available and valid for international comparisons. Low levels of literacy, and education in general, can impede the economic development of a country in the current rapidly changing, technology-driven world.

Location This entry identifies the country's regional location, neighboring countries, and adjacent bodies of water.

Major aquifers This entry lists the major (mega) aquifer system(s) that underlie a country, keeping in mind that many of these mega aquifers are so large that they extend under multiple countries. More than 30% of freshwater is held in underground aquifers. There is great variation in the size of such aquifers, but a limited number of very large aquifer systems contain a majority of the World's groundwater volume in storage.

Major infectious diseases This entry lists major infectious diseases likely to be encountered in countries where the risk of such diseases is assessed to be very high as compared to the United States. These infectious diseases represent risks to US Government personnel traveling to the specified country for a period of less than three years. The *degree of risk* is assessed by considering the foreign nature of these infectious diseases, their severity, and the probability of being affected by the diseases present. The diseases listed do not necessarily represent the total disease burden experienced by the local population.

The risk to an individual traveler varies considerably by the specific location, visit duration, type of activities, type of accommodations, time of year, and other factors. Consultation with a travel medicine physician is needed to evaluate individual risk and recommend appropriate preventive measures such as vaccines.

Diseases are organized into the following six exposure categories shown in italics *and listed in typical descending order of risk.* Note: The sequence of exposure categories listed in individual country entries may vary according to local conditions.

food or waterborne diseases acquired through eating or drinking:

Hepatitis A - viral disease that interferes with the functioning of the liver; spread through consumption of food or water contaminated with fecal matter, principally in areas of poor sanitation; victims exhibit fever, jaundice, and diarrhea; 15% of victims will experience prolonged symptoms over 6-9 months; vaccine available.

Hepatitis E - water-borne viral disease that interferes with the functioning of the liver; most commonly spread through fecal contamination of drinking water; victims exhibit jaundice, fatigue, abdominal pain, and dark colored urine.

Typhoid fever - bacterial disease spread through contact with food or water contaminated by fecal matter or sewage; victims exhibit sustained high fevers; left untreated, mortality rates can reach 20%.

vector-borne diseases acquired through the bite of an infected arthropod:

Malaria - caused by single-cell parasitic protozoa *Plasmodium*; transmitted to humans via the bite of the female *Anopheles* mosquito; parasites multiply in the liver attacking red blood cells resulting in cycles of fever, chills, and sweats accompanied by anemia; death due to damage to vital organs and interruption of blood supply to the brain; endemic in 85, mostly tropical, countries with 95% of cases and the majority of 0.4-0.6 million estimated annual deaths occurring in sub-Saharan Africa (six countries – Nigeria, the Democratic Republic of the Congo, Uganda, Mozambique, Angola and Burkina Faso – accounted for just over half of all malaria deaths globally in 2020).

Dengue fever - mosquito-borne (*Aedes aegypti*) viral disease associated with urban environments; manifests as sudden onset of fever and severe headache; occasionally produces shock and hemorrhage leading to death in 5% of cases.

Yellow fever - mosquito-borne (in urban areas *Aedes aegypti*) viral disease associated with urban environments; severity ranges from influenza-like symptoms to severe hepatitis and hemorrhagic fever; occurs only in tropical South America and sub-Saharan Africa, where most cases are reported; fatality rate is less than 20%.

Japanese Encephalitis - mosquito-borne (*Culex tritaeniorhynchus*) viral disease associated with rural areas in Asia; acute encephalitis can progress to paralysis, coma, and death; fatality rates 30%.

African Trypanosomiasis - caused by the parasitic protozoa *Trypanosoma*; transmitted to humans via the bite of bloodsucking tsetse flies; infection leads to malaise and irregular fevers and, in advanced cases when the parasites invade the central nervous system, coma and death; endemic in 36 countries of sub-Saharan Africa; cattle and wild animals act as reservoir hosts for the parasites.

Cutaneous Leishmaniasis - caused by the parasitic protozoa *leishmania*; transmitted to humans via the bite of sandflies; results in skin lesions that may become chronic; endemic in 88 countries; 90% of cases occur in Iran, Afghanistan, Syria, Saudi Arabia, Brazil, and Peru; wild and domesticated animals as well as humans can act as reservoirs of infection.

Plague - bacterial disease transmitted by fleas normally associated with rats; person-to-person airborne transmission also possible; recent plague epidemics occurred in areas of Asia, Africa, and South America associated with rural areas or small towns and villages; manifests as fever, headache, and painfully swollen lymph nodes; disease progresses rapidly and without antibiotic treatment leads to pneumonic form with a death rate in excess of 50%.

Crimean-Congo hemorrhagic fever - tick-borne viral disease; infection may also result from exposure to infected animal blood or tissue; geographic distribution includes Africa, Asia, the Middle East, and Eastern Europe; sudden onset of fever, headache, and muscle aches followed by hemorrhaging in the bowels, urine, nose, and gums; mortality rate is approximately 30%.

Rift Valley fever - viral disease affecting domesticated animals and humans; transmission is by mosquito and other biting insects; infection may also occur through handling of infected meat or contact with blood; geographic distribution includes eastern and southern Africa where cattle and sheep are raised; symptoms are generally mild with fever and some liver abnormalities, but the disease may progress to hemorrhagic fever, encephalitis, or ocular disease; fatality rates are low at about 1% of cases.

Chikungunya - mosquito-borne (*Aedes aegypti*) viral disease associated with urban environments, similar to Dengue Fever; characterized by sudden onset of fever, rash, and severe joint pain usually lasting 3-7 days, some cases result in persistent arthritis.

water-contact diseases acquired through swimming or wading in freshwater lakes, streams, and rivers:

Leptospirosis - bacterial disease that affects animals and humans; infection occurs through contact with water, food, or soil contaminated by animal urine; symptoms include high fever, severe headache, vomiting, jaundice, and diarrhea; untreated, the disease can result in kidney damage, liver failure, meningitis, or respiratory distress; fatality rates are low but left untreated recovery can take months.

Schistosomiasis - caused by parasitic trematode flatworm *Schistosoma*; fresh water snails act as intermediate host and release larval form of parasite that penetrates the skin of people exposed to contaminated water; worms mature and reproduce in the blood vessels, liver, kidneys, and intestines releasing eggs, which become trapped in tissues triggering an immune response; may manifest as either urinary or intestinal disease resulting in decreased work or learning capacity; mortality, while generally low, may occur in advanced cases usually due to bladder cancer; endemic in 74 developing countries with 80% of infected people living in sub-Saharan Africa; humans act as the reservoir for this parasite.

aerosolized dust or soil-contact disease acquired through inhalation of aerosols contaminated with rodent urine:

Lassa fever - viral disease carried by rats of the genus *Mastomys*; endemic in portions of West Africa; infection occurs through direct contact with or consumption of food contaminated by rodent urine or fecal matter containing virus particles; fatality rate can reach 50% in epidemic outbreaks.

respiratory disease acquired through close contact with an infectious person:

Meningococcal meningitis - bacterial disease causing an inflammation of the lining of the brain and spinal cord; one of the most important bacterial pathogens is *Neisseria meningitidis* because of its potential to cause epidemics; symptoms include stiff neck, high fever, headaches, and vomiting; bacteria are transmitted from person to person by respiratory droplets and facilitated by close and prolonged contact resulting from crowded living conditions, often with a seasonal distribution; death occurs in 5-15% of cases, typically within 24-48 hours of onset of symptoms; highest burden of meningococcal disease occurs in the hyperendemic region of sub-Saharan Africa known as the "Meningitis Belt" which stretches from Senegal east to Ethiopia.

animal-contact disease acquired through direct contact with local animals:

Rabies - viral disease of mammals usually transmitted through the bite of an infected animal, most commonly dogs; virus affects the central nervous system causing brain alteration and death; symptoms initially are non-specific fever and headache progressing to neurological symptoms; death occurs within days of the onset of symptoms.

Major lakes (area sq km) This entry describes one of the two major surface hydrological features of a country: large localized water bodies termed lakes (the other feature is rivers). The entry contains a list of major natural lakes, defined as having an area of 500 sq km or greater. Taken together with major rivers, these features constitute the primary sources of surface freshwater.

Major ocean currents This field describes the major ocean currents found in the ocean basins. Oceanic currents describe the movement of water from one location to another. Currents are generally measured in meters per second or in knots (1 knot = 1.85 kilometers per hour or 1.15 miles per hour). Oceanic currents are driven by three main factors:

1. The rise and fall of the *tides*. Tides create ocean currents, which are strongest near the shore, but also extend into bays and estuaries along the coast. These are called "tidal currents." Tidal currents change in a very regular pattern and can be predicted for future dates. In some locations, strong tidal currents can travel at speeds of eight knots or more.
2. *Wind*. Winds drive currents that are at or near the ocean's surface. Near coastal areas winds tend to drive currents on a localized scale and can result in phenomena like coastal upwelling. On a more global scale, in the open ocean, winds drive currents that circulate water for thousands of miles throughout the ocean basins.
3. *Thermohaline circulation*. This is a circulatory process driven by density differences in water due to temperature (thermo) and salinity (haline) variations in different parts of the ocean. Currents driven by thermohaline circulation occur at both deep and shallow ocean levels and move much more slowly than tidal or surface currents.

Currents affect the Earth's climate by driving warm water from the Equator and cold water from the poles around the Earth.

Major rivers (by length in km) This entry describes one of the two major surface hydrological features of a country: large flowing bodies of water termed rivers (the other feature is lakes). The entry includes a list of major rivers, defined as having a length of 1,000 km or greater. These rivers constitute major drainage basins or watersheds that capture the flow of the majority of surface water flow. Taken together with major lakes, these features constitute the primary sources of surface freshwater.

In instances where a river flows through more than one country, a note has been added to the field to indicate the country where the river starts and the country where a river ends. [s] after country name indicates river source; [m] after country name indicates river mouth.

Major urban areas - population This entry provides the population of the capital and up to six major cities defined as urban agglomerations with populations of at least 750,000 people. An *urban agglomeration* is defined as comprising the city or town proper and also the suburban fringe or thickly settled territory lying outside of, but adjacent to, the boundaries of the city. For smaller countries, lacking urban centers of 750,000 or more, only the population of the capital is presented.

Major watersheds (area sq km) This entry lists the major watersheds or catchment areas of major rivers in a country in terms of their area in sq km. Most of the watersheds listed have an area of at least 500,000 sq km, although some smaller but significant watersheds are also included. The watersheds are listed by the ocean into which they drain. When that drainage occurs other than into the ocean proper, italics are used to identify the constituent part of an ocean (e.g., *Black Sea*). However, some watersheds, known as *endorheic basins*, drain internally with no external flow to the ocean. An example of an endorheic basin is the Caspian Sea, the World's largest lake. Given the size of the largest watersheds, they frequently occur across more than one country.

Map description A short description of the country map.

Map references This entry includes the name of the *Factbook* reference map on which a country may be found. Note that boundary representations on these maps are not necessarily authoritative. The entry on **Geographic coordinates** may be helpful in finding some smaller countries.

Marine fisheries This entry describes the major fisheries in the world's oceans in terms of the area covered, their ranking in terms of the global catch, the main producing countries, and the principal species caught. The information is provided by the Fisheries and Aquaculture Department of the UN Food and Agriculture Organization (FAO).

Maritime claims This entry includes the following claims, the definitions of which are excerpted from the United Nations Convention on the Law of the Sea (UNCLOS), which alone contains the full and definitive descriptions:

territorial sea - the sovereignty of a coastal state extends beyond its land territory and internal waters to an adjacent belt of sea, described as the territorial sea in the UNCLOS (Part II); this sovereignty extends to the air space over the territorial sea as well as its underlying seabed and subsoil; every state has the right to establish the breadth of its territorial sea up to a limit not exceeding 12 nautical miles; the normal baseline for measuring the breadth of the territorial sea is the mean low-water line along the coast as marked on large-scale charts officially recognized by the coastal state; where the coasts of two states are opposite or adjacent to each other, neither state is entitled to extend its territorial sea beyond the median line, every point of which is equidistant from the nearest points on the baseline from which the territorial seas of both states are measured; the UNCLOS describes specific rules for archipelagic states.

contiguous zone - according to the UNCLOS (Article 33), this is a zone contiguous to a coastal state's territorial sea, over which it may exercise the control necessary to: prevent infringement of its customs, fiscal, immigration, or sanitary laws and regulations within its territory or territorial sea; punish infringement of the above laws and regulations committed within its territory or territorial sea; the contiguous zone may not extend beyond 24 nautical miles from the baselines from which the breadth of the territorial sea is measured (e.g., the US has claimed a 12-nautical mile contiguous zone in addition to its 12-nautical mile territorial sea); where the coasts of two states are opposite or adjacent to each other, neither state is entitled to extend its contiguous zone beyond the median line, every point of which is equidistant from the nearest points on the baseline from which the contiguous zone of both states are measured.

exclusive economic zone (EEZ) - the UNCLOS (Part V) defines the EEZ as a zone beyond and adjacent to the territorial sea in which a coastal state has: sovereign rights for the purpose of exploring and exploiting, conserving and managing the natural resources, whether living or non-living, of the waters superjacent to the seabed and of the seabed and its subsoil, and with regard to other activities for the economic exploitation and exploration of the zone, such as the production of energy from the water, currents, and winds; jurisdiction with regard to the establishment and use of artificial islands, installations, and structures; marine scientific research; the protection and preservation of the marine environment; the outer limit of the exclusive economic zone shall not exceed 200 nautical miles from the baselines from which the breadth of the territorial sea is measured.

continental shelf - the UNCLOS (Article 76) defines the continental shelf of a coastal state as comprising the seabed and subsoil of the submarine areas that extend beyond its territorial sea throughout the natural prolongation of its land territory to the outer edge of the continental margin, or to a distance of 200 nautical miles from the baselines from which the breadth of the territorial sea is measured where the outer edge of the continental margin does not extend up to that distance; the continental margin comprises the submerged prolongation of the landmass of the coastal state, and consists of the seabed and subsoil of the shelf, the slope and the rise; wherever the continental margin extends beyond 200 nautical miles from the baseline, coastal states may extend their claim to a distance not to exceed 350 nautical miles from the baseline or 100 nautical miles from the 2,500-meter isobath, which is a line connecting points of 2,500 meters in depth; it does not include the deep ocean floor with its oceanic ridges or the subsoil thereof.

exclusive fishing zone - while this term is not used in the UNCLOS, some states (e.g., the United Kingdom) have chosen not to claim an EEZ but rather to claim jurisdiction over the living resources off their coast; in such cases, the term exclusive fishing zone is often used; the breadth of this zone is normally the same as the EEZ or 200 nautical miles.

Maritime threats This entry describes the threat of piracy, as defined in Article 101, UN Convention on the Law of the Sea (UNCLOS), or armed robbery against ships, as defined in Resolution A. 1025 (26) adopted on 2 December 2009 at the 26th Assembly Session of the International Maritime Organization. The entry includes the number of ships on the high seas or in territorial waters that were boarded or attacked by pirates, and the number of crewmen abducted or killed, as compiled by the International Maritime Bureau. Information is also supplied on the geographical range of attacks.

Maternal mortality ratio The maternal mortality ratio (MMR) is the annual number of female deaths per 100,000 live births from any cause related to or aggravated by pregnancy or its management (excluding accidental or incidental causes). The MMR includes deaths during pregnancy, childbirth, or within 42 days of termination of pregnancy, irrespective of the duration and site of the pregnancy, for a specified year.

Median age This entry is the age that divides a population into two numerically equal groups; that is, half the people are younger than this age and half are older. It is a single index that summarizes the age distribution of a population. Currently, the median age ranges from a low of about 15 in Niger and Uganda to 40 or more in several European countries and Japan. See the entry for "Age structure" for the importance of a young versus an older age structure and, by implication, a low versus a higher median age.

Member states This entry, which appears only in the European Union, Government category, provides a listing of all of the European Union member countries, as well as their associated overseas countries and territories.

Merchant marine This entry provides the total and the number of each type of privately or publicly owned commercial ship for each country; military ships are not included; the five ships by type include: *bulk carrier* - for cargo such as coal, grain, cement, ores, and gravel; *container ship* - for loads in truck-size containers, a transportation system called containerization; *general cargo* - also referred to as break-bulk containers - for a wide variety of packaged merchandise, such as textiles, furniture and machinery; *oil tanker* - for crude oil and petroleum products; *other* - includes chemical carriers, dredgers, liquefied natural gas (LNG) carriers, refrigerated cargo ships called reefers, tugboats, passenger vessels (cruise and ferry), and offshore supply ships

Military This category includes the entries dealing with a country's military structure, manpower, and expenditures.

Military - note This entry includes miscellaneous military information of significance not included elsewhere.

Military and security forces This entry lists the military and security forces subordinate to defense ministries or the equivalent (typically ground, naval, air, and marine forces), as well as those belonging to interior ministries or the equivalent (typically gendarmeries, border/coast guards, paramilitary police, and other internal security forces).

Military and security service personnel strengths This entry provides estimates of military and security services personnel strengths. The numbers are based on a wide-range of publicly available information. Unless otherwise noted, military estimates focus on the major services (army, navy, air force, and where applicable, gendarmeries) and do not account for activated reservists or delineate military service members assigned to joint staffs or defense ministries.

Military deployments This entry lists military forces deployed to other countries or territories abroad. *The World Factbook* defines deployed as a permanently stationed force or a temporary deployment of greater than six months. Deployments smaller than 100 personnel or paramilitaries, police, contractors, mercenaries, or proxy forces are not included. Numbers provided are estimates only and should be considered paper strengths, not necessarily the current number of troops on the ground. In addition, some estimates, such as those by the US military, are significantly influenced by deployment policies, contingencies, or world events and may change suddenly. Where available, the organization or mission that at least some of the forces are deployed under is listed. The following terms and abbreviations are used throughout the entry:

AMISOM - Africa Union (AU) Mission in Somalia; UN-supported, AU-operated peacekeeping mission
BATUS - British Army Training Unit Suffield, Canada
BATUK - British Army Training Unit, Kenya
CSTO - Collective Security Treaty Organization
ECOMIG - ECOWUS Mission in The Gambia; Africa Union-European Union peacekeeping, stabilization, and training mission in Gambia
EUTM - European Union Training Mission
EUFOR - European Union Force Bosnia and Herzegovina (also known as Operation Althea)
EuroCorps - European multi-national corps headquartered in Strasbourg, France, consisting of troops from Belgium, France, Germany, Luxembourg, and Spain; Greece, Italy, Poland, Romania and Turkey are Associated Nations of EuroCorps
G5 Joint Force - G5 Sahel Cross-Border Joint Force comprised of troops from Burkina Faso, Chad, Mali, Mauritania, and Niger
KFOR - the Kosovo Force; a NATO-led international peacekeeping force in Kosovo
MFO - Multinational Force & Observers Sinai, headquartered in Rome
MINUSCA - United Nations Multidimensional Integrated Stabilization Mission in the Central African Republic
MINUSMA - United Nations Multidimensional Integrated Stabilization Mission in Mali
MNJTF - Multinational Joint Task Force Against Boko Haram comprised of troops from Benin, Cameroon, Chad, Niger, and Nigeria with the mission of fighting Boko Haram in the Lake Chad Basin
MONUSCO - United Nations Organization Stabilization Mission in the Democratic Republic of the Congo
NATO - North American Treaty Organization, headquartered in Brussels, Belgium
Operation Barkhane - French-led counterinsurgency and counterterrorism mission in the Sahel alongside the G5 Joint Force; headquartered in N'Djamena, Chad and supported by Canada, Denmark, Estonia, the European Union, Germany, Spain, the United Kingdom, and the US
Operation Inherent Resolve - US-led coalition to counter the Islamic State in Iraq and Syria and provide assistance and training to Iraqi security forces
UNAFIL - United Nations Interim Force in Lebanon
UNAMID - African Union - United Nations Hybrid Operation in Darfur, Sudan
UNDOF - United Nations Disengagement Observer Force, Golan (Israel-Syria border)
UNFICYP - United Nations Peacekeeping Force in Cyprus
UNISFA - United Nations Interim Security Force for Abyei (Sudan-South Sudan border)
UNMISS - United Nations Mission in the Republic of South Sudan
UNSOM - United Nations Assistance Mission in Somalia

Military equipment inventories and acquisitions This entry provides basic information on each country's military equipment inventories, as well as how they acquire their equipment; it is intended to show broad trends in major military equipment holdings, such as tanks and other armored vehicles, air defense systems, artillery, naval ships, helicopters, and fixed-wing aircraft. Arms acquisition information is an overview of major arms suppliers over a specific period of time, including second-hand arms delivered as aid, with a focus on major weapons systems. It is based on the type and number of weapon systems ordered and delivered and the financial value of the deal. For some countries, general information on domestic defense industry capabilities is provided.

Military expenditures This entry gives estimates on spending on defense programs for the most recent year available as a percent of gross domestic product (GDP). For countries with no military forces, this figure can include expenditures on public security and police.

Military service age and obligation This entry gives the required ages for voluntary or conscript military service and the length of service obligation.

Money figures All money figures are expressed in contemporaneous US dollars unless otherwise indicated.

Mother's mean age at first birth This entry provides the mean (average) age of mothers at the birth of their first child. It is a useful indicator for gauging the success of family planning programs aiming to reduce maternal mortality, increase contraceptive use – particularly among married and unmarried adolescents – delay age at first marriage, and improve the health of newborns.

National air transport system This entry includes four subfields describing the air transport system of a given country in terms of both structure and performance. The first subfield, *number of registered air carriers*, indicates the total number of air carriers registered with the country's national aviation authority and issued an air operator certificate as required by the Convention on International Civil Aviation. The second subfield, *inventory of registered aircraft operated by air carriers*, lists the total number of aircraft operated by all registered air carriers in the country. The last two subfields measure the performance of the air transport system in terms of both passengers and freight. The subfield, *annual passenger traffic on registered air carriers*, includes the total number of passengers carried by air carriers registered in the country, including both domestic and international passengers, in a given year. The last subfield, *annual freight traffic on registered air carriers*, includes the volume of freight, express, and diplomatic bags carried by registered air carriers and measured in metric tons times kilometers traveled. Freight ton-kilometers equal the sum of the products obtained by multiplying the number of tons of freight, express, and diplomatic bags carried on each flight stage by the stage distance (operation of an aircraft from takeoff to its next landing). For statistical purposes, freight includes express and diplomatic bags but not passenger baggage.

National anthem A generally patriotic musical composition - usually in the form of a song or hymn of praise - that evokes and eulogizes the history, traditions, or struggles of a nation or its people. National anthems can be officially recognized as a national song by a country's constitution or by an enacted law, or simply by tradition. Although most anthems contain lyrics, some do not.

National heritage World Heritage Sites are designated by the United Nations Educational, Scientific, and Cultural Organization (UNESCO), which seeks to encourage the identification, protection, and preservation of cultural, historic, scientific, and natural heritage sites around the world considered to be of outstanding value to humanity. This entry includes two subfields: *total World Heritage Sites* and *selected World Heritage Site locales*. The former consists of natural sites, cultural sites, and mixed (natural and cultural) sites in a country; the latter presents a representative sample of the sites found within a country.

National holiday This entry gives the primary national day of celebration - usually independence day.

National symbol(s) A national symbol is a faunal, floral, or other abstract representation - or some distinctive object - that over time has come to be closely identified with a country or entity. Not all countries have national symbols; a few countries have more than one.

Nationality This entry provides the identifying terms for citizens - *noun* and *adjective*.

Natural gas This field refers to a country's natural gas *production*, *consumption*, *exports*, *imports*, and *proven reserves*. *Proven reserves* are those quantities of natural gas that have been analyzed as commercially recoverable in the future based on known reservoirs and assuming current economic conditions. All data reflect only dry natural gas and exclude non-hydrocarbon gases, as well as vented, flared, and reinjected natural gas. Data are reported using cubic meters.

Natural gas - production This entry is the total natural gas produced in cubic meters (cu m). The discrepancy between the amount of natural gas produced and/or imported and the amount consumed and/or exported is due to the omission of stock changes and other complicating factors.

Natural hazards This entry lists potential natural disasters. For countries where volcanic activity is common, a *volcanism* subfield highlights historically active volcanoes.

Natural resources This entry lists a country's mineral, petroleum, hydropower, and other resources of commercial importance, such as rare earth elements (REEs). In general, products appear only if they make a significant contribution to the economy, or are likely to do so in the future.

Net migration rate This entry includes the figure for the difference between the number of persons entering and leaving a country during the year per 1,000 persons (based on midyear population). An excess of persons entering the country is referred to as net immigration (e.g., 3.56 migrants/1,000 population); an excess of persons leaving the country as net emigration (e.g., -9.26 migrants/1,000 population). The net migration rate indicates the contribution of migration to the overall level of population change. The net migration rate does not distinguish between economic migrants, refugees, and other types of migrants nor does it distinguish between lawful migrants and undocumented migrants.

Obesity - adult prevalence rate This entry gives the percent of a country's population considered to be obese. Obesity is defined as an adult having a Body Mass Index (BMI) greater to or equal to 30.0. BMI is calculated by taking a person's weight in kg and dividing it by the person's squared height in meters.

Ocean currents This entry provides information on ocean currents, which are the continuous, predictable, and directional movements of seawater driven by a number of forces acting upon the water including gravity, wind (Coriolis Effect), and water density (temperature and salinity differences). Depth contours, shoreline configurations, and interactions with other currents can all influence a current's direction and strength. Ocean currents move primarily in a horizontal direction.

Ocean volume This entry provides the estimated volume of each of the oceans in millions of cubic kilometers and the percent of the World Ocean total volume.

People - note This entry includes miscellaneous demographic information of significance not included elsewhere.

People and Society This category includes entries dealing with national identity (including ethnicities, languages, and religions), demography (a variety of population statistics) and societal characteristics (health and education indicators).

Personal Names - Capitalization The *Factbook* capitalizes the surname or family name of individuals for the convenience of our users who are faced with a world of different cultures and naming conventions. The need for capitalization, bold type, underlining, italics, or some other indicator of the individual's surname is apparent in the following examples: MAO Zedong, Fidel CASTRO Ruz, George W. BUSH, and TUNKU SALAHUDDIN Abdul Aziz Shah ibni Al-Marhum Sultan Hisammuddin Alam Shah. By knowing the surname, a short form without all capital letters can be used with confidence as in President Castro, Chairman Mao, President Bush, or Sultan Tunku Salahuddin. The same system of capitalization is extended to the names of leaders with surnames that are not commonly used such as King CHARLES III. For Vietnamese names, the given name is capitalized because officials are referred to by their given name rather than by their surname. For example, the president of Vietnam is Nguyen Xuan PHUC. His surname is Nguyen, but he is referred to by his given name - President PHUC.

Personal Names - Spelling The romanization of personal names in the *Factbook* normally follows the same transliteration system used by the US Board on Geographic Names for spelling place names. At times, however, a foreign leader expressly indicates a preference for, or the media or official documents regularly use, a romanized spelling that differs from the transliteration derived from the US Government standard. In such cases, the *Factbook* uses the alternative spelling.

Personal Names - Titles The *Factbook* capitalizes any valid title (or short form of it) immediately preceding a person's name. A title standing alone is not capitalized. Examples: President PUTIN and President BIDEN are chiefs of state. In Russia, the president is chief of state and the premier is the head of the government, while in the US, the president is both chief of state and head of government.

Petroleum See entries under **Refined petroleum products**.

Petroleum products See entries under **Refined petroleum products**.

Physicians density This entry gives the number of medical doctors (physicians), including generalist and specialist medical practitioners, per 1,000 of the population. Medical doctors are defined as doctors that study, diagnose, treat, and prevent illness, disease, injury, and other physical and mental impairments in humans through the application of modern medicine. They also plan, supervise, and evaluate care and treatment plans by other health care providers. The World Health Organization estimates that fewer than 2.3 health workers (physicians, nurses, and midwives only) per 1,000 would be insufficient to achieve coverage of primary healthcare needs.

Pipelines This entry gives the lengths and types of pipelines for transporting products like natural gas, crude oil, or petroleum products.

Piracy Piracy is defined by the 1982 United Nations Convention on the Law of the Sea as any illegal act of violence, detention, or depredation directed against a ship, aircraft, persons, or property in a place outside the jurisdiction of any State. Such criminal acts committed in the territorial waters of a littoral state are generally considered to be armed robbery against ships. Information on piracy may be found, where applicable, under **Maritime threats**.

Political parties and leaders This entry includes a listing of significant political parties, coalitions, and electoral lists as of each country's last legislative election, unless otherwise noted. kParties that do not win a seat in national elections are usually not included.

Political structure This entry, which appears only in the European Union, Government category, provides a definition for the entity that is the European Union.

Population This entry gives an estimate from the US Bureau of the Census based on statistics from population censuses, vital statistics registration systems, or sample surveys pertaining to the recent past and on assumptions about future trends. The total population presents one overall measure of the potential impact of the country on the world and within its region. Note: Starting with the 1993 *Factbook*, demographic estimates for some countries (mostly African) have explicitly taken into account the effects of the growing impact of the HIV/AIDS epidemic. These countries are currently: The Bahamas, Benin, Botswana, Brazil, Burkina Faso, Burma, Burundi, Cambodia, Cameroon, Central African Republic, Democratic Republic of the Congo, Republic of the Congo, Cote d'Ivoire, Ethiopia, Gabon, Ghana, Guyana, Haiti, Honduras, Kenya, Lesotho, Malawi, Mozambique, Namibia, Nigeria, Rwanda, South Africa, Swaziland, Tanzania, Thailand, Togo, Uganda, Zambia, and Zimbabwe.

Population below poverty line National estimates of the percentage of the population falling below the poverty line are based on surveys of sub-groups, with the results weighted by the number of people in each group. Definitions of poverty vary considerably among nations. For example, rich nations generally employ more generous standards of poverty than poor nations.

Population distribution This entry provides a summary description of the population dispersion within a country. While it may suggest population density, it does not provide density figures.

Population growth rate The average annual percent change in the population, resulting from a surplus (or deficit) of births over deaths and the balance of migrants entering and leaving a country. The rate may be positive or negative. The growth rate is a factor in determining how great a burden would be imposed on a country by the changing needs of its people for infrastructure (e.g., schools, hospitals, housing, roads), resources (e.g., food, water, electricity), and jobs. Rapid population growth can be seen as threatening by neighboring countries.

Population pyramid A population pyramid illustrates the age and sex structure of a country's population and may provide insights about political and social stability, as well as economic development. The population is distributed along the horizontal axis, with males shown on the left and females on the right. The male and female populations are broken down into 5-year age groups represented as horizontal bars along the vertical axis, with the youngest age groups at the bottom and the oldest at the top. The shape of the population pyramid gradually evolves over time based on fertility, mortality, and international migration trends.

Some distinctive types of population pyramids are:

- A **youthful distribution** has a broad base and narrow peak and is characterized by a high proportion of children and low proportion of the elderly. This population distribution results from high fertility, high mortality, low life expectancy, and high population growth. It is typical of developing countries where female education and contraceptive use are low and health care and sanitation are poor.
- A **transitional distribution** is caused by declining fertility and mortality rates, increasing life expectancy, and slowing population growth. The population has a larger proportion of working-age people relative to children and the elderly and produces a barrel-shaped pyramid, where the mid-section bulges and the base and top are narrower. The large proportion of working-age people can create a "demographic bonus" if it is educated and productively employed.
- A **mature distribution** has fairly balanced proportions of the population in the child, working-age, and elderly age groups and will gradually form an inverted triangle population pyramid as population growth continues to fall or ceases and the proportion of older people increases. Low fertility, low mortality, and high life expectancy - made possible by the availability of advanced healthcare, family planning, sanitation, and education - lead to aging populations in industrialized countries.

Ports and terminals This entry lists major ports and terminals primarily on the basis of the amount of cargo tonnage shipped through the facilities on an annual basis. In some instances, the number of containers handled or ship visits were also considered. Most ports service multiple classes of vessels including bulk carriers (dry and liquid), break bulk cargoes (goods loaded individually in bags, boxes, crates, or drums; sometimes palletized), containers, roll-on/roll-off, and passenger ships. The listing leads off with *major seaports* handling all types of cargo. Inland *river/lake ports* are listed separately along with the river or lake name. Ports configured specifically to handle bulk cargoes are designated as *oil terminals* or *dry bulk cargo ports*. *LNG terminals* handle liquefied natural gas (LNG) and are differentiated as either export, where the gas is chilled to a liquid state to reduce its volume for transport on specialized gas carriers, or import, where the off-loaded LNG undergoes a regasification process before entering pipelines for distribution. As break bulk cargoes are largely transported by containers today, the entry also includes a listing of major *container ports* with the corresponding throughput measured in twenty-foot equivalent units (TEUs) referring to a standard container size. Some ports are significant for handling passenger traffic and are listed as *cruise/ferry ports*. In addition to commercial traffic, many seaports also provide important military infrastructure such as naval bases or dockyards.

Preliminary statement This entry, which appears only in the European Union, Introduction category, provides an explanation and justification for the inclusion of a separate European Union geographic entity.

Principality A sovereign state ruled by a monarch with the title of prince; principalities were common in the past, but today only three remain: Liechtenstein, Monaco, and the co-principality of Andorra.

Public debt This entry records the cumulative total of all government borrowings less repayments that are denominated in a country's home currency. Public debt should not be confused with external debt, which reflects the foreign currency liabilities of both the private and public sector and must be financed out of foreign exchange earnings.

Railways This entry states the *total* route length of the railway network and of its component parts by gauge, which is the measure of the distance between the inner sides of the load-bearing rails. The four typical types of gauges are: *broad, standard, narrow,* and *dual*. Other gauges are listed in a *note*. Some 60% of the world's railways use the standard gauge of 1.4 m (4.7 ft). Gauges vary by country and sometimes within countries. The choice of gauge during initial construction was mainly in response to local conditions and the intent of the builder. Narrow-gauge railways were cheaper to build and could negotiate sharper curves, broad-gauge railways gave greater stability and permitted higher speeds. Standard-gauge railways were a compromise between narrow and broad gauges.

Rare earth elements Rare earth elements or REEs are 17 chemical elements that are critical in many of today's high-tech industries. They include lanthanum, cerium, praseodymium, neodymium, promethium, samarium, europium, gadolinium, terbium, dysprosium, holmium, erbium, thulium, ytterbium, lutetium, scandium, and yttrium. Typical applications for REEs include batteries in hybrid cars, fiber optic cables, flat panel displays, and permanent magnets, as well as some defense and medical products.

Real GDP (purchasing power parity) This entry gives the gross domestic product (GDP) or value of all final goods and services produced within a nation in a given year. A nation's GDP at purchasing power parity (PPP) exchange rates is the sum value of all goods and services produced in the country valued at prices prevailing in the United States in the year noted. This is the measure most economists prefer when looking at per-capita welfare and when comparing living conditions or use of resources across countries. The measure is difficult to compute, as a US dollar value has to be assigned to all goods and services in the country regardless of whether these goods and services have a direct equivalent in the United States (for example, the value of an ox-cart or non-US military equipment); as a result, PPP estimates for some countries are based on a small and sometimes different set of goods and services. In addition, many countries do not formally participate in the World Bank's PPP project that calculates these measures, so the resulting GDP estimates for these countries may lack precision. For many developing countries, PPP-based GDP measures are multiples of the official exchange rate (OER) measure. The differences between the OER- and PPP-denominated GDP values for most of the wealthy industrialized countries are generally much smaller.

Real GDP growth rate This entry gives a country's real GDP annual growth rate, adjusted for seasonal unemployment and inflation. A country's growth rate is year-over-year, and not compounded.

Real GDP per capita This entry shows real GDP, divided by population as of 1 July for the same year.

Reference maps This section includes world and regional maps.

Refined petroleum products - consumption This entry is the country's total consumption of refined petroleum products, in barrels per day (bbl/day). The discrepancy between the amount of refined petroleum products produced and/or imported and the amount consumed and/or exported is due to the omission of stock changes, refinery gains, and other complicating factors.

Refined petroleum products - exports This entry is the country's total exports of refined petroleum products, in barrels per day (bbl/day).

Refined petroleum products - imports This entry is the country's total imports of refined petroleum products, in barrels per day (bbl/day).

Refined petroleum products - production This entry is the country's total output of refined petroleum products, in barrels per day (bbl/day). The discrepancy between the amount of refined petroleum products produced and/or imported and the amount consumed and/or exported is due to the omission of stock changes, refinery gains, and other complicating factors.

Refugees and internally displaced persons This entry includes those persons residing in a country as *refugees, internally displaced persons (IDPs)*, or *stateless persons*. Each country's refugee entry includes only countries of origin that are the source of refugee populations of 5,000 or more. The definition of a *refugee* according to a UN Convention is "a person who is outside his/her country of nationality or habitual residence; has a well-founded fear of persecution because of his/her race, religion, nationality, membership in a particular social group or political opinion; and is unable or unwilling to avail himself/herself of the protection of that country, or to return there, for fear of persecution." The UN established the Office of the UN High Commissioner for Refugees (UNHCR) in 1950 to handle refugee matters worldwide. The UN Relief and Works Agency for Palestine Refugees in the Near East (UNRWA) has a different operational definition for a Palestinian refugee: "a person whose normal place of residence was Palestine during the period 1 June 1946 to 15 May 1948 and who lost both home and means of livelihood as a result of the 1948 conflict." The term *internally displaced person* is not specifically covered in the 1951 UN Convention Relating to the Status of Refugees; it is used to describe people who have fled their homes for reasons similar to refugees, but who remain within their own national territory and are subject to the laws of that state. A *stateless person* is defined as someone who is not considered a national by any state under the operation of its law, according to the 1954 UN Convention Relating to the Status of Stateless Persons.

Religions This entry is an ordered listing of religions by adherents starting with the largest group and sometimes includes the percent of total population. The core characteristics and beliefs of the world's major religions are described below.

Baha'i - Founded by Mirza Husayn-Ali (known as Baha'u'llah) in Iran in 1852, Baha'i faith emphasizes monotheism and believes in one eternal transcendent God. Its guiding focus is to encourage the unity of all peoples on the earth so that justice and peace may be achieved on earth. Baha'i revelation contends the prophets of major world religions reflect some truth or element of the divine, believes all were manifestations of God given to specific communities in specific times, and that Baha'u'llah is an additional prophet meant to call all humankind. Bahais are an open community, located worldwide, with the greatest concentration of believers in South Asia.

Buddhism - Religion or philosophy inspired by the 5th century B.C. teachings of Siddhartha Gautama (also known as Gautama Buddha "the enlightened one"). Buddhism focuses on the goal of spiritual enlightenment centered on an understanding of Gautama Buddha's Four Noble Truths on the nature of suffering, and on the Eightfold Path of spiritual and moral practice, to break the cycle of suffering of which we are a part. Buddhism ascribes to a karmic system of rebirth. Several schools and sects of Buddhism exist, differing often on the nature of the Buddha, the extent to which enlightenment can be achieved (for one or for all) and by whom (religious orders or laity).

Basic Groupings

Theravada Buddhism: The oldest Buddhist school, Theravada is practiced mostly in Sri Lanka, Cambodia, Laos, Burma, and Thailand, with minority representation elsewhere in Asia and the West. Theravadans follow the Pali Canon of Buddha's teachings, and believe that one may escape the cycle of rebirth, worldly attachment, and suffering for oneself; this process may take one or several lifetimes.

Mahayana Buddhism, including subsets Zen and Tibetan (Lamaistic) Buddhism: Forms of Mahayana Buddhism are common in East Asia and Tibet, and parts of the West. Mahayanas have additional scriptures beyond the Pali Canon and believe the Buddha is eternal and still teaching. Unlike Theravada Buddhism, Mahayana schools maintain the Buddha-nature is present in all beings and all will ultimately achieve enlightenment.

Hoa Hao: a minority tradition of Buddhism practiced in Vietnam that stresses lay participation, primarily by peasant farmers; it eschews expensive ceremonies and temples and relocates the primary practices into the home.

Christianity - Descending from Judaism, Christianity's central belief maintains Jesus of Nazareth is the promised messiah of the Hebrew Scriptures, and that his life, death, and resurrection are salvific for the world. Christianity is one of the three monotheistic

Abrahamic faiths, along with Islam and Judaism, which traces its spiritual lineage to Abraham of the Hebrew Scriptures. Its sacred texts include the Hebrew Bible and the New Testament (or the Christian Gospels).

Basic Groupings

Catholicism (or Roman Catholicism): This is the oldest established western Christian church and the world's largest single religious body. It is supranational, and recognizes a hierarchical structure with the Pope, or Bishop of Rome, as its head, located at the Vatican. Catholics believe the Pope is the divinely ordered head of the Church from a direct spiritual legacy of Jesus' apostle Peter. Catholicism is comprised of 23 particular Churches, or Rites - one Western (Roman or Latin-Rite) and 22 Eastern. The Latin Rite is by far the largest, making up about 98% of Catholic membership. Eastern-Rite Churches, such as the Maronite Church and the Ukrainian Catholic Church, are in communion with Rome although they preserve their own worship traditions and their immediate hierarchy consists of clergy within their own rite. The Catholic Church has a comprehensive theological and moral doctrine specified for believers in its catechism, which makes it unique among most forms of Christianity.

The Church of Jesus Christ of Latter-day Saints: The Church was organized in 1830 and teaches that it is the restoration of Jesus Christ's original church. It embraces salvation through Christ, personal revelation, and has an open canon, including the King James Bible and the Book of Mormon, which is another testament of Christ's divinity. The Book of Mormon maintains there was an appearance of Jesus in the New World following the Christian account of his resurrection, and that the Americas are uniquely blessed continents. The Church has a centralized doctrine and leadership structure, but has volunteer, lay clergy who oversee local congregations in 176 countries and territories.

Jehovah's Witnesses structure their faith on the Christian Bible, but their rejection of the Trinity is distinct from mainstream Christianity. They believe that a Kingdom of God, the Theocracy, will emerge following Armageddon and usher in a new earthly society. Adherents are required to evangelize and to follow a strict moral code.

Orthodox Christianity: The oldest established eastern form of Christianity, the Holy Orthodox Church, has a ceremonial head in the Bishop of Constantinople (Istanbul), also known as a Patriarch, but its various regional forms (e.g., Greek Orthodox, Russian Orthodox, Serbian Orthodox, Ukrainian Orthodox) are autocephalous (independent of Constantinople's authority, and have their own Patriarchs). Orthodox churches are highly nationalist and ethnic. The Orthodox Christian faith shares many theological tenets with the Roman Catholic Church, but diverges on some key premises and does not recognize the governing authority of the Pope.

Protestant Christianity: Protestant Christianity originated in the 16th century as an attempt to reform Roman Catholicism's practices, dogma, and theology. It encompasses several forms or denominations which are extremely varied in structure, beliefs, relationship to national governments, clergy, and governance. Many protestant theologies emphasize the primary role of scripture in their faith, advocating individual interpretation of Christian texts without the mediation of a final religious authority such as the Roman Pope. The oldest Protestant denominations include Lutheranism, Calvinism (Presbyterianism), and Anglican Christianity (Episcopalianism), which have established liturgies, governing structure, and formal clergy. Other variants on Protestant Christianity, including Pentecostal movements and independent churches, may lack one or more of these elements, and their leadership and beliefs are individualized and dynamic.

Hinduism - Originating in the Vedic civilization of India (second and first millennium B.C.), Hinduism is an extremely diverse set of beliefs and practices with no single founder or religious authority. Hinduism has many scriptures; the Vedas, the Upanishads, and the Bhagavad-Gita are among some of the most important. Hindus may worship one or many deities, usually with prayer rituals within their own home. The most common figures of devotion are the gods Vishnu, Shiva, and a mother goddess, Devi. Most Hindus believe the soul, or *atman*, is eternal, and goes through a cycle of birth, death, and rebirth (*samsara*) determined by one's positive or negative karma, or the consequences of one's actions. The goal of religious life is to learn to act so as to finally achieve liberation (*moksha*) of one's soul, escaping the rebirth cycle.

Islam - One of the three monotheistic Abrahamic faiths, Islam originated with the teachings of Muhammad in the 7th century. Muslims believe Muhammad is the final of all religious prophets (beginning with Abraham) and that the Qu'ran, which is the Islamic scripture, was revealed to him by God. Islam derives from the word submission, and obedience to God is a primary theme in this religion. In order to live an Islamic life, believers must follow the five pillars, or tenets, of Islam, which are the testimony of faith (*shahada*), daily prayer (*salah*), giving alms (*zakah*), fasting during Ramadan (*sawm*), and the pilgrimage to Mecca (*hajj*).

Basic Groupings

The two primary branches of Islam are Sunni and Shia, which split from each other over a religio-political leadership dispute about the rightful successor to Muhammad. The Shia believe Muhammad's cousin and son-in-law, Ali, was the only divinely ordained Imam (religious leader), while the Sunni maintain the first three caliphs after Muhammad were also legitimate authorities. In modern Islam, Sunnis and Shia continue to have different views of acceptable schools of Islamic jurisprudence, and who is a proper Islamic religious authority. Islam also has an active mystical branch, Sufism, with various Sunni and Shia subsets.

Sunni Islam accounts for over 87-90% of the world's Muslim population. It recognizes the Abu Bakr as the first caliph after Muhammad. Sunni has four schools of Islamic doctrine and law - Hanafi, Maliki, Shafi'i, and Hanbali - which uniquely interpret the *Hadith*, or recorded oral traditions of Muhammad. A Sunni Muslim may elect to follow any one of these schools, as all are considered equally valid.

Shia Islam represents 10-13% of Muslims worldwide, and its distinguishing feature is its reverence for Ali as an infallible, divinely inspired leader, and as the first Imam of the Muslim community after Muhammad. A majority of Shia are known as "Twelvers," because they believe that the 11 familial successor imams after Muhammad culminate in a 12th Imam (al-Mahdi) who is hidden in the world and will reappear at its end to redeem the righteous.

Variants

Ismaili faith: A sect of Shia Islam, its adherents are also known as "Seveners," because they believe that the rightful seventh Imam in Islamic leadership was Isma'il, the elder son of Imam Jafar al-Sadiq. Ismaili tradition awaits the return of the seventh Imam as the Mahdi, or Islamic messianic figure. Ismailis are located in various parts of the world, particularly South Asia and the Levant.

Alawi faith: Another Shia sect of Islam, the name reflects followers' devotion to the religious authority of Ali. Alawites are a closed, secretive religious group who assert they are Shia Muslims, although outside scholars speculate their beliefs may have a syncretic mix with other faiths originating in the Middle East. Alawis live mostly in Syria, Lebanon, and Turkey.

Druze faith: A highly secretive tradition and a closed community that derives from the Ismaili sect of Islam; its core beliefs are thought to emphasize a combination of Gnostic principles believing that the Fatimid caliph, al-Hakin, is the one who embodies the key aspects of goodness of the universe, which are, the intellect, the word, the soul, the preceder, and the follower. The Druze have a key presence in Syria, Lebanon, and Israel.

Jainism - Originating in India, Jain spiritual philosophy believes in an eternal human soul, the eternal universe, and a principle of "the own nature of things." It emphasizes compassion for all living things, seeks liberation of the human soul from reincarnation through enlightenment, and values personal responsibility due to the belief in the immediate consequences of one's behavior. Jain philosophy teaches non-violence and prescribes vegetarianism for monks and laity alike; its adherents are a highly influential religious minority in Indian society.

Judaism - One of the first known monotheistic religions, likely dating to between 2000-1500 B.C., Judaism is the native faith of the Jewish people, based upon the belief in a covenant of responsibility between a sole omnipotent creator God and Abraham, the patriarch of Judaism's Hebrew Bible, or *Tanakh*. Divine revelation of principles and prohibitions in the Hebrew Scriptures form the basis of Jewish law, or *halakhah*, which is a key component of the faith. While there are extensive traditions of Jewish halakhic and theological discourse, there is no final dogmatic authority in the tradition. Local communities have their own religious leadership. Modern Judaism has three basic categories of faith: Orthodox, Conservative, and Reform/Liberal. These differ in their views and observance of Jewish law, with the Orthodox representing the most traditional practice, and Reform/Liberal communities the most accommodating of individualized interpretations of Jewish identity and faith.
Shintoism - A native animist tradition of Japan, Shinto practice is based upon the premise that every being and object has its own spirit or *kami*. Shinto practitioners worship several particular *kamis*, including the *kamis* of nature, and families often have shrines to their ancestors' *kamis*. Shintoism has no fixed tradition of prayers or prescribed dogma, but is characterized by individual ritual. Respect for the *kamis* in nature is a key Shinto value. Prior to the end of World War II, Shinto was the state religion of Japan, and bolstered the cult of the Japanese emperor.
Sikhism - Founded by the Guru Nanak (born 1469), Sikhism believes in a non-anthropomorphic, supreme, eternal, creator God; centering one's devotion to God is seen as a means of escaping the cycle of rebirth. Sikhs follow the teachings of Nanak and nine subsequent gurus. Their scripture, the Guru Granth Sahib - also known as the Adi Granth - is considered the living Guru, or final authority of Sikh faith and theology. Sikhism emphasizes equality of humankind and disavows caste, class, or gender discrimination.
Taoism - Chinese philosophy or religion based upon Lao Tzu's Tao Te Ching, which centers on belief in the Tao, or the way, as the flow of the universe and the nature of things. Taoism encourages a principle of non-force, or wu-wei, as the means to live harmoniously with the Tao. Taoists believe the esoteric world is made up of a perfect harmonious balance and nature, while in the manifest world - particularly in the body - balance is distorted. The Three Jewels of the Tao - compassion, simplicity, and humility - serve as the basis for Taoist ethics.
Zoroastrianism - Originating from the teachings of Zoroaster in about the 9th or 10th century B.C., Zoroastrianism may be the oldest continuing creedal religion. Its key beliefs center on a transcendent creator God, Ahura Mazda, and the concept of free will. The key ethical tenets of Zoroastrianism expressed in its scripture, the Avesta, are based on a dualistic worldview where one may prevent chaos if one chooses to serve God and exercises good thoughts, good words, and good deeds. Zoroastrianism is generally a closed religion and members are almost always born to Zoroastrian parents. Prior to the spread of Islam, Zoroastrianism dominated greater Iran. Today, though a minority, Zoroastrians remain primarily in Iran, India (where they are known as Parsi), and Pakistan.
Traditional beliefs
Animism: the belief that non-human entities contain souls or spirits.
Badimo: a form of ancestor worship of the Tswana people of Botswana.
Confucianism: an ideology that humans are perfectible through self-cultivation and self-creation; developed from teachings of the Chinese philosopher Confucius. Confucianism has strongly influenced the culture and beliefs of East Asian countries, including China, Japan, Korea, Singapore, Taiwan, and Vietnam.
Inuit beliefs: a form of shamanism (see below) based on the animistic principles of the Inuit or Eskimo peoples.
Kirant: the belief system of the Kirat, a people who live mainly in the Himalayas of Nepal. It is primarily a form of polytheistic shamanism, but includes elements of animism and ancestor worship.
Pagan is a blanket term used to describe many unconnected belief practices throughout history, usually in reference to religions outside of the Abrahamic category (monotheistic faiths including Judaism, Christianity, and Islam).
Shamanism: beliefs and practices promoting communication with the spiritual world. Shamanistic beliefs are organized around a shaman or medicine man who - as an intermediary between the human and spirit world - is believed to be able to heal the sick (by healing their souls), communicate with the spirit world, and help souls into the afterlife through the practice of entering a trance. In shaman-based religions, the shaman is also responsible for leading sacred rites.
Spiritualism: the belief that souls and spirits communicate with the living usually through intermediaries called mediums.
Syncretic (fusion of diverse religious beliefs and practices)
Cao Dai: a nationalistic Vietnamese sect, officially established in 1926, that draws practices and precepts from Confucianism, Taoism, Buddhism, and Catholicism.
Chondogyo: or the religion of the Heavenly Way, is based on Korean shamanism, Buddhism, and Korean folk traditions, with some elements drawn from Christianity. Formulated in the 1860s, it holds that God lives in all of us and strives to convert society into a paradise on earth, populated by believers transformed into intelligent moral beings with a high social conscience.
Kimbanguism: a puritan form of the Baptist denomination founded by Simon Kimbangu in the 1920s in what is now the Democratic Republic of Congo. Adherents believe that salvation comes through Jesus' death and resurrection, like Christianity, but additionally that living a spiritually pure life following strict codes of conduct is required for salvation.
Modekngei: a hybrid of Christianity and ancient Palauan culture and oral traditions founded around 1915 on the island of Babeldaob. Adherents simultaneously worship Jesus Christ and Palauan goddesses.
Rastafarianism: an afro-centrist ideology and movement based on Christianity that arose in Jamaica in the 1930s; it believes that Haile Selassie I, Emperor of Ethiopia from 1930-74, was the incarnation of the second coming of Jesus.
Santeria: practiced in Cuba, the merging of the Yoruba religion of Nigeria with Roman Catholicism and native Indian traditions. Its practitioners believe that each person has a destiny and eventually transcends to merge with the divine creator and source of all energy, Olorun.
Voodoo/Vodun: a form of spirit and ancestor worship combined with some Christian faiths, especially Catholicism. Haitian and Louisiana Voodoo, which have included more Catholic practices, are separate from West African Vodun, which has retained a focus on spirit worship.
Non-religious
Agnosticism: the belief that most things are unknowable. In regard to religion, it is usually characterized as neither a belief nor non-belief in a deity.
Atheism: the belief that there are no deities of any kind.

Reserves of foreign exchange and gold This entry gives the dollar value for the stock of all financial assets that are available to the central monetary authority for use in meeting a country's balance of payments needs as of the end-date of the period specified. This category includes not only foreign currency and gold, but also a country's holdings of Special Drawing Rights in the International Monetary Fund, and its reserve position in the Fund.

Revenue from coal This entry refers to the economic profits, expressed as a percentage of a country's GDP, from the extraction of coal. These profits equal coal gross revenues minus cost(s) to extract the coal. Other sources may refer to this field as coal rents.

Revenue from forest resources This entry refers to the economic profits, expressed as a percentage of a country's GDP, from the harvesting of forests (e.g., lumber and timber industries). These profits equal forest gross revenues minus costs to harvest the forest. Other sources may refer to this field as forest rents.

Roadways This entry gives the *total* length of the road network and includes the length of the *paved* and *unpaved* portions.

Sanitation facility access This entry provides information about access to improved or unimproved sanitation facilities available to segments of the population of a country. *Improved* sanitation - use of any of the following facilities: flush or pour-flush to a piped sewer system, septic tank or pit latrine; ventilated improved pit (VIP) latrine; pit latrine with slab; or a composting toilet. *Unimproved* sanitation - use of any of the following facilities: flush or pour-flush not piped to a sewer system, septic tank or pit latrine; pit latrine without a slab or open pit; bucket; hanging toilet or hanging latrine; shared facilities of any type; no facilities; or bush or field.

School life expectancy (primary to tertiary education) School life expectancy (SLE) is the total number of years of schooling (primary to tertiary) that a child can expect to receive, assuming that the probability of his or her being enrolled in school at any particular future age is equal to the current enrollment ratio at that age. Caution must be maintained when utilizing this indicator in international comparisons. For example, a year or grade completed in one country is not necessarily the same in terms of educational content or quality as a year or grade completed in another country. SLE represents the expected number of years of schooling that will be completed, including years spent repeating one or more grades.

Sex ratio This entry includes the number of males for each female in five age groups - *at birth, under 15 years, 15-64 years, 65 years and over*, and for the *total population*. Sex ratio at birth has recently emerged as an indicator of certain kinds of sex discrimination in some countries. For instance, high sex ratios at birth in some Asian countries are now attributed to sex-selective abortion and infanticide due to a strong preference for sons. This will affect future marriage patterns and fertility patterns. Eventually, it could cause unrest among young adult males who are unable to find partners.

Smart City A smart city uses communication and information technology, a wide range of sensors, and data analysis, to improve operational activities, share information, and optimize the quality of life for its citizens. Everyday enhancements may include more effective linkups of urban services, increased safety and security, more efficient resource consumption (and a concomitant reduction in costs), environmental initiatives, and better disaster preparation and response. The vast amount of data collected does present concerns over intrusiveness and can be used to monitor the everyday lives of citizens.

Stateless person Statelessness is the condition whereby an individual is not considered a national by any country. Stateless people are denied basic rights, such as access to employment, housing, education, healthcare, and pensions, and they may be unable to vote, own property, open a bank account, or legally register a marriage or birth. They may also be vulnerable to arbitrary treatment and human trafficking. In at least 30 states, women cannot pass their nationality on to their children. In these countries, if a child's father is foreign, stateless, or absent, the child usually becomes stateless. Estimates of the number of stateless people are inherently imprecise because few countries have procedures to identify them; the UN approximates that there are at least 10 million stateless people worldwide. Stateless people are counted in a country's overall population figure if they have lived there for a year.

Suffrage This entry gives the age at enfranchisement and whether the right to vote is universal or restricted.

Taxes and other revenues This entry records total taxes and other revenues received by the national government during the time period indicated, expressed as a percent of GDP. Taxes include personal and corporate income taxes, value added taxes, excise taxes, and tariffs. Other revenues include social contributions - such as payments for social security and hospital insurance - grants, and net revenues from public enterprises. Normalizing the data, by dividing total revenues by GDP, enables easy comparisons across countries, and provides an average rate at which all income (GDP) is paid to the national level government for the supply of public goods and services.

Telecommunication systems This entry includes a brief general assessment of a country's telecommunications system with details on the domestic and international components. The following terms and abbreviations are used throughout the entry:

2G - is short for second-generation cellular network. After 2G was launched, the previous mobile wireless network systems were retroactively dubbed 1G. While radio signals on 1G networks are analog, radio signals on 2G networks are digital. Both systems use digital signaling to connect the radio towers (which listen to the devices) to the rest of the mobile system.

3G - is the third generation of wireless mobile telecommunications technology. It is the upgrade for 2.5G and 2.5G GPRS networks, for faster data transfer. This increased speed is based on a set of standards used for mobile devices and mobile telecommunications use services and networks that comply with the International Mobile Telecommunications-2000 (IMT-2000) specifications by the International Telecommunication Union. 3G finds application in wireless voice telephony, mobile Internet access, fixed wireless Internet access, video calls, and mobile TV.

4G - is the fourth generation of broadband cellular network technology, succeeding 3G. The first-release Long Term Evolution (LTE) standard was commercially deployed in Oslo, Norway, and Stockholm, Sweden in 2009, and has since been deployed throughout most parts of the world. Applications, include enhanced mobile web access, IP telephony, high-definition mobile TV, and video conferencing.

5G - is the fifth generation technology standard for cellular networks, which cellular phone companies began deploying worldwide in 2019; it is the planned successor to the 4G networks which provide connectivity to most current cellphones. Like its predecessors, 5G networks are cellular networks, in which the service area is divided into small geographical areas called cells. All 5G wireless devices in a cell are connected to the Internet and telephone network by radio waves through a local antenna in the cell. The main advantage of the new networks is that they will have greater bandwidth, allowing higher download speeds, eventually up to 10 gigabits per second (Gbit/s). Due to the increased bandwidth, the expectation is that the new networks will not just serve cellphones like existing cellular networks, but also be used as general Internet service providers for laptops and desktop computers, competing with existing ISPs such as cable Internet. Existing 4G cellphones will not be able to use the new networks, which will require new 5G-enabled wireless devices.

ADSL - Asymmetric Digital Subscriber Line (ADSL) is a type of digital subscriber line (DSL) that allows faster data transmission via copper service phone lines to a home or business. ADSL provides an "always on" connection and higher speeds than dial-up Internet can provide. In ADSL, bandwidth and bit rate (i.e., speed) are asymmetric, meaning greater toward the customer (downstream) than the reverse (upstream).

AngoSat 2 - geostationary communications satellite for ground communication and broadcasting infrastructure in Angola, operated by Angosat and built by the Russian company ISS Reshetnev.

Arabsat - Arab Satellite Communications Organization (Riyadh, Saudi Arabia).

Cellular telephone system - the telephones in this system are radio transceivers, with each instrument having its own private radio frequency and sufficient radiated power to reach the booster station in its area (cell), from which the telephone signal is fed to a telephone exchange.

Central American Microwave System - a trunk microwave radio relay system that links the countries of Central America and Mexico with each other.

Coaxial cable - a multichannel communication cable consisting of a central conducting wire, surrounded by and insulated from a cylindrical conducting shell; a large number of telephone channels can be made available within the insulated space by the use of a large number of carrier frequencies.

DSL - Digital Subscriber Line (DSL) is a family of technologies that are used to transmit digital data over telephone lines.

e-services - Electronic services rely on information and communication technologies (ICT); the three main components of e-services are the service provider, service receiver (or customer), and the channel for delivery, generally the Internet. E-services have expanded to e-health, e-commerce, e-fleet, and e-government, among other services. E-services are also linked to the development of IoT and smart city technology.

ECOWAS telecommunications - Economic Community of West African States regional telecommunications development program, focused on broadband infrastructure, landing of submarine cables, and the establishment of a single liberalized telecoms market.

Eutelsat - European Telecommunications Satellite Organization (Paris).

Fiber-optic cable - a multichannel communications cable using a thread of optical glass fibers as a transmission medium in which the signal (voice, video, etc.) is in the form of a coded pulse of light.

FTTX - Fiber to the x (FTTX) is a generic term for any broadband network architecture using optical fiber to provide all or part of the local loop used for last mile telecommunications. As fiber optic cables are able to carry much more data than copper cables, especially over long distances, copper telephone networks built in the 20th century are being replaced by fiber. FTTX is a general term for several configurations of fiber deployment, broadly organized into two groups: FTTN and FTTP /H/B. Fiber to the node (FTTN), also referred to as Fiber to the neighborhood, delivers fiber to within 300m (1,000 ft) of a customer's premises. Fiber to the premises (FTTP) can be further categorized as fiber to the home (FTTH) or fiber to the building/business (FTTB). FTTN (and FTTC, fiber to the curb (to less than 300m (1,000 ft of a customer's premises)) are seen as interim steps toward full FTTP.

Galileo - Chartered in 2016, Galileo is a global navigation satellite system (GNSS) created by the European Union through the European Space Agency (ESA), and operated by the European Union Agency for the Space Programme (EUSPA). Headquartered in Prague, Czechia, it has two ground operations centers: one in Fucino, Italy, and the other in Oberpfaffenhofen, Germany. The project is named after the Italian astronomer Galileo Galilei and aims to provide an independent high-precision positioning system. Galileo provides a global search and rescue (SAR) function as part of the MEOSAR system.

GPON - stands for Gigabyte Passive Optical Networks, which are networks that rely on optical cables to deliver information from a single feeding fiber from a provider - to multiple destinations - via the use of splitters. GPONs are currently the leading form of Passive Optical Networks (PON) and offer up to a 1:64 ratio on a single fiber. As opposed to a standard copper wire in most networks, GPONs are 95% more energy efficient.

GSM - a global system for mobile (cellular) communications devised by the Groupe Special Mobile of the pan-European standardization organization, Conference Europeanne des Posts et Telecommunications (CEPT) in 1982.

HF - high frequency; any radio frequency in the 3,000- to 30,000-kHz range.

HSPA - High Speed Packet Access (HSPA) is an amalgamation of two mobile protocols, High Speed Downlink Packet Access (HSDPA) and High Speed Uplink Packet Access (HSUPA), that extends and improves the performance of existing 3G mobile telecommunication networks using the Wideband Code Division Multiple Access (WCDMA) protocols. A further improved 3rd Generation Partnership Project (3GPP) standard, Evolved High Speed Packet Access (also known as HSPA+), was released late in 2008 with subsequent worldwide adoption beginning in 2010. The newer standard allows bit-rates to reach as high as 337 Mbit/s in the downlink and 34 Mbit/s in the uplink. However, these speeds are rarely achieved in practice.

ICT - Information and communications technology (ICT) encompasses the capture, storage, retrieval, processing, display, representation, presentation, organization, management, security, transfer, and interchange of data and information; includes all categories of ubiquitous technology used for the gathering, storing, transmitting, retrieving, or processing of information.

Inmarsat - International Maritime Satellite Organization is a British satellite telecommunications company, offering global mobile services. It provides telephone and data services to users worldwide, via portable or mobile terminals that communicate with ground stations through 13 geostationary telecommunications satellites. Inmarsat's network provides communications services to a range of governments, aid agencies, media outlets, and businesses (especially in the shipping, airline, and mining industries) with a need to communicate in remote regions or where there is no reliable terrestrial network.

Intelsat - Intelsat Corporation (formerly International Telecommunications Satellite Organization, INTEL-SAT, INTELSAT) is a communications satellite services provider.

Intersputnik - International Organization of Space Communications (Moscow); first established in the former Soviet Union and the East European countries, it is now marketing its services worldwide with earth stations in North America, Africa, and East Asia.

IP - Internet Protocol is a communications protocol for computers connected to a network, especially the Internet, specifying the format for addresses and units of transmitted data; data traversing the Internet is divided into smaller pieces, called packets.

IoT - the Internet of Things is a system of interrelated computing devices, mechanical, and digital machines provided with unique identifiers (UIDs) and the ability to transfer data over a network without requiring human-to-human or human-to-computer interaction.

Iridium - the Iridium satellite constellation provides L band (long wavelength band) voice and data information coverage to satellite phones, pagers, and integrated transceivers over the entire surface of the earth. Iridium Communications owns and operates the constellation, additionally selling equipment and access to its services.

ITU - the International Telecommunication Union (ITU) is a United Nations specialized agency that is responsible for issues that concern information and communication technologies. Founded in 1865, the ITU is the oldest global international organization. The ITU coordinates the shared global use of the radio spectrum, promotes international cooperation in assigning satellite orbits, works to improve telecommunication infrastructure in the developing world, and assists in the development and coordination of worldwide technical standards. The ITU is also active in the areas of broadband Internet, latest-generation wireless technologies, aeronautical and maritime navigation, radio astronomy, satellite-based meteorology, convergence in fixed-mobile phone, Internet access, data, voice, TV broadcasting, and next-generation networks.

IXP - an Internet exchange point (IXP) is a physical location through which Internet infrastructure companies such as Internet service providers (ISPs) and content delivery networks (CDNs) connect with each other.

Kacific 1 - Kacific Broadband Satellites Group (Kacific) is a satellite operator providing high-speed broadband Internet service for the South East Asia and Pacific Islands regions. Its first Ka-band HTS satellite, Kacific1, was designed and built by Boeing and launched into geostationary orbit in December 2019.

Landline - communication wire or cable of any sort that is installed on poles or buried in the ground.

LTE - Long-Term Evolution (LTE) is a standard for wireless broadband communication for mobile devices and data terminals Based on the GSM/EDGE and UMTS/HSPA technologies, it increases communication capacity and speed using a different radio interface together with core network improvements.

LTE Advanced - (aka LTE A) is a mobile communication standard and a major enhancement of the Long Term Evolution (LTE) standard. It was submitted as a candidate 4G in late 2009 as meeting the requirements of the IMT-Advanced standard, and was standardized by the 3rd Generation Partnership Project (3GPP) in March 2011 as 3GPP Release 10.

LTE-TDD & LTE-FDD - There are two major differences between LTE-TDD and LTE-FDD: how data is uploaded and downloaded, and what frequency spectra the networks are deployed in. While LTE-FDD uses paired frequencies to upload and download data, LTE-TDD uses a single frequency, alternating between uploading and downloading data through time. The ratio between uploads and downloads on a LTE-TDD network can be changed dynamically, depending on whether more data needs to be sent or received. LTE-TDD and LTE-FDD also operate on different frequency bands, with LTE-TDD working better at higher frequencies, and LTE-FDD working better at lower frequencies.

M-commerce - short for mobile commerce, m-commerce is the use of wireless handheld devices like cellphones and tablets to conduct commercial transactions online, including the purchase and sale of products, online banking, and paying bills.

MNO - a mobile network operator (MNO), also known as a wireless service provider, wireless carrier, cellular company, or mobile network carrier, is a provider of wireless communications services that owns or controls all the elements necessary to sell and deliver services to an end user including radio spectrum allocation, wireless network infrastructure, back haul infrastructure, billing, customer care, provisioning computer systems, and marketing and repair organizations.

MNP - mobile number portability

MVNO - a mobile virtual network operator (MVNO) does not own the wireless network infrastructure over which it provides services to its customers. A MVNO enters into a business agreement with a mobile network operator (MNO) to obtain bulk access to network services at wholesale rates, then sets retail prices independently.

Medarabtel - the Middle East Telecommunications Project of the International Telecommunications Union (ITU) providing a modern telecommunications network, primarily by microwave radio relay, linking Algeria, Djibouti, Egypt, Jordan, Libya, Morocco, Saudi Arabia, Somalia, Sudan, Syria, Tunisia, and Yemen; it was initially started in Morocco in 1970 by the Arab Telecommunications Union (ATU) and was known at that time as the Middle East Mediterranean Telecommunications Network.

Microwave radio relay - transmission of long distance telephone calls and television programs by highly directional radio microwaves that are received and sent on from one booster station to another on an optical path.

NB-IoT - narrowband Internet of Things is a low-power, wide-area network (LPWAN) radio technology. NB-IoT improves the power consumption of user devices, system capacity, and spectrum efficiency.

NGN - The next-generation network is the evolution and migration of fixed and mobile network infrastructures from distinct, proprietary networks to converged networks on an IP. One network transports all information and services (voice, data, and media) by encapsulating these into IP packets, similar to those used on the Internet. The result is unrestricted, consistent and ubiquitous access for users to different service providers.

NMT - Nordic Mobile Telephone; NMT is a first generation (1G) mobile cellular phone system based on analog technology that was developed jointly by the national telecommunications authorities of the Nordic countries (Denmark, Finland, Iceland, Norway, and Sweden). NMT-450 analog networks have been replaced with digital networks using the same cellular frequencies.

Orbita - a Russian television service; also the trade name of a packet-switched digital telephone network.

PanAmSat - PanAmSat Corporation (Greenwich, CT) was a satellite service provider.

Radio telephone communications - the two-way transmission and reception of sounds by broadcast radio on authorized frequencies using telephone handsets.

Satellite communication system - a communication system consisting of two or more earth stations and at least one satellite that provide long distance transmission of voice, data, and television; the system usually serves as a trunk connection between telephone exchanges; if the earth stations are in the same country, it is a domestic system.

Satellite earth station - a communications facility with a microwave radio transmitting and receiving antenna, and receiving and transmitting equipment required for communicating with satellites.

Satellite link - a radio connection between a satellite and an earth station permitting communication between them, either one-way (down link from satellite to earth station - television receive-only transmission) or two-way (telephone channels).

SHF - super high frequency; any radio frequency in the 3,000- to 30,000-MHz range.

Shortwave - radio frequencies (from 1.605 to 30 MHz) that fall above the commercial broadcast band and are used for communication over long distances.

SIM card - subscriber identity/identification module card, is a small, removable integrated circuit used in a mobile phone to store data unique to the user, such as an identification number, passwords, phone numbers, and messages.

Solidaridad - geosynchronous satellites in Mexico's system of international telecommunications in the Western Hemisphere.

Spectrum - spectrum management is the allocation and regulation of the electromagnetic spectrum into radio frequency (RF) bands, a procedure normally carried out by governments in most countries. Because radio propagation does not stop at national boundaries, governments have sought to harmonise the allocation of RF bands and their standardization. A spectrum auction is a process whereby a government uses an auction system to sell the rights to transmit signals over specific bands of the electromagnetic spectrum and to assign scarce spectrum resources.

Submarine cable - a cable designed for service under water.

TE North - A submarine cable linking Egypt with France, with a branching unit to Cyprus, developed by Alcatel-Lucent.

Telecommunication (telecom) - is the exchange of signs, signals, messages, words, images and sounds, or information of any nature by wire, radio, optical, or other electromagnetic systems (i.e., via the use of technology). Telecommunication occurs through a transmission medium, such as over physical media, for example, over electrical cable, or via electromagnetic radiation through space such as radio or light.

Teledensity - (telephone density) is the number of telephone connections for every hundred individuals living within an area. It varies widely between nations and also between urban and rural areas within a country. Telephone density correlates closely with the per capita GDP of an area, and is also used as an indicator of the purchasing power of the middle class of a country or specific region.

Telefax - facsimile service between subscriber stations via the public switched telephone network or the international Datel network.

Telegraph - a telecommunications system designed for unmodulated electric impulse transmission.

Telephony - is the field of technology involving the development, application, and deployment of telecommunication services for the purpose of electronic transmission of voice, fax, or data, between distant parties. The history of telephony is intimately linked to the invention and development of the telephone.

Telex - a communication service involving teletypewriters connected by wire through automatic exchanges.

Trans-Caspian cable - Trans-Caspian Fiber Optic (TCFO) submarine cable; a project between AzerTelecom in Azerbaijan, KazTransCom of Kazakhstan, and Turkmentelekom in Turkmenistan for the construction of a fiber-optic cable in the Caspian Sea.

Tropospheric scatter - a form of microwave radio transmission in which the troposphere is used to scatter and reflect a fraction of the incident radio waves back to earth. Powerful, highly directional antennas are used to transmit and receive the microwave signals. Reliable over-the-horizon communications are realized for distances up to 600 miles in a single hop; additional hops can extend the range of this system for very long distances.

Trunk network - a network of switching centers, connected by multichannel trunk lines.

UHF - ultra high frequency; any radio frequency in the 300- to 3,000-MHz range.

VHF - very high frequency; any radio frequency in the 30- to 300-MHz range.

VNO - A virtual network operator (VNO) is a management services provider and a network services reseller of other telecommunication service providers. VNOs do not possess a telecom network infrastructure; however, they provide telecom services by acquiring the required capacity from other telecom carriers. These network providers are classified as virtual because they offer network services to clients without possessing the actual network. VNOs usually lease bandwidth at agreed wholesale rates from different telecom providers and then offer solutions to their direct customers.

VOD - or video on demand is a video media distribution system that allows users to access video entertainment without a traditional video entertainment device and without the constraints of a typical static broadcasting schedule.

Voice over Internet Protocol - VoIP, also called IP telephony, refers to the delivery of voice communications and multimedia sessions over Internet Protocol (IP) networks, such as the Internet. The terms Internet telephony, broadband telephony, and broadband phone service specifically refer to the provisioning of communications services (voice, fax, text-messaging, voice-messaging) over the public Internet, rather than via the public switched telephone network (PSTN), also known as plain old telephone service (POTS).

VSAT - a VSAT (very-small-aperture terminal) is a two-way satellite ground station with a dish antenna that is smaller than 3.8 meters. The majority of VSAT antennas range from 75 cm to 1.2 m. Data rates, generally, range from 4 kbit/s up to 16 Mbit/s.

WACS - the West Africa Cable System is a submarine communications cable linking South Africa with the UK along the west coast of Africa and Europe; constructed by Alcatel-Lucent. The cable consists of four fiber pairs and is 14,530 Km in length with 14 landing points – 12 along the western coast of Africa and 2 in Europe – with termination in London, UK.

WiMAX - stands for Worldwide Interoperability for Microwave Access; it is a family of wireless broadband communication standards based on the IEEE 802.16 set of standards, which provide multiple physical layer (PHY) and Media Access Control (MAC) options.

Telephone numbers All telephone numbers in *The World Factbook* consist of the country code in brackets, the city or area code (where required) in parentheses, and the local number. The one component that is not presented is the international access code, which varies from country to country. For example, an international direct dial telephone call placed from the US to Madrid, Spain, would be as follows: 011 [34] (1) 577-xxxx, where 011 is the international access code for station-to-station calls; 01 is for calls other than station-to-station calls, [34] is the country code for Spain, (1) is the city code for Madrid, 577 is the local exchange, and xxxx is the local telephone number. An international direct dial telephone call placed from another country to the US would be as follows: international access code + [1] (202) 939-xxxx, where [1] is the country code for the US, (202) is the area code for Washington, DC, 939 is the local exchange, and xxxx is the local telephone number.

Telephones - fixed lines This entry gives the *total* number of fixed telephone lines in use, as well as the number of *subscriptions per 100 inhabitants.*

Telephones - mobile cellular This entry gives the *total* number of mobile cellular telephone subscribers, as well as the number of *subscriptions per 100 inhabitants.* Note that because of the ubiquity of mobile phone use in developed countries, the number of subscriptions per 100 inhabitants can exceed 100.

Terminology Due to the highly structured nature of the *Factbook* database, some collective generic terms have to be used. For example, the word **Country** in the **Country name** entry refers to a wide variety of dependencies, areas of special sovereignty, uninhabited islands, and other entities in addition to the traditional countries or independent states. **Military** is also used as an umbrella term for various civil defense, security, and defense activities in many entries. The **Independence** entry includes the usual colonial independence dates and former ruling states as well as other significant nationhood dates such as the traditional founding date or the date of unification, federation, confederation, establishment, or state succession that are not strictly independence dates. Dependent areas have the nature of their dependency status noted in this same entry.

Terrain This entry contains a brief description of the topography of a country.

Terrorist group(s) This entry provides a list of US State Department-designated Foreign Terrorist Organizations (FTO) that are assessed to maintain a presence in each country. This includes cases where sympathizers, supporters, or associates of designated FTOs have carried out attacks or been arrested by security forces for terrorist-type activities in the country. See Appendix T for details on each FTO.

Time difference This entry is expressed in *The World Factbook* in two ways. First, it is stated as the difference in hours between the capital of an entity and **Coordinated Universal Time (UTC)** during Standard Time. Additionally, the difference in time between the capital of an entity and that observed in Washington, D.C. is also provided. Note that the time difference assumes both locations are simultaneously observing Standard Time or Daylight Saving Time.

Time zones Ten countries (Australia, Brazil, Canada, Indonesia, Kazakhstan, Mexico, New Zealand, Russia, Spain, and the United States) and the island of Greenland observe more than one official time depending on the number of designated time zones within their boundaries. An illustration of time zones throughout the world and within countries can be seen in the Standard Time Zones of the World map included in the **Reference Maps** section of *The World Factbook.*

Tobacco use This entry measures the age standardized prevalence of tobacco use, whether smoked or smokeless or both, among persons 15 years and older for the total population, and separately for the male and female populations.

Total fertility rate This entry gives a figure for the average number of children that would be born per woman if all women lived to the end of their childbearing years and bore children according to a given fertility rate at each age. The total fertility rate (TFR) is a more direct measure of the level of fertility than the crude birth rate, since it refers to births per woman. This indicator shows the potential for population change in the country. A rate of two children per woman is considered the replacement rate for a population, resulting in relative stability in terms of total numbers. Rates above two children indicate populations growing in size and whose median age is declining. Higher rates may also indicate difficulties for families, in some situations, to feed and educate their children and for women to enter the labor force. Rates below two children indicate populations decreasing in size and growing older. Global fertility rates are in general decline and this trend is most pronounced in industrialized countries, especially Western Europe, where populations are projected to decline dramatically over the next 50 years.

Total renewable water resources This entry provides the long-term average water availability for a country measured in cubic meters per year of precipitation, recharged ground water, and surface inflows from surrounding countries. Total renewable water resources provides the water total available to a country but does not include water resource totals that have been reserved for upstream or downstream countries through international agreements. Note that these values are averages and do not accurately reflect the total available in any given year. Annual available resources can vary greatly due to short-term and long-term climatic and weather variations.

Total water withdrawal This entry provides the annual quantity of water in cubic meters withdrawn for municipal, industrial, and agricultural purposes. Municipal sector use refers to the annual quantity of water withdrawn primarily for direct use by the population through the public distribution network. Industrial sector use refers to the annual quantity of self-supplied water withdrawn for industrial purposes. Agricultural sector use refers to the annual quantity of self-supplied water withdrawn for irrigation, livestock, and aquaculture purposes.

Trafficking in persons Trafficking in persons is modern-day slavery, involving victims who are forced, defrauded, or coerced into labor or sexual exploitation. The International Labor Organization (ILO), the UN agency charged with addressing labor standards, employment, and social protection issues, estimated in 2016 that 24.9 million people worldwide were victims of forced labor, bonded labor, forced child labor, sexual servitude, and involuntary servitude. Human trafficking is a multi-dimensional threat, depriving people of their human rights and freedoms, risking global health, promoting social breakdown, inhibiting development by depriving countries of their human capital, and helping fuel the growth of organized crime. In 2000, the US Congress passed the Trafficking Victims Protection Act (TVPA), reauthorized several times (the latest in (2019), which provides tools for the US to combat trafficking in persons, both domestically and abroad. One of the law's key components is the creation of the US Department of State's annual *Trafficking in Persons Report*, which assesses the government response (i.e., the *current situation*) in some 150 countries with a significant number of victims trafficked across their borders who are recruited, harbored, transported, provided, or obtained for forced labor or sexual exploitation. Countries in the annual report are rated in three tiers, based on government efforts to combat trafficking. The countries identified in this entry are those listed in the annual *Trafficking in Persons Report* as 'Tier 2 Watch List' or 'Tier 3' based on the following *tier rating* definitions:

Tier 2 Watch List countries do not fully comply with the minimum standards for the elimination of trafficking but are making significant efforts to do so, and meet one of the following criteria:
1. they display high or significantly increasing number of victims,
2. they have failed to provide evidence of increasing efforts to combat trafficking in persons, or,
3. they have committed to take action over the next year.

Tier 3 countries neither satisfy the minimum standards for the elimination of trafficking nor demonstrate a significant effort to do so. Countries in this tier are subject to potential non-humanitarian and non-trade sanctions.

Transnational issues This category includes four entries - **Disputes - international, Refugees and internally displaced persons, Trafficking in persons**, and **Illicit drugs** - that deal with current issues going beyond national boundaries.

Transportation This category includes the entries dealing with the means for movement of people and goods.

Transportation - note This entry includes miscellaneous transportation information of significance not included elsewhere.

Unemployment rate This entry contains the percent of the labor force that is without jobs. Substantial underemployment might be noted.

Unemployment, youth ages 15-24 This entry gives the percent of the total labor force ages 15-24 unemployed during a specified year.

Union name This entry, which appears only in the European Union, Government category, provides the full name and abbreviation for the European Union.

Urbanization This entry provides two measures of the degree of urbanization of a population. The first, *urban population*, describes the percentage of the total population living in urban areas, as defined by the country. The second, *rate of urbanization*, describes the projected average rate of change of the size of the urban population over the given period of time. It is possible for a country with a 100% urban population to still display a change in the rate of urbanization (up or down). For example, a population of 100,000 that is 100% urban can change in size to 110,000 or 90,000 but remain 100% urban.

Additionally, the World entry includes a list of the *ten largest urban agglomerations*. An *urban agglomeration* is defined as comprising the city or town proper and also the suburban fringe or thickly settled territory lying outside of, but adjacent to, the boundaries of the city.

UTC (Coordinated Universal Time) See entry for Coordinated Universal Time.

Waste and recycling This entry provides the amount of municipal solid waste a country produces annually and the amount of that waste that is recycled. Municipal solid waste consists of everyday items that are used and thrown away, including product packaging, furniture, clothing, bottles, food scraps, newspapers, grass clippings, appliances, paint, and batteries. Municipal solid waste - often referred to as trash or garbage - comes from homes, schools, hospitals, and businesses. Recycling is the process of collecting and processing materials that would otherwise be thrown away as trash and turning them into new products. Recycling benefits both communities and the environment.

This entry includes three subfields: *annual amount of municipal solid waste generated* (tons), *annual amount of municipal solid waste recycled* (tons), and *percent of municipal solid waste recycled*.

Waterways This entry gives the total length of navigable rivers, canals, and other inland bodies of water.

Years All year references are for the calendar year (CY) unless indicated as fiscal year (FY). The calendar year is an accounting period of 12 months from 1 January to 31 December. The fiscal year is an accounting period of 12 months other than 1 January to 31 December.

THE HUMAN WORLD

POPULATION

World – 7,772,850,805 (2022 est.)

Most populous countries (in millions) (2022 est.)
1. China 1410.5
2. India 1389.6
3. US 337.3
4. Indonesia 277.3
5. Pakistan 242.9
6. Nigeria 225.1
7. Brazil 217.2
8. Bangladesh 165.7
9. Russia 142
10. Japan 124.2

Least populous countries (2022 est.)
1. Holy See (Vatican City) 1,000
2. Niue 2,000
3. Nauru 9,811
4. Tuvalu 11,544
5. Palau 21,695
6. Monaco 31,400
7. San Marino 34,682
8. Liechtenstein 39,711
9. Dominica 74,629
10. Marshall Islands 79,906

Most densely populated countries (population per sq km) (2022 est.)
1. Monaco 15,700
2. Singapore 8,352
3. Bahrain 2,027
4. Malta 1,469
5. Maldives 1,309
6. Bangladesh 1,273
7. Barbados 704
8. Mauritius 644
9. San Marino 569
10. South Korea 535

Least densely populated countries (population per sq km) (2022 est.)
1. Mongolia 2.1
2. Namibia 3.3
3. Australia 3.4
4. Iceland 3.6
5. Guyana 4
6. Mauritania 4
7. Libya 4.1
8. Suriname 4.1
9. Botswana 4.2
10. Canada 4.2

Largest urban agglomerations (in millions) (2020 est.)
1. Tokyo (Japan) 37.4
2. New Delhi (India) 30.3
3. Shanghai (China) 27.1
4. Sao Paulo (Brazil) 22.0
5. Mexico City (Mexico) 21.8
6. Dhaka (Bangladesh) 21.0
7. Cairo (Egypt) 20.9
8. Beijing (China) 20.5
9. Mumbai (India) 20.4
10. Osaka (Japan) 19.2

Highest population growth rate (2022 est.)
1. Syria 5.91%
2. South Sudan 4.91%
3. Niger 3.66%
4. Burundi 3.63%
5. Equatorial Guinea 3.5%
6. Angola 3.36%
7. Benin 3.34%
8. Uganda 3.27%
9. Democratic Republic of the Congo 3.14%
10. Chad 3.09%

Lowest population growth rate (2022 est.)
1. Moldova -1.12%
2. Latvia -1.11%
3. Romania -1.09%
4. Lithuania -1.04%
5. Serbia -0.75
6. Estonia -0.71%
7. Micronesia -0.67%
8. Bulgaria -0.67%
9. Ukraine -0.5
10. Croatia -0.47

Highest life expectancy at birth (2022 est.)
1. Monaco 89.5
2. Singapore 86.4
3. Japan 84.8
4. San Marino 83.9
5. Canada 83.8
6. Iceland 83.6
7. Andorra 83.4
8. Israel 83.4
9. Switzerland 83.2
10. Malta 83.2

Lowest life expectancy at birth (2022 est.)
1. Afghanistan 53.7
2. Central African Republic 55.5
3. Somalia 55.7
4. Mozambique 57.1
5. Sierra Leone 58.8
6. Chad 59.2
7. South Sudan 59.2
8. Lesotho 59.6
9. Eswatini 59.7
10. Niger 60.1

Highest total fertility rate (children per woman) (2022 est.)
1. Niger 6.82
2. Angola 5.83
3. Democratic Republic of Congo 5.63
4. Mali 5.54
5. Chad 5.46
6. Benin 5.43
7. Uganda 5.36
8. South Sudan 5.32
9. Somalia 5.31
10. Burundi 5.03

Lowest total fertility rate (children per woman) (2022 est.)
1. Taiwan 1.08
2. South Korea 1.1
3. Singapore 1.16
4. Macau 1.22
5. Italy 1.22
6. Hong Kong 1.22
7. Puerto Rico 1.24
8. Spain 1.27
9. Montserrat 1.32
10. Mauritius 1.35

Highest number of people living with HIV/AIDS (millions) (2020 est.)

1. South Africa 7.8
2. India 2.3
3. Mozambique 2.1
4. Nigeria 1.7
5. Tanzania 1.7
6. Zambia 1.5
7. Kenya 1.4
8. Uganda 1.4
9. Zimbabwe 1.3
10. Russia 1

Largest urban agglomerations (in millions) (2020 est.)

1. Tokyo (Japan) 37.4
2. New Delhi (India) 30.3
3. Shanghai (China) 27.1
4. Sao Paulo (Brazil) 22.0
5. Mexico City (Mexico) 21.8
6. Dhaka (Bangladesh) 21.0
7. Cairo (Egypt) 20.9
8. Beijing (China) 20.5
9. Mumbai (India) 20.4
10. Osaka (Japan) 19.2

LANGUAGES

Most spoken languages globally (2020 est.)

1. English 16.5%
2. Mandarin Chinese 14.6%
3. Hindi 8.3%
4. Spanish 7%
5. French 3.6%
6. Arabic 3.6%
7. Bengali 3.4%
8. Russian 3.4%
9. Portuguese 3.3%
10. Indonesia 2.6%

Most spoken first languages globally (2018 est.)

1. Mandarin Chinese 12.3%
2. Spanish 6%
3. English 5.1%
4. Arabic 5.1%
5. Hindi 3.5%
6. Bengali 3.3%
7. Portuguese 3%
8. Russian 2.1%
9. Japanese 1.7%

THE CONNECTED WORLD

AIRPORTS

Busiest Airports by Passengers (2022)

1. Hartsfield–Jackson Atlanta International Airport (ATL) 75,704,760
2. Dallas Fort Worth International Airport (DFW) 62,465,756
3. Denver International Airport (DEN) 58,828,552
4. O'Hare International Airport (ORD) 54,020,399
5. Los Angeles International Airport (LAX) 48,007,284
6. Charlotte Douglas International Airport (CLT) 43,302,230
7. Orlando International Airport (MCO) 40,351,068
8. Guangzhou Baiyun International Airport (CAN) 40,259,401
9. Chengdu Shuangliu International Airport (CTU) 40,117,496
10. Las Vegas McCarran International Airport (LAS) 39,754,366

Busiest Airports for Cargo (metric tons) (2022)

1. Hong Kong International Airport (HKG) 5,025,495
2. Memphis International Airport (MEM) 4,480,465
3. Shanghai Pudong International Airport (PVG) 3,982,616
4. Ted Stevens Anchorage International Airport (ANC) 3,555,160
5. Incheon International Airport (ICN) 3,329,292
6. Louisville Muhammad Ali International Airport (SDF) 3,052,269
7. Taiwan Taoyuan International Airport (TPE) 2,812,065
8. Los Angeles International Airport (LAX) 2,691,830
9. Doha Hamad International Airport (DOH) 2,620,095
10. Tokyo Narita International Airport (NRT) 2,644.074

RAILWAYS - ROADWAYS

Longest Railroad Networks (kilometers) (2022)

1. United States 250,000 km
2. China 124,000 km
3. Russia 85,500 km
4. India 65,000 km
5. Canada 48,000 km
6. Germany 41,000 km
7. Australia 40,000 km
8. Argentina 36,000 km
9. South Africa 31,000 km
10. France 29,000 km

Longest Road Networks (kilometers) (2022)

1. United States 6,803,479 km
2. India 6,371,847 km
3. China 5,918,000 km
4. Brazil 2,000,000 km
5. Russia 1,529,373 km
6. France 1,053,215 km
7. Canada 1,042,300
8. Australia 873,573 km
9. Mexico 817,576 km
10. South Africa 750,000 km

WATERWAYS

Total Waterways 2,293,412 (kilometers) (2017 est.)

Longest Waterways (rivers, canals, other navigable inland bodies of water).

1. Russia 317,505 km
2. Brazil 153,348 km
3. China 138,357
4. United States 40,230 km
5. Indonesia 21,579 km
6. India 20,175 km
7. Columbia 18,000 km
8. Vietnam 17,702 km
9. Democratic Republic of the Congo 15,000 km
10. Myanmar 12,800 km

MERCHANT MARINES

Total worldwide: 98,202 Fleet Strength (2022 est.)

Largest Merchant Marines

1. Indonesia 10,427
2. Panama 7,980
3. China 6,662
4. Japan 5,201
5. United States 3,627
6. Liberia 3,492
7. Singapore 3,321
8. Russia 2,873
9. Vietnam 1,926
10. South Korea 1,904

PORTS

Top Container Ports by Twenty-foot Equivalent Units Throughput (TEUs) (2020)

1. Shanghai (China) 43,500,000
2. Singapore (Singapore) 36,600,000
3. Ningbo-Zhoushan (China) 28,720,000
4. Shenzhen (China) 26,550,000
5. Guangzhou (China) 23,190,000
6. Qingdao (China) 22,000,000
7. Busan (South Korea) 21,590,000
8. Hong Kong (China) 20,070,000
9. Tianjin (China) 18,350,000
10. Rotterdam (Netherlands) 14,350,000

INTERNET

- Total Internet users worldwide – 4.9 billion (2022 est.)
- Percent of world population actively using the Internet – 69%
- Percent of the world population that have never used the Internet – 31%
- Total number of people worldwide that have never used the Internet or have access to it – 3.0 billion

Internet users by country (in millions) (2022)

1. China 1000
2. India 658
3. US 307.2
4. Indonesia 204.7
5. Brazil 165.3
6. Russia 129.8
7. Japan 118.3
8. Nigeria 109.2
9. Mexico 96.9
10. Germany 78

Broadband fixed subscriptions

Total worldwide – 1.23 billion

Subscriptions per 100 inhabitants – 17

AUTOMOBILE PRODUCTION BY COUNTRY

(2021 est.)

1. China 26.08 million vehicles
2. United States 9.17 million vehicles
3. Japan 7.85 million vehicles
4. India 4.40 million vehicles
5. South Korea 3.46 million vehicles
6. Germany 3.31 million vehicles
7. Mexico 3.15 million vehicles
8. Brazil 2.25 million vehicles
9. Spain 2.11 million vehicles
10. Thailand 1.69 million vehicles

SATELLITES BY COUNTRY

There are about 4,550 satellites in orbit (2022 est.)

1. US 2,804
2. China 467
3. United Kingdom 349
4. Russia 168
5. Japan 93

TELEPHONES

- Fixed lines – total subscriptions worldwide – 901,317,598 (2020 est.)
- Fixed lines – subscriptions per 100 inhabitants – 11 (2020 est.)
- Mobile cellular – total subscriptions 7.8 billion – (2020 est.)
- Mobile cellular – subscriptions per 100 inhabitants – 106 (2020 est.)

TELEPHONE SUBSCRIPTIONS

Fixed subscriptions (2020 est.)

1. China 181,908,000
2. United States 101,526,000
3. Japan 61,978,594
4. Germany 38,300,000
5. France 37,759,000
6. United Kingdom 32,037,000
7. Brazil 30,653,813
8. Iran 29,093,587
9. Russian Federation 25,892,405
10. Mexico 24,500,456

Mobile Cellular subscriptions (2020 est.)

1. China 1,718,411,000
2. India 1,153,709,832
3. Indonesia 355,620,388
4. United States 351,477,000
5. Russian Federation 238,733,217
6. Brazil 205,834,781
7. Nigeria 204,228,678
8. Japan 195,054,893
9. Bangladesh 176,279,465
10. Pakistan 175,624,364

SOCIAL MEDIA USAGE BY COUNTRY

Average daily social media usage of Internet users worldwide is 146 minutes (2021 est.)

1. Philippines 248 minutes
2. Brazil 226 minutes
3. Nigeria 222 minutes
4. Columbia 221 minutes
5. South Africa 217 minutes
6. Argentina 205 minutes
7. Mexico 205 minutes
8. Indonesia 200 minutes
9. Ghana 200 minutes
10. Saudi Arabia 196 minutes

THE ECONOMIC WORLD

NATIONAL ACCOUNTS

Largest Real GDP – Purchasing Power Parity Economies (in 2017 USD) (2020 est. unless noted)

1. China — $23.01 trillion
2. US — $19.85 trillion
3. India — $8.44 trillion
4. Japan — $5.22 trillion (2019 est.)
5. Germany — $4.24 trillion
6. Russia — $3.88 trillion
7. Indonesia — $3.13 trillion
8. Brazil — $2.99 trillion
9. France — $2.83 trillion
10. United Kingdom — $2.78 trillion

Highest Real GDP – PPP per capita Economies (in 2017 USD) (2020 est. unless noted)

1. Liechtenstein — $139,100
2. Monaco — $115,700 (2015 est.)
3. Luxembourg — $110,300
4. Singapore — $93,400
5. Ireland — $89,700
6. Qatar — $85,300
7. Isle of Man — $84,600 (2014 est.)
8. Bermuda — $81,800 (2019 est.)
9. Cayman Islands — $73,600 (2019 est.)
10. Falkland Islands — $70,800 (2015 est.)

Lowest Real GDP – PPP per capita Economies (in 2017 USD) (2020 est.)

1. Burundi — $700
2. Somalia — $800
3. Central African Republic — $900
4. Democratic Republic of the Congo — $1,100
5. Niger — $1,200
6. Mozambique — $1,200
7. Liberia — $1,400
8. Malawi — $1,500
9. Madagascar — $1,500
10. Chad — $1,500

ECONOMIC EQUITY

Most Equal Family Income Distribution Countries (using Gini Index coefficients) (2020 est. unless noted)

1. Slovakia — 23.2 (2019 est.)
2. Belarus — 24.4
3. Slovenia — 24.4 (2019 est.)
4. Armenia — 25.2
5. Czechia — 25.3 (2019 est.)
6. Ukraine — 25.6
7. Moldova — 26.0 (2019 est.)
8. United Arab Emirates — 26.0 (2018 est.)
9. Iceland — 26.1 (2017 est.)
10. Azerbaijan — 26.6 (2005 est.)

INTERNATIONAL TRADE

Global Trade Data

Agricultural Products (2020 est.)
Exports: 1.49 trillion
Imports: 1.54 trillion

Merchandise Trade: 46.3% of all trade (2021 est.)
Exports: 22.4 trillion
Imports: 22.6 trillion

Trade in Services: 11.8% of all trade (2021 est.)
Exports: 6.04 trillion
Imports: 5.56 trillion

Largest Exporting Economies (2021 est.)

1. China — $3.36 trillion
2. US — $1.75 trillion
3. Germany — $1.63 trillion
4. Japan — $757.07 billion
5. Netherlands — $693.80 billion

Largest Importing Economies (2021 est.)

1. US — $2.93 trillion
2. China — $2.68 trillion
3. Germany — $1.42 trillion
4. Japan — $772.28 billion
5. France — $714.84 billion

Largest Re-Exporting Economies (2021 est.)

1. US — $274.54 billion
2. United Arab Emirates — $123.63 billion
3. Canada — $39.26 billion
4. United Kingdom — $21.33 billion
5. Italy — $14.77 billion

Largest Re-Importing Economies (2021 est.)

1. China — $156.82 billion
2. Switzerland — $11.02 billion
3. Italy — $4.41 billion
4. United Kingdom — $4.35 billion
5. Canada — $3.73 billion

INFLATION (2021 EST.)

Highest Inflation Economies (2021 est. unless noted)

1. Sudan — 383%
2. Lebanon — 155%
3. Zimbabwe — 99%
4. Suriname — 59%
5. Iran — 31% (2020 est.)
6. Ethiopia — 27%
7. Zambia — 22%
8. Turkey — 20%
9. Nigeria — 17%
10. Haiti — 17%

LABOR

Global Labor Force Participation Rate (2021 est.): 59%

Largest Labor Forces (2021 est.)

1. China — 792.08 million
2. India — 471.30 million
3. US — 164.79 million
4. Indonesia — 139.16 million
5. Brazil — 99.43 million
6. Pakistan — 73.78 million
7. Russia — 71.77 million
8. Bangladesh — 69.82 million
9. Japan — 68.22 million
10. Nigeria — 64.48 million

Highest Labor Force Participation Rates (2021 est.)

1. Qatar — 87%
2. Solomon Islands — 85%
3. Madagascar — 85%

4. Zimbabwe 84%
5. Tanzania 83%
6. Rwanda 82%
7. North Korea 82%
8. Cambodia 80%
9. Nepal 80%
10. Ethiopia 78%

Lowest Labor Force Participation Rates (2021 est.)
1. Djibouti 31%
2. Somalia 34%
3. Yemen 37%
4. Jordan 38%
5. Moldova 39%

Highest Child Labor Force Participation Rates (2021 est.)
1. Ethiopia 45%
2. Burkina Faso 42%
3. Chad 39%
4. Cameroon 39%
5. Togo 39%

Lowest Female Labor Force Participation Rates (2021 est.)
1. Yemen 6%
2. Iraq 11%
3. Jordan 13%
4. Iran 14%
5. Afghanistan 15%

UNEMPLOYMENT

Global Unemployment Rate (2021 est.): 6.2%

Highest Unemployment Rates (2021 est.)
1. South Africa 37%
2. Djibouti 28%
3. Eswatini 26%
4. Gaza Strip/West Bank 25%
5. Botswana 25%

FINANCES & FISCAL HEALTH

Economies with Highest Central Government Debt (2020 est.)
1. Sudan 273% of GDP
2. Greece 226% of GDP
3. Japan 221% of GDP
4. Eritrea 185% of GDP
5. Cyprus 162% of GDP
6. Cape Verde 158% of GDP
7. Singapore 155% of GDP
8. Italy 151% of GDP
9. Lebanon 150% of GDP
10. Barbados 150% of GDP

Highest Credit Rating Economies (as of 2022 based on the top 3 debt auditing agencies)
- Australia
- Denmark
- Germany
- Luxembourg
- Netherlands
- Norway
- Singapore
- Sweden
- Switzerland

Economies with Lowest Central Government Debt (2020 est.)
1. Brunei 3% of GDP
2. Tuvalu 7% of GDP
3. Afghanistan 7% of GDP
4. Kuwait 12% of GDP
5. Switzerland 13% of GDP

Fastest Growing Economies by Annual Growth (2021 est.)
1. Libya 31%
2. Maldives 31%
3. Guyana 20%
4. Macau 18%
5. Panama 15%

PERSONAL REMITTANCES

Global Remittances (2020 est.): $653 billion (0.8% of all GDP)

Most Remittance-Dependent Economies (2020 est.)
1. Tonga 39.0% of GDP
2. Kyrgyzstan 31.1% of GDP
3. Tajikistan 26.9% of GDP
4. Lebanon 25.6% of GDP
5. Samoa 25.3% of GDP
6. Somalia 24.9% of GDP
7. Nepal 24.3% of GDP
8. El Salvador 24.1% of GDP
9. Haiti 23.8% of GDP
10. Honduras 23.5% of GDP

THE ENERGY WORLD

ELECTRICITY

Worldwide electricity access: 90% (2019 est.)
- **Urban areas:** 96% (2019 est.)
- **Rural areas:** 85% (2019 est.)

Largest installed generating capacities (in kW) (2020 est.)
1. China 2.22 billion
2. US 1.14 billion
3. India 432.77 million
4. Japan 348.67 million
5. Russia 276.46 million
6. Germany 248.27 million
7. Brazil 195.04 million
8. Canada 153.25 million
9. France 138.61 million
10. South Korea 135.79 million

Highest electricity consumers (in kWh) (2020 est.)
1. China 6.88 trillion
2. US 3.90 trillion
3. India 1.23 trillion
4. Russia 942.90 billion
5. Japan 903.70 billion

Largest electricity exporters (in kWh) (2020 est.)
1. Canada 67.20 billion
2. Germany 66.93 billion
3. France 64.43 billion
4. Sweden 36.82 billion
5. Switzerland 32.55 billion

Largest electricity importers (in kWh) (2020 est.)

1. US 61.45 billion
2. Germany 48.05 billion
3. Italy 39.79 billion
4. Thailand 29.55 billion
5. Switzerland 26.99 billion

ENERGY CONSUMPTION

Highest energy consumption per capita (in Btu/person) (2019 est.)

1. Qatar 723.58 million
2. Singapore 639.95 million
3. Bahrain 547.98 million
4. United Arab Emirates 471.79 million
5. Brunei 415.18 million
6. Canada 403.70 million
7. Kuwait 381.99 million
8. Norway 333.83 million
9. Turkmenistan 330.51 million
10. Luxembourg 310.07 million
11. US 304.41 million
12. Saudi Arabia 296.95 million
13. Oman 292.02 million
14. Malta 267.74 million
15. South Korea 242.35 million

CARBON DIOXIDE EMISSIONS

Worldwide CO_2 emissions: 35.55 billion metric tonnes (2019 est.)

Highest CO_2 emitters (in metric tonnes) (2019 est.)

1. China 10.77 billion
2. US 5.14 billion
3. India 2.31 billion
4. Russia 1.85 billion
5. Japan 1.10 billion
6. Germany 726.88 million
7. South Korea 686.95 million
8. Iran 646.04 million
9. Canada 612.08 million
10. Saudi Arabia 579.93 million
11. Indonesia 563.54 million
12. South Africa 470.36 million
13. Mexico 463.74 million
14. Brazil 456.67 million
15. Australia 417.87 million

Percent of CO_2 emissions from top 15 emitters: 75.4%

COAL

Largest proven coal reserves (in metric tons) (2019 est.)

1. US 228.66 billion
2. Russia 162.17 billion
3. Australia 149.08 billion
4. China 141.60 billion
5. India 105.93 billion
6. Indonesia 39.89 billion
7. Germany 35.90 billion
8. Ukraine 34.38 billion
9. Poland 26.93 billion
10. Kazakhstan 25.61 billion

Highest coal consumers (in metric tons) (2020 est.)

1. China 4.51 billion
2. India 883.98 million
3. US 441.97 million
4. Russia 266.04 million
5. Japan 210.88 million

Largest coal exporters (in metric tons) (2020 est.)

1. Indonesia 409.89 million
2. Australia 390.81 million
3. Russia 224.32 million
4. South Africa 74.97 million
5. Colombia 69.86 million

Largest coal importers (in metric tons) (2020 est.)

1. China 307.05 million
2. India 219.21 million
3. Japan 174.49 million
4. South Korea 123.78 million
5. Taiwan 63.52 million

PETROLEUM

Largest proven crude oil reserves (in barrels) (2021 est.)

1. Venezuela 303.81 billion
2. Saudi Arabia 258.60 billion
3. Iran 208.60 billion
4. Canada 170.30 billion
5. Iraq 145.02 billion
6. Kuwait 101.50 billion
7. United Arab Emirates 97.80 billion
8. Russia 80.00 billion
9. Libya 48.36 billion
10. US 47.11 billion

Highest refined petroleum consumers (in barrels/day) (2020 est.)

1. US 20.54 million
2. China 14.01 million
3. India 4.92 million
4. Japan 3.74 million
5. Russia 3.70 million

Largest crude oil exporters (in barrels/day) (2019 est.)

1. Saudi Arabia 7.34 million
2. Russia 5.20 million
3. Iraq 3.98 million
4. Canada 3.18 million
5. United Arab Emirates 2.43 million

Largest crude oil importers (in barrels/day) (2018 est.)

1. China 9.24 million
2. US 7.77 million
3. India 4.53 million
4. South Korea 3.03 million
5. Japan 3.01 million

NATURAL GAS

Largest proven natural gas reserves (in m^3) (2021 est.)

1. Russia 47.81 trillion
2. Iran 33.99 trillion
3. Qatar 23.86 trillion
4. US 13.18 trillion
5. Turkmenistan 11.33 trillion
6. Saudi Arabia 9.42 trillion
7. China 6.65 trillion
8. United Arab Emirates 6.09 trillion
9. Nigeria 5.76 trillion
10. Venezuela 5.67 trillion

Highest natural gas consumers (in m^3) (2021 est.)

1. US 857.54 billion
2. Russia 460.61 billion
3. China 306.58 billion
4. Iran 220.70 billion
5. Canada 124.50 billion

Largest natural gas exporters (in m³) (2021 est.)

1. Russia 250.85 billion
2. US 188.40 billion
3. Qatar 126.75 billion
4. Norway 107.34 billion
5. Australia 101.77 billion

Largest natural gas importers (in m³) (2020 est.)

1. China 131.61 billion
2. Japan 105.26 billion
3. Germany 83.12 billion
4. US 79.51 billion
5. Italy 70.91 billion

THE PHYSICAL WORLD

- **Dimensions of Planet Earth**
  - Surface Area – 510.072 million sq km
  - Land surface – 148.94 million sq km (29.1% of Earth's surface)
  - Water surface – 361.9 million sq km (70.9% of Earth's surface)
  - Equatorial circumference – 40,075 km
  - Polar circumference – 40,008 km
  - Equatorial diameter – 12,756 km
  - Polar diameter – 12,714 km
  - Mean elevation – 840 m
- **Earth Superlatives**
  - Greatest tidal range – 16.3 m Bay of Fundy, Canada
  - Deepest gorge – 4,360 m Colca river, Peru
  - Longest gorge – 350 km Grand Canyon, US
  - Deepest lake – 1,742 m Lake Baikal, Russia
  - Highest navigable lake – 3,810 m Lake Titicaca, Peru/Bolivia
  - Longest cave system – 650 km Mammoth Cave, US
  - Longest glacier – 515 km Lambert-Fisher Ice Passage, Antarctica
  - Deepest depression – -403 m Dead Sea, Israel/Jordan
  - Highest point: Mount Everest 8,849 m
  - Lowest point:
    - Land – Denman Glacier (Antarctica) more than -3,500 m
    - Ocean – Challenger Deep – 10,924 m, Mariana Trench, (Pacific Ocean)
- **Seven Continental Landmasses**
  - Asia 44,568,500 sq km;
  - Africa 30,065,000 sq km;
  - North America 24,473,000 sq km;
  - South America 17,819,000 sq km;
  - Antarctica 14,200,000 sq km;
  - Europe 9,948,000 sq km;
  - Australia 7,741,220 sq km
- **Ten Largest Islands**
  1. Greenland 2,166,086 sq km;
  2. New Guinea (Indonesia, Papua New Guinea) 785,753 sq km;
  3. Borneo (Brunei, Indonesia, Malaysia) 751,929 sq km;
  4. Madagascar 587,713 sq km;
  5. Baffin Island (Canada) 507,451 sq km;
  6. Sumatra (Indonesia) 472,784 sq km;
  7. Honshu (Japan) 227,963 sq km;
  8. Victoria Island (Canada) 217,291 sq km;
  9. Great Britain (United Kingdom) 209,331 sq km;
  10. Ellesmere Island (Canada) 196,236 sq km

CLIMATE

Five Driest Places on Earth (Average Annual Precipitation)

1. McMurdo Dry Valleys, Antarctica 0 mm (0 in)
2. Arica, Chile 0.76 mm (0.03 in)
3. Al Kufrah, Libya 0.86 mm (0.03 in)
4. Aswan, Egypt 0.86 mm (0.03 in)
5. Luxor, Egypt 0.86 mm (0.03 in)

Five Wettest Places on Earth (Average Annual Precipitation)

1. Mawsynram, India 11,871 mm (467.4 in)
2. Cherrapunji, India 11,777 mm (463.7 in)
3. Tutunendo, Colombia 11,770 mm (463.4 in)
4. Cropp River, New Zealand 11,516 mm (453.4 in)
5. San Antonia de Ureca, Equatorial Guinea 10,450 mm (411.4 in)

Five Coldest Places on Earth (Lowest Average Monthly Temperature)

1. Verkhoyansk, Russia (Siberia) -47°C (-53°F) January
2. Oymyakon, Russia (Siberia) -46°C (-52°F) January
3. Eureka, Canada -38.4°C (-37.1°F) February
4. Isachsen, Canada -36°C (-32.8°F) February
5. Alert, Canada -34°C (-28°F) February

Five Hottest Places on Earth (Highest Average Monthly Temperature)

1. Death Valley, US (California) 39°C (101°F) July
2. Iranshahr, Iran 38.3°C (100.9°F) June
3. Ouallene, Algeria 38°C (100.4°F) July
4. Kuwait City, Kuwait 37.7°C (100°F) July
5. Medina, Saudi Arabia 36°C (97°F) July

TERRAIN

Highest point on each continent

Asia - Mount Everest (China-Nepal) 8,849 m;
South America - Cerro Aconcagua (Argentina) 6,960 m;
North America - Denali (Mount McKinley) (United States) 6,190 m;
Africa - Kilimanjaro (Tanzania) 5,895 m;
Europe - El'brus (Russia) 5,633 m;
Antarctica - Vinson Massif 4,897 m;
Australia - Mount Kosciuszko 2,229 m

Lowest point on each continent

Antarctica - Denman Glacier more than -3,500 m;
Asia - Dead Sea (Israel-Jordan) -431 m;
Africa - Lac Assal (Djibouti) -155 m;
South America - Laguna del Carbon (Argentina) -105 m;
North America - Death Valley (United States) -86 m;
Europe - Caspian Sea (Azerbaijan-Kazakhstan-Russia) -28 m;
Australia - Lake Eyre -15 m

Ten Largest Natural Lakes:

1. Caspian Sea (Azerbaijan, Iran, Kazakhstan, Russia, Turkmenistan) 374,000 sq km;
2. Lake Superior (Canada, United States) 82,100 sq km;
3. Lake Victoria (Kenya, Tanzania, Uganda) 62,940 sq km;
4. Lake Huron (Canada, United States) 59,600 sq km;
5. Lake Michigan (United States) 57,750 sq km;
6. Lake Tanganyika (Burundi, Democratic Republic of the Congo, Tanzania, Zambia) 32,000 sq km;
7. Great Bear Lake (Canada) 31,328 sq km;
8. Lake Baikal (Russia) 31,500 sq km;
9. Lake Malawi (Malawi, Mozambique, Tanzania) 22,490 sq km;
10. Great Slave Lake (Canada) 28,568 sq km

Ten Longest Rivers:

1. Nile (Africa) 6,650 km;
2. Amazon (South America) 6,436 km;
3. Yangtze (Asia) 6,300 km;
4. Mississippi-Missouri (North America) 6,275 km;
5. Yenisey-Angara (Asia) 5,539 km;
6. Huang He/Yellow (Asia) 5,464 km;
7. Ob-Irtysh (Asia) 5,410 km;
8. Congo (Africa) 4,700 km;
9. Amur (Asia) 4,444 km;
10. Lena (Asia) 4,400 km

FIVE OCEANS OF THE WORLD

Area (% of total World Ocean area)

Pacific – 168,723,000 sq km (46.6%)
Atlantic – 85,133,000 sq km (23.5%)
Indian – 70,560,000 sq km (19.5%)
Southern – 21,960,000 sq km (6.1%)
Arctic – 15,558,000 sq km (4.3%)

Volume (% of total World Ocean volume)

Pacific – 669,880,000 cu km (50.1%)
Atlantic – 310,410,000 cu km (23.3%)
Indian – 264,000,000 cu km (19.8%)
Southern – 71,800,000 cu km (5.4%)
Arctic – 18,750,000 cu km (1.4%)

Average Depth

Pacific – 4,080 m
Indian – 3,741 m
Atlantic – 3,646 m
Southern – 3,270 m
Arctic – 1,205 m

Deepest Points

Pacific – Mariana Trench -10,924 m Challenger Deep
Indian – Java Trench -7,192 m unnamed deep
Atlantic – Puerto Rico Trench -8,605 m unnamed deep
Southern – South Sandwich Trench -7,434 m unnamed deep
Arctic – Molloy Deep -5,577 m

AFGHANISTAN

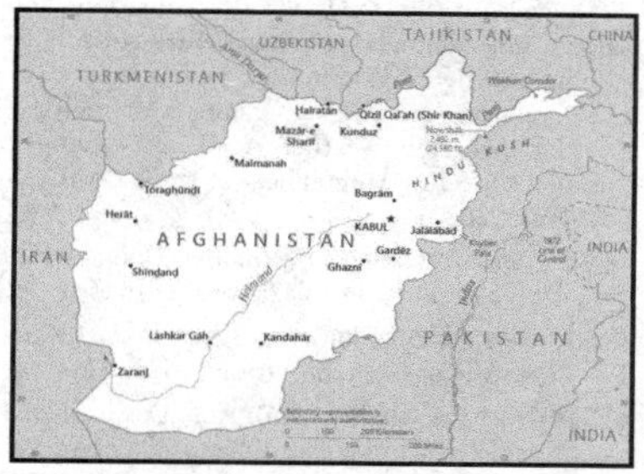

INTRODUCTION

Background: Ahmad Shah DURRANI unified the Pashtun tribes and founded Afghanistan in 1747. The country served as a buffer between the British and Russian Empires until it won independence from notional British control in 1919. A brief experiment in increased democracy ended in a 1973 coup and a 1978 communist countercoup. The Soviet Union invaded in 1979 to support the tottering Afghan communist regime, touching off a long and destructive war. The USSR withdrew in 1989 under relentless pressure by internationally supported anti-communist mujahidin rebels. A series of subsequent civil wars saw Kabul finally fall in 1996 to the Taliban, a hardline Pakistani-sponsored movement that emerged in 1994 to end the country's civil war and anarchy. Following the 11 September 2001 terrorist attacks, a US, Allied, and anti-Taliban Northern Alliance military action toppled the Taliban for sheltering Usama BIN LADIN.

A UN-sponsored Bonn Conference in 2001 established a process for political reconstruction that included the adoption of a new constitution, a presidential election in 2004, and National Assembly elections in 2005. In December 2004, Hamid KARZAI became the first democratically elected president of Afghanistan and was reelected in August 2009. In February 2020, the US and the Taliban signed the "US-Taliban Agreement," which contained commitments by the US related to the withdrawal from Afghanistan of military forces of the US, its allies, and Coalition partners, as well as commitments by the Taliban related to counterterrorism, among other topics. Following a US drawdown of virtually all of its troops, a summer 2021 Taliban offensive quickly overran the country and the Taliban took over Kabul in August of 2021.

GEOGRAPHY

Location: Southern Asia, north and west of Pakistan, east of Iran

Geographic coordinates: 33 00 N, 65 00 E

Map references: Asia

Area: *total:* 652,230 sq km
land: 652,230 sq km
water: 0 sq km
country comparison to the world: 43

Area - comparative: almost six times the size of Virginia; slightly smaller than Texas

Land boundaries: *total:* 5,987 km
border countries (6): China 91 km; Iran 921 km; Pakistan 2,670 km; Tajikistan 1,357 km; Turkmenistan 804 km; Uzbekistan 144 km

Coastline: 0 km (landlocked)

Maritime claims: none (landlocked)

Climate: arid to semiarid; cold winters and hot summers

Terrain: mostly rugged mountains; plains in north and southwest

Elevation: *highest point:* Noshak 7,492 m
lowest point: Amu Darya 258 m
mean elevation: 1,884 m

Natural resources: natural gas, petroleum, coal, copper, chromite, talc, barites, sulfur, lead, zinc, iron ore, salt, precious and semiprecious stones, arable land

Land use: *agricultural land:* 58.1% (2018 est.)
arable land: 11.8% (2018)
permanent crops: 0.3% (2018)
permanent pasture: 46% (2018)
forest: 1.8% (2018 est.)
other: 40.1% (2018)

Irrigated land: 32,080 sq km (2012)

Major lakes (area sq km): *salt water lake(s):* Ab-e Istadah-ye Muqur (endorheic basin) - 520 sq km

Major rivers (by length in km): Amu Darya (shared with Tajikistan [s], Turkmenistan, and Uzbekistan [m]) - 2,620 km; Helmand river source (shared with Iran) - 1,130 km

note – [s] after country name indicates river source; [m] after country name indicates river mouth

Major watersheds (area sq km):

Indian Ocean drainage: Indus (1,081,718 sq km)

Internal *(endorheic basin)* drainage: Amu Darya (534,739 sq km); Tarim Basin (1,152,448 sq km)

Population distribution: populations tend to cluster in the foothills and periphery of the rugged Hindu Kush range; smaller groups are found in many of the country's interior valleys; in general, the east is more densely settled, while the south is sparsely populated

Natural hazards: damaging earthquakes occur in Hindu Kush mountains; flooding; droughts

Geography - note: landlocked; the Hindu Kush mountains that run northeast to southwest divide the northern provinces from the rest of the country; the highest peaks are in the northern Vakhan (Wakhan Corridor)

PEOPLE AND SOCIETY

Population: 38,346,720 (2022 est.)
country comparison to the world: 37

Nationality: *noun:* Afghan(s)
adjective: Afghan

Ethnic groups: Current, reliable statistical data on ethnicity in Afghanistan are not available; Afghanistan's 2004 Constitution cited Pashtun, Tajik, Hazara, Uzbek, Turkman, Baluch, Pachaie, Nuristani, Aymaq, Arab, Qirghiz, Qizilbash, Gujur, and Brahwui ethnicities; Afghanistan has dozens of other small ethnic groups

Languages: Afghan Persian or Dari (official, lingua franca) 77%, Pashto (official) 48%, Uzbeki 11%, English 6%, Turkmani 3%, Urdu 3%, Pachaie 1%, Nuristani 1%, Arabic 1%, Balochi 1%, other <1% (2020 est.)
major-language sample(s):
کتاب حقایق جهان، مرجعی ضروری برای اطلاعات اولیه (Dari)
د دنیا د حقائېقو کتاب، بنیادی معلوماتو لپاره ضروری سرچینه- (Pashto)
note 1: percentages sum to more than 100% because many people are multilingual
note 2: Uzbeki, Turkmani, Pachaie, Nuristani, Balochi, and Pamiri are the third official languages in areas where the majority speaks them

Religions: Muslim 99.7% (Sunni 84.7 - 89.7%, Shia 10 - 15%), other <0.3% (2009 est.)

Age structure: *0-14 years:* 40.62% (male 7,562,703/female 7,321,646)
15-24 years: 21.26% (male 3,960,044/female 3,828,670)
25-54 years: 31.44% (male 5,858,675/female 5,661,887)
55-64 years: 4.01% (male 724,597/female 744,910)
65 years and over: 2.68% (male 451,852/female 528,831) (2020 est.)

Dependency ratios: *total dependency ratio:* 88.8
youth dependency ratio: 75.3
elderly dependency ratio: 4.8
potential support ratio: 21 (2020 est.)

Median age: *total:* 19.5 years
male: 19.4 years
female: 19.5 years (2020 est.)
country comparison to the world: 201

Population growth rate: 2.3% (2022 est.)
country comparison to the world: 32

Birth rate: 35.46 births/1,000 population (2022 est.)
country comparison to the world: 15

Death rate: 12.33 deaths/1,000 population (2022 est.)
country comparison to the world: 13

Net migration rate: -0.1 migrant(s)/1,000 population (2022 est.)
country comparison to the world: 103

Population distribution: populations tend to cluster in the foothills and periphery of the rugged Hindu Kush range; smaller groups are found in many of the country's interior valleys; in general, the east is more densely settled, while the south is sparsely populated

Urbanization: *urban population:* 26.6% of total population (2022)
rate of urbanization: 3.34% annual rate of change (2020-25 est.)

Major urban areas - population: 4.458 million KABUL (capital) (2022)

Sex ratio: *at birth:* 1.05 male(s)/female
0-14 years: 1.03 male(s)/female
15-24 years: 1.03 male(s)/female
25-54 years: 1.03 male(s)/female
55-64 years: 0.97 male(s)/female
65 years and over: 0.7 male(s)/female
total population: 1.03 male(s)/female (2022 est.)

Mother's mean age at first birth: 19.9 years (2015 est.)
note: data represents median age at first birth among women 25-49

Maternal mortality ratio: 638 deaths/100,000 live births (2017 est.)

country comparison to the world: 11

Infant mortality rate: *total:* 104.89 deaths/1,000 live births
male: 113.33 deaths/1,000 live births
female: 96.03 deaths/1,000 live births (2022 est.)
country comparison to the world: 1

Life expectancy at birth: *total population:* 53.65 years
male: 52.1 years
female: 55.28 years (2022 est.)
country comparison to the world: 227

Total fertility rate: 4.62 children born/woman (2022 est.)
country comparison to the world: 15

Contraceptive prevalence rate: 18.9% (2018)
note: percent of women aged 12-49

Drinking water source: *improved: urban:* 100% of population
rural: 68.3% of population
total: 76.5% of population
unimproved: urban: 0% of population
rural: 31.7% of population
total: 23.5% of population (2020 est.)

Current health expenditure: 13.2% of GDP (2019)

Physicians density: 0.25 physicians/1,000 population (2020)

Hospital bed density: 0.4 beds/1,000 population (2017)

Sanitation facility access: *improved: urban:* 88.2% of population
rural: 52% of population
total: 61.4% of population
unimproved: urban: 11.8% of population
rural: 48% of population
total: 38.6% of population (2020 est.)

HIV/AIDS - adult prevalence rate: (2020 est.) <.1%

Major infectious diseases: *degree of risk:* intermediate (2020)
food or waterborne diseases: bacterial diarrhea, hepatitis A, and typhoid fever
vectorborne diseases: Crimea-Congo hemorrhagic fever, malaria
note: Afghanistan is one of two countries with endemic wild polio virus (the other is Pakistan) and considered high risk for international spread of the disease; before any international travel, anyone unvaccinated, incompletely vaccinated, or with an unknown polio vaccination status should complete the routine polio vaccine series; before travel to any high-risk destination, the US Centers for Disease Control and Prevention (CDC) recommends that adults who previously completed the full, routine polio vaccine series receive a single, lifetime booster dose of polio vaccine

Obesity - adult prevalence rate: 5.5% (2016)
country comparison to the world: 176

Alcohol consumption per capita: *total:* 0.01 liters of pure alcohol (2019 est.)
beer: 0 liters of pure alcohol (2019 est.)
wine: 0 liters of pure alcohol (2019 est.)
spirits: 0.01 liters of pure alcohol (2019 est.)
other alcohols: 0 liters of pure alcohol (2019 est.)
country comparison to the world: 183

Tobacco use: *total:* 23.3% (2020 est.)
male: 39.4% (2020 est.)
female: 7.2% (2020 est.)
country comparison to the world: 62

Children under the age of 5 years underweight: 19.1% (2018)
country comparison to the world: 22

Child marriage: *women married by age 15:* 4.2%
women married by age 18: 28.3% (2017 est.)

Education expenditures: 3.2% of GDP (2019 est.)
country comparison to the world: 138

Literacy: *definition:* age 15 and over can read and write
total population: 37.3%
male: 52.1%
female: 22.6% (2021)

School life expectancy (primary to tertiary education): *total:* 10 years
male: 13 years
female: 8 years (2018)

Unemployment, youth ages 15-24: *total:* 16.2%
male: 14.5%
female: 21.1% (2020)

ENVIRONMENT

Environment - current issues: limited natural freshwater resources; inadequate supplies of potable water; soil degradation; overgrazing; deforestation (much of the remaining forests are being cut down for fuel and building materials); desertification; air and water pollution in overcrowded urban areas

Environment - international agreements: *party to:* Biodiversity, Climate Change, Climate Change-Kyoto Protocol, Climate Change-Paris Agreement, Comprehensive Nuclear Test Ban, Desertification, Endangered Species, Environmental Modification, Hazardous Wastes, Marine Dumping-London Convention, Nuclear Test Ban, Ozone Layer Protection
signed, but not ratified: Law of the Sea, Marine Life Conservation

Air pollutants: *particulate matter emissions:* 53.17 micrograms per cubic meter (2016 est.)
carbon dioxide emissions: 8.67 megatons (2016 est.)
methane emissions: 90.98 megatons (2020 est.)

Climate: arid to semiarid; cold winters and hot summers

Land use: *agricultural land:* 58.1% (2018 est.)
arable land: 11.8% (2018)
permanent crops: 0.3% (2018)
permanent pasture: 46% (2018)
forest: 1.8% (2018 est.)
other: 40.1% (2018)

Urbanization: *urban population:* 26.6% of total population (2022)
rate of urbanization: 3.34% annual rate of change (2020-25 est.)

Revenue from forest resources: *forest revenues:* 0.2% of GDP (2018 est.)
country comparison to the world: 93

Revenue from coal: *coal revenues:* 0.45% of GDP (2018 est.)
country comparison to the world: 12

Food insecurity: *severe localized food insecurity: due to civil conflict, population displacement, and economic slowdown* - between November 2021 and March 2022, during the winter lean season, the food insecurity situation was expected to deteriorate and the number of people in "Crisis" or above was likely to increase to 22.8 million, about 35% more than during the same season in 2020/21; following the developments of August 2021 in the country, the international aid flows, an important element of public spending, were halted; the food security situation and agricultural livelihoods in the country is likely to significantly deteriorate in the coming months due to cumulative and cascading impact of multiple shocks, including weather, conflict, economic crisis and the lingering effects of the COVID-19 pandemic (2022)

Waste and recycling: *municipal solid waste generated annually:* 5,628,525 tons (2016 est.)

Major lakes (area sq km): *salt water lake(s):* Ab-e Istadah-ye Muqur (endorheic basin) - 520 sq km

Major rivers (by length in km): Amu Darya (shared with Tajikistan [s], Turkmenistan, and Uzbekistan [m]) - 2,620 km; Helmand river source (shared with Iran) - 1,130 km
note – [s] after country name indicates river source; [m] after country name indicates river mouth

Major watersheds (area sq km):

Indian Ocean drainage: Indus (1,081,718 sq km)

Internal *(endorheic basin)* drainage: Amu Darya (534,739 sq km); Tarim Basin (1,152,448 sq km)

Total water withdrawal: *municipal:* 203.4 million cubic meters (2017 est.)
industrial: 169.5 million cubic meters (2017 est.)
agricultural: 20 billion cubic meters (2017 est.)

Total renewable water resources: 65.33 billion cubic meters (2017 est.)

GOVERNMENT

Country name: *conventional long form:* formerly Islamic Republic of Afghanistan
conventional short form: Afghanistan
local long form: formerly Jamhuri-ye Islami-ye Afghanistan
local short form: Afghanistan
former: Islamic Republic of Afghanistan
etymology: the name "Afghan" originally referred to the Pashtun people (today it is understood to include all the country's ethnic groups), while the suffix "-stan" means "place of" or "country"; so Afghanistan literally means the "Land of the Afghans"

Government type: the United States does not recognize the Taliban government

Capital: *name:* Kabul
geographic coordinates: 34 31 N, 69 11 E
time difference: UTC+4.5 (9.5 hours ahead of Washington, DC, during Standard Time)
daylight saving time: does not observe daylight savings time
etymology: named for the Kabul River, but the river's name is of unknown origin

Administrative divisions: 34 provinces (welayat, singular - welayat); Badakhshan, Badghis, Baghlan, Balkh, Bamyan, Daykundi, Farah, Faryab, Ghazni, Ghor, Helmand, Herat, Jowzjan, Kabul, Kandahar, Kapisa, Khost, Kunar, Kunduz, Laghman, Logar, Nangarhar, Nimroz, Nuristan, Paktika, Paktiya, Panjshir, Parwan, Samangan, Sar-e Pul, Takhar, Uruzgan, Wardak, Zabul

Independence: 19 August 1919 (from UK control over Afghan foreign affairs)

National holiday: Independence Day, 19 August (1919)

Constitution: *history:* last ratified in 2004
amendments: formerly proposed by a commission formed by presidential decree followed by the convention of a Grand Council (Loya Jirga) decreed by the president; passage requires at least two-thirds majority vote of the Loya Jirga membership and endorsement by the president

Legal system: before the Taliban's takeover of Kabul in August 2021, Afghanistan had a mixed legal system of civil, customary, and Islamic (sharia) law; after August 2021, the Taliban's so-called "interim government" has claimed to be implementing its own interpretation of Islamic law, partially based on the Hanafi school of Islamic jurisprudence.
(2021)

International law organization participation: has not submitted an ICJ jurisdiction declaration; formerly accepted ICCt jurisdiction

Citizenship: *citizenship by birth:* no
citizenship by descent only: at least one parent must have been born in - and continuously lived in - Afghanistan
dual citizenship recognized: no
residency requirement for naturalization: 5 years

Suffrage: 18 years of age; universal

Executive branch: *chief of state:* president (vacant); note – before 15 August, 2021, the president was both chief of state and head of government; President Ashraf GHANI departed the country on 15 August 2021; on 7 September 2021, the Taliban announced Mullah Mohammad HASSAN Akhund as the so-called "acting Prime Minister" of a so-called "interim government"; as of November 2021, the group had announced three acting so-called "Deputy Prime Ministers": Mullah Abdul Ghani BERADER, Mullah Abdul Salam HANAFI, and Maulawi Abdul KABIR
head of government: president (vacant); note - President Ashraf GHANI departed the country on 15 August 2021; on 7 September 2021, the Taliban announced Mullah Mohammad HASSAN Akhund as the acting Prime Minister of an interim Taliban government; the US does not recognize the Taliban government; as of November 2021, the group had announced three acting Deputy Prime Ministers: Mullah Abdul Ghani BERADER, Mullah Abdul Salam HANAFI, and Maulawi Abdul KABIR
cabinet: before 15 August 2021, the cabinet formerly consisted of 25 ministers appointed by the president, approved by the National Assembly; the Taliban have announced a so-called "cabinet" which includes 33 ministries
elections/appointments: the 2004 Afghan constitution directed that the president should be elected by majority popular vote for a 5-year term (eligible for a second term); election last held on 28 September 2019
election results: no elections have been held since 2019; in that election, Ashraf GHANI was declared winner by the Independent Election Commission on 18 February 2020; the IEC declared Ashraf GHANI the winner with 50.6% of the vote, Abdullah ABDULLAH, Dr. 39.5%, other 0.9%

Legislative branch: *description:* before 15 August, 2021, Afghanistan had a bicameral National Assembly that consisted of a House of Elders and a House of People; since August 15, the Taliban's so-called "interim government" has not purported to announce the formation of a legislative branch
elections: before 15 August, 2021: House of Elders - district councils - held within 5 days of installation; provincial councils - within 15 days of installation; and presidential appointees - within 2 weeks after the presidential inauguration; note - in early 2016, former President Ashraf Ghani extended their mandate until parliamentary and district elections could be held; former House of People - last held on 20 October 2018
election results: before 15 August 2021, House of Elders - percent of vote by party - NA; seats by party - NA; composition - men 85, women 17, percent of women 16.7% before 15 August 2021, House of People - percent of vote by party NA; seats by party - NA; composition - men 179, women 69, percent of women 27.7%; note - total National Assembly percent of women 24.4%

Judicial branch: *highest court(s):* the Taliban's so-called "interim government" has a "Supreme Court" (consisting of a supreme court chief and an unknown number of justices); before 15 August, 2021, Afghanistan had a Supreme Court (consisting of a supreme court chief and 8 justices organized into criminal, public security, civil, and commercial divisions)
judge selection and term of office: the court chief and justices were appointed by the president with the approval of the Wolesi Jirga; court chief and justices served single 10-year terms
subordinate courts: before 15 August 2021, consisted of Appeals Courts; Primary Courts; and Special Courts for issues including narcotics, security, property, family, and juveniles

Political parties and leaders: the Taliban's so-called "interim government" includes mostly Taliban members and not other political parties; before 15 August, 2021, the Ministry of Justice had licensed 72 political parties as of April 2019

International organization participation: before 15 August, 2021, Afghanistan was a member or participant in the following organizations: ADB, CICA, CP, ECO, EITI (candidate country), FAO, G-77, IAEA, IBRD, ICAO, ICC (NGOs), ICCt, ICRM, IDA, IDB, IFAD, IFC, IFRCS, ILO, IMF, Interpol, IOC, IOM, IPU, ISO (correspondent), ITSO, ITU, ITUC (NGOs), MIGA, NAM, OIC, OPCW, OSCE (partner), SAARC, SACEP, SCO (dialogue member), UN, UNAMA, UNCTAD, UNESCO, UNHCR, UNIDO, UNWTO, UPU, WCO, WFTU (NGOs), WHO, WIPO, WMO, WTO

Diplomatic representation in the US: *chief of mission:* the Afghan Embassy closed in March 2022
chancery: 2341 Wyoming Avenue NW, Washington, DC 20008
telephone: [1] (202) 483-6410
FAX: [1] (202) 483-6488
email address and website:
info@afghanembassy.us
https://www.afghanembassy.us/

Diplomatic representation from the US: *chief of mission:* Ambassador (vacant); Charge d'Affaires: Ian McCARY (since August 2021); note – since 15 August 2021, the United States has not yet made a decision whether to recognize the Taliban or any other entity as the Government of Afghanistan
embassy: Embassy Kabul, operations have been suspended; Department of State's Afghanistan Affairs Unit operates from Doha, Qatar.

Flag description: three equal vertical bands of black (hoist side), red, and green, with the national emblem in white centered on the red band and slightly overlapping the other 2 bands; the center of the emblem features a mosque with pulpit and flags on either side, below the mosque are Eastern Arabic numerals for the solar year 1298 (1919 in the Gregorian calendar, the year of Afghan independence from the UK); this central image is circled by a border consisting of sheaves of wheat on the left and right, in the upper-center is an Arabic inscription of the Shahada (Muslim creed) below which are rays of the rising sun over the Takbir (Arabic expression meaning "God is great"), and at bottom center is a scroll bearing the name Afghanistan; black signifies the past, red is for the blood shed for independence, and green can represent either hope for the future, agricultural prosperity, or Islam
note 1: the United States has not recognized the Taliban or any other entity as the government of Afghanistan and, accordingly, continues to display the flag of Afghanistan as set forth in the country's constitution of 2004
note 2: Afghanistan had more changes to its national flag in the 20th century - 19 by one count - than any other country; the colors black, red, and green appeared on most of them

National symbol(s): lion; national colors: red, green, black

National anthem: *name:* "Milli Surood" (National Anthem)
lyrics/music: Abdul Bari JAHANI/Babrak WASA
note: adopted 2006

National heritage: *total World Heritage Sites:* 2 (both cultural)
selected World Heritage Site locales: Minaret of Jam; Buddhas of Bamyan
note: the monumental 6th- and 7th-century statues were destroyed by the Taliban in 2001

ECONOMY

Economic overview: Prior to 2001, Afghanistan was an extremely poor, landlocked, and foreign aid-dependent country. Increased domestic economic activity occurred following the US-led invasion, as well as significant international economic development assistance. This increased activity expanded access to water, electricity, sanitation, education, and health services, and fostered consistent growth in government revenues since 2014. While international security forces have been drawing down since 2012, with much higher U.S. forces' drawdowns occurring since 2017, economic progress continues, albeit uneven across sectors and key economic indicators. After recovering from the 2018 drought and growing 3.9% in 2019, political instability, expiring international financial commitments, and the COVID-19 pandemic have wrought significant adversity on the Afghan economy, with a projected 5% contraction.

Current political parties' power-sharing agreement following the September 2019 presidential elections as well as ongoing Taliban attacks and peace talks have led to Afghan economic instability. This instability, coupled with expiring international grant and assistance, endangers recent fiscal gains and has led to more internally displaced persons. In November 2020, Afghanistan secured $12 billion in additional international aid for 2021-2025, much of which is conditional upon Taliban peace progress.

Additionally, Afghanistan continues to experience influxes of repatriating Afghanis, mostly from Iran, significantly straining economic and security institutions.

Afghanistan's trade deficit remains at approximately 31% of GDP and is highly dependent on financing through grants and aid. While Afghan agricultural growth remains consistent, recent industrial and services growth have been enormously impacted by COVID-19 lockdowns and trade cessations. While trade with the People's Republic of China has rapidly expanded in recent years, Afghanistan still relies heavily upon India and Pakistan as export partners but is more diverse in its import partners. Furthermore, Afghanistan still struggles to effectively enforce business contracts, facilitate easy tax collection, and enable greater international trade for domestic enterprises.

Current Afghan priorities focus on the following goals:

— Securing international economic agreements, many of which are contingent on Taliban peace progress;
— Increasing exports to $2 billion USD by 2023;
— Continuing to expand government revenue collection;
— Countering corruption and navigating challenges from the power-sharing agreement; and
— Developing a strong private sector that can empower the economy.

Real GDP (purchasing power parity): $77.04 billion (2020 est.)
$78.56 billion (2019 est.)
$75.6 billion (2018 est.)
note: data are in 2017 dollars
country comparison to the world: 97

Real GDP growth rate: 2.7% (2017 est.)
2.2% (2016 est.)
1% (2015 est.)
country comparison to the world: 105

Real GDP per capita: $2,000 (2020 est.)
$2,100 (2019 est.)
$2,000 (2018 est.)
note: data are in 2017 dollars
country comparison to the world: 214

GDP (official exchange rate): $20.24 billion (2017 est.)

Inflation rate (consumer prices): 5% (2017 est.)
4.4% (2016 est.)
country comparison to the world: 180

GDP - composition, by sector of origin: *agriculture:* 23% (2016 est.)
industry: 21.1% (2016 est.)
services: 55.9% (2016 est.)
note: data exclude opium production

GDP - composition, by end use: *household consumption:* 81.6% (2016 est.)
government consumption: 12% (2016 est.)
investment in fixed capital: 17.2% (2016 est.)
investment in inventories: 30% (2016 est.)
exports of goods and services: 6.7% (2016 est.)
imports of goods and services: -47.6% (2016 est.)

Agricultural products: wheat, milk, grapes, vegetables, potatoes, watermelons, melons, rice, onions, apples

Industries: small-scale production of bricks, textiles, soap, furniture, shoes, fertilizer, apparel, food products, non-alcoholic beverages, mineral water, cement; handwoven carpets; natural gas, coal, copper

Industrial production growth rate: -1.9% (2016 est.)
country comparison to the world: 181

Labor force: 8.478 million (2017 est.)
country comparison to the world: 58

Labor force - by occupation: *agriculture:* 44.3%
industry: 18.1%
services: 37.6% (2017 est.)

Unemployment rate: 23.9% (2017 est.)
22.6% (2016 est.)
country comparison to the world: 195

Unemployment, youth ages 15-24: *total:* 16.2%
male: 14.5%
female: 21.1% (2020)
country comparison to the world: 99

Population below poverty line: 54.5% (2016 est.)

Gini Index coefficient - distribution of family income: 29.4 (2008)
country comparison to the world: 153

Household income or consumption by percentage share: *lowest 10%:* 3.8%
highest 10%: 24% (2008)

Budget: *revenues:* 2.276 billion (2017 est.)
expenditures: 5.328 billion (2017 est.)

Budget surplus (+) or deficit (-): -15.1% (of GDP) (2017 est.)
country comparison to the world: 217

Public debt: 7% of GDP (2017 est.)
7.8% of GDP (2016 est.)
country comparison to the world: 202

Taxes and other revenues: 11.2% (of GDP) (2017 est.)
country comparison to the world: 210

Fiscal year: 21 December - 20 December

Current account balance: $1.014 billion (2017 est.)
$1.409 billion (2016 est.)
country comparison to the world: 49

Exports: $1.48 billion (2020 est.)
$1.52 billion (2019 est.)
$1.61 billion (2018 est.)
note: Data are in current year dollars and do not include illicit exports or re-exports.
country comparison to the world: 164

Exports - partners: United Arab Emirates 45%, Pakistan 24%, India 22%, China 1% (2019)

Exports - commodities: gold, grapes, opium, fruits and nuts, insect resins, cotton, handwoven carpets, soapstone, scrap metal (2019)

Imports: $6.98 billion (2020 est.) note: data are in current year dollars
$7.37 billion (2019 est.) note: data are in current year dollars
$7.98 billion (2018 est.) note: data are in current year dollars
country comparison to the world: 125

Imports - partners: United Arab Emirates 23%, Pakistan 17%, India 13%, China 9%, United States 9%, Uzbekistan 7%, Kazakhstan 6% (2019)

Imports - commodities: wheat flours, broadcasting equipment, refined petroleum, rolled tobacco, aircraft parts, synthetic fabrics (2019)

Reserves of foreign exchange and gold: $7.187 billion (31 December 2017 est.)
$6.901 billion (31 December 2015 est.)
country comparison to the world: 85

Debt - external: $284 million (FY10/11)
country comparison to the world: 185

Exchange rates: afghanis (AFA) per US dollar -
7.87 (2017 est.)
68.03 (2016 est.)
67.87 (2015)
61.14 (2014 est.)
57.25 (2013 est.)

ENERGY

Electricity access: *electrification - total population:* 99% (2018)
electrification - urban areas: 100% (2018)
electrification - rural areas: 98% (2018)

Electricity: *installed generating capacity:* 776,000 kW (2020 est.)
consumption: 5,913,090,000 kWh (2019 est.)
exports: 0 kWh (2019 est.)
imports: 4.912 billion kWh (2019 est.)
transmission/distribution losses: 61.6 million kWh (2019 est.)

Electricity generation sources: *fossil fuels:* 15.9% of total installed capacity (2020 est.)
solar: 5.1% of total installed capacity (2020 est.)
hydroelectricity: 79.1% of total installed capacity (2020 est.)

Coal: *production:* 2.096 million metric tons (2020 est.)
consumption: 2.096 million metric tons (2020 est.)
proven reserves: 66 million metric tons (2019 est.)

Petroleum: *total petroleum production:* 0 bbl/day (2021 est.)
refined petroleum consumption: 24,300 bbl/day (2019 est.)
crude oil estimated reserves: 0 barrels (2021 est.)

Refined petroleum products - imports: 34,210 bbl/day (2015 est.)
country comparison to the world: 97

Natural gas: *production:* 80.193 million cubic meters (2020 est.)
consumption: 80.193 million cubic meters (2020 est.)
proven reserves: 49.554 billion cubic meters (2021 est.)

Carbon dioxide emissions: 7.893 million metric tonnes of CO2 (2019 est.)
from coal and metallurgical coke: 4.158 million metric tonnes of CO2 (2019 est.)
from petroleum and other liquids: 3.468 million metric tonnes of CO2 (2019 est.)
from consumed natural gas: 267,000 metric tonnes of CO2 (2019 est.)
country comparison to the world: 117

Energy consumption per capita: 3.227 million Btu/person (2019 est.)
country comparison to the world: 180

COMMUNICATIONS

Telephones - fixed lines: *total subscriptions:* 145,787 (2020 est.)

subscriptions per 100 inhabitants: (2020 est.) less than 1
country comparison to the world: 126

Telephones - mobile cellular: *total subscriptions:* 22,678,024 (2020 est.)
subscriptions per 100 inhabitants: 58 (2020 est.)
country comparison to the world: 53

Telecommunication systems: *general assessment:* the return of the Taliban to power in August 2021 following the American-led withdrawal of security forces has thrown the telecom sector into disarray; Afghanistan was near the bottom of the world's rankings in terms of its telecom market maturity, but it had been making some positive progress toward establishing widespread coverage over the prior decade under civilian administration; after the first Taliban regime was toppled in 2001, considerable foreign investment along with open competition in the telecom sector resulted in the transformation of the mobile market; the first mobile network was set up in 2002, and by 2020 coverage had reached 90%; mobile penetration rates, too, had climbed from zero to almost 100% by the time a new insurgency kicked off in 2019 that was closely followed by the start of the Covid-19 pandemic; both events caused a drop in subscriber numbers and in revenue for the mobile operators; it was additional costs involved with repairing and replacing network infrastructure destroyed by the Taliban in the build up to their takeover that put a strain on the operators' finances; with increased levels of risk and uncertainty now associated with running a telecom company in the embattled state (2021)
domestic: before 15 August 2021, less than 1 per 100 for fixed-line teledensity; 58 per 100 for mobile-cellular; an increasing number of Afghans utilize mobile-cellular phone networks (2021)
international: country code - 93; multiple VSAT's provide international and domestic voice and data connectivity (2019)

Broadcast media: since 15 August 2021, independent media outlets have decreased in number due to financial hardships, departure of staff from the country, and restrictions placed by the Taliban; media workers report self-censoring criticism of the Taliban; before 15 August 2021, the former Afghan Government-owned broadcaster, Radio Television Afghanistan (RTA), operated a series of radio and television stations in Kabul and the provinces and the country had an estimated 174 private radio stations and 83 TV stations; television and radio are key media platforms; only about a fifth of Afghans in urban areas use the internet, mostly through smartphones, and young adults are significantly more likely to use the internet (2021)

Internet country code: .af

Internet users: *total:* 7,007,101 (2020 est.)
percent of population: 18% (2020 est.)
country comparison to the world: 76

Broadband - fixed subscriptions: *total:* 26,570 (2020 est.)
subscriptions per 100 inhabitants: 0.1 (2020 est.)
country comparison to the world: 157

TRANSPORTATION

National air transport system: *number of registered air carriers:* 3 (2020)
inventory of registered aircraft operated by air carriers: 13
annual passenger traffic on registered air carriers: 1,722,612 (2018)
annual freight traffic on registered air carriers: 29.56 million (2018) mt-km

Civil aircraft registration country code prefix: YA

Airports: *total:* 46 (2021)
country comparison to the world: 94

Airports - with paved runways: *total:* 29
over 3,047 m: 4
2,438 to 3,047 m: 8
1,524 to 2,437 m: 12
914 to 1,523 m: 2
under 914 m: 3 (2021)

Airports - with unpaved runways: *total:* 17
2,438 to 3,047 m: 1
1,524 to 2,437 m: 7
914 to 1,523 m: 4
under 914 m: 5 (2021)

Heliports: 1 (2021)

Pipelines: 466 km gas (2013)

Roadways: *total:* 34,903 km (2017)
paved: 17,903 km (2017)
unpaved: 17,000 km (2017)
country comparison to the world: 92

Waterways: 1,200 km (2011) (chiefly Amu Darya, which handles vessels up to 500 DWT)
country comparison to the world: 62

Ports and terminals: *river port(s):* Hairatan, Qizil Qal`ah (Amu Darya)

MILITARY AND SECURITY

Military and security forces: as of 2022, the Taliban had established a de facto Ministry of Defense and named commanders and deputy commanders for 8 regional corps; in December 2021, it announced the formation of a police force (2022)

Military expenditures: 3.3% of GDP (2019) (approximately $2.35 billion)
3.2% of GDP (2018) (approximately $2.31 billion)
3.3% of GDP (2017) (approximately $2.34 billion)
3.1% of GDP (2016) (approximately $2.6 billion)
2.9% of GDP (2015) (approximately $2.22 billion)
country comparison to the world: 27

Military and security service personnel strengths: in May 2022, the de facto Ministry of Defense announced that approximately 130,000 troops had been recruited for a new "National Army" (2022)
note: as of 2022, there were also up to 10,000 foreign fighters in Afghanistan, most of whom were aligned with the Taliban

Military equipment inventories and acquisitions: the Taliban military/security forces are armed largely with equipment captured from the Afghan National Defense and Security Forces (ANDSF) when the central government in Kabul collapsed in 2021 (2022)

Military service age and obligation: not available
note: the Taliban dismissed nearly all women from the former Afghan Government security forces, except those serving in detention facilities and assisting with body searches

Military - note: as of 2022, the Taliban's primary security threats included ISIS-Khorasan and anti-Taliban resistance elements known as the National Resistance Front and Afghanistan Freedom Front

TERRORISM

Terrorist group(s): Haqqani Taliban Network; Harakat ul-Mujahidin; Harakat ul-Jihad-i-Islami; Islamic Jihad Union; Islamic Movement of Uzbekistan; Islamic State of Iraq and ash-Sham-Khorasan Province (ISIS-K); Islamic Revolutionary Guard Corps (IRGC)/Qods Force; Jaish-e-Mohammed; Jaysh al Adl (Jundallah); Lashkar i Jhangvi; Lashkar-e Tayyiba; al-Qa'ida; al- Qa'ida in the Indian Subcontinent (AQIS); Tehrik-e-Taliban Pakistan (TTP)
note 1: as of mid-2022, TTP was reportedly the largest component of foreign terrorist fighters in Afghanistan, with an estimated 3-4,000 armed fighters operating primarily along the Afghanistan-Pakistan border

TRANSNATIONAL ISSUES

Disputes - international: *Afghanistan-China:* None identified
Afghanistan-Iran: Afghan and Iranian commissioners have discussed boundary monument densification and resurvey; Iran protests Afghanistan's restricting flow of dammed Helmand River tributaries during drought
Afghanistan-Pakistan: Pakistan has built fences in some portions of its border with Afghanistan which remains open in some areas to terrorist and other illegal activities. Their alignments may not always be in conformance with Durand Line and original surveyed definitions of the boundary.
Afghanistan-Tajikistan: None identified
Afghanistan-Turkmenistan: None identified
Afghanistan-Uzbekistan: None identified. Boundary follows Amu Darya river as delimited in the Afghan-Soviet treaties and not by the river's current course. The boundary was delimited and possibly demarcated during Soviet times (pre-1991). No current negotiations between Afghanistan and Uzbekistan to redelimit the boundary have been identified.

Russia remains concerned about the smuggling of poppy derivatives from Afghanistan through Central Asian countries

Refugees and internally displaced persons: *refugees (country of origin):* 72,188 (Pakistan) (mid-year 2021)
IDPs: 4.314 million (mostly Pashtuns and Kuchis displaced in the south and west due to natural disasters and political instability) (2021)

Trafficking in persons: *current situation:* human traffickers exploit domestic and foreign victims and returning Afghan migrants and exploit Afghan victims abroad; internal trafficking is more prevalent than transnational trafficking; traffickers exploit men, women, and a large number of children domestically; victims are subjected to forced labor in agriculture, brick kilns, carpet weaving, domestic servitude, commercial sex, begging, poppy cultivation and harvesting, salt mining, transnational drug smuggling, and truck driving; Afghan security forces and non-state armed groups, including the pro-government militias and the Taliban, continue to unlawfully recruit and use child soldiers; sexual

exploitation of boys remains pervasive nationwide, and traffickers subject some boys to sexual exploitation abroad
tier rating: Tier 3 — Afghanistan does not fully comply with the minimum standards for the elimination of trafficking in persons and is not making significant efforts to do so; the government decreased law enforcement efforts against civilian and official perpetrators of trafficking, and officials complicit in recruitment and use of child soldiers and the sexual exploitation of boys continued to operate with impunity; authorities continued to arrest, detain, and penalize many trafficking victims, including punishing sex trafficking victims for "moral crimes"; the judiciary remained underfunded, understaffed, and undertrained (2020)

Illicit drugs: the world's largest producer of illicit opiates, but it is not a major supplier to the United States; 215,000 hectares (ha) of opium poppy cultivated in Afghanistan in 2020; also produces methamphetamine and cannabis products; one of the highest domestic substance abuse rates in the world (2022)

AKROTIRI

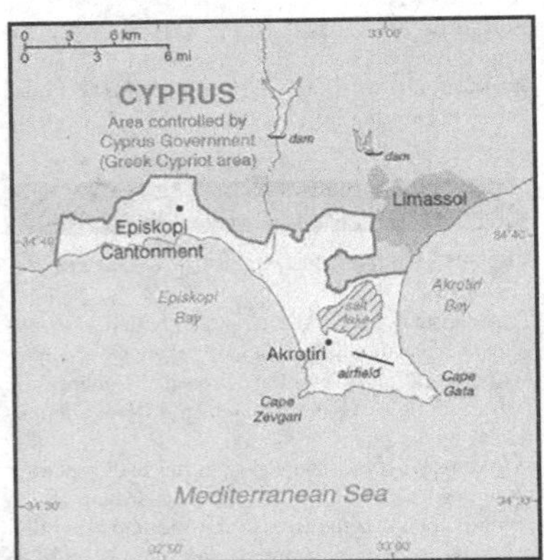

INTRODUCTION

Background: By terms of the 1960 Treaty of Establishment that created the independent Republic of Cyprus, the UK retained full sovereignty and jurisdiction over two areas of almost 254 square kilometers - Akrotiri and Dhekelia. The southernmost and smaller of the two is the Akrotiri Sovereign Base Area, which is also referred to as the Western Sovereign Base Area.

GEOGRAPHY

Location: Eastern Mediterranean, peninsula on the southwest coast of Cyprus

Geographic coordinates: 34 37 N, 32 58 E

Map references: Middle East

Area: *total:* 123 sq km
note: includes a salt lake and wetlands
country comparison to the world: 223

Area - comparative: about 0.7 times the size of Washington, DC

Land boundaries: *total:* 48 km
border countries (1): Cyprus 48 km

Coastline: 56.3 km

Climate: temperate; Mediterranean with hot, dry summers and cool winters

Geography - note: British extraterritorial rights also extended to several small off-post sites scattered across Cyprus; of the Sovereign Base Area (SBA) land, 60% is privately owned and farmed, 20% is owned by the Ministry of Defense, and 20% is SBA Crown land

PEOPLE AND SOCIETY

Population: (2020) approximately 18,195 on the Sovereign Base Areas of Akrotiri and Dhekelia including 11,000 Cypriots and 7,195 Service and UK-based contract personnel and dependents

Languages: English, Greek
major-language sample(s): Το Παγκόσμιο Βιβλίο Δεδομένων, η απαραίτητη πηγή βασικών πληροφοριών. (Greek)

ENVIRONMENT

Environment - current issues: hunting around the salt lake; note - breeding place for loggerhead and green turtles; only remaining colony of griffon vultures is on the base

Climate: temperate; Mediterranean with hot, dry summers and cool winters

GOVERNMENT

Country name: *conventional long form:* none
conventional short form: Akrotiri
etymology: named for the village that lies within the Western Sovereign Base Area on Cyprus

Dependency status: a special form of UK overseas territory; administered by an administrator who is also the Commander, British Forces Cyprus

Capital: *name:* Episkopi Cantonment (base administrative center for Akrotiri and Dhekelia)
geographic coordinates: 34 40 N, 32 51 E
time difference: UTC+2 (7 hours ahead of Washington, DC, during Standard Time)
daylight saving time: +1hr, begins last Sunday in March; ends last Sunday in October
etymology: "Episkopi" means "episcopal" in Greek and stems from the fact that the site previously served as the bishop's seat of an Orthodox diocese

Constitution: *history:* presented 3 August 1960, effective 16 August 1960 (The Sovereign Base Areas of Akrotiri and Dhekelia Order in Council 1960 serves as a basic legal document)
amendments: amended 1966

Legal system: laws applicable to the Cypriot population are, as far as possible, the same as the laws of the Republic of Cyprus; note - the Sovereign Base Area Administration has its own court system to deal with civil and criminal matters

Executive branch: *chief of state:* King CHARLES III (since 8 September 2022)
head of government: Administrator Air Vice-Marshal Peter J.M. SQUIRES (since 1 September 2022); note -administrator reports to the British Ministry of Defense and is also Commander, British Forces Cyprus (BFC); the chief officer, an appointed civilian, is responsible for the day-to-day running of the civil government of the Sovereign Base Areas
elections/appointments: the monarchy is hereditary; administrator appointed by the monarch on the advice of the Ministry of Defense

Judicial branch: *highest court(s):* Senior Judges' Court (consists of several visiting judges from England and Wales)
judge selection and term of office: see entry for United Kingdom
subordinate courts: Resident Judges' Court; Courts Martial

Diplomatic representation in the US: none (overseas territory of the UK)

Diplomatic representation from the US: *embassy:* none (overseas territory of the UK)

Flag description: the flag of the UK is used

National anthem: *note:* as a UK area of special sovereignty, "God Save the King" is official (see United Kingdom)

ECONOMY

Economic overview: Economic activity is limited to providing services to the military and their families located in Akrotiri. All food and manufactured goods must be imported.

Exchange rates: *note:* uses the euro

COMMUNICATIONS

Broadcast media: British Forces Broadcast Service (BFBS) provides multi-channel satellite TV service as well as BFBS radio broadcasts to the Akrotiri Sovereign Base Area

TRANSPORTATION

Airports: *total:* 1 (2021)
country comparison to the world: 209

Airports - with paved runways: *2,438 to 3,047 m:* 1 (2021)

MILITARY AND SECURITY

Military - note: defense is the responsibility of the UK; Akrotiri (aka the Western Sovereign Base Area) has a full Royal Air Force base, headquarters for British Forces Cyprus, and the Episkopi Cantonment

TRANSNATIONAL ISSUES

Illicit drugs: NA

ALBANIA

INTRODUCTION

Background: Albania declared its independence from the Ottoman Empire in 1912, but was conquered by Italy in 1939 and occupied by Germany in 1943. Communist partisans took over the country in 1944. Albania allied itself first with the USSR (until 1960), and then with China (to 1978). In the early 1990s, Albania ended 46 years of isolated communist rule and established a multiparty democracy. The transition has proven challenging as successive governments have tried to deal with high unemployment, widespread corruption, dilapidated infrastructure, powerful organized crime networks, and combative political opponents.

Albania has made progress in its democratic development since it first held multiparty elections in 1991, but deficiencies remain. Most of Albania's post-communist elections were marred by claims of electoral fraud; however, international observers judged elections to be largely free and fair since the restoration of political stability following the collapse of pyramid schemes in 1997. Albania joined NATO in April 2009 and in June 2014 became an EU candidate. Albania in April 2017 received a European Commission recommendation to open EU accession negotiations following the passage of historic EU-mandated justice reforms in 2016. Although Albania's economy continues to grow, it has slowed, and the country is still one of the poorest in Europe. A large informal economy and a weak energy and transportation infrastructure remain obstacles.

GEOGRAPHY

Location: Southeastern Europe, bordering the Adriatic Sea and Ionian Sea, between Greece to the south and Montenegro and Kosovo to the north

Geographic coordinates: 41 00 N, 20 00 E

Map references: Europe

Area: *total:* 28,748 sq km
land: 27,398 sq km
water: 1,350 sq km
country comparison to the world: 144

Area - comparative: slightly smaller than Maryland

Land boundaries: *total:* 691 km
border countries (4): Greece 212 km; Kosovo 112 km; Macedonia 181 km; Montenegro 186 km

Coastline: 362 km

Maritime claims: *territorial sea:* 12 nm
continental shelf: 200-m depth or to the depth of exploitation

Climate: mild temperate; cool, cloudy, wet winters; hot, clear, dry summers; interior is cooler and wetter

Terrain: mostly mountains and hills; small plains along coast

Elevation: *highest point:* Maja e Korabit (Golem Korab) 2,764 m
lowest point: Adriatic Sea 0 m
mean elevation: 708 m

Natural resources: petroleum, natural gas, coal, bauxite, chromite, copper, iron ore, nickel, salt, timber, hydropower, arable land

Land use: *agricultural land:* 42.8% (2018 est.)
arable land: 22.3% (2018 est.)
permanent crops: 3% (2018 est.)
permanent pasture: 17.4% (2018 est.)
forest: 28.8% (2018 est.)
other: 28.2% (2018 est.)

Irrigated land: 3,537 sq km (2014)

Major lakes (area sq km): *fresh water lake(s):* Lake Scutari (shared with Montenegro) - 400 sq km
note - largest lake in the Balkans

Major watersheds (area sq km):

Atlantic Ocean drainage: *(Black Sea)* Danube (795,656 sq km)

Population distribution: a fairly even distribution, with somewhat higher concentrations of people in the western and central parts of the country

Natural hazards: destructive earthquakes; tsunamis occur along southwestern coast; floods; drought

Geography - note: strategic location along Strait of Otranto (links Adriatic Sea to Ionian Sea and Mediterranean Sea)

PEOPLE AND SOCIETY

Population: 3,095,344 (2022 est.)
country comparison to the world: 136

Nationality: *noun:* Albanian(s)
adjective: Albanian

Ethnic groups: Albanian 82.6%, Greek 0.9%, other 1% (including Vlach, Romani, Macedonian, Montenegrin, and Egyptian), unspecified 15.5% (2011 est.)
note: data represent population by ethnic and cultural affiliation

Languages: Albanian 98.8% (official - derived from Tosk dialect), Greek 0.5%, other 0.6% (including Macedonian, Romani, Vlach, Turkish, Italian, and Serbo-Croatian), unspecified 0.1% (2011 est.)
major-language sample(s): Libri i fakteve boterore, burim i pa zevendesueshem per informacione elementare. (Albanian)

Religions: Muslim 56.7%, Roman Catholic 10%, Orthodox 6.8%, atheist 2.5%, Bektashi (a Sufi order) 2.1%, other 5.7%, unspecified 16.2% (2011 est.)
note: all mosques and churches were closed in 1967 and religious observances prohibited; in November 1990, Albania began allowing private religious practice

Age structure: *0-14 years:* 17.6% (male 284,636/female 256,474)
15-24 years: 15.39% (male 246,931/female 226,318)
25-54 years: 42.04% (male 622,100/female 670,307)
55-64 years: 11.94% (male 178,419/female 188,783)
65 years and over: 13.03% (male 186,335/female 214,276) (2020 est.)

Dependency ratios: *total dependency ratio:* 46.9
youth dependency ratio: 25.3
elderly dependency ratio: 21.6
potential support ratio: 4.6 (2020 est.)

Median age: *total:* 34.3 years
male: 32.9 years
female: 35.7 years (2020 est.)
country comparison to the world: 91

Population growth rate: 0.22% (2022 est.)
country comparison to the world: 179

Birth rate: 12.69 births/1,000 population (2022 est.)
country comparison to the world: 143

Death rate: 7.31 deaths/1,000 population (2022 est.)
country comparison to the world: 111

Net migration rate: -3.23 migrant(s)/1,000 population (2022 est.)
country comparison to the world: 184

Population distribution: a fairly even distribution, with somewhat higher concentrations of people in the western and central parts of the country

Urbanization: *urban population:* 63.8% of total population (2022)
rate of urbanization: 1.29% annual rate of change (2020-25 est.)

Major urban areas - population: 512,000 TIRANA (capital) (2022)

Sex ratio: *at birth:* 1.07 male(s)/female
0-14 years: 1.1 male(s)/female
15-24 years: 1.11 male(s)/female
25-54 years: 0.92 male(s)/female
55-64 years: 0.92 male(s)/female
65 years and over: 0.66 male(s)/female
total population: 0.97 male(s)/female (2022 est.)

Mother's mean age at first birth: 26.6 years (2020 est.)

Maternal mortality ratio: 15 deaths/100,000 live births (2017 est.)
country comparison to the world: 136

Infant mortality rate: *total:* 10.82 deaths/1,000 live births
male: 11.85 deaths/1,000 live births
female: 9.71 deaths/1,000 live births (2022 est.)
country comparison to the world: 131

Life expectancy at birth: *total population:* 79.47 years
male: 76.8 years
female: 82.33 years (2022 est.)
country comparison to the world: 61

Total fertility rate: 1.54 children born/woman (2022 est.)
country comparison to the world: 194

Contraceptive prevalence rate: 46% (2017/18)

Drinking water source: *improved: urban:* 97.3% of population
rural: 96.4% of population
total: 97% of population
unimproved: urban: 2.7% of population
rural: 3.6% of population
total: 3% of population (2020 est.)

Current health expenditure: 5.2% of GDP (2018)

Physicians density: 1.88 physicians/1,000 population (2020)

Hospital bed density: 2.9 beds/1,000 population (2013)

Sanitation facility access: *improved: urban:* 99.8% of population
rural: 100% of population
total: 99.9% of population
unimproved: urban: 0.2% of population
rural: 0.5% of population
total: 0.1% of population (2020 est.)

HIV/AIDS - adult prevalence rate: (2020 est.) <.1

Obesity - adult prevalence rate: 21.7% (2016)
country comparison to the world: 85

Alcohol consumption per capita: *total:* 4.4 liters of pure alcohol (2019 est.)
beer: 1.75 liters of pure alcohol (2019 est.)
wine: 1.15 liters of pure alcohol (2019 est.)
spirits: 1.43 liters of pure alcohol (2019 est.)
other alcohols: 0.08 liters of pure alcohol (2019 est.)
country comparison to the world: 90

Tobacco use: *total:* 22.4% (2020 est.)
male: 38.8% (2020 est.)
female: 6% (2020 est.)
country comparison to the world: 69

Children under the age of 5 years underweight: 1.5% (2017/18)
country comparison to the world: 118

Child marriage: *women married by age 15:* 1.4%
women married by age 18: 11.8%
men married by age 18: 1.2% (2018 est.)

Education expenditures: 3.9% of GDP (2019 est.)
country comparison to the world: 105

Literacy: *definition:* age 15 and over can read and write
total population: 98.1%
male: 98.5%
female: 97.8% (2018)

School life expectancy (primary to tertiary education): *total:* 15 years
male: 14 years
female: 15 years (2020)

Unemployment, youth ages 15-24: *total:* 27%
male: 27.8%
female: 25.9% (2019 est.)

ENVIRONMENT

Environment - current issues: deforestation; soil erosion; water pollution from industrial and domestic effluents; air pollution from industrial and power plants; loss of biodiversity due to lack of resources for sound environmental management

Environment - international agreements: *party to:* Air Pollution, Air Pollution-Nitrogen Oxides, Air Pollution-Sulphur 85, Biodiversity, Climate Change, Climate Change-Kyoto Protocol, Climate Change-Paris Agreement, Comprehensive Nuclear Test Ban, Desertification, Endangered Species, Hazardous Wastes, Law of the Sea, Ozone Layer Protection, Ship Pollution, Tropical Timber 2006, Wetlands
signed, but not ratified: none of the selected agreements

Air pollutants: *particulate matter emissions:* 17.87 micrograms per cubic meter (2016 est.)
carbon dioxide emissions: 4.54 megatons (2016 est.)
methane emissions: 2.55 megatons (2020 est.)

Climate: mild temperate; cool, cloudy, wet winters; hot, clear, dry summers; interior is cooler and wetter

Land use: *agricultural land:* 42.8% (2018 est.)
arable land: 22.3% (2018 est.)
permanent crops: 3% (2018 est.)
permanent pasture: 17.4% (2018 est.)
forest: 28.8% (2018 est.)
other: 28.2% (2018 est.)

Urbanization: *urban population:* 63.8% of total population (2022)
rate of urbanization: 1.29% annual rate of change (2020-25 est.)

Revenue from forest resources: *forest revenues:* 0.18% of GDP (2018 est.)
country comparison to the world: 95

Revenue from coal: *coal revenues:* 0.03% of GDP (2018 est.)
country comparison to the world: 34

Waste and recycling: *municipal solid waste generated annually:* 1,142,964 tons (2015 est.)

Major lakes (area sq km): *fresh water lake(s):* Lake Scutari (shared with Montenegro) - 400 sq km
note - largest lake in the Balkans

Major watersheds (area sq km): *Atlantic Ocean drainage: (Black Sea)* Danube (795,656 sq km)

Total water withdrawal: *municipal:* 283 million cubic meters (2017 est.)
industrial: 231.8 million cubic meters (2017 est.)
agricultural: 905 million cubic meters (2017 est.)

Total renewable water resources: 30.2 billion cubic meters (2017 est.)

GOVERNMENT

Country name: *conventional long form:* Republic of Albania
conventional short form: Albania
local long form: Republika e Shqiperise
local short form: Shqiperia
former: People's Socialist Republic of Albania
etymology: the English-language country name seems to be derived from the ancient Illyrian tribe of the Albani; the native name "Shqiperia" is derived from the Albanian word "Shqiponje" ("Eagle") and is popularly interpreted to mean "Land of the Eagles"

Government type: parliamentary republic

Capital: *name:* Tirana (Tirane)
geographic coordinates: 41 19 N, 19 49 E
time difference: UTC+1 (6 hours ahead of Washington, DC, during Standard Time)
daylight saving time: +1hr, begins last Sunday in March; ends last Sunday in October
etymology: the name Tirana first appears in a 1418 Venetian document; the origin of the name is unclear, but may derive from Tirkan Fortress, whose ruins survive on the slopes of Dajti mountain and which overlooks the city

Administrative divisions: 12 counties (qarqe, singular - qark); Berat, Diber, Durres, Elbasan, Fier, Gjirokaster, Korce, Kukes, Lezhe, Shkoder, Tirane, Vlore

Independence: 28 November 1912 (from the Ottoman Empire)

National holiday: Independence Day, 28 November (1912), also known as Flag Day

Constitution: *history:* several previous; latest approved by the Assembly 21 October 1998, adopted by referendum 22 November 1998, promulgated 28 November 1998
amendments: proposed by at least one fifth of the Assembly membership; passage requires at least a two-thirds majority vote by the Assembly; referendum required only if approved by two thirds of the Assembly; amendments approved by referendum effective upon declaration by the president of the republic; amended several times, last in 2020

Legal system: civil law system except in the northern rural areas where customary law known as the "Code of Leke" is still present

International law organization participation: has not submitted an ICJ jurisdiction declaration; accepts ICCt jurisdiction

Citizenship: *citizenship by birth:* no
citizenship by descent only: at least one parent must be a citizen of Albania
dual citizenship recognized: yes
residency requirement for naturalization: 5 years

Suffrage: 18 years of age; universal

Executive branch: *chief of state:* President of the Republic Bajram BEGAJ (since 24 July 2022)
head of government: Prime Minister Edi RAMA (since 10 September 2013); Deputy Prime Minister Arben AHMETAJ (since 18 September 2021)
cabinet: Council of Ministers proposed by the prime minister, nominated by the president, and approved by the Assembly
elections/appointments: president indirectly elected by the Assembly for a 5-year term (eligible for a second term); a candidate needs three-fifths majority vote of the Assembly in 1 of 3 rounds or a simple majority in 2 additional rounds to become president; election last held in 4 rounds on 16, 23, and 30 May and 4 June 2022 (next election to be held in 2027); prime minister appointed by the president on the proposal of the majority party or coalition of parties in the Assembly
election results: 2022: Bajram BEGAJ elected president in the fourth round; Assembly vote - 78-4, opposition parties boycotted
2017: Ilir META elected president in the fourth round; Assembly vote - 87-2

Legislative branch: *description:* unicameral Assembly or Kuvendi (140 seats; members directly elected in multi-seat constituencies by proportional representation vote to serve 4-year terms)
elections: last held on 25 April 2021 (next to be held in 2025)
election results: percent of vote by party/coalition - PS 48.7%, PD-Alliance for Change 39.4%, LSI 6.8%, PSD 2.3%, other 2.8%; seats by party/coalition - PS 74, PD-Alliance for Change 59, LSI 4, PSD 3; composition - men 93, women 47, percent of women 33.6%

Judicial branch: *highest court(s):* Supreme Court (consists of 19 judges, including the chief justice); Constitutional Court (consists of 9 judges, including the chairman)

judge selection and term of office: Supreme Court judges appointed by the High Judicial Council with the consent of the president to serve single 9-year terms; Supreme Court chairman is elected for a single 3-year term by the court members; appointments of Constitutional Court judges are rotated among the president, Parliament, and Supreme Court from a list of pre-qualified candidates (each institution selects 3 judges), to serve single 9-year terms; candidates are pre-qualified by a randomly selected body of experienced judges and prosecutors; Constitutional Court chairman is elected by the court members for a single, renewable 3-year term
subordinate courts: Courts of Appeal; Courts of First Instance; specialized courts: Court for Corruption and Organized Crime, Appeals Court for Corruption and Organized Crime (responsible for corruption, organized crime, and crimes of high officials)

Political parties and leaders: Alliance for Change (electoral coalition led by PD)
Democratic Party or PD [Enkelejd ALIBEAJ, interim leader]
Party for Justice, Integration and Unity or PDIU [Shpetim IDRIZI] (part of the Alliance for Change)
Social Democratic Party or PSD [Tom DOSHI]
Socialist Movement for Integration or LSI [Monika KRYEMADHI]
Socialist Party or PS [Edi RAMA]

International organization participation: BSEC, CD, CE, CEI, EAPC, EBRD, EITI (compliant country), FAO, IAEA, IBRD, ICAO, ICC (national committees), ICCt, ICRM, IDA, IDB, IFAD, IFC, IFRCS, ILO, IMF, IMO, Interpol, IOC, IOM, IPU, ISO (correspondent), ITU, ITUC (NGOs), MIGA, NATO, OAS (observer), OIC, OIF, OPCW, OSCE, PCA, SELEC, UN, UNCTAD, UNESCO, UNIDO, UNWTO, UPU, WCO, WFTU (NGOs), WHO, WIPO, WMO, WTO

Diplomatic representation in the US: *chief of mission:* Ambassador Floreta LULI-FABER (since 18 May 2015)
chancery: 2100 S Street NW, Washington, DC 20008
telephone: [1] (202) 223-4942
FAX: [1] (202) 628-7342
email address and website:
embassy.washington@mfa.gov.al
http://www.ambasadat.gov.al/usa/en
consulate(s) general: New York

Diplomatic representation from the US: *chief of mission:* Ambassador Yuri KIM (since 27 January 2020)
embassy: Rruga Stavro Vinjau, No. 14, Tirana
mailing address: 9510 Tirana Place, Washington DC 20521-9510
telephone: [355] 4 2247-285
FAX: [355] 4 2232-222
email address and website:
ACSTirana@state.gov
https://al.usembassy.gov/

Flag description: red with a black two-headed eagle in the center; the design is claimed to be that of 15th-century hero Georgi Kastrioti SKANDERBEG, who led a successful uprising against the Ottoman Turks that resulted in a short-lived independence for some Albanian regions (1443-78); an unsubstantiated explanation for the eagle symbol is the tradition that Albanians see themselves as descendants of the eagle; they refer to themselves as "Shqiptare," which translates as "sons of the eagle"

National symbol(s): black double-headed eagle; national colors: red, black

National anthem: *name:* "Hymni i Flamurit" (Hymn to the Flag)
lyrics/music: Aleksander Stavre DRENOVA/ Ciprian PORUMBESCU
note: adopted 1912

National heritage: *total World Heritage Sites:* 4 (2 cultural, 1 natural, 1 mixed)
selected World Heritage Site locales: Butrint (c); Historic Berat and Gjirokastër (c); Primeval Beech Forests (n); Lake Ohrid Region (m)

ECONOMY

Economic overview: Albania, a formerly closed, centrally planned state, is a developing country with a modern open-market economy. Albania managed to weather the first waves of the global financial crisis but, the negative effects of the crisis caused a significant economic slowdown. Since 2014, Albania's economy has steadily improved and economic growth reached 3.8% in 2017. However, close trade, remittance, and banking sector ties with Greece and Italy make Albania vulnerable to spillover effects of possible debt crises and weak growth in the euro zone.

Remittances, a significant catalyst for economic growth, declined from 12-15% of GDP before the 2008 financial crisis to 5.8% of GDP in 2015, mostly from Albanians residing in Greece and Italy. The agricultural sector, which accounts for more than 40% of employment but less than one quarter of GDP, is limited primarily to small family operations and subsistence farming, because of a lack of modern equipment, unclear property rights, and the prevalence of small, inefficient plots of land. Complex tax codes and licensing requirements, a weak judicial system, endemic corruption, poor enforcement of contracts and property issues, and antiquated infrastructure contribute to Albania's poor business environment making attracting foreign investment difficult. Since 2015, Albania has launched an ambitious program to increase tax compliance and bring more businesses into the formal economy. In July 2016, Albania passed constitutional amendments reforming the judicial system in order to strengthen the rule of law and to reduce deeply entrenched corruption.

Albania's electricity supply is uneven despite upgraded transmission capacities with neighboring countries. However, the government has recently taken steps to stem non-technical losses and has begun to upgrade the distribution grid. Better enforcement of electricity contracts has improved the financial viability of the sector, decreasing its reliance on budget support. Also, with help from international donors, the government is taking steps to improve the poor road and rail networks, a long standing barrier to sustained economic growth.

Inward foreign direct investment has increased significantly in recent years as the government has embarked on an ambitious program to improve the business climate through fiscal and legislative reforms. The government is focused on the simplification of licensing requirements and tax codes, and it entered into a new arrangement with the IMF for additional financial and technical support. Albania's three-year IMF program, an extended fund facility arrangement, was successfully concluded in February 2017. The Albanian Government has strengthened tax collection amid moderate public wage and pension increases in an effort to reduce its budget deficit. The country continues to face high public debt, exceeding its former statutory limit of 60% of GDP in 2013 and reaching 72% in 2016.

Real GDP (purchasing power parity): $37.73 billion (2020 est.)
$39.02 billion (2019 est.)
$38.19 billion (2018 est.)
note: data are in 2017 dollars
country comparison to the world: 122

Real GDP growth rate: 2.24% (2019 est.)
4.07% (2018 est.)
3.8% (2017 est.)
country comparison to the world: 124

Real GDP per capita: $13,300 (2020 est.)
$13,700 (2019 est.)
$13,300 (2018 est.)
note: data are in 2017 dollars
country comparison to the world: 115

GDP (official exchange rate): $15.273 billion (2019 est.)

Inflation rate (consumer prices): 1.4% (2019 est.)
2% (2018 est.)
1.9% (2017 est.)
country comparison to the world: 78

Credit ratings:

Moody's rating: B1 (2007)

Standard & Poors rating: B+ (2016)
note: The year refers to the year in which the current credit rating was first obtained.

GDP - composition, by sector of origin: *agriculture:* 21.7% (2017 est.)
industry: 24.2% (2017 est.)
services: 54.1% (2017 est.)

GDP - composition, by end use: *household consumption:* 78.1% (2017 est.)
government consumption: 11.5% (2017 est.)
investment in fixed capital: 25.2% (2017 est.)
investment in inventories: 0.2% (2017 est.)
exports of goods and services: 31.5% (2017 est.)
imports of goods and services: -46.6% (2017 est.)

Agricultural products: milk, maize, tomatoes, potatoes, watermelons, wheat, grapes, cucumbers, onions, apples

Industries: food; footwear, apparel and clothing; lumber, oil, cement, chemicals, mining, basic metals, hydropower

Industrial production growth rate: 6.8% (2017 est.)
country comparison to the world: 31

Labor force: 1.104 million (2020 est.)
country comparison to the world: 139

Labor force - by occupation: *agriculture:* 41.4%
industry: 18.3%
services: 40.3% (2017 est.)

Unemployment rate: 5.83% (2019 est.)
6.32% (2018 est.)
note: these official rates may not include those working at near-subsistence farming
country comparison to the world: 96

Unemployment, youth ages 15-24: *total:* 27%
male: 27.8%
female: 25.9% (2019 est.)
country comparison to the world: 42

Population below poverty line: 14.3% (2012 est.)

Gini Index coefficient - distribution of family income: 33.2 (2017 est.)
30 (2008 est.)
country comparison to the world: 129

Household income or consumption by percentage share: *lowest 10%:* 4.1%
highest 10%: 19.6% (2015 est.)

Budget: *revenues:* 3.614 billion (2017 est.)
expenditures: 3.874 billion (2017 est.)

Budget surplus (+) or deficit (-): -2% (of GDP) (2017 est.)
country comparison to the world: 103

Public debt: 71.8% of GDP (2017 est.)
73.2% of GDP (2016 est.)
country comparison to the world: 46

Taxes and other revenues: 27.6% (of GDP) (2017 est.)
country comparison to the world: 99

Fiscal year: calendar year

Current account balance: -$908 million (2017 est.)
-$899 million (2016 est.)
country comparison to the world: 142

Exports: $3.47 billion (2020 est.)
$4.82 billion (2019 est.)
$4.78 billion (2018 est.)
note: Data are in current year dollars and do not include illicit exports or re-exports.
country comparison to the world: 140

Exports - partners: Italy 45%, Spain 8%, Germany 6%, Greece 5%, France 4%, China 4% (2019)

Exports - commodities: leather footwear and parts, crude petroleum, iron alloys, clothing, electricity, perfumes (2019)

Imports: $5.67 billion (2020 est.) note: data are in current year dollars
$6.93 billion (2019 est.) note: data are in current year dollars
$6.85 billion (2018 est.) note: data are in current year dollars
country comparison to the world: 133

Imports - partners: Italy 28%, Greece 12%, China 11%, Turkey 9%, Germany 5% (2019)

Imports - commodities: refined petroleum, cars, tanned hides, packaged medical supplies, footwear parts (2019)

Reserves of foreign exchange and gold: $3.59 billion (31 December 2017 est.)
$3.109 billion (31 December 2016 est.)
country comparison to the world: 103

Debt - external: $9.311 billion (2019 est.)
$9.547 billion (2018 est.)
country comparison to the world: 116

Exchange rates: leke (ALL) per US dollar -
102.43 (2020 est.)
111.36 (2019 est.)
108.57 (2018 est.)
125.96 (2014 est.)
105.48 (2013 est.)

ENERGY

Electricity access: *electrification - total population:* 100% (2020)

Electricity: *installed generating capacity:* 2.531 million kW (2020 est.)
consumption: 6,527,980,000 kWh (2019 est.)
exports: 963 million kWh (2020 est.)
imports: 3.239 billion kWh (2020 est.)
transmission/distribution losses: 1.054 billion kWh (2019 est.)

Electricity generation sources:
solar: 0.6% of total installed capacity (2020 est.)
hydroelectricity: 99.4% of total installed capacity (2020 est.)

Coal: *production:* 9,000 metric tons (2020 est.)
consumption: 119,000 metric tons (2020 est.)
exports: 0 metric tons (2020 est.)
imports: 110,000 metric tons (2020 est.)
proven reserves: 522 million metric tons (2019 est.)

Petroleum: *total petroleum production:* 16,100 bbl/day (2021 est.)
refined petroleum consumption: 26,400 bbl/day (2019 est.)
crude oil and lease condensate exports: 10,500 bbl/day (2018 est.)
crude oil and lease condensate imports: 0 bbl/day (2018 est.)
crude oil estimated reserves: 150 million barrels (2021 est.)

Refined petroleum products - production: 5,638 bbl/day (2015 est.)
country comparison to the world: 103

Refined petroleum products - exports: 3,250 bbl/day (2015 est.)
country comparison to the world: 98

Refined petroleum products - imports: 26,660 bbl/day (2015 est.)
country comparison to the world: 103

Natural gas: *production:* 42.05 million cubic meters (2019 est.)
consumption: 42.05 million cubic meters (2019 est.)
proven reserves: 5.692 billion cubic meters (2021 est.)

Carbon dioxide emissions: 3.794 million metric tonnes of CO2 (2019 est.)
from coal and metallurgical coke: 235,000 metric tonnes of CO2 (2019 est.)
from petroleum and other liquids: 3.482 million metric tonnes of CO2 (2019 est.)
from consumed natural gas: 78,000 metric tonnes of CO2 (2019 est.)
country comparison to the world: 144

Energy consumption per capita: 38.442 million Btu/person (2019 est.)
country comparison to the world: 110

COMMUNICATIONS

Telephones - fixed lines: *total subscriptions:* 223,469 (2020 est.)
subscriptions per 100 inhabitants: 8 (2020 est.)
country comparison to the world: 120

Telephones - mobile cellular: *total subscriptions:* 2,618,880 (2020 est.)
subscriptions per 100 inhabitants: 91 (2020 est.)
country comparison to the world: 144

Telecommunication systems: *general assessment:* Albania's small telecom market has experienced some significant changes in recent years; upgrades were made to the fixed-line infrastructure to support broadband services; fixed-line telephony use and penetration in Albania is declining steadily as subscribers migrate to mobile solutions; the mobile sector is well provided with LTE networks, while operators have invested in 5G; some of these efforts have been made in conjunction with neighboring Kosovo, with the intention of a seamless 5G corridor along the highway connecting the two countries; the country has long sought accession to the European Union (EU) which has benefited its telecoms sector through closer scrutiny of its regulatory regime and through the injection of funding to help modernize infrastructure (2021)
domestic: fixed-line approximately 8 per 100, teledensity continues to decline due to heavy use of mobile-cellular telephone services; mobile-cellular telephone use is widespread and generally effective, 91 per 100 for mobile-cellular (2020)
international: country code - 355; submarine cables for the Adria 1 and Italy-Albania provide connectivity to Italy, Croatia, and Greece; a combination submarine cable and land fiber-optic system, provides additional connectivity to Bulgaria, Macedonia, and Turkey; international traffic carried by fiber-optic cable and, when necessary, by microwave radio relay from the Tirana exchange to Italy and Greece (2019)

Broadcast media: Albania has more than 65 TV stations, including several that broadcast nationally; Albanian TV broadcasts are also available to Albanian-speaking populations in neighboring countries; many viewers have access to Italian and Greek TV broadcasts via terrestrial reception; Albania's TV stations have begun a government-mandated conversion from analog to digital broadcast; the government has pledged to provide analog-to-digital converters to low-income families affected by this decision; cable TV service is available; 2 public radio networks and roughly 78 private radio stations; several international broadcasters are available (2019)

Internet country code: .al

Internet users: *total:* 2,043,251 (2020 est.)
percent of population: 72% (2020 est.)
country comparison to the world: 127

Broadband - fixed subscriptions: *total:* 508,937 (2020 est.)
subscriptions per 100 inhabitants: 18 (2020 est.)
country comparison to the world: 91

TRANSPORTATION

National air transport system: *number of registered air carriers:* 2 (2020)
inventory of registered aircraft operated by air carriers: 5
annual passenger traffic on registered air carriers: 303,137 (2018)

Civil aircraft registration country code prefix: ZA

Airports: *total:* 3 (2021)
country comparison to the world: 190

Airports - with paved runways: *total:* 3
2,438 to 3,047 m: 2
1,524 to 2,437 m: 1 (2021)

Pipelines: 498 km gas (a majority of the network is in disrepair and parts of it are missing), 249 km oil (2015)

Railways: *total:* 677 km (2015) (447 km of major railway lines and 230 km of secondary lines)
standard gauge: 677 km (2015) 1.435-m gauge
country comparison to the world: 103

Roadways: *total:* 3,945 km (2018)
country comparison to the world: 156

Waterways: 41 km (2011) (on the Bojana River)
country comparison to the world: 114

Merchant marine: *total:* 70
by type: general cargo 47, oil tanker 1, other 22 (2021)
country comparison to the world: 103

Ports and terminals: *major seaport(s):* Durres, Sarande, Shengjin, Vlore

MILITARY AND SECURITY

Military and security forces: Republic of Albania Armed Forces (Forcat e Armatosura të Republikës së Shqipërisë (FARSH)): Land Forces, Navy Forces (includes Coast Guard), Air Forces

Ministry of Interior: Guard of the Republic, State Police (includes the Border and Migration Police) (2022)
note: the State Police are primarily responsible for internal security, while the Guard of the Republic protects senior state officials, foreign dignitaries, and certain state properties

Military expenditures: 1.6% of GDP (2022 est.)
1.4% of GDP (2021)
1.3% of GDP (2020)
1.5% of GDP (2019) (approximately $360 million)
1.3% of GDP (2018) (approximately $330 million)
country comparison to the world: 84

Military and security service personnel strengths: approximately 7,000 total active duty personnel (5,000 Army; 1,500 Navy; 500 Air Force) (2022)

Military equipment inventories and acquisitions: the Albanian military was previously equipped with mostly Soviet-era weapons that were sold or destroyed; its inventory now includes a mix of mostly donated and second-hand European and US equipment; since 2010, it has received limited amounts of equipment from France, Germany, and the US (2021)

Military service age and obligation: 19 is the legal minimum age for voluntary military service; 18 is the legal minimum age in case of general/partial compulsory mobilization; conscription abolished 2010 (2021)
note: as of 2020, women comprised about 14% of the military's full-time personnel, including 20% of the officers

Military - note: Albania became a member of NATO in 2009; as of 2022, Greece and Italy were providing NATO's air policing mission for Albania

TERRORISM

Terrorist group(s): Islamic Revolutionary Guard Corps/Qods Force; Islamic State of Iraq and ash-Sham (ISIS)

TRANSNATIONAL ISSUES

Disputes - international: none

Refugees and internally displaced persons: *stateless persons:* 1,528 (mid-year 2021)
note: 40,186 estimated refugee and migrant arrivals (January 2015-October 2022)

Illicit drugs: active transshipment point for Albanian narco-trafficking organizations moving illicit drugs such as cocaine and heroin from Turkey and countries in South America and Asia throughout Europe; significant source country for cannabis production

ALGERIA

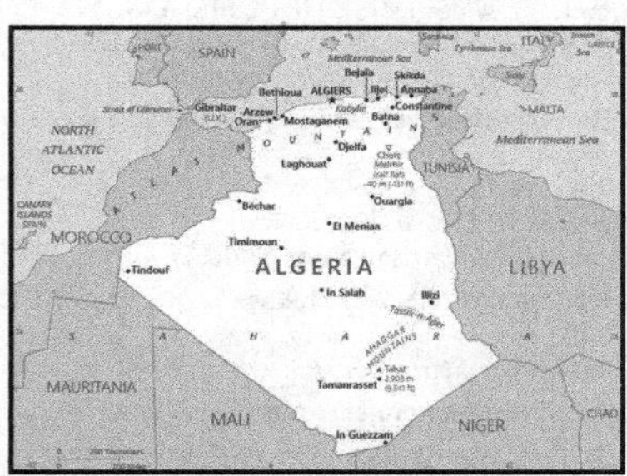

INTRODUCTION

Background: Algeria has known many empires and dynasties starting with the ancient Numidians (3rd century B.C.), Phoenicians, Carthaginians, Romans, Vandals, Byzantines, over a dozen different Arab and Berber dynasties, Spaniards, and Ottoman Turks. It was under the latter that the Barbary pirates operated from North Africa and preyed on shipping beginning in roughly 1500, peaking in the early to mid-17th century, until finally subdued by the French capture of Algiers in 1830. The French southward conquest of the entirety of Algeria proceeded throughout the 19th century and was marked by many atrocities. The country was heavily colonized by the French in the late 19th and early 20th centuries. A bloody eight-year struggle culminated in Algerian independence in 1962.

Algeria's primary political party, the National Liberation Front (FLN), was established in 1954 as part of the struggle for independence and has since largely dominated politics, though it is falling out of favor with the youth. The Government of Algeria in 1988 instituted a multi-party system in response to public unrest, but the surprising first round success of the Islamic Salvation Front (FIS) in the December 1991 legislative elections led the Algerian army to intervene and postpone the second round of elections to prevent what the secular elite feared would be an extremist-led government from assuming power. The army began a crackdown on the FIS that spurred FIS supporters to begin attacking government targets. Fighting escalated into an insurgency, which saw intense violence from 1992-98, resulting in over 100,000 deaths – many attributed to indiscriminate massacres of villagers by extremists. The government gained the upper hand by the late-1990s, and FIS's armed wing, the Islamic Salvation Army, disbanded in January 2000. FIS membership is illegal.

Former president Abdelaziz BOUTEFLIKA, with the backing of the military, won the presidency in 1999 in an election that was boycotted by several candidates protesting alleged fraud, and won subsequent elections in 2004, 2009, and 2014. Protests broke out across the country in late February 2019 against President BOUTEFLIKA's decision to seek a fifth term. BOUTEFLIKA resigned in April 2019, and in December 2019, Algerians elected former Prime Minister Abdelmadjid TEBBOUNE as the country's new president. A longtime FLN member, TEBBOUNE ran for president as an independent. In 2020, Algeria held a constitutional referendum, which President TEBBOUNE enacted in January 2021. Subsequent reforms to the national electoral law introduced open list voting to curb corruption. The new law also eliminated gender quotas in Parliament, and the June 2021 legislative elections saw female representation plummet. Local elections took place in November 2021. The referendum, parliamentary elections, and local elections saw record low voter turnout. Since 2014, Algeria's reliance on hydrocarbon revenues to fund the government and finance the large subsidies for the population has fallen under stress because of declining oil prices.

GEOGRAPHY

Location: Northern Africa, bordering the Mediterranean Sea, between Morocco and Tunisia

Geographic coordinates: 28 00 N, 3 00 E

Map references: Africa

Area: *total:* 2,381,740 sq km
land: 2,381,740 sq km
water: 0 sq km
country comparison to the world: 11

Area - comparative: slightly less than 3.5 times the size of Texas

Land boundaries: *total:* 6,734 km
border countries (6): Libya 989 km; Mali 1,359 km; Mauritania 460 km; Morocco 1,941 km; Niger 951 km; Tunisia 1,034 km

Coastline: 998 km

Maritime claims: *territorial sea:* 12 nm
contiguous zone: 24 nm
exclusive fishing zone: 32-52 nm

Climate: arid to semiarid; mild, wet winters with hot, dry summers along coast; drier with cold winters and hot summers on high plateau; sirocco is a hot, dust/sand-laden wind especially common in summer

Terrain: mostly high plateau and desert; Atlas Mountains in the far north and Hoggar Mountains in the south; narrow, discontinuous coastal plain

Elevation: *highest point:* Tahat 2,908 m
lowest point: Chott Melrhir -40 m
mean elevation: 800 m

Natural resources: petroleum, natural gas, iron ore, phosphates, uranium, lead, zinc

Land use: *agricultural land:* 17.4% (2018 est.)
arable land: 3.2% (2018 est.)
permanent crops: 0.4% (2018 est.)
permanent pasture: 13.8% (2018 est.)
forest: 0.8% (2018 est.)
other: 81.8% (2018 est.)

Irrigated land: 13,600 sq km (2014)

Major watersheds (area sq km):

Atlantic Ocean drainage: Niger (2,261,741 sq km)

Internal *(endorheic basin)* drainage: Lake Chad (2,497,738 sq km)

Major aquifers: Lullemeden-Irhazer Aquifer System, Murzuk-Djado Basin, North Western Sahara Aquifer, Taoudeni-Tanezrouft Basin

Population distribution: the vast majority of the populace is found in the extreme northern part of the country along the Mediterranean Coast as shown in this population distribution map

Natural hazards: mountainous areas subject to severe earthquakes; mudslides and floods in rainy season; droughts

Geography - note: largest country in Africa but 80% desert; canyons and caves in the southern Hoggar Mountains and in the barren Tassili n'Ajjer area in the southeast of the country contain numerous examples of prehistoric art - rock paintings and carvings depicting human activities and wild and domestic animals (elephants, giraffes, cattle) - that date to the African Humid Period, roughly 11,000 to 5,000 years ago, when the region was completely vegetated

PEOPLE AND SOCIETY

Population: 44,178,884 (2022 est.)
country comparison to the world: 34

Nationality: *noun:* Algerian(s)
adjective: Algerian

Ethnic groups: Arab-Berber 99%, European less than 1%
note: although almost all Algerians are Berber in origin (not Arab), only a minority identify themselves as primarily Berber, about 15% of the total population; these people live mostly in the mountainous region of Kabylie east of Algiers and several other communities; the Berbers are also Muslim but identify with their Berber rather than Arab cultural heritage; Berbers have long agitated, sometimes violently, for autonomy; the government is unlikely to grant autonomy but has officially recognized Berber languages and introduced them into public schools

Languages: Arabic (official), French (lingua franca), Berber or Tamazight (official); dialects include Kabyle Berber (Taqbaylit), Shawiya Berber (Tacawit), Mzab Berber, Tuareg Berber (Tamahaq)
major-language sample(s):
كتاب حقائق العالم، المصدر الذي لا يمكن الاستغناء عنه للمعلومات الأساسية
(Arabic)

Religions: Muslim (official; predominantly Sunni) 99%, other (includes Christian, Jewish, Ahmadi Muslims, Shia Muslims, Ibadi Muslims) <1% (2012 est.)

Demographic profile: For the first two thirds of the 20th century, Algeria's high fertility rate caused its population to grow rapidly. However, about a decade after independence from France in 1962, the total fertility rate fell dramatically from 7 children per woman in the 1970s to about 2.4 in 2000, slowing Algeria's population growth rate by the late 1980s. The lower fertility rate was mainly the result of women's rising age at first marriage (virtually all Algerian children being born in wedlock) and to a lesser extent the wider use of contraceptives. Later marriages and a preference for smaller families are attributed to increases in women's education and participation in the labor market; higher unemployment; and a shortage of housing forcing multiple generations to live together. The average woman's age at first marriage increased from about 19 in the mid-1950s to 24 in the mid-1970s to 30.5 in the late 1990s.

Algeria's fertility rate experienced an unexpected upturn in the early 2000s, as the average woman's age at first marriage dropped slightly. The reversal in fertility could represent a temporary fluctuation in marriage age or, less likely, a decrease in the steady rate of contraceptive use.

Thousands of Algerian peasants - mainly Berber men from the Kabylia region - faced with land dispossession and economic hardship under French rule migrated temporarily to France to work in manufacturing and mining during the first half of the 20th century. This movement accelerated during World War I, when Algerians filled in for French factory workers or served as soldiers. In the years following independence, low-skilled Algerian workers and Algerians who had supported the French (known as Harkis) emigrated en masse to France. Tighter French immigration rules and Algiers' decision to cease managing labor migration to France in the 1970s limited legal emigration largely to family reunification.

Not until Algeria's civil war in the 1990s did the country again experience substantial outmigration. Many Algerians legally entered Tunisia without visas claiming to be tourists and then stayed as workers. Other Algerians headed to Europe seeking asylum, although France imposed restrictions. Sub-Saharan African migrants came to Algeria after its civil war to work in agriculture and mining. In the 2000s, a wave of educated Algerians went abroad seeking skilled jobs in a wider range of destinations, increasing their presence in North America and Spain. At the same time, legal foreign workers principally from China and Egypt came to work in Algeria's construction and oil sectors. Illegal migrants from Sub-Saharan Africa, particularly Malians, Nigeriens, and Gambians, continue to come to Algeria in search of work or to use it as a stepping stone to Libya and Europe.

Since 1975, Algeria also has been the main recipient of Sahrawi refugees from the ongoing conflict in Western Sahara (today part of Morocco). More than 100,000 Sahrawis are estimated to be living in five refugee camps in southwestern Algeria near Tindouf.

Age structure: *0-14 years:* 29.58% (male 6,509,490/female 6,201,450)
15-24 years: 13.93% (male 3,063,972/female 2,922,368)
25-54 years: 42.91% (male 9,345,997/female 9,091,558)
55-64 years: 7.41% (male 1,599,369/female 1,585,233)
65 years and over: 6.17% (male 1,252,084/female 1,401,357) (2020 est.)

Dependency ratios: *total dependency ratio:* 60.1
youth dependency ratio: 49.3
elderly dependency ratio: 10.8
potential support ratio: 9.3 (2020 est.)

Median age: *total:* 28.9 years
male: 28.6 years
female: 29.3 years (2020 est.)
country comparison to the world: 139

Population growth rate: 1.34% (2022 est.)
country comparison to the world: 71

Birth rate: 18.52 births/1,000 population (2022 est.)
country comparison to the world: 78

Death rate: 4.32 deaths/1,000 population (2022 est.)
country comparison to the world: 207

Net migration rate: -0.82 migrant(s)/1,000 population (2022 est.)
country comparison to the world: 138

Population distribution: the vast majority of the populace is found in the extreme northern part of the country along the Mediterranean Coast as shown in this population distribution map

Urbanization: *urban population:* 74.8% of total population (2022)
rate of urbanization: 1.99% annual rate of change (2020-25 est.)

Major urban areas - population: 2.854 million ALGIERS (capital), 922,000 Oran (2022)

Sex ratio: *at birth:* 1.05 male(s)/female
0-14 years: 1.05 male(s)/female
15-24 years: 1.05 male(s)/female
25-54 years: 1.03 male(s)/female
55-64 years: 1 male(s)/female
65 years and over: 0.75 male(s)/female
total population: 1.03 male(s)/female (2022 est.)

Maternal mortality ratio: 112 deaths/100,000 live births (2017 est.)
country comparison to the world: 68

Infant mortality rate: *total:* 19.72 deaths/1,000 live births
male: 21.77 deaths/1,000 live births
female: 17.55 deaths/1,000 live births (2022 est.)
country comparison to the world: 82

Life expectancy at birth: *total population:* 78.03 years
male: 76.57 years
female: 79.57 years (2022 est.)
country comparison to the world: 77

Total fertility rate: 2.51 children born/woman (2022 est.)
country comparison to the world: 68

Contraceptive prevalence rate: 53.6% (2018/19)

Drinking water source: *improved: urban:* 99.6% of population
rural: 98.8% of population
total: 99.4% of population
unimproved: urban: 0.4% of population
rural: 1.2% of population
total: 0.6% of population (2020 est.)

Current health expenditure: 6.2% of GDP (2019)

Physicians density: 1.72 physicians/1,000 population (2018)

Hospital bed density: 1.9 beds/1,000 population (2015)

Sanitation facility access: *improved: urban:* 98.3% of population
rural: 91.3% of population
total: 96.5% of population
unimproved: urban: 1.7% of population
rural: 8.7% of population
total: 3.5% of population (2020 est.)

HIV/AIDS - adult prevalence rate: (2020 est.) <0.1%

Obesity - adult prevalence rate: 27.4% (2016)
country comparison to the world: 38

Alcohol consumption per capita: *total:* 0.59 liters of pure alcohol (2019 est.)
beer: 0.31 liters of pure alcohol (2019 est.)
wine: 0.2 liters of pure alcohol (2019 est.)
spirits: 0.08 liters of pure alcohol (2019 est.)

other alcohols: 0 liters of pure alcohol (2019 est.)
country comparison to the world: 160

Tobacco use: *total:* 21% (2020 est.)
male: 41.3% (2020 est.)
female: 0.7% (2020 est.)
country comparison to the world: 80

Children under the age of 5 years underweight: 2.7% (2018/19)
country comparison to the world: 100

Child marriage: *women married by age 15:* 0%
women married by age 18: 3.8% (2019 est.)

Education expenditures: 6.1% of GDP (2019 est.)
country comparison to the world: 30

Literacy: *definition:* age 15 and over can read and write
total population: 81.4%
male: 87.4%
female: 75.3% (2018)

School life expectancy (primary to tertiary education): *total:* 14 years
male: 14 years
female: 15 years (2011)

Unemployment, youth ages 15-24: *total:* 39.3%
male: 33.1%
female: 82% (2017 est.)

ENVIRONMENT

Environment - current issues: air pollution in major cities; soil erosion from overgrazing and other poor farming practices; desertification; dumping of raw sewage, petroleum refining wastes, and other industrial effluents is leading to the pollution of rivers and coastal waters; Mediterranean Sea, in particular, becoming polluted from oil wastes, soil erosion, and fertilizer runoff; inadequate supplies of potable water

Environment - international agreements: *party to:* Biodiversity, Climate Change, Climate Change-Kyoto Protocol, Climate Change-Paris Agreement, Comprehensive Nuclear Test Ban, Desertification, Endangered Species, Environmental Modification, Hazardous Wastes, Law of the Sea, Ozone Layer Protection, Ship Pollution, Wetlands
signed, but not ratified: Nuclear Test Ban

Air pollutants: *particulate matter emissions:* 35.17 micrograms per cubic meter (2016 est.)
carbon dioxide emissions: 150.01 megatons (2016 est.)
methane emissions: 49.94 megatons (2020 est.)

Climate: arid to semiarid; mild, wet winters with hot, dry summers along coast; drier with cold winters and hot summers on high plateau; sirocco is a hot, dust/sand-laden wind especially common in summer

Land use: *agricultural land:* 17.4% (2018 est.)
arable land: 3.2% (2018 est.)
permanent crops: 0.4% (2018 est.)
permanent pasture: 13.8% (2018 est.)
forest: 0.8% (2018 est.)
other: 81.8% (2018 est.)

Urbanization: *urban population:* 74.8% of total population (2022)
rate of urbanization: 1.99% annual rate of change (2020-25 est.)

Revenue from forest resources: *forest revenues:* 0.1% of GDP (2018 est.)
country comparison to the world: 110

Revenue from coal: *coal revenues:* 0% of GDP (2018 est.)
country comparison to the world: 53

Waste and recycling: *municipal solid waste generated annually:* 12,378,740 tons (2016 est.)
municipal solid waste recycled annually: 990,299 tons (2013 est.)
percent of municipal solid waste recycled: 8% (2013 est.)

Major watersheds (area sq km):

Atlantic Ocean drainage: Niger (2,261,741 sq km)

Internal *(endorheic basin)* drainage: Lake Chad (2,497,738 sq km)

Major aquifers: Lullemeden-Irhazer Aquifer System, Murzuk-Djado Basin, North Western Sahara Aquifer, Taoudeni-Tanezrouft Basin

Total water withdrawal: *municipal:* 3.6 billion cubic meters (2017 est.)
industrial: 191 million cubic meters (2017 est.)
agricultural: 6.671 billion cubic meters (2017 est.)

Total renewable water resources: 11.67 billion cubic meters (2017 est.)

GOVERNMENT

Country name: *conventional long form:* People's Democratic Republic of Algeria
conventional short form: Algeria
local long form: Al Jumhuriyah al Jaza'iriyah ad Dimuqratiyah ash Sha'biyah
local short form: Al Jaza'ir
etymology: the country name derives from the capital city of Algiers

Government type: presidential republic

Capital: *name:* Algiers
geographic coordinates: 36 45 N, 3 03 E
time difference: UTC+1 (6 hours ahead of Washington, DC, during Standard Time)
etymology: name derives from the Arabic "al-Jazair" meaning "the islands" and refers to the four islands formerly off the coast but joined to the mainland since 1525

Administrative divisions: 58 provinces (wilayas, singular - wilaya); Adrar, Ain Defla, Ain Temouchent, Alger, Annaba, Batna, Bechar, Bejaia, Beni Abbes, Biskra, Blida, Bordj Badji Mokhtar, Bordj Bou Arreridj, Bouira, Boumerdes, Chlef, Constantine, Djanet, Djelfa, El Bayadh, El Meghaier, El Meniaa, El Oued, El Tarf, Ghardaia, Guelma, Illizi, In Guezzam, In Salah, Jijel, Khenchela, Laghouat, Mascara, Medea, Mila, Mostaganem, M'Sila, Naama, Oran, Ouargla, Ouled Djellal, Oum el Bouaghi, Relizane, Saida, Setif, Sidi Bel Abbes, Skikda, Souk Ahras, Tamanrasset, Tebessa, Tiaret, Timimoun, Tindouf, Tipaza, Tissemsilt, Tizi Ouzou, Tlemcen, Touggourt

Independence: 5 July 1962 (from France)

National holiday: Independence Day, 5 July (1962); Revolution Day, 1 November (1954)

Constitution: *history:* several previous; latest approved by referendum November 2020
amendments: proposed by the president of the republic or through the president with the support of three fourths of the members of both houses of Parliament in joint session; passage requires approval by both houses, approval by referendum, and promulgation by the president; the president can forego a referendum if the Constitutional Council determines the proposed amendment does not conflict with basic constitutional principles; articles including the republican form of government, the integrity and unity of the country, and fundamental citizens' liberties and rights cannot be amended; amended 2002, 2008, 2016; last in 2020

Legal system: mixed legal system of French civil law and Islamic law; judicial review of legislative acts in ad hoc Constitutional Council composed of various public officials including several Supreme Court justices

International law organization participation: has not submitted an ICJ jurisdiction declaration; non-party state to the ICCt

Citizenship: *citizenship by birth:* no
citizenship by descent only: the mother must be a citizen of Algeria
dual citizenship recognized: no
residency requirement for naturalization: 7 years

Suffrage: 18 years of age; universal

Executive branch: *chief of state:* President Abdelmadjid TEBBOUNE (since 12 December 2019)
head of government: Prime Minister Ayman BENABDERRAHMANE (since 7 July 2021)
cabinet: Cabinet of Ministers appointed by the president
elections/appointments: president directly elected by absolute majority popular vote in two rounds if needed for a 5-year term (eligible for a second term); election last held on 12 December 2019 (next to be held in 2024); prime minister nominated by the president after consultation with the majority party in Parliament
election results: 2019: Abdelmadjid TEBBOUNE (FLN) 58.1%, Abdelkader BENGRINA (El-Bina) 17.4%, Ali BENFLIS (Talaie El Hurriyet) 10.6%, Azzedine MIHOUBI (National Democratic Rally, RND) 7.3%, Abdelaziz BELAID (Front El Mustakbal, FM) 6.7%
2014: Abdelaziz BOUTEFLIKA reelected president for a fourth term; percent of vote - Abdelaziz BOUTEFLIKA (FLN) 81.5%, Ali BENFLIS (FLN) 12.2%, Abdelaziz BELAID (Future Front) 3.4%, other 2.9%

Legislative branch: *description:* bicameral Parliament or Barlaman consists of:
Council of the Nation or Majlis al-Umma (174 seats; two-thirds of members indirectly elected by simple majority vote by an electoral college composed of local assemblies within each wilaya, and one-third of members appointed by the president; members serve 6-year terms with one-half of the membership renewed every 3 years)

National People's Assembly or al-Majlis al-Sha'abi al-Watani (407 seats including 8 seats for Algerian diaspora); members directly elected in multi-seat constituencies by open-list proportional representation vote to serve 5-year terms); note - in March 2021, President TEBBOUNE ordered the number of Assembly seats be reduced to 407 from 462
elections:
Council of the Nation - last held on 5 February 2022 (next election NA)

National People's Assembly - snap election held on 12 June 2021 (next to be held on 12 June 2026)
election results:

Council of the Nation - percent of vote by party - NA; seats by party - FLN 54, RND 22, Future Front 7, National Construction Movement 5, FFS 4, other 6, independent 18, appointed 58; composition - NA

National People's Assembly - percent of vote by party - NA; seats by party - FLN 98, MSP 65, RND 58, (Future Front) 48, Movement of National Construction 39, other 15, independent 84; composition - men 374, women 33, percent of women 8.1%; note - total Parliament percent of women 7.3%

Judicial branch: *highest court(s):* Supreme Court or Le Cour Suprême, (consists of 150 judges organized into 8 chambers: Civil, Commercial and Maritime, Criminal, House of Offenses and Contraventions, House of Petitions, Land, Personal Status, and Social; Constitutional Council (consists of 12 members including the court chairman and deputy chairman); note - Algeria's judicial system does not include sharia courts
judge selection and term of office: Supreme Court judges appointed by the High Council of Magistracy, an administrative body presided over by the president of the republic, and includes the republic vice-president and several members; judges appointed for life; Constitutional Council members - 4 appointed by the president of the republic, 2 each by the 2 houses of Parliament, 2 by the Supreme Court, and 2 by the Council of State; Council president and members appointed for single 6-year terms with half the membership renewed every 3 years
subordinate courts: appellate or wilaya courts; first instance or daira tribunals

Political parties and leaders: Algerian National Front or FNA [Moussa TOUATI]
Algerian Popular Movement or MPA [Amara BENYOUNES]
Algerian Rally or RA [Ali ZAGHDOUD]
Algeria's Hope Rally or TAJ [Fatma Zohra ZEROUATI]
Democratic and Social Movement or MDS [Fethi GHARES]
Dignity or El Karama [Mohamed DAOUI]
El-Bina (Harakat El-Binaa El-Watani) [Abdelkader BENGRINA]
El-Islah [Filali GHOUINI]
Ennour El Djazairi Party (Algerian Radiance Party) or PED [Badreddine BELBAZ]
Front for Justice and Development or El Adala [Abdallah DJABALLAH]
Future Front or El Mostakbel [Abdelaziz BELAID]
Islamic Renaissance Movement or Ennahda Movement [Mohamed DOUIBI]
Justice and Development Front or FJD [Abdellah DJABALLAH]
Movement for National Reform or Islah [Filali GHOUINI]
Movement of Society for Peace or MSP [Abderrazak MAKRI]
National Construction Movement (Harakat Al-bina' Al-watanii) [Abdelkader BENGRINA]
National Democratic Rally (Rassemblement National Democratique) or RND [Tayeb ZITOUNI]
National Front for Social Justice or FNJS [Khaled BOUNEDJEMA]
National Liberation Front or FLN [Abou El Fadhel BAADJI]
National Party for Solidarity and Development or PNSD [Dalila YALAQUI]
National Reform Movement or Islah [Djahid YOUNSI]
National Republican Alliance or ANR [Belkacem SAHLI]
New Dawn Party (El-Fajr El-Jadid) [Tahar BENBAIBECHE]
New Generation (Jil Jadid) [Soufiane DJILALI]
Oath of 1954 or Ahd 54 [Ali Fawzi REBAINE]
Party of Justice and Liberty or PLJ [Djamel Ben ZIADI]
Rally for Culture and Democracy or RCD [Mohcine BELABBAS]
Socialist Forces Front or FFS [Youcef AOUCHICHE]
Union for Change and Progress or UCP [Zoubida ASSOUL]
Union of Democratic and Social Forces or UFDS [Noureddine BAHBOUH]
Vanguard of Liberties (Talaie El Hurriyet) [Abdelkader SAADI]
Workers Party or PT [Louisa HANOUNE]
Youth Party or PJ [Hamana BOUCHARMA]
note: a law banning political parties based on religion was enacted in March 1997

International organization participation: ABEDA, AfDB, AFESD, AMF, AMU, AU, BIS, CAEU, CD, FAO, G-15, G-24, G-77, IAEA, IBRD, ICAO, ICC (national committees), ICRM, IDA, IDB, IFAD, IFC, IFRCS, IHO, ILO, IMF, IMO, IMSO, Interpol, IOC, IOM, IPU, ISO, ITSO, ITU, ITUC (NGOs), LAS, MIGA, MONUSCO, NAM, OAPEC, OAS (observer), OIC, OPCW, OPEC, OSCE (partner), UN, UNCTAD, UNESCO, UNHCR, UNIDO, UNITAR, UNWTO, UPU, WCO, WHO, WIPO, WMO, WTO (observer)

Diplomatic representation in the US: *chief of mission:* Ambassador Ahmed BOUTACHE (since 26 October 2021)
chancery: 2118 Kalorama Road NW, Washington, DC 20008
telephone: [1] (202) 265-2800
FAX: [1] (202) 986-5906
email address and website:
mail@algerianembassy.org
https://www.algerianembassy.org/
consulate(s) general: New York

Diplomatic representation from the US: *chief of mission:* Ambassador Elizabeth Moore AUBIN (since 9 February 2022)
embassy: 05 Chemin Cheikh Bachir, Ibrahimi, El-Biar 16030, Alger
mailing address: 6030 Algiers Place, Washington DC 20521-6030
telephone: [213] (0) 770-08-2000
FAX: [213] (0) 770-08-2299
email address and website:
ACSAlgiers@state.gov
https://dz.usembassy.gov/

Flag description: two equal vertical bands of green (hoist side) and white; a red, five-pointed star within a red crescent centered over the two-color boundary; the colors represent Islam (green), purity and peace (white), and liberty (red); the crescent and star are also Islamic symbols, but the crescent is more closed than those of other Muslim countries because Algerians believe the long crescent horns bring happiness

National symbol(s): five-pointed star between the extended horns of a crescent moon, fennec fox; national colors: green, white, red

National anthem: *name:* "Kassaman" (We Pledge)
lyrics/music: Mufdi ZAKARIAH/Mohamed FAWZI
note: adopted 1962; ZAKARIAH wrote "Kassaman" as a poem while imprisoned in Algiers by French colonial forces

National heritage: *total World Heritage Sites:* 7 (6 cultural, 1 mixed)
selected World Heritage Site locales: Beni Hammad Fort (c); Djémila (c); Casbah of Algiers (c); M'zab Valley (c); Tassili n'Ajjer (m); Timgad (c); Tipasa (c)

ECONOMY

Economic overview: Algeria's economy remains dominated by the state, a legacy of the country's socialist post-independence development model. In recent years the Algerian Government has halted the privatization of state-owned industries and imposed restrictions on imports and foreign involvement in its economy, pursuing an explicit import substitution policy.

Hydrocarbons have long been the backbone of the economy, accounting for roughly 30% of GDP, 60% of budget revenues, and nearly 95% of export earnings. Algeria has the 10th-largest reserves of natural gas in the world - including the 3rd-largest reserves of shale gas - and is the 6th-largest gas exporter. It ranks 16th in proven oil reserves. Hydrocarbon exports enabled Algeria to maintain macroeconomic stability, amass large foreign currency reserves, and maintain low external debt while global oil prices were high. With lower oil prices since 2014, Algeria's foreign exchange reserves have declined by more than half and its oil stabilization fund has decreased from about $20 billion at the end of 2013 to about $7 billion in 2017, which is the statutory minimum.

Declining oil prices have also reduced the government's ability to use state-driven growth to distribute rents and fund generous public subsidies, and the government has been under pressure to reduce spending. Over the past three years, the government has enacted incremental increases in some taxes, resulting in modest increases in prices for gasoline, cigarettes, alcohol, and certain imported goods, but it has refrained from reducing subsidies, particularly for education, healthcare, and housing programs.

Algiers has increased protectionist measures since 2015 to limit its import bill and encourage domestic production of non-oil and gas industries. Since 2015, the government has imposed additional restrictions on access to foreign exchange for imports, and import quotas for specific products, such as cars. In January 2018 the government imposed an indefinite suspension on the importation of roughly 850 products, subject to periodic review.

President BOUTEFLIKA announced in fall 2017 that Algeria intends to develop its non-conventional energy resources. Algeria has struggled to develop non-hydrocarbon industries because of heavy regulation and an emphasis on state-driven growth. Algeria has not increased non-hydrocarbon exports, and hydrocarbon exports have declined because of field depletion and increased domestic demand.

Real GDP (purchasing power parity): $468.4 billion (2020 est.)
$495.56 billion (2019 est.)
$491.63 billion (2018 est.)
note: data are in 2017 dollars
country comparison to the world: 42

Real GDP growth rate: 1.4% (2017 est.)

3.2% (2016 est.)
3.7% (2015 est.)
country comparison to the world: 157

Real GDP per capita: $10,700 (2020 est.)
$11,500 (2019 est.)
$11,600 (2018 est.)
note: data are in 2017 dollars
country comparison to the world: 138

GDP (official exchange rate): $169.912 billion (2019 est.)

Inflation rate (consumer prices): 1.9% (2019 est.)
4.2% (2018 est.)
5.6% (2017 est.)
country comparison to the world: 104

Credit ratings: *note:* The year refers to the year in which the current credit rating was first obtained.

GDP - composition, by sector of origin: *agriculture:* 13.3% (2017 est.)
industry: 39.3% (2017 est.)
services: 47.4% (2017 est.)

GDP - composition, by end use: *household consumption:* 42.7% (2017 est.)
government consumption: 20.2% (2017 est.)
investment in fixed capital: 38.1% (2017 est.)
investment in inventories: 11.2% (2017 est.)
exports of goods and services: 23.6% (2017 est.)
imports of goods and services: -35.8% (2017 est.)

Agricultural products: potatoes, wheat, milk, watermelons, barley, onions, tomatoes, oranges, dates, vegetables

Industries: petroleum, natural gas, light industries, mining, electrical, petrochemical, food processing

Industrial production growth rate: 0.6% (2017 est.)
country comparison to the world: 164

Labor force: 10.859 million (2017 est.)
country comparison to the world: 48

Labor force - by occupation: *agriculture:* 10.8%
industry: 30.9%
services: 58.4% (2011 est.)

Unemployment rate: 11.7% (2017 est.)
10.5% (2016 est.)
country comparison to the world: 160

Unemployment, youth ages 15-24: *total:* 39.3%
male: 33.1%
female: 82% (2017 est.)
country comparison to the world: 14

Population below poverty line: 5.5% (2011 est.)

Gini Index coefficient - distribution of family income: 27.6 (2011 est.)
country comparison to the world: 161

Household income or consumption by percentage share: *lowest 10%:* 2.8%
highest 10%: 26.8% (1995)

Budget: *revenues:* 54.15 billion (2017 est.)
expenditures: 70.2 billion (2017 est.)

Budget surplus (+) or deficit (-): -9.6% (of GDP) (2017 est.)
country comparison to the world: 207

Public debt: 27.5% of GDP (2017 est.)
20.4% of GDP (2016 est.)
note: data cover central government debt as well as debt issued by subnational entities and intra-governmental debt
country comparison to the world: 170

Taxes and other revenues: 32.3% (of GDP) (2017 est.)
country comparison to the world: 67

Fiscal year: calendar year

Current account balance: -$22.1 billion (2017 est.)
-$26.47 billion (2016 est.)
country comparison to the world: 198

Exports: $38.32 billion (2019 est.)
$44.39 billion (2018 est.)
note: Data are in current year dollars and do not include illicit exports or re-exports.
country comparison to the world: 67

Exports - partners: Italy 13%, France 13%, Spain 12%, United States 7%, United Kingdom 7%, India 5%, South Korea 5% (2019)

Exports - commodities: crude petroleum, natural gas, refined petroleum, fertilizers, ammonia (2019)

Imports: $54.26 billion (2019 est.) note: data are in current year dollars
$60.05 billion (2018 est.) note: data are in current year dollars
country comparison to the world: 56

Imports - partners: China 18%, France 14%, Italy 8%, Spain 8%, Germany 5%, Turkey 5% (2019)

Imports - commodities: refined petroleum, wheat, packaged medical supplies, milk, vehicle parts (2019)

Reserves of foreign exchange and gold: $97.89 billion (31 December 2017 est.)
$114.7 billion (31 December 2016 est.)
country comparison to the world: 26

Debt - external: $5.574 billion (2019 est.)
$5.666 billion (2018 est.)
country comparison to the world: 130

Exchange rates: Algerian dinars (DZD) per US dollar -
131.085 (2020 est.)
119.775 (2019 est.)
118.4617 (2018 est.)
100.691 (2014 est.)
80.579 (2013 est.)

ENERGY

Electricity access: *electrification - total population:* 99.4% (2019)
electrification - urban areas: 99.6% (2019)
electrification - rural areas: 97% (2019)

Electricity: *installed generating capacity:* 21.694 million kW (2020 est.)
consumption: 66.646 billion kWh (2019 est.)
exports: 673 million kWh (2019 est.)
imports: 531 million kWh (2019 est.)
transmission/distribution losses: 9.897 billion kWh (2019 est.)

Electricity generation sources: *fossil fuels:* 98.9% of total installed capacity (2020 est.)
solar: 0.9% of total installed capacity (2020 est.)
hydroelectricity: 0.1% of total installed capacity (2020 est.)

Coal: *production:* 0 metric tons (2020 est.)
consumption: 85,000 metric tons (2020 est.)
exports: 0 metric tons (2020 est.)
imports: 85,000 metric tons (2020 est.)
proven reserves: 59 million metric tons (2019 est.)

Petroleum: *total petroleum production:* 1,414,800 bbl/day (2021 est.)
refined petroleum consumption: 450,500 bbl/day (2019 est.)
crude oil and lease condensate exports: 633,500 bbl/day (2018 est.)
crude oil and lease condensate imports: 4,100 bbl/day (2018 est.)
crude oil estimated reserves: 12.2 billion barrels (2021 est.)

Refined petroleum products - production: 627,900 bbl/day (2015 est.)
country comparison to the world: 29

Refined petroleum products – exports: 578,800 bbl/day (2015 est.)
country comparison to the world: 15

Refined petroleum products - imports: 82,930 bbl/day (2015 est.)
country comparison to the world: 61

Natural gas: *production:* 87,853,976,000 cubic meters (2019 est.)
consumption: 46,945,035,000 cubic meters (2019 est.)
exports: 42,667,386,000 cubic meters (2019 est.)
imports: 0 cubic meters (2021 est.)
proven reserves: 4,503,900,000,000 cubic meters (2021 est.)

Carbon dioxide emissions: 151.633 million metric tonnes of CO_2 (2019 est.)
from coal and metallurgical coke: 352,000 metric tonnes of CO_2 (2019 est.)
from petroleum and other liquids: 57.867 million metric tonnes of CO_2 (2019 est.)
from consumed natural gas: 93.414 million metric tonnes of CO_2 (2019 est.)
country comparison to the world: 34

Energy consumption per capita: 61.433 million Btu/person (2019 est.)
country comparison to the world: 91

COMMUNICATIONS

Telephones - fixed lines: *total subscriptions:* 4,784,306 (2020 est.)
subscriptions per 100 inhabitants: 11 (2020 est.)
country comparison to the world: 31

Telephones - mobile cellular: *total subscriptions:* 45,555,673 (2020 est.)
subscriptions per 100 inhabitants: 104 (2020 est.)
country comparison to the world: 33

Telecommunication systems: *general assessment:* Algeria has a steadily developing telecom infrastructure with growth encouraged by supportive regulatory measures and by government policies aimed at delivering serviceable internet connections across the country; mobile broadband is largely based on 3G and LTE, and the data rates are also low in global terms; LTE is available in all provinces, investment is required from the mobile network operators (MNOs) to improve the quality of service; the state has previously been hesitant to commit to 5G, instead encouraging the MNOs to undertake upgrades to LTE infrastructure before investing in commercial 5G services; in March 2022, the state is in the process of freeing up the requisite spectrum to enable the MNOs to launch 5G services sometime this year; fixed internet speeds remain slow (2022)
domestic: a limited network of fixed-lines with a teledensity of slightly less than 11 telephones per

100 persons has been offset by the rapid increase in mobile-cellular subscribership; mobile-cellular teledensity was approximately 104 telephones per 100 persons in 2020 (2020)
international: country code - 213; ALPAL-2 is a submarine telecommunications cable system in the Mediterranean Sea linking Algeria and the Spanish Balearic island of Majorca; ORVAL is a submarine cable to Spain; landing points for the TE North/TGN-Eurasia/SEACOM/SeaMeWe-4 fiber-optic submarine cable system that provides links to Europe, the Middle East, and Asia; MED cable connecting Algeria with France; microwave radio relay to Italy, France, Spain, Morocco, and Tunisia; Algeria part of the 4,500 Km terrestrial Trans Sahara Backbone network which connects to other fiber networks in the region; Alcomstat-1 satellite offering telemedicine network (2020)

Broadcast media: state-run Radio-Television Algerienne operates the broadcast media and carries programming in Arabic, Berber dialects, and French; use of satellite dishes is widespread, providing easy access to European and Arab satellite stations; state-run radio operates several national networks and roughly 40 regional radio stations

Internet country code: .dz

Internet users: *total:* 27,626,157 (2020 est.)
percent of population: 63% (2020 est.)
country comparison to the world: 33

Broadband - fixed subscriptions: *total:* 3,790,459 (2020 est.)
subscriptions per 100 inhabitants: 9 (2020 est.)
country comparison to the world: 40

TRANSPORTATION

National air transport system: *number of registered air carriers:* 3 (2020)
inventory of registered aircraft operated by air carriers: 87
annual passenger traffic on registered air carriers: 6,442,442 (2018)
annual freight traffic on registered air carriers: 28.28 million (2018) mt-km

Civil aircraft registration country code prefix: 7T

Airports: *total:* 149 (2021)
country comparison to the world: 36

Airports - with paved runways: *total:* 67
over 3,047 m: 14
2,438 to 3,047 m: 27
1,524 to 2,437 m: 18
914 to 1,523 m: 6
under 914 m: 2 (2021)

Airports - with unpaved runways: *total:* 82
2,438 to 3,047 m: 2
1,524 to 2,437 m: 16
914 to 1,523 m: 36
under 914 m: 28 (2021)

Heliports: 4 (2022)

Pipelines: 2,600 km condensate, 16,415 km gas, 3,447 km liquid petroleum gas, 7,036 km oil, 144 km refined products (2013)

Railways: *total:* 3,973 km (2014)
standard gauge: 2,888 km (2014) 1.432-m gauge (283 km electrified)
narrow gauge: 1,085 km (2014) 1.055-m gauge
country comparison to the world: 50

Roadways: *total:* 104,000 km (2015)
paved: 71,656 km (2015)
unpaved: 32,344 km (2015)
country comparison to the world: 45

Merchant marine: *total:* **114**
by type: bulk carrier 1, container ship 2, general cargo 11, oil tanker 11, other 89 (2021)
country comparison to the world: 84

Ports and terminals: *major seaport(s):* Algiers, Annaba, Arzew, Bejaia, Djendjene, Jijel, Mostaganem, Oran, Skikda
LNG terminal(s) (export): Arzew, Bethioua, Skikda

MILITARY AND SECURITY

Military and security forces: Algerian People's National Army (ANP): Land Forces, Naval Forces (includes Coast Guard), Air Forces, Territorial Air Defense Forces, Republican Guard (under ANP but responsible to the President), National Gendarmerie; Ministry of Interior: General Directorate of National Security (national police) (2022)

Military expenditures: 5.6% of GDP (2021 est.)
6.7% of GDP (2020 est.)
6% of GDP (2019) (approximately $19.2 billion)
5.5% of GDP (2018) (approximately $17.9 billion)
5.9% of GDP (2017) (approximately $18.8 billion)
country comparison to the world: 6

Military and security service personnel strengths: approximately 140,000 ANP personnel (120,000 Army; 6,000 Navy; 14,000 Air Force); approximately 130,000 National Gendarmerie; approximately 200,000 General Directorate of National Security (2022)

Military equipment inventories and acquisitions: the ANP's inventory includes mostly Russian-sourced equipment; since 2010, Algeria has received arms from a variety of countries, with Russia as the leading supplier (2022)

Military service age and obligation: 18 is the legal minimum age for voluntary military service for men and women; 19-30 years of age for compulsory service for men (all Algerian men must register at age 17); conscript service obligation reduced from 18 to 12 months in 2014 (2022)
note: as of 2020, conscripts comprised an estimated 70% of the military

Military - note: the ANP has played a large role in the country's politics since independence in 1962, including coups in 1965 and 1991; it was a key backer of BOUTEFLIKA's election in 1999 and remained a center of power during his 20-year rule; the military was instrumental in BOUTEFLIKA's resignation in 2019 when it withdrew support and called for him to be removed from office

the ANP traditionally has focused on internal stability and on Morocco where relations as of 2022 remained tense over Western Sahara and Algerian accusations that Morocco supports the Movement for the Autonomy of Kabylie (MAK), a separatist group in Algeria's Kabylie region; however, following the Arab Spring events of 2011 and a series of cross- border terrorist attacks emanating from Mali in 2012-2013, particularly the 2013 attack on a commercial gas plant by al- Qa'ida-linked terrorists that resulted in the deaths of 35 hostages and 29 jihadists, it has made a concerted effort to beef up security along its other borders and promote regional security cooperation; since 2013, additional Army and paramilitary forces were deployed to the borders with Tunisia, Libya, Niger, and Mali to interdict and deter cross-border attacks by Islamic militant groups; in addition, Algeria has provided security assistance to some neighboring countries, particularly Tunisia, and conducted joint military/counter-terrorism operations (2022)

TERRORISM

Terrorist group(s): al-Qa'ida in the Islamic Maghreb (AQIM); Islamic State of Iraq and ash-Sham (ISIS) – Algeria; al-Mulathamun Battalion (al-Mourabitoun)

TRANSNATIONAL ISSUES

Disputes - international: *Algeria-Morocco:* the Algerian-Moroccan land border remains closed; Algeria's border with Morocco remains an irritant to bilateral relations, each nation accusing the other of harboring militants and arms smuggling; the National Liberation Front's (FLN) assertions of a claim to Chirac Pastures in southeastern Morocco remain a dormant dispute
Algeria-Libya: dormant dispute includes Libyan claims of about 32,000 sq km still reflected on its maps of southeastern Algeria
Algeria-Mali: none identified
Algeria-Mauritania: none identified
Algeria-Niger: none identified
Algeria-Tunisia: none identified

Refugees and internally displaced persons: *refugees (country of origin):* more than 100,000 (Sahrawi, mostly living in Algerian-sponsored camps in the southwestern Algerian town of Tindouf) (2018); 6,750 (Syria) (mid-year 2021)

Trafficking in persons: *current situation:* human traffickers exploit domestic and foreign victims; Algerian women and girls are vulnerable to sex trafficking due to financial problems or after running away from home; undocumented sub-Saharan migrants are vulnerable to labor and sex trafficking and are exploited in restaurants, houses, and informal worksites; sub-Saharan men and women needing more funds for their onward journey to Europe work illegally in construction and commercial sex and are vulnerable to sex trafficking and debt bondage; foreign women and girls, mainly from sub-Saharan Africa, are subject to sex trafficking in bars and informal brothels; criminal begging rings that exploit sub-Saharan African migrant children are common
tier rating: Tier 3 — Algeria does not fully comply with the minimum standards for the elimination of trafficking and is not making significant efforts to do so; authorities prosecuted fewer traffickers and identified fewer victims compared to last year and convicted no traffickers; the government continued to lack effective procedures and mechanisms to screen for, identify, and refer potential victims to protective services and punished some potential victims for unlawful acts traffickers forced them to commit; the government took some steps to combat trafficking, including prosecuting some traffickers, identifying some victims, and continuing to implement its 2019-2021 national anti-trafficking action plan (2020)

Illicit drugs: NA

AMERICAN SAMOA

INTRODUCTION

Background: Tutuila was settled by 1000 B.C. and the island served as a refuge for exiled chiefs and defeated warriors from the other Samoan islands. The Manu'a Islands developed its own traditional chiefdom that maintained its autonomy by controlling oceanic trade. In 1722, Dutch explorer Jacob ROGGEVEEN was the first European to sail through the Manu'a Islands, and he was followed by French explorer Louis Antoine DE BOUGAINVILLE in 1768. Whalers and missionaries arrived in American Samoa in the 1830s, but American and European traders tended to favor the port in Apia - now in independent Samoa - over the smaller and less-developed Pago Pago on Tutuila. In the mid-1800s, a dispute arose in Samoa over control of the Samoan archipelago, with different chiefs gaining support from Germany, the UK, and the US. In 1872, the high chief of Tutuila offered the US exclusive rights to Pago Pago in return for US protection, but the US rejected this offer. As fighting resumed, the US agreed to the chief's request in 1878 and set up a coaling station at Pago Pago. In 1899, with continued disputes over succession, Germany and the US agreed to divide the Samoan islands, while the UK withdrew its claims in exchange for parts of the Solomon Islands. Local chiefs on Tutuila formally ceded their land to the US in 1900, followed by the chief of Manu'a in 1904. The territory was officially named "American Samoa" in 1911.

The US administered the territory through the Department of the Navy, and in 1918, the naval governor instituted strict quarantine rules to prevent the spread of the Spanish flu, allowing American Samoa to avoid the deadly infection that ravaged the then-New Zealand administered territory of Samoa. In 1949, there was an attempt to organize the territory, granting it formal self-government, but local chiefs helped defeat the measure in the US Congress. Administration was transferred to the Department of the Interior in 1951, and in 1967, American Samoa adopted a constitution that provides significant protections for traditional Samoan land tenure rules, language, and culture. In 1977, after four attempts, voters approved a measure to directly elect their governor. Nevertheless, American Samoa officially remains an unorganized territory and people born in American Samoa are US nationals instead of US citizens, a status many American Samoans prefer.

GEOGRAPHY

Location: Oceania, group of islands in the South Pacific Ocean, about halfway between Hawaii and New Zealand

Geographic coordinates: 14 20 S, 170 00 W

Map references: Oceania

Area: *total:* 224 sq km
land: 224 sq km
water: 0 sq km
note: includes Rose Atoll and Swains Island
country comparison to the world: 215

Area - comparative: slightly larger than Washington, DC

Land boundaries: *total:* 0 km

Coastline: 116 km

Maritime claims: *territorial sea:* 12 nm
exclusive economic zone: 200 nm

Climate: tropical marine, moderated by southeast trade winds; annual rainfall averages about 3 m; rainy season (November to April), dry season (May to October); little seasonal temperature variation

Terrain: five volcanic islands with rugged peaks and limited coastal plains, two coral atolls (Rose Atoll, Swains Island)

Elevation: *highest point:* Lata Mountain 964 m
lowest point: Pacific Ocean 0 m

Natural resources: pumice, pumicite

Land use: *agricultural land:* 24.5% (2018 est.)
arable land: 15% (2018 est.)
permanent crops: 9.5% (2018 est.)
permanent pasture: 0% (2018 est.)
forest: 75.5% (2018 est.)
other: 0% (2018 est.)

Irrigated land: 0 sq km (2012)

Natural hazards: cyclones common from December to March
volcanism: limited volcanic activity on the Ofu and Olosega Islands; neither has erupted since the 19th century

Geography - note: Pago Pago has one of the best natural deepwater harbors in the South Pacific Ocean, sheltered by shape from rough seas and protected by peripheral mountains from high winds; strategic location in the South Pacific Ocean

PEOPLE AND SOCIETY

Population: 45,443 (2022 est.)
country comparison to the world: 210

Nationality: *noun:* American Samoan(s) (US nationals)
adjective: American Samoan

Ethnic groups: Pacific Islander 92.6% (includes Samoan 88.9%, Tongan 2.9%, other .8%), Asian 3.6% (includes Filipino 2.2%, other 1.4%), mixed 2.7%, other 1.2% (2010 est.)
note: data represent population by ethnic origin or race

Languages: Samoan 88.6% (closely related to Hawaiian and other Polynesian languages), English 3.9%, Tongan 2.7%, other Pacific islander 3%, other 1.8% (2010 est.)
note: most people are bilingual

Religions: Christian 98.3%, other <1%, unaffiliated <1% (2020 est.)

Age structure: *0-14 years:* 27.76% (male 7,063/female 6,662)
15-24 years: 18.16% (male 4,521/female 4,458)
25-54 years: 37.49% (male 9,164/female 9,370)
55-64 years: 9.69% (male 2,341/female 2,447)
65 years and over: 6.9% (male 1,580/female 1,831) (2020 est.)

Median age: *total:* 27.2 years
male: 26.7 years
female: 27.7 years (2020 est.)
country comparison to the world: 149

Population growth rate: -1.92% (2022 est.)
country comparison to the world: 236

Birth rate: 16.7 births/1,000 population (2022 est.)
country comparison to the world: 95

Death rate: 6.1 deaths/1,000 population (2022 est.)
country comparison to the world: 154

Net migration rate: -29.8 migrant(s)/1,000 population (2022 est.)
country comparison to the world: 231

Urbanization: *urban population:* 87.2% of total population (2022)
rate of urbanization: 0.26% annual rate of change (2020-25 est.)

Major urban areas - population: 49,000 PAGO PAGO (capital) (2018)

Sex ratio: *at birth:* 1.06 male(s)/female
0-14 years: 1.06 male(s)/female
15-24 years: 1.02 male(s)/female
25-54 years: 0.97 male(s)/female
55-64 years: 0.96 male(s)/female
65 years and over: 0.69 male(s)/female
total population: 0.99 male(s)/female (2022 est.)

Infant mortality rate: *total:* 10.06 deaths/1,000 live births
male: 12.14 deaths/1,000 live births
female: 7.86 deaths/1,000 live births (2022 est.)
country comparison to the world: 137

Life expectancy at birth: *total population:* 75.32 years
male: 72.83 years
female: 77.97 years (2022 est.)
country comparison to the world: 124

Total fertility rate: 2.21 children born/woman (2022 est.)
country comparison to the world: 85

ENVIRONMENT

Environment - current issues: limited supply of drinking water; pollution; waste disposal; coastal and stream alteration; soil erosion

Climate: tropical marine, moderated by southeast trade winds; annual rainfall averages about 3 m; rainy season (November to April), dry season (May to October); little seasonal temperature variation

Land use: *agricultural land:* 24.5% (2018 est.)
arable land: 15% (2018 est.)
permanent crops: 9.5% (2018 est.)
permanent pasture: 0% (2018 est.)
forest: 75.5% (2018 est.)
other: 0% (2018 est.)

Urbanization: *urban population:* 87.2% of total population (2022)
rate of urbanization: 0.26% annual rate of change (2020-25 est.)

Revenue from forest resources: *forest revenues:* 0% of GDP (2018 est.)
country comparison to the world: 159

Revenue from coal: *coal revenues:* 0% of GDP (2018 est.)
country comparison to the world: 54

Waste and recycling: *municipal solid waste generated annually:* 18,989 tons (2016 est.)

GOVERNMENT

Country name: *conventional long form:* American Samoa
conventional short form: American Samoa
former: Eastern Samoa
abbreviation: AS
etymology: the meaning of Samoa is disputed; some modern explanations are that the "sa" connotes "sacred" and "moa" indicates "center," so the name can mean "Holy Center"; alternatively, some assertions state that it can mean "place of the sacred moa bird" of Polynesian mythology; the name, however, may go back to Proto-Polynesian (PPn) times (before 1000 B.C.); a plausible PPn reconstruction has the first syllable as "sa'a" meaning "tribe or people" and "moa" meaning "deep sea or ocean" to convey the meaning "people of the deep sea"

Government type: unincorporated, unorganized Territory of the US with local self-government; republican form of territorial government with separate executive, legislative, and judicial branches

Dependency status: unincorporated, unorganized Territory of the US; administered by the Office of Insular Affairs, US Department of the Interior

Capital: *name:* Pago Pago
geographic coordinates: 14 16 S, 170 42 W
time difference: UTC-11 (6 hours behind Washington, DC, during Standard Time)
note: pronounced pahn-go pahn-go

Administrative divisions: none (territory of the US); there are no first-order administrative divisions as defined by the US Government, but there are 3 districts and 2 islands* at the second order; Eastern, Manu'a, Rose Island*, Swains Island*, Western

Independence: none (territory of the US)

National holiday: Flag Day, 17 April (1900)

Constitution: *history:* adopted 17 October 1960; revised 1 July 1967
amendments: proposed by either house of the Legislative Assembly; passage requires three-fifths majority vote by the membership of each house, approval by simple majority vote in a referendum, approval by the US Secretary of the Interior, and only by an act of the US Congress; amended several times, last in 2021

Legal system: mixed legal system of US common law and customary law

Citizenship: see United States

Note: in accordance with US Code Title 8, Section 1408, persons born in American Samoa are US nationals but not US citizens

Suffrage: 18 years of age; universal

Executive branch: *chief of state:* President Joseph R. BIDEN Jr. (since 20 January 2021); Vice President Kamala D. HARRIS (since 20 January 2021)
head of government: Governor Lemanu Peleti MAUGA (since 3 January 2021)
cabinet: Cabinet consists of 12 department directors appointed by the governor with the consent of the Legislature or Fono
elections/appointments: president and vice president indirectly elected on the same ballot by an Electoral College of 'electors' chosen from each state to serve a 4-year term (eligible for a second term); under the US Constitution, residents of unincorporated territories, such as American Samoa, do not vote in elections for US president and vice president; however, they may vote in Democratic and Republican presidential primary elections; governor and lieutenant governor directly elected on the same ballot by absolute majority popular vote in 2 rounds if needed for a 4-year term (eligible for a second term); election last held on 3 November 2020 (next to be held in November 2024)
election results: Lemanu Peleti MAUGA elected governor in first round; percent of vote - Lemanu Peleti MAUGA (independent) 60.3%, Gaoteote Palaie TOFAU (independent) 21.9%, I'aulualo Fa'afetai TALIA (independent) 12.3%

Legislative branch: *description:* bicameral Legislature or Fono consists of:
Senate (18 seats; members indirectly selected by regional governing councils to serve 4-year terms)
House of Representatives (21 seats; 20 members directly elected by simple majority vote and 1 decided by public meeting on Swains Island; members serve 2-year terms)
elections:
Senate - last held on 3 November 2020 (next to be held in November 2024)
House of Representatives - last held on 3 November 2020 (next to be held in November 2024)
election results:
Senate - percent of vote by party - NA; seats by party - independent 18; composition - men 17, women 1; percent of women 5.6%
House of Representatives - percent of vote by party - NA; seats by party - NA; composition - men 20, women 1; percent of women 4.8%; note total Legislature percent of women 5.1%
5
note: American Samoa elects 1 member by simple majority vote to serve a 2-year term as a delegate to the US House of Representatives; the delegate can vote when serving on a committee and when the House meets as the Committee of the Whole House, but not when legislation is submitted for a "full floor" House vote; election of delegate last held on 3 November 2020 (next to be held in November 2022); Amata Coleman RADEWAGEN elected delegate; Amata Coleman RADEWAGEN (Republican Party) 83.5%, Oreta CHRICHTON (Democratic Party) 14.4%, Meleagi SUITONU-CHAPMAN (Democratic Party) 2.1%

Judicial branch: *highest court(s):* High Court of American Samoa (consists of the chief justice, associate chief justice, and 6 Samoan associate judges and organized into trial, family, drug, and appellate divisions); note - American Samoa has no US federal courts
judge selection and term of office: chief justice and associate chief justice appointed by the US Secretary of the Interior to serve for life; Samoan associate judges appointed by the governor to serve for life
subordinate courts: district and village courts

Political parties and leaders: Democratic Party [T'ia REID, chairman]
Republican Party [Taulapapa William SWORD, chairman]

International organization participation: AOSIS (observer), Interpol (subbureau), IOC, PIF (observer), SPC

Diplomatic representation in the US: none (territory of the US)

Diplomatic representation from the US: *embassy:* none (territory of the US)

Flag description: blue, with a white triangle edged in red that is based on the fly side and extends to the hoist side; a brown and white American bald eagle flying toward the hoist side is carrying 2 traditional Samoan symbols of authority, a war club known as a "fa'alaufa'i" (upper; left talon), and a coconut-fiber fly whisk known as a "fue" (lower; right talon); the combination of symbols broadly mimics that seen on the US Great Seal and reflects the relationship between the US and American Samoa

National symbol(s): a fue (coconut fiber fly whisk; representing wisdom) crossed with a to'oto'o (staff; representing authority); national colors: red, white, blue

National anthem: *name:* "Amerika Samoa" (American Samoa)
lyrics/music: Mariota Tiumalu TUIASOSOPO/ Napoleon Andrew TUITELELEAPAGA
note: local anthem adopted 1950; as a territory of the United States, "The Star-Spangled Banner" is official (see United States)

ECONOMY

Economic overview: American Samoa s a traditional Polynesian economy in which more than 90% of the land is communally owned. Economic activity is strongly linked to the US with which American Samoa conducts most of its commerce. Tuna fishing and processing are the backbone of the private sector with processed fish products as the primary exports. The fish processing business accounted for 15.5% of employment in 2015.

In late September 2009, an earthquake and the resulting tsunami devastated American Samoa and nearby Samoa, disrupting transportation and power generation, and resulting in about 200 deaths. The US Federal Emergency Management Agency oversaw a relief program of nearly $25 million. Transfers from the US Government add substantially to American Samoa's economic well-being.

Attempts by the government to develop a larger and broader economy are restrained by Samoa's remote location, its limited transportation, and its devastating hurricanes. Tourism has some potential as a source of income and jobs.

Real GDP (purchasing power parity): $658 million (2016 est.)
$674.9 million (2015 est.)
$666.9 billion (2014 est.)
note: data are in 2016 US dollars
country comparison to the world: 211

Real GDP growth rate: -2.5% (2016 est.)
1.2% (2015 est.)
1% (2014 est.)
country comparison to the world: 207

Real GDP per capita: $11,200 (2016 est.)
$11,300 (2015 est.)
$11,200 (2014 est.)
country comparison to the world: 134

GDP (official exchange rate): $658 million (2016 est.)

Inflation rate (consumer prices): -0.5% (2015 est.)
1.4% (2014 est.)
country comparison to the world: 12

GDP - composition, by sector of origin: *agriculture:* 27.4% (2012)
industry: 12.4% (2012)
services: 60.2% (2012)

GDP - composition, by end use: *household consumption:* 66.4% (2016 est.)
government consumption: 49.7% (2016 est.)
investment in fixed capital: 7.3% (2016 est.)
investment in inventories: 5.1% (2016 est.)
exports of goods and services: 65% (2016 est.)
imports of goods and services: -93.5% (2016 est.)

Agricultural products: bananas, coconuts, vegetables, taro, breadfruit, yams, copra, pineapples, papayas; dairy products, livestock

Industries: tuna canneries (largely supplied by foreign fishing vessels), handicrafts

Labor force: 17,850 (2015 est.)
country comparison to the world: 212

Labor force - by occupation: *industry:* 15.5%
services: 46.4% (2015 est.)

Unemployment rate: 29.8% (2005)
country comparison to the world: 206

Budget: *revenues:* 249 million (2016 est.)
expenditures: 262.5 million (2016 est.)

Budget surplus (+) or deficit (-): -2.1% (of GDP) (2016 est.)
country comparison to the world: 107

Public debt: 12.2% of GDP (2016 est.)
country comparison to the world: 197

Taxes and other revenues: 37.8% (of GDP) (2016 est.)
country comparison to the world: 53

Fiscal year: 1 October - 30 September

Exports: $428 million (2016 est.)
$427 million (2015 est.)
note: Data are in current year dollars and do not include illicit exports or re-exports.
country comparison to the world: 192

Exports - partners: Australia 25%, Ghana 19%, Indonesia 15.6%, Burma 10.4%, Portugal 5.1% (2017)

Exports - commodities: canned tuna

Imports: $615 million (2016 est.)
$657 million (2015 est.)
country comparison to the world: 198

Imports - partners: Fiji 10.7%, Singapore 10.4%, NZ 10.4%, South Korea 9.3%, Samoa 8.2%, Kenya 6.4%, Australia 5.2% (2017)

Imports - commodities: raw materials for canneries, food, petroleum products, machinery and parts

Exchange rates: the US dollar is used

ENERGY

Electricity: *installed generating capacity:* 47,000 kW (2020 est.)
consumption: 151 million kWh (2019 est.)
exports: 0 kWh (2020 est.)
imports: 0 kWh (2020 est.)
transmission/distribution losses: 12 million kWh (2019 est.)

Electricity generation sources: *fossil fuels:* 100% of total installed capacity (2020 est.)

Petroleum: *total petroleum production:* 0 bbl/day (2021 est.)
refined petroleum consumption: 2,300 bbl/day (2019 est.)

Refined petroleum products - imports: 2,346 bbl/day (2015 est.)
country comparison to the world: 188

Carbon dioxide emissions: 355,000 metric tonnes of CO2 (2019 est.)
from petroleum and other liquids: 355,000 metric tonnes of CO2 (2019 est.)

Energy consumption per capita: 88.796 million Btu/person (2019 est.)
country comparison to the world: 65

COMMUNICATIONS

Telephones - fixed lines: *total subscriptions:* 10,000 (2020 est.)
subscriptions per 100 inhabitants: 18 (2020 est.)
country comparison to the world: 191

Telephones - mobile cellular: *total subscriptions:* 2,250 (2009 est.)
subscriptions per 100 inhabitants: 4 (2009 est.)
country comparison to the world: 223

Telecommunication systems: *general assessment:* American Samoa Telecommunications Authority, ASTCA, supplies telecommunication services to the residents of the American Samoan islands, a territory of the United States, which are found in a remote area of the Pacific Ocean; the primary system between the islands consists of fiber-optic cables and satellite connections; over Independence Day weekend 2021, the undersea fiber-optic cable linking the Tutuila and Manu'a Islands failed, completely stranding the Manu'a Islands from all telecommunication services; telecommunication services were restored to the people of Manu'a islands through microwave link between Tutuila to the Manu'a Islands; the link is now providing a steady 1Gbps backhaul most of the time of the year with 600Mbps at four 9's availability, over this extremely long distance (2022)
domestic: nearly 18 per 100 fixed-line teledensity (2020)
international: country code - 1-684; landing points for the ASH, Southern Cross NEXT and Hawaiki providing connectivity to New Zealand, Australia, American Samoa, Hawaii, California, and SAS connecting American Samoa with Samoa; satellite earth station - 1 (Intelsat-Pacific Ocean) (2019)

Broadcast media: 3 TV stations; multi-channel pay TV services are available; about a dozen radio stations, some of which are repeater stations

Internet country code: as

Internet users: *total:* 17,147 (2020 est.)
percent of population: 31% (2020 est.)
country comparison to the world: 214

TRANSPORTATION

Airports: *total:* 3 (2021)
country comparison to the world: 191

Airports - with paved runways: *total:* 3
over 3,047 m: 1
914 to 1,523 m: 1
under 914 m: 1 (2021)

Roadways: *total:* 241 km (2016)
country comparison to the world: 205

Ports and terminals: *major seaport(s):* Pago Pago

MILITARY AND SECURITY

Military - note: defense is the responsibility of the US

TRANSNATIONAL ISSUES

Disputes - international: none identified

ANDORRA

INTRODUCTION

Background: The Moorish invasion of Spain in the 8th century and subsequent incursions into France were finally stemmed at the Pyrenees by Frankish King Charlemagne, who in 795 created the Hispanic March, a series of buffer states to keep the Muslim Moors from advancing into Christian France. The landlocked Principality of Andorra, one of the smallest states in Europe and nestled high in the Pyrenees between the French and Spanish borders, is the last independent survivor of these March states. For 715 years, from 1278 to 1993, Andorrans lived under a unique coprincipality, ruled by French and Spanish leaders (from 1607 onward, the French chief of state and the Bishop of Urgell). In 1993, this feudal system was modified with the introduction of a modern constitution; the co-princes remained as titular heads of

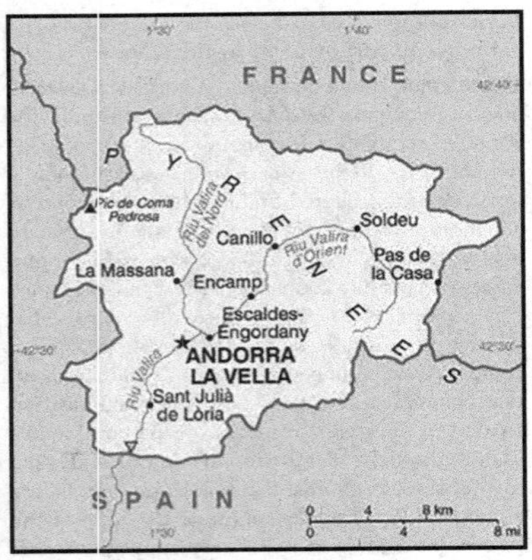

state, but the government transformed into a parliamentary democracy.

Andorra has become a popular tourist destination visited by approximately 8 million people each year drawn by the winter sports, summer climate, and duty-free shopping. Andorra has also become a wealthy international commercial center because of its mature banking sector and low taxes. As part of its effort to modernize its economy, Andorra has opened to foreign investment, and engaged in other reforms, such as advancing tax initiatives aimed at supporting a broader infrastructure. Although not a member of the EU, Andorra enjoys a special relationship with the bloc that is governed by various customs and cooperation agreements and uses the euro as its national currency.

GEOGRAPHY

Location: Southwestern Europe, Pyrenees mountains, on the border between France and Spain

Geographic coordinates: 42 30 N, 1 30 E

Map references: Europe

Area: *total:* 468 sq km
land: 468 sq km
water: 0 sq km
country comparison to the world: 195

Area - comparative: 2.5 times the size of Washington, DC

Land boundaries: *total:* 118 km
border countries (2): France 55 km; Spain 63 km

Coastline: 0 km (landlocked)

Maritime claims: none (landlocked)

Climate: temperate; snowy, cold winters and warm, dry summers

Terrain: rugged mountains dissected by narrow valleys

Elevation: *highest point:* Pic de Coma Pedrosa 2,946 m
lowest point: Riu Runer 840 m
mean elevation: 1,996 m

Natural resources: hydropower, mineral water, timber, iron ore, lead

Land use: *agricultural land:* 40% (2018 est.)
arable land: 1.7% (2018 est.)
permanent crops: 0% (2018 est.)
permanent pasture: 38.3% (2018 est.)
forest: 34% (2018 est.)
other: 26% (2018 est.)

Irrigated land: 0 sq km (2012)

Population distribution: population is unevenly distributed and is concentrated in the seven urbanized valleys that make up the country's parishes (political administrative divisions)

Natural hazards: avalanches

Geography - note: landlocked; straddles a number of important crossroads in the Pyrenees

PEOPLE AND SOCIETY

Population: 85,560 (2022 est.)
country comparison to the world: 199

Nationality: *noun:* Andorran(s)
adjective: Andorran

Ethnic groups: Andorran 48.3%, Spanish 24.8%, Portuguese 11.2%, French 4.5%, Argentine 1.4%, other 9.8% (2021 est.)
note: data represent population by nationality

Languages: Catalan (official), French, Castilian, Portuguese

Religions: Christian (predominantly Roman Catholic) 89.5, other 8.8%, unaffiliated 1.7% (2020 est.)

Age structure: *0-14 years:* 13.37% (male 5,901/female 5,551)
15-24 years: 10.16% (male 4,474/female 4,227)
25-54 years: 43.19% (male 18,857/female 18,131)
55-64 years: 15.91% (male 7,184/female 6,443)
65 years and over: 17.36% (male 7,544/female 7,323) (2020 est.)

Median age: *total:* 46.2 years
male: 46.3 years
female: 46.1 years (2020 est.)
country comparison to the world: 6

Population growth rate: -0.1% (2022 est.)
country comparison to the world: 203

Birth rate: 6.88 births/1,000 population (2022 est.)
country comparison to the world: 226

Death rate: 7.92 deaths/1,000 population (2022 est.)
country comparison to the world: 96

Net migration rate: 0 migrant(s)/1,000 population (2022 est.)
country comparison to the world: 82

Population distribution: population is unevenly distributed and is concentrated in the seven urbanized valleys that make up the country's parishes (political administrative divisions)

Urbanization: *urban population:* 87.8% of total population (2022)
rate of urbanization: 0.11% annual rate of change (2020-25 est.)

Major urban areas - population: 23,000 ANDORRA LA VELLA (capital) (2018)

Sex ratio: *at birth:* 1.07 male(s)/female
0-14 years: 1.06 male(s)/female
15-24 years: 1.04 male(s)/female
25-54 years: 1.05 male(s)/female
55-64 years: 1.1 male(s)/female
65 years and over: 0.9 male(s)/female
total population: 1.05 male(s)/female (2022 est.)

Mother's mean age at first birth: 32.8 years (2019)

Infant mortality rate: *total:* 3.44 deaths/1,000 live births
male: 3.54 deaths/1,000 live births
female: 3.34 deaths/1,000 live births (2022 est.)
country comparison to the world: 198

Life expectancy at birth: *total population:* 83.42 years
male: 81.2 years
female: 85.79 years (2022 est.)
country comparison to the world: 9

Total fertility rate: 1.45 children born/woman (2022 est.)
country comparison to the world: 209

Drinking water source: *improved: urban:* 100% of population
rural: 100% of population
total: 100% of population

Current health expenditure: 6.7% of GDP (2019)

Physicians density: 3.33 physicians/1,000 population (2015)

Hospital bed density: 2.5 beds/1,000 population

Sanitation facility access: *improved: urban:* 100% of population
rural: 100% of population
total: 100% of population

Obesity - adult prevalence rate: 25.6% (2016)
country comparison to the world: 49

Alcohol consumption per capita: *total:* 10.99 liters of pure alcohol (2019 est.)
beer: 3.59 liters of pure alcohol (2019 est.)
wine: 4.98 liters of pure alcohol (2019 est.)
spirits: 2.32 liters of pure alcohol (2019 est.)
other alcohols: 0 liters of pure alcohol (2019 est.)
country comparison to the world: 12

Tobacco use: *total:* 31.8% (2020 est.)
male: 35.3% (2020 est.)
female: 28.3% (2020 est.)
country comparison to the world: 21

Education expenditures: 3.2% of GDP (2019 est.)
country comparison to the world: 139

Literacy: *definition:* age 15 and over can read and write
total population: 100%
male: 100%
female: 100% (2016)

ENVIRONMENT

Environment - current issues: deforestation; overgrazing of mountain meadows contributes to soil erosion; air pollution; wastewater treatment and solid waste disposal

Environment - international agreements: *party to:* Biodiversity, Climate Change, Climate Change-Paris Agreement, Comprehensive Nuclear Test Ban, Desertification, Hazardous Wastes, Ozone Layer Protection, Wetlands
signed, but not ratified: none of the selected agreements

Air pollutants: *particulate matter emissions:* 9.95 micrograms per cubic meter (2016 est.)
carbon dioxide emissions: 0.47 megatons (2016 est.)
methane emissions: 0.05 megatons (2020 est.)

Climate: temperate; snowy, cold winters and warm, dry summers

Land use: *agricultural land:* 40% (2018 est.)
arable land: 1.7% (2018 est.)
permanent crops: 0% (2018 est.)
permanent pasture: 38.3% (2018 est.)
forest: 34% (2018 est.)
other: 26% (2018 est.)

Urbanization: *urban population:* 87.8% of total population (2022)

rate of urbanization: 0.11% annual rate of change (2020-25 est.)

Revenue from forest resources: *forest revenues:* 0% of GDP (2018 est.)
country comparison to the world: 160

Waste and recycling: *municipal solid waste generated annually:* 43,000 tons (2012 est.)

Total renewable water resources: 315.6 million cubic meters (2017 est.)

GOVERNMENT

Country name: *conventional long form:* Principality of Andorra
conventional short form: Andorra
local long form: Principat d'Andorra
local short form: Andorra
etymology: the origin of the country's name is obscure; the name may derive from the Arabic "ad-darra" meaning "the forest," a reference to its location as part of the Spanish March (defensive buffer zone) against the invading Moors in the 8th century; an alternate explanation is that the name originates from a Navarrese word "andurrial" meaning "shrubcovered land"

Government type: parliamentary democracy (since March 1993) that retains its chiefs of state in the form of a co-principality; the two princes are the President of France and Bishop of Seu d'Urgell, Spain

Capital: *name:* Andorra la Vella
geographic coordinates: 42 30 N, 1 31 E
time difference: UTC+1 (6 hours ahead of Washington, DC during Standard Time)
daylight saving time: +1hr, begins last Sunday in March; ends last Sunday in October
etymology: translates as "Andorra the Old" in Catalan

Administrative divisions: 7 parishes (parroquies, singular - parroquia); Andorra la Vella, Canillo, Encamp, Escaldes-Engordany, La Massana, Ordino, Sant Julia de Loria

Independence: 1278 (formed under the joint sovereignty of the French Count of Foix and the Spanish Bishop of Urgell)

National holiday: Our Lady of Meritxell Day, 8 September (1278)

Constitution: *history:* drafted 1991, approved by referendum 14 March 1993, effective 28 April 1993
amendments: proposed by the coprinces jointly or by the General Council; passage requires at least a two-thirds majority vote by the General Council, ratification in a referendum, and sanctioning by the coprinces

Legal system: mixed legal system of civil and customary law with the influence of canon (religious) law

International law organization participation: has not submitted an ICJ jurisdiction declaration; accepts ICCt jurisdiction

Citizenship: *citizenship by birth:* no
citizenship by descent only: the mother must be an Andorran citizen or the father must have been born in Andorra and both parents maintain permanent residence in Andorra
dual citizenship recognized: no
residency requirement for naturalization: 25 years

Suffrage: 18 years of age; universal

Executive branch: *chief of state:* Co-prince Emmanuel MACRON (since 14 May 2017); represented by Patrick STROZDA (since 14 May 2017); and Co-prince Archbishop Joan-Enric VIVES i Sicilia (since 12 May 2003); represented by Josep Maria MAURI (since 20 July 2012)
head of government: Xaviar Espot ZAMORA (since 16 May 2019)
cabinet: Executive Council of 12 ministers designated by the head of government
elections/appointments: head of government indirectly elected by the General Council (Andorran parliament), formally appointed by the co-princes for a 4-year term; election last held on 7 April 2019 (next to be held in April 2023); the leader of the majority party in the General Council is usually elected head of government
election results: 2019: Xaviar Espot ZAMORA (DA) elected head of government; percent of General Council vote - 60.7%
2015: Antoni MARTI elected head of government; percent of General Council vote - 58.3%

Legislative branch: *description:* unicameral General Council of the Valleys or Consell General de les Valls (a minimum of 28 seats; 14 members directly elected in two-seat constituencies (7 parishes) by simple majority vote and 14 directly elected in a single national constituency by proportional representation vote; members serve 4-year terms); note - voters cast two separate ballots - one for a national list and one for a parish list
elections: last held on 7 April 2019 (next to be held in April 2023)
election results: percent of vote by party - DA 35.1%, PS 30.6%, L'A 12.5%, Third Way/Lauredian Union 10.4%, other 11.4%; seats by party - DA 11, PS 7, L'A 4, Third Way/Lauredian Union 4, other 2; composition - men 15, women 13, percent of women 46.4%

Judicial branch: *highest court(s):* Supreme Court of Justice of Andorra or Tribunal Superior de la Justicia d'Andorra (consists of the court president and 8 judges organized into civil, criminal, and administrative chambers); Constitutional Court or Tribunal Constitucional (consists of 4 magistrates)
judge selection and term of office: Supreme Court president and judges appointed by the Supreme Council of Justice, a 5-member judicial policy and administrative body appointed 1 each by the coprinces, 1 by the General Council, 1 by the executive council president, and 1 by the courts; judges serve 6-year renewable terms; Constitutional magistrates - 2 appointed by the coprinces and 2 by the General Council; magistrates' appointments limited to 2 consecutive 8-year terms
subordinate courts: Tribunal of Judges or Tribunal de Batlles; Tribunal of the Courts or Tribunal de Corts

Political parties and leaders: Democrats for Andorra or DA [Xaviar ESPOT ZAMORA]
Liberals of Andorra or L'A [Jordi GALLARDO FERNANDEZ]
Social Democracy and Progress or SDP [Victor NAUDI ZAMORA]
Social Democratic Party or PS [Susanna VELA]
Third Way/Lauredian Union [Josep PINTAT FORNE]
United for the Progress of Andorra or UPA [Alfons CLAVERA ARIZTI]
note: Andorra has several smaller parties at the parish level (one is Lauredian Union)

International organization participation: CE, FAO, ICAO, ICC (NGOs), ICCt, ICRM, IFRCS, Interpol, IOC, IPU, ITU, OIF, OPCW, OSCE, UN, UNCTAD, UNESCO, Union Latina, UNWTO, WCO, WHO, WIPO, WTO (observer)

Diplomatic representation in the US: *chief of mission:* Ambassador Elisenda VIVES BALMANA (since 2 March 2016)
chancery: 2 United Nations Plaza, 27th Floor, New York, NY 10017
telephone: [1] (212) 750-8064; [1] (212) 750-8065
FAX: [1] (212) 750-6630
email address and website:
contact@andorraun.org

Diplomatic representation from the US: *embassy:* the US does not have an embassy in Andorra; the US ambassador to Spain is accredited to Andorra; US interests in Andorra are represented by the US Consulate General's office in Barcelona (Spain); mailing address: Paseo Reina Elisenda de Montcada, 23, 08034 Barcelona, Espana; telephone: [34] (93) 280-22-27; FAX: [34] (93) 280-61-75; email address: Barcelonaacs@state.gov

Flag description: three vertical bands of blue (hoist side), yellow, and red, with the national coat of arms centered in the yellow band; the latter band is slightly wider than the other 2 so that the ratio of band widths is 8:9:8; the coat of arms features a quartered shield with the emblems of (starting in the upper left and proceeding clockwise): Urgell, Foix, Bearn, and Catalonia; the motto reads VIRTUS UNITA FORTIOR (Strength United is Stronger); the flag combines the blue and red French colors with the red and yellow of Spain to show Franco-Spanish protection
note: similar to the flags of Chad and Romania, which do not have a national coat of arms in the center, and the flag of Moldova, which does bear a national emblem

National symbol(s): red cow (breed unspecified); national colors: blue, yellow, red

National anthem: *name:* "El Gran Carlemany" (The Great Charlemagne)
lyrics/music: Joan BENLLOCH i VIVO/Enric MARFANY BONS
note: adopted 1921; the anthem provides a brief history of Andorra in a first person narrative

National heritage: *total World Heritage Sites:* 1 (cultural)
selected World Heritage Site locales: Madriu-Perafita-Claror Valley

ECONOMY

Economic overview: Andorra has a developed economy and a free market, with per capita income above the European average and above the level of its neighbors, Spain and France. The country has developed a sophisticated infrastructure including a one-of-a-kind micro-fiber-optic network for the entire country. Tourism, retail sales, and finance comprise more than three-quarters of GDP. Duty-free shopping for some products and the country's summer and winter resorts attract millions of visitors annually. Andorra uses the euro and is effectively subject to the monetary policy of the European Central Bank. Andorra's comparative advantage as a tax haven eroded when the borders of neighboring France and Spain opened and the government eased bank secrecy laws under pressure from the EU and OECD.

Agricultural production is limited - only about 5% of the land is arable - and most food has to be imported, making the economy vulnerable to changes in fuel and food prices. The principal livestock is sheep. Manufacturing output and exports consist mainly of perfumes and cosmetic products, products of the printing industry, electrical machinery and equipment, clothing, tobacco products, and furniture. Andorra is a member of the EU Customs Union and is treated as an EU member for trade in manufactured goods (no tariffs) and as a non-EU member for agricultural products.

To provide incentives for growth and diversification in the economy, the Andorran government began sweeping economic reforms in 2006. The Parliament approved three laws to complement the first phase of economic openness: on companies (October 2007), on business accounting (December 2007), and on foreign investment (April 2008 and June 2012). From 2011 to 2015, the Parliament also approved direct taxes in the form of taxes on corporations, on individual incomes of residents and non-residents, and on capital gains, savings, and economic activities. These regulations aim to establish a transparent, modern, and internationally comparable regulatory framework, in order to attract foreign investment and businesses that offer higher value added.

Real GDP (purchasing power parity): $3.327 billion (2015 est.)
$3.363 billion (2014 est.)
$3.273 billion (2013 est.)
note: data are in 2012 US dollars
country comparison to the world: 189

Real GDP growth rate: -1.1% (2015 est.)
1.4% (2014 est.)
-0.1% (2013 est.)
country comparison to the world: 199

Real GDP per capita: $49,900 (2015 est.)
$51,300 (2014 est.)
$50,300 (2013 est.)
country comparison to the world: 28

GDP (official exchange rate): $2.712 billion (2016 est.)

Inflation rate (consumer prices): -0.9% (2015 est.)
-0.1% (2014 est.)
country comparison to the world: 6

Credit ratings:

Fitch rating: BBB+ (2018)

Standard & Poors rating: BBB (2017)
note: The year refers to the year in which the current credit rating was first obtained.

GDP - composition, by sector of origin: *agriculture:* 11.9% (2015 est.)
industry: 33.6% (2015 est.)
services: 54.5% (2015 est.)

Agricultural products: small quantities of rye, wheat, barley, oats, vegetables, tobacco, sheep, cattle

Industries: tourism (particularly skiing), banking, timber, furniture

Labor force: 39,750 (2016)
country comparison to the world: 195

Labor force - by occupation: *agriculture:* 0.5%
industry: 4.4%
services: 95.1% (2015)

Unemployment rate: 3.7% (2016 est.)
4.1% (2015 est.)
country comparison to the world: 53

Budget: *revenues:* 1.872 billion (2016)
expenditures: 2.06 billion (2016)

Budget surplus (+) or deficit (-): -6.9% (of GDP) (2016)
country comparison to the world: 192

Public debt: 41% of GDP (2014 est.)
41.4% of GDP (2013 est.)
country comparison to the world: 122

Taxes and other revenues: 69% (of GDP) (2016)
country comparison to the world: 5

Fiscal year: calendar year

Exports: $78.71 million (2015 est.)
$79.57 million (2014 est.)
note: Data are in current year dollars and do not include illicit exports or re-exports.
country comparison to the world: 211

Exports - partners: Spain 40%, France 19%, United States 11%, Mauritania 5% (2019)

Exports - commodities: integrated circuits, medical supplies, essential oils, cars, tanned hides (2019)

Imports: $1.257 billion (2015 est.)
$1.264 billion (2014 est.)
country comparison to the world: 182

Imports - partners: Spain 71%, France 17% (2019)

Imports - commodities: cars, refined petroleum, perfumes, shaving products, liquors (2019)

Debt - external: $0 (2016)
country comparison to the world: 203

Exchange rates: euros (EUR) per US dollar -
0.885 (2017 est.)
0.903 (2016 est.)
0.9214 (2015 est.)
0.885 (2014 est.)
0.7634 (2013 est.)

ENERGY

Electricity access: *electrification - total population:* 100% (2020)

Refined petroleum products - production: 0 bbl/day (2016)
country comparison to the world: 112

COMMUNICATIONS

Telephones - fixed lines: *total subscriptions:* 40,000 (2020 est.)
subscriptions per 100 inhabitants: 52 (2020 est.)
country comparison to the world: 162

Telephones - mobile cellular: *total subscriptions:* 94,000 (2020 est.)
subscriptions per 100 inhabitants: 122 (2020 est.)
country comparison to the world: 193

Telecommunication systems: *general assessment:* Andorra has a modern telecommunications system with microwave radio relay connections between the exchanges and land line circuits to France and Spain (2020)
domestic: about 52 per 100 fixed-line, 122 per 100 mobile-cellular (2020)
international: country code - 376; landline circuits to France and Spain; modern system with microwave radio relay connections between exchanges (2019)

Broadcast media: 1 public TV station and 2 public radio stations; about 10 commercial radio stations; good reception of radio and TV broadcasts from stations in France and Spain; upgraded to terrestrial digital TV broadcasting in 2007; roughly 25 international TV channels available (2019)

Internet country code: .ad

Internet users: *total:* 71,084 (2020 est.)
percent of population: 92% (2020 est.)
country comparison to the world: 187

Broadband - fixed subscriptions: *total:* 37,000 (2020 est.)
subscriptions per 100 inhabitants: 48 (2020 est.)
country comparison to the world: 146

TRANSPORTATION

Civil aircraft registration country code prefix: C3

Roadways: *total:* 320 km (2019)
country comparison to the world: 201

MILITARY AND SECURITY

Military and security forces: no regular military forces; Police Corps of Andorra

Military - note: defense is the responsibility of France and Spain

TRANSNATIONAL ISSUES

Disputes - international: *Andorra-France:* none identified
Andorra-Spain: none identified

ANGOLA

INTRODUCTION

Background: From the late 14th to the mid 19th century a Kingdom of Kongo stretched across central Africa from present-day northern Angola into the current Congo republics. It traded heavily with the Portuguese who, beginning in the 16th century, established coastal colonies and trading posts and introduced Christianity. By the 19th century, Portuguese settlement had spread to the interior; in 1914, Portugal abolished the last vestiges of the Kongo Kingdom and Angola became a Portuguese colony.

Angola scores low on human development indexes despite using its large oil reserves to rebuild since the end of a 27- year civil war in

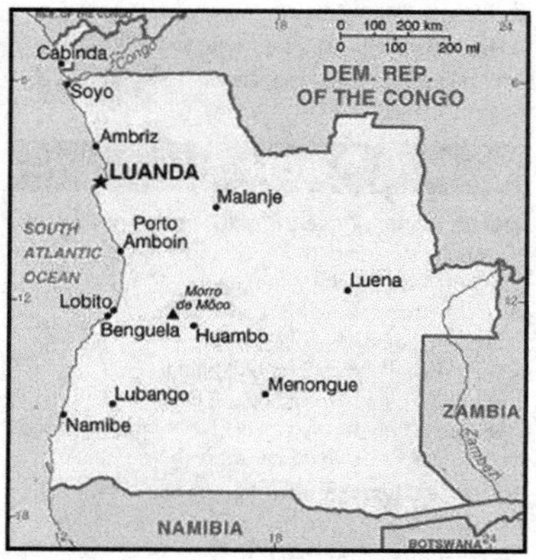

2002. Fighting between the Popular Movement for the Liberation of Angola (MPLA), led by Jose Eduardo DOS SANTOS, and the National Union for the Total Independence of Angola (UNITA), led by Jonas SAVIMBI, followed independence from Portugal in 1975. Peace seemed imminent in 1992 when Angola held national elections, but fighting picked up again in 1993. Up to 1.5 million lives may have been lost - and 4 million people displaced - during the more than a quarter century of fighting. SAVIMBI's death in 2002 ended UNITA's insurgency and cemented the MPLA's hold on power. DOS SANTOS stepped down from the presidency in 2017, having led the country since 1979. He pushed through a new constitution in 2010. Joao LOURENCO was elected president in August 2017 and became president of the MPLA in September 2018.

GEOGRAPHY

Location: Southern Africa, bordering the South Atlantic Ocean, between Namibia and Democratic Republic of the Congo

Geographic coordinates: 12 30 S, 18 30 E

Map references: Africa

Area: *total:* 1,246,700 sq km
land: 1,246,700 sq km
water: 0 sq km
country comparison to the world: 24

Area - comparative: about eight times the size of Georgia; slightly less than twice the size of Texas

Land boundaries: *total:* 5,369 km
border countries (4): Democratic Republic of the Congo 2,646 km (of which 225 km is the boundary of discontiguous Cabinda Province); Republic of the Congo 231 km; Namibia 1,427 km; Zambia 1,065 km

Coastline: 1,600 km

Maritime claims: *territorial sea:* 12 nm
contiguous zone: 24 nm
exclusive economic zone: 200 nm

Climate: semiarid in south and along coast to Luanda; north has cool, dry season (May to October) and hot, rainy season (November to April)

Terrain: narrow coastal plain rises abruptly to vast interior plateau

Elevation: *highest point:* Moca 2,620 m
lowest point: Atlantic Ocean 0 m
mean elevation: 1,112 m

Natural resources: petroleum, diamonds, iron ore, phosphates, copper, feldspar, gold, bauxite, uranium

Land use: *agricultural land:* 45.7% (2018 est.)
arable land: 3.9% (2018 est.)
permanent crops: 0.3% (2018 est.)
permanent pasture: 41.5% (2018 est.)
forest: 54.3% (2018 est.)

Irrigated land: 860 sq km (2014)

Major rivers (by length in km): Zambezi (shared with Zambia [s], Namibia, Botswana, Zimbabwe, and Mozambique [m]) - 2,740 km; Okavango river source (shared with Namibia and Botswana [m]) - 1,600 km
note – [s] after country name indicates river source; [m] after country name indicates river mouth

Major watersheds (area sq km):
Atlantic Ocean drainage: Congo (3,730,881 sq km)
Indian Ocean drainage: Zambezi (1,332,412 sq km)
Internal *(endorheic basin)* drainage: Okavango Basin (863,866 sq km)

Major aquifers: Congo Basin, Upper Kalahari-Cuvelai-Upper Zambezi Basin

Population distribution: most people live in the western half of the country; urban areas account for the highest concentrations of people, particularly the capital of Luanda as shown in this population distribution map

Natural hazards: locally heavy rainfall causes periodic flooding on the plateau

Geography - note: the province of Cabinda is an exclave, separated from the rest of the country by the Democratic Republic of the Congo

PEOPLE AND SOCIETY

Population: 34,795,287 (2022 est.)
country comparison to the world: 42

Nationality: *noun:* Angolan(s)
adjective: Angolan

Ethnic groups: Ovimbundu 37%, Kimbundu 25%, Bakongo 13%, Mestico (mixed European and native African) 2%, European 1%, other 22%

Languages: Portuguese 71.2% (official), Umbundu 23%, Kikongo 8.2%, Kimbundu 7.8%, Chokwe 6.5%, Nhaneca 3.4%, Nganguela 3.1%, Fiote 2.4%, Kwanhama 2.3%, Muhumbi 2.1%, Luvale 1%, other 3.6%; note - data represent most widely spoken languages; shares sum to more than 100% because some respondents gave more than one answer on the census (2014 est.)

Religions: Roman Catholic 41.1%, Protestant 38.1%, other 8.6%, none 12.3% (2014 est.)

Demographic profile: More than two decades after the end of Angola's 27-year civil war, the country still faces a variety of socioeconomic problems, including poverty, high maternal and child mortality, and illiteracy. Despite the country's rapid post-war economic growth based on oil production, about 40 percent of Angolans live below the poverty line and unemployment is widespread, especially among the large young-adult population. Only about 70% of the population is literate, and the rate drops to around 60% for women. The youthful population - about 45% are under the age of 15 - is expected to continue growing rapidly with a fertility rate of more than 5 children per woman and a low rate of contraceptive use. Fewer than half of women deliver their babies with the assistance of trained health care personnel, which contributes to Angola's high maternal mortality rate.

Of the estimated 550,000 Angolans who fled their homeland during its civil war, most have returned home since 2002. In 2012, the UN assessed that conditions in Angola had been stable for several years and invoked a cessation of refugee status for Angolans. Following the cessation clause, some of those still in exile returned home voluntarily through UN repatriation programs, and others integrated into host countries.

Age structure: *0-14 years:* 47.83% (male 7,758,636/female 7,797,869)
15-24 years: 18.64% (male 2,950,999/female 3,109,741)
25-54 years: 27.8% (male 4,301,618/female 4,740,463)
55-64 years: 3.43% (male 523,517/female 591,249)
65 years and over: 2.3% (male 312,197/female 436,050) (2020 est.)

Dependency ratios: *total dependency ratio:* 94.5
youth dependency ratio: 90.2
elderly dependency ratio: 4.3
potential support ratio: 23.5 (2020 est.)

Median age: *total:* 15.9 years
male: 15.4 years
female: 16.4 years (2020 est.)
country comparison to the world: 225

Population growth rate: 3.36% (2022 est.)
country comparison to the world: 6

Birth rate: 41.8 births/1,000 population (2022 est.)
country comparison to the world: 2

Death rate: 8.01 deaths/1,000 population (2022 est.)
country comparison to the world: 88

Net migration rate: -0.19 migrant(s)/1,000 population (2022 est.)
country comparison to the world: 108

Population distribution: most people live in the western half of the country; urban areas account for the highest concentrations of people, particularly the capital of Luanda as shown in this population distribution map

Urbanization: *urban population:* 68.1% of total population (2022)
rate of urbanization: 4.04% annual rate of change (2020-25 est.)

Major urban areas - population: 8.952 million LUANDA (capital), 914,000 Lubango, 862,000 Cabinda, Benguela 777,000 (2022)

Sex ratio: *at birth:* 1.03 male(s)/female
0-14 years: 1 male(s)/female
15-24 years: 0.95 male(s)/female
25-54 years: 0.91 male(s)/female
55-64 years: 0.89 male(s)/female
65 years and over: 0.59 male(s)/female
total population: 0.95 male(s)/female (2022 est.)

Mother's mean age at first birth: 19.4 years (2015/16 est.)
note: data represents median age at first birth among women 20-49

Maternal mortality ratio: 241 deaths/100,000 live births (2017 est.)
country comparison to the world: 45

Infant mortality rate: *total:* 58.86 deaths/1,000 live births
male: 64.11 deaths/1,000 live births
female: 53.46 deaths/1,000 live births (2022 est.)
country comparison to the world: 12

Life expectancy at birth: *total population:* 62.11 years
male: 60.05 years
female: 64.24 years (2022 est.)
country comparison to the world: 214

Total fertility rate: 5.83 children born/woman (2022 est.)
country comparison to the world: 2

Contraceptive prevalence rate: 13.7% (2015/16)

Drinking water source: *improved: urban:* 81.3% of population
rural: 36.5% of population
total: 66.5% of population
unimproved: urban: 18.7% of population
rural: 63.5% of population
total: 33.5% of population (2020 est.)

Current health expenditure: 2.5% of GDP (2019)

Physicians density: 0.21 physicians/1,000 population (2018)

Sanitation facility access: *improved: urban:* 93.7% of population
rural: 30.3% of population
total: 72.7% of population
unimproved: urban: 6.3% of population
rural: 69.7% of population
total: 27.3% of population (2020 est.)

HIV/AIDS - adult prevalence rate: 1.8% (2020 est.)
country comparison to the world: 24

Major infectious diseases: *degree of risk:* very high (2020)
food or waterborne diseases: bacterial and protozoal diarrhea, hepatitis A, typhoid fever
vectorborne diseases: dengue fever, malaria
water contact diseases: schistosomiasis
animal contact diseases: rabies

Obesity - adult prevalence rate: 8.2% (2016)
country comparison to the world: 154

Alcohol consumption per capita: *total:* 5.84 liters of pure alcohol (2019 est.)
beer: 3.78 liters of pure alcohol (2019 est.)
wine: 0.72 liters of pure alcohol (2019 est.)
spirits: 1.27 liters of pure alcohol (2019 est.)
other alcohols: 0.08 liters of pure alcohol (2019 est.)
country comparison to the world: 73

Children under the age of 5 years underweight: 19% (2015/16)
country comparison to the world: 25

Child marriage: *women married by age 15:* 7.9%
women married by age 18: 30.3%
men married by age 18: 6% (2016 est.)

Education expenditures: 1.8% of GDP (2019 est.)
country comparison to the world: 181

Literacy: *definition:* age 15 and over can read and write
total population: 71.1%
male: 82%
female: 60.7% (2015)

School life expectancy (primary to tertiary education): *total:* 10 years
male: 12 years
female: 7 years (2011)

Unemployment, youth ages 15-24: *total:* 17.3%
male: 17.9%
female: 16.7% (2014 est.)

ENVIRONMENT

Environment - current issues: overuse of pastures and subsequent soil erosion attributable to population pressures; desertification; deforestation of tropical rain forest, in response to both international demand for tropical timber and to domestic use as fuel, resulting in loss of biodiversity; soil erosion contributing to water pollution and siltation of rivers and dams; inadequate supplies of potable water

Environment - international agreements: *party to:* Biodiversity, Climate Change, Climate Change-Kyoto Protocol, Climate Change-Paris Agreement, Comprehensive Nuclear Test Ban, Desertification, Endangered Species, Hazardous Wastes, Law of the Sea, Marine Dumping-London Protocol, Ozone Layer Protection, Ship Pollution
signed, but not ratified: none of the selected agreements

Air pollutants: *particulate matter emissions:* 27.95 micrograms per cubic meter (2016 est.)
carbon dioxide emissions: 34.69 megatons (2016 est.)
methane emissions: 23.28 megatons (2020 est.)

Climate: semiarid in south and along coast to Luanda; north has cool, dry season (May to October) and hot, rainy season (November to April)

Land use: *agricultural land:* 45.7% (2018 est.)
arable land: 3.9% (2018 est.)
permanent crops: 0.3% (2018 est.)
permanent pasture: 41.5% (2018 est.)
forest: 54.3% (2018 est.)

Urbanization: *urban population:* 68.1% of total population (2022)
rate of urbanization: 4.04% annual rate of change (2020-25 est.)

Revenue from forest resources: *forest revenues:* 0.36% of GDP (2018 est.)
country comparison to the world: 74

Revenue from coal: *coal revenues:* 0% of GDP (2018 est.)
country comparison to the world: 55

Major infectious diseases: *degree of risk:* very high (2020)
food or waterborne diseases: bacterial and protozoal diarrhea, hepatitis A, typhoid fever
vectorborne diseases: dengue fever, malaria
water contact diseases: schistosomiasis
animal contact diseases: rabies

Waste and recycling: *municipal solid waste generated annually:* 4,213,644 tons (2012 est.)

Major rivers (by length in km): Zambezi (shared with Zambia [s], Namibia, Botswana, Zimbabwe, and Mozambique [m]) - 2,740 km; Okavango river source (shared with Namibia and Botswana [m]) - 1,600 km
note – [s] after country name indicates river source; [m] after country name indicates river mouth

Major watersheds (area sq km):

Atlantic Ocean drainage: Congo (3,730,881 sq km)

Indian Ocean drainage: Zambezi (1,332,412 sq km)

Internal *(endorheic basin)* drainage: Okavango Basin (863,866 sq km)

Major aquifers: Congo Basin, Upper Kalahari-Cuvelai-Upper Zambezi Basin

Total water withdrawal: *municipal:* 319.5 million cubic meters (2017 est.)
industrial: 239.6 million cubic meters (2017 est.)
agricultural: 146.7 million cubic meters (2017 est.)

Total renewable water resources: 148.4 billion cubic meters (2017 est.)

GOVERNMENT

Country name: *conventional long form:* Republic of Angola
conventional short form: Angola
local long form: Republica de Angola
local short form: Angola
former: People's Republic of Angola
etymology: name derived by the Portuguese from the title "ngola" held by kings of the Ndongo (Ndongo was a kingdom in what is now northern Angola)

Government type: presidential republic

Capital: *name:* Luanda
geographic coordinates: 8 50 S, 13 13 E
time difference: UTC+1 (6 hours ahead of Washington, DC, during Standard Time)
daylight saving time: does not observe daylight savings time
etymology: originally named "Sao Paulo da Assuncao de Loanda" (Saint Paul of the Assumption of Loanda), which over time was shortened and corrupted to just Luanda

Administrative divisions: 18 provinces (provincias, singular - provincia); Bengo, Benguela, Bie, Cabinda, Cuando Cubango, Cuanza-Norte, Cuanza-Sul, Cunene, Huambo, Huila, Luanda, Lunda-Norte, Lunda-Sul, Malanje, Moxico, Namibe, Uige, Zaire

Independence: 11 November 1975 (from Portugal)

National holiday: Independence Day, 11 November (1975)

Constitution: *history:* previous 1975, 1992; latest passed by National Assembly 21 January 2010, adopted 5 February 2010
amendments: proposed by the president of the republic or supported by at least one third of the National Assembly membership; passage requires at least two-thirds majority vote of the Assembly subject to prior Constitutional Court review if requested by the president of the republic

Legal system: civil legal system based on Portuguese civil law; no judicial review of legislation

International law organization participation: has not submitted an ICJ jurisdiction declaration; non-party state to the ICCt

Citizenship: *citizenship by birth:* no
citizenship by descent only: at least one parent must be a citizen of Angola
dual citizenship recognized: no
residency requirement for naturalization: 10 years

Suffrage: 18 years of age; universal

Executive branch: *chief of state:* President Joao Manuel Goncalves LOURENCO (since 15 September 2022); Vice President Bornito De Sousa Baltazar DIOGO (since 15 September 2022); note - the president is both chief of state and head of government
head of government: President Joao Manuel Goncalves LOURENCO (since 15 September 2022); Vice President Bornito De Sousa Baltazar DIOGO (since 15 September 2022)
cabinet: Council of Ministers appointed by the president

elections/appointments: the candidate of the winning party or coalition in the last legislative election becomes the president; president serves a 5-year term (eligible for a second consecutive or discontinuous term); last held on 24 August 2022 (next to be held on 24 August 2027) (2022)
election results: Joao Manuel Goncalves LOURENCO (MPLA) elected president by then winning party following the 24 August 2022 general election

Legislative branch: *description:* unicameral National Assembly or Assembleia Nacional (220 seats; members directly elected in a single national constituency and in multi-seat constituencies by closed list proportional representation vote; members serve 5-year terms)
elections: last held on 24 August 2022 (next to be held on 24 August 2027)
election results: percent of vote by party - MPLA 51.1%, UNITA 43.9%, PRS 1.1%, FNLA 1.1%, PHA 1%, other 1.7%; seats by party - MPLA 124, UNITA 90, PRS 2, FNLA 2; PHA-2; composition - men 146, women 74, percent of women 33.6%

Judicial branch: *highest court(s):* Supreme Court or Supremo Tribunal de Justica (consists of the court president, vice president, and a minimum of 16 judges); Constitutional Court or Tribunal Constitucional (consists of 11 judges)
judge selection and term of office: Supreme Court judges appointed by the president upon recommendation of the Supreme Judicial Council, an 18-member body chaired by the president; judge tenure NA; Constitutional Court judges - 4 nominated by the president, 4 elected by National Assembly, 2 elected by Supreme National Council, 1 elected by competitive submission of curricula; judges serve single 7-year terms
subordinate courts: provincial and municipal courts

Political parties and leaders: Broad Convergence for the Salvation of Angola Electoral Coalition or CASA-CE [Manuel FERNANDES]
National Front for the Liberation of Angola or FNLA; note - party has two factions; one led by Lucas NGONDA; the other by Ngola KABANGU
National Union for the Total Independence of Angola or UNITA [Adalberto Costa JUNIOR] (largest opposition party) Popular Movement for the Liberation of Angola or MPLA [Joao LOURENCO]; note- ruling party in power since 1975 Social Renewal Party or PRS [Benedito DANIEL]

International organization participation: ACP, AfDB, AU, CEMAC, CPLP, FAO, G-77, IAEA, IBRD, ICAO, ICRM, IDA, IFAD, IFC, IFRCS, ILO, IMF, IMO, Interpol, IOC, IOM, IPU, ISO (correspondent), ITSO, ITU, ITUC (NGOs), MIGA, NAM, OAS (observer), OPEC, SADC, UN, UNCTAD, UNESCO, UNIDO, Union Latina, UNWTO, UPU, WCO, WFTU (NGOs), WHO, WIPO, WMO, WTO

Diplomatic representation in the US: *chief of mission:* Ambassador Joaquim do Espirito SANTO (since 16 September 2019)
chancery: 2100-2108 16th Street NW, Washington, DC 20009
telephone: [1] (202) 785-1156
FAX: [1] (202) 822-9049
email address and website:
info@angola.org
https://angola.org/
consulate(s) general: Houston, New York

Diplomatic representation from the US: *chief of mission:* Ambassador Tulinabo S. MUSHINGI, (since 9 March 2022)
embassy: Rua Houari Boumedienne, #32, Luanda
mailing address: 2550 Luanda Place, Washington, DC 20521-2550
telephone: [244] (222) 64-1000
FAX: [244] (222) 64-1000
email address and website:
Consularluanda@state.gov
https://ao.usembassy.gov/

Flag description: two equal horizontal bands of red (top) and black with a centered yellow emblem consisting of a five-pointed star within half a cogwheel crossed by a machete (in the style of a hammer and sickle); red represents liberty and black the African continent; the symbols characterize workers and peasants

National symbol(s): Palanca Negra Gigante (giant black sable antelope); national colors: red, black, yellow

National anthem: *name:* "Angola Avante" (Forward Angola)
lyrics/music: Manuel Rui Alves MONTEIRO/Rui Alberto Vieira Dias MINGAO
note: adopted 1975

National heritage: *total World Heritage Sites:* 1 (cultural)
selected World Heritage Site locales: Mbanza-Kongo

ECONOMY

Economic overview: Angola's economy is overwhelmingly driven by its oil sector. Oil production and its supporting activities contribute about 50% of GDP, more than 70% of government revenue, and more than 90% of the country's exports; Angola is an OPEC member and subject to its direction regarding oil production levels. Diamonds contribute an additional 5% to exports. Subsistence agriculture provides the main livelihood for most of the people, but half of the country's food is still imported.

Increased oil production supported growth averaging more than 17% per year from 2004 to 2008. A postwar reconstruction boom and resettlement of displaced persons led to high rates of growth in construction and agriculture as well. Some of the country's infrastructure is still damaged or undeveloped from the 27-year-long civil war (1975-2002). However, the government since 2005 has used billions of dollars in credit from China, Brazil, Portugal, Germany, Spain, and the EU to help rebuild Angola's public infrastructure. Land mines left from the war still mar the countryside, and as a result, the national military, international partners, and private Angolan firms all continue to remove them.

The global recession that started in 2008 stalled Angola's economic growth and many construction projects stopped because Luanda accrued billions in arrears to foreign construction companies when government revenue fell. Lower prices for oil and diamonds also resulted in GDP falling 0.7% in 2016. Angola formally abandoned its currency peg in 2009 but reinstituted it in April 2016 and maintains an overvalued exchange rate. In late 2016, Angola lost the last of its correspondent relationships with foreign banks, further exacerbating hard currency problems. Since 2013 the central bank has consistently spent down reserves to defend the kwanza, gradually allowing a 40% depreciation since late 2014. Consumer inflation declined from 325% in 2000 to less than 9% in 2014, before rising again to above 30% from 2015-2017.

Continued low oil prices, the depreciation of the kwanza, and slower than expected growth in non-oil GDP have reduced growth prospects, although several major international oil companies remain in Angola. Corruption, especially in the extractive sectors, is a major long-term challenge that poses an additional threat to the economy.

Real GDP (purchasing power parity): $203.71 billion (2020 est.)
$212.29 billion (2019 est.)
$213.62 billion (2018 est.)
note: data are in 2017 dollars
country comparison to the world: 67

Real GDP growth rate: -2.5% (2017 est.)
-2.6% (2016 est.)
0.9% (2015 est.)
country comparison to the world: 208

Real GDP per capita: $6,200 (2020 est.)
$6,700 (2019 est.)
$6,900 (2018 est.)
note: data are in 2017 dollars
country comparison to the world: 161

GDP (official exchange rate): $97.261 billion (2019 est.)

Inflation rate (consumer prices): 17.2% (2019 est.)
20.3% (2018 est.)
32.1% (2017 est.)
country comparison to the world: 217

Credit ratings:

Fitch rating: CCC (2020)

Moody's rating: Caa1 (2020)

Standard & Poors rating: CCC+ (2020)
note: The year refers to the year in which the current credit rating was first obtained.

GDP - composition, by sector of origin: *agriculture:* 10.2% (2011 est.)
industry: 61.4% (2011 est.)
services: 28.4% (2011 est.)

GDP - composition, by end use: *household consumption:* 80.6% (2017 est.)
government consumption: 15.6% (2017 est.)
investment in fixed capital: 10.3% (2017 est.)
investment in inventories: -1.2% (2017 est.)
exports of goods and services: 25.4% (2017 est.)
imports of goods and services: -30.7% (2017 est.)

Agricultural products: cassava, bananas, maize, sweet potatoes, pineapples, sugar cane, potatoes, citrus fruit, vegetables, cabbage

Industries: petroleum; diamonds, iron ore, phosphates, feldspar, bauxite, uranium, and gold; cement; basic metal products; fish processing; food processing, brewing, tobacco products, sugar; textiles; ship repair

Industrial production growth rate: 2.5% (2017 est.)
country comparison to the world: 115

Labor force: 12.51 million (2017 est.)
country comparison to the world: 44

Labor force - by occupation: *agriculture:* 85%
industry: 15% (2015 est.)
industry and services: 15% (2003 est.)

Unemployment rate: 6.6% (2016 est.)
country comparison to the world: 105

Unemployment, youth ages 15-24: *total:* 17.3%

male: 17.9%
female: 16.7% (2014 est.)
country comparison to the world: 93

Population below poverty line: 32.3% (2018 est.)

Gini Index coefficient - distribution of family income: 51.3 (2018 est.)
country comparison to the world: 11

Household income or consumption by percentage share: *lowest 10%:* 0.6%
highest 10%: 44.7% (2000)

Budget: *revenues:* 37.02 billion (2017 est.)
expenditures: 45.44 billion (2017 est.)

Budget surplus (+) or deficit (-): -6.7% (of GDP) (2017 est.)
country comparison to the world: 189

Public debt: 65% of GDP (2017 est.)
75.3% of GDP (2016 est.)
country comparison to the world: 60

Taxes and other revenues: 29.3% (of GDP) (2017 est.)
country comparison to the world: 83

Fiscal year: calendar year

Current account balance: -$1.254 billion (2017 est.)
-$4.834 billion (2016 est.)
country comparison to the world: 154

Exports: $21 billion (2020 est.)
$35.18 billion (2019 est.)
$41.39 billion (2018 est.)
note: Data are in current year dollars and do not include illicit exports or re-exports.
country comparison to the world: 80

Exports - partners: China 62%, India 10%, United Arab Emirates 4%, Portugal 3%, Spain 3% (2019)

Exports - commodities: crude petroleum, diamonds, natural gas, refined petroleum, ships (2019)

Imports: $15.12 billion (2020 est.) note: data are in current year dollars
$22.3 billion (2019 est.) note: data are in current year dollars
$25.89 billion (2018 est.) note: data are in current year dollars
country comparison to the world: 96

Imports - partners: China 22%, Portugal 15%, Nigeria 6%, Belgium 6%, United States 5%, South Africa 5%, Brazil 5% (2019)

Imports - commodities: refined petroleum, scrap vessels, meat, rice, palm oil (2019)

Reserves of foreign exchange and gold: $17.29 billion (31 December 2017 est.)
$23.74 billion (31 December 2016 est.)
country comparison to the world: 63

Debt - external: $42.08 billion (31 December 2017 est.)
$27.14 billion (31 December 2016 est.)
country comparison to the world: 74

Exchange rates: kwanza (AOA) per US dollar -
172.6 (2017 est.)
163.656 (2016 est.)
163.656 (2015 est.)
120.061 (2014 est.)
98.303 (2013 est.)

ENERGY

Electricity access: *electrification - total population:* 43% (2019)
electrification - urban areas: 61% (2019)
electrification - rural areas: 6% (2019)

Electricity: *installed generating capacity:* 7.344 million kW (2020 est.)
consumption: 11.815 billion kWh (2019 est.)
exports: 0 kWh (2019 est.)
imports: 0 kWh (2019 est.)
transmission/distribution losses: 1.741 billion kWh (2019 est.)

Electricity generation sources: *fossil fuels:* 28.4% of total installed capacity (2020 est.)
solar: 0.1% of total installed capacity (2020 est.)
hydroelectricity: 70.1% of total installed capacity (2020 est.)
biomass and waste: 1.4% of total installed capacity (2020 est.)

Petroleum: *total petroleum production:* 1,197,600 bbl/day (2021 est.)
refined petroleum consumption: 133,400 bbl/day (2019 est.)
crude oil and lease condensate exports: 1,367,400 bbl/day (2018 est.)
crude oil and lease condensate imports: 0 bbl/day (2018 est.)
crude oil estimated reserves: 7.783 billion barrels (2021 est.)

Refined petroleum products - production: 53,480 bbl/day (2015 est.)
country comparison to the world: 80

Refined petroleum products - exports: 30,340 bbl/day (2015 est.)
country comparison to the world: 62

Refined petroleum products - imports: 111,600 bbl/day (2015 est.)
country comparison to the world: 50

Natural gas: *production:* 6,767,715,000 cubic meters (2019 est.)
consumption: 860.887 million cubic meters (2019 est.)
exports: 5,877,945,000 cubic meters (2019 est.)
imports: 0 cubic meters (2021 est.)
proven reserves: 343.001 billion cubic meters (2021 est.)

Carbon dioxide emissions: 19.362 million metric tonnes of CO_2 (2019 est.)
from coal and metallurgical coke: 0 metric tonnes of CO_2 (2019 est.)
from petroleum and other liquids: 17.673 million metric tonnes of CO_2 (2019 est.)
from consumed natural gas: 1.689 million metric tonnes of CO_2 (2019 est.)
country comparison to the world: 84

Energy consumption per capita: 11.693 million Btu/person (2019 est.)
country comparison to the world: 147

COMMUNICATIONS

Telephones - fixed lines: *total subscriptions:* 119,164 (2020 est.)
subscriptions per 100 inhabitants: (2020 est.) less than 1
country comparison to the world: 132

Telephones - mobile cellular: *total subscriptions:* 14,645,050 (2020 est.)
subscriptions per 100 inhabitants: 45 (2020 est.)
country comparison to the world: 70

Telecommunication systems: *general assessment:* Angola's telecom sector in recent years has benefited from political stability, which has encouraged foreign investment in the sector; the government and regulator have also set in train mechanisms to open up the telecom sector to new competitors, mobile services were launched in April 2022; the MNOs were slow to develop LTE services, instead relying on their GSM and 3G network capabilities; there has been slow progress in LTE network development, with only a small proportion of the country covered by network infrastructure; the Ministry of Telecommunications in early 2021 set up a 5G hub to assess 5G user cases; the regulator in November 2021 granted licenses to various companies offering 5G services, with spectrum in the 3.3-3.7GHz range having been set aside for such services (2022)
domestic: only about one fixed-line per 100 persons; mobile-cellular teledensity about 45 telephones per 100 persons (2020)
international: country code - 244; landing points for the SAT-3/WASC, WACS, ACE and SACS fiber-optic submarine cable that provides connectivity to other countries in west Africa, Brazil, Europe and Asia; satellite earth stations - 29, Angosat-2 satellite expected by 2021 (2019)

Broadcast media: state controls all broadcast media with nationwide reach; state-owned Televisao Popular de Angola (TPA) provides terrestrial TV service on 2 channels; a third TPA channel is available via cable and satellite; TV subscription services are available; state-owned Radio Nacional de Angola (RNA) broadcasts on 5 stations; about a half-dozen private radio stations broadcast locally

Internet country code: .ao

Internet users: *total:* 11,831,857 (2020 est.)
percent of population: 36% (2020 est.)
country comparison to the world: 51

Broadband - fixed subscriptions: *total:* 230,610 (2020 est.)
subscriptions per 100 inhabitants: 0.7 (2020 est.)
country comparison to the world: 116

TRANSPORTATION

National air transport system: *number of registered air carriers:* 10 (2020)
inventory of registered aircraft operated by air carriers: 55
annual passenger traffic on registered air carriers: 1,516,628 (2018)
annual freight traffic on registered air carriers: 78.16 million (2018) mt-km

Civil aircraft registration country code prefix: D2

Airports: *total:* 102 (2021)
country comparison to the world: 54

Airports - with paved runways: *total:* 32
over 3,047 m: 8
2,438 to 3,047 m: 8
1,524 to 2,437 m: 10
914 to 1,523 m: 6 (2021)

Airports - with unpaved runways: *total:* 70
over 3,047 m: 2
2,438 to 3,047 m: 2
1,524 to 2,437 m: 17
914 to 1,523 m: 27
under 914 m: 22 (2021)

Heliports: 1 (2021)

Pipelines: 352 km gas, 85 km liquid petroleum gas, 1,065 km oil, 5 km oil/gas/water (2013)

Railways: *total:* 2,852 km (2014)
narrow gauge: 2,729 km (2014) 1.067-m gauge
123 km 0.600-mm gauge
country comparison to the world: 63

Roadways: *total:* 26,000 km (2018)
paved: 13,600 km (2018)
unpaved: 12,400 km (2018)
country comparison to the world: 102

Waterways: 1,300 km (2011)
country comparison to the world: 57

Merchant marine: *total:* 54
by type: general cargo 13, oil tanker 8, other 33 (2021)
country comparison to the world: 117

Ports and terminals: *major seaport(s):* Cabinda, Lobito, Luanda, Namibe
LNG terminal(s) (export): Angola Soyo

MILITARY AND SECURITY

Military and security forces: Angolan Armed Forces (Forcas Armadas Angolanas, FAA): Army, Navy (Marinha de Guerra Angola, MGA), Angolan National Air Force (Forca Aerea Nacional Angolana, FANA; under operational control of the Army); Rapid Reaction Police (paramilitary) (2022)

Military expenditures: 1.4% of GDP (2021 est.)
1.7% of GDP (2020 est.)
1.8% of GDP (2019 est.) (approximately $2.7 billion)
2.1% of GDP (2018 est.) (approximately $3.02 billion)
2.6% of GDP (2017 est.) (approximately $3.65 billion)
country comparison to the world: 95

Military and security service personnel strengths: approximately 101,000 active troops (95,000 Army; 1,000 Navy; 5,000 Air Force); estimated 10,000 Rapid Reaction Police (2022)

Military equipment inventories and acquisitions: most Angolan military weapons and equipment are of Russian, Soviet, or Warsaw Pact origin; since 2010, Russia has been the principal supplier of military hardware to Angola (2021)

Military service age and obligation: 20-45 years of age for compulsory and 18-45 years for voluntary military service for men (registration at age 18 is mandatory); 20-45 years of age for voluntary service for women; 2-year conscript service obligation; Angolan citizenship required; the Navy is entirely staffed with volunteers (2021)

Military - note: the Angolan Armed Forces were created in 1991 under the Bicesse Accords signed between the Angolan Government and the National Union for the Total Independence of Angola (UNITA)

the Angolan Armed Forces are responsible for external security but also have domestic security responsibilities, including border security, expulsion of irregular migrants, and small-scale actions against groups like the Front for the Liberation of the Enclave of Cabinda separatists in Cabinda (2022)

Maritime threats: the International Maritime Bureau reports the territorial waters of Angola are a risk for armed robbery against ships; in 2021, four attacks against commercial vessels were reported, a decrease from the six attacks in 2020; most of these occurred in the main port of Luanda while ships were berthed or at anchor

TRANSNATIONAL ISSUES

Disputes - international: *Angola-Democratic Republic of Congo (DRC):* DRC accuses Angola of shifting monuments
Angola-Namibia: none identified
Angola-Republic of Congo: (Kabinda Exclave) none identified
Angola-Zambia: because the straight-line segments along the left bank (Zambian side) of the Cuando/Kwando River do not conform with the physical alignment of the unstable shoreline, Zambian residents in some areas have settled illegally on sections of shoreline that fall on the Angolan side of the boundary

Refugees and internally displaced persons: *refugees (country of origin):* 37,159 (Democratic Republic of the Congo) (refugees and asylum seekers), 9,272 (Guinea), 6,357 (Cote d'Ivoire), 5,725 (Mauritania) (2022)

Illicit drugs: used as a transshipment point for cocaine destined for Western Europe and other African states, particularly South Africa

ANGUILLA

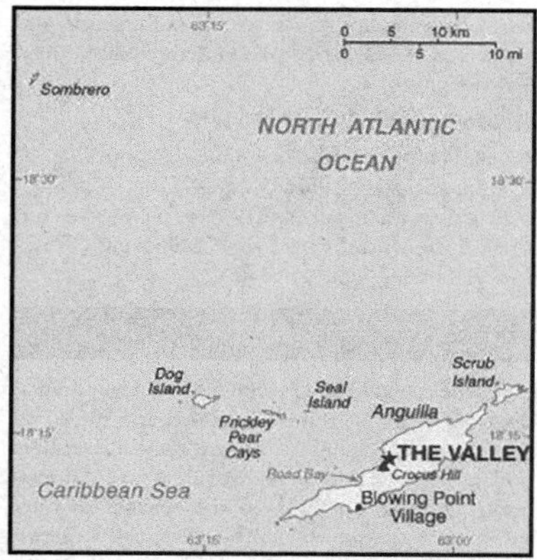

INTRODUCTION

Background: Colonized by English settlers from Saint Kitts in 1650, Anguilla was administered by Great Britain until the early 19th century, when the island - against the wishes of the inhabitants - was incorporated into a single British dependency along with Saint Kitts and Nevis. Several attempts at separation failed. In 1971, two years after a revolt, Anguilla was finally allowed to secede; this arrangement was formally recognized in 1980, with Anguilla becoming a separate British dependency. On 7 September 2017, the island suffered extensive damage from Hurricane Irma, particularly to communications and residential and business infrastructure.

GEOGRAPHY

Location: Caribbean, islands between the Caribbean Sea and North Atlantic Ocean, east of Puerto Rico

Geographic coordinates: 18 15 N, 63 10 W

Map references: Central America and the Caribbean

Area: *total:* 91 sq km
land: 91 sq km
water: 0 sq km
country comparison to the world: 226

Area - comparative: about one-half the size of Washington, DC

Land boundaries: *total:* 0 km

Coastline: 61 km

Maritime claims: *territorial sea:* 12 nm
exclusive economic zone: 200 nm
exclusive fishing zone: 200 nm

Climate: tropical; moderated by northeast trade winds

Terrain: flat and low-lying island of coral and limestone

Elevation: *highest point:* Crocus Hill 73 m
lowest point: Caribbean Sea 0 m

Natural resources: salt, fish, lobster

Land use: *agricultural land:* 0% (2018 est.)
forest: 61.1% (2018 est.)
other: 38.9% (2018 est.)

Irrigated land: 0 sq km (2012)

Population distribution: most of the population is concentrated in The Valley in the center of the island; settlmement is fairly uniform in the southwest, but rather sparce in the northeast

Natural hazards: frequent hurricanes and other tropical storms (July to October)

Geography - note: the most northerly of the Leeward Islands in the Lesser Antilles

PEOPLE AND SOCIETY

Population: 18,741 (2022 est.)
country comparison to the world: 219

Nationality: *noun:* Anguillan(s)
adjective: Anguillan

Ethnic groups: African/Black 85.3%, Hispanic 4.9%, mixed 3.8%, White 3.2%, East Indian/Indian 1%, other 1.6%, unspecified 0.3% (2011 est.)
note: data represent population by ethnic origin

Languages: English (official)

Religions: Protestant 73.2% (includes Anglican 22.7%, Methodist 19.4%, Pentecostal 10.5%, Seventh Day Adventist 8.3%, Baptist 7.1%, Church of God 4.9%, Presbyterian 0.2%, Brethren 0.1%), Roman Catholic 6.8%, Jehovah's Witness 1.1%, other Christian 10.9%, other 3.2%, unspecified 0.3%, none 4.5% (2011 est.)

Age structure: *0-14 years:* 21.63% (male 1,991/female 1,922)
15-24 years: 13.9% (male 1,269/female 1,246)
25-54 years: 42.27% (male 3,428/female 4,218)
55-64 years: 12.42% (male 993/female 1,254)

65 years and over: 9.78% (male 874/female 895) (2020 est.)

Median age: *total:* 35.7 years
male: 33.7 years
female: 37.6 years (2020 est.)
country comparison to the world: 81

Population growth rate: 1.8% (2022 est.)
country comparison to the world: 51

Birth rate: 12.01 births/1,000 population (2022 est.)
country comparison to the world: 156

Death rate: 4.64 deaths/1,000 population (2022 est.)
country comparison to the world: 204

Net migration rate: 10.67 migrant(s)/1,000 population (2022 est.)
country comparison to the world: 8

Population distribution: most of the population is concentrated in The Valley in the center of the island; settlmement is fairly uniform in the southwest, but rather sparce in the northeast

Urbanization: *urban population:* 100% of total population (2022)
rate of urbanization: 0.47% annual rate of change (2020-25 est.)

Major urban areas - population: 1,000 THE VALLEY (capital) (2018)

Sex ratio: *at birth:* 1.03 male(s)/female
0-14 years: 1.03 male(s)/female
15-24 years: 1.02 male(s)/female
25-54 years: 0.82 male(s)/female
55-64 years: 0.77 male(s)/female
65 years and over: 0.88 male(s)/female
total population: 0.89 male(s)/female (2022 est.)

Infant mortality rate: *total:* 3.07 deaths/1,000 live births
male: 4.01 deaths/1,000 live births
female: 2.1 deaths/1,000 live births (2022 est.)
country comparison to the world: 211

Life expectancy at birth: *total population:* 82.2 years
male: 79.59 years
female: 84.89 years (2022 est.)
country comparison to the world: 26

Total fertility rate: 1.72 children born/woman (2022 est.)
country comparison to the world: 161

Drinking water source: *improved: urban:* 97.5% of population
total: 97.5% of population
unimproved: urban: 2.5% of population
total: 2.5% of population (2017 est.)

Sanitation facility access: *improved: urban:* 99.1% of population
total: 99.1% of population
unimproved: urban: 0.9% of population
total: 0.9% of population (2017 est.)

Education expenditures: 3.6% of GDP (2018 est.)
country comparison to the world: 115

ENVIRONMENT

Environment - current issues: supplies of potable water sometimes cannot meet increasing demand largely because of poor distribution system

Climate: tropical; moderated by northeast trade winds

Land use: *agricultural land:* 0% (2018 est.)
arable land: 0% (2018 est.)
permanent crops: 0% (2018 est.)
permanent pasture: 0% (2018 est.)
forest: 61.1% (2018 est.)
other: 38.9% (2018 est.)

Urbanization: *urban population:* 100% of total population (2022)
rate of urbanization: 0.47% annual rate of change (2020-25 est.)

GOVERNMENT

Country name: *conventional long form:* none
conventional short form: Anguilla
etymology: the name Anguilla means "eel" in various Romance languages (Spanish, Italian, Portuguese, French) and likely derives from the island's lengthy shape

Government type: parliamentary democracy (House of Assembly); self-governing overseas territory of the UK

Dependency status: overseas territory of the UK

Capital: *name:* The Valley
geographic coordinates: 18 13 N, 63 03 W
time difference: UTC-4 (1 hour ahead of Washington, DC, during Standard Time)
etymology: name derives from the capital's location between several hills

Administrative divisions: none (overseas territory of the UK)

Independence: none (overseas territory of the UK)

National holiday: Anguilla Day, 30 May (1967)

Constitution: *history:* several previous; latest 1 April 1982
amendments: amended 1990, 2012, 2017, 2019

Legal system: common law based on the English model

Citizenship: see United Kingdom

Suffrage: 18 years of age; universal

Executive branch: *chief of state:* King CHARLES III (since 8 September 2022); represented by Governor Dileeni DANIEL-SELVARATNAM (since 18 January 2021)
head of government: Premier Dr. Ellis WEBSTER (since 30 June 2020); note - starting in 2019, the title of head of government was changed to premier from chief minister of Anguilla
cabinet: Executive Council appointed by the governor from among elected members of the House of Assembly
elections/appointments: the monarchy is hereditary; governor appointed by the monarch; following legislative elections, the leader of the majority party or majority coalition usually appointed premier by the governor

Legislative branch: *description:* unicameral House of Assembly (11 seats; 7 members directly elected in single-seat constituencies by simple majority vote, 2 appointed by the governor, and 2 ex officio members - the attorney general and deputy governor; members serve five-year terms)
elections: last held on 29 June 2020 (next to be held in 2025)
election results: percent of vote by party - NA; seats by party - APM 7, AUF 4; composition - men 8, women 3, percent of women 27.3%

Judicial branch: *highest court(s):* the Eastern Caribbean Supreme Court (ECSC) is the superior court of the Organization of Eastern Caribbean States; the ECSC - headquartered on St. Lucia - consists of the Court of Appeal - headed by the chief justice and 4 judges - and the High Court with 18 judges; the Court of Appeal is itinerant, travelling to member states on a schedule to hear appeals from the High Court and subordinate courts; High Court judges reside in the member states, though none on Anguilla
judge selection and term of office: Eastern Caribbean Supreme Court chief justice appointed by Her Majesty, Queen ELIZABETH II; other justices and judges appointed by the Judicial and Legal Services Commission; Court of Appeal justices appointed for life with mandatory retirement at age 65; High Court judges appointed for life with mandatory retirement at age 62
subordinate courts: Magistrate's Court; Juvenile Court

Political parties and leaders: Anguilla Progressive Movement or APM [Dr. Ellis WEBSTER]; (formerly Anguilla United Movement or AUM)
Anguilla United Front or AUF [Cora RICHARDSON-HODGE]

International organization participation: Caricom (associate), CDB, Interpol (subbureau), OECS, UNESCO (associate), UPU

Diplomatic representation in the US: none (overseas territory of the UK)

Diplomatic representation from the US: *embassy:* none (overseas territory of the UK); alternate contact is the US Embassy in Barbados [1] (246) 227-4000

Flag description: blue, with the flag of the UK in the upper hoist-side quadrant and the Anguillan coat of arms centered in the outer half of the flag; the coat of arms depicts three orange dolphins in an interlocking circular design on a white background with a turquoise-blue field below; the white in the background represents peace; the blue base symbolizes the surrounding sea, as well as faith, youth, and hope; the three dolphins stand for endurance, unity, and strength

National symbol(s): dolphin

National anthem: *name:* "God Bless Anguilla"
lyrics/music: Alex RICHARDSON
note: local anthem adopted 1981; as an overseas territory of the United Kingdom, "God Save the King" is official (see United Kingdom)

ECONOMY

Economic overview: Anguilla has few natural resources, is unsuited for agriculture, and the economy depends heavily on luxury tourism, offshore banking, lobster fishing, and remittances from emigrants. Increased activity in the tourism industry has spurred the growth of the construction sector contributing to economic growth. Anguillan officials have put substantial effort into developing the offshore financial sector, which is small but growing. In the medium term, prospects for the economy will depend largely on the recovery of the tourism sector and, therefore, on revived income growth in the industrialized nations as well as on favorable weather conditions.

Real GDP (purchasing power parity): $175.4 million (2009 est.)
$191.7 million (2008 est.)
$108.9 million (2004 est.)
country comparison to the world: 221

Real GDP growth rate: -8.5% (2009 est.)

country comparison to the world: 220

Real GDP per capita: $12,200 (2008 est.)
country comparison to the world: 126
GDP (official exchange rate)
$175.4 million (2009 est.)

Inflation rate (consumer prices): 1.3% (2017 est.)
-0.6% (2016 est.)
country comparison to the world: 76

GDP - composition, by sector of origin: *agriculture:* 3% (2017 est.)
industry: 10.5% (2017 est.)
services: 86.4% (2017 est.)

GDP - composition, by end use: *household consumption:* 74.1% (2017 est.)
government consumption: 18.3% (2017 est.)
investment in fixed capital: 26.8% (2017 est.)
investment in inventories: 0% (2017 est.)
exports of goods and services: 48.2% (2017 est.)
imports of goods and services: -67.4% (2017 est.)

Agricultural products: small quantities of tobacco, vegetables; cattle raising

Industries: tourism, boat building, offshore financial services

Industrial production growth rate: 4% (2017 est.)
country comparison to the world: 75

Labor force: 6,049 (2001)
country comparison to the world: 218

Labor force - by occupation: *agriculture:* 74.1%
industry: 3%
services: 18%
agriculture/fishing/forestry/mining: 4% (2000 est.)
manufacturing: 3% (2000 est.)
construction: 18% (2000 est.)
transportation and utilities: 10% (2000 est.)
commerce: 36% (2000 est.)

Unemployment rate: 8% (2002)
country comparison to the world: 124

Population below poverty line: 23% (2002 est.)

Budget: *revenues:* 81.92 million (2017 est.)
expenditures: 80.32 million (2017 est.)
Budget surplus (+) or deficit (-)
0.9% (of GDP) (2017 est.)
country comparison to the world: 34

Public debt: 20.1% of GDP (2015 est.)
20.8% of GDP (2014 est.)
country comparison to the world: 189

Taxes and other revenues: 46.7% (of GDP) (2017 est.)
country comparison to the world: 19

Fiscal year: 1 April - 31 March

Current account balance: -$23.2 million (2017 est.)
-$25.3 million (2016 est.)
country comparison to the world: 73

Exports: $7.9 million (2017 est.)
$3.9 million (2016 est.)
note: Data are in current year dollars and do not include illicit exports or re-exports.
country comparison to the world: 219

Exports - commodities: lobster, fish, livestock, salt, concrete blocks, rum

Imports: $186.2 million (2017 est.)
$170.1 million (2016 est.)
country comparison to the world: 211

Imports - commodities: fuels, foodstuffs, manufactures, chemicals, trucks, textiles

Reserves of foreign exchange and gold: $76.38 million (31 December 2017 est.)
$48.14 million (31 December 2015 est.)
country comparison to the world: 183

Debt - external: $41.04 million (31 December 2013)
$8.8 million (1998)
country comparison to the world: 195

Exchange rates: East Caribbean dollars (XCD) per US dollar -
2.7 (2017 est.)
2.7 (2016 est.)
2.7 (2015 est.)
2.7 (2014 est.)
2.7 (2013 est.)

COMMUNICATIONS

Telephones - fixed lines: *total subscriptions:* 6,000 (2018 est.)
subscriptions per 100 inhabitants: 42 (2018 est.)
country comparison to the world: 200

Telephones - mobile cellular: *total subscriptions:* 26,000 (2018 est.)
subscriptions per 100 inhabitants: 182 (2018 est.)
country comparison to the world: 212

Telecommunication systems: *general assessment:* in the telecom sector, with declines seen in subscriber numbers (particularly for prepaid mobile services — the mainstay of short-term visitors) and revenue; fixed and mobile broadband services are two areas that have benefited from the crisis to a small extent as employees and students have resorted to working from home, but their contribution to the sector has been insufficient to offset steep falls in other areas of the market; one area of the telecom market that does not yet appear poised for growth is 5G mobile; governments, regulators, and even the mobile network operators have shown that they have little appetite for investing in 5G opportunities at the present time; network expansion and enhancements remain concentrated around improving LTE coverage; until the economies and markets stabilize, and overseas visitors return there is unlikely to be much momentum towards implementing 5G capabilities anywhere in the region (2021)
domestic: fixed-line teledensity is about 42 per 100 persons; mobile-cellular teledensity is roughly 182 per 100 persons (2018)
international: country code - 1-264; landing points for the SSCS, ECFS, GCN and Southern Caribbean Fiber with submarine cable links to Caribbean islands and to the US; microwave radio relay to island of Saint Martin/Sint Maarten (2019)

Broadcast media: 1 private TV station; multi-channel cable TV subscription services are available; about 10 radio stations, one of which is government-owned

Internet country code: .ai

Internet users: *total:* 12,489 (2019 est.)
percent of population: 82% (2019 est.)
country comparison to the world: 215

Broadband - fixed subscriptions: *total:* 5,000 (2018 est.)
subscriptions per 100 inhabitants: 35 (2018 est.)
country comparison to the world: 186

TRANSPORTATION

National air transport system: *number of registered air carriers:* 2 (2020)
inventory of registered aircraft operated by air carriers: 4

Civil aircraft registration country code prefix: VP-A

Airports: *total:* 1 (2021)
country comparison to the world: 210

Airports - with paved runways: *total:* 1
1,524 to 2,437 m: 1 (2021)

Roadways: *total:* 175 km (2004)
paved: 82 km (2004)
unpaved: 93 km (2004)
country comparison to the world: 209

Merchant marine: *total:* 2
by type: other 2 (2021)
country comparison to the world: 173

Ports and terminals: *major seaport(s):* Blowing Point, Road Bay

MILITARY AND SECURITY

Military - note: defense is the responsibility of the UK

TRANSNATIONAL ISSUES

Disputes - international: none identified

Illicit drugs: transshipment point for South American narcotics destined for the US and Europe

ANTARCTICA

INTRODUCTION

Background: Speculation over the existence of a "southern land" was not confirmed until the early 1820s when British and American commercial operators and British and Russian national expeditions began exploring the Antarctic Peninsula region and other areas south of the Antarctic Circle. Not until 1840 was it established that Antarctica was indeed a continent and not merely a group of islands or an area of ocean. Several exploration "firsts" were achieved in the early 20th century, but generally the area saw little human activity. Following World War II, however, the continent experienced an upsurge in scientific research. A number of countries have set up a range of year-round and seasonal stations, camps, and refuges to support scientific research in Antarctica. Seven have made territorial claims and two maintain the basis for a claim, but most countries do not recognize these claims. In order to form a legal framework for the activities of nations on the

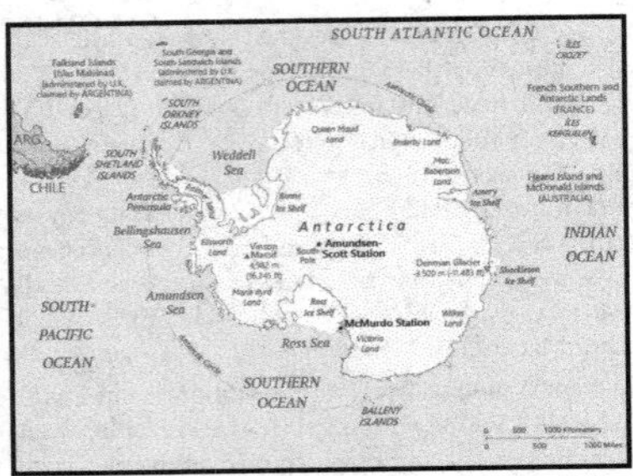

continent, an Antarctic Treaty was negotiated that neither denies nor gives recognition to existing territorial claims; signed in 1959, it entered into force in 1961. Also relevant to Antarctic governance are the Environmental Protocol to the Antarctic Treaty and the Convention for the Conservation of Antarctic Marine Living Resources.

GEOGRAPHY

Location: continent mostly south of the Antarctic Circle

Geographic coordinates: 90 00 S, 0 00 E

Map references: Antarctic Region

Area: *total:* 14.2 million sq km
land: 14.2 million sq km (285,000 sq km ice-free, 13.915 million sq km ice-covered) (est.)
note: fifth-largest continent, following Asia, Africa, North America, and South America, but larger than Australia and the subcontinent of Europe
country comparison to the world: 2

Area - comparative: slightly less than 1.5 times the size of the US

Land boundaries: 0
note: see entry on Disputes - international

Coastline: 17,968 km

Maritime claims: Australia, Chile, and Argentina claim Exclusive Economic Zone (EEZ) rights or similar over 200 nm extensions seaward from their continental claims, but like the claims themselves, these zones are not accepted by other countries; 22 of 29 Antarctic Treaty consultative parties have made no claims to Antarctic territory, although Russia and the United States have reserved the right to do so, and no country can make a new claim; also see the Disputes - international entry

Climate: the coldest, windiest, and driest continent on Earth; severe low temperatures vary with latitude, elevation, and distance from the ocean; East Antarctica is colder than West Antarctica because of its higher elevation; Antarctic Peninsula has the most moderate climate; higher temperatures occur in January along the coast and average slightly below freezing; summers characterized by continuous daylight, while winters bring continuous darkness; persistent high pressure over the interior brings dry, subsiding air that results in very little cloud cover

Terrain: about 99% thick continental ice sheet and 1% barren rock, with average elevations between 2,000 and 4,000 m; mountain ranges up to nearly 5,000 m; ice-free coastal areas include parts of southern Victoria Land, Wilkes Land, the Antarctic Peninsula area, and parts of Ross Island on McMurdo Sound; glaciers form ice shelves along about half of the coastline, and floating ice shelves constitute 11% of the area of the continent

Elevation: *highest point:* Vinson Massif 4,892 m
lowest point: Denman Glacier more than -3,500 m (-11,500 ft) below sea level
mean elevation: 2,300 m
note: the lowest known land point in Antarctica is hidden in the Denman Glacier; at its surface is the deepest ice yet discovered and the world's lowest elevation not under seawater

Natural resources: iron ore, chromium, copper, gold, nickel, platinum and other minerals, and coal and hydrocarbons have been found in small noncommercial quantities; mineral exploitation except for scientific research is banned by the Environmental Protocol to the Antarctic Treaty; krill, icefish, toothfish, and crab have been taken by commercial fisheries, which are managed through the Commission for the Conservation of Antarctic Living Marine Resources (CCAMLR)

Land use: *agricultural land:* 0% (2018 est.)

Natural hazards: katabatic (gravity-driven) winds blow coastward from the high interior; frequent blizzards form near the foot of the plateau; cyclonic storms form over the ocean and move clockwise along the coast; large icebergs may calve from ice shelf
volcanism: volcanic activity on Deception Island and isolated areas of West Antarctica; other seismic activity rare and weak

Geography - note: the coldest, windiest, highest (on average), and driest continent; during summer, more solar radiation reaches the surface at the South Pole than is received at the Equator in an equivalent period

mostly uninhabitable, 99% of the land area is covered by the Antarctic ice sheet, the largest single mass of ice on earth covering an area of 14 million sq km (5.4 million sq mi) and containing 26.5 million cu km (6.4 million cu mi) of ice (this is almost 62% of all of the world's fresh water); if all this ice were converted to liquid water, one estimate is that it would be sufficient to raise the height of the world's oceans by 58 m (190 ft)

PEOPLE AND SOCIETY

Population: no indigenous inhabitants, but there are both year-round and summer-only staffed research stations
note: 54 countries have signed the 1959 Antarctic Treaty; 30 of those operate through their National Antarctic Program a number of seasonal-only (summer) and year-round research stations on the continent and its nearby islands south of 60 degrees south latitude (the region covered by the Antarctic Treaty); the population engaging in and supporting science or managing and protecting the Antarctic region varies from approximately 5,000 in summer to 1,100 in winter; in addition, approximately 1,000 personnel, including ship's crew and scientists doing onboard research, are present in the waters of the treaty region

as of 2017, peak summer (December-February) maximum capacity in scientific stations - 4,877 total; Argentina 601, Australia 243, Belarus 12, Belgium 40, Brazil 66, Bulgaria 22, Chile 433, China 166, Czechia 20, Ecuador 34, Finland 17, France 90, France and Italy jointly 80, Germany 104, India 113, Italy 120, Japan 130, South Korea 130, Netherlands 10, NZ 86, Norway 70, Peru 30, Poland 40, Russia 335, South Africa 80, Spain 98, Sweden 20, Ukraine 24, UK 196, US 1,399, Uruguay 68 (2017)

winter (June-August) maximum capacity in scientific station - 1,036 total; Argentina 221, Australia 52, Brazil 15, Chile 114, China 32, France 24, France and Italy jointly 13, Germany 9, India 48, Japan 40, Netherlands 10, South Korea 25, NZ 11, Norway 7, Poland 16, Russia 125, South Africa 15, Ukraine 12, UK 44, US 215, Uruguay 8 (2017)

research stations operated within the Antarctic Treaty area (south of 60 degrees south latitude) by National Antarctic Programs year-round stations - approximately 40 total; Argentina 6, Australia 3, Brazil 1, Chile 6, China 2, France 1, France and Italy jointly 1, Germany 1, India 2, Japan 1, Netherlands 1, South Korea 2, NZ 1, Norway 1, Poland 1, Russia 5, South Africa 1, Ukraine 1, UK 2, US 3, Uruguay 2 (2017)

a range of seasonal-only (summer) stations, camps, and refuges - Argentina, Australia, Belarus, Belgium, Bulgaria, Brazil, Chile, China, Czechia, Ecuador, Finland, France, Germany, India, Italy, Japan, Netherlands, South Korea, New Zealand, Norway, Peru, Poland, Russia, South Africa, Spain, Sweden, Ukraine, UK, US, and Uruguay (2017)

in addition, during the austral summer some nations have numerous occupied locations such as tent camps, summerlong temporary facilities, and mobile traverses in support of research

ENVIRONMENT

Environment - current issues: the discovery of a large Antarctic ozone hole in the earth's stratosphere (the ozone layer) - first announced in 1985 - spurred the signing of the Montreal Protocol in 1987, an international agreement phasing out the use of ozone-depleting chemicals; the ozone layer prevents most harmful wavelengths of ultra-violet (UV) light from passing through the earth's atmosphere; ozone depletion has been shown to harm a variety of Antarctic marine plants and animals (plankton); in 2016, a gradual trend toward "healing" of the ozone hole was reported; since the 1990s, satellites have shown accelerating ice loss driven by ocean change; although considerable uncertainty remains, scientists are increasing our understanding and ability to model potential impacts of ice loss

Climate: the coldest, windiest, and driest continent on Earth; severe low temperatures vary with latitude, elevation, and distance from the ocean; East Antarctica is colder than West Antarctica because of its higher elevation; Antarctic Peninsula has the most moderate climate; higher temperatures occur in January along the coast and average slightly below freezing; summers characterized by continuous daylight, while winters bring continuous darkness; persistent high pressure over the interior brings dry, subsiding air that results in very little cloud cover

GOVERNMENT

Country name: *conventional long form:* none
conventional short form: Antarctica

etymology: name derived from two Greek words meaning "opposite to the Arctic" or "opposite to the north"

Government type: Antarctic Treaty Summary - the Antarctic region is governed by a system known as the Antarctic Treaty system; the system includes: 1. the Antarctic Treaty, signed on 1 December 1959 and entered into force on 23 June 1961, which establishes the legal framework for the management of Antarctica, 2. Measures, Decisions, and Resolutions adopted at Antarctic Treaty Consultative Meetings, 3. The Convention for the Conservation of Antarctic Seals (1972), 4. The Convention for the Conservation of Antarctic Marine Living Resources (1980), and 5. The Protocol on Environmental Protection to the Antarctic Treaty (1991); the Antarctic Treaty Consultative Meetings operate by consensus (not by vote) of all consultative parties at annual Treaty meetings; by January 2022, there were 54 treaty member nations: 29 consultative and 25 non-consultative; consultative (decision-making) members include the seven nations that claim portions of Antarctica as national territory (some claims overlap) and 22 non-claimant nations; the US and Russia have reserved the right to make claims; the US does not recognize the claims of others; Antarctica is administered through meetings of the consultative member nations; measures adopted at these meetings are carried out by these member nations (with respect to their own nationals and operations) in accordance with their own national laws; the years in parentheses indicate when a consultative membernation acceded to the Treaty and when it was accepted as a consultative member, while no date indicates the country was an original 1959 treaty signatory; claimant nations are - Argentina, Australia, Chile, France, NZ, Norway, and the UK; nonclaimant consultative nations are - Belgium, Brazil (1975/1983), Bulgaria (1978/1998), China (1983/1985), Czechia (1962/2014), Ecuador (1987/1990), Finland (1984/1989), Germany (1979/1981), India (1983/1983), Italy (1981/1987), Japan, South Korea (1986/1989), Netherlands (1967/1990), Peru (1981/1989), Poland (1961/1977), Russia, South Africa, Spain (1982/1988), Sweden (1984/1988), Ukraine (1992/2004), Uruguay (1980/1985), and the US; non-consultative members, with year of accession in parentheses, are - Austria (1987), Belarus (2006), Canada (1988), Colombia (1989), Cuba (1984), Denmark (1965), Estonia (2001), Greece (1987), Guatemala (1991), Hungary (1984), Iceland (2015), Kazakhstan (2015), North Korea (1987), Malaysia (2011), Monaco (2008), Mongolia (2015), Pakistan (2012), Papua New Guinea (1981), Portugal (2010), Romania (1971), Slovakia (1962/1993), Slovenia (2019), Switzerland (1990), Turkey (1996), and Venezuela (1999); note - Czechoslovakia acceded to the Treaty in 1962 and separated into the Czech Republic and Slovakia in 1993; Article 1 - area to be used for peaceful purposes only; military activity, such as weapons testing, is prohibited, but military personnel and equipment may be used for scientific research or any other peaceful purpose; Article 2 - freedom of scientific investigation and cooperation shall continue; Article 3 - free exchange of information and personnel, cooperation with the UN and other international agencies; Article 4 - does not recognize, dispute, or establish territorial claims and no new claims shall be asserted while the treaty is in force; Article 5 - prohibits nuclear explosions or disposal of radioactive wastes; Article 6 - includes under the treaty all land and ice shelves south of 60 degrees 00 minutes south and reserves high seas rights; Article 7 - treaty-state observers have free access, including aerial observation, to any area and may inspect all stations, installations, and equipment; advance notice of all expeditions and of the introduction of military personnel must be given; Article 8 - allows for jurisdiction over observers and scientists by their own states; Article 9 - frequent consultative meetings take place among member nations; Article 10 - treaty states will discourage activities by any country in Antarctica that are contrary to the treaty; Article 11 - disputes to be settled peacefully by the parties concerned or, ultimately, by the International Court of Justice; Articles 12, 13, 14 - deal with upholding, interpreting, and amending the treaty among involved nations; other agreements - some 200 measures adopted at treaty consultative meetings and approved by governments; the Protocol on Environmental Protection to the Antarctic Treaty was signed 4 October 1991 and entered into force 14 January 1998; this agreement provides for the protection of the Antarctic environment and includes five annexes that have entered into force: 1) environmental impact assessment, 2) conservation of Antarctic fauna and flora, 3) waste disposal and waste management, 4) prevention of marine pollution, 5) area protection and management; a sixth annex addressing liability arising from environmental emergencies has yet to enter into force; the Protocol prohibits all activities relating to mineral resources except scientific research; a permanent Antarctic Treaty Secretariat was established in 2004 in Buenos Aires, Argentina

Legal system: Antarctica is administered through annual meetings - known as Antarctic Treaty Consultative Meetings - which include consultative member nations, non-consultative member nations, observer organizations, and expert organizations; decisions from these meetings are carried out by these member nations (with respect to their own nationals and operations) in accordance with their own national laws; more generally, the Antarctic Treaty area, that is to all areas between 60 and 90 degrees south latitude, is subject to a number of relevant legal instruments and procedures adopted by the states party to the Antarctic Treaty; note - US law, including certain criminal offenses by or against US nationals, such as murder, may apply extraterritoriality; some US laws directly apply to Antarctica; for example, the Antarctic Conservation Act, 16 U.S.C. section 2401 et seq., provides civil and criminal penalties for the following activities unless authorized by regulation or statute: the taking of native mammals or birds; the introduction of nonindigenous plants and animals; entry into specially protected areas; the discharge or disposal of pollutants; and the importation into the US of certain items from Antarctica; violation of the Antarctic Conservation Act carries penalties of up to $10,000 in fines and one year in prison; the National Science Foundation and Department of Justice share enforcement responsibilities; Public Law 95-541, the US Antarctic Conservation Act of 1978, as amended in 1996, requires expeditions from the US to Antarctica to notify, in advance, the Office of Oceans and Polar Affairs, Room 2665, Department of State, Washington, DC 20520, which reports such plans to other nations as required by the Antarctic Treaty; for more information, contact antarctica@state.gov

Flag description: unofficial; a True South flag, created in 2018, has quickly become popular for its simple yet elegant design and has been used by various National Antarctic Programs, Antarctic nonprofits, and expedition teams; the flag's meaning is described as: horizontal stripes of navy and white represent the long days and nights at Antarctica's extreme latitude; in the center, a lone white peak erupts from a field of snow and ice, echoing those of the bergs, mountains, and pressure ridges that define the Antarctic horizon; the long shadow it casts forms the unmistakable shape of a compass arrow pointed south, an homage to the continent's legacy of exploration; together, the two center shapes create a diamond, symbolizing the hope that Antarctica will continue to be a center of peace, discovery, and cooperation for generations to come

ECONOMY

Economic overview: Scientific undertakings rather than commercial pursuits are the predominant human activity in Antarctica. Offshore fishing and tourism, both based abroad, account for Antarctica's limited economic activity.

Antarctic Fisheries, within the area covered by the Convention on Conservation of Antarctic Marine Living Resources currently target Patagonian toothfish, Antarctic toothfish, mackerel icefish and Antarctic krill. The Commission for the Conservation of Antarctic Marine Living Resources (CCAMLR) manages these fisheries using the ecosystem-based and precautionary approach. The Commission's objective is conservation of Antarctic marine living resources and it regulates the fisheries based on the level of information available, and maintaining existing ecological relationships. While Illegal, Unreported and Unregulated (IUU) fishing has declined in the Convention area since 1990, it remains a concern

A total of 73,670 tourists visited the Antarctic Treaty area in the 2019-2020 Antarctic summer, 32 percent greater than the 55,489 visitors in 2018-2019. These estimates were provided to the Antarctic Treaty by the International Association of Antarctica Tour Operators and do not include passengers on overflights. Nearly all of the tourists were passengers on commercial ships and several yachts that make trips during the summer.

ENERGY

Carbon dioxide emissions: 28,000 metric tonnes of CO_2 (2019 est.)
from petroleum and other liquids: 28,000 metric tonnes of CO_2 (2019 est.)
country comparison to the world: 214

COMMUNICATIONS

Telecommunication systems: *general assessment:* scientists with the United States Antarctic Program at McMurdo Station have now got their hands on a Starlink terminal of their own, where it is said to be improving connectivity as they carry out their research; this was made possible through laser links between the SpaceX satellites in orbit that eliminate the need for ground stations at the poles, and makes

Antarctica the seventh and final continent to receive Starlink internet coverage (2022)
domestic: commercial cellular networks operating in a small number of locations (2019)
international: country code - none allocated; via satellite (including mobile Inmarsat and Iridium systems) to and from all research stations, ships, aircraft, and most field parties

Internet country code: .aq

Internet users: *total:* 4,400 (2016 est.)
percent of population: 100% (2016 est.)
country comparison to the world: 222

TRANSPORTATION

Airports: *total:* 17 (2021)
country comparison to the world: 141

Airports - with unpaved runways: *total:* 17
over 3,047 m: 4
2,438 to 3,047 m: 2
1,524 to 2,437 m: 2
914 to 1,523 m: 5
under 914 m: 4 (2021)

Heliports: 53 (2021)
note: all year-round and seasonal stations operated by National Antarctic Programs stations have some kind of helicopter landing facilities, prepared (helipads) or unprepared

Ports and terminals: most coastal stations have sparse and intermittent offshore anchorages; a few stations have basic wharf facilities

Transportation - note: US coastal stations include McMurdo (77 51 S, 166 40 E) and Palmer (64 43 S, 64 03 W); government use only; all ships are subject to inspection in accordance with Article 7, Antarctic Treaty; relevant legal instruments and authorization procedures adopted by the states parties to the Antarctic Treaty regulating the Antarctic Treaty area have to be complied with (see "Legal System"); The Hydrographic Commission on Antarctica (HCA), a commission of the International Hydrographic Organization (IHO), is responsible for hydrographic surveying and nautical charting matters in Antarctic Treaty area; it coordinates and facilitates provision of accurate and appropriate charts and other aids to navigation in support of safety of navigation in region; membership of HCA is open to any IHO Member State whose government has acceded to the Antarctic Treaty and which contributes resources or data to IHO Chart coverage of the area

MILITARY AND SECURITY

Military - note: the Antarctic Treaty of 1961 prohibits any measures of a military nature, such as the establishment of military bases and fortifications, the carrying out of military maneuvers, or the testing of any type of weapon; it permits the use of military personnel or equipment for scientific research or for any other peaceful purposes

TRANSNATIONAL ISSUES

Disputes - international: the Antarctic Treaty freezes, and most states do not recognize, the land and maritime territorial claims made by Argentina, Australia, Chile, France, New Zealand, Norway, and the UK (some overlapping) for three-fourths of the continent; the US and Russia reserve the right to make claims

ANTIGUA AND BARBUDA

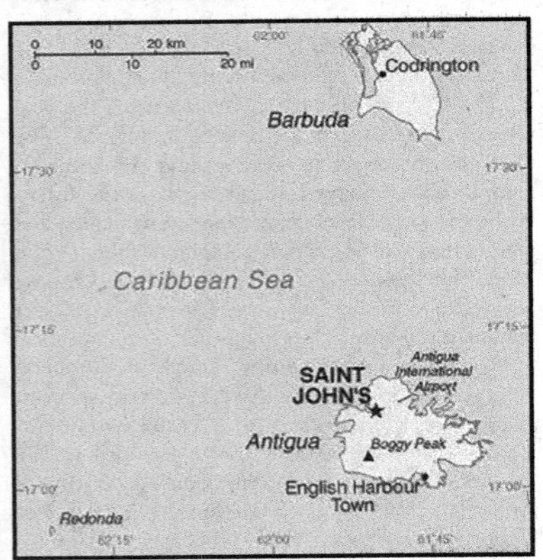

INTRODUCTION

Background: The Siboney were the first people to inhabit the islands of Antigua and Barbuda in 2400 B.C., but Arawak Indians populated the islands when Christopher COLUMBUS landed on his second voyage in 1493. Early Spanish and French settlements were succeeded by an English colony in 1667. Slavery, to provide labor on the sugar plantations on Antigua, was abolished in 1834. The islands became an independent state within the British Commonwealth of Nations in 1981. On 6 September 2017, Hurricane Irma passed over the island of Barbuda devastating the island and forcing the evacuation of the population to Antigua. Almost all of the structures on Barbuda were destroyed and the vegetation stripped, but Antigua was spared the worst.

GEOGRAPHY

Location: Caribbean, islands between the Caribbean Sea and the North Atlantic Ocean, east-southeast of Puerto Rico

Geographic coordinates: 17 03 N, 61 48 W

Map references: Central America and the Caribbean

Area: *total:* 443 sq km (Antigua 280 sq km; Barbuda 161 sq km)
land: 443 sq km
water: 0 sq km
note: includes Redonda, 1.6 sq km
country comparison to the world: 200

Area - comparative: 2.5 times the size of Washington, DC

Land boundaries: *total:* 0 km

Coastline: 153 km

Maritime claims: *territorial sea:* 12 nm
contiguous zone: 24 nm
exclusive economic zone: 200 nm
continental shelf: 200 nm or to the edge of the continental margin

Climate: tropical maritime; little seasonal temperature variation

Terrain: mostly low-lying limestone and coral islands, with some higher volcanic areas

Elevation: *highest point:* Mount Obama 402 m
lowest point: Caribbean Sea 0 m

Natural resources: NEGL; pleasant climate fosters tourism

Land use: *agricultural land:* 20.5% (2018 est.)
arable land: 9% (2018 est.)
permanent crops: 2.3% (2018 est.)
permanent pasture: 9% (2018 est.)
forest: 18.8% (2018 est.)
other: 60.8% (2018 est.)

Irrigated land: 1.3 sq km (2012)

Population distribution: the island of Antigua is home to approximately 97% of the population; nearly the entire population of Barbuda lives in Codrington

Natural hazards: hurricanes and tropical storms (July to October); periodic droughts

Geography - note: Antigua has a deeply indented shoreline with many natural harbors and beaches; Barbuda has a large western harbor

PEOPLE AND SOCIETY

Population: 100,335 (2022 est.)
country comparison to the world: 196

Nationality: *noun:* Antiguan(s), Barbudan(s)
adjective: Antiguan, Barbudan

Ethnic groups: African descent 87.3%, mixed 4.7%, Hispanic 2.7%, White 1.6%, other 2.7%, unspecified 0.9% (2011 est.)
note: data represent population by ethnic group

Languages: English (official), Antiguan creole

Religions: Protestant 68.3% (Anglican 17.6%, Seventh Day Adventist 12.4%, Pentecostal 12.2%, Moravian 8.3%, Methodist 5.6%, Wesleyan Holiness 4.5%, Church of God 4.1%, Baptist 3.6%), Roman Catholic 8.2%, other 12.2%, unspecified 5.5%, none 5.9% (2011 est.)

Age structure: *0-14 years:* 22.52% (male 11,243/female 10,871)
15-24 years: 16.15% (male 7,891/female 7,961)
25-54 years: 41.68% (male 18,757/female 22,167)
55-64 years: 10.74% (male 4,693/female 5,848)
65 years and over: 8.91% (male 3,736/female 5,012) (2020 est.)

Dependency ratios: *total dependency ratio:* 45.3
youth dependency ratio: 31.8
elderly dependency ratio: 13.6
potential support ratio: 7.4 (2020 est.)

Median age: *total:* 32.7 years

male: 30.7 years
female: 34.4 years (2020 est.)
country comparison to the world: 106

Population growth rate: 1.15% (2022 est.)
country comparison to the world: 82

Birth rate: 15.16 births/1,000 population (2022 est.)
country comparison to the world: 115

Death rate: 5.65 deaths/1,000 population (2022 est.)
country comparison to the world: 176

Net migration rate: 2.03 migrant(s)/1,000 population (2022 est.)
country comparison to the world: 49

Population distribution: the island of Antigua is home to approximately 97% of the population; nearly the entire population of Barbuda lives in Codrington

Urbanization: *urban population:* 24.3% of total population (2022)
rate of urbanization: 0.87% annual rate of change (2020-25 est.)

Major urban areas - population: 21,000 SAINT JOHN'S (capital) (2018)

Sex ratio: *at birth:* 1.05 male(s)/female
0-14 years: 1.03 male(s)/female
15-24 years: 0.99 male(s)/female
25-54 years: 0.85 male(s)/female
55-64 years: 0.8 male(s)/female
65 years and over: 0.64 male(s)/female
total population: 0.89 male(s)/female (2022 est.)

Infant mortality rate: *total:* 14.3 deaths/1,000 live births
male: 17.27 deaths/1,000 live births
female: 11.17 deaths/1,000 live births (2022 est.)
country comparison to the world: 106

Life expectancy at birth: *total population:* 77.8 years
male: 75.63 years
female: 80.08 years (2022 est.)
country comparison to the world: 83

Total fertility rate: 1.95 children born/woman (2022 est.)
country comparison to the world: 114

Drinking water source: *improved: total:* 96.7% of population
unimproved: total: 3.2% of population (2017 est.)

Current health expenditure: 4.4% of GDP (2019)

Physicians density: 2.76 physicians/1,000 population (2017)

Hospital bed density: 2.9 beds/1,000 population (2017)

Sanitation facility access: *improved: total:* 91.7% of population
unimproved: total: 8.1% of population (2017 est.)

HIV/AIDS - adult prevalence rate: 1.1% (2018 est.)
country comparison to the world: 37

Obesity - adult prevalence rate: 18.9% (2016)
country comparison to the world: 113

Alcohol consumption per capita: *total:* 11.88 liters of pure alcohol (2019 est.)
beer: 2.97 liters of pure alcohol (2019 est.)
wine: 3.95 liters of pure alcohol (2019 est.)
spirits: 4.55 liters of pure alcohol (2019 est.)
other alcohols: 0.41 liters of pure alcohol (2019 est.)
country comparison to the world: 6

Education expenditures: 3.3% of GDP (2020 est.)
country comparison to the world: 135

Literacy: *definition:* age 15 and over has completed five or more years of schooling
total population: 99%
male: 98.4%
female: 99.4% (2015)

School life expectancy (primary to tertiary education): *total:* 15 years
male: 14 years
female: 16 years (2012)

ENVIRONMENT

Environment - current issues: water management - a major concern because of limited natural freshwater resources - is further hampered by the clearing of trees to increase crop production, causing rainfall to run off quickly

Environment - international agreements: *party to:* Biodiversity, Climate Change, Climate Change-Kyoto Protocol, Climate Change-Paris Agreement, Comprehensive Nuclear Test Ban, Desertification, Endangered Species, Environmental Modification, Hazardous Wastes, Law of the Sea, Marine Dumping-London Convention, Marine Dumping-London Protocol, Nuclear Test Ban, Ozone Layer Protection, Ship Pollution, Wetlands, Whaling
signed, but not ratified: none of the selected agreements

Air pollutants: *particulate matter emissions:* 17.92 micrograms per cubic meter (2016 est.)
carbon dioxide emissions: 0.56 megatons (2016 est.)
methane emissions: 0.22 megatons (2020 est.)

Climate: tropical maritime; little seasonal temperature variation

Land use: *agricultural land:* 20.5% (2018 est.)
arable land: 9% (2018 est.)
permanent crops: 2.3% (2018 est.)
permanent pasture: 9% (2018 est.)
forest: 18.8% (2018 est.)
other: 60.8% (2018 est.)

Urbanization: *urban population:* 24.3% of total population (2022)
rate of urbanization: 0.87% annual rate of change (2020-25 est.)

Revenue from forest resources: *forest revenues:* 0% of GDP (2018 est.)
country comparison to the world: 161

Revenue from coal: *coal revenues:* 0% of GDP (2018 est.)
country comparison to the world: 56

Waste and recycling: *municipal solid waste generated annually:* 30,585 tons (2012 est.)

Total water withdrawal: *municipal:* 7.2 million cubic meters (2017 est.)
industrial: 2.5 million cubic meters (2017 est.)
agricultural: 1.8 million cubic meters (2017 est.)

Total renewable water resources: 52 million cubic meters (2017 est.)

GOVERNMENT

Country name: *conventional long form:* none
conventional short form: Antigua and Barbuda
etymology: "antiguo" is Spanish for "ancient" or "old"; the island was discovered by Christopher COLUMBUS in 1493 and, according to tradition, named by him after the church of Santa Maria la Antigua (Old Saint Mary's) in Seville; "barbuda" is Spanish for "bearded" and the adjective may refer to the alleged beards of the indigenous people or to the island's bearded fig trees

Government type: parliamentary democracy under a constitutional monarchy; a Commonwealth realm

Capital: *name:* Saint John's
geographic coordinates: 17 07 N, 61 51 W
time difference: UTC-4 (1 hour ahead of Washington, DC, during Standard Time)
etymology: named after Saint John the Apostle

Administrative divisions: 6 parishes and 2 dependencies*; Barbuda*, Redonda*, Saint George, Saint John, Saint Mary, Saint Paul, Saint Peter, Saint Philip

Independence: 1 November 1981 (from the UK)

National holiday: Independence Day, 1 November (1981)

Constitution: *history:* several previous; latest presented 31 July 1981, effective 31 October 1981 (The Antigua and Barbuda Constitution Order 1981)
amendments: proposed by either house of Parliament; passage of amendments to constitutional sections such as citizenship, fundamental rights and freedoms, the establishment, power, and authority of the executive and legislative branches, the Supreme Court Order, and the procedure for amending the constitution requires approval by at least two-thirds majority vote of the membership of both houses, approval by at least two-thirds majority in a referendum, and assent to by the governor general; passage of other amendments requires only two-thirds majority vote by both houses; amended 2009, 2011, 2018

Legal system: common law based on the English model

International law organization participation: has not submitted an ICJ jurisdiction declaration; accepts ICCt jurisdiction

Citizenship: *citizenship by birth:* yes
citizenship by descent only: yes
dual citizenship recognized: yes
residency requirement for naturalization: 7 years

Suffrage: 18 years of age; universal

Executive branch: *chief of state:* King CHARLES III (since 8 September 2022); represented by Governor General Rodney WILLIAMS (since 14 August 2014)
head of government: Prime Minister Gaston BROWNE (since 13 June 2014)
cabinet: Council of Ministers appointed by the governor general on the advice of the prime minister
elections/appointments: the monarchy is hereditary; governor general appointed by the monarch on the advice of the prime minister; following legislative elections, the leader of the majority party or majority coalition usually appointed prime minister by the governor general

Legislative branch: *description:* bicameral Parliament consists of:
Senate (17 seats; members appointed by the governor general)
House of Representatives (18 seats; members directly elected in single-seat constituencies by simple majority vote to serve 5-year terms)
elections:
Senate - last appointed on 26 March 2018 (next NA)
House of Representatives - last held on 21 March 2018 (next to be held in March 2023)
election results:

Senate - composition - men 8, women 9, percent of women 52.9%
House of Representatives - percent of vote by party - ABLP 59.4%, UPP 37.2%, BPM 1.4%, other 1.9% ; seats by party - ABLP 15, UPP 1, BPM 1; composition - men 16, women 2, percent of women 11.1%; note - total Parliament percent of women 31.4%

Judicial branch: *highest court(s):* the Eastern Caribbean Supreme Court (ECSC) is the superior court of the Organization of Eastern Caribbean States; the ECSC - headquartered on St. Lucia - consists of the Court of Appeal - headed by the chief justice and 4 judges - and the High Court with 18 judges; the Court of Appeal is itinerant, travelling to member states on a schedule to hear appeals from the High Court and subordinate courts; High Court judges reside in the member states, with 2 assigned to Antigua and Barbuda
judge selection and term of office: chief justice of Eastern Caribbean Supreme Court appointed by the Her Majesty, Queen ELIZABETH II; other justices and judges appointed by the Judicial and Legal Services Commission; Court of Appeal justices appointed for life with mandatory retirement at age 65; High Court judges appointed for life with mandatory retirement at age 62
subordinate courts: Industrial Court; Magistrates' Courts

Political parties and leaders: Antigua Labor Party or ABLP [Gaston BROWNE]
Barbuda People's Movement or BPM [Trevor WALKER]
Democratic National Alliance or DNA [Joanne MASSIAH]
Go Green for Life or GGL [Owen GEORGE]
United Progressive Party or UPP [Harold LOVELL]

International organization participation: ACP, AOSIS, C, Caricom, CDB, CELAC, FAO, G-77, IBRD, ICAO, ICC (NGOs), ICCt, ICRM, IDA, IFAD, IFC, IFRCS, ILO, IMF, IMO, IMSO, Interpol, IOC, IOM, ISO (subscriber), ITU, ITUC (NGOs), MIGA, NAM (observer), OAS, OECS, OPANAL, OPCW, Petrocaribe, UN, UNCTAD, UNESCO, UPU, WFTU (NGOs), WHO, WIPO, WMO, WTO

Diplomatic representation in the US: *chief of mission:* Ambassador Sir Ronald SANDERS (since 17 September 2015)
chancery: 3234 Prospect Street NW, Washington, DC 20007
telephone: [1] (202) 362-5122
FAX: [1] (202) 362-5225
email address and website:
embantbar@aol.com
consulate(s) general: Miami, New York

Diplomatic representation from the US: *embassy:* the US does not have an embassy in Antigua and Barbuda; the US Ambassador to Barbados is accredited to Antigua and Barbuda; [1] (246) 227-4000

Flag description: red, with an inverted isosceles triangle based on the top edge of the flag; the triangle contains three horizontal bands of black (top), light blue, and white, with a yellow rising sun in the black band; the sun symbolizes the dawn of a new era, black represents the African heritage of most of the population, blue is for hope, and red is for the dynamism of the people; the "V" stands for victory; the successive yellow, blue, and white coloring is also meant to evoke the country's tourist attractions of sun, sea, and sand

National symbol(s): fallow deer; national colors: red, white, blue, black, yellow

National anthem: *name:* Fair Antigua, We Salute Thee
lyrics/music: Novelle Hamilton RICHARDS/Walter Garnet Picart CHAMBERS
note: adopted 1967; as a Commonwealth country, in addition to the national anthem, "God Save the King" serves as the royal anthem (see United Kingdom)

National heritage: *total World Heritage Sites:* 1 (cultural)
selected World Heritage Site locales: Antigua Naval Dockyard

ECONOMY

Economic overview: Tourism continues to dominate Antigua and Barbuda's economy, accounting for nearly 60% of GDP and 40% of investment. The dual-island nation's agricultural production is focused on the domestic market and constrained by a limited water supply and a labor shortage stemming from the lure of higher wages in tourism and construction. Manufacturing comprises enclave-type assembly for export with major products being bedding, handicrafts, and electronic components.

Like other countries in the region, Antigua's economy was severely hit by effects of the global economic recession in 2009. The country suffered from the collapse of its largest private sector employer, a steep decline in tourism, a rise in debt, and a sharp economic contraction between 2009 and 2011. Antigua has not yet returned to its pre-crisis growth levels. Barbuda suffered significant damages after hurricanes Irma and Maria passed through the Caribbean in 2017.

Prospects for economic growth in the medium term will continue to depend on tourist arrivals from the US, Canada, and Europe and could be disrupted by potential damage from natural disasters. The new government, elected in 2014 and led by Prime Minister Gaston Browne, continues to face significant fiscal challenges. The government places some hope in a new Citizenship by Investment Program, to both reduce public debt levels and spur growth, and a resolution of a WTO dispute with the US.

Real GDP (purchasing power parity): $1.76 billion (2020 est.)
$2.09 billion (2019 est.)
$2.02 billion (2018 est.)
note: data are in 2017 dollars
country comparison to the world: 198

Real GDP growth rate: 2.8% (2017 est.)
5.3% (2016 est.)
4.1% (2015 est.)
country comparison to the world: 102

Real GDP per capita: $18,000 (2020 est.)
$21,500 (2019 est.)
$21,000 (2018 est.)
note: data are in 2017 dollars
country comparison to the world: 94

GDP (official exchange rate): $1.524 billion (2017 est.)

Inflation rate (consumer prices): 2.5% (2017 est.)
-0.5% (2016 est.)
country comparison to the world: 126

GDP - composition, by sector of origin: *agriculture:* 1.8% (2017 est.)
industry: 20.8% (2017 est.)
services: 77.3% (2017 est.)

GDP - composition, by end use: *household consumption:* 53.5% (2017 est.)
government consumption: 15.2% (2017 est.)
investment in fixed capital: 23.9% (2017 est.)
investment in inventories: 0.1% (2017 est.)
exports of goods and services: 73.9% (2017 est.)
imports of goods and services: -66.5% (2017 est.)

Agricultural products: tropical fruit, milk, mangoes/guavas, melons, tomatoes, pineapples, lemons, limes, eggplants, onions

Industries: tourism, construction, light manufacturing (clothing, alcohol, household appliances)

Industrial production growth rate: 6.8% (2017 est.)
country comparison to the world: 32

Labor force: 30,000 (1991)
country comparison to the world: 203

Labor force - by occupation: *agriculture:* 7%
industry: 11%
services: 82% (1983 est.)

Unemployment rate: 11% (2014 est.)
country comparison to the world: 155

Budget: *revenues:* 298.2 million (2017 est.)
expenditures: 334 million (2017 est.)

Budget surplus (+) or deficit (-): -2.4% (of GDP) (2017 est.)
country comparison to the world: 112

Public debt: 86.8% of GDP (2017 est.)
86.2% of GDP (2016 est.)
country comparison to the world: 30

Taxes and other revenues: 19.6% (of GDP) (2017 est.)
country comparison to the world: 154

Fiscal year: 1 April - 31 March

Current account balance: -$112 million (2017 est.)
$2 million (2016 est.)
country comparison to the world: 89

Exports: $1.15 billion (2018 est.)
$56.5 million (2016 est.)
note: Data are in current year dollars and do not include illicit exports or re-exports.
country comparison to the world: 174

Exports - partners: Poland 37%, Suriname 33%, United Arab Emirates 8% (2019)

Exports - commodities: ships, refined petroleum, precious/semi-precious metal scraps, rice, corn (2019)

Imports: $1.12 billion (2018 est.) note: data are in current year dollars
$503.4 million (2016 est.)
country comparison to the world: 187

Imports - partners: United States 39%, Poland 16%, China 7% (2019)

Imports - commodities: refined petroleum, ships, cars, precious/semi-precious metals, recreational boats (2019)

Debt - external: $441.2 million (31 December 2012)
$458 million (June 2010)
country comparison to the world: 180

Exchange rates: East Caribbean dollars (XCD) per US dollar -

2.7 (2017 est.)
2.7 (2013 est.)

ENERGY

Electricity access: *electrification - total population:* 100% (2020)

Electricity: *installed generating capacity:* 117,000 kW (2020 est.)
consumption: 278 million kWh (2019 est.)
exports: 0 kWh (2020 est.)
imports: 0 kWh (2020 est.)
transmission/distribution losses: 65 million kWh (2019 est.)

Electricity generation sources: *fossil fuels:* 95.4% of total installed capacity (2020 est.)
solar: 4.6% of total installed capacity (2020 est.)

Petroleum: *total petroleum production:* 0 bbl/day (2021 est.)
refined petroleum consumption: 5,000 bbl/day (2019 est.)

Refined petroleum products - exports: 91 bbl/day (2015 est.)
country comparison to the world: 119

Refined petroleum products - imports: 5,065 bbl/day (2015 est.)
country comparison to the world: 172

Carbon dioxide emissions: 729,000 metric tonnes of CO_2 (2019 est.)
from petroleum and other liquids: 729,000 metric tonnes of CO_2 (2019 est.)
country comparison to the world: 182

Energy consumption per capita: 107.154 million Btu/person (2019 est.)
country comparison to the world: 52

COMMUNICATIONS

Telephones - fixed lines: *total subscriptions:* 27,000 (2020 est.)
subscriptions per 100 inhabitants: 28 (2020 est.)
country comparison to the world: 170

Telephones - mobile cellular: *total subscriptions:* 184,000 (2020 est.)
subscriptions per 100 inhabitants: 188 (2020 est.)
country comparison to the world: 184

Telecommunication systems: *general assessment:* the telecom sector has seen a decline in subscriber numbers (particularly for prepaid mobile services the mainstay of short term visitors) and revenue; fixed and mobile broadband services are two areas that have benefited from the crisis as employees and students have resorted to working from home; one area of the telecom market that is not prepared for growth is 5G mobile; governments, regulators, and even the mobile network operators have shown that they have not been investing in 5G opportunities at the present time; network expansion and enhancements remain concentrated around improving LTE coverage (2021)
domestic: fixed-line teledensity roughly 28 per 100 persons; mobile-cellular teledensity is about 188 per 100 persons (2020)
international: country code - 1-268; landing points for the ECFS and Southern Caribbean Fiber submarine cable systems with links to other islands in the eastern Caribbean; satellite earth stations - 1 Intelsat (Atlantic Ocean) (2019)

Broadcast media: state-controlled Antigua and Barbuda Broadcasting Service (ABS) operates 1 TV station; multi-channel cable TV subscription services are available; ABS operates 1 radio station; roughly 15 radio stations, some broadcasting on multiple frequencies

Internet country code: .ag

Internet users: *total:* 73,807 (2019 est.)
percent of population: 76% (2019 est.)
country comparison to the world: 185

Broadband - fixed subscriptions: *total:* 8,000 (2020 est.)
subscriptions per 100 inhabitants: 8 (2020 est.)
country comparison to the world: 181

TRANSPORTATION

National air transport system: *number of registered air carriers:* 1 (2020)
inventory of registered aircraft operated by air carriers: 10
annual passenger traffic on registered air carriers: 580,174 (2018)
annual freight traffic on registered air carriers: 290,000 (2018) mt-km

Civil aircraft registration country code prefix: V2

Airports: *total:* 3 (2021)
country comparison to the world: 192

Airports - with paved runways: *total:* 2
2,438 to 3,047 m: 1
under 914 m: 1 (2021)

Airports - with unpaved runways: *total:* 1
under 914 m: 1 (2021)

Roadways: *total:* 1,170 km (2011)
paved: 386 km (2011)
unpaved: 784 km (2011)
country comparison to the world: 180

Merchant marine: *total:* 677
by type: bulk carrier 24, container ship 123, general cargo 473, oil tanker 2, other 55 (2021)
country comparison to the world: 35

Ports and terminals: *major seaport(s):* Saint John's

MILITARY AND SECURITY

Military and security forces: Antigua and Barbuda Defense Force (ABDF): Coast Guard and the Antigua and Barbuda Regiment (2022)

Military expenditures: not available

Military and security service personnel strengths: approximately 200 active military personnel (2022)

Military equipment inventories and acquisitions: the ABDF's equipment inventory is limited to small arms, light weapons, and soft-skin vehicles; the Coast Guard maintains ex-US patrol vessels and some smaller boats (2022)

Military service age and obligation: 18-23 years of age for voluntary military service for both men and women; no conscription (2022)

Military - note: has been a member of the Caribbean Regional Security System (RSS) since its creation in 1982; RSS signatories (Barbados, Dominica, Grenada, Saint Kitts, Saint Lucia, and Saint Vincent and the Grenadines) agreed to prepare contingency plans and assist one another, on request, in national emergencies, prevention of smuggling, search and rescue, immigration control, fishery protection, customs and excise control, maritime policing duties, protection of offshore installations, pollution control, national and other disasters, and threats to national security (2022)

TRANSNATIONAL ISSUES

Disputes - international: none identified

Illicit drugs: a transit point for cocaine and marijuana destined for North America, Europe, and elsewhere in the Caribbean

ARCTIC OCEAN

INTRODUCTION

Background: The Arctic Ocean is the smallest of the world's five oceans (after the Pacific Ocean, Atlantic Ocean, Indian Ocean, and the Southern Ocean). The Northwest Passage (US and Canada) and Northern Sea Route (Norway and Russia) are two important seasonal waterways. In recent years the polar ice pack has receded in the summer allowing for increased navigation and raising the possibility of future sovereignty and shipping disputes among the six countries bordering the Arctic Ocean (Canada, Denmark (Greenland), Iceland, Norway, Russia, US).

GEOGRAPHY

Location: body of water between Europe, Asia, and North America, mostly north of the Arctic Circle

Geographic coordinates: 90 00 N, 0 00 E

Map references: Arctic Region

Area: *total:* 15.558 million sq km
note: includes Barents Sea, Beaufort Sea, Chukchi Sea, East Siberian Sea, Greenland Sea, Kara Sea, Laptev Sea, Northwest Passage, Norwegian Sea, and other tributary water bodies

Area - comparative: slightly less than 1.5 times the size of the US

Coastline: 45,389 km

Climate: polar climate characterized by persistent cold and relatively narrow annual temperature range; winters characterized by continuous darkness, cold and stable weather conditions, and clear skies;

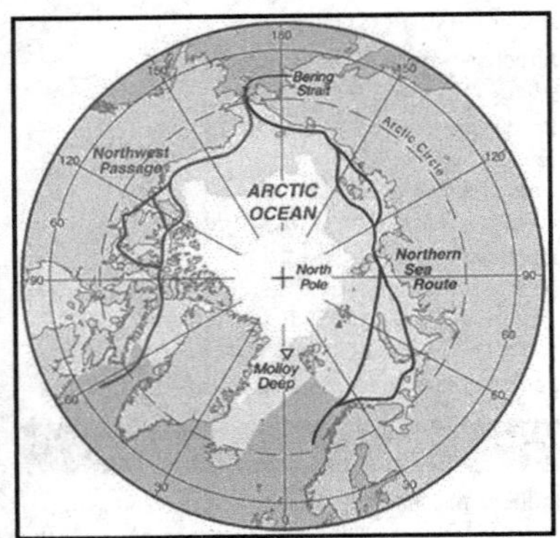

summers characterized by continuous daylight, damp and foggy weather, and weak cyclones with rain or snow

Ocean volume: *ocean volume:* 18.75 million cu km
percent of World Ocean total volume: 1.4%

Major ocean currents: two major, slow-moving, wind-driven currents (drift streams) dominate: a clockwise drift pattern in the Beaufort Gyre in the western part of the Arctic Ocean and a nearly straight line Transpolar Drift Stream that moves eastward across the ocean from the New Siberian Islands (Russia) to the Fram Strait (between Greenland and Svalbard); sea ice that lies close to the center of the gyre can complete a 360 degree circle in about 2 years, while ice on the gyre periphery will complete the same circle in about 7-8 years; sea ice in the Transpolar Drift crosses the ocean in about 3 years

Elevation: *highest point:* sea level
lowest point: Molloy Deep -5,577 m
mean depth: -1,205 m

Natural resources: sand and gravel aggregates, placer deposits, polymetallic nodules, oil and gas fields, fish, marine mammals (seals and whales)

Natural hazards: ice islands occasionally break away from northern Ellesmere Island; icebergs calved from glaciers in western Greenland and extreme northeastern Canada; permafrost in islands; virtually ice locked from October to June; ships subject to superstructure icing from October to May

Geography - note: major chokepoint is the southern Chukchi Sea (northern access to the Pacific Ocean via the Bering Strait); strategic location between North America and Russia; shortest marine link between the extremes of eastern and western Russia; floating research stations operated by the US and Russia; maximum snow cover in March or April about 20 to 50 centimeters over the frozen ocean; snow cover lasts about 10 months

ENVIRONMENT

Environment - current issues: climate change; changes in biodiversity; water pollution from use of toxic chemicals; endangered marine species include walruses and whales; fragile ecosystem slow to change and slow to recover from disruptions or damage; thinning polar icepack

Marine fisheries: the Arctic fishery region (Region 18) is the smallest in the world with a catch of only 515 mt in 2019, although the Food and Agriculture Organization assesses that some Arctic catches are reported in adjacent regions; Russia and Canada were historically the major producers; in 2017, Canada, Denmark (Greenland), Iceland, Norway, Russia, and the US, along with the People's Republic of China, the European Union, Japan, and the Republic of Korea, agreed to a 16 year ban on fishing in the Central Arctic Ocean to allow for time to study the ecological system of these waters

Regional fisheries bodies: International Council for the Exploration of the Seas

Climate: polar climate characterized by persistent cold and relatively narrow annual temperature range; winters characterized by continuous darkness, cold and stable weather conditions, and clear skies; summers characterized by continuous daylight, damp and foggy weather, and weak cyclones with rain or snow

GOVERNMENT

Country name: *etymology:* the name Arctic comes from the Greek word "arktikos" meaning "near the bear" or "northern," and that word derives from "arktos," meaning "bear"; the name refers either to the constellation Ursa Major, the "Great Bear," which is prominent in the northern celestial sphere, or to the constellation Ursa Minor, the "Little Bear," which contains Polaris, the North (Pole) Star

ECONOMY

Economic overview: Economic activity is limited to the exploitation of natural resources, including petroleum, natural gas, fish, and seals.

TRANSPORTATION

Ports and terminals: *major seaport(s):* Churchill (Canada), Murmansk (Russia), Prudhoe Bay (US)

Transportation - note: sparse network of air, ocean, river, and land routes; the Northwest Passage (North America) and Northern Sea Route (Eurasia) are important seasonal waterways

TRANSNATIONAL ISSUES

Disputes - international: record summer melting of sea ice in the Arctic has renewed interest in maritime shipping lanes and sea floor exploration
Canada-US: dispute how to divide the Beaufort Sea and the status of the Northwest Passage but continue to work cooperatively to survey the Arctic continental shelf
Canada-Denmark (Greenland)-Norway: have made submissions to the UN Commission on the Limits of the Continental shelf (CLCS)
Norway-Russia: signed a comprehensive maritime boundary agreement in 2010; Russia has augmented its 2001 CLCS submission:

ARGENTINA

INTRODUCTION

Background: In 1816, the United Provinces of the Rio Plata declared their independence from Spain. After Bolivia, Paraguay, and Uruguay went their separate ways, the area that remained became Argentina. The country's population and culture were heavily shaped by immigrants from throughout Europe, with Italy and Spain providing the largest percentage of newcomers from 1860 to 1930. Up until about the mid-20th century, much of Argentina's history was dominated by periods of internal political unrest and conflict between civilian and military factions.

After World War II, an era of populism under former President Juan Domingo PERON - the founder of the Peronist political movement and direct and indirect military interference in subsequent governments was followed by a military junta that took power in 1976. Democracy returned in 1983 after a failed bid to seize the Falkland Islands (Islas Malvinas) by force, and has persisted despite numerous challenges, the most formidable of which was a severe economic crisis in 2001-02 that led to violent public protests and the successive resignations of several presidents. The years 2003-15 saw Peronist rule by Nestor KIRCHNER (2003-07) and his spouse Cristina FERNANDEZ DE KIRCHNER (2007-15), who oversaw several years of strong economic growth (2003-11) followed by a gradual deterioration in the government's fiscal situation and eventual economic stagnation and isolation. Argentina underwent a brief period of economic reform and international reintegration under Mauricio MACRI (2015-19), but a recession in 2018-19 and frustration with MACRI's economic policies ushered in a new Peronist government in 2019 led by President Alberto FERNANDEZ and Vice President FERNANDEZ DE KIRCHNER. Presidential elections will take place next in 2023.

GEOGRAPHY

Location: Southern South America, bordering the South Atlantic Ocean, between Chile and Uruguay

Geographic coordinates: 34 00 S, 64 00 W

Map references: South America

Area: *total:* 2,780,400 sq km
land: 2,736,690 sq km
water: 43,710 sq km
country comparison to the world: 9

Area - comparative: slightly less than three-tenths the size of the US

Land boundaries: *total:* 11,968 km

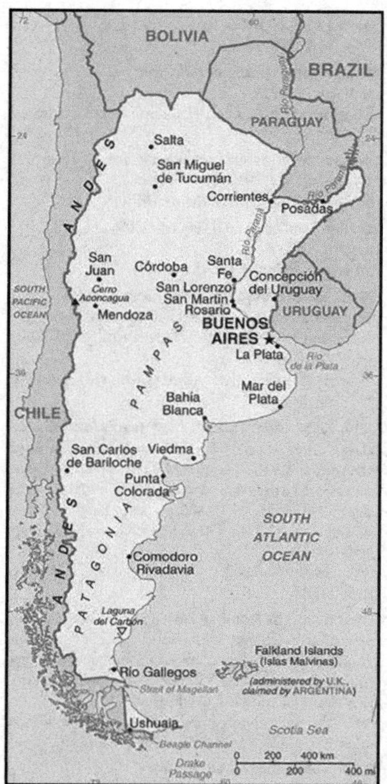

border countries (5): Bolivia 942 km; Brazil 1,263 km; Chile 6,691 km; Paraguay 2,531 km; Uruguay 541 km

Coastline: 4,989 km

Maritime claims: *territorial sea:* 12 nm
contiguous zone: 24 nm
exclusive economic zone: 200 nm
continental shelf: 200 nm or to the edge of the continental margin

Climate: mostly temperate; arid in southeast; subantarctic in southwest

Terrain: rich plains of the Pampas in northern half, flat to rolling plateau of Patagonia in south, rugged Andes along western border

Elevation: *highest point:* Cerro Aconcagua (located in the northwestern corner of the province of Mendoza; highest point in South America) 6,962 m
lowest point: Laguna del Carbon (located between Puerto San Julian and Comandante Luis Piedra Buena in the province of Santa Cruz) -105 m
mean elevation: 595 m

Natural resources: fertile plains of the pampas, lead, zinc, tin, copper, iron ore, manganese, petroleum, uranium, arable land

Land use: *agricultural land:* 53.9% (2018 est.)
arable land: 13.9% (2018 est.)
permanent crops: 0.4% (2018 est.)
permanent pasture: 39.6% (2018 est.)
forest: 10.7% (2018 est.)
other: 35.4% (2018 est.)

Irrigated land: 23,600 sq km (2012)

Major lakes (area sq km): *fresh water lake(s):* Lago Buenos Aires (shared with Chile) - 2,240 sq km; Lago Argentino - 1,410 sq km; Lago Viedma - 1,090 sq km; Lago San Martin (shared with Chile) - 1,010 sq km; Lago Colhue Huapi - 800 sq km; Lago Fagnano (shared with Chile) - 590 sq km; Lago Nahuel Huapi - 550 sq km
salt water lake(s): Laguna Mar Chiquita - 1,850 sq km;

Major rivers (by length in km): Rio de la Plata/Parana river mouth (shared with Brazil [s], Paraguay, and Uruguay) - 4,880 km; Paraguay (shared with Brazil [s], and Paraguay [m]) - 2,549 km; Uruguay (shared with Brazil [s] and Uruguay [m]) - 1,610 km
note – [s] after country name indicates river source; [m] after country name indicates river mouth

Major watersheds (area sq km):

Atlantic Ocean drainage: Paraná (2,582,704 sq km)

Major aquifers: Guarani Aquifer System

Population distribution: one-third of the population lives in Buenos Aires; pockets of agglomeration occur throughout the northern and central parts of the country; Patagonia to the south remains sparsely populated

Natural hazards: San Miguel de Tucuman and Mendoza areas in the Andes subject to earthquakes; pamperos are violent windstorms that can strike the pampas and northeast; heavy flooding in some areas
volcanism: volcanic activity in the Andes Mountains along the Chilean border; Copahue (2,997 m) last erupted in 2000; other historically active volcanoes include Llullaillaco, Maipo, Planchon-Peteroa, San Jose, Tromen, Tupungatito, and Viedma

Geography - note: *note 1:* second-largest country in South America (after Brazil); strategic location relative to sea lanes between the South Atlantic and the South Pacific Oceans (Strait of Magellan, Beagle Channel, Drake Passage); diverse geophysical landscapes range from tropical climates in the north to tundra in the far south; Cerro Aconcagua is the Western Hemisphere's tallest mountain, while Laguna del Carbon is the lowest point in the Western Hemisphere; shares Iguazu Falls, the world's largest waterfalls system, with Brazil
note 2: southeast Bolivia and northwest Argentina seem to be the original development site for peanuts

PEOPLE AND SOCIETY

Population: 46,245,668 (2022 est.)
country comparison to the world: 32

Nationality: *noun:* Argentine(s)
adjective: Argentine

Ethnic groups: European (mostly Spanish and Italian descent) and Mestizo (mixed European and Amerindian ancestry) 97.2%, Amerindian 2.4%, African descent 0.4% (2010 est.)

Languages: Spanish (official), Italian, English, German, French, indigenous (Mapudungun, Quechua)
major-language sample(s):
La Libreta Informativa del Mundo, la fuente indispensable de información básica. (Spanish)

Religions: Roman Catholic 62.9%, Evangelical 15.3% (Pentecostal 13%, other Evangelical 2.3%), Jehovah's Witness and Church of Jesus Christ 1.4%, other 1.2% (includes Muslim, Jewish), none 18.9% (includes agnostic and atheist), unspecified 0.3% (2019 est.)

Demographic profile: Argentina's population continues to grow but at a slower rate because of its steadily declining birth rate. Argentina's fertility decline began earlier than in the rest of Latin America, occurring most rapidly between the early 20th century and the 1950s, and then becoming more gradual. Life expectancy has been improving, most notably among the young and the poor. While the population under age 15 is shrinking, the youth cohort - ages 15-24 - is the largest in Argentina's history and will continue to bolster the working-age population. If this large working-age population is well-educated and gainfully employed, Argentina is likely to experience an economic boost and possibly higher per capita savings and investment. Although literacy and primary school enrollment are nearly universal, grade repetition is problematic and secondary school completion is low. Both of these issues vary widely by region and socioeconomic group.

Argentina has been primarily a country of immigration for most of its history, welcoming European immigrants (often providing needed low-skilled labor) after its independence in the 19th century and attracting especially large numbers from Spain and Italy. More than 7 million European immigrants are estimated to have arrived in Argentina between 1880 and 1930, when it adopted a more restrictive immigration policy. European immigration also began to wane in the 1930s because of the global depression. The inflow rebounded temporarily following WWII and resumed its decline in the 1950s when Argentina's military dictators tightened immigration rules and European economies rebounded. Regional migration increased, however, supplying low-skilled workers escaping economic and political instability in their home countries. As of 2015, immigrants made up almost 5% of Argentina's population, the largest share in South America. Migration from neighboring countries accounted for approximately 80% of Argentina's immigrant population in 2015.

The first waves of highly skilled Argentine emigrant workers headed mainly to the United States and Spain in the 1960s and 1970s, driven by economic decline and repressive military dictatorships. The 2008 European economic crisis drove the return migration of some Argentinean and other Latin American nationals, as well as the immigration of Europeans to South America, where Argentina was a key recipient. In 2015, Argentina received the highest number of legal migrants in Latin America and the Caribbean. The majority of its migrant inflow came from Paraguay and Bolivia.

Age structure: *0-14 years:* 24.02% (male 5,629,188/female 5,294,723)
15-24 years: 15.19% (male 3,539,021/female 3,367,321)
25-54 years: 39.6% (male 9,005,758/female 9,002,931)
55-64 years: 9.07% (male 2,000,536/female 2,122,699)
65 years and over: 12.13% (male 2,331,679/female 3,185,262) (2020 est.)

Dependency ratios: *total dependency ratio:* 56.5
youth dependency ratio: 38.1
elderly dependency ratio: 17.7
potential support ratio: 5.6 (2020 est.)

Median age: *total:* 32.4 years

male: 31.1 years
female: 33.6 years (2020 est.)
country comparison to the world: 110

Population growth rate: 0.82% (2022 est.)
country comparison to the world: 113

Birth rate: 15.58 births/1,000 population (2022 est.)
country comparison to the world: 106

Death rate: 7.32 deaths/1,000 population (2022 est.)
country comparison to the world: 110

Net migration rate: -0.08 migrant(s)/1,000 population (2022 est.)
country comparison to the world: 102

Population distribution: one-third of the population lives in Buenos Aires; pockets of agglomeration occur throughout the northern and central parts of the country; Patagonia to the south remains sparsely populated

Urbanization: *urban population:* 92.3% of total population (2022)
rate of urbanization: 0.97% annual rate of change (2020-25 est.)

Major urban areas - population: 15.370 million BUENOS AIRES (capital), 1.598 million Cordoba, 1.574 million Rosario, 1.209 million Mendoza, 1.014 million San Miguel de Tucuman, 904,000 La Plata (2022)

Sex ratio: *at birth:* 1.07 male(s)/female
0-14 years: 1.06 male(s)/female
15-24 years: 1.06 male(s)/female
25-54 years: 1 male(s)/female
55-64 years: 0.94 male(s)/female
65 years and over: 0.57 male(s)/female
total population: 0.98 male(s)/female (2022 est.)

Maternal mortality ratio: 39 deaths/100,000 live births (2017 est.)
country comparison to the world: 101

Infant mortality rate: *total:* 9.35 deaths/1,000 live births
male: 10.35 deaths/1,000 live births
female: 8.28 deaths/1,000 live births (2022 est.)
country comparison to the world: 141

Life expectancy at birth: *total population:* 78.31 years
male: 75.23 years
female: 81.59 years (2022 est.)
country comparison to the world: 74

Total fertility rate: 2.18 children born/woman (2022 est.)
country comparison to the world: 89

Contraceptive prevalence rate: 70.1% (2019/20)

Drinking water source: *improved: urban:* 99.8% of population
unimproved: urban: 0.2% of population

Current health expenditure: 9.5% of GDP (2019)

Physicians density: 4.06 physicians/1,000 population (2020)

Hospital bed density: 5 beds/1,000 population (2017)

Sanitation facility access: *improved: urban:* 100% of population

HIV/AIDS - adult prevalence rate: 0.4% (2020 est.)
country comparison to the world: 71

Major infectious diseases: *note:* widespread ongoing transmission of a respiratory illness caused by the novel coronavirus (COVID-19) is occurring throughout Argentina; as of 18 August 2022, Argentina has reported a total of 9,633,732 cases of COVID-19 or 21,315.55 cumulative cases of COVID-19 per 100,000 population with a total of 129,566 cumulative deaths or 286.67 cumulative deaths per 100,000 population; as of 17 August 2022, 91.07% of the population has received at least one dose of COVID-19 vaccine

Obesity - adult prevalence rate: 28.3% (2016)
country comparison to the world: 30

Alcohol consumption per capita: *total:* 7.95 liters of pure alcohol (2019 est.)
beer: 3.62 liters of pure alcohol (2019 est.)
wine: 2.88 liters of pure alcohol (2019 est.)
spirits: 0.72 liters of pure alcohol (2019 est.)
other alcohols: 0.72 liters of pure alcohol (2019 est.)
country comparison to the world: 45

Tobacco use: *total:* 24.5% (2020 est.)
male: 29.4% (2020 est.)
female: 19.6% (2020 est.)
country comparison to the world: 53

Children under the age of 5 years underweight: 1.7% (2018/19)
country comparison to the world: 115

Education expenditures: 4.8% of GDP (2019 est.)
country comparison to the world: 72

Literacy: *definition:* age 15 and over can read and write
total population: 99%
male: 98.9%
female: 99.1% (2018)

School life expectancy (primary to tertiary education): *total:* 18 years
male: 17 years
female: 19 years (2019)

Unemployment, youth ages 15-24: *total:* 30.2%
male: 26.8%
female: 35% (2020 est.)

ENVIRONMENT

Environment - current issues: environmental problems (urban and rural) typical of an industrializing economy such as deforestation, soil degradation (erosion, salinization), desertification, air pollution, and water pollution

Environment - international agreements: *party to:* Antarctic-Environmental Protection, Antarctic-Marine Living Resources, Antarctic Seals, Antarctic Treaty, Biodiversity, Climate Change, Climate Change-Kyoto Protocol, Climate Change-Paris Agreement, Comprehensive Nuclear Test Ban, Desertification, Endangered Species, Environmental Modification, Hazardous Wastes, Law of the Sea, Marine Dumping-London Convention, Nuclear Test Ban, Ozone Layer Protection, Ship Pollution, Wetlands, Whaling
signed, but not ratified: Marine Dumping-London Protocol, Marine Life Conservation

Air pollutants: *particulate matter emissions:* 11.83 micrograms per cubic meter (2016 est.)
carbon dioxide emissions: 201.35 megatons (2016 est.)
methane emissions: 120.66 megatons (2020 est.)

Climate: mostly temperate; arid in southeast; subantarctic in southwest

Land use: *agricultural land:* 53.9% (2018 est.)
arable land: 13.9% (2018 est.)
permanent crops: 0.4% (2018 est.)
permanent pasture: 39.6% (2018 est.)
forest: 10.7% (2018 est.)
other: 35.4% (2018 est.)

Urbanization: *urban population:* 92.3% of total population (2022)
rate of urbanization: 0.97% annual rate of change (2020-25 est.)

Revenue from forest resources: *forest revenues:* 0.09% of GDP (2018 est.)
country comparison to the world: 115

Revenue from coal: *coal revenues:* 0% of GDP (2018 est.)
country comparison to the world: 57

Waste and recycling: *municipal solid waste generated annually:* 17,910,550 tons (2014 est.)
municipal solid waste recycled annually: 1,074,633 tons (2010 est.)
percent of municipal solid waste recycled: 6% (2010 est.)

Major lakes (area sq km): *fresh water lake(s):* Lago Buenos Aires (shared with Chile) - 2,240 sq km; Lago Argentino - 1,410 sq km; Lago Viedma - 1,090 sq km; Lago San Martin (shared with Chile) - 1,010 sq km; Lago Colhue Huapi - 800 sq km; Lago Fagnano (shared with Chile) - 590 sq km; Lago Nahuel Huapi - 550 sq km
salt water lake(s): Laguna Mar Chiquita - 1,850 sq km;

Major rivers (by length in km): Rio de la Plata/Parana river mouth (shared with Brazil [s], Paraguay, and Uruguay) - 4,880 km; Paraguay (shared with Brazil [s], and Paraguay [m]) - 2,549 km; Uruguay (shared with Brazil [s] and Uruguay [m]) - 1,610 km
note – [s] after country name indicates river source; [m] after country name indicates river mouth

Major watersheds (area sq km):
Atlantic Ocean drainage: Paraná (2,582,704 sq km)

Major aquifers: Guarani Aquifer System

Total water withdrawal: *municipal:* 5.85 billion cubic meters (2017 est.)
industrial: 4 billion cubic meters (2017 est.)
agricultural: 27.93 billion cubic meters (2017 est.)

Total renewable water resources: 876.24 billion cubic meters (2017 est.)

GOVERNMENT

Country name: *conventional long form:* Argentine Republic
conventional short form: Argentina
local long form: Republica Argentina
local short form: Argentina
etymology: originally the area was referred to as Tierra Argentina, i.e., "Land beside the Silvery River" or "silvery land," which referred to the massive estuary in the east of the country, the Rio de la Plata (River of Silver); over time the name shortened to simply Argentina or "silvery"

Government type: presidential republic

Capital: *name:* Buenos Aires
geographic coordinates: 34 36 S, 58 22 W
time difference: UTC-3 (2 hours ahead of Washington, DC, during Standard Time)
etymology: the name translates as "fair winds" in Spanish and derives from the original designation of the settlement that would become the present-day city, "Santa Maria del Buen Aire" (Saint Mary of the Fair Winds)

Administrative divisions: 23 provinces (provincias, singular - provincia) and 1 autonomous city*; Buenos Aires, Catamarca, Chaco, Chubut, Ciudad Autonoma de Buenos Aires*, Cordoba, Corrientes, Entre Rios, Formosa, Jujuy, La Pampa, La Rioja, Mendoza, Misiones, Neuquen, Rio Negro, Salta, San Juan, San Luis, Santa Cruz, Santa Fe, Santiago del Estero, Tierra del Fuego - Antartida e Islas del Atlantico Sur (Tierra del Fuego - Antarctica and the South Atlantic Islands), Tucuman
note: the US does not recognize any claims to Antarctica

Independence: 9 July 1816 (from Spain)

National holiday: Revolution Day (May Revolution Day), 25 May (1810)

Constitution: *history:* several previous; latest effective 11 May 1853
amendments: a declaration of proposed amendments requires two-thirds majority vote by both houses of the National Congress followed by approval by an ad hoc, multi-member constitutional convention; amended several times, last significant amendment in 1994

Legal system: civil law system based on West European legal systems; note - in mid-2015, Argentina adopted a new civil code, replacing the old one in force since 1871

International law organization participation: has not submitted an ICJ jurisdiction declaration; accepts ICCt jurisdiction

Citizenship: *citizenship by birth:* yes
citizenship by descent only: yes
dual citizenship recognized: yes
residency requirement for naturalization: 2 years

Suffrage: 18-70 years of age; universal and compulsory; 16-17 years of age - optional for national elections

Executive branch: *chief of state:* President Alberto Angel FERNANDEZ (since 10 December 2019); Vice President Cristina FERNANDEZ DE KIRCHNER (since 10 December 2019); note - the president is both chief of state and head of government
head of government: President Alberto Angel FERNANDEZ (since 10 December 2019); Vice President Cristina FERNANDEZ DE KIRCHNER (since 10 December 2019)
cabinet: Cabinet appointed by the president
elections/appointments: president and vice president directly elected on the same ballot by qualified majority vote (to win, a candidate must receive at least 45% of votes or 40% of votes and a 10-point lead over the second place candidate; if neither occurs, a second round is held); the president serves a 4-year term (eligible for a second consecutive term); election last held on 27 October 2019 (next to be held in October 2023)
election results:
2019: Alberto Angel FERNANDEZ elected president; percent of vote - Alberto Angel FERNANDEZ (TODOS) 48.1%, Mauricio MACRI (PRO) 40.4%, Roberto LAVAGNA (independent) 6.2%, other 5.3%
2015: Mauricio MACRI elected president in second round; percent of vote in first round - Daniel SCIOLI (PJ) 37.1%, Mauricio MACRI (PRO) 34.2%, Sergio MASSA (FR/PJ) 21.4%, other 7.3%; percent of vote in second round - Mauricio MACRI (PRO) 51.4%, Daniel SCIOLI (PJ) 48.6%

Legislative branch: *description:* bicameral National Congress or Congreso Nacional consists of:
Senate or Senado (72 seats; members directly elected on a provincial basis with 2 seats awarded to the party with the most votes and 1 seat to the party with the second highest number of votes; members serve 6-year terms with one-third of the membership renewed every 2 years)
Chamber of Deputies or Cámara de Diputados (257 seats; members directly elected in multi-seat constituencies by party-list proportional representation vote using the D'Hondt method; members serve 4-year terms with one-half of the membership renewed every 2 years)
elections:
Senate - last held on 14 November 2021 (next to be held 29 October 2023)
Chamber of Deputies - last held on 14 November 2021 (next to be held 29 October 2023)
election results:
Senate - percent of vote by bloc or party - NA; seats by bloc or party - FdT 35, JxC 33, other 4; composition (as of February 2022) men 41, women 31, percent of women 43.1%
Chamber of Deputies - percent of vote by bloc or party - NA; seats by bloc or party - FdT 118, JxC 116, FIT-U 4, other: 19; composition (as of February 2022) - men 142, women 115, percent of women 44.7%; note - total National Congress percent of women 44.4%

Judicial branch: *highest court(s):* Supreme Court or Corte Suprema (consists of the court president, vice president, 2 judges, 1 vacancy)
judge selection and term of office: judges nominated by the president and approved by the Senate; ministers can serve until mandatory retirement at age 75; extensions beyond 75 require renomination by the president and approval by the Senate
subordinate courts: federal level appellate, district, and territorial courts; provincial level supreme, appellate, and first instance courts

Political parties and leaders: Avanza Libertad or AL [Jose Luis ESPERT]
Civic Coalition ARI or CC-ARI [Elisa CARRIO, Maximiliano FERRARO]
Federal Consensus or CF [Roberto LAVAGNA, Juan Manuel URTUBEY]
Frente Civico por Santiago (Civic Front for Santiago) [Gerardo ZAMORA]
Frente de Izquierda (Workers' Left Front) or FIT-U [Nicolas DEL CANO, Miriam BREGMAN] (coalition of leftist parties in lower house; includes PTS, PO, and MST)
Frente de la Concordia Misionero (Front for the Renewal of Social Concord) or FRCS [Carlos Eduardo ROVIRA]
Frente de Todos (Everyone's Front) or FdT [Alberto FERNANDEZ] (includes FR, La Campora, and PJ); note - ruling coalition since 2019; includes several national and provincial Peronist political parties:
Frente Renovador (Renewal Front) or FR [Sergio MASSA, Pablo MIROLO]
Generacion por un Encuentro Nacional (Generation for a National Encounter) or GEN [Margarita STOLBIZER]
Hacemos por Cordoba (We do for Cordoba) or HC [Juan SCHIARETTI]
Juntos por el Cambio (Together for Change) or JxC [Horacio Rodríguez LARRETA] (includes CC-ARI, PRO, and UCR); note - primary opposition coalition since 2019
Juntos Somos Rio Negro (Together We Are Rio Negro) or JSRN [Alberto WERETILNECK]
Justicialist Party or PJ [Alberto Angel FERNANDEZ]
La Campora [Maximo KIRCHNER]
La Libertad Avanza or LLA [Javier MILEI]
Movimiento Popular Neuquino (Neuquen People's Movement) or MPN [Omar GUTIERREZ]
Partido Socialista or PS [Monica Haydee FEIN]
Propuesta Republicana or PRO [Mauricio MACRI]
Radical Civic Union or UCR [Gerardo MORALES]
Socialist Workers' Party or PTS [Nicolas DEL CANO]
Unidad Federal (coalition of provencial parties in the lower house; includes FRCS and JSRN)
Workers' Party or PO [Gabriel SOLANO]
Workers' Socialist Movement or MST [Alejandro BODART]
Vamos con Vos (Let's Go with You) or VcV [Florencio RANDAZZO]

International organization participation: AfDB (nonregional member), Australia Group, BCIE, BIS, CAN (associate), CD, CELAC, FAO, FATF, G-15, G-20, G-24, G-77, IADB, IAEA, IBRD, ICAO, ICC (national committees), ICCt, ICRM, IDA, IFAD, IFC, IFRCS, IHO, ILO, IMF, IMO, IMSO, Interpol, IOC, IOM, IPU, ISO, ITSO, ITU, ITUC (NGOs), LAES, LAIA, Mercosur, MIGA, MINURSO, MINUSTAH, NAM (observer), NSG, OAS, OPANAL, OPCW, Paris Club (associate), PCA, PROSUR, SICA (observer), UN, UNASUR, UNCTAD, UNESCO, UNFICYP, UNHCR, UNHRC, UNIDO, Union Latina (observer), UNTSO, UNWTO, UPU, Wassenaar Arrangement, WCO, WFTU (NGOs), WHO, WIPO, WMO, WTO, ZC

Diplomatic representation in the US: *chief of mission:* Ambassador Jorge Martin Arturo ARGUELLO (since 6 February 2020)
chancery: 1600 New Hampshire Avenue NW, Washington, DC 20009
telephone: [1] (202) 238-6400
FAX: [1] (202) 332-3171
email address and website:
eeeuu@mrecic.gov.ar
https://eeeuu.cancilleria.gob.ar/en
consulate(s) general: Atlanta, Chicago, Houston, Los Angeles, Miami, New York, Washington, DC

Diplomatic representation from the US: *chief of mission:* Ambassador Marc Robert STANLEY (since 24 January 2022)
embassy: Avenida Colombia 4300, (C1425GMN) Buenos Aires
mailing address: 3130 Buenos Aires Place, Washington DC 20521-3130
telephone: [54] (11) 5777-4533
FAX: [54] (11) 5777-4240
email address and website:
buenosaires-acs@state.gov
https://ar.usembassy.gov/

Flag description: three equal horizontal bands of sky blue (top), white, and sky blue; centered in the white band is a radiant yellow sun with a human face (delineated in brown) known as the Sun of May; the colors represent the clear skies and snow of the Andes; the sun symbol commemorates the appearance of the sun through cloudy skies on 25 May 1810 during the first mass demonstration in favor of independence; the sun features are those of Inti, the Inca god of the sun

National symbol(s): Sun of May (a sun-with-face symbol); national colors: sky blue, white

National anthem: *name:* "Himno Nacional Argentino" (Argentine National Anthem)

lyrics/music: Vicente LOPEZ y PLANES/Jose Blas PARERA
note: adopted 1813; Vicente LOPEZ was inspired to write the anthem after watching a play about the 1810 May Revolution against Spain

National heritage: *total World Heritage Sites:* 11 (6 cultural, 5 natural)
selected World Heritage Site locales: Los Glaciares National Park (n); Jesuit Missions of the Guaranis (c); Iguazú National Park (n); Cueva de las Manos (c); Valdés Península (n); Ischigualasto/Talampaya National Parks (n); Jesuit Block and Estancias of Córdoba (c); Quebrada de Humahuaca (c); Qhapaq Ñan/Andean Road System (c)

ECONOMY

Economic overview: Argentina benefits from rich natural resources, a highly literate population, an export-oriented agricultural sector, and a diversified industrial base. Although one of the world's wealthiest countries 100 years ago, Argentina suffered during most of the 20th century from recurring economic crises, persistent fiscal and current account deficits, high inflation, mounting external debt, and capital flight.

Cristina FERNANDEZ DE KIRCHNER succeeded her husband as president in late 2007, and in 2008 the rapid economic growth of previous years slowed sharply as government policies held back exports and the world economy fell into recession. In 2010 the economy rebounded strongly, but slowed in late 2011 even as the government continued to rely on expansionary fiscal and monetary policies, which kept inflation in the double digits.

In order to deal with these problems, the government expanded state intervention in the economy: it nationalized the oil company YPF from Spain's Repsol, expanded measures to restrict imports, and further tightened currency controls in an effort to bolster foreign reserves and stem capital flight. Between 2011 and 2013, Central Bank foreign reserves dropped $21.3 billion from a high of $52.7 billion. In July 2014, Argentina and China agreed on an $11 billion currency swap; the Argentine Central Bank has received the equivalent of $3.2 billion in Chinese yuan, which it counts as international reserves.

With the election of President Mauricio MACRI in November 2015, Argentina began a historic political and economic transformation, as his administration took steps to liberalize the Argentine economy, lifting capital controls, floating the peso, removing export controls on some commodities, cutting some energy subsidies, and reforming the country's official statistics. Argentina negotiated debt payments with holdout bond creditors, continued working with the IMF to shore up its finances, and returned to international capital markets in April 2016.

In 2017, Argentina's economy emerged from recession with GDP growth of nearly 3.0%. The government passed important pension, tax, and fiscal reforms. And after years of international isolation, Argentina took on several international leadership roles, including hosting the World Economic Forum on Latin America and the World Trade Organization Ministerial Conference, and is set to assume the presidency of the G-20 in 2018.

Real GDP (purchasing power parity): $893.31 billion (2020 est.)
$991.52 billion (2019 est.)
$1,012,670,000,000 (2018 est.)
note: data are in 2017 dollars
country comparison to the world: 27

Real GDP growth rate: -2.03% (2019 est.)
-2.53% (2018 est.)
2.83% (2017 est.)
country comparison to the world: 204

Real GDP per capita: $19,700 (2020 est.)
$22,100 (2019 est.)
$22,800 (2018 est.)
note: data are in 2017 dollars
country comparison to the world: 86

GDP (official exchange rate): $447.467 billion (2019 est.)

Inflation rate (consumer prices): 25.7% (2017 est.)
26.5% (2016 est.)
note: data are derived from private estimates
country comparison to the world: 220

Credit ratings:

Fitch rating: CCC (2020)

Moody's rating: Ca (2020)

Standard & Poors rating: CCC+ (2020)
note: The year refers to the year in which the current credit rating was first obtained.

GDP - composition, by sector of origin: *agriculture:* 10.8% (2017 est.)
industry: 28.1% (2017 est.)
services: 61.1% (2017 est.)

GDP - composition, by end use: *household consumption:* 65.9% (2017 est.)
government consumption: 18.2% (2017 est.)
investment in fixed capital: 14.8% (2017 est.)
investment in inventories: 3.7% (2017 est.)
exports of goods and services: 11.2% (2017 est.)
imports of goods and services: -13.8% (2017 est.)

Agricultural products: maize, soybeans, wheat, sugar cane, milk, barley, sunflower seed, beef, grapes, potatoes

Industries: food processing, motor vehicles, consumer durables, textiles, chemicals and petrochemicals, printing, metallurgy, steel

Industrial production growth rate: 2.7% (2017 est.)
note: based on private sector estimates
country comparison to the world: 111

Labor force: 18 million (2017 est.)
note: urban areas only
country comparison to the world: 31

Labor force - by occupation: *agriculture:* 5.3%
industry: 28.6%
services: 66.1% (2017 est.)

Unemployment rate: 9.84% (2019 est.)
9.18% (2018 est.)
country comparison to the world: 145

Unemployment, youth ages 15-24: *total:* 30.2%
male: 26.8%
female: 35% (2020 est.)
country comparison to the world: 33

Population below poverty line: 35.5% (2019 est.)

Gini Index coefficient - distribution of family income: 41.4 (2018 est.)
45.8 (2009)
country comparison to the world: 51

Household income or consumption by percentage share: *lowest 10%:* 1.8%
highest 10%: 31% (2017 est.)

Budget: *revenues:* 120.6 billion (2017 est.)
expenditures: 158.6 billion (2017 est.)

Budget surplus (+) or deficit (-): -6% (of GDP) (2017 est.)
country comparison to the world: 182

Public debt: 57.6% of GDP (2017 est.)
55% of GDP (2016 est.)
country comparison to the world: 77

Taxes and other revenues: 18.9% (of GDP) (2017 est.)
country comparison to the world: 157

Fiscal year: calendar year

Current account balance: -$3.997 billion (2019 est.)
-$27.049 billion (2018 est.)
country comparison to the world: 178

Exports: $64.18 billion (2020 est.)
$79.29 billion (2019 est.)
$77.07 billion (2018 est.)
note: Data are in current year dollars and do not include illicit exports or re-exports.
country comparison to the world: 51

Exports - partners: Brazil 16%, China 11%, United States 7%, Chile 5% (2019)

Exports - commodities: soybean products, corn, delivery trucks, wheat, frozen meat, gold (2019)

Imports: $52.14 billion (2020 est.) note: data are in current year dollars
$66.28 billion (2019 est.) note: data are in current year dollars
$86.78 billion (2018 est.) note: data are in current year dollars
country comparison to the world: 57

Imports - partners: Brazil 21%, China 18%, US 14%, Germany 6% (2019)

Imports - commodities: cars, refined petroleum, vehicle parts, natural gas, soybeans (2019)

Reserves of foreign exchange and gold: $55.33 billion (31 December 2017 est.)
$38.43 billion (31 December 2016 est.)
country comparison to the world: 38

Debt - external: $278.524 billion (2019 est.)
$261.949 billion (2018 est.)
country comparison to the world: 33

Exchange rates: Argentine pesos (ARS) per US dollar -
82.034 (2020 est.)
59.96559 (2019 est.)
37.23499 (2018 est.)
9.23 (2014 est.)
8.08 (2013 est.)

ENERGY

Electricity access: *electrification - total population:* 99% (2020)
electrification - urban areas: 99% (2020)
electrification - rural areas: 85% (2020)

Electricity: *installed generating capacity:* 44.731 million kW (2020 est.)
consumption: 121,563,940,000 kWh (2020 est.)
exports: 261 million kWh (2020 est.)
imports: 7.802 billion kWh (2020 est.)
transmission/distribution losses: 20.74 billion kWh (2020 est.)

Electricity generation sources: *fossil fuels:* 65.8% of total installed capacity (2020 est.)
nuclear: 7.3% of total installed capacity (2020 est.)
solar: 1% of total installed capacity (2020 est.)
wind: 6.8% of total installed capacity (2020 est.)

hydroelectricity: 17.6% of total installed capacity (2020 est.)
biomass and waste: 1.5% of total installed capacity (2020 est.)

Coal: *production:* 829,000 metric tons (2020 est.)
consumption: 1.55 million metric tons (2020 est.)
exports: 4,000 metric tons (2020 est.)
imports: 990,000 metric tons (2020 est.)
proven reserves: 500 million metric tons (2019 est.)

Petroleum: *total petroleum production:* 690,200 bbl/day (2021 est.)
refined petroleum consumption: 680,000 bbl/day (2019 est.)
crude oil and lease condensate exports: 59,100 bbl/day (2018 est.)
crude oil and lease condensate imports: 11,400 bbl/day (2018 est.)
crude oil estimated reserves: 2,482,700,000 barrels (2021 est.)

Refined petroleum products - production: 669,800 bbl/day (2015 est.)
country comparison to the world: 26

Refined petroleum products - exports: 58,360 bbl/day (2015 est.)
country comparison to the world: 51

Refined petroleum products - imports: 121,400 bbl/day (2015 est.)
country comparison to the world: 49

Natural gas: *production:* 41,194,148,000 cubic meters (2020 est.)
consumption: 49,476,585,000 cubic meters (2019 est.)
exports: 691.241 million cubic meters (2019 est.)
imports: 6,865,323,000 cubic meters (2019 est.)
proven reserves: 396.464 billion cubic meters (2021 est.)

Carbon dioxide emissions: 193.205 million metric tonnes of CO_2 (2019 est.)
from coal and metallurgical coke: 2.122 million metric tonnes of CO_2 (2019 est.)
from petroleum and other liquids: 94.208 million metric tonnes of CO_2 (2019 est.)
from consumed natural gas: 96.875 million metric tonnes of CO_2 (2019 est.)
country comparison to the world: 32

Energy consumption per capita: 79.083 million Btu/person (2019 est.)
country comparison to the world: 77

COMMUNICATIONS

Telephones - fixed lines: *total subscriptions:* 7,356,165 (2020 est.)
subscriptions per 100 inhabitants: 16 (2020 est.)
country comparison to the world: 21

Telephones - mobile cellular: *total subscriptions:* 54,763,900 (2020 est.)
subscriptions per 100 inhabitants: 121 (2020 est.)
country comparison to the world: 29

Telecommunication systems: *general assessment:* Argentina's ongoing problem with hyperinflation continues to distort the telecom market's performance, which shows strong growth in revenue but only modest gains in subscriber numbers each year; the fixed broadband segment has penetration levels only slightly higher than the fixed-line teledensity; nearly a quarter of the country's broadband connections are via DSL, although fiber is starting claim an increasing share of that market as networks expand across most of the main cities; mobile broadband continues to be the preferred platform for internet access, supported by high mobile penetration levels and nationwide LTE coverage; the first 5G service was launched in February 2021 using refarmed LTE frequencies; the anticipated 5G spectrum auctions should drive even stronger uptake in mobile broadband services; while the various fixed, mobile, and cable operators push to expand and enhance their services, the government is also making an active contribution towards boosting broadband connectivity around the country; its national connectivity plan 'Plan Conectar', launched in September 2020, provides funding for a range of programs to increase coverage; in August 2021, the telecom regulator announced the release funding to help operators accelerate the rollout of their broadband infrastructure and services (2021)
domestic: roughly 16 per 100 fixed-line and 121 per 100 mobile-cellular; microwave radio relay, fiber-optic cable, and a domestic satellite system with 40 earth stations serve the trunk network (2020)
international: country code - 54; landing points for the UNISUR, Bicentenario, Atlantis-2, SAm-1, and SAC, Tannat, Malbec and ARBR submarine cable systems that provide links to Europe, Africa, South and Central America, and US; satellite earth stations - 112 (2019)

Broadcast media: government owns a TV station and radio network; more than two dozen TV stations and hundreds of privately owned radio stations; high rate of cable TV subscription usage (2022)

Internet country code: .ar

Internet users: *total:* 39,024,016 (2020 est.)
percent of population: 86% (2020 est.)
country comparison to the world: 26

Broadband - fixed subscriptions: *total:* 9,571,562 (2020 est.)
subscriptions per 100 inhabitants: 21 (2020 est.)
country comparison to the world: 20

TRANSPORTATION

National air transport system: *number of registered air carriers:* 6 (2020)
inventory of registered aircraft operated by air carriers: 107
annual passenger traffic on registered air carriers: 18,081,937 (2018)
annual freight traffic on registered air carriers: 311.57 million (2018) mt-km

Civil aircraft registration country code prefix: LV

Airports: *total:* 916 (2021)
country comparison to the world: 6

Airports - with paved runways: *total:* 161
over 3,047 m: 4
2,438 to 3,047 m: 29
1,524 to 2,437 m: 65
914 to 1,523 m: 53
under 914 m: 10 (2021)

Airports - with unpaved runways: *total:* 977
over 3,047 m: 1
2,438 to 3,047 m: 1
1,524 to 2,437 m: 43
914 to 1,523 m: 484
under 914 m: 448 (2021)

Heliports: 2 (2021)

Pipelines: 29,930 km gas, 41 km liquid petroleum gas, 6,248 km oil, 3,631 km refined products (2013)

Railways: *total:* 36,917.4 km (2014)
standard gauge: 2,745.1 km (2014) 1.435-m gauge (41.1 km electrified)
narrow gauge: 7,523.3 km (2014) 1.000-m gauge
broad gauge: 26,391 km (2014) 1.676-m gauge (149 km electrified)
258 km 0.750-mm gauge
country comparison to the world: 6

Roadways: *total:* 281,290 km (2017)
paved: 117,616 km (2017)
unpaved: 163,674 km (2017)
country comparison to the world: 21

Waterways: 11,000 km (2012)
country comparison to the world: 13

Merchant marine: *total:* 202
by type: container ship 1,bulk carrier 1 general cargo 8, oil tanker 33, other 159 (2021)
country comparison to the world: 66

Ports and terminals: *major seaport(s):* Bahia Blanca, Buenos Aires, La Plata, Punta Colorada, Ushuaia
container port(s) (TEUs): Buenos Aires (1,485,328) (2019)
LNG terminal(s) (import): Bahia Blanca
river port(s): Arroyo Seco, Rosario, San Lorenzo-San Martin (Parana)

MILITARY AND SECURITY

Military and security forces: Armed Forces of the Argentine Republic (Fuerzas Armadas de la República Argentina): Argentine Army (Ejercito Argentino, EA), Navy of the Argentine Republic (Armada Republica, ARA; includes naval aviation and naval infantry), Argentine Air Force (Fuerza Aerea Argentina, FAA); Ministry of Security: Gendarmería Nacional Argentina (National Gendarmerie), Coast Guard (Prefectura Naval) (2022)

Military expenditures: 0.8% of GDP (2021 est.)
0.8% of GDP (2020)
0.7% of GDP (2019) (approximately $5 billion)
0.8% of GDP (2018) (approximately $5.3 billion)
0.9% of GDP (2017) (approximately $5.95 billion)
country comparison to the world: 139

Military and security service personnel strengths: approximately 82,000 active duty personnel (50,000 Army; 18,000 Navy, including about 3,500 marines); 14,000 Air Force); estimated 20,000 Gendarmerie (2022)

Military equipment inventories and acquisitions: the inventory of Argentina's armed forces is a mix of domestically-produced and mostly older imported weapons, largely from Europe and the US; since 2010, France and the US are the leading suppliers of equipment; Argentina has an indigenous defense industry that produces air, land, and sea systems (2022)

Military service age and obligation: 18-24 years of age for voluntary military service for men and women; conscription suspended in 1995; citizens can still be drafted in times of crisis, national emergency, or war, or if the Defense Ministry is unable to fill all vacancies to keep the military functional (2022)
note – as of 2021, women comprised over 21% of the active duty military

Military deployments: 250 Cyprus (UNFICYP) (May 2022)

Military - note: the Army and Navy were both created in 1810 during the Argentine War of

Independence, while the Air Force was established in 1945; the military coups d'état in 1930, 1943, 1955, 1962, 1966, and 1976; the 1976 coup, aka the "National Reorganization Process," marked the beginning of the so-called "Dirty War," a period of state-sponsored terrorism that saw the deaths or disappearances of thousands of Argentinians; the defeat in the 1983 Falklands War led to the downfall of the military junta
Argentina has Major Non-NATO Ally (MNNA) status with the US; MNNA is a designation under US law that provides foreign partners with certain benefits in the areas of defense trade and security cooperation; while MNNA status provides military and economic privileges, it does not entail any security commitments (2022)

TERRORISM

Terrorist group(s): Hizballah

TRANSNATIONAL ISSUES

Disputes - international: *Argentina-Bolivia:* Contraband smuggling, human trafficking, and illegal narcotic trafficking are problems in the porous areas of the border with Bolivia
Argentina-Brazil: Uncontested dispute between Brazil and Uruguay over Braziliera/Brasiliera Island in the Quarai/Cuareim River leaves the tripoint with Argentina in question.
Argentina-Chile: The joint boundary commission, established by Chile and Argentina in 2001 has yet to map and demarcate the delimited boundary in the inhospitable Andean Southern Ice Field (Campo de Hielo Sur).
Argentina-Paraguay: None identified
Argentina-Uruguay: In 2010, the ICJ ruled in favor of Uruguay's operation of two paper mills on the Uruguay River, which forms the border with Argentina; the two countries formed a joint pollution monitoring regime. Isla de Martín Garcia situated in the Rio de la Plata estuary is wholly within Uruguayan territorial waters but up to its low tide mark, the island is Argentinian territory. The island is accorded unrestricted access rights.
Argentina-United Kingdom: Argentina continues to assert its claims to the UK-administered Falkland Islands (Islas Malvinas), South Georgia, and the South Sandwich Islands in its constitution, forcibly occupying the Falklands in 1982, but in 1995 agreed to no longer seek settlement by force; UK continues to reject Argentine requests for sovereignty talks.

Refugees and internally displaced persons: *refugees (country of origin):* 170,517 (Venezuela) (economic and political crisis; includes Venezuelans who have claimed asylum, are recognized as refugees, or have received alternative legal stay) (2021)

Illicit drugs: counterfeiting, drug trafficking, and other smuggling offenses along the northern border; some money laundering organizations in the Tri-Border Area may have links to the terrorist organization Hizballah; a large producer of chemical precursors

ARMENIA

INTRODUCTION

Background: Armenia prides itself on being the first nation to formally adopt Christianity (early 4th century). Despite periods of autonomy, over the centuries Armenia came under the sway of various empires including the Roman, Byzantine, Arab, Persian, and Ottoman. During World War I in the western portion of Armenia, the Ottoman Empire instituted a policy of forced resettlement coupled with other harsh practices that resulted in at least 1 million Armenian deaths - actions widely recognized as constituting genocide. The eastern area of Armenia was ceded by the Ottomans to Russia in 1828; this portion declared its independence in 1918, but was conquered by the Soviet Red Army in 1920.

Armenia remains involved in the protracted struggle with Azerbaijan over control of Nagorno-Karabakh, a primarily ethnic Armenian region that Moscow recognized in 1923 as an autonomous oblast within Soviet Azerbaijan. In the late Soviet period, a separatist movement developed that sought to end Azerbaijani control over the region. Fighting over Nagorno-Karabakh began in 1988 and escalated after Armenia and Azerbaijan attained independence from the Soviet Union in 1991. By the time a cease-fire took effect in May 1994, separatists, with Armenian support, controlled Nagorno-Karabakh and seven surrounding Azerbaijani territories. Following the Second Nagorno-Karabakh War in September-November 2020, Armenia lost control over much of the territory it had captured a quarter century earlier. Under the terms of a cease-fire agreement signed in November 2020, Armenia returned to Azerbaijan the remaining territories it occupied and some parts of the Nagorno-Karabakh region, including the key city that Armenians call Shushi and Azerbaijanis call Shusha.

Turkey closed the common border with Armenia in 1993 in support of Azerbaijan in its conflict with Armenia over control of Nagorno- Karabakh and surrounding areas, further hampering Armenian economic growth. In 2009, Armenia and Turkey signed Protocols normalizing relations between the two countries, but neither country ratified the Protocols, and Armenia officially withdrew from the Protocols in March 2018. In 2015, Armenia joined the Eurasian Economic Union alongside Russia, Belarus, Kazakhstan, and Kyrgyzstan. In November 2017, Armenia signed a Comprehensive and Enhanced Partnership Agreement (CEPA) with the EU.

In spring 2018, former President of Armenia (2008-18) Serzh SARGSIAN of the Republican Party of Armenia (RPA) tried to extend his time in power by becoming prime minister, prompting popular protests that became known as the "Velvet Revolution" after SARGSIAN was forced to resign. The leader of the protests, Civil Contract party chief Nikol PASHINYAN, was elected by the National Assembly as the new prime minister on 8 May 2018. PASHINYAN's party prevailed in an early legislative election in December 2018, and he was reelected as prime minister.

GEOGRAPHY

Location: Southwestern Asia, between Turkey (to the west) and Azerbaijan; note - Armenia views itself as part of Europe; geopolitically, it can be classified as falling within Europe, the Middle East, or both

Geographic coordinates: 40 00 N, 45 00 E

Map references: Asia

Area: *total:* 29,743 sq km
land: 28,203 sq km
water: 1,540 sq km
country comparison to the world: 142

Area - comparative: slightly smaller than Maryland

Land boundaries: *total:* 1,570 km
border countries (4): Azerbaijan 996 km; Georgia 219 km; Iran 44 km; Turkey 311 km

Coastline: 0 km (landlocked)

Maritime claims: none (landlocked)

Climate: highland continental, hot summers, cold winters

Terrain: Armenian Highland with mountains; little forest land; fast flowing rivers; good soil in Aras River valley

Elevation: *highest point:* Aragats Lerrnagagat' 4,090 m
lowest point: Debed River 400 m
mean elevation: 1,792 m

Natural resources: small deposits of gold, copper, molybdenum, zinc, bauxite

Land use: *agricultural land:* 59.7% (2018 est.)
arable land: 15.8% (2018 est.)
permanent crops: 1.9% (2018 est.)
permanent pasture: 42% (2018 est.)
forest: 9.1% (2018 est.)
other: 31.2% (2018 est.)

Irrigated land: 2,740 sq km (2012)

Major lakes (area sq km): *fresh water lake(s):* Lake Sevan - 1,360 sq km

Population distribution: most of the population is located in the northern half of the country; the capital of Yerevan is home to more than five times as many people as Gyumri, the second largest city in the country

Natural hazards: occasionally severe earthquakes; droughts

Geography - note: landlocked in the Lesser Caucasus Mountains; Sevana Lich (Lake Sevan) is the largest lake in this mountain range

PEOPLE AND SOCIETY

Population: 3,000,756 (2022 est.)
country comparison to the world: 138

Nationality: *noun:* Armenian(s)
adjective: Armenian

Ethnic groups: Armenian 98.1%, Yezidi (Kurd) 1.2%, other 0.7% (2011 est.)

Languages: Armenian (official) 97.9%, Kurdish (spoken by Yezidi minority) 1%, other 1%; note - Russian is widely spoken (2011 est.)
major-language sample(s):
Աշխարհի Փաստագիրք, Անփոխարինելի Աղբյուր Հիմնական Տեղեկատվության. (Armenian)

Religions: Armenian Apostolic 92.6%, Evangelical 1%, other 2.4%, none 1.1%, unspecified 2.9% (2011 est.)

Demographic profile: Armenia's population peaked at nearly 3.7 million in the late 1980s but has declined sharply since independence in 1991, to just over 3 million in 2021, largely as a result of its decreasing fertility rate, increasing death rate, and negative net emigration rate. The total fertility rate (the average number of children born per woman) first fell below the 2.1 replacement level in the late 1990s and has hovered around 1.6-1.65 for over 15 years. In an effort to increase the country's birth rate, the government has expanded its child benefits, including a substantial increase in the lump sum payment for having a first and second child and a boost in the monthly payment to mothers of children under two. Reversing net negative migration, however, remains the biggest obstacle to stabilizing or increasing population growth. Emigration causes Armenia not only lose individuals but also the children they might have.

The emigration of a significant number of working-age people combined with decreased fertility and increased life expectancy is causing the elderly share of Armenia's population to grow. The growing elderly population will put increasing pressure on the government's ability to fund the pension system, health care, and other services for seniors. Improving education, creating more jobs (particularly in the formal sector), promoting labor market participation, and increasing productivity would mitigate the financial impact of supporting a growing elderly population.

Armenia has a long history of migration, some forced and some voluntary. Its large diaspora is diverse and dispersed around the world. Widely varying estimates suggest the Armenian diaspora may number anywhere from 5-9 million, easily outnumbering the number of Armenians living in Armenia. Armenians forged communities abroad from ancient Egypt, Greece and Rome to Russia and to the Americas, where they excelled as craftsmen, merchants, and in other occupations.

Several waves of Armenian migration occurred in the 20th century. In the aftermath of the 1915 Armenian genocide, hundreds of thousands of survivors fled to communities in the Caucasus (including present day Armenia), Lebanon, Syria, Iran, Europe, and Russia and established new communities in Africa and the Americas. In the 1930s, the Soviets deported thousands of Armenians to Siberia and Central Asia. After World War II, the Soviets encouraged the Armenian diaspora in France, the Middle East, and Iran to return the Armenian homeland in order to encourage population growth after significant losses in the male workforce during the war.

Following Armenian independence in 1991, the economic downturn and high unemployment prompted hundreds of thousands of Armenians to seek better economic opportunities primarily in Russia but also in the US, former Soviet states, and Europe. In the early 1990s, hundreds of thousands of Armenians fled from Azerbaijan to Armenia because of the ongoing Nagorno-Karabakh conflict, but many of them then emigrated again, mainly to Russia and the US. When the economy became more stable in the late 1990s, permanent emigration slowed, but Armenians continued to seek temporary seasonal work in Russia. The remittances families receive from relatives working abroad is vital to Armenian households and the country's economy.

Age structure: *0-14 years:* 18.64% (male 297,320/female 265,969)
15-24 years: 11.63% (male 184,258/female 167,197)
25-54 years: 43.04% (male 639,101/female 661,421)
55-64 years: 14.08% (male 195,754/female 229,580)
65 years and over: 12.6% (male 154,117/female 226,607) (2020 est.)

Dependency ratios: *total dependency ratio:* 48.4
youth dependency ratio: 30.9
elderly dependency ratio: 17.5
potential support ratio: 5.7 (2020 est.)

Median age: *total:* 36.6 years
male: 35.1 years
female: 38.3 years (2020 est.)
country comparison to the world: 78

Population growth rate: -0.38% (2022 est.)
country comparison to the world: 220

Birth rate: 11.1 births/1,000 population (2022 est.)
country comparison to the world: 166

Death rate: 9.51 deaths/1,000 population (2022 est.)
country comparison to the world: 47

Net migration rate: -5.36 migrant(s)/1,000 population (2022 est.)
country comparison to the world: 206

Population distribution: most of the population is located in the northern half of the country; the capital of Yerevan is home to more than five times as many people as Gyumri, the second largest city in the country

Urbanization: *urban population:* 63.6% of total population (2022)
rate of urbanization: 0.23% annual rate of change (2020-25 est.)

Major urban areas - population: 1.092 million YEREVAN (capital) (2022)

Sex ratio: *at birth:* 1.08 male(s)/female
0-14 years: 1.11 male(s)/female
15-24 years: 1.11 male(s)/female
25-54 years: 0.99 male(s)/female
55-64 years: 0.85 male(s)/female
65 years and over: 0.65 male(s)/female
total population: 0.95 male(s)/female (2022 est.)

Mother's mean age at first birth: 25.2 years (2019 est.)

Maternal mortality ratio: 26 deaths/100,000 live births (2017 est.)
country comparison to the world: 119

Infant mortality rate: *total:* 12.18 deaths/1,000 live births
male: 13.72 deaths/1,000 live births
female: 10.51 deaths/1,000 live births (2022 est.)
country comparison to the world: 115

Life expectancy at birth: *total population:* 76.13 years
male: 72.86 years
female: 79.68 years (2022 est.)
country comparison to the world: 106

Total fertility rate: 1.65 children born/woman (2022 est.)
country comparison to the world: 175

Contraceptive prevalence rate: 57.1% (2015/16)

Drinking water source: *improved: urban:* 100% of population
rural: 100% of population
total: 100% of population

Current health expenditure: 11.3% of GDP (2019)

Physicians density: 4.4 physicians/1,000 population (2017)

Hospital bed density: 4.2 beds/1,000 population (2014)

Sanitation facility access: *improved: urban:* 100% of population
rural: 84.6% of population
total: 94.4% of population
unimproved: urban: 0% of population
rural: 15.4% of population
total: 5.6% of population (2020 est.)

HIV/AIDS - adult prevalence rate: 0.2% (2020 est.)
country comparison to the world: 94

Obesity - adult prevalence rate: 20.2% (2016)
country comparison to the world: 101

Alcohol consumption per capita: *total:* 3.77 liters of pure alcohol (2019 est.)
beer: 0.52 liters of pure alcohol (2019 est.)
wine: 0.46 liters of pure alcohol (2019 est.)
spirits: 2.78 liters of pure alcohol (2019 est.)
other alcohols: 0.01 liters of pure alcohol (2019 est.)
country comparison to the world: 99

Tobacco use: *total:* 25.5% (2020 est.)
male: 49.4% (2020 est.)
female: 1.5% (2020 est.)
country comparison to the world: 45

Children under the age of 5 years underweight: 2.6% (2015/16)
country comparison to the world: 101

Child marriage: *women married by age 15:* 0%
women married by age 18: 5.3%
men married by age 18: 0.4% (2016 est.)

Education expenditures: 2.7% of GDP (2020 est.)
country comparison to the world: 162

Literacy: *definition:* age 15 and over can read and write
total population: 99.8%
male: 99.8%
female: 99.7% (2020)

School life expectancy (primary to tertiary education): *total:* 13 years
male: 13 years
female: 14 years (2020)

Unemployment, youth ages 15-24: *total:* 32.6%
male: 31.2%
female: 34.4% (2019 est.)

ENVIRONMENT

Environment - current issues: soil pollution from toxic chemicals such as DDT; deforestation; pollution of Hrazdan and Aras Rivers; the draining of Sevana Lich (Lake Sevan), a result of its use as a source for hydropower, threatens drinking water supplies; restart of Metsamor nuclear power plant in spite of its location in a seismically active zone

Environment - international agreements: *party to:* Air Pollution, Biodiversity, Climate Change, Climate Change-Kyoto Protocol, Climate Change-Paris Agreement, Comprehensive Nuclear Test Ban, Desertification, Endangered Species, Environmental Modification, Hazardous Wastes, Law of the Sea, Nuclear Test Ban, Ozone Layer Protection, Wetlands: signed, but not ratified: Air Pollution-Heavy Metals, Air Pollution-Multi-effect Protocol, Air Pollution-Persistent Organic Pollutants

Air pollutants: *particulate matter emissions:* 30.48 micrograms per cubic meter (2016 est.)
carbon dioxide emissions: 5.16 megatons (2016 est.)
methane emissions: 2.91 megatons (2020 est.)

Climate: highland continental, hot summers, cold winters

Land use: *agricultural land:* 59.7% (2018 est.)
arable land: 15.8% (2018 est.)
permanent crops: 1.9% (2018 est.)
permanent pasture: 42% (2018 est.)
forest: 9.1% (2018 est.)
other: 31.2% (2018 est.)

Urbanization: *urban population:* 63.6% of total population (2022)
rate of urbanization: 0.23% annual rate of change (2020-25 est.)

Revenue from forest resources: *forest revenues:* 0.28% of GDP (2018 est.)
country comparison to the world: 82

Revenue from coal: *coal revenues:* 0% of GDP (2018 est.)
country comparison to the world: 58

Waste and recycling: *municipal solid waste generated annually:* 492,800 tons (2014 est.)

Major lakes (area sq km): *fresh water lake(s):* Lake Sevan - 1,360 sq km

Total water withdrawal: *municipal:* 616.4 million cubic meters (2017 est.)
industrial: 122.4 million cubic meters (2017 est.)
agricultural: 2.127 billion cubic meters (2017 est.)

Total renewable water resources: 7.77 billion cubic meters (2017 est.)

GOVERNMENT

Country name: *conventional long form:* Republic of Armenia
conventional short form: Armenia
local long form: Hayastani Hanrapetut'yun
local short form: Hayastan
former: Armenian Soviet Socialist Republic, Armenian Republic
etymology: the etymology of the country's name remains obscure; according to tradition, the country is named after Hayk, the legendary patriarch of the Armenians and the great-great-grandson of Noah; Hayk's descendant, Aram, purportedly is the source of the name Armenia

Government type: parliamentary democracy; note - constitutional changes adopted in December 2015 transformed the government to a parliamentary system

Capital: *name:* Yerevan
geographic coordinates: 40 10 N, 44 30 E
time difference: UTC+4 (9 hours ahead of Washington, DC, during Standard Time)
etymology: name likely derives from the ancient Urartian fortress of Erebuni established on the current site of Yerevan in 782 B.C. and whose impressive ruins still survive

Administrative divisions: 11 provinces (marzer, singular - marz); Aragatsotn, Ararat, Armavir, Geghark'unik', Kotayk', Lorri, Shirak, Syunik', Tavush, Vayots' Dzor, Yerevan

Independence: 21 September 1991 (from the Soviet Union); notable earlier dates: 321 B.C. (Kingdom of Armenia established under the Orontid Dynasty), A.D. 884 (Armenian Kingdom reestablished under the Bagratid Dynasty); 1198 (Cilician Kingdom established); 28 May 1918 (Democratic Republic of Armenia declared)

National holiday: Independence Day, 21 September (1991)

Constitution: *history:* previous 1915, 1978; latest adopted 5 July 1995
amendments: proposed by the president of the republic or by the National Assembly; passage requires approval by the president, by the National Assembly, and by a referendum with at least 25% registered voter participation and more than 50% of votes; constitutional articles on the form of government and democratic procedures are not amendable; amended 2005, 2015, last in 2020; note - a constitutional referendum originally scheduled for 4 May 2020 was indefinitely postponed due to the COVID-19 pandemic that began in early 2020, the Nagorno-Karabakh war in the fall of 2020, and the postwar political crisis of early 2021

Legal system: civil law system

International law organization participation: has not submitted an ICJ jurisdiction declaration; non-party state to the ICCt

Citizenship: *citizenship by birth:* no
citizenship by descent only: at least one parent must be a citizen of Armenia
dual citizenship recognized: yes
residency requirement for naturalization: 3 years

Suffrage: 18 years of age; universal

Executive branch: *chief of state:* President Vahagn KHACHATURYAN (since 13 March 2022)
head of government: Prime Minister Nikol PASHINYAN (since 10 September 2021); Deputy Prime Ministers Mher GRIGORYAN (since 3 August 2021) and Hambardzum MATEVOSYAN (since 25 November 2021); note - Prime Minister Nikol PASHINYAN resigned on 25 April 2021; he was reappointed by the president on 2 August 2021 and sworn in on 10 September 2021
cabinet: Council of Ministers appointed by the prime minister
elections/appointments: president indirectly elected by the National Assembly in 3 rounds if needed for a single 7-year term; election last held on 2-3 March 2022; prime minister elected by majority vote in 2 rounds if needed by the National Assembly; election last held 2 August 2021; the next parliamentary elections are expected to be held in Armenia by 2026
election results:
2022: Vahagn KHACHATURYAN elected president in second round; note - Vahagn KHACHATURYAN ran unopposed and won the Assembly vote 71-0
2018: Armen SARKISSIAN elected president in first round; note - Armen SARKISSIAN ran unopposed and won the Assembly vote 90-10
note: Nikol PASHINYAN was first elected prime minister on 8 May 2018 and reelected on January 2019; in response to a political crisis that followed Armenia's defeat in the Second Nagorno-Karabakh War in late 2020, PASHINYAN called an early legislative election for June 2021; his party won the election and PASHINYAN was elected to the prime ministership for a third time; his election was confirmed by the president on 2 August 2021, and he was sworn in on 10 September 2021

Legislative branch: *description:* unicameral National Assembly (Parliament) or Azgayin Zhoghov (minimum 101 seats, with additional seats allocated as necessary and generally changing with each parliamentary convocation; current - 107; members directly elected in single-seat constituencies by closed party-list proportional representation vote; members serve 5-year terms; four mandates are reserved for national minorities; no more than 70% of the top membership of a party list can belong to the same sex; political parties must meet a 5% threshold and alliances a 7% threshold to win seats; at least three parties must be seated in the parliament)
elections: last held early on 20 June 2021 (next to be held in June 2026)
election results: percent of vote by party - Civil Contract 53.9%, Armenia Alliance 21.0%, I Have Honour Alliance 5.2%; seats by party - Civil Contract 71 of 107 seats, Armenia Alliance 29, I Have Honour Alliance 7; composition (as of February 2022) - men 69, women 38, percent of women 35.5%

Judicial branch: *highest court(s):* Court of Cassation (consists of the Criminal Chamber with a chairman and 5 judges and the Civil and Administrative Chamber with a chairman and 10 judges – with both civil and administrative specializations); Constitutional Court (consists of 9 judges)
judge selection and term of office: Court of Cassation judges nominated by the Supreme Judicial Council, a 10- member body of selected judges and legal scholars; judges appointed by the president; judges can serve until age 65; Constitutional Court judges - 4 appointed by the president, and 5 elected by the National Assembly; judges can serve until age 70
subordinate courts: criminal and civil appellate courts; administrative appellate court; first instance courts; specialized administrative and bankruptcy courts

Political parties and leaders: 5165 National Conservative Movement Party [Karin TONOYAN]
Alliance of Democrats [Arman BABAJANYAN]
Armenia Alliance or HD [Robert KOCHARYAN] (alliance of the Armenian Revolutionary Federation and the Reborn Armenia Party)
Armenian National Congress or ANC [Levon TER-PETROSSIAN] (bloc of independent and opposition parties)
Bright Armenia [Edmon MARUKYAN]
Civil Contract or KP [Nikol PASHINYAN]
Homeland of Armenians [Artak GALSTYAN]
Homeland Party [Artur VANETSYAN]

I Have Honor Alliance (alliance of the RPA and the Homeland Party, [Serzh SARGSIAN and Artur VANETSYAN]
Liberal Party [Samvel BABAYAN]
National Democratic Party [Vahe GASPARYAN]
Prosperous Armenia or BHK [Gagik TSARUKYAN]
Republic Party (Hanrapetutyun Party) [Aram SARGSYAN]
Republican Party of Armenia or RPA [Serzh SARGSIAN]

International organization participation: ADB, BSEC, CD, CE, CIS, CSTO, EAEC (observer), EAEU, EAPC, EBRD, FAO, GCTU, IAEA, IBRD, ICAO, ICC (NGOs), ICRM, IDA, IFAD, IFC, IFRCS, ILO, IMF, Interpol, IOC, IOM, IPU, ISO, ITSO, ITU, MIGA, NAM (observer), OAS (observer), OIF, OPCW, OSCE, PFP, UN, UNCTAD, UNESCO, UNHRC, UNIDO, UNIFIL, UNWTO, UPU, WCO, WFTU (NGOs), WHO, WIPO, WMO, WTO

Diplomatic representation in the US: *chief of mission:* Ambassador Lilit MAKUNTS (since 15 September 2021)
chancery: 2225 R Street NW, Washington, DC 20008
telephone: [1] (202) 319-1976
FAX: [1] (202) 319-2982
email address and website:
armembassyusa@mfa.am
https://usa.mfa.am/en/
consulate(s) general: Glendale (CA)

Diplomatic representation from the US: *chief of mission:* Ambassador Lynne M. TRACEY (since 5 March 2019)
embassy: 1 American Ave., Yerevan 0082
mailing address: 7020 Yerevan Place, Washington, DC 20521-7020
telephone: [374] (10) 464-700
FAX: [374] (10) 464-742
email address and website:
acsyerevan@state.gov
https://am.usembassy.gov/

Flag description: three equal horizontal bands of red (top), blue, and orange; the color red recalls the blood shed for liberty, blue the Armenian skies as well as hope, and orange the land and the courage of the workers who farm it

National symbol(s): Mount Ararat, eagle, lion; national colors: red, blue, orange

National anthem: *name:* "Mer Hayrenik" (Our Fatherland)
lyrics/music: Mikael NALBANDIAN/Barsegh KANACHYAN
note: adopted 1991; based on the anthem of the Democratic Republic of Armenia (1918-1922) but with different lyrics

National heritage: *total World Heritage Sites:* 3 (3 cultural)
selected World Heritage Site locales: Monasteries of Haghpat and Sanahin; Monastery of Geghard and the Upper Azat Valley; Cathedral and Churches of Echmiatsin

ECONOMY

Economic overview: Under the old Soviet central planning system, Armenia developed a modern industrial sector, supplying machine tools, textiles, and other manufactured goods to sister republics, in exchange for raw materials and energy. Armenia has since switched to small-scale agriculture and away from the large agro industrial complexes of the Soviet era. Armenia has only two open trade borders - Iran and Georgia - because its borders with Azerbaijan and Turkey have been closed since 1991 and 1993, respectively, as a result of Armenia's ongoing conflict with Azerbaijan over the separatist Nagorno-Karabakh region.

Armenia joined the World Trade Organization in January 2003. The government has made some improvements in tax and customs administration in recent years, but anti-corruption measures have been largely ineffective. Armenia will need to pursue additional economic reforms and strengthen the rule of law in order to raise its economic growth and improve economic competitiveness and employment opportunities, especially given its economic isolation from Turkey and Azerbaijan.

Armenia's geographic isolation, a narrow export base, and pervasive monopolies in important business sectors have made it particularly vulnerable to volatility in the global commodity markets and the economic challenges in Russia. Armenia is particularly dependent on Russian commercial and governmental support, as most key Armenian infrastructure is Russian-owned and/or managed, especially in the energy sector. Remittances from expatriates working in Russia are equivalent to about 12-14% of GDP. Armenia joined the Russia-led Eurasian Economic Union in January 2015, but has remained interested in pursuing closer ties with the EU as well, signing a Comprehensive and Enhanced Partnership Agreement with the EU in November 2017. Armenia's rising government debt is leading Yerevan to tighten its fiscal policies – the amount is approaching the debt to GDP ratio threshold set by national legislation.

Real GDP (purchasing power parity): $37.31 billion (2020 est.)
$40.38 billion (2019 est.)
$37.53 billion (2018 est.)
note: data are in 2017 dollars
country comparison to the world: 125

Real GDP growth rate: 7.5% (2017 est.)
0.3% (2016 est.)
3.3% (2015 est.)
country comparison to the world: 11

Real GDP per capita: $12,600 (2020 est.)
$13,700 (2019 est.)
$12,700 (2018 est.)
note: data are in 2017 dollars
country comparison to the world: 118

GDP (official exchange rate): $13.694 billion (2019 est.)

Inflation rate (consumer prices): 1.4% (2019 est.)
2.5% (2018 est.)
0.9% (2017 est.)
country comparison to the world: 79

Credit ratings:

Fitch rating: B+ (2020)

Moody's rating: Ba3 (2019)
note: The year refers to the year in which the current credit rating was first obtained.

GDP - composition, by sector of origin: *agriculture:* 16.7% (2017 est.)
industry: 28.2% (2017 est.)
services: 54.8% (2017 est.)

GDP - composition, by end use: *household consumption:* 76.7% (2017 est.)
government consumption: 14.2% (2017 est.)
investment in fixed capital: 17.3% (2017 est.)
investment in inventories: 4.1% (2017 est.)
exports of goods and services: 38.1% (2017 est.)
imports of goods and services: -50.4% (2017 est.)

Agricultural products: milk, potatoes, grapes, vegetables, tomatoes, watermelons, wheat, apples, cabbages, barley

Industries: brandy, mining, diamond processing, metal-cutting machine tools, forging and pressing machines, electric motors, knitted wear, hosiery, shoes, silk fabric, chemicals, trucks, instruments, microelectronics, jewelry, software, food processing

Industrial production growth rate: 5.4% (2017 est.)
country comparison to the world: 51

Labor force: 1.507 million (2017 est.)
country comparison to the world: 128

Labor force - by occupation: *agriculture:* 36.3%
industry: 17%
services: 46.7% (2013 est.)

Unemployment rate: 18.9% (2017 est.)
18.8% (2016 est.)
country comparison to the world: 186

Unemployment, youth ages 15-24: *total:* 32.6%
male: 31.2%
female: 34.4% (2019 est.)
country comparison to the world: 29

Population below poverty line: 26.4% (2019 est.)

Gini Index coefficient - distribution of family income: 34.4 (2018 est.)
31.5 (2013 est.)
country comparison to the world: 112

Household income or consumption by percentage share: *lowest 10%:* 3.5%
highest 10%: 25.7% (2014)

Budget: *revenues:* 2.644 billion (2017 est.)
expenditures: 3.192 billion (2017 est.)

Budget surplus (+) or deficit (-): -4.8% (of GDP) (2017 est.)
country comparison to the world: 167

Public debt: 53.5% of GDP (2017 est.)
51.9% of GDP (2016 est.)
country comparison to the world: 89

Taxes and other revenues: 22.9% (of GDP) (2017 est.)
country comparison to the world: 130

Fiscal year: calendar year

Current account balance: -$328 million (2017 est.)
-$238 million (2016 est.)
country comparison to the world: 111

Exports: $3.82 billion (2020 est.)
$5.64 billion (2019 est.)
$4.91 billion (2018 est.)
note: Data are in current year dollars and do not include illicit exports or re-exports.
country comparison to the world: 136

Exports - partners: Russia 22%, Switzerland 20%, China 7%, Bulgaria 6%, Iraq 5%, Serbia 5%, Netherlands 5%, Germany 5% (2019)

Exports - commodities: copper ore, gold, tobacco, liquors, iron alloys (2019)

Imports: $5 billion (2020 est.) note: data are in current year dollars
$7.47 billion (2019 est.) note: data are in current year dollars
$6.61 billion (2018 est.) note: data are in current year dollars
country comparison to the world: 138

Imports - partners: Russia 29%, China 10%, Georgia 8%, Iran 6%, Turkey 5% (2019)

Imports - commodities: natural gas, cars, refined petroleum, broadcasting equipment, diamonds (2019)

Reserves of foreign exchange and gold: $2.314 billion (31 December 2017 est.)
$2.204 billion (31 December 2016 est.)
country comparison to the world: 119

Debt - external: $11.637 billion (2019 est.)
$10.785 billion (2018 est.)
country comparison to the world: 111

Exchange rates: drams (AMD) per US dollar -
487.9 (2017 est.)
480.49 (2016 est.)
480.49 (2015 est.)
477.92 (2014 est.)
415.92 (2013 est.)

ENERGY

Electricity access: *electrification - total population:* 100% (2020)

Electricity: *installed generating capacity:* 3.633 million kW (2020 est.)
consumption: 5,758,470,000 kWh (2019 est.)
exports: 1.251 billion kWh (2020 est.)
imports: 320 million kWh (2020 est.)
transmission/distribution losses: 548 million kWh (2019 est.)

Electricity generation sources: *fossil fuels:* 40.6% of total installed capacity (2020 est.)
nuclear: 34.8% of total installed capacity (2020 est.)
solar: 0.3% of total installed capacity (2020 est.)
hydroelectricity: 24.3% of total installed capacity (2020 est.)

Coal: *production:* 0 metric tons (2020 est.)
consumption: 12,000 metric tons (2020 est.)
exports: 0 metric tons (2020 est.)
imports: 12,000 metric tons (2020 est.)
proven reserves: 163 million metric tons (2019 est.)

Petroleum: *total petroleum production:* 0 bbl/day (2021 est.)
refined petroleum consumption: 10,900 bbl/day (2019 est.)

Refined petroleum products - imports: 7,145 bbl/day (2015 est.)
country comparison to the world: 158

Natural gas: *production:* 0 cubic meters (2021 est.)
consumption: 2,537,497,000 cubic meters (2019 est.)
exports: 0 cubic meters (2021 est.)
imports: 2,514,220,000 cubic meters (2019 est.)
proven reserves: 0 cubic meters (2021 est.)

Carbon dioxide emissions: 6.354 million metric tonnes of CO_2 (2019 est.)
from coal and metallurgical coke: 12,000 metric tonnes of CO_2 (2019 est.)
from petroleum and other liquids: 1.364 million metric tonnes of CO_2 (2019 est.)
from consumed natural gas: 4.978 million metric tonnes of CO_2 (2019 est.)
country comparison to the world: 130

Energy consumption per capita: 53.019 million Btu/person (2019 est.)
country comparison to the world: 98

COMMUNICATIONS

Telephones - fixed lines: *total subscriptions:* 427,539 (2020 est.)
subscriptions per 100 inhabitants: 14 (2020 est.)
country comparison to the world: 99

Telephones - mobile cellular: *total subscriptions:* 3,488,797 (2020 est.)
subscriptions per 100 inhabitants: 118 (2020 est.)
country comparison to the world: 135

Telecommunication systems: *general assessment:* Armenia's telecom sector was able to post in the mobile and broadband segments; its fixed-line penetration continues to slide downwards, with the rollout of fiber networks which have encouraged the increase in bundled services; the fixed broadband market remains undeveloped due to the lack of underlying infrastructure outside the main cities (2021)
domestic: roughly 14 per 100 fixed-line and 118 per 100 mobile-cellular; reliable fixed-line and mobile-cellular services are available across Yerevan and in major cities and towns; mobile-cellular coverage available in most rural areas (2020)
international: country code - 374; Yerevan is connected to the Caucasus Cable System fiber-optic cable through Georgia and Iran to Europe; additional international service is available by microwave radio relay and landline connections to the other countries of the Commonwealth of Independent States, through the Moscow international switch, and by satellite to the rest of the world; satellite earth stations - 3 (2019)

Broadcast media: Armenia's government-run Public Television network operates alongside 100 privately owned TV stations that provide local to near nationwide coverage; three Russian TV companies are broadcast in Armenia under interstate agreements; subscription cable TV services are available in most regions; several major international broadcasters are available, including CNN; Armenian TV completed conversion from analog to digital broadcasting in late 2016; Public Radio of Armenia is a national, state-run broadcast network that operates alongside 18 privately owned radio stations
(2019)

Internet country code: .am

Internet users: *total:* 2,288,566 (July 2022 est.)
percent of population: 77% (July 2022 est.)
country comparison to the world: 125

Broadband - fixed subscriptions: *total:* 430,407 (2020 est.)
subscriptions per 100 inhabitants: 15 (2020 est.)
country comparison to the world: 95

TRANSPORTATION

National air transport system: *number of registered air carriers:* 3 (2020)
inventory of registered aircraft operated by air carriers: 5

Civil aircraft registration country code prefix: EK

Airports: *total:* 7 (2021)
country comparison to the world: 165

Airports - with paved runways: *total:* 10
over 3,047 m: 2
2,438 to 3,047 m: 2
1,524 to 2,437 m: 4
914 to 1,523 m: 2 (2021)

Airports - with unpaved runways: *total:* 1
914 to 1,523 m: 1 (2021)

Pipelines: 3,838 km gas (high and medium pressure) (2017)

Railways: *total:* 780 km (2014)
broad gauge: 780 km (2014) 1.520-m gauge (780 km electrified)
note: 726 km operational
country comparison to the world: 98

Roadways: *total:* 7,700 km (2019)
urban: 3,780 km
non-urban: 3,920 km
country comparison to the world: 140

MILITARY AND SECURITY

Military and security forces: Armenian Armed Forces: Armenian Army (includes land, air, air defense forces) (2022)

Military expenditures: 4.4% of GDP (2021 est.)
5% of GDP (2020 est.)
5.3% of GDP (2019 est.) (approximately $1.82 billion)
4.6% of GDP (2018 est.) (approximately 1.6 billion)
4.4% of GDP (2017 est.) (approximately $1.43 billion)
country comparison to the world: 14

Military and security service personnel strengths: approximately 45,000 active troops (42,000 ground; 3,000 air/defense) (2022)

Military equipment inventories and acquisitions: the inventory of the Armenian Armed Forces includes mostly Russian and Soviet-era equipment (2022)

Military service age and obligation: 18-27 for voluntary/contract (men and women) or compulsory (men) military service; contract military service is 3-12 months or 3 or 5 years; conscripts serve 24 months; men under the age of 36, who have not previously served as contract servicemen and are registered in the reserve, as well as women, regardless of whether they are registered in the reserve can be enrolled in contractual military service; all citizens aged 27 to 50 are registered in the military reserve and may be called to serve if mobilization is declared (2022)
note: as of 2021, conscripts comprised about half of the military's active personnel; as of 2018, women made up about 13% of the active duty military

Military - note: since November 2020, Russia has deployed about 2,000 peacekeeping troops to the area in and around Nagorno- Karabakh as part of a cease-fire agreement between Armenia and Azerbaijan; fighting erupted between the two countries over the Nagorno-Karabakh region in September of 2020; Nagorno-Karabakh lies within Azerbaijan but has been under control of ethnic Armenian forces (the "Nagorno-Karabakh Defense Army") backed by Armenia since a separatist war there ended in 1994; six weeks of fighting resulted in about 6,500 deaths and ended after Armenia ceded swaths of Nagorno-Karabakh territory; tensions remained high into 2022, and both sides have accused the other of provocations since the fighting ended; Armenia has accused Azerbaijani forces of a series of border intrusions and of seizing pockets of territory

Armenia has been a member of the Collective Security Treaty Organization (CSTO) since 1994 and contributes troops to CSTO's rapid reaction force

TRANSNATIONAL ISSUES

Disputes - international: local border forces struggle to control the illegal transit of goods and people across the porous, undemarcated Armenian, Azerbaijani, and Georgian borders
Armenia-Azerbaijan: The dispute over the break-away Nagorno-Karabakh region and the Armenian military occupation of surrounding lands in Azerbaijan remains the primary focus of regional instability. Residents have evacuated the former Soviet-era small ethnic enclaves in Armenia and Azerbaijan.
Armenia-Georgia: Georgians restrict Armenian access into Samtse-Javakheti ethnic Armenian areas. Armenia has made no claims to the region.
Armenia-Iran: None identified
Armenia-Turkey: In 2009, Swiss mediators facilitated an accord reestablishing diplomatic ties between Armenia and Turkey, but neither side has ratified the agreement and the rapprochement effort has faltered, in part due to resistance from Azerbaijan. The border has been closed since 1993, and no diplomatic relations established after Armenian independence. In 2022, Turkey and Armenia have agreed to move forward with efforts to normalize relations.

Turkish authorities have complained that blasting from quarries in Armenia might be damaging the ruins of Ani, an ancient city on the high ridge overlooking the Arpaçay valley on the opposite shore.

Refugees and internally displaced persons: *refugees (country of origin):* 38,774 (Azerbaijan), 5,205 (Syria - ethnic Armenians) (mid-year 2021)
stateless persons: 892 (mid-year 2021)

Illicit drugs: a transit country for illicit drugs with its location between source countries Afghanistan and Iran and the markets of Europe and Russia

ARUBA

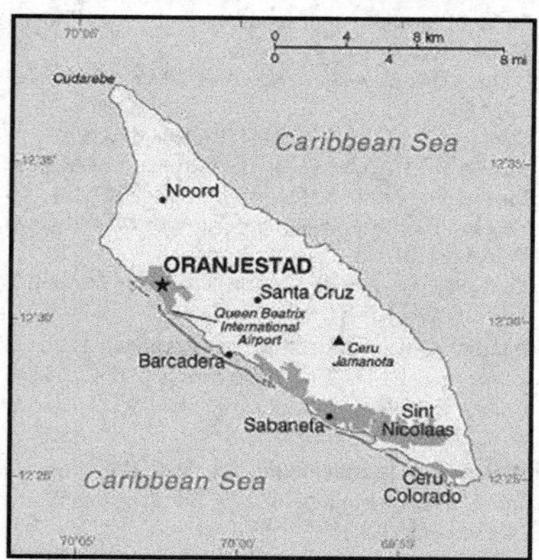

INTRODUCTION

Background: Discovered and claimed for Spain in 1499, Aruba was acquired by the Dutch in 1636. The island's economy has been dominated by three main industries. A 19th century gold rush was followed by prosperity brought on by the opening in 1924 of an oil refinery. The last decades of the 20th century saw a boom in the tourism industry. Aruba seceded from the Netherlands Antilles in 1986 and became a separate, semi-autonomous member of the Kingdom of the Netherlands. Movement toward full independence was halted at Aruba's request in 1990.

GEOGRAPHY

Location: Caribbean, island in the Caribbean Sea, north of Venezuela

Geographic coordinates: 12 30 N, 69 58 W

Map references: Central America and the Caribbean

Area: *total:* 180 sq km
land: 180 sq km
water: 0 sq km
country comparison to the world: 217

Area - comparative: slightly larger than Washington, DC

Land boundaries: *total:* 0 km

Coastline: 68.5 km

Maritime claims: *territorial sea:* 12 nm
exclusive economic zone: 200 nm

Climate: tropical marine; little seasonal temperature variation

Terrain: flat with a few hills; scant vegetation

Elevation: *highest point:* Ceru Jamanota 188 m
lowest point: Caribbean Sea 0 m

Natural resources: NEGL; white sandy beaches foster tourism

Land use: *agricultural land:* 11.1% (2018 est.)
arable land: 11.1% (2018 est.)
permanent crops: 0% (2018 est.)
permanent pasture: 0% (2018 est.)
forest: 2.3% (2018 est.)
other: 86.6% (2018 est.)

Population distribution: most residents live in or around Oranjestad and San Nicolaas; most settlments tend to be located on the less mountainous western side of the island

Natural hazards: hurricanes; lies outside the Caribbean hurricane belt and is rarely threatened

Geography - note: a flat, riverless island renowned for its white sand beaches; its tropical climate is moderated by constant trade winds from the Atlantic Ocean; the temperature is almost constant at about 27 degrees Celsius (81 degrees Fahrenheit)

PEOPLE AND SOCIETY

Population: 122,320 (2022 est.)
country comparison to the world: 188

Nationality: *noun:* Aruban(s)
adjective: Aruban; Dutch

Ethnic groups: Aruban 66%, Colombian 9.1%, Dutch 4.3%, Dominican 4.1%, Venezuelan 3.2%, Curacaoan 2.2%, Haitian 1.5%, Surinamese 1.2%, Peruvian 1.1%, Chinese 1.1%, other 6.2% (2010 est.)
note: data represent population by country of birth

Languages: Papiamento (official) (a creole language that is a mixture of Portuguese, Spanish, Dutch, English, and, to a lesser extent, French, as well as elements of African languages and the language of the Arawak) 69.4%, Spanish 13.7%, English (widely spoken) 7.1%, Dutch (official) 6.1%, Chinese 1.5%, other 1.7%, unspecified 0.4% (2010 est.)

Religions: Roman Catholic 75.3%, Protestant 4.9% (includes Methodist 0.9%, Adventist 0.9%, Anglican 0.4%, other Protestant 2.7%), Jehovah's Witness 1.7%, other 12%, none 5.5%, unspecified 0.5% (2010 est.)

Age structure: *0-14 years:* 17.55% (male 10,524/female 10,437)
15-24 years: 12.06% (male 7,231/female 7,175)
25-54 years: 40.54% (male 23,387/female 25,029)
55-64 years: 14.79% (male 8,285/female 9,383)
65 years and over: 15.05% (male 7,064/female 10,913) (2020 est.)

Dependency ratios: *total dependency ratio:* 47
youth dependency ratio: 25.6
elderly dependency ratio: 21.5
potential support ratio: 4.7 (2020 est.)

Median age: *total:* 39.9 years
male: 38.2 years
female: 41.5 years (2020 est.)
country comparison to the world: 53

Population growth rate: 1.14% (2022 est.)
country comparison to the world: 83

Birth rate: 11.82 births/1,000 population (2022 est.)
country comparison to the world: 158

Death rate: 8.62 deaths/1,000 population (2022 est.)
country comparison to the world: 72

Net migration rate: 8.18 migrant(s)/1,000 population (2022 est.)
country comparison to the world: 11

Population distribution: most residents live in or around Oranjestad and San Nicolaas; most settlments tend to be located on the less mountainous western side of the island

Urbanization: *urban population:* 44.1% of total population (2022)
rate of urbanization: 0.77% annual rate of change (2020-25 est.)

Major urban areas - population: 30,000 ORANJESTAD (capital) (2018)

Sex ratio: *at birth:* 1.02 male(s)/female
0-14 years: 1.01 male(s)/female
15-24 years: 1 male(s)/female
25-54 years: 0.94 male(s)/female
55-64 years: 0.87 male(s)/female
65 years and over: 0.52 male(s)/female
total population: 0.9 male(s)/female (2022 est.)

Infant mortality rate: *total:* 12.09 deaths/1,000 live births
male: 16.46 deaths/1,000 live births

female: 7.63 deaths/1,000 live births (2022 est.)
country comparison to the world: 117

Life expectancy at birth: *total population:* 78.01 years
male: 74.93 years
female: 81.15 years (2022 est.)
country comparison to the world: 78

Total fertility rate: 1.83 children born/woman (2022 est.)
country comparison to the world: 138

Drinking water source: *improved: urban:* 98.1% of population
rural: 98.1% of population
total: 98.1% of population
unimproved: urban: 1.9% of population
rural: 1.9% of population
total: 1.9% of population (2015 est.)

Sanitation facility access: *improved: urban:* 97.7% of population
rural: 97.7% of population
total: 97.7% of population
unimproved: urban: 2.3% of population
rural: 2.3% of population
total: 2.3% of population (2015 est.)

Education expenditures: 5.5% of GDP (2016 est.)
country comparison to the world: 40

Literacy: *definition:* age 15 and over can read and write
total population: 97.8%
male: 97.8%
female: 97.8% (2018)

School life expectancy (primary to tertiary education): *total:* 14 years
male: 13 years
female: 14 years (2012)

ENVIRONMENT

Environment - current issues: difficulty in properly disposing of waste produced by large numbers of tourists; waste burning that occurs in the landfill causes air pollution and poses an environmental and health risk; ocean environmental damage due to plastic pollution

Air pollutants: *carbon dioxide emissions:* 0.88 megatons (2016 est.)

Climate: tropical marine; little seasonal temperature variation

Land use: *agricultural land:* 11.1% (2018 est.)
arable land: 11.1% (2018 est.)
permanent crops: 0% (2018 est.)
permanent pasture: 0% (2018 est.)
forest: 2.3% (2018 est.)
other: 86.6% (2018 est.)

Urbanization: *urban population:* 44.1% of total population (2022)
rate of urbanization: 0.77% annual rate of change (2020-25 est.)

Revenue from forest resources: *forest revenues:* 0% of GDP (2017 est.)
country comparison to the world: 162

Waste and recycling: *municipal solid waste generated annually:* 88,132 tons (2013 est.)
municipal solid waste recycled annually: 9,695 tons (2013 est.)
percent of municipal solid waste recycled: 11% (2013 est.)

GOVERNMENT

Country name: *conventional long form:* Country of Aruba
conventional short form: Aruba
local long form: Land Aruba (Dutch); Pais Aruba (Papiamento)
local short form: Aruba
etymology: the origin of the island's name is unclear; according to tradition, the name comes from the Spanish phrase "oro huba" (there was gold), but in fact no gold was ever found on the island; another possibility is the native word "oruba," which means "well-situated"

Government type: parliamentary democracy; part of the Kingdom of the Netherlands

Dependency status: constituent country of the Kingdom of the Netherlands; full autonomy in internal affairs obtained in 1986 upon separation from the Netherlands Antilles; Dutch Government responsible for defense and foreign affairs

Capital: *name:* Oranjestad
geographic coordinates: 12 31 N, 70 02 W
time difference: UTC-4 (1 hour ahead of Washington, DC, during Standard Time)
etymology: translates as "orange town" in Dutch; the city is named after William I (1533-1584), Prince of Orange, the first ruler of the Netherlands

Administrative divisions: none (part of the Kingdom of the Netherlands)
note: Aruba is one of four constituent countries of the Kingdom of the Netherlands; the other three are the Netherlands, Curacao, and Sint Maarten

Independence: none (part of the Kingdom of the Netherlands)

National holiday: National Anthem and Flag Day, 18 March (1976)

Constitution: *history:* previous 1947, 1955; latest drafted and approved August 1985, enacted 1 January 1986 (regulates governance of Aruba but is subordinate to the Charter for the Kingdom of the Netherlands); in 1986, Aruba became a semiautonomous entity within the Kingdom of the Netherlands

Legal system: civil law system based on the Dutch civil code

Citizenship: see the Netherlands

Suffrage: 18 years of age; universal

Executive branch: *chief of state:* King WILLEM-ALEXANDER of the Netherlands (since 30 April 2013); represented by Governor General Alfonso BOEKHOUDT (since 1 January 2017)
head of government: Prime Minister Evelyn WEVER-CROES (since 17 November 2017)
cabinet: Council of Ministers elected by the Legislature (Staten)
elections/appointments: the monarchy is hereditary; governor general appointed by the monarch for a 6-year term; prime minister and deputy prime minister indirectly elected by the Staten for 4-year term; election last held on 25 June 2021 (next to be held by June 2026)
election results: as leader of the majority party of the ruling coalition, Evelyn WEVER-CROES (MEP) elected prime minister; percent of legislative vote - NA

Legislative branch: *description:* unicameral Legislature or Staten (21 seats; members directly elected in a single nationwide constituency by proportional representation vote; members serve 4-year terms)
elections: last held on 25 June 2021 (next to be held in June 2025)
election results: percent of vote by party MEP 35.3%, AVP 31.3%, ROOTS 9.4%, MAS 8%, Accion21 5.8%; seats by party - MEP 9, AVP 7, ROOTS 2, MAS 2, Accion21 1; composition - men 13, women 8, percent of women 38.1%

Judicial branch: *highest court(s):* Joint Court of Justice of Aruba, Curacao, Sint Maarten, and of Bonaire, Sint Eustatius and Saba or "Joint Court of Justice" (sits as a 3-judge panel); final appeals heard by the Supreme Court in The Hague, Netherlands
judge selection and term of office: Joint Court judges appointed for life by the monarch
subordinate courts: Court in First Instance

Political parties and leaders: Accion21 [Miguel MANSUR]
Aruban People's Party or AVP [Michiel "Mike" EMAN]
Democratic Network or RED [Ricardo CROES]
Movimiento Aruba Soberano (Aruban Sovereignty Movement) or MAS [Marisol LOPEZ-TROMP]
People's Electoral Movement Party or MEP [Evelyn WEVER-CROES]
Pueblo Orguyoso y Respeta or POR [Alan Howell]
RAIZ (ROOTS) [Ursell ARENDS]

International organization participation: Caricom (observer), FATF, ILO, IMF, Interpol, IOC, ITUC (NGOs), UNESCO (associate), UNWTO (associate), UPU

Diplomatic representation in the US: *chief of mission:* none (represented by the Kingdom of the Netherlands)

Diplomatic representation from the US: *embassy:* the US does not have an embassy in Aruba; the Consul General to Curacao is accredited to Aruba

Flag description: blue, with two narrow, horizontal, yellow stripes across the lower portion and a red, four-pointed star outlined in white in the upper hoist-side corner; the star represents Aruba and its red soil and white beaches, its four points the four major languages (Papiamento, Dutch, Spanish, English) as well as the four points of a compass, to indicate that its inhabitants come from all over the world; the blue symbolizes Caribbean waters and skies; the stripes represent the island's two main "industries": the flow of tourists to the sun-drenched beaches and the flow of minerals from the earth

National symbol(s): Hooiberg (Haystack) Hill; national colors: blue, yellow, red, white

National anthem: *name:* "Aruba Deshi Tera" (Aruba Precious Country)
lyrics/music: Juan Chabaya 'Padu' LAMPE/Rufo Inocencio WEVER
note: local anthem adopted 1986; as part of the Kingdom of the Netherlands, "Het Wilhelmus" is official (see Netherlands)

ECONOMY

Economic overview: Tourism, petroleum bunkering, hospitality, and financial and business services are the mainstays of the small open Aruban economy.

Tourism accounts for a majority of economic activity; as of 2017, over 2 million tourists visited Aruba annually, with the large majority (80-85%) of those from the US. The rapid growth of the tourism sector has resulted in a substantial expansion of other activities. Construction continues to boom, especially in the hospitality sector.

Aruba is heavily dependent on imports and is making efforts to expand exports to improve its trade balance. Almost all consumer and capital goods are imported, with the US, the Netherlands, and Panama being the major suppliers.

In 2016, Citgo Petroleum Corporation, an indirect wholly owned subsidiary of Petroleos de Venezuela SA, and the Government of Aruba signed an agreement to restart Valero Energy Corp.'s former 235,000-b/d refinery. Tourism and related industries have continued to grow, and the Aruban Government is working to attract more diverse industries. Aruba's banking sector continues to be a strong sector; unemployment has significantly decreased.

Real GDP (purchasing power parity): $4.158 billion (2017 est.)
$4.05 billion (2017 est.)
$4.107 billion (2016 est.)
country comparison to the world: 182

Real GDP growth rate: 1.2% (2017 est.)
-0.1% (2016 est.)
-0.4% (2015 est.)
country comparison to the world: 165

Real GDP per capita: $37,500 (2017 est.)
$38,442 (2017 est.)
$37,300 (2016 est.)
country comparison to the world: 49

GDP (official exchange rate): $2.7 billion (2017 est.)

Inflation rate (consumer prices): -0.5% (2017 est.)
-0.9% (2016 est.)
country comparison to the world: 13

Credit ratings:

Fitch rating: BB (2020)

Standard & Poors rating: BBB+ (2013)
note: The year refers to the year in which the current credit rating was first obtained.

GDP - composition, by sector of origin: *agriculture:* 0.4% (2002 est.)
industry: 33.3% (2002 est.)
services: 66.3% (2002 est.)

GDP - composition, by end use: *household consumption:* 60.3% (2014 est.)
government consumption: 25.3% (2015 est.)
investment in fixed capital: 22.3% (2014 est.)
investment in inventories: 0% (2015 est.)
exports of goods and services: 70.5% (2015 est.)
imports of goods and services: -76.6% (2015 est.)

Agricultural products: aloes; livestock; fish

Industries: tourism, petroleum transshipment facilities, banking

Labor force: 51,610 (2007 est.)
note: of the 51,610 workers aged 15 and over in the labor force, 32,252 were born in Aruba and 19,353 came from abroad; foreign workers are 38% of the employed population
country comparison to the world: 190

Labor force - by occupation: *note:* most employment is in wholesale and retail trade, followed by hotels and restaurants

Unemployment rate: 7.7% (2016 est.)
country comparison to the world: 120

Budget: *revenues:* 681.6 million (2017 est.)
expenditures: 755.5 million (2017 est.)

Budget surplus (+) or deficit (-): -2.7% (of GDP) (2017 est.)
country comparison to the world: 118

Public debt: 86% of GDP (2017 est.)
84.7% of GDP (2016 est.)
country comparison to the world: 31

Taxes and other revenues: 25.2% (of GDP) (2017 est.)
country comparison to the world: 118

Fiscal year: calendar year

Current account balance: $22 million (2017 est.)
$133 million (2016 est.)
country comparison to the world: 59

Exports: $1.45 billion (2020 est.)
$2.56 billion (2019 est.)
$2.56 billion (2018 est.)
note: Data are in current year dollars and do not include illicit exports or re-exports.
country comparison to the world: 165

Exports - partners: Malaysia 57%, United States 11%, Netherlands 6%, Jordan 6%, Venezuela 5% (2019)

Exports - commodities: refined petroleum, liquors, scrap iron, soap, tobacco (2019)

Imports: $1.67 billion (2020 est.) note: data are in current year dollars
$2.24 billion (2019 est.) note: data are in current year dollars
$2.27 billion (2018 est.) note: data are in current year dollars
country comparison to the world: 178

Imports - partners: United States 48%, Netherlands 16% (2019)

Imports - commodities: refined petroleum, jewelry, cars, vehicle parts, tobacco products (2019)

Reserves of foreign exchange and gold: $921.8 million (31 December 2017 est.)
$828 million (31 December 2015 est.)
country comparison to the world: 134

Debt - external: $693.2 million (31 December 2014 est.)
$666.4 million (31 December 2013 est.)
country comparison to the world: 173

Exchange rates: Aruban guilders/florins per US dollar -
1.79 (2017 est.)
1.79 (2016 est.)
1.79 (2015 est.)
1.79 (2014 est.)
1.79 (2013 est.)

ENERGY

Electricity access: *electrification - total population:* 100% (2020)

Electricity: *installed generating capacity:* 296,000 kW (2020 est.)
consumption: 909.442 million kWh (2019 est.)
exports: 0 kWh (2020 est.)
imports: 0 kWh (2020 est.)
transmission/distribution losses: 10.27 million kWh (2019 est.)

Electricity generation sources: *fossil fuels:* 83.3% of total installed capacity (2020 est.)
solar: 1.2% of total installed capacity (2020 est.)
wind: 15.4% of total installed capacity (2020 est.)

Petroleum: *total petroleum production:* 0 bbl/day (2021 est.)
refined petroleum consumption: 8,100 bbl/day (2019 est.)

Refined petroleum products - imports: 7,891 bbl/day (2015 est.)
country comparison to the world: 153

Carbon dioxide emissions: 1.254 million metric tonnes of CO2 (2019 est.)
from petroleum and other liquids: 1.254 million metric tonnes of CO2 (2019 est.)
country comparison to the world: 168

Energy consumption per capita: 174.629 million Btu/person (2019 est.)
country comparison to the world: 26

COMMUNICATIONS

Telephones - fixed lines: *total subscriptions:* 35,000 (2020 est.)
subscriptions per 100 inhabitants: 33 (2020 est.)
country comparison to the world: 167

Telephones - mobile cellular: *total subscriptions:* 141,000 (2020 est.)
subscriptions per 100 inhabitants: 132 (2020 est.)
country comparison to the world: 188

Telecommunication systems: *general assessment:* the telecom sector has seen a decline in subscriber numbers (particularly for prepaid mobile services the mainstay of short term visitors) and revenue; fixed and mobile broadband services are two areas that have benefited from the crisis as employees and students have resorted to working from home; one area of the telecom market that is not prepared for growth is 5G mobile; governments, regulators, and even the mobile network operators have shown that they have not been investing in 5G opportunities at the present time; network expansion and enhancements remain concentrated around improving LTE coverage (2021)
domestic: 33 per 100 fixed-line telephone subscriptions and 132 per 100 mobile-cellular (2020)
international: country code - 297; landing points for the PAN-AM, PCCS, Deep Blue Cable, and Alonso de Ojeda submarine telecommunications cable system that extends from Trinidad and Tobago, Florida, Puerto Ricco, Jamaica, Guyana, Sint Eustatius & Saba, Suriname, Dominican Republic, BVI, USVI, Haiti, Cayman Islands, the Netherlands Antilles, through Aruba to Panama, Venezuela, Colombia, Ecuador, Peru and Chile; extensive interisland microwave radio relay links (2019)

Broadcast media: 2 commercial TV stations; cable TV subscription service provides access to foreign channels; about 19 commercial radio stations broadcast (2017)

Internet country code: .aw

Internet users: *total:* 103,121 (2019 est.)
percent of population: 97% (2019 est.)
country comparison to the world: 180

Broadband - fixed subscriptions: *total:* 19,000 (2020 est.)
subscriptions per 100 inhabitants: 18 (2020 est.)
country comparison to the world: 167

TRANSPORTATION

National air transport system: *number of registered air carriers:* 3 (2020)
inventory of registered aircraft operated by air carriers: 19

annual passenger traffic on registered air carriers: 274,280 (2018)

Civil aircraft registration country code prefix: P4

Airports: *total:* 1 (2021)
country comparison to the world: 211

Airports - with paved runways: *total:* 1
2,438 to 3,047 m: 1 (2021)

Roadways: *total:* 1,000 km (2010)
country comparison to the world: 186

Merchant marine: *total:* 1
by type: other 1 (2021)
country comparison to the world: 179

Ports and terminals: *major seaport(s):* Barcadera, Oranjestad
oil terminal(s): Sint Nicolaas
cruise port(s): Oranjestad

MILITARY AND SECURITY

Military and security forces: no regular military forces; Aruban Militia (ARUMIL) (2022)

Military - note: defense is the responsibility of the Kingdom of the Netherlands; the Aruba security services focus on organized crime and terrorism; the Dutch Government controls foreign and defense policy; the Dutch Caribbean Coast Guard (DCCG) provides maritime security

TRANSNATIONAL ISSUES

Disputes - international: none identified

Refugees and internally displaced persons: *refugees (country of origin):* 17,000 (Venezuela) (2021)

Trafficking in persons: *current situation:* human traffickers exploit domestic and foreign victims; foreign men and women are subject to forced labor in Aruba's services and construction sectors; Venezuelans overstaying visas are at risk of forced labor in domestic service, construction, and commercial sex; Chinese men and women and Indian men are subject to forced labor in retail businesses and domestic service; managers of some Chinese-owned grocery stores and restaurants exploit children through sex trafficking and forced labor
tier rating: Tier 2 Watch List — Aruba does not fully meet the minimum standards for the elimination of trafficking but is making significant efforts to do so; the government provided officials with anti-trafficking training, continued an awareness campaign, and continued to implement the 2018-2022 national action plan; however, officials investigated fewer trafficking cases and did not report prosecuting or convicting any traffickers; efforts were hindered by the conflation of trafficking with migrant smuggling; authorities also did not report identifying any victims, including Venezuelan migrants and refugees, who are vulnerable to trafficking (2020)

Illicit drugs: northbound transshipment point for cocaine from Colombia and Venezuela; Cocaine shipped to the United States, other Caribbean islands, Africa, and Europe

ASHMORE AND CARTIER ISLANDS

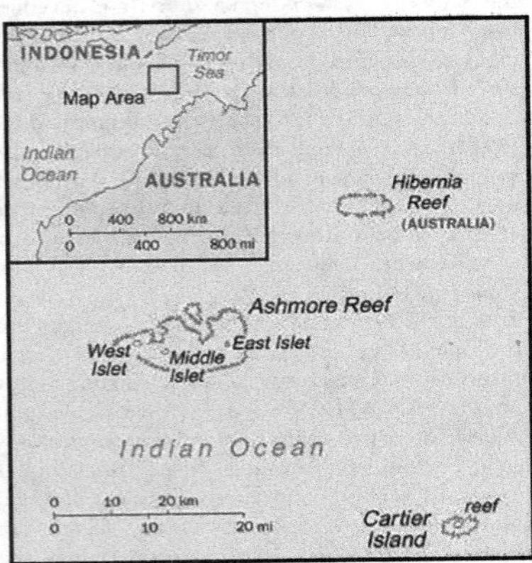

INTRODUCTION

Background: Indonesian fishermen have long fished in the area around Ashmore Reef and Cartier Island. British explorers were the first Europeans to see Cartier Island and Ashmore Reef in 1800 and 1811, respectively. American whalers frequently sailed by the islands in the 1850s and later settled to mine the phosphate deposits on Ashmore Reef, which were exhausted by 1891. The UK disputed US access to Ashmore Reef and formally annexed it in 1878. Cartier Island was annexed in 1909. In 1931, the UK transferred the islands to Australia, which accepted them in 1934 as part of Western Australia. In 1938, Australia transferred governance to the Northern Territory. During World War II, the islands saw several Allied ship visits and post-war, Cartier Island became a bombing range. In 1978, governance of Ashmore and Cartier Islands was moved to the federal government. Ashmore Reef and Cartier Island became marine reserves in 1983 and 2000 respectively.

In 1974, Australia and Indonesia signed a memorandum of understanding (MOU) to allow Indonesian fishermen to continue fishing around the islands. The MOU also allows Indonesian fishermen to visit the graves of past fishermen, replenish their fresh water, and shelter in the West Island Lagoon of Ashmore Reef. In the 1990s, Indonesia challenged Australia's claims to the islands, which was settled in a maritime boundary treaty in 1997. The islands were a popular first point of contact for migrants and refugees seeking to enter Australia, so in 2001, Australia declared the islands outside the Australian migration zone.

GEOGRAPHY

Location: Southeastern Asia, islands in the Indian Ocean, midway between northwestern Australia and Timor island; Ashmore Reef is 840 km west of Darwin and 610 km north of Broome; Cartier Islet is 70 km east of Ashmore Reef

Geographic coordinates: 12 25 S, 123 20 E
note – Ashmore Reef - 12 14 S, 123 05 E; Cartier Islet - 12 32 S, 123 32 E

Map references: Southeast Asia

Area: *total:* 5 sq km
land: 5 sq km
water: 0 sq km
note: includes Ashmore Reef (West, Middle, and East Islets) and Cartier Island
country comparison to the world: 249

Area - comparative: about eight times the size of the National Mall in Washington, DC

Land boundaries: *total:* 0 km

Coastline: 74.1 km

Maritime claims: *territorial sea:* 12 nm
contiguous zone: 24 nm
continental shelf: 200-m depth or to the depth of exploitation
exclusive fishing zone: 200 nm

Climate: tropical

Terrain: low with sand and coral

Elevation: *highest point:* Cartier Island 5 m
lowest point: Indian Ocean 0 m

Natural resources: fish

Land use: *agricultural land:* 0% (2018 est.)

Natural hazards: surrounded by shoals and reefs that can pose maritime hazards

Geography - note: Ashmore Reef National Nature Reserve established in August 1983; Cartier Island Marine Reserve established in 2000

PEOPLE AND SOCIETY

Population: (July 2021 est.) no indigenous inhabitants
note: Indonesian fishermen are allowed access to the lagoon and fresh water at Ashmore Reef's West Island; access to East and Middle Islands is by permit only

Population growth rate: 0.32% (2021 est.)
country comparison to the world: 165

ENVIRONMENT

Environment - current issues: illegal killing of protected wildlife by traditional Indonesian fisherman, as well as fishing by non-traditional Indonesian vessels, are ongoing problems; sea level rise, changes in sea temperature, and ocean acidification are concerns; marine debris

Climate: tropical

Land use: *agricultural land:* 0% (2018 est.)

GOVERNMENT

Country name: *conventional long form:* Territory of Ashmore and Cartier Islands
conventional short form: Ashmore and Cartier Islands
etymology: named after British Captain Samuel ASHMORE, who first sighted his namesake island in 1811, and after the ship Cartier, from which the second island was discovered in 1800

Dependency status: territory of Australia; administered from Canberra by the Department of Regional Australia, Local Government, Arts and Sport

Legal system: the laws of the Commonwealth of Australia and the laws of the Northern Territory of Australia, where applicable, apply

Citizenship: see Australia

Diplomatic representation in the US: none (territory of Australia)

Diplomatic representation from the US: *embassy:* none (territory of Australia)

Flag description: the flag of Australia is used

ECONOMY

Economic overview: no economic activity

TRANSPORTATION

Ports and terminals: none; offshore anchorage only

MILITARY AND SECURITY

Military - note: defense is the responsibility of Australia; periodic visits by the Royal Australian Navy and Royal Australian Air Force

TRANSNATIONAL ISSUES

Disputes - international: *Australia-Indonesia:* Australia has closed parts of the Ashmore and Cartier reserve to Indonesian traditional fishing; Indonesian groups challenge Australia's claim to Ashmore Reef

Illicit drugs: NA

ATLANTIC OCEAN

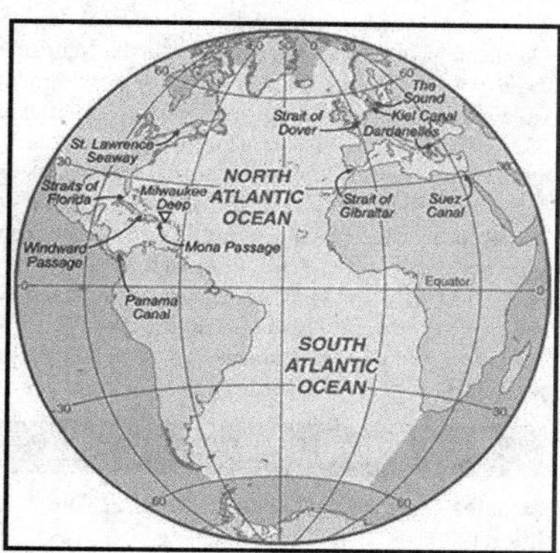

INTRODUCTION

Background: The Atlantic Ocean is the second largest of the world's five oceans (after the Pacific Ocean, but larger than the Indian Ocean, Southern Ocean, and Arctic Ocean). The Kiel Canal (Germany), Oresund (Denmark-Sweden), Bosporus (Turkey), Strait of Gibraltar (Morocco-Spain), and the Saint Lawrence Seaway (Canada-US) are important strategic access waterways. The decision by the International Hydrographic Organization in the spring of 2000 to delimit a fifth world ocean, the Southern Ocean, removed the portion of the Atlantic Ocean south of 60 degrees south latitude.

GEOGRAPHY

Location: body of water between Africa, Europe, the Arctic Ocean, the Americas, and the Southern Ocean

Geographic coordinates: 0 00 N, 25 00 W

Map references: Political Map of the World

Area: *total:* 85.133 million sq km
note: includes Baffin Bay, Baltic Sea, Black Sea, Caribbean Sea, Davis Strait, Denmark Strait, part of the Drake Passage, Hudson Bay, Hudson Strait, Gulf of Mexico, Labrador Sea, Mediterranean Sea, North Sea, almost all of the Scotia Sea, and other tributary water bodies

Area - comparative: about 7.5 times the size of the US

Coastline: 111,866 km

Climate: tropical cyclones (hurricanes) develop off the coast of Africa near Cabo Verde and move westward into the Caribbean Sea; hurricanes can occur from May to December but are most frequent from August to November

Ocean volume: *ocean volume:* 310,410,900 cu km
percent of World Ocean total volume: 23.3%

Major ocean currents: clockwise North Atlantic Gyre consists of the northward flowing, warm Gulf Stream in the west, the eastward flowing North Atlantic Current in the north, the southward flowing cold Canary Current in the east, and the westward flowing North Equatorial Current in the south; the counterclockwise South Atlantic Gyre composed of the southward flowing warm Brazil Current in the west, the eastward flowing South Atlantic Current in the south, the northward flowing cold Benguela Current in the east, and the westward flowing South Equatorial Current in the north

Elevation: *highest point:* sea level
lowest point: Puerto Rico Trench -8,605 m
mean depth: -3,646 m

Natural resources: oil and gas fields, fish, marine mammals (seals and whales), sand and gravel aggregates, placer deposits, polymetallic nodules, precious stones

Natural hazards: icebergs common in Davis Strait, Denmark Strait, and the northwestern Atlantic Ocean from February to August and have been spotted as far south as Bermuda and the Madeira Islands; ships subject to superstructure icing in extreme northern Atlantic from October to May; persistent fog can be a maritime hazard from May to September; hurricanes (May to December)

Geography - note: major chokepoints include the Dardanelles, Strait of Gibraltar, access to the Panama and Suez Canals; strategic straits include the Strait of Dover, Straits of Florida, Mona Passage, The Sound (Oresund), and Windward Passage; the Equator divides the Atlantic Ocean into the North Atlantic Ocean and South Atlantic Ocean

ENVIRONMENT

Environment - current issues: endangered marine species include the manatee, seals, sea lions, turtles, and whales; unsustainable exploitation of fisheries (over fishing, bottom trawling, drift net fishing, discards, catch of non-target species); pollution (maritime transport, discharges, offshore drilling, oil spills); municipal sludge pollution off eastern US, southern Brazil, and eastern Argentina; oil pollution in Caribbean Sea, Gulf of Mexico, Lake Maracaibo, Mediterranean Sea, and North Sea; industrial waste and municipal sewage pollution in Baltic Sea, North Sea, and Mediterranean Sea

Marine fisheries: the Atlantic Ocean fisheries are the second most important in the world accounting for 26.4%, or 21,063,495 mt, of the global catch in 2019; of the seven regions delineated by the Food and Agriculture Organization in the Atlantic basin, the most important include the following:

Northeast Atlantic region (Region 27) is the fourth most important in the world producing 10.2% of the global catch or 8,116,507 mt in 2019; the region encompasses the waters north of 36º North latitude and east of 40º West longitude with the major producers including Norway (3,528,240 mt), Russia (1,044,153 mt), Iceland (933,019 mt), UK (823,669 mt), and Denmark (641,927 mt); the region includes the historically important fishing grounds of the North Sea, the Baltic Sea, and the Atlantic waters between Greenland, Iceland, and the British Isles; the principal catches include Atlantic cod, haddock, saithe (pollock), Blue Whiting, herring, and mackerel; not all fish caught are for human consumption, half of fish catches in the North Sea are processed as fish oil or fish meal, which are used in animal fodder

Eastern Central Atlantic region (Region 34) is the second most important Atlantic fishery, and sixth largest in the world producing more than 6.8% of the global catch or 5,397,726 mt in 2019; the region encompasses the waters between 36º North and 6º South latitude and east of 40º West longitude off the west coast of Africa with the major producers including Morocco (1,419,872 mt), Mauritania (705,850 mt), Senegal (472,571 mt), Nigeria (451,768 mt), Ghana (303,001 mt), Cameroon (265,969 mt), and Sierra Leone (200,000 mt); the principal catches include pilchard, sardinellas, shad, and mackerel

Northwest Atlantic region (Region 21) is the third most important Atlantic fishery and eighth in the world producing 2% of the global catch and 1,679,512 mt in 2019; it encompasses the waters north of 35º North latitude and west of 42º West longitude including the important fishing grounds over the continental shelf of North America such as the Grand Banks, the Georges Bank, and the Flemish Cap, as well as Baffin Bay with the major producers including the US (927,777 mt), Canada (615,651 mt), and Greenland (179,990 mt); the principal catches include sea scallops, prawns, lobster, herring, and menhaden

Mediterranean and Black Sea region (Region 37) is a minor fishing region representing 1.7% or 1,385,190 mt of the world's total capture in 2019; the region encompasses all waters east of the Strait of Gibraltar with the major producers including Turkey (686,650 mt), Italy (281,212 mt), Tunisia (129,325 mt), Spain (119,759 mt), and Russia (72,279 mt); the principal catches include European anchovy, European pilchard, Gobies, and clams

Regional fisheries bodies: Commission for the Conservation of Southern Bluefin Tuna, Fishery Committee for the Eastern Central Atlantic, Fisheries Committee for the West Central Gulf of Guinea, General Fisheries Commission for the Mediterranean, International Commission for the Conservation of Atlantic Tunas, International Council for the Exploration of the Seas, Northwest Atlantic Fisheries Organization, North Atlantic Salmon Conservation Organization, North East Atlantic Fisheries Commission, Southeast Atlantic Fisheries Organization, Western Central Atlantic Fishery Commission

Climate: tropical cyclones (hurricanes) develop off the coast of Africa near Cabo Verde and move westward into the Caribbean Sea; hurricanes can occur from May to December but are most frequent from August to November

GOVERNMENT

Country name: *etymology:* name derives from the Greek description of the waters beyond the Strait of Gibraltar, Atlantis thalassa, meaning "Sea of Atlas"

ECONOMY

Economic overview: The Atlantic Ocean provides some of the world's most heavily trafficked sea routes, between and within the Eastern and Western Hemispheres. Other economic activity includes the exploitation of natural resources, e.g., fishing, dredging of aragonite sands (The Bahamas), and production of crude oil and natural gas (Caribbean Sea, Gulf of Mexico, and North Sea).

TRANSPORTATION

Ports and terminals: *major seaport(s):* Alexandria (Egypt), Algiers (Algeria), Antwerp (Belgium), Barcelona (Spain), Buenos Aires (Argentina), Casablanca (Morocco), Colon (Panama), Copenhagen (Denmark), Dakar (Senegal), Gdansk (Poland), Hamburg (Germany), Helsinki (Finland), Las Palmas (Canary Islands, Spain), Le Havre (France), Lisbon (Portugal), London (UK), Marseille (France), Montevideo (Uruguay), Montreal (Canada), Naples (Italy), New Orleans (US), New York (US), Oran (Algeria), Oslo (Norway), Peiraiefs or Piraeus (Greece), Rio de Janeiro (Brazil), Rotterdam (Netherlands), Saint Petersburg (Russia), Stockholm (Sweden)

Transportation - note: Kiel Canal and Saint Lawrence Seaway are two important waterways; significant domestic commercial and recreational use of Intracoastal Waterway on central and south Atlantic seaboard and Gulf of Mexico coast of US; the International Maritime Bureau reports the territorial waters of littoral states and offshore Atlantic waters as high risk for piracy and armed robbery against ships, particularly in the Gulf of Guinea off West Africa; in 2014, 41 commercial vessels were attacked in the Gulf of Guinea with 5 hijacked and 144 crew members taken hostage; hijacked vessels are often disguised and cargoes stolen; crews have been robbed and stores or cargoes stolen

MILITARY AND SECURITY

Maritime threats: the International Maritime Bureau reports the territorial and offshore waters in the Niger Delta and Gulf of Guinea remain a very high risk for piracy and armed robbery of ships; in 2021, there were 34 reported incidents of piracy and armed robbery at sea in the Gulf of Guinea region; although a significant decrease from the total number of 81 incidents in 2020, it included the one hijacking and three of five ships fired upon worldwide; while boarding and attempted boarding to steal valuables from ships and crews are the most common types of incidents, almost a third of all incidents involve a hijacking and/or kidnapping; in 2021, 57 crew members were kidnapped in seven separate incidents in the Gulf of Guinea, representing 100% of kidnappings worldwide; Nigerian pirates in particular are well armed and very aggressive, operating as far as 200 nm offshore; the Maritime Administration of the US Department of Transportation has issued a Maritime Advisory (2022-001 - Gulf of Guinea-Piracy/Armed Robbery/Kidnapping for Ransom) effective 4 January 2022, which states in part, "Piracy, armed robbery, and kidnapping for ransom continue to serve as significant threats to US-flagged vessels transiting or operating in the Gulf of Guinea;" South American ports in Brazil and Colombia, as well as Caribbean ports in Mexico and Haiti continue to be affected by the crime of armed robbery against ships with 15 incidents reported in 2021 compared to 17 in 2020 with most of these occurring while berthed or anchored

TRANSNATIONAL ISSUES

Disputes - international: some maritime disputes (see littoral states)

AUSTRALIA

INTRODUCTION

Background: Aboriginal Australians arrived on the continent at least 60,000 years ago and developed complex hunter-gatherer societies and oral histories. Dutch navigators led by Abel TASMAN were the first Europeans to land in Australia in 1606, and they mapped the western and northern coasts. They named the continent New Holland but made no attempts to permanently settle it. In 1770, English captain James COOK sailed to the east coast of Australia, named it New South Wales, and claimed it for Great Britain. In 1788 and 1825, Great Britain established New South Wales and then Tasmania as penal colonies respectively. Great Britain and Ireland sent more than 150,000 convicts to Australia before ending the practice in 1868. As Europeans began settling areas away from the coasts, they came into more direct contact with Aboriginal Australians. Europeans also cleared land for agriculture, impacting Aboriginal Australians' ways of life. These issues, along with disease and a policy in the 1900s that forcefully removed Aboriginal children from their parents, reduced the Aboriginal Australian population from more than 700,000 pre-European contact to a low of 74,000 in 1933.

Four additional colonies were established in Australia in the mid-1800s: Western Australia (1829), South Australia (1836), Victoria (1851), and Queensland (1859). Gold rushes beginning in the 1850s brought thousands of new immigrants to New South Wales and Victoria, helping to reorient Australia away from its penal colony roots. In the second half of the 1800s, the colonies were all gradually granted self-government, and in 1901, they federated and became the Commonwealth of Australia. Australia contributed more than 400,000 troops to Allied efforts during World War I, and Australian troops played a large role in the defeat of Japanese troops in the Pacific in World War II. Australia severed most constitutional links with the UK in 1942, and in 1951 signed the Australia, New Zealand, and US (ANZUS) Treaty, cementing its military alliance with the United States. In 2021, Australia, the UK, and the US announced the AUKUS enhanced trilateral security partnership to maintain and expand the three countries' edge in military capabilities and critical technologies. Australia's post-war economy boomed and by the 1970s, racial policies that prevented most non-Whites from immigrating to Australia were removed, greatly increasing Asian immigration to the country. In recent decades, Australia has become an internationally competitive, advanced market economy due in large part to economic reforms adopted in the 1980s and its proximity to East and Southeast Asia.

In the early 2000s, Australian politics became unstable with frequent attempts to oust party leaders, including five changes of prime minister between 2010 and 2018. As a result, both major parties instituted rules to make it harder to remove a party leader.

GEOGRAPHY

Location: Oceania, continent between the Indian Ocean and the South Pacific Ocean

Geographic coordinates: 27 00 S, 133 00 E

Map references: Oceania

Area: *total:* 7,741,220 sq km
land: 7,682,300 sq km
water: 58,920 sq km
note: includes Lord Howe Island and Macquarie Island
country comparison to the world: 7

Area - comparative: slightly smaller than the US contiguous 48 states

Land boundaries: *total:* 0 km

Coastline: 25,760 km

Maritime claims: *territorial sea:* 12 nm
contiguous zone: 24 nm
exclusive economic zone: 200 nm
continental shelf: 200 nm or to the edge of the continental margin

Climate: generally arid to semiarid; temperate in south and east; tropical in north

Terrain: mostly low plateau with deserts; fertile plain in southeast

Elevation: *highest point:* Mount Kosciuszko 2,228 m
lowest point: Lake Eyre -15 m
mean elevation: 330 m

Natural resources: alumina, coal, iron ore, copper, tin, gold, silver, uranium, nickel, tungsten, rare earth elements, mineral sands, lead, zinc, diamonds, opals, natural gas, petroleum; note - Australia is the world's largest net exporter of coal accounting for 29% of global coal exports; as well, Australia is by far the world's largest supplier of opals

Land use: *agricultural land:* 46.65% (2018 est.)
arable land: 4.03% (2018 est.)
permanent crops: 0.04% (2018 est.)
permanent pasture: 42.58% (2018 est.)
forest: 17.42% (2018 est.)
other: 33.42% (2018 est.)

Irrigated land: 25,460 sq km (2014)

Major lakes (area sq km): *fresh water lake(s):* Lake Alexandrina - 570 sq km
salt water lake(s): Lake Eyre - 9,690 sq km; Lake Torrens (ephemeral) - 5,780 sq km; Lake Gairdner - 4,470 sq km; Lake Mackay (ephemeral) - 3,494 sq km; Lake Frome - 2,410 sq km; Lake Amadeus (ephemeral) - 1,032 sq km

Major rivers (by length in km): River Murray - 2,508 km; Darling River - 1,545 km; Murrumbidgee River - 1,485 km; Lachlan River - 1,339 km; Cooper Creek - 1,113 km; Flinders River - 1,004 km

Major watersheds (area sq km):

Indian Ocean drainage: *(Great Australian Bight)* Murray-Darling (1,050,116 sq km)

Internal *(endorheic basin)* drainage: Lake Eyre (1,212,198 sq km)

Major aquifers: Great Artesian Basin, Canning Basin

Population distribution: population is primarily located on the periphery, with the highest concentration of people residing in the east and southeast; a secondary population center is located in and around Perth in the west; of the States and Territories, New South Wales has, by far, the largest population; the interior, or "outback", has a very sparse population

Natural hazards: cyclones along the coast; severe droughts; forest fires
volcanism: volcanic activity on Heard and McDonald Islands

Geography - note: *note 1:* world's smallest continent but sixth-largest country; the largest country in Oceania, the largest country entirely in the Southern Hemisphere, and the largest country without land borders
note 2: the Great Dividing Range that runs along eastern Australia is that continent's longest mountain range and the third-longest land-based range in the world; the term "Great Dividing Range" refers to the fact that the mountains form a watershed crest from which all of the rivers of eastern Australia flow – east, west, north, and south
note 3: Australia is the only continent without glaciers; it is the driest inhabited continent on earth, making it particularly vulnerable to the challenges of climate change; the invigorating sea breeze known as the "Fremantle Doctor" affects the city of Perth on the west coast and is one of the most consistent winds in the world; Australia is home to 10% of the world's biodiversity, and a great number of its flora and fauna exist nowhere else in the world

PEOPLE AND SOCIETY

Population: 26,141,369 (2022 est.)
country comparison to the world: 54

Nationality: *noun:* Australian(s)
adjective: Australian

Ethnic groups: English 36.1%, Australian 33.5%, Irish 11.0%, Scottish 9.3%, Chinese 5.6%, Italian 4.6%, German 4.5%, Aboriginal and Torres Strait Islander 2.8%, Indian 2.8%, Greek 1.8%, Dutch 1.6%
(2016 est.)
note: data represent self-identified ancestry, with the option of reporting two ancestries

Languages: English 72.7%, Mandarin 2.5%, Arabic 1.4%, Cantonese 1.2%, Vietnamese 1.2%, Italian 1.2%, Greek 1%, other 14.8%, unspecified 6.5% (2016 est.)
note: data represent language spoken at home

Religions: Protestant 23.1% (Anglican 13.3%, Uniting Church 3.7%, Presbyterian and Reformed 2.3%, Baptist 1.5%, Pentecostal 1.1%, Lutheran .7%, other Protestant .5%), Roman Catholic 22.6%, other Christian 4.2%, Muslim 2.6%, Buddhist 2.4%, Orthodox 2.3% (Eastern Orthodox 2.1%, Oriental Orthodox .2%), Hindu 1.9%, other 1.3%, none 30.1%, unspecified 9.6% (2016 est.)

Age structure: *0-14 years:* 18.72% (male 2,457,418/female 2,309,706)
15-24 years: 12.89% (male 1,710,253/female 1,572,794)
25-54 years: 41.15% (male 5,224,840/female 5,255,041)
55-64 years: 11.35% (male 1,395,844/female 1,495,806)
65 years and over: 15.88% (male 1,866,761/female 2,177,996) (2020 est.)

Dependency ratios: *total dependency ratio:* 55.1
youth dependency ratio: 29.9
elderly dependency ratio: 25.1
potential support ratio: 4 (2020 est.)

Median age: *total:* 37.5 years
male: 36.5 years
female: 38.5 years (2020 est.)
country comparison to the world: 69

Population growth rate: 1.25% (2022 est.)
country comparison to the world: 74

Birth rate: 12.3 births/1,000 population (2022 est.)
country comparison to the world: 150

Death rate: 6.77 deaths/1,000 population (2022 est.)
country comparison to the world: 127

Net migration rate: 6.93 migrant(s)/1,000 population (2022 est.)
country comparison to the world: 14

Population distribution: population is primarily located on the periphery, with the highest concentration of people residing in the east and southeast; a secondary population center is located in and around Perth in the west; of the States and Territories, New South Wales has, by far, the largest population; the interior, or "outback", has a very sparse population

Urbanization: *urban population:* 86.5% of total population (2022)
rate of urbanization: 1.27% annual rate of change (2020-25 est.)
note: data include Christmas Island, Cocos Islands, and Norfolk Island

Major urban areas - population: 5.151 million Melbourne, 5.057 million Sydney, 2.472 million Brisbane, 2.093 million Perth, 1.356 million Adelaide, 467,000 CANBERRA (capital) (2022)

Sex ratio: *at birth:* 1.06 male(s)/female
0-14 years: 1.07 male(s)/female
15-24 years: 1.09 male(s)/female
25-54 years: 1 male(s)/female
55-64 years: 0.93 male(s)/female
65 years and over: 0.72 male(s)/female
total population: 0.99 male(s)/female (2022 est.)

Mother's mean age at first birth: 28.7 years (2019 est.)

Maternal mortality ratio: 6 deaths/100,000 live births (2017 est.)
country comparison to the world: 159

Infant mortality rate: *total:* 3.01 deaths/1,000 live births
male: 3.24 deaths/1,000 live births
female: 2.76 deaths/1,000 live births (2022 est.)
country comparison to the world: 213

Life expectancy at birth: *total population:* 83.09 years
male: 80.93 years
female: 85.36 years (2022 est.)
country comparison to the world: 14

Total fertility rate: 1.73 children born/woman (2022 est.)
country comparison to the world: 159

Contraceptive prevalence rate: 66.9% (2015/16)
note: percent of women aged 18-44

Drinking water source: *improved: urban:* 100% of population
rural: 100% of population
total: 100% of population

Current health expenditure: 9.9% of GDP (2019)

Physicians density: 4.13 physicians/1,000 population (2020)

Hospital bed density: 3.8 beds/1,000 population (2016)

Sanitation facility access: *improved: total:* 100% of population *unimproved: total:* 0% of population (2020 est.)

HIV/AIDS - adult prevalence rate: 0.1% (2020 est.)
country comparison to the world: 118

Obesity - adult prevalence rate: 29% (2016)
country comparison to the world: 27

Alcohol consumption per capita: *total:* 9.51 liters of pure alcohol (2019 est.)
beer: 3.71 liters of pure alcohol (2019 est.)
wine: 3.67 liters of pure alcohol (2019 est.)
spirits: 1.32 liters of pure alcohol (2019 est.)
other alcohols: 0.81 liters of pure alcohol (2019 est.)
country comparison to the world: 27

Tobacco use: *total:* 13.6% (2020 est.)
male: 15.6% (2020 est.)
female: 11.5% (2020 est.)
country comparison to the world: 113

Education expenditures: 5.1% of GDP (2018 est.)
country comparison to the world: 56

School life expectancy (primary to tertiary education): *total:* 22 years
male: 21 years
female: 22 years (2019)

Unemployment, youth ages 15-24: *total:* 14.3%
male: 15.3%
female: 13.2% (2020 est.)

ENVIRONMENT

Environment - current issues: soil erosion from overgrazing, deforestation, industrial development, urbanization, and poor farming practices; limited natural freshwater resources; soil salinity rising due to the use of poor quality water; drought, desertification; clearing for agricultural purposes threatens the natural habitat of many unique animal and plant species; disruption of the fragile ecosystem has resulted in significant floral extinctions; the Great Barrier Reef off the northeast coast, the largest coral reef in the world, is threatened by increased shipping and its popularity as a tourist site; overfishing, pollution, and invasive species are also problems

Environment - international agreements: *party to:* Antarctic-Environmental Protection, Antarctic-Marine Living Resources, Antarctic Seals, Antarctic Treaty, Biodiversity, Climate Change, Climate Change-Kyoto Protocol, Climate Change-Paris Agreement, Comprehensive Nuclear Test Ban, Desertification, Endangered Species, Environmental Modification, Hazardous Wastes, Law of the Sea, Marine Dumping-London Convention, Marine Dumping-London Protocol, Marine Life Conservation, Nuclear Test Ban, Ozone Layer Protection, Ship Pollution, Tropical Timber 2006, Wetlands, Whaling
signed, but not ratified: none of the selected agreements

Air pollutants: *particulate matter emissions:* 7.19 micrograms per cubic meter (2016 est.)
carbon dioxide emissions: 375.91 megatons (2016 est.)
methane emissions: 105.01 megatons (2020 est.)

Climate: generally arid to semiarid; temperate in south and east; tropical in north

Land use: *agricultural land:* 46.65% (2018 est.)
arable land: 4.03% (2018 est.)
permanent crops: 0.04% (2018 est.)
permanent pasture: 42.58% (2018 est.)
forest: 17.42% (2018 est.)
other: 33.42% (2018 est.)

Urbanization: *urban population:* 86.5% of total population (2022)
rate of urbanization: 1.27% annual rate of change (2020-25 est.)
note: data include Christmas Island, Cocos Islands, and Norfolk Island

Revenue from forest resources: *forest revenues:* 0.13% of GDP (2018 est.)
country comparison to the world: 105

Revenue from coal: *coal revenues:* 0.78% of GDP (2018 est.)
country comparison to the world: 7

Waste and recycling: *municipal solid waste generated annually:* 13.345 million tons (2015 est.)
municipal solid waste recycled annually: 5,618,245 tons (2015 est.)
percent of municipal solid waste recycled: 42.1% (2015 est.)

Major lakes (area sq km): *fresh water lake(s):* Lake Alexandrina - 570 sq km
salt water lake(s): Lake Eyre - 9,690 sq km; Lake Torrens (ephemeral) - 5,780 sq km; Lake Gairdner - 4,470 sq km; Lake Mackay (ephemeral) - 3,494 sq km; Lake Frome - 2,410 sq km; Lake Amadeus (ephemeral) - 1,032 sq km

Major rivers (by length in km): River Murray - 2,508 km; Darling River - 1,545 km; Murrumbidgee River - 1,485 km; Lachlan River - 1,339 km; Cooper Creek - 1,113 km; Flinders River - 1,004 km

Major watersheds (area sq km):

Indian Ocean drainage: *(Great Australian Bight)* Murray-Darling (1,050,116 sq km)

Internal *(endorheic basin)* drainage: Lake Eyre (1,212,198 sq km)

Major aquifers: Great Artesian Basin, Canning Basin

Total water withdrawal: *municipal:* 3.392 billion cubic meters (2017 est.)
industrial: 2.662 billion cubic meters (2017 est.)
agricultural: 10.5 billion cubic meters (2017 est.)

Total renewable water resources: 492 billion cubic meters (2017 est.)

GOVERNMENT

Country name: *conventional long form:* Commonwealth of Australia
conventional short form: Australia
etymology: the name Australia derives from the Latin "australis" meaning "southern"; the Australian landmass was long referred to as "Terra Australis" or the Southern Land

Government type: federal parliamentary democracy under a constitutional monarchy; a Commonwealth realm

Capital: *name:* Canberra
geographic coordinates: 35 16 S, 149 08 E
time difference: UTC+10 (14 hours ahead of Washington, DC, during Standard Time)
daylight saving time: +1hr, begins first Sunday in October; ends first Sunday in April
time zone note: Australia has four time zones, including Lord Howe Island (UTC+10:30)
etymology: the name is claimed to derive from either Kambera or Camberry, which are names corrupted from the original native designation for the area "Nganbra" or "Nganbira"

Administrative divisions: 6 states and 2 territories*; Australian Capital Territory*, New South Wales, Northern Territory*, Queensland, South Australia, Tasmania, Victoria, Western Australia

Dependent areas: Ashmore and Cartier Islands, Christmas Island, Cocos (Keeling) Islands, Coral Sea Islands, Heard Island and McDonald Islands, Norfolk Island

Independence: 1 January 1901 (from the federation of UK colonies)

National holiday: Australia Day (commemorates the arrival of the First Fleet of Australian settlers), 26 January (1788); ANZAC Day (commemorates the anniversary of the landing of troops of the Australian and New Zealand Army Corps during World War I at Gallipoli, Turkey), 25 April (1915)

Constitution: *history:* approved in a series of referenda from 1898 through 1900 and became law 9 July 1900, effective 1 January 1901
amendments: proposed by Parliament; passage requires approval of a referendum bill by absolute majority vote in both houses of Parliament, approval in a referendum by a majority of voters in at least four states and in the territories, and Royal Assent; proposals that would reduce a state's representation in either house or change a state's boundaries require that state's approval prior to Royal Assent; amended several times, last in 1977

Legal system: common law system based on the English model

International law organization participation: accepts compulsory ICJ jurisdiction with reservations; accepts ICCt jurisdiction

Citizenship: *citizenship by birth:* no
citizenship by descent only: at least one parent must be a citizen or permanent resident of Australia
dual citizenship recognized: yes
residency requirement for naturalization: 4 years

Suffrage: 18 years of age; universal and compulsory

Executive branch: *chief of state:* King CHARLES III (since 8 September 2022); represented by Governor General David HURLEY (since 1 July 2019)
head of government: Prime Minister Anthony ALBANESE (since 23 May 2022)
cabinet: Cabinet nominated by the prime minister from among members of Parliament and sworn in by the governor general
elections/appointments: the monarchy is hereditary; governor general appointed by the monarch on the recommendation of the prime minister; following legislative elections, the leader of the majority party or majority coalition is sworn in as prime minister by the governor general

Legislative branch: *description:* bicameral Federal Parliament consists of:
Senate (76 seats; 12 members from each of the 6 states and 2 each from the 2 mainland territories; members directly elected in multi-seat constituencies by proportional representation vote; members serve 6-year terms with one-half of state membership renewed every 3 years and territory membership renewed every 3 years)
House of Representatives (151 seats; members directly elected in single-seat constituencies by majority preferential vote; members serve terms of up to 3 years)
elections:

Senate - last held on 21 May 2022 (next to be held on May 2025)
House of Representatives - last held on 21 May 2022 (next to be held on May 2025)
election results:
Senate (initial results) - percent of vote by party - Liberal/National coalition 32.13%, ALP 29.81%, The Greens 13.85%, One Nation 4.38%, Lambie Network .26%; seats by party - Liberal/National coalition 29, ALP 21, The Greens 9, One Nation 1, Lambie Network 1, undecided 14
House of Representatives (initial results) - percent of vote by party - ALP 32.83%, Liberal/National coalition 35.77%, The Greens 11.85%, Katter's Australian Party 0.4%, Centre Alliance 0.24%, independents 5.52%; seats by party - ALP 76, Liberal/National Coalition 57, The Greens 4, Katter's Australian Party 1, Centre Alliance 1, independent 10, undecided 2

Judicial branch: *highest court(s):* High Court of Australia (consists of 7 justices, including the chief justice); note - each of the 6 states, 2 territories, and Norfolk Island has a Supreme Court; the High Court is the final appellate court beyond the state and territory supreme courts
judge selection and term of office: justices appointed by the governor-general in council for life with mandatory retirement at age 70
subordinate courts: subordinate courts: at the federal level: Federal Court; Federal Circuit and Family Court of Australia; *at the state and territory level:* Local Court - New South Wales; Magistrates' Courts – Victoria, Queensland, South Australia, Western Australia, Tasmania, Northern Territory, Australian Capital Territory; District Courts – New South Wales, Queensland, South Australia, Western Australia; County Court – Victoria; Family Court – Western Australia; Court of Petty Sessions – Norfolk Island

Political parties and leaders: Australian Greens Party or The Greens [Adam BANDT]
Australian Labor Party or ALP [Anthony ALBANESE]
Liberal Party of Australia [Peter DUTTON]
The Nationals [David LITTLEPROUD]
Pauline Hanson's One Nation or PHON or ONP [Pauline HANSON]

International organization participation: ADB, ANZUS, APEC, ARF, ASEAN (dialogue partner), Australia Group, BIS, C, CD, CP, EAS, EBRD, EITI (implementing country), FAO, FATF, G-20, IAEA, IBRD, ICAO, ICC (national committees), ICCt, ICRM, IDA, IEA, IFC, IFRCS, IHO, ILO, IMF, IMO, IMSO, Interpol, IOC, IOM, IPU, ISO, ITSO, ITU, ITUC (NGOs), MIGA, NEA, NSG, OECD, OPCW, OSCE (partner), Pacific Alliance (observer), Paris Club, PCA, PIF, SAARC (observer), Quad, SICA (observer), Sparteca, SPC, UN, UNCTAD, UNESCO, UNHCR, UNMISS, UNMIT, UNRWA, UNTSO, UNWTO, UPU, Wassenaar Arrangement, WCO, WFTU (NGOs), WHO, WIPO, WMO, WTO, ZC

Diplomatic representation in the US: *chief of mission:* Ambassador Arthur SINODINOS (since 6 February 2020)
chancery: 1601 Massachusetts Avenue NW, Washington, DC 20036
telephone: [1] (202) 797-3000
FAX: [1] (202) 797-3168
email address and website:
https://usa.embassy.gov.au/
consulate(s) general: Chicago, Honolulu, Houston, Los Angeles, New York, San Francisco

Diplomatic representation from the US: *chief of mission:* Ambassador Caroline KENNEDY (since 25 July 2022)
embassy: Moonah Place, Yarralumla, Australian Capital Territory 2600
mailing address: 7800 Canberra Place, Washington DC 20512-7800
telephone: [61] (02) 6214-5600
FAX: [61] (02) 9373-9184
email address and website:
AskEmbassyCanberra@state.gov
https://au.usembassy.gov/
consulate(s) general: Melbourne, Perth, Sydney

Flag description: blue with the flag of the UK in the upper hoist-side quadrant and a large seven-pointed star in the lower hoist-side quadrant known as the Commonwealth or Federation Star, representing the federation of the colonies of Australia in 1901; the star depicts one point for each of the six original states and one representing all of Australia's internal and external territories; on the fly half is a representation of the Southern Cross constellation in white with one small, five pointed star and four larger, seven-pointed stars

National symbol(s): Commonwealth Star (seven-pointed Star of Federation), golden wattle tree (Acacia pycnantha Benth), kangaroo, emu; national colors: green, gold

Commonwealth Coat of Arms:

National anthem: *name:* Advance Australia Fair
lyrics/music: Peter Dodds McCORMICK
note 1: adopted 1984; although originally written in the late 19th century, the anthem was not used for all official occasions until 1984; as a Commonwealth country, in addition to the national anthem, "God Save the King" serves as the royal anthem (see United Kingdom)
note 2: the well-known and much-loved bush ballad "Waltzing Matilda" is often referred to as Australia's unofficial national anthem; the original lyrics were written in 1895 by Australian poet Banjo PATERSON, and were first published as sheet music in 1903; since 2012, a Waltzing Matilda Day has been held annually on 6 April, the anniversary of the first performance of the song in 1895

National heritage: *total World Heritage Sites:* 20 (4 cultural, 12 natural, 4 mixed); note - includes one site on Heard Island and McDonald Islands
selected World Heritage Site locales: Great Barrier Reef (n); Greater Blue Mountains Area (n); Fraser Island (n); Gondwana Rainforests (n); Lord Howe Island Group (n); Royal Exhibition Building and Carlton Gardens (c); Shark Bay (n); Sydney Opera House (c); Uluru-Kata Tjuta National Park (m); Kakadu National Park (m)

ECONOMY

Economic overview: Australia is an open market with minimal restrictions on imports of goods and services. The process of opening up has increased productivity, stimulated growth, and made the economy more flexible and dynamic. Australia plays an active role in the WTO, APEC, the G20, and other trade forums. Australia's free trade agreement (FTA) with China entered into force in 2015, adding to existing FTAs with the Republic of Korea, Japan, Chile, Malaysia, New Zealand, Singapore, Thailand, and the US, and a regional FTA with ASEAN and New Zealand. Australia continues to negotiate bilateral agreements with Indonesia, as well as larger agreements with its Pacific neighbors and the Gulf Cooperation Council countries, and an Asia-wide Regional Comprehensive Economic Partnership that includes the 10 ASEAN countries and China, Japan, Korea, New Zealand, and India.

Australia is a significant exporter of natural resources, energy, and food. Australia's abundant and diverse natural resources attract high levels of foreign investment and include extensive reserves of coal, iron, copper, gold, natural gas, uranium, and renewable energy sources. A series of major investments, such as the US$40 billion Gorgon Liquid Natural Gas Project, will significantly expand the resources sector.

For nearly two decades up till 2017, Australia had benefited from a dramatic surge in its terms of trade. As export prices increased faster than import prices, the economy experienced continuous growth, low unemployment, contained inflation, very low public debt, and a strong and stable financial system. Australia entered 2018 facing a range of growth constraints, principally driven by the sharp fall in global prices of key export commodities. Demand for resources and energy from Asia and especially China is growing at a slower pace and sharp drops in export prices have impacted growth.

Real GDP (purchasing power parity): $1,250,900,000,000 (2020 est.)
$1,254,480,000,000 (2019 est.)
$1,227,940,000,000 (2018 est.)
note: data are in 2017 dollars
country comparison to the world: 18

Real GDP growth rate: 1.84% (2019 est.)
2.77% (2018 est.)
2.45% (2017 est.)
country comparison to the world: 145

Real GDP per capita: $48,700 (2020 est.)
$49,500 (2019 est.)
$49,200 (2018 est.)
note: data are in 2017 dollars
country comparison to the world: 30

GDP (official exchange rate): $1,390,790,000,000 (2019 est.)

Inflation rate (consumer prices): 1.6% (2019 est.)
1.9% (2018 est.)
1.9% (2017 est.)
country comparison to the world: 91

Credit ratings:

Fitch rating: AAA (2011)

Moody's rating: Aaa (2002)

Standard & Poors rating: AAA (2003)
note: The year refers to the year in which the current credit rating was first obtained.

GDP - composition, by sector of origin: *agriculture:* 3.6% (2017 est.)
industry: 25.3% (2017 est.)
services: 71.2% (2017 est.)

GDP - composition, by end use: *household consumption:* 56.9% (2017 est.)
government consumption: 18.4% (2017 est.)
investment in fixed capital: 24.1% (2017 est.)
investment in inventories: 0.1% (2017 est.)
exports of goods and services: 21.5% (2017 est.)
imports of goods and services: -21% (2017 est.)

Agricultural products: sugar cane, wheat, barley, milk, rapeseed, beef, cotton, grapes, poultry, potatoes

Industries: mining, industrial and transportation equipment, food processing, chemicals, steel

Industrial production growth rate: 1.4% (2017 est.)
country comparison to the world: 144

Labor force: 12.568 million (2020 est.)
country comparison to the world: 43

Labor force - by occupation: *agriculture:* 3.6%
industry: 21.1%
services: 75.3% (2009 est.)

Unemployment rate: 5.16% (2019 est.)
5.29% (2018 est.)
country comparison to the world: 83

Unemployment, youth ages 15-24: *total:* 14.3%
male: 15.3%
female: 13.2% (2020 est.)
country comparison to the world: 112

Gini Index coefficient - distribution of family income:
34.4 (2014 est.)
35.2 (1994)
country comparison to the world: 113

Household income or consumption by percentage share: *lowest 10%:* 2%
highest 10%: 25.4% (1994)

Budget: *revenues:* 490 billion (2017 est.)
expenditures: 496.9 billion (2017 est.)

Budget surplus (+) or deficit (-): -0.5% (of GDP) (2017 est.)
country comparison to the world: 60

Public debt: 40.8% of GDP (2017 est.)
40.6% of GDP (2016 est.)
country comparison to the world: 123

Taxes and other revenues: 35.5% (of GDP) (2017 est.)
country comparison to the world: 61

Fiscal year: 1 July - 30 June

Current account balance: $8.146 billion (2019 est.)
-$29.777 billion (2018 est.)
country comparison to the world: 27

Exports: $299.04 billion (2020 est.)
$342.43 billion (2019 est.)
$327.32 billion (2018 est.)
note: Data are in current year dollars and do not include illicit exports or re-exports.
country comparison to the world: 23

Exports - partners: China 39%, Japan 15%, South Korea 7%, India 5% (2019)

Exports - commodities: iron ore, coal, natural gas, gold, aluminum oxide (2019)

Imports: $249.07 billion (2020 est.) note: data are in current year dollars
$295.46 billion (2019 est.) note: data are in current year dollars
$310.23 billion (2018 est.) note: data are in current year dollars
country comparison to the world: 23

Imports - partners: China 25%, United States 12%, Japan 7%, Germany 5%, Thailand 5% (2019)

Imports - commodities: refined petroleum, cars, crude petroleum, broadcasting equipment, delivery trucks (2019)

Reserves of foreign exchange and gold: $66.58 billion (31 December 2017 est.)
$55.07 billion (31 December 2016 est.)
country comparison to the world: 33

Debt - external: $3,115,913,000,000 (2019 est.)
$2,837,818,000,000 (2018 est.)
country comparison to the world: 8

Exchange rates: Australian dollars (AUD) per US dollar -
1.34048 (2020 est.)
1.46402 (2019 est.)
1.38552 (2018 est.)
1.3291 (2014 est.)
1.1094 (2013 est.)

ENERGY

Electricity access: *electrification - total population:* 100% (2020)

Electricity: *installed generating capacity:* 82.517 million kW (2020 est.)
consumption: 237,388,272,000 kWh (2019 est.)
exports: 0 kWh (2020 est.)
imports: 0 kWh (2020 est.)
transmission/distribution losses: 12,607,778,000 kWh (2019 est.)

Electricity generation sources: *fossil fuels:* 75.4% of total installed capacity (2020 est.)
solar: 8.6% of total installed capacity (2020 est.)
wind: 8.4% of total installed capacity (2020 est.)
hydroelectricity: 6.2% of total installed capacity (2020 est.)
biomass and waste: 1.4% of total installed capacity (2020 est.)

Coal: *production:* 504.051 million metric tons (2020 est.)
consumption: 99.048 million metric tons (2020 est.)
exports: 390.808 million metric tons (2020 est.)
imports: 583,000 metric tons (2020 est.)
proven reserves: 149.079 billion metric tons (2019 est.)

Petroleum: *total petroleum production:* 442,500 bbl/day (2021 est.)
refined petroleum consumption: 1,174,100 bbl/day (2019 est.)
crude oil and lease condensate exports: 197,700 bbl/day (2018 est.)
crude oil and lease condensate imports: 356,900 bbl/day (2018 est.)
crude oil estimated reserves: 2.446 billion barrels (2021 est.)

Refined petroleum products - production: 462,500 bbl/day (2017 est.)
country comparison to the world: 35

Refined petroleum products - exports: 64,120 bbl/day (2017 est.)
country comparison to the world: 48

Refined petroleum products - imports: 619,600 bbl/day (2017 est.)
country comparison to the world: 12

Natural gas: *production:* 142,104,321,000 cubic meters (2020 est.)
consumption: 41,905,381,000 cubic meters (2020 est.)
exports: 101,766,728,000 cubic meters (2020 est.)
imports: 6,295,646,000 cubic meters (2020 est.)
proven reserves: 3,228,115,000,000 cubic meters (2021 est.)

Carbon dioxide emissions: 417.87 million metric tonnes of CO_2 (2019 est.)
from coal and metallurgical coke: 162.26 million metric tonnes of CO_2 (2019 est.)
from petroleum and other liquids: 158.668 million metric tonnes of CO_2 (2019 est.)
from consumed natural gas: 96.942 million metric tonnes of CO_2 (2019 est.)
country comparison to the world: 15

Energy consumption per capita: 241.004 million Btu/person (2019 est.)
country comparison to the world: 16

COMMUNICATIONS

Telephones - fixed lines: *total subscriptions:* 6.2 million (2020 est.)
subscriptions per 100 inhabitants: 24 (2020 est.)
country comparison to the world: 23

Telephones - mobile cellular: *total subscriptions:* 27.453 million (2020 est.)
subscriptions per 100 inhabitants: 108 (2020 est.)
country comparison to the world: 48

Telecommunication systems: *general assessment:* the Australian telecom market since 2020 has been impacted by the pandemic, which forced many people to school and work from home and thus adopt fixed-line broadband services; internet traffic, both fixed and mobile, increased substantially as a result; in the fixed sector, there is an ongoing migration from copper-based platforms to fiber; the extension of fixed wireless access will mean that up to 120,000 premises currently dependent on satellite broadband will be able to access 5G-based fixed services; the fixed-line market has been falling steadily over the past five years; in the Australian fixed broadband market, there is a dynamic shift among customers to fiber networks; the DSL sector is steadily shrinking while subscribers on HFC infrastructure will continue to be provided by existing cable, with a steady migration to full fiber connectivity (2022)
domestic: 24 per 100 fixed-line telephone subscriptions and 108 per 100 mobile-cellular; more subscribers to mobile services than there are people; 90% of all mobile device sales are now smartphones, growth in mobile traffic brisk (2020)
international: country code - 61; landing points for more than 20 submarine cables including: the SeaMeWe-3 optical telecommunications submarine cable with links to Asia, the Middle East, and Europe; the INDIGO-Central, INDIGO West and ASC, North West Cable System, Australia-Papua New Guinea cable, CSCS, PPC-1, Gondwana-1, SCCN, Hawaiki, TGA, Basslink, Bass Strait-1, Bass Strait-2, JGA-S, with links to other Australian cities, New Zealand and many countries in southeast Asia, US and Europe; the H2 Cable, AJC, Telstra Endeavor, Southern Cross NEXT with links to Japan, Hong Kong, and other Pacific Ocean countries as well as the US; satellite earth stations - 10 Intelsat (4 Indian Ocean and 6 Pacific Ocean), 2 Inmarsat, 2 Globalstar, 5 other (2019)

Broadcast media: the Australian Broadcasting Corporation (ABC) runs multiple national and local radio networks and TV stations, as well as ABC Australia, a TV service that broadcasts in the Asia-Pacific region and is the main public broadcaster; Special Broadcasting Service (SBS), a second large public broadcaster, operates radio and TV networks broadcasting in multiple languages; several large national commercial TV networks, a large number of local commercial TV stations, and hundreds of commercial radio stations are accessible; cable and satellite systems are available (2022)

Internet country code: .au

Internet users: *total:* 23,123,940 (2020 est.)
percent of population: 90% (2020 est.)
country comparison to the world: 36

Broadband - fixed subscriptions: *total:* 9,099,619 (2020 est.)
subscriptions per 100 inhabitants: 36 (2020 est.)
country comparison to the world: 23

TRANSPORTATION

National air transport system: *number of registered air carriers:* 25 (2020)
inventory of registered aircraft operated by air carriers: 583
annual passenger traffic on registered air carriers: 75,667,645 (2018)
annual freight traffic on registered air carriers: 2,027,640,000 (2018) mt-km

Civil aircraft registration country code prefix: VH

Airports: *total:* 418 (2021)
country comparison to the world: 19

Airports - with paved runways: *total:* 349
over 3,047 m: 11
2,438 to 3,047 m: 14
1,524 to 2,437 m: 155
914 to 1,523 m: 155
under 914 m: 14 (2021)

Airports - with unpaved runways: *total:* 131
1,524 to 2,437 m: 16
914 to 1,523 m: 101
under 914 m: 14 (2021)

Heliports: 1 (2021)

Pipelines: 637 km condensate/gas, 30,054 km gas, 240 km liquid petroleum gas, 3,609 km oil, 110 km oil/gas/water, 72 km refined products (2013)

Railways: *total:* 33,011 km (2015)
standard gauge: 17,446 km (2015) 1.435-m gauge (650 km electrified)
narrow gauge: 12,318 km (2015) 1.067-m gauge (2,075.5 km electrified)
broad gauge: 3,247 km (2015) 1.600-m gauge (372 km electrified)
country comparison to the world: 8

Roadways: *total:* 873,573 km (2015)
urban: 145,928 km (2015)
non-urban: 727,645 km (2015)
country comparison to the world: 9

Waterways: 2,000 km (2011) (mainly used for recreation on Murray and Murray-Darling River systems)
country comparison to the world: 44

Merchant marine: *total:* 581
by type: bulk carrier 2, general cargo 76, oil tanker 7, other 496 (2021)
country comparison to the world: 40

Ports and terminals: *major seaport(s):*
Indian Ocean: Adelaide, Darwin, Fremantle, Geelong, Melbourne
Pacific Ocean: Brisbane, Cairns, Gladstone, Hobart, Newcastle, Port Port Kembla, Sydney
container port(s) (TEUs): Melbourne (2,967,315), Sydney (2,572,714) (2019)
LNG terminal(s) (export): Australia Pacific, Barrow Island, Burrup (Pluto), Curtis Island, Darwin, Karratha, Bladin Point (Ichthys), Gladstone, Prelude (offshore FLNG), Wheatstone
dry bulk cargo port(s): Dampier (iron ore), Dalrymple Bay (coal), Hay Point (coal), Port Hedland (iron ore), Port Walcott (iron ore)

MILITARY AND SECURITY

Military and security forces: Australian Defense Force (ADF): Australian Army, Royal Australian Navy, Royal Australian Air Force (2022)
note: the Army includes a Special Operations Command, while the Navy includes a Naval Aviation Force

Military expenditures: 2% of GDP (2022 est.)
2.1% of GDP (2021)
2.1% of GDP (2020)
2% of GDP (2019) (approximately $31.5 billion)
1.9% of GDP (2018) (approximately $29.8 billion)
country comparison to the world: 55

Military and security service personnel strengths: approximately 60,000 active troops (30,000 Army; 15,000 Navy; 15,000 Air Force) (2022)

Military equipment inventories and acquisitions: the Australian military's inventory includes a mix of domestically-produced and imported Western weapons systems; since 2015, the US is the largest supplier of arms; the Australian defense industry produces a variety of land and sea weapons platforms; the defense industry also participates in joint development and production ventures with other Western countries, including the US and Canada (2022)

Military service age and obligation: 17 years of age for voluntary military service (with parental consent); no conscription (abolished 1973); women allowed to serve in all roles, including combat arms, since 2013 (2022)
note 1: foreign nationals who are permanent residents, particularly New Zealanders, or those who have applied for citizenship or overseas candidates who have appropriate experience and qualifications from an overseas military can apply to join the ADF
note 2: in 2020-2021, women comprised nearly 20% of the military

Military deployments: *note:* since the 1990s, Australia has deployed more than 30,000 personnel on nearly 100 UN peacekeeping and coalition military operations, including in Cambodia, Rwanda, the Solomon Islands, Somalia, and East Timor

Military - note: Australia has been part of the Australia, New Zealand, and US Security (ANZUS) Treaty since 1951; Australia is also a member of the Five Powers Defense Arrangements (FPDA), a series of mutual assistance agreements reached in 1971 embracing Australia, Malaysia, New Zealand, Singapore, and the UK; the FPDA commits the members to consult with one another in the event or threat of an armed attack on any of the members and to mutually decide what measures should be taken, jointly or separately; there is no specific obligation to intervene militarily

Australia has a long-standing military relationship with the US; Australian and US forces first fought together in France in 1918 at the Battle of Hamel, and have fought together in every major US conflict since; Australia and the US signed an agreement in 2014 that allowed for closer bi-lateral defense and security cooperation, including annual rotations of US Marines and enhanced rotations of US Air Force aircraft to Australia; Australian military forces train often with US forces; Australia has Major Non-NATO Ally (MNNA) status with the US, a designation under US law that provides foreign partners with certain benefits in the areas of defense trade and security cooperation: Australia also has long-standing defense and security ties to the UK, including a Defense and Security Cooperation Treaty signed in 2013; in 2020, Australia and the UK signed a memorandum of understanding to cooperate on the building of a next generation of frigates for their respective navies; the Australia-UK Ministerial Consultations (AUKMIN) is their premier bilateral forum on foreign policy, defense, and security issues

in 2021, Australia, the UK, and the US announced an enhanced trilateral security partnership called "AUKUS" which would build on existing bilateral ties, including deeper integration of defense and security-related science, technology, industrial bases, and supply chains, as well as deeper cooperation on a range of defense and security capabilities; the first initiative under AUKUS was a commitment to support Australia in acquiring conventionally armed nuclear-powered submarines for the Royal Australian Navy (2022)

TERRORISM

Terrorist group(s): Islamic State of Iraq and ash-Sham (ISIS)

TRANSNATIONAL ISSUES

Disputes - international: *Australia-Indonesia (Maritime Boundary):* All borders between Indonesia and Australia have been agreed upon bilaterally, but a 1997 treaty that would settle the last of their maritime and EEZ boundary has yet to be ratified by Indonesia's legislature. Indonesian groups challenge Australia's claim to Ashmore Reef. Australia closed parts of the Ashmore and Cartier reserve to Indonesian traditional fishing.
Australia-Timor-Leste (Maritime Boundary): In 2007, Australia and Timor-Leste agreed to a 50-year development zone and revenue sharing arrangement and deferred a maritime boundary.

Refugees and internally displaced persons: *refugees (country of origin):* 12,701 (Iran), 10,108 (Afghanistan), 5,400 (Pakistan) (mid-year 2021)
stateless persons: 5,770 (mid-year 2021)

Illicit drugs: Tasmania is one of the world's major suppliers of licit opiate products; government maintains strict controls over areas of opium poppy cultivation and output of poppy straw concentrate; major consumer of cocaine and amphetamines

AUSTRIA

INTRODUCTION

Background: Once the center of power for the large Austro-Hungarian Empire, Austria was reduced to a small republic after its defeat in World War I. Following annexation by Nazi Germany in 1938 and subsequent occupation by the victorious Allies in 1945, Austria's status remained unclear for a decade. A State Treaty signed in 1955 ended the occupation, recognized Austria's independence, and forbade unification with Germany. A constitutional law that same year declared the country's "perpetual neutrality" as a condition for Soviet military withdrawal. The Soviet Union's collapse in 1991 and Austria's entry into the EU in 1995 have altered the meaning of this neutrality. A prosperous, democratic country, Austria entered the EU Economic and Monetary Union in 1999.

GEOGRAPHY

Location: Central Europe, north of Italy and Slovenia

Geographic coordinates: 47 20 N, 13 20 E

Map references: Europe

Area: *total:* 83,871 sq km
land: 82,445 sq km
water: 1,426 sq km
country comparison to the world: 114

Area - comparative: about the size of South Carolina; slightly more than two-thirds the size of Pennsylvania

Land boundaries: *total:* 2,524 km
border countries (8): Czech Republic 402 km; Germany 801 km; Hungary 321 km; Italy 404 km; Liechtenstein 34 km; Slovakia 105 km; Slovenia 299 km; Switzerland 158 km

Coastline: 0 km (landlocked)

Maritime claims: none (landlocked)

Climate: temperate; continental, cloudy; cold winters with frequent rain and some snow in lowlands and snow in mountains; moderate summers with occasional showers

Terrain: mostly mountains (Alps) in the west and south; mostly flat or gently sloping along the eastern and northern margins

Elevation: *highest point:* Grossglockner 3,798 m
lowest point: Neusiedler See 115 m
mean elevation: 910 m

Natural resources: oil, coal, lignite, timber, iron ore, copper, zinc, antimony, magnesite, tungsten, graphite, salt, hydropower

Land use: *agricultural land:* 38.4% (2018 est.)
arable land: 16.5% (2018 est.)
permanent crops: 0.8% (2018 est.)
permanent pasture: 21.1% (2018 est.)
forest: 47.2% (2018 est.)
other: 14.4% (2018 est.)

Irrigated land: 1,170 sq km (2012)

Major lakes (area sq km): *fresh water lake(s):* Lake Constance (shared with Switzerland and Germany) - 540 sq km

Major rivers (by length in km): Danube (shared with Germany [s], Slovakia, Czechia, Hungary, Croatia, Serbia, Bulgaria, Ukraine, Moldova, and Romania [m]) - 2,888 km
note – [s] after country name indicates river source; [m] after country name indicates river mouth

Major watersheds (area sq km):

Atlantic Ocean drainage: Rhine-Maas (198,735 sq km), *(Black Sea)* Danube (795,656 sq km)

Population distribution: the northern and eastern portions of the country are more densely populated; nearly two-thirds of the populace lives in urban areas

Natural hazards: landslides; avalanches; earthquakes

Geography - note: *note 1:* landlocked; strategic location at the crossroads of central Europe with many easily traversable Alpine passes and valleys; major river is the Danube; population is concentrated on eastern lowlands because of steep slopes, poor soils, and low temperatures elsewhere
note 2: the world's largest and longest ice cave system at 42 km (26 mi) is the Eisriesenwelt (Ice Giants World) inside the Hochkogel mountain near Werfen, about 40 km south of Salzburg; ice caves are bedrock caves that contain year-round ice formations; they differ from glacial caves, which are transient and are formed by melting ice and flowing water within and under glaciers

PEOPLE AND SOCIETY

Population: 8,913,088 (2022 est.)
country comparison to the world: 99

Nationality: *noun:* Austrian(s)
adjective: Austrian

Ethnic groups: Austrian 80.8%, German 2.6%, Bosnian and Herzegovinian 1.9%, Turkish 1.8%, Serbian 1.6%, Romanian 1.3%, other 10% (2018 est.)
note: data represent population by country of birth

Languages: German (official nationwide) 88.6%, Turkish 2.3%, Serbian 2.2%, Croatian (official in Burgenland) 1.6%, other (includes Slovene, official in southern Carinthia, and Hungarian, official in Burgenland) 5.3% (2001 est.)
major-language sample(s):
Das World Factbook, die unverzichtbare Quelle für grundlegende Informationen. (German)

Religions: Catholic 57%, Eastern Orthodox 8.7%, Muslim 7.9%, Evangelical Christian 3.3%, other/none/unspecified 23.1% (2018 est.)
note: data on Muslim is a 2016 estimate; data on other/none/unspecified are from 2012-2018 estimates

Age structure: *0-14 years:* 14.01% (male 635,803/female 605,065)
15-24 years: 10.36% (male 466,921/female 451,248)
25-54 years: 41.35% (male 1,831,704/female 1,831,669)
55-64 years: 14.41% (male 635,342/female 641,389)
65 years and over: 19.87% (male 768,687/female 991,621) (2020 est.)

Dependency ratios: *total dependency ratio:* 50.6
youth dependency ratio: 21.7
elderly dependency ratio: 28.9
potential support ratio: 3.5 (2020 est.)

Median age: *total:* 44.5 years
male: 43.1 years
female: 45.8 years (2020 est.)
country comparison to the world: 14

Population growth rate: 0.32% (2022 est.)
country comparison to the world: 166

Birth rate: 9.45 births/1,000 population (2022 est.)
country comparison to the world: 193

Death rate: 9.85 deaths/1,000 population (2022 est.)
country comparison to the world: 38

Net migration rate: 3.55 migrant(s)/1,000 population (2022 est.)
country comparison to the world: 35

Population distribution: the northern and eastern portions of the country are more densely populated; nearly two-thirds of the populace lives in urban areas

Urbanization: *urban population:* 59.3% of total population (2022)
rate of urbanization: 0.68% annual rate of change (2020-25 est.)

Major urban areas - population: 1.960 million VIENNA (capital) (2022)

Sex ratio: *at birth:* 1.05 male(s)/female
0-14 years: 1.05 male(s)/female
15-24 years: 1.03 male(s)/female
25-54 years: 1 male(s)/female
55-64 years: 0.99 male(s)/female
65 years and over: 0.65 male(s)/female
total population: 0.96 male(s)/female (2022 est.)

Mother's mean age at first birth: 29.7 years (2020 est.)

Maternal mortality ratio: 5 deaths/100,000 live births (2017 est.)
country comparison to the world: 163

Infant mortality rate: *total:* 3.24 deaths/1,000 live births
male: 3.65 deaths/1,000 live births
female: 2.81 deaths/1,000 live births (2022 est.)
country comparison to the world: 205

Life expectancy at birth: *total population:* 82.27 years
male: 79.64 years
female: 85.04 years (2022 est.)
country comparison to the world: 25

Total fertility rate: 1.51 children born/woman (2022 est.)
country comparison to the world: 199

Contraceptive prevalence rate: 79% (2019)
note: percent of women aged 16-49

Drinking water source: *improved: urban:* 100% of population
rural: 100% of population
total: 100% of population

Current health expenditure: 10.4% of GDP (2019)

Physicians density: 5.29 physicians/1,000 population (2020)

Hospital bed density: 7.3 beds/1,000 population (2018)

Sanitation facility access: *improved: urban:* 100% of population
rural: 100% of population
total: 100% of population

HIV/AIDS - adult prevalence rate: 0.1% (2017 est.)
country comparison to the world: 119

Obesity - adult prevalence rate: 20.1% (2016)
country comparison to the world: 105

Alcohol consumption per capita: *total:* 11.9 liters of pure alcohol (2019 est.)
beer: 6.3 liters of pure alcohol (2019 est.)
wine: 3.7 liters of pure alcohol (2019 est.)
spirits: 1.9 liters of pure alcohol (2019 est.)
other alcohols: 0 liters of pure alcohol (2019 est.)
country comparison to the world: 5

Tobacco use: *total:* 26.4% (2020 est.)
male: 27.7% (2020 est.)
female: 25% (2020 est.)
country comparison to the world: 42

Education expenditures: 5.2% of GDP (2018 est.)
country comparison to the world: 53

School life expectancy (primary to tertiary education): *total:* 16 years
male: 16 years
female: 16 years (2019)

Unemployment, youth ages 15-24: *total:* 10.5%
male: 11.3%
female: 9.5% (2020 est.)

ENVIRONMENT

Environment - current issues: some forest degradation caused by air and soil pollution; soil pollution results from the use of agricultural chemicals; air pollution results from emissions by coal- and oil-fired power stations and industrial plants and from trucks transiting Austria between northern and southern Europe; water pollution; the Danube, as well as some of Austria's other rivers and lakes, are threatened by pollution

Environment - international agreements: *party to:* Air Pollution, Air Pollution-Heavy Metals, Air Pollution-Nitrogen Oxides, Air Pollution-Persistent Organic Pollutants, Air Pollution-Sulphur 85, Air Pollution-Sulphur 94, Air Pollution-Volatile Organic Compounds, Antarctic Treaty, Biodiversity, Climate Change, Climate Change-Kyoto Protocol, Climate Change-Paris Agreement, Comprehensive Nuclear Test Ban, Desertification, Endangered Species, Environmental Modification, Hazardous Wastes, Law of the Sea, Nuclear Test Ban, Ozone Layer Protection, Ship Pollution, Tropical Timber 2006, Wetlands, Whaling
signed, but not ratified: Air Pollution-Multi-effect Protocol, Antarctic-Environmental Protection

Air pollutants: *particulate matter emissions:* 12.43 micrograms per cubic meter (2016 est.)
carbon dioxide emissions: 61.45 megatons (2016 est.)
methane emissions: 6.34 megatons (2020 est.)

Climate: temperate; continental, cloudy; cold winters with frequent rain and some snow in lowlands and snow in mountains; moderate summers with occasional showers

Land use: *agricultural land:* 38.4% (2018 est.)
arable land: 16.5% (2018 est.)
permanent crops: 0.8% (2018 est.)
permanent pasture: 21.1% (2018 est.)
forest: 47.2% (2018 est.)
other: 14.4% (2018 est.)

Urbanization: *urban population:* 59.3% of total population (2022)
rate of urbanization: 0.68% annual rate of change (2020-25 est.)

Revenue from forest resources: *forest revenues:* 0.07% of GDP (2018 est.)
country comparison to the world: 122

Revenue from coal: *coal revenues:* 0% of GDP (2018 est.)
country comparison to the world: 59

Waste and recycling: *municipal solid waste generated annually:* 4.836 million tons (2015 est.)
municipal solid waste recycled annually: 1,240,918 tons (2015 est.)
percent of municipal solid waste recycled: 25.7% (2015 est.)

Major lakes (area sq km): *fresh water lake(s):* Lake Constance (shared with Switzerland and Germany) - 540 sq km

Major rivers (by length in km): Danube (shared with Germany [s], Slovakia, Czechia, Hungary, Croatia, Serbia, Bulgaria, Ukraine, Moldova, and Romania [m]) - 2,888 km
note – [s] after country name indicates river source; [m] after country name indicates river mouth

Major watersheds (area sq km):

Atlantic Ocean drainage: Rhine-Maas (198,735 sq km), *(Black Sea)* Danube (795,656 sq km)

Total water withdrawal: *municipal:* 720 million cubic meters (2017 est.)
industrial: 2.695 billion cubic meters (2017 est.)
agricultural: 77.1 million cubic meters (2017 est.)

Total renewable water resources: 77.7 billion cubic meters (2017 est.)

GOVERNMENT

Country name: *conventional long form:* Republic of Austria
conventional short form: Austria
local long form: Republik Oesterreich
local short form: Oesterreich
etymology: the name Oesterreich means "eastern realm" or "eastern march" and dates to the 10th century; the designation refers to the fact that Austria was the easternmost extension of Bavaria, and, in fact, of all the Germans; the word Austria is a Latinization of the German name

Government type: federal parliamentary republic

Capital: *name:* Vienna
geographic coordinates: 48 12 N, 16 22 E
time difference: UTC+1 (6 hours ahead of Washington, DC, during Standard Time)
daylight saving time: +1hr, begins last Sunday in March; ends last Sunday in October
etymology: the origin of the name is disputed but may derive from early Celtic settlements of the area; a possible reconstructed Celtic name from several centuries B.C. is Vedunia (meaning "forest stream"); under Roman settlement, beginning around 15 B.C., the name became Vindobona (likely from the Celtic *windo*, meaning "white, fair, or bright" and *bona* meaning "base, fortification, or settlement" to give a connotation of "white settlement" or "white fort"); archeological remains of the latter survive at many sites in the center of Vienna

Administrative divisions: 9 states (Bundeslaender, singular - Bundesland); Burgenland, Kaernten (Carinthia), Niederoesterreich (Lower Austria), Oberoesterreich (Upper Austria), Salzburg, Steiermark (Styria), Tirol (Tyrol), Vorarlberg, Wien (Vienna)

Independence: *no official date of independence:* 976 (Margravate of Austria established); 17 September 1156 (Duchy of Austria founded); 6 January 1453 (Archduchy of Austria acknowledged); 11 August 1804 (Austrian Empire proclaimed); 30 March 1867 (Austro-Hungarian dual monarchy established); 12 November 1918 (First Republic proclaimed); 27 April 1945 (Second Republic proclaimed)

National holiday: National Day (commemorates passage of the law on permanent neutrality), 26 October (1955)

Constitution: *history:* several previous; latest adopted 1 October 1920, revised 1929, replaced May 1934, replaced by German Weimar constitution in 1938 following German annexation, reinstated 1 May 1945
amendments: proposed through laws designated "constitutional laws" or through the constitutional process if the amendment is part of another law; approval required by at least a two-thirds majority vote by the National Assembly and the presence of one half of the members; a referendum is required only if requested by one third of the National Council or Federal Council membership; passage by referendum requires absolute majority vote; amended many times, last in 2020

Legal system: civil law system; judicial review of legislative acts by the Constitutional Court

International law organization participation: accepts compulsory ICJ jurisdiction; accepts ICCt jurisdiction

Citizenship: *citizenship by birth:* no
citizenship by descent only: at least one parent must be a citizen of Austria
dual citizenship recognized: no
residency requirement for naturalization: 10 years

Suffrage: 16 years of age; universal

Executive branch: *chief of state:* President Alexander VAN DER BELLEN (since 26 January 2017); note - President Alexander VAN DER BELLEN was re-elected to a second six year term on 9 October 2022
head of government: Chancellor Karl NEHAMMER (since 6 December 2021); note - Chancellor

Alexander SCHALLENBERG resigned on 2 December 2021
cabinet: Council of Ministers chosen by the president on the advice of the chancellor
elections/appointments: president directly elected by absolute majority popular vote in 2 rounds if needed for a 6-year term (eligible for a second term); elections last held on 24 April 2016 (first round), 22 May 2016 (second round, which was annulled), and 4 December 2016 (second round re-vote) (next election to be held on 9 October 2022); chancellor appointed by the president but determined by the majority coalition parties in the Federal Assembly; vice chancellor appointed by the president on the advice of the chancellor
election results: 2016: Alexander VAN DER BELLEN elected in second round; percent of vote in first round - Norbert HOFER (FPOe) 35.1%, Alexander VAN DER BELLEN (independent, allied with the Greens) 21.3%, Irmgard GRISS (independent) 18.9%, Rudolf HUNDSTORFER (SPOe) 11.3%, Andreas KHOL (OeVP) 11.1%, Richard LUGNER (independent) 2.3%; percent of vote in second round re-vote - Alexander VAN DER BELLEN 53.8%, Norbert HOFER 46.2%
2010: Heinz FISCHER re-elected; percent of vote - Heinz FISCHER 79.3%, Barbara ROSENKRANZ 15.2%, Rudolf GEHRING 5.4%

Legislative branch: *description:* bicameral Federal Assembly or Bundesversammlung consists of:
Federal Council or Bundesrat (61 seats; members appointed by state parliaments with each state receiving 3 to 12 seats in proportion to its population; members serve 5- or 6-year terms)
National Council or Nationalrat (183 seats; members directly elected in single-seat constituencies by proportional representation vote; members serve 5-year terms)
elections: Federal Council - last appointed in 2021
National Council - last held on 29 September 2019 (next to be held in 2024); note - election was originally scheduled for 2022, but President VAN DER BELLEN called for an early election
election results: Federal Council - percent of vote by party - OeVP 42.6%, SPOe 31.2%. FPOe 16.4%, The Greens 8.2%, NEOS 1.6%; seats by party - OeVP 26, SPOe 19, FPOe 10, The Greens 5, NEOS 1; composition (as of March 2022) - men 36, women 25, percent of women 41%
National Council - percent of vote by party - OeVP 37.5%, SPOe 21.2%, FPOe 16.2%, The Greens 13.9%, NEOS 8.1%, other 3.1%; seats by party - OeVP 71, SPOe 40, FPOe 31, The Greens 26, NEOS 15; composition (as of March 2022) - men 107, women 76, percent of women 41.5%

Judicial branch: *highest court(s):* Supreme Court of Justice or Oberster Gerichtshof (consists of 85 judges organized into 17 senates or panels of 5 judges each); Constitutional Court or Verfassungsgerichtshof (consists of 20 judges including 6 substitutes; Administrative Court or Verwaltungsgerichtshof - 2 judges plus other members depending on the importance of the case)
judge selection and term of office: Supreme Court judges nominated by executive branch departments and appointed by the president; judges serve for life; Constitutional Court judges nominated by several executive branch departments and approved by the president; judges serve for life; Administrative Court judges recommended by executive branch departments and appointed by the president; terms of judges and members determined by the president
subordinate courts: Courts of Appeal (4); Regional Courts (20); district courts (120); county courts

Political parties and leaders: Austrian People's Party or OeVP [Karl NEHAMMER]
Communist Party of Austria or KPOe [Mirko MESSNER]
Freedom Party of Austria or FPOe [Herbert KICKI]
The Greens - The Green Alternative [Werner KOGLER]
NEOS - The New Austria and Liberal Forum [Beate MEINL-REISINGER]
Social Democratic Party of Austria or SPOe [Pamela RENDI-WAGNER]

International organization participation: ADB (nonregional member), AfDB (nonregional member), Australia Group, BIS, BSEC (observer), CD, CE, CEI, CERN, EAPC, EBRD, ECB, EIB, EMU, ESA, EU, FAO, FATF, G-9, IADB, IAEA, IBRD, ICAO, ICC (national committees), ICCt, ICRM, IDA, IEA, IFAD, IFC, IFRCS, IGAD (partners), ILO, IMF, IMO, Interpol, IOC, IOM, IPU, ISO, ITSO, ITU, ITUC (NGOs), MIGA, MINURSO, NEA, NSG, OAS (observer), OECD, OIF (observer), OPCW, OSCE, Paris Club, PCA, PFP, Schengen Convention, SELEC (observer), UN, UNCTAD, UNESCO, UNFICYP, UNHCR, UNIDO, UNIFIL, UNTSO, UNWTO, UPU, Wassenaar Arrangement, WCO, WFTU (NGOs), WHO, WIPO, WMO, WTO, ZC

Diplomatic representation in the US: *chief of mission:* Ambassador Martin WEISS (since 6 January 2020)
chancery: 3524 International Court NW, Washington, DC 20008-3035
telephone: [1] (202) 895-6700
FAX: [1] (202) 895-6750
email address and website:
washington-ka@bmeia.gv.at
https://www.austria.org/
consulate(s) general: Los Angeles, New York, Washington
consulate(s): Chicago

Diplomatic representation from the US: *chief of mission:* Ambassador Victoria Reggie KENNEDY (since 12 January 2022)
embassy: Boltzmanngasse 16, 1090, Vienna
mailing address: 9900 Vienna Place, Washington DC 20521-9900
telephone: [43] (1) 31339-0
FAX: [43] (1) 310-06-82
email address and website:
ConsulateVienna@state.gov
https://at.usembassy.gov/

Flag description: three equal horizontal bands of red (top), white, and red; the flag design is certainly one of the oldest - if not the oldest - national banners in the world; according to tradition, in 1191, following a fierce battle in the Third Crusade, Duke Leopold V of Austria's white tunic became completely blood-spattered; upon removal of his wide belt or sash, a white band was revealed; the red-white-red color combination was subsequently adopted as his banner

National symbol(s): eagle, edelweiss, Alpine gentian; national colors: red, white

National anthem: *name:* "Bundeshymne" (Federal Hymn)
lyrics/music: Paula von PRERADOVIC/Wolfgang Amadeus MOZART or Johann HOLZER (disputed)
note 1: adopted 1947; the anthem is also known as "Land der Berge, Land am Strome" (Land of the Mountains, Land by the River); Austria adopted a new national anthem after World War II to replace the former imperial anthem composed by Franz Josef HAYDN, which had been appropriated by Germany in 1922 and was thereafter associated with the Nazi regime; a gender-neutral version of the lyrics was adopted by the Austrian Federal Assembly in fall 2011 and became effective 1 January 2012
note 2: the beloved waltz "The Blue Danube" ("An der schoenen, blauen Donau"), composed in 1866 by the Austrian composer Johann STRAUSS II, is consistently referred to as Austria's unofficial national anthem

National heritage: *total World Heritage Sites:* 12 (11 cultural, 1 natural)
selected World Heritage Site locales: Historic Salzburg (c); Palace and Gardens of Schönbrunn (c); Halstadt– Dachstein/Salzkammergut Cultural Landscape (c); Semmering railway (c); Historic Graz and Schloss Eggenberg (c); Wachau Cultural Landscape (c); Historic Vienna (c); Fertő/Neusiedlersee Cultural Landscape (c); Baden bei Wien (c); Primeval Beech Forests - Dürrenstein, Kalkalpen (n)

ECONOMY

Economic overview: Austria is a well-developed market economy with skilled labor force and high standard of living. It is closely tied to other EU economies, especially Germany's, but also the US', its third-largest trade partner. Its economy features a large service sector, a sound industrial sector, and a small, but highly developed agricultural sector.

Austrian economic growth strengthened in 2017, with a 2.9% increase in GDP. Austrian exports, accounting for around 60% of the GDP, were up 8.2% in 2017. Austria's unemployment rate fell by 0.3% to 5.5%, which is low by European standards, but still at its second highest rate since the end of World War II, driven by an increased number of refugees and EU migrants entering the labor market.

Austria's fiscal position compares favorably with other euro-zone countries. The budget deficit stood at a low 0.7% of GDP in 2017 and public debt declined again to 78.4% of GDP in 2017, after reaching a post-war high 84.6% in 2015. The Austrian government has announced it plans to balance the fiscal budget in 2019. Several external risks, such as Austrian banks' exposure to Central and Eastern Europe, the refugee crisis, and continued unrest in Russia/Ukraine, eased in 2017, but are still a factor for the Austrian economy. Exposure to the Russian banking sector and a deep energy relationship with Russia present additional risks.

Austria elected a new pro-business government in October 2017 that campaigned on promises to reduce bureaucracy, improve public sector efficiency, reduce labor market protections, and provide positive investment incentives.

Real GDP (purchasing power parity): $463.12 billion (2020 est.)
$495.8 billion (2019 est.)
$488.86 billion (2018 est.)
note: data are in 2017 dollars
country comparison to the world: 43

Real GDP growth rate: 1.42% (2019 est.)
2.58% (2018 est.)
2.4% (2017 est.)
country comparison to the world: 155

Real GDP per capita: $51,900 (2020 est.)
$55,800 (2019 est.)
$55,300 (2018 est.)
note: data are in 2017 dollars
country comparison to the world: 25

GDP (official exchange rate): $445.025 billion (2019 est.)

Inflation rate (consumer prices): 1.5% (2019 est.)
2% (2018 est.)
2% (2017 est.)
country comparison to the world: 86

Credit ratings:

Fitch rating: AA+ (2015)

Moody's rating: Aa1 (2016)

Standard & Poors rating: AA+ (2012)
note: The year refers to the year in which the current credit rating was first obtained.

GDP - composition, by sector of origin: *agriculture:* 1.3% (2017 est.)
industry: 28.4% (2017 est.)
services: 70.3% (2017 est.)

GDP - composition, by end use: *household consumption:* 52.1% (2017 est.)
government consumption: 19.5% (2017 est.)
investment in fixed capital: 23.5% (2017 est.)
investment in inventories: 1.6% (2017 est.)
exports of goods and services: 54.2% (2017 est.)
imports of goods and services: -50.7% (2017 est.)

Agricultural products: milk, maize, sugar beet, wheat, barley, potatoes, pork, triticale, grapes, apples

Industries: construction, machinery, vehicles and parts, food, metals, chemicals, lumber and paper, electronics, tourism

Industrial production growth rate: 6.5% (2017 est.)
country comparison to the world: 35

Labor force: 3.739 million (2020 est.)
country comparison to the world: 94

Labor force - by occupation: *agriculture:* 0.7%
industry: 25.2%
services: 74.1% (2017 est.)

Unemployment rate: 7.35% (2019 est.)
7.7% (2018 est.)
country comparison to the world: 117

Unemployment, youth ages 15-24: *total:* 10.5%
male: 11.3%
female: 9.5% (2020 est.)
country comparison to the world: 136

Population below poverty line: 13.3% (2018 est.)

Gini Index coefficient - distribution of family income: 29.7 (2017 est.)
30.5 (2014)
country comparison to the world: 150

Household income or consumption by percentage share: *lowest 10%:* 2.8%
highest 10%: 23.5% (2012 est.)

Budget: *revenues:* 201.7 billion (2017 est.)
expenditures: 204.6 billion (2017 est.)

Budget surplus (+) or deficit (-): -0.7% (of GDP) (2017 est.)
country comparison to the world: 67

Public debt: 78.6% of GDP (2017 est.)
83.6% of GDP (2016 est.)
note: this is general government gross debt, defined in the Maastricht Treaty as consolidated general government gross debt at nominal value, outstanding at the end of the year; it covers the following categories of government liabilities (as defined in ESA95): currency and deposits (AF.2), securities other than shares excluding financial derivatives (AF.3, excluding AF.34), and loans (AF.4); the general government sector comprises the sub-sectors of central government, state government, local government and social security funds; as a percentage of GDP, the GDP used as a denominator is the gross domestic product in current year prices
country comparison to the world: 37

Taxes and other revenues: 48.3% (of GDP) (2017 est.)
country comparison to the world: 18

Fiscal year: calendar year

Current account balance: $12.667 billion (2019 est.)
$5.989 billion (2018 est.)
country comparison to the world: 21

Exports: $226.79 billion (2020 est.)
$247.17 billion (2019 est.)
$253.3 billion (2018 est.)
note: Data are in current year dollars and do not include illicit exports or re-exports.
country comparison to the world: 28

Exports - partners: Germany 28%, United States 7%, Italy 6%, Switzerland 5% (2019)

Exports - commodities: cars, packaged medical supplies, vehicle parts, medical vaccines/cultures, flavored water (2019)

Imports: $211.85 billion (2020 est.) note: data are in current year dollars
$232.8 billion (2019 est.) note: data are in current year dollars
$238.79 billion (2018 est.) note: data are in current year dollars
country comparison to the world: 29

Imports - partners: Germany 39%, Italy 7%, Czechia 5% (2019)

Imports - commodities: cars, vehicle parts, broadcasting equipment, refined petroleum, packaged medical supplies (2019)

Reserves of foreign exchange and gold: $21.57 billion (31 December 2017 est.)
$23.36 billion (31 December 2016 est.)
country comparison to the world: 57

Debt - external: $688.434 billion (2019 est.)
$686.196 billion (2018 est.)
country comparison to the world: 19

Exchange rates: euros (EUR) per US dollar -
0.828 (2020 est.)
0.903 (2019 est.)
0.878 (2018 est.)
0.885 (2014 est.)
0.763 (2013 est.)

ENERGY

Electricity access: *electrification - total population:* 100% (2020)

Electricity: *installed generating capacity:* 28.376 million kW (2020 est.)
consumption: 69,905,200,000 kWh (2020 est.)
exports: 22,918,265,000 kWh (2020 est.)
imports: 24.522 billion kWh (2020 est.)
transmission/distribution losses: 3.192 billion kWh (2020 est.)

Electricity generation sources: *fossil fuels:* 17.4% of total installed capacity (2020 est.)
solar: 2.8% of total installed capacity (2020 est.)
wind: 9.4% of total installed capacity (2020 est.)
hydroelectricity: 62.9% of total installed capacity (2020 est.)
biomass and waste: 7.4% of total installed capacity (2020 est.)

Coal: *production:* 1.327 million metric tons (2020 est.)
consumption: 4.899 million metric tons (2020 est.)
exports: 1,000 metric tons (2020 est.)
imports: 3.667 million metric tons (2020 est.)
proven reserves: 0 metric tons (2019 est.)

Petroleum: *total petroleum production:* 20,100 bbl/day (2021 est.)
refined petroleum consumption: 278,700 bbl/day (2019 est.)
crude oil and lease condensate exports: 0 bbl/day (2018 est.)
crude oil and lease condensate imports: 168,300 bbl/day (2018 est.)
crude oil estimated reserves: 35.2 million barrels (2021 est.)

Refined petroleum products - production: 186,500 bbl/day (2017 est.)
country comparison to the world: 54

Refined petroleum products - exports: 49,960 bbl/day (2017 est.)
country comparison to the world: 55

Refined petroleum products - imports: 135,500 bbl/day (2017 est.)
country comparison to the world: 42

Natural gas: *production:* 924.515 million cubic meters (2019 est.)
consumption: 9,207,632,000 cubic meters (2019 est.)
exports: 2,800,248,000 cubic meters (2019 est.)
imports: 14,114,028,000 cubic meters (2019 est.)
proven reserves: 5.04 billion cubic meters (2021 est.)

Carbon dioxide emissions: 65.54 million metric tonnes of CO_2 (2019 est.)
from coal and metallurgical coke: 10.508 million metric tonnes of CO_2 (2019 est.)
from petroleum and other liquids: 37.336 million metric tonnes of CO_2 (2019 est.)
from consumed natural gas: 17.695 million metric tonnes of CO_2 (2019 est.)
country comparison to the world: 52

Energy consumption per capita: 171.299 million Btu/person (2019 est.)
country comparison to the world: 28

COMMUNICATIONS

Telephones - fixed lines: *total subscriptions:* 3,786,725 (2020 est.)
subscriptions per 100 inhabitants: 42 (2020 est.)
country comparison to the world: 35

Telephones - mobile cellular: *total subscriptions:* 10,717,445 (2020 est.)
subscriptions per 100 inhabitants: 119 (2020 est.)
country comparison to the world: 85

Telecommunication systems: *general assessment:* mature telecom market; the mobile market benefits from a growing number of Mobile Virtual Network Operators; the telcos as well as the government and regulator have been focused on delivering improved telecom infrastructure; the government has a program to provide a national gigabit service by 2030, delivered by private enterprise though with some state funding; this is based on fiber networks supported by 5G, with the Mobile Network Operators able to expand the reach of their 5G services following auctions held in March 2019 and September 2020; the fixed-line broadband market is still dominated by the DSL sector, while the cable broadband sector has held a steady share of connections in recent years; the fiber sector was slow to develop, and although fiber remains low there are plans to build out the network infrastructure (2021)
domestic: developed and efficient; 42 per 100 fixed-line for households, 174 per 100 for companies; roughly 119 per 100 mobile-cellular; broadband: 138 per 100 on smartphones; roughly 29 per 100 fixed broadband and 107 per 100 mobile broadband (2020)
international: country code - 43; earth stations available in the Astra, Intelsat, Eutelsat satellite systems (2019)

Broadcast media: worldwide cable and satellite TV are available; the public incumbent ORF competes with three other major, several regional domestic, and up to 400 international TV stations; TV coverage is in principle 100%, but only 90% use broadcast media; Internet streaming not only complements, but increasingly replaces regular TV stations (2019)

Internet country code: .at

Internet users: *total:* 7,846,840 (2020 est.)
percent of population: 88% (2020 est.)
country comparison to the world: 73

Broadband - fixed subscriptions: *total:* 2.606 million (2020 est.)
subscriptions per 100 inhabitants: 29 (2020 est.)
country comparison to the world: 49

Communications - note: *note 1:* the Austrian National Library contains important collections of the Imperial Library of the Holy Roman Empire and of the Austrian Empire, as well as of the Austrian Republic; among its more than 12 million items are outstanding holdings of rare books, maps, globes, papyrus, and music; its Globe Museum is the only one in the world
note 2: on 1 October 1869, Austria-Hungary introduced the world's first postal card - postal stationery with an imprinted stamp indicating the prepayment of postage; simple and cheap (sent for a fraction of the cost of a regular letter), postal cards became an instant success, widely produced in the millions worldwide
note 3: Austria followed up with the creation of the world's first commercial picture postcards - cards bearing a picture or photo to which postage is affixed - in May 1871; sent from Vienna, the image served as a souvenir of the city; together, postal cards and post cards served as the world's e-mails of the late 19th and early 20th centuries
note 4: Austria was also an airmail pioneer; from March to October of 1918, it conducted the world's first regular (daily) airmail service - between the imperial cities of Vienna, Krakow, and Lemberg - a combined distance of some 650 km (400 mi) (earlier airmail services had been set up in a few parts of the world but only for short stretches, and none lasted beyond a few days or weeks); an expansion of the route in June of 1918 allowed private mail to be flown to Kyiv, in newly independent Ukraine, which made the route the world's first regular international airmail service (covering a distance of some 1,200 km; 750 mi)

TRANSPORTATION

National air transport system: *number of registered air carriers:* 11 (2020)
inventory of registered aircraft operated by air carriers: 130
annual passenger traffic on registered air carriers: 12,935,505 (2018)
annual freight traffic on registered air carriers: 373.51 million (2018) mt-km

Civil aircraft registration country code prefix: OE

Airports: *total:* 50 (2021)
country comparison to the world: 90

Airports - with paved runways: *total:* 24
over 3,047 m: 1
2,438 to 3,047 m: 5
1,524 to 2,437 m: 1
914 to 1,523 m: 4
under 914 m: 13 (2021)

Airports - with unpaved runways: *total:* 28
1,524 to 2,437 m: 1
914 to 1,523 m: 3
under 914 m: 24 (2021)

Heliports: 1 (2021)

Pipelines: 1,888 km gas, 594 km oil, 157 km refined products (2017)

Railways: *total:* 5,300 km (2018) (2017)
standard gauge: 5,300 km 1.435-m gauge (3,826 km electrified) (2016)
country comparison to the world: 36

Roadways: *total:* 137,039 km (2018)
paved: 137,039 km (2018) (includes 2,232 km of expressways)
country comparison to the world: 39

Waterways: 358 km (2011)
country comparison to the world: 98

Merchant marine: *total:* 1
by type: other 1 (2021)
country comparison to the world: 180

Ports and terminals: *river port(s):* Enns, Krems, Linz, Vienna (Danube)

MILITARY AND SECURITY

Military and security forces: Austrian Armed Forces: Land Forces, Air Forces, Cyber Forces, Special Forces (2022)

Military expenditures: 0.9% of GDP (2021 est.)
0.7% of GDP (2020)
0.7% of GDP (2019) (approximately $3.78 billion)
0.7% of GDP (2018) (approximately $3.82 billion)
0.8% of GDP (2017) (approximately $3.71 billion)
country comparison to the world: 136

Military and security service personnel strengths: approximately 25,000 active duty personnel (20,000 Army; 5,000 Air Force) (2022)

Military equipment inventories and acquisitions: the Austrian military's inventory includes a mix of domestically-produced and imported weapons systems from European countries and the US; the Austrian defense industry produces a range of equipment and partners with other countries (2021)

Military service age and obligation: registration requirement at age 17, the legal minimum age for voluntary military service; men above the age of 18 are subject to compulsory military service; women may volunteer; compulsory service is for 6 months, or optionally, alternative civil/community service (Zivildienst) for 9 months (2022)
note 1: as of 2019, women made up about 4% of the military's full-time personnel
note 2: in a January 2013 referendum, a majority of Austrians voted in favor of retaining the system of compulsory military service (with the option of alternative/non-military service) instead of switching to a professional army system; approximately 40% of those liable to compulsory service have opted in favor of alternative civil/community service

Military deployments: 170 Bosnia-Herzegovina (EUFOR stabilization force); 300 Kosovo (NATO/KFOR); 200 Lebanon (UNIFIL) (Aug 2022)

Military - note: Austria is constitutionally non-aligned but is an EU member and actively participates in EU peacekeeping and crisis management operations under the Common Security and Defense Policy; Austria is not a member of NATO but joined NATO's Partnership for Peace framework in 1995 and participates in NATO-led crisis management and peacekeeping operations; as of 2022, more than 100,000 Austrian military and civilian personnel had taken part in more than 50 international peace support and humanitarian missions since 1960 (2022)

TERRORISM

Terrorist group(s): Islamic State of Iraq and ash-Sham (ISIS)

TRANSNATIONAL ISSUES

Disputes - international: none identified

Refugees and internally displaced persons: *refugees (country of origin):* 57,887 (Syria), 41,037 (Afghanistan), 9,661 (Iraq), 8,212 (Somalia), 7,046 (Iran), 7,003 (Russia) (mid-year 2021); 86,903 (Ukraine) (as of 22 November 2022)
stateless persons: 3,229 (mid-year 2021)

Illicit drugs: transshipment point for Southwest Asian heroin and South American cocaine destined for Western Europe; increasing consumption of European-produced synthetic drugs

AZERBAIJAN

INTRODUCTION

Background: Azerbaijan - a secular nation with a majority-Turkic and majority-Shia Muslim population - was briefly independent (from 1918 to 1920) following the collapse of the Russian Empire; it was subsequently incorporated into the Soviet Union for seven decades. Azerbaijan remains involved in the protracted Nagorno-Karabakh conflict with Armenia. Nagorno-Karabakh was a primarily ethnic Armenian region that Moscow recognized in 1923 as an autonomous oblast within Soviet Azerbaijan. In the late Soviet period, a separatist movement developed which sought to end Azerbaijani control over the region. Fighting over Nagorno-Karabakh began in 1988 and escalated after Armenia and Azerbaijan attained independence from the Soviet Union in 1991. By the time a ceasefire took effect in May 1994, separatists, with Armenian support, controlled Nagorno-Karabakh and seven surrounding Azerbaijani territories.

Under the terms of a cease-fire agreement following Azerbaijan's victory in the Second Nagorno-Karabakh War that took place from September-November 2020, Armenia returned to Azerbaijan the remaining territories it had occupied and also the southern part of Nagorno-Karabakh, including the culturally and historically important city that Azerbaijanis call Shusha and Armenians call Shushi. Despite Azerbaijan's territorial gains, peace in the region remains elusive because of unsettled issues concerning the delimitation of borders, the opening of regional transportation and communication links, the status of ethnic enclaves near border regions, and the final status of the Nagorno-Karabakh region. Russian peacekeepers deployed to Nagorno-Karabakh to supervise the cease-fire for a minimum five-year term have not prevented the outbreak of sporadic, low-level military clashes along the Azerbaijan-Armenia border in 2021.

In the three decades following its independence in 1991, Azerbaijan has succeeded in significantly reducing the poverty rate and has directed revenues from its oil and gas production to develop the country's infrastructure. However, corruption remains a burden on the economy, and Western observers and members of the country's political opposition have accused the government of authoritarianism, pointing to elections that are neither free nor fair, state control of the media, and the systematic abuse of human rights targeting individuals and groups who are perceived as threats to the administration. The country's leadership has remained in the ALIYEV family since Heydar ALIYEV, formerly the most highly ranked Azerbaijani member of the Communist Party during the Soviet period, became president in the midst of the first Nagorno-Karabakh War in 1993. Heydar ALIYEV groomed his son to succeed him, and Ilham ALIYEV subsequently became president in 2003. As a result of two national referendums that eliminated presidential term limits and extended the presidential term from 5 to 7 years, President ALIYEV secured a fourth term in April 2018 in an election that international observers noted had serious shortcomings. Reforms are underway to diversify the country's economy away from its dependence on oil and gas; additional reforms are needed to address weaknesses in government institutions, particularly in the education and health sectors, and the court system.

GEOGRAPHY

Location: Southwestern Asia, bordering the Caspian Sea, between Iran and Russia, with a small European portion north of the Caucasus range

Geographic coordinates: 40 30 N, 47 30 E

Map references: Asia

Area: *total:* 86,600 sq km
land: 82,629 sq km
water: 3,971 sq km
note: includes the exclave of Naxcivan Autonomous Republic and the Nagorno-Karabakh region; the region's autonomy was abolished by Azerbaijani Supreme Soviet on 26 November 1991
country comparison to the world: 113

Area - comparative: about three-quarters the size of Pennsylvania; slightly smaller than Maine

Land boundaries: *total:* 2,468 km
border countries (5): Armenia 996 km; Georgia 428 km; Iran 689 km; Russia 338 km; Turkey 17 km

Coastline: 0 km (landlocked); note - Azerbaijan borders the Caspian Sea (713 km)

Maritime claims: none (landlocked)

Climate: dry, semiarid steppe

Terrain: large, flat Kur-Araz Ovaligi (Kura-Araks Lowland, much of it below sea level) with Great Caucasus Mountains to the north, Qarabag Yaylasi (Karabakh Upland) to the west; Baku lies on Abseron Yasaqligi (Apsheron Peninsula) that juts into Caspian Sea

Elevation: *highest point:* Bazarduzu Dagi 4,466 m
lowest point: Caspian Sea -28 m
mean elevation: 384 m

Natural resources: petroleum, natural gas, iron ore, nonferrous metals, bauxite

Land use: *agricultural land:* 57.6% (2018 est.)
arable land: 22.8% (2018 est.)
permanent crops: 2.7% (2018 est.)
permanent pasture: 32.1% (2018 est.)
forest: 11.3% (2018 est.)
other: 31.1% (2018 est.)

Irrigated land: 14,277 sq km (2012)

Major lakes (area sq km): *salt water lake(s):* Caspian Sea (shared with Iran, Russia, Turkmenistan, and Kazakhstan) - 374,000 sq km

Population distribution: highest population density is found in the far eastern area of the country, in and around Baku; apart from smaller urbanized areas, the rest of the country has a fairly light and evenly distributed population

Natural hazards: droughts

Geography - note: both the main area of the country and the Naxcivan exclave are landlocked

PEOPLE AND SOCIETY

Population: 10,353,296 (2022 est.)
country comparison to the world: 90

Nationality: *noun:* Azerbaijani(s)
adjective: Azerbaijani

Ethnic groups: Azerbaijani 91.6%, Lezghin 2%, Russian 1.3%, Armenian 1.3%, Talysh 1.3%, other 2.4% (2009 est.)
note: the Nagorno-Karabakh region, which is part of Azerbaijan on the basis of the borders recognized when the Soviet Union dissolved in 1991, is populated almost entirely by ethnic Armenians; Azerbaijan has over 80 ethnic groups

Languages: Azerbaijani (Azeri) (official) 92.5%, Russian 1.4%, Armenian 1.4%, other 4.7% (2009 est.)
major-language sample(s): Dünya fakt kitabı, əsas məlumatlar üçün əvəz olunmaz mənbədir (Azerbaijani)
note: Russian is widely spoken

Religions: Muslim 97.3% (predominantly Shia), Christian 2.6%, other <0.1, unaffiliated <0.1 (2020 est.)
note: religious affiliation for the majority of Azerbaijanis is largely nominal, percentages for actual practicing adherents are probably much lower

Demographic profile: Azerbaijan's citizenry has over 80 ethnic groups. The far eastern part of the country has the highest population density, particularly in and around Baku. Apart from smaller urbanized areas, the rest of the country has a fairly light and evenly distributed population. Approximately 57% of the country's inhabitants lives in urban areas. While the population is continuing to grow, it is in the early stages of aging. The declining fertility rate – which has decreased from about 5.5 children per woman in the 1950s to less than the 2.1 replacement level in 2022 – combined with increasing life expectancy has resulted in the elderly making up a larger share of Azerbaijan's populace. The percentage of elderly residents and the slowed growth and eventual shrinkage of the working-age population could put pressure on the country's pension and healthcare systems.

Age structure: *0-14 years:* 22.84% (male 1,235,292/female 1,095,308)
15-24 years: 13.17% (male 714,718/female 629,494)

25-54 years: 45.29% (male 2,291,600/female 2,330,843)
55-64 years: 11.41% (male 530,046/female 634,136)
65 years and over: 7.29% (male 289,604/female 454,769) (2020 est.)

Dependency ratios: *total dependency ratio:* 43.4
youth dependency ratio: 33.7
elderly dependency ratio: 9.7
potential support ratio: 10.3 (2020 est.)

Median age: *total:* 32.6 years
male: 31.1 years
female: 34.2 years (2020 est.)
country comparison to the world: 108

Population growth rate: 0.67% (2022 est.)
country comparison to the world: 131

Birth rate: 13.59 births/1,000 population (2022 est.)
country comparison to the world: 133

Death rate: 6.92 deaths/1,000 population (2022 est.)
country comparison to the world: 119

Net migration rate: 0 migrant(s)/1,000 population (2022 est.)
country comparison to the world: 83

Population distribution: highest population density is found in the far eastern area of the country, in and around Baku; apart from smaller urbanized areas, the rest of the country has a fairly light and evenly distributed population

Urbanization: *urban population:* 57.2% of total population (2022)
rate of urbanization: 1.38% annual rate of change (2020-25 est.)
note: data include Nagorno-Karabakh

Major urban areas - population: 2.401 million BAKU (capital) (2022)

Sex ratio: *at birth:* 1.06 male(s)/female
0-14 years: 1.11 male(s)/female
15-24 years: 1.15 male(s)/female
25-54 years: 0.99 male(s)/female
55-64 years: 0.82 male(s)/female
65 years and over: 0.49 male(s)/female
total population: 0.98 male(s)/female (2022 est.)

Mother's mean age at first birth: 24 years (2019 est.)

Maternal mortality ratio: 26 deaths/100,000 live births (2017 est.)
country comparison to the world: 120

Infant mortality rate: *total:* 23.51 deaths/1,000 live births
male: 24.62 deaths/1,000 live births
female: 22.33 deaths/1,000 live births (2022 est.)
country comparison to the world: 70

Life expectancy at birth: *total population:* 74.15 years
male: 71.08 years
female: 77.41 years (2022 est.)
country comparison to the world: 142

Total fertility rate: 1.86 children born/woman (2022 est.)
country comparison to the world: 133

Drinking water source: *improved: urban:* 100% of population
rural: 93.3% of population
total: 97.1% of population
unimproved: urban: 0% of population
rural: 6.7% of population
total: 2.9% of population (2020 est.)

Current health expenditure: 4% of GDP (2019)

Physicians density: 3.17 physicians/1,000 population (2019)

Hospital bed density: 4.8 beds/1,000 population (2014)

Sanitation facility access: *improved: urban:* 100% of population
unimproved: urban: 0% of population

HIV/AIDS - adult prevalence rate: 0.1% (2020 est.)
country comparison to the world: 120

Obesity - adult prevalence rate: 19.9% (2016)
country comparison to the world: 106

Alcohol consumption per capita: *total:* 1.38 liters of pure alcohol (2019 est.)
beer: 0.36 liters of pure alcohol (2019 est.)
wine: 0.06 liters of pure alcohol (2019 est.)
spirits: 0.94 liters of pure alcohol (2019 est.)
other alcohols: 0.01 liters of pure alcohol (2019 est.)
country comparison to the world: 142

Tobacco use: *total:* 24% (2020 est.)
male: 47.9% (2020 est.)
female: 0.1% (2020 est.)
country comparison to the world: 56

Children under the age of 5 years underweight: 4.9% (2013)
country comparison to the world: 78

Education expenditures: 2.7% of GDP (2019 est.)
country comparison to the world: 163

Literacy: *definition:* age 15 and over can read and write
total population: 99.8%
male: 99.9%
female: 99.7% (2019)

School life expectancy (primary to tertiary education): *total:* 14 years
male: 13 years
female: 14 years (2020)

Unemployment, youth ages 15-24: *total:* 12.4%
male: 10.9%
female: 14.2% (2019 est.)

ENVIRONMENT

Environment - current issues: local scientists consider the Abseron Yasaqligi (Apsheron Peninsula) (including Baku and Sumqayit) and the Caspian Sea to be the ecologically most devastated area in the world because of severe air, soil, and water pollution; soil pollution results from oil spills, from the use of DDT pesticide, and from toxic defoliants used in the production of cotton; surface and underground water are polluted by untreated municipal and industrial wastewater and agricultural run-off

Environment - international agreements: *party to:* Air Pollution, Biodiversity, Climate Change, Climate Change-Kyoto Protocol, Climate Change-Paris Agreement, Comprehensive Nuclear Test Ban, Desertification, Endangered Species, Hazardous Wastes, Law of the Sea, Marine Dumping-London Convention, Ozone Layer Protection, Ship Pollution, Wetlands
signed, but not ratified: none of the selected agreements

Air pollutants: *particulate matter emissions:* 18.2 micrograms per cubic meter (2016 est.)
carbon dioxide emissions: 37.62 megatons (2016 est.)
methane emissions: 44.87 megatons (2020 est.)

Climate: dry, semiarid steppe

Land use: *agricultural land:* 57.6% (2018 est.)
arable land: 22.8% (2018 est.)
permanent crops: 2.7% (2018 est.)
permanent pasture: 32.1% (2018 est.)
forest: 11.3% (2018 est.)
other: 31.1% (2018 est.)

Urbanization: *urban population:* 57.2% of total population (2022)
rate of urbanization: 1.38% annual rate of change (2020-25 est.)
note: data include Nagorno-Karabakh

Revenue from forest resources: *forest revenues:* 0.02% of GDP (2018 est.)
country comparison to the world: 138

Revenue from coal: *coal revenues:* 0% of GDP (2018 est.)
country comparison to the world: 60

Waste and recycling: *municipal solid waste generated annually:* 2,930,349 tons (2015 est.)

Major lakes (area sq km): *salt water lake(s):* Caspian Sea (shared with Iran, Russia, Turkmenistan, and Kazakhstan) - 374,000 sq km

Total water withdrawal: *municipal:* 449.6 million cubic meters (2017 est.)
industrial: 3.062 billion cubic meters (2017 est.)
agricultural: 9.27 billion cubic meters (2017 est.)

Total renewable water resources: 34.675 billion cubic meters (2017 est.)

GOVERNMENT

Country name: *conventional long form:* Republic of Azerbaijan
conventional short form: Azerbaijan
local long form: Azarbaycan Respublikasi
local short form: Azarbaycan
former: Azerbaijan Soviet Socialist Republic
etymology: the name translates as "Land of Fire" and refers to naturally occurring surface fires on ancient oil pools or from natural gas discharges

Government type: presidential republic

Capital: *name:* Baku (Baki, Baky)
geographic coordinates: 40 23 N, 49 52 E
time difference: UTC+4 (9 hours ahead of Washington, DC, during Standard Time)
daylight saving time: does not observe daylight savings time
etymology: the name derives from the Persian designation of the city "bad-kube" meaning "wind-pounded city" and refers to the harsh winds and severe snow storms that can hit the city
note: at approximately 28 m below sea level, Baku's elevation makes it the lowest capital city in the world

Administrative divisions: 66 districts (rayonlar; rayon - singular), 11 cities (saharlar; sahar - singular);
rayons: Abseron, Agcabadi, Agdam, Agdas, Agstafa, Agsu, Astara, Babak, Balakan, Barda, Beylaqan, Bilasuvar, Cabrayil, Calilabad, Culfa, Daskasan, Fuzuli, Gadabay, Goranboy, Goycay, Goygol, Haciqabul, Imisli, Ismayilli, Kalbacar, Kangarli, Kurdamir, Lacin, Lankaran, Lerik, Masalli, Neftcala, Oguz, Ordubad, Qabala, Qax, Qazax, Qobustan, Quba, Qubadli, Qusar, Saatli, Sabirabad, Sabran, Sadarak, Sahbuz, Saki, Salyan, Samaxi, Samkir, Samux, Sarur, Siyazan, Susa, Tartar, Tovuz, Ucar, Xacmaz, Xizi, Xocali, Xocavand, Yardimli, Yevlax, Zangilan, Zaqatala, Zardab

cities: Baku, Ganca, Lankaran, Mingacevir, Naftalan, Naxcivan (Nakhichevan), Saki, Sirvan, Sumqayit, Xankandi, Yevlax

Independence: 30 August 1991 (declared from the Soviet Union); 18 October 1991 (adopted by the Supreme Council of Azerbaijan)

National holiday: Republic Day (founding of the Democratic Republic of Azerbaijan), 28 May (1918)

Constitution: *history:* several previous; latest adopted 12 November 1995
amendments: proposed by the president of the republic or by at least 63 members of the National Assembly; passage requires at least 95 votes of Assembly members in two separate readings of the draft amendment six months apart and requires presidential approval after each of the two Assembly votes, followed by presidential signature; constitutional articles on the authority, sovereignty, and unity of the people cannot be amended; amended 2002, 2009, 2016

Legal system: civil law system

International law organization participation: has not submitted an ICJ jurisdiction declaration; non-party state to the ICCt

Citizenship: *citizenship by birth:* yes
citizenship by descent only: yes
dual citizenship recognized: no
residency requirement for naturalization: 5 years

Suffrage: 18 years of age; universal

Executive branch: *chief of state:* President Ilham ALIYEV (since 31 October 2003); First Vice President Mehriban ALIYEVA (since 21 February 2017)
head of government: Prime Minister Ali ASADOV (since 8 October 2019); First Deputy Prime Minister Yaqub EYYUBOV (since June 2006)
cabinet: Council of Ministers appointed by the president and confirmed by the National Assembly
elections/appointments: president directly elected by absolute majority popular vote in 2 rounds (if needed) for a 7-year term; a single individual is eligible for unlimited terms; election last held on 11 April 2018 (next to be held in 2025); prime minister and first deputy prime minister appointed by the president and confirmed by the National Assembly; note - a constitutional amendment approved in a September 2016 referendum expanded the presidential term from 5 to 7 years; a separate constitutional amendment approved in the same referendum also introduced the post of first vice-president and additional vice-presidents, who are directly appointed by the president
election results: Ilham ALIYEV reelected president (11 April 2018) in first round; percent of vote - Ilham ALIYEV (YAP) 86%, Zahid ORUJ (independent) 3.1%, other 10.9%
note: OSCE observers noted shortcomings in the election, including a restrictive political environment, limits on fundamental freedoms, a lack of genuine competition, and ballot box stuffing

Legislative branch: *description:* unicameral National Assembly or Milli Mejlis (125 seats; members directly elected in single-seat constituencies by simple majority vote to serve 5-year terms)
elections: last held early on 9 February 2020 (next to be held in 2025)
election results: percent of vote by party - NA; seats by party - YAP 69, CSP 3, AVP 1, CUP 1, ADMP 1, PDR 1, Great Order 1, National Front Party 1, REAL 1, VP 1, Whole Azerbaijan Popular Front 1, party unknown 1, independent 41; composition - men 103, women 22, percent of women 17.6%

Judicial branch: *highest court(s):* Supreme Court (consists of the chairman, vice chairman, and 23 judges in plenum sessions and organized into civil, economic affairs, criminal, and rights violations chambers); Constitutional Court (consists of 9 judges)
judge selection and term of office: Supreme Court judges nominated by the president and appointed by the Milli Majlis; judges appointed for 10 years; Constitutional Court chairman and deputy chairman appointed by the president; other court judges nominated by the president and appointed by the Milli Majlis to serve single 15-year terms
subordinate courts: Courts of Appeal (replaced the Economic Court in 2002); district and municipal courts

Political parties and leaders: Azerbaijan Democratic Enlightenment Party or ADMP [Elshan MASAYEV]
Civic Solidarity Party or VHP [Sabir RUSTAMKHANLI]
Civic Unity Party or CUP [Sabir HAJIYEV]
Great Order Party [Fazil MUSTAFA]
Islamic Party of Azerbaijan or AiP [Mavsum SAMADOV]
Musavat [Arif HAJILI]
Popular Front Party [Ali KARIMLI]
Motherland Party or AVP [Fazail AGAMALI]
National Front Party [Razi NURULLAYEV]
National Revival Movement Party [Faraj GULIYEV]
Party for Democratic Reforms or PDR [Asim MOLLAZADE]
Republican Alternative Party or REAL [Ilgar MAMMADOV]
Social Democratic Party [Ayaz MUTALIBOV]
Social Prosperity Party [Asli KAZIMOVA]
Unity Party or VP [Tahir KARIMLI]
Whole Azerbaijan Popular Front Party [Gudrat HASANGULIYEV]
New Azerbaijan Party (Yeni Azərbaycan Partiyasi) or YAP [Ilham ALIYEV]

International organization participation: ADB, BSEC, CD, CE, CICA, CIS, EAPC, EBRD, ECO, FAO, GCTU, GUAM, IAEA, IBRD, ICAO, ICC (NGOs), ICRM, IDA, IDB, IFAD, IFC, IFRCS, ILO, IMF, IMO, Interpol, IOC, IOM, IPU, ISO, ITSO, ITU, ITUC (NGOs), MIGA, NAM, OAS (observer), OIC, OPCW, OSCE, PFP, UN, UNCTAD, UNESCO, UNHCR, UNIDO, UNWTO, UPU, WCO, WFTU (NGOs), WHO, WIPO, WMO, WTO (observer)

Diplomatic representation in the US: *chief of mission:* Ambassador Kahzar IBRAHIM (since 15 September 2021)
chancery: 2741 34th Street NW, Washington, DC 20008
telephone: [1] (202) 337-3500
FAX: [1] (202) 337-5911
email address and website:
azerbaijan@azembassy.us; consul@azembassy.us
https://washington.mfa.gov.az/en
consulate(s) general: Los Angeles

Diplomatic representation from the US: *chief of mission:* Ambassador Lee LITZENBERGER (since 12 March 2019)
embassy: 111 Azadlig Avenue, AZ1007 Baku
mailing address: 7050 Baku Place, Washington, DC 20521-7050
telephone: [994] (12) 488-3300
FAX: [994] (12) 488-3330
email address and website:
BakuACS@state.gov
https://az.usembassy.gov/

Flag description: three equal horizontal bands of sky blue (top), red, and green; a vertical crescent moon and an eight-pointed star in white are centered in the red band; the blue band recalls Azerbaijan's Turkic heritage, red stands for modernization and progress, and green refers to Islam; the crescent moon and star are a Turkic insignia; the eight star points represent the eight Turkic peoples of the world

National symbol(s): flames of fire; national colors: blue, red, green

National anthem: *name:* "Azerbaijan Marsi" (March of Azerbaijan)
lyrics/music: Ahmed JAVAD/Uzeyir HAJIBEYOV
note: adopted 1992; although originally written in 1919 during a brief period of independence, "Azerbaijan Marsi" did not become the official anthem until after the dissolution of the Soviet Union

National heritage: *total World Heritage Sites:* 3 (all cultural)
selected World Heritage Site locales: Walled City of Baku; Gobustan Rock Art Cultural Landscape; Historic Center of Sheki

ECONOMY

Economic overview: Prior to the decline in global oil prices since 2014, Azerbaijan's high economic growth was attributable to rising energy exports and to some non-export sectors. Oil exports through the Baku-Tbilisi-Ceyhan Pipeline, the Baku-Novorossiysk, and the Baku-Supsa Pipelines remain the main economic driver, but efforts to boost Azerbaijan's gas production are underway. The expected completion of the geopolitically important Southern Gas Corridor (SGC) between Azerbaijan and Europe will open up another source of revenue from gas exports. First gas to Turkey through the SGC is expected in 2018 with project completion expected by 2020-21.

Declining oil prices caused a 3.1% contraction in GDP in 2016, and a 0.8% decline in 2017, highlighted by a sharp reduction in the construction sector. The economic decline was accompanied by higher inflation, a weakened banking sector, and two sharp currency devaluations in 2015. Azerbaijan's financial sector continued to struggle. In May 2017, Baku allowed the majority state-owed International Bank of Azerbaijan (IBA), the nation's largest bank, to default on some of its outstanding debt and file for restructuring in Azerbaijani courts; IBA also filed in US and UK bankruptcy courts to have its restructuring recognized in their respective jurisdictions.

Azerbaijan has made limited progress with market-based economic reforms. Pervasive public and private sector corruption and structural economic inefficiencies remain a drag on long-term growth, particularly in non-energy sectors. The government has, however, made efforts to combat corruption, particularly in customs and government services. Several other obstacles impede Azerbaijan's economic progress, including the need for more foreign investment in the non-energy sector and the continuing conflict with Armenia over the Nagorno-Karabakh region. While trade with Russia and the other former

Soviet republics remains important, Azerbaijan has expanded trade with Turkey and Europe and is seeking new markets for non-oil/gas exports - mainly in the agricultural sector - with Gulf Cooperation Council member countries, the US, and others. It is also improving Baku airport and the Caspian Sea port of Alat for use as a regional transportation and logistics hub.

Long-term prospects depend on world oil prices, Azerbaijan's ability to develop export routes for its growing gas production, and its ability to improve the business environment and diversify the economy. In late 2016, the president approved a strategic roadmap for economic reforms that identified key non-energy segments of the economy for development, such as agriculture, logistics, information technology, and tourism. In October 2017, the long-awaited Baku-Tbilisi-Kars railway, stretching from the Azerbaijani capital to Kars in north-eastern Turkey, began limited service.

Real GDP (purchasing power parity): $138.51 billion (2020 est.)
$144.74 billion (2019 est.)
$141.24 billion (2018 est.)
note: data are in 2017 dollars
country comparison to the world: 77

Real GDP growth rate: 0.1% (2017 est.)
-3.1% (2016 est.)
0.6% (2015 est.)
country comparison to the world: 188

Real GDP per capita: $13,700 (2020 est.)
$14,400 (2019 est.)
$14,200 (2018 est.)
note: data are in 2017 dollars
country comparison to the world: 112

GDP (official exchange rate): $48.104 billion (2019 est.)

Inflation rate (consumer prices): 2.6% (2019 est.)
2.3% (2018 est.)
12.8% (2017 est.)
country comparison to the world: 128

Credit ratings:

Fitch rating: BB+ (2016)

Moody's rating: Ba2 (2017)

Standard & Poors rating: BB+ (2016)
note: The year refers to the year in which the current credit rating was first obtained.

GDP - composition, by sector of origin: *agriculture:* 6.1% (2017 est.)
industry: 53.5% (2017 est.)
services: 40.4% (2017 est.)

GDP - composition, by end use: *household consumption:* 57.6% (2017 est.)
government consumption: 11.5% (2017 est.)
investment in fixed capital: 23.6% (2017 est.)
investment in inventories: 0.5% (2017 est.)
exports of goods and services: 48.7% (2017 est.)
imports of goods and services: -42% (2017 est.)

Agricultural products: milk, wheat, potatoes, barley, tomatoes, watermelons, cotton, apples, maize, onions

Industries: petroleum and petroleum products, natural gas, oilfield equipment; steel, iron ore; cement; chemicals and petrochemicals; textiles

Industrial production growth rate: -3.8% (2017 est.)
country comparison to the world: 191

Labor force: 4.939 million (2019 est.)
country comparison to the world: 79

Labor force - by occupation: *agriculture:* 37%
industry: 14.3%
services: 48.9% (2014)

Unemployment rate: 5% (2017 est.)
5% (2016 est.)
country comparison to the world: 79

Unemployment, youth ages 15-24: *total:* 12.4%
male: 10.9%
female: 14.2% (2019 est.)
country comparison to the world: 122

Population below poverty line: 4.9% (2015 est.)

Gini Index coefficient - distribution of family income: 33.7 (2008)
36.5 (2001)
country comparison to the world: 121

Household income or consumption by percentage share: *lowest 10%:* 3.4%
highest 10%: 27.4% (2008)

Budget: *revenues:* 9.556 billion (2017 est.)
expenditures: 10.22 billion (2017 est.)

Budget surplus (+) or deficit (-): -1.6% (of GDP) (2017 est.)
country comparison to the world: 93

Public debt: 54.1% of GDP (2017 est.)
50.7% of GDP (2016 est.)
country comparison to the world: 85

Taxes and other revenues: 23.5% (of GDP) (2017 est.)
country comparison to the world: 126

Fiscal year: calendar year

Current account balance: $1.685 billion (2017 est.)
-$1.363 billion (2016 est.)
country comparison to the world: 44

Exports: $15.21 billion (2020 est.)
$23.63 billion (2019 est.)
$25.48 billion (2018 est.)
note: Data are in current year dollars and do not include illicit exports or re-exports.
country comparison to the world: 91

Exports - partners: Italy 28%, Turkey 15%, Israel 7%, Germany 5%, India 5% (2017)

Exports - commodities: crude petroleum, natural gas, refined petroleum, tomatoes, gold (2019)

Imports: $15.54 billion (2020 est.) note: data are in current year dollars
$17.71 billion (2019 est.) note: data are in current year dollars
$17.71 billion (2018 est.) note: data are in current year dollars
country comparison to the world: 95

Imports - partners: United Kingdom 17%, Russia 17%, Turkey 12%, China 6% (2019)

Imports - commodities: gold, cars, refined petroleum, wheat, packaged medical supplies (2019)

Reserves of foreign exchange and gold: $6.681 billion (31 December 2017 est.)
$7.142 billion (31 December 2016 est.)
country comparison to the world: 88

Debt - external: $17.41 billion (31 December 2017 est.)
$13.83 billion (31 December 2016 est.)
country comparison to the world: 99

Exchange rates: Azerbaijani manats (AZN) per US dollar -
1.723 (2017 est.)
1.5957 (2016 est.)
1.5957 (2015 est.)
1.0246 (2014 est.)
0.7844 (2013 est.)

ENERGY

Electricity access: *electrification - total population:* 100% (2020)

Electricity: *installed generating capacity:* 7.677 million kW (2020 est.)
consumption: 21,026,630,000 kWh (2019 est.)
exports: 1.491 billion kWh (2020 est.)
imports: 137 million kWh (2020 est.)
transmission/distribution losses: 2.226 billion kWh (2019 est.)

Electricity generation sources: *fossil fuels:* 94.2% of total installed capacity (2020 est.)
solar: 0.2% of total installed capacity (2020 est.)
wind: 0.4% of total installed capacity (2020 est.)
hydroelectricity: 4.4% of total installed capacity (2020 est.)
biomass and waste: 0.8% of total installed capacity (2020 est.)

Coal: *production:* 0 metric tons (2020 est.)
consumption: 19,000 metric tons (2020 est.)
exports: 0 metric tons (2020 est.)
imports: 19,000 metric tons (2020 est.)
proven reserves: 0 metric tons (2019 est.)

Petroleum: *total petroleum production:* 711,700 bbl/day (2021 est.)
refined petroleum consumption: 107,500 bbl/day (2019 est.)
crude oil and lease condensate exports: 679,900 bbl/day (2018 est.)
crude oil and lease condensate imports: 0 bbl/day (2018 est.)
crude oil estimated reserves: 7 billion barrels (2021 est.)

Refined petroleum products - production: 138,900 bbl/day (2015 est.)
country comparison to the world: 61

Refined petroleum products - exports: 46,480 bbl/day (2015 est.)
country comparison to the world: 57

Refined petroleum products - imports: 5,576 bbl/day (2015 est.)
country comparison to the world: 168

Natural gas: *production:* 23,075,077,000 cubic meters (2019 est.)
consumption: 11,467,681,000 cubic meters (2019 est.)
exports: 11,586,357,000 cubic meters (2019 est.)
imports: 1,233,225,000 cubic meters (2019 est.)
proven reserves: 1,699,008,000,000 cubic meters (2021 est.)

Carbon dioxide emissions: 35.389 million metric tonnes of CO_2 (2019 est.)
from coal and metallurgical coke: 29,000 metric tonnes of CO_2 (2019 est.)
from petroleum and other liquids: 12.863 million metric tonnes of CO_2 (2019 est.)
from consumed natural gas: 22.497 million metric tonnes of CO_2 (2019 est.)
country comparison to the world: 72

Energy consumption per capita: 64.416 million Btu/person (2019 est.)
country comparison to the world: 86

COMMUNICATIONS

Telephones - fixed lines: *total subscriptions:* 1,652,688 (2020 est.)
subscriptions per 100 inhabitants: 16 (2020 est.)
country comparison to the world: 59

Telephones - mobile cellular: *total subscriptions:* 10,344,300 (2020 est.)
subscriptions per 100 inhabitants: 102 (2020 est.)
country comparison to the world: 87

Telecommunication systems: *general assessment:* in spite of the telecom sector being one of the major contributors to Azerbaijan's non-oil GDP, overall development, growth, and investment in the sector has been held back by years of political and civil unrest coupled with endemic corruption; mobile penetration rates reached 100% as far back as 2011 but have largely stagnated since then; the Mobile Network Operators (MNOs) are slowly extending the reach of their LTE networks around the country, and this increased coverage (along with access to faster data-based services) is expected to produce a moderate resurgence for both mobile and mobile broadband over the next few years as customers migrate from 3G to 4G. 5G services are still some ways off, as the demand for high-speed data and fast broadband can easily be met by existing capacity on LTE networks; fixed-line teledensity continues to drop down each year as customers consolidate their telecommunications services around the mobile platform; the rate of decline is comparatively slower than other countries, since Azerbaijan has a relatively high proportion of (87%) of fixed-line broadband customers still on DSL; fiber is gradually being rolled out in urban areas, and this makes up the bulk of the growth being seen in the overall fixed broadband market; DSL's predominance, however, will serve to keep Azerbaijan's average access speeds in the sub-10Mbps range for the foreseeable future (2020)
domestic: teledensity of some 16 fixed-lines per 100 persons; mobile-cellular teledensity of 102 telephones per 100 persons; satellite service connects Baku to a modern switch in its exclave of Naxcivan (Nakhchivan) (2020)
international: country code - 994; the TAE fiber-optic link transits Azerbaijan providing international connectivity to neighboring countries; the old Soviet system of cable and microwave is still serviceable; satellite earth stations - 2 (2019)

Broadcast media: 3 state-run and 1 public TV channels; 4 domestic commercial TV stations and about 15 regional TV stations; cable TV services are available in Baku; 1 state-run and 1 public radio network operating; a small number of private commercial radio stations broadcasting; local FM relays of Baku commercial stations are available in many localities; note - all broadcast media is pro-government, and most private broadcast media outlets are owned by entities directly linked to the government

Internet country code: .az

Internet users: *total:* 8,745,304 (2022 est.)
percent of population: 85% (2022 est.)
country comparison to the world: 61

Broadband - fixed subscriptions: *total:* 1,995,474 (2020 est.)
subscriptions per 100 inhabitants: 20 (2020 est.)
country comparison to the world: 58

TRANSPORTATION

National air transport system: *number of registered air carriers:* 42 (2020)
inventory of registered aircraft operated by air carriers: 44
annual passenger traffic on registered air carriers: 2,279,546 (2018)
annual freight traffic on registered air carriers: 44.09 million (2018) mt-km

Civil aircraft registration country code prefix: 4K

Airports: *total:* 23 (2021)
country comparison to the world: 132

Airports - with paved runways: *total:* 30
over 3,047 m: 5
2,438 to 3,047 m: 5
1,524 to 2,437 m: 13
914 to 1,523 m: 4
under 914 m: 3 (2021)

Airports - with unpaved runways: *total:* 7
under 914 m: 7 (2021)

Heliports: 1 (2021)

Pipelines: 89 km condensate, 3,890 km gas, 2,446 km oil (2013)

Railways: *total:* 2,944.3 km (2017)
broad gauge: 2,944.3 km (2017) 1.520-m gauge (approx. 1,767 km electrified)
country comparison to the world: 62

Roadways: *total:* 24,981 km (2013)
note: total roadway length has increased significantly and continues to grow due to the recovery of Armenian-held territories and related reconstruction efforts. No updated figure is currently available.
country comparison to the world: 104

Merchant marine: *total:* 305
by type: general cargo 38, oil tanker 43, other 224 (2021)
country comparison to the world: 54

Ports and terminals: *major seaport(s):* Baku (Baki) located on the Caspian Sea

MILITARY AND SECURITY

Military and security forces: Azerbaijan Armed Forces: Land Forces (Combined Arms Army), Air Forces, Navy Forces; Ministry of Internal Affairs: State Border Service (includes Coast Guard), Internal Security Troops (2022)

Military expenditures: 5.2% of GDP (2021 est.)
5.4% of GDP (2020 est.)
3.8% of GDP (2019 est.) (approximately $3.4 billion)
3.6% of GDP (2018 est.) (approximately $3.2 billion)
3.8% of GDP (2017 est.) (approximately $3.26 billion)
country comparison to the world: 9

Military and security service personnel strengths: information varies; approximately 65,000 active armed forces (55,000 Army; 2,000 Navy; 8,000 Air Force); approximately 15,000 Ministry of Internal Affairs troops (2022)

Military equipment inventories and acquisitions: the military's inventory is comprised mostly of Russian and Soviet-era weapons systems with a small mix of equipment from other countries, including Israel and Turkey (2022)

Military service age and obligation: 18-35 years of age for compulsory military service for men; 17-35 years of age for voluntary service for men and women (2022)
note: as of 2018, women made up an estimated 3% of the active duty military

Military - note: since November 2020, Russia has deployed about 2,000 peacekeeping troops to the area in and around Nagorno- Karabakh as part of a ceasefire agreement between Armenia and Azerbaijan; fighting erupted between the two countries over the Nagorno-Karabakh region in September of 2020; Nagorno-Karabakh lies within Azerbaijan but has been under control of ethnic Armenian forces (the "Nagorno-Karabakh Defense Army") backed by Armenia since a separatist war there ended in 1994; six weeks of fighting resulted in about 6,500 deaths and ended after Armenia ceded swaths of Nagorno-Karabakh territory; tensions remained high in 2022, and both sides have accused the other of provocations since the fighting ended; Armenia has accused Azerbaijani forces of a series of border intrusions and of seizing pockets of territory

TERRORISM

Terrorist group(s): Islamic State of Iraq and ash-Sham (ISIS); Islamic Revolutionary Guard Corps (IRGC)/Qods Force

TRANSNATIONAL ISSUES

Disputes - international: Local border forces struggle to control the illegal transit of goods and people across the porous, undemarcated Armenian, Azerbaijani, and Georgian borders.
Armenia-Azerbaijan: The dispute over the breakaway Nagorno-Karabakh region and the Armenian military occupation of surrounding lands in Azerbaijan remains the primary focus of regional instability. Residents have evacuated the former Soviet-era small ethnic enclaves in Armenia and Azerbaijan.
Azerbaijan-Georgia: A joint boundary commission agrees on most of the alignment, leaving only small areas at certain crossing points in dispute. Consequently, the two states have yet to agree on a delimitation or demarcation of their common boundary. One area of contention is where the international boundary should run through the 6th-13th Century David-Gareja monastery complex.
Azerbaijan-Iran: none identified
Azerbaijan-Russia: Russia complains of cross-border smuggling.
Azerbaijan-Turkey: none identified
Caspian Sea (Maritime Boundary): Azerbaijan, Kazakhstan, and Russia ratified the Caspian seabed delimitation treaties based on equidistance, while Iran continues to insist on a one-fifth slice of the sea. Bilateral talks continue with Turkmenistan on dividing the seabed and contested oilfields in the middle of the Caspian.

Refugees and internally displaced persons: *IDPs:* 655,000 (conflict with Armenia over Nagorno-Karabakh; IDPs are mainly ethnic Azerbaijanis but also include ethnic Kurds, Russians, and Turks predominantly from occupied territories around Nagorno-Karabakh; includes IDPs' descendants, returned IDPs, and people living in insecure areas and excludes people displaced by natural disasters; around half the IDPs live in the capital Baku) (2021)
stateless persons: 3,585 (mid-year 2021)

Illicit drugs: limited illicit cultivation of cannabis and opium poppy, mostly for CIS consumption; small government eradication program; transit point for Southwest Asian opiates bound for Russia and to a lesser extent the rest of Europe

BAHAMAS, THE

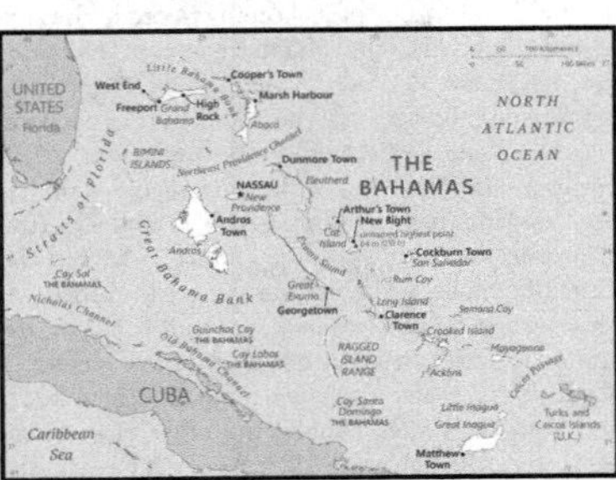

INTRODUCTION

Background: Lucayan Indians inhabited the islands when Christopher COLUMBUS first set foot in the New World on San Salvador in 1492. British settlement of the islands began in 1647; the islands became a colony in 1783. Piracy thrived in the 17th and 18th centuries because of The Bahamas close proximity to shipping lanes. Since attaining independence from the UK in 1973, The Bahamas has prospered through tourism, international banking, and investment management, which comprise up to 85% of GDP. Because of its proximity to the US - the nearest Bahamian landmass being only 80 km (50 mi) from Florida - the country is a major transshipment point for illicit trafficking, particularly to the US mainland, as well as Europe. US law enforcement agencies cooperate closely with The Bahamas, and the US Coast Guard assists Bahamian authorities in maritime security and law enforcement through Operation Bahamas, Turks and Caicos, or OPBAT.

GEOGRAPHY

Location: chain of islands in the North Atlantic Ocean, southeast of Florida, northeast of Cuba; note - although The Bahamas does not border the Caribbean Sea, geopolitically it is often designated as a Caribbean nation

Geographic coordinates: 24 15 N, 76 00 W

Map references: Central America and the Caribbean

Area: *total:* 13,880 sq km
land: 10,010 sq km
water: 3,870 sq km
country comparison to the world: 160

Area - comparative: slightly smaller than Connecticut

Land boundaries: *total:* 0 km

Coastline: 3,542 km

Maritime claims: *territorial sea:* 12 nm
exclusive economic zone: 200 nm

Climate: tropical marine; moderated by warm waters of Gulf Stream

Terrain: long, flat coral formations with some low rounded hills

Elevation: *highest point:* 1.3 km NE of Old Bight on Cat Island 64 m
lowest point: Atlantic Ocean 0 m

Natural resources: salt, aragonite, timber, arable land

Land use: *agricultural land:* 1.4% (2018 est.)
arable land: 0.8% (2018 est.)
permanent crops: 0.4% (2018 est.)
permanent pasture: 0.2% (2018 est.)
forest: 51.4% (2018 est.)
other: 47.2% (2018 est.)

Irrigated land: 10 sq km (2012)

Population distribution: most of the population lives in urban areas, with two-thirds living on New Providence Island where Nassau is located

Natural hazards: hurricanes and other tropical storms cause extensive flood and wind damage

Geography - note: strategic location adjacent to US and Cuba; extensive island chain of which 30 are inhabited

PEOPLE AND SOCIETY

Population: 355,608 (2022 est.)
country comparison to the world: 178

Nationality: *noun:* Bahamian(s)
adjective: Bahamian

Ethnic groups: African descent 90.6%, White 4.7%, mixed 2.1%, other 1.9%, unspecified 0.7% (2010 est.)
note: data represent population by racial group

Languages: English (official), Creole (among Haitian immigrants)

Religions: Protestant 69.9% (includes Baptist 34.9%, Anglican 13.7%, Pentecostal 8.9% Seventh Day Adventist 4.4%, Methodist 3.6%, Church of God 1.9%, Brethren 1.6%, other Protestant .9%), Roman Catholic 12%, other Christian 13% (includes Jehovah's Witness 1.1%), other 0.6%, none 1.9%, unspecified 2.6% (2010 est.)

Age structure: *0-14 years:* 21.7% (male 38,811/female 37,719)
15-24 years: 14.91% (male 26,636/female 25,945)
25-54 years: 43.56% (male 76,505/female 77,119)
55-64 years: 10.75% (male 17,508/female 20,391)
65 years and over: 9.08% (male 12,587/female 19,434) (2021 est.)

Dependency ratios: *total dependency ratio:* 41.5
youth dependency ratio: 30.6
elderly dependency ratio: 11
potential support ratio: 9.1 (2020 est.)

Median age: *total:* 32.8 years
male: 31.7 years
female: 34 years (2020 est.)
country comparison to the world: 104

Population growth rate: 0.82% (2022 est.)
country comparison to the world: 114

Birth rate: 14.64 births/1,000 population (2022 est.)
country comparison to the world: 118

Death rate: 6.41 deaths/1,000 population (2022 est.)
country comparison to the world: 139

Net migration rate: 0 migrant(s)/1,000 population (2022 est.)
country comparison to the world: 84

Population distribution: most of the population lives in urban areas, with two-thirds living on New Providence Island where Nassau is located

Urbanization: *urban population:* 83.5% of total population (2022)
rate of urbanization: 1.02% annual rate of change (2020-25 est.)

Major urban areas - population: 280,000 NASSAU (capital) (2018)

Sex ratio: *at birth:* 1.03 male(s)/female
0-14 years: 1.03 male(s)/female
15-24 years: 1.03 male(s)/female
25-54 years: 0.99 male(s)/female
55-64 years: 0.86 male(s)/female
65 years and over: 0.5 male(s)/female
total population: 0.95 male(s)/female (2022 est.)

Maternal mortality ratio: 70 deaths/100,000 live births (2017 est.)
country comparison to the world: 83

Infant mortality rate: *total:* 12.78 deaths/1,000 live births
male: 13.22 deaths/1,000 live births
female: 12.33 deaths/1,000 live births (2022 est.)
country comparison to the world: 111

Life expectancy at birth: *total population:* 76.13 years
male: 73.2 years
female: 79.14 years (2022 est.)
country comparison to the world: 107

Total fertility rate: 1.98 children born/woman (2022 est.)
country comparison to the world: 111

Drinking water source: *improved: total:* 98.9% of population
unimproved: total: 1.1% of population (2017 est.)

Current health expenditure: 5.8% of GDP (2019)

Physicians density: 1.94 physicians/1,000 population (2017)

Hospital bed density: 3 beds/1,000 population (2017)

Sanitation facility access: *improved: total:* 98.2% of population
unimproved: total: 1.8% of population (2017 est.)

HIV/AIDS - adult prevalence rate: 1.2% (2020 est.)
country comparison to the world: 34

Obesity - adult prevalence rate: 31.6% (2016)
country comparison to the world: 21

Alcohol consumption per capita: *total:* 9.48 liters of pure alcohol (2019 est.)
beer: 3.66 liters of pure alcohol (2019 est.)
wine: 1.43 liters of pure alcohol (2019 est.)
spirits: 4.08 liters of pure alcohol (2019 est.)
other alcohols: 0.31 liters of pure alcohol (2019 est.)
country comparison to the world: 28

Tobacco use: *total:* 10.6% (2020 est.)
male: 18.8% (2020 est.)
female: 2.4% (2020 est.)
country comparison to the world: 134

Education expenditures: 2.5% of GDP (2020 est.)
country comparison to the world: 167

Unemployment, youth ages 15-24
total: 25.8%
male: 20.8%
female: 31.6% (2016 est.)

ENVIRONMENT

Environment - current issues: coral reef decay; solid waste disposal

Environment - international agreements: *party to:* Biodiversity, Climate Change, Climate Change-Kyoto Protocol, Climate Change-Paris Agreement,

Comprehensive Nuclear Test Ban, Desertification, Endangered Species, Hazardous Wastes, Law of the Sea, Nuclear Test Ban, Ozone Layer Protection, Ship Pollution, Wetlands
signed, but not ratified: none of the selected agreements

Air pollutants: *particulate matter emissions:* 17.56 micrograms per cubic meter (2016 est.)
carbon dioxide emissions: 1.79 megatons (2016 est.)
methane emissions: 0.23 megatons (2020 est.)

Climate: tropical marine; moderated by warm waters of Gulf Stream

Land use: *agricultural land:* 1.4% (2018 est.)
arable land: 0.8% (2018 est.)
permanent crops: 0.4% (2018 est.)
permanent pasture: 0.2% (2018 est.)
forest: 51.4% (2018 est.)
other: 47.2% (2018 est.)

Urbanization: *urban population:* 83.5% of total population (2022)
rate of urbanization: 1.02% annual rate of change (2020-25 est.)

Revenue from forest resources: *forest revenues:* 0.01% of GDP (2018 est.)
country comparison to the world: 146

Revenue from coal: *coal revenues:* 0% of GDP (2018 est.)
country comparison to the world: 61

Waste and recycling: *municipal solid waste generated annually:* 264,000 tons (2015 est.)

Total water withdrawal: *municipal:* 31 million cubic meters (2017 est.)

Total renewable water resources: 700 million cubic meters (2017 est.)

GOVERNMENT

Country name: *conventional long form:* Commonwealth of The Bahamas
conventional short form: The Bahamas
etymology: name derives from the Spanish "baha mar," meaning "shallow sea," which describes the shallow waters of the Bahama Banks

Government type: parliamentary democracy under a constitutional monarchy; a Commonwealth realm

Capital: *name:* Nassau
geographic coordinates: 25 05 N, 77 21 W
time difference: UTC-5 (same time as Washington, DC, during Standard Time)
daylight saving time: +1hr, begins second Sunday in March; ends first Sunday in November
etymology: named after William III (1650-1702), king of England, Scotland, and Ireland, who was a member of the House of Nassau

Administrative divisions: 31 districts; Acklins Islands, Berry Islands, Bimini, Black Point, Cat Island, Central Abaco, Central Andros, Central Eleuthera, City of Freeport, Crooked Island and Long Cay, East Grand Bahama, Exuma, Grand Cay, Harbour Island, Hope Town, Inagua, Long Island, Mangrove Cay, Mayaguana, Moore's Island, North Abaco, North Andros, North Eleuthera, Ragged Island, Rum Cay, San Salvador, South Abaco, South Andros, South Eleuthera, Spanish Wells, West Grand Bahama

Independence: 10 July 1973 (from the UK)

National holiday: Independence Day, 10 July (1973)

Constitution: *history:* previous 1964 (preindependence); latest adopted 20 June 1973, effective 10 July 1973
amendments: proposed as an "Act" by Parliament; passage of amendments to articles such as the organization and composition of the branches of government requires approval by at least two-thirds majority of the membership of both houses of Parliament and majority approval in a referendum; passage of amendments to constitutional articles such as fundamental rights and individual freedoms, the powers, authorities, and procedures of the branches of government, or changes to the Bahamas Independence Act 1973 requires approval by at least three-fourths majority of the membership of both houses and majority approval in a referendum; amended many times, last in 2016

Legal system: common law system based on the English model

International law organization participation: has not submitted an ICJ jurisdiction declaration; non-party state to the ICCt

Citizenship: *citizenship by birth:* no
citizenship by descent only: at least one parent must be a citizen of The Bahamas
dual citizenship recognized: no
residency requirement for naturalization: 6-9 years

Suffrage: 18 years of age; universal

Executive branch: *chief of state:* King CHARLES III (since 8 September 2022); represented by Governor General Cornelius A. SMITH (since 28 June 2019)
head of government: Prime Minister Philip DAVIS (since 17 September 2021)
cabinet: Cabinet appointed by governor general on recommendation of prime minister
elections/appointments: the monarchy is hereditary; governor general appointed by the monarch on the advice of the prime minister; following legislative elections, the leader of the majority party or majority coalition usually appointed prime minister by the governor general; the prime minister recommends the deputy prime minister

Legislative branch: *description:* bicameral Parliament consists of:
Senate (16 seats; members appointed by the governor general - 9 selected on the advice of the prime minister, 4 on the advice of the leader of the opposition party, and 3 on the advice of the prime minister in consultation with the opposition leader; members serve 5-year terms)
House of Assembly (39 seats; members directly elected in single-seat constituencies by simple majority vote to serve 5-year terms)
elections:
Senate - last appointments on 24 May 2017 (next appointments in 2022)
House of Assembly - last held on 16 September 2021 (next to be held by September 2026)
election results:
Senate - appointed; composition as of March 2022 - men 12, women 4, percent of women 25%
House of Assembly - percent of vote by party - PLP 52.5%, FNM 36.2%; seats by party - PLP 32, FNM 7; composition as of March 2022 - men 32, women 7, percent of women 18%; note - total Parliament percent of women 20%
note: the government may dissolve the parliament and call elections at any time

Judicial branch: *highest court(s):* Court of Appeal (consists of the court president and 4 justices, organized in 3-member panels); Supreme Court (consists of the chief justice and a maximum of 11 and a minimum of 2 justices)
judge selection and term of office: Court of Appeal president and Supreme Court chief justice appointed by the governor-general on the advice of the prime minister after consultation with the leader of the opposition party; other Court of Appeal and Supreme Court justices appointed by the governor general upon recommendation of the Judicial and Legal Services Commission, a 5-member body headed by the chief justice; Court of Appeal justices appointed for life with mandatory retirement normally at age 68 but can be extended until age 70; Supreme Court justices appointed for life with mandatory retirement normally at age 65 but can be extended until age 67
subordinate courts: Industrial Tribunal; Stipendiary and Magistrates' Courts; Family Island Administrators
note: The Bahamas is a member of the 15-member Caribbean Community but is not party to the agreement establishing the Caribbean Court of Justice as its highest appellate court; the Judicial Committee of the Privy Council (in London) serves as the final court of appeal for The Bahamas

Political parties and leaders: Democratic National Alliance or DNA [Arinthia KOMOLAFE]
Free National Movement or FNM [Michael PINTARD]
Progressive Liberal Party or PLP [Philip "Brave" DAVIS]

International organization participation: ACP, AOSIS, C, Caricom, CDB, CELAC, FAO, G-77, IADB, IAEA, IBRD, ICAO, ICC (NGOs), ICRM, IDA, IFAD, IFC, IFRCS, ILO, IMF, IMO, IMSO, Interpol, IOC, IOM, ISO (correspondent), ITSO, ITU, LAES, MIGA, NAM, OAS, OPANAL, OPCW, Petrocaribe, UN, UNCTAD, UNESCO, UNIDO, UNWTO, UPU, WCO, WHO, WIPO, WMO, WTO (observer)

Diplomatic representation in the US: *chief of mission:* Ambassador Wendall Kermith JONES (since 19 April 2022)
chancery: 600 New Hampshire Ave NW, Suite 530, Washington, DC 20037
telephone: [1] (202) 319-2660
FAX: [1] (202) 319-2668
email address and website:
embassy@bahamasembdc.org
https://www.bahamasembdc.org/
consulate(s) general: Atlanta, Miami, New York, Washington, DC

Diplomatic representation from the US: chief of mission: Ambassador (vacant); Charge d' Affaires Usha E. PITTS (since 1 January 2021)
embassy: 42 Queen Street, Nassau
mailing address: 3370 Nassau Place, Washington, DC 20521-3370
telephone: [1] (242) 322-1181
FAX: [1] (242) 356-7174
email address and website:
acsnassau@state.gov
https://bs.usembassy.gov/

Flag description: three equal horizontal bands of aquamarine (top), gold, and aquamarine, with a black equilateral triangle based on the hoist side; the band colors represent the golden beaches of the islands surrounded by the aquamarine sea; black represents the vigor and force of a united people, while the pointing triangle indicates the enterprise and determination of the Bahamian people to develop the rich resources of land and sea

National symbol(s): blue marlin, flamingo, Yellow Elder flower; national colors: aquamarine, yellow, black

National anthem: *name:* "March On, Bahamaland!"
lyrics/music: Timothy GIBSON
note: adopted 1973; as a Commonwealth country, in addition to the national anthem, "God Save the King" serves as the royal anthem (see United Kingdom)

ECONOMY

Economic overview: The Bahamas has the second highest per capita GDP in the English-speaking Caribbean with an economy heavily dependent on tourism and financial services. Tourism accounts for approximately 50% of GDP and directly or indirectly employs half of the archipelago's labor force. Financial services constitute the second-most important sector of the Bahamian economy, accounting for about 15% of GDP. Manufacturing and agriculture combined contribute less than 7% of GDP and show little growth, despite government incentives aimed at those sectors. The new government led by Prime Minister Hubert MINNIS has prioritized addressing fiscal imbalances and rising debt, which stood at 75% of GDP in 2016. Large capital projects like the Baha Mar Casino and Hotel are driving growth. Public debt increased in 2017 in large part due to hurricane reconstruction and relief financing. The primary fiscal balance was a deficit of 0.4% of GDP in 2016. The Bahamas is the only country in the Western Hemisphere that is not a member of the World Trade Organization.

Real GDP (purchasing power parity): $12.1 billion (2020 est.)
$14.45 billion (2019 est.)
$14.28 billion (2018 est.)
note: data are in 2017 dollars
country comparison to the world: 158

Real GDP growth rate: 1.4% (2017 est.)
-1.7% (2016 est.)
1% (2015 est.)
country comparison to the world: 158

Real GDP per capita: $30,800 (2020 est.)
$37,100 (2019 est.)
$37,000 (2018 est.)
note: data are in 2017 dollars
country comparison to the world: 64

GDP (official exchange rate): $12.16 billion (2017 est.)

Inflation rate (consumer prices): 1.4% (2017 est.)
-0.3% (2016 est.)
country comparison to the world: 80

Credit ratings:

Moody's rating: *Ba2 (2020)*

Standard & Poors rating: BB- (2020)
note: The year refers to the year in which the current credit rating was first obtained.

GDP - composition, by sector of origin: *agriculture:* 2.3% (2017 est.)
industry: 7.7% (2017 est.)
services: 90% (2017 est.)

GDP - composition, by end use: *household consumption:* 68% (2017 est.)
government consumption: 13% (2017 est.)
investment in fixed capital: 26.3% (2017 est.)
investment in inventories: 0.7% (2017 est.)
exports of goods and services: 33.7% (2017 est.)
imports of goods and services: -41.8% (2017 est.)

Agricultural products: sugar cane, grapefruit, vegetables, bananas, tomatoes, poultry, tropical fruit, oranges, coconuts, mangoes/guavas

Industries: tourism, banking, oil bunkering, maritime industries, transshipment and logistics, salt, aragonite, pharmaceuticals

Industrial production growth rate: 5.8% (2017 est.)
country comparison to the world: 44

Labor force: 196,900 (2013 est.)
country comparison to the world: 171

Labor force - by occupation: *agriculture:* 3%
industry: 11%
services: 49%
tourism: 37% (2011 est.)

Unemployment rate: 10.1% (2017 est.)
12.2% (2016 est.)
country comparison to the world: 148

Unemployment, youth ages 15-24: *total:* 25.8%
male: 20.8%
female: 31.6% (2016 est.)
country comparison to the world: 51

Population below poverty line: 9.3% (2010 est.)

Household income or consumption by percentage share: *lowest 10%:* 1%
highest 10%: 22% (2007 est.)

Budget: *revenues:* 2.139 billion (2017 est.)
expenditures: 2.46 billion (2017 est.)

Budget surplus (+) or deficit (-): -2.6% (of GDP) (2017 est.)
country comparison to the world: 115

Public debt: 54.6% of GDP (2017 est.)
50.5% of GDP (2016 est.)
country comparison to the world: 80

Taxes and other revenues: 17.6% (of GDP) (2017 est.)
country comparison to the world: 166

Fiscal year: 1 July - 30 June

Current account balance: -$1.909 billion (2017 est.)
-$868 million (2016 est.)
country comparison to the world: 166

Exports: $1.69 billion (2020 est.)
$5.14 billion (2019 est.)
$4.75 billion (2018 est.)
note: Data are in current year dollars and do not include illicit exports or re-exports.
country comparison to the world: 160

Exports - partners: Poland 32%, United States 17%, Ecuador 9%, China 6%, Japan 5% (2019)

Exports - commodities: ships, refined petroleum, nitrogen compounds, crustaceans, styrene polymers (2019)

Imports: $3.64 billion (2020 est.) note: data are in current year dollars
$4.91 billion (2019 est.) note: data are in current year dollars
$5.12 billion (2018 est.) note: data are in current year dollars
country comparison to the world: 153

Imports - partners: United States 31%, South Korea 29%, Japan 14% (2019)

Imports - commodities: ships, refined petroleum, crude petroleum, recreational boats, cars (2019)

Reserves of foreign exchange and gold: $1.522 billion (31 December 2017 est.)
$1.002 billion (31 December 2016 est.)
country comparison to the world: 125

Debt - external: $17.56 billion (31 December 2013 est.)
$16.35 billion (31 December 2012 est.)
country comparison to the world: 98

Exchange rates: Bahamian dollars (BSD) per US dollar -
1 (2017 est.)
1 (2016 est.)
1 (2015 est.)
1 (2014 est.)
1 (2013 est.)

ENERGY

Electricity access: *electrification - total population:* 100% (2020)

Electricity: *installed generating capacity:* 578,000 kW (2020 est.)
consumption: 2,103,248,000 kWh (2019 est.)
exports: 0 kWh (2019 est.)
imports: 0 kWh (2020 est.)
transmission/distribution losses: 245,000 kWh (2019 est.)

Electricity generation sources: *fossil fuels:* 99.8% of total installed capacity (2020 est.)
solar: 0.2% of total installed capacity (2020 est.)

Petroleum: total petroleum production: 0 bbl/day (2021 est.)
refined petroleum consumption: 25,800 bbl/day (2019 est.)

Refined petroleum products – imports: 19,150 bbl/day (2015 est.)
country comparison to the world: 123

Natural gas: *production:* 0 cubic meters (2021 est.)
consumption: 4.417 million cubic meters (2019 est.)
exports: 0 cubic meters (2021 est.)
imports: 4.417 million cubic meters (2019 est.)
proven reserves: 0 cubic meters (2021 est.)

Carbon dioxide emissions: 3.984 million metric tonnes of CO2 (2019 est.)
from coal and metallurgical coke: 0 metric tonnes of CO2 (2019 est.)
from petroleum and other liquids: 3.976 million metric tonnes of CO2 (2019 est.)
from consumed natural gas: 7,000 metric tonnes of CO2 (2019 est.)
country comparison to the world: 142

Energy consumption per capita: 140.505 million Btu/person (2019 est.)
country comparison to the world: 37

COMMUNICATIONS

Telephones - fixed lines: *total subscriptions:* 91,000 (2020 est.)
subscriptions per 100 inhabitants: 23 (2020 est.)
country comparison to the world: 139

Telephones - mobile cellular: *total subscriptions:* 466,000 (2020 est.)
subscriptions per 100 inhabitants: 119 (2020 est.)
country comparison to the world: 175

Telecommunication systems: *general assessment:* the telecom sector has seen a decline in subscriber numbers (particularly for prepaid mobile services the mainstay of short term visitors) and revenue; fixed and mobile broadband services are two areas

that have benefited from the crisis as employees and students have resorted to working from home (2021)
domestic: 23 per 100 fixed-line, 119 per 100 mobile-cellular (2020)
international: country code - 1-242; landing points for the ARCOS-1, BICS, Bahamas 2-US, and BDSN fiber-optic submarine cables that provide links to South and Central America, parts of the Caribbean, and the US; satellite earth stations - 2; the Bahamas Domestic Submarine Network links all of the major islands; (2019)

Broadcast media: The Bahamas has 4 major TV providers that provide service to all major islands in the archipelago; 1 TV station is operated by government-owned, commercially run Broadcasting Corporation of the Bahamas (BCB) and competes freely with 4 privately owned TV stations; multi-channel cable TV subscription service is widely available; there are 32 licensed broadcast (radio) service providers, 31 are privately owned FM radio stations operating on New Providence, Grand Bahama Island, Abaco Island, and on smaller islands in the country; the BCB operates a multi-channel radio broadcasting network that has national coverage; the sector is regulated by the Utilities Regulation and Competition Authority (2019)

Internet country code: .bs

Internet users: *total:* 342,126 (2020 est.)
percent of population: 87% (2020 est.)
country comparison to the world: 169

Broadband - fixed subscriptions: *total:* 83,000 (2020 est.)
subscriptions per 100 inhabitants: 21 (2020 est.)
country comparison to the world: 130

TRANSPORTATION

National air transport system: *number of registered air carriers:* 5 (2020)
inventory of registered aircraft operated by air carriers: 35
annual passenger traffic on registered air carriers: 1,197,116 (2018)
annual freight traffic on registered air carriers: 160,000 (2018) mt-km

Civil aircraft registration country code prefix: C6

Airports: *total:* 54 (2021)
country comparison to the world: 85

Airports - with paved runways: *total:* 24
over 3,047 m: 2
2,438 to 3,047 m: 2
1,524 to 2,437 m: 13
914 to 1,523 m: 7 (2021)

Airports - with unpaved runways: *total:* 37
1,524 to 2,437 m: 4
914 to 1,523 m: 16
under 914 m: 17 (2021)

Heliports: 1 (2021)

Roadways: *total:* 2,700 km (2011)
paved: 1,620 km (2011)
unpaved: 1,080 km (2011)
country comparison to the world: 167

Merchant marine: *total:* 1,323
by type: bulk carrier 333, container ship 45, general cargo 64, oil tanker 224, other 657 (2021)
country comparison to the world: 19

Ports and terminals: *major seaport(s):* Freeport, Nassau, South Riding Point
cruise port(s): Nassau
container port(s) (TEUs): Freeport (1,396,568) (2019)

MILITARY AND SECURITY

Military and security forces: Royal Bahamas Defense Force (RBDF): includes land, air, maritime elements (2022)
note: the RBDF is primarily responsible for external security but also provides security at a detention center for migrants and performs some domestic security functions, such as guarding embassies; the Royal Bahamas Police Force (RBPF) maintains internal security; both the RBDF and the RBPF report to the minister of national security

Military expenditures: 0.8% of GDP (2022 est.)
0.9% of GDP (2021)
0.9% of GDP (2020)
0.7% of GDP (2019)
0.7% of GDP (2018)
country comparison to the world: 140

Military and security service personnel strengths: approximately 1,500 active RBDF personnel (2022)

Military equipment inventories and acquisitions: most of the RBDF's major equipment inventory is supplied by the Netherlands (2022)

Military service age and obligation: 18 years of age for voluntary male and female service; no conscription (2022)

Military - note: the RBDF was established in 1980; its primary responsibilities are disaster relief, maritime security, and counter-narcotics operations; it is a naval force, but includes a lightly-armed marine infantry/commando squadron for base and internal security, as well as a few light non-combat aircraft; the maritime element has coastal patrol craft and patrol boats; the RBDF maintains training relationships with the UK and the US (2022)

TRANSNATIONAL ISSUES

Disputes - international: *The Bahamas-US (Maritime Boundary):* In declaring its archipelagic waters and 200 nm EEZ in 1993 legislation, The Bahamas did not delimit the outer limits of the EEZ; but in areas where EEZs overlap with neighbors, The Bahamas agreed to equidistance as a line of separation. However, The Bahamas has yet to define maritime boundaries with any of its neighbors, including the United States, whose Florida coast lays about 70 nm from Grand Bahama Island.

Illicit drugs: a significant transit point for illegal drugs bound for the United States; illicit production of marijuana continues

BAHRAIN

INTRODUCTION

Background: In 1783, the Sunni AL-KHALIFA family took power in Bahrain. In order to secure these holdings, it entered into a series of treaties with the UK during the 19th century that made Bahrain a British protectorate. The archipelago attained its independence in 1971. A steady decline in oil production and reserves since 1970 prompted Bahrain to take steps to diversify its economy, in the process developing petroleum processing and refining, aluminum production, and hospitality and retail sectors. It has also endeavored to become a leading regional banking center, especially with respect to Islamic finance. Bahrain's small size, central location among Gulf countries, economic dependence on Saudi Arabia, and proximity to Iran require it to play a delicate balancing act in foreign affairs among its larger neighbors. Its foreign policy activities usually fall in line with Saudi Arabia and the UAE.

The Sunni royal family has long struggled to manage relations with its large Shia-majority population. In early 2011, amid Arab uprisings elsewhere in the region, the Bahraini Government confronted similar pro-democracy and reform protests at home with police and military action, including deploying Gulf Cooperation Council security forces to Bahrain. Failed political talks prompted opposition political societies to boycott 2014 legislative and municipal council elections. In 2018, a law preventing members of political societies dissolved by the courts from participating in elections effectively sidelined the majority of opposition figures from taking part in national elections. As a result, most members of parliament are independents. Ongoing dissatisfaction with the political status quo continues to factor into sporadic clashes between demonstrators and security forces. On 15 September 2020, Bahrain and the United Arab Emirates signed peace agreements (the Abraham Accords) with Israel – brokered by the

US – in Washington DC. Bahrain and the UAE thus became the third and fourth Middle Eastern countries, along with Egypt and Jordan, to recognize Israel.

GEOGRAPHY

Location: Middle East, archipelago in the Persian Gulf, east of Saudi Arabia

Geographic coordinates: 26 00 N, 50 33 E

Map references: Middle East

Area: *total:* 760 sq km
land: 760 sq km
water: 0 sq km
country comparison to the world: 187

Area - comparative: 3.5 times the size of Washington, DC

Land boundaries: *total:* 0 km

Coastline: 161 km

Maritime claims: *territorial sea:* 12 nm
contiguous zone: 24 nm
continental shelf: extending to boundaries to be determined

Climate: arid; mild, pleasant winters; very hot, humid summers

Terrain: mostly low desert plain rising gently to low central escarpment

Elevation: *highest point:* Jabal ad Dukhan 135 m
lowest point: Persian Gulf 0 m

Natural resources: oil, associated and nonassociated natural gas, fish, pearls

Land use: *agricultural land:* 11.3% (2018 est.)
arable land: 2.1% (2018 est.)
permanent crops: 3.9% (2018 est.)
permanent pasture: 5.3% (2018 est.)
forest: 0.7% (2018 est.)
other: 88% (2018 est.)

Irrigated land: 40 sq km (2012)

Major aquifers: Arabian Aquifer System

Population distribution: smallest population of the Gulf States, but urbanization rate exceeds 90%; largest settlement concentration is found on the far northern end of the island in and around Manamah and Al Muharraq

Natural hazards: periodic droughts; dust storms

Geography - note: close to primary Middle Eastern petroleum sources; strategic location in Persian Gulf, through which much of the Western world's petroleum must transit to reach open ocean

PEOPLE AND SOCIETY

Population: 1,540,558 (2022 est.)
note: immigrants make up approximately 45% of the total population, according to UN data (2019)
country comparison to the world: 155

Nationality: *noun:* Bahraini(s)
adjective: Bahraini

Ethnic groups: Bahraini 46%, Asian 45.5%, other Arab 4.7%, African 1.6%, European 1%, other 1.2% (includes Gulf Co-operative country nationals, North and South Americans, and Oceanians) (2010 est.)

Languages: Arabic (official), English, Farsi, Urdu
major-language sample(s):
العالم، المصدر الذي لا يمكن الاستغناء عنه للمعلومات الأساسية
كتاب حقائق (Arabic)

Religions: Muslim 73.7%, Christian 9.3%, Jewish 0.1%, other 16.9% (2017 est.)

Age structure: *0-14 years:* 18.45% (male 141,039/female 136,687)
15-24 years: 15.16% (male 129,310/female 98,817)
25-54 years: 56.14% (male 550,135/female 294,778)
55-64 years: 6.89% (male 64,761/female 38,870)
65 years and over: 3.36% (male 25,799/female 24,807) (2020 est.)

Dependency ratios: *total dependency ratio:* 26.5
youth dependency ratio: 23.1
elderly dependency ratio: 3.4
potential support ratio: 29.8 (2020 est.)

Median age: *total:* 32.9 years
male: 34.4 years
female: 30.3 years (2020 est.)
country comparison to the world: 102

Population growth rate: 0.88% (2022 est.)
country comparison to the world: 108

Birth rate: 12.4 births/1,000 population (2022 est.)
country comparison to the world: 147

Death rate: 2.82 deaths/1,000 population (2022 est.)
country comparison to the world: 226

Net migration rate: -0.82 migrant(s)/1,000 population (2022 est.)
country comparison to the world: 139

Population distribution: smallest population of the Gulf States, but urbanization rate exceeds 90%; largest settlement concentration is found on the far northern end of the island in and around Manamah and Al Muharraq

Urbanization: *urban population:* 89.7% of total population (2022)
rate of urbanization: 1.99% annual rate of change (2020-25 est.)

Major urban areas - population: 689,000 MANAMA (capital) (2022)

Sex ratio: *at birth:* 1.03 male(s)/female
0-14 years: 1.03 male(s)/female
15-24 years: 1.29 male(s)/female
25-54 years: 1.86 male(s)/female
55-64 years: 1.61 male(s)/female
65 years and over: 0.83 male(s)/female
total population: 1.52 male(s)/female (2022 est.)

Maternal mortality ratio: 14 deaths/100,000 live births (2017 est.)
country comparison to the world: 137

Infant mortality rate: *total:* 10.19 deaths/1,000 live births
male: 11.97 deaths/1,000 live births
female: 8.37 deaths/1,000 live births (2022 est.)
country comparison to the world: 136

Life expectancy at birth: *total population:* 79.9 years
male: 77.63 years
female: 82.24 years (2022 est.)
country comparison to the world: 52

Total fertility rate: 1.67 children born/woman (2022 est.)
country comparison to the world: 172

Drinking water source: *improved: total:* 100% of population
unimproved: total: 0% of population (2020 est.)

Current health expenditure: 4% of GDP (2019)

Physicians density: 0.93 physicians/1,000 population (2015)

Hospital bed density: 1.7 beds/1,000 population (2017)

Sanitation facility access: *improved: total:* 100% of population
unimproved: total: 0% of population (2020 est.)

HIV/AIDS - adult prevalence rate: (2017 est.) <.1%

Obesity - adult prevalence rate: 29.8% (2016)
country comparison to the world: 25

Alcohol consumption per capita: *total:* 1.18 liters of pure alcohol (2019 est.)
beer: 0.4 liters of pure alcohol (2019 est.)
wine: 0.11 liters of pure alcohol (2019 est.)
spirits: 0.66 liters of pure alcohol (2019 est.)
other alcohols: 0.01 liters of pure alcohol (2019 est.)
country comparison to the world: 147

Tobacco use: *total:* 14.9% (2020 est.)
male: 25.3% (2020 est.)
female: 4.5% (2020 est.)
country comparison to the world: 104

Education expenditures: 2.3% of GDP (2017 est.)
country comparison to the world: 172

Literacy: *definition:* age 15 and over can read and write
total population: 97.5%
male: 99.9%
female: 94.9% (2018)

School life expectancy (primary to tertiary education): *total:* 16 years
male: 16 years
female: 17 years (2019)

Unemployment, youth ages 15-24: *total:* 5.3%
male: 2.6%
female: 12.2% (2012 est.)

ENVIRONMENT

Environment - current issues: desertification resulting from the degradation of limited arable land, periods of drought, and dust storms; coastal degradation (damage to coastlines, coral reefs, and sea vegetation) resulting from oil spills and other discharges from large tankers, oil refineries, and distribution stations; lack of freshwater resources (groundwater and seawater are the only sources for all water needs); lowered water table leaves aquifers vulnerable to saline contamination; desalinization provides some 90% of the country's freshwater

Environment - international agreements: *party to:* Biodiversity, Climate Change, Climate Change-Kyoto Protocol, Climate Change-Paris Agreement, Comprehensive Nuclear Test Ban, Desertification, Endangered Species, Hazardous Wastes, Law of the Sea, Ozone Layer Protection, Ship Pollution, Wetlands
signed, but not ratified: none of the selected agreements

Air pollutants: *particulate matter emissions:* 69.04 micrograms per cubic meter (2016 est.)
carbon dioxide emissions: 31.69 megatons (2016 est.)
methane emissions: 15.47 megatons (2020 est.)

Climate: arid; mild, pleasant winters; very hot, humid summers

Land use: *agricultural land:* 11.3% (2018 est.)
arable land: 2.1% (2018 est.)
permanent crops: 3.9% (2018 est.)
permanent pasture: 5.3% (2018 est.)
forest: 0.7% (2018 est.)
other: 88% (2018 est.)

Urbanization: *urban population:* 89.7% of total population (2022)
rate of urbanization: 1.99% annual rate of change (2020-25 est.)

Revenue from forest resources: *forest revenues:* 0% of GDP (2018 est.)
country comparison to the world: 163

Revenue from coal: *coal revenues:* 0% of GDP (2018 est.)
country comparison to the world: 62

Waste and recycling: *municipal solid waste generated annually:* 951,943 tons (2016 est.)
municipal solid waste recycled annually: 76,155 tons (2012 est.)
percent of municipal solid waste recycled: 8% (2012 est.)

Major aquifers: Arabian Aquifer System

Total water withdrawal: *municipal:* 275.6 million cubic meters (2017 est.)
industrial: 14.1 million cubic meters (2017 est.)
agricultural: 144.7 million cubic meters (2017 est.)

Total renewable water resources: 116 million cubic meters (2017 est.)

GOVERNMENT

Country name: *conventional long form:* Kingdom of Bahrain
conventional short form: Bahrain
local long form: Mamlakat al Bahrayn
local short form: Al Bahrayn
former: Dilmun, Tylos, Awal, Mishmahig, Bahrayn, State of Bahrain
etymology: the name means "the two seas" in Arabic and refers to the water bodies surrounding the archipelago

Government type: constitutional monarchy

Capital: *name:* Manama
geographic coordinates: 26 14 N, 50 34 E
time difference: UTC+3 (8 hours ahead of Washington, DC, during Standard Time)
etymology: name derives from the Arabic "al-manama" meaning "place of rest" or "place of dreams"

Administrative divisions: 4 governorates (muhafazat, singular - muhafazah); Asimah (Capital), Janubiyah (Southern), Muharraq, Shamaliyah (Northern)
note: each governorate administered by an appointed governor

Independence: 15 August 1971 (from the UK)

National holiday: National Day, 16 December (1971); note - 15 August 1971 was the date of independence from the UK, 16 December 1971 was the date of independence from British protection

Constitution: *history:* adopted 14 February 2002
amendments: proposed by the king or by at least 15 members of either chamber of the National Assembly followed by submission to an Assembly committee for review and, if approved, submitted to the government for restatement as drafts; passage requires a two-thirds majority vote by the membership of both chambers and validation by the king; constitutional articles on the state religion (Islam), state language (Arabic), and the monarchy and "inherited rule" cannot be amended; amended 2012, 2017

Legal system: mixed legal system of Islamic (sharia) law, English common law, Egyptian civil, criminal, and commercial codes; customary law

International law organization participation: has not submitted an ICJ jurisdiction declaration; non-party state to the ICCt

Citizenship: *citizenship by birth:* no
citizenship by descent only: the father must be a citizen of Bahrain
dual citizenship recognized: no
residency requirement for naturalization: 25 years; 15 years for Arab nationals

Suffrage: 20 years of age; universal

Executive branch: *chief of state:* King HAMAD bin Isa Al-Khalifa (since 6 March 1999); Crown Prince SALMAN bin Hamad Al-Khalifa (born 21 October 1969)
head of government: Prime Minister Crown Prince SALMAN bin Hamad Al-Khalifa (since 11 November 2020); Deputy Prime Minister and Minister for Infrastructure KHALID bin Abdallah Al Khalifa (since 13 June 2022)
cabinet: Cabinet appointed by the monarch
elections/appointments: the monarchy is hereditary; prime minister appointed by the monarch

Legislative branch: *description:* bicameral National Assembly consists of:
Consultative Council or Majlis al-Shura (40 seats; members appointed by the king)
Council of Representatives or Majlis al-Nuwab (40 seats; members directly elected in single-seat constituencies by absolute majority vote in 2 rounds if needed; members serve 4-year renewable terms)
elections:
Consultative Council - last appointments on 12 December 2018 (next NA)
Council of Representatives - first round for 9 members held on 24 November 2018; second round for remaining 31 members held on 1 December 2018 (next to be held on 12 November 2022)
election results:
Consultative Council - composition - men 31, women 9, percent of women 22.5%
Council of Representatives (for 2018 election) - percent of vote by society - NA; seats by society - Islamic Al-Asalah (Sunni Salafi) 3, Minbar al-Taqadumi (Communist) 2, National Unity Gathering (Sunni progovernment) 1, National Islamic Minbar (Sunni Muslim Brotherhood) 1, independent 33; composition - men 34, women 6, percent of women 15%; note - total National Assembly percent of women 19%

Judicial branch: *highest court(s):* Court of Cassation (consists of the chairman and 3 judges); Supreme Court of Appeal (consists of the chairman and 3 judges); Constitutional Court (consists of the president and 6 members); High Sharia Court of Appeal (court sittings include the president and at least one judge)
judge selection and term of office: Court of Cassation judges appointed by royal decree and serve for a specified tenure; Constitutional Court president and members appointed by the Higher Judicial Council, a body chaired by the monarch and includes judges from the Court of Cassation, sharia law courts, and Civil High Courts of Appeal; members serve 9-year terms; High Sharia Court of Appeal member appointments by royal decree for a specified tenure
subordinate courts: Civil High Courts of Appeal; middle and lower civil courts; High Sharia Court of Appeal; Senior Sharia Court; Administrative Courts of Appeal; military courts
note: the judiciary of Bahrain is divided into civil law courts and sharia law courts; sharia courts (involving personal status and family law) are further divided into Sunni Muslim and Shia Muslim; the Courts are supervised by the Supreme Judicial Council.

Political parties and leaders: *note:* political parties are prohibited, but political societies were legalized under a July 2005 law

International organization participation: ABEDA, AFESD, AMF, CAEU, CICA, FAO, G-77, GCC, IAEA, IBRD, ICAO, ICC (national committees), ICRM, IDA, IDB, IFC, IFRCS, IHO, ILO, IMF, IMO, IMSO, Interpol, IOC, IOM (observer), IPU, ISO, ITSO, ITU, ITUC (NGOs), LAS, MIGA, NAM, OAPEC, OIC, OPCW, PCA, UN, UNCTAD, UNESCO, UNIDO, UNWTO, UPU, WCO, WFTU (NGOs), WHO, WIPO, WMO, WTO

Diplomatic representation in the US: *chief of mission:* Ambassador Abdulla bin Rashid AL KHALIFA (since 21 July 2017)
chancery: 3502 International Drive NW, Washington, DC 20008
telephone: [1] (202) 342-1111
FAX: [1] (202) 362-2192
email address and website:
ambsecretary@bahrainembassy.org
mofa.gov.bh
consulate(s) general: New York

Diplomatic representation from the US: *chief of mission:* Ambassador Steven C. BONDY (since 9 February 2022)
embassy: Building 979, Road 3119 (next to Al-Ahli Sports Club), Block 331, Zinj District, P.O. Box 26431, Manama
mailing address: 6210 Manama Place, Washington DC 20521-6210
telephone: [973] 17-242700
FAX: [973] 17-272594
email address and website:
ManamaConsular@state.gov
https://bh.usembassy.gov/

Flag description: red, the traditional color for flags of Persian Gulf states, with a white serrated band (five white points) on the hoist side; the five points represent the five pillars of Islam
note: until 2002, the flag had eight white points, but this was reduced to five to avoid confusion with the Qatari flag

National symbol(s): a red field surmounted by a white serrated band with five white points; national colors: red, white

National anthem: *name:* "Bahrainona" (Our Bahrain)
lyrics/music: unknown
note: adopted 1971; although Mohamed Sudqi AYYASH wrote the original lyrics, they were changed in 2002 following the transformation of Bahrain from an emirate to a kingdom

National heritage: *total World Heritage Sites:* 3 (all cultural)
selected World Heritage Site locales: Dilmun Burial Mounds; Qal'at al-Bahrain – Ancient Harbor and Capital of Dilmun; Bahrain Pearling Path

ECONOMY

Economic overview: Oil and natural gas play a dominant role in Bahrain's economy. Despite the

Government's past efforts to diversify the economy, oil still comprises 85% of Bahraini budget revenues. In the last few years lower world energy prices have generated sizable budget deficits - about 10% of GDP in 2017 alone. Bahrain has few options for covering these deficits, with low foreign assets and fewer oil resources compared to its GCC neighbors. The three major US credit agencies downgraded Bahrain's sovereign debt rating to "junk" status in 2016, citing persistently low oil prices and the government's high debt levels. Nevertheless, Bahrain was able to raise about $4 billion by issuing foreign currency denominated debt in 2017.

Other major economic activities are production of aluminum - Bahrain's second biggest export after oil and gas –finance, and construction. Bahrain continues to seek new natural gas supplies as feedstock to support its expanding petrochemical and aluminum industries. In April 2018 Bahrain announced it had found a significant oil field off the country's west coast, but is still assessing how much of the oil can be extracted profitably.

In addition to addressing its current fiscal woes, Bahraini authorities face the long-term challenge of boosting Bahrain's regional competitiveness — especially regarding industry, finance, and tourism — and reconciling revenue constraints with popular pressure to maintain generous state subsidies and a large public sector. Since 2015, the government lifted subsidies on meat, diesel, kerosene, and gasoline and has begun to phase in higher prices for electricity and water. As part of its diversification plans, Bahrain implemented a Free Trade Agreement (FTA) with the US in August 2006, the first FTA between the US and a Gulf state. It plans to introduce a Value Added Tax (VAT) by the end of 2018.

Real GDP (purchasing power parity): $69.65 billion (2020 est.)
$73.95 billion (2019 est.)
$72.51 billion (2018 est.)
note: data are in 2017 dollars
country comparison to the world: 104

Real GDP growth rate: 2.49% (2019 est.)
13.89% (2018 est.)
3.85% (2017 est.)
country comparison to the world: 115

Real GDP per capita: $40,900 (2020 est.)
$45,100 (2019 est.)
$46,200 (2018 est.)
note: data are in 2017 dollars
country comparison to the world: 42

GDP (official exchange rate) :$38.472 billion (2019 est.)

Inflation rate (consumer prices): 1.4% (2017 est.)
2.8% (2016 est.)
country comparison to the world: 81

Credit ratings:

Fitch rating: *B+ (2020)*

Moody's rating: B2 (2018)

Standard & Poors rating: B+ (2017)
note: The year refers to the year in which the current credit rating was first obtained.

GDP - composition, by sector of origin: *agriculture:* 0.3% (2017 est.)
industry: 39.3% (2017 est.)
services: 60.4% (2017 est.)

GDP - composition, by end use: *household consumption:* 45.8% (2017 est.)
government consumption: 15.5% (2017 est.)
investment in fixed capital: 26.1% (2017 est.)
investment in inventories: 0.4% (2017 est.)
exports of goods and services: 80.2% (2017 est.)
imports of goods and services: -67.9% (2017 est.)

Agricultural products: mutton, dates, milk, poultry, tomatoes, fruit, sheep offals, sheep skins, eggs, pumpkins

Industries: petroleum processing and refining, aluminum smelting, iron pelletization, fertilizers, Islamic and offshore banking, insurance, ship repairing, tourism

Industrial production growth rate: 0.6% (2017 est.)
country comparison to the world: 165

Labor force: 831,600 (2017 est.)
note: excludes unemployed; 44% of the population in the 15-64 age group is non-national
country comparison to the world: 144

Labor force - by occupation: *agriculture:* 1%
industry: 32%
services: 67% (2004 est.)

Unemployment rate: 3.6% (2017 est.)
3.7% (2016 est.)
note: official estimate; actual rate is higher
country comparison to the world: 50

Unemployment, youth ages 15-24: *total:* 5.3%
male: 2.6%
female: 12.2% (2012 est.)
country comparison to the world: 167

Budget: *revenues:* 5.854 billion (2017 est.)
expenditures: 9.407 billion (2017 est.)

Budget surplus (+) or deficit (-): -10.1% (of GDP) (2017 est.)
country comparison to the world: 211

Public debt: 88.5% of GDP (2017 est.)
81.4% of GDP (2016 est.)
country comparison to the world: 26

Taxes and other revenues: 16.6% (of GDP) (2017 est.)
country comparison to the world: 176

Fiscal year: calendar year

Current account balance: -$1.6 billion (2017 est.)
-$1.493 billion (2016 est.)
country comparison to the world: 162

Exports: $30.1 billion (2018 est.)
$26.762 billion (2017 est.)
note: Data are in current year dollars and do not include illicit exports or re-exports.
country comparison to the world: 70

Exports - partners: United Arab Emirates 31%, Saudi Arabia 12%, Japan 8%, United States 8% (2019)

Exports - commodities: refined petroleum, aluminum and plating, crude petroleum, iron ore, gold (2019)

Imports: $27.19 billion (2018 est.) note: data are in current year dollars
$22.132 billion (2017 est.)
country comparison to the world: 73

Imports - partners: United Arab Emirates 27%, China 11%, Saudi Arabia 7%, United States 5%, Brazil 5%, Japan 5%, India 5% (2019)

Imports - commodities: cars, iron ore, jewelry, gold, gas turbines (2019)

Reserves of foreign exchange and gold: $2.349 billion (31 December 2017 est.)
$3.094 billion (31 December 2016 est.)
country comparison to the world: 118

Debt - external: $52.15 billion (31 December 2017 est.)
$42.55 billion (31 December 2016 est.)
country comparison to the world: 66

Exchange rates: Bahraini dinars (BHD) per US dollar -
0.37705 (2020 est.)
0.37705 (2019 est.)
0.377 (2018 est.)
0.376 (2014 est.)
0.376 (2013 est.)

ENERGY

Electricity access: *electrification - total population:* 100% (2020)

Electricity: *installed generating capacity:* 6.982 million kW (2020 est.)
consumption: 31,038,250,000 kWh (2019 est.)
exports: 447 million kWh (2019 est.)
imports: 652 million kWh (2019 est.)
transmission/distribution losses: 611 million kWh (2019 est.)

Electricity generation sources: *fossil fuels:* 100% of total installed capacity (2020 est.)

Petroleum: total petroleum production: 185,300 bbl/day (2021 est.)
refined petroleum consumption: 73,200 bbl/day (2019 est.)
crude oil and lease condensate exports: 0 bbl/day (2018 est.)
crude oil and lease condensate imports: 228,800 bbl/day (2018 est.)
crude oil estimated reserves: 186.5 million barrels (2021 est.)

Refined petroleum products - production: 274,500 bbl/day (2015 est.)
country comparison to the world: 45

Refined petroleum products - exports: 245,300 bbl/day (2015 est.)
country comparison to the world: 30

Refined petroleum products - imports: 14,530 bbl/day (2015 est.)
country comparison to the world: 136

Natural gas: *production:* 18,271,840,000 cubic meters (2019 est.)
consumption: 18,251,140,000 cubic meters (2019 est.)
exports: 0 cubic meters (2021 est.)
imports: 0 cubic meters (2021 est.)
proven reserves: 81.382 billion cubic meters (2021 est.)

Carbon dioxide emissions: 43.112 million metric tonnes of CO_2 (2019 est.)
from petroleum and other liquids: 7.308 million metric tonnes of CO_2 (2019 est.)
from consumed natural gas: 35.804 million metric tonnes of CO_2 (2019 est.)
country comparison to the world: 61

Energy consumption per capita: 547.976 million Btu/person (2019 est.)
country comparison to the world: 3

COMMUNICATIONS

Telephones - fixed lines: *total subscriptions:* 274,106 (2020 est.)
subscriptions per 100 inhabitants: 16 (2020 est.)
country comparison to the world: 112

Telephones - mobile cellular: *total subscriptions:* 1,748,672 (2020 est.)

subscriptions per 100 inhabitants: 103 (2020 est.)
country comparison to the world: 155

Telecommunication systems: *general assessment:* Bahrain continues to develop its telecoms sector in a bid to develop its long-term Economic Vision 2030 strategy; this is a multi-faceted strategy aimed at developing a digital transformation across numerous sectors, including e-government, e-health, e-commerce, and e-banking; 5G services have become widely available since they were launched in 2020; Bahrain's telecom sector by the Fourth National Telecommunications Plan (initiated in 2016) which focuses on fiber optic infrastructure deployment and establishing affordable prices for high-speed access (2022)
domestic: approximately 16 per 100 fixed-line and 103 per 100 mobile-cellular; modern fiber-optic integrated services; digital network with rapidly expanding mobile-cellular telephones (2020)
international: country code - 973; landing points for the FALCON, Tata TGN-Gulf, GBICS/MENA, and FOG submarine cable network that provides links to Asia, the Middle East, and Africa; tropospheric scatter to Qatar and UAE; microwave radio relay to Saudi Arabia; satellite earth station - 1 (2019)

Broadcast media: state-run Bahrain Radio and Television Corporation (BRTC) operates 5 terrestrial TV networks and several radio stations; satellite TV systems provide access to international broadcasts; 1 private FM station directs broadcasts to Indian listeners; radio and TV broadcasts from countries in the region are available (2019)

Internet country code: .bh

Internet users: *total:* 170,158 (2020 est.)
percent of population: 100% (2020 est.)
country comparison to the world: 177

Broadband - fixed subscriptions: *total:* 148,928 (2020 est.)
subscriptions per 100 inhabitants: 9 (2020 est.)
country comparison to the world: 123

TRANSPORTATION

National air transport system: *number of registered air carriers:* 6 (2020)
inventory of registered aircraft operated by air carriers: 42
annual passenger traffic on registered air carriers: 5,877,003 (2018)
annual freight traffic on registered air carriers: 420.98 million (2018) mt-km

Civil aircraft registration country code prefix: A9C

Airports: *total:* 4 (2021)
country comparison to the world: 183

Airports - with paved runways: *total:* 4
over 3,047 m: 3
914 to 1,523 m: 1 (2021)

Heliports: 1 (2021)

Pipelines: 20 km gas, 54 km oil (2013)

Roadways: *total:* 4,122 km (2010)
paved: 3,392 km (2010)
unpaved: 730 km (2010)
country comparison to the world: 152

Merchant marine: *total:* 205
by type: general cargo 12, oil tanker 4, other 189 (2021)
country comparison to the world: 65

Ports and terminals: *major seaport(s):* Mina' Salman, Sitrah

MILITARY AND SECURITY

Military and security forces: Bahrain Defense Force (BDF): Royal Bahraini Army (includes the Royal Guard), Royal Bahraini Navy, Royal Bahraini Air Force; Ministry of Interior: National Guard, Special Security Forces Command (SSFC), Coast Guard (2022)
note: the Royal Guard is officially under the command of the Army, but exercises considerable autonomy; the National Guard's primary mission is to guard critical infrastructure such as the airport and oil fields; while the Guard is under the Ministry of Interior, it reports directly to the king

Military expenditures: 3.6% of GDP (2021 est.)
4.2% of GDP (2020 est.)
4% of GDP (2019 est.) (approximately $2.09 billion)
4% of GDP (2018 est.) (approximately $2.08 billion)
4.2% of GDP (2017 est.) (approximately $2.18 billion)
country comparison to the world: 22

Military and security service personnel strengths: information varies; approximately 10,000 active personnel (7,500 Army; 1,000 Navy; 1,500 Air Force); approximately 3,000 National Guard (2022)

Military equipment inventories and acquisitions: the inventory of the Bahrain Defense force consists of a mix of equipment acquired from a wide variety of suppliers; since 2010, the US is the leading supplier of arms to Bahrain (2022)

Military service age and obligation: 18 years of age for voluntary military service; 15 years of age for non-commissioned officers, technicians, and cadets; no conscription (2022)
note: the BDF hires foreign nationals, Sunni Muslims primarily from Arabic countries and Pakistan, to serve under contract; as of 2020, foreigners were estimated to comprise as much as 80% of the military; the policy has become a controversial issue with the primarily Shia population; during the 2011, the BDF reportedly deployed mostly foreign personnel against protesters

Military - note: Bahrain hosts the US Naval Forces Central Command (USNAVCENT; established 1983), which includes the US 5th Fleet, several subordinate naval task forces, and the Combined Maritime Forces (established 2002), a coalition of more than 30 nations providing maritime security for regional shipping lanes; in 2018, the UK opened a naval support base in Bahrain

in addition to the US and UK, Bahrain maintains close security ties to Saudi Arabia and the United Arab Emirates (UAE); both Saudi Arabia and the UAE sent forces to Bahrain to assist with internal security following the 2011 uprising; in 2015, Bahrain joined the Saudi Arabia-led military action to try to restore the Government of Yemen that was ousted by Iranian-backed Huthi rebels, supplying a few hundred troops and combat aircraft

Bahrain has Major Non-NATO Ally (MNNA) status with the US; MNNA is a designation under US law that provides foreign partners with certain benefits in the areas of defense trade and security cooperation; while MNNA status provides military and economic privileges, it does not entail any security commitments (2022)

TERRORISM

Terrorist group(s): al-Ashtar Brigades; Islamic Revolutionary Guard Corps/Qods Force
note 1: in addition to the al-Ashtar Brigades and the IRGC/Qods Force, Saraya al-Mukhtar (aka The Mukhtar Brigade) is an Iran-backed terrorist organization based in Bahrain, reportedly receiving financial and logistic support from the IRGC; Saraya al-Mukhtar's self-described goal is to depose the Bahraini Government with the intention of paving the way for Iran to exert greater influence in Bahrain; the group was designated by the US as a Specially Designated Global Terrorist in Dec 2020

TRANSNATIONAL ISSUES

Disputes - international: none identified

BANGLADESH

INTRODUCTION

Background: The huge delta region formed at the confluence of the Ganges and Brahmaputra River systems - now referred to as Bangladesh - was a loosely incorporated outpost of various empires centered on the Gangetic plain for much of the first millennium A.D. Muslim conversions and settlement in the region began in the 10th century, primarily from Arab and Persian traders and preachers. Europeans established trading posts in the area in the 16th century. Eventually the area known as Bengal, primarily Hindu in the western section and mostly Muslim in the eastern half, became part of British India. Partition in 1947 resulted in an eastern wing of Pakistan in the Muslim-majority area, which became East Pakistan. Calls for greater autonomy and animosity between the eastern and western wings of Pakistan led to a Bengali independence movement. That movement, led by the Awami League (AL) and supported by India, won the independence war for Bangladesh in 1971.

The post-independence AL government faced daunting challenges and in 1975 it was overthrown by the military, triggering a series of military coups that resulted in a military-backed government and subsequent creation of the Bangladesh Nationalist Party (BNP) in 1978. That government also ended in a coup in 1981, followed by military-backed rule until democratic elections occurred in 1991. The BNP and AL have alternated in power since 1991, with the exception of a military-backed, emergency caretaker regime that suspended parliamentary

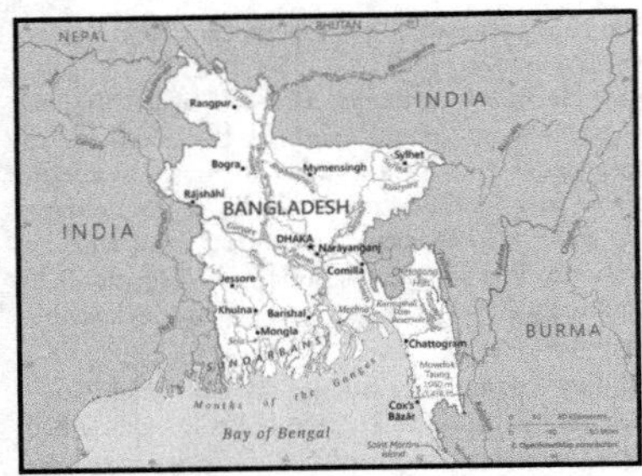

elections planned for January 2007 in an effort to reform the political system and root out corruption. That government returned the country to fully democratic rule in December 2008 with the election of the AL and Prime Minister Sheikh HASINA. In January 2014, the incumbent AL won the national election by an overwhelming majority after the BNP boycotted the election, which extended HASINA's term as prime minister. In December 2018, HASINA secured a third consecutive term (fourth overall) with the AL coalition securing 96% of available seats, amid widespread claims of election irregularities. With the help of international development assistance, Bangladesh has reduced the poverty rate from over half of the population to less than a third, achieved Millennium Development Goals for maternal and child health, and made great progress in food security since independence. The economy has grown at an annual average of about 6% for the last two decades. In 2021 the UN approved a resolution to allow Bangladesh to officially graduate from least-developed-country (LDC) status in 2026, based on World Bank criteria.

GEOGRAPHY

Location: Southern Asia, bordering the Bay of Bengal, between Burma and India

Geographic coordinates: 24 00 N, 90 00 E

Map references: Asia

Area: *total:* 148,460 sq km
land: 130,170 sq km
water: 18,290 sq km
country comparison to the world: 94

Area - comparative: slightly larger than Pennsylvania and New Jersey combined; slightly smaller than Iowa

Land boundaries: *total:* 4,413 km
border countries (2): Burma 271 km; India 4,142 km

Coastline: 580 km

Maritime claims: *territorial sea:* 12 nm
contiguous zone: 18 nm
exclusive economic zone: 200 nm
continental shelf: to the outer limits of the continental margin

Climate: tropical; mild winter (October to March); hot, humid summer (March to June); humid, warm rainy monsoon (June to October)

Terrain: mostly flat alluvial plain; hilly in southeast

Elevation: *highest point:* Mowdok Taung 1,060 m
lowest point: Indian Ocean 0 m
mean elevation: 85 m

Natural resources: natural gas, arable land, timber, coal

Land use: *agricultural land:* 70.1% (2018 est.)
arable land: 59% (2018 est.)
permanent crops: 6.5% (2018 est.)
permanent pasture: 4.6% (2018 est.)
forest: 11.1% (2018 est.)
other: 18.8% (2018 est.)

Irrigated land: 53,000 sq km (2012)

Major rivers (by length in km): Brahmaputra river mouth (shared with China [s] and India) - 3,969 km; Ganges river mouth (shared with India [s]) - 2,704 km
note – [s] after country name indicates river source; [m] after country name indicates river mouth

Major watersheds (area sq km): Indian Ocean drainage: Brahmaputra (651,335 sq km), Ganges (1,016,124 sq km)

Major aquifers: Indus-Ganges-Brahmaputra Basin

Natural hazards: droughts; cyclones; much of the country routinely inundated during the summer monsoon season

Geography - note: most of the country is situated on deltas of large rivers flowing from the Himalayas: the Ganges unites with the Jamuna (main channel of the Brahmaputra) and later joins the Meghna to eventually empty into the Bay of Bengal

PEOPLE AND SOCIETY

Population: 165,650,475 (2022 est.)
country comparison to the world: 8

Nationality: *noun:* Bangladeshi(s)
adjective: Bangladeshi

Ethnic groups: Bengali at least 98.9%, other indigenous ethnic groups 1.1% (2011 est.)
note: Bangladesh's government recognizes 27 indigenous ethnic groups under the 2010 Cultural Institution for Small Anthropological Groups Act; other sources estimate there are about 75 ethnic groups; critics of the 2011 census claim that it underestimates the size of Bangladesh's ethnic population

Languages: Bangla 98.8% (official, also known as Bengali), other 1.2% (2011 est.)
major-language sample(s):
বিশ্ব ফেসবুক, মৌলিক তথ্যের অপরিহার্য উৎস (Bangla)

Religions: Muslim 88.4%, other 11.6% (2020 est.)

Age structure: *0-14 years:* 26.48% (male 21,918,651/female 21,158,574)
15-24 years: 18.56% (male 15,186,470/female 15,001,950)
25-54 years: 40.72% (male 31,694,267/female 34,535,643)
55-64 years: 7.41% (male 5,941,825/female 6,115,856)
65 years and over: 6.82% (male 5,218,206/female 5,879,411) (2020 est.)

Dependency ratios: *total dependency ratio:* 47
youth dependency ratio: 39.3
elderly dependency ratio: 7.7
potential support ratio: 13 (2020 est.)

Median age: *total:* 27.9 years
male: 27.1 years
female: 28.6 years (2020 est.)
country comparison to the world: 143

Population growth rate: 0.93% (2022 est.)
country comparison to the world: 101

Birth rate: 17.69 births/1,000 population (2022 est.)
country comparison to the world: 86

Death rate: 5.47 deaths/1,000 population (2022 est.)
country comparison to the world: 183

Net migration rate: -2.9 migrant(s)/1,000 population (2022 est.)
country comparison to the world: 179

Urbanization: *urban population:* 39.7% of total population (2022)
rate of urbanization: 2.88% annual rate of change (2020-25 est.)

Major urban areas - population: 22.478 million DHAKA (capital), 5.253 million Chittagong, 950,000 Khulna, 942,000 Rajshahi, 928,000 Sylhet, Bogra 864,000 (2022)

Sex ratio: *at birth:* 1.04 male(s)/female
0-14 years: 1.04 male(s)/female
15-24 years: 1.02 male(s)/female
25-54 years: 0.92 male(s)/female
55-64 years: 0.96 male(s)/female
65 years and over: 0.73 male(s)/female
total population: 0.96 male(s)/female (2022 est.)

Mother's mean age at first birth: 18.6 years (2017/18 est.)
note: data represents median age at first birth among women 20-49

Maternal mortality ratio: 173 deaths/100,000 live births (2017 est.)
country comparison to the world: 53

Infant mortality rate: *total:* 30.35 deaths/1,000 live births
male: 32.96 deaths/1,000 live births
female: 27.63 deaths/1,000 live births (2022 est.)
country comparison to the world: 51

Life expectancy at birth: *total population:* 74.7 years
male: 72.52 years
female: 76.96 years (2022 est.)
country comparison to the world: 133

Total fertility rate: 2.09 children born/woman (2022 est.)
country comparison to the world: 95

Contraceptive prevalence rate: 62.7% (2019)

Drinking water source: *improved: urban:* 99% of population
rural: 98.7% of population
total: 98.9% of population
unimproved: urban: 1% of population
rural: 1.3% of population
total: 1.1% of population (2020 est.)

Current health expenditure: 2.5% of GDP (2019)

Physicians density: 0.67 physicians/1,000 population (2020)

Hospital bed density: 0.8 beds/1,000 population (2016)

Sanitation facility access: *improved: urban:* 85.3% of population
rural: 73.5% of population
total: 78% of population
unimproved: urban: 14.7% of population
rural: 26.5% of population
total: 22% of population (2020 est.)

HIV/AIDS - adult prevalence rate: (2018 est.) <.1%

Major infectious diseases: *degree of risk:* high (2020)
food or waterborne diseases: bacterial and protozoal diarrhea, hepatitis A and E, and typhoid fever
vectorborne diseases: dengue fever and malaria are high risks in some locations
water contact diseases: leptospirosis

animal contact diseases: rabies
note: widespread ongoing transmission of a respiratory illness caused by the novel coronavirus (COVID-19) is occurring throughout Bangladesh; as of 18 August 2022, Bangladesh has reported a total of 2,009,434 cases of COVID-19 or 1,220.13 cumulative cases of COVID-19 per 100,000 population with a total of 29,314 cumulative deaths or a rate of 17.8 cumulative deaths per 100,000 population; as of 17 August 2022, 76.89% of the population has received at least one dose of COVID-19 vaccine

Obesity - adult prevalence rate: 3.6% (2016)
country comparison to the world: 191

Alcohol consumption per capita: *total:* 0 liters of pure alcohol (2019 est.)
beer: 0 liters of pure alcohol (2019 est.)
wine: 0 liters of pure alcohol (2019 est.)
spirits: 0 liters of pure alcohol (2019 est.)
other alcohols: 0 liters of pure alcohol (2019 est.)
country comparison to the world: 185

Tobacco use: *total:* 34.7% (2020 est.)
male: 52.2% (2020 est.)
female: 17.1% (2020 est.)
country comparison to the world: 17

Children under the age of 5 years underweight: 22.6% (2019)
country comparison to the world: 16

Child marriage: *women married by age 15:* 15.5%
women married by age 18: 51.4% (2019 est.)

Education expenditures: 1.3% of GDP (2019 est.)
country comparison to the world: 186

Literacy: *definition:* age 15 and over can read and write
total population: 74.9%
male: 77.8%
female: 72% (2020)

School life expectancy (primary to tertiary education): *total:* 12 years
male: 12 years
female: 13 years (2020)

Unemployment, youth ages 15-24: *total:* 12.8%
male: 10.8%
female: 16.8% (2017 est.)

ENVIRONMENT

Environment - current issues: many people are landless and forced to live on and cultivate flood-prone land; waterborne diseases prevalent in surface water; water pollution, especially of fishing areas, results from the use of commercial pesticides; ground water contaminated by naturally occurring arsenic; intermittent water shortages because of falling water tables in the northern and central parts of the country; soil degradation and erosion; deforestation; destruction of wetlands; severe overpopulation with noise pollution

Environment - international agreements: *party to:* Biodiversity, Climate Change, Climate Change-Kyoto Protocol, Climate Change-Paris Agreement, Comprehensive Nuclear Test Ban, Desertification, Endangered Species, Environmental Modification, Hazardous Wastes, Law of the Sea, Nuclear Test Ban, Ozone Layer Protection, Ship Pollution, Wetlands
signed, but not ratified: none of the selected agreements

Air pollutants: *particulate matter emissions:* 58.33 micrograms per cubic meter (2016 est.)
carbon dioxide emissions: 84.25 megatons (2016 est.)
methane emissions: 59.3 megatons (2020 est.)

Climate: tropical; mild winter (October to March); hot, humid summer (March to June); humid, warm rainy monsoon (June to October)

Land use: *agricultural land:* 70.1% (2018 est.)
arable land: 59% (2018 est.)
permanent crops: 6.5% (2018 est.)
permanent pasture: 4.6% (2018 est.)
forest: 11.1% (2018 est.)
other: 18.8% (2018 est.)

Urbanization: *urban population:* 39.7% of total population (2022)
rate of urbanization: 2.88% annual rate of change (2020-25 est.)

Revenue from forest resources: *forest revenues:* 0.08% of GDP (2018 est.)
country comparison to the world: 117

Revenue from coal: *coal revenues:* 0.02% of GDP (2018 est.)
country comparison to the world: 42

Food insecurity: *severe localized food insecurity: due to economic constraints* - losses in income and remittances caused by the COVID-19 pandemic and its containment measures led to an increase in poverty; in 2022, food insecurity is expected to increase and remain at high levels due to the impact of recent shocks, including floods that occurred in mid-May 2022 in the northeastern parts of the country and the elevated international prices of energy, fuel and food, which have been transmitted to the domestic markets (2022)

Waste and recycling: *municipal solid waste generated annually:* 14,778,497 tons (2012 est.)

Major rivers (by length in km)
Brahmaputra river mouth (shared with China [s] and India) - 3,969 km; Ganges river mouth (shared with India [s]) - 2,704 km
note – [s] after country name indicates river source; [m] after country name indicates river mouth

Major watersheds (area sq km)
Indian Ocean drainage: Brahmaputra (651,335 sq km), Ganges (1,016,124 sq km)

Major aquifers: Indus-Ganges-Brahmaputra Basin

Total water withdrawal: *municipal:* 3.6 billion cubic meters (2017 est.)
industrial: 770 million cubic meters (2017 est.)
agricultural: 31.5 billion cubic meters (2017 est.)

Total renewable water resources: 1.227 trillion cubic meters (2017 est.)

GOVERNMENT

Country name: *conventional long form:* People's Republic of Bangladesh
conventional short form: Bangladesh
local long form: Gana Prajatantri Bangladesh
local short form: Bangladesh
former: East Bengal, East Pakistan
etymology: the name - a compound of the Bengali words "Bangla" (Bengal) and "desh" (country) - means "Country of Bengal"

Government type: parliamentary republic

Capital: *name:* Dhaka
geographic coordinates: 23 43 N, 90 24 E
time difference: UTC+6 (11 hours ahead of Washington, DC, during Standard Time)
etymology: the origins of the name are unclear, but some sources state that the city's site was originally called "dhakka," meaning "watchtower," and that the area served as a watch-station for Bengal rulers

Administrative divisions: 8 divisions; Barishal, Chattogram, Dhaka, Khulna, Mymensingh, Rajshahi, Rangpur, Sylhet

Independence: 16 December 1971 (from Pakistan)

National holiday: Independence Day, 26 March (1971); Victory Day, 16 December (1971); note - 26 March 1971 is the date of the Awami League's declaration of an independent Bangladesh, and 16 December (Victory Day) memorializes the military victory over Pakistan and the official creation of the state of Bangladesh

Constitution: *history:* previous 1935, 1956, 1962 (preindependence); latest enacted 4 November 1972, effective 16 December 1972, suspended March 1982, restored November 1986
amendments: proposed by the House of the Nation; approval requires at least two-thirds majority vote of the House membership and assent of the president of the republic; amended many times, last in 2018

Legal system: mixed legal system of mostly English common law and Islamic law

International law organization participation: has not submitted an ICJ jurisdiction declaration; accepts ICCt jurisdiction

Citizenship: *citizenship by birth:* no
citizenship by descent only: at least one parent must be a citizen of Bangladesh
dual citizenship recognized: yes, but limited to select countries
residency requirement for naturalization: 5 years

Suffrage: 18 years of age; universal

Executive branch: *chief of state:* President Abdul HAMID (since 24 April 2013); note - Abdul HAMID served as acting president following the death of Zillur RAHMAN in March 2013; HAMID was subsequently indirectly elected by the National Parliament and sworn in 24 April 2013
head of government: Prime Minister Sheikh HASINA Wazed (since 6 January 2009)
cabinet: Cabinet selected by the prime minister, appointed by the president
elections/appointments: president indirectly elected by the National Parliament for a 5-year term (eligible for a second term); election last held on 7 February 2018 (next to be held by 2023); the president appoints as prime minister the majority party leader in the National Parliament
election results: 2018: President Abdul HAMID (AL) reelected by the National Parliament unopposed for a second term; Sheikh HASINA reappointed prime minister as leader of the majority AL party following parliamentary elections in 2018

Legislative branch: *description:* unicameral House of the Nation or Jatiya Sangsad (350 seats; 300 members in single-seat territorial constituencies directly elected by simple majority vote; 50 members - reserved for women only - indirectly elected by the elected members by proportional representation vote using single transferable vote; all members serve 5-year terms)
elections: last held on 30 December 2018 (next to be held in December 2023)

election results: percent of vote by party - NA; seats by party as of February 2022 - AL 299, JP 27, BNP 7, other 10, independent 4; composition - men 277, women 73, percent of women 20.9%

Judicial branch: *highest court(s):* Supreme Court of Bangladesh (organized into the Appellate Division with 7 justices and the High Court Division with 99 justices)
judge selection and term of office: chief justice and justices appointed by the president; justices serve until retirement at age 67
subordinate courts: civil courts include: Assistant Judge's Court; Joint District Judge's Court; Additional District Judge's Court; District Judge's Court; criminal courts include: Court of Sessions; Court of Metropolitan Sessions; Metropolitan Magistrate Courts; Magistrate Court; special courts/tribunals

Political parties and leaders: Awami League or AL [Sheikh HASINA]
Bangladesh Jamaat-i-Islami or JIB [Shafiqur RAHMAN]
Bangladesh Nationalist Front or BNF [S. M. Abul Kalam AZAD]
Bangladesh Nationalist Party or BNP [Tarique RAHMAN, acting chairperson; Khaleda ZIA]
Bangladesh Tariqat Federation or BTF [Syed Nozibul Bashar MAIZBHANDARI]
Jatiya Party or JP (Ershad faction) [Rowshan ERSHAD]
Jatiya Party or JP (Manju faction) [Anwar Hossain MANJU]
Liberal Democratic Party or LDP [Oli AHMED]
National Socialist Party (Jatiya Samajtantrik Dal) or JSD [Hasanul Haque INU]
Workers Party or WP [Rashed Khan MENON]

International organization participation: ADB, ARF, BIMSTEC, C, CD, CICA (observer), CP, D-8, FAO, G-77, IAEA, IBRD, ICAO, ICC (national committees), ICRM, IDA, IDB, IFAD, IFC, IFRCS, IHO, ILO, IMF, IMO, IMSO, Interpol, IOC, IOM, IPU, ISO, ITSO, ITU, ITUC (NGOs), MIGA, MINURSO, MINUSMA, MONUSCO, NAM, OIC, OPCW, PCA, SAARC, SACEP, UN, UNAMID, UNCTAD, UNESCO, UNHCR, UNIDO, UNISFA, UNIFIL, UNMIL, UNMISS, UNOCI, UNWTO, UPU, WCO, WFTU (NGOs), WHO, WIPO, WMO, WTO

Diplomatic representation in the US: *chief of mission:* Ambassador M Shahidul ISLAM (since 17 February 2021)
chancery: 3510 International Drive NW, Washington, DC 20008
telephone: [1] (202) 244-0183
FAX: [1] (202) 244-2771; [1] (202) 244 7830
email address and website:
mission.washington@mofa.gov.bd
http://www.bdembassyusa.org/
consulate(s) general: Los Angeles, New York

Diplomatic representation from the US: *chief of mission:* Ambassador Peter HAAS (since 15 March 2022)
embassy: Madani Avenue, Baridhara, Dhaka - 1212
mailing address: 6120 Dhaka Place, Washington DC 20521-6120
telephone: [880] (2) 5566-2000
FAX: [880] (2) 5566-2907
email address and website:
DhakaACS@state.gov
https://bd.usembassy.gov/

Flag description: green field with a large red disk shifted slightly to the hoist side of center; the red disk represents the rising sun and the sacrifice to achieve independence; the green field symbolizes the lush vegetation of Bangladesh

National symbol(s): Bengal tiger, water lily; national colors: green, red

National anthem: *name:* "Amar Shonar Bangla" (My Golden Bengal)
lyrics/music: Rabindranath TAGORE
note: adopted 1971; Rabindranath TAGORE, a Nobel laureate, also wrote India's national anthem

National heritage: *total World Heritage Sites:* 3 (2 cultural, 1 natural)
selected World Heritage Site locales: Bagerhat Historic Mosque (c); Ruins of the Buddhist Vihara at Paharpur (c); Sundarbans (n)

ECONOMY

Economic overview: Bangladesh's economy has grown roughly 6% per year since 2005 despite prolonged periods of political instability, poor infrastructure, endemic corruption, insufficient power supplies, and slow implementation of economic reforms. Although more than half of GDP is generated through the services sector, almost half of Bangladeshis are employed in the agriculture sector, with rice as the single-most-important product.

Garments, the backbone of Bangladesh's industrial sector, accounted for more than 80% of total exports in FY 2016-17. The industrial sector continues to grow, despite the need for improvements in factory safety conditions. Steady export growth in the garment sector, combined with $13 billion in remittances from overseas Bangladeshis, contributed to Bangladesh's rising foreign exchange reserves in FY 2016-17. Recent improvements to energy infrastructure, including the start of liquefied natural gas imports in 2018, represent a major step forward in resolving a key growth bottleneck.

Real GDP (purchasing power parity): $793.49 billion (2020 est.)
$775.08 billion (2019 est.)
$716.65 billion (2018 est.)
note: data are in 2017 dollars
country comparison to the world: 31

Real GDP growth rate: 7.4% (2017 est.)
7.2% (2016 est.)
6.8% (2015 est.)
country comparison to the world: 12

Real GDP per capita: $4,800 (2020 est.)
$4,800 (2019 est.)
$4,400 (2018 est.)
note: data are in 2017 dollars
country comparison to the world: 175

GDP (official exchange rate): $329.545 billion (2020 est.)

Inflation rate (consumer prices): 5.5% (2019 est.)
5.5% (2018 est.)
5.6% (2017 est.)
country comparison to the world: 187

Credit ratings:

Fitch rating: *BB- (2014)*

Moody's rating: Ba3 (2012)

Standard & Poors rating: BB- (2010)
note: The year refers to the year in which the current credit rating was first obtained.

GDP - composition, by sector of origin: *agriculture:* 14.2% (2017 est.)
industry: 29.3% (2017 est.)
services: 56.5% (2017 est.)

GDP - composition, by end use: *household consumption:* 68.7% (2017 est.)
government consumption: 6% (2017 est.)
investment in fixed capital: 30.5% (2017 est.)
investment in inventories: 1% (2017 est.)
exports of goods and services: 15% (2017 est.)
imports of goods and services: -20.3% (2017 est.)

Agricultural products: rice, potatoes, maize, sugar cane, milk, vegetables, onions, jute, mangoes/guavas, wheat

Industries: jute, cotton, garments, paper, leather, fertilizer, iron and steel, cement, petroleum products, tobacco, pharmaceuticals, ceramics, tea, salt, sugar, edible oils, soap and detergent, fabricated metal products, electricity, natural gas

Industrial production growth rate: 10.2% (2017 est.)
country comparison to the world: 15

Labor force: 66.64 million (2017 est.)
note: extensive migration of labor to Saudi Arabia, Kuwait, UAE, Oman, Qatar, and Malaysia
country comparison to the world: 7

Labor force - by occupation: *agriculture:* 42.7%
industry: 20.5%
services: 36.9% (2016 est.)

Unemployment rate: 4.4% (2017 est.)
4.4% (2016 est.)
note: about 40% of the population is underemployed; many persons counted as employed work only a few hours a week and at low wages
country comparison to the world: 64

Unemployment, youth ages 15-24: *total:* 12.8%
male: 10.8%
female: 16.8% (2017 est.)
country comparison to the world: 119

Population below poverty line: 24.3% (2016 est.)

Gini Index coefficient - distribution of family income: 32.4 (2016 est.)
33.2 (2005)
country comparison to the world: 139

Household income or consumption by percentage share: *lowest 10%:* 4%
highest 10%: 27% (2010 est.)

Budget: *revenues:* 25.1 billion (2017 est.)
expenditures: 33.5 billion (2017 est.)

Budget surplus (+) or deficit (-): -3.2% (of GDP) (2017 est.)
country comparison to the world: 137

Public debt: 33.1% of GDP (2017 est.)
33.3% of GDP (2016 est.)
country comparison to the world: 159

Taxes and other revenues: 9.6% (of GDP) (2017 est.)
country comparison to the world: 214

Fiscal year: 1 July - 30 June

Current account balance: -$5.322 billion (2017 est.)
$1.391 billion (2016 est.)
country comparison to the world: 185

Exports: $38.78 billion (2020 est.)
$44.96 billion (2019 est.)
$44.13 billion (2018 est.)
note: Data are in current year dollars and do not include illicit exports or re-exports.
country comparison to the world: 66

Exports - partners: United States 15%, Germany 14%, United Kingdom 8%, Spain 7%, France 7% (2019)

Exports - commodities: clothing, knitwear, leather footwear (2019)

Imports: $57.26 billion (2020 est.) note: data are in current year dollars
$64.23 billion (2019 est.) note: data are in current year dollars
$65.59 billion (2018 est.) note: data are in current year dollars
country comparison to the world: 54

Imports - partners: China 31%, India 15%, Singapore 5% (2019)

Imports - commodities: refined petroleum, cotton, natural gas, scrap iron, wheat (2019)

Reserves of foreign exchange and gold: $33.42 billion (31 December 2017 est.)
$32.28 billion (31 December 2016 est.)
country comparison to the world: 49

Debt - external: $50.26 billion (31 December 2017 est.)
$41.85 billion (31 December 2016 est.)
country comparison to the world: 68

Exchange rates: taka (BDT) per US dollar -
84.75 (2020 est.)
85 (2019 est.)
83.715 (2018 est.)
77.947 (2014 est.)
77.614 (2013 est.)

ENERGY

Electricity access: *electrification - total population:* 83% (2019)
electrification - urban areas: 93% (2019)
electrification - rural areas: 77% (2019)

Electricity: *installed generating capacity:* 18.461 million kW (2020 est.)
consumption: 76,849,877,000 kWh (2019 est.)
exports: 0 kWh (2019 est.)
imports: 6.786 billion kWh (2019 est.)
transmission/distribution losses: 9.537 billion kWh (2019 est.)

Electricity generation sources: *fossil fuels:* 98.6% of total installed capacity (2020 est.)
solar: 0.6% of total installed capacity (2020 est.)
hydroelectricity: 0.8% of total installed capacity (2020 est.)

Coal: *production:* 1.016 million metric tons (2020 est.)
consumption: 9.345 million metric tons (2020 est.)
exports: 0 metric tons (2020 est.)
imports: 8.329 million metric tons (2020 est.)
proven reserves: 293 million metric tons (2019 est.)

Petroleum: *total petroleum production:* 13,500 bbl/day (2021 est.)
refined petroleum consumption: 122,500 bbl/day (2019 est.)
crude oil and lease condensate exports: 0 bbl/day (2018 est.)
crude oil and lease condensate imports: 21,600 bbl/day (2018 est.)
crude oil estimated reserves: 28 million barrels (2021 est.)

Refined petroleum products - production: 26,280 bbl/day (2015 est.)
country comparison to the world: 86

Refined petroleum products - exports: 901 bbl/day (2015 est.)
country comparison to the world: 108

Refined petroleum products - imports: 81,570 bbl/day (2015 est.)
country comparison to the world: 63

Natural gas: *production:* 28,629,927,000 cubic meters (2019 est.)
consumption: 31,268,968,000 cubic meters (2019 est.)
exports: 0 cubic meters (2021 est.)
imports: 2,639,041,000 cubic meters (2019 est.)
proven reserves: 126.293 billion cubic meters (2021 est.)

Carbon dioxide emissions: 96.18 million metric tonnes of CO2 (2019 est.)
from coal and metallurgical coke: 16.538 million metric tonnes of CO2 (2019 est.)
from petroleum and other liquids: 18.535 million metric tonnes of CO2 (2019 est.)
from consumed natural gas: 61.107 million metric tonnes of CO2 (2019 est.)
country comparison to the world: 44

Energy consumption per capita: 9.917 million Btu/person (2019 est.)
country comparison to the world: 155

COMMUNICATIONS

Telephones - fixed lines: *total subscriptions:* 1,390,048 (2020 est.)
subscriptions per 100 inhabitants: 1 (2020 est.)
country comparison to the world: 65

Telephones - mobile cellular: *total subscriptions:* 176,279,465 (2020 est.)
subscriptions per 100 inhabitants: 107 (2020 est.)
country comparison to the world: 9

Telecommunication systems: *general assessment:* Bangladesh's economic resurgence over the last decade took a battering in 2020 and 2021 as a result of the Covid-19 pandemic; the country had been on track to move off the United Nation's Least Developed Countries list by 2026, however the crisis may have pushed that back a few years; the telecommunications sector experienced a set of challenges, with mobile data usage exploding at the same time as many consumers were being forced to curb their spending in other areas; the demand on data grew so large and so rapidly that Bangladesh came close to running out of bandwidth; at the start of 2020, Bangladesh was consuming around 900Gb/s on average, well below the 2,642GB/s capacity of its submarine cables; this ballooned to over 2,300Gb/s during the pandemic; Bangladesh was looking forward to adding 7,200Gb/s capacity when the SEA-ME-WE-6 submarine cable goes into service in mid-2024, but the sudden upsurge in downloads is forcing state-run company Bangladesh Submarine Cable Company Limited (BSCCL) to scramble to find alternatives before the country's internet supply is maxed out; the increased demand during the Covid-19 crisis also put pressure on the country's existing mobile networks, already under strain as a result of strong growth in the mobile broadband market coupled with significant untapped potential for mobile services in general across the country; this led to premium prices being paid at auction for spectrum in the 1800MHz and 2100MHz bands, most of which will be used to enhance and expand LTE services; a 5G spectrum auction had been anticipated for 2020, but low interest from the MNOs in going down that path when there are still so many areas waiting for LTE access means that 5G will likely be deferred until 2023 (2021)
domestic: fixed-line teledensity remains less than 1 per 100 persons; mobile-cellular telephone subscribership has been increasing rapidly and now exceeds 107 per 100 persons; mobile subscriber growth is anticipated over the next five years to 2023 (2020)
international: country code - 880; landing points for the SeaMeWe-4 and SeaMeWe-5 fiber-optic submarine cable system that provides links to Europe, the Middle East, and Asia; satellite earth stations - 6; international radiotelephone communications and landline service to neighboring countries (2019)

Broadcast media: state-owned Bangladesh Television (BTV) broadcasts throughout the country. Some channels, such as BTV World, operate via satellite. The government also owns a medium wave radio channel and some private FM radio broadcast news channels. Of the 41 Bangladesh approved TV stations, 26 are currently being used to broadcast. Of those, 23 operate under private management via cable distribution. Collectively, TV channels can reach more than 50 million people across the country.

Internet country code: .bd

Internet users: *total:* 41,172,346 (2020 est.)
percent of population: 25% (2020 est.)
country comparison to the world: 24

Broadband - fixed subscriptions: *total:* 10,052,819 (2020 est.)
subscriptions per 100 inhabitants: 6 (2020 est.)
country comparison to the world: 19

TRANSPORTATION

National air transport system: *number of registered air carriers:* 6 (2020)
inventory of registered aircraft operated by air carriers: 30
annual passenger traffic on registered air carriers: 5,984,155 (2018)
annual freight traffic on registered air carriers: 63.82 million (2018) mt-km

Civil aircraft registration country code prefix: S2

Airports: *total:* 18 (2021)
country comparison to the world: 137

Airports - with paved runways: *total:* 16
over 3,047 m: 2
2,438 to 3,047 m: 2
1,524 to 2,437 m: 6
914 to 1,523 m: 1
under 914 m: 5 (2021)

Airports - with unpaved runways: *total:* 2
1,524 to 2,437 m: 1
under 914 m: 1 (2021)

Heliports: 3 (2021)

Pipelines: 2,950 km gas (2013)

Railways: *total:* 2,460 km (2014)
narrow gauge: 1,801 km (2014) 1.000-m gauge
broad gauge: 659 km (2014) 1.676-m gauge
country comparison to the world: 68

Roadways: *total:* 369,105 km (2018)
paved: 110,311 km (2018)
unpaved: 258,794 km (2018)
country comparison to the world: 20

Waterways: 8,370 km (2011) (includes up to 3,060 km of main cargo routes; network reduced to 5,200 km in the dry season)
country comparison to the world: 18

Merchant marine: *total:* 468
by type: bulk carrier 48, container ship 6, general cargo 140, oil tanker 144, other 130 (2021)
country comparison to the world: 44

Ports and terminals: *major seaport(s):* Chattogram (Chittagong)

container port(s) (TEUs): Chattogram (Chittagong) (3,088,187) (2019)
river port(s): Mongla Port (Sela River)

MILITARY AND SECURITY

Military and security forces: Armed Forces of Bangladesh (aka Bangladesh Defense Force): Bangladesh Army, Bangladesh Navy, Bangladesh Air Force; Ministry of Home Affairs: Border Guard Bangladesh (BGB), Bangladesh Coast Guard, Rapid Action Battalion (RAB), Ansars, Village Defense Party (VDP) (2022)
note 1: the Armed Forces of Bangladesh are jointly administered by the Ministry of Defense (MOD) and the Armed Forces Division (AFD), both under the Prime Minister's Office; the AFD has ministerial status and parallel functions with MOD; the AFD is a joint coordinating headquarters for the three services and also functions as a joint command center during wartime; to coordinate policy, the prime minister and the president are advised by a six-member board, which includes the three service chiefs of staff, the principal staff officer of the AFD, and the military secretaries to the prime minister and president
note 2: the RAB, Ansars, and VDP are paramilitary organizations for internal security; the RAB is a joint task force founded in 2004 and composed of members of the police, Army, Navy, Air Force, and Border Guards seconded to the RAB from their respective units; its mandate includes internal security, intelligence gathering related to criminal activities, and government-directed investigations

Military expenditures: 1.1% of GDP (2022 est.)
1.2% of GDP (2021 est.)
1.3% of GDP (2020)
1.4% of GDP (2019) (approximately $5.12 billion)
1.4% of GDP (2018) (approximately $4.57 billion)
country comparison to the world: 121

Military and security service personnel strengths: information varies; approximately 165,000 total active personnel (135,000 Army; 15,000 Navy; 15,000 Air Force) (2022)

Military equipment inventories and acquisitions: much of the military's inventory is comprised of Chinese- and Russian-origin equipment, with a smaller mix from a variety of other suppliers; since 2010, China has been the leading provider of arms to Bangladesh; as of 2022, Bangladesh was undertaking a large defense modernization program, with a focus on naval acquisitions (2022)

Military service age and obligation: 16-21 years of age for voluntary military service; Bangladeshi nationality and 10th grade education required; officers: 17-21 years of age, Bangladeshi nationality, and 12th grade education required (2022)

Military deployments: 1,375 Central African Republic (MINUSCA); 1,625 Democratic Republic of the Congo (MONUSCO; plus about 190 police); 120 Lebanon (UNIFIL); 1,100 Mali (MINUSMA; plus about 280 police); 1,600 South Sudan (UNMISS); 180 Sudan (UNISFA) (May 2022)

Military - note: the military's chief areas of focus are border, economic exclusion zone, and domestic security; the Army maintains a large domestic security presence in the Chittagong Hills area where it conducted counterinsurgency operations against tribal guerrillas from the 1970s until the late 1990s; since 2009, the military has been in a force-wide expansion and modernization program known as Forces Goal 2030 (2022)

Maritime threats: the International Maritime Bureau reports the territorial waters of Bangladesh remain a risk for armed robbery against ships; there were no attacks reported in 2021 as opposed to four ships that were boarded in 2020

TERRORISM

Terrorist group(s): Harakat ul-Jihad-i-Islami/ Bangladesh; Islamic State of Iraq and ash-Sham in Bangladesh (ISB); al-Qa'ida; al-Qa'ida in the Indian Subcontinent (AQIS)

TRANSNATIONAL ISSUES

Disputes - international: *Bangladesh-Burma:* Burmese border authorities are constructing a 200 km (124 mi) wire fence designed to deter illegal cross-border transit and tensions from the military build-up along border.
Bangladesh-India: Bangladesh referred its maritime boundary claims with Burma and India to the International Tribunal on the Law of the Sea; Indian Prime Minister Singh's September 2011 visit to Bangladesh resulted in the signing of a Protocol to the 1974 Land Boundary Agreement between India and Bangladesh, which had called for the settlement of longstanding boundary disputes over undemarcated areas and the exchange of territorial enclaves, but which had never been implemented.

Refugees and internally displaced persons: *refugees (country of origin)*: 943,529 (Burma) (2022) (includes an estimated 773,972 Rohingya refugees who have fled conflict since 25 August 2017)
IDPs: 427,000 (conflict, development, human rights violations, religious persecution, natural disasters) (2021)
stateless persons: 889,704 (mid-year 2021)

Illicit drugs: transit country for illegal drugs produced in neighboring countries; does not manufacture precursor chemicals with the exception of sulphuric acid, hydrochloric acid, and toluene

BARBADOS

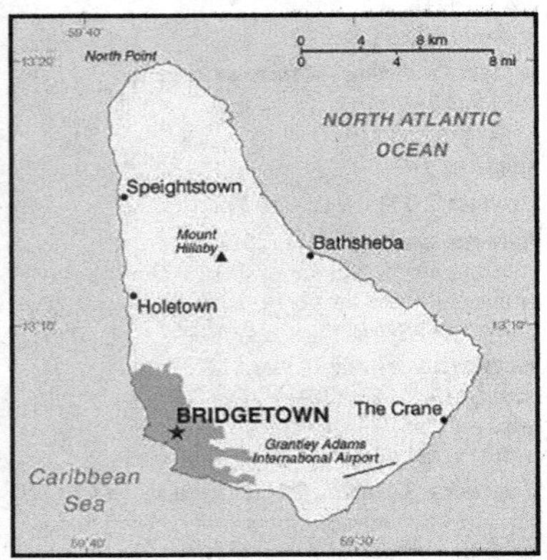

INTRODUCTION

Background: The island was uninhabited when first settled by the British in 1627. African slaves worked the sugar plantations established on the island, which initially dominated the Caribbean sugar industry. By 1720, Barbados was no longer a dominant force within the sugar industry, having been surpassed by the Leeward Islands and Jamaica. Slavery was abolished in 1834. The Barbadian economy remained heavily dependent on sugar, rum, and molasses production through most of the 20th century. The gradual introduction of social and political reforms in the 1940s and 1950s led to complete independence from the UK in 1966. In the 1990s, tourism and manufacturing surpassed the sugar industry in economic importance. Barbados became a republic on 30 November 2021, with the former Governor-General Sandra MASON elected as the first president. Barbados plans to create a new constitution in 2022.

GEOGRAPHY

Location: Caribbean, island in the North Atlantic Ocean, northeast of Venezuela

Geographic coordinates: 13 10 N, 59 32 W

Map references: Central America and the Caribbean

Area: *total:* 430 sq km
land: 430 sq km
water: 0 sq km
country comparison to the world: 201

Area - comparative: 2.5 times the size of Washington, DC

Land boundaries: *total:* 0 km

Coastline: 97 km

Maritime claims: *territorial sea:* 12 nm
exclusive economic zone: 200 nm

Climate: tropical; rainy season (June to October)

Terrain: relatively flat; rises gently to central highland region

Elevation: *highest point:* Mount Hillaby 336 m
lowest point: Atlantic Ocean 0 m

Natural resources: petroleum, fish, natural gas

Land use: *agricultural land:* 32.6% (2018 est.)
arable land: 25.6% (2018 est.)
permanent crops: 2.3% (2018 est.)
permanent pasture: 4.7% (2018 est.)
forest: 19.4% (2018 est.)
other: 48% (2018 est.)

Irrigated land: 50 sq km (2012)

Population distribution: most densely populated country in the eastern Caribbean; approximately one-third live in urban areas

Natural hazards: infrequent hurricanes; periodic landslides

Geography - note: easternmost Caribbean island

PEOPLE AND SOCIETY

Population: 302,674 (2022 est.)
country comparison to the world: 180

Nationality: *noun:* Barbadian(s) or Bajan (colloquial)
adjective: Barbadian or Bajan (colloquial)

Ethnic groups: African descent 92.4%, mixed 3.1%, White 2.7%, East Indian 1.3%, other 0.2%, unspecified 0.3% (2010 est.)

Languages: English (official), Bajan (English-based creole language, widely spoken in informal settings)

Religions: Protestant 66.4% (includes Anglican 23.9%, other Pentecostal 19.5%, Adventist 5.9%, Methodist 4.2%, Wesleyan 3.4%, Nazarene 3.2%, Church of God 2.4%, Baptist 1.8%, Moravian 1.2%, other Protestant 0.9%), Roman Catholic 3.8%, other Christian 5.4% (includes Jehovah's Witness 2.0%, other 3.4%), Rastafarian 1%, other 1.5%, none 20.6%, unspecified 1.2% (2010 est.)

Age structure: *0-14 years:* 17.49% (male 25,762/female 25,764)
15-24 years: 12.34% (male 18,024/female 18,330)
25-54 years: 42.69% (male 62,655/female 63,093)
55-64 years: 13.91% (male 19,533/female 21,430)
65 years and over: 13.57% (male 16,398/female 23,571) (2020 est.)

Dependency ratios: *total dependency ratio:* 50.3
youth dependency ratio: 25.2
elderly dependency ratio: 25.1
potential support ratio: 4 (2020 est.)

Median age: *total:* 39.5 years
male: 38.4 years
female: 40.7 years (2020 est.)
country comparison to the world: 55

Population growth rate: 0.26% (2022 est.)
country comparison to the world: 172

Birth rate: 10.83 births/1,000 population (2022 est.)
country comparison to the world: 174

Death rate: 7.96 deaths/1,000 population (2022 est.)
country comparison to the world: 93

Net migration rate: -0.29 migrant(s)/1,000 population (2022 est.)
country comparison to the world: 116

Population distribution: most densely populated country in the eastern Caribbean; approximately one-third live in urban areas

Urbanization: *urban population:* 31.3% of total population (2022)
rate of urbanization: 0.46% annual rate of change (2020-25 est.)

Major urban areas - population: 89,000 BRIDGETOWN (capital) (2018)

Sex ratio: *at birth:* 1.01 male(s)/female
0-14 years: 1 male(s)/female
15-24 years: 0.98 male(s)/female
25-54 years: 0.98 male(s)/female
55-64 years: 0.92 male(s)/female
65 years and over: 0.55 male(s)/female
total population: 0.93 male(s)/female (2022 est.)

Maternal mortality ratio: 27 deaths/100,000 live births (2017 est.)
country comparison to the world: 115

Infant mortality rate: *total:* 10 deaths/1,000 live births
male: 11.58 deaths/1,000 live births
female: 8.41 deaths/1,000 live births (2022 est.)
country comparison to the world: 139

Life expectancy at birth: *total population:* 78.55 years
male: 75.79 years
female: 81.35 years (2022 est.)
country comparison to the world: 69

Total fertility rate: 1.7 children born/woman (2022 est.)
country comparison to the world: 167

Contraceptive prevalence rate: 59.2% (2012)

Drinking water source: *improved: total:* 98.8% of population
unimproved: total: 2% of population (2020 est.)

Current health expenditure: 6.3% of GDP (2019)

Physicians density: 2.49 physicians/1,000 population (2017)

Hospital bed density: 6 beds/1,000 population (2017)

Sanitation facility access: *improved: total:* 100% of population
unimproved: total: 0% of population (2020 est.)

HIV/AIDS - adult prevalence rate: 1.1% (2019 est.)
country comparison to the world: 38

Obesity - adult prevalence rate: 23.1% (2016)
country comparison to the world: 67

Alcohol consumption per capita: *total:* 9.94 liters of pure alcohol (2019 est.)
beer: 3.66 liters of pure alcohol (2019 est.)
wine: 1.36 liters of pure alcohol (2019 est.)
spirits: 4.75 liters of pure alcohol (2019 est.)
other alcohols: 0.17 liters of pure alcohol (2019 est.)
country comparison to the world: 22

Tobacco use: *total:* 8.5% (2020 est.)
male: 15% (2020 est.)
female: 1.9% (2020 est.)
country comparison to the world: 142

Children under the age of 5 years underweight: 3.5% (2012)
country comparison to the world: 90

Education expenditures: 4.3% of GDP (2020 est.)
country comparison to the world: 89

Literacy: *definition:* age 15 and over can read and write
total population: 99.6%
male: 99.6%
female: 99.6% (2014)

School life expectancy (primary to tertiary education): *total:* 15 years
male: 14 years
female: 17 years (2011)

Unemployment, youth ages 15-24: *total:* 26%
male: 30.3%
female: 21.2% (2019 est.)

ENVIRONMENT

Environment - current issues: pollution of coastal waters from waste disposal by ships; soil erosion; illegal solid waste disposal threatens contamination of aquifers

Environment - international agreements: *party to:* Biodiversity, Climate Change, Climate Change-Kyoto Protocol, Climate Change-Paris Agreement, Comprehensive Nuclear Test Ban, Desertification, Endangered Species, Hazardous Wastes, Law of the Sea, Marine Dumping-London Convention, Marine Dumping-London Protocol, Ozone Layer Protection, Ship Pollution, Wetlands
signed, but not ratified: none of the selected agreements

Air pollutants: *particulate matter emissions:* 22.24 micrograms per cubic meter (2016 est.)
carbon dioxide emissions: 1.28 megatons (2016 est.)
methane emissions: 2.35 megatons (2020 est.)

Climate: tropical; rainy season (June to October)

Land use: *agricultural land:* 32.6% (2018 est.)
arable land: 25.6% (2018 est.)
permanent crops: 2.3% (2018 est.)
permanent pasture: 4.7% (2018 est.)
forest: 19.4% (2018 est.)
other: 48% (2018 est.)

Urbanization: *urban population:* 31.3% of total population (2022)
rate of urbanization: 0.46% annual rate of change (2020-25 est.)

Revenue from forest resources: *forest revenues:* 0.01% of GDP (2018 est.)
country comparison to the world: 147

Revenue from coal: *coal revenues:* 0% of GDP (2018 est.)
country comparison to the world: 63

Waste and recycling: *municipal solid waste generated annually:* 174,815 tons (2011 est.)
municipal solid waste recycled annually: 15,733 tons (2015 est.)
percent of municipal solid waste recycled: 9% (2015 est.)

Total water withdrawal: *municipal:* 20 million cubic meters (2017 est.)
industrial: 6.2 million cubic meters (2017 est.)
agricultural: 54.8 million cubic meters (2017 est.)

Total renewable water resources: 80 million cubic meters (2017 est.)

GOVERNMENT

Country name: *conventional long form:* none
conventional short form: Barbados
etymology: the name derives from the Portuguese "as barbadas," which means "the bearded ones" and can refer either to the long, hanging roots of the island's bearded fig trees or to the alleged beards of the native Carib inhabitants

Government type: parliamentary republic; a Commonwealth realm

Capital: *name:* Bridgetown
geographic coordinates: 13 06 N, 59 37 W
time difference: UTC-4 (1 hour ahead of Washington, DC, during Standard Time)
etymology: named after a bridge constructed over the swampy area (known as the Careenage) around the Constitution River that flows through the center of Bridgetown

Administrative divisions: 11 parishes and 1 city*; Bridgetown*, Christ Church, Saint Andrew, Saint George, Saint James, Saint John, Saint Joseph, Saint Lucy, Saint Michael, Saint Peter, Saint Philip, Saint Thomas

Independence: 30 November 1966 (from the UK)

National holiday: Independence Day, 30 November (1966)

Constitution: *history:* adopted 22 November 1966, effective 30 November 1966; Constitution (Amendment) (No. 2) Bill, 2021 establishes Barbados as a republic and revokes the earlier Order in Council
amendments: proposed by Parliament; passage of amendments to constitutional sections such as citizenship, fundamental rights and freedoms, and the organization and authorities of the branches of government requires two-thirds majority vote by the membership of both houses of Parliament; passage of other amendments only requires a majority vote of both houses; amended several times, last in 2021
note: following the transition to a republic in November 2021, the Government of Barbados in February 2022 began the process of establishing a constitution commission to review a new draft constitution

Legal system: English common law; no judicial review of legislative acts

International law organization participation: accepts compulsory ICJ jurisdiction with reservations; accepts ICCt jurisdiction

Citizenship: *citizenship by birth:* yes
citizenship by descent only: yes
dual citizenship recognized: yes
residency requirement for naturalization: 5 years

Suffrage: 18 years of age; universal

Executive branch: *chief of state:* President Sandra MASON (since 30 November 2021)
head of government: Prime Minister Mia MOTTLEY (since 25 May 2018)
cabinet: Cabinet appointed by the president on the advice of the prime minister
elections/appointments: the president is elected by an electoral college of both Houses of Parliament for a four year renewable term; election last held 20 October 2021; following legislative elections, the leader of the majority party or leader of the majority coalition usually appointed prime minister by the president; the prime minister recommends the deputy prime minister
election results: Sandra MASON elected as first president on 20 October 2021

Legislative branch: *description:* bicameral Parliament consists of:
Senate (21 seats - 18 for current term; members appointed by the president - 12 on the advice of the prime minister, 2 on the advice of the opposition leader, and 7 at the discretion of the president)
House of Assembly (30 seats; members directly elected in single-seat constituencies by simple majority vote to serve 5-year terms)
elections:
Senate - last appointments on 4 February 2022 (next appointments in February 2027)
House of Assembly - last held on 19 January 2022 (next to be held in January 2027)
election results:
Senate - appointed; composition as of March 2022- men 10, women 8, percent of women 44.4%
House of Assembly - percent of vote by party - BLP 69%, DLP 26.5%, other 4.5%; seats by party - BLP 30; composition as of March 2022 - men 22, women 8, percent of women 26.7%; note - total Parliament percent of women 33.3%
note: tradition dictates that the election is held within 5 years of the last election, but constitutionally it is 5 years from the first seating of Parliament plus a 90-day grace period

Judicial branch: *highest court(s):* Supreme Court (consists of the High Court with 8 justices) and the Court of Appeal (consists of the High Court chief justice and president of the court and 4 justices; note - in 2005, Barbados acceded to the Caribbean Court of Justice as the final court of appeal, replacing that of the Judicial Committee of the Privy Council (in London)
judge selection and term of office: Supreme Court chief justice appointed by the president on the recommendation of the prime minister and opposition leader of Parliament; other justices appointed by the president on the recommendation of the Judicial and Legal Service Commission, a 5-member independent body consisting of the Supreme Court chief justice, the commission head, and presidential appointees recommended by the prime minister; justices serve until mandatory retirement at age 65
subordinate courts: Magistrates' Courts

Political parties and leaders: Alliance Party for Progress or APP [Joseph ATHERLEY]
Barbados Labor Party or BLP [Mia MOTTLEY]
Democratic Labor Party or DLP [Ronnie YEARWOOD]

International organization participation: ACP, AOSIS, C, Caricom, CDB, CELAC, FAO, G-77, IADB, IBRD, ICAO, ICCt, ICRM, IDA, IFAD, IFC, IFRCS, ILO, IMF, IMO, Interpol, IOC, ISO, ITSO, ITU, ITUC (NGOs), LAES, MIGA, NAM, OAS, OPANAL, OPCW, UN, UNCTAD, UNESCO, UNHCR, UNIDO, UPU, WCO, WFTU (NGOs), WHO, WIPO, WMO, WTO

Diplomatic representation in the US: *chief of mission:* Ambassador Noel Anderson LYNCH (since 11 January 2019)
chancery: 2144 Wyoming Avenue NW, Washington, DC 20008
telephone: [1] (202) 939-9200
FAX: [1] (202) 332-7467
email address and website:
washington@foreign.gov.bb
consulate(s) general: Miami, New York
Diplomatic representation from the US
chief of mission: Ambassador Linda S. TAGLIALATELA (since 1 February 2016) note - also accredited to Antigua and Barbuda, Dominica, Grenada, Saint Kitts and Nevis, Saint Lucia, and Saint Vincent and the Grenadines
embassy: Wildey Business Park, St. Michael BB 14006, Barbados, W.I.
mailing address: 3120 Bridgetown Place, Washington DC 20521-3120
telephone: (246) 227-4000
FAX: (246) 431-0179
email address and website:
BridgetownACS@state.gov
https://bb.usembassy.gov/

Flag description: three equal vertical bands of ultramarine blue (hoist side), gold, and ultramarine blue with the head of a black trident centered on the gold band; the band colors represent the blue of the sea and sky and the gold of the beaches; the trident head represents independence and a break with the past (the colonial coat of arms contained a complete trident)

National symbol(s): Neptune's trident, pelican, Red Bird of Paradise flower (also known as Pride of Barbados); national colors: blue, yellow, black

National anthem: *name:* "The National Anthem of Barbados"
lyrics/music: Irving BURGIE/C. Van Roland EDWARDS
note: adopted 1966; the anthem is also known as "In Plenty and In Time of Need"

National heritage: *total World Heritage Sites:* 1 (cultural)
selected World Heritage Site locales: Historic Bridgetown and its Garrison

ECONOMY

Economic overview: Barbados is the wealthiest and one of the most developed countries in the Eastern Caribbean and enjoys one of the highest per capita incomes in the region. Historically, the Barbadian economy was dependent on sugarcane cultivation and related activities. However, in recent years the economy has diversified into light industry and tourism. Offshore finance and information services are important foreign exchange earners, boosted by being in the same time zone as eastern US financial centers and by a relatively highly educated workforce. Following the 2008-09 recession, external vulnerabilities such as fluctuations in international oil prices have hurt economic growth, raised Barbados' already high public debt to GDP ratio - which stood at 105% of GDP in 2016 - and cut into its international reserves.

Real GDP (purchasing power parity): $3.7 billion (2020 est.)
$4.49 billion (2019 est.)
$4.49 billion (2018 est.)
note: data are in 2017 dollars
country comparison to the world: 185

Real GDP growth rate: -0.2% (2017 est.)
2.3% (2016 est.)
2.2% (2015 est.)
country comparison to the world: 195

Real GDP per capita: $12,900 (2020 est.)
$15,600 (2019 est.)
$15,700 (2018 est.)
note: data are in 2017 dollars
country comparison to the world: 117

GDP (official exchange rate): $4.99 billion (2017 est.)

Inflation rate (consumer prices): 4.4% (2017 est.)
1.5% (2016 est.)
country comparison to the world: 174

Credit ratings:

Moody's rating: Caa1 (2019)

Standard & Poors rating: B- (2019)
note: The year refers to the year in which the current credit rating was first obtained.

GDP - composition, by sector of origin: *agriculture:* 1.5% (2017 est.)
industry: 9.8% (2017 est.)
services: 88.7% (2017 est.)

GDP - composition, by end use: *household consumption:* 84.2% (2017 est.)
government consumption: 13.4% (2017 est.)
investment in fixed capital: 17.6% (2017 est.)
investment in inventories: 0.2% (2017 est.)
exports of goods and services: 31.6% (2017 est.)
imports of goods and services: -47% (2017 est.)

Agricultural products: sugar cane, poultry, vegetables, milk, eggs, pork, coconuts, pulses, sweet potatoes, tropical fruit

Industries: tourism, sugar, light manufacturing, component assembly for export

Industrial production growth rate: 2.4% (2017 est.)
country comparison to the world: 119

Labor force: 144,000 (2017 est.)
country comparison to the world: 175

Labor force - by occupation: *agriculture:* 10%
industry: 15%
services: 75% (1996 est.)

Unemployment rate: 10.1% (2017 est.)
9.9% (2016 est.)
country comparison to the world: 149

Unemployment, youth ages 15-24: *total:* 26%
male: 30.3%
female: 21.2% (2019 est.)
country comparison to the world: 49

Budget: *revenues:* 1.466 billion (2017 est.) (2013 est.)
expenditures: 1.664 billion (2017 est.)

Budget surplus (+) or deficit (-): -4% (of GDP) (2017 est.)
country comparison to the world: 155

Public debt: 157.3% of GDP (2017 est.)
149.1% of GDP (2016 est.)
country comparison to the world: 3

Taxes and other revenues: 29.4% (of GDP) (2017 est.)
country comparison to the world: 82

Fiscal year: 1 April - 31 March

Current account balance: -$189 million (2017 est.)
-$206 million (2016 est.)
country comparison to the world: 97

Exports: $485.4 million (2017 est.)
$516.9 million (2016 est.)
note: Data are in current year dollars and do not include illicit exports or re-exports.
country comparison to the world: 190

Exports - partners: US 21%, Poland 14%, Jamaica 8%, Guyana 6%,Trinidad and Tobago 6% (2019)

Exports - commodities: rums and other hard liquor, ships, orthopedic appliances, cement, packaged medicines (2019)

Imports: $1.52 billion (2017 est.)
$1.541 billion (2016 est.)
country comparison to the world: 179

Imports - partners: United States 35%, Trinidad and Tobago 14%, China 9%, Netherlands 5% (2019)

Imports - commodities: refined petroleum, ships, cars, shipping containers, packaged medicines (2019)

Reserves of foreign exchange and gold: $264.5 million (31 December 2017 est.)
$341.8 million (31 December 2016 est.)
country comparison to the world: 169

Debt - external: $4.49 billion (2010 est.)
$668 million (2003 est.)
country comparison to the world: 137

Exchange rates: Barbadian dollars (BBD) per US dollar -
2 (2017 est.)
2 (2016 est.)
2 (2015 est.)
2 (2014 est.)
2 (2013 est.)
note: the Barbadian dollar is pegged to the US dollar

ENERGY

Electricity access: *electrification - total population:* 100% (2020)

Electricity: *installed generating capacity:* 311,000 kW (2020 est.)
consumption: 1 billion kWh (2019 est.)
exports: 0 kWh (2019 est.)
imports: 0 kWh (2019 est.)
transmission/distribution losses: 20 million kWh (2019 est.)

Electricity generation sources: *fossil fuels:* 95.9% of total installed capacity (2020 est.)
solar: 4.1% of total installed capacity (2020 est.)

Petroleum: *total petroleum production:* 1,000 bbl/day (2021 est.)
refined petroleum consumption: 10,800 bbl/day (2019 est.)
crude oil and lease condensate exports: 700 bbl/day (2018 est.)
crude oil and lease condensate imports: 0 bbl/day (2018 est.)
crude oil estimated reserves: 2 million barrels (2021 est.)

Refined petroleum products - imports: 10,630 bbl/day (2015 est.)
country comparison to the world: 147

Natural gas: *production:* 14.923 million cubic meters (2019 est.)
consumption: 20.954 million cubic meters (2019 est.)
exports: 0 cubic meters (2021 est.)
imports: 6.031 million cubic meters (2019 est.)
proven reserves: 113 million cubic meters (2021 est.)

Carbon dioxide emissions: 1.703 million metric tonnes of CO2 (2019 est.)
from coal and metallurgical coke: 0 metric tonnes of CO2 (2019 est.)
from petroleum and other liquids: 1.662 million metric tonnes of CO2 (2019 est.)
from consumed natural gas: 41,000 metric tonnes of CO2 (2019 est.)
country comparison to the world: 163

Energy consumption per capita: 83.723 million Btu/person (2019 est.)
country comparison to the world: 68

COMMUNICATIONS

Telephones - fixed lines: *total subscriptions:* 128,000 (2020 est.)
subscriptions per 100 inhabitants: 45 (2020 est.)
country comparison to the world: 130

Telephones - mobile cellular: *total subscriptions:* 295,000 (2020 est.)
subscriptions per 100 inhabitants: 103 (2020 est.)
country comparison to the world: 179

Telecommunication systems: *general assessment:* the telecom sector has seen a decline in subscriber numbers (particularly for prepaid mobile services the mainstay of short term visitors) and revenue; fixed and mobile broadband services are two areas that have benefited from the crisis as employees and students have resorted to working from home; one area of the telecom market that is not prepared for growth is 5G mobile; governments, regulators, and even the mobile network operators have shown that they have not been investing in 5G opportunities at the present time; network expansion and enhancements remain concentrated around improving LTE coverage (2021)
domestic: fixed-line teledensity of roughly 45 per 100 persons; mobile-cellular telephone density about 103 per 100 persons (2020)
international: country code - 1-246; landing points for the ECFS and Southern Caribbean Fiber submarine cable with links to 15 other islands in the eastern Caribbean extending from the British Virgin Islands to Trinidad and Puerto Ricco; satellite earth stations - 1 (Intelsat - Atlantic Ocean); tropospheric scatter to Trinidad and Saint Lucia (2019)

Broadcast media: government-owned Caribbean Broadcasting Corporation (CBC) operates the lone terrestrial TV station; CBC also operates a multi-channel cable TV subscription service; roughly a dozen radio stations, consisting of a CBC-operated network operating alongside privately owned radio stations (2019)

Internet country code: .bb

Internet users: *total:* 235,357 (2019 est.)
percent of population: 82% (2019 est.)
country comparison to the world: 173

Broadband - fixed subscriptions: *total:* 128,000 (2020 est.)
subscriptions per 100 inhabitants: 45 (2020 est.)
country comparison to the world: 125

TRANSPORTATION

Civil aircraft registration country code prefix: 8P

Airports: *total:* 1 (2021)
country comparison to the world: 212

Airports - with paved runways: *total:* 1
over 3,047 m: 1 (2021)

Pipelines: 33 km gas, 64 km oil, 6 km refined products (2013)

Roadways: *total:* 1,700 km (2015)
paved: 1,700 km (2015)
country comparison to the world: 173

Merchant marine: *total:* 165
by type: bulk carrier 46, general cargo 103, other 16 (2021)
country comparison to the world: 71

Ports and terminals: *major seaport(s):* Bridgetown

MILITARY AND SECURITY

Military and security forces: Barbados Defense Force: The Barbados Regiment, The Barbados Coast Guard (2022)

Military expenditures: 0.8% of GDP (2022 est.)
0.9% of GDP (2021 est.)
0.9% of GDP (2020 est.)
0.8% of GDP (2019 est.) (approximately $35 million)
0.8% of GDP (2018 est.) (approximately $40 million)
country comparison to the world: 141

Military and security service personnel strengths: approximately 600 active personnel (2022)

Military equipment inventories and acquisitions: the Netherlands provide the BDF's major equipment inventory (maritime patrol boats) (2022)

Military service age and obligation: voluntary service only (men and women); 17 years, 9 months to 17 years, 11 months with letter of consent from a parent or guardian, or be in the age range of 18-25 years at the start of recruit training; citizens of Barbados by descent or naturalization (2022)

Military - note: Barbados has been a member of the Caribbean Regional Security System (RSS) since its creation in 1982; RSS signatories (Antigua and Barbuda, Dominica, Grenada, Saint Kitts and Nevis, Saint Lucia, and Saint Vincent and the

Grenadines) agreed to prepare contingency plans and assist one another, on request, in national emergencies, prevention of smuggling, search and rescue, immigration control, fishery protection, customs and excise control, maritime policing duties, protection of off-shore installations, pollution control, national and other disasters, and threats to national security; the RSS is headquartered in Barbados (2022)

TRANSNATIONAL ISSUES

Disputes - international: *Barbados-Venezuela (Maritime Boundary):* Barbados joins other Caribbean states and the United Kingdom to counter Venezuela's claim that Aves Island, a large sandbar with some vegetation, sustains human habitation or economic life, the criteria under the UN Convention on the Law of the Sea (UNCLOS), Article 121, which would permit Venezuela to extend its EEZ/continental shelf over a large portion of the eastern Caribbean Sea. The dispute hampers hydrocarbon prospecting and creation of exploration blocks.
Barbados-Trinidad and Tobago (Maritime Boundary): Barbados and Trinidad and Tobago abide by the April 2006 Permanent Court of Arbitration decision delimiting a maritime boundary and limiting catches of flying fish in Trinidad and Tobago's exclusive economic zone.

Illicit drugs: a transit point for cocaine and marijuana destined for North America, Europe, and elsewhere in the Caribbean

BELARUS

INTRODUCTION

Background: After seven decades as a constituent republic of the USSR, Belarus attained its independence in 1991. It has retained closer political and economic ties to Russia than have any of the other former Soviet republics. Belarus and Russia signed a treaty on a two-state union on 8 December 1999 envisioning greater political and economic integration. Although Belarus agreed to a framework to carry out the accord, serious implementation has yet to take place and current negotiations on further integration have been contentious. Since his election in July 1994 as the country's first and only directly elected president, Alyaksandr LUKASHENKA has steadily consolidated his power through authoritarian means and a centralized economic system. Government restrictions on political and civil freedoms, freedom of speech and the press, peaceful assembly, and religion have remained in place. Restrictions on political freedoms have grown increasingly strained following the disputed presidential election in August 2020. The election results sparked large-scale protests as members of the opposition and civil society criticized the election's validity. Alyaksandr LUKASHENKA has remained in power as the disputed winner of the presidential election after quelling protests in late 2020.

GEOGRAPHY

Location: Eastern Europe, east of Poland

Geographic coordinates: 53 00 N, 28 00 E

Map references: Europe

Area: *total:* 207,600 sq km
land: 202,900 sq km
water: 4,700 sq km
country comparison to the world: 86

Area - comparative: slightly less than twice the size of Kentucky; slightly smaller than Kansas

Land boundaries: *total:* 3,599 km
border countries (5): Latvia 161 km; Lithuania 640 km; Poland 375 km; Russia 1,312 km; Ukraine 1,111 km

Coastline: 0 km (landlocked)

Maritime claims: none (landlocked)

Climate: cold winters, cool and moist summers; transitional between continental and maritime

Terrain: generally flat with much marshland

Elevation: *highest point:* Dzyarzhynskaya Hara 346 m
lowest point: Nyoman River 90 m
mean elevation: 160 m

Natural resources: timber, peat deposits, small quantities of oil and natural gas, granite, dolomitic limestone, marl, chalk, sand, gravel, clay

Land use: *agricultural land:* 43.7% (2018 est.)
arable land: 27.2% (2018 est.)
permanent crops: 0.6% (2018 est.)
permanent pasture: 15.9% (2018 est.)
forest: 42.7% (2018 est.)
other: 13.6% (2018 est.)

Irrigated land: 1,140 sq km (2012)

Major rivers (by length in km): Dnieper (shared with Russia [s] and Ukraine [m]) - 2,287 km
note – [s] after country name indicates river source; [m] after country name indicates river mouth

Major watersheds (area sq km): Atlantic Ocean drainage: *(Black Sea)* Dnieper (533,966 sq km)

Population distribution: a fairly even distribution throughout most of the country, with urban areas attracting larger and denser populations

Natural hazards: large tracts of marshy land

Geography - note: landlocked; glacial scouring accounts for the flatness of Belarusian terrain and for its 11,000 lakes

PEOPLE AND SOCIETY

Population: 9,413,505 (2022 est.)
country comparison to the world: 96

Nationality: *noun:* Belarusian(s)
adjective: Belarusian

Ethnic groups: Belarusian 83.7%, Russian 8.3%, Polish 3.1%, Ukrainian 1.7%, other 2.4%, unspecified 0.9% (2009 est.)

Languages: Russian (official) 70.2%, Belarusian (official) 23.4%, other 3.1% (includes small Polish- and Ukrainian-speaking minorities), unspecified 3.3% (2009 est.)
major-language sample(s):
Книга фактов о мире – незаменимый источник базовой информации. (Russian)

Religions: Orthodox 48.3%, Catholic 7.1%, other 3.5%, non-believers 41.1% (2011 est.)

Age structure: *0-14 years:* 16.09% (male 784,231/female 740,373)
15-24 years: 9.59% (male 467,393/female 441,795)
25-54 years: 43.94% (male 2,058,648/female 2,105,910)
55-64 years: 14.45% (male 605,330/female 763,972)
65 years and over: 15.93% (male 493,055/female 1,017,211) (2020 est.)

Dependency ratios: *total dependency ratio:* 48.9
youth dependency ratio: 25.7
elderly dependency ratio: 23.2
potential support ratio: 4.3 (2020 est.)

Median age: *total:* 40.9 years
male: 38 years
female: 43.9 years (2020 est.)
country comparison to the world: 48

Population growth rate: -0.31% (2022 est.)
country comparison to the world: 217

Birth rate: 9.08 births/1,000 population (2022 est.)
country comparison to the world: 200

Death rate: 12.88 deaths/1,000 population (2022 est.)
country comparison to the world: 9

Net migration rate: 0.72 migrant(s)/1,000 population (2022 est.)
country comparison to the world: 71

Population distribution: a fairly even distribution throughout most of the country, with urban areas attracting larger and denser populations

Urbanization: *urban population:* 80.3% of total population (2022)
rate of urbanization: 0.28% annual rate of change (2020-25 est.)

Major urban areas - population: 2.049 million MINSK (capital) (2022)

Sex ratio: *at birth:* 1.06 male(s)/female
0-14 years: 1.06 male(s)/female
15-24 years: 1.06 male(s)/female
25-54 years: 0.98 male(s)/female
55-64 years: 0.79 male(s)/female
65 years and over: 0.35 male(s)/female

total population: 0.87 male(s)/female (2022 est.)

Mother's mean age at first birth: 26.8 years (2019 est.)

Maternal mortality ratio: 2 deaths/100,000 live births (2017 est.)
country comparison to the world: 181

Infant mortality rate: *total:* 3.27 deaths/1,000 live births
male: 3.72 deaths/1,000 live births
female: 2.79 deaths/1,000 live births (2022 est.)
country comparison to the world: 203

Life expectancy at birth: *total population:* 74.28 years
male: 68.9 years
female: 79.97 years (2022 est.)
country comparison to the world: 138

Total fertility rate: 1.51 children born/woman (2022 est.)
country comparison to the world: 200

Contraceptive prevalence rate: 52.6% (2019)

Drinking water source: *improved: urban:* 100% of population
rural: 99.6% of population
total: 99.9% of population
unimproved: urban: 0% of population
rural: 0.4% of population
total: 0.1% of population (2020 est.)

Current health expenditure: 5.9% of GDP (2019)

Physicians density: 4.54 physicians/1,000 population (2019)

Hospital bed density: 10.8 beds/1,000 population (2014)

Sanitation facility access: *improved: urban:* 99.9% of population
rural: 98.3% of population
total: 99.5% of population
unimproved: urban: 0.1% of population
rural: 1.7% of population
total: 0.5% of population (2020 est.)

HIV/AIDS - adult prevalence rate: 0.5% (2020 est.)
country comparison to the world: 62

Obesity - adult prevalence rate: 24.5% (2016)
country comparison to the world: 58

Alcohol consumption per capita: *total:* 10.57 liters of pure alcohol (2019 est.)
beer: 2.26 liters of pure alcohol (2019 est.)
wine: 0.98 liters of pure alcohol (2019 est.)
spirits: 4.67 liters of pure alcohol (2019 est.)
other alcohols: 2.66 liters of pure alcohol (2019 est.)
country comparison to the world: 18

Tobacco use: *total:* 30.5% (2020 est.)
male: 47.4% (2020 est.)
female: 13.5% (2020 est.)
country comparison to the world: 30

Child marriage: *women married by age 15:* 0.1%
women married by age 18: 4.7%
men married by age 18: 1.6% (2019 est.)

Education expenditures: 5% of GDP (2020 est.)
country comparison to the world: 62

Literacy: *definition:* age 15 and over can read and write
total population: 99.9%
male: 99.9%
female: 99.9% (2019)

School life expectancy (primary to tertiary education): *total:* 15 years
male: 15 years
female: 16 years (2018)

Unemployment, youth ages 15-24: *total:* 12.4%
male: 14.3%
female: 10.2% (2020 est.)

ENVIRONMENT

Environment - current issues: soil pollution from pesticide use; southern part of the country contaminated with fallout from 1986 nuclear reactor accident at Chornobyl' in northern Ukraine

Environment - international agreements: *party to:* Air Pollution, Air Pollution-Nitrogen Oxides, Air Pollution-Sulphur 85, Antarctic-Environmental Protection, Antarctic Treaty, Biodiversity, Climate Change, Climate Change-Kyoto Protocol, Climate Change-Paris Agreement, Comprehensive Nuclear Test Ban, Desertification, Endangered Species, Environmental Modification, Hazardous Wastes, Law of the Sea, Marine Dumping-London Convention, Nuclear Test Ban, Ozone Layer Protection, Ship Pollution, Wetlands
signed, but not ratified: none of the selected agreements

Air pollutants: *particulate matter emissions:* 18.06 micrograms per cubic meter (2016 est.)
carbon dioxide emissions: 58.28 megatons (2016 est.)
methane emissions: 17.19 megatons (2020 est.)

Climate: cold winters, cool and moist summers; transitional between continental and maritime

Land use: *agricultural land:* 43.7% (2018 est.)
arable land: 27.2% (2018 est.)
permanent crops: 0.6% (2018 est.)
permanent pasture: 15.9% (2018 est.)
forest: 42.7% (2018 est.)
other: 13.6% (2018 est.)

Urbanization: *urban population:* 80.3% of total population (2022)
rate of urbanization: 0.28% annual rate of change (2020-25 est.)

Revenue from forest resources: *forest revenues:* 1.02% of GDP (2018 est.)
country comparison to the world: 52

Revenue from coal: *coal revenues:* 0% of GDP (2018 est.)
country comparison to the world: 64

Waste and recycling: *municipal solid waste generated annually:* 4.28 million tons (2015 est.)
municipal solid waste recycled annually: 684,800 tons (2016 est.)
percent of municipal solid waste recycled: 16% (2016 est.)

Major rivers (by length in km): Dnieper (shared with Russia [s] and Ukraine [m]) - 2,287 km
note – [s] after country name indicates river source; [m] after country name indicates river mouth

Major watersheds (area sq km): Atlantic Ocean drainage: *(Black Sea)* Dnieper (533,966 sq km)

Total water withdrawal: *municipal:* 523 million cubic meters (2017 est.)
industrial: 443 million cubic meters (2017 est.)
agricultural: 431 million cubic meters (2017 est.)

Total renewable water resources: 57.9 billion cubic meters (2017 est.)

GOVERNMENT

Country name: *conventional long form:* Republic of Belarus
conventional short form: Belarus
local long form: Respublika Byelarus' (Belarusian)/ Respublika Belarus' (Russian)
local short form: Byelarus' (Belarusian)/ Belarus' (Russian)
former: Belorussian (Byelorussian) Soviet Socialist Republic
etymology: the name is a compound of the Belarusian words "bel" (white) and "Rus" (the Old East Slavic ethnic designation) to form the meaning White Rusian or White Ruthenian

Government type: presidential republic in name, although in fact a dictatorship

Capital: *name:* Minsk
geographic coordinates: 53 54 N, 27 34 E
time difference: UTC+2 (7 hours ahead of Washington, DC, during Standard Time)
etymology: the origin of the name is disputed; Minsk may originally have been located 16 km to the southwest, on the banks of Menka River; remnants of a 10th-century settlement on the banks of the Menka have been found

Administrative divisions: 6 regions (voblastsi, singular - voblasts') and 1 municipality* (horad); Brest, Homyel' (Gomel'), Horad Minsk* (Minsk City), Hrodna (Grodno), Mahilyow (Mogilev), Minsk, Vitsyebsk (Vitebsk)
note: administrative divisions have the same names as their administrative centers; Russian spelling provided for reference when different from Belarusian

Independence: 25 August 1991 (from the Soviet Union)

National holiday: Independence Day, 3 July (1944); note - 3 July 1944 was the date Minsk was liberated from German troops, 25 August 1991 was the date of independence from the Soviet Union

Constitution: *history:* several previous; latest drafted between late 1991 and early 1994, signed 15 March 1994
amendments: proposed by the president of the republic through petition to the National Assembly or by petition of least 150,000 eligible voters; approval required by at least two-thirds majority vote in both chambers or by simple majority of votes cast in a referendum; amended 1996, 2004

Legal system: civil law system; note - nearly all major codes (civil, civil procedure, criminal, criminal procedure, family, and labor) were revised and came into force in 1999 and 2000

International law organization participation: has not submitted an ICJ jurisdiction declaration; non-party state to the ICCt

Citizenship: *citizenship by birth:* no
citizenship by descent only: at least one parent must be a citizen of Belarus
dual citizenship recognized: no
residency requirement for naturalization: 7 years

Suffrage: 18 years of age; universal

Executive branch: *chief of state:* President Alyaksandr LUKASHENKA (since 20 July 1994)
head of government: Prime Minister Raman HALOWCHENKA (since 4 June 2020); First Deputy Prime Minister Mikalay SNAPKOW (since 4 June 2020); Deputy Prime Ministers Uladzimir

KUKHARAW, Ihar PETRYSHENKA (since 18 August 2018), Yuryy NAZARAW (since 3 March 2020), Alyaksandr SUBOTSIN (since 4 June 2020)
cabinet: Council of Ministers appointed by the president
elections/appointments: president directly elected by absolute majority popular vote in 2 rounds if needed for a 5-year term (no term limits); first election took place on 23 June and 10 July 1994; according to the 1994 constitution, the next election should have been held in 1999; however, Alyaksandr LUKASHENKA extended his term to 2001 via a November 1996 referendum; subsequent election held on 9 September 2001; an October 2004 referendum ended presidential term limits and allowed the President LUKASHENKA to run and win in a third (19 March 2006), fourth (19 December 2010), fifth (11 October 2015), and sixth (9 August 2020); next election to be held in (2025); prime minister and deputy prime ministers appointed by the president and approved by the National Assembly
election results: Alyaksandr LUKASHENKA reelected president (9 August 2022); percent of vote - Alyaksandr LUKASHENKA (independent) 80.1%, Svyatlana TSIKHANOWSKAYA (independent) 10.1%, other 9.8%; note - widespread street protests erupted following announcement of the election results amid allegations of voter fraud
Alyaksandr LUKASHENKA president (11 October 2015); percent of vote - Alyaksandr LUKASHENKA (independent) 84.1%, Tatsyana KARATKEVICH 4.4%, Sergey GAYDUKEVICH 3.3%, other 8.2%.

Legislative branch: *description:* bicameral National Assembly or Natsyyalny Skhod consists of:
Council of the Republic or Savet Respubliki (64 seats; 56 members indirectly elected by regional and Minsk city councils and 8 members appointed by the president; members serve 4-year terms)
House of Representatives or Palata Pradstawnikow (110 seats; members directly elected in single-seat constituencies by absolute majority vote in 2 rounds if needed; members serve 4-year terms)
elections:
Council of the Republic - indirect election last held on 7 November 2019
House of Representatives - last held on 17 November 2019 (next to be held in 2023); OSCE observers determined that the election was neither free nor impartial and that vote counting was problematic in a number of polling stations; pro-LUKASHENKA candidates won every seat; international observers determined that the previous elections, on 28 September 2008, 23 September 2012, and 11 September 2016 also fell short of democratic standards, with pro-LUKASHENKA candidates winning every, or virtually every, seat
election results:
Council of the Republic - percent of vote by party - NA; seats by party - NA; composition - NA
House of Representatives - percent of vote by party - NA; seats by party - KPB 11, Republican Party of Labor and Justice 6, BPP 2, LDP 1, BAP 1, independent 89; composition - men 66, women 44, percent of women 40%
note: the US does not recognize the legitimacy of the National Assembly

Judicial branch: *highest court(s):* Supreme Court (consists of the chairman and deputy chairman and organized into several specialized panels, including economic and military; number of judges set by the president of the republic and the court chairman); Constitutional Court (consists of 12 judges, including a chairman and deputy chairman)
judge selection and term of office: Supreme Court judges appointed by the president with the consent of the Council of the Republic; judges initially appointed for 5 years and evaluated for life appointment; Constitutional Court judges - 6 appointed by the president and 6 elected by the Council of the Republic; the presiding judge directly elected by the president and approved by the Council of the Republic; judges can serve for 11 years with an age limit of 70
subordinate courts: oblast courts; Minsk City Court; town courts; Minsk city and oblast economic courts

Political parties and leaders: *pro-government parties:* Belarusian Agrarian Party or BAP [Mikhail RUSY]
Belarusian Patriotic Party or BPP [Mikalay ULAKHOVICH]
Belarusian Social Sport Party or BSSP [Uladzimir ALEKSANDROVICH]
Communist Party of Belarus or KPB [Alyaksey SOKOL]
Liberal Democratic Party or LDP [Aleh GAYDUKEVICH]
Republican Party [Uladzimir BELAZOR]
Republican Party of Labor and Justice [Alyaksandr STSYAPANAW]
Social Democratic Party of Popular Accord [Syarhey YERMAK]
opposition parties: Belarusian Christian Democracy Party [Paval SEVYARYNETS, Volha KAVALKOVA, Vital RYMASHEWSKI] (unregistered)
Belarusian Party of the Green [Dzimtry KUCHUK]
Belarusian Party of the Left "Just World" [Syarhey KALYAKIN]
Belarusian Social-Democratic Assembly of BSDH [Syarhey CHERACHEN]
Belarusian Social Democratic Party ("Assembly") or BSDPH [Ihar BARYSAW]
Belarusian Social Democratic Party (People's Assembly) or BSDP [Mikalay STATKEVICH] (unregistered)
BPF Party [Ryhor KASTUSYOW]
Christian Conservative Party or BPF [Zyanon PAZNYAK]
United Civic Party or UCP [Mikalay KAZLOW]

International organization participation: BSEC (observer), CBSS (observer), CEI, CIS, CSTO, EAEC, EAEU, EAPC, EBRD, FAO, GCTU, IAEA, IBRD, ICAO, ICC (NGOs), ICRM, IDA, IFC, IFRCS, ILO, IMF, IMSO, Interpol, IOC, IOM, IPU, ISO, ITU, ITUC (NGOs), MIGA, NAM, NSG, OPCW, OSCE, PCA, PFP, SCO (dialogue member), UN, UNCTAD, UNESCO, UNIDO, UNIFIL, UNWTO, UPU, WCO, WFTU (NGOs), WHO, WIPO, WMO, WTO (observer), ZC

Diplomatic representation in the US: *chief of mission:* Ambassador (vacant; recalled by Belarus in 2008); Charge d'Affaires Pavel SHIDLOVSKY (since 9 August 2022)
chancery: 1619 New Hampshire Avenue NW, Washington, DC 20009
telephone: [1] (202) 986-1606
FAX: [1] (202) 986-1805
email address and website:
usa@mfa.gov.by

Diplomatic representation from the US: *chief of mission:* Ambassador Julie FISHER (since 23 December 2020)
embassy: 46 Starovilenskaya Street, Minsk 220002
mailing address: 7010 Minsk Place, Washington DC 20521-7010
telephone:[375](17)210-12-83/217-73-47/217-73-48
FAX: [375] (17) 334-78-53
email address and website:
ConsularMinsk@state.gov
https://by.usembassy.gov/

Flag description: red horizontal band (top) and green horizontal band one-half the width of the red band; a white vertical stripe on the hoist side bears Belarusian national ornamentation in red; the red band color recalls past struggles from oppression, the green band represents hope and the many forests of the country

National symbol(s): no clearly defined current national symbol, the mounted knight known as Pahonia (the Chaser) is the traditional Belarusian symbol; national colors: green, red, white

National anthem: *name:* "My, Bielarusy" (We Belarusians)
lyrics/music: Mikhas KLIMKOVICH and Uladzimir KARYZNA/Nester SAKALOUSKI
note: music adopted 1955, lyrics adopted 2002; after the fall of the Soviet Union, Belarus kept the music of its Soviet-era anthem but adopted new lyrics; also known as "Dziarzauny himn Respubliki Bielarus" (State Anthem of the Republic of Belarus)

National heritage: *total World Heritage Sites:* 4 (3 cultural, 1 natural)
selected World Heritage Site locales: Białowieża Forest (n); Mir Castle Complex (c); Architectural, Residential, and Cultural Complex of the Radziwill Family at Nesvizh (c)

ECONOMY

Economic overview: As part of the former Soviet Union, Belarus had a relatively well-developed industrial base, but it is now outdated, inefficient, and dependent on subsidized Russian energy and preferential access to Russian markets. The country's agricultural base is largely dependent on government subsidies. Following the collapse of the Soviet Union, an initial burst of economic reforms included privatization of state enterprises, creation of private property rights, and the acceptance of private entrepreneurship, but by 1994 the reform effort dissipated. About 80% of industry remains in state hands, and foreign investment has virtually disappeared. Several businesses have been renationalized. State-owned entities account for 70-75% of GDP, and state banks make up 75% of the banking sector.

Economic output declined for several years following the break-up of the Soviet Union, but revived in the mid-2000s. Belarus has only small reserves of crude oil and imports crude oil and natural gas from Russia at subsidized, below market, prices. Belarus derives export revenue by refining Russian crude and selling it at market prices. Russia and Belarus have had serious disagreements over prices and quantities for Russian energy. Beginning in early 2016, Russia claimed Belarus began accumulating debt – reaching $740 million by April 2017 – for paying below the agreed price for Russian natural gas and Russia cut back its export of crude oil as a result of the debt. In April 2017, Belarus agreed to pay its gas debt and Russia restored the flow of crude.

New non-Russian foreign investment has been limited in recent years, largely because of an unfavorable financial climate. In 2011, a financial crisis lead to a nearly three-fold devaluation of the Belarusian ruble. The Belarusian economy has continued to struggle under the weight of high external debt servicing payments and a trade deficit. In mid-December 2014, the devaluation of the Russian ruble triggered a near 40% devaluation of the Belarusian ruble.

Belarus's economy stagnated between 2012 and 2016, widening productivity and income gaps between Belarus and neighboring countries. Budget revenues dropped because of falling global prices on key Belarusian export commodities. Since 2015, the Belarusian government has tightened its macro-economic policies, allowed more flexibility to its exchange rate, taken some steps towards price liberalization, and reduced subsidized government lending to state-owned enterprises. Belarus returned to modest growth in 2017, largely driven by improvement of external conditions and Belarus issued sovereign debt for the first time since 2011, which provided the country with badly-needed liquidity, and issued $600 million worth of Eurobonds in February 2018, predominantly to US and British investors.

Real GDP (purchasing power parity): $179.97 billion (2020 est.)
$181.61 billion (2019 est.)
$179.1 billion (2018 est.)
note: data are in 2017 dollars
country comparison to the world: 70

Real GDP growth rate: 1.22% (2019 est.)
3.17% (2018 est.)
2.53% (2017 est.)
country comparison to the world: 164

Real GDP per capita: $19,100 (2020 est.)
$19,300 (2019 est.)
$18,900 (2018 est.)
note: data are in 2017 dollars
country comparison to the world: 90

GDP (official exchange rate): $63.168 billion (2019 est.)

Inflation rate (consumer prices): 5.6% (2019 est.)
4.8% (2018 est.)
6% (2017 est.)
country comparison to the world: 189

Credit ratings:

Fitch rating: B (2018)

Moody's rating: B3 (2018)

Standard & Poors rating: B (2017)
note: The year refers to the year in which the current credit rating was first obtained.

GDP - composition, by sector of origin: *agriculture:* 8.1% (2017 est.)
industry: 40.8% (2017 est.)
services: 51.1% (2017 est.)

GDP - composition, by end use: *household consumption:* 54.8% (2017 est.)
government consumption: 14.6% (2017 est.)
investment in fixed capital: 24.9% (2017 est.)
investment in inventories: 5.7% (2017 est.)
exports of goods and services: 67% (2017 est.)
imports of goods and services: -67% (2017 est.)

Agricultural products: milk, potatoes, sugar beet, wheat, triticale, barley, maize, rye, rapeseed, poultry
Industries
metal-cutting machine tools, tractors, trucks, earthmovers, motorcycles, synthetic fibers, fertilizer, textiles, refrigerators, washing machines and other household appliances

Industrial production growth rate: 5.6% (2017 est.)
country comparison to the world: 47

Labor force: 4.381 million (2016 est.)
country comparison to the world: 86

Labor force - by occupation: *agriculture:* 9.7%
industry: 23.4%
services: 66.8% (2015 est.)

Unemployment rate: 0.8% (2017 est.)
1% (2016 est.)
note: official registered unemployed; large number of underemployed workers
country comparison to the world: 6

Unemployment, youth ages 15-24: *total:* 12.4%
male: 14.3%
female: 10.2% (2020 est.)
country comparison to the world: 123

Population below poverty line: 5% (2019 est.)

Gini Index coefficient - distribution of family income: 25.2 (2018 est.)
21.7 (1998)
country comparison to the world: 169

Household income or consumption by percentage share: *lowest 10%:* 3.8%
highest 10%: 21.9% (2008)

Budget: *revenues:* 22.15 billion (2017 est.)
expenditures: 20.57 billion (2017 est.)

Budget surplus (+) or deficit (-): 2.9% (of GDP) (2017 est.)
country comparison to the world: 14

Public debt: 53.4% of GDP (2017 est.)
53.5% of GDP (2016 est.)
country comparison to the world: 90

Taxes and other revenues: 40.7% (of GDP) (2017 est.)
country comparison to the world: 35

Fiscal year: calendar year

Current account balance: -$931 million (2017 est.)
-$1.669 billion (2016 est.)
country comparison to the world: 143

Exports: $37.04 billion (2020 est.)
$41.97 billion (2019 est.)
$42.27 billion (2018 est.)
note: Data are in current year dollars and do not include illicit exports or re-exports.
country comparison to the world: 69

Exports - partners: Russia 42%, Ukraine 13%, United Kingdom 7% (2019)

Exports - commodities: refined petroleum, fertilizers, cheese, delivery trucks, crude petroleum (2019)

Imports: $35.16 billion (2020 est.) note: data are in current year dollars
$42.38 billion (2019 est.) note: data are in current year dollars
$41.34 billion (2018 est.) note: data are in current year dollars
country comparison to the world: 68

Imports - partners: Russia 57%, China 7%, Poland 5%, Germany 5%, Ukraine 5% (2019)

Imports - commodities: crude petroleum, natural gas, cars and vehicle parts, packaged medicines, broadcasting equipment (2019)

Reserves of foreign exchange and gold: $7.315 billion (31 December 2017 est.)
$4.927 billion (31 December 2016 est.)
country comparison to the world: 84

Debt - external: $39.847 billion (2019 est.)
$39.297 billion (2018 est.)
country comparison to the world: 76

Exchange rates: Belarusian rubles (BYB/BYR) per US dollar -
1.9 (2017 est.)
2 (2016 est.)
2 (2015 est.)
15,926 (2014 est.)
10,224.1 (2013 est.)

ENERGY

Electricity access: *electrification - total population:* 100% (2020)

Electricity: *installed generating capacity:* 11.36 million kW (2020 est.)
consumption: 32,665,500,000 kWh (2019 est.)
exports: 4.777 billion kWh (2020 est.)
imports: 4.277 billion kWh (2020 est.)
transmission/distribution losses: 2.711 billion kWh (2019 est.)

Electricity generation sources: *fossil fuels:* 95.8% of total installed capacity (2020 est.)
nuclear: 0.9% of total installed capacity (2020 est.)
solar: 0.5% of total installed capacity (2020 est.)
wind: 0.5% of total installed capacity (2020 est.)
hydroelectricity: 1.1% of total installed capacity (2020 est.)
biomass and waste: 1.2% of total installed capacity (2020 est.)

Coal: *production:* 0 metric tons (2020 est.)
consumption: 621,000 metric tons (2020 est.)
exports: 1.574 million metric tons (2020 est.)
imports: 2.117 million metric tons (2020 est.)
proven reserves: 0 metric tons (2019 est.)

Petroleum: *total petroleum production:* 34,300 bbl/day (2021 est.)
refined petroleum consumption: 134,600 bbl/day (2019 est.)
crude oil and lease condensate exports: 32,200 bbl/day (2018 est.)
crude oil and lease condensate imports: 383,200 bbl/day (2018 est.)
crude oil estimated reserves: 198 million barrels (2021 est.)

Refined petroleum products - production: 477,200 bbl/day (2015 est.)
country comparison to the world: 34

Refined petroleum products - exports: 351,200 bbl/day (2015 est.)
country comparison to the world: 25

Refined petroleum products - imports: 14,630 bbl/day (2015 est.)
country comparison to the world: 135

Natural gas: *production:* 68.951 million cubic meters (2019 est.)
consumption: 18,639,590,000 cubic meters (2019 est.)
exports: 0 cubic meters (2021 est.)
imports: 18,673,429,000 cubic meters (2019 est.)
proven reserves: 2.832 billion cubic meters (2021 est.)

Carbon dioxide emissions: 54.695 million metric tonnes of CO2 (2019 est.)
from coal and metallurgical coke: 1.623 million metric tonnes of CO2 (2019 est.)
from petroleum and other liquids: 16.856 million metric tonnes of CO2 (2019 est.)
from consumed natural gas: 36.217 million metric tonnes of CO2 (2019 est.)
country comparison to the world: 56

Energy consumption per capita: 102.558 million Btu/person (2019 est.)
country comparison to the world: 56

COMMUNICATIONS

Telephones - fixed lines: *total subscriptions:* 4,406,560 (2020 est.)
subscriptions per 100 inhabitants: 47 (2020 est.)
country comparison to the world: 33

Telephones - mobile cellular: *total subscriptions:* 11,704,084 (2020 est.)
subscriptions per 100 inhabitants: 124 (2020 est.)
country comparison to the world: 80

Telecommunication systems: *general assessment:* the Government of Belarus has successfully promoted the migration to an all-IP platform as part of a wider effort towards a digital transformation for the economy; the state-supported infrastructure operator beCloud has built an extensive fiber network, which reaches all but the smallest settlements in the country; Belarus has the second-highest fiber subscription rate in Europe, behind only Iceland; LTE coverage is almost universal, while considerable progress has also been made in developing 5G services (2021)
domestic: fixed-line teledensity is improving although rural areas continue to be underserved, approximately 47 per 100 fixed-line; mobile-cellular teledensity now roughly 124 telephones per 100 persons (2020)
international: country code - 375; Belarus is landlocked and therefore a member of the Trans-European Line (TEL), Trans-Asia-Europe (TAE) fiber-optic line, and has access to the Trans-Siberia Line (TSL); 3 fiber-optic segments provide connectivity to Latvia, Poland, Russia, and Ukraine; worldwide service is available to Belarus through this infrastructure; additional analog lines to Russia; Intelsat, Eutelsat, and Intersputnik earth stations; almost 31,000 base stations in service in 2019 (2020)

Broadcast media: 7 state-controlled national TV channels; Polish and Russian TV broadcasts are available in some areas; state-run Belarusian Radio operates 5 national networks and an external service; Russian and Polish radio broadcasts are available (2019)

Internet country code: .by

Internet users: *total:* 8,027,601 (July 2022 est.)
percent of population: 85% (July 2022 est.)
country comparison to the world: 71

Broadband - fixed subscriptions: *total:* 3,255,552 (2020 est.)
subscriptions per 100 inhabitants: 35 (2020 est.)
country comparison to the world: 44

TRANSPORTATION

National air transport system: *number of registered air carriers:* 2 (2020)
inventory of registered aircraft operated by air carriers: 30
annual passenger traffic on registered air carriers: 2,760,168 (2018)
annual freight traffic on registered air carriers: 1.9 million (2018) mt-km

Civil aircraft registration country code prefix: EW

Airports: *total:* 65 (2021)
country comparison to the world: 75

Airports - with paved runways: *total:* 33
over 3,047 m: 1
2,438 to 3,047 m: 20
1,524 to 2,437 m: 4
914 to 1,523 m: 1
under 914 m: 7 (2021)

Airports - with unpaved runways: *total:* 32
over 3,047 m: 1
1,524 to 2,437 m: 1
914 to 1,523 m: 2
under 914 m: 28 (2021)

Heliports: 1 (2021)

Pipelines: 5,386 km gas, 1,589 km oil, 1,730 km refined products (2013)

Railways: *total:* 5,528 km (2014)
standard gauge: 25 km (2014) 1.435-m gauge
broad gauge: 5,503 km (2014) 1.520-m gauge (874 km electrified)
country comparison to the world: 33

Roadways: *total:* 86,600 km (2017)
country comparison to the world: 55

Waterways: 2,500 km (2011) (major rivers are the west-flowing Western Dvina and Neman Rivers and the south-flowing Dnepr River and its tributaries, the Berezina, Sozh, and Pripyat Rivers)
country comparison to the world: 37

Merchant marine: *total:* 4
by type: other 4 (2021)
country comparison to the world: 167

Ports and terminals: *river port(s):* Mazyr (Prypyats')

MILITARY AND SECURITY

Military and security forces: Belarus Armed Forces: Army, Air and Air Defense Force, Special Operations Force, Special Troops (electronic warfare, signals, engineers, biological/chemical/nuclear protection troops, etc); Ministry of Interior: State Border Troops, Militia, Internal Troops (2022)

Military expenditures: 1.2% of GDP (2021 est.)
1.5% of GDP (2020 est.)
1.5% of GDP (2019 est.) (approximately $2.11 billion)
1.5% of GDP (2018 est.) (approximately $2.05 billion)
1.5% of GDP (2017 est.) (approximately $1.98 billion)
country comparison to the world: 110

Military and security service personnel strengths: approximately 45,000 active duty troops; information on the individual services varies, but reportedly includes about 25,000 Army, 15,000 Air/Air Defense, and 5,000 Special Operations forces (2022)

Military equipment inventories and acquisitions: the inventory of the Belarus Armed Forces is comprised mostly of Russian/Soviet-origin equipment, and since 2010 Russia has been the leading provider of arms; Belarus's defense industry manufactures some equipment (mostly modernized Soviet designs), including vehicles, guided weapons, and electronic warfare systems (2021)

Military service age and obligation: 18-27 years of age for compulsory military or alternative service; conscript service obligation is 12-18 months, depending on academic qualifications, and 24-36 months for alternative service, also depending on academic qualifications; 17- year-olds are eligible to become cadets at military higher education institutes, where they are classified as military personnel (2022)
note: conscripts can be assigned to the military, to the Ministry of Interior as internal or border troops, or to the Ministry of Labor and Social Protection (alternative service); as of 2020, conscripts comprised an estimated 40% of the military

Military - note: Belarus has close security ties with Russia, including an integrated air and missile defense system, joint training exercises, and the establishment of three joint training centers since 2020 (1 in Belarus, 2 in Russia); Russia has been the principal supplier of arms to Belarus, and Belarusian troops reportedly train on Russian equipment; Russia leases from Belarus a strategic ballistic missile defense site operated by Russian Aerospace Forces and a global communications facility for the Russian Navy; in 2020, the countries signed an agreement allowing for close security cooperation between the Belarusian Ministry of Interior and the Russian National Guard, including protecting public order and key government facilities, and combating extremism and terrorism; in 2022, Belarus allowed Russian military forces to stage on its territory for its invasion of Ukraine
Belarus has been a member of the Collective Security Treaty Organization (CSTO) since 1994 and contributes an airborne brigade to CSTO's rapid reaction force (KSOR) (2022)

TRANSNATIONAL ISSUES

Disputes - international: *Belarus-Latvia:* Boundary demarcated with Latvia.
Belarus-Lithuania: Boundary demarcated with Lithuania.
Belarus-Poland: As a member state that forms part of the EU's external border, Poland has implemented strict Schengen border rules to restrict illegal immigration and trade along its border with Belarus.

Refugees and internally displaced persons: *refugees (country of origin):* 16,433 (Ukraine) (as of 22 November 2022)
stateless persons: 6,104 (mid-year 2021)

Trafficking in persons: *current situation:* human traffickers exploit domestic and foreign victims and exploit Belarusians abroad; the majority of trafficking victims are men subjected to forced labor; most Belarusian victims are trafficked in Belarus and Russia, but also in Poland, Turkey, and other Eurasian and Middle Eastern countries; the government continued to subject factory workers, civil servants, and students to state-sponsored forced labor harvesting crops on state-owned farms or cleaning streets
tier rating: Tier 3 — Belarus does not fully meet the minimum standards for the elimination of trafficking because of a government policy or pattern of government-sponsored forced labor in public works projects and the agricultural sector; however, authorities convicted traffickers under its trafficking statute for the first time in eight years, increased training for law enforcement officers, and confirmed significantly more victims; the government adopted a national action plan to protect minors from sexual violence and exploitation (2020)

Illicit drugs: limited cultivation of opium poppy and cannabis, mostly for the domestic market; transshipment point for illicit drugs to and via Russia, and to the Baltics and Western Europe; a small and lightly regulated financial center; anti-moneylaundering legislation does not meet international standards and was weakened further when know-your-customer requirements were curtailed in 2008; few investigations or prosecutions of money-laundering activities

BELGIUM

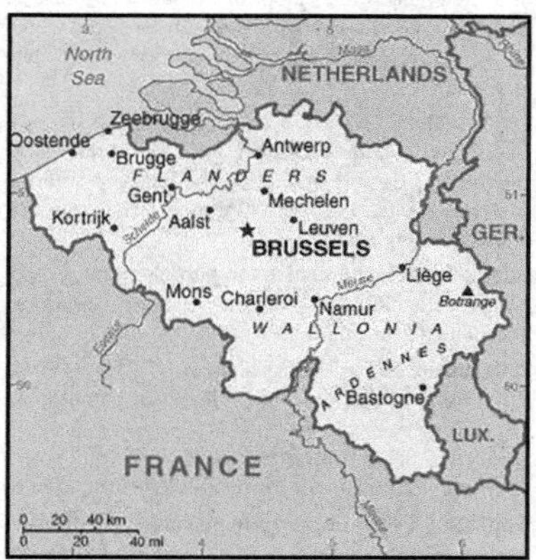

INTRODUCTION

Background: Belgium became independent from the Netherlands in 1830; it was occupied by Germany during World Wars I and II. The country prospered in the past half century as a modern, technologically advanced European state and member of NATO and the EU. In recent years, political divisions between the Dutch-speaking Flemish of the north and the French-speaking Walloons of the south have led to constitutional amendments granting these regions formal recognition and autonomy. The capital city of Brussels is home to numerous international organizations, including the EU and NATO.

GEOGRAPHY

Location: Western Europe, bordering the North Sea, between France and the Netherlands

Geographic coordinates: 50 50 N, 4 00 E

Map references: Europe

Area: *total:* 30,528 sq km
land: 30,278 sq km
water: 250 sq km
country comparison to the world: 140

Area - comparative: about the size of Maryland

Land boundaries: *total:* 1,297 km
border countries (4): France 556 km; Germany 133 km; Luxembourg 130 km; Netherlands 478 km

Coastline: 66.5 km

Maritime claims: *territorial sea:* 12 nm
contiguous zone: 24 nm
exclusive economic zone: geographic coordinates define outer limit
continental shelf: median line with neighbors

Climate: temperate; mild winters, cool summers; rainy, humid, cloudy

Terrain: flat coastal plains in northwest, central rolling hills, rugged mountains of Ardennes Forest in southeast

Elevation: *highest point:* Botrange 694 m
lowest point: North Sea 0 m
mean elevation: 181 m

Natural resources: construction materials, silica sand, carbonates, arable land

Land use: *agricultural land:* 44.1% (2018 est.)
arable land: 27.2% (2018 est.)
permanent crops: 0.8% (2018 est.)
permanent pasture: 16.1% (2018 est.)
forest: 22.4% (2018 est.)
other: 33.5% (2018 est.)

Irrigated land: 230 sq km (2012)

Major watersheds (area sq km): Atlantic Ocean drainage: Seine (78,919 sq km), Rhine-Maas (198,735 sq km)

Population distribution: most of the population concentrated in the northern two-thirds of the country; the southeast is more thinly populated; considered to have one of the highest population densities in the world; approximately 97% live in urban areas

Natural hazards: flooding is a threat along rivers and in areas of reclaimed coastal land, protected from the sea by concrete dikes

Geography - note: crossroads of Western Europe; most West European capitals are within 1,000 km of Brussels, the seat of both the EU and NATO

PEOPLE AND SOCIETY

Population: 11,847,338 (2022 est.)
country comparison to the world: 81

Nationality: *noun:* Belgian(s)
adjective: Belgian

Ethnic groups: Belgian 75.2%, Italian 4.1%, Moroccan 3.7%, French 2.4%, Turkish 2%, Dutch 2%, other 10.6% (2012 est.)

Languages: Dutch (official) 60%, French (official) 40%, German (official) less than 1%
major-language sample(s): Het Wereld Feitenboek, een omnisbare bron van informatie. (Dutch)
The World Factbook, une source indispensable d'informations de base. (French)

Religions: Roman Catholic 57.1%, Protestant 2.3%, other Christian, 2.8%, Muslim 6.8%, other 1.7%, atheist 9.1%, nonbeliever/agnostic 20.2% (2018 est.)

Age structure: *0-14 years:* 17.22% (male 1,033,383/female 984,624)
15-24 years: 11.2% (male 670,724/female 642,145)
25-54 years: 39.23% (male 2,319,777/female 2,278,450)
55-64 years: 13.14% (male 764,902/female 775,454)
65 years and over: 19.21% (male 988,148/female 1,263,109) (2020 est.)

Dependency ratios: *total dependency ratio:* 57
youth dependency ratio: 26.7
elderly dependency ratio: 30.2
potential support ratio: 3.3 (2020 est.)

Median age: *total:* 41.6 years
male: 40.4 years
female: 42.8 years (2020 est.)
country comparison to the world: 44

Population growth rate: 0.57% (2022 est.)
country comparison to the world: 148

Birth rate: 10.95 births/1,000 population (2022 est.)
country comparison to the world: 170

Death rate: 9.64 deaths/1,000 population (2022 est.)
country comparison to the world: 41

Net migration rate: 4.38 migrant(s)/1,000 population (2022 est.)
country comparison to the world: 26

Population distribution: most of the population concentrated in the northern two-thirds of the country; the southeast is more thinly populated; considered to have one of the highest population densities in the world; approximately 97% live in urban areas

Urbanization: *urban population:* 98.2% of total population (2022)
rate of urbanization: 0.38% annual rate of change (2020-25 est.)

Major urban areas - population: 2.110 million BRUSSELS (capital), 1.053 million Antwerp (2022)

Sex ratio: *at birth:* 1.05 male(s)/female
0-14 years: 1.05 male(s)/female
15-24 years: 1.05 male(s)/female
25-54 years: 1.02 male(s)/female
55-64 years: 0.99 male(s)/female
65 years and over: 0.65 male(s)/female
total population: 0.97 male(s)/female (2022 est.)

Mother's mean age at first birth: 29.2 years (2020 est.)

Maternal mortality ratio: 5 deaths/100,000 live births (2017 est.)
country comparison to the world: 164

Infant mortality rate: *total:* 3.19 deaths/1,000 live births
male: 3.63 deaths/1,000 live births
female: 2.73 deaths/1,000 live births (2022 est.)
country comparison to the world: 207

Life expectancy at birth: *total population:* 81.86 years
male: 79.25 years
female: 84.59 years (2022 est.)
country comparison to the world: 32

Total fertility rate: 1.77 children born/woman (2022 est.)
country comparison to the world: 149

Contraceptive prevalence rate: 66.7% (2018)

Drinking water source: *improved: urban:* 100% of population
rural: 100% of population
total: 100% of population

Current health expenditure: 10.7% of GDP (2019)

Physicians density: 6.08 physicians/1,000 population (2020)

Hospital bed density: 5.6 beds/1,000 population (2019)

Sanitation facility access: *improved: urban:* 100% of population
rural: 100% of population
total: 100% of population

Obesity - adult prevalence rate: 22.1% (2016)
country comparison to the world: 81

Alcohol consumption per capita: *total:* 9.15 liters of pure alcohol (2019 est.)
beer: 4.35 liters of pure alcohol (2019 est.)
wine: 3.41 liters of pure alcohol (2019 est.)
spirits: 1.09 liters of pure alcohol (2019 est.)
other alcohols: 0.3 liters of pure alcohol (2019 est.)

country comparison to the world: 34

Tobacco use: *total:* 23.4% (2020 est.)
male: 25.8% (2020 est.)
female: 21% (2020 est.)
country comparison to the world: 61

Children under the age of 5 years underweight: 1% (2014/15)
country comparison to the world: 121

Education expenditures: 6.4% of GDP (2018 est.)
country comparison to the world: 26

School life expectancy (primary to tertiary education): *total:* 20 years
male: 19 years
female: 21 years (2019)

Unemployment, youth ages 15-24: *total:* 15.3%
male: 15.5%
female: 15.1% (2020 est.)

ENVIRONMENT

Environment - current issues: *intense pressures from human activities:* urbanization, dense transportation network, industry, extensive animal breeding and crop cultivation; air and water pollution also have repercussions for neighboring countries

Environment - international agreements: *party to:* Air Pollution, Air Pollution-Heavy Metals, Air Pollution-Multi-effect Protocol, Air Pollution-Nitrogen Oxides, Air Pollution-Persistent Organic Pollutants, Air Pollution-Sulphur 85, Air Pollution-Sulphur 94, Air Pollution-Volatile Organic Compounds, Antarctic-Environmental Protection, Antarctic-Marine Living Resources, Antarctic Seals, Antarctic Treaty, Biodiversity, Climate Change, Climate Change-Kyoto Protocol, Climate Change-Paris Agreement, Comprehensive Nuclear Test Ban, Desertification, Endangered Species, Environmental Modification, Hazardous Wastes, Law of the Sea, Marine Dumping-London Convention, Marine Dumping-London Protocol, Marine Life Conservation, Nuclear Test Ban, Ozone Layer Protection, Ship Pollution, Tropical Timber 2006, Wetlands, Whaling
signed, but not ratified: none of the selected agreements

Air pollutants: *particulate matter emissions:* 12.88 micrograms per cubic meter (2016 est.)
carbon dioxide emissions: 96.89 megatons (2016 est.)
methane emissions: 7.78 megatons (2020 est.)

Climate: temperate; mild winters, cool summers; rainy, humid, cloudy

Land use: *agricultural land:* 44.1% (2018 est.)
arable land: 27.2% (2018 est.)
permanent crops: 0.8% (2018 est.)
permanent pasture: 16.1% (2018 est.)
forest: 22.4% (2018 est.)
other: 33.5% (2018 est.)

Urbanization: *urban population:* 98.2% of total population (2022)
rate of urbanization: 0.38% annual rate of change (2020-25 est.)

Revenue from forest resources: *forest revenues:* 0.02% of GDP (2018 est.)
country comparison to the world: 139

Revenue from coal: *coal revenues:* 0% of GDP (2018 est.)
country comparison to the world: 65

Waste and recycling: *municipal solid waste generated annually:* 4.708 million tons (2015 est.)
municipal solid waste recycled annually: 1,614,985 tons (2015 est.)
percent of municipal solid waste recycled: 34.3% (2015 est.)

Major watersheds (area sq km): Atlantic Ocean drainage: Seine (78,919 sq km), Rhine-Maas (198,735 sq km)

Total water withdrawal: *municipal:* 739 million cubic meters (2017 est.)
industrial: 3.21 billion cubic meters (2017 est.)
agricultural: 45 million cubic meters (2017 est.)

Total renewable water resources: 18.3 billion cubic meters (2017 est.)

GOVERNMENT

Country name: *conventional long form:* Kingdom of Belgium
conventional short form: Belgium
local long form: Royaume de Belgique (French)/ Koninkrijk Belgie (Dutch)/Koenigreich Belgien (German)
local short form: Belgique/Belgie/Belgien
etymology: the name derives from the Belgae, an ancient Celtic tribal confederation that inhabited an area between the English Channel and the west bank of the Rhine in the first centuries B.C.

Government type: federal parliamentary democracy under a constitutional monarchy

Capital: *name:* Brussels
geographic coordinates: 50 50 N, 4 20 E
time difference: UTC+1 (6 hours ahead of Washington, DC, during Standard Time)
daylight saving time: +1hr, begins last Sunday in March; ends last Sunday in October
etymology: may derive from the Old Dutch *bruoc/ broek*, meaning "marsh" and *sella/zele/sel* signifying "home" to express the meaning "home in the marsh"

Administrative divisions: 3 regions (French: regions, singular - region; Dutch: gewesten, singular - gewest); Brussels-Capital Region, also known as Brussels Hoofdstedelijk Gewest (Dutch), Region de Bruxelles-Capitale (French long form), Bruxelles-Capitale (French short form); Flemish Region (Flanders), also known as Vlaams Gewest (Dutch long form), Vlaanderen (Dutch short form), Region Flamande (French long form), Flandre (French short form); Walloon Region (Wallonia), also known as Region Wallone (French long form), Wallonie (French short form), Waals Gewest (Dutch long form), Wallonie (Dutch short form)
note: as a result of the 1993 constitutional revision that furthered devolution into a federal state, there are now three levels of government (federal, regional, and linguistic community) with a complex division of responsibilities; the 2012 sixth state reform transferred additional competencies from the federal state to the regions and linguistic communities

Independence: 4 October 1830 (a provisional government declared independence from the Netherlands); 21 July 1831 (King LEOPOLD I ascended to the throne)

National holiday: Belgian National Day (ascension to the throne of King LEOPOLD I), 21 July (1831)

Constitution: *history:* drafted 25 November 1830, approved 7 February 1831, entered into force 26 July 1831, revised 14 July 1993 (creating a federal state)
amendments: "revisions" proposed as declarations by the federal government in accord with the king or by Parliament followed by dissolution of Parliament and new elections; adoption requires two-thirds majority vote of a two-thirds quorum in both houses of the next elected Parliament; amended many times, last in 2019

Legal system: civil law system based on the French Civil Code; note - Belgian law continues to be modified in conformance with the legislative norms mandated by the European Union; judicial review of legislative acts

International law organization participation: accepts compulsory ICJ jurisdiction with reservations; accepts ICCt jurisdiction

Citizenship: *citizenship by birth:* no
citizenship by descent only: at least one parent must be a citizen of Belgium
dual citizenship recognized: yes
residency requirement for naturalization: 5 years

Suffrage: 18 years of age; universal and compulsory

Executive branch: *chief of state:* King PHILIPPE (since 21 July 2013); Heir Apparent Princess ELISABETH (daughter of the monarch, born 25 October 2001)
head of government: Prime Minister Alexander DE CROO (since 1 October 2020); Deputy Prime Ministers Vincent Van QUICKENBORNE (since 1 October 2020), Sophie WILMES (since 1 October 2020), Vincent VAN PETEGHEM (since 1 October 2020), Frank VANDENBROUCKE (since 1 October 2020), Pierre-Yves DERMAGNE (since 1 October 2020), Petra DE SUTTER (since 1 October 2020), Georges GILKINET (since 1 October 2020)
cabinet: Council of Ministers formally appointed by the monarch
elections/appointments: the monarchy is hereditary and constitutional; following legislative elections, the leader of the majority party or majority coalition usually appointed prime minister by the monarch and approved by Parliament

Legislative branch: *description:* bicameral Parliament consists of:
Senate or Senaat (in Dutch), Senat (in French) (60 seats; 50 members indirectly elected by the community and regional parliaments based on their election results, and 10 elected by the 50 other senators; members serve 5-year terms) Chamber of Representatives or Kamer van Volksvertegenwoordigers (in Dutch), Chambre des Representants (in French) (150 seats; members directly elected in multi-seat constituencies by proportional representation vote; members serve 5-year terms)
elections:
Senate - last held 26 May 2019 (next to be held in 2024)
Chamber of Representatives - last held on 26 May 2019 (next to be held in 2024); note - elections coincided with the EU elections
election results:
Senate - percent of vote by party - N-VA 15%, VB 12%, PS 12%, MR 12%, CD&V 8.3%, Open VLD 8.3%, Ecolo 15%, SP.A 6.7%, CDH 3.3%, PVDA-PTB 8.3%; seats by party - N-VA 9, VB 7, PS 7, MR 7, CD&V 5, Open VLD 5, Ecolo 9, SP.A 4, CDH 2, PVDA-PTB 5; composition as of March 2022 - men 31, women 29, percent of women 48.3% Chamber of Representatives - percent of vote by party - N-VA 16.7%, VB 12%, PS 13.3%, CD&V 8%, PVDA-PTB 8%, Open VLD 8%, MR 9.3%, SP.A 6%, Ecolo 8.7%,

Green 5.3%, CDH 3.3%, Defi 1.3%; seats by party - N-VA 25, VB 18, PS 20, CD&V 12, PVDA+PTB 12, Open VLD 12, MR 14, SP.A 9, Ecolo 13, Green 8, CDH 5, Defi 2; composition as of March 2022 - men 87, women 63, percent of women 42%; note - overall Parliament percent of women 43.8%
note: the 1993 constitutional revision that further devolved Belgium into a federal state created three levels of government (federal, regional, and linguistic community) with a complex division of responsibilities; this reality leaves six governments, each with its own legislative assembly; changes above occurred since the sixth state reform

Judicial branch: *highest court(s):* Constitutional Court or Grondwettelijk Hof (in Dutch) and Cour Constitutionelle (in French) (consists of 12 judges - 6 Dutch-speaking and 6 French-speaking); Supreme Court of Justice or Hof van Cassatie (in Dutch) and Cour de Cassation (in French) (court organized into 3 chambers: civil and commercial; criminal; social, fiscal, and armed forces; each chamber includes a Dutch division and a French division, each with a chairperson and 5-6 judges)
judge selection and term of office: Constitutional Court judges appointed by the monarch from candidates submitted by Parliament; judges appointed for life with mandatory retirement at age 70; Supreme Court judges appointed by the monarch from candidates submitted by the High Council of Justice, a 44-member independent body of judicial and non-judicial members; judges appointed for life
subordinate courts: Courts of Appeal; regional courts; specialized courts for administrative, commercial, labor, immigration, and audit issues; magistrate's courts; justices of the peace

Political parties and leaders:

Flemish parties: Christian Democratic and Flemish or CD&V [Sammy MAHDI]
Forward [Conner ROUSSEAU] (formerly Social Progressive Alternative or SP.A)
Groen or Green [Nadia NAJI and Jeremie VANEECKHOUT] (formerly AGALEV, Flemish Greens)
New Flemish Alliance or N-VA [Bart DE WEVER]
Open Flemish Liberals and Democrats or Open VLD [Egbert LACHAERT]
Vlaams Belang (Flemish Interest) or VB [Tom VAN GRIEKEN]

Francophone parties:: Ecolo (Francophone Greens) [Jean-Marc NOLLET and Rajae MAOUANE]
Francophone Federalist Democrats or Defi [Francois DE SMET]
Les Engages [Maxine PREVOT] (formerly Humanist and Democratic Center or CDH)
People's Party or PP [Mischael MODRIKAMEN] (dissolved 18 June 2019)
Reform Movement or MR [George-Louis BOUCHEZ]
Socialist Party or PS [Paul MAGNETTE]
Workers' Party or PVDA-PTB [Raoul HEDEBOUW]

International organization participation: ADB (nonregional members), AfDB (nonregional members), Australia Group, Benelux, BIS, CD, CE, CERN, EAPC, EBRD, ECB, EIB, EITI (implementing country), EMU, ESA, EU, FAO, FATF, G-9, G-10, IADB, IAEA, IBRD, ICAO, ICC (national committees), ICCt, ICRM, IDA, IEA, IFAD, IFC, IFRCS, IGAD (partners), IHO, ILO, IMF, IMO, IMSO, Interpol, IOC, IOM, IPU, ISO, ITSO, ITU, ITUC (NGOs), MIGA, MONUSCO, NATO, NEA, NSG, OAS (observer), OECD, OIF, OPCW, OSCE, Pacific Alliance (observer), Paris Club, PCA, Schengen Convention, SELEC (observer), UN, UNCTAD, UNESCO, UNHCR, UNIDO, UNIFIL, UNRWA, UNTSO, UPU, Wassenaar Arrangement, WCO, WHO, WIPO, WMO, WTO, ZC

Diplomatic representation in the US: *chief of mission:* Ambassador Jean-Arthur REGIBEAU (since 17 September 2020)
chancery: 1430 K Street NW, Washington DC 20005
telephone: [1] (202) 333-6900
FAX: [1] (202) 338-4960
email address and website:
Washington@diplobel.fed.be
https://unitedstates.diplomatie.belgium.be/en
consulate(s) general: Atlanta, Los Angeles, New York

Diplomatic representation from the US: *chief of mission:* Ambassador Michael ADLER (since 15 March 2022)
embassy: 27 Boulevard du Regent [Regentlaan], B-1000 Brussels
mailing address: 7600 Brussels Place, Washington DC 20521-7600
telephone: [32] (2) 811-4000
FAX: [32] (2) 811-4500
email address and website:
uscitizenBrussels@state.gov
https://be.usembassy.gov/

Flag description: three equal vertical bands of black (hoist side), yellow, and red; the vertical design was based on the flag of France; the colors are those of the arms of the duchy of Brabant (yellow lion with red claws and tongue on a black field)

National symbol(s): golden rampant lion; national colors: red, black, yellow

National anthem: *name:* "La Brabanconne" (The Song of Brabant)
lyrics/music: Louis-Alexandre DECHET [French] and Victor CEULEMANS [Dutch]/Francois VAN CAMPENHOUT
note: adopted 1830; according to legend, Louis-Alexandre DECHET, an actor at the theater in which the revolution against the Netherlands began, wrote the lyrics with a group of young people in a Brussels cafe

National heritage: *total World Heritage Sites:* 15 (14 cultural, 1 natural)
selected World Heritage Site locales: Belfries of Belgium (c); Historic Brugge (c); The Grand Place, Brussels (c); Major Town Houses of Victor Horta (c); Notre-Dame Cathedral, Tournai (c); Spa, Liege (c); Primeval Beech Forests - Sonian Wood (n); Stoclet Palace (c)

ECONOMY

Economic overview: Belgium's central geographic location and highly developed transport network have helped develop a well-diversified economy, with a broad mix of transport, services, manufacturing, and high tech. Service and high-tech industries are concentrated in the northern Flanders region while the southern region of Wallonia is home to industries like coal and steel manufacturing. Belgium is completely reliant on foreign sources of fossil fuels, and the planned closure of its seven nuclear plants by 2025 should increase its dependence on foreign energy. Its role as a regional logistical hub makes its economy vulnerable to shifts in foreign demand, particularly with EU trading partners. Roughly three-quarters of Belgium's trade is with other EU countries, and the port of Zeebrugge conducts almost half its trade with the United Kingdom alone, leaving Belgium's economy vulnerable to the outcome of negotiations on the UK's exit from the EU.

Belgium's GDP grew by 1.7% in 2017 and the budget deficit was 1.5% of GDP. Unemployment stood at 7.3%, however the unemployment rate is lower in Flanders than Wallonia, 4.4% compared to 9.4%, because of industrial differences between the regions. The economy largely recovered from the March 2016 terrorist attacks that mainly impacted the Brussels region tourist and hospitality industry. Prime Minister Charles MICHEL's center-right government has pledged to further reduce the deficit in response to EU pressure to decrease Belgium's high public debt of about 104% of GDP, but such efforts would also dampen economic growth. In addition to restrained public spending, low wage growth and higher inflation promise to curtail a more robust recovery in private consumption.

The government has pledged to pursue a reform program to improve Belgium's competitiveness, including changes to labor market rules and welfare benefits. These changes have generally made Belgian wages more competitive regionally, but have raised tensions with trade unions, which have called for extended strikes. In 2017, Belgium approved a tax reform plan to ease corporate rates from 33% to 29% by 2018 and down to 25% by 2020. The tax plan also included benefits for innovation and SMEs, intended to spur competitiveness and private investment.

Real GDP (purchasing power parity): $557.11 billion (2020 est.)
$594.47 billion (2019 est.)
$584.05 billion (2018 est.)
note: data are in 2017 dollars
country comparison to the world: 36

Real GDP growth rate: 1.41% (2019 est.)
1.49% (2018 est.)
1.9% (2017 est.)
country comparison to the world: 156

Real GDP per capita: $48,200 (2020 est.)
$51,700 (2019 est.)
$51,100 (2018 est.)
note: data are in 2017 dollars
country comparison to the world: 31

GDP (official exchange rate): $533.028 billion (2019 est.)

Inflation rate (consumer prices): 1.4% (2019 est.)
2% (2018 est.)
2.1% (2017 est.)
country comparison to the world: 82

Credit ratings:

Fitch rating: AA- (2016)

Moody's rating: Aa3 (2011)

Standard & Poors rating: AA (2011)
note: The year refers to the year in which the current credit rating was first obtained.

GDP - composition, by sector of origin: *agriculture:* 0.7% (2017 est.)
industry: 22.1% (2017 est.)
services: 77.2% (2017 est.)

GDP - composition, by end use: *household consumption:* 51.2% (2017 est.)
government consumption: 23.4% (2017 est.)
investment in fixed capital: 23.3% (2017 est.)

investment in inventories: 1.3% (2017 est.)
exports of goods and services: 85.1% (2017 est.)
imports of goods and services: -84.4% (2017 est.)

Agricultural products: sugar beets, milk, potatoes, wheat, pork, lettuce, poultry, maize, barley, pears

Industries: engineering and metal products, motor vehicle assembly, transportation equipment, scientific instruments, processed food and beverages, chemicals, pharmaceuticals, base metals, textiles, glass, petroleum

Industrial production growth rate: 0.2% (2017 est.)
country comparison to the world: 168

Labor force: 4.122 million (2020 est.)
country comparison to the world: 88

Labor force - by occupation: *agriculture:* 1.3%
industry: 18.6%
services: 80.1% (2013 est.)

Unemployment rate: 5.36% (2019 est.)
5.96% (2018 est.)
country comparison to the world: 86

Unemployment, youth ages 15-24: *total:* 15.3%
male: 15.5%
female: 15.1% (2020 est.)
country comparison to the world: 106

Population below poverty line: 14.8% (2018 est.)

Gini Index coefficient - distribution of family income: 27.4 (2017 est.)
28.7 (1996)
country comparison to the world: 163

Household income or consumption by percentage share: *lowest 10%:* 3.4%
highest 10%: 28.4% (2006)

Budget: *revenues:* 253.5 billion (2017 est.)
expenditures: 258.6 billion (2017 est.)

Budget surplus (+) or deficit (-): -1% (of GDP) (2017 est.)
country comparison to the world: 74

Public debt: 103.4% of GDP (2017 est.)
106% of GDP (2016 est.)
note: data cover general government debt and include debt instruments issued (or owned) by government entities other than the treasury; the data include treasury debt held by foreign entities; the data include debt issued by subnational entities, as well as intra-governmental debt; intra-governmental debt consists of treasury borrowings from surpluses in the social funds, such as for retirement, medical care, and unemployment; debt instruments for the social funds are not sold at public auctions; general government debt is defined by the Maastricht definition and calculated by the National Bank of Belgium as consolidated gross debt; the debt is defined in European Regulation EC479/2009 concerning the implementation of the protocol on the excessive deficit procedure annexed to the Treaty on European Union (Treaty of Maastricht) of 7 February 1992; the sub-sectors of consolidated gross debt are: federal government, communities and regions, local government, and social security funds
country comparison to the world: 13

Taxes and other revenues: 51.3% (of GDP) (2017 est.)
country comparison to the world: 15

Fiscal year: calendar year

Current account balance: $1.843 billion (2019 est.)
-$4.135 billion (2018 est.)
country comparison to the world: 41

Exports: $414.79 billion (2020 est.)
$436.3 billion (2019 est.)
$451.25 billion (2018 est.)
note: Data are in current year dollars and do not include illicit exports or re-exports.
country comparison to the world: 17

Exports - partners: Germany 17%, France 14%, Netherlands 13%, United Kingdom 8%, United States 6%, Italy 5% (2019)

Exports - commodities: cars and vehicle parts, refined petroleum, packaged medicines, medical cultures/vaccines, diamonds, natural gas (2019)

Imports: $412.85 billion (2020 est.) note: data are in current year dollars
$433.04 billion (2019 est.) note: data are in current year dollars
$452.53 billion (2018 est.) note: data are in current year dollars
country comparison to the world: 15

Imports - partners: Netherlands 16%, Germany 13%, France 10%, United States 8%, Ireland 5%, China 5% (2019)

Imports - commodities: cars, refined petroleum, packaged medicines, medical cultures/vaccines, diamonds, natural gas (2019)

Reserves of foreign exchange and gold: $26.16 billion (31 December 2017 est.)
$24.1 billion (31 December 2015 est.)
country comparison to the world: 54

Debt - external: $1,317,513,000,000 (2019 est.)
$1,332,358,000,000 (2018 est.)
country comparison to the world: 17

Exchange rates: euros (EUR) per US dollar -
0.828 (2020 est.)
0.903 (2019 est.)
0.878 (2018 est.)
0.885 (2014 est.)
0.763 (2013 est.)

ENERGY

Electricity access: *electrification - total population:* 100% (2020)

Electricity: *installed generating capacity:* 26.929 million kW (2020 est.)
consumption: 81,171,300,000 kWh (2020 est.)
exports: 14.053 billion kWh (2020 est.)
imports: 13.394 billion kWh (2020 est.)
transmission/distribution losses: 3.444 billion kWh (2020 est.)

Electricity generation sources: *fossil fuels:* 33.1% of total installed capacity (2020 est.)
nuclear: 38.1% of total installed capacity (2020 est.)
solar: 5.8% of total installed capacity (2020 est.)
wind: 15% of total installed capacity (2020 est.)
hydroelectricity: 0.3% of total installed capacity (2020 est.)
biomass and waste: 7.7% of total installed capacity (2020 est.)

Coal: *production:* 1.105 million metric tons (2020 est.)
consumption: 4.167 million metric tons (2020 est.)
exports: 504,000 metric tons (2020 est.)
imports: 3.467 million metric tons (2020 est.)
proven reserves: 0 metric tons (2019 est.)

Petroleum: *total petroleum production:* 11,400 bbl/day (2021 est.)
refined petroleum consumption: 642,300 bbl/day (2019 est.)
crude oil and lease condensate exports: 0 bbl/day (2018 est.)
crude oil and lease condensate imports: 666,700 bbl/day (2018 est.)
crude oil estimated reserves: 0 barrels (2021 est.)

Refined petroleum products - production: 731,700 bbl/day (2017 est.)
country comparison to the world: 25

Refined petroleum products - exports: 680,800 bbl/day (2017 est.)
country comparison to the world: 12

Refined petroleum products - imports: 601,400 bbl/day (2017 est.)
country comparison to the world: 14

Natural gas: *production:* 0 cubic meters (2021 est.)
consumption: 18,171,598,000 cubic meters (2019 est.)
exports: 3,942,860,000 cubic meters (2019 est.)
imports: 22,606,066,000 cubic meters (2019 est.)
proven reserves: 0 cubic meters (2021 est.)

Carbon dioxide emissions: 128.247 million metric tonnes of CO2 (2019 est.)
from coal and metallurgical coke: 10.301 million metric tonnes of CO2 (2019 est.)
from petroleum and other liquids: 83.474 million metric tonnes of CO2 (2019 est.)
from consumed natural gas: 34.472 million metric tonnes of CO2 (2019 est.)
country comparison to the world: 37

Energy consumption per capita: 234.216 million Btu/person (2019 est.)
country comparison to the world: 17

COMMUNICATIONS

Telephones - fixed lines: *total subscriptions:* 3,634,639 (2020 est.)
subscriptions per 100 inhabitants: 31 (2020 est.)
country comparison to the world: 36

Telephones - mobile cellular: *total subscriptions:* 11,529,728 (2020 est.)
subscriptions per 100 inhabitants: 99 (2020 est.)
country comparison to the world: 81

Telecommunication systems: *general assessment:* mobile networks have been upgraded to support growing mobile data use among subscribers, with near-comprehensive LTE coverage; operators have also trialed 5G in preparation for launching services; the auction of 5G-suitable spectrum has been delayed to the beginning of 2022, while the onerous restrictions on radiation have meant that some 5G trials have been suspended; there is effective competition in Belgium between the DSL and cable platforms, while in recent years government support has also encouraged investment in fiber networks; in a bid to encourage investment in under served areas, the regulator in 2018 amended the conditions by which market players grant wholesale access to copper and fiber infrastructure; in May 2019 it opened a further consultation on cost models for access to the networks of cablecos and fiber infrastructure (2021)
domestic: about 31 per 100 fixed-line and 99 per 100 mobile-cellular; nationwide mobile-cellular telephone system; extensive cable network; limited microwave radio relay network (2020)
international: country code - 32; landing points for Concerto, UK-Belgium, Tangerine, and SeaMeWe-3, submarine cables that provide links to Europe, the Middle East, Australia, and Asia; satellite earth stations - 7 (Intelsat - 3) (2019)

Broadcast media: a segmented market with the three major communities (Flemish-, French-, and German-speaking) each having responsibility for their own broadcast media; multiple TV channels exist for each community; additionally, in excess of 90% of households are connected to cable and can access broadcasts of TV stations from neighboring countries; each community has a public radio network coexisting with private broadcasters

Internet country code: .be

Internet users: *total:* 10,620,701 (2020 est.)
percent of population: 92% (2020 est.)
country comparison to the world: 54

Broadband - fixed subscriptions: *total:* 4,734,210 (2020 est.)
subscriptions per 100 inhabitants: 41 (2020 est.)
country comparison to the world: 34

TRANSPORTATION

National air transport system: *number of registered air carriers:* 7 (2020)
inventory of registered aircraft operated by air carriers: 117
annual passenger traffic on registered air carriers: 13,639,487 (2018)
annual freight traffic on registered air carriers: 1,285,340,000 (2018) mt-km

Civil aircraft registration country code prefix: OO

Airports: *total:* 41 (2021)
country comparison to the world: 102

Airports - with paved runways: *total:* 26
over 3,047 m: 6
2,438 to 3,047 m: 9
1,524 to 2,437 m: 2
914 to 1,523 m: 1
under 914 m: 8 (2021)

Airports - with unpaved runways: *total:* 15
under 914 m: 15 (2021)

Heliports: 1 (2021)

Pipelines: 3,139 km gas, 154 km oil, 535 km refined products (2013)

Railways: *total:* 3,592 km (2014)
standard gauge: 3,592 km (2014) 1.435-m gauge (2,960 km electrified)
country comparison to the world: 55

Roadways: *total:* 118,414 km (2015)
paved: 118,414 km (2015) (includes 1,747 km of expressways)
country comparison to the world: 41

Waterways: 2,043 km (2012) (1,528 km in regular commercial use)
country comparison to the world: 43

Merchant marine: *total:* 201
by type: bulk carrier 19, container ship 7, general cargo 16, oil tanker 21, other 138 (2021)
country comparison to the world: 68

Ports and terminals: *major seaport(s):* Oostende, Zeebrugge
container port(s) (TEUs): Antwerp (11,860,204) (2019)
LNG terminal(s) (import): Zeebrugge
river port(s): Antwerp, Gent (Schelde River) Brussels (Senne River) Liege (Meuse River)

MILITARY AND SECURITY

Military and security forces: Belgian Armed Forces: Land Component, Marine (Naval) Component, Air Component, Medical Service (2022)

Military expenditures: 1.2% of GDP (2022 est.)
1.1% of GDP (2021)
1% of GDP (2020)
0.9% of GDP (2019) (approximately $5.54 billion)
0.9% of GDP (2018) (approximately $5.43 billion)
country comparison to the world: 111

Military and security service personnel strengths: approximately 25,000 active duty personnel (10,000 Land Component; 1,500 Marine Component; 5,000 Air Force Component; 1,500 Medical Service; 7,000 other, including joint staff, support, and training schools) (2022)

Military equipment inventories and acquisitions: the Belgian Armed Forces have a mix of weapons systems from European countries, Israel, and the US; since 2010, several European nations have been the leading suppliers of armaments; Belgium has an export-focused defense industry that focuses on components and subcontracting (2021)

Military service age and obligation: 18 years of age for voluntary military service for men and women; conscription abolished in 1995 (2022)
note 1: in 2020, women comprised about 9% of the military's full-time personnel
note 2: foreign nationals 18-34 years of age who speak Dutch or French and are citizens of EU countries, Iceland, Lichtenstein, Norway, and Switzerland may apply to join the military

Military deployments: 125 France (contributing member of EuroCorps); 250 Romania (NATO) (2022)
note: in response to Russia's 2022 invasion of Ukraine, some NATO countries, including Belgium, have sent additional troops and equipment to the battlegroups deployed in NATO territory in eastern Europe

Military - note: Belgium is a member of NATO and was one of the original 12 countries to sign the North Atlantic Treaty (also known as the Washington Treaty) in 1949; Belgium hosts the NATO headquarters in Brussels

in 2015, Belgium, the Netherlands, and Luxembourg signed an agreement to conduct joint air policing of their territories; under the agreement, which went into effect in January of 2017, the Belgian and Dutch Air Forces trade responsibility for patrolling the skies over the three countries

in 2018, the Defense Ministers of Belgium, Denmark and the Netherlands signed a Memorandum of Understanding (MOU) for the creation of a Composite Special Operations Component Command (C-SOCC); the C-SOCC was declared operational in December 2020

TERRORISM

Terrorist group(s): Islamic Revolutionary Guard Corps/Qods Force; Islamic State of Iraq and ash-Sham (ISIS)

TRANSNATIONAL ISSUES

Disputes - international: none identified

Refugees and internally displaced persons: *refugees (country of origin):* 18,493 (Syria), 5,094 (Iraq) (2020); 60,241 (Ukraine) (as of 22 November 2022)
stateless persons: 1,159 (mid-year 2021)

Illicit drugs: a primary entry point for cocaine smuggled into Europe; also a transit point for precursor chemicals from China for amphetamine and MDMA (ecstasy) production labs in Belgium; a transit country for new psychoactive substances (NPS); increasing number of amphetamine and ecstasy production labs in Belgium; heroin also transits through Belgium.

BELIZE

INTRODUCTION

Background: Belize was the site of several Mayan city states until their decline at the end of the first millennium A.D. The British and Spanish disputed the region in the 17th and 18th centuries; it formally became the colony of British Honduras in 1862. Territorial disputes between the UK and Guatemala delayed the independence of Belize until 1981. Guatemala refused to recognize the new nation until 1992 and the two countries are involved in an ongoing border dispute. Both nations have voted to send the dispute for final resolution to the International Court of Justice. Tourism has become the mainstay of the economy. Current concerns include the country's heavy foreign debt burden, high crime rates, high unemployment combined with a majority youth population, growing involvement in the Mexican and South American drug trade, and one of the highest HIV/AIDS prevalence rates in Central America.

GEOGRAPHY

Location: Central America, bordering the Caribbean Sea, between Guatemala and Mexico

Geographic coordinates: 17 15 N, 88 45 W

Map references: Central America and the Caribbean

Area: *total:* 22,966 sq km
land: 22,806 sq km
water: 160 sq km
country comparison to the world: 151

Area - comparative: slightly smaller than Massachusetts

Land boundaries: *total:* 542 km
border countries (2): Guatemala 266 km; Mexico 276 km

Coastline: 386 km

Maritime claims: *territorial sea:* 12 nm in the north, 3 nm in the south; note - from the mouth of the Sarstoon River to Ranguana Cay, Belize's territorial

sea is 3 nm; according to Belize's Maritime Areas Act, 1992, the purpose of this limitation is to provide a framework for negotiating a definitive agreement on territorial differences with Guatemala
exclusive economic zone: 200 nm

Climate: tropical; very hot and humid; rainy season (May to November); dry season (February to May)

Terrain: flat, swampy coastal plain; low mountains in south

Elevation: *highest point:* Doyle's Delight 1,124 m
lowest point: Caribbean Sea 0 m
mean elevation: 173 m

Natural resources: arable land potential, timber, fish, hydropower

Land use: *agricultural land:* 6.9% (2018 est.)
arable land: 3.3% (2018 est.)
permanent crops: 1.4% (2018 est.)
permanent pasture: 2.2% (2018 est.)
forest: 60.6% (2018 est.)
other: 32.5% (2018 est.)

Irrigated land: 35 sq km (2012)

Population distribution: approximately 25% to 30% of the population lives in the former capital, Belize City; over half of the overall population is rural; population density is slightly higher in the north and east

Natural hazards: frequent, devastating hurricanes (June to November) and coastal flooding (especially in south)

Geography - note: only country in Central America without a coastline on the North Pacific Ocean

PEOPLE AND SOCIETY

Population: 412,387 (2022 est.)
country comparison to the world: 175

Nationality: *noun:* Belizean(s)
adjective: Belizean

Ethnic groups: Mestizo 52.9%, Creole 25.9%, Maya 11.3%, Garifuna 6.1%, East Indian 3.9%, Mennonite 3.6%, White 1.2%, Asian 1%, other 1.2%, unknown 0.3% (2010 est.)
note: percentages add up to more than 100% because respondents were able to identify more than one ethnic origin

Languages: English 62.9% (official), Spanish 56.6%, Creole 44.6%, Maya 10.5%, German 3.2%, Garifuna 2.9%, other 1.8%, unknown 0.5%; note - shares sum to more than 100% because some respondents gave more than one answer on the census (2010 est.)
major-language sample(s): The World Factbook, the indispensable source for basic information. (English)
La Libreta Informativa del Mundo, la fuente indispensable de información básica. (Spanish)

Religions: Roman Catholic 40.1%, Protestant 31.5% (includes Pentecostal 8.4%, Seventh Day Adventist 5.4%, Anglican 4.7%, Mennonite 3.7%, Baptist 3.6%, Methodist 2.9%, Nazarene 2.8%), Jehovah's Witness 1.7%, other 10.5% (includes Baha'i, Buddhist, Hindu, Church of Jesus Christ, Muslim, Rastafarian, Salvation Army), unspecified 0.6%, none 15.5% (2010 est.)

Demographic profile: Migration continues to transform Belize's population. About 16% of Belizeans live abroad, while immigrants constitute approximately 15% of Belize's population. Belizeans seeking job and educational opportunities have preferred to emigrate to the United States rather than former colonizer Great Britain because of the United States' closer proximity and stronger trade ties with Belize. Belizeans also emigrate to Canada, Mexico, and English-speaking Caribbean countries. The emigration of a large share of Creoles (Afro-Belizeans) and the influx of Central American immigrants, mainly Guatemalans, Salvadorans, and Hondurans, has changed Belize's ethnic composition. Mestizos have become the largest ethnic group, and Belize now has more native Spanish speakers than English or Creole speakers, despite English being the official language. In addition, Central American immigrants are establishing new communities in rural areas, which contrasts with the urbanization trend seen in neighboring countries. Recently, Chinese, European, and North American immigrants have become more frequent.

Immigration accounts for an increasing share of Belize's population growth rate, which is steadily falling due to fertility decline. Belize's declining birth rate and its increased life expectancy are creating an aging population. As the elderly population grows and nuclear families replace extended households, Belize's government will be challenged to balance a rising demand for pensions, social services, and healthcare for its senior citizens with the need to reduce poverty and social inequality and to improve sanitation.

Age structure: *0-14 years:* 32.57% (male 66,454/female 63,700)
15-24 years: 19% (male 39,238/female 36,683)
25-54 years: 37.72% (male 73,440/female 77,300)
55-64 years: 6.18% (male 12,235/female 12,444)
65 years and over: 4.53% (male 8,781/female 9,323) (2020 est.)

Dependency ratios: *total dependency ratio:* 52
youth dependency ratio: 44.4
elderly dependency ratio: 7.6
potential support ratio: 13.1 (2020 est.)

Median age: *total:* 23.9 years
male: 23 years
female: 24.8 years (2020 est.)
country comparison to the world: 172

Population growth rate: 1.64% (2022 est.)
country comparison to the world: 58

Birth rate: 21.28 births/1,000 population (2022 est.)
country comparison to the world: 64

Death rate: 3.94 deaths/1,000 population (2022 est.)
country comparison to the world: 216

Net migration rate: -0.96 migrant(s)/1,000 population (2022 est.)
country comparison to the world: 143

Population distribution: approximately 25% to 30% of the population lives in the former capital, Belize City; over half of the overall population is rural; population density is slightly higher in the north and east

Urbanization: *urban population:* 46.4% of total population (2022)
rate of urbanization: 2.3% annual rate of change (2020-25 est.)

Major urban areas - population: 23,000 BELMOPAN (capital) (2018)

Sex ratio: *at birth:* 1.05 male(s)/female
0-14 years: 1.04 male(s)/female
15-24 years: 1.12 male(s)/female
25-54 years: 0.93 male(s)/female
55-64 years: 0.96 male(s)/female
65 years and over: 0.78 male(s)/female
total population: 1 male(s)/female (2022 est.)

Maternal mortality ratio: 36 deaths/100,000 live births (2017 est.)
country comparison to the world: 104

Infant mortality rate: *total:* 11.15 deaths/1,000 live births
male: 12.36 deaths/1,000 live births
female: 9.88 deaths/1,000 live births (2022 est.)
country comparison to the world: 130

Life expectancy at birth: *total population:* 75.82 years
male: 74.23 years
female: 77.5 years (2022 est.)
country comparison to the world: 114

Total fertility rate: 2.62 children born/woman (2022 est.)
country comparison to the world: 64

Contraceptive prevalence rate: 51.4% (2015/16)

Drinking water source: *improved: urban:* 100% of population
rural: 99.4% of population
total: 99.7% of population
unimproved: urban: 0% of population
rural: 0.6% of population
total: 0.3% of population (2020 est.)

Current health expenditure: 6% of GDP (2019)

Physicians density: 1.08 physicians/1,000 population (2018)

Hospital bed density: 1 beds/1,000 population (2017)

Sanitation facility access: *improved: urban:* 99.1% of population
rural: 95.7% of population
total: 97.3% of population
unimproved: urban: 0.9% of population
rural: 4.3% of population
total: 2.7% of population (2020 est.)

HIV/AIDS - adult prevalence rate: 1.2% (2020 est.)
country comparison to the world: 35

Obesity - adult prevalence rate: 24.1% (2016)
country comparison to the world: 60

Alcohol consumption per capita: *total:* 5.93 liters of pure alcohol (2019 est.)
beer: 3.88 liters of pure alcohol (2019 est.)
wine: 0.68 liters of pure alcohol (2019 est.)
spirits: 1.19 liters of pure alcohol (2019 est.)
other alcohols: 0.17 liters of pure alcohol (2019 est.)

country comparison to the world: 72

Tobacco use: *total:* 8.5% (2020 est.)
male: 15.1% (2020 est.)
female: 1.8% (2020 est.)
country comparison to the world: 143

Children under the age of 5 years underweight: 4.6% (2015/16)
country comparison to the world: 81

Child marriage: *women married by age 15:* 6.3%
women married by age 18: 33.5%
men married by age 18: 22.2% (2016 est.)

Education expenditures: 7.9% of GDP (2020 est.)
country comparison to the world: 11

School life expectancy (primary to tertiary education): *total:* 13 years
male: 13 years
female: 13 years (2020)

Unemployment, youth ages 15-24: *total:* 19.3%
male: 12.7%
female: 28.5% (2019 est.)

ENVIRONMENT

Environment - current issues: deforestation; water pollution, including pollution of Belize's Barrier Reef System, from sewage, industrial effluents, agricultural runoff; inability to properly dispose of solid waste

Environment - international agreements: *party to:* Biodiversity, Climate Change, Climate Change-Kyoto Protocol, Climate Change-Paris Agreement, Comprehensive Nuclear Test Ban, Desertification, Endangered Species, Hazardous Wastes, Law of the Sea, Ozone Layer Protection, Ship Pollution, Wetlands, Whaling
signed, but not ratified: none of the selected agreements

Air pollutants: *particulate matter emissions:* 21.23 micrograms per cubic meter (2016 est.)
carbon dioxide emissions: 0.57 megatons (2016 est.)
methane emissions: 0.55 megatons (2020 est.)

Climate: tropical; very hot and humid; rainy season (May to November); dry season (February to May)

Land use: *agricultural land:* 6.9% (2018 est.)
arable land: 3.3% (2018 est.)
permanent crops: 1.4% (2018 est.)
permanent pasture: 2.2% (2018 est.)
forest: 60.6% (2018 est.)
other: 32.5% (2018 est.)

Urbanization: *urban population:* 46.4% of total population (2022)
rate of urbanization: 2.3% annual rate of change (2020-25 est.)

Revenue from forest resources: *forest revenues:* 0.31% of GDP (2018 est.)
country comparison to the world: 79

Revenue from coal: *coal revenues:* 0% of GDP (2018 est.)
country comparison to the world: 66

Waste and recycling: *municipal solid waste generated annually:* 101,379 tons (2015 est.)

Total water withdrawal: *municipal:* 11.4 million cubic meters (2017 est.)
industrial: 21.2 million cubic meters (2017 est.)
agricultural: 68.4 million cubic meters (2017 est.)

Total renewable water resources: 21.734 billion cubic meters (2017 est.)

GOVERNMENT

Country name: *conventional long form:* none
conventional short form: Belize
former: British Honduras
etymology: may be named for the Belize River, whose name possibly derives from the Maya word "belix," meaning "muddy-watered"

Government type: parliamentary democracy (National Assembly) under a constitutional monarchy; a Commonwealth realm

Capital: *name:* Belmopan
geographic coordinates: 17 15 N, 88 46 W
time difference: UTC-6 (1 hour behind Washington, DC, during Standard Time)
etymology: the decision to move the capital of the country inland to higher and more stable land was made in the 1960s; the name chosen for the new city was formed from the union of two words: "Belize," the name of the longest river in the country, and "Mopan," one of the rivers in the area of the new capital that empties into the Belize River

Administrative divisions: 6 districts; Belize, Cayo, Corozal, Orange Walk, Stann Creek, Toledo

Independence: 21 September 1981 (from the UK)

National holiday: Battle of St. George's Caye Day (National Day), 10 September (1798); Independence Day, 21 September (1981)

Constitution: *history:* previous 1954, 1963 (preindependence); latest signed and entered into force 21 September 1981
amendments: proposed and adopted by two-thirds majority vote of the National Assembly House of Representatives except for amendments relating to rights and freedoms, changes to the Assembly, and to elections and judiciary matters, which require at least three-quarters majority vote of the House; both types of amendments require assent of the governor general; amended several times, last in 2017

Legal system: English common law

International law organization participation: has not submitted an ICJ jurisdiction declaration; accepts ICCt jurisdiction

Citizenship: *citizenship by birth:* yes
citizenship by descent only: yes
dual citizenship recognized: yes
residency requirement for naturalization: 5 years

Suffrage: 18 years of age; universal

Executive branch: *chief of state:* King CHARLES III (since 8 September 2022); represented by Governor Froyla TZALAM (since 27 May 2021)
head of government: Prime Minister Juan Antonio BRICENO (since 12 November 2020); Deputy Prime Minister Cordel HYDE (since 16 November 2020)
cabinet: Cabinet appointed by the governor general on the advice of the prime minister from among members of the National Assembly
elections/appointments: the monarchy is hereditary; governor general appointed by the monarch; following legislative elections, the leader of the majority party or majority coalition usually appointed prime minister by the governor general; prime minister recommends the deputy prime minister

Legislative branch: *description:* bicameral National Assembly consists of:
Senate (14 seats, including the president); members appointed by the governor general - 6 on the advice of the prime minister, 3 on the advice of the leader of the opposition, and 1 each on the advice of the Belize Council of Churches and Evangelical Association of Churches, the Belize Chamber of Commerce and Industry and the Belize Better Business Bureau, non-governmental organizations in good standing, and the National Trade Union Congress and the Civil Society Steering Committee; Senate president elected from among the Senate members or from outside the Senate; members serve 5-year terms
House of Representatives (31 seats; members directly elected in single-seat constituencies by simple majority vote to serve 5-year terms)
elections:
Senate - last appointed 11 November 2020 (next appointments in November 2025)
House of Representatives - last held on 11 November 2020 (next to be held in November 2025)
election results: Senate - all members appointed; composition as of March 2022 - composition - men 9, women 5, percent of women 35.7%
House of Representatives - percent of vote by party - PUP 59.6%, UDP 38.8%, other 1.6%; seats by party - PUP 26, UDP 5; composition as of March 2022 - men 27, women 4, percent of women 12.9%; note - total percent of women in the National Assembly 20%

Judicial branch: *highest court(s):* Supreme Court of Judicature (consists of the Court of Appeal with the court president and 3 justices, and the Supreme Court with the chief justice and 10 justices); note - in 2010, Belize acceded to the Caribbean Court of Justice as the final court of appeal, replacing that of the Judicial Committee of the Privy Council in London
judge selection and term of office: Court of Appeal president and justices appointed by the governor-general upon advice of the prime minister after consultation with the National Assembly opposition leader; justices' tenures vary by terms of appointment; Supreme Court chief justice appointed by the governor-general upon the advice of the prime minister and the National Assembly opposition leader; other judges appointed by the governor-general upon the advice of the Judicial and Legal Services Section of the Public Services Commission and with the concurrence of the prime minister after consultation with the National Assembly opposition leader; judges can be appointed beyond age 65 but must retire by age 75; in 2013, the Supreme Court chief justice overturned a constitutional amendment that had restricted Court of Appeal judge appointments to as short as 1 year
subordinate courts: Magistrates' Courts; Family Court

Political parties and leaders: Belize Progressive Party or BPP [Wil MAHEIA] (formed in 2015 from a merger of the People's National Party, elements of the Vision Inspired by the People, and other smaller political groups)
People's United Party or PUP [Juan Antonio "Johnny" BRICENO]
United Democratic Party or UDP [Dean Oliver Barrow and Patrick FABER]
Vision Inspired by the People or VIP [Hubert ENRIQUEZ]

International organization participation: ACP, AOSIS, C, Caricom, CD, CDB, CELAC, FAO, G-77, IADB, IAEA, IBRD, ICAO, ICC (NGOs), ICRM, IDA, IFAD, IFC, IFRCS, ILO, IMF, IMO,

Interpol, IOC, IOM, ITU, LAES, MIGA, NAM, OAS, OPANAL, OPCW, PCA, Petrocaribe, SICA, UN, UNCTAD, UNESCO, UNIDO, UPU, WCO, WHO, WIPO, WMO, WTO

Diplomatic representation in the US: *chief of mission:* Ambassador Lynn Raymond YOUNG (since 7 July 2021)
chancery: 2535 Massachusetts Avenue NW, Washington, DC 20008-2826
telephone: [1] (202) 332-9636
FAX: [1] (202) 332-6888
email address and website:
reception.usa@mfa.gov.bz
https://www.belizeembassyusa.mfa.gov.bz/
consulate(s) general: Los Angeles, New York (consular services temporarily suspended beginning 18 December 2020)
consulate(s): Miami

Diplomatic representation from the US: *chief of mission:* Ambassador (vacant); Charge d'Affaires Leyla MOSES-ONES (since August 2021)
embassy: Floral Park Road, Belmopan, Cayo
mailing address: 3050 Belmopan Place, Washington DC 20521-3050
telephone: (501) 822-4011
FAX: (501) 822-4012
email address and website:
ACSBelize@state.gov
https://bz.usembassy.gov/

Flag description: royal blue with a narrow red stripe along the top and the bottom edges; centered is a large white disk bearing the coat of arms; the coat of arms features a shield flanked by two workers in front of a mahogany tree with the related motto SUB UMBRA FLOREO (I Flourish in the Shade) on a scroll at the bottom, all encircled by a green garland of 50 mahogany leaves; the colors are those of the two main political parties: blue for the PUP and red for the UDP; various elements of the coat of arms - the figures, the tools, the mahogany tree, and the garland of leaves - recall the logging industry that led to British settlement of Belize
note: Belize's flag is the only national flag that depicts human beings; two British overseas territories, Montserrat and the British Virgin Islands, also depict humans

National symbol(s): Baird's tapir (a large, browsing, forest-dwelling mammal), keel-billed toucan, Black Orchid; national colors: red, blue

National anthem: *name:* Land of the Free
lyrics/music: Samuel Alfred HAYNES/Selwyn Walford YOUNG
note: adopted 1981; as a Commonwealth country, in addition to the national anthem, "God Save the King" serves as the royal anthem (see United Kingdom)

National heritage: *total World Heritage Sites:* 1 (natural)
selected World Heritage Site locales: Belize Barrier Reef Reserve System

ECONOMY

Economic overview: Tourism is the number one foreign exchange earner in this small economy, followed by exports of sugar, bananas, citrus, marine products, and crude oil.

The government's expansionary monetary and fiscal policies, initiated in September 1998, led to GDP growth averaging nearly 4% in 1999-2007, but GPD growth has averaged only 2.1% from 2007-2016, with 2.5% growth estimated for 2017. Belize's dependence on energy imports makes it susceptible to energy price shocks.

Although Belize has the third highest per capita income in Central America, the average income figure masks a huge income disparity between rich and poor, and a key government objective remains reducing poverty and inequality with the help of international donors. High unemployment, a growing trade deficit and heavy foreign debt burden continue to be major concerns. Belize faces continued pressure from rising sovereign debt, and a growing trade imbalance.

Real GDP (purchasing power parity): $2.43 billion (2020 est.)
$2.83 billion (2019 est.)
$2.78 billion (2018 est.)
note: data are in 2017 dollars
country comparison to the world: 191

Real GDP growth rate: 0.8% (2017 est.)
-0.5% (2016 est.)
3.8% (2015 est.)
country comparison to the world: 176

Real GDP per capita: $6,100 (2020 est.)
$7,300 (2019 est.)
$7,300 (2018 est.)
note: data are in 2017 dollars
country comparison to the world: 162

GDP (official exchange rate): $1.854 billion (2017 est.)

Inflation rate (consumer prices): 1.1% (2017 est.)
0.7% (2016 est.)
country comparison to the world: 68

Credit ratings:

Moody's rating: Caa3 (2020)

Standard & Poors rating: CCC+ (2020)
note: The year refers to the year in which the current credit rating was first obtained.

GDP - composition, by sector of origin: *agriculture:* 10.3% (2017 est.)
industry: 21.6% (2017 est.)
services: 68% (2017 est.)

GDP - composition, by end use: *household consumption:* 75.1% (2017 est.)
government consumption: 15.2% (2017 est.)
investment in fixed capital: 22.5% (2017 est.)
investment in inventories: 1.2% (2017 est.)
exports of goods and services: 49.1% (2017 est.)
imports of goods and services: -63.2% (2017 est.)

Agricultural products: sugar care, oranges, bananas, maize, poultry, rice, sorghum, papayas, grapefruit, soybeans

Industries: garment production, food processing, tourism, construction, oil

Industrial production growth rate: -0.6% (2017 est.)
country comparison to the world: 172

Labor force: 120,500 (2008 est.)
note: shortage of skilled labor and all types of technical personnel
country comparison to the world: 179

Labor force - by occupation: *agriculture:* 10.2%
industry: 18.1%
services: 71.7% (2007 est.)

Unemployment rate: 9% (2017 est.)
8% (2016 est.)
country comparison to the world: 138

Unemployment, youth ages 15-24: *total:* 19.3%
male: 12.7%
female: 28.5% (2019 est.)
country comparison to the world: 82

Population below poverty line: 41% (2013 est.)

Budget: *revenues:* 553.5 million (2017 est.)
expenditures: 572 million (2017 est.)

Budget surplus (+) or deficit (-): -1% (of GDP) (2017 est.)
country comparison to the world: 75

Public debt: 99% of GDP (2017 est.)
95.9% of GDP (2016 est.)
country comparison to the world: 17

Taxes and other revenues: 29.9% (of GDP) (2017 est.)
country comparison to the world: 78

Fiscal year: 1 April - 31 March

Current account balance: -$143 million (2017 est.)
-$163 million (2016 est.)
country comparison to the world: 92

Exports: $710 million (2020 est.)
$1.1 billion (2019 est.)
$1.07 billion (2018 est.)
note: Data are in current year dollars and do not include illicit exports or re-exports.
country comparison to the world: 185

Exports - partners: United Kingdom 27%, United States 24%, Spain 6%, Jamaica 5%, Ireland 5% (2019)

Exports - commodities: raw sugar, bananas, fruit juice, fish products, crude petroleum (2019)

Imports: $900 million (2020 est.) note: data are in current year dollars
$1.2 billion (2019 est.) note: data are in current year dollars
$1.16 billion (2018 est.) note: data are in current year dollars
country comparison to the world: 192

Imports - partners: United States 36%, China 13%, Mexico 12%, Guatemala 10% (2019)

Imports - commodities: refined petroleum, cigarettes, recreational boats, natural gas, cars (2019)

Reserves of foreign exchange and gold: $312.1 million (31 December 2017 est.)
$376.7 million (31 December 2016 est.)
country comparison to the world: 167

Debt - external: $1.315 billion (31 December 2017 est.)
$1.338 billion (31 December 2016 est.)
country comparison to the world: 162

Exchange rates: Belizean dollars (BZD) per US dollar -
2 (2017 est.)
2 (2016 est.)
2 (2015 est.)
2 (2014 est.)
2 (2013 est.)

ENERGY

Electricity access: *electrification - total population:* 99.5% (2018)
electrification - urban areas: 98.2% (2018)
electrification - rural areas: 100% (2018)

Electricity: *installed generating capacity:* 204,000 kW (2020 est.)
consumption: 992.305 million kWh (2019 est.)

exports: 0 kWh (2019 est.)
imports: 240 million kWh (2019 est.)
transmission/distribution losses: 80.3 million kWh (2019 est.)

Electricity generation sources: *fossil fuels:* 63.6% of total installed capacity (2020 est.)
solar: 0.2% of total installed capacity (2020 est.)
hydroelectricity: 13.4% of total installed capacity (2020 est.)
biomass and waste: 22.9% of total installed capacity (2020 est.)

Petroleum: *total petroleum production:* 1,300 bbl/day (2021 est.)
refined petroleum consumption: 3,900 bbl/day (2019 est.)
crude oil and lease condensate exports: 1,200 bbl/day (2018 est.)
crude oil and lease condensate imports: 0 bbl/day (2018 est.)
crude oil estimated reserves: 6.7 million barrels (2021 est.)

Refined petroleum products - production: 36 bbl/day (2015 est.)
country comparison to the world: 109

Refined petroleum products - exports: 0 bbl/day (2015 est.)
country comparison to the world: 130

Refined petroleum products - imports: 4,161 bbl/day (2015 est.)
country comparison to the world: 176

Carbon dioxide emissions: 541,000 metric tonnes of CO2 (2019 est.)
from petroleum and other liquids: 541,000 metric tonnes of CO2 (2019 est.)
country comparison to the world: 188

Energy consumption per capita: 31.552 million Btu/person (2019 est.)
country comparison to the world: 120

COMMUNICATIONS

Telephones - fixed lines: *total subscriptions:* 19,000 (2020 est.)
subscriptions per 100 inhabitants: 5 (2020 est.)
country comparison to the world: 175

Telephones - mobile cellular: *total subscriptions:* 264,000 (2020 est.)
subscriptions per 100 inhabitants: 66 (2020 est.)
country comparison to the world: 181

Telecommunication systems: *general assessment:* Belize's fixed-line teledensity and mobile penetration remain lower than average for the region, a legacy of insufficient market competition and under investment in telecoms services; a significant investment in infrastructure, launching an LTE-A service at the end of 2016 and in mid-2017 completing a submarine cable to Ambergris Caye, enabling it to launch an FttP service in San Pedro; the nfrastructure has been updated from the legacy copper to fiber; investments have been made to provide high speed broadband to 80% of residences across Belize. (2021)
domestic: roughly 5 per 100 fixed-line and mobile-cellular teledensity of 66 per 100 persons; mobile sector accounting for over 90% of all phone subscriptions (2020)
international: country code - 501; landing points for the ARCOS and SEUL fiber-optic telecommunications submarine cable that provides links to South and Central America, parts of the Caribbean, and the US; satellite earth station - 8 (Intelsat - 2, unknown - 6) (2019)

Broadcast media: 8 privately owned TV stations; multi-channel cable TV provides access to foreign stations; about 25 radio stations broadcasting on roughly 50 different frequencies; state-run radio was privatized in 1998 (2019)

Internet country code: .bz

Internet users: *total:* 202,787 (2020 est.)
percent of population: 51% (2020 est.)
country comparison to the world: 176

Broadband - fixed subscriptions: *total:* 36,000 (2020 est.)
subscriptions per 100 inhabitants: 9 (2020 est.)
country comparison to the world: 147

TRANSPORTATION

National air transport system: *number of registered air carriers:* 2 (2020)
inventory of registered aircraft operated by air carriers: 28
annual passenger traffic on registered air carriers: 1,297,533 (2018)
annual freight traffic on registered air carriers: 3.78 million (2018) mt-km

Civil aircraft registration country code prefix: V3

Airports: *total:* 47 (2021)
country comparison to the world: 91

Airports - with paved runways: *total:* 6
2,438 to 3,047 m: 1
914 to 1,523 m: 2
under 914 m: 3 (2021)

Airports - with unpaved runways: *total:* 41
2,438 to 3,047 m: 1
914 to 1,523 m: 11
under 914 m: 29 (2021)

Roadways: *total:* 3,281 km (2017)
paved: 601 km (2017)
unpaved: 2,680 km (2017)
country comparison to the world: 160

Waterways: 825 km (2011) (navigable only by small craft)
country comparison to the world: 77

Merchant marine: *total:* 813
by type: bulk carrier 54, container ship 1, general cargo 428, oil tanker 70, other 260 (2021)
country comparison to the world: 29

Ports and terminals: *major seaport(s):* Belize City, Big Creek

MILITARY AND SECURITY

Military and security forces: Belize Defense Force (BDF): Army, Air Wing; Belize Coast Guard (2022)
note: the Ministry of National Defense and Border Security is responsible for oversight of the BDF and the Coast Guard, while the Ministry of Home Affairs and New Growth Industries has responsibility for police and prisons

Military expenditures: 1.2% of GDP (2022 est.)
1.3% of GDP (2021 est.)
1.5% of GDP (2020 est.)
1.4% of GDP (2019 est.) (approximately $35 million)
1.4% of GDP (2018 est.) (approximately $35 million)
country comparison to the world: 112

Military and security service personnel strengths: approximately 1,300 BDF personnel; approximately 300 Belize Coast Guard (2022)

Military equipment inventories and acquisitions: the BDF's inventory is limited and consists mostly of UK- and US-origin equipment (2022)

Military service age and obligation: 18 years of age for voluntary military service; laws allow for conscription only if volunteers are insufficient, but conscription has never been implemented; volunteers typically outnumber available positions by 3:1; initial service obligation 12 years (2022)

Military - note: the BDF traces its history back to the Prince Regent Royal Honduras Militia, a volunteer force established in 1817; the BDF was established in 1978 from the disbanded Police Special Force and the Belize Volunteer Guard to assist the resident British forces with the defense of Belize against Guatemala

the British Army has maintained a presence in Belize since its independence; as of 2022, the presence consisted of a small training support unit that provides jungle training to troops from the UK and international partners

TRANSNATIONAL ISSUES

Disputes - international: *Belize-Guatemala:* Demarcated but insecure boundary due to Guatemala's claims to more than half of Belizean territory. Line of Adjacency operates in lieu of an international boundary to control influx of Guatemalan squatters onto Belizean territory. Smuggling, narcotics trafficking, and human trafficking for sexual exploitation and debt bondage are all problems. Belize lacks resources to detect and extradite impoverished Guatemalan peasants squatting in Belizean rain forests in the remote border areas. At present, Belize and Honduras 12-nm territorial sea claims close off Guatemalan access to Caribbean in the Bahia de Amatique. Maritime boundary remains unresolved pending further negotiation.
Belize-Honduras: Honduras claims the Belizean-administered Sapodilla Cays off the coast of Belize in its constitution, but agreed to a joint ecological park around the cays should Guatemala consent to a maritime corridor in the Caribbean under the OAS-sponsored 2002 Belize-Guatemala Differendum.
Belize-Mexico: Belize and Mexico are working to solve minor border demarcation discrepancies arising from inaccuracies in the 1898 border treaty. Transshipment of illegal narcotics, smuggling, human trafficking, illegal immigration, and the growing of marijuana in very low population areas are all issues in the region today.

Illicit drugs: a transit country for illegal drugs, mainly cocaine, originating from countries in South America; low domestic drug consumption problem outside of recreational cannabis

BENIN

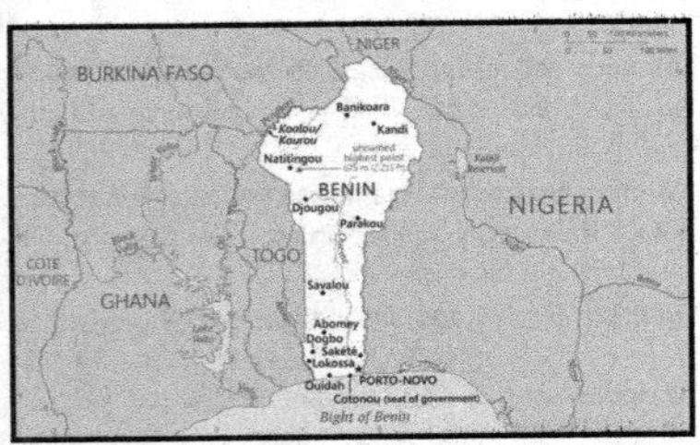

INTRODUCTION

Background: Present day Benin is comprised of about 42 ethnic groups, including the Yoruba in the southeast, who migrated from what is now Nigeria in the 12th century; the Dendi in the north-central area, who came from Mali in the 16th century; the Bariba and the Fula in the northeast; the Ottamari in the Atakora mountains; the Fon in the area around Abomey in the south-central area; and the Mina, Xueda, and Aja, who came from Togo, on the coast. The Kingdom of Dahomey emerged on the Abomey plateau in the 17th century and was a regional power for much of the 18th and 19th centuries. Dahomey had an organized domestic economy, international trade with Europeans, and a highly organized military. The growth of Dahomey coincided with the growth of the Atlantic slave trade, and it became known as a major source of enslaved people. France began to control the coastal areas of Dahomey in the second half of the 19th century; the entire kingdom was conquered by 1894. French Dahomey achieved independence in 1960; it changed its name to the Republic of Benin in 1975.

A succession of military governments ended in 1972 with the rise to power of Mathieu KEREKOU and the establishment of a government based on Marxist-Leninist principles. A move to representative government began in 1989. Two years later, free elections ushered in former Prime Minister Nicephore SOGLO as president, marking the first successful transfer of power in Africa from a dictatorship to a democracy. KEREKOU was returned to power by elections held in 1996 and 2001, though some irregularities were alleged. KEREKOU stepped down at the end of his second term in 2006 and was succeeded by Thomas YAYI Boni, a political outsider and independent, who won a second five-year term in March 2011. Patrice TALON, a wealthy businessman, took office in 2016; the space for pluralism, dissent, and free expression has narrowed under his administration. TALON won a second term in April 2021.

GEOGRAPHY

Location: Western Africa, bordering the Bight of Benin, between Nigeria and Togo

Geographic coordinates: 9 30 N, 2 15 E

Map references: Africa

Area: *total:* 112,622 sq km
land: 110,622 sq km
water: 2,000 sq km
country comparison to the world: 102

Area - comparative: slightly smaller than Pennsylvania

Land boundaries: *total:* 2,123 km
border countries (4): Burkina Faso 386 km; Niger 277 km; Nigeria 809 km; Togo 651 km

Coastline: 121 km

Maritime claims: *territorial sea:* 200 nm; note: the US does not recognize this claim
continental shelf: 200 nm
exclusive fishing zone: 200 nm

Climate: tropical; hot, humid in south; semiarid in north

Terrain: mostly flat to undulating plain; some hills and low mountains

Elevation: *highest point:* unnamed elevation 675 m; located 2.5 km southeast of the town of Kotopounga
lowest point: Atlantic Ocean 0 m
mean elevation: 273 m

Natural resources: small offshore oil deposits, limestone, marble, timber

Land use: *agricultural land:* 31.3% (2018 est.)
arable land: 22.9% (2018 est.)
permanent crops: 3.5% (2018 est.)
permanent pasture: 4.9% (2018 est.)
forest: 40% (2018 est.)
other: 28.7% (2018 est.)

Irrigated land: 230 sq km (2012)

Major watersheds (area sq km): Atlantic Ocean drainage: Niger (2,261,741 sq km), Volta (410,991 sq km)

Population distribution: the population is primarily located in the south, with the highest concentration of people residing in and around the cities on the Atlantic coast; most of the north remains sparsely populated with higher concentrations of residents in the west at shown in this population distribution map

Natural hazards: hot, dry, dusty harmattan wind may affect north from December to March

Geography - note: sandbanks create difficult access to a coast with no natural harbors, river mouths, or islands

PEOPLE AND SOCIETY

Population: 13,754,688 (2022 est.)
country comparison to the world: 74

Nationality: *noun:* Beninese (singular and plural)
adjective: Beninese

Ethnic groups: Fon and related 38.4%, Adja and related 15.1%, Yoruba and related 12%, Bariba and related 9.6%, Fulani and related 8.6%, Ottamari and related 6.1%, Yoa-Lokpa and related 4.3%, Dendi and related 2.9%, other 0.9%, foreigner 1.9% (2013 est.)

Languages: 55 languages; French (official); Fon (a Gbe language) and Yoruba are the most important indigenous languages in the south; half a dozen regionally important languages in the north, including Bariba (once counted as a Gur language) and Fulfulde

Religions: Muslim 27.7%, Roman Catholic 25.5%, Protestant 13.5% (Celestial 6.7%, Methodist 3.4%, other Protestant 3.4%), Vodoun 11.6%, other Christian 9.5%, other traditional religions 2.6%, other 2.6%, none 5.8% (2013 est.)

Demographic profile: Benin has a youthful age structure – almost 65% of the population is under the age of 25 – which is bolstered by high fertility and population growth rates. Benin's total fertility has been falling over time but remains high, declining from almost 7 children per women in 1990 to 4.8 in 2016. Benin's low contraceptive use and high unmet need for contraception contribute to the sustained high fertility rate. Although the majority of Beninese women use skilled health care personnel for antenatal care and delivery, the high rate of maternal mortality indicates the need for more access to high quality obstetric care.

Poverty, unemployment, increased living costs, and dwindling resources increasingly drive the Beninese to migrate. An estimated 4.4 million, more than 40%, of Beninese live abroad. Virtually all Beninese emigrants move to West African countries, particularly Nigeria and Cote d'Ivoire. Of the less than 1% of Beninese emigrants who settle in Europe, the vast majority live in France, Benin's former colonial ruler.

With about 40% of the population living below the poverty line, many desperate parents resort to sending their children to work in wealthy households as domestic servants (a common practice known as vidomegon), mines, quarries, or agriculture domestically or in Nigeria and other neighboring countries, often under brutal conditions. Unlike in other West African countries, where rural people move to the coast, farmers from Benin's densely populated southern and northwestern regions move to the historically sparsely populated central region to pursue agriculture. Immigrants from West African countries came to Benin in increasing numbers between 1992 and 2002 because of its political stability and porous borders.

Age structure: *0-14 years:* 45.56% (male 2,955,396/female 2,906,079)
15-24 years: 20.36% (male 1,300,453/female 1,318,880)
25-54 years: 28.54% (male 1,735,229/female 1,935,839)
55-64 years: 3.15% (male 193,548/female 211,427)
65 years and over: 2.39% (male 140,513/female 167,270) (2020 est.)

Dependency ratios: *total dependency ratio:* 82.6
youth dependency ratio: 76.6
elderly dependency ratio: 6
potential support ratio: 16.7 (2020 est.)

Median age: *total:* 17 years
male: 16.4 years
female: 17.6 years (2020 est.)
country comparison to the world: 218

Population growth rate: 3.34% (2022 est.)
country comparison to the world: 7

Birth rate: 41.15 births/1,000 population (2022 est.)
country comparison to the world: 3

Death rate: 8.01 deaths/1,000 population (2022 est.)
country comparison to the world: 89

Net migration rate: 0.24 migrant(s)/1,000 population (2022 est.)
country comparison to the world: 76

Population distribution: the population is primarily located in the south, with the highest concentration of people residing in and around the cities on the Atlantic coast; most of the north remains sparsely populated with higher concentrations of residents in the west at shown in this population distribution map

Urbanization: *urban population:* 49.5% of total population (2022)
rate of urbanization: 3.74% annual rate of change (2020-25 est.)

Major urban areas - population: 285,000 PORTO-NOVO (capital) (2018); 1.189 million Abomey-Calavi, 709,000 COTONOU (seat of government) (2022)

Sex ratio: *at birth:* 1.05 male(s)/female
0-14 years: 1.02 male(s)/female
15-24 years: 1 male(s)/female
25-54 years: 0.9 male(s)/female
55-64 years: 0.91 male(s)/female
65 years and over: 0.72 male(s)/female
total population: 0.97 male(s)/female (2022 est.)

Mother's mean age at first birth: 20.5 years (2017/18 est.)
note: data represents median age at first birth among women 25-49

Maternal mortality ratio: 397 deaths/100,000 live births (2017 est.)
country comparison to the world: 27

Infant mortality rate: *total:* 55.76 deaths/1,000 live births
male: 60.79 deaths/1,000 live births
female: 50.48 deaths/1,000 live births (2022 est.)
country comparison to the world: 15

Life expectancy at birth: *total population:* 62.21 years
male: 60.39 years
female: 64.14 years (2022 est.)
country comparison to the world: 213

Total fertility rate: 5.43 children born/woman (2022 est.)
country comparison to the world: 6

Contraceptive prevalence rate: 15.5% (2017/18)

Drinking water source: *improved: urban:* 79% of population
rural: 70.8% of population
total: 74.7% of population
unimproved: urban: 21% of population
rural: 29.2% of population
total: 25.3% of population (2020 est.)

Current health expenditure: 2.4% of GDP (2019)

Physicians density: 0.07 physicians/1,000 population (2019)

Hospital bed density: 0.5 beds/1,000 population

Sanitation facility access: *improved: urban:* 56.3% of population
rural: 18.1% of population
total: 36.6% of population
unimproved: urban: 43.7% of population
rural: 81.9% of population
total: 63.4% of population (2020 est.)

HIV/AIDS - adult prevalence rate: 0.9% (2020 est.)
country comparison to the world: 46

Major infectious diseases: *degree of risk:* very high (2020)
food or waterborne diseases: bacterial and protozoal diarrhea, hepatitis A, and typhoid fever
vectorborne diseases: dengue fever and malaria
animal contact diseases: rabies
respiratory diseases: meningococcal meningitis
note: on 21 March 2022, the US Centers for Disease Control and Prevention (CDC) issued a Travel Alert for polio in Africa; Benin is currently considered a high risk to travelers for circulating vaccine-derived polioviruses (cVDPV); vaccine-derived poliovirus (VDPV) is a strain of the weakened poliovirus that was initially included in oral polio vaccine (OPV) and *that has changed over time and behaves more like the wild or naturally occurring virus;* this means it can be spread more easily to people who are unvaccinated against polio and who come in contact with the stool or respiratory secretions, such as from a sneeze, of an "infected" person who received oral polio vaccine; the CDC recommends that before any international travel, anyone unvaccinated, incompletely vaccinated, or with an unknown polio vaccination status should complete the routine polio vaccine series; before travel to any high-risk destination, the CDC recommends that adults who previously completed the full, routine polio vaccine series receive a single, lifetime booster dose of polio vaccine

Obesity - adult prevalence rate: 9.6% (2016)
country comparison to the world: 142

Alcohol consumption per capita: *total:* 1.25 liters of pure alcohol (2019 est.)
beer: 0.81 liters of pure alcohol (2019 est.)
wine: 0.02 liters of pure alcohol (2019 est.)
spirits: 0.2 liters of pure alcohol (2019 est.)
other alcohols: 0.22 liters of pure alcohol (2019 est.)
country comparison to the world: 145

Tobacco use: *total:* 6.9% (2020 est.)
male: 11.8% (2020 est.)
female: 1.9% (2020 est.)
country comparison to the world: 156

Children under the age of 5 years underweight: 16.8% (2017/18)
country comparison to the world: 31

Child marriage: *women married by age 15:* 9.4%
women married by age 18: 30.6%
men married by age 18: 4.8% (2018 est.)

Education expenditures: 3% of GDP (2019 est.)
country comparison to the world: 149

Literacy: *definition:* age 15 and over can read and write
total population: 42.4%
male: 54%
female: 31.1% (2018)

School life expectancy (primary to tertiary education): *total:* 13 years
male: 14 years
female: 11 years (2016)

Unemployment, youth ages 15-24: *total:* 3.9%
male: 3.2%
female: 4.5% (2018 est.)

ENVIRONMENT

Environment - current issues: inadequate supplies of potable water; water pollution; poaching threatens wildlife populations; deforestation; desertification (the spread of the desert into agricultural lands in the north is accelerated by regular droughts)

Environment - international agreements: *party to:* Biodiversity, Climate Change, Climate Change-Kyoto Protocol, Climate Change-Paris Agreement, Comprehensive Nuclear Test Ban, Desertification, Endangered Species, Environmental Modification, Hazardous Wastes, Law of the Sea, Marine Dumping-London Convention, Nuclear Test Ban, Ozone Layer Protection, Ship Pollution, Tropical Timber 2006, Wetlands, Whaling
signed, but not ratified: none of the selected agreements

Air pollutants: *particulate matter emissions:* 33.11 micrograms per cubic meter (2016 est.)
carbon dioxide emissions: 6.48 megatons (2016 est.)
methane emissions: 5.8 megatons (2020 est.)

Climate: tropical; hot, humid in south; semiarid in north

Land use: *agricultural land:* 31.3% (2018 est.)
arable land: 22.9% (2018 est.)
permanent crops: 3.5% (2018 est.)
permanent pasture: 4.9% (2018 est.)
forest: 40% (2018 est.)
other: 28.7% (2018 est.)

Urbanization: *urban population:* 49.5% of total population (2022)
rate of urbanization: 3.74% annual rate of change (2020-25 est.)

Revenue from forest resources: *forest revenues:* 2.24% of GDP (2018 est.)
country comparison to the world: 31

Revenue from coal: *coal revenues:* 0% of GDP (2018 est.)
country comparison to the world: 67

Waste and recycling: *municipal solid waste generated annually:* 685,936 tons (1993 est.)
municipal solid waste recycled annually: 171,484 tons (2005 est.)
percent of municipal solid waste recycled: 25% (2005 est.)

Major watersheds (area sq km): Atlantic Ocean drainage: Niger (2,261,741 sq km), Volta (410,991 sq km)

Total water withdrawal: *municipal:* 145 million cubic meters (2017 est.)
industrial: 30 million cubic meters (2017 est.)
agricultural: 59 million cubic meters (2017 est.)

Total renewable water resources: 26.39 billion cubic meters (2017 est.)

GOVERNMENT

Country name: *conventional long form:* Republic of Benin
conventional short form: Benin
local long form: Republique du Benin
local short form: Benin
former: Dahomey, People's Republic of Benin
etymology: named for the Bight of Benin, the body of water on which the country lies

Government type: presidential republic

Capital: *name:* Porto-Novo (constitutional capital); Cotonou (seat of government)
geographic coordinates: 6 29 N, 2 37 E
time difference: UTC+1 (6 hours ahead of Washington, DC, during Standard Time)
etymology: the name Porto-Novo is Portuguese for "new port"; Cotonou means "by the river of death" in the native Fon language

Administrative divisions: 12 departments; Alibori, Atacora, Atlantique, Borgou, Collines, Couffo, Donga, Littoral, Mono, Oueme, Plateau, Zou

Independence: 1 August 1960 (from France)

National holiday: Independence Day, 1 August (1960)

Constitution: *history:* previous 1946, 1958 (preindependence); latest adopted by referendum 2 December 1990, promulgated 11 December 1990
amendments: proposed concurrently by the president of the republic (after a decision in the Council of Ministers) and the National Assembly; consideration of drafts or proposals requires at least three-fourths majority vote of the Assembly membership; passage requires approval in a referendum unless approved by at least four-fifths majority vote of the Assembly membership; constitutional articles affecting territorial sovereignty, the republican form of government, and secularity of Benin cannot be amended; amended 2019

Legal system: civil law system modeled largely on the French system and some customary law

International law organization participation: has not submitted an ICJ jurisdiction declaration; accepts ICCt jurisdiction

Citizenship: *citizenship by birth:* no
citizenship by descent only: at least one parent must be a citizen of Benin
dual citizenship recognized: yes
residency requirement for naturalization: 10 years

Suffrage: 18 years of age; universal

Executive branch: *chief of state:* President Patrice TALON (since 6 April 2016); note - the president is both chief of state and head of government
head of government: President Patrice TALON (since 6 April 2016); prime minister position abolished
cabinet: Council of Ministers appointed by the president
elections/appointments: president directly elected by absolute majority popular vote in 2 rounds if needed for a 5-year term (eligible for a second term); last held on 11 April 2021 (next to be held in April 2026)
election results: Patrice TALON elected to a second term; percent of vote - Patrice TALON (independent) 86.4%, Alassane SOUMANOU (FCBE) 11.3%, other 2.3% (2021)

Legislative branch: *description:* unicameral National Assembly or Assemblee Nationale (83 seats - current 81; members directly elected in multi-seat constituencies by proportional representation vote; members serve 4-year terms)
elections: last held on 28 April 2019 (next to be held in April 2023)
election results: percent of vote by party - Union Progressiste 56.2%, Bloc Republicain 43.8%; seats by party - Union Progressiste 47, Bloc Republicain 36; composition as of February 2022 - men 75, women 6, percent of women 7.4%

Judicial branch: *highest court(s):* Supreme Court or Cour Supreme (consists of the chief justice and 16 justices organized into an administrative division, judicial chamber, and chamber of accounts); Constitutional Court or Cour Constitutionnelle (consists of 7 members, including the court president); High Court of Justice (consists of the Constitutional Court members, 6 members appointed by the National Assembly, and the Supreme Court president); note - jurisdiction of the High Court of Justice is limited to cases of high treason by the national president or members of the government while in office
judge selection and term of office: Supreme Court president and judges appointed by the president of the republic upon the advice of the National Assembly; judges appointed for single renewable 5-year terms; Constitutional Court members - 4 appointed by the National Assembly and 3 by the president of the republic; members appointed for single renewable 5-year terms; other members of the High Court of Justice elected by the National Assembly; member tenure NA
subordinate courts: Court of Appeal or Cour d'Appel; district courts; village courts; Assize courts

Political parties and leaders: African Movement for Development and Progress or MADEP [Sefou FAGBOHOUN]
Alliance for a Triumphant Benin or ABT [Abdoulaye BIO TCHANE]
Benin Renaissance or RB [Lehady SOGLO]
Cowrie Force for an Emerging Benin or FCBE [Yayi BONI]
Democratic Renewal Party or PRD [Adrien HOUNGBEDJI]
National Alliance for Development and Democracy or AND [Valentin Aditi HOUDE]
New Consciousness Rally or NC [Pascal KOUPAKI]
Patriotic Awakening or RP [Janvier YAHOUEDEOU]
Social Democrat Party or PSD [Emmanuel GOLOU]
Sun Alliance or AS [Sacca LAFIA]
Union Makes the Nation or UN [Adrien HOUNGBEDJI] (includes PRD, MADEP)
United Democratic Forces or FDU [Mathurin NAGO]
note: approximately 20 additional minor parties

International organization participation: ACP, AfDB, AU, CD, ECOWAS, Entente, FAO, FZ, G-77, IAEA, IBRD, ICAO, ICCt, ICRM, IDA, IDB, IFAD, IFC, IFRCS, ILO, IMF, IMO, Interpol, IOC, IOM, IPU, ISO, ITSO, ITU, ITUC (NGOs), MIGA, MINUSMA, MNJTF, MONUSCO, NAM, OAS (observer), OIC, OIF, OPCW, PCA, UN, UNAMID, UNCTAD, UNESCO, UNHCR, UNHRC, UNIDO, UNISFA, UNMIL, UNMISS, UNOCI, UNWTO, UPU, WADB (regional), WAEMU, WCO, WFTU (NGOs), WHO, WIPO, WMO, WTO

Diplomatic representation in the US: *chief of mission:* Ambassador Jean Claude Felix DO REGO (since 17 July 2020)
chancery: 2124 Kalorama Road NW, Washington, DC 20008
telephone: [1] (202) 232-6656; [1] (202) 232-2611
FAX: [1] (202) 265-1996
email address and website:
ambassade.washington@gouv.bj
https://beninembassy.us/

Diplomatic representation from the US: *chief of mission:* Ambassador Brian SHUKAN (since 5 May 2022)
embassy: 01 BP 2012, Cotonou
mailing address:
2120 Cotonou Place, Washington DC 20521-2120
telephone: [229] 21-30-06-50
FAX: [229] 21-30-03-84
email address and website:
ACSCotonou@state.gov
https://bj.usembassy.gov/

Flag description: two equal horizontal bands of yellow (top) and red (bottom) with a vertical green band on the hoist side; green symbolizes hope and revival, yellow wealth, and red courage
note: uses the popular Pan-African colors of Ethiopia

National symbol(s): *leopard; national colors:* green, yellow, red

National anthem: *name:* "L'Aube Nouvelle" (The Dawn of a New Day)
lyrics/music: Gilbert Jean DAGNON
note: adopted 1960

National heritage: *total World Heritage Sites:* 2 (1 cultural, 1 natural)
selected World Heritage Site locales: Royal Palaces of Abomey (c); W-Arly-Pendjari Complex (n)

ECONOMY

Economic overview: The free market economy of Benin has grown consecutively for four years, though growth slowed in 2017, as its close trade links to Nigeria expose Benin to risks from volatile commodity prices. Cotton is a key export commodity, with export earnings significantly impacted by the price of cotton in the broader market. The economy began deflating in 2017, with the consumer price index falling 0.8%.

During the first two years of President TALON's administration, which began in April 2016, the government has followed an ambitious action plan to kickstart development through investments in infrastructure, education, agriculture, and governance. Electricity generation, which has constrained Benin's economic growth, has increased and blackouts have been considerably reduced. Private foreign direct investment is small, and foreign aid accounts for a large proportion of investment in infrastructure projects.

Benin has appealed for international assistance to mitigate piracy against commercial shipping in its territory, and has used equipment from donors effectively against such piracy. Pilferage has significantly dropped at the Port of Cotonou, though the port is still struggling with effective implementation of the International Ship and Port Facility Security (ISPS) Code. Projects included in Benin's $307 million Millennium Challenge Corporation (MCC) first compact (2006-11) were designed to increase investment and private sector activity by improving key institutional and physical infrastructure. The four projects focused on access to land, access to financial services, access to justice, and access to markets (including modernization of the port). The Port of Cotonou is a major contributor to Benin's economy, with revenues projected to account for more than 40% of Benin's national budget.

Benin will need further efforts to upgrade infrastructure, stem corruption, and expand access to foreign markets to achieve its potential. In September 2015, Benin signed a second MCC Compact for $375 million that entered into force in June 2017 and is designed to strengthen the national utility service provider, attract private sector investment, fund infrastructure investments in electricity generation and distribution, and develop off-grid electrification for poor and unserved households. As part of the Government of Benin's action plan to spur growth, Benin passed public private partnership legislation in 2017 to attract more foreign investment, place more emphasis on tourism, facilitate the development of new food processing systems and agricultural products, encourage new information and communication technology, and establish Independent Power Producers. In April 2017, the IMF approved a three year $150.4 million Extended Credit Facility agreement to maintain debt sustainability and boost donor confidence.

Real GDP (purchasing power parity): $40.29 billion (2020 est.)
$38.79 billion (2019 est.)
$36.3 billion (2018 est.)
note: data are in 2017 dollars
country comparison to the world: 119

Real GDP growth rate: 5.6% (2017 est.)
4% (2016 est.)
2.1% (2015 est.)
country comparison to the world: 33

Real GDP per capita: $3,300 (2020 est.)
$3,300 (2019 est.)
$3,200 (2018 est.)
note: data are in 2017 dollars
country comparison to the world: 192

GDP (official exchange rate): $10.315 billion (2018 est.)

Inflation rate (consumer prices): -0.8% (2019 est.)
1.7% (2018 est.)
0% (2017 est.)
country comparison to the world: 8

Credit ratings:

Fitch rating: B (2019)

Moody's rating: B2 (2019)

Standard & Poors rating: B+ (2018)
note: The year refers to the year in which the current credit rating was first obtained.

GDP - composition, by sector of origin: *agriculture:* 26.1% (2017 est.)
industry: 22.8% (2017 est.)
services: 51.1% (2017 est.)

GDP - composition, by end use: *household consumption:* 70.5% (2017 est.)
government consumption: 13.1% (2017 est.)
investment in fixed capital: 27.6% (2017 est.)
investment in inventories: 0% (2017 est.)
exports of goods and services: 31.6% (2017 est.)
imports of goods and services: -43% (2017 est.)

Agricultural products: cassava, yams, maize, cotton, oil palm fruit, rice, pineapples, tomatoes, vegetables, soybeans

Industries: textiles, food processing, construction materials, cement

Industrial production growth rate: 3% (2017 est.)
country comparison to the world: 101

Labor force: 3.662 million (2007 est.)
country comparison to the world: 97

Unemployment rate: 1% (2014 est.)
country comparison to the world: 8

Unemployment, youth ages 15-24: *total:* 3.9%
male: 3.2%
female: 4.5% (2018 est.)
country comparison to the world: 172

Population below poverty line: 38.5% (2019 est.)

Gini Index coefficient - distribution of family income: 47.8 (2015 est.)
country comparison to the world: 20

Household income or consumption by percentage share: *lowest 10%:* 3.1%
highest 10%: 29% (2003)

Budget: *revenues:* 1.578 billion (2017 est.)
expenditures: 2.152 billion (2017 est.)

Budget surplus (+) or deficit (-): -6.2% (of GDP) (2017 est.)
country comparison to the world: 186

Public debt: 54.6% of GDP (2017 est.)
49.7% of GDP (2016 est.)
country comparison to the world: 81

Taxes and other revenues: 17.1% (of GDP) (2017 est.)
country comparison to the world: 171

Fiscal year: calendar year

Current account balance: -$1.024 billion (2017 est.)
-$808 million (2016 est.)
country comparison to the world: 147

Exports: $3.58 billion (2019 est.)
$3.85 billion (2018 est.)
note: Data are in current year dollars and do not include illicit exports or re-exports.
country comparison to the world: 138

Exports - partners: Nigeria 25%, Bangladesh 14%, United Arab Emirates 14%, India 13%, China 8%, Vietnam 5% (2019)

Exports - commodities: cotton, refined petroleum, gold, cashews, copper (2019)

Imports: $4.31 billion (2019 est.) note: data are in current year dollars
$4.67 billion (2018 est.) note: data are in current year dollars
$5.035 billion (2017 est.)
country comparison to the world: 146

Imports - partners: China 28%, Thailand 9%, India 8%, Togo 6%, United States 5% (2019)

Imports - commodities: rice, cars, palm oil, electricity, cotton (2019)

Reserves of foreign exchange and gold: $698.9 million (31 December 2017 est.)
$57.5 million (31 December 2016 est.)
country comparison to the world: 141

Debt - external: $2.804 billion (31 December 2017 est.)
$2.476 billion (31 December 2016 est.)
country comparison to the world: 145

Exchange rates: Communaute Financiere Africaine francs (XOF) per US dollar -
605.3 (2017 est.)
593.01 (2016 est.)
593.01 (2015 est.)
591.45 (2014 est.)
494.42 (2013 est.)

ENERGY

Electricity access: *electrification - total population:* 33% (2019)
electrification - urban areas: 58% (2019)
electrification - rural areas: 9% (2019)

Electricity: *installed generating capacity:* 475,000 kW (2020 est.)
consumption: 524.08 million kWh (2020 est.)
exports: 2 million kWh (2020 est.)
imports: 646 million kWh (2020 est.)
transmission/distribution losses: 346 million kWh (2020 est.)

Electricity generation sources: *fossil fuels:* 96.9% of total installed capacity (2020 est.)
solar: 3.1% of total installed capacity (2020 est.)

Coal: *production:* 0 metric tons (2020 est.)
consumption: 78,000 metric tons (2020 est.)
exports: 0 metric tons (2020 est.)
imports: 78,000 metric tons (2020 est.)
proven reserves: 0 metric tons (2019 est.)

Petroleum: *total petroleum production:* 0 bbl/day (2021 est.)
refined petroleum consumption: 46,300 bbl/day (2019 est.)
crude oil estimated reserves: 8 million barrels (2021 est.)

Refined petroleum products - production: 0 bbl/day (2015 est.)
country comparison to the world: 118

Refined petroleum products - exports: 1,514 bbl/day (2015 est.)
country comparison to the world: 107

Refined petroleum products - imports: 38,040 bbl/day (2015 est.)
country comparison to the world: 93

Natural gas: *production:* 0 cubic meters (2021 est.)
consumption: 19.057 million cubic meters (2019 est.)
exports: 0 cubic meters (2021 est.)
imports: 19.057 million cubic meters (2019 est.)
proven reserves: 1.133 billion cubic meters (2021 est.)

Carbon dioxide emissions: 6.903 million metric tonnes of CO2 (2019 est.)
from coal and metallurgical coke: 274,000 metric tonnes of CO2 (2019 est.)
from petroleum and other liquids: 6.592 million metric tonnes of CO2 (2019 est.)
from consumed natural gas: 37,000 metric tonnes of CO2 (2019 est.)
country comparison to the world: 126

Energy consumption per capita: 8.468 million Btu/person (2019 est.)
country comparison to the world: 159

COMMUNICATIONS

Telephones - fixed lines: *total subscriptions:* 32,386 (2020 est.)
subscriptions per 100 inhabitants: (2020 est.) less than 1
country comparison to the world: 169

Telephones - mobile cellular: *total subscriptions:* 11,140,891 (2020 est.)
subscriptions per 100 inhabitants: 92 (2020 est.)
country comparison to the world: 83

Telecommunication systems: *general assessment:* Benin's telecom market continues to be restricted by the poor condition of the country's fixed-line infrastructure; this has hampered the development of fixed-line voice and internet services, and there is negligible revenue derived from these sectors; mobile networks account for almost all internet connections, and also carry most voice traffic; there is promise for considerable change in the mobile sector; slow progress is being made in developing competition in the mobile sector; in May 2021 the government sought foreign companies to bid for a fourth mobile license; improved international internet connectivity has contributed to a reduction in end-user pricing, and provided the potential to transform many areas of the country's economy, bringing a greater proportion of the population into the orbit of internet commerce and connectivity; a 2,000km fiber project started in 2016 was finally completed in mid-2021, prompting the government to secure a loan to build additional fiber infrastructure connecting four of the country's 12 departments (2022)

domestic: fixed-line teledensity only about 1 per 100 persons; spurred by the presence of multiple mobile-cellular providers, cellular telephone subscribership has increased rapidly, nearing 92 per 100 persons (2020)
international: country code - 229; landing points for the SAT-3/WASC and ACE fiber-optic submarine cable that provides connectivity to Europe, and most West African countries; satellite earth stations - 7 (Intelsat-Atlantic Ocean) (2019)

Broadcast media: state-run Office de Radiodiffusion et de Television du Benin (ORTB) operates a TV station providing a wide broadcast reach; several privately owned TV stations broadcast from Cotonou; satellite TV subscription service is available; state-owned radio, under ORTB control, includes a national station supplemented by a number of regional stations; substantial number of privately owned radio broadcast stations; transmissions of a few international broadcasters are available on FM in Cotonou (2019)

Internet country code: .bj

Internet users: *total:* 3,152,032 (2020 est.)
percent of population: 26% (2020 est.)
country comparison to the world: 111

Broadband - fixed subscriptions: *total:* 29,981 (2020 est.)
subscriptions per 100 inhabitants: 0.3 (2020 est.)
country comparison to the world: 155

TRANSPORTATION

National air transport system: *number of registered air carriers:* 1 (2015)
inventory of registered aircraft operated by air carriers: 1 (2015)
annual passenger traffic on registered air carriers: 112,392 (2015)
annual freight traffic on registered air carriers: 805,347 (2015) mt-km

Civil aircraft registration country code prefix: TY

Airports: *total:* 6 (2021)
country comparison to the world: 172

Airports - with paved runways: *total:* 1
1,524 to 2,437 m: 1 (2021)

Airports - with unpaved runways: *total:* 5
2,438 to 3,047 m: 2
1,524 to 2,437 m: 1
914 to 1,523 m: 2 (2021)

Pipelines: 134 km gas

Railways: *total:* 438 km (2014)
narrow gauge: 438 km (2014) 1.000-m gauge
country comparison to the world: 116

Roadways: *total:* 16,000 km (2006)
paved: 1,400 km (2006)
unpaved: 14,600 km (2006)
country comparison to the world: 120

Waterways: 150 km (2011) (seasonal navigation on River Niger along northern border)
country comparison to the world: 111

Merchant marine: *total:* 6
by type: other 6 (2021)
country comparison to the world: 163

Ports and terminals: *major seaport(s):* Cotonou
LNG terminal(s) (import): Cotonou

MILITARY AND SECURITY

Military and security forces: Benin Armed Forces (Forces Armees Beninoises, FAB): Army, Navy, Air Force; Ministry of Interior and Public Security: Republican Police (Police Republicaine, DGPR) (2022)

Military expenditures: 0.7% of GDP (2021 est.)
0.5% of GDP (2020 est.)
0.5% of GDP (2019 est.) (approximately $130 million)
0.7% of GDP (2018 est.) (approximately $140 million)
0.9% of GDP (2017 est.) (approximately $160 million)
country comparison to the world: 147

Military and security service personnel strengths: approximately 7,000 active duty BDF troops; estimated 5,000 Republican Police (2022)

Military equipment inventories and acquisitions: the FAB is equipped with a small mix of mostly older French and Soviet-era equipment (2021)

Military service age and obligation: 18-35 years of age for voluntary and selective compulsory military service; a higher education diploma is required; both sexes are eligible for military service; conscript service is 18 months (2022)

Military deployments: 260 (plus about 160 police) Mali (MINUSMA) (May 2022)

Military - note: as of 2022, a key focus for the security forces of Benin was countering infiltrations into the country by terrorist groups tied to al-Qa'ida and the Islamic State of Iraq and ash-Sham (ISIS) operating just over the border from north Benin in Burkina Faso and Niger; in May 2022, the Benin Government said it was "at war" with terrorism after suffering a series of attacks from these groups; in addition, the FAB participated in the Multinational Joint Task Force (MNJTF) along with Cameroon, Chad, Niger, and Nigeria against Boko Haram and other terrorist groups operating in the general area of the Lake Chad Basin and along Nigeria's northeast border

the FAB has a close working relationship with the Belgian armed forces; the Belgians offer military advice, training, and second-hand equipment donations, and deploy to Benin for limited military exercises (2022)

Maritime threats: the International Maritime Bureau reports the territorial and offshore waters in the Niger Delta and Gulf of Guinea remain a very high risk for piracy and armed robbery of ships; in 2021, there were 34 reported incidents of piracy and armed robbery at sea in the Gulf of Guinea region; although a significant decrease from the total number of 81 incidents in 2020, it included the one hijacking and three of five ships fired upon worldwide; while boarding and attempted boarding to steal valuables from ships and crews are the most common types of incidents, almost a third of all incidents involve a hijacking and/or kidnapping; in 2021, 57 crew members were kidnapped in seven separate incidents in the Gulf of Guinea, representing 100% of kidnappings worldwide; Nigerian pirates in particular are well armed and very aggressive, operating as far as 200 nm offshore; the Maritime Administration of the US Department of Transportation has issued a Maritime Advisory (2022-001 - Gulf of Guinea-Piracy/Armed Robbery/Kidnapping for Ransom) effective 4 January 2022, which states in part, "Piracy, armed robbery, and kidnapping for ransom continue to serve as significant threats to US-flagged vessels transiting or operating in the Gulf of Guinea"

TERRORISM

Terrorist group(s): al-Qa'ida (Jama'at Nusrat al Islam wal Muslimeen); Islamic State in the Greater Sahara (ISIS-GS); Boko Haram

TRANSNATIONAL ISSUES

Disputes - international: *Benin-Burkina Faso:* Benin retains a border dispute with Burkina Faso near the town of Koualau/Kourou.
Benin-Togo: Talks continue between Benin and Togo on funding the Adjarala hydroelectric dam on the Mona River.
Benin-Niger: The location of Benin-Niger-Nigeria tripoint is unresolved.

Illicit drugs: a significant transit and departure country for cocaine shipments in Africa destined for Europe

BERMUDA

INTRODUCTION

Background: Bermuda was first settled in 1609 by shipwrecked English colonists heading for Virginia. Self-governing since 1620, Bermuda is the oldest and most populous of the British overseas territories. Vacationing to the island to escape North American winters first developed in Victorian times. Tourism continues to be important to the island's economy, although international business has overtaken it in recent years. Bermuda has also developed into a highly successful offshore financial center. A referendum on independence from the UK was soundly defeated in 1995.

GEOGRAPHY

Location: North America, group of islands in the North Atlantic Ocean, east of South Carolina (US)

Geographic coordinates: 32 20 N, 64 45 W

Map references: North America

Area: *total:* 54 sq km
land: 54 sq km
water: 0 sq km
country comparison to the world: 230

Area - comparative: about one-third the size of Washington, DC

Land boundaries: *total:* 0 km

Coastline: 103 km

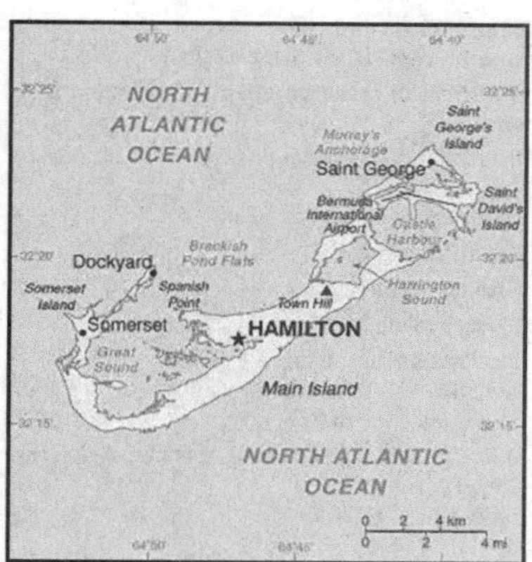

Maritime claims: *territorial sea:* 12 nm
exclusive economic zone: 200 nm
exclusive fishing zone: 200 nm

Climate: subtropical; mild, humid; gales, strong winds common in winter

Terrain: low hills separated by fertile depressions

Elevation: *highest point:* Town Hill 79 m
lowest point: Atlantic Ocean 0 m

Natural resources: limestone, pleasant climate fostering tourism

Land use: *agricultural land:* 14.8% (2018 est.)
arable land: 14.8% (2018 est.)
permanent crops: 0% (2018 est.)
permanent pasture: 0% (2018 est.)
forest: 20% (2018 est.)
other: 65.2% (2018 est.)

Population distribution: relatively even population distribution throughout

Natural hazards: hurricanes (June to November)

Geography - note: consists of about 138 coral islands and islets with ample rainfall, but no rivers or freshwater lakes; some land was leased by the US Government from 1941 to 1995

PEOPLE AND SOCIETY

Population: 72,337 (2022 est.)
country comparison to the world: 202

Nationality: *noun:* Bermudian(s)
adjective: Bermudian

Ethnic groups: African descent 52%, White 31%, mixed 9%, Asian 4%, other 4% (2010 est.)

Languages: English (official), Portuguese

Religions: Protestant 46.2% (includes Anglican 15.8%, African Methodist Episcopal 8.6%, Seventh Day Adventist 6.7, Pentecostal 3.5%, Methodist 2.7%, Presbyterian 2.0%, Church of God 1.6%, Baptist 1.2%, Salvation Army 1.1%, Brethren 1.0%, other Protestant 2.0%), Roman Catholic 14.5%, Jehovah's Witness 1.3%, other Christian 9.1%, Muslim 1%, other 3.9%, none 17.8%, unspecified 6.2% (2010 est.)

Age structure: *0-14 years:* 16.7% (male 6,053/female 5,928)
15-24 years: 11.88% (male 4,290/female 4,235)
25-54 years: 35.31% (male 12,758/female 12,575)
55-64 years: 16.37% (male 5,560/female 6,185)
65 years and over: 19.74% (male 6,032/female 8,134) (2020 est.)

Median age: *total:* 43.6 years
male: 41.6 years
female: 45.7 years (2020 est.)
country comparison to the world: 23

Population growth rate: 0.34% (2022 est.)
country comparison to the world: 163

Birth rate: 11.03 births/1,000 population (2022 est.)
country comparison to the world: 167

Death rate: 9.11 deaths/1,000 population (2022 est.)
country comparison to the world: 56

Net migration rate: 1.49 migrant(s)/1,000 population (2022 est.)
country comparison to the world: 59

Population distribution: relatively even population distribution throughout

Urbanization: *urban population:* 100% of total population (2022)
rate of urbanization: -0.2% annual rate of change (2020-25 est.)

Major urban areas - population: 10,000 HAMILTON (capital) (2018)

Sex ratio: *at birth:* 1.05 male(s)/female
0-14 years: 1.05 male(s)/female
15-24 years: 1.06 male(s)/female
25-54 years: 1.02 male(s)/female
55-64 years: 0.91 male(s)/female
65 years and over: 0.6 male(s)/female
total population: 0.95 male(s)/female (2022 est.)

Infant mortality rate: *total:* 2.19 deaths/1,000 live births
male: 2.51 deaths/1,000 live births
female: 1.86 deaths/1,000 live births (2022 est.)
country comparison to the world: 221

Life expectancy at birth: *total population:* 82.04 years
male: 78.96 years
female: 85.28 years (2022 est.)
country comparison to the world: 28

Total fertility rate: 1.9 children born/woman (2022 est.)
country comparison to the world: 125

Drinking water source: *improved: urban:* 99.9% of population
total: 99.9% of population
unimproved: urban: 0.1% of population
total: 0.1% of population (2020)

Sanitation facility access: *improved: urban:* 99.9% of population
total: 99.9% of population
unimproved: urban: 0.1% of population
total: 0.1% of population (2020)

Education expenditures: 1.3% of GDP (2017 est.)
country comparison to the world: 187

School life expectancy (primary to tertiary education): *total:* 13 years
male: 12 years
female: 13 years (2015)

Unemployment, youth ages 15-24: *total:* 29.3%
male: 29.7%
female: 29% (2014 est.)

ENVIRONMENT

Environment - current issues: dense population and heavy vehicle traffic create serious congestion and air pollution problems; water resources scarce (most obtained as rainwater or from wells); solid waste disposal; hazardous waste disposal; sewage disposal; overfishing; oil spills

Air pollutants: *carbon dioxide emissions:* 0.61 megatons (2016 est.)

Climate: subtropical; mild, humid; gales, strong winds common in winter

Land use: *agricultural land:* 14.8% (2018 est.)
arable land: 14.8% (2018 est.)
permanent crops: 0% (2018 est.)
permanent pasture: 0% (2018 est.)
forest: 20% (2018 est.)
other: 65.2% (2018 est.)

Urbanization: *urban population:* 100% of total population (2022)
rate of urbanization: -0.2% annual rate of change (2020-25 est.)

Waste and recycling: *municipal solid waste generated annually:* 82,000 tons (2012 est.)
municipal solid waste recycled annually: 1,640 tons (2012 est.)
percent of municipal solid waste recycled: 2% (2012 est.)

GOVERNMENT

Country name: *conventional long form:* none
conventional short form: Bermuda
former: Somers Islands
etymology: the islands making up Bermuda are named after Juan de BERMUDEZ, an early 16th century Spanish sea captain and the first European explorer of the archipelago

Government type: Overseas Territory of the UK with limited self-government; parliamentary democracy

Dependency status: overseas territory of the UK

Capital: *name:* Hamilton
geographic coordinates: 32 17 N, 64 47 W
time difference: UTC-4 (1 hour ahead of Washington, DC, during Standard Time)
daylight saving time: +1hr, begins second Sunday in March; ends first Sunday in November
etymology: named after Henry HAMILTON (ca. 1734-1796) who served as governor of Bermuda from 1788-1794

Administrative divisions: 9 parishes and 2 municipalities*; Devonshire, Hamilton, Hamilton*, Paget, Pembroke, Saint George*, Saint George's, Sandys, Smith's, Southampton, Warwick

Independence: none (overseas territory of the UK)

National holiday: Bermuda Day, 24 May; note - formerly known as Victoria Day, Empire Day, and Commonwealth Day

Constitution: *history:* several previous (dating to 1684); latest entered into force 8 June 1968 (Bermuda Constitution Order 1968)
amendments: proposal procedure - NA; passage by an Order in Council in the UK; amended several times, last in 2012

Legal system: English common law

International law organization participation: has not submitted an ICJ jurisdiction declaration; non-party state to the ICCt

Citizenship: *citizenship by birth:* no
citizenship by descent only: at least one parent must be a citizen of the UK

dual citizenship recognized: yes
residency requirement for naturalization: 10 years

Suffrage: 18 years of age; universal

Executive branch: *chief of state:* King CHARLES III (since 8 September 2022); represented by Governor Rena LALGIE (since 14 December 2020)
head of government: Premier David BURT (since 19 July 2017)
cabinet: Cabinet nominated by the premier, appointed by the governor
elections/appointments: the monarchy is hereditary; governor appointed by the monarch; following legislative elections, the leader of the majority party or majority coalition usually appointed premier by the governor

Legislative branch: *description:* bicameral Parliament consists of:
Senate (11 seats; 3 members appointed by the governor, 5 by the premier, and 3 by the opposition party; members serve 5-year terms) and the House of Assembly (36 seats; members directly elected in single-seat constituencies by simple majority vote to serve up to 5-year terms)
House of Assembly (36 seats; members directly elected in single-seat constituencies by simple majority vote to serve up to 5-year terms)
elections:
Senate - last appointments in August 2017 (next appointments in 2022)
House of Assembly - last held on 1 October 2020 (next to be held not later than 2025)
election results: Senate - composition as of March 2022 - men 5, women 6, percent of women 54.5%
House of Assembly - percent of vote by party - PLP 62.1%, OBA 32.3%, other 5.4%, independent 0.2%; seats by party - PLP 30, OBA 6; composition as of March 2022 - men 28, women 8, percent of women 22.2%; note - total Parliament percent of women as of March 2022 - 29.8%

Judicial branch: *highest court(s):* Court of Appeal (consists of the court president and at least 2 justices); Supreme Court (consists of the chief justice, 4 puisne judges, and 1 associate justice); note - the Judicial Committee of the Privy Council (in London) is the court of final appeal
judge selection and term of office: Court of Appeal justice appointed by the governor; justice tenure by individual appointment; Supreme Court judges nominated by the Judicial and Legal Services Commission and appointed by the governor; judge tenure based on terms of appointment
subordinate courts: commercial court (began in 2006); magistrates' courts

Political parties and leaders: Free Democratic Movement or FDM [Marc A. R. BEAN]
One Bermuda Alliance or OBA [N. H. Cole SIMONS]
Progressive Labor Party or PLP [E. David BURT]

International organization participation: Caricom (associate), ICC (NGOs), Interpol (subbureau), IOC, ITUC (NGOs), UPU, WCO

Diplomatic representation in the US: none (overseas territory of the UK)

Diplomatic representation from the US: *chief of mission:* Consul General Karen GRISSETTE (since 6 July 2021)
embassy: US Consulate Bermuda, 16 Middle Road, Devonshire, DV 03, Bermuda
mailing address: 5300 Hamilton Place, Washington, DC 20520-5300
telephone: (441) 295-1342
FAX: (441) 295-1592
email address and website:
HamiltonConsulate@state.gov
https://bm.usconsulate.gov/
consulate(s) general: 16 Middle Road, Devonshire DV O3

Flag description: red, with the flag of the UK in the upper hoist-side quadrant and the Bermudian coat of arms (a white shield with a red lion standing on a green grassy field holding a scrolled shield showing the sinking of the ship Sea Venture off Bermuda in 1609) centered on the outer half of the flag; it was the shipwreck of the vessel, filled with English colonists originally bound for Virginia, that led to the settling of Bermuda
note: the flag is unusual in that it is only British overseas territory that uses a red ensign, all others use blue

National symbol(s): red lion

Coat of arms of Bermuda:

National anthem: *name:* Hail to Bermuda
lyrics/music: Bette JOHNS
note: serves as a local anthem; as a territory of the United Kingdom, "God Save the King" is official (see United Kingdom)

National heritage: *total World Heritage Sites:* 1 (cultural); note - excerpted from the UK entry
selected World Heritage Site locales: Historic Town of St George and Related Fortifications

ECONOMY

Economic overview: International business, which consists primarily of insurance and other financial services, is the real bedrock of Bermuda's economy, consistently accounting for about 85% of the island's GDP. Tourism is the country's second largest industry, accounting for about 5% of Bermuda's GDP but a much larger share of employment. Over 80% of visitors come from the US and the sector struggled in the wake of the global recession of 2008-09. Even the financial sector has lost roughly 5,000 high-paying expatriate jobs since 2008, weighing heavily on household consumption and retail sales. Bermuda must import almost everything. Agriculture and industry are limited due to the small size of the island.

Bermuda's economy returned to negative growth in 2016, reporting a contraction of 0.1% GDP, after growing by 0.6% in 2015. Unemployment reached 7% in 2016 and 2017, public debt is growing and exceeds $2.4 billion, and the government continues to work on attracting foreign investment. Still, Bermuda enjoys one of the highest per capita incomes in the world.

Real GDP (purchasing power parity): $5.23 billion (2019 est.) note: data are in 2017 dollars
$5.2 billion (2018 est.) note: data are in 2017 dollars
$5.227 billion (2017 est.)
country comparison to the world: 175

Real GDP growth rate: -0.1% (2016 est.)
0.6% (2015 est.)
-0.3% (2014 est.)
country comparison to the world: 194

Real GDP per capita: $81,800 (2019 est.) note: data are in 2017 dollars
$81,400 (2018 est.) note: data are in 2017 dollars
$81,835 (2017 est.)
country comparison to the world: 8

GDP (official exchange rate): $6.127 billion (2016 est.)

Inflation rate (consumer prices): 1.9% (2017 est.)
1.4% (2016 est.)
country comparison to the world: 105

Credit ratings:

Fitch rating: *N/A (2015)*

Moody's rating: A2 (2016)

Standard & Poors rating: A+ (2015)
note: The year refers to the year in which the current credit rating was first obtained.

GDP - composition, by sector of origin: *agriculture:* 0.9% (2017 est.)
industry: 5.3% (2017 est.)
services: 93.8% (2017 est.)

GDP - composition, by end use: *household consumption:* 51.3% (2017 est.)
government consumption: 15.7% (2017 est.)
investment in fixed capital: 13.7% (2017 est.)
investment in inventories: 0% (2017 est.)
exports of goods and services: 49.8% (2017 est.)
imports of goods and services: -30.4% (2017 est.)

Agricultural products: bananas, vegetables, citrus, flowers; dairy products, honey

Industries: international business, tourism, light manufacturing

Industrial production growth rate: 2% (2017 est.)
country comparison to the world: 129

Labor force: 33,480 (2016 est.)
country comparison to the world: 201

Labor force - by occupation: *agriculture:* 2%
industry: 13%
services: 85% (2016 est.)

Unemployment rate: 7% (2017 est.)
7% (2016 est.)
country comparison to the world: 113

Unemployment, youth ages 15-24: *total:* 29.3%
male: 29.7%
female: 29% (2014 est.)
country comparison to the world: 37

Population below poverty line: 11% (2008 est.)

Budget: *revenues:* 999.2 million (2017 est.)
expenditures: 1.176 billion (2017 est.)

Budget surplus (+) or deficit (-): -2.9% (of GDP) (2017 est.)
country comparison to the world: 127

Public debt: 43% of GDP (FY14/15)
country comparison to the world: 117

Taxes and other revenues: 16.3% (of GDP) (2017 est.)
country comparison to the world: 183

Fiscal year: 1 April - 31 March

Current account balance: $818.6 million (2017 est.)
$763 million (2016 est.)
country comparison to the world: 52

Exports: $1.59 billion (2019 est.)
$1.59 billion (2018 est.)
note: Data are in current year dollars and do not include illicit exports or re-exports.
country comparison to the world: 163

Exports - partners: Jamaica 49.1%, Luxembourg 36.1%, US 4.9% (2017)

Exports - commodities: re-exports of pharmaceuticals

Imports: $2.23 billion (2019 est.) note: data are in current year dollars
$2.2 billion (2018 est.) note: data are in current year dollars
country comparison to the world: 171

Imports - partners: United States 44%, South Korea 17%, Germany 10%, Canada 8% (2019)

Imports - commodities: ships, refined petroleum, postage stamps, recreational boats, aircraft (2019)

Debt - external: $2.515 billion (2017 est.)
$2.435 billion (2015 est.)
country comparison to the world: 149

Exchange rates: Bermudian dollars (BMD) per US dollar -
1 (2020 est.)
1 (2019 est.)
1 (2018 est.)

ENERGY

Electricity access: *electrification - total population:* 100% (2020)

Electricity: *installed generating capacity:* 172,000 kW (2020 est.)
consumption: 533.434 million kWh (2019 est.)
exports: 0 kWh (2020 est.)
imports: 0 kWh (2020 est.)
transmission/distribution losses: 41 million kWh (2019 est.)

Electricity generation sources: *fossil fuels:* 100% of total installed capacity (2020 est.)

Petroleum: *total petroleum production:* 0 bbl/day (2021 est.)
refined petroleum consumption: 5,200 bbl/day (2019 est.)

Refined petroleum products - imports: 3,939 bbl/day (2015 est.)
country comparison to the world: 178

Carbon dioxide emissions: 796,000 metric tonnes of CO_2 (2019 est.)
from petroleum and other liquids: 796,000 metric tonnes of CO_2 (2019 est.)
country comparison to the world: 180

Energy consumption per capita: 176.312 million Btu/person (2019 est.)
country comparison to the world: 24

COMMUNICATIONS

Telephones - fixed lines: *total subscriptions:* 25,000 (2020 est.)
subscriptions per 100 inhabitants: 40 (2020 est.)
country comparison to the world: 172

Telephones - mobile cellular: *total subscriptions:* 68,000 (2020 est.)
subscriptions per 100 inhabitants: 109 (2020 est.)
country comparison to the world: 200

Telecommunication systems: *general assessment:* the telecom sector has seen a decline in subscriber numbers (particularly for prepaid mobile services the mainstay of short term visitors) and revenue; fixed and mobile broadband services are two areas that have benefited from the crisis as employees and students have resorted to working from home; one area of the telecom market that is not prepared for growth is 5G mobile; governments, regulators, and even the mobile network operators have shown that they have not been investing in 5G opportunities at the present time; network expansion and enhancements remain concentrated around improving LTE coverage (2021)
domestic: the system has a high fixed-line teledensity nearing 40 per 100, coupled with a mobile-cellular teledensity of roughly 109 per 100 persons (2020)
international: country code - 1-441; landing points for the GlobeNet, Gemini Bermuda, CBUS, and the CB-1 submarine cables to the Caribbean, South America and the US; satellite earth stations - 3 (2019)

Broadcast media: 3 TV stations; cable and satellite TV subscription services are available; roughly 13 radio stations operating

Internet country code: .bm

Internet users: *total:* 62,625 (2020 est.)
percent of population: 98% (2020 est.)
country comparison to the world: 192

Broadband - fixed subscriptions: *total:* 23,000 (2020 est.)
subscriptions per 100 inhabitants: 37 (2020 est.)
country comparison to the world: 163

TRANSPORTATION

Civil aircraft registration country code prefix: VP-B

Airports: *total:* 1 (2021)
country comparison to the world: 213

Airports - with paved runways: *total:* 1
2,438 to 3,047 m: 1 (2021)

Roadways: *total:* 447 km (2010)
paved: 447 km (2010)
note: 225 km public roads; 222 km private roads
country comparison to the world: 197

Merchant marine: *total:* 147
by type: container ship 12, oil tanker 18, other 117 (2021)
country comparison to the world: 75

Ports and terminals: *major seaport(s):* Hamilton, Ireland Island, Saint George

MILITARY AND SECURITY

Military and security forces: Royal Bermuda Regiment; Bermuda Police Service (2022)
note: the Royal Bermuda Regiment is a reserve multi-role battalion that carries out two primary functions – providing military aid to civil authorities and humanitarian and disaster relief

Military and security service personnel strengths: the Royal Bermuda Regiment has about 350 troops (2022)

Military equipment inventories and acquisitions: the Regiment is equipped with small arms (2021)

Military service age and obligation: men and women who are Commonwealth citizens and 18-45 years of age can volunteer for the Bermuda Regiment; service is for a minimum period of three years and two months from the date of enlistment; service can be extended only by volunteering or an executive order from the Governor; annual training commitment is about 30 days a year, which includes a two-week camp, weekends, and drill nights (2022)

Military - note: defense is the responsibility of the UK

TRANSNATIONAL ISSUES

Disputes - international: none identified

BHUTAN

INTRODUCTION

Background: Following Britain's victory in the 1865 Duar War, Britain and Bhutan signed the Treaty of Sinchulu, under which Bhutan would receive an annual subsidy in exchange for ceding land to British India. Ugyen WANGCHUCK - who had served as the de facto ruler of an increasingly unified Bhutan and had improved relations with the British toward the end of the 19th century - was named king in 1907. Three years later, a treaty was signed whereby the British agreed not to interfere in Bhutanese internal affairs, and Bhutan allowed Britain to direct its foreign affairs. Bhutan negotiated a similar arrangement with independent India in 1949. The Indo-Bhutanese Treaty of Friendship returned to Bhutan a small piece of the territory annexed by the British, formalized the annual subsidies the country received, and defined India's responsibilities in defense and foreign relations. Under a succession of modernizing monarchs beginning in the 1950s, Bhutan joined the UN in 1971 and slowly continued its engagement beyond its borders.

In 2005, King Jigme Singye WANGCHUCK unveiled the draft of Bhutan's first constitution - which introduced major democratic reforms - and held a national referendum for its approval. The King abdicated the throne in 2006 in favor of his son, Jigme Khesar Namgyel WANGCHUCK. In 2007, India and Bhutan renegotiated their treaty, eliminating the clause that stated that Bhutan would be "guided by" India in conducting its foreign policy, although Thimphu continues to coordinate closely with New Delhi. In 2008, Bhutan held its first parliamentary election in accordance with the constitution. Bhutan experienced a peaceful turnover of power following a parliamentary election in 2013, which resulted in the defeat of the incumbent party. In 2018, the incumbent party again lost the parliamentary election. Of the more than 100,000 ethnic Nepali - predominantly Lhotshampa - refugees who fled or were forced out of Bhutan in the 1990s, about 6,500 remain displaced in Nepal.

GEOGRAPHY

Location: Southern Asia, between China and India

Geographic coordinates: 27 30 N, 90 30 E

Map references: Asia

Area: *total:* 38,394 sq km
land: 38,394 sq km
water: 0 sq km
country comparison to the world: 136

Area - comparative: slightly larger than Maryland; about one-half the size of Indiana

Land boundaries: *total:* 1,136 km
border countries (2): China 477 km; India 659 km

Coastline: 0 km (landlocked)

Maritime claims: none (landlocked)

Climate: varies; tropical in southern plains; cool winters and hot summers in central valleys; severe winters and cool summers in Himalayas

Terrain: mostly mountainous with some fertile valleys and savanna

Elevation: *highest point:* Gangkar Puensum 7,570 m
lowest point: Drangeme Chhu 97 m
mean elevation: 2,220 m

Natural resources: timber, hydropower, gypsum, calcium carbonate

Land use: *agricultural land:* 13.6% (2018 est.)
arable land: 2.6% (2018 est.)
permanent crops: 0.3% (2018 est.)
permanent pasture: 10.7% (2018 est.)
forest: 85.5% (2018 est.)
other: 0.9% (2018 est.)

Irrigated land: 320 sq km (2012)

Natural hazards: violent storms from the Himalayas are the source of the country's Bhutanese name, which translates as Land of the Thunder Dragon; frequent landslides during the rainy season

Geography - note: landlocked; strategic location between China and India; controls several key Himalayan mountain passes

PEOPLE AND SOCIETY

Population: 867,775 (2022 est.)
country comparison to the world: 165

Nationality: *noun:* Bhutanese (singular and plural)
adjective: Bhutanese

Ethnic groups: Ngalop (also known as Bhote) 50%, ethnic Nepali 35% (predominantly Lhotshampas), indigenous or migrant tribes 15%

Languages: Sharchopkha 28%, Dzongkha (official) 24%, Lhotshamkha 22%, other 26% (includes foreign languages) (2005 est.)

Religions: Lamaistic Buddhist 75.3%, Indian- and Nepali-influenced Hinduism 22.1%, other 2.6% (2005 est.)

Age structure: *0-14 years:* 24.52% (male 98,113/female 93,740)
15-24 years: 17.77% (male 70,768/female 68,211)
25-54 years: 44.72% (male 184,500/female 165,374)
55-64 years: 6.39% (male 26,714/female 23,280)
65 years and over: 6.6% (male 26,797/female 24,821) (2020 est.)

Dependency ratios: *total dependency ratio:* 45.1
youth dependency ratio: 36.1
elderly dependency ratio: 9
potential support ratio: 11.1 (2020 est.)

Median age: *total:* 29.1 years
male: 29.6 years
female: 28.6 years (2020 est.)
country comparison to the world: 136

Population growth rate: 0.97% (2022 est.)
country comparison to the world: 98

Birth rate: 15.94 births/1,000 population (2022 est.)
country comparison to the world: 102

Death rate: 6.22 deaths/1,000 population (2022 est.)
country comparison to the world: 148

Net migration rate: 0 migrant(s)/1,000 population (2022 est.)
country comparison to the world: 85

Urbanization: *urban population:* 43.7% of total population (2022)
rate of urbanization: 2.52% annual rate of change (2020-25 est.)

Major urban areas - population: 203,000 THIMPHU (capital) (2018)

Sex ratio: *at birth:* 1.05 male(s)/female
0-14 years: 1.05 male(s)/female
15-24 years: 1.04 male(s)/female
25-54 years: 1.12 male(s)/female
55-64 years: 1.13 male(s)/female
65 years and over: 0.97 male(s)/female
total population: 1.08 male(s)/female (2022 est.)

Maternal mortality ratio: 183 deaths/100,000 live births (2017 est.)
country comparison to the world: 51

Infant mortality rate: *total:* 27.04 deaths/1,000 live births
male: 27.22 deaths/1,000 live births
female: 26.86 deaths/1,000 live births (2022 est.)
country comparison to the world: 61

Life expectancy at birth: *total population:* 72.31 years
male: 71.19 years
female: 73.49 years (2022 est.)
country comparison to the world: 161

Total fertility rate: 1.79 children born/woman (2022 est.)
country comparison to the world: 147

Drinking water source: *improved: urban:* 99.5% of population
rural: 100% of population
total: 99.8% of population
unimproved: urban: 0.5% of population
rural: 0% of population
total: 0.2% of population (2020 est.)

Current health expenditure: 3.6% of GDP (2019)

Physicians density: 0.5 physicians/1,000 population (2020)

Hospital bed density: 1.7 beds/1,000 population (2012)

Sanitation facility access: *improved: urban:* 90.8% of population
rural: 83.1% of population
total: 86.4% of population
unimproved: urban: 9.2% of population
rural: 16.9% of population
total: 13.6% of population (2020 est.)

HIV/AIDS - adult prevalence rate: 0.2% (2020 est.)
country comparison to the world: 95

Obesity - adult prevalence rate: 6.4% (2016)
country comparison to the world: 167

Alcohol consumption per capita: *total:* 0.07 liters of pure alcohol (2019 est.)
beer: 0.01 liters of pure alcohol (2019 est.)
wine: 0.05 liters of pure alcohol (2019 est.)
spirits: 0 liters of pure alcohol (2019 est.)
other alcohols: 0 liters of pure alcohol (2019 est.)
country comparison to the world: 179

Education expenditures: 6.9% of GDP (2018 est.)
country comparison to the world: 20

Literacy: *definition:* age 15 and over can read and write
total population: 66.6%
male: 75%
female: 57.1% (2017)

School life expectancy (primary to tertiary education): *total:* 13 years
male: 13 years
female: 13 years (2018)

Unemployment, youth ages 15-24: *total:* 10.7%
male: 8.2%
female: 12.7% (2015 est.)

ENVIRONMENT

Environment - current issues: soil erosion; limited access to potable water; wildlife conservation; industrial pollution; waste disposal

Environment - international agreements: *party to:* Biodiversity, Climate Change, Climate Change-Kyoto Protocol, Climate Change-Paris Agreement, Desertification, Endangered Species, Hazardous Wastes, Nuclear Test Ban, Ozone Layer Protection, Wetlands
signed, but not ratified: Law of the Sea

Air pollutants: *particulate matter emissions:* 35.32 micrograms per cubic meter (2016 est.)
carbon dioxide emissions: 1.26 megatons (2016 est.)
methane emissions: 1.11 megatons (2020 est.)

Climate: varies; tropical in southern plains; cool winters and hot summers in central valleys; severe winters and cool summers in Himalayas

Land use: *agricultural land:* 13.6% (2018 est.)
arable land: 2.6% (2018 est.)
permanent crops: 0.3% (2018 est.)
permanent pasture: 10.7% (2018 est.)
forest: 85.5% (2018 est.)
other: 0.9% (2018 est.)

Urbanization: *urban population:* 43.7% of total population (2022)

rate of urbanization: 2.52% annual rate of change (2020-25 est.)

Revenue from forest resources: *forest revenues:* 1.89% of GDP (2018 est.)
country comparison to the world: 37

Revenue from coal: *coal revenues:* 0% of GDP (2018 est.)
country comparison to the world: 68

Waste and recycling: *municipal solid waste generated annually:* 111,314 tons (2007 est.)
municipal solid waste recycled annually: 957 tons (2016 est.)
percent of municipal solid waste recycled: 0.9% (2016 est.)

Total water withdrawal: *municipal:* 17 million cubic meters (2017 est.)
industrial: 3 million cubic meters (2017 est.)
agricultural: 318 million cubic meters (2017 est.)

Total renewable water resources: 78 billion cubic meters (2017 est.)

GOVERNMENT

Country name: *conventional long form:* Kingdom of Bhutan
conventional short form: Bhutan
local long form: Druk Gyalkhap
local short form: Druk Yul
etymology: named after the Bhotia, the ethnic Tibetans who migrated from Tibet to Bhutan; "Bod" is the Tibetan name for their land; the Bhutanese name "Druk Yul" means "Land of the Thunder Dragon"

Government type: constitutional monarchy

Capital: *name:* Thimphu
geographic coordinates: 27 28 N, 89 38 E
time difference: UTC+6 (11 hours ahead of Washington, DC, during Standard Time)
etymology: the origins of the name are unclear; the traditional explanation, dating to the 14th century, is that *thim* means "dissolve" and *phu* denotes "high ground" to express the meaning of "dissolving high ground," in reference to a local deity that dissolved before a traveler's eyes, becoming a part of the rock on which the present city stands

Administrative divisions: 20 districts (dzongkhag, singular and plural); Bumthang, Chhukha, Dagana, Gasa, Haa, Lhuentse, Mongar, Paro, Pemagatshel, Punakha, Samdrup Jongkhar, Samtse, Sarpang, Thimphu, Trashigang, Trashi Yangtse, Trongsa, Tsirang, Wangdue Phodrang, Zhemgang

Independence: 17 December 1907 (became a unified kingdom under its first hereditary king); 8 August 1949 (Treaty of Friendship with India maintains Bhutanese independence)

National holiday: National Day (Ugyen WANGCHUCK became first hereditary king), 17 December (1907)

Constitution: *history:* previous governing documents were various royal decrees; first constitution drafted November 2001 to March 2005, ratified 18 July 2008
amendments: proposed as a motion by simple majority vote in a joint session of Parliament; passage requires at least a three-fourths majority vote in a joint session of the next Parliament and assent by the king

Legal system: civil law based on Buddhist religious law

International law organization participation: has not submitted an ICJ jurisdiction declaration; non-party state to the ICCt

Citizenship: *citizenship by birth:* no
citizenship by descent only: the father must be a citizen of Bhutan
dual citizenship recognized: no
residency requirement for naturalization: 10 years

Suffrage: 18 years of age; universal

Executive branch: *chief of state:* King Jigme Khesar Namgyel WANGCHUCK (since 14 December 2006); note - King Jigme Singye WANGCHUCK abdicated the throne on 14 December 2006 to his son
head of government: Prime Minister Lotay TSHERING (since 7 November 2018)
cabinet: Council of Ministers or Lhengye Zhungtshog members nominated by the monarch in consultation with the prime minister and approved by the National Assembly; members serve 5-year terms
elections/appointments: the monarchy is hereditary but can be removed by a two-thirds vote of Parliament; leader of the majority party in Parliament is nominated as the prime minister, appointed by the monarch

Legislative branch: *description:* bicameral Parliament or Chi Tshog consists of:
non-partisan National Council or Gyelyong Tshogde (25 seats; 20 members directly elected in single-seat constituencies by simple majority vote and 5 members appointed by the king; members serve 5-year terms)
National Assembly or Tshogdu (47 seats; members directly elected in single-seat constituencies in a two-round majoritarian voting system; members serve 5-year terms)
elections:
National Council election last held on 20 April 2018 (next to be held in 2023)
National Assembly - first round held on 15 September 2018 and second round held on 18 October 2018 (next to be held in 2023)
election results:
National Council - seats by party - independent 20 (all candidates ran as independents); composition - men 23, women 2, percent of women 8%
National Assembly - first round - percent of vote by party - DNT 31.9%, DPT 30.9%, PDP 27.4%, BKP 9.8%; second round - percent of vote by party - NA; seats by party - DNT 30, DPT 17; composition - men 40, women 7, percent of women 14.9%; note - total Parliament percent of women 12.5%

Judicial branch: *highest court(s):* Supreme Court (consists of the chief justice and 4 associate justices); note - the Supreme Court has sole jurisdiction in constitutional matters
judge selection and term of office: Supreme Court chief justice appointed by the monarch upon the advice of the National Judicial Commission, a 4-member body to include the Legislative Committee of the National Assembly, the attorney general, the Chief Justice of Bhutan and the senior Associate Justice of the Supreme Court; other judges (drangpons) appointed by the monarch from among the High Court judges selected by the National Judicial Commission; chief justice serves a 5-year term or until reaching age 65 years, whichever is earlier; the 4 other judges serve 10-year terms or until age 65, whichever is earlier
subordinate courts: High Court (first appellate court); District or Dzongkhag Courts; sub-district or Dungkhag Courts

Political parties and leaders: Bhutan Kuen-Nyam Party
Bhutan Peace and Prosperity Party (Druk Phuensum Tshogpa) or DPT [Dorji WANGDI] (Druk Chirwang Tshogpa or DCT merged with DPT in March 2018)
People's Democratic Party or PDP [Tshering TOBGAY]
United Party of Bhutan (Druk Nyamrup Tshogpa) or DNT [Lotay TSHERING]

International organization participation: ADB, BIMSTEC, CP, FAO, G-77, IBRD, ICAO, IDA, IFAD, IFC, IMF, Interpol, IOC, IOM (observer), IPU, ISO (correspondent), ITSO, ITU, MIGA, NAM, OPCW, SAARC, SACEP, UN, UNCTAD, UNESCO, UNIDO, UNISFA, UNTSO, UNWTO, UPU, WCO, WHO, WIPO, WMO, WTO (observer)

Diplomatic representation in the US: *chief of mission:* Ambassador Doma TSHERING (since 13 September 2017)
note – also the Permanent Representative to the UN
telephone: [1] (212) 682-2268
FAX: [1] (212) 661-0551
email address and website: email - consulate.pmbny@mfa.gov.bt
web address - https://www.mfa.gov.bt/pmbny/
consulate(s) general: New York
embassy: 343 East 43rd Street, New York, NY 10017
note – the Permanent Mission to the UN for Bhutan has consular jurisdiction in the US

Diplomatic representation from the US: *embassy:* none; frequent informal contact is maintained via the US embassy in New Delhi (India) and Bhutan's Permanent Mission to the UN

Flag description: divided diagonally from the lower hoist-side corner; the upper triangle is yellow and the lower triangle is orange; centered along the dividing line is a large black and white dragon facing away from the hoist side; the dragon, called the Druk (Thunder Dragon), is the emblem of the nation; its white color stands for purity and the jewels in its claws symbolize wealth; the background colors represent spiritual and secular powers within Bhutan: the orange is associated with Buddhism, while the yellow denotes the ruling dynasty

National symbol(s): thunder dragon known as Druk Gyalpo; national colors: orange, yellow

National anthem: *name:* "Druk tsendhen" (The Thunder Dragon Kingdom)
lyrics/music: Gyaldun Dasho Thinley DORJI/Aku TONGMI
note: adopted 1953

ECONOMY

Economic overview: Bhutan's small economy is based largely on hydropower, agriculture, and forestry, which provide the main livelihood for more than half the population. Because rugged mountains dominate the terrain and make the building of roads and other infrastructure difficult and expensive, industrial production is primarily of the cottage industry type. The economy is closely aligned with India's through strong trade and monetary links and is dependent on India for financial assistance and migrant laborers for development projects, especially for road construction. Bhutan signed a pact in December 2014 to expand duty-free trade with Bangladesh.

Multilateral development organizations administer most educational, social, and environment programs, and take into account the government's desire to protect the country's environment and cultural traditions. For example, the government is cautious in its expansion of the tourist sector, restricting visits to environmentally conscientious tourists. Complicated controls and uncertain policies in areas such as industrial licensing, trade, labor, and finance continue to hamper foreign investment.

Bhutan's largest export - hydropower to India - could spur sustainable growth in the coming years if Bhutan resolves chronic delays in construction. Bhutan's hydropower exports comprise 40% of total exports and 25% of the government's total revenue. Bhutan currently taps only 6.5% of its 24,000-megawatt hydropower potential and is behind schedule in building 12 new hydropower dams with a combined capacity of 10,000 megawatts by 2020 in accordance with a deal signed in 2008 with India. The high volume of imported materials to build hydropower plants has expanded Bhutan's trade and current account deficits. Bhutan also signed a memorandum of understanding with Bangladesh and India in July 2017 to jointly construct a new hydropower plant for exporting electricity to Bangladesh.

Real GDP (purchasing power parity): $8.42 billion (2020 est.)
$9.03 billion (2019 est.)
$8.56 billion (2018 est.)
note: data are in 2017 dollars
country comparison to the world: 166

Real GDP growth rate: 7.4% (2017 est.)
7.3% (2016 est.)
6.2% (2015 est.)
country comparison to the world: 13

Real GDP per capita: $10,900 (2020 est.)
$11,800 (2019 est.)
$11,300 (2018 est.)
note: data are in 2017 dollars
country comparison to the world: 136

GDP (official exchange rate): $2.405 billion (2017 est.)

Inflation rate (consumer prices): 5.8% (2017 est.)
7.6% (2016 est.)
country comparison to the world: 191

GDP - composition, by sector of origin: *agriculture:* 16.2% (2017 est.)
industry: 41.8% (2017 est.)
services: 42% (2017 est.)

GDP - composition, by end use: *household consumption:* 58% (2017 est.)
government consumption: 16.8% (2017 est.)
investment in fixed capital: 47.2% (2017 est.)
investment in inventories: 0% (2017 est.)
exports of goods and services: 26% (2017 est.)
imports of goods and services: -48% (2017 est.)

Agricultural products: milk, rice, maize, potatoes, roots/tubers, oranges, areca nuts, chillies/peppers, spices, ginger

Industries: cement, wood products, processed fruits, alcoholic beverages, calcium carbide, tourism

Industrial production growth rate: 6.3% (2017 est.)
country comparison to the world: 36

Labor force: 397,900 (2017 est.)
note: major shortage of skilled labor
country comparison to the world: 159

Labor force - by occupation: *agriculture:* 58%
industry: 20%
services: 22% (2015 est.)

Unemployment rate: 3.2% (2017 est.)
3.2% (2016 est.)
country comparison to the world: 45

Unemployment, youth ages 15-24: *total:* 10.7%
male: 8.2%
female: 12.7% (2015 est.)
country comparison to the world: 133

Population below poverty line: 8.2% (2017 est.)

Gini Index coefficient - distribution of family income: 37.4 (2017 est.)
38.1 (2007)
country comparison to the world: 80

Household income or consumption by percentage share: *lowest 10%:* 2.8%
highest 10%: 30.6% (2012)

Budget: *revenues:* 655.3 million (2017 est.)
expenditures: 737.4 million (2017 est.)
note: the Government of India finances nearly one-quarter of Bhutan's budget expenditures

Budget surplus (+) or deficit (-): -3.4% (of GDP) (2017 est.)
country comparison to the world: 142

Public debt: 106.3% of GDP (2017 est.)
114.2% of GDP (2016 est.)
country comparison to the world: 12

Taxes and other revenues: 27.2% (of GDP) (2017 est.)
country comparison to the world: 101

Fiscal year: 1 July - 30 June

Current account balance: -$547 million (2017 est.)
-$621 million (2016 est.)
country comparison to the world: 123

Exports: $790 million (2020 est.)
$780 million (2019 est.)
$790 million (2018 est.)
note: Data are in current year dollars and do not include illicit exports or re-exports.
country comparison to the world: 183

Exports - partners: India 94% (2019)

Exports - commodities: iron alloys, dolomite, refined iron, cement, silicon carbides (2019)

Imports: *$1.19 billion (2020 est.) note:* data are in current year dollars
$1.23 billion (2019 est.) note: data are in current year dollars
$1.25 billion (2018 est.) note: data are in current year dollars
country comparison to the world: 185

Imports - partners: India 85%, Thailand 5% (2019)

Imports - commodities: refined petroleum, iron products, delivery trucks, cars, wood charcoal (2019)

Reserves of foreign exchange and gold: $1.206 billion (31 December 2017 est.)
$1.127 billion (31 December 2016 est.)
country comparison to the world: 129

Debt - external: $2.671 billion (31 December 2017 est.)
$2.355 billion (31 December 2016 est.)
country comparison to the world: 147

Exchange rates: ngultrum (BTN) per US dollar -
64.97 (2017 est.)
67.2 (2016 est.)
67.2 (2015 est.)
64.15 (2014 est.)
61.03 (2013 est.)

ENERGY

Electricity access: *electrification - total population:* 100% (2020)

Electricity: *installed generating capacity:* 2.334 million kW (2020 est.)
consumption: 4,314,890,000 kWh (2019 est.)
exports: 4.6 billion kWh (2019 est.)
imports: 22.85 million kWh (2019 est.)
transmission/distribution losses: 60 million kWh (2019 est.)

Electricity generation sources: *hydroelectricity:* 100% of total installed capacity (2020 est.)

Coal: *production:* 174,000 metric tons (2020 est.)
consumption: 211,000 metric tons (2020 est.)
exports: 0 metric tons (2020 est.)
imports: 37,000 metric tons (2020 est.)
proven reserves: 0 metric tons (2019 est.)

Petroleum: *total petroleum production:* 0 bbl/day (2021 est.)
refined petroleum consumption: 4,400 bbl/day (2019 est.)

Refined petroleum products - imports: 3,120 bbl/day (2015 est.)
country comparison to the world: 183

Carbon dioxide emissions: 934,000 metric tonnes of CO2 (2019 est.)
from coal and metallurgical coke: 328,000 metric tonnes of CO2 (2019 est.)
from petroleum and other liquids: 606,000 metric tonnes of CO2 (2019 est.)
country comparison to the world: 174

Energy consumption per capita: 100.135 million Btu/person (2019 est.)
country comparison to the world: 59

COMMUNICATIONS

Telephones - fixed lines: *total subscriptions:* 22,987 (2020 est.)
subscriptions per 100 inhabitants: 3 (2020 est.)
country comparison to the world: 173

Telephones - mobile cellular: *total subscriptions:* 745,137 (2020 est.)
subscriptions per 100 inhabitants: 97 (2020 est.)
country comparison to the world: 167

Telecommunication systems: *general assessment:* the small land-locked Kingdom of Bhutan has only recently emerged from decades of isolation from the modern world; that, and its mountainous terrain, left the country far back in the field in terms of teledensity as well as access to the Internet; over the last decade, the country has undergone a significant transformation due to the opening of its borders, liberalization of its telecom sector, and the active support from the government towards increased competition in the mobile, broadband, and ISP segments; the relatively widespread availability of the mobile platform has caused an explosion in mobile broadband subscriber numbers, growing from zero to over 100% penetration in just ten years (between 2010 and 2019).; the onset of the Covid-19 crisis

in 2020 caused the subscription rates to drop back a little; growth is projected to return in 2022 (along with the broader mobile market) as the overall economy recovers; the government opens up more to foreign investment, trade, and tourism; and network expansion continues – the recent (December 2021) launch of 5G services by both of the country's mobile operators being particularly noteworthy (2022)
domestic: approximately 3 to 100 fixed-line and 97 to 100 mobile cellular; domestic service inadequate, notably in rural areas (2020)
international: country code - 975; international telephone and telegraph service via landline and microwave relay through India; satellite earth station - 1 Intelsat

Broadcast media: state-owned TV station established in 1999; cable TV service offers dozens of Indian and other international channels; first radio station, privately launched in 1973, is now state-owned; 5 private radio stations are currently broadcasting (2012)

Internet country code: .bt

Internet users: *total:* 416,671 (2020 est.)
percent of population: 54% (2020 est.)
country comparison to the world: 162

Broadband - fixed subscriptions: *total:* 3,189 (2020 est.)
subscriptions per 100 inhabitants: 0.4 (2020 est.)
country comparison to the world: 192

TRANSPORTATION

National air transport system: *number of registered air carriers:* 2 (2020)
inventory of registered aircraft operated by air carriers: 6
annual passenger traffic on registered air carriers: 275,849 (2018)
annual freight traffic on registered air carriers: 690,000 (2018) mt-km

Civil aircraft registration country code prefix: A5

Airports: *total:* 2 (2021)
country comparison to the world: 196

Airports - with paved runways: *total:* 2
1,524 to 2,437 m: 1
914 to 1,523 m: 1 (2021)

Airports - with unpaved runways: *total:* 1
914 to 1,523 m: 1 (2012)

Roadways: *total:* 12,205 km (2017)
urban: 437 km (2017)
country comparison to the world: 132

MILITARY AND SECURITY

Military and security forces: Royal Bhutan Army (includes Royal Bodyguard and an air wing); National Militia; Ministry of Home and Cultural Affairs: Royal Bhutan Police (2022)
note: the Royal Bhutan Police (RBP) agency is responsible for internal security; the Army is responsible for external threats but also has responsibility for some internal security functions, including conducting counterinsurgency operations, guarding forests, and providing security for prominent persons

Military and security service personnel strengths: the Royal Bhutan Army has an estimated 8,000 personnel (2022)

Military equipment inventories and acquisitions: India has provided most of the Royal Bhutan Army's equipment (2022)

Military service age and obligation: 18 years of age for voluntary military service; no conscription; militia training is compulsory for males aged 20-25, over a 3-year period; in 2021, the Royal Bhutan Army graduated from a year-long training course the first batch of 150 women to be allowed to serve in combat roles; previously, women were allowed to serve in medical and other non-combat roles (2022)

Military - note: India is responsible for military training, arms supplies, and the air defense of Bhutan (2022)

TRANSNATIONAL ISSUES

Disputes - international: *Bhutan-China:* Lacking any treaty describing the boundary, Bhutan and China continue negotiations to establish a common boundary alignment to resolve territorial disputes arising from substantial cartographic discrepancies, the most contentious of which lie in Bhutan's west along China's Chumbi salient.
Bhutan-India: none identified

Trafficking in persons: *current situation:* human traffickers exploit domestic and foreign victims in Bhutan and Bhutanese abroad; some traffickers posing as recruiters use the lure of well-paying jobs overseas to exploit Bhutanese citizens for forced labor; some Bhutanese working in hospitality, retail, and service industries in the Gulf states and India, Thailand, and the UK reported trafficking indicators, including illegal recruitment fees, wage deductions, restricted movement, passport retention, and non-payment of wages; Bhutanese women and girls working as domestics, caregivers, and entertainers are subject to sex and labor trafficking domestically; Bhutanese and Indian women may be forced to work in hotels, massage parlors, and nightclubs, while male Indian workers face unauthorized deductions and non-payment of wages in the construction and hydropower sectors
tier rating:
Tier 2 Watch List — Bhutan does not fully meet the minimum standards for the elimination of trafficking but is making significant efforts to do so; among its accomplishments, Bhutan convicted one trafficker, appealed the dismissal of trafficking charges in a second case, finalized and disseminated standard operating procedures for victim identification and referral, and initiated an investigation into reports of labor exploitation; the government also continued to work with an international organization on anti-trafficking training and public awareness events; however, Bhutanese courts continued to dismiss and refile on lesser charges human trafficking cases due to inconsistencies between Bhutanese law and the international definition of trafficking; additionally, authorities did not identify any trafficking victims during the reporting period and did not provide protective services to Bhutanese victims of forced labor abroad (2020)

BOLIVIA

INTRODUCTION

Background: Bolivia, named after independence fighter Simon BOLIVAR, broke away from Spanish rule in 1825. Much of its subsequent history has consisted of a series of coups and countercoups, with the last coup occurring in 1978. Democratic civilian rule was established in 1982, but leaders have faced problems of deep-seated poverty, social unrest, and illegal drug production.

In December 2005, Bolivians elected Movement Toward Socialism leader Evo MORALES president - by the widest margin of any leader since the restoration of civilian rule in 1982 - after he ran on a promise to change the country's traditional political class and empower the nation's poor and indigenous majority. In December 2009 and October 2014, President MORALES easily won reelection. His party maintained control of the legislative branch of the government, which has allowed him to continue his "process of change." In February 2016, MORALES narrowly lost a referendum to approve a constitutional amendment that would have allowed him to compete in the 2019 presidential election. However, a 2017 Supreme Court ruling stating that term limits violate human rights provided the justification for MORALES to be chosen by his party to run again in 2019. MORALES attempted to claim victory in the October 2019 election, but widespread allegations of electoral fraud, rising violence, and pressure from the military ultimately forced him to flee the country. An interim government, led by President Jeanine ANEZ Chavez, prepared new elections that took place in October 2020; President Luis Alberto ARCE Catacora took office the following month.

GEOGRAPHY

Location: Central South America, southwest of Brazil

Geographic coordinates: 17 00 S, 65 00 W

Map references: South America

Area: *total:* 1,098,581 sq km
land: 1,083,301 sq km
water: 15,280 sq km
country comparison to the world: 29

Area - comparative: slightly less than three times the size of Montana

Land boundaries: *total:* 7,252 km
border countries (5): Argentina 942 km; Brazil 3,403 km; Chile 942 km; Paraguay 753 km; Peru 1,212 km

Coastline: 0 km (landlocked)

Maritime claims: none (landlocked)

Climate: varies with altitude; humid and tropical to cold and semiarid

Terrain: rugged Andes Mountains with a highland plateau (Altiplano), hills, lowland plains of the Amazon Basin

Elevation: *highest point:* Nevado Sajama 6,542 m
lowest point: Rio Paraguay 90 m
mean elevation: 1,192 m

Natural resources: tin, natural gas, petroleum, zinc, tungsten, antimony, silver, iron, lead, gold, timber, hydropower

Land use: *agricultural land:* 34.3% (2018 est.)
arable land: 3.6% (2018 est.)
permanent crops: 0.2% (2018 est.)
permanent pasture: 30.5% (2018 est.)
forest: 52.5% (2018 est.)
other: 13.2% (2018 est.)

Irrigated land: 3,000 sq km (2012)

Major lakes (area sq km): *fresh water lake(s):* Lago Titicaca (shared with Peru) - 8,030 sq km
salt water lake(s): Lago Poopo - 1,340 sq km

Major watersheds (area sq km): Atlantic Ocean drainage: Amazon (6,145,186 sq km), Paraná (2,582,704 sq km)

Major aquifers: Amazon Basin

Population distribution: a high altitude plain in the west between two cordillera of the Andes, known as the Altiplano, is the focal area for most of the population; a dense settlement pattern is also found in and around the city of Santa Cruz, located on the eastern side of the Andes

Natural hazards: flooding in the northeast (March to April)
volcanism: volcanic activity in Andes Mountains on the border with Chile; historically active volcanoes in this region are Irruputuncu (5,163 m), which last erupted in 1995, and the Olca-Paruma volcanic complex (5,762 m to 5,167 m)

Geography - note: *note 1:* landlocked; shares control of Lago Titicaca, world's highest navigable lake (elevation 3,805 m), with Peru
note 2: the southern regions of Peru and the extreme northwestern part of Bolivia are considered to be the place of origin for the common potato, while southeast Bolivia and northwest Argentina seem to be the original development site for peanuts

PEOPLE AND SOCIETY

Population: 12,054,379 (2022 est.)
country comparison to the world: 79

Nationality: *noun:* Bolivian(s)
adjective: Bolivian

Ethnic groups: Mestizo (mixed White and Amerindian ancestry) 68%, Indigenous 20%, White 5%, Cholo/Chola 2%, African descent 1%, other 1%, unspecified 3%; 44% of respondents indicated feeling part of some indigenous group, predominantly Quechua or Aymara (2009 est.)
note: results among surveys vary based on the wording of the ethnicity question and the available response choices; the 2001 national census did not provide "Mestizo" as a response choice, resulting in a much higher proportion of respondents identifying themselves as belonging to one of the available indigenous ethnicity choices; the use of "Mestizo" and "Cholo" varies among response choices in surveys, with surveys using the terms interchangeably, providing one or the other as a response choice, or providing the two as separate response choices

Languages: Spanish (official) 60.7%, Quechua (official) 21.2%, Aymara (official) 14.6%, Guarani (official) 0.6%, other native languages 0.4%, foreign languages 2.4%, none 0.1%; note - Bolivia's 2009 constitution designates Spanish and all indigenous languages as official; 36 indigenous languages are specified, including a few that are extinct (2001 est.)
major-language sample(s): La Libreta Informativa del Mundo, la fuente indispensable de información básica. (Spanish)

Religions: Roman Catholic 70%, Evangelical 14.5%, Adventist 2.5%, Church of Jesus Christ 1.2%, agnostic 0.3%, atheist 0.8%, other 3.5%, none 6.6%, unspecified 0.6% (2018 est.)

Demographic profile: Bolivia ranks at or near the bottom among Latin American countries in several areas of health and development, including poverty, education, fertility, malnutrition, mortality, and life expectancy. On the positive side, more children are being vaccinated and more pregnant women are getting prenatal care and having skilled health practitioners attend their births.

Bolivia's income inequality is the highest in Latin America and one of the highest in the world. Public education is of poor quality, and educational opportunities are among the most unevenly distributed in Latin America, with girls and indigenous and rural children less likely to be literate or to complete primary school. The lack of access to education and family planning services helps to sustain Bolivia's high fertility rate—approximately three children per woman. Bolivia's lack of clean water and basic sanitation, especially in rural areas, contributes to health problems.

Between 7% and 16% of Bolivia's population lives abroad (estimates vary in part because of illegal migration). Emigrants primarily seek jobs and better wages in Argentina (the principal destination), the US, and Spain. In recent years, more restrictive immigration policies in Europe and the US have increased the flow of Bolivian emigrants to neighboring countries. Fewer Bolivians migrated to Brazil in 2015 and 2016 because of its recession; increasing numbers have been going to Chile, mainly to work as miners.

Age structure: *0-14 years:* 30.34% (male 1,799,925/female 1,731,565)
15-24 years: 19.21% (male 1,133,120/female 1,103,063)
25-54 years: 38.68% (male 2,212,096/female 2,289,888)
55-64 years: 6.06% (male 323,210/female 382,139)
65 years and over: 5.71% (male 291,368/female 373,535) (2020 est.)

Dependency ratios: *total dependency ratio:* 60.5
youth dependency ratio: 48.5
elderly dependency ratio: 12
potential support ratio: 8.3 (2020 est.)

Median age: *total:* 25.3 years
male: 24.5 years
female: 26 years (2020 est.)
country comparison to the world: 160

Population growth rate: 1.12% (2022 est.)
country comparison to the world: 87

Birth rate: 18.61 births/1,000 population (2022 est.)
country comparison to the world: 75

Death rate: 6.48 deaths/1,000 population (2022 est.)
country comparison to the world: 138

Net migration rate: -0.98 migrant(s)/1,000 population (2022 est.)
country comparison to the world: 145

Population distribution: a high altitude plain in the west between two cordillera of the Andes, known as the Altiplano, is the focal area for most of the population; a dense settlement pattern is also found in and around the city of Santa Cruz, located on the eastern side of the Andes

Urbanization: *urban population:* 70.8% of total population (2022)
rate of urbanization: 1.87% annual rate of change (2020-25 est.)

Major urban areas - population: 1.908 million LA PAZ (capital), 1.784 million Santa Cruz, 1.369 million Cochabamba (2022); 278,000 Sucre (constitutional capital) (2018)

Sex ratio: *at birth:* 1.05 male(s)/female
0-14 years: 1.04 male(s)/female
15-24 years: 1.03 male(s)/female
25-54 years: 1.01 male(s)/female
55-64 years: 0.97 male(s)/female
65 years and over: 0.72 male(s)/female
total population: 1.01 male(s)/female (2022 est.)

Mother's mean age at first birth: 21.1 years (2008 est.)
note: data represents median age at first birth among women 25-49

Maternal mortality ratio: 155 deaths/100,000 live births (2017 est.)
country comparison to the world: 56

Infant mortality rate: *total:* 22.28 deaths/1,000 live births
male: 24.5 deaths/1,000 live births
female: 19.95 deaths/1,000 live births (2022 est.)
country comparison to the world: 72

Life expectancy at birth: *total population:* 72.5 years
male: 71.04 years
female: 74.02 years (2022 est.)
country comparison to the world: 153

Total fertility rate: 2.33 children born/woman (2022 est.)
country comparison to the world: 77

Contraceptive prevalence rate: 66.5% (2016)

Drinking water source: *improved: urban:* 99.2% of population
rural: 80.2% of population
total: 93.5% of population
unimproved: urban: 0.8% of population
rural: 19.8% of population
total: 6.5% of population (2020 est.)

Current health expenditure: 6.9% of GDP (2019)

Physicians density: 1.03 physicians/1,000 population (2017)

Hospital bed density: 1.3 beds/1,000 population (2017)

Sanitation facility access: *improved: urban:* 97.8% of population
rural: 48.4% of population
total: 83.1% of population
unimproved: urban: 2.2% of population
rural: 51.6% of population
total: 16.9% of population (2020 est.)

HIV/AIDS - adult prevalence rate: 0.2% (2020 est.)
country comparison to the world: 96

Major infectious diseases: *degree of risk:* very high (2020)
food or waterborne diseases: bacterial diarrhea and hepatitis A
vectorborne diseases: dengue fever and malaria

Obesity - adult prevalence rate: 20.2% (2016)
country comparison to the world: 102

Alcohol consumption per capita: *total:* 2.98 liters of pure alcohol (2019 est.)
beer: 2.22 liters of pure alcohol (2019 est.)
wine: 0.14 liters of pure alcohol (2019 est.)
spirits: 0.54 liters of pure alcohol (2019 est.)
other alcohols: 0.08 liters of pure alcohol (2019 est.)
country comparison to the world: 115

Tobacco use: *total:* 12.7% (2020 est.)
male: 20.5% (2020 est.)
female: 4.8% (2020 est.)
country comparison to the world: 120

Children under the age of 5 years underweight: 3.4% (2016)
country comparison to the world: 91

Child marriage: *women married by age 15:* 3.4%
women married by age 18: 19.7%
men married by age 18: 5.2% (2016 est.)

Education expenditures: 7.3% of GDP (2014 est.)
country comparison to the world: 17

Literacy: *definition:* age 15 and over can read and write
total population: 92.5%
male: 96.5%
female: 88.6% (2015)

Unemployment, youth ages 15-24: *total:* 16.1%
male: 15.7%
female: 16.6% (2020 est.)

ENVIRONMENT

Environment - current issues: the clearing of land for agricultural purposes and the international demand for tropical timber are contributing to deforestation; soil erosion from overgrazing and poor cultivation methods (including slash-and-burn agriculture); desertification; loss of biodiversity; industrial pollution of water supplies used for drinking and irrigation

Environment - international agreements: *party to:* Biodiversity, Climate Change, Climate Change-Kyoto Protocol, Climate Change-Paris Agreement, Comprehensive Nuclear Test Ban, Desertification, Endangered Species, Hazardous Wastes, Law of the Sea, Marine Dumping-London Convention, Nuclear Test Ban, Ozone Layer Protection, Ship Pollution, Wetlands,
signed, but not ratified: Environmental Modification, Marine Life Conservation

Air pollutants: *particulate matter emissions:* 20.24 micrograms per cubic meter (2016 est.)
carbon dioxide emissions: 21.61 megatons (2016 est.)
methane emissions: 21.01 megatons (2020 est.)

Climate: varies with altitude; humid and tropical to cold and semiarid

Land use: *agricultural land:* 34.3% (2018 est.)
arable land: 3.6% (2018 est.)
permanent crops: 0.2% (2018 est.)
permanent pasture: 30.5% (2018 est.)
forest: 52.5% (2018 est.)
other: 13.2% (2018 est.)

Urbanization: *urban population:* 70.8% of total population (2022)
rate of urbanization: 1.87% annual rate of change (2020-25 est.)

Revenue from forest resources: *forest revenues:* 0.33% of GDP (2018 est.)
country comparison to the world: 78

Revenue from coal: *coal revenues:* 0% of GDP (2018 est.)
country comparison to the world: 69

Major infectious diseases: *degree of risk:* very high (2020)
food or waterborne diseases: bacterial diarrhea and hepatitis A
vectorborne diseases: dengue fever and malaria

Waste and recycling: *municipal solid waste generated annually:* 2,219,052 tons (2015 est.)
municipal solid waste recycled annually: 268,727 tons (2015 est.)
percent of municipal solid waste recycled: 12.1% (2015 est.)

Major lakes (area sq km): *fresh water lake(s):* Lago Titicaca (shared with Peru) - 8,030 sq km
salt water lake(s): Lago Poopo - 1,340 sq km

Major watersheds (area sq km): Atlantic Ocean drainage: Amazon (6,145,186 sq km), Paraná (2,582,704 sq km)

Major aquifers: Amazon Basin

Total water withdrawal: *municipal:* 136 million cubic meters (2017 est.)
industrial: 32 million cubic meters (2017 est.)
agricultural: 1.92 billion cubic meters (2017 est.)

Total renewable water resources: 574 billion cubic meters (2017 est.)

GOVERNMENT

Country name: *conventional long form:* Plurinational State of Bolivia
conventional short form: Bolivia
local long form: Estado Plurinacional de Bolivia
local short form: Bolivia
etymology: the country is named after Simon BOLIVAR, a 19th-century leader in the South American wars for independence

Government type: presidential republic

Capital: *name:* La Paz (administrative capital); Sucre (constitutional [legislative and judicial] capital)
geographic coordinates: 16 30 S, 68 09 W
time difference: UTC-4 (1 hour ahead of Washington, DC, during Standard Time)
etymology: La Paz is a shortening of the original name of the city, Nuestra Senora de La Paz (Our Lady of Peace); Sucre is named after Antonio Jose de SUCRE (1795-1830), military hero in the independence struggle from Spain and the second president of Bolivia
note: at approximately 3,630 m above sea level, La Paz's elevation makes it the highest capital city in the world

Administrative divisions: 9 departments (departamentos, singular - departamento); Beni, Chuquisaca, Cochabamba, La Paz, Oruro, Pando, Potosi, Santa Cruz, Tarija

Independence: 6 August 1825 (from Spain)

National holiday: Independence Day, 6 August (1825)

Constitution: *history:* many previous; latest drafted 6 August 2006 to 9 December 2008, approved by referendum 25 January 2009, effective 7 February 2009
amendments: proposed through public petition by at least 20% of voters or by the Plurinational Legislative Assembly; passage requires approval by at least two-thirds majority vote of the total membership of the Assembly and approval in a referendum; amended 2013

Legal system: civil law system with influences from Roman, Spanish, canon (religious), French, and indigenous law

International law organization participation: has not submitted an ICJ jurisdiction declaration; accepts ICCt jurisdiction

Citizenship: *citizenship by birth:* yes
citizenship by descent only: yes
dual citizenship recognized: yes
residency requirement for naturalization: 3 years

Suffrage: 18 years of age; universal and compulsory

Executive branch: *chief of state:* President Luis Alberto ARCE Catacora (since 8 November 2020); Vice President David CHOQUEHUANCA Cespedes (since 8 November 2020); note - the president is both chief of state and head of government
head of government: President Luis Alberto ARCE Catacora (since 8 November 2020); Vice President David CHOQUEHUANCA Cespedes (since 8 November 2020)
cabinet: Cabinet appointed by the president
elections/appointments: president and vice president directly elected on the same ballot one of 3 ways: candidate wins at least 50% of the vote, or at least 40% of the vote and 10% more than the next highest candidate; otherwise a second round is held and the winner determined by simple majority vote; president and vice president are elected by majority vote to serve a 5-year term; no term limits (changed from two consecutive term limit by Constitutional Court in late 2017); election last held on 18 October 2020 (next to be held in October 2025)

election results:
2020: Luis Alberto ARCE Catacora elected president; percent of vote - Luis Alberto ARCE Catacora (MAS) 55.1%; Carlos Diego MESA Gisbert (CC) 28.8%; Luis Fernando CAMACHO Vaca (Creemos) 14%; other 2.1%
2018: Juan Evo MORALES Ayma reelected president; percent of vote - Juan Evo MORALES Ayma (MAS) 61%; Samuel DORIA MEDINA Arana (UN) 24.5%; Jorge QUIROGA Ramirez (POC) 9.1%; other 5.4%; note - MORALES resigned from office on 10 November 2019 over alleged election rigging; resignations of all his constitutionally designated successors followed, including the Vice President, President of the Senate, President of the Chamber of Deputies, and First Vice President of the Senate, leaving the Second Vice President of the Senate, Jeanine ANEZ Chavez, the highest-ranking official still in office; her appointment to the presidency was endorsed by Bolivia's Constitutional Court, and she served as interim president until the 8 November 2020 inauguration of Luis Alberto ARCE Catacora, who was winner of the 18 October 2020 presidential election

Legislative branch: *description:* bicameral Plurinational Legislative Assembly or Asamblea Legislativa Plurinacional consists of:
Chamber of Senators or Camara de Senadores (36 seats; members directly elected in multi-seat constituencies by party-list proportional representation vote; members serve 5-year terms)
Chamber of Deputies or Camara de Diputados (130 seats; 70 members directly elected in single-seat constituencies by simple majority vote, 53 directly elected in single-seat constituencies by closed party-list proportional representation vote, and 7 (apportioned to non-contiguous, rural areas in 7 of the 9 states) directly elected in single-seat constituencies by simple majority vote; members serve 5-year terms)
elections:
Chamber of Senators - last held on 18 October 2020 (next to be held in 2025)
Chamber of Deputies - last held on 18 October 2020 (next to be held in 2025)
election results:
Chamber of Senators - percent of vote by party - NA; seats by party - MAS 21, ACC 11, Creemos 4; composition as of March 2022 - men 16, women 20, percent of women 55.6%
Chamber of Deputies - percent of vote by party - NA; seats by party - MAS 75, ACC 39, Creemos 16; composition as of March 2022 - men 70, women 60, percent of women 46.2%; note - total Plurinational Legislative Assembly percent of women as of March 2022 - 48.2%

Judicial branch: *highest court(s):* Supreme Court or Tribunal Supremo de Justicia (consists of 12 judges or ministros organized into civil, penal, social, and administrative chambers); Plurinational Constitutional Tribunal (consists of 7 primary and 7 alternate magistrates); Plurinational Electoral Organ (consists of 7 members and 6 alternates); National Agro-Environment Court (consists of 5 primary and 5 alternate judges; Council of the Judiciary (consists of 3 primary and 3 alternate judges)
judge selection and term of office: Supreme Court, Plurinational Constitutional Tribunal, National Agro-Environmental Court, and Council of the Judiciary candidates pre-selected by the Plurinational Legislative Assembly and elected by direct popular vote; judges elected for 6-year terms; Plurinational Electoral Organ judges appointed - 6 by the Legislative Assembly and 1 by the president of the republic; members serve single 6-year terms
subordinate courts: National Electoral Court; District Courts (in each of the 9 administrative departments); agro-environmental lower courts

Political parties and leaders: Community Citizen Alliance or ACC [Carlos Diego MESA Gisbert]
Movement Toward Socialism or MAS [Juan Evo MORALES Ayma]
National Unity or UN [Samuel DORIA MEDINA Auza]
Revolutionary Left Front or FRI [Edgar GUZMAN Jauregui]
Social Democrat Movement or MDS [Ruben COSTAS Aguilera]
We Believe or Creemos [Luis Fernando CAMACHO Vaca]
note: We Believe or Creemos [Luis Fernando CAMACHO Vaca] is a coalition comprised of several opposition parties that participated in the 2020 election, which includes the Christian Democratic Party (PDC) and Solidarity Civic Unity (UCS)

International organization participation: CAN, CD, CELAC, FAO, G-77, IADB, IAEA, IBRD, ICAO, ICC (national committees), ICCt, ICRM, IDA, IFAD, IFC, IFRCS, ILO, IMF, IMO, Interpol, IOC, IOM, IPU, ISO (correspondent), ITSO, ITU, LAES, LAIA, Mercosur (associate), MIGA, MINUSTAH, MONUSCO, NAM, OAS, OPANAL, OPCW, PCA, UN, UN Security Council (temporary), UNAMID, UNASUR, UNCTAD, UNESCO, UNHRC, UNIDO, Union Latina, UNISFA, UNMIL, UNMISS, UNOCI, UNWTO, UPU, WCO, WFTU (NGOs), WHO, WIPO, WMO, WTO

Diplomatic representation in the US: *chief of mission:* Ambassador (vacant); Charge d'Affaires Maysa Rossana URENA MENACHO (since 1 September 2022)
chancery: 3014 Massachusetts Ave., NW, Washington, DC 20008
telephone: [1] (202) 483-4410
FAX: [1] (202) 328-3712
email address and website:
embolivia.wdc@gmail.com
consulate(s) general: Houston, Los Angeles, Maple Grove (MN), Miami, New York, Washington, DC

Diplomatic representation from the US: *chief of mission:* Ambassador (vacant); Charge d'Affaires Charisse PHILLIPS (since August 2020)
embassy: Avenida Arce 2780, La Paz
mailing address: 3220 La Paz Place, Washington DC 20512-3220
telephone: [591] (2) 216-8000
FAX: [591] (2) 216-8111
email address and website:
ConsularLaPazACS@state.gov
https://bo.usembassy.gov/
note: in September 2008, the Bolivian Government expelled the US Ambassador to Bolivia, Philip GOLDBERG, and both countries have yet to reinstate their ambassadors

Flag description: three equal horizontal bands of red (top), yellow, and green with the coat of arms centered on the yellow band; red stands for bravery and the blood of national heroes, yellow for the nation's mineral resources, and green for the fertility of the land
note: similar to the flag of Ghana, which has a large black five-pointed star centered in the yellow band; in 2009, a presidential decree made it mandatory for a so-called wiphala - a square, multi-colored flag representing the country's indigenous peoples - to be used alongside the traditional flag

National symbol(s): *llama, Andean condor, two national flowers:* the cantuta and the patuju; national colors: red, yellow, green

National anthem: *name:* "Cancion Patriotica" (Patriotic Song)
lyrics/music: Jose Ignacio de SANJINES/Leopoldo Benedetto VINCENTI
note: adopted 1852

National heritage: *total World Heritage Sites:* 7 (6 cultural, 1 natural)
selected World Heritage Site locales: City of Potosi (c); El Fuerte de Samaipata (c); Historic Sucre (c); Jesuit Missions of Chiquitos (c); Noel Kempff Mercado National Park (n); Tiahuanacu (c); Qhapaq Ñan/Andean Road System (c)

ECONOMY

Economic overview: Bolivia is a resource rich country with strong growth attributed to captive markets for natural gas exports – to Brazil and Argentina. However, the country remains one of the least developed countries in Latin America because of state-oriented policies that deter investment.

Following an economic crisis during the early 1980s, reforms in the 1990s spurred private investment, stimulated economic growth, and cut poverty rates. The period 2003-05 was characterized by political instability, racial tensions, and violent protests against plans - subsequently abandoned - to export Bolivia's newly discovered natural gas reserves to large Northern Hemisphere markets. In 2005-06, the government passed hydrocarbon laws that imposed significantly higher royalties and required foreign firms then operating under risk-sharing contracts to surrender all production to the state energy company in exchange for a predetermined service fee; the laws engendered much public debate. High commodity prices between 2010 and 2014 sustained rapid growth and large trade surpluses with GDP growing 6.8% in 2013 and 5.4% in 2014. The global decline in oil prices that began in late 2014 exerted downward pressure on the price Bolivia receives for exported gas and resulted in lower GDP growth rates - 4.9% in 2015 and 4.3% in 2016 - and losses in government revenue as well as fiscal and trade deficits.

A lack of foreign investment in the key sectors of mining and hydrocarbons, along with conflict among social groups, pose challenges for the Bolivian economy. In 2015, President Evo MORALES expanded efforts to court international investment and boost Bolivia's energy production capacity. MORALES passed an investment law and promised not to nationalize additional industries in an effort to improve the investment climate. In early 2016, the Government of Bolivia approved the 2016-2020 National Economic and Social Development Plan aimed at maintaining growth of 5% and reducing poverty.

Real GDP (purchasing power parity): $92.59 billion (2020 est.)
$100.45 billion (2019 est.)
$98.27 billion (2018 est.)
note: data are in 2017 dollars

country comparison to the world: 93

Real GDP growth rate: 2.22% (2019 est.)
4.23% (2018 est.)
4.19% (2017 est.)
country comparison to the world: 127

Real GDP per capita: $7,900 (2020 est.)
$8,700 (2019 est.)
$8,700 (2018 est.)
note: data are in 2017 dollars
country comparison to the world: 152

GDP (official exchange rate): $40.822 billion (2019 est.)

Inflation rate (consumer prices): 1.8% (2019 est.)
2.2% (2018 est.)
2.8% (2017 est.)
country comparison to the world: 98

Credit ratings:

Fitch rating: B (2020)

Moody's rating: B2 (2020)

Standard & Poors rating: B+ (2020)
note: The year refers to the year in which the current credit rating was first obtained.

GDP - composition, by sector of origin: *agriculture:* 13.8% (2017 est.)
industry: 37.8% (2017 est.)
services: 48.2% (2017 est.)

GDP - composition, by end use: *household consumption:* 67.7% (2017 est.)
government consumption: 17% (2017 est.)
investment in fixed capital: 21.3% (2017 est.)
investment in inventories: 3.8% (2017 est.)
exports of goods and services: 21.7% (2017 est.)
imports of goods and services: -31.3% (2017 est.)

Agricultural products: sugar cane, soybeans, potatoes, maize, sorghum, rice, milk, plantains, poultry, bananas

Industries: mining, smelting, electricity, petroleum, food and beverages, handicrafts, clothing, jewelry

Industrial production growth rate: 2.2% (2017 est.)
country comparison to the world: 123

Labor force: 5.719 million (2016 est.)
country comparison to the world: 71

Labor force - by occupation: *agriculture:* 29.4%
industry: 22%
services: 48.6% (2015 est.)

Unemployment rate: 4% (2017 est.)
4% (2016 est.)
note: data are for urban areas; widespread underemployment
country comparison to the world: 58

Unemployment, youth ages 15-24: *total:* 16.1%
male: 15.7%
female: 16.6% (2020 est.)
country comparison to the world: 100

Population below poverty line: 37.2% (2019 est.)

Gini Index coefficient - distribution of family income: 42.2 (2018 est.)
57.9 (1999)
country comparison to the world: 46

Household income or consumption by percentage share: *lowest 10%:* 0.9%
highest 10%: 36.1% (2014 est.)

Budget: *revenues:* 15.09 billion (2017 est.)
expenditures: 18.02 billion (2017 est.)

Budget surplus (+) or deficit (-): -7.8% (of GDP) (2017 est.)
country comparison to the world: 196

Public debt: 49% of GDP (2017 est.)
44.9% of GDP (2016 est.)
note: data cover general government debt and includes debt instruments issued by government entities other than the treasury; the data include treasury debt held by foreign entities; the data include debt issued by subnational entities
country comparison to the world: 104

Taxes and other revenues: 39.9% (of GDP) (2017 est.)
country comparison to the world: 39

Fiscal year: calendar year

Current account balance: -$2.375 billion (2017 est.)
-$1.932 billion (2016 est.)
country comparison to the world: 171

Exports: $7.55 billion (2020 est.)
$10.26 billion (2019 est.)
$10.35 billion (2018 est.)
note: Data are in current year dollars and do not include illicit exports or re-exports.
country comparison to the world: 110

Exports - partners: Argentina 16%, Brazil 15%, United Arab Emirates 12%, India 10%, United States 6%, South Korea 5%, Peru 5%, Colombia 5% (2019)

Exports - commodities: natural gas, gold, zinc, soybean oil and soy products, tin, silver, lead (2019)

Imports: $8.27 billion (2020 est.) note: data are in current year dollars
$11.95 billion (2019 est.) note: data are in current year dollars
$12.44 billion (2018 est.) note: data are in current year dollars
country comparison to the world: 116

Imports - partners: Brazil 22%, Chile 15%, China 13%, Peru 11%, Argentina 8%, United States 7% (2017)

Imports - commodities: cars, refined petroleum, delivery trucks, iron, buses (2019)

Reserves of foreign exchange and gold: $10.26 billion (31 December 2017 est.)
$10.08 billion (31 December 2016 est.)
country comparison to the world: 74

Debt - external: $12.81 billion (31 December 2017 est.)
$7.268 billion (31 December 2016 est.)
country comparison to the world: 107

Exchange rates: bolivianos (BOB) per US dollar -
6.91 (2020 est.)
6.91 (2019 est.)
6.91 (2018 est.)
6.91 (2014 est.)
6.91 (2013 est.)

ENERGY

Electricity access: *electrification - total population:* 93% (2019)
electrification - urban areas: 99.3% (2019)
electrification - rural areas: 79% (2019)

Electricity: *installed generating capacity:* 3.834 million kW (2020 est.)
consumption: 8,756,690,000 kWh (2019 est.)
exports: 0 kWh (2019 est.)
imports: 0 kWh (2019 est.)
transmission/distribution losses: 1.227 billion kWh (2019 est.)

Electricity generation sources: *fossil fuels:* 64.4% of total installed capacity (2020 est.)
solar: 2.6% of total installed capacity (2020 est.)
wind: 0.7% of total installed capacity (2020 est.)
hydroelectricity: 30.5% of total installed capacity (2020 est.)
biomass and waste: 1.8% of total installed capacity (2020 est.)

Coal: *proven reserves:* 1 million metric tons (2019 est.)

Petroleum: *total petroleum production:* 65,400 bbl/day (2021 est.)
refined petroleum consumption: 87,800 bbl/day (2019 est.)
crude oil estimated reserves: 240.9 million barrels (2021 est.)

Refined petroleum products - production: 65,960 bbl/day (2015 est.)
country comparison to the world: 75

Refined petroleum products - exports: 9,686 bbl/day (2015 est.)
country comparison to the world: 82

Refined petroleum products - imports: 20,620 bbl/day (2015 est.)
country comparison to the world: 118

Natural gas: *production:* 15,328,422,000 cubic meters (2019 est.)
consumption: 2,918,839,000 cubic meters (2019 est.)
exports: 11,818,215,000 cubic meters (2019 est.)
imports: 0 cubic meters (2021 est.)
proven reserves: 302.99 billion cubic meters (2021 est.)

Carbon dioxide emissions: 17.786 million metric tonnes of CO_2 (2019 est.)
from petroleum and other liquids: 12.071 million metric tonnes of CO_2 (2019 est.)
from consumed natural gas: 5.715 million metric tonnes of CO_2 (2019 est.)
country comparison to the world: 89

Energy consumption per capita: 27.094 million Btu/person (2019 est.)
country comparison to the world: 126

COMMUNICATIONS

Telephones - fixed lines: *total subscriptions:* 598,082 (2020 est.)
subscriptions per 100 inhabitants: 5 (2020 est.)
country comparison to the world: 87

Telephones - mobile cellular: *total subscriptions:* 11,804,343 (2020 est.)
subscriptions per 100 inhabitants: 101 (2020 est.)
country comparison to the world: 79

Telecommunication systems: *general assessment:* the structure of Bolivia's fixed telecom market is different from most other countries; local services are primarily provided by 15 telecom cooperatives; these are non-profit-making companies privately owned and controlled by their users; since the market was liberalized, the cooperatives have also provided long-distance telephony, while several also offer broadband and pay TV service; they have invested in network upgrades in a bid to improve services for customers, and to expand their footprints; Bolivia has a multi-carrier system wherein consumers can choose a long-distance carrier for each call by dialing the carrier's prefix; several operators have also adopted fixed-wireless technologies, and some rent

fiber-optic capacity; the fixed broadband services remain expensive, though the cost of bandwidth is only a fraction of what it was only a few years ago; services are still unavailable in many rural and remote areas, and even in some of the major urban areas; being a landlocked country, Bolivia had no direct access to submarine cable networks, and relies on satellite services or terrestrial links across neighboring countries; in September 2020 a new cable running via Peru, has increased capacity and contributed to a dramatic fall in end-user prices; fixed broadband services are fast migrating from DSL to fiber, while there are also cable broadband services available in some major cities; in 2007 the focus was on providing telecom services in rural areas under a project known as 'Territory with Total Coverage'; this project aims to increase telecom coverage through mobile rather than through fixed networks; Bolivia has almost twenty times as many mobile phone subscribers as fixed line connections, and the trend towards fixed-mobile substitution continues; all the mobile companies offer 3G and LTE services; due to the poor quality, high cost, and poor reach of DSL, mobile networks have become the principal platform for voice services and data access; by early 2021 companies' networks reached more than 95% of the population; about 92% of all internet accesses are via smartphones (2021)
domestic: 5 per 100 fixed-line, mobile-cellular telephone use expanding rapidly and teledensity stands at 101 per 100 persons; most telephones are concentrated in La Paz, Santa Cruz, and other capital cities (2020)
international: country code - 591; Bolivia has no direct access to submarine cable networks and must therefore connect to the rest of the world either via satellite or through terrestrial links across neighboring countries; satellite earth station - 1 Intelsat (Atlantic Ocean) (2019)

Broadcast media: large number of radio and TV stations broadcasting with private media outlets dominating; state-owned and private radio and TV stations generally operating freely, although both pro-government and anti-government groups have attacked media outlets in response to their reporting (2019)

Internet country code: .bo

Internet users: *total:* 7,003,817 (2020 est.)
percent of population: 60% (2020 est.)
country comparison to the world: 77

Broadband - fixed subscriptions: *total:* 931,918 (2020 est.)
subscriptions per 100 inhabitants: 8 (2020 est.)
country comparison to the world: 76

TRANSPORTATION

National air transport system: *number of registered air carriers:* 7 (2020)
inventory of registered aircraft operated by air carriers: 39
annual passenger traffic on registered air carriers: 4,122,113 (2018)
annual freight traffic on registered air carriers: 13.73 million (2018) mt-km

Civil aircraft registration country code prefix: CP

Airports: *total:* 855 (2021)
country comparison to the world: 7

Airports - with paved runways: *total:* 21
over 3,047 m: 5
2,438 to 3,047 m: 4
1,524 to 2,437 m: 6
914 to 1,523 m: 6 (2021)

Airports - with unpaved runways: *total:* 834
over 3,047 m: 1
2,438 to 3,047 m: 4
1,524 to 2,437 m: 47
914 to 1,523 m: 151
under 914 m: 631 (2021)

Pipelines: 5,457 km gas, 51 km liquid petroleum gas, 2,511 km oil, 1,627 km refined products (2013)

Railways: *total:* 3,960 km (2019)
narrow gauge: 3,960 km (2014) 1.000-m gauge
country comparison to the world: 51

Roadways: *total:* 90,568 km (2017)
paved: 9,792 km (2017)
unpaved: 80,776 km (2017)
country comparison to the world: 53

Waterways: 10,000 km (2012) (commercially navigable almost exclusively in the northern and eastern parts of the country)
country comparison to the world: 15

Merchant marine: *total:* 45
by type: general cargo 29, oil tanker 2, other 14 (2021)
country comparison to the world: 121

Ports and terminals: *river port(s):* Puerto Aguirre (Paraguay/Parana)
note: Bolivia has free port privileges in maritime ports in Argentina, Brazil, Chile, and Paraguay

MILITARY AND SECURITY

Military and security forces: Bolivian Armed Forces: Bolivian Army (Ejercito de Boliviano, EB), Bolivian Naval Force (Fuerza Naval Boliviana, FNB), Bolivian Air Force (Fuerza Aerea Boliviana, FAB); Ministry of Government: National Police (Policía Nacional de Bolivia, PNB) (2022)
note: the PNB includes two paramilitary forces, the Anti-Narcotics Special Forces (Fuerza Especial de Lucha Contra el Narcotráfico, FELCN) and the Anti-Terrorist Group (GAT); the PNB is part of the reserves for the Armed Forces; the police and military share responsibility for border enforcement

Military expenditures: 1.4% of GDP (2021 est.)
1.4% of GDP (2020 est.)
1.4% of GDP (2019 est.) (approximately $980 million)
1.5% of GDP (2018 est.) (approximately $1 billion)
1.5% of GDP (2017 est.) (approximately $1.01 billion)
country comparison to the world: 96

Military and security service personnel strengths: information varies widely; approximately 40,000 active troops (28,000 Army; 5,000 Navy; 7,000 Air Force); note - a considerable portion of the Navy personnel are marines and naval police; approximately 40,000 National Police (2022)

Military equipment inventories and acquisitions: the Bolivian Armed Forces are equipped with a mix of mostly older Brazilian, Chinese, European, and US equipment; since 2010, China and France have been the leading suppliers of military hardware to Bolivia (2022)

Military service age and obligation: compulsory for all men between the ages of 18 and 22; men can volunteer from the age of 16, women from 18; service is for 12 months; Search and Rescue service can be substituted for citizens who have reached the age of compulsory military service; duration of this service is 24 months (2022)
note: foreign nationals 18-22 residing in Bolivia may join the armed forces; joining speeds the process of acquiring Bolivian citizenship by naturalization

Military - note: Bolivia has a small naval force for patrolling some 5,000 miles of navigable rivers to combat narcotics trafficking and smuggling, provide disaster relief, and deliver supplies to remote rural areas, as well as for maintaining a presence on Lake Titicaca; the Navy also exists in part to cultivate a maritime tradition and as a reminder of Bolivia's desire to regain the access to the Pacific Ocean that the country lost to Chile in the War of the Pacific (1879-1884); every year on 23 March, the Navy participates in parades and government ceremonies commemorating the Día Del Mar (Day of the Sea) holiday that remembers the loss (2022)

TRANSNATIONAL ISSUES

Disputes - international: Contraband smuggling, human trafficking, and illegal narcotic trafficking are problems in the porous areas of its border regions with all of its neighbors (Argentina, Brazil, Chile, Paraguay, and Peru).
Bolivia-Chile: Despite tariff-free access to ports in southern Peru and northern Chile, Bolivia persists with its long-standing claims to regain sovereign access to the Pacific Ocean.
Bolivia-Peru: Despite tariff-free access to ports in southern Peru and northern Chile, Bolivia persists with its long-standing claims to regain sovereign access to the Pacific Ocean. Smuggling of archaeological artifacts from Peru to Bolivia, illegal timber and narcotics smuggling, human trafficking, and falsified documents are current issues.
Bolivia-Brazil: The Roboré Accord of March 29, 1958 placed the long-disputed Isla Suárez/Ilha de Guajará-Mirim, a fluvial island on the Río Mamoré, between the two towns of Guajará-Mirim (Brazil) and Guayaramerin (Bolivia), under Bolivian administration but did not resolve the sovereignty dispute
Bolivia-Argentina: Contraband smuggling, human trafficking, and illegal narcotic trafficking are problems in the porous areas of the border.
Bolivia-Paraguay: On April 27, 2009, the president of Argentina hosted the presidents of Bolivia and Paraguay together with representatives of the fiver other guarantor states -- Brazil, Chile, Peru, the United States, and Uruguay -- to the signing for the Final Record of the Boundary Commission in execution of the 1938 Peace Treaty between Bolivia and Paraguay.

Refugees and internally displaced persons: *refugees (country of origin):* 12,400 (Venezuela) (2022)

Illicit drugs: third-largest source country of cocaine and a major transit for Peruvian cocaine; in 2020 coca cultivation totaled 39,400 hectares (ha); illicit drug consumption is low in Bolivia; most cocaine is exported to other Latin American countries, such as Brazil, Paraguay, and Argentina, for domestic consumption, or for onward transit to West Africa and Europe, not the United States

BOSNIA AND HERZEGOVINA

INTRODUCTION

Background: Bosnia and Herzegovina declared sovereignty in October 1991 and independence from the former Yugoslavia on 3 March 1992 after a referendum boycotted by ethnic Serbs. The Bosnian Serbs - supported by neighboring Serbia and Montenegro - responded with armed resistance aimed at partitioning the republic along ethnic lines and joining Serb-held areas to form a "Greater Serbia." In March 1994, Bosniaks and Croats reduced the number of warring factions from three to two by signing an agreement creating a joint Bosniak-Croat Federation of Bosnia and Herzegovina. On 21 November 1995, in Dayton, Ohio, the warring parties initialed a peace agreement that ended three years of interethnic civil strife (the final agreement was signed in Paris on 14 December 1995).

The Dayton Peace Accords retained Bosnia and Herzegovina's international boundaries and created a multiethnic and democratic government charged with conducting foreign, diplomatic, and fiscal policy. Also recognized was a second tier of government composed of two entities roughly equal in size: the predominantly Bosniak-Bosnian Croat Federation of Bosnia and Herzegovina and the predominantly Bosnian Serb-led Republika Srpska (RS). The Federation and RS governments are responsible for overseeing most government functions. Additionally, the Dayton Accords established the Office of the High Representative to oversee the implementation of the civilian aspects of the agreement. The Peace Implementation Council at its conference in Bonn in 1997 also gave the High Representative the authority to impose legislation and remove officials, the so-called "Bonn Powers." An original NATO-led international peacekeeping force (IFOR) of 60,000 troops assembled in 1995 was succeeded over time by a smaller, NATO-led Stabilization Force (SFOR). In 2004, European Union peacekeeping troops (EUFOR) replaced SFOR. Currently, EUFOR deploys around 600 troops in theater in a security assistance and training capacity.

GEOGRAPHY

Location: Southeastern Europe, bordering the Adriatic Sea and Croatia

Geographic coordinates: 44 00 N, 18 00 E

Map references: Europe

Area: *total:* 51,197 sq km
land: 51,187 sq km
water: 10 sq km
country comparison to the world: 128

Area - comparative: slightly smaller than West Virginia

Land boundaries: *total:* 1,543 km
border countries (3): Croatia 956 km; Montenegro 242 km; Serbia 345 km

Coastline: 20 km

Maritime claims: NA

Climate: hot summers and cold winters; areas of high elevation have short, cool summers and long, severe winters; mild, rainy winters along coast

Terrain: mountains and valleys

Elevation: *highest point:* Maglic 2,386 m
lowest point: Adriatic Sea 0 m
mean elevation: 500 m

Natural resources: coal, iron ore, antimony, bauxite, copper, lead, zinc, chromite, cobalt, manganese, nickel, clay, gypsum, salt, sand, timber, hydropower

Land use: *agricultural land:* 42.2% (2018 est.)
arable land: 19.7% (2018 est.)
permanent crops: 2% (2018 est.)
permanent pasture: 20.5% (2018 est.)
forest: 42.8% (2018 est.)
other: 15% (2018 est.)

Irrigated land: 30 sq km (2012)

Major watersheds (area sq km): Atlantic Ocean drainage: *(Black Sea)* Danube (795,656 sq km)

Population distribution: the northern and central areas of the country are the most densely populated

Natural hazards: destructive earthquakes

Geography - note: within Bosnia and Herzegovina's recognized borders, the country is divided into a joint Bosniak/Croat Federation (about 51% of the territory) and the Bosnian Serb-led Republika Srpska or RS (about 49% of the territory); the region called Herzegovina is contiguous to Croatia and Montenegro, and traditionally has been settled by an ethnic Croat majority in the west and an ethnic Serb majority in the east

PEOPLE AND SOCIETY

Population: 3,816,459 (2022 est.)
country comparison to the world: 130

Nationality: *noun:* Bosnian(s), Herzegovinian(s)
adjective: Bosnian, Herzegovinian

Ethnic groups: Bosniak 50.1%, Serb 30.8%, Croat 15.4%, other 2.7%, not declared/no answer 1% (2013 est.)
note: Republika Srpska authorities dispute the methodology and refuse to recognize the results; Bosniak has replaced Muslim as an ethnic term in part to avoid confusion with the religious term Muslim - an adherent of Islam

Languages: Bosnian (official) 52.9%, Serbian (official) 30.8%, Croatian (official) 14.6%, other 1.6%, no answer 0.2% (2013 est.)
major-language sample(s): Knjiga svjetskih činjenica, neophodan izvor osnovnih informacija. (Bosnian/Montenegrin)
Knjiga svetskih činjenica, neophodan izvor osnovnih informacija. (Serbian)
Knjiga svjetskih činjenica, nužan izvor osnovnih informacija. (Croatian)

Religions: Muslim 50.7%, Orthodox 30.7%, Roman Catholic 15.2%, atheist 0.8%, agnostic 0.3%, other 1.2%, undeclared/no answer 1.1% (2013 est.)

Age structure: *0-14 years:* 13.18% (male 261,430/female 244,242)
15-24 years: 10.83% (male 214,319/female 201,214)
25-54 years: 44.52% (male 859,509/female 848,071)
55-64 years: 15.24% (male 284,415/female 300,168)
65 years and over: 16.22% (male 249,624/female 372,594) (2020 est.)

Dependency ratios: *total dependency ratio:* 48
youth dependency ratio: 21.5
elderly dependency ratio: 26.5
potential support ratio: 3.8 (2020 est.)

Median age: *total:* 43.3 years
male: 41.6 years
female: 44.8 years (2020 est.)
country comparison to the world: 27

Population growth rate: -0.22% (2022 est.)
country comparison to the world: 212

Birth rate: 8.41 births/1,000 population (2022 est.)
country comparison to the world: 214

Death rate: 10.26 deaths/1,000 population (2022 est.)
country comparison to the world: 32

Net migration rate: -0.38 migrant(s)/1,000 population (2022 est.)
country comparison to the world: 122

Population distribution: the northern and central areas of the country are the most densely populated

Urbanization: *urban population:* 49.8% of total population (2022)
rate of urbanization: 0.61% annual rate of change (2020-25 est.)

Major urban areas - population: 344,000 SARAJEVO (capital) (2022)

Sex ratio: *at birth:* 1.07 male(s)/female
0-14 years: 1.07 male(s)/female
15-24 years: 1.06 male(s)/female
25-54 years: 1.02 male(s)/female
55-64 years: 0.96 male(s)/female
65 years and over: 0.42 male(s)/female
total population: 0.95 male(s)/female (2022 est.)

Mother's mean age at first birth: 27.7 years (2019 est.)

Maternal mortality ratio: 10 deaths/100,000 live births (2017 est.)
country comparison to the world: 143

Infant mortality rate: *total:* 5.21 deaths/1,000 live births
male: 5.34 deaths/1,000 live births
female: 5.07 deaths/1,000 live births (2022 est.)

country comparison to the world: 173

Life expectancy at birth: *total population:* 77.98 years
male: 75.02 years
female: 81.15 years (2022 est.)
country comparison to the world: 81

Total fertility rate: 1.36 children born/woman (2022 est.)
country comparison to the world: 216

Contraceptive prevalence rate: 45.8% (2011/12)

Drinking water source: *improved: urban:* 99.9% of population
rural: 100% of population
total: 99.9% of population
unimproved: urban: 0.1% of population
rural: 0% of population
total: 0.1% of population (2020 est.)

Current health expenditure: 9.1% of GDP (2019)

Physicians density: 2.16 physicians/1,000 population (2015)

Hospital bed density: 3.5 beds/1,000 population (2014)

Sanitation facility access: *improved: urban:* 99.5% of population
unimproved: urban: 0.5% of population

HIV/AIDS - adult prevalence rate: (2018) <.1%

Obesity - adult prevalence rate: 17.9% (2016)
country comparison to the world: 118

Alcohol consumption per capita: *total:* 5.46 liters of pure alcohol (2019 est.)
beer: 4.19 liters of pure alcohol (2019 est.)
wine: 0.47 liters of pure alcohol (2019 est.)
spirits: 0.62 liters of pure alcohol (2019 est.)
other alcohols: 0.17 liters of pure alcohol (2019 est.)
country comparison to the world: 80

Tobacco use: *total:* 35% (2020 est.)
male: 42% (2020 est.)
female: 28% (2020 est.)
country comparison to the world: 15

Children under the age of 5 years underweight: 1.6% (2012)
country comparison to the world: 116

Literacy: *definition:* age 15 and over can read and write
total population: 98.5%
male: 99.5%
female: 97.5% (2015)

School life expectancy (primary to tertiary education): *total:* 14 years
male: 14 years
female: 15 years (2014)

Unemployment, youth ages 15-24: *total:* 36.6%
male: 32.5%
female: 42.8% (2020 est.)

ENVIRONMENT

Environment - current issues: air pollution; deforestation and illegal logging; inadequate wastewater treatment and flood management facilities; sites for disposing of urban waste are limited; land mines left over from the 1992-95 civil strife are a hazard in some areas

Environment - international agreements: *party to:* Air Pollution, Biodiversity, Climate Change, Climate Change-Kyoto Protocol, Climate Change-Paris Agreement, Comprehensive Nuclear Test Ban, Desertification, Endangered Species, Hazardous Wastes, Law of the Sea, Marine Life Conservation, Nuclear Test Ban, Ozone Layer Protection, Wetlands
signed, but not ratified: none of the selected agreements

Air pollutants: *particulate matter emissions:* 27.25 micrograms per cubic meter (2016 est.)
carbon dioxide emissions: 21.85 megatons (2016 est.)
methane emissions: 2.92 megatons (2020 est.)

Climate: hot summers and cold winters; areas of high elevation have short, cool summers and long, severe winters; mild, rainy winters along coast

Land use: *agricultural land:* 42.2% (2018 est.)
arable land: 19.7% (2018 est.)
permanent crops: 2% (2018 est.)
permanent pasture: 20.5% (2018 est.)
forest: 42.8% (2018 est.)
other: 15% (2018 est.)

Urbanization: *urban population:* 49.8% of total population (2022)
rate of urbanization: 0.61% annual rate of change (2020-25 est.)

Revenue from forest resources: *forest revenues:* 0.49% of GDP (2018 est.)
country comparison to the world: 66

Revenue from coal: *coal revenues:* 0.34% of GDP (2018 est.)
country comparison to the world: 17

Waste and recycling: *municipal solid waste generated annually:* 1,248,718 tons (2015 est.)
municipal solid waste recycled annually: 12 tons (2015 est.)
percent of municipal solid waste recycled: 0% (2015 est.)

Major watersheds (area sq km): *Atlantic Ocean drainage: (Black Sea)* Danube (795,656 sq km)

Total water withdrawal: *municipal:* 360.8 million cubic meters (2017 est.)
industrial: 71.8 million cubic meters (2017 est.)

Total renewable water resources: 37.5 billion cubic meters (2017 est.)

GOVERNMENT

Country name: *conventional long form:* none
conventional short form: Bosnia and Herzegovina
local long form: none
local short form: Bosna i Hercegovina
former: People's Republic of Bosnia and Herzegovina, Socialist Republic of Bosnia and Herzegovina
abbreviation: BiH
etymology: the larger northern territory is named for the Bosna River; the smaller southern section takes its name from the German word "herzog," meaning "duke," and the ending "-ovina," meaning "land," forming the combination denoting "dukedom"

Government type: parliamentary republic

Capital: *name:* Sarajevo
geographic coordinates: 43 52 N, 18 25 E
time difference: UTC+1 (6 hours ahead of Washington, DC, during Standard Time)
daylight saving time: +1hr, begins last Sunday in March; ends last Sunday in October
etymology: the name derives from the Turkish noun *saray*, meaning "palace" or "mansion," and the term *ova*, signifying "plain(s)," to give a meaning of "palace plains" or "the plains about the palace"

Administrative divisions: 3 first-order administrative divisions - Brcko District (Brcko Distrikt) (ethnically mixed), Federation of Bosnia and Herzegovina (Federacija Bosne i Hercegovine) (predominantly Bosniak-Croat), Republika Srpska (predominantly Serb)

Independence: 1 March 1992 (from Yugoslavia); note - referendum for independence completed on 1 March 1992; independence declared on 3 March 1992

National holiday: Independence Day, 1 March (1992) and Statehood Day, 25 November (1943) - both observed in the Federation of Bosnia and Herzegovina entity; Victory Day, 9 May (1945) and Dayton Agreement Day, 21 November (1995) - both observed in the Republika Srpska entity
note: there is no national-level holiday

Constitution: *history:* 14 December 1995 (constitution included as part of the Dayton Peace Accords); note - each of the political entities has its own constitution
amendments: decided by the Parliamentary Assembly, including a two-thirds majority vote of members present in the House of Representatives; the constitutional article on human rights and fundamental freedoms cannot be amended; amended several times, last in 2009

Legal system: civil law system; Constitutional Court review of legislative acts

International law organization participation: has not submitted an ICJ jurisdiction declaration; accepts ICCt jurisdiction

Citizenship: *citizenship by birth:* no
citizenship by descent only: at least one parent must be a citizen of Bosnia and Herzegovina
dual citizenship recognized: yes, provided there is a bilateral agreement with the other state
residency requirement for naturalization: 8 years

Suffrage: 18 years of age, 16 if employed; universal

Executive branch: *chief of state:* Chairman of the Presidency Zeljka CVIJANOVIC (chairman since 16 November 2022; presidency member since 16 November 2022 - Serb seat); Zeljko KOMSIC (presidency member since 20 November 2018 - Croat seat); Denis BECIROVIC (presidency member since 16 November 2022 - Bosniak seat)
head of government: Chairman of the Council of Ministers Zoran TEGELTIJA (since 5 December 2019)
cabinet: Council of Ministers nominated by the council chairman, approved by the state-level House of Representatives
elections/appointments: 3-member presidency (1 Bosniak and 1 Croat elected from the Federation of Bosnia and Herzegovina and 1 Serb elected from the Republika Srpska) directly elected by simple majority popular vote for a 4-year term (eligible for a second term, but then ineligible for 4 years); the presidency chairpersonship rotates every 8 months with the new member of the presidency elected with the highest number of votes starting the new mandate as chair; election last held on 2 October 2022 (next to be held in October 2026); the chairman of the Council of Ministers appointed by the presidency and confirmed by the state-level House of Representatives

election results: *2022:* percent of vote Denis BECIROVIC - (SDP BiH) 57.4% - Bosniak seat; Zeljko KOMSIC (DF) 55.8% - Croat seat; Zeljka CVIJANOVIC (SNSD) 51.7% - Serb seat
2018: percent of vote - Milorad DODIK (SNSD) 53.9% - Serb seat; Zeljko KOMSIC (DF) 52.6% - Croat seat; Sefik DZAFEROVIC (SDA) 36.6% - Bosniak seat
2014: percent of vote - Mladen IVANIC (PDP) 48.7% - Serb seat; Dragan COVIC (HDZ-BiH) 52.2% - Croat seat; Bakir IZETBEGOVIC (SDA) 32.9% - Bosniak seat
note: President of the Federation of Bosnia and Herzegovina Marinko CAVARA (since 9 February 2015); Vice Presidents Melika MAHMUTBEGOVIC (since 9 February 2015), Milan DUNOVIC (since 9 February 2015); President of the Republika Srpska Zeljka CVIJANOVIC (since 18 November 2018); Vice Presidents Ramiz SALKIC (since 24 November 2014), Josip JERKOVIC (since 24 November 2014)

Legislative branch: *description:* bicameral Parliamentary Assembly or Skupstina consists of:
House of Peoples or Dom Naroda (15 seats - 5 Bosniak, 5 Croat, 5 Serb; members designated by the Federation of Bosnia and Herzegovina's House of Peoples and the Republika Srpska's National Assembly to serve 4-year terms) House of Representatives or Predstavnicki Dom (42 seats to include 28 seats allocated to the Federation of Bosnia and Herzegovina and 14 to the Republika Srpska; members directly elected by proportional representation vote to serve 4-year terms); note - the Federation of Bosnia and Herzegovina has a bicameral legislature that consists of the House of Peoples (58 seats - 17 Bosniak, 17 Croat, 17 Serb, 7 other) and the House of Representatives (98 seats; members directly elected by proportional representation vote to serve 4-year terms); Republika Srpska's unicameral legislature is the National Assembly (83 directly elected delegates serve 4-year terms)
elections: House of Peoples - last held on 2 October 2022 (next to be held in 2026)
House of Representatives - last held on 2 October 2022 (next to be held in 2026)
election results: House of Peoples - percent of vote by coalition/party - NA; seats by coalition/party - NA; composition - men 12, women 3, percent of women 20%
House of Representatives - percent of vote by party/coalition - SDA 17.2%, SNSD 16.3%, HDZ BiH 8.8%, SDP 8.2%, SDS 7.1%, DF-GS 6.4%, NiP 5%, PDP 4.6%, NS/HC 3.1%, NES 3%, For Justice and Order 2.1%, DEMOS 1.9%, US 1.6%, BHI KF 1.3%, other 13.4%; seats by party/coalition - SDA 9, SNSD 6, SDP 5, HDZ BiH 4, DF-GS 3, NiP 3, SDS 2, PDP 2, NS/HC 2, NES 2, For Justice and Order 1, DEMOS 1, US 1, BHI KF 1; composition - men 31, women 11, percent of women 26.2%; note - total Parliamentary Assembly percent of women 24.6%

Judicial branch: *highest court(s):* Bosnia and Herzegovina (BiH) Constitutional Court (consists of 9 members); Court of BiH (consists of 44 national judges and 7 international judges organized into 3 divisions - Administrative, Appellate, and Criminal, which includes a War Crimes Chamber)
judge selection and term of office: BiH Constitutional Court judges - 4 selected by the Federation of Bosnia and Herzegovina House of Representatives, 2 selected by the Republika Srpska's National Assembly, and 3 non-Bosnian judges selected by the president of the European Court of Human Rights; Court of BiH president and national judges appointed by the High Judicial and Prosecutorial Council; Court of BiH president appointed for renewable 6-year term; other national judges appointed to serve until age 70; international judges recommended by the president of the Court of BiH and appointed by the High Representative for Bosnia and Herzegovina; international judges appointed to serve until age 70
subordinate courts: the Federation has 10 cantonal courts plus a number of municipal courts; the Republika Srpska has a supreme court, 5 district courts, and a number of municipal courts

Political parties and leaders: Alliance for a Better Future of BiH or SBB BiH [Fahrudin RADONCIC]
Alliance of Independent Social Democrats or SNSD [Milorad DODIK]
Alternative Party for Democratic Activity or A-SDA [Nermin OGRESEVIC] (merged with Independent Bosnian Herzegovinian List to form NES)
Bosnian-Herzegovinian Initiative or BHI KF [Fuad KASUMOVIC]
Civic Alliance or GS [Reuf BAJROVIC]
Croat Peasants' Party or HSS [Mario KARAMATIC]
Croatian Christian Democratic Union of Bosnia and Herzegovina or HKDU [Ivanka BARIC]
Croatian Democratic Union or HDU [Miro GRABOVAC-TITAN]
Croatian Democratic Union of Bosnia and Herzegovina or HDZ-BiH [Dragan COVIC]
Croatian Democratic Union 1990 or HDZ-1990 [Ilija CVITANOVIC]
Croatian Party of Rights dr. Ante Starcevic or HSP-AS Bih [Stanko PRIMORAC]
Democratic Alliance or DEMOS [Nedeljko CUBRILOVIC]
Democratic Front of DF [Zeljko KOMSIC]
Democratic Peoples' Alliance or DNS [Nenad NESIC]
For Justice and Order [Nebojsa VUKANOVIC]
Independent Bloc or NB [Senad SEPIC]
Movement for Democratic Action or PDA [Elzina PIRIC]
National Democratic Movement or NDP [Dragan CAVIC]
Our Party or NS/HC [Edin FORTO]
Party for Democratic Action or SDA [Bakir IZETBEGOVIC]
Party of Democratic Progress or PDP [Branislav BORENOVIC]
People and Justice Party or NiP [Elmedin KONAKOVIC]
People's European Union of Bosnia and Herzegovina or NES [Nermin OGRESEVIC]
Progressive Srpska or NS [Goran DORDIC]
Serb Democratic Party or SDS [Mirko SAROVIC]
Serb Radical Party-Dr. Vojislav Seselj or SRS-VS [Vojislav SESELJ] (merged with PDP)
Social Democratic Party or SDP [Nermin NIKSIC]
Socialist Party or SP [Petar DOKIC]
United Srpska or US [Nenad STEVANDIC]

International organization participation: BIS, CD, CE, CEI, EAPC, EBRD, FAO, G-77, IAEA, IBRD, ICAO, ICC (NGOs), ICCt, ICRM, IDA, IFAD, IFC, IFRCS, ILO, IMF, IMO, IMSO, Interpol, IOC, IOM, IPU, ISO, ITSO, ITU, ITUC (NGOs), MIGA, MINUSMA, MONUSCO, NAM (observer), OAS (observer), OIC (observer), OIF (observer), OPCW, OSCE, PFP, SELEC, UN, UNCTAD, UNESCO, UNIDO, UNWTO, UPU, WCO, WHO, WIPO, WMO, WTO (observer)

Diplomatic representation in the US: *chief of mission:* Ambassador Bojan VUJIC (since 16 September 2019)
chancery: 2109 E Street NW, Washington, DC 20037
telephone: [1] (202) 337-1500
FAX: [1] (202) 337-1502
email address and website:
consularaffairs@bhembassy; info@bhembassy.org
http://www.bhembassy.org/index.html
consulate(s) general: Chicago, New York

Diplomatic representation from the US: *chief of mission:* Ambassador Michael J. MURPHY (since 23 February 2022)
embassy: 1 Robert C. Frasure Street, 71000 Sarajevo
mailing address: 7130 Sarajevo Place, Washington DC 20521-7130
telephone: [387] (33) 704-000
FAX: [387] (33) 659-722
email address and website:
sarajevoACS@state.gov
https://ba.usembassy.gov/
branch office(s): Banja Luka, Mostar

Flag description: a wide blue vertical band on the fly side with a yellow isosceles triangle abutting the band and the top of the flag; the remainder of the flag is blue with seven full five-pointed white stars and two half stars top and bottom along the hypotenuse of the triangle; the triangle approximates the shape of the country and its three points stand for the constituent peoples - Bosniaks, Croats, and Serbs; the stars represent Europe and are meant to be continuous (thus the half stars at top and bottom); the colors (white, blue, and yellow) are often associated with neutrality and peace, and traditionally are linked with Bosnia
note: one of several flags where a prominent component of the design reflects the shape of the country; other such flags are those of Brazil, Eritrea, and Vanuatu

National symbol(s): *golden lily; national colors:* blue, yellow, white

National anthem: *name:* "Drzavna himna Bosne i Hercegovine" (The National Anthem of Bosnia and Herzegovina)
lyrics/music: none officially/Dusan SESTIC
note: music adopted 1999; lyrics proposed in 2008 and others in 2016 were not approved

National heritage: *total World Heritage Sites:* 4 (3 cultural, 1 natural)
selected World Heritage Site locales: Old Bridge Area of Mostar (c); Mehmed Paša Sokolović Bridge (c); Stećci Medieval Tombstones Graveyards (c); Primeval Beech Forests - Janj Forest (n)

ECONOMY

Economic overview: Bosnia and Herzegovina has a transitional economy with limited market reforms. The economy relies heavily on the export of metals, energy, textiles, and furniture as well as on remittances and foreign aid. A highly decentralized government hampers economic policy coordination and reform, while excessive bureaucracy and a segmented market discourage foreign investment. The economy is among the least competitive in the region. Foreign banks, primarily from Austria and Italy, control much of the banking sector, though the largest bank is a private domestic one. The konvertibilna marka (convertible mark) - the national currency introduced in 1998 - is pegged to the euro through a currency board arrangement, which has maintained confidence in the currency and has facilitated reliable trade links with European partners. Bosnia and Herzegovina became a full member of the Central European Free Trade Agreement in September 2007. In 2016, Bosnia began a three-year IMF loan program, but it has struggled to meet the economic reform benchmarks required to receive all funding installments.

Bosnia and Herzegovina's private sector is growing slowly, but foreign investment dropped sharply after 2007 and remains low. High unemployment remains the most serious macroeconomic problem. Successful implementation of a value-added tax in 2006 provided a steady source of revenue for the government and helped rein in gray-market activity, though public perceptions of government corruption and misuse of taxpayer money has encouraged a large informal economy to persist. National-level statistics have improved over time, but a large share of economic activity remains unofficial and unrecorded.

Bosnia and Herzegovina's top economic priorities are: acceleration of integration into the EU; strengthening the fiscal system; public administration reform; World Trade Organization membership; and securing economic growth by fostering a dynamic, competitive private sector.

Real GDP (purchasing power parity): $47.05 billion (2020 est.)
$49.17 billion (2019 est.)
$47.82 billion (2018 est.)
note: data are in 2017 dollars
country comparison to the world: 114

Real GDP growth rate: 3% (2017 est.)
3.2% (2016 est.)
3.1% (2015 est.)
country comparison to the world: 97

Real GDP per capita: $14,300 (2020 est.)
$14,900 (2019 est.)
$14,400 (2018 est.)
note: data are in 2017 dollars
country comparison to the world: 109

GDP (official exchange rate): $20.078 billion (2019 est.)

Inflation rate (consumer prices): 1.2% (2017 est.)
-1.1% (2016 est.)
country comparison to the world: 73

Credit ratings:

Moody's rating: B3 (2012)

Standard & Poors rating: B (2011)
note: The year refers to the year in which the current credit rating was first obtained.

GDP - composition, by sector of origin: *agriculture:* 6.8% (2017 est.)
industry: 28.9% (2017 est.)
services: 64.3% (2017 est.)

GDP - composition, by end use: *household consumption:* 77.4% (2017 est.)
government consumption: 20% (2017 est.)
investment in fixed capital: 16.6% (2017 est.)
investment in inventories: 2.3% (2017 est.)
exports of goods and services: 38.7% (2017 est.)
imports of goods and services: -55.1% (2017 est.)

Agricultural products: maize, milk, vegetables, potatoes, wheat, plums/sloes, apples, barley, cabbages, poultry

Industries: steel, coal, iron ore, lead, zinc, manganese, bauxite, aluminum, motor vehicle assembly, textiles, tobacco products, wooden furniture, ammunition, domestic appliances, oil refining

Industrial production growth rate: 3% (2017 est.)
country comparison to the world: 102

Labor force: 806,000 (2020 est.)
country comparison to the world: 145

Labor force - by occupation: *agriculture:* 18%
industry: 30.4%
services: 51.7% (2017 est.)

Unemployment rate: 33.28% (2019 est.)
35.97% (2018 est.)
note: official rate; actual rate is lower as many technically unemployed persons work in the gray economy
country comparison to the world: 210

Unemployment, youth ages 15-24: *total:* 36.6%
male: 32.5%
female: 42.8% (2020 est.)
country comparison to the world: 22

Population below poverty line: 16.9% (2015 est.)

Gini Index coefficient - distribution of family income: 33 (2011 est.)
33.1 (2007)
country comparison to the world: 130

Household income or consumption by percentage share: *lowest 10%:* 2.9%
highest 10%: 25.8% (2011 est.)

Budget: *revenues:* 7.993 billion (2017 est.)
expenditures: 7.607 billion (2017 est.)

Budget surplus (+) or deficit (-): 2.1% (of GDP) (2017 est.)
country comparison to the world: 15

Public debt: 39.5% of GDP (2017 est.)
44.1% of GDP (2016 est.)
note: data cover general government debt and includes debt instruments issued (or owned) by government entities other than the treasury; the data include treasury debt held by foreign entities; the data include debt issued by subnational entities, as well as intra-governmental debt; intra-governmental debt consists of treasury borrowings from surpluses in the social funds, such as for retirement, medical care, and unemployment; debt instruments for the social funds are not sold at public auctions.
country comparison to the world: 130

Taxes and other revenues: 44% (of GDP) (2017 est.)
country comparison to the world: 26

Fiscal year: calendar year

Current account balance: -$873 million (2017 est.)
-$821 million (2016 est.)
country comparison to the world: 138

Exports: $6.81 billion (2020 est.)
$8.17 billion (2019 est.)
$8.57 billion (2018 est.)
note: Data are in current year dollars and do not include illicit exports or re-exports.
country comparison to the world: 116

Exports - partners: Germany 14%, Italy 12%, Croatia 11%, Serbia 11%, Austria 9%, Slovenia 8% (2019)

Exports - commodities: electricity, seating, leather shoes, furniture, insulated wiring (2019)

Imports: $9.71 billion (2020 est.) note: data are in current year dollars
$11.15 billion (2019 est.) note: data are in current year dollars
$11.55 billion (2018 est.) note: data are in current year dollars
country comparison to the world: 107

Imports - partners: Croatia 15%, Serbia 13%, Germany 10%, Italy 9%, Slovenia 7%, China 6% (2019)

Imports - commodities: refined petroleum, cars, packaged medicines, coal, electricity (2019)

Reserves of foreign exchange and gold: $6.474 billion (31 December 2017 est.)
$5.137 billion (31 December 2016 est.)
country comparison to the world: 90

Debt - external: $10.87 billion (31 December 2017 est.)
$10.64 billion (31 December 2016 est.)
country comparison to the world: 113

Exchange rates: konvertibilna markas (BAM) per US dollar -
1.729 (2017 est.)
1.7674 (2016 est.)
1.7674 (2015 est.)
1.7626 (2014 est.)
1.4718 (2013 est.)

ENERGY

Electricity access: *electrification - total population:* 100% (2020)

Electricity: *installed generating capacity:* 4.775 million kW (2020 est.)
consumption: 11,657,450,000 kWh (2019 est.)
exports: 7.316 billion kWh (2020 est.)
imports: 3.266 billion kWh (2020 est.)
transmission/distribution losses: 1.257 billion kWh (2019 est.)

Electricity generation sources: *fossil fuels:* 62.8% of total installed capacity (2020 est.)
solar: 0.3% of total installed capacity (2020 est.)
wind: 1.5% of total installed capacity (2020 est.)
hydroelectricity: 35.4% of total installed capacity (2020 est.)
biomass and waste: 0.1% of total installed capacity (2020 est.)

Coal: *production:* 6.966 million metric tons (2020 est.)
consumption: 7.752 million metric tons (2020 est.)
exports: 525,000 metric tons (2020 est.)
imports: 1.366 million metric tons (2020 est.)
proven reserves: 2.264 billion metric tons (2019 est.)

Petroleum: *total petroleum production:* 0 bbl/day (2021 est.)
refined petroleum consumption: 34,700 bbl/day (2019 est.)
crude oil and lease condensate exports: 0 bbl/day (2018 est.)
crude oil and lease condensate imports: 13,900 bbl/day (2018 est.)
crude oil estimated reserves: 0 barrels (2021 est.)

Refined petroleum products - production: 0 bbl/day (2015 est.)
country comparison to the world: 121

Refined petroleum products - exports: 4,603 bbl/day (2015 est.)
country comparison to the world: 92

Refined petroleum products - imports: 18,280 bbl/day (2015 est.)
country comparison to the world: 129

Natural gas: *production:* 0 cubic meters (2021 est.)

consumption: 218.266 million cubic meters (2019 est.)
exports: 0 cubic meters (2021 est.)
imports: 218.266 million cubic meters (2019 est.)
proven reserves: 0 cubic meters (2021 est.)

Carbon dioxide emissions: 16.209 million metric tonnes of CO2 (2019 est.)
from coal and metallurgical coke: 10.923 million metric tonnes of CO2 (2019 est.)
from petroleum and other liquids: 4.871 million metric tonnes of CO2 (2019 est.)
from consumed natural gas: 415,000 metric tonnes of CO2 (2019 est.)
country comparison to the world: 95

Energy consumption per capita: 71.815 million Btu/person (2019 est.)
country comparison to the world: 83

COMMUNICATIONS

Telephones - fixed lines: *total subscriptions:* 706,135 (2020 est.)
subscriptions per 100 inhabitants: 22 (2020 est.)
country comparison to the world: 83

Telephones - mobile cellular: *total subscriptions:* 3,509,674 (2020 est.)
subscriptions per 100 inhabitants: 107 (2020 est.)
country comparison to the world: 134

Telecommunication systems: *general assessment:* the telecom market has been liberalized and a regulatory framework created based on the EU's regulatory framework for communications; although Bosnia-Herzegovina remains an EU candidate country, in July 2017 it applied amended mobile roaming charges to fit in with changes introduced across the Union; further roaming agreements were made in 2019 with other western Balkan countries; the fixed-line broadband network is comparatively underdeveloped, with the result that investments made in mobile upgrades to facilitate broadband connectivity in the country to a greater extent than is common elsewhere in Europe; internet services are available; DSL and cable are the main platforms for fixed-line connectivity, while fiber broadband as yet has only a small market presence; the three MNOs, each affiliated with one of the incumbent fixed-line operators, provide national coverage with 3G, though LTE coverage is only about 89%; their upgraded networks are helping to support broadband in rural areas where fixed-line infrastructure is insufficient; mobile data and mobile broadband offers will provide future revenue growth given the limited potential of mobile voice services; the MNOs tested LTE services under trial licenses from 2013, commercial launches were delayed until the award of spectrum in early 2019; the regulator stipulated that licenses must provide national coverage within five years; trials of 5G technology have been undertaken, though there are no plans to launch services commercially in the short term, given that the MNOs can continue to exploit the capacity of their existing LTE networks (2021)
domestic: fixed-line teledensity roughly 22 per 100 persons and mobile-cellular subscribership stands at 107 telephones per 100 persons (2020)
international: country code - 387; no satellite earth stations

Broadcast media: *3 public TV broadcasters:* Radio and TV of Bosnia and Herzegovina, Federation TV (operating 2 networks), and Republika Srpska Radio-TV; a local commercial network of 5 TV stations; 3 private, near-national TV stations and dozens of small independent TV broadcasting stations; 3 large public radio broadcasters and many private radio stations (2019)

Internet country code: .ba

Internet users: *total:* 2,394,995 (2020 est.)
percent of population: 73% (2020 est.)
country comparison to the world: 123

Broadband - fixed subscriptions: *total:* 770,424 (2020 est.)
subscriptions per 100 inhabitants: 24 (2020 est.)
country comparison to the world: 78

TRANSPORTATION

National air transport system: *number of registered air carriers:* 1 (2020)
inventory of registered aircraft operated by air carriers: 1
annual passenger traffic on registered air carriers: 7,070 (2015)
annual freight traffic on registered air carriers: 87 (2015) mt-km

Civil aircraft registration country code prefix: T9

Airports: *total:* 24 (2021)
country comparison to the world: 129

Airports - with paved runways: *total:* 7
2,438 to 3,047 m: 4
1,524 to 2,437 m: 1
under 914 m: 2 (2021)

Airports - with unpaved runways: *total:* 17
1,524 to 2,437 m: 1
914 to 1,523 m: 5
under 914 m: 11 (2021)

Heliports: 6 (2021)

Pipelines: 147 km gas, 9 km oil (2013)

Railways: *total:* 965 km (2014)
standard gauge: 965 km (2014) 1.435-m gauge (565 km electrified)
country comparison to the world: 90

Roadways: *total:* 22,926 km (2010)
paved: 19,426 km (2010) (4,652 km of interurban roads)
unpaved: 3,500 km (2010)
country comparison to the world: 108

Waterways: 990 km (2022) (Sava River on northern border; open to shipping but use limited)
country comparison to the world: 70

Ports and terminals: *river port(s):* Bosanska Gradiska, Bosanski Brod, Bosanski Samac, Brcko, Orasje (Sava River)

MILITARY AND SECURITY

Military and security forces: Armed Forces of Bosnia and Herzegovina (AFBiH or Oruzanih Snaga Bosne i Hercegovine, OSBiH): Operations Command (includes Army, Air, and Air Defense units), Support Command (2022)

Military expenditures: 0.9% of GDP (2021 est.)
0.9% of GDP (2020)
0.8% of GDP (2019) (approximately $370 million)
0.9% of GDP (2018) (approximately $370 million)
0.9% of GDP (2017) (approximately $360 million)
country comparison to the world: 137

Military and security service personnel strengths: approximately 9,000 active duty personnel (2022)

Military equipment inventories and acquisitions: the military's inventory includes mainly Soviet-era weapons systems with a small and varied mix of older European and US equipment (2021)

Military service age and obligation: 18 years of age for voluntary military service; mandatory retirement at age 35 or after 15 years of service for junior enlisted personnel, mandatory retirement at age 50 and 30 years of service for non-commissioned officers, mandatory retirement at age 55 and 30 years of service for all commissioned officers; conscription abolished in 2005 (2021)
note: as of 2019, women made up about 7% of the military's full-time personnel

Military - note: the Armed Forces of Bosnia and Herzegovina (AFBiH) are comprised of the former Bosnian-Croat Army of the Federation of Bosnia and Herzegovina (Vojska Federacije Bosne i Hercegovin, VF) and the Bosnian-Serb Republic of Serbia Army (Vojska Republike Srpske, VRS); the two forces were unified under the 2003 Law on Defense, which also established the country's Ministry of Defense

the European Union Force Bosnia and Herzegovina (EUFOR) has operated in the country to oversee implementation of the Dayton/Paris Agreement since taking over from NATO's Stabilization Force (SFOR) in 2004; in addition to its security mission, EUFOR supports the overall EU comprehensive strategy for Bosnia and Herzegovina and the efforts of the AFBiH to attain NATO standards; as of 2022, it had about 600 troops from 19 countries

Bosnia and Herzegovina joined NATO's Partnership for Peace (PfP) program in 2007 and was invited to join NATO's Membership Action Plan in 2010; as of 2022, NATO maintained a military headquarters in Sarajevo with the mission of assisting Bosnia and Herzegovina with the PfP program and promoting closer integration with NATO, as well as providing logistics and other support to EUFOR

TERRORISM

Terrorist group(s): Islamic Revolutionary Guard Corps/Qods Force

TRANSNATIONAL ISSUES

Disputes - international: *Bosnia and Herzegovina-Serbia:* Serbia delimited about half of the boundary with Bosnia and Herzegovina, but sections along the Drina River remain in dispute.
Bosnia and Herzegovina-Croatia: none identified
Bosnia and Herzegovina-Montenegro: none identified

Refugees and internally displaced persons: *refugees (country of origin):* 5,112 (Croatia) (2020)
IDPs: 92,000 (Bosnian Croats, Serbs, and Bosniaks displaced by inter-ethnic violence, human rights violations, and armed conflict during the 1992-95 war) (2021)
stateless persons: 149 (mid-year 2021)
note: 108,942 estimated refugee and migrant arrivals (January 2015-November 2022)

Illicit drugs: drug trafficking groups are major players in the procurement and transportation of large quantities of cocaine destined for European markets

BOTSWANA

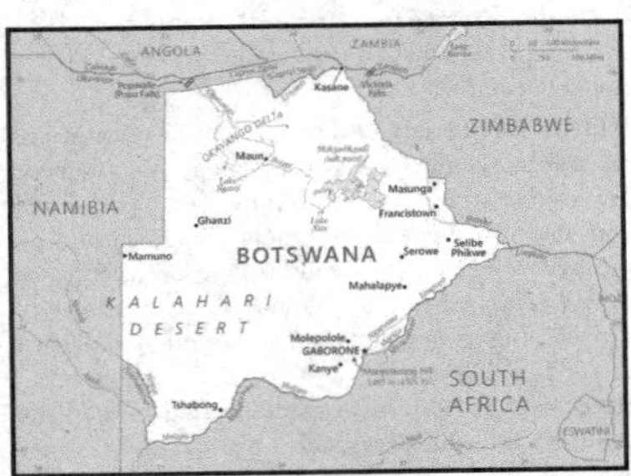

INTRODUCTION

Background: Seeking to stop the incorporation of their land into Rhodesia (Zimbabwe) or the Union of South Africa, in 1885, three tribal chiefs traveled to Great Britain and successfully lobbied the British Government to put "Bechuanaland" under UK protection. Upon independence in 1966, the British protectorate of Bechuanaland adopted the new name of Botswana. More than five decades of uninterrupted civilian leadership, progressive social policies, and significant capital investment have created one of the most stable economies in Africa. The ruling Botswana Democratic Party has won every national election since independence; President Mokgweetsi Eric MASISI assumed the presidency in April 2018 following the retirement of former President Ian KHAMA due to constitutional term limits. MASISI won his first election as president in October 2019, and he is Botswana's fifth president since independence. Mineral extraction, principally diamond mining, dominates economic activity, though tourism is a growing sector due to the country's conservation practices and extensive nature preserves. Botswana has one of the world's highest rates of HIV/AIDS infection, but also one of Africa's most progressive and comprehensive programs for dealing with the disease.

GEOGRAPHY

Location: Southern Africa, north of South Africa

Geographic coordinates: 22 00 S, 24 00 E

Map references: Africa

Area: *total:* 581,730 sq km
land: 566,730 sq km
water: 15,000 sq km
country comparison to the world: 50

Area - comparative: slightly smaller than Texas; almost four times the size of Illinois

Land boundaries: *total:* 4,347.15 km
border countries (4): Namibia 1,544 km; South Africa 1,969 km; Zambia 0.15 km; Zimbabwe 834 km

Coastline: 0 km (landlocked)

Maritime claims: none (landlocked)

Climate: semiarid; warm winters and hot summers

Terrain: predominantly flat to gently rolling tableland; Kalahari Desert in southwest

Elevation: *highest point:* Manyelanong Hill 1,495 m
lowest point: junction of the Limpopo and Shashe Rivers 513 m
mean elevation: 1,013 m

Natural resources: diamonds, copper, nickel, salt, soda ash, potash, coal, iron ore, silver

Land use: *agricultural land:* 45.8% (2018 est.)
arable land: 0.6% (2018 est.)
permanent crops: 0% (2018 est.)
permanent pasture: 45.2% (2018 est.)
forest: 19.8% (2018 est.)
other: 34.4% (2018 est.)

Irrigated land: 20 sq km (2012)

Major rivers (by length in km): Zambezi (shared with Zambia [s]), Angola, Namibia, Zimbabwe, and Mozambique [m]) - 2,740 km; Limpopo (shared with South Africa [s], Zimbabwe, and Mozambique [m]) - 1,800 km; Okavango river mouth (shared with Angola [s], and Namibia) - 1,600 km
note – [s] after country name indicates river source; [m] after country name indicates river mouth

Major watersheds (area sq km): Atlantic Ocean drainage: Orange (941,351 sq km)

Indian Ocean drainage: Zambezi (1,332,412 sq km) Internal *(endorheic basin)* drainage: Okavango Basin (863,866 sq km)

Major aquifers: Lower Kalahari-Stampriet Basin, Upper Kalahari-Cuvelai-Upper Zambezi Basin

Population distribution: the population is primarily concentrated in the east with a focus in and around the captial of Gaborone, and the far central-eastern city of Francistown; population density remains low in other areas in the country, especially in the Kalahari to the west as shown in this population distribution map

Natural hazards: periodic droughts; seasonal August winds blow from the west, carrying sand and dust across the country, which can obscure visibility

Geography - note: landlocked; population concentrated in the southern and eastern parts of the country

PEOPLE AND SOCIETY

Population: 2,384,246 (2022 est.)
country comparison to the world: 145

Nationality: *noun:* Motswana (singular), Batswana (plural)
adjective: Motswana (singular), Batswana (plural)

Ethnic groups: Tswana (or Setswana) 79%, Kalanga 11%, Basarwa 3%, other, including Kgalagadi and people of European ancestry 7%

Languages: Setswana 77.3%, Sekalanga 7.4%, Shekgalagadi 3.4%, English (official) 2.8%, Zezuru/Shona 2%, Sesarwa 1.7%, Sembukushu 1.6%, Ndebele 1%, other 2.8% (2011 est.)

Religions: Christian 79.1%, Badimo 4.1%, other 1.4% (includes Baha'i, Hindu, Muslim, Rastafarian), none 15.2%, unspecified 0.3% (2011 est.)

Demographic profile: Botswana has experienced one of the most rapid declines in fertility in Sub-Saharan Africa. The total fertility rate has fallen from more than 5 children per woman in the mid 1980s to approximately 2.4 in 2013. The fertility reduction has been attributed to a host of factors, including higher educational attainment among women, greater participation of women in the workforce, increased contraceptive use, later first births, and a strong national family planning program. Botswana was making significant progress in several health indicators, including life expectancy and infant and child mortality rates, until being devastated by the HIV/AIDs epidemic in the 1990s.

Today Botswana has the third highest HIV/AIDS prevalence rate in the world at approximately 22%, however comprehensive and effective treatment programs have reduced HIV/AIDS-related deaths. The combination of declining fertility and increasing mortality rates because of HIV/AIDS is slowing the population aging process, with a narrowing of the youngest age groups and little expansion of the oldest age groups. Nevertheless, having the bulk of its population (about 60%) of working age will only yield economic benefits if the labor force is healthy, educated, and productively employed.

Batswana have been working as contract miners in South Africa since the 19th century. Although Botswana's economy improved shortly after independence in 1966 with the discovery of diamonds and other minerals, its lingering high poverty rate and lack of job opportunities continued to push workers to seek mining work in southern African countries. In the early 1970s, about a third of Botswana's male labor force worked in South Africa (lesser numbers went to Namibia and Zimbabwe). Not until the 1980s and 1990s, when South African mining companies had reduced their recruitment of foreign workers and Botswana's economic prospects had improved, were Batswana increasingly able to find job opportunities at home.

Most Batswana prefer life in their home country and choose cross-border migration on a temporary basis only for work, shopping, visiting family, or tourism. Since the 1970s, Botswana has pursued an open migration policy enabling it to recruit thousands of foreign workers to fill skilled labor shortages. In the late 1990s, Botswana's prosperity and political stability attracted not only skilled workers but small numbers of refugees from neighboring Angola, Namibia, and Zimbabwe.

Age structure: *0-14 years:* 30.54% (male 357,065/female 350,550)
15-24 years: 18.31% (male 208,824/female 215,462)
25-54 years: 39.67% (male 434,258/female 484,922)
55-64 years: 5.92% (male 59,399/female 77,886)
65 years and over: 5.56% (male 53,708/female 75,159) (2020 est.)

Dependency ratios: *total dependency ratio:* 61.1
youth dependency ratio: 53.8
elderly dependency ratio: 7.3
potential support ratio: 13.8 (2020 est.)

Median age: *total:* 25.7 years
male: 24.5 years
female: 26.7 years (2020 est.)
country comparison to the world: 157

Population growth rate: 1.4% (2022 est.)
country comparison to the world: 68

Birth rate: 20.28 births/1,000 population (2022 est.)
country comparison to the world: 70

Death rate: 9.05 deaths/1,000 population (2022 est.)
country comparison to the world: 59

Net migration rate: 2.81 migrant(s)/1,000 population (2022 est.)
country comparison to the world: 41

Population distribution: the population is primarily concentrated in the east with a focus in and around the captial of Gaborone, and the far central-eastern city of Francistown; population density remains low in other areas in the country, especially in the Kalahari to the west as shown in this population distribution map

Urbanization: *urban population:* 72.2% of total population (2022)
rate of urbanization: 2.47% annual rate of change (2020-25 est.)

Major urban areas - population: 269,000 GABORONE (capital) (2018)

Sex ratio: *at birth:* 1.03 male(s)/female
0-14 years: 1.02 male(s)/female
15-24 years: 0.96 male(s)/female
25-54 years: 0.9 male(s)/female
55-64 years: 0.79 male(s)/female
65 years and over: 0.6 male(s)/female
total population: 0.92 male(s)/female (2022 est.)

Maternal mortality ratio: 144 deaths/100,000 live births (2017 est.)
country comparison to the world: 59

Infant mortality rate: *total:* 25.18 deaths/1,000 live births
male: 27.54 deaths/1,000 live births
female: 22.75 deaths/1,000 live births (2022 est.)
country comparison to the world: 67

Life expectancy at birth: *total population:* 65.64 years
male: 63.6 years
female: 67.74 years (2022 est.)
country comparison to the world: 200

Total fertility rate: 2.39 children born/woman (2022 est.)
country comparison to the world: 74

Contraceptive prevalence rate: 67.4% (2017)

Drinking water source: *improved: urban:* 98.1% of population
rural: 96.9% of population
total: 99.4% of population
unimproved: urban: 0.2% of population
rural: 3.1% of population
total: 0.6% of population (2020 est.)

Current health expenditure: 6.1% of GDP (2019)

Physicians density: 0.38 physicians/1,000 population (2018)

Hospital bed density: 1.8 beds/1,000 population

Sanitation facility access: *improved: urban:* 94.9% of population
rural: 63% of population
total: 85.6% of population
unimproved: urban: 5.1% of population
rural: 37% of population
total: 14.4% of population (2020 est.)

HIV/AIDS - adult prevalence rate: 19.9% (2020 est.)
country comparison to the world: 3

Major infectious diseases: *degree of risk:* high (2020)
food or waterborne diseases: bacterial diarrhea, hepatitis A, and typhoid fever
vectorborne diseases: malaria

Obesity - adult prevalence rate: 18.9% (2016)
country comparison to the world: 114

Alcohol consumption per capita: *total:* 5.98 liters of pure alcohol (2019 est.)
beer: 2.93 liters of pure alcohol (2019 est.)
wine: 0.46 liters of pure alcohol (2019 est.)
spirits: 0.96 liters of pure alcohol (2019 est.)
other alcohols: 1.64 liters of pure alcohol (2019 est.)
country comparison to the world: 71

Tobacco use: *total:* 19.4% (2020 est.)
male: 30.4% (2020 est.)
female: 8.3% (2020 est.)
country comparison to the world: 90

Education expenditures: 6.9% of GDP (2019 est.)
country comparison to the world: 21

Literacy: *definition:* age 15 and over can read and write
total population: 88.5%
male: 88%
female: 88.9% (2015)

School life expectancy (primary to tertiary education): *total:* 13 years
male: 13 years
female: 13 years (2013)

Unemployment, youth ages 15-24: *total:* 46.2%
male: 44.9%
female: 47.8% (2020 est.)

ENVIRONMENT

Environment - current issues: overgrazing; desertification; limited freshwater resources; air pollution

Environment - international agreements: *party to:* Biodiversity, Climate Change, Climate Change-Kyoto Protocol, Climate Change-Paris Agreement, Desertification, Endangered Species, Hazardous Wastes, Law of the Sea, Nuclear Test Ban, Ozone Layer Protection, Wetlands
signed, but not ratified: none of the selected agreements

Air pollutants: *particulate matter emissions:* 21.24 micrograms per cubic meter (2016 est.)
carbon dioxide emissions: 6.34 megatons (2016 est.)
methane emissions: 5.73 megatons (2020 est.)

Climate: semiarid; warm winters and hot summers

Land use: *agricultural land:* 45.8% (2018 est.)
arable land: 0.6% (2018 est.)
permanent crops: 0% (2018 est.)
permanent pasture: 45.2% (2018 est.)
forest: 19.8% (2018 est.)
other: 34.4% (2018 est.)

Urbanization: *urban population:* 72.2% of total population (2022)
rate of urbanization: 2.47% annual rate of change (2020-25 est.)

Revenue from forest resources: *forest revenues:* 0.23% of GDP (2018 est.)
country comparison to the world: 88

Revenue from coal: *coal revenues:* 0.45% of GDP (2018 est.)
country comparison to the world: 13

Waste and recycling: *municipal solid waste generated annually:* 210,854 tons (2010 est.)
municipal solid waste recycled annually: 2,109 tons (2005 est.)
percent of municipal solid waste recycled: 1% (2005 est.)

Major rivers (by length in km): Zambezi (shared with Zambia [s]), Angola, Namibia, Zimbabwe, and Mozambique [m]) - 2,740 km; Limpopo (shared with South Africa [s], Zimbabwe, and Mozambique [m]) - 1,800 km; Okavango river mouth (shared with Angola [s], and Namibia) - 1,600 km
note – [s] after country name indicates river source; [m] after country name indicates river mouth

Major watersheds (area sq km): Atlantic Ocean drainage: Orange (941,351 sq km)
Indian Ocean drainage: Zambezi (1,332,412 sq km)
Internal *(endorheic basin)* drainage: Okavango Basin (863,866 sq km)

Major aquifers: Lower Kalahari-Stampriet Basin, Upper Kalahari-Cuvelai-Upper Zambezi Basin

Total water withdrawal: *municipal:* 100.6 million cubic meters (2017 est.)
industrial: 23.4 million cubic meters (2017 est.)
agricultural: 69 million cubic meters (2017 est.)

Total renewable water resources: 12.24 billion cubic meters (2017 est.)

GOVERNMENT

Country name: *conventional long form:* Republic of Botswana
conventional short form: Botswana
local long form: Republic of Botswana
local short form: Botswana
former: Bechuanaland
etymology: the name Botswana means "Land of the Tswana" - referring to the country's major ethnic group

Government type: parliamentary republic

Capital: *name:* Gaborone
geographic coordinates: 24 38 S, 25 54 E
time difference: UTC+2 (7 hours ahead of Washington, DC, during Standard Time)
etymology: named after GABORONE (ca. 1825-1931), a revered kgosi (chief) of the Tlokwa tribe, part of the larger Tswana ethnic group

Administrative divisions: 10 districts and 6 town councils*; Central, Chobe, Francistown*, Gaborone*, Ghanzi, Jwaneng*, Kgalagadi, Kgatleng, Kweneng, Lobatse*, North East, North West, Selebi-Phikwe*, South East, Southern, Sowa Town*

Independence: 30 September 1966 (from the UK)

National holiday: Independence Day (Botswana Day), 30 September (1966)

Constitution: *history:* previous 1960 (preindependence); latest adopted March 1965, effective 30 September 1966
amendments: proposed by the National Assembly; passage requires approval in two successive Assembly votes with at least two-thirds majority in the final vote; proposals to amend constitutional provisions on fundamental rights and freedoms, the structure and branches of government, and public services also requires approval by majority vote in a referendum and assent by the president of the republic; amended several times, last in 2016

Legal system: mixed legal system of civil law influenced by the Roman-Dutch model and also customary and common law

International law organization participation: accepts compulsory ICJ jurisdiction with reservations; accepts ICCt jurisdiction

Citizenship: *citizenship by birth:* no

citizenship by descent only: at least one parent must be a citizen of Botswana
dual citizenship recognized: no
residency requirement for naturalization: 10 years

Suffrage: 18 years of age; universal

Executive branch: *chief of state:* President Mokgweetse Eric MASISI (since 1 April 2018); Vice President Slumber TSOGWANE (since 4 April 2018); note - the president is both chief of state and head of government
head of government: President Mokgweetse Eric MASISI (since 1 April 2018); Vice President Slumber TSOGWANE (since 4 April 2018);
cabinet: Cabinet appointed by the president
elections/appointments: president indirectly elected by the National Assembly for a 5-year term (eligible for a second term); election last held on 23 October 2019 (next to be held in 2024 October); vice president appointed by the president
election results: President Seretse Khama Ian KHAMA (since 1 April 2008) stepped down on 1 April 2018 having completed the constitutionally mandated 10-year term limit; upon his retirement, then Vice President MASISI became president; national elections held on 23 October 2019 gave MASISI'S BPD 38 seats in the National Assembly which then selected MASISI as President (2019)

Legislative branch: *description:* unicameral Parliament consists of the National Assembly (63 seats; 57 members directly elected in single-seat constituencies by simple majority vote, 4 nominated by the president and indirectly elected by simple majority vote by the rest of the National Assembly, and 2 ex-officio members - the president and attorney general; elected members serve 5-year terms); note - the House of Chiefs (Ntlo ya Dikgosi), an advisory body to the National Assembly, consists of 35 members - 8 hereditary chiefs from Botswana's principal tribes, 22 indirectly elected by the chiefs, and 5 appointed by the president; the House of Chiefs consults on issues including powers of chiefs, customary courts, customary law, tribal property, and constitutional amendments
elections: last held on 23 October 2019 (next to be held in October 2024)
election results: percent of vote by party - BDP 52.7%, UDC 35.9%, BPF 4.4%, AP 5.1%, other 1.7%; seats by party - BDP 38, UDC 15, BPF 3, AP 1; composition as of February 2022 - men 56, women 7, percent of women 11.1%

Judicial branch: *highest court(s):* Court of Appeal, High Court (each consists of a chief justice and a number of other judges as prescribed by the Parliament)
judge selection and term of office: Court of Appeal and High Court chief justices appointed by the president and other judges appointed by the president upon the advice of the Judicial Service Commission; all judges appointed to serve until age 70
subordinate courts: Industrial Court (with circuits scheduled monthly in the capital city and in 3 districts); Magistrates Courts (1 in each district); Customary Court of Appeal; Paramount Chief's Court/Urban Customary Court; Senior Chief's Representative Court; Chief's Representative's Court; Headman's Court

Political parties and leaders: Alliance of Progressives or AP [Ndaba GAOLATHE]
Botswana Congress Party or BCP [Dumelang SALESHANDO]
Botswana Democratic Party or BDP [Mokgweetsi MASISI]
Botswana Movement for Democracy or BMD [Sidney PILANE]
Botswana National Front or BNF [Duma BOKO]
Botswana Patriotic Front or BPF [Biggie BUTALE]
Botswana Peoples Party or BPP [Motlatsi MOLAPISI]
Real Alternative Party or RAP [Gaontebale MOKGOSI]
Umbrella for Democratic Change or UDC [Duma BOKO] (various times the coalition has included the BMD, BPP, BCP and BNF) (2019)

International organization participation: ACP, AfDB, AU, C, CD, FAO, G-77, IAEA, IBRD, ICAO, ICCt, ICRM, IDA, IFAD, IFC, IFRCS, ILO, IMF, Interpol, IOC, IOM, IPU, ISO, ITSO, ITU, ITUC (NGOs), MIGA, NAM, OPCW, SACU, SADC, UN, UNCTAD, UNESCO, UNIDO, UNWTO, UPU, WCO, WFTU (NGOs), WHO, WIPO, WMO, WTO

Diplomatic representation in the US: *chief of mission:* Ambassador Onkokame Kitso MOKAILA (since 17 September 2020)
chancery: 1531-1533 New Hampshire Avenue NW, Washington, DC 20036
telephone: [1] (202) 244-4990
FAX: [1] (202) 244-4164
email address and website:
info@botswanaembassy.org
http://www.botswanaembassy.org/
consulate(s) general: Atlanta

Diplomatic representation from the US: *chief of mission:* Ambassador (vacant); Charge d'Affaires Amanda S. JACOBSEN
embassy: Embassy Drive, Government Enclave (off Khama Crescent), Gaborone
mailing address: 2170 Gabarone Place, Washington DC 20521-2170
telephone: [267] 395-3982
FAX: [267] 318-0232
email address and website:
ConsularGabarone@state.gov
https://bw.usembassy.gov/

Flag description: light blue with a horizontal white-edged black stripe in the center; the blue symbolizes water in the form of rain, while the black and white bands represent racial harmony

National symbol(s): *zebra; national colors:* light blue, white, black

National anthem: *name:* "Fatshe leno la rona" (Our Land)
lyrics/music: Kgalemang Tumedisco MOTSETE
note: adopted 1966

National heritage: *total World Heritage Sites:* 2 (1 cultural, 1 natural)
selected World Heritage Site locales: Tsodilo Hills (c); Okavango Delta (n)

ECONOMY

Economic overview: Until the beginning of the global recession in 2008, Botswana maintained one of the world's highest economic growth rates since its independence in 1966. Botswana recovered from the global recession in 2010, but only grew modestly until 2017, primarily due to a downturn in the global diamond market, though water and power shortages also played a role. Through fiscal discipline and sound management, Botswana has transformed itself from one of the poorest countries in the world five decades ago into a middle-income country with a per capita GDP of approximately $18,100 in 2017. Botswana also ranks as one of the least corrupt and best places to do business in Sub-Saharan Africa.

Because of its heavy reliance on diamond exports, Botswana's economy closely follows global price trends for that one commodity. Diamond mining fueled much of Botswana's past economic expansion and currently accounts for one-quarter of GDP, approximately 85% of export earnings, and about one-third of the government's revenues. In 2017, Diamond exports increased to the highest levels since 2013 at about 22 million carats of output, driving Botswana's economic growth to about 4.5% and increasing foreign exchange reserves to about 45% of GDP. De Beers, a major international diamond company, signed a 10-year deal with Botswana in 2012 and moved its rough stone sorting and trading division from London to Gaborone in 2013. The move was geared to support the development of Botswana's nascent downstream diamond industry.

Tourism is a secondary earner of foreign exchange and many Batswana engage in tourism-related services, subsistence farming, and cattle rearing. According to official government statistics, unemployment is around 20%, but unofficial estimates run much higher. The prevalence of HIV/AIDS is second highest in the world and threatens the country's impressive economic gains.

Real GDP (purchasing power parity): $37.72 billion (2020 est.)
$40.95 billion (2019 est.)
$39.75 billion (2018 est.)
note: data are in 2017 dollars
country comparison to the world: 123

Real GDP growth rate: 2.4% (2017 est.)
4.3% (2016 est.)
-1.7% (2015 est.)
country comparison to the world: 118

Real GDP per capita: $16,000 (2020 est.)
$17,800 (2019 est.)
$17,600 (2018 est.)
note: data are in 2017 dollars
country comparison to the world: 104

GDP (official exchange rate): $18.335 billion (2019 est.)

Inflation rate (consumer prices): 2.7% (2019 est.)
3.2% (2018 est.)
3.2% (2017 est.)
country comparison to the world: 133

Credit ratings:

Moody's rating: A2 (2020)

Standard & Poors rating: BBB+ (2020)
note: The year refers to the year in which the current credit rating was first obtained.

GDP - composition, by sector of origin: *agriculture:* 1.8% (2017 est.)
industry: 27.5% (2017 est.)
services: 70.6% (2017 est.)

GDP - composition, by end use: *household consumption:* 48.5% (2017 est.)
government consumption: 18.4% (2017 est.)
investment in fixed capital: 29% (2017 est.)
investment in inventories: -1.8% (2017 est.)

exports of goods and services: 39.8% (2017 est.)
imports of goods and services: -33.9% (2017 est.)

Agricultural products: milk, roots/tubers, vegetables, sorghum, beef, game meat, watermelons, cabbages, goat milk, onions

Industries: diamonds, copper, nickel, salt, soda ash, potash, coal, iron ore, silver; beef processing; textiles

Industrial production growth rate: -4.2% (2017 est.)
country comparison to the world: 193

Labor force: 1.177 million (2017 est.)
country comparison to the world: 135

Unemployment rate: 20% (2013 est.)
17.8% (2009 est.)
country comparison to the world: 189

Unemployment, youth ages 15-24: *total:* 46.2%
male: 44.9%
female: 47.8% (2020 est.)
country comparison to the world: 8

Population below poverty line: 19.3% (2009 est.)

Gini Index coefficient - distribution of family income: 53.3 (2015 est.)
63 (1993)
country comparison to the world: 9

Budget: *revenues:* 5.305 billion (2017 est.)
expenditures: 5.478 billion (2017 est.)

Budget surplus (+) or deficit (-): -1% (of GDP) (2017 est.)
country comparison to the world: 76

Public debt: 14% of GDP (2017 est.)
15.6% of GDP (2016 est.)
country comparison to the world: 195

Taxes and other revenues: 30.5% (of GDP) (2017 est.)
country comparison to the world: 75

Fiscal year: 1 April - 31 March

Current account balance: $2.146 billion (2017 est.)
$2.147 billion (2016 est.)
country comparison to the world: 38

Exports: $6.16 billion (2019 est.)
$7.53 billion (2018 est.)
note: Data are in current year dollars and do not include illicit exports or re-exports.
country comparison to the world: 118

Exports - partners: India 21%, Belgium 19%, United Arab Emirates 19%, South Africa 9%, Israel 7%, Hong Kong 6%, Singapore 5% (2019)

Exports - commodities: diamonds, insulated wiring, gold, beef, carbonates (2019)

Imports: $7.44 billion (2019 est.) note: data are in current year dollars
$7.31 billion (2018 est.) note: data are in current year dollars
country comparison to the world: 121

Imports - partners: South Africa 58%, Namibia 9%, Canada 7% (2019)

Imports - commodities: diamonds, refined petroleum, cars, delivery trucks, electricity (2019)

Reserves of foreign exchange and gold: $7.491 billion (31 December 2017 est.)
$7.189 billion (31 December 2016 est.)
country comparison to the world: 82

Debt - external: $2.187 billion (31 December 2017 est.)
$2.421 billion (31 December 2016 est.)
country comparison to the world: 151

Exchange rates: pulas (BWP) per US dollar -
10.90512 (2020 est.)
10.81081 (2019 est.)
10.60446 (2018 est.)
10.1263 (2014 est.)
8.9761 (2013 est.)

ENERGY

Electricity access: *electrification - total population:* 59% (2019)
electrification - urban areas: 71% (2019)
electrification - rural areas: 29% (2019)

Electricity: *installed generating capacity:* 766,000 kW (2020 est.)
consumption: 3,515,900,000 kWh (2019 est.)
exports: 0 kWh (2019 est.)
imports: 1.101 billion kWh (2019 est.)
transmission/distribution losses: 631 million kWh (2019 est.)

Electricity generation sources: *fossil fuels:* 99.8% of total installed capacity (2020 est.)
solar: 0.2% of total installed capacity (2020 est.)

Coal: *production:* 1.876 million metric tons (2020 est.)
consumption: 1.416 million metric tons (2020 est.)
exports: 497,000 metric tons (2020 est.)
imports: 0 metric tons (2020 est.)
proven reserves: 1.66 billion metric tons (2019 est.)

Petroleum: *total petroleum production:* 0 bbl/day (2021 est.)
refined petroleum consumption: 21,700 bbl/day (2019 est.)

Refined petroleum products - imports: 21,090 bbl/day (2015 est.)
country comparison to the world: 116

Carbon dioxide emissions: 5.965 million metric tonnes of CO_2 (2019 est.)
from coal and metallurgical coke: 2.922 million metric tonnes of CO_2 (2019 est.)
from petroleum and other liquids: 3.042 million metric tonnes of CO_2 (2019 est.)
country comparison to the world: 131

Energy consumption per capita: 34.095 million Btu/person (2019 est.)
country comparison to the world: 117

COMMUNICATIONS

Telephones - fixed lines: *total subscriptions:* 140,003 (2020 est.)
subscriptions per 100 inhabitants: 6 (2020 est.)
country comparison to the world: 128

Telephones - mobile cellular: *total subscriptions:* 3,829,408 (2020 est.)
subscriptions per 100 inhabitants: 163 (2020 est.)
country comparison to the world: 131

Telecommunication systems: *general assessment:* effective regulatory reform has made Botswana's telecom market one of the most liberalized in the region; there is a service-neutral licensing regime adapted to the convergence of technologies and services, and several operators now compete in all telecom sectors; Botswana has one of the highest mobile penetration rates in Africa; in a bid to generate new revenue streams and secure market share, the three mobile network operators have entered the underdeveloped broadband sector by adopting of 3G, LTE, and WiMAX technologies; in the fixed-line broadband market they compete with a large number of ISPs, some of which have rolled out their own wireless access infrastructure; the landlocked country depends on satellites for international bandwidth, and on other countries for transit capacity to the landing points of international submarine cables; the landing of additional cables in the region in recent years has improved the competitive situation in this sector, while prices for connectivity have fallen dramatically (2022)
domestic: fixed-line teledensity has declined in recent years and now stands at roughly 6 telephones per 100 persons; mobile-cellular teledensity is roughly 163 telephones per 100 persons (2020)
international: country code - 267; international calls are made via satellite, using international direct dialing; 2 international exchanges; digital microwave radio relay links to Namibia, Zambia, Zimbabwe, and South Africa; satellite earth station - 1 Intelsat (Indian Ocean)

Broadcast media: 2 TV stations - 1 state-owned and 1 privately owned; privately owned satellite TV subscription service is available; 2 state-owned national radio stations; 4 privately owned radio stations broadcast locally (2019)

Internet country code: .bw

Internet users: *total:* 1,505,040 (2020 est.)
percent of population: 64% (2020 est.)
country comparison to the world: 135

Broadband - fixed subscriptions: *total:* 259,525 (2020 est.)
subscriptions per 100 inhabitants: 11 (2020 est.)
country comparison to the world: 111

TRANSPORTATION

National air transport system: *number of registered air carriers:* 1 (2020)
inventory of registered aircraft operated by air carriers: 6
annual passenger traffic on registered air carriers: 253,417 (2018)
annual freight traffic on registered air carriers: 110,000 (2018) mt-km

Civil aircraft registration country code prefix: A2

Airports: *total:* 74 (2021)
country comparison to the world: 70

Airports - with paved runways: *total:* 10
over 3,047 m: 2
2,438 to 3,047 m: 1
1,524 to 2,437 m: 6
914 to 1,523 m: 1 (2021)

Airports - with unpaved runways: *total:* 64
1,524 to 2,437 m: 5
914 to 1,523 m: 46
under 914 m: 13 (2021)

Railways: *total:* 888 km (2014)
narrow gauge: 888 km (2014) 1.067-m gauge
country comparison to the world: 95

Roadways: *total:* 31,747 km (2017)
paved: 9,810 km (2017)
unpaved: 21,937 km (2017)
country comparison to the world: 94

MILITARY AND SECURITY

Military and security forces: Botswana Defense Force (BDF): Ground Forces Command, Air Arm Command, Defense Logistics Command (2022)
note: both the BDF and the Botswana Police Service report to the Ministry of Defense, Justice, and Security

Military expenditures: 3% of GDP (2021 est.)
3% of GDP (2020 est.)
2.8% of GDP (2019) (approximately $760 million)
2.8% of GDP (2018) (approximately $730 million)
2.9% of GDP (2017) (approximately $740 million)
country comparison to the world: 31

Military and security service personnel strengths: approximately 9,000 active BDF personnel (2022)

Military equipment inventories and acquisitions: the BDF has a mix of foreign-supplied and mostly older weapons and equipment, largely from Europe (2021)

Military service age and obligation: 18 is the legal minimum age for voluntary military service for men and women; no conscription (2022)

Military - note: Bechuanaland/Botswana did not have a permanent military during colonial times, with the British colonial administrators relying instead on small, lightly armed constabularies such as the Bechuanaland Mounted Police, the Bechuanaland Border Police, and by the early 1960s, the Police Mobile Unit (PMU); after independence in 1966, Botswana militarized the PMU and gave it responsibility for the country's defense rather than create a conventional military force; however, turmoil in neighboring countries and numerous cross-border incursions by Rhodesian and South African security forces in the 1960s and 1970s demonstrated that the PMU was inadequate for defending the country and led to the establishment of the Botswana Defense Force (BDF) in 1977; as of 2022, the BDF's primary missions included securing territorial integrity/border security and internal duties such as disaster relief and anti-poaching

Botswana participates in the Southern African Development Community (SADC) Standby Force, and in 2021-2022 contributed nearly 300 troops to the SADC's effort to help the Mozambique Government suppress an insurgency (2022)

TRANSNATIONAL ISSUES

Disputes - international: none identified

BOUVET ISLAND

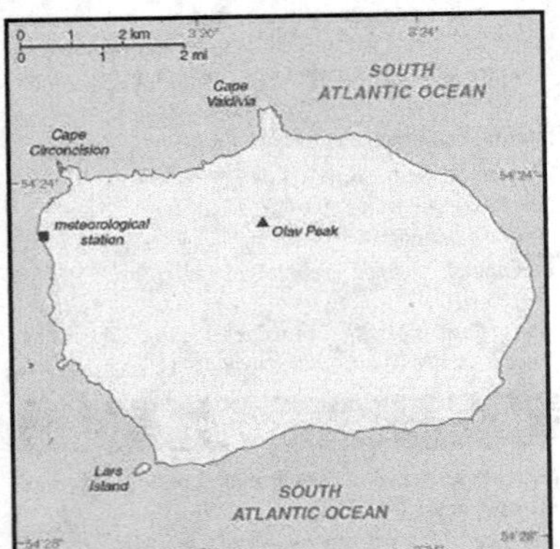

INTRODUCTION

Background: This uninhabited, volcanic, Antarctic island is almost entirely covered by glaciers making it difficult to approach; it is recognized as the most remote island on Earth. (It is furthest in distance from any other point of land, 1,639 km from Antarctica.) Bouvet Island was discovered in 1739 by a French naval officer after whom it is named. No claim was made until 1825, when the British flag was raised. A few expeditions visited the island in the late 19th century. In 1929, the UK waived its claim in favor of Norway, which had occupied the island two years previously. In 1971, Norway designated Bouvet Island and the adjacent territorial waters a nature reserve. Since 1977, Norway has run an automated meteorological station and studied foraging strategies and distribution of fur seals and penguins on the island. In February 2006, an earthquake weakened the station's foundation causing it to be blown out to sea in a winter storm. Norway erected a new research station in 2014 that can hold six people for periods of two to four months.

GEOGRAPHY

Location: island in the South Atlantic Ocean, southwest of the Cape of Good Hope (South Africa)

Geographic coordinates: 54 26 S, 3 24 E

Map references: Antarctic Region

Area: *total:* 49 sq km
land: 49 sq km
water: 0 sq km
country comparison to the world: 232

Area - comparative: about 0.3 times the size of Washington, DC

Land boundaries: *total:* 0 km

Coastline: 29.6 km

Maritime claims: *territorial sea:* 4 nm

Climate: antarctic

Terrain: volcanic; coast is mostly inaccessible

Elevation: *highest point:* Olavtoppen (Olav Peak) 780 m
lowest point: South Atlantic Ocean 0 m

Natural resources: none

Land use: *agricultural land:* 0% (2018 est.)
arable land: 0% (2018 est.)
permanent crops: 0% (2018 est.)
permanent pasture: 0% (2018 est.)
forest: 0% (2018 est.)
other: 100% (2018 est.)

Natural hazards: occasional volcanism, rock slides; harsh climate, surrounded by pack ice in winter

Geography - note: almost entirely covered by glacial ice (93%); declared a nature reserve by Norway; the distance from Bouvet Island to Norway is 12,776 km, which is almost one-third the circumference of the earth

PEOPLE AND SOCIETY

Population: uninhabited

ENVIRONMENT

Environment - current issues: none; almost entirely ice covered

Climate: antarctic

Land use: *agricultural land:* 0% (2018 est.)
arable land: 0% (2018 est.)
permanent crops: 0% (2018 est.)
permanent pasture: 0% (2018 est.)
forest: 0% (2018 est.)
other: 100% (2018 est.)

GOVERNMENT

Country name: *conventional long form:* none
conventional short form: Bouvet Island
etymology: named after the French naval officer Jean-Baptiste Charles BOUVET who discovered the island in 1739
note: pronounced boo-vay i-land

Dependency status: territory of Norway; administered by the Polar Department of the Ministry of Justice and Oslo Police

Legal system: the laws of Norway apply where applicable

Flag description: the flag of Norway is used

ECONOMY

Economic overview: no economic activity; declared a nature reserve

COMMUNICATIONS

Internet country code: .bv

Communications - note: has an automated meteorological station

TRANSPORTATION

Ports and terminals: none; offshore anchorage only

MILITARY AND SECURITY

Military - note: defense is the responsibility of Norway

TRANSNATIONAL ISSUES

Disputes - international: none identified

BRAZIL

INTRODUCTION

Background: Following more than three centuries under Portuguese rule, Brazil gained its independence in 1822, maintaining a monarchical system of government until the abolition of slavery in 1888 and the subsequent proclamation of a republic by the military in 1889. Brazilian coffee exporters politically dominated the country until populist leader Getulio VARGAS rose to power in 1930. VARGAS governed over various versions of democratic and authoritarian regimes from 1930 to 1945. Democratic rule returned (including a democratically elected VARGAS administration from 1951 to 1955) and lasted until 1964, when the military overthrew President Joao GOULART. The military regime censored journalists and repressed and tortured dissidents in the late 1960s and early 1970s. The dictatorship lasted until 1985, when the military regime peacefully ceded power to civilian rulers, and the Brazilian Congress passed its current constitution in 1989.

By far the largest and most populous country in South America, Brazil continues to pursue industrial and agricultural growth and development of its interior. Having successfully weathered a period of global financial difficulty in the late 20th century, under President Luiz Inacio LULA da Silva (2003-2010) Brazil was seen as one of the world's strongest emerging markets and a contributor to global growth. The awarding of the 2014 FIFA World Cup and 2016 Summer Olympic Games, the first ever to be held in South America, was symbolic of the country's rise. However, from about 2013 to 2016, Brazil was plagued by a sagging economy, high unemployment, and high inflation, only emerging from recession in 2017. Former President Dilma ROUSSEFF (2011-2016) was removed from office in 2016 by Congress for having committed impeachable acts against Brazil's budgetary laws, and her vice president, Michel TEMER, served the remainder of her second term. A money-laundering investigation, Operation Lava Jato, uncovered a vast corruption scheme and prosecutors charged several high-profile Brazilian politicians with crimes. Former-President LULA was convicted of accepting bribes and served jail time (2018-19), although his conviction was overturned in early 2021. LULA's revival became complete in October 2022 when he narrowly defeated incumbent Jair BOLSONARO (2019-2022) in the presidential election. LULA will assume the office on 1 January 2023.

GEOGRAPHY

Location: Eastern South America, bordering the Atlantic Ocean

Geographic coordinates: 10 00 S, 55 00 W

Map references: South America

Area: *total:* 8,515,770 sq km
land: 8,358,140 sq km
water: 157,630 sq km
note: includes Arquipelago de Fernando de Noronha, Atol das Rocas, Ilha da Trindade, Ilhas Martin Vaz, and Penedos de Sao Pedro e Sao Paulo
country comparison to the world: 6

Area - comparative: slightly smaller than the US

Land boundaries: *total:* 16,145 km
border countries (10): Argentina 1,263 km; Bolivia 3,403 km; Colombia 1,790 km; French Guiana 649 km; Guyana 1,308 km; Paraguay 1,371 km; Peru 2,659 km; Suriname 515 km; Uruguay 1,050 km; Venezuela 2,137 km

Coastline: 7,491 km

Maritime claims: *territorial sea:* 12 nm
contiguous zone: 24 nm
exclusive economic zone: 200 nm
continental shelf: 200 nm or to edge of the continental margin

Climate: mostly tropical, but temperate in south

Terrain: mostly flat to rolling lowlands in north; some plains, hills, mountains, and narrow coastal belt

Elevation: *highest point:* Pico da Neblina 2,994 m
lowest point: Atlantic Ocean 0 m
mean elevation: 320 m

Natural resources: alumina, bauxite, beryllium, gold, iron ore, manganese, nickel, niobium, phosphates, platinum, tantalum, tin, rare earth elements, uranium, petroleum, hydropower, timber

Land use: *agricultural land:* 32.9% (2018 est.)
arable land: 8.6% (2018 est.)
permanent crops: 0.8% (2018 est.)
permanent pasture: 23.5% (2018 est.)
forest: 61.9% (2018 est.)
other: 5.2% (2018 est.)

Irrigated land: 54,000 sq km (2012)

Major lakes (area sq km): *fresh water lake(s):* Lagoa dos Patos - 10,140 sq km
salt water lake(s): Lagoa Mirim (shared with Uruguay) - 2,970 sq km

Major rivers (by length in km): Amazon river mouth (shared with Peru [s]) - 6,400 km; Rio de la Plata/Parana river source (shared with Paraguay, Argentina, and Uruguay [m]) - 4,880 km; Tocantins - 3,650 km; Sao Francisco - 3,180 km; Paraguay river source (shared with Argentina and Paraguay [m]) - 2,549 km; Rio Negro river mouth (shared with Colombia [s] and Venezuela) - 2,250 km; Uruguay river source (shared with Argentina and Uruguay [m]) - 1,610 km
note – [s] after country name indicates river source; [m] after country name indicates river mouth

Major watersheds (area sq km): Atlantic Ocean drainage: Amazon (6,145,186 sq km), Orinoco (953,675 sq km), Paraná (2,582,704 sq km), São Francisco (617,814 sq km), Tocantins (764,213 sq km)

Major aquifers: Amazon Basin, Guarani Aquifer System, Maranhao Basin

Population distribution: the vast majority of people live along, or relatively near, the Atlantic coast in the east; the population core is in the southeast, anchored by the cities of Sao Paolo, Brasilia, and Rio de Janeiro

Natural hazards: recurring droughts in northeast; floods and occasional frost in south

Geography - note: *note 1:* largest country in South America and in the Southern Hemisphere; shares common boundaries with every South American country except Chile and Ecuador; most of the Pantanal, the world's largest tropical wetland, extends through the west central part of the country; shares Iguazu Falls, the world's largest waterfalls system, with Argentina
note 2: cassava (manioc) the sixth most important food crop in the world - after maize, rice, wheat, potatoes, and soybeans - seems to have originated in the west-central part of Brazil; pineapples are probably indigenous to the southern Brazil-Paraguay region
note 3: Rocas Atoll, located off the northeast coast of Brazil, is the only atoll in the South Atlantic.

Rocas Atoll:

PEOPLE AND SOCIETY

Population: 217,240,060 (2022 est.)
country comparison to the world: 7

Nationality: *noun:* Brazilian(s)
adjective: Brazilian

Ethnic groups: White 47.7%, mixed 43.1%, Black 7.6%, Asian 1.1%, Indigenous 0.4% (2010 est.)

Languages: Portuguese (official and most widely spoken language); note - less common languages include Spanish (border areas and schools), German, Italian, Japanese, English, and a large number of minor Amerindian languages
major-language sample(s): O Livro de Fatos Mundiais, a fonte indispensável para informação básica. (Brazilian Portuguese)

Religions: Roman Catholic 64.6%, other Catholic 0.4%, Protestant 22.2% (includes Adventist 6.5%, Assembly of God 2.0%, Christian Congregation of Brazil 1.2%, Universal Kingdom of God 1.0%, other Protestant 11.5%), other Christian 0.7%, Spiritist 2.2%, other 1.4%, none 8%, unspecified 0.4% (2010 est.)

Demographic profile: Brazil's rapid fertility decline since the 1960s is the main factor behind the country's slowing population growth rate, aging population, and fast-paced demographic transition. Brasilia has not taken full advantage of its large working-age population to develop its human capital and strengthen its social and economic institutions but is funding a study abroad program to bring advanced skills back to the country. The current favorable age structure will begin to shift around 2025, with the labor force shrinking and the elderly starting to compose an increasing share of the total population. Well-funded public pensions have nearly wiped out poverty among the elderly, and Bolsa Familia and other social programs have lifted tens of millions out of poverty. More than half of Brazil's population is considered middle class, but poverty and income inequality levels remain high; the Northeast, North, and Center-West, women, and black, mixed race, and indigenous populations are disproportionately affected. Disparities in opportunities foster social exclusion and contribute to Brazil's high crime rate, particularly violent crime in cities and favelas (slums).

Brazil has traditionally been a net recipient of immigrants, with its southeast being the prime destination. After the importation of African slaves was outlawed in the mid-19th century, Brazil sought Europeans (Italians, Portuguese, Spaniards, and Germans) and later Asians (Japanese) to work in agriculture, especially coffee cultivation. Recent immigrants come mainly from Argentina, Chile, and Andean countries (many are unskilled illegal migrants) or are returning Brazilian nationals. Since Brazil's economic downturn in the 1980s, emigration to the United States, Europe, and Japan has been rising but is negligible relative to Brazil's total population. The majority of these emigrants are well-educated and middle-class. Fewer Brazilian peasants are emigrating to neighboring countries to take up agricultural work.

Age structure: *0-14 years:* 21.11% (male 22,790,634/female 21,907,018)
15-24 years: 16.06% (male 17,254,363/female 16,750,581)
25-54 years: 43.83% (male 46,070,240/female 46,729,640)
55-64 years: 9.78% (male 9,802,995/female 10,911,140)
65 years and over: 9.21% (male 8,323,344/female 11,176,018) (2020 est.)

Dependency ratios: *total dependency ratio:* 43.5
youth dependency ratio: 29.7
elderly dependency ratio: 13.8
potential support ratio: 7.3 (2020 est.)

Median age: *total:* 33.2 years
male: 32.3 years
female: 34.1 years (2020 est.)
country comparison to the world: 101

Population growth rate: 0.7% (2022 est.)
country comparison to the world: 128

Birth rate: 13.96 births/1,000 population (2022 est.)
country comparison to the world: 127

Death rate: 6.81 deaths/1,000 population (2022 est.)
country comparison to the world: 125

Net migration rate: -0.19 migrant(s)/1,000 population (2022 est.)
country comparison to the world: 109

Population distribution: the vast majority of people live along, or relatively near, the Atlantic coast in the east; the population core is in the southeast, anchored by the cities of Sao Paolo, Brasilia, and Rio de Janeiro

Urbanization: *urban population:* 87.6% of total population (2022)
rate of urbanization: 0.87% annual rate of change (2020-25 est.)

Major urban areas - population: 22.430 million Sao Paulo, 13.634 million Rio de Janeiro, 6.194 million Belo Horizonte, 4.804 million BRASILIA (capital), 4.220 million Recife, 4.185 million Porto Alegre (2022)

Sex ratio: *at birth:* 1.05 male(s)/female
0-14 years: 1.04 male(s)/female
15-24 years: 1.03 male(s)/female
25-54 years: 0.98 male(s)/female
55-64 years: 0.9 male(s)/female
65 years and over: 0.58 male(s)/female
total population: 0.97 male(s)/female (2022 est.)

Maternal mortality ratio: 60 deaths/100,000 live births (2017 est.)
country comparison to the world: 88

Infant mortality rate: *total:* 13.31 deaths/1,000 live births
male: 14.75 deaths/1,000 live births
female: 11.8 deaths/1,000 live births (2022 est.)
country comparison to the world: 109

Life expectancy at birth: *total population:* 75.92 years
male: 72.5 years
female: 79.5 years (2022 est.)
country comparison to the world: 112

Total fertility rate: 1.8 children born/woman (2022 est.)
country comparison to the world: 144

Contraceptive prevalence rate: 80.5% (2019)

Drinking water source: *improved: urban:* 99.8% of population
rural: 96.9% of population
total: 99.4% of population
unimproved: urban: 0.2% of population
rural: 3.1% of population
total: 0.6% of population (2020 est.)

Current health expenditure: 9.6% of GDP (2019)

Physicians density: 2.31 physicians/1,000 population (2019)

Hospital bed density: 2.1 beds/1,000 population (2017)

Sanitation facility access: *improved: urban:* 94.1% of population
rural: 63.6% of population
total: 90.2% of population
unimproved: urban: 5.9% of population
rural: 36.4% of population
total: 9.8% of population (2020 est.)

HIV/AIDS - adult prevalence rate: 0.6% (2020 est.)
country comparison to the world: 57

Major infectious diseases: *degree of risk:* very high (2020)
food or waterborne diseases: bacterial diarrhea and hepatitis A
vectorborne diseases: dengue fever and malaria
water contact diseases: schistosomiasis
note: widespread ongoing transmission of a respiratory illness caused by the novel coronavirus (COVID-19) is occurring throughout Brazil; as of 18 August 2022, Brazil has reported a total of 34,201,280 cases of COVID-19 or 16,090.22 cumulative cases of COVID-19 per 100,000 population with a total of 681,763 cumulative deaths or a rate 320.74 cumulative deaths per 100,000 population; as of 17 August 2022, 86.79% of the population has received at least one dose of COVID-19 vaccine

Obesity - adult prevalence rate: 22.1% (2016)
country comparison to the world: 82

Alcohol consumption per capita: *total:* 6.12 liters of pure alcohol (2019 est.)
beer: 3.84 liters of pure alcohol (2019 est.)
wine: 0.24 liters of pure alcohol (2019 est.)
spirits: 2 liters of pure alcohol (2019 est.)
other alcohols: 0.04 liters of pure alcohol (2019 est.)
country comparison to the world: 68

Tobacco use: *total:* 12.8% (2020 est.)
male: 16.2% (2020 est.)
female: 9.4% (2020 est.)
country comparison to the world: 118

Education expenditures: 6.1% of GDP (2018 est.)
country comparison to the world: 31

Literacy: *definition:* age 15 and over can read and write
total population: 93.2%
male: 93%
female: 93.4% (2018)

School life expectancy (primary to tertiary education): *total:* 16 years
male: 15 years
female: 16 years (2019)

Unemployment, youth ages 15-24: *total:* 31.3%
male: 27.5%
female: 36.3% (2020 est.)

ENVIRONMENT

Environment - current issues: deforestation in Amazon Basin destroys the habitat and endangers a multitude of plant and animal species indigenous to the area; illegal wildlife trade; illegal poaching; air and water pollution in Rio de Janeiro, Sao Paulo, and several other large cities; land degradation and water pollution caused by improper mining activities; wetland degradation; severe oil spills

Environment - international agreements: *party to:* Antarctic-Environmental Protection, Antarctic-Marine Living Resources, Antarctic Seals, Antarctic Treaty, Biodiversity, Climate Change, Climate Change-Kyoto Protocol, Climate Change-Paris Agreement, Comprehensive Nuclear Test Ban, Desertification, Endangered Species, Environmental Modification, Hazardous Wastes, Law of the Sea, Marine Dumping-London Convention, Nuclear Test Ban, Ozone Layer Protection, Ship Pollution, Tropical Timber 2006, Wetlands, Whaling
signed, but not ratified: Marine Dumping-London Protocol

Air pollutants: *particulate matter emissions:* 11.49 micrograms per cubic meter (2016 est.)
carbon dioxide emissions: 462.3 megatons (2016 est.)
methane emissions: 401.83 megatons (2020 est.)

Climate: mostly tropical, but temperate in south

Land use: *agricultural land:* 32.9% (2018 est.)
arable land: 8.6% (2018 est.)
permanent crops: 0.8% (2018 est.)
permanent pasture: 23.5% (2018 est.)
forest: 61.9% (2018 est.)
other: 5.2% (2018 est.)

Urbanization: *urban population:* 87.6% of total population (2022)
rate of urbanization: 0.87% annual rate of change (2020-25 est.)

Revenue from forest resources: *forest revenues:* 0.62% of GDP (2018 est.)
country comparison to the world: 61

Revenue from coal: *coal revenues:* 0.01% of GDP (2018 est.)
country comparison to the world: 46

Waste and recycling: *municipal solid waste generated annually:* 79,889,010 tons (2015 est.)
municipal solid waste recycled annually: 1,118,446 tons (2014 est.)

percent of municipal solid waste recycled: 1.4% (2014 est.)

Major lakes (area sq km): *fresh water lake(s):* Lagoa dos Patos - 10,140 sq km
salt water lake(s): Lagoa Mirim (shared with Uruguay) - 2,970 sq km

Major rivers (by length in km): Amazon river mouth (shared with Peru [s]) - 6,400 km; Rio de la Plata/Parana river source (shared with Paraguay, Argentina, and Uruguay [m]) - 4,880 km; Tocantins - 3,650 km; Sao Francisco - 3,180 km; Paraguay river source (shared with Argentina and Paraguay [m]) - 2,549 km; Rio Negro river mouth (shared with Colombia [s] and Venezuela) - 2,250 km; Uruguay river source (shared with Argentina and Uruguay [m]) - 1,610 km
note – [s] after country name indicates river source; [m] after country name indicates river mouth

Major watersheds (area sq km): Atlantic Ocean drainage: Amazon (6,145,186 sq km), Orinoco (953,675 sq km), Paraná (2,582,704 sq km), São Francisco (617,814 sq km), Tocantins (764,213 sq km)

Major aquifers: Amazon Basin, Guarani Aquifer System, Maranhao Basin

Total water withdrawal: *municipal:* 16.74 billion cubic meters (2017 est.)
industrial: 9.511 billion cubic meters (2017 est.)
agricultural: 39.43 billion cubic meters (2017 est.)

Total renewable water resources: 8.647 trillion cubic meters (2017 est.)

GOVERNMENT

Country name: *conventional long form:* Federative Republic of Brazil
conventional short form: Brazil
local long form: Republica Federativa do Brasil
local short form: Brasil
etymology: the country name derives from the brazilwood tree that used to grow plentifully along the coast of Brazil and that was used to produce a deep red dye

Government type: federal presidential republic

Capital: *name:* Brasilia
geographic coordinates: 15 47 S, 47 55 W
time difference: UTC-3 (2 hours ahead of Washington, DC, during Standard Time)
time zone note: Brazil has four time zones, including one for the Fernando de Noronha Islands
etymology: name bestowed on the new capital of Brazil upon its inauguration in 1960; previous Brazilian capitals had been Salvador from 1549 to 1763 and Rio de Janeiro from 1763 to 1960

Administrative divisions: 26 states (estados, singular - estado) and 1 federal district* (distrito federal); Acre, Alagoas, Amapa, Amazonas, Bahia, Ceara, Distrito Federal*, Espirito Santo, Goias, Maranhao, Mato Grosso, Mato Grosso do Sul, Minas Gerais, Para, Paraiba, Parana, Pernambuco, Piaui, Rio de Janeiro, Rio Grande do Norte, Rio Grande do Sul, Rondonia, Roraima, Santa Catarina, Sao Paulo, Sergipe, Tocantins

Independence: 7 September 1822 (from Portugal)

National holiday: Independence Day, 7 September (1822)

Constitution: *history:* several previous; latest ratified 5 October 1988
amendments: proposed by at least one third of either house of the National Congress, by the president of the republic, or by simple majority vote by more than half of the state legislative assemblies; passage requires at least three-fifths majority vote by both houses in each of two readings; constitutional provisions affecting the federal form of government, separation of powers, suffrage, or individual rights and guarantees cannot be amended; amended many times, last in 2021

Legal system: civil law; note - a new civil law code was enacted in 2002 replacing the 1916 code

International law organization participation: has not submitted an ICJ jurisdiction declaration; accepts ICCt jurisdiction

Citizenship: *citizenship by birth:* yes
citizenship by descent only: yes
dual citizenship recognized: yes
residency requirement for naturalization: 4 years

Suffrage: voluntary between 16 to 18 years of age, over 70, and if illiterate; compulsory between 18 to 70 years of age; note - military conscripts by law cannot vote

Executive branch: *chief of state:* President Jair BOLSONARO (since 1 January 2019); Vice President Antonio Hamilton Martins MOURAO (since 1 January 2019); note - the president is both chief of state and head of government
head of government: President Jair BOLSONARO (since 1 January 2019); Vice President Antonio Hamilton Martins MOURAO (since 1 January 2019)
cabinet: Cabinet appointed by the president
elections/appointments: president and vice president directly elected on the same ballot by absolute majority popular vote in 2 rounds if needed for a single 4-year term (eligible for an immediate second term, and additional terms after a one-term break); election last held on 2 October 2022 with runoff on 30 October 2022 (next to be held on 4 October 2026)
election results:
2022: Luiz Inacio LULA da Silva elected president in second round; percent of vote in first round - Luiz Inacio LULA da Silva (PT) 48.4%, Jair BOLSONARO (PSL) 43.2%, Simone TEBET (MDB) 4.2%, Ciro GOMES (PDT) 3%, other 1.2%; percent of vote in second round - Luiz Inacio LULA da Silva (PT) 50.9%, Jair BOLSONARO (PSL) 49.1%; note - LULA will take office 1 January 2023
2018: Jair BOLSONARO elected president in second round; percent of vote in first round - Jair BOLSONARO (PSL) 46%, Fernando HADDAD (PT) 29.3%, Ciro GOMEZ (PDT) 12.5%, Geraldo ALCKMIN (PSDB) 4.8%, other 7.4%; percent of vote in second round - Jair BOLSONARO (PSL) 55.1%, Fernando HADDAD (PT) 44.9%
2014: Dilma ROUSSEFF reelected president in second round; percent of vote in second round - Dilma ROUSSEFF (PT) 51.6%, Aecio NEVES (PSDB) 48.4%; note - on 12 May 2016, Brazil's Senate voted to hold an impeachment trial of President Dilma ROUSSEFF, who was then suspended from her executive duties; Vice President Michel TEMER took over as acting president; on 31 August 2016 the Senate voted 61-20 in favor of conviction and her removal from office; TEMER served as president for the remainder of ROUSSEFF's term, which ended 1 January 2019

Legislative branch: *description:* bicameral National Congress or Congresso Nacional consists of:
Federal Senate or Senado Federal (81 seats; 3 members each from 26 states and 3 from the federal district directly elected in multi-seat constituencies by simple majority vote to serve 8-year terms, with one-third and two-thirds of the membership elected alternately every 4 years)
Chamber of Deputies or Camara dos Deputados (513 seats; members directly elected in multi-seat constituencies by party-list proportional representation vote to serve 4-year terms)
elections:
Federal Senate - last held on 2 October 2022 for one-third of the Senate (next to be held on 4 October 2026 for two-thirds of the Senate)
Chamber of Deputies - last held on 2 October 2022 (next to be held on 4 October 2026)
election results:
Federal Senate - percent of vote by party - NA; seats by party - PL 8, Brazil Union 5, PT 4, Progressistas 3, PSD 2, Republican 2, MBD 1, PSB 1, PSC 1; note - complete Federal Senate compostion after 2022 election - PL 13, Brazil Union 12, MBD 10, PSD 10, PT 9, Progressistas 7, Podemos 6, PSDB 4, Republicans 3, PDT 2, Cidadania 1, PSB 1, PSC 1, PROS 1, REDE 1
Chamber of Deputies - percent of vote by party - NA; seats by party - PL 99, PT 67, Brazil Union 59, PP 47, MDB 42, PSD 42, Republicans 41, PDT 17, PSB 14, PSDB 13, Podemos 12, PSOL 12, Avante 7, PCdoB 6, PSC 6, PV 6, Cidadania 5, Patriota 4, PROS 4, SD 4, NOVO 3, REDE 2, PTB 1

Judicial branch: *highest court(s):* Supreme Federal Court or Supremo Tribunal Federal (consists of 11 justices)
judge selection and term of office: justices appointed by the president and approved by the Federal Senate; justices appointed to serve until mandatory retirement at age 75
subordinate courts: Tribunal of the Union, Federal Appeals Court, Superior Court of Justice, Superior Electoral Court, regional federal courts; state court system

Political parties and leaders: Act (Agir) [Daniel TOURINHO] (formerly Christian Labor Party or PTC)
Avante [Luis Henrique de Oliveira RESENDE] (formerly Labor Party of Brazil or PTdoB)
Brazil Union (Uniao Brasil); note - founded from a merger between the Democrats (DEM) and the Social Liberal Party (PSL)
Brazilian Communist Party or PCB [Astrogildo PEREIRA]
Brazilian Democratic Movement or MDB [Luiz Felipe Baleia TENUTO Rossi]
Brazilian Labor Party or PTB [Kassyo Santos RAMOS]
Brazilian Renewal Labor Party or PRTB [Aiceia RODRIGUES and Hamilton MOURAO]
Brazilian Labor Party or PTB
Brazilian Social Democracy Party or PSDB [Bruno ARAUJO]
Brazilian Socialist Party or PSB [Carlos Roberto SIQUEIRA de Barros]
Christian Democracy or DC [Jose Maria EYMAEL] (formerly Christian Social
Cidadania [Roberto Joao Pereira FREIRE] (formerly Popular Socialist Party or PPS)
Communist Party of Brazil or PCdoB [Luciana SANTOS]
Democratic Labor Party or PDT [Carlos LUPI]
Democratic Party or PSDC
Democrats or DEM [Jose AGRIPINO] (formerly Liberal Front Party or PFL); note - dissolved in February 2022
Green Party or PV [Jose Luiz PENNA]

Liberal Party or PL [Luciano BIVAR and Antonio de RUEDA] (formerly Party of the Republic or PR)
National Mobilization Party or PMN [Antonio Carlos Bosco MASSAROLLO]
New Party or NOVO [Eduardo RIBEIRO]
Patriota [Adilson BAROSSO Oliveira] (formerly National Ecologic Party or PEN)
Podemos [Renata ABREU] (formerly National Labor Party or PTN)
Progressive Party (Progressistas) or PP [Ciro NOGUEIRA]
Republican Social Order Party or PROS [Euripedes JUNIOR]
Republicans (Republicanos) [Marcos Antonio PEREIRA] (formerly Brazilian Republican Party or PRB)
Social Christian Party or PSC [Everaldo Dias PEREIRA]
Social Democratic Party or PSD [Alfredo COATIT Neto]
Social Liberal Party or PSL [Luciano Caldas BIVAR]
Socialism and Freedom Party or PSOL [Juliano MEDEIROS]
Solidarity or SD [Paulinho DA FORCA]
Sustainability Network or REDE [Marina SILVA]
United Socialist Workers' Party or PSTU [Jose Maria DE ALMEIDA]
Workers' Cause Party or PCO [Rui Costa PIMENTA]
Workers' Party or PT [Gleisi HOFFMANN]

International organization participation: AfDB (nonregional member), BIS, BRICS, CAN (associate), CD, CELAC, CPLP, FAO, FATF, G-15, G-20, G-24, G-5, G-77, IADB, IAEA, IBRD, ICAO, ICC (national committees), ICCt, ICRM, IDA, IFAD, IFC, IFRCS, IHO, ILO, IMF, IMO, IMSO, Interpol, IOC, IOM, IPU, ISO, ITSO, ITU, ITUC (NGOs), LAES, LAIA, LAS (observer), Mercosur, MIGA, MINURSO, MINUSTAH, MONUSCO, NAM (observer), NSG, OAS, OECD (enhanced engagement), OPANAL, OPCW, Paris Club (associate), PCA, PROSUR, SICA (observer), UN, UNASUR, UNCTAD, UNESCO, UNFICYP, UNHCR, UNHRC, UNIDO, UNISFA, UNIFIL, Union Latina, UNISFA, UNITAR, UNMIL, UNMISS, UNOCI, UNRWA, UNWTO, UPU, WCO, WFTU (NGOs), WHO, WIPO, WMO, WTO

Diplomatic representation in the US: *chief of mission:* Ambassador Nestor Jose FORSTER, Jr. (since 23 December 2020)
chancery: 3006 Massachusetts Avenue NW, Washington, DC 20008
telephone: [1] (202) 238-2700
FAX: [1] (202) 238-2827
email address and website:
http://washington.itamaraty.gov.br/en-us/Main.xml
consulate(s) general: Atlanta, Boston, Chicago, Hartford (CT), Houston, Los Angeles, Miami, New York, San Francisco, Washington, DC

Diplomatic representation from the US: *chief of mission:* Ambassador (vacant); Charge d'Affaires Douglas A. KONEFF (since July 2021)
embassy: SES - Avenida das Nacoes, Quadra 801, Lote 3, 70403-900 - Brasilia, DF
mailing address: 7500 Brasilia Place, Washington DC 20521-7500
telephone: [55] (61) 3312-7000
FAX: [55] (61) 3225-9136
email address and website:
BrasilliaACS@state.gov
https://br.usembassy.gov/
consulate(s) general: Recife, Porto Alegre, Rio de Janeiro, Sao Paulo
branch office(s): Belo Horizonte

Flag description: green with a large yellow diamond in the center bearing a blue celestial globe with 27 white five-pointed stars; the globe has a white equatorial band with the motto ORDEM E PROGRESSO (Order and Progress); the current flag was inspired by the banner of the former Empire of Brazil (1822-1889); on the imperial flag, the green represented the House of Braganza of Pedro I, the first Emperor of Brazil, while the yellow stood for the Habsburg Family of his wife; on the modern flag the green represents the forests of the country and the yellow rhombus its mineral wealth (the diamond shape roughly mirrors that of the country); the blue circle and stars, which replaced the coat of arms of the original flag, depict the sky over Rio de Janeiro on the morning of 15 November 1889 - the day the Republic of Brazil was declared; the number of stars has changed with the creation of new states and has risen from an original 21 to the current 27 (one for each state and the Federal District)
note: one of several flags where a prominent component of the design reflects the shape of the country; other such flags are those of Bosnia and Herzegovina, Eritrea, and Vanuatu

National symbol(s): Southern Cross constellation; national colors: green, yellow, blue

National anthem: *name:* "Hino Nacional Brasileiro" (Brazilian National Anthem)
lyrics/music: Joaquim Osorio Duque ESTRADA/ Francisco Manoel DA SILVA
note: music adopted 1890, lyrics adopted 1922; the anthem's music, composed in 1822, was used unofficially for many years before it was adopted

National heritage: *total World Heritage Sites:* 23 (15 cultural, 7 natural, 1 mixed)
selected World Heritage Site locales: Brasilia (c); Historic Salvador de Bahia (c); Historic Ouro Preto (c); Historic Olinda (c); Iguaçu National Park (n); Jesuit Missions of the Guaranis (c); Rio de Janeiro: Carioca Landscapes (c); Central Amazon Conservation Complex (n); Atlantic Forest South-East Reserves (n); Paraty and Ilha Grande – Culture and Biodiversity (m)

ECONOMY

Economic overview: Brazil is the eighth-largest economy in the world, but is recovering from a recession in 2015 and 2016 that ranks as the worst in the country's history. In 2017, Brazil`s GDP grew 1%, inflation fell to historic lows of 2.9%, and the Central Bank lowered benchmark interest rates from 13.75% in 2016 to 7%.

The economy has been negatively affected by multiple corruption scandals involving private companies and government officials, including the impeachment and conviction of Former President Dilma ROUSSEFF in August 2016. Sanctions against the firms involved — some of the largest in Brazil — have limited their business opportunities, producing a ripple effect on associated businesses and contractors but creating opportunities for foreign companies to step into what had been a closed market.

The succeeding TEMER administration has implemented a series of fiscal and structural reforms to restore credibility to government finances. Congress approved legislation in December 2016 to cap public spending. Government spending growth had pushed public debt to 73.7% of GDP at the end of 2017, up from over 50% in 2012. The government also boosted infrastructure projects, such as oil and natural gas auctions, in part to raise revenues. Other economic reforms, proposed in 2016, aim to reduce barriers to foreign investment, and to improve labor conditions. Policies to strengthen Brazil's workforce and industrial sector, such as local content requirements, have boosted employment, but at the expense of investment.

Brazil is a member of the Common Market of the South (Mercosur), a trade bloc that includes Argentina, Paraguay and Uruguay - Venezuela's membership in the organization was suspended In August 2017. After the Asian and Russian financial crises, Mercosur adopted a protectionist stance to guard against exposure to volatile foreign markets and it currently is negotiating Free Trade Agreements with the European Union and Canada.

Real GDP (purchasing power parity): $2,989,430,000,000 (2020 est.)
$3,115,910,000,000 (2019 est.)
$3,072,550,000,000 (2018 est.)
note: data are in 2017 dollars
country comparison to the world: 8

Real GDP growth rate: 1.13% (2019 est.)
1.2% (2018 est.)
1.62% (2017 est.)
country comparison to the world: 168

Real GDP per capita: $14,100 (2020 est.)
$14,800 (2019 est.)
$14,700 (2018 est.)
note: data are in 2017 dollars
country comparison to the world: 110

GDP (official exchange rate): $1,877,942,000,000 (2019 est.)

Inflation rate (consumer prices): 3.7% (2019 est.)
3.6% (2018 est.)
3.4% (2017 est.)
country comparison to the world: 157

Credit ratings:

Fitch rating: *BB- (2018)*

Moody's rating: Ba2 (2016)

Standard & Poors rating: BB- (2018)
note: The year refers to the year in which the current credit rating was first obtained.

GDP - composition, by sector of origin: *agriculture:* 6.6% (2017 est.)
industry: 20.7% (2017 est.)
services: 72.7% (2017 est.)

GDP - composition, by end use: *household consumption:* 63.4% (2017 est.)
government consumption: 20% (2017 est.)
investment in fixed capital: 15.6% (2017 est.)
investment in inventories: -0.1% (2017 est.)
exports of goods and services: 12.6% (2017 est.)
imports of goods and services: -11.6% (2017 est.)

Agricultural products: sugar cane, soybeans, maize, milk, cassava, oranges, poultry, rice, beef, cotton

Industries: textiles, shoes, chemicals, cement, lumber, iron ore, tin, steel, aircraft, motor vehicles and parts, other machinery and equipment

Industrial production growth rate: 0% (2017 est.)
country comparison to the world: 169

Labor force: 86.621 million (2020 est.)
country comparison to the world: 5

Labor force - by occupation: *agriculture:* 9.4%
industry: 32.1%

services: 58.5% (2017 est.)

Unemployment rate: 11.93% (2019 est.)
12.26% (2018 est.)
country comparison to the world: 164

Unemployment, youth ages 15-24: *total:* 31.3%
male: 27.5%
female: 36.3% (2020 est.)
country comparison to the world: 32

Population below poverty line: 4.2% (2016 est.)
note: approximately 4% of the population are below the "extreme" poverty line

Gini Index coefficient - distribution of family income: 53.9 (2018 est.)
54 (2004)
country comparison to the world: 7

Household income or consumption by percentage share: *lowest 10%:* 0.8%
highest 10%: 43.4% (2016 est.)

Budget: *revenues:* 733.7 billion (2017 est.)
expenditures: 756.3 billion (2017 est.)

Budget surplus (+) or deficit (-): -1.1% (of GDP) (2017 est.)
country comparison to the world: 82

Public debt: 84% of GDP (2017 est.)
78.4% of GDP (2016 est.)
country comparison to the world: 32

Taxes and other revenues: 35.7% (of GDP) (2017 est.)
country comparison to the world: 57

Fiscal year: calendar year

Current account balance: -$50.927 billion (2019 est.)
-$41.54 billion (2018 est.)
country comparison to the world: 203

Exports: $239.18 billion (2020 est.)
$260.07 billion (2019 est.)
$274.9 billion (2018 est.)
note: Data are in current year dollars and do not include illicit exports or re-exports.
country comparison to the world: 27

Exports - partners: China 28%, United States 13% (2019)

Exports - commodities: soybeans, crude petroleum, iron, corn, wood pulp products (2019)

Imports: $227.44 billion (2020 est.) note: data are in current year dollars
$269.02 billion (2019 est.) note: data are in current year dollars
$267.52 billion (2018 est.) note: data are in current year dollars
country comparison to the world: 27

Imports - partners: China 21%, United States 18%, Germany 6%, Argentina 6% (2019)

Imports - commodities: refined petroleum, vehicle parts, crude petroleum, integrated circuits, pesticides (2019)

Reserves of foreign exchange and gold: $374 billion (31 December 2017 est.)
$367.5 billion (31 December 2016 est.)
country comparison to the world: 10

Debt - external: $681.336 billion (2019 est.)
$660.693 billion (2018 est.)
country comparison to the world: 20

Exchange rates: reals (BRL) per US dollar -
5.12745 (2020 est.)
4.14915 (2019 est.)
3.862 (2018 est.)
3.3315 (2014 est.)
2.3535 (2013 est.)

ENERGY

Electricity access: *electrification - total population:* 100% (2020)

Electricity: *installed generating capacity:* 195.037 million kW (2020 est.)
consumption: 540,997,340,000 kWh (2020 est.)
exports: 395 million kWh (2020 est.)
imports: 25.113 billion kWh (2020 est.)
transmission/distribution losses: 105.727 billion kWh (2020 est.)

Electricity generation sources: *fossil fuels:* 11.8% of total installed capacity (2020 est.)
nuclear: 2.3% of total installed capacity (2020 est.)
solar: 1.7% of total installed capacity (2020 est.)
wind: 9.2% of total installed capacity (2020 est.)
hydroelectricity: 65.8% of total installed capacity (2020 est.)
biomass and waste: 9.2% of total installed capacity (2020 est.)

Coal: *production:* 13.993 million metric tons (2020 est.)
consumption: 31.841 million metric tons (2020 est.)
exports: 16,000 metric tons (2020 est.)
imports: 19.217 million metric tons (2020 est.)
proven reserves: 6.596 billion metric tons (2019 est.)

Petroleum: *total petroleum production:* 3,629,100 bbl/day (2021 est.)
refined petroleum consumption: 3,142,300 bbl/day (2019 est.)
crude oil and lease condensate exports: 1,123,300 bbl/day (2018 est.)
crude oil and lease condensate imports: 186,200 bbl/day (2018 est.)
crude oil estimated reserves: 12,714,600,000 barrels (2021 est.)

Refined petroleum products - production: 2.811 million bbl/day (2015 est.)
country comparison to the world: 7

Refined petroleum products - exports: 279,000 bbl/day (2015 est.)
country comparison to the world: 28

Refined petroleum products - imports: 490,400 bbl/day (2015 est.)
country comparison to the world: 17

Natural gas: *production:* 25,395,979,000 cubic meters (2019 est.)
consumption: 35,253,198,000 cubic meters (2019 est.)
exports: 0 cubic meters (2021 est.)
imports: 9,724,017,000 cubic meters (2019 est.)
proven reserves: 363.984 billion cubic meters (2021 est.)

Carbon dioxide emissions: 456.67 million metric tonnes of CO_2 (2019 est.)
from coal and metallurgical coke: 63.53 million metric tonnes of CO_2 (2019 est.)
from petroleum and other liquids: 328.824 million metric tonnes of CO_2 (2019 est.)
from consumed natural gas: 64.316 million metric tonnes of CO_2 (2019 est.)
country comparison to the world: 14

Energy consumption per capita: 59.444 million Btu/person (2019 est.)
country comparison to the world: 93

COMMUNICATIONS

Telephones - fixed lines: *total subscriptions:* 30,653,813 (2020 est.)
subscriptions per 100 inhabitants: 14 (2020 est.)
country comparison to the world: 7

Telephones - mobile cellular: *total subscriptions:* 205,834,781 (2020 est.)
subscriptions per 100 inhabitants: 97 (2020 est.)
country comparison to the world: 6

Telecommunication systems: *general assessment:* Brazil is one of the largest mobile and broadband markets in Latin America with healthy competition and pricing; the development of 5G, was scheduled for March 2020 but was delayed due to interference issues with satellite TV broadcasts and the pandemic; the auction was completed November 2021; the licenses are obliged to provide 5G services to all capital cities by July 2022, as well as about 35,500km of the national highway network; the country also has one of the largest fixed line broadband markets in Latin America, though broadband subscriptions is only slightly above the regional average, trailing behind Chile, Argentina, and Uruguay; amendments to the licensing regime adopted in October 2019 also require that ISPs which have switched to authorizations invest money saved from lighter regulations in the expansion of broadband services; the fixed line broadband market has seen rapid growth for a number of years, with a growing focus on fiber broadband; in 2019 the number of fiber accesses overtook DSL connections; the country is a key landing point for a number of important submarine cables connecting to the US, Central and South America, the Caribbean, Europe, and Africa; several new cable systems are due to come into service through to 2022, which will increase bandwidth and push down broadband prices for end-users; investments have also been made into terrestrial fiber cables between Brazil, Argentina, and Chile (2021)
domestic: fixed-line connections stand at roughly 14 per 100 persons; less-expensive mobile-cellular technology has been a major impetus broadening telephone service to the lower-income segments of the population with mobile-cellular teledensity roughly 97 per 100 persons (2020)
international: country code - 55; landing points for a number of submarine cables, including Malbec, ARBR, Tamnat, SAC, SAm-1, Atlantis -2, Seabras-1, Monet, EllaLink, BRUSA, GlobeNet, AMX-1, Brazilian Festoon, Bicentenario, Unisur, Junior, Americas -II, SAE x1, SAIL, SACS and SABR that provide direct connectivity to South and Central America, the Caribbean, the US, Africa, and Europe; satellite earth stations - 3 Intelsat (Atlantic Ocean), 1 Inmarsat (Atlantic Ocean region east), connected by microwave relay system to Mercosur Brazilsat B3 satellite earth station; satellites is a major communication platform, as it is almost impossible to lay fiber optic cable in the thick vegetation (2019)

Broadcast media: state-run Radiobras operates a radio and a TV network; more than 1,000 radio stations and more than 100 TV channels operating - mostly privately owned; private media ownership highly concentrated (2022)

Internet country code: .br

Internet users: *total:* 172,173,121 (2020 est.)
percent of population: 81% (2020 est.)
country comparison to the world: 4

Broadband - fixed subscriptions: *total:* 36,344,670 (2020 est.)
subscriptions per 100 inhabitants: 17 (2020 est.)
country comparison to the world: 4

TRANSPORTATION

National air transport system: *number of registered air carriers:* 9 (2020)
inventory of registered aircraft operated by air carriers: 443
annual passenger traffic on registered air carriers: 102,109,977 (2018)
annual freight traffic on registered air carriers: 1,845,650,000 (2018) mt-km

Civil aircraft registration country code prefix: PP

Airports: *total:* 4,093 (2021)
country comparison to the world: 2

Airports - with paved runways: *total:* 698
over 3,047 m: 7
2,438 to 3,047 m: 27
1,524 to 2,437 m: 179
914 to 1,523 m: 436 (2017)
under 914 m: 49 (2021)

Airports - with unpaved runways: *total:* 3,395
1,524 to 2,437 m: 92
914 to 1,523 m: 1,619
under 914 m: 1,684 (2021)

Heliports: 13 (2021)

Pipelines: 5,959 km refined petroleum product (1,165 km distribution, 4,794 km transport), 11,696 km natural gas (2,274 km distribution, 9,422 km transport), 1,985 km crude oil (distribution), 77 km ethanol/petrochemical (37 km distribution, 40 km transport) (2016)

Railways: *total:* 29,849.9 km (2014)
standard gauge: 194 km (2014) 1.435-m gauge
narrow gauge: 23,341.6 km (2014) 1.000-m gauge (24 km electrified)
broad gauge: 5,822.3 km (2014) 1.600-m gauge (498.3 km electrified)
dual gauge: 492 km (2014) 1.600-1.000-m gauge
country comparison to the world: 9

Roadways: *total:* 2 million km (2018)
paved: 246,000 km (2018)
unpaved: 1.754 million km (2018)
country comparison to the world: 4

Waterways: 50,000 km (2012) (most in areas remote from industry and population)
country comparison to the world: 2

Merchant marine: *total:* 864
by type: bulk carrier 11, container ship 19, general cargo 42, oil tanker 31, other 761 (2021)
country comparison to the world: 27

Ports and terminals: *major seaport(s):* Belem, Itajai, Paranagua, Rio Grande, Rio de Janeiro, Santos, Sao Sebastiao, Tubarao
oil terminal(s): DTSE/Gegua oil terminal, Ilha Grande (Gebig), Guaiba Island terminal, Guamare oil terminal
container port(s) (TEUs): Itajai (1,223,262), Paranagua (865,110), Santos (4,165,248) (2019)
LNG terminal(s) (import): Pecem, Rio de Janiero
river port(s): Manaus (Amazon)
dry bulk cargo port(s): Sepetiba ore terminal, Tubarao

MILITARY AND SECURITY

Military and security forces: Brazilian Armed Forces (Forças Armadas Brasileiras): Brazilian Army (Exercito Brasileiro, EB), Brazilian Navy (Marinha do Brasil, MB, includes Naval Aviation (Aviacao Naval Brasileira) and Marine Corps (Corpo de Fuzileiros Navais)), Brazilian Air Force (Forca Aerea Brasileira, FAB) (2022)

Military expenditures: 1.3% of GDP (2021 est.)
1.4% of GDP (2020)
1.4% of GDP (2019) (approximately $35.6 billion)
1.5% of GDP (2018) (approximately $36 billion)
1.4% of GDP (2017) (approximately $34.4 billion)
country comparison to the world: 102

Military and security service personnel strengths: approximately 360,000 active military personnel (220,000 Army; 70,000 Navy; 70,000 Air Force) (2022)

Military equipment inventories and acquisitions: the Brazilian military's inventory consists of a mix of domestically-produced and imported weapons, largely from Europe and the US; since 2010, the US and several European countries are the leading suppliers of military equipment to Brazil; Brazil's defense industry is capable of designing and manufacturing equipment for all three military services and for export; it also jointly produces equipment with other countries (2022)

Military service age and obligation: 18-45 years of age for compulsory military service for men (women exempted); only 5-10% of those inducted are required to serve; conscript service obligation is 10-12 months; 17-45 years of age for voluntary service (2022)
note: in 2020, women comprised approximately 9% of the Brazilian military

Military - note: the origins of Brazil's military stretch back to the 1640s
the three national police forces – the Federal Police, Federal Highway Police, and Federal Railway Police – have domestic security responsibilities and report to the Ministry of Justice and Public Security (Ministry of Justice); there are two distinct units within the state police forces: the civil police, which performs an investigative role, and the military police, charged with maintaining law and order in the states and the Federal District; despite the name, military police forces report to the Ministry of Justice, not the Ministry of Defense; the National Public Security Force (Forca Nacional de Seguranca Publica or SENASP) is a national police force made up of Military Police from various states; the armed forces also have some domestic security responsibilities and report to the Ministry of Defense

Brazil has Major Non-NATO Ally (MNNA) status with the US; MNNA is a designation under US law that provides foreign partners with certain benefits in the areas of defense trade and security cooperation; while MNNA status provides military and economic privileges, it does not entail any security commitments (2022)

Maritime threats: the International Maritime Bureau reports the territorial waters of Brazil are a risk for armed robbery against ships; in 2021, three attacks against commercial vessels were reported, a decrease from the seven attacks in 2020; all of these occurred in the port of Macapa while ships were berthed or at anchor

TERRORISM

Terrorist group(s): Hizballah (2022)

TRANSNATIONAL ISSUES

Disputes - international: *Brazil-Bolivia:* The Roboré Accord of March 29, 1958 placed the long-disputed Isla Suárez/Ilha de Guajará-Mirim, a fluvial island on the Río Mamoré, between the two towns of Guajará-Mirim (Brazil) and Guayaramerin (Bolivia), under Bolivian administration but did not resolve the sovereignty dispute
Brazil-Colombia: Contraband smuggling (narcotics and arms), illegal migration, trafficking in animals, plants, lumber, illegal exploitation of mineral resources, Colombian (FARC) insurgent incursions in the area remain problematic issues.
Brazil-Uruguay: The uncontested boundary dispute between Brazil and Uruguay over over Arroyo de la Invernada triangle and sovereignty over Isla Brasilera leaves the tripoint with Argentina in question. Smuggling of firearms and narcotics continues to be an issue along the Uruguay-Brazil border.
Brazil-Venezuela: Colombian-organized illegal narcotics and paramilitary activities penetrate Brazil's border region with Venezuela.

Refugees and internally displaced persons: *refugees (country of origin):* 261,441 (Venezuela) (economic and political crisis; includes Venezuelans who have claimed asylum, are recognized as refugees, or received alternative legal stay) (2020)
IDPs: 21,000
stateless persons: 14 (mid-year 2021)

Illicit drugs: a significant transit and destination country for cocaine; most of the cocaine enters Brazil from neighboring producing countries Bolivia, Colombia, and Peru then goes to West Africa and Europe, but an increasing percentage feeds substantial domestic drug consumption; second-largest consumer of cocaine hydrochloride and cocaine-derivative products in the world

BRITISH INDIAN OCEAN TERRITORY

INTRODUCTION

Background: Formerly administered as part of the British Crown Colony of Mauritius, the British Indian Ocean Territory (BIOT) was established as an overseas territory of the UK in 1965. A number of the islands of the territory were later transferred to the Seychelles when it attained independence in 1976. Subsequently, BIOT has consisted only of the six main island groups comprising the Chagos Archipelago. Only Diego Garcia, the largest and most southerly of the islands, is inhabited. It contains a joint UK-US naval support facility and hosts one of four dedicated ground antennas that assist in the operation of the Global Positioning

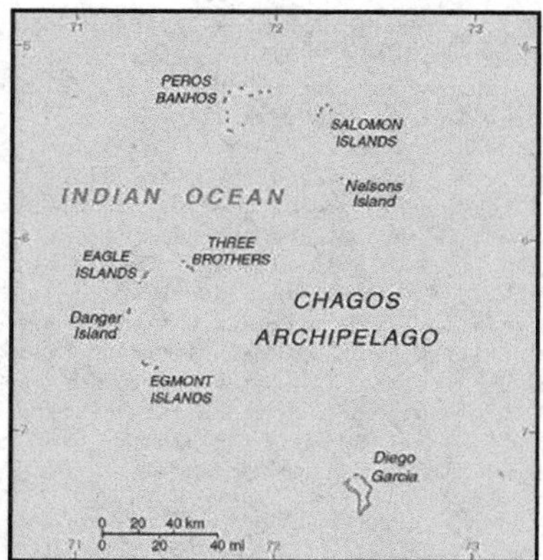

System (GPS) navigation system (the others are on Kwajalein (Marshall Islands), at Cape Canaveral, Florida (US), and on Ascension Island (Saint Helena, Ascension, and Tristan da Cunha)). The US Air Force also operates a telescope array on Diego Garcia as part of the Ground-Based Electro-Optical Deep Space Surveillance System (GEODSS) for tracking orbital debris, which can be a hazard to spacecraft and astronauts.

Between 1967 and 1973, former agricultural workers, earlier residents in the islands, were relocated primarily to Mauritius, but also to the Seychelles. Negotiations between 1971 and 1982 resulted in the establishment of a trust fund by the British Government as compensation for the displaced islanders, known as Chagossians. Beginning in 1998, the islanders pursued a series of lawsuits against the British Government seeking further compensation and the right to return to the territory. In 2006 and 2007, British court rulings invalidated the immigration policies contained in the 2004 BIOT Constitution Order that had excluded the islanders from the archipelago, but upheld the special military status of Diego Garcia. In 2008, the House of Lords, as the final court of appeal in the UK, ruled in favor of the British Government by overturning the lower court rulings and finding no right of return for the Chagossians. In March 2015, the Permanent Court of Arbitration unanimously held that the marine protected area that the UK declared around the Chagos Archipelago in April 2010 was in violation of the UN Convention on the Law of the Sea.

In February 2019, the International Court of Justice ruled in an advisory opinion that Britain's decolonization of Mauritius was not completed lawfully because of continued Chagossian claims. A non-binding May 2019 UN General Assembly vote demanded that Britain end its "colonial administration" of the Chagos Archipelago and that it be returned to Mauritius. UK officials defend Britain's sovereignty over the islands and argue that the issue is a bilateral dispute between Mauritius and the UK that does not warrant international intervention.

GEOGRAPHY

Location: archipelago in the Indian Ocean, south of India, about halfway between Africa and Indonesia

Geographic coordinates: 6 00 S, 71 30 E;note - Diego Garcia 7 20 S, 72 25 E

Map references: Political Map of the World

Area: *total:* 60 sq km
land: 60 sq km (44 Diego Garcia)
water: 54,340 sq km
note: includes the entire Chagos Archipelago of 55 islands

Area - comparative: land area is about one-third the size of Washington, DC

Land boundaries: *total:* 0 km

Coastline: 698 km

Maritime claims: *territorial sea:* 12 nm

Environment (Protection and Preservation) Zone: 200 nm

Climate: tropical marine; hot, humid, moderated by trade winds

Terrain: flat and low coral atolls (most areas do not exceed two m in elevation); sits atop the submarine volcanic Chagos- Laccadive Ridge

Elevation: *highest point:* ocean-side dunes on Diego Garcia 9 m
lowest point: Indian Ocean 0 m

Natural resources: coconuts, fish, sugarcane

Land use: *agricultural land:* 0% (2018 est.)
arable land: 0% (2018 est.)
permanent crops: 0% (2018 est.)
permanent pasture: 0% (2018 est.)
forest: 0% (2018 est.)
other: 100% (2018 est.)

Natural hazards: none; located outside routes of Indian Ocean cyclones

Geography - note: *note 1:* archipelago of 55 islands; Diego Garcia, the largest and southernmost island, occupies a strategic location in the central Indian Ocean; the island is the site of a joint US-UK military facility
note 2: Diego Garcia is the only inhabited island of the BIOT and one of only two British territories where traffic drives on the right, the other being Gibraltar

PEOPLE AND SOCIETY

Population: no indigenous inhabitants
note: approximately 1,200 former agricultural workers resident in the Chagos Archipelago, often referred to as Chagossians or Ilois, were relocated to Mauritius and the Seychelles in the 1960s and 1970s; approximately 3,000 UK and US military personnel and civilian contractors living on the island of Diego Garcia (2018)

ENVIRONMENT

Environment - current issues: wastewater discharge into the lagoon on Diego Garcia

Climate: tropical marine; hot, humid, moderated by trade winds

Land use: *agricultural land:* 0% (2018 est.)
arable land: 0% (2018 est.)
permanent crops: 0% (2018 est.)
permanent pasture: 0% (2018 est.)
forest: 0% (2018 est.)
other: 100% (2018 est.)

GOVERNMENT

Country name: *conventional long form:* British Indian Ocean Territory
conventional short form: none
abbreviation: BIOT
etymology: self-descriptive name specifying the territory's affiliation and location

Dependency status: overseas territory of the UK; administered by a commissioner, resident in the Foreign, Commonwealth, and Development Office in London

Legal system: the laws of the UK apply where applicable

Executive branch: *chief of state:* King CHARLES III (since 8 September 2022)
head of government: Commissioner Paul CANDLER (since 8 July 2021); Administrator Kit PYMAN; note - both reside in the UK and are represented by Commander Steven R. DRYSDALE, RN, commanding British Forces on Diego Garcia (since 19 February 2021)
cabinet: NA
elections/appointments: the monarchy is hereditary; commissioner and administrator appointed by the monarch

International organization participation: UPU

Diplomatic representation in the US: none (overseas territory of the UK)

Diplomatic representation from the US: *embassy:* none (overseas territory of the UK)

Flag description: white with six blue wavy horizontal stripes; the flag of the UK is in the upper hoist-side quadrant; the striped section bears a palm tree and yellow crown (the symbols of the territory) centered on the outer half of the flag; the wavy stripes represent the Indian Ocean; although not officially described, the six blue stripes may stand for the six main atolls of the archipelago

National anthem: *note:* as an overseas territory of the United Kingdom, "God Save the King" is official (see United Kingdom)

ECONOMY

Economic overview: All economic activity is concentrated on the largest island of Diego Garcia, where a joint UK-US military facility is located. Construction projects and various services needed to support the military installation are performed by military and contract employees from the UK, Mauritius, the Philippines, and the US. Some of the natural resources found in this territory include coconuts, fish, and sugarcane.

Exchange rates: the US dollar is used

COMMUNICATIONS

Telecommunication systems: *general assessment:* separate facilities for military and public needs are available (2018)
domestic: all commercial telephone services are available, including connection to the Internet (2018)
international: country code (Diego Garcia) - 246; landing point for the SAFE submarine cable that provides direct connectivity to Africa, Asia and near-by Indian Ocean island countries; international telephone service is carried by satellite (2019)

Broadcast media: Armed Forces Radio and Television Service (AFRTS) broadcasts over 3 separate frequencies for US and UK military personnel stationed on the islands

Internet country code: .io

Communications - note: Diego Garcia hosts one of four dedicated ground antennas that assist in the operation of the Global Positioning System (GPS) navigation system (the others are on Kwajalein (Marshall Islands), at Cape Canaveral, Florida (US), and on Ascension Island (Saint Helena, Ascension, and Tristan da Cunha))

TRANSPORTATION

Airports: *total:* 1 (2021)

Airports - with paved runways: *total:* 1
over 3,047 m: 1 (2021)

Roadways: *note:* short section of paved road between port and airfield on Diego Garcia

Ports and terminals: *major seaport(s):* Diego Garcia

MILITARY AND SECURITY

Military and security forces: no regular military forces

Military - note: defense is the responsibility of the UK; in November 2016, the UK extended the US lease on Diego Garcia until December 2036

TRANSNATIONAL ISSUES

Disputes - international: Mauritius and Seychelles claim the Chagos Islands; negotiations between 1971 and 1982 resulted in the establishment of a trust fund by the British Government as compensation for the displaced islanders, known as Chagossians, who were evicted between 1967-73; in 2001, the former inhabitants of the archipelago were granted UK citizenship and the right of return; in 2006 and 2007, British court rulings invalidated the immigration policies contained in the 2004 BIOT Constitution Order that had excluded the islanders from the archipelago; in 2008, a House of Lords' decision overturned lower court rulings, once again denying the right of return to Chagossians; in addition, the UK created the world's largest marine protection area around the Chagos islands prohibiting the extraction of any natural resources therein

BRITISH VIRGIN ISLANDS

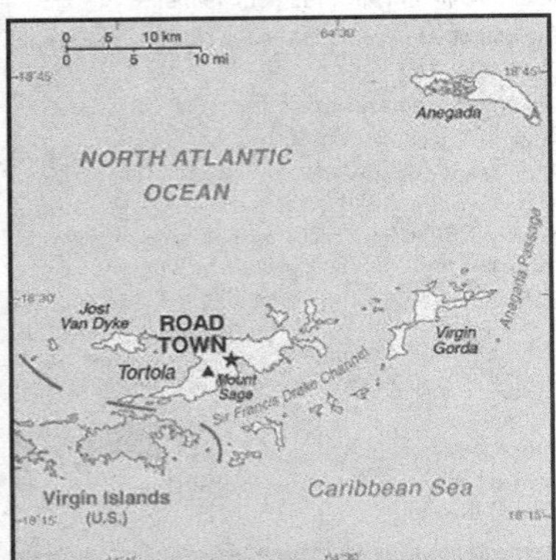

INTRODUCTION

Background: First inhabited by Arawak and later by Carib Indians, the Virgin Islands were settled by the Dutch in 1648 and then annexed by the English in 1672. The islands were part of the British colony of the Leeward Islands (1872-1960); they were granted autonomy in 1967. The economy is closely tied to the larger and more populous US Virgin Islands to the west; the US dollar is the legal currency. On 6 September 2017, Hurricane Irma devastated the island of Tortola. An estimated 80% of residential and business structures were destroyed or damaged, communications disrupted, and local roads rendered impassable.

GEOGRAPHY

Location: Caribbean, between the Caribbean Sea and the North Atlantic Ocean, east of Puerto Rico

Geographic coordinates: 18 30 N, 64 30 W

Map references: Central America and the Caribbean

Area: *total:* 151 sq km
land: 151 sq km
water: 0 sq km
note: comprised of 16 inhabited and more than 20 uninhabited islands; includes the islands of Tortola, Anegada, Virgin Gorda, Jost van Dyke

Area - comparative: about 0.9 times the size of Washington, DC

Land boundaries: *total:* 0 km

Coastline: 80 km

Maritime claims: territorial sea: 12 nm
exclusive fishing zone: 200 nm

Climate: subtropical; humid; temperatures moderated by trade winds

Terrain: coral islands relatively flat; volcanic islands steep, hilly

Elevation: *highest point:* Mount Sage 521 m
lowest point: Caribbean Sea 0 m

Natural resources: NEGL; pleasant climate, beaches foster tourism

Land use: *agricultural land:* 46.7% (2018 est.)
arable land: 6.7% (2018 est.)
permanent crops: 6.7% (2018 est.)
permanent pasture: 33.3% (2018 est.)
forest: 24.3% (2018 est.)
other: 29% (2018 est.)

Population distribution: a fairly even distribution throughout the inhabited islands, with the largest islands of Tortola, Anegada, Virgin Gorda, and Jost Van Dyke having the largest populations

Natural hazards: hurricanes and tropical storms (July to October)

Geography - note: strong ties to nearby US Virgin Islands and Puerto Rico

PEOPLE AND SOCIETY

Population: 38,632 (2022 est.)

Nationality: *noun:* British Virgin Islander(s)
adjective: British Virgin Islander

Ethnic groups: African/Black 76.3%, Latino 5.5%, White 5.4%, mixed 5.3%, Indian 2.1%, East Indian 1.6%, other 3%, unspecified 0.8% (2010 est.)

Languages: English (official)

Religions: Protestant 70.2% (Methodist 17.6%, Church of God 10.4%, Anglican 9.5%, Seventh Day Adventist 9.0%, Pentecostal 8.2%, Baptist 7.4%, New Testament Church of God 6.9%, other Protestant 1.2%), Roman Catholic 8.9%, Jehovah's Witness 2.5%, Hindu 1.9%, other 6.2%, none 7.9%, unspecified 2.4% (2010 est.)

Age structure: *0-14 years:* 16.48% (male 3,088/female 3,156)
15-24 years: 12.22% (male 2,212/female 2,418)
25-54 years: 47.84% (male 8,476/female 9,652)
55-64 years: 12.83% (male 2,242/female 2,521)
65 years and over: 10.63% (male 1,921/female 2,105) (2021 est.)

Median age: *total:* 37.2 years
male: 37 years
female: 37.5 years (2020 est.)

Population growth rate: 1.91% (2022 est.)

Birth rate: 10.95 births/1,000 population (2022 est.)

Death rate: 5.38 deaths/1,000 population (2022 est.)

Net migration rate: 13.56 migrant(s)/1,000 population (2022 est.)

Population distribution: a fairly even distribution throughout the inhabited islands, with the largest islands of Tortola, Anegada, Virgin Gorda, and Jost Van Dyke having the largest populations

Urbanization: *urban population:* 49.3% of total population (2022)
rate of urbanization: 1.73% annual rate of change (2020-25 est.)

Major urban areas - population: 15,000 ROAD TOWN (capital) (2018)

Sex ratio: *at birth:* 1.05 male(s)/female
0-14 years: 0.98 male(s)/female
15-24 years: 0.92 male(s)/female
25-54 years: 0.88 male(s)/female
55-64 years: 0.93 male(s)/female
65 years and over: 0.76 male(s)/female
total population: 0.91 male(s)/female (2022 est.)

Infant mortality rate: *total:* 14.16 deaths/1,000 live births
male: 16.89 deaths/1,000 live births
female: 11.28 deaths/1,000 live births (2022 est.)

Life expectancy at birth: *total population:* 79.67 years
male: 78.17 years
female: 81.25 years (2022 est.)

Total fertility rate: 1.35 children born/woman (2022 est.)

Drinking water source: *improved: total:* 99.9% of population
unimproved: total: 0.1% of population (2020 est.)

Sanitation facility access: *improved: urban:* 97.5% of population
rural: 97.5% of population
total: 97.5% of population
unimproved: urban: 2.5% of population
rural: 2.5% of population
total: 2.5% of population (2015 est.)

Education expenditures: 2.9% of GDP (2019 est.)

Literacy: School life expectancy (primary to tertiary education): *total:* 12 years
male: 12 years
female: 12 years (2018)

ENVIRONMENT

Environment - current issues: limited natural freshwater resources except for a few seasonal streams and springs on Tortola; most of the islands' water supply comes from desalination plants; sewage and mining/industry waste contribute to water pollution, threatening coral reefs

Air pollutants: *carbon dioxide emissions:* 0.21 megatons (2016 est.)

Climate: subtropical; humid; temperatures moderated by trade winds

Land use: *agricultural land:* 46.7% (2018 est.)
arable land: 6.7% (2018 est.)
permanent crops: 6.7% (2018 est.)
permanent pasture: 33.3% (2018 est.)
forest: 24.3% (2018 est.)
other: 29% (2018 est.)

Urbanization: *urban population:* 49.3% of total population (2022)
rate of urbanization: 1.73% annual rate of change (2020-25 est.)

Waste and recycling: *municipal solid waste generated annually:* 21,099 tons (2000 est.)

GOVERNMENT

Country name: *conventional long form:* none
conventional short form: British Virgin Islands
abbreviation: BVI
etymology: the myriad islets, cays, and rocks surrounding the major islands reminded explorer Christopher COLUMBUS in 1493 of Saint Ursula and her 11,000 virgin followers (Santa Ursula y las Once Mil Virgenes), which over time shortened to the Virgins (las Virgenes)

Government type: Overseas Territory of the UK with limited self-government; parliamentary democracy

Dependency status: overseas territory of the UK; internal self-governing

Capital: *name:* Road Town
geographic coordinates: 18 25 N, 64 37 W
time difference: UTC-4 (1 hour ahead of Washington, DC, during Standard Time)
etymology: name refers to the nautical term "roadstead" or "roads," a body of water less sheltered than a harbor but where ships can lie reasonably safely at anchor sheltered from rip currents, spring tides, or ocean swells

Administrative divisions: none (overseas territory of the UK)

Independence: none (overseas territory of the UK)

National holiday: Territory Day, 1 July (1956)

Constitution: *history:* several previous; latest effective 15 June 2007 (The Virgin Islands Constitution Order 2007)
amendments: initiated by any elected member of the House of Assembly; passage requires simple majority vote by the elected members of the Assembly and assent by the governor on behalf of the monarch; amended 2015

Legal system: English common law

Citizenship: see United Kingdom

Suffrage: 18 years of age; universal

Executive branch: *chief of state:* King CHARLES III (since 8 September 2022); represented by Governor John J. RANKIN (since 29 January 2021)
head of government: Premier Dr. Natalio WHEATLEY (since 5 May 2022)
cabinet: Executive Council appointed by the governor from members of the House of Assembly
elections/appointments: the monarchy is hereditary; governor appointed by the monarch; following legislative elections, the leader of the majority party or majority coalition usually appointed premier by the governor
note: on 5 May 2022, Premier Andrew FAHIE removed by a no confidence vote in House of Assembly following his arrest on drug trafficking and money laundering charges on 28 April 2022; Premier Dr. Natalio WHEATLEY sworn in as premier on 5 May 2022

Legislative branch: *description:* unicameral House of Assembly (15 seats; 13 members - 9 in single-seat constituencies and 4 at-large seats directly elected by simple majority vote and 2 ex-officio members - the attorney general and the speaker - chosen from outside the House; members serve 4-year terms)
elections: last held on 25 February 2019 (next to be held in 2023)
election results: percent of vote by party - VIP 46.5%, NDP 28.2%, PVIM 17.4%, PU 8%; seats by party - VIP 8, NDP 3, PVIM 1, PU 1; composition as of March 2022 - men 11, women 4, percent of women 26.7%

Judicial branch: *highest court(s):* the Eastern Caribbean Supreme Court (ECSC) is the superior court of the Organization of Eastern Caribbean States; the ECSC - headquartered on St. Lucia - consists of the Court of Appeal - headed by the chief justice and 4 judges - and the High Court with 18 judges; the Court of Appeal is itinerant, traveling to member states on a schedule to hear appeals from the High Court and subordinate courts; High Court judges reside in the member states, with 3 in the British Virgin Islands
judge selection and term of office: Eastern Caribbean Supreme Court chief justice appointed by Her Majesty, Queen ELIZABETH II; other justices and judges appointed by the Judicial and Legal Services Commission; Court of Appeal justices appointed for life with mandatory retirement at age 65; High Court judges appointed for life with mandatory retirement at age 62
subordinate courts: Magistrates' Courts

Political parties and leaders: National Democratic Party or NDP [Marlon PENN]
Progressive Virgin Islands Movement or PVIM [Ronnie SKELTON]
Progressives United or PU [Julian FRASER]
Virgin Islands Party or VIP [Natalio WHEATLEY]

International organization participation: Caricom (associate), CDB, Interpol (subbureau), IOC, OECS, UNESCO (associate), UPU

Diplomatic representation in the US: none (overseas territory of the UK)

Diplomatic representation from the US: *embassy:* none (overseas territory of the UK)

Flag description: blue with the flag of the UK in the upper hoist-side quadrant and the Virgin Islander coat of arms centered in the outer half of the flag; the coat of arms depicts a woman flanked on either side by a vertical column of six oil lamps above a scroll bearing the Latin word VIGILATE (Be Watchful); the islands were named by COLUMBUS in 1493 in honor of Saint Ursula and her 11 virgin followers (some sources say 11,000) who reputedly were martyred by the Huns in the 4th or 5th century; the figure on the banner holding a lamp represents the saint; the other lamps symbolize her followers

National symbol(s): zenaida dove, white cedar flower; national colors: yellow, green, red, white, blue

National anthem: *note:* as an overseas territory of the United Kingdom, "God Save the King" is official (see United Kingdom)

ECONOMY

Economic overview: The economy, one of the most stable and prosperous in the Caribbean, is highly dependent on tourism, which generates an estimated 45% of the national income. More than 934,000 tourists, mainly from the US, visited the islands in 2008. Because of traditionally close links with the US Virgin Islands, the British Virgin Islands has used the US dollar as its currency since 1959.

Livestock raising is the most important agricultural activity; poor soils limit the islands' ability to meet domestic food requirements.

In the mid-1980s, the government began offering offshore registration to companies wishing to incorporate in the islands, and incorporation fees now generate substantial revenues. Roughly 400,000 companies were on the offshore registry by yearend 2000. The adoption of a comprehensive insurance law in late 1994, which provides a blanket of confidentiality with regulated statutory gateways for investigation of criminal offenses, made the British Virgin Islands even more attractive to international business.

Real GDP (purchasing power parity): $500 million (2017 est.)
$490.2 million (2016 est.)
$481.1 million (2015 est.)

Real GDP growth rate: 2% (2017 est.)
1.9% (2016 est.)
1.8% (2015 est.)

Real GDP per capita: $34,200 (2017 est.)

GDP (official exchange rate): $1.028 billion (2017 est.)

Inflation rate (consumer prices): 1.1% (2017 est.)
1.1% (2016 est.)

GDP - composition, by sector of origin: *agriculture:* 0.2% (2017 est.)
industry: 6.8% (2017 est.)
services: 93.1% (2017 est.)

GDP - composition, by end use: *household consumption:* 25.1% (2017 est.)
government consumption: 7.5% (2017 est.)
investment in fixed capital: 21.7% (2017 est.)
investment in inventories: 20.4% (2017 est.)
exports of goods and services: 94.7% (2017 est.)
imports of goods and services: -69.4% (2017 est.)

Agricultural products: fruits, vegetables; livestock, poultry; fish

Industries: tourism, light industry, construction, rum, concrete block, offshore banking center

Industrial production growth rate: 1.1% (2017 est.)

Labor force: 12,770 (2004)

Labor force - by occupation: *agriculture:* 0.6%
industry: 40%
services: 59.4% (2005)

Unemployment rate: 2.9% (2015 est.)

Budget: *revenues:* 400 million (2017 est.)
expenditures: 400 million (2017 est.)

Budget surplus (+) or deficit (-): 0% (of GDP) (2017 est.)

Taxes and other revenues: 38.9% (of GDP) (2017 est.)

Fiscal year: 1 April - 31 March

Current account balance: $362.6 million (2011 est.)
$279.8 million (2010 est.)

Exports: $23 million (2017 est.)
$23 million (2015 est.)
note: Data are in current year dollars and do not include illicit exports or re-exports.

Exports - partners: Malta 30%, Seychelles 29%, Switzerland 14% (2019)

Exports - commodities: recreational boats, aircraft, diamonds, paintings, precious stones (2019)

Imports: $300 million (2017 est.)
$210 million (2016 est.)

Imports - partners: Germany 32%, United States 22%, Italy 9%, France 7%, Seychelles 7% (2019)

Imports - commodities: recreational boats, aircraft, refined petroleum, cars, furniture (2019)

Debt - external: $36.1 million (1997)

Exchange rates: the US dollar is used

ENERGY

Electricity access: *electrification - total population:* 100% (2020)

Electricity: *installed generating capacity:* 33,000 kW (2020 est.)
consumption: 116.298 million kWh (2019 est.)
exports: 0 kWh (2020 est.)
imports: 0 kWh (2020 est.)
transmission/distribution losses: 22.5 million kWh (2019 est.)

Electricity generation sources: *fossil fuels:* 98.8% of total installed capacity (2020 est.)
solar: 0.2% of total installed capacity (2020 est.)
wind: 1% of total installed capacity (2020 est.)

Petroleum: *total petroleum production:* 0 bbl/day (2021 est.)
refined petroleum consumption: 1,200 bbl/day (2019 est.)

Refined petroleum products - imports: 1,227 bbl/day (2015 est.)

Carbon dioxide emissions: 173,000 metric tonnes of CO_2 (2019 est.)
from petroleum and other liquids: 173,000 metric tonnes of CO_2 (2019 est.)

Energy consumption per capita: 80.136 million Btu/person (2019 est.)

COMMUNICATIONS

Telephones - fixed lines: *total subscriptions:* 7,000 (2020 est.)
subscriptions per 100 inhabitants: 23 (2020 est.)

Telephones - mobile cellular: *total subscriptions:* 35,163 (2020 est.)
subscriptions per 100 inhabitants: 116 (2020 est.)

Telecommunication systems: *general assessment:* the telecom sector has seen a decline in subscriber numbers (particularly for prepaid mobile services the mainstay of short term visitors) and revenue; fixed and mobile broadband services are two areas that have benefited from the crisis as employees and students have resorted to working from home; one major casualty may be the region's second largest telco operator, Digicel; the company filed for bankruptcy in the US in April 2020; it continues to operate in all of its Caribbean markets as it seeks to refinance billions of dollars of debt; the other major telco, regional incumbent Cable & Wireless Communications (CWC), is experiencing similar drops in subscriber numbers and revenue; CWC is expanding and enhancing its fixed and mobile networks in many of the countries it serves around the Caribbean, despite many locations being small islands with very small populations; one area of the telecom market that is not prepared for growth is 5G mobile; governments, regulators, and even the mobile network operators have shown that they have not been investing in 5G opportunities at the present time; network expansion and enhancements remain concentrated around improving LTE coverage. (2021)
domestic: fixed-line connections exceed 23 per 100 persons and mobile cellular subscribership is roughly 116 per 100 persons (2020)
international: country code - 1-284; landing points for PCCS, ECFS, CBUS, Deep Blue Cable, East-West, PAN-AM, Americas-1, Southern Caribbean Fiber, Columbus- IIb, St Thomas - St Croix System, Taino-Carib, and Americas INorth via submarine cable to Caribbean, Central and South America, and US (2019)

Broadcast media: 1 private TV station; multi-channel TV is available from cable and satellite subscription services; about a half-dozen private radio stations

Internet country code: .vg

Internet users: *total:* 23,585 (2020 est.)
percent of population: 78% (2020 est.)

Broadband - fixed subscriptions: *total:* 6,738 (2020 est.)
subscriptions per 100 inhabitants: 22 (2020 est.)

TRANSPORTATION

Civil aircraft registration country code prefix: VP-L

Airports: *total:* 4 (2021)

Airports - with paved runways: *total:* 2
914 to 1,523 m: 1
under 914 m: 1 (2021)

Airports - with unpaved runways: *total:* 2
914 to 1,523 m: 2 (2021)

Roadways: *total:* 200 km (2007)
paved: 200 km (2007)

Merchant marine: *total:* 30
by type: general cargo 3, other 27 (2021)

Ports and terminals: *major seaport(s):* Road Harbor

MILITARY AND SECURITY

Military - note: defense is the responsibility of the UK

TRANSNATIONAL ISSUES

Disputes - international: none

Illicit drugs: transshipment point for South American narcotics destined for the US and Europe; large offshore financial center makes it vulnerable to money laundering

BRUNEI

INTRODUCTION

Background: The Sultanate of Brunei's influence peaked between the 15th and 17th centuries when its control extended over coastal areas of northwest Borneo and the southern Philippines. Brunei subsequently entered a period of decline brought on by internal strife over royal succession, colonial expansion of European powers, and piracy. In 1888, Brunei became a British protectorate; independence was achieved in 1984. The same family has ruled Brunei for over six centuries.

Brunei benefits from extensive petroleum and natural gas fields, the source of one of the highest per capita GDPs in the world. In 2017, Brunei celebrated the 50th anniversary of the Sultan Hassanal BOLKIAH's accession to the throne.

GEOGRAPHY

Location: Southeastern Asia, along the northern coast of the island of Borneo, bordering the South China Sea and Malaysia

Geographic coordinates: 4 30 N, 114 40 E

Map references: Southeast Asia

Area: *total:* 5,765 sq km
land: 5,265 sq km
water: 500 sq km
country comparison to the world: 172

Area - comparative: slightly smaller than Delaware

Land boundaries: *total:* 266 km
border countries (1): Malaysia 266 km

Coastline: 161 km

Maritime claims: *territorial sea:* 12 nm
exclusive economic zone: 200 nm or to median line

Climate: tropical; hot, humid, rainy

Terrain: flat coastal plain rises to mountains in east; hilly lowland in west

Elevation: *highest point:* Bukit Pagon 1,850 m
lowest point: South China Sea 0 m
mean elevation: 478 m

Natural resources: petroleum, natural gas, timber

Land use: *agricultural land:* 2.5% (2018 est.)
arable land: 0.8% (2018 est.)
permanent crops: 1.1% (2018 est.)
permanent pasture: 0.6% (2018 est.)
forest: 71.8% (2018 est.)
other: 25.7% (2018 est.)

Irrigated land: 10 sq km (2012)

Natural hazards: typhoons, earthquakes, and severe flooding are rare

Geography - note: close to vital sea lanes through South China Sea linking Indian and Pacific Oceans; two parts physically separated by Malaysia; the eastern part, the Temburong district, is an exclave and is almost an enclave within Malaysia

PEOPLE AND SOCIETY

Population: 478,054 (2022 est.)
note: immigrants make up approximately 26% of the total population, according to UN data (2019)
country comparison to the world: 173

Nationality: *noun:* Bruneian(s)
adjective: Bruneian

Ethnic groups: Malay 65.8%, Chinese 10.2%, other 24% (2020 est.)

Languages: Malay (Bahasa Melayu) (official), English, Chinese dialects
major-language sample(s): Buku Fakta Dunia, sumber yang diperlukan untuk maklumat asas. (Malay)

Religions: Muslim (official) 80.9%, Christian 7.1%, Buddhist 7.1%, other (includes indigenous beliefs) 5% (2016 est.)

Demographic profile: Brunei is a small, oil-rich sultanate of less than half a million people, making it the smallest country in Southeast Asia by population. Its total fertility rate – the average number of births per woman – has been steadily declining over the last few decades, from over 3.5 in the 1980s to below replacement level today at nearly 1.8. The trend is due to women's increased years of education and participation in the workforce, which have resulted in later marriages and fewer children. Yet, the population continues to grow because of the large number of women of reproductive age and a reliance on foreign labor – mainly from Malaysia, Thailand, the Philippines, Indonesia, and South Asian countries – to fill low-skilled jobs.

Brunei is officially Muslim, and Malay is the official language. The country follows an official Malay national ideology, Malay Islamic Monarchy, which promotes Malay language and culture, Islamic values, and the monarchy. Only seven of Brunei's native groups are recognized in the constitution and are defined as "Malay" – Brunei Malays, Belait, Kedayan, Dusun, Bisayak, Lun Bawang, and Sama-Baiau. Together they make up about 66% percent of the population and are referred to as the Bumiputera. The Bumiputera are entitled to official privileges, including land ownership, access to certain types of employment (Royal Brunei Armed Forces and Brunei Shell Petroleum), easier access to higher education, and better job opportunities in the civil service.

Brunei's Chinese population descends from migrants who arrived when Brunei was a British protectorate (1888 and 1984). They are prominent in the non-state commercial sector and account for approximately 10% of the population. Most Bruneian Chinese are permanent residents rather than citizens despite roots going back several generations. Many are stateless and are denied rights granted to citizens, such as land ownership, subsidized health care, and free secondary and university education. Because of the discriminatory policies, the number of Chinese in Brunei has shrunk considerably in the last 50 years. Native ethnic groups that are not included in the Bumiputera are not recognized in the constitution and are not officially identified as "Malay" or automatically granted citizenship. Foreign workers constitute some quarter of the labor force.

Age structure: *0-14 years:* 22.41% (male 53,653/female 50,446)
15-24 years: 16.14% (male 37,394/female 37,559)
25-54 years: 47.21% (male 103,991/female 115,291)
55-64 years: 8.34% (male 19,159/female 19,585)
65 years and over: 5.9% (male 13,333/female 14,067) (2020 est.)

Dependency ratios: *total dependency ratio:* 38.7
youth dependency ratio: 31
elderly dependency ratio: 7.7
potential support ratio: 12.9 (2020 est.)

Median age: *total:* 31.1 years
male: 30.5 years
female: 31.8 years (2020 est.)
country comparison to the world: 116

Population growth rate: 1.45% (2022 est.)
country comparison to the world: 66

Birth rate: 16.14 births/1,000 population (2022 est.)
country comparison to the world: 101

Death rate: 3.79 deaths/1,000 population (2022 est.)
country comparison to the world: 218

Net migration rate: 2.18 migrant(s)/1,000 population (2022 est.)
country comparison to the world: 48

Urbanization: *urban population:* 78.9% of total population (2022)
rate of urbanization: 1.44% annual rate of change (2020-25 est.)

Major urban areas - population: 241,000 BANDAR SERI BEGAWAN (capital) (2011)
note: the boundaries of the capital city were expanded in 2007, greatly increasing the city area; the population of the capital increased tenfold

Sex ratio: *at birth:* 1.05 male(s)/female
0-14 years: 1.06 male(s)/female
15-24 years: 1 male(s)/female
25-54 years: 0.89 male(s)/female
55-64 years: 0.94 male(s)/female
65 years and over: 0.74 male(s)/female
total population: 0.95 male(s)/female (2022 est.)

Maternal mortality ratio: 31 deaths/100,000 live births (2017 est.)
country comparison to the world: 109

Infant mortality rate: *total:* 10.52 deaths/1,000 live births
male: 12.88 deaths/1,000 live births
female: 8.05 deaths/1,000 live births (2022 est.)
country comparison to the world: 134

Life expectancy at birth: *total population:* 78.38 years
male: 76.01 years
female: 80.86 years (2022 est.)
country comparison to the world: 72

Total fertility rate: 1.74 children born/woman (2022 est.)
country comparison to the world: 157

Drinking water source: *improved: urban:* 99.7% of population
total: 99.9% of population
unimproved: urban: 0.4% of population
rural: 0% of population
total: 0.1% of population (2020)

Current health expenditure: 2.2% of GDP (2019)

Physicians density: 1.61 physicians/1,000 population (2017)

Hospital bed density: 2.9 beds/1,000 population (2017)

Obesity - adult prevalence rate: 14.1% (2016)
country comparison to the world: 129

Alcohol consumption per capita: *total:* 0.69 liters of pure alcohol (2019 est.)
beer: 0.66 liters of pure alcohol (2019 est.)
wine: 0.04 liters of pure alcohol (2019 est.)
spirits: 0 liters of pure alcohol (2019 est.)
other alcohols: 0 liters of pure alcohol (2019 est.)
country comparison to the world: 157

Tobacco use: *total:* 16.2% (2020 est.)
male: 30% (2020 est.)
female: 2.3% (2020 est.)
country comparison to the world: 100

Education expenditures: 4.4% of GDP (2016 est.)
country comparison to the world: 86

Literacy: *definition:* age 15 and over can read and write
total population: 97.2%
male: 98.1%
female: 93.4% (2018)

School life expectancy (primary to tertiary education): *total:* 14 years
male: 14 years
female: 14 years (2020)

Unemployment, youth ages 15-24: *total:* 21.4%
male: 19%
female: 25.8% (2019 est.)

ENVIRONMENT

Environment - current issues: no major environmental problems, but air pollution control is becoming a concern; seasonal trans-boundary haze from forest fires in Indonesia

Environment - international agreements: *party to:* Biodiversity, Climate Change, Climate Change-Kyoto Protocol, Climate Change-Paris Agreement, Comprehensive Nuclear Test Ban, Desertification, Endangered Species, Hazardous Wastes, Law of the Sea, Ozone Layer Protection, Ship Pollution
signed, but not ratified: none of the selected agreements

Air pollutants: *particulate matter emissions:* 5.78 micrograms per cubic meter (2016 est.)
carbon dioxide emissions: 7.66 megatons (2016 est.)
methane emissions: 8.4 megatons (2020 est.)

Climate: tropical; hot, humid, rainy

Land use: *agricultural land:* 2.5% (2018 est.)
arable land: 0.8% (2018 est.)
permanent crops: 1.1% (2018 est.)
permanent pasture: 0.6% (2018 est.)
forest: 71.8% (2018 est.)
other: 25.7% (2018 est.)

Urbanization: *urban population:* 78.9% of total population (2022)
rate of urbanization: 1.44% annual rate of change (2020-25 est.)

Revenue from forest resources: *forest revenues:* 0.05% of GDP (2018 est.)
country comparison to the world: 127

Revenue from coal: *coal revenues:* 0% of GDP (2018 est.)
country comparison to the world: 70

Waste and recycling: *municipal solid waste generated annually:* 216,253 tons (2016 est.)

Total water withdrawal: *municipal:* 151.5 million cubic meters (2017 est.)
agricultural: 5.3 million cubic meters (2017 est.)

Total renewable water resources: 8.5 billion cubic meters (2017 est.)

GOVERNMENT

Country name: *conventional long form:* Brunei Darussalam
conventional short form: Brunei
local long form: Negara Brunei Darussalam
local short form: Brunei
etymology: derivation of the name is unclear; according to legend, MUHAMMAD SHAH, who would become the first sultan of Brunei, upon discovering what would become Brunei exclaimed "Baru nah," which roughly translates as "there" or "that's it"

Government type: absolute monarchy or sultanate

Capital: *name:* Bandar Seri Begawan
geographic coordinates: 4 53 N, 114 56 E
time difference: UTC+8 (13 hours ahead of Washington, DC, during Standard Time)
etymology: named in 1970 after Sultan Omar Ali SAIFUDDIEN III (1914-1986; "The Father of Independence") who adopted the title of "Seri Begawan" (approximate meaning "honored lord") upon his abdication in 1967; "bandar" in Malay means "town" or "city"; the capital had previously been called Bandar Brunei (Brunei Town)

Administrative divisions: 4 districts (daerah-daerah, singular - daerah); Belait, Brunei dan Muara, Temburong, Tutong

Independence: 1 January 1984 (from the UK)

National holiday: National Day, 23 February (1984); note - 1 January 1984 was the date of independence from the UK, 23 February 1984 was the date of independence from British protection; the Sultan's birthday, 15 June

Constitution: *history:* drafted 1954 to 1959, signed 29 September 1959; note - some constitutional provisions suspended since 1962 under a State of Emergency, others suspended since independence in 1984
amendments: proposed by the monarch; passage requires submission to the Privy Council for Legislative Council review and finalization takes place by proclamation; the monarch can accept or reject changes to the original proposal provided by the Legislative Council; amended several times, last in 2010

Legal system: mixed legal system based on English common law and Islamic law; note - in April 2019, the full sharia penal codes came into force and apply to Muslims and partly to non-Muslims in parallel with present common law codes

International law organization participation: has not submitted an ICJ jurisdiction declaration; non-party state to the ICC

Citizenship: *citizenship by birth:* no
citizenship by descent only: the father must be a citizen of Brunei
dual citizenship recognized: no
residency requirement for naturalization: 12 years

Suffrage: 18 years of age for village elections; universal

Executive branch: *chief of state:* Sultan and Prime Minister Sir HASSANAL Bolkiah (since 5 October 1967); note - the monarch is both chief of state and head of government
head of government: Sultan and Prime Minister Sir HASSANAL Bolkiah (since 5 October 1967)
cabinet: Council of Ministers appointed and presided over by the monarch; note - 4 additional advisory councils appointed by the monarch are the Religious Council, Privy Council for constitutional issues, Council of Succession, and Legislative Council; Sultan and Prime Minister Sir HASSANAL Bolkiah is also Minister of Finance, Defense, and Foreign Affairs and Trade
elections/appointments: none; the monarchy is hereditary

Legislative branch: *description:* unicameral Legislative Council or Majlis Mesyuarat Negara Brunei (33 seats; 20 members appointed by the sultan from ex-officio cabinet ministers, titled people, and prominent citizens in public service and various professional fields and 13 members from 4 multi-seat constituencies, and 3 ex-officio members - the speaker and first and second secretaries
elections: January 2017 - appointed by the sultan
election results: NA; composition (as of February 2022) - men 30, women 3, percent of women 9.1%

Judicial branch: *highest court(s):* Supreme Court (consists of the Court of Appeal and the High Court, each with a chief justice and 2 judges); Sharia Court (consists the Court of Appeals and the High Court); note - Brunei has a dual judicial system of secular and sharia (religious) courts; the Judicial Committee of Privy Council (in London) serves as the final appellate court for civil cases only
judge selection and term of office: Supreme Court judges appointed by the monarch to serve until age 65, and older if approved by the monarch; Sharia Court judges appointed by the monarch for life
subordinate courts: Intermediate Court; Magistrates' Courts; Juvenile Court; small claims courts; lower sharia courts

Political parties and leaders: National Development Party or NDP [YASSIN Affendi]
note: Brunei National Solidarity Party or PPKB [Abdul LATIF bin Chuchu] and People's Awareness Party or PAKAR [Awang Haji MAIDIN bin Haji Ahmad] were deregistered in 2007; parties are small and have limited activity

International organization participation: ADB, APEC, ARF, ASEAN, C, CP, EAS, FAO, G-77, IAEA, IBRD, ICAO, ICC (NGOs), ICRM, IDA, IFRCS, ILO, IMF, IMO, IMSO, Interpol, IOC, ISO (correspondent), ITSO, ITU, NAM, OIC, OPCW, UN, UNCTAD, UNESCO, UNIFIL, UNWTO, UPU, WCO, WHO, WIPO, WMO, WTO

Diplomatic representation in the US: *chief of mission:* Ambassador Dato Paduka Haji Serbini bin Haji ALI (since 28 January 2016)
chancery: 3520 International Court NW, Washington, DC 20008
telephone: [1] (202) 237-1838
FAX: [1] (202) 885-0560
email address and website:
info@bruneiembassy.org
http://www.bruneiembassy.org/index.html
consulate(s): New York

Diplomatic representation from the US: *chief of mission:* Ambassador Caryn R. McCLELLAND (since December 2021)
embassy: Simpang 336-52-16-9, Jalan Duta, Bandar Seri Begawan, BC4115
mailing address: 4020 Bandar Seri Begawan Place, Washington DC 20521-4020
telephone: (673) 238-7400
FAX: (673) 238-7533
email address and website:
ConsularBrunei@state.gov
https://bn.usembassy.gov/

Flag description: yellow with two diagonal bands of white (top, almost double width) and black starting from the upper hoist side; the national emblem in red is superimposed at the center; yellow is the color of royalty and symbolizes the sultanate; the white and black bands denote Brunei's chief ministers; the emblem includes five main components: a swallow-tailed flag, the royal umbrella representing the monarchy, the wings of four feathers symbolizing justice, tranquility, prosperity, and peace, the two upraised hands signifying the government's pledge to preserve and promote the welfare of the people, and the crescent moon denoting Islam, the state religion; the state motto "Always render service with God's guidance" appears in yellow Arabic script on the crescent; a ribbon below the crescent reads "Brunei, the Abode of Peace"

National symbol(s): *royal parasol; national colors:* yellow, white, black

National anthem: *name:* "Allah Peliharakan Sultan" (God Bless His Majesty)
lyrics/music: Pengiran Haji Mohamed YUSUF bin Pengiran Abdul Rahim/Awang Haji BESAR bin Sagap
note: adopted 1951

ECONOMY

Economic overview: Brunei is an energy-rich sultanate on the northern coast of Borneo in Southeast

Asia. Brunei boasts a well-educated, largely English-speaking population; excellent infrastructure; and a stable government intent on attracting foreign investment. Crude oil and natural gas production account for approximately 65% of GDP and 95% of exports, with Japan as the primary export market.

Per capita GDP is among the highest in the world, and substantial income from overseas investment supplements income from domestic hydrocarbon production. Bruneian citizens pay no personal income taxes, and the government provides free medical services and free education through the university level.

The Bruneian Government wants to diversify its economy away from hydrocarbon exports to other industries such as information and communications technology and halal manufacturing, permissible under Islamic law. Brunei's trade increased in 2016 and 2017, following its regional economic integration in the ASEAN Economic Community, and the expected ratification of the Trans-Pacific Partnership trade agreement.

Real GDP (purchasing power parity): $27.23 billion (2020 est.)
$26.91 billion (2019 est.)
$25.9 billion (2018 est.)
note: data are in 2017 dollars
country comparison to the world: 140

Real GDP growth rate: 1.3% (2017 est.)
-2.5% (2016 est.)
-0.4% (2015 est.)
country comparison to the world: 161

Real GDP per capita: $62,200 (2020 est.)
$62,100 (2019 est.)
$60,400 (2018 est.)
note: data are in 2017 dollars
country comparison to the world: 14

GDP (official exchange rate): $12.13 billion (2017 est.)

Inflation rate (consumer prices): -0.2% (2017 est.)
-0.7% (2016 est.)
country comparison to the world: 16

GDP - composition, by sector of origin: *agriculture:* 1.2% (2017 est.)
industry: 56.6% (2017 est.)
services: 42.3% (2017 est.)

GDP - composition, by end use: *household consumption:* 25% (2017 est.)
government consumption: 24.8% (2017 est.)
investment in fixed capital: 32.6% (2017 est.)
investment in inventories: 8.5% (2017 est.)
exports of goods and services: 45.9% (2017 est.)
imports of goods and services: -36.8% (2017 est.)

Agricultural products: poultry, eggs, fruit, cassava, bananas, legumes, cucumbers, rice, pineapples, beef

Industries: petroleum, petroleum refining, liquefied natural gas, construction, agriculture, aquaculture, transportation

Industrial production growth rate: 1.5% (2017 est.)
country comparison to the world: 142

Labor force: 203,600 (2014 est.)
country comparison to the world: 168

Labor force - by occupation: *agriculture:* 4.2%
industry: 62.8%
services: 33% (2008 est.)

Unemployment rate: 6.9% (2017 est.)
6.9% (2016 est.)
country comparison to the world: 109

Unemployment, youth ages 15-24: *total:* 21.4%
male: 19%
female: 25.8% (2019 est.)
country comparison to the world: 66

Budget: *revenues:* 2.245 billion (2017 est.)
expenditures: 4.345 billion (2017 est.)

Budget surplus (+) or deficit (-): -17.3% (of GDP) (2017 est.)
country comparison to the world: 218

Public debt: 2.8% of GDP (2017 est.)
3% of GDP (2016 est.)
country comparison to the world: 207

Taxes and other revenues: 18.5% (of GDP) (2017 est.)
country comparison to the world: 158

Fiscal year: 1 April - 31 March

Current account balance: $2.021 billion (2017 est.)
$1.47 billion (2016 est.)
country comparison to the world: 40

Exports: $7.83 billion (2019 est.)
$7.04 billion (2018 est.)
note: Data are in current year dollars and do not include illicit exports or re-exports.
country comparison to the world: 106

Exports - partners: Japan 34%, Australia 12%, Singapore 10%, India 8%, Malaysia 8%, Thailand 7%, China 6%, South Korea 5% (2019)

Exports - commodities: natural gas, crude petroleum, refined petroleum, industrial alcohols, industrial hydrocarbons (2019)

Imports: $6.81 billion (2019 est.) note: data are in current year dollars
$5.68 billion (2018 est.) note: data are in current year dollars
country comparison to the world: 126

Imports - partners: Singapore 18%, China 14%, Malaysia 12%, Nigeria 5%, United Arab Emirates 5%, United States 5% (2019)

Imports - commodities: crude petroleum, refined petroleum, cars, tug boats, valves (2019)

Reserves of foreign exchange and gold: $3.488 billion (31 December 2017 est.)
$3.366 billion (31 December 2015 est.)
country comparison to the world: 105

Debt - external: $0 (2014)
$0 (2013)
note: public external debt only; private external debt unavailable
country comparison to the world: 204

Exchange rates: Bruneian dollars (BND) per US dollar -
1.33685 (2020 est.)
1.35945 (2019 est.)
1.3699 (2018 est.)
1.3749 (2014 est.)
1.267 (2013 est.)

ENERGY

Electricity access: *electrification - total population:* 100% (2020)

Electricity: *installed generating capacity:* 1.261 million kW (2020 est.)
consumption: 4,140,140,000 kWh (2019 est.)
exports: 0 kWh (2019 est.)
imports: 0 kWh (2019 est.)
transmission/distribution losses: 497 million kWh (2019 est.)

Electricity generation sources: *fossil fuels:* 100% of total installed capacity (2020 est.)
solar: 0.1% of total installed capacity (2020 est.)

Petroleum: *total petroleum production:* 107,300 bbl/day (2021 est.)
refined petroleum consumption: 18,800 bbl/day (2019 est.)
crude oil and lease condensate exports: 103,100 bbl/day (2018 est.)
crude oil and lease condensate imports: 0 bbl/day (2018 est.)
crude oil estimated reserves: 1.1 billion barrels (2021 est.)

Refined petroleum products - production: 10,310 bbl/day (2015 est.)
country comparison to the world: 100

Refined petroleum products - exports: 0 bbl/day (2015 est.)
country comparison to the world: 135

Refined petroleum products - imports: 6,948 bbl/day (2015 est.)
country comparison to the world: 159

Natural gas: *production:* 12,498,299,000 cubic meters (2020 est.)
consumption: 4,166,987,000 cubic meters (2020 est.)
exports: 7,774,406,000 cubic meters (2020 est.)
imports: 0 cubic meters (2021 est.)
proven reserves: 260.515 billion cubic meters (2021 est.)

Carbon dioxide emissions: 9.956 million metric tonnes of CO2 (2019 est.)
from petroleum and other liquids: 2.387 million metric tonnes of CO2 (2019 est.)
from consumed natural gas: 7.569 million metric tonnes of CO2 (2019 est.)
country comparison to the world: 107

Energy consumption per capita: 415.184 million Btu/person (2019 est.)
country comparison to the world: 5

COMMUNICATIONS

Telephones - fixed lines: *total subscriptions:* 103,885 (2020 est.)
subscriptions per 100 inhabitants: 24 (2020 est.)
country comparison to the world: 136

Telephones - mobile cellular: *total subscriptions:* 526,589 (2020 est.)
subscriptions per 100 inhabitants: 123 (2020 est.)
country comparison to the world: 173

Telecommunication systems: *general assessment:* Brunei's mobile market experienced drop-off in subscriber numbers in 2020; in 2022 there was a concerted effort to build out the fixed-line infrastructure while progressing towards introducing 5G mobile services; Brunei's fixed-line market is one of the few countries in the world to have displayed significant growth rather than a decline in teledensity in the last few years; this upward trend is set to continue as the new Unified National Network (UNN) works diligently to expand and enhance the fixed-line infrastructure around the country; strong growth was also seen in the fixed broadband space, on the back of those same infrastructure developments that are part of the Brunei Vision 2035 initiative; fixed broadband is starting from a relatively low base by international standards and is still only at 18%, leaving lots of room for growth; mobile and mobile broadband, on the other hand, are still suffering from the market contractions first felt in 2020; Brunei's 2G

GSM network is shut down, with the spectrum to be reallocated to 3G, 4G, and potentially 5G use (2021)
domestic: every service available; nearly 24 per 100 fixed-line, 120 per 100 mobile-cellular (2020)
international: country code - 673; landing points for the SEA-ME-WE-3, SJC, AAG, Lubuan-Brunei Submarine Cable via optical telecommunications submarine cables that provides links to Asia, the Middle East, Southeast Asia, Africa, Australia, and the US; satellite earth stations - 2 Intelsat (1 Indian Ocean and 1 Pacific Ocean) (2019)

Broadcast media: state-controlled Radio Television Brunei (RTB) operates 5 channels; 3 Malaysian TV stations are available; foreign TV broadcasts are available via satellite systems; RTB operates 5 radio networks and broadcasts on multiple frequencies; British Forces Broadcast Service (BFBS) provides radio broadcasts on 2 FM stations; some radio broadcast stations from Malaysia are available via repeaters

Internet country code: .bn

Internet users: *total:* 415,609 (2020 est.)
percent of population: 95% (2020 est.)
country comparison to the world: 163

Broadband - fixed subscriptions: *total:* 71,078 (2020 est.)
subscriptions per 100 inhabitants: 16 (2020 est.)
country comparison to the world: 134

TRANSPORTATION

National air transport system: *number of registered air carriers:* 1 (2020)
inventory of registered aircraft operated by air carriers: 10
annual passenger traffic on registered air carriers: 1,234,455 (2018)
annual freight traffic on registered air carriers: 129.35 million (2018) mt-km

Civil aircraft registration country code prefix: V8

Airports: *total:* 1 (2021)
country comparison to the world: 215

Airports - with paved runways: *over 3,047 m:* 1 (2021)

Heliports: 3 (2021)

Pipelines: 33 km condensate, 86 km condensate/gas, 628 km gas, 492 km oil (2013)

Roadways: *total:* 2,976 km (2014)
paved: 2,559 km (2014)
unpaved: 417 km (2014)
country comparison to the world: 163

Waterways: 209 km (2012) (navigable by craft drawing less than 1.2 m; the Belait, Brunei, and Tutong Rivers are major transport links)
country comparison to the world: 106

Merchant marine: *total:* 96
by type: general cargo 18, oil tanker 3, other 75 (2021)
country comparison to the world: 90

Ports and terminals: *major seaport(s):* Muara
oil terminal(s): Lumut, Seria
LNG terminal(s) (export): Lumut

MILITARY AND SECURITY

Military and security forces: Royal Brunei Armed Forces: Land Force, Navy, Air Force, Joint Force (2022)
note: the Gurkha Reserve Unit (GRU) under the Ministry of Defense is a special guard force for the Sultan, the royal family, and the country's oil installations

Military expenditures: 3.1% of GDP (2021 est.)
3.7% of GDP (2020 est.)
3.1% of GDP (2019) (approximately $870 million)
2.7% of GDP (2018) (approximately $720 million)
2.8% of GDP (2017) (approximately $750 million)
country comparison to the world: 30

Military and security service personnel strengths: approximately 6,000 total active troops (4,000 Army; 1,000 Navy; 1,000 Air Force) (2022)

Military equipment inventories and acquisitions: the Brunei imports nearly all of its military equipment and weapons systems and has a variety of suppliers, including the US and several European countries (2021)

Military service age and obligation: 17 years of age for voluntary military service; non-Malays are ineligible to serve (2022)
note: the Gurkha Reserve Unit (GRU) employs about 500 Gurkhas from Nepal, the majority of whom are veterans of the British Army and the Singapore Police Force who have joined the GRU as a second career

Military - note: the Royal Brunei Armed Forces were formed in 1961 with British support as the Brunei Malay Regiment; "Royal" was added as an honorary title in 1965; the military was given its current title in 1984

Brunei has a long-standing defense relationship with the United Kingdom and hosts a British Army garrison, which includes a Gurkha battalion and a jungle warfare school; Brunei also hosts a Singaporean military training base (2022)

TRANSNATIONAL ISSUES

Disputes - international: per Letters of Exchange signed in 2009, Malaysia in 2010 ceded two hydrocarbon concession blocks to Brunei in exchange for Brunei's sultan dropping claims to the Limbang corridor, which divides Brunei; nonetheless, Brunei claims a maritime boundary extending as far as a median with Vietnam, thus asserting an implicit claim to Louisa Reef

Refugees and internally displaced persons: *stateless persons:* 20,863 (mid-year 2021); note - thousands of stateless persons, often ethnic Chinese, are permanent residents and their families have lived in Brunei for generations; obtaining citizenship is difficult and requires individuals to pass rigorous tests on Malay culture, customs, and language; stateless residents receive an International Certificate of Identity, which enables them to travel overseas; the government is considering changing the law prohibiting non- Bruneians, including stateless permanent residents, from owning land

Trafficking in persons: *current situation:* human traffickers exploit foreign victims in Brunei; some men and women who migrate to Brunei to work as domestics or in retail or construction are subject to involuntary servitude, debt-based coercion, contract switching, non-payment of wages, passport confiscation, physical abuse, or confinement; some female migrants entering Brunei on tourist visas are forced into prostitution; some traffickers use Brunei as a transit point for victims used for sex and labor trafficking in Malaysia and Indonesia
tier rating: Tier 2 Watch List — Brunei does not fully meet the minimum standards for the elimination of trafficking but is making significant efforts to do so; the government enacted the 2019 Trafficking in Persons Order, which criminalized sex and labor trafficking and separated trafficking crimes from migrant smuggling crimes; the government formalized its interagency anti-trafficking in persons committee; instituted a committee to review foreign worker recruitment practices, ratified the ASEAN Convention against Trafficking in Persons, and acceded to the UN TIP Protocol; however, authorities did not formally identify any trafficking cases, did not initiate any new trafficking prosecutions, and did not convict any traffickers; trafficking victims continued to be detained, deported, and charged with crimes without law enforcement determining if they were forced to commit the illegal acts by traffickers; the government again did not allocate money to a fund established in 2004 for victim compensation and repatriation; a draft national action plan to combat trafficking was not completed for the sixth consecutive year (2020)

Illicit drugs: drug trafficking and illegally importing controlled substances are serious offenses in Brunei and carry a mandatory death penalty

BULGARIA

INTRODUCTION

Background: The Bulgars, a Central Asian Turkic tribe, merged with the local Slavic inhabitants in the late 7th century to form the first Bulgarian state. In succeeding centuries, Bulgaria struggled with the Byzantine Empire to assert its place in the Balkans, but by the end of the 14th century the country was overrun by the Ottoman Turks. Northern Bulgaria attained autonomy in 1878 and all of Bulgaria became independent from the Ottoman Empire in 1908. Having fought on the losing side in both World Wars, Bulgaria fell within the Soviet sphere of influence and became a People's Republic in 1946. Communist domination ended in 1990, when Bulgaria held its first multiparty election since World War II and began the contentious process of moving toward political democracy and a market economy while combating inflation, unemployment, corruption, and crime. The country joined NATO in 2004 and the EU in 2007.

GEOGRAPHY

Location: Southeastern Europe, bordering the Black Sea, between Romania and Turkey

Geographic coordinates: 43 00 N, 25 00 E

Map references: Europe

Area: *total:* 110,879 sq km
land: 108,489 sq km
water: 2,390 sq km
country comparison to the world: 105

Area - comparative: almost identical in size to Virginia; slightly larger than Tennessee

Land boundaries: *total:* 1,806 km
border countries (5): Greece 472 km; Macedonia 162 km; Romania 605 km; Serbia 344 km; Turkey 223 km

Coastline: 354 km

Maritime claims: *territorial sea:* 12 nm
contiguous zone: 24 nm
exclusive economic zone: 200 nm

Climate: temperate; cold, damp winters; hot, dry summers

Terrain: mostly mountains with lowlands in north and southeast

Elevation: *highest point:* Musala 2,925 m
lowest point: Black Sea 0 m
mean elevation: 472 m

Natural resources: bauxite, copper, lead, zinc, coal, timber, arable land

Land use: *agricultural land:* 46.9% (2018 est.)
arable land: 29.9% (2018 est.)
permanent crops: 1.5% (2018 est.)
permanent pasture: 15.5% (2018 est.)
forest: 36.7% (2018 est.)
other: 16.4% (2018 est.)

Irrigated land: 1,020 sq km (2012)

Major rivers (by length in km): Danube (shared with Germany [s], Austria, Slovakia, Czechia, Hungary, Croatia, Serbia, Ukraine, Moldova, and Romania [m]) - 2,888 km
note – [s] after country name indicates river source; [m] after country name indicates river mouth

Major watersheds (area sq km): Atlantic Ocean drainage: *(Black Sea)* Danube (795,656 sq km)

Population distribution: a fairly even distribution throughout most of the country, with urban areas attracting larger populations

Natural hazards: earthquakes; landslides

Geography - note: strategic location near Turkish Straits; controls key land routes from Europe to Middle East and Asia

PEOPLE AND SOCIETY

Population: 6,873,253 (2022 est.)
country comparison to the world: 107

Nationality: *noun:* Bulgarian(s)
adjective: Bulgarian

Ethnic groups: Bulgarian 76.9%, Turkish 8%, Romani 4.4%, other 0.7% (including Russian, Armenian, and Vlach), other (unknown) 10% (2011 est.)
note: Romani populations are usually underestimated in official statistics and may represent 9–11% of Bulgaria's population

Languages: Bulgarian (official) 76.8%, Turkish 8.2%, Romani 3.8%, other 0.7%, unspecified 10.5% (2011 est.)
major-language sample(s):
Световен Алманах, незаменимият източник за основна информация. (Bulgarian)

Religions: Eastern Orthodox 59.4%, Muslim 7.8%, other (including Catholic, Protestant, Armenian Apostolic Orthodox, and Jewish) 1.7%, none 3.7%, unspecified 27.4% (2011 est.)

Age structure: *0-14 years:* 14.52% (male 520,190/ female 491,506)
15-24 years: 9.4% (male 340,306/female 314,241)
25-54 years: 42.87% (male 1,538,593/female 1,448,080)
55-64 years: 13.15% (male 433,943/female 482,474)
65 years and over: 20.06% (male 562,513/female 835,053) (2020 est.)

Dependency ratios: *total dependency ratio:* 56.6
youth dependency ratio: 23
elderly dependency ratio: 33.6
potential support ratio: 3 (2020 est.)

Median age: *total:* 43.7 years
male: 41.9 years
female: 45.6 years (2020 est.)
country comparison to the world: 20

Population growth rate: -0.67% (2022 est.)
country comparison to the world: 226

Birth rate: 8.05 births/1,000 population (2022 est.)
country comparison to the world: 216

Death rate: 14.41 deaths/1,000 population (2022 est.)
country comparison to the world: 5

Net migration rate: -0.29 migrant(s)/1,000 population (2022 est.)
country comparison to the world: 117

Population distribution: a fairly even distribution throughout most of the country, with urban areas attracting larger populations

Urbanization: *urban population:* 76.4% of total population (2022)
rate of urbanization: -0.28% annual rate of change (2020-25 est.)

Major urban areas - population: 1.287 million SOFIA (capital) (2022)

Sex ratio: *at birth:* 1.06 male(s)/female
0-14 years: 1.06 male(s)/female
15-24 years: 1.08 male(s)/female
25-54 years: 1.07 male(s)/female
55-64 years: 0.91 male(s)/female
65 years and over: 0.72 male(s)/female
total population: 0.95 male(s)/female (2022 est.)

Mother's mean age at first birth: 26.4 years (2020 est.)

Maternal mortality ratio: 10 deaths/100,000 live births (2017 est.)
country comparison to the world: 144

Infant mortality rate: *total:* 7.98 deaths/1,000 live births
male: 9.02 deaths/1,000 live births
female: 6.88 deaths/1,000 live births (2022 est.)
country comparison to the world: 150

Life expectancy at birth: *total population:* 75.57 years
male: 72.36 years
female: 78.97 years (2022 est.)
country comparison to the world: 120

Total fertility rate: 1.5 children born/woman (2022 est.)
country comparison to the world: 202

Drinking water source: *improved: urban:* 99.5% of population
rural: 97.4% of population
total: 99% of population
unimproved: urban: 0.5% of population
rural: 2.6% of population
total: 1% of population (2020 est.)

Current health expenditure: 7.1% of GDP (2019)

Physicians density: 4.2 physicians/1,000 population (2018)

Hospital bed density: 7.5 beds/1,000 population (2017)

Sanitation facility access: *improved: urban:* 100% of population
rural: 100% of population
total: 100% of population

HIV/AIDS - adult prevalence rate: (2019 est.) <.1%

Obesity - adult prevalence rate: 25% (2016)
country comparison to the world: 53

Alcohol consumption per capita: *total:* 11.18 liters of pure alcohol (2019 est.)
beer: 4.44 liters of pure alcohol (2019 est.)
wine: 1.72 liters of pure alcohol (2019 est.)
spirits: 4.96 liters of pure alcohol (2019 est.)
other alcohols: 0.06 liters of pure alcohol (2019 est.)
country comparison to the world: 9

Tobacco use: *total:* 39% (2020 est.)
male: 40.9% (2020 est.)
female: 37.1% (2020 est.)
country comparison to the world: 7

Children under the age of 5 years underweight: 1.9% (2014)
country comparison to the world: 111

Education expenditures: 4.1% of GDP (2017 est.)
country comparison to the world: 98

Literacy: *definition:* age 15 and over can read and write
total population: 98.4%
male: 98.7%
female: 98.1% (2015)

School life expectancy (primary to tertiary education): *total:* 14 years
male: 14 years
female: 14 years (2019)

Unemployment, youth ages 15-24: *total:* 14.2%
male: 14.6%
female: 13.7% (2020 est.)

ENVIRONMENT

Environment - current issues: air pollution from industrial emissions; rivers polluted from raw sewage, heavy metals, detergents; deforestation; forest damage from air pollution and resulting acid rain; soil contamination from heavy metals from metallurgical plants and industrial wastes

Environment - international agreements: *party to:* Air Pollution, Air Pollution-Heavy Metals, Air Pollution-Multi-effect Protocol, Air Pollution-Nitrogen Oxides, Air Pollution-Persistent Organic Pollutants, Air Pollution-Sulphur 85, Air Pollution-Sulphur 94, Air Pollution-Volatile Organic Compounds, Antarctic-Environmental Protection, Antarctic-Marine Living Resources, Antarctic Treaty, Biodiversity, Climate Change, Climate Change-Kyoto Protocol, Climate Change-Paris Agreement, Comprehensive Nuclear Test Ban, Desertification, Endangered Species, Environmental Modification, Hazardous Wastes, Law of the Sea, Marine Dumping- London Convention, Marine Dumping-London Protocol, Nuclear Test Ban, Ozone Layer Protection, Ship Pollution, Tropical Timber 2006, Wetlands, Whaling
signed, but not ratified: none of the selected agreements

Air pollutants: *particulate matter emissions:* 18.82 micrograms per cubic meter (2016 est.)
carbon dioxide emissions: 41.71 megatons (2016 est.)
methane emissions: 6.77 megatons (2020 est.)

Climate: temperate; cold, damp winters; hot, dry summers

Land use: *agricultural land:* 46.9% (2018 est.)
arable land: 29.9% (2018 est.)
permanent crops: 1.5% (2018 est.)
permanent pasture: 15.5% (2018 est.)
forest: 36.7% (2018 est.)
other: 16.4% (2018 est.)

Urbanization: *urban population:* 76.4% of total population (2022)
rate of urbanization: -0.28% annual rate of change (2020-25 est.)

Revenue from forest resources: *forest revenues:* 0.22% of GDP (2018 est.)
country comparison to the world: 89

Revenue from coal: *coal revenues:* 0.14% of GDP (2018 est.)
country comparison to the world: 23

Waste and recycling: *municipal solid waste generated annually:* 3.011 million tons (2015 est.)
municipal solid waste recycled annually: 572,993 tons (2015 est.)
percent of municipal solid waste recycled: 19% (2015 est.)

Major rivers (by length in km): Danube (shared with Germany [s], Austria, Slovakia, Czechia, Hungary, Croatia, Serbia, Ukraine, Moldova, and Romania [m]) - 2,888 km
note – [s] after country name indicates river source; [m] after country name indicates river mouth

Major watersheds (area sq km): Atlantic Ocean drainage: *(Black Sea)* Danube (795,656 sq km)

Total water withdrawal: *municipal:* 882 million cubic meters (2017 est.)
industrial: 3.942 billion cubic meters (2017 est.)
agricultural: 834.5 million cubic meters (2017 est.)

Total renewable water resources: 21.3 billion cubic meters (2017 est.)

GOVERNMENT

Country name: *conventional long form:* Republic of Bulgaria
conventional short form: Bulgaria
local long form: Republika Bulgaria
local short form: Bulgaria
former: Kingdom of Bulgaria, People's Republic of Bulgaria
etymology: named after the Bulgar tribes who settled the lower Balkan region in the 7th century A.D.

Government type: parliamentary republic

Capital: *name:* Sofia
geographic coordinates: 42 41 N, 23 19 E
time difference: UTC+2 (7 hours ahead of Washington, DC, during Standard Time)
daylight saving time: +1hr, begins last Sunday in March; ends last Sunday in October
etymology: named after the Saint Sofia Church in the city, parts of which date back to the 4th century A.D.

Administrative divisions: 28 provinces (oblasti, singular - oblast); Blagoevgrad, Burgas, Dobrich, Gabrovo, Haskovo, Kardzhali, Kyustendil, Lovech, Montana, Pazardzhik, Pernik, Pleven, Plovdiv, Razgrad, Ruse, Shumen, Silistra, Sliven, Smolyan, Sofia, Sofia-Grad (Sofia City), Stara Zagora, Targovishte, Varna, Veliko Tarnovo, Vidin, Vratsa, Yambol

Independence: 3 March 1878 (as an autonomous principality within the Ottoman Empire); 22 September 1908 (complete independence from the Ottoman Empire)

National holiday: Liberation Day, 3 March (1878)

Constitution: *history:* several previous; latest drafted between late 1990 and early 1991, adopted 13 July 1991
amendments: proposed by the National Assembly or by the president of the republic; passage requires three-fourths majority vote of National Assembly members in three ballots; signed by the National Assembly chairperson; note - under special circumstances, a "Grand National Assembly" is elected with the authority to write a new constitution and amend certain articles of the constitution, including those affecting basic civil rights and national sovereignty; passage requires at least two-thirds majority vote in each of several readings; amended several times, last in 2015

Legal system: civil law

International law organization participation: accepts compulsory ICJ jurisdiction with reservations; accepts ICCt jurisdiction

Citizenship: *citizenship by birth:* no
citizenship by descent only: at least one parent must be a citizen of Bulgaria
dual citizenship recognized: yes
residency requirement for naturalization: 5 years

Suffrage: 18 years of age; universal

Executive branch: *chief of state:* President Rumen RADEV (since 22 January 2017); Vice President Iliana IOTOVA (since 22 January 2017)
head of government: Prime Minister Gulub DONEV (since 2 August 2022); note - Prime Minister DONEV leads a caretaker government until snap elections are held on 2 October 2022
cabinet: Council of Ministers nominated by the prime minister, elected by the National Assembly
elections/appointments: president and vice president elected on the same ballot by absolute majority popular vote in 2 rounds if needed for a 5-year term (eligible for a second term); election last held on 14 and 21 November 2021 (next to be held in fall 2026); chairman of the Council of Ministers (prime minister) elected by the National Assembly; deputy prime ministers nominated by the prime minister, elected by the National Assembly
election results: 2021: Rumen RADEV reelected president in second round; percent of vote in the first round - Rumen RADEV (independent) 49.4%, Anastas GERDZHIKOV (independent) 22.8%, Mustafa KARADAYI (DPS) 11.6%, Kostadin KOSTADINOV (Revival) 3.9%, Lozan PANOV (independent) 3.7%, other 8.6%; percent of vote in the second round - Rumen RADEV 66.7%, Anastas GERDZHIKOV 31.8%, neither 1.5%
2016: Rumen RADEV elected president in second round; percent of vote in the second round - Rumen RADEV (independent, supported by Bulgarian Socialist Party) 59.4%, Tsetska TSACHEVA (GERB) 36.2%, neither 4.5%
2011: Rosen PLEVNELIEV elected president in the second round; percent of vote in the second round - Rosen PLEVNELIEV (independent) 52.6%, Ivailo KALFIN (BSP) 47.4%

Legislative branch: *description:* unicameral National Assembly or Narodno Sabranie (240 seats; members directly elected in multi-seat constituencies by proportional representation vote to serve 4-year terms)
elections: last held on 2 October 2022 (next election to be held in 2026)
election results: percent of vote by party/coalition - GERB-SDS 24.5%, PP 19.5%, DPS 13.3%, Revival 9.8%, BSP for Bulgaria 9%, DB 7.2%, BV 4.5%, other 12.2%; seats by party/coalition GERB-SDS 67, PP 53, DPS 36, Revival 27, BSP for Bulgaria 25, DB 20, BV 12; composition - men NA, women NA, percent of women NA%

Judicial branch: *highest court(s):* Supreme Court of Cassation (consists of a chairman and approximately 72 judges organized into penal, civil, and commercial colleges); Supreme Administrative Court (organized into 2 colleges with various panels of 5 judges each); Constitutional Court (consists of 12 justices); note - Constitutional Court resides outside the judiciary
judge selection and term of office: Supreme Court of Cassation and Supreme Administrative judges elected by the Supreme Judicial Council or SJC (consists of 25 members with extensive legal experience) and appointed by the president; judges can serve until mandatory retirement at age 65; Constitutional Court justices elected by the National Assembly and appointed by the president and the SJC; justices appointed for 9-year terms with renewal of 4 justices every 3 years
subordinate courts: appeals courts; regional and district courts; administrative courts; courts martial

Political parties and leaders: Agrarian People's Union or ZNS [Roumen YONCHEV]
BSP for Bulgaria [Korneliya NINOVA] (alliance of BSP, PKT, New Dawn, Ecoglasnost)
Bulgaria of the Citizens or DBG [Dimitar DELCHEV]
Bulgarian Agrarian People's Union or BZNS [Nikolay NENCHEV]
Bulgarian Rise or BV [Stefan YANEV]
Bulgarian Socialist Party or BSP [Korneliya NINOVA]
Citizens for the European Development of Bulgaria or GERB [Boyko BORISOV] (alliance with SDS)
Democratic Bulgaria or DB (alliance of Yes! Bulgaria, DSB, and The Greens) [Atanas ATANASOV, Hristo IVANOV]
Democrats for a Strong Bulgaria or DSB [Atanas ATANASOV]

Ecoglasnost [Emil GEORGIEV]
Green Movement or The Greens [Borislav SANDOV, Vladislav PENEV]
Middle European Class or SEC [Konstantin BACHIISKI]
Movement for Rights and Freedoms or DPS [Mustafa KARADAYI]
Movement 21 or D21 [Tatyana DONCHEVA]
New Dawn [Mincho MINCHEV]
Political Club Thrace or PKT [Stefan NACHEZ]
Political Movement "Social Democrats" or PDS [Elena NONEVA]
Revival [Kostadin KOSTADINOV]
Stand Up.BG or IS.BG [Maya MONOLOVA]
Stand Up.BG, We Are Coming! or IBG-NI [Maya MONOLOVA, Nikolay HADZHIGENOV] (coalition of IS.BG, D21, DBG, ENP, and ZNS)
There is Such a People or ITN [Slavi TRIFONOV]
United People's Party or ENP [Valentina VASILEVA-FILADELFEVS]
Union of Democratic Forces or SDS [Rumen HRISTOV] (alliance with GERB)
Yes! Bulgaria [Hristo IVANOV]
Volt Bulgaria or Volt [Nastimir ANANIEV]
We Continue the Change of PP [Kiril PETKOV and Asen VASILEV] (electoral alliance of PP, PDS, SEC, and Volt)

International organization participation: Australia Group, BIS, BSEC, CD, CE, CEI, CERN, EAPC, EBRD, ECB, EIB, EU, FAO, G- 9, IAEA, IBRD, ICAO, ICC (national committees), ICCt, ICRM, IDA, IFC, IFRCS, IHO (pending member), ILO, IMF, IMO, IMSO, Interpol, IOC, IOM, IPU, ISO, ITU, ITUC (NGOs), MIGA, NATO, NSG, OAS (observer), OIF, OPCW, OSCE, PCA, SELEC, UN, UNCTAD, UNESCO, UNHCR, UNIDO, UNMIL, UNWTO, UPU, Wassenaar Arrangement, WCO, WFTU (NGOs), WHO, WIPO, WMO, WTO, ZC

Diplomatic representation in the US: *chief of mission:* Ambassador Georgi Velikov PANAYOTOV (since 7 June 2022)
chancery: 1621 22nd Street NW, Washington, DC 20008
telephone: [1] (202) 387-0174; [1] (202) 299-0273, [1] (202) 483-1386
FAX: [1] (202) 234-7973
email address and website:
office@bulgaria-embassy.org; Embassy.Washington@mfa.bg
https://www.bulgaria-embassy.org/en/homepage/
consulate(s) general: Chicago, Los Angeles, New York

Diplomatic representation from the US: *chief of mission:* Ambassador Herro MUSTAFA (since 18 October 2019)
embassy: 16, Kozyak Street, Sofia 1408
mailing address: 5740 Sofia Place, Washington, DC 20521-5740
telephone: [359] (2) 937-5100
FAX: [359] (2) 937-5320
email address and website:
acs_sofia@state.gov
https://bg.usembassy.gov/

Flag description: three equal horizontal bands of white (top), green, and red; the pan-Slavic white-blue-red colors were modified by substituting a green band (representing freedom) for the blue
note: the national emblem, formerly on the hoist side of the white stripe, has been removed

National symbol(s): *lion; national colors:* white, green, red

National anthem: *name:* "Mila Rodino" (Dear Homeland)
lyrics/music: Tsvetan Tsvetkov RADOSLAVOV
note: adopted 1964; composed in 1885 by a student en route to fight in the Serbo-Bulgarian War

National heritage: *total World Heritage Sites:* 10 (7 cultural, 3 natural)
selected World Heritage Site locales: Boyana Church (c); Madara Rider (c); Thracian Tomb of Kazanlak (c); Rock- Hewn Churches of Ivanovo (c); Rila Monastery (c); Ancient City of Nessebar (c); Thracian Tomb of Sveshtari (c); Srebarna Nature Reserve (n); Pirin National Park (n); Primeval Beech Forests of the Carpathians (n)

ECONOMY

Economic overview: Bulgaria, a former communist country that entered the EU in 2007, has an open economy that historically has demonstrated strong growth, but its per-capita income remains the lowest among EU members and its reliance on energy imports and foreign demand for its exports makes its growth sensitive to external market conditions.

The government undertook significant structural economic reforms in the 1990s to move the economy from a centralized, planned economy to a more liberal, market-driven economy. These reforms included privatization of state-owned enterprises, liberalization of trade, and strengthening of the tax system - changes that initially caused some economic hardships but later helped to attract investment, spur growth, and make gradual improvements to living conditions. From 2000 through 2008, Bulgaria maintained robust, average annual real GDP growth in excess of 6%, which was followed by a deep recession in 2009 as the financial crisis caused domestic demand, exports, capital inflows and industrial production to contract, prompting the government to rein in spending. Real GDP growth remained slow - less than 2% annually - until 2015, when demand from EU countries for Bulgarian exports, plus an inflow of EU development funds, boosted growth to more than 3%. In recent years, strong domestic demand combined with low international energy prices have contributed to Bulgaria's economic growth approaching 4% and have also helped to ease inflation. Bulgaria's prudent public financial management contributed to budget surpluses both in 2016 and 2017.

Bulgaria is heavily reliant on energy imports from Russia, a potential vulnerability, and is a participant in EU-backed efforts to diversify regional natural gas supplies. In late 2016, the Bulgarian Government provided funding to Bulgaria's National Electric Company to cover the $695 million compensation owed to Russian nuclear equipment manufacturer Atomstroyexport for the cancellation of the Belene Nuclear Power Plant project, which the Bulgarian Government terminated in 2012. As of early 2018, the government was floating the possibility of resurrecting the Belene project. The natural gas market, dominated by state-owned Bulgargaz, is also almost entirely supplied by Russia. Infrastructure projects such as the Inter-Connector Greece-Bulgaria and Inter-Connector Bulgaria-Serbia, which would enable Bulgaria to have access to non-Russian gas, have either stalled or made limited progress. In 2016, the Bulgarian Government established the State eGovernment Agency. This new agency is responsible for the electronic governance, coordinating national policies with the EU, and strengthening cybersecurity.

Despite a favorable investment regime, including low, flat corporate income taxes, significant challenges remain. Corruption in public administration, a weak judiciary, low productivity, lack of transparency in public procurements, and the presence of organized crime continue to hamper the country's investment climate and economic prospects.

Real GDP (purchasing power parity): $155.06 billion (2020 est.)
$161.78 billion (2019 est.)
$156.02 billion (2018 est.)
note: data are in 2017 dollars
country comparison to the world: 74

Real GDP growth rate: 3.39% (2019 est.)
3.2% (2018 est.)
3.5% (2017 est.)
country comparison to the world: 89

Real GDP per capita: $22,400 (2020 est.)
$23,200 (2019 est.)
$22,200 (2018 est.)
note: data are in 2017 dollars
country comparison to the world: 83

GDP (official exchange rate): $68.49 billion (2019 est.)

Inflation rate (consumer prices): 3.1% (2019 est.)
2.8% (2018 est.)
2% (2017 est.)
country comparison to the world: 147

Credit ratings:

Fitch rating: BBB (2017)

Moody's rating: Baa1 (2020)

Standard & Poors rating: BBB (2019)
note: The year refers to the year in which the current credit rating was first obtained.

GDP - composition, by sector of origin: *agriculture:* 4.3% (2017 est.)
industry: 28% (2017 est.)
services: 67.4% (2017 est.)

GDP - composition, by end use: *household consumption:* 61.6% (2017 est.)
government consumption: 16% (2017 est.)
investment in fixed capital: 19.2% (2017 est.)
investment in inventories: 1.7% (2017 est.)
exports of goods and services: 66.3% (2017 est.)
imports of goods and services: -64.8% (2017 est.)

Agricultural products: wheat, maize, sunflower seed, milk, barley, rapeseed, potatoes, grapes, tomatoes, watermelons

Industries: electricity, gas, water; food, beverages, tobacco; machinery and equipment, automotive parts, base metals, chemical products, coke, refined petroleum, nuclear fuel; outsourcing centers

Industrial production growth rate: 3.6% (2017 est.)
country comparison to the world: 80

Labor force: 3.113 million (2020 est.)
note: number of employed persons
country comparison to the world: 102

Labor force - by occupation: *agriculture:* 6.8%
industry: 26.6%
services: 66.6% (2016 est.)

Unemployment rate: 5.66% (2019 est.)
6.18% (2018 est.)
country comparison to the world: 91

Unemployment, youth ages 15-24: *total:* 14.2%
male: 14.6%
female: 13.7% (2020 est.)

country comparison to the world: 113

Population below poverty line: 23.8% (2019 est.)

Gini Index coefficient - distribution of family income: 40.4 (2017 est.)
38.3 (2016)
country comparison to the world: 60

Household income or consumption by percentage share: *lowest 10%:* 1.9%
highest 10%: 31.2% (2017)

Budget: *revenues:* 20.35 billion (2017 est.)
expenditures: 19.35 billion (2017 est.)

Budget surplus (+) or deficit (-): 1.8% (of GDP) (2017 est.)
country comparison to the world: 16

Public debt: 23.9% of GDP (2017 est.)
27.4% of GDP (2016 est.)
note: defined by the EU's Maastricht Treaty as consolidated general government gross debt at nominal value, outstanding at the end of the year in the following categories of government liabilities: currency and deposits, securities other than shares excluding financial derivatives, and loans; general government sector comprises the subsectors: central government, state government, local government, and social security funds
country comparison to the world: 181

Taxes and other revenues: 35.7% (of GDP) (2017 est.)
country comparison to the world: 58

Fiscal year: calendar year

Current account balance: $2.06 billion (2019 est.)
$611 million (2018 est.)
country comparison to the world: 39

Exports: $39.27 billion (2020 est.)
$44.04 billion (2019 est.)
$43.52 billion (2018 est.)
note: Data are in current year dollars and do not include illicit exports or re-exports.
country comparison to the world: 64

Exports - partners: Germany 16%, Romania 8%, Italy 7%, Turkey 7%, Greece 6% (2019)

Exports - commodities: refined petroleum, packaged medicines, copper, wheat, electricity (2019)

Imports: $38.07 billion (2020 est.) note: data are in current year dollars
$41.84 billion (2019 est.) note: data are in current year dollars
$41.91 billion (2018 est.) note: data are in current year dollars
country comparison to the world: 65

Imports - partners: Germany 11%, Russia 9%, Italy 7%, Romania 7%, Turkey 7% (2019)

Imports - commodities: crude petroleum, copper, cars, packaged medicines, refined petroleum (2019)

Reserves of foreign exchange and gold: $28.38 billion (31 December 2017 est.)
$25.13 billion (31 December 2016 est.)
country comparison to the world: 51

Debt - external: $39.059 billion (2019 est.)
$41.139 billion (2018 est.)
country comparison to the world: 77

Exchange rates: leva (BGN) per US dollar -
1.61885 (2020 est.)
1.7669 (2019 est.)
1.7172 (2018 est.)
1.7644 (2014 est.)
1.4742 (2013 est.)

ENERGY

Electricity access: *electrification - total population:* 100% (2020)

Electricity: *installed generating capacity:* 11.097 million kW (2020 est.)
consumption: 30,905,170,000 kWh (2019 est.)
exports: 7.115 billion kWh (2020 est.)
imports: 3.707 billion kWh (2020 est.)
transmission/distribution losses: 2.767 billion kWh (2019 est.)

Electricity generation sources: *fossil fuels:* 36.5% of total installed capacity (2020 est.)
nuclear: 44.7% of total installed capacity (2020 est.)
solar: 4% of total installed capacity (2020 est.)
wind: 4% of total installed capacity (2020 est.)
hydroelectricity: 9.1% of total installed capacity (2020 est.)
biomass and waste: 1.9% of total installed capacity (2020 est.)

Coal: *production:* 22.298 million metric tons (2020 est.)
consumption: 23.213 million metric tons (2020 est.)
exports: 35,000 metric tons (2020 est.)
imports: 675,000 metric tons (2020 est.)
proven reserves: 2.366 billion metric tons (2019 est.)

Petroleum: *total petroleum production:* 4,500 bbl/day (2021 est.)
refined petroleum consumption: 97,800 bbl/day (2019 est.)
crude oil and lease condensate exports: 0 bbl/day (2018 est.)
crude oil and lease condensate imports: 119,800 bbl/day (2018 est.)
crude oil estimated reserves: 15 million barrels (2021 est.)

Refined petroleum products - production: 144,300 bbl/day (2015 est.)
country comparison to the world: 60

Refined petroleum products - exports: 92,720 bbl/day (2015 est.)
country comparison to the world: 45

Refined petroleum products - imports: 49,260 bbl/day (2015 est.)
country comparison to the world: 83

Natural gas: *production:* 62.439 million cubic meters (2020 est.)
consumption: 2,929,401,000 cubic meters (2019 est.)
exports: 2.747 million cubic meters (2020 est.)
imports: 2,950,157,000 cubic meters (2019 est.)
proven reserves: 5.663 billion cubic meters (2021 est.)

Carbon dioxide emissions: 38.373 million metric tonnes of CO2 (2019 est.)
from coal and metallurgical coke: 20.483 million metric tonnes of CO2 (2019 est.)
from petroleum and other liquids: 12.248 million metric tonnes of CO2 (2019 est.)
from consumed natural gas: 5.642 million metric tonnes of CO2 (2019 est.)
country comparison to the world: 67

Energy consumption per capita: 103.924 million Btu/person (2019 est.)
country comparison to the world: 55

COMMUNICATIONS

Telephones - fixed lines: *total subscriptions:* 872,757 (2020 est.)
subscriptions per 100 inhabitants: 13 (2020 est.)
country comparison to the world: 77

Telephones - mobile cellular: *total subscriptions:* 7,945,739 (2020 est.)
subscriptions per 100 inhabitants: 114 (2020 est.)
country comparison to the world: 98

Telecommunication systems: *general assessment:* Bulgaria's telecom market was for some years affected by the difficult macroeconomic climate, as well as by relatively high unemployment and a shrinking population; these factors continue to slow investments in the sector, though revenue growth has returned since 2019; there still remains pressure on revenue growth, with consumers migrating from fixed-line voice telephony to mobile and VoIP alternatives, while the volume of SMS and MMS traffic has been affected by the growing use of alternative OTT messaging services; investing in network upgrades and its development of services based on 5G have stimulated other market players to invest in their own service provision; by the end of 2022 about 70% of the population is expected to be covered by 5G; the broadband market in Bulgaria enjoys excellent cross-platform competition; the share of the market held by DSL has fallen steadily as a result of customers being migrated to fiber networks; by early 2021 about 65% of fixed-line broadband subscribers were on fiber infrastructure; Bulgaria joins the U.S. State Department's Clean Network initiative in a bid to protect its 5G communications networks (2022)
domestic: fixed-line over 13 per 100 persons, mobile-cellular teledensity, fostered by multiple service providers, is over 114 telephones per 100 persons (2020)
international: country code - 359; Caucasus Cable System via submarine cable provides connectivity to Ukraine, Georgia and Russia; a combination submarine cable and land fiber-optic system provides connectivity to Italy, Albania, and Macedonia; satellite earth stations - 3 (1 Intersputnik in the Atlantic Ocean region, 2 Intelsat in the Atlantic and Indian Ocean regions) (2019)

Broadcast media: 4 national terrestrial TV stations with 1 state-owned and 3 privately owned; a vast array of TV stations are available from cable and satellite TV providers; state-owned national radio broadcasts over 3 networks; large number of private radio stations broadcasting, especially in urban areas

Internet country code: .bg

Internet users: *total:* 4,853,811 (2020 est.)
percent of population: 70% (2020 est.)
country comparison to the world: 92

Broadband - fixed subscriptions: *total:* 2,115,053 (2020 est.)
subscriptions per 100 inhabitants: 30 (2020 est.)
country comparison to the world: 56

TRANSPORTATION

National air transport system: *number of registered air carriers:* 8 (2020)
inventory of registered aircraft operated by air carriers: 44
annual passenger traffic on registered air carriers: 1,022,645 (2018)
annual freight traffic on registered air carriers: 1.38 million (2018) mt-km

Civil aircraft registration country code prefix: LZ

Airports: *total:* 68 (2021)

country comparison to the world: 72

Airports - with paved runways: *total:* 57
over 3,047 m: 2
2,438 to 3,047 m: 17
1,524 to 2,437 m: 12
under 914 m: 26 (2021)

Airports - with unpaved runways: *total:* 11
914 to 1,523 m: 2
under 914 m: 9 (2021)

Heliports: 1 (2021)

Pipelines: 2,765 km gas, 346 km oil, 378 km refined products (2017)

Railways: *total:* 5,114 km (2014)
standard gauge: 4,989 km (2014) 1.435-m gauge (2,880 km electrified)
narrow gauge: 125 km (2014) 0.760-m gauge
country comparison to the world: 37

Roadways: *total:* 19,512 km (2011)
paved: 19,235 km (2011) (includes 458 km of expressways)
unpaved: 277 km (2011)
note: does not include Category IV local roads
country comparison to the world: 115

Waterways: 470 km (2009)
country comparison to the world: 91

Merchant marine: *total:* 79
by type: bulk carrier 4, general cargo 14, oil tanker 8, other 53 (2021)
country comparison to the world: 99

Ports and terminals: *major seaport(s):* Burgas, Varna (Black Sea)

MILITARY AND SECURITY

Military and security forces: *Bulgarian Armed Forces:* Land Forces (Army), Naval Forces, Bulgarian Air Forces (Voennovazdushni Sili, VVS), Joint Special Forces; Ministry of Interior: Border Guards (2022)

Military expenditures: 1.7% of GDP (2022 est.)
1.6% of GDP (2021)
1.6% of GDP (2020)
3.1% of GDP (2019) (approximately $2.95 billion)
1.5% of GDP (2018) (approximately $1.72 billion)
country comparison to the world: 76

Military and security service personnel strengths: approximately 28,000 active duty personnel (17,000 Army; 4,000 Navy; 7,000 Air Force) (2022)

Military equipment inventories and acquisitions: the military's inventory consists primarily of Soviet-era equipment, although in recent years Bulgaria has procured limited amounts of more modern weapons systems from some Western countries (2022)

Military service age and obligation: 18 years of age for voluntary military service; conscription ended in 2007; service obligation 6-9 months (2022)
note 1: in 2021, women comprised about 17% of the Bulgarian military's full-time personnel
note 2: in 2020, Bulgaria announced a program to allow every citizen up to the age of 40 to join the armed forces for 6 months of military service in the voluntary reserve

Military - note: Bulgaria became a member of NATO in 2004; Bulgaria conducts its own air policing mission, but because of Russian aggression in the Black Sea region, NATO allies have sent detachments of fighters to augment the Bulgarian Air Force since 2014 (2022)

TERRORISM

Terrorist group(s): Islamic State of Iraq and ash-Sham (ISIS); Islamic Revolutionary Guard Corps/ Qods Force

TRANSNATIONAL ISSUES

Disputes - international: none

Refugees and internally displaced persons: *refugees (country of origin):* 19,014 (Syria) (mid-year 2021); 51,864 (Ukraine) (as of 22 November 2022)
stateless persons: 1,143 (mid-year 2021)
note: 83,250 estimated refugee and migrant arrivals (January 2015-September 2022); Bulgaria is predominantly a transit country

Illicit drugs: source country for amphetamine tablets

BURKINA FASO

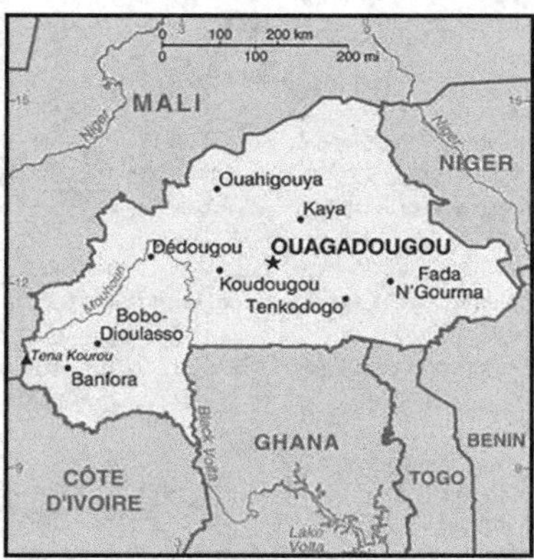

INTRODUCTION

Background: Many of Burkina Faso's ethnic groups arrived in the region between the 12th and 15th centuries. The Gurma and Mossi peoples established several of the largest kingdoms in the area and used horse-mounted warriors in military campaigns. Of the various Mossi kingdoms, the most powerful were Ouagadougou and Yatenga. In the late 19th century, European states competed for control of the region. France eventually conquered the area and established it as a French protectorate.

The area achieved independence from France in 1960 and changed its name to Burkina Faso in 1984. Repeated military coups were common in the country's first few decades. The last successful coup occurred in 1987 when Blaise COMPAORE deposed the former president, established a government, and ruled for 27 years. In October 2014, COMPAORE resigned following protests against his repeated efforts to amend the constitution's two-term presidential limit. An interim administration led a year-long transition period organizing presidential and legislative elections. In November 2015, Roch Marc Christian KABORE was elected president; he was reelected in November 2020.

Terrorist groups - including groups affiliated with Al-Qa'ida and the Islamic State - began attacks in the country in 2016 and conducted attacks in the capital in 2016, 2017, and 2018. By late 2021, insecurity in Burkina Faso had displaced 1.4 million people and led to significant jumps in humanitarian needs and food insecurity. In addition to terrorism, the country faces a myriad of problems including high population growth, recurring drought, pervasive and perennial food insecurity, and limited natural resources. It is one of the world's poorest countries.

GEOGRAPHY

Location: Western Africa, north of Ghana

Geographic coordinates: 13 00 N, 2 00 W

Map references: Africa

Area: *total:* 274,200 sq km
land: 273,800 sq km
water: 400 sq km

Area - comparative: slightly larger than Colorado

Land boundaries: *total:* 3,611 km
border countries (6): Benin 386 km; Cote d'Ivoire 545 km; Ghana 602 km; Mali 1325 km; Niger 622 km; Togo 131 km

Coastline: 0 km (landlocked)

Maritime claims: none (landlocked)

Climate: three climate zones including a hot tropical savanna with a short rainy season in the southern half, a tropical hot semi-arid steppe climate typical of the Sahel region in the northern half, and small area of hot desert in the very north of the country bordering the Sahara Desert

Terrain: mostly flat to dissected, undulating plains; hills in the west and southeast; occupies an extensive plateau with savanna that is grassy in the north and gradually gives way to sparse forests in the south

Elevation: *highest point:* Tena Kourou 749 m
lowest point: Mouhoun (Black Volta) River 200 m
mean elevation: 297 m

Natural resources: gold, manganese, zinc, limestone, marble, phosphates, pumice, salt

Land use: *agricultural land:* 44.2% (2018 est.)
arable land: 22% (2018 est.)
permanent crops: 37% (2018 est.)
permanent pasture: 21.93% (2018 est.)
forest: 19.3% (2018 est.)
other: 36.5% (2018 est.)

Irrigated land: 550 sq km (2016)

Major rivers (by length in km): Volta river source (shared with Ghana [m]) - 1,600 km
note – [s] after country name indicates river source; [m] after country name indicates river mouth

Major watersheds (area sq km): Atlantic Ocean drainage: Niger (2,261,741 sq km), Volta (410,991 sq km)

Population distribution: Most of the population is located in the center and south. Nearly one-third of the population lives in cities. The capital and largest city is Ouagadougou (Ouaga), with a population of 1.8 million as shown in this population distribution map
(2019)

Natural hazards: recurring droughts

Geography - note: landlocked savanna cut by the three principal rivers of the Black, Red, and White Voltas

PEOPLE AND SOCIETY

Population: 21,935,389 (2022 est.)

Nationality: *noun:* Burkinabe (singular and plural)
adjective: Burkinabe

Ethnic groups: Mossi 52%, Fulani 8.4%, Gurma 7%, Bobo 4.9%, Gurunsi 4.6%, Senufo 4.5%, Bissa 3.7%, Lobi 2.4%, Dagara 2.4%, Tuareg/Bella 1.9%, Dioula 0.8%, unspecified/no answer 0.3%, other 7.2% (2010 est.)

Languages: French (official), native African languages belonging to Sudanic family spoken by 90% of the population

Religions: Muslim 63.2%, Roman Catholic 24.6%, Protestant 6.9%, traditional/animist 4.2%, none 0.7%, unspecified 0.4% (2017-18 est.)

Demographic profile: Burkina Faso has a young age structure – the result of declining mortality combined with steady high fertility – and continues to experience rapid population growth, which is putting increasing pressure on the country's limited arable land. More than 65% of the population is under the age of 25, and the population is growing at 3% annually. Mortality rates, especially those of infants and children, have decreased because of improved health care, hygiene, and sanitation, but women continue to have an average of almost 6 children. Even if fertility were substantially reduced, today's large cohort entering their reproductive years would sustain high population growth for the foreseeable future. Only about a third of the population is literate and unemployment is widespread, dampening the economic prospects of Burkina Faso's large working-age population.

Migration has traditionally been a way of life for Burkinabe, with seasonal migration being replaced by stints of up to two years abroad. Cote d'Ivoire remains the top destination, although it has experienced periods of internal conflict. Under French colonization, Burkina Faso became a main labor source for agricultural and factory work in Cote d'Ivoire. Burkinabe also migrated to Ghana, Mali, and Senegal for work between the world wars. Burkina Faso attracts migrants from Cote d'Ivoire, Ghana, and Mali, who often share common ethnic backgrounds with the Burkinabe. Despite its food shortages and high poverty rate, Burkina Faso has become a destination for refugees in recent years and hosts about 26,000 Malian refugees as of July 2022.
(2018)

Age structure: *0-14 years:* 43.58% (male 4,606,350/female 4,473,951)
15-24 years: 20.33% (male 2,121,012/female 2,114,213)
25-54 years: 29.36% (male 2,850,621/female 3,265,926)
55-64 years: 3.57% (male 321,417/female 423,016)
65 years and over: 3.16% (male 284,838/female 374,057) (2020 est.)

Dependency ratios: *total dependency ratio:* 87.9
youth dependency ratio: 83.4
elderly dependency ratio: 4.5
potential support ratio: 22.1 (2020 est.)

Median age: *total:* 17.9 years
male: 17 years
female: 18.7 years (2020 est.)

Population growth rate: 2.53% (2022 est.)

Birth rate: 33.57 births/1,000 population (2022 est.)

Death rate: 7.71 deaths/1,000 population (2022 est.)

Net migration rate: -0.61 migrant(s)/1,000 population (2022 est.)

Population distribution: Most of the population is located in the center and south. Nearly one-third of the population lives in cities. The capital and largest city is Ouagadougou (Ouaga), with a population of 1.8 million as shown in this population distribution map
(2019)

Urbanization: *urban population:* 31.9% of total population (2022)
rate of urbanization: 4.75% annual rate of change (2020-25 est.)

Major urban areas - population: 3.056 million OUAGADOUGOU (capital), 1.074 million Bobo-Dioulasso (2022)

Sex ratio: *at birth:* 1.03 male(s)/female
0-14 years: 1.03 male(s)/female
15-24 years: 1.01 male(s)/female
25-54 years: 0.86 male(s)/female
55-64 years: 0.75 male(s)/female
65 years and over: 0.66 male(s)/female
total population: 0.96 male(s)/female (2022 est.)

Mother's mean age at first birth: 19.4 years (2010 est.)
note: data represents median age at first birth among women 25-29

Maternal mortality ratio: 320 deaths/100,000 live births (2017 est.)

Infant mortality rate: *total:* 49.42 deaths/1,000 live births
male: 53.7 deaths/1,000 live births
female: 45.02 deaths/1,000 live births (2022 est.)

Life expectancy at birth: *total population:* 63.44 years
male: 61.63 years
female: 65.31 years (2022 est.)

Total fertility rate: 4.27 children born/woman (2022 est.)

Contraceptive prevalence rate: 35.3% (2020/21)

Drinking water source: *improved: urban:* 94.7% of population
rural: 71.3% of population
total: 78.5% of population
unimproved: urban: 5.3% of population
rural: 28.7% of population
total: 21.5% of population (2020 est.)

Current health expenditure: 5.5% of GDP (2019)

Physicians density: 0.09 physicians/1,000 population (2019)

Hospital bed density: 0.4 beds/1,000 population

Sanitation facility access: *improved: urban:* 90.8% of population
rural: 37.7% of population
total: 54% of population
unimproved: urban: 9.2% of population
rural: 62.3% of population
total: 46% of population (2020 est.)

HIV/AIDS - adult prevalence rate: 0.7% (2020 est.)

Major infectious diseases: *degree of risk:* very high (2020)
food or waterborne diseases: bacterial and protozoal diarrhea, hepatitis A, and typhoid fever
vectorborne diseases: dengue fever and malaria
water contact diseases: schistosomiasis
animal contact diseases: rabies
respiratory diseases: meningococcal meningitis
note: on 21 March 2022, the US Centers for Disease Control and Prevention (CDC) issued a Travel Alert for polio in Africa; Burkina Faso is currently considered a high risk to travelers for circulating vaccine-derived polioviruses (cVDPV); vaccine-derived poliovirus (VDPV) is a strain of the weakened poliovirus that was initially included in oral polio vaccine (OPV) and *that has changed over time and behaves more like the wild or naturally occurring virus;* this means it can be spread more easily to people who are unvaccinated against polio and who come in contact with the stool or respiratory secretions, such as from a sneeze, of an "infected" person who received oral polio vaccine; the CDC recommends that before any international travel, anyone unvaccinated, incompletely vaccinated, or with an unknown polio vaccination status should complete the routine polio vaccine series; before travel to any high-risk destination, the CDC recommends that adults who previously completed the full, routine polio vaccine series receive a single, lifetime booster dose of polio vaccine

Obesity - adult prevalence rate: 5.6% (2016)

Alcohol consumption per capita: *total:* 7.28 liters of pure alcohol (2019 est.)
beer: 1 liters of pure alcohol (2019 est.)
wine: 0.08 liters of pure alcohol (2019 est.)
spirits: 0.31 liters of pure alcohol (2019 est.)
other alcohols: 5.88 liters of pure alcohol (2019 est.)

Tobacco use: *total:* 14.3% (2020 est.)
male: 22.1% (2020 est.)
female: 6.4% (2020 est.)

Children under the age of 5 years underweight: 16.4% (2019)

Education expenditures: 5.8% of GDP (2019 est.)

Literacy: *definition:* age 15 and over can read and write
total population: 39.3%
male: 49.2%
female: 31% (2018)

School life expectancy (primary to tertiary education): *total:* 9 years
male: 9 years
female: 9 years (2020)

Unemployment, youth ages 15-24: *total:* 8.6%
male: 8.9%
female: 8.4% (2019)

ENVIRONMENT

Environment - current issues: recent droughts and desertification severely affecting agricultural activities, population distribution, and the economy; overgrazing; soil degradation; deforestation (2019)

Environment - international agreements: *party to:* Biodiversity, Climate Change, Climate

Change-Kyoto Protocol, Climate Change-Paris Agreement, Comprehensive Nuclear Test Ban, Desertification, Endangered Species, Hazardous Wastes, Law of the Sea, Marine Life Conservation, Ozone Layer Protection, Wetlands
signed, but not ratified: Nuclear Test Ban

Air pollutants: *particulate matter emissions:* 36.78 micrograms per cubic meter (2016 est.)
carbon dioxide emissions: 3.42 megatons (2016 est.)
methane emissions: 12.85 megatons (2020 est.)

Climate: three climate zones including a hot tropical savanna with a short rainy season in the southern half, a tropical hot semi-arid steppe climate typical of the Sahel region in the northern half, and small area of hot desert in the very north of the country bordering the Sahara Desert

Land use: *agricultural land:* 44.2% (2018 est.)
arable land: 22% (2018 est.)
permanent crops: 37% (2018 est.)
permanent pasture: 21.93% (2018 est.)
forest: 19.3% (2018 est.)
other: 36.5% (2018 est.)

Urbanization: *urban population:* 31.9% of total population (2022)
rate of urbanization: 4.75% annual rate of change (2020-25 est.)

Revenue from forest resources: *forest revenues:* 4.54% of GDP (2018 est.)

Revenue from coal: *coal revenues:* 0% of GDP (2018 est.)

Food insecurity: *severe localized food insecurity: due to civil insecurity in the north* - according to the latest analysis, 3.45 million people are projected to be food insecure and in need of humanitarian assistance between June and August 2022; in Centre-Nord and Sahel regions, insecurity continues to cause population displacements and, as of March 2022, about 1.85 million people had been displaced and required assistance; domestic cereal production in 2021 was estimated at a below-average level due to effects of adverse weather and civil conflict, further aggravating conditions; abnormally high prices of food are also a contributory factor that have constrained access to food; the coup d'état that occurred in January 2022 is an additional factor that could increase civil insecurity and further stress food insecurity conditions (2022)

Waste and recycling: *municipal solid waste generated annually:* 2,575,251 tons (2015 est.)
municipal solid waste recycled annually: 309,030 tons (2005 est.)
percent of municipal solid waste recycled: 12% (2005 est.)

Major rivers (by length in km): Volta river source (shared with Ghana [m]) - 1,600 km
note – [s] after country name indicates river source; [m] after country name indicates river mouth

Major watersheds (area sq km): Atlantic Ocean drainage: Niger (2,261,741 sq km), Volta (410,991 sq km)

Total water withdrawal: *municipal:* 375.6 million cubic meters (2017 est.)
industrial: 21.7 million cubic meters (2017 est.)
agricultural: 420.7 million cubic meters (2017 est.)

Total renewable water resources: 13.5 billion cubic meters (2017 est.)

GOVERNMENT

Country name: *conventional long form:* none
conventional short form: Burkina Faso
local long form: none
local short form: Burkina Faso
former: Upper Volta, Republic of Upper Volta
etymology: name translates as "Land of the Honest (Incorruptible) Men"

Government type: presidential republic

Capital: *name:* Ouagadougou
geographic coordinates: 12 22 N, 1 31 W
time difference: UTC 0 (5 hours ahead of Washington, DC, during Standard Time)
etymology: Ouagadougou is a Francophone spelling of the native name "Wogodogo," meaning "where people get honor and respect"

Administrative divisions: 13 regions; Boucle du Mouhoun, Cascades, Centre, Centre-Est, Centre-Nord, Centre-Ouest, Centre-Sud, Est, Hauts-Bassins, Nord, Plateau-Central, Sahel, Sud-Ouest

Independence: 5 August 1960 (from France)

National holiday: Republic Day, 11 December (1958); note - commemorates the day that Upper Volta became an autonomous republic in the French Community

Constitution: *history:* several previous; latest approved by referendum 2 June 1991, adopted 11 June 1991, temporarily suspended late October to mid-November 2014; initial draft of a new constitution to usher in the new republic was completed in January 2017 and a final draft was submitted to the government in December 2017; a constitutional referendum originally scheduled for adoption in March 2019 was postponed; on 1 March 2022 a transition charter was adopted, allowing military authorities to rule for three years and barring transitional President Lt. Col. Paul-Henri Sandaogo DAMIBA from being an electoral candidate after the transition
amendments: proposed by the president, by a majority of National Assembly membership, or by petition of at least 30,000 eligible voters submitted to the Assembly; passage requires at least three-fourths majority vote in the Assembly; failure to meet that threshold requires majority voter approval in a referendum; constitutional provisions on the form of government, the multiparty system, and national sovereignty cannot be amended; amended several times

Legal system: civil law based on the French model and customary law; in mid-2019, the National Assembly amended the penal code

International law organization participation: has not submitted an ICJ jurisdiction declaration; accepts ICCt jurisdiction

Citizenship: *citizenship by birth:* no
citizenship by descent only: at least one parent must be a citizen of Burkina Faso
dual citizenship recognized: yes
residency requirement for naturalization: 10 years

Suffrage: 18 years of age; universal

Executive branch: *chief of state:* transitional President Capt Ibrahim TRAORE (since 30 September 2022); note - on 30 September 2022, a military junta led by TRAORE, took power and ousted President Lt. Col. Paul-Henri Sandaogo DAMIBA and took over as head of the Patriotic Movement for Safeguard and Restoration.
head of government: Prime Minister Albert OUEDRAOGO (since 3 March 2022); note - transitional President Lt. Col. DAMIBA appointed OUEDRAOGO Prime Minister on 3 March 2022; the position had been vacant since 24 January 2022 when the military ousted former Prime Minister Lassina ZERBO
cabinet: Council of Ministers appointed by the president on the recommendation of the prime minister
elections/appointments: president elected by absolute majority popular vote in 2 rounds if needed for a 5-year term (eligible for a second); last held on 22 November 2020 (next to be held in November 2025); prime minister appointed by the president with consent of the National Assembly; note - on 1 March 2022 a transition charter was adopted, allowing military authorities to rule for three years and barring transitional President Lt. Col. Paul-Henri Sandaogo DAMIBA from being an electoral candidate after the transition.
election results: *2020:* Roch Marc Christian KABORE reelected president in first round; percent of vote - Roch Marc Christian KABORE (MPP) 57.9%, Eddie KOMBOIGO (CDP) 15.5%, Zephirin DIABRE (UPC)12.5%, other 14.1%
2015: Roch Marc Christian KABORE elected president in first round; percent of vote - Roch Marc Christian KABORE (MPP) 53.5%, Zephirin DIABRE (UPC) 29.6%, Tahirou BARRY (PAREN) 3.1%, Benewende Stanislas SANKARA (UNIRMS) 2.8%, other 10.9%

Legislative branch: *description:* unicameral National Assembly (127 seats; 111 members directly elected in 13 multi-seat constituencies by party-list proportional representation vote and 26 members elected in a nationwide constituency by proportional representation vote; all member serve 5-year terms)
elections: last held on 22 November 2020 (next to be held in November 2025)
election results: percent of vote by party - MPP 34.6%, CDP 13.3%, UPC 10.2%, NTD 5.6%, other 36.3%; seats by party - MPP 56, CDP 20, NTD 13, UPC 12, other 26; composition as of October 2021 - men 119, women 8, percent of women 6.3%

Judicial branch: *highest court(s):* Supreme Court of Appeals or Cour de Cassation (consists of NA judges); Council of State (consists of NA judges); Constitutional Council or Conseil Constitutionnel (consists of the council president and 9 members)
judge selection and term of office: Supreme Court judge appointments mostly controlled by the president of Burkina Faso; judges have no term limits; Council of State judge appointment and tenure NA; Constitutional Council judges appointed by the president of Burkina Faso upon the proposal of the minister of justice and the president of the National Assembly; judges appointed for 9-year terms with one-third of membership renewed every 3 years
subordinate courts: Appeals Court; High Court; first instance tribunals; district courts; specialized courts relating to issues of labor, children, and juveniles; village (customary) courts

Political parties and leaders: Act Together [Kadre OUEDRAOGO]
African Democratic Rally/Alliance for Democracy and Federation or ADF/RDA [Gilbert Noel OUEDRAOGO]
Congress for Democracy and Progress or CDP [Eddie KOMBOIGO]
Convergence for Progress and Solidarity-Generation 3 or CPS-G3
Movement for the Future Burkina Faso or MBF
National Convention for Progress or CNP
New Era for Democracy or NTD [Vincent DABILGOU]
Pan-African Alliance for Refoundation or APR

Party for Democracy and Socialism/Metba or PDS/Metba [Philippe OUEDRAOGO]
Party for Development and Change or PDC [Aziz SEREME]
Patriotic Rally for Integrity or RPI
Peoples Movement for Progress or MPP [Roch Marc Christian KABORE]
Progressives United for Renewal or PUR
Union for Progress and Reform or UPC [Zephirin DIABRE]
Union for Rebirth - Sankarist Party or UNIR-PS [Benewende Stanislas SANKARA]
note: only parties with seats in the National Assembly included

International organization participation: ACP, AfDB, AU, CD, ECOWAS, EITI (compliant country), Entente, FAO, FZ, G-77, IAEA, IBRD, ICAO, ICC (NGOs), ICCt, ICRM, IDA, IDB, IFAD, IFC, IFRCS, ILO, IMF, Interpol, IOC, IOM, IPU, ISO, ITSO, ITU, ITUC (NGOs), MIGA, MINUSMA, MONUSCO, NAM, OIC, OIF, OPCW, PCA, UN, UNAMID, UNCTAD, UNESCO, UNIDO, UNISFA, UNITAR, UNWTO, UPU, WADB (regional), WAEMU, WCO, WFTU (NGOs), WHO, WIPO, WMO, WTO

Diplomatic representation in the US: *chief of mission:* Charge d'Affaires Boulmonli Leonard LOMBO (since 15 April 2022)
chancery: 2340 Massachusetts Avenue NW, Washington, DC 20008
telephone: [1] (202) 332-5577
FAX: [1] (202) 667-1882
email address and website:
contact@burkina-usa.org
https://burkina-usa.org/

Diplomatic representation from the US: *chief of mission:* Ambassador Sandra E. CLARK (since 25 September 2020)
embassy: Secteur 15, Ouaga 2000, Avenue Sembene Ousmane, Rue 15.873, Ouagadougou
mailing address: 2440 Ouagadougou Place, Washington, DC 20521-2440
telephone: (226) 25-49-53-00
FAX: (226) 25-49-56-23
email address and website:
ouagaACS@state.gov
https://bf.usembassy.gov/

Flag description: two equal horizontal bands of red (top) and green with a yellow five-pointed star in the center; red recalls the country's struggle for independence, green is for hope and abundance, and yellow represents the country's mineral wealth
note: uses the popular Pan-African colors of Ethiopia

National symbol(s): *white stallion; national colors:* red, yellow, green

National anthem: *name:* "Le Ditanye" (Anthem of Victory)
lyrics/music: Thomas SANKARA
note: adopted 1974; also known as "Une Seule Nuit" (One Single Night); written by the country's former president, an avid guitar player

National heritage: *total World Heritage Sites:* 3 (2 cultural, 1 natural)
selected World Heritage Site locales: Ruins of Loropéni (c); Ancient Ferrous Metallurgy Sites (c); W-Arly-Pendjari Complex (n)

ECONOMY

Economic overview: Burkina Faso is a poor, landlocked country that depends on adequate rainfall. Irregular patterns of rainfall, poor soil, and the lack of adequate communications and other infrastructure contribute to the economy's vulnerability to external shocks. About 80% of the population is engaged in subsistence farming and cotton is the main cash crop. The country has few natural resources and a weak industrial base.

Cotton and gold are Burkina Faso's key exports - gold has accounted for about three-quarters of the country's total export revenues. Burkina Faso's economic growth and revenue depends largely on production levels and global prices for the two commodities. The country has seen an upswing in gold exploration, production, and exports.

In 2016, the government adopted a new development strategy, set forth in the 2016-2020 National Plan for Economic and Social Development, that aims to reduce poverty, build human capital, and to satisfy basic needs. A new three-year IMF program (2018-2020), approved in 2018, will allow the government to reduce the budget deficit and preserve critical spending on social services and priority public investments.

While the end of the political crisis has allowed Burkina Faso's economy to resume positive growth, the country's fragile security situation could put these gains at risk. Political insecurity in neighboring Mali, unreliable energy supplies, and poor transportation links pose long-term challenges.

Real GDP (purchasing power parity): $45.16 billion (2020 est.)
$44.27 billion (2019 est.)
$41.88 billion (2018 est.)
note: data are in 2017 dollars

Real GDP growth rate: 6.4% (2017 est.)
5.9% (2016 est.)
3.9% (2015 est.)

Real GDP per capita: $2,200 (2020 est.)
$2,200 (2019 est.)
$2,100 (2018 est.)
note: data are in 2017 dollars

GDP (official exchange rate): $14.271 billion (2018 est.)

Inflation rate (consumer prices): -3.2% (2019 est.)
1.9% (2018 est.)
1.4% (2017 est.)

Credit ratings:

Standard & Poors rating: *B (2017)*
note: The year refers to the year in which the current credit rating was first obtained.

GDP - composition, by sector of origin: *agriculture:* 31% (2017 est.)
industry: 23.9% (2017 est.)
services: 44.9% (2017 est.)

GDP - composition, by end use: *household consumption:* 56.5% (2017 est.)
government consumption: 23.9% (2017 est.)
investment in fixed capital: 24.6% (2017 est.)
investment in inventories: 1% (2017 est.)
exports of goods and services: 28.4% (2017 est.)
imports of goods and services: -34.4% (2017 est.)

Agricultural products: sorghum, maize, millet, cotton, cow peas, sugar cane, groundnuts, rice, sesame seed, vegetables

Industries: cotton lint, beverages, agricultural processing, soap, cigarettes, textiles, gold

Industrial production growth rate: 10.4% (2017 est.)

Labor force: 8.501 million (2016 est.)
note: a large part of the male labor force migrates annually to neighboring countries for seasonal employment

Labor force - by occupation: *agriculture:* 90%
industry and services: 10% (2000 est.)

Unemployment rate: 77% (2004)

Unemployment, youth ages 15-24: *total:* 8.6%
male: 8.9%
female: 8.4% (2019)

Population below poverty line: 41.4% (2018 est.)

Gini Index coefficient - distribution of family income: 35.3 (2014 est.)
48.2 (1994)

Household income or consumption by percentage share: *lowest 10%:* 2.9%
highest 10%: 32.2% (2009 est.)

Budget: *revenues:* 2.666 billion (2017 est.)
expenditures: 3.655 billion (2017 est.)

Budget surplus (+) or deficit (-): -7.9% (of GDP) (2017 est.)

Public debt: 38.1% of GDP (2017 est.)
38.3% of GDP (2016 est.)

Taxes and other revenues: 21.2% (of GDP) (2017 est.)

Fiscal year: calendar year

Current account balance: -$1.019 billion (2017 est.)
-$820 million (2016 est.)

Exports: $4.47 billion (2019 est.)
$4.51 billion (2018 est.)
note: Data are in current year dollars and do not include illicit exports or re-exports.

Exports - partners: Switzerland 59%, India 21% (2019)

Exports - commodities: gold, cotton, zinc, cashews, sesame seeds (2019)

Imports: $5.02 billion (2019 est.) note: data are in current year dollars
$5.17 billion (2018 est.) note: data are in current year dollars
$5.3 billion (2017 est.)

Imports - partners: Cote d'Ivoire 15%, China 9%, Ghana 8%, France 8%, India 6%, United States 5% (2019)

Imports - commodities: refined petroleum, delivery trucks, packaged medicines, electricity, aircraft (2019)

Reserves of foreign exchange and gold: $49 million (31 December 2017 est.)
$50.9 million (31 December 2016 est.)

Debt - external: $3.056 billion (31 December 2017 est.)
$2.88 billion (31 December 2016 est.)

Exchange rates: Communaute Financiere Africaine francs (XOF) per US dollar -
605.3 (2017 est.)
593.01 (2016 est.)
593.01 (2015 est.)
591.45 (2014 est.)
494.42 (2013 est.)

ENERGY

Electricity access: *electrification - total population:* 22% (2019)
electrification - urban areas: 69% (2019)
electrification - rural areas: 2% (2019)

Electricity: *installed generating capacity:* 392,000 kW (2020 est.)
consumption: 2,033,520,000 kWh (2019 est.)
exports: 0 kWh (2019 est.)
imports: 600 million kWh (2019 est.)
transmission/distribution losses: 248 million kWh (2019 est.)

Electricity generation sources: *fossil fuels:* 89.4% of total installed capacity (2020 est.)
solar: 3.3% of total installed capacity (2020 est.)
hydroelectricity: 6.9% of total installed capacity (2020 est.)
biomass and waste: 0.4% of total installed capacity (2020 est.)

Petroleum: *total petroleum production:* 0 bbl/day (2021 est.)
refined petroleum consumption: 30,800 bbl/day (2019 est.)

Refined petroleum products - imports: 23,580 bbl/day (2015 est.)

Carbon dioxide emissions: 4.444 million metric tonnes of CO2 (2019 est.)
from petroleum and other liquids: 4.444 million metric tonnes of CO2 (2019 est.)

Energy consumption per capita: 3.23 million Btu/person (2019 est.)

COMMUNICATIONS

Telephones - fixed lines: *total subscriptions:* 75,039 (2020 est.)
subscriptions per 100 inhabitants: (2020 est.) less than 1

Telephones - mobile cellular: *total subscriptions:* 22,117,218 (2020 est.)
subscriptions per 100 inhabitants: 106 (2020 est.)

Telecommunication systems: *general assessment:* Burkina Faso's telecom sector in recent years has made some gains in providing the necessary infrastructure and bandwidth to support telecom services; an IXP completed in September 2020 increased international bandwidth capacity by a third, while in mid-2021 the government was able to start the second phase of a national fiber backbone project; this will link the capital city to an addition 145 municipalities, and provide additional connectivity to terrestrial cables in neighboring countries; the activities of the militants in side areas of the country jeopardize overall security, and render it difficult for the telcos to safeguard their networks and equipment; Burkina Faso joins G5 Sahel countries to eliminate roaming fees (2022)
domestic: fixed-line connections stand at less than 1 per 100 persons; mobile-cellular usage nearly 106 per 100, with multiple providers there is competition and the hope for growth from a low base; Internet penetration is 16% (2020)
international: country code - 226; satellite earth station - 1 Intelsat (Atlantic Ocean)

Broadcast media: since the official inauguration of Terrestrial Digital Television (TNT) in December 2017, Burkina Faso now has 14 digital TV channels among which 2 are state-owned; there are more than 140 radio stations (commercial, religious, community) available throughout the country including a national and regional state-owned network; the state-owned Radio Burkina and the private Radio Omega are among the most widespread stations and both include broadcasts in French and local languages (2019)

Internet country code: .bf

Internet users: *total:* 4,598,721 (2020 est.)
percent of population: 22% (2020 est.)

Broadband - fixed subscriptions: *total:* 13,979 (2020 est.)
subscriptions per 100 inhabitants: 0.1 (2020 est.)

TRANSPORTATION

National air transport system: *number of registered air carriers:* 1 (2020)
inventory of registered aircraft operated by air carriers: 3
annual passenger traffic on registered air carriers: 151,531 (2018)
annual freight traffic on registered air carriers: 100,000 (2018) mt-km

Civil aircraft registration country code prefix: XT

Airports: *total:* 23 (2021)

Airports - with paved runways: *total:* 2
over 3,047 m: 1
2,438 to 3,047 m: 1 (2021)

Airports - with unpaved runways: *total:* 21
1,524 to 2,437 m: 3
914 to 1,523 m: 13
under 914 m: 5 (2021)

Railways: *total:* 622 km (2014)
narrow gauge: 622 km (2014) 1.000-m gauge
note: another 660 km of this railway extends into Cote d'Ivoire

Roadways: *total:* 15,304 km (2014)
paved: 3,642 km (2014)
unpaved: 11,662 km (2014)

MILITARY AND SECURITY

Military and security forces: Armed Forces of Burkina Faso (FABF): Army of Burkina Faso (L'Armee de Terre, LAT), Air Force of Burkina Faso (Force Aerienne de Burkina Faso, FABF), National Gendarmerie; Volunteers for the Defense of the Fatherland (VDP) (2022)
note 1: the National Gendarmerie officially reports to the Ministry of Defense, but usually operates in support of the Ministry of Security and the Ministry of Justice; Gendarmerie troops are typically integrated with Army forces in antiterrorism operations
note 2: the VDP is a civilian defense force established in 2019 to act as auxiliaries to the Army in the fight against militants; the volunteers receive two weeks of training and typically assist with carrying out surveillance, information-gathering, and escort duties

Military expenditures: 2.4% of GDP (2021 est.)
2.4% of GDP (2020 est.)
2.2% of GDP (2019 est.) (approximately $450 million)
1.9% of GDP (2018 est.) (approximately $370 million)
1.4% of GDP (2017 est.) (approximately $260 million)

Military and security service personnel strengths: approximately 13,000 personnel (8,000 Army; 500 Air Force; 4,500 National Gendarmerie) (2022)
note 1: in 2019, the Burkina Faso Government announced an initial strength goal for the VDF of 15,000 members, but in October 2022 announced plans to recruit up to 50,000 VDF volunteers
note 2: in 2022, Burkina Faso announced a special recruitment for 3,000 additional soldiers to assist with its fight against terrorist groups operating in the country

Military equipment inventories and acquisitions: the FABF has a mix of foreign-supplied weapons; since 2010, it has received limited amounts of mostly donated secondhand equipment from a variety of countries (2022)

Military service age and obligation: 18-26 years of age for voluntary military service; no conscription; women may serve in supporting roles (2022)

Military deployments: 650 (plus about 180 police) Mali (MINUSMA) (May 2022)
note: Burkina Faso is part of a four (formerly five)-nation anti-jihadist task force known as the G4 Sahel Group, set up in 2014 with Chad, Mali (withdrew in 2022), Mauritania, and Niger; it has committed 550 troops and 100 gendarmes to the force; as of 2020, defense forces from each of the participating states were allowed to pursue terrorist fighters up to 100 km into neighboring countries; the force is backed by France, the UN, and the US

Military - note: including the most recent in October 2022, the military has conducted eight coups since 1960; as of 2022, the military was also actively engaged in combat operations with terrorist groups linked to al-Qa'ida and the Islamic State of Iraq and ash-Sham (ISIS), particularly in the northern and eastern regions; in the north, Jama'at Nusrat al-Islam wal-Muslimin (JNIM), a coalition of al-Qa'ida linked militant groups, has exploited ethnic tensions and perceptions of state neglect, as well as grievances over corruption, patronage politics, social stratification, and land disputes; in 2022, JNIM conducted attacks in 10 of the country's 13 provinces; most of the attacks were assessed to be by the Macina Liberation Front (FLM) of the JNIM coalition; the ISIS-Greater Sahara (ISIS-GS) terrorist group operated in the eastern part of the country; in 2022, an estimated 40% of the country was not under government control (2022)

TERRORISM

Terrorist group(s): Ansarul Islam; Islamic State of Iraq and ash-Sham in the Greater Sahara (ISIS-GS); al-Mulathamun Battalion (al-Mourabitoun); Jama'at Nusrat al-Islam wal-Muslimin (JNIM)

TRANSNATIONAL ISSUES

Disputes - international: adding to illicit cross-border activities, Burkina Faso has issues concerning unresolved boundary alignments with its neighbors; demarcation is currently underway with Mali; the dispute with Niger was referred to the ICJ in 2010, and a dispute over several villages with Benin persists; Benin retains a border dispute with Burkina Faso around the town of Koualau/Kourou

Refugees and internally displaced persons: *refugees (country of origin):* 33,611 (Mali) (2022)

IDPs: 1,761,915 (2022)

BURMA

INTRODUCTION

Background: Burma, colonized by Britain in the 19th century and granted independence post-World War II, contains ethnic Burman and scores of other ethnic and religious minority groups that have all resisted external efforts to consolidate control of the country throughout its history, extending to the several minority groups today that possess independent fighting forces and control pockets of territory. Burman and armed ethnic minorities fought off-and-on until military Gen. NE WIN seized power in 1962. He ruled Burma until 1988 when a military junta took control. In 1990, the junta permitted an election but then rejected the results when the main opposition National League for Democracy (NLD) and its leader AUNG SAN SUU KYI (ASSK) won in a landslide. The junta placed ASSK under house arrest for much of the next 20 years, until November 2010. In 2007, rising fuel prices in Burma led pro-democracy activists and Buddhist monks to launch a "Saffron Revolution" consisting of large protests against the ruling junta, which violently suppressed the movement by killing an unknown number of participants and arresting thousands. The regime prevented new elections until it had drafted a constitution designed to preserve its control; it passed the new constitution in its 2008 referendum, days after Cyclone Nargis killed at least 138,000. The junta conducted an election in 2010, but the NLD boycotted the vote, and the military's Union Solidarity and Development Party easily won; international observers denounced the election as flawed.

With former or current military officers installed in its most senior positions, Burma began a halting process of political and economic reforms. Officials freed prisoners, brokered ceasefires with ethnic armed organizations (EAOs), amended courts, expanded civil liberties, brought ASSK into government in 2012, and permitted the NLD in 2015 to take power after a sweeping electoral win.

However, Burma's first credibly elected civilian government, with ASSK as the de facto head of state, faced strong headwinds after five decades of military dictatorship. The NLD government drew international criticism for blocking investigations of Burma's military for operations, which the US Department of State determined constituted genocide, on its Rohingya population that killed thousands and forced more than 770,000 Rohingya to flee into neighboring Bangladesh. The military did not support an NLD pledge in 2019 to examine reforming the military's 2008 constitution. When the 2020 elections resulted in further NLD gains, the military denounced them as fraudulent. This challenge led Commander-in-Chief Sr. General MIN AUNG HLAING (MAH) to launch a coup in February 2021 that has left Burma reeling with the return to authoritarian rule, the detention of ASSK and thousands of pro-democracy actors, and renewed brutal repression against protestors, widespread violence, and economic decline.

Since the coup and subsequent crackdown, lawmakers elected in the November 2020 election and members of parliament ousted by the military have formed a shadow National Unity Government (NUG). Members of the NUG include representatives from the NLD, ethnic minority groups, civil society, and other minor parties. In May 2021, the NUG announced the formation of an an armed wing called the People's Defense Force, and in September announced the start of an insurgency against the military junta that has continued into 2022.

GEOGRAPHY

Location: Southeastern Asia, bordering the Andaman Sea and the Bay of Bengal, between Bangladesh and Thailand

Geographic coordinates: 22 00 N, 98 00 E

Map references: Southeast Asia

Area: *total:* 676,578 sq km
land: 653,508 sq km
water: 23,070 sq km
country comparison to the world: 42

Area - comparative: slightly smaller than Texas

Land boundaries: *total:* 6,522 km
border countries (5): Bangladesh 271 km; China 2,129 km; India 1,468 km; Laos 238 km; Thailand 2,416 km

Coastline: 1,930 km

Maritime claims: *territorial sea:* 12 nm
contiguous zone: 24 nm
exclusive economic zone: 200 nm
continental shelf: 200 nm or to the edge of the continental margin

Climate: tropical monsoon; cloudy, rainy, hot, humid summers (southwest monsoon, June to September); less cloudy, scant rainfall, mild temperatures, lower humidity during winter (northeast monsoon, December to April)

Terrain: central lowlands ringed by steep, rugged highlands

Elevation: *highest point:* Gamlang Razi 5,870 m
lowest point: Andaman Sea/Bay of Bengal 0 m
mean elevation: 702 m

Natural resources: petroleum, timber, tin, antimony, zinc, copper, tungsten, lead, coal, marble, limestone, precious stones, natural gas, hydropower, arable land

Land use: *agricultural land:* 19.2% (2018 est.)
arable land: 16.5% (2018 est.)
permanent crops: 2.2% (2018 est.)
permanent pasture: 0.5% (2018 est.)
forest: 48.2% (2018 est.)
other: 32.6% (2018 est.)

Irrigated land: 22,950 sq km (2012)

Major rivers (by length in km): Mekong (shared with China [s], Laos, Thailand, Cambodia, and Vietnam [m]) - 4,350 km; Salween river mouth (shared with China [s] and Thailand) - 3,060 km; Irrawaddy river mouth (shared with China [s]) - 2,809 km; Chindwin - 1,158 km
note – [s] after country name indicates river source; [m] after country name indicates river mouth

Major watersheds (area sq km): Indian Ocean drainage: Brahmaputra (651,335 sq km), Ganges (1,016,124 sq km), Irrawaddy (413,710 sq km), Salween (271,914 sq km)

Pacific Ocean drainage: Mekong (805,604 sq km)

Population distribution: population concentrated along coastal areas and in general proximity to the shores of the Irrawaddy River; the extreme north is relatively underpopulated

Natural hazards: destructive earthquakes and cyclones; flooding and landslides common during rainy season (June to September); periodic droughts

Geography - note: strategic location near major Indian Ocean shipping lanes; the north-south flowing Irrawaddy River is the country's largest and most important commercial waterway

PEOPLE AND SOCIETY

Population: 57,526,449 (2022 est.)
country comparison to the world: 25

Nationality: *noun:* Burmese (singular and plural)
adjective: Burmese

Ethnic groups: Burman (Bamar) 68%, Shan 9%, Karen 7%, Rakhine 4%, Chinese 3%, Indian 2%, Mon 2%, other 5%
note: government recognizes 135 indigenous ethnic groups

Languages: Burmese (official)
major-language sample(s):
ကမ္ဘာ့အချက်အလက်စာအုပ်- အခြေခံအချက်အလက်တွေအတွက် မရှိမဖြစ်တဲ့ အရင်းအမြစ်
(Burmese)

note: minority ethnic groups use their own languages

Religions: Buddhist 87.9%, Christian 6.2%, Muslim 4.3%, Animist 0.8%, Hindu 0.5%, other 0.2%, none 0.1% (2014 est.)
note: religion estimate is based on the 2014 national census, including an estimate for the non-enumerated population of Rakhine State, which is assumed to mainly affiliate with the Islamic faith; as of December 2019, Muslims probably make up less than 3% of Burma's total population due to the large outmigration of the Rohingya population since 2017

Demographic profile: Burma's 2014 national census – the first in more than 30 years – revealed that the country's total population is approximately 51.5 million, significantly lower than the Burmese Government's prior estimate of 61 million. The Burmese Government assumed that the 2% population growth rate between 1973 and 1983 remained constant and that emigration was zero, ignoring later sample surveys showing declining fertility rates and substantial labor migration abroad in recent decades. These factors reduced the estimated average annual growth rate between 2003 and 2014 to about .9%. Among Southeast Asian countries, Burma's life expectancy is among the lowest and its infant and maternal mortality rates are among the highest. The large difference in life expectancy between women and men has resulted in older age cohorts consisting of far more women than men.

Burma's demographic transition began in the 1950s, when mortality rates began to drop. Fertility did not start to decrease until the 1960s, sustaining high population growth until the decline accelerated in the 1980s. The birth rate has held fairly steady from 2000 until today. Since the 1970s, the total fertility rate (TFR) has fallen more than 60%, from almost 6 children per woman to 2.2 in 2016. The reduced TFR is largely a result of women marrying later and more women never marrying, both being associated with greater educational attainment and labor force participation among women. TFR, however, varies regionally, between urban and rural areas, by educational attainment, and among ethnic groups, with fertility lowest in urban areas (where it is below replacement level).

The shift in Burma's age structure has been slow (45% of the population is still under 25 years of age) and uneven among its socioeconomic groups. Any economic boost from the growth of the working-age population is likely to take longer to develop, to have a smaller impact, and to be distributed unequally. Rural poverty and unemployment continue to drive high levels of internal and international migration. The majority of labor migration is internal, mainly from rural to urban areas. The new government's growing regional integration, reforms, and improved diplomatic relations are increasing the pace of international migration and destination choices. As many as 4-5 million Burmese, mostly from rural areas and several ethnic groups, have taken up unskilled jobs abroad in agriculture, fishing, manufacturing, and domestic service. Thailand is the most common destination, hosting about 70% of Burma's international migrants, followed by Malaysia, China, and Singapore.

Burma is a patchwork of more than 130 religious and ethnic groups, distinguishing it as one of the most diverse countries in the region. Ethnic minorities face substantial discrimination, and the Rohingya, the largest Muslim group, are arguably the most persecuted population in the country. The Burmese Government and the Buddhist majority see the Rohingya as a threat to identity, competitors for jobs and resources, terrorists, and some still resent them for their alliance with Burma's British colonizers during its 19th century. Since at least the 1960s, they have been subjected to systematic human rights abuses, violence, marginalization, and disenfranchisement, which authorities continue to deny. Despite living in Burma for centuries, many Burmese see the Rohingya as illegal Bengali immigrants and refer to them Bengalis. As a result, the Rohingya have been classified as foreign residents and stripped of their citizenship, rendering them one of the largest stateless populations in the world.

Hundreds of thousands of Burmese from various ethnic groups have been internally displaced (an estimated 644,000 as of year-end 2016) or have fled to neighboring countries over the decades because of persecution, armed conflict, rural development projects, drought, and natural disasters. Bangladesh has absorbed the most refugees from Burma, with an estimated 33,000 officially recognized and 200,000 to 500,000 unrecognized Rohingya refugees, as of 2016. An escalation in violation has caused a surge in the inflow of Rohingya refugees since late August 2017, raising the number to an estimated 870,000. As of June 2017, another approximately 132,500 refugees, largely Rohingya and Chin, were living in Malaysia, and more than 100,000, mostly Karen, were housed in camps along the Burma-Thailand border.

Age structure: *0-14 years:* 25.97% (male 7,524,869/female 7,173,333)
15-24 years: 17% (male 4,852,122/female 4,769,412)
25-54 years: 42.76% (male 11,861,971/female 12,337,482)
55-64 years: 8.22% (male 2,179,616/female 2,472,681)
65 years and over: 6.04% (male 1,489,807/female 1,928,778) (2020 est.)

Dependency ratios: *total dependency ratio:* 46.5
youth dependency ratio: 37.3
elderly dependency ratio: 9.1
potential support ratio: 10.9 (2020 est.)

Median age: *total:* 29.2 years
male: 28.3 years
female: 30 years (2020 est.)
country comparison to the world: 133

Population growth rate: 0.78% (2022 est.)
country comparison to the world: 118

Birth rate: 16.34 births/1,000 population (2022 est.)
country comparison to the world: 99

Death rate: 7.13 deaths/1,000 population (2022 est.)
country comparison to the world: 115

Net migration rate: -1.37 migrant(s)/1,000 population (2022 est.)
country comparison to the world: 156

Population distribution: population concentrated along coastal areas and in general proximity to the shores of the Irrawaddy River; the extreme north is relatively underpopulated

Urbanization: *urban population:* 31.8% of total population (2022)
rate of urbanization: 1.85% annual rate of change (2020-25 est.)

Major urban areas - population: 5.514 million RANGOON (Yangon) (capital), 1.501 million Mandalay (2022)

Sex ratio: *at birth:* 1.06 male(s)/female
0-14 years: 1.05 male(s)/female
15-24 years: 1.02 male(s)/female
25-54 years: 0.96 male(s)/female
55-64 years: 0.89 male(s)/female
65 years and over: 0.63 male(s)/female
total population: 0.97 male(s)/female (2022 est.)

Mother's mean age at first birth: 24.7 years (2015/16 est.)
note: data represents median age at first birth among women 25-49

Maternal mortality ratio: 250 deaths/100,000 live births (2017 est.)
country comparison to the world: 42

Infant mortality rate: *total:* 32.94 deaths/1,000 live births
male: 36.18 deaths/1,000 live births
female: 29.52 deaths/1,000 live births (2022 est.)
country comparison to the world: 44

Life expectancy at birth: *total population:* 69.92 years
male: 68.27 years
female: 71.67 years (2022 est.)
country comparison to the world: 172

Total fertility rate: 2.02 children born/woman (2022 est.)
country comparison to the world: 104

Contraceptive prevalence rate: 52.2% (2015/16)

Drinking water source: *improved: urban:* 95.4% of population
rural: 80.7% of population
total: 85.3% of population
unimproved: urban: 4.6% of population
rural: 19.3% of population
total: 14.7% of population (2020 est.)

Current health expenditure: 4.7% of GDP (2019)

Physicians density: 0.74 physicians/1,000 population (2019)

Hospital bed density: 1 beds/1,000 population (2017)

Sanitation facility access: *improved: urban:* 93.9% of population
rural: 81.3% of population
total: 85.2% of population
unimproved: urban: 6.1% of population
rural: 18.7% of population
total: 14.8% of population (2020 est.)

HIV/AIDS - adult prevalence rate: 0.6% (2019 est.)
country comparison to the world: 58

Major infectious diseases: *degree of risk:* very high (2020)
food or waterborne diseases: bacterial and protozoal diarrhea, hepatitis A, and typhoid fever
vectorborne diseases: dengue fever, malaria, and Japanese encephalitis
animal contact diseases: rabies

Obesity - adult prevalence rate: 5.8% (2016)
country comparison to the world: 172

Alcohol consumption per capita: *total:* 2.06 liters of pure alcohol (2019 est.)
beer: 0.5 liters of pure alcohol (2019 est.)
wine: 0.02 liters of pure alcohol (2019 est.)
spirits: 1.55 liters of pure alcohol (2019 est.)
other alcohols: 0 liters of pure alcohol (2019 est.)
country comparison to the world: 128

Tobacco use: *total:* 44.1% (2020 est.)
male: 68.5% (2020 est.)
female: 19.7% (2020 est.)
country comparison to the world: 2

Children under the age of 5 years underweight: 19.1% (2017/18)
country comparison to the world: 23

Child marriage: *women married by age 15:* 1.9%
women married by age 18: 16%
men married by age 18: 5% (2016 est.)

Education expenditures: 2% of GDP (2019 est.)
country comparison to the world: 178

Literacy: *definition:* age 15 and over can read and write
total population: 89.1%
male: 92.4%
female: 86.3% (2019)

School life expectancy (primary to tertiary education): *total:* 11 years
male: 10 years
female: 11 years (2018)

Unemployment, youth ages 15-24: *total:* 1.5%
male: 1.4%
female: 1.6% (2019 est.)

ENVIRONMENT

Environment - current issues: deforestation; industrial pollution of air, soil, and water; inadequate sanitation and water treatment contribute to disease; rapid depletion of the country's natural resources

Environment - international agreements: *party to:* Biodiversity, Climate Change, Climate Change-Kyoto Protocol, Climate Change-Paris Agreement, Comprehensive Nuclear Test Ban, Desertification, Endangered Species, Hazardous Wastes, Law of the Sea, Nuclear Test Ban, Ozone Layer Protection, Ship Pollution, Tropical Timber 2006, Wetlands
signed, but not ratified: none of the selected agreements

Air pollutants: *particulate matter emissions:* 34.69 micrograms per cubic meter (2016 est.)
carbon dioxide emissions: 25.28 megatons (2016 est.)
methane emissions: 42.2 megatons (2020 est.)

Climate: tropical monsoon; cloudy, rainy, hot, humid summers (southwest monsoon, June to September); less cloudy, scant rainfall, mild temperatures, lower humidity during winter (northeast monsoon, December to April)

Land use: *agricultural land:* 19.2% (2018 est.)
arable land: 16.5% (2018 est.)
permanent crops: 2.2% (2018 est.)
permanent pasture: 0.5% (2018 est.)
forest: 48.2% (2018 est.)
other: 32.6% (2018 est.)

Urbanization: *urban population:* 31.8% of total population (2022)
rate of urbanization: 1.85% annual rate of change (2020-25 est.)

Revenue from forest resources: *forest revenues:* 1.69% of GDP (2018 est.)
country comparison to the world: 38

Revenue from coal: *coal revenues:* 0.01% of GDP (2018 est.)
country comparison to the world: 47

Food insecurity: *severe localized food insecurity: due to conflict, political instability, and economic constraints* - the political crisis, following the military takeover on 1 February 2021, resulted in increased tensions and unrest throughout the country; the current uncertain political situation may further compromise the fragile situation of vulnerable households and the Rohingya IDPs residing in the country; armed conflict between the military and non-state armed groups led to population displacements, disrupted agricultural activities and limited access for humanitarian support especially in Rakhine, Chin, Kachin, Kayin, Kayah and Shan states; income losses and a decline in remittances, due to the impact of the COVID-19 pandemic, have affected the food security situation of vulnerable households; domestic prices of Emata rice, the most consumed variety in the country, were at high levels in May 2022, constraining access to a key staple food (2022)

Waste and recycling: *municipal solid waste generated annually:* 4,677,307 tons (2000 est.)

Major rivers (by length in km): Mekong (shared with China [s], Laos, Thailand, Cambodia, and Vietnam [m]) - 4,350 km; Salween river mouth (shared with China [s] and Thailand) - 3,060 km; Irrawaddy river mouth (shared with China [s]) - 2,809 km; Chindwin - 1,158 km
note – [s] after country name indicates river source; [m] after country name indicates river mouth

Major watersheds (area sq km): Indian Ocean drainage: Brahmaputra (651,335 sq km), Ganges (1,016,124 sq km), Irrawaddy (413,710 sq km), Salween (271,914 sq km)

Pacific Ocean drainage: Mekong (805,604 sq km)

Total water withdrawal: *municipal:* 3.323 billion cubic meters (2017 est.)
industrial: 498.4 million cubic meters (2017 est.)
agricultural: 29.57 billion cubic meters (2017 est.)

Total renewable water resources: 1.168 trillion cubic meters (2017 est.)

GOVERNMENT

Country name: *conventional long form:* Union of Burma
conventional short form: Burma
local long form: Pyidaungzu Thammada Myanma Naingngandaw (translated as the Republic of the Union of Myanmar)
local short form: Myanma Naingngandaw
former: Socialist Republic of the Union of Burma, Union of Myanmar
etymology: both "Burma" and "Myanmar" derive from the name of the majority Burman (Bamar) ethnic group
note: since 1989 the military authorities in Burma and the deposed parliamentary government have promoted the name Myanmar as a conventional name for their state; the US Government has not officially adopted the name

Government type: parliamentary republic

Capital: *name:* Rangoon (aka Yangon, continues to be recognized as the primary Burmese capital by the US Government); Nay Pyi Taw is the administrative capital
geographic coordinates: 16 48 N, 96 10 E
time difference: UTC+6.5 (11.5 hours ahead of Washington, DC, during Standard Time)
etymology: Rangoon/Yangon derives from the Burmese words *yan* and *koun*, which mean "enemies" and "expelled" respectively and provide the meaning of "end of strife"; Nay Pyi Taw translates as: "Great City of the Sun" or "Abode of Kings"

Administrative divisions: 7 regions (taing-myar, singular - taing), 7 states (pyi ne-myar, singular - pyi ne), 1 union territory
regions: Ayeyarwady (Irrawaddy), Bago, Magway, Mandalay, Sagaing, Tanintharyi, Yangon (Rangoon)
states: Chin, Kachin, Kayah, Karen, Mon, Rakhine, Shan
union territory: Nay Pyi Taw

Independence: 4 January 1948 (from the UK)

National holiday: Independence Day, 4 January (1948); Union Day, 12 February (1947)

Constitution: *history:* previous 1947, 1974 (suspended until 2008); latest drafted 9 April 2008, approved by referendum 29 May 2008
amendments: proposals require at least 20% approval by the Assembly of the Union membership; passage of amendments to sections of the constitution on basic principles, government structure, branches of government, state emergencies, and amendment procedures requires 75% approval by the Assembly and approval in a referendum by absolute majority of registered voters; passage of amendments to other sections requires only 75% Assembly approval; military granted 25% of parliamentary seats by default; amended 2015

Legal system: mixed legal system of English common law (as introduced in codifications designed for colonial India) and customary law

International law organization participation: has not submitted an ICJ jurisdiction declaration; non-party state to the ICCt

Citizenship: *citizenship by birth:* no
citizenship by descent only: both parents must be citizens of Burma
dual citizenship recognized: no
residency requirement for naturalization: none
note: an applicant for naturalization must be the child or spouse of a citizen

Suffrage: 18 years of age; universal

Executive branch: *chief of state:* Prime Minister, State Administration Council (SAC) Chair, Sr. Gen. MIN AUNG HLAING (since 1 August 2021); note - MIN AUNG HLAING self-appointed himself to the role of prime minister of a "caretaker" provisional government that subsumed the SAC on 1 August 2021; the SAC, chaired by MIN AUNG HLAING, has served as the executive governing body since 2 February 2021, following the 1 February 2021 military takeover of the government and the declaration of a state of emergency and still exists under the provisional government according to state media
head of government: Prime Minister, State Administration Council (SAC) Chair, Sr. Gen. MIN AUNG HLAING (since 1 August 2021); MIN AUNG HLAING self-appointed himself to the role of prime minister of a "caretaker" provisional government that subsumed the SAC on 1 August 2021
cabinet: Cabinet appointments shared by the president and the commander-in-chief; note - after 1 February, the military junta replaced the cabinet
elections/appointments: prior to the military takeover, president was indirectly elected by simple majority vote by the full Assembly of the Union from among 3 vice-presidential candidates nominated by the Presidential Electoral College (consists of members of the lower and upper houses and military members); the other 2 candidates become vice presidents (president elected for a 5-year term); election last held on 28 March 2018; the military junta pledged to hold new elections in 2023
election results: 2018: WIN MYINT elected president in an indirect by-election held on 28 March 2018 after the resignation of HTIN KYAW; Assembly of the Union vote - WIN MYINT (NLD) 403, MYINT SWE (USDP) 211, HENRY VAN THIO (NLD) 18, 4 votes canceled (636 votes cast); note

- WIN MYINT and other key leaders of the ruling NLD party were placed under arrest following the military takeover on 1 February 2021
2016: Assembly of the Union vote - HTIN KYAW elected president; HTIN KYAW (NLD) 360, MYINT SWE (USDP) 213, HENRY VAN THIO (NLD) 79 (652 votes cast)
state counsellor: State Counselor AUNG SAN SUU KYI (since 6 April 2016); note - under arrest since 1 February 2021 (has been sentenced to 26 years in prison as of October 2022); formerly served as minister of foreign affairs and minister for the office of the president
note: a parliamentary bill creating the position of "state counsellor" was signed into law by former President HTIN KYAW on 6 April 2016; a state counsellor serves the equivalent term of the president and is similar to a prime minister in that the holder acts as a link between the parliament and the executive branch

Legislative branch: *description:* bicameral Assembly of the Union or Pyidaungsu consists of:
House of Nationalities or Amyotha Hluttaw, (224 seats; 168 members directly elected in single-seat constituencies by absolute majority vote with a second round if needed and 56 appointed by the military; members serve 5-year terms) House of Representatives or Pyithu Hluttaw, (440 seats, currently 433; 330 members directly elected in single-seat constituencies by simple majority vote and 110 appointed by the military; members serve 5-year terms); note - on 1 February 2021, the military dissolved the Assembly of the Union; the State Administration Council (SAC) governs in place of the Assembly of the Union
elections: House of Nationalities - last held on 8 November 2020 (next to be held in 2025)
House of Representatives - last held on 8 November 2020 (next to be held in 2025); note - the military junta overturned the results of the 8 November legislative elections
election results: House of Nationalities - percent of vote by party - NLD 61.6%, USDP 3.1%, ANP 1.8%, MUP 1.3%, KySDP 1.3%, other 5.9%, military appointees 25%; seats by party - NLD 138, USDP 7, ANP 4, MUP 3, KySPD 3, SNLD 2, TNP 2, other 2, canceled due to insurgency 7, military appointees 56
House of Representatives - percent of vote by party - NLD 58.6%, USDP 5.9%, SNLD 3.0%, other 7.5%, military 25%; seats by party - NLD 258, USDP 26, SNLD 13, ANP 4, PNO 3, TNP 3, MUP 2, KySPD 2, other 4, canceled due to insurgency 15, military appointees 110

Judicial branch: *highest court(s):* Supreme Court of the Union (consists of the chief justice and 7-11 judges)
judge selection and term of office: chief justice and judges nominated by the president, with approval of the Lower House, and appointed by the president; judges normally serve until mandatory retirement at age 70
subordinate courts: High Courts of the Region; High Courts of the State; Court of the Self-Administered Division; Court of the Self-Administered Zone; district and township courts; special courts (for juvenile, municipal, and traffic offenses); courts martial

Political parties and leaders: Arakan National Party or ANP [THAR TUN HLA]
Democratic Party or DP [U THU WAI]
Kayah State Democratic Party or KySDP
Kayin People's Party or KPP [TUN AUNG MYINT]
Kokang Democracy and Unity Party or KDUP [LUO XINGGUANG]
La Hu National Development Party or LHNDP [KYA HAR SHAL]
Lisu National Development Party or LNDP [U ARKI DAW]
Mon Unity Party (formed in 2019 from the All Mon Region Democracy Party and Mon National Party)
National Democratic Force or NDF [KHIN MAUNG SWE]
National League for Democracy or NLD [AUNG SAN SUU KYI]
National Unity Party or NUP [U HAN SHWE]
Pa-O National Organization or PNO [AUNG KHAM HTI]
People's Party [KO KO GYI]
Shan Nationalities Democratic Party or SNDP [SAI AI PAO]
Shan Nationalities League for Democracy or SNLD
Ta'ang National Party or TNP [AIK MONE]
Tai-Leng Nationalities Development Party or TNDP [U SAI HTAY AUNG]
Union Solidarity and Development Party or USDP [THAN HTAY]
Unity and Democracy Party of Kachin State or UDPKS [U KHAT HTEIN NAN]
Wa Democratic Party or WDP [KHUN HTUN LU]
Wa National Unity Party or WNUP [NYI PALOTE]
Zomi Congress for Democracy or ZCD [PU CIN SIAN THANG]
numerous smaller parties

International organization participation: ADB, ARF, ASEAN, BIMSTEC, CP, EAS, EITI (candidate country), FAO, G-77, IAEA, IBRD, ICAO, ICRM, IDA, IFAD, IFC, IFRCS, IHO, ILO, IMF, IMO, Interpol, IOC, IOM, IPU, ISO (correspondent), ITU, ITUC (NGOs), NAM, OPCW (signatory), SAARC (observer), UN, UNCTAD, UNESCO, UNIDO, UNWTO, UPU, WCO, WHO, WIPO, WMO, WTO

Diplomatic representation in the US: *chief of mission:* Ambassador (vacant); Charge d'Affaires HTWE Hteik Tin Lwin (since 5 February 2022)
chancery: 2300 S Street NW, Washington, DC 20008
telephone: [1] (202) 332-3344; [1] (202) 332-4250
FAX: [1] (202) 332-4351
email address and website:
pyi.thayar@verizon.net; washington-embassy@mofa.gov.mm
http://www.mewashingtondc.com/wordpress/
consulate(s) general: Los Angeles, New York

Diplomatic representation from the US: *chief of mission:* Ambassador Thomas J. VAJDA (since 19 January 2021)
embassy: 110 University Avenue, Kamayut Township, Rangoon
mailing address: 4250 Rangoon Place, Washington DC 20521-4250
telephone: [95] (1) 753-6509
FAX: [95] (1) 751-1069
email address and website:
ACSRangoon@state.gov
https://mm.usembassy.gov/

Flag description: design consists of three equal horizontal stripes of yellow (top), green, and red; centered on the green band is a large white five-pointed star that partially overlaps onto the adjacent colored stripes; the design revives the triband colors used by Burma from 1943-45, during the Japanese occupation

National symbol(s): *chinthe (mythical lion); national colors:* yellow, green, red, white

National anthem: *name:* "Kaba Ma Kyei" (Till the End of the World, Myanmar)
lyrics/music: SAYA TIN
note: adopted 1948; Burma is among a handful of non-European nations that have anthems rooted in indigenous traditions; the beginning portion of the anthem is a traditional Burmese anthem before transitioning into a Western-style orchestrated work

National heritage: *total World Heritage Sites:* 2 (both cultural)
selected World Heritage Site locales: Pyu Ancient Cities; Bagan

ECONOMY

Economic overview: Since Burma began the transition to a civilian-led government in 2011, the country initiated economic reforms aimed at attracting foreign investment and reintegrating into the global economy. Burma established a managed float of the Burmese kyat in 2012, granted the Central Bank operational independence in July 2013, enacted a new anti-corruption law in September 2013, and granted licenses to 13 foreign banks in 2014-16. State Counsellor AUNG SAN SUU KYI and the ruling National League for Democracy, who took power in March 2016, have sought to improve Burma's investment climate following the US sanctions lift in October 2016 and reinstatement of Generalized System of Preferences trade benefits in November 2016. In October 2016, Burma passed a foreign investment law that consolidates investment regulations and eases rules on foreign ownership of businesses.

Burma's economic growth rate recovered from a low growth under 6% in 2011 but has been volatile between 6% and 8% between 2014 and 2018. Burma's abundant natural resources and young labor force have the potential to attract foreign investment in the energy, garment, information technology, and food and beverage sectors. The government is focusing on accelerating agricultural productivity and land reforms, modernizing and opening the financial sector, and developing transportation and electricity infrastructure. The government has also taken steps to improve transparency in the mining and oil sectors through publication of reports under the Extractive Industries Transparency Initiative (EITI) in 2016 and 2018.

Despite these improvements, living standards have not improved for the majority of the people residing in rural areas. Burma remains one of the poorest countries in Asia – approximately 26% of the country's 51 million people live in poverty. The isolationist policies and economic mismanagement of previous governments have left Burma with poor infrastructure, endemic corruption, underdeveloped human resources, and inadequate access to capital, which will require a major commitment to reverse. The Burmese Government has been slow to address impediments to economic development such as unclear land rights, a restrictive trade licensing system, an opaque revenue collection system, and an antiquated banking system.

Real GDP (purchasing power parity): $247.24 billion (2020 est.)
$274.69 billion (2019 est.)
$270.11 billion (2018 est.)
note: data are in 2017 dollars
country comparison to the world: 61

Real GDP growth rate: 6.8% (2017 est.)
5.9% (2016 est.)
7% (2015 est.)
country comparison to the world: 20

Real GDP per capita: $4,500 (2020 est.)
$5,100 (2019 est.)
$5,000 (2018 est.)
note: data are in 2017 dollars
country comparison to the world: 178

GDP (official exchange rate): $76.606 billion (2019 est.)

Inflation rate (consumer prices): 8.8% (2019 est.)
6.8% (2018 est.)
4.6% (2017 est.)
country comparison to the world: 202

GDP - composition, by sector of origin: *agriculture:* 24.1% (2017 est.)
industry: 35.6% (2017 est.)
services: 40.3% (2017 est.)

GDP - composition, by end use: *household consumption:* 59.2% (2017 est.)
government consumption: 13.8% (2017 est.)
investment in fixed capital: 33.5% (2017 est.)
investment in inventories: 1.5% (2017 est.)
exports of goods and services: 21.4% (2017 est.)
imports of goods and services: -28.6% (2017 est.)

Agricultural products: rice, sugar cane, beans, vegetables, milk, maize, poultry, groundnuts, fruit, plantains

Industries: agricultural processing; wood and wood products; copper, tin, tungsten, iron; cement, construction materials pharmaceuticals; fertilizer; oil and natural gas; garments; jade and gems

Industrial production growth rate: 8.9% (2017 est.)
country comparison to the world: 20

Labor force: 22.3 million (2017 est.)
country comparison to the world: 25

Labor force - by occupation: *agriculture:* 70%
industry: 7%
services: 23% (2001 est.)

Unemployment rate: 4% (2017 est.)
4% (2016 est.)
country comparison to the world: 59

Unemployment, youth ages 15-24: *total:* 1.5%
male: 1.4%
female: 1.6% (2019 est.)
country comparison to the world: 181

Population below poverty line: 24.8% (2017 est.)

Gini Index coefficient - distribution of family income: 30.7 (2017 est.)
country comparison to the world: 146

Household income or consumption by percentage share: *lowest 10%:* 2.8%
highest 10%: 32.4% (1998)

Budget: *revenues:* 9.108 billion (2017 est.)
expenditures: 11.23 billion (2017 est.)

Budget surplus (+) or deficit (-): -3.2% (of GDP) (2017 est.)
country comparison to the world: 138

Public debt: 33.6% of GDP (2017 est.)
35.7% of GDP (2016 est.)
country comparison to the world: 156

Taxes and other revenues: 13.5% (of GDP) (2017 est.)
country comparison to the world: 205

Fiscal year: 1 April - 31 March

Current account balance: $240 million (2019 est.)
-$2.398 billion (2018 est.)
country comparison to the world: 56

Exports: $17.52 billion (2019 est.)
$15.73 billion (2018 est.)
note: Data are in current year dollars and do not include illicit exports or re-exports.
country comparison to the world: 88

Exports - partners: China 24%, Thailand 24%, Japan 7%, Germany 5% (2019)

Exports - commodities: natural gas, clothing products, rice, copper, dried legumes (2019)

Imports: $17.36 billion (2019 est.) note: data are in current year dollars
$18.66 billion (2018 est.) note: data are in current year dollars
note: import figures are grossly underestimated due to the value of consumer goods, diesel fuel, and other products smuggled in from Thailand, China, Malaysia, and India
country comparison to the world: 93

Imports - partners: China 43%, Thailand 15%, Singapore 12%, Indonesia 5% (2019)

Imports - commodities: refined petroleum, broadcasting equipment, fabrics, motorcycles, packaged medicines (2019)

Reserves of foreign exchange and gold: $4.924 billion (31 December 2017 est.)
$4.63 billion (31 December 2016 est.)
country comparison to the world: 95

Debt - external: $6.594 billion (31 December 2017 est.)
$8.2 billion (31 December 2016 est.)
country comparison to the world: 126

Exchange rates: kyats (MMK) per US dollar -
1,361.9 (2017 est.)
1,234.87 (2016 est.)
1,234.87 (2015 est.)
1,162.62 (2014 est.)
984.35 (2013 est.)

ENERGY

Electricity access: *electrification - total population:* 51% (2019)
electrification - urban areas: 76% (2019)
electrification - rural areas: 39% (2019)

Electricity: *installed generating capacity:* 7.247 million kW (2020 est.)
consumption: 20,474,380,000 kWh (2019 est.)
exports: 1.002 billion kWh (2019 est.)
imports: 0 kWh (2019 est.)
transmission/distribution losses: 3.405 billion kWh (2019 est.)

Electricity generation sources: *fossil fuels:* 52.6% of total installed capacity (2020 est.)
solar: 0.1% of total installed capacity (2020 est.)
hydroelectricity: 47.3% of total installed capacity (2020 est.)
tide and wave: 0% of total installed capacity (2020 est.)
geothermal: 0% of total installed capacity (2020 est.)
biomass and waste: 0% of total installed capacity (2020 est.)

Coal: *production:* 1.468 million metric tons (2020 est.)
consumption: 1.981 million metric tons (2020 est.)
exports: 1,000 metric tons (2020 est.)
imports: 514,000 metric tons (2020 est.)
proven reserves: 6 million metric tons (2019 est.)

Petroleum: *total petroleum production:* 7,800 bbl/day (2021 est.)
refined petroleum consumption: 146,200 bbl/day (2019 est.)
crude oil and lease condensate exports: 4,700 bbl/day (2018 est.)
crude oil and lease condensate imports: 0 bbl/day (2018 est.)
crude oil estimated reserves: 139 million barrels (2021 est.)

Refined petroleum products - production: 13,330 bbl/day (2017 est.)
country comparison to the world: 97

Refined petroleum products - exports: 0 bbl/day (2015 est.)
country comparison to the world: 137

Refined petroleum products - imports: 102,600 bbl/day (2015 est.)
country comparison to the world: 53

Natural gas: *production:* 17,710,912,000 cubic meters (2019 est.)
consumption: 3,612,431,000 cubic meters (2019 est.)
exports: 14,188,161,000 cubic meters (2019 est.)
imports: 475.156 million cubic meters (2020 est.)
proven reserves: 637.128 billion cubic meters (2021 est.)

Carbon dioxide emissions: 31.848 million metric tonnes of CO2 (2019 est.)
from coal and metallurgical coke: 3.881 million metric tonnes of CO2 (2019 est.)
from petroleum and other liquids: 20.832 million metric tonnes of CO2 (2019 est.)
from consumed natural gas: 7.134 million metric tonnes of CO2 (2019 est.)
country comparison to the world: 75

Energy consumption per capita: 10.679 million Btu/person (2019 est.)
country comparison to the world: 154

COMMUNICATIONS

Telephones - fixed lines: *total subscriptions:* 523,951 (2020 est.)
subscriptions per 100 inhabitants: 1 (2020 est.)
country comparison to the world: 92

Telephones - mobile cellular: *total subscriptions:* 78,548,329 (2020 est.)
subscriptions per 100 inhabitants: 144 (2020 est.)
country comparison to the world: 21

Telecommunication systems: *general assessment:* Burma, one of the least developed telecom markets in Asia, saw growth in mobile and broadband services through foreign competition and roll out of 4G and 5G networks; infrastructure development challenged by flooding, unreliable electricity, inefficient bureaucracy, and corruption; digital divide affects rural areas; fixed broadband remains low due to number of fixed-lines and near saturation of the mobile platform; healthy m-banking platform; tests for NB-IoT; benefit from launch of regional satellite; government utilizes intermittent censorship and shut-down of Internet in political crisis (2020)
domestic: fixed-line is just under 1 per 100, while mobile-cellular is roughly 144 per 100 (2020)
international: country code - 95; landing points for the SeaMeWe-3, SeaMeWe-5, AAE-1 and Singapore-Myanmar optical telecommunications submarine cable that provides links to Asia, the Middle East, Africa, Southeast Asia, Australia and

Europe; satellite earth stations - 2, Intelsat (Indian Ocean) and ShinSat (2019)

Broadcast media: government controls all domestic broadcast media; 2 state-controlled TV stations with 1 of the stations controlled by the armed forces; 2 pay-TV stations are joint state-private ventures; access to satellite TV is limited; 1 state-controlled domestic radio station and 9 FM stations that are joint state-private ventures; transmissions of several international broadcasters are available in parts of Burma; the Voice of America (VOA), Radio Free Asia (RFA), BBC Burmese service, the Democratic Voice of Burma (DVB), and Radio Australia use shortwave to broadcast in Burma; VOA, RFA, and DVB produce daily TV news programs that are transmitted by satellite to audiences in Burma; in March 2017, the government granted licenses to 5 private broadcasters, allowing them digital free-to-air TV channels to be operated in partnership with government-owned Myanmar Radio and Television (MRTV) and will rely upon MRTV's transmission infrastructure; following the February 2021 military coup, the regime revoked the media licenses of most independent outlets, including the free-to-air licenses for DVB and Mizzima (2022)

Internet country code: .mm

Internet users: *total:* 19,043,428 (2020 est.)
percent of population: 35% (2020 est.)
country comparison to the world: 40

Broadband - fixed subscriptions: *total:* 688,185 (2020 est.)
subscriptions per 100 inhabitants: 1 (2020 est.)
country comparison to the world: 81

TRANSPORTATION

National air transport system: *number of registered air carriers:* 8 (2020)
inventory of registered aircraft operated by air carriers: 42
annual passenger traffic on registered air carriers: 3,407,788 (2018)
annual freight traffic on registered air carriers: 4.74 million (2018) mt-km

Civil aircraft registration country code prefix: XY

Airports: *total:* 64 (2021)
country comparison to the world: 76

Airports - with paved runways: *total:* 36
over 3,047 m: 12
2,438 to 3,047 m: 11
1,524 to 2,437 m: 12
under 914 m: 1 (2021)

Airports - with unpaved runways: *total:* 28
over 3,047 m: 1
1,524 to 2,437 m: 4
914 to 1,523 m: 10
under 914 m: 13 (2021)

Heliports: 11 (2021)

Pipelines: 3,739 km gas, 1321 km oil (2017)

Railways: *total:* 5,031 km (2008)
narrow gauge: 5,031 km (2008) 1.000-m gauge
country comparison to the world: 40

Roadways: *total:* 157,000 km (2013)
paved: 34,700 km (2013)
unpaved: 122,300 km (2013)
country comparison to the world: 33

Waterways: 12,800 km (2011)
country comparison to the world: 11

Merchant marine: *total:* 95
by type: bulk carrier 2, general cargo 39, oil tanker 5, other 49 (2021)
country comparison to the world: 92

Ports and terminals: *major seaport(s):* Mawlamyine (Moulmein), Sittwe
river port(s): Rangoon (Yangon) (Rangoon River)

MILITARY AND SECURITY

Military and security forces: *Burmese Defense Service (Tatmadaw):* Army (Tatmadaw Kyi), Navy (Tatmadaw Yay), Air Force (Tatmadaw Lay); People's Militia; Ministry of Home Affairs: People's Police Force; Border Guard Forces/Police (2022)
note: under the 2008 constitution, the Tatmadaw controls appointments of senior officials to lead the Ministry of Defense, the Ministry of Border Affairs, and the Ministry of Home Affairs; in March 2022, a new law gave the commander-in-chief of the Tatmadaw the authority to appoint or remove the head of the police force

Military expenditures: 3.4% of GDP (2021 est.)
3% of GDP (2020 est.)
4.1% of GDP (2019 est.) (approximately $7.7 billion)
4.4% of GDP (2018 est.) (approximately $8.1 billion)
4.7% of GDP (2017 est.) (approximately $7.8 billion)
country comparison to the world: 26

Military and security service personnel strengths: estimates vary widely, from approximately 300,000 to as many as 400,000 active duty personnel (2022)

Military equipment inventories and acquisitions: the Burmese military inventory is comprised mostly of older Chinese and Russian/Soviet-era equipment with a smaller mix of more modern acquisitions; since 2010, China and Russia have been the leading suppliers of military hardware; Burma has a limited defense industry, including a growing shipbuilding capability (2022)

Military service age and obligation: 18-35 years of age (men) and 18-27 years of age (women) for voluntary military service; no conscription (a 2010 law reintroducing conscription has not yet entered into force); 2-year service obligation; male (ages 18-45) and female (ages 18-35) professionals (including doctors, engineers, mechanics) serve up to 3 years; service terms may be stretched to 5 years in an officially declared emergency (2021)

Military - note: since the country's founding, the armed forces have been heavily involved in domestic politics, running the country for five decades following a military coup in 1962; prior to the 2021 coup, the military already controlled three key security ministries (Defense, Border, and Home Affairs), one of two vice presidential appointments, 25% of the parliamentary seats, and had a proxy political party, the Union Solidarity and Development Party (USDP)

as of 2022, the military owned and operated two business conglomerates that had over 100 subsidiaries and close ties to other companies; the business activities of these conglomerates included banking and insurance, hotels, tourism, jade and ruby mining, timber, construction, real estate, and the production of palm oil, sugar, soap, cement, beverages, drinking water, coal, and gas; some of the companies supplied goods and services to the military, such as food, clothing, insurance, and cellphone service; the military also managed a film industry, publishing houses, and television stations

as of 2022, the military's primary operational focus was internal security, particularly attempts to quell a growing armed insurgency against the 2021 coup and operations against ethnic-based separatist groups; these operations have resulted in numerous civilian casualties, human rights abuses, and internal displacement--ethnic-based armed groups have been fighting for self-rule against the Burmese Government since the country's 1948 independence; as of 2022, there were approximately 20 such groups operating in Burma with strengths of a few hundred up to more than 20,000 estimated fighters; some were organized along military lines with "brigades" and "divisions" and armed with heavy weaponry, including artillery; they reportedly controlled an estimated one-third of the country's territory, primarily in the border regions; key groups included the United Wa State Army, Karen National Union, Kachin Independence Army, Arakan Army, Ta'ang National Liberation Army, and the Myanmar Nationalities Democratic Alliance Army

as of 2022, Burma also had a large number of other armed militias which took many different forms and varied in allegiances and size; most were pro-military junta and associated with the Burmese military (Tatmadaw); some were integrated within the Tatmadaw's command structure as Border Guard Forces (BGF); the BGF were organized as 325- man battalions, which included a mix of militia forces, ethnic armed groups, and government soldiers; they were armed, supplied, and paid by the Tatmadaw; other pro-military government militias were not integrated within the Tatmadaw command structure but received direction from the military and were recognized as government militias; the amount of support they received from the Tatmadaw varied depending on local security conditions; the third type of pro-government militias were small community-based units that were armed, coordinated, and trained by local Tatmadaw forces and activated as needed; as of 2022, the military junta government was raising new militia units to help combat the popular uprising

in mid-2022, the rebel National Unity Government claimed its armed wing, the People's Defense Force (PDF), had more than 60,000 fighters organized into battalions; in addition, several armed ethnic groups have added their support to antijunta resistance groups or joined forces with local units of the PDF (2022)

TRANSNATIONAL ISSUES

Disputes - international: over half of Burma's population consists of diverse ethnic groups who have substantial numbers of kin in neighboring countries; Bangladesh struggles to accommodate 912,000 Rohingya, Burmese Muslim minority from Rakhine State, living as refugees in Cox's Bazar; Burmese border authorities are constructing a 200 km (124 mi) wire fence designed to deter illegal cross-border transit and tensions from the military build-up along border with Bangladesh in 2010; Bangladesh referred its maritime boundary claims with Burma and India to the International Tribunal on the Law of the Sea; Burmese forces attempting to dig in to the largely autonomous Shan State to rout local militias tied to the drug trade, prompts local residents to periodically flee into neighboring Yunnan Province in China; fencing along the India-Burma international border at Manipur's Moreh town is in progress to check illegal drug trafficking and movement of militants; over 100,000 mostly Karen refugees and asylum seekers fleeing civil strife, political upheaval, and economic stagnation in Burma were living in remote camps in Thailand near the border as of May 2017

Refugees and internally displaced persons: *IDPs:* 671,011 (government offensives against armed ethnic minority groups near its borders with China and Thailand, natural disasters, forced land evictions) (2021)
stateless persons: 600,000 (mid-year 2021); note - Rohingya Muslims, living predominantly in Rakhine State, are Burma's main group of stateless people; the Burmese Government does not recognize the Rohingya as a "national race" and stripped them of their citizenship under the 1982 Citizenship Law, categorizing them as "non-nationals" or "foreign residents;" under the Rakhine State Action Plan drafted in October 2014, the Rohingya must demonstrate their family has lived in Burma for at least 60 years to qualify for a lesser naturalized citizenship and the classification of Bengali or be put in detention camps and face deportation; native-born but non-indigenous people, such as Indians, are also stateless; the Burmese Government does not grant citizenship to children born outside of the country to Burmese parents who left the country illegally or fled persecution, such as those born in Thailand; the number of stateless persons has decreased dramatically because hundreds of thousands of Rohingya have fled to Bangladesh since 25 August 2017 to escape violence

Trafficking in persons: *current situation:* human traffickers exploit men, women, and children through forced labor, and women and children in sex trafficking in Burma and abroad; Burmese men are forced to work domestically and abroad in fishing, manufacturing, forestry, agriculture, and construction; fishermen are lured into forced labor in remote waters and offshore by recruitment agencies in Burma and Southeast Asia; Burmese women increasingly are lured to China for marriage under false pretenses and are subjected to sex trafficking, forced concubinage and childbearing, and forced domestic labor; men, women, and children in ethnic minority areas are at increased risk of sex trafficking and forced labor in farming, manufacturing, and construction; men and boys are recruited locally by traffickers for forced labor in oil palm, banana, and rubber plantations, in mining, fishing, and bamboo, teak, rice, and sugarcane harvesting; some military personnel, civilian brokers, border guard officials, and ethnic armed groups continue to recruit child soldiers, particularly in conflict areas
tier rating: Tier 3 — Burma does not fully meet the minimum standards for the elimination of trafficking and is not making significant efforts to do so; authorities increased the investigation and prosecution of trafficking crimes, including those involving officials, and the investigation of forced labor in the fishing sector; the government identified and referred more victims to care and enacted legislation enhancing protections for child victims; however, a policy or pattern of forced labor existed; the use of children in labor and support roles by the military increased in conflict zones in Rakhine and Shan States; displacement resulting from military conflict made Rohingya and other ethnic groups vulnerable to human trafficking; the constitutionally guaranteed power of the military continued to limit the government's ability to address forced adult labor and child soldier recruitment; although authorities allocated increased funding to victim protection, most services to trafficking victims were provided by NGOs and foreign donors (2020)

Illicit drugs: a major source of illicit methamphetamine and opiates; illicit import of precursor chemicals from China increased production and trafficking of synthetic drugs; second-largest opium poppy cultivator in Asia, with an estimated 20,200 hectares grown in 2019; "Yaba," a tablet containing methamphetamine, caffeine, and other stimulants, is produced in Burma and trafficked regionally; ethnic armed organizations, military-affiliated militias, and transnational criminal organizations oversee billion dollar drug production and trafficking industry; drugs produced in Burma are trafficked beyond Southeast Asia to Australia, New Zealand, and Japan; not a major source or transit country for drugs entering the United States
(2021)

BURUNDI

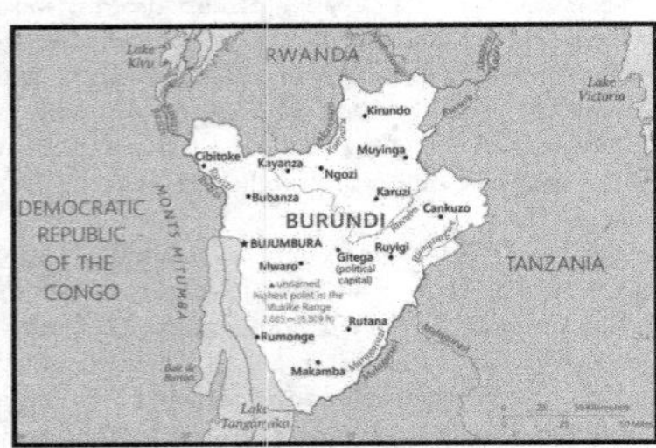

INTRODUCTION

Background: Established in the 1600s, the Burundi Kingdom has had borders similar to those of modern Burundi since the 1800s. Burundi's two major ethnic groups, the majority Hutu and minority Tutsi, share a common language and culture and largely lived in peaceful cohabitation under Tutsi monarchs in pre-colonial Burundi. Regional, class, and clan distinctions contributed to social status in the Burundi Kingdom, yielding a complex class structure. German colonial rule in the late 19th and early 20th centuries and Belgian rule after World War I preserved Burundi's monarchy. Seeking to simplify administration, Belgian colonial officials reduced the number of chiefdoms and eliminated most Hutu chiefs from positions of power. In 1961, the Burundian Tutsi king's oldest son, Louis RWAGASORE was murdered by a competing political faction shortly before he was set to become prime minister, triggering increased political competition that contributed to later instability. Burundi gained its independence from Belgium in 1962 as the Kingdom of Burundi.

Revolution in neighboring Rwanda stoked ethnic polarization as the Tutsi increasingly feared violence and loss of political power. A failed Hutu-led coup in 1965 triggered a purge of Hutu officials and set the stage for Tutsi officers to overthrow the monarchy in 1966 and establish a Tutsi-dominated republic. A Hutu rebellion in 1972 that resulted in the death of several thousand Tutsi civilians sparked a brutal crackdown on Hutu civilians by the Tutsi-led military, which ultimately killed 100,000-200,000 people. International pressure led to a new constitution in 1992 and democratic elections in June 1993. Burundi's first democratically elected president, Hutu Melchior NDADAYE, was assassinated in October 1993 after only 100 days in office by Tutsi military officers fearing Hutu domination, sparking a civil war. His successor, Cyprien NTARYAMIRA, died when the Rwandan president's plane he was traveling on was shot down in April 1994, which triggered the Rwandan genocide and further entrenched ethnic conflict in Burundi. The internationally brokered Arusha Agreement, signed in 2000, and subsequent cease-fire agreements with armed movements ended the 1993-2005 civil war. Burundi's second democratic elections were held in 2005, resulting in the election of Pierre NKURUNZIZA as president. He was reelected in 2010 and again in 2015 after a controversial court decision allowed him to circumvent a term limit. President Evariste NDAYISHIMIYE - from NKURUNZIZA's ruling party - was elected in 2020.

GEOGRAPHY

Location: Central Africa, east of the Democratic Republic of the Congo, west of Tanzania

Geographic coordinates: 3 30 S, 30 00 E

Map references: Africa

Area: *total:* 27,830 sq km
land: 25,680 sq km
water: 2,150 sq km
country comparison to the world: 146

Area - comparative: slightly smaller than Maryland

Land boundaries: *total:* 1,140 km
border countries (3): Democratic Republic of the Congo 236 km; Rwanda 315 km; Tanzania 589 km

Coastline: 0 km (landlocked)

Maritime claims: none (landlocked)

Climate: equatorial; high plateau with considerable altitude variation (772 m to 2,670 m above sea level); average annual temperature varies with altitude from 23 to 17 degrees Celsius but is generally moderate as the average altitude is about 1,700 m; average annual rainfall is about 150 cm; two wet seasons (February to May and September to November), and two dry seasons (June to August and December to January)

Terrain: hilly and mountainous, dropping to a plateau in east, some plains

Elevation: *highest point:* unnamed elevation on Mukike Range 2,685 m
lowest point: Lake Tanganyika 772 m
mean elevation: 1,504 m

Natural resources: nickel, uranium, rare earth oxides, peat, cobalt, copper, platinum, vanadium, arable land, hydropower, niobium, tantalum, gold, tin, tungsten, kaolin, limestone

Land use: *agricultural land:* 73.3% (2018 est.)
arable land: 38.9% (2018 est.)
permanent crops: 15.6% (2018 est.)
permanent pasture: 18.8% (2018 est.)
forest: 6.6% (2018 est.)

other: 20.1% (2018 est.)

Irrigated land: 230 sq km (2012)

Major lakes (area sq km): *fresh water lake(s):* Lake Tanganyika (shared with Democratic Republic of Congo, Tanzania, and Zambia) - 32,000 sq km

Major watersheds (area sq km): Atlantic Ocean drainage: Congo (3,730,881 sq km), *(Mediterranean Sea)* Nile (3,254,853 sq km)

Population distribution: one of Africa's most densely populated countries; concentrations tend to be in the north and along the northern shore of Lake Tanganyika in the west; most people live on farms near areas of fertile volcanic soil as shown in this population distribution map

Natural hazards: flooding; landslides; drought

Geography - note: landlocked; straddles crest of the Nile-Congo watershed; the Kagera, which drains into Lake Victoria, is the most remote headstream of the White Nile

PEOPLE AND SOCIETY

Population: 12,696,478 (2022 est.)
country comparison to the world: 77

Nationality: *noun:* Burundian(s)
adjective: Burundian

Ethnic groups: Hutu, Tutsi, Twa (Pygmy)

Languages: Kirundi only 29.7% (official); French only 0.3% (official); Swahili only 0.2%; English only 0.1% (official); Kirundi and French 8.4%; Kirundi, French, and English 2.4%, other language combinations 2%, unspecified 56.9% (2008 est.)
major-language sample(s): Igitabo Mpuzamakungu c'ibimenyetso bifatika, isoko ntabanduka ku nkuru z'urufatiro. (Kirundi)
note: data represent languages read and written by people 10 years of age or older; spoken Kirundi is nearly universal

Religions: Roman Catholic 58.6%, Protestant 35.3% (includes Adventist 2.7% and other Protestant 32.6%), Muslim 3.4%, other 1.3%, none 1.3% (2016-17 est.)

Demographic profile: Burundi is a densely populated country with a high population growth rate, factors that combined with land scarcity and poverty place a large share of its population at risk of food insecurity. About 90% of the population relies on subsistence agriculture. Subdivision of land to sons, and redistribution to returning refugees, results in smaller, overworked, and less productive plots. Food shortages, poverty, and a lack of clean water contribute to a 60% chronic malnutrition rate among children. A lack of reproductive health services has prevented a significant reduction in Burundi's maternal mortality and fertility rates, which are both among the world's highest. With two-thirds of its population under the age of 25 and a birth rate of about 6 children per woman, Burundi's population will continue to expand rapidly for decades to come, putting additional strain on a poor country.

Historically, migration flows into and out of Burundi have consisted overwhelmingly of refugees from violent conflicts. In the last decade, more than a half million Burundian refugees returned home from neighboring countries, mainly Tanzania. Reintegrating the returnees has been problematic due to their prolonged time in exile, land scarcity, poor infrastructure, poverty, and unemployment. Repatriates and existing residents (including internally displaced persons) compete for limited land and other resources. To further complicate matters, international aid organizations reduced their assistance because they no longer classified Burundi as a post-conflict country. Conditions have deteriorated since renewed violence erupted in April 2015, causing another outpouring of refugees. In addition to refugee out-migration, Burundi has hosted thousands of refugees from neighboring countries, mostly from the Democratic Republic of the Congo and lesser numbers from Rwanda.

Age structure: *0-14 years:* 43.83% (male 2,618,868/female 2,581,597)
15-24 years: 19.76% (male 1,172,858/female 1,171,966)
25-54 years: 29.18% (male 1,713,985/female 1,748,167)
55-64 years: 4.17% (male 231,088/female 264,131)
65 years and over: 3.06% (male 155,262/female 207,899) (2020 est.)

Dependency ratios: *total dependency ratio:* 91
youth dependency ratio: 86.4
elderly dependency ratio: 4.5
potential support ratio: 22 (2020 est.)

Median age: *total:* 17.7 years
male: 17.4 years
female: 18 years (2020 est.)
country comparison to the world: 217

Population growth rate: 3.63% (2022 est.)
country comparison to the world: 4

Birth rate: 35.17 births/1,000 population (2022 est.)
country comparison to the world: 16

Death rate: 5.96 deaths/1,000 population (2022 est.)
country comparison to the world: 161

Net migration rate: 7.09 migrant(s)/1,000 population (2022 est.)
country comparison to the world: 12

Population distribution: one of Africa's most densely populated countries; concentrations tend to be in the north and along the northern shore of Lake Tanganyika in the west; most people live on farms near areas of fertile volcanic soil as shown in this population distribution map

Urbanization: *urban population:* 14.4% of total population (2022)
rate of urbanization: 5.43% annual rate of change (2020-25 est.)

Major urban areas - population: 1.139 million BUJUMBURA (capital) (2022)

Sex ratio: *at birth:* 1.03 male(s)/female
0-14 years: 1.02 male(s)/female
15-24 years: 1 male(s)/female
25-54 years: 0.98 male(s)/female
55-64 years: 0.88 male(s)/female
65 years and over: 0.62 male(s)/female
total population: 0.99 male(s)/female (2022 est.)

Mother's mean age at first birth: 21.5 years (2016/17 est.)
note: data represents median age at first birth among women 25-49

Maternal mortality ratio: 548 deaths/100,000 live births (2017 est.)
country comparison to the world: 16

Infant mortality rate: *total:* 37.84 deaths/1,000 live births
male: 42.02 deaths/1,000 live births
female: 33.54 deaths/1,000 live births (2022 est.)
country comparison to the world: 35

Life expectancy at birth: *total population:* 67.42 years
male: 65.32 years
female: 69.59 years (2022 est.)
country comparison to the world: 190

Total fertility rate: 5.03 children born/woman (2022 est.)
country comparison to the world: 10

Contraceptive prevalence rate: 28.5% (2016/17)

Drinking water source: *improved: urban:* 98.7% of population
rural: 78.9% of population
total: 81.6% of population
unimproved: urban: 1.3% of population
rural: 21.1% of population
total: 18.4% of population (2020 est.)

Current health expenditure: 8% of GDP (2019)

Physicians density: 0.07 physicians/1,000 population (2020)

Hospital bed density: 0.8 beds/1,000 population (2014)

Sanitation facility access: *improved: urban:* 87.4% of population
rural: 53.7% of population
total: 58.4% of population
unimproved: urban: 12.6% of population
rural: 46.3% of population
total: 41.6% of population (2020 est.)

HIV/AIDS - adult prevalence rate: 1% (2020 est.)
country comparison to the world: 42

Major infectious diseases: *degree of risk:* very high (2020)
food or waterborne diseases: bacterial and protozoal diarrhea, hepatitis A, and typhoid fever
vectorborne diseases: malaria and dengue fever
water contact diseases: schistosomiasis
animal contact diseases: rabies

Obesity - adult prevalence rate: 5.4% (2016)
country comparison to the world: 178

Alcohol consumption per capita: *total:* 4.07 liters of pure alcohol (2019 est.)
beer: 1.84 liters of pure alcohol (2019 est.)
wine: 0 liters of pure alcohol (2019 est.)
spirits: 0 liters of pure alcohol (2019 est.)
other alcohols: 2.23 liters of pure alcohol (2019 est.)
country comparison to the world: 95

Tobacco use: *total:* 11.8% (2020 est.)
male: 17.4% (2020 est.)
female: 6.1% (2020 est.)
country comparison to the world: 123

Children under the age of 5 years underweight: 27% (2018/19)
country comparison to the world: 9

Child marriage: *women married by age 15:* 2.8%
women married by age 18: 19%
men married by age 18: 1.4% (2017 est.)

Education expenditures: 5.1% of GDP (2018 est.)
country comparison to the world: 57

Literacy: *definition:* age 15 and over can read and write
total population: 68.4%
male: 76.3%
female: 61.2% (2017)

School life expectancy (primary to tertiary education): *total:* 11 years
male: 11 years
female: 11 years (2018)

Unemployment, youth ages 15-24: *total:* 2.9%
male: 4.4%
female: 2% (2014 est.)

ENVIRONMENT

Environment - current issues: soil erosion as a result of overgrazing and the expansion of agriculture into marginal lands; deforestation (little forested land remains because of uncontrolled cutting of trees for fuel); habitat loss threatens wildlife populations

Environment - international agreements: *party to:* Biodiversity, Climate Change, Climate Change-Kyoto Protocol, Climate Change-Paris Agreement, Comprehensive Nuclear Test Ban, Desertification, Endangered Species, Hazardous Wastes, Ozone Layer Protection, Wetlands
signed, but not ratified: Law of the Sea, Nuclear Test Ban

Air pollutants: *particulate matter emissions:* 35.61 micrograms per cubic meter (2016 est.)
carbon dioxide emissions: 0.5 megatons (2016 est.)
methane emissions: 1.42 megatons (2020 est.)

Climate: equatorial; high plateau with considerable altitude variation (772 m to 2,670 m above sea level); average annual temperature varies with altitude from 23 to 17 degrees Celsius but is generally moderate as the average altitude is about 1,700 m; average annual rainfall is about 150 cm; two wet seasons (February to May and September to November), and two dry seasons (June to August and December to January)

Land use: *agricultural land:* 73.3% (2018 est.)
arable land: 38.9% (2018 est.)
permanent crops: 15.6% (2018 est.)
permanent pasture: 18.8% (2018 est.)
forest: 6.6% (2018 est.)
other: 20.1% (2018 est.)

Urbanization: *urban population:* 14.4% of total population (2022)
rate of urbanization: 5.43% annual rate of change (2020-25 est.)

Revenue from forest resources: *forest revenues:* 10.31% of GDP (2018 est.)
country comparison to the world: 3

Revenue from coal: *coal revenues:* 0% of GDP (2018 est.)
country comparison to the world: 72

Food insecurity: *widespread lack of access: due to the effects of weather* - about 646,000 people are estimated to be severely food insecure between June and September 2022; the main drivers are poor rains in May in some central and southern eastern areas that affected pulses production, the socio-economic impact of the COVID-19 pandemic, and high food prices due to elevated fuel prices inflating transport costs (2022)

Waste and recycling: *municipal solid waste generated annually:* 1,872,016 tons (2002 est.)

Major lakes (area sq km): *fresh water lake(s):* Lake Tanganyika (shared with Democratic Republic of Congo, Tanzania, and Zambia) - 32,000 sq km

Major watersheds (area sq km): *Atlantic Ocean drainage:* Congo (3,730,881 sq km), *(Mediterranean Sea)* Nile (3,254,853 sq km)

Total water withdrawal: *municipal:* 43.1 million cubic meters (2017 est.)
industrial: 15 million cubic meters (2017 est.)
agricultural: 222 million cubic meters (2017 est.)

Total renewable water resources: 12.536 billion cubic meters (2017 est.)

GOVERNMENT

Country name: *conventional long form:* Republic of Burundi
conventional short form: Burundi
local long form: Republique du Burundi (French)/ Republika y'u Burundi (Kirundi)
local short form: Burundi
former: Urundi, German East Africa, Ruanda-Urundi, Kingdom of Burundi
etymology: name derived from the pre-colonial Kingdom of Burundi (17th-19th century)

Government type: presidential republic

Capital: *name:* Gitega (political capital), Bujumbura (commercial capital); note - in January 2019, the Burundian parliament voted to make Gitega the political capital of the country while Bujumbura would remain its economic capital; as of 2022, the government's move to Gitega remains incomplete
geographic coordinates: 3 25 S, 29 55 E
time difference: UTC+2 (7 hours ahead of Washington, DC, during Standard Time)
etymology: the naming origins for both Gitega and Bujumbura are obscure; Bujumbura's name prior to independence in 1962 was Usumbura

Administrative divisions: 18 provinces; Bubanza, Bujumbura Mairie, Bujumbura Rural, Bururi, Cankuzo, Cibitoke, Gitega, Karuzi, Kayanza, Kirundo, Makamba, Muramvya, Muyinga, Mwaro, Ngozi, Rumonge, Rutana, Ruyigi

Independence: 1 July 1962 (from UN trusteeship under Belgian administration)

National holiday: Independence Day, 1 July (1962)

Constitution: *history:* several previous, ratified by referendum 28 February 2005
amendments: proposed by the president of the republic after consultation with the government or by absolute majority support of the membership in both houses of Parliament; passage requires at least two-thirds majority vote by the Senate membership and at least four-fifths majority vote by the National Assembly; the president can opt to submit amendment bills to a referendum; constitutional articles including those on national unity, the secularity of Burundi, its democratic form of government, and its sovereignty cannot be amended; amended 2018 (amendments extended the presidential term from 5 to 7 years, reintroduced the position of prime minister, and reduced the number of vice presidents from 2 to 1)

Legal system: mixed legal system of Belgian civil law and customary law

International law organization participation: has not submitted an ICJ jurisdiction declaration; withdrew from ICCt in October 2017

Citizenship: *citizenship by birth:* no
citizenship by descent only: the father must be a citizen of Burundi
dual citizenship recognized: no
residency requirement for naturalization: 10 years

Suffrage: 18 years of age; universal

Executive branch: *chief of state:* President Evariste NDAYISHIMIYE (since 18 June 2020); Vice President Prosper BAZOMBANZA (since 24 June 2020); note - the president is both chief of state and head of government
head of government: President Evariste NDAYISHIMIYE (since 18 June 2020); Vice President Prosper BAZOMBANZA (since 24 June 2020); Prime Minister Gervais NDIRAKOBUCA (since 7 September 2022)
cabinet: Council of Ministers appointed by president
elections/appointments: president directly elected by absolute majority popular vote in 2 rounds if needed for a 7-year term (eligible for a second term); election last held on 20 May 2020 (next to be held in 2027); vice presidents nominated by the president, endorsed by Parliament; note - a 2018 constitutional referendum effective for the 2020 election, increased the presidential term from 5 to 7 years with a 2-consecutive-term limit, reinstated the position of the prime minister position, and reduced the number of vice presidents from 2 to 1
election results: *2020:* Evariste NDAYISHIMIYE elected president; percent of vote - Evariste NDAYISHIMIYE (CNDDFDD) 71.5%, Agathon RWASA (CNL) 25.2%, Gaston SINDIMWO (UPRONA) 1.7%, OTHER 1.6%

Legislative branch: *description:* bicameral Parliament or Parlement consists of:
Senate or Inama Nkenguzamateka (39 seats in the July 2020 election); 36 members indirectly elected by an electoral college of provincial councils using a three-round voting system, which requires a two-thirds majority vote in the first two rounds and simple majority vote for the two leading candidates in the final round; 3 seats reserved for Twas, and 30% of all votes reserved for women; members serve 5-year terms)
National Assembly or Inama Nshingamateka (123 seats in the May 2020 election; 100 members directly elected in multiseat constituencies by proportional representation vote and 23 co-opted members; 60% of seats allocated to Hutu and 40% to Tutsi; 3 seats reserved for Twas; 30% of total seats reserved for women; members serve 5-year terms)
elections:
Senate - last held on 20 July 2020 (next to be held in 2025)
National Assembly - last held on 20 May 2020 (next to be held in 2025)
election results: Senate - percent of vote by party - CNDD-FDD 87.2%, Twa 7.7%, CNL 2.6%, UPRONA 2.6%; seats by party - CNDD-FDD 34, CNL 1, UPRONA 1, Twa 3; composition - men 23, women 16, percent of women 37.2% National Assembly - percent of vote by party - CNDD-FDD 70.9%, CNL 23.4%, UPRONA 2.5%, other (co-opted Twa) 3.2%; seats by party - CNDD-FDD 86, CNL 32, UPRONA 2, Twa 3; composition - men 76, women 47, percent of women 38.2%; note - total Parliament percent of women 38%

Judicial branch: *highest court(s):* Supreme Court (consists of 9 judges and organized into judicial, administrative, and cassation chambers); Constitutional Court (consists of 7 members)
judge selection and term of office: Supreme Court judges nominated by the Judicial Service Commission, a 15- member independent body of judicial and legal profession officials), appointed by the president and confirmed by the Senate; judge tenure NA; Constitutional Court judges appointed by the president and confirmed by the Senate and serve 6-year nonrenewable terms
subordinate courts: Courts of Appeal; County Courts; Courts of Residence; Martial Court; Court Against Corruption; Commercial Court

Political parties and leaders: Front for Democracy in Burundi-Nyakuri or FRODEBU-Nyakuri [Keffa NIBIZI]

Front for Democracy in Burundi-Sahwanya or FRODEBU-Sahwanya [Pierre Claver NAHIMANA]
National Congress for Liberty or CNL [Agathon RWASA]
National Council for the Defense of Democracy - Front for the Defense of Democracy or CNDD-FDD [Evariste NDAYISHIMIYE]
National Liberation Forces or FNL [Jacques BIGITIMANA]
Union for National Progress (Union pour le Progress Nationale) or UPRONA [Abel GASHATSI]

International organization participation: ACP, AfDB, ATMIS, AU, CEMAC, CEPGL, CICA, COMESA, EAC, FAO, G-77, IBRD, ICAO, ICCt, ICRM, IDA, IFAD, IFC, IFRCS, ILO, IMF, Interpol, IOC, IOM, IPU, ISO (correspondent), ITU, ITUC (NGOs), MIGA, NAM, OIF, OPCW, UN, UNAMID, UNCTAD, UNESCO, UNIDO, UNISFA, UNWTO, UPU, WCO, WHO, WIPO, WMO, WTO

Diplomatic representation in the US: *chief of mission:* Ambassador Jean de Dieu NDIKUMANA (since 7 July 2021)
chancery: 2233 Wisconsin Avenue NW, Washington, DC 20007
telephone: [1] (202) 342-2574
FAX: [1] (202) 342-2578
email address and website:
burundiembusadc@gmail.com
https://burundiembassy-usa.com/index.php

Diplomatic representation from the US: *chief of mission:* Ambassador Melanie Harris HIGGINS (since 2 March 2021)
embassy: B.P. 1720, Avenue Des Etats-Unis, Bujumbura
mailing address: 2100 Bujumbura Place, Washington DC 20521-2100
telephone: [257] 22-207-000
FAX: [257] 22-222-926
email address and website:
BujumburaC@state.gov
https://bi.usembassy.gov/

Flag description: divided by a white diagonal cross into red panels (top and bottom) and green panels (hoist side and fly side) with a white disk superimposed at the center bearing three red six-pointed stars outlined in green arranged in a triangular design (one star above, two stars below); green symbolizes hope and optimism, white purity and peace, and red the blood shed in the struggle for independence; the three stars in the disk represent the three major ethnic groups: Hutu, Twa, Tutsi, as well as the three elements in the national motto: unity, work, progress

National symbol(s): *lion; national colors:* red, white, green

National anthem: *name:* "Burundi Bwacu" (Our Beloved Burundi)
lyrics/music: Jean-Baptiste NTAHOKAJA/Marc BARENGAYABO
note: adopted 1962

ECONOMY

Economic overview: Burundi is a landlocked, resource-poor country with an underdeveloped manufacturing sector. Agriculture accounts for over 40% of GDP and employs more than 90% of the population. Burundi's primary exports are coffee and tea, which account for more than half of foreign exchange earnings, but these earnings are subject to fluctuations in weather and international coffee and tea prices, Burundi is heavily dependent on aid from bilateral and multilateral donors, as well as foreign exchange earnings from participation in the African Union Mission to Somalia (AMISOM). Foreign aid represented 48% of Burundi's national income in 2015, one of the highest percentages in Sub-Saharan Africa, but this figure decreased to 33.5% in 2016 due to political turmoil surrounding President NKURUNZIZA's bid for a third term. Burundi joined the East African Community (EAC) in 2009.

Burundi faces several underlying weaknesses – low governmental capacity, corruption, a high poverty rate, poor educational levels, a weak legal system, a poor transportation network, and overburdened utilities – that have prevented the implementation of planned economic reforms. The purchasing power of most Burundians has decreased as wage increases have not kept pace with inflation, which reached approximately 18% in 2017.

Real GDP growth dropped precipitously following political events in 2015 and has yet to recover to pre-conflict levels. Continued resistance by donors and the international community will restrict Burundi's economic growth as the country deals with a large current account deficit.

Real GDP (purchasing power parity): $8.69 billion (2020 est.)
$8.67 billion (2019 est.)
$8.51 billion (2018 est.)
note: data are in 2017 dollars
country comparison to the world: 165

Real GDP growth rate: 0% (2017 est.)
-1% (2016 est.)
-4% (2015 est.)
country comparison to the world: 192

Real GDP per capita: $700 (2020 est.)
$800 (2019 est.)
$800 (2018 est.)
note: data are in 2017 dollars
country comparison to the world: 229

GDP (official exchange rate): $3.027 billion (2019 est.)

Inflation rate (consumer prices): -0.6% (2019 est.)
-2.5% (2018 est.)
15.9% (2017 est.)
country comparison to the world: 10

GDP - composition, by sector of origin: *agriculture:* 39.5% (2017 est.)
industry: 16.4% (2017 est.)
services: 44.2% (2017 est.)

GDP - composition, by end use: *household consumption:* 83% (2017 est.)
government consumption: 20.8% (2017 est.)
investment in fixed capital: 16% (2017 est.)
investment in inventories: 0% (2017 est.)
exports of goods and services: 5.5% (2017 est.)
imports of goods and services: -25.3% (2017 est.)

Agricultural products: cassava, bananas, sweet potatoes, plantains, beans, vegetables, potatoes, cashew nuts, maize, taro

Industries: light consumer goods (sugar, shoes, soap, beer); cement, assembly of imported components; public works construction; food processing (fruits)

Industrial production growth rate: -2% (2017 est.)
country comparison to the world: 182

Labor force: 5.012 million (2017 est.)
country comparison to the world: 78

Labor force - by occupation: *agriculture:* 93.6%
industry: 2.3%
services: 4.1% (2002 est.)

Unemployment, youth ages 15-24: *total:* 2.9%
male: 4.4%
female: 2% (2014 est.)
country comparison to the world: 177

Population below poverty line: 64.6% (2014 est.)

Gini Index coefficient - distribution of family income: 38.6 (2013 est.)
country comparison to the world: 71

Household income or consumption by percentage share: *lowest 10%:* 4.1%
highest 10%: 28% (2006)

Budget: *revenues:* 536.7 million (2017 est.)
expenditures: 729.6 million (2017 est.)

Budget surplus (+) or deficit (-): -5.7% (of GDP) (2017 est.)
country comparison to the world: 177

Public debt: 51.7% of GDP (2017 est.)
48.4% of GDP (2016 est.)
country comparison to the world: 96

Taxes and other revenues: 15.8% (of GDP) (2017 est.)
country comparison to the world: 186

Fiscal year: calendar year

Current account balance: -$418 million (2017 est.)
-$411 million (2016 est.)
country comparison to the world: 118

Exports: $290 million (2018 est.)
$283 million (2018 est.)
$315 million (2017 est.)
note: Data are in current year dollars and do not include illicit exports or re-exports.
country comparison to the world: 200

Exports - partners: United Arab Emirates 50%, Democratic Republic of the Congo 7% (2019)

Exports - commodities: gold, coffee, tea, raw earth metal ores, wheat flours (2019)

Imports: $910 million (2018 est.) note: data are in current year dollars
$927 million (2018 est.)
$1.295 billion (2017 est.)
country comparison to the world: 191

Imports - partners: China 14%, Saudi Arabia 14%, India 9%, Kenya 7%, United Arab Emirates 7%, Tanzania 5%, Zambia 5% (2019)

Imports - commodities: refined petroleum, packaged medicines, cement, raw sugar, cars (2019)

Reserves of foreign exchange and gold: $97.4 million (31 December 2017 est.)
$95.17 million (31 December 2016 est.)
country comparison to the world: 181

Debt - external: $610.9 million (31 December 2017 est.)
$622.4 million (31 December 2016 est.)
country comparison to the world: 174

Exchange rates: Burundi francs (BIF) per US dollar -
1,945 (2020 est.)
1,876.25 (2019 est.)
1,800.495 (2018 est.)
1,571.9 (2014 est.)
1,546.7 (2013 est.)

ENERGY

Electricity access: *electrification - total population:* 11% (2019)
electrification - urban areas: 66% (2019)

electrification - rural areas: 2% (2019)

Electricity: *installed generating capacity:* 100,000 kW (2020 est.)
consumption: 440.774 million kWh (2019 est.)
exports: 0 kWh (2019 est.)
imports: 100 million kWh (2019 est.)
transmission/distribution losses: 15.96 million kWh (2019 est.)

Electricity generation sources: *fossil fuels:* 33.3% of total installed capacity (2020 est.)
solar: 2.3% of total installed capacity (2020 est.)
hydroelectricity: 62.8% of total installed capacity (2020 est.)
biomass and waste: 1.7% of total installed capacity (2020 est.)

Petroleum: *total petroleum production:* 0 bbl/day (2021 est.)
refined petroleum consumption: 5,000 bbl/day (2019 est.)

Refined petroleum products - imports: 1,374 bbl/day (2015 est.)
country comparison to the world: 195

Carbon dioxide emissions: 715,000 metric tonnes of CO_2 (2019 est.)
from petroleum and other liquids: 715,000 metric tonnes of CO_2 (2019 est.)
country comparison to the world: 183

Energy consumption per capita: 1.087 million Btu/person (2019 est.)
country comparison to the world: 194

COMMUNICATIONS

Telephones - fixed lines: *total subscriptions:* 18,300 (2020 est.)
subscriptions per 100 inhabitants: (2020 est.) less than 1
country comparison to the world: 177

Telephones - mobile cellular: *total subscriptions:* 6,631,151 (2020 est.)
subscriptions per 100 inhabitants: 56 (2020 est.)
country comparison to the world: 111

Telecommunication systems: *general assessment:* Burundi provides an attractive telecom market given its high population density and existing low subscription rates for all services; one downside for investors is that the country has a very low economic output, disposable income is also very low, and fixed-line infrastructure is poor outside the main urban areas; this is a greater motivation for investors to focus on improving mobile networks than in expanding fixed-line infrastructure; to overcome difficulties associated with the poor telecom infrastructure, the government has supported a number of prominent telcos building a national fiber backbone network; this network offers onward connectivity to submarine cable infrastructure landings in Kenya and Tanzania; the first sections of this network were switched on in early 2014, and additional provinces have since been connected; in addition, the government in early 2018 kick-started the Burundi Broadband project, which aims to deliver national connectivity by 2025; based on this improved infrastructure the government and ITU have developed an ICT strategy to make use of telecoms to promote the country's socio-economic development through to 2028; progress made by Tanzania with its own national backbone network has benefited Burundi, which has been provided with onward connectivity to most countries in the region; International bandwidth capacity has continued to increase in recent years, including a 38% increase in the nine months to September 2021, resulting in lower retail prices for consumers; two of the mobile operators have launched 3G and LTE services to capitalize on the growing demand for internet access; the number of mobile subscribers increased 7% in the third quarter of 2021, quarter-onquarter; similar growth is expected for the next two years at least, which will help bring the mobile level closer to the average for the region (2022)
domestic: telephone density one of the lowest in the world; fixed-line connections stand at less than 1 per 100 persons; mobile-cellular usage is about 56 per 100 persons (2020)
international: country code - 257; satellite earth station - 1 Intelsat (Indian Ocean); the government, supported by the World Bank, has backed a joint venture with a number of prominent telecoms to build a national fiber backbone network, offering onward connectivity to submarine cable infrastructure landings in Kenya and Tanzania (2019)

Broadcast media: state-controlled Radio Television Nationale de Burundi (RTNB) operates a TV station and a national radio network; 3 private TV stations and about 10 privately owned radio stations; transmissions of several international broadcasters are available in Bujumbura (2019)

Internet country code: .bi

Internet users: *total:* 1,070,170 (2020 est.)
percent of population: 9% (2020 est.)
country comparison to the world: 145

Broadband - fixed subscriptions: *total:* 4,230 (2020 est.)
subscriptions per 100 inhabitants: 0.04 (2020 est.)
country comparison to the world: 190

TRANSPORTATION

Civil aircraft registration country code prefix: 9U

Airports: *total:* 7 (2021)
country comparison to the world: 166

Airports - with paved runways: *total:* 1
over 3,047 m: 1 (2021)

Airports - with unpaved runways: *total:* 6
914 to 1,523 m: 4
under 914 m: 2 (2021)

Heliports: 1 (2021)

Roadways: *total:* 12,322 km (2016)
paved: 1,500 km (2016)
unpaved: 10,822 km (2016)
country comparison to the world: 130

Waterways: 673 km (2022) (mainly on Lake Tanganyika between Bujumbura, Burundi's principal port, and lake ports in Tanzania, Zambia, and the Democratic Republic of the Congo)
country comparison to the world: 83

Ports and terminals: *lake port(s):* Bujumbura (Lake Tanganyika)

MILITARY AND SECURITY

Military and security forces: National Defense Forces (Forces de Defense Nationale, FDN): Army (includes maritime wing, air wing); Ministry of Public Security: National Police (Police Nationale du Burundi) (2022)

Military expenditures: 2% of GDP (2021 est.)
2.1% of GDP (2020 est.)
3% of GDP (2019 est.) (approximately $120 million)
2.3% of GDP (2018 est.) (approximately $100 million)
2.1% of GDP (2017 est.) (approximately $95 million)
country comparison to the world: 56

Military and security service personnel strengths: approximately 30,000 active duty troops, the majority of which are ground forces (2022)

Military equipment inventories and acquisitions: the FDN is armed mostly with weapons from Russia and the former Soviet Union, with some Western equipment, largely from France; since 2010, the FDN has received small amounts of mostly second-hand equipment from China, South Africa, and the US (2021)

Military service age and obligation: 18 years of age for voluntary military service (2021)

Military deployments: 760 Central African Republic (MINUSCA); 5,400 Somalia (ATMIS) (2022)

Military - note: in addition to its foreign deployments, the FDN was focused on internal security missions, particularly against rebel groups opposed to the regime such as National Forces of Liberation (FNL), the Resistance for the Rule of Law-Tabara (aka RED Tabara), and Popular Forces of Burundi (FPB or FOREBU); these groups were based in the neighboring Democratic Republic of Congo and have carried out sporadic attacks in Burundi (2022)

TRANSNATIONAL ISSUES

Disputes - international: cross-border conflicts persist among Tutsi, Hutu, other ethnic groups, associated political rebels, armed gangs, and various government forces in the Great Lakes region
Burundi-Rwanda: Burundi's Ngozi province and Rwanda's Butare province dispute the two-kilometer-square hilly farmed area of Sabanerwa in the Rukurazi Valley where the Akanyaru/Kanyaru River shifted its course southward after heavy rains in 1965 around Kibinga Hill in Rwanda's Butare Province

Refugees and internally displaced persons: *refugees (country of origin):* 85,470 (Democratic Republic of the Congo) (refugees and asylum seekers) (2022)

IDPs: 84,791 (some ethnic Tutsis remain displaced from intercommunal violence that broke out after the 1993 coup and fighting between government forces and rebel groups; violence since April 2015) (2022)
stateless persons: 767 (mid-year 2021)

CABO VERDE

INTRODUCTION

Background: The uninhabited islands were discovered and colonized by the Portuguese in the 15th century; Cabo Verde subsequently became a trading center for African slaves and later an important coaling and resupply stop for whaling and transatlantic shipping. The fusing of European and various African cultural traditions is reflected in Cabo Verde's Krioulo language, music, and pano textiles. Following independence in 1975, and a tentative interest in unification with Guinea-Bissau, a one-party system was established and maintained until multi-party elections were held in 1990. Cabo Verde continues to sustain one of Africa's most stable democratic governments and one of its most stable economies, maintaining a currency formerly pegged to the Portuguese escudo and then the euro since 1998. Repeated droughts during the second half of the 20th century caused significant hardship and prompted heavy emigration. As a result, Cabo Verde's expatriate population - concentrated in Boston and Western Europe - is greater than its domestic one. Most Cabo Verdeans have both African and Portuguese antecedents. Cabo Verde's population descends from its first permanent inhabitants in the late 15th-century – a preponderance of West African slaves, a small share of Portuguese colonists, and even fewer Italians and Spaniards. Among the nine inhabited islands, population distribution is variable. Islands in the east are very dry and are home to the country's growing tourism industry. The more western islands receive more precipitation and support larger populations, but agriculture and livestock grazing have damaged their soil fertility and vegetation. For centuries, the country's overall population size has fluctuated significantly, as recurring periods of famine and epidemics have caused high death tolls and emigration. In November 2021, Jose Maria NEVES was sworn in as Cabo Verde's latest president.

GEOGRAPHY

Location: Western Africa, group of islands in the North Atlantic Ocean, west of Senegal

Geographic coordinates: 16 00 N, 24 00 W

Map references: Africa

Area: *total:* 4,033 sq km
land: 4,033 sq km
water: 0 sq km
country comparison to the world: 175

Area - comparative: slightly larger than Rhode Island

Land boundaries: *total:* 0 km

Coastline: 965 km

Maritime claims: *territorial sea:* 12 nm
contiguous zone: 24 nm
exclusive economic zone: 200 nm
measured from claimed archipelagic baselines

Climate: temperate; warm, dry summer; precipitation meager and erratic

Terrain: steep, rugged, rocky, volcanic

Elevation: *highest point:* Mt. Fogo (a volcano on Fogo Island) 2,829 m
lowest point: Atlantic Ocean 0 m

Natural resources: salt, basalt rock, limestone, kaolin, fish, clay, gypsum

Land use: *agricultural land:* 18.6% (2018 est.)
arable land: 11.7% (2018 est.)
permanent crops: 0.7% (2018 est.)
permanent pasture: 6.2% (2018 est.)
forest: 21% (2018 est.)
other: 60.4% (2018 est.)

Irrigated land: 35 sq km (2012)

Population distribution: among the nine inhabited islands, population distribution is variable; islands in the east are very dry and are only sparsely settled to exploit their extensive salt deposits; the more southerly islands receive more precipitation and support larger populations, but agriculture and livestock grazing have damaged the soil fertility and vegetation; approximately half of the population lives on Sao Tiago Island, which is the location of the capital of Praia; Mindelo, on the northern island of Sao Vicente, also has a large urban population as shown in this population distribution map

Natural hazards: prolonged droughts; seasonal harmattan wind produces obscuring dust; volcanically and seismically active

volcanism: Fogo (2,829 m), which last erupted in 1995, is Cabo Verde's only active volcano

Geography - note: strategic location 500 km from west coast of Africa near major north-south sea routes; important communications station; important sea and air refueling site; one of four North Atlantic archipelagos that make up Macaronesia; the others are Azores (Portugal), Canary Islands (Spain), and Madeira (Portugal)

PEOPLE AND SOCIETY

Population: 596,707 (2022 est.)
country comparison to the world: 172

Nationality: *noun:* Cabo Verdean(s)
adjective: Cabo Verdean

Ethnic groups: Creole (Mulatto) 71%, African 28%, European 1%

Languages: Portuguese (official), Krioulo (a Portuguese-based Creole language with two main dialects spoken in Cabo Verde and in the Cabo Verdean diaspora worldwide)

Religions: Roman Catholic 77.3%, Protestant 4.6% (includes Church of the Nazarene 1.7%, Adventist 1.5%, Assembly of God 0.9%, Universal Kingdom of God 0.4%, and God and Love 0.1%), other Christian 3.4% (includes Christian Rationalism 1.9%, Jehovah's Witness 1%, and New Apostolic 0.5%), Muslim 1.8%, other 1.3%, none 10.8%, unspecified 0.7% (2010 est.)

Demographic profile: Cabo Verde's population descends from its first permanent inhabitants in the late 15th-century - a preponderance of West African slaves, a small share of Portuguese colonists, and even fewer Italians, Spaniards, and Portuguese Jews. Over the centuries, the country's overall population size has fluctuated significantly, as recurring periods of famine and epidemics have caused high death tolls and emigration.

Labor migration historically reduced Cabo Verde's population growth and still provides a key source of income through remittances. Expatriates probably outnumber Cabo Verde's resident population, with most families having a member abroad. Cabo Verdeans have settled in the US, Europe, Africa, and South America. The largest diaspora community in New Bedford, Massachusetts, dating to the early 1800s, is a byproduct of the transatlantic whaling industry. Cabo Verdean men fleeing poverty at home joined the crews of US whaling ships that stopped in the islands. Many settled in New Bedford and stayed in the whaling or shipping trade, worked in the textile or cranberry industries, or operated their own transatlantic packet ships that transported compatriots to the US. Increased Cabo Verdean emigration to the US coincided with the gradual and eventually complete abolition of slavery in the archipelago in 1878.

During the same period, Portuguese authorities coerced Cabo Verdeans to go to Sao Tome and Principe and other Portuguese colonies in Africa to work as indentured laborers on plantations. In the 1920s, when the US implemented immigration quotas, Cabo Verdean emigration shifted toward Portugal, West Africa (Senegal), and South America (Argentina). Growing numbers of Cabo Verdean labor migrants headed to Western Europe in the 1960s and 1970s. They filled unskilled jobs in Portugal, as many Portuguese sought out work opportunities in the more prosperous economies of northwest Europe. Cabo Verdeans eventually expanded their emigration to the Netherlands, where they worked in the shipping industry. Migration to the US resumed under relaxed migration laws. Cabo Verdean women also began migrating to southern Europe to become domestic workers, a trend that continues today and has shifted the gender balance of Cabo Verdean emigration.

Emigration has declined in more recent decades due to the adoption of more restrictive migration policies in destination countries. Reduced emigration along with a large youth population, decreased mortality rates, and increased life expectancies, has boosted population growth, putting further pressure on domestic employment and resources. In addition, Cabo Verde has attracted increasing numbers of migrants in recent decades, consisting primarily of people from West Africa, Portuguese-speaking African countries, Portugal, and China. Since the 1990s, some West African migrants have used Cabo Verde as a stepping stone for illegal migration to Europe.

Age structure: *0-14 years:* 27.95% (male 82,010/ female 81,012)
15-24 years: 18.69% (male 54,521/female 54,504)

25-54 years: 40.76% (male 115,811/female 121,923)
55-64 years: 7.12% (male 18,939/female 22,597)
65 years and over: 5.48% (male 12,037/female 19,901) (2020 est.)

Dependency ratios: *total dependency ratio:* 49
youth dependency ratio: 41.8
elderly dependency ratio: 7.1
potential support ratio: 14 (2020 est.)

Median age: *total:* 26.8 years
male: 25.9 years
female: 27.6 years (2020 est.)
country comparison to the world: 151

Population growth rate: 1.21% (2022 est.)
country comparison to the world: 76

Birth rate: 18.49 births/1,000 population (2022 est.)
country comparison to the world: 79

Death rate: 5.8 deaths/1,000 population (2022 est.)
country comparison to the world: 168

Net migration rate: -0.57 migrant(s)/1,000 population (2022 est.)
country comparison to the world: 126

Population distribution: among the nine inhabited islands, population distribution is variable; islands in the east are very dry and are only sparsely settled to exploit their extensive salt deposits; the more southerly islands receive more precipitation and support larger populations, but agriculture and livestock grazing have damaged the soil fertility and vegetation; approximately half of the population lives on Sao Tiago Island, which is the location of the capital of Praia; Mindelo, on the northern island of Sao Vicente, also has a large urban population as shown in this population distribution map

Urbanization: *urban population:* 67.5% of total population (2022)
rate of urbanization: 1.83% annual rate of change (2020-25 est.)

Major urban areas - population: 168,000 PRAIA (capital) (2018)

Sex ratio: *at birth:* 1.03 male(s)/female
0-14 years: 1.01 male(s)/female
15-24 years: 1 male(s)/female
25-54 years: 0.95 male(s)/female
55-64 years: 0.86 male(s)/female
65 years and over: 0.52 male(s)/female
total population: 0.95 male(s)/female (2022 est.)

Maternal mortality ratio: 58 deaths/100,000 live births (2017 est.)
country comparison to the world: 91

Infant mortality rate: *total:* 23.53 deaths/1,000 live births
male: 27.64 deaths/1,000 live births
female: 19.29 deaths/1,000 live births (2022 est.)
country comparison to the world: 69

Life expectancy at birth: *total population:* 73.75 years
male: 71.41 years
female: 76.15 years (2022 est.)
country comparison to the world: 144

Total fertility rate: 2.13 children born/woman (2022 est.)
country comparison to the world: 92

Contraceptive prevalence rate: 55.8% (2018)

Drinking water source: *improved: urban:* 100% of population
rural: 90% of population
total: 96.7% of population
unimproved: urban: 0% of population
rural: 10% of population
total: 3.3% of population (2020 est.)

Current health expenditure: 4.9% of GDP (2019)

Physicians density: 0.83 physicians/1,000 population (2018)

Hospital bed density: 2.1 beds/1,000 population

Sanitation facility access: *improved: urban:* 91.7% of population
rural: 73.3% of population
total: 85.6% of population
unimproved: urban: 8.3% of population
rural: 26.7% of population
total: 14.4% of population (2020 est.)

HIV/AIDS - adult prevalence rate: 0.5% (2020 est.)
country comparison to the world: 63

Obesity - adult prevalence rate: 11.8% (2016)
country comparison to the world: 134

Alcohol consumption per capita: *total:* 4.7 liters of pure alcohol (2019 est.)
beer: 2.28 liters of pure alcohol (2019 est.)
wine: 1.82 liters of pure alcohol (2019 est.)
spirits: 0.6 liters of pure alcohol (2019 est.)
other alcohols: 0 liters of pure alcohol (2019 est.)
country comparison to the world: 85

Tobacco use: *total:* 11.4% (2020 est.)
male: 17.3% (2020 est.)
female: 5.4% (2020 est.)
country comparison to the world: 127

Education expenditures: 4.7% of GDP (2019 est.)
country comparison to the world: 74

Literacy: *definition:* age 15 and over can read and write
total population: 86.8%
male: 91.7%
female: 82% (2015)

School life expectancy (primary to tertiary education): *total:* 13 years
male: 12 years
female: 13 years (2018)

Unemployment, youth ages 15-24: *total:* 50.4%
male: 41.4%
female: 65.3% (2019)

ENVIRONMENT

Environment - current issues: deforestation due to demand for firewood; water shortages; prolonged droughts and improper use of land (overgrazing, crop cultivation on hillsides lead to desertification and erosion); environmental damage has threatened several species of birds and reptiles; illegal beach sand extraction; overfishing

Environment - international agreements: *party to:* Biodiversity, Climate Change, Climate Change-Kyoto Protocol, Climate Change-Paris Agreement, Comprehensive Nuclear Test Ban, Desertification, Endangered Species, Environmental Modification, Hazardous Wastes, Law of the Sea, Marine Dumping-London Convention, Nuclear Test Ban, Ozone Layer Protection, Ship Pollution, Wetlands
signed, but not ratified: none of the selected agreements

Air pollutants: *particulate matter emissions:* 31.99 micrograms per cubic meter (2016 est.)
carbon dioxide emissions: 0.54 megatons (2016 est.)
methane emissions: 0.13 megatons (2020 est.)

Climate: temperate; warm, dry summer; precipitation meager and erratic

Land use: *agricultural land:* 18.6% (2018 est.)
arable land: 11.7% (2018 est.)
permanent crops: 0.7% (2018 est.)
permanent pasture: 6.2% (2018 est.)
forest: 21% (2018 est.)
other: 60.4% (2018 est.)

Urbanization: *urban population:* 67.5% of total population (2022)
rate of urbanization: 1.83% annual rate of change (2020-25 est.)

Revenue from forest resources: *forest revenues:* 0.38% of GDP (2018 est.)
country comparison to the world: 72

Revenue from coal: *coal revenues:* 0% of GDP (2018 est.)
country comparison to the world: 73

Waste and recycling: *municipal solid waste generated annually:* 132,555 tons (2012 est.)

Total water withdrawal: *municipal:* 1.6 million cubic meters (2017 est.)
industrial: 400,000 cubic meters (2017 est.)
agricultural: 25 million cubic meters (2017 est.)

Total renewable water resources: 300 million cubic meters (2017 est.)

GOVERNMENT

Country name: *conventional long form:* Republic of Cabo Verde
conventional short form: Cabo Verde
local long form: Republica de Cabo Verde
local short form: Cabo Verde
etymology: the name derives from Cap-Vert (Green Cape) on the Senegalese coast, the westernmost point of Africa and the nearest mainland to the islands

Government type: parliamentary republic

Capital: *name:* Praia
geographic coordinates: 14 55 N, 23 31 W
time difference: UTC-1 (4 hours ahead of Washington, DC, during Standard Time)
etymology: the earlier Portuguese name was Villa de Praia ("Village of the Beach"); it became just Praia in 1974 (prior to full independence in 1975)

Administrative divisions: 22 municipalities (concelhos, singular - concelho); Boa Vista, Brava, Maio, Mosteiros, Paul, Porto Novo, Praia, Ribeira Brava, Ribeira Grande, Ribeira Grande de Santiago, Sal, Santa Catarina, Santa Catarina do Fogo, Santa Cruz, Sao Domingos, Sao Filipe, Sao Lourenco dos Orgaos, Sao Miguel, Sao Salvador do Mundo, Sao Vicente, Tarrafal, Tarrafal de Sao Nicolau

Independence: 5 July 1975 (from Portugal)

National holiday: Independence Day, 5 July (1975)

Constitution: *history:* previous 1981; latest effective 25 September 1992
amendments: proposals require support of at least four fifths of the active National Assembly membership; amendment drafts require sponsorship of at least one third of the active Assembly membership; passage requires at least two-thirds majority vote by the Assembly membership; constitutional sections, including those on national independence, form of government, political pluralism, suffrage, and human rights and liberties, cannot be amended; revised 1995, 1999, 2010

Legal system: civil law system of Portugal

International law organization participation: as not submitted an ICJ jurisdiction declaration; accepts ICCt jurisdiction

Citizenship: *citizenship by birth:* no
citizenship by descent only: at least one parent must be a citizen of Cabo Verde
dual citizenship recognized: yes
residency requirement for naturalization: 5 years

Suffrage: 18 years of age; universal

Executive branch: *chief of state:* President Jose Maria NEVES (since 9 November 2021)
head of government: Prime Minister Ulisses CORREIA E. SILVA (since 22 April 2016)
cabinet: Council of Ministers appointed by the president on the recommendation of the prime minister
elections/appointments: president directly elected by absolute majority popular vote in 2 rounds if needed for a 5-year term (eligible for a second term); election last held on 17 October 2021 (next to be held in October 2026); prime minister nominated by the National Assembly and appointed by the president (2021)
election results: election results: 2020: Jose Maria NEVES elected president; percent of vote - Jose Maria NEVES (PAICV) 51.7%, Carlos VEIGA (MPD) 42.4%, Casimiro DE PINA (Independent) 1.8%, Fernando Rocha DELGADO (Independent) 1.4%, Helio SANCHES (independent) 1.14%, Gilson ALVES (independent) 0.8%, Joaquim MONTEIRO (independent) 3.4%
election results: 2015: Jorge Carlos FONSECA reelected president; percent of vote - Jorge Carlos FONSECA (MPD) 74.1%, Albertino GRACA (independent) 22.5%, other 3% (2021)
African Party for the Independence of Cape Verde (APICV):
Movement for Democracy (MFD)

Legislative branch: *description:* unicameral National Assembly or Assembleia Nacional (72 seats; members directly elected in multi-seat constituencies by proportional representation vote; members serve 5-year terms)
elections: last held on 18 April 2021 (next to be held in April 2026) (2021)
election results: percent of vote by party MPD 50.2%, PAICV 39.6%, UCID 9.0%; seats by party - MPD 38, PAICV 30, UCID 4; composition - men 44, women 28, percent of women 37.5% (2021)

Judicial branch: *highest court(s):* Supreme Court of Justice (consists of the chief justice and at least 7 judges and organized into civil, criminal, and administrative sections)
judge selection and term of office: judge appointments - 1 by the president of the republic, 1 elected by the National Assembly, and 3 by the Superior Judicial Council (SJC), a 16-member independent body chaired by the chief justice and includes the attorney general, 8 private citizens, 2 judges, 2 prosecutors, the senior legal inspector of the Attorney General's office, and a representative of the Ministry of Justice; chief justice appointed by the president of the republic from among peers of the Supreme Court of Justice and in consultation with the SJC; judges appointed for life
subordinate courts: appeals courts, first instance (municipal) courts; audit, military, and fiscal and customs courts

Political parties and leaders: African Party for Independence of Cabo Verde or PAICV [Jose Maria NEVES]
Democratic and Independent Cabo Verdean Union or UCID [Joao DOS SANTOS LUIS]
Democratic Christian Party or PDC [Manuel RODRIGUES]
Democratic Renewal Party or PRD [Victor FIDALGO]
Movement for Democracy or MPD [Ulisses CORREIA E SILVA]
Party for Democratic Convergence or PCD [Dr. Eurico MONTEIRO]
Party of Work and Solidarity or PTS [Anibal MEDINA]
Social Democratic Party or PSD [Joao ALEM]

International organization participation: ACP, AfDB, AOSIS, AU, CD, CPLP, ECOWAS, FAO, G-77, IAEA, IBRD, ICAO, ICCt (signatory), ICRM, IDA, IFAD, IFC, IFRCS, ILO, IMF, IMO, Interpol, IOC, IOM, IPU, ITSO, ITU, ITUC (NGOs), MIGA, NAM, OIF, OPCW, UN, UNCTAD, UNESCO, UNIDO, Union Latina, UNWTO, UPU, WCO, WHO, WIPO, WMO, WTO

Diplomatic representation in the US: *chief of mission:* Ambassador Jose Luis do Livramento MONTEIRO ALVES DE BRITO (since 23 December 2020)
chancery: 3415 Massachusetts Avenue NW, Washington, DC 20007
telephone: [1] (202) 965-6820
FAX: [1] (202) 965-1207
email address and website:
embassy@caboverdeus.net
https://www.embcv-usa.gov.cv/
consulate(s) general: Boston

Diplomatic representation from the US: *chief of mission:* Ambassador John "Jeff" DAIGLE (since 10 September 2019)
embassy: Rua Abilio Macedo 6, Praia
mailing address: 2460 Praia Place, Washington DC 20521-2460
telephone: [238] 260-8900
FAX: [238] 261-1355
email address and website:
PraiaConsular@state.gov
https://cv.usembassy.gov/

Flag description: five unequal horizontal bands; the top-most band of blue - equal to one half the width of the flag - is followed by three bands of white, red, and white, each equal to 1/12 of the width, and a bottom stripe of blue equal to one quarter of the flag width; a circle of 10 yellow, five-pointed stars is centered on the red stripe and positioned 3/8 of the length of the flag from the hoist side; blue stands for the sea and the sky, the circle of stars represents the 10 major islands united into a nation, the stripes symbolize the road to formation of the country through peace (white) and effort (red)

National symbol(s): ten, five-pointed, yellow stars; national colors: blue, white, red, yellow

National anthem: *name:* "Cantico da Liberdade" (Song of Freedom)
lyrics/music: Amilcar Spencer LOPES/Adalberto Higino Tavares SILVA
note: adopted 1996

National heritage: *total World Heritage Sites:* 1 (cultural)
selected World Heritage Site locales: Cidade Velha; Historic Center of Ribeira Grande

ECONOMY

Economic overview: Cabo Verde's economy depends on development aid, foreign investment, remittances, and tourism. The economy is service-oriented with commerce, transport, tourism, and public services accounting for about three-fourths of GDP. Tourism is the mainstay of the economy and depends on conditions in the euro-zone countries. Cabo Verde annually runs a high trade deficit financed by foreign aid and remittances from its large pool of emigrants; remittances as a share of GDP are one of the highest in Sub-Saharan Africa.

Although about 40% of the population lives in rural areas, the share of food production in GDP is low. The island economy suffers from a poor natural resource base, including serious water shortages, exacerbated by cycles of long-term drought, and poor soil for growing food on several of the islands, requiring it to import most of what it consumes. The fishing potential, mostly lobster and tuna, is not fully exploited.

Economic reforms are aimed at developing the private sector and attracting foreign investment to diversify the economy and mitigate high unemployment. The government's elevated debt levels have limited its capacity to finance any shortfalls.

Real GDP (purchasing power parity): $3.36 billion (2020 est.)
$3.94 billion (2019 est.)
$3.73 billion (2018 est.)
note: data are in 2017 dollars
country comparison to the world: 188

Real GDP growth rate: 4% (2017 est.)
4.7% (2016 est.)
1% (2015 est.)
country comparison to the world: 73

Real GDP per capita: $6,000 (2020 est.)
$7,200 (2019 est.)
$6,900 (2018 est.)
note: data are in 2017 dollars
country comparison to the world: 165

GDP (official exchange rate): $1.971 billion (2019 est.)

Inflation rate (consumer prices): 1.1% (2019 est.)
1.2% (2018 est.)
0.7% (2017 est.)
country comparison to the world: 70

Credit ratings:

Fitch rating: B- (2020)

Standard & Poors rating: B (2013)
note: The year refers to the year in which the current credit rating was first obtained.

GDP - composition, by sector of origin: *agriculture:* 8.9% (2017 est.)
industry: 17.5% (2017 est.)
services: 73.7% (2017 est.)

GDP - composition, by end use: *household consumption:* 50.1% (2017 est.)
government consumption: 18.3% (2017 est.)
investment in fixed capital: 32.2% (2017 est.)
investment in inventories: 1.9% (2017 est.)
exports of goods and services: 48.6% (2017 est.)
imports of goods and services: -51.1% (2017 est.)

Agricultural products: sugar cane, tomatoes, bananas, cabbages, coconuts, cassava, pulses, vegetables, milk, goat milk

Industries: food and beverages, fish processing, shoes and garments, salt mining, ship repair

Industrial production growth rate: 2.9% (2017 est.)
country comparison to the world: 107

Labor force: 196,100 (2007 est.)
country comparison to the world: 172

Unemployment rate: 9% (2017 est.)

9% (2016 est.)
country comparison to the world: 139

Unemployment, youth ages 15-24:
total: 50.4%
male: 41.4%
female: 65.3% (2019)
country comparison to the world: 4

Population below poverty line: 35% (2015 est.)

Gini Index coefficient - distribution of family income: 42.4 (2015 est.)
country comparison to the world: 45

Household income or consumption by percentage share: *lowest 10%:* 1.9%
highest 10%: 40.6% (2000)

Budget: *revenues:* 493.5 million (2017 est.)
expenditures: 546.7 million (2017 est.)

Budget surplus (+) or deficit (-): -3% (of GDP) (2017 est.)
country comparison to the world: 131

Public debt: 125.8% of GDP (2017 est.)
127.6% of GDP (2016 est.)
country comparison to the world: 8

Taxes and other revenues: 27.8% (of GDP) (2017 est.)
country comparison to the world: 98

Fiscal year: calendar year

Current account balance: -$109 million (2017 est.)
-$40 million (2016 est.)
country comparison to the world: 88

Exports: $420 million (2020 est.)
$1 billion (2019 est.)
$960 million (2018 est.)
note: Data are in current year dollars and do not include illicit exports or re-exports.
country comparison to the world: 193

Exports - partners: Spain 65%, Portugal 14%, Italy 8% (2019)

Exports - commodities: processed and frozen fish, mollusks, clothing, scrap iron (2019)

Imports: $1.02 billion (2020 est.) note: data are in current year dollars
$1.29 billion (2019 est.) note: data are in current year dollars
$1.34 billion (2018 est.) note: data are in current year dollars
country comparison to the world: 188

Imports - partners: Portugal 36%, Netherlands 16%, Spain 11%, China 6% (2019)

Imports - commodities: refined petroleum, delivery trucks, coal tar oil, cars, rice (2019)

Reserves of foreign exchange and gold: $617.4 million (31 December 2017 est.)
$572.7 million (31 December 2016 est.)
country comparison to the world: 145

Debt - external: $1.713 billion (31 December 2017 est.)
$1.688 billion (31 December 2016 est.)
country comparison to the world: 155

Exchange rates: Cabo Verdean escudos (CVE) per US dollar –
101.8 (2017 est.)
99.688 (2016 est.)
99.688 (2015 est.)
99.426 (2014 est.)
83.114 (2013 est.)

ENERGY

Electricity access: *electrification - total population:* 96% (2019)
electrification - urban areas: 99% (2019)
electrification - rural areas: 89% (2019)

Electricity: *installed generating capacity:* 205,000 kW (2020 est.)
consumption: 436.854 million kWh (2019 est.)
exports: 0 kWh (2019 est.)
imports: 0 kWh (2019 est.)
transmission/distribution losses: 32.146 million kWh (2019 est.)

Electricity generation sources: *fossil fuels:* 80.2% of total installed capacity (2020 est.)
solar: 2% of total installed capacity (2020 est.)
wind: 17.8% of total installed capacity (2020 est.)

Petroleum: *total petroleum production:* 0 bbl/day (2021 est.)
refined petroleum consumption: 6,500 bbl/day (2019 est.)

Refined petroleum products - imports: 5,607 bbl/day (2015 est.)
country comparison to the world: 166

Carbon dioxide emissions: 1.002 million metric tonnes of CO2 (2019 est.)
from petroleum and other liquids: 1.002 million metric tonnes of CO2 (2019 est.)
country comparison to the world: 173

Energy consumption per capita: 26.539 million Btu/person (2019 est.)
country comparison to the world: 128

COMMUNICATIONS

Telephones - fixed lines: *total subscriptions:* 57,668 (2020 est.)
subscriptions per 100 inhabitants: 10 (2020 est.)
country comparison to the world: 154

Telephones - mobile cellular: *total subscriptions:* 544,729 (2020 est.)
subscriptions per 100 inhabitants: 98 (2020 est.)
country comparison to the world: 172

Telecommunication systems: *general assessment:* LTE reaches almost 40% of the population; regulator awards commercial 4G licenses and starts 5G pilot; govt. extends USD 25 million for submarine fiber-optic cable project linking Africa to Portugal and Brazil (2020)
domestic: a little over 10 per 100 fixed-line teledensity and nearly 98 per 100 mobile-cellular; fiber-optic ring, completed in 2001, links all islands providing Internet access and ISDN services; cellular service introduced in 1998; broadband services launched early in the decade (2020)
international: country code - 238; landing points for the Atlantis-2, EllaLink, Cabo Verde Telecom Domestic Submarine Cable Phase 1,2, 3 and WACS fiber-optic transatlantic telephone cable that provides links to South America, Africa, and Europe; HF radiotelephone to Senegal and Guinea-Bissau; satellite earth station - 1 Intelsat (Atlantic Ocean) (2019)

Broadcast media: state-run TV and radio broadcast network plus a growing number of private broadcasters; Portuguese public TV and radio services for Africa are available; transmissions of a few international broadcasters are available (2019)

Internet country code: .cv

Internet users: *total:* 361,392 (2020 est.)
percent of population: 65% (2020 est.)
country comparison to the world: 167

Broadband - fixed subscriptions: *total:* 24,839 (2020 est.)
subscriptions per 100 inhabitants: 5 (2020 est.)
country comparison to the world: 160

TRANSPORTATION

National air transport system: *number of registered air carriers:* 2 (2020)
inventory of registered aircraft operated by air carriers: 5
annual passenger traffic on registered air carriers: 140,429 (2018)
annual freight traffic on registered air carriers: 1,728,152 (2015) mt-km

Civil aircraft registration country code prefix: D4

Airports: *total:* 9 (2021)
country comparison to the world: 156

Airports - with paved runways total: 9
over 3,047 m: 1
1,524 to 2,437 m: 3
914 to 1,523 m: 3
under 914 m: 2 (2021)

Roadways: *total:* 1,350 km (2013)
*paved:*932 km (2013)
*unpaved:*418 km (2013)
country comparison to the world: 176

Merchant marine: *total:* 46
by type: general cargo 16, oil tanker 3, other 27 (2021)
country comparison to the world: 120

Ports and terminals: *major seaport(s):* Porto Grande

MILITARY AND SECURITY

Military and security forces: Cabo Verdean Armed Forces (FACV): Army (also called the National Guard, GN; includes a small air component), Cabo Verde Coast Guard (Guardia Costeira de Cabo Verde, GCCV); Ministry of Internal Affairs: National Police (2022)

Military expenditures: 0.5% of GDP (2021 est.)
0.5% of GDP (2020 est.)
0.5% of GDP (2019 est.) (approximately $20 million)
0.5% of GDP (2018 est.) (approximately $20 million)
0.5% of GDP (2017 est.) (approximately $20 million)
country comparison to the world: 157

Military and security service personnel strengths: approximately 1,200 personnel including about 100 in the Coast Guard (2022)

Military equipment inventories and acquisitions: the FACV has a limited amount of mostly dated and second-hand equipment, largely from China, some European countries, and the former Soviet Union (2022)

Military service age and obligation: 18-35 years of age for male and female selective compulsory military service; 2-years conscript service obligation; 17 years of age for voluntary service (with parental consent) (2022)

Military - note: as of 2022, the FACV/National Guard was mostly a ground force with 2 infantry battalions and a small air component with a maritime patrol squadron; the Coast Guard had a few coastal patrol craft and patrol boats

TRANSNATIONAL ISSUES

Disputes - international: none

Refugees and internally displaced persons: *stateless persons:* 115 (mid-year 2021)

Illicit drugs: Cabo Verde is a transit hub for cocaine, marijuana, and other drugs trafficked from Latin America to Europe; marijuana, cocaine, hashish, heroin, and methamphetamine are the most frequently consumed drugs in Cabo Verde

CAMBODIA

INTRODUCTION

Background: Most Cambodians consider themselves to be Khmers, descendants of the Angkor Empire that extended over much of Southeast Asia and reached its zenith between the 10th and 13th centuries. Attacks by the Thai and Cham (from present-day Vietnam) weakened the empire, ushering in a long period of decline. The king placed the country under French protection in 1863, and it became part of French Indochina in 1887. Following Japanese occupation in World War II, Cambodia gained full independence from France in 1953. In April 1975, after a seven-year struggle, communist Khmer Rouge forces captured Phnom Penh and evacuated all cities and towns. At least 1.5 million Cambodians died from execution, forced hardships, or starvation during the Khmer Rouge regime under POL POT. A December 1978 Vietnamese invasion drove the Khmer Rouge into the countryside, began a 10-year Vietnamese occupation, and touched off 20 years of civil war.

The 1991 Paris Peace Accords mandated democratic elections and a cease-fire, which was not fully respected by the Khmer Rouge. UN-sponsored elections in 1993 helped restore some semblance of normalcy under a coalition government. Factional fighting in 1997 ended the first coalition government, but a second round of national elections in 1998 led to the formation of another coalition government and renewed political stability. The remaining elements of the Khmer Rouge surrendered in early 1999. Some of the surviving Khmer Rouge leaders were tried for crimes against humanity by a hybrid UN-Cambodian tribunal supported by international assistance. In 2018, the tribunal heard its final cases, but it remains in operation to hear appeals. Elections in July 2003 were relatively peaceful, but it took one year of negotiations between contending political parties before a coalition government was formed. In October 2004, King Norodom SIHANOUK abdicated the throne and his son, Prince Norodom SIHAMONI, was selected to succeed him. Local (Commune Council) elections were held in Cambodia in 2012, with little of the violence that preceded prior elections. National elections in July 2013 were disputed, with the opposition - the Cambodia National Rescue Party (CNRP) - boycotting the National Assembly. The political impasse was ended nearly a year later, with the CNRP agreeing to enter parliament in exchange for commitments by the ruling Cambodian People's Party (CPP) to undertake electoral and legislative reforms. The CNRP made further gains in local commune elections in June 2017, accelerating sitting Prime Minister HUN SEN's efforts to marginalize the CNRP before national elections in 2018. HUN SEN arrested CNRP President KEM SOKHA in September 2017. The Supreme Court dissolved the CNRP in November 2017 and banned its leaders from participating in politics for at least five years. The CNRP's seats in the National Assembly were redistributed to smaller, less influential opposition parties, while all of the CNRP's 5,007 seats in the commune councils throughout the country were reallocated to the CPP. With the CNRP banned, the CPP swept the 2018 national elections, winning all 125 National Assembly seats and effectively turning the country into a one-party state.

Cambodia has strong and growing economic and political ties with its large neighbor to the north, China. More than 53% of foreign investment in the country in 2021 came from China, and Beijing has provided over $15 billion in financial assistance since the 1990s. China accounted for 443 percent of Cambodia's foreign debt in 2021. The CPP also partly sees Chinese support as a counterbalance to Thailand and Vietnam and to international criticism of the CPP's human rights and antidemocratic record.

GEOGRAPHY

Location: Southeastern Asia, bordering the Gulf of Thailand, between Thailand, Vietnam, and Laos

Geographic coordinates: 13 00 N, 105 00 E

Map references: Southeast Asia

Area: *total:* 181,035 sq km
land: 176,515 sq km
water: 4,520 sq km
country comparison to the world: 90

Area - comparative: one and a half times the size of Pennsylvania; slightly smaller than Oklahoma

Land boundaries: *total:* 2,530 km
border countries (3): Laos 555 km; Thailand 817 km; Vietnam 1158 km

Coastline: 443 km

Maritime claims: *territorial sea:* 12 nm
contiguous zone: 24 nm
exclusive economic zone: 200 nm
continental shelf: 200 nm

Climate: tropical; rainy, monsoon season (May to November); dry season (December to April); little seasonal temperature variation

Terrain: mostly low, flat plains; mountains in southwest and north

Elevation: *highest point:* Phnum Aoral 1,810 m
lowest point: Gulf of Thailand 0 m
mean elevation: 126 m

Natural resources: oil and gas, timber, gemstones, iron ore, manganese, phosphates, hydropower potential, arable land

Land use: *agricultural land:* 32.1% (2018 est.)
arable land: 22.7% (2018 est.)
permanent crops: 0.9% (2018 est.)
permanent pasture: 8.5% (2018 est.)
forest: 56.5% (2018 est.)
other: 11.4% (2018 est.)

Irrigated land: 3,540 sq km (2012)

Major lakes (area sq km): *fresh water lake(s):* Tonle Sap - 2,700-16,000 sq km

Major rivers (by length in km): Mekong (shared with China [s], Burma, Thailand, Laos, and Vietnam [m]) - 4,350 km
note – [s] after country name indicates river source; [m] after country name indicates river mouth

Major watersheds (area sq km): Pacific Ocean drainage: Mekong (805,604 sq km)

Population distribution: population concentrated in the southeast, particularly in and around the capital of Phnom Penh; further distribution is linked closely to the Tonle Sap and Mekong Rivers

Natural hazards: monsoonal rains (June to November); flooding; occasional droughts

Geography - note: a land of paddies and forests dominated by the Mekong River and Tonle Sap (Southeast Asia's largest freshwater lake)

PEOPLE AND SOCIETY

Population: 16,713,015 (2022 est.)
country comparison to the world: 72

Nationality: *noun:* Cambodian(s)
adjective: Cambodian

Ethnic groups: Khmer 95.4%, Cham 2.4%, Chinese 1.5%, other 0.7% (2019-20 est.)

Languages: Khmer (official) 95.8%, minority languages 2.9%, Chinese 0.6%, Vietnamese 0.5%, other 0.2% (2019 est.)
major-language sample(s):
សៀវភៅហេតុការណនៅលើពិភពលោក។
ទីតាំងពត៌មានមូលដានគ្រឹះយាងសំខាន់។. (Khmer)

Religions: Buddhist (official) 97.1%, Muslim 2%, Christian 0.3%, other 0.5% (2019 est.)

Demographic profile: Cambodia is a predominantly rural country with among the most ethnically and religiously homogenous populations in Southeast Asia: more than 95% of its inhabitants are Khmer and more than 95% are Buddhist. The population's size and age structure shrank and then rebounded during the 20th century as a result of conflict and mass death. During the Khmer Rouge regime between 1975 and 1979 as many as 1.5 to 2 million people are estimated to have been killed or died as a result of starvation, disease, or overwork - a loss of about 25% of the population. At the same time, emigration was high, and the fertility rate sharply declined. In the 1980s, after the overthrow of the Khmer Rouge, fertility nearly doubled and reached pre-Khmer Rouge levels of close to 7 children per woman, reflecting in part higher infant survival rates. The baby boom was followed by a sustained fertility decline starting in the early 1990s, eventually decreasing from 3.8 in 2000 to 2.9 in 2010, although the rate varied by income, education, and rural versus urban location. Despite continuing fertility reduction, Cambodia still has a youthful population that is likely to maintain population growth through population momentum. Improvements have also been made in mortality, life expectancy, and contraceptive prevalence, although reducing malnutrition among children remains stalled. Differences in health indicators are pronounced between urban and rural areas, which experience greater poverty.

Cambodia is predominantly a country of migration, driven by the search for work, education, or marriage. Internal migration is more prevalent than international migration, with rural to urban migration being the most common, followed by rural to rural migration. Urban migration focuses on the pursuit of unskilled or semi-skilled jobs in Phnom Penh, with men working mainly in the construction industry and women working in garment factories. Most Cambodians who migrate abroad do so illegally using brokers because it is cheaper and faster than through formal channels, but doing so puts them at risk of being trafficked for forced labor or sexual exploitation. Young Cambodian men and women migrate short distances across the Thai border using temporary passes to work in agriculture, while others migrate long distances primarily into Thailand and Malaysia for work in agriculture, fishing, construction, manufacturing, and domestic service. Cambodia was a refugee sending country in the 1970s and 1980s as a result of the brutality of the Khmer Rouge regime, its ousting by the Vietnamese invasion, and the resultant civil war. Tens of thousands of Cambodians fled to Thailand; more than 100,000 were resettled in the US in the 1980s. Cambodia signed a multi-million dollar agreement with Australia in 2014 to voluntarily resettle refugees seeking shelter in Australia. However, the deal has proven to be a failure because of poor conditions and a lack of support services for the few refugees willing to accept the offer.

Age structure: *0-14 years:* 30.18% (male 2,582,427/female 2,525,619)
15-24 years: 17.28% (male 1,452,784/female 1,472,769)
25-54 years: 41.51% (male 3,442,051/female 3,584,592)
55-64 years: 6.44% (male 476,561/female 612,706)
65 years and over: 4.59% (male 287,021/female 490,454) (2020 est.)

Dependency ratios: *total dependency ratio:* 55.7
youth dependency ratio: 48.2
elderly dependency ratio: 7.6
potential support ratio: 13.2 (2020 est.)

Median age: *total:* 26.4 years
male: 25.6 years
female: 27.2 years (2020 est.)
country comparison to the world: 153

Population growth rate: 1.08% (2022 est.)
country comparison to the world: 89

Birth rate: 19.29 births/1,000 population (2022 est.)
country comparison to the world: 73

Death rate: 5.76 deaths/1,000 population (2022 est.)
country comparison to the world: 171

Net migration rate: -2.7 migrant(s)/1,000 population (2022 est.)
country comparison to the world: 175

Population distribution: population concentrated in the southeast, particularly in and around the capital of Phnom Penh; further distribution is linked closely to the Tonle Sap and Mekong Rivers

Urbanization: *urban population:* 25.1% of total population (2022)
rate of urbanization: 3.06% annual rate of change (2020-25 est.)

Major urban areas - population: 2.211 million PHNOM PENH (capital) (2022)

Sex ratio: *at birth:* 1.05 male(s)/female
0-14 years: 1.02 male(s)/female
15-24 years: 0.97 male(s)/female
25-54 years: 0.94 male(s)/female
55-64 years: 0.81 male(s)/female
65 years and over: 0.51 male(s)/female
total population: 0.94 male(s)/female (2022 est.)

Mother's mean age at first birth: 22.4 years (2014 est.)
note: data represents median age at first birth among women 25-49

Maternal mortality ratio: 160 deaths/100,000 live births (2017 est.)
country comparison to the world: 55

Infant mortality rate: *total:* 29.58 deaths/1,000 live births
male: 33.13 deaths/1,000 live births
female: 25.87 deaths/1,000 live births (2022 est.)
country comparison to the world: 54

Life expectancy at birth: *total population:* 70.65 years
male: 68.79 years
female: 72.59 years (2022 est.)
country comparison to the world: 168

Total fertility rate: 2.24 children born/woman (2022 est.)
country comparison to the world: 81

Contraceptive prevalence rate: 56.3% (2014)

Drinking water source: *improved: urban:* 99.3% of population
rural: 80.6% of population
total: 85.1% of population
unimproved: urban: 0.7% of population
rural: 19.4% of population
total: 14.9% of population (2020 est.)

Current health expenditure: 7% of GDP (2019)

Physicians density: 0.19 physicians/1,000 population (2014)

Hospital bed density: 1.9 beds/1,000 population (2016)

Sanitation facility access: *improved: urban:* 100% of population
rural: 69.3% of population
total: 76.8% of population
unimproved: urban: 0% of population
rural: 30.7% of population
total: 23.2% of population (2020 est.)

HIV/AIDS - adult prevalence rate: 0.5% (2020 est.)
country comparison to the world: 64

Major infectious diseases: *degree of risk:* very high (2020)
food or waterborne diseases: bacterial diarrhea, hepatitis A, and typhoid fever
vectorborne diseases: dengue fever, Japanese encephalitis, and malaria

Obesity - adult prevalence rate: 3.9% (2016)
country comparison to the world: 188

Alcohol consumption per capita: *total:* 4.56 liters of pure alcohol (2019 est.)
beer: 4.12 liters of pure alcohol (2019 est.)
wine: 0.03 liters of pure alcohol (2019 est.)
spirits: 0.41 liters of pure alcohol (2019 est.)
other alcohols: 0 liters of pure alcohol (2019 est.)
country comparison to the world: 87

Tobacco use: *total:* 21.1% (2020 est.)
male: 36.1% (2020 est.)
female: 6% (2020 est.)
country comparison to the world: 78

Children under the age of 5 years underweight: 24.1% (2014)
country comparison to the world: 12

Education expenditures: 2.2% of GDP (2018 est.)
country comparison to the world: 175

Literacy: *definition:* age 15 and over can read and write
total population: 80.5%
male: 86.5%
female: 75% (2015)

School life expectancy (primary to tertiary education): *total:* 11 years
male: 11 years
female: 10 years

Unemployment, youth ages 15-24: *total:* 2.5%
male: 2.7%
female: 2.3% (2019 est.)

ENVIRONMENT

Environment - current issues: illegal logging activities throughout the country and strip mining for gems in the western region along the border with Thailand have resulted in habitat loss and declining biodiversity (in particular, destruction of mangrove swamps threatens natural fisheries); soil erosion; in rural areas, most of the population does not have access to potable water; declining fish stocks because of illegal fishing and overfishing; coastal ecosystems choked by sediment washed loose from deforested areas inland

Environment - international agreements: *party to:* Biodiversity, Climate Change, Climate Change-Kyoto Protocol, Climate Change-Paris Agreement, Comprehensive Nuclear Test Ban, Desertification, Endangered Species, Hazardous Wastes, Marine Life Conservation, Ozone Layer Protection, Ship Pollution, Tropical Timber 2006, Wetlands, Whaling
signed, but not ratified: Law of the Sea

Air pollutants: *particulate matter emissions:* 23.98 micrograms per cubic meter (2016 est.)
carbon dioxide emissions: 9.92 megatons (2016 est.)
methane emissions: 14.88 megatons (2020 est.)

Climate: tropical; rainy, monsoon season (May to November); dry season (December to April); little seasonal temperature variation

Land use: *agricultural land:* 32.1% (2018 est.)
arable land: 22.7% (2018 est.)
permanent crops: 0.9% (2018 est.)
permanent pasture: 8.5% (2018 est.)
forest: 56.5% (2018 est.)
other: 11.4% (2018 est.)

Urbanization: *urban population:* 25.1% of total population (2022)
rate of urbanization: 3.06% annual rate of change (2020-25 est.)

Revenue from forest resources forest revenues: 0.84% of GDP (2018 est.)
country comparison to the world: 57

Revenue from coal: *coal revenues:* 0% of GDP (2018 est.)
country comparison to the world: 74

Waste and recycling: *municipal solid waste generated annually:* 1.089 million tons (2014 est.)

Major lakes (area sq km): *fresh water lake(s):* Tonle Sap - 2,700-16,000 sq km

Major rivers (by length in km): Mekong (shared with China [s], Burma, Thailand, Laos, and Vietnam [m]) - 4,350 km
note - [s] after country name indicates river source; [m] after country name indicates river mouth

Major watersheds (area sq km): Pacific Ocean drainage: Mekong (805,604 sq km)

Total water withdrawal: *municipal:* 98 million cubic meters (2017 est.)
industrial: 33 million cubic meters (2017 est.)
agricultural: 2.053 billion cubic meters (2017 est.)

Total renewable water resources: 476.1 billion cubic meters (2017 est.)

GOVERNMENT

Country name: *conventional long form:* Kingdom of Cambodia
conventional short form: Cambodia
local long form: Preahreacheanachakr Kampuchea (phonetic transliteration)
local short form: Kampuchea
former: Khmer Republic, Democratic Kampuchea, People's Republic of Kampuchea, State of Cambodia
etymology: the English name Cambodia is an anglicization of the French Cambodge, which is the French transliteration of the native name Kampuchea

Government type: parliamentary constitutional monarchy

Capital: *name:* Phnom Penh
geographic coordinates: 11 33 N, 104 55 E
time difference: UTC+7 (12 hours ahead of Washington, DC, during Standard Time)
etymology: Phnom Penh translates as "Penh's Hill" in Khmer; the city takes its name from the present Wat Phnom (Hill Temple), the tallest religious structure in the city, whose establishment, according to legend, was inspired in the 14th century by a pious nun, Daun PENH

Administrative divisions: 24 provinces (khett, singular and plural) and 1 municipality (krong, singular and plural)
provinces: Banteay Meanchey, Battambang, Kampong Cham, Kampong Chhnang, Kampong Speu, Kampong Thom, Kampot, Kandal, Kep, Koh Kong, Kratie, Mondolkiri, Oddar Meanchey, Pailin, Preah Sihanouk, Preah Vihear, Prey Veng, Pursat, Ratanakiri, Siem Reap, Stung Treng, Svay Rieng, Takeo, Tbong Khmum
municipalities: Phnom Penh (Phnum Penh)

Independence: 9 November 1953 (from France)

National holiday: Independence Day, 9 November (1953)

Constitution: *history:* previous 1947; latest promulgated 21 September 1993
amendments: proposed by the monarch, by the prime minister, or by the president of the National Assembly if supported by one fourth of the Assembly membership; passage requires two-thirds majority of the Assembly membership; constitutional articles on the multiparty democratic form of government and the monarchy cannot be amended; amended 1999, 2008, 2014, 2018, and 2021

Legal system: civil law system (influenced by the UN Transitional Authority in Cambodia) customary law, Communist legal theory, and common law

International law organization participation: accepts compulsory ICJ jurisdiction with reservations; accepts ICCt jurisdiction

Citizenship: *citizenship by birth:* no
citizenship by descent only: at least one parent must be a citizen of Cambodia
dual citizenship recognized: yes
residency requirement for naturalization: 7 years

Suffrage: 18 years of age; universal

Executive branch: *chief of state:* King Norodom SIHAMONI (since 29 October 2004)
head of government: Prime Minister HUN SEN (since 14 January 1985)
cabinet: Council of Ministers named by the prime minister and appointed by the monarch
elections/appointments: monarch chosen by the 9-member Royal Council of the Throne from among all eligible males of royal descent; following legislative elections, a member of the majority party or majority coalition named prime minister by the Chairman of the National Assembly and appointed by the monarch

Legislative branch: *description:* bicameral Parliament of Cambodia consists of:
Senate (62 seats; 58 indirectly elected by parliamentarians and commune councils, 2 indirectly elected by the National Assembly, and 2 appointed by the monarch; members serve 6-year terms)
National Assembly (125 seats; members directly elected in multi-seat constituencies by proportional representation vote; members serve 5-year terms)
elections:
Senate - last held on 25 February 2018 (next to be held in 2024); National Assembly - last held on 29 July 2018 (next to be held in July 2023)
election results:
Senate - percent of vote by party - CPP 96%, FUNCINPEC 2.4%, KNUP 1.6%; seats by party - CPP 58; composition -men 53, women 9, percent of women 14.5%
National Assembly - percent of vote by party - CPP 76.9%, FUNCINPEC 5.9%, LDP 4.9%, Khmer Will Party 3.4%, other 8.9%; seats by party - CPP 125; composition - men 100, women 25, percent of women 20%; note - total Parliament of Cambodia percent of women 18.2%

Judicial branch: *highest court(s):* Supreme Council (organized into 5- and 9-judge panels and includes a court chief and deputy chief); Constitutional Court (consists of 9 members); note - in 1997, the Cambodian Government requested UN assistance in establishing trials to prosecute former Khmer Rouge senior leaders for crimes against humanity committed during the 1975-1979 Khmer Rouge regime; the Extraordinary Chambers of the Courts of Cambodia (also called the Khmer Rouge Tribunal) was established in 2006 and began hearings for the first case in 2009; court proceedings remain ongoing in 2021
judge selection and term of office: Supreme Court and Constitutional Council judge candidates recommended by the Supreme Council of Magistracy, a 17-member body chaired by the monarch and includes other high-level judicial officers; judges of both courts appointed by the monarch; Supreme Court judges appointed for life; Constitutional Council judges appointed for 9-year terms with one-third of the court renewed every 3 years
subordinate courts: Appellate Court; provincial and municipal courts; Military Court

Political parties and leaders: Candlelight Party or CP (the latest incarnation of the Sam Rainsy Party or SRP and the former Human Rights Party or HRP, which joined to form the Cambodia National Rescue Party or CNRP in 2012; the CNRP was dissolved in 2017)
Cambodian People's Party or CPP [HUN SEN]
Khmer Will Party [KONG MONIKA]
Khmer National Unity Party or KNUP (an offshoot of FUNCINPEC) [NHEK BUN CHHAY]
League for Democracy Party or LDP [KHEM Veasna]
National United Front for Independent, Neutral, Peaceful, and Cooperative Cambodia or FUNCINPEC [Prince NORODOM CHAKRAVUTH]
note - other minor parties that registered for the 2022 commune-level elections included: Cambodia National Love Party, Cambodia Nationality Party, Cambodian Youth Party, Cambodia Reform Party, Kampucheaniyum Party, Grassroots Democratic Party, Khmer United Party, Beehive Social Democratic Party, Cambodia Indigenous People's Democracy Party, Ekpheap Cheat Khmer Party, Reaksmey Khemara Party, Khmer Economic Development Party (2022)
note: following the 2017 commune election, the CPP-led government arrested the CNRP president Kem SOKHA for treason, dissolved the party on similar grounds, and forced most of its senior leadership into exile, where the party's former president, Sam RAINSY, had been living since late 2015; as of March 2022, a total of 17 political parties had registered to run in the June 2022 commune-level elections, and opposition parties, particularly the Candlelight Party, continued to report, intimidation, harassment, and arrests by the Cambodian Government

International organization participation: ADB, ARF, ASEAN, CICA, EAS, FAO, G-77, IAEA, IBRD, ICAO, ICRM, IDA, IFAD, IFC, IFRCS, ILO, IMF, IMO, Interpol, IOC, IOM, IPU, ISO (correspondent), ITU, MINUSMA, MIGA, NAM, OIF, OPCW, PCA, UN, UNAMID, UNCTAD, UNESCO, UNIDO, UNIFIL, UNISFA, UNMISS, UNWTO, UPU, WCO, WFTU (NGOs), WHO, WIPO, WMO, WTO

Diplomatic representation in the US: *chief of mission:* Ambassador KEO Chhea (since 19 April 2022)

chancery: 4530 16th Street NW, Washington, DC 20011
telephone: [1] (202) 726-7742
FAX: [1] (202) 726-8381
email address and website:
camemb.usa@mfaic.gov
https://www.embassyofcambodiadc.org/

Diplomatic representation from the US: *chief of mission:* Ambassador W. Patrick MURPHY (since 23 October 2019)
embassy: #1, Street 96, Sangkat Wat Phnom, Khan Daun Penh, Phnom Penh
mailing address: 4540 Phnom Penh Place, Washington DC 20521-4540
telephone: [855] (23) 728-000
FAX: [855] (23) 728-700
email address and website:
ACSPhnomPenh@state.gov
https://kh.usembassy.gov/

Flag description: three horizontal bands of blue (top), red (double width), and blue with a white, three-towered temple, representing Angkor Wat, outlined in black in the center of the red band; red and blue are traditional Cambodian colors
note: only national flag to prominently incorporate an actual identifiable building into its design (a few other national flags - those of Afghanistan, San Marino, Portugal, and Spain - show small generic buildings as part of their coats of arms on the flag)

National symbol(s): Angkor Wat temple, kouprey (wild ox); national colors: red, blue

National anthem: *name:* "Nokoreach" (Royal Kingdom)
lyrics/music: CHUON NAT/F. PERRUCHOT and J. JEKYLL
note: adopted 1941, restored 1993; the anthem, based on a Cambodian folk tune, was restored after the defeat of the Communist regime

National heritage: *total World Heritage Sites:* 3 (all cultural)
selected World Heritage Site locales: Angkor; Temple of Preah Vihear; Sambor Prei Kuk

ECONOMY

Economic overview: Cambodia has experienced strong economic growth over the last decade; GDP grew at an average annual rate of over 8% between 2000 and 2010 and about 7% since 2011. The tourism, garment, construction and real estate, and agriculture sectors accounted for the bulk of growth. Around 700,000 people, the majority of whom are women, are employed in the garment and footwear sector. An additional 500,000 Cambodians are employed in the tourism sector, and a further 200,000 people in construction. Tourism has continued to grow rapidly with foreign arrivals exceeding 2 million per year in 2007 and reaching 5.6 million visitors in 2017. Mining also is attracting some investor interest and the government has touted opportunities for mining bauxite, gold, iron and gems.

Still, Cambodia remains one of the poorest countries in Asia, and long-term economic development remains a daunting challenge, inhibited by corruption, limited human resources, high income inequality, and poor job prospects. According to the Asian Development Bank (ADB), the percentage of the population living in poverty decreased to 13.5% in 2016. More than 50% of the population is less than 25 years old. The population lacks education and productive skills, particularly in the impoverished countryside, which also lacks basic infrastructure.

The World Bank in 2016 formally reclassified Cambodia as a lower middle-income country as a result of continued rapid economic growth over the past several years. Cambodia's graduation from a low-income country will reduce its eligibility for foreign assistance and will challenge the government to seek new sources of financing. The Cambodian Government has been working with bilateral and multilateral donors, including the Asian Development Bank, the World Bank and IMF, to address the country's many pressing needs; more than 20% of the government budget will come from donor assistance in 2018. A major economic challenge for Cambodia over the next decade will be fashioning an economic environment in which the private sector can create enough jobs to handle Cambodia's demographic imbalance.

Textile exports, which accounted for 68% of total exports in 2017, have driven much of Cambodia's growth over the past several years. The textile sector relies on exports to the United States and European Union, and Cambodia's dependence on its comparative advantage in textile production is a key vulnerability for the economy, especially because Cambodia has continued to run a current account deficit above 9% of GDP since 2014.

Real GDP (purchasing power parity): $70.08 billion (2020 est.)
$72.36 billion (2019 est.)
$67.59 billion (2018 est.)
note: data are in 2017 dollars
country comparison to the world: 102

Real GDP growth rate: 6.9% (2017 est.)
7% (2016 est.)
7% (2015 est.)
country comparison to the world: 18

Real GDP per capita: $4,200 (2020 est.)
$4,400 (2019 est.)
$4,200 (2018 est.)
note: data are in 2017 dollars
country comparison to the world: 180

GDP (official exchange rate): $22.09 billion (2017 est.)

Inflation rate (consumer prices): 2.9% (2017 est.)
3% (2016 est.)
country comparison to the world: 145

Credit ratings
Moody's rating: *B2 (2007)*

Standard & Poors rating: N/A (2014)
note: The year refers to the year in which the current credit rating was first obtained.

GDP - composition, by sector of origin: *agriculture:* 25.3% (2017 est.)
industry: 32.8% (2017 est.)
services: 41.9% (2017 est.)

GDP - composition, by end use: *household consumption:* 76% (2017 est.)
government consumption: 5.4% (2017 est.)
investment in fixed capital: 21.8% (2017 est.)
investment in inventories: 1.2% (2017 est.)
exports of goods and services: 68.6% (2017 est.)
imports of goods and services: -73% (2017 est.)

Agricultural products: cassava, rice, maize, vegetables, sugar cane, soybeans, rubber, oil palm fruit, bananas, pork

Industries: tourism, garments, construction, rice milling, fishing, wood and wood products, rubber, cement, gem mining, textiles

Industrial production growth rate: 10.6% (2017 est.)
country comparison to the world: 11

Labor force: 8.913 million (2017 est.)
country comparison to the world: 52

Labor force - by occupation: *agriculture:* 48.7%
industry: 19.9%
services: 31.5% (2013 est.)

Unemployment rate: 0.3% (2017 est.)
0.2% (2016 est.)
note: high underemployment, according to official statistics
country comparison to the world: 2

Unemployment, youth ages 15-24: *total:* 2.5%
male: 2.7%
female: 2.3% (2019 est.)
country comparison to the world: 178

Population below poverty line: 16.5% (2016 est.)

Gini Index coefficient - distribution of family income: 37.9 (2008 est.)
41.9 (2004 est.)
country comparison to the world: 75

Household income or consumption by percentage share: *lowest 10%:* 2%
highest 10%: 28% (2013 est.)

Budget: *revenues:* 3.947 billion (2017 est.)
expenditures: 4.354 billion (2017 est.)

Budget surplus (+) or deficit (-): -1.8% (of GDP) (2017 est.)
country comparison to the world: 97

Public debt: 30.4% of GDP (2017 est.)
29.1% of GDP (2016 est.)
country comparison to the world: 165

Taxes and other revenues: 17.9% (of GDP) (2017 est.)
country comparison to the world: 164

Fiscal year: calendar year

Current account balance: -$1.871 billion (2017 est.)
-$1.731 billion (2016 est.)
country comparison to the world: 165

Exports: $19.4 billion (2020 est.)
$21.07 billion (2019 est.)
$18.41 billion (2018 est.)
note: Data are in current year dollars and do not include illicit exports or re-exports.
country comparison to the world: 84

Exports - partners: United States 21%, Singapore 8%, Thailand 8%, Germany 7%, Japan 6%, China 5%, Canada 5%, United Kingdom 5% (2019)

Exports - commodities: clothing, precious metal scraps, trunks/cases, gold, leather footwear (2019)

Imports: $23.12 billion (2020 est.) note: data are in current year dollars
$25.52 billion (2019 est.) *note:* data are in current year dollars
$21.86 billion (2018 est.) *note:* data are in current year dollars
country comparison to the world: 77

Imports - partners: China 27%, Thailand 25%, Vietnam 15%, Singapore 8% (2019)

Imports - commodities: refined petroleum, clothing, gold, cars, flavored water (2019)

Reserves of foreign exchange and gold: $12.2 billion (31 December 2017 est.)
$9.122 billion (31 December 2016 est.)
country comparison to the world: 69

Debt - external: $11.87 billion (31 December 2017 est.)

$10.3 billion (31 December 2016 est.)
country comparison to the world: 108

Exchange rates: riels (KHR) per US dollar
-4,055 (2017 est.)
4.058.7 (2016 est.)
4.058.7 (2015 est.)
4.067.8 (2014 est.)
4,037.5 (2013 est.)

ENERGY

Electricity access: *electrification - total population:* 75% (2019)
electrification - urban areas: 100% (2019)
electrification - rural areas: 67% (2019)

Electricity: *installed generating capacity:* 2.954 million kW (2020 est.)
consumption: 10,288,340,000 kWh (2019 est.)
exports: 0 kWh (2019 est.)
imports: 3.063 billion kWh (2019 est.)
transmission/distribution losses: 1.187 billion kWh (2019 est.)

Electricity generation sources: *fossil fuels:* 52% of total installed capacity (2020 est.)
solar: 1.2% of total installed capacity (2020 est.)
hydroelectricity: 45.6% of total installed capacity (2020 est.)
biomass and waste: 1.2% of total installed capacity (2020 est.)

Coal: *production:* 0 metric tons (2020 est.)
consumption: 2.974 million metric tons (2020 est.)
exports: 0 metric tons (2020 est.)
imports: 3.311 million metric tons (2020 est.)
proven reserves: 0 metric tons (2019 est.)

Petroleum: *total petroleum production:* 0 bbl/day (2021 est.)
refined petroleum consumption: 64,100 bbl/day (2019 est.)

Refined petroleum products - imports: 43,030 bbl/day (2015 est.)
country comparison to the world: 86

Carbon dioxide emissions: 13.844 million metric tonnes of CO2 (2019 est.)
from coal and metallurgical coke: 4.837 million metric tonnes of CO2 (2019 est.)
from petroleum and other liquids: 9.007 million metric tonnes of CO2 (2019 est.)
country comparison to the world: 98

Energy consumption per capita: 13.629 million Btu/person (2019 est.)
country comparison to the world: 142

COMMUNICATIONS

Telephones - fixed lines: *total subscriptions:* 55,603 (2020 est.)
subscriptions per 100 inhabitants: (2020 est.) less than 1
country comparison to the world: 155

Telephones - mobile cellular: *total subscriptions:* 21,086,791 (2020 est.)
subscriptions per 100 inhabitants: 126 (2020 est.)
country comparison to the world: 59

Telecommunication systems: *general assessment:* Cambodia's mobile-dominated telecoms sector spent much of 2020 battling two major challenges: the global pandemic, and the government's retraction of trial licenses for the rollout of 5G; citing concerns about waste and inefficiency occurring if each operator built a separate 5G infrastructure in order to maximize their own network's coverage (and, presumably, to capture greater market share), the regulator withdrew the licenses that the operators had been using for their 5G trials; this was despite all of the operators having already announced a successful completion of their trials; more than a year later, the market is still waiting on the government to release its 5G policy and roadmap, along with the allocation of spectrum and approvals to permit commercial operation; there is little expectation of any further progress happening before the start of 2022; the mobile network operators have maintained their focus and investment strategies on upgrading and expanding their existing LTE networks around the country, and to 5G-enable their base stations; when the 5G market eventually arrives, the underlying infrastructure will at least be ready to support a rapid adoption of the higher-value applications and services; the mobile market fell back slightly during 2020 and 2021 (in terms of total subscriber numbers) as the Covid-19 crisis wore on, but it remains in relatively good health as mobile users increased their data usage over the period; the mobile broadband market experienced a small but very rare contraction in 2020, although rates were already very high in this area; there is likely to be a quick rebound to previous levels once economic conditions stabilize, followed by a modest rates of growth over the next five years; the number of fixed telephony lines in service continues to fall sharply as customers migrate to mobile platforms for both voice and data; the lack of any widespread fixed-line infrastructure has had a flow-on effect in the fixed-line broadband market, a sector that also remains largely under-developed (2021)
domestic: fixed-line connections stand at less than 1 per 100 persons; mobile-cellular usage, aided by competition among service providers, is about 130 per 100 persons (2020)
international: country code - 855; landing points for MCT and AAE-1 via submarine cables providing communication to Asia, the Middle East, Europe and Africa; satellite earth station - 1 Intersputnik (Indian Ocean region) (2019)

Broadcast media: mixture of state-owned, joint public-private, and privately owned broadcast media; 27 TV broadcast stations with most operating on multiple channels, including 1 state-operated station broadcasting from multiple locations, 11 stations either jointly operated or privately owned with some broadcasting from several locations; multi-channel cable and satellite systems are available (2019); 84 radio broadcast stations - 1 state-owned broadcaster with multiple stations and a large mixture of public and private broadcasters; one international broadcaster is available (2019) as well as one Chinese joint venture television station with the Ministry of Interior; several television and radio operators broadcast online only (often via Facebook) (2019)

Internet country code: .kh

Internet users: *total:* 5,440,559 (2019 est.)
percent of population: 33% (2019 est.)
country comparison to the world: 84

Broadband - fixed subscriptions: *total:* 233,732 (2020 est.) Slowly increase as focus is on mobile internet
subscriptions per 100 inhabitants: 1 (2020 est.)
country comparison to the world: 114

TRANSPORTATION

National air transport system: *number of registered air carriers:* 6 (2020)
inventory of registered aircraft operated by air carriers: 25
annual passenger traffic on registered air carriers: 1,411,059 (2018)
annual freight traffic on registered air carriers: 680,000 (2018) mt-km

Civil aircraft registration country code prefix: XU

Airports: *total:* 16 (2021)
country comparison to the world: 142

Airports - with paved runways: *total:* 6
2,438 to 3,047 m: 3
1.524 to 2,437 m: 2
914 to 1,523 m: 1 (2021)

Airports - with unpaved runways: *total:* 10
1.524 to 2,437 m: 2
914 to 1,523 m: 7
under 914 m: 1 (2021)

Heliports: 1 (2021)

Railways: *total:* 642 km (2014)
narrow gauge: 642 km (2014) 1.000-m gauge
note: under restoration
country comparison to the world: 107

Roadways: *total:* 47,263 km (2013)
paved: 12,239 km (2013)
unpaved: 35,024 km (2013)
country comparison to the world: 83

Waterways: 3,700 km (2012) (mainly on Mekong River)
country comparison to the world: 30

Merchant marine: *total:* 245
by type: container ship 2, general cargo 162, oil tanker 18, other 63 (2021)
country comparison to the world: 60

Ports and terminals: *major seaport(s):* Sihanoukville (Kampong Saom)
river port(s): Phnom Penh (Mekong)

MILITARY AND SECURITY

Military and security forces: *Royal Cambodian Armed Forces (RCAF):* Royal Cambodian Army, Royal Khmer Navy, Royal Cambodian Air Force, Royal Gendarmerie; the National Committee for Maritime Security (performs Coast Guard functions and has representation from military and civilian agencies); Ministry of Interior: Cambodian National Police (2022)

Military expenditures: 2.5% of GDP (2021 est.)
2.5% of GDP (2020 est.)
2.2% of GDP (2019 est.) (approximately $1.2 billion)
2.2% of GDP (2018 est.) (approximately $1.13 billion)
2.1% of GDP (2017 est.) (approximately $1.02 billion)
country comparison to the world: 38

Military and security service personnel strengths: information varies; approximately 100,000 total active troops including less than 5,000 Navy and Air Force personnel; approximately 10,000 Gendarmerie (2022)

Military equipment inventories and acquisitions: the RCAF is armed largely with older Chinese and Russian-origin equipment; since 2010, it has received limited amounts of more modern equipment from a variety of suppliers, particularly China (2022) *note:* in December 2021, the US Government halted arms-related trade with Cambodia, citing deepening Chinese military influence, corruption, and human rights abuses by the government and armed forces; the policy of denial applied to licenses or other approvals for exports and imports of defense articles and defense services destined for or originating in Cambodia, with exceptions (on a case-by-case basis) related to conventional weapons destruction and humanitarian demining activities

Military service age and obligation: 18 is the legal minimum age for compulsory and voluntary military service (conscription only selectively enforced since 1993); women may volunteer (2022)
note: in 2018, women made up an estimated 6% of the active duty military and 88 women held the rank of general

Military deployments: 225 Central African Republic (MINUSCA); 180 Lebanon (UNIFIL); 290 Mali (MINUSMA) (May 2022)

Military - note: the Royal Cambodian Armed Forces (RCAF) was re-established in 1993 under the first coalition government from the merger of the Cambodian Government's military forces (Cambodian People's Armed Forces) and the two noncommunist resistance forces (Sihanoukist National Army, aka National Army for Khmer Independence, and the Khmer People's National Liberation Armed Forces); thousands of communist Khmer Rouge fighters began surrendering by 1994 under a government amnesty program and the last of the Khmer Rouge forces (National Army of Democratic Kampuchea) were demobilized or absorbed into the RCAF in 1999

Cambodia was once one of the most land mined countries in the world; by the early 1990s, various aid organizations estimated there were 8 to 10 million landmines scattered throughout the country; the mines were laid during Cambodia's decades-long war by the Cambodian army, the Vietnamese, the Khmer Rouge, the non-communist fighters, and US forces; part of Cambodia's defense policy is demining the territory with the intent of having the entire country cleared of unexploded ordnances by 2035; over 1 million landmines and over 3 million explosives were discovered and removed from 1992 to 2018 (2022)

TRANSNATIONAL ISSUES

Disputes - international: Cambodia-Laos: Cambodia is concerned that Laos' extensive upstream dam construction will affect Cambodian waters downstream

Cambodia-Thailand Cambodia and Thailand have agreed to maintain peace along the border regardless of the decision of the International Court of Justice (ICJ) over territorial dispute near Cambodia's Preah Vihear Temple; the ICJ decision of 11 November 2013 determined that Cambodia had sovereignty over the whole territory of the promontory of Preah Vihear; the border disputes do not involve large amounts of territory, and most of the issues were settled by the Nov. 11,2013 ICJ ruling

Cambodia-Vietnam: issues include casinos built in Cambodia near the border (gambling and prostitution); narcotics (criminals, crime, and abuse); trafficking of women and children, petrol smuggling into Cambodia from Vietnam, illegal logging, and illegal migration; a positive development is the special economic Zone in Bavet, Svay Rieng Province, Cambodia that is being developed by the Manhattan (Svay Rieng) International Group of Taiwan

Refugees and internally displaced persons: *stateless persons:* 57,444 (mid-year 2021)

Trafficking in persons: *current situation:* human traffickers exploit Cambodian men, women, and children in forced labor and sex trafficking in Cambodia and abroad, and foreign nationals are trafficked in Cambodia; Cambodian adults and children migrate to other countries in the region or increasingly to the Middle East where traffickers force them to work in agriculture, fishing, construction, manufacturing, and domestic servitude; significant numbers of Cambodian men and boys are subject to forced labor on Thai ships in international waters and may experience physical abuse, nonpayment or underpayment of wages, and confinement at sea for years; brick kiln owners exploit thousands of Cambodians, including children, through debt-based coercion; children from poor families are vulnerable to forced labor, often with the complicity of their parents, in domestic servitude, forced begging, or street vending in Thailand and Vietnam; Cambodian and ethnic Vietnamese women and girls from rural areas move to cities and tourist areas where they are sex trafficked
tier rating: Tier 2 Watch List — Cambodia does not fully meet the minimum standards for the elimination of trafficking but is making significant efforts to do so; authorities continued to prosecute and convict traffickers and utilized new victim identification and data collection technologies; the government enacted a five-year national action plan to combat human trafficking; however, corruption continued to impede law enforcement efforts, criminal proceedings, and services to victims; some corrupt officials may have profited directly from sex and labor trafficking or accepted bribes to dismiss charges or reduce sentences; insufficient judicial monitoring systems enabled suspected traffickers to flee before trial; authorities failed to issue formal guidance allowing the use of undercover techniques in anti-trafficking investigations (2020)

Illicit drugs: manufacture of methamphetamine expanding due to transnational crime syndicates moving from China to evade the law; drugs destined for Australia, Japan, New Zealand and the Republic of Korea and the rest of East and South-East Asia (2021)

CAMEROON

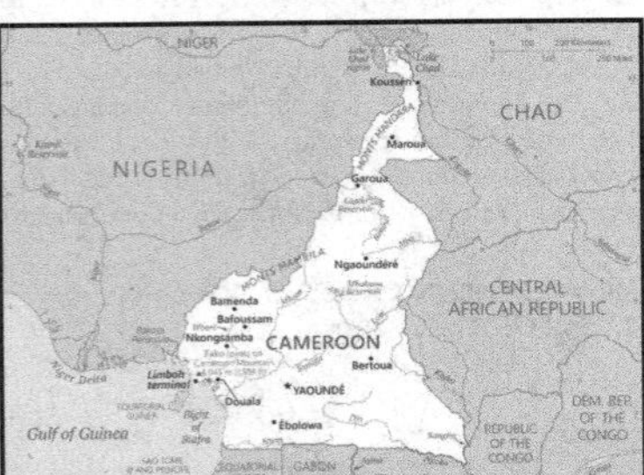

INTRODUCTION

Background: Much of the area of present-day Cameroon was ruled by powerful chiefdoms before becoming a German colony in 1884 known as Kamerun. After World War I, the territory was divided between France and the UK as League of Nations mandates. French Cameroon became independent in 1960 as the Republic of Cameroon. The following year the southern portion of neighboring British Cameroon voted to merge with the new country to form the Federal Republic of Cameroon. In 1972, a new constitution replaced the federation with a unitary state, the United Republic of Cameroon. The country has generally enjoyed stability, which has enabled the development of agriculture, roads, and railways, as well as a petroleum industry. Despite slow movement toward democratic reform, political power remains firmly in the hands of President Paul BIYA.

GEOGRAPHY

Location: Central Africa, bordering the Bight of Biafra, between Equatorial Guinea and Nigeria

Geographic coordinates: 6 00 N, 12 00 E

Map references: Africa

Area: *total:* 475,440 sq km
land: 472,710 sq km
water: 2,730 sq km
country comparison to the world: 56

Area - comparative: slightly larger than California; about four times the size of Pennsylvania

Land boundaries: *total:* 5,018 km
border countries (6): Central African Republic 901 km; Chad 1,116 km; Republic of the Congo 494 km; Equatorial Guinea 183 km; Gabon 349 km; Nigeria 1975 km

Coastline: 402 km

Maritime claims: *territorial sea:* 12 nm
contiguous zone: 24 nm

Climate: varies with terrain, from tropical along coast to semiarid and hot in north

Terrain: diverse, with coastal plain in southwest, dissected plateau in center, mountains in west, plains in north

Elevation: *highest point:* Fako on Mont Cameroun 4,045 m
lowest point: Atlantic Ocean 0 m
mean elevation: 667 m

Natural resources: petroleum, bauxite, iron ore, timber, hydropower

Land use: *agricultural land:* 20.6% (2018 est.)
arable land: 13.1% (2018 est.)
permanent crops: 3.3% (2018 est.)
permanent pasture: 4.2% (2018 est.)

forest: 41.7% (2018 est.)
other: 37.7% (2018 est.)

Irrigated land: 290 sq km (2012)

Major lakes (area sq km): *fresh water lake(s):* Lake Chad (endorheic lake shared with Niger, Nigeria, and Chad) - 10,360-25,900 sq km note - area varies by season and year to year

Major watersheds (area sq km): Atlantic Ocean drainage: Congo (3,730,881 sq km), Niger (2,261,741 sq km)

Internal (endorheic basin) drainage: Lake Chad (2,497,738 sq km)

Major aquifers: Lake Chad Basin

Population distribution: population concentrated in the west and north, with the interior of the country sparsely populated as shown in this population distribution map

Natural hazards: volcanic activity with periodic releases of poisonous gases from Lake Nyos and Lake Monoun volcanoes
volcanism: Mt. Cameroon (4,095 m), which last erupted in 2000, is the most frequently active volcano in West Africa; lakes in Oku volcanic field have released fatal levels of gas on occasion, killing some 1,700 people in 1986

Geography - note: sometimes referred to as the hinge of Africa because of its central location on the continent and its position at the west-south juncture of the Gulf of Guinea; throughout the country there are areas of thermal springs and indications of current or prior volcanic activity; Mount Cameroon, the highest mountain in Sub-Saharan west Africa, is an active volcano

PEOPLE AND SOCIETY

Population: 29,321,637 (2022 est.)
country comparison to the world: 51

Nationality: *noun:* Cameroonian(s)
adjective: Cameroonian

Ethnic groups: Bamileke-Bamu 24.3%, Beti/Bassa, Mbam 21.6%, Biu-Mandara 14.6%, Arab-Choa/Hausa/Kanuri 11%, Adamawa-Ubangi, 9.8%, Grassfields 7.7%, Kako, Meka/Pygmy 3.3%, Cotier/Ngoe/Oroko 2.7%, Southwestern Bantu 0.7%, foreign/other ethnic group 4.5% (2018 est.)

Languages: 24 major African language groups, English (official), French (official)
major-language sample(s): The World Factbook, the indispensable source for basic information. (English)

The World Factbook, une source indispensable d'informations de base. (French)

Religions: Roman Catholic 38.3%, Protestant 25.5%, other Christian 6.9%, Muslim 24.4%, animist 2.2%, other 0.5%, none 2.2% (2018 est.)

Demographic profile: Cameroon has a large youth population, with more than 60% of the populace under the age of 25. Fertility is falling but remains at a high level, especially among poor, rural, and uneducated women, in part because of inadequate access to contraception. Life expectancy remains low at about 55 years due to the prevalence of HIV and AIDs and an elevated maternal mortality rate, which has remained high since 1990. Cameroon, particularly the northern region, is vulnerable to food insecurity largely because of government mismanagement, corruption, high production costs, inadequate infrastructure, and natural disasters. Despite economic growth in some regions, poverty is on the rise, and is most prevalent in rural areas, which are especially affected by a shortage of jobs, declining incomes, poor school and health care infrastructure, and a lack of clean water and sanitation. Underinvestment in social safety nets and ineffective public financial management also contribute to Cameroon's high rate of poverty. The activities of Boko Haram, other armed groups, and counterinsurgency operations have worsened food insecurity in the Far North region.

International migration has been driven by unemployment (including fewer government jobs), poverty, the search for educational opportunities, and corruption. The US and Europe are preferred destinations, but, with tighter immigration restrictions in these countries, young Cameroonians are increasingly turning to neighboring states, such as Gabon and Nigeria, South Africa, other parts of Africa, and the Near and Far East. Cameroon's limited resources make it dependent on UN support to host more than 490,000 refugees and asylum seekers as of September 2022. These refugees and asylum seekers are primarily from the Central African Republic and Nigeria. Internal and external displacement have grown dramatically in recent years. Boko Haram's attacks and counterattacks by government forces in the Far North since 2014 have increased the number of internally displaced people. Armed conflict between separatists and Cameroon's military in the Northwest and Southwest since 2016 have displaced hundreds of thousands of the country's Anglophone minority.

Age structure: *0-14 years:* 42.34% (male 5,927,640/female 5,820,226)
15-24 years: 20.04% (male 2,782,376/female 2,776,873)
25-54 years: 30.64% (male 4,191,151/female 4,309,483)
55-64 years: 3.87% (male 520,771/female 552,801)
65 years and over: 3.11% (male 403,420/female 460,248) (2020 est.)

Dependency ratios: *total dependency ratio:* 81.1
youth dependency ratio: 76.2
elderly dependency ratio: 4.9
potential support ratio: 20.3 (2020 est.)

Median age: *total:* 18.5 years
male: 18.2 years
female: 18.8 years (2020 est.)
country comparison to the world: 209

Population growth rate: 2.75% (2022 est.)
country comparison to the world: 15

Birth rate: 35.53 births/1,000 population (2022 est.)
country comparison to the world: 14

Death rate: 7.73 deaths/1,000 population (2022 est.)
country comparison to the world: 101

Net migration rate: -0.31 migrant(s)/1,000 population (2022 est.)
country comparison to the world: 119

Population distribution: population concentrated in the west and north, with the interior of the country sparsely populated as shown in this population distribution map

Urbanization: *urban population:* 58.7% of total population (2022)
rate of urbanization: 3.43% annual rate of change (2020-25 est.)

Major urban areas - population: 4.164 million YAOUNDE (capital), 3.927 million Douala (2022)

Sex ratio: *at birth:* 1.03 male(s)/female
0-14 years: 1.02 male(s)/female
15-24 years: 1 male(s)/female
25-54 years: 0.97 male(s)/female
55-64 years: 0.94 male(s)/female
65 years and over: 0.74 male(s)/female
total population: 0.99 male(s)/female (2022 est.)

Mother's mean age at first birth: 20.1 years (2018 est.)
note: data represents median age at first birth among women 25-49

Maternal mortality ratio: 529 deaths/100,000 live births (2017 est.)
country comparison to the world: 18

Infant mortality rate: *total:* 48.73 deaths/1,000 live births
male: 53.58 deaths/1,000 live births
female: 43.73 deaths/1,000 live births (2022 est.)
country comparison to the world: 22

Life expectancy at birth: *total population:* 63.27 years
male: 61.49 years
female: 65.09 years (2022 est.)
country comparison to the world: 210

Total fertility rate: 4.55 children born/woman (2022 est.)
country comparison to the world: 19

Contraceptive prevalence rate: 19.3% (2018)

Drinking water source: *improved: urban:* 95.1% of population
rural: 56.2% of population
total: 78.6% of population
unimproved: urban: 4.9% of population
rural: 43.8% of population
total: 21.4% of population (2020 est.)

Current health expenditure: 3.6% of GDP (2019)

Physicians density: 0.13 physicians/1,000 population (2019)

Hospital bed density: 1.3 beds/1,000 population

Sanitation facility access: *improved: urban:* 83.2% of population
rural: 27.7% of population
total: 59.7% of population
unimproved: urban: 16.8% of population
rural: 72.3% of population
total: 40.3% of population (2020 est.)

HIV/AIDS - adult prevalence rate: 3% (2020 est.)
country comparison to the world: 15

Major infectious diseases: degree of risk: very high (2020)
food or waterborne diseases: bacterial and protozoal diarrhea, hepatitis A, and typhoid fever
vectorborne diseases: malaria and dengue fever
water contact diseases: schistosomiasis
animal contact diseases: rabies
respiratory diseases: meningococcal meningitis
note: on 21 March 2022, the US Centers for Disease Control and Prevention (CDC) issued a Travel Alert for polio in Africa; Cameroon is currently considered a high risk to travelers for circulating vaccine-derived polioviruses (cVDPV); vaccine-derived poliovirus (VDPV) is a strain of the weakened poliovirus that was initially included in oral polio vaccine (OPV) and that has changed over time and behaves more like the wild or naturally occurring virus; this means it can be spread more easily to people who are unvaccinated against polio and who come in contact with the stool or respiratory secretions, such as from a sneeze, of an "infected" person who received oral polio vaccine; the CDC recommends that before any international travel, anyone unvaccinated,

incompletely vaccinated, or with an unknown polio vaccination status should complete the routine polio vaccine series; before travel to any high-risk destination, the CDC recommends that adults who previously completed the full, routine polio vaccine series receive a single, lifetime booster dose of polio vaccine

Obesity - adult prevalence rate: 11.4% (2016)
country comparison to the world: 135

Alcohol consumption per capita: *total:* 4.09 liters of pure alcohol (2019 est.)
beer: 2.36 liters of pure alcohol (2019 est.)
wine: 0.16 liters of pure alcohol (2019 est.)
spirits: 0.01 liters of pure alcohol (2019 est.)
other alcohols: 1.56 liters of pure alcohol (2019 est.)
country comparison to the world: 93

Tobacco use: *total:* 7.3% (2020 est.)
male: 13.2% (2020 est.)
female: 1.4% (2020 est.)
country comparison to the world: 155

Children under the age of 5 years underweight: 11% (2018/19)
country comparison to the world: 55

Child marriage: *women married by age 15:* 10.7%
women married by age 18: 29.8%
men married by age 18: 2.9% (2018 est.)

Education expenditures: 3.1% of GDP (2019 est.)
country comparison to the world: 143

Literacy: *definition:* age 15 and over can read and write
total population: 77.1%
male: 82.6%
female: 71.6% (2018)

School life expectancy (primary to tertiary education): *total:* 12 years
male: 13 years
female: 11 years (2016)

Unemployment, youth ages 15-24: *total:* 6.3%
male: 5.8%
female: 6.8% (2014 est.)

ENVIRONMENT

Environment - current issues: waterborne diseases are prevalent; deforestation and overgrazing result in erosion, desertification, and reduced quality of pastureland; poaching; overfishing; overhunting

Environment - international agreements: *party to:* Biodiversity, Climate Change, Climate Change-Kyoto Protocol, Climate Change-Paris Agreement, Comprehensive Nuclear Test Ban, Desertification, Endangered Species, Environmental Modification, Hazardous Wastes, Law of the Sea, Ozone Layer Protection, Ship Pollution, Tropical Timber 2006, Wetlands, Whaling
signed, but not ratified: Nuclear Test Ban

Air pollutants: *particulate matter emissions:* 65.26 micrograms per cubic meter (2016 est.)
carbon dioxide emissions: 8.29 megatons (2016 est.)
methane emissions: 30.71 megatons (2020 est.)

Climate: varies with terrain, from tropical along coast to semiarid and hot in north

Land use: *agricultural land:* 20.6% (2018 est.)
arable land: 13.1% (2018 est.)
permanent crops: 3.3% (2018 est.)
permanent pasture: 4.2% (2018 est.)
forest: 41.7% (2018 est.)
other: 37.7% (2018 est.)

Urbanization: *urban population:* 58.7% of total population (2022)
rate of urbanization: 3.43% annual rate of change (2020-25 est.)

Revenue from forest resources: *forest revenues:* 2.5% of GDP (2018 est.)
country comparison to the world: 27

Revenue from coal: *coal revenues:* 0% of GDP (2018 est.)
country comparison to the world: 75

Food insecurity: *severe localized food insecurity:* due to civil insecurity and population displacements - according to a March 2022 analysis, about 2.4 million people are projected to be severely food insecure between June and August 2022; this is mainly the result of conflict, sociopolitical unrest and high food prices (2022)

Waste and recycling: municipal solid waste generated annually: 3,270,617 tons (2013 est.)
municipal solid waste recycled annually: 13,082 tons (2009 est.)
percent of municipal solid waste recycled: 0.4% (2009 est.)

Major lakes (area sq km): *fresh water lake(s):* Lake Chad (endorheic lake shared with Niger, Nigeria, and Chad) - 10,360-25,900 sq km note - area varies by season and year to year

Major watersheds (area sq km): Atlantic Ocean drainage: Congo (3,730,881 sq km), Niger (2,261,741 sq km)

Internal (endorheic basin) drainage: Lake Chad (2,497,738 sq km)

Major aquifers: Lake Chad Basin

Total water withdrawal: *municipal:* 246.8 million cubic meters (2017 est.)
industrial: 104.6 million cubic meters (2017 est.)
agricultural: 737 million cubic meters (2017 est.)

Total renewable water resources: 283.15 billion cubic meters (2017 est.)

GOVERNMENT

Country name: *conventional long form:* Republic of Cameroon
conventional short form: Cameroon
local long form: Republique du Cameroun (French)/ Republic of Cameroon (English)
local short form: Cameroun/Cameroon
former: Kamerun, French Cameroon, British Cameroon, Federal Republic of Cameroon, United Republic of Cameroon
etymology: in the 15th century, Portuguese explorers named the area near the mouth of the Wouri River the Rio dos Camaroes (River of Prawns) after the abundant shrimp in the water; over time the designation became Cameroon in English; this is the only instance where a country is named after a crustacean

Government type: presidential republic

Capital: *name:* Yaounde
geographic coordinates: 3 52 N, 11 31 E
time difference: UTC+1 (6 hours ahead of Washington, DC, during Standard Time)
etymology: founded as a German colonial settlement of Jaunde in 1888 and named after the local Yaunde (Ewondo) people

Administrative divisions: 10 regions (regions, singular - region); Adamaoua, Centre, East (Est), Far North (Extreme-Nord), Littoral, North (Nord), North-West (Nord-Ouest), West (Ouest), South (Sud), South-West (Sud-Ouest)

Independence: 1 January 1960 (from French-administered UN trusteeship)

National holiday: State Unification Day (National Day), 20 May (1972)

Constitution: *history:* several previous; latest effective 18 January 1996
amendments: proposed by the president of the republic or by Parliament; amendment drafts require approval of at least one third of the membership in either house of Parliament; passage requires absolute majority vote of the Parliament membership; passage of drafts requested by the president for a second reading in Parliament requires two-thirds majority vote of its membership; the president can opt to submit drafts to a referendum, in which case passage requires a simple majority; constitutional articles on Cameroon's unity and territorial integrity and its democratic principles cannot be amended; amended 2008

Legal system: mixed legal system of English common law, French civil law, and customary law

International law organization participation: accepts compulsory ICJ jurisdiction; non-party state to the ICCt

Citizenship: *citizenship by birth:* no
citizenship by descent only: at least one parent must be a citizen of Cameroon
dual citizenship recognized: no
residency requirement for naturalization: 5 years

Suffrage: 20 years of age; universal

Executive branch: *chief of state:* President Paul BIYA (since 6 November 1982)
head of government: Prime Minister Joseph Dion NGUTE (since 4 January 2019); Deputy Prime Minister Amadou ALI (since 2014)
cabinet: Cabinet proposed by the prime minister, appointed by the president
elections/appointments: president directly elected by simple majority popular vote for a 7-year term (no term limits); election last held on 7 October 2018 (next to be held in October 2025); prime minister appointed by the president
election results: Paul BIYA reelected president; percent of vote - Paul BIYA (CPDM) 71.3%, Maurice KAMTO (MRC) 14.2%, Cabral LIBII (Univers) 6.3%, other 8.2% (2018)

Legislative branch: description: bicameral Parliament or Parlement consists of:

Senate or Senat (100 seats; 70 members indirectly elected by regional councils and 30 appointed by the president; members serve 5-year terms)

National Assembly or Assemblee Nationale (180 seats; members directly elected in multi-seat constituencies by simple majority vote to serve 5-year terms)
elections: Senate - last held on 25 March 2018 (next to be held in 2023)

National Assembly - last held on 9 February 2020 (current term extended by president); note - the Constitutional Court has ordered a partial rerun of elections in the English speaking areas; date to be determined
election results: Senate - percent of vote by party - CDPM 81.1%, SDF 8.6%, UNDP 5.8%, UDC 1.16%, other 2.8%; seats by party - CPDM 63, SDF 7; composition as of March 2022 - men 74, women 26, percent of women 26%

National Assembly - percent of vote by party - NA; seats by party - CPDM 139, UNDP 7, SDF 5, PCRN 5, UDC 4, FSNC 3, MDR 2, Union of Socialist Movements 2; 13 vacant; composition as of March 2022 - men 119, women 61, percent of women 33.9%; note - total Parliament percent of women 31.1%

Judicial branch: *highest court(s):* Supreme Court of Cameroon (consists of 9 titular and 6 surrogate judges and organized into judicial, administrative, and audit chambers); Constitutional Council (consists of 11 members)
judge selection and term of office: Supreme Court judges appointed by the president with the advice of the Higher Judicial Council of Cameroon, a body chaired by the president and includes the minister of justice, selected magistrates, and representatives of the National Assembly; judge term NA; Constitutional Council members appointed by the president for single 9-year terms
subordinate courts: Parliamentary Court of Justice (jurisdiction limited to cases involving the president and prime minister); appellate and first instance courts; circuit and magistrates' courts

Political parties and leaders: Alliance for Democracy and Development [Marcel YONDO]
Cameroon People's Democratic Movement or CPDM [Paul BIYA]
Cameroon People's Party or CPP [Edith Kah WALLA]
Cameroon Renaissance Movement or MRC [Maurice KAMTO]
Cameroonian Democratic Union or UDC [Adamou Ndam NJOYA]
Cameroonian Party for National Reconciliation or PCRN [Cabral LIBII]
Front for the National Salvation of Cameroon or FSNC [Issa Tchiroma BAKARY]
Movement for the Defense of the Republic or MDR [Dakole DAISSALA]
Movement for the Liberation and Development of Cameroon or MLDC [Marcel YONDO]
National Union for Democracy and Progress or UNDP [Maigari BELLO BOUBA]
Progressive Movement or MP [Jean-Jacques EKINDI]
Social Democratic Front or SDF [John FRU NDI]
Union of Peoples of Cameroon or UPC [Provisionary Management Bureau] [Cecil ODHIAMBO]
Union of Socialist Movements

International organization participation: ACP, AfDB, AU, BDEAC, C, CEMAC, EITI (compliant country), FAO, FZ, G-77, IAEA, IBRD, ICAO, ICRM, IDA, IDB, IFAD, IFC, IFRCS, IHO, ILO, IMF, IMO, IMSO, Interpol, IOC, IOM, IPU, ISO, ITSO, ITU, ITUC (NGOs), LCBC, MIGA, MNJTF, MONUSCO, NAM, OIC, OIF, OPCW, PCA, UN, UNCTAD, UNESCO, UNHCR, UNHRC, UNIDO, UNOCI, UNWTO, UPU, WCO, WFTU (NGOs), WHO, WIPO, WMO, WTO

Diplomatic representation in the US: *chief of mission:* Ambassador Henri ETOUNDI ESSOMBA (since 27 June 2016)
chancery: 2349 Massachusetts Avenue NW, Washington, DC 20008
telephone: [1] (202) 265-8790
FAX: [1] (202) 387-3826
email address and website:
cs@cameroonembassyusa.org
https://www.cameroonembassyusa.org/mainFolder/index.html

Diplomatic representation from the US: *chief of mission:* Ambassador Christopher J. LAMORA (since 21 March 2022)
embassy: Avenue Rosa Parks, Yaoundé
mailing address: 2520 Yaounde Place, Washington, DC 20521-2520
telephone: [237] 22251-4000/[237] 22220-1500
FAX: [237] 22220-1500, Ext. 4531
email address and website:
YaoundeACS@state.gov
https://cm.usembassy.gov/
branch office(s): Douala

Flag description: three equal vertical bands of green (hoist side), red, and yellow, with a yellow five-pointed star centered in the red band; the vertical tricolor recalls the flag of France; red symbolizes unity, yellow the sun, happiness, and the savannahs in the north, and green hope and the forests in the south; the star is referred to as the "star of unity"
note: uses the popular Pan-African colors of Ethiopia

National symbol(s): lion; national colors: green, red, yellow

National anthem: *name:* "O Cameroun, Berceau de nos Ancetres" (O Cameroon, Cradle of Our Forefathers)
lyrics/music: Rene Djam AFAME, Samuel Minkio BAMBA, Moise Nyatte NKO'O [French], Benard Nsokika FONLON [English]/Rene Djam AFAME
note: adopted 1957; Cameroon's anthem, also known as "Chant de Ralliement" (The Rallying Song), has been used unofficially since 1948 and officially adopted in 1957; the anthem has French and English versions whose lyrics differ

National heritage: total World Heritage Sites: 2 (both natural)
selected World Heritage Site locales: Dja Faunal Reserve; Sangha Trinational Forest

ECONOMY

Economic overview: Cameroon's market-based, diversified economy features oil and gas, timber, aluminum, agriculture, mining and the service sector. Oil remains Cameroon's main export commodity, and despite falling global oil prices, still accounts for nearly 40% of exports. Cameroon's economy suffers from factors that often impact underdeveloped countries, such as stagnant per capita income, a relatively inequitable distribution of income, a top-heavy civil service, endemic corruption, continuing inefficiencies of a large parastatal system in key sectors, and a generally unfavorable climate for business enterprise.

Since 1990, the government has embarked on various IMF and World Bank programs designed to spur business investment, increase efficiency in agriculture, improve trade, and recapitalize the nation's banks. The IMF continues to press for economic reforms, including increased budget transparency, privatization, and poverty reduction programs. The Government of Cameroon provides subsidies for electricity, food, and fuel that have strained the federal budget and diverted funds from education, healthcare, and infrastructure projects, as low oil prices have led to lower revenues.

Cameroon devotes significant resources to several large infrastructure projects currently under construction, including a deep seaport in Kribi and the Lom Pangar Hydropower Project. Cameroon's energy sector continues to diversify, recently opening a natural gas-powered electricity generating plant. Cameroon continues to seek foreign investment to improve its inadequate infrastructure, create jobs, and improve its economic footprint, but its unfavorable business environment remains a significant deterrent to foreign investment.

Real GDP (purchasing power parity): $94.94 billion (2020 est.)
$94.25 billion (2019 est.)
$90.87 billion (2018 est.)
note: data are in 2017 dollars
country comparison to the world: 92

Real GDP growth rate: 3.5% (2017 est.)
4.6% (2016 est.)
5.7% (2015 est.)
country comparison to the world: 84

Real GDP per capita: $3,600 (2020 est.)
$3,600 (2019 est.)
$3,600 (2018 est.)
note: data are in 2017 dollars
country comparison to the world: 189

GDP (official exchange rate): $34.99 billion (2017 est.)

Inflation rate (consumer prices): 2.4% (2019 est.)
1% (2018 est.)
0.6% (2017 est.)
country comparison to the world: 123

Credit ratings: *Fitch rating:* B (2006)

Moody's rating: B2 (2016)

Standard & Poors rating: B- (2020)
note: The year refers to the year in which the current credit rating was first obtained.

GDP - composition, by sector of origin: *agriculture:* 16.7% (2017 est.)
industry: 26.5% (2017 est.)
services: 56.8% (2017 est.)

GDP - composition, by end use: *household consumption:* 66.3% (2017 est.)
government consumption: 11.8% (2017 est.)
investment in fixed capital: 21.6% (2017 est.)
investment in inventories: -0.3% (2017 est.)
exports of goods and services: 21.6% (2017 est.)
imports of goods and services: -20.9% (2017 est.)

Agricultural products: cassava, plantains, maize, oil palm fruit, taro, sugar cane, sorghum, tomatoes, bananas, vegetables

Industries: petroleum production and refining, aluminum production, food processing, light consumer goods, textiles, lumber, ship repair

Industrial production growth rate: 3.3% (2017 est.)
country comparison to the world: 94

Labor force: 9.912 million (2017 est.)
country comparison to the world: 50

Labor force - by occupation: *agriculture:* 70%
industry: 13%
services: 17% (2001 est.)

Unemployment rate: 4.3% (2014 est.)
30% (2001 est.)
country comparison to the world: 63

Unemployment, youth ages 15-24: *total:* 6.3%
male: 5.8%
female: 6.8% (2014 est.)
country comparison to the world: 164

Population below poverty line: 37.5% (2014 est.)

Gini Index coefficient - distribution of family income: 46.5 (2014 est.)
46.6 (2014 est.)
country comparison to the world: 22

Household income or consumption by percentage share: *lowest 10%:* 37.5%
highest 10%: 35.4% (2001)

Budget: *revenues:* 5.363 billion (2017 est.)
expenditures: 6.556 billion (2017 est.)

Budget surplus (+) or deficit (-): -3.4% (of GDP) (2017 est.)

country comparison to the world: 143

Public debt: 36.9% of GDP (2017 est.)
32.5% of GDP (2016 est.)
country comparison to the world: 143

Taxes and other revenues: 15.3% (of GDP) (2017 est.)
country comparison to the world: 191

Fiscal year: 1 July - 30 June

Current account balance: -$932 million (2017 est.)
-$1.034 billion (2016 est.)
country comparison to the world: 144

Exports: $7.73 billion (2019 est.)
$7.3 billion (2018 est.)
note: Data are in current year dollars and do not include illicit exports or re-exports.
country comparison to the world: 107

Exports - partners: China 17%, Netherlands 14%, Italy 9%, United Arab Emirates 8%, India 7%, United States 6%, Belgium 6%, Spain 5%, France 5% (2019)

Exports - commodities: crude petroleum, cocoa beans, lumber, gold, natural gas, bananas (2019)

Imports: $9.09 billion (2019 est.) note: data are in current year dollars
$8.42 billion (2018 est.) note: data are in current year dollars
country comparison to the world: 110

Imports - partners: China 28%, Nigeria 15%, France 9%, Belgium 6% (2019)

Imports - commodities: crude petroleum, scrap vessels, rice, special purpose ships, packaged medicines (2019)

Reserves of foreign exchange and gold: $3.235 billion (31 December 2017 est.)
$2.26 billion (31 December 2016 est.)
country comparison to the world: 107

Debt - external: $9.375 billion (31 December 2017 est.)
$7.364 billion (31 December 2016 est.)
country comparison to the world: 114

Exchange rates: Cooperation Financiere en Afrique Centrale francs (XAF) per US dollar -
605.3 (2017 est.)
593.01 (2016 est.)
593.01 (2015 est.)
591.45 (2014 est.)
494.42 (2013 est.)

ENERGY

Electricity access: *electrification - total population:* 70% (2019)
electrification - urban areas: 98% (2019)
electrification - rural areas: 32% (2019)

Electricity: *installed generating capacity:* 1.754 million kW (2020 est.)
consumption: 6,508,840,000 kWh (2019 est.)
exports: 0 kWh (2019 est.)
imports: 19 million kWh (2019 est.)
transmission/distribution losses: 1.864 billion kWh (2019 est.)

Electricity generation sources: *fossil fuels:* 32.5% of total installed capacity (2020 est.)
solar: 0.2% of total installed capacity (2020 est.)
hydroelectricity: 67.3% of total installed capacity (2020 est.)

Petroleum: *total petroleum production:* 63,200 bbl/day (2021 est.)
refined petroleum consumption: 37,900 bbl/day (2019 est.)
crude oil and lease condensate exports: 62,200 bbl/day (2018 est.)
crude oil and lease condensate imports: 20,200 bbl/day (2018 est.)
crude oil estimated reserves: 200 million barrels (2021 est.)

Refined petroleum products - production: 39,080 bbl/day (2015 est.)
country comparison to the world: 82

Refined petroleum products - exports: 8,545 bbl/day (2015 est.)
country comparison to the world: 84

Refined petroleum products - imports: 14,090 bbl/day (2015 est.)
country comparison to the world: 138

Natural gas: *production:* 2,678,486,000 cubic meters (2019 est.)
consumption: 986.189 million cubic meters (2019 est.)
exports: 1,603,156,000 cubic meters (2019 est.)
imports: 0 cubic meters (2021 est.)
proven reserves: 135.071 billion cubic meters (2021 est.)

Carbon dioxide emissions: 7.105 million metric tonnes of CO_2 (2019 est.)
from petroleum and other liquids: 5.171 million metric tonnes of CO_2 (2019 est.)
from consumed natural gas: 1.935 million metric tonnes of CO_2 (2019 est.)
country comparison to the world: 125

Energy consumption per capita: 6.187 million Btu/person (2019 est.)
country comparison to the world: 167

COMMUNICATIONS

Telephones - fixed lines: *total subscriptions:* 964,378 (2020 est.)

subscriptions per 100 inhabitants: 4 (2020 est.)
country comparison to the world: 74

Telephones - mobile cellular total subscriptions: 22,350,310 (2020 est.)

subscriptions per 100 inhabitants: 84 (2020 est.)
country comparison to the world: 55

Telecommunication systems: *general assessment:* Cameroon was for many years one of the few countries in Africa with only two competing mobile operators; the investment programs among operators over the next few years will considerably boost mobile broadband services in rural areas of the country, many of which are under served by fixed-line infrastructure; the government has also been supportive, having launched its 'Cameroon Digital 2020' program, aimed at improving connectivity nationally; improved submarine and terrestrial cable connectivity has substantially increased international bandwidth, in turn leading to reductions in access prices for consumers; other projects such as Acceleration of the Digital Transformation of Cameroon are aimed at developing the digital economy (2022)
domestic: only a little above 3 per 100 persons for fixed-line subscriptions; mobile-cellular usage has increased sharply, reaching a subscribership base of roughly 95 per 100 persons (2020)
international: country code - 237; landing points for the SAT-3/WASC, SAIL, ACE, NCSCS, Ceiba-2, and WACS fiberoptic submarine cable that provides connectivity to Europe, South America, and West Africa; satellite earth stations - 2 Intelsat (Atlantic Ocean) (2019)

Broadcast media: government maintains tight control over broadcast media; state-owned Cameroon Radio Television (CRTV), broadcasting on both a TV and radio network, was the only officially recognized and fully licensed broadcaster until August 2007, when the government finally issued licenses to 2 private TV broadcasters and 1 private radio broadcaster; about 70 privately owned, unlicensed radio stations operating but are subject to closure at any time; foreign news services required to partner with state-owned national station (2019)

Internet country code: .cm

Internet users: *total:* 10,087,428 (2020 est.)
percent of population: 38% (2020 est.)
country comparison to the world: 55

Broadband - fixed subscriptions: *total:* 722,579 (2020 est.)
subscriptions per 100 inhabitants: 3 (2020 est.)
country comparison to the world: 79

TRANSPORTATION

National air transport system: *number of registered air carriers:* 1 (2020)
inventory of registered aircraft operated by air carriers: 3
annual passenger traffic on registered air carriers: 265,136 (2018)
annual freight traffic on registered air carriers: 70,000 (2018) mt-km

Civil aircraft registration country code prefix: TJ

Airports: *total:* 33 (2021)
country comparison to the world: 111

Airports - with paved runways: *total:* 11
over 3,047 m: 2
2,438 to 3,047 m: 5
1,524 to 2,437 m: 3
914 to 1,523 m: 1 (2021)

Airports - with unpaved runways: *total:* 22
1,524 to 2,437 m: 4
914 to 1,523 m: 10
under 914 m: 8 (2021)

Pipelines: 53 km gas, 5 km liquid petroleum gas, 1,107 km oil, 35 km water (2013)

Railways: *total:* 987 km (2014)
narrow gauge: 987 km (2014) 1.000-m gauge
note: railway connections generally efficient but limited; rail lines connect major cities of Douala, Yaounde, Ngaoundere, and Garoua; passenger and freight service provided by CAMRAIL
country comparison to the world: 89

Roadways: *total:* 77,589 km (2016)
paved: 5,133 km (2016)
unpaved: 72,456 km (2016)
country comparison to the world: 64

Waterways: (2010) (major rivers in the south, such as the Wouri and the Sanaga, are largely non-navigable; in the north, the Benue, which connects through Nigeria to the Niger River, is navigable in the rainy season only to the port of Garoua)

Merchant marine: *total:* 94
by type: bulk carrier 3, container ship 1 ,general cargo 35, oil tanker 24, other 31 (2021)
country comparison to the world: 93

Ports and terminals: *oil terminal(s):* Limboh Terminal
river port(s): Douala (Wouri)

Garoua (Benoue)

MILITARY AND SECURITY

Military and security forces: *Cameroon Armed Forces (Forces Armees Camerounaises, FAC):* Army (L'Armee de Terre), Navy (Marine Nationale Republique, MNR, includes naval infantry), Air Force (Armee de l'Air du Cameroun, AAC), Rapid Intervention Battalion (Bataillons d'Intervention Rapide or BIR), National Gendarmerie, Presidential Guard (2022)
note 1 : the National Police and the National Gendarmerie are responsible for internal security; the Police report to the General Delegation of National Security, while the Gendarmerie reports to the Secretariat of State for Defense in charge of the Gendarmerie
note 2: the Rapid Intervention Battalion (BIR) maintains its own command and control structure and reports directly to the president; the BIR is structured as a large brigade with up to 9 battalions, detachments, or groups consisting of infantry, airborne/airmobile, amphibious, armored reconnaissance, counterterrorism, and support elements, such as artillery and intelligence

Military expenditures: 1% of GDP (2021 est.)
1% of GDP (2020 est.)
1.4% of GDP (2019 est.) (approximately $710 million)
1.4% of GDP (2018 est.) (approximately $710 million)
1.5% of GDP (2017 est.) (approximately $710 million)
country comparison to the world: 126

Military and security service personnel strengths: information varies; approximately 40,000 active-duty troops; (25,000 ground forces, including the Rapid Intervention Battalion/BIR and Presidential Guard; 2,000 Navy; 1,000 Air Force; 12,000 Gendarmerie) (2022)
note: the BIR has approximately 5,000 personnel

Military equipment inventories and acquisitions: the FAC inventory includes a wide mix of mostly older or second-hand Chinese, Russian, and Western equipment, with a limited quantity of more modern weapons; since 2010, China has been the leading supplier of armaments to the FAC (2021)

Military service age and obligation: 18-23 years of age for male and female voluntary military service; no conscription; high school graduation required; service obligation 4 years (2021)

Military deployments: 750 (plus about 350 police) Central African Republic (MINUSCA) (May 2022)
note: Cameroon has committed approximately 2,000-2,500 troops to the Multinational Joint Task Force (MNJTF) against Boko Haram and other terrorist groups operating in the general area of the Lake Chad Basin and along Nigeria's northeast border; national MNJTF troop contingents are deployed within their own country territories, although cross-border operations occur occasionally

Military - note: as of 2022, the FAC was largely focused on the threat from the terrorist group Boko Haram along its frontiers with Nigeria and Chad (Far North region) and an insurgency from armed Anglophone separatist groups in the North-West and South-West regions (as of early 2022, this internal conflict has left an estimated 4,000 civilians dead and over 700,000 people displaced since fighting started in 2016); in addition, the FAC often deployed units to the border region with the Central African Republic to counter intrusions from armed militias and bandits

Maritime threats: the International Maritime Bureau reports the territorial and offshore waters in the Niger Delta and Gulf of Guinea remain a very high risk for piracy and armed robbery of ships; in 2021, there were 34 reported incidents of piracy and armed robbery at sea in the Gulf of Guinea region; although a significant decrease from the total number of 81 incidents in 2020, it included the one hijacking and three of five ships fired upon worldwide; while boarding and attempted boarding to steal valuables from ships and crews are the most common types of incidents, almost a third of all incidents involve a hijacking and/or kidnapping; in 2021,57 crew members were kidnapped in seven separate incidents in the Gulf of Guinea, representing 100% of kidnappings worldwide; Nigerian pirates in particular are well armed and very aggressive, operating as far as 200 nm offshore; the Maritime Administration of the US Department of Transportation has issued a Maritime Advisory (2022-001 - Gulf of Guinea-Piracy/Armed Robbery/Kidnapping for Ransom) effective 4 January 2022, which states in part, "Piracy, armed robbery, and kidnapping for ransom continue to serve as significant threats to US-flagged vessels transiting or operating in the Gulf of Guinea"

TERRORISM

Terrorist group(s): Boko Haram; Islamic State of Iraq and ash-Sham - West Africa
note: details about the history, aims, leadership, organization, areas of operation, tactics, targets, weapons, size, and sources of support of the group(s) appear(s) in Appendix-T

TRANSNATIONAL ISSUES

Disputes - international: Joint Border Commission with Nigeria reviewed 2002 ICJ ruling on the entire boundary and bilaterally resolved differences, including June 2006 Greentree Agreement that immediately ceded sovereignty of the Bakassi Peninsula to Cameroon with a full phase-out of Nigerian control and patriation of residents in 2008; Cameroon and Nigeria agreed on maritime delimitation in March 2008; sovereignty dispute between Equatorial Guinea and Cameroon over an island at the mouth of the Ntem River; only Nigeria and Cameroon have heeded the Lake Chad Commission's admonition to ratify the delimitation treaty, which also includes the Chad-Niger and Niger-Nigeria boundaries

Refugees and internally displaced persons: refugees (country of origin): 353,362 (Central African Republic), 138,107 (Nigeria) (2022)

IDPs: 975,786 (2022) (includes far north, northwest, and southwest)

Trafficking in persons: *current situation:* human traffickers exploit domestic and foreign victims in Cameroon and Cameroonians abroad; deteriorating economic and education conditions and diminished police and judicial presence caused by conflict in the Northwest and Southwest has left displaced persons vulnerable to trafficking; parents may be lured by promises of education or a better life for their children in urban areas, and then the children are subject to forced labor and sex trafficking; teenagers and adolescents may be lured to cities with promises of employment and then become victims of forced labor and sex trafficking; children from neighboring countries are forced to work in spare parts shops or cattle grazing by business owners and herders; Cameroonians, often from rural areas, are exploited in forced labor and sex trafficking in the Middle East, Europe, the United States, and African countries
tier rating: Tier 2 Watch List — Cameroon does not meet the minimum standards for the elimination of trafficking, but is making significant efforts to do so; authorities investigated at least nine suspected trafficking cases, identified 77 victims, and provided some training on trafficking indicators to officials and teachers; however, officials prosecuted and convicted fewer traffickers; standard operating procedures for the identification and referral of trafficking victims were not implemented, and officials were not trained on the measures; the government did not report referring trafficking victims to government institutions for vulnerable children, but NGO-funded centers provided care for an unknown number of child victims; 2012 anti-trafficking legislation addressing victim and witness protection in conformity with international law was not passed for the eighth consecutive year (2020)

CANADA

INTRODUCTION

Background: A land of vast distances and rich natural resources, Canada became a self-governing dominion in 1867, while retaining ties to the British crown. Canada gained legislative independence from Britain in 1931 and formalized its constitutional independence from the UK when it passed the Canada Act in 1982. Economically and technologically, the nation has developed in parallel with the US, its neighbor to the south across the world's longest international border. Canada faces the political challenges of meeting public demands for quality improvements in health care, education, social services, and economic competitiveness, as well as responding to the particular concerns of predominantly francophone Quebec. Canada also aims to develop its diverse energy resources while maintaining its commitment to the environment.

GEOGRAPHY

Location: Northern North America, bordering the North Atlantic Ocean on the east, North Pacific

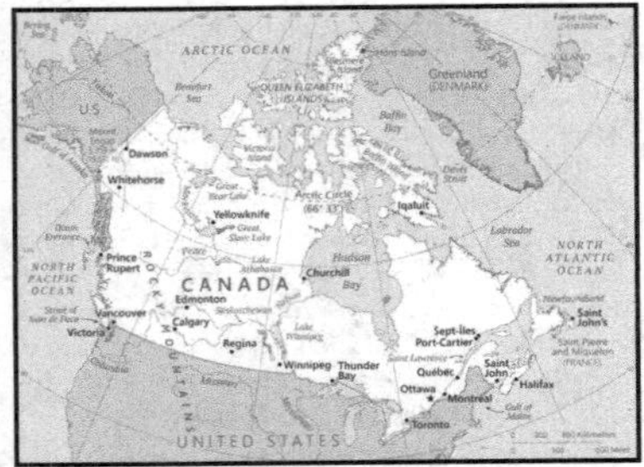

Ocean on the west, and the Arctic Ocean on the north, north of the conterminous US

Geographic coordinates: 60 00 N, 95 00 W

Map references: North America

Area: *total:* 9,984,670 sq km
land: 9,093,507 sq km
water: 891,163 sq km
country comparison to the world: 3

Area - comparative: slightly larger than the US

Land boundaries: *total:* 8,891 km
border countries (1): US 8,891 km (includes 2,475 km with Alaska)
note: Canada is the world's largest country that borders only one country

Coastline: 202,080 km
note: the Canadian Arctic Archipelago - consisting of 36,563 islands, several of them some of the world's largest -contributes to Canada easily having the longest coastline in the world

Maritime claims: *territorial sea:* 12 nm
contiguous zone: 24 nm
exclusive economic zone: 200 nm
continental shelf: 200 nm or to the edge of the continental margin

Climate: varies from temperate in south to subarctic and arctic in north

Terrain: mostly plains with mountains in west, lowlands in southeast

Elevation: *highest point:* Mount Logan 5,959 m
lowest point: Atlantic/Pacific/Arctic Oceans 0 m
mean elevation: 487 m

Natural resources: bauxite, iron ore, nickel, zinc, copper, gold, lead, uranium, rare earth elements, molybdenum, potash, diamonds, silver, fish, timber, wildlife, coal, petroleum, natural gas, hydropower

Land use: *agricultural land:* 6.8% (2018 est.)
arable land: 4.7% (2018 est.)
permanent crops: 0.5% (2018 est.)
permanent pasture: 1.6% (2018 est.)
forest: 34.1% (2018 est.)
other: 59.1% (2018 est.)

Irrigated land: 8,700 sq km (2012)

Major lakes (area sq km): *fresh water lake(s):* Huron* - 35,972 sq km; Great Bear Lake - 31,328 sq km; Superior* - 28,754 sq km; Great Slave Lake - 28,568 sq km; Lake Winnipeg - 24,387 sq km; Erie* - 12,776 sq km; Ontario* - 9,790 sq km; Lake Athabasca -7,935 sq km; Reindeer Lake - 6,650 sq km; Nettilling Lake - 5,542 sq km
note - Great Lakes area shown as Canadian waters*

Major rivers (by length in km): Mackenzie - 4, 241 km; Yukon river source (shared with the US [m]) - 3,185 km; Saint Lawrence river mouth (shared with US) - 3,058 km; Nelson - 2,570 km; Columbia river source (shared with the US [m]) - 1,953 km; Churchill - 1,600 km; Fraser - 1,368 km; Ottawa - 1,271 km; Athabasca - 1,231 km; North Saskatchewan - 1,220 km; Liard - 1,115 km
note – [s] after country name indicates river source; [m] after country name indicates river mouth
Major watersheds (area sq km): Atlantic Ocean drainage: Mississippi* (Gulf of Mexico) (3,202,185 sq km, Canada only 32,000 sq km), Nelson (Hudson Bay) (1,093,141 sq km), Saint Lawrence* (1,049,636 sq km, Canada only 839,200 sq km)
Arctic Ocean drainage: Mackenzie (1,706,388 sq km)
Pacific Ocean drainage: Yukon* (847,620 sq km, Canada only 823,800 sq km), Columbia* (657,501 sq km, Canada only 103,000 sq km)
*note - watersheds shared with the US shown with **

Major aquifers: Northern Great Plains Aquifer

Population distribution: *vast majority of Canadians are positioned in a discontinuous band within approximately 300 km of the southern border with the United States; the most populated province is Ontario, followed by Quebec and British Columbia*

Natural hazards: continuous permafrost in north is a serious obstacle to development; cyclonic storms form east of the Rocky Mountains, a result of the mixing of air masses from the Arctic, Pacific, and North American interior, and produce most of the country's rain and snow east of the mountains
volcanism: the vast majority of volcanoes in Western Canada's Coast Mountains remain dormant

Geography - note: *note 1:* second-largest country in world (after Russia) and largest in the Americas; strategic location between Russia and US via north polar route; approximately 90% of the population is concentrated within 160 km (100 mi) of the US border
note 2: Canada has more fresh water than any other country and almost 9% of Canadian territory is water; Canada has at least 2 million and possibly over 3 million lakes - that is more than all other countries combined

PEOPLE AND SOCIETY

Population: 38,232,593 (2022 est.)
country comparison to the world: 38

Nationality: *noun:* Canadian(s)
adjective: Canadian

Ethnic groups: Canadian 32.3%, English 18.3%, Scottish 13.9%, French 13.6%, Irish 13.4%, German 9.6%, Chinese 5.1%, Italian 4.6%, North American Indian 4.4%, East Indian 4%, Ukrainian 3.9%, other 47.7% (2016 est.)
note: percentages add up to more than 100% because respondents were able to identify more than one ethnic origin

Languages: English (official) 58.7%, French (official) 22%, Punjabi 1.4%, Italian 1.3%, Spanish 1.3%, German 1.3%, Cantonese 1.2%, Tagalog 1.2%, Arabic 1.1%, other 10.5% (2011 est.)
major-language sample(s): The World Factbook, the indispensable source for basic information. (English)

The World Factbook, une source indispensable d'informations de base. (French)

Religions: Catholic 39% (includes Roman Catholic 38.8%, other Catholic .2%), Protestant 20.3% (includes United Church 6.1%, Anglican 5%, Baptist 1.9%, Lutheran 1.5%, Pentecostal 1.5%, Presbyterian 1.4%, other Protestant 2.9%), Orthodox 1.6%, other Christian 6.3%, Muslim 3.2%, Hindu 1.5%, Sikh 1.4%, Buddhist 1.1%, Jewish 1%, other 0.6%, none 23.9% (2011 est.)

Age structure: *0-14 years:* 15.99% (male 3,094,008/female 2,931,953)
15-24 years: 11.14% (male 2,167,013/female 2,032,064)
25-54 years: 39.81% (male 7,527,554/female 7,478,737)
55-64 years: 14.08% (male 2,624,474/female 2,682,858)
65 years and over: 18.98% (male 3,274,298/female 3,881,126) (2020 est.)

Dependency ratios: *total dependency ratio:* 51.2
youth dependency ratio: 23.9
elderly dependency ratio: 27.4
potential support ratio: 3.7 (2020 est.)

Median age: *total:* 41.8 years
male: 40.6 years
female: 42.9 years (2020 est.)
country comparison to the world: 40

Population growth rate: 0.75% (2022 est.)
country comparison to the world: 122

Birth rate: 10.17 births/1,000 population (2022 est.)
country comparison to the world: 186

Death rate: 8.12 deaths/1,000 population (2022 est.)
country comparison to the world: 81

Net migration rate: 5.46 migrant(s)/1,000 population (2022 est.)
country comparison to the world: 21

Population distribution: vast majority of Canadians are positioned in a discontinuous band within approximately 300 km of the southern border with the United States; the most populated province is Ontario, followed by Quebec and British Columbia

Urbanization: *urban population:* 81.8% of total population (2022)
rate of urbanization: 0.95% annual rate of change (2020-25 est.)

Major urban areas - population: 6.313 million Toronto, 4.277 million Montreal, 2.632 million Vancouver, 1.611 million Calgary, 1.519 million Edmonton, 1.423 million OTTAWA (capital) (2022)

Sex ratio: *at birth:* 1.05 male(s)/female
0-14 years: 1.06 male(s)/female
15-24 years: 1.06 male(s)/female
25-54 years: 1.01 male(s)/female
55-64 years: 0.98 male(s)/female
65 years and over: 0.75 male(s)/female
total population: 0.98 male(s)/female (2022 est.)

Mother's mean age at first birth: 29.4 years (2019 est.)

Maternal mortality ratio: 10 deaths/100,000 live births (2017 est.)
country comparison to the world: 145

Infant mortality rate: *total:* 4.38 deaths/1,000 live births
male: 4.66 deaths/1,000 live births
female: 4.08 deaths/1,000 live births (2022 est.)
country comparison to the world: 184

Life expectancy at birth: *total population:* 83.8 years
male: 81.52 years
female: 86.21 years (2022 est.)

country comparison to the world: 6

Total fertility rate: 1.57 children born/woman (2022 est.)
country comparison to the world: 191

Drinking water source: *improved: urban:* 99.3% of population
rural: 99.1% of population
total: 99.2% of population
unimproved: urban: 0.7% of population
rural: 0.9% of population
total: 0.8% of population (2020 est.)

Current health expenditure: 10.8% of GDP (2019)

Physicians density: 2.44 physicians/1,000 population (2019)

Hospital bed density: 2.5 beds/1,000 population (2019)

Sanitation facility access: *improved: urban:* 99.1% of population
rural: 98.9% of population
total: 99% of population
unimproved: urban: 0.9% of population
rural: 1.1% of population
total: 1% of population (2020 est.)

Obesity - adult prevalence rate: 29.4% (2016)
country comparison to the world: 26

Alcohol consumption per capita: *total:* 8 liters of pure alcohol (2019 est.)
beer: 3.5 liters of pure alcohol (2019 est.)
wine: 2 liters of pure alcohol (2019 est.)
spirits: 2.1 liters of pure alcohol (2019 est.)
other alcohols: 0.4 liters of pure alcohol (2019 est.)
country comparison to the world: 44

Tobacco use: *total:* 13% (2020 est.)
male: 15.3% (2020 est.)
female: 10.7% (2020 est.)
country comparison to the world: 117

Education expenditures: 5.3% of GDP (2011 est.)
country comparison to the world: 48

School life expectancy (primary to tertiary education): *total:* 16 years
male: 16 years
female: 17 years (2019)

Unemployment, youth ages 15-24: *total:* 20.2%
male: 20.9%
female: 19.4% (2020 est.)

ENVIRONMENT

Environment - current issues: metal smelting, coal-burning utilities, and vehicle emissions impacting agricultural and forest productivity; air pollution and resulting acid rain severely affecting lakes and damaging forests; ocean waters becoming contaminated due to agricultural, industrial, mining, and forestry activities

Environment - international agreements: *party to:* Air Pollution, Air Pollution-Heavy Metals, Air Pollution-Multi-effect Protocol, Air Pollution-Nitrogen Oxides, Air Pollution-Persistent Organic Pollutants, Air Pollution-Sulphur 85, Air Pollution-Sulphur 94, Antarctic-Environmental Protection, Antarctic-Marine Living Resources, Antarctic Treaty, Biodiversity, Climate Change, Climate Change-Paris Agreement, Comprehensive Nuclear Test Ban, Desertification, Endangered Species, Environmental Modification, Hazardous Wastes, Law of the Sea, Marine Dumping-London Convention, Marine Dumping-London Protocol, Nuclear Test Ban, Ozone Layer Protection, Ship Pollution, Wetlands
signed, but not ratified: Air Pollution-Volatile Organic Compounds, Marine Life Conservation

Air pollutants: *particulate matter emissions:* 6.48 micrograms per cubic meter (2016 est.)
carbon dioxide emissions: 544.89 megatons (2016 est.)
methane emissions: 101.82 megatons (2020 est.)

Climate: varies from temperate in south to subarctic and arctic in north

Land use: *agricultural land:* 6.8% (2018 est.)
arable land: 4.7% (2018 est.)
permanent crops: 0.5% (2018 est.)
permanent pasture: 1.6% (2018 est.)
forest: 34.1% (2018 est.)
other: 59.1% (2018 est.)

Urbanization: *urban population:* 81.8% of total population (2022)
rate of urbanization: 0.95% annual rate of change (2020-25 est.)

Revenue from forest resources: *forest revenues:* 0.08% of GDP (2018 est.)
country comparison to the world: 118

Revenue from coal: *coal revenues:* 0.08% of GDP (2018 est.)
country comparison to the world: 27

Waste and recycling: *municipal solid waste generated annually:* 25,103,034 tons (2014 est.)
municipal solid waste recycled annually: 5,168,715 tons (2008 est.)
percent of municipal solid waste recycled: 20.6% (2008 est.)

Major lakes (area sq km): *fresh water lake(s):* Huron* - 35,972 sq km; Great Bear Lake - 31,328 sq km; Superior* - 28,754 sq km; Great Slave Lake - 28,568 sq km; Lake Winnipeg - 24,387 sq km; Erie* - 12,776 sq km; Ontario* - 9,790 sq km; Lake Athabasca -7,935 sq km; Reindeer Lake - 6,650 sq km; Nettilling Lake - 5,542 sq km
note - Great Lakes area shown as Canadian waters*

Major rivers (by length in km): Mackenzie - 4, 241 km; Yukon river source (shared with the US [m]) - 3,185 km; Saint Lawrence river mouth (shared with US) - 3,058 km; Nelson - 2,570 km; Columbia river source (shared with the US [m]) - 1,953 km; Churchill - 1,600 km; Fraser - 1,368 km; Ottawa - 1,271 km; Athabasca - 1,231 km; North Saskatchewan - 1,220 km; Liard - 1,115 km
note – [s] after country name indicates river source; [m] after country name indicates river mouth

Major watersheds (area sq km): Atlantic Ocean drainage: Mississippi* (Gulf of Mexico) (3,202,185 sq km, Canada only 32,000 sq km), Nelson (Hudson Bay) (1,093,141 sq km), Saint Lawrence* (1,049,636 sq km, Canada only 839,200 sq km)

Arctic Ocean drainage: Mackenzie (1,706,388 sq km)

Pacific Ocean drainage: Yukon* (847,620 sq km, Canada only 823,800 sq km), Columbia* (657,501 sq km, Canada only 103,000 sq km)
*note - watersheds shared with the US shown with **

Major aquifers: Northern Great Plains Aquifer

Total water withdrawal: *municipal:* 4.888 billion cubic meters (2017 est.)
industrial: 28.07 billion cubic meters (2017 est.)
agricultural: 2.639 billion cubic meters (2017 est.)

Total renewable water resources: 2.902 trillion cubic meters (2017 est.)

GOVERNMENT

Country name: *conventional long form:* none
conventional short form: Canada
etymology: the country name likely derives from the St. Lawrence Iroquoian word "kanata" meaning village or settlement

Government type: federal parliamentary democracy (Parliament of Canada) under a constitutional monarchy; a Commonwealth realm; federal and state authorities and responsibilities regulated in constitution

Capital: *name:* Ottawa
geographic coordinates: 45 25 N, 75 42 W
time difference: UTC-5 (same time as Washington, DC, during Standard Time)
daylight saving time: +1 hr, begins second Sunday in March; ends first Sunday in November
time zone note: Canada has six time zones
etymology: the city lies on the south bank of the Ottawa River, from which it derives its name; the river name comes from the Algonquin word "adawe" meaning "to trade" and refers to the indigenous peoples who used the river as a trade highway

Administrative divisions: 10 provinces and 3 territories*; Alberta, British Columbia, Manitoba, New Brunswick, Newfoundland and Labrador, Northwest Territories*, Nova Scotia, Nunavut*, Ontario, Prince Edward Island, Quebec, Saskatchewan, Yukon*

Independence: 1 July 1867 (union of British North American colonies); 11 December 1931 (recognized by UK per Statute of Westminster)

National holiday: Canada Day, 1 July (1867)

Constitution: *history:* consists of unwritten and written acts, customs, judicial decisions, and traditions dating from 1763; the written part of the constitution consists of the Constitution Act of 29 March 1867, which created a federation of four provinces, and the Constitution Act of 17 April 1982
amendments: proposed by either house of Parliament or by the provincial legislative assemblies; there are 5 methods for passage though most require approval by both houses of Parliament, approval of at least two thirds of the provincial legislative assemblies and assent and formalization as a proclamation by the governor general in council; the most restrictive method is reserved for amendments affecting fundamental sections of the constitution, such as the office of the monarch or the governor general, and the constitutional amendment procedures, which require unanimous approval by both houses and by all the provincial assemblies, and assent of the governor general in council; amended 11 times, last in 2011 (Fair Representation Act, 2011)

Legal system: common law system except in Quebec, where civil law based on the French civil code prevails

International law organization participation: accepts compulsory ICJ jurisdiction with reservations; accepts ICCt jurisdiction

Citizenship: *citizenship by birth:* yes
citizenship by descent only: yes
dual citizenship recognized: yes
residency requirement for naturalization: minimum of 3 of last 5 years resident in Canada

Suffrage: 18 years of age; universal

Executive branch: *chief of state:* King CHARLES III (since 8 September 2022); represented by Governor General Mary SIMON (since 6 July 2021)

head of government: Prime Minister Justin Pierre James TRUDEAU (Liberal Party) (since 4 November 2015)
cabinet: Federal Ministry chosen by the prime minister usually from among members of his/her own party sitting in Parliament
elections/appointments: the monarchy is hereditary; governor general appointed by the monarch on the advice of the prime minister for a 5-year term; following legislative elections, the leader of the majority party or majority coalition in the House of Commons generally designated prime minister by the governor general
note: the governor general position is largely ceremonial

Legislative branch: description: bicameral Parliament or Parlement consists of:
Senate or Senat (105 seats; members appointed by the governor general on the advice of the prime minister and can serve until age 75)
House of Commons or Chambre des Communes (338 seats; members directly elected in single-seat constituencies by simple majority vote with terms up to 4 years)
elections: Senate - appointed; latest appointments in July 2021
House of Commons - last held on 20 September 2021 (next to be held on or before 20 October 2025)
election results:
Senate - composition as of May 2022 - men 47, women 45, percent of women 48.9%
House of Commons - percent of vote by party - CPC 33.7%, Liberal Party 32.6%, NDP 17.8%, Bloc Quebecois 7.7%, Greens 2.3%, other 5.9%; seats by party - Liberal Party 159, CPC 119, NDP 25, Bloc Quebecois 32, Greens 2, independent 1 ; composition as of May 2022 - men 235, women 103, percent of women 30.5%; note - total Parliament percent of women 34.4%

Judicial branch: *highest court(s):* Supreme Court of Canada (consists of the chief justice and 8 judges); note - in 1949, Canada abolished all appeals beyond its Supreme Court, which prior to that time, were heard by the Judicial Committee of the Privy Council (in London)
judge selection and term of office: chief justice and judges appointed by the prime minister in council; all judges appointed for life with mandatory retirement at age 75
subordinate courts: federal level: Federal Court of Appeal; Federal Court; Tax Court; federal administrative tribunals; Courts Martial; provincial/territorial level: provincial superior, appeals, first instance, and specialized courts; note - in 1999, the Nunavut Court - a circuit court with the power of a provincial superior court, as well as a territorial court - was established to serve isolated settlements

Political parties and leaders: Bloc Quebecois [Yves-Francois BLANCHET]
Conservative Party of Canada or CPC [Candice BERGEN (interim)]
Green Party [Amita KUTTNER (interim)]
Liberal Party [Justin TRUDEAU]
New Democratic Party or NDP [Jagmeet SINGH]
People's Party of Canada [Maxime BERNIER]

International organization participation: ADB (nonregional member), AfDB (nonregional member), APEC, Arctic Council, ARF, ASEAN (dialogue partner), Australia Group, BIS, C, CD, CDB, CE (observer), EAPC, EBRD, EITI (implementing country), FAO, FATF, G-7, G-8, G-10, G-20, IADB, IAEA, IBRD, ICAO, ICC (national committees), ICCt, ICRM, IDA, IEA, IFAD, IFC, IFRCS, IGAD (partners), IHO, ILO, IMF, IMO, IMSO, Interpol, IOC, IOM, IPU, ISO, ITSO, ITU, ITUC (NGOs), MIGA, MINUSTAH, MONUSCO, NAFTA, NATO, NEA, NSG, OAS, OECD, OIF, OPCW, OSCE, Pacific Alliance (observer), Paris Club, PCA, PIF (partner), UN, UNCTAD, UNESCO, UNFICYP, UNHCR, UNMISS, UNRWA, UNTSO, UPU, USMCA, Wassenaar Arrangement, WCO, WFTU (NGOs), WHO, WIPO, WMO, WTO, ZC

Diplomatic representation in the US: *chief of mission:* Ambassador Kirsten HILLMAN (since 17 July 2020)
chancery: 501 Pennsylvania Avenue NW, Washington, DC 20001
telephone: [1] (844) 880-6519
FAX: [1] (202) 682-7738
email address and website:
ccs.scc@international.gc.ca
https://www.international.gc.ca/country-pays/us-eu/washington.aspx?lang=eng
consulate(s) general: Atlanta, Boston, Chicago, Dallas, Denver, Detroit, Los Angeles, Miami, Minneapolis, New York, San Francisco/Silicon Valley, Seattle
trade office(s): Houston, Palo Alto (CA), San Diego; note - there are trade offices in the Consulates General

Diplomatic representation from the US: *chief of mission:* Ambassador David L. COHEN (since December 2021)
embassy: 490 Sussex Drive, Ottawa, Ontario K1N 1G8
mailing address: 5480 Ottawa Place, Washington DC 20521-5480
telephone: [1] (613) 238-5335
FAX: [1] (613) 241-7845
email address and website:
OttawaNIV@state.gov
https://ca.usembassy.gov/
consulate(s) general: Calgary, Halifax, Montreal, Quebec City, Toronto, Vancouver
consulate(s): Winnipeg

Flag description: two vertical bands of red (hoist and fly side, half width) with white square between them; an 11 -pointed red maple leaf is centered in the white square; the maple leaf has long been a Canadian symbol

National symbol(s): maple leaf, beaver; national colors: red, white

National anthem: *name:* "O Canada"
lyrics/music: Adolphe-Basile ROUTHIER [French], Robert Stanley WEIR [English]/Calixa LAVALLEE
note: adopted 1980; originally written in 1880, "O Canada" served as an unofficial anthem many years before its official adoption; the anthem has French and English versions whose lyrics differ; as a Commonwealth realm, in addition to the national anthem, "God Save the King" serves as the royal anthem (see United Kingdom)

National heritage: *total World Heritage Sites:* 20 (9 cultural, 10 natural, 1 mixed) (2021)
selected World Heritage Site locales: L'Anse aux Meadows (c); Canadian Rocky Mountain Parks (n); Dinosaur Provincial Park (n); Historic District of Old Quebec (c); Old Town Lunenburg (c); Wood Buffalo National Park (n); Head-Smashed-In Buffalo Jump (c); Gros Morne National Park (n); Pimachiowin Aki (m)

ECONOMY

Economic overview: Canada resembles the US in its market-oriented economic system, pattern of production, and high living standards. Since World War II, the impressive growth of the manufacturing, mining, and service sectors has transformed the nation from a largely rural economy into one primarily industrial and urban. Canada has a large oil and natural gas sector with the majority of crude oil production derived from oil sands in the western provinces, especially Alberta. Canada now ranks third in the world in proved oil reserves behind Venezuela and Saudi Arabia and is the world's seventh-largest oil producer.

The 1989 Canada-US Free Trade Agreement and the 1994 North American Free Trade Agreement (which includes Mexico) dramatically increased trade and economic integration between the US and Canada. Canada and the US enjoy the world's most comprehensive bilateral trade and investment relationship, with goods and services trade totaling more than $680 billion in 2017, and two-way investment stocks of more than $800 billion. Over three-fourths of Canada's merchandise exports are destined for the US each year. Canada is the largest foreign supplier of energy to the US, including oil, natural gas, and electric power, and a top source of US uranium imports.

Given its abundant natural resources, highly skilled labor force, and modern capital stock, Canada enjoyed solid economic growth from 1993 through 2007. The global economic crisis of 2007-08 moved the Canadian economy into sharp recession by late 2008, and Ottawa posted its first fiscal deficit in 2009 after 12 years of surplus. Canada's major banks emerged from the financial crisis of 2008-09 among the strongest in the world, owing to the financial sector's tradition of conservative lending practices and strong capitalization. Canada's economy posted strong growth in 2017 at 3%, but most analysts are projecting Canada's economic growth will drop back closer to 2% in 2018.

Real GDP (purchasing power parity):
$1,742,790,000,000 (2020 est.)
$1,842,330,000,000 (2019 est.)
$1,808,660,000,000 (2018 est.)
note: data are in 2017 dollars
country comparison to the world: 15

Real GDP growth rate: 1.66% (2019 est.)
2.02% (2018 est.)
3.17% (2017 est.)
country comparison to the world: 148

Real GDP per capita: $45,900 (2020 est.)
$49,000 (2019 est.)
$48,800 (2018 est.)
note: data are in 2017 dollars
country comparison to the world: 34

GDP (official exchange rate): $1,741,865,000,000 (2019 est.)

Inflation rate (consumer prices): 1.9% (2019 est.)
2.2% (2018 est.)
1.5% (2017 est.)
country comparison to the world: 106

Credit ratings: *Fitch rating:* AA+ (2020)

Moody's rating: Aaa (2002)

Standard & Poors rating: AAA (2002)
note: The year refers to the year in which the current credit rating was first obtained.

GDP - composition, by sector of origin: *agriculture:* 1.6% (2017 est.)

industry: 28.2% (2017 est.)
services: 70.2% (2017 est.)

GDP - composition, by end use: *household consumption:* 57.8% (2017 est.)
government consumption: 20.8% (2017 est.)
investment in fixed capital: 23% (2017 est.)
investment in inventories: 0.7% (2017 est.)
exports of goods and services: 30.9% (2017 est.)
imports of goods and services: -33.2% (2017 est.)

Agricultural products: wheat, rapeseed, maize, barley, milk, soybeans, potatoes, oats, peas, pork

Industries: transportation equipment, chemicals, processed and unprocessed minerals, food products, wood and paper products, fish products, petroleum, natural gas

Industrial production growth rate: 4.9% (2017 est.)
country comparison to the world: 60

Labor force: 18.136 million (2020 est.)
country comparison to the world: 30

Labor force - by occupation: *agriculture:* 2%
industry: 13%
services: 6%
industry and services: 76%
manufacturing: 3% (2006 est.)

Unemployment rate: 5.67% (2019 est.)
5.83% (2018 est.)
country comparison to the world: 92

Unemployment, youth ages 15-24: *total:* 20.2%
male: 20.9%
female: 19.4% (2020 est.)
country comparison to the world: 76

Population below poverty line: 9.4% (2008 est.)
note: this figure is the Low Income Cut-Off, a calculation that results in higher figures than found in many comparable economies; Canada does not have an official poverty line

Gini Index coefficient - distribution of family income: 33.3 (2017 est.)
31.5 (1994)
country comparison to the world: 128

Household income or consumption by percentage share: lowest 10%: 2.6%
highest 10%: 24.8% (2000)

Budget: revenues: 649.6 billion (2017 est.)
expenditures: 665.7 billion (2017 est.)

Budget surplus (+) or deficit (-): -1% (of GDP) (2017 est.)
country comparison to the world: 77

Public debt: 89.7% of GDP (2017 est.)
91.1% of GDP (2016 est.)
note: figures are for gross general government debt, as opposed to net federal debt; gross general government debt includes both intragovernmental debt and the debt of public entities at the sub-national level
country comparison to the world: 25

Taxes and other revenues: 39.3% (of GDP) (2017 est.)
country comparison to the world: 48

Fiscal year: 1 April - 31 March

Current account balance: -$35.425 billion (2019 est.)
-$42.862 billion (2018 est.)
country comparison to the world: 201

Exports: $477.31 billion (2020 est.)
$555.83 billion (2019 est.)
$556.89 billion (2018 est.)
note: Data are in current year dollars and do not include illicit exports or re-exports.
country comparison to the world: 14

Exports - partners: US 73% (2019)

Exports - commodities: crude petroleum, cars and vehicle parts, gold, refined petroleum, natural gas (2019)

Imports: $510.29 billion (2020 est.) note: data are in current year dollars
$583.6 billion (2019 est.) note: data are in current year dollars
$589.55 billion (2018 est.) note: data are in current year dollars
country comparison to the world: 10

Imports - partners: US 57%, China 11%, Mexico 5% (2019)

Imports - commodities: cars and vehicle parts, delivery trucks, crude petroleum, refined petroleum (2019)

Reserves of foreign exchange and gold: $86.68 billion (31 December 2017 est.)
$82.72 billion (31 December 2016 est.)
country comparison to the world: 28

Debt - external: $2,124,887,000,000 (2019 est.)
$1,949,796,000,000 (2018 est.)
country comparison to the world: 12

Exchange rates: Canadian dollars (CAD) per US dollar –
1.28035 (2020 est.)
1.3228 (2019 est.)
1.32925 (2018 est.)
1.2788 (2014 est.)
1.0298 (2013 est.)

ENERGY

Electricity access: *electrification - total population:* 100% (2020)

Electricity: *installed generating capacity:* 153.251 million kW (2020 est.)
consumption: 539.695 billion kWh (2020 est.)
exports: 67.2 billion kWh (2020 est.)
imports: 9.8 billion kWh (2020 est.)
transmission/distribution losses: 32.937 billion kWh (2020 est.)

Electricity generation sources: *fossil fuels:* 16.5% of total installed capacity (2020 est.)
nuclear: 14.7% of total installed capacity (2020 est.)
solar: 0.7% of total installed capacity (2020 est.)
wind: 5.7% of total installed capacity (2020 est.)
hydroelectricity: 60.8% of total installed capacity (2020 est.)
biomass and waste: 1.6% of total installed capacity (2020 est.)

Coal: *production:* 48.328 million metric tons (2020 est.)
consumption: 25.642 million metric tons (2020 est.)
exports: 32.026 million metric tons (2020 est.)
imports: 7.577 million metric tons (2020 est.)
proven reserves: 6.582 billion metric tons (2019 est.)

Petroleum: *total petroleum production:* 5,468,100 bbl/day (2021 est.)
refined petroleum consumption: 2,629,300 bbl/day (2019 est.)
crude oil and lease condensate exports: 3.177 million bbl/day (2018 est.)
crude oil and lease condensate imports: 793,800 bbl/day (2018 est.)
crude oil estimated reserves: 170.3 billion barrels (2021 est.)

Refined petroleum products - production: 2.009 million bbl/day (2017 est.)
country comparison to the world: 10

Refined petroleum products - exports: 1.115 million bbl/day (2017 est.)
country comparison to the world: 8

Refined petroleum products - imports: 405,700 bbl/day (2017 est.)
country comparison to the world: 21

Natural gas: *production:* 178,723,494,000 cubic meters (2019 est.)
consumption: 124,502,315,000 cubic meters (2019 est.)
exports: 76,094,066,000 cubic meters (2019 est.)
imports: 28,026,440,000 cubic meters (2019 est.)
proven reserves: 2,067,126,000,000 cubic meters (2021 est.)

Carbon dioxide emissions: 612.084 million metric tonnes of CO2 (2019 est.)
from coal and metallurgical coke: 56.087 million metric tonnes of CO2 (2019 est.)
from petroleum and other liquids: 311.336 million metric tonnes of CO2 (2019 est.)
from consumed natural gas: 244.66 million metric tonnes of CO2 (2019 est.)
country comparison to the world: 9

Energy consumption per capita: 403.7 million Btu/person (2019 est.)
country comparison to the world: 6

COMMUNICATIONS

Telephones - fixed lines: *total subscriptions:* 13.34 million (2020 est.)
subscriptions per 100 inhabitants: 35 (2020 est.)
country comparison to the world: 15

Telephones - mobile cellular: *total subscriptions:* 32.36 million (2020 est.)
subscriptions per 100 inhabitants: 86 (2020 est.)
country comparison to the world: 45

Telecommunication systems: *general assessment:* the Canadian telecom market continues to show steady development as operators invest in network upgrades; much of the investment among telcos has been channelled into LTE infrastructure to capitalize on consumer demand for mobile data services, while there has also been further investment in 5G; investment programs have also been supported by regulatory efforts to ensure that operators have spectrum available to develop 5G services; an investment in fixed-line infrastructure, focused on FttP and, among cable broadband providers; government policy has encouraged the extension of broadband to rural and regional areas, with the result that services are almost universally available and the emphasis now is on improving service speeds to enable the entire population to benefit from the digital economy and society; cable broadband is the principal access platform, followed by DSL; the mobile rate remains comparatively low by international standards; Canadians have provided for LTE and LTE-A infrastructure; despite topographical challenges and the remoteness of many areas, the major players effectively offer 99% population coverage with LTE; operators now provide up to 70% population coverage with 5G (2022)
domestic: Nearly 37 per 100 fixed-line and 96 per 100 mobile-cellular teledensity; domestic satellite system with about 300 earth stations (2020)
international: country code - 1 ; landing points for the Nunavut Undersea Fiber Optic Network System, Greenland Connect, Persona, GTT Atlantic, and Express, KetchCan 1 Submarine Fiber Cable system, St Pierre and Miquelon Cable submarine cables providing links to the US and Europe; satellite earth

stations - 7 (5 Intelsat - 4 Atlantic Ocean and 1 Pacific Ocean, and 2 Intersputnik - Atlantic Ocean region) (2019)

Broadcast media: 2 public TV broadcasting networks, 1 in English and 1 in French, each with a large number of network affiliates; several private-commercial networks also with multiple network affiliates; overall, about 150 TV stations; multi-channel satellite and cable systems provide access to a wide range of stations including US stations; mix of public and commercial radio broadcasters with the Canadian Broadcasting Corporation (CBC), the public radio broadcaster, operating 4 radio networks, Radio Canada International, and radio services to indigenous populations in the north; roughly 1,119 licensed radio stations (2016)

Internet country code: .ca

Internet users: *total:* 36,896,088 (2020 est.)
percent of population: 97% (2020 est.)
country comparison to the world: 27

Broadband - fixed subscriptions: *total:* 15,825,813 (2020 est.)
subscriptions per 100 inhabitants: 42 (2020 est.)
country comparison to the world: 16

TRANSPORTATION

National air transport system: *number of registered air carriers:* 51 (2020)
inventory of registered aircraft operated by air carriers: 879
annual passenger traffic on registered air carriers: 89.38 million (2018)
annual freight traffic on registered air carriers: 3,434,070,000 (2018) mt-km

Civil aircraft registration country code prefix: C

Airports: *total:* 1,467 (2021)
country comparison to the world: 4

Airports - with paved runways: *total:* 523
over 3,047 m: 21
2,438 to 3,047 m: 19
1.524 to 2,437 m: 147
914 to 1,523 m: 257
under 914 m: 79 (2021)

Airports - with unpaved runways: *total:* 944
1.524 to 2,437 m: 75
914 to 1,523 m: 385
*under 914 m:*484(2021)

Heliports: 26 (2021)

Pipelines: 840,000 km oil and gas (2020)

Railways: *total:* 49,422 km (2021) note: 129 km electrified (2021)
standard gauge: 49,422 km (2021) 1.435-m gauge
country comparison to the world: 5

Roadways: *total:* 1,042,300 km (2011)
paved: 415,600 km (2011) (includes 17,000 km of expressways)
unpaved: 626,700 km (2011)
country comparison to the world: 8

Waterways: 636 km (2011) (Saint Lawrence Seaway of 3,769 km, including the Saint Lawrence River of 3,058 km, shared with United States)
country comparison to the world: 85

Merchant marine: *total:* 679
by type: bulk carrier 22, container ship 1, general cargo 66, oil tanker 15, other 575 (2021)
country comparison to the world: 34

Ports and terminals: *major seaport(s):* Halifax, Saint John (New Brunswick), Vancouver
oil terminal(s): Lower Lakes terminal
container port(s) (TEUs): Montreal (1,745,244), Vancouver (3,398,860) (2019)

LNG terminal(s) (import): Saint John
river and lake port(s): Montreal, Quebec City, Sept-Isles (St. Lawrence)
dry bulk cargo port(s): Port-Cartier (iron ore and grain),
Fraser River Port (Fraser) Hamilton (Lake Ontario)

MILITARY AND SECURITY

Military and security forces: Canadian Forces: Canadian Army, Royal Canadian Navy, Royal Canadian Air Force, Canadian Joint Operations Command, Canadian Special Operations Forces Command; Primary Reserve (army, air, naval reserves); Coast Guard (Department of Fisheries and Oceans) (2022)
note: the Army reserves include the Canadian Rangers, which provides a limited presence in Canada's northern, coastal, and isolated areas for sovereignty, public safety, and surveillance roles

Military expenditures: 1.4% of GDP (2021 est.)
1.4% of GDP (2020)
1.3% of GDP (2019) (approximately $26 billion)
1.3% of GDP (2018) (approximately $25.7 billion)
1.4% of GDP (2017) (approximately $27.6 billion)
country comparison to the world: 97

Military and security service personnel strengths: approximately 70,000 active armed forces personnel (23,000 Army; 12,000 Navy; 12,000 Air Force; 23,000 other) (2022)
note: the Army also has approximately 19,000 part-time volunteer soldiers in the Reserve Force, including about 5,500 Rangers

Military equipment inventories and acquisitions: the CAF's inventory is a mix of domestically-produced equipment and imported weapons systems from Australia, Europe, Israel, and the US; since 2010, the leading supplier has been the US; Canada's defense industry develops, maintains, and produces a range of equipment, including aircraft, combat vehicles, naval vessels, and associated components (2022)

Military service age and obligation: 17 years of age for voluntary male and female military service (with parental consent); 16 years of age for Reserve and Military College applicants; Canadian citizenship or permanent residence status required; maximum 34 years of age; service obligation 3-9 years (2022)
note 1: Canada opened up all military occupations to women in 2001 ; in 2020, women comprised about 16% of the CAF

Military deployments: the CAF has nearly 1,400 military personnel forward deployed for NATO air, land, and sea missions in the European theater, including up to 650 troops in Latvia and 140 in Romania (2022)
note: in response to Russia's 2022 invasion of Ukraine, some NATO countries, including Canada, have sent additional troops and equipment to the battlegroups deployed in NATO territory in eastern Europe

Military - note: Canada is a member of NATO and was one of the original 12 countries to sign the North Atlantic Treaty (also known as the Washington Treaty) in 1949

Canada is part of the North American Aerospace Defense Command (NORAD; established 1958); NORAD is a Canada-US bi-national military command responsible for monitoring and defending North American airspace; traditionally, a Canadian Armed Forces officer has served as the deputy commander of NORAD

Canada's defense relationship with the US extends back to the Ogdensburg Declaration of 1940, when the two countries formally agreed on military cooperation, including the establishment of the Permanent Joint Board on Defense (PJBD), which continued to be the highest-level bilateral defense forum between Canada and the US as of 2022

British troops withdrew from Canada in 1871 as part of the UK-US Treaty of Washington; following the withdrawal, the first Canadian militia, known as the Royal Canadian Regiment, was organized in 1883 to protect Canadian territory and defend British interests abroad, which it did in the South African War (1899-1902), Canada's first overseas conflict; militia units formed the backbone of the more than 425,000 Canadian soldiers that went to Europe during World War I in what was called the Canadian Expeditionary Force; the Royal Canadian Navy was created in 1910, while the Canadian Air Force was established in 1920 and became the Royal Canadian Air Force in 1924; the Canadian Army was officially founded in 1942; a unified Canadian Armed Forces was created in 1968

TERRORISM

Terrorist group(s): Islamic State of Iraq and ash-Sham (ISIS); Hizballah
note: details about the history, aims, leadership, organization, areas of operation, tactics, targets, weapons, size, and sources of support of the group(s) appear(s) in Appendix-T

TRANSNATIONAL ISSUES

Disputes - international: managed maritime boundary disputes with the US at Dixon Entrance, Beaufort Sea, Strait of Juan de Fuca, and the Gulf of Maine, including the disputed Machias Seal Island and North Rock; Canada and the United States dispute how to divide the Beaufort Sea and the status of the Northwest Passage but continue to work cooperatively to survey the Arctic continental shelf; US works closely with Canada to intensify security measures for monitoring and controlling legal and illegal movement of people, transport, and commodities across the international border; sovereignty dispute with Denmark over Hans Island in the Kennedy Channel between Ellesmere Island and Greenland; commencing the collection of technical evidence for submission to the Commission on the Limits of the Continental Shelf in support of claims for continental shelf beyond 200 nm from its declared baselines in the Arctic, as stipulated in Article 76, paragraph 8, of the UN Convention on the Law of the Sea

Refugees and internally displaced persons: *refugees (country of origin):* 22,400 (Venezuela) (refugees and migrants) (2020); 9,883 (Nigeria), 7,571 (Turkey), 7,385 (Iran), 6,965 (Pakistan), 6,287 (China), 5,244 (Colombia) (mid-year 2021)
stateless persons: 3,823 (mid-year 2021)

Illicit drugs: illicit production of fentanyl primarily for Canada's domestic drug market with at least small quantities smuggled to the US; complex laboratories setup for fentanyl production have been found and Mexican traffickers present in the country; Canada legalized marijuana in 2018

CAYMAN ISLANDS

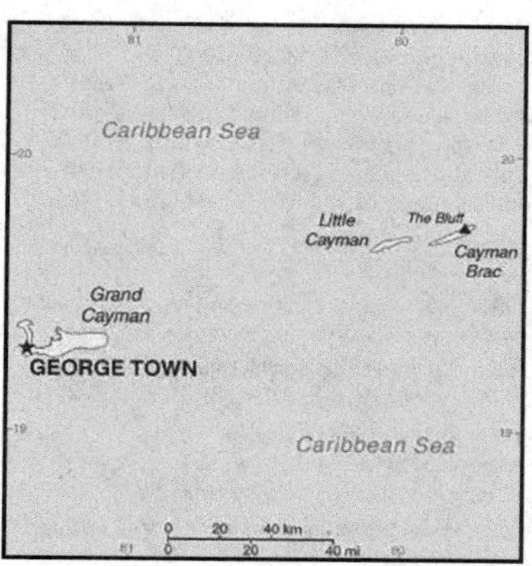

INTRODUCTION

Background: The Cayman Islands were colonized from Jamaica by the British during the 18th and 19th centuries and were administered by Jamaica after 1863. In 1959, the islands became a territory within the Federation of the West Indies. When the Federation dissolved in 1962, the Cayman Islands chose to remain a British dependency. The territory has transformed itself into a significant offshore financial center.

GEOGRAPHY

Location: Caribbean, three-island group (Grand Cayman, Cayman Brac, Little Cayman) in Caribbean Sea, 240 km south of Cuba and 268 km northwest of Jamaica

Geographic coordinates: 19 30 N, 80 30 W

Map references: Central America and the Caribbean

Area: *total:* 264 sq km
land: 264 sq km
water: 0 sq km
country comparison to the world: 210

Area - comparative: 1.5 times the size of Washington, DC

Land boundaries: *total:* 0 km

Coastline: 160 km

Maritime claims: *territorial sea:* 12 nm
exclusive economic zone: 200 nm
exclusive fishing zone: 200 nm

Climate: tropical marine; warm, rainy summers (May to October) and cool, relatively dry winters (November to April)

Terrain: low-lying limestone base surrounded by coral reefs

Elevation: *highest point:* 1 km SW of The Bluff on Cayman Brac 50 m
lowest point: Caribbean Sea 0 m

Natural resources: fish, climate and beaches that foster tourism

Land use: *agricultural land:* 11.2% (2018 est.)
arable land: 0.8% (2018 est.)
permanent crops: 2.1% (2018 est.)
permanent pasture: 8.3% (2018 est.)
forest: 52.9% (2018 est.)
other: 35.9% (2018 est.)

Population distribution: majority of the population resides on Grand Cayman

Natural hazards: hurricanes (July to November)

Geography - note: important location between Cuba and Central America

PEOPLE AND SOCIETY

Population: 64,309 (2022 est.)
note: most of the population lives on Grand Cayman
country comparison to the world: 204

Nationality: *noun:* Caymanian(s)
adjective: Caymanian

Ethnic groups: mixed 40%, White 20%, African descent 20%, expatriates of various ethnic groups 20%

Languages: English (official) 90.9%, Spanish 4%, Filipino 3.3%, other 1.7%, unspecified 0.1% (2010 est.)

Religions: Protestant 67.8% (includes Church of God 22.6%, Seventh Day Adventist 9.4%, Presbyterian/United Church 8.6%, Baptist 8.3%, Pentecostal 7.1%, non-denominational 5.3%, Anglican 4.1%, Wesleyan Holiness 2.4%), Roman Catholic 14.1%, Jehovah's Witness 1.1%, other 7%, none 9.3%, unspecified 0.7% (2010 est.)

Age structure: *0-14 years:* 17.75% (male 5,535/female 5,457)
15-24 years: 11.86% (male 3,673/female 3,675)
25-54 years: 41.37% (male 12,489/female 13,140)
55-64 years: 14.78% (male 4,398/female 4,755)
65 years and over: 14.24% (male 4,053/female 4,769) (2020 est.)

Median age: *total:* 40.5 years
male: 39.7 years
female: 41.2 years (2020 est.)
country comparison to the world: 51

Population growth rate: 1. 83% (2022 est.)
country comparison to the world: 49

Birth rate: 11. 69 births/1,000 population (2022 est.)
country comparison to the world: 159

Death rate: 5.97 deaths/1,000 population (2022 est.)
country comparison to the world: 160

Net migration rate: 12.56 migrant(s)/1,000 population (2022 est.)
note: major destination for Cubans trying to migrate to the US
country comparison to the world: 6

Population distribution: majority of the population resides on Grand Cayman

Urbanization: *urban population:* 100% of total population (2022)
rate of urbanization: 1.13% annual rate of change (2020-25 est.)

Major urban areas - population: 35,000 GEORGE TOWN (capital) (2018)

Sex ratio: *at birth:* 1.02 male(s)/female
0-14 years: 1.01 male(s)/female
15-24 years: 1 male(s)/female
25-54 years: 0.95 male(s)/female
55-64 years: 0.94 male(s)/female
65 years and over: 0.7 male(s)/female
total population: 0.95 male(s)/female (2022 est.)

Infant mortality rate: *total:* 7.65 deaths/1,000 live births
male: 9.26 deaths/1,000 live births
female: 6.01 deaths/1,000 live births (2022 est.)
country comparison to the world: 154

Life expectancy at birth: *total population:* 82.04 years
male: 79.35 years
female: 84.79 years (2022 est.)
country comparison to the world: 29

Total fertility rate: 1.82 children born/woman (2022 est.)
country comparison to the world: 140

Drinking water source: *improved: urban:* 97.4% of population
total: 97.4% of population
unimproved: urban: 2.6% of population
total: 2.6% of population (2015 est.)

Sanitation facility access: *improved: urban:* 95.6% of population
total: 95.6% of population
unimproved: urban: 4.4% of population
total: 4.4% of population (2015 est.)

Unemployment, youth ages 15-24: *total:* 13.8%
male: 16.4%
female: 11.4% (2015 est.)

ENVIRONMENT

Environment - current issues: no natural freshwater resources; drinking water supplies are met by reverse osmosis desalination plants and rainwater catchment; trash washing up on the beaches or being deposited there by residents; no recycling or waste treatment facilities; deforestation (trees being cut down to create space for commercial use)

Air pollutants: *carbon dioxide emissions:* 0.55 megatons (2016 est.)

Climate: tropical marine; warm, rainy summers (May to October) and cool, relatively dry winters (November to April)

Land use: *agricultural land:* 11.2% (2018 est.)
arable land: 0.8% (2018 est.)
permanent crops: 2.1% (2018 est.)
permanent pasture: 8.3% (2018 est.)
forest: 52.9% (2018 est.)
other: 35.9% (2018 est.)

Urbanization: *urban population:* 100% of total population (2022)
rate of urbanization: 1.13% annual rate of change (2020-25 est.)

Revenue from forest resources: *forest revenues:* 0% of GDP (2018 est.)
country comparison to the world: 164

Revenue from coal: *coal revenues:* 0% of GDP (2018 est.)
country comparison to the world: 76

Waste and recycling: *municipal solid waste generated annually:* 60,000 tons (2014 est.)
municipal solid waste recycled annually: 12,600 tons (2013 est.)
percent of municipal solid waste recycled: 21% (2013 est.)

GOVERNMENT

Country name: *conventional long form:* none
conventional short form: Cayman Islands

etymology: the islands' name comes from the native Carib word "caiman," describing the marine crocodiles living there

Government type: parliamentary democracy; self-governing overseas territory of the UK

Dependency status: overseas territory of the UK

Capital: *name:* George Town (on Grand Cayman)
geographic coordinates: 19 18 N, 81 23 W
time difference: UTC-5 (same time as Washington, DC, during Standard Time)
etymology: named after English King GEORGE III (1738-1820)

Administrative divisions: 6 districts; Bodden Town, Cayman Brac and Little Cayman, East End, George Town, North Side, West Bay

Independence: none (overseas territory of the UK)

National holiday: Constitution Day, the first Monday in July (1959)

Constitution: *history:* several previous; latest approved 10 June 2009, entered into force 6 November 2009 (The Cayman Islands Constitution Order 2009)
amendments: amended 2016, 2020

Legal system: English common law and local statutes

Citizenship: see United Kingdom

Suffrage: 18 years of age; universal

Executive branch: *chief of state:* King CHARLES III (since 8 September 2022); represented by Governor Martyn ROPER (since 29 October 2018)
head of government: Premier Wayne PANTON (since 21 April 2021)
cabinet: Cabinet selected from the Parliament and appointed by the governor on the advice of the premier
elections/appointments: the monarchy is hereditary; governor appointed by the monarch; following legislative elections, the leader of the majority party or majority coalition appointed premier by the governor

Legislative branch: *description:* unicameral Parliament (21 seats; 19 members directly elected by majority vote and 2 ex officio members -the deputy governor and attorney general - appointed by the governor; members serve 4-year terms)
elections: last held on 14 April 2021 (next to be held on 2025)
election results: percent of vote by party - independent 79.1%, PPM 19.6%; seats by party - independent 12, PPM 7; composition of elected members - men 15, women 4, percent of women 21.1%; ex-officio members - men 2

Judicial branch: *highest court(s):* Court of Appeal (consists of the court president and at least 2 judges); Grand Court (consists of the court president and at least 2 judges); note - appeals beyond the Court of Appeal are heard by the Judicial Committee of the Privy Council (in London)
judge selection and term of office: Court of Appeal and Grand Court judges appointed by the governor on the advice of the Judicial and Legal Services Commission, an 8-member independent body consisting of governor appointees, Court of Appeal president, and attorneys; Court of Appeal judges' tenure based on their individual instruments of appointment; Grand Court judges normally appointed until retirement at age 65 but can be extended until age 70
subordinate courts: Summary Court

Political parties and leaders: Cayman Islands Peoples Party or CIPP [Ezzard MILLER]
People's Progressive Movement or PPM [Roy McTAGGART]

International organization participation: Caricom (associate), CDB, Interpol (subbureau), IOC, UNESCO (associate), UPU

Diplomatic representation in the US: none (overseas territory of the UK)

Diplomatic representation from the US: *embassy:* none (overseas territory of the UK); consular services provided through the US Embassy in Jamaica

Flag description: a blue field with the flag of the UK in the upper hoist-side quadrant and the Caymanian coat of arms centered on the outer half of the flag; the coat of arms includes a crest with a pineapple, representing the connection with Jamaica, and a turtle, representing Cayman's seafaring tradition, above a shield bearing a golden lion, symbolizing Great Britain, below which are three green stars (representing the three islands) surmounting white and blue wavy lines representing the sea; a scroll below the shield bears the motto HE HATH FOUNDED IT UPON THE SEAS

National symbol(s): green sea turtle

National anthem: *name:* "Beloved Isle Cayman"
lyrics/music: Leila E. ROSS
note: adopted 1993; served as an unofficial anthem since 1930; as an overseas territory of the United Kingdom, in addition to the local anthem, "God Save the King" is official (see United Kingdom)

ECONOMY

Economic overview: With no direct taxation, the islands are a thriving offshore financial center. More than 65,000 companies were registered in the Cayman Islands as of 2017, including more than 280 banks, 700 insurers, and 10,500 mutual funds. A stock exchange was opened in 1997. Nearly 90% of the islands' food and consumer goods must be imported. The Caymanians enjoy a standard of living comparable to that of Switzerland.

Tourism is also a mainstay, accounting for about 70% of GDP and 75% of foreign currency earnings. The tourist industry is aimed at the luxury market and caters mainly to visitors from North America. Total tourist arrivals exceeded 2.1 million in 2016, with more than three-quarters from the US.

Real GDP (purchasing power parity): $4.78 billion (2019 est.) note: data are in 2017 dollars
$4.61 billion (2018 est.) note: data are in 2017 dollars
$4.409 billion (2017 est.)
country comparison to the world: 179

Real GDP growth rate: 1.7% (2014 est.)
1.2% (2013 est.)
1.6% (2012 est.)
country comparison to the world: 147

Real GDP per capita: $73,600 (2019 est.) *note:* data are in 2017 dollars
$71,800 (2018 est.) note: data are in 2017 dollars
$69,573 (2017 est.)
country comparison to the world: 9

GDP (official exchange rate): $2.25 billion (2008 est.)

Inflation rate (consumer prices): 2% (2017 est.)
-0.6% (2016 est.)
country comparison to the world: 109

Credit ratings: Moody's rating: Aa3 (1997)
note: The year refers to the year in which the current credit rating was first obtained.

GDP - composition, by sector of origin: *agriculture:* 0.3% (2017 est.)
industry: 7.4% (2017 est.)
services: 92.3% (2017 est.)

GDP - composition, by end use: *household consumption:* 62.3% (2017 est.)
government consumption: 14.5% (2017 est.)
investment in fixed capital: 22.1% (2017 est.)
investment in inventories: 0.1% (2017 est.)
exports of goods and services: 65.4% (2017 est.)
imports of goods and services: -64.2% (2017 est.)

Agricultural products: vegetables, fruit; livestock; turtle farming

Industries: tourism, banking, insurance and finance, construction, construction materials, furniture

Industrial production growth rate: 2.2% (2017 est.)
country comparison to the world: 124

Labor force: 39,000 (2007 est.)
note: nearly 55% are non-nationals
country comparison to the world: 196

Labor force - by occupation: *agriculture:* 1.9%
industry: 19.1%
services: 79% (2008 est.)

Unemployment rate: 4% (2008)
4.4% (2004)
country comparison to the world: 60

Unemployment, youth ages 15-24: *total:* 13.8%
male: 16.4%
female: 11.4% (2015 est.)
country comparison to the world: 115

Budget: *revenues:* 874.5 million (2017 est.)
expenditures: 766.6 million (2017 est.)

Budget surplus (+) or deficit (-): 4.8% (of GDP) (2017 est.)
country comparison to the world: 7

Taxes and other revenues: 38.9% (of GDP) (2017 est.)
country comparison to the world: 51

Fiscal year: 1 April - 31 March

Current account balance: -$492.6 million (2017 est.)
-$493.5 million (2016 est.)
country comparison to the world: 121

Exports: $4.13 billion (2019 est.)
$3.96 billion (2018 est.)
note: Data are in current year dollars and do not include illicit exports or re-exports.
country comparison to the world: 132

Exports - partners: Netherlands 82%, Spain 11% (2019)

Exports - commodities: recreational boats, gold, broadcasting equipment, sulfates, collector's items (2019)

Imports: $2.7 billion (2019 est.) note: data are in current year dollars
$2.52 billion (2018 est.) note: data are in current year dollars
country comparison to the world: 162

Imports - partners: Netherlands 56%, United States 18%, Italy 8%, Switzerland 5% (2019)

Imports - commodities: recreational boats, ships, gold, refined petroleum, cars (2019)

Exchange rates: Caymanian dollars (KYD) per US dollar -
0.82 (2017 est.)
0.82 (2016 est.)
0.82 (2015 est.)
0.82 (2014 est.)
0.83 (2013 est.)

ENERGY

Electricity access: *electrification - total population:* 100% (2020)

Electricity: *installed generating capacity:* 174,000 kW (2020 est.)
consumption: 655.165 million kWh (2019 est.)
exports: 0 kWh (2020 est.)
imports: 0 kWh (2020 est.)
transmission/distribution losses: 40 million kWh (2019 est.)

Electricity generation sources: *fossil fuels:* 97.6% of total installed capacity (2020 est.)
solar: 2.4% of total installed capacity (2020 est.)

Petroleum: *total petroleum production:* 0 bbl/day (2021 est.)
refined petroleum consumption: 5,500 bbl/day (2019 est.)

Refined petroleum products - imports: 4,285 bbl/day (2015 est.)
country comparison to the world: 175

Carbon dioxide emissions: 808,000 metric tonnes of CO_2 (2019 est.)
from petroleum and other liquids: 808,000 metric tonnes of CO_2 (2019 est.)
country comparison to the world: 178

Energy consumption per capita: 175.578 million Btu/person (2019 est.)
country comparison to the world: 25

COMMUNICATIONS

Telephones - fixed lines: *total subscriptions:* 36,000 (2020 est.)
subscriptions per 100 inhabitants: 55 (2020 est.)
country comparison to the world: 166

Telephones - mobile cellular: *total subscriptions:* 100,000 (2020 est.)
subscriptions per 100 inhabitants: 152 (2020 est.)
country comparison to the world: 190

Telecommunication systems: *general assessment:* the telecom sector has seen a decline in subscriber numbers (particularly for prepaid mobile services the mainstay of short term visitors) and revenue; fixed and mobile broadband services are two areas that have benefited from the crisis as employees and students have resorted to working from home; one area of the telecom market that is not prepared for growth is 5G mobile; governments, regulators, and even the mobile network operators have shown that they have not been investing in 5G opportunities at the present time; network expansion and enhancements remain concentrated around improving LTE coverage (2021)
domestic: introduction of competition in the mobile-cellular market in 2004 boosted subscriptions; nearly 55 per 100 fixed-line and 152 per 100 mobile-cellular (2020)
international: country code - 1 -345; landing points for the Maya-1, Deep Blue Cable, and the Cayman-Jamaica Fiber System submarine cables that provide links to the US and parts of Central and South America; satellite earth station - 1 Intelsat (Atlantic Ocean) (2019)

Broadcast media: 4 TV stations; cable and satellite subscription services offer a variety of international programming; government-owned Radio Cayman operates 2 networks broadcasting on 5 stations; 10 privately owned radio stations operate alongside Radio Cayman

Internet country code: .ky

Internet users: *total:* 53,233 (2020 est.)
percent of population: 81% (2020 est.)
country comparison to the world: 194

Broadband - fixed subscriptions: *total:* 3,200 (2020 est.)
subscriptions per 100 inhabitants: 49 (2020 est.)
country comparison to the world: 191

TRANSPORTATION

National air transport system: *number of registered air carriers:* 1 (2020)
inventory of registered aircraft operated by air carriers: 6

Civil aircraft registration country code prefix: VP-C

Airports
total: 3 (2021)
country comparison to the world: 193

Airports - with paved runways: *total:* 3
1,524 to 2,437 m: 2
914 to 1,523 m: 1 (2021)

Airports - with unpaved runways: *total:* 1
914 to 1,523 m: 1 (2012)

Roadways: *total:* 785 km (2007)
paved: 785 km (2007)
country comparison to the world: 189

Merchant marine: *total:* 160
by type: bulk carrier 32, container ship 1, general cargo 1, oil tanker 23, other 103 (2021)
country comparison to the world: 73

Ports and terminals: *major seaport(s):* Cayman Brac, George Town

MILITARY AND SECURITY

Military and security forces: no regular military forces; Royal Cayman Islands Police Service

Military - note: defense is the responsibility of the UK

TRANSNATIONAL ISSUES

Disputes - international: none

Illicit drugs: major offshore financial center vulnerable to drug trafficking money laundering

CENTRAL AFRICAN REPUBLIC

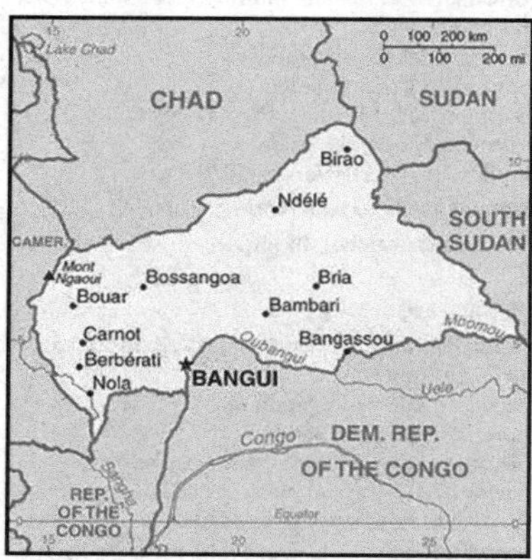

INTRODUCTION

Background: The Central African Republic (CAR) is a perennially weak state that sits at the crossroads of ethnic and linguistic groups in the center of the African continent. Among the last areas of Sub-Saharan Africa to be drawn into the world economy, its introduction into trade networks around the early 1700s fostered significant competition among its population. The local population sought to benefit from the lucrative Atlantic, trans-Saharan, and Indian Ocean trade in enslaved people and ivory. Slave raids aided by the local populations fostered animosity between ethnic groups that remains today. The territory was established as a French colony named Ubangui-Shari in 1903, and France modeled its administration of the colony after the Belgian Congo, subcontracting control of the territory to private companies that collected rubber and ivory. Although France banned the domestic slave trade in CAR in the 1910s, the private companies continued to exploit the population through forced labor. The colony of Ubangi-Shari gained independence from France as the Central African Republic in August 1960, but the death of independence leader Barthelemy BOGANDA six months prior led to an immediate struggle for power.

CAR's political history has since been marred by a series of coups, the first of which brought Jean-Bedel BOKASSA to power in 1966. BOKaSsA's regime was characterized by widespread corruption and an intolerance of opposition, which manifested in the disappearances of many who challenged BOKASSA's rule. In an effort to prolong his mandate, he named himself emperor in 1976 and changed the country's name to the Central African Empire. His regime's economic mismanagement culminated in widespread student protests in early 1979 that were violently suppressed by security forces. BOKASSA, rumored to have participated in the killing of some young students after the protests, fell out of favor with the international community and was overthrown in a French-backed coup in 1979. After BOKASSA's departure, the country's name once again became the Central African Republic.

CAR's fifth coup in March 2013 unseated President Francois BOZIZE after a mainly Muslim rebel coalition named the Seleka seized the capital and forced BOZIZE, who himself had taken power in a coup in 2003, to flee the country. Widespread abuses by the Seleka spurred the formation of mainly Christian self-defense groups that called themselves the anti-Balaka, which have also committed human rights abuses against Muslim populations in retaliation. Since the rise of the self-defense groups, conflict in CAR has become increasingly ethnoreligious-based, although focused on identity as opposed to religious ideology. Elections organized by a transitional government in early 2016 installed independent candidate Faustin-Archange TOUADERA as president; he was reelected in December 2020. A peace agreement signed in February 2019 between the government and the main armed factions has had little effect, and armed groups remain in control of large swaths of the country's territory.

GEOGRAPHY

Location: Central Africa, north of Democratic Republic of the Congo

Geographic coordinates: 7 00 N, 21 00 E

Map references: Africa

Area: *total:* 622,984 sq km
land: 622,984 sq km
water: 0 sq km
country comparison to the world: 47

Area - comparative: slightly smaller than Texas; about four times the size of Georgia

Land boundaries: *total:* 5,920 km
border countries (5): Cameroon 901 km; Chad 1556 km; Democratic Republic of the Congo 1,747 km, Republic of the Congo 487 km; South Sudan 1055 km; Sudan 174 km

Coastline: 0 km (landlocked)

Maritime claims: none (landlocked)

Climate: tropical; hot, dry winters; mild to hot, wet summers

Terrain: vast, flat to rolling plateau; scattered hills in northeast and southwest

Elevation: *highest point:* Mont Ngaoui 1,410 m

lowest point: Oubangui River 335 m
mean elevation: 635 m

Natural resources: diamonds, uranium, timber, gold, oil, hydropower

Land use: *agricultural land:* 8.1% (2018 est.)
arable land: 2.9% (2018 est.)
permanent crops: 0.1% (2018 est.)
permanent pasture: 5.1% (2018 est.)
forest: 36.2% (2018 est.)
other: 55.7% (2018 est.)

Irrigated land: 10 sq km (2012)

Major rivers (by length in km): Ubangi river [s] (shared with Democratic Republic of Congo and Republic of Congo [m]) - 2,270 km
note – [s] after country name indicates river source; [m] after country name indicates river mouth

Major watersheds (area sq km): Atlantic Ocean drainage: Congo (3,730,881 sq km), (Mediterranean Sea) Nile (3,254,853 sq km)

Internal (endorheic basin) drainage: Lake Chad (2,497,738 sq km)

Major aquifers: Congo Basin, Lake Chad Basin

Population distribution: majority of residents live in the western and central areas of the country, especially in and around the capital of Bangui as shown in this population distribution map

Natural hazards: hot, dry, dusty harmattan winds affect northern areas; floods are common

Geography - note: landlocked; almost the precise center of Africa

PEOPLE AND SOCIETY

Population: 5,454,533 (2022 est.)
country comparison to the world: 119

Nationality: *noun:* Central African(s)
adjective: Central African

Ethnic groups: Baya 28.8%, Banda 22.9%, Mandjia 9.9%, Sara 7.9%, M'Baka-Bantu 7.9%, Arab-Fulani (Peul) 6%, Mbum 6%, Ngbanki 5.5%, Zande-Nzakara 3%, other Central African Republic ethnic groups 2%, non-Central African Republic ethnic groups .1% (2003 est.)

Languages: French (official), Sangho (lingua franca and national language), tribal languages

Religions: Christian 89%, Muslim 9%, folk religion 1%, unaffiliated 1% (2020 est.)
note: animistic beliefs and practices strongly influence the Christian majority

Demographic profile: The Central African Republic's (CAR) humanitarian crisis has worsened since the coup of March 2013. CAR's high mortality rate and low life expectancy are attributed to elevated rates of preventable and treatable diseases (including malaria and malnutrition), an inadequate health care system, precarious food security, and armed conflict. Some of the worst mortality rates are in western CAR's diamond mining region, which has been impoverished because of government attempts to control the diamond trade and the fall in industrial diamond prices. To make matters worse, the government and international donors have reduced health funding in recent years. The CAR's weak educational system and low literacy rate have also suffered as a result of the country's ongoing conflict. Schools are closed, qualified teachers are scarce, infrastructure, funding, and supplies are lacking and subject to looting, and many students and teachers have been displaced by violence.

Rampant poverty, human rights violations, unemployment, poor infrastructure, and a lack of security and stability have led to forced displacement internally and externally. Since the political crisis that resulted in CAR's March 2013 coup began in December 2012, approximately 600,000 people have fled to Chad, the Democratic Republic of the Congo, and other neighboring countries, while another estimated 600,000 were displaced internally as of October 2019. The UN has urged countries to refrain from repatriating CAR refugees amid the heightened lawlessness. (2019)

Age structure: *0-14 years:* 39.49% (male 1,188,682/ female 1,176,958)
15-24 years: 19.89% (male 598,567/female 593,075)
25-54 years: 32.95% (male 988,077/female 986,019)
55-64 years: 4.32% (male 123,895/female 134,829)
65 years and over: 3.35% (male 78,017/female 122,736) (2020 est.)

Dependency ratios: *total dependency ratio:* 86.4
youth dependency ratio: 81.1
elderly dependency ratio: 5.2
potential support ratio: 19.2 (2020 est.)

Median age: *total:* 20 years
male: 19.7 years
female: 20.3 years (2020 est.)
country comparison to the world: 194

Population growth rate: 1. 78% (2022 est.)
country comparison to the world: 52

Birth rate: 32.79 births/1,000 population (2022 est.)
country comparison to the world: 23

Death rate: 11. 76 deaths/1,000 population (2022 est.)
country comparison to the world: 16

Net migration rate: -3.22 migrant(s)/1,000 population (2022 est.)
country comparison to the world: 183

Population distribution: majority of residents live in the western and central areas of the country, especially in and around the capital of Bangui as shown in this population distribution map

Urbanization: *urban population:* 43.1% of total population (2022)
rate of urbanization: 3.32% annual rate of change (2020-25 est.)

Major urban areas - population: 933,000 BANGUI (capital) (2022)

Sex ratio: *at birth:* 1.03 male(s)/female
0-14 years: 1.05 male(s)/female
15-24 years: 1.08 male(s)/female
25-54 years: 0.89 male(s)/female
55-64 years: 1.04 male(s)/female
65 years and over: 0.64 male(s)/female
total population: 0.99 male(s)/female (2022 est.)

Maternal mortality ratio: 829 deaths/100,000 live births (2017 est.)
country comparison to the world: 5

Infant mortality rate: *total:* 82.97 deaths/1,000 live births
male: 89.03 deaths/1,000 live births
female: 76.73 deaths/1,000 live births (2022 est.)
country comparison to the world: 3

Life expectancy at birth: *total population:* 55.52 years
male: 54.19 years
female: 56.88 years (2022 est.)
country comparison to the world: 226

Total fertility rate: 4.04 children born/woman (2022 est.)
country comparison to the world: 27

Contraceptive prevalence rate: 17.8% (2019)

Drinking water source: *improved: urban:* 83.9% of population
rural: 47.5% of population
total: 62.9% of population
unimproved: urban: 16.1% of population
rural: 52.5% of population
total: 37.1% of population (2020 est.)

Current health expenditure: 7.8% of GDP (2019)

Physicians density: 0.07 physicians/1,000 population (2018)

Hospital bed density: 1 beds/1,000 population (2011)

Sanitation facility access: *improved: urban:* 53.8% of population
rural: 12.4% of population
total: 29.9% of population
unimproved: urban: 46.2% of population
rural: 87.6% of population
total: 70.1% of population (2020 est.)

HIV/AIDS - adult prevalence rate: 2.9% (2020 est.)
country comparison to the world: 18

Major infectious diseases: degree of risk: very high (2020)
food or waterborne diseases: bacterial and protozoal diarrhea, hepatitis A and E, and typhoid fever
vectorborne diseases: malaria and dengue fever
water contact diseases: schistosomiasis

animal contact diseases: rabies
respiratory diseases: meningococcal meningitis
note: on 21 March 2022, the US Centers for Disease Control and Prevention (CDC) issued a Travel Alert for polio in Africa; the Central African Republic is currently considered a high risk to travelers for circulating vaccine-derived polioviruses (cVDPV); vaccine-derived poliovirus (VDPV) is a strain of the weakened poliovirus that was initially included in oral polio vaccine (OPV) and that has changed over time and behaves more like the wild or naturally occurring virus; this means it can be spread more easily to people who are unvaccinated against polio and who come in contact with the stool or respiratory secretions, such as from a sneeze, of an "infected" person who received oral polio vaccine; the CDC recommends that before any international travel, anyone unvaccinated, incompletely vaccinated, or with an unknown polio vaccination status should complete the routine polio vaccine series; before travel to any high-risk destination, the CDC recommends that adults who previously completed the full, routine polio vaccine series receive a single, lifetime booster dose of polio vaccine

Obesity - adult prevalence rate: 7.5% (2016)
country comparison to the world: 159

Alcohol consumption per capita: *total:* 0.94 liters of pure alcohol (2019 est.)
beer: 0.55 liters of pure alcohol (2019 est.)
wine: 0.04 liters of pure alcohol (2019 est.)
spirits: 0.02 liters of pure alcohol (2019 est.)
other alcohols: 0.33 liters of pure alcohol (2019 est.)
country comparison to the world: 152

Children under the age of 5 years underweight: 20.5% (2019)
country comparison to the world: 19

Child marriage: *women married by age 15:* 25.8%
women married by age 18: 61%
men married by age 18: 17.1% (2019 est.)

Education expenditures: 1.8% of GDP (2019 est.)
country comparison to the world: 182

Literacy: *definition:* age 15 and over can read and write
total population: 37.4%
male: 49.5%
female: 25.8% (2018)

School life expectancy (primary to tertiary education): *total:* 7 years
male: 8 years
female: 6 years (2012)

ENVIRONMENT

Environment - current issues: water pollution; tap water is not potable; poaching and mismanagement have diminished the country's reputation as one of the last great wildlife refuges; desertification; deforestation; soil erosion

Environment - international agreements: *party to:* Biodiversity, Climate Change, Climate Change-Kyoto Protocol, Climate Change-Paris Agreement, Comprehensive Nuclear Test Ban, Desertification, Endangered Species, Hazardous Wastes, Nuclear Test Ban, Ozone Layer Protection, Tropical Timber 2006, Wetlands
signed, but not ratified: Law of the Sea

Air pollutants: *particulate matter emissions:* 49.5 micrograms per cubic meter (2016 est.)
carbon dioxide emissions: 0.3 megatons (2016 est.)
methane emissions: 22.44 megatons (2020 est.)

Climate: tropical; hot, dry winters; mild to hot, wet summers

Land use: *agricultural land:* 8.1% (2018 est.)
arable land: 2.9% (2018 est.)
permanent crops: 0.1% (2018 est.)
permanent pasture: 5.1% (2018 est.)
forest: 36.2% (2018 est.)
other: 55.7% (2018 est.)

Urbanization: *urban population:* 43.1% of total population (2022)
rate of urbanization: 3.32% annual rate of change (2020-25 est.)

Revenue from forest resources: *forest revenues:* 8.99% of GDP (2018 est.)
country comparison to the world: 5

Revenue from coal: *coal revenues:* 0% of GDP (2018 est.)
country comparison to the world: 77

Food insecurity: *exceptional shortfall in aggregate food production/supplies:* due to internal conflict - persisting conflicts and displacements are expected to continue affecting agricultural activities and limit farmers' access to crop growing areas and inputs, with a negative impact on 2022 crop production; according to an analysis issued in April 2022, the number of severely food insecure people in "Crisis" and above were estimated at 2.2 million between April and August 2022, mainly due to high levels of civil insecurity, population displacements and high food prices (2022)

Waste and recycling: municipal solid waste generated annually: 1,105,983 tons (2014 est.)

Major rivers (by length in km): Ubangi river [s] (shared with Democratic Republic of Congo and Republic of Congo [m]) - 2,270 km
note – [s] after country name indicates river source; [m] after country name indicates river mouth

Major watersheds (area sq km): Atlantic Ocean drainage: Congo (3,730,881 sq km), (Mediterranean Sea) Nile (3,254,853 sq km)

Internal (endorheic basin) drainage: Lake Chad (2,497,738 sq km)

Major aquifers: Congo Basin, Lake Chad Basin

Total water withdrawal: *municipal:* 60.1 million cubic meters (2017 est.)
industrial: 12 million cubic meters (2017 est.)
agricultural: 400,000 cubic meters (2017 est.)

Total renewable water resources: 141 billion cubic meters (2017 est.)

GOVERNMENT

Country name: *conventional long form:* Central African Republic
conventional short form: none
local long form: Republique Centrafricaine
local short form: none
former: Ubangi-Shari, Central African Empire
abbreviation: CAR
etymology: self-descriptive name specifying the country's location on the continent; "Africa" is derived from the Roman designation of the area corresponding to present-day Tunisia "Africa terra," which meant "Land of the Afri" (the tribe resident in that area), but which eventually came to mean the entire continent

Government type: presidential republic

Capital: *name:* Bangui
geographic coordinates: 4 22 N, 18 35 E
time difference: UTC+1 (6 hours ahead of Washington, DC, during Standard Time)
etymology: established as a French settlement in 1889 and named after its location on the northern bank of the Ubangi River; the Ubangi itself was named from the native word for the "rapids" located beside the outpost, which marked the end of navigable water north from Brazzaville

Administrative divisions: 14 prefectures (prefectures, singular - prefecture), 2 economic prefectures* (prefectures economiques, singular -prefecture economique), and 1 commune**; Bamingui-Bangoran, Bangui**, Basse-Kotto, Haute-Kotto, Haut-Mbomou, Kemo, Lobaye, Mambere-Kadei, Mbomou, Nana-Grebizi*, Nana-Mambere, Ombella-Mpoko, Ouaka, Ouham, Ouham-Pende, Sangha-Mbaere*, Vakaga

Independence: 13 August 1960 (from France)

National holiday: Republic Day, 1 December (1958)

Constitution: *history:* several previous; latest (interim constitution) approved by the Transitional Council 30 August 2015, adopted by referendum 13-14 December 2015, ratified 27 March 2016
amendments: proposals require support of the government, two thirds of the National Council of Transition, and assent by the "Mediator of the Central African" crisis; passage requires at least three-fourths majority vote by the National Council membership; non-amendable constitutional provisions include those on the secular and republican form of government, fundamental rights and freedoms, amendment procedures, or changes to the authorities of various high-level executive, parliamentary, and judicial officials

Legal system: civil law system based on the French model

International law organization participation: has not submitted an ICJ jurisdiction declaration; accepts ICCt jurisdiction

Citizenship: citizenship by birth: no
citizenship by descent only: least one parent must be a citizen of the Central African Republic
dual citizenship recognized: yes
residency requirement for naturalization: 35 years

Suffrage: 18 years of age; universal

Executive branch: *chief of state:* President Faustin-Archange TOUADERA (since 30 March 2016)
head of government: Prime Minister Felix MOLOUA (since 7 February 2022); note - Prime Minister Henri-Marie DONDRA resigned on 2 February 2022
cabinet: Council of Ministers appointed by the president
elections/appointments: under the 2015 constitution, the president is elected by universal direct suffrage for a period of 5 years (eligible for a second term); election last held 27 December 2020 (next to be held in December 2025); note -Central African Republic held presidential and partial legislative elections on December 27, 2020; voting was disrupted in some areas, so those constituencies held the first round of their legislative elections on March 14, 2021 while some of the constituencies that did vote on December 27, 2020 held runoff elections for their legislators.
election results: 2020/2021: Faustin-Archange TOUADERA reelected president in first round;

percent of vote - Faustin-Archange TOUADERA (independent) 53.9%, Anicet Georges DOLOGUELE (URCA) 21%, other 25.1%
2015: Faustin-Archange TOUADERA elected president in the second round; percent of vote in first round - Anicet-Georges DOLOGUELE (URCA) 23.7%, Faustin-Archange TOUADERA (independent) 19.1%, Desire KOLINGBA (RDC) 12%, Martin ZIGUELE (MLPC) 11.4%, other 33.8%; percent of vote in second round - Faustin-Archange TOUADERA 62.7%, Anicet-Georges DOLOGUELE 37.3%

Legislative branch: description: unicameral National Assembly or Assemblee Nationale (140 seats; members directly elected in single-seat constituencies by absolute majority vote with a second round if needed; members serve 5-year terms)
elections: first round last held on 27 December 2020; note - on election day, voting in many electoral areas was disrupted by armed groups; on 13 February 2021, President TOUADERA announced that a new first round of elections will be held on 27 February for those areas controlled by armed groups and second round on 14 March
election results: December 2015 election: percent of vote by party - NA; seats by party - UNDP 16, URCA 11, RDC 8, MLPC 10, KNK 7, other 28, independent 60; composition as of March 2022 - men 122, women 18, percent of women 12.9%

Judicial branch: *highest court(s):* Supreme Court or Cour Supreme (consists of NA judges); Constitutional Court (consists of 9 judges, at least 3 of whom are women)
judge selection and term of office: Supreme Court judges appointed by the president; Constitutional Court judge appointments - 2 by the president, 1 by the speaker of the National Assembly, 2 elected by their peers, 2 are advocates elected by their peers, and 2 are law professors elected by their peers; judges serve 7-year non-renewable terms
subordinate courts: high courts; magistrates' courts

Political parties and leaders: African Party for Radical Transformation and Integration of States or PATRIE [Crepin MBOLI-GOUMBA]
Central African Democratic Rally or RDC [Desire KOLINGBA]
Movement for the Liberation of the Central African People or MLPC [Martin ZIGUELE]
National Convergence (also known as Kwa Na Kwa or KNK) [Francois BOZIZE]
National Movement of Independents or MOUNI
National Union for Democracy and Progress or UNDP [Michel AMINE]
National Union of Republican Democrats or UNADER
Party for Democratic Governance or PGD
Path of Hope [Karim MECKASSOUA]
Union for Central African Renewal or URCA [Anicet-Georges DOLOGUELE]
United Hearts Movement or MCU [Faustin-Archange TOUADERA]
note: only parties with seats in the Parliament included

International organization participation: ACP, AfDB, AU, BDEAC, CEMAC, EITI (compliant country) (suspended), FAO, FZ, G-77, IAEA, IBRD, ICAO, ICCt, ICRM, IDA, IFAD, IFC, IFRCS, ILO, IMF, Interpol, IOC, IOM, ITSO, ITU, ITUC (NGOs), LCBC, MIGA, NAM, OIC (observer), OIF, OPCW, UN, UNCTAD, UNESCO, UNIDO, UNWTO, UPU, WCO, WHO, WIPO, WMO, WTO

Diplomatic representation in the US: *chief of mission:* Ambassador Martial NDOUBOU (since 17 September 2018)
chancery: 2704 Ontario Road NW, Washington, DC 20009
telephone: [1] (202) 483-7800
FAX: [1] (202) 332-9893
email address and website:
pc@usrcaembassy.org
https://www.usrcaembassy.org/

Diplomatic representation from the US: *chief of mission:* Ambassador Patricia A. MAHONEY (since 8 April 2022)
embassy: Avenue David Dacko, Bangui
mailing address: 2060 Bangui Place, Washington DC 20521-2060
telephone: [236] 2161-0200
FAX: [236] 2161-4494
email address and website: https://cf.usembassy.gov/

Flag description: four equal horizontal bands of blue (top), white, green, and yellow with a vertical red band in center; a yellow five-pointed star to the hoist side of the blue band; banner combines the Pan-African and French flag colors; red symbolizes the blood spilled in the struggle for independence, blue represents the sky and freedom, white peace and dignity, green hope and faith, and yellow tolerance; the star represents aspiration towards a vibrant future

National symbol(s): elephant; national colors: blue, white, green, yellow, red

National anthem: *name:* "La Renaissance" (The Renaissance)
lyrics/music: Barthelemy BOGANDA/Herbert PEPPER
note: adopted 1960; Barthelemy BOGANDA wrote the anthem's lyrics and was the first prime minister of the autonomous French territory

National heritage: *total World Heritage Sites:* 2 (natural)
selected World Heritage Site locales: Manovo-Gounda St. Floris National Park; Sangha Trinational Forest

ECONOMY

Economic overview: Subsistence agriculture, together with forestry and mining, remains the backbone of the economy of the Central African Republic (CAR), with about 60% of the population living in outlying areas. The agricultural sector generates more than half of estimated GDP, although statistics are unreliable in the conflict-prone country. Timber and diamonds account for most export earnings, followed by cotton. Important constraints to economic development include the CAR's landlocked geography, poor transportation system, largely unskilled work force, and legacy of misdirected macroeconomic policies. Factional fighting between the government and its opponents remains a drag on economic revitalization. Distribution of income is highly unequal and grants from the international community can only partially meet humanitarian needs. CAR shares a common currency with the Central African Monetary Union. The currency is pegged to the Euro.

Since 2009, the IMF has worked closely with the government to institute reforms that have resulted in some improvement in budget transparency, but other problems remain. The government's additional spending in the run-up to the 2011 election worsened CAR's fiscal situation. In 2012, the World Bank approved $125 million in funding for transport infrastructure and regional trade, focused on the route between CAR's capital and the port of Douala in Cameroon. In July 2016, the IMF approved a three-year extended credit facility valued at $116 million; in mid-2017, the IMF completed a review of CAR's fiscal performance and broadly approved of the government's management, although issues with revenue collection, weak government capacity, and transparency remain. The World Bank in late 2016 approved a $20 million grant to restore basic fiscal management, improve transparency, and assist with economic recovery.

Participation in the Kimberley Process, a commitment to remove conflict diamonds from the global supply chain, led to a partially lifted the ban on diamond exports from CAR in 2015, but persistent insecurity is likely to constrain real GDP growth.

Real GDP (purchasing power parity): $4.483 billion (2019 est.)
$4.354 billion (2018 est.)
$4.195 billion (2017 est.)
note: data are in 2017 dollars
country comparison to the world: 180

Real GDP growth rate: 4.3% (2017 est.)
4.5% (2016 est.)
4.8% (2015 est.)
country comparison to the world: 66

Real GDP per capita: $900 (2020 est.)
$900 (2019 est.)
$900 (2018 est.)
note: data are in 2017 dollars
country comparison to the world: 227

GDP (official exchange rate): $1.937 billion (2017 est.)

Inflation rate (consumer prices): 2.7% (2019 est.)
1.6% (2018 est.)
4.2% (2017 est.)
country comparison to the world: 134

GDP - composition, by sector of origin: *agriculture:* 43.2% (2017 est.)
industry: 16% (2017 est.)
services: 40.8% (2017 est.)

GDP - composition, by end use: *household consumption:* 95.3% (2017 est.)
government consumption: 8.5% (2017 est.)
investment in fixed capital: 13.7% (2017 est.)
investment in inventories: 0% (2017 est.)
exports of goods and services: 12% (2017 est.)
imports of goods and services: -29.5% (2017 est.)

Agricultural products: cassava, yams, groundnuts, taro, bananas, sugar cane, beef, maize, plantains, milk

Industries: gold and diamond mining, logging, brewing, sugar refining

Industrial production growth rate: 3.9% (2017 est.)
country comparison to the world: 77

Labor force: 2.242 million (2017 est.)
country comparison to the world: 119

Unemployment rate: 6.9% (2017 est.)
country comparison to the world: 110

Population below poverty line: 62% (2008 est.)

Gini Index coefficient - distribution of family income

43.6 (2003 est.): 61.3 (1993)

country comparison to the world: 38

Household income or consumption by percentage share: *lowest 10%:* 2.1%
highest 10%: 33% (2003)

Budget: revenues: 282.9 million (2017 est.)
expenditures: 300.1 million (2017 est.)

Budget surplus (+) or deficit (-): -0.9% (of GDP) (2017 est.)
country comparison to the world: 71

Public debt: 52.9% of GDP (2017 est.)

56% of GDP (2016 est.): *country comparison to the world:* 93

Taxes and other revenues: 14.6% (of GDP) (2017 est.)
country comparison to the world: 198

Fiscal year: calendar year

Current account balance: -$163 million (2017 est.)
-$97 million (2016 est.)
country comparison to the world: 95

Exports: $113.7 million (2017 est.)
$101.5 million (2016 est.)
note: Data are in current year dollars and do not include illicit exports or re-exports.
country comparison to the world: 208

Exports - partners: China 41%, United Arab Emirates 19%, France 7% (2019)

Exports - commodities: lumber, gold, diamonds, sea vessels, cocoa paste (2019)

Imports: $393.1 million (2017 est.)
$342.2 million (2016 est.)
country comparison to the world: 207

Imports - partners: India 18%, France 12%, United States 11%, China 9%, Netherlands 7%, Belgium 7%, Malta 6% (2019)

Imports - commodities: refined petroleum, packaged medicines, natural gas, broadcasting equipment, second-hand clothing (2019)

Reserves of foreign exchange and gold: $304.3 million (31 December 2017 est.)
$252.5 million (31 December 2016 est.)
country comparison to the world: 168

Debt - external: $779.9 million (31 December 2017 est.)
$691.5 million (31 December 2016 est.)
country comparison to the world: 171

Exchange rates: Cooperation Financiere en Afrique Centrale francs (XAF) per US dollar -
605.3 (2017 est.)
593.01 (2016 est.)
593.01 (2015 est.)
591.45 (2014 est.)
494.42 (2013 est.)

ENERGY

Electricity access: *electrification - total population:* 3% (2019)
electrification - urban areas: 7% (2019)
electrification - rural areas: 0.4% (2019)

Electricity: *installed generating capacity:* 38,000 kW (2020 est.)
consumption: 140.44 million kWh (2019 est.)
exports: 0 kWh (2019 est.)
imports: 0 kWh (2019 est.)
transmission/distribution losses: 10.5 million kWh (2019 est.)

Electricity generation sources: *fossil fuels:* 0.7% of total installed capacity (2020 est.)
hydroelectricity: 99.3% of total installed capacity (2020 est.)

Coal: proven reserves: 3 million metric tons (2019 est.)

Petroleum: *total petroleum production:* 0 bbl/day (2021 est.)
refined petroleum consumption: 2,000 bbl/day (2019 est.)

Refined petroleum products - imports: 2,799 bbl/day (2015 est.)
country comparison to the world: 185

Carbon dioxide emissions: 285,000 metric tonnes of CO2 (2019 est.)
from petroleum and other liquids: 285,000 metric tonnes of CO2 (2019 est.)
country comparison to the world: 198

Energy consumption per capita: 1.121 million Btu/person (2019 est.)
country comparison to the world: 193

COMMUNICATIONS

Telephones - fixed lines: *total subscriptions:* 2,000 (2020 est.)
subscriptions per 100 inhabitants: (2020 est.) less than 1
country comparison to the world: 214

Telephones - mobile cellular: *total subscriptions:* 1.831 million (2020 est.)
subscriptions per 100 inhabitants: 38 (2020 est.)
country comparison to the world: 153

Telecommunication systems: *general assessment:* given the poor fixed-line infrastructure in most countries across Africa, voice and data services across the region are greatly dependent on mobile networks; in the majority of markets, including those with better developed fixed infrastructure such as South Africa, Nigeria, and Kenya, up to 98% of all voice and data connections are via mobile networks; during the last two to three years, national governments and telecom regulators have striven to improve fixed infrastructure with the wider aim of developing economic growth based on digital services and connectivity; this work is principally focused on delivering fiber-based connectivity; since the amount of copper infrastructure (DSL or HFC) used for broadband is so negligible, governments and private firms, including telcos are investing in fiber rather than in older technologies; while supporting broadband to premises, health centers, and government buildings, the new fiber infrastructure is mainly being deployed to provide mobile platforms and to support the rapid growth in data traffic (2022)
domestic: very limited telephone service with less than 1 fixed-line connection per 100 persons; with the presence of multiple providers mobile-cellular service has reached nearly 38 per 100 mobile-cellular subscribers; cellular usage is increasing from a low base; most fixed-line and mobile-cellular telephone services are concentrated in Bangui (2020)
international: country code - 236; satellite earth station - 1 Intelsat (Atlantic Ocean)

Broadcast media: government-owned network, Radiodiffusion Television Centrafricaine, provides limited domestic TV broadcasting; state-owned radio network is supplemented by a small number of privately owned broadcast stations as well as a few community radio stations; transmissions of at least 2 international broadcasters are available (2017)

Internet country code: .cf

Internet users: *total:* 482,976 (2020 est.)
percent of population: 10% (2020 est.)
country comparison to the world: 158

Broadband - fixed subscriptions: *total:* 499 (2019 est.) Data available for 2019 only.
subscriptions per 100 inhabitants: 0.01 (2019 est.)
country comparison to the world: 210

TRANSPORTATION

National air transport system: *number of registered air carriers:* 2 (2020)
inventory of registered aircraft operated by air carriers: 2
annual passenger traffic on registered air carriers: 46,364 (2015)
annual freight traffic on registered air carriers: 0 (2015) mt-km

Civil aircraft registration country code prefix: TL

Airports: *total:* 39 (2021)
country comparison to the world: 106

Airports - with paved runways: *total:* 1
2,438 to 3,047 m: 1 (2021)

Airports - with unpaved runways: *total:* 37
2,438 to 3,047 m: 1
1,524 to 2,437 m: 11
914 to 1,523 m: 19
under 914 m: 6 (2021)

Roadways: *total:* 24,000 km (2018)
paved: 700 km (2018)
unpaved: 23,300 km (2018)
country comparison to the world: 105

Waterways: 2,800 km (2011) (the primary navigable river is the Ubangi, which joins the River Congo; it was the traditional route for the export of products because it connected with the Congo-Ocean railway at Brazzaville; because of the warfare on both sides of the River Congo from 1997, importers and exporters preferred routes through Cameroon)
country comparison to the world: 36

Ports and terminals: *river port(s):* Bangui (Oubangui)

Nola (Sangha): MILITARY AND SECURITY

Military and security forces: Central African Armed Forces (Forces Armees Centrafricaines, FACA): Army (includes an air squadron, Escadrille Centrafricaine); Ministry of Interior: National Gendarmerie (Gendarmerie Nationale), National Police (2022)
note: in 2019-2021, the CAR created three Mixed Special Security units (Unités Spéciales Mixtes de Sécurité or USMS), regionally based battalion-sized units comprised of about 40% government and 60% rebel soldiers created to provide security along transportation corridors and at mining sites; the units are intended to be transitional in nature with a scheduled deployment time of two years

Military expenditures: 1.8% of GDP (2021 est.)
1.8% of GDP (2020 est.)
1.7% of GDP (2019 est.) (approximately $50 million)
1.4% of GDP (2018 est.) (approximately $40 million)
1.4% of GDP (2017 est.) (approximately $40 million)
country comparison to the world: 69

Military and security service personnel strengths: information varies; approximately 8,000 FACA troops; up to 2,000 Gendarmerie; approximately 2,000 Mixed Special Security Units (2022)

Military equipment inventories and acquisitions: the FACA is lightly and poorly armed with mostly outdated weapons; since 2010, it has received small amounts of second-hand equipment from China, Russia, and Ukraine (2021)
note: since 2013, CAR has been under a UNSC arms embargo; the embargo bans all supplies of arms and related materiel to the country except to the CAR security forces if approved in advance by the relevant UN Sanctions Committee

Military service age and obligation: 18 years of age for military service; no conscription (2021)

Military - note: the 2013 coup resulted in the institutional collapse of the FACA; its forces were overwhelmed and forced to flee to neighboring countries; it has been estimated that only 10% of the FACA returned after the coup, and it has struggled to rebuild in the years of instability since; the European Union, France, Russia, the UN, and the US have provided various levels of security assistance in 2018, the UN Security Council approved Russian security assistance for the CAR to help train and advise FACA personnel, as well as transport them to operational areas, provide logistical support, and assist with medical evacuation; Russia sent private military contractors, and as of early 2022, as many as 2,000 were providing assistance to the FACA, as well as performing other security roles such as guarding mines and government officials; some Russian contractors and the CAR forces they supported have been accused of carrying out indiscriminate killings, using excessive force against civilians, and looting the UN Multidimensional Integrated Stabilization Mission in the Central African Republic (MINUSCA) has operated in the country since 2014; its peacekeeping mission includes providing security, protecting civilians, facilitating humanitarian assistance, disarming and demobilizing armed groups, and supporting the country's fragile transitional government; in November 2019, the UN Security Council extended the mandate of the MINUSCA peacekeeping mission another year; as of mid-2022, MINUSCA had nearly 15,000 total personnel

the European Union Training Mission in the Central African Republic (EUTM-RCA) has operated in the country since 2016, providing advice, training, and educational programs to the country's security forces (2022)

TRANSNATIONAL ISSUES

Disputes - international: Central African Republic-South Sudan: periodic violent skirmishes persist among related pastoral populations along the border with South Sudan over water and grazing rights

Central African Republic-Sudan: periodic violent skirmishes persist among related pastoral populations along the border with Sudan over water and grazing rights

Refugees and internally displaced persons: *refugees (country of origin):* 6,351 (Democratic Republic of Congo) (2022)

IDPs: 484,335 (clashes between army and rebel groups since 2005; tensions between ethnic groups) (2022)

CHAD

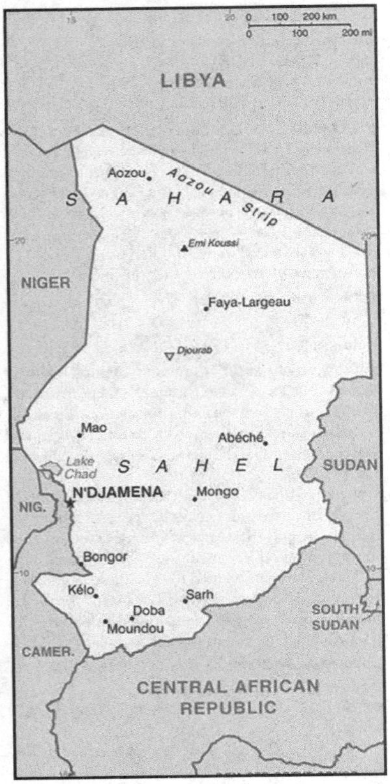

INTRODUCTION

Background: Chad emerged from a collection of powerful states that controlled the Sahelian belt starting around the 9th century. These states focused on controlling trans-Saharan trade routes and profited mostly from the slave trade. The Kanem-Bornu Empire, centered around the Lake Chad Basin, existed between the 9th and 19th centuries, and during its peak, the empire controlled territory stretching from southern Chad to southern Libya and included portions of modern-day Algeria, Cameroon, Nigeria, Niger, and Sudan. The Sudanese warlord Rabih AZ-ZUBAYR used an army comprised largely of slaves to conquer the Kanem-Bornu Empire in the late 19th century. In southeastern Chad, the Bagirmi and Ouaddai (Wadai) kingdoms emerged in the 15th and 16th centuries and lasted until the arrival of the French in the 19th and 20th centuries. France began moving into the region in the late 1880s and defeated the Bagirmi kingdom in 1897, Rabih AZ-ZUBAYR in 1900, and the Ouddai kingdom in 1909. In the arid regions of northern Chad and southern Libya, an Islamic order called the Sanusiyya (Sanusi) relied heavily on the trans-Saharan slave trade and had upwards of 3 million followers by the 1880s. The French arrived in the region in the early 1900s and defeated the Sanusiyya in 1910 after years of intermittent war. By 1910, France had incorporated the northern arid region, the Lake Chad Basin, and southeastern Chad into French Equatorial Africa.

Chad achieved its independence in 1960 and saw three decades of instability, oppressive rule, civil war, and a Libyan invasion. With the help of the French military and several African countries, Chadian leaders expelled Libyan forces during the 1987 "Toyota War," so named for the use of Toyota pickup trucks as fighting vehicles. In 1990, Chadian general Idriss DEBY led a rebellion against President Hissene HABRE. Under DEBY, Chad drafted and approved a constitution and held elections in 1996. DEBY led the country until April 2021 when he was killed during a rebel incursion. Shortly after his death, a group of military officials - led by former President DEBY's son, Mahamat Idriss DEBY - took control of the government. The military officials dismissed the National Assembly, suspended the Constitution, and formed a Transitional Military Council while pledging to hold democratic elections in October 2022.

Chad faces widespread poverty, an economy severely weakened by low international oil prices, and rebel and terrorist-led insurgencies in the Lake Chad Basin. Additionally, northern Chad has seen several waves of rebellions since 1998. In late 2015, the government imposed a state of emergency in the Lake Chad Basin following multiple attacks by the terrorist group Boko Haram, now known as ISIS-West Africa. In mid-2015, Boko Haram conducted bombings in N'Djamena. In late 2019, the Chadian government also declared a state of emergency in the Sila and Ouaddai regions bordering Sudan and in the Tibesti region bordering Niger where rival ethnic groups are still fighting. The army has suffered heavy losses to Islamic terror groups in the Lake Chad Basin. In March 2020, Islamic militants attacked a Chadian military camp in the Lake Chad Basin and killed nearly 100 soldiers; it was the deadliest attack in the history of the Chadian military.

GEOGRAPHY

Location: Central Africa, south of Libya

Geographic coordinates: 15 00 N, 19 00 E

Map references: Africa

Area: *total:* 1.284 million sq km
land: 1,259,200 sq km
water: 24,800 sq km
country comparison to the world: 22

Area - comparative: almost nine times the size of New York state; slightly more than three times the size of California

Land boundaries: *total:* 6,406 km
border countries (6): Cameroon 1,116 km; Central African Republic 1,556 km; Libya 1,050 km; Niger 1,196 km; Nigeria 85 km; Sudan 1,403 km

Coastline: 0 km (landlocked)

Maritime claims: none (landlocked)

Climate: tropical in south, desert in north

Terrain: broad, arid plains in center, desert in north, mountains in northwest, lowlands in south

Elevation: *highest point:* Emi Koussi 3,445 m
lowest point: Djourab 160 m
mean elevation: 543 m

Natural resources: petroleum, uranium, natron, kaolin, fish (Lake Chad), gold, limestone, sand and gravel, salt

Land use: *agricultural land:* 39.6% (2018 est.)
arable land: 3.9% (2018 est.)
permanent crops: 0% (2018 est.)
permanent pasture: 35.7% (2018 est.)
forest: 9.1% (2018 est.)
other: 51.3% (2018 est.)

Irrigated land: 300 sq km (2012)

Major lakes (area sq km): fresh water lake(s): Lake Chad (endorheic lake shared with Niger, Nigeria, and Cameroon) - 10,360-25,900 sq km note - area varies by season and year to year

Major watersheds (area sq km): Atlantic Ocean drainage: Niger (2,261,741 sq km)

Internal (endorheic basin) drainage: Lake Chad (2,497,738 sq km)

Major aquifers: Lake Chad Basin, Nubian Aquifer System

Population distribution: the population is unevenly distributed due to contrasts in climate and physical geography; the highest density is found in the southwest, particularly around Lake Chad and points south; the dry Saharan zone to the north is the least densely populated as shown in this population distribution map

Natural hazards: hot, dry, dusty harmattan winds occur in north; periodic droughts; locust plagues

Geography - note: *note 1:* Chad is the largest of Africa's 16 landlocked countries
note 2: not long ago - geologically speaking - what is today the Sahara was green savannah teeming with wildlife; during the African Humid Period, roughly 11,000 to 5,000 years ago, a vibrant animal community, including elephants, giraffes, hippos, and antelope lived there; the last remnant of the "Green Sahara" exists in the Lakes of Ounianga (oo-nee-ahn-ga) in northern Chad, a series of 18 interconnected freshwater, saline, and hypersaline lakes now protected as a World Heritage site
note 3: Lake Chad, the most significant water body in the Sahel, is a remnant of a former inland sea, paleolake Mega-Chad; at its greatest extent, sometime before 5000 B.C., Lake Mega-Chad was the largest of four Saharan paleolakes that existed during the African Humid Period; it covered an area of about 400,000 sq km (150,000 sq mi), roughly the size of today's Caspian Sea

PEOPLE AND SOCIETY

Population: 17,963,211 (2022 est.)
country comparison to the world: 67

Nationality: *noun:* Chadian(s)
adjective: Chadian

Ethnic groups: Sara (Ngambaye/Sara/Madjingaye/Mbaye) 30.5%, Kanembu/Bornu/Buduma 9.8%, Arab 9.7%, Wadai/Maba /Masalit/Mimi 7%, Gorane 5.8%, Masa/Musseye/Musgum 4.9%, Bulala/Medogo/Kuka 3.7%, Marba/Lele/Mesme 3.5%, Mundang 2.7%, Bidiyo/Migaama/Kenga/Dangleat 2.5%, Dadjo/Kibet/Muro 2.4%, Tupuri/Kera 2%, Gabri/Kabalaye /Nanchere/Somrai 2%, Fulani/Fulbe/Bodore 1.8%, Karo/Zime/Peve 1.3%, Baguirmi/Barma 1.2%, Zaghawa/Bideyat/Kobe 1.1%, Tama/Assongori/Mararit 1.1%, Mesmedje/Massalat/Kadjakse 0.8%, other Chadian ethnicities 3.4%, Chadians of foreign ethnicities 0.9%, foreign nationals 0.3%, unspecified 1.7% (2014-15 est.)

Languages: French (official), Arabic (official), Sara (in south), more than 120 different languages and dialects
major-language sample(s): The World Factbook, une source indispensable d'informations de base. (French)
كتاب حقائق العالم، المصدر الذي لا يمكن الاستغناء عنه للمعلومات الأساسية
(Arabic)

RELIGIONS

Muslim 52.1%, Protestant 23.9%, Roman Catholic 20%, animist 0.3%, other Christian 0.2%, none 2.8%, unspecified 0.7% (2014-15 est.)

Demographic profile: Despite the start of oil production in 2003, 40% of Chad's population lives below the poverty line. The population will continue to grow rapidly because of the country's very high fertility rate and large youth cohort – more than 65% of the populace is under the age of 25 – although the mortality rate is high and life expectancy is low. Chad has the world's third highest maternal mortality rate. Among the primary risk factors are poverty, anemia, rural habitation, high fertility, poor education, and a lack of access to family planning and obstetric care. Impoverished, uneducated adolescents living in rural areas are most affected. To improve women's reproductive health and reduce fertility, Chad will need to increase women's educational attainment, job participation, and knowledge of and access to family planning. Only about a quarter of women are literate, less than 5% use contraceptives, and more than 40% undergo genital cutting.

As of October 2017, more than 320,000 refugees from Sudan and more than 75,000 from the Central African Republic strain Chad's limited resources and create tensions in host communities. Thousands of new refugees fled to Chad in 2013 to escape worsening violence in the Darfur region of Sudan. The large refugee populations are hesitant to return to their home countries because of continued instability. Chad was relatively stable in 2012 in comparison to other states in the region, but past fighting between government forces and opposition groups and inter-communal violence have left nearly 60,000 of its citizens displaced in the eastern part of the country.

Age structure: *0-14 years:* 47.43% (male 4,050,505/female 3,954,413)
15-24 years: 19.77% (male 1,676,495/female 1,660,417)
25-54 years: 27.14% (male 2,208,181/female 2,371,490)
55-64 years: 3.24% (male 239,634/female 306,477)
65 years and over: 2.43% (male 176,658/female 233,087) (2020 est.)

Dependency ratios: *total dependency ratio:* 96
youth dependency ratio: 91.1
elderly dependency ratio: 4.9
potential support ratio: 20.4 (2020 est.)

Median age: *total:* 16.1 years
male: 15.6 years
female: 16.5 years (2020 est.)
country comparison to the world: 223

Population growth rate: 3.09% (2022 est.)
country comparison to the world: 10

Birth rate: 40.45 births/1,000 population (2022 est.)
country comparison to the world: 6

Death rate: 9.45 deaths/1,000 population (2022 est.)
country comparison to the world: 49

Net migration rate: -0.13 migrant(s)/1,000 population (2022 est.)
country comparison to the world: 105

Population distribution: the population is unevenly distributed due to contrasts in climate and physical geography; the highest density is found in the southwest, particularly around Lake Chad and points south; the dry Saharan zone to the north is the least densely populated as shown in this population distribution map

Urbanization: *urban population:* 24.1% of total population (2022)
rate of urbanization: 4.1% annual rate of change (2020-25 est.)

Major urban areas - population: 1.533 million N'DJAMENA (capital) (2022)

Sex ratio: *at birth:* 1.04 male(s)/female
0-14 years: 1.02 male(s)/female
15-24 years: 1.01 male(s)/female
25-54 years: 0.92 male(s)/female
55-64 years: 0.77 male(s)/female
65 years and over: 0.69 male(s)/female
total population: 0.98 male(s)/female (2022 est.)

Mother's mean age at first birth: 18.1 years (2014/15 est.)
note: data represents median age at first birth among women 20-49

Maternal mortality ratio: 1,140 deaths/100,000 live births (2017 est.)
country comparison to the world: 2

Infant mortality rate: *total:* 65.48 deaths/1,000 live births
male: 71.21 deaths/1,000 live births
female: 59.52 deaths/1,000 live births (2022 est.)
country comparison to the world: 7

Life expectancy at birth: *total population:* 59.15 years
male: 57.32 years
female: 61.06 years (2022 est.)
country comparison to the world: 222

Total fertility rate: 5.46 children born/woman (2022 est.)
country comparison to the world: 5

Contraceptive prevalence rate: 8.1% (2019)

Drinking water source: *improved: urban:* 90.2% of population
rural: 51.9% of population
total: 60.9% of population
unimproved: urban: 9.8% of population
rural: 48.1% of population
total: 39.1% of population (2020 est.)

Current health expenditure: 4.4% of GDP (2019)

Physicians density: 0.06 physicians/1,000 population (2020)

Sanitation facility access: *improved: urban:* 57.5% of population
rural: 4.9% of population
total: 17.3% of population
unimproved: urban: 42.5% of population
rural: 95.1% of population
total: 82.7% of population (2020 est.)

HIV/AIDS - adult prevalence rate: 1.1% (2020 est.)
country comparison to the world: 39

Major infectious diseases: *degree of risk:* very high (2020)
food or waterborne diseases: bacterial and protozoal diarrhea, hepatitis A and E, and typhoid fever
vectorborne diseases: malaria and dengue fever
water contact diseases: schistosomiasis
animal contact diseases: rabies
respiratory diseases: meningococcal meningitis
note: on 21 March 2022, the US Centers for Disease Control and Prevention (CDC) issued a Travel Alert for polio in Africa; Chad is currently considered a high risk to travelers for circulating vaccine-derived polioviruses (cVDPV); vaccine-derived poliovirus (VDPV) is a strain of the weakened poliovirus that was initially included in oral polio vaccine (OPV) and that has changed over time and behaves more like the wild or naturally occurring virus; this means it can be spread more easily to people who are unvaccinated against polio and who come in contact with the stool or respiratory secretions, such as from a sneeze, of an "infected" person who received oral polio vaccine; the CDC recommends that before any international travel, anyone unvaccinated, incompletely vaccinated, or with an unknown polio vaccination status should complete the routine polio vaccine series; before travel to any high-risk destination, the CDC recommends that adults who previously completed the full, routine polio vaccine series receive a single, lifetime booster dose of polio vaccine

Obesity - adult prevalence rate: 6.1% (2016)
country comparison to the world: 170

Alcohol consumption per capita: *total:* 0.55 liters of pure alcohol (2019 est.)
beer: 0.37 liters of pure alcohol (2019 est.)
wine: 0.01 liters of pure alcohol (2019 est.)
spirits: 0.01 liters of pure alcohol (2019 est.)
other alcohols: 0.16 liters of pure alcohol (2019 est.)
country comparison to the world: 162

Tobacco use: *total:* 8.3% (2020 est.)
male: 13.8% (2020 est.)
female: 2.7% (2020 est.)
country comparison to the world: 146

Children under the age of 5 years underweight: 29.2% (2019)
country comparison to the world: 7

Child marriage: *women married by age 15:* 24.2%
women married by age 18: 60.6%
men married by age 18: 8.1% (2019 est.)

Education expenditures: 2.4% of GDP (2019 est.)
country comparison to the world: 171

Literacy: *definition:* age 15 and over can read and write French or Arabic
total population: 22.3%
male: 31.3%
female: 14% (2016)

School life expectancy (primary to tertiary education): *total:* 7 years
male: 9 years
female: 6 years (2015)

Unemployment, youth ages 15-24: *total:* 1.5%
male: 2.4%
female: 0.7% (2018)

ENVIRONMENT

Environment - current issues: inadequate supplies of potable water; improper waste disposal in rural areas and poor farming practices contribute to soil and water pollution; desertification

Environment - international agreements: *party to:* Biodiversity, Climate Change, Climate Change-Kyoto Protocol, Climate Change-Paris Agreement, Comprehensive Nuclear Test Ban, Desertification, Endangered Species, Hazardous Wastes, Law of the Sea, Nuclear Test Ban, Ozone Layer Protection, Wetlands
signed, but not ratified: Marine Dumping-London Convention

Air pollutants: *particulate matter emissions:* 53.01 micrograms per cubic meter (2016 est.)
carbon dioxide emissions: 1.02 megatons (2016 est.)
methane emissions: 30.69 megatons (2020 est.)

Climate: tropical in south, desert in north

Land use: *agricultural land:* 39.6% (2018 est.)
arable land: 3.9% (2018 est.)
permanent crops: 0% (2018 est.)
permanent pasture: 35.7% (2018 est.)
forest: 9.1% (2018 est.)
other: 51.3% (2018 est.)

Urbanization: *urban population:* 24.1% of total population (2022)
rate of urbanization: 4.1% annual rate of change (2020-25 est.)

Revenue from forest resources: *forest revenues:* 3.81% of GDP (2018 est.)
country comparison to the world: 19

Revenue from coal: *coal revenues:* 0% of GDP (2018 est.)
country comparison to the world: 78

Food insecurity: *widespread lack of access:* due to civil insecurity and shortfall in cereal production - according to the latest analysis, about 2.1 million people are projected to be in "Crisis" and above, between June and August 2022 due to persisting insecurity in Lac and Tibesti regions that disrupted livelihood activities and caused population displacements, as well as a below-average cereal production in 2021 (2022)

Waste and recycling: *municipal solid waste generated annually:* 1,358,851 tons (2010 est.)

Major lakes (area sq km): *fresh water lake(s):* Lake Chad (endorheic lake shared with Niger, Nigeria, and Cameroon) - 10,360-25,900 sq km note - area varies by season and year to year

Major watersheds (area sq km): Atlantic Ocean drainage: Niger (2,261,741 sq km)

Internal (endorheic basin) drainage: Lake Chad (2,497,738 sq km)

Major aquifers: Lake Chad Basin, Nubian Aquifer System

Total water withdrawal: *municipal:* 103.7 million cubic meters (2017 est.)
industrial: 103.7 million cubic meters (2017 est.)
agricultural: 672.2 million cubic meters (2017 est.)

Total renewable water resources: 45.7 billion cubic meters (2017 est.)

GOVERNMENT

Country name: conventional long form: Republic of Chad
conventional short form: Chad
local long form: Republique du Tchad/Jumhuriyat Tshad
local short form: Tchad/Tshad
etymology: named for Lake Chad, which lies along the country's western border; the word "tsade" means "large body of water" or "lake" in several local native languages
note: the only country whose name is composed of a single syllable with a single vowel

Government type: presidential republic

Capital: *name:* N'Djamena
geographic coordinates: 12 06 N, 15 02 E
time difference: UTC+1 (6 hours ahead of Washington, DC, during Standard Time)
etymology: name taken from the Arab name of a nearby village, Nijamina, meaning "place of rest"

Administrative divisions: 23 provinces (provinces, singular - province); Barh-El-Gazel, Batha, Borkou, Chari-Baguirmi, Ennedi-Est, Ennedi-Ouest, Guera, Hadjer-Lamis, Kanem, Lac, Logone Occidental, Logone Oriental, Mandoul, Mayo-Kebbi-Est, Mayo-Kebbi-Ouest, Moyen-Chari, N'Djamena, Ouaddai, Salamat, Sila, Tandjile, Tibesti, Wadi-Fira

Independence: 11 August 1960 (from France)

National holiday: Independence Day, 11 August (1960)

Constitution: *history:* several previous; latest approved 30 April 2018 by the National Assembly, entered into force 4 May 2018; suspended 21 April 2021 and remained so through April 2022
amendments: proposed as a revision by the president of the republic after a Council of Ministers (cabinet) decision or by the National Assembly; approval for consideration of a revision requires at least three-fifths majority vote by the Assembly; passage requires approval by referendum or at least two-thirds majority vote by the Assembly

Legal system: mixed legal system of civil and customary law

International law organization participation: has not submitted an ICJ jurisdiction declaration; accepts ICCt jurisdiction

Citizenship: *citizenship by birth:* no
citizenship by descent only: both parents must be citizens of Chad
dual citizenship recognized: Chadian law does not address dual citizenship
residency requirement for naturalization: 15 years

Suffrage: 18 years of age; universal

Executive branch: *chief of state:* Interim President Mahamat Idriss DEBY (since 20 April 2021); note - on 20 April 2021, newly reelected President Idriss DEBY Itno, Lt. Gen. died of injuries he sustained following clashes between government forces he was commanding and insurgents in the northern part of the country; following his death, Mahamat Idriss DEBY took control of the country and dismissed the Chadian parliament, establishing a Transitional Military Council and promising elections within eighteen months
head of government: Interim Prime Minister Albert Pahimi PADACKE (since 26 April 2021); note - PADACKE was appointed interim prime minister by the Transitional Military Council led by Mahamat Idriss DEBY
cabinet: Council of Ministers
elections/appointments: president directly elected by absolute majority popular vote in 2 rounds if needed for a 5-year term (no term limits); election last held on 11 April 2021; note - on 20 April 2021, military officials suspended the Constitution and formed a Transitional Military Council, pledging to hold democratic elections in October 2022

election results: 2021: Lt. Gen. Idriss DEBY Itno reelected; percent of vote - Lt. Gen. Idriss DEBY (MPS) 79.3%, Pahimi PADACKET Albert (RNDT) 10.3%, Lydie BEASSEMDA (Party for Democracy and Independence) 3.2%, other 7.2%
2016: Lt. Gen. Idriss DEBY Itno reelected president in first round; percent of vote - Lt. Gen. Idriss DEBY (MPS) 61.6%, Saleh KEBZABO (UNDR) 12.8%, Laokein Kourayo MEDAR (CTPD) 10.7%, Djimrangar DADNADJI (CAP-SUR) 5.1%, other 9.8%

Legislative branch: *description:* formerly a unicameral National Assembly or Assemblée Nationale (188 seats; 163 directly elected in multiseat constituencies by proportional representation vote and 25 directly elected in single-seat constituencies by absolute majority vote with a second round if needed; members serve 4-year terms); note - on 5 October 2021, Interim President Mahamat Idriss DEBY installed 93 members of an interim parliament, called the National Transitional Council (NTC), replacing the National Assembly which was disbanded after he took control of the country on 20 April 2021; according to DEBY, the NTC will act as a national assembly of transition until the country's next elections take place
elections: members of the so called "National Transitional Council" were installed by Interim President DEBY on 5 October 2021 (next parliamentary elections to be held September 2022)
election results: percent of vote by party - NA; seats by party - NA; composition - men 64, women 29, percent of women 31.2%
note: the National Assembly mandate was extended to 2020, reportedly due to a lack of funding for the scheduled 2015 election; the MPS has held a majority in the NA since 1997

Judicial branch: *highest court(s):* Supreme Court (consists of the chief justice, 3 chamber presidents, and 12 judges or councilors and divided into 3 chambers); Constitutional Council (consists of 3 judges and 6 jurists)
judge selection and term of office: Supreme Court chief justice selected by the president; councilors - 8 designated by the president and 7 by the speaker of the National Assembly; chief justice and councilors appointed for life; Constitutional Council judges - 2 appointed by the president and 1 by the speaker of the National Assembly; jurists - 3 each by the president and by the speaker of the National Assembly; judges appointed for 9-year terms
subordinate courts: High Court of Justice; Courts of Appeal; tribunals; justices of the peace

Political parties and leaders: Chadian Convention for Peace and Development or CTPD [Laoukein Kourayo MEDARD]
Federation Action for the Republic or FAR [Ngarledjy YORONGAR]
National Rally for Development and Progress or Viva-RNDP [Dr. Nouradine Delwa Kassire COUMAKOYE]
National Union for Democracy and Renewal or UNDR [Saleh KEBZABO]
Party for Unity and Reconstruction or PUR
Patriotic Salvation Movement or MPS [formerly Idriss DEBY]
Rally for Democracy and Progress or RDP [Mahamat Allahou TAHER]
Rally of Chadian Nationalists/Awakening or RNDT/Le Reveil [Albert Pahimi PADACKE]
Social Democratic Party for a Change-over of Power or PDSA [Malloum YOBODA]
Union for Democracy and the Republic or UDR
Union for Renewal and Democracy or URD [Felix Romadoumngar NIALBE]
note 1: 19 additional parties each contributed one member
note 2: only parties with at least two seats in the last elected National Assembly (February 2011) included
note: on 5 October 2021, Interim President Mahamat Idriss DEBY appointed 93 members to the interim National Transitional Council (NTC); 30% of the NTC members were retained from parties previously represented in the National Assembly

International organization participation: ACP, AfDB, AU, BDEAC, CEMAC, EITI (compliant country), FAO, FZ, G-77, IAEA, IBRD, ICAO, ICCt, ICRM, IDA, IDB, IFAD, IFC, IFRCS, ILO, IMF, Interpol, IOC, IOM, IPU, ITSO, ITU, ITUC (NGOs), LCBC, MIGA, MINUSMA, MNJTF, NAM, OIC, OIF, OPCW, UN, UNCTAD, UNESCO, UNIDO, UNOCI, UNWTO, UPU, WCO, WHO, WIPO, WMO, WTO

Diplomatic representation in the US: *chief of mission:* Ambassador Koutou NGOTE GALI (since 22 June 2018)
chancery: 2401 Massachusetts Avenue NW, Washington, DC 20008
telephone: [1] (202) 652-1312
FAX: [1] (202) 265-1937
email address and website:
info@chadembassy.us
https://chadembassy.us/

Diplomatic representation from the US: *chief of mission:* Ambassador (vacant); Charge d'Affaires Ellen THORBURN (since 8 November 2021)
embassy: Rond-Point Chagoua, B.P. 413, N'Djamena
mailing address: 2410 N'Djamena Place, Washington DC 20521-2410
telephone: [235] 2251-5017
FAX: [235] 2253-9102
email address and website:
NdjamenaACS@state.gov
https://td.usembassy.gov/

Flag description: three equal vertical bands of blue (hoist side), gold, and red; the flag combines the blue and red French (former colonial) colors with the red and yellow (gold) of the Pan-African colors; blue symbolizes the sky, hope, and the south of the country, which is relatively well-watered; gold represents the sun, as well as the desert in the north of the country; red stands for progress, unity, and sacrifice
note: almost identical to the flag of Romania but with a darker shade of blue; also similar to the flags of Andorra and Moldova, both of which have a national coat of arms centered in the yellow band; design based on the flag of France

National symbol(s): goat (north), lion (south); national colors: blue, yellow, red

National anthem: *name:* "La Tchadienne" (The Chadian)
lyrics/music: Louis GIDROL and his students/Paul VILLARD
note: adopted 1960

National heritage: *total World Heritage Sites:* 2 (1 natural, 1 mixed)
selected World Heritage Site locales: Lakes of Ounianga (n); Ennedi Massif: Natural and Cultural Landscape (m)

ECONOMY

Economic overview: Chad's landlocked location results in high transportation costs for imported goods and dependence on neighboring countries. Oil and agriculture are mainstays of Chad's economy. Oil provides about 60% of export revenues, while cotton, cattle, livestock, and gum arabic provide the bulk of Chad's non-oil export earnings. The services sector contributes less than one-third of GDP and has attracted foreign investment mostly through telecommunications and banking.

Nearly all of Chad's fuel is provided by one domestic refinery, and unanticipated shutdowns occasionally result in shortages. The country regulates the price of domestic fuel, providing an incentive for black market sales.

Although high oil prices and strong local harvests supported the economy in the past, low oil prices now stress Chad's fiscal position and have resulted in significant government cutbacks. Chad relies on foreign assistance and foreign capital for most of its public and private sector investment. Investment in Chad is difficult due to its limited infrastructure, lack of trained workers, extensive government bureaucracy, and corruption. Chad obtained a three-year extended credit facility from the IMF in 2014 and was granted debt relief under the Heavily Indebted Poor Countries Initiative in April 2015.

In 2018, economic policy will be driven by efforts that started in 2016 to reverse the recession and to repair damage to public finances and exports. The government is implementing an emergency action plan to counterbalance the drop in oil revenue and to diversify the economy. Chad's national development plan (NDP) cost just over $9 billion with a financing gap of $6.7 billion. The NDP emphasized the importance of private sector participation in Chad's development, as well as the need to improve the business environment, particularly in priority sectors such as mining and agriculture.

The Government of Chad reached a deal with Glencore and four other banks on the restructuring of a $1.45 billion oil-backed loan in February 2018, after a long negotiation. The new terms include an extension of the maturity to 2030 from 2022, a two-year grace period on principal repayments, and a lower interest rate of the London Inter-bank Offer Rate (Libor) plus 2% - down from Libor plus 7.5%. The original Glencore loan was to be repaid with crude oil assets, however, Chad's oil sales were hit by the downturn in the price of oil. Chad had secured a $312 million credit from the IMF in June 2017, but release of those funds hinged on restructuring the Glencore debt. Chad had already cut public spending to try to meet the terms of the IMF program, but that prompted strikes and protests in a country where nearly 40% of the population lives below the poverty line. Multinational partners, such as the African Development Bank, the EU, and the World Bank are likely to continue budget support in 2018, but Chad will remain at high debt risk, given its dependence on oil revenue and pressure to spend on subsidies and security.

Real GDP (purchasing power parity): $24.97 billion (2020 est.)
$25.19 billion (2019 est.)
$24.4 billion (2018 est.)
note: data are in 2017 dollars
country comparison to the world: 144

Real GDP growth rate: -3.1% (2017 est.)
-6.4% (2016 est.)
1.8% (2015 est.)
country comparison to the world: 211

Real GDP per capita: $1,500 (2020 est.)
$1,600 (2019 est.)

$1,600 (2018 est.)
note: data are in 2017 dollars
country comparison to the world: 220

GDP (official exchange rate): $10.912 billion (2019 est.)

Inflation rate (consumer prices): -0.9% (2019 est.)
4.2% (2018 est.)
-1.5% (2017 est.)
country comparison to the world: 7

GDP - composition, by sector of origin: *agriculture:* 52.3% (2017 est.)
industry: 14.7% (2017 est.)
services: 33.1% (2017 est.)

GDP - composition, by end use: *household consumption:* 75.1% (2017 est.)
government consumption: 4.4% (2017 est.)
investment in fixed capital: 24.1% (2017 est.)
investment in inventories: 0.7% (2017 est.)
exports of goods and services: 35.1% (2017 est.)
imports of goods and services: -39.4% (2017 est.)

Agricultural products: sorghum, groundnuts, millet, yams, cereals, sugar cane, beef, maize, cotton, cassava

Industries: oil, cotton textiles, brewing, natron (sodium carbonate), soap, cigarettes, construction materials

Industrial production growth rate: -4% (2017 est.)
country comparison to the world: 192

Labor force: 5.654 million (2017 est.)
country comparison to the world: 72

Labor force - by occupation: *agriculture:* 80%
industry: 20% (2006 est.)

Unemployment, youth ages 15-24: *total:* 1.5%
male: 2.4%
female: 0.7% (2018)
country comparison to the world: 182

Population below poverty line: 42.3% (2018 est.)

Gini Index coefficient - distribution of family income: 43.3 (2011 est.)
country comparison to the world: 40

Household income or consumption by percentage share: *lowest 10%:* 2.6%
highest 10%: 30.8% (2003)

Budget: *revenues:* 1.337 billion (2017 est.)
expenditures: 1.481 billion (2017 est.)

Budget surplus (+) or deficit (-): -1.5% (of GDP) (2017 est.)
country comparison to the world: 89

Public debt: 52.5% of GDP (2017 est.)
52.4% of GDP (2016 est.)
country comparison to the world: 94

Taxes and other revenues: 13.5% (of GDP) (2017 est.)
country comparison to the world: 206

Fiscal year: calendar year

Current account balance: -$558 million (2017 est.)
-$926 million (2016 est.)
country comparison to the world: 124

Exports: $2.464 billion (2017 est.)
$2.187 billion (2016 est.)
note: Data are in current year dollars and do not include illicit exports or re-exports.
country comparison to the world: 148

Exports - partners: China 32%, United Arab Emirates 21%, India 19%, United States 10%, France 6%, Germany 5% (2019)

Exports - commodities: crude petroleum, gold, livestock, sesame seeds, gum arabic, insect resins (2019)

Imports: $2.16 billion (2017 est.)
$1.997 billion (2016 est.)
country comparison to the world: 173

Imports - partners: China 29%, United Arab Emirates 16%, France 10%, United States 8%, India 5% (2019)

Imports - commodities: delivery trucks, paints, packaged medicines, aircraft, broadcasting equipment (2019)

Reserves of foreign exchange and gold: $22.9 million (31 December 2017 est.)
$20.92 million (31 December 2016 est.)
country comparison to the world: 190

Debt - external: $1.724 billion (31 December 2017 est.)
$1.281 billion (31 December 2016 est.)
country comparison to the world: 154

Exchange rates: Cooperation Financiere en Afrique Centrale francs (XAF) per US dollar -
605.3 (2017 est.)
593.01 (2016 est.)
593.01 (2015 est.)
591.45 (2014 est.)
494.42 (2013 est.)

ENERGY

Electricity access: *electrification - total population:* 9% (2019)
electrification - urban areas: 32% (2019)
electrification - rural areas: 1% (2019)

Electricity: *installed generating capacity:* 87,000 kW (2020 est.)
consumption: 188.46 million kWh (2019 est.)
exports: 0 kWh (2019 est.)
imports: 0 kWh (2019 est.)
transmission/distribution losses: 111 million kWh (2019 est.)

Electricity generation sources: *fossil fuels:* 96.8% of total installed capacity (2020 est.)
wind: 3.2% of total installed capacity (2020 est.)

Petroleum: *total petroleum production:* 87,900 bbl/day (2021 est.)
refined petroleum consumption: 12,600 bbl/day (2019 est.)
crude oil and lease condensate exports: 116,000 bbl/day (2018 est.)
crude oil and lease condensate imports: 0 bbl/day (2018 est.)
crude oil estimated reserves: 1.5 billion barrels (2021 est.)

Refined petroleum products - imports: 2,285 bbl/day (2015 est.)
country comparison to the world: 189

Carbon dioxide emissions: 1.771 million metric tonnes of CO2 (2019 est.)
from petroleum and other liquids: 1.771 million metric tonnes of CO2 (2019 est.)
country comparison to the world: 162

Energy consumption per capita: 1.575 million Btu/person (2019 est.)
country comparison to the world: 190

COMMUNICATIONS

Telephones - fixed lines: *total subscriptions:* 5,340 (2020 est.)
subscriptions per 100 inhabitants: (2020 est.) less than 1
country comparison to the world: 204

Telephones - mobile cellular: *total subscriptions:* 8,687,151 (2020 est.)
subscriptions per 100 inhabitants: 53 (2020 est.)
country comparison to the world: 95

Telecommunication systems: *general assessment:* the telecom infrastructure is particularly poor; fixed, mobile and internet is well below African averages; Chad's telecom market offers some potential for investors to develop services given the low starting base; the country's first 3G/LTE mobile license was awarded in April 2014; Chad finally gained access to international fiber bandwidth in 2012 its national backbone infrastructure remains underdeveloped; the World Bank-funded Central African Backbone (CAB) project takes in Chad, while the country is also party to a Trans-Saharan Backbone project which will link a fiber cable to Nigeria and Algeria (2022)
domestic: fixed-line connections less than 1 per 100 persons; mobile-cellular subscribership base of about 53 per 100 persons (2020)
international: country code - 235; satellite earth station - 1 Intelsat (Atlantic Ocean)

Broadcast media: 1 state-owned TV station; 2 privately-owned TV stations; state-owned radio network, Radiodiffusion Nationale Tchadienne (RNT), operates national and regional stations; over 10 private radio stations; some stations rebroadcast programs from international broadcasters (2017)

Internet country code: .td

Internet users: *total:* 1,642,586 (2020 est.)
percent of population: 10% (2020 est.)
country comparison to the world: 133

TRANSPORTATION

National air transport system: *number of registered air carriers:* 2 (2020)
inventory of registered aircraft operated by air carriers: 3

Civil aircraft registration country code prefix: TT

Airports: *total:* 59 (2021)
country comparison to the world: 81

Airports - with paved runways: *total:* 9
over 3,047 m: 2
2,438 to 3,047 m: 4
1,524 to 2,437 m: 2
under 914 m: 1 (2021)

Airports - with unpaved runways: *total:* 50
over 3,047 m: 1
2,438 to 3,047 m: 2
1,524 to 2,437 m: 14
914 to 1,523 m: 22
under 914 m: 11 (2021)

Pipelines: 582 km oil (2013)

Roadways: *total:* 40,000 km (2018)
note: consists of 25,000 km of national and regional roads and 15,000 km of local roads; 206 km of urban roads are paved
country comparison to the world: 88

Waterways: 12,400 km (2022) (Chari and Logone Rivers are navigable only in wet season) Chari is 11,400 km Legone is 1,000 km
country comparison to the world: 12

MILITARY AND SECURITY

Military and security forces: Chadian National Army (Armee Nationale du Tchad, ANT): Ground Forces (l'Armee de Terre, AdT), Chadian Air Force (l'Armee de l'Air Tchadienne, AAT), General Direction of

the Security Services of State Institutions (Direction Generale des Services de Securite des Institutions de l'Etat, GDSSIE); National Gendarmerie; Ministry of Public Security and Immigration: National Nomadic Guard of Chad (GNNT), Chadian National Police (2022)
note: the GDSSIE, formerly known as the Republican Guard, is the presidential guard force and is considered to be Chad's elite military unit; it is reportedly a division-size unit with infantry, armor, and special forces/anti-terrorism regiments (known as the Special Anti-Terrorist Group or SATG, aka Division of Special Anti-Terrorist Groups or DGSAT)

Military expenditures: 2.5% of GDP (2021 est.)
2.9% of GDP (2020 est.)
2% of GDP (2019 est.) (approximately $320 million)
2% of GDP (2018 est.) (approximately $310 million)
2% of GDP (2017 est.) (approximately $310 million)
country comparison to the world: 39

Military and security service personnel strengths: limited and varied information; estimated to have up to 35,000 active ANT personnel (25-30,000 Ground Forces; 300 Air Force; approximately 5,000 GDSSIE); approximately 5,000 National Gendarmerie; approximately 3,000 Nomadic Guard (2022)

Military equipment inventories and acquisitions: the ANT is mostly armed with older or second-hand equipment from Belgium, France, Russia, and the former Soviet Union; since 2010, it has received equipment, including donations, from more than 10 countries, including China, Italy, Ukraine, and the US (2021)

Military service age and obligation: 20 is the legal minimum age for compulsory military service for men with an 18-36 month service obligation (information varies); women are subject to 12 months of compulsory military or civic service at age 21; 18-35 for voluntary service; soldiers released from active duty are in the reserves until the age of 50 (2022)

Military deployments: 1,450 Mali (MINUSMA) (May 2022)
note 1: Chad has committed approximately 1,000-1,500 troops to the Multinational Joint Task Force (MNJTF) against Boko Haram and other terrorist groups operating in the general area of the Lake Chad Basin and along Nigeria's northeast border; national MNJTF troop contingents are deployed within their own territories, although cross-border operations are conducted periodically; in 2019, Chad sent more than 1,000 troops to Nigeria's Borno State to fight Boko Haram as part of the MNJTF mission
note 2: Chad is also part of a four (formerly five)-nation anti-jihadist task force known as the G4 Sahel Group, set up in 2014 with Chad, Mali (withdrew in 2022), Mauritania, and Niger; it has committed 550 troops and 100 gendarmes to the force; as of 2020, defense forces from each of the participating states were allowed to pursue terrorist fighters up to 100 km into neighboring countries; the force is backed by France, the UN, and the US

Military - note: as of 2022, the ANT was chiefly focused on counterterrorism and counterinsurgency operations; it was engaged with the Boko Haram (BH) and the Islamic State in West Africa (ISWA) terrorist groups in the Lake Chad Basin area (primarily the Lac Province) and in the Sahel, particularly the tri-border area with Burkina Faso, Mali, and Niger; in addition, the ANT was conducting operations against internal anti-government militias and armed dissident groups several rebel groups operate in northern Chad from bases in southern Libya, including the FACT (Front pour le Changement et la Concorde au Tchad), the Military Command Council for the Salvation of the Republic le Conseil de Commandement Militaire pour le salut de la République or CCSMR), the Union of Forces for Democracy and Development (le Union des Forces pour la Démocratie et le Développement or UFDD), and the Union of Resistance Forces (le Union des Forces de la Résistance UFR); former Chadian President Idriss DEBY was killed in April 2021 during fighting in the northern part of the country between the FACT and the Chadian Army; some armed groups, including the UFDD and UFR, signed an accord in August 2022 in return for the release of prisoners, amnesty, and an end to hostilities between the Chadian Government and these armed factions; however, other armed groups, including the FACT and CCSMR, refused to join the accord (2022)

TERRORISM

Terrorist group(s): Boko Haram; Islamic State of Iraq and ash-Sham - West Africa (ISIS-WA)

TRANSNATIONAL ISSUES

Disputes - international: since 2003, ad hoc armed militia groups and the Sudanese military have driven hundreds of thousands of Darfur residents into Chad; Chad wishes to be a helpful mediator in resolving the Darfur conflict, and in 2010 established a joint border monitoring force with Sudan, which has helped to reduce cross-border banditry and violence; only Nigeria and Cameroon have heeded the Lake Chad Commission's admonition to ratify the delimitation treaty, which also includes the Chad-Niger and Niger-Nigeria boundaries

Refugees and internally displaced persons: refugees (country of origin): 394,666 (Sudan), 124,491 (Central African Republic), 35,907 (Cameroon), 20,257 (Nigeria) (2022)

IDPs: 381,289 (majority are in the east) (2022)

Trafficking in persons: current situation: human traffickers exploit domestic and foreign victims in Chad and Chadians abroad; most trafficking is internal; some children are sent by their parents to relatives or intermediaries to receive education, an apprenticeship, goods, or money and are then forced to work in domestic service or cattle herding; children are also forced to work in agriculture, gold mines, charcoal vending, and fishing, and those attending Koranic schools are forced into begging and street vending; girls from rural areas who search for work in larger towns are exploited in sex trafficking and domestic servitude; terrorist groups abduct children to serve as soldiers, suicide bombers, brides, and forced laborers
tier rating: Tier 2 Watch List – Chad does not fully meet the minimum standards for the elimination of trafficking but is making significant efforts to do so; one trafficker was convicted, the first under a 2018 law, but the government did not report investigating or prosecuting alleged traffickers, including complicit government officials; the government adopted a formal Road Map to implement its 2108 National Action Plan but did not report executing it; authorities did not identify any victims and have not drafted victim identification and referral procedures; the government continued to make no effort to raise awareness on trafficking (2020)

Illicit drugs: NA

CHILE

INTRODUCTION

Background: Indigenous groups inhabited central and southern Chile for several thousands of years, living in mixed pastoralist and settled communities, ending with the Inca ruling the north of the country for nearly a century prior to the arrival of the Spanish in the 16th century. The Captaincy General of Chile was founded by the Spanish in 1541, lasting until Chile declared its independence in 1810. The subsequent struggle became tied to other South American independence conflicts, with a decisive victory over the Spanish not being achieved until 1818. In the War of the Pacific (1879-83), Chile defeated Peru and Bolivia to win its current northernmost regions. By the 1880s, the Chilean central government cemented its control over the central and southern regions inhabited by Mapuche Indigenous peoples. Between 1891 and 1973, a series of elected governments succeeded each other until the three-year-old Marxist government of Salvador ALLENDE was overthrown in 1973 by a military coup led by General Augusto PINOCHET, who ruled until a democratically elected president was inaugurated in 1990. Economic reforms, maintained consistently since the 1980s, contributed to steady growth, reduced poverty rates by over half, and helped secure the country's commitment to democratic and representative government. Chile has increasingly assumed regional and international leadership roles befitting its status as a stable, democratic nation.

GEOGRAPHY

Location: Southern South America, bordering the South Pacific Ocean, between Argentina and Peru

Geographic coordinates: 30 00 S, 71 00 W

Map references: South America

Area: *total:* 756,102 sq km
land: 743,812 sq km
water: 12,290 sq km
note: includes Easter Island (Isla de Pascua) and Isla Sala y Gomez
country comparison to the world: 39

Area - comparative: slightly smaller than twice the size of Montana

Land boundaries: *total:* 7,801 km

border countries (3): Argentina 6,691 km; Bolivia 942 km; Peru 168 km

Coastline: 6,435 km

Maritime claims: *territorial sea:* 12 nm
contiguous zone: 24 nm
exclusive economic zone: 200 nm
continental shelf: 200/350 nm

Climate: temperate; desert in north; Mediterranean in central region; cool and damp in south

Terrain: low coastal mountains, fertile central valley, rugged Andes in east

Elevation: *highest point:* Nevado Ojos del Salado 6,893 m (highest volcano in the world)
lowest point: Pacific Ocean 0 m
mean elevation: 1,871 m

Natural resources: copper, timber, iron ore, nitrates, precious metals, molybdenum, hydropower

Land use: *agricultural land:* 21.1% (2018 est.)
arable land: 1.7% (2018 est.)
permanent crops: 0.6% (2018 est.)
permanent pasture: 18.8% (2018 est.)
forest: 21.9% (2018 est.)
other: 57% (2018 est.)

Irrigated land: 11,100 sq km (2012)

Major lakes (area sq km): *fresh water lake(s):* Lago General Carrera (shared with Argentina) - 2,240 sq km; Lago O'Higgins (shared with Argentina) - 1,010 sq km; Lago Llanquihue - 800 sq km; Lago Fagnano (shared with Argentina) - 590 sq km

Population distribution: 90% of the population is located in the middle third of the country around the capital of Santiago; the far north (anchored by the Atacama Desert) and the extreme south are relatively underpopulated

Natural hazards: severe earthquakes; active volcanism; tsunamis
volcanism: significant volcanic activity due to more than three-dozen active volcanoes along the Andes Mountains; Lascar (5,592 m), which last erupted in 2007, is the most active volcano in the northern Chilean Andes; Llaima (3,125 m) in central Chile, which last erupted in 2009, is another of the country's most active; Chaiten's 2008 eruption forced major evacuations; other notable historically active volcanoes include Cerro Hudson, Calbuco, Copahue, Guallatiri, Llullaillaco, Nevados de Chillan, Puyehue, San Pedro, and Villarrica; see note 2 under "Geography - note"

Geography - note: *note 1* : the longest north-south trending country in the world, extending across 39 degrees of latitude; strategic location relative to sea lanes between the Atlantic and Pacific Oceans (Strait of Magellan, Beagle Channel, Drake Passage)
note 2: Chile is one of the countries along the Ring of Fire, a belt of active volcanoes and earthquake epicenters bordering the Pacific Ocean; up to 90% of the world's earthquakes and some 75% of the world's volcanoes occur within the Ring of Fire
note 3: the Atacama Desert - the driest desert in the world - spreads across the northern part of the country; Ojos del Salado (6,893 m) in the Atacama Desert is the highest active volcano in the world, Chile's tallest mountain, and the second highest in the Western Hemisphere and the Southern Hemisphere - its small crater lake (at 6,390 m) is the world's highest lake

PEOPLE AND SOCIETY

Population: 18,430,408 (2022 est.)
country comparison to the world: 66

Nationality: *noun:* Chilean(s)
adjective: Chilean

Ethnic groups: White and non-Indigenous 88.9%, Mapuche 9.1%, Aymara 0.7%, other Indigenous groups 1% (includes Rapa Nui, Likan Antai, Quechua, Colla, Diaguita, Kawesqar, Yagan or Yamana), unspecified 0.3% (2012 est.)

Languages: Spanish 99.5% (official), English 10.2%, Indigenous 1% (includes Mapudungun, Aymara, Quechua, Rapa Nui), other 2.3%, unspecified 0.2%; note - shares sum to more than 100% because some respondents gave more than one answer on the census (2012 est.)
major-language sample(s): La Libreta Informativa del Mundo, la fuente indispensable de información básica. (Spanish)

Religions: Roman Catholic 60%, Evangelical 18%, atheist or agnostic 4%, none 17% (2018 est.)

Demographic profile: Chile is in the advanced stages of demographic transition and is becoming an aging society - with fertility below replacement level, low mortality rates, and life expectancy on par with developed countries. Nevertheless, with its dependency ratio nearing its low point, Chile could benefit from its favorable age structure. It will need to keep its large working-age population productively employed, while preparing to provide for the needs of its growing proportion of elderly people, especially as women - the traditional caregivers -increasingly enter the workforce. Over the last two decades, Chile has made great strides in reducing its poverty rate, which is now lower than most Latin American countries. However, its severe income inequality ranks as the worst among members of the Organization for Economic Cooperation and Development. Unequal access to quality education perpetuates this uneven income distribution.

Chile has historically been a country of emigration but has slowly become more attractive to immigrants since transitioning to democracy in 1990 and improving its economic stability (other regional destinations have concurrently experienced deteriorating economic and political conditions). Most of Chile's small but growing foreign-born population consists of transplants from other Latin American countries, especially Peru.

Age structure: *0-14 years:* 19.79% (male 1,836,240/female 1,763,124)
15-24 years: 13.84% (male 1,283,710/female 1,233,238)
25-54 years: 42.58% (male 3,882,405/female 3,860,700)
55-64 years: 11.98% (male 1,034,049/female 1,145,022)
65 years and over: 11.81% (male 902,392/female 1,245,890) (2020 est.)

Birth rate: 12.75 births/1,000 population (2022 est.)
country comparison to the world: 141

Death rate: 6.52 deaths/1,000 population (2022 est.)
country comparison to the world: 136

Net migration rate: 0.33 migrant(s)/1,000 population (2022 est.)
country comparison to the world: 75

Population distribution: 90% of the population is located in the middle third of the country around the capital of Santiago; the far north (anchored by the Atacama Desert) and the extreme south are relatively underpopulated

Urbanization: *urban population:* 87.9% of total population (2022)
rate of urbanization: 0.78% annual rate of change (2020-25 est.)

Major urban areas - population: 6.857 million SANTIAGO (capital), 1.000 million Valparaiso, 902,000 Concepcion (2022)

Sex ratio: *at birth:* 1.04 male(s)/female
0-14 years: 1.04 male(s)/female
15-24 years: 1.04 male(s)/female
25-54 years: 1.01 male(s)/female
55-64 years: 0.91 male(s)/female
65 years and over: 0.56 male(s)/female
total population: 0.97 male(s)/female (2022 est.)

Maternal mortality ratio: 13 deaths/100,000 live births (2017 est.)
country comparison to the world: 138

Infant mortality rate: *total:* 6.55 deaths/1,000 live births
male: 7.12 deaths/1,000 live births
female: 5.95 deaths/1,000 live births (2022 est.)
country comparison to the world: 165

Life expectancy at birth: *total population:* 79.79 years
male: 76.8 years
female: 82.92 years (2022 est.)
country comparison to the world: 54

Total fertility rate: 1.76 children born/woman (2022 est.)
country comparison to the world: 151

Contraceptive prevalence rate: 76.3% (2015/16)

Drinking water source: *improved: urban:* 100% of population
rural: 100% of population
total: 100% of population

Current health expenditure: 9.3% of GDP (2019)

Physicians density: 2.84 physicians/1,000 population (2020)

Hospital bed density: 2.1 beds/1,000 population (2018)

Sanitation facility access: *improved: urban:* 100% of population
rural: 100% of population
total: 100% of population

HIV/AIDS - adult prevalence rate: 0.6% (2020 est.)
country comparison to the world: 59

Obesity - adult prevalence rate: 28% (2016)
country comparison to the world: 32

Alcohol consumption per capita: *total:* 7.8 liters of pure alcohol (2019 est.)
beer: 2.76 liters of pure alcohol (2019 est.)
wine: 2.61 liters of pure alcohol (2019 est.)
spirits: 2.43 liters of pure alcohol (2019 est.)
other alcohols: 0 liters of pure alcohol (2019 est.)
country comparison to the world: 47

Tobacco use: *total:* 29.2% (2020 est.)
male: 31.6% (2020 est.)
female: 26.8% (2020 est.)
country comparison to the world: 34

Children under the age of 5 years underweight

0.5% (2014): *country comparison to the world:* 126

Education expenditures: 5.4% of GDP (2018 est.)
country comparison to the world: 41

Literacy: *definition:* age 15 and over can read and write
total population: 96.4%
male: 96.3%
female: 96.3% (2017)

School life expectancy (primary to tertiary education): *total:* 17 years
male: 17 years
female: 17 years (2019)

Unemployment, youth ages 15-24: *total:* 24.9%
male: 23.7%
female: 26.6% (2020 est.)

ENVIRONMENT

Environment - current issues: air pollution from industrial and vehicle emissions; water pollution from raw sewage; noise pollution; improper garbage disposal; soil degradation; widespread deforestation and mining threaten the environment; wildlife conservation

Environment - international agreements: *party to:* Antarctic-Environmental Protection, Antarctic-Marine Living Resources, Antarctic Seals, Antarctic Treaty, Biodiversity, Climate Change, Climate Change-Kyoto Protocol, Climate Change-Paris Agreement, Comprehensive Nuclear Test Ban, Desertification, Endangered Species, Environmental Modification, Hazardous Wastes, Law of the Sea, Marine Dumping-London Convention, Marine Dumping-London Protocol, Nuclear Test Ban, Ozone Layer Protection, Ship Pollution, Wetlands, Whaling
signed, but not ratified: none of the selected agreements

Air pollutants: particulate matter emissions: 21.03 micrograms per cubic meter (2016 est.)
carbon dioxide emissions: 85.82 megatons (2016 est.)
methane emissions: 15.97 megatons (2020 est.)

Climate: temperate; desert in north; Mediterranean in central region; cool and damp in south

Land use: *agricultural land:* 21.1% (2018 est.)
arable land: 1.7% (2018 est.)
permanent crops: 0.6% (2018 est.)
permanent pasture: 18.8% (2018 est.)
forest: 21.9% (2018 est.)
other: 57% (2018 est.)

Urbanization: *urban population:* 87.9% of total population (2022)
rate of urbanization: 0.78% annual rate of change (2020-25 est.)

Revenue from forest resources: *forest revenues:* 0.49% of GDP (2018 est.)
country comparison to the world: 67

Revenue from coal: *coal revenues:* 0.01% of GDP (2018 est.)
country comparison to the world: 48

Waste and recycling: *municipal solid waste generated annually:* 6.517 million tons (2009 est.)
municipal solid waste recycled annually: 24,113 tons (2009 est.)
percent of municipal solid waste recycled: 0.4% (2009 est.)

Major lakes (area sq km): *fresh water lake(s):* Lago General Carrera (shared with Argentina) - 2,240 sq km; Lago O'Higgins (shared with Argentina) - 1,010 sq km; Lago Llanquihue - 800 sq km; Lago Fagnano (shared with Argentina) - 590 sq km

Total water withdrawal: *municipal:* 1.267 billion cubic meters (2017 est.)
industrial: 4.744 billion cubic meters (2017 est.)
agricultural: 29.42 billion cubic meters (2017 est.)

Total renewable water resources: 923.06 billion cubic meters (2017 est.)

GOVERNMENT

Country name: *conventional long form:* Republic of Chile
conventional short form: Chile
local long form: Republica de Chile
local short form: Chile
etymology: derivation of the name is unclear, but it may come from the Mapuche word "chilli" meaning "limit of the earth" or from the Quechua "chiri" meaning "cold"

Government type: presidential republic

Capital: *name:* Santiago; note - Valparaiso is the seat of the national legislature
geographic coordinates: 33 27 S, 70 40 W
time difference: UTC-3 (2 hours ahead of Washington, DC, during Standard Time)
daylight saving time: +1 hr, begins second Sunday in August; ends second Sunday in May; note - Punta Arenas observes DST throughout the year
time zone note: Chile has three time zones: the continental portion at UTC-3; the southern Magallanes region, which does not use daylight savings time and remains at UTC-3 for the summer months; and Easter Island at UTC-5
etymology: Santiago is named after the biblical figure Saint James (ca. A.D. 3-44), patron saint of Spain, but especially revered in Galicia; "Santiago" derives from the local Galician evolution of the Vulgar Latin "Sanctu Iacobu"; Valparaiso derives from the Spanish "Valle Paraiso" meaning "Paradise Valley"

Administrative divisions: 16 regions (regiones, singular - region); Aysen, Antofagasta, Araucania, Arica y Parinacota, Atacama, Biobio, Coquimbo, Libertador General Bernardo O'Higgins, Los Lagos, Los Rios, Magallanes y de la Antartica Chilena (Magallanes and Chilean Antarctica), Maule, Nuble, Region Metropolitana (Santiago), Tarapaca, Valparaiso
note: the US does not recognize any claims to Antarctica

Independence: 18 September 1810 (from Spain)

National holiday: Independence Day, 18 September (1810)

Constitution: *history:* many previous; latest adopted 11 September 1980, effective 11 March 1981 ; a referendum held on 25 October 2020 approved forming a convention to draft a new constitution, and on 15-16 May 2021, a referendum was held to elect members to the convention; the convention will finalize in July 2022, and Chileans will vote on the new constitution in a 4 September referendum
amendments: proposed by members of either house of the National Congress or by the president of the republic; passage requires at least three-fifths majority vote of the membership in both houses and approval by the president; passage of amendments to constitutional articles, such as the republican form of government, basic rights and freedoms, the Constitutional Tribunal, electoral justice, the Council of National Security, or the constitutional amendment process, requires at least two-third majority vote by both houses of Congress and approval by the president; the president can opt to hold a referendum when Congress and the president disagree on an amendment; amended many times, last in 2020

Legal system: civil law system influenced by several West European civil legal systems; judicial review of legislative acts by the Constitutional Tribunal

International law organization participation: has not submitted an ICJ jurisdiction declaration; accepts ICCt jurisdiction

Citizenship: *citizenship by birth:* yes
citizenship by descent only: yes
dual citizenship recognized: yes
residency requirement for naturalization: 5 years

Suffrage: 18 years of age; universal

Executive branch: *chief of state:* President Gabriel BORIC (since 11 March 2022); note - the president is both chief of state and head of government
head of government: President Gabriel BORIC (since 11 March 2022)
cabinet: Cabinet appointed by the president
elections/appointments: president directly elected by absolute majority popular vote in 2 rounds if needed for a single 4-year term; election last held on 21 November 2021 with a runoff held on 19 December 2021 (next to be held on 23 November 2025 with runoff if needed on 20 December)
election results:
2021: Gabriel BORIC elected president in second round; percent of vote in first round - Jose Antonio

KAST (FSC) 27.9%; Gabriel BORIC (AD) 25.8%; Franco PARISI (PDG) 12.8%; Sebastian SICHEL (ChP+) 12.8%; Yasna PROVOSTE (New Social Pact) 11.6%; other 9.1%; percent of vote in second round - Gabriel BORIC (AD) 55.9%; Jose Antonio KAST (FSC) 44.1%

2017: Sebastian PINERA Echenique elected president in second round; percent of vote in first round - Sebastian PINERA Echenique (independent) 36.6%; Alejandro GUILLIER (independent) 22.7%; Beatriz SANCHEZ (independent) 20.3%; Jose Antonio KAST (independent) 7.9%; Carolina GOIC (PdC) 5.9%; Marco ENRIQUEZ-OMINAMI (PRO) 5.7%; other 0.9%; percent of vote in second round - Sebastian PINERA Echenique 54.6%, Alejandro GUILLIER 45.4%

Legislative branch: *description:* bicameral National Congress or Congreso Nacional consists of:

Senate or Senado (50 seats); members directly elected in multi-seat constituencies by open party-list proportional representation vote to serve 8-year terms with one-half of the membership renewed every 4 years)

Chamber of Deputies or Camara de Diputados (155 seats; members directly elected in multi-seat constituencies by open party-list proportional representation vote to serve 4-year terms)

elections:

Senate - last held on 21 November 2021 (next to be held on 23 November 2025)

Chamber of Deputies - last held on 21 November 2021 (next to be held on 23 November 2025)

election results:

Senate - percent of vote by party - NA; seats by party - ChP+ 12 (RN 5, UDI 5, EVOPOLI 2), NPS 8 (PS 4, PPD 2, PDC 2), PLR 1, AD 4 (PCCh 2, FREVS 2) independent 2; note - total composition of the Senate as of 1 May 2022: seats by party - ChP+ 24 (RN 12, UDI 9, EVOPOLI 3), NPS 18 (PS 7, PPD 6, PDC 5), AD 6 (PCCh 2, FREVS 2, RD 2), PLR 1, independent 1 ; composition - men 38, women 12, percent of women 24%

Chamber of Deputies - percent of vote by party - NA; seats by party - ChP+ 53 (RN 25, UDI 23, EVOPOLI 4, PRI 1), AD 37 (PCCh 12, CS 9, RD 8, Commons 6, FREVS 2), NPS 37 (PS 13, PDC 8, PPD 7, PL 4, PRSD 4, CIU 1), FSC 15 (PLR 14, PCC 1), PDG 6, PH 3, PEV 2, IU 1, independent 1 ; composition - men 100, women 55, percent of women 35.5%; note - overall National Congress percent of women 32.7%

Judicial branch: *highest court(s):* Supreme Court or Corte Suprema (consists of a court president and 20 members or ministros); Constitutional Court (consists of 10 members and is independent of the rest of the judiciary); Elections Qualifying Court (consists of 5 members)

judge selection and term of office: Supreme Court president and judges (ministers) appointed by the president of the republic and ratified by the Senate from lists of candidates provided by the court itself; judges appointed for life with mandatory retirement at age 70; Constitutional Court members appointed - 3 by the Supreme Court, 3 by the president of the republic, 2 by the Chamber of Deputies, and 2 by the Senate; members serve 9-year terms with partial membership replacement every 3 years (the court reviews constitutionality of legislation); Elections Qualifying Court members appointed by lottery - 1 by the former president or vice president of the Senate and 1 by the former president or vice president of the Chamber of Deputies, 2 by the Supreme Court, and 1 by the Appellate Court of Valparaiso; members appointed for 4-year terms

subordinate courts: Courts of Appeal; oral criminal tribunals; military tribunals; local police courts; specialized tribunals and courts in matters such as family, labor, customs, taxes, and electoral affairs

Political parties and leaders

Approve Dignity (Apruebo Dignidad) coalition or AD (includes PC, FA, and FREVS) [Gabriel BORIC]
Broad Front Coalition (Frente Amplio) or FA (includes RD, CS, and Comunes) [Gonzalo WINTER]
Broad Social Movement of Leftist Citizens (includes former MAS and Izquierda Ciudadana) [Fernando ZAMORANO]
Chile We Can Do More or ChP+ [Sebastian SICHEL] (coalition includes EVOPOLI, PRI, RN, UDI)
Christian Conservative Party or PCC [Antaris VARELA]
Christian Democratic Party or PDC [Carmen FREI Ruiz-Tagle]
Christian Social Front or FSC [Jose Antonio KAST] (includes PCC, PLR)
Citizens or CIU [María Ignacia GOMEZ Martinez]
Commons (Comunes) [Jorge RAMIREZ]
Communist Party of Chile or PCCh [Guillermo TEILLIER del Valle]
Democratic Revolution or RD [Margarita PORTUGUEZ]
Green Ecological Party or PEV [Felix GONZALEZ] (dissolved 7 February 2022)
Humanist Party or PH [Octavio GONZALEZ]
Independent Democratic Union or UDI [Javier MACAYA]
Independent Regionalist Democratic Party or PRI [Hugo ORTIZ de Filippi]
Liberal Party (Partido Liberal de Chile) or PL [Patricio MORALES]
National Renewal or RN [Francisco CHAHUAN]
New Social Pact or NPS [Yasna PROVOSTE] (includes PDC, PL, PPD, PRSD, PS)
Party for Democracy or PPD [Natalia PERGIENTILI Domenech]
Party of the People or PDG [Franco Aldo PARISI Fernandez]
Political Evolution or EVOpOli [Luz POBLETE Coddou]
Radical Social Democratic Party or PRSD [Carlos MALDONADO Curti]
Republican Party or PLR [Rojo EDWARDS]
Social Convergence or CS [Alondra ARELLANO Hernandez]
Social Green Regionalist Federation or FREVS [Flavia TORREALBA Diaz]
Socialist Party or PS [Alvaro Antonio ELIZALDE Soto]
United Independents or IU [Cristian Alejandro CONTRERAS Radovic]

International organization participation: APEC, BIS, CAN (associate), CD, CELAC, FAO, G-15, G-77, IADB, IAEA, IBRD, ICAO, ICC (national committees), ICCt, ICRM, IDA, IFAD, IFC, IFRCS, IHO, ILO, IMF, IMO, IMSO, Interpol, IOC, IOM, IPU, ISO, ITSO, ITU, ITUC (NGOs), LAES, LAIA, Mercosur (associate), MIGA, MINUSTAH, NAM, OAS, OeCd (enhanced engagement), OPANAL, OPCW, Pacific Alliance, PCA, PROSUR, SICA (observer), UN, UNASUR, UNCTAD, UNESCO, UNFICYP, UNHCR, UNIDO, Union Latina, UNMOGIP, UNTSO, UNWTO, UPU, WCO, WFTU (NGOs), WHO, WIPO, WMO, WTO

Diplomatic representation in the US: *chief of mission:* Ambassador Juan Gabriel VALDES Soublette (since 7 June 2022)
chancery: 1732 Massachusetts Avenue NW, Washington, DC 20036
telephone: [1] (202) 785-1746
FAX: [1] (202) 887-5579
email address and website:
echile.eeuu@minrel.gob.cl
https://chile.gob.cl/estados-unidos/en/
consulate(s) general: Chicago, Houston, Los Angeles, Miami, New York, San Francisco

Diplomatic representation from the US: *chief of mission:* Ambassador (vacant); Charge d'Affaires Richard H. GLENN (since August 2020)
embassy: Avenida Andres Bello 2800, Las Condes, Santiago
mailing address: 3460 Santiago Place, Washington DC 20521-3460
telephone: [56] (2) 2330-3000
FAX: [56] (2) 2330-3710
email address and website:
SantiagoUSA@state.gov
https://cl.usembassy.gov/

Flag description: two equal horizontal bands of white (top) and red; a blue square the same height as the white band at the hoist-side end of the white band; the square bears a white five-pointed star in the center representing a guide to progress and honor; blue symbolizes the sky, white is for the snow-covered Andes, and red represents the blood spilled to achieve independence

note: design influenced by the US flag

National symbol(s): huemul (mountain deer), Andean condor; national colors: red, white, blue

National anthem: *name:* "Himno Nacional de Chile" (National Anthem of Chile)
lyrics/music: Eusebio LILLO Robles and Bernardo DE VERA y Pintado/Ramon CARNICER y Battle
note: music adopted 1828, original lyrics adopted 1818, adapted lyrics adopted 1847; under Augusto PINOCHET's military rule, a verse glorifying the army was added; however, as a protest, some citizens refused to sing this verse; it was removed when democracy was restored in 1990

National heritage: *total World Heritage Sites:* 7 (all cultural)
selected World Heritage Site locales: Rapa Nui National Park; Churches of Chiloe; Historic Valparaiso; Humberstone and Santa Laura Saltpeter Works; Sewell Mining Town; Qhapaq Ñan/Andean Road System; Chinchorro archeological sites

ECONOMY

Economic overview: Chile has a market-oriented economy characterized by a high level of foreign trade and a reputation for strong financial institutions and sound policy that have given it the strongest sovereign bond rating in South America. Exports of goods and services account for approximately one-third of GDP, with commodities making up some 60% of total exports. Copper is Chile's top export and provides 20% of government revenue.

From 2003 through 2013, real growth averaged almost 5% per year, despite a slight contraction in 2009 that resulted from the global financial crisis. Growth slowed to an estimated 1.4% in 2017. A continued drop in copper prices prompted Chile to experience its third consecutive year of slow growth.

Chile deepened its longstanding commitment to trade liberalization with the signing of a free trade agreement with the US, effective 1 January 2004. Chile has 26 trade agreements covering 60 countries including agreements with the EU, Mercosur, China, India, South Korea, and Mexico. In May 2010, Chile signed the OECD Convention, becoming the first South American country to join the OECD. In October 2015, Chile signed the Trans-Pacific Partnership trade agreement, which was finalized as the Comprehensive and Progressive Trans-Pacific Partnership (CPTPP) and signed at a ceremony in Chile in March 2018.

The Chilean Government has generally followed a countercyclical fiscal policy, under which it accumulates surpluses in sovereign wealth funds during periods of high copper prices and economic growth, and generally allows deficit spending only during periods of low copper prices and growth. As of 31 October 2016, those sovereign wealth funds - kept mostly outside the country and separate from Central Bank reserves - amounted to more than $23.5 billion. Chile used these funds to finance fiscal stimulus packages during the 2009 economic downturn.

In 2014, then-President Michelle BACHELET introduced tax reforms aimed at delivering her campaign promise to fight inequality and to provide access to education and health care. The reforms are expected to generate additional tax revenues equal to 3% of Chile's GDP, mostly by increasing corporate tax rates to OECD averages.

Real GDP (purchasing power parity): $445.88 billion (2020 est.)
$473.19 billion (2019 est.)
$468.77 billion (2018 est.)
note: data are in 2017 dollars
country comparison to the world: 45

Real GDP growth rate: 1.03% (2019 est.)
4% (2018 est.)
1.41% (2017 est.)
country comparison to the world: 170

Real GDP per capita: $23,300 (2020 est.)
$25,000 (2019 est.)
$25,000 (2018 est.)
note: data are in 2017 dollars
country comparison to the world: 81

GDP (official exchange rate): $282.655 billion (2019 est.)

Inflation rate (consumer prices): 2.2% (2019 est.)
2.7% (2018 est.)
2.1% (2017 est.)
country comparison to the world: 115

Credit ratings: *Fitch rating:* A- (2020)

Moody's rating: A1 (2018)

Standard & Poors rating: A+ (2017)
note: The year refers to the year in which the current credit rating was first obtained.

GDP - composition, by sector of origin: *agriculture:* 4.2% (2017 est.)
industry: 32.8% (2017 est.)
services: 63% (2017 est.)

GDP - composition, by end use: *household consumption:* 62.3% (2017 est.)
government consumption: 14% (2017 est.)
investment in fixed capital: 21.5% (2017 est.)
investment in inventories: 0.5% (2017 est.)
exports of goods and services: 28.7% (2017 est.)
imports of goods and services: -27% (2017 est.)

Agricultural products: grapes, apples, wheat, sugar beet, milk, potatoes, tomatoes, maize, poultry, pork

Industries: copper, lithium, other minerals, foodstuffs, fish processing, iron and steel, wood and wood products, transport equipment, cement, textiles

Industrial production growth rate: -0.4% (2017 est.)
country comparison to the world: 170

Labor force: 7.249 million (2020 est.)
country comparison to the world: 63

Labor force - by occupation: *agriculture:* 9.2%
industry: 23.7%
services: 67.1% (2013)

Unemployment rate: 7.22% (2019 est.)
7.33% (2018 est.)
country comparison to the world: 116

Unemployment, youth ages 15-24: *total:* 24.9%
male: 23.7%
female: 26.6% (2020 est.)
country comparison to the world: 56

Population below poverty line: 8.6% (2017 est.)

Gini Index coefficient - distribution of family income: 44.4 (2017 est.)
57.1 (2000)
country comparison to the world: 33

Household income or consumption by percentage share: *lowest 10%:* 1.7%
highest 10%: 41.5% (2013 est.)

Budget: *revenues:* 57.75 billion (2017 est.)
expenditures: 65.38 billion (2017 est.)

Budget surplus (+) or deficit (-): -2.8% (of GDP) (2017 est.)
country comparison to the world: 124

Public debt: 23.6% of GDP (2017 est.)
21% of GDP (2016 est.)
country comparison to the world: 182

Taxes and other revenues: 20.8% (of GDP) (2017 est.)
country comparison to the world: 145

Fiscal year: calendar year

Current account balance: -$10.933 billion (2019 est.)
-$10.601 billion (2018 est.)
country comparison to the world: 193

Exports: $79.8 billion (2020 est.)
$78.02 billion (2019 est.)
$84.65 billion (2018 est.)
note: Data are in current year dollars and do not include illicit exports or re-exports.
country comparison to the world: 46

Exports - partners: China 32%, United States 14%, Japan 9%, South Korea 7% (2019)

Exports - commodities: copper, wood pulp, fish fillets, pitted fruits, wine (2019)

Imports: *$66.43 billion (2020 est.) note:* data are in current year dollars
$80.17 billion (2019 est.) note: data are in current year dollars
$85.11 billion (2018 est.) note: data are in current year dollars
country comparison to the world: 50

Imports - partners: China 24%, United States 20%, Brazil 8%, Germany 5%, Argentina 5% (2019)

Imports - commodities: refined petroleum, crude petroleum, cars, broadcasting equipment, delivery trucks (2019)

Reserves of foreign exchange and gold: $38.98 billion (31 December 2017 est.)
$40.49 billion (31 December 2016 est.)
country comparison to the world: 44

Debt - external: $193.298 billion (2019 est.)
$181.089 billion (2018 est.)
country comparison to the world: 39

Exchange rates: Chilean pesos (CLP) per US dollar -
738.81 (2020 est.)
770.705 (2019 est.)
674.25 (2018 est.)
658.93 (2014 est.)
570.37 (2013 est.)

ENERGY

Electricity access: *electrification - total population:* 100% (2020)

Electricity: *installed generating capacity:* 29.808 million kW (2020 est.)
consumption: 75.302 billion kWh (2020 est.)
exports: 0 kWh (2020 est.)
imports: 0 kWh (2020 est.)
transmission/distribution losses: 4.62 billion kWh (2020 est.)

Electricity generation sources: *fossil fuels:* 51.9% of total installed capacity (2020 est.)
solar: 9.5% of total installed capacity (2020 est.)
wind: 6.9% of total installed capacity (2020 est.)
hydroelectricity: 26% of total installed capacity (2020 est.)
geothermal: 0.3% of total installed capacity (2020 est.)
biomass and waste: 5.4% of total installed capacity (2020 est.)

Coal: *production:* 542,000 metric tons (2020 est.)
consumption: 10.573 million metric tons (2020 est.)
exports: 134,000 metric tons (2020 est.)
imports: 10.607 million metric tons (2020 est.)
proven reserves: 1.181 billion metric tons (2019 est.)

Petroleum: *total petroleum production:* 11,900 bbl/day (2021 est.)
refined petroleum consumption: 361,700 bbl/day (2019 est.)
crude oil and lease condensate exports: 0 bbl/day (2018 est.)
crude oil and lease condensate imports: 172,700 bbl/day (2018 est.)
crude oil estimated reserves: 150 million barrels (2021 est.)

Refined petroleum products - production: 216,200 bbl/day (2017 est.)
country comparison to the world: 49

Refined petroleum products - exports: 7,359 bbl/day (2017 est.)
country comparison to the world: 87

Refined petroleum products - imports: 166,400 bbl/day (2017 est.)
country comparison to the world: 38

Natural gas: *production:* 1,109,962,000 cubic meters (2020 est.)
consumption: 6,558,312,000 cubic meters (2020 est.)
exports: 0 cubic meters (2021 est.)
imports: 4,602,471,000 cubic meters (2020 est.)
proven reserves: 97.976 billion cubic meters (2021 est.)

Carbon dioxide emissions: 88.333 million metric tonnes of CO2 (2019 est.)
from coal and metallurgical coke: 24.217 million metric tonnes of CO2 (2019 est.)
from petroleum and other liquids: 51.228 million metric tonnes of CO2 (2019 est.)

from consumed natural gas: 12.888 million metric tonnes of CO2 (2019 est.)
country comparison to the world: 47

Energy consumption per capita: 81.953 million Btu/person (2019 est.)
country comparison to the world: 72

COMMUNICATIONS

Telephones - fixed lines: *total subscriptions:* 2,567,938 (2020 est.)
subscriptions per 100 inhabitants: 13 (2020 est.)
country comparison to the world: 50

Telephones - mobile cellular: *total subscriptions:* 25,068,249 (2020 est.)
subscriptions per 100 inhabitants: 131 (2020 est.)
country comparison to the world: 51

Telecommunication systems: *general assessment:* the market for fixed and mobile telephony is highly competitive and rapidly evolving; the mobile rate is among the highest in South America; LTE infrastructure is extensive and 5G spectrum auctions which took place in February 2021 are expected to prompt the deployment of 5G networks by the end of the year, following extensive trials held by the MNOs; fixed broadband is relatively high for the region, with services among the fastest and least expensive in Latin America; government initiatives such as the National Fiber Optic project and Fibra Óptica Austral are providing high-capacity connectivity across the country and will further increase fixed-line broadband; there is a strong focus on fiber broadband, with the number of fiber subscribers having increased 61.7% in 2020, year-on-year; technological improvements have allowed operators to provide a variety of services via their networks, giving rise to a number of bundled packages at competitive prices, including access to video on demand services which in turn is increasing fixed-line broadband; traditional fixed-line teledensity continues to fall as consumers switch to mobile networks and to fixed broadband for voice and data connectivity; more than 8,300 schools receive free broadband as part of the 'Connectivity for Education 2030' project (2021)
domestic: number of fixed-line connections have dropped to about 13 per 100 in recent years as mobile-cellular usage continues to increase, reaching 131 telephones per 100 persons; domestic satellite system with 3 earth stations (2020)
international: country code - 56; landing points for the Pan-Am, Prat, SAm-1, American Movil-Telxius West Coast Cable, FOS Quellon-Chacabuco, Fibra Optical Austral, SAC and Curie submarine cables providing links to the US, Caribbean and to Central and South America; satellite earth stations - 2 Intelsat (Atlantic Ocean) (2019)

Broadcast media: national and local terrestrial TV channels, coupled with extensive cable TV networks; the state-owned Television Nacional de Chile (TVN) network is self-financed through commercial advertising revenues and is not under direct government control; large number of privately owned TV stations; about 250 radio stations

Internet country code: .cl

Internet users: *total:* 16,822,264 (2020 est.)
percent of population: 88% (2020 est.)
country comparison to the world: 43

Broadband - fixed subscriptions: *total:* 3,763,826 (2020 est.)
subscriptions per 100 inhabitants: 20 (2020 est.)
country comparison to the world: 41

TRANSPORTATION

National air transport system: *number of registered air carriers:* 9 (2020)
inventory of registered aircraft operated by air carriers: 173
annual passenger traffic on registered air carriers: 19,517,185 (2018)
annual freight traffic on registered air carriers: 1,226,440,000 (2018) mt-km

Civil aircraft registration country code prefix: CC

Airports: *total:* 481 (2021)
country comparison to the world: 14

Airports - with paved runways: *total:* 90
over 3,047 m: 5
2,438 to 3,047 m: 7
1,524 to 2,437 m: 23
914 to 1,523 m: 31
under 914 m: 24 (2021)

Airports - with unpaved runways: *total:* 391
2,438 to 3,047 m: 5
1,524 to 2,437 m: 11
914 to 1,523 m: 56
*under 914 m:*319 (2021)

Heliports: 1 (2021)

Pipelines: 3,160 km gas, 781 km liquid petroleum gas, 985 km oil, 722 km refined products (2013)

Railways: *total:* 7,281.5 km (2014)
narrow gauge: 3,853.5 km (2014) 1.000-m gauge
broad gauge: 3,428 km (2014) 1.676-m gauge (1,691 km electrified)
country comparison to the world: 30

Roadways: *total:* 77,801 km (2016)
country comparison to the world: 62

Merchant marine: *total:* 231
by type: bulk carrier 6, container ship 5, general cargo 58, oil tanker 14, other 148 (2021)
country comparison to the world: 64

Ports and terminals: *major seaport(s):* Coronel, Huasco, Lirquen, Puerto Ventanas, San Antonio, San Vicente, Valparaiso
container port(s) (TEUs): San Antonio (1,709,635), Valparaiso (898,715) (2019)

LNG terminal(s) (import): Mejillones, Quintero

MILITARY AND SECURITY

Military and security forces: Armed Forces of Chile (Fuerzas Armadas de Chile): Chilean Army (Ejército de Chile), Chilean Navy (Armada de Chile, includes marine units and coast guard or Maritime Territory and Merchant Marine Directorate (Directemar)), Chilean Air Force (Fuerza Aerea de Chile, FACh); Ministry of the Interior and Public Security: Carabineros de Chile (National Police Force) (2022)
note: the Carabineros de Chile are responsible to both the Ministry of Defense and the Ministry of the Interior

Military expenditures: 2% of GDP (2021 est.)
2% of GDP (2020)
1.9% of GDP (2019) (approximately $7.33 billion)
1.9% of GDP (2018) (approximately $7.2 billion)
2% of GDP (2017) (approximately $7.1 billion)
country comparison to the world: 57

Military and security service personnel strengths: approximately 70,000 active armed forces personnel (40,000 Army; 20,000 Navy; 10,000 Air Force); approximately 50,000 Carabineros (2022)

Military equipment inventories and acquisitions: the Chilean military inventory is comprised of a wide mix of mostly Western equipment and some domestically-produced systems; since 2010, it has received military hardware from nearly 15 countries with Germany and the US as the leading suppliers; Chile's defense industry has capabilities in military aircraft, ships, and vehicles (2022)

Military service age and obligation: 18-45 years of age for voluntary male and female military service; selective compulsory service (there are usually enough volunteers to make compulsory service unnecessary); service obligation is a minimum of 12 months for Army and 22 months for Navy and Air Force (2022)
note: as of 2021, women comprised approximately 18% of the armed forces

Military - note: the Chilean Army was founded in 1810, but traces its origins back to the Army of the Kingdom of Chile, which was established by the Spanish Crown in the early 1600s; the Navy traces its origins to 1817; it was first led by a British officer and its first ships were largely crewed by American, British, and Irish sailors; by the 1880s, the Chilean Navy was one of the most powerful in the Americas, and included the world's first protected cruiser (a ship with an armored deck to protect vital machine spaces); Chile's military aviation was inaugurated in 1913 with the creation of a military aviation school (2022)

TRANSNATIONAL ISSUES

Disputes - international: Chile and Peru rebuff Bolivia's reactivated claim to restore the Atacama corridor, ceded to Chile in 1884, but Chile has offered instead unrestricted but not sovereign maritime access through Chile to Bolivian natural gas; Chile rejects Peru's unilateral legislation to change its latitudinal maritime boundary with Chile to an equidistance line with a southwestern axis favoring Peru; in October 2007, Peru took its maritime complaint with Chile to the ICJ; territorial claim in Antarctica (Chilean Antarctic Territory) partially overlaps Argentine and British claims; the joint boundary commission, established by Chile and Argentina in 2001, has yet to map and demarcate the delimited boundary in the inhospitable Andean Southern Ice Field (Campo de Hielo Sur)

Refugees and internally displaced persons: refugees (country of origin): 448,138 (Venezuela) (economic and political crisis; includes Venezuelans who have claimed asylum or have received alternative legal stay) (2020)

Illicit drugs: transshipment country for cocaine destined for Europe and the region; some money laundering activity, especially through the Iquique Free Trade Zone; imported precursors passed on to Bolivia; domestic cocaine consumption is rising, making Chile a significant consumer of cocaine

CHINA

INTRODUCTION

Background: China's historical civilization dates to at least 13th century B.C., first under the Shang (to 1046 B.C.) and then the Zhou (1046-221 B.C) dynasties. The imperial era of China began in 221 B.C. under the Qin Dynasty and lasted until the fall of the Qing Dynasty in 1912. During this period, China alternated between periods of unity and disunity under a succession of imperial dynasties. In the 19th century, the Qing Dynasty suffered heavily from overextension by territorial conquest, insolvency, civil war, imperialism, military defeats, and foreign expropriation of ports and infrastructure. It collapsed following the Revolution of 1911, and China became a republic under SUN Yat-sen of the Kuomintang (KMT or Nationalist) Party. However, the republic was beset by division, warlordism, and continued foreign intervention. In the late 1920s, a civil war erupted between the ruling KMT-controlled government led by CHIANG Kai-shek, and the Chinese Communist Party (CCP). Japan occupied much of northeastern China in the early 1930s, and then launched a full-scale invasion of the country in 1937. The resulting eight years of warfare devastated the country and cost up to 20 million Chinese lives by the time of Japan's defeat in 1945. The Nationalist-Communist civil war continued with renewed intensity following the end of World War II and culminated with a CCP victory in 1949, under the leadership of MAO Zedong.

MAO and the CCP established an autocratic socialist system that, while ensuring the PRC's sovereignty, imposed strict controls over everyday life and launched agricultural, economic, political, and social policies - such as the Great Leap Forward (1958-1962) and the Cultural Revolution (1966-1976) - that cost the lives of millions of people. MAO died in 1976. Beginning in 1978, subsequent leaders DENG Xiaoping, JIANG Zemin, and HU Jintao focused on market-oriented economic development and opening up the country to foreign trade, while maintaining the rule of the CCP. Since the change, China has been among the world's fastest growing economies, with real gross domestic product averaging over 9% growth annually through 2021, lifting an estimated 800 million people out of poverty, and dramatically improving overall living standards. By 2011, the PRC's economy was the second largest in the world. The growth, however, has created considerable social displacement, adversely affected the country's environment, and reduced the country's natural resources. Current leader XI Jinping has continued these policies, but also has maintained tight political controls. Over the past decade, China has also increased its global outreach, including military deployments, participation in international organizations, and initiating a global connectivity initiative in 2013 called the "Belt and Road Initiative" (BRI). While many nations have signed on to BRI agreements to attract PRC investment, others have balked at the opaque lending behavior; weak environment, social, and governance (ESG) standards; and other practices that undermine local governance and foster corruption associated with some BRI-linked projects. XI Jinping assumed the positions of General Secretary of the Chinese Communist Party and Chairman of the Central Military Commission in 2012 and President in 2013. In March 2018, the PRC's National People's Congress passed an amendment abolishing presidential term limits, opening the door for XI to seek a third five-year term in 2023.

GEOGRAPHY

Location: Eastern Asia, bordering the East China Sea, Korea Bay, Yellow Sea, and South China Sea, between North Korea and Vietnam

Geographic coordinates: 35 00 N, 105 00 E

Map references: Asia

Area: *total:* 9,596,960 sq km
land: 9,326,410 sq km
water: 270,550 sq km
country comparison to the world: 5

Area - comparative: slightly smaller than the US

Land boundaries: *total:* 22,457 km
border countries (14): Afghanistan 91 km; Bhutan 477 km; Burma 2,129 km; India 2,659 km; Kazakhstan 1,765 km; North Korea 1,352 km; Kyrgyzstan 1,063 km; Laos 475 km; Mongolia 4,630 km; Nepal 1,389 km; Pakistan 438 km; Russia (northeast) 4,133 km and Russia (northwest) 46 km; Tajikistan 477 km; Vietnam 1,297 km

Coastline: 14,500 km

Maritime claims: *territorial sea:* 12 nm
contiguous zone: 24 nm
exclusive economic zone: 200 nm
continental shelf: 200 nm or to the edge of the continental margin

Climate: extremely diverse; tropical in south to subarctic in north

Terrain: mostly mountains, high plateaus, deserts in west; plains, deltas, and hills in east

Elevation: *highest point:* Mount Everest (highest peak in Asia and highest point on earth above sea level) 8,849 m
lowest point: Turpan Pendi (Turfan Depression) -154 m
mean elevation: 1,840 m

Natural resources: coal, iron ore, helium, petroleum, natural gas, arsenic, bismuth, cobalt, cadmium, ferrosilicon, gallium, germanium, hafnium, indium, lithium, mercury, tantalum, tellurium, tin, titanium, tungsten, antimony, manganese, magnesium, molybdenum, selenium, strontium, vanadium, magnetite, aluminum, lead, zinc, rare earth elements, uranium, hydropower potential (world's largest), arable land

Land use: *agricultural land:* 54.7% (2018 est.)
arable land: 11.3% (2018 est.)
permanent crops: 1.6% (2018 est.)
permanent pasture: 41.8% (2018 est.)
forest: 22.3% (2018 est.)
other: 23% (2018 est.)

Irrigated land: 690,070 sq km (2012)

Major lakes (area sq km): *fresh water lake(s):* Dongting Hu - 3,100 sq km; Poyang Hu - 3,350 sq km; Hongze Hu - 2,700 sq km; Tai Hu - 2,210 sq km; Hulun Nur - 1,590
salt water lake(s): Quinghai Hu - 4,460 sq km; Nam Co - 2,500 sq km; Siling Co - 1,860 sq km; Tangra Yumco - 1,400 sq km; Bosten Hu 1,380 sq km

Major rivers (by length in km): Yangtze - 6,300 km; Huang He - 5,464 km; Amur river source (shared with Mongolia and Russia [m]) - 4,444 km; Mekong river source (shared with Burma, Laos, Thailand, Cambodia, and Vietnam [m]) - 4,350 km; Brahmaputra river source (shared with India and Bangladesh [m]) - 3,969 km; Indus river source (shared with India and Pakistan [m]) -3,610 km; Salween river source (shared with Thailand and Burma [m]) - 3,060 km; Irrawaddy river source (shared with Burma [m]) - 2,809 km; Pearl (shared with Vietnam [s]) - 2,200 km; Red river source (shared with Vietnam [m]) - 1,149 km
note – [s] after country name indicates river source; [m] after country name indicates river mouth

Major watersheds (area sq km): *Pacific Ocean drainage:* Amur (1,929,955 sq km), Huang He (944,970 sq km), Mekong (805,604 sq km), Yangtze (1,722,193 sq km)

Indian Ocean drainage: Brahmaputra (651,335 sq km), Ganges (1,016,124 sq km), Indus (1,081,718 sq km), Irrawaddy (413,710 sq km), Salween (271,914 sq km)

Arctic Ocean drainage: Ob (2,972,493 sq km)

Internal (endorheic basin) drainage: Tarim Basin (1,152,448 sq km), Amu Darya (534,739 sq km), Syr Darya (782,617 sq km), Lake Balkash (510,015 sq km)

Major aquifers: North China Aquifer System (Huang Huai Hai Plain), Song-Liao Plain, Tarim Basin

Population distribution: overwhelming majority of the population is found in the eastern half of the country; the west, with its vast mountainous and desert areas, remains sparsely populated; though ranked first in the world in total population, overall density is less than that of many other countries in Asia and Europe; high population density is found along the Yangtze and Yellow River valleys, the Xi Jiang River delta, the Sichuan Basin (around Chengdu), in and around Beijing, and the industrial area around Shenyang

Natural hazards: frequent typhoons (about five per year along southern and eastern coasts); damaging floods; tsunamis; earthquakes; droughts; land subsidence
volcanism: China contains some historically active volcanoes including Changbaishan (also known as Baitoushan, Baegdu, or P'aektu-san), Hainan Dao, and Kunlun although most have been relatively inactive in recent centuries

Geography - note: *note 1:* world's fourth largest country (after Russia, Canada, and US) and largest country situated entirely in Asia; Mount Everest

on the border with Nepal is the world's tallest peak above sea level
note 2: the largest cave chamber in the world is the Miao Room, in the Gebihe cave system at China's Ziyun Getu He Chuandong National Park, which encloses some 10.78 million cu m (380.7 million cu ft) of volume; the world's largest sinkhole is the Xiaoxhai Tiankeng sinkhole in Chongqing Municipality, which is 660 m deep, with a volume of 130 million cu m
note 3: China appears to have been the center of domestication for two of the world's leading cereal crops: millet in the north along the Yellow River and rice in the south along the lower or middle Yangtze River

PEOPLE AND SOCIETY

Population: 1,410,539,758 (2022 est.)
country comparison to the world: 1

Nationality: *noun:* Chinese (singular and plural)
adjective: Chinese

Ethnic groups: Han Chinese 91.1%, ethnic minorities 8.9% (includes Zhang, Hui, Manchu, Uighur, Miao, Yi, Tujia, Tibetan, Mongol, Dong, Buyei, Yao, Bai, Korean, Hani, Li, Kazakh, Dai, and other nationalities) (2021 est.)
note: the PRC officially recognizes 56 ethnic groups

Languages: Standard Chinese or Mandarin (official; Putonghua, based on the Beijing dialect), Yue (Cantonese), Wu (Shanghainese), Minbei (Fuzhou), Minnan (Hokkien-Taiwanese), Xiang, Gan, Hakka dialects, minority languages (see Ethnic groups entry); note - Zhuang is official in Guangxi Zhuang, Yue is official in Guangdong, Mongolian is official in Nei Mongol, Uighur is official in Xinjiang Uygur, Kyrgyz is official in Xinjiang Uygur, and Tibetan is official in Xizang (Tibet)
major-language sample(s):
世界概況 — 不可缺少的基本消息來源 (Standard Chinese)

Religions: folk religion 21.9%, Buddhist 18.2%, Christian 5.1%, Muslim 1.8%, Hindu < 0.1%, Jewish < 0.1%, other 0.7% (includes Daoist (Taoist)), unaffiliated 52.1% (2021 est.)
note: officially atheist

Age structure: *0-14 years:* 17.29% (male 129,296,339/female 111,782,427)
15-24 years: 11.48% (male 86,129,841/female 73,876,148)
25-54 years: 46.81% (male 333,789,731/female 318,711,557)
55-64 years: 12.08% (male 84,827,645/female 83,557,507)
65 years and over: 12.34% (male 81,586,490/female 90,458,292) (2020 est.)

Dependency ratios: *total dependency ratio:* 42.2
youth dependency ratio: 25.2
elderly dependency ratio: 17
potential support ratio: 5.9 (2020 est.)
note: data do not include Hong Kong, Macau, and Taiwan

Median age: *total:* 38.4 years
male: 37.5 years
female: 39.4 years (2020 est.)
country comparison to the world: 62

Population growth rate: 0.19% (2022 est.)
country comparison to the world: 180

Birth rate: 9.93 births/1,000 population (2022 est.)
country comparison to the world: 189

Death rate: 7.9 deaths/1,000 population (2022 est.)
country comparison to the world: 97

Net migration rate: -0.11 migrant(s)/1,000 population (2022 est.)
country comparison to the world: 104

Population distribution: overwhelming majority of the population is found in the eastern half of the country; the west, with its vast mountainous and desert areas, remains sparsely populated; though ranked first in the world in total population, overall density is less than that of many other countries in Asia and Europe; high population density is found along the Yangtze and Yellow River valleys, the Xi Jiang River delta, the Sichuan Basin (around Chengdu), in and around Beijing, and the industrial area around Shenyang

Urbanization: *urban population:* 63.6% of total population (2022)
rate of urbanization: 1.78% annual rate of change (2020-25 est.)
note: data do not include Hong Kong and Macau

Major urban areas - population: 28.517 million Shanghai, 21.333 million BEIJING (capital), 16.875 million Chongqing, 14.012 million Tianjin, 13.965 million Guangzhou, 12.831 million Shenzhen (2022)

Sex ratio: *at birth:* 1.1 male(s)/female
0-14 years: 1.15 male(s)/female
15-24 years: 1.16 male(s)/female
25-54 years: 1.05 male(s)/female
55-64 years: 1 male(s)/female
65 years and over: 0.68 male(s)/female
total population: 1.04 male(s)/female (2022 est.)

Maternal mortality ratio: 29 deaths/100,000 live births (2017 est.)
country comparison to the world: 111

Infant mortality rate: *total:* 6.76 deaths/1,000 live births
male: 7.19 deaths/1,000 live births
female: 6.3 deaths/1,000 live births (2022 est.)
country comparison to the world: 160

Life expectancy at birth: *total population:* 77.72 years
male: 75 years
female: 80.7 years (2022 est.)
country comparison to the world: 85

Total fertility rate: 1.45 children born/woman (2022 est.)
country comparison to the world: 210

Contraceptive prevalence rate: 84.5% (2017)

Drinking water source: *improved: urban:* 97.3% of population
rural: 91.5% of population
total: 95.1% of population
unimproved: urban: 2.7% of population
rural: 8.5% of population
total: 4.9% of population (2020 est.)

Current health expenditure: 5.4% of GDP (2019)

Physicians density: 2.23 physicians/1,000 population (2019)

Hospital bed density: 4.3 beds/1,000 population (2017)

Sanitation facility access: *improved: urban:* 97.6% of population
rural: 90.6% of population
total: 94.9% of population
unimproved: urban: 2.4% of population
rural: 9.4% of population
total: 5.1% of population (2020 est.)

Major infectious diseases: *degree of risk:* high (2020)
food or waterborne diseases: bacterial diarrhea, hepatitis A, and typhoid fever
vectorborne diseases: Crimean-Congo hemorrhagic fever, Japanese encephalitis
soil contact diseases: hantaviral hemorrhagic fever with renal syndrome (HFRS)
note: a new coronavirus is causing an outbreak of respiratory illness (COVID-19) in China; illness with this virus has ranged from mild to severe with fatalities reported; the US Department of State has issued a do not travel advisory for China due to COVID-19; the Centers for Disease Control and Prevention has also recommended against travel to China and published additional guidance at https://wwwnc.cdc.gov/travel/notices/warning/novel-coronavirus-china; the US Department of Homeland Security has issued instructions requiring US passengers who have been in China to travel through select airports where the US Government has implemented enhanced screening procedures; as of 18 August 2022, China has reported a total of 6,041,468 cases of COVID-19 or 410.62 cumulative cases of COVID-19 per 100,000 population with a total of 24,322 cumulative deaths or a rate 1.65 cumulative deaths per 100,000 population; as of 9 August 2022, 91.27% of the population has received at least one dose of COVID-19 vaccine

Obesity - adult prevalence rate: 6.2% (2016)
country comparison to the world: 169

Alcohol consumption per capita: *total:* 4.48 liters of pure alcohol (2019 est.)
beer: 1.66 liters of pure alcohol (2019 est.)
wine: 0.18 liters of pure alcohol (2019 est.)
spirits: 2.63 liters of pure alcohol (2019 est.)
other alcohols: 0 liters of pure alcohol (2019 est.)
country comparison to the world: 89

Tobacco use: *total:* 25.6% (2020 est.)
male: 49.4% (2020 est.)
female: 1.7% (2020 est.)
country comparison to the world: 44

Children under the age of 5 years underweight: 2.4% (2013)
country comparison to the world: 103

Education expenditures: 3.5% of GDP (2018 est.)
country comparison to the world: 123

Literacy: *definition:* age 15 and over can read and write
total population: 96.8%
male: 98.5%
female: 95.2% (2018)

School life expectancy (primary to tertiary education): *total:* 14 years
male: 14 years
female: 14 years (2015)

People - note: in October 2015, the Chinese Government announced that it would change its rules to allow all couples to have two children, loosening a 1979 mandate that restricted many couples to one child; the new policy was implemented on 1 January 2016 to address China's rapidly aging population and future economic needs

ENVIRONMENT

Environment - current issues: air pollution (greenhouse gases, sulfur dioxide particulates) from reliance on coal produces acid rain; China is the world's largest single emitter of carbon dioxide from the burning of fossil fuels; water shortages, particularly in the north; water pollution from untreated wastes; coastal destruction due to land reclamation, industrial development, and aquaculture; deforestation and habitat destruction; poor land management leads to soil erosion, landslides, floods, droughts, dust storms, and desertification; trade in endangered species

Environment - international agreements: party to: Antarctic-Environmental Protection, Antarctic-Marine Living Resources, Antarctic Treaty, Biodiversity, Climate Change, Climate Change-Kyoto Protocol, Climate Change-Paris Agreement, Desertification, Endangered Species, Environmental Modification, Hazardous Wastes, Law of the Sea, Marine Dumping-London Convention, Marine Dumping-London Protocol, Ozone Layer Protection, Ship Pollution, Tropical Timber 2006, Wetlands, Whaling
signed, but not ratified: Comprehensive Nuclear Test Ban

Air pollutants: *particulate matter emissions:* 49.16 micrograms per cubic meter (2016 est.)
carbon dioxide emissions: 9,893.04 megatons (2016 est.)
methane emissions: 1,490.24 megatons (2020 est.)

Climate: extremely diverse; tropical in south to subarctic in north

Land use: *agricultural land:* 54.7% (2018 est.)
arable land: 11.3% (2018 est.)
permanent crops: 1.6% (2018 est.)
permanent pasture: 41.8% (2018 est.)
forest: 22.3% (2018 est.)
other: 23% (2018 est.)

Urbanization: *urban population:* 63.6% of total population (2022)
rate of urbanization: 1.78% annual rate of change (2020-25 est.)
note: data do not include Hong Kong and Macau

Revenue from forest resources: *forest revenues:* 0.08% of GDP (2018 est.)
country comparison to the world: 119

Revenue from coal: *coal revenues:* 0.57% of GDP (2018 est.)
country comparison to the world: 9

Waste and recycling: municipal solid waste generated annually: 210 million tons (2015 est.)

Major lakes (area sq km): *fresh water lake(s):* Dongting Hu - 3,100 sq km; Poyang Hu - 3,350 sq km; Hongze Hu - 2,700 sq km; Tai Hu - 2,210 sq km; Hulun Nur - 1,590
salt water lake(s): Quinghai Hu - 4,460 sq km; Nam Co - 2,500 sq km; Siling Co - 1,860 sq km; Tangra Yumco - 1,400 sq km; Bosten Hu 1,380 sq km

Major rivers (by length in km): Yangtze - 6,300 km; Huang He - 5,464 km; Amur river source (shared with Mongolia and Russia [m]) - 4,444 km; Mekong river source (shared with Burma, Laos, Thailand, Cambodia, and Vietnam [m]) - 4,350 km; Brahmaputra river source (shared with India and Bangladesh [m]) - 3,969 km; Indus river source (shared with India and Pakistan [m]) -3,610 km; Salween river source (shared with Thailand and Burma [m]) - 3,060 km; Irrawaddy river source (shared with Burma [m]) - 2,809 km; Pearl (shared with Vietnam [s]) - 2,200 km; Red river source (shared with Vietnam [m]) - 1,149 km
note – [s] after country name indicates river source; [m] after country name indicates river mouth

Major watersheds (area sq km): *Pacific Ocean drainage:* Amur (1,929,955 sq km), Huang He (944,970 sq km), Mekong (805,604 sq km), Yangtze (1,722,193 sq km)

Indian Ocean drainage: Brahmaputra (651,335 sq km), Ganges (1,016,124 sq km), Indus (1,081,718 sq km), Irrawaddy (413,710 sq km), Salween (271,914 sq km)

Arctic Ocean drainage: Ob (2,972,493 sq km)

Internal (endorheic basin) drainage: Tarim Basin (1,152,448 sq km), Amu Darya (534,739 sq km), Syr Darya (782,617 sq km), Lake Balkash (510,015 sq km)

Major aquifers: North China Aquifer System (Huang Huai Hai Plain), Song-Liao Plain, Tarim Basin

Total water withdrawal: *municipal:* 79.4 billion cubic meters (2017 est.)
industrial: 133.5 billion cubic meters (2017 est.)
agricultural: 385.2 billion cubic meters (2017 est.)

Total renewable water resources: 2.84 trillion cubic meters (2017 est.)

GOVERNMENT

Country name: *conventional long form:* People's Republic of China
conventional short form: China
local long form: Zhonghua Renmin Gongheguo
local short form: Zhongguo
abbreviation: PRC
etymology: English name derives from the Qin (Chin) rulers of the 3rd century B.C., who comprised the first imperial dynasty of ancient China; the Chinese name Zhongguo translates as "Central Nation" or "Middle Kingdom"

Government type: communist party-led state

Capital: *name:* Beijing
geographic coordinates: 39 55 N, 116 23 E
time difference: UTC+8 (13 hours ahead of Washington, DC, during Standard Time)
time zone note: China is the largest country (in terms of area) with just one time zone; before 1949 it was divided into five
etymology: the Chinese meaning is "Northern Capital"

Administrative divisions: 23 provinces (sheng, singular and plural), 5 autonomous regions (zizhiqu, singular and plural), 4 municipalities (shi, singular and plural), and two special administrative regions (tebie xingzhengqu, singular and plural)
provinces: Anhui, Fujian, Gansu, Guangdong, Guizhou, Hainan, Hebei, Heilongjiang, Henan, Hubei, Hunan, Jiangsu, Jiangxi, Jilin, Liaoning, Qinghai, Shaanxi, Shandong, Shanxi, Sichuan, Yunnan, Zhejiang; (see note on Taiwan)
autonomous regions: Guangxi, Nei Mongol (Inner Mongolia), Ningxia, Xinjiang Uyghur, Xizang (Tibet)
municipalities: Beijing, Chongqing, Shanghai, Tianjin
special administrative regions: Hong Kong, Macau
note: China considers Taiwan its 23rd province; see separate entries for the special administrative regions of Hong Kong and Macau

Independence: 1 October 1949 (People's Republic of China established); notable earlier dates: 221 B.C. (unification under the Qin Dynasty); 1 January 1912 (Qing Dynasty replaced by the Republic of China)

National holiday: National Day (anniversary of the founding of the People's Republic of China), 1 October (1949)

Constitution: *history:* several previous; latest promulgated 4 December 1982
amendments: proposed by the Standing Committee of the National People's Congress or supported by more than one fifth of the National People's Congress membership; passage requires more than two-thirds majority vote of the Congress membership; amended several times, last in 2018

Legal system: civil law influenced by Soviet and continental European civil law systems; legislature retains power to interpret statutes; note - on 28 May 2020, the National People's Congress adopted the PRC Civil Code, which codifies personal relations and property relations

International law organization participation: has not submitted an ICJ jurisdiction declaration; non-party state to the ICCt

Citizenship: *citizenship by birth:* no
citizenship by descent only: least one parent must be a citizen of China
dual citizenship recognized: no
residency requirement for naturalization: while naturalization is theoretically possible, in practical terms it is extremely difficult; residency is required but not specified

Suffrage: 18 years of age; universal

Executive branch: *chief of state:* President XI Jinping (since 14 March 2013); Vice President WANG Qishan (since 17 March 2018)
head of government: Premier LI Keqiang (since 16 March 2013); Executive Vice Premiers HAN Zheng (since 19 March 2018), SUN Chunlan (since 19 March 2018), LIU He (since 19 March 2018), HU Chunhua (since 19 March 2018)
cabinet: State Council appointed by National People's Congress
elections/appointments: president and vice president indirectly elected by National People's Congress (no term limits); election last held on 17 March 2018 (next to be held in March 2023); premier nominated by president, confirmed by National People's Congress
election results: 2018: XI Jinping reelected president; National People's Congress vote - 2,970 (unanimously); WANG Qishan elected vice president with 2,969 votes
2013: XI Jinping elected president; National People's Congress vote - 2,952; LI Yuanchao elected vice president with 2,839 votes
note - in March 2018, the PRC's National People's Congress passed an amendment abolishing presidential term limits, opening the door for XI to seek a third five-year term in 2023

Legislative branch: *description:* unicameral National People's Congress or Quanguo Renmin Daibiao Dahui (maximum of 3,000 seats; members indirectly elected by municipal, regional, and provincial people's congresses, and the People's Liberation Army; members serve 5-year terms); note - in practice, only members of the Chinese Communist Party (CCP), its 8 allied independent parties, and CCP-approved independent candidates are elected
elections: last held in December 2017-February 2018 (next to be held in late 2022 to early 2023)
election results: percent of vote - NA; seats by party - NA; composition - men 2,238, women 742, percent of women 24.9%

Judicial branch: *highest court(s):* Supreme People's Court (consists of over 340 judges, including the chief justice and 13 grand justices organized into a

civil committee and tribunals for civil, economic, administrative, complaint and appeal, and communication and transportation cases)
judge selection and term of office: chief justice appointed by the People's National Congress (NPC); limited to 2 consecutive 5-year-terms; other justices and judges nominated by the chief justice and appointed by the Standing Committee of the NPC; term of other justices and judges determined by the NPC
subordinate courts: Higher People's Courts; Intermediate People's Courts; District and County People's Courts; Autonomous Region People's Courts; International Commercial Courts; Special People's Courts for military, maritime, transportation, and forestry issues

Political parties and leaders: Chinese Communist Party or CCP [XI Jinping]
note: China has 8 nominally independent small parties controlled by the CCP

International organization participation: ADB, AfDB (nonregional member), APEC, Arctic Council (observer), ARF, ASEAN (dialogue partner), BIS, BRICS, CDB, CICA, EAS, FAO, FATF, G-20, G-24 (observer), G-5, G-77, IADB, IAEA, IBRD, ICAO, ICC (national committees), ICRM, IDA, IFAD, IFC, IFRCS, IHO, ILO, IMF, IMO, IMSO, Interpol, IOC, IOM (observer), IPU, ISO, ITSO, ITU, LAIA (observer), MIGA, MINURSO, MINUSMA, MONUSCO, NAM (observer), NSG, OAS (observer), OPCW, Pacific Alliance (observer), PCA, PIF (partner), SAARC (observer), SCO, SICA (observer), UN, UNAMID, UNCTAD, UNESCO, UNFICYP, UNHCR, UNHRC, UNIDO, UNIFIL, UNISFA, UNMIL, UNMISS, UNOCI, UN Security Council (permanent), UNTSO, UNWTO, UPU, WCO, WHO, WIPO, WMO, WTO, ZC

Diplomatic representation in the US: *chief of mission:* Ambassador QIN Gang (since 15 Sep 2021)
chancery: 3505 International Place NW, Washington, DC 20008
telephone: [1] (202) 495-2266
FAX: [1] (202) 495-2138
email address and website:
chinaemppress_us@mfa.gov.cn
http://www.china-embassy.org/eng/
consulate(s) general: Chicago, Los Angeles, New York, San Francisco; note - the US ordered closure of the Houston consulate in late July 2020

Diplomatic representation from the US: *chief of mission:* Ambassador Nicholas BURNS (since 2 April 2022)
embassy: 55 An Jia Lou Road, Chaoyang District, Beijing 100600
mailing address: 7300 Beijing Place, Washington DC 20521-7300
telephone: [86] (10) 8531-3000
FAX: [86] (10) 8531-4200
email address and website:
BeijingACS@state.gov
https://china.usembassy-china.org.cn/
consulate(s) general: Guangzhou, Shanghai, Shenyang, Wuhan; note - the Chinese Government ordered closure of the US consulate in Chengdu in late July 2020

Flag description: red with a large yellow five-pointed star and four smaller yellow five-pointed stars (arranged in a vertical arc toward the middle of the flag) in the upper hoist-side corner; the color red represents revolution, while the stars symbolize the four social classes - the working class, the peasantry, the urban petty bourgeoisie, and the national bourgeoisie (capitalists) -united under the Communist Party of China

National symbol(s): dragon, giant panda; national colors: red, yellow

National anthem: *name:* "Yiyongjun Jinxingqu" (The March of the Volunteers)
lyrics/music: TIAN Han/NIE Er
note: adopted 1949; the anthem, though banned during the Cultural Revolution, is more commonly known as "Zhongguo Guoge" (Chinese National Song); it was originally the theme song to the 1935 Chinese movie, "Sons and Daughters in a Time of Storm"

National heritage: total World Heritage Sites: 56 (14 natural, 38 cultural, 4 mixed)
selected World Heritage Site locales: Imperial Palaces of the Ming and Qing Dynasties (c); Mausoleum of the First Qin Emperor (c); The Great Wall (c); Summer Palace (c); Jiuzhaigou Valley (n); Potala Palace (c); Ancient Pingyao (c); Historic Macau (c); Dengfeng (c); Grand Canal (c); Mount Huangshan (m)

Government - note: in 2018, the Beijing established an investigatory National Supervisory Commission to oversee all state employees

ECONOMY

Economic overview: Since the late 1970s, China has moved from a closed, centrally planned system to a more market-oriented one that plays a major global role. China has implemented reforms in a gradualist fashion, resulting in efficiency gains that have contributed to a more than tenfold increase in GDP since 1978. Reforms began with the phaseout of collectivized agriculture, and expanded to include the gradual liberalization of prices, fiscal decentralization, increased autonomy for state enterprises, growth of the private sector, development of stock markets and a modern banking system, and opening to foreign trade and investment. China continues to pursue an industrial policy, state support of key sectors, and a restrictive investment regime. From 2013 to 2017, China had one of the fastest growing economies in the world, averaging slightly more than 7% real growth per year. Measured on a purchasing power parity (PPP) basis that adjusts for price differences, China in 2017 stood as the largest economy in the world, surpassing the US in 2014 for the first time in modern history. China became the world's largest exporter in 2010, and the largest trading nation in 2013. Still, China's per capita income is below the world average.

In July 2005 moved to an exchange rate system that references a basket of currencies. From mid-2005 to late 2008, the renminbi (RMB) appreciated more than 20% against the US dollar, but the exchange rate remained virtually pegged to the dollar from the onset of the global financial crisis until June 2010, when Beijing announced it would resume a gradual appreciation. From 2013 until early 2015, the renminbi held steady against the dollar, but it depreciated 13% from mid-2015 until end-2016 amid strong capital outflows; in 2017 the RMB resumed appreciating against the dollar – roughly 7% from end-of-2016 to end-of-2017. In 2015, the People's Bank of China announced it would continue to carefully push for full convertibility of the renminbi, after the currency was accepted as part of the IMF's special drawing rights basket. However, since late 2015 Beijing has strengthened capital controls and oversight of overseas investments to better manage the exchange rate and maintain financial stability.

Beijing faces numerous economic challenges including: (a) reducing its high domestic savings rate and correspondingly low domestic household consumption; (b) managing its high corporate debt burden to maintain financial stability; (c) controlling off-balance sheet local government debt used to finance infrastructure stimulus; (d) facilitating higher-wage job opportunities for the aspiring middle class, including rural migrants and college graduates, while maintaining competitiveness; (e) dampening speculative investment in the real estate sector without sharply slowing the economy; (f) reducing industrial overcapacity; and (g) raising productivity growth rates through the more efficient allocation of capital and state-support for innovation. Economic development has progressed further in coastal provinces than in the interior, and by 2016 more than 169.3 million migrant workers and their dependents had relocated to urban areas to find work. One consequence of China's population control policy known as the "one-child policy" - which was relaxed in 2016 to permit all families to have two children - is that China is now one of the most rapidly aging countries in the world. Deterioration in the environment - notably air pollution, soil erosion, and the steady fall of the water table, especially in the North - is another longterm problem. China continues to lose arable land because of erosion and urbanization. Beijing is seeking to add energy production capacity from sources other than coal and oil, focusing on natural gas, nuclear, and clean energy development. In 2016, China ratified the Paris Agreement, a multilateral agreement to combat climate change, and committed to peak its carbon dioxide emissions between 2025 and 2030.

The government's 13th Five-Year Plan, unveiled in March 2016, emphasizes the need to increase innovation and boost domestic consumption to make the economy less dependent on government investment, exports, and heavy industry. However, China has made more progress on subsidizing innovation than rebalancing the economy. Beijing has committed to giving the market a more decisive role in allocating resources, but its policies continue to favor state-owned enterprises and emphasize stability. Beijing in 2010 pledged to double China's GDP by 2020, and the 13th Five Year Plan includes annual economic growth targets of at least 6.5% through 2020 to achieve that goal. In recent years, China has renewed its support for state-owned enterprises in sectors considered important to "economic security," explicitly looking to foster globally competitive industries. Beijing also has undermined some market-oriented reforms by reaffirming the "dominant" role of the state in the economy, a stance that threatens to discourage private initiative and make the economy less efficient over time. The slight acceleration in economic growth in 2017—the first such uptick since 2010—gives Beijing more latitude to pursue its economic reforms, focusing on financial sector deleveraging and its Supply-Side Structural Reform agenda, first announced in late 2015.

Real GDP (purchasing power parity):
$23,009,780,000,000 (2020 est.)
$22,492,450,000,000 (2019 est.)

$21,229,360,000,000 (2018 est.)
note: data are in 2017 dollars
country comparison to the world: 1

Real GDP growth rate: 6.14% (2019 est.)
6.75% (2018 est.)
6.92% (2017 est.)
country comparison to the world: 26

Real GDP per capita: $16,400 (2020 est.)
$16,100 (2019 est.)
$15,200 (2018 est.)
note: data are in 2017 dollars
country comparison to the world: 102

GDP (official exchange rate): $14,327,359,000,000 (2019 est.)
note: because China's exchange rate is determined by fiat rather than by market forces, the official exchange rate measure of GDP is not an accurate measure of China's output; GDP at the official exchange rate substantially understates the actual level of China's output vis-a-vis the rest of the world; in China's situation, GDP at purchasing power parity provides the best measure for comparing output across countries

Inflation rate (consumer prices): 2.8% (2019 est.)
2% (2018 est.)
1.5% (2017 est.)
country comparison to the world: 138

Credit ratings: *Fitch rating:* A+ (2007)

Moody's rating: A1 (2017)

Standard & Poors rating: A+ (2017)
note: The year refers to the year in which the current credit rating was first obtained.

GDP - composition, by sector of origin: *agriculture:* 7.9% (2017 est.)
industry: 40.5% (2017 est.)
services: 51.6% (2017 est.)

GDP - composition, by end use: *household consumption:* 39.1% (2017 est.)
government consumption: 14.5% (2017 est.)
investment in fixed capital: 42.7% (2017 est.)
investment in inventories: 1.7% (2017 est.)
exports of goods and services: 20.4% (2017 est.)
imports of goods and services: -18.4% (2017 est.)

Agricultural products: maize, rice, vegetables, wheat, sugar cane, potatoes, cucumbers, tomatoes, watermelons, sweet potatoes

Industries: world leader in gross value of industrial output; mining and ore processing, iron, steel, aluminum, and other metals, coal; machine building; armaments; textiles and apparel; petroleum; cement; chemicals; fertilizer; consumer products (including footwear, toys, and electronics); food processing; transportation equipment, including automobiles, railcars and locomotives, ships, aircraft; telecommunications equipment, commercial space launch vehicles, satellites

Industrial production growth rate: 6.1% (2017 est.)
country comparison to the world: 40

Labor force: 774.71 million (2019 est.)
note: by the end of 2012, China's working age population (15-64 years) was 1.004 billion
country comparison to the world: 1

Labor force - by occupation: *agriculture:* 27.7%
industry: 28.8%
services: 43.5% (2016 est.)

Unemployment rate: 3.64% (2019 est.)
3.84% (2018 est.)
note: data are for registered urban unemployment, which excludes private enterprises and migrants
country comparison to the world: 52

Population below poverty line: 0.6% (2019 est.)

Gini Index coefficient - distribution of family income: 38.5 (2016 est.)
46.2 (2015 est.)
country comparison to the world: 73

Household income or consumption by percentage share: *lowest 10%:* 2.1%
highest 10%: 31.4% (2012)
note: data are for urban households only

Budget: *revenues:* 2.553 trillion (2017 est.)
expenditures: 3.008 trillion (2017 est.)

Budget surplus (+) or deficit (-): -3.8% (of GDP) (2017 est.)
country comparison to the world: 152

Public debt: 47% of GDP (2017 est.)
44.2% of GDP (2016 est.)
note: official data; data cover both central and local government debt, including debt officially recognized by China's National Audit Office report in 2011; data exclude policy bank bonds, Ministry of Railway debt, and China Asset Management Company debt
country comparison to the world: 111

Taxes and other revenues: 21.3% (of GDP) (2017 est.)
country comparison to the world: 141

Fiscal year: calendar year

Current account balance: $141.335 billion (2019 est.)
$25.499 billion (2018 est.)
country comparison to the world: 3

Exports: $2,732,370,000,000 (2020 est.)
$2.631 trillion (2019 est.)
$2,651,010,000,000 (2018 est.)
note: Data are in current year dollars and do not include illicit exports or re-exports.
country comparison to the world: 1

Exports - partners: United States 17%, Hong Kong 10%, Japan 6% (2019)

Exports - commodities: broadcasting equipment, computers, integrated circuits, office machinery and parts, telephones (2019)

Imports: $2,362,690,000,000 (2020 est.) note: data are in current year dollars
$2,499,150,000,000 (2019 est.) note: data are in current year dollars
$2,563,100,000,000 (2018 est.) note: data are in current year dollars
country comparison to the world: 2

Imports - partners: South Korea 9%, Japan 8%, Australia 7%, Germany 7%, US 7%, Taiwan 6% (2019)

Imports - commodities: crude petroleum, integrated circuits, iron, natural gas, cars, gold (2019)

Reserves of foreign exchange and gold: $3.236 trillion (31 December 2017 est.)
$3.098 trillion (31 December 2016 est.)
country comparison to the world: 1

Debt - external: $2,027,950,000,000 (2019 est.)
$1,935,206,000,000 (2018 est.)
country comparison to the world: 13

Exchange rates: Renminbi yuan (RMB) per US dollar -
6.5374 (2020 est.)
7.0403 (2019 est.)
6.8798 (2018 est.)
6.1434 (2014 est.)
6.1958 (2013 est.)

ENERGY

Electricity access: *electrification - total population:* 100% (2020)

Electricity: *installed generating capacity:* 2,217,925,000 kW (2020 est.)
consumption: 6,875,088,640,000 kWh (2019 est.)
exports: 21.655 billion kWh (2019 est.)
imports: 4.858 billion kWh (2019 est.)
transmission/distribution losses: 333.01 billion kWh (2019 est.)

Electricity generation sources: *fossil fuels:* 66% of total installed capacity (2020 est.)
nuclear: 4.8% of total installed capacity (2020 est.)
solar: 3.5% of total installed capacity (2020 est.)
wind: 6.2% of total installed capacity (2020 est.)
hydroelectricity: 17.8% of total installed capacity (2020 est.)
biomass and waste: 1.6% of total installed capacity (2020 est.)

Coal: *production:* 4,314,681,000 metric tons (2020 est.)
consumption: 4,506,387,000 metric tons (2020 est.)
exports: 6.652 million metric tons (2020 est.)
imports: 307.047 million metric tons (2020 est.)
proven reserves: 141.595 billion metric tons (2019 est.)

Petroleum: *total petroleum production:* 4,712,200 bbl/day (2021 est.)
refined petroleum consumption: 14,007,500 bbl/day (2019 est.)
crude oil and lease condensate exports: 52,500 bbl/day (2018 est.)
crude oil and lease condensate imports: 9,238,100 bbl/day (2018 est.)
crude oil estimated reserves: 26,022,600,000 barrels (2021 est.)

Refined petroleum products - production: 11.51 million bbl/day (2015 est.)
country comparison to the world: 2

Refined petroleum products - exports: 848,400 bbl/day (2015 est.)
country comparison to the world: 9

Refined petroleum products - import: 1.16 million bbl/day (2015 est.)
country comparison to the world: 4

Natural gas: *production:* 179,317,495,000 cubic meters (2019 est.)
consumption: 306,576,649,000 cubic meters (2019 est.)
exports: 3,548,831,000 cubic meters (2019 est.)
imports: 131,608,161,000 cubic meters (2019 est.)
proven reserves: 6,654,250,000,000 cubic meters (2021 est.)

Carbon dioxide emissions: 10,773,248,000 metric tonnes of CO2 (2019 est.)
from coal and metallurgical coke: 8,652,419,000 metric tonnes of CO2 (2019 est.)
from petroleum and other liquids: 1,520,552,000 metric tonnes of CO2 (2019 est.)
from consumed natural gas: 600.276 million metric tonnes of CO2 (2019 est.)
country comparison to the world: 1

Energy consumption per capita: 105.687 million Btu/person (2019 est.)
country comparison to the world: 54

COMMUNICATIONS

Telephones - fixed lines: *total subscriptions:* 181.908 million (2020 est.)
subscriptions per 100 inhabitants: 13 (2020 est.)
country comparison to the world: 1

Telephones - mobile cellular: *total subscriptions:* 1.72 billion (2020 est.)
subscriptions per 100 inhabitants: 119 (2020 est.)
country comparison to the world: 1

Telecommunication systems: *general assessment:* China has the largest Internet market in the world with almost all subscribers accessing Internet through mobile devices; market is driven through government-allied investment; fast-developing data center market; government aims to provide universal and affordable broadband coverage through market competition and private investment in state-controlled enterprises; 3G and LTE subscribers will migrate to 5G aiming for 2 million 5G base stations by the end of 2022; government strengthens IoT policies to boost economic growth; China is pushing development of smart cities beyond Beijing; Beijing residents carry virtual card integrating identity, social security, health, and education documents; government controls gateways to global Internet through censorship, surveillance, and shutdowns; major exporter of broadcasting equipment worldwide (2022)
domestic: nearly 13 per 100 fixed line and 118 per 100 mobile-cellular; a domestic satellite system with several earth stations has been in place since 2018 (2020)
international: country code - 86; landing points for the RJCN, EAC-C2C, TPE, APCN-2, APG, NCP, TEA, SeaMeWe-3, SJC2, Taiwan Strait Express-1, AAE-1, APCN-2, AAG, FEA, FLAG and TSE submarine cables providing connectivity to Asia, the Middle East, Europe, and the US; satellite earth stations - 7 (5 Intelsat - 4 Pacific Ocean and 1 Indian Ocean; 1 Intersputnik - Indian Ocean region; and 1 Inmarsat - Pacific and Indian Ocean regions) (2019)

Broadcast media: all broadcast media are owned by, or affiliated with, the Chinese Communisty Party (CCP) or a government agency; no privately owned TV or radio stations; state-run Chinese Central TV, provincial, and municipal stations offer more than 2,000 channels; the Central Propaganda Department as well as local (provincial, municipal) sends directives to all domestic media outlets to guide its reporting with the government maintaining authority to approve all programming; foreign-made TV programs must be approved/censored prior to broadcast; increasingly, PRC nationals turn to online platforms (Bilibili, Tencent Video, iQiyi, etc) to access PRC and international films and television shows. Video platforms have to abide by regulations issued by the Cyberspace Administration of China (CAC), which align with censorship policies from CCP propaganda authorities. (2022)

Internet country code: .cn

Internet users: *total:* 987 million (2020 est.)
percent of population: 70% (2020 est.)
country comparison to the world: 1

Broadband - fixed subscriptions: *total:* 483,549,500 (2020 est.)
subscriptions per 100 inhabitants: 34 (2020 est.)
country comparison to the world: 1

TRANSPORTATION

National air transport system: *number of registered air carriers:* 56 (2020)
inventory of registered aircraft operated by air carriers: 2,890
annual passenger traffic on registered air carriers: 436,183,969 (2018)
annual freight traffic on registered air carriers: 611,439,830 (2018) mt-km

Civil aircraft registration country code prefix: B

Airports: *total:* 507 (2021)
country comparison to the world: 13

Airports - with paved runways: *total:* 510
over 3,047 m: 87
2,438 to 3,047 m: 187
1,524 to 2,437 m: 109
914 to 1,523 m: 43
under 914 m: 84 (2021)

Airports - with unpaved runways: *total:* 23
over 3,047 m: 2
2,438 to 3,047 m: 0
1,524 to 2,437 m: 1
914 to 1,523 m: 7
under 914 m: 13 (2021)

Heliports: 39 (2021)

Pipelines: 76,000 km gas, 30,400 km crude oil, 27,700 km refined petroleum products, 797,000 km water (2018)

Railways: *total:* 150,000 km (2021) 1.435-m gauge (100,000 km electrified); 104,0000 traditional, 40,000 high-speed
country comparison to the world: 2

Roadways: *total:* 5.2 million km (2020)
paved: 4.578 million km (2020) (includes 168000 km of expressways)
unpaved: 622,000 km (2017)
country comparison to the world: 3

Waterways: 27,700 km (2020) (navigable waterways)
country comparison to the world: 6

Merchant marine: *total:* 6,662
by type: bulk carrier 1,558, container ship 341, general cargo 957, oil tanker 1,061, other 2,745 (2021)
country comparison to the world: 3

Ports and terminals: *major seaport(s):* Dalian, Ningbo, Qingdao, Qinhuangdao, Shanghai, Shenzhen, Tianjin
container port(s) (TEUs): Dalian (8,760,000), Guangzhou (23,236,200), Ningbo (27,530,000), Qingdao (21,010,000), Shanghai (43,303,000), Shenzhen (25,770,000), Tianjin (17,264,000) (2019)

LNG terminal(s) (import): Fujian, Guangdong, Jiangsu, Shandong, Shanghai, Tangshan, Zhejiang
river port(s): Guangzhou (Pearl)

Transportation - note: seven of the world's ten largest container ports are in China

MILITARY AND SECURITY

Military and security forces: *People's Liberation Army (PLA):* Ground Forces, Navy (PLAN, includes marines and naval aviation), Air Force (PLAAF, includes airborne forces), Rocket Force (strategic missile force), and Strategic Support Force (information, electronic, and cyber warfare, as well as space forces); People's Armed Police (PAP, includes Coast Guard, Border Defense Force, Internal Security Forces); PLA Reserve Force (2022)
note 1: the Strategic Support Force includes the Space Systems Department, which is responsible for nearly all PLA space operations, including space launch and support, space surveillance, space information support, space telemetry, tracking, and control, and space warfare
note 2: the PAP is a paramilitary police component of China's armed forces that is under the command of the Central Military Commission (CMC) and charged with internal security, law enforcement, counterterrorism, and maritime rights protection
note 3: in 2018, the Coast Guard was moved from the State Oceanic Administration to the PAP; in 2013, China merged four of its five major maritime law enforcement agencies – the China Marine Surveillance (CMS), Maritime Police, Fishery Law Enforcement (FLE), and Anti-Smuggling Police – into a unified coast guard

Military expenditures: 1.5% of GDP (2021 est.)
1.7% of GDP (2020 est.)
1.7% of GDP (2019) (approximately $290 billion)
1.7% of GDP (2018) (approximately $265 billion)
1.8% of GDP (2017) (approximately $260 billion)
country comparison to the world: 88

Military and security service personnel strengths: approximately 2 million active duty troops (approximately 1 million Ground; 250,000 Navy/Marines; 350-400,000 Air Force; 120,000 Rocket Forces; 150-175,000 Strategic Support Forces); estimated 600-650,000 People's Armed Police (2022)

Military equipment inventories and acquisitions: the PLA is outfitted primarily with a wide mix of older and modern domestically-produced systems heavily influenced by technology derived from other countries; Russia has been the top supplier of foreign military equipment since 2010; China has a large defense-industrial sector capable of producing advanced weapons systems across all military domains (2022)
note: the PLA is in the midst of a decades-long modernization effort; in 2017, President XI set three developmental goals for the force - becoming a mechanized force with increased information and strategic capabilities by 2020, a fully modernized force by 2035, and a world-class military by mid-century

Military service age and obligation: 18-22 years of age for men for selective compulsory military service, with a 2-year service obligation; women 18-19 years of age who are high school graduates and meet requirements for specific military jobs are subject to conscription; women may also volunteer; all officers are volunteers (2022)
note: the PLA's conscription system functions as a levy; the PLA establishes the number of conscripts needed, which produces quotas for the provinces; each province provides a set number of soldiers or sailors; if the number of volunteers fails to meet quotas, the local governments may compel individuals to enter military service

Military deployments: 425 Mali (MINUSMA); 225 Democratic Republic of the Congo (MONUSCO); 420 Lebanon (UNIFIL); 1,050 South Sudan (UNMISS); up to 2,000 Djibouti (May 2022)

Military - note: established in 1927, the PLA is the military arm of the ruling Chinese Communist Party (CCP), which oversees the PLA through its Central Military Commission; the Central Military Commission is China's top military decision making body the PRC's internal security forces consist primarily of the Ministry of Public Security (MPS), the Ministry of State Security (MSS), the People's Armed Police (PAP), and the militia; the PLA support the internal security forces as necessary:

the MPS controls the civilian national police, which serves as the first-line force for public order; its primary mission is domestic law enforcement and maintaining order, including anti-rioting and anti-terrorism

the MSS is the PRC's main civilian intelligence and counterintelligence service

the PAP is a paramilitary component (or adjunct) of the PLA; its primary missions include internal security, maintaining public order, maritime security, and assisting the PLA in times of war; it is under the command of the Central Military Commission (CMC); the China Coast Guard (CCG) administratively falls under the PAP; the CCG has a variety of missions, such as maritime sovereignty enforcement, surveillance, resource protection, anti-smuggling, and general law enforcement

the militia is an armed reserve of civilians which serves as an auxiliary and reserve force for the PLA upon mobilization; it is distinct from the PLA's reserve forces; militia units are organized around towns, villages, urban sub-districts, and enterprises, and vary widely in composition and mission; they have dual civilian-military command structures; a key component of the militia are the local maritime forces, commonly referred to as the People's Armed Forces Maritime Militia (PAFMM); the PAFMM consists of mariners (and their vessels) who receive training, equipment, and other forms of support from the Navy and CCG (although the PAFMM remains separate from both) to perform tasks such as maritime patrolling, surveillance and reconnaissance, emergency/disaster response, transportation, search and rescue, and auxiliary tasks in support of naval operations in wartime; the PAFMM's tasks are often conducted in conjunction or coordination with the Navy and the CCG; it has been used to assert Beijing's maritime claims in the Sea of Japan and South China Sea (2022)

TRANSNATIONAL ISSUES

Disputes - international: China and India continue their security and foreign policy dialogue started in 2005 related to a number of boundary disputes across the 2,000 mile shared border; India does not recognize Pakistan's 1964 ceding to China of the Aksai Chin, a territory designated as part of the princely state of Kashmir by the British Survey of India in 1865; China claims most of the Indian state Arunachal Pradesh to the base of the Himalayas, but the US recognizes the state of Arunachal Pradesh as Indian territory; Bhutan and China continue negotiations to establish a common boundary alignment to resolve territorial disputes arising from substantial cartographic discrepancies, the most contentious of which lie in Bhutan's west along China's Chumbi salient; Chinese maps show an international boundary symbol (the so-called "nine-dash line") off the coasts of the littoral states of the South China Sea, where China has interrupted Vietnamese hydrocarbon exploration; China asserts sovereignty over Scarborough Reef along with the Philippines and Taiwan, and over the Spratly Islands together with Malaysia, the Philippines, Taiwan, Vietnam, and Brunei; the 2002 Declaration on the Conduct of Parties in the South China Sea eased tensions in the Spratlys, and in 2017 China and ASEAN began confidential negotiations for an updated Code of Conduct for the South China Sea designed not to settle territorial disputes but establish rules and norms in the region; this still is not the legally binding code of conduct sought by some parties; Vietnam and China continue to expand construction of facilities in the Spratlys and in early 2018 China began deploying advanced military systems to disputed Spratly outposts; China occupies some of the Paracel Islands also claimed by Vietnam and Taiwan; the Japanese-administered Senkaku Islands are also claimed by China and Taiwan; certain islands in the Yalu and Tumen Rivers are in dispute with North Korea; North Korea and China seek to stem illegal migration to China by North Koreans, fleeing privation and oppression; China and Russia have demarcated the once disputed islands at the Amur and Ussuri confluence and in the Argun River in accordance with their 2004 Agreement; China and Tajikistan have begun demarcating the revised boundary agreed to in the delimitation of 2002; the decade-long demarcation of the China-Vietnam land boundary was completed in 2009; citing environmental, cultural, and social concerns, China has reconsidered construction of 13 dams on the Salween River, but energy-starved Burma, with backing from Thailand, continues to consider building five hydro-electric dams downstream despite regional and international protests

Refugees and internally displaced persons: refugees (country of origin): 303,107 (Vietnam), undetermined (North Korea) (mid-year 2021)

IDPs: undetermined (2021)

Trafficking in persons: *current situation:* human traffickers exploit domestic and foreign victims in China and Chinese people abroad; Chinese men, women, and children are victims of forced labor and sex trafficking in at least 60 countries; traffickers also use China as a transit point to subject foreign individuals to trafficking in other countries throughout Asia and in international maritime industries; state-sponsored forced labor is intensifying under the government's mass detention and political indoctrination campaign against Muslim minorities in the Xinjiang Uyghur Autonomous Region; well-organized criminal syndicates and local gangs subject Chinese women and girls to sex trafficking within China; women and girls from South Asia, Southeast Asia, and several countries in Africa experience forced labor in domestic service, forced concubinism leading to forced childbearing, and sex trafficking via forced and fraudulent marriage to Chinese men; African and Asian men reportedly experience conditions indicative of forced labor aboard Chinese-flagged fishing vessels; many North Korean refugees and asylum-seekers living in China illegally are particularly vulnerable to trafficking
tier rating: Tier 3 — China does not fully meet the minimum standards for elimination of trafficking and is not making significant efforts to do so; the government prosecuted and convicted some traffickers and continued to cooperate with international authorities to address forced and fraudulent marriages in China; however, there was a government policy or pattern of widespread forced labor, including the continued mass arbitrary detention of more than one million Uyghurs, ethnic Kazakhs, ethnic Kyrgyz, and other Muslims in the Xinjiang Uyghur Autonomous Region; the government did not report any investigations, prosecutions, or convictions of law enforcement officials allegedly complicit despite continued reports of officials benefiting from, permitting, or directly facilitating sex trafficking; authorities did not report identifying any trafficking victims or referring them to protective services; it is likely that law enforcement arrested and detained unidentified trafficking victims for crimes traffickers compelled them to commit; for the third consecutive year, the government did not report the extent to which it funded anti-trafficking activities in furtherance of the 2013-2020 National Action Plan on Combating Human Trafficking (2020)

Illicit drugs: a major source of precursor chemicals, new psychoactive substances (NPS), and synthetic drugs, including fentanyl precursors and methamphetamine; PRC criminal organizations, transnational crime, and organizations from Mexico and Southeast Asia traffic licit precursor chemical components and illicit finished drugs within the PRC as well as to international markets; significant illicit drug consumption of methamphetamine and ketamine; a major destination and transit country for heroin produced in neighboring countries; the PRC remains a major source of NPS sold in North America and Europe (2021)

CHRISTMAS ISLAND

INTRODUCTION

Background: Although Europeans sighted the island as early as 1615, it was only named in 1643 by English Captain William MYNORS for the day of its rediscovery. Another English ship sailed by the island in 1688 and found it uninhabited. Attempts to explore the island over the next two centuries were hampered by steep cliffs and dense jungle. Phosphate discovery on the island in 1887, lead to the UK annexing it the following year. In 1898, the Christmas Island Phosphate Company brought in 200 Chinese indentured servants to work the mines, along with Malays, Sikhs, and a small number of Europeans. The UK administered Christmas Island from Singapore.

Japan invaded the island in 1942, but islanders sabotaged Japanese mining operations, making the mines relatively unproductive. After World War II, Australia and New Zealand bought the Christmas Island Phosphate Company, and in 1958, the UK transferred sovereignty from Singapore to Australia in exchange for $20 million for the loss of future phosphate income. In 1980, Australia set up the Christmas Island National Park and expanded its boundaries throughout the 1980s until it covered more than 60% of the Island's territory. The

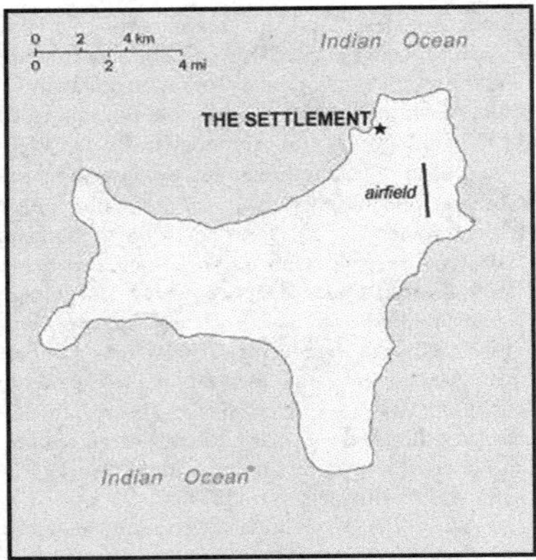

phosphate mine was closed in 1987 because of environmental concerns and Australia has rejected several efforts to reopen it.

In the 1980s, boats of asylum seekers started landing on Christmas Island and the migrants claimed refugee status since they were on Australian territory. In 2001, Australia declared Christmas Island outside the Australian migration zone and built an immigration detention center on the island. Completed in 2008, the controversial detention center was officially closed in 2018, but then reopened in early 2019. In 2020, the center served as a coronavirus quarantine facility for Australian citizens evacuated from China.

GEOGRAPHY

Location: Southeastern Asia, island in the Indian Ocean, south of Indonesia

Geographic coordinates: 10 30 S, 105 40 E

Map references: Southeast Asia

Area: *total:* 135 sq km
land: 135 sq km
water: 0 sq km

Area - comparative: about three-quarters the size of Washington, DC

Land boundaries: *total:* 0 km

Coastline: 138.9 km

Maritime claims: *territorial sea:* 12 nm
contiguous zone: 12 nm
exclusive fishing zone: 200 nm

Climate: tropical with a wet season (December to April) and dry season; heat and humidity moderated by trade winds

Terrain: steep cliffs along coast rise abruptly to central plateau

Elevation: *highest point:* Murray Hill 361 m
lowest point: Indian Ocean 0 m

Natural resources: phosphate, beaches

Land use: *agricultural land:* 0% (2018 est.)
other: 100% (2018 est.)

Population distribution: majority of the population lives on the northern tip of the island

Natural hazards: the narrow fringing reef surrounding the island can be a maritime hazard

Geography - note: located along major sea lanes of the Indian Ocean

PEOPLE AND SOCIETY

Population: 2,205 (2016 est.)

Nationality: *noun:* Christmas Islander(s)
adjective: Christmas Island

Ethnic groups: Chinese 70%, European 20%, Malay 10% (2001)
note: no indigenous population

Languages: English (official) 27.6%, Mandarin 17.2%, Malay 17.1%, Cantonese 3.9%, Min Nan 1.6%, Tagalog 1%, other 4.5%, unspecified 27.1% (2016 est.)
note: data represent language spoken at home

Religions: Muslim 19.4%, Buddhist 18.3%, Roman Catholic 8.8%, Protestant 6.5% (includes Anglican 3.6%, Uniting Church 1.2%, other 1.7%), other Christian 3.3%, other 0.6%, none 15.3%, unspecified 27.7% (2016 est.)

Age structure: *0-14 years:* 12.79% (male 147/female 135)
15-24 years: 12.2% (male 202/female 67)
25-54 years: 57.91% (male 955/female 322)
55-64 years: 11.66% (male 172/female 85)
65 years and over: 5.44% (male 84/female 36) (2017 est.)

Population growth rate: 1.11% (2014 est.)

Population distribution: majority of the population lives on the northern tip of the island

ENVIRONMENT

Environment - current issues: loss of rainforest; impact of phosphate mining

Climate: tropical with a wet season (December to April) and dry season; heat and humidity moderated by trade winds

Land use: *agricultural land:* 0% (2018 est.)
other: 100% (2018 est.)

GOVERNMENT

Country name: *conventional long form:* Territory of Christmas Island
conventional short form: Christmas Island
etymology: named by English Captain William MYNORS for the day of its rediscovery, Christmas Day (25 December 1643); the island had been sighted by Europeans as early as 1615

Government type: non-self-governing overseas territory of Australia

Dependency status: non-self governing territory of Australia; administered from Canberra by the Department of Infrastructure, Transport, Cities & Regional Development

Capital: *name:* The Settlement (Flying Fish Cove)
geographic coordinates: 10 25 S, 105 43 E
time difference: UTC+7 (12 hours ahead of Washington, DC, during Standard Time)
etymology: self-descriptive name for the main locus of population

Administrative divisions: none (territory of Australia)

Independence: none (territory of Australia)

National holiday: Australia Day (commemorates the arrival of the First Fleet of Australian settlers), 26 January (1788)

Constitution: *history:* 1 October 1958 (Christmas Island Act 1958)
amendments: amended many times, last in 2020

Legal system: legal system is under the authority of the governor general of Australia and Australian law

Citizenship: see Australia

Suffrage: 18 years of age

Executive branch: chief of state: King CHARLES III (since 8 September 2022); represented by Governor General of the Commonwealth of Australia General David HURLEY (since 1 July 2019)
head of government: Acting Administrator Sarah VANDENBROEK (since 4 October 2022)
cabinet: NA
elections/appointments: the monarchy is hereditary; governor general appointed by the monarch on the recommendation of the Australian prime minister; administrator appointed by the governor general of Australia for a 2-year term and represents the monarch and Australia

Legislative branch: *description:* unicameral Christmas Island Shire Council (9 seats; members directly elected by simple majority vote to serve 4-year terms)
elections: held every 2 years with half the members standing for election; last held in October 2021 (next to be held in October 2023)
election results: percent of vote - NA; seats by party - independent 9; composition as of 17 October 2021 - men 8, women 1, percent of women 11.1%

Judicial branch: *highest court(s):* under the terms of the Territorial Law Reform Act 1992, Western Australia provides court services as needed for the island, including the Supreme Court and subordinate courts (District Court, Magistrate Court, Family Court, Children's Court, and Coroners' Court)

Political parties and leaders: none

International organization participation: none

Diplomatic representation in the US: none (territory of Australia)

Diplomatic representation from the US: embassy: none (territory of Australia)

Flag description: territorial flag; divided diagonally from upper hoist to lower fly; the upper triangle is green with a yellow image of the Golden Bosun Bird superimposed; the lower triangle is blue with the Southern Cross constellation, representing Australia, superimposed; a centered yellow disk displays a green map of the island
note: the flag of Australia is used for official purposes

National symbol(s): golden bosun bird

National anthem: note: as a territory of Australia, "Advance Australia Fair" remains official as the national anthem, while "God Save the King" serves as the royal anthem (see Australia)

ECONOMY

Economic overview: The main economic activities on Christmas Island are the mining of low grade phosphate, limited tourism, the provision of government services and, since 2005, the construction and operation of the Immigration Detention Center. The government sector includes administration, health, education, policing, customs, quarantine, and defense.

Industries: tourism, phosphate extraction (near depletion)

Fiscal year: 1 July - 30 June

Exports - partners: Malaysia 36%, New Zealand 21%, Indonesia 20%, Australia 10% (2019)

Exports - commodities: calcium phosphates, fertilizers, valves, air pumps, industrial printers (2019)

Imports - partners: Australia 80%, United States 7%, Canada 5% (2019)

Imports - commodities: refined petroleum, cars, iron structures, aircraft, crustaceans (2019)

Exchange rates: Australian dollars (AUD) per US dollar -
1.311 (2017 est.)
1.3442 (2016 est.)
1.3442 (2015)
1.3291 (2014 est.)
1.1094 (2013 est.)

COMMUNICATIONS

Telecommunication systems: *general assessment:* internet access on Christmas Island is provided by satellite; improvements through the Regional Connectivity Program to the macro and small cell mobile sites will provide new and improved mobile, voice and data connectivity for residents and visitors; the upgrade will also support local businesses and community facilities, enabling increased residential access to essential services such as telehealth and education (2022)
domestic: improvements to Christmas Island include an upgrade to the macro cell base stations and deploy a new macro cell base station at the airport (2022)
international: international code - 61 8; ASC submarine cable to Singapore and Australia; satellite earth station - 1 (Intelsat provides telephone and telex service) (2019)

Broadcast media: 1 community radio station; satellite broadcasts of several Australian radio and TV stations (2017)

Internet country code: .cx

Internet users: *total:* 790 (2016 est.)
percent of population: 36% (2016 est.)

TRANSPORTATION

Airports: *total:* 1 (2021)

Airports - with paved runways: *total:* 1
1,524 to 2,437 m: 1 (2021)

Railways: *total:* 18 km (2017)
standard gauge: 18 km (2017) 1.435-m (not in operation)
note: the 18-km Christmas Island Phosphate Company Railway between Flying Fish Cove and South Point was decommissioned in 1987; some tracks and scrap remain in place

Roadways: *total:* 142 km (2011)
paved: 32 km (2011)
*unpaved:*110 km (2011)

Ports and terminals: *major seaport(s):* Flying Fish Cove

MILITARY AND SECURITY

Military - note: defense is the responsibility of Australia

TRANSNATIONAL ISSUES

Disputes - international: none

CLIPPERTON ISLAND

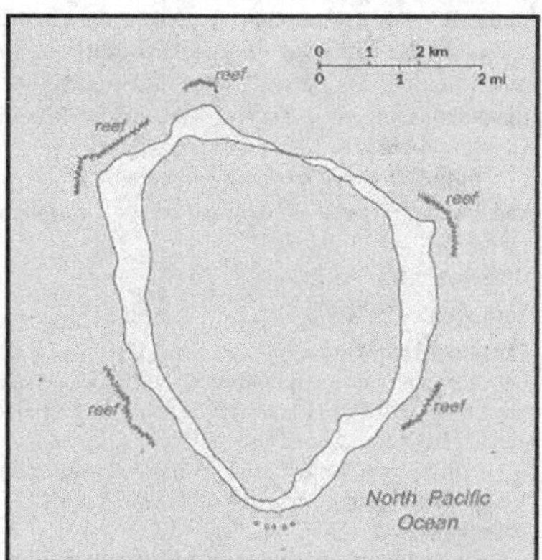

INTRODUCTION

Background: This isolated atoll was named for John CLIPPERTON, an English pirate who was rumored to have made it his hideout early in the 18th century. Annexed by France in 1855 and claimed by the US, it was seized by Mexico in 1897. Arbitration eventually awarded the island to France in 1931, which took possession in 1935.

GEOGRAPHY

Location: Middle America, atoll in the North Pacific Ocean, 1,120 km southwest of Mexico

Geographic coordinates: 10 17 N, 109 13 W

Map references: Political Map of the World

Area: *total:* 6 sq km
land: 6 sq km
water: 0 sq km

Area - comparative: about 12 times the size of The Mall in Washington, DC

Land boundaries: *total:* 0 km

Coastline: 11.1 km

Maritime claims: *territorial sea:* 12 nm
exclusive economic zone: 200 nm

Climate: tropical; humid, average temperature 20-32 degrees Celsius, wet season (May to October)

Terrain: coral atoll

Elevation: *highest point:* Rocher Clipperton 29 m
lowest point: Pacific Ocean 0 m

Natural resources: fish

Land use: *agricultural land:* 0% (2018 est.)
forest: 0% (2018 est.)
other: 100% (2018 est.)

Natural hazards: subject to tropical storms and hurricanes from May to October

Geography - note: the atoll reef is approximately 12 km (7.5 mi) in circumference; an attempt to colonize the atoll in the early 20th century ended in disaster and was abandoned in 1917

PEOPLE AND SOCIETY

Population: uninhabited

ENVIRONMENT

Environment - current issues: no natural resources, guano deposits depleted; the ring-shaped atoll encloses a stagnant fresh-water lagoon

Climate: tropical; humid, average temperature 20-32 degrees Celsius, wet season (May to October)

Land use: *agricultural land:* 0% (2018 est.)
forest: 0% (2018 est.)
other: 100% (2018 est.)

GOVERNMENT

Country name: *conventional long form:* none
conventional short form: Clipperton Island
local long form: none
local short form: Ile Clipperton
former: sometimes referred to as Ile de la Passion or Atoll Clipperton
etymology: named after an 18th-century English pirate who supposedly used the island as a base

Dependency status: possession of France; administered directly by the Minister of Overseas France

Legal system: the laws of France apply

Flag description: the flag of France is used

ECONOMY

Economic overview: Although 115 species of fish have been identified in the territorial waters of Clipperton Island, tuna fishing is the only economically viable species.

TRANSPORTATION

Ports and terminals: none; offshore anchorage only

MILITARY AND SECURITY

Military - note: defense is the responsibility of France

TRANSNATIONAL ISSUES

Disputes - international: none

COCOS (KEELING) ISLANDS

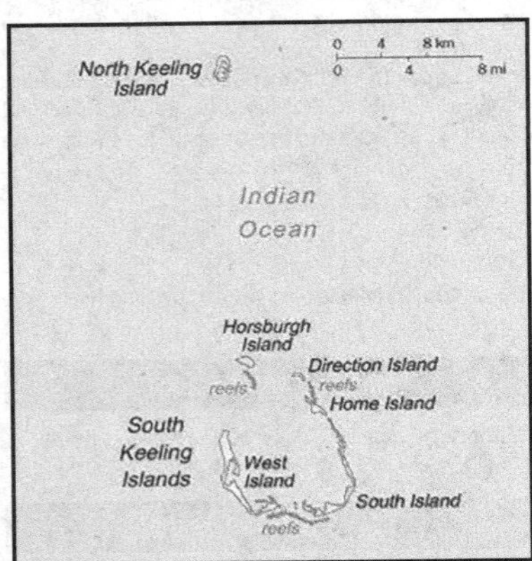

INTRODUCTION

Background: British captain William KEELING discovered Cocos (Keeling) Islands in 1609, and they were named the Cocos Islands in 1622 for their coconut trees. Some maps began referring to them as the Keeling Islands in 1703. In 1825, Scottish trader John CLUNIES-ROSS was trying to get to Christmas Island but was blown off-course and landed on Cocos (Keeling) Islands. The next year, a British trader hired John's brother to bring slaves and a harem of Malay women to create the first permanent settlement on the island. By the 1830s, the Clunies-Ross family had firmly established themselves as the leaders of the islands and they ruled Cocos (Keeling) Islands in a feudal style until 1978.

The UK annexed the islands in 1857 and administered them from Ceylon after 1878 and from Singapore after 1886. Cocos (Keeling) Islands hosted a cable relaying station and was attacked by the Germans in World War I. The Japanese similarly attacked the islands in World War II. The UK transferred the islands to Australia in 1955, which officially named the islands the Cocos (Keeling) Islands, and in 1978, Australia bought all the land held by the Clunies-Ross family, ending their control of the islands' governance. In a referendum in 1984, most islanders voted to integrate with Australia, and Western Australian laws have applied on the islands since 1992.

GEOGRAPHY

Location: Southeastern Asia, group of islands in the Indian Ocean, southwest of Indonesia, about halfway between Australia and Sri Lanka

Geographic coordinates: 12 30 S, 96 50 E

Map references: Southeast Asia

Area: *total:* 14 sq km
land: 14 sq km
water: 0 sq km
note: includes the two main islands of West Island and Home Island
country comparison to the world: 240

Area - comparative: about 24 times the size of The Mall in Washington, DC

Land boundaries: *total:* 0 km

Coastline: 26 km

Maritime claims: *territorial sea:* 12 nm
exclusive fishing zone: 200 nm

Climate: tropical with high humidity, moderated by the southeast trade winds for about nine months of the year

Terrain: flat, low-lying coral atolls

Elevation: *highest point:* South Point on South Island 9 m
lowest point: Indian Ocean 0 m

Natural resources: fish

Land use: *agricultural land:* 0% (2018 est.)
forest: 0% (2018 est.)
other: 100% (2018 est.)

Population distribution: only Home Island and West Island are populated

Natural hazards: cyclone season is October to April

Geography - note: *note 1:* there are 27 coral islands in the group; apart from North Keeling Island, which lies 30 km north of the main group, the islands form a horseshoe-shaped atoll surrounding a lagoon; North Keeling Island was declared a national park in 1995 and is administered by Parks Australia; the population on the two inhabited islands generally is split between the ethnic Europeans on West Island and the ethnic Malays on Home Island; the islands are thickly covered with coconut palms and other vegetation
note 2: site of a World War I naval battle in November 1914 between the Australian light cruiser HMAS Sydney and the German raider SMS Emden; after being heavily damaged in the engagement, the Emden was beached by her captain on North Keeling Island

PEOPLE AND SOCIETY

Population: 596 (July 2014 est.)
country comparison to the world: 236

Nationality: *noun:* Cocos Islander(s)
adjective: Cocos Islander

Ethnic groups Europeans, Cocos Malays: Languages Malay (Cocos dialect) 68.8%, English 22.3%, unspecified 8.9%; *note* - data represent language spoken at home (2016 est.)
major-language sample(s): Buku Fakta Dunia, sumber yang diperlukan untuk maklumat asas. (Malay)

Religions: Muslim (predominantly Sunni) 75%, Anglican 3.5%, Roman Catholic 2.2%, none 12.9%, unspecified 6.3% (2016 est.)

Death rate: 8.89 deaths/1,000 population (2021 est.)
country comparison to the world: 63

Population distribution: only Home Island and West Island are populated

ENVIRONMENT

Environment - current issues: freshwater resources are limited to rainwater accumulations in natural underground reservoirs; illegal fishing a concern

Climate: tropical with high humidity, moderated by the southeast trade winds for about nine months of the year

Land use: *agricultural land:* 0% (2018 est.)
forest: 0% (2018 est.)
other: 100% (2018 est.)

GOVERNMENT

Country name: *conventional long form:* Territory of Cocos (Keeling) Islands
conventional short form: Cocos (Keeling) Islands
etymology: the name refers to the abundant coconut trees on the islands and to English Captain William KEELING, the first European to sight the islands in 1609

Government type: non-self-governing overseas territory of Australia

Dependency status: non-self governing territory of Australia; administered from Canberra by the Department of Infrastructure, Transport, Cities & Regional Development

Capital: *name:* West Island
geographic coordinates: 12 10 S, 96 50 E
time difference: UTC+6.5 (11.5 hours ahead of Washington, DC, during Standard Time)

Administrative divisions: none (territory of Australia)

Independence: none (territory of Australia)

National holiday: Australia Day (commemorates the arrival of the First Fleet of Australian settlers), 26 January (1788)

Constitution: *history:* 23 November 1955 (Cocos (Keeling) Islands Act 1955)
amendments: amended many times, last in 2020

Legal system: common law based on the Australian model

Citizenship: see Australia

Suffrage: 18 years of age

Executive branch: *chief of state:* King CHARLES III (since 8 September 2022); represented by Governor General of the Commonwealth of Australia General David HURLEY (since 1 July 2019)
head of government: Acting Administrator Sarah VANDENBROEK (since 4 October 2022)
cabinet: NA
elections/appointments: the monarchy is hereditary; governor general appointed by the monarch on the recommendation of the Australian prime minister; administrator appointed by the governor general for a 2-year term and represents the monarch and Australia

Legislative branch: description: unicameral Cocos (Keeling) Islands Shire Council (7 seats; members directly elected by simple majority vote to serve 4-year terms with 4 members renewed every 2 years)
elections: last held on 16 October 2021 (next to be held in October 2023)
election results: percent of vote by party - NA; seats by party - NA; composition - men 4, women 3, percent of women 42.9%

Judicial branch: *highest court(s):* under the terms of the Territorial Law Reform Act 1992, Western Australia provides court services as needed for the island including the Supreme Court and subordinate courts (District Court, Magistrate Court, Family Court, Children's Court, and Coroners' Court)

Political parties and leaders: none

International organization participation: none

Diplomatic representation in the US: none (territory of Australia)

Diplomatic representation from the US: embassy: none (territory of Australia)

Flag description: the flag of Australia is used

National anthem: *note:* as a territory of Australia, "Advance Australia Fair" remains official as the national anthem, while "God Save the King" serves as the royal anthem (see Australia)

ECONOMY

Economic overview: Coconuts, grown throughout the islands, are the sole cash crop. Small local gardens and fishing contribute to the food supply, but additional food and most other necessities must be imported from Australia. There is a small tourist industry.

Real GDP growth rate: 1% (2003)
country comparison to the world: 171

Agricultural products: vegetables, bananas, pawpaws, coconuts

Industries: copra products, tourism

Labor force - by occupation: *note:* the Cocos Islands Cooperative Society Ltd. employs construction workers, stevedores, and lighterage workers; tourism is the other main source of employment

Unemployment rate: 0.1% (2011)
60% (2000 est.)
country comparison to the world: 1

Fiscal year: 1 July - 30 June

Exports - partners: United States 57%, Ireland 15% (2019)

Exports - commodities: computers, packaged medicines, precious metal watches, office machinery/parts, chemical analysis instruments (2019)

Imports - partners: Australia 73%, United Arab Emirates 15%, Netherlands 5% (2019)

Imports - commodities: gold, x-ray equipment, cars, prefabricated buildings, packaged medicines (2019)

Exchange rates: Australian dollars (AUD) per US dollar -
1.311 (2017 est.)
1.3442 (2016 est.)
1.3442 (2015)
1.3291 (2014)
1.1094 (2013)

COMMUNICATIONS

Telecommunication systems: *general assessment:* telephone service is part of the Australian network; an operational local mobile-cellular network available; wireless Internet connectivity available
domestic: local area code - 08
international: international code - 61 8; telephone, telex, and facsimile communications with Australia and elsewhere via satellite; satellite earth station - 1 (Intelsat)

Broadcast media: 1 local radio station staffed by community volunteers; satellite broadcasts of several Australian radio and TV stations available (2017)

Internet country code: .cc

TRANSPORTATION

Airports: *total:* 1 (2021)
country comparison to the world: 217

Airports - with paved runways: *total:* 1
2,438 to 3,047 m: 1 (2021)

Roadways: *total:* 22 km (2007)
paved: 10 km (2007)
unpaved: 12 km (2007)
country comparison to the world: 221

Ports and terminals: *major seaport(s):* Port Refuge

MILITARY AND SECURITY

Military - note: defense is the responsibility of Australia

TRANSNATIONAL ISSUES

Disputes - international: none

COLOMBIA

INTRODUCTION

Background: Colombia was one of the three countries that emerged after the dissolution of Gran Colombia in 1830 (the others are Ecuador and Venezuela). A decades-long conflict between government forces, paramilitaries, and antigovernment insurgent groups heavily funded by the drug trade, principally the Revolutionary Armed Forces of Colombia (FARC), escalated during the 1990s. More than 31,000 former United Self Defense Forces of Colombia (AUC) paramilitaries demobilized by the end of 2006, and the AUC as a formal organization ceased to operate. In the wake of the paramilitary demobilization, illegal armed groups arose, whose members include some former paramilitaries. After four years of formal peace negotiations, the Colombian Government signed a final peace accord with the FARC in November 2016, which was subsequently ratified by the Colombian Congress. The accord calls for members of the FARC to demobilize, disarm, and reincorporate into society and politics. The accord also committed the Colombian Government to create three new institutions to form a 'comprehensive system for truth, justice, reparation, and non-repetition,' to include a truth commission, a special unit to coordinate the search for those who disappeared during the conflict, and a 'Special Jurisdiction for Peace' to administer justice for conflict-related crimes. Despite decades of internal conflict and drug-related security challenges, Colombia maintains relatively strong and independent democratic institutions characterized by peaceful, transparent elections and the protection of civil liberties.

GEOGRAPHY

Location: Northern South America, bordering the Caribbean Sea, between Panama and Venezuela, and bordering the North Pacific Ocean, between Ecuador and Panama

Geographic coordinates: 4 00 N, 72 00 W

Map references: South America

Area: *total:* 1,138,910 sq km
land: 1,038,700 sq km
water: 100,210 sq km
note: includes Isla de Malpelo, Roncador Cay, and Serrana Bank
country comparison to the world: 27

Area - comparative: slightly less than twice the size of Texas

Land boundaries: *total:* 6,672 km
border countries (5): Brazil 1,790 km; Ecuador 708 km; Panama 339 km; Peru 1,494 km; Venezuela 2,341 km

Coastline: 3,208 km (Caribbean Sea 1,760 km, North Pacific Ocean 1,448 km)

Maritime claims: *territorial sea:* 12 nm
exclusive economic zone: 200 nm
continental shelf: 200-m depth or to the depth of exploitation

Climate: tropical along coast and eastern plains; cooler in highlands

Terrain: flat coastal lowlands, central highlands, high Andes Mountains, eastern lowland plains (Llanos)

Elevation: *highest point:* Pico Cristobal Colon 5,730 m
lowest point: Pacific Ocean 0 m
mean elevation: 593 m

Natural resources: petroleum, natural gas, coal, iron ore, nickel, gold, copper, emeralds, hydropower

Land use: *agricultural land:* 37.5% (2018 est.)
arable land: 1.4% (2018 est.)
permanent crops: 1.6% (2018 est.)
permanent pasture: 34.5% (2018 est.)
forest: 54.4% (2018 est.)
other: 8.1% (2018 est.)

Irrigated land: 10,900 sq km (2012)

Major rivers (by length in km): Rio Negro river source (shared with Venezuela and Brazil [m]) - 2,250 km; Orinoco (shared with Venezuela [s]) - 2,101 km
note – [s] after country name indicates river source; [m] after country name indicates river mouth

Major watersheds (area sq km): Atlantic Ocean drainage: Amazon (6,145,186 sq km), Orinoco (953,675 sq km)

Major aquifers: Amazon Basin

Population distribution: the majority of people live in the north and west where agricultural opportunities and natural resources are found; the vast grasslands of the llanos to the south and east, which make up approximately 60% of the country, are sparsely populated

Natural hazards: highlands subject to volcanic eruptions; occasional earthquakes; periodic droughts
volcanism: Galeras (4,276 m) is one of Colombia's most active volcanoes, having erupted in 2009 and 2010 causing major evacuations; it has been deemed a Decade Volcano by the International Association of Volcanology and Chemistry of the Earth's Interior, worthy of study due to its explosive history and close proximity to human populations; Nevado del Ruiz (5,321 m), 129 km (80 mi) west of Bogota, erupted in 1985 producing lahars (mudflows) that killed 23,000 people; the volcano last erupted in 1991; additionally, after 500 years of dormancy, Nevado del Huila reawakened in 2007 and has experienced frequent eruptions since then; other historically active volcanoes include Cumbal, Dona Juana, Nevado del Tolima, and Purace

Geography - note: only South American country with coastlines on both the North Pacific Ocean and Caribbean Sea

PEOPLE AND SOCIETY

Population: 49,059,221 (2022 est.)
country comparison to the world: 29

Nationality: *noun:* Colombian(s)
adjective: Colombian

Ethnic groups: Mestizo and White 87.6%, Afro-Colombian (includes Mulatto, Raizal, and Palenquero) 6.8%, Amerindian 4.3%, unspecified 1.4% (2018 est.)

Languages: Spanish (official) and 65 Amerindian languages
major-language sample(s): La Libreta Informativa del Mundo, la fuente indispensable de información básica. (Spanish)

Religions: Christian 92.3% (predominantly Roman Catholic), other 1%, unspecified 6.7% (2020 est.)

Demographic profile: Colombia is in the midst of a demographic transition resulting from steady declines in its fertility, mortality, and population growth rates. The birth rate has fallen from more than 6 children per woman in the 1960s to just above replacement level today as a result of increased literacy, family planning services, and urbanization. However, income inequality is among the worst in the world, and more than a third of the population lives below the poverty line.

Colombia experiences significant legal and illegal economic emigration and refugee outflows. Large-scale labor emigration dates to the 1960s; the United States and, until recently, Venezuela have been the main host countries. Emigration to Spain picked up in the 1990s because of its economic growth, but this flow has since diminished because of Spain's ailing economy and high unemployment. Colombia has been the largest source of Latin American refugees in Latin America, nearly 400,000 of whom live primarily in Venezuela and Ecuador. Venezuela's political and economic crisis since 2015, however, has created a reverse flow, consisting largely of Colombians returning home.

Forced displacement continues to be prevalent because of violence among guerrillas, paramilitary groups, and Colombian security forces. Afro-Colombian and indigenous populations are disproportionately affected. Even with the Colombian Government's December 2016 peace agreement with the Revolutionary Armed Forces of Colombia (FARC), the risk of displacement remains as other rebel groups fill the void left by the FARC. Between 1985 and September 2017, nearly 7.6 million persons have been internally displaced, the highest total in the world. These estimates may undercount actual numbers because many internally displaced persons are not registered. Historically, Colombia also has one of the world's highest levels of forced disappearances. About 30,000 cases have been recorded over the last four decades—although the number is likely to be much higher—including human rights activists, trade unionists, Afro-Colombians, indigenous people, and farmers in rural conflict zones.

Because of political violence and economic problems, Colombia received limited numbers of immigrants during the 19th and 20th centuries, mostly from the Middle East, Europe, and Japan. More recently, growth in the oil, mining, and manufacturing sectors has attracted increased labor migration; the primary source countries are Venezuela, the US, Mexico, and Argentina. Colombia has also become a transit area for illegal migrants from Africa, Asia, and the Caribbean -- especially Haiti and Cuba -- who are en route to the US or Canada.

Age structure: *0-14 years:* 23.27% (male 5,853,351/female 5,567,196)
15-24 years: 16.38% (male 4,098,421/female 3,939,870)
25-54 years: 42.04% (male 10,270,516/female 10,365,423)
55-64 years: 9.93% (male 2,307,705/female 2,566,173)
65 years and over: 8.39% (male 1,725,461/female 2,390,725) (2020 est.)

Dependency ratios: *total dependency ratio:* 45.4
youth dependency ratio: 32.3
elderly dependency ratio: 13.2
potential support ratio: 7.6 (2020 est.)

Median age: *total:* 31.2 years
male: 30.2 years
female: 32.2 years (2020 est.)
country comparison to the world: 115

Population growth rate: 0.59% (2022 est.)
country comparison to the world: 146

Birth rate: 15.21 births/1,000 population (2022 est.)
country comparison to the world: 114

Death rate: 7.73 deaths/1,000 population (2022 est.)
country comparison to the world: 102

Net migration rate: -1.58 migrant(s)/1,000 population (2022 est.)
country comparison to the world: 159

Population distribution: the majority of people live in the north and west where agricultural opportunities and natural resources are found; the vast grasslands of the llanos to the south and east, which make up approximately 60% of the country, are sparsely populated

Urbanization: *urban population:* 82% of total population (2022)
rate of urbanization: 1.01% annual rate of change (2020-25 est.)

Major urban areas - population: 11.344 million BOGOTA (capital), 4.068 million Medellin, 2.837 million Cali, 2.325 million Barranquilla, 1.366 million Bucaramanga, 1.079 million Cartagena (2022)

Sex ratio: *at birth:* 1.05 male(s)/female
0-14 years: 1.05 male(s)/female
15-24 years: 1.04 male(s)/female
25-54 years: 0.94 male(s)/female
55-64 years: 0.85 male(s)/female
65 years and over: 0.65 male(s)/female
total population: 0.96 male(s)/female (2022 est.)

Mother's mean age at first birth: 21.7 years (2015 est.)
note: data represents median age at first birth among women 25-49

Maternal mortality ratio: 83 deaths/100,000 live births (2017 est.)
country comparison to the world: 78

Infant mortality rate: *total:* 11.65 deaths/1,000 live births
male: 13.07 deaths/1,000 live births
female: 10.15 deaths/1,000 live births (2022 est.)
country comparison to the world: 122

Life expectancy at birth: *total population:* 74.89 years
male: 71.27 years
female: 78.69 years (2022 est.)
country comparison to the world: 130

Total fertility rate: 1.95 children born/woman (2022 est.)
country comparison to the world: 115

Contraceptive prevalence rate: 81% (2015/16)

Drinking water source: *improved: urban:* 100% of population
rural: 87.5% of population
total: 97.7% of population
unimproved: urban: 0% of population
rural: 12.5% of population
total: 2.3% of population (2020 est.)

Current health expenditure: 7.7% of GDP (2019)

Physicians density: 2.33 physicians/1,000 population (2020)

Hospital bed density: 1.7 beds/1,000 population (2018)

Sanitation facility access: *improved: urban:* 99.1% of population
rural: 87.7% of population
total: 97% of population
unimproved: urban: 0.9% of population
rural: 12.3% of population
total: 3% of population (2020 est.)

HIV/AIDS - adult prevalence rate: 0.4% (2020 est.)
country comparison to the world: 72

Major infectious diseases: *degree of risk:* high (2020)
food or waterborne diseases: bacterial diarrhea
vectorborne diseases: dengue fever, malaria, and yellow fever
note: widespread ongoing transmission of a respiratory illness caused by the novel coronavirus (COVID-19) is occurring throughout Colombia; as of 18 August 2022, Columbia has reported a total of 6,286,392 cases of COVID-19 or 12,354.62 cumulative cases of COVID-19 per 100,000 population with a total of 141,287 cumulative deaths or a rate 277.67 cumulative deaths per 100,000 population; as of 29 July 2022, 82.64% of the population has received at least one dose of COVID-19 vaccine

Obesity - adult prevalence rate: 22.3% (2016)
country comparison to the world: 78

Alcohol consumption per capita: *total:* 4.09 liters of pure alcohol (2019 est.)
beer: 3.09 liters of pure alcohol (2019 est.)
wine: 0.06 liters of pure alcohol (2019 est.)
spirits: 0.92 liters of pure alcohol (2019 est.)
other alcohols: 0.02 liters of pure alcohol (2019 est.)
country comparison to the world: 94

Tobacco use: *total:* 8.5% (2020 est.)
male: 12.4% (2020 est.)
female: 4.6% (2020 est.)
country comparison to the world: 144

Children under the age of 5 years underweight: 3.7% (2015/16)
country comparison to the world: 87

Education expenditures: 4.5% of GDP (2019 est.)
country comparison to the world: 82

Literacy: *definition:* age 15 and over can read and write
total population: 95.6%
male: 95.4%
female: 95.9% (2020)

School life expectancy (primary to tertiary education): *total:* 14 years
male: 14 years
female: 15 years (2019)

Unemployment, youth ages 15-24: *total:* 25.8%
male: 20.7%
female: 33% (2020 est.)

ENVIRONMENT

Environment - current issues: deforestation resulting from timber exploitation in the jungles of the Amazon and the region of Chocó; illicit drug crops grown by peasants in the national parks; soil erosion; soil and water quality damage from overuse of pesticides; air pollution, especially in Bogota, from vehicle emissions

Environment - international agreements: party to: Antarctic-Environmental Protection, Antarctic Treaty, Biodiversity, Climate Change, Climate Change-Kyoto Protocol, Climate Change-Paris Agreement, Comprehensive Nuclear Test Ban, Desertification, Endangered Species, Hazardous Wastes, Marine Life Conservation, Nuclear Test Ban, Ozone Layer Protection, Ship Pollution, Tropical Timber 2006, Wetlands, Whaling
signed, but not ratified: Law of the Sea

Air pollutants: particulate matter emissions: 15.24 micrograms per cubic meter (2016 est.)
carbon dioxide emissions: 97.81 megatons (2016 est.)
methane emissions: 81.52 megatons (2020 est.)

Climate: tropical along coast and eastern plains; cooler in highlands

Land use: *agricultural land:* 37.5% (2018 est.)
arable land: 1.4% (2018 est.)
permanent crops: 1.6% (2018 est.)
permanent pasture: 34.5% (2018 est.)
forest: 54.4% (2018 est.)
other: 8.1% (2018 est.)

Urbanization: *urban population:* 82% of total population (2022)
rate of urbanization: 1.01% annual rate of change (2020-25 est.)

Revenue from forest resources: *forest revenues:* 0.1% of GDP (2018 est.)
country comparison to the world: 111

Revenue from coal: *coal revenues:* 0.75% of GDP (2018 est.)
country comparison to the world: 8

Waste and recycling: *municipal solid waste generated annually:* 12,150,120 tons (2011 est.)
municipal solid waste recycled annually: 2,089,821 tons (2013 est.)
percent of municipal solid waste recycled: 17.2% (2013 est.)

Major rivers (by length in km): Rio Negro river source (shared with Venezuela and Brazil [m]) - 2,250 km; Orinoco (shared with Venezuela [s]) - 2,101 km
note – [s] after country name indicates river source; [m] after country name indicates river mouth

Major watersheds (area sq km): Atlantic Ocean drainage: Amazon (6,145,186 sq km), Orinoco (953,675 sq km)

Major aquifers: Amazon Basin

Total water withdrawal: *municipal:* 3.49 billion cubic meters (2017 est.)
industrial: 3.73 billion cubic meters (2017 est.)
agricultural: 6.391 billion cubic meters (2017 est.)

Total renewable water resources: 2.36 trillion cubic meters (2017 est.)

GOVERNMENT

Country name: *conventional long form:* Republic of Colombia
conventional short form: Colombia
local long form: Republica de Colombia
local short form: Colombia
etymology: the country is named after explorer Christopher COLUMBUS

Government type: presidential republic

Capital: *name:* Bogota
geographic coordinates: 4 36 N, 74 05 W
time difference: UTC-5 (same time as Washington, DC, during Standard Time)
etymology: originally referred to as "Bacata," meaning "enclosure outside of the farm fields," by the indigenous Muisca

Administrative divisions: 32 departments (departamentos, singular - departamento) and 1 capital district* (distrito capital); Amazonas, Antioquia, Arauca, Atlantico, Bogota*, Bolivar, Boyaca, Caldas, Caqueta, Casanare, Cauca, Cesar, Choco, Cordoba, Cundinamarca, Guainia, Guaviare, Huila, La Guajira, Magdalena, Meta, Narino, Norte de Santander, Putumayo, Quindio, Risaralda, Archipielago de San Andres, Providencia y Santa Catalina (colloquially San Andres y Providencia), Santander, Sucre, Tolima, Valle del Cauca, Vaupes, Vichada

Independence: 20 July 1810 (from Spain)

National holiday: Independence Day, 20 July (1810)

Constitution: *history:* several previous; latest promulgated 4 July 1991
amendments: proposed by the government, by Congress, by a constituent assembly, or by public petition; passage requires a majority vote by Congress in each of two consecutive sessions; passage of amendments to constitutional articles on citizen rights, guarantees, and duties also require approval in a referendum by over one half of voters and participation of over one fourth of citizens registered to vote; amended many times, last in 2020

Legal system: civil law system influenced by the Spanish and French civil codes

International law organization participation: has not submitted an ICJ jurisdiction declaration; accepts ICCt jurisdiction

Citizenship: *citizenship by birth:* no
citizenship by descent only: least one parent must be a citizen or permanent resident of Colombia
dual citizenship recognized: yes
residency requirement for naturalization: 5 years

Suffrage: 18 years of age; universal

Executive branch: *chief of state:* President Gustavo Francisco PETRO Urrego (since 7 August 2022); Vice President Francia Elena MARQUEZ Mina (since 7 August 2022); the president is both chief of state and head of government
head of government: President Gustavo Francisco PETRO Urrego (since 7 August 2022); Vice President Francia Elena MARQUEZ Mina (since 7 August 2022)
cabinet: Cabinet appointed by the president
elections/appointments: president directly elected by absolute majority vote in 2 rounds if needed for a single 4-year term; election last held on 29 May 2022 with a runoff held on 19 June 2022 (next to be held on 31 May 2026); note -political reform in 2015 eliminated presidential reelection
election results:
2022: Gustavo Francisco PETRO Urrego elected president in second round; percent of vote in first round - Gustavo Francisco PETRO Urrego (PHxC) 40.3%, Rodolfo HERNANDEZ Suarez (LIGA) 28.2%, Federico GUTIERREZ (Team for Colombia / CREEMOS) 23.9%, other 7.6%; percent of vote in second round - Gustavo Francisco PETRO Urrego (PHxC) 50.4%, Rodolfo HERNANDEZ Suarez (LIGA) 47.3%
2018: Ivan DUQUE Marquez elected president in second round; percent of vote - Ivan DUQUE Marquez (CD) 54%, Gustavo PETRO (Humane Colombia) 41.8%, other/blank/invalid 4.2%

Legislative branch: description: bicameral Congress or Congreso consists of:
Senate or Senado (108 seats; 100 members elected in a single nationwide constituency by party-list proportional representation vote, 2 members elected in a special nationwide constituency for indigenous communities, 5 members of the Commons political party, formerly the People's Alternative Revolutionary Force (FARC), for 2 legislative terms only: 2018-2022 and 2022-2026 as per the 2016 peace accord, and 1 seat reserved for the runner-up presidential candidate in the recent election; all members serve 4-year terms)

Chamber of Representatives or Camara de Representantes (188 seats; 162 members elected in multi-seat constituencies by party-list proportional representation vote, 2 members elected in a special nationwide constituency for Afro-Colombians, 1 member elected by Colombians residing abroad, 1 member elected in a special nationwide constituency for the indigenous communities, 5 members of the Commons political party for two legislative terms only: 2018-2022 and 2022-2026 as per the 2016 peace accord, 16 seats for rural conflict victims for two legislative terms only: 2022-2026 and 2026-2030, and 1 seat reserved for the runner-up vice presidential candidate in the recent election; all members serve 4-year terms)

elections:
Senate - last held on 13 March 2022 (next to be held in March 2026)
Chamber of Representatives - last held on 13 March 2022 (next to be held in March 2026)
election results:
Senate - percent of vote by party - NA; seats by party - PHxC 16, PC 16, PL 15, Green Alliance and Center Hope Coalition 14, CD 14, CR 11, U Party 10, MIRA–Colombia Free and Just Coalition 4; composition - men 75, women 33, percent of women 31%
Chamber of Representatives - percent of vote by party - NA; seats by party - PL 33, PHxC 28, PC 27, CR 18, CD 16, U Party 16, Green Alliance 14, League of Anticorruption Governors 2, others 34; composition - men 136, women 52, percent of women 28%; total Congress percent of women 29%

Judicial branch: *highest court(s):* Supreme Court of Justice or Corte Suprema de Justicia (consists of the Civil-Agrarian and Labor Chambers each with 7 judges, and the Penal Chamber with 9 judges); Constitutional Court (consists of 9 magistrates); Council of State (consists of 27 judges); Superior Judiciary Council (consists of 13 magistrates)
judge selection and term of office: Supreme Court judges appointed by the Supreme Court members from candidates submitted by the Superior Judiciary Council; judges elected for individual 8-year terms; Constitutional Court magistrates -nominated by the president, by the Supreme Court, and elected by the Senate; judges elected for individual 8-year terms; Council of State members appointed by the State Council plenary from lists nominated by the Superior Judiciary Council
subordinate courts: Superior Tribunals (appellate courts for each of the judicial districts); regional courts; civil municipal courts; Superior Military Tribunal; first instance administrative courts

Political parties and leaders: Alternative Democratic Pole or PDA [Alexander LOPEZ Maya]
Citizens Option (Opcion Ciudadana) or OC [Angel ALIRIO Moreno] (formerly known as the National Integration Party or PIN)
The Commons (formerly People's Alternative Revolutionary Force or FARC) [Rodrigo LONDONO Echeverry]
Conservative Party or PC [Carlos Andres TRUJILLO]
Democratic Center Party or CD [Alvaro URIBE Velez]
Fair and Free Colombia (Colombia Justa Libres) [Eduardo Canas Estrada and Ricardo Arias Mora]
Green Alliance [Claudia LOPEZ Hernandez]
Historic Pact for Colombia or PHxC (coalition composed of several left-leaning political parties and social movements)
Humane Colombia [Gustavo PETRO]
Independent Movement of Absolute Renovation or MIRA [Carlos Eduardo GUEVARA]
League of Anti-Corruption Rulers or LIGA [Rodolfo HERNANDEZ Suarez]
Liberal Party or PL [Cesar GAVIRIA]
People's Alternative Revolutionary Force or FARC [Rodrigo LONDONO Echeverry]
Radical Change or CR [German VARGAS Lleras]
Team for Colombia - also known as the Experience Coalition or Coalition of the Regions (coalition composed of center-right and right-wing parties)
Union Party for the People or U Party [Dilian Francisca TORO]
We Believe Colombia or CREEMOS [Federico GUTIERREZ]
note: Colombia has numerous smaller political parties and movements

International organization participation: BCIE, BIS, CAN, Caricom (observer), CD, CDB, CELAC, EITI (candidate country), FAO, G-3, G-24, G-77, IADB, IAEA, IBRD, ICAO, ICC (national committees), ICCt, ICRM, IDA, IFAD, IFC, IFRCS, IHO, ILO, IMF, IMO, IMSO, Interpol, IOC, IOM, IPU, ISO, ITSO, ITU, ITUC (NGOs), LAES, LAIA, Mercosur (associate), MIGA, NAM, OAS, OPANAL, OPCW, Pacific Alliance, PCA, PROSUR, UN, UNASUR, UNCTAD, UNESCO, UNHCR, UNIDO, Union Latina, UNWTO, UPU, WCO, WFTU (NGOs), WHO, WIPO, WMO, WTO

Diplomatic representation in the US: *chief of mission:* Ambassador Luis Gilberto MURILLO URRUTIA (since 16 September 2022)
chancery: 1724 Massachusetts Avenue NW, Washington, DC 20036
telephone: [1] (202) 387-8338
FAX: [1] (202) 232-8643
email address and website:
eestadosunidos@cancilleria.gov.co
https://www.colombiaemb.org/
consulate(s) general: Atlanta, Houston, Los Angeles, Miami, New York, Newark (NJ), Orlando, San Juan (Puerto Rico), Washington, DC
consulate(s): Boston, Chicago, San Francisco

Diplomatic representation from the US: *chief of mission:* Ambassador (vacant); Charge d'Affaires Francisco L. PALMIERI (since 1 June 2022)
embassy: Carrera 45, No. 24B-27, Bogota
mailing address: 3030 Bogota Place, Washington DC 20521-3030
telephone: [57] (1) 275-2000
FAX: [57] (1) 275-4600
email address and website:
ACSBogota@state.gov
https://co.usembassy.gov/

Flag description: three horizontal bands of yellow (top, double-width), blue, and red; the flag retains the three main colors of the banner of Gran Colombia, the short-lived South American republic that broke up in 1830; various interpretations of the colors exist and include: yellow for the gold in Colombia's land, blue for the seas on its shores, and red for the blood spilled in attaining freedom; alternatively, the colors have been described as representing more elemental concepts such as sovereignty and justice (yellow), loyalty and vigilance (blue), and valor and generosity (red); or simply the principles of liberty, equality, and fraternity
note: similar to the flag of Ecuador, which is longer and bears the Ecuadorian coat of arms superimposed in the center

National symbol(s): *Andean condor; national colors:* yellow, blue, red

National anthem: *name:* "Himno Nacional de la Republica de Colombia" (National Anthem of the Republic of Colombia)
lyrics/music: Rafael NUNEZ/Oreste SINDICI
note: adopted 1920; the anthem was created from an inspirational poem written by President Rafael NUNEZ

National heritage: *total World Heritage Sites:* 9 (6 cultural, 2 natural, 1 mixed)
selected World Heritage Site locales: Chiribiquete National Park (m); Coffee Cultural Landscape of Colombia (c); Historic Center of Santa Cruz de Mompox (c); Los Katíos National Park (n); Malpelo Fauna and Flora Sanctuary (n); Tierradentro National Archeological Park (c); San Agustín Archaeological Park (c); Colonial Cartagena (c); Qhapaq Ñan/Andean Road System (c)

ECONOMY

Economic overview: Colombia heavily depends on energy and mining exports, making it vulnerable to fluctuations in commodity prices. Colombia is Latin America's fourth largest oil producer and the world's fourth largest coal producer, third largest coffee exporter, and second largest cut flowers exporter. Colombia's economic development is hampered by inadequate infrastructure, poverty, narcotrafficking, and an uncertain security situation, in addition to dependence on primary commodities (goods that have little value-added from processing or labor inputs).

Colombia's economy slowed in 2017 because of falling world market prices for oil and lower domestic oil production due to insurgent attacks on pipeline infrastructure. Although real GDP growth averaged 4.7% during the past decade, it fell to an estimated 1.8% in 2017. Declining oil prices also have contributed to reduced government revenues. In 2016, oil revenue dropped below 4% of the federal budget and likely remained below 4% in 2017. A Western credit rating agency in December 2017 downgraded Colombia's sovereign credit rating to BBB-, because of weaker-than-expected growth and increasing external debt. Colombia has struggled to address local referendums against foreign investment, which have slowed its expansion, especially in the oil and mining sectors. Colombia's FDI declined by 3% to $10.2 billion between January and September 2017.

Colombia has signed or is negotiating Free Trade Agreements (FTA) with more than a dozen countries; the US-Colombia FTA went into effect in May 2012. Colombia is a founding member of the Pacific Alliance—a regional trade block formed in 2012 by Chile, Colombia, Mexico, and Peru to promote regional trade and economic integration. The Colombian government took steps in 2017 to address several bilateral trade irritants with the US, including those on truck scrappage, distilled spirits, pharmaceuticals, ethanol imports, and labor rights. Colombia hopes to accede to the Organization for Economic Cooperation and Development.

Real GDP (purchasing power parity): $683.94 billion (2020 est.)
$734.22 billion (2019 est.)
$710.89 billion (2018 est.)
note: data are in 2017 dollars
country comparison to the world: 32

Real GDP growth rate: 3.26% (2019 est.)
2.51% (2018 est.)
1.36% (2017 est.)
country comparison to the world: 91

Real GDP per capita: $13,400 (2020 est.)
$14,600 (2019 est.)
$14,300 (2018 est.)
note: data are in 2017 dollars
country comparison to the world: 114

GDP (official exchange rate): $323.255 billion (2019 est.)

Inflation rate (consumer prices): 3.5% (2019 est.)
3.2% (2018 est.)

4.3% (2017 est.)
country comparison to the world: 154

Credit ratings: *Fitch rating:* BBB- (2020)

Moody's rating: Baa2 (2014)

Standard & Poors rating: BBB- (2017)
note: The year refers to the year in which the current credit rating was first obtained.

GDP - composition, by sector of origin: *agriculture:* 7.2% (2017 est.)
industry: 30.8% (2017 est.)
services: 62.1% (2017 est.)

GDP - composition, by end use: *household consumption:* 68.2% (2017 est.)
government consumption: 14.8% (2017 est.)
investment in fixed capital: 22.2% (2017 est.)
investment in inventories: 0.2% (2017 est.)
exports of goods and services: 14.6% (2017 est.)
imports of goods and services: -19.7% (2017 est.)

Agricultural products: sugar cane, milk, oil palm fruit, potatoes, rice, bananas, cassava leaves, plantains, poultry, maize

Industries: textiles, food processing, oil, clothing and footwear, beverages, chemicals, cement; gold, coal, emeralds

Industrial production growth rate: -2.2% (2017 est.)
country comparison to the world: 185

Labor force: 19.309 million (2020 est.)
country comparison to the world: 28

Labor force - by occupation: *agriculture:* 17%
industry: 21%
services: 62% (2011 est.)

Unemployment rate: 10.5% (2019 est.)
9.68% (2018 est.)
country comparison to the world: 153

Unemployment, youth ages 15-24: *total:* 25.8%
male: 20.7%
female: 33% (2020 est.)
country comparison to the world: 52

Population below poverty line: 35.7% (2019 est.)

Gini Index coefficient - distribution of family income: 50.4 (2018 est.)
53.5 (2014)
country comparison to the world: 15

Household income or consumption by percentage share: *lowest 10%:* 1.2%
highest 10%: 39.6% (2015 est.)

Budget: *revenues:* 83.35 billion (2017 est.)
expenditures: 91.73 billion (2017 est.)

Budget surplus (+) or deficit (-): -2.7% (of GDP) (2017 est.)
country comparison to the world: 119

Public debt: 49.4% of GDP (2017 est.)
49.8% of GDP (2016 est.)
note: data cover general government debt, and includes debt instruments issued (or owned) by government entities other than the treasury; the data include treasury debt held by foreign entities; the data include debt issued by subnational entities
country comparison to the world: 102

Taxes and other revenues: 26.5% (of GDP) (2017 est.)
country comparison to the world: 109

Fiscal year: calendar year

Current account balance: -$13.748 billion (2019 est.)
-$13.118 billion (2018 est.)
country comparison to the world: 196

Exports: $39.14 billion (2020 est.)
$52.96 billion (2019 est.)
$55.06 billion (2018 est.)
note: Data are in current year dollars and do not include illicit exports or re-exports.
country comparison to the world: 65

Exports - partners: United States 31%, China 11%, Panama 6%, Ecuador 5% (2019)

Exports - commodities: crude petroleum, coal, refined petroleum, coffee, gold (2019)

Imports: $51.56 billion (2020 est.) note: data are in current year dollars
$65.83 billion (2019 est.) note: data are in current year dollars
$64.56 billion (2018 est.) note: data are in current year dollars
country comparison to the world: 58

Imports - partners: United States 27%, China 20%, Mexico 7%, Brazil 6% (2019)

Imports - commodities: refined petroleum, cars, broadcasting equipment, packaged medicines, corn (2019)

Reserves of foreign exchange and gold: $47.13 billion (31 December 2017 est.)
$46.18 billion (31 December 2016 est.)
country comparison to the world: 42

Debt - external: $135.644 billion (2019 est.)
$128.238 billion (2018 est.)
country comparison to the world: 47

Exchange rates: Colombian pesos (COP) per US dollar -
3,457.93 (2020 est.)
3,416.5 (2019 est.)
3,147.43 (2018 est.)
2,001 (2014 est.)
2,001.1 (2013 est.)

ENERGY

Electricity access: *electrification - total population:* 97% (2019)
electrification - urban areas: 100% (2019)
electrification - rural areas: 86% (2019)

Electricity: *installed generating capacity:* 19.769 million kW (2020 est.)
consumption: 69,856,680,000 kWh (2019 est.)
exports: 251 million kWh (2020 est.)
imports: 1.302 billion kWh (2020 est.)
transmission/distribution losses: 5.724 billion kWh (2019 est.)

Electricity generation sources: *fossil fuels:* 32.9% of total installed capacity (2020 est.)
solar: 0.3% of total installed capacity (2020 est.)
wind: 0.1% of total installed capacity (2020 est.)
hydroelectricity: 65.7% of total installed capacity (2020 est.)
biomass and waste: 1% of total installed capacity (2020 est.)

Coal: *production:* 51.395 million metric tons (2020 est.)
consumption: 8.547 million metric tons (2020 est.)
exports: 69.861 million metric tons (2020 est.)
imports: 79,000 metric tons (2020 est.)
proven reserves: 4.554 billion metric tons (2019 est.)

Petroleum: *total petroleum production:* 756,400 bbl/day (2021 est.)
refined petroleum consumption: 352,400 bbl/day (2019 est.)
crude oil and lease condensate exports: 481,300 bbl/day (2018 est.)
crude oil and lease condensate imports: 0 bbl/day (2018 est.)
crude oil estimated reserves: 2.036 billion barrels (2021 est.)

Refined petroleum products - production: 303,600 bbl/day (2015 est.)
country comparison to the world: 41

Refined petroleum products - exports: 56,900 bbl/day (2015 est.)
country comparison to the world: 52

Refined petroleum products - imports: 57,170 bbl/day (2015 est.)
country comparison to the world: 74

Natural gas: *production:* 11,305,086,000 cubic meters (2020 est.)
consumption: 11,708,232,000 cubic meters (2020 est.)
exports: 0 cubic meters (2020 est.)
imports: 403.146 million cubic meters (2020 est.)
proven reserves: 87.782 billion cubic meters (2021 est.)

Carbon dioxide emissions: 81.007 million metric tonnes of CO2 (2019 est.)
from coal and metallurgical coke: 12.666 million metric tonnes of CO2 (2019 est.)
from petroleum and other liquids: 47.679 million metric tonnes of CO2 (2019 est.)
from consumed natural gas: 20.662 million metric tonnes of CO2 (2019 est.)
country comparison to the world: 48

Energy consumption per capita: 34.703 million Btu/person (2019 est.)
country comparison to the world: 116

COMMUNICATIONS

Telephones - fixed lines: *total subscriptions:* 7,248,026 (2020 est.)
subscriptions per 100 inhabitants: 14 (2020 est.)
country comparison to the world: 22

Telephones - mobile cellular: *total subscriptions:* 67,672,570 (2020 est.)
subscriptions per 100 inhabitants: 133 (2020 est.)
country comparison to the world: 25

Telecommunication systems: *general assessment:* the telecom sector had a solid year thanks to positive performances in the fixed-line broadband, mobile broadband, and mobile voice and data markets; the fixed-line penetration remained stable by the end of 2020, though began to increase into 2021 as a result of the particular demands on households resulting from government measures associated with addressing the pandemic; the mobile market reached a penetration rate of 136% (an increase of over three percentage points on 2019) and managed to keep the same upward growth trajectory that it has sustained over the last ten years; the fixed-line broadband market also expanded, with the number of subscribers increasing 11.4%, and with revenue increasing 9.9% thanks to increased data usage as many customers were forced to work or study from home during the year; the mobile broadband market was the standout performer in 2020, with a 13% increase in the number of subscribers year-on-year, the penetration rate is relatively low compared to other Latin American countries; most significant of all was the surge in mobile broadband traffic a 51% increase over the previous year (2022)

domestic: fixed-line connections stand at about 14 per 100 persons; mobile cellular telephone subscribership is 133 per 100 persons; Partners Telecom Colombia's (WOM) market entrance in June 2021 increased competition among cellular service providers and is resulting in falling local and international calling rates and contributing to the steep decline in the market share of fixed-line services; domestic satellite system with 41 earth stations (2021)
international: country code - 57; landing points for the SAC, Maya-1, SAIT, ACROS, AMX-1, CFX-1, PCCS, Deep Blue Cable, Globe Net, PAN-AM, SAm-1 submarine cable systems providing links to the US, parts of the Caribbean, and Central and South America; satellite earth stations - 10 (6 Intelsat, 1 Inmarsat, 3 fully digitalized international switching centers) (2019)

Broadcast media: combination of state-owned and privately owned broadcast media provide service; more than 500 radio stations and many national, regional, and local TV stations (2019)

Internet country code: .co

Internet users: *total:* 35,618,019 (2020 est.)
percent of population: 70% (2020 est.)
country comparison to the world: 28

Broadband - fixed subscriptions: *total:* 7,764,772 (2020 est.)
subscriptions per 100 inhabitants: 15 (2020 est.)
country comparison to the world: 28

TRANSPORTATION

National air transport system: *number of registered air carriers:* 12 (2020)
inventory of registered aircraft operated by air carriers: 157
annual passenger traffic on registered air carriers: 33,704,037 (2018)
annual freight traffic on registered air carriers: 1,349,450,000 (2018) mt-km

Civil aircraft registration country code prefix: HJ, HK

Airports: *total:* 836 (2021)
country comparison to the world: 8

Airports - with paved runways: *total:* 121
over 3,047 m: 2
2,438 to 3,047 m: 9
1,524 to 2,437 m: 39
914 to 1,523 m: 53
under 914 m: 18 (2021)

Airports - with unpaved runways: *total:* 715
over 3,047 m: 1
1,524 to 2,437 m: 25
914 to 1,523 m: 201
*under 914 m:*488 (2021)

Heliports: 3 (2021)

Pipelines: 4,991 km gas, 6,796 km oil, 3,429 km refined products (2013)

Railways: *total:* 2,141 km (2019)
standard gauge: 150 km (2019) 1.435-m gauge
narrow gauge: 1,991 km (2019) 0.914-m gauge
country comparison to the world: 72

Roadways: *total:* 205,379 km (2019)
country comparison to the world: 26

Waterways: 24,725 km (2019) (18,225 km navigable; the most important waterway, the River Magdalena, of which 1,092 km is navigable, is dredged regularly to ensure safe passage of cargo vessels and container barges)
country comparison to the world: 7

Merchant marine: *total:* 122
by type: general cargo 23, oil tanker 7, other 92 (2021)
country comparison to the world: 80

Ports and terminals: *major seaport(s):* Atlantic Ocean (Caribbean) - Cartagena, Santa Marta, Turbo

Pacific Ocean - Buenaventura: *oil terminal(s):* Covenas offshore terminal
container port(s) (TEUs): Buenaventura (1,121,267), Cartagena (2,995,031) (2019)
river port(s): Barranquilla (Rio Magdalena)
dry bulk cargo port(s): Puerto Bolivar (coal)

Pacific Ocean - Buenaventura

MILITARY AND SECURITY

Military and security forces: *Military Forces of Colombia (Fuerzas Militares de Colombia):* National Army (Ejercito Nacional), Republic of Colombia Navy (Armada Republica de Colombia, ARC; includes Coast Guard), Colombian Air Force (Fuerza Aerea de Colombia, FAC); Colombian National Police (PNC; civilian force that is under the jurisdiction of the Ministry of Defense) (2022)

Military expenditures: 3% of GDP (2021 est.)
3% of GDP (2020 est.)
3.1% of GDP (2019) (approximately $19.6 billion)
3.1% of GDP (2018) (approximately $18.6 billion)
3.2% of GDP (2017) (approximately $18.3 billion)
country comparison to the world: 32

Military and security service personnel strengths: approximately 260,000 total active troops (200,000 Army; 45,000 Navy, including about 20,000 marines; 14,000 Air Force); approximately 170,000 National Police (2022)

Military equipment inventories and acquisitions: the Colombian military inventory includes a wide mix of equipment from a variety of suppliers, including Canada, Europe, Israel, South Korea, and the US; Germany, Israel, and the US have been the leading suppliers of military hardware since 2010; Colombia's defense industry is active in producing air, land, and naval platforms (2022)

Military service age and obligation: 18-24 years of age for compulsory (men) and voluntary (men and women) military service; conscript service obligation is 18 months; conscripted soldiers reportedly include regular soldiers (conscripts without a high school degree), drafted high school graduates (bachilleres), and rural (campesino) soldiers who serve in their home regions (2022)
note: in 2020, conscripts reportedly comprised about 50% of the Colombian military's active force with approximately 60-90,000 conscripts brought into the military annually

Military deployments: 275 Egypt (MFO) (2022)

Military - note: as of 2022, the Colombian Armed Forces were primarily focused on internal security, particularly counter-narcotics, counter-terrorism, and counterinsurgency operations against drug traffickers, militants from several factions of the Revolutionary Armed Forces of Colombia (FARC) and National Liberation Army (ELN) terrorist/guerrilla organizations, and other illegal armed groups; the Colombian Government signed a peace agreement with the FARC in 2016, but some former members (known as dissidents) have returned to fighting (note - these dissident groups include the designated terrorist groups Revolutionary Armed Forces of Colombia - People's Army or FARC-EP and Segunda Marquetalia; see Appendix T); the Colombian military resumed operations against FARC dissidents and their successor paramilitary groups in late 2019; in 2017, the Colombian Government initiated formal peace talks with the ELN, but in January 2019, the government suspended the peace talks shortly after the ELN exploded a car bomb at the National Police Academy in Bogotá and resumed counter-terrorism/counterinsurgency operations against the group; operations against the FARC dissident groups and the ELN continued into 2022, although the Colombian Government resumed talks with ELN in November 2022; the military was also focused on the security challenges posed by its neighbor, Venezuela, where instability has attracted narcotics traffickers and both the ELN and FARC dissidents, including FARC-EP and Segunda Marquetalia, operate openly

Maritime threats: the International Maritime Bureau reports the territorial waters of Colombia are a risk for armed robbery against ships; in 2021, six attacks against commercial vessels were reported, an increase over the single attack in 2020; most of these occurred in the main port of Cartagena while ships were berthed or at anchor

TERRORISM

Terrorist group(s): National Liberation Army (ELN); Revolutionary Armed Forces of Colombia - People's Army (FARC-EP); Segunda Marquetalia
note: details about the history, aims, leadership, organization, areas of operation, tactics, targets, weapons, size, and sources of support of the group(s) appear(s) in Appendix-T

TRANSNATIONAL ISSUES

Disputes - international: in December 2007, ICJ allocated San Andres, Providencia, and Santa Catalina islands to Colombia under 1928 Treaty but did not rule on 82 degrees W meridian as maritime boundary with Nicaragua; managed dispute with Venezuela over maritime boundary and Venezuelan-administered Los Monjes Islands near the Gulf of Venezuela; Colombian-organized illegal narcotics, guerrilla, and paramilitary activities penetrate all neighboring borders and have caused Colombian citizens to flee mostly into neighboring countries; Colombia, Honduras, Nicaragua, Jamaica, and the US assert various claims to Bajo Nuevo and Serranilla Bank

Refugees and internally displaced persons: refugees (country of origin): 1,842,390 (Venezuela) (economic and political crisis; includes Venezuelans who have claimed asylum, are recognized as refugees, or received alternative legal stay) (2022)

IDPs: 8,258,460 (conflict between government and illegal armed groups and drug traffickers since 1985) (2022)
stateless persons: 11 (mid-year 2021)

Illicit drugs: Colombia is the world's top cocaine producer; exports and is a source of heroin and marijuana; coca cultivation was estimated at 245,000 hectares (ha) in 2020; potential pure cocaine production reached 1,010 metric tons in 2020

COMOROS

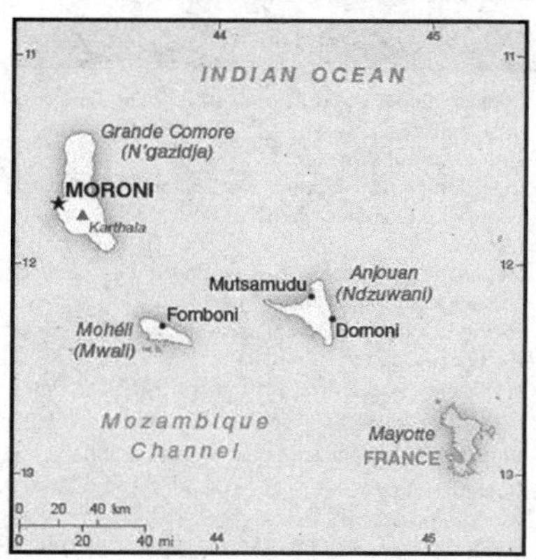

INTRODUCTION

Background: The archipelago of the Comoros in the Indian Ocean, composed of the islands of Mayotte, Anjouan, Moheli, and Grande Comore declared independence from France on 6 July 1975. Residents of Mayotte voted to remain in France, and France now has classified it as a department of France. Since independence, Comoros has endured political instability through realized and attempted coups. In 1997, the islands of Anjouan and Moheli declared independence from Comoros. In 1999, military chief Col. AZALI Assoumani seized power of the entire government in a bloodless coup; he initiated the 2000 Fomboni Accords, a power-sharing agreement in which the federal presidency rotates among the three islands, and each island maintains its local government. AZALI won the 2002 federal presidential election as president of the Union of the Comoros from Grande Comore Island, which held the first four-year term. AZALI stepped down in 2006 and President Ahmed Abdallah Mohamed SAMBI was elected as president from Anjouan. In 2007, Mohamed BACAR effected Anjouan's de-facto secession from the Union of the Comoros, refusing to step down when Comoros' other islands held legitimate elections in July. The African Union (AU) initially attempted to resolve the political crisis by applying sanctions and a naval blockade to Anjouan, but in March 2008 the AU and Comoran soldiers seized the island. The island's inhabitants generally welcomed the move. In 2009, the Comorian population approved a constitutional referendum extending the term of the president from four years to five years. In May 2011, Ikililou DHOININE won the presidency in peaceful elections widely deemed to be free and fair. In closely contested elections in 2016, former President AZALI Assoumani won a second term, when the rotating presidency returned to Grande Comore. A new July 2018 constitution removed the presidential term limits and the requirement for the presidency to rotate between the three main islands. In August 2018, President AZALI formed a new government and subsequently ran and was elected president in March 2019.

GEOGRAPHY

Location: Southern Africa, group of islands at the northern mouth of the Mozambique Channel, about two-thirds of the way between northern Madagascar and northern Mozambique

Geographic coordinates: 12 10 S, 44 15 E

Map references: Africa

Area: *total:* 2,235 sq km
land: 2,235 sq km
water: 0 sq km
country comparison to the world: 179

Area - comparative: slightly more than 12 times the size of Washington, DC

Land boundaries: *total:* 0 km

Coastline: 340 km

Maritime claims: *territorial sea:* 12 nm
exclusive economic zone: 200 nm

Climate: tropical marine; rainy season (November to May)

Terrain: volcanic islands, interiors vary from steep mountains to low hills

Elevation: *highest point:* Karthala 2,360 m
lowest point: Indian Ocean 0 m

Natural resources: fish

Land use: *agricultural land:* 84.4% (2018 est.)
arable land: 46.7% (2018 est.)
permanent crops: 29.6% (2018 est.)
permanent pasture: 8.1% (2018 est.)
forest: 1.4% (2018 est.)
other: 14.2% (2018 est.)

Irrigated land: 1.3 sq km (2012)

Population distribution: the capital city of Maroni, located on the western side of the island of Grande Comore, is the country's largest city; however, of the three islands that comprise Comoros, it is Anjouan that is the most densely populated as shown in this population distribution map

Natural hazards: cyclones possible during rainy season (December to April); volcanic activity on Grand Comore
volcanism: Karthala (2,361 m) on Grand Comore Island last erupted in 2007; a 2005 eruption forced thousands of people to be evacuated and produced a large ash cloud

Geography - note: important location at northern end of Mozambique Channel; the only Arab League country that lies entirely in the Southern Hemisphere

PEOPLE AND SOCIETY

Population: 876,437 (2022 est.)
country comparison to the world: 164

Nationality: *noun:* Comoran(s)
adjective: Comoran

Ethnic groups: Antalote, Cafre, Makoa, Oimatsaha, Sakalava

Languages: Arabic (official), French (official), Shikomoro (official; similar to Swahili) (Comorian)

Religions: Sunni Muslim 98%, other (including Shia Muslim, Roman Catholic, Jehovah's Witness, Protestant) 2%
note: Sunni Islam is the state religion

Demographic profile: Comoros' population is a melange of Arabs, Persians, Indonesians, Africans, and Indians, and the much smaller number of Europeans that settled on the islands between the 8th and 19th centuries, when they served as a regional trade hub. The Arab and Persian influence is most evident in the islands' overwhelmingly Muslim majority – about 98% of Comorans are Sunni Muslims. The country is densely populated, averaging nearly 350 people per square mile, although this varies widely among the islands, with Anjouan being the most densely populated.

Given the large share of land dedicated to agriculture and Comoros' growing population, habitable land is becoming increasingly crowded. The combination of increasing population pressure on limited land and resources, widespread poverty, and poor job prospects motivates thousands of Comorans each year to attempt to illegally migrate using small fishing boats to the neighboring island of Mayotte, which is a French territory. The majority of legal Comoran migration to France came after Comoros' independence from France in 1975, with the flow peaking in the mid-1980s.

At least 150,000 to 200,000 people of Comoran citizenship or descent live abroad, mainly in France, where they have gone seeking a better quality of life, job opportunities, higher education (Comoros has no universities), advanced health care, and to finance elaborate traditional wedding ceremonies (aada). Remittances from the diaspora are an economic mainstay, in 2013 representing approximately 25% of Comoros' GDP and significantly more than the value of its exports of goods and services (only 15% of GDP). Grand Comore, Comoros' most populous island, is both the primary source of emigrants and the main recipient of remittances. Most remittances are spent on private consumption, but this often goes toward luxury goods and the aada and does not contribute to economic development or poverty reduction. Although the majority of the diaspora is now French-born with more distant ties to Comoros, it is unclear whether they will sustain the current level of remittances.

Age structure: *0-14 years:* 36.68% (male 154,853/female 155,602)
15-24 years: 20.75% (male 85,208/female 90,422)
25-54 years: 33.99% (male 136,484/female 151,178)
55-64 years: 4.49% (male 17,237/female 20,781)
65 years and over: 4.08% (male 15,437/female 19,079) (2020 est.)

Dependency ratios: *total dependency ratio:* 75.5
youth dependency ratio: 67.4
elderly dependency ratio: 5.4
potential support ratio: 18.6 (2020 est.)

Median age: *total:* 20.9 years
male: 20.2 years
female: 21.5 years (2020 est.)
country comparison to the world: 188

Population growth rate: 1.37% (2022 est.)
country comparison to the world: 70

Birth rate: 22.52 births/1,000 population (2022 est.)
country comparison to the world: 55

Death rate: 6.55 deaths/1,000 population (2022 est.)
country comparison to the world: 135

Net migration rate: -2.25 migrant(s)/1,000 population (2022 est.)
country comparison to the world: 172

Population distribution: the capital city of Maroni, located on the western side of the island of Grande Comore, is the country's largest city; however, of the three islands that comprise Comoros, it is Anjouan that is the most densely populated as shown in this population distribution map

Urbanization: *urban population:* 29.9% of total population (2022)
rate of urbanization: 2.97% annual rate of change (2020-25 est.)

Major urban areas - population: 62,000 MORONI (capital) (2018)

Sex ratio: *at birth:* 1.03 male(s)/female
0-14 years: 1 male(s)/female
15-24 years: 0.95 male(s)/female
25-54 years: 0.91 male(s)/female
55-64 years: 0.85 male(s)/female
65 years and over: 0.76 male(s)/female
total population: 0.94 male(s)/female (2022 est.)

Mother's mean age at first birth: 23 years (2012 est.)
note: data represents median age at first birth among women 25-49

Maternal mortality ratio: 273 deaths/100,000 live births (2017 est.)
country comparison to the world: 40

Infant mortality rate: *total:* 57.1 deaths/1,000 live births
male: 67.17 deaths/1,000 live births
female: 46.73 deaths/1,000 live births (2022 est.)
country comparison to the world: 13

Life expectancy at birth: *total population:* 67.2 years
male: 64.93 years
female: 69.54 years (2022 est.)
country comparison to the world: 192

Total fertility rate: 2.78 children born/woman (2022 est.)
country comparison to the world: 56

Contraceptive prevalence rate: 19.4% (2012)

Drinking water source: *improved: urban:* 97.4% of population
rural: 88.5% of population
total: 91% of population
unimproved: urban: 2.6% of population
rural: 11.5% of population
total: 8.9% of population (2017 est.)

Current health expenditure: 5.2% of GDP (2019)

Physicians density: 0.26 physicians/1,000 population (2018)

Sanitation facility access: *improved: urban:* 62.4% of population
rural: 43.6% of population
total: 49% of population
unimproved: urban: 37.6% of population
rural: 56.4% of population
total: 51% of population (2017 est.)

HIV/AIDS - adult prevalence rate: (2020 est.) <0.1%

Obesity - adult prevalence rate: 7.8% (2016)
country comparison to the world: 157

Alcohol consumption per capita: *total:* 0.18 liters of pure alcohol (2019 est.)
beer: 0.04 liters of pure alcohol (2019 est.)
wine: 0.07 liters of pure alcohol (2019 est.)
spirits: 0.07 liters of pure alcohol (2019 est.)
other alcohols: 0 liters of pure alcohol (2019 est.)
country comparison to the world: 173

Tobacco use: *total:* 20.3% (2020 est.)
male: 29.5% (2020 est.)
female: 11.1% (2020 est.)
country comparison to the world: 83

Children under the age of 5 years underweight: 16.9% (2012)
country comparison to the world: 30

Education expenditures: 2.5% of GDP (2015 est.)
country comparison to the world: 168

Literacy: *definition:* age 15 and over can read and write
total population: 58.8%
male: 64.6%
female: 53% (2018)

School life expectancy (primary to tertiary education): *total:* 11 years
male: 11 years
female: 11 years (2014)

Unemployment, youth ages 15-24: *total:* 19.5%
male: 20%
female: 18.8% (2014)

ENVIRONMENT

Environment - current issues: deforestation; soil degradation and erosion results from forest loss and from crop cultivation on slopes without proper terracing; marine biodiversity affected as soil erosion leads to the silting of coral reefs

Environment - international agreements: party to: Biodiversity, Climate Change, Climate Change-Kyoto Protocol, Climate Change-Paris Agreement, Comprehensive Nuclear Test Ban, Desertification, Endangered Species, Hazardous Wastes, Law of the Sea, Ozone Layer Protection, Ship Pollution, Wetlands

signed, but not ratified: none of the selected agreements

Air pollutants: particulate matter emissions: 18.6 micrograms per cubic meter (2016 est.)
carbon dioxide emissions: 0.2 megatons (2016 est.)
methane emissions: 0.19 megatons (2020 est.)

Climate: tropical marine; rainy season (November to May)

Land use: *agricultural land:* 84.4% (2018 est.)
arable land: 46.7% (2018 est.)
permanent crops: 29.6% (2018 est.)
permanent pasture: 8.1% (2018 est.)
forest: 1.4% (2018 est.)
other: 14.2% (2018 est.)

Urbanization: *urban population:* 29.9% of total population (2022)
rate of urbanization: 2.97% annual rate of change (2020-25 est.)

Revenue from forest resources: *forest revenues:* 1.39% of GDP (2018 est.)
country comparison to the world: 46

Revenue from coal: *coal revenues:* 0% of GDP (2018 est.)
country comparison to the world: 79

Waste and recycling: *municipal solid waste generated annually:* 91,013 tons (2015 est.)

Total water withdrawal: *municipal:* 4.8 million cubic meters (2017 est.)
industrial: 500,000 cubic meters (2017 est.)
agricultural: 4.7 million cubic meters (2017 est.)

Total renewable water resources: 1.2 billion cubic meters (2017 est.)

GOVERNMENT

Country name: *conventional long form:* Union of the Comoros
conventional short form: Comoros
local long form: Udzima wa Komori (Comorian)/ Union des Comores (French)/ Al Ittihad al Qumuri (Arabic)
local short form: Komori (Comorian)/ Les Comores (French)/ Juzur al Qamar (Arabic)
former: Comorian State, Federal Islamic Republic of the Comoros
etymology: name derives from the Arabic designation "Juzur al Qamar" meaning "Islands of the Moon"

Government type: federal presidential republic

Capital: *name:* Moroni
geographic coordinates: 11 42 S, 43 14 E
time difference: UTC+3 (8 hours ahead of Washington, DC, during Standard Time)
etymology: Moroni derives from "mroni," which means "at the river" in Shingazidja, the Comorian language spoken on Grande Comore (N'gazidja)

Administrative divisions: 3 islands; Anjouan (Ndzuwani), Grande Comore (N'gazidja), Moheli (Mwali)

Independence: 6 July 1975 (from France)

National holiday: Independence Day, 6 July (1975)

Constitution: *history:* previous 1996, 2001; newest adopted 30 July 2018
amendments: proposed by the president of the union or supported by at least one third of the Assembly of the Union membership; adoption requires approval by at least three-quarters majority of the total Assembly membership or approval in a referendum
note: a referendum held on 30 July 2018 - boycotted by the opposition - overwhelmingly approved a new constitution that allows for 2 consecutive 5-year presidential terms and revises the rotating presidency within the islands

Legal system: mixed legal system of Islamic religious law, the French civil code of 1975, and customary law

International law organization participation: has not submitted an ICJ jurisdiction declaration; accepts ICCt jurisdiction

Citizenship: *citizenship by birth:* no
citizenship by descent only: at least one parent must be a citizen of the Comoros
dual citizenship recognized: no
residency requirement for naturalization: 10 years

Suffrage: 18 years of age; universal

Executive branch: *chief of state:* President AZALI Assoumani (since 26 May 2016); note - the president is both chief of state and head of government
head of government: President AZALI Assoumani (since 26 May 2016)
cabinet: Council of Ministers appointed by the president
elections/appointments: president directly elected by simple majority popular vote in 2 rounds for a 5-year term (eligible for a second term); election last held on 24 March 2019 (next to be held in 2024)
election results: 2019: AZALI Assoumani (CRC) elected president in first round - AZALI Assoumani (CRC) 60.8%, Ahamada MAHAMOUDOU (PJ)

14.6%, Mouigni Baraka Said SOILIHI (Independent) 5.6%, other 19%
2016: AZALI Assoumani (CRC) elected president in the second round; percent of vote in first round - Mohamed Ali SOILIHI (UPDC) 17.6%, Mouigni BARAKA (RDC) 15.1%, AZALI Assoumani (CRC) 15%, Fahmi Said IBRAHIM (PEC) 14.5%, other 37.8%; percent of vote in second round - AZALI Assoumani (CRC) 41.4%, Mohamed Ali SOILIHI (UPDC) 39.7%; Mouigni BARAKA (RDC) 19%

Legislative branch: *description:* unicameral Assembly of the Union (33 seats; 24 members directly elected by absolute majority vote in 2 rounds if needed and 9 members indirectly elected by the 3 island assemblies; members serve 5-year terms) (2017)
elections: last held on 19 January 2020 with a runoff on 23 February 2020 (next to be held in 2025) (2020)
election results: seats by party -1st round - Boycotting parties 16, Independent 3, CRC 2, RDC 2, RADHI 1, Orange party 0; note - 9 additional seats filled by the 3 island assemblies; 2nd round - CRC 20, Orange Party 2, Independents 2; composition for elected members as of 2022 - men 20, women 4, percent of women 16.7% (2019)

Judicial branch: *highest court(s):* Supreme Court or Cour Supreme (consists of 7 judges)
judge selection and term of office: Supreme Court judges - selection and term of office NA
subordinate courts: Court of Appeals (in Moroni); Tribunal de premiere instance; island village (community) courts; religious courts

Political parties and leaders: only parties with seats in the Assembly of the Union listed:
Convention for the Renewal of the Comoros or CRC [AZALI Assoumani]
Orange Party [Mohamed DAOUDOU]
Independents (2018)

International organization participation: ACP, AfDB, AMF, AOSIS, AU, CAEU (candidates), COMESA, FAO, FZ, G-77, IBRD, ICAO, ICCt, ICRM, IDA, IDB, IFAD, IFC, IFRCS, ILO, IMF, IMO, IMSO, InOC, Interpol, IOC, IOM, ITSO, ITU, ITUC (NGOs), LAS, MIGA, NAM, OIC, OIF, OPCW, UN, UNCTAD, UNESCO, UNIDO, UPU, WCO, WHO, WIPO, WMO, WTO (observer)

Diplomatic representation in the US: *chief of mission:* Ambassador Issimail CHANFI (since 23 December 2020)
chancery: Mission to the UN, 866 United Nations Plaza, Suite 495, New York, NY 10017
telephone: [1] (212) 750-1637
FAX: [1] (212) 750-1657
email address and website:
comoros@un.int
https://www.un.int/comoros/

Diplomatic representation from the US: *embassy:* the US does not have an embassy in Comoros; the US Ambassador to Madagascar is accredited to Comoros

Flag description: four equal horizontal bands of yellow (top), white, red, and blue, with a green isosceles triangle based on the hoist; centered within the triangle is a vertical white crescent moon with the convex side facing the hoist and four white, five-pointed stars placed vertically in a line between the points of the crescent; the horizontal bands and the four stars represent the four main islands of the archipelago - Mwali, N'gazidja, Ndzuwani, and Mahore (Mayotte - department of France, but claimed by Comoros)
note: the crescent, stars, and color green are traditional symbols of Islam

National symbol(s): four five-pointed stars and crescent moon; national colors: green, white

National anthem: *name:* "Udzima wa ya Masiwa" (The Union of the Great Islands)
lyrics/music: Said Hachim SIDI ABDEREMANE/ Said Hachim SIDI ABDEREMANE and Kamildine ABDALLAH
note: adopted 1978

ECONOMY

Economic overview: One of the world's poorest and smallest economies, the Comoros is made up of three islands that are hampered by inadequate transportation links, a young and rapidly increasing population, and few natural resources. The low educational level of the labor force contributes to a subsistence level of economic activity and a heavy dependence on foreign grants and technical assistance. Agriculture, including fishing, hunting, and forestry, accounts for about 50% of GDP, employs a majority of the labor force, and provides most of the exports. Export income is heavily reliant on the three main crops of vanilla, cloves, and ylang ylang (perfume essence); and the Comoros' export earnings are easily disrupted by disasters such as fires and extreme weather. Despite agriculture's importance to the economy, the country imports roughly 70% of its food; rice, the main staple, and other dried vegetables account for more than 25% of imports. Remittances from about 300,000 Comorans contribute about 25% of the country's GDP. France, Comoros's colonial power, remains a key trading partner and bilateral donor.

Comoros faces an education system in need of upgrades, limited opportunities for private commercial and industrial enterprises, poor health services, limited exports, and a high population growth rate. Recurring political instability, sometimes initiated from outside the country, and an ongoing electricity crisis have inhibited growth. The government, elected in mid-2016, has moved to improve revenue mobilization, reduce expenditures, and improve electricity access, although the public sector wage bill remains one of the highest in Sub-Saharan Africa. In mid-2017, Comoros joined the Southern African Development Community with 15 other regional member states.

Real GDP (purchasing power parity): $2.73 billion (2020 est.)
$2.6 billion (2019 est.)
$2.55 billion (2018 est.)
note: data are in 2017 dollars
country comparison to the world: 190

Real GDP growth rate: 2.7% (2017 est.)
2.2% (2016 est.)
1% (2015 est.)
country comparison to the world: 106

Real GDP per capita: $3,100 (2020 est.)
$3,100 (2019 est.)
$3,100 (2018 est.)
note: data are in 2017 dollars
country comparison to the world: 196

GDP (official exchange rate): $1.186 billion (2019 est.)

Inflation rate (consumer prices): 1% (2017 est.)
1.8% (2016 est.)
country comparison to the world: 63

GDP - composition, by sector of origin: *agriculture:* 47.7% (2017 est.)
industry: 11.8% (2017 est.)
services: 40.5% (2017 est.)

GDP - composition, by end use: household consumption: 92.6% (2017 est.)
government consumption: 20.4% (2017 est.)
investment in fixed capital: 20% (2017 est.)
investment in inventories: -3.1% (2017 est.)
exports of goods and services: 17.2% (2017 est.)
imports of goods and services: -47.1% (2017 est.)

Agricultural products: coconuts, cassava, rice, bananas, pulses nes, milk, taro, sweet potatoes, maize, cloves

Industries: fishing, tourism, perfume distillation

Industrial production growth rate: 1% (2017 est.)
country comparison to the world: 154

Labor force: 278,500 (2016 est.)
country comparison to the world: 165

Labor force - by occupation: *agriculture:* 80%
industry: 20% (1996 est.)
industry and services: 20% (1996 est.)

Unemployment rate: 6.5% (2014 est.)
country comparison to the world: 102

Unemployment, youth ages 15-24: *total:* 19.5%
male: 20%
female: 18.8% (2014)
country comparison to the world: 80

Population below poverty line: 42.4% (2013 est.)

Gini Index coefficient - distribution of family income: 45.3 (2014 est.)
country comparison to the world: 29

Household income or consumption by percentage share: *lowest 10%:* 0.9%
highest 10%: 55.2% (2004)

Budget: *revenues:* 165.2 million (2017 est.)
expenditures: 207.3 million (2017 est.)

Budget surplus (+) or deficit (-): -6.5% (of GDP) (2017 est.)
country comparison to the world: 188

Public debt: 32.4% of GDP (2017 est.)
27.7% of GDP (2016 est.)
country comparison to the world: 160

Taxes and other revenues: 25.3% (of GDP) (2017 est.)
country comparison to the world: 117

Fiscal year: calendar year

Current account balance: -$27 million (2017 est.)
-$45 million (2016 est.)
country comparison to the world: 74

Exports: $140 million (2019 est.)
$150 million (2018 est.)
note: Data are in current year dollars and do not include illicit exports or re-exports.
country comparison to the world: 206

Exports - partners: France 32%, India 23%, Germany 10%, Turkey 9%, Madagascar 7% (2019)

Exports - commodities: cloves, essential oils, vacuum flask, vanilla, scrap vessels (2019)

Imports: $350 million (2019 est.) note: data are in current year dollars

$360 million (2018 est.) note: data are in current year dollars
country comparison to the world: 208

Imports - partners: China 22%, United Arab Emirates 16%, France 11%, Pakistan 9%, India 6% (2019)

Imports - commodities: rice, chicken products, refined petroleum, cement, cars (2019)

Reserves of foreign exchange and gold: $208 million (31 December 2017 est.)
$159.5 million (31 December 2016 est.)
country comparison to the world: 173

Debt - external: $199.8 million (31 December 2017 est.)
$132 million (31 December 2016 est.)
country comparison to the world: 189

Exchange rates: Comoran francs (KMF) per US dollar -
458.2 (2017 est.)
444.76 (2016 est.)
444.76 (2015 est.)
443.6 (2014 est.)
370.81 (2013 est.)

ENERGY

Electricity access: *electrification - total population:* 70% (2019)
electrification - urban areas: 89% (2019)
electrification - rural areas: 62% (2019)

Electricity: *installed generating capacity:* 35,000 kW (2020 est.)
consumption: 96.248 million kWh (2019 est.)
exports: 0 kWh (2019 est.)
imports: 0 kWh (2019 est.)
transmission/distribution losses: 6.048 million kWh (2019 est.)

Electricity generation sources: *fossil fuels:* 100% of total installed capacity (2020 est.)

Petroleum: *total petroleum production:* 0 bbl/day (2021 est.)
refined petroleum consumption: 2,200 bbl/day (2019 est.)

Refined petroleum products - imports: 1,241 bbl/day (2015 est.)
country comparison to the world: 197

Carbon dioxide emissions: 326,000 metric tonnes of CO2 (2019 est.)
from petroleum and other liquids: 326,000 metric tonnes of CO2 (2019 est.)
country comparison to the world: 195

Energy consumption per capita: 5.346 million Btu/person (2019 est.)
country comparison to the world: 170

COMMUNICATIONS

Telephones - fixed lines: *total subscriptions:* 7,573 (2020 est.)
subscriptions per 100 inhabitants: 1 (2020 est.)
country comparison to the world: 193

Telephones - mobile cellular: *total subscriptions:* 781,579 (2020 est.)
subscriptions per 100 inhabitants: 90 (2020 est.)
country comparison to the world: 166

Telecommunication systems: *general assessment:* Qatar launched a special program for the construction of a wireless network to inter connect the 3 islands of the archipelago; telephone service limited to the islands' few towns (2020)
domestic: fixed-line connections less than 1 per 100 persons; mobile-cellular usage about 90 per 100 persons; 2 companies provide domestic and international mobile service and wireless data (2020)
international: country code - 269; landing point for the EASSy, Comoros Domestic Cable System, Avassa, and FLY-LION3 fiber-optic submarine cable system connecting East Africa with Europe; HF radiotelephone communications to Madagascar and Reunion (2019)

Broadcast media: national state-owned TV station and a TV station run by Anjouan regional government; national state-owned radio; regional governments on the islands of Grande Comore and Anjouan each operate a radio station; a few independent and small community radio stations operate on the islands of Grande Comore and Moheli, and these two islands have access to Mayotte Radio and French TV

Internet country code: .km

Internet users: *total:* 69,568 (2020 est.)
percent of population: 8% (2020 est.)
country comparison to the world: 188

Broadband - fixed subscriptions: *total:* 1,066 (2020 est.)
subscriptions per 100 inhabitants: 0.1 (2020 est.)
country comparison to the world: 201

TRANSPORTATION

National air transport system: *number of registered air carriers:* 2 (2020)
inventory of registered aircraft operated by air carriers: 9

Civil aircraft registration country code prefix: D6

Airports: *total:* 4 (2021)
country comparison to the world: 185

Airports - with paved runways: *total:* 4
2,438 to 3,047 m: 1
914 to 1,523 m: 3 (2021)

Roadways: *total:* 880 km (2002)
*paved:*673 km (2002)
unpaved: 207 km (2002)
country comparison to the world: 188

Merchant marine: *total:* 236
by type: bulk carrier 8, container ship 7, general cargo 112, oil tanker 31, other 78 (2021)
country comparison to the world: 63

Ports and terminals: *major seaport(s):* Moroni, Moutsamoudou

MILITARY AND SECURITY

Military and security forces: National Army for Development (l'Armee Nationale de Developpement, AND): Comoran Security Force (also called Comoran Defense Force (Force Comorienne de Defense, FCD), includes Gendarmerie); Ministry of Interior: Coast Guard, Federal Police, National Directorate of Territorial Safety (2022)
note: when the Gendarmerie serves as the judicial police, it reports to the Minister of Justice

Military and security service personnel strengths: estimated 600 Defense Force personnel; estimated 500 Federal Police (2022)

Military equipment inventories and acquisitions: the defense forces are lightly armed with a mix of mostly older equipment from a variety of countries, including France, Italy, Russia, and the US (2021)

Military service age and obligation: 18 years of age for 2-year voluntary military service for men and women; no conscription (2021)

Military - note: the security forces are limited in capabilities to performing search and rescue operations and maintaining internal security; a defense treaty with France provides naval resources for protection of territorial waters, training of Comoran military personnel, and air surveillance; France maintains a small maritime base and a Foreign Legion contingent on neighboring Mayotte (2022)

TRANSNATIONAL ISSUES

Disputes - international: claims French-administered Mayotte and challenges France's and Madagascar's claims to Banc du Geyser, a drying reef in the Mozambique Channel; in May 2008, African Union forces assisted the Comoros military in recapturing Anjouan Island from rebels who seized it in 2001

Trafficking in persons: *current situation:* human traffickers may exploit domestic and foreign victims in Comoros and Comorians abroad; some Comorian and Malagasy women are subject to forced labor in the Middle East; adults and children may be forced to work in agriculture, construction, or as domestics in Mayotte; children abandoned by parents who left to seek jobs abroad are vulnerable to exploitation in domestic service, vending, baking, fishing, and agriculture; children from poor families whose parents place them with a relative or acquaintance for educational opportunities are vulnerable to domestic servitude and physical and sexual abuse; some children in Koranic schools may experience forced labor in agriculture or domestic servitude; inadequate border controls; government corruption, and international crime networks leave Comorians vulnerable to international trafficking
tier rating:
Tier 3 — Comoros does not fully meet the minimum standards for the elimination of trafficking is not making significant efforts to do so; the Anti-Trafficking Task Force met for the first time since 2017 and began drafting a national action plan for combatting trafficking; the government took steps to ratify the 2000 UN TIP Protocol and supported centers that identify and provide care to victims of crime, would include trafficking victims; however, authorities continued to lack an understanding of trafficking and did not make any anti-trafficking law enforcement efforts; the government did not investigate, prosecute, or convict any alleged traffickers or officials suspected of complicity in trafficking; the government did not develop any standing operating procedures for identifying trafficking victims and referring them to limited care providers; no public awareness campaigns were conducted (2020)

CONGO, DEMOCRATIC REPUBLIC OF THE

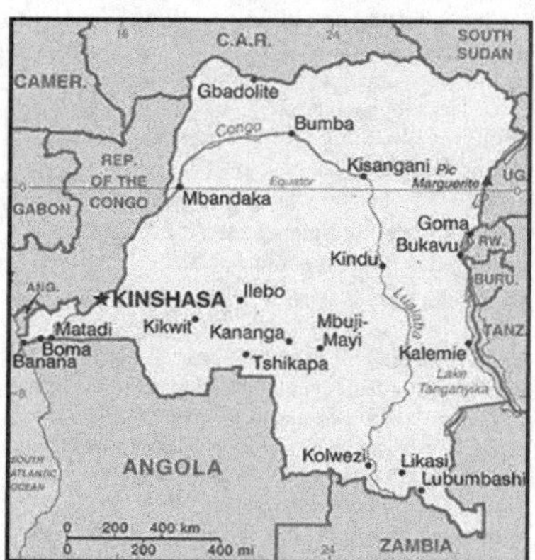

INTRODUCTION

Background: The Kingdom of Kongo ruled the area around the mouth of the Congo River from the 14th to 19th centuries. To the center and east, the Kingdoms of Luba and Lunda ruled from the 16th and 17th centuries to the 19th century. In the 1870s, European exploration of the Congo Basin, sponsored by King LEOPOLD II of Belgium, eventually allowed the ruler to acquire rights to the Congo territory and to make it his private property under the name of the Congo Free State. During the Free State, the king's colonial military forced the local population to produce rubber. From 1885 to 1908, millions of Congolese people died as a result of disease and exploitation. International condemnation finally forced LEOPOLD to cede the land to Belgium, creating the Belgian Congo.

The Republic of the Congo gained its independence from Belgium in 1960, but its early years were marred by political and social instability. Col. Joseph MOBUTU seized power and declared himself president in a November 1965 coup. He subsequently changed his name - to MOBUTU Sese Seko - as well as that of the country - to Zaire. MOBUTU retained his position for 32 years through several sham elections, as well as through brutal force. Ethnic strife and civil war, touched off by a massive inflow of refugees in 1994 from conflict in Rwanda and Burundi, led in May 1997 to the toppling of the MOBUTU regime by a rebellion backed by Rwanda and Uganda and fronted by Laurent KABILA. KABILA renamed the country the Democratic Republic of the Congo (DRC), but in August 1998 his regime was itself challenged by a second insurrection again backed by Rwanda and Uganda. Troops from Angola, Chad, Namibia, Sudan, and Zimbabwe intervened to support KABILA's regime. In January 2001, KABILA was assassinated and his son, Joseph KABILA, was named head of state. In October 2002, the new president was successful in negotiating the withdrawal of Rwandan forces occupying the eastern DRC; two months later, the Pretoria Accord was signed by all remaining warring parties to end the fighting and establish a government of national unity. Presidential, National Assembly, and provincial elections took place in 2006, with Joseph KABILA elected to office.

National elections were held in November 2011 and disputed results allowed Joseph KABILA to be reelected to the presidency. While the DRC constitution barred President KABILA from running for a third term, the DRC Government delayed national elections originally slated for November 2016, to 30 December 2018. This failure to hold elections as scheduled fueled significant civil and political unrest, with sporadic street protests by KABILA's opponents and exacerbation of tensions in the tumultuous eastern DRC regions. Presidential, legislative, and provincial elections were held in late December 2018 and early 2019 across most of the country. The DRC Government canceled presidential elections in the cities of Beni and Butembo (citing concerns over an ongoing Ebola outbreak in the region) as well as Yumbi (which had recently experienced heavy violence).

Opposition candidate Felix TSHISEKEDI was announced the election winner on 10 January 2019 and inaugurated two weeks later. This was the first transfer of power to an opposition candidate without significant violence or a coup since the DRC's independence.

The DRC, particularly in the East, continues to experience violence perpetrated by more than 100 armed groups active in the region, including the Allied Democratic Forces, the Democratic Forces for the Liberation of Rwanda, and assorted Mai Mai militias. The UN Organization Stabilization Mission in the DRC (MONUSCO) has operated in the region since 1999 and is the largest and most expensive UN peacekeeping mission in the world.

GEOGRAPHY

Location: Central Africa, northeast of Angola

Geographic coordinates: 0 00 N, 25 00 E

Map references: Africa

Area: *total:* 2,344,858 sq km
land: 2,267,048 sq km
water: 77,810 sq km
country comparison to the world: 12

Area - comparative: slightly less than one-fourth the size of the US

Land boundaries: *total:* 11,027 km
border countries (9): Angola 2,646 km (of which 225 km is the boundary of Angola's discontiguous Cabinda Province); Burundi 236 km; Central African Republic 1,747 km; Republic of the Congo 1,775 km; Rwanda 221 km; South Sudan 714 km; Tanzania 479 km; Uganda 877 km; Zambia 2,332 km

Coastline: 37 km

Maritime claims: *territorial sea:* 12 nm
exclusive economic zone: since 2011, the DRC has had a Common Interest Zone agreement with Angola for the mutual development of off-shore resources

Climate: tropical; hot and humid in equatorial river basin; cooler and drier in southern highlands; cooler and wetter in eastern highlands; north of Equator - wet season (April to October), dry season (December to February); south of Equator - wet season (November to March), dry season (April to October)

Terrain: vast central basin is a low-lying plateau; mountains in east

Elevation: *highest point:* Pic Marguerite on Mont Ngaliema (Mount Stanley) 5,110 m
lowest point: Atlantic Ocean 0 m
mean elevation: 726 m

Natural resources: cobalt, copper, niobium, tantalum, petroleum, industrial and gem diamonds, gold, silver, zinc, manganese, tin, uranium, coal, hydropower, timber

Land use: *agricultural land:* 11.4% (2018 est.)
arable land: 3.1% (2018 est.)
permanent crops: 0.3% (2018 est.)
permanent pasture: 8% (2018 est.)
forest: 67.9% (2018 est.)
other: 20.7% (2018 est.)

Irrigated land: 110 sq km (2012)

Major lakes (area sq km): *fresh water lake(s):* Lake Tanganyika (shared with Burundi, Tanzania, and Zambia) - 32,000 sq km; Lake Albert (shared with Uganda) - 5,590 sq km; Lake Mweru (shared with Zambia) - 4,350 sq km; Lac Mai-Ndombe - 2,300 sq km; Lake Kivu (shared with Rwanda) - 2,220 sq km; Lake Edward (shared with Uganda) - 2,150 sq km; Lac Tumba - 500 sq km; Lac Upemba - 530 sq km

Major rivers (by length in km): Congo river mouth (shared with Zambia [s], Angola, and Republic of Congo) - 4,700 km; Ubangi river mouth (shared with Central African Republic [s] and Republic of Congo) - 2,270 km
note – [s] after country name indicates river source; [m] after country name indicates river mouth

Major watersheds (area sq km): Atlantic Ocean drainage: Congo (3,730,881 sq km), (Mediterranean Sea) Nile (3,254,853 sq km)

Indian Ocean drainage: Zambezi (1,332,412 sq km)

Major aquifers: Congo Basin

Population distribution: urban clusters are spread throughout the country, particularly in the northeast along the border with Uganda, Rwanda, and Burundi; the largest city is the capital, Kinshasha, located in the west along the Congo River; the south is least densely populated as shown in this population distribution map

Natural hazards: periodic droughts in south; Congo River floods (seasonal); active volcanoes in the east along the Great Rift Valley
volcanism: Nyiragongo (3,470 m), which erupted in 2002 and is experiencing ongoing activity, poses a major threat to the city of Goma, home to a quarter million people; the volcano produces unusually fast-moving lava, known to travel up to 100 km /hr; Nyiragongo has been deemed a Decade Volcano by the International Association of Volcanology and Chemistry of the Earth's Interior, worthy of study due to its explosive history and close proximity to human populations; its neighbor, Nyamuragira, which erupted in 2010, is Africa's most active volcano; Visoke is the only other historically active volcano

Geography - note: *note 1:* second largest country in Africa (after Algeria) and largest country in Sub-Saharan Africa; straddles the equator; dense tropical rain forest in central river basin and eastern highlands; the narrow strip of land that controls the lower Congo River is the DRC's only outlet to the South Atlantic Ocean *note 2:* because of its speed, cataracts, rapids, and turbulence the Congo River, most of which flows through the DRC, has never been accurately measured along much of its length; nonetheless, it is conceded to be the deepest river in the world; estimates of its greatest depth vary between 220 and 250 meters

PEOPLE AND SOCIETY

Population: 108,407,721 (2022 est.)
country comparison to the world: 14

Nationality: *noun:* Congolese (singular and plural)
adjective: Congolese or Congo

Ethnic groups: more than 200 African ethnic groups of which the majority are Bantu; the four largest tribes - Mongo, Luba, Kongo (all Bantu), and the Mangbetu-Azande (Hamitic) - make up about 45% of the population

Languages: French (official), Lingala (a lingua franca trade language), Kingwana (a dialect of Kiswahili or Swahili), Kikongo, Tshiluba
major-language sample(s): Buku oyo ya bosembo ya Mokili Mobimba Ezali na Makanisi ya Liboso Mpenza. (Lingala)

Religions: Roman Catholic 29.9%, Protestant 26.7%, other Christian 36.5%, Kimbanguist 2.8%, Muslim 1.3%, other (includes syncretic sects and indigenous beliefs) 1.2%, none 1.3%, unspecified 0.2% (2014 est.)

Demographic profile: Despite a wealth of fertile soil, hydroelectric power potential, and mineral resources, the Democratic Republic of the Congo (DRC) struggles with many socioeconomic problems, including high infant and maternal mortality rates, malnutrition, poor vaccination coverage, lack of access to improved water sources and sanitation, and frequent and early fertility. Ongoing conflict, mismanagement of resources, and a lack of investment have resulted in food insecurity; almost 30% of children under the age of 5 are malnourished. The overall coverage of basic public services – education, health, sanitation, and potable water – is very limited and piecemeal, with substantial regional and rural/urban disparities. Fertility remains high at more than 5 children per woman and is likely to remain high because of the low use of contraception and the cultural preference for larger families.

The DRC is a source and host country for refugees. Between 2012 and 2014, more than 119,000 Congolese refugees returned from the Republic of Congo to the relative stability of northwest DRC, but more than 850,000 Congolese refugees and asylum seekers were hosted by neighboring countries as of December 2021. In addition, an estimated 5.5 million Congolese were internally displaced as of July 2022, the vast majority fleeing violence between rebel group and Congolese armed forces. Thousands of refugees have come to the DRC from neighboring countries, including Rwanda, the Central African Republic, South Sudan, and Burundi.

Age structure: 0-14 years: 46.38% (male 23,757,297/female 23,449,057)

15-24 years: 19.42% (male 9,908,686/female 9,856,841)

25-54 years: 28.38% (male 14,459,453/female 14,422,912)

55-64 years: 3.36% (male 1,647,267/female 1,769,429)

65 years and over: 2.47% (male 1,085,539/female 1,423,782) (2020 est.)

Dependency ratios: *total dependency ratio:* 95.4
youth dependency ratio: 89.5
elderly dependency ratio: 5.9
potential support ratio: 17 (2020 est.)

Median age: *total:* 16.7 years
male: 16.5 years
female: 16.8 years (2020 est.)
country comparison to the world: 222

Population growth rate: 3.14% (2022 est.)
country comparison to the world: 9

Birth rate: 40.08 births/1,000 population (2022 est.)
country comparison to the world: 7

Death rate: 7.94 deaths/1,000 population (2022 est.)
country comparison to the world: 95

Net migration rate: -0.71 migrant(s)/1,000 population (2022 est.)
country comparison to the world: 131

Population distribution: urban clusters are spread throughout the country, particularly in the northeast along the border with Uganda, Rwanda, and Burundi; the largest city is the capital, Kinshasha, located in the west along the Congo River; the south is least densely populated as shown in this population distribution map

Urbanization: *urban population:* 46.8% of total population (2022)
rate of urbanization: 4.33% annual rate of change (2020-25 est.)

Major urban areas - population: 15.628 million KINSHASA (capital), 2.765 million Mbuji-Mayi, 2.695 million Lubumbashi, 1.593 million Kananga, 1.366 million Kisangani, 1.190 million Bukavu (2022)

Sex ratio: *at birth:* 1.03 male(s)/female
0-14 years: 1.01 male(s)/female
15-24 years: 1.01 male(s)/female
25-54 years: 1 male(s)/female
55-64 years: 0.94 male(s)/female
65 years and over: 0.6 male(s)/female
total population: 1 male(s)/female (2022 est.)

Mother's mean age at first birth: 19.9 years (2013/14 est.)
note: data represents median age at first birth among women 20-49

Maternal mortality ratio: 473 deaths/100,000 live births (2017 est.)
country comparison to the world: 23

Infant mortality rate: *total:* 60.85 deaths/1,000 live births
male: 66.49 deaths/1,000 live births
female: 55.03 deaths/1,000 live births (2022 est.)
country comparison to the world: 10

Life expectancy at birth: *total population:* 61.83 years
male: 60.03 years
female: 63.69 years (2022 est.)
country comparison to the world: 216

Total fertility rate: 5.63 children born/woman (2022 est.)
country comparison to the world: 3

Contraceptive prevalence rate: 28.1% (2017/18)

Drinking water source: *improved: urban:* 88.8% of population
rural: 34.7% of population
total: 59.4% of population
unimproved: urban: 11.2% of population
rural: 65.3% of population
total: 40.6% of population (2020 est.)

Current health expenditure: 3.5% of GDP (2019)

Physicians density: 0.38 physicians/1,000 population (2018)

Sanitation facility access: *improved: urban:* 53.4% of population
rural: 20.5% of population
total: 35.5% of population
unimproved: urban: 46.6% of population
rural: 79.5% of population
total: 64.5% of population (2020 est.)

HIV/AIDS - adult prevalence rate: 0.7% (2020 est.)
country comparison to the world: 55

Major infectious diseases: *degree of risk:* very high (2020)
food or waterborne diseases: bacterial and protozoal diarrhea, hepatitis A, and typhoid fever
vectorborne diseases: malaria, dengue fever, and trypanosomiasis-gambiense (African sleeping sickness)
water contact diseases: schistosomiasis
animal contact diseases: rabies
note: on 21 March 2022, the US Centers for Disease Control and Prevention (CDC) issued a Travel Alert for polio in Africa; the Democratic Republic of the Congo is currently considered a high risk to travelers for circulating vaccine-derived polioviruses (cVDPV); vaccine-derived poliovirus (VDPV) is a strain of the weakened poliovirus that was initially included in oral polio vaccine (OPV) and that has changed over time and behaves more like the wild or naturally occurring virus; this means it can be spread more easily to people who are unvaccinated against polio and who come in contact with the stool or respiratory secretions, such as from a sneeze, of an "infected" person who received oral polio vaccine; the CDC recommends that before any international travel, anyone unvaccinated, incompletely vaccinated, or with an unknown polio vaccination status should complete the routine polio vaccine series; before travel to any high-risk destination, the CDC recommends that adults who previously completed the full, routine polio vaccine series receive a single, lifetime booster dose of polio vaccine

Obesity - adult prevalence rate: 6.7% (2016)
country comparison to the world: 164

Alcohol consumption per capita: *total:* 0.56 liters of pure alcohol (2019 est.)
beer: 0.5 liters of pure alcohol (2019 est.)
wine: 0.01 liters of pure alcohol (2019 est.)
spirits: 0.05 liters of pure alcohol (2019 est.)
other alcohols: 0 liters of pure alcohol (2019 est.)
country comparison to the world: 161

Tobacco use: *total:* 12.8% (2020 est.)
male: 22.7% (2020 est.)
female: 2.9% (2020 est.)
country comparison to the world: 119

Children under the age of 5 years underweight: 23.1% (2017/18)
country comparison to the world: 13

Child marriage: *women married by age 15:* 0%
women married by age 18: 0.1%
men married by age 18: 0% (2017 est.)

Education expenditures: 1.5% of GDP (2017 est.)
country comparison to the world: 184

Literacy: *definition:* age 15 and over can read and write French, Lingala, Kingwana, or Tshiluba
total population: 77%
male: 88.5%
female: 66.5% (2016)

School life expectancy (primary to tertiary education): *total:* 11 years
male: 10 years
female: 9 years (2013)

Unemployment, youth ages 15-24: *total:* 8.7%
male: 11.3%
female: 6.8% (2012 est.)

ENVIRONMENT

Environment - current issues: poaching threatens wildlife populations; water pollution; deforestation (forests endangered by fires set to clear the land for agricultural purposes; forests also used as a source of fuel); soil erosion; mining (diamonds, gold, coltan - a mineral used in creating capacitors for electronic devices) causing environmental damage

Environment - international agreements: *party to:* Biodiversity, Climate Change, Climate Change-Kyoto Protocol, Climate Change-Paris Agreement, Comprehensive Nuclear Test Ban, Desertification, Endangered Species, Hazardous Wastes, Law of the Sea, Marine Dumping-London Convention, Nuclear Test Ban, Ozone Layer Protection, Tropical Timber 2006, Wetlands
signed, but not ratified: Environmental Modification

Air pollutants: *particulate matter emissions:* 37.62 micrograms per cubic meter (2016 est.)
carbon dioxide emissions: 2.02 megatons (2016 est.)
methane emissions: 61.24 megatons (2020 est.)

Climate: tropical; hot and humid in equatorial river basin; cooler and drier in southern highlands; cooler and wetter in eastern highlands; north of Equator - wet season (April to October), dry season (December to February); south of Equator - wet season (November to March), dry season (April to October)

Land use: *agricultural land:* 11.4% (2018 est.)
arable land: 3.1% (2018 est.)
permanent crops: 0.3% (2018 est.)
permanent pasture: 8% (2018 est.)
forest: 67.9% (2018 est.)
other: 20.7% (2018 est.)

Urbanization: *urban population:* 46.8% of total population (2022)
rate of urbanization: 4.33% annual rate of change (2020-25 est.)

Revenue from forest resources: *forest revenues:* 8.72% of GDP (2018 est.)
country comparison to the world: 6

Revenue from coal: *coal revenues:* 0% of GDP (2018 est.)
country comparison to the world: 80

Food insecurity: *widespread lack of access:* due to internal conflict in eastern regions and economic downturn - given the recent escalation of conflicts in the eastern provinces and the consequent population displacement, the magnitude and severity of acute food insecurity may exceed the projected levels; additionally, elevated staple food prices, both domestically and globally, pose a further risk to food insecurity (2022)

Waste and recycling: *municipal solid waste generated annually:* 14,385,226 tons (2016 est.)
municipal solid waste recycled annually: 704,876 tons (2005 est.)
percent of municipal solid waste recycled: 4.9% (2005 est.)

Major lakes (area sq km): *fresh water lake(s):* Lake Tanganyika (shared with Burundi, Tanzania, and Zambia) - 32,000 sq km; Lake Albert (shared with Uganda) - 5,590 sq km; Lake Mweru (shared with Zambia) - 4,350 sq km; Lac Mai-Ndombe - 2,300 sq km; Lake Kivu (shared with Rwanda) - 2,220 sq km; Lake Edward (shared with Uganda) - 2,150 sq km; Lac Tumba - 500 sq km; Lac Upemba - 530 sq km

Major rivers (by length in km): Congo river mouth (shared with Zambia [s], Angola, and Republic of Congo) - 4,700 km; Ubangi river mouth (shared with Central African Republic [s] and Republic of Congo) - 2,270 km
note – [s] after country name indicates river source; [m] after country name indicates river mouth

Major watersheds (area sq km): *Atlantic Ocean drainage:* Congo (3,730,881 sq km), (Mediterranean Sea) Nile (3,254,853 sq km)

Indian Ocean drainage: Zambezi (1,332,412 sq km)

Major aquifers: Congo Basin

Total water withdrawal: *municipal:* 464.9 million cubic meters (2017 est.)
industrial: 146.8 million cubic meters (2017 est.)
agricultural: 71.9 million cubic meters (2017 est.)

Total renewable water resources: 1.283 trillion cubic meters (2017 est.)

GOVERNMENT

Country name: *conventional long form:* Democratic Republic of the Congo
conventional short form: DRC
local long form: Republique Democratique du Congo
local short form: RDC
former: Congo Free State, Belgian Congo, Congo/Leopoldville, Congo/Kinshasa, Zaire
abbreviation: DRC (or DROC)
etymology: named for the Congo River, most of which lies within the DRC; the river name derives from Kongo, a Bantu kingdom that occupied its mouth at the time of Portuguese discovery in the late 15th century and whose name stems from its people the Bakongo, meaning "hunters"

Government type: semi-presidential republic

Capital: *name:* Kinshasa
geographic coordinates: 4 19 S, 15 18 E
time difference: UTC+1 (6 hours ahead of Washington, DC, during Standard Time)
time zone note: the DRC has two time zones
etymology: founded as a trading post in 1881 and named Leopoldville in honor of King LEOPOLD II of the Belgians, who controlled the Congo Free State, the vast central African territory that became the Democratic Republic of the Congo in 1960; in 1966, Leopoldville was renamed Kinshasa, after a village of that name that once stood near the site

Administrative divisions: 26 provinces (provinces, singular - province); Bas-Uele (Lower Uele), Equateur, Haut-Katanga (Upper Katanga), Haut-Lomami (Upper Lomami), Haut-Uele (Upper Uele), Ituri, Kasai, Kasai-Central, Kasai-Oriental (East Kasai), Kinshasa, Kongo Central, Kwango, Kwilu, Lomami, Lualaba, Mai-Ndombe, Maniema, Mongala, Nord-Kivu (North Kivu), Nord-Ubangi (North Ubangi), Sankuru, Sud-Kivu (South Kivu), Sud-Ubangi (South Ubangi), Tanganyika, Tshopo, Tshuapa

Independence: 30 June 1960 (from Belgium)

National holiday: Independence Day, 30 June (1960)

Constitution: *history:* several previous; latest adopted 13 May 2005, approved by referendum 18-19 December 2005, promulgated 18 February 2006
amendments: proposed by the president of the republic, by the government, by either house of Parliament, or by public petition; agreement on the substance of a proposed bill requires absolute majority vote in both houses; passage requires a referendum only if both houses in joint meeting fail to achieve three-fifths majority vote; constitutional articles, including the form of government, universal suffrage, judicial independence, political pluralism, and personal freedoms, cannot be amended; amended 2011

Legal system: civil law system primarily based on Belgian law, but also customary and tribal law

International law organization participation: accepts compulsory ICJ jurisdiction with reservations; accepts ICCt jurisdiction

Citizenship: *citizenship by birth:* no
citizenship by descent only: at least one parent must be a citizen of the Democratic Republic of the Congo
dual citizenship recognized: no
residency requirement for naturalization: 5 years

Suffrage: 18 years of age; universal and compulsory

Executive branch: *chief of state:* President Felix TSHISEKEDI (since 24 January 2019)
head of government: Prime Minister Anatole Collinet MAKOSSO (since 12 May 2021); Deputy Prime Ministers Jose MAKILA, Leonard She OKITUNDU, Henri MOVA Sankanyi (since February 2018)
cabinet: Ministers of State appointed by the president
elections/appointments: president directly elected by simple majority vote for a 5-year term (eligible for a second term); election last held on 30 December 2018 (next to be held in December 2023); prime minister appointed by the president
election results: Felix TSHISEKEDI elected president; percent of vote - Felix TSHISEKEDI (UDPS) 38.6%, Martin FAYULU (Lamuka coalition) 34.8%, Emmanuel Ramazani SHADARY (PPRD) 23.9%, other 2.7%; note - election marred by serious voting irregularities (2018)

Legislative branch: *description:* bicameral Parliament or Parlement consists of:
Senate (109 seats; 109 members to include 108 indirectly elected by provincial assemblies by proportional representation vote to serve 5-year terms and a former president, appointed for life)
National Assembly (500 seats; 439 members directly elected in multi-seat constituencies by proportional representation vote and 61 directly elected in single-seat constituencies by simple majority vote; members serve 5-year terms)
elections: Senate - last held on 14 March 2019

National Assembly - last held on 30 December 2018 (first round), 31 March 2019 (second round): *election results:* Senate - percent of vote by party - NA; seats by party - PPRD 22, MLC 14, FR 7, RCD 7, PDC 6, CDC 3, MSR 3, PALU 2, other 18, independent 26; composition as of 2022 - men 83, women 26, percent of women 23.9% National Assembly - percent of vote by party - NA; seats by party - PPRD 62, UDPS 41, PPPD 29, MSR 27, MLC 22, PALU 19, UNC 17, ARC 16, AFDC 15, ECT 11, RRC 11, other 214 (includes numerous political parties that won 10 or fewer seats and 2 constituencies where voting was halted), independent 16; composition as of 2022

- men 436, women 64, percent of women 12.8%; total Parliament percent of women 14.8%

Judicial branch: *highest court(s):* Court of Cassation or Cour de Cassation (consists of 26 justices and organized into legislative and judiciary sections); Constitutional Court (consists of 9 judges)
judge selection and term of office: Court of Cassation judges nominated by the Judicial Service Council, an independent body of public prosecutors and selected judges of the lower courts; judge tenure NA; Constitutional Court judges - 3 nominated by the president, 3 by the Judicial Service Council, and 3 by the legislature; judges appointed by the president to serve 9-year non-renewable terms with one-third of the membership renewed every 3 years
subordinate courts: State Security Court; Court of Appeals (organized into administrative and judiciary sections); Tribunal de Grande; magistrates' courts; customary courts

Political parties and leaders: Christian Democrat Party or PDC [Jose ENDUNDO]
Congolese Rally for Democracy or RCD [Azarias RUBERWA]
Convention of Christian Democrats or CDC
Engagement for Citizenship and Development or ECiDe [Martin FAYULU]
Forces of Renewal or FR [Mbusa NYAMWISI]
Lamuka coalition [Martin FAYULU] (includes ECiDe, MLC, Together for Change, CNB, and, Nouvel Elan)
Movement for the Liberation of the Congo or MLC [Jean-Pierre BEMBA]
Nouvel Elan [Adolphe MUZITO]
Our Congo or CNB ("Congo Na Biso") [Freddy MATUNGULU]
People's Party for Reconstruction and Democracy or PPRD [Henri MOVA Sakanyi]
Social Movement for Renewal or MSR [Pierre LUMBI]
Together for Change ("Ensemble") [Moise KATUMBI]
Unified Lumumbist Party or PALU
Union for the Congolese Nation or UNC [Vital KAMERHE]
Union for Democracy and Social Progress or UDPS [Felix TSHISEKEDI]

International organization participation: ACP, AfDB, AU, CEMAC, CEPGL, COMESA, EITI (compliant country), FAO, G-24, G-77, IAEA, IBRD, ICAO, ICC (NGOs), ICCt, ICRM, IDA, IFAD, IFC, IFRCS, IHO, ILO, IMF, IMO, Interpol, IOC, IOM, IPU, ISO, ITSO, ITU, ITUC (NGOs), LCBC (observer), MIGA, NAM, OIF, OPCW, PCA, SADC, UN, UNCTAD, UNESCO, UNHCR, UNIDO, UNWTO, UPU, WCO, WFTU (NGOs), WHO, WIPO, WMO, WTO

Diplomatic representation in the US: *chief of mission:* Ambassador Marie-Hélène MATHEY-BOO (since 6 June 2022)
chancery: 1100 Connecticut Avenue NW, Suite 725, Washington DC 20036
telephone: [1] (202) 234-7690; [1] (202) 234-7691
FAX: [1] (202) 234-2609
email address and website:
https://www.ambardcusa.org/
representative office: New York

Diplomatic representation from the US: *chief of mission:* Ambassador Michael A. HAMMER (since 22 December 2018)
embassy: 310 Avenue des Aviateurs, Kinshasa, Gombe
mailing address: 2220 Kinshasa Place, Washington DC 20521-2220
telephone: [243] 081 556-0151
FAX: [243] 81 556-0175
email address and website:
ACSKinshasa@state.gov
https://cd.usembassy.gov/

Flag description: sky blue field divided diagonally from the lower hoist corner to upper fly corner by a red stripe bordered by two narrow yellow stripes; a yellow, five-pointed star appears in the upper hoist corner; blue represents peace and hope, red the blood of the country's martyrs, and yellow the country's wealth and prosperity; the star symbolizes unity and the brilliant future for the country

National symbol(s): *leopard; national colors:* sky blue, red, yellow

National anthem: *name:* "Debout Congolaise" (Arise Congolese)
lyrics/music: Joseph LUTUMBA/Simon-Pierre BOKA di Mpasi Londi
note: adopted 1960; replaced when the country was known as Zaire; but readopted in 1997

National heritage: *total World Heritage Sites:* 5 (all natural)
selected World Heritage Site locales: Garamba National Park; Kahuzi-Biega National Park; Okapi Wildlife Reserve; Salonga National Park; Virunga National Park

ECONOMY

Economic overview: The economy of the Democratic Republic of the Congo - a nation endowed with vast natural resource wealth - continues to perform poorly. Systemic corruption since independence in 1960, combined with countrywide instability and intermittent conflict that began in the early-90s, has reduced national output and government revenue, and increased external debt. With the installation of a transitional government in 2003 after peace accords, economic conditions slowly began to improve as the government reopened relations with international financial institutions and international donors, and President KABILA began implementing reforms. Progress on implementing substantive economic reforms remains slow because of political instability, bureaucratic inefficiency, corruption, and patronage, which also dampen international investment prospects.

Renewed activity in the mining sector, the source of most export income, boosted Kinshasa's fiscal position and GDP growth until 2015, but low commodity prices have led to slower growth, volatile inflation, currency depreciation, and a growing fiscal deficit. An uncertain legal framework, corruption, and a lack of transparency in government policy are long-term problems for the large mining sector and for the economy as a whole. Much economic activity still occurs in the informal sector and is not reflected in GDP data.

Poverty remains widespread in DRC, and the country failed to meet any Millennium Development Goals by 2015. DRC also concluded its program with the IMF in 2015. The price of copper – the DRC's primary export - plummeted in 2015 and remained at record lows during 2016-17, reducing government revenues, expenditures, and foreign exchange reserves, while inflation reached nearly 50% in mid-2017 – its highest level since the early 2000s.

Real GDP (purchasing power parity): $96.03 billion (2020 est.)
$95.29 billion (2019 est.)
$91.29 billion (2018 est.)
note: data are in 2017 dollars
country comparison to the world: 91

Real GDP growth rate: 3.4% (2017 est.)
2.4% (2016 est.)
6.9% (2015 est.)
country comparison to the world: 87

Real GDP per capita: $1,100 (2020 est.)
$1,100 (2019 est.)
$1,100 (2018 est.)
note: data are in 2017 dollars
country comparison to the world: 226

GDP (official exchange rate): $47.16 billion (2019 est.)

Inflation rate (consumer prices): 41.5% (2017 est.)
18.2% (2016 est.)
country comparison to the world: 223

Credit ratings: Moody's rating: Caa1 (2019)

Standard & Poors rating: CCC+ (2017)
note: The year refers to the year in which the current credit rating was first obtained.

GDP - composition, by sector of origin: *agriculture:* 19.7% (2017 est.)
industry: 43.6% (2017 est.)
services: 36.7% (2017 est.)

GDP - composition, by end use: *household consumption:* 78.5% (2017 est.)
government consumption: 12.7% (2017 est.)
investment in fixed capital: 15.9% (2017 est.)
investment in inventories: 0% (2017 est.)
exports of goods and services: 25.7% (2017 est.)
imports of goods and services: -32.8% (2017 est.)

Agricultural products: cassava, plantains, sugar cane, maize, oil palm fruit, rice, roots/tubers nes, bananas, sweet potatoes, groundnuts

Industries: mining (copper, cobalt, gold, diamonds, coltan, zinc, tin, tungsten), mineral processing, consumer products (textiles, plastics, footwear, cigarettes), metal products, processed foods and beverages, timber, cement, commercial ship repair

Industrial production growth rate: 1.6% (2017 est.)
country comparison to the world: 140

Labor force: 20.692 million (2012 est.)
country comparison to the world: 26

Unemployment, youth ages 15-24: *total:* 8.7%
male: 11.3%
female: 6.8% (2012 est.)
country comparison to the world: 147

Population below poverty line: 63% (2014 est.)

Gini Index coefficient - distribution of family income 42.1 (2012 est.): *country comparison to the world:* 47

Household income or consumption by percentage share: *lowest 10%:* 2.3%
highest 10%: 34.7% (2006)

Budget: *revenues:* 4.634 billion (2017 est.)
expenditures: 5.009 billion (2017 est.)

Budget surplus (+) or deficit (-): -0.9% (of GDP) (2017 est.)
country comparison to the world: 72

Public debt: 18.1% of GDP (2017 est.)
19.3% of GDP (2016 est.)
country comparison to the world: 192

Taxes and other revenues: 11.2% (of GDP) (2017 est.)
country comparison to the world: 211

Fiscal year: calendar year

Current account balance: -$200 million (2017 est.)
-$1.215 billion (2016 est.)
country comparison to the world: 99

Exports: $13.93 billion (2020 est.)
$15.17 billion (2019 est.)
$16.08 billion (2018 est.)
note: Data are in current year dollars and do not include illicit exports or re-exports.
country comparison to the world: 94

Exports - partners: China 53%, United Arab Emirates 11%, Saudi Arabia 6%, South Korea 5% (2019)

Exports - commodities: copper, cobalt, crude petroleum, diamonds (2019)

Imports: *$14.56 billion (2020 est.) note:* data are in current year dollars
$16.89 billion (2019 est.) *note:* data are in current year dollars
$17.77 billion (2018 est.) *note:* data are in current year dollars
country comparison to the world: 97

Imports - partners: China 29%, South Africa 15%, Zambia 12%, Rwanda 5%, Belgium 5%, India 5% (2019)

Imports - commodities: packaged medicines, refined petroleum, sulfuric acid, stone processing machines, delivery trucks (2019)

Reserves of foreign exchange and gold: $457.5 million (31 December 2017 est.)
$708.2 million (31 December 2016 est.)
country comparison to the world: 155

Debt - external: $4.963 billion (31 December 2017 est.)
$5.35 billion (31 December 2016 est.)
country comparison to the world: 134

Exchange rates: Congolese francs (CDF) per US dollar -
1,546.8 (2017 est.)
1,010.3 (2016 est.)
1,010.3 (2015 est.)
925.99 (2014 est.)
925.23 (2013 est.)

ENERGY

Electricity access: *electrification - total population:* 9% (2019)
electrification - urban areas: 19% (2019)
electrification - rural areas: 0.4% (2019)

Electricity: *installed generating capacity:* 2.919 million kW (2020 est.)
consumption: 7,181,700,000 kWh (2019 est.)
exports: 248 million kWh (2019 est.)
imports: 385 million kWh (2019 est.)
transmission/distribution losses: 2.142 billion kWh (2019 est.)

Electricity generation sources: *fossil fuels:* 0.1% of total installed capacity (2020 est.)
solar: 0.1% of total installed capacity (2020 est.)
hydroelectricity: 99.6% of total installed capacity (2020 est.)
biomass and waste: 0.3% of total installed capacity (2020 est.)

Coal: *production:* 0 metric tons (2020 est.)
consumption: 10,000 metric tons (2020 est.)
exports: 0 metric tons (2020 est.)
imports: 10,000 metric tons (2020 est.)
proven reserves: 88 million metric tons (2019 est.)

Petroleum: *total petroleum production:* 22,000 bbl/day (2021 est.)
refined petroleum consumption: 17,900 bbl/day (2019 est.)
crude oil and lease condensate exports: 21,300 bbl/day (2018 est.)
crude oil and lease condensate imports: 0 bbl/day (2018 est.)
crude oil estimated reserves: 180 million barrels (2021 est.)

Refined petroleum products - production: 0 bbl/day (2017 est.)
country comparison to the world: 132

Refined petroleum products - exports: 0 bbl/day (2015 est.)
country comparison to the world: 145

Refined petroleum products - imports: 21,140 bbl/day (2015 est.)
country comparison to the world: 115

Natural gas: *production:* 368,000 cubic meters (2019 est.)
consumption: 368,000 cubic meters (2019 est.)
exports: 0 cubic meters (2021 est.)
imports: 0 cubic meters (2021 est.)
proven reserves: 991 million cubic meters (2021 est.)

Carbon dioxide emissions: 2.653 million metric tonnes of CO2 (2019 est.)
from coal and metallurgical coke: 44,000 metric tonnes of CO2 (2019 est.)
from petroleum and other liquids: 2.608 million metric tonnes of CO2 (2019 est.)
from consumed natural gas: 1,000 metric tonnes of CO2 (2019 est.)
country comparison to the world: 151

Energy consumption per capita: 1.371 million Btu/person (2019 est.)
country comparison to the world: 192

COMMUNICATIONS

Telephones - mobile cellular: *total subscriptions:* 40,798,396 (2020 est.)
subscriptions per 100 inhabitants: 46 (2020 est.)
country comparison to the world: 38

Telecommunication systems: *general assessment:* the telecom system remains one of the least developed in the region; the government can only loosely regulate the sector; the investment made in infrastructure is derived from donor countries or from the efforts of foreign (particularly Chinese) companies and banks; efforts have been made to improve the regulation of the telecom sector; the limited fixed-line infrastructure has become the principal providers of basic telecom services; the development of the DRC's internet and broadband market has been held back by the poorly developed national and international infrastructure; the country was finally connected to international bandwidth through the WACS submarine cable in 2013; breakages in the WACS cable have exposed the vulnerability of international bandwidth, which is still limited; the Equiano submarine cable, and has also completed a 5,000km cable running through the DRC to link to cable systems landing in countries facing the Atlantic and Indian Oceans; the first commercial LTE networks were launched in May 2018 soon after LTE licenses were issued; mobile operators are keen to develop mobile data services, capitalizing on the growth of smartphones usage; there has been some progress with updating technologies, most of the GSM network has been upgraded to 3G by 2021 (2022)
domestic: inadequate fixed-line infrastructure with fixed-line connections less than 1 per 100 persons; mobile-cellular subscriptions over 46 per 100 persons (2020)
international: country code - 243; ACE and WACS submarine cables to West and South Africa and Europe; satellite earth station - 1 Intelsat (Atlantic Ocean) (2019)

Broadcast media: state-owned TV broadcast station with near national coverage; more than a dozen privately owned TV stations - 2 with near national coverage; 2 state-owned radio stations are supplemented by more than 100 private radio stations; transmissions of at least 2 international broadcasters are available

Internet country code: .cd

Internet users: *total:* 12,538,597 (2020 est.)
percent of population: 14% (2020 est.)
country comparison to the world: 49

Broadband - fixed subscriptions: *total:* 31,000 (2020 est.)
subscriptions per 100 inhabitants: 0.03 (2020 est.)
country comparison to the world: 152

TRANSPORTATION

National air transport system: *number of registered air carriers:* 8 (2020)
inventory of registered aircraft operated by air carriers: 13
annual passenger traffic on registered air carriers: 932,043 (2018)
annual freight traffic on registered air carriers: 890,000 (2018) mt-km

Civil aircraft registration country code prefix: 9Q

Airports: *total:* 198 (2021)
country comparison to the world: 28

Airports - with paved runways: *total:* 26
over 3,047 m: 3
2,438 to 3,047 m: 3
1,524 to 2,437 m: 17
914 to 1,523 m: 2
under 914 m: 1 (2021)

Airports - with unpaved runways: *total:* 172
1,524 to 2,437 m: 20
914 to 1,523 m: 87
under 914 m: 65 (2021)

Heliports: 1 (2021)

Pipelines: 62 km gas, 77 km oil, 756 km refined products (2013)

Railways: *total:* 4,007 km (2014)
narrow gauge: 3,882 km (2014) 1.067-m gauge (858 km electrified)
125 1.000-mm gauge
country comparison to the world: 48

Roadways: *total:* 152,373 km (2015)
paved: 3,047 km (2015)
unpaved: 149,326 km (2015)
urban: 7,400 km (2015)
non-urban: 144,973 km
country comparison to the world: 34

Waterways: 15,000 km (2011) (including the Congo River, its tributaries, and unconnected lakes)

country comparison to the world: 9

Merchant marine: *total:* 22
by type: general cargo 4, oil tanker 2, other 16 (2021)
country comparison to the world: 145

Ports and terminals: *major seaport(s):* Banana
river or lake port(s): Boma, Bumba, Kinshasa, Kisangani, Matadi, Mbandaka (Congo); Kindu (Lualaba); Bukavu, Goma (Lake Kivu); Kalemie (Lake Tanganyika)

MILITARY AND SECURITY

Military and security forces: Armed Forces of the Democratic Republic of the Congo (Forces d'Armees de la Republique Democratique du Congo, FARDC): Land Forces, National Navy (La Marine Nationale), Congolese Air Force (Force Aerienne Congolaise, FAC); Republican Guard; Ministry of Interior: Congolese National Police, Directorate General for Migration (2022)
note: the Republican Guard is a division-size element consisting of approximately 5 regiments; it is regarded as the country's best equipped and trained military unit and is under the direct control of the president

Military expenditures: 0.7% of GDP (2021 est.)
0.7% of GDP (2020 est.)
0.9% of GDP (2019 est.) (approximately $570 million)
0.8% of GDP (2018 est.) (approximately $520 million)
0.9% of GDP (2017 est.) (approximately $550 million)
country comparison to the world: 148

Military and security service personnel strengths: limited and widely varied information; approximately 100,000 active troops (mostly Army, but includes several thousand Navy and Air Force personnel, as well as about 10,000 Republican Guard; note - Navy personnel includes naval infantry) (2022)

Military equipment inventories and acquisitions: the FARDC is equipped mostly with a mix of second-hand Russian and Soviet-era weapons acquired from former Warsaw Pact nations; most equipment was acquired between 1970 and 2000; in recent years, Ukraine has been the largest supplier of arms to the FARDC (2021)

Military service age and obligation: 18-45 years of age for voluntary military service for men and women; 18-45 years of age for compulsory military service for men; it is unclear how much conscription is used (2021)
note: in eastern Congo, fighters from armed groups, and in some cases government security forces, have been accused of forced recruitment of child soldiers

Military - note: the modern FARDC was created out of the armed factions of the two Congo wars of 1996-1997 and 1998-2003; as part of the peace accords that ended the last war, the largest rebel groups were incorporated into the FARDC; many armed groups, however, continue to fight and as of 2022, there were over 100 illegal armed groups operating in the country by some estimates; as of 2022, the FARDC was actively engaged in combat operations against numerous armed groups, particularly in the eastern provinces of Ituri, North Kivu, and South Kivu, although there was also violence in Maniema, Kasai, Kasai Central, and Tanganyika provinces; the military is widely assessed as being unable to provide adequate security throughout the country due to insufficient training, poor morale and leadership, ill-discipline and corruption, low equipment readiness, a fractious ethnic makeup, and the sheer size of the country and diversity of armed rebel groups

as of 2022, one of the primary armed groups the FARDC was conducting operations against was the March 23 Movement (M23, aka Congolese Revolutionary Army), which resumed attacks, largely against civilians, in the DRC province of North Kivu in 2022 after having been defeated in 2013 by FARDC and UN forces; the M23's resurgence has raised tensions between the DRC and Rwanda, as the DRC Government claims Rwanda backs the M23, which it has labeled a terrorist group, charges that the Rwandan Government has denied; M23 attacks and fighting between the FARDC and M23 in 2022 has led to the displacement of more than 200,000 people; UN troops were supporting the FARDC's operations against M23

the United Nations Organization Stabilization Mission in the Democratic Republic of the Congo (MONUSCO) has operated in the central and eastern parts of the country since 1999; as of mid-2022, MONUSCO had around 15,000 personnel; MONUSCO includes a Force Intervention Brigade (FIB; 3 infantry battalions, plus artillery and special forces), the first ever UN peacekeeping force specifically tasked to carry out targeted offensive operations to neutralize and disarm groups considered a threat to state authority and civilian security (2022)

TERRORISM

Terrorist group(s): Islamic State of Iraq and ash-Sham – Democratic Republic of the Congo (ISIS-DRC)
note: details about the history, aims, leadership, organization, areas of operation, tactics, targets, weapons, size, and sources of support of the group(s) appear(s) in Appendix-T

TRANSNATIONAL ISSUES

Disputes - international: heads of the Great Lakes states and UN pledged in 2004 to abate tribal, rebel, and militia fighting in the region, including northeast Congo, where the UN Organization Mission in the Democratic Republic of the Congo (MONUC), organized in 1999, maintains over 16,500 uniformed peacekeepers

Democratic Republic of Congo(DRC)-Republic of the Congo: the location of the boundary in the broad Congo River is indefinite except in the Pool Malebo/Stanley Pool area

Democratic Republic of Congo(DRC)-Uganda: Uganda rejects the DRC claim to Margherita Peak in the Rwenzori mountains and considers it a boundary divide; there is tension and violence on Lake Albert over prospective oil reserves at the mouth of the Semliki River

Democratic Republic of Congo(DRC)-Zambia: boundary commission continues discussions over Congolese-administered triangle of land on the right bank of the Lunkinda River claimed by Zambia near the DRC village of Pweto

Democratic Republic of Congo(DRC)-Angola: DRC accuses Angola of shifting monuments

Refugees and internally displaced persons: *refugees (country of origin):* 212,120 (Central African Republic), 209,798 (Rwanda), 56,653 (South Sudan) (refugees and asylum seekers), 41,836 (Burundi) (2022)

IDPs: 5.53 million (fighting between government forces and rebels since mid-1990s; conflict in Kasai region since 2016) (2022)

Trafficking in persons: *current situation:* human traffickers exploit domestic and foreign victims in Democratic Republic of the Congo and Congolese abroad; most trafficking is internal and involves the forced labor of men, women, and children in artisanal mining, agriculture, domestic servitude, sex trafficking, or child recruitment by armed groups; some traffickers are family members or others who promise victims or victims' families educational or job opportunities and instead force victims to work as domestic servants, street vendors, gang members, or in commercial sex; some Congolese women and girls who migrate to other countries in Africa or the Middle East are exploited in sex trafficking or forced labor in agriculture, diamond mines, or domestic service; they may be fraudulently recruited by traffickers with false promises of jobs or education
tier rating: Tier 2 Watch List — The Democratic Republic of the Congo (DRC) does not fully meet the minimum standards for the elimination of trafficking but is making significant efforts to do so; the DRC was upgraded to Tier 2 Watch List because of several accomplishments; the government drafted and launched its first national anti-trafficking action plan; authorities increased law enforcement efforts, including investigating and prosecuting more trafficking crimes; a number of traffickers were convicted, including a high-ranking army officer and the leader of an armed group; however, authorities continued to lack standard operating procedures for identifying victims and referring them to care; there were credible allegations that the army abducted women and girls for sexual slavery and recruited and used child soldiers (2020)

Illicit drugs: country of origin of methamphetamine destined for overseas markets

CONGO, REPUBLIC OF THE

INTRODUCTION

Background: Upon independence in 1960, the former French region of Middle Congo became the Republic of the Congo. A quarter century of experimentation with Marxism was abandoned in 1990 and a democratically elected government took office in 1992. A two-year civil war that ended in 1999 restored former Marxist President Denis SASSOU-Nguesso, who had ruled from 1979 to 1992, and sparked a short period of ethnic and political unrest that was resolved by a peace

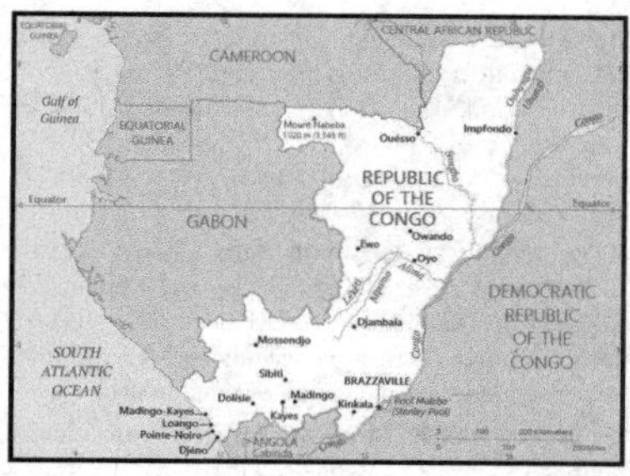

agreement in late 1999. A new constitution adopted three years later provided for a multi-party system and a seven-year presidential term, and elections arranged shortly thereafter installed SASSOU-Nguesso. Following a year of renewed fighting, President SASSOU-Nguesso and southern-based rebel groups agreed to a final peace accord in March 2003. SASSOU-Nguesso was reeelected in 2009 and, after passing a referendum allowing him to run for a third term, was reelected again in 2016. The Republic of Congo is one of Africa's largest petroleum producers, but with declining production it will need new offshore oil finds to sustain its oil earnings over the long term.

GEOGRAPHY

Location: Central Africa, bordering the South Atlantic Ocean, between Angola and Gabon

Geographic coordinates: 1 00 S, 15 00 E

Map references: Africa

Area: *total:* 342,000 sq km
land: 341,500 sq km
water: 500 sq km
country comparison to the world: 65

Area - comparative: slightly smaller than Montana; about twice the size of Florida

Land boundaries: *total:* 5,554 km
border countries (5): Angola 231 km; Cameroon 494 km; Central African Republic 487 km; Democratic Republic of the Congo 1,775 km; Gabon 2,567 km

Coastline: 169 km

Maritime claims: *territorial sea:* 12 nm
contiguous zone: 24 nm
exclusive economic zone: 200 nm

Climate: tropical; rainy season (March to June); dry season (June to October); persistent high temperatures and humidity; particularly enervating climate astride the Equator

Terrain: coastal plain, southern basin, central plateau, northern basin

Elevation: *highest point:* Mont Nabeba 1,020 m
lowest point: Atlantic Ocean 0 m
mean elevation: 430 m

Natural resources: petroleum, timber, potash, lead, zinc, uranium, copper, phosphates, gold, magnesium, natural gas, hydropower

Land use: *agricultural land:* 31.1% (2018 est.)
arable land: 1.6% (2018 est.)
permanent crops: 0.2% (2018 est.)
permanent pasture: 29.3% (2018 est.)
forest: 65.6% (2018 est.)
other: 3.3% (2018 est.)

Irrigated land: 20 sq km (2012)

Major rivers (by length in km): Ubangi (shared with Central African Republic [s] and Democratic Republic of Congo [m]) - 2,270 km
note – [s] after country name indicates river source; [m] after country name indicates river mouth

Major watersheds (area sq km): Atlantic Ocean drainage: Congo (3,730,881 sq km)

Major aquifers: Congo Basin

Population distribution: the population is primarily located in the south, in and around the capital of Brazzaville as shown in this population distribution map

Natural hazards: seasonal flooding

Geography - note: about 70% of the population lives in Brazzaville, Pointe-Noire, or along the railroad between them

PEOPLE AND SOCIETY

Population: 5,546,307 (2022 est.)
country comparison to the world: 118

Nationality: *noun:* Congolese (singular and plural)
adjective: Congolese or Congo

Ethnic groups: Kongo 40.5%, Teke 16.9%, Mbochi 13.1%, foreigner 8.2%, Sangha 5.6%, Mbere/Mbeti/Kele 4.4%, Punu 4.3%, Pygmy 1.6%, Oubanguiens 1.6%, Duma 1.5%, Makaa 1.3%, other and unspecified 1% (2014-15 est.)

Languages: French (official), French Lingala and Monokutuba (lingua franca trade languages), many local languages and dialects (of which Kikongo is the most widespread)
major-language sample(s):
Buku oyo ya bosembo ya Mokili Mobimba Ezali na Makanisi ya Liboso Mpenza. (Lingala)

Religions: Roman Catholic 33.1%, Awakening Churches/Christian Revival 22.3%, Protestant 19.9%, Salutiste 2.2%, Muslim 1.6%, Kimbanguiste 1.5%, other 8.1%, none 11.3% (2007 est.)

Demographic profile: The Republic of the Congo is one of the most urbanized countries in Africa, with nearly 70% of Congolese living in urban areas. The population is concentrated in the southwest of the country, mainly in the capital Brazzaville, Pointe-Noire, and along the railway line that connects the two. The tropical jungles in the north of the country are sparsely populated. Most Congolese are Bantu, and most belong to one of four main ethnic groups, the Kongo, Teke, Mbochi, and Sangha, which consist of over 70 subgroups.

The Republic of Congo is in the early stages of a demographic transition, whereby a population shifts from high fertility and mortality rates to low fertility and mortality rates associated with industrialized societies. Its total fertility rate (TFR), the average number of children born per woman, remains high at 4.4. While its TFR has steadily decreased, the progress slowed beginning in about 1995. The slowdown in fertility reduction has delayed the demographic transition and Congo's potential to reap a demographic dividend, the economic boost that can occur when the share of the working-age population is larger than the dependent age groups.

The TFR differs significantly between urban and rural areas – 3.7 in urban areas versus 6.5 in rural areas. The TFR also varies among regions. The urban regions of Brazzaville and Pointe-Noire have much lower TFRs than other regions, which are predominantly or completely rural. The gap between desired fertility and actual fertility is also greatest in rural areas. Rural families may have more children to contribute to agricultural production and/or due to a lack of information about and access to contraception. Urban families may prefer to have fewer children because raising them is more expensive and balancing work and childcare may be more difficult. The number of births among teenage girls, the frequency of giving birth before the age of fifteen, and a lack of education are the most likely reasons for higher TFRs in rural areas. Although 90% of school-age children are enrolled in primary school, repetition and dropout rates are high and the quality of education is poor. Congolese women with no or little education start having children earlier and have more children in total than those with at least some secondary education.

Age structure: *0-14 years:* 41.57% (male 1,110,484/female 1,089,732)
15-24 years: 17.14% (male 454,981/female 452,204)
25-54 years: 33.5% (male 886,743/female 886,312)
55-64 years: 4.59% (male 125,207/female 117,810)
65 years and over: 3.2% (male 75,921/female 93,676) (2020 est.)

Dependency ratios: *total dependency ratio:* 78.7
youth dependency ratio: 73.7
elderly dependency ratio: 4.9
potential support ratio: 20.3 (2020 est.)

Median age: *total:* 19.5 years
male: 19.3 years
female: 19.7 years (2020 est.)
country comparison to the world: 202

Population growth rate: 2.34% (2022 est.)
country comparison to the world: 30

Birth rate: 31.82 births/1,000 population (2022 est.)
country comparison to the world: 26

Death rate: 8.38 deaths/1,000 population (2022 est.)
country comparison to the world: 76

Net migration rate: 0 migrant(s)/1,000 population (2022 est.)
country comparison to the world: 86

Population distribution: the population is primarily located in the south, in and around the capital of Brazzaville as shown in this population distribution map

Urbanization: *urban population:* 68.7% of total population (2022)
rate of urbanization: 3.19% annual rate of change (2020-25 est.)

Major urban areas - population: 2.553 million BRAZZAVILLE (capital), 1.295 million Pointe-Noire (2022)

Sex ratio: *at birth:* 1.03 male(s)/female
0-14 years: 1.02 male(s)/female
15-24 years: 1.01 male(s)/female
25-54 years: 1.01 male(s)/female
55-64 years: 1.08 male(s)/female
65 years and over: 0.66 male(s)/female
total population: 1.01 male(s)/female (2022 est.)

Mother's mean age at first birth: 19.6 years (2011/12 est.)
note: data represents median age at first birth among women 20-49

Maternal mortality ratio: 378 deaths/100,000 live births (2017 est.)
country comparison to the world: 29

Infant mortality rate: *total:* 47.93 deaths/1,000 live births
male: 52.39 deaths/1,000 live births

female: 43.34 deaths/1,000 live births (2022 est.)
country comparison to the world: 24

Life expectancy at birth: *total population:* 62.1 years
male: 60.65 years
female: 63.61 years (2022 est.)
country comparison to the world: 215

Total fertility rate: 4.36 children born/woman (2022 est.)
country comparison to the world: 21

Contraceptive prevalence rate: 30.1% (2014/15)

Drinking water source: *improved: urban:* 97.5% of population
rural: 56.4% of population
total: 84.2% of population
unimproved: urban: 2.5% of population
rural: 43.6% of population
total: 15.8% of population (2020 est.)

Current health expenditure: 2.1% of GDP (2019)

Physicians density: 0.1 physicians/1,000 population (2018)

Sanitation facility access: *improved: urban:* 73.4% of population
rural: 15.1% of population
total: 54.7% of population
unimproved: urban: 26.6% of population
rural: 84.9% of population
total: 45.3% of population (2020 est.)

HIV/AIDS - adult prevalence rate: 3.3% (2020 est.)
country comparison to the world: 14

Major infectious diseases: *degree of risk:* very high (2020)
food or waterborne diseases: bacterial and protozoal diarrhea, hepatitis A, and typhoid fever
vectorborne diseases: malaria and dengue fever
water contact diseases: schistosomiasis
animal contact diseases: rabies
note: on 21 March 2022, the US Centers for Disease Control and Prevention (CDC) issued a Travel Alert for polio in Africa; the Republic of the Congo is currently considered a high risk to travelers for circulating vaccine-derived polioviruses (cVDPV); vaccine-derived poliovirus (VDPV) is a strain of the weakened poliovirus that was initially included in oral polio vaccine (OPV) and *that has changed over time and behaves more like the wild or naturally occurring virus;* this means it can be spread more easily to people who are unvaccinated against polio and who come in contact with the stool or respiratory secretions, such as from a sneeze, of an "infected" person who received oral polio vaccine; the CDC recommends that before any international travel, anyone unvaccinated, incompletely vaccinated, or with an unknown polio vaccination status should complete the routine polio vaccine series; before travel to any high-risk destination, the CDC recommends that adults who previously completed the full, routine polio vaccine series receive a single, lifetime booster dose of polio vaccine

Obesity - adult prevalence rate: 9.6% (2016)
country comparison to the world: 143

Alcohol consumption per capita: *total:* 5.74 liters of pure alcohol (2019 est.)
beer: 5.11 liters of pure alcohol (2019 est.)
wine: 0.1 liters of pure alcohol (2019 est.)
spirits: 0.52 liters of pure alcohol (2019 est.)
other alcohols: 0.01 liters of pure alcohol (2019 est.)
country comparison to the world: 75

Tobacco use: *total:* 14.5% (2020 est.)
male: 26.8% (2020 est.)
female: 2.1% (2020 est.)
country comparison to the world: 105

Children under the age of 5 years underweight: 12.3% (2014/15)
country comparison to the world: 47

Child marriage: *women married by age 15:* 8.4%
women married by age 18: 29.1%
men married by age 18: 5.6% (2018 est.)

Education expenditures: 3.9% of GDP (2019 est.)
country comparison to the world: 106

Literacy: *definition:* age 15 and over can read and write
total population: 80.3%
male: 86.1%
female: 74.6% (2018)

School life expectancy (primary to tertiary education): *total:* 11 years
male: 11 years
female: 11 years (2012)

ENVIRONMENT

Environment - current issues: air pollution from vehicle emissions; water pollution from raw sewage; tap water is not potable; deforestation; wildlife protection

Environment - international agreements: *party to:* Biodiversity, Climate Change, Climate Change-Kyoto Protocol, Climate Change-Paris Agreement, Desertification, Endangered Species, Hazardous Wastes, Law of the Sea, Marine Dumping-London Protocol, Ozone Layer Protection, Ship Pollution, Tropical Timber 2006, Wetlands
signed, but not ratified: none of the selected agreements

Air pollutants: *particulate matter emissions:* 38.67 micrograms per cubic meter (2016 est.)
carbon dioxide emissions: 3.28 megatons (2016 est.)
methane emissions: 2.24 megatons (2020 est.)

Climate: tropical; rainy season (March to June); dry season (June to October); persistent high temperatures and humidity; particularly enervating climate astride the Equator

Land use: *agricultural land:* 31.1% (2018 est.)
arable land: 1.6% (2018 est.)
permanent crops: 0.2% (2018 est.)
permanent pasture: 29.3% (2018 est.)
forest: 65.6% (2018 est.)
other: 3.3% (2018 est.)

Urbanization: *urban population:* 68.7% of total population (2022)
rate of urbanization: 3.19% annual rate of change (2020-25 est.)

Revenue from forest resources: *forest revenues:* 3.17% of GDP (2018 est.)
country comparison to the world: 23

Revenue from coal: *coal revenues:* 0% of GDP (2018 est.)
country comparison to the world: 81

Food insecurity: *severe localized food insecurity: due to refugee influx* - as of 30 April 2022, about 29,100 refugees from the Central African Republic and 22,100 from the Democratic Republic of the Congo were residing in the country, mostly in Likouala and Plateaux departments; host communities face food shortages and limited livelihood opportunities, and refugees' food security is essentially dependent on continued humanitarian assistance (2022)

Waste and recycling: *municipal solid waste generated annually:* 451,200 tons (1993 est.)
municipal solid waste recycled annually: 118,214 tons (2005 est.)
percent of municipal solid waste recycled: 26.2% (2005 est.)

Major rivers (by length in km): Ubangi (shared with Central African Republic [s] and Democratic Republic of Congo [m]) - 2,270 km
note – [s] after country name indicates river source; [m] after country name indicates river mouth

Major watersheds (area sq km): Atlantic Ocean drainage: Congo (3,730,881 sq km)

Major aquifers: Congo Basin

Total water withdrawal: *municipal:* 63.7 million cubic meters (2017 est.)
industrial: 24 million cubic meters (2017 est.)
agricultural: 4 million cubic meters (2017 est.)

Total renewable water resources: 832 billion cubic meters (2017 est.)

GOVERNMENT

Country name: *conventional long form:* Republic of the Congo
conventional short form: Congo (Brazzaville)
local long form: Republique du Congo
local short form: Congo
former: French Congo, Middle Congo, People's Republic of the Congo, Congo/Brazzaville
etymology: named for the Congo River, which makes up much of the country's eastern border; the river name derives from Kongo, a Bantu kingdom that occupied its mouth at the time of Portuguese discovery in the late 15th century and whose name stems from its people the Bakongo, meaning "hunters"

Government type: presidential republic

Capital: *name:* Brazzaville
geographic coordinates: 4 15 S, 15 17 E
time difference: UTC+1 (6 hours ahead of Washington, DC, during Standard Time)
etymology: named after the Italian-born French explorer and humanitarian, Pierre Savorgnan de BRAZZA (1852-1905), who promoted French colonial interests in central Africa and worked against slavery and the abuse of African laborers

Administrative divisions: 12 departments (departments, singular - department); Bouenza, Brazzaville, Cuvette, Cuvette-Ouest, Kouilou, Lekoumou, Likouala, Niari, Plateaux, Pointe-Noire, Pool, Sangha

Independence: 15 August 1960 (from France)

National holiday: Independence Day, 15 August (1960)

Constitution: *history:* several previous; latest approved by referendum 25 October 2015
amendments: proposed by the president of the republic or by Parliament; passage of presidential proposals requires Supreme Court review followed by approval in a referendum; such proposals may also be submitted directly to Parliament, in which case passage requires at least three-quarters majority vote of both houses in joint session; proposals by Parliament require three-fourths majority vote of both houses in joint session; constitutional articles including those affecting the country's territory, republican form of government, and secularity of the state are not amendable

Legal system: mixed legal system of French civil law and customary law

International law organization participation: has not submitted an ICJ jurisdiction declaration; accepts ICCt jurisdiction

Citizenship: *citizenship by birth:* no
citizenship by descent only: at least one parent must be a citizen of the Republic of the Congo
dual citizenship recognized: no
residency requirement for naturalization: 10 years

Suffrage: 18 years of age; universal

Executive branch: *chief of state:* President Denis SASSOU-Nguesso (since 25 October 1997)
head of government: Prime Minister Clement MOUAMBA (since 24 April 2016); note - a constitutional referendum held in 2015 approved the change of the head of government from the president to the prime minister (2019)
cabinet: Council of Ministers appointed by the president
elections/appointments: president directly elected by absolute majority popular vote in 2 rounds if needed for a 5-year term (eligible for 2 additional terms); election last held on 21 March 2021 (next to be held on 21 March 2026)
election results:
Denis SASSOU-Nguesso reelected president in the first round; percent of vote - Denis SASSOU-Nguesso (PCT) 88.4%, Guy Price Parfait KOLELAS (MCDDI) 8.0%, other 3.6% (2021)

Legislative branch: *description:* bicameral Parliament or Parliament consists of:
Senate (72 seats; members indirectly elected by local, district, and regional councils by simple majority vote to serve 6-year terms) note- the Senate is renewed in its entirety following a constitutional reform implemented in 2015 ending the renewal by half
National Assembly (151 seats; members directly elected in single-seat constituencies by absolute majority popular vote in 2 rounds if needed; members serve 5-year terms) (2022)
elections:
Senate - last held on 31 August 2017 (next to be held in 2023)
National Assembly - last held on 10 and 31 July 2022 (next to be held in July 2027) (2022)
election results:
Senate - percent of vote by party - NA; seats by party - PCT 46, independent 12, MAR 2, RDPS 2, UPADS 2, DRD 1, FP 1, MCDDI 1, PRL 1, Pulp 1, PUR 1, RC 1; composition - men 58, women 14, percent of women 19.4%
National Assembly - percent of vote by party - NA; seats by party - PCT 112, UPADS 7, UDH-YUKI 7, MAR 4, RLP 2, CLUB 2002 2, DRR 2, RDPS 2, PAC 1, MSD 1, MDP 1, CPR 1, PPRD 1, CR 1, MCDDI 1, independent 6; composition -men 134, women 17, percent of women 11.3%; note - total Parliament percent of women 13.9%
National Assembly - percent of vote by party - NA; seats by party - PCT 96, UPADS 8, MCDDI 4, other 23 (less than 4 seats) independent 20; composition - men 134, women 17, percent of women 11.3%; note - total Parliament percent of women 13.9% (2022)

Judicial branch: *highest court(s):* Supreme Court or Cour Supreme (consists of NA judges); Constitutional Court (consists of 9 members); note - a High Court of Justice, outside the judicial authority, tries cases involving treason by the president of the republic
judge selection and term of office: Supreme Court judges elected by Parliament and serve until age 65; Constitutional Court members appointed by the president of the republic - 3 directly by the president and 6 nominated by Parliament; members appointed for renewable 9-year terms with one-third of the membership renewed every 3 years
subordinate courts: Court of Audit and Budgetary Discipline; courts of appeal; regional and district courts; employment tribunals; juvenile courts

Political parties and leaders: Alliance of the Presidential Majority or AMP
Action Movement for Renewal or MAR [Roland BOUITI-VIAUDO]
Citizen's Rally or RC [Claude Alphonse NSILOU]
Congolese Labour Party or PCT [Denis SASSOU-Nguesso]
Congolese Movement for Democracy and Integral Development or MCDDI [VACANT]
Movement for Unity, Solidarity, and Work or MUST [Claudine MUNARI]
Pan-African Union for Social Development or UPADS [Pascal Tsaty MABIALA]
Party for the Unity and the Republic or PUR [Wilfrid NGUESSO]
Patriotic Union for Democracy and Progress or UPDP [Auguste-Celestin GONGARD NKOUA]
Perspectives and Realities Club or CPR [Aimé Hydevert MOUAGNI]
Rally for Democracy and Social Progress or RDPS [Jean-Pierre Thystère TCHICAYA]
Republican and Liberal Party or PRL [Bonaventure MIZIDY]
Union of Democratic Forces or UDF [Josué Rodrigue NGOUONIMBA]
Union for Democracy and Republic or UDR [Guy Kinfoussia ROMAIN]
Union for the Republic or UR [Michel Bidimbou POUELA]

International organization participation: ACP, AfDB, AU, BDEAC, CEMAC, EITI (compliant country), FAO, FZ, G-77, IAEA, IBRD, ICAO, ICCt, ICRM, IDA, IFAD, IFC, IFRCS, ILO, IMF, IMO, Interpol, IOC, IOM, IPU, ISO (correspondent), ITSO, ITU, ITUC (NGOs), LCBC (observer), MIGA, NAM, OIF, OPCW, UN, UNCTAD, UNESCO, UNHCR, UNIDO, UNITAR, UNWTO, UPU, WCO, WFTU (NGOs), WHO, WIPO, WMO, WTO

Diplomatic representation in the US: *chief of mission:* Ambassador Serge MOMBOULI (since 31 July 2001)
chancery: 1720 16th Street NW, Washington, DC 20009
telephone: [1] (202) 726-5500
FAX: [1] (202) 726-1860
email address and website:
info@ambacongo-us.org
http://www.ambacongo-us.org/en-us/home.aspx
consulate(s): New Orleans

Diplomatic representation from the US: *chief of mission:* Ambassador Eugene S. YOUNG (since 30 March 2022)
embassy: 70-83 Section D, Boulevard Denis Sassou N'Guesso, Brazzaville
mailing address: 2090 Brazzaville Place, Washington DC 20521-2090
telephone: [242] 06 612-2000, [242] 05 387-9700
email address and website:
BrazzavilleACS@state.gov
https://cg.usembassy.gov/

Flag description: divided diagonally from the lower hoist side by a yellow band; the upper triangle (hoist side) is green and the lower triangle is red; green symbolizes agriculture and forests, yellow the friendship and nobility of the people, red is unexplained but has been associated with the struggle for independence
note: uses the popular Pan-African colors of Ethiopia

National symbol(s): lion, elephant; national colors: green, yellow, red

National anthem: *name:* "La Congolaise" (The Congolese)
lyrics/music: Jacques TONDRA and Georges KIBANGHI/Jean ROYER and Joseph SPADILIERE
note: originally adopted 1959, restored 1991

National heritage: *total World Heritage Sites:* 1 (natural)
selected World Heritage Site locales: Sangha Trinational Forest

ECONOMY

Economic overview: The Republic of the Congo's economy is a mixture of subsistence farming, an industrial sector based largely on oil and support services, and government spending. Oil has supplanted forestry as the mainstay of the economy, providing a major share of government revenues and exports. Natural gas is increasingly being converted to electricity rather than being flared, greatly improving energy prospects. New mining projects, particularly iron ore, which entered production in late 2013, may add as much as $1 billion to annual government revenue. The Republic of the Congo is a member of the Central African Economic and Monetary Community (CEMAC) and shares a common currency – the Central African Franc – with five other member states in the region.

The current administration faces difficult economic challenges of stimulating recovery and reducing poverty. The drop in oil prices that began in 2014 has constrained government spending; lower oil prices forced the government to cut more than $1 billion in planned spending. The fiscal deficit amounted to 11% of GDP in 2017. The government's inability to pay civil servant salaries has resulted in multiple rounds of strikes by many groups, including doctors, nurses, and teachers. In the wake of a multi-year recession, the country reached out to the IMF in 2017 for a new program; the IMF noted that the country's continued dependence on oil, unsustainable debt, and significant governance weakness are key impediments to the country's economy. In 2018, the country's external debt level will approach 120% of GDP. The IMF urged the government to renegotiate debts levels to sustainable levels before it agreed to a new macroeconomic adjustment package.

Real GDP (purchasing power parity): $19.03 billion (2020 est.)
$20.68 billion (2019 est.)
$20.63 billion (2018 est.)
note: data are in 2017 dollars
country comparison to the world: 153

Real GDP growth rate: -3.1% (2017 est.)
-2.8% (2016 est.)
2.6% (2015 est.)
country comparison to the world: 212

Real GDP per capita: $3,400 (2020 est.)
$3,800 (2019 est.)
$3,900 (2018 est.)
note: data are in 2017 dollars
country comparison to the world: 191

GDP (official exchange rate): $8.718 billion (2017 est.)

Inflation rate (consumer prices): 2.2% (2019 est.)
1.1% (2018 est.)
0.4% (2017 est.)
country comparison to the world: 116

Credit ratings:

Fitch rating: CCC (2019)

Moody's rating: Caa2 (2018)

Standard & Poors rating: CCC+ (2020)
note: The year refers to the year in which the current credit rating was first obtained.

GDP - composition, by sector of origin: *agriculture:* 9.3% (2017 est.)
industry: 51% (2017 est.)
services: 39.7% (2017 est.)

GDP - composition, by end use: *household consumption:* 47.6% (2017 est.)
government consumption: 9.6% (2017 est.)
investment in fixed capital: 42.5% (2017 est.)
investment in inventories: 0.1% (2017 est.)
exports of goods and services: 62.9% (2017 est.)
imports of goods and services: -62.7% (2017 est.)

Agricultural products: cassava, sugar cane, oil palm fruit, cassava leaves, bananas, plantains, roots/tubers, game meat, vegetables, mangoes/guavas

Industries: petroleum extraction, cement, lumber, brewing, sugar, palm oil, soap, flour, cigarettes

Industrial production growth rate: -3% (2017 est.)
country comparison to the world: 187

Labor force: 2.055 million (2016 est.)
country comparison to the world: 121

Labor force - by occupation: *agriculture:* 35.4%
industry: 20.6%
services: 44% (2005 est.)

Unemployment rate: 36% (2014 est.)
country comparison to the world: 212

Population below poverty line: 40.9% (2011 est.)

Gini Index coefficient - distribution of family income: 48.9 (2011 est.)
country comparison to the world: 17

Household income or consumption by percentage share: *lowest 10%:* 2.1%
highest 10%: 37.1% (2005)

Budget: *revenues:* 1.965 billion (2017 est.)
expenditures: 2.578 billion (2017 est.)

Budget surplus (+) or deficit (-): -7% (of GDP) (2017 est.)
country comparison to the world: 194

Public debt: 130.8% of GDP (2017 est.)
128.7% of GDP (2016 est.)
country comparison to the world: 7

Taxes and other revenues: 22.5% (of GDP) (2017 est.)
country comparison to the world: 132

Fiscal year: calendar year

Current account balance: -$1.128 billion (2017 est.)
-$5.735 billion (2016 est.)
country comparison to the world: 148

Exports: $4.193 billion (2017 est.)
$4.116 billion (2016 est.)
note: Data are in current year dollars and do not include illicit exports or re-exports.
country comparison to the world: 130

Exports - partners: China 49%, United Arab Emirates 15%, India 6%, Italy 5% (2019)

Exports - commodities: crude petroleum, copper, lumber, ships, refined petroleum (2019)

Imports: $2.501 billion (2017 est.)
$5.639 billion (2016 est.)
country comparison to the world: 164

Imports - partners: China 15%, France 12%, Belgium 6%, Angola 5% (2019)

Imports - commodities: ships, chicken products, refined petroleum, processed fish, packaged medicines (2019)

Reserves of foreign exchange and gold: $505.7 million (31 December 2017 est.)
$727.1 million (31 December 2016 est.)
country comparison to the world: 151

Debt - external: $4.605 billion (31 December 2017 est.)
$4.721 billion (31 December 2016 est.)
country comparison to the world: 136

Exchange rates: Cooperation Financiere en Afrique Centrale francs (XAF) per US dollar -
579.8 (2017 est.)
593.01 (2016 est.)
593.01 (2015 est.)
591.45 (2014 est.)
494.42 (2013 est.)

ENERGY

Electricity access: *electrification - total population:* 72% (2019)
electrification - urban areas: 89% (2019)
electrification - rural areas: 36% (2019)

Electricity: *installed generating capacity:* 629,000 kW (2020 est.)
consumption: 2,065,580,000 kWh (2019 est.)
exports: 44 million kWh (2019 est.)
imports: 23 million kWh (2019 est.)
transmission/distribution losses: 1.623 billion kWh (2019 est.)

Electricity generation sources: *fossil fuels:* 70.1% of total installed capacity (2020 est.)
hydroelectricity: 29.9% of total installed capacity (2020 est.)

Petroleum: *total petroleum production:* 270,900 bbl/day (2021 est.)
refined petroleum consumption: 12,600 bbl/day (2019 est.)
crude oil and lease condensate exports: 331,700 bbl/day (2018 est.)
crude oil and lease condensate imports: 0 bbl/day (2018 est.)
crude oil estimated reserves: 2.882 billion barrels (2021 est.)

Refined petroleum products - production: 15,760 bbl/day (2015 est.)
country comparison to the world: 93

Refined petroleum products - exports: 5,766 bbl/day (2015 est.)
country comparison to the world: 89

Refined petroleum products - imports: 7,162 bbl/day (2015 est.)
country comparison to the world: 156

Natural gas: *production:* 1,400,209,000 cubic meters (2019 est.)
consumption: 1,400,209,000 cubic meters (2019 est.)
exports: 0 cubic meters (2021 est.)
imports: 0 cubic meters (2021 est.)
proven reserves: 283.989 billion cubic meters (2021 est.)

Carbon dioxide emissions: 4.523 million metric tonnes of CO_2 (2019 est.)
from coal and metallurgical coke: 0 metric tonnes of CO_2 (2019 est.)
from petroleum and other liquids: 1.777 million metric tonnes of CO_2 (2019 est.)
from consumed natural gas: 2.747 million metric tonnes of CO_2 (2019 est.)
country comparison to the world: 138

Energy consumption per capita: 16.156 million Btu/person (2019 est.)
country comparison to the world: 139

COMMUNICATIONS

Telephones - fixed lines: *total subscriptions:* 17,000 (2020 est.)
subscriptions per 100 inhabitants: (2020 est.) less than 1
country comparison to the world: 179

Telephones - mobile cellular: *total subscriptions:* 4.89 million (2020 est.)
subscriptions per 100 inhabitants: 89 (2020 est.)
country comparison to the world: 122

Telecommunication systems: *general assessment:* suffering from economic challenges of stimulating recovery and reducing poverty; primary network consists of microwave radio relay and coaxial cable with services barely adequate for government use; key exchanges are in Brazzaville, Pointe-Noire, and Loubomo; intercity lines frequently out of order; youth are seeking the Internet more than their parents and often gain access through cyber cafes; only the most affluent have Internet access in their homes; operator has plans to upgrade national broadband through fiber link to West Africa Cable System (WACS) landing station at Pointe-Noire with connections to Angola and DRC; fiber network project with aims to connect north and south regions; DRC operator added fiber link between Brazzaville and Kinshasa (2020)
domestic: fixed-line infrastructure inadequate, providing less than 1 fixed-line connection per 100 persons; mobile-cellular 89 per 100 persons (2020)
international: country code - 242; WACS submarine cables to Europe and Western and South Africa; satellite earth station - 1 Intelsat (Atlantic Ocean) (2019)

Broadcast media: 1 state-owned TV and 3 state-owned radio stations; several privately owned TV and radio stations; satellite TV service is available; rebroadcasts of several international broadcasters are available

Internet country code: .cg

Internet users: *total:* 484,245 (2019 est.)
percent of population: 9% (2019 est.)
country comparison to the world: 157

Broadband - fixed subscriptions: *total:* 1,000 (2020 est.)
subscriptions per 100 inhabitants: 0.02 (2020 est.)
country comparison to the world: 202

TRANSPORTATION

National air transport system: *number of registered air carriers:* 3 (2020)
inventory of registered aircraft operated by air carriers: 12
annual passenger traffic on registered air carriers: 333,899 (2018)

annual freight traffic on registered air carriers: 4.6 million (2018) mt-km

Civil aircraft registration country code prefix: TN

Airports: *total:* 27 (2021)
country comparison to the world: 123

Airports - with paved runways: *total:* 8
over 3,047 m: 2
2,438 to 3,047 m: 1
1,524 to 2,437 m: 5 (2021)

Airports - with unpaved runways: *total:* 19
1,524 to 2,437 m: 8
914 to 1,523 m: 9
under 914 m: 2 (2021)

Pipelines: 232 km gas, 4 km liquid petroleum gas, 982 km oil (2013)

Railways: *total:* 510 km (2014)
narrow gauge: 510 km (2014) 1.067-m gauge
country comparison to the world: 112

Roadways: *total:* 23,324 km (2017)
paved: 3,111 km (2017)
unpaved: 20,213 km (2017)
note: road network in Congo is composed of 23,324 km of which 17,000 km are classified as national, departmental, and routes of local interest: 6,324 km are non-classified routes
country comparison to the world: 107

Waterways: 1,120 km (2011) (commercially navigable on Congo and Oubangui Rivers above Brazzaville; there are many ferries across the river to Kinshasa; the Congo south of Brazzaville-Kinshasa to the coast is not navigable because of rapids, necessitating a rail connection to Pointe-Noire; other rivers are used for local traffic only)
country comparison to the world: 65

Merchant marine: *total:* 11
by type: general cargo 1, oil tanker 1, other 9 (2021)
country comparison to the world: 153

Ports and terminals: *major seaport(s):* Pointe-Noire
oil terminal(s): Djeno
river port(s): Brazzaville (Congo)
Impfondo (Oubangui) Ouesso (Sangha) Oyo (Alima)

MILITARY AND SECURITY

Military and security forces: Congolese Armed Forces (Forces Armees Congolaises, FAC): Army, Navy, Congolese Air Force, Gendarmerie (2022)

Military expenditures: 2.5% of GDP (2021 est.)
3.2% of GDP (2020 est.)
2.3% of GDP (2019 est.) (approximately $350 million)
2.1% of GDP (2018 est.) (approximately $330 million)
3.6% of GDP (2017 est.) (approximately $580 million)
country comparison to the world: 40

Military and security service personnel strengths: approximately 12,000 active duty troops (8,000 Army; 800 Navy; 1,000 Air Force; 2,000 Gendarmerie) (2022)

Military equipment inventories and acquisitions: the FAC is armed with mostly aging Russian and Soviet-era weapons, with a smaller mix of French and South African equipment; the leading supplier of arms to the FAC since 2010 is South Africa (2021)

Military service age and obligation: 18 years of age for voluntary military service for men and women; conscription ended in 1969 (2021)

Military - note: as of 2022, the FAC had limited capabilities due to obsolescent and poorly maintained equipment and low levels of training; its primary focus was internal security; since its creation in 1961, the FAC has had a turbulent history; it has been sidelined by some national leaders in favor of personal militias, endured an internal rebellion (1996), and clashed with various rebel groups and political or ethnic militias (1993-1996, 2002-2005, 2017); during the 1997-1999 civil war, the military generally split along ethnic lines, with most northern officers supporting eventual winner SASSOU-Nguesso, and most southerners backing the rebels; others joined ethnic-based factions loyal to regional warlords; forces backing SASSOU-Nguesso were supported by Angolan troops and received some French assistance; the FAC also has undergone at least three reorganizations that included the incorporation of former rebel combatants and various ethnic and political militias; in recent years, France has provided some advice and training, and a military cooperation agreement was signed with Russia in 2019

TRANSNATIONAL ISSUES

Disputes - international: *Republic of the Congo-Democratic Republic of Congo(DRC):* the location of the boundary in the broad Congo River is indefinite except in the Pool Malebo/Stanley Pool area
Republic of the Congo-Angola: (Kabinda Exclave) None identified

Refugees and internally displaced persons: *refugees (country of origin):* 29,229 (Central African Republic), 22,150 (Democratic Republic of the Congo) (refugees and asylum seekers) (2022)
IDPs: 159,830 (multiple civil wars since 1992) (2022)

COOK ISLANDS

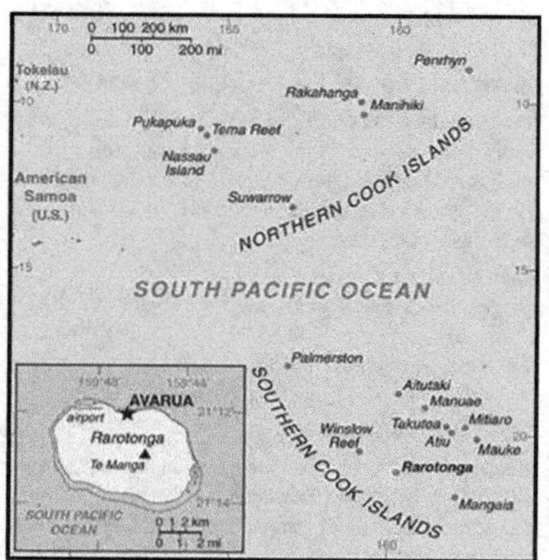

INTRODUCTION

Background: Polynesians from Tahiti were probably the first people to settle Rarotonga around A.D. 900. Over time, Samoans and Tongans also settled in Rarotonga, and Rarotongans voyaged to the northern Cook Islands, settling Manihiki and Rakahanga. Pukapuka and Penrhyn in the northern Cook Islands were settled directly from Samoa. Prior to European contact, there was considerable travel and trade between inhabitants of the different islands and atolls but they were not united in a single political entity. Spanish navigators were the first Europeans to spot the northern Cook Islands in 1595 followed by the first landing in 1606. The Cook Islands remained free of further European contact until the 1760s, and in 1773, British explorer James COOK saw Manuae in the southern Cook Islands. The islands were named after COOK in the 1820s by Russian mapmakers. English missionary activity during the 1820s and 1830s banned singing and dancing and converted most of the population.

Fearing France would militarily occupy the islands like it did in Tahiti, Rarotongans asked the UK for protectorate status in the 1840s and 1860s, which the UK ignored. In 1888, Queen MAKEA TAKAU of Rarotonga formally petitioned for protectorate status, which the UK reluctantly agreed to. In 1901, the UK placed Rarotonga and the rest of the islands in the New Zealand Colony and in 1915, the Cook Islands Act organized the Cook Islands into one political entity. It remained a protectorate until 1965, when New Zealand granted the Cook Islands self-government status. The Cook Islands has a great deal of local autonomy and is an independent member of international organizations, but it is in free association with New Zealand, which is responsible for defense and foreign affairs. Economic opportunities in the Cook Islands are sparse, and more Cook Islanders live in New Zealand than in the Cook Islands.

In a referendum in 1994, voters chose to keep the name Cook Islands rather than changing to a Maori name for the islands. The issue was revived in 2019, but after being poorly received by the diaspora in New Zealand, the government decided to retain the name Cook Islands but to provide a Maori name alongside it. The Maori name has not yet been determined.

GEOGRAPHY

Location: Oceania, group of islands in the South Pacific Ocean, about halfway between Hawaii and New Zealand

Geographic coordinates: 21 14 S, 159 46 W

Map references: Oceania

Area: *total:* 236 sq km
land: 236 sq km
water: 0 sq km
country comparison to the world: 214

Area - comparative: 1.3 times the size of Washington, DC

Land boundaries: *total:* 0 km

Coastline: 120 km

Maritime claims: *territorial sea:* 12 nm
exclusive economic zone: 200 nm
continental shelf: 200 nm or to the edge of the continental margin

Climate: tropical oceanic; moderated by trade winds; a dry season from April to November and a more humid season from December to March

Terrain: low coral atolls in north; volcanic, hilly islands in south

Elevation: *highest point:* Te Manga 652 m
lowest point: Pacific Ocean 0 m

Natural resources: coconuts (copra)

Land use: *agricultural land:* 8.4% (2018 est.)
arable land: 4.2% (2018 est.)
permanent crops: 4.2% (2018 est.)
permanent pasture: 0% (2018 est.)
forest: 64.6% (2018 est.)
other: 27% (2018 est.)

Population distribution: most of the population is found on the island of Rarotonga

Natural hazards: tropical cyclones (November to March)

Geography - note: the northern Cook Islands are seven low-lying, sparsely populated, coral atolls; the southern Cook Islands, where most of the population lives, consist of eight elevated, fertile, volcanic isles, including the largest, Rarotonga, at 67 sq km

PEOPLE AND SOCIETY

Population: 8,128 (2022 est.)
note: the Cook Islands' Ministry of Finance & Economic Management estimated the resident population to have been 11,700 in September 2016
country comparison to the world: 223

Nationality: *noun:* Cook Islander(s)
adjective: Cook Islander

Ethnic groups: Cook Island Maori (Polynesian) 81.3%, part Cook Island Maori 6.7%, other 11.9% (2011 est.)

Languages: English (official) 86.4%, Cook Islands Maori (Rarotongan) (official) 76.2%, other 8.3% (2011 est.)
note: shares sum to more than 100% because some respondents gave more than one answer on the census

Religions: Protestant 62.8% (Cook Islands Christian Church 49.1%, Seventh Day Adventist 7.9%, Assemblies of God 3.7%, Apostolic Church 2.1%), Roman Catholic 17%, Church of Jesus Christ 4.4%, other 8%, none 5.6%, no response 2.2% (2011 est.)

Age structure: *0-14 years:* 18.69% (male 797/female 722)
15-24 years: 13.9% (male 606/female 524)
25-54 years: 37.66% (male 1,595/female 1,634)
55-64 years: 15.69% (male 711/female 564)
65 years and over: 14.74% (male 584/female 614) (2022 est.)

Median age: *total:* 38.3 years
male: 37.8 years
female: 38.7 years (2020 est.)
country comparison to the world: 64

Population growth rate: -2.39% (2022 est.)
country comparison to the world: 237

Birth rate: 12.55 births/1,000 population (2022 est.)
country comparison to the world: 145

Death rate: 9.1 deaths/1,000 population (2022 est.)
country comparison to the world: 57

Net migration rate: -27.31 migrant(s)/1,000 population (2022 est.)
country comparison to the world: 230

Population distribution: most of the population is found on the island of Rarotonga

Urbanization: *urban population:* 75.9% of total population (2022)
rate of urbanization: 0.52% annual rate of change (2020-25 est.)

Sex ratio: *at birth:* 1.04 male(s)/female
0-14 years: 1.1 male(s)/female
15-24 years: 1.16 male(s)/female
25-54 years: 0.96 male(s)/female
55-64 years: 1.26 male(s)/female
65 years and over: 0.73 male(s)/female
total population: 1.06 male(s)/female (2022 est.)

Infant mortality rate: *total:* 15.93 deaths/1,000 live births
male: 20.02 deaths/1,000 live births
female: 11.62 deaths/1,000 live births (2022 est.)
country comparison to the world: 95

Life expectancy at birth: *total population:* 77.14 years
male: 74.32 years
female: 80.11 years (2022 est.)
country comparison to the world: 94

Total fertility rate: 2.07 children born/woman (2022 est.)
country comparison to the world: 96

Drinking water source: *improved: total:* 100% of population
unimproved: total: 0% of population (2020 est.)

Current health expenditure: 3.1% of GDP (2019)

Physicians density: 1.41 physicians/1,000 population (2014)

Sanitation facility access: *improved: total:* 99.1% of population
unimproved: total: 0.9% of population (2020 est.)

Major infectious diseases: *degree of risk:* high (2020)
food or waterborne diseases: bacterial diarrhea
vectorborne diseases: malaria

Obesity - adult prevalence rate: 55.9% (2016)
country comparison to the world: 2

Alcohol consumption per capita: *total:* 12.97 liters of pure alcohol (2019 est.)
beer: 3.62 liters of pure alcohol (2019 est.)
wine: 2.28 liters of pure alcohol (2019 est.)
spirits: 7.07 liters of pure alcohol (2019 est.)
other alcohols: 0 liters of pure alcohol (2019 est.)
country comparison to the world: 1

Tobacco use: *total:* 24% (2020 est.)
male: 27.7% (2020 est.)
female: 20.3% (2020 est.)
country comparison to the world: 57

Education expenditures: 3.5% of GDP (2019 est.)
country comparison to the world: 124

School life expectancy (primary to tertiary education): *total:* 15 years
male: 15 years
female: 14 years (2012)

ENVIRONMENT

Environment - current issues: limited land presents solid and liquid waste disposal problems; soil destruction and deforestation; environmental degradation due to indiscriminate use of pesticides; improper disposal of pollutants; overfishing and destructive fishing practices; over dredging of lagoons and coral rubble beds; unregulated building

Environment - international agreements: *party to:* Antarctic-Marine Living Resources, Biodiversity, Climate Change, Climate Change-Kyoto Protocol, Climate Change-Paris Agreement, Comprehensive Nuclear Test Ban, Desertification, Hazardous Wastes, Law of the Sea, Ozone Layer Protection, Ship Pollution
signed, but not ratified: none of the selected agreements

Air pollutants: *particulate matter emissions:* 12.03 micrograms per cubic meter (2016 est.)

Climate: tropical oceanic; moderated by trade winds; a dry season from April to November and a more humid season from December to March

Land use: *agricultural land:* 8.4% (2018 est.)
arable land: 4.2% (2018 est.)
permanent crops: 4.2% (2018 est.)
permanent pasture: 0% (2018 est.)
forest: 64.6% (2018 est.)
other: 27% (2018 est.)

Urbanization: *urban population:* 75.9% of total population (2022)
rate of urbanization: 0.52% annual rate of change (2020-25 est.)

Total renewable water resources: 0 cubic meters (2017 est.)

GOVERNMENT

Country name: *conventional long form:* none
conventional short form: Cook Islands
former: Hervey Islands
etymology: named after Captain James COOK, the British explorer who visited the islands in 1773 and 1777

Government type: parliamentary democracy

Dependency status: self-governing in free association with New Zealand; Cook Islands is fully responsible for internal affairs; New Zealand retains responsibility for external affairs and defense in consultation with the Cook Islands

Capital: *name:* Avarua
geographic coordinates: 21 12 S, 159 46 W
time difference: UTC-10 (5 hours behind Washington, DC, during Standard Time)
etymology: translates as "two harbors" in Maori

Administrative divisions: none

Independence: none (became self-governing in free association with New Zealand on 4 August 1965 with the right at any time to move to full independence by unilateral action)

National holiday: Constitution Day, the first Monday in August (1965)

Constitution: *history:* 4 August 1965 (Cook Islands Constitution Act 1964)
amendments: proposed by Parliament; passage requires at least two-thirds majority vote by the Parliament membership in each of several readings and assent of the chief of state's representative;

passage of amendments relating to the chief of state also requires two-thirds majority approval in a referendum; amended many times, last in 2004

Legal system: common law similar to New Zealand common law

International law organization participation: has not submitted an ICJ jurisdiction declaration (New Zealand normally retains responsibility for external affairs); accepts ICCt jurisdiction

Suffrage: 18 years of age; universal

Executive branch: *chief of state:* King CHARLES III (since 8 September 2022); represented by Sir Tom J. MARSTERS (since 9 August 2013); New Zealand High Commissioner Ms Tui DEWES (since October 2020)
head of government: Prime Minister Mark BROWN (since 1 October 2020)
cabinet: Cabinet chosen by the prime minister
elections/appointments: the monarchy is hereditary; UK representative appointed by the monarch; New Zealand high commissioner appointed by the New Zealand Government; following legislative elections, the leader of the majority party or majority coalition usually becomes prime minister

Legislative branch: *description:* unicameral Parliament, formerly the Legislative Assembly (24 seats; members directly elected in single-seat constituencies by simple majority vote to serve 4-year terms); note - the House of Ariki, a 24-member parliamentary body of traditional leaders appointed by the Queen's representative serves as a consultative body to the Parliament
elections:
last held on 14 June 2018 (next to be held by 2022)
election results:
percent of vote by party - NA; seats by party - Demo 11, CIP 10, One Cook Islands Movement 1, independent 2; composition - men 17, women 7, percent of women 17.7%

Judicial branch: *highest court(s):* Court of Appeal (consists of the chief justice and 3 judges of the High Court); High Court (consists of the chief justice and at least 4 judges and organized into civil, criminal, and land divisions); note - appeals beyond the Cook Islands Court of Appeal are heard by the Judicial Committee of the Privy Council (in London)
judge selection and term of office: High Court chief justice appointed by the Queen's Representative on the advice of the Executive Council tendered by the prime minister; other judges appointed by the Queen's Representative, on the advice of the Executive Council tendered by the chief justice, High Court chief justice, and the minister of justice; chief justice and judges appointed for 3-year renewable terms
subordinate courts: justices of the peace

Political parties and leaders: Cook Islands Party or CIP [Mark BROWN]
Democratic Party or Demo [Tina BROWNE]
One Cook Islands Movement [Teina BISHOP]

International organization participation: ACP, ADB, AOSIS, FAO, ICAO, ICCt, ICRM, IFAD, IFRCS, IMO, IMSO, IOC, ITUC (NGOs), OPCW, PIF, Sparteca, SPC, UNESCO, UPU, WHO, WMO

Diplomatic representation in the US: none (self-governing in free association with New Zealand)

Diplomatic representation from the US: *embassy:* none (self-governing in free association with New Zealand)

Flag description: blue with the flag of the UK in the upper hoist-side quadrant and a large circle of 15 white five-pointed stars (one for every island) centered in the outer half of the flag

National symbol(s): a circle of 15, five-pointed, white stars on a blue field, Tiare maori (Gardenia taitensis) flower; national colors: green, white

National anthem: *name:* "Te Atua Mou E" (To God Almighty)
lyrics/music: Tepaeru Te RITO/Thomas DAVIS
note: adopted 1982; as prime minister, Sir Thomas DAVIS composed the anthem; his wife, a tribal chief, wrote the lyrics

ECONOMY

Economic overview: Like many other South Pacific island nations, the Cook Islands' economic development is hindered by the isolation of the country from foreign markets, the limited size of domestic markets, lack of natural resources, periodic devastation from natural disasters, and inadequate infrastructure. Agriculture, employing more than one-quarter of the working population, provides the economic base with major exports of copra and citrus fruit. Black pearls are the Cook Islands' leading export. Manufacturing activities are limited to fruit processing, clothing, and handicrafts. Trade deficits are offset by remittances from emigrants and by foreign aid overwhelmingly from New Zealand. In the 1980s and 1990s, the country became overextended, maintaining a bloated public service and accumulating a large foreign debt. Subsequent reforms, including the sale of state assets, the strengthening of economic management, the encouragement of tourism, and a debt restructuring agreement, have rekindled investment and growth. The government is targeting fisheries and seabed mining as sectors for future economic growth.

Real GDP (purchasing power parity): $299.9 million (2016 est.)
$183.2 million (2015 est.)
country comparison to the world: 216

Real GDP growth rate: 0.1% (2005 est.)
country comparison to the world: 189

Real GDP per capita: $16,700 (2016 est.)
$9,100 (2005 est.)
country comparison to the world: 101

GDP (official exchange rate): $299.9 million (2016 est.)

Inflation rate (consumer prices): 2.2% (2011 est.)
country comparison to the world: 117

GDP - composition, by sector of origin: *agriculture:* 5.1% (2010 est.)
industry: 12.7% (2010 est.)
services: 82.1% (2010 est.)

Agricultural products: vegetables, coconuts, roots/tubers, cassava, papayas, tomatoes, pork, fruit, sweet potatoes, mangoes/guavas

Industries: fishing, fruit processing, tourism, clothing, handicrafts

Industrial production growth rate: 1% (2002)
country comparison to the world: 155

Labor force: 6,820 (2001)
country comparison to the world: 217

Labor force - by occupation: *agriculture:* 29%
industry: 15%
services: 56% (1995)

Unemployment rate: 13.1% (2005)
country comparison to the world: 169

Budget: *revenues:* 86.9 million (2010)
expenditures: 77.9 million (2010)

Budget surplus (+) or deficit (-): 3% (of GDP) (2010 est.)
country comparison to the world: 13

Taxes and other revenues: 29% (of GDP) (2010 est.)
country comparison to the world: 86

Fiscal year: 1 April - 31 March

Current account balance: $26.67 million (2005)
country comparison to the world: 58

Exports: $3.125 million (2011 est.)
$5.163 million (2010 est.)
note: Data are in current year dollars and do not include illicit exports or re-exports.
country comparison to the world: 222

Exports - partners: Japan 37%, Thailand 21%, France 17% (2019)

Exports - commodities: fish products, recreational boats, precious metal scraps, fruit juice, chemical analysis instruments (2019)

Imports: $109.3 million (2011 est.)
$90.62 million (2010 est.)
country comparison to the world: 216

Imports - partners: New Zealand 41%, China 21%, Italy 12%, Fiji 10% (2019)

Imports - commodities: ships, refined petroleum, recreational boats, cars, flavored water (2019)

Debt - external: $141 million (1996 est.)
country comparison to the world: 191

Exchange rates: NZ dollars (NZD) per US dollar -
1.416 (2017 est.)
1.4341 (2016 est.)
1.4341 (2015 est.)
1.441 (2014 est.)
1.4279 (2013 est.)

ENERGY

Electricity: *installed generating capacity:* 18,000 kW (2020 est.)
consumption: 38.729 million kWh (2019 est.)
exports: 0 kWh (2020 est.)
imports: 0 kWh (2020 est.)
transmission/distribution losses: 3 million kWh (2019 est.)

Electricity generation sources: *fossil fuels:* 70% of total installed capacity (2020 est.)
solar: 30% of total installed capacity (2020 est.)

Petroleum: *total petroleum production:* 0 bbl/day (2021 est.)
refined petroleum consumption: 800 bbl/day (2019 est.)

Refined petroleum products - imports: 611 bbl/day (2015 est.)
country comparison to the world: 204

Carbon dioxide emissions: 114,000 metric tonnes of CO2 (2019 est.)
from petroleum and other liquids: 114,000 metric tonnes of CO2 (2019 est.)
country comparison to the world: 208

Energy consumption per capita: 0 Btu/person (2019 est.)
country comparison to the world: 197

COMMUNICATIONS

Telephones - fixed lines: *total subscriptions:* 6,576 (2018 est.)

subscriptions per 100 inhabitants: 38 (2018 est.)
country comparison to the world: 198

Telephones - mobile cellular: *total subscriptions:* 14,539 (2018 est.)
subscriptions per 100 inhabitants: 83 (2018 est.)
country comparison to the world: 217

Telecommunication systems: *general assessment:* demand for mobile broadband is increasing due to mobile services being the primary and most widespread source for Internet access across the region; Telecom Cook Islands offers international direct dialing, Internet, email, and fax; individual islands are connected by a combination of satellite earth stations, microwave systems, and VHF and HF radiotelephone (2020)
domestic: service is provided by small exchanges connected to subscribers by open-wire, cable, and fiber-optic cable; nearly 38 per 100 fixed-line and about 83 per 100 mobile-cellular (2019)
international: country code - 682; the Manatua submarine cable to surrounding islands of Niue, Samoa, French Polynesia and other Cook Islands, the topography of the South Pacific region has made Internet connectivity a serious issue for many of the remote islands; submarine fiber-optic networks are expensive to build and maintain; satellite earth station - 1 Intelsat (Pacific Ocean) (2019)

Broadcast media: 1 privately owned TV station broadcasts from Rarotonga providing a mix of local news and overseas-sourced programs (2019)

Internet country code: .ck

Internet users: *total:* 9,476 (2019 est.)
percent of population: 54% (2019 est.)
country comparison to the world: 216

Broadband - fixed subscriptions: *total:* 2,700 (2018 est.)
subscriptions per 100 inhabitants: 15 (2018 est.)
country comparison to the world: 195

TRANSPORTATION

National air transport system: *number of registered air carriers:* 1 (2020)
inventory of registered aircraft operated by air carriers: 6

Civil aircraft registration country code prefix: E5

Airports: *total:* 11 (2021)
country comparison to the world: 153

Airports - with paved runways: *total:* 1
1,524 to 2,437 m: 1 (2021)

Airports - with unpaved runways: *total:* 10
1,524 to 2,437 m: 2
914 to 1,523 m: 7
under 914 m: 1 (2021)

Roadways: *total:* 295 km (2018)
*paved:*207 km (2018)
*unpaved:*88 km (2018)
country comparison to the world: 202

Merchant marine: *total:* 194
by type: bulk carrier 19, container ship 1, general cargo 57, oil tanker 54, other 63 (2021)
country comparison to the world: 69

Ports and terminals: *major seaport(s):* Avatiu

MILITARY AND SECURITY

Military and security forces: no regular military forces; Cook Islands Police Service

Military - note: defense is the responsibility of New Zealand in consultation with the Cook Islands and at its request

the Cook Islands have a "shiprider" agreement with the US, which allows local maritime law enforcement officers to embark on US Coast Guard (USCG) and US Navy (USN) vessels, including to board and search vessels suspected of violating laws or regulations within its designated exclusive economic zone (EEZ) or on the high seas; "shiprider" agreements also enable USCG personnel and USN vessels with embarked USCG law enforcement personnel to work with host nations to protect critical regional resources (2022)

TRANSNATIONAL ISSUES

Disputes - international: none

CORAL SEA ISLANDS

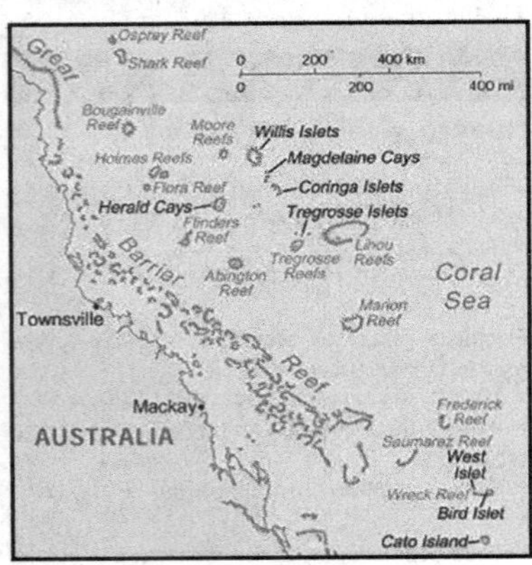

INTRODUCTION

Background: The widely scattered islands were first charted in 1803, but they were too small to host any permanent human habitation. The 1870s and 1880s, saw attempts at guano mining, but these were soon abandoned. The islands became an Australian territory in 1969 and its boundaries were extended in 1997. A small meteorological staff has operated on the Willis Islets since 1921, and several other islands host unmanned weather stations, beacons, and lighthouses. Much of the territory lies within marine national nature reserves.

GEOGRAPHY

Location: Oceania, islands in the Coral Sea, northeast of Australia

Geographic coordinates: 18 00 S, 152 00 E

Map references: Oceania

Area: *total:* 3 sq km less than
land: 3 sq km less than
water: 0 sq km
note: includes numerous small islands and reefs scattered over a sea area of about 780,000 sq km (300,000 sq mi) with the Willis Islets the most important
country comparison to the world: 252

Area - comparative: about four times the size of the National Mall in Washington, DC

Land boundaries: *total:* 0 km

Coastline: 3,095 km

Maritime claims: *territorial sea:* 3 nm
exclusive fishing zone: 200 nm

Climate: tropical

Terrain: sand and coral reefs and islands (cays)

Elevation: *highest point:* unnamed location on Cato Island 9 m
lowest point: Pacific Ocean 0 m

Natural resources: fish

Land use: *agricultural land:* 0% (2018 est.)
other: 100% (2018 est.)

Natural hazards: occasional tropical cyclones

Geography - note: important nesting area for birds and turtles

PEOPLE AND SOCIETY

Population: (July 2021 est.) no indigenous inhabitants
note: there is a staff of four at the meteorological station on Willis Island

ENVIRONMENT

Environment - current issues: no permanent fresh-water resources; damaging activities include coral mining, destructive fishing practices (overfishing, blast fishing)

Climate: tropical

Land use: *agricultural land:* 0% (2018 est.)
other: 100% (2018 est.)

GOVERNMENT

Country name: *conventional long form:* Coral Sea Islands Territory
conventional short form: Coral Sea Islands
etymology: self-descriptive name to reflect the islands' position in the Coral Sea off the northeastern coast of Australia

Dependency status: territory of Australia; administered from Canberra by the Department of Regional Australia, Local Government, Arts and Sport

Legal system: the common law legal system of Australia applies where applicable

Citizenship: see Australia

Diplomatic representation in the US: none (territory of Australia)

Diplomatic representation from the US: *embassy:* none (territory of Australia)

Flag description: the flag of Australia is used

ECONOMY

Economic overview: no economic activity

COMMUNICATIONS

Communications - note: automatic weather stations on many of the isles and reefs relay data to the mainland

TRANSPORTATION

Ports and terminals: none; offshore anchorage only

MILITARY AND SECURITY

Military - note: defense is the responsibility of Australia

TRANSNATIONAL ISSUES

Disputes - international: none

COSTA RICA

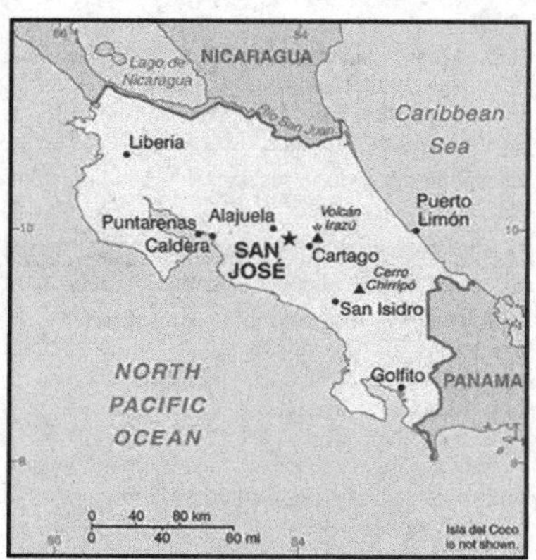

INTRODUCTION

Background: Although explored by the Spanish early in the 16th century, initial attempts at colonizing Costa Rica proved unsuccessful due to a combination of factors, including disease from mosquito-infested swamps, brutal heat, resistance by indigenous populations, and pirate raids. It was not until 1563 that a permanent settlement of Cartago was established in the cooler, fertile central highlands. The area remained a colony for some two and a half centuries. In 1821, Costa Rica became one of several Central American provinces that jointly declared their independence from Spain. Two years later it joined the United Provinces of Central America, but this federation disintegrated in 1838, at which time Costa Rica proclaimed its sovereignty and independence. Since the late 19th century, only two brief periods of violence have marred the country's democratic development. On 1 December 1948, Costa Rica dissolved its armed forces. Although it still maintains a large agricultural sector, Costa Rica has expanded its economy to include strong technology and tourism industries. The standard of living is relatively high. Land ownership is widespread.

GEOGRAPHY

Location: Central America, bordering both the Caribbean Sea and the North Pacific Ocean, between Nicaragua and Panama

Geographic coordinates: 10 00 N, 84 00 W

Map references: Central America and the Caribbean

Area: *total:* 51,100 sq km
land: 51,060 sq km
water: 40 sq km
note: includes Isla del Coco
country comparison to the world: 129

Area - comparative: slightly smaller than West Virginia

Land boundaries: *total:* 661 km
border countries (2): Nicaragua 313 km; Panama 348 km

Coastline: 1,290 km

Maritime claims: *territorial sea:* 12 nm
exclusive economic zone: 200 nm
continental shelf: 200 nm

Climate: tropical and subtropical; dry season (December to April); rainy season (May to November); cooler in highlands

Terrain: coastal plains separated by rugged mountains including over 100 volcanic cones, of which several are major active volcanoes

Elevation: *highest point:* Cerro Chirripo 3,819 m
lowest point: Pacific Ocean 0 m
mean elevation: 746 m

Natural resources: hydropower

Land use: *agricultural land:* 37.1% (2018 est.)
arable land: 4.9% (2018 est.)
permanent crops: 6.7% (2018 est.)
permanent pasture: 25.5% (2018 est.)
forest: 51.5% (2018 est.)
other: 11.4% (2018 est.)

Irrigated land: 1,015 sq km (2012)

Population distribution: roughly half of the nation's population resides in urban areas; the capital of San Jose is the largest city and home to approximately one-fifth of the population

Natural hazards: occasional earthquakes, hurricanes along Atlantic coast; frequent flooding of lowlands at onset of rainy season and landslides; active volcanoes
volcanism: Arenal (1,670 m), which erupted in 2010, is the most active volcano in Costa Rica; a 1968 eruption destroyed the town of Tabacon; Irazu (3,432 m), situated just east of San Jose, has the potential to spew ash over the capital city as it did between 1963 and 1965; other historically active volcanoes include Miravalles, Poas, Rincon de la Vieja, and Turrialba

Geography - note: four volcanoes, two of them active, rise near the capital of San Jose in the center of the country; one of the volcanoes, Irazu, erupted destructively in 1963-65

PEOPLE AND SOCIETY

Population: 5,204,411 (2022 est.)
country comparison to the world: 124

Nationality: *noun:* Costa Rican(s)
adjective: Costa Rican

Ethnic groups: White or Mestizo 83.6%, Mulatto 6.7%, Indigenous 2.4%, Black or African descent 1.1%, other 1.1%, none 2.9%, unspecified 2.2% (2011 est.)

Languages: Spanish (official), English
major-language sample(s):
La Libreta Informativa del Mundo, la fuente indispensable de información básica. (Spanish)

Religions: Roman Catholic 47.5%, Evangelical and Pentecostal 19.8%, Jehovah's Witness 1.4%, other Protestant 1.2%, other 3.1%, none 27% (2021 est.)

Demographic profile: Costa Rica's political stability, high standard of living, and well-developed social benefits system set it apart from its Central American neighbors. Through the government's sustained social spending - almost 20% of GDP annually - Costa Rica has made tremendous progress toward achieving its goal of providing universal access to education, healthcare, clean water, sanitation, and electricity. Since the 1970s, expansion of these services has led to a rapid decline in infant mortality, an increase in life expectancy at birth, and a sharp decrease in the birth rate. The average number of children born per women has fallen from about 7 in the 1960s to 3.5 in the early 1980s to below replacement level today. Costa Rica's poverty rate is lower than in most Latin American countries, but it has stalled at around 20% for almost two decades.

Costa Rica is a popular regional immigration destination because of its job opportunities and social programs. Almost 9% of the population is foreign-born, with Nicaraguans comprising nearly three-quarters of the foreign population. Many Nicaraguans who perform unskilled seasonal labor enter Costa Rica illegally or overstay their visas, which continues to be a source of tension. Less than 3% of Costa Rica's population lives abroad. The overwhelming majority of expatriates have settled in the United States after completing a university degree or in order to work in a highly skilled field.

Age structure: *0-14 years:* 22.08% (male 575,731/female 549,802)
15-24 years: 15.19% (male 395,202/female 379,277)
25-54 years: 43.98% (male 1,130,387/female 1,111,791)
55-64 years: 9.99% (male 247,267/female 261,847)
65 years and over: 8.76% (male 205,463/female 241,221) (2020 est.)

Dependency ratios: *total dependency ratio:* 45.1
youth dependency ratio: 30.2
elderly dependency ratio: 14.9
potential support ratio: 6.7 (2020 est.)

Median age: *total:* 32.6 years
male: 32.1 years
female: 33.1 years (2020 est.)
country comparison to the world: 109

Population growth rate: 1.01% (2022 est.)
country comparison to the world: 95

Birth rate: 14.28 births/1,000 population (2022 est.)
country comparison to the world: 121

Death rate: 4.91 deaths/1,000 population (2022 est.)
country comparison to the world: 198

Net migration rate: 0.77 migrant(s)/1,000 population (2022 est.)
country comparison to the world: 69

Population distribution: roughly half of the nation's population resides in urban areas; the capital of San Jose is the largest city and home to approximately one-fifth of the population

Urbanization: *urban population:* 82% of total population (2022)
rate of urbanization: 1.5% annual rate of change (2020-25 est.)

Major urban areas - population: 1.441 million SAN JOSE (capital) (2022)

Sex ratio: *at birth:* 1.05 male(s)/female
0-14 years: 1.05 male(s)/female
15-24 years: 1.04 male(s)/female
25-54 years: 1.02 male(s)/female
55-64 years: 0.94 male(s)/female
65 years and over: 0.64 male(s)/female
total population: 1 male(s)/female (2022 est.)

Maternal mortality ratio: 27 deaths/100,000 live births (2017 est.)
country comparison to the world: 116

Infant mortality rate: *total:* 8.39 deaths/1,000 live births
male: 9.45 deaths/1,000 live births
female: 7.28 deaths/1,000 live births (2022 est.)
country comparison to the world: 144

Life expectancy at birth: *total population:* 79.64 years
male: 76.99 years
female: 82.43 years (2022 est.)
country comparison to the world: 58

Total fertility rate: 1.86 children born/woman (2022 est.)
country comparison to the world: 134

Contraceptive prevalence rate: 70.9% (2018)

Drinking water source: *improved: urban:* 100% of population
rural: 100% of population
total: 100% of population

Current health expenditure: 7.3% of GDP (2019)

Physicians density: 3.3 physicians/1,000 population (2020)

Hospital bed density: 1.1 beds/1,000 population (2019)

Sanitation facility access: *improved: urban:* 99% of population
rural: 97.1% of population
total: 98.7% of population
unimproved: urban: 1% of population
rural: 2.9% of population
total: 1.3% of population (2020 est.)

HIV/AIDS - adult prevalence rate: 0.4% (2020 est.)
country comparison to the world: 73

Major infectious diseases: *degree of risk:* intermediate (2020)
food or waterborne diseases: bacterial diarrhea
vectorborne diseases: dengue fever

Obesity - adult prevalence rate: 25.7% (2016)
country comparison to the world: 48

Alcohol consumption per capita: *total:* 3.07 liters of pure alcohol (2019 est.)
beer: 2.17 liters of pure alcohol (2019 est.)
wine: 0.15 liters of pure alcohol (2019 est.)
spirits: 0.36 liters of pure alcohol (2019 est.)
other alcohols: 0.39 liters of pure alcohol (2019 est.)
country comparison to the world: 112

Tobacco use: *total:* 8.8% (2020 est.)
male: 12.9% (2020 est.)
female: 4.6% (2020 est.)
country comparison to the world: 140

Children under the age of 5 years underweight: 2.9% (2018)
country comparison to the world: 97

Child marriage: *women married by age 15:* 2%
women married by age 18: 17.1% (2018 est.)

Education expenditures: 6.7% of GDP (2020 est.)
country comparison to the world: 24

Literacy: *definition:* age 15 and over can read and write
total population: 97.9%
male: 97.8%
female: 97.9% (2018)

School life expectancy (primary to tertiary education): *total:* 17 years
male: 16 years
female: 17 years (2019)

Unemployment, youth ages 15-24: *total:* 40.7%
male: 34%
female: 50.9% (2020 est.)

ENVIRONMENT

Environment - current issues: deforestation and land use change, largely a result of the clearing of land for cattle ranching and agriculture; soil erosion; coastal marine pollution; fisheries protection; solid waste management; air pollution

Environment - international agreements: *party to:* Biodiversity, Climate Change, Climate Change-Kyoto Protocol, Climate Change-Paris Agreement, Comprehensive Nuclear Test Ban, Desertification, Endangered Species, Environmental Modification, Hazardous Wastes, Law of the Sea, Marine Dumping-London Convention, Nuclear Test Ban, Ozone Layer Protection, Tropical Timber 2006, Wetlands, Whaling
signed, but not ratified: Marine Life Conservation

Air pollutants: *particulate matter emissions:* 15.85 micrograms per cubic meter (2016 est.)
carbon dioxide emissions: 8.02 megatons (2016 est.)
methane emissions: 5.61 megatons (2020 est.)

Climate: tropical and subtropical; dry season (December to April); rainy season (May to November); cooler in highlands

Land use: *agricultural land:* 37.1% (2018 est.)
arable land: 4.9% (2018 est.)
permanent crops: 6.7% (2018 est.)
permanent pasture: 25.5% (2018 est.)
forest: 51.5% (2018 est.)
other: 11.4% (2018 est.)

Urbanization: *urban population:* 82% of total population (2022)
rate of urbanization: 1.5% annual rate of change (2020-25 est.)

Revenue from forest resources: *forest revenues:* 0.82% of GDP (2018 est.)
country comparison to the world: 58

Revenue from coal: *coal revenues:* 0% of GDP (2018 est.)
country comparison to the world: 82

Waste and recycling: *municipal solid waste generated annually:* 1.46 million tons (2014 est.)
municipal solid waste recycled annually: 18,396 tons (2014 est.)
percent of municipal solid waste recycled: 1.3% (2014 est.)

Total water withdrawal: *municipal:* 652 million cubic meters (2017 est.)
industrial: 240 million cubic meters (2017 est.)
agricultural: 2.302 billion cubic meters (2017 est.)

Total renewable water resources: 113 billion cubic meters (2017 est.)

GOVERNMENT

Country name: *conventional long form:* Republic of Costa Rica
conventional short form: Costa Rica
local long form: Republica de Costa Rica
local short form: Costa Rica
etymology: the name means "rich coast" in Spanish and was first applied in the early colonial period of the 16th century

Government type: presidential republic

Capital: *name:* San Jose
geographic coordinates: 9 56 N, 84 05 W
time difference: UTC-6 (1 hour behind Washington, DC, during Standard Time)
etymology: named in honor of Saint Joseph

Administrative divisions: 7 provinces (provincias, singular - provincia); Alajuela, Cartago, Guanacaste, Heredia, Limon, Puntarenas, San Jose

Independence: 15 September 1821 (from Spain)

National holiday: Independence Day, 15 September (1821)

Constitution: *history:* many previous; latest effective 8 November 1949
amendments: proposals require the signatures of at least 10 Legislative Assembly members or petition of at least 5% of qualified voters; consideration of proposals requires two-thirds majority approval in each of three readings by the Assembly, followed by preparation of the proposal as a legislative bill and its approval by simple majority of the Assembly; passage requires at least two-thirds majority vote of the Assembly membership; a referendum is required only if approved by at least two thirds of the Assembly; amended many times, last in 2020

Legal system: civil law system based on Spanish civil code; judicial review of legislative acts in the Supreme Court

International law organization participation: accepts compulsory ICJ jurisdiction; accepts ICCt jurisdiction

Citizenship: *citizenship by birth:* yes
citizenship by descent only: yes
dual citizenship recognized: yes
residency requirement for naturalization: 7 years

Suffrage: 18 years of age; universal and compulsory

Executive branch: *chief of state:* President Rodrigo CHAVES Robles (since 8 May 2022); First Vice President Stephan BRUNNER Neibig (since 8 May 2022); Second Vice President Mary Denisse MUNIVE Angermuller (since 8 May 2022); note - the president is both chief of state and head of government
head of government: President Rodrigo CHAVES Robles (since 8 May 2022); First Vice President Stephan BRUNNER Neibig (since 8 May 2022); Second Vice President Mary Denisse MUNIVE Angermuller (since 8 May 2022)
cabinet: Cabinet selected by the president
elections/appointments: president and vice presidents directly elected on the same ballot by modified majority popular vote (40% threshold) for a 4-year term (eligible for non-consecutive terms); election last held on 6 February 2022 with a runoff on 3 April 2022 (next to be held in February 2026 with a runoff in April 2026)
election results:
2022: Rodrigo CHAVES Robles elected president in second round; percent of vote in first round - Jose Maria FIGUERES Olsen (PLN) 27.3%, Rodrigo CHAVES Robles (PPSD) 16.8%, Fabricio ALVARADO Munoz (PNR) 14.9%, Eliecer FEINZAIG Mintz (PLP) 12.4%, Lineth SABORIO Chaverri (PUSC) 12.4%, Jose Maria VILLALTA Florez-Estrada 8.7% (PFA), other 7.5%; percent of vote in second round - Rodrigo CHAVES Robles (PPSD) 52.8%, Jose Maria FIGUERES Olsen (PLN) 47.2%
2018: Carlos ALVARADO Quesada elected president in second round; percent of vote in first round - Fabricio ALVARADO Munoz (PRN) 25%; Carlos ALVARADO Quesada (PAC) 21.6%; Antonio ALVAREZ (PLN) 18.6%; Rodolfo PIZA (PUSC) 16%; Juan Diego CASTRO (PIN) 9.5%; Rodolfo HERNANDEZ (PRS) 4.9%, other 4.4%; percent of vote in second round - Carlos ALVARADO Quesada (PAC) 60.7%; Fabricio ALVARADO Munoz (PRN) 39.3%

Legislative branch: *description:* unicameral Legislative Assembly or Asamblea Legislativa (57 seats; members directly elected in multi-seat constituencies - corresponding to the country's 7 provinces - by closed party-list proportional representation vote; members serve 4-year terms)
elections:
last held on 6 February 2022 (next to be held in February 2026)
election results:
percent of vote by party - PLN 24.8%, PPSD 15%, PUSC 11.4%, PNR 10.1%, PLP 9.1%, 8.3%, other 21.3%; seats by party - PLN 19, PPSD 10, PUSC 9, PNR 7, PLP 6, PFA 6; composition - men 30, women 27, percent of women 47.4%

Judicial branch: *highest court(s):* Supreme Court of Justice (consists of 22 judges organized into 3 cassation chambers each with 5 judges and the Constitutional Chamber with 7 judges)
judge selection and term of office: Supreme Court of Justice judges elected by the National Assembly for 8-year terms with renewal decided by the National Assembly
subordinate courts: appellate courts; trial courts; first instance and justice of the peace courts; Superior Electoral Tribunal

Political parties and leaders: Accessibility Without Exclusion or PASE [Oscar Andres LOPEZ Arias]
Broad Front (Frente Amplio) or PFA [Ana Patricia MORA Castellanos]
Christian Democratic Alliance or ADC [Mario REDONDO Poveda]
Citizen Action Party or PAC [Marta Eugenia SOLANO Arias]
Costa Rican Renewal Party or PRC [Justo OROZCO Alvarez]
Liberal Progressive Party or PLP [Eliecer FEINZAIG Mintz]
Libertarian Movement Party or ML [Victor Danilo CUBERO Corrales]
National Integration Party or PIN [Walter MUNOZ Cespedes]
National Liberation Party or PLN [Kattia RIVERA Soto]
National Restoration Party or PRN [Carlos Luis AVENDANO Calvo]
New Generation or PNG [Rodolfo SOLIS Herrera]
New Republic Party or PNR [Francisco Javier PRENDAS Rodriguez]
Patriotic Alliance [Jorge ARAYA Westover]
Social Christian Republican Party or PRS [Otto ROBERTO Vargas]
Social Christian Unity Party or PUSC of UNIDAD [Randall QUIROS Bustamante]
Social Democratic Progress Party or PPSD [Luz Mary ALPIZAR Loaiza]

International organization participation: BCIE, CACM, CD, CELAC, FAO, G-77, IADB, IAEA, IBRD, ICAO, ICC (national committees), ICCt, ICRM, IDA, IFAD, IFC, IFRCS, ILO, IMF, IMO, IMSO, Interpol, IOC, IOM, IPU, ISO, ITSO, ITU, ITUC (NGOs), LAES, LAIA (observer), MIGA, NAM (observer), OAS, OIF (observer), OPANAL, OPCW, Pacific Alliance (observer), PCA, SICA, UN, UNCTAD, UNESCO, UNHCR, UNIDO, Union Latina, UNWTO, UPU, WCO, WFTU (NGOs), WHO, WIPO, WMO, WTO

Diplomatic representation in the US: *chief of mission:* Ambassador Fernando LLORCA Castro (since 17 September 2018)
chancery: 2114 S Street NW, Washington, DC 20008
telephone: [1] (202) 499-2984
FAX: [1] (202) 265-4795
email address and website:
embcr-us@rree.go.cr
http://www.costarica-embassy.org/index.php?q=node/21
consulate(s) general: Atlanta, Chicago, Houston, Los Angeles, Miami, New York, Washington DC
honorary consulate(s): San Juan (Puerto Rico), Saint Paul (MN), Tucson (AZ)

Diplomatic representation from the US: *chief of mission:* Ambassador Cynthia A. TELLES (since 11 March 2022)
embassy: Calle 98 Via 104, Pavas, San Jose
mailing address: 3180 St. George's Place, Washington DC 20521-3180
telephone: [506] 2519-2000
FAX: [506] 2519-2305
email address and website:
acssanjose@state.gov
https://cr.usembassy.gov/

Flag description: five horizontal bands of blue (top), white, red (double width), white, and blue, with the coat of arms in a white elliptical disk placed toward the hoist side of the red band; Costa Rica retained the earlier blue-white-blue flag of Central America until 1848 when, in response to revolutionary activity in Europe, it was decided to incorporate the French colors into the national flag and a central red stripe was added; today the blue color is said to stand for the sky, opportunity, and perseverance, white denotes peace, happiness, and wisdom, while red represents the blood shed for freedom, as well as the generosity and vibrancy of the people
note: somewhat resembles the flag of North Korea; similar to the flag of Thailand but with the blue and red colors reversed

National symbol(s): yiguirro (clay-colored robin); national colors: blue, white, red

National anthem: *name:* "Himno Nacional de Costa Rica" (National Anthem of Costa Rica)
lyrics/music: Jose Maria ZELEDON Brenes/Manuel Maria GUTIERREZ
note: adopted 1949; the anthem's music was originally written for an 1853 welcome ceremony for diplomatic missions from the US and UK; the lyrics were added in 1903

National heritage: *total World Heritage Sites:* 4 (1 cultural, 3 natural)
selected World Heritage Site locales: Guanacaste Conservation Area (n); Cocos Island National Park (n); Precolumbian Stone Spheres (c); La Amistad International Park (n)

ECONOMY

Economic overview: Since 2010, Costa Rica has enjoyed strong and stable economic growth - 3.8% in 2017. Exports of bananas, coffee, sugar, and beef are the backbone of its commodity exports. Various industrial and processed agricultural products have broadened exports in recent years, as have high value-added goods, including medical devices. Costa Rica's impressive biodiversity also makes it a key destination for ecotourism.

Foreign investors remain attracted by the country's political stability and relatively high education levels, as well as the incentives offered in the free-trade zones; Costa Rica has attracted one of the highest levels of foreign direct investment per capita in Latin America. The US-Central American-Dominican Republic Free Trade Agreement (CAFTA-DR), which became effective for Costa Rica in 2009, helped increase foreign direct investment in key sectors of the economy, including insurance and telecommunication. However, poor infrastructure, high energy costs, a complex bureaucracy, weak investor protection, and uncertainty of contract enforcement impede greater investment.

Costa Rica's economy also faces challenges due to a rising fiscal deficit, rising public debt, and relatively low levels of domestic revenue. Poverty has remained around 20-25% for nearly 20 years, and the government's strong social safety net has eroded due to increased constraints on its expenditures. Costa Rica's credit rating was downgraded from stable to negative in 2015 and again in 2017, upping pressure on lending rates - which could hurt small business, on the budget deficit - which could hurt infrastructure development, and on the rate of return on investment - which could soften foreign direct investment (FDI). Unlike the rest of Central America, Costa Rica is not highly dependent on remittances - which represented just 1 % of GDP in 2016, but instead relies on FDI -which accounted for 5.1% of GDP.

Real GDP (purchasing power parity): $100.25 billion (2020 est.)
$105.02 billion (2019 est.)

$102.79 billion (2018 est.)
note: data are in 2017 dollars
country comparison to the world: 88

Real GDP growth rate: 3.3% (2017 est.)
4.2% (2016 est.)
3.6% (2015 est.)
country comparison to the world: 90

Real GDP per capita: $19,700 (2020 est.)
$20,800 (2019 est.)
$20,600 (2018 est.)
note: data are in 2017 dollars
country comparison to the world: 87

GDP (official exchange rate): $61.855 billion (2019 est.)

Inflation rate (consumer prices): 2% (2019 est.)
2.2% (2018 est.)
1.6% (2017 est.)
country comparison to the world: 110

Credit ratings:

Fitch rating: B (2020)

Moody's rating: B2 (2020)

Standard & Poors rating: B (2020)
note: The year refers to the year in which the current credit rating was first obtained.

GDP - composition, by sector of origin: *agriculture:* 5.5% (2017 est.)
industry: 20.6% (2017 est.)
services: 73.9% (2017 est.)

GDP - composition, by end use: *household consumption:* 64.2% (2017 est.)
government consumption: 17.3% (2017 est.)
investment in fixed capital: 17.1% (2017 est.)
investment in inventories: 1% (2017 est.)
exports of goods and services: 33.3% (2017 est.)
imports of goods and services: -32.9% (2017 est.)

Agricultural products: sugar cane, pineapples, bananas, milk, oil palm fruit, fruit, oranges, watermelons, cassava, rice

Industries: medical equipment, food processing, textiles and clothing, construction materials, fertilizer, plastic products

Industrial production growth rate: 1.3% (2017 est.)
country comparison to the world: 147

Labor force: 1.843 million (2020 est.)
note: official estimate; excludes Nicaraguans living in Costa Rica
country comparison to the world: 123

Labor force - by occupation: *agriculture:* 14%
industry: 22%
services: 64% (2006 est.)

Unemployment rate: 8.1% (2017 est.)
9.5% (2016 est.)
country comparison to the world: 127

Unemployment, youth ages 15-24: *total:* 40.7%
male: 34%
female: 50.9% (2020 est.)
country comparison to the world: 11

Population below poverty line: 21% (2019 est.)

Gini Index coefficient - distribution of family income: 48 (2018 est.)
49.2 (2013)
country comparison to the world: 19

Household income or consumption by percentage share: *lowest 10%:* 1.5%
highest 10%: 36.9% (2014 est.)

Budget: *revenues:* 8.357 billion (2017 est.)
expenditures: 11.92 billion (2017 est.)

Budget surplus (+) or deficit (-): -6.1% (of GDP) (2017 est.)
country comparison to the world: 185

Public debt: 48.9% of GDP (2017 est.)
44.9% of GDP (2016 est.)
country comparison to the world: 105

Taxes and other revenues: 14.3% (of GDP) (2017 est.)
country comparison to the world: 200

Fiscal year: calendar year

Current account balance: -$1.692 billion (2017 est.)
-$1.326 billion (2016 est.)
country comparison to the world: 163

Exports: $21.2 billion (2019 est.)
$20.53 billion (2018 est.)
note: Data are in current year dollars and do not include illicit exports or re-exports.
country comparison to the world: 79

Exports - partners: United States 38%, Netherlands 6%, Belgium 5%, Guatemala 5%, Panama 5% (2019)

Exports - commodities: medical instruments, bananas, tropical fruits, orthopedic appliances, food preparations (2019)

Imports: $19.39 billion (2019 est.) note: data are in current year dollars
$19.64 billion (2018 est.) note: data are in current year dollars
country comparison to the world: 86

Imports - partners: United States 41%, China 13%, Mexico 7% (2019)

Imports - commodities: refined petroleum, broadcasting equipment, cars, medical instruments, packaged medicines (2019)

Reserves of foreign exchange and gold: $7.15 billion (31 December 2017 est.)
$7.574 billion (31 December 2016 est.)
country comparison to the world: 86

Debt - external: $29.589 billion (2019 est.)
$28.553 billion (2018 est.)
country comparison to the world: 85

Exchange rates: Costa Rican colones (CRC) per US dollar -
573.5 (2017 est.)
544.74 (2016 est.)
544.74 (2015 est.)
534.57 (2014 est.)
538.32 (2013 est.)

ENERGY

Electricity access: *electrification - total population:* 100% (2020)

Electricity: *installed generating capacity:* 3.674 million kW (2020 est.)
consumption: 10,072,472,000 kWh (2019 est.)
exports: 712 million kWh (2019 est.)
imports: 733 million kWh (2019 est.)
transmission/distribution losses: 1,321,498,000 kWh (2019 est.)

Electricity generation sources: *fossil fuels:* 0.2% of total installed capacity (2020 est.)
solar: 0.6% of total installed capacity (2020 est.)
wind: 12.5% of total installed capacity (2020 est.)
hydroelectricity: 71.1% of total installed capacity (2020 est.)
geothermal: 14.5% of total installed capacity (2020 est.)
biomass and waste: 1.2% of total installed capacity (2020 est.)

Petroleum: *total petroleum production:* 400 bbl/day (2021 est.)
refined petroleum consumption: 63,300 bbl/day (2019 est.)

Refined petroleum products - imports: 51,320 bbl/day (2015 est.)
country comparison to the world: 80

Carbon dioxide emissions: 8.115 million metric tonnes of CO2 (2019 est.)
from coal and metallurgical coke: 1,000 metric tonnes of CO2 (2019 est.)
from petroleum and other liquids: 8.114 million metric tonnes of CO2 (2019 est.)
country comparison to the world: 111

Energy consumption per capita: 44.899 million Btu/person (2019 est.)
country comparison to the world: 103

COMMUNICATIONS

Telephones - fixed lines: *total subscriptions:* 559,882 (2020 est.)
subscriptions per 100 inhabitants: 11 (2020 est.)
country comparison to the world: 90

Telephones - mobile cellular: *total subscriptions:* 7,512,370 (2020 est.)
subscriptions per 100 inhabitants: 147 (2020 est.)
country comparison to the world: 100

Telecommunication systems: *general assessment:* the fixed broadband market is one of the few parts of Costa Rica's telecom sector to experience solid growth in recent years, both in size and revenue; the country's fiber network expanded by 56% in 2020, reaching about 176,200km; fixed-line broadband traffic volume also increased by more than 30%, year-on-year; other areas of the market have proven relatively lack luster, with slow or even negative growth; some of this can be attributed to the economic and social impacts of the pandemic, but the fixed-line and mobile sectors have both been struggling to produce decent results since well before the start of the crisis; the rollout of 5G network infrastructure in Costa Rica is unlikely to occur to any scale before 2023, but this may be one of the few remaining areas of opportunity open to investors outside of fixed-line internet and pay TV services (2021)
domestic: roughly 11 per 100 fixed-line and 148 per 100 mobile-cellular; point-to-point and point-to-multi-point microwave, fiber-optic, and coaxial cable link rural areas; Internet service is available (2020)
international: country code - 506; landing points for the ARCOS-1, MAYA-1, and the PAC submarine cables that provide links to South and Central America, parts of the Caribbean, and the US; connected to Central American Microwave System; satellite earth stations - 2 Intelsat (Atlantic Ocean) (2019)

Broadcast media: over two dozen privately owned TV stations and 1 publicly owned TV station nationwide; cable network services are widely available; more than 100 privately owned radio stations and a public radio network (2022)

Internet country code: .cr

Internet users: *total:* 4,126,232 (2020 est.)
percent of population: 81% (2020 est.)
country comparison to the world: 100

Broadband - fixed subscriptions: *total:* 992,725 (2020 est.)

subscriptions per 100 inhabitants: 20 (2020 est.)
country comparison to the world: 74

TRANSPORTATION

National air transport system: *number of registered air carriers:* 1 (2020)
inventory of registered aircraft operated by air carriers: 39
annual passenger traffic on registered air carriers: 1,948,546 (2018)
annual freight traffic on registered air carriers: 11.13 million (2018) mt-km

Civil aircraft registration country code prefix: TI

Airports: *total:* 161 (2021)
country comparison to the world: 34

Airports - with paved runways: *total:* 47
2,438 to 3,047 m: 2
1,524 to 2,437 m: 2
914 to 1,523 m: 27
under 914 m: 16 (2021)

Airports - with unpaved runways: *total:* 114
914 to 1,523 m: 18
under 914 m: 96 (2021)

Pipelines: 662 km refined products (2013)

Railways: *total:* 278 km (2014)
narrow gauge: 278 km (2014) 1.067-m gauge
note: the entire rail network fell into disrepair and out of use at the end of the 20th century; since 2005, certain sections of rail have been rehabilitated
country comparison to the world: 123

Roadways: *total:* 5,035 km (2017)
country comparison to the world: 147

Waterways: 730 km (2011) (seasonally navigable by small craft)
country comparison to the world: 80

Merchant marine: *total:* 11
by type: other 11 (2021)
country comparison to the world: 154

Ports and terminals: *major seaport(s):* Atlantic Ocean (Caribbean) - Puerto Limon
Pacific Ocean - Caldera

MILITARY AND SECURITY

Military and security forces: no regular military forces; Ministry of Public Security: the Public Force (Fuerza Pública (National Police)), Air Surveillance Service (Servicio de Vigilancia Aérea), National Coast Guard Service (Servicio Nacional de Guardacostas), Border Police (Policia de Fronteras); Ministry of Presidency: Directorate of Intelligence and Security (DIS), Special Intervention Unit (UEI) (2022)
note: Costa Rica's armed forces were constitutionally abolished in 1949

Military expenditures: 0.7% of GDP (2021 est.)
0.7% of GDP (2020 est.)
0.7% of GDP (2019) (approximately $630 million)
0.7% of GDP (2018) (approximately $610 million)
0.7% of GDP (2017) (approximately $600 million)
country comparison to the world: 149

Military and security service personnel strengths: 12,500 Public Force personnel; approximately 500-600 Air, 500-600 Coast Guard, and 300-400 Border Police personnel (2022)

Military equipment inventories and acquisitions: the Public Force is lightly armed with an inventory that includes mostly second-hand US equipment (2022)

Military - note: Costa Rica relies on specialized paramilitary units within the Ministry of Public Security (MPS) for internal security missions and countering transnational threats such as narcotics smuggling and organized crime, as well as for participating in regional security operations and exercises; MPS forces have received advisory and training support from both Colombia and the US; since 2012, the US has also provided some military equipment, including aircraft and patrol boats (2022)

TRANSNATIONAL ISSUES

Disputes - international: Costa Rica and Nicaragua regularly file border dispute cases over the delimitations of the San Juan River and the northern tip of Calero Island to the International Court of Justice (ICJ); in 2009, the ICJ ruled that Costa Rican vessels carrying out police activities could not use the river, but official Costa Rican vessels providing essential services to riverside inhabitants and Costa Rican tourists could travel freely on the river; in 2011, the ICJ provisionally ruled that both countries must remove personnel from the disputed area; in 2013, the ICJ rejected Nicaragua's 2012 suit to halt Costa Rica's construction of a highway paralleling the river on the grounds of irreparable environmental damage; in 2013, the ICJ, regarding the disputed territory, ordered that Nicaragua should refrain from dredging or canal construction and refill and repair damage caused by trenches connecting the river to the Caribbean and upheld its 2010 ruling that Nicaragua must remove all personnel; in early 2014, Costa Rica brought Nicaragua to the ICJ over offshore oil concessions in the disputed region

Refugees and internally displaced persons: *refugees (country of origin):* 29,906 (Venezuela) (economic and political crisis; includes Venezuelans who have claimed asylum, are recognized as refugees, or received alternative legal stay) (2021)
stateless persons: 205 (mid-year 2021)

Illicit drugs: significant transit country for drugs entering the United States; a growing drug consumption problem; drugs warehoused in Costa Rica end up in the local market where criminal organizations use cocaine as payment for services.

COTE D'IVOIRE

INTRODUCTION

Background: Various small kingdoms ruled the area of Cote d'Ivoire between the 15th and 19th centuries, when European explorers arrived and then began to expand their presence. In 1844, France established a protectorate. During this period, many of these kingdoms and tribes fought to maintain their cultural identities - some well into the 20th century. For example, the Sanwi kingdom - originally founded in the 17th century - tried to break away from Cote d'Ivoire and establish an independent state in 1969.

Cote d'Ivoire achieved independence from France in 1960 but has maintained close ties with France. The export and production of cocoa and foreign investment drove economic growth that led Cote d'Ivoire to become one of the most prosperous states in West Africa. In December 1999, a military coup overthrew the government. In late 2000, junta leader Robert GUEI held rigged elections and declared himself the winner. Popular protests forced him to step aside, and Laurent GBAGBO was elected. In September 2002, Ivoirian dissidents and members of the military launched a failed coup that developed into a civil war. In 2003, a cease-fire resulted in rebels holding the north, the government holding the south, and peacekeeping forces occupying a buffer zone in the middle. In March 2007, President GBAGBO and former rebel leader Guillaume SORO signed an agreement in which SORO joined GBAGBO's government as prime minister. The two agreed to reunite the country by dismantling the buffer zone, integrating rebel forces into the national armed forces, and holding elections. In November 2010, Alassane Dramane OUATTARA won the presidential election, but GBAGBO refused to hand over power, resulting in five months of violent conflict. In April 2011, after widespread fighting, GBAGBO was formally forced from office by armed OUATTARA supporters and UN and French forces. In 2015, OUATTARA won a second term. In October 2020, OUATTARA won a controversial third presidential term, despite a two-term limit in the Ivoirian constitution, in an election boycotted by the opposition. Through political compromise with OUATTARA, the opposition did participate peacefully in March 2021 legislative elections and won a substantial minority of seats. Also in March 2021, the International Criminal Court in The Hague ruled on a final acquittal for GBAGBO, who was on trial for crimes against humanity, paving the way for GBAGBO's June 2021 return to Abidjan. GBAGBO has publicly met with President OUATTARA since his return in June 2021 as a demonstration of political reconciliation. The next presidential election is scheduled for 2025.

GEOGRAPHY

Location: Western Africa, bordering the North Atlantic Ocean, between Ghana and Liberia

Geographic coordinates: 8 00 N, 5 00 W

Map references: Africa

Area: *total:* 322,463 sq km
land: 318,003 sq km
water: 4,460 sq km

Area - comparative: slightly larger than New Mexico

Land boundaries: *total:* 3,458 km
border countries (5): Burkina Faso 545 km; Ghana 720 km; Guinea 816 km; Liberia 778 km; Mali 599 km

Coastline: 515 km

Maritime claims: *territorial sea:* 12 nm
exclusive economic zone: 200 nm
continental shelf: 200 nm

Climate: tropical along coast, semiarid in far north; three seasons - warm and dry (November to March), hot and dry (March to May), hot and wet (June to October)

Terrain: mostly flat to undulating plains; mountains in northwest

Elevation: *highest point:* Monts Nimba 1,752 m
lowest point: Gulf of Guinea 0 m
mean elevation: 250 m

Natural resources: petroleum, natural gas, diamonds, manganese, iron ore, cobalt, bauxite, copper, gold, nickel, tantalum, silica sand, clay, cocoa beans, coffee, palm oil, hydropower

Land use: *agricultural land:* 64.8% (2018 est.)
arable land: 9.1% (2018 est.)
permanent crops: 14.2% (2018 est.)
permanent pasture: 41.5% (2018 est.)
forest: 32.7% (2018 est.)
other: 2.5% (2018 est.)

Irrigated land: 730 sq km (2012)

Major lakes (area sq km): *salt water lake(s):* Lagune Aby - 780 sq km

Major watersheds (area sq km): Atlantic Ocean drainage: Niger (2,261,741 sq km), Volta (410,991 sq km)

Population distribution: the population is primarily located in the forested south, with the highest concentration of people residing in and around the cities on the Atlantic coast; most of the northern savanna remains sparsely populated with higher concentrations located along transportation corridors as shown in this population distribution map

Natural hazards: coast has heavy surf and no natural harbors; during the rainy season torrential flooding is possible

Geography - note: most of the inhabitants live along the sandy coastal region; apart from the capital area, the forested interior is sparsely populated

PEOPLE AND SOCIETY

Population: 28,713,423 (2022 est.)

Nationality: *noun:* Ivoirian(s)
adjective: Ivoirian

Ethnic groups: Akan 28.9%, Voltaique or Gur 16.1%, Northern Mande 14.5%, Kru 8.5%, Southern Mande 6.9%, unspecified 0.9%, non-Ivoirian 24.2% (2014 est.)

Languages: French (official), 60 native dialects of which Dioula is the most widely spoken
major-language sample(s):
The World Factbook, une source indispensable d'informations de base. (French)

Religions: Muslim 42.9%, Catholic 17.2%, Evangelical 11.8%, Methodist 1.7%, other Christian 3.2%, animist 3.6%, other religion 0.5%, none 19.1% (2014 est.)
note: the majority of foreign migrant workers are Muslim (72.7%) and Christian (17.7%)

Demographic profile: Cote d'Ivoire's population is likely to continue growing for the foreseeable future because almost 60% of the populace is younger than 25, the total fertility rate is holding steady at about 3.5 children per woman, and contraceptive use is under 20%. The country will need to improve education, health care, and gender equality in order to turn its large and growing youth cohort into human capital. Even prior to 2010 unrest that shuttered schools for months, access to education was poor, especially for women. The lack of educational attainment contributes to Cote d'Ivoire's high rates of unskilled labor, adolescent pregnancy, and HIV/AIDS prevalence.

Following its independence in 1960, Cote d'Ivoire's stability and the blossoming of its labor-intensive cocoa and coffee industries in the southwest made it an attractive destination for migrants from other parts of the country and its neighbors, particularly Burkina Faso. The HOUPHOUET-BOIGNY administration continued the French colonial policy of encouraging labor immigration by offering liberal land ownership laws. Foreigners from West Africa, Europe (mainly France), and Lebanon composed about 25% of the population by 1998.

Ongoing economic decline since the 1980s and the power struggle after HOUPHOUET-BOIGNY's death in 1993 ushered in the politics of "Ivoirite," institutionalizing an Ivoirian identity that further marginalized northern Ivoirians and scapegoated immigrants. The hostile Muslim north-Christian south divide snowballed into a 2002 civil war, pushing tens of thousands of foreign migrants, Liberian refugees, and Ivoirians to flee to war-torn Liberia or other regional countries and more than a million people to be internally displaced. Subsequently, violence following the contested 2010 presidential election prompted some 250,000 people to seek refuge in Liberia and other neighboring countries and again internally displaced as many as a million people. By July 2012, the majority had returned home, but ongoing inter-communal tension and armed conflict continue to force people from their homes.

Age structure: *0-14 years:* 38.53% (male 5,311,971/female 5,276,219)
15-24 years: 20.21% (male 2,774,374/female 2,779,012)
25-54 years: 34.88% (male 4,866,957/female 4,719,286)
55-64 years: 3.53% (male 494,000/female 476,060)
65 years and over: 2.85% (male 349,822/female 433,385) (2020 est.)

Dependency ratios: *total dependency ratio:* 79.8
youth dependency ratio: 74.6
elderly dependency ratio: 5.2
potential support ratio: 19.3 (2020 est.)

Median age: *total:* 20.3 years
male: 20.3 years
female: 20.3 years (2020 est.)

Population growth rate: 2.19% (2022 est.)

Birth rate: 28.3 births/1,000 population (2022 est.)

Death rate: 7.6 deaths/1,000 population (2022 est.)

Net migration rate: 1.18 migrant(s)/1,000 population (2022 est.)

Population distribution: the population is primarily located in the forested south, with the highest concentration of people residing in and around the cities on the Atlantic coast; most of the northern savanna remains sparsely populated with higher concentrations located along transportation corridors as shown in this population distribution map

Urbanization: *urban population:* 52.7% of total population (2022)
rate of urbanization: 3.38% annual rate of change (2020-25 est.)

Major urban areas - population: 231,000 YAMOUSSOUKRO (capital) (2018), 5.516 million ABIDJAN (seat of government) (2022)

Sex ratio: *at birth:* 1.03 male(s)/female
0-14 years: 1.06 male(s)/female
15-24 years: 1.07 male(s)/female
25-54 years: 1.06 male(s)/female
55-64 years: 0.97 male(s)/female
65 years and over: 0.58 male(s)/female
total population: 0.97 male(s)/female (2022 est.)

Mother's mean age at first birth: 19.6 years (2011/12 est.)
note: data represents median age at first birth among women 20-49

Maternal mortality ratio: 617 deaths/100,000 live births (2017 est.)

Infant mortality rate: *total:* 55.67 deaths/1,000 live births
male: 62.99 deaths/1,000 live births
female: 48.13 deaths/1,000 live births (2022 est.)

Life expectancy at birth: *total population:* 62.26 years
male: 60.07 years
female: 64.52 years (2022 est.)

Total fertility rate: 3.53 children born/woman (2022 est.)

Contraceptive prevalence rate: 27.8% (2020)

Drinking water source: *improved: urban:* 89.9% of population
rural: 69.1% of population
total: 79.8% of population
unimproved: urban: 10.1% of population
rural: 30.9% of population
total: 20.2% of population (2020 est.)

Current health expenditure: 3.3% of GDP (2019)

Physicians density: 0.16 physicians/1,000 population (2019)

Sanitation facility access: *improved: urban:* 77.8% of population
rural: 35% of population
total: 57.1% of population
unimproved: urban: 22.2% of population
rural: 65% of population
total: 42.9% of population (2020 est.)

HIV/AIDS - adult prevalence rate: 2.1% (2020 est.)

Major infectious diseases: *degree of risk:* very high (2020)
food or waterborne diseases: bacterial diarrhea, hepatitis A, and typhoid fever
vectorborne diseases: malaria, dengue fever, and yellow fever
water contact diseases: schistosomiasis
animal contact diseases: rabies
respiratory diseases: meningococcal meningitis

Obesity - adult prevalence rate: 10.3% (2016)

Alcohol consumption per capita: *total:* 1.7 liters of pure alcohol (2019 est.)
beer: 1.13 liters of pure alcohol (2019 est.)
wine: 0.33 liters of pure alcohol (2019 est.)
spirits: 0.2 liters of pure alcohol (2019 est.)
other alcohols: 0.04 liters of pure alcohol (2019 est.)

Tobacco use: *total:* 9.4% (2020 est.)
male: 17.9% (2020 est.)
female: 0.9% (2020 est.)

Children under the age of 5 years underweight: 12.8% (2016)

Child marriage: *women married by age 15:* 7%
women married by age 18: 27%
men married by age 18: 3.5% (2016 est.)

Education expenditures: 3.7% of GDP (2019 est.)

Literacy: *definition:* age 15 and over can read and write
total population: 89.9%
male: 93.1%
female: 86.7% (2019)

School life expectancy (primary to tertiary education): *total:* 10 years
male: 11 years
female: 10 years (2019)

Unemployment, youth ages 15-24: *total:* 5.5%
male: 4.7%
female: 6.5% (2017 est.)

ENVIRONMENT

Environment - current issues: deforestation (most of the country's forests - once the largest in West Africa - have been heavily logged); water pollution from sewage, and from industrial, mining, and agricultural effluents

Environment - international agreements: *party to:* Biodiversity, Climate Change, Climate Change-Kyoto Protocol, Climate Change-Paris Agreement, Comprehensive Nuclear Test Ban, Desertification, Endangered Species, Hazardous Wastes, Law of the Sea, Marine Dumping-London Convention, Nuclear Test Ban, Ozone Layer Protection, Ship Pollution, Tropical Timber 2006, Wetlands, Whaling
signed, but not ratified: none of the selected agreements

Air pollutants: *particulate matter emissions:* 23.72 micrograms per cubic meter (2016 est.)
carbon dioxide emissions: 9.67 megatons (2016 est.)
methane emissions: 10.3 megatons (2020 est.)

Climate: tropical along coast, semiarid in far north; three seasons - warm and dry (November to March), hot and dry (March to May), hot and wet (June to October)

Land use: *agricultural land:* 64.8% (2018 est.)
arable land: 9.1% (2018 est.)
permanent crops: 14.2% (2018 est.)
permanent pasture: 41.5% (2018 est.)
forest: 32.7% (2018 est.)
other: 2.5% (2018 est.)

Urbanization: *urban population:* 52.7% of total population (2022)
rate of urbanization: 3.38% annual rate of change (2020-25 est.)

Revenue from forest resources: *forest revenues:* 2.04% of GDP (2016 est.)

Revenue from coal: *coal revenues:* 0% of GDP (2018 est.)

Waste and recycling: *municipal solid waste generated annually:* 4,440,814 tons (2010 est.)
municipal solid waste recycled annually: 133,224 tons (2005 est.)
percent of municipal solid waste recycled: 3% (2005 est.)

Major lakes (area sq km): *salt water lake(s):* Lagune Aby - 780 sq km

Major watersheds (area sq km): Atlantic Ocean drainage: Niger (2,261,741 sq km), Volta (410,991 sq km)

Total water withdrawal: *municipal:* 320 million cubic meters (2017 est.)
industrial: 242 million cubic meters (2017 est.)
agricultural: 600 million cubic meters (2017 est.)

Total renewable water resources: 84.14 billion cubic meters (2017 est.)

GOVERNMENT

Country name: *conventional long form:* Republic of Cote d'Ivoire
conventional short form: Cote d'Ivoire
local long form: Republique de Cote d'Ivoire
local short form: Cote d'Ivoire
former: Ivory Coast
etymology: name reflects the intense ivory trade that took place in the region from the 15th to 17th centuries
note: pronounced coat-div-whar

Government type: presidential republic

Capital: *name:* Yamoussoukro (legislative capital), Abidjan (administrative capital); note - although Yamoussoukro has been the official capital since 1983, Abidjan remains the administrative capital as well as the officially designated economic capital; the US, like other countries, maintains its Embassy in Abidjan
geographic coordinates: 6 49 N, 5 16 W
time difference: UTC 0 (5 hours ahead of Washington, DC, during Standard Time)
etymology: Yamoussoukro is named after Queen YAMOUSSOU, who ruled in the village of N'Gokro in 1929 at the time of French colonization; the village was renamed Yamoussoukro, the suffix "-kro" meaning "town" in the native Baoule language; Abidjan's name supposedly comes from a misunderstanding; tradition states that an old man carrying branches met a European explorer who asked for the name of the nearest village; the man, not understanding and terrified by this unexpected encounter, fled shouting "min-chan m'bidjan," which in the Ebrie language means: "I return from cutting leaves"; the explorer, thinking that his question had been answered, recorded the name of the locale as Abidjan; a different version has the first colonists asking native women the name of the place and getting a similar response

Administrative divisions: 12 districts and 2 autonomous districts*; Abidjan*, Bas-Sassandra, Comoe, Denguele, Goh-Djiboua, Lacs, Lagunes, Montagnes, Sassandra-Marahoue, Savanes, Vallee du Bandama, Woroba, Yamoussoukro*, Zanzan

Independence: 7 August 1960 (from France)

National holiday: Independence Day, 7 August (1960)

Constitution: *history:* previous 1960, 2000; latest draft completed 24 September 2016, approved by the National Assembly 11 October 2016, approved by referendum 30 October 2016, promulgated 8 November 2016
amendments: proposed by the president of the republic or by Parliament; consideration of drafts or proposals requires an absolute majority vote by the parliamentary membership; passage of amendments affecting presidential elections, presidential term of office and vacancies, and amendment procedures requires approval by absolute majority in a referendum; passage of other proposals by the president requires at least four-fifths majority vote by Parliament; constitutional articles on the sovereignty of the state and its republican and secular form of government cannot be amended; amended 2020

Legal system: civil law system based on the French civil code; judicial review of legislation held in the Constitutional Chamber of the Supreme Court

International law organization participation: accepts compulsory ICJ jurisdiction with reservations; accepts ICCt jurisdiction

Citizenship: *citizenship by birth:* no
citizenship by descent only: at least one parent must be a citizen of Cote d'Ivoire
dual citizenship recognized: no
residency requirement for naturalization: 5 years

Suffrage: 18 years of age; universal

Executive branch: *chief of state:* President Alassane Dramane OUATTARA (since 4 December 2010); Vice President Tiémoko Meyliet KONE (since 19 April 2022); note - Vice President Tiémoko Meyliet KONE was appointed by President Alassane Dramane OUATTARA before a Congressional meeting on 19 April 2022
head of government: Prime Minister Patrick ACHI (since 19 April 2022); note - Prime Minister ACHI resigned on 13 April 2022 and was reappointed by President Alassane Dramane OUATTARA before a Congressional meeting on 19 April 2022
cabinet: Council of Ministers appointed by the president
elections/appointments: president directly elected by absolute majority popular vote in 2 rounds if needed for a single renewable 5-year term ; election last held on 31 October 2020 (next to be held in October 2025); vice president elected on same ballot as president; prime minister appointed by the president; note – because President OUATTARA promulgated the new constitution during his second term, he has claimed that the clock is reset on term limits, allowing him to run for up to two additional terms
election results:
Alassane OUATTARA reelected president; percent of vote - Alassane OUATTARA (RDR) 94.3%, Kouadio Konan BERTIN (PDCI-RDA) 2.0%, other 3.7% (2020)

Legislative branch: *description:* bicameral Parliament consists of:
Senate or Senat (99 seats; 66 members indirectly elected by the National Assembly and members of municipal, autonomous districts, and regional councils, and 33 members appointed by the president; members serve 5-year terms)
National Assembly (255 seats - 254 for 2021-2026 term; members directly elected in single- and multi-seat constituencies by simple majority vote to serve 5-year terms)
elections:
Senate - first ever held on 25 March 2018 (next to be held on 31 March 2023)

National Assembly - last held on 6 March 2021 (next to be held on 31 March 2026)
election results:
Senate - percent by party NA; seats by party - RHDP 50, independent 16; composition - men 80, women 19, percent of women 19.2%
National Assembly - percent of vote by party - RHDP 49.2%, PDCI-RRA-EDS 16.5%, DPIC 6%, TTB 2.1%, IPF 2%, other seats 24.2%; seats by party - RHDP, 137, PDCI-RRA-EDS 50, DPIC 23, EDS 8, TTB 8, IPF 2, independent 26; composition - men 218, women 36, percent of women 14.2%; note - total Parliament percent of women 15.6%

Judicial branch: *highest court(s):* Supreme Court or Cour Supreme (organized into Judicial, Audit, Constitutional, and Administrative Chambers; consists of the court president, 3 vice presidents for the Judicial, Audit, and Administrative chambers, and 9 associate justices or magistrates)
judge selection and term of office: judges nominated by the Superior Council of the Magistrature, a 7-member body consisting of the national president (chairman), 3 "bench" judges, and 3 public prosecutors; judges appointed for life
subordinate courts: Courts of Appeal (organized into civil, criminal, and social chambers); first instance courts; peace courts

Political parties and leaders: African Peoples' Party-Cote d'Ivoire or PPA-CI [Laurent GBAGBO]
Democratic Party of Cote d'Ivoire or PDCI [Henri Konan BEDIE]
Ivorian Popular Front or FPI [Pascal Affi N'GUESSAN]
Liberty and Democracy for the Republic or LIDER [Mamadou KOULIBALY]
Movement of the Future Forces or MFA [Innocent Augustin ANAKY KOBENA]
Pan-African Congress for People's Justice and Equality or COJEP [Charles BLE GOUDE]
Rally of Houphouetists for Democracy and Peace or RHDP [Alassane Dramane OUATTARA]
Rally of the Republicans or RDR [Henriette DIABATE]
Together for Democracy and Sovereignty or EDS [Georges Armand OUEGNIN]
Together to Build (UDPCI, FPI, and allies) [Toikeuse MABRI]
Union for Cote d'Ivoire or UPCI [Gnamien KONAN]
Union for Democracy and Peace in Cote d'Ivoire or UDPCI [Albert Toikeusse MABRI]

International organization participation: ACP, AfDB, AU, ECOWAS, EITI (compliant country), Entente, FAO, FZ, G-24, G-77, IAEA, IBRD, ICAO, ICC, ICCt, ICRM, IDA, IDB, IFAD, IFC, IFRCS, ILO, IMF, IMO, Interpol, IOC, IOM, IPU, ISO, ITSO, ITU, ITUC (NGOs), MIGA, MINUSMA, MONUSCO, NAM, OIC, OIF, OPCW, UN, UNCTAD, UNESCO, UNHCR, UNHRC, UNIDO, Union Latina, UN Security Council (temporary), UNWTO, UPU, WADB (regional), WAEMU, WCO, WFTU (NGOs), WHO, WIPO, WMO, WTO

Diplomatic representation in the US: *chief of mission:* Ambassador Ibrahima TOURE (since 13 January 2022)
chancery: 2424 Massachusetts Avenue NW, Washington, DC 20008
telephone: [1] (202) 797-0300
FAX: [1] (202) 462-9444
email address and website:
info@ambacidc.org
https://ambaciusa.org/#

Diplomatic representation from the US: *chief of mission:* Ambassador Richard K. BELL (since 10 October 2019)
embassy: B.P. 730 Abidjan Cidex 03
mailing address: 2010 Abidjan Place, Washington DC 20521-2010
telephone: [225] 27-22-49-40-00
FAX: [225] 27-22-49-43-23
email address and website:
AbjAmCit@state.gov
https://ci.usembassy.gov/

Flag description: three equal vertical bands of orange (hoist side), white, and green; orange symbolizes the land (savannah) of the north and fertility, white stands for peace and unity, green represents the forests of the south and the hope for a bright future
note: similar to the flag of Ireland, which is longer and has the colors reversed - green (hoist side), white, and orange; also similar to the flag of Italy, which is green (hoist side), white, and red; design was based on the flag of France

National symbol(s): elephant; national colors: orange, white, green

National anthem: *name:* "L'Abidjanaise" (Song of Abidjan)
lyrics/music: Mathieu EKRA, Joachim BONY, and Pierre Marie COTY/Pierre Marie COTY and Pierre Michel PANGO
note: adopted 1960; although the nation's capital city moved from Abidjan to Yamoussoukro in 1983, the anthem still owes its name to the former capital

National heritage: *total World Heritage Sites:* 5 (2 cultural, 3 natural)
selected World Heritage Site locales: Comoé National Park (n); Historic Grand-Bassam (c); Mount Nimba Strict Nature Reserve (n); Sudanese-style Mosques (c); Taï National Park (n)

ECONOMY

Economic overview: For the last 5 years Cote d'Ivoire's growth rate has been among the highest in the world. Cote d'Ivoire is heavily dependent on agriculture and related activities, which engage roughly two-thirds of the population. Cote d'Ivoire is the world's largest producer and exporter of cocoa beans and a significant producer and exporter of coffee and palm oil. Consequently, the economy is highly sensitive to fluctuations in international prices for these products and to climatic conditions. Cocoa, oil, and coffee are the country's top export revenue earners, but the country has targeted agricultural processing of cocoa, cashews, mangoes, and other commodities as a high priority. Mining gold and exporting electricity are growing industries outside agriculture.
Following the end of more than a decade of civil conflict in 2011, Cote d'Ivoire has experienced a boom in foreign investment and economic growth. In June 2012, the IMF and the World Bank announced $4.4 billion in debt relief for Cote d'Ivoire under the Highly Indebted Poor Countries Initiative.

Real GDP (purchasing power parity): $136.48 billion (2020 est.)
$134.05 billion (2019 est.)
$126.19 billion (2018 est.)
note: data are in 2017 dollars

Real GDP growth rate: 7.8% (2017 est.)
8.3% (2016 est.)
8.8% (2015 est.)

Real GDP per capita: $5,200 (2020 est.)
$5,200 (2019 est.)
$5,000 (2018 est.)
note: data are in 2017 dollars

GDP (official exchange rate): $42.498 billion (2018 est.)

Inflation rate (consumer prices): -1.1% (2019 est.)
0.3% (2018 est.)
0.6% (2017 est.)

Credit ratings:

Fitch rating: B+ (2015)

Moody's rating: Ba3 (2015)
note: The year refers to the year in which the current credit rating was first obtained.

GDP - composition, by sector of origin: *agriculture:* 20.1% (2017 est.)
industry: 26.6% (2017 est.)
services: 53.3% (2017 est.)

GDP - composition, by end use: *household consumption:* 61.7% (2017 est.)
government consumption: 14.9% (2017 est.)
investment in fixed capital: 22.4% (2017 est.)
investment in inventories: 0.3% (2017 est.)
exports of goods and services: 30.8% (2017 est.)
imports of goods and services: -30.1% (2017 est.)

Agricultural products: yams, cassava, cocoa, oil palm fruit, sugar cane, rice, plantains, maize, cashew nuts, rubber

Industries: foodstuffs, beverages; wood products, oil refining, gold mining, truck and bus assembly, textiles, fertilizer, building materials, electricity

Industrial production growth rate: 4.2% (2017 est.)

Labor force: 8.747 million (2017 est.)

Labor force - by occupation: *agriculture:* 68% (2007 est.)

Unemployment rate: 9.4% (2013 est.)

Unemployment, youth ages 15-24: *total:* 5.5%
male: 4.7%
female: 6.5% (2017 est.)

Population below poverty line: 39.5% (2018 est.)

Gini Index coefficient - distribution of family income: 41.5 (2015 est.)
36.7 (1995)

Household income or consumption by percentage share: *lowest 10%:* 2.2%
highest 10%: 31.8% (2008)

Budget: *revenues:* 7.749 billion (2017 est.)
expenditures: 9.464 billion (2017 est.)

Budget surplus (+) or deficit (-): -4.2% (of GDP) (2017 est.)

Public debt: 47% of GDP (2017 est.)
47% of GDP (2016 est.)

Taxes and other revenues: 19.1% (of GDP) (2017 est.)

Fiscal year: calendar year

Current account balance: -$1.86 billion (2017 est.)
-$414 million (2016 est.)

Exports: $13.79 billion (2019 est.)
$13.08 billion (2018 est.)
note: Data are in current year dollars and do not include illicit exports or re-exports.

Exports - partners: Netherlands 10%, United States 6%, France 6%, Spain 5%, Malaysia 5%, Switzerland 5%, Germany 5%, Vietnam 5% (2019)

Exports - commodities: cocoa beans, gold, rubber, refined petroleum, crude petroleum (2019)

Imports: $12.88 billion (2019 est.) note: data are in current year dollars
$13.18 billion (2018 est.) note: data are in current year dollars

Imports - partners: China 18%, Nigeria 13%, France 11% (2019)

Imports - commodities: crude petroleum, rice, frozen fish, refined petroleum, packaged medicines (2019)

Reserves of foreign exchange and gold: $6.257 billion (31 December 2017 est.)
$4.935 billion (31 December 2016 est.)

Debt - external: $13.07 billion (31 December 2017 est.)
$11.02 billion (31 December 2016 est.)

Exchange rates: Communaute Financiere Africaine francs (XOF) per US dollar -
594.3 (2017 est.)
593.01 (2016 est.)
593.01 (2015 est.)
591.45 (2014 est.)
494.42 (2013 est.)

ENERGY

Electricity access: *electrification - total population:* 76% (2019)
electrification - urban areas: 99% (2019)
electrification - rural areas: 51% (2019)

Electricity: *installed generating capacity:* 2.197 million kW (2020 est.)
consumption: 5,924,320,000 kWh (2019 est.)
exports: 1.178 billion kWh (2019 est.)
imports: 172 million kWh (2019 est.)
transmission/distribution losses: 1.957 billion kWh (2019 est.)

Electricity generation sources: *fossil fuels:* 75.6% of total installed capacity (2020 est.)
solar: 0.2% of total installed capacity (2020 est.)
wind: 0% of total installed capacity (2020 est.)
hydroelectricity: 24.2% of total installed capacity (2020 est.)

Petroleum: *total petroleum production:* 33,000 bbl/day (2021 est.)
refined petroleum consumption: 56,500 bbl/day (2019 est.)
crude oil and lease condensate exports: 30,200 bbl/day (2018 est.)
crude oil and lease condensate imports: 69,200 bbl/day (2018 est.)
crude oil estimated reserves: 100 million barrels (2021 est.)

Refined petroleum products - production: 69,360 bbl/day (2017 est.)

Refined petroleum products - exports: 31,450 bbl/day (2015 est.)

Refined petroleum products - imports: 7,405 bbl/day (2015 est.)

Natural gas: *production:* 2,424,768,000 cubic meters (2019 est.)
consumption: 2,424,768,000 cubic meters (2019 est.)
exports: 0 cubic meters (2021 est.)
imports: 0 cubic meters (2021 est.)
proven reserves: 28.317 billion cubic meters (2021 est.)

Carbon dioxide emissions: 11.88 million metric tonnes of CO2 (2019 est.)
from petroleum and other liquids: 7.332 million metric tonnes of CO2 (2019 est.)
from consumed natural gas: 4.548 million metric tonnes of CO2 (2019 est.)

Energy consumption per capita: 8.225 million Btu/person (2019 est.)

COMMUNICATIONS

Telephones - fixed lines: *total subscriptions:* 264,073 (2020 est.)
subscriptions per 100 inhabitants: 1 (2020 est.)

Telephones - mobile cellular: *total subscriptions:* 40,095,246 (2020 est.)
subscriptions per 100 inhabitants: 152 (2020 est.)

Telecommunication systems: *general assessment:* in recent years the government of Ivory Coast has helped develop a competitive telecom sector focused on the provision of converged services, thus allowing operators to offer fixed-line and mobile services under a universal services license regime; the fixed internet and broadband sectors remain underdeveloped; this is a legacy of poor international connectivity, which resulted in high wholesale prices, limited bandwidth, and a lack of access for alternative operators to international infrastructure; these limitations were addressed following the landing of a second cable in November 2011; Orange Group has also launched its 20,000km Djoliba cable system, reaching across eight countries in the region, while the 2Africa submarine cable is being developed by a consortium of companies; with a landing station providing connectivity to Côte d'Ivoire, the system is expected to be completed in late 2023 (2022)
domestic: 1 per 100 fixed-line teledensity; with multiple mobile-cellular service providers competing in the market, mobile subscriptions have increased to 152 per 100 persons (2020)
international: country code - 225; landing point for the SAT-3/WASC, ACE, MainOne, and WACS fiber-optic submarine cable that provides connectivity to Europe and South and West Africa; satellite earth stations - 2 Intelsat (1 Atlantic Ocean and 1 Indian Ocean) (2019)

Broadcast media: state-controlled Radiodiffusion Television Ivoirieinne (RTI) is made up of 2 radio stations (Radio Cote d'Ivoire and Frequence2) and 2 television stations (RTI1 and RTI2), with nationwide coverage, broadcasts mainly in French; after 2011 post-electoral crisis, President OUATTARA's administration reopened RTI Bouake', the broadcaster's office in Cote d'Ivoire's 2nd largest city, where facilities were destroyed during the 2002 rebellion; Cote d'Ivoire is also home to 178 proximity radio stations, 16 religious radio stations, 5 commercial radio stations, and 5 international radios stations, according to the Haute Autorite' de la Communication Audiovisuelle (HACA); govt now runs radio UNOCIFM, a radio station previously owned by the UN Operation in Cote d'Ivoire; in Dec 2016, the govt announced 4 companies had been granted licenses to operate -Live TV, Optimum Media Cote d'Ivoire, the Audiovisual Company of Cote d'Ivoire (Sedaci), and Sorano-CI, out of the 4 companies only one has started operating (2019)

Internet country code: .ci

Internet users: *total:* 9,496,179 (2020 est.)
percent of population: 36% (2020 est.)

Broadband - fixed subscriptions: *total:* 260,097 (2020 est.)
subscriptions per 100 inhabitants: 1 (2020 est.)

TRANSPORTATION

National air transport system: *number of registered air carriers:* 1 (2020)
inventory of registered aircraft operated by air carriers: 10
annual passenger traffic on registered air carriers: 779,482 (2018)
annual freight traffic on registered air carriers: 5.8 million (2018) mt-km

Civil aircraft registration country code prefix: TU

Airports: *total:* 27 (2021)

Airports - with paved runways: *total:* 7
over 3,047 m: 1
2,438 to 3,047 m: 2
1,524 to 2,437 m: 4 (2021)

Airports - with unpaved runways: *total:* 20
1,524 to 2,437 m: 6
914 to 1,523 m: 11
under 914 m: 3 (2021)

Heliports: 1 (2021)

Pipelines: 101 km condensate, 256 km gas, 118 km oil, 5 km oil/gas/water, 7 km water (2013)

Railways: *total:* 660 km (2008)
narrow gauge: 660 km (2008) 1.000-m gauge
note: an additional 622 km of this railroad extends into Burkina Faso

Roadways: *total:* 81,996 km (2007)
paved: 6,502 km (2007)
unpaved: 75,494 km (2007)
note: includes intercity and urban roads; another 20,000 km of dirt roads are in poor condition and 150,000 km of dirt roads are impassable

Waterways: 980 km (2011) (navigable rivers, canals, and numerous coastal lagoons)

Merchant marine: *total:* 25
by type: oil tanker 2, other 23 (2021)

Ports and terminals: *major seaport(s):* Abidjan, San-Pedro
oil terminal(s): Espoir Offshore Terminal

MILITARY AND SECURITY

Military and security forces: Armed Forces of Cote d'Ivoire (Forces Armees de Cote d'Ivoire, FACI; aka Republican Forces of Ivory Coast, FRCI): Army, Navy, Cote Air Force, Special Forces; National Gendarmerie (under the Ministry of Defense); Ministry of Security and Civil Protection: National Police; Coordination Center for Operational Decisions (a mix of police, gendarmerie, and FACI personnel for assisting police in providing security in some large cities) (2022)

Military expenditures: 1.1% of GDP (2021 est.)
1.1% of GDP (2020 est.)
1.1% of GDP (2019 est.) (approximately $710 million)
1.2% of GDP (2018 est.) (approximately $780 million)
1.1% of GDP (2017 est.) (approximately $720 million)

Military and security service personnel strengths: approximately 25,000 active troops (23,000 Army, including about 2,000 Special Forces; 1,000 Navy; 1,000 Air Force); 5-10,000 Gendarmerie (2022)

Military equipment inventories and acquisitions: the inventory of the FACI consists mostly of older or second-hand equipment, typically of French or Soviet-era origin; Cote d'Ivoire was under a partial UN arms embargo from 2004 to 2016; since 2016, it has received limited amounts of mostly second-hand equipment from several countries, including France (2022)

Military service age and obligation: 18-25 years of age for compulsory and voluntary male and female military service; conscription is not enforced; voluntary recruitment of former rebels into the new national army is restricted to ages 22-29 (2022)

Military deployments: 850 Mali (MINUSMA) (2022)

Military - note: the military has mutinied several times since the late 1990s, most recently in 2017, and has had a large role in the country's political turmoil; as of 2022, the FACI was focused on internal security and the growing threat posed by Islamic militants associated with the al-Qa'ida in the Islamic Maghreb (AQIM) terrorist group operating across the border in Burkina Faso; AQIM militants conducted significant attacks in the country in 2016 and 2020; Côte d'Ivoire since 2016 has stepped up border security and completed building a joint counter-terrorism training center with France near Abidjan in 2020 the UN maintained a 9,000-strong peacekeeping force in Cote d'Ivoire (UNOCI) from 2004 until 2017 (2022)

Maritime threats: the International Maritime Bureau reports the territorial and offshore waters in the Niger Delta and Gulf of Guinea remain a very high risk for piracy and armed robbery of ships; in 2021, there were 34 reported incidents of piracy and armed robbery at sea in the Gulf of Guinea region; although a significant decrease from the total number of 81 incidents in 2020, it included the one hijacking and three of five ships fired upon worldwide; while boarding and attempted boarding to steal valuables from ships and crews are the most common types of incidents, almost a third of all incidents involve a hijacking and/or kidnapping; in 2021, 57 crew members were kidnapped in seven separate incidents in the Gulf of Guinea, representing 100% of kidnappings worldwide; Nigerian pirates in particular are well armed and very aggressive, operating as far as 200 nm offshore; the Maritime Administration of the US Department of Transportation has issued a Maritime Advisory (2022-001 - Gulf of Guinea-Piracy/Armed Robbery/Kidnapping for Ransom) effective 4 January 2022, which states in part, "Piracy, armed robbery, and kidnapping for ransom continue to serve as significant threats to US-flagged vessels transiting or operating in the Gulf of Guinea"

TERRORISM

Terrorist group(s): al-Qa'ida in the Islamic Maghreb (AQIM); Jama'at Nusrat al Islam wal Muslimeen (JNIM)

TRANSNATIONAL ISSUES

Disputes - international: disputed maritime border between Cote d'Ivoire and Ghana

Refugees and internally displaced persons: IDPs: 302,000 (post-election conflict in 2010-11, as well as civil war from 2002-04; land disputes; most pronounced in western and southwestern regions) (2021)

stateless persons: 952,969 (mid-year 2021); note - many Ivoirians lack documentation proving their nationality, which prevent them from accessing education and healthcare; birth on Ivorian soil does not automatically result in citizenship; disputes over citizenship and the associated rights of the large population descended from migrants from neighboring countries is an ongoing source of tension and contributed to the country's 2002 civil war; some observers believe the government's mass naturalizations of thousands of people over the last couple of years is intended to boost its electoral support base; the government in October 2013 acceded to international conventions on statelessness and in August 2013 reformed its nationality law, key steps to clarify the nationality of thousands of residents; since the adoption of the Abidjan Declaration to eradicate statelessness in West Africa in February 2015, 6,400 people have received nationality papers in Cote d'Ivoire; in September 2020, Cote d'Ivoire adopted Africa's first statelessness determination procedure to regularize the status of stateless people

Illicit drugs: illicit producer of cannabis, mostly for local consumption; utility as a narcotic transshipment point to Europe reduced by ongoing political instability; while rampant corruption and inadequate supervision leave the banking system vulnerable to money laundering, the lack of a developed financial system limits the country's utility as a major money-laundering center

CROATIA

INTRODUCTION

Background: The lands that today comprise Croatia were part of the Austro-Hungarian Empire until the close of World War I. In 1918, the Croats, Serbs, and Slovenes formed a kingdom known after 1929 as Yugoslavia. Following World War II, Yugoslavia became a federal independent communist state consisting of six socialist republics under the strong hand of Marshal Josip Broz, aka TITO. Although Croatia declared its independence from Yugoslavia in 1991, it took four years of sporadic, but often bitter, fighting before occupying Yugoslav forces, dominated by Serb officers, were mostly cleared from Croatian lands, along with a majority of Croatia's ethnic Serb population. Under UN supervision, the last Serb-held enclave in eastern Slavonia was returned to Croatia in 1998. The country joined NATO in April 2009 and the EU in July 2013.

GEOGRAPHY

Location: Southeastern Europe, bordering the Adriatic Sea, between Bosnia and Herzegovina and Slovenia

Geographic coordinates: 45 10 N, 15 30 E

Map references: Europe

Area: *total:* 56,594 sq km
land: 55,974 sq km
water: 620 sq km

Area - comparative: slightly smaller than West Virginia

Land boundaries: *total:* 2,237 km
border countries (5): Bosnia and Herzegovina 956 km; Hungary 348 km; Montenegro 19 km; Serbia 314 km; Slovenia 600 km

Coastline: 5,835 km (mainland 1,777 km, islands 4,058 km)

Maritime claims: *territorial sea:* 12 nm
continental shelf: 200-m depth or to the depth of exploitation

Climate: Mediterranean and continental; continental climate predominant with hot summers and cold winters; mild winters, dry summers along coast

Terrain: geographically diverse; flat plains along Hungarian border, low mountains and highlands near Adriatic coastline and islands

Elevation: *highest point:* Dinara 1,831 m
lowest point: Adriatic Sea 0 m
mean elevation: 331 m

Natural resources: oil, some coal, bauxite, low-grade iron ore, calcium, gypsum, natural asphalt, silica, mica, clays, salt, hydropower

Land use: *agricultural land:* 23.7% (2018 est.)
arable land: 16% (2018 est.)
permanent crops: 1.5% (2018 est.)
permanent pasture: 6.2% (2018 est.)
forest: 34.4% (2018 est.)
other: 41.9% (2018 est.)

Irrigated land: 240 sq km (2012)

Major rivers (by length in km): Danube (shared with Germany [s], Austria, Slovakia, Czechia, Hungary, Serbia, Bulgaria, Ukraine, Moldova, and Romania [m]) - 2,888 km
note – [s] after country name indicates river source; [m] after country name indicates river mouth

Major watersheds (area sq km): Atlantic Ocean drainage: *(Black Sea)* Danube (795,656 sq km)

Population distribution: more of the population lives in the northern half of the country, with approximately a quarter of the populace residing in and around the capital of Zagreb; many of the islands are sparsely populated

Natural hazards: destructive earthquakes

Geography - note: controls most land routes from Western Europe to Aegean Sea and Turkish Straits; most Adriatic Sea islands lie off the coast of Croatia - some 1,200 islands, islets, ridges, and rocks

PEOPLE AND SOCIETY

Population: 4,188,853 (2022 est.)

Nationality: *noun:* Croat(s), Croatian(s)
adjective: Croatian
note: the French designation of "Croate" to Croatian mercenaries in the 17th century eventually became "Cravate" and later came to be applied to the soldiers' scarves - the cravat; Croatia celebrates Cravat Day every 18 October

Ethnic groups: Croat 90.4%, Serb 4.4%, other 4.4% (including Bosniak, Hungarian, Slovene, Czech, and Romani), unspecified 0.8% (2011 est.)

Languages: Croatian (official) 95.6%, Serbian 1.2%, other 3% (including Hungarian, Czech, Slovak, and Albanian), unspecified 0.2% (2011 est.)
major-language sample(s):
Knjiga svjetskih činjenica, nužan izvor osnovnih informacija. (Croatian)

Religions: Roman Catholic 86.3%, Orthodox 4.4%, Muslim 1.5%, other 1.5%, unspecified 2.5%, not religious or atheist 3.8% (2011 est.)

Age structure: *0-14 years:* 14.16% (male 308,668/female 289,996)
15-24 years: 10.76% (male 233,602/female 221,495)
25-54 years: 39.77% (male 841,930/female 839,601)
55-64 years: 14.24% (male 290,982/female 310,969)
65 years and over: 21.06% (male 364,076/female 526,427) (2020 est.)

Dependency ratios: *total dependency ratio:* 55.7
youth dependency ratio: 22.6
elderly dependency ratio: 33.1
potential support ratio: 3 (2020 est.)

Median age: *total:* 43.9 years
male: 42 years
female: 45.9 years (2020 est.)

Population growth rate: -0.47% (2022 est.)

Birth rate: 8.65 births/1,000 population (2022 est.)

Death rate: 12.88 deaths/1,000 population (2022 est.)

Net migration rate: -0.5 migrant(s)/1,000 population (2022 est.)

Population distribution: more of the population lives in the northern half of the country, with approximately a quarter of the populace residing in and around the capital of Zagreb; many of the islands are sparsely populated

Urbanization: *urban population:* 58.2% of total population (2022)
rate of urbanization: 0.05% annual rate of change (2020-25 est.)

Major urban areas - population: 684,000 ZAGREB (capital) (2022)

Sex ratio: *at birth:* 1.06 male(s)/female
0-14 years: 1.01 male(s)/female
15-24 years: 1 male(s)/female
25-54 years: 1.03 male(s)/female
55-64 years: 1.04 male(s)/female
65 years and over: 0.67 male(s)/female
total population: 1.01 male(s)/female (2022 est.)

Mother's mean age at first birth: 29 years (2020 est.)

Maternal mortality ratio: 8 deaths/100,000 live births (2017 est.)

Infant mortality rate: *total:* 8.74 deaths/1,000 live births
male: 8.52 deaths/1,000 live births
female: 8.98 deaths/1,000 live births (2022 est.)

Life expectancy at birth: *total population:* 77.22 years
male: 74.1 years
female: 80.53 years (2022 est.)

Total fertility rate: 1.45 children born/woman (2022 est.)

Drinking water source: *improved: total:* 100% of population
unimproved: total: 0% of population (2020 est.)

Current health expenditure: 7% of GDP (2019)

Physicians density: 3.47 physicians/1,000 population (2019)

Hospital bed density: 5.5 beds/1,000 population (2017)

Sanitation facility access: *improved: urban:* 99.5% of population
rural: 98.4% of population
total: 99% of population
unimproved: urban: 0.5% of population
rural: 1.6% of population
total: 1% of population (2020 est.)

HIV/AIDS - adult prevalence rate: (2020 est.) <.1%

Major infectious diseases: *degree of risk:* intermediate (2020)
vectorborne diseases: tickborne encephalitis

Obesity - adult prevalence rate: 24.4% (2016)

Alcohol consumption per capita: *total:* 9.64 liters of pure alcohol (2019 est.)
beer: 4.75 liters of pure alcohol (2019 est.)
wine: 3.52 liters of pure alcohol (2019 est.)
spirits: 1.37 liters of pure alcohol (2019 est.)
other alcohols: 0.36 liters of pure alcohol (2019 est.)

Tobacco use: *total:* 36.9% (2020 est.)
male: 37.6% (2020 est.)
female: 36.1% (2020 est.)

Education expenditures: 3.9% of GDP (2017 est.)

Literacy: *definition:* age 15 and over can read and write
total population: 99.3%
male: 99.7%
female: 98.9% (2015)

School life expectancy (primary to tertiary education): *total:* 15 years
male: 14 years
female: 16 years (2019)

Unemployment, youth ages 15-24: *total:* 21.1%
male: 18.7%
female: 25% (2020 est.)

ENVIRONMENT

Environment - current issues: air pollution improving but still a concern in urban settings and in emissions arriving from neighboring countries; surface water pollution in the Danube River Basin

Environment - international agreements: *party to:* Air Pollution, Air Pollution-Heavy Metals, Air Pollution-Multi-effect Protocol, Air Pollution-Nitrogen Oxides, Air Pollution-Persistent Organic Pollutants, Air Pollution-Sulphur 94, Air Pollution-Volatile Organic Compounds, Biodiversity, Climate Change, Climate Change-Kyoto Protocol, Climate Change-Paris Agreement, Comprehensive Nuclear Test Ban, Desertification, Endangered Species, Hazardous Wastes, Law of the Sea, Marine Dumping-London Convention, Nuclear Test Ban, Ozone Layer Protection, Ship Pollution, Tropical Timber 2006, Wetlands, Whaling
signed, but not ratified: none of the selected agreements

Air pollutants: *particulate matter emissions:* 17.03 micrograms per cubic meter (2016 est.)
carbon dioxide emissions: 17.49 megatons (2016 est.)
methane emissions: 3.98 megatons (2020 est.)

Climate: Mediterranean and continental; continental climate predominant with hot summers and cold winters; mild winters, dry summers along coast

Land use: *agricultural land:* 23.7% (2018 est.)
arable land: 16% (2018 est.)
permanent crops: 1.5% (2018 est.)
permanent pasture: 6.2% (2018 est.)
forest: 34.4% (2018 est.)
other: 41.9% (2018 est.)

Urbanization: *urban population:* 58.2% of total population (2022)
rate of urbanization: 0.05% annual rate of change (2020-25 est.)

Revenue from forest resources: *forest revenues:* 0.26% of GDP (2018 est.)

Revenue from coal: *coal revenues:* 0% of GDP (2018 est.)

Waste and recycling: *municipal solid waste generated annually:* 1.654 million tons (2015 est.)
municipal solid waste recycled annually: 269,933 tons (2015 est.)
percent of municipal solid waste recycled: 16.3% (2015 est.)

Major rivers (by length in km): Danube (shared with Germany [s], Austria, Slovakia, Czechia, Hungary, Serbia, Bulgaria, Ukraine, Moldova, and Romania [m]) - 2,888 km
note – [s] after country name indicates river source; [m] after country name indicates river mouth

Major watersheds (area sq km): Atlantic Ocean drainage: *(Black Sea)* Danube (795,656 sq km)

Total water withdrawal: *municipal:* 455 million cubic meters (2017 est.)
industrial: 184 million cubic meters (2017 est.)
agricultural: 76 million cubic meters (2017 est.)

Total renewable water resources: 105.5 billion cubic meters (2017 est.)

GOVERNMENT

Country name: *conventional long form:* Republic of Croatia
conventional short form: Croatia
local long form: Republika Hrvatska
local short form: Hrvatska
former: People's Republic of Croatia, Socialist Republic of Croatia
etymology: name derives from the Croats, a Slavic tribe who migrated to the Balkans in the 7th century A.D.

Government type: parliamentary republic

Capital: *name:* Zagreb
geographic coordinates: 45 48 N, 16 00 E
time difference: UTC+1 (6 hours ahead of Washington, DC, during Standard Time)

daylight saving time: +1 hr, begins last Sunday in March; ends last Sunday in October
etymology: the name seems to be related to "digging"; archeologists suggest that the original settlement was established beyond a water-filled hole or *graba* and that the name derives from this; *za* in Slavic means "beyond"; the overall meaning may be "beyond the trench (fault, channel, ditch)"

Administrative divisions: 20 counties (zupanije, zupanija - singular) and 1 city* (grad - singular) with special county status; Bjelovarsko-Bilogorska (Bjelovar-Bilogora), Brodsko-Posavska (Brod-Posavina), Dubrovacko-Neretvanska (Dubrovnik-Neretva), Istarska (Istria), Karlovacka (Karlovac), Koprivnicko-Krizevacka (Koprivnica-Krizevci), Krapinsko-Zagorska (Krapina-Zagorje), Licko-Senjska (Lika-Senj), Medimurska (Medimurje), Osjecko-Baranjska (Osijek-Baranja), Pozesko-Slavonska (Pozega-Slavonia), Primorsko-Goranska (Primorje-Gorski Kotar), Sibensko-Kninska (Sibenik-Knin), Sisacko-Moslavacka (Sisak-Moslavina), Splitsko-Dalmatinska (Split-Dalmatia), Varazdinska (Varazdin), Viroviticko-Podravska (Virovitica-Podravina), Vukovarsko-Srijemska (Vukovar-Syrmia), Zadarska (Zadar), Zagreb*, Zagrebacka (Zagreb county)

Independence: 25 June 1991 (from Yugoslavia); note - 25 June 1991 was the day the Croatian parliament voted for independence; following a three-month moratorium to allow the European Community to solve the Yugoslav crisis peacefully, parliament adopted a decision on 8 October 1991 to sever constitutional relations with Yugoslavia; notable earlier dates: ca. 925 (Kingdom of Croatia established); 1 December 1918 (Kingdom of Serbs, Croats, and Slovenes (Yugoslavia) established)

National holiday: Statehood Day (National Day), 30 May (1990); note - marks the day in 1990 that the first modern multi-party Croatian parliament convened

Constitution: *history:* several previous; latest adopted 22 December 1990
amendments: proposed by at least one fifth of the Assembly membership, by the president of the republic, by the Government of Croatia, or through petition by at least 10% of the total electorate; proceedings to amend require majority vote by the Assembly; passage requires two-thirds majority vote by the Assembly; passage by petition requires a majority vote in a referendum and promulgation by the Assembly; amended several times, last in 2014

Legal system: civil law system influenced by legal heritage of Austria-Hungary; note - Croatian law was fully harmonized with the European Community acquis as of the June 2010 completion of EU accession negotiations

International law organization participation: has not submitted an ICJ jurisdiction declaration; accepts ICCt jurisdiction

Citizenship: *citizenship by birth:* no
citizenship by descent only: at least one parent must be a citizen of Croatia
dual citizenship recognized: yes
residency requirement for naturalization: 5 years

Suffrage: 18 years of age; universal

Executive branch: *chief of state:* President Zoran MILANOVIC (since 18 February 2020)
head of government: Prime Minister Andrej PLENKOVIC (since 19 October 2016); Deputy Prime Ministers Damir KRSTICEVIC (since 19 October 2016), Predrag STROMAR (since 9 June 2017), Marija Pejcinovic BURIC (since 19 June 2017), and Tomislav TOLUSIC (since 25 May 2018)
cabinet: Council of Ministers named by the prime minister and approved by the Assembly
elections/appointments: president directly elected by absolute majority popular vote in 2 rounds if needed for a 5-year term (eligible for a second term); election last held on 22 December 2019 with a runoff on 5 January 2020 (next to be held in 2024); the leader of the majority party or majority coalition usually appointed prime minister by the president and approved by the Assembly
election results:
2019: Zoran MILANOVIC elected president in second round; percent of vote in second round - Zoran MILANOVIC (SDP) 52.7%, Kolinda GRABAR-KITAROVIC (HDZ) 47.3%
2015: Kolinda GRABAR-KITAROVIC elected president in second round; percent of vote in second round - Kolinda GRABAR-KITAROVIC (HDZ) 50.7%, Ivo JOSIPOVIC (Forward Croatia Progressive Alliance) 49.3%

Legislative branch: *description:* unicameral Assembly or Hrvatski Sabor (151 seats; 140 members in 10 multi-seat constituencies and 3 members in a single constituency for Croatian diaspora directly elected by proportional representation vote using the D'Hondt method with a 5% threshold; an additional 8 members elected from a nationwide constituency by simple majority by voters belonging to minorities recognized by Croatia; the Serb minority elects 3 Assembly members, the Hungarian and Italian minorities elect 1 each, the Czech and Slovak minorities elect 1 jointly, and all other minorities elect 2; all members serve 4-year terms
elections:
early election held on 5 July 2020 (next to be held by 2024)
election results:
percent of vote by coalition/party - HDZ-led coalition 37.3%, Restart coalition 24.9%, DPMS-led coalition 10.9%, MOST 7.4%, Green-Left coalition 7%, P-F-SSIP 4%, HNS-LD 1.3%, NS-R 1%, other 6.2%; number of seats by coalition/party - HDZ-led coalition 66, Restart coalition 41, DPMS-led coalition 16, MOST 8, Green-Left coalition 7, P-F-SSIP 3, HNS-LD 1, NS-R 1, national minorities 8; composition as of January 2021 - men 103, women 48, percent of women 31.8%
note: seats by party as of March 2021 - HDZ 62, SDP 33, DP 9, Most 6, Croatian Sovereignists 4, We Can! 4, IDS 3, SDSS 3, HSS 2, HSLS 2, BZH 1, Center 1, FOKUS 1, GLAS 1, HDS 1, HSU 1, NL 1, Reformists 1, SSIP 1, RF 1, independent 12

Judicial branch: *highest court(s):* Supreme Court (consists of the court president and vice president, 25 civil department justices, and 16 criminal department justices)
judge selection and term of office: president of Supreme Court nominated by the president of Croatia and elected by the Sabor for a 4-year term; other Supreme Court justices appointed by the National Judicial Council; all judges serve until age 70
subordinate courts: Administrative Court; county, municipal, and specialized courts; note - there is an 11-member Constitutional Court with jurisdiction limited to constitutional issues but is outside of the judicial system

Political parties and leaders: Bloc for Croatia or BLOK or BZH [Zlatko HASANBEGOVIC]
The Bridge or Most [Bozo PETROV] (formerly the Bridge of Independent Lists)
Center or Centar [Ivica PULJAK] (formerly Pametno and Party with a First and Last Name or SSIP)
Civic Liberal Alliance or GLAS [Ankar Mrak TARITAS]
Croatian Demochristian Party or HDS [Goran DODIG]
Croatian Democratic Alliance of Slavonia and Baranja or HDSSB [Branimir GLAVAS]
Croatian Democratic Union or HDZ [Andrej PLENKOVIC]
Croatian Democratic Union-led coalition (includes HSLS, HDS, HDSSB)
Croatian Party of Pensioners or HSU [Veselko GABRICEVIC]
Croatian Peasant Party or HSS [Kreso BELJAK]
Croatian People's Party - Liberal Democrats or HNS-LD [Stjepan CURAJ]
Croatian Social Liberal Party or HSLS [Dario HREBAK]
Croatian Sovereignists or HS [Marijan PAVLICEK]
Focus on the Important or Focus [Davor NADI]
Green-Left coalition [collective leadership] (includes MOZEMO!, NL)
Homeland Movement or DP [Ivan PENAVA] (also known as Miroslav Škoro Homeland Movement or DPMS)
Independent Democratic Serb Party or SDSS [Milorad PUPOVAC]
Istrian Democratic Assembly or IDS [Dalibor PAUS]
New Left or NL [Ivana KEKIN]
People's Party - Reformists or NS-R [Radimir CACIC]
Restart Coalition (includes SDP, HSS, HSU, GLAS, IDS, NS-R)
Social Democratic Party of Croatia or SDP [Peda GRBIN]
We Can! or Mozemo! [collective leadership]
Workers' Front or RF [collective leadership]

International organization participation: Australia Group, BIS, BSEC (observer), CD, CE, CEI, EAPC, EBRD, ECB, EMU, EU, FAO, G-11, IADB, IAEA, IBRD, ICAO, ICC (national committees), ICCt, ICRM, IDA, IFAD, IFC, IFRCS, IHO, ILO, IMF, IMO, IMSO, Interpol, IOC, IOM, IPU, ISO, ITSO, ITU, ITUC (NGOs), MIGA, MINURSO, NAM (observer), NATO, NSG, OAS (observer), OIF (observer), OPCW, OSCE, PCA, SELEC, UN, UNCTAD, UNESCO, UNFICYP, UNHCR, UNIDO, UNIFIL, UNMIL, UNMOGIP, UNWTO, UPU, Wassenaar Arrangement, WCO, WHO, WIPO, WMO, WTO, ZC

Diplomatic representation in the US: *chief of mission:* Ambassador Pjer SIMUNOVIC (since 8 September 2017)
chancery: 2343 Massachusetts Avenue NW, Washington, DC 20008
telephone: [1] (202) 588-5899
FAX: [1] (202) 588-8936; [1] (202) 588-8937
email address and website:
washington@mvep.hr
http://us.mvep.hr/en/
consulate(s) general: Chicago, Los Angeles, New York, Seattle (WA), Washington, DC
consulate(s): Anchorage (AL), Houston, Kansas City (MO), New Orleans, Pittsburgh (PA)

Diplomatic representation from the US: *chief of mission:* Ambassador (vacant); Charge d'Affaires Mark FLEMING (since May 2021)
embassy: Ulica Thomasa Jeffersona 2, 10010 Zagreb
mailing address: 5080 Zagreb Place, Washington DC 20521-5080
telephone: [385] (1) 661-2200
FAX: [385] (1) 661-8933
email address and website:
ZagrebACS@state.gov
https://hr.usembassy.gov/

Flag description: three equal horizontal bands of red (top), white, and blue - the Pan-Slav colors - superimposed by the Croatian coat of arms; the coat of arms consists of one main shield (a checkerboard of 13 red and 12 silver (white) fields) surmounted by five smaller shields that form a crown over the main shield; the five small shields represent five historic regions (from left to right): Croatia, Dubrovnik, Dalmatia, Istria, and Slavonia
note: the Pan-Slav colors were inspired by the 19th-century flag of Russia

National symbol(s): red-white checkerboard; national colors: red, white, blue

National anthem: *name:* "Lijepa nasa domovino" (Our Beautiful Homeland)
lyrics/music: Antun MIHANOVIC/Josip RUNJANIN
note: adopted in 1972 while still part of Yugoslavia; "Lijepa nasa domovino," whose lyrics were written in 1835, served as an unofficial anthem beginning in 1891

National heritage: *total World Heritage Sites:* 10 (8 cultural, 2 natural)
selected World Heritage Site locales: Plitvice Lakes National Park (n); Historic Split (c); Old City of Dubrovnik (c); Euphrasian Basilica; Historic Trogir (c); Šibenik Cathedral (c); Stari Grad Plain (c); Zadar and Fort St. Nikola Venetian Defense Works (c); Primeval Beech Forests (n); Stećci Medieval Tombstones Graveyards (c)

ECONOMY

Economic overview: Though still one of the wealthiest of the former Yugoslav republics, Croatia's economy suffered badly during the 1991-95 war. The country's output during that time collapsed, and Croatia missed the early waves of investment in Central and Eastern Europe that followed the fall of the Berlin Wall. Between 2000 and 2007, however, Croatia's economic fortunes began to improve with moderate but steady GDP growth between 4% and 6%, led by a rebound in tourism and credit-driven consumer spending. Inflation over the same period remained tame and the currency, the kuna, stable.

Croatia experienced an abrupt slowdown in the economy in 2008; economic growth was stagnant or negative in each year between 2009 and 2014, but has picked up since the third quarter of 2014, ending 2017 with an average of 2.8% growth. Challenges remain including uneven regional development, a difficult investment climate, an inefficient judiciary, and loss of educated young professionals seeking higher salaries elsewhere in the EU. In 2016, Croatia revised its tax code to stimulate growth from domestic consumption and foreign investment. Income tax reduction began in 2017, and in 2018 various business costs were removed from income tax calculations. At the start of 2018, the government announced its economic reform plan, slated for implementation in 2019.

Tourism is one of the main pillars of the Croatian economy, comprising 19.6% of Croatia's GDP Croatia is working to become a regional energy hub, and is undertaking plans to open a floating liquefied natural gas (LNG) regasification terminal by the end of 2019 or early in 2020 to import LNG for re-distribution in southeast Europe.

Croatia joined the EU on July 1, 2013, following a decade-long accession process. Croatia has developed a plan for Eurozone accession, and the government projects Croatia will adopt the Euro by 2024. In 2017, the Croatian government decreased public debt to 78% of GDP, from an all-time high of 84% in 2014, and realized a 0.8% budget surplus - the first surplus since independence in 1991. The government has also sought to accelerate privatization of non-strategic assets with mixed success. Croatia's economic recovery is still somewhat fragile; Croatia's largest private company narrowly avoided collapse in 2017, thanks to a capital infusion from an American investor. Restructuring is ongoing, and projected to finish by mid-July 2018.

Real GDP (purchasing power parity): $107.11 billion (2020 est.)
$116.89 billion (2019 est.)
$113.64 billion (2018 est.)
note: data are in 2017 dollars

Real GDP growth rate: 2.94% (2019 est.)
2.7% (2018 est.)
3.14% (2017 est.)

Real GDP per capita: $26,500 (2020 est.)
$28,800 (2019 est.)
$27,800 (2018 est.)
note: data are in 2017 dollars

GDP (official exchange rate): $60.687 billion (2019 est.)

Inflation rate (consumer prices): 0.7% (2019 est.)
1.4% (2018 est.)
1.1% (2017 est.)

Credit ratings:

Fitch rating: BBB- (2019)

Moody's rating: Ba1 (2020)

Standard & Poors rating: BBB- (2019)
note: The year refers to the year in which the current credit rating was first obtained.

GDP - composition, by sector of origin: *agriculture:* 3.7% (2017 est.)
industry: 26.2% (2017 est.)
services: 70.1% (2017 est.)

GDP - composition, by end use: *household consumption:* 57.3% (2017 est.)
government consumption: 19.5% (2017 est.)
investment in fixed capital: 20% (2017 est.)
investment in inventories: 0% (2017 est.)
exports of goods and services: 51.1% (2017 est.)
imports of goods and services: -48.8% (2017 est.)

Agricultural products: maize, wheat, sugar beet, milk, barley, soybeans, potatoes, pork, grapes, sunflower seed

Industries: chemicals and plastics, machine tools, fabricated metal, electronics, pig iron and rolled steel products, aluminum, paper, wood products, construction materials, textiles, shipbuilding, petroleum and petroleum refining, food and beverages, tourism

Industrial production growth rate: 1.2% (2017 est.)

Labor force: 1.656 million (2020 est.)

Labor force - by occupation: *agriculture:* 1.9%
industry: 27.3%
services: 70.8% (2017 est.)

Unemployment rate: 8.07% (2019 est.)
9.86% (2018 est.)

Unemployment, youth ages 15-24: *total:* 21.1%
male: 18.7%
female: 25% (2020 est.)

Population below poverty line: 18.3% (2018 est.)

Gini Index coefficient - distribution of family income: 30.4 (2017 est.)
32.1 (2014 est.)

Household income or consumption by percentage share: *lowest 10%:* 2.7%
highest 10%: 23% (2015 est.)

Budget: *revenues:* 25.24 billion (2017 est.)
expenditures: 24.83 billion (2017 est.)

Budget surplus (+) or deficit (-): 0.8% (of GDP) (2017 est.)

Public debt: 77.8% of GDP (2017 est.)
82.3% of GDP (2016 est.)

Taxes and other revenues: 46.1% (of GDP) (2017 est.)

Fiscal year: calendar year

Current account balance: $1.597 billion (2019 est.)
$1 billion (2018 est.)

Exports: $23.66 billion (2020 est.)
$31.07 billion (2019 est.)
$30.71 billion (2018 est.)
note: Data are in current year dollars and do not include illicit exports or re-exports.

Exports - partners: Italy 13%, Germany 13%, Slovenia 10%, Bosnia and Herzegovina 9%, Austria 6%, Serbia 5% (2019)

Exports - commodities: refined petroleum, packaged medicines, cars, medical cultures/vaccines, lumber (2019)

Imports: $27.59 billion (2020 est.) note: data are in current year dollars
$31.39 billion (2019 est.) note: data are in current year dollars
$31.32 billion (2018 est.) note: data are in current year dollars

Imports - partners: Italy 14%, Germany 14%, Slovenia 11%, Hungary 7%, Austria 6% (2019)

Imports - commodities: crude petroleum, cars, refined petroleum, packaged medicines, electricity (2019)

Reserves of foreign exchange and gold: $18.82 billion (31 December 2017 est.)
$14.24 billion (31 December 2016 est.)

Debt - external: $48.263 billion (2019 est.)
$51.176 billion (2018 est.)

Exchange rates: kuna (HRK) per US dollar -
6.2474 (2020 est.)
6.72075 (2019 est.)
6.48905 (2018 est.)
6.8583 (2014 est.)
5.7482 (2013 est.)

ENERGY

Electricity access: *electrification - total population:* 100% (2020)

Electricity: *installed generating capacity:* 4.94 million kW (2020 est.)
consumption: 16,790,680,000 kWh (2019 est.)
exports: 5.852 billion kWh (2020 est.)
imports: 10.491 billion kWh (2020 est.)

transmission/distribution losses: 1.659 billion kWh (2019 est.)

Electricity generation sources: *fossil fuels:* 41% of total installed capacity (2020 est.)
solar: 0.9% of total installed capacity (2020 est.)
wind: 16.1% of total installed capacity (2020 est.)
hydroelectricity: 31.8% of total installed capacity (2020 est.)
geothermal: 0.9% of total installed capacity (2020 est.)
biomass and waste: 9.3% of total installed capacity (2020 est.)

Coal: *production:* 0 metric tons (2020 est.)
consumption: 643,000 metric tons (2020 est.)
exports: 2,000 metric tons (2020 est.)
imports: 644,000 metric tons (2020 est.)
proven reserves: 0 metric tons (2019 est.)

Petroleum: *total petroleum production:* 12,200 bbl/day (2021 est.)
refined petroleum consumption: 71,500 bbl/day (2019 est.)
crude oil and lease condensate exports: 0 bbl/day (2018 est.)
crude oil and lease condensate imports: 65,200 bbl/day (2018 est.)
crude oil estimated reserves: 71 million barrels (2021 est.)

Refined petroleum products - production: 74,620 bbl/day (2015 est.)

Refined petroleum products - exports: 40,530 bbl/day (2015 est.)

Refined petroleum products - imports: 35,530 bbl/day (2015 est.)

Natural gas: *production:* 851.005 million cubic meters (2020 est.)
consumption: 3,009,113,000 cubic meters (2020 est.)
exports: 34.462 million cubic meters (2020 est.)
imports: 2,131,802,000 cubic meters (2020 est.)
proven reserves: 24.919 billion cubic meters (2021 est.)

Carbon dioxide emissions: 16.752 million metric tonnes of CO2 (2019 est.)
from coal and metallurgical coke: 1.674 million metric tonnes of CO2 (2019 est.)
from petroleum and other liquids: 9.4 million metric tonnes of CO2 (2019 est.)
from consumed natural gas: 5.678 million metric tonnes of CO2 (2019 est.)

Energy consumption per capita: 89.733 million Btu/person (2019 est.)

COMMUNICATIONS

Telephones - fixed lines: *total subscriptions:* 1,299,329 (2020 est.)
subscriptions per 100 inhabitants: 32 (2020 est.)

Telephones - mobile cellular: *total subscriptions:* 4,375,699 (2020 est.)
subscriptions per 100 inhabitants: 107 (2020 est.)

Telecommunication systems: *general assessment:* the mobile market is served by three MNOs, supplemented by a number of MVNOs; the network operators have focused on improving ARPU by encouraging prepaid subscribers to migrate to postpaid plans, and on developing revenue from mobile data services; 5G services are widely available, though the sector will only show its full potential later in 2021 following the award of licenses in several bands; this will contribute towards the government's national broadband plan to 2027, which is tied to the EC's two allied projects aimed at providing gigabit connectivity by the end of 2025; the broadband sector benefits from effective competition between the DSL and cable platforms, while there are also numerous fiber deployments in urban areas; the number of FttP subscribers broached 134,000 in March 2021. (2021)
domestic: fixed-line teledensity has dropped somewhat to about 32 per 100 persons; mobile-cellular telephone subscriptions are about 107 per 100 (2020)
international: country code - 385; the ADRIA-1 submarine cable provides connectivity to Albania and Greece; digital international service is provided through the main switch in Zagreb; Croatia participates in the Trans-Asia-Europe fiber-optic project, which consists of 2 fiber-optic trunk connections with Slovenia and a fiber-optic trunk line from Rijeka to Split and Dubrovnik (2019)

Broadcast media: the national state-owned public broadcaster, Croatian Radiotelevision, operates 4 terrestrial TV networks, a satellite channel that rebroadcasts programs for Croatians living abroad, and 6 regional TV centers; 2 private broadcasters operate national terrestrial networks; 29 privately owned regional TV stations; multi-channel cable and satellite TV subscription services are available; state-owned public broadcaster operates 4 national radio networks and 23 regional radio stations; 2 privately owned national radio networks and 117 local radio stations (2019)

Internet country code: .hr

Internet users: *total:* 3,157,190 (2020 est.)
percent of population: 78% (2020 est.)

Broadband - fixed subscriptions: *total:* 1,030,973 (2020 est.)
subscriptions per 100 inhabitants: 25 (2020 est.)

TRANSPORTATION

National air transport system: *number of registered air carriers:* 2 (2020)
inventory of registered aircraft operated by air carriers: 18
annual passenger traffic on registered air carriers: 2,093,577 (2018)
annual freight traffic on registered air carriers: 530,000 (2018) mt-km

Civil aircraft registration country code prefix: 9A

Airports: *total:* 69 (2021)

Airports - with paved runways: *total:* 24
over 3,047 m: 2
2,438 to 3,047 m: 6
1,524 to 2,437 m: 3
914 to 1,523 m: 3
under 914 m: 10 (2021)

Airports - with unpaved runways: *total:* 45
1,524 to 2,437 m: 1
914 to 1,523 m: 6
under 914 m: 38 (2021)

Heliports: 1 (2021)

Pipelines: 2,410 km gas, 610 km oil (2011)

Railways: *total:* 2,722 km (2014)
standard gauge: 2,722 km (2014) 1.435-m gauge (980 km electrified)

Roadways: *total:* 26,958 km (2015) (includes 1,416 km of expressways)

Waterways: 4,714 km (2022) Danube 2,859 km, Sava 562 km, Drava 505 km, Neretva 20 km, Bosut 151 km, Kupa 296 km, Mura 53 km, Korana 134 km, Lonja 134 km

Merchant marine: *total:* 354
by type: bulk carrier 14, general cargo 32, oil tanker 16, other 292 (2021)

Ports and terminals: *major seaport(s):* Ploce, Rijeka, Sibenik, Split
oil terminal(s): Omisalj

LNG terminal(s) (import): Krk Island
river port(s): Vukovar (Danube)

MILITARY AND SECURITY

Military and security forces: Armed Forces of the Republic of Croatia (Oruzane Snage Republike Hrvatske, OSRH): Ground Forces (Hrvatska Kopnena Vojska, HKoV), Naval Forces (Hrvatska Ratna Mornarica, HRM; includes Coast Guard), Air Force and Air Defense Forces; Military Police Force (2022)

Military expenditures: 2% of GDP (2022 est.)
2.2% of GDP (2021)
1.7% of GDP (2020)
1.6% of GDP (2019) (approximately $1.62 billion)
1.6% of GDP (2018) (approximately $1.52 billion)

Military and security service personnel strengths: approximately 15,000 active duty personnel (10,000 Army; 1,500 Navy; 1,500 Air force; 2,000 joint/other) (2022)

Military equipment inventories and acquisitions: the inventory of the Croatian Armed Forces consists mostly of Soviet-era equipment, although in recent years, it has acquired a limited amount of more modern weapon systems from Western suppliers, including Finland, Germany, and the US (2021)

Military service age and obligation: 18-27 years of age for voluntary military service; conscription abolished in 2008 (2022)
note: as of 2019, women comprised about 13% of the military's full-time personnel

Military deployments 130 Kosovo (KFOR/NATO) (2022)
note: in response to Russia's 2022 invasion of Ukraine, some NATO countries have sent additional troops and equipment to the battlegroups deployed in NATO territory in eastern Europe

Military - note: Croatia joined NATO in 2009

TRANSNATIONAL ISSUES

Disputes - international: dispute remains with Bosnia and Herzegovina over several small sections of the boundary related to maritime access that hinders ratification of the 1999 border agreement; since the breakup of Yugoslavia in the early 1990s, Croatia and Slovenia have each claimed sovereignty over Piranski Bay and four villages, and Slovenia has objected to Croatia's claim of an exclusive economic zone in the Adriatic Sea; in 2009, however Croatia and Slovenia signed a binding international arbitration agreement to define their disputed land and maritime borders, which led to Slovenia lifting its objections to Croatia joining the EU; Slovenia continues to impose a hard border Schengen regime with Croatia, which joined the EU in 2013 but has not yet fulfilled Schengen requirements

Refugees and internally displaced persons: *refugees (country of origin)*: 19,134 (Ukraine) (as of 22 November 2022)
stateless persons: 2,910 (mid-year 2021)
note: 771,932 estimated refugee and migrant arrivals (January 2015-October 2022)

Illicit drugs: drug trafficking groups are major players in the procurement and transportation of large quantities of cocaine destined for European markets

CUBA

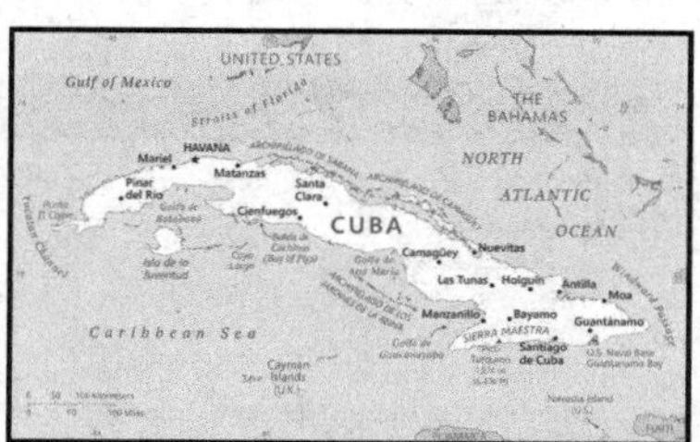

INTRODUCTION

Background: The native Amerindian population of Cuba began to decline after the arrival of Christopher COLUMBUS in 1492 and following its development as a Spanish colony during the next several centuries. Large numbers of African slaves were imported to work the coffee and sugar plantations, and Havana became the launching point for the annual treasure fleets bound for Spain from Mexico and Peru. Spanish rule eventually provoked an independence movement and occasional rebellions were harshly suppressed. US intervention during the Spanish-American War in 1898 assisted the Cubans in overthrowing Spanish rule. The Treaty of Paris established Cuban independence from Spain in 1898 and, following three-and-a-half years of subsequent US military rule, Cuba became an independent republic in 1902 after which the island experienced a string of governments mostly dominated by the military and corrupt politicians. Fidel CASTRO led a rebel army to victory in 1959; his authoritarian rule held the subsequent regime together for nearly five decades. He handed off the presidency in February 2008 to his younger brother Raul CASTRO. Cuba's communist revolution, with Soviet support, was exported throughout Latin America and Africa during the 1960s, 1970s, and 1980s. Miguel DIAZ-CANEL Bermudez, hand-picked by Raul CASTRO to succeed him, was approved as president by the National Assembly and took office on 19 April 2018. DIAZ-CANEL was appointed First Secretary of the Communist Party on 19 April 2021 following the retirement of Raul CASTRO, and continues to serve as both president and first secretary.

Cuba traditionally and consistently portrays the US embargo, in place since 1961, as the source of its difficulties. As a result of efforts begun in December 2014 to reestablish diplomatic relations with the Cuban Government, which were severed in January 1961, the US and Cuba reopened embassies in their respective countries in July 2015. The embargo remains in place, and the relationship between the US and Cuba remains tense.

Illicit migration of Cuban nationals to the US via maritime and overland routes has been a longstanding challenge. On 12 January 2017, the US and Cuba signed a Joint Statement ending the so-called "wet-foot, dry-foot" policy – by which Cuban nationals who reached US soil were permitted to stay. Irregular Cuban maritime migration has dropped significantly since FY 2016, when migrant interdictions at sea topped 5,000, but land border crossings continue. In FY 2021, the US Coast Guard interdicted 838 Cuban nationals at sea. Also in FY 2021, 39,303 Cuban nationals presented themselves at various land border ports of entry throughout the US.

GEOGRAPHY

Location: Caribbean, island between the Caribbean Sea and the North Atlantic Ocean, 150 km south of Key West, Florida

Geographic coordinates: 21 30 N, 80 00 W

Map references: Central America and the Caribbean

Area: *total:* 110,860 sq km
land: 109,820 sq km
water: 1,040 sq km
country comparison to the world: 106

Area - comparative: slightly smaller than Pennsylvania

Land boundaries: *total:* 28.5 km
border countries (1): US Naval Base at Guantanamo Bay 28.5 km
note: Guantanamo Naval Base is leased by the US and remains part of Cuba

Coastline: 3,735 km

Maritime claims: *territorial sea:* 12 nm
contiguous zone: 24 nm
exclusive economic zone: 200 nm

Climate: tropical; moderated by trade winds; dry season (November to April); rainy season (May to October)

Terrain: mostly flat to rolling plains, with rugged hills and mountains in the southeast

Elevation: *highest point:* Pico Turquino 1,974 m
lowest point: Caribbean Sea 0 m
mean elevation: 108 m

Natural resources: cobalt, nickel, iron ore, chromium, copper, salt, timber, silica, petroleum, arable land

Land use: *agricultural land:* 60.3% (2018 est.)
arable land: 33.8% (2018 est.)
permanent crops: 3.6% (2018 est.)
permanent pasture: 22.9% (2018 est.)
forest: 27.3% (2018 est.)
other: 12.4% (2018 est.)

Irrigated land: 8,700 sq km (2012)

Population distribution: large population clusters found throughout the country, the more significant ones being in the larger towns and cities, particularly the capital of Havana

Natural hazards: the east coast is subject to hurricanes from August to November (in general, the country averages about one hurricane every other year); droughts are common

Geography - note: largest country in Caribbean and westernmost island of the Greater Antilles

PEOPLE AND SOCIETY

Population: 11,008,112 (2022 est.)
country comparison to the world: 84

Nationality: *noun:* Cuban(s)
adjective: Cuban

Ethnic groups: White 64.1%, Mulatto or mixed 26.6%, Black 9.3% (2012 est.)
note: data represent racial self-identification from Cuba's 2012 national census

Languages: Spanish (official)
major-language sample(s):
La Libreta Informativa del Mundo, la fuente indispensable de información básica. (Spanish)

Religions: Christian 58.9%, folk religion 17.6%, Buddhist <1%, Hindu <1%, Jewish <1%, Muslim <1%, other <1%, none 23.2% (2020 est.)
note: folk religions include religions of African origin, spiritualism, and others intermingled with Catholicism or Protestantism; data is estimative because no authoritative source on religious affiliation exists for Cuba

Age structure: *0-14 years:* 16.34% (male 929,927/female 877,035)
15-24 years: 11.81% (male 678,253/female 627,384)
25-54 years: 41.95% (male 2,335,680/female 2,303,793)
55-64 years: 14.11% (male 760,165/female 799,734)
65 years and over: 15.8% (male 794,743/female 952,348) (2020 est.)

Dependency ratios: *total dependency ratio:* 46.7
youth dependency ratio: 23.3
elderly dependency ratio: 23.3
potential support ratio: 4.3 (2020 est.)

Median age: *total:* 42.1 years
male: 40.2 years
female: 43.8 years (2020 est.)
country comparison to the world: 37

Population growth rate: -0.21% (2022 est.)
country comparison to the world: 211

Birth rate: 10.11 births/1,000 population (2022 est.)
country comparison to the world: 188

Death rate: 9.29 deaths/1,000 population (2022 est.)
country comparison to the world: 51

Net migration rate: -2.92 migrant(s)/1,000 population (2022 est.)
country comparison to the world: 180

Population distribution: large population clusters found throughout the country, the more significant ones being in the larger towns and cities, particularly the capital of Havana

Urbanization: *urban population:* 77.4% of total population (2022)

rate of urbanization: 0.19% annual rate of change (2020-25 est.)

Major urban areas - population: 2.146 million HAVANA (capital) (2022)

Sex ratio: *at birth:* 1.06 male(s)/female
0-14 years: 1.06 male(s)/female
15-24 years: 1.06 male(s)/female
25-54 years: 1.01 male(s)/female
55-64 years: 0.93 male(s)/female
65 years and over: 0.51 male(s)/female
total population: 0.93 male(s)/female (2022 est.)

Maternal mortality ratio: 36 deaths/100,000 live births (2017 est.)
country comparison to the world: 105

Infant mortality rate: *total:* 4.13 deaths/1,000 live births
male: 4.65 deaths/1,000 live births
female: 3.57 deaths/1,000 live births (2022 est.)
country comparison to the world: 187

Life expectancy at birth: *total population:* 79.64 years
male: 77.29 years
female: 82.14 years (2022 est.)
country comparison to the world: 59

Total fertility rate: 1.71 children born/woman (2022 est.)
country comparison to the world: 163

Contraceptive prevalence rate: 69% (2019)

Drinking water source: *improved: urban:* 98.9% of population
rural: 97% of population
total: 98.5% of population
unimproved: urban: 1.1% of population
rural: 3% of population
total: 1.5% of population (2020 est.)

Current health expenditure: 11.3% of GDP (2019)

Physicians density: 8.42 physicians/1,000 population (2018)

Hospital bed density: 5.3 beds/1,000 population (2017)

Sanitation facility access: *improved: urban:* 94.8% of population
rural: 87% of population
total: 93% of population
unimproved: urban: 5.2% of population
rural: 13% of population
total: 7% of population (2017 est.)

HIV/AIDS - adult prevalence rate: 0.4% (2020 est.)
country comparison to the world: 74

Major infectious diseases: *degree of risk:* intermediate (2020)
food or waterborne diseases: bacterial diarrhea and hepatitis A
vectorborne diseases: dengue fever

Obesity - adult prevalence rate: 24.6% (2016)
country comparison to the world: 56

Alcohol consumption per capita: *total:* 4.7 liters of pure alcohol (2019 est.)
beer: 1.77 liters of pure alcohol (2019 est.)
wine: 0.23 liters of pure alcohol (2019 est.)
spirits: 2.69 liters of pure alcohol (2019 est.)
other alcohols: 0.01 liters of pure alcohol (2019 est.)
country comparison to the world: 86

Tobacco use: *total:* 17.9% (2020 est.)
male: 25.5% (2020 est.)
female: 10.3% (2020 est.)
country comparison to the world: 92

Children under the age of 5 years underweight: 2.4% (2019)
country comparison to the world: 104

Child marriage: *women married by age 15:* 4.8%
women married by age 18: 29.4%
men married by age 18: 5.9% (2019 est.)

Literacy: *definition:* age 15 and over can read and write
total population: 99.8%
male: 99.9%
female: 99.8% (2015)

School life expectancy (primary to tertiary education): *total:* 14 years
male: 14 years
female: 15 years (2020)

People - note: illicit emigration is a continuing problem; Cubans attempt to depart the island and enter the US using homemade rafts, alien smugglers, direct flights, or falsified visas; Cubans also use non-maritime routes to enter the US including direct flights to Miami and overland via the southwest border; the number of Cubans migrating to the US surged after the announcement of normalization of US-Cuban relations in late December 2014 but has decreased since the end of the so-called "wet-foot, dry-foot" policy on 12 January 2017

ENVIRONMENT

Environment - current issues: soil degradation and desertification (brought on by poor farming techniques and natural disasters) are the main environmental problems; biodiversity loss; deforestation; air and water pollution

Environment - international agreements: *party to:* Antarctic Treaty, Biodiversity, Climate Change, Climate Change-Kyoto Protocol, Climate Change-Paris Agreement, Comprehensive Nuclear Test Ban, Desertification, Endangered Species, Environmental Modification, Hazardous Wastes, Law of the Sea, Marine Dumping-London Convention, Ozone Layer Protection, Ship Pollution, Wetlands
signed, but not ratified: Marine Life Conservation

Air pollutants: *particulate matter emissions:* 18.37 micrograms per cubic meter (2016 est.)
carbon dioxide emissions: 28.28 megatons (2016 est.)
methane emissions: 9.3 megatons (2020 est.)

Climate: tropical; moderated by trade winds; dry season (November to April); rainy season (May to October)

Land use: *agricultural land:* 60.3% (2018 est.)
arable land: 33.8% (2018 est.)
permanent crops: 3.6% (2018 est.)
permanent pasture: 22.9% (2018 est.)
forest: 27.3% (2018 est.)
other: 12.4% (2018 est.)

Urbanization: *urban population:* 77.4% of total population (2022)
rate of urbanization: 0.19% annual rate of change (2020-25 est.)

Revenue from forest resources: *forest revenues:* 0.06% of GDP (2018 est.)
country comparison to the world: 124

Revenue from coal: *coal revenues:* 0% of GDP (2018 est.)
country comparison to the world: 85

Waste and recycling: *municipal solid waste generated annually:* 2,692,692 tons (2007 est.)
municipal solid waste recycled annually: 255,536 tons (2015 est.)
percent of municipal solid waste recycled: 9.5% (2015 est.)

Total water withdrawal: *municipal:* 1.7 billion cubic meters (2017 est.)
industrial: 740 million cubic meters (2017 est.)
agricultural: 4.519 billion cubic meters (2017 est.)

Total renewable water resources: 38.12 billion cubic meters (2017 est.)

GOVERNMENT

Country name: *conventional long form:* Republic of Cuba
conventional short form: Cuba
local long form: Republica de Cuba
local short form: Cuba
etymology: name derives from the Taino Indian designation for the island "coabana" meaning "great place"

Government type: communist state

Capital: *name:* Havana
geographic coordinates: 23 07 N, 82 21 W
time difference: UTC-5 (same time as Washington, DC, during Standard Time)
daylight saving time: +1hr, begins second Sunday in March; ends first Sunday in November; note - Cuba has been known to alter the schedule of DST on short notice in an attempt to conserve electricity for lighting
etymology: the sites of Spanish colonial cities often retained their original Taino names; Habana, the Spanish name for the city, may be based on the name of a local Taino chief, HABAGUANEX

Administrative divisions: 15 provinces (provincias, singular - provincia) and 1 special municipality* (municipio especial); Artemisa, Camaguey, Ciego de Avila, Cienfuegos, Granma, Guantanamo, Holguin, Isla de la Juventud*, La Habana, Las Tunas, Matanzas, Mayabeque, Pinar del Rio, Sancti Spiritus, Santiago de Cuba, Villa Clara

Independence: 20 May 1902 (from Spain 10 December 1898; administered by the US from 1898 to 1902); not acknowledged by the Cuban Government as a day of independence

National holiday: Triumph of the Revolution (Liberation Day), 1 January (1959)

Constitution: *history:* several previous; latest drafted 14 July 2018, approved by the National Assembly 22 December 2018, approved by referendum 24 February 2019
amendments: proposed by the National Assembly of People's Power; passage requires approval of at least two-thirds majority of the National Assembly membership; amendments to constitutional articles on the authorities of the National Assembly, Council of State, or any rights and duties in the constitution also require approval in a referendum; constitutional articles on the Cuban political, social, and economic system cannot be amended

Legal system: civil law system based on Spanish civil code

International law organization participation: has not submitted an ICJ jurisdiction declaration; non-party state to the ICCt

Citizenship: *citizenship by birth:* yes
citizenship by descent only: yes
dual citizenship recognized: no

residency requirement for naturalization: unknown

Suffrage: 16 years of age; universal

Executive branch: *chief of state:* President Miguel DIAZ-CANEL Bermudez (since 19 April 2018); Vice President Salvador Antonio VALDES Mesa (since 10 October 2019)
head of government: Prime Minister Manuel MARRERO Cruz (since 21 December 2019); Deputy Prime Ministers Ramiro VALDES Menendez, Ines Maria CHAPMAN Waugh, Jorge Luis TAPIA Fonseca, Alejandro GIL Fernandez, Ricardo CABRISAS Ruiz (since 21 December 2019), and Jorge Luis PERDOMO DI-LELLA (since 20 April 2021)
cabinet: Council of Ministers proposed by the president and appointed by the National Assembly
elections/appointments: president and vice president indirectly elected by the National Assembly for a 5-year term (may be reelected for another 5-year term); election last held on 10 October 2019 (next to be held NA)
election results:
2019: Miguel DIAZ-CANEL Bermudez (PCC) elected president; percent of National Assembly vote - 98.8%; Salvador Antonio VALDES Mesa (PCC) elected vice president; percent of National Assembly vote - 98.1%
2018: Miguel DIAZ-CANEL Bermudez (PCC) elected president; percent of National Assembly vote - 98.8%; Salvador Antonio VALDES Mesa (PCC) elected vice president; percent of National Assembly vote - 100%
note - on 19 April 2018, DIAZ-CANEL succeeded Raul CASTRO as president of the Councils of State and Ministers; on 10 October 2019 he was elected to the newly created position of President of the Republic, which replaced the position of President of the Councils of State and Ministers

Legislative branch: *description:* unicameral National Assembly of People's Power or Asamblea Nacional del Poder Popular (605 seats; (586 seats filled in 2021); members directly elected by absolute majority vote; members serve 5-year terms); note 1 - the National Candidature Commission submits a slate of approved candidates; to be elected, candidates must receive more than 50% of valid votes otherwise the seat remains vacant or the Council of State can declare another election; note 2 -in July 2019, the National Assembly passed a law which reduces the number of members from 605 to 474, effective with the 2023 general election
elections:
last held on 11 March 2018 (next to be held in early 2023)
election results:
Cuba's Communist Party is the only legal party, and officially sanctioned candidates run unopposed; composition (as of June 2021) - men 273, women 313, percent of women 53.4%

Judicial branch: *highest court(s):* People's Supreme Court (consists of court president, vice president, 41 professional justices, and NA lay judges); organization includes the State Council, criminal, civil, administrative, labor, crimes against the state, and military courts)
judge selection and term of office: professional judges elected by the National Assembly are not subject to a specific term; lay judges nominated by workplace collectives and neighborhood associations and elected by municipal or provincial assemblies; lay judges appointed for 5-year terms and serve up to 30 days per year
subordinate courts: People's Provincial Courts; People's Regional Courts; People's Courts

Political parties and leaders: Cuban Communist Party or PCC [Miguel DIAZ-CANEL Bermudez]

International organization participation: ACP, ALBA, AOSIS, CELAC, EAEU (observer), FAO, G-77, IAEA, ICAO, ICC (national committees), ICRM, IFAD, IFRCS, IHO, ILO, IMO, IMSO, Interpol, IOC, IOM (observer), IPU, ISO, ITSO, ITU, LAES, LAIA, NAM, OAS (excluded from formal participation since 1962), OPANAL, OPCW, PCA, Petrocaribe, PIF (partner), UN, UNCTAD, UNESCO, UNHRC, UNIDO, Union Latina, UNWTO, UPU, WCO, WFTU (NGOs), WHO, WIPO, WMO, WTO

Diplomatic representation in the US: *chief of mission:* Ambassador (vacant); Charge d'Affaires Lianys TORRES RIVERA (since 14 January 2021)
chancery: 2630 16th Street NW, Washington, DC 20009
telephone: [1] (202) 797-8515 through 8518
FAX: [1] (202) 797-8521
email address and website:
recepcion@usadc.embacuba.cu
http://misiones.minrex.gob.cu/en/usa

Diplomatic representation from the US: *chief of mission:* Ambassador (vacant); Charge d'Affaires Timothy ZUNIGA-BROWN (since 31 July 2020)
embassy: Calzada between L & M Streets, Vedado, Havana
mailing address: 3200 Havana Place, Washington DC 20521-3200
telephone: [53] (7) 839-4100
FAX: [53] (7) 839-4247
email address and website:
acshavana@state.gov
https://cu.usembassy.gov/

Flag description: five equal horizontal bands of blue (top, center, and bottom) alternating with white; a red equilateral triangle based on the hoist side bears a white, five-pointed star in the center; the blue bands refer to the three old divisions of the island: central, occidental, and oriental; the white bands describe the purity of the independence ideal; the triangle symbolizes liberty, equality, and fraternity, while the red color stands for the blood shed in the independence struggle; the white star, called La Estrella Solitaria (the Lone Star) lights the way to freedom and was taken from the flag of Texas
note: design similar to the Puerto Rican flag, with the colors of the bands and triangle reversed

National symbol(s): royal palm; national colors: red, white, blue

National anthem: *name:* "La Bayamesa" (The Bayamo Song)
lyrics/music: Pedro FIGUEREDO
note: adopted 1940; Pedro FIGUEREDO first performed "La Bayamesa" in 1868 during the Ten Years War against the Spanish; a leading figure in the uprising, FIGUEREDO was captured in 1870 and executed by a firing squad; just prior to the fusillade he is reputed to have shouted, "Morir por la Patria es vivir" (To die for the country is to live), a line from the anthem

National heritage: *total World Heritage Sites:* 9 (7 cultural, 2 natural)
selected World Heritage Site locales: Old Havana (c); Trinidad and the Valley de los Ingenios (c); San Pedro de la Roca Castle (c); Desembarco del Granma National Park (n); Viñales Valley (c); Archaeological Landscape of the First Coffee Plantations (c); Alejandro de Humboldt National Park (n); Historic Cienfuegos (c); Historic Camagüey (c)

ECONOMY

Economic overview: The government continues to balance the need for loosening its socialist economic system against a desire for firm political control. In April 2011, the government held the first Cuban Communist Party Congress in almost 13 years, during which leaders approved a plan for wide-ranging economic changes. Since then, the government has slowly and incrementally implemented limited economic reforms, including allowing Cubans to buy electronic appliances and cell phones, stay in hotels, and buy and sell used cars. The government has cut state sector jobs as part of the reform process, and it has opened up some retail services to "self-employment," leading to the rise of so-called "cuentapropistas" or entrepreneurs. More than 500,000 Cuban workers are currently registered as self-employed.

The Cuban regime has updated its economic model to include permitting the private ownership and sale of real estate and new vehicles, allowing private farmers to sell agricultural goods directly to hotels, allowing the creation of non-agricultural cooperatives, adopting a new foreign investment law, and launching a "Special Development Zone" around the Mariel port.

Since 2016, Cuba has attributed slowed economic growth in part to problems with petroleum product deliveries from Venezuela. Since late 2000, Venezuela provided petroleum products to Cuba on preferential terms, supplying at times nearly 100,000 barrels per day. Cuba paid for the oil, in part, with the services of Cuban personnel in Venezuela, including some 30,000 medical professionals.

Real GDP (purchasing power parity): $137 billion (2017 est.)
$134.8 billion (2016 est.)
$134.2 billion (2015 est.)
note: data are in 2016 US dollars
country comparison to the world: 78

Real GDP growth rate: 1.6% (2017 est.)
0.5% (2016 est.)
4.4% (2015 est.)
country comparison to the world: 150

Real GDP per capita: $12,300 (2016 est.)
$12,200 (2015 est.)
$12,100 (2014 est.)
note: data are in 2016 US dollars
country comparison to the world: 122

GDP (official exchange rate): $93.79 billion (2017 est.)
note: data are in Cuban Pesos at 1 CUP = 1 US$; official exchange rate

Inflation rate (consumer prices): 5.5% (2017 est.)
4.5% (2016 est.)
country comparison to the world: 188

Credit ratings: Moody's rating: Caa2 (2014)
note: The year refers to the year in which the current credit rating was first obtained.

GDP - composition, by sector of origin: *agriculture:* 4% (2017 est.)
industry: 22.7% (2017 est.)

services: 73.4% (2017 est.)

GDP - composition, by end use: *household consumption:* 57% (2017 est.)
government consumption: 31.6% (2017 est.)
investment in fixed capital: 9.6% (2017 est.)
investment in inventories: 0% (2017 est.)
exports of goods and services: 14.6% (2017 est.)
imports of goods and services: -12.7% (2017 est.)

Agricultural products: sugar cane, cassava, vegetables, plantains, sweet potatoes, tomatoes, milk, pumpkins, mangoes/guavas, rice

Industries: petroleum, nickel, cobalt, pharmaceuticals, tobacco, construction, steel, cement, agricultural machinery, sugar

Industrial production growth rate: -1.2% (2017 est.)
country comparison to the world: 179

Labor force: 4.691 million (2017 est.)
note: state sector 72.3%, non-state sector 27.7%
country comparison to the world: 83

Labor force - by occupation: *agriculture:* 18%
industry: 10%
services: 72% (2016 est.)

Unemployment rate: 2.6% (2017 est.)
2.4% (2016 est.)
note: data are official rates; unofficial estimates are about double
country comparison to the world: 30

Budget: *revenues:* 54.52 billion (2017 est.)
expenditures: 64.64 billion (2017 est.)

Budget surplus (+) or deficit (-): -10.8% (of GDP) (2017 est.)
country comparison to the world: 214

Public debt: 47.7% of GDP (2017 est.)
42.7% of GDP (2016 est.)
country comparison to the world: 110

Taxes and other revenues: 58.1% (of GDP) (2017 est.)
country comparison to the world: 8

Fiscal year: calendar year

Current account balance: $985.4 million (2017 est.)
$2.008 billion (2016 est.)
country comparison to the world: 50

Exports: $2.63 billion (2017 est.)
$2.546 billion (2016 est.)
note: Data are in current year dollars and do not include illicit exports or re-exports.
country comparison to the world: 146

Exports - partners: China 38%, Spain 11%, Netherlands 5%, Germany 5% (2019)

Exports - commodities: cigars, raw sugar, nickel products, rum, zinc (2019)

Imports: $11.06 billion (2017 est.)
$10.28 billion (2016 est.)
country comparison to the world: 101

Imports - partners: Spain 19%, China 15%, Italy 6%, Canada 5%, Russia 5%, United States 5%, Brazil 5% (2019)

Imports - commodities: poultry meat, wheat, soybean products, corn, concentrated milk (2019)

Reserves of foreign exchange and gold: $11.35 billion (31 December 2017 est.)
$12.3 billion (31 December 2016 est.)
country comparison to the world: 72

Debt - external: $30.06 billion (31 December 2017 est.)
$29.89 billion (31 December 2016 est.)
country comparison to the world: 83

Exchange rates: Cuban pesos (CUP) per US dollar -
1 (2017 est.)
1 (2016 est.)
1 (2015 est.)
1 (2014 est.)
22.7 (2013 est.)

ENERGY

Electricity access: *electrification - total population:* 100% (2020)

Electricity: *installed generating capacity:* 7.479 million kW (2020 est.)
consumption: 16,097,460,000 kWh (2019 est.)
exports: 0 kWh (2020 est.)
imports: 0 kWh (2020 est.)
transmission/distribution losses: 3.429 billion kWh (2019 est.)

Electricity generation sources: *fossil fuels:* 95.5% of total installed capacity (2020 est.)
solar: 1.4% of total installed capacity (2020 est.)
wind: 0.1% of total installed capacity (2020 est.)
hydroelectricity: 0.3% of total installed capacity (2020 est.)
biomass and waste: 2.7% of total installed capacity (2020 est.)

Coal: *production:* 0 metric tons (2020 est.)
consumption: 4,000 metric tons (2020 est.)
exports: 0 metric tons (2020 est.)
imports: 4,000 metric tons (2020 est.)
proven reserves: 0 metric tons (2019 est.)

Petroleum: *total petroleum production:* 38,400 bbl/day (2021 est.)
refined petroleum consumption: 164,100 bbl/day (2019 est.)
crude oil and lease condensate exports: 0 bbl/day (2018 est.)
crude oil and lease condensate imports: 48,500 bbl/day (2018 est.)
crude oil estimated reserves: 124 million barrels (2021 est.)

Refined petroleum products - production: 104,100 bbl/day (2015 est.)
country comparison to the world: 67

Refined petroleum products - exports: 24,190 bbl/day (2015 est.)
country comparison to the world: 69

Refined petroleum products - imports: 52,750 bbl/day (2015 est.)
country comparison to the world: 78

Natural gas: *production:* 976.023 million cubic meters (2019 est.)
consumption: 976.023 million cubic meters (2019 est.)
exports: 0 cubic meters (2021 est.)
imports: 0 cubic meters (2021 est.)
proven reserves: 70.792 billion cubic meters (2021 est.)

Carbon dioxide emissions: 16.478 million metric tonnes of CO_2 (2019 est.)
from coal and metallurgical coke: 28,000 metric tonnes of CO_2 (2019 est.)
from petroleum and other liquids: 14.636 million metric tonnes of CO_2 (2019 est.)
from consumed natural gas: 1.814 million metric tonnes of CO_2 (2019 est.)
country comparison to the world: 94

Energy consumption per capita: 32.785 million Btu/person (2019 est.)
country comparison to the world: 119

COMMUNICATIONS

Telephones - fixed lines: *total subscriptions:* 1,502,230 (2020 est.)
subscriptions per 100 inhabitants: 13 (2020 est.)
country comparison to the world: 62

Telephones - mobile cellular: *total subscriptions:* 6,661,763 (2020 est.)
subscriptions per 100 inhabitants: 59 (2020 est.)
country comparison to the world: 110

Telecommunication systems: *general assessment:* internet availability has increased substantially over the past few years, but only about 64 percent of Cubans have Internet access, and even fewer Cubans--about 60 percent of the population--have access to cell phone service; in 2021 the Cuban Government passed a decree that strengthened its authority to censor Internet and telephonic communications; state control of the telecom sector hinders development; Cuba has the lowest mobile phone and Internet subscription rates in the region; fixed-line density is also very low; thaw of US-Cuba relations encouraged access to services, such as Wi-Fi hot spots; access to sites is controlled and censored; DSL and Internet are available in Havana, though costs are too high for most Cubans; international investment and agreement to improve Internet access through cost-free and direct connection between networks (2021)
domestic: fixed-line density remains low at a little over 13 per 100 inhabitants; mobile-cellular service has expanded to about 59 per 100 persons (2020)
international: country code - 53; the ALBA-1, GTMO-1, and GTMO-PR fiber-optic submarine cables link Cuba, Jamaica, and Venezuela; satellite earth station - 1 Intersputnik (Atlantic Ocean region) (2019)

Broadcast media: *government owns and controls all broadcast media:* five national TV channels (Cubavision, Tele Rebelde, Multivision, Educational Channel 1 and 2), two international channels (Cubavision Internacional and Caribe), 16 regional TV stations, 6 national radio networks, and multiple regional stations; the Cuban Government beams over the Radio-TV Marti signal; although private ownership of electronic media is prohibited, several online independent news sites exist; those that are not openly critical of the government are often tolerated; the others are blocked by the government; there are no independent TV channels, but several outlets have created strong audiovisual content (El Toque, for example); a community of young Youtubers is also growing, mostly with channels about sports, technology and fashion; Christian denominations are creating original video content to distribute via social media (2019)

Internet country code: .cu

Internet users: *total:* 8,381,696 (2020 est.)
percent of population: 74% (2020 est.)
note: private citizens are prohibited from buying computers or accessing the Internet without special authorization; foreigners may access the Internet in large hotels but are subject to firewalls; some Cubans buy illegal passwords on the black market or take advantage of public outlets

to access limited email and the government-controlled "intranet"; issues relating to COVID-19 impact research into internet adoption, so actual internet user figures may be different than published numbers suggest
country comparison to the world: 65

Broadband - fixed subscriptions: *total:* 231,654 (2020 est.)
subscriptions per 100 inhabitants: 2 (2020 est.)
country comparison to the world: 115

TRANSPORTATION

National air transport system: *number of registered air carriers:* 4 (2020)
inventory of registered aircraft operated by air carriers: 18
annual passenger traffic on registered air carriers: 560,754 (2018)
annual freight traffic on registered air carriers: 17.76 million (2018) mt-km

Civil aircraft registration country code prefix: CU

Airports: *total:* 133 (2021)
country comparison to the world: 41

Airports - with paved runways: *total:* 64
over 3,047 m: 7
2,438 to 3,047 m: 10
1,524 to 2,437 m: 16
914 to 1,523 m: 4
under 914 m: 27 (2021)

Airports - with unpaved runways: *total:* 69
914 to 1,523 m: 11
under 914 m: 58 (2021)

Pipelines: 41 km gas, 230 km oil (2013)

Railways: *total:* 8,367 km (2017)
standard gauge: 8,195 km (2017) 1.435-m gauge (124 km electrified)
narrow gauge: 172 km (2017) 1.000-m gauge
note: As of 2013, 70 km of standard gauge and 12 km of narrow gauge track were not for public use
country comparison to the world: 26

Roadways: *total:* 60,000 km (2015)
paved: 20,000 km (2001)
unpaved: 40,000 km (2001)
country comparison to the world: 75

Waterways: 240 km (2011) (almost all navigable inland waterways are near the mouths of rivers)
country comparison to the world: 103

Merchant marine: *total:* 59
by type: general cargo 12, oil tanker 7, other 40 (2021)
country comparison to the world: 113

Ports and terminals: *major seaport(s):* Antilla, Cienfuegos, Guantanamo, Havana, Matanzas, Mariel, Nuevitas Bay, Santiago de Cuba

MILITARY AND SECURITY

Military and security forces: Revolutionary Armed Forces (Fuerzas Armadas Revolucionarias, FAR): Revolutionary Army (Ejercito Revolucionario, ER), Revolutionary Navy (Marina de Guerra Revolucionaria, MGR, includes Marine Corps), Revolutionary Air and Air Defense Forces (Defensas Anti-Aereas y Fuerza Aerea Revolucionaria, DAAFAR); Paramilitary forces: Youth Labor Army (Ejercito Juvenil del Trabajo, EJT), Territorial Militia Troops (Milicia de Tropas de Territoriales, MTT), Civil Defense Force; Ministry of Interior: Border Guards, State Security, National Revolutionary Police (2022)

Military expenditures: 4.2% of GDP (2020 est.)
3.2% of GDP (2019 est.) (approximately $5.9 billion)
2.9% of GDP (2018 est.) (approximately $5.6 billion)
2.9% of GDP (2017 est.) (approximately $5.5 billion)
3.1% of GDP (2016 est.) (approximately $5.5 billion)
country comparison to the world: 15

Military and security service personnel strengths: limited available information; estimated 50,000 active personnel (approximately 40,000 Army; 3,000 Navy; 8,000 Air Force) (2022)

Military equipment inventories and acquisitions: the Cuban military inventory is comprised of aging Russian and Soviet-era equipment; the last recorded arms delivery to Cuba was by Russia in 2004; in 2019, Russia approved a loan for approximately $43-50 million for Cuba's purchase of spare parts and armored vehicles (2022)

Military service age and obligation: 17-28 years of age for compulsory (men) and voluntary (men and women) military service; conscripts serve for two years (2022)

Military - note: the FAR has a large role in the Cuban economy through several military owned and operated conglomerates, including such sectors as banking, hotels, industry, retail, transportation, and tourism (2022)

TRANSNATIONAL ISSUES

Disputes - international: US Naval Base at Guantanamo Bay is leased to US and only mutual agreement or US abandonment of the facility can terminate the lease

Trafficking in persons: *current situation:* human traffickers exploit domestic and foreign victims in Cuba and Cubans abroad; individuals are forced or coerced into participating and threatened to stay in labor export programs, most notably foreign medical missions; sex trafficking and sex tourism occur within Cuba; traffickers exploit Cubans in sex trafficking and forced labor in South America, the Caribbean, Asia, Africa, the Mediterranean, and the US; foreigners from Africa and Asia are subject to sex trafficking and forced labor in Cuba to pay off travel debts; the government uses high school students in some rural areas to harvest crops without pay, claiming that the work is voluntary
tier rating:
Tier 3 — Cuba does not fully meet the minimum standards for the elimination of trafficking and is not making significant efforts to do so; the government made some efforts to investigate, prosecute, and convict sex traffickers and sex tourists and identified and provided assistance to some victims; however, no efforts were made to address forced labor; there was a government policy or pattern to profit from labor export programs with strong indications of forced labor, particularly in foreign medical missions; authorities did not protect potential trafficking victims, leaving them at risk of being detained or charged for crimes their traffickers forced them to commit (2020)

Illicit drugs: Cuba is not a major consumer, producer, or transit point of illicit drugs; strict policing on smuggling, production and consumption; prescription drug abuse is increasing

CURACAO

INTRODUCTION

Background: The original Arawak Indian settlers who arrived on the island from South America in about A.D. 1000, were largely enslaved by the Spanish early in the 16th century and forcibly relocated to other colonies where labor was needed. Curacao was seized by the Dutch from the Spanish in 1634. Once the center of the Caribbean slave trade, Curacao was hard hit economically by the Dutch abolition of slavery in 1863. Its prosperity (and that of neighboring Aruba) was restored in the early 20th century with the construction of the Isla Refineria to service the newly discovered Venezuelan oilfields. In 1954, Curacao and several other Dutch Caribbean colonies were reorganized as the Netherlands Antilles, part of the Kingdom of the Netherlands. In referenda in 2005 and 2009, the citizens of Curacao voted to become a self-governing country within the Kingdom of the Netherlands. The change in status became effective in October 2010 with the dissolution of the Netherlands Antilles.

GEOGRAPHY

Location: Caribbean, an island in the Caribbean Sea, 55 km off the coast of Venezuela

Geographic coordinates: 12 10 N, 69 00 W

Map references: Central America and the Caribbean

Area: *total:* 444 sq km
land: 444 sq km
water: 0 sq km

Area - comparative: more than twice the size of Washington, DC

Land boundaries: 0

Coastline: 364 km

Maritime claims: *territorial sea:* 12 nm
exclusive economic zone: 200 nm

Climate: tropical marine climate, ameliorated by northeast trade winds, results in mild temperatures; semiarid with average rainfall of 60 cm/year

Terrain: generally low, hilly terrain

Elevation: *highest point:* Mt. Christoffel 372 m
lowest point: Caribbean Sea 0 m

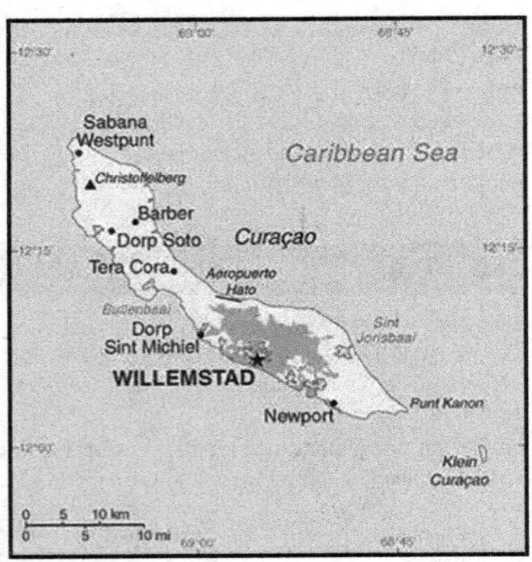

Natural resources: calcium phosphates, protected harbors, hot springs

Land use: *agricultural land:* 10% (2018 est.)
arable land: 10% (2018)
other: 90% (2018 est.)

Population distribution: largest concentration on the island is Willemstad; smaller settlements near the coast can be found throughout the island, particularly in the northwest

Natural hazards: Curacao is south of the Caribbean hurricane belt and is rarely threatened

Geography - note: Curacao is a part of the Windward Islands (southern) group in the Lesser Antilles

PEOPLE AND SOCIETY

Population: 152,379 (2022 est.)

Nationality: *noun:* Curacaoan
adjective: Curacaoan; Dutch

Ethnic groups: Curacaoan 75.4%, Dutch 6%, Dominican 3.6%, Colombian 3%, Bonairean, Sint Eustatian, Saban 1.5%, Haitian 1.2%, Surinamese 1.2%, Venezuelan 1.1%, Aruban 1.1%, other 5%, unspecified 0.9% (2011 est.)

Languages: Papiamento (official) (a creole language that is a mixture of Portuguese, Spanish, Dutch, English, and, to a lesser extent, French, as well as elements of African languages and the language of the Arawak) 80%, Dutch (official) 8.8%, Spanish 5.6%, English (official) 3.1%, other 2.3%, unspecified 0.3% (2011 est.)
note: data represent most spoken language in household

Religions: Roman Catholic 72.8%, Pentecostal 6.6%, Protestant 3.2%, Adventist 3%, Jehovah's Witness 2%, Evangelical 1.9%, other 3.8%, none 6%, unspecified 0.6% (2011 est.)

Age structure: *0-14 years:* 19.68% (male 15,227/female 14,553)
15-24 years: 13.38% (male 10,438/female 9,806)
25-54 years: 36.55% (male 27,733/female 27,589)
55-64 years: 13.88% (male 9,130/female 11,873)
65 years and over: 16.52% (male 10,127/female 14,869) (2020 est.)

Dependency ratios: *total dependency ratio:* 55.9
youth dependency ratio: 28.3
elderly dependency ratio: 27.5
potential support ratio: 3.6 (2020 est.)

Median age: *total:* 36.7 years
male: 34.4 years
female: 39.5 years (2020 est.)

Population growth rate: 0.32% (2022 est.)

Birth rate: 13.2 births/1,000 population (2022 est.)

Death rate: 8.71 deaths/1,000 population (2022 est.)

Net migration rate: -1.31 migrant(s)/1,000 population (2022 est.)

Population distribution: largest concentration on the island is Willemstad; smaller settlements near the coast can be found throughout the island, particularly in the northwest

Urbanization: *urban population:* 89% of total population (2022)
rate of urbanization: 0.57% annual rate of change (2020-25 est.)

Major urban areas - population: 144,000 WILLEMSTAD (capital) (2018)

Sex ratio: *at birth:* 1.05 male(s)/female
0-14 years: 1.06 male(s)/female
15-24 years: 1.08 male(s)/female
25-54 years: 1.02 male(s)/female
55-64 years: 0.95 male(s)/female
65 years and over: 0.69 male(s)/female
total population: 0.99 male(s)/female (2022 est.)

Infant mortality rate: *total:* 7.88 deaths/1,000 live births
male: 8.69 deaths/1,000 live births
female: 7.02 deaths/1,000 live births (2022 est.)

Life expectancy at birth: *total population:* 79.42 years
male: 77.09 years
female: 81.87 years (2022 est.)

Total fertility rate: 1.98 children born/woman (2022 est.)

Drinking water source: *improved: total:* 100% of population
unimproved: total: 0% of population (2017)

Sanitation facility access: *improved: total:* 100% of population
unimproved: total: 0% of population (2017)

Education expenditures: 4.9% of GDP (2013 est.)

School life expectancy (primary to tertiary education): *total:* 17 years
male: 18 years
female: 18 years (2013)

Unemployment, youth ages 15-24: *total:* 29.3%
male: 25.4%
female: 34.5% (2018 est.)

ENVIRONMENT

Environment - current issues: problems in waste management that threaten environmental sustainability on the island include pollution of marine areas from domestic sewage, inadequate sewage treatment facilities, industrial effluents and agricultural runoff, the mismanagement of toxic substances, and ineffective regulations; the refinery in Sint Anna Bay, at the eastern edge of Willemstad's large natural harbor, processes heavy crude oil from Venezuela; it has caused significant environmental damage to the surrounding area because of neglect and a lack of strict environmental controls; the release of noxious fumes and potentially hazardous particles causes schools downwind to regularly close

Air pollutants: *carbon dioxide emissions:* 5.39 megatons (2016 est.)

Climate: tropical marine climate, ameliorated by northeast trade winds, results in mild temperatures; semiarid with average rainfall of 60 cm/year

Land use: *agricultural land:* 10% (2018 est.)
arable land: 10% (2018)
other: 90% (2018 est.)

Urbanization: *urban population:* 89% of total population (2022)
rate of urbanization: 0.57% annual rate of change (2020-25 est.)

Revenue from forest resources: *forest revenues:* 0% of GDP (2018 est.)

Revenue from coal: *coal revenues:* 0% of GDP (2018 est.)

Waste and recycling: *municipal solid waste generated annually:* 24,704 tons (2013 est.)
municipal solid waste recycled annually: 494 tons (2013 est.)
percent of municipal solid waste recycled: 2% (2013 est.)

GOVERNMENT

Country name: *conventional long form:* Country of Curacao
conventional short form: Curacao
local long form: Land Curacao (Dutch)/ Pais Korsou (Papiamento)
local short form: Curacao (Dutch)/ Korsou (Papiamento)
former: Netherlands Antilles; Curacao and Dependencies
etymology: the most plausible name derivation is that the island was designated Isla de la Curacion (Spanish meaning "Island of the Cure" or "Island of Healing") or Ilha da Curacao (Portuguese meaning the same) to reflect the locale's function as a recovery stop for sick crewmen

Government type: parliamentary democracy

Dependency status: constituent country within the Kingdom of the Netherlands; full autonomy in internal affairs granted in 2010; Dutch Government responsible for defense and foreign affairs

Capital: *name:* Willemstad
geographic coordinates: 12 06 N, 68 55 W
time difference: UTC-4 (1 hour ahead of Washington, DC, during Standard Time)
etymology: named after Prince WILLIAM II of Orange (1626-1650), who served as stadtholder (Dutch head of state) from 1647 to 1650, shortly after the the Dutch captured Curacao from the Spanish in 1634

Administrative divisions: none (part of the Kingdom of the Netherlands)
note: Curacao is one of four constituent countries of the Kingdom of the Netherlands; the other three are the Netherlands, Aruba, and Sint Maarten

Independence: none (part of the Kingdom of the Netherlands)

National holiday: King's Day (birthday of King WILLEM-ALEXANDER), 27 April (1967); note - King's or Queen's Day are observed on the ruling monarch's birthday; celebrated on 26 April if 27 April is a Sunday

Constitution: *history:* previous 1947, 1955; latest adopted 5 September 2010, entered into force 10

October 2010 (regulates governance of Curacao but is subordinate to the Charter for the Kingdom of the Netherlands); note - in October 2010, with the dissolution of the Netherlands Antilles, Curacao became a semi-autonomous entity within the Kingdom of the Netherlands

Legal system: based on Dutch civil law

Citizenship: see the Netherlands

Suffrage: 18 years of age; universal

Executive branch: *chief of state:* King WILLEM-ALEXANDER of the Netherlands (since 30 April 2013); represented by Governor Lucille A. GEORGE-WOUT (since 4 November 2013)
head of government: Prime Minister Gilmar PISAS (since 14 June 2021)
cabinet: Cabinet sworn-in by the governor
elections/appointments: the monarch is hereditary; governor appointed by the monarch; following legislative elections, the leader of the majority party usually elected prime minister by the Parliament of Curacao; last election 19 March 2021 (next to be held in 2025)

Legislative branch: *description:* unicameral Parliament of Curacao (21 seats; members directly elected by party-list proportional representation vote to serve 4-year terms)
elections:
last held on 19 March 2021 (next to be held in 2025)
election results:
percent of vote by party - MFK 28.1%, PAR 14.1%, PNP 12.6%, MAN 6.5%, KEM 5.4%, TPK 5.3%; seats by party - MFK 9, PAR 4, PNP 4, MAN 2, KEM 1, TPK 1; composition - NA

Judicial branch: *highest court(s):* Joint Court of Justice of Aruba, Curacao, Sint Maarten, and of Bonaire, Sint Eustatius and Saba or "Joint Court of Justice" (sits as a 3-judge panel); final appeals heard by the Supreme Court, in The Hague, Netherlands
judge selection and term of office: Joint Court judges appointed by the monarch for life
subordinate courts: first instance courts, appeals court; specialized courts

Political parties and leaders: Korsou di Nos Tur or KdnT [Amparo dos SANTOS]
Korsou Esun Miho or KEM [Michelangelo MARTINES]
Movementu Futuro Korsou or MFK [Gilmar PISAS]
Movementu Progresivo or MP [Marylin MOSES]
Movishon Antia Nobo or MAN [Hensley KOEIMAN]
Partido Antia Restruktura or PAR [Eugene RHUGGENAATH]
Partido Inovashon Nashonal or PIN [Suzanne CAMELIA-ROMER]
Partido Nashonal di Pueblo or PNP [Ruthmilda LARMONIE-CECILIA]
Pueblo Soberano or PS [Ben WHITEMAN]
Trabou pa Kòrsou or TPK [Rennox CALMES]
Un Korsou Hustu [Omayra LEEFLANG]

International organization participation: Caricom (observer), FATF, ILO, ITU, UNESCO (associate), UPU

Diplomatic representation in the US: none (represented by the Kingdom of the Netherlands)

Diplomatic representation from the US: *chief of mission:* Consul General Margy BOND (since January 2022); note - also accredited to Aruba and Sint Maarten
embassy: P.O. Box 158, J.B. Gorsiraweg 1
mailing address: 3160 Curacao Place, Washington DC 20521-3160
telephone: [599] (9) 461-3066
FAX: [599] (9) 461-6489
email address and website:
ACSCuracao@state.gov
https://cw.usconsulate.gov/

Flag description: *on a blue field a horizontal yellow band somewhat below the center divides the flag into proportions of 5:1:2;* two five-pointed white stars - the smaller above and to the left of the larger - appear in the canton; the blue of the upper and lower sections symbolizes the sky and sea respectively; yellow represents the sun; the stars symbolize Curacao and its uninhabited smaller sister island of Klein Curacao; the five star points signify the five continents from which Curacao's people derive

National symbol(s): laraha (citrus tree); national colors: blue, yellow, white

National anthem: *name:* "Himmo di Korsou" (Anthem of Curacao)
lyrics/music: Guillermo ROSARIO, Mae HENRIQUEZ, Enrique MULLER, Betty DORAN/ Frater Candidus NOWENS, Errol "El Toro" COLINA
note: adapted 1978; the lyrics, originally written in 1899, were rewritten in 1978 to make them less colonial in nature

National heritage: *total World Heritage Sites:* 1 (cultural); note - excerpted from the Netherlands entry
selected World Heritage Site locales: Historic Willemstad

ECONOMY

Economic overview: Most of Curacao's GDP results from services. Tourism, petroleum refining and bunkering, offshore finance, and transportation and communications are the mainstays of this small island economy, which is closely tied to the outside world. Curacao has limited natural resources, poor soil, and inadequate water supplies, and budgetary problems complicate reform of the health and education systems. Although GDP grew only slightly during the past decade, Curacao enjoys a high per capita income and a well-developed infrastructure compared to other countries in the region.

Curacao has an excellent natural harbor that can accommodate large oil tankers, and the port of Willemstad hosts a free trade zone and a dry dock. Venezuelan state-owned oil company PdVSA, under a contract in effect until 2019, leases the single refinery on the island from the government, directly employing some 1,000 people. Most of the oil for the refinery is imported from Venezuela and most of the refined products are exported to the US and Asia. Almost all consumer and capital goods are imported, with the US, the Netherlands, and Venezuela being the major suppliers.

The government is attempting to diversify its industry and trade. Curacao is an Overseas Countries and Territories (OCT) of the European Union. Nationals of Curacao are citizens of the European Union, even though it is not a member. Based on its OCT status, products that originate in Curacao have preferential access to the EU and are exempt from import duties. Curacao is a beneficiary of the Caribbean Basin Initiative and, as a result, products originating in Curacao can be imported tax free into the US if at least 35% has been added to the value of these products in Curacao. The island has state-of-the-art information and communication technology connectivity with the rest of the world, including a Tier IV datacenter. With several direct satellite and submarine optic fiber cables, Curacao has one of the best Internet speeds and reliability in the Western Hemisphere.

Real GDP (purchasing power parity): $3.86 billion (2019 est.) note: data are in 2017 dollars
$3.99 billion (2018 est.) note: data are in 2017 dollars
$4.08 billion (2017 est.)

Real GDP growth rate: 3.6% (2012 est.)
2% (2011 est.)
0.1% (2010 est.)

Real GDP per capita: $24,500 (2019 est.) note: data are in 2017 dollars
$25,100 (2018 est.) note: data are in 2017 dollars
$25,475 (2017 est.)

GDP (official exchange rate): $5.6 billion (2012 est.)

Inflation rate (consumer prices): 2.6% (2013 est.)
2.8% (2012 est.)

GDP - composition, by sector of origin: *agriculture:* 0.7% (2012 est.)
industry: 15.5% (2012 est.)
services: 83.8% (2012 est.)

GDP - composition, by end use: *household consumption:* 66.9% (2016 est.)
government consumption: 33.6% (2016 est.)
investment in fixed capital: 19.4% (2016 est.)
investment in inventories: 0% (2016 est.)
exports of goods and services: 17.5% (2016 est.)
imports of goods and services: -37.5% (2016 est.)

Agricultural products: aloe, sorghum, peanuts, vegetables, tropical fruit

Industries: tourism, petroleum refining, petroleum transshipment, light manufacturing, financial and business services

Labor force: 73,010 (2013)

Labor force - by occupation: *agriculture:* 1.2%
industry: 16.9%
services: 81.8% (2008 est.)

Unemployment rate: 13% (2013 est.)
9.8% (2011 est.)

Unemployment, youth ages 15-24: *total:* 29.3%
male: 25.4%
female: 34.5% (2018 est.)

Budget surplus (+) or deficit (-): -0.4% (of GDP) (2012 est.)

Public debt: 33.2% of GDP (2012 est.)
40.6% of GDP (2011 est.)

Taxes and other revenues: 16.6% (of GDP) (2012 est.)

Current account balance: -$400 million (2011 est.)
-$600 million (2010 est.)

Exports: $1.77 billion (2019 est.)
$1.93 billion (2018 est.)
note: Data are in current year dollars and do not include illicit exports or re-exports.

Exports - partners: Switzerland 27%, United States 17%, Spain 14%, Ecuador 7%, India 7%, Antigua and Barbuda 5% (2019)

Exports - commodities: gold, precious metal scraps, petroleum coke, frozen fish, coal tar oil (2019)

Imports: $2.33 billion (2019 est.) note: data are in current year dollars
$2.75 billion (2018 est.) note: data are in current year dollars

Imports - partners: United States 35%, Netherlands 24%, China 5% (2019)

Imports - commodities: refined petroleum, cars, crude petroleum, packaged medicines, perfumes (2019)

Reserves of foreign exchange and gold: $0 (31 December 2017 est.)

Exchange rates: Netherlands Antillean guilders (ANG) per US dollar -
1.79 (2017 est.)
1.79 (2016 est.)
1.79 (2015 est.)
1.79 (2014 est.)
1.79 (2013 est.)

ENERGY

Electricity access: *electrification - total population:* 100% (2020)

Refined petroleum products - production: 189,800 bbl/day (2015 est.)

Refined petroleum products - exports: 167,500 bbl/day (2015 est.)

Refined petroleum products - imports: 45,800 bbl/day (2015 est.)

COMMUNICATIONS

Telephones - fixed lines: *total subscriptions:* 54,000 (2020 est.)
subscriptions per 100 inhabitants: 33 (2020 est.)

Telephones - mobile cellular: *total subscriptions:* 182,000 (2020 est.)
subscriptions per 100 inhabitants: 111 (2020 est.)

Telecommunication systems: *general assessment:* fully automatic modern telecommunications system; telecom sector across the Caribbean region continues to be one of the growth areas; given the lack of economic diversity in the region, with a high dependence on tourism and activities such as fisheries and offshore financial services the telecom sector contributes greatly to the GDP (2020)
domestic: roughly 33 per 100 users for fixed-line and 111 per 100 users for cellular-mobile, majority of the islanders have Internet; market revenue has been affected in recent quarters as a result of competition and regulatory measures on termination rates and roaming tariffs (2020)
international: country code - +599, PCCS submarine cable system to US, Caribbean and Central and South America (2019)

Broadcast media: government-run TeleCuracao operates a TV station and a radio station; 2 other privately owned TV stations and several privately owned radio stations (2019)

Internet country code: .cw

Internet users: *total:* 107,060 (2019 est.)
percent of population: 68% (2019 est.)

Broadband - fixed subscriptions: *total:* 55,000 (2020 est.)
subscriptions per 100 inhabitants: 34 (2020 est.)

TRANSPORTATION

National air transport system: *number of registered air carriers:* 2 (2020)
inventory of registered aircraft operated by air carriers: 11

Civil aircraft registration country code prefix: PJ

Airports: *total:* 1 (2021)

Airports - with paved runways: *total:* 1
over 3,047 m: 1 (2021)

Roadways: *total:* 550 km

Merchant marine: *total:* 63
by type: general cargo 6, oil tanker 1, other 56 (2021)

Ports and terminals: *major seaport(s):* Willemstad
oil terminal(s): Bullen Baai (Curacao Terminal)
bulk cargo port(s): Fuik Bay (phosphate rock)

MILITARY AND SECURITY

Military and security forces: no regular military forces; Curaçao Militia (CURMIL) (2022)

Military - note: defense is the responsibility of the Kingdom of the Netherlands; the Dutch Government controls foreign and defense policy; the Dutch Caribbean Coast Guard (DCCG) provides maritime security (2022)

TRANSNATIONAL ISSUES

Refugees and internally displaced persons: *refugees (country of origin):* 14,200 (Venezuela) (2021)

Trafficking in persons: *current situation:* human traffickers exploit domestic and foreign victims in Curacao; undocumented migrants, including the growing population of Venezuelans, are vulnerable to sex and labor trafficking; Curacaoan and foreign women and girls, mostly Dominican and Venezuelan, are exploited in sex trafficking; migrants from other Caribbean countries, South America, China, and India are subject to forced labor in construction, domestic servitude, landscaping, minimarkets, retail, and restaurants
tier rating: Tier 2 Watch List — Curacao does not fully meet the minimum standards for the elimination of trafficking but it is making significant efforts to do so; the government prosecuted and convicted more traffickers than in the previous reporting period; however, authorities identified fewer victims, and assistance to victims was contingent upon their cooperation with law enforcement in prosecuting traffickers; victims who were in the country illegally, including Venezuelans, were at risk of deportation if they did not participate in trials against their traffickers; the government did not operate centers for trafficking victims but provided some funding to NGOs and international organizations to care for victims (2020)

Illicit drugs: northbound transshipment points for cocaine from Colombia and Venezuela; cocaine is transported to the United States, other Caribbean islands, Africa, and Europe

CYPRUS

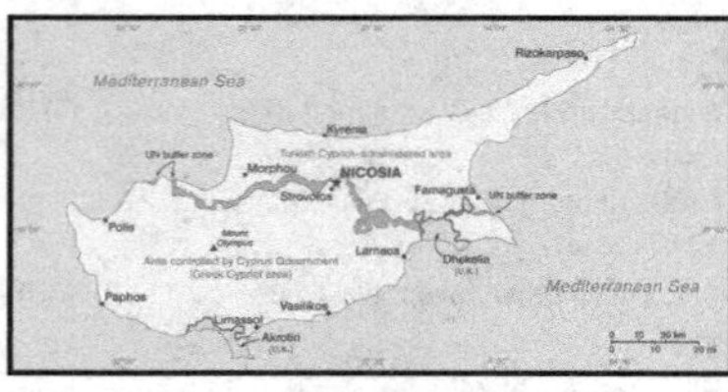

INTRODUCTION

Background: A former British colony, Cyprus became independent in 1960 following years of resistance to British rule. Tensions between the Greek Cypriot majority and Turkish Cypriot minority communities came to a head in December 1963, when violence broke out in the capital of Nicosia. Despite the deployment of UN peacekeepers in 1964, sporadic intercommunal violence continued, forcing most Turkish Cypriots into enclaves throughout the island. In 1974, a Greek Government-sponsored attempt to overthrow the elected president of Cyprus was met by military intervention from Turkey, which soon controlled more than a third of the island. In 1983, the Turkish Cypriot administered area declared itself the "Turkish Republic of Northern Cyprus" ("TRNC"), but it is recognized only by Turkey. An UN-mediated agreement, the Annan Plan, failed to win approval by both communities in 2004. In February 2014, after a hiatus of nearly two years, the leaders of the two communities resumed formal discussions under UN auspices aimed at reuniting the divided island. The most recent round of negotiations to reunify the island were suspended in July 2017 after failure to achieve a breakthrough. The entire island entered the EU on 1 May 2004, although the EU acquis - the body of common rights and obligations - applies only to the areas under the internationally recognized government, and is suspended in the "TRNC." However, individual Turkish Cypriots able to document their eligibility for Republic of Cyprus citizenship legally enjoy the same rights accorded to other citizens of EU states.

GEOGRAPHY

Location: Middle East, island in the Mediterranean Sea, south of Turkey; note - Cyprus views itself as part of Europe; geopolitically, it can be classified as falling within Europe, the Middle East, or both

Geographic coordinates: 35 00 N, 33 00 E

Map references: Middle East

Area: *total:* 9,251 sq km (of which 3,355 sq km are in north Cyprus)
land: 9,241 sq km
water: 10 sq km
country comparison to the world: 169

Area - comparative: about 0.6 times the size of Connecticut

Land boundaries: *total:* 156 km
border sovereign base areas: Akrotiri 48 km; Dhekelia 108 km

Coastline: 648 km

Maritime claims: *territorial sea:* 12 nm
contiguous zone: 24 nm
continental shelf: 200-m depth or to the depth of exploitation

Climate: temperate; Mediterranean with hot, dry summers and cool winters

Terrain: central plain with mountains to north and south; scattered but significant plains along southern coast

Elevation: *highest point:* Mount Olympus 1,951 m
lowest point: Mediterranean Sea 0 m
mean elevation: 91 m

Natural resources: copper, pyrites, asbestos, gypsum, timber, salt, marble, clay earth pigment

Land use: *agricultural land:* 13.4% (2018 est.)
arable land: 9.8% (2018 est.)
permanent crops: 3.2% (2018 est.)
permanent pasture: 0.4% (2018 est.)
forest: 18.8% (2018 est.)
other: 67.8% (2018 est.)

Irrigated land: 460 sq km (2012)

Population distribution: *population concentrated in central Nicosia and in the major cities of the south:* Paphos, Limassol, and Larnaca

Natural hazards: moderate earthquake activity; droughts

Geography - note: the third largest island in the Mediterranean Sea (after Sicily and Sardinia); several small Cypriot enclaves exist within the Dhekelia Sovereign Base Area

PEOPLE AND SOCIETY

Population: 1,295,102 (2022 est.)
country comparison to the world: 159

Nationality: *noun:* Cypriot(s)
adjective: Cypriot

Ethnic groups: Greek 98.8%, other 1% (includes Maronite, Armenian, Turkish-Cypriot), unspecified 0.2% (2011 est.)
note: data represent only the Greek-Cypriot citizens in the Republic of Cyprus

Languages: Greek (official) 80.9%, Turkish (official) 0.2%, English 4.1%, Romanian 2.9%, Russian 2.5%, Bulgarian 2.2%, Arabic 1.2%, Filipino 1.1%, other 4.3%, unspecified 0.6%; note - data represent only the Republic of Cyprus (2011 est.)
major-language sample(s):
Το Παγκόσμιο Βιβλίο Δεδομένων, η απαραίτητη πηγή βασικών πληροφοριών. (Greek)

Religions: Orthodox Christian 89.1%, Roman Catholic 2.9%, Protestant/Anglican 2%, Muslim 1.8%, Buddhist 1%, other (includes Maronite, Armenian Church, Hindu) 1.4%, unknown 1.1%, none/atheist 0.6% (2011 est.)
note: data represent only the government-controlled area of Cyprus

Age structure: *0-14 years:* 15.69% (male 102,095/female 96,676)
15-24 years: 12.29% (male 84,832/female 70,879)
25-54 years: 47.12% (male 316,710/female 280,167)
55-64 years: 11.92% (male 72,476/female 78,511)
65 years and over: 12.97% (male 71,053/female 93,277) (2020 est.)

Dependency ratios: *total dependency ratio:* 44.9
youth dependency ratio: 24
elderly dependency ratio: 20.9
potential support ratio: 4.8 (2020 est.)
note: data represent the whole country

Median age: *total:* 37.9 years
male: 36.7 years
female: 39.4 years (2020 est.)
country comparison to the world: 65

Population growth rate: 1.06% (2022 est.)
country comparison to the world: 90

Birth rate: 10.57 births/1,000 population (2022 est.)
country comparison to the world: 180

Death rate: 6.94 deaths/1,000 population (2022 est.)
country comparison to the world: 118

Net migration rate: 6.96 migrant(s)/1,000 population (2022 est.)
country comparison to the world: 13

Population distribution: *population concentrated in central Nicosia and in the major cities of the south:* Paphos, Limassol, and Larnaca

Urbanization: *urban population:* 66.9% of total population (2022)
rate of urbanization: 0.76% annual rate of change (2020-25 est.)

Major urban areas - population: 269,000 NICOSIA (capital) (2018)

Sex ratio: *at birth:* 1.05 male(s)/female
0-14 years: 1.05 male(s)/female
15-24 years: 1.05 male(s)/female
25-54 years: 1.02 male(s)/female
55-64 years: 0.78 male(s)/female
65 years and over: 0.55 male(s)/female
total population: 0.93 male(s)/female (2022 est.)

Mother's mean age at first birth: 30 years (2020 est.)
note: data represents only government-controlled areas

Maternal mortality ratio: 6 deaths/100,000 live births (2017 est.)
country comparison to the world: 160

Infant mortality rate: *total:* 8.36 deaths/1,000 live births
male: 10.22 deaths/1,000 live births
female: 6.41 deaths/1,000 live births (2022 est.)
country comparison to the world: 145

Life expectancy at birth: *total population:* 79.74 years
male: 76.93 years
female: 82.68 years (2022 est.)
country comparison to the world: 55

Total fertility rate: 1.48 children born/woman (2022 est.)
country comparison to the world: 205

Drinking water source: *improved: urban:* 99.7% of population
rural: 99.8% of population
total: 99.8% of population
unimproved: urban: 0.3% of population
rural: 0.2% of population
total: 0.2% of population (2020 est.)

Current health expenditure: 7% of GDP (2019)

Physicians density: 3.14 physicians/1,000 population (2019)

Hospital bed density: 3.4 beds/1,000 population (2017)

Sanitation facility access: *improved: urban:* 99.7% of population
rural: 98.8% of population
total: 99.4% of population
unimproved: urban: 0.3% of population
rural: 1.2% of population
total: 0.6% of population (2020 est.)

HIV/AIDS - adult prevalence rate: 0.1% (2017 est.)
country comparison to the world: 121

Obesity - adult prevalence rate: 21.8% (2016)
country comparison to the world: 84

Alcohol consumption per capita: *total:* 9.59 liters of pure alcohol (2019 est.)
beer: 2.85 liters of pure alcohol (2019 est.)
wine: 2.72 liters of pure alcohol (2019 est.)
spirits: 4.02 liters of pure alcohol (2019 est.)
other alcohols: 0 liters of pure alcohol (2019 est.)
country comparison to the world: 26

Tobacco use: *total:* 35.1% (2020 est.)
male: 47% (2020 est.)
female: 23.2% (2020 est.)
country comparison to the world: 14

Education expenditures: 5.8% of GDP (2017 est.)
country comparison to the world: 37

Literacy: *definition:* age 15 and over can read and write
total population: 99.1%
male: 99.5%
female: 98.7% (2015)

School life expectancy (primary to tertiary education): *total:* 16 years
male: 16 years
female: 16 years (2019)

Unemployment, youth ages 15-24: *total:* 18.2%
male: 24.4%
female: 12.3% (2020 est.)

People - note: demographic data for Cyprus represent the population of the government-controlled area and the area administered by Turkish Cypriots, unless otherwise indicated

ENVIRONMENT

Environment - current issues: water resource problems (no natural reservoir catchments, seasonal disparity in rainfall, sea water intrusion to island's largest aquifer, increased salination in the north); water pollution from sewage, industrial wastes, and pesticides; coastal degradation; erosion; loss of wildlife habitats from urbanization

Environment - international agreements: *party to:* Air Pollution, Air Pollution-Heavy Metals, Air Pollution-Multi-effect Protocol, Air Pollution-Nitrogen Oxides, Air Pollution-Persistent Organic Pollutants, Air Pollution-Sulphur 94, Biodiversity, Climate Change, Climate Change-Kyoto Protocol, Climate Change-Paris Agreement, Comprehensive Nuclear Test Ban, Desertification, Endangered Species, Environmental Modification, Hazardous Wastes, Law of the Sea, Marine Dumping-London Convention, Nuclear Test Ban, Ozone Layer

Protection, Ship Pollution, Tropical Timber 2006, Wetlands, Whaling
signed, but not ratified: none of the selected agreements

Air pollutants: *particulate matter emissions:* 16.79 micrograms per cubic meter (2016 est.)
carbon dioxide emissions: 6.63 megatons (2016 est.)
methane emissions: 0.86 megatons (2020 est.)

Climate: temperate; Mediterranean with hot, dry summers and cool winters

Land use: *agricultural land:* 13.4% (2018 est.)
arable land: 9.8% (2018 est.)
permanent crops: 3.2% (2018 est.)
permanent pasture: 0.4% (2018 est.)
forest: 18.8% (2018 est.)
other: 67.8% (2018 est.)

Urbanization: *urban population:* 66.9% of total population (2022)
rate of urbanization: 0.76% annual rate of change (2020-25 est.)

Revenue from forest resources: *forest revenues:* 0% of GDP (2018 est.)
country comparison to the world: 166

Revenue from coal: *coal revenues:* 0% of GDP (2018 est.)
country comparison to the world: 87

Waste and recycling: *municipal solid waste generated annually:* 541,000 tons (2015 est.)
municipal solid waste recycled annually: 72,007 tons (2015 est.)
percent of municipal solid waste recycled: 13.3% (2015 est.)

Total water withdrawal: *municipal:* 110 million cubic meters (2017 est.)
industrial: 17 million cubic meters (2017 est.)
agricultural: 184 million cubic meters (2017 est.)

Total renewable water resources: 780 million cubic meters (2017 est.)

GOVERNMENT

Country name: *conventional long form:* Republic of Cyprus
conventional short form: Cyprus
local long form: Kypriaki Dimokratia (Greek)/ Kibris Cumhuriyeti (Turkish)
local short form: Kypros (Greek)/ Kibris (Turkish)
etymology: the derivation of the name "Cyprus" is unknown, but the extensive mining of copper metal on the island in antiquity gave rise to the Latin word "cuprum" for copper
note: the Turkish Cypriot community, which administers the northern part of the island, refers to itself as the "Turkish Republic of Northern Cyprus" or "TRNC" ("Kuzey Kibris Turk Cumhuriyeti" or "KKTC")

Government type: Republic of Cyprus - presidential republic; self-declared "Turkish Republic of Northern Cyprus" (TRNC) - parliamentary republic with enhanced presidency
note: a separation of the two main ethnic communities inhabiting the island began following the outbreak of communal strife in 1963; this separation was further solidified when a Greek military-junta-supported coup attempt prompted the Turkish military intervention in July 1974 that gave the Turkish Cypriots de facto control in the north; Greek Cypriots control the only internationally recognized government on the island; on 15 November 1983, then Turkish Cypriot "President" Rauf DENKTAS declared independence and the formation of the "TRNC," which is recognized only by Turkey

Capital: *name:* Nicosia (Lefkosia/Lefkosa)
geographic coordinates: 35 10 N, 33 22 E
time difference: UTC+2 (7 hours ahead of Washington, DC, during Standard Time)
daylight saving time: +1hr, begins last Sunday in March; ends last Sunday in October
etymology: a mispronunciation of the city's Greek name Lefkosia and its Turkish name Lefkosa, both of which mean "White City"; the Greek name may derive from the Greek phrase "leuke ousia" ("white estate")

Administrative divisions: 6 districts; Ammochostos (Famagusta; all but a small part located in the Turkish Cypriot community), Keryneia (Kyrenia; the only district located entirely in the Turkish Cypriot community), Larnaka (Larnaca; with a small part located in the Turkish Cypriot community), Lefkosia (Nicosia; a small part administered by Turkish Cypriots), Lemesos (Limassol), Pafos (Paphos); note - the 5 "districts" of the "Turkish Republic of Northern Cyprus" are Gazimagusa (Famagusta), Girne (Kyrenia), Guzelyurt (Morphou), Iskele (Trikomo), Lefkosa (Nicosia)

Independence: 16 August 1960 (from the UK); note - Turkish Cypriots proclaimed self-rule on 13 February 1975 and independence in 1983, but these proclamations are recognized only by Turkey

National holiday: Independence Day, 1 October (1960); note - Turkish Cypriots celebrate 15 November (1983) as "Republic Day"

Constitution: *history:* ratified 16 August 1960; note - in 1963, the constitution was partly suspended as Turkish Cypriots withdrew from the government; Turkish-held territory in 1983 was declared the "Turkish Republic of Northern Cyprus" ("TRNC"); in 1985, the "TRNC" approved its own constitution
amendments: constitution of the Republic of Cyprus - proposed by the House of Representatives; passage requires at least two-thirds majority vote of the total membership of the "Greek Community" and the "Turkish Community"; however, all seats of Turkish Cypriot members have remained vacant since 1964; amended many times, last in 2020; constitution of the "Turkish Republic of Northern Cyprus" - proposed by at least 10 members of the "Assembly of the Republic"; passage requires at least two-thirds majority vote of the total Assembly membership and approval by referendum; amended 2014

Legal system: mixed legal system of English common law and civil law with European law supremacy

International law organization participation: accepts compulsory ICJ jurisdiction with reservations; accepts ICCt jurisdiction

Citizenship: *citizenship by birth:* no
citizenship by descent only: at least one parent must be a citizen of Cyprus
dual citizenship recognized: yes
residency requirement for naturalization: 7 years

Suffrage: 18 years of age; universal

Executive branch: *chief of state:* President Nikos ANASTASIADIS (since 28 February 2013); the president is both chief of state and head of government; note - vice presidency reserved for a Turkish Cypriot, but vacant since 1974 because Turkish Cypriots do not participate in the Republic of Cyprus Government
head of government: President Nikos ANASTASIADIS (since 28 February 2013)
cabinet: Council of Ministers appointed by the president; note - under the 1960 constitution, 3 of the ministerial posts reserved for Turkish Cypriots, appointed by the vice president; positions currently filled by Greek Cypriots
elections/appointments: president directly elected by absolute majority popular vote in 2 rounds if needed for a 5-year term; election last held on 28 January 2018 with a runoff on 4 February 2018 (next to be held in February 2023)
election results:
2018: Nikos ANASTASIADIS reelected president in second round; percent of vote in first round - Nikos ANASTASIADIS (DISY) 35.5%, Stavros MALAS (AKEL) 30.2%, Nicolas PAPADOPOULOS (DIKO) 25.7%, other 8.6%; percent of vote in second round - Nikos ANASTASIADIS 56%, Stavros MALAS 44%
2013: Nikos ANASTASIADIS elected president in second round; percent of vote in first round - Nikos ANASTASIADIS 45.5% (DISY), Stavros MALAS 26.9% (AKEL), Georgos LILLIKAS 24.9% (SP), other 2.7%; percent of vote in second round - Nikos ANASTASIADIS 57.5%, Savros MALAS 42.5%
note: the first round of the TRNC presidential election, originally scheduled for 26 April 2020, was postponed to 11 October 2020 due to the COVID-19 pandemic; the second round was held on 18 October 2020; percent of vote in the first round - Ersin TATAR (UBP) 32.4%, Mustafa AKINCI (independent) 29.8%, Tufan ERHURMAN (RTP) 21.7%, Kudret OZERSAY (independent) 5.7%, Erhan ARIKLI (YDP) 5.4%, Serdar DENKTAS (independent) 4.2%, other 0.8%; percent of vote in the second round - Ersin TATAR 51.7%, Mustafa AKINCI 48.3%

Legislative branch: *description:* area under government control: unicameral House of Representatives or Vouli Antiprosopon (80 seats; 56 assigned to Greek Cypriots, 24 to Turkish Cypriots, but only those assigned to Greek Cypriots are filled; members directly elected by both proportional representation and preferential vote; members serve 5-year terms); area administered by Turkish Cypriots: unicameral "Assembly of the Republic" or Cumhuriyet Meclisi (50 seats; members directly elected to 5-year terms by proportional representation system using a hybrid d'Hondt method with voter preferences for individual candidates
elections:
area under government control: last held on 30 May 2021 (next to be held in 2026); area administered by Turkish Cypriots: last held on 23 January 2022 (next to be held in 2027)
election results:
area under government control: House of Representatives - percent of vote by party/coalition - DISY 27.8%, AKEL 22.3%, DIKO 11.3%, ELAM 6.8%, EDEK-SP 6.7%, DiPa 6.1%, Movement of Ecologists - Citizens' Cooperation 4.4%, other 14.6%; seats by party/coalition - DISY 17, AKEL 15, DIKO 9, ELAM 4, EDEK-SP 4, DiPa 4, Movement of Ecologists - Citizens' Cooperation 3; area administered by Turkish Cypriots - "Assembly of the Republic" -percent of vote by party - UBP 39.5%,

CTP 32%, DP 7.4%, HP 6.7%, YDP 6.4%, other 8%; seats by party - UBP 24, CTP 18, DP 3, HP 3, YDP 2

Judicial branch: *highest court(s):* Supreme Court of Cyprus (consists of 13 judges, including the court president); note - the highest court in the "TRNC" is the "Supreme Court" (consists of 8 "judges," including the "court president")
judge selection and term of office: Republic of Cyprus Supreme Court judges appointed by the president of the republic upon the recommendation of the Supreme Court judges; judges can serve until age 68; "TRNC Supreme Court" judges appointed by the "Supreme Council of Judicature," a 12-member body of judges, the attorney general, appointees by the president of the "TRNC," and by the "Legislative Assembly," and members elected by the bar association; judge tenure NA
subordinate courts: Republic of Cyprus district courts; Assize Courts; Administrative Court; specialized courts for issues relating to family, industrial disputes, the military, and rent control; "TRNC Assize Courts"; "district and family courts"

Political parties and leaders: *area under government control:*
Citizens' Alliance or SP [Giorgos LILLIKAS] (dissolved 2 December 2021)
Democratic Front or DiPa [Marios GAROYIAN]
Democratic Party or DIKO [Nikolas PAPADOPOULOS]
Democratic Rally or DISY [Averof NEOPHYTOU]
Movement of Ecologists - Citizens' Alliance [Charalambos THEOPEMPTOU]
Movement of Social Democrats EDEK [Marinos SIZOPOULOS]
National Popular Front or ELAM [Christos CHRISTOU]
Progressive Party of the Working People or AKEL (Communist Party) [Stefanos STEFANOU]
Solidarity Movement [Eleni THEOCHAROUS]
area administered by Turkish Cypriots:
Communal Democracy Party or TDP [Mine ATLI]
Communal Liberation Party - New Forces or TKP-YG [Mehmet CAKICI]
Cyprus Socialist Party or KSP [Mehmet BIRINCI]
Democratic Party or DP [Fikri ATAOGLU]
National Democratic Party or NDP [Buray BUSKUVUTCU]
National Unity Party or UBP [Faiz SUCUOGLU]
New Cyprus Party or YKP [Murat KANATLI]
People's Party or HP [Kudret OZERSAY]
Rebirth Party or YDP [Erhan ARIKLI]
Republican Turkish Party or CTP [Tufan ERHURMAN]
United Cyprus Party or BKP [Izzet IZCAN]

International organization participation: Australia Group, C, CD, CE, EBRD, ECB, EIB, EMU, EU, FAO, IAEA, IBRD, ICAO, ICC (national committees), ICCt, ICRM, IDA, IFAD, IFC, IFRCS, IHO, ILO, IMF, IMO, IMSO, Interpol, IOC, IOM, IPU, ISO, ITSO, ITU, ITUC (NGOs), MIGA, NAM, NSG, OAS (observer), OIF, OPCW, OSCE, PCA, UN, UNCTAD, UNESCO, UNHCR, UNIDO, UNIFIL, UNWTO, UPU, WCO, WFTU (NGOs), WHO, WIPO, WMO, WTO

Diplomatic representation in the US: *chief of mission:* Ambassador Marios LYSIOTIS (since 17 September 2018)
chancery: 2211 R Street NW, Washington, DC 20008
telephone: [1] (202) 462-5772
FAX: [1] (202) 483-6710
email address and website:
info@cyprusembassy.net
https://www.cyprusembassy.net/
consulate(s) general: New York
honorary consulate(s): Atlanta, Chicago, Houston, Kirkland (WA), Los Angeles, New Orleans, San Francisco
note: representative of the Turkish Cypriot community in the US is Mustafa LAKADAMYALI; office at 1667 K Street NW, Washington, DC; telephone [1] (202) 887-6198

Diplomatic representation from the US: *chief of mission:* Ambassador Judith Gail GARBER (since 18 March 2019)
embassy: Metochiou and Ploutarchou Street, 2407, Engomi, Nicosia
mailing address: 5450 Nicosia Place, Washington DC 20521-5450
telephone: [357] (22) 393939
FAX: [357] (22) 780944
email address and website:
ACSNicosia@state.gov
https://cy.usembassy.gov/

Flag description: centered on a white field is a copper-colored silhouette of the island (the island has long been famous for its copper deposits) above two olive-green-colored, crossed olive branches; the branches symbolize the hope for peace and reconciliation between the Greek and Turkish communities
note: one of only two national flags that uses a map as a design element; the flag of Kosovo is the other
note: the "Turkish Republic of Northern Cyprus" flag retains the white field of the Cyprus national flag but displays narrow horizontal red stripes positioned a small distance from the top and bottom edges between which are centered a red crescent and a red five-pointed star; the banner is modeled after the Turkish national flag but with the colors reversed

National symbol(s): Cypriot mouflon (wild sheep), white dove; national colors: blue, white

National anthem: *name:* "Ymnos eis tin Eleftherian" (Hymn to Liberty)
lyrics/music: Dionysios SOLOMOS/Nikolaos MANTZAROS
note: adopted 1960; Cyprus adopted the Greek national anthem as its own; the Turkish Cypriot community in Cyprus uses the anthem of Turkey

National heritage: *total World Heritage Sites:* 3 (all cultural)
selected World Heritage Site locales: Paphos; Painted Churches in the Troodos Region; Choirokoitia

ECONOMY

Economic overview: The area of the Republic of Cyprus under government control has a market economy dominated by a services sector that accounts for more than four-fifths of GDP. Tourism, finance, shipping, and real estate have traditionally been the most important services. Cyprus has been a member of the EU since May 2004 and adopted the euro as its national currency in January 2008.

During the first five years of EU membership, the Cyprus economy grew at an average rate of about 4%, with unemployment between 2004 and 2008 averaging about 4%. However, the economy tipped into recession in 2009 as the ongoing global financial crisis and resulting low demand hit the tourism and construction sectors. An overextended banking sector with excessive exposure to Greek debt added to the contraction. Cyprus' biggest two banks were among the largest holders of Greek bonds in Europe and had a substantial presence in Greece through bank branches and subsidiaries. Following numerous downgrades of its credit rating, Cyprus lost access to international capital markets in May 2011. In July 2012, Cyprus became the fifth euro-zone government to request an economic bailout program from the European Commission, European Central Bank and the International Monetary Fund - known collectively as the "Troika."

Shortly after the election of President Nikos ANASTASIADES in February 2013, Cyprus reached an agreement with the Troika on a $13 billion bailout that triggered a two-week bank closure and the imposition of capital controls that remained partially in place until April 2015. Cyprus' two largest banks merged and the combined entity was recapitalized through conversion of some large bank deposits to shares and imposition of losses on bank bondholders. As with other EU countries, the Troika conditioned the bailout on passing financial and structural reforms and privatizing state-owned enterprises. Despite downsizing and restructuring, the Cypriot financial sector remains burdened by the largest stock of non-performing loans in the euro zone, equal to nearly half of all loans. Since the bailout, Cyprus has received positive appraisals by the Troika and outperformed fiscal targets but has struggled to overcome political opposition to bailout-mandated legislation, particularly regarding privatizations. The rate of non-performing loans (NPLs) is still very high at around 49%, and growth would accelerate if Cypriot banks could increase the pace of resolution of the NPLs.

In October 2013, a US-Israeli consortium completed preliminary appraisals of hydrocarbon deposits in Cyprus' exclusive economic zone (EEZ), which estimated gross mean reserves of about 130 billion cubic meters. Though exploration continues in Cyprus' EEZ, no additional commercially exploitable reserves have been identified. Developing offshore hydrocarbon resources remains a critical component of the government's economic recovery efforts, but development has been delayed as a result of regional developments and disagreements about exploitation methods.

Real GDP (purchasing power parity): $33.67 billion (2020 est.)
$35.48 billion (2019 est.)
$34.42 billion (2018 est.)
note: data are in 2017 dollars
country comparison to the world: 131

Real GDP growth rate: 3.08% (2019 est.)
5.25% (2018 est.)
5.16% (2017 est.)
country comparison to the world: 96

Real GDP per capita: $37,700 (2020 est.)
$40,200 (2019 est.)
$39,600 (2018 est.)
note: data are in 2017 dollars
country comparison to the world: 48

GDP (official exchange rate): $24.946 billion (2019 est.)

Inflation rate (consumer prices): 0.2% (2019 est.)

1.4% (2018 est.)
0.5% (2017 est.)
country comparison to the world: 25

Credit ratings:

Fitch rating: BBB- (2018)

Moody's rating: Ba2 (2018)

Standard & Poors rating: BBB- (2018)
note: The year refers to the year in which the current credit rating was first obtained.

GDP - composition, by sector of origin: *agriculture:* 2% (2017 est.)
industry: 12.5% (2017 est.)
services: 85.5% (2017 est.)

GDP - composition, by end use: *household consumption:* 68.7% (2017 est.)
government consumption: 14.9% (2017 est.)
investment in fixed capital: 21.1% (2017 est.)
investment in inventories: -0.7% (2017 est.)
exports of goods and services: 63.8% (2017 est.)
imports of goods and services: -67.8% (2017 est.)

Agricultural products: milk, potatoes, pork, sheep milk, goat milk, barley, wheat, poultry, olives, tangerines/mandarins

Industries: tourism, food and beverage processing, cement and gypsum, ship repair and refurbishment, textiles, light chemicals, metal products, wood, paper, stone and clay products

Industrial production growth rate: 13.4% (2017 est.)
country comparison to the world: 5

Labor force: 416,000 (2019 est.)
country comparison to the world: 158

Labor force - by occupation: *agriculture:* 3.8%
industry: 15.2%
services: 81% (2014 est.)

Unemployment rate: 7.07% (2019 est.)
8.37% (2018 est.)
country comparison to the world: 115

Unemployment, youth ages 15-24: *total:* 18.2%
male: 24.4%
female: 12.3% (2020 est.)
country comparison to the world: 87

Population below poverty line: 14.7% (2018 est.)

Gini Index coefficient - distribution of family income:
31.4 (2017 est.)
32.4 (2013 est.)
country comparison to the world: 144

Household income or consumption by percentage share: *lowest 10%:* 3.3%
highest 10%: 28.8% (2014)

Budget: *revenues:* 8.663 billion (2017 est.)
expenditures: 8.275 billion (2017 est.)

Budget surplus (+) or deficit (-): 1.8% (of GDP) (2017 est.)
country comparison to the world: 17

Public debt: 97.5% of GDP (2017 est.)
106.6% of GDP (2016 est.)
note: data cover general government debt and include debt instruments issued (or owned) by government entities other than the treasury; the data include treasury debt held by foreign entities; the data exclude debt issued by subnational entities, as well as intragovernmental debt; intragovernmental debt consists of treasury borrowings from surpluses in the social funds, such as for retirement, medical care, and unemployment
country comparison to the world: 19

Taxes and other revenues: 39.9% (of GDP) (2017 est.)
country comparison to the world: 40

Fiscal year: calendar year

Current account balance: -$1.578 billion (2019 est.)
-$958 million (2018 est.)
country comparison to the world: 161

Exports: $16.1 billion (2020 est.)
$17.92 billion (2019 est.)
$19.02 billion (2018 est.)
note: Data are in current year dollars and do not include illicit exports or re-exports.
country comparison to the world: 90

Exports - partners: India 9%, Greece 9%, Libya 8%, United Kingdom 7% (2019)

Exports - commodities: ships, refined petroleum, packaged medicines, cheese, crude petroleum (2019)

Imports: $17.58 billion (2020 est.) note: data are in current year dollars
$18.2 billion (2019 est.) note: data are in current year dollars
$18.6 billion (2018 est.) note: data are in current year dollars
country comparison to the world: 91

Imports - partners: Greece 16%, Italy 10%, Turkey 8%, Russia 5%, Germany 5%, United Kingdom 5%, China 5% (2019)

Imports - commodities: refined petroleum, ships, cars, coal tar oil, packaged medicines (2019)

Reserves of foreign exchange and gold: $888.2 million (31 December 2017 est.)
$817.7 million (31 December 2016 est.)
country comparison to the world: 136

Debt - external: $213.19 billion (2019 est.)
$231.885 billion (2018 est.)
country comparison to the world: 37

Exchange rates: euros (EUR) per US dollar -
0.82771 (2020 est.)
0.90338 (2019 est.)
0.87789 (2018 est.)
0.885 (2014 est.)
0.7634 (2013 est.)

Economy of the area administered by Turkish Cypriots:

Economy - overview: Even though the whole of the island is part of the EU, implementation of the EU "acquis communautaire" has been suspended in the area administered by Turkish Cypriots, known locally as the "Turkish Republic of Northern Cyprus" ("TRNC"), until political conditions permit the reunification of the island. The market-based economy of the "TRNC" is roughly one-fifth the size of its southern neighbor and is likewise dominated by the service sector with a large portion of the population employed by the government. In 2012 - the latest year for which data are available - the services sector, which includes the public sector, trade, tourism, and education, contributed 58.7% to economic output. In the same year, light manufacturing and agriculture contributed 2.7% and 6.2%, respectively. Manufacturing is limited mainly to food and beverages, furniture and fixtures, construction materials, metal and non-metal products, textiles and clothing. The "TRNC" maintains few economic ties with the Republic of Cyprus outside of trade in construction materials. Since its creation, the "TRNC" has heavily relied on financial assistance from Turkey, which supports the "TRNC" defense, telecommunications, water and postal services. The Turkish Lira is the preferred currency, though foreign currencies are widely accepted in business transactions. The "TRNC" remains vulnerable to the Turkish market and monetary policy because of its use of the Turkish Lira. The "TRNC" weathered the European financial crisis relatively unscathed - compared to the Republic of Cyprus - because of the lack of financial sector development, the health of the Turkish economy, and its separation from the rest of the island. The "TRNC" economy experienced growth estimated at 2.8% in 2013 and 2.3% in 2014 and is projected to grow 3.8% in 2015.;

GDP (purchasing power parity): $1.829 billion (2007 est.)

GDP - real growth rate: 2.3% (2014 est.)
2.8% (2013 est.)

GDP - per capita: $11,700 (2007 est.)

GDP - composition by sector: agriculture: 6.2%,; industry: 35.1%,; services: 58.7% (2012 est.)

Labor force: 95,030 (2007 est.)

Labor force - by occupation: agriculture: 14.5%,; industry: 29%,; services: 56.5% (2004)

Unemployment rate: 9.4% (2005 est.)

Inflation rate: 11.4% (2006)

Budget: revenues: $2.5 billion,; expenditures: $2.5 billion (2006)

Agriculture - products: citrus fruit, dairy, potatoes, grapes, olives, poultry, lamb

Industries: foodstuffs, textiles, clothing, ship repair, clay, gypsum, copper, furniture

Industrial production growth rate: -0.3% (2007 est.)

Electricity production: 998.9 million kWh (2005)

Electricity consumption: 797.9 million kWh (2005)

Exports: $68.1 million, f.o.b. (2007 est.)

Export - commodities: citrus, dairy, potatoes, textiles

Export - partners: Turkey 40%; direct trade between the area administered by Turkish Cypriots and the area under government control remains limited

Imports: $1.2 billion, f.o.b. (2007 est.)

Import - commodities: vehicles, fuel, cigarettes, food, minerals, chemicals, machinery

Import - partners: Turkey 60%; direct trade between the area administered by Turkish Cypriots and the area under government control remains limited

Currency (code): Turkish new lira (YTL)

Exchange rates: Turkish new lira per US dollar:; 1.9 (2013); 1.8 (2012); 1.668 (2011); 1.5026 (2010); 1.55 (2009)

ENERGY

Electricity access: *electrification - total population:* 100% (2020)

Electricity: *installed generating capacity:* 1.881 million kW (2020 est.)
consumption: 4.733 billion kWh (2019 est.)
exports: 0 kWh (2019 est.)
imports: 0 kWh (2019 est.)
transmission/distribution losses: 184 million kWh (2019 est.)

Electricity generation sources: *fossil fuels:* 86.8% of total installed capacity (2020 est.)
solar: 6.9% of total installed capacity (2020 est.)
wind: 5.1% of total installed capacity (2020 est.)
biomass and waste: 1.3% of total installed capacity (2020 est.)

Petroleum: *total petroleum production:* 0 bbl/day (2021 est.)
refined petroleum consumption: 54,400 bbl/day (2019 est.)

Refined petroleum products - exports: 500 bbl/day (2015 est.)
country comparison to the world: 110

Refined petroleum products - imports: 49,240 bbl/day (2015 est.)
country comparison to the world: 84

Carbon dioxide emissions: 8.024 million metric tonnes of CO2 (2019 est.)
from petroleum and other liquids: 8.024 million metric tonnes of CO2 (2019 est.)
country comparison to the world: 113

Energy consumption per capita: 133.92 million Btu/person (2019 est.)
country comparison to the world: 40

COMMUNICATIONS

Telephones - fixed lines: *total subscriptions:* 311,439 (2020 est.)
subscriptions per 100 inhabitants: 35 (2020 est.)
country comparison to the world: 107

Telephones - mobile cellular: *total subscriptions:* 1,239,960 (2020 est.)
subscriptions per 100 inhabitants: 140 (2020 est.)
country comparison to the world: 160

Telecommunication systems: *general assessment:* Cyprus suffered from the effects of the pandemic in 2020 and 2021, when the tourism sector was essentially closed; during 2022, there have been adverse effects caused by Russia's invasion of Ukraine, which has resulted in a dramatic drop in the number of Russian tourists entering the country; the mobile market is served by four mobile network operators; the number of mobile subscribers fell in 2020, largely the result of subscribers scaling back on multiple SIM cards as an economic measure; the broadband market continues to develop steadily, providing the country with one of the highest broadband penetration rates in the region; DSL remains the dominant access platform, accounting for about two-thirds of fixed broadband connections; although fiber infrastructure in Cyprus is minimal (supported by the government and regulator) to extend an FttP service to about 200,000 premises; as a result, the number of DSL subscribers is set to fall steadily in coming years as customers are migrated to the fiber platform (2021)
domestic: fixed-line about 35 per 100 and about 140 per 100 for mobile-cellular teledensity; open-wire, fiber-optic cable, and microwave radio relay (2020)
international: country code - 357 (area administered by Turkish Cypriots uses the country code of Turkey - 90); a number of submarine cables, including the SEA-ME-WE-3, CADMOS, MedNautilus Submarine System, POSEIDON, TE North/TGN-Eurasia/SEACOM/Alexandros/Medes, UGARIT, Aphrodite2, Hawk, Lev Submarine System, and Tamares combine to provide connectivity to Europe, the Middle East, Africa, Asia, Australia, and Southeast Asia; Turcyos-1 and Turcyos-2 submarine cable in Turkish North Cyprus link to Turkey; tropospheric scatter; satellite earth stations - 8 (3 Intelsat - 1 Atlantic Ocean and 2 Indian Ocean, 2 Eutelsat, 2 Intersputnik, and 1 Arabsat) (2019)

Broadcast media: mixture of state and privately run TV and radio services; the public broadcaster operates 2 TV channels and 4 radio stations; 6 private TV broadcasters, satellite and cable TV services including telecasts from Greece and Turkey, and a number of private radio stations are available; in areas administered by Turkish Cypriots, there are 2 public TV stations, 4 public radio stations, and 7 privately owned TV and 21 radio broadcast stations plus 6 radio and 4 TV channels of local universities, plus 1 radio station of military, security forces and 1 radio station of civil defense cooperation, as well as relay stations from Turkey (2019)

Internet country code: .cy

Internet users: *total:* 1,098,699 (2020 est.)
percent of population: 91% (2020 est.)
country comparison to the world: 143

Broadband - fixed subscriptions: *total:* 332,080 (2020 est.)
subscriptions per 100 inhabitants: 37 (2020 est.)
country comparison to the world: 103

TRANSPORTATION

National air transport system: *number of registered air carriers:* 2 (2020)
inventory of registered aircraft operated by air carriers: 6
annual passenger traffic on registered air carriers: 401,408 (2018)
annual freight traffic on registered air carriers: 20,000 (2018) mt-km

Civil aircraft registration country code prefix: 5B

Airports: *total:* 15 (2021)
country comparison to the world: 145

Airports - with paved runways: *total:* 13
2,438 to 3,047 m: 7
1,524 to 2,437 m: 2
914 to 1,523 m: 3
under 914 m: 1 (2021)

Airports - with unpaved runways: *total:* 2
under 914 m: 2 (2021)

Heliports: 9 (2021)

Roadways: *total:* 12,901 km (2016)
government control: 12,901 km (2016) (includes 272 km of expressways)
paved: 8,631 km (2016)
unpaved: 4,270 km (2016)

Turkish Cypriot control: 7,000 km (2011)
country comparison to the world: 128

Merchant marine: *total:* 1,051
by type: bulk carrier 269, container ship 182, general cargo 197, oil tanker 59, other 344 (2021)
country comparison to the world: 25

Ports and terminals: *major seaport(s):* area under government control: Larnaca, Limassol, Vasilikos
area administered by Turkish Cypriots: Famagusta, Kyrenia

MILITARY AND SECURITY

Military and security forces: Republic of Cyprus: Cypriot National Guard (Ethniki Froura, EF; includes Army Land Forces, Naval Command, Air Command) (2022)

Military expenditures: 2% of GDP (2021 est.)
1.8% of GDP (2020 est.)
1.6% of GDP (2019) (approximately $610 million)
1.8% of GDP (2018) (approximately $650 million)
1.6% of GDP (2017) (approximately $540 million)
country comparison to the world: 59

Military and security service personnel strengths: approximately 13,000 total active duty personnel (2022)

Military equipment inventories and acquisitions: the inventory of the Cypriot National Guard is a mix of Soviet-era and some more modern weapons systems; since 2010, it has received equipment from several countries, including France, Israel, Russia, and Serbia (2021)

Military service age and obligation: Cypriot National Guard (CNG): 18-50 years of age for compulsory military service for all Greek Cypriot males; 17 years of age for voluntary service; 14-month service obligation (2022)
note: the CNG accepts all foreign nationals of at least partial Cypriot descent under age 32 as volunteers; dual citizenship Cypriot origin citizens, who were born in Cyprus or abroad, have the obligation to serve in the CNG on repatriation, regardless of whether or not they possess a foreign citizenship; a person is considered as having Cypriot origin where a grandparent or parent was/is a Cypriot citizen

Military - note: the United Nations Peacekeeping Force in Cyprus (UNFICYP) was set up in 1964 to prevent further fighting between the Greek Cypriot and Turkish Cypriot communities on the island and bring about a return to normal conditions; the UNFICYP mission had about 800 personnel as of mid-2022

TERRORISM

Terrorist group(s): Islamic State of Iraq and ash-Sham (ISIS)

TRANSNATIONAL ISSUES

Disputes - international: hostilities in 1974 divided the island into two de facto autonomous entities, the internationally recognized Cypriot Government and a Turkish-Cypriot community (north Cyprus); the 1,000-strong UN Peacekeeping Force in Cyprus (UNFICYP) has served in Cyprus since 1964 and maintains the buffer zone between north and south; on 1 May 2004, Cyprus entered the EU still divided, with the EU's body of legislation and standards (acquis communitaire) suspended in the north; Turkey protests Cypriot Government creating hydrocarbon blocks and maritime boundary with Lebanon in March 2007

Refugees and internally displaced persons: *refugees (country of origin):* 9,820 (Syria) (mid-year 2021); 14,336 (Ukraine) (as of 15 November 2022)

IDPs: 242,000 (both Turkish and Greek Cypriots; many displaced since 1974) (2021)
stateless persons: 66 (mid-year 2021)
note: 46,379 estimated refugee and migrant arrivals (January 2015-October 2022)

Illicit drugs: vulnerable to money laundering from illegal drugs

CZECHIA

INTRODUCTION

Background: At the close of World War I, the Czechs and Slovaks of the former Austro-Hungarian Empire merged to form Czechoslovakia, a parliamentarian democracy. During the interwar years, having rejected a federal system, the new country's predominantly Czech leaders were frequently preoccupied with meeting the increasingly strident demands of other ethnic minorities within the republic, most notably the Slovaks, the Sudeten Germans, and the Ruthenians (Ukrainians). On the eve of World War II, Nazi Germany occupied the territory that today comprises Czechia, and Slovakia became an independent state allied with Germany. After the war, a reunited but truncated Czechoslovakia (less Ruthenia) fell within the Soviet sphere of influence when the pro-Soviet Communist party staged a coup in February 1948. In 1968, an invasion by fellow Warsaw Pact troops ended the efforts of the country's leaders to liberalize communist rule and create "socialism with a human face," ushering in a period of repression known as "normalization." The peaceful "Velvet Revolution" swept the Communist Party from power at the end of 1989 and inaugurated a return to democratic rule and a market economy. On 1 January 1993, the country underwent a nonviolent "velvet divorce" into its two national components, the Czech Republic and Slovakia. The Czech Republic joined NATO in 1999 and the European Union in 2004. The country formally added the short-form name Czechia in 2016, while also continuing to use the full form name, the Czech Republic.

GEOGRAPHY

Location: Central Europe, between Germany, Poland, Slovakia, and Austria

Geographic coordinates: 49 45 N, 15 30 E

Map references: Europe

Area: *total:* 78,867 sq km
land: 77,247 sq km
water: 1,620 sq km
country comparison to the world: 116

Area - comparative: about two-thirds the size of Pennsylvania; slightly smaller than South Carolina

Land boundaries: *total:* 2,046 km
border countries (4): Austria 402 km; Germany 704 km; Poland 699 km; Slovakia 241 km

Coastline: 0 km (landlocked)

Maritime claims: none (landlocked)

Climate: temperate; cool summers; cold, cloudy, humid winters

Terrain: Bohemia in the west consists of rolling plains, hills, and plateaus surrounded by low mountains; Moravia in the east consists of very hilly country

Elevation: *highest point:* Snezka 1,602 m
lowest point: Labe (Elbe) River 115 m
mean elevation: 433 m

Natural resources: hard coal, soft coal, kaolin, clay, graphite, timber, arable land

Land use: *agricultural land:* 54.8% (2018 est.)
arable land: 41% (2018 est.)
permanent crops: 1% (2018 est.)
permanent pasture: 12.8% (2018 est.)
forest: 34.4% (2018 est.)
other: 10.8% (2018 est.)

Irrigated land: 320 sq km (2012)

Major rivers (by length in km): Danube (shared with Germany [s], Austria, Slovakia, Hungary, Croatia, Serbia, Bulgaria, Ukraine, Moldova, and Romania [m]) - 2,888 km; Elbe river source (shared with Germany [m]) - 1,252 km
note – [s] after country name indicates river source; [m] after country name indicates river mouth

Major watersheds (area sq km): Atlantic Ocean drainage: *(Black Sea)* Danube (795,656 sq km)

Population distribution: a fairly even distribution throughout most of the country, but the northern and eastern regions tend to have larger urban concentrations

Natural hazards: flooding

Geography - note: *note 1:* landlocked; strategically located astride some of oldest and most significant land routes in Europe; Moravian Gate is a traditional military corridor between the North European Plain and the Danube in central Europe
note 2: the Hranice Abyss in Czechia is the world's deepest surveyed underwater cave at 404 m (1,325 ft); its survey is not complete and it could end up being some 800-1,200 m deep

PEOPLE AND SOCIETY

Population: 10,705,384 (2022 est.)
country comparison to the world: 86

Nationality: *noun:* Czech(s)
adjective: Czech

Ethnic groups: Czech 57.3%, Moravian 3.4%, other 7.7%, unspecified 31.6% (2021 est.)
note: includes only persons with one ethnicity

Languages: Czech (official) 88.4%, Slovak 1.5%, other 2.6%, unspecified 7.2%
note: includes only persons with one mother tongue (2021 est.)
major-language sample(s):
World Fackbook, nepostradatelný zdroj základních informací. (Czech)

Religions: Roman Catholic 7%, other believers belonging to a church or religious society 6% (includes Evangelical United Brethren Church and Czechoslovak Hussite Church), believers unaffiliated with a religious society 9.1%, none 47.8%, unspecified 30.1% (2021 est.)

Age structure: *0-14 years:* 15.17% (male 834,447/female 789,328)
15-24 years: 9.2% (male 508,329/female 475,846)
25-54 years: 43.29% (male 2,382,899/female 2,249,774)
55-64 years: 12.12% (male 636,357/female 660,748)
65 years and over: 20.23% (male 907,255/female 1,257,515) (2020 est.)

Dependency ratios: *total dependency ratio:* 56
youth dependency ratio: 24.6
elderly dependency ratio: 31.4
potential support ratio: 3.2 (2020 est.)

Median age: *total:* 43.3 years
male: 42 years
female: 44.7 years (2020 est.)
country comparison to the world: 28

Population growth rate: 0.02% (2022 est.)
country comparison to the world: 193

Birth rate: 8.59 births/1,000 population (2022 est.)
country comparison to the world: 212

Death rate: 10.74 deaths/1,000 population (2022 est.)
country comparison to the world: 25

Net migration rate: 2.32 migrant(s)/1,000 population (2022 est.)
country comparison to the world: 47

Population distribution: a fairly even distribution throughout most of the country, but the northern and eastern regions tend to have larger urban concentrations

Urbanization: *urban population:* 74.4% of total population (2022)
rate of urbanization: 0.2% annual rate of change (2020-25 est.)

Major urban areas - population: 1.318 million PRAGUE (capital) (2022)

Sex ratio: *at birth:* 1.05 male(s)/female
0-14 years: 1.06 male(s)/female
15-24 years: 1.19 male(s)/female
25-54 years: 1.14 male(s)/female
55-64 years: 0.93 male(s)/female
65 years and over: 0.61 male(s)/female
total population: 1.05 male(s)/female (2022 est.)

Mother's mean age at first birth: 28.5 years (2020 est.)

Maternal mortality ratio: 3 deaths/100,000 live births (2017 est.)
country comparison to the world: 176

Infant mortality rate: *total:* 2.4 deaths/1,000 live births
male: 2.59 deaths/1,000 live births
female: 2.19 deaths/1,000 live births (2022 est.)
country comparison to the world: 218

Life expectancy at birth: *total population:* 79.73 years
male: 76.8 years

female: 82.82 years (2022 est.)
country comparison to the world: 56

Total fertility rate: 1.49 children born/woman (2022 est.)
country comparison to the world: 204

Drinking water source: *improved: urban:* 99.9% of population
rural: 99.8% of population
total: 99.9% of population
unimproved: urban: 0.1% of population
rural: 0.2% of population
total: 0.1% of population (2020 est.)

Current health expenditure: 7.8% of GDP (2019)

Physicians density: 4.15 physicians/1,000 population (2020)

Hospital bed density: 6.6 beds/1,000 population (2018)

Sanitation facility access: *improved: urban:* 100% of population
rural: 100% of population
total: 100% of population

HIV/AIDS - adult prevalence rate: (2018 est.) <.1%

Obesity - adult prevalence rate: 26% (2016)
country comparison to the world: 46

Alcohol consumption per capita: *total:* 12.73 liters of pure alcohol (2019 est.)
beer: 6.77 liters of pure alcohol (2019 est.)
wine: 2.73 liters of pure alcohol (2019 est.)
spirits: 3.24 liters of pure alcohol (2019 est.)
other alcohols: 0 liters of pure alcohol (2019 est.)
country comparison to the world: 3

Tobacco use: *total:* 30.7% (2020 est.)
male: 35% (2020 est.)
female: 26.4% (2020 est.)
country comparison to the world: 28

Education expenditures: 4.3% of GDP (2018 est.)
country comparison to the world: 90

Literacy: *total population:* 99%
male: 99%
female: 99% (2011)

School life expectancy (primary to tertiary education): *total:* 16 years
male: 16 years
female: 17 years (2019)

Unemployment, youth ages 15-24: *total:* 8%
male: 7.2%
female: 9.2% (2020 est.)

ENVIRONMENT

Environment - current issues: air and water pollution in areas of northwest Bohemia and in northern Moravia around Ostrava present health risks; acid rain damaging forests; land pollution caused by industry, mining, and agriculture

Environment - international agreements: *party to:* Air Pollution, Air Pollution-Heavy Metals, Air Pollution-Multi-effect Protocol, Air Pollution-Nitrogen Oxides, Air Pollution-Persistent Organic Pollutants, Air Pollution-Sulphur 85, Air Pollution-Sulphur 94, Air Pollution-Volatile Organic Compounds, Antarctic-Environmental Protection, Antarctic Treaty, Biodiversity, Climate Change, Climate Change-Kyoto Protocol, Climate Change-Paris Agreement, Comprehensive Nuclear Test Ban, Desertification, Endangered Species, Environmental Modification, Hazardous Wastes, Law of the Sea, Nuclear Test Ban, Ozone Layer Protection, Ship Pollution, Tropical Timber 2006, Wetlands, Whaling
signed, but not ratified: none of the selected agreements

Air pollutants: *particulate matter emissions:* 15.15 micrograms per cubic meter (2016 est.)
carbon dioxide emissions: 102.22 megatons (2016 est.)
methane emissions: 13.11 megatons (2020 est.)

Climate: temperate; cool summers; cold, cloudy, humid winters

Land use: *agricultural land:* 54.8% (2018 est.)
arable land: 41% (2018 est.)
permanent crops: 1% (2018 est.)
permanent pasture: 12.8% (2018 est.)
forest: 34.4% (2018 est.)
other: 10.8% (2018 est.)

Urbanization: *urban population:* 74.4% of total population (2022)
rate of urbanization: 0.2% annual rate of change (2020-25 est.)

Revenue from forest resources: *forest revenues:* 0.17% of GDP (2017 est.)
country comparison to the world: 97

Revenue from coal: *coal revenues:* 0.14% of GDP (2018 est.)
country comparison to the world: 24

Waste and recycling: *municipal solid waste generated annually:* 3.337 million tons (2015 est.)
municipal solid waste recycled annually: 850,935 tons (2015 est.)
percent of municipal solid waste recycled: 25.5% (2015 est.)

Major rivers (by length in km): Danube (shared with Germany [s], Austria, Slovakia, Hungary, Croatia, Serbia, Bulgaria, Ukraine, Moldova, and Romania [m]) - 2,888 km; Elbe river source (shared with Germany [m]) - 1,252 km
note – [s] after country name indicates river source; [m] after country name indicates river mouth

Major watersheds (area sq km): Atlantic Ocean drainage: *(Black Sea)* Danube (795,656 sq km)

Total water withdrawal: *municipal:* 616.6 million cubic meters (2017 est.)
industrial: 967.2 million cubic meters (2017 est.)
agricultural: 46.6 million cubic meters (2017 est.)

Total renewable water resources: 13.15 billion cubic meters (2017 est.)

GOVERNMENT

Country name: *conventional long form:* Czech Republic
conventional short form: Czechia
local long form: Ceska republika
local short form: Cesko
etymology: name derives from the Czechs, a West Slavic tribe who rose to prominence in the late 9th century A.D.; the country officially adopted the English short-form name of Czechia on 1 July 2016

Government type: parliamentary republic

Capital: *name:* Prague
geographic coordinates: 50 05 N, 14 28 E
time difference: UTC+1 (6 hours ahead of Washington, DC, during Standard Time)
daylight saving time: +1hr, begins last Sunday in March; ends last Sunday in October
etymology: the name may derive from an old Slavic root "praga" or "prah", meaning "ford", and refer to the city's origin at a crossing point of the Vltava (Moldau) River

Administrative divisions: 13 regions (kraje, singular - kraj) and 1 capital city* (hlavni mesto); Jihocesky (South Bohemia), Jihomoravsky (South Moravia), Karlovarsky (Karlovy Vary), Kralovehradecky (Hradec Kralove), Liberecky (Liberec), Moravskoslezsky (Moravia-Silesia), Olomoucky (Olomouc), Pardubicky (Pardubice), Plzensky (Pilsen), Praha (Prague)*, Stredocesky (Central Bohemia), Ustecky (Usti), Vysocina (Highlands), Zlinsky (Zlin)

Independence: 1 January 1993 (Czechoslovakia split into the Czech Republic and Slovakia); note - although 1 January is the day the Czech Republic came into being, the Czechs commemorate 28 October 1918, the day the former Czechoslovakia declared its independence from the Austro-Hungarian Empire, as their independence day

National holiday: Czechoslovak Founding Day, 28 October (1918)

Constitution: *history:* previous 1960; latest ratified 16 December 1992, effective 1 January 1993
amendments: passage requires at least three-fifths concurrence of members present in both houses of Parliament; amended several times, last in 2021

Legal system: new civil code enacted in 2014, replacing civil code of 1964 - based on former Austro-Hungarian civil codes and socialist theory - and reintroducing former Czech legal terminology

International law organization participation: has not submitted an ICJ jurisdiction declaration; accepts ICCt jurisdiction

Citizenship: *citizenship by birth:* no
citizenship by descent only: at least one parent must be a citizen of Czechia
dual citizenship recognized: no
residency requirement for naturalization: 5 years

Suffrage: 18 years of age; universal

Executive branch: *chief of state:* President Milos ZEMAN (since 8 March 2013)
head of government: Prime Minister Petr FIALA (since 17 December 2021); First Deputy Prime Minister Vit RAKUSAN (since 17 December 2021), Deputy Prime Ministers Marian JURECKA, Ivan BARTOS, Vlastimil VALEK (all since 17 December 2021)
cabinet: Cabinet appointed by the president on the recommendation of the prime minister
elections/appointments: president directly elected by absolute majority popular vote in 2 rounds if needed for a 5-year term (limited to 2 consecutive terms); elections last held on 12-13 January 2018 with a runoff on 26-27 January 2018 (next to be held in January 2023); prime minister appointed by the president for a 4-year term
election results:
2018: Milos ZEMAN reelected president in the second round; percent of vote - Milos ZEMAN (SPO) 51.4%, Jiri DRAHOS (independent) 48.6%
2013: Milos ZEMAN elected president; percent of vote - Milos ZEMAN (SPO) 54.8%, Karel SCHWARZENBERG (TOP 09) 45.2%

Legislative branch: *description:* bicameral Parliament or Parlament consists of:
Senate or Senat (81 seats; members directly elected in single-seat constituencies by absolute majority

vote in 2 rounds if needed; members serve 6-year terms with one-third of the membership renewed every 2 years)
Chamber of Deputies or Poslanecka Snemovna (200 seats; members directly elected in 14 multi-seat constituencies by proportional representation vote with a 5% threshold required to fill a seat; members serve 4-year terms)
elections:
Senate - last held in 2 rounds on 23-24 September and 30 September and 1 October 2022 (next to be held in October 2024)
Chamber of Deputies - last held on 8-9 October 2021 (next to be held by October 2025)
election results:
Senate - percent of vote by party - seats by party - ODS 23, STAN 15, KDU-CSL 12, ANO 5, TOP 09 6, CSSD 1, SEN 21 4, Pirates 2, minor parties with one seat each 9, independents 1
Chamber of Deputies - percent of vote by party – SPOLU 27.8%, Action of Dissatisfied Persons (ANO)27.1%, Pirates and Mayors of Independents (STAN) 15.6%, Freedom and Direct Democracy 9.6%, other 19.9%; seats by party - Action of Dissatisfied Persons 72, SPOLU 71, Pirates and Mayors 37, Freedom and Direct Democracy 20

Judicial branch: *highest court(s):* Supreme Court (organized into Civil Law and Commercial Division, and Criminal Division each with a court chief justice, vice justice, and several judges); Constitutional Court (consists of 15 justices); Supreme Administrative Court (consists of 36 judges, including the court president and vice president, and organized into 6-, 7-, and 9-member chambers)
judge selection and term of office: Supreme Court judges proposed by the Chamber of Deputies and appointed by the president; judges appointed for life; Constitutional Court judges appointed by the president and confirmed by the Senate; judges appointed for 10-year, renewable terms; Supreme Administrative Court judges selected by the president of the Court; unlimited terms
subordinate courts: High Court; regional and district courts

Political parties and leaders: Christian Democratic Union-Czechoslovak People's Party or KDU-CSL [Marian JURECKA]
Civic Democratic Party or ODS [Petr FIALA]
Communist Party of Bohemia and Moravia or KSCM [Katerina KONECNA]
Czech Social Democratic Party or CSSD [Michal SMARDA]
Freedom and Direct Democracy or SPD [Tomio OKAMURA]
Mayors and Independents or STAN [Vit RAKUSAN]
Mayors for the Liberec Region [Martin PUTA]
Movement of Dissatisfied Citizens or ANO [Andrej BABIS]
Party of Free Citizens Svobodni [Libor VONDRACEK]
Pirate Party or Pirates [Ivan BARTOS]
Senator 21 [Vaclav LASKA]
Tradition Responsibility Prosperity 09 or TOP 09 [Marketa PEKAROVA ADAMOVA]

International organization participation: Australia Group, BIS, BSEC (observer), CD, CE, CEI, CERN, EAPC, EBRD, ECB, EIB, ESA, EU, FAO, IAEA, IBRD, ICAO, ICC (national committees), ICCt, ICRM, IDA, IEA, IFC, IFRCS, ILO, IMF, IMO, IMSO, Interpol, IOC, IOM, IPU, ISO, ITSO, ITU, ITUC (NGOs), MIGA, MONUSCO, NATO, NEA, NSG, OAS (observer), OECD, OIF (observer), OPCW, OSCE, PCA, Schengen Convention, SELEC, UN, UNCTAD, UNESCO, UNHCR, UNHRC, UNIDO, UNWTO, UPU, Wassenaar Arrangement, WCO, WFTU (NGOs), WHO, WIPO, WMO, WTO, ZC

Diplomatic representation in the US: *chief of mission:* Ambassador Miloslav STASEK (since 16 September 2022)
chancery: 3900 Spring of Freedom Lane NW, Washington, DC 20008-3803
telephone: [1] (202) 274-9100
FAX: [1] (202) 966-8540
email address and website:
washington@embassy.mzv.cz
https://www.mzv.cz/washington/
consulate(s) general: Chicago, Los Angeles, New York

Diplomatic representation from the US: *chief of mission:* Ambassador (vacant); Charge d'Affaires Christy AGOR (since 18 August 2022)
embassy: Trziste 15, 118 01 Praha 1 - Mala Strana
mailing address: 5630 Prague Place, Washington DC 20521-5630
telephone: [420] 257-022-000
FAX: [420] 257-022-809
email address and website:
ACSPrg@state.gov
https://cz.usembassy.gov/

Flag description: two equal horizontal bands of white (top) and red with a blue isosceles triangle based on the hoist side
note: combines the white and red colors of Bohemia with blue from the arms of Moravia; is identical to the flag of the former Czechoslovakia

National symbol(s): silver (or white), double-tailed, rampant lion; national colors: white, red, blue

National anthem: *name:* "Kde domov muj?" (Where is My Home?)
lyrics/music: Josef Kajetan TYL/Frantisek Jan SKROUP
note: adopted 1993; the anthem was originally written as incidental music to the play "Fidlovacka" (1834), it soon became very popular as an unofficial anthem of the Czech nation; its first verse served as the official Czechoslovak anthem beginning in 1918, while the second verse (Slovak) was dropped after the split of Czechoslovakia in 1993

National heritage: *total World Heritage Sites:* 16 (all cultural)
selected World Heritage Site locales: Historic Prague; Historic Telč; Historic Český Krumlov; Lednice-Valtice Cultural Landscape; Historic Kutná Hora; Holy Trinity Column, Olomouc; Karlovy Vary Spa

ECONOMY

Economic overview: Czechia is a prosperous market economy that boasts one of the highest GDP growth rates and lowest unemployment levels in the EU, but its dependence on exports makes economic growth vulnerable to contractions in external demand. Czechia's exports comprise some 80% of GDP and largely consist of automobiles, the country's single largest industry. Czechia acceded to the EU in 2004 but has yet to join the euro-zone. While the flexible koruna helps Czechia weather external shocks, it was one of the world's strongest performing currencies in 2017, appreciating approximately 16% relative to the US dollar after the central bank (Czech National Bank -CNB) ended its cap on the currency's value in early April 2017, which it had maintained since November 2013. The CNB hiked rates in August and November 2017 - the first rate changes in nine years - to address rising inflationary pressures brought by strong economic growth and a tight labor market.

Since coming to power in 2014, the new government has undertaken some reforms to try to reduce corruption, attract investment, and improve social welfare programs, which could help increase the government's revenues and improve living conditions for Czechs. The government introduced in December 2016 an online tax reporting system intended to reduce tax evasion and increase revenues. The government also plans to remove labor market rigidities to improve the business climate, bring procurement procedures in line with EU best practices, and boost wages. The country's low unemployment rate has led to steady increases in salaries, and the government is facing pressure from businesses to allow greater migration of qualified workers, at least from Ukraine and neighboring Central European countries.

Long-term challenges include dealing with a rapidly aging population, a shortage of skilled workers, a lagging education system, funding an unsustainable pension and health care system, and diversifying away from manufacturing and toward a more high-tech, services-based, knowledge economy.

Real GDP (purchasing power parity): $409.97 billion (2020 est.)
$434.31 billion (2019 est.)
$424.48 billion (2018 est.)
note: data are in 2017 dollars
country comparison to the world: 47

Real GDP growth rate: 2.27% (2019 est.)
3.18% (2018 est.)
5.35% (2017 est.)
country comparison to the world: 123

Real GDP per capita: $38,300 (2020 est.)
$40,700 (2019 est.)
$39,900 (2018 est.)
note: data are in 2017 dollars
country comparison to the world: 46

GDP (official exchange rate): $250.631 billion (2019 est.)

Inflation rate (consumer prices): 2.8% (2019 est.)
2.1% (2018 est.)
2.4% (2017 est.)
country comparison to the world: 139

Credit ratings:

Fitch rating: AA- (2018)

Moody's rating: Aa3 (2019)

Standard & Poors rating: AA- (2011)
note: The year refers to the year in which the current credit rating was first obtained.

GDP - composition, by sector of origin: *agriculture:* 2.3% (2017 est.)
industry: 36.9% (2017 est.)
services: 60.8% (2017 est.)

GDP - composition, by end use: *household consumption:* 47.4% (2017 est.)
government consumption: 19.2% (2017 est.)
investment in fixed capital: 24.7% (2017 est.)
investment in inventories: 1.1% (2017 est.)
exports of goods and services: 79.9% (2017 est.)
imports of goods and services: -72.3% (2017 est.)

Agricultural products: wheat, sugar beet, milk, barley, rapeseed, potatoes, maize, pork, triticale, poultry

Industries: motor vehicles, metallurgy, machinery and equipment, glass, armaments

Industrial production growth rate: 7.5% (2017 est.)
country comparison to the world: 27

Labor force: 5.222 million (2020 est.)
country comparison to the world: 75

Labor force - by occupation: *agriculture:* 2.8%
industry: 38%
services: 59.2% (2015)

Unemployment rate: 2.8% (2019 est.)
3.18% (2018 est.)
country comparison to the world: 33

Unemployment, youth ages 15-24: *total:* 8%
male: 7.2%
female: 9.2% (2020 est.)
country comparison to the world: 155

Population below poverty line: 10.1% (2018 est.)

Gini Index coefficient - distribution of family income: 24.9 (2017 est.)
25.1 (2014)
country comparison to the world: 171

Household income or consumption by percentage share: *lowest 10%:* 4.1%
highest 10%: 21.7% (2015 est.)

Budget: *revenues:* 87.37 billion (2017 est.)
expenditures: 83.92 billion (2017 est.)

Budget surplus (+) or deficit (-): 1.6% (of GDP) (2017 est.)
country comparison to the world: 19

Public debt: 34.7% of GDP (2017 est.)
36.8% of GDP (2016 est.)
country comparison to the world: 153

Taxes and other revenues: 40.5% (of GDP) (2017 est.)
country comparison to the world: 37

Fiscal year: calendar year

Current account balance: -$678 million (2019 est.)
$1.259 billion (2018 est.)
country comparison to the world: 130

Exports: $174.92 billion (2020 est.)
$186.54 billion (2019 est.)
$191.69 billion (2018 est.)
note: Data are in current year dollars and do not include illicit exports or re-exports.
country comparison to the world: 34

Exports - partners: Germany 31%, Slovakia 7%, Poland 6%, France 5% (2019)

Exports - commodities: cars and vehicle parts, computers, broadcasting equipment, office machinery/parts, seating (2019)

Imports: $157.95 billion (2020 est.) note: data are in current year dollars
$171.43 billion (2019 est.) note: data are in current year dollars
$176.78 billion (2018 est.) note: data are in current year dollars
country comparison to the world: 34

Imports - partners: Germany 27%, China 12%, Poland 9%, Slovakia 5% (2019)

Imports - commodities: broadcasting equipment, cars and vehicle parts, office machinery/parts, computers, packaged medicines (2019)

Reserves of foreign exchange and gold: $148 billion (31 December 2017 est.)
$85.73 billion (31 December 2016 est.)
country comparison to the world: 19

Debt - external: $191.871 billion (2019 est.)
$200.197 billion (2018 est.)
country comparison to the world: 40

Exchange rates: koruny (CZK) per US dollar -
21.76636 (2020 est.)
23.0629 (2019 est.)
22.71439 (2018 est.)
24.599 (2014 est.)
20.758 (2013 est.)

ENERGY

Electricity access: *electrification - total population:* 100% (2020)

Electricity: *installed generating capacity:* 22.485 million kW (2020 est.)
consumption: 60.814 billion kWh (2020 est.)
exports: 23.521 billion kWh (2020 est.)
imports: 13.368 billion kWh (2020 est.)
transmission/distribution losses: 4.117 billion kWh (2020 est.)

Electricity generation sources: *fossil fuels:* 47% of total installed capacity (2020 est.)
nuclear: 37.6% of total installed capacity (2020 est.)
solar: 3% of total installed capacity (2020 est.)
wind: 0.9% of total installed capacity (2020 est.)
hydroelectricity: 4.5% of total installed capacity (2020 est.)
biomass and waste: 7% of total installed capacity (2020 est.)

Coal: *production:* 33.806 million metric tons (2020 est.)
consumption: 37.212 million metric tons (2020 est.)
exports: 1.885 million metric tons (2020 est.)
imports: 3.795 million metric tons (2020 est.)
proven reserves: 2.927 billion metric tons (2019 est.)

Petroleum: *total petroleum production:* 6,300 bbl/day (2021 est.)
refined petroleum consumption: 219,500 bbl/day (2019 est.)
crude oil and lease condensate exports: 400 bbl/day (2018 est.)
crude oil and lease condensate imports: 150,200 bbl/day (2018 est.)
crude oil estimated reserves: 15 million barrels (2021 est.)

Refined petroleum products - production: 177,500 bbl/day (2017 est.)
country comparison to the world: 56

Refined petroleum products - exports: 52,200 bbl/day (2017 est.)
country comparison to the world: 54

Refined petroleum products - imports: 83,860 bbl/day (2017 est.)
country comparison to the world: 60

Natural gas: *production:* 189.185 million cubic meters (2020 est.)
consumption: 8,815,133,000 cubic meters (2020 est.)
exports: 0 cubic meters (2020 est.)
imports: 7,590,318,000 cubic meters (2020 est.)
proven reserves: 3.964 billion cubic meters (2021 est.)

Carbon dioxide emissions: 99.533 million metric tonnes of CO2 (2019 est.)
from coal and metallurgical coke: 57.268 million metric tonnes of CO2 (2019 est.)
from petroleum and other liquids: 25.526 million metric tonnes of CO2 (2019 est.)
from consumed natural gas: 16.739 million metric tonnes of CO2 (2019 est.)
country comparison to the world: 43

Energy consumption per capita: 161.972 million Btu/person (2019 est.)
country comparison to the world: 30

COMMUNICATIONS

Telephones - fixed lines: *total subscriptions:* 1,335,224 (2020 est.)
subscriptions per 100 inhabitants: 12 (2020 est.)
country comparison to the world: 66

Telephones - mobile cellular: *total subscriptions:* 12,999,812 (2020 est.)
subscriptions per 100 inhabitants: 121 (2020 est.)
country comparison to the world: 75

Telecommunication systems: *general assessment:* the telecom market has attracted investment from among the key regional telcos; telcos in the Czech Republic have become multi-service providers, offering a full range of fixed and mobile services; the auction has enabled the licensees to expand the reach of their 5G networks; this process has also been assisted by them closing down 3G networks and reforming spectrum for 5G and LTE use (2021)
domestic: roughly 12 fixed-telephone subscriptions per 100 inhabitants and mobile telephone usage of about 121 per 100 inhabitants (2020)
international: country code - 420; satellite earth stations - 6 (2 Intersputnik - Atlantic and Indian Ocean regions, 1 Intelsat, 1 Eutelsat, 1 Inmarsat, 1 Globalstar) (2019)

Broadcast media: 22 TV stations operate nationally, with 17 of them in private hands; publicly operated Czech Television has 5 national channels; throughout the country, there are some 350 TV channels in operation, many through cable, satellite, and IPTV subscription services; 63 radio broadcasters are registered, operating over 80 radio stations, including 7 multiregional radio stations or networks; publicly operated broadcaster Czech Radio operates 4 national, 14 regional, and 4 Internet stations; both Czech Radio and Czech Television are partially financed through a license fee (2019)

Internet country code: .cz

Internet users: *total:* 9,323,428 (July 2022 est.)
percent of population: 86.8% (July 2022 est.)
country comparison to the world: 59

Broadband - fixed subscriptions: *total:* 3,845,426 (2020 est.)
subscriptions per 100 inhabitants: 36 (2020 est.)
country comparison to the world: 39

TRANSPORTATION

National air transport system: *number of registered air carriers:* 4 (2020)
inventory of registered aircraft operated by air carriers: 48
annual passenger traffic on registered air carriers: 5,727,200 (2018)
annual freight traffic on registered air carriers: 25.23 million (2018) mt-km

Civil aircraft registration country code prefix: OK

Airports: *total:* 128 (2021)
country comparison to the world: 45

Airports - with paved runways: *total:* 41
over 3,047 m: 2
2,438 to 3,047 m: 9
1,524 to 2,437 m: 12
914 to 1,523 m: 2
under 914 m: 16 (2021)

Airports - with unpaved runways: *total:* 87
1,524 to 2,437 m: 1
914 to 1,523 m: 25
under 914 m: 61 (2021)

Heliports: 1 (2021)

Pipelines: 7,160 km gas, 675 km oil, 94 km refined products (2016)

Railways: *total:* 9,408 km (2017)
standard gauge: 9,385 km (2017) 1.435-m gauge (3,218 km electrified)
narrow gauge: 23 km (2017) 0.760-m gauge
country comparison to the world: 24

Roadways: *total:* 55,744 km (2019) (includes urban and category I, II, III roads)
paved: 55,744 km (2019) (includes 1,252 km of expressways)
country comparison to the world: 81

Waterways: 664 km (2010) (principally on Elbe, Vltava, Oder, and other navigable rivers, lakes, and canals)
country comparison to the world: 84

Ports and terminals: *river port(s):* Prague (Vltava) Decin, Usti nad Labem (Elbe)

MILITARY AND SECURITY

Military and security forces: Czech Armed Forces: Land Forces; Air Forces; Cyber Forces; Special Forces (2022)

Military expenditures: 1.3% of GDP (2022 est.)
1.4% of GDP (2021)
1.3% of GDP (2020)
1.2% of GDP (2019) (approximately $4.05 billion)
1.1% of GDP (2018) (approximately $3.8 billion)
country comparison to the world: 103

Military and security service personnel strengths: approximately 26,000 active personnel (20,000 Army; 6,000 Air Force) (2022)

Military equipment inventories and acquisitions: the Czech military has a mix of Soviet-era and more modern equipment, mostly of Western European origin; since 2010, the leading suppliers of military equipment to Czechia have been Austria and Spain; Czechia has a considerable domestic defense industry; during the Cold War, Czechoslovakia was a major supplier of tanks, armored personnel carriers, military trucks, and trainer aircraft (2021)
note: in 2019, Czechia announced a modernization plan to acquire more equipment that was compliant with NATO standards, including aircraft from the US and armored vehicles from Germany and Sweden, as well as domestically-produced arms

Military service age and obligation: 18-28 years of age for voluntary military service for men and women; conscription abolished 2004 (2022)
note: as of 2019, women comprised about 13% of the military's full-time personnel

Military deployments: up to 130 Lithuania (NATO); 130 Slovakia (NATO) (2022)
note: in response to Russia's invasion of Ukraine, some NATO countries have sent additional troops and equipment to the battlegroups deployed in NATO territory in eastern Europe

Military - note: Czechia joined NATO in 1999; Czechia, Hungary, and Poland were invited to begin accession talks at NATO's Madrid Summit in 1997, and in March 1999 they became the first former members of the Warsaw Pact to join the Alliance

TRANSNATIONAL ISSUES

Disputes - international: none

Refugees and internally displaced persons: *refugees (country of origin):* 462,622 (Ukraine) (as of 22 November 2022)
stateless persons: 1,498 (mid-year 2021)

Illicit drugs: manufacture of methamphetamine continues to be mostly based on pseudoephedrine from Poland or Turkey.

DENMARK

INTRODUCTION

Background: Once the seat of Viking raiders and later a major north European power, Denmark has evolved into a modern, prosperous nation that is participating in the general political and economic integration of Europe. It joined NATO in 1949 and the EEC (now the EU) in 1973. However, the country has opted out of certain elements of the EU's Maastricht Treaty, including the European Economic and Monetary Union, European defense cooperation, and justice and home affairs issues.

GEOGRAPHY

Location: Northern Europe, bordering the Baltic Sea and the North Sea, on a peninsula north of Germany (Jutland); also includes several major islands (Sjaelland, Fyn, and Bornholm)

Geographic coordinates: 56 00 N, 10 00 E

Map references: Europe

Area: *total:* 43,094 sq km
land: 42,434 sq km
water: 660 sq km
note: includes the island of Bornholm in the Baltic Sea and the rest of metropolitan Denmark (the Jutland Peninsula, and the major islands of Sjaelland and Fyn), but excludes the Faroe Islands and Greenland country
comparison to the world: 133

Area - comparative: slightly less than twice the size of Massachusetts; about two-thirds the size of West Virginia

Land boundaries: *total:* 140 km
border countries (1): Germany 140 km

Coastline: 7,314 km

Maritime claims: *territorial sea:* 12 nm
contiguous zone: 24 nm
exclusive economic zone: 200 nm
continental shelf: 200-m depth or to the depth of exploitation

Climate: temperate; humid and overcast; mild, windy winters and cool summers

Terrain: low and flat to gently rolling plains

Elevation: *highest point:* Store Mollehoj 171 m
lowest point: Lammefjord -7 m
mean elevation: 34 m

Natural resources: petroleum, natural gas, fish, arable land, salt, limestone, chalk, stone, gravel and sand

Land use: *agricultural land:* 63.4% (2018 est.)
arable land: 58.9% (2018 est.)
permanent crops: 0.1% (2018 est.)
permanent pasture: 4.4% (2018 est.)
forest: 12.9% (2018 est.)
other: 23.7% (2018 est.)

Irrigated land: 4,350 sq km (2012)

Population distribution: with excellent access to the North Sea, Skagerrak, Kattegat, and the Baltic Sea, population centers tend to be along coastal areas, particularly in Copenhagen and the eastern side of the country's mainland

Natural hazards: flooding is a threat in some areas of the country (e.g., parts of Jutland, along the southern coast of the island of Lolland) that are protected from the sea by a system of dikes

Geography - note: composed of the Jutland Peninsula and a group of more than 400 islands (Danish Archipelago); controls Danish Straits (Skagerrak and Kattegat) linking Baltic and North Seas; about one-quarter of the population lives in greater Copenhagen

PEOPLE AND SOCIETY

Population: 5,920,767 (2022 est.)
country comparison to the world: 114

Nationality: *noun:* Dane(s)
adjective: Danish

Ethnic groups: Danish (includes Greenlandic (who are predominantly Inuit) and Faroese) 85.6%, Turkish 1.1%, other 13.3% (largest groups are Polish, Syrian, Romanian, German, and Iraqi) (2022 est.)
note: data represent population by ancestry

Languages: Danish, Faroese, Greenlandic (an Inuit dialect), German (small minority); note - English is the predominant second language
major-language sample(s):
Verdens Faktabog, den uundværlig kilde til grundlæggende oplysninger. (Danish)

Religions: Evangelical Lutheran (official) 74.7%, Muslim 5.5%, other/none/unspecified (denominations of less than 1% each in descending order of size include Roman Catholic, Jehovah's Witness, Serbian Orthodox Christian, Jewish, Baptist, Buddhist, Church of Jesus Christ, Pentecostal, and nondenominational Christian) 19.8% (2019 est.)

Age structure: *0-14 years:* 16.42% (male 494,806/female 469,005)
15-24 years: 12.33% (male 370,557/female 352,977)
25-54 years: 38.71% (male 1,149,991/female 1,122,016)
55-64 years: 12.63% (male 370,338/female 371,149)
65 years and over: 19.91% (male 538,096/female 630,475) (2020 est.)

Dependency ratios: *total dependency ratio:* 57.3
youth dependency ratio: 25.6
elderly dependency ratio: 31.7
potential support ratio: 3.2 (2020 est.)

Median age: *total:* 42 years
male: 40.9 years
female: 43.1 years (2020 est.)
country comparison to the world: 38

Population growth rate: 0.44% (2022 est.)
country comparison to the world: 158

Birth rate: 11.22 births/1,000 population (2022 est.)
country comparison to the world: 164

Death rate: 9.52 deaths/1,000 population (2022 est.)
country comparison to the world: 45

Net migration rate: 2.73 migrant(s)/1,000 population (2022 est.)
country comparison to the world: 42

Population distribution: with excellent access to the North Sea, Skagerrak, Kattegat, and the Baltic Sea, population centers tend to be along coastal areas, particularly in Copenhagen and the eastern side of the country's mainland

Urbanization: *urban population:* 88.4% of total population (2022)
rate of urbanization: 0.54% annual rate of change (2020-25 est.)

Major urban areas - population: 1.370 million COPENHAGEN (capital) (2022)

Sex ratio: *at birth:* 1.07 male(s)/female
0-14 years: 1.06 male(s)/female
15-24 years: 1.05 male(s)/female
25-54 years: 1.03 male(s)/female
55-64 years: 1 male(s)/female
65 years and over: 0.7 male(s)/female
total population: 0.99 male(s)/female (2022 est.)

Mother's mean age at first birth: 29.8 years (2020 est.)

Maternal mortality ratio: 4 deaths/100,000 live births (2017 est.)
country comparison to the world: 172

Infant mortality rate: *total:* 3.04 deaths/1,000 live births
male: 3.49 deaths/1,000 live births
female: 2.56 deaths/1,000 live births (2022 est.)
country comparison to the world: 212

Life expectancy at birth: *total population:* 81.66 years
male: 79.74 years
female: 83.71 years (2022 est.)
country comparison to the world: 36

Total fertility rate: 1.77 children born/woman (2022 est.)
country comparison to the world: 150

Drinking water source: *improved: urban:* 100% of population
rural: 100% of population
total: 100% of population

Current health expenditure: 10% of GDP (2019)

Physicians density: 4.23 physicians/1,000 population (2018)

Hospital bed density: 2.6 beds/1,000 population (2019)

Sanitation facility access: *improved: urban:* 100% of population
rural: 100% of population
total: 100% of population

HIV/AIDS - adult prevalence rate: 0.1% (2020 est.)
country comparison to the world: 122

Obesity - adult prevalence rate: 19.7% (2016)
country comparison to the world: 109

Alcohol consumption per capita: *total:* 9.16 liters of pure alcohol (2019 est.)
beer: 3.42 liters of pure alcohol (2019 est.)
wine: 4.08 liters of pure alcohol (2019 est.)
spirits: 1.66 liters of pure alcohol (2019 est.)
other alcohols: 0 liters of pure alcohol (2019 est.)
country comparison to the world: 33

Tobacco use: *total:* 17.5% (2020 est.)
male: 17.8% (2020 est.)
female: 17.1% (2020 est.)
country comparison to the world: 97

Education expenditures: 7.8% of GDP (2017 est.)
country comparison to the world: 12

School life expectancy (primary to tertiary education): *total:* 19 years
male: 18 years
female: 19 years (2019)

Unemployment, youth ages 15-24: *total:* 11.6%
male: 12.6%
female: 10.6% (2020 est.)

ENVIRONMENT

Environment - current issues: air pollution, principally from vehicle and power plant emissions; nitrogen and phosphorus pollution of the North Sea; drinking and surface water becoming polluted from animal wastes and pesticides; much of country's household and industrial waste is recycled

Environment - international agreements: *party to:* Air Pollution, Air Pollution-Heavy Metals, Air Pollution-Multi-effect Protocol, Air Pollution-Nitrogen Oxides, Air Pollution-Persistent Organic Pollutants, Air Pollution-Sulphur 85, Air Pollution-Sulphur 94, Air Pollution-Volatile Organic Compounds, Antarctic Treaty, Biodiversity, Climate Change, Climate Change-Kyoto Protocol, Climate Change-Paris Agreement, Comprehensive Nuclear Test Ban, Desertification, Endangered Species, Environmental Modification, Hazardous Wastes, Law of the Sea, Marine Dumping-London Convention, Marine Dumping-London Protocol, Marine Life Conservation, Nuclear Test Ban, Ozone Layer Protection, Ship Pollution, Tropical Timber 2006, Wetlands, Whaling
signed, but not ratified: Antarctic-Environmental Protection

Air pollutants: *particulate matter emissions:* 10.12 micrograms per cubic meter (2016 est.)
carbon dioxide emissions: 31.79 megatons (2016 est.)
methane emissions: 6.54 megatons (2020 est.)

Climate: temperate; humid and overcast; mild, windy winters and cool summers

Land use: *agricultural land:* 63.4% (2018 est.)
arable land: 58.9% (2018 est.)
permanent crops: 0.1% (2018 est.)
permanent pasture: 4.4% (2018 est.)
forest: 12.9% (2018 est.)
other: 23.7% (2018 est.)

Urbanization: *urban population:* 88.4% of total population (2022)
rate of urbanization: 0.54% annual rate of change (2020-25 est.)

Revenue from forest resources: *forest revenues:* 0.02% of GDP (2018 est.)
country comparison to the world: 140

Revenue from coal: *coal revenues:* 0% of GDP (2018 est.)
country comparison to the world: 88

Waste and recycling: *municipal solid waste generated annually:* 4.485 million tons (2015 est.)
municipal solid waste recycled annually: 1,223,060 tons (2015 est.)
percent of municipal solid waste recycled: 27.3% (2015 est.)

Total water withdrawal: *municipal:* 381.5 million cubic meters (2017 est.)
industrial: 32.9 million cubic meters (2017 est.)
agricultural: 326.7 million cubic meters (2017 est.)

Total renewable water resources: 6 billion cubic meters (2017 est.)

GOVERNMENT

Country name: *conventional long form:* Kingdom of Denmark
conventional short form: Denmark
local long form: Kongeriget Danmark
local short form: Danmark
etymology: the name derives from the words "Dane(s)" and "mark"; the latter referring to a march (borderland) or forest

Government type: parliamentary constitutional monarchy

Capital: *name:* Copenhagen
geographic coordinates: 55 40 N, 12 35 E
time difference: UTC+1 (6 hours ahead of Washington, DC, during Standard Time)
daylight saving time: +1hr, begins last Sunday in March; ends last Sunday in October; note - applies to continental Denmark only, not to its North Atlantic components
etymology: name derives from the city's Danish appellation Kobenhavn, meaning "Merchant's Harbor"

Administrative divisions: metropolitan Denmark - 5 regions (regioner, singular - region); Hovedstaden (Capital), Midtjylland (Central Jutland), Nordjylland (North Jutland), Sjaelland (Zealand), Syddanmark (Southern Denmark)

Independence: ca. 965 (unified and Christianized under Harald I GORMSSON); 5 June 1849 (became a parliamentary constitutional monarchy)

National holiday: Constitution Day, 5 June (1849); note - closest equivalent to a national holiday

Constitution: *history:* several previous; latest adopted 5 June 1953
amendments: proposed by the Folketing with consent of the government; passage requires approval by the next Folketing following a general election, approval by simple majority vote of at least 40% of voters in a referendum, and assent of the chief of state; changed several times, last in 2009 (Danish Act of Succession)

Legal system: civil law; judicial review of legislative acts

International law organization participation: accepts compulsory ICJ jurisdiction with reservations; accepts ICCt jurisdiction

Citizenship: *citizenship by birth:* no
citizenship by descent only: at least one parent must be a citizen of Denmark
dual citizenship recognized: yes
residency requirement for naturalization: 7 years

Suffrage: 18 years of age; universal

Executive branch: *chief of state:* Queen MARGRETHE II (since 14 January 1972); Heir Apparent Crown Prince FREDERIK (elder son of the monarch, born on 26 May 1968)
head of government: Prime Minister Mette FREDERIKSEN (since 27 June 2019)
cabinet: Council of State appointed by the monarch
elections/appointments: the monarchy is hereditary; following legislative elections, the leader of the majority party or majority coalition usually appointed prime minister by the monarch

Legislative branch: *description:* unicameral People's Assembly or Folketing (179 seats, including 2 each representing Greenland and the Faroe Islands; members directly elected in multi-seat constituencies by party-list proportional representation vote; members serve 4-year terms unless the Folketing is dissolved earlier)
elections:
last held on 1 November 2022 (next to be held on 31 October 2026)
election results:
percent of vote by party - SDP 27.5%, V 13.3%, M 9.3%, E 8.1%, DF 2.6%, SLP 3.8%, SF 8.3%, EL 5.1%, C 5.5%, AP 3.3%, NB 3.3%, LA 8.1%; seats by party - SDP 50, V 23, M 16, E 14, DF 5, SLP 7, SF 15, EL 9, C 10, AP 6, NB 6, LA 14; composition
5 June 2019: percent of vote by party - SDP 27.4%, V 24.6%, DF 9.1%, SLP 9.1%, SF 8%, EL 7.4%, C 6.9%, AP 2.9%, NB 2.3%, LA 2.3%; seats by party - SDP 48, V 43, DF 16, SLP 16, SF 14, EL 13, C 12, AP 5, NB 4, LA 4; composition (as of September 2021) - men 108, women 71 (includes 2 from Greenland), percent of women 39.7%

Judicial branch: *highest court(s):* Supreme Court (consists of the court president and 18 judges)
judge selection and term of office: judges appointed by the monarch upon the recommendation of the Minister of Justice, with the advice of the Judicial Appointments Council, a 6-member independent body of judges and lawyers; judges appointed for life with retirement at age 70
subordinate courts: Special Court of Indictment and Revision; 2 High Courts; Maritime and Commercial Court; county courts

Political parties and leaders: The Alternative AP [Franciska ROSENKILDE]
Conservative People's Party or DKF or C [Soren PAPE POULSEN]
Danish People's Party or DF or O [Morten MESSERSCHMIDT]
Denmark Democrats or E [Inger STOJBERG]
Green Left or SF or F [Pia OLSEN DYHR] (formerly Socialist People's Party or SF or F)
Liberal Alliance or LA or I [Alex VANOPSLAGH]
Liberal Party (Venstre) or V [Jakob ELLEMANN-JENSEN]
Moderates or M [Lars Lokke RASMUSSEN]
New Right Party or NB or D [Ann Pernille VERMUND TVEDE]
Red-Green Alliance (Unity List) or EL [collective leadership, Mai VILLADSEN, spokesperson]
Social Democrats or SDP or A [Mette FREDERIKSEN]
Social Liberal Party or SLP or B [Sofie CARSTEN NIELSEN]

International organization participation: ADB (nonregional member), AfDB (nonregional member), Arctic Council, Australia Group, BIS, CBSS, CD, CE, CERN, EAPC, EBRD, ECB, EIB, EITI (implementing country), ESA, EU, FAO, FATF, G-9, IADB, IAEA, IBRD, ICAO, ICC (national committees), ICCt, ICRM, IDA, IEA, IFAD, IFC, IFRCS, IGAD (partners), IHO, ILO, IMF, IMO, IMSO, Interpol, IOC, IOM, IPU, ISO, ITSO, ITU, ITUC (NGOs), MIGA, MINUSMA, NATO, NC, NEA, NIB, NSG, OAS (observer), OECD, OPCW, OSCE, Paris Club, PCA, Schengen Convention, UN, UNCTAD, UNESCO, UNHCR, UNIDO, UNMIL, UNMISS, UNRWA, UNTSO, UPU, Wassenaar Arrangement, WCO, WHO, WIPO, WMO, WTO, ZC

Diplomatic representation in the US: *chief of mission:* Ambassador Christina Markus LASSEN (since 16 September 2022)
chancery: 3200 Whitehaven Street NW, Washington, DC 20008
telephone: [1] (202) 234-4300
FAX: [1] (202) 328-1470
email address and website:
wasamb@um.dk
https://usa.um.dk/en
consulate(s) general: Chicago, Houston, New York, Silicon Valley (CA)

Diplomatic representation from the US: *chief of mission:* Ambassador Alan LEVENTHAL (since 1 July 2022)
embassy: Dag Hammarskjolds Alle 24, 2100 Kobenhavn 0
mailing address: 5280 Copenhagen Place, Washington DC 20521-5280
telephone: [45] 33-41-71-00
FAX: [45] 35-43-02-23
email address and website:
CopenhagenACS@state.gov
https://dk.usembassy.gov/

Flag description: red with a white cross that extends to the edges of the flag; the vertical part of the cross is shifted to the hoist side; the banner is referred to as the Dannebrog (Danish flag) and is one of the oldest national flags in the world; traditions as to the origin of the flag design vary, but the best known is a legend that the banner fell from the sky during an early-13th century battle; caught up by the Danish king before it ever touched the earth, this heavenly talisman inspired the royal army to victory; in actuality, the flag may derive from a crusade banner or ensign
note: the shifted cross design element was subsequently adopted by the other Nordic countries of Finland, Iceland, Norway, and Sweden, as well as by the Faroe Islands

National symbol(s): lion, mute swan; national colors: red, white

National anthem: *name:* "Der er et yndigt land" (There is a Lovely Country); "Kong Christian" (King Christian)
lyrics/music: Adam Gottlob OEHLENSCHLAGER/ Hans Ernst KROYER; Johannes EWALD/unknown
note: Denmark has two national anthems with equal status; "Der er et yndigt land," adopted 1844, is a national anthem, while "Kong Christian," adopted 1780, serves as both a national and royal anthem; "Kong Christian" is also known as "Kong Christian stod ved hojen mast" (King Christian Stood by the Lofty Mast) and "Kongesangen" (The King's Anthem); within Denmark, the royal anthem is played only when royalty is present and is usually followed by the national anthem; when royalty is not present, only the national anthem is performed; outside Denmark, the royal anthem is played, unless the national anthem is requested

National heritage: *total World Heritage Sites:* 10 (7 cultural, 3 natural); note - includes three sites in Greenland
selected World Heritage Site locales: Denmark: Mounds, Runic Stones, and Church at Jelling (c); Roskilde Cathedral (c); Kronborg Castle (c); Wadden Sea (n); Stevns Klint (n); Christiansfeld, Moravian Church Settlement (c); Par force hunting landscape, North Zealand (c); Greenland: Ilulissat Icefjord (n); Kujataa, Norse and Inuit Farming (c); Aasivissuit-Nipisat, Inuit Hunting Ground (c)

ECONOMY

Economic overview: This thoroughly modern market economy features advanced industry with world-leading firms in pharmaceuticals, maritime shipping, and renewable energy, and a high-tech agricultural sector. Danes enjoy a high standard of living, and the Danish economy is characterized by extensive government welfare measures and an equitable distribution of income. An aging population will be a long-term issue.

Denmark's small open economy is highly dependent on foreign trade, and the government strongly supports trade liberalization. Denmark is a net exporter of food, oil, and gas and enjoys a comfortable balance of payments surplus, but depends on imports of raw materials for the manufacturing sector.

Denmark is a member of the EU but not the eurozone. Despite previously meeting the criteria to join the European Economic and Monetary Union, Denmark has negotiated an opt-out with the EU and is not required to adopt the euro.

Denmark is experiencing a modest economic expansion. The economy grew by 2.0% in 2016 and 2.1% in 2017. The expansion is expected to decline slightly in 2018. Unemployment stood at 5.5% in 2017, based on the national labor survey. The labor market was tight in 2017, with corporations experiencing some difficulty finding appropriately-skilled workers to fill billets. The Danish Government offers extensive programs to train unemployed persons to work in sectors that need qualified workers.

Denmark maintained a healthy budget surplus for many years up to 2008, but the global financial crisis swung the budget balance into deficit. Since 2014 the balance has shifted between surplus and deficit. In 2017 there was a surplus of 1.0%. The government projects a lower deficit in 2018 and 2019 of 0.7%, and public debt (EMU debt) as a share of GDP is expected to decline to 35.6% in 2018 and 34.8% in 2019. The Danish Government plans to address increasing municipal, public housing and integration spending in 2018.

Real GDP (purchasing power parity): $326.2 billion (2020 est.)
$335.36 billion (2019 est.)
$326.07 billion (2018 est.)
note: data are in 2017 dollars
country comparison to the world: 53

Real GDP growth rate: 2.85% (2019 est.)
2.18% (2018 est.)
2.83% (2017 est.)
country comparison to the world: 101

Real GDP per capita: $55,900 (2020 est.)
$57,700 (2019 est.)
$56,300 (2018 est.)
note: data are in 2017 dollars
country comparison to the world: 20

GDP (official exchange rate): $350.037 billion (2019 est.)

Inflation rate (consumer prices): 0.7% (2019 est.)
0.8% (2018 est.)
1.1% (2017 est.)
country comparison to the world: 52

Credit ratings:

Fitch rating: AAA (2003)

Moody's rating: Aaa (1999)

Standard & Poors rating: AAA (2001)
note: The year refers to the year in which the current credit rating was first obtained.

GDP - composition, by sector of origin: *agriculture:* 1.3% (2017 est.)
industry: 22.9% (2017 est.)
services: 75.8% (2017 est.)

GDP - composition, by end use household consumption: 48% (2017 est.)
government consumption: 25.2% (2017 est.)
investment in fixed capital: 20% (2017 est.)
investment in inventories: -0.2% (2017 est.)
exports of goods and services: 54.5% (2017 est.)
imports of goods and services: -47.5% (2017 est.)

Agricultural products: milk, wheat, barley, potatoes, sugar beet, pork, rye, rapeseed, oats, poultry

Industries: wind turbines, pharmaceuticals, medical equipment, shipbuilding and refurbishment, iron, steel, nonferrous metals, chemicals, food processing, machinery and transportation equipment, textiles and clothing, electronics, construction, furniture and other wood products

Industrial production growth rate: 2.5% (2017 est.)
country comparison to the world: 116

Labor force: 2.736 million (2020 est.)
country comparison to the world: 107

Labor force - by occupation: *agriculture:* 2.4%
industry: 18.3%
services: 79.3% (2016 est.)

Unemployment rate: 3.05% (2019 est.)
3.07% (2018 est.)
country comparison to the world: 40

Unemployment, youth ages 15-24: *total:* 11.6%
male: 12.6%
female: 10.6% (2020 est.)
country comparison to the world: 127

Population below poverty line: 12.5% (2018 est.)

Gini Index coefficient - distribution of family income: 28.7 (2017 est.)
27.5 (2010 est.)
country comparison to the world: 157

Household income or consumption by percentage share: *lowest 10%:* 9%
highest 10%: 23.4% (2016 est.)

Budget: *revenues:* 172.5 billion (2017 est.)
expenditures: 168.9 billion (2017 est.)

Budget surplus (+) or deficit (-): 1.1% (of GDP) (2017 est.)
country comparison to the world: 30

Public debt: 35.3% of GDP (2017 est.)
37.9% of GDP (2016 est.)
note: data cover general government debt and include debt instruments issued (or owned) by government entities other than the treasury; the data include treasury debt held by foreign entities; the

data include debt issued by subnational entities, as well as intra-governmental debt; intragovernmental debt consists of treasury borrowings from surpluses in the social funds, such as for retirement, medical care, and unemployment; debt instruments for the social funds are not sold at public auctions
country comparison to the world: 151

Taxes and other revenues: 53% (of GDP) (2017 est.)
country comparison to the world: 12

Fiscal year: calendar year

Current account balance: $30.935 billion (2019 est.)
$24.821 billion (2018 est.)
country comparison to the world: 12

Exports: $191.53 billion (2020 est.) note: data are in current year dollars
$204.14 billion (2019 est.) note: data are in current year dollars
$200.81 billion (2018 est.) note: data are in current year dollars
country comparison to the world: 31

Exports - partners: Germany 14%, United States 11%, Sweden 10%, United Kingdom 7%, Norway 6%, Netherlands 5%, China 5% (2019)

Exports - commodities: packaged medicines, electric generators, pork, refined petroleum, medical cultures/vaccines (2019)

Imports: $170.33 billion (2020 est.) note: data are in current year dollars
$178.44 billion (2019 est.) note: data are in current year dollars
$179.95 billion (2018 est.) note: data are in current year dollars
country comparison to the world: 32

Imports - partners: Germany 21%, Sweden 11%, Netherlands 8%, China 7% (2019)

Imports - commodities: cars, refined petroleum, packaged medicines, crude petroleum, broadcasting equipment (2019)

Reserves of foreign exchange and gold: $75.25 billion (31 December 2017 est.)
$64.25 billion (31 December 2016 est.)
country comparison to the world: 30

Debt - external: $504.808 billion (2019 est.)
$517.972 billion (2018 est.)
country comparison to the world: 24

Exchange rates: Danish kroner (DKK) per US dollar -
6.16045 (2020 est.)
6.7506 (2019 est.)
6.5533 (2018 est.)
6.7236 (2014 est.)
5.6125 (2013 est.)

ENERGY

Electricity access: *electrification - total population:* 100% (2020)

Electricity: *installed generating capacity:* 17.655 million kW (2020 est.)
consumption: 33.081 billion kWh (2020 est.)
exports: 12.694 billion kWh (2020 est.)
imports: 18.891 billion kWh (2020 est.)
transmission/distribution losses: 1.573 billion kWh (2020 est.)

Electricity generation sources: *fossil fuels:* 14.8% of total installed capacity (2020 est.)
solar: 4.2% of total installed capacity (2020 est.)
wind: 57.5% of total installed capacity (2020 est.)
hydroelectricity: 0.1% of total installed capacity (2020 est.)
biomass and waste: 23.5% of total installed capacity (2020 est.)

Coal: *production:* 0 metric tons (2020 est.)
consumption: 1.249 million metric tons (2020 est.)
exports: 194,000 metric tons (2020 est.)
imports: 1.122 million metric tons (2020 est.)
proven reserves: 0 metric tons (2019 est.)

Petroleum: *total petroleum production:* 69,000 bbl/day (2021 est.)
refined petroleum consumption: 165,400 bbl/day (2019 est.)
crude oil and lease condensate exports: 56,700 bbl/day (2018 est.)
crude oil and lease condensate imports: 95,200 bbl/day (2018 est.)
crude oil estimated reserves: 441 million barrels (2021 est.)

Refined petroleum products - production: 183,900 bbl/day (2017 est.)
country comparison to the world: 55

Refined petroleum products - exports: 133,700 bbl/day (2017 est.)
country comparison to the world: 38

Refined petroleum products - imports: 109,700 bbl/day (2017 est.)
country comparison to the world: 51

Natural gas: *production:* 1,314,636,000 cubic meters (2020 est.)
consumption: 2,188,096,000 cubic meters (2020 est.)
exports: 1,700,594,000 cubic meters (2020 est.)
imports: 2,645,893,000 cubic meters (2020 est.)
proven reserves: 29.534 billion cubic meters (2021 est.)

Carbon dioxide emissions: 33.85 million metric tonnes of CO2 (2019 est.)
from coal and metallurgical coke: 3.455 million metric tonnes of CO2 (2019 est.)
from petroleum and other liquids: 24.621 million metric tonnes of CO2 (2019 est.)
from consumed natural gas: 5.775 million metric tonnes of CO2 (2019 est.)
country comparison to the world: 73

Energy consumption per capita: 124.163 million Btu/person (2019 est.)
country comparison to the world: 43

COMMUNICATIONS

Telephones - fixed lines: *total subscriptions:* 734,436 (2020 est.)
subscriptions per 100 inhabitants: 13 (2020 est.)
country comparison to the world: 79

Telephones - mobile cellular: *total subscriptions:* 7,252,675 (2020 est.)
subscriptions per 100 inhabitants: 125 (2020 est.)
country comparison to the world: 103

Telecommunication systems: *general assessment:* Denmark has one of the highest broadband subscription rates globally, with a near universal availability of super fast connections; extensive cable and DSL infrastructure has been supported by a progressive regulatory regime which has encouraged operator access to both copper and fiber networks; fiber networks have a fast-growing footprint, while a number of community and metropolitan schemes have supplemented TDC NET's own commitments to build out fiber nationally; a number of wholesale fiber schemes have also added to the wider availability of fiber broadband; the reach of LTE infrastructure is comprehensive, while the Mobile Network Operators by mid-2021 had also provided about 90% population coverage with 5G; services based on 5G were initially launched using trial 3.5GHz licenses; the multi-spectrum auction held in April 2021 has enabled them to improve the resilience and capacity of 5G; all MNOs are engaged in closing down their 3G networks and repurposing spectrum for LTE and 5G use (2021)
domestic: fixed-line roughly 16 per 100 and about 123 per 100 for mobile-cellular subscriptions (2020)
international: country code - 45; landing points for the NSC, COBRAcable, CANTAT-3, DANICE, Havfrue/AEC-2, TAT-14m Denmark-Norway-5 & 6, Skagenfiber West & East, GC1, GC2, GC3, GC-KPN, Kattegat 1 & 2 & 3, Energinet Lyngsa-Laeso, Energinet Laeso-Varberg, Fehmarn Balt, Baltica, German-Denmark 2 & 3, Ronne-Rodvig, Denmark-Sweden 15 & 16 & 17 & 18, IP-Only Denmark-Sweden, Scandinavian South, Scandinavian Ring North, Danica North, 34 series of fiber-optic submarine cables link Denmark with Canada, Faroe Islands, Germany, Iceland, Netherlands, Norway, Poland, Russia, Sweden, US, and, UK; satellite earth stations - 18 (6 Intelsat, 10 Eutelsat, 1 Orion, 1 Inmarsat (Blaavand-Atlantic-East)); note - the Nordic countries (Denmark, Finland, Iceland, Norway, and Sweden) share the Danish earth station and the Eik, Norway, station for worldwide Inmarsat access (2019)

Broadcast media: strong public-sector TV presence with state-owned Danmarks Radio (DR) operating 6 channels and publicly owned TV2 operating roughly a half-dozen channels; broadcasts of privately owned stations are available via satellite and cable feed; DR operates 4 nationwide FM radio stations, 10 digital audio broadcasting stations, and 14 web-based radio stations; 140 commercial and 187 community (non-commercial) radio stations (2019)

Internet country code: .dk

Internet users: *total:* 5,656,462 (2020 est.)
percent of population: 97% (2020 est.)
country comparison to the world: 82

Broadband - fixed subscriptions: *total:* 2,590,282 (2020 est.)
subscriptions per 100 inhabitants: 45 (2020 est.)
country comparison to the world: 51

TRANSPORTATION

National air transport system: *number of registered air carriers:* 10 (2020)
inventory of registered aircraft operated by air carriers: 76
annual passenger traffic on registered air carriers: 582,011 (2015)
annual freight traffic on registered air carriers: 0 (2015) mt-km

Civil aircraft registration country code prefix: OY

Airports: *total:* 80 (2021)
country comparison to the world: 68

Airports - with paved runways: *total:* 28
over 3,047 m: 2
2,438 to 3,047 m: 7
1,524 to 2,437 m: 5
914 to 1,523 m: 12
under 914 m: 2 (2021)

Airports - with unpaved runways: *total:* 52
914 to 1,523 m: 5
under 914 m: 47 (2021)

Pipelines: 1,536 km gas, 330 km oil (2015)

Railways: *total:* 3,476 km (2017)
standard gauge: 3,476 km (2017) 1.435-m gauge (1,756 km electrified)
country comparison to the world: 57

Roadways: *total:* 74,558 km (2017)
paved: 74,558 km (2017) (includes 1,205 km of expressways)
country comparison to the world: 65

Waterways: 400 km (2010)
country comparison to the world: 96

Merchant marine: *total:* 717
by type: bulk carrier 8, container ship 148, general cargo 68, oil tanker 105, other 388 (2021)
country comparison to the world: 33

Ports and terminals: *major seaport(s):* Baltic Sea - Aarhus, Copenhagen, Fredericia, Kalundborg
cruise port(s): Copenhagen
river port(s): Aalborg (Langerak)
dry bulk cargo port(s): Ensted (coal)
North Sea - Esbjerg,

MILITARY AND SECURITY

Military and security forces: Danish Armed Forces (Forsvaret): Royal Danish Army, Royal Danish Navy, Royal Danish Air Force, Danish Home Guard (Reserves) (2022)
note: the Danish military maintains a Joint Arctic Command with the mission of protecting the sovereignty of the Kingdom of Denmark in the Arctic Region, including the Faroe Islands and Greenland; the command also conducts maritime pollution prevention, environmental monitoring, fishery inspections, search and rescue, hydrographical surveys, and provides support to governmental science missions

Military expenditures: 1.4% of GDP (2022 est.)
1.4% of GDP (2021)
1.4% of GDP (2020)
1.3% of GDP (2019) (approximately $5.02 billion)
1.3% of GDP (2018) (approximately $4.8 billion)
country comparison to the world: 98

Military and security service personnel strengths: approximately 17,000 active duty personnel (10,000 Army; 3,500 Navy; 3,500 Air Force) (2022)

Military equipment inventories and acquisitions: the Danish military inventory is comprised of a mix of modern European, US, and domestically-produced equipment; the US has been the largest supplier of military equipment to Denmark since 2010; the Danish defense industry is active in the production of naval vessels, defense electronics, and subcomponents of larger weapons systems, such as the US F-35 fighter aircraft (2022)

Military service age and obligation: 18 years of age for compulsory and voluntary military service; conscripts serve an initial training period that varies from 4 to 12 months depending on specialization; former conscripts are assigned to mobilization units; women eligible to volunteer for military service; in addition to full time employment, the Danish military offers reserve contracts in all three branches (2022)
note 1: women have been able serve in all military occupations, including combat arms, since 1988; as of 2019, they made up about 8% of the military's full-time personnel; conscientious objectors can choose to instead serve 6 months in a non-military position, for example in Beredskabsstyrelsen (dealing with non-military disasters like fires, flood, pollution, etc.) or overseas foreign aid work
note 2: foreigners who have lived in Denmark for at least 1 year or in another EU country for 6 years may apply to join the armed forces, provided they are fluent in Danish
note 2: Denmark has had compulsory military service since 1849

Military deployments: approximately 220 Estonia (NATO); approximately 750 Latvia (NATO); approximately 100 Middle East/Iraq (NATO) (2022)
note: in response to Russia's 2022 invasion of Ukraine, some NATO countries, including Denmark, have sent additional troops and equipment to the battlegroups deployed in NATO territory in eastern Europe

Military - note: Denmark is a member of NATO and was one of the original 12 countries to sign the North Atlantic Treaty (also known as the Washington Treaty) in 1949

Denmark is a member of the EU and voted to join the EU's Common Defense and Security Policy in a June 2022 referendum

the Danish Armed Forces cooperate closely with the militaries of other Nordic countries through the Nordic Defense Cooperation (NORDEFCO), which consists of Denmark, Finland, Iceland, Norway, and Sweden; areas of cooperation include armaments, education, human resources, training and exercises, and operations; NORDEFCO was established in 2009

in 2018, the Defense Ministers of Belgium, Denmark and the Netherlands signed a Memorandum of Understanding (MOU) for the creation of a Composite Special Operations Component Command (C-SOCC); the C-SOCC was declared operational in December 2020 (2022)

TERRORISM

Terrorist group(s): Islamic State of Iraq and ash-Sham (ISIS); Islamic Revolutionary Guard Corps/ Qods Force

TRANSNATIONAL ISSUES

Disputes - international: Iceland, the UK, and Ireland dispute Denmark's claim that the Faroe Islands' continental shelf extends beyond 200 nm; sovereignty dispute with Canada over Hans Island in the Kennedy Channel between Ellesmere Island and Greenland; Denmark (Greenland) and Norway have made submissions to the Commission on the Limits of the Continental Shelf (CLCS) and Russia is collecting additional data to augment its 2001 CLCS submission

Refugees and internally displaced persons: *refugees (country of origin):* 19,833 (Syria), 5,634 (Eritrea) (mid-year 2021); 36,983 (Ukraine) (as of 15 November 2022)
stateless persons: 11,608 (mid-year 2021)

DHEKELIA

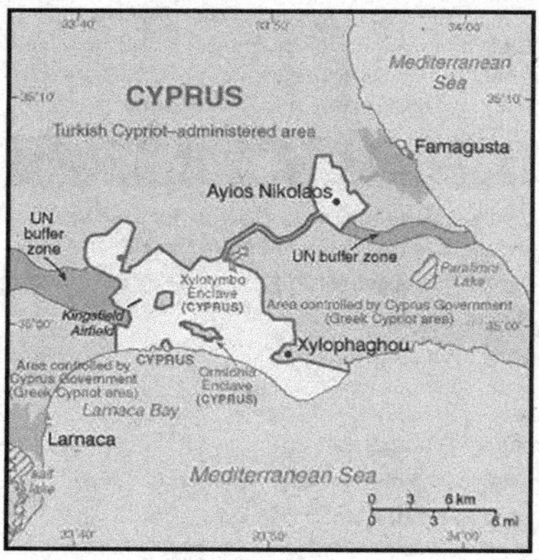

INTRODUCTION

Background: By terms of the 1960 Treaty of Establishment that created the independent Republic of Cyprus, the UK retained full sovereignty and jurisdiction over two areas of almost 254 square kilometers - Akrotiri and Dhekelia. The larger of these is the Dhekelia Sovereign Base Area, which is also referred to as the Eastern Sovereign Base Area.

GEOGRAPHY

Location: Eastern Mediterranean, on the southeast coast of Cyprus near Famagusta

Geographic coordinates: 34 59 N, 33 45 E

Map references: Middle East

Area: *total:* 131 sq km
note: area surrounds three Cypriot enclaves
country comparison to the world: 222

Area - comparative: about three-quarters the size of Washington, DC

Land boundaries: *total:* 108 km
border countries (1): Cyprus 108 km

Coastline: 27.5 km

Climate: temperate; Mediterranean with hot, dry summers and cool winters

Geography - note: British extraterritorial rights also extended to several small off-post sites scattered across Cyprus; several small Cypriot enclaves exist within the Sovereign Base Area (SBA); of the SBA land, 60% is privately owned and farmed, 20% is owned by the Ministry of Defense, and 20% is SBA Crown land

PEOPLE AND SOCIETY

Population: approximately 15,500 on the Sovereign Base Areas of Akrotiri and Dhekelia including 9,700 Cypriots and 5,800 Service and UK-based contract personnel and dependents

Languages: English, Greek
major-language sample(s):
Το Παγκόσμιο Βιβλίο Δεδομένων, η απαραίτητη πηγή βασικών πληροφοριών. (Greek)

ENVIRONMENT

Environment - current issues: netting and trapping of small migrant songbirds in the spring and autumn

Climate: temperate; Mediterranean with hot, dry summers and cool winters

GOVERNMENT

Country name: *conventional long form:* none
conventional short form: Dhekelia

Dependency status: a special form of UK overseas territory; administered by an administrator who is also the Commander, British Forces Cyprus

Capital: *name:* Episkopi Cantonment (base administrative center for Akrotiri and Dhekelia); located in Akrotiri
geographic coordinates: 34 40 N, 32 51 E
time difference: UTC+2 (7 hours ahead of Washington, DC, during Standard Time)
daylight saving time: +1hr, begins last Sunday in March; ends last Sunday in October
etymology: "Episkopi" means "episcopal" in Greek and stems from the fact that the site previously served as the bishop's seat of an Orthodox diocese

Constitution: *history:* presented 3 August 1960, effective 16 August 1960 (The Sovereign Base Areas of Akrotiri and Dhekelia Order in Council 1960, serves as a basic legal document); amended 1966

Legal system: laws applicable to the Cypriot population are, as far as possible, the same as the laws of the Republic of Cyprus; note -the Sovereign Base Area Administration has its own court system to deal with civil and criminal matters

Executive branch: *chief of state:* King CHARLES III (since 8 September 2022)
head of government: Administrator Air Vice-Marshal Peter J.M. SQUIRES (since 1 September 2022); note - the administrator reports to the British Ministry of Defense and is also Commander, British Forces Cyprus (BFC); the chief officer, an appointed civilian, is responsible for the day-to-day running of the civil government of the Sovereign Base Areas
elections/appointments: the monarchy is hereditary; administrator appointed by the monarch on the advice of the Ministry of Defense

Judicial branch: *highest court(s):* Senior Judges' Court (consists of several visiting judges from England and Wales)
judge selection and term of office: see entry for United Kingdom
subordinate courts: Resident Judges' Court; military courts

Diplomatic representation in the US: none (overseas territory of the UK)

Diplomatic representation from the US: none (overseas territory of the UK)

Flag description: the flag of the UK is used

National anthem: *note:* as a United Kingdom area of special sovereignty, "God Save the King" is official (see United Kingdom)

ECONOMY

Economic overview: Economic activity is limited to providing services to the military and their families located in Dhekelia. All food and manufactured goods must be imported.

Industries: none

Exchange rates: *note:* uses the euro

COMMUNICATIONS

Broadcast media: British Forces Broadcast Service (BFBS) provides multi-channel satellite TV service as well as BFBS radio broadcasts to the Dhekelia Sovereign Base

MILITARY AND SECURITY

Military - note: defense of Dhekelia (aka Eastern Sovereign Base Area) is the responsibility of the UK; includes Dhekelia Garrison and Ayios Nikolaos Station connected by a roadway

DJIBOUTI

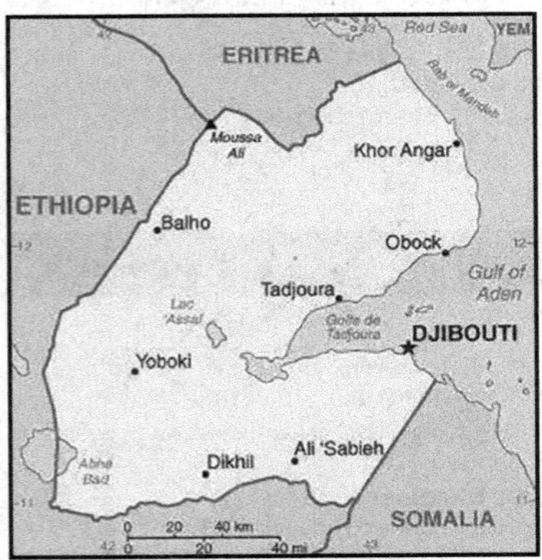

INTRODUCTION

Background: The region of present-day Djibouti was the site of the medieval Ifat and Adal Sultanates. In the late 19th century, treaties signed by the Afar sultans with the French allowed the latter to establish the colony of French Somaliland in 1862. The French signed additional treaties with the ethnic Somali in 1885.

Tension between the ethnic Afar and Somali populations increased over time, as the ethnic Somalis perceived that the French unfairly favored the Afar and gave them disproportionate influence in local governance. In 1958, the French held a referendum that provided residents of French Somaliland the option to either continue their association with France or to join neighboring Somalia as it established its independence. The ethnic Somali protested the vote, because French colonial leaders did not recognize many Somali as residents, which gave the Afar outsized influence in the decision to uphold ties with France. After a second referendum in 1967, the French changed the territory's name to the French Territory of the Afars and the Issas, in part to underscore their relationship with the ethnic Afar and downplay the significance of the ethnic Somalis. A final referendum in 1977 established Djibouti as an independent nation and granted ethnic Somalis Djiboutian nationality, formally resetting the balance of power between the majority ethnic Somalis and minority ethnic Afar residents. Upon independence, the country was named after its capital city of Djibouti. Hassan Gouled APTIDON, an ethnic Somali leader, installed an authoritarian one-party state and proceeded to serve as president until 1999. Unrest between the Afar minority and Somali majority culminated in a civil war during the 1990s that ended in 2001 with a peace accord between Afar rebels and the Somali Issa-dominated government. In 1999, Djibouti's first multiparty presidential election resulted in the election of Ismail Omar GUELLEH as president; he was reelected to a second term in 2005 and extended his tenure in office via a constitutional amendment, which allowed him to serve his third and fourth terms, and to begin a fifth term in 2021.

Djibouti occupies a strategic geographic location at the intersection of the Red Sea and the Gulf of Aden. Its ports handle 95% of Ethiopia's trade. Djibouti's ports also service transshipments between Europe, the Middle East, and Asia. The government holds longstanding ties to France, which maintains a military presence in the country, as does the US, Japan, Italy, Germany, Spain, and China.

GEOGRAPHY

Location: Eastern Africa, bordering the Gulf of Aden and the Red Sea, between Eritrea and Somalia

Geographic coordinates: 11 30 N, 43 00 E

Map references: Africa

Area: *total:* 23,200 sq km
land: 23,180 sq km
water: 20 sq km
country comparison to the world: 150

Area - comparative: slightly smaller than New Jersey

Land boundaries: *total:* 528 km

border countries (3): Eritrea 125 km; Ethiopia 342 km; Somalia 61 km

Coastline: 314 km

Maritime claims: *territorial sea:* 12 nm
contiguous zone: 24 nm
exclusive economic zone: 200 nm

Climate: desert; torrid, dry

Terrain: coastal plain and plateau separated by central mountains

Elevation: *highest point:* Moussa Ali 2,021 m
lowest point: Lac Assal -155 m
mean elevation: 430 m

Natural resources: potential geothermal power, gold, clay, granite, limestone, marble, salt, diatomite, gypsum, pumice, petroleum

Land use: *agricultural land:* 73.4% (2018 est.)
arable land: 0.1% (2018 est.)
permanent crops: 0% (2018 est.)
permanent pasture: 73.3% (2018 est.)
forest: 0.2% (2018 est.)
other: 26.4% (2018 est.)

Irrigated land: 10 sq km (2012)

Major lakes (area sq km): *salt water lake(s):* Abhe Bad/Abhe Bid Hayk (shared with Ethiopia) - 780 sq km

Population distribution: most densely populated areas are in the east; the largest city is Djibouti, with a population over 600,000; no other city in the country has a total population over 50,000 as shown in this population distribution map

Natural hazards: earthquakes; droughts; occasional cyclonic disturbances from the Indian Ocean bring heavy rains and flash floods
volcanism: experiences limited volcanic activity; Ardoukoba (298 m) last erupted in 1978; Manda-Inakir, located along the Ethiopian border, is also historically active

Geography - note: strategic location near world's busiest shipping lanes and close to Arabian oilfields; terminus of rail traffic into Ethiopia; mostly wasteland; Lac Assal (Lake Assal) is the lowest point in Africa and the saltiest lake in the world

PEOPLE AND SOCIETY

Population: 957,273 (2022 est.)
country comparison to the world: 162

Nationality: *noun:* Djiboutian(s)
adjective: Djiboutian

Ethnic groups: Somali 60%, Afar 35%, other 5% (mostly Yemeni Arab, also French, Ethiopian, and Italian)

Languages: French (official), Arabic (official), Somali, Afar

Religions: Sunni Muslim 94% (nearly all Djiboutians), other 6% (mainly foreign-born residents - Shia Muslim, Christian, Hindu, Jewish, Baha'i, and atheist)

Demographic profile: Djibouti is a poor, predominantly urban country, characterized by high rates of illiteracy, unemployment, and childhood malnutrition. More than 75% of the population lives in cities and towns (predominantly in the capital, Djibouti). The rural population subsists primarily on nomadic herding. Prone to droughts and floods, the country has few natural resources and must import more than 80% of its food from neighboring countries or Europe. Health care, particularly outside the capital, is limited by poor infrastructure, shortages of equipment and supplies, and a lack of qualified personnel. More than a third of health care recipients are migrants because the services are still better than those available in their neighboring home countries. The nearly universal practice of female genital cutting reflects Djibouti's lack of gender equality and is a major contributor to obstetrical complications and its high rates of maternal and infant mortality. A 1995 law prohibiting the practice has never been enforced.

Because of its political stability and its strategic location at the confluence of East Africa and the Gulf States along the Gulf of Aden and the Red Sea, Djibouti is a key transit point for migrants and asylum seekers heading for the Gulf States and beyond. Each year some hundred thousand people, mainly Ethiopians and some Somalis, journey through Djibouti, usually to the port of Obock, to attempt a dangerous sea crossing to Yemen. However, with the escalation of the ongoing Yemen conflict, Yemenis began fleeing to Djibouti in March 2015, with almost 20,000 arriving by August 2017. Most Yemenis remain unregistered and head for Djibouti City rather than seeking asylum at one of Djibouti's three spartan refugee camps. Djibouti has been hosting refugees and asylum seekers, predominantly Somalis and lesser numbers of Ethiopians and Eritreans, at camps for 20 years, despite lacking potable water, food shortages, and unemployment.

Age structure: *0-14 years:* 29.97% (male 138,701/female 137,588)
15-24 years: 20.32% (male 88,399/female 98,955)
25-54 years: 40.73% (male 156,016/female 219,406)
55-64 years: 5.01% (male 19,868/female 26,307)
65 years and over: 3.97% (male 16,245/female 20,319) (2020 est.)

Dependency ratios: *total dependency ratio:* 50.6
youth dependency ratio: 43.6
elderly dependency ratio: 7.1
potential support ratio: 14.1 (2020 est.)

Median age: *total:* 24.9 years
male: 23 years
female: 26.4 years (2020 est.)
country comparison to the world: 163

Population growth rate: 1.97% (2022 est.)
country comparison to the world: 42

Birth rate: 22.25 births/1,000 population (2022 est.)
country comparison to the world: 58

Death rate: 7.12 deaths/1,000 population (2022 est.)
country comparison to the world: 116

Net migration rate: 4.59 migrant(s)/1,000 population (2022 est.)
country comparison to the world: 24

Population distribution: most densely populated areas are in the east; the largest city is Djibouti, with a population over 600,000; no other city in the country has a total population over 50,000 as shown in this population distribution map

Urbanization: *urban population:* 78.4% of total population (2022)
rate of urbanization: 1.56% annual rate of change (2020-25 est.)

Major urban areas - population: 591,000 DJIBOUTI (capital) (2022)

Sex ratio: *at birth:* 1.03 male(s)/female
0-14 years: 1.01 male(s)/female
15-24 years: 0.9 male(s)/female
25-54 years: 0.7 male(s)/female
55-64 years: 0.72 male(s)/female
65 years and over: 0.65 male(s)/female
total population: 0.83 male(s)/female (2022 est.)

Maternal mortality ratio: 248 deaths/100,000 live births (2017 est.)
country comparison to the world: 43

Infant mortality rate: *total:* 46.89 deaths/1,000 live births
male: 54.14 deaths/1,000 live births
female: 39.43 deaths/1,000 live births (2022 est.)
country comparison to the world: 25

Life expectancy at birth: *total population:* 65.3 years
male: 62.72 years
female: 67.96 years (2022 est.)
country comparison to the world: 203

Total fertility rate: 2.15 children born/woman (2022 est.)
country comparison to the world: 91

Contraceptive prevalence rate: 19% (2012)

Drinking water source: *improved: urban:* 99.7% of population
rural: 59.3% of population
total: 90.8% of population
unimproved: urban: 0.3% of population
rural: 40.7% of population
total: 9.2% of population (2020 est.)

Current health expenditure: 1.8% of GDP (2019)

Physicians density: 0.22 physicians/1,000 population (2014)

Hospital bed density: 1.4 beds/1,000 population (2017)

Sanitation facility access: *improved: urban:* 87.7% of population
rural: 24.2% of population
total: 73.8% of population
unimproved: urban: 12.3% of population
rural: 75.8% of population
total: 26.2% of population (2020 est.)

HIV/AIDS - adult prevalence rate: 0.8% (2020 est.)
country comparison to the world: 51

Major infectious diseases: *degree of risk:* high (2020)
food or waterborne diseases: bacterial and protozoal diarrhea, hepatitis A, and typhoid fever
vectorborne diseases: dengue fever
note: on 21 March 2022, the US Centers for Disease Control and Prevention (CDC) issued a Travel Alert for polio in Africa; Djibouti is currently considered a high risk to travelers for circulating vaccine-derived polioviruses (cVDPV); vaccine-derived poliovirus (VDPV) is a strain of the weakened poliovirus that was initially included in oral polio vaccine (OPV) and *that has changed over time and behaves more like the wild or naturally occurring virus;* this means it can be spread more easily to people who are unvaccinated against polio and who come in contact with the stool or respiratory secretions, such as from a sneeze, of an "infected" person who received oral polio vaccine; the CDC recommends that before any international travel, anyone unvaccinated, incompletely vaccinated, or with an unknown polio vaccination status should complete the routine polio vaccine series; before travel to any high-risk destination, the CDC recommends that adults who

previously completed the full, routine polio vaccine series receive a single, lifetime booster dose of polio vaccine

Obesity - adult prevalence rate: 13.5% (2016)
country comparison to the world: 131

Alcohol consumption per capita: *total:* 0.21 liters of pure alcohol (2019 est.)
beer: 0.05 liters of pure alcohol (2019 est.)
wine: 0.02 liters of pure alcohol (2019 est.)
spirits: 0.14 liters of pure alcohol (2019 est.)
other alcohols: 0 liters of pure alcohol (2019 est.)
country comparison to the world: 172

Children under the age of 5 years underweight: 29.9% (2012)
country comparison to the world: 6

Education expenditures: 3.6% of GDP (2018 est.)
country comparison to the world: 116

Literacy: School life expectancy (primary to tertiary education): *total:* 7 years
male: 7 years
female: 7 years (2011)

Unemployment, youth ages 15-24: *total:* 73%
male: 72%
female: 74.6% (2017)

ENVIRONMENT

Environment - current issues: inadequate supplies of potable water; water pollution; limited arable land; deforestation (forests threatened by agriculture and the use of wood for fuel); desertification; endangered species

Environment - international agreements: *party to:* Biodiversity, Climate Change, Climate Change-Kyoto Protocol, Climate Change-Paris Agreement, Comprehensive Nuclear Test Ban, Desertification, Endangered Species, Hazardous Wastes, Law of the Sea, Ozone Layer Protection, Ship Pollution, Wetlands
signed, but not ratified: none of the selected agreements

Air pollutants: *particulate matter emissions:* 40.38 micrograms per cubic meter (2016 est.)
carbon dioxide emissions: 0.62 megatons (2016 est.)
methane emissions: 0.52 megatons (2020 est.)

Climate: desert; torrid, dry

Land use: *agricultural land:* 73.4% (2018 est.)
arable land: 0.1% (2018 est.)
permanent crops: 0% (2018 est.)
permanent pasture: 73.3% (2018 est.)
forest: 0.2% (2018 est.)
other: 26.4% (2018 est.)

Urbanization: *urban population:* 78.4% of total population (2022)
rate of urbanization: 1.56% annual rate of change (2020-25 est.)

Revenue from forest resources: *forest revenues:* 0.26% of GDP (2018 est.)
country comparison to the world: 86

Revenue from coal: *coal revenues:* 0% of GDP (2018 est.)
country comparison to the world: 89

Food insecurity: *widespread lack of access: due to unfavorable weather and high food prices* - about 132,000 people were estimated to be severely food insecure between March and June 2022 mainly due to insufficient rains in 2021 and 2022, which affected rangelands and pastoral livelihoods, and high food prices (2022)

Waste and recycling: *municipal solid waste generated annually:* 114,997 tons (2002 est.)

Major lakes (area sq km): *salt water lake(s):* Abhe Bad/Abhe Bid Hayk (shared with Ethiopia) - 780 sq km

Total water withdrawal: *municipal:* 16 million cubic meters (2017 est.)
industrial: 0 cubic meters (2017 est.)
agricultural: 3 million cubic meters (2017 est.)

Total renewable water resources: 300 million cubic meters (2017 est.)

GOVERNMENT

Country name: *conventional long form:* Republic of Djibouti
conventional short form: Djibouti
local long form: Republique de Djibouti (French)/ Jumhuriyat Jibuti (Arabic)
local short form: Djibouti (French)/ Jibuti (Arabic)
former: French Somaliland, French Territory of the Afars and Issas
etymology: the country name derives from the capital city of Djibouti

Government type: presidential republic

Capital: *name:* Djibouti
geographic coordinates: 11 35 N, 43 09 E
time difference: UTC+3 (8 hours ahead of Washington, DC, during Standard Time)
etymology: the origin of the name is disputed; multiple descriptions, possibilities, and theories have been proposed

Administrative divisions: 6 districts (cercles, singular - cercle); Ali Sabieh, Arta, Dikhil, Djibouti, Obock, Tadjourah

Independence: 27 June 1977 (from France)

National holiday: Independence Day, 27 June (1977)

Constitution: *history:* approved by referendum 4 September 1992
amendments: proposed by the president of the republic or by the National Assembly; Assembly consideration of proposals requires assent of at least one third of the membership; passage requires a simple majority vote by the Assembly and approval by simple majority vote in a referendum; the president can opt to bypass a referendum if adopted by at least two-thirds majority vote of the Assembly; constitutional articles on the sovereignty of Djibouti, its republican form of government, and its pluralist form of democracy cannot be amended; amended 2006, 2008, 2010

Legal system: mixed legal system based primarily on the French civil code (as it existed in 1997), Islamic religious law (in matters of family law and successions), and customary law

International law organization participation: accepts compulsory ICJ jurisdiction with reservations; accepts ICCt jurisdiction

Citizenship: *citizenship by birth:* no
citizenship by descent only: the mother must be a citizen of Djibouti
dual citizenship recognized: no
residency requirement for naturalization: 10 years

Suffrage: 18 years of age; universal

Executive branch: *chief of state:* President Ismail Omar GUELLEH (since 8 May 1999)
head of government: Prime Minister Abdoulkader Kamil MOHAMED (since 1 April 2013)
cabinet: Council of Ministers appointed by the prime minister
elections/appointments: president directly elected by absolute majority popular vote in 2 rounds if needed for a 5-year term; election last held on 9 April 2021 (next to be held in April 2026); prime minister appointed by the president
election results:
2021: Ismail Omar GUELLEH reelected president for a fifth term; percent of vote - Ismail Omar GUELLEH (RPP) 97.4%, Zakaria Ismael FARAH (MDEND) 2.7%
2016: Ismail Omar GUELLEH reelected president for a fourth term; percent of vote - Ismail Omar GUELLEH (RPP) 87%, Omar Elmi KHAIREH (CDU) 7.3%, other 5.6%

Legislative branch: *description:* unicameral National Assembly or Assemblee Nationale, formerly the Chamber of Deputies (65 seats; members directly elected in multi-seat constituencies by party-list proportional representation vote; members serve 5-year terms)
elections:
last held on 23 February 2018 (next to be held in February 2023)
election results:
percent of vote by party - NA; seats by party - UMP 57, UDJ-PDD 7, CDU 1; composition - men 48, women 17, percent of women 26.2%

Judicial branch: *highest court(s):* Supreme Court or Cour Supreme (consists of NA magistrates); Constitutional Council (consists of 6 magistrates)
judge selection and term of office: Supreme Court magistrates appointed by the president with the advice of the Superior Council of the Magistracy (CSM), a 10-member body consisting of 4 judges, 3 members (non parliamentarians and judges) appointed by the president, and 3 appointed by the National Assembly president or speaker; magistrates appointed for life with retirement at age 65; Constitutional Council magistrate appointments - 2 by the president of the republic, 2 by the president of the National Assembly, and 2 by the CSM; magistrates appointed for 8-year, nonrenewable terms
subordinate courts: High Court of Appeal; 5 Courts of First Instance; customary courts; State Court (replaced sharia courts in 2003)

Political parties and leaders: Center for United Democrats or CDU [Ahmed Mohamed YOUSSOUF, chairman]
Democratic Renewal Party or PRD [Abdillahi HAMARITEH]
Djibouti Development Party or PDD [Mohamed Daoud CHEHEM]
Front for Restoration of Unity and Democracy (Front pour la Restauration de l'Unite Democratique) or FRUD [Ali Mohamed DAOUD]
Movement for Democratic Renewal and Development or MRD (previously Democratic Renewal Party or PRD) [Daher Ahmed FARAH]
National Democratic Party or PND [Aden Robleh AWALEH]
People's Rally for Progress or RPP [Ismail Omar GUELLEH] (governing party)
Peoples Social Democratic Party or PPSD [Hasna Moumin BAHDON]

Republican Alliance for Democracy or ARD [Aden Mohamed ABDOU]
Union for Democracy and Justice or UDJ [Ilya Ismail GUEDI Hared]
Union for the Presidential Majority coalition or UMP [collective leadership] (electoral coalition includes RPP, FRUD, PPSD, and UPR)
Union for National Salvation coalition or USN [collective leadership] (electoral coalition includes ARD, PRD, PDD, UDJ, and PND)
Union of Reform Partisans or UPR [Ibrahim Daoud CHEHEM]
note: only parties with seats in the National Assembly included

International organization participation: ACP, AfDB, AFESD, AMF, ATMIS, AU, CAEU (candidates), COMESA, FAO, G-77, IBRD, ICAO, ICCt, ICRM, IDA, IDB, IFAD, IFC, IFRCS, IGAD, ILO, IMF, IMO, Interpol, IOC, IOM, IPU, ITU, ITUC (NGOs), LAS, MIGA, MINURSO, NAM, OIC, OIF, OPCW, UN, UNCTAD, UNESCO, UNHCR, UNIDO, UNWTO, UPU, WCO, WFTU (NGOs), WHO, WIPO, WMO, WTO

Diplomatic representation in the US: *chief of mission:* Ambassador Mohamed Siad DOUALEH (28 January 2016)
chancery: 1156 15th Street NW, Suite 515, Washington, DC 20005
telephone: [1] (202) 331-0270
FAX: [1] (202) 331-0302
email address and website:
info@djiboutiembassyus.org
https://www.djiboutiembassyus.org/

Diplomatic representation from the US: *chief of mission:* Ambassador Jonathan Goodale PRATT (since 22 February 2021)
embassy: Lot 350-B Haramouss, B.P. 185
mailing address: 2150 Djibouti Place, Washington DC 20521-2150
telephone: [253] 21-45-30-00
FAX: [253] 21-45-31-29
email address and website:
DjiboutiACS@state.gov
https://dj.usembassy.gov/

Flag description: two equal horizontal bands of light blue (top) and light green with a white isosceles triangle based on the hoist side bearing a red five-pointed star in the center; blue stands for sea and sky and the Issa Somali people; green symbolizes earth and the Afar people; white represents peace; the red star recalls the struggle for independence and stands for unity

National symbol(s): red star; national colors: light blue, green, white, red

National anthem: *name:* "Jabuuti" (Djibouti)
lyrics/music: Aden ELMI/Abdi ROBLEH
note: adopted 1977

ECONOMY

Economic overview: Djibouti's economy is based on service activities connected with the country's strategic location as a deepwater port on the Red Sea. Three-fourths of Djibouti's inhabitants live in the capital city; the remainder are mostly nomadic herders. Scant rainfall and less than 4% arable land limits crop production to small quantities of fruits and vegetables, and most food must be imported.

Djibouti provides services as both a transit port for the region and an international transshipment and refueling center. Imports, exports, and reexports represent 70% of port activity at Djibouti's container terminal. Reexports consist primarily of coffee from landlocked neighbor Ethiopia. Djibouti has few natural resources and little industry. The nation is, therefore, heavily dependent on foreign assistance to support its balance of payments and to finance development projects. An official unemployment rate of nearly 40% - with youth unemployment near 80% - continues to be a major problem. Inflation was a modest 3% in 2014-2017, due to low international food prices and a decline in electricity tariffs.

Djibouti's reliance on diesel-generated electricity and imported food and water leave average consumers vulnerable to global price shocks, though in mid-2015 Djibouti passed new legislation to liberalize the energy sector. The government has emphasized infrastructure development for transportation and energy and Djibouti – with the help of foreign partners, particularly China – has begun to increase and modernize its port capacity. In 2017, Djibouti opened two of the largest projects in its history, the Doraleh Port and Djibouti-Addis Ababa Railway, funded by China as part of the "Belt and Road Initiative," which will increase the country's ability to capitalize on its strategic location.

Real GDP (purchasing power parity): $5.42 billion (2020 est.)
$5.39 billion (2019 est.)
$5 billion (2018 est.)
note: data are in 2017 dollars
country comparison to the world: 174

Real GDP growth rate: 6.7% (2017 est.)
6.5% (2016 est.)
6.5% (2015 est.)
country comparison to the world: 22

Real GDP per capita: $5,500 (2020 est.)
$5,500 (2019 est.)
$5,200 (2018 est.)
note: data are in 2017 dollars
country comparison to the world: 167

GDP (official exchange rate): $3.323 billion (2019 est.)

Inflation rate (consumer prices): 0.7% (2017 est.)
2.7% (2016 est.)
country comparison to the world: 53

GDP - composition, by sector of origin: *agriculture:* 2.4% (2017 est.)
industry: 17.3% (2017 est.)
services: 80.2% (2017 est.)

GDP - composition, by end use: *household consumption:* 56.5% (2017 est.)
government consumption: 29.2% (2017 est.)
investment in fixed capital: 41.8% (2017 est.)
investment in inventories: 0.3% (2017 est.)
exports of goods and services: 38.6% (2017 est.)
imports of goods and services: -66.4% (2017 est.)

Agricultural products: vegetables, milk, beef, camel milk, lemons, limes, goat meat, mutton, beans, tomatoes

Industries: construction, agricultural processing, shipping

Industrial production growth rate: 2.7% (2017 est.)
country comparison to the world: 112

Labor force: 294,600 (2012)
country comparison to the world: 163

Unemployment rate: 40% (2017 est.)
60% (2014 est.)
country comparison to the world: 214

Unemployment, youth ages 15-24: *total:* 73%
male: 72%
female: 74.6% (2017)
country comparison to the world: 1

Population below poverty line: 21.1% (2017 est.)

Gini Index coefficient - distribution of family income: 41.6 (2017 est.)
country comparison to the world: 49

Household income or consumption by percentage share: *lowest 10%:* 2.4%
highest 10%: 30.9% (2002)

Budget: *revenues:* 717 million (2017 est.)
expenditures: 899.2 million (2017 est.)

Budget surplus (+) or deficit (-): -9% (of GDP) (2017 est.)
country comparison to the world: 205

Public debt: 31.8% of GDP (2017 est.)
33.7% of GDP (2016 est.)
country comparison to the world: 161

Taxes and other revenues: 35.3% (of GDP) (2017 est.)
country comparison to the world: 62

Fiscal year: calendar year

Current account balance: -$280 million (2017 est.)
-$178 million (2016 est.)
country comparison to the world: 105

Exports: $5.15 billion (2019 est.) note: data are in current year dollars
$4.56 billion (2018 est.) note: data are in current year dollars
country comparison to the world: 125

Exports - partners: Saudi Arabia 42%, India 15%, China 14%, Egypt 5%, South Korea 5% (2019)

Exports - commodities: various animals, chlorides, dried legumes, industrial fatty acids/oils, coffee, chickpeas (2019)

Imports: $4.76 billion (2019 est.) note: data are in current year dollars
$4.19 billion (2018 est.) note: data are in current year dollars
country comparison to the world: 140

Imports - partners: China 43%, United Arab Emirates 15%, India 7%, Turkey 5% (2019)

Imports - commodities: refined petroleum, fertilizers, iron sheeting, cars, palm oil (2019)

Reserves of foreign exchange and gold: $547.7 million (31 December 2017 est.)
$398.5 million (31 December 2016 est.)
country comparison to the world: 148

Debt - external: $1.954 billion (31 December 2017 est.)
$1.519 billion (31 December 2016 est.)
country comparison to the world: 153

Exchange rates: Djiboutian francs (DJF) per US dollar -177.7 (2017 est.)
177.72 (2016 est.)
177.72 (2015 est.)
177.72 (2014 est.)
177.72 (2013 est.)

ENERGY

Electricity access: *electrification - total population:* 42% (2019)
electrification - urban areas: 54% (2019)
electrification - rural areas: 1% (2019)

Electricity: *installed generating capacity:* 130,000 kW (2020 est.)
consumption: -62.6 million kWh (2019 est.)
exports: 0 kWh (2019 est.)
imports: 0 kWh (2019 est.)
transmission/distribution losses: 120 million kWh (2019 est.)

Electricity generation sources: *fossil fuels:* 98.2% of total installed capacity (2020 est.)
solar: 1.8% of total installed capacity (2020 est.)

Petroleum: *total petroleum production:* 0 bbl/day (2021 est.)
refined petroleum consumption: 4,300 bbl/day (2019 est.)

Refined petroleum products - exports: 403 bbl/day (2015 est.)
country comparison to the world: 112

Refined petroleum products - imports: 6,692 bbl/day (2015 est.)
country comparison to the world: 161

Carbon dioxide emissions: 610,000 metric tonnes of CO_2 (2019 est.)
from petroleum and other liquids: 610,000 metric tonnes of CO_2 (2019 est.)
country comparison to the world: 185

Energy consumption per capita: 8.869 million Btu/person (2019 est.)
country comparison to the world: 158

COMMUNICATIONS

Telephones - fixed lines: *total subscriptions:* 38,866 (2020 est.)
subscriptions per 100 inhabitants: 4 (2020 est.)
country comparison to the world: 164

Telephones - mobile cellular: *total subscriptions:* 434,035 (2020 est.)
subscriptions per 100 inhabitants: 44 (2020 est.)
country comparison to the world: 176

Telecommunication systems: *general assessment:* Djibouti remains one of the last bastions where the national telco has a monopoly on all telecom services, including fixed lines, mobile, internet, and broadband; despite the country benefiting from its location as a hub for international submarine cables, prices for telecom services remain relatively high, and out of reach for a number of customers, weighing on market advancement; the Djibouti government is aiming to sell a minority stake in the incumbent telco (retaining some control of decisions) while securing the financial backing and the management acumen of a foreign operator; this is part of a larger plan to modernize the country's economy more generally; the state expects to conduct a sale of up to 40% of the company to an international investor by the end 2022 (2022)
domestic: about 4 per 100 fixed-line teledensity and nearly 44 per 100 mobile-cellular; Djibouti Telecom (DT) is the sole provider of telecommunications services and utilizes mostly a microwave radio relay network; fiber-optic cable is installed in the capital; rural areas connected via wireless local loop radio systems; mobile cellular coverage is primarily limited to the area in and around Djibouti city (2020)
international: country code - 253; landing points for the SEA-ME-WE-3 & 5, EASSy, Aden-Djibouti, Africa-1, DARE-1, EIG, MENA, Bridge International, PEACE Cable, and SEACOM fiber-optic submarine cable systems providing links to Asia, the Middle East, Europe, Southeast Asia, Australia and Africa; satellite earth stations - 2 (1 Intelsat - Indian Ocean and 1 Arabsat) (2019)

Broadcast media: state-owned Radiodiffusion-Television de Djibouti operates the sole terrestrial TV station, as well as the only 2 domestic radio networks; no private TV or radio stations; transmissions of several international broadcasters are available (2019)

Internet country code: .dj

Internet users: *total:* 582,921 (2020 est.)
percent of population: 59% (2020 est.)
country comparison to the world: 153

Broadband - fixed subscriptions: *total:* 25,053 (2020 est.)
subscriptions per 100 inhabitants: 3 (2020 est.)
country comparison to the world: 159

TRANSPORTATION

National air transport system: *number of registered air carriers:* 2 (2020)
inventory of registered aircraft operated by air carriers: 4

Civil aircraft registration country code prefix: J2

Airports: *total:* 13 (2021)
country comparison to the world: 151

Airports - with paved runways: *total:* 3
over 3,047 m: 1
2,438 to 3,047 m: 1
1,524 to 2,437 m: 1 (2021)

Airports - with unpaved runways: *total:* 10
1,524 to 2,437 m: 1
914 to 1,523 m: 7
under 914 m: 2 (2021)

Railways: *total:* 97 km (2017) (Djibouti segment of the 756 km Addis Ababa-Djibouti railway)
standard gauge: 97 km (2017) 1.435-m gauge
country comparison to the world: 127

Roadways: *total:* 2,893 km (2013)
country comparison to the world: 164

Merchant marine: *total:* 33
by type: bulk carrier 1, container ship 1, general cargo 2, oil tanker 8, other 21 (2021)
country comparison to the world: 131

Ports and terminals: *major seaport(s):* Djibouti

MILITARY AND SECURITY

Military and security forces: Djibouti Armed Forces (FAD): Army, Navy, Air Force; Djibouti Coast Guard; Ministry of Interior: National Gendarmerie, National Police (2022)
note: the National Police is responsible for security within Djibouti City and has primary control over immigration and customs procedures for all land border-crossing points, while the National Gendarmerie is responsible for all security outside of Djibouti City, as well as for protecting critical infrastructure within the city, such as the international airport

Military expenditures: 3.5% of GDP (2019 est.) (approximately $180 million)
3.5% of GDP (2018 est.) (approximately $160 million)
3.3% of GDP (2017 est.) (approximately $150 million)
2.7% of GDP (2016 est.) (approximately $120 million)
2.5% of GDP (2015 est.) (approximately $110 million)
country comparison to the world: 23

Military and security service personnel strengths: approximately 10,000 active troops (8,000 Army; 250 Naval; 250 Air; 1,500 Gendarmerie) (2022)

Military equipment inventories and acquisitions: the FAD is armed largely with older French and Soviet-era weapons systems; since 2010, it has received limited amounts of mostly second-hand equipment from a variety of countries, including China and the US (2021)

Military service age and obligation: 18 years of age for voluntary military service for men and women; 16-25 years of age for voluntary military training; no conscription (2021)

Military deployments: 960 Somalia (ATMIS) (2022)

Military - note: as of 2022, China, France, Italy, Japan, and the US maintained bases in Djibouti for regional military missions, including counterterrorism, counter-piracy, crisis response, and security assistance (note – France has multiple bases and hosts troop contingents from Germany and Spain); the EU and NATO have also maintained a presence to support multinational naval counter-piracy operations and maritime training efforts; in 2017, Djibouti and Saudi Arabia announced plans for the Saudis to build a military base there, although no start date was announced

Maritime threats: the International Maritime Bureau's (IMB) Piracy Reporting Center (PRC) received one incident of piracy and armed robbery in 2021 for the Horn of Africa; while there were no recorded incidents, the IMB PRC warned that Somali pirates continue to possess the capacity to carry out attacks in the Somali basin and wider Indian Ocean; in particular, the report warns that, "Masters and crew must remain vigilant and cautious when transiting these waters."; the presence of several naval task forces in the Gulf of Aden and additional anti-piracy measures on the part of ship operators, including the use of on-board armed security teams, contributed to the drop in incidents; the EU naval mission, Operation ATALANTA, continues its operations in the Gulf of Aden and Indian Ocean through 2022; naval units from China, India, Japan, Pakistan, South Korea, the US, and other countries also operate in conjunction with EU forces; China has established a base in Djibouti to support its deployed naval units in the Horn of Africa

TERRORISM

Terrorist group(s): al-Shabaab

TRANSNATIONAL ISSUES

Disputes - international: *Djibouti-Somalia:* Djibouti maintains economic ties and border accords with "Somaliland" leadership while maintaining some political ties to various factions in Somalia;

Djibouti-Eritrea: in 2008, Eritrean troops moved across the border on Ras Doumera peninsula and occupied Doumera Island with undefined sovereignty in the Red Sea; the Eritrean occupation of remote Doumeira Island and portions peninsula persists unabated as of September 2009; porous boundary over largely uninhabited areas provides access for smuggling and other illegal activities; as of 7 June 2010, Qatar was mediating Eritrea-Djibouti border dispute,

Djibouti-Ethiopia: While Djibouti has had significant issues along its border with neighbors such as Somalia and Eritrea, the Ethiopia-Djibouti relationship has been relatively harmonious; diplomatic relations between the two countries were initially established in 1984; historically, there is co-ownership of the Addis Ababa-Djibout railways and acts as a symbol of the healthy bi-lateral partnership between both Ethiopia and Djibouti; in 1991 a Treaty of Friendship and Cooperation was signed by the two countries; Ethiopia uses the Port of Djibouti as a major hub for export and import of goods since 1998; after establishing independence, there have been no major disputes along this border.

Refugees and internally displaced persons: *refugees (country of origin):* 5,972 (Yemen) (mid-year 2021); 14,227 (Somalia) (2021)

DOMINICA

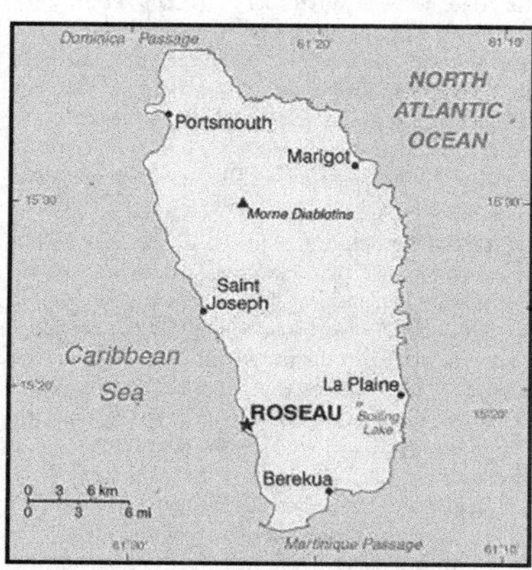

INTRODUCTION

Background: Dominica was the last of the Caribbean islands to be colonized by Europeans due chiefly to the fierce resistance of the native Caribs. France ceded possession to Great Britain in 1763, which colonized the island in 1805. Slavery ended in 1833 and in 1835 the first three men of African descent were elected to the legislative assembly of Dominica. In 1871, Dominica became part first of the British Leeward Islands and then the British Windward Islands until 1958. In 1967, Dominica became an associated state of the UK, and formally took responsibility for its internal affairs. In 1980, two years after independence, Dominica's fortunes improved when a corrupt and tyrannical administration was replaced by that of Mary Eugenia CHARLES, the first female prime minister in the Caribbean, who remained in office for 15 years. On 18 September 2017, Hurricane Maria passed over the island, causing extensive damage to structures, roads, communications, and the power supply, and largely destroying critical agricultural areas.

GEOGRAPHY

Location: Caribbean, island between the Caribbean Sea and the North Atlantic Ocean, about halfway between Puerto Rico and Trinidad and Tobago

Geographic coordinates: 15 25 N, 61 20 W

Map references: Central America and the Caribbean

Area: *total:* 751 sq km
land: 751 sq km
water: NEGL
country comparison to the world: 188

Area - comparative: slightly more than four times the size of Washington, DC

Land boundaries: *total:* 0 km

Coastline: 148 km

Maritime claims: *territorial sea:* 12 nm
contiguous zone: 24 nm
exclusive economic zone: 200 nm

Climate: tropical; moderated by northeast trade winds; heavy rainfall

Terrain: rugged mountains of volcanic origin

Elevation: *highest point:* Morne Diablotins 1,447 m
lowest point: Caribbean Sea 0 m

Natural resources: timber, hydropower, arable land

Land use: *agricultural land:* 34.7% (2018 est.)
arable land: 8% (2018 est.)
permanent crops: 24% (2018 est.)
permanent pasture: 2.7% (2018 est.)
forest: 59.2% (2018 est.)
other: 6.1% (2018 est.)

Population distribution: population is mosly clustered along the coast, with roughly a third living in the parish of St. George, in or around the capital of Roseau; the volcanic interior is sparsely populated

Natural hazards: flash floods are a constant threat; destructive hurricanes can be expected during the late summer months

volcanism: Dominica was the last island to be formed in the Caribbean some 26 million years ago, it lies in the middle of the volcanic island arc of the Lesser Antilles that extends from the island of Saba in the north to Grenada in the south; of the 16 volcanoes that make up this arc, five are located on Dominica, more than any other island in the Caribbean: Morne aux Diables (861 m), Morne Diablotins (1,430 m), Morne Trois Pitons (1,387 m), Watt Mountain (1,224 m), which last erupted in 1997, and Morne Plat Pays (940 m); the two best known volcanic features on Dominica, the Valley of Desolation and the Boiling Lake thermal areas, lie on the flanks of Watt Mountain and both are popular tourist destinations

Geography - note: known as "The Nature Island of the Caribbean" due to its spectacular, lush, and varied flora and fauna, which are protected by an extensive natural park system; the most mountainous of the Lesser Antilles, its volcanic peaks are cones of lava craters and include Boiling Lake, the second-largest, thermally active lake in the world

PEOPLE AND SOCIETY

Population: 74,629 (2022 est.)
country comparison to the world: 201

Nationality: *noun:* Dominican(s)
adjective: Dominican

Ethnic groups: African descent 84.5%, mixed 9%, Indigenous 3.8%, other 2.1%, unspecified 0.6% (2011 est.)

Languages: English (official), French patois

Religions: Roman Catholic 52.7%, Protestant 29.7% (includes Seventh Day Adventist 6.7%, Pentecostal 6.1%, Baptist 5.2%, Christian Union Church 3.9%, Methodist 2.6%, Gospel Mission 2.1%, other Protestant 3.1%), Jehovah's Witness 1.3%, Rastafarian 1.1%, other 4.3%, none 9.4%, unspecified 1.4% (2011 est.)

Age structure: *0-14 years:* 21.41% (male 8,135/female 7,760)
15-24 years: 13.15% (male 5,017/female 4,746)
25-54 years: 42.79% (male 16,133/female 15,637)
55-64 years: 10.53% (male 4,089/female 3,731)
65 years and over: 12.12% (male 4,128/female 4,867) (2020 est.)

Median age: *total:* 34.9 years
male: 34.4 years
female: 35.5 years (2020 est.)
country comparison to the world: 87

Population growth rate: 0.05% (2022 est.)
country comparison to the world: 190

Birth rate: 13.91 births/1,000 population (2022 est.)
country comparison to the world: 130

Death rate: 8.11 deaths/1,000 population (2022 est.)
country comparison to the world: 84

Net migration rate: -5.31 migrant(s)/1,000 population (2022 est.)
country comparison to the world: 205

Population distribution: population is mosly clustered along the coast, with roughly a third living in the parish of St. George, in or around the capital of Roseau; the volcanic interior is sparsely populated

Urbanization: *urban population:* 71.7% of total population (2022)
rate of urbanization: 0.84% annual rate of change (2020-25 est.)

Major urban areas - population: 15,000 ROSEAU (capital) (2018)

Sex ratio: *at birth:* 1.05 male(s)/female
0-14 years: 1.05 male(s)/female
15-24 years: 1.06 male(s)/female
25-54 years: 1.04 male(s)/female
55-64 years: 1.06 male(s)/female
65 years and over: 0.68 male(s)/female
total population: 1.02 male(s)/female (2022 est.)

Infant mortality rate: *total:* 11.27 deaths/1,000 live births
male: 15.28 deaths/1,000 live births
female: 7.07 deaths/1,000 live births (2022 est.)
country comparison to the world: 127

Life expectancy at birth: *total population:* 78.21 years
male: 75.25 years
female: 81.31 years (2022 est.)
country comparison to the world: 76

Total fertility rate: 2.02 children born/woman (2022 est.)
country comparison to the world: 105

Drinking water source: *improved: urban:* 95.7% of population
unimproved: urban: 4.3% of population

Current health expenditure: 5.5% of GDP (2019)

Physicians density: 1.1 physicians/1,000 population (2018)

Hospital bed density: 3.8 beds/1,000 population

HIV/AIDS - adult prevalence rate: 0.6% (2018 est.)
country comparison to the world: 60

Obesity - adult prevalence rate: 27.9% (2016)
country comparison to the world: 33

Alcohol consumption per capita: *total:* 6.32 liters of pure alcohol (2019 est.)
beer: 1.64 liters of pure alcohol (2019 est.)
wine: 0.29 liters of pure alcohol (2019 est.)
spirits: 4.39 liters of pure alcohol (2019 est.)
other alcohols: 0 liters of pure alcohol (2019 est.)
country comparison to the world: 67

Education expenditures: 5% of GDP (2020 est.)
country comparison to the world: 63

People - note: 3,000-3,500 Kalinago (Carib) still living on Dominica are the only pre-Columbian population remaining in the Caribbean; only 70-100 may be "pure" Kalinago because of years of integration into the broader population

ENVIRONMENT

Environment - current issues: water shortages a continuing concern; pollution from agrochemicals and from untreated sewage; forests endangered by the expansion of farming; soil erosion; pollution of the coastal zone by agricultural and industrial chemicals, and untreated sewage

Environment - international agreements: *party to:* Biodiversity, Climate Change, Climate Change-Kyoto Protocol, Climate Change-Paris Agreement, Desertification, Endangered Species, Environmental Modification, Hazardous Wastes, Law of the Sea, Ozone Layer Protection, Ship Pollution, Whaling
signed, but not ratified: none of the selected agreements

Air pollutants: *particulate matter emissions:* 18.17 micrograms per cubic meter (2016 est.)
carbon dioxide emissions: 0.18 megatons (2016 est.)
methane emissions: 0.04 megatons (2020 est.)

Climate: tropical; moderated by northeast trade winds; heavy rainfall

Land use: *agricultural land:* 34.7% (2018 est.)
arable land: 8% (2018 est.)
permanent crops: 24% (2018 est.)
permanent pasture: 2.7% (2018 est.)
forest: 59.2% (2018 est.)
other: 6.1% (2018 est.)

Urbanization: *urban population:* 71.7% of total population (2022)
rate of urbanization: 0.84% annual rate of change (2020-25 est.)

Revenue from forest resources: *forest revenues:* 0.03% of GDP (2018 est.)
country comparison to the world: 133

Revenue from coal: *coal revenues:* 0% of GDP (2018 est.)
country comparison to the world: 90

Waste and recycling: *municipal solid waste generated annually:* 13,176 tons (2013 est.)

Total water withdrawal: *municipal:* 19 million cubic meters (2017 est.)
industrial: 0 cubic meters (2017 est.)
agricultural: 1 million cubic meters (2017 est.)

Total renewable water resources: 200 million cubic meters (2017 est.)

GOVERNMENT

Country name: *conventional long form:* Commonwealth of Dominica
conventional short form: Dominica
etymology: the island was named by explorer Christopher COLUMBUS for the day of the week on which he spotted it, Sunday ("Domingo" in Latin), 3 November 1493

Government type: parliamentary republic

Capital: *name:* Roseau
geographic coordinates: 15 18 N, 61 24 W
time difference: UTC-4 (1 hour ahead of Washington, DC, during Standard Time)
etymology: the name is French for "reed"; the first settlement was named after the river reeds that grew in the area

Administrative divisions: 10 parishes; Saint Andrew, Saint David, Saint George, Saint John, Saint Joseph, Saint Luke, Saint Mark, Saint Patrick, Saint Paul, Saint Peter

Independence: 3 November 1978 (from the UK)

National holiday: Independence Day, 3 November (1978)

Constitution: *history:* previous 1967 (preindependence); latest presented 25 July 1978, entered into force 3 November 1978
amendments: proposed by the House of Assembly; passage of amendments to constitutional sections such as fundamental rights and freedoms, the government structure, and constitutional amendment procedures requires approval by three fourths of the Assembly membership in the final reading of the amendment bill, approval by simple majority in a referendum, and assent of the president; amended several times, last in 2015

Legal system: common law based on the English model

International law organization participation: accepts compulsory ICJ jurisdiction; accepts ICCt jurisdiction

Citizenship: *citizenship by birth:* yes
citizenship by descent only: yes
dual citizenship recognized: yes
residency requirement for naturalization: 5 years

Suffrage: 18 years of age; universal

Executive branch: *chief of state:* President Charles A. SAVARIN (since 2 October 2013)
head of government: Prime Minister Roosevelt SKERRIT (since 8 January 2004)
cabinet: Cabinet appointed by the president on the advice of the prime minister
elections/appointments: president nominated by the prime minister and leader of the opposition party and elected by the House of Assembly for a 5-year term (eligible for a second term); election last held on 1 October 2018 (next to be held in October 2023); prime minister appointed by the president
election results:
Charles A. SAVARIN (DLP) reelected president unopposed

Legislative branch: *description:* unicameral House of Assembly (32 seats; 21 representatives directly elected in single-seat constituencies by simple majority vote, 9 senators appointed by the president - 5 on the advice of the prime minister, and 4 on the advice of the leader of the opposition party, plus 2 ex-officio members - the house speaker and the attorney general; members serve 5-year terms)
elections:
last held on 6 December 2019 (next to be held in 2024); note - tradition dictates that the election is held within 5 years of the last election, but technically it is 5 years from the first seating of parliament plus a 90-day grace period
election results:
percent of vote by party - DLP 59.0%, UWP 41.0%; seats by party - DLP 18, UWP 3; composition -men 21, women 11, percent of women 34.4%

Judicial branch: *highest court(s):* the Eastern Caribbean Supreme Court (ECSC) is the superior court of the Organization of Eastern Caribbean States; the ECSC - headquartered on St. Lucia - consists of the Court of Appeal - headed by the chief justice and 4 judges - and the High Court with 18 judges; the Court of Appeal is itinerant, traveling to member states on a schedule to hear appeals from the High Court and subordinate courts; High Court judges reside in the member states, with 2 in Dominica; note - in 2015, Dominica acceded to the Caribbean Court of Justice as final court of appeal, replacing that of the Judicial Committee of the Privy Council, in London
judge selection and term of office: chief justice of Eastern Caribbean Supreme Court appointed by the Her Majesty, Queen ELIZABETH II; other justices and judges appointed by the Judicial and Legal Services Commission, an independent body of judicial officials; Court of Appeal justices appointed for life with mandatory retirement at age 65; High Court judges appointed for life with mandatory retirement at age 62
subordinate courts: Court of Summary Jurisdiction; magistrates' courts

Political parties and leaders: Dominica Freedom Party or DFP [Bernard HURTAULT]
Dominica Labor Party or DLP [Roosevelt SKERRIT]

Dominica United Workers Party or UWP [Lennox LINTON]

International organization participation: ACP, AOSIS, C, Caricom, CD, CDB, CELAC, Commonwealth of Nations, ECCU, FAO, G-77, IAEA, IBRD, ICCt, ICRM, IDA, IFAD, IFC, IFRCS, ILO, IMF, IMO, Interpol, IOC, ISO (correspondent), ITU, ITUC (NGOs), MIGA, NAM, OAS, OECS, OIF, OPANAL, OPCW, Petrocaribe, UN, UNCTAD, UNESCO, UNIDO, UPU, WFTU, WHO, WIPO, WMO, WTO

Diplomatic representation in the US: *chief of mission:* Ambassador (vacant); Charge d'Affaires Judith-Anne ROLLE (since 16 December 2021)
chancery: 3216 New Mexico Avenue NW, Washington, DC 20016
telephone: [1] (202) 364-6781
FAX: [1] (202) 364-6791
email address and website: mail.embdomdc@gmail.com
consulate(s) general: New York

Diplomatic representation from the US: *embassy:* the US does not have an embassy in Dominica; the US Ambassador to Barbados is accredited to Dominica

Flag description: green with a centered cross of three equal bands - the vertical part is yellow (hoist side), black, and white and the horizontal part is yellow (top), black, and white; superimposed in the center of the cross is a red disk bearing a Sisserou parrot, unique to Dominica, encircled by 10 green, five-pointed stars edged in yellow; the 10 stars represent the 10 administrative divisions (parishes); green symbolizes the island's lush vegetation; the triple-colored cross represents the Christian Trinity; the yellow color denotes sunshine, the main agricultural products (citrus and bananas), and the native Carib Indians; black is for the rich soil and the African heritage of most citizens; white signifies rivers, waterfalls, and the purity of aspirations; the red disc stands for social justice

National symbol(s): Sisserou parrot, Carib Wood flower; national colors: green, yellow, black, white, red

National anthem: *name:* "Isle of Beauty"
lyrics/music: Wilfred Oscar Morgan POND/Lemuel McPherson CHRISTIAN
note: adopted 1967

National heritage: *total World Heritage Sites:* 1 (natural)
selected World Heritage Site locales: Pitons Management Area

ECONOMY

Economic overview: The Dominican economy was dependent on agriculture - primarily bananas - in years past, but increasingly has been driven by tourism, as the government seeks to promote Dominica as an "ecotourism" destination. However, Hurricane Maria, which passed through the island in September 2017, destroyed much of the country's agricultural sector and caused damage to all of the country's transportation and physical infrastructure. Before Hurricane Maria, the government had attempted to foster an offshore financial industry and planned to sign agreements with the private sector to develop geothermal energy resources. At a time when government finances are fragile, the government's focus has been to get the country back in shape to service cruise ships. The economy contracted in 2015 and recovered to positive growth in 2016 due to a recovery of agriculture and tourism. Dominica suffers from high debt levels, which increased from 67% of GDP in 2010 to 77% in 2016. Dominica is one of five countries in the East Caribbean that have citizenship by investment programs whereby foreigners can obtain passports for a fee and revenue from this contribute to government budgets.

Real GDP (purchasing power parity): $710 million (2020 est.)
$850 million (2019 est.)
$830 million (2018 est.)
note: data are in 2017 dollars
country comparison to the world: 209

Real GDP growth rate: -4.7% (2017 est.)
2.6% (2016 est.)
-3.7% (2015 est.)
country comparison to the world: 217

Real GDP per capita: $9,900 (2020 est.)
$11,900 (2019 est.)
$11,500 (2018 est.)
note: data are in 2017 dollars
country comparison to the world: 141

GDP (official exchange rate): $557 million (2017 est.)

Inflation rate (consumer prices): 0.6% (2017 est.)
0% (2016 est.)
country comparison to the world: 46

GDP - composition, by sector of origin: *agriculture:* 22.3% (2017 est.)
industry: 12.6% (2017 est.)
services: 65.1% (2017 est.)

GDP - composition, by end use: *household consumption:* 60.6% (2017 est.)
government consumption: 26.2% (2017 est.)
investment in fixed capital: 21.5% (2017 est.)
investment in inventories: 0% (2017 est.)
exports of goods and services: 54.4% (2017 est.)
imports of goods and services: -62.7% (2017 est.)

Agricultural products: bananas, yams, grapefruit, taro, milk, coconuts, oranges, yautia, plantains, sugar cane
note: forest and fishery potential not exploited

Industries: soap, coconut oil, tourism, copra, furniture, cement blocks, shoes

Industrial production growth rate: -13% (2017 est.)
country comparison to the world: 199

Labor force: 25,000 (2000 est.)
country comparison to the world: 207

Labor force - by occupation: *agriculture:* 40%
industry: 32%
services: 28% (2002 est.)

Unemployment rate: 23% (2000 est.)
country comparison to the world: 193

Population below poverty line: 29% (2009 est.)

Budget: *revenues:* 227.8 million (2017 est.)
expenditures: 260.4 million (2017 est.)

Budget surplus (+) or deficit (-): -5.9% (of GDP) (2017 est.)
country comparison to the world: 181

Public debt: 82.7% of GDP (2017 est.)
71.7% of GDP (2016 est.)
country comparison to the world: 33

Taxes and other revenues: 40.9% (of GDP) (2017 est.)
country comparison to the world: 34

Fiscal year: 1 July - 30 June

Current account balance: -$70 million (2017 est.)
$5 million (2016 est.)
country comparison to the world: 83

Exports: $160 million (2018 est.) note: data are in current year dollars
$43.7 million (2016 est.)
country comparison to the world: 205

Exports - partners: Saudi Arabia 47%, Qatar 5% (2019)

Exports - commodities: medical instruments, pharmaceuticals, low-voltage protection equipment, tropical fruits, bandages (2019)

Imports: $430 million (2018 est.) note: data are in current year dollars
$188.4 million (2016 est.)
country comparison to the world: 205

Imports - partners: United States 57%, Nigeria 11%, China 6%, Italy 5% (2019)

Imports - commodities: refined petroleum, natural gas, crude petroleum, recreational boats, cars (2019)

Reserves of foreign exchange and gold: $212.3 million (31 December 2017 est.)
$221.9 million (31 December 2016 est.)
country comparison to the world: 172

Debt - external: $280.4 million (31 December 2017 est.)
$314.2 million (31 December 2015 est.)
country comparison to the world: 186

Exchange rates: East Caribbean dollars (XCD) per US dollar -
2.7 (2017 est.)
2.7 (2016 est.)
2.7 (2015 est.)
2.7 (2014 est.)
2.7 (2013 est.)

ENERGY

Electricity access: *electrification - total population:* 100% (2020)

Electricity: *installed generating capacity:* 42,000 kW (2020 est.)
consumption: 82.078 million kWh (2019 est.)
exports: 0 kWh (2019 est.)
imports: 0 kWh (2019 est.)
transmission/distribution losses: 8.1 million kWh (2019 est.)

Electricity generation sources: *fossil fuels:* 74.8% of total installed capacity (2020 est.)
solar: 0.1% of total installed capacity (2020 est.)
wind: 0.6% of total installed capacity (2020 est.)
hydroelectricity: 24.5% of total installed capacity (2020 est.)

Petroleum: *total petroleum production:* 0 bbl/day (2021 est.)
refined petroleum consumption: 1,200 bbl/day (2019 est.)

Refined petroleum products - imports: 1,237 bbl/day (2015 est.)
country comparison to the world: 198

Carbon dioxide emissions: 182,000 metric tonnes of CO2 (2019 est.)
from petroleum and other liquids: 182,000 metric tonnes of CO2 (2019 est.)
country comparison to the world: 203

Energy consumption per capita: 37.513 million Btu/person (2019 est.)
country comparison to the world: 111

COMMUNICATIONS

Telephones - fixed lines: *total subscriptions:* 1,000 (2020 est.)
subscriptions per 100 inhabitants: 1 (2020 est.)
country comparison to the world: 218

Telephones - mobile cellular: *total subscriptions:* 76,000 (2020 est.)
subscriptions per 100 inhabitants: 106 (2020 est.)
country comparison to the world: 196

Telecommunication systems: *general assessment:* the telecom sector has seen a decline in subscriber numbers (particularly for prepaid mobile services the mainstay of short term visitors) and revenue; fixed and mobile broadband services are two areas that have benefited from the crisis as employees and students have resorted to working from home; one area of the telecom market that is not prepared for growth is 5G mobile; governments, regulators, and even the mobile network operators have shown that they have not been investing in 5G opportunities at the present time; network expansion and enhancements remain concentrated around improving LTE coverage (2021)
domestic: fixed-line connections continue to decline slowly with only two active operators providing about 4 fixed-line connections per 100 persons; subscribership among the three mobile-cellular providers is about 106 per 100 persons (2020)
international: country code - 1-767; landing points for the ECFS and the Southern Caribbean Fiber submarine cables providing connectivity to other islands in the eastern Caribbean extending from the British Virgin Islands to Trinidad and to the US; microwave radio relay and SHF radiotelephone links to Martinique and Guadeloupe; VHF and UHF radiotelephone links to Saint Lucia (2019)

Broadcast media: no terrestrial TV service available; subscription cable TV provider offers some locally produced programming plus channels from the US, Latin America, and the Caribbean; state-operated radio broadcasts on 6 stations; privately owned radio broadcasts on about 15 stations (2019)

Internet country code: .dm

Internet users: *total:* 50,266 (2019 est.)
percent of population: 70% (2019 est.)
country comparison to the world: 196

Broadband - fixed subscriptions: *total:* 16,000 (2020 est.)
subscriptions per 100 inhabitants: 22 (2020 est.)
country comparison to the world: 172

TRANSPORTATION

Civil aircraft registration country code prefix: J7

Airports: *total:* 2 (2021)
country comparison to the world: 197

Airports - with paved runways: *total:* 2
1,524 to 2,437 m: 1
914 to 1,523 m: 1 (2021)

Roadways: *total:* 1,512 km (2018)
paved: 762 km (2018)
*unpaved:*750 km (2018)
country comparison to the world: 174

Merchant marine: *total:* 93
by type: general cargo 30, oil tanker 19, other 44 (2021)
country comparison to the world: 95

Ports and terminals: *major seaport(s):* Portsmouth, Roseau

MILITARY AND SECURITY

Military and security forces: no regular military forces; Commonwealth of Dominica Police Force (includes Coast Guard) under the Ministry of Justice, Immigration, and National Security (2022)

Military - note: Dominica has been a member of the Caribbean Regional Security System (RSS) since its creation in 1982; RSS signatories (Antigua and Barbuda, Barbados, Grenada, St. Kitts, St. Lucia, and St. Vincent and the Grenadines) agreed to prepare contingency plans and assist one another, on request, in national emergencies, prevention of smuggling, search and rescue, immigration control, fishery protection, customs and excise control, maritime policing duties, protection of off-shore installations, pollution control, national and other disasters, and threats to national security (2022)

TRANSNATIONAL ISSUES

Disputes - international: Dominica is the only Caribbean state to challenge Venezuela's sovereignty claim over Aves Island and joins the other island nations in challenging whether the feature sustains human habitation, a criterion under the UN Convention on the Law of the Sea, which permits Venezuela to extend its EEZ and continental shelf claims over a large portion of the eastern Caribbean Sea

Illicit drugs: a transit point for cocaine and marijuana destined for North America, Europe, and elsewhere in the Caribbean

DOMINICAN REPUBLIC

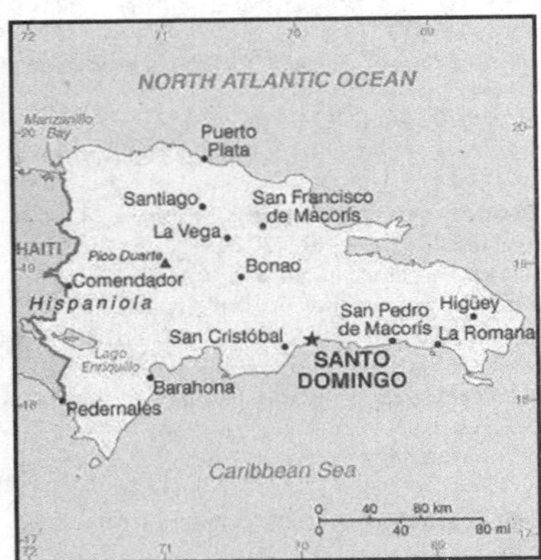

INTRODUCTION

Background: The Taino - indigenous inhabitants of Hispaniola prior to the arrival of Europeans - divided the island into five chiefdoms and territories. Christopher COLUMBUS explored and claimed the island on his first voyage in 1492; it became a springboard for Spanish conquest of the Caribbean and the American mainland. In 1697, Spain recognized French dominion over the western third of the island, which in 1804 became Haiti. The remainder of the island, by then known as Santo Domingo, sought to gain its own independence in 1821 but was conquered and ruled by the Haitians for 22 years; it finally attained independence as the Dominican Republic in 1844. In 1861, the Dominicans voluntarily returned to the Spanish Empire, but two years later they launched a war that restored independence in 1865. A legacy of unsettled, mostly non-representative rule followed, capped by the dictatorship of Rafael Leonidas TRUJILLO from 1930 to 1961. Juan BOSCH was elected president in 1962 but was deposed in a military coup in 1963. In 1965, the US led an intervention in the midst of a civil war sparked by an uprising to restore BOSCH. In 1966, Joaquin BALAGUER defeated BOSCH in the presidential election. BALAGUER maintained a tight grip on power for most of the next 30 years when international reaction to flawed elections forced him to curtail his term in 1996. Since then, regular competitive elections have been held in which opposition candidates have won the presidency. Former President Leonel FERNANDEZ Reyna (first term 1996-2000) won election to a new term in 2004 following a constitutional amendment allowing presidents to serve more than one term, and was later reelected to a second consecutive term. Following the two-term presidency of Danilo MEDINA Sanchez (2012-2020), Luis Rodolfo ABINADER Corona was elected president in July 2020.

GEOGRAPHY

Location: Caribbean, eastern two-thirds of the island of Hispaniola, between the Caribbean Sea and the North Atlantic Ocean, east of Haiti

Geographic coordinates: 19 00 N, 70 40 W

Map references: Central America and the Caribbean

Area: *total:* 48,670 sq km
land: 48,320 sq km
water: 350 sq km
country comparison to the world: 131

Area - comparative: slightly more than twice the size of New Jersey

Land boundaries: *total:* 376 km

border countries (1): Haiti 376 km

Coastline: 1,288 km

Maritime claims: *territorial sea:* 12 nm
contiguous zone: 24 nm
exclusive economic zone: 200 nm
continental shelf: 200 nm or to the edge of the continental margin
measured from claimed archipelagic straight baselines

Climate: tropical maritime; little seasonal temperature variation; seasonal variation in rainfall

Terrain: rugged highlands and mountains interspersed with fertile valleys

Elevation: *highest point:* Pico Duarte 3,098 m
lowest point: Lago Enriquillo -46 m
mean elevation: 424 m

Natural resources: nickel, bauxite, gold, silver, arable land

Land use: *agricultural land:* 51.5% (2018 est.)
arable land: 16.6% (2018 est.)
permanent crops: 10.1% (2018 est.)
permanent pasture: 24.8% (2018 est.)
forest: 40.8% (2018 est.)
other: 7.7% (2018 est.)

Irrigated land: 3,070 sq km (2012)

Major lakes (area sq km): *salt water lake(s):* Lago de Enriquillo - 500 sq km

Population distribution: coastal development is significant, especially in the southern coastal plains and the Cibao Valley, where population density is highest; smaller population clusters exist in the interior mountains (Cordillera Central)

Natural hazards: lies in the middle of the hurricane belt and subject to severe storms from June to October; occasional flooding; periodic droughts

Geography - note: shares island of Hispaniola with Haiti (eastern two-thirds makes up the Dominican Republic, western one-third is Haiti); the second largest country in the Antilles (after Cuba); geographically diverse with the Caribbean's tallest mountain, Pico Duarte, and lowest elevation and largest lake, Lago Enriquillo

PEOPLE AND SOCIETY

Population: 10,694,700 (2022 est.)
country comparison to the world: 87

Nationality: *noun:* Dominican(s)
adjective: Dominican

Ethnic groups: mixed 70.4% (Mestizo/Indio 58%, Mulatto 12.4%), Black 15.8%, White 13.5%, other 0.3% (2014 est.)
note: respondents self-identified their race; the term "indio" in the Dominican Republic is not associated with people of indigenous ancestry but people of mixed ancestry or skin color between light and dark

Languages: Spanish (official)
major-language sample(s):
La Libreta Informativa del Mundo, la fuente indispensable de información básica. (Spanish)

Religions: Roman Catholic 44.3%, Evangelical 13%, Protestant 7.9%, Adventist 1.4%, other 1.8%, atheist 0.2%, none 29.4%, unspecified 2% (2018 est.)

Age structure: *0-14 years:* 26.85% (male 1,433,166/female 1,385,987)
15-24 years: 18.15% (male 968,391/female 937,227)
25-54 years: 40.54% (male 2,168,122/female 2,088,926)
55-64 years: 8.17% (male 429,042/female 428,508)
65 years and over: 6.29% (male 310,262/female 350,076) (2020 est.)

Dependency ratios: *total dependency ratio:* 53.8
youth dependency ratio: 42.2
elderly dependency ratio: 11.6
potential support ratio: 8.6 (2020 est.)

Median age: *total:* 27.9 years
male: 27.8 years
female: 28.1 years (2020 est.)
country comparison to the world: 144

Population growth rate: 0.91% (2022 est.)
country comparison to the world: 106

Birth rate: 18.03 births/1,000 population (2022 est.)
country comparison to the world: 81

Death rate: 6.29 deaths/1,000 population (2022 est.)
country comparison to the world: 147

Net migration rate: -2.68 migrant(s)/1,000 population (2022 est.)
country comparison to the world: 174

Population distribution: coastal development is significant, especially in the southern coastal plains and the Cibao Valley, where population density is highest; smaller population clusters exist in the interior mountains (Cordillera Central)

Urbanization: *urban population:* 83.8% of total population (2022)
rate of urbanization: 1.64% annual rate of change (2020-25 est.)

Major urban areas - population: 3.458 million SANTO DOMINGO (capital) (2022)

Sex ratio: *at birth:* 1.04 male(s)/female
0-14 years: 1.03 male(s)/female
15-24 years: 1.03 male(s)/female
25-54 years: 1.04 male(s)/female
55-64 years: 1 male(s)/female
65 years and over: 0.73 male(s)/female
total population: 1.02 male(s)/female (2022 est.)

Mother's mean age at first birth: 20.9 years (2013 est.)
note: data represents median age at first birth among women 25-49

Maternal mortality ratio: 95 deaths/100,000 live births (2017 est.)
country comparison to the world: 71

Infant mortality rate: *total:* 21.18 deaths/1,000 live births
male: 23.51 deaths/1,000 live births
female: 18.76 deaths/1,000 live births (2022 est.)
country comparison to the world: 78

Life expectancy at birth: *total population:* 72.56 years
male: 70.86 years
female: 74.33 years (2022 est.)
country comparison to the world: 151

Total fertility rate: 2.21 children born/woman (2022 est.)
country comparison to the world: 86

Contraceptive prevalence rate: 62.8% (2019)

Drinking water source: *improved: urban:* 98.3% of population
rural: 91.7% of population
total: 97.2% of population
unimproved: urban: 1.7% of population
rural: 8.3% of population
total: 2.8% of population (2020 est.)

Current health expenditure: 5.9% of GDP (2019)

Physicians density: 1.45 physicians/1,000 population (2019)

Hospital bed density: 1.6 beds/1,000 population (2017)

Sanitation facility access: *improved: urban:* 97.4% of population
rural: 91.3% of population
total: 96.3% of population
unimproved: urban: 2.6% of population
rural: 8.7% of population
total: 3.7% of population (2020 est.)

HIV/AIDS - adult prevalence rate: 0.9% (2020 est.)
country comparison to the world: 47

Major infectious diseases: *degree of risk:* high (2020)
food or waterborne diseases: bacterial diarrhea, hepatitis A, and typhoid fever
vectorborne diseases: dengue fever

Obesity - adult prevalence rate: 27.6% (2016)
country comparison to the world: 37

Alcohol consumption per capita: *total:* 5.56 liters of pure alcohol (2019 est.)
beer: 3.15 liters of pure alcohol (2019 est.)
wine: 0.17 liters of pure alcohol (2019 est.)
spirits: 2.18 liters of pure alcohol (2019 est.)
other alcohols: 0.06 liters of pure alcohol (2019 est.)
country comparison to the world: 78

Tobacco use: *total:* 10.6% (2020 est.)
male: 14.6% (2020 est.)
female: 6.5% (2020 est.)
country comparison to the world: 135

Children under the age of 5 years underweight: 4% (2013)
country comparison to the world: 85

Education expenditures: 4% of GDP (2019 est.)
country comparison to the world: 102

Literacy: *definition:* age 15 and over can read and write
total population: 93.8%
male: 93.8%
female: 93.8% (2016)

School life expectancy (primary to tertiary education): *total:* 14 years
male: 14 years
female: 15 years (2017)

Unemployment, youth ages 15-24: *total:* 14.9%
male: 11.6%
female: 20.7% (2020 est.)

ENVIRONMENT

Environment - current issues: water shortages; soil eroding into the sea damages coral reefs; deforestation

Environment - international agreements: *party to:* Biodiversity, Climate Change, Climate Change-Kyoto Protocol, Climate Change-Paris Agreement, Comprehensive Nuclear Test Ban, Desertification, Endangered Species, Hazardous Wastes, Law of the Sea, Marine Dumping-London Convention, Marine Life Conservation, Nuclear Test Ban, Ozone Layer Protection, Ship Pollution, Wetlands, Whaling
signed, but not ratified: none of the selected agreements

Air pollutants: *particulate matter emissions:* 12.95 micrograms per cubic meter (2016 est.)
carbon dioxide emissions: 25.26 megatons (2016 est.)
methane emissions: 8.1 megatons (2020 est.)

Climate: tropical maritime; little seasonal temperature variation; seasonal variation in rainfall

Land use: *agricultural land:* 51.5% (2018 est.)
arable land: 16.6% (2018 est.)
permanent crops: 10.1% (2018 est.)
permanent pasture: 24.8% (2018 est.)
forest: 40.8% (2018 est.)
other: 7.7% (2018 est.)

Urbanization: *urban population:* 83.8% of total population (2022)
rate of urbanization: 1.64% annual rate of change (2020-25 est.)

Revenue from forest resources: *forest revenues:* 0.03% of GDP (2018 est.)
country comparison to the world: 134

Revenue from coal: *coal revenues:* 0% of GDP (2018 est.)
country comparison to the world: 91

Waste and recycling: *municipal solid waste generated annually:* 4,063,910 tons (2015 est.)
municipal solid waste recycled annually: 333,241 tons (2015 est.)
percent of municipal solid waste recycled: 8.2% (2015 est.)

Major lakes (area sq km): *salt water lake(s):* Lago de Enriquillo - 500 sq km

Total water withdrawal: *municipal:* 855 million cubic meters (2017 est.)
industrial: 659.9 million cubic meters (2017 est.)
agricultural: 7.563 billion cubic meters (2017 est.)

Total renewable water resources: 23.5 billion cubic meters (2017 est.)

GOVERNMENT

Country name: *conventional long form:* Dominican Republic
conventional short form: The Dominican
local long form: Republica Dominicana
local short form: La Dominicana
former: Santo Domingo (the capital city's name formerly applied to the entire country)
etymology: the country name derives from the capital city of Santo Domingo (Saint Dominic)

Government type: presidential republic

Capital: *name:* Santo Domingo
geographic coordinates: 18 28 N, 69 54 W
time difference: UTC-4 (1 hour ahead of Washington, DC, during Standard Time)
etymology: named after Saint Dominic de GUZMAN (1170-1221), founder of the Dominican Order

Administrative divisions: 10 regions (regiones, singular - region); Cibao Nordeste, Cibao Noroeste, Cibao Norte, Cibao Sur, El Valle, Enriquillo, Higuamo, Ozama, Valdesia, Yuma

Independence: 27 February 1844 (from Haiti)

National holiday: Independence Day, 27 February (1844)

Constitution: *history:* many previous (38 total); latest proclaimed 13 June 2015
amendments: proposed by a special session of the National Congress called the National Revisory Assembly; passage requires at least two-thirds majority approval by at least one half of those present in both houses of the Assembly; passage of amendments to constitutional articles, such as fundamental rights and guarantees, territorial composition, nationality, or the procedures for constitutional reform, also requires approval in a referendum

Legal system: civil law system based on the French civil code; Criminal Procedures Code modified in 2004 to include important elements of an accusatory system

International law organization participation: accepts compulsory ICJ jurisdiction; accepts ICCt jurisdiction

Citizenship: *citizenship by birth:* no
citizenship by descent only: at least one parent must be a citizen of the Dominican Republic
dual citizenship recognized: yes
residency requirement for naturalization: 2 years

Suffrage: 18 years of age; universal and compulsory; married persons regardless of age can vote; note - members of the armed forces and national police by law cannot vote

Executive branch: *chief of state:* President Luis Rodolfo ABINADER Corona (since 16 August 2020); Vice President Raquel PENA de Antuna (since 16 August 2020); note - the president is both chief of state and head of government
head of government: President Luis Rodolfo ABINADER Corona (since 16 August 2020); Vice President Raquel PENA de Antuna (since 16 August 2020); note - the president is both chief of state and head of government
cabinet: Cabinet nominated by the president
elections/appointments: president and vice president directly elected on the same ballot by absolute vote in 2 rounds if needed for a 4-year term (eligible for a maximum of two consecutive terms); election last held on 5 July 2020 (next to be held in 2024); note - the 2020 election was rescheduled from 17 May to 5 July 2020 due to COVID-19 pandemic
election results:
2020: Luis Rodolfo ABINADER Corona elected president in first round; percent of vote - Luis Rodolfo ABINADER Corona (PRM) 52.5%, Gonzalo CASTILLO Terrero (PLD) 37.5%, Leonel Antonio FERNANDEZ Reyna (FP) 8.9% other 1.1%
2016: Danilo MEDINA Sanchez reelected president; percent of vote - Danilo MEDINA Sanchez (PLD) 61.7%, Luis Rodolfo ABINADER Corona (PRM) 35%, other 3.3%; Margarita CEDENO DE FERNANDEZ (PLD) reelected vice president

Legislative branch: *description:* bicameral National Congress or Congreso Nacional consists of:
Senate or Senado (32 seats; 26 members directly elected in single-seat constituencies by simple majority vote, and 6 members indirectly elected based upon province-wide party plurality votes for its candidates to the Chamber of Deputies; all members serve 4-year terms; note - in 2019, the Central Election Commission changed the electoral system for seats in26 constituencies to direct simple majority but retained indirect election for the remaining 6 constituencies; previously all 32 members were indirectly elected; the change had been challenged by the ruling and opposition parties)
House of Representatives or Camara de Diputados (190 seats; 178 members directly elected in multi-seat constituencies by closed party-list proportional representation vote using the D'Hondt method, 5 members in a nationwide constituency and 7 diaspora members directly elected by simple majority vote; members serve 4-year terms)
elections:
Senate - last held on 5 July 2020 (next to be held 2024)
House of Representatives - last held on 5 July 2020 (next to be held in 2024); note - the 2020 election was rescheduled from 17 May to 5 July 2020 due to COVID-19 pandemic
election results:
Senate - percent of vote by party - NA; seats by party - PRM 17, PLD 6, PRSC 6, BIS 1, DXC 1, FP 1; composition - men 28, women 4, percent of women 12.5%
House of Representatives - percent of vote by party - NA; seats by party - PRM 86, PLD 75, PRSC 6, PRD 4, Broad Front 3, FP 3, AP 2, APD 2, BIS 2, DXC 2, other 5; composition - men 137, women 53, percent of women 27.9%; note -total National Congress percent of women 25.7%

Judicial branch: *highest court(s):* Supreme Court of Justice or Suprema Corte de Justicia (consists of a minimum of 16 magistrates); Constitutional Court or Tribunal Constitucional (consists of 13 judges); note - the Constitutional Court was established in 2010 by constitutional amendment
judge selection and term of office: Supreme Court and Constitutional Court judges appointed by the National Council of the Judiciary comprised of the president, the leaders of both chambers of congress, the president of the Supreme Court, and a non-governing party congressional representative; Supreme Court judges appointed for 7-year terms; Constitutional Court judges appointed for 9-year terms
subordinate courts: courts of appeal; courts of first instance; justices of the peace; special courts for juvenile, labor, and land cases; Contentious Administrative Court for cases filed against the government

Political parties and leaders: Alliance for Democracy or APD
Broad Front (Frente Amplio) [Fidel SANTANA]
Country Alliance or AP [Guillermo Antonio MORENO Garcia]
Dominican Liberation Party or PLD [Danilo MEDINA Sánchez]
Dominican Revolutionary Party or PRD [Miguel VARGAS Maldonado]
Dominicans For Change or DXC [Manuel OVIEDO Estrada]
Institutional Social Democratic Bloc or BIS
Liberal Reformist Party or PRL (formerly the Liberal Party of the Dominican Republic or PLRD)
Modern Revolutionary Party or PRM [Luis ABINADER]
National Progressive Front or FNP [Vinicio CASTILLO, Pelegrin CASTILLO]
People's Force or FP [Leonel FERNANDEZ Reyna]
Social Christian Reformist Party or PRSC [Federico Augusto "Quique" ANTUN Batile]

International organization participation: ACP, AOSIS, BCIE, Caricom (observer), CD, CELAC, FAO, G-77, IADB, IAEA, IBRD, ICAO, ICC (national committees), ICCt, ICRM, IDA, IFAD, IFC, IFRCS, IHO, ILO, IMF, IMO, Interpol, IOC, IOM, IPU, ISO (correspondent), ITSO, ITU, ITUC (NGOs), LAES, LAIA, MIGA, MINUSMA, NAM, OAS, OIF (observer), OPANAL, OPCW, Pacific

Alliance (observer), PCA, Petrocaribe, SICA (associated member), UN, UNCTAD, UNESCO, UNIDO, Union Latina, UNWTO, UPU, WCO, WFTU (NGOs), WHO, WIPO, WMO, WTO

Diplomatic representation in the US: *chief of mission:* Ambassador Sonia GUZMAN (since 18 January 2021)
chancery: 1715 22nd Street NW, Washington, DC 20008
telephone: [1] (202) 332-6280
FAX: [1] (202) 265-8057
email address and website:
embassy@drembassyusa.org
http://drembassyusa.org/
consulate(s) general: Boston, Chicago, Glendale (CA), Mayaguez (Puerto Rico), Miami, New Orleans, New York, San Juan (Puerto Rico)
consulate(s): San Francisco

Diplomatic representation from the US: *chief of mission:* Ambassador (vacant); Charge d'Affaires Robert W. THOMAS (since 20 January 2021)
embassy: Av. Republica de Colombia #57, Santo Domingo
mailing address: 3470 Santo Domingo Place, Washington DC 20521-3470
telephone: (809) 567-7775
email address and website:
SDOAmericans@state.gov
https://do.usembassy.gov/

Flag description: a centered white cross that extends to the edges divides the flag into four rectangles - the top ones are ultramarine blue (hoist side) and vermilion red, and the bottom ones are vermilion red (hoist side) and ultramarine blue; a small coat of arms featuring a shield supported by a laurel branch (left) and a palm branch (right) is at the center of the cross; above the shield a blue ribbon displays the motto, DIOS, PATRIA, LIBERTAD (God, Fatherland, Liberty), and below the shield, REPUBLICA DOMINICANA appears on a red ribbon; in the shield a bible is opened to a verse that reads "Y la verdad nos hara libre" (And the truth shall set you free); blue stands for liberty, white for salvation, and red for the blood of heroes

National symbol(s): palmchat (bird); national colors: red, white, blue

National anthem: *name:* "Himno Nacional" (National Anthem)
lyrics/music: Emilio PRUD'HOMME/Jose REYES
note: adopted 1934; also known as "Quisqueyanos valientes" (Valient Sons of Quisqueye); the anthem never refers to the people as Dominican but rather calls them "Quisqueyanos," a reference to the indigenous name of the island

National heritage: *total World Heritage Sites:* 1 (cultural)
selected World Heritage Site locales: Colonial City of Santo Domingo

ECONOMY

Economic overview: The Dominican Republic was for most of its history primarily an exporter of sugar, coffee, and tobacco, but over the last three decades the economy has become more diversified as the service sector has overtaken agriculture as the economy's largest employer, due to growth in construction, tourism, and free trade zones. The mining sector has also played a greater role in the export market since late 2012 with the commencement of the extraction phase of the Pueblo Viejo Gold and Silver mine, one of the largest gold mines in the world.

For the last 20 years, the Dominican Republic has been one of the fastest growing economies in Latin America. The economy rebounded from the global recession in 2010-16, and the fiscal situation is improving. A tax reform package passed in November 2012, a reduction in government spending, and lower energy costs helped to narrow the central government budget deficit from 6.6% of GDP in 2012 to 2.6% in 2016, and public debt is declining. Marked income inequality, high unemployment, and underemployment remain important long-term challenges; the poorest half of the population receives less than one-fifth of GDP, while the richest 10% enjoys nearly 40% of GDP.

The economy is highly dependent upon the US, the destination for approximately half of exports and the source of 40% of imports. Remittances from the US amount to about 7% of GDP, equivalent to about a third of exports and two-thirds of tourism receipts. The Central America-Dominican Republic Free Trade Agreement came into force in March 2007, boosting investment and manufacturing exports.

Real GDP (purchasing power parity): $184.45 billion (2020 est.)
$197.74 billion (2019 est.)
$188.23 billion (2018 est.)
note: data are in 2017 dollars
country comparison to the world: 68

Real GDP growth rate: 4.6% (2017 est.)
6.6% (2016 est.)
7% (2015 est.)
country comparison to the world: 57

Real GDP per capita: $17,000 (2020 est.)
$18,400 (2019 est.)
$17,700 (2018 est.)
note: data are in 2017 dollars
country comparison to the world: 98

GDP (official exchange rate): $88.956 billion (2019 est.)

Inflation rate (consumer prices): 1.8% (2019 est.)
3.5% (2018 est.)
3.2% (2017 est.)
country comparison to the world: 99

Credit ratings:

Fitch rating: BB- (2016)

Moody's rating: Ba3 (2017)

Standard & Poors rating: BB- (2015)
note: The year refers to the year in which the current credit rating was first obtained.

GDP - composition, by sector of origin: *agriculture:* 5.6% (2017 est.)
industry: 33% (2017 est.)
services: 61.4% (2017 est.)

GDP - composition, by end use: *household consumption:* 69.3% (2017 est.)
government consumption: 12.2% (2017 est.)
investment in fixed capital: 21.9% (2017 est.)
investment in inventories: -0.1% (2017 est.)
exports of goods and services: 24.8% (2017 est.)
imports of goods and services: -28.1% (2017 est.)

Agricultural products: sugar cane, bananas, papayas, rice, plantains, milk, avocados, fruit, pineapples, coconuts

Industries: tourism, sugar processing, gold mining, textiles, cement, tobacco, electrical components, medical devices

Industrial production growth rate: 3.1% (2017 est.)
country comparison to the world: 99

Labor force: 4.732 million (2017 est.)
country comparison to the world: 81

Labor force - by occupation: *agriculture:* 14.4%
industry: 20.8% (2014)
services: 64.7% (2014 est.)

Unemployment rate: 5.1% (2017 est.)
5.5% (2016 est.)
country comparison to the world: 81

Unemployment, youth ages 15-24: *total:* 14.9%
male: 11.6%
female: 20.7% (2020 est.)
country comparison to the world: 108

Population below poverty line: 21% (2019 est.)

Gini Index coefficient - distribution of family income: 43.7 (2018 est.)
45.7 (2012 est.)
country comparison to the world: 36

Household income or consumption by percentage share: *lowest 10%:* 1.9%
highest 10%: 37.4% (2013 est.)

Budget: *revenues:* 11.33 billion (2017 est.)
expenditures: 13.62 billion (2017 est.)

Budget surplus (+) or deficit (-): -3% (of GDP) (2017 est.)
country comparison to the world: 132

Public debt: 37.2% of GDP (2017 est.)
34.6% of GDP (2016 est.)
country comparison to the world: 140

Taxes and other revenues: 14.9% (of GDP) (2017 est.)
country comparison to the world: 194

Fiscal year: calendar year

Current account balance: -$165 million (2017 est.)
-$815 million (2016 est.)
country comparison to the world: 96

Exports: $14.44 billion (2020 est.) note: data are in current year dollars
$20.51 billion (2019 est.) note: data are in current year dollars
$20.05 billion (2018 est.) note: data are in current year dollars
country comparison to the world: 93

Exports - partners: United States 54%, Switzerland 8%, Canada 5%, India 5%, China 5% (2019)

Exports - commodities: gold, medical instruments, cigars, low-voltage protection equipment, bananas (2019)

Imports: $20.19 billion (2020 est.) note: data are in current year dollars
$24.53 billion (2019 est.) note: data are in current year dollars
$24.11 billion (2018 est.) note: data are in current year dollars
country comparison to the world: 82

Imports - partners: United States 50%, China 13% (2019)

Imports - commodities: refined petroleum, cars, jewelry, natural gas, broadcasting equipment (2019)

Reserves of foreign exchange and gold: $6.873 billion (31 December 2017 est.)
$6.134 billion (31 December 2016 est.)

country comparison to the world: 87

Debt - external: $23.094 billion (2019 est.)
$21.198 billion (2018 est.)
country comparison to the world: 90

Exchange rates: Dominican pesos (DOP) per US dollar -
47.42 (2017 est.)
46.078 (2016 est.)
46.078 (2015 est.)
45.052 (2014 est.)
43.556 (2013 est.)

ENERGY

Electricity access: *electrification - total population:* 100% (2020)

Electricity: *installed generating capacity:* 5.674 million kW (2020 est.)
consumption: 16,330,980,000 kWh (2019 est.)
exports: 0 kWh (2019 est.)
imports: 0 kWh (2019 est.)
transmission/distribution losses: 2.576 billion kWh (2019 est.)

Electricity generation sources: *fossil fuels:* 93.4% of total installed capacity (2020 est.)
solar: 1.5% of total installed capacity (2020 est.)
wind: 3.2% of total installed capacity (2020 est.)
hydroelectricity: 0.7% of total installed capacity (2020 est.)
biomass and waste: 1.2% of total installed capacity (2020 est.)

Coal: *production:* 0 metric tons (2020 est.)
consumption: 1.791 million metric tons (2020 est.)
exports: 0 metric tons (2020 est.)
imports: 2.359 million metric tons (2020 est.)
proven reserves: 0 metric tons (2019 est.)

Petroleum: *total petroleum production:* 0 bbl/day (2021 est.)
refined petroleum consumption: 148,200 bbl/day (2019 est.)
crude oil and lease condensate exports: 0 bbl/day (2018 est.)
crude oil and lease condensate imports: 24,900 bbl/day (2018 est.)
crude oil estimated reserves: 0 barrels (2021 est.)

Refined petroleum products - production: 16,060 bbl/day (2015 est.)
country comparison to the world: 92

Refined petroleum products - exports: 0 bbl/day (2015 est.)
country comparison to the world: 149

Refined petroleum products - imports: 108,500 bbl/day (2015 est.)
country comparison to the world: 52

Natural gas: *production:* 0 cubic meters (2021 est.)
consumption: 1,602,759,000 cubic meters (2019 est.)
exports: 28.657 million cubic meters (2019 est.)
imports: 1,586,449,000 cubic meters (2019 est.)
proven reserves: 0 cubic meters (2021 est.)

Carbon dioxide emissions: 26.808 million metric tonnes of CO2 (2019 est.)
from coal and metallurgical coke: 4.713 million metric tonnes of CO2 (2019 est.)
from petroleum and other liquids: 18.951 million metric tonnes of CO2 (2019 est.)
from consumed natural gas: 3.144 million metric tonnes of CO2 (2019 est.)
country comparison to the world: 77

Energy consumption per capita: 39.016 million Btu/person (2019 est.)
country comparison to the world: 109

COMMUNICATIONS

Telephones - fixed lines: *total subscriptions:* 1,155,493 (2020 est.)
subscriptions per 100 inhabitants: 11 (2020 est.)
country comparison to the world: 72

Telephones - mobile cellular: *total subscriptions:* 8,989,587 (2020 est.)
subscriptions per 100 inhabitants: 83 (2020 est.)
country comparison to the world: 94

Telecommunication systems: *general assessment:* the Dominican Republic's telecom sector continued its solid form throughout 2020 and into 2021, shrugging off the economic turmoil unleashed by the Covid-19 pandemic to maintain a decade-long run of low but positive growth across all areas of the market; the Dominican Republic remains behind most of its counterparts in the Latin American region, especially in terms of fixed-line network coverage; mobile subscriptions are on par with the regional average, but at subscription levels of around 88% there is still ample opportunity for growth; in terms of growth, the standout winner was once again the mobile broadband segment; the market is expected to see close to 8% growth in 2021, building further on the gains it already made in 2020 when lock downs and work-from-home rules encouraged many people to find ways to upgrade their internet access and performance; the limited coverage of fixed-line broadband networks makes mobile the first, if not only, choice for most people in the country (2021)
domestic: fixed-line teledensity is about 11 per 100 persons; multiple providers of mobile-cellular service with a subscribership of nearly 83 per 100 persons (2020)
international: country code - 1-809; 1-829; 1-849; landing point for the ARCOS-1, Antillas 1, AMX-1, SAm-1, East-West, Deep Blue Cable and the Fibralink submarine cables that provide links to South and Central America, parts of the Caribbean, and US; satellite earth station - 1 Intelsat (Atlantic Ocean) (2019)

Broadcast media: combination of state-owned and privately owned broadcast media; 1 state-owned TV network and a number of private TV networks; networks operate repeaters to extend signals throughout country; combination of state-owned and privately owned radio stations with more than 300 radio stations operating (2019)

Internet country code: .do

Internet users: *total:* 8,352,886 (2020 est.)
percent of population: 77% (2020 est.)
country comparison to the world: 66

Broadband - fixed subscriptions: *total:* 1,031,858 (2020 est.)
subscriptions per 100 inhabitants: 10 (2020 est.)
country comparison to the world: 72

TRANSPORTATION

National air transport system: *number of registered air carriers:* 1 (2020)
inventory of registered aircraft operated by air carriers: 6

Civil aircraft registration country code prefix: HI

Airports: *total:* 36 (2021)
country comparison to the world: 108

Airports - with paved runways: *total:* 16
over 3,047 m: 3
2,438 to 3,047 m: 4
1,524 to 2,437 m: 4
914 to 1,523 m: 4
under 914 m: 1 (2021)

Airports - with unpaved runways: *total:* 20
1,524 to 2,437 m: 1
914 to 1,523 m: 1
under 914 m: 18 (2021)

Heliports: 1 (2021)

Pipelines: 27 km gas, 103 km oil (2013)

Railways: *total:* 496 km (2014)
standard gauge: 354 km (2014) 1.435-m gauge
narrow gauge: 142 km (2014) 0.762-m gauge
country comparison to the world: 114

Roadways: *total:* 19,705 km (2002)
paved: 9,872 km (2002)
unpaved: 9,833 km (2002)
country comparison to the world: 113

Merchant marine: *total:* 38
by type: container ship 1, general cargo 2, oil tanker 1, other 34 (2021)
country comparison to the world: 126

Ports and terminals: *major seaport(s):* Puerto Haina, Puerto Plata, Santo Domingo
oil terminal(s): Punta Nizao oil terminal

LNG terminal(s) (import): Andres LNG terminal (Boca Chica)

MILITARY AND SECURITY

Military and security forces: Armed Forces of the Dominican Republic: Army (Ejercito Nacional, EN), Navy (Marina de Guerra, MdG; includes naval infantry), Dominican Air Force (Fuerza Aerea Dominicana, FAD) (2022)
note: in addition to the military, the Ministry of Armed Forces directs the Airport Security Authority and Civil Aviation, Port Security Authority, the Tourist Security Corps, and Border Security Corps; the National Police (Policia Nacional) are under the Ministry of Interior

Military expenditures: 0.7% of GDP (2022 est.)
0.7% of GDP (2021 est.)
0.8% of GDP (2020 est.)
0.7% of GDP (2019 est.) (approximately $1.43 billion)
0.7% of GDP (2018 est.) (approximately $1.33 billion)
country comparison to the world: 150

Military and security service personnel strengths: information varies; approximately 60,000 active personnel (30,000 Army; 13,000 Navy; 17,000 Air Force); approximately 30,000 National Police (2022)

Military equipment inventories and acquisitions: the military is lightly armed with an inventory consisting mostly of older US equipment with limited quantities of material from other countries (2022)

Military service age and obligation: 17-21 years of age for voluntary military service (men and women); recruits must have completed primary school and be Dominican Republic citizens (2022) *note:* as of 2021, women made up approximately 20% of the active duty military

Military - note: the military is primarily focused on countering illegal immigration and refugees along its 350-kilometer-long border with Haiti and interdicting air and maritime narcotics trafficking, as well as disaster relief (2022)

TRANSNATIONAL ISSUES

Disputes - international: Haitian migrants cross the porous border into the Dominican Republic to find work; illegal migrants from the Dominican Republic cross the Mona Passage each year to Puerto Rico to find better work

Refugees and internally displaced persons: *refugees (country of origin):* 115,283 (Venezuela) (economic and political crisis; includes Venezuelans who have claimed asylum or have received alternative legal stay) (2021)

stateless persons: 133,770 (2016); note - a September 2013 Constitutional Court ruling revoked the citizenship of those born after 1929 to immigrants without proper documentation, even though the constitution at the time automatically granted citizenship to children born in the Dominican Republic and the 2010 constitution provides that constitutional provisions cannot be applied retroactively; the decision overwhelmingly affected people of Haitian descent whose relatives had come to the Dominican Republic since the 1890s as a cheap source of labor for sugar plantations; a May 2014 law passed by the Dominican Congress regularizes the status of those with birth certificates but will require those without them to prove they were born in the Dominican Republic and to apply for naturalization; the government has issued documents to thousands of individuals who may claim citizenship under this law, but no official estimate has been released

Illicit drugs: a major transshipment point for cocaine transiting through the Caribbean

ECUADOR

INTRODUCTION

Background: What is now Ecuador formed part of the northern Inca Empire until the Spanish conquest in 1533. Quito became a seat of Spanish colonial government in 1563 and part of the Viceroyalty of New Granada in 1717. The territories of the Viceroyalty - New Granada (Colombia), Venezuela, and Quito - gained their independence between 1819 and 1822 and formed a federation known as Gran Colombia. When Quito withdrew in 1830, the traditional name was changed in favor of the "Republic of the Equator." Between 1904 and 1942, Ecuador lost territories in a series of conflicts with its neighbors. A border war with Peru that flared in 1995 was resolved in 1999. Although Ecuador marked 30 years of civilian governance in 2004, the period was marred by political instability. Protests in Quito contributed to the mid-term ouster of three of Ecuador's last four democratically elected presidents. In late 2008, voters approved a new constitution, Ecuador's 20th since gaining independence. Guillermo LASSO was elected president in April 2021 becoming the country's first center-right president in nearly two decades when he took office the following month.

GEOGRAPHY

Location: Western South America, bordering the Pacific Ocean at the Equator, between Colombia and Peru

Geographic coordinates: 2 00 S, 77 30 W

Map references: South America

Area: *total:* 283,561 sq km
land: 276,841 sq km
water: 6,720 sq km
note: includes Galapagos Islands
country comparison to the world: 75

Area - comparative: slightly smaller than Nevada

Land boundaries: *total:* 2,237 km
border countries (2): Colombia 708 km; Peru 1529 km

Coastline: 2,237 km

Maritime claims: *territorial sea:* 12 nm
exclusive economic zone: 200 nm
continental shelf: 200 nm
note: Ecuador has declared its right to extend its continental shelf to 350 nm measured from the baselines of the Galapagos Archipelago

Climate: tropical along coast, becoming cooler inland at higher elevations; tropical in Amazonian jungle lowlands

Terrain: coastal plain (costa), inter-Andean central highlands (sierra), and flat to rolling eastern jungle (oriente)

Elevation: *highest point:* Chimborazo 6,267
lowest point: Pacific Ocean 0 m
mean elevation: 1,117 m
note: because the earth is not a perfect sphere and has an equatorial bulge, the highest point on the planet farthest from its center is Mount Chimborazo not Mount Everest, which is merely the highest peak above sea level

Natural resources: petroleum, fish, timber, hydropower

Land use: *agricultural land:* 29.7% (2018 est.)
arable land: 4.7% (2018 est.)
permanent crops: 5.6% (2018 est.)
permanent pasture: 19.4% (2018 est.)
forest: 38.9% (2018 est.)
other: 31.4% (2018 est.)

Irrigated land: 15,000 sq km (2012)

Major watersheds (area sq km): Atlantic Ocean drainage: Amazon (6,145,186 sq km)

Population distribution: nearly half of the population is concentrated in the interior in the Andean intermontane basins and valleys, with large concentrations also found along the western coastal strip; the rainforests of the east remain sparsely populated

Natural hazards: frequent earthquakes; landslides; volcanic activity; floods; periodic droughts
volcanism: volcanic activity concentrated along the Andes Mountains; Sangay (5,230 m), which erupted in 2010, is mainland Ecuador's most active volcano; other historically active volcanoes in the Andes include Antisana, Cayambe, Chacana, Cotopaxi, Guagua Pichincha, Reventador, Sumaco, and Tungurahua; Fernandina (1,476 m), a shield volcano that last erupted in 2009, is the most active of the many Galapagos volcanoes; other historically active Galapagos volcanoes include Wolf, Sierra Negra, Cerro Azul, Pinta, Marchena, and Santiago

Geography - note: *note 1:* Cotopaxi in Andes is highest active volcano in world
note 2: genetic research indicates that the cherry-sized tomato originated in Ecuador without any human domestication; later domestication in Mexico transformed the plant into the large modern tomato; archeological research indicates that the cacao tree, whose seeds are used to make chocolate and which was long thought to have originated in Mesoamerica, was first domesticated in the upper Amazon region of northwest South America - present-day Ecuador - about 3,300 B.C.

PEOPLE AND SOCIETY

Population: 17,289,554 (2022 est.)
country comparison to the world: 71

Nationality: *noun:* Ecuadorian(s)
adjective: Ecuadorian

Ethnic groups: Mestizo (mixed Amerindian and White) 71.9%, Montubio 7.4%, Amerindian 7%, White 6.1%, Afroecuadorian 4.3%, Mulatto 1.9%, Black 1%, other 0.4% (2010 est.)

Languages: Spanish (Castilian) 93% (official), Quechua 4.1%, other indigenous 0.7%, foreign 2.2%; note - (Quechua and Shuar are official languages of intercultural relations; other indigenous languages are in official use by indigenous peoples in the areas they inhabit) (2010 est.)
major-language sample(s):
La Libreta Informativa del Mundo, la fuente indispensable de información básica. (Spanish)

Religions: Roman Catholic 68.8%, Evangelical 15.4%, Adventist 1.2%, Jehovah's Witness 1%, other 1.3%, agnostic or atheist 1.4%, none 10.1%, don't know/no response 1% (2020 est.)
note: data represent persons at least 16 years of age from five Ecuadoran cities

Demographic profile: Ecuador's high poverty and income inequality most affect indigenous, mixed race, and rural populations. The government has increased its social spending to ameliorate these problems, but critics question the efficiency and implementation of its national development plan. Nevertheless, the conditional cash transfer program, which requires participants' children to attend school and have medical check-ups, has helped improve educational attainment and healthcare among poor children. Ecuador is stalled at above replacement level fertility and the population most likely will keep growing rather than stabilize.

An estimated 2 to 3 million Ecuadorians live abroad, but increased unemployment in key receiving countries - Spain, the United States, and Italy - is slowing emigration and increasing the likelihood of returnees to Ecuador. The first large-scale emigration of Ecuadorians occurred between 1980 and 2000, when an economic crisis drove Ecuadorians from southern provinces to New York City, where they had trade contacts. A second, nationwide wave of emigration in the late 1990s was caused by another economic downturn, political instability, and a currency crisis. Spain was the logical destination because of its shared language and the wide availability of low-skilled, informal jobs at a time when increased border surveillance made illegal migration to the US difficult. Ecuador has a small but growing immigrant population and is Latin America's top recipient of refugees; 98% are neighboring Colombians fleeing violence in their country.

Age structure: *0-14 years:* 25.82% (male 2,226,240/female 2,138,219)
15-24 years: 17.8% (male 1,531,545/female 1,478,222)
25-54 years: 40.31% (male 3,333,650/female 3,480,262)
55-64 years: 7.92% (male 647,718/female 691,759)
65 years and over: 8.15% (male 648,761/female 728,491) (2020 est.)

Dependency ratios: *total dependency ratio:* 53.8
youth dependency ratio: 42.1
elderly dependency ratio: 11.7
potential support ratio: 8.6 (2020 est.)

Median age: *total:* 28.8 years

male: 28 years
female: 29.6 years (2020 est.)
country comparison to the world: 140

Population growth rate: 1.13% (2022 est.)
country comparison to the world: 85

Birth rate: 16.45 births/1,000 population (2022 est.)
country comparison to the world: 98

Death rate: 5.17 deaths/1,000 population (2022 est.)
country comparison to the world: 189

Net migration rate: 0 migrant(s)/1,000 population (2022 est.)
country comparison to the world: 87

Population distribution: nearly half of the population is concentrated in the interior in the Andean intermontane basins and valleys, with large concentrations also found along the western coastal strip; the rainforests of the east remain sparsely populated

Urbanization: *urban population:* 64.6% of total population (2022)
rate of urbanization: 1.62% annual rate of change (2020-25 est.)

Major urban areas - population: 3.092 million Guayaquil, 1.928 million QUITO (capital) (2022)

Sex ratio: *at birth:* 1.05 male(s)/female
0-14 years: 1.04 male(s)/female
15-24 years: 1.04 male(s)/female
25-54 years: 0.96 male(s)/female
55-64 years: 0.92 male(s)/female
65 years and over: 0.78 male(s)/female
total population: 0.98 male(s)/female (2022 est.)

Maternal mortality ratio: 59 deaths/100,000 live births (2017 est.)
country comparison to the world: 90

Infant mortality rate: *total:* 18.13 deaths/1,000 live births
male: 21.7 deaths/1,000 live births
female: 14.39 deaths/1,000 live births (2022 est.)
country comparison to the world: 90

Life expectancy at birth: *total population:* 78 years
male: 75.06 years
female: 81.1 years (2022 est.)
country comparison to the world: 79

Total fertility rate: 2.04 children born/woman (2022 est.)
country comparison to the world: 101

Contraceptive prevalence rate: 77.9% (2018/19)
note: percent of women aged 15-50

Drinking water source: *improved: urban:* 100% of population
rural: 87.1% of population
total: 95.4% of population
unimproved: urban: 0% of population
rural: 12.9% of population
total: 4.6% of population (2020 est.)

Current health expenditure: 7.8% of GDP (2019)

Physicians density: 2.22 physicians/1,000 population (2017)

Hospital bed density: 1.4 beds/1,000 population (2016)

Sanitation facility access: *improved: urban:* 100% of population
rural: 96.9% of population
total: 98.9% of population
unimproved: urban: 0% of population
rural: 3.1% of population
total: 1.1% of population (2020 est.)

HIV/AIDS - adult prevalence rate: 0.3% (2020 est.)
country comparison to the world: 80

Major infectious diseases: *degree of risk:* high (2020)
food or waterborne diseases: bacterial diarrhea, hepatitis A, and typhoid fever
vectorborne diseases: dengue fever and malaria

Obesity - adult prevalence rate: 19.9% (2016)
country comparison to the world: 107

Alcohol consumption per capita: *total:* 3.05 liters of pure alcohol (2019 est.)
beer: 2.32 liters of pure alcohol (2019 est.)
wine: 0.09 liters of pure alcohol (2019 est.)
spirits: 0.61 liters of pure alcohol (2019 est.)
other alcohols: 0.03 liters of pure alcohol (2019 est.)
country comparison to the world: 114

Tobacco use: *total:* 11.3% (2020 est.)
male: 18.4% (2020 est.)
female: 4.2% (2020 est.)
country comparison to the world: 128

Children under the age of 5 years underweight: 5.2% (2018/19)
country comparison to the world: 76

Child marriage: *women married by age 15:* 3.8%
women married by age 18: 22.2% (2018 est.)

Education expenditures: 4.1% of GDP (2020 est.)
country comparison to the world: 99

Literacy: *definition:* age 15 and over can read and write
total population: 93.6%
male: 94.8%
female: 92.5% (2020)

School life expectancy (primary to tertiary education): *total:* 15 years
male: 14 years
female: 15 years (2019)

Unemployment, youth ages 15-24: *total:* 11.1%
male: 8.7%
female: 15.4% (2020 est.)

ENVIRONMENT

Environment - current issues: deforestation; soil erosion; desertification; water pollution; pollution from oil production wastes in ecologically sensitive areas of the Amazon Basin and Galapagos Islands

Environment - international agreements: *party to:* Antarctic-Environmental Protection, Antarctic Treaty, Biodiversity, Climate Change, Climate Change-Kyoto Protocol, Climate Change-Paris Agreement, Comprehensive Nuclear Test Ban, Desertification, Endangered Species, Hazardous Wastes, Law of the Sea, Nuclear Test Ban, Ozone Layer Protection, Ship Pollution, Tropical Timber 2006, Wetlands, Whaling
signed, but not ratified: none of the selected agreements

Air pollutants: *particulate matter emissions:* 14.91 micrograms per cubic meter (2016 est.)
carbon dioxide emissions: 41.15 megatons (2016 est.)
methane emissions: 23.51 megatons (2020 est.)

Climate: tropical along coast, becoming cooler inland at higher elevations; tropical in Amazonian jungle lowlands

Land use: *agricultural land:* 29.7% (2018 est.)
arable land: 4.7% (2018 est.)
permanent crops: 5.6% (2018 est.)
permanent pasture: 19.4% (2018 est.)
forest: 38.9% (2018 est.)
other: 31.4% (2018 est.)

Urbanization: *urban population:* 64.6% of total population (2022)
rate of urbanization: 1.62% annual rate of change (2020-25 est.)

Revenue from forest resources: *forest revenues:* 0.27% of GDP (2018 est.)
country comparison to the world: 83

Revenue from coal: *coal revenues:* 0% of GDP (2018 est.)
country comparison to the world: 92

Waste and recycling: *municipal solid waste generated annually:* 5,297,211 tons (2015 est.)
municipal solid waste recycled annually: 683,340 tons (2015 est.)
percent of municipal solid waste recycled: 12.9% (2015 est.)

Major watersheds (area sq km): Atlantic Ocean drainage: Amazon (6,145,186 sq km)

Total water withdrawal: *municipal:* 1.293 billion cubic meters (2017 est.)
industrial: 549 million cubic meters (2017 est.)
agricultural: 8.076 billion cubic meters (2017 est.)

Total renewable water resources: 442.4 billion cubic meters (2017 est.)

GOVERNMENT

Country name: *conventional long form:* Republic of Ecuador
conventional short form: Ecuador
local long form: Republica del Ecuador
local short form: Ecuador
etymology: the country's position on the globe, straddling the Equator, accounts for its Spanish name

Government type: presidential republic

Capital: *name:* Quito
geographic coordinates: 0 13 S, 78 30 W
time difference: UTC-5 (same time as Washington, DC, during Standard Time)
time zone note: Ecuador has two time zones, including the Galapagos Islands (UTC-6)
etymology: named after the Quitu, a Pre-Columbian indigenous people credited with founding the city; the name is also a combination of two Tsafiki words: *quitso* (meaning "center" or "half") + *to* or *tu* ("the world"); the combination roughly translates as "center of the world" and reflects the fact that native peoples recognized that at the two annual equinoxes, the overhead sun in that area (only about 20 km (12 mi) north of the equator) did not display any shade and thus must be in the middle of the world

Administrative divisions: 24 provinces (provincias, singular - provincia); Azuay, Bolivar, Canar, Carchi, Chimborazo, Cotopaxi, El Oro, Esmeraldas, Galapagos, Guayas, Imbabura, Loja, Los Rios, Manabi, Morona-Santiago, Napo, Orellana, Pastaza, Pichincha, Santa Elena, Santo Domingo de los Tsachilas, Sucumbios, Tungurahua, Zamora-Chinchipe

Independence: 24 May 1822 (from Spain)

National holiday: Independence Day (independence of Quito), 10 August (1809)

Constitution: *history:* many previous; latest approved 20 October 2008
amendments: proposed by the president of the republic through a referendum, by public petition of at least 1% of registered voters, or by agreement of at least one-third membership of the National

Assembly; passage requires two separate readings a year apart and approval by at least two-thirds majority vote of the Assembly, and approval by absolute majority in a referendum; amendments such as changes to the structure of the state, constraints on personal rights and guarantees, or constitutional amendment procedures are not allowed; amended 2011, 2015, 2018

Legal system: civil law based on the Chilean civil code with modifications; traditional law in indigenous communities

International law organization participation: has not submitted an ICJ jurisdiction declaration; accepts ICCt jurisdiction

Citizenship: *citizenship by birth:* yes
citizenship by descent only: yes
dual citizenship recognized: no
residency requirement for naturalization: 3 years

Suffrage: 18-65 years of age; universal and compulsory; 16-18, over 65, and other eligible voters, voluntary

Executive branch: *chief of state:* President Guillermo LASSO Mendoza (since 24 May 2021); Vice President Alfredo Enrique BORRERO Vega (since 24 May 2021); the president is both chief of state and head of government
head of government: President Guillermo LASSO Mendoza (since 24 May 2021); Vice President Alfredo Enrique BORRERO Vega (since 24 May 2021)
cabinet: Cabinet appointed by the president
elections/appointments: president and vice president directly elected on the same ballot by absolute majority popular vote in 2 rounds if needed for a 4-year term (eligible for a second term); election last held on 7 February 2021 with a runoff on 11 April 2021 (next to be held in February 2025)
election results:
2021: Guillermo LASSO Mendoza elected president; first round election results: percent of vote - Andres ARAUZ (UNES) 32.72%, Guillermo LASSO Mendoza (CREO) 19.74%, Yaku PEREZ Guartambel (MUPP) 19.38%, Xavier HERVAS Mora (Independent) 15.68%, other 12.48%; second round election results: percent of vote - Guillermo LASSO Mendoza (CREO) 52.5%, Andres ARAUZ (UNES) 47.5%
2017: Lenin MORENO Garces elected president in second round; percent of vote - Lenin MORENO Garces (Alianza PAIS Movement) 51.1%, Guillermo LASSO (CREO) 48.9%

Legislative branch: *description:* unicameral National Assembly or Asamblea Nacional (137 seats; 116 members directly elected in single- seat constituencies by simple majority vote, 15 members directly elected in a single nationwide constituency by proportional representation vote, and 6 directly elected in multi-seat constituencies for Ecuadorians living abroad by simple majority vote; members serve 4-year terms); note - all Assembly members have alternates from the same party who cast votes when a primary member is absent, resigns, or is removed from office
elections:
last held on 7 February 2021 (next scheduled in February 2025)
election results:
percent of vote by party - UNES 32.21%, MUPP 16.81%, ID 11.98%, PSC 9.73%, CREO 9.65%, MC-PSE 3.76%, other 15.86%; seats by party - UNES 49, MUPP 27, ID 18, PSC 18, CREO 12, MC-PSE 2, independents 3, other 8; composition as of March 2022 - men 84, women 53, percent of women 38.7%; note - defections by members of National Assembly are commonplace, resulting in frequent changes in the numbers of seats held by the various parties

Judicial branch: *highest court(s):* National Court of Justice or Corte Nacional de Justicia (consists of 21 judges, including the chief justice and organized into 5 specialized chambers); Constitutional Court or Corte Constitucional (consists of the court president and 8 judges)
judge selection and term of office: candidates for the National Court of Justice evaluated and appointed justices by the Judicial Council, a 9-member independent body of law professionals; justices elected for 9-year, non-renewable terms, with one-third of the membership renewed every 3 years; candidates for the Constitutional Court evaluated and appointed judges by a 6-member independent body of law professionals; judges appointed for 4-year renewable terms
subordinate courts: provincial courts (one for each province except Galapagos); fiscal, criminal, and administrative tribunals; Election Dispute Settlement Courts; cantonal courts

Political parties and leaders: Avanza Party or AVANZA [Javier ORTI Torres]
Central Democratic Movement or CD [Jimmy JAIRALA]
Citizen Revolution Movement or MRC or RC5 [Rafael CORREA]
Creating Opportunities Movement or CREO [Guillermo LASSO]
Democratic Left or ID [Rodrigo BORJA Cevallos]
Forward Ecuador Movement [Alvaro NOBOA]
Pachakutik Plurinational Unity Movement or MUPP [Marlon Rene SANTI Gualinga]
Patriotic Society Party or PSP [Lucio Edwin GUTIERREZ Borbua]
Popular Democracy Movement or MPD [Luis VILLACIS]
Social Christian Party or PSC [Jaime NEBOT Saadi]
Socialist Party [Gustavo VALLEJO]
Society United for More Action or SUMA [Guillermo CELI]

International organization participation: CAN, CD, CELAC, FAO, G-11, G-77, IADB, IAEA, IBRD, ICAO, ICC (national committees), ICCt, ICRM, IDA, IFAD, IFC, IFRCS, IHO, ILO, IMF, IMO, Interpol, IOC, IOM, IPU, ISO, ITSO, ITU, ITUC (NGOs), LAES, LAIA, Mercosur (associate), MIGA, MINUSTAH, NAM, OAS, OPANAL, OPCW, OPEC, Pacific Alliance (observer), PCA, PROSUR, SICA (observer), UN, UNAMID, UNASUR, UNCTAD, UNESCO, UNHCR, UNIDO, Union Latina, UNISFA, UNMIL, UNMISS, UNOCI, UNWTO, UPU, WCO, WFTU (NGOs), WHO, WIPO, WMO, WTO

Diplomatic representation in the US: *chief of mission:* Ambassador Ivonne Leila Juez De A-BAKI (since 6 February 2020)
chancery: 2535 15th Street NW, Washington, DC 20009
telephone: [1] (202) 234-7200
FAX: [1] (202) 333-2893
email address and website:
embassy@ecuador.org
http://www.ecuador.org/
consulate(s) general: Atlanta, Chicago, Houston, Los Angeles, Miami, Minneapolis, New Haven (CT), New Orleans, New York, Newark (NJ), Phoenix, San Francisco

Diplomatic representation from the US: *chief of mission:* Ambassador Michael J. FITZPATRICK (since 3 July 2019)
embassy: E12-170 Avenida Avigiras y Avenida Eloy Alfaro, Quito
mailing address: 3420 Quito Place, Washington DC 20521-3420
telephone: [593] (2) 398-5000
email address and website:
ACSQuito@state.gov
https://ec.usembassy.gov/
consulate(s) general: Guayaquil

Flag description: three horizontal bands of yellow (top, double width), blue, and red with the coat of arms superimposed at the center of the flag; the flag retains the three main colors of the banner of Gran Colombia, the South American republic that broke up in 1830; the yellow color represents sunshine, grain, and mineral wealth, blue the sky, sea, and rivers, and red the blood of patriots spilled in the struggle for freedom and justice
note: similar to the flag of Colombia, which is shorter and does not bear a coat of arms

National symbol(s): Andean condor; national colors: yellow, blue, red

National anthem: *name:* "Salve, Oh Patria!" (We Salute You, Our Homeland)
lyrics/music: Juan Leon MERA/Antonio NEUMANE
note: adopted 1948; Juan Leon MERA wrote the lyrics in 1865; only the chorus and second verse are sung

National heritage: *total World Heritage Sites:* 5 (3 cultural, 2 natural)
selected World Heritage Site locales: Historic Quito (c); Galápagos Islands (n); Historic Cuenca (c); Qhapaq Ñan/Andean Road System (c); Sangay National Park (n)

ECONOMY

Economic overview: Ecuador is substantially dependent on its petroleum resources, which accounted for about a third of the country's export earnings in 2017. Remittances from overseas Ecuadorian are also important.

In 1999/2000, Ecuador's economy suffered from a banking crisis that lead to some reforms, including adoption of the US dollar as legal tender. Dollarization stabilized the economy, and positive growth returned in most of the years that followed. China has become Ecuador's largest foreign lender since 2008 and now accounts for 77.7% of the Ecuador's bilateral debt. Various economic policies under the CORREA administration, such as an announcement in 2017 that Ecuador would terminate 13 bilateral investment treaties - including one with the US, generated economic uncertainty and discouraged private investment.

Faced with a 2013 trade deficit of $1.1 billion, Ecuador imposed tariff surcharges from 5% to 45% on an estimated 32% of imports. Ecuador's economy fell into recession in 2015 and remained in recession in 2016. Declining oil prices and exports forced the CORREA administration to cut government oulays. Foreign investment in Ecuador is low as a result of the unstable regulatory environment and weak rule of law.

n April of 2017, Lenin MORENO was elected President of Ecuador by popular vote. His immediate challenge was to reengage the private sector to improve cash flow in the country. Ecuador's economy returned to positive, but sluggish, growth. In early 2018, the MORENO administration held a public referendum on seven economic and political issues in a move counter to CORREA-administration policies, reduce corruption, strengthen democracy, and revive employment and the economy. The referendum resulted in repeal of taxes associated with recovery from the earthquake of 2016, reduced restrictions on metal mining in the Yasuni Intangible Zone - a protected area, and several political reforms.

Real GDP (purchasing power parity): $182.24 billion (2020 est.)
$197.55 billion (2019 est.)
$197.53 billion (2018 est.)
note: data are in 2017 dollars
country comparison to the world: 69

Real GDP growth rate: 0.06% (2019 est.)
1.29% (2018 est.)
2.37% (2017 est.)
country comparison to the world: 191

Real GDP per capita: $10,300 (2020 est.)
$11,400 (2019 est.)
$11,600 (2018 est.)
note: data are in 2017 dollars
country comparison to the world: 139

GDP (official exchange rate): $107.436 billion (2019 est.)

Inflation rate (consumer prices): 0.2% (2019 est.)
-0.2% (2018 est.)
0.4% (2017 est.)
country comparison to the world: 26

Credit ratings:

Fitch rating: B- (2020)

Moody's rating: Caa3 (2020)

Standard & Poors rating: B- (2020)
note: The year refers to the year in which the current credit rating was first obtained.

GDP - composition, by sector of origin: *agriculture:* 6.7% (2017 est.)
industry: 32.9% (2017 est.)
services: 60.4% (2017 est.)

GDP - composition, by end use: *household consumption:* 60.7% (2017 est.)
government consumption: 14.4% (2017 est.)
investment in fixed capital: 24.3% (2017 est.)
investment in inventories: 1% (2017 est.)
exports of goods and services: 20.8% (2017 est.)
imports of goods and services: -21.3% (2017 est.)

Agricultural products: sugar cane, bananas, milk, oil palm fruit, maize, rice, plantains, poultry, cocoa, potatoes

Industries: petroleum, food processing, textiles, wood products, chemicals

Industrial production growth rate: -0.6% (2017 est.)
note: excludes oil refining
country comparison to the world: 173

Labor force: 8.086 million (2017 est.)
country comparison to the world: 59

Labor force - by occupation: *agriculture:* 26.1%
industry: 18.4%
services: 55.5% (2017 est.)

Unemployment rate: 5.71% (2019 est.)
5.26% (2018 est.)
country comparison to the world: 94

Unemployment, youth ages 15-24: *total:* 11.1%
male: 8.7%
female: 15.4% (2020 est.)
country comparison to the world: 130

Population below poverty line: 25% (2019 est.)

Gini Index coefficient - distribution of family income: 45.4 (2018 est.)
48.5 (December 2017)
note: data are for urban households only
country comparison to the world: 28

Household income or consumption by percentage share: *lowest 10%:* 1.4%
highest 10%: 35.4% (2012 est.)
note: data are for urban households only

Budget: *revenues:* 33.43 billion (2017 est.)
expenditures: 38.08 billion (2017 est.)

Budget surplus (+) or deficit (-): -4.5% (of GDP) (2017 est.)
country comparison to the world: 164

Public debt: 45.4% of GDP (2017 est.)
43.2% of GDP (2016 est.)
country comparison to the world: 114

Taxes and other revenues: 32% (of GDP) (2017 est.)
country comparison to the world: 69

Fiscal year: calendar year

Current account balance: -$53 million (2019 est.)
-$1.328 billion (2018 est.)
country comparison to the world: 79

Exports: $22.23 billion (2020 est.) note: data are in current year dollars
$26.12 billion (2019 est.) note: data are in current year dollars
$25.38 billion (2018 est.) note: data are in current year dollars
country comparison to the world: 77

Exports - partners: United States 30%, China 13%, Panama 8%, Chile 7% (2019)

Exports - commodities: crude petroleum, crustaceans, bananas, fish, refined petroleum (2019)

Imports: $19.89 billion (2020 est.) note: data are in current year dollars
$25.89 billion (2019 est.) note: data are in current year dollars
$26.29 billion (2018 est.) note: data are in current year dollars
country comparison to the world: 84

Imports - partners: United States 22%, China 18%, Colombia 9%, Panama 5% (2019)

Imports - commodities: refined petroleum, coal tar oil, cars, packaged medicines, soybean products (2019)

Reserves of foreign exchange and gold: $2.395 billion (31 December 2017 est.)
$4.259 billion (31 December 2016 est.)
country comparison to the world: 116

Debt - external: $50.667 billion (2019 est.)
$43.224 billion (2018 est.)
country comparison to the world: 67

Exchange rates: 25,000 (2020 est.)
25,000 (2019 est.)
25,000 (2018 est.)
the US dollar became Ecuador's currency in 2001

ENERGY

Electricity access: *electrification - total population:* 97% (2019)
electrification - urban areas: 100% (2019)
electrification - rural areas: 93% (2019)

Electricity: *installed generating capacity:* 9.354 million kW (2020 est.)
consumption: 26,353,430,000 kWh (2019 est.)
exports: 1.826 billion kWh (2019 est.)
imports: 6 million kWh (2019 est.)
transmission/distribution losses: 4.303 billion kWh (2019 est.)

Electricity generation sources: *fossil fuels:* 21% of total installed capacity (2020 est.)
solar: 0.1% of total installed capacity (2020 est.)
wind: 0.2% of total installed capacity (2020 est.)
hydroelectricity: 77.2% of total installed capacity (2020 est.)
biomass and waste: 1.5% of total installed capacity (2020 est.)

Coal: *proven reserves:* 24 million metric tons (2019 est.)

Petroleum: *total petroleum production:* 478,000 bbl/day (2021 est.)
refined petroleum consumption: 259,000 bbl/day (2019 est.)
crude oil and lease condensate exports: 349,400 bbl/day (2018 est.)
crude oil and lease condensate imports: 0 bbl/day (2018 est.)
crude oil estimated reserves: 8.273 billion barrels (2021 est.)

Refined petroleum products - production: 137,400 bbl/day (2015 est.)
country comparison to the world: 62

Refined petroleum products - exports: 25,870 bbl/day (2015 est.)
country comparison to the world: 66

Refined petroleum products - imports: 153,900 bbl/day (2015 est.)
country comparison to the world: 40

Natural gas: *production:* 342.407 million cubic meters (2019 est.)
consumption: 342.407 million cubic meters (2019 est.)
proven reserves: 10.902 billion cubic meters (2021 est.)

Carbon dioxide emissions: 36.051 million metric tonnes of CO2 (2019 est.)
from coal and metallurgical coke: 45,000 metric tonnes of CO2 (2019 est.)
from petroleum and other liquids: 35.329 million metric tonnes of CO2 (2019 est.)
from consumed natural gas: 677,000 metric tonnes of CO2 (2019 est.)
country comparison to the world: 70

Energy consumption per capita: 42.564 million Btu/person (2019 est.)
country comparison to the world: 104

COMMUNICATIONS

Telephones - fixed lines: *total subscriptions:* 2,063,044 (2020)
subscriptions per 100 inhabitants: 12 (2020 est.)
country comparison to the world: 56

Telephones - mobile cellular: *total subscriptions:* 15,485,366 (2020 est.)
subscriptions per 100 inhabitants: 88 (2020 est.)
country comparison to the world: 66

Telecommunication systems: *general assessment:* Ecuador has a small telecom market dominated by the mobile sector; the evolution of the market has

been influenced by the poor fixed-line infrastructure, which has stymied the development of fixed-line broadband services; to some extent poor infrastructure has been the result of topographical challenges which have rendered the cost of deploying networks to remote and mountainous areas prohibitive; although Ecuador has several fixed-line operators and a large number of ISPs, the state-owned incumbent leads the fixed-line market, and thus also the fixed broadband market; thus far the MVNO sector has been slow to develop, partly because the incumbent operators also have their low-cost brands and thus there is little business case for new market entrants; the government is keen to advance and improve teledensity; from 2022, additional revenue will be earmarked for programs aimed at expanding the reach of internet and mobile services in rural areas of the country; Ecuador lacks a national 5G roadmap; the mobile operators have conducted several 5G pilots, but no progress has been made on allocation spectrum for 5G, or on developing strategies to encourage investment in the sector (2022)
domestic: according to 2021 statistics from the Ministry of Telecommunications and Information Society, 50 percent of Ecuadorian homes do not have access to fixed internet; Ecuador's telecoms regulator is currently evaluating and reorganizing the 3.5GHz, 2.5 GHz, 700 MHz and AWS spectrum for future government tenders; 2G/3G technologies have a 91.11 percent of penetration and 4G technologies has 60.74 percent (2021); fixed-line teledensity is about 12 per 100 persons; mobile-cellular service with a subscribership of nearly 88 per 100 persons (2021)
international: country code - 593; landing points for the SPSC (Mistral Submarine Cable), Panamerican Cable System (PAN-AM), Pacific Caribbean Cable System (PCCS), America Movil-Telxius West Coast Cable and SAm-1 submarine (SAm-1) cables that provide links to South and Central America, and extending onward to the Caribbean and the US; satellite earth station - 1 Intelsat (Atlantic Ocean) (2019)

Broadcast media: *the Communication Council, an official entity, carried out a media registry in Ecuador in December 2020. It registered 956 media outlets, 89% are private, 5% are public and 6% belong to small communities. The government controls most of the 44 public media, this includes national media and multiple local radio stations. In addition, of the 956 registered media, 58% are radio and 18% print. Two provinces have the largest number of media outlets:* Guayas has 172 media outlets and Pichincha has 130 media outlets. (2020) so also sent to the National Assembly a new regulation proposal that is still under discussion. (2022)

Internet country code: .ec

Internet users: *total:* 11,467,989 (2020 est.)
percent of population: 65% (2020 est.)
according to 2021 statistics from Ecuador's Ministry of Telecommunications and Information Society, 50% of homes do not have access to fixed internet
country comparison to the world: 52

Broadband - fixed subscriptions: *total:* 2,371,297 (2020 est.)
subscriptions per 100 inhabitants: 13 (2020 est.)
country comparison to the world: 55

TRANSPORTATION

National air transport system: *number of registered air carriers:* 7 (2020)
inventory of registered aircraft operated by air carriers: 35
annual passenger traffic on registered air carriers: 5,365,261 (2018)
annual freight traffic on registered air carriers: 64.2 million (2018) mt-km

Civil aircraft registration country code prefix: HC

Airports: *total:* 432 (2021)
country comparison to the world: 18

Airports - with paved runways: *total:* 104
over 3,047 m: 4
2,438 to 3,047 m: 5
1,524 to 2,437 m: 18
914 to 1,523 m: 26
under 914 m: 51 (2021)

Airports - with unpaved runways: *total:* 328
914 to 1,523 m: 37
under 914 m: 291 (2021)

Heliports: 2 (2021)

Pipelines: 485 km extra heavy crude, 123 km gas, 2,131 km oil, 1,526 km refined products (2017)

Railways: *total:* 965 km (2022)
narrow gauge: 965 km (2022) 1.067-m gauge
note: passenger service limited to certain sections of track, mostly for tourist trains
country comparison to the world: 91

Roadways: *total:* 43,950 km (2022)
paved: 8,895 km (2022)
unpaved: 35,055 km (2022)
country comparison to the world: 86

Waterways: 1,500 km (2012) (most inaccessible)
country comparison to the world: 55

Merchant marine: *total:* 145
by type: container ship 1, general cargo 7, oil tanker 27, other 110 (2021)
country comparison to the world: 77

Ports and terminals: *major seaport(s):* Esmeraldas, Manta, Puerto Bolivar
container port(s) (TEUs): Guayaquil (1,680,751) (2019)
river port(s): Guayaquil (Guayas)

MILITARY AND SECURITY

Military and security forces: Ecuadorian Armed Forces: the Ecuadorian Army (Ejército Ecuatoriano), Ecuadorian Navy (Armada del Ecuador, Fuerza Naval del Ecuador, FNE; includes naval infantry, naval aviation, coast guard), Ecuadorian Air Force (Fuerza Aerea Ecuatoriana, FAE) (2022)
note: the National Police of Ecuador (Policía Nacional del Ecuador) is under the Ministry of Government

Military expenditures: 2% of GDP (2021 est.)
2.3% of GDP (2020 est.)
2.2% of GDP (2019) (approximately $2.98 billion)
2.4% of GDP (2018) (approximately $3.14 billion)
2.4% of GDP (2017) (approximately $3.1 billion)
country comparison to the world: 60

Military and security service personnel strengths: approximately 40,000 active military personnel (25,000 Army; 9,000 Navy; 6,000 Air Force) (2022)

Military equipment inventories and acquisitions: the military's equipment inventory is mostly older and derived from a wide variety of sources; since 2010, Ecuador has received limited amounts of military equipment from more than 15 countries, including Brazil, China, Russia, and the US (2022)

Military service age and obligation: 18 years of age for selective conscript military service, although conscription was suspended in 2008; 18 years of age for voluntary military service; Ecuadorian birth requirement; 1-year service obligation; females have been allowed to serve in all branches since 2012 (2022)
note: in 2017, women made up an estimated 3% of the military

Military - note: border conflicts with Peru dominated the military's focus until the late 1990s; as of 2022, border security remained a priority, but in more recent years, security challenges have shifted towards counterinsurgency and counter-narcotics operations, particularly in the northern border area where violence and other criminal activity related to terrorism, insurgency, and narco-trafficking in Colombia, as well as refugees from Venezuela, has spilled over the border; troop deployments along the border with Colombia were scaled back following the 2016 signing of a peace agreement between the Colombian Government and the Revolutionary Armed Forces of Colombia (FARC) terrorist group (see Appendix T), but recent violence associated with FARC dissidents to the agreement have led Ecuador and Colombia to reinforce their shared border; since 2012, the Ecuadorian Government has also expanded the military's role in general public security and counter-narcotics operations, in part due to rising violence, police corruption, and police ineffectiveness

the military has had a large role in Ecuador's political history; it ruled the country from 1963-1966 and 1972-1979, and supported a dictatorship in 1970-1972; during the 1980s, the military remained loyal to the civilian government, but civilian-military relations were at times tenuous, and the military had considerable autonomy from civilian oversight; it was involved in coup attempts in 2000 and 2010

Maritime threats: the International Maritime Bureau continues to report the territorial and offshore waters of Ecuador as at risk for piracy and armed robbery against ships; vessels, including commercial shipping and pleasure craft, have been attacked and hijacked both at anchor and while underway; crews have been robbed and stores or cargoes stolen; there has been a slight decrease with four attacks reported in 2021 and five in 2020; one ship was boarded while underway and two ships were fired upon

TRANSNATIONAL ISSUES

Disputes - international: organized illegal narcotics operations in Colombia penetrate across Ecuador's shared border

Refugees and internally displaced persons: *refugees (country of origin):* 65,854 (Colombia) (refugees and asylum seekers) (2021); 513,900 (Venezuela) (economic and political crisis; includes Venezuelans who have claimed asylum, are recognized as refugees, or have received alternative legal stay) (2022)

Illicit drugs: Ecuador is a major transit country for illicit drugs such as cocaine, heroin and chemical precursors to process cocaine from Colombia and Peru; not a major drug producing country

EGYPT

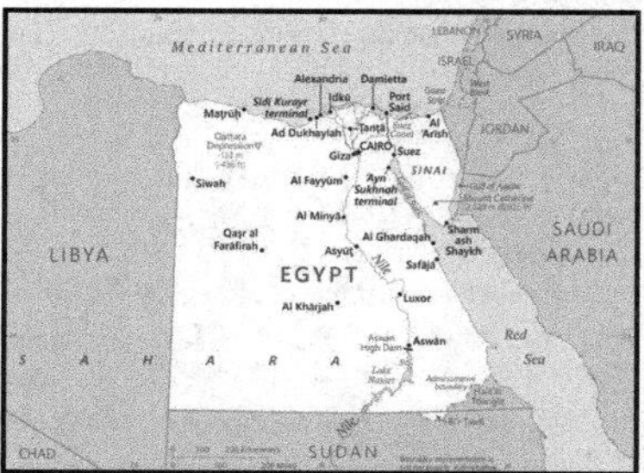

INTRODUCTION

Background: The regularity and richness of the annual Nile River flood, coupled with semi-isolation provided by deserts to the east and west, allowed for the development of one of the world's great civilizations. A unified kingdom arose circa 3200 B.C., and a series of dynasties ruled in Egypt for the next three millennia. The last native dynasty fell to the Persians in 341 B.C., who in turn were replaced by the Greeks, Romans, and Byzantines. It was the Arabs who introduced Islam and the Arabic language in the 7th century and who ruled for the next six centuries. A local military caste, the Mamluks took control about 1250 and continued to govern after the conquest of Egypt by the Ottoman Turks in 1517. Completion of the Suez Canal in 1869 elevated Egypt as an important world transportation hub. Ostensibly to protect its investments, Britain seized control of Egypt's government in 1882, but nominal allegiance to the Ottoman Empire continued until 1914. Partially independent from the UK in 1922, Egypt acquired full sovereignty from Britain in 1952. The completion of the Aswan High Dam in 1971 and the resultant Lake Nasser have reaffirmed the time-honored place of the Nile River in the agriculture and ecology of Egypt. A rapidly growing population (the largest in the Arab world), limited arable land, and dependence on the Nile all continue to overtax resources and stress society. The government has struggled to meet the demands of Egypt's fast-growing population as it implements large-scale infrastructure projects, energy cooperation, and foreign direct investment appeals.

Inspired by the 2010 Tunisian revolution, Egyptian opposition groups led demonstrations and labor strikes countrywide, culminating in President Hosni MUBARAK's ouster in 2011. Egypt's military assumed national leadership until a new legislature was in place in early 2012; later that same year, Muhammad MURSI won the presidential election. Following protests throughout the spring of 2013 against MURSI's government and the Muslim Brotherhood, the Egyptian Armed Forces intervened and removed MURSI from power in July 2013 and replaced him with interim president Adly MANSOUR. Simultaneously, the government began enacting laws to limit freedoms of assembly and expression. In January 2014, voters approved a new constitution by referendum and in May 2014 elected former defense minister Abdelfattah ELSISI president. Egypt elected a new legislature in December 2015, its first House of Representatives since 2012. ELSISI was reelected to a second four-year term in March 2018. In April 2019, Egypt approved via national referendum a set of constitutional amendments extending ELSISI's term in office through 2024 and possibly through 2030 if reelected for a third term. The amendments would also allow future presidents up to two consecutive six-year terms in office, reestablish an upper legislative house, allow for one or more vice presidents, establish a 25% quota for female legislators, reaffirm the military's role as guardian of Egypt, and expand presidential authority to appoint the heads of judicial councils. Successful legislative elections were held in October-November 2020, having been delayed for six months.

GEOGRAPHY

Location: Northern Africa, bordering the Mediterranean Sea, between Libya and the Gaza Strip, and the Red Sea north of Sudan, and includes the Asian Sinai Peninsula

Geographic coordinates: 27 00 N, 30 00 E

Map references: Africa

Area: *total:* 1,001,450 sq km
land: 995,450 sq km
water: 6,000 sq km
country comparison to the world: 31

Area - comparative: more than eight times the size of Ohio; slightly more than three times the size of New Mexico

Land boundaries: *total:* 2,612 km
border countries (4): Gaza Strip 13 km; Israel 208 km; Libya 1,115 km; Sudan 1,276 km

Coastline: 2,450 km

Maritime claims: *territorial sea:* 12 nm
contiguous zone: 24 nm
exclusive economic zone: 200 nm or the equidistant median line with Cyprus
continental shelf: 200 nm

Climate: desert; hot, dry summers with moderate winters

Terrain: vast desert plateau interrupted by Nile valley and delta

Elevation: *highest point:* Mount Catherine 2,629 m
lowest point: Qattara Depression -133 m
mean elevation: 321 m

Natural resources: petroleum, natural gas, iron ore, phosphates, manganese, limestone, gypsum, talc, asbestos, lead, rare earth elements, zinc

Land use: *agricultural land:* 3.6% (2018 est.)
arable land: 2.8% (2018 est.)
permanent crops: 0.8% (2018 est.)
permanent pasture: 0% (2018 est.)
forest: 0.1% (2018 est.)
other: 96.3% (2018 est.)

Irrigated land: 36,500 sq km (2012)

Major lakes (area sq km): *salt water lake(s):* Lake Manzala - 1,360 sq km
note - largest of Nile Delta lakes

Major rivers (by length in km): Nile river mouth (shared with Rwanda [s], Tanzania, Uganda, South Sudan, and Sudan) - 6,650 km

note – [s] after country name indicates river source; [m] after country name indicates river mouth

Major watersheds (area sq km): Atlantic Ocean drainage: *(Mediterranean Sea)* Nile (3,254,853 sq km)

Major aquifers: Nubian Aquifer System

Population distribution: approximately 95% of the population lives within 20 km of the Nile River and its delta; vast areas of the country remain sparsely populated or uninhabited as shown in this population distribution map

Natural hazards: periodic droughts; frequent earthquakes; flash floods; landslides; hot, driving windstorms called khamsin occur in spring; dust storms; sandstorms

Geography - note: *note:* controls Sinai Peninsula, the only land bridge between Africa and remainder of Eastern Hemisphere; controls Suez Canal, a sea link between Indian Ocean and Mediterranean Sea; size, and juxtaposition to Israel, establish its major role in Middle Eastern geopolitics; dependence on upstream neighbors; dominance of Nile basin issues; prone to influxes of refugees from Sudan and the Palestinian territories

PEOPLE AND SOCIETY

Population: 107,770,524 (2022 est.)
country comparison to the world: 15

Nationality: *noun:* Egyptian(s)
adjective: Egyptian

Ethnic groups: Egyptian 99.7%, other 0.3% (2006 est.)
note: data represent respondents by nationality

Languages: Arabic (official), English, and French widely understood by educated classes
major-language sample(s):
كتاب حقائق العالم، أفضل مصدر للمعلومات الأساسية (Arabic)

Religions: Muslim (predominantly Sunni) 90%, Christian (majority Coptic Orthodox, other Christians include Armenian Apostolic, Catholic, Maronite, Orthodox, and Anglican) 10%

Demographic profile: Egypt is the most populous country in the Arab world and the third most populous country in Africa, behind Nigeria and Ethiopia. Most of the country is desert, so about 95% of the population is concentrated in a narrow strip of fertile land along the Nile River, which represents only about 5% of Egypt's land area. Egypt's rapid population growth – 46% between 1994 and 2014 – stresses limited natural resources, jobs, housing, sanitation, education, and health care.

Although the country's total fertility rate (TFR) fell from roughly 5.5 children per woman in 1980 to just over 3 in the late 1990s, largely as a result of state-sponsored family planning programs, the population growth rate dropped more modestly because of decreased mortality rates and longer life expectancies. During the last decade, Egypt's TFR decline stalled for several years and then reversed, reaching 3.6 in 2011, and has plateaued the last few years. Contraceptive use has held steady at about 60%, while preferences for larger families and early marriage may have strengthened in the wake of the recent 2011 revolution. The large cohort of women of or nearing childbearing age will sustain high population growth for the foreseeable future (an effect called population momentum).

Nevertheless, post-MUBARAK governments have not made curbing population growth a priority. To increase contraceptive use and to prevent further overpopulation will require greater government commitment and substantial social change, including encouraging smaller families and better educating and empowering women. Currently, literacy, educational attainment, and labor force participation rates are much lower for women than men. In addition, the prevalence of violence against women, the lack of female political representation, and the perpetuation of the nearly universal practice of female genital cutting continue to keep women from playing a more significant role in Egypt's public sphere.

Population pressure, poverty, high unemployment, and the fragmentation of inherited land holdings have historically motivated Egyptians, primarily young men, to migrate internally from rural and smaller urban areas in the Nile Delta region and the poorer rural south to Cairo, Alexandria, and other urban centers in the north, while a much smaller number migrated to the Red Sea and Sinai areas. Waves of forced internal migration also resulted from the 1967 Arab-Israeli War and the floods caused by the completion of the Aswan High Dam in 1970. Limited numbers of students and professionals emigrated temporarily prior to the early 1970s, when economic problems and high unemployment pushed the Egyptian Government to lift restrictions on labor migration. At the same time, high oil revenues enabled Saudi Arabia, Iraq, and other Gulf states, as well as Libya and Jordan, to fund development projects, creating a demand for unskilled labor (mainly in construction), which attracted tens of thousands of young Egyptian men.

Between 1970 and 1974 alone, Egyptian migrants in the Gulf countries increased from approximately 70,000 to 370,000. Egyptian officials encouraged legal labor migration both to alleviate unemployment and to generate remittance income (remittances continue to be one of Egypt's largest sources of foreign currency and GDP). During the mid-1980s, however, depressed oil prices resulting from the Iran-Iraq War, decreased demand for low-skilled labor, competition from less costly South Asian workers, and efforts to replace foreign workers with locals significantly reduced Egyptian migration to the Gulf States. The number of Egyptian migrants dropped from a peak of almost 3.3 million in 1983 to about 2.2 million at the start of the 1990s, but numbers gradually recovered.

In the 2000s, Egypt began facilitating more labor migration through bilateral agreements, notably with Arab countries and Italy, but illegal migration to Europe through overstayed visas or maritime human smuggling via Libya also rose. The Egyptian Government estimated there were 6.5 million Egyptian migrants in 2009, with roughly 75% being temporary migrants in other Arab countries (Libya, Saudi Arabia, Jordan, Kuwait, and the United Arab Emirates) and 25% being predominantly permanent migrants in the West (US, UK, Italy, France, and Canada).

During the 2000s, Egypt became an increasingly important transit and destination country for economic migrants and asylum seekers, including Palestinians, East Africans, and South Asians and, more recently, Iraqis and Syrians. Egypt draws many refugees because of its resettlement programs with the West; Cairo has one of the largest urban refugee populations in the world. Many East African migrants are interned or live in temporary encampments along the Egypt-Israel border, and some have been shot and killed by Egyptian border guards.

Age structure: *0-14 years:* 33.62% (male 18,112,550/female 16,889,155)
15-24 years: 18.01% (male 9,684,437/female 9,071,163)
25-54 years: 37.85% (male 20,032,310/female 19,376,847)
55-64 years: 6.08% (male 3,160,438/female 3,172,544)
65 years and over: 4.44% (male 2,213,539/female 2,411,457) (2020 est.)

Dependency ratios: *total dependency ratio:* 64.6
youth dependency ratio: 55.8
elderly dependency ratio: 8.8
potential support ratio: 11.4 (2020 est.)

Median age: *total:* 24.1 years
male: 23.8 years
female: 24.5 years (2020 est.)
country comparison to the world: 166

Population growth rate: 1.68% (2022 est.)
country comparison to the world: 56

Birth rate: 21.46 births/1,000 population (2022 est.)
country comparison to the world: 63

Death rate: 4.32 deaths/1,000 population (2022 est.)
country comparison to the world: 208

Net migration rate: -0.31 migrant(s)/1,000 population (2022 est.)
country comparison to the world: 120

Population distribution: approximately 95% of the population lives within 20 km of the Nile River and its delta; vast areas of the country remain sparsely populated or uninhabited as shown in this population distribution map

Urbanization: *urban population:* 43% of total population (2022)
rate of urbanization: 1.9% annual rate of change (2020-25 est.)

Major urban areas - population: 21.750 million CAIRO (capital), 5.484 million Alexandria, 764,000 Bur Sa'id (2022)

Sex ratio: *at birth:* 1.06 male(s)/female
0-14 years: 1.06 male(s)/female
15-24 years: 1.06 male(s)/female
25-54 years: 1.06 male(s)/female
55-64 years: 1.08 male(s)/female
65 years and over: 0.89 male(s)/female
total population: 1.06 male(s)/female (2022 est.)

Mother's mean age at first birth: 22.6 years (2014 est.)
note: data represents median age at first birth among women 25-49

Maternal mortality ratio: 37 deaths/100,000 live births (2017 est.)
country comparison to the world: 102

Infant mortality rate: *total:* 17.7 deaths/1,000 live births
male: 18.69 deaths/1,000 live births
female: 16.64 deaths/1,000 live births (2022 est.)
country comparison to the world: 93

Life expectancy at birth: *total population:* 74.45 years
male: 73.26 years
female: 75.72 years (2022 est.)
country comparison to the world: 136

Total fertility rate: 2.88 children born/woman (2022 est.)
country comparison to the world: 52

Contraceptive prevalence rate: 58.5% (2014)

Drinking water source: *improved: urban:* 99.7% of population
rural: 99.7% of population
total: 99.7% of population
unimproved: urban: 0.3% of population
rural: 0.3% of population
total: 0.3% of population (2020 est.)

Current health expenditure: 4.7% of GDP (2019)

Physicians density: 0.75 physicians/1,000 population (2019)

Hospital bed density: 1.4 beds/1,000 population (2017)

Sanitation facility access: *improved: urban:* 99.9% of population
rural: 98.2% of population
total: 98.9% of population
unimproved: urban: 0.1% of population
rural: 1.8% of population
total: 1.1% of population (2020 est.)

HIV/AIDS - adult prevalence rate: (2020 est.) <.1%

Major infectious diseases: *degree of risk:* intermediate (2020)
food or waterborne diseases: bacterial diarrhea, hepatitis A, and typhoid fever
water contact diseases: schistosomiasis

Obesity - adult prevalence rate: 32% (2016)
country comparison to the world: 18

Alcohol consumption per capita: *total:* 0.14 liters of pure alcohol (2019 est.)
beer: 0.09 liters of pure alcohol (2019 est.)
wine: 0.01 liters of pure alcohol (2019 est.)
spirits: 0.04 liters of pure alcohol (2019 est.)
other alcohols: 0 liters of pure alcohol (2019 est.)
country comparison to the world: 175

Tobacco use: *total:* 24.3% (2020 est.)
male: 48.1% (2020 est.)
female: 0.4% (2020 est.)
country comparison to the world: 54

Children under the age of 5 years underweight: 7% (2014)
country comparison to the world: 68

Education expenditures: 3.9% of GDP (2015 est.)
country comparison to the world: 108

Literacy: *definition:* age 15 and over can read and write
total population: 71.2%
male: 76.5%
female: 65.5% (2017)

School life expectancy (primary to tertiary education): *total:* 14 years
male: 14 years
female: 14 years (2018)

Unemployment, youth ages 15-24: *total:* 19.2%
male: 12.2%
female: 49.3% (2019 est.)

ENVIRONMENT

Environment - current issues: agricultural land being lost to urbanization and windblown sands; increasing soil salination below Aswan High Dam; desertification; oil pollution threatening coral reefs, beaches, and marine habitats; other water pollution from agricultural pesticides, raw sewage, and industrial effluents; limited natural freshwater resources away from the Nile, which is the only perennial water source; rapid growth in population overstraining the Nile and natural resources

Environment - international agreements: *party to:* Biodiversity, Climate Change, Climate Change-Kyoto Protocol, Climate Change-Paris Agreement, Desertification, Endangered Species, Environmental Modification, Hazardous Wastes, Law of the Sea, Marine Dumping- London Convention, Marine Dumping-London Protocol, Nuclear Test Ban, Ozone Layer Protection, Ship Pollution, Wetlands
signed, but not ratified: Comprehensive Nuclear Test Ban

Air pollutants: *particulate matter emissions:* 79.28 micrograms per cubic meter (2016 est.)
carbon dioxide emissions: 238.56 megatons (2016 est.)
methane emissions: 59.68 megatons (2020 est.)

Climate: desert; hot, dry summers with moderate winters

Land use: *agricultural land:* 3.6% (2018 est.)
arable land: 2.8% (2018 est.)
permanent crops: 0.8% (2018 est.)
permanent pasture: 0% (2018 est.)
forest: 0.1% (2018 est.)
other: 96.3% (2018 est.)

Urbanization: *urban population:* 43% of total population (2022)
rate of urbanization: 1.9% annual rate of change (2020-25 est.)

Revenue from forest resources: *forest revenues:* 0.15% of GDP (2018 est.)
country comparison to the world: 100

Waste and recycling: *municipal solid waste generated annually:* 21 million tons (2012 est.)
municipal solid waste recycled annually: 2.625 million tons (2013 est.)
percent of municipal solid waste recycled: 12.5% (2013 est.)

Major lakes (area sq km): *salt water lake(s):* Lake Manzala - 1,360 sq km
note - largest of Nile Delta lakes

Major rivers (by length in km): Nile river mouth (shared with Rwanda [s], Tanzania, Uganda, South Sudan, and Sudan) - 6,650 km
note – [s] after country name indicates river source; [m] after country name indicates river mouth

Major watersheds (area sq km): Atlantic Ocean drainage: *(Mediterranean Sea)* Nile (3,254,853 sq km)

Major aquifers: Nubian Aquifer System

Total water withdrawal: *municipal:* 10.75 billion cubic meters (2017 est.)
industrial: 5.4 billion cubic meters (2017 est.)
agricultural: 61.35 billion cubic meters (2017 est.)

Total renewable water resources: 57.5 billion cubic meters (2017 est.)

GOVERNMENT

Country name: *conventional long form:* Arab Republic of Egypt
conventional short form: Egypt
local long form: Jumhuriyat Misr al-Arabiyah
local short form: Misr
former: United Arab Republic (with Syria)
etymology: the English name "Egypt" derives from the ancient Greek name for the country "Aigyptos"; the Arabic name "Misr" can be traced to the ancient Akkadian "misru" meaning border or frontier

Government type: presidential republic

Capital: *name:* Cairo
geographic coordinates: 30 03 N, 31 15 E
time difference: UTC+2 (7 hours ahead of Washington, DC, during Standard Time)
etymology: from the Arabic "al-Qahira," meaning "the victorious"

Administrative divisions: 27 governorates (muhafazat, singular - muhafazat); Ad Daqahliyah, Al Bahr al Ahmar (Red Sea), Al Buhayrah, Al Fayyum, Al Gharbiyah, Al Iskandariyah (Alexandria), Al Isma'iliyah (Ismailia), Al Jizah (Giza), Al Minufiyah, Al Minya, Al Qahirah (Cairo), Al Qalyubiyah, Al Uqsur (Luxor), Al Wadi al Jadid (New Valley), As Suways (Suez), Ash Sharqiyah, Aswan, Asyut, Bani Suwayf, Bur Sa'id (Port Said), Dumyat (Damietta), Janub Sina' (South Sinai), Kafr ash Shaykh, Matruh, Qina, Shamal Sina' (North Sinai), Suhaj

Independence: 28 February 1922 (from UK protectorate status; the military-led revolution that began on 23 July 1952 led to a republic being declared on 18 June 1953 and all British troops withdrawn on 18 June 1956); note - it was ca. 3200 B.C. that the Two Lands of Upper (southern) and Lower (northern) Egypt were first united politically

National holiday: Revolution Day, 23 July (1952)

Constitution: *history:* several previous; latest approved by a constitutional committee in December 2013, approved by referendum held on 14-15 January 2014, ratified by interim president on 19 January 2014
amendments: proposed by the president of the republic or by one fifth of the House of Representatives members; a decision to accept the proposal requires majority vote by House members; passage of amendment requires a two-thirds majority vote by House members and passage by majority vote in a referendum; articles of reelection of the president and principles of freedom are not amendable unless the amendment "brings more guarantees;" amended 2019

Legal system: mixed legal system based on Napoleonic civil and penal law, Islamic religious law, and vestiges of colonial-era laws; judicial review of the constitutionality of laws by the Supreme Constitutional Court

International law organization participation: accepts compulsory ICJ jurisdiction with reservations; non-party state to the ICCt

Citizenship: *citizenship by birth:* no
citizenship by descent only: if the father was born in Egypt
dual citizenship recognized: only with prior permission from the government
residency requirement for naturalization: 10 years

Suffrage: 18 years of age; universal and compulsory

Executive branch: *chief of state:* President Abdelfattah ELSISI (since 8 June 2014)
head of government: Prime Minister Mostafa MADBOULY (since 7 June 2018)
cabinet: Cabinet ministers nominated by the executive branch and approved by the House of Representatives
elections/appointments: president elected by absolute majority popular vote in 2 rounds if needed for a 6-year term (eligible for 3 consecutive terms); election last held on 26-28 March 2018 (next to be held in 2024); prime minister appointed by the president, approved by the House of Representatives; note - following a constitutional amendment approved by referendum in April 2019, the presidential term was extended from 4 to 6 years and eligibility extended to 3 consecutive terms
election results:
2018: Abdelfattah ELSISI reelected president in first round; percent of valid votes cast - Abdelfattah ELSISI (independent) 97.1%, Moussa Mostafa MOUSSA (El Ghad Party) 2.9%; note - more than 7% of ballots cast were deemed invalid

Legislative branch: *description:* bicameral Parliament consists of:
Senate (Majlis Al-Shiyoukh) (300 seats; 100 members elected in single seat constituencies, 100 elected by closed party-list system, and 100 appointed by the president; note - the upper house, previously the Shura Council, was eliminated in the 2014 constitution, reestablished as the Senate, following passage in a 2019 constitutional referendum and approved by the House of Representatives in June 2020
House of Representatives (Majlis Al-Nowaab) (596 seats; 448 members directly elected by individual candidacy system, 120 members - with quotas for women, youth, Christians and workers - elected in party-list constituencies by simple majority popular vote, and 28 members appointed by the president; members of both houses serve 5-year terms
elections:
Senate - first round held on 11-12 August 2020 (9-10 August for diaspora); second round held on 8-9 September (6-7 September for diaspora) (next to be held in 2025)
House of Representatives - last held 24-25 October and 7-8 November 2020) (next to be held in 2025)
election results:
Senate - percent of vote by party - NA; seats by party - Nation's Future Party 100, independent 100; composition - men 260, women 40, percent of women 13.3%
House of Representatives (2020) - percent of vote by party - NA; seats by party - Nation's Future Party 316, Republican People's Party 50, New Wafd Party 26, Homeland Defenders Party 23, Modern Egypt Party 11, Reform and Development Party 9, Al-Nour Party 7, Egyptian Conference Party 7, Egyptian Freedom Party 7, Egyptian Social Democratic Party 7, Tagammu 6, Justice Party 2, Etradet Geel Party 1, independent 124; composition - men 428, women 164, percent of women 27.5%; note - total Parliament percent of women 22.8%

Judicial branch: *highest court(s):* Supreme Constitutional Court (SCC) (consists of the court president and 10 justices); the SCC serves as the final court of arbitration on the constitutionality of laws and conflicts between lower courts regarding jurisdiction and rulings; Court of Cassation (CC) (consists of the court president and 550 judges organized in circuits with cases heard by panels of 5 judges); the CC is the highest appeals body for civil and criminal cases, also known as "ordinary justices"; Supreme Administrative Court (SAC) (consists of the court president and NA judges and organized in circuits with cases heard by panels of 5 judges); the SAC is the highest court of the State Council
judge selection and term of office: under the 2014 constitution, all judges and justices selected

and appointed by the Supreme Judiciary Council and approved as a formality by the president of the Republic; judges appointed for life; under the 2019 amendments, the president has the power to appoint heads of judiciary authorities and courts, the prosecutor general, and the head of the Supreme Constitutional Court
subordinate courts: Courts of Appeal; Courts of First Instance; courts of limited jurisdiction; Family Court (established in 2004)

Political parties and leaders: Al-Nour [Yunis MAKHYUN]
Arab Democratic Nasserist Party [El Etehad el Masri el ARABI]
Congress Party [Omar Al-Mokhtar SEMIDA]
Conservative Party [El Mohafezin]
Democratic Peace Party [Ahmed FADALY]
Egyptian National Movement Party [Gen. Raouf EL SAYED]
Egyptian Social Democratic Party [Farid ZAHRAN]
El Ghad Party [Moussa Mostafa MOUSSA]
El Serh El Masry el Hor [Tarek Ahmed Abbas NADIM]
Eradet Geel Party [Tayseer MATAR]
Free Egyptians Party [Essam KHALIL]
Freedom Party [Mamdouuh HASSAN]
Justice Party
Homeland's Protector Party [Lt. Gen. (retired) Galal AL-HARIDI]
Modern Egypt Party [Nabil DEIBIS]
My Homeland Egypt Party [Gen. Seif El Islam ABDEL BARY]
Nation's Future Party (Mostaqbal Watan) [Abdel Wahab Abdel RAZEQ]
National Progressive Unionist (Tagammu) Party [Sayed Abdel AAL]
Reform and Development Party [Mohamad Anwar al-SADAT]
Republican People's Party [Hazim AMR]
Revolutionary Guards Party [Magdy EL-SHARIF]
Wafd Party [Abdel Sanad YAMAMA]

International organization participation: ABEDA, AfDB, AFESD, AMF, AU, BSEC (observer), CAEU, CD, CICA, COMESA, D-8, EBRD, FAO, G-15, G-24, G-77, IAEA, IBRD, ICAO, ICC (national committees), ICRM, IDA, IDB, IFAD, IFC, IFRCS, IHO, ILO, IMF, IMO, IMSO, Interpol, IOC, IOM, IPU, ISO, ITSO, ITU, LAS, LCBC (observer), MIGA, MINURSO, MINUSMA, MONUSCO, NAM, OAPEC, OAS (observer), OIC, OIF, OSCE (partner), PCA, UN, UNAMID, UNCTAD, UNESCO, UNHCR, UNIDO, UNISFA, UNMISS, UNOCI, UNRWA, UNWTO, UPU, WCO, WFTU (NGOs), WHO, WIPO, WMO, WTO

Diplomatic representation in the US: *chief of mission:* Ambassador Motaz Mounir ZAHRAN (since 17 September 2020)
chancery: 3521 International Court NW, Washington, DC 20008
telephone: [1] (202) 895-5400; [1] (202) 895-5408
FAX: [1] (202) 244-5131
email address and website:
consulate@egyptembassy.net
https://www.egyptembassy.net/
consulate(s) general: Chicago, Houston, Los Angeles, New York

Diplomatic representation from the US: *chief of mission:* Ambassador (vacant); Charge d'Affaires Daniel RUBINSTEIN (since 23 August 2022)
embassy: 5 Tawfik Diab St., Garden City, Cairo
mailing address: 7700 Cairo Place, Washington DC 20512-7700
telephone: [20-2] 2797-3300
FAX: [20-2] 2797-3200
email address and website:
ConsularCairoACS@state.gov
https://eg.usembassy.gov/
consulate(s) general: Alexandria

Flag description: three equal horizontal bands of red (top), white, and black; the national emblem (a gold Eagle of Saladin facing the hoist side with a shield superimposed on its chest above a scroll bearing the name of the country in Arabic) centered in the white band; the band colors derive from the Arab Liberation flag and represent oppression (black), overcome through bloody struggle (red), to be replaced by a bright future (white)
note: similar to the flag of Syria, which has two green stars in the white band; Iraq, which has an Arabic inscription centered in the white band; and Yemen, which has a plain white band

National symbol(s): golden eagle, white lotus; national colors: red, white, black

National anthem: *name:* "Bilady, Bilady, Bilady" (My Homeland, My Homeland, My Homeland)
lyrics/music: Younis-al QADI/Sayed DARWISH
note: adopted 1979; the current anthem, less militaristic than the previous one, was created after the signing of the 1979 peace treaty with Israel; Sayed DARWISH, commonly considered the father of modern Egyptian music, composed the anthem

National heritage: *total World Heritage Sites:* 7 (6 cultural, 1 natural)
selected World Heritage Site locales: Memphis and its Necropolis (c); Ancient Thebes with its Necropolis (c); Nubian Monuments (c); Saint Catherine Area (c); Abu Mena (c); Historic Cairo (c); Wadi Al-Hitan (Whale Valley) (n)

ECONOMY

Economic overview: Occupying the northeast corner of the African continent, Egypt is bisected by the highly fertile Nile valley where most economic activity takes place. Egypt's economy was highly centralized during the rule of former President Gamal Abdel NASSER but opened up considerably under former Presidents Anwar EL-SADAT and Mohamed Hosni MUBARAK. Agriculture, hydrocarbons, manufacturing, tourism, and other service sectors drove the country's relatively diverse economic activity.

Despite Egypt's mixed record for attracting foreign investment over the past two decades, poor living conditions and limited job opportunities have contributed to public discontent. These socioeconomic pressures were a major factor leading to the January 2011 revolution that ousted MUBARAK. The uncertain political, security, and policy environment since 2011 has restricted economic growth and failed to alleviate persistent unemployment, especially among the young.

In late 2016, persistent dollar shortages and waning aid from its Gulf allies led Cairo to turn to the IMF for a 3-year, $12 billion loan program. To secure the deal, Cairo floated its currency, introduced new taxes, and cut energy subsidies - all of which pushed inflation above 30% for most of 2017, a high that had not been seen in a generation. Since the currency float, foreign investment in Egypt's high interest treasury bills has risen exponentially, boosting both dollar availability and central bank reserves. Cairo will be challenged to obtain foreign and local investment in manufacturing and other sectors without a sustained effort to implement a range of business reforms.

Real GDP (purchasing power parity): $1,223,040,000,000 (2020 est.)
$1,180,890,000,000 (2019 est.)
$1,118,720,000,000 (2018 est.)
note: data are in 2017 dollars
country comparison to the world: 20

Real GDP growth rate: 4.2% (2017 est.)
4.3% (2016 est.)
4.4% (2015 est.)
country comparison to the world: 68

Real GDP per capita: $12,000 (2020 est.)
$11,800 (2019 est.)
$11,400 (2018 est.)
note: data are in 2017 dollars
country comparison to the world: 128

GDP (official exchange rate): $323.763 billion (2019 est.)

Inflation rate (consumer prices): 9.3% (2019 est.)
14.4% (2018 est.)
29.6% (2017 est.)
country comparison to the world: 205

Credit ratings:
Fitch rating: B+ (2019)
Moody's rating: B2 (2019)
Standard & Poors rating: B (2018)
note: The year refers to the year in which the current credit rating was first obtained.

GDP - composition, by sector of origin: *agriculture:* 11.7% (2017 est.)
industry: 34.3% (2017 est.)
services: 54% (2017 est.)

GDP - composition, by end use: *household consumption:* 86.8% (2017 est.)
government consumption: 10.1% (2017 est.)
investment in fixed capital: 14.8% (2017 est.)
investment in inventories: 0.5% (2017 est.)
exports of goods and services: 16.3% (2017 est.)
imports of goods and services: -28.5% (2017 est.)

Agricultural products: sugar cane, sugar beets, wheat, maize, tomatoes, rice, potatoes, oranges, onions, milk

Industries: textiles, food processing, tourism, chemicals, pharmaceuticals, hydrocarbons, construction, cement, metals, light manufactures

Industrial production growth rate: 3.5% (2017 est.)
country comparison to the world: 84

Labor force: 24.113 million (2020 est.)
country comparison to the world: 23

Labor force - by occupation: *agriculture:* 25.8%
industry: 25.1%
services: 49.1% (2015 est.)

Unemployment rate: 7.86% (2019 est.)
12.7% (2016 est.)
country comparison to the world: 122

Unemployment, youth ages 15-24: *total:* 19.2%
male: 12.2%
female: 49.3% (2019 est.)
country comparison to the world: 84

Population below poverty line: 32.5% (2017 est.)

Gini Index coefficient - distribution of family income: 31.5 (2017 est.)
29.8 (2012)
country comparison to the world: 143

Household income or consumption by percentage share: *lowest 10%:* 4%
highest 10%: 26.6% (2008)

Budget: *revenues:* 42.32 billion (2017 est.)
expenditures: 62.61 billion (2017 est.)

Budget surplus (+) or deficit (-): -8.6% (of GDP) (2017 est.)
country comparison to the world: 202

Public debt: 103% of GDP (2017 est.)
96.8% of GDP (2016 est.)
note: data cover central government debt and include debt instruments issued (or owned) by government entities other than the treasury; the data include treasury debt held by foreign entities; the data include debt issued by subnational entities, as well as intragovernmental debt; intragovernmental debt consists of treasury borrowings from surpluses in the social funds, such as for retirement, medical care, and unemployment; debt instruments for the social funds are sold at public auctions
country comparison to the world: 14

Taxes and other revenues: 17.9% (of GDP) (2017 est.)
country comparison to the world: 165

Fiscal year: 1 July - 30 June

Current account balance: -$8.915 billion (2019 est.)
-$7.682 billion (2018 est.)
country comparison to the world: 190

Exports: $40.1 billion (2020 est.) note: data are in current year dollars
$53.52 billion (2019 est.) note: data are in current year dollars
$51.62 billion (2018 est.) note: data are in current year dollars
country comparison to the world: 62

Exports - partners: United States 9%, United Arab Emirates 6%, Italy 6%, Turkey 6%, Saudi Arabia 6%, India 5% (2019)

Exports - commodities: crude petroleum, refined petroleum, gold, natural gas, fertilizers (2019)

Imports: $72.48 billion (2020 est.) note: data are in current year dollars
$78.95 billion (2019 est.) note: data are in current year dollars
$76.33 billion (2018 est.) note: data are in current year dollars
country comparison to the world: 47

Imports - partners: China 15%, Russia 7%, United States 6%, Saudi Arabia 6%, Germany 5%, Turkey 5% (2019)

Imports - commodities: refined petroleum, wheat, crude petroleum, cars, packaged medicines (2019)

Reserves of foreign exchange and gold: $35.89 billion (31 December 2017 est.)
$23.2 billion (31 December 2016 est.)
country comparison to the world: 47

Debt - external: $109.238 billion (2019 est.)
$92.638 billion (2018 est.)
country comparison to the world: 53

Exchange rates: Egyptian pounds (EGP) per US dollar -
15.69 (2020 est.)
16.14 (2019 est.)
17.90999 (2018 est.)
7.7133 (2014 est.)
7.08 (2013 est.)

ENERGY

Electricity access: *electrification - total population:* 100% (2020)

Electricity: *installed generating capacity:* 59.826 million kW (2020 est.)
consumption: 149,079,120,000 kWh (2019 est.)
exports: 360 million kWh (2019 est.)
imports: 74 million kWh (2019 est.)
transmission/distribution losses: 33.623 billion kWh (2019 est.)

Electricity generation sources: *fossil fuels:* 88.7% of total installed capacity (2020 est.)
solar: 1% of total installed capacity (2020 est.)
wind: 2.5% of total installed capacity (2020 est.)
hydroelectricity: 7.7% of total installed capacity (2020 est.)
biomass and waste: 0.2% of total installed capacity (2020 est.)

Coal: *production:* 262,000 metric tons (2020 est.)
consumption: 2.31 million metric tons (2020 est.)
exports: 86,000 metric tons (2020 est.)
imports: 2.134 million metric tons (2020 est.)
proven reserves: 16 million metric tons (2019 est.)

Petroleum: *total petroleum production:* 660,800 bbl/day (2021 est.)
refined petroleum consumption: 810,200 bbl/day (2019 est.)
crude oil and lease condensate exports: 204,100 bbl/day (2018 est.)
crude oil and lease condensate imports: 117,400 bbl/day (2018 est.)
crude oil estimated reserves: 3.3 billion barrels (2021 est.)

Refined petroleum products - production: 547,500 bbl/day (2015 est.)
country comparison to the world: 31

Refined petroleum products - exports: 47,360 bbl/day (2015 est.)
country comparison to the world: 56

Refined petroleum products - imports: 280,200 bbl/day (2015 est.)
country comparison to the world: 26

Natural gas: *production:* 64,292,955,000 cubic meters (2019 est.)
consumption: 58,176,781,000 cubic meters (2019 est.)
exports: 5,009,100,000 cubic meters (2019 est.)
imports: 83.563 million cubic meters (2019 est.)
proven reserves: 1,783,958,000,000 cubic meters (2021 est.)

Carbon dioxide emissions: 235.137 million metric tonnes of CO2 (2019 est.)
from coal and metallurgical coke: 8.728 million metric tonnes of CO2 (2019 est.)
from petroleum and other liquids: 112.281 million metric tonnes of CO2 (2019 est.)
from consumed natural gas: 114.128 million metric tonnes of CO2 (2019 est.)
country comparison to the world: 29

Energy consumption per capita: 40.063 million Btu/person (2019 est.)
country comparison to the world: 106

COMMUNICATIONS

Telephones - fixed lines: *total subscriptions:* 9,858,331 (2020 est.)
subscriptions per 100 inhabitants: 10 (2020 est.)
country comparison to the world: 18

Telephones - mobile cellular: *total subscriptions:* 95,357,427 (2020 est.)
subscriptions per 100 inhabitants: 93 (2020 est.)
country comparison to the world: 18

Telecommunication systems: *general assessment:* Egypt's large telecom market is supported by a population of about 108 million and benefits from effective competition in most sectors; a liberal regulatory regime allows for unified licenses which permit operators to offer fixed-line as well as mobile services; in recent years the government has developed a number of digital migration projects aimed at increasing average broadband speeds, delivering fiber broadband to about 60% of the population, developing an in-house satellite program, and creating a knowledge-based economy through the greater adoption of ICTs; the New Administrative Capital being built is only one of more than a dozen smart city projects, which together are stimulating investment in 5G and fiber broadband, as well as the adoption of IoT and AI solutions; the country endeavors to be a significant ICT hub in the North Africa and Middle East regions; Egypt's mature mobile market has one of the highest subscription rates in Africa; progress in the adoption of mobile data services has been hampered by the lack of sufficient spectrum; the regulator in September 2020 made available 60MHz in the 2.6GHz band, though the spectrum was not allocated until late 2021; the additional spectrum will go far to enabling the MNOs to improve the quality of mobile broadband services offered; further 5G trials are to be held later in 2022, focused on the New Administrative Capital; the international cable infrastructure remains an important asset for Egypt, which benefits from its geographical position; Telecom Egypt has become one of the largest concerns in this segment, being a participating member in numerous cable systems; in mid-2021 the telco announced plans to build the Hybrid African Ring Path system, connecting a number of landlocked countries in Africa with Italy, France, and Portugal; the system will partly use the company's existing terrestrial and sub sea cable networks (2022)
domestic: fixed-line roughly 10 per 100, mobile-cellular 93 per 100 (2020)
international: country code - 20; landing points for Aletar, Africa-1, FEA, Hawk, IMEWE, and the SEA-ME-WE-3 & 4 submarine cable networks linking to Asia, Africa, the Middle East, and Australia ; satellite earth stations - 4 (2 Intelsat - Atlantic Ocean and Indian Ocean, 1 Arabsat, and 1 Inmarsat); tropospheric scatter to Sudan; microwave radio relay to Israel; a participant in Medarabtel (2019)

Broadcast media: mix of state-run and private broadcast media; state-run TV operates 2 national and 6 regional terrestrial networks, as well as a few satellite channels; dozens of private satellite channels and a large number of Arabic satellite channels are available for free; some limited satellite services are also available via subscription; state-run radio operates about 30 stations belonging to 8 networks;

privately-owned radio includes 8 major stations, 4 of which belong to 1 network (2019)

Internet country code: .eg

Internet users: *total:* 73,680,770 (2020 est.)
percent of population: 72% (2020 est.)
country comparison to the world: 12

Broadband - fixed subscriptions: *total:* 9,349,469 (2020 est.)
subscriptions per 100 inhabitants: 9 (2020 est.)
country comparison to the world: 22

Communications - note: one of the largest and most famous libraries in the ancient world was the Great Library of Alexandria in Egypt (founded about 295 B.C., it may have survived in some form into the 5th century A.D.); seeking to resurrect the great center of learning and communication, the Egyptian Government in 2002 inaugurated the Bibliotheca Alexandrina, an Egyptian National Library on the site of the original Great Library, which commemorates the original archive and also serves as a center of cultural and scientific excellence

TRANSPORTATION

National air transport system: *number of registered air carriers:* 14 (2020)
inventory of registered aircraft operated by air carriers: 101
annual passenger traffic on registered air carriers: 12,340,832 (2018)
annual freight traffic on registered air carriers: 437.63 million (2018) mt-km

Civil aircraft registration country code prefix: SU

Airports: *total:* 83 (2021)
country comparison to the world: 65

Airports - with paved runways: *total:* 72
over 3,047 m: 15
2,438 to 3,047 m: 36
1,524 to 2,437 m: 15
under 914 m: 6 (2021)

Airports - with unpaved runways: *total:* 11
2,438 to 3,047 m: 1
1,524 to 2,437 m: 3
914 to 1,523 m: 4
under 914 m: 3 (2021)

Heliports: 7 (2021)

Pipelines: 486 km condensate, 74 km condensate/gas, 7,986 km gas, 957 km liquid petroleum gas, 5,225 km oil, 37 km oil/gas/water, 895 km refined products, 65 km water (2013)

Railways: *total:* 5,085 km (2014)
standard gauge: 5,085 km (2014) 1.435-m gauge (62 km electrified)
country comparison to the world: 39

Roadways: *total:* 65,050 km (2018)
paved: 48,000 km (2018)
unpaved: 17,050 km (2018)
country comparison to the world: 73

Waterways: 3,500 km (2018) (includes the Nile River, Lake Nasser, Alexandria-Cairo Waterway, and numerous smaller canals in Nile Delta; the Suez Canal (193.5 km including approaches) is navigable by oceangoing vessels drawing up to 17.68 m)
country comparison to the world: 31

Merchant marine: *total:* 421
by type: bulk carrier 14, container ship 8, general cargo 27, oil tanker 40, other 332 (2021)
country comparison to the world: 46

Ports and terminals: *major seaport(s):* Mediterranean Sea - Alexandria, Damietta, El Dekheila, Port Said
oil terminal(s): Ain Sukhna terminal, Sidi Kerir terminal
container port(s) (TEUs): Port Said (East) (3,816,084) (2019)

LNG terminal(s) (export): Damietta, Idku (Abu Qir Bay), Sumed
Gulf of Suez - Suez

MILITARY AND SECURITY

Military and security forces: Egyptian Armed Forces (EAF): Army (includes Republican Guard), Navy (includes Coast Guard), Air Force, Air Defense Command, Border Guard Forces; Interior Ministry: Public Security Sector Police, the Central Security Force, National Security Sector (2022)
note 1: the Public Security Sector Police are responsible for law enforcement nationwide; the Central Security Force protects infrastructure and is responsible for crowd control; the National Security Sector is responsible for internal security threats and counterterrorism along with other security services
note 2: in addition to its external defense duties, the EAF also has a mandate to assist police in protecting vital infrastructure during a state of emergency; military personnel were granted full arrest authority in 2011 but normally only use this authority during states of emergency and "periods of significant turmoil"

Military expenditures: 1.3% of GDP (2021 est.)
1.3% of GDP (2020)
1.3% of GDP (2019) (approximately $15.8 billion)
1.4% of GDP (2018) (approximately $15.9 billion)
1.6% of GDP (2017) (approximately $16.7 billion)
country comparison to the world: 104

Military and security service personnel strengths: information varies; approximately 450,000 active duty personnel (325,000 Army; 18,000 Navy; 30,000 Air Force; 75,000 Air Defense Command); approximately 300,000 Central Security Forces personnel (2022)

Military equipment inventories and acquisitions: the EAF's inventory is comprised of a mix of domestically produced, imported Soviet-era, and more modern, particularly Western, weapons systems; in recent years, the EAF has embarked on an extensive equipment modernization program with major purchases from a variety of suppliers; since 2010, the leading suppliers of military hardware to Egypt have been France, Russia, and the US; Egypt has an established defense industry that produces a range of products from small arms to armored vehicles and naval vessels; it also has licensed and co-production agreements with several countries, including the US (2022)

Military service age and obligation: voluntary enlistment possible from age 16 for men and women; 18-30 years of age for conscript service for men; service obligation 14-36 months, followed by a 9-year reserve obligation; active service length depends on education; high school drop-outs serve for the full 36 months, while college graduates serve for lesser periods of time, depending on their education (2022)
note: as of 2020, conscripts were estimated to comprise over half of the military, as well as a considerable portion of the Central Security Force

Military deployments: 1,000 Central African Republic (MINUSCA); 1,075 Mali (MINUSMA) (May 2022)

Military - note: since 2011, the Egyptian Armed Forces, police, and other security forces have been actively engaged in counterinsurgency and counter-terrorism operations in the North Sinai governorate against several militant groups, particularly the Islamic State of Iraq and ash-Sham – Sinai Province; as of 2022, Egypt had tens of thousands of military troops, police, and other security personnel deployed in the Sinai for internal security duties; in addition, tribal militias were assisting Egyptian security forces

the military has a large stake in the civilian economy, including running banks, businesses, gas stations, shipping lines, and utilities, and producing consumer and industrial goods, importing commodities, and building and managing infrastructure projects, such as bridges, roads, hospitals, and housing; the various enterprises are reportedly profitable enough to make the armed forces largely self-funded

Egypt has Major Non-NATO Ally (MNNA) status with the US; MNNA is a designation under US law that provides foreign partners with certain benefits in the areas of defense trade and security cooperation; while MNNA status provides military and economic privileges, it does not entail any security commitments

the Multinational Force & Observers (MFO) has operated in the Sinai since 1982 as a peacekeeping and monitoring force to supervise the implementation of the security provisions of the 1979 Egyptian-Israeli Treaty of Peace; the MFO is an independent international organization, created by agreement between Egypt and Israel; as of 2022, it was composed of about 1,150 troops from 13 countries; Colombia, Fiji, and the US were the leading providers of troops to the MFO (2022)

TERRORISM

Terrorist group(s): Army of Islam; Islamic State of Iraq and ash-Sham – Sinai Province (ISIS-SP); al-Qa'ida

TRANSNATIONAL ISSUES

Disputes - international: Sudan claims but Egypt de facto administers security and economic development of Halaib region north of the 22nd parallel boundary; Egypt no longer shows its administration of the Bir Tawil trapezoid in Sudan on its maps; Gazan breaches in the security wall with Egypt in January 2008 highlight difficulties in monitoring the Sinai border

Refugees and internally displaced persons: *refugees (country of origin):* 70,022 (West Bank and Gaza Strip) (mid-year 2021); 144,683 (Syria), 52,446 (Sudan) (refugees and asylum seekers), 20,970 (South Sudan) (refugees and asylum seekers), 21,105 (Eritrea) (refugees and asylum seekers), 15,585 (Ethiopia) (refugees and asylum seekers), 10,025 (Yemen) (refugees and asylum seekers), 6,815 (Iraq) (refugees and asylum seekers), 6,802 (Somalia) (refugees and asylum seekers) (2022)
stateless persons: 7 (mid-year 2021)

Illicit drugs: major source of precursor chemicals used in the production of illicit narcotics

EL SALVADOR

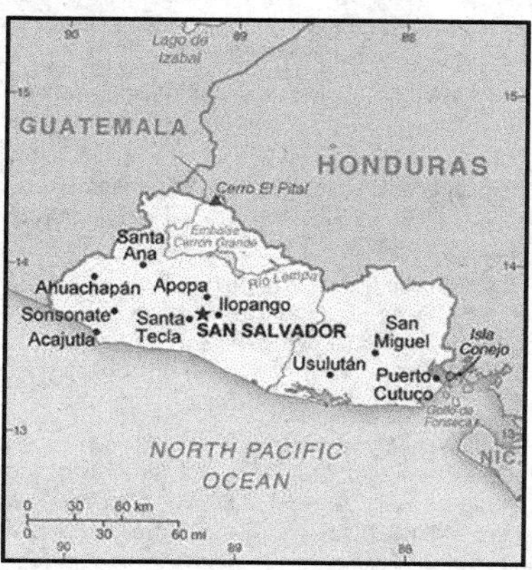

INTRODUCTION

Background: El Salvador achieved independence from Spain in 1821 and from the Central American Federation in 1839. A 12-year civil war, which cost about 75,000 lives, was brought to a close in 1992 when the government and leftist rebels signed a treaty that provided for military and political reforms. El Salvador is beset by one of the world's highest homicide rates and pervasive criminal gangs.

GEOGRAPHY

Location: Central America, bordering the North Pacific Ocean, between Guatemala and Honduras

Geographic coordinates: 13 50 N, 88 55 W

Map references: Central America and the Caribbean

Area: *total:* 21,041 sq km
land: 20,721 sq km
water: 320 sq km
country comparison to the world: 153

Area - comparative: about the same size as New Jersey

Land boundaries: *total:* 590 km
border countries (2): Guatemala 199 km; Honduras 391 km

Coastline: 307 km

Maritime claims: *territorial sea:* 12 nm
contiguous zone: 24 nm
exclusive economic zone: 200 nm

Climate: tropical; rainy season (May to October); dry season (November to April); tropical on coast; temperate in uplands

Terrain: mostly mountains with narrow coastal belt and central plateau

Elevation: *highest point:* Cerro El Pital 2,730 m
lowest point: Pacific Ocean 0 m
mean elevation: 442 m

Natural resources: hydropower, geothermal power, petroleum, arable land

Land use: *agricultural land:* 74.7% (2018 est.)
arable land: 33.1% (2018 est.)
permanent crops: 10.9% (2018 est.)
permanent pasture: 30.7% (2018 est.)
forest: 13.6% (2018 est.)
other: 11.7% (2018 est.)

Irrigated land: 452 sq km (2012)

Population distribution: athough it is the smallest country in land area in Central America, El Salvador has a population that is 18 times larger than Belize; at least 20% of the population lives abroad; high population density country-wide, with particular concentration around the capital of San Salvador

Natural hazards: known as the Land of Volcanoes; frequent and sometimes destructive earthquakes and volcanic activity; extremely susceptible to hurricanes
volcanism: significant volcanic activity; San Salvador (1,893 m), which last erupted in 1917, has the potential to cause major harm to the country's capital, which lies just below the volcano's slopes; San Miguel (2,130 m), which last erupted in 2002, is one of the most active volcanoes in the country; other historically active volcanoes include Conchaguita, Ilopango, Izalco, and Santa Ana

Geography - note: smallest Central American country and only one without a coastline on the Caribbean Sea

PEOPLE AND SOCIETY

Population: 6,568,745 (2022 est.)
country comparison to the world: 109

Nationality: *noun:* Salvadoran(s)
adjective: Salvadoran

Ethnic groups: Mestizo 86.3%, White 12.7%, Amerindian 0.2% (includes Lenca, Kakawira, Nahua-Pipil), Black 0.1%, other 0.6% (2007 est.)

Languages: Spanish (official), Nawat (among some Amerindians)
major-language sample(s):
La Libreta Informativa del Mundo, la fuente indispensable de información básica. (Spanish)

Religions: Roman Catholic 50%, Protestant 36%, other 2%, none 12% (2014 est.)

Demographic profile: El Salvador is the smallest and most densely populated country in Central America. It is well into its demographic transition, experiencing slower population growth, a decline in its number of youths, and the gradual aging of its population. The increased use of family planning has substantially lowered El Salvador's fertility rate, from approximately 6 children per woman in the 1970s to replacement level today. A 2008 national family planning survey showed that female sterilization remained the most common contraception method in El Salvador - its sterilization rate is among the highest in Latin America and the Caribbean - but that the use of injectable contraceptives is growing. Fertility differences between rich and poor and urban and rural women are narrowing.

Salvadorans fled during the 1979 to 1992 civil war mainly to the United States but also to Canada and to neighboring Mexico, Guatemala, Honduras, Nicaragua, and Costa Rica. Emigration to the United States increased again in the 1990s and 2000s as a result of deteriorating economic conditions, natural disasters (Hurricane Mitch in 1998 and earthquakes in 2001), and family reunification. At least 20% of El Salvador's population lives abroad. The remittances they send home account for close to 20% of GDP, are the second largest source of external income after exports, and have helped reduce poverty.

Age structure: *0-14 years:* 25.83% (male 857,003/female 817,336)
15-24 years: 18.82% (male 619,368/female 600,501)
25-54 years: 40.51% (male 1,221,545/female 1,404,163)
55-64 years: 7.23% (male 198,029/female 270,461)
65 years and over: 7.6% (male 214,717/female 277,979) (2020 est.)

Dependency ratios: *total dependency ratio:* 54.4
youth dependency ratio: 41.1
elderly dependency ratio: 13.4
potential support ratio: 7.5 (2020 est.)

Median age: *total:* 27.7 years
male: 26.2 years
female: 29.3 years (2020 est.)
country comparison to the world: 145

Population growth rate: 0.57% (2022 est.)
country comparison to the world: 149

Birth rate: 17.87 births/1,000 population (2022 est.)
country comparison to the world: 84

Death rate: 5.91 deaths/1,000 population (2022 est.)
country comparison to the world: 163

Net migration rate: -6.29 migrant(s)/1,000 population (2022 est.)
country comparison to the world: 211

Population distribution: athough it is the smallest country in land area in Central America, El Salvador has a population that is 18 times larger than Belize; at least 20% of the population lives abroad; high population density country-wide, with particular concentration around the capital of San Salvador

Urbanization: *urban population:* 74.8% of total population (2022)
rate of urbanization: 1.33% annual rate of change (2020-25 est.)

Major urban areas - population: 1.111 million SAN SALVADOR (capital) (2022)

Sex ratio: *at birth:* 1.05 male(s)/female
0-14 years: 1.05 male(s)/female
15-24 years: 1.03 male(s)/female
25-54 years: 0.87 male(s)/female
55-64 years: 0.72 male(s)/female
65 years and over: 0.68 male(s)/female
total population: 0.92 male(s)/female (2022 est.)

Mother's mean age at first birth: 20.8 years (2008 est.)
note: data represents median age at first birth among women 25-29

Maternal mortality ratio: 46 deaths/100,000 live births (2017 est.)
country comparison to the world: 95

Infant mortality rate: *total:* 12.14 deaths/1,000 live births
male: 13.79 deaths/1,000 live births
female: 10.41 deaths/1,000 live births (2022 est.)
country comparison to the world: 116

Life expectancy at birth: *total population:* 75.37 years
male: 71.88 years
female: 79.04 years (2022 est.)
country comparison to the world: 123

Total fertility rate: 2.05 children born/woman (2022 est.)
country comparison to the world: 99

Contraceptive prevalence rate: 71.9% (2014)

Drinking water source: *improved: urban:* 99.6% of population
rural: 94.2% of population
total: 98.2% of population
unimproved: urban: 0.4% of population
rural: 5.8% of population
total: 1.8% of population (2020 est.)

Current health expenditure: 7.2% of GDP (2019)

Physicians density: 2.87 physicians/1,000 population (2018)

Hospital bed density: 1.2 beds/1,000 population (2017)

Sanitation facility access: *improved: urban:* 100% of population
rural: 97.1% of population
total: 99.2% of population
unimproved: urban: 0% of population
rural: 2.9% of population
total: 0.8% of population (2020 est.)

HIV/AIDS - adult prevalence rate: 0.5% (2020 est.)
country comparison to the world: 65

Major infectious diseases: *degree of risk:* high (2020)
food or waterborne diseases: bacterial and protozoal diarrhea
vectorborne diseases: dengue fever

Obesity - adult prevalence rate: 24.6% (2016)
country comparison to the world: 57

Alcohol consumption per capita: *total:* 2.94 liters of pure alcohol (2019 est.)
beer: 1.5 liters of pure alcohol (2019 est.)
wine: 0.06 liters of pure alcohol (2019 est.)
spirits: 1.37 liters of pure alcohol (2019 est.)
other alcohols: 0 liters of pure alcohol (2019 est.)
country comparison to the world: 116

Tobacco use: *total:* 7.9% (2020 est.)
male: 14.1% (2020 est.)
female: 1.7% (2020 est.)
country comparison to the world: 151

Children under the age of 5 years underweight: 5% (2014)
country comparison to the world: 77

Education expenditures: 3.4% of GDP (2019 est.)
country comparison to the world: 129

Literacy: *definition:* age 15 and over can read and write
total population: 89.1%
male: 91.3%
female: 87.3% (2019)

School life expectancy (primary to tertiary education): *total:* 12 years
male: 12 years
female: 12 years (2018)

Unemployment, youth ages 15-24: *total:* 10%
male: 8.3%
female: 12.8% (2019)

ENVIRONMENT

Environment - current issues: deforestation; soil erosion; water pollution; contamination of soils from disposal of toxic wastes

Environment - international agreements: *party to:* Biodiversity, Climate Change, Climate Change-Kyoto Protocol, Climate Change-Paris Agreement, Comprehensive Nuclear Test Ban, Desertification, Endangered Species, Hazardous Wastes, Nuclear Test Ban, Ozone Layer Protection, Ship Pollution, Wetlands
signed, but not ratified: Law of the Sea

Air pollutants: *particulate matter emissions:* 23.42 micrograms per cubic meter (2016 est.)
carbon dioxide emissions: 7.17 megatons (2016 est.)
methane emissions: 4.71 megatons (2020 est.)

Climate: tropical; rainy season (May to October); dry season (November to April); tropical on coast; temperate in uplands

Land use: *agricultural land:* 74.7% (2018 est.)
arable land: 33.1% (2018 est.)
permanent crops: 10.9% (2018 est.)
permanent pasture: 30.7% (2018 est.)
forest: 13.6% (2018 est.)
other: 11.7% (2018 est.)

Urbanization: *urban population:* 74.8% of total population (2022)
rate of urbanization: 1.33% annual rate of change (2020-25 est.)

Revenue from forest resources: *forest revenues:* 0.6% of GDP (2018 est.)
country comparison to the world: 62

Revenue from coal: *coal revenues:* 0% of GDP (2018 est.)
country comparison to the world: 93

Waste and recycling: *municipal solid waste generated annually:* 1,648,996 tons (2010 est.)

Total water withdrawal: *municipal:* 474 million cubic meters (2017 est.)
industrial: 213 million cubic meters (2017 est.)
agricultural: 1.431 billion cubic meters (2017 est.)

Total renewable water resources: 26.27 billion cubic meters (2017 est.)

GOVERNMENT

Country name: *conventional long form:* Republic of El Salvador
conventional short form: El Salvador
local long form: Republica de El Salvador
local short form: El Salvador
etymology: name is an abbreviation of the original Spanish conquistador designation for the area "Provincia de Nuestro Senor Jesus Cristo, el Salvador del Mundo" (Province of Our Lord Jesus Christ, the Saviour of the World), which became simply "El Salvador" (The Savior)

Government type: presidential republic

Capital: *name:* San Salvador
geographic coordinates: 13 42 N, 89 12 W
time difference: UTC-6 (1 hour behind Washington, DC, during Standard Time)
etymology: Spanish for "Holy Savior" (referring to Jesus Christ)

Administrative divisions: 14 departments (departamentos, singular - departamento); Ahuachapan, Cabanas, Chalatenango, Cuscatlan, La Libertad, La Paz, La Union, Morazan, San Miguel, San Salvador, San Vicente, Santa Ana, Sonsonate, Usulutan

Independence: 15 September 1821 (from Spain)

National holiday: Independence Day, 15 September (1821)

Constitution: *history:* many previous; latest drafted 16 December 1983, enacted 23 December 1983
amendments: proposals require agreement by absolute majority of the Legislative Assembly membership; passage requires at least two-thirds majority vote of the Assembly; constitutional articles on basic principles, and citizen rights and freedoms cannot be amended; amended 2003, 2009, 2014

Legal system: civil law system with minor common law influence; judicial review of legislative acts in the Supreme Court

International law organization participation: has not submitted an ICJ jurisdiction declaration; non-party state to the ICCt

Citizenship: *citizenship by birth:* yes
citizenship by descent only: yes
dual citizenship recognized: yes
residency requirement for naturalization: 5 years

Suffrage: 18 years of age; universal

Executive branch: *chief of state:* President Nayib Armando BUKELE Ortez (since 1 June 2019); Vice President Felix Augusto Antonio ULLOA Garay (since 1 June 2019); note - the president is both chief of state and head of government
head of government: President Nayib Armando BUKELE Ortez (since 1 June 2019); Vice President Felix Augusto Antonio ULLOA Garay (since 1 June 2019)
cabinet: Council of Ministers selected by the president
elections/appointments: president and vice president directly elected on the same ballot by absolute majority popular vote in 2 rounds if needed for a single 5-year term; election last held on 3 February 2019 (next to be held on February 2024)
election results:
2019: Nayib Armando BUKELE Ortez elected president - Nayib Armando BUKELE Ortez (GANA) 53.1%, Carlos CALLEJA Hakker (ARENA) 31.72%, Hugo MARTINEZ (FMLN) 14.41%, other 0.77%
2014: Salvador SANCHEZ CEREN elected president in second round; percent of vote in first round - Salvador SANCHEZ CEREN (FMLN) 48.9%, Norman QUIJANO (ARENA) 39%, Antonio SACA (CN) 11.4%, other 0.7%; percent of vote in second round - Salvador SANCHEZ CEREN 50.1%, Norman QUIJANO 49.9%

Legislative branch: *description:* unicameral Legislative Assembly or Asamblea Legislativa (84 seats; members directly elected in multi-seat constituencies and a single nationwide constituency by proportional representation vote to serve 3-year terms)
elections:
last held on 28 February 2021 (next to be held in 2024)
election results:
percent of vote by party - NI 66.46%, ARENA 12.18%, FMLN 6.91%, GANA 5.29%, PCN 4.08%, NT 1.7%, PDC 1.7%, V 1.01%; seats by party - NI 56, ARENA 14, GANA 5, FMLN 4, PCN 2, PDC 1, NT 1, V 1; composition - men 61, women 23, percent of women 27.4%

Judicial branch: *highest court(s):* Supreme Court or Corte Suprema de Justicia (consists of 15 judges, including its president, and 15 substitute judges organized into Constitutional, Civil, Penal, and Administrative Conflict Chambers)
judge selection and term of office: judges elected by the Legislative Assembly on the recommendation of both the National Council of the Judicature, an independent body elected by the Legislative Assembly,

and the Bar Association; judges elected for 9-year terms, with renewal of one-third of membership every 3 years; consecutive reelection is allowed
subordinate courts: Appellate Courts; Courts of First Instance; Courts of Peace

Political parties and leaders: Christian Democratic Party or PDC [Reynaldo CARBALLO]
Farabundo Marti National Liberation Front or FMLN [Oscar ORTIZ]
Great Alliance for National Unity or GANA [Nelson GUARDADO]
National Coalition Party or PCN [Manuel RODRIGUEZ]
Nationalist Republican Alliance or ARENA [Erick SALGUERO]
New Ideas (Nuevas Ideas) or NI [Xavier Zablah BUKELE]
Our Time (Nuestro Tiempo) or NT [Juan VALIENTE]
Vamos or V [Josue ALVARADO Flores]

International organization participation: BCIE, CACM, CD, CELAC, FAO, G-11, G-77, IADB, IAEA, IBRD, ICAO, ICC (national committees), ICRM, IDA, IFAD, IFC, IFRCS, ILO, IMF, IMO, Interpol, IOC, IOM, IPU, ISO (correspondent), ITSO, ITU, ITUC (NGOs), LAES, LAIA (observer), MIGA, MINURSO, MINUSTAH, NAM (observer), OAS, OPANAL, OPCW, Pacific Alliance (observer), PCA, Petrocaribe, SICA, UN, UNCTAD, UNESCO, UNIDO, UNIFIL, Union Latina, UNISFA, UNMISS, UNOCI, UNWTO, UPU, WCO, WFTU (NGOs), WHO, WIPO, WMO, WTO

Diplomatic representation in the US: *chief of mission:* Ambassador Carmen Milena MAYORGA VALERA (since 23 December 2020)
chancery: 1400 16th Street NW, Suite 100, Washington, DC 20036
telephone: [1] (202) 595-7500
FAX: [1] (202) 232-3763
email address and website:
correo@elsalvador.org
consulate(s) general: Atlanta, Boston, Brentwood (NY), Charlotte, Chicago, Dallas, Denver, Houston, Las Vegas (NV), Loreado (TX), Los Angeles, McAllen (TX), New York, San Bernardino (CA), San Francisco, Tucson (AZ), Washington (DC), Woodbridge (VA)

Diplomatic representation from the US: *chief of mission:* Ambassador (vacant); Charge d'Affaires Patrick H. VENTRELL
embassy: Final Boulevard Santa Elena, Antiguo Cuscatlan, La Libertad, San Salvador
mailing address: 3450 San Salvador Place, Washington, DC 20521-3450
telephone: [503] 2501-2999
FAX: [503] 2501-2150
email address and website:
ACSSanSal@state.gov
https://sv.usembassy.gov/

Flag description: three equal horizontal bands of cobalt blue (top), white, and cobalt blue with the national coat of arms centered in the white band; the coat of arms features a round emblem encircled by the words REPUBLICA DE EL SALVADOR EN LA AMERICA CENTRAL; the banner is based on the former blue-white-blue flag of the Federal Republic of Central America; the blue bands symbolize the Pacific Ocean and the Caribbean Sea, while the white band represents the land between the two bodies of water, as well as peace and prosperity
note: similar to the flag of Nicaragua, which has a different coat of arms centered in the white band; also similar to the flag of Honduras, which has five blue stars arranged in an X pattern centered in the white band

National symbol(s): turquoise-browed motmot (bird); national colors: blue, white

National anthem: *name:* "Himno Nacional de El Salvador" (National Anthem of El Salvador)
lyrics/music: Juan Jose CANAS/Juan ABERLE
note: officially adopted 1953, in use since 1879; at 4:20 minutes, the anthem of El Salvador is one of the world's longest

National heritage: *total World Heritage Sites:* 1 (cultural)
selected World Heritage Site locales: Joya de Cerén Archaeological Site

ECONOMY

Economic overview: The smallest country in Central America geographically, El Salvador has the fourth largest economy in the region. With the global recession, real GDP contracted in 2009 and economic growth has since remained low, averaging less than 2% from 2010 to 2014, but recovered somewhat in 2015-17 with an average annual growth rate of 2.4%. Remittances accounted for approximately 18% of GDP in 2017 and were received by about a third of all households.

In 2006, El Salvador was the first country to ratify the Dominican Republic-Central American Free Trade Agreement, which has bolstered the export of processed foods, sugar, and ethanol, and supported investment in the apparel sector amid increased Asian competition. In September 2015, El Salvador kicked off a five-year $277 million second compact with the Millennium Challenge Corporation - a US Government agency aimed at stimulating economic growth and reducing poverty - to improve El Salvador's competitiveness and productivity in international markets.

The Salvadoran Government maintained fiscal discipline during reconstruction and rebuilding following earthquakes in 2001 and hurricanes in 1998 and 2005, but El Salvador's public debt, estimated at 59.3% of GDP in 2017, has been growing over the last several years.

Real GDP (purchasing power parity): $52.26 billion (2020 est.)
$56.77 billion (2019 est.)
$55.31 billion (2018 est.)
note: data are in 2017 dollars
country comparison to the world: 110

Real GDP growth rate: 2.3% (2017 est.)
2.6% (2016 est.)
2.4% (2015 est.)
country comparison to the world: 120

Real GDP per capita: $8,100 (2020 est.)
$8,800 (2019 est.)
$8,600 (2018 est.)
note: data are in 2017 dollars
country comparison to the world: 150

GDP (official exchange rate): $27.023 billion (2019 est.)

Inflation rate (consumer prices): 0% (2019 est.)
1% (2018 est.)
1% (2017 est.)
country comparison to the world: 19

Credit ratings:

Fitch rating: B- (2017)

Moody's rating: B3 (2018)

Standard & Poors rating: B- (2018)
note: The year refers to the year in which the current credit rating was first obtained.

GDP - composition, by sector of origin: *agriculture:* 12% (2017 est.)
industry: 27.7% (2017 est.)
services: 60.3% (2017 est.)

GDP - composition, by end use: *household consumption:* 84.5% (2017 est.)
government consumption: 15.8% (2017 est.)
investment in fixed capital: 16.9% (2017 est.)
investment in inventories: 0% (2017 est.)
exports of goods and services: 27.6% (2017 est.)
imports of goods and services: -44.9% (2017 est.)

Agricultural products: sugar cane, maize, milk, poultry, sorghum, beans, coconuts, eggs, apples, oranges

Industries: food processing, beverages, petroleum, chemicals, fertilizer, textiles, furniture, light metals

Industrial production growth rate: 3.6% (2017 est.)
country comparison to the world: 81

Labor force: 2.908 million (2019 est.)
country comparison to the world: 105

Labor force - by occupation: *agriculture:* 21%
industry: 20%
services: 58% (2011 est.)

Unemployment rate: 7% (2017 est.)
6.9% (2016 est.)
note: data are official rates; but underemployment is high
country comparison to the world: 114

Unemployment, youth ages 15-24: *total:* 10%
male: 8.3%
female: 12.8% (2019)
country comparison to the world: 139

Population below poverty line: 22.8% (2019 est.)

Gini Index coefficient - distribution of family income: 38.6 (2018 est.)
38 (2014)
country comparison to the world: 72

Household income or consumption by percentage share: *lowest 10%:* 2.2%
highest 10%: 32.3% (2014 est.)

Budget: *revenues:* 5.886 billion (2017 est.)
expenditures: 6.517 billion (2017 est.)

Budget surplus (+) or deficit (-): -2.5% (of GDP) (2017 est.)
country comparison to the world: 114

Public debt: 67.9% of GDP (2017 est.)
66.4% of GDP (2016 est.)
note: El Salvador's total public debt includes non-financial public sector debt, financial public sector debt, and central bank debt
country comparison to the world: 55

Taxes and other revenues: 23.7% (of GDP) (2017 est.)
country comparison to the world: 123

Fiscal year: calendar year

Current account balance: -$501 million (2017 est.)
-$500 million (2016 est.)
country comparison to the world: 122

Exports: $6.29 billion (2020 est.) note: data are in current year dollars
$7.98 billion (2019 est.) note: data are in current year dollars
$7.56 billion (2018 est.) note: data are in current year dollars

country comparison to the world: 117

Exports - partners: United States 40%, Guatemala 15%, Honduras 15%, Nicaragua 6% (2019)

Exports - commodities: textiles and apparel, electrical capacitors, plastic lids, raw sugar, toilet paper (2019)

Imports: $10.82 billion (2020 est.) note: data are in current year dollars
$12.45 billion (2019 est.) note: data are in current year dollars
$12.32 billion (2018 est.) note: data are in current year dollars
country comparison to the world: 102

Imports - partners: United States 30%, China 14%, Guatemala 13%, Mexico 8%, Honduras 6% (2019)

Imports - commodities: refined petroleum, packaged medicines, clothing, broadcasting equipment, natural gas (2019)

Reserves of foreign exchange and gold: $3.567 billion (31 December 2017 est.)
$3.238 billion (31 December 2016 est.)
country comparison to the world: 104

Debt - external: $17.24 billion (2019 est.)
$16.712 billion (2018 est.)
country comparison to the world: 100

Exchange rates: *note:* the US dollar is used as a medium of exchange and circulates freely in the economy
1 (2017 est.)

ENERGY

Electricity access: *electrification - total population:* 97% (2019)
electrification - urban areas: 99% (2019)
electrification - rural areas: 93% (2019)

Electricity: *installed generating capacity:* 2.586 million kW (2020 est.)
consumption: 6,443,200,000 kWh (2019 est.)
exports: 158 million kWh (2019 est.)
imports: 1.45 billion kWh (2019 est.)
transmission/distribution losses: 795.8 million kWh (2019 est.)

Electricity generation sources: *fossil fuels:* 28.2% of total installed capacity (2020 est.)
solar: 7.5% of total installed capacity (2020 est.)
hydroelectricity: 30% of total installed capacity (2020 est.)
geothermal: 22.2% of total installed capacity (2020 est.)
biomass and waste: 12.1% of total installed capacity (2020 est.)

Coal: *production:* 0 metric tons (2020 est.)
consumption: 1,000 metric tons (2020 est.)
exports: 0 metric tons (2020 est.)
imports: 1,000 metric tons (2020 est.)
proven reserves: 0 metric tons (2019 est.)

Petroleum: *total petroleum production:* 0 bbl/day (2021 est.)
refined petroleum consumption: 59,100 bbl/day (2019 est.)

Refined petroleum products - exports: 347 bbl/day (2015 est.)
country comparison to the world: 115

Refined petroleum products - imports: 49,280 bbl/day (2015 est.)
country comparison to the world: 82

Carbon dioxide emissions: 7.632 million metric tonnes of CO2 (2019 est.)
from coal and metallurgical coke: 2,000 metric tonnes of CO2 (2019 est.)
from petroleum and other liquids: 7.63 million metric tonnes of CO2 (2019 est.)
country comparison to the world: 122

Energy consumption per capita: 24.124 million Btu/person (2019 est.)
country comparison to the world: 131

COMMUNICATIONS

Telephones - fixed lines: *total subscriptions:* 894,000 (2020 est.)
subscriptions per 100 inhabitants: 14 (2020 est.)
country comparison to the world: 75

Telephones - mobile cellular: *total subscriptions:* 9.949 million (2020 est.)
subscriptions per 100 inhabitants: 153 (2020 est.)
country comparison to the world: 90

Telecommunication systems: *general assessment:* El Salvador is the smallest country in central America geographically, it has the fourth largest economy in the region; the country's telecom sector has been restricted by poor infrastructure and unequal income distribution; there have been organizational delays which have slowed the development of telecom services; El Salvador's fixed-line teledensity is substantially lower than the Latin American and Caribbean average; there has been a significant drop in the number of fixed lines since 2010, particularly in 2017, largely due to the substitution for mobile-only alternatives; about 94% of all telephony lines in the country are on mobile networks; mobile subscriptions are remarkably high considering El Salvador's economic indicators, being about a third higher than average for Latin America and the Caribbean; the country was one of the last in the region to provide LTE services, mainly due to the inadequate provision of suitable spectrum; the multi-spectrum auction conducted at the end of 2019 has allowed MNOs to improve the reach and quality of their service offerings; El Salvador's telecom legislation is one of the more liberal in Latin America, encouraging competition in most areas and permitting foreign investment; there are no regulations which promote wholesale broadband; the only effective cross-platform competition in the broadband market comes from the few cable operators; there has been some market consolidation in recent years (2021)
domestic: fixed-line services, roughly 14 per 100, has slowed in the face of mobile-cellular competition now at 153 subscribers per 100 inhabitants (2020)
international: country code - 503; satellite earth station - 1 Intelsat (Atlantic Ocean); connected to Central American Microwave System (2019)

Broadcast media: multiple privately owned national terrestrial TV networks, supplemented by cable TV networks that carry international channels; hundreds of commercial radio broadcast stations and two known government-owned radio broadcast station; transition to digital transmission to begin in 2018 along with adaptation of the Japanese-Brazilian Digital Standard (ISDB-T) (2022)

Internet country code: .sv

Internet users: *total:* 3,567,410 (2020 est.)
percent of population: 55% (2020 est.)
country comparison to the world: 107

Broadband - fixed subscriptions: *total:* 586,000 (2020 est.)
subscriptions per 100 inhabitants: 9 (2020 est.)
country comparison to the world: 87

TRANSPORTATION

National air transport system: *number of registered air carriers:* 1 (2020)
inventory of registered aircraft operated by air carriers: 13
annual passenger traffic on registered air carriers: 2,545,105 (2018)
annual freight traffic on registered air carriers: 10.73 million (2018) mt-km

Civil aircraft registration country code prefix: YS

Airports: *total:* 68 (2021)
country comparison to the world: 73

Airports - with paved runways: *total:* 5
over 3,047 m: 1
1,524 to 2,437 m: 1
914 to 1,523 m: 2
under 914 m: 1 (2021)

Airports - with unpaved runways: *total:* 63
1,524 to 2,437 m: 1
914 to 1,523 m: 11
under 914 m: 51 (2021)

Heliports: 2 (2021)

Railways: *total:* 12.5 km (2014)
narrow gauge: 12.5 km (2014) 0.914-mm gauge
country comparison to the world: 135

Roadways: *total:* 9,012 km (2017)
paved: 5,341 km (2017)
unpaved: 3,671 km (2017)
country comparison to the world: 138

Waterways: 422 km (2022) (Rio Lempa River is partially navigable by small craft)
country comparison to the world: 95

Merchant marine: *total:* 2
by type: other 2 (2021)
country comparison to the world: 174

Ports and terminals: *major seaport(s):* Puerto Cutuco
oil terminal(s): Acajutla offshore terminal

MILITARY AND SECURITY

Military and security forces: the Armed Force of El Salvador (La Fuerza Armada de El Salvador, FAES): Army of El Salvador (Ejercito de El Salvador, ES), Navy of El Salvador (Fuerza Naval de El Salvador, FNES), Salvadoran Air Force (Fuerza Aerea Salvadorena, FAS); Ministry of Justice and Public Security: National Civil Police (Policia Nacional Civil, PNC) (2022)
note: in 2016, El Salvador created a combined Army commando and National Civil Police unit to combat criminal gang violence

Military expenditures: 1.2% of GDP (2021 est.)
1.2% of GDP (2020)
1.2% of GDP (2019) (approximately $570 million)
1.1% of GDP (2018) (approximately $540 million)
1% of GDP (2017) (approximately $500 million)
country comparison to the world: 113

Military and security service personnel strengths: approximately 21,000 active military personnel (17,000 Army; 2,000 Navy; 2,000 Air Force) (2022)
note: in 2021, El Salvador announced intentions to double the size of the military, although no time frame was given

Military equipment inventories and acquisitions: the FAES is dependent on a mix of mostly older imported platforms, largely from the US; since 2010, the FAES has received small amounts of equipment from several countries, including Chile, Israel, Spain, and the US (2022)

Military service age and obligation: 18 years of age for selective compulsory military service; 16-22 years of age for voluntary male or female service; service obligation is 12 months, with 11 months for officers and non-commissioned officers (2022)
note: as of 2016, women made up about 6% of the active duty military

Military deployments: 175 Mali (MINUSMA) (May 2022)

Military - note: the National Civilian Police (Ministry of Justice and Public Security) is responsible for maintaining public security, while the Ministry of Defense is responsible for maintaining national security; the constitution separates public security and military functions, but allows the president to use the armed forces in exceptional circumstances to maintain internal peace and public security; in November 2019, President BUKELE signed a decree authorizing military involvement in police duties to combat gang violence, organized crime, and narcotics trafficking, as well as assisting with border security; as of 2022, a considerable portion of the Army was deployed in support of the National Police (2022)

TRANSNATIONAL ISSUES

Disputes - international: *El Salvador-Honduras:* International Court of Justice (ICJ) ruled on the delimitation of "bolsones" (disputed areas) along the El Salvador-Honduras border in 1992 with final settlement by the parties in 2006 after an Organization of American States survey and a further ICJ ruling in 2003; the 1992 ICJ ruling advised a tripartite resolution to a maritime boundary in the Gulf of Fonseca with consideration of Honduran access to the Pacific; El Salvador continues to claim tiny Conejo Island, not mentioned in the ICJ ruling, off Honduras in the Gulf of Fonseca.

Refugees and internally displaced persons: IDPs: 71,500 (2021)

Illicit drugs: a transit country for illicit drugs destined for the United States

EQUATORIAL GUINEA

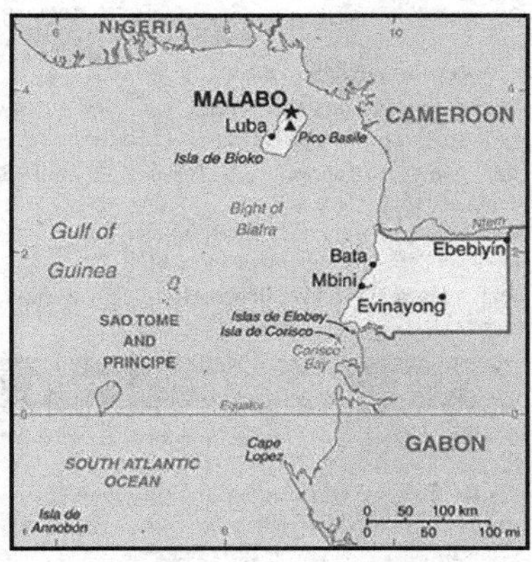

INTRODUCTION

Background: Equatorial Guinea gained independence in 1968 after 190 years of Spanish rule; it is one of the smallest countries in Africa consisting of a mainland territory and five inhabited islands. The capital of Malabo is located on the island of Bioko, approximately 25 km from the Cameroonian coastline in the Gulf of Guinea. Between 1968 and 1979, autocratic President Francisco MACIAS NGUEMA virtually destroyed all of the country's political, economic, and social institutions before being deposed by his nephew Teodoro OBIANG NGUEMA MBASOGO in a violent coup. President OBIANG has ruled since October 1979 and has been elected several times, most recently in 2016. Although nominally a constitutional democracy since 1991, presidential and legislative elections since 1996 have been considered flawed. The president exerts almost total control over the political system and has placed legal and bureaucratic barriers that hinder political opposition. Equatorial Guinea experienced rapid economic growth in the early years of the 21st century due to the discovery of large offshore oil reserves in 1996. Production peaked in late 2004 and has slowly declined since, although aggressive searches for new oilfields continue. Despite the country's economic windfall from oil production, resulting in massive increases in government revenue in past years, generally lower global oil prices since 2014 and depreciating oil fields have placed significant strain on the state budget. While oil revenues have mainly been used for the development of infrastructure, corruption has hindered socio-economic development and there have been limited improvements in the population's living standards. Equatorial Guinea continues to seek to diversify its economy and to increase foreign investment. The country hosts major regional and international conferences and continues to seek a greater role in international affairs, and leadership in the sub-region.

GEOGRAPHY

Location: Central Africa, bordering the Bight of Biafra, between Cameroon and Gabon

Geographic coordinates: 2 00 N, 10 00 E

Map references: Africa

Area: *total:* 28,051 sq km
land: 28,051 sq km
water: 0 sq km
country comparison to the world: 145

Area - comparative: slightly smaller than Maryland

Land boundaries: *total:* 528 km
border countries (2): Cameroon 183 km; Gabon 345 km

Coastline: 296 km

Maritime claims: *territorial sea:* 12 nm
exclusive economic zone: 200 nm

Climate: tropical; always hot, humid

Terrain: coastal plains rise to interior hills; islands are volcanic

Elevation: *highest point:* Pico Basile 3,008 m
lowest point: Atlantic Ocean 0 m
mean elevation: 577 m

Natural resources: petroleum, natural gas, timber, gold, bauxite, diamonds, tantalum, sand and gravel, clay

Land use: *agricultural land:* 10.1% (2018 est.)
arable land: 4.3% (2018 est.)
permanent crops: 2.1% (2018 est.)
permanent pasture: 3.7% (2018 est.)
forest: 57.5% (2018 est.)
other: 32.4% (2018 est.)

Population distribution: only two large cities over 30,000 people (Bata on the mainland, and the capital Malabo on the island of Bioko); small communities are scattered throughout the mainland and the five inhabited islands as shown in this population distribution map

Natural hazards: violent windstorms; flash floods
volcanism: Santa Isabel (3,007 m), which last erupted in 1923, is the country's only historically active volcano; Santa Isabel, along with two dormant volcanoes, form Bioko Island in the Gulf of Guinea

Geography - note: insular and continental regions widely separated; despite its name, no part of the Equator passes through Equatorial Guinea; the mainland part of the country is located just north of the Equator

PEOPLE AND SOCIETY

Population: 1,679,172 (2022 est.)
country comparison to the world: 154

Nationality: *noun:* Equatorial Guinean(s) or Equatoguinean(s)
adjective: Equatorial Guinean or Equatoguinean

Ethnic groups: Fang 85.7%, Bubi 6.5%, Mdowe 3.6%, Annobon 1.6%, Bujeba 1.1%, other 1.4% (1994 est.)

Languages: Spanish (official) 67.6%, other (includes Fang, Bubi, Portuguese (official), French (official), Portuguese-based Creoles spoken in Ano Bom) 32.4% (1994 est.)
major-language sample(s):
La Libreta Informativa del Mundo, la fuente indispensable de información básica. (Spanish)

Religions: Roman Catholic 88%, Protestant 5%, Muslim 2%, other 5% (animist, Baha'i, Jewish) (2015 est.)

Demographic profile: Equatorial Guinea is one of the smallest and least populated countries in continental Africa and is the only independent African country where Spanish is an official language. Despite a boom in oil production in the 1990s, authoritarianism, corruption, and resource mismanagement have concentrated the benefits among a small elite. These practices have perpetuated income inequality and unbalanced development, such as low public spending on education and health care. Unemployment remains problematic because the oil-dominated economy employs a small labor force dependent on skilled foreign workers. The agricultural sector, Equatorial Guinea's main employer, continues to deteriorate because of a lack of investment and the migration of rural workers to urban areas. About three-quarters of the population lives below the poverty line.

Equatorial Guinea's large and growing youth population – about 60% are under the age of 25 – is particularly affected because job creation in the non-oil sectors is limited, and young people often do not have the skills needed in the labor market. Equatorial Guinean children frequently enter school late, have poor attendance, and have high drop-out rates. Thousands of Equatorial Guineans fled across the border to Gabon in the 1970s to escape the dictatorship of Francisco MACIAS NGUEMA; smaller numbers have followed in the decades since. Continued inequitable economic growth and high youth unemployment increases the likelihood of ethnic and regional violence.

Age structure: *0-14 years:* 38.73% (male 164,417/female 159,400)
15-24 years: 19.94% (male 84,820/female 81,880)
25-54 years: 32.72% (male 137,632/female 135,973)
55-64 years: 4.69% (male 17,252/female 22,006)
65 years and over: 3.92% (male 13,464/female 19,334) (2020 est.)

Dependency ratios: *total dependency ratio:* 64.4
youth dependency ratio: 60.5
elderly dependency ratio: 3.9
potential support ratio: 25.5 (2020 est.)

Median age: *total:* 20.3 years
male: 19.9 years
female: 20.7 years (2020 est.)
country comparison to the world: 191

Population growth rate: 3.5% (2022 est.)
country comparison to the world: 5

Birth rate: 29.95 births/1,000 population (2022 est.)
country comparison to the world: 30

Death rate: 8.95 deaths/1,000 population (2022 est.)
country comparison to the world: 62

Net migration rate: 13.96 migrant(s)/1,000 population (2022 est.)
country comparison to the world: 3

Population distribution: only two large cities over 30,000 people (Bata on the mainland, and the capital Malabo on the island of Bioko); small communities are scattered throughout the mainland and the five inhabited islands as shown in this population distribution map

Urbanization: *urban population:* 74% of total population (2022)
rate of urbanization: 3.62% annual rate of change (2020-25 est.)

Major urban areas - population: 297,000 MALABO (capital) (2018)

Sex ratio: *at birth:* 1.03 male(s)/female
0-14 years: 1.08 male(s)/female
15-24 years: 1.21 male(s)/female
25-54 years: 1.21 male(s)/female
55-64 years: 1.17 male(s)/female
65 years and over: 0.87 male(s)/female
total population: 1.15 male(s)/female (2022 est.)

Maternal mortality ratio: 301 deaths/100,000 live births (2017 est.)
country comparison to the world: 37

Infant mortality rate: *total:* 78.33 deaths/1,000 live births
male: 84.23 deaths/1,000 live births
female: 72.25 deaths/1,000 live births (2022 est.)
country comparison to the world: 4

Life expectancy at birth: *total population:* 63.7 years
male: 61.44 years
female: 66.03 years (2022 est.)
country comparison to the world: 206

Total fertility rate: 4.26 children born/woman (2022 est.)
country comparison to the world: 24

Drinking water source: *improved: urban:* 81.7% of population
rural: 32.1% of population
total: 67.6% of population
unimproved: urban: 18.3% of population
rural: 67.9% of population
total: 32.4% of population (2017 est.)

Current health expenditure: 3.1% of GDP (2019)

Physicians density: 0.4 physicians/1,000 population (2017)

Sanitation facility access: *improved: urban:* 81.2% of population
rural: 63.4% of population
total: 76.2% of population
unimproved: urban: 18.8% of population
rural: 36.6% of population
total: 23.8% of population (2020 est.)

HIV/AIDS - adult prevalence rate: 7.3% (2020 est.)
country comparison to the world: 10

Major infectious diseases: *degree of risk:* very high (2020)
food or waterborne diseases: bacterial and protozoal diarrhea, hepatitis A, and typhoid fever
vectorborne diseases: malaria and dengue fever
animal contact diseases: rabies

Obesity - adult prevalence rate: 8% (2016)
country comparison to the world: 156

Alcohol consumption per capita: *total:* 6.11 liters of pure alcohol (2019 est.)
beer: 3.83 liters of pure alcohol (2019 est.)
wine: 1.24 liters of pure alcohol (2019 est.)
spirits: 0.99 liters of pure alcohol (2019 est.)
other alcohols: 0.05 liters of pure alcohol (2019 est.)
country comparison to the world: 69

Children under the age of 5 years underweight: 5.6% (2011)
country comparison to the world: 73

Literacy: *definition:* age 15 and over can read and write
total population: 95.3%
male: 97.4%
female: 93% (2015)

ENVIRONMENT

Environment - current issues: deforestation (forests are threatened by agricultural expansion, fires, and grazing); desertification; water pollution (tap water is non-potable); wildlife preservation

Environment - international agreements: *party to:* Biodiversity, Climate Change, Climate Change-Kyoto Protocol, Climate Change-Paris Agreement, Desertification, Endangered Species, Hazardous Wastes, Law of the Sea, Marine Dumping-London Convention, Nuclear Test Ban, Ozone Layer Protection, Ship Pollution, Wetlands
signed, but not ratified: Comprehensive Nuclear Test Ban

Air pollutants: *particulate matter emissions:* 45.9 micrograms per cubic meter (2016 est.)
carbon dioxide emissions: 5.65 megatons (2016 est.)
methane emissions: 11.21 megatons (2020 est.)

Climate: tropical; always hot, humid

Land use: *agricultural land:* 10.1% (2018 est.)
arable land: 4.3% (2018 est.)
permanent crops: 2.1% (2018 est.)
permanent pasture: 3.7% (2018 est.)
forest: 57.5% (2018 est.)
other: 32.4% (2018 est.)

Urbanization: *urban population:* 74% of total population (2022)
rate of urbanization: 3.62% annual rate of change (2020-25 est.)

Revenue from forest resources: *forest revenues:* 1.52% of GDP (2018 est.)
country comparison to the world: 42

Revenue from coal: *coal revenues:* 0% of GDP (2018 est.)
country comparison to the world: 94

Waste and recycling: *municipal solid waste generated annually:* 198,443 tons (2016 est.)

Total water withdrawal: *municipal:* 15.8 million cubic meters (2017 est.)
industrial: 3 million cubic meters (2017 est.)
agricultural: 1 million cubic meters (2017 est.)

Total renewable water resources: 26 billion cubic meters (2017 est.)

GOVERNMENT

Country name: *conventional long form:* Republic of Equatorial Guinea
conventional short form: Equatorial Guinea
local long form: Republica de Guinea Ecuatorial (Spanish)/ Republique de Guinee Equatoriale (French)
local short form: Guinea Ecuatorial (Spanish)/ Guinee Equatoriale (French)
former: Spanish Guinea
etymology: the country is named for the Guinea region of West Africa that lies along the Gulf of Guinea and stretches north to the Sahel; the "equatorial" refers to the fact that the country lies just north of the Equator

Government type: presidential republic

Capital: *name:* Malabo; note - Malabo is on the island of Bioko; in 2017, some governmental offices began to move to a new capital of Ciudad de la Paz (formerly referred to as Oyala) on the mainland near Djibloho, but a lack of funds has halted progress on construction
geographic coordinates: 3 45 N, 8 47 E
time difference: UTC+1 (6 hours ahead of Washington, DC, during Standard Time)
etymology: named after King MALABO (Malabo Lopelo Melaka) (1837–1937), the last king of the Bubi, the ethnic group indigenous to the island of Bioko; the name of the new capital, Ciudad de la Paz, translates to "City of Peace" in Spanish

Administrative divisions: 8 provinces (provincias, singular - provincia); Annobon, Bioko Norte,

Bioko Sur, Centro Sur, Djibloho, Kie-Ntem, Litoral, Wele-Nzas

Independence: 12 October 1968 (from Spain)

National holiday: Independence Day, 12 October (1968)

Constitution: *history:* previous 1968, 1973, 1982; approved by referendum 17 November 1991
amendments: proposed by the president of the republic or supported by three fourths of the membership in either house of the National Assembly; passage requires three-fourths majority vote by both houses of the Assembly and approval in a referendum if requested by the president; amended several times, last in 2012

Legal system: mixed system of civil and customary law

International law organization participation: accepts compulsory ICJ jurisdiction; accepts ICCt jurisdiction

Citizenship: *citizenship by birth:* no
citizenship by descent only: at least one parent must be a citizen of Equatorial Guinea
dual citizenship recognized: no
residency requirement for naturalization: 10 years

Suffrage: 18 years of age; universal

Executive branch: *chief of state:* President Brig. Gen. (Ret.) Teodoro OBIANG Nguema Mbasogo (since 3 August 1979 when he seized power in a military coup); Vice President Teodoro Nguema OBIANG Mangue (since 2012)
head of government: Prime Minister Francisco Pascual Eyegue OBAMA Asue (since 23 June 2016); First Deputy Prime Minister Clemente Engonga NGUEMA Onguene (since 23 June 2016); Second Deputy Prime Minister Angel MESIE Mibuy (since 5 February 2018); Third Deputy Prime Minister Alfonso Nsue MOKUY (since 23 June 2016)
cabinet: Council of Ministers appointed by the president and overseen by the prime minister
elections/appointments: president directly elected by simple majority popular vote for a 7-year term (eligible for a second term); election last held on 24 April 2016 (next to be held in 2023); prime minister and deputy prime ministers appointed by the president
election results:
Teodoro OBIANG Nguema Mbasogo reelected president; percent of vote - Teodoro OBIANG Nguema Mbasogo (PDGE) 93.5%, other 6.5% (2016)

Legislative branch: *description:* bicameral National Assembly or Asemblea Nacional consists of:
Senate or Senado (70 seats statutory, 72 seats for current term; 55 members directly elected in multi-seat constituencies by closed party-list proportional representation vote, 15 appointed by the president, and 2 ex-officio) Chamber of Deputies or Camara de los Diputados (100 seats; members directly elected in multi-seat constituencies by closed party-list proportional representation vote to serve 5-year terms)
elections:
Senate - last held on 12 November 2017 (next to be held in 2022/2023)
Chamber of Deputies - last held on 12 November 2017 (next to be held in 2022/2023)
election results:
Senate - percent of vote by party - NA; elected seats by party - PDGE and aligned coalition 70; composition (including 2 ex-officio) - men 60, women 12, percent of women 16.7%
Chamber of Deputies - percent of vote by party - NA; seats by party - PDGE 99, CI 1; composition - men 78, women 22, percent of women 22%; note - total National Assembly percent of women 18.8%

Judicial branch: *highest court(s):* Supreme Court of Justice (consists of the chief justice - who is also chief of state - and 9 judges organized into civil, criminal, commercial, labor, administrative, and customary sections); Constitutional Court (consists of the court president and 4 members)
judge selection and term of office: Supreme Court judges appointed by the president for 5-year terms; Constitutional Court members appointed by the president, 2 of whom are nominated by the Chamber of Deputies; note - judges subject to dismissal by the president at any time
subordinate courts: Court of Guarantees; military courts; Courts of Appeal; first instance tribunals; district and county tribunals

Political parties and leaders: Convergence Party for Social Democracy or CPDS [Andres ESONO ONDO]
Democratic Party for Equatorial Guinea or PDGE [Teodoro Obiang NGUEMA MBASOGO]
Juntos Podemos (coalition includes CPDS, FDR, UDC)
National Congress of Equatorial Guinea [Agustin MASOKO ABEGUE]
National Democratic Party [Benedicto OBIANG MANGUE]
National Union for Democracy [Thomas MBA MONABANG]
Popular Action of Equatorial Guinea or APGE [Carmelo MBA BACALE]
Popular Union or UP [Daniel MARTINEZ AYECABA]
Center Right Union or UCD [Avelino MOCACHE MEHENGA]

International organization participation: ACP, AfDB, AU, BDEAC, CEMAC, CPLP, FAO, Francophonie, FZ, G-77, IBRD, ICAO, ICRM, IDA, IFAD, IFC, IFRCS, ILO, IMF, IMO, Interpol, IOC, IPU, ITSO, ITU, MIGA, NAM, OAS (observer), OIF, OPCW, UN, UNCTAD, UNESCO, UNIDO, , UNWTO, UPU, WHO, WIPO, WTO (observer)

Diplomatic representation in the US: *chief of mission:* Ambassador Miguel Ntutumu EVUNA Andeme (since 23 February 2015)
chancery: 2020 16th Street NW, Washington, DC 20009
telephone: [1] (202) 518-5700
FAX: [1] (202) 518-5252
email address and website:
info@egembassydc.com
https://www.egembassydc.com/
consulate(s) general: Houston

Diplomatic representation from the US: *chief of mission:* Ambassador David R. GILMOUR (since 24 May 2022)
embassy: Malabo II Highway (between the Headquarters of Sonagas and the offices of the United Nations), Malabo
mailing address: 2320 Malabo Place, Washington, DC 20521-2520
telephone: [240] 333 09-57-41
email address and website:
Malaboconsular@state.gov
https://gq.usembassy.gov/

Flag description: three equal horizontal bands of green (top), white, and red, with a blue isosceles triangle based on the hoist side and the coat of arms centered in the white band; the coat of arms has six yellow six-pointed stars (representing the mainland and five offshore islands) above a gray shield bearing a silk-cotton tree and below which is a scroll with the motto UNIDAD, PAZ, JUSTICIA (Unity, Peace, Justice); green symbolizes the jungle and natural resources, blue represents the sea that connects the mainland to the islands, white stands for peace, and red recalls the fight for independence

National symbol(s): silk cotton tree; national colors: green, white, red, blue

National anthem: *name:* "Caminemos pisando la senda" (Let Us Tread the Path)
lyrics/music: Atanasio Ndongo MIYONO/Atanasio Ndongo MIYONO or Ramiro Sanchez LOPEZ (disputed)
note: adopted 1968

ECONOMY

Economic overview: Exploitation of oil and gas deposits, beginning in the 1990s, has driven economic growth in Equatorial Guinea; a recent rebasing of GDP resulted in an upward revision of the size of the economy by approximately 30%. Forestry and farming are minor components of GDP. Although preindependence Equatorial Guinea counted on cocoa production for hard currency earnings, the neglect of the rural economy since independence has diminished the potential for agriculture-led growth. Subsistence farming is the dominant form of livelihood. Declining revenue from hydrocarbon production, high levels of infrastructure expenditures, lack of economic diversification, and corruption have pushed the economy into decline in recent years and limited improvements in the general population's living conditions. Equatorial Guinea's real GDP growth has been weak in recent years, averaging -0.5% per year from 2010 to 2014, because of a declining hydrocarbon sector. Inflation remained very low in 2016, down from an average of 4% in 2014.

As a middle income country, Equatorial Guinea is now ineligible for most low-income World Bank and the IMF funding. The government has been widely criticized for its lack of transparency and misuse of oil revenues and has attempted to address this issue by working toward compliance with the Extractive Industries Transparency Initiative. US foreign assistance to Equatorial Guinea is limited in part because of US restrictions pursuant to the Trafficking Victims Protection Act.

Equatorial Guinea hosted two economic diversification symposia in 2014 that focused on attracting investment in five sectors: agriculture and animal ranching, fishing, mining and petrochemicals, tourism, and financial services. Undeveloped mineral resources include gold, zinc, diamonds, columbite-tantalite, and other base metals. In 2017 Equatorial Guinea signed a preliminary agreement with Ghana to sell liquefied natural gas (LNG); as oil production wanes, the government believes LNG could provide a boost to revenues, but it will require large investments and long lead times to develop.

Real GDP (purchasing power parity): $23.86 billion (2020 est.)
$25.09 billion (2019 est.)
$26.68 billion (2018 est.)

note: data are in 2017 dollars
country comparison to the world: 146

Real GDP growth rate: -3.2% (2017 est.)
-8.6% (2016 est.)
-9.1% (2015 est.)
country comparison to the world: 213

Real GDP per capita: $17,000 (2020 est.)
$18,500 (2019 est.)
$20,400 (2018 est.)
note: data are in 2017 dollars
country comparison to the world: 99

GDP (official exchange rate): $10.634 billion (2019 est.)

Inflation rate (consumer prices): 1.2% (2019 est.)
1.3% (2018 est.)
0.7% (2017 est.)
country comparison to the world: 74

GDP - composition, by sector of origin: *agriculture:* 2.5% (2017 est.)
industry: 54.6% (2017 est.)
services: 42.9% (2017 est.)

GDP - composition, by end use: *household consumption:* 50% (2017 est.)
government consumption: 21.8% (2017 est.)
investment in fixed capital: 10.2% (2017 est.)
investment in inventories: 0.1% (2017 est.)
exports of goods and services: 56.9% (2017 est.)
imports of goods and services: -39% (2017 est.)

Agricultural products: sweet potatoes, cassava, roots/tubers nes, plantains, oil palm fruit, bananas, coconuts, coffee, cocoa, eggs

Industries: petroleum, natural gas, sawmilling

Industrial production growth rate: -6.9% (2017 est.)
country comparison to the world: 197

Labor force: 195,200 (2007 est.)
country comparison to the world: 173

Unemployment rate: 8.6% (2014 est.)
22.3% (2009 est.)
country comparison to the world: 132

Population below poverty line: 44% (2011 est.)

Budget: *revenues:* 2.114 billion (2017 est.)
expenditures: 2.523 billion (2017 est.)

Budget surplus (+) or deficit (-): -3.3% (of GDP) (2017 est.)
country comparison to the world: 141

Public debt: 37.4% of GDP (2017 est.)
43.3% of GDP (2016 est.)
country comparison to the world: 139

Taxes and other revenues: 16.9% (of GDP) (2017 est.)
country comparison to the world: 173

Fiscal year: calendar year

Current account balance: -$738 million (2017 est.)
-$1.457 billion (2016 est.)
country comparison to the world: 136

Exports: $8.776 billion (2019 est.)
$8.914 billion (2018 est.)
$9.94 billion (2017 est.)
country comparison to the world: 104

Exports - partners: China 34%, India 19%, Spain 11%, United States 7% (2019)

Exports - commodities: crude petroleum, natural gas, industrial alcohols, lumber, veneer sheeting (2019)

Imports: $6.245 billion (2019 est.)
$6.129 billion (2018 est.)
$5.708 billion (2017 est.)
country comparison to the world: 128

Imports - partners: United States 22%, Spain 19%, China 12%, United Kingdom 6%, United Arab Emirates 5% (2019)

Imports - commodities: gas turbines, beer, ships, industrial machinery, excavation machinery (2019)

Reserves of foreign exchange and gold: $45.5 million (31 December 2017 est.)
$62.31 million (31 December 2016 est.)
country comparison to the world: 188

Debt - external: $1.211 billion (31 December 2017 est.)
$1.074 billion (31 December 2016 est.)
country comparison to the world: 163

Exchange rates: Cooperation Financiere en Afrique Centrale francs (XAF) per US dollar -
605.3 (2017 est.)
593.01 (2016 est.)
593.01 (2015 est.)
591.45 (2014 est.)
494.42 (2013 est.)

ENERGY

Electricity access: *electrification - total population:* 67% (2019)
electrification - urban areas: 75% (2019)
electrification - rural areas: 45% (2019)

Electricity: *installed generating capacity:* 349,000 kW (2020 est.)
consumption: 1,002,960,000 kWh (2019 est.)
exports: 0 kWh (2019 est.)
imports: 0 kWh (2019 est.)
transmission/distribution losses: 183 million kWh (2019 est.)

Electricity generation sources: *fossil fuels:* 89.4% of total installed capacity (2020 est.)
hydroelectricity: 10.6% of total installed capacity (2020 est.)

Petroleum: *total petroleum production:* 142,600 bbl/day (2021 est.)
refined petroleum consumption: 22,300 bbl/day (2019 est.)
crude oil and lease condensate exports: 184,500 bbl/day (2018 est.)
crude oil and lease condensate imports: 0 bbl/day (2018 est.)
crude oil estimated reserves: 1.1 billion barrels (2021 est.)

Refined petroleum products - imports: 5,094 bbl/day (2015 est.)
country comparison to the world: 171

Natural gas: *production:* 4,569,369,000 cubic meters (2019 est.)
consumption: 1,080,003,000 cubic meters (2019 est.)
exports: 3,568,030,000 cubic meters (2019 est.)
imports: 0 cubic meters (2021 est.)
proven reserves: 139.007 billion cubic meters (2021 est.)

Carbon dioxide emissions: 4.528 million metric tonnes of CO2 (2019 est.)
from petroleum and other liquids: 2.409 million metric tonnes of CO2 (2019 est.)
from consumed natural gas: 2.119 million metric tonnes of CO2 (2019 est.)
country comparison to the world: 137

Energy consumption per capita: 57.596 million Btu/person (2019 est.)
country comparison to the world: 95

COMMUNICATIONS

Telephones - fixed lines: *total subscriptions:* 11,000 (2020 est.)
subscriptions per 100 inhabitants: 1 (2020 est.)
country comparison to the world: 190

Telephones - mobile cellular: *total subscriptions:* 645,000 (2020 est.)
subscriptions per 100 inhabitants: 46 (2020 est.)
country comparison to the world: 169

Telecommunication systems: *general assessment:* the telecom service is forecasted to register a growth of more than 6% during the period of 2022-2026; mobile data is the largest contributor to total service revenue in 2021, followed by mobile voice, fixed broadband, mobile messaging, and fixed voice; the launch of the international submarine cable ACE, which connects 13 West African countries with Europe, will improve international capacity, bringing opportunities to data center providers; 4G network expansion and 4G service promotion will allow consumers and businesses to leverage 4G services (2022)
domestic: fixed-line density is less than 1 per 100 persons and mobile-cellular subscribership is roughly 46 per 100 (2020)
international: country code - 240; landing points for the ACE, Ceiba-1, and Ceiba-2 submarine cables providing communication from Bata and Malabo, Equatorial Guinea to numerous Western African and European countries; satellite earth station - 1 Intelsat (Indian Ocean) (2019)

Broadcast media: the state maintains control of broadcast media with domestic broadcast media limited to 1 state-owned TV station, 1 private TV station owned by the president's eldest son (who is the Vice President), 1 state-owned radio station, and 1 private radio station owned by the president's eldest son; satellite TV service is available; transmissions of multiple international broadcasters are generally accessible (2019)

Internet country code: .gq

Internet users: *total:* 352,555 (2019 est.)
percent of population: 26% (2019 est.)
country comparison to the world: 168

Broadband - fixed subscriptions: *total:* 1,000 (2020 est.)
subscriptions per 100 inhabitants: 0.1 (2020 est.)
country comparison to the world: 203

TRANSPORTATION

National air transport system: *number of registered air carriers:* 6 (2020)
inventory of registered aircraft operated by air carriers: 15
annual passenger traffic on registered air carriers: 466,435 (2018)
annual freight traffic on registered air carriers: 350,000 (2018) mt-km

Civil aircraft registration country code prefix: 3C

Airports: *total:* 7 (2021)
country comparison to the world: 167

Airports - with paved runways: *total:* 6
over 3,047 m: 1
2,438 to 3,047 m: 2
1,524 to 2,437 m: 1
under 914 m: 2 (2021)

Airports - with unpaved runways: *total:* 1
2,438 to 3,047 m: 1 (2021)

Pipelines: 42 km condensate, 5 km condensate/gas, 79 km gas, 71 km oil (2013)

Roadways: *total:* 2,880 km (2017)
country comparison to the world: 165

Merchant marine: *total:* 42
by type: bulk carrier 1, general cargo 8, oil tanker 6, other 27 (2021)
country comparison to the world: 123

Ports and terminals: *major seaport(s):* Bata, Luba, Malabo

LNG terminal(s) (export): Bioko Island

MILITARY AND SECURITY

Military and security forces: Equatorial Guinea Armed Forces (Fuerzas Armadas de Guinea Ecuatorial, FAGE): Equatorial Guinea National Guard (Guardia Nacional de Guinea Ecuatorial, GNGE (Army)), Navy, Air Force; Gendarmerie (2022)
note: the Gendarmerie reports to the Ministry of National Defense and is responsible for security outside cities and for special events; military personnel also fulfill some police functions in border areas, sensitive sites, and high-traffic areas

Military expenditures: 1.3% of GDP (2021 est.)
1.5% of GDP (2020 est.)
1.5% of GDP (2019 est.) (approximately $270 million)
1.1% of GDP (2018 est.) (approximately $230 million)
1.1% of GDP (2017 est.) (approximately $250 million)
country comparison to the world: 105

Military and security service personnel strengths: approximately 1,500 active duty troops; approximately 500 Gendarmerie (2022)

Military equipment inventories and acquisitions: the FAGE is armed with mostly older (typically Soviet-era) and second-hand weapons systems; in recent years, it has sought to modernize its naval inventory; Ukraine has been the leading provider of equipment since 2010 (2021)

Military service age and obligation: 18 years of age for selective compulsory military service, although conscription is rare in practice; 2-year service obligation; women hold only administrative positions in the Navy (2021)

Military - note: as of 2022, the FAGE's National Guard (Army) had only three small infantry battalions with limited combat capabilities; the country has invested heavily in naval capabilities in the 2010s to protect its oil installations and combat piracy and crime in the Gulf of Guinea; while the Navy was small, it was well-equipped with an inventory that included a light frigate and a corvette, as well as several off-shore patrol boats; the Air Force possessed only a few operational combat aircraft and ground attack-capable helicopters

Maritime threats: the International Maritime Bureau reports the territorial and offshore waters in the Niger Delta and Gulf of Guinea remain a very high risk for piracy and armed robbery of ships; in 2021, there were 34 reported incidents of piracy and armed robbery at sea in the Gulf of Guinea region; although a significant decrease from the total number of 81 incidents in 2020, it included the one hijacking and three of five ships fired upon worldwide; while boarding and attempted boarding to steal valuables from ships and crews are the most common types of incidents, almost a third of all incidents involve a hijacking and/or kidnapping; in 2021, 57 crew members were kidnapped in seven separate incidents in the Gulf of Guinea, representing 100% of kidnappings worldwide; Nigerian pirates in particular are well armed and very aggressive, operating as far as 200 nm offshore; the Maritime Administration of the US Department of Transportation has issued a Maritime Advisory (2022-001 - Gulf of Guinea-Piracy/Armed Robbery/Kidnapping for Ransom) effective 4 January 2022, which states in part, "Piracy, armed robbery, and kidnapping for ransom continue to serve as significant threats to US-flagged vessels transiting or operating in the Gulf of Guinea"

TRANSNATIONAL ISSUES

Disputes - international: *Equatorial Guinea-Cameroon:* in 2002, ICJ ruled on an equidistance settlement of Cameroon-Equatorial Guinea-Nigeria maritime boundary in the Gulf of Guinea, but a dispute between Equatorial Guinea and Cameroon over an island at the mouth of the Ntem River and imprecisely defined maritime coordinates in the ICJ decision delayed final delimitation
Equatorial Guinea-Gabon: UN urged Equatorial Guinea and Gabon to resolve the sovereignty dispute over Gabon-occupied Mbane and lesser islands and to create a maritime boundary in the hydrocarbon-rich Corisco Bay

Trafficking in persons: *current situation:* human traffickers exploit domestic and foreign victims in Equatorial Guinea and Equatoguineans abroad; the majority of trafficking victims are subjected to forced domestic service and commercial sex in cities, particularly in the hospitality and restaurant sector; local and foreign women, including Latin Americans, are exploited in commercial sex domestically, while some Equatoguinean women are sex trafficked in Spain; some children from rural areas have been forced into domestic servitude; children from nearby countries are forced to labor as domestic workers, market workers, vendors, and launderers; individuals recruited from African countries and temporary workers from Brazil, the Dominican Republic, and Venezuela are sometimes exploited in forced labor and sex trafficking
tier rating:
Tier 2 Watch List — Equatorial Guinea does not fully meet the minimum standards for the elimination of trafficking but is making significant efforts to do so; authorities investigated, and for the first time since 2010, initiated the prosecution of alleged human traffickers; the government partnered with an international organization to provide training for more than 700 officials and civil society actors; authorities developed and implemented formal screening procedures to identify victims within vulnerable populations, an effort that had stalled for five years; however, the government still has not convicted a trafficker or any complicit government employees under its 2004 anti-trafficking law; a lack of training among judicial officials has resulted in potential trafficking crimes being tried under related statutes; victim services remained inadequate; authorities did not report referring any trafficking victims to government housing that was supposed to serve as temporary shelter (2020)

ERITREA

INTRODUCTION

Background: After independence from Italian colonial control in 1941 and 10 years of British administrative control, the UN established Eritrea as an autonomous region within the Ethiopian federation in 1952. Ethiopia's full annexation of Eritrea as a province 10 years later sparked a violent 30-year struggle for independence that ended in 1991 with Eritrean rebels defeating government forces. Eritreans overwhelmingly approved independence in a 1993 referendum. ISAIAS Afwerki has been Eritrea's only president since independence; his rule, particularly since 2001, has been highly autocratic and repressive. His government has created a highly militarized society by pursuing an unpopular program of mandatory conscription into national service – divided between military and civilian service – of indefinite length. A two-and-a-half-year border war with Ethiopia that erupted in 1998 ended under UN auspices in December 2000. A subsequent 2007 Eritrea-Ethiopia Boundary Commission (EEBC) demarcation was rejected by Ethiopia. More than a decade of a tense "no peace, no war" stalemate ended in 2018 after the newly elected Ethiopian prime minister accepted the EEBC's 2007 ruling, and the two countries signed declarations of peace and friendship. Following the July 2018 peace agreement with Ethiopia, Eritrean leaders engaged in intensive diplomacy around the Horn of Africa, bolstering regional peace, security, and cooperation, as well as brokering rapprochements between governments and opposition groups. In November 2018, the UN Security Council lifted an arms embargo that had been imposed on Eritrea since 2009, after the UN Somalia-Eritrea Monitoring Group reported they had not found evidence of Eritrean support in recent years for Al-Shabaab. The country's rapprochement with Ethiopia has led to a steady resumption of economic ties, with increased air transport, trade, tourism, and port activities, but the economy remains agriculture-dependent, and Eritrea is still one of Africa's poorest nations. Despite the country's improved relations with its neighbors, ISAIAS has not let up on repression and conscription and militarization continue.

GEOGRAPHY

Location: Eastern Africa, bordering the Red Sea, between Djibouti and Sudan

Geographic coordinates: 15 00 N, 39 00 E

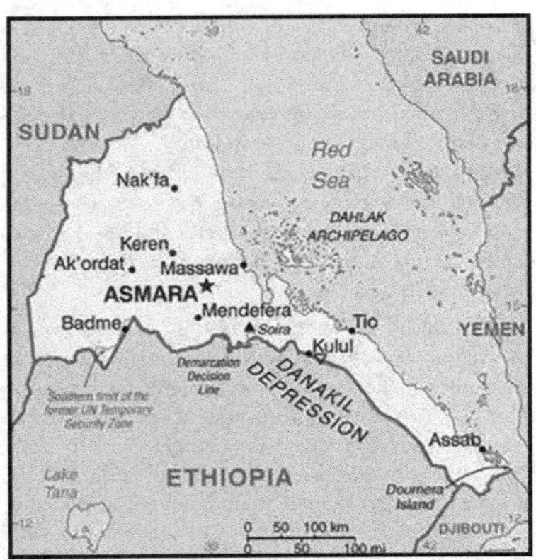

Map references: Africa

Area: *total:* 117,600 sq km
land: 101,000 sq km
water: 16,600 sq km
country comparison to the world: 101

Area - comparative: slightly smaller than Pennsylvania

Land boundaries: *total:* 1,840 km
border countries (3): Djibouti 125 km; Ethiopia 1,033 km; Sudan 682 km

Coastline: 2,234 km (mainland on Red Sea 1,151 km, islands in Red Sea 1,083 km)

Maritime claims: *territorial sea:* 12 nm

Climate: hot, dry desert strip along Red Sea coast; cooler and wetter in the central highlands (up to 61 cm of rainfall annually, heaviest June to September); semiarid in western hills and lowlands

Terrain: dominated by extension of Ethiopian north-south trending highlands, descending on the east to a coastal desert plain, on the northwest to hilly terrain and on the southwest to flat-to-rolling plains

Elevation: *highest point:* Soira 3,018 m
lowest point: near Kulul within the Danakil Depression -75 m
mean elevation: 853 m

Natural resources: gold, potash, zinc, copper, salt, possibly oil and natural gas, fish

Land use: *agricultural land:* 75.1% (2018 est.)
arable land: 6.8% (2018 est.)
permanent crops: 0% (2018 est.)
permanent pasture: 68.3% (2018 est.)
forest: 15.1% (2018 est.)
other: 9.8% (2018 est.)

Irrigated land: 210 sq km (2012)

Population distribution: density is highest in the center of the country in and around the cities of Asmara (capital) and Keren; smaller settlements exist in the north and south as shown in this population distribution map

Natural hazards: frequent droughts, rare earthquakes and volcanoes; locust swarms
volcanism: Dubbi (1,625 m), which last erupted in 1861, was the country's only historically active volcano until Nabro (2,218 m) came to life on 12 June 2011

Geography - note: strategic geopolitical position along world's busiest shipping lanes; Eritrea retained the entire coastline of Ethiopia along the Red Sea upon de jure independence from Ethiopia on 24 May 1993

PEOPLE AND SOCIETY

Population: 6,209,262 (2022 est.)
country comparison to the world: 111

Nationality: *noun:* Eritrean(s)
adjective: Eritrean

Ethnic groups: Tigrinya 50%, Tigre 30%, Saho 4%, Afar 4%, Kunama 4%, Bilen 3%, Hedareb/Beja 2%, Nara 2%, Rashaida 1% (2021 est.)
note: data represent Eritrea's nine recognized ethnic groups

Languages: Tigrinya (official), Arabic (official), English (official), Tigre, Kunama, Afar, other Cushitic languages

Religions: Eritrean Orthodox, Roman Catholic, Evangelical Lutheran, Sunni Muslim

Demographic profile: Eritrea is a persistently poor country that has made progress in some socioeconomic categories but not in others. Education and human capital formation are national priorities for facilitating economic development and eradicating poverty. To this end, Eritrea has made great strides in improving adult literacy – doubling the literacy rate over the last 20 years – in large part because of its successful adult education programs. The overall literacy rate was estimated to be almost 74% in 2015; more work needs to be done to raise female literacy and school attendance among nomadic and rural communities. Subsistence farming fails to meet the needs of Eritrea's growing population because of repeated droughts, dwindling arable land, overgrazing, soil erosion, and a shortage of farmers due to conscription and displacement. The government's emphasis on spending on defense over agriculture and its lack of foreign exchange to import food also contribute to food insecurity.

Eritrea has been a leading refugee source country since at least the 1960s, when its 30-year war for independence from Ethiopia began. Since gaining independence in 1993, Eritreans have continued migrating to Sudan, Ethiopia, Yemen, Egypt, or Israel because of a lack of basic human rights or political freedom, educational and job opportunities, or to seek asylum because of militarization.

Eritrea's large diaspora has been a source of vital remittances, funding its war for independence and providing 30% of the country's GDP annually since it became independent.

In the last few years, Eritreans have increasingly been trafficked and held hostage by Bedouins in the Sinai Desert, where they are victims of organ harvesting, rape, extortion, and torture. Some Eritrean trafficking victims are kidnapped after being smuggled to Sudan or Ethiopia, while others are kidnapped from within or around refugee camps or crossing Eritrea's borders. Eritreans composed approximately 90% of the conservatively estimated 25,000-30,000 victims of Sinai trafficking from 2009-2013, according to a 2013 consultancy firm report.

Age structure: *0-14 years:* 38.23% (male 1,169,456/female 1,155,460)
15-24 years: 20.56% (male 622,172/female 627,858)
25-54 years: 33.42% (male 997,693/female 1,034,550)
55-64 years: 3.8% (male 105,092/female 125,735)
65 years and over: 4% (male 99,231/female 143,949) (2020 est.)

Dependency ratios: *total dependency ratio:* 83.9
youth dependency ratio: 75.6
elderly dependency ratio: 8.3
potential support ratio: 12.1 (2020 est.)

Median age: *total:* 20.3 years
male: 19.7 years
female: 20.8 years (2020 est.)
country comparison to the world: 192

Population growth rate: 1.03% (2022 est.)
country comparison to the world: 93

Birth rate: 27.04 births/1,000 population (2022 est.)
country comparison to the world: 40

Death rate: 6.69 deaths/1,000 population (2022 est.)
country comparison to the world: 130

Net migration rate: -10.11 migrant(s)/1,000 population (2022 est.)
country comparison to the world: 221

Population distribution: density is highest in the center of the country in and around the cities of Asmara (capital) and Keren; smaller settlements exist in the north and south as shown in this population distribution map

Urbanization: *urban population:* 42.6% of total population (2022)
rate of urbanization: 3.67% annual rate of change (2020-25 est.)

Major urban areas - population: 1.035 million ASMARA (capital) (2022)

Sex ratio: *at birth:* 1.03 male(s)/female
0-14 years: 1.01 male(s)/female
15-24 years: 0.99 male(s)/female
25-54 years: 0.96 male(s)/female
55-64 years: 0.88 male(s)/female
65 years and over: 0.67 male(s)/female
total population: 0.97 male(s)/female (2022 est.)

Mother's mean age at first birth: 21.3 years (2010 est.)
note: data represents median age at first birth among women 25-29

Maternal mortality ratio: 480 deaths/100,000 live births (2017 est.)
country comparison to the world: 21

Infant mortality rate: *total:* 41.5 deaths/1,000 live births
male: 48.36 deaths/1,000 live births
female: 34.44 deaths/1,000 live births (2022 est.)
country comparison to the world: 30

Life expectancy at birth: *total population:* 66.85 years
male: 64.25 years
female: 69.53 years (2022 est.)
country comparison to the world: 195

Total fertility rate: 3.58 children born/woman (2022 est.)
country comparison to the world: 35

Drinking water source: *improved: urban:* 73.2% of population
rural: 53.3% of population
total: 57.8% of population
unimproved: urban: 26.8% of population
rural: 46.7% of population
total: 42.2% of population (2015 est.)

Current health expenditure: 4.5% of GDP (2019)

Physicians density: 0.08 physicians/1,000 population (2020)

Hospital bed density: 0.7 beds/1,000 population (2011)

Sanitation facility access: *improved: urban:* 44.5% of population
rural: 7.3% of population
total: 15.7% of population
unimproved: urban: 55.5% of population
rural: 92.7% of population
total: 84.3% of population (2017 est.)

HIV/AIDS - adult prevalence rate: 0.5% (2020 est.)
country comparison to the world: 66

Major infectious diseases: *degree of risk:* high (2020)
food or waterborne diseases: bacterial diarrhea, hepatitis A, and typhoid fever
vectorborne diseases: malaria and dengue fever

Obesity - adult prevalence rate: 5% (2016)
country comparison to the world: 183

Alcohol consumption per capita: *total:* 0.93 liters of pure alcohol (2019 est.)
beer: 0.42 liters of pure alcohol (2019 est.)
wine: 0 liters of pure alcohol (2019 est.)
spirits: 0 liters of pure alcohol (2019 est.)
other alcohols: 0.51 liters of pure alcohol (2019 est.)
country comparison to the world: 153

Tobacco use: *total:* 7.5% (2020 est.)
male: 14.7% (2020 est.)
female: 0.2% (2020 est.)
country comparison to the world: 153

Literacy: *definition:* age 15 and over can read and write
total population: 76.6%
male: 84.4%
female: 68.9% (2018)

School life expectancy (primary to tertiary education): *total:* 8 years
male: 8 years
female: 7 years (2015)

ENVIRONMENT

Environment - current issues: deforestation; desertification; soil erosion; overgrazing

Environment - international agreements: *party to:* Biodiversity, Climate Change, Climate Change-Kyoto Protocol, Comprehensive Nuclear Test Ban, Desertification, Endangered Species, Hazardous Wastes, Ozone Layer Protection, Whaling
signed, but not ratified: Climate Change-Paris Agreement

Air pollutants: *particulate matter emissions:* 42.4 micrograms per cubic meter (2016 est.)
carbon dioxide emissions: 0.71 megatons (2016 est.)
methane emissions: 4.48 megatons (2020 est.)

Climate: hot, dry desert strip along Red Sea coast; cooler and wetter in the central highlands (up to 61 cm of rainfall annually, heaviest June to September); semiarid in western hills and lowlands

Land use: *agricultural land:* 75.1% (2018 est.)
arable land: 6.8% (2018 est.)
permanent crops: 0% (2018 est.)
permanent pasture: 68.3% (2018 est.)
forest: 15.1% (2018 est.)
other: 9.8% (2018 est.)

Urbanization: *urban population:* 42.6% of total population (2022)
rate of urbanization: 3.67% annual rate of change (2020-25 est.)

Waste and recycling: *municipal solid waste generated annually:* 726,957 tons (2011 est.)

Total water withdrawal: *municipal:* 31 million cubic meters (2017 est.)
industrial: 1 million cubic meters (2017 est.)
agricultural: 550 million cubic meters (2017 est.)

Total renewable water resources: 7.315 billion cubic meters (2017 est.)

GOVERNMENT

Country name: *conventional long form:* State of Eritrea
conventional short form: Eritrea
local long form: Hagere Ertra
local short form: Ertra
former: Eritrea Autonomous Region in Ethiopia
etymology: the country name derives from the ancient Greek appellation "Erythra Thalassa" meaning Red Sea, which is the major water body bordering the country

Government type: presidential republic

Capital: *name:* Asmara
geographic coordinates: 15 20 N, 38 56 E
time difference: UTC+3 (8 hours ahead of Washington, DC, during Standard Time)
etymology: the name means "they [women] made them unite," which according to Tigrinya oral tradition refers to the women of the four clans in the Asmara area who persuaded their menfolk to unite and defeat their common enemy; the name has also been translated as "live in peace"

Administrative divisions: 6 regions (zobatat, singular - zoba); 'Anseba, Debub (South), Debubawi K'eyyih Bahri (Southern Red Sea), Gash-Barka, Ma'ikel (Central), Semienawi K'eyyih Bahri (Northern Red Sea)

Independence: 24 May 1993 (from Ethiopia)

National holiday: Independence Day, 24 May (1991)

Constitution: *history:* ratified by the Constituent Assembly 23 May 1997 (not fully implemented)
amendments: proposed by the president of Eritrea or by assent of at least one half of the National Assembly membership; passage requires at least an initial three-quarters majority vote by the Assembly and, after one year, final passage by at least four-fifths majority vote by the Assembly

Legal system: mixed legal system of civil, customary, and Islamic religious law

International law organization participation: has not submitted an ICJ jurisdiction declaration; non-party state to the ICCt

Citizenship: *citizenship by birth:* no
citizenship by descent only: at least one parent must be a citizen of Eritrea
dual citizenship recognized: no
residency requirement for naturalization: 20 years

Suffrage: 18 years of age; universal

Executive branch: *chief of state:* President ISAIAS Afwerki (since 8 June 1993); note - the president is both chief of state and head of government and is head of the State Council and National Assembly
head of government: President ISAIAS Afwerki (since 8 June 1993)
cabinet: State Council appointed by the president
elections/appointments: president indirectly elected by the National Assembly for a 5-year term (eligible for a second term); the only election was held on 8 June 1993, following independence from Ethiopia (next election postponed indefinitely)
election results:
1993: ISAIAS Afwerki elected president by the transitional National Assembly; percent of National Assembly vote - ISAIAS Afwerki (PFDJ) 95%, other 5%

Legislative branch: *description:* unicameral National Assembly (Hagerawi Baito) (150 seats; 75 members indirectly elected by the ruling party and 75 directly elected by simple majority vote; members serve 5-year terms)
elections:
in May 1997, following the adoption of the new constitution, 75 members of the PFDJ Central Committee (the old Central Committee of the EPLF), 60 members of the 527-member Constituent Assembly, which had been established in 1997 to discuss and ratify the new constitution, and 15 representatives of Eritreans living abroad were formed into a Transitional National Assembly to serve as the country's legislative body until countrywide elections to form a National Assembly were held; although only 75 of 150 members of the Transitional National Assembly were elected, the constitution stipulates that once past the transition stage, all members of the National Assembly will be elected by secret ballot of all eligible voters; National Assembly elections scheduled for December 2001 were postponed indefinitely due to the war with Ethiopia, and as of late 2021, there was no sitting legislative body (2021)
election results:
NA

Judicial branch: *highest court(s):* High Court (consists of 20 judges and organized into civil, commercial, criminal, labor, administrative, and customary sections)
judge selection and term of office: High Court judges appointed by the president
subordinate courts: regional/zonal courts; community courts; special courts; sharia courts (for issues dealing with Muslim marriage, inheritance, and family); military courts

Political parties and leaders: People's Front for Democracy and Justice or PFDJ [ISAIAS Afwerki] (the only party recognized by the government)

International organization participation: ACP, AfDB, AU, COMESA, FAO, G-77, IAEA, IBRD, ICAO, ICC (NGOs), IDA, IFAD, IFC, IFRCS (observer), ILO, IMF, IMO, Interpol, IOC, ISO (correspondent), ITU, ITUC (NGOs), LAS (observer), MIGA, NAM, OPCW, PCA, UN, UNCTAD, UNESCO, UNHRC, UNIDO, UNWTO, UPU, WCO, WFTU (NGOs), WHO, WIPO, WMO

Diplomatic representation in the US: *chief of mission:* Ambassador (vacant); Charge d'Affaires Berhane Gebrehiwet SOLOMON (since 15 March 2011)
chancery: 1708 New Hampshire Avenue NW, Washington, DC 20009
telephone: [1] (202) 319-1991
FAX: [1] (202) 319-1304
email address and website:
embassyeritrea@embassyeritrea.org
https://us.embassyeritrea.org/

Diplomatic representation from the US: *chief of mission:* Ambassador (vacant); Charge d'Affaires Steven C. WALKER (since December 2019)
embassy: 179 Alaa Street, Asmara
mailing address: 7170 Asmara Place, Washington DC 20521-7170
telephone: [291] (1) 12-00-04

FAX: [291] (1) 12-75-84
email address and website:
consularasmara@state.gov
https://er.usembassy.gov/

Flag description: red isosceles triangle (based on the hoist side) dividing the flag into two right triangles; the upper triangle is green, the lower one is blue; a gold wreath encircling a gold olive branch is centered on the hoist side of the red triangle; green stands for the country's agriculture economy, red signifies the blood shed in the fight for freedom, and blue symbolizes the bounty of the sea; the wreath-olive branch symbol is similar to that on the first flag of Eritrea from 1952; the shape of the red triangle broadly mimics the shape of the country
note: one of several flags where a prominent component of the design reflects the shape of the country; other such flags are those of Bosnia and Herzegovina, Brazil, and Vanuatu

National symbol(s): camel; national colors: green, red, blue

National anthem: *name:* "Ertra, Ertra, Ertra" (Eritrea, Eritrea, Eritrea)
lyrics/music: SOLOMON Tsehaye Beraki/ Isaac Abraham MEHAREZGI and ARON Tekle Tesfatsion
note: adopted 1993; upon independence from Ethiopia

National heritage: *total World Heritage Sites:* 1 (cultural)
selected World Heritage Site locales: Asmara: A Modernist African City

ECONOMY

Economic overview: Since formal independence from Ethiopia in 1993, Eritrea has faced many economic problems, including lack of financial resources and chronic drought. Eritrea has a command economy under the control of the sole political party, the People's Front for Democracy and Justice. Like the economies of many African nations, a large share of the population - nearly 80% in Eritrea - is engaged in subsistence agriculture, but the sector only produces a small share of the country's total output. Mining accounts for the lion's share of output.

The government has strictly controlled the use of foreign currency by limiting access and availability; new regulations in 2013 aimed at relaxing currency controls have had little economic effect. Few large private enterprises exist in Eritrea and most operate in conjunction with government partners, including a number of large international mining ventures, which began production in 2013. In late 2015, the Government of Eritrea introduced a new currency, retaining the name nakfa, and restricted the amount of hard currency individuals could withdraw from banks per month. The changeover has resulted in exchange fluctuations and the scarcity of hard currency available in the market.

While reliable statistics on Eritrea are difficult to obtain, erratic rainfall and the large percentage of the labor force tied up in military service continue to interfere with agricultural production and economic development. Eritrea's harvests generally cannot meet the food needs of the country without supplemental grain purchases. Copper, potash, and gold production are likely to continue to drive limited economic growth and government revenue over the next few years, but military spending will continue to compete with development and investment plans.

Real GDP (purchasing power parity): $9.702 billion (2017 est.)
$8.953 billion (2016 est.)
$8.791 billion (2015 est.)
note: data are in 2017 dollars
country comparison to the world: 163

Real GDP growth rate: 5% (2017 est.)
1.9% (2016 est.)
2.6% (2015 est.)
country comparison to the world: 46

Real GDP per capita: $1,600 (2017 est.)
$1,500 (2016 est.)
$1,500 (2015 est.)
note: data are in 2017 dollars
country comparison to the world: 217

GDP (official exchange rate): $5.813 billion (2017 est.)

Inflation rate (consumer prices): 9% (2017 est.)
9% (2016 est.)
country comparison to the world: 203

GDP - composition, by sector of origin: *agriculture:* 11.7% (2017 est.)
industry: 29.6% (2017 est.)
services: 58.7% (2017 est.)

GDP - composition, by end use: *household consumption:* 80.9% (2017 est.)
government consumption: 24.3% (2017 est.)
investment in fixed capital: 6.4% (2017 est.)
investment in inventories: 0.1% (2017 est.)
exports of goods and services: 10.9% (2017 est.)
imports of goods and services: -22.5% (2017 est.)

Agricultural products: sorghum, milk, vegetables, barley, cereals, pulses nes, roots/tubers nes, wheat, millet, beef

Industries: food processing, beverages, clothing and textiles, light manufacturing, salt, cement

Industrial production growth rate: 5.4% (2017 est.)
country comparison to the world: 52

Labor force: 2.71 million (2017 est.)
country comparison to the world: 108

Labor force - by occupation: *agriculture:* 80%
industry: 20% (2004 est.)

Unemployment rate: 5.8% (2017 est.)
10% (2016 est.)
country comparison to the world: 95

Population below poverty line: 50% (2004 est.)

Budget: *revenues:* 2.029 billion (2017 est.)
expenditures: 2.601 billion (2017 est.)

Budget surplus (+) or deficit (-): -9.8% (of GDP) (2017 est.)
country comparison to the world: 209

Public debt: 131.2% of GDP (2017 est.)
132.8% of GDP (2016 est.)
country comparison to the world: 6

Taxes and other revenues: 34.9% (of GDP) (2017 est.)
country comparison to the world: 64

Fiscal year: calendar year

Current account balance: -$137 million (2017 est.)
-$105 million (2016 est.)
country comparison to the world: 91

Exports: $624.3 million (2017 est.)
$485.4 million (2016 est.)
country comparison to the world: 187

Exports - partners: China 62%, South Korea 28.3% (2017)

Exports - commodities: gold and other minerals, livestock, sorghum, textiles, food, small industry manufactures

Imports: $1.127 billion (2017 est.)
$1.048 billion (2016 est.)
country comparison to the world: 186

Imports - partners: UAE 14.5%, China 13.2%, Saudi Arabia 13.2%, Italy 12.9%, Turkey 5.6%, South Africa 4.6% (2017)

Imports - commodities: machinery, petroleum products, food, manufactured goods

Reserves of foreign exchange and gold: $236.7 million (31 December 2017 est.)
$218.4 million (31 December 2016 est.)
country comparison to the world: 171

Debt - external: $792.7 million (31 December 2017 est.)
$875.6 million (31 December 2016 est.)
country comparison to the world: 170

Exchange rates: nakfa (ERN) per US dollar -
15.38 (2017 est.)
15.375 (2016 est.)
15.375 (2015 est.)
15.375 (2014 est.)
15.375 (2013 est.)

ENERGY

Electricity access: *electrification - total population:* 47% (2019)
electrification - urban areas: 95% (2019)
electrification - rural areas: 13% (2019)

Electricity: *installed generating capacity:* 228,000 kW (2020 est.)
consumption: 394.46 million kWh (2019 est.)
exports: 0 kWh (2019 est.)
imports: 0 kWh (2019 est.)
transmission/distribution losses: 61 million kWh (2019 est.)

Electricity generation sources: *fossil fuels:* 93.8% of total installed capacity (2020 est.)
solar: 5.7% of total installed capacity (2020 est.)
wind: 0.5% of total installed capacity (2020 est.)

Petroleum: *total petroleum production:* 0 bbl/day (2021 est.)
refined petroleum consumption: 5,200 bbl/day (2019 est.)

Refined petroleum products - imports: 3,897 bbl/day (2015 est.)
country comparison to the world: 179

Carbon dioxide emissions: 798,000 metric tonnes of CO_2 (2019 est.)
from petroleum and other liquids: 798,000 metric tonnes of CO_2 (2019 est.)
country comparison to the world: 179

Energy consumption per capita: 3.217 million Btu/person (2019 est.)
country comparison to the world: 182

COMMUNICATIONS

Telephones - fixed lines: *total subscriptions:* 66,000 (2020 est.)
subscriptions per 100 inhabitants: 2 (2020 est.)
country comparison to the world: 150

Telephones - mobile cellular: *total subscriptions:* 1.801 million (2020 est.)
subscriptions per 100 inhabitants: 51 (2020 est.)
country comparison to the world: 154

Telecommunication systems: *general assessment:* Eritrea's telecom sector operates under a state-owned monopoly for fixed and mobile services; as a result of such restrictions on competition, the country has the least developed telecommunications market in Africa; mobile penetration stands at only about 20%, while fixed-line internet use barely registers; this is exacerbated by the very low use of computers, with only about 4% of households having a computer, and most of these being in the capital, Asmara; the 3G network continues to rollout which provides basic internet access to the majority or Eritreans; investment in telecom infrastructure is still required to improve the quality of services; the government has embarked on a work program to do exactly that, specifically aimed at extending services to remote areas, improving the quality of services, and ensuring that more telecoms infrastructure is supported by solar power to compensate for the poor state of the electricity network; additional foreign investment in telecom infrastructure, as well as introduction of more competition, would help transform what remains a virtually untapped market (2022)
domestic: fixed-line subscribership is less than 2 per 100 persons and mobile-cellular is just over 51 per 100 (2020)
international: country code - 291 (2019)

Broadcast media: government controls broadcast media with private ownership prohibited; 1 state-owned TV station; state-owned radio operates 2 networks; purchases of satellite dishes and subscriptions to international broadcast media are permitted (2019)

Internet country code: .er

Internet users: *total:* 53,200 (2019 est.)
percent of population: 1% (2019 est.)
country comparison to the world: 195

Broadband - fixed subscriptions: *total:* 5,000 (2020 est.)
subscriptions per 100 inhabitants: 0.1 (2020 est.)
country comparison to the world: 187

TRANSPORTATION

National air transport system: *number of registered air carriers:* 1 (2020)
inventory of registered aircraft operated by air carriers: 1
annual passenger traffic on registered air carriers: 102,729 (2018)

Civil aircraft registration country code prefix: E3

Airports: *total:* 13 (2021)
country comparison to the world: 152

Airports - with paved runways: *total:* 4
over 3,047 m: 2
2,438 to 3,047 m: 2 (2021)

Airports - with unpaved runways: *total:* 9
over 3,047 m: 1
2,438 to 3,047 m: 1
1,524 to 2,437 m: 5
914 to 1,523 m: 2 (2021)

Heliports: 1 (2021)

Railways: *total:* 306 km (2018)
narrow gauge: 306 km (2018) 0.950-m gauge
country comparison to the world: 121

Roadways: *total:* 16,000 km (2018)
paved: 1,600 km (2000)
unpaved: 14,400 km (2000)
country comparison to the world: 121

Merchant marine: *total:* 9
by type: general cargo 4, oil tanker 1, other 4 (2021)
country comparison to the world: 157

Ports and terminals: *major seaport(s):* Assab, Massawa

MILITARY AND SECURITY

Military and security forces: Eritrean Defense Forces (EDF): Eritrean Ground Forces, Eritrean Navy, Eritrean Air Force (includes Air Defense Force); Hizbawi Serawit (aka People's Army or People's Militia) (2022)

Military expenditures: 10% of GDP (2019 est.) (approximately $640 million)
10.2% of GDP (2018 est.) (approximately $630 million)
10.3% of GDP (2017 est.) (approximately $630 million)
10.4% of GDP (2016 est.) (approximately $640 million)
10.6% of GDP (2015 est.) (approximately $600 million)
country comparison to the world: 1

Military and security service personnel strengths: limited available information; estimated 150,000-200,000 personnel, including about 2,000 in the naval and air forces (2022)

Military equipment inventories and acquisitions: the EDF inventory is comprised primarily of older Russian and Soviet-era systems; Eritrea was under a UN arms embargo from 2009 to 2018; from the 1990s to 2008, Russia was the leading supplier of arms to Eritrea; in 2019, Eritrea expressed interest in purchasing Russian arms, including missile boats, helicopters, and small arms (2021)

Military service age and obligation: Eritrea mandates military service for all citizens between the ages of 18 and 40 (18-27 for women if conscripted); 18- month conscript service obligation, which includes 4-6 months of military training and 12 months of military or other national service (military service is most common); in practice, military service is often extended indefinitely; citizens up to the age of 55 eligible for recall during mobilization (2022)
note: as of 2020, women were estimated to make up as much as 30% of the Eritrean military

Military - note: since the country's independence in 1991, the Eritrean military has participated in numerous conflicts, including the Hanish Island Crisis with Yemen (1995), the First Congo War (1996-1997), the Second Sudanese Civil War (1996-1998), the Eritrea-Ethiopia War (1998-2000), the Djiboutian-Eritrean border conflict (2008), and the Tigray War (2020-2022) (2022)

TRANSNATIONAL ISSUES

Disputes - international: Eritrea and Ethiopia agreed to abide by 2002 Ethiopia-Eritrea Boundary Commission's (EEBC) delimitation decision, but neither party responded to the revised line detailed in the November 2006 EEBC Demarcation Statement; Sudan accuses Eritrea of supporting eastern Sudanese rebel groups; in 2008, Eritrean troops moved across the border on Ras Doumera peninsula and occupied Doumera Island with undefined sovereignty in the Red Sea

Trafficking in persons: *current situation:* human traffickers export domestic victims in Eritrea or abroad; National Service is mandatory at age 18 and may take a variety of forms, including military service and physical labor but also government office jobs and teaching; Eritreans who flee the country, usually with the aim of reaching Europe, seek the help of paid smugglers and are vulnerable to trafficking when they cross the border clandestinely into Sudan, Ethiopia, and to a lesser extent Djibouti; Eritreans are subject to forced labor and sex trafficking mainly in Sudan, Ethiopia, and Libya
tier rating: Tier 3 — Eritrea does not fully meet the minimum standards for the elimination of trafficking and is not making significant efforts to do so; the government engaged in critical bilateral and multilateral partnerships to build its capacity for anti-trafficking initiatives; officials participated in a UN-sponsored regional anti-trafficking workshop and committed to produce a regional plan of action to combat trafficking; however, a government policy or pattern of forced labor existed; the government continued to subject its nationals to forced labor in its compulsory national service and citizen militia by forcing them to serve indefinitely or for arbitrary periods; authorities did not report any trafficking investigations, prosecutions, or convictions, including complicit government employees, nor did they report identifying victims and referring them to care; the government has no action plan to combat human trafficking (2020)

ESTONIA

INTRODUCTION

Background: After centuries of Danish, Swedish, German, and Russian rule, Estonia attained independence in 1918. Forcibly incorporated into the USSR in 1940 - an action never recognized by the US and many other countries - it regained its freedom in 1991 with the collapse of the Soviet Union. Since the last Russian troops left in 1994, Estonia has been free to promote economic and political ties with the West. It joined both NATO and the EU in the spring of 2004, formally joined the OECD in late 2010, and adopted the euro as its official currency on 1 January 2011.

GEOGRAPHY

Location: Eastern Europe, bordering the Baltic Sea and Gulf of Finland, between Latvia and Russia

Geographic coordinates: 59 00 N, 26 00 E

Map references: Europe

Area: *total:* 45,228 sq km
land: 42,388 sq km
water: 2,840 sq km
note: includes 1,520 islands in the Baltic Sea
country comparison to the world: 132

Area - comparative: about twice the size of New Jersey

Land boundaries: *total:* 657 km
border countries (2): Latvia 333 km; Russia 324 km

Coastline: 3,794 km

Maritime claims: *territorial sea:* 12 nm
exclusive economic zone: limits as agreed to by Estonia, Finland, Latvia, Sweden, and Russia

Climate: maritime; wet, moderate winters, cool summers

Terrain: marshy, lowlands; flat in the north, hilly in the south

Elevation: *highest point:* Suur Munamagi 318 m
lowest point: Baltic Sea 0 m
mean elevation: 61 m

Natural resources: oil shale, peat, rare earth elements, phosphorite, clay, limestone, sand, dolomite, arable land, sea mud

Land use: *agricultural land:* 22.2% (2018 est.)
arable land: 14.9% (2018 est.)
permanent crops: 0.1% (2018 est.)
permanent pasture: 7.2% (2018 est.)
forest: 52.1% (2018 est.)
other: 25.7% (2018 est.)

Irrigated land: 40 sq km (2012)

Population distribution: a fairly even distribution throughout most of the country, with urban areas attracting larger and denser populations

Natural hazards: sometimes flooding occurs in the spring

Geography - note: the mainland terrain is flat, boggy, and partly wooded; offshore lie more than 1,500 islands

PEOPLE AND SOCIETY

Population: 1,211,524 (2022 est.)
country comparison to the world: 160

Nationality: *noun:* Estonian(s)
adjective: Estonian

Ethnic groups: Estonian 68.7%, Russian 24.8%, Ukrainian 1.7%, Belarusian 1%, Finn 0.6%, other 1.6%, unspecified 1.6% (2011 est.)

Languages: Estonian (official) 68.5%, Russian 29.6%, Ukrainian 0.6%, other 1.2%, unspecified 0.1% (2011 est.)

Religions: Orthodox 16.2%, Lutheran 9.9%, other Christian (including Methodist, Seventh Day Adventist, Roman Catholic, Pentecostal) 2.2%, other 0.9%, none 54.1%, unspecified 16.7% (2011 est.)

Age structure: *0-14 years:* 16.22% (male 102,191/female 97,116)
15-24 years: 8.86% (male 56,484/female 52,378)
25-54 years: 40.34% (male 252,273/female 243,382)
55-64 years: 13.58% (male 76,251/female 90,576)
65 years and over: 21% (male 89,211/female 168,762) (2020 est.)

Dependency ratios: *total dependency ratio:* 58.4
youth dependency ratio: 26.1
elderly dependency ratio: 32.3
potential support ratio: 3.1 (2020 est.)

Median age: *total:* 43.7 years
male: 40.4 years
female: 47 years (2020 est.)
country comparison to the world: 21

Population growth rate: -0.71% (2022 est.)
country comparison to the world: 228

Birth rate: 8.75 births/1,000 population (2022 est.)
country comparison to the world: 208

Death rate: 13.1 deaths/1,000 population (2022 est.)
country comparison to the world: 8

Net migration rate: -2.79 migrant(s)/1,000 population (2022 est.)
country comparison to the world: 177

Population distribution: a fairly even distribution throughout most of the country, with urban areas attracting larger and denser populations

Urbanization: *urban population:* 69.6% of total population (2021)
rate of urbanization: -0.03% annual rate of change (2020-25 est.)

Major urban areas - population: 452,000 TALLINN (capital) (2022)

Sex ratio: *at birth:* 1.05 male(s)/female
0-14 years: 1.05 male(s)/female
15-24 years: 1.08 male(s)/female
25-54 years: 1.05 male(s)/female
55-64 years: 0.85 male(s)/female
65 years and over: 0.42 male(s)/female
total population: 0.89 male(s)/female (2022 est.)

Mother's mean age at first birth: 28.2 years (2020 est.)

Maternal mortality ratio: 9 deaths/100,000 live births (2017 est.)
country comparison to the world: 147

Infant mortality rate: *total:* 3.42 deaths/1,000 live births
male: 3.29 deaths/1,000 live births
female: 3.56 deaths/1,000 live births (2022 est.)
country comparison to the world: 200

Life expectancy at birth: *total population:* 77.88 years
male: 73.25 years
female: 82.73 years (2022 est.)
country comparison to the world: 82

Total fertility rate: 1.61 children born/woman (2022 est.)
country comparison to the world: 182

Drinking water source: *improved: urban:* 100% of population
total: 99.6% of population
unimproved: urban: 0% of population
total: 0.4% of population (2020 est.)

Current health expenditure: 6.7% of GDP (2019)

Physicians density: 3.47 physicians/1,000 population (2019)

Hospital bed density: 4.6 beds/1,000 population (2018)

Sanitation facility access: *improved: urban:* 99.8% of population
rural: 100% of population
total: 99.8% of population
unimproved: urban: 0.2% of population
rural: 0% of population
total: 0.2% of population (2020 est.)

HIV/AIDS - adult prevalence rate: 0.8% (2020 est.)
country comparison to the world: 52

Major infectious diseases: *degree of risk:* intermediate (2020)
vectorborne diseases: tickborne encephalitis

Obesity - adult prevalence rate: 21.2% (2016)
country comparison to the world: 92

Alcohol consumption per capita: *total:* 11.65 liters of pure alcohol (2019 est.)
beer: 4 liters of pure alcohol (2019 est.)
wine: 1.92 liters of pure alcohol (2019 est.)
spirits: 4.6 liters of pure alcohol (2019 est.)
other alcohols: 1.13 liters of pure alcohol (2019 est.)
country comparison to the world: 7

Tobacco use: *total:* 29.7% (2020 est.)
male: 36.3% (2020 est.)
female: 23% (2020 est.)
country comparison to the world: 32

Children under the age of 5 years underweight: 0.4% (2013/15)
country comparison to the world: 128

Education expenditures: 5.2% of GDP (2018 est.)
country comparison to the world: 54

Literacy: *definition:* age 15 and over can read and write
total population: 99.8%
male: 99.8%
female: 99.8% (2015)

School life expectancy (primary to tertiary education): *total:* 16 years
male: 15 years
female: 17 years (2019)

Unemployment, youth ages 15-24: *total:* 17.9%
male: 17.4%
female: 18.4% (2020 est.)

ENVIRONMENT

Environment - current issues: air polluted with sulfur dioxide from oil-shale burning power plants in northeast; however, the amounts of pollutants emitted into the air have fallen dramatically and the pollution load of wastewater at purification plants has decreased substantially due to improved technology and environmental monitoring; Estonia has more than 1,400 natural and manmade lakes, the smaller of which in agricultural areas need to be monitored; coastal seawater is polluted in certain locations

Environment - international agreements: *party to:* Air Pollution, Air Pollution-Heavy Metals, Air Pollution-Nitrogen Oxides, Air Pollution-Persistent

Organic Pollutants, Air Pollution-Sulphur 85, Air Pollution-Volatile Organic Compounds, Antarctic Treaty, Biodiversity, Climate Change, Climate Change-Kyoto Protocol, Climate Change-Paris Agreement, Comprehensive Nuclear Test Ban, Desertification, Endangered Species, Environmental Modification, Hazardous Wastes, Law of the Sea, Marine Dumping-London Protocol, Ozone Layer Protection, Ship Pollution, Tropical Timber 2006, Wetlands, Whaling
signed, but not ratified: none of the selected agreements

Air pollutants: *particulate matter emissions:* 6.74 micrograms per cubic meter (2016 est.)
carbon dioxide emissions: 16.59 megatons (2016 est.)
methane emissions: 0.99 megatons (2020 est.)

Climate: maritime; wet, moderate winters, cool summers

Land use: *agricultural land:* 22.2% (2018 est.)
arable land: 14.9% (2018 est.)
permanent crops: 0.1% (2018 est.)
permanent pasture: 7.2% (2018 est.)
forest: 52.1% (2018 est.)
other: 25.7% (2018 est.)

Urbanization: *urban population:* 69.6% of total population (2021)
rate of urbanization: -0.03% annual rate of change (2020-25 est.)

Revenue from forest resources: *forest revenues:* 0.85% of GDP (2018 est.)
country comparison to the world: 55

Revenue from coal: *coal revenues:* 0% of GDP (2018 est.)
country comparison to the world: 95

Waste and recycling: *municipal solid waste generated annually:* 473,000 tons (2015 est.)
municipal solid waste recycled annually: 117,020 tons (2015 est.)
percent of municipal solid waste recycled: 24.7% (2015 est.)

Total water withdrawal: *municipal:* 59.4 million cubic meters (2017 est.)
industrial: 1.721 billion cubic meters (2017 est.)
agricultural: 4.5 million cubic meters (2017 est.)

Total renewable water resources: 12.806 billion cubic meters (2017 est.)

GOVERNMENT

Country name: *conventional long form:* Republic of Estonia
conventional short form: Estonia
local long form: Eesti Vabariik
local short form: Eesti
former: Estonian Soviet Socialist Republic (while occupied by the USSR)
etymology: the country name may derive from the Aesti, an ancient people who lived along the eastern Baltic Sea in the first centuries A.D.

Government type: parliamentary republic

Capital: *name:* Tallinn
geographic coordinates: 59 26 N, 24 43 E
time difference: UTC+2 (7 hours ahead of Washington, DC, during Standard Time)
daylight saving time: +1hr, begins last Sunday in March; ends last Sunday in October
etymology: the Estonian name is generally believed to be derived from "Taani-linn" (originally meaning "Danish castle", now "Danish town") after a stronghold built in the area by the Danes; it could also have come from "tali-linn" ("winter castle" or "winter town") or "talu-linn" ("home castle" or "home town")

Administrative divisions: 15 urban municipalities (linnad, singular - linn), 64 rural municipalities (vallad, singular vald)
urban municipalities: Haapsalu, Keila, Kohtla-Jarve, Loksa, Maardu, Narva, Narva-Joesuu, Paide, Parnu, Rakvere, Sillamae, Tallinn, Tartu, Viljandi, Voru
rural municipalities: Alutaguse, Anija, Antsla, Elva, Haademeeste, Haljala, Harku, Hiiumaa, Jarva, Joelahtme, Jogeva, Johvi, Kadrina, Kambja, Kanepi, Kastre, Kehtna, Kihnu, Kiili, Kohila, Kose, Kuusalu, Laane-Harju, Laane-Nigula, Laaneranna, Luganuse, Luunja, Marjamaa, Muhu, Mulgi, Mustvee, Noo, Otepaa, Peipsiaare, Pohja-Parnumaa, Pohja- Sakala, Poltsamaa, Polva, Raasiku, Rae, Rakvere, Räpina, Rapla, Rouge, Ruhnu, Saarde, Saaremaa, Saku, Saue, Setomaa, Tapa, Tartu, Toila, Tori, Torva, Turi, Vaike-Maarja, Valga, Viimsi, Viljandi, Vinni, Viru-Nigula, Vormsi, Voru

Independence: 24 February 1918 (from Soviet Russia); 20 August 1991 (declared from the Soviet Union); 6 September 1991 (recognized by the Soviet Union)

National holiday: Independence Day, 24 February (1918); note - 24 February 1918 was the date Estonia declared its independence from Soviet Russia and established its statehood; 20 August 1991 was the date it declared its independence from the Soviet Union restoring its statehood

Constitution: *history:* several previous; latest adopted 28 June 1992, entered into force 3 July 1992
amendments: proposed by at least one-fifth of Parliament members or by the president of the republic; passage requires three readings of the proposed amendment and a simple majority vote in two successive memberships of Parliament; passage of amendments to the "General Provisions" and "Amendment of the Constitution" chapters requires at least three-fifths majority vote by Parliament to conduct a referendum and majority vote in a referendum; amended several times, last in 2015

Legal system: civil law system

International law organization participation: accepts compulsory ICJ jurisdiction with reservations; accepts ICCt jurisdiction

Citizenship: *citizenship by birth:* no
citizenship by descent only: at least one parent must be a citizen of Estonia
dual citizenship recognized: no
residency requirement for naturalization: 5 years

Suffrage: 18 years of age; universal; age 16 for local elections

Executive branch: *chief of state:* President Alar KARIS (since 11 October 2021)
head of government: Prime Minister Kaja KALLAS (since 26 January 2021)
cabinet: Cabinet appointed by the prime minister, approved by Parliament
elections/appointments:
president indirectly elected by Parliament for a 5-year term (eligible for a second term); if a candidate does not secure two thirds of the votes after 3 rounds of balloting, then an electoral college consisting of Parliament members and local council members elects the president, choosing between the 2 candidates with the highest number of votes; election last held on 30-31 August 2021 (next to be held in 2026); in a first round of voting on 30 August, parliament failed to elect a president; in a second round on 31 August, the sole candidate, Alar KARIS, received 72 votes of 101 votes (there were 8 blank votes and 21 electors not present); prime minister nominated by the president and approved by Parliament
election results:
2021: Alar KARIS elected president; parliamentary vote Alar KARIS (independent) 72 of 101 votes; KALLAS is Estonia's first female prime minister
2016: Kersti KALJULAID is indirectly elected president with 81 of 98 votes in parliament (17 ballots blank). She is sworn in on October 10 as the first female head of state of Estonia.

Legislative branch: *description:* unicameral Parliament or Riigikogu (101 seats; members directly elected in multi-seat constituencies by open- list proportional representation vote to serve 4-year terms)
elections:
last held on 3 March 2019 (next to be held in March 2023)
election results:
percent of vote by party - RE 28.9%, K 23.1%, EKRE 17.8%, Pro Patria 11.4%, SDE 9.8%, other 9%; seats by party - RE 34, K 26, EKRE 19, Pro Patria 12, SDE 10; composition - men 75, women 26, percent of women 25.7%

Judicial branch: *highest court(s):* Supreme Court (consists of 19 justices, including the chief justice, and organized into civil, criminal, administrative, and constitutional review chambers)
judge selection and term of office: the chief justice is proposed by the president of the republic and appointed by the Riigikogu; other justices proposed by the chief justice and appointed by the Riigikogu; justices appointed for life
subordinate courts: circuit (appellate) courts; administrative, county, city, and specialized courts

Political parties and leaders: Center Party of Estonia (Keskerakond) or K [Juri RATAS]
Estonia 200 [Kristina KALLAS]
Estonian Conservative People's Party (Konservatiivne Rahvaerakond) or EKRE [Martin HELME]
Estonian Reform Party (Reformierakond) or RE [Kaja KALLAS]
Pro Patria (Isamaa) [Helir-Valdor SEEDER]
Social Democratic Party or SDE [Lauri LAANEMETS]

International organization participation: Australia Group, BA, BIS, CBSS, CD, CE, EAPC, EBRD, ECB, EIB, EMU, ESA (cooperating state), EU, FAO, IAEA, IBRD, ICAO, ICC (national committees), ICCt, ICRM, IDA, IEA, IFAD, IFC, IFRCS, IHO, ILO, IMF, IMO, Interpol, IOC, IOM, IPU, ISO, ITSO, ITU, ITUC (NGOs), MIGA, MINUSMA, NATO, NIB, NSG, OAS (observer), OECD, OIF (observer), OPCW, OSCE, PCA, Schengen Convention, UN, UNCTAD, UNESCO, UNHCR, UNTSO, UPU, Wassenaar Arrangement, WCO, WHO, WIPO, WMO, WTO

Diplomatic representation in the US: *chief of mission:* Ambassador Kristjan PRIKK (since 7 July 2021)
chancery: 1990 K Street NW, Washington, DC 20006
telephone: [1] (202) 588-0101

FAX: [1] (202) 588-0108
email address and website:
Embassy.Washington@mfa.ee
https://washington.mfa.ee/
consulate(s) general: New York, San Francisco

Diplomatic representation from the US: *chief of mission:* Ambassador (vacant); Charge d'Affaires Brian RORAFF (since July 2019)
embassy: Kentmanni 20, 15099 Tallinn
mailing address: 4530 Tallinn Place, Washington DC 20521-4530
telephone: [372] 668-8100
FAX: [372] 668-8265
email address and website:
acstallinn@state.gov
https://ee.usembassy.gov/

Flag description: three equal horizontal bands of blue (top), black, and white; various interpretations are linked to the flag colors; blue represents faith, loyalty, and devotion, while also reminiscent of the sky, sea, and lakes of the country; black symbolizes the soil of the country and the dark past and suffering endured by the Estonian people; white refers to the striving towards enlightenment and virtue, and is the color of birch bark and snow, as well as summer nights illuminated by the midnight sun

National symbol(s): barn swallow, cornflower; national colors: blue, black, white

National anthem: *name:* "Mu isamaa, mu onn ja room" (My Native Land, My Pride and Joy)
lyrics/music: Johann Voldemar JANNSEN/Fredrik PACIUS
note: adopted 1920, though banned between 1940 and 1990 under Soviet occupation; the anthem, used in Estonia since 1869, shares the same melody as Finland's but has different lyrics

National heritage: *total World Heritage Sites:* 2 (both cultural)
selected World Heritage Site locales: Historic Center (Old Town) of Tallinn; Struve Geodetic Arc

ECONOMY

Economic overview: Estonia, a member of the EU since 2004 and the euro zone since 2011, has a modern market-based economy and one of the higher per capita income levels in Central Europe and the Baltic region, but its economy is highly dependent on trade, leaving it vulnerable to external shocks. Estonia's successive governments have pursued a free market, pro-business economic agenda, and sound fiscal policies that have resulted in balanced budgets and the lowest debt-to-GDP ratio in the EU.

The economy benefits from strong electronics and telecommunications sectors and strong trade ties with Finland, Sweden, Germany, and Russia. The economy's 4.9% GDP growth in 2017 was the fastest in the past six years, leaving the Estonian economy in its best position since the financial crisis 10 years ago. For the first time in many years, labor productivity increased faster than labor costs in 2017. Inflation also rose in 2017 to 3.5% alongside increased global prices for food and energy, which make up a large share of Estonia's consumption.

Estonia is challenged by a shortage of labor, both skilled and unskilled, although the government has amended its immigration law to allow easier hiring of highly qualified foreign workers, and wage growth that outpaces productivity gains. The government is also pursuing efforts to boost productivity growth with a focus on innovations that emphasize technology start-ups and e-commerce.

Real GDP (purchasing power parity): $47.44 billion (2020 est.)
$48.87 billion (2019 est.)
$46.54 billion (2018 est.)
note: data are in 2017 dollars
country comparison to the world: 113

Real GDP growth rate: 5% (2019 est.)
4.36% (2018 est.)
5.51% (2017 est.)
country comparison to the world: 48

Real GDP per capita: $35,600 (2020 est.)
$36,800 (2019 est.)
$35,200 (2018 est.)
note: data are in 2017 dollars
country comparison to the world: 54

GDP (official exchange rate): $31.461 billion (2019 est.)

Inflation rate (consumer prices): 2.2% (2019 est.)
3.4% (2018 est.)
3.4% (2017 est.)
country comparison to the world: 118

Credit ratings:

Fitch rating: AA- (2018)

Moody's rating: A1 (2002)

Standard & Poors rating: AA- (2011)
note: The year refers to the year in which the current credit rating was first obtained.

GDP - composition, by sector of origin: *agriculture:* 2.8% (2017 est.)
industry: 29.2% (2017 est.)
services: 68.1% (2017 est.)

GDP - composition, by end use: *household consumption:* 50.3% (2017 est.)
government consumption: 20.4% (2017 est.)
investment in fixed capital: 24% (2017 est.)
investment in inventories: 2.2% (2017 est.)
exports of goods and services: 77.2% (2017 est.)
imports of goods and services: -74% (2017 est.)

Agricultural products: wheat, milk, barley, rapeseed, rye, oats, peas, potatoes, pork, triticale

Industries: food, engineering, electronics, wood and wood products, textiles; information technology, telecommunications

Industrial production growth rate: 9.5% (2017 est.)
country comparison to the world: 17

Labor force: 648,000 (2020 est.)
country comparison to the world: 151

Labor force - by occupation: *agriculture:* 2.7%
industry: 20.5%
services: 76.8% (2017 est.)

Unemployment rate: 4.94% (2019 est.)
4.73% (2018 est.)
country comparison to the world: 74

Unemployment, youth ages 15-24: *total:* 17.9%
male: 17.4%
female: 18.4% (2020 est.)
country comparison to the world: 90

Population below poverty line: 21.7% (2018 est.)

Gini Index coefficient - distribution of family income: 30.4 (2017 est.)
35.6 (2014)
country comparison to the world: 149

Household income or consumption by percentage share: *lowest 10%:* 2.3%
highest 10%: 25.6% (2015)

Budget: *revenues:* 10.37 billion (2017 est.)
expenditures: 10.44 billion (2017 est.)

Budget surplus (+) or deficit (-): -0.3% (of GDP) (2017 est.)
country comparison to the world: 52

Public debt: 9% of GDP (2017 est.)
9.4% of GDP (2016 est.)
note: data cover general government debt and include debt instruments issued (or owned) by government entities, including sub-sectors of central government, state government, local government, and social security funds
country comparison to the world: 199

Taxes and other revenues: 39.9% (of GDP) (2017 est.)
country comparison to the world: 41

Fiscal year: calendar year

Current account balance: $616 million (2019 est.)
$280 million (2018 est.)
country comparison to the world: 53

Exports: $21.69 billion (2020 est.) note: data are in current year dollars
$22.94 billion (2019 est.) note: data are in current year dollars
$22.69 billion (2018 est.) note: data are in current year dollars
country comparison to the world: 78

Exports - partners: Finland 13%, Sweden 9%, Latvia 8%, Russia 8%, United States 7%, Lithuania 6%, Germany 6% (2019)

Exports - commodities: broadcasting equipment, refined petroleum, coal tar oil, cars, prefabricated buildings (2019)

Imports: $21.73 billion (2020 est.) note: data are in current year dollars
$21.68 billion (2019 est.) note: data are in current year dollars
$21.89 billion (2018 est.) note: data are in current year dollars
country comparison to the world: 80

Imports - partners: Russia 12%, Germany 10%, Finland 9%, Lithuania 7%, Latvia 7%, Sweden 6%, Poland 6%, China 6% (2019)

Imports - commodities: cars, refined petroleum, coal tar oil, broadcasting equipment, packaged medicines (2019)

Reserves of foreign exchange and gold: $345 million (31 December 2017 est.)
$352.2 million (31 December 2016 est.)
country comparison to the world: 164

Debt - external: $23.944 billion (2019 est.)
$23.607 billion (2018 est.)
country comparison to the world: 89

Exchange rates: euros (EUR) per US dollar -
0.82771 (2020 est.)
0.90338 (2019 est.)
0.87789 (2018 est.)
0.885 (2014 est.)
0.7634 (2013 est.)

ENERGY

Electricity access: *electrification - total population:* 100% (2020)

Electricity: *installed generating capacity:* 3.03 million kW (2020 est.)

consumption: 9.172 billion kWh (2020 est.)
exports: 3.722 billion kWh (2020 est.)
imports: 7.367 billion kWh (2020 est.)
transmission/distribution losses: 375 million kWh (2020 est.)

Electricity generation sources: *fossil fuels:* 55.8% of total installed capacity (2020 est.)
solar: 2% of total installed capacity (2020 est.)
wind: 14.3% of total installed capacity (2020 est.)
hydroelectricity: 0.7% of total installed capacity (2020 est.)
biomass and waste: 27.2% of total installed capacity (2020 est.)

Coal: *production:* 0 metric tons (2020 est.)
consumption: 3,000 metric tons (2020 est.)
exports: 0 metric tons (2020 est.)
imports: 3,000 metric tons (2020 est.)
proven reserves: 0 metric tons (2019 est.)

Petroleum: *total petroleum production:* 21,800 bbl/day (2021 est.)
refined petroleum consumption: 27,500 bbl/day (2019 est.)
crude oil and lease condensate exports: 0 bbl/day (2018 est.)
crude oil and lease condensate imports: 0 bbl/day (2018 est.)
crude oil estimated reserves: 0 barrels (2021 est.)

Refined petroleum products - production: 0 bbl/day (2017 est.)
country comparison to the world: 141

Refined petroleum products - exports: 27,150 bbl/day (2017 est.)
country comparison to the world: 64

Refined petroleum products - imports: 35,520 bbl/day (2017 est.)
country comparison to the world: 95

Natural gas: *production:* 0 cubic meters (2021 est.)
consumption: 417.106 million cubic meters (2020 est.)
exports: 0 cubic meters (2021 est.)
imports: 417.276 million cubic meters (2020 est.)
proven reserves: 0 cubic meters (2021 est.)

Carbon dioxide emissions: 4.924 million metric tonnes of CO_2 (2019 est.)
from coal and metallurgical coke: 44,000 metric tonnes of CO_2 (2019 est.)
from petroleum and other liquids: 3.979 million metric tonnes of CO_2 (2019 est.)
from consumed natural gas: 901,000 metric tonnes of CO_2 (2019 est.)
country comparison to the world: 135

Energy consumption per capita: 76.329 million Btu/person (2019 est.)
country comparison to the world: 80

COMMUNICATIONS

Telephones - fixed lines: *total subscriptions:* 304,728 (2020 est.)
subscriptions per 100 inhabitants: 23 (2020 est.)
country comparison to the world: 109

Telephones - mobile cellular: *total subscriptions:* 1,925,789 (2020 est.)
subscriptions per 100 inhabitants: 145 (2020 est.)
country comparison to the world: 149

Telecommunication systems: *general assessment:* the competitive telecom market continues to progress with a range of regulatory measures which have enabled alternative operators to chip away at the fixed-line market share; fixed-line infrastructure upgrades have been focused on fiber, and the legacy DSL network has gradually been replaced; limited commercial 5G deployments have been made though an expansion of service availability awaits the delayed auction of spectrum in the 3.5GHz band, which is expected to be held later in 2021 (2021)
domestic: just under 23 per 100 for fixed-line subscribership and approximately 145 per 100 for mobile-cellular; substantial fiber-optic cable systems carry telephone, TV, and radio traffic in the digital mode; Internet services are widely available; schools and libraries are connected to the Internet, a large percentage of the population files income tax returns online, and online voting - in local and parliamentary elections - has climbed steadily since first being introduced in 2005; a large percent of Estonian households have broadband access (2020)
international: country code - 372; landing points for the EE-S-1, EESF-3, Baltic Sea Submarine Cable, FEC and EESF-2 fiber-optic submarine cables to other Estonia points, Finland, and Sweden; 2 international switches are located in Tallinn (2019)

Broadcast media: the publicly owned broadcaster, Eesti Rahvusringhaaling (ERR), operates 3 TV channels and 5 radio networks; growing number of private commercial radio stations broadcasting nationally, regionally, and locally; fully transitioned to digital television in 2010; national private TV channels expanding service; a range of channels are aimed at Russian-speaking viewers; in 2016, there were 42 on-demand services available in Estonia, including 19 pay TVOD and SVOD services; roughly 85% of households accessed digital television services

Internet country code: .ee

Internet users: *total:* 1,276,521 (July 2022 est.)
percent of population: 96.1% (July 2022 est.)
country comparison to the world: 141

Broadband - fixed subscriptions: *total:* 415,610 (2020 est.)
subscriptions per 100 inhabitants: 31 (2020 est.)
country comparison to the world: 96

TRANSPORTATION

National air transport system: *number of registered air carriers:* 3 (2020)
inventory of registered aircraft operated by air carriers: 14
annual passenger traffic on registered air carriers: 31,981 (2018)

Civil aircraft registration country code prefix: ES

Airports: *total:* 18 (2021)
country comparison to the world: 138

Airports - with paved runways: *total:* 13
over 3,047 m: 2
2,438 to 3,047 m: 8
1,524 to 2,437 m: 2
914 to 1,523 m: 1 (2021)

Airports - with unpaved runways: *total:* 5
1,524 to 2,437 m: 1
914 to 1,523 m: 1
under 914 m: 3 (2021)

Heliports: 1 (2021)

Pipelines: 2,360 km gas (2016)

Railways: *total:* 2,146 km (2016)
broad gauge: 2,146 km (2016) 1.520-m and 1.524-m gauge (132 km electrified)
note: includes 1,510 km public and 636 km non-public railway
country comparison to the world: 71

Roadways: *total:* 58,412 km (2011) (includes urban roads)
paved: 10,427 km (2011) (includes 115 km of expressways)
unpaved: 47,985 km (2011)
country comparison to the world: 78

Waterways: 335 km (2011) (320 km are navigable year-round)
country comparison to the world: 99

Merchant marine: *total:* 68
by type: general cargo 2, oil tanker 4, other 62 (2021)
country comparison to the world: 106

Ports and terminals: *major seaport(s):* Kuivastu, Kunda, Muuga, Parnu Reid, Sillamae, Tallinn

MILITARY AND SECURITY

Military and security forces: Estonian Defense Forces: Land Forces, Navy, Air Force, Estonian Defense League (Reserves) (2022)

Military expenditures: 2.35% of GDP (2022 est.)
2.2% of GDP (2021)
2.4% of GDP (2020)
2% of GDP (2019) (approximately $850 million)
2% of GDP (2018) (approximately $800 million)
country comparison to the world: 47

Military and security service personnel strengths: approximately 7,000 active duty personnel; approximately 15,000 Defense League (2022)

Military equipment inventories and acquisitions: the Estonian military has a limited inventory of Soviet-era and some more recently acquired modern weapons systems, largely from western European countries, particularly France and the Netherlands (2021)

Military service age and obligation: 18-27 for compulsory military or governmental service for men; conscript service requirement 8-11 months depending on education; non-commissioned officers, reserve officers, and specialists serve 11 months; women can volunteer, and as of 2018 could serve in any military branch (2022)
note 1: conscripts comprise approximately 3,000-3,300 of the Estonian military's 7,000 active duty personnel and serve in all branches, except for the Air Force, which does not have conscripts; after conscript service, reservists are called up for training every 5 years; Estonia has had conscription since 1991
note 2: the Estonian Defense Forces rely largely on reservists who have completed compulsory conscription in the previous 10 years to fill out its active duty and Territorial Defense units during a crisis; a total of approximately 230,000 Estonians are enrolled in the mobilization registry
note 3: in 2020, women comprised about 10% of the full-time professional military force

Military - note: Estonia became a member of NATO in 2004
since 2017, Estonia has hosted a UK-led multi-national NATO ground force battlegroup as part of the Alliance's Enhanced Forward Presence initiative; NATO has provided air protection for Estonia since 2004 through its Air Policing mission; NATO member countries that possess air combat capabilities voluntarily contribute to the mission on 4-month rotations; NATO fighter aircraft have been hosted at Estonia's Ämari Air Base since 2014 (2022)

TRANSNATIONAL ISSUES

Disputes - international: Russia and Estonia in May 2005 signed a technical border agreement, but Russia in June 2005 recalled its signature after the Estonian parliament added to its domestic ratification act a historical preamble referencing the Soviet occupation and Estonia's pre-war borders under the 1920 Treaty of Tartu; Russia contends that the preamble allows Estonia to make territorial claims on Russia in the future, while Estonian officials deny that the preamble has any legal impact on the treaty text; Russia demands better treatment of the Russian-speaking population in Estonia; as a member state that forms part of the EU's external border, Estonia implements strict Schengen border rules with Russia

Refugees and internally displaced persons: *refugees (country of origin):* 62,239 (Ukraine) (as of 15 November 2022)
stateless persons: 71,873 (mid-year 2021); note - following independence in 1991, automatic citizenship was restricted to those who were Estonian citizens prior to the 1940 Soviet occupation and their descendants; thousands of ethnic Russians remained stateless when forced to choose between passing Estonian language and citizenship tests or applying for Russian citizenship; one reason for demurring on Estonian citizenship was to retain the right of visa-free travel to Russia; stateless residents can vote in local elections but not general elections; stateless parents who have been lawful residents of Estonia for at least five years can apply for citizenship for their children before they turn 15 years old

Illicit drugs: producer of synthetic drugs; important transshipment zone for cannabis, cocaine, opiates, and synthetic drugs since joining the European Union and the Schengen Accord; potential money laundering related to organized crime and drug trafficking is a concern, as is possible use of the gambling sector to launder funds; major use of opiates and ecstasy

ESWATINI

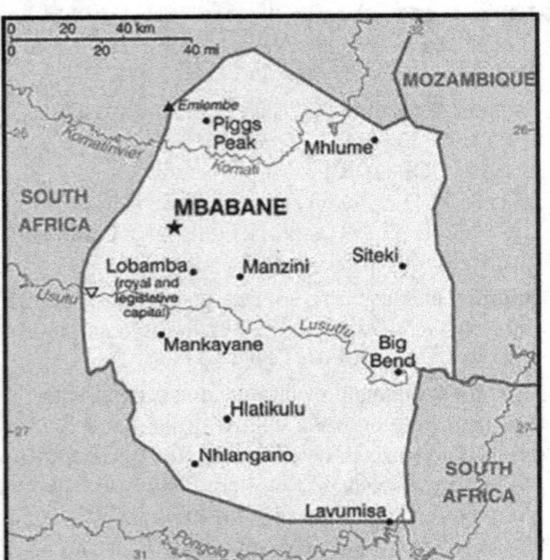

INTRODUCTION

Background: Autonomy for Eswatini was guaranteed by the British in the late 19th century; independence was granted in 1968. A new constitution came into effect in 2006, which included provisions for a more independent parliament and judiciary, but the legal status of political parties remains unclear. King MSWATI III renamed the country from Swaziland to Eswatini in April 2018. Despite its classification as a lower-middle income country, Eswatini suffers from severe poverty and high unemployment. Eswatini has the world's highest HIV/AIDS prevalence rate, although recent years have shown marked declines in new infections.

GEOGRAPHY

Location: Southern Africa, between Mozambique and South Africa

Geographic coordinates: 26 30 S, 31 30 E

Map references: Africa

Area: *total:* 17,364 sq km
land: 17,204 sq km
water: 160 sq km

Area - comparative: slightly smaller than New Jersey

Land boundaries: *total:* 546 km
border countries (2): Mozambique 108 km; South Africa 438 km

Coastline: 0 km (landlocked)

Maritime claims: none (landlocked)

Climate: varies from tropical to near temperate

Terrain: mostly mountains and hills; some moderately sloping plains

Elevation: *highest point:* Emlembe 1,862 m
lowest point: Great Usutu River 21 m
mean elevation: 305 m

Natural resources: asbestos, coal, clay, cassiterite, hydropower, forests, small gold and diamond deposits, quarry stone, and talc

Land use: *agricultural land:* 68.3% (2018 est.)
arable land: 9.8% (2018 est.)
permanent crops: 0.8% (2018 est.)
permanent pasture: 57.7% (2018 est.)
forest: 31.7% (2018 est.)
other: 0% (2018 est.)

Irrigated land: 500 sq km (2012)

Population distribution: because of its mountainous terrain, the population distribution is uneven throughout the country, concentrating primarily in valleys and plains as shown in this population distribution map

Natural hazards: drought

Geography - note: landlocked; almost completely surrounded by South Africa

PEOPLE AND SOCIETY

Population: 1,121,761 (2022 est.)

Nationality: *noun:* liSwati (singular), emaSwati (plural); note - former term, Swazi(s), still used among English speakers
adjective: Swati; note - former term, Swazi, still used among English speakers

Ethnic groups: predominantly Swazi; smaller populations of other African ethnic groups, including the Zulu, as well as people of European ancestry

Languages: English (official, used for government business), siSwati (official)

Religions: Christian 90% (Zionist - a blend of Christianity and indigenous ancestral worship - 40%, Roman Catholic 20%, other 30% - includes Anglican, Methodist, Church of Jesus Christ, Jehovah's Witness), Muslim 2%, other 8% (includes Baha'i, Buddhist, Hindu, indigenous, Jewish) (2015 est.)

Demographic profile: Eswatini, a small, predominantly rural, landlocked country surrounded by South Africa and Mozambique, suffers from severe poverty and the world's highest HIV/AIDS prevalence rate. A weak and deteriorating economy, high unemployment, rapid population growth, and an uneven distribution of resources all combine to worsen already persistent poverty and food insecurity, especially in rural areas. Erratic weather (frequent droughts and intermittent heavy rains and flooding), overuse of small plots, the overgrazing of cattle, and outdated agricultural practices reduce crop yields and further degrade the environment, exacerbating Eswatini's poverty and subsistence problems. Eswatini's extremely high HIV/AIDS prevalence rate – more than 28% of adults have the disease – compounds these issues. Agricultural production has declined due to HIV/AIDS, as the illness causes households to lose manpower and to sell livestock and other assets to pay for medicine and funerals.

Swazis, mainly men from the country's rural south, have been migrating to South Africa to work in coal, and later gold, mines since the late 19th century. Although the number of miners abroad has never been high in absolute terms because of Eswatini's small population, the outflow has had important social and economic repercussions. The peak of mining employment in South Africa occurred during the 1980s. Cross-border movement has accelerated since the 1990s, as increasing unemployment has pushed more Swazis to look for work in South Africa (creating a "brain drain" in the health and educational sectors); southern Swazi men have continued to pursue mining, although the industry has downsized. Women now make up an increasing share of migrants and dominate cross-border trading in handicrafts, using the proceeds to purchase goods back in Eswatini. Much of today's migration, however, is not work-related but focuses on visits to family and friends, tourism, and shopping.

Age structure: *0-14 years:* 33.63% (male 185,640/female 185,808)
15-24 years: 18.71% (male 98,029/female 108,654)
25-54 years: 39.46% (male 202,536/female 233,275)
55-64 years: 4.36% (male 20,529/female 27,672)
65 years and over: 3.83% (male 15,833/female 26,503) (2020 est.)

Dependency ratios: *total dependency ratio:* 70.8
youth dependency ratio: 64
elderly dependency ratio: 6.9

potential support ratio: 14.6 (2020 est.)

Median age: *total:* 23.7 years
male: 22.5 years
female: 24.7 years (2020 est.)

Population growth rate: 0.75% (2022 est.)

Birth rate: 23.35 births/1,000 population (2022 est.)

Death rate: 9.71 deaths/1,000 population (2022 est.)

Net migration rate: -6.16 migrant(s)/1,000 population (2022 est.)

Population distribution: because of its mountainous terrain, the population distribution is uneven throughout the country, concentrating primarily in valleys and plains as shown in this population distribution map

Urbanization: *urban population:* 24.6% of total population (2022)
rate of urbanization: 2.42% annual rate of change (2020-25 est.)

Major urban areas - population: 68,000 MBABANE (capital) (2018)

Sex ratio: *at birth:* 1.03 male(s)/female
0-14 years: 1 male(s)/female
15-24 years: 0.91 male(s)/female
25-54 years: 0.87 male(s)/female
55-64 years: 0.73 male(s)/female
65 years and over: 0.48 male(s)/female
total population: 0.9 male(s)/female (2022 est.)

Maternal mortality ratio: 437 deaths/100,000 live births (2017 est.)

Infant mortality rate: *total:* 39.63 deaths/1,000 live births
male: 43.89 deaths/1,000 live births
female: 35.25 deaths/1,000 live births (2022 est.)

Life expectancy at birth: *total population:* 59.69 years
male: 57.62 years
female: 61.81 years (2022 est.)

Total fertility rate: 2.44 children born/woman (2022 est.)

Contraceptive prevalence rate: 66.1% (2014)

Drinking water source: *improved: urban:* 97.5% of population
rural: 74.8% of population
total: 80.3% of population
unimproved: urban: 2.5% of population
rural: 25.2% of population
total: 19.7% of population (2020 est.)

Current health expenditure: 6.8% of GDP (2019)

Physicians density: 0.14 physicians/1,000 population (2020)

Hospital bed density: 2.1 beds/1,000 population (2011)

Sanitation facility access: *improved: urban:* 92.3% of population
rural: 83.9% of population
total: 85.9% of population
unimproved: urban: 7.7% of population
rural: 16.1% of population
total: 14.1% of population (2020 est.)

HIV/AIDS - adult prevalence rate: 26.8% (2020 est.)

Major infectious diseases: *degree of risk:* intermediate (2020)
food or waterborne diseases: bacterial diarrhea, hepatitis A, and typhoid fever
vectorborne diseases: malaria
water contact diseases: schistosomiasis

Obesity - adult prevalence rate: 16.5% (2016)

Alcohol consumption per capita: *total:* 7.68 liters of pure alcohol (2019 est.)
beer: 2.45 liters of pure alcohol (2019 est.)
wine: 0.06 liters of pure alcohol (2019 est.)
spirits: 0 liters of pure alcohol (2019 est.)
other alcohols: 5.17 liters of pure alcohol (2019 est.)

Tobacco use: *total:* 9.2% (2020 est.)
male: 16.5% (2020 est.)
female: 1.8% (2020 est.)

Children under the age of 5 years underweight: 5.8% (2014)

Education expenditures: 5.3% of GDP (2020 est.)

Literacy: *definition:* age 15 and over can read and write
total population: 88.4%
male: 88.3%
female: 88.5% (2018)

School life expectancy (primary to tertiary education): *total:* 13 years
male: 13 years
female: 12 years (2013)

Unemployment, youth ages 15-24: *total:* 47.1%
male: 44.2%
female: 50% (2016)

ENVIRONMENT

Environment - current issues: limited supplies of potable water; wildlife populations being depleted because of excessive hunting; population growth, deforestation, and overgrazing lead to soil erosion and soil degradation

Environment - international agreements: *party to:* Biodiversity, Climate Change, Climate Change-Kyoto Protocol, Climate Change-Paris Agreement, Comprehensive Nuclear Test Ban, Desertification, Endangered Species, Hazardous Wastes, Law of the Sea, Nuclear Test Ban, Ozone Layer Protection, Wetlands
signed, but not ratified: none of the selected agreements

Air pollutants: *particulate matter emissions:* 16.26 micrograms per cubic meter (2016 est.)
carbon dioxide emissions: 1.16 megatons (2016 est.)
methane emissions: 1.9 megatons (2020 est.)

Climate: varies from tropical to near temperate

Land use: *agricultural land:* 68.3% (2018 est.)
arable land: 9.8% (2018 est.)
permanent crops: 0.8% (2018 est.)
permanent pasture: 57.7% (2018 est.)
forest: 31.7% (2018 est.)
other: 0% (2018 est.)

Urbanization: *urban population:* 24.6% of total population (2022)
rate of urbanization: 2.42% annual rate of change (2020-25 est.)

Revenue from forest resources: *forest revenues:* 2.25% of GDP (2018 est.)

Revenue from coal: *coal revenues:* 0.1% of GDP (2018 est.)

Food insecurity: *severe localized food insecurity: due to higher staple food prices* - the price of maize meal, the key food staple, increased in the first five months of 2022 and, as of May 2022, were 3 percent higher on a yearly basis; wheat flour prices were also at record highs in May 2022; this mainly reflects the elevated global prices and the country's high dependence on imported wheat to satisfy national consumption needs (2022)

Waste and recycling: *municipal solid waste generated annually:* 218,199 tons (2016 est.)

Total water withdrawal: *municipal:* 41.3 million cubic meters (2017 est.)
industrial: 20.7 million cubic meters (2017 est.)
agricultural: 1.006 billion cubic meters (2017 est.)

Total renewable water resources: 4.51 billion cubic meters (2017 est.)

GOVERNMENT

Country name: *conventional long form:* Kingdom of Eswatini
conventional short form: Eswatini
local long form: Umbuso weSwatini
local short form: eSwatini
former: Swaziland
etymology: the country name derives from 19th century King MSWATI II, under whose rule Swati territory was expanded and unified
note: pronounced ay-swatini or eh-swatini

Government type: absolute monarchy

Capital: *name:* Mbabane (administrative capital); Lobamba (royal and legislative capital)
geographic coordinates: 26 19 S, 31 08 E
time difference: UTC+2 (7 hours ahead of Washington, DC, during Standard Time)
etymology: named after a Swati chief, Mbabane KUNENE, who lived in the area at the onset of British settlement

Administrative divisions: 4 regions; Hhohho, Lubombo, Manzini, Shiselweni

Independence: 6 September 1968 (from the UK)

National holiday: Independence Day (Somhlolo Day), 6 September (1968)

Constitution: *history:* previous 1968, 1978; latest signed by the king 26 July 2005, effective 8 February 2006
amendments: proposed at a joint sitting of both houses of Parliament; passage requires majority vote by both houses and/or majority vote in a referendum, and assent of the king; passage of amendments affecting "specially entrenched" constitutional provisions requires at least three-fourths majority vote by both houses, passage by simple majority vote in a referendum, and assent of the king; passage of "entrenched" provisions requires at least two-thirds majority vote of both houses, passage in a referendum, and assent of the king

Legal system: mixed legal system of civil, common, and customary law

International law organization participation: accepts compulsory ICJ jurisdiction with reservations; non-party state to the ICCt

Citizenship: *citizenship by birth:* no
citizenship by descent only: both parents must be citizens of Eswatini
dual citizenship recognized: no
residency requirement for naturalization: 5 years

Suffrage: 18 years of age

Executive branch: *chief of state:* King MSWATI III (since 25 April 1986)
head of government: Prime Minister Cleopas DLAMINI (since since 19 July 2021); Deputy Prime Minister Themba MASUKU (since 6 November 2018)

cabinet: Cabinet recommended by the prime minister, confirmed by the monarch; at least one-half of the cabinet membership must be appointed from among elected members of the House of Assembly
elections/appointments: the monarchy is hereditary; prime minister appointed by the monarch from among members of the House of Assembly

Legislative branch: *description:* bicameral Parliament (Libandla) consists of:
Senate (30 seats; 20 members appointed by the monarch and 10 indirectly elected by simple majority vote by the House of Assembly; members serve 5-year terms)
House of Assembly (70 seats statutory, current 74; 59 members directly elected in single-seat constituencies or tinkhundla by absolute majority vote in 2 rounds if needed, 10 members appointed by the monarch, 4 women elected by the members if representation of elected women is less than 30%, and 1 ex-officio member - the attorney general; members serve 5-year terms)
elections:
Senate - last held on 23 October 2018 (next to be held - 31 October 2023)
House of Assembly - last held on 21 September 2018 (next to be held in 2023)
election results:
Senate - percent of seats by party - NA; seats by party - NA; composition - men 18, women 12, percent of women 40%
House of Assembly - percent of vote by party - NA; seats by party - independent 59; composition - men 65, women 9, percent of women 12.2%; note - total Parliament percent of women 20.2%

Judicial branch: *highest court(s):* Supreme Court (consists of the chief justice and at least 4 justices) and the High Court (consists of the chief justice - ex officio - and 4 justices); note - the Supreme Court has jurisdiction in all constitutional matters
judge selection and term of office: justices of the Supreme Court and High Court appointed by the monarch on the advice of the Judicial Service Commission (JSC), a judicial advisory body consisting of the Supreme Court Chief Justice, 4 members appointed by the monarch, and the chairman of the Civil Service Commission; justices of both courts eligible for retirement at age 65 with mandatory retirement at age 75
subordinate courts: magistrates' courts; National Swazi Courts for administering customary/traditional laws (jurisdiction restricted to customary law for Swazi citizens)

Political parties and leaders: political parties exist but conditions for their operations, particularly in elections, are undefined, legally unclear, or culturally restricted; the following are considered political associations:
African United Democratic Party or AUDP [Sibusiso DLAMINI]
Ngwane National Liberatory Congress or NNLC [Sibongile MAZIBUKO]
People's United Democratic Movement or PUDEMO [Mlungisi MAKHANYA]
Swazi Democratic Party or SWADEPA [Jan SITHOLE]

International organization participation: ACP, AfDB, AU, C, COMESA, FAO, G-77, IAEA, IBRD, ICAO, ICRM, IDA, IFAD, IFC, IFRCS, ILO, IMF, IMO, Interpol, IOC, IOM, ISO (correspondent), ITSO, ITU, ITUC (NGOs), MIGA, NAM, OPCW, PCA, SACU, SADC, UN, UNCTAD, UNESCO, UNIDO, UNWTO, UPU, WCO, WHO, WIPO, WMO, WTO

Diplomatic representation in the US: *chief of mission:* Ambassador Kennedy Fitzgerald GROENING (7 June 2022)
chancery: 1712 New Hampshire Avenue NW, Washington, DC 20009
telephone: [1] (202) 234-5002
FAX: [1] (202) 234-8254
email address and website:
embassy@swaziland-usa.com; swaziland@compuserve.com

Diplomatic representation from the US: *chief of mission:* Ambassador Jeanne M. MALONEY (since 4 March 2021)
embassy: Corner of MR 103 and Cultural Center Drive, Ezulwini, P.O. Box D202, The Gables, H106
mailing address: 2350 Mbabane Place, Washington DC 20521-2350
telephone: (268) 2417-9000
FAX: [268] 2416-3344
email address and website:
ConsularMbabane@state.gov
https://sz.usembassy.gov/

Flag description: three horizontal bands of blue (top), red (triple width), and blue; the red band is edged in yellow; centered in the red band is a large black and white shield covering two spears and a staff decorated with feather tassels, all placed horizontally; blue stands for peace and stability, red represents past struggles, and yellow the mineral resources of the country; the shield, spears, and staff symbolize protection from the country's enemies, while the black and white of the shield are meant to portray black and white people living in peaceful coexistence

National symbol(s): lion, elephant; national colors: blue, yellow, red

National anthem: *name:* "Nkulunkulu Mnikati wetibusiso temaSwati" (Oh God, Bestower of the Blessings of the Swazi)
lyrics/music: Andrease Enoke Fanyana SIMELANE/ David Kenneth RYCROFT
note: adopted 1968; uses elements of both ethnic Swazi and Western music styles

ECONOMY

Economic overview: A small, landlocked kingdom, Eswatini is bordered in the north, west and south by the Republic of South Africa and by Mozambique in the east. Eswatini depends on South Africa for a majority of its exports and imports. Eswatini's currency is pegged to the South African rand, effectively relinquishing Eswatini's monetary policy to South Africa. The government is dependent on customs duties from the Southern African Customs Union (SACU) for almost half of its revenue. Eswatini is a lower middle income country. As of 2017, more than one-quarter of the adult population was infected by HIV/AIDS; Eswatini has the world's highest HIV prevalence rate, a financial strain and source of economic instability.

The manufacturing sector diversified in the 1980s and 1990s, but manufacturing has grown little in the last decade. Sugar and soft drink concentrate are the largest foreign exchange earners, although a drought in 2015-16 decreased sugar production and exports. Overgrazing, soil depletion, drought, and floods are persistent problems. Mining has declined in importance in recent years. Coal, gold, diamond, and quarry stone mines are small scale, and the only iron ore mine closed in 2014. With an estimated 28% unemployment rate, Eswatini's need to increase the number and size of small and medium enterprises and to attract foreign direct investment is acute.

Eswatini's national development strategy, which expires in 2022, prioritizes increases in infrastructure, agriculture production, and economic diversification, while aiming to reduce poverty and government spending. Eswatini's revenue from SACU receipts are likely to continue to decline as South Africa pushes for a new distribution scheme, making it harder for the government to maintain fiscal balance without introducing new sources of revenue.

Real GDP (purchasing power parity): $9.74 billion (2020 est.)
$9.9 billion (2019 est.)
$9.68 billion (2018 est.)
note: data are in 2017 dollars

Real GDP growth rate: 1.6% (2017 est.)
1.4% (2016 est.)
0.4% (2015 est.)

Real GDP per capita: $8,400 (2020 est.)
$8,600 (2019 est.)
$8,500 (2018 est.)
note: data are in 2017 dollars

GDP (official exchange rate): $4.484 billion (2019 est.)

Inflation rate (consumer prices): 6.2% (2017 est.)
7.8% (2016 est.)

Credit ratings: Moody's rating: B3 (2020)
note: The year refers to the year in which the current credit rating was first obtained.

GDP - composition, by sector of origin: *agriculture:* 6.5% (2017 est.)
industry: 45% (2017 est.)
services: 48.6% (2017 est.)

GDP - composition, by end use: *household consumption:* 64% (2017 est.)
government consumption: 21.3% (2017 est.)
investment in fixed capital: 13.4% (2017 est.)
investment in inventories: -0.1% (2017 est.)
exports of goods and services: 47.9% (2017 est.)
imports of goods and services: -46.3% (2017 est.)

Agricultural products: sugar cane, maize, roots/tubers nes, grapefruit, oranges, milk, beef, potatoes, vegetables, bananas

Industries: soft drink concentrates, coal, forestry, sugar processing, textiles, and apparel

Industrial production growth rate: 5.6% (2017 est.)

Labor force: 427,900 (2016 est.)

Labor force - by occupation: *agriculture:* 10.7%
industry: 30.4%
services: 58.9% (2014 est.)

Unemployment rate: 28% (2014 est.)
28% (2013 est.)

Unemployment, youth ages 15-24: *total:* 47.1%
male: 44.2%
female: 50% (2016)

Population below poverty line: 58.9% (2016 est.)

Gini Index coefficient - distribution of family income: 54.6 (2016 est.)

Household income or consumption by percentage share: *lowest 10%:* 1.7%
highest 10%: 40.1% (2010 est.)

Budget: *revenues:* 1.263 billion (2017 est.)
expenditures: 1.639 billion (2017 est.)

Budget surplus (+) or deficit (-): -8.5% (of GDP) (2017 est.)

Public debt: 28.4% of GDP (2017 est.)
25.5% of GDP (2016 est.)

Taxes and other revenues: 28.6% (of GDP) (2017 est.)

Fiscal year: 1 April - 31 March

Current account balance: $604 million (2017 est.)
$642 million (2016 est.)

Exports: $1.81 billion (2020 est.) note: data are in current year dollars
$2.07 billion (2019 est.) note: data are in current year dollars
$1.9 billion (2018 est.) note: data are in current year dollars

Exports - partners: South Africa 94% (2017)

Exports - commodities: soft drink concentrates, sugar, timber, cotton yarn, refrigerators, citrus, and canned fruit

Imports: $1.7 billion (2020 est.) note: data are in current year dollars
$1.93 billion (2019 est.) note: data are in current year dollars
$2.07 billion (2018 est.) note: data are in current year dollars

Imports - partners: South Africa 81.6%, China 5.2% (2017)

Imports - commodities: motor vehicles, machinery, transport equipment, foodstuffs, petroleum products, chemicals

Reserves of foreign exchange and gold: $563.1 million (31 December 2017 est.)
$564.4 million (31 December 2016 est.)

Debt - external: $535 million (2019 est.)
$456 million (2018 est.)

Exchange rates: emalangeni per US dollar -
14.44 (2017 est.)
14.6924 (2016 est.)
14.6924 (2015 est.)
12.7581 (2014 est.)
10.8469 (2013 est.)

ENERGY

Electricity access: *electrification - total population:* 90% (2019)
electrification - urban areas: 98% (2019)
electrification - rural areas: 87% (2019)

Electricity: *installed generating capacity:* 286,000 kW (2020 est.)
consumption: 1,448,308,000 kWh (2019 est.)
exports: 0 kWh (2019 est.)
imports: 942 million kWh (2019 est.)
transmission/distribution losses: 154.7 million kWh (2019 est.)

Electricity generation sources: *fossil fuels:* 44.1% of total installed capacity (2020 est.)
solar: 0.2% of total installed capacity (2020 est.)
hydroelectricity: 24.8% of total installed capacity (2020 est.)
biomass and waste: 31% of total installed capacity (2020 est.)

Coal: *production:* 108,000 metric tons (2020 est.)
consumption: 169,000 metric tons (2020 est.)
exports: 163,000 metric tons (2020 est.)
imports: 135,000 metric tons (2020 est.)
proven reserves: 144 million metric tons (2019 est.)

Petroleum: *total petroleum production:* 0 bbl/day (2021 est.)
refined petroleum consumption: 6,000 bbl/day (2019 est.)

Refined petroleum products - production: 0 bbl/day (2015 est.)

Refined petroleum products - exports: 0 bbl/day (2015 est.)

Refined petroleum products - imports: 5,279 bbl/day (2015 est.)

Natural gas: *production:* 0 cubic meters (2021 est.)
consumption: 0 cubic meters (2021 est.)
exports: 0 cubic meters (2021 est.)
imports: 0 cubic meters (2021 est.)
proven reserves: 0 cubic meters (2021 est.)

Carbon dioxide emissions: 1.224 million metric tonnes of CO2 (2019 est.)
from coal and metallurgical coke: 350,000 metric tonnes of CO2 (2019 est.)
from petroleum and other liquids: 875,000 metric tonnes of CO2 (2019 est.)
from consumed natural gas: 0 metric tonnes of CO2 (2019 est.)

Energy consumption per capita: 19.371 million Btu/person (2019 est.)

COMMUNICATIONS

Telephones - fixed lines: *total subscriptions:* 39,000 (2020 est.)
subscriptions per 100 inhabitants: 3 (2020 est.)

Telephones - mobile cellular: *total subscriptions:* 1.243 million (2020 est.)
subscriptions per 100 inhabitants: 107 (2020 est.)

Telecommunication systems: *general assessment:* Eswatini was one of the last countries in the world to open up its telecom market to competition; until 2011 the state-owned Eswatini Posts and Telecommunications also acted as the industry regulator and had a stake in the country's sole mobile network; a new independent regulatory authority was established in late 2013 and has since embarked on significant changes to the sector; mobile market subscriptions have been affected by the common use among subscribers when they use SIM cards from different networks in order to access cheaper on-net calls; subscriber growth has slowed in recent years, but was expected to have reached 8% in 2021, as people adapted to the changing needs for connectivity caused by the pandemic; the internet sector has been open to competition with a small number of licensed ISPs; DSL services were introduced in 2008, development of the sector has been hampered by the limited fixed-line infrastructure and by a lack of competition in the access and backbone networks; Eswatini is landlocked and so depends on neighboring countries for international bandwidth; this has meant that access pricing is relatively high, and market subscriptions remains relatively low; prices have fallen recently in line with greater bandwidth availability resulting from several new submarine cable systems which have reached the region in recent years; in September 2020 a terrestrial cable linked Mozambique with Eswatini and South Africa (2022)
domestic: Eswatini has 2 mobile-cellular providers; communication infrastructure has a geographic coverage of about 90% and a rising subscriber base; fixed-line stands at nearly 3 per 100 and mobile-cellular teledensity roughly 107 telephones per 100 persons; telephone system consists of carrier-equipped, open-wire lines and low-capacity, microwave radio relay (2020)
international: country code - 268; satellite earth station - 1 Intelsat (Atlantic Ocean)

Broadcast media: 1 state-owned TV station; satellite dishes are able to access South African providers; state-owned radio network with 3 channels; 1 private radio station (2019)

Internet country code: .sz

Internet users: *total:* 539,623 (2019 est.)
percent of population: 47% (2019 est.)

Broadband - fixed subscriptions: *total:* 12,000 (2020 est.)
subscriptions per 100 inhabitants: 1 (2020 est.)

TRANSPORTATION

Civil aircraft registration country code prefix: 3DC

Airports: *total:* 14 (2021)

Airports - with paved runways: *total:* 2
over 3,047 m: 1
2,438 to 3,047 m: 1 (2021)

Airports - with unpaved runways: *total:* 12
914 to 1,523 m: 5
under 914 m: 7 (2021)

Railways: *total:* 301 km (2014)
narrow gauge: 301 km (2014) 1.067-m gauge

Roadways: *total:* 3,769 km (2019)

MILITARY AND SECURITY

Military and security forces: Umbutfo Eswatini Defense Force (UEDF): Army (includes a small air wing) (2022)

Military expenditures: 1.7% of GDP (2021 est.)
1.8% of GDP (2020 est.)
1.9% of GDP (2019 est.) (approximately $140 million)
2.1% of GDP (2018 est.) (approximately $150 million)
2.1% of GDP (2017 est.) (approximately $140 million)

Military and security service personnel strengths: approximately 3,000 active duty personnel (2022)

Military equipment inventories and acquisitions: the UEDF is lightly armed with mostly South African material; it has received small amounts of second-hand equipment since 2010 (2021)

Military service age and obligation: 18-30 years of age for voluntary military service for men and women; no conscription (2021)

Military - note: the UEDF was originally created in 1973 as the Royal Swaziland Defense Force; the UEDF's primary mission is external security but it also has domestic security responsibilities, including protecting members of the royal family; the king is the UEDF commander in chief and holds the position of minister of defense, although the UEDF reports to the Army commander and principal undersecretary of defense for day-to-day operations; the Royal Eswatini Police Service (REPS) is responsible for maintaining internal security as well as migration and border crossing enforcement; it is under the prime minister, although the king is the force's titular commissioner in chief (2022)

TRANSNATIONAL ISSUES

Disputes - international: in 2006, Swati king advocated resorting to ICJ to claim parts of Mpumalanga and KwaZulu-Natal from South Africa

ETHIOPIA

INTRODUCTION

Background: Unique among African countries, the ancient Ethiopian monarchy maintained its freedom from colonial rule with the exception of a short-lived Italian occupation from 1936 to 1941. In 1974, a military junta, the Derg, deposed Emperor Haile SELASSIE (who had ruled since 1930) and established a socialist state. Torn by bloody coups, uprisings, wide-scale drought, and massive refugee problems, the regime was finally toppled in 1991 by a coalition of rebel forces, the Ethiopian People's Revolutionary Democratic Front (EPRDF). A constitution was adopted in 1994, and Ethiopia's first multiparty elections were held in 1995.

A border war with Eritrea in the late 1990s ended with a peace treaty in December 2000. In November 2007, the Eritrea- Ethiopia Border Commission (EEBC) issued specific coordinates as virtually demarcating the border and pronounced its work finished. Alleging that the EEBC acted beyond its mandate in issuing the coordinates, Ethiopia did not accept them and maintained troops in previously contested areas pronounced by the EEBC as belonging to Eritrea. This intransigence resulted in years of heightened tension between the two countries. In August 2012, longtime leader Prime Minister MELES Zenawi died in office and was replaced by his Deputy Prime Minister HAILEMARIAM Desalegn, marking the first peaceful transition of power in decades. Following a wave of popular dissent and anti-government protest that began in 2015, HAILEMARIAM resigned in February 2018 and ABIY Ahmed Ali took office in April 2018 as Ethiopia's first ethnic Oromo prime minister. In June 2018, ABIY announced Ethiopia would accept the border ruling of 2000, prompting rapprochement between Ethiopia and Eritrea that was marked with a peace agreement in July 2018 and a reopening of the border in September 2018. In November 2019, Ethiopia's nearly 30-year ethnic-based ruling coalition - the EPRDF - merged into a single unity party called the Prosperity Party, however, one of the four constituent parties (the Tigray Peoples Liberation Front or TPLF) refused to join.

In November 2020, a military conflict erupted between forces aligned with the Tigrayan People's Liberation Front (TPLF) and Ethiopia's national military, the Ethiopian National Defense Force. The conflict, which has continued into 2022, has exacerbated ethnic violence and has largely centered in Tigray, Amhara, and Afar regional states.

GEOGRAPHY

Location: Eastern Africa, west of Somalia

Geographic coordinates: 8 00 N, 38 00 E

Map references: Africa

Area: *total:* 1,104,300 sq km
land: 1,096,570 sq km
water: 7,730 sq km
note: area numbers are approximate since a large portion of the Ethiopia-Somalia border is undefined
country comparison to the world: 28

Area - comparative: slightly less than twice the size of Texas

Land boundaries: *total:* 5,925 km
border countries (6): Djibouti 342 km; Eritrea 1,033 km; Kenya 867 km; Somalia 1,640 km; South Sudan 1,299 km; Sudan 744 km

Coastline: 0 km (landlocked)

Maritime claims: none (landlocked)

Climate: tropical monsoon with wide topographic-induced variation

Terrain: high plateau with central mountain range divided by Great Rift Valley

Elevation: *highest point:* Ras Dejen 4,550 m
lowest point: Danakil Depression -125 m
mean elevation: 1,330 m

Natural resources: small reserves of gold, platinum, copper, potash, natural gas, hydropower

Land use: *agricultural land:* 36.3% (2018 est.)
arable land: 15.2% (2018 est.)
permanent crops: 1.1% (2018 est.)
permanent pasture: 20% (2018 est.)
forest: 12.2% (2018 est.)
other: 51.5% (2018 est.)

Irrigated land: 2,900 sq km (2012)

Major lakes (area sq km): *fresh water lake(s):* Lake Tana - 3,600 sq km; Abaya Hayk - 1,160 sq km; Ch'amo Hayk - 550 sq km
salt water lake(s): Lake Turkana (shared with Kenya) - 6,400 sq km; Abhe Bid Hayk/Abhe Bad (shared with Djibouti) - 780 sq km;

Major rivers (by length in km): Blue Nile river source (shared with Sudan [m]) - 1,600 km
note – [s] after country name indicates river source; [m] after country name indicates river mouth

Major watersheds (area sq km): Atlantic Ocean drainage: *(Mediterranean Sea)* Nile (3,254,853 sq km)

Major aquifers: Ogaden-Juba Basin, Sudd Basin (Umm Ruwaba Aquifer)

Population distribution: highest density is found in the highlands of the north and middle areas of the country, particularly around the centrally located capital city of Addis Ababa; the far east and southeast are sparsely populated as shown in this population distribution map

Natural hazards: geologically active Great Rift Valley susceptible to earthquakes, volcanic eruptions; frequent droughts
volcanism: volcanic activity in the Great Rift Valley; Erta Ale (613 m), which has caused frequent lava flows in recent years, is the country's most active volcano; Dabbahu became active in 2005, forcing evacuations; other historically active volcanoes include Alayta, Dalaffilla, Dallol, Dama Ali, Fentale, Kone, Manda Hararo, and Manda-Inakir

Geography - note: *note 1:* landlocked - entire coastline along the Red Sea was lost with the de jure independence of Eritrea on 24 May 1993; Ethiopia is, therefore, the most populous landlocked country in the world; the Blue Nile, the chief headstream of the Nile by water volume, rises in T'ana Hayk (Lake Tana) in northwest Ethiopia
note 2: three major crops may have originated in Ethiopia: coffee (almost certainly), grain sorghum, and castor bean

PEOPLE AND SOCIETY

Population: 113,656,596 (2022 est.)
country comparison to the world: 13

Nationality: *noun:* Ethiopian(s)
adjective: Ethiopian

Ethnic groups: Oromo 35.8%, Amhara 24.1%, Somali 7.2%, Tigray 5.7%, Sidama 4.1%, Guragie 2.6%, Welaita 2.3%, Afar 2.2%, Silte 1.3%, Kefficho 1.2%, other 13.5% (2022 est.)

Languages: Oromo (official working language in the State of Oromiya) 33.8%, Amharic (official national language) 29.3%, Somali (official working language of the State of Sumale) 6.2%, Tigrigna (Tigrinya) (official working language of the State of Tigray) 5.9%, Sidamo 4%, Wolaytta 2.2%, Gurage 2%, Afar (official working language of the State of Afar) 1.7%,

Hadiyya 1.7%, Gamo 1.5%, Gedeo 1.3%, Opuuo 1.2%, Kafa 1.1%, other 8.1%, English (major foreign language taught in schools), Arabic (2007 est.)
major-language sample(s):
Kitaaba Addunyaa Waan Qabataamaatiif - Kan Madda Odeeffannoo bu'uraawaatiif baay'ee barbaachisaa ta'e. (Oromo)
የአለም አውነታ መጽሐፍ፣ ለመሠረታዊ መረጃ አጅግ አስፈላጊ የሆነ ምንጭ:: (Amharic)

Religions: Ethiopian Orthodox 43.8%, Muslim 31.3%, Protestant 22.8%, Catholic 0.7%, traditional 0.6%, other 0.8% (2016 est.)

Demographic profile: Ethiopia is a predominantly agricultural country – nearly 80% of the population lives in rural areas – that is in the early stages of demographic transition. Infant, child, and maternal mortality have fallen sharply over the past decade, but the total fertility rate has declined more slowly and the population continues to grow. The rising age of marriage and the increasing proportion of women remaining single have contributed to fertility reduction. While the use of modern contraceptive methods among married women has increased significantly from 6 percent in 2000 to 27 percent in 2012, the overall rate is still quite low.

Ethiopia's rapid population growth is putting increasing pressure on land resources, expanding environmental degradation, and raising vulnerability to food shortages. With about 40 percent of the population below the age of 15 and a fertility rate of 4 children per woman (and even higher in rural areas), Ethiopia will have to make further progress in meeting its family planning needs if it is to achieve the age structure necessary for reaping a demographic dividend in the coming decades.

Poverty, drought, political repression, and forced government resettlement have driven Ethiopia's internal and external migration since the 1960s. Before the 1974 revolution, only small numbers of the Ethiopian elite went abroad to study and then returned home, but under the brutal Derg regime thousands fled the country, primarily as refugees. Between 1982 and 1991 there was a new wave of migration to the West for family reunification. Since the defeat of the Derg in 1991, Ethiopians have migrated to escape violence among some of the country's myriad ethnic groups or to pursue economic opportunities. Internal and international trafficking of women and children for domestic work and prostitution is a growing problem.

Age structure: *0-14 years:* 39.81% (male 21,657,152/female 21,381,628)
15-24 years: 19.47% (male 10,506,144/female 10,542,128)
25-54 years: 32.92% (male 17,720,540/female 17,867,298)
55-64 years: 4.42% (male 2,350,606/female 2,433,319)
65 years and over: 3.38% (male 1,676,478/female 1,977,857) (2020 est.)

Dependency ratios: *total dependency ratio:* 76.8
youth dependency ratio: 70.6
elderly dependency ratio: 6.3
potential support ratio: 16 (2020 est.)

Median age: *total:* 19.8 years
male: 19.6 years
female: 20.1 years (2020 est.)
country comparison to the world: 197

Population growth rate: 2.46% (2022 est.)
country comparison to the world: 25

Birth rate: 30.49 births/1,000 population (2022 est.)
country comparison to the world: 29

Death rate: 5.7 deaths/1,000 population (2022 est.)
country comparison to the world: 173

Net migration rate: -0.19 migrant(s)/1,000 population (2022 est.)
country comparison to the world: 110

Population distribution: highest density is found in the highlands of the north and middle areas of the country, particularly around the centrally located capital city of Addis Ababa; the far east and southeast are sparsely populated as shown in this population distribution map

Urbanization: *urban population:* 22.7% of total population (2022)
rate of urbanization: 4.4% annual rate of change (2020-25 est.)

Major urban areas - population: 5.228 million ADDIS ABABA (capital) (2022)

Sex ratio: *at birth:* 1.03 male(s)/female
0-14 years: 1.01 male(s)/female
15-24 years: 1 male(s)/female
25-54 years: 0.99 male(s)/female
55-64 years: 0.96 male(s)/female
65 years and over: 0.68 male(s)/female
total population: 0.99 male(s)/female (2022 est.)

Mother's mean age at first birth: 19.3 years (2019 est.)
note: data represents median age at first birth among women 20-49

Maternal mortality ratio: 401 deaths/100,000 live births (2017 est.)
country comparison to the world: 26

Infant mortality rate: *total:* 33.51 deaths/1,000 live births
male: 38.33 deaths/1,000 live births
female: 28.55 deaths/1,000 live births (2022 est.)
country comparison to the world: 42

Life expectancy at birth: *total population:* 68.25 years
male: 66.12 years
female: 70.44 years (2022 est.)
country comparison to the world: 183

Total fertility rate: 3.99 children born/woman (2022 est.)
country comparison to the world: 28

Contraceptive prevalence rate: 37.7% (2020)

Drinking water source: *improved: urban:* 98.5% of population
rural: 70.2% of population
total: 76.4% of population
unimproved: urban: 1.5% of population
rural: 29.8% of population
total: 23.6% of population (2020 est.)

Current health expenditure: 3.2% of GDP (2019)

Physicians density: 0.11 physicians/1,000 population (2020)

Hospital bed density: 0.3 beds/1,000 population (2016)

Sanitation facility access: *improved: urban:* 52.5% of population
rural: 8.1% of population
total: 17.7% of population
unimproved: urban: 47.5% of population
rural: 91.9% of population
total: 82.3% of population (2020 est.)

HIV/AIDS - adult prevalence rate: 0.9% (2020 est.)
country comparison to the world: 48

Major infectious diseases: *degree of risk:* very high (2020)
food or waterborne diseases: bacterial and protozoal diarrhea, hepatitis A, and typhoid fever
vectorborne diseases: malaria and dengue fever
water contact diseases: schistosomiasis
animal contact diseases: rabies
respiratory diseases: meningococcal meningitis
note: on 21 March 2022, the US Centers for Disease Control and Prevention (CDC) issued a Travel Alert for polio in Africa; Ethiopia is currently considered a high risk to travelers for circulating vaccine-derived polioviruses (cVDPV); vaccine-derived poliovirus (VDPV) is a strain of the weakened poliovirus that was initially included in oral polio vaccine (OPV) and *that has changed over time and behaves more like the wild or naturally occurring virus*; this means it can be spread more easily to people who are unvaccinated against polio and who come in contact with the stool or respiratory secretions, such as from a sneeze, of an "infected" person who received oral polio vaccine; the CDC recommends that before any international travel, anyone unvaccinated, incompletely vaccinated, or with an unknown polio vaccination status should complete the routine polio vaccine series; before travel to any high-risk destination, CDC recommends that adults who previously completed the full, routine polio vaccine series receive a single, lifetime booster dose of polio vaccine

Obesity - adult prevalence rate: 4.5% (2016)
country comparison to the world: 185

Alcohol consumption per capita: *total:* 1.16 liters of pure alcohol (2019 est.)
beer: 0.92 liters of pure alcohol (2019 est.)
wine: 0 liters of pure alcohol (2019 est.)
spirits: 0.2 liters of pure alcohol (2019 est.)
other alcohols: 0.03 liters of pure alcohol (2019 est.)
country comparison to the world: 149

Tobacco use: *total:* 5.1% (2020 est.)
male: 8.8% (2020 est.)
female: 1.3% (2020 est.)
country comparison to the world: 161

Children under the age of 5 years underweight: 21.1% (2019)
country comparison to the world: 17

Child marriage: *women married by age 15:* 14.1%
women married by age 18: 40.3%
men married by age 18: 5% (2016 est.)

Education expenditures: 5.1% of GDP (2018 est.)
country comparison to the world: 58

Literacy: *definition:* age 15 and over can read and write
total population: 51.8%
male: 57.2%
female: 44.4% (2017)

School life expectancy (primary to tertiary education): *total:* 9 years
male: 8 years
female: 8 years (2012)

Unemployment, youth ages 15-24: *total:* 3.5%
male: 2.7%
female: 4.5% (2013 est.)

ENVIRONMENT

Environment - current issues: deforestation; overgrazing; soil erosion; desertification; loss of biodiversity; water shortages in some areas from water-intensive farming and poor management; industrial pollution and pesticides contribute to air, water, and soil pollution

Environment - international agreements: *party to:* Biodiversity, Climate Change, Climate Change-Kyoto Protocol, Climate Change-Paris Agreement, Comprehensive Nuclear Test Ban, Desertification, Endangered Species, Hazardous Wastes, Ozone Layer Protection
signed, but not ratified: Environmental Modification, Law of the Sea, Nuclear Test Ban

Air pollutants: *particulate matter emissions:* 34.36 micrograms per cubic meter (2016 est.)
carbon dioxide emissions: 14.87 megatons (2016 est.)
methane emissions: 114.21 megatons (2020 est.)

Climate: tropical monsoon with wide topographic-induced variation

Land use: *agricultural land:* 36.3% (2018 est.)
arable land: 15.2% (2018 est.)
permanent crops: 1.1% (2018 est.)
permanent pasture: 20% (2018 est.)
forest: 12.2% (2018 est.)
other: 51.5% (2018 est.)

Urbanization: *urban population:* 22.7% of total population (2022)
rate of urbanization: 4.4% annual rate of change (2020-25 est.)

Revenue from forest resources: *forest revenues:* 5.81% of GDP (2018 est.)
country comparison to the world: 11

Revenue from coal: *coal revenues:* 0% of GDP (2018 est.)
country comparison to the world: 96

Food insecurity: *widespread lack of access: due to conflict in Tigray Region, drought conditions in southeastern areas, high food prices* - The difficult and worsening food security situation is the result of multiple shocks affecting food availability and access including: the conflict in northern Tigray Region and in adjacent areas of Amhara and Afar regions, which began in November 2020; in Tigray region alone, 5.3 million people are estimated to be severely food insecure; the failure of the March-May 2022 "Gu-Genna" rains in southern pastoral areas of southern Oromiya Region and southern Somali Region, exacerbated drought conditions prevailing since late 2020, causing severe crop and livestock losses; severe macroeconomic challenges including insufficient foreign currency reserves and the continuous depreciation of the national currency, as a result, inflation is at very high levels, with the year-on-year food inflation rate estimated at 35.5 percent in July, one the highest of the last decade; these difficulties are exacerbated by the ripple effects of the Ukraine war, which triggered hikes in international prices of wheat, fuel and fertilizers (2022)

Waste and recycling: *municipal solid waste generated annually:* 6,532,787 tons (2015 est.)

Major lakes (area sq km): *fresh water lake(s):* Lake Tana - 3,600 sq km; Abaya Hayk - 1,160 sq km; Ch'amo Hayk - 550 sq km
salt water lake(s): Lake Turkana (shared with Kenya) - 6,400 sq km; Abhe Bid Hayk/Abhe Bad (shared with Djibouti) - 780 sq km;

Major rivers (by length in km): Blue Nile river source (shared with Sudan [m]) - 1,600 km

note – [s] after country name indicates river source; [m] after country name indicates river mouth

Major watersheds (area sq km): Atlantic Ocean drainage: *(Mediterranean Sea)* Nile (3,254,853 sq km)

Major aquifers: Ogaden-Juba Basin, Sudd Basin (Umm Ruwaba Aquifer)

Total water withdrawal: *municipal:* 810 million cubic meters (2017 est.)
industrial: 51.1 million cubic meters (2017 est.)
agricultural: 9.687 billion cubic meters (2017 est.)

Total renewable water resources: 122 billion cubic meters (2017 est.)

GOVERNMENT

Country name: *conventional long form:* Federal Democratic Republic of Ethiopia
conventional short form: Ethiopia
local long form: Ityop'iya Federalawi Demokrasiyawi Ripeblik
local short form: Ityop'iya
former: Abyssinia, Italian East Africa
abbreviation: FDRE
etymology: the country name derives from the Greek word "Aethiopia," which in classical times referred to lands south of Egypt in the Upper Nile region

Government type: federal parliamentary republic

Capital: *name:* Addis Ababa
geographic coordinates: 9 02 N, 38 42 E
time difference: UTC+3 (8 hours ahead of Washington, DC, during Standard Time)
etymology: the name in Amharic means "new flower" and was bestowed on the city in 1889, three years after its founding

Administrative divisions: 11 ethnically based regional states (kililoch, singular - kilil) and 2 chartered cities* (astedader akabibiwach, singular - astedader akabibi); Adis Abeba* (Addis Ababa), Afar, Amara (Amhara), Binshangul Gumuz, Dire Dawa*, Gambela Hizboch (Gambela Peoples), Hareri Hizb (Harari People), Oromiya (Oromia), Sidama, Sumale (Somali), Tigray, YeDebub Biheroch Bihereseboch na Hizboch (Southern Nations, Nationalities and Peoples), YeDebub M'irab Ityop'iya Hizboch (Southwest Ethiopia Peoples)

Independence: oldest independent country in Africa and one of the oldest in the world - at least 2,000 years (may be traced to the Aksumite Kingdom, which coalesced in the first century B.C.)

National holiday: Derg Downfall Day (defeat of MENGISTU regime), 28 May (1991)

Constitution: *history:* several previous; latest drafted June 1994, adopted 8 December 1994, entered into force 21 August 1995
amendments: proposals submitted for discussion require two-thirds majority approval in either house of Parliament or majority approval of one-third of the State Councils; passage of amendments other than constitutional articles on fundamental rights and freedoms and the initiation and amendment of the constitution requires two-thirds majority vote in a joint session of Parliament and majority vote by two thirds of the State Councils; passage of amendments affecting rights and freedoms and amendment procedures requires two-thirds majority vote in each house of Parliament and majority vote by all the State Councils

Legal system: civil law system

International law organization participation: has not submitted an ICJ jurisdiction declaration; non-party state to the ICCt

Citizenship: *citizenship by birth:* no
citizenship by descent only: at least one parent must be a citizen of Ethiopia
dual citizenship recognized: no
residency requirement for naturalization: 4 years

Suffrage: 18 years of age; universal

Executive branch: *chief of state:* President SAHLE-WORK Zewde (since 25 October 2018)
head of government: Prime Minister ABIY Ahmed Ali (since April 2018); Deputy Prime Minister DEMEKE Mekonnen Hassen (since 29 November 2012)
cabinet: Council of Ministers selected by the prime minister and approved by the House of People's Representatives
elections/appointments: president indirectly elected by both chambers of Parliament for a 6-year term (eligible for a second term); election held on 21 June 2021 and 30 September 2021 (the scheduled 29 August 2020 election was postponed by Prime Minister ABIY due to the COVID-19 pandemic); prime minister designated by the majority party following legislative elections
election results:
2021: SAHLE-WORK elected president during joint session of Parliament, vote - 659 (unanimous); ABIY confirmed Prime Minister by House of Peoples' Representatives (4 October 2021)
2018: SAHLE-WORK elected president during joint session of Parliament, vote - 659 (unanimous); note - snap election held on 25 October 2018 due to resignation of President MULATA Teshome
note: SAHLE-WORK Zewde is the first female elected head of state in Ethiopia; she is currently the only female president in Africa.

Legislative branch: *description:* bicameral Parliament consists of:
House of Federation or Yefedereshein Mikir Bete (153 seats maximum; 144 seats current; members indirectly elected by state assemblies to serve 5-year terms)
House of People's Representatives or Yehizb Tewokayoch Mekir Bete (547 seats maximum; 470 seats current; members directly elected in single-seat constituencies by simple majority vote; 22 seats reserved for minorities; all members serve 5-year terms)
elections:
House of Federation - last held 4 October 2021 (next expected 31 October 2026)
House of People's Representatives - last held in two parts on 21 June 2021 and 30 September 2021 (next election expected 30 June 2026)
election results:
House of Federation - percent of vote by coalition/party - NA; seats by coalition/party - NA; composition - men 100, women 44, percent of women 30.6%
House of Representatives - percent of vote by coalition/party - NA; seats by coalition/party - Prosperity Party 454, NAMA 5, EZEMA 4, Gedeo People's Democratic organization 2, Kucha People Democratic Party 1, independent 4; composition - men 275, women 195, percent of women 41.5%; note - total Parliament percent of women 38.9%
notes: House of Federation is responsible for interpreting the constitution and federal-regional issues

and the House of People's Representatives is responsible for passing legislation; percent of vote percentages are calculated on the number of members actually seated versus on the constitutional maximums

Judicial branch: *highest court(s):* Federal Supreme Court (consists of 11 judges); note - the House of Federation has jurisdiction for all constitutional issues
judge selection and term of office: president and vice president of Federal Supreme Court recommended by the prime minister and appointed by the House of People's Representatives; other Supreme Court judges nominated by the Federal Judicial Administrative Council (a 10-member body chaired by the president of the Federal Supreme Court) and appointed by the House of People's Representatives; judges serve until retirement at age 60
subordinate courts: federal high courts and federal courts of first instance; state court systems (mirror structure of federal system); sharia courts and customary and traditional courts

Political parties and leaders: House of People's Representatives:
Ethiopian Citizens for Social Justice and Democracy or EZEMA [BERHANU Nega]
Gedeo People's Democratic Party
Independent
Kucha People Democratic Party
National Movement of Amhara or NAMA
Prosperity Party or PP
note: Ethiopia has over fifty national-level and regional-level political parties. The ruling party, the Prosperity Party, was created by Prime Minister ABIY in November 2019 from member parties of the former Ethiopian People's Revolutionary Democratic Front (EPRDF), which included the Amhara Democratic Party (ADP), Oromo Democratic Party (ODP), Southern Ethiopian People's Democratic Movement (SEPDM), plus other EPRDF-allied parties such as the Afar National Democratic Party (ANDP), Benishangul Gumuz People's Democratic Party (BGPDP), Gambella People's Democratic Movement (GPDM), Somali People's Democratic Party (SPDP), and the Harari National League (HNL). Once the Prosperity Party was created, the various ethnically-based parties that comprised or were affiliated with the EPRDF were subsequently disbanded; in January 2021, the Ethiopian electoral board de-registered the Tigray People's Liberation Front or TPLF; national level parties are qualified to register candidates in multiple regions across Ethiopia; regional parties can register candidates for both national and regional parliaments, but only in one region of Ethiopia

International organization participation: ACP, AfDB, ATMIS, AU, COMESA, EITI (candidate country), FAO, G-24, G-77, IAEA, IBRD, ICAO, ICRM, IDA, IFAD, IFC, IFRCS, IGAD, ILO, IMF, IMO, Interpol, IOC, IOM, IPU, ISO, ITSO, ITU, ITUC (NGOs), MIGA, NAM, OPCW, PCA, UN, UNAMID, UNCTAD, UNESCO, UNHCR, UNIDO, UNISFA, UNMIL, UNOCI, UNWTO, UPU, WCO, WFTU (NGOs), WHO, WIPO, WMO, WTO (observer)

Diplomatic representation in the US: *chief of mission:* Ambassador SELESHI Bekele Awulachew (since 7 June 2022)
chancery: 3506 International Drive NW, Washington, DC 20008
telephone: [1] (202) 364-1200
FAX: [1] (202) 587-0195
email address and website:
ethiopia@ethiopianembassy.org
https://ethiopianembassy.org/
consulate(s) general: Los Angeles
consulate(s): New York

Diplomatic representation from the US: *chief of mission:* Ambassador (vacant); Charge d'Affaires Ambassador Tracey Ann JACOBSON (since 25 February 2022)
embassy: Entoto Street, P.O. Box 1014, Addis Ababa
mailing address: 2030 Addis Ababa Place, Washington DC 20521-2030
telephone: [251] 111-30-60-00
FAX: [251] 111-24-24-01
email address and website:
AddisACS@state.gov
https://et.usembassy.gov/

Flag description: three equal horizontal bands of green (top), yellow, and red, with a yellow pentagram and single yellow rays emanating from the angles between the points on a light blue disk centered on the three bands; green represents hope and the fertility of the land, yellow symbolizes justice and harmony, while red stands for sacrifice and heroism in the defense of the land; the blue of the disk symbolizes peace and the pentagram represents the unity and equality of the nationalities and peoples of Ethiopia
note: Ethiopia is the oldest independent country in Africa, and the three main colors of her flag (adopted ca. 1895) were so often appropriated by other African countries upon independence that they became known as the Pan-African colors; the emblem in the center of the current flag was added in 1996

National symbol(s): Abyssinian lion (traditional), yellow pentagram with five rays of light on a blue field (promoted by current government); national colors: green, yellow, red

National anthem: *name:* "Whedefit Gesgeshi Woud Enat Ethiopia" (March Forward, Dear Mother Ethiopia)
lyrics/music: DEREJE Melaku Mengesha/ SOLOMON Lulu
note: adopted 1992

National heritage: *total World Heritage Sites:* 9 (8 cultural, 1 natural)
selected World Heritage Site locales: Rock-Hewn Churches, Lalibela (c); Simien National Park (n); Fasil Ghebbi, Gondar Region (c); Axum (c); Lower Valley of the Awash (c); Lower Valley of the Omo (c); Tiya (c); Harar Jugol, the Fortified Historic Town (c); Konso Cultural Landscape (c)

ECONOMY

Economic overview: Ethiopia - the second most populous country in Africa - is a one-party state with a planned economy. For more than a decade before 2016, GDP grew at a rate between 8% and 11% annually – one of the fastest growing states among the 188 IMF member countries. This growth was driven by government investment in infrastructure, as well as sustained progress in the agricultural and service sectors. More than 70% of Ethiopia's population is still employed in the agricultural sector, but services have surpassed agriculture as the principal source of GDP.

Ethiopia has the lowest level of income-inequality in Africa and one of the lowest in the world, with a Gini coefficient comparable to that of the Scandinavian countries. Yet despite progress toward eliminating extreme poverty, Ethiopia remains one of the poorest countries in the world, due both to rapid population growth and a low starting base. Changes in rainfall associated with world-wide weather patterns resulted in the worst drought in 30 years in 2015-16, creating food insecurity for millions of Ethiopians.

The state is heavily engaged in the economy. Ongoing infrastructure projects include power production and distribution, roads, rails, airports and industrial parks. Key sectors are state-owned, including telecommunications, banking and insurance, and power distribution. Under Ethiopia's constitution, the state owns all land and provides long-term leases to tenants. Title rights in urban areas, particularly Addis Ababa, are poorly regulated, and subject to corruption.

Ethiopia's foreign exchange earnings are led by the services sector - primarily the state-run Ethiopian Airlines - followed by exports of several commodities. While coffee remains the largest foreign exchange earner, Ethiopia is diversifying exports, and commodities such as gold, sesame, khat, livestock and horticulture products are becoming increasingly important. Manufacturing represented less than 8% of total exports in 2016, but manufacturing exports should increase in future years due to a growing international presence.

The banking, insurance, telecommunications, and micro-credit industries are restricted to domestic investors, but Ethiopia has attracted roughly $8.5 billion in foreign direct investment (FDI), mostly from China, Turkey, India and the EU; US FDI is $567 million. Investment has been primarily in infrastructure, construction, agriculture/horticulture, agricultural processing, textiles, leather and leather products.

To support industrialization in sectors where Ethiopia has a comparative advantage, such as textiles and garments, leather goods, and processed agricultural products, Ethiopia plans to increase installed power generation capacity by 8,320 MW, up from a capacity of 2,000 MW, by building three more major dams and expanding to other sources of renewable energy. In 2017, the government devalued the birr by 15% to increase exports and alleviate a chronic foreign currency shortage in the country.

Real GDP (purchasing power parity): $264.05 billion (2020 est.)
$248.97 billion (2019 est.)
$229.76 billion (2018 est.)
note: data are in 2017 dollars
country comparison to the world: 58

Real GDP growth rate: 10.9% (2017 est.)
8% (2016 est.)
10.4% (2015 est.)
country comparison to the world: 4

Real GDP per capita: $2,300 (2020 est.)
$2,200 (2019 est.)
$2,100 (2018 est.)
note: data are in 2017 dollars
country comparison to the world: 205

GDP (official exchange rate): $92.154 billion (2019 est.)

Inflation rate (consumer prices): 15.7% (2019 est.)
13.9% (2018 est.)
10.8% (2017 est.)
country comparison to the world: 216

Credit ratings:

Fitch rating: B (2014)

Moody's rating: B2 (2020)

Standard & Poors rating: B (2014)
note: The year refers to the year in which the current credit rating was first obtained.

GDP - composition, by sector of origin: *agriculture:* 34.8% (2017 est.)
industry: 21.6% (2017 est.)
services: 43.6% (2017 est.)

GDP - composition, by end use: *household consumption:* 69.6% (2017 est.)
government consumption: 10% (2017 est.)
investment in fixed capital: 43.5% (2017 est.)
investment in inventories: -0.1% (2017 est.)
exports of goods and services: 8.1% (2017 est.)
imports of goods and services: -31.2% (2017 est.)

Agricultural products: maize, cereals, wheat, sorghum, milk, barley, sweet potatoes, roots/tubers nes, sugar cane, millet

Industries: food processing, beverages, textiles, leather, garments, chemicals, metals processing, cement

Industrial production growth rate: 10.5% (2017 est.)
country comparison to the world: 13

Labor force: 52.82 million (2017 est.)
country comparison to the world: 12

Labor force - by occupation: *agriculture:* 72.7%
industry: 7.4%
services: 19.9% (2013 est.)

Unemployment rate: 17.5% (2012 est.)
18% (2011 est.)
country comparison to the world: 184

Unemployment, youth ages 15-24: *total:* 3.5%
male: 2.7%
female: 4.5% (2013 est.)
country comparison to the world: 175

Population below poverty line: 23.5% (2015 est.)

Gini Index coefficient - distribution of family income: 35 (2015 est.)
30 (2000)
country comparison to the world: 106

Household income or consumption by percentage share: *lowest 10%:* 4.1%
highest 10%: 25.6% (2005)

Budget: *revenues:* 11.24 billion (2017 est.)
expenditures: 13.79 billion (2017 est.)

Budget surplus (+) or deficit (-): -3.2% (of GDP) (2017 est.)
country comparison to the world: 139

Public debt: 54.2% of GDP (2017 est.)
53.2% of GDP (2016 est.)
country comparison to the world: 83

Taxes and other revenues: 13.9% (of GDP) (2017 est.)
country comparison to the world: 203

Fiscal year: 8 July - 7 July

Current account balance: -$6.551 billion (2017 est.)
-$6.574 billion (2016 est.)
country comparison to the world: 186

Exports: $7.62 billion (2018 est.) note: data are in current year dollars
$2.814 billion (2016 est.)
country comparison to the world: 109

Exports - partners: China 17%, United States 16%, United Arab Emirates 8%, Saudi Arabia 6%, South Korea 5%, Germany 5% (2019)

Exports - commodities: coffee, sesame seeds, gold, cut flowers, zinc (2019)

Imports: $19.93 billion (2018 est.) note: data are in current year dollars
$14.69 billion (2016 est.)
country comparison to the world: 83

Imports - partners: China 27%, India 9%, United Arab Emirates 9%, France 9%, United Kingdom 7% (2019)

Imports - commodities: aircraft, gas turbines, packaged medicines, electric filament, cars (2019)

Reserves of foreign exchange and gold: $3.013 billion (31 December 2017 est.)
$3.022 billion (31 December 2016 est.)
country comparison to the world: 110

Debt - external: $27.27 billion (2019 est.)
$26.269 billion (2018 est.)
country comparison to the world: 87

Exchange rates: birr (ETB) per US dollar -
25 (2017 est.)
21.732 (2016 est.)
21.732 (2015 est.)
21.55 (2014 est.)
19.8 (2013 est.)

ENERGY

Electricity access: *electrification - total population:* 47% (2019)
electrification - urban areas: 96% (2019)
electrification - rural areas: 34% (2019)

Electricity: *installed generating capacity:* 4.856 million kW (2020 est.)
consumption: 9,778,100,000 kWh (2019 est.)
exports: 1 billion kWh (2019 est.)
imports: 0 kWh (2019 est.)
transmission/distribution losses: 3.374 billion kWh (2019 est.)

Electricity generation sources: *solar:* 0.1% of total installed capacity (2020 est.)
wind: 3.8% of total installed capacity (2020 est.)
hydroelectricity: 95.8% of total installed capacity (2020 est.)
biomass and waste: 0.3% of total installed capacity (2020 est.)

Coal: *production:* 0 metric tons (2020 est.)
consumption: 689,000 metric tons (2020 est.)
exports: 0 metric tons (2020 est.)
imports: 528,000 metric tons (2020 est.)
proven reserves: 0 metric tons (2019 est.)

Petroleum: *total petroleum production:* 0 bbl/day (2021 est.)
refined petroleum consumption: 107,900 bbl/day (2019 est.)
crude oil estimated reserves: 400,000 barrels (2021 est.)

Refined petroleum products - imports: 69,970 bbl/day (2015 est.)
country comparison to the world: 67

Natural gas: *proven reserves:* 24.919 billion cubic meters (2021 est.)

Carbon dioxide emissions: 16.798 million metric tonnes of CO2 (2019 est.)
from coal and metallurgical coke: 1.474 million metric tonnes of CO2 (2019 est.)
from petroleum and other liquids: 15.324 million metric tonnes of CO2 (2019 est.)
country comparison to the world: 92

Energy consumption per capita: 3.219 million Btu/person (2019 est.)
country comparison to the world: 181

COMMUNICATIONS

Telephones - fixed lines: *total subscriptions:* 1.252 million (2020 est.)
subscriptions per 100 inhabitants: 1 (2020 est.)
country comparison to the world: 68

Telephones - mobile cellular: *total subscriptions:* 44.5 million (2020 est.)
subscriptions per 100 inhabitants: 39 (2020 est.)
country comparison to the world: 34

Telecommunication systems: *general assessment:* has been one of the last in Africa to allow its national telco a monopoly on all telecom services including fixed, mobile, internet and data communications; this has stifled innovation, restricted network expansion, and limited the scope of services on offer; the World Bank in early 2021 provided a $200 million loan to help develop the country's digital transformation, while the government has embarked on its 2020-2030 program as well as its Digital Ethiopia 2025 strategy, both aimed at making better use of digital technologies to promote socioeconomic development (2021)
domestic: fixed-line subscriptions at about 1 per 100 while mobile-cellular stands at a little over 39 per 100; the number of mobile telephones is increasing steadily (2020)
international: country code - 251; open-wire to Sudan and Djibouti; microwave radio relay to Kenya and Djibouti; 2 domestic satellites provide the national trunk service; satellite earth stations - 3 Intelsat (1 Atlantic Ocean and 2 Pacific Ocean) (2016)

Broadcast media: 6 public TV stations broadcasting nationally and 10 public radio broadcasters; 7 private radio stations and 19 community radio stations (2017)

Internet country code: .et

Internet users: *total:* 27,591,260 (2020 est.)
percent of population: 24% (2020 est.)
country comparison to the world: 34

Broadband - fixed subscriptions: *total:* 212,000 (2020 est.)
subscriptions per 100 inhabitants: 0.2 (2020 est.)
country comparison to the world: 118

TRANSPORTATION

National air transport system: *number of registered air carriers:* 1 (2020)
inventory of registered aircraft operated by air carriers: 75
annual passenger traffic on registered air carriers: 11,501,244 (2018)
annual freight traffic on registered air carriers: 2,089,280,000 (2018) mt-km

Civil aircraft registration country code prefix: ET

Airports: *total:* 57 (2021)
country comparison to the world: 82

Airports - with paved runways: *total:* 17
over 3,047 m: 3
2,438 to 3,047 m: 8
1,524 to 2,437 m: 4
under 914 m: 2 (2021)

Airports - with unpaved runways: *total:* 40
2,438 to 3,047 m: 3
1,524 to 2,437 m: 9
914 to 1,523 m: 20
under 914 m: 8 (2021)

Railways: *total:* 659 km (2017) (Ethiopian segment of the 756 km Addis Ababa-Djibouti railroad)
standard gauge: 659 km (2017) 1.435-m gauge
note: electric railway with redundant power supplies; under joint control of Djibouti and Ethiopia and managed by a Chinese contractor
country comparison to the world: 105

Roadways: *total:* 120,171 km (2018)
country comparison to the world: 40

Merchant marine: *total:* 11
by type: general cargo 9, oil tanker 2 (2020)
country comparison to the world: 155

Ports and terminals: Ethiopia is landlocked and uses the ports of Djibouti in Djibouti and Berbera in Somalia

MILITARY AND SECURITY

Military and security forces: Ethiopian National Defense Force (ENDF): Ground Forces, Ethiopian Air Force (Ye Ityopya Ayer Hayl, ETAF); Ministry of Peace: Ethiopian Federal Police (EFP) (2022)
note 1: in 2020 the Ethiopian Government announced it had re-established a navy, which had been disbanded in 1996; in March 2019, Ethiopia signed a defense cooperation agreement with France which stipulated that France would support the establishment of an Ethiopian navy, which would reportedly be based out of Djibouti
note 2: in 2018, Ethiopia established a Republican Guard military unit responsible to the Prime Minister for protecting senior officials
note 3: each of the states have regional and/or a "special" paramilitary security and police forces that report to regional civilian authorities and operate separately from federal forces; local militias operate across the country in loose and varying coordination with these regional security and police forces, the ENDF, and the EFP; there have been some calls for these regional paramilitary forces to be incorporated into the ENDF and EFP

Military expenditures: 0.5% of GDP (2021 est.)
0.5% of GDP (2020 est.)
0.6% of GDP (2019 est.) (approximately $970 million)
0.6% of GDP (2018 est.) (approximately $950 million)
0.7% of GDP (2017 est.) (approximately $930 million)
country comparison to the world: 158

Military and security service personnel strengths: information varies; prior to the 2020-21 Tigray conflict, approximately 150,000 active duty troops, including about 3,000 Air Force personnel (no personnel numbers available for the newly-established Navy) (2022)

Military equipment inventories and acquisitions: the ENDF's inventory is comprised mostly of Soviet-era equipment from the 1970s; since 2010, the ENDF has received arms from a variety of countries, with China, Russia, and Ukraine as the leading suppliers; Ethiopia has a modest industrial defense base centered on small arms and production of armored vehicles (2021)

Military service age and obligation: 18-22 years of age for voluntary military service (although the military may, when necessary, recruit a person more than 22 years old); no compulsory military service, but the military can conduct callups when necessary and compliance is compulsory (2022)
note: in November 2021, the Ethiopian Government issued a nationwide state of emergency that enabled officials to order military-age citizens to undergo training and accept military duty in support of the Tigray conflict; the order also recalled retired military officers to active duty

Military deployments: 5-10,000 Somalia (4,500 for ATMIS; the remainder under a bilateral agreement with Somalia; note - bilateral figures are prior to the conflict with Tigray); 250 Sudan (UNISFA); 1,475 South Sudan (UNMISS) (2022)

Military - note: since November 2020, the Government of Ethiopia has been engaged in a protracted military conflict with the Tigray People's Liberation Front (TPLF), the former governing party of the Tigray Region; the government deemed a TPLF attack on Ethiopia military forces as a domestic terrorism incident and launched a military offensive in response; the TPLF asserted that its actions were self-defense in the face of planned Ethiopian Government action to remove it from the provincial government; the Ethiopian Government sent large elements of the ENDF into Tigray to remove the TPLF and invited militia and paramilitary forces from the states of Afar and Amara, as well as the military forces of Eritrea, to assist; the fighting included heavy civilian and military casualties with widespread abuses reported; in March 2022, the Ethiopian Government declared a truce to facilitate the flow of humanitarian aid into the Tigray region; the TPLF reciprocated with a truce of its own; however, fighting between the TPLF and the Ethiopian Government resumed in August 2022; the two sides agreed to another cease-fire in November 2022

the military forces of the Tigray regional government are known as the Tigray Defense Force (TDF); the TDF is comprised of state paramilitary forces, local militia, and troops that defected from the ENDF; it was reported to have up to 250,000 fighters at the start of the conflict

in 2022, the ENDF was also engaged in counterinsurgency operations against anti-government militants in several other states; the largest was in Oromya (Oromia) against the Oromo Liberation Army (OLA; aka Shene), an insurgent group that claimed to be fighting for greater autonomy for the Oromo, Ethiopia's largest ethnic group; the OLA was a member of a coalition of eight anti-government factions known as the United Front of Ethiopia and Confederalist Forces (UFEFCF); formed in 2021, the UFEFCF included the TPLF, as well as rebel groups of variable sizes from several regions of the country; the OLA has also clashed with ethnic militias (aka Fano) from the neighboring state of Amara

in July 2022, militants from the Somalia-based terrorist group al-Shabaab launched an incursion into Ethiopia's Somali (Sumale) region, attacking villages and security forces; the Ethiopian Government claimed that regional security forces killed hundreds of Shabaab fighters and subsequently deployed additional ENDF troops into Somalia's Gedo region to prevent further such incursions (2022)

TERRORISM

Terrorist group(s): al-Shabaab; Islamic Revolutionary Guard Corps (IRGC)/Qods Force

TRANSNATIONAL ISSUES

Disputes - international: *Ethiopia-Eritrea:* Eritrea and Ethiopia agreed to abide by the 2002 Eritrea-Ethiopia Boundary Commission's (EEBC) delimitation decision, but neither party responded to the revised line detailed in the November 2006 EEBC Demarcation Statement
Ethiopia-Somalia: While border clashes continue in the al-Fashqa (Fashaga) area, the US views the 1902 boundary treaty between Ethiopia and Sudan as being in force; the undemarcated former British administrative line has little meaning as a political separation to rival clans within Ethiopia's Ogaden and southern Somalia's Oromo region; Ethiopian forces invaded southern Somalia and routed Islamist courts from Mogadishu in January 2007; "Somaliland" secessionists provide port facilities in Berbera and trade ties to landlocked Ethiopia;
Ethiopia-Sudan: Ethiopia's construction of a large dam (the Grand Ethiopian Renaissance Dam) on the Blue Nile since 2011 has become a focal point of relations with Egypt and Sudan; as of 2020, four years of three-way talks between the three capitals over operating the dam and filling its reservoir had made little progress; Ethiopia began filling the dam in July 2020; civil unrest in eastern Sudan has hampered efforts to demarcate the porous boundary with Ethiopia

Refugees and internally displaced persons: *refugees (country of origin):* 407,382 (South Sudan), 251,126 (Somalia), 162,011 (Eritrea), 48,445 (Sudan) (2022)

IDPs: 2.72 million (includes conflict- and climate-induced IDPs, excluding unverified estimates from the Amhara region; border war with Eritrea from 1998-2000; ethnic clashes; and ongoing fighting between the Ethiopian military and separatist rebel groups in the Somali and Oromia regions; natural disasters; intercommunal violence; most IDPs live in Sumale state) (2022)

Illicit drugs: transit hub for heroin originating in Southwest and Southeast Asia and destined for Europe, as well as cocaine destined for markets in southern Africa; cultivates qat (khat) for local use and regional export, principally to Djibouti and Somalia (legal in all three countries); the lack of a well-developed financial system limits the country's utility as a money laundering center

EUROPEAN UNION

INTRODUCTION

Preliminary statement: The evolution of what is today the European Union (EU) from a regional economic agreement among six neighboring states in 1951 to today's hybrid intergovernmental and supranational organization of 27 countries across the European continent stands as an unprecedented phenomenon in the annals of history. Dynastic unions for territorial consolidation were long the norm in Europe; on a few occasions even country-level unions were arranged - the Polish-Lithuanian Commonwealth and the Austro-Hungarian Empire were examples. For such a large number of nation-states to cede some of their sovereignty to an overarching entity is unique.

Although the EU is not a federation in the strict sense, it is far more than a free-trade association such as ASEAN or Mercosur, and it has certain attributes associated with independent nations: its own flag, currency (for some members), and law-making abilities, as well as diplomatic representation and a common foreign and security policy in its dealings with external partners.

Thus, inclusion of basic intelligence on the EU has been deemed appropriate as a separate entity in The World Factbook.

Background: Following the two devastating World Wars in the first half of the 20th century, a number of far-sighted European leaders in the late 1940s sought a response to the overwhelming desire for peace and reconciliation on the continent. In 1950, the French Foreign Minister Robert SCHUMAN proposed pooling the production of coal and steel in Western Europe and setting up an organization for that purpose that would bring France and the Federal Republic of Germany together and would be open to other countries as well. The following year, the European Coal and Steel Community (ECSC) was set up when six members - Belgium, France, West Germany, Italy, Luxembourg, and the Netherlands - signed the Treaty of Paris.

The ECSC was so successful that within a few years the decision was made to integrate other elements of the member states' economies. In 1957, envisioning an "ever closer union," the Treaties of Rome were signed creating the European Economic Community (EEC) and the European Atomic Energy Community (Euratom), and the six member states strove to eliminate trade barriers among themselves by forming a common market. In 1967, the institutions of all three communities were formally merged into the European Community (EC), creating a single Commission, a single Council of Ministers, and the body known today as the European Parliament. Members of the European Parliament were initially selected by national parliaments, but in 1979 the first direct elections were undertaken and have been held every five years since.

In 1973, the first enlargement of the EC took place with the addition of Denmark, Ireland, and the UK. The 1980s saw further membership expansion with Greece joining in 1981 and Spain and Portugal in 1986. The 1992 Treaty of Maastricht laid the basis for further forms of cooperation in foreign and defense policy, in judicial and internal affairs, and in the creation of an economic and monetary union - including a common currency. This further integration created the European Union (EU), at the time standing alongside the EC. In 1995, Austria, Finland, and Sweden joined the EU/EC, raising the total number of member states to 15.

A new currency, the euro, was launched in world money markets on 1 January 1999; it became the unit of exchange for all EU member states except Denmark, Sweden, and the UK. In 2002, citizens of those 12 countries began using euro banknotes and coins. Ten new countries joined the EU in 2004 - Cyprus, the Czech Republic, Estonia, Hungary, Latvia, Lithuania, Malta, Poland, Slovakia, and Slovenia. Bulgaria and Romania joined in 2007 and Croatia in 2013, but the UK withdrew in 2020. Current membership stands at 27. (Seven of the new countries - Cyprus, Estonia, Latvia, Lithuania, Malta, Slovakia, and Slovenia - have now adopted the euro, bringing total euro-zone membership to 19.)

In an effort to ensure that the EU could function efficiently with an expanded membership, the Treaty of Nice (concluded in 2000; entered into force in 2003) set forth rules to streamline the size and procedures of EU institutions. An effort to establish a "Constitution for Europe," growing out of a Convention held in 2002-2003, foundered when it was rejected in referenda in France and the Netherlands in 2005. A subsequent effort in 2007 incorporated many of the features of the rejected draft Constitutional Treaty while also making a number of substantive and symbolic changes. The new treaty, referred to as the Treaty of Lisbon, sought to amend existing treaties rather than replace them. The treaty was approved at the EU intergovernmental conference of member states held in Lisbon in December 2007, after which the process of national ratifications began. In October 2009, an Irish referendum approved the Lisbon Treaty (overturning a previous rejection) and cleared the way for an ultimate unanimous endorsement. Poland and the Czech Republic ratified soon after. The Lisbon Treaty came into force on 1 December 2009 and the EU officially replaced and succeeded the EC. The Lisbon Treaty's provisions are part of the basic consolidated versions of the Treaty on European Union and the Treaty on the Functioning of the European Union now governing what remains a very specific integration project.

UK citizens on 23 June 2016 narrowly voted to leave the EU; the formal exit took place on 31 January 2020. The EU and UK negotiated and ratified a Withdrawal Agreement that included a status quo transition period through December 2020, when the follow-on EU-UK Trade and Cooperation Agreement was concluded.

GEOGRAPHY

Location: Europe between the North Atlantic Ocean in the west and Russia, Belarus, and Ukraine to the east

Map references: Europe

Area: *total:* 4,236,351 sq km
rank by area (sq km):
1. France (includes five overseas regions) 643,801
2. Spain 505,370
3. Sweden 450,295
4. Germany 357,022
5. Finland 338,145
6. Poland 312,685
7. Italy 301,340
8. Romania 238,391
9. Greece 131,957
10. Bulgaria 110,879
11. Hungary 93,028
12. Portugal 92,090
13. Austria 83,871
14. Czechia 78,867
15. Ireland 70,273
16. Lithuania 65,300
17. Latvia 64,589
18. Croatia 56,594
19. Slovakia 49,035
20. Estonia 45,228
21. Denmark 43,094
22. Netherlands 41,543
23. Belgium 30,528
24. Slovenia 20,273
25. Cyprus 9,251
26. Luxembourg 2,586
27. Malta 316

Area - comparative: less than one-half the size of the US

Land boundaries: *total:* 13,770 km
border countries (20): Albania 212 km; Andorra 118 km; Belarus 1,176 km; Bosnia and Herzegovina 956 km; Holy See 3 km; Liechtenstein 34 km; North Macedonia 396 km; Moldova 683 km; Monaco 6 km; Montenegro 19 km; Norway 2,375 km; Russia 2,435 km; San Marino 37 km; Serbia 1,353 km; Switzerland 1,729 km; Turkey 415 km; United Kingdom 499 km; Ukraine 1,324 km; note - the Brexit Withdrawal Agreement (2020) commits the United Kingdom (UK) to maintain an open border in Ireland, so the border between Northern Ireland (UK) and the Republic of Ireland is only *de jure* and is not a hard border; the *de facto* border is the Irish Sea between the islands of Ireland and Great Britain
note: data for European continent only

Coastline: 53,563.9 km

Climate: cold temperate; potentially subarctic in the north to temperate; mild wet winters; hot dry summers in the south

Terrain: fairly flat along Baltic and Atlantic coasts; mountainous in the central and southern areas

Elevation: *highest point:* Mont Blanc, France 4,810 m
lowest point: Zuidplaspolder, Netherlands -7 m

Natural resources: iron ore, natural gas, petroleum, coal, copper, lead, zinc, bauxite, uranium, potash, salt, hydropower, arable land, timber, fish

Irrigated land: 154,539.82 sq km (2011 est.)

Population distribution: population distribution varies considerably from country to country, but tends to follow a pattern of coastal and river settlement, with urban agglomerations forming large hubs facilitating large scale housing, industry, and commerce; the area in and around the Netherlands, Belgium, and Luxembourg (known collectively as Benelux), is the most densely populated area in the EU

Natural hazards: flooding along coasts; avalanches in mountainous area; earthquakes in the south; volcanic eruptions in Italy; periodic droughts in Spain; ice floes in the Baltic Sea region

PEOPLE AND SOCIETY

Population: (July 2022 est.) 450,858,381
rank by population:
1 Germany - 84,316,622;
2 France - 68,305,148;
3 Italy - 61,095,551;
4 Spain - 47,163,418;
5 Poland - 38,093,101;
6 Romania - 18,519,899;
7 Netherlands - 17,400,824;
8 Belgium - 11,847,338;
9 Czechia - 10,705,384;
10 Greece - 10,533,871;
11 Sweden - 10,483,647;
12 Portugal - 10,242,081;
13 Hungary - 9,699,577;
14 Austria - 8,913,088;
15 Bulgaria - 6,873,253;
16 Denmark - 5,920,767;
17 Finland - 5,601,547;
18 Slovakia - 5,431,252;
19 Ireland - 5,275,004;
20 Croatia - 4,188,853;
21 Lithuania - 2,683,546;
22 Slovenia - 2,101,208;
23 Latvia - 1,842,226;
24 Cyprus - 1,295,102;
25 Estonia - 1,211,524;
26 Luxembourg - 650,364;
27 Malta - 464,186 (July 2022 est.)

Languages: Bulgarian, Croatian, Czech, Danish, Dutch, English, Estonian, Finnish, French, German, Greek, Hungarian, Irish, Italian, Latvian, Lithuanian, Maltese, Polish, Portuguese, Romanian, Slovak, Slovene, Spanish, Swedish
note: only the 24 official languages are listed; German, the major language of Germany and Austria, is the most widely spoken mother tongue - about 16% of the EU population; English is the most widely spoken foreign language - about 29% of the EU population is conversant with it; English is an official language in Ireland and Malta and thus remained an official EU language after the UK left the bloc (2020)

Religions: Roman Catholic 41%, Orthodox 10%, Protestant 9%, other Christian 4%, Muslim 2%, other 4% (includes Jewish, Sikh, Buddhist, Hindu), atheist 10%, non-believer/agnostic 17%, unspecified 3% (2019 est.)

Age structure: *0-14 years:* 15.05% (male 34,978,216/female 33,217,600)
15-24 years: 10.39% (male 24,089,260/female 22,990,579)
25-54 years: 40.54% (male 92,503,000/female 91,144,596)
55-64 years: 13.52% (male 29,805,200/female 31,424,172)
65 years and over: 20.5% (male 39,834,507/female 53,020,673) (2020 est.)

Median age: *total:* 44 years
male: 42.6 years
female: 45.5 years (2020 est.)

Population growth rate: (2021 est.) 0.10%

Birth rate: (2020 est.) 9.5 births/1,000 population

Death rate: (2021 est.) 10.7 deaths/1,000 population

Net migration rate: -2.85 migrant(s)/1,000 population

Population distribution: population distribution varies considerably from country to country, but tends to follow a pattern of coastal and river settlement, with urban agglomerations forming large hubs facilitating large scale housing, industry, and commerce; the area in and around the Netherlands, Belgium, and Luxembourg (known collectively as Benelux), is the most densely populated area in the EU

Sex ratio: *at birth:* 1.06 male(s)/female
0-14 years: 1.05 male(s)/female
15-24 years: 1.05 male(s)/female
25-54 years: 1.01 male(s)/female
55-64 years: 0.95 male(s)/female
65 years and over: 0.75 male(s)/female
total population: 0.95 male(s)/female (2020 est.)

Infant mortality rate: *total:* 3.47 deaths/1,000 live births
male: 3.32 deaths/1,000 live births
female: 3.62 deaths/1,000 live births (2021 est.)

Life expectancy at birth: *total population:* 77.63 years
male: 72.98 years
female: 82.51 years (2021 est.)

Total fertility rate: (2021 est.) 1.62 children born/woman

Current health expenditure: 9.9% of GDP (2016)

Major infectious diseases: *note:* widespread ongoing transmission of a respiratory illness caused by the novel coronavirus (COVID-19) is occurring regionally; the US Department of Homeland Security has issued instructions requiring US passengers who have been in the European Union's Schengen Area (comprised of the following 26 European states: Austria, Belgium, Czech Republic, Denmark, Estonia, Finland, France, Germany, Greece, Hungary, Iceland, Italy, Latvia, Liechtenstein, Lithuania, Luxembourg, Malta, Netherlands, Norway, Poland, Portugal, Slovakia, Slovenia, Spain, Sweden, and Switzerland) to travel through select airports where the US Government has implemented enhanced screening procedures

Education expenditures: 4.7% of GDP (2019 est.)

Unemployment, youth ages 15-24: *total:* 18.7%
male: 18.5%
female: 19.2% (2020 est.)

ENVIRONMENT

Environment - current issues: various forms of air, soil, and water pollution; see individual country entries

Environment - international agreements: *party to:* Air Pollution, Air Pollution-Heavy Metals, Air Pollution-Multi-effect Protocol, Air Pollution-Nitrogen Oxides, Air Pollution-Persistent Organic Pollutants, Air Pollution-Sulphur 94, Antarctic-Marine Living Resources, Biodiversity, Climate Change, Climate Change-Kyoto Protocol, Climate Change-Paris Agreement, Desertification, Endangered Species, Hazardous Wastes, Law of the Sea, Ozone Layer Protection, Tropical Timber 2006
signed, but not ratified: Air Pollution-Volatile Organic Compounds

Air pollutants: *carbon dioxide emissions:* 2,881.62 megatons (2016 est.)

Climate: cold temperate; potentially subarctic in the north to temperate; mild wet winters; hot dry summers in the south

Revenue from forest resources: *forest revenues:* 0.05% of GDP (2018 est.)

Revenue from coal: *coal revenues:* 0.02% of GDP (2018 est.)

Total renewable water resources: 2,057.8 cubic meters (2011)

GOVERNMENT

Union name: *conventional long form:* European Union
abbreviation: EU

Political structure: a hybrid and unique intergovernmental and supranational organization

Capital: *name:* Brussels (Belgium), Strasbourg (France), Luxembourg, Frankfurt (Germany); note - the European Council, a gathering of the EU heads of state and/or government, and the Council of the European Union, a ministerial-level body of 10 formations, meet in Brussels, Belgium, except for Council meetings held in Luxembourg in April, June, and October; the European Parliament meets in Brussels and Strasbourg, France, and has administrative offices in Luxembourg; the Court of Justice of the European Union is located in Luxembourg; and the European Central Bank is located in Frankfurt, Germany
geographic coordinates: (Brussels) 50 50 N, 4 20 E
time difference: UTC+1 (6 hours ahead of Washington, DC, during Standard Time)
daylight saving time: +1hr, begins last Sunday in March; ends last Sunday in October
time zone note: the 27 European Union countries spread across three time zones; a proposal has been put forward to do away with daylight savings time in all EU member states

Member states: 27 countries: Austria, Belgium, Bulgaria, Croatia, Cyprus, Czechia, Denmark, Estonia, Finland, France, Germany, Greece, Hungary, Ireland, Italy, Latvia, Lithuania, Luxembourg, Malta, Netherlands, Poland, Portugal, Romania, Slovakia, Slovenia, Spain, Sweden; note - candidate countries: Albania, Moldova, Montenegro, North Macedonia, Serbia, Turkey, Ukraine

there are 13 overseas countries and territories (OCTs) (1 with Denmark [Greenland], 6 with France [French Polynesia, French Southern and Antarctic Lands, New Caledonia, Saint Barthelemy, Saint Pierre and Miquelon, Wallis and Futuna], and 6 with the Netherlands [Aruba, Bonaire, Curacao, Saba, Sint Eustatius, Sint Maarten]), all are part of the Overseas Countries and Territories Association (OCTA)
note: there are non-European OCTs having special relations with Denmark, France, and the Netherlands (list is annexed to the Treaty on the Functioning of the European Union), that are associated with the EU to promote their economic and social development; member states apply to their trade with OCTs the same treatment as they accord each other pursuant to the treaties; OCT nationals are in principle

EU citizens, but these countries are neither part of the EU, nor subject to the EU

Independence: 7 February 1992 (Maastricht Treaty signed establishing the European Union); 1 November 1993 (Maastricht Treaty entered into force)
note: the Treaties of Rome, signed on 25 March 1957 and subsequently entered into force on 1 January 1958, created the European Economic Community and the European Atomic Energy Community; a series of subsequent treaties have been adopted to increase efficiency and transparency, to prepare for new member states, and to introduce new areas of cooperation - such as a single currency; the Treaty of Lisbon, signed on 13 December 2007 and entered into force on 1 December 2009 is the most recent of these treaties and is intended to make the EU more democratic, more efficient, and better able to address global problems with one voice

National holiday: Europe Day (also known as Schuman Day), 9 May (1950); note - the day in 1950 that Robert SCHUMAN proposed the creation of what became the European Coal and Steel Community, the progenitor of today's European Union, with the aim of achieving a united Europe

Constitution: *history:* none; note - the EU legal order relies primarily on two consolidated texts encompassing all provisions as amended from a series of past treaties: the Treaty on European Union (TEU), as modified by the 2009 Lisbon Treaty states in Article 1 that "the HIGH CONTRACTING PARTIES establish among themselves a EUROPEAN UNION ... on which the Member States confer competences to attain objectives they have in common"; Article 1 of the TEU states further that the EU is "founded on the present Treaty and on the Treaty on the Functioning of the European Union (hereinafter referred to as 'the Treaties')," both possessing the same legal value; Article 6 of the TEU provides that a separately adopted Charter of Fundamental Rights of the European Union "shall have the same legal value as the Treaties"
amendments: European Union treaties can be amended in several ways: 1) Ordinary Revision Procedure (for key amendments to the treaties); initiated by an EU country's government, by the European Parliament, or by the European Commission; following adoption of the proposal by the European Council, a convention is formed of national government representatives to review the proposal and subsequently a conference of government representatives also reviews the proposal; passage requires ratification by all EU member states; 2) Simplified Revision Procedure (for amendment of EU internal policies and actions); passage of a proposal requires unanimous European Council vote following European Council consultation with the European Commission, the European Parliament, and the European Central Bank (if the amendment concerns monetary matters) and requires ratification by all EU member states; 3) Passerelle Clause (allows the alteration of a legislative procedure without a formal amendment of the treaties); 4) Flexibility Clause (permits the EU to decide in subject areas where EU competences have not been explicitly granted in the Treaties but are necessary to the attainment of the objectives set out in the Treaty); note - the Treaty of Lisbon (signed in December 2007 and effective in December 2009) amended the two treaties that formed the EU - the Maastricht Treaty (1993) and the Treaty of Rome (1958), known in updated form as the Treaty on the Functioning of the European Union

Legal system: unique supranational law system in which, according to an interpretive declaration of member-state governments appended to the Treaty of Lisbon, "the Treaties and the law adopted by the Union on the basis of the Treaties have primacy over the law of Member States" under conditions laid down in the case law of the Court of Justice; key principles of EU law include fundamental rights as guaranteed by the Charter of Fundamental Rights and as resulting from constitutional traditions common to the EU's 27 member states; EU law is divided into 'primary' and 'secondary' legislation; primary legislation is derived from the consolidated versions of the Treaty on European Union and the Treaty on the Functioning of the European Union and are the basis for all EU action; secondary legislation - which includes directives, regulations, and decisions - is derived from the principles and objectives set out in the treaties

Suffrage: 18 years of age (16 years in Austria); universal; voting for the European Parliament is permitted in each member state

Executive branch: under the EU treaties there are three distinct institutions, each of which conducts functions that may be regarded as executive in nature:
European Council - brings together heads of state and government, along with the president of the European Commission, and meets at least four times a year; its aim is to provide the impetus for the development of the Union and to issue general policy guidelines; the Treaty of Lisbon established the position of "permanent" (full-time) president of the European Council; leaders of the EU member states appoint the president for a 2 1/2 year term, renewable once; the president's responsibilities include chairing the EU summits and providing policy and organizational continuity; the current president is Charles MICHEL (Belgium), since 1 December 2019, succeeding Donald TUSK (Poland; 2014 - 2019)
Council of the European Union - consists of ministers of each EU member state and meets regularly in 10 different configurations depending on the subject matter; it conducts policymaking and coordinating functions as well as legislative functions; ministers of EU member states chair meetings of the Council of the EU based on a 6-month rotating presidency except for the meetings of EU Foreign Ministers in the Foreign Affairs Council that are chaired by the High Representative for Foreign Affairs and Security Policy
European Commission - headed by a College of Commissioners comprised of 27 members (one from each member country) including the president; each commissioner is responsible for one or more policy areas; the Commission's main responsibilities include the sole right to initiate EU legislation (except for foreign and security/defense policy), promoting the general interest of the EU, acting as "guardian of the Treaties" by monitoring the application of EU law, implementing/executing the EU budget, managing programs, negotiating on the EU's behalf in core policy areas such as trade, and ensuring the Union's external representation in some policy areas; its current president is Ursula VON DER LEYEN (Germany) elected on 16 July 2019 (took office on 1 December 2019); the president of the European Commission is nominated by the European Council and formally "elected" by the European Parliament; the Commission president allocates specific responsibilities among the members of the College (appointed by common accord of the member state governments in consultation with the president-elect); the European Parliament confirms the entire Commission for a 5-year term.
note: for external representation and foreign policy making, leaders of the EU member states appointed Joseph BORRELL (Spain) as the High Representative of the European Union for Foreign Affairs and Security Policy; BORRELL took office on 1 December 2019, succeeding Federica MOGHERINI (Italy (2014 - 2019); the High Representative's concurrent appointment as Vice President of the European Commission was meant to bring more coherence to the EU's foreign policy (horizontally, between policies managed by the Commission that are particularly relevant for EU external relations, such as trade, humanitarian aid and crisis management, neighborhood policy and enlargement; and vertically, between member-state capitals and the EU); the High Representative helps develop and implement the EU's Common Foreign and Security Policy and Common Security and Defense Policy components, chairs the Foreign Affairs Council, represents and acts for the Union in many international contexts, and oversees the European External Action Service, the diplomatic corps of the EU, established on 1 December 2010

Legislative branch: *description:* two legislative bodies consisting of the Council of the European Union (27 seats; ministers representing the 27 member states) and the European Parliament (705 seats; seats allocated among member states roughly in proportion to population size; members elected by proportional representation to serve 5-year terms); note - the European Parliament President, David SASSOLI, was elected in July 2019 by a majority of fellow members of the European Parliament (MEPs) and represents the Parliament within the EU and internationally; the Council of the EU and the MEPs share responsibilities for adopting the bulk of EU legislation, normally acting in co-decision on Commission proposals (but not in the area of Common Foreign and Security Policy, which is governed by consensus of the EU member state governments)
elections:
last held on 23-26 May 2019 (next to be held in May 2024)
election results:
percent of vote - NA; seats by party (as of 31 August 2022) - EPP 176, S&D 145, RE 103, ID 65, Greens/EFA 71, ECR 64, GUE-NGL 39, non-attached 42; Parliament composition - men 428, women 277, percent of women 39.3%; note - composition of the European Council - men 23, women 4, percent of women 11.1%; total Council and Parliament percent of women 38.3%

Judicial branch: *highest court(s):* Court of Justice of the European Union, which includes the Court of Justice (informally known as the European Court of Justice or ECJ) and the General Court (consists of 27 judges, one drawn from each member state; the ECJ includes 11 Advocates General while the General Court can include additional judges; both the ECJ and the General Court may sit in a "Grand Chamber" of 15 judges in special cases but usually in chambers of 3 to 5 judges
judge selection and term of office: judges appointed by the common consent of the member states to serve 6-year renewable terms

note: the ECJ is the supreme judicial authority of the EU; it ensures that EU law is interpreted and applied uniformly throughout the EU, resolves disputed issues among the EU institutions and with member states, and reviews issues and opinions regarding questions of EU law referred by member state courts

Political parties and leaders: European United Left-Nordic Green Left or GUE/NGL [Manon AUBRY and Martin SCHIRDEWAN]
European Conservatives and Reformists or ECR [Raffaele FITTO and Ryszard LEGUTKO]
European Greens/European Free Alliance or Greens/EFA [Ska KELLER and Philippe LAMBERTS]
European People's Party or EPP [Manfred WEBER]
Identity and Democracy Party or ID [Marco ZANNI]
Progressive Alliance of Socialists and Democrats or S&D [Iratxe GARCIA]
Renew Europe or RE [Stephane SEJOURNE](successor to Alliance of Liberals and Democrats for Europe or ALDE)

International organization participation: ARF, ASEAN (dialogue member), Australian Group, BIS, BSEC (observer), CBSS, CERN, EBRD, FAO, FATF, G-8, G-10, G-20, IDA, IEA, IGAD (partners), LAIA (observer), NSG (observer), OAS (observer), OECD, PIF (partner), SAARC (observer), SICA (observer), UN (observer), UNRWA (observer), WCO, WTO, ZC (observer)

Diplomatic representation in the US: *chief of mission:* Ambassador Stavros LAMBRINIDIS (since 1 March 2019)
chancery: 2175 K Street NW, Suite 800, Washington, DC 20037
telephone: [1] (202) 862-9500
FAX: [1] (202) 429-1766

Diplomatic representation from the US: *chief of mission:* Ambassador Mark GITENSTEIN (since 24 January 2022)
embassy: Zinnerstraat - 13 - Rue Zinner, B-1000 Brussels
mailing address: use embassy street address
telephone: [32] (2) 811-4100
email address and website:
https://useu.usmission.gov/

Flag description: a blue field with 12 five-pointed gold stars arranged in a circle in the center; blue represents the sky of the Western world, the stars are the peoples of Europe in a circle, a symbol of unity; the number of stars is fixed

National symbol(s): a circle of 12, five-pointed, golden yellow stars on a blue field; union colors: blue, yellow

National anthem: *name:* "Ode to Joy"
lyrics/music: no lyrics/Ludwig VAN BEETHOVEN, arranged by Herbert VON KARAJAN
note: official EU anthem since 1985; the anthem is meant to represent all of Europe rather than just the organization, conveying ideas of peace, freedom, and unity

ECONOMY

Economic overview: The 27 member states that make up the EU have adopted an internal single market with free movement of goods, services, capital, and labor. The EU, which is also a customs union, aims to bolster Europe's trade position and its political and economic weight in international affairs.

Despite great differences in per capita income among member states (from $28,000 to $109,000) and in national attitudes toward issues like inflation, debt, and foreign trade, the EU has achieved a high degree of coordination of monetary and fiscal policies. A common currency – the euro – circulates among 19 of the member states that make up the European Economic and Monetary Union (EMU). Eleven member states introduced the euro as their common currency on 1 January 1999 (Greece did so two years later). Since 2004, 13 states acceded to the EU. Of the 13, Slovenia (2007), Cyprus and Malta (2008), Slovakia (2009), Estonia (2011), Latvia (2014), and Lithuania (2015) have adopted the euro; seven other member states - excluding Denmark, which has a formal opt-out - are required by EU treaties to adopt the common currency upon meeting fiscal and monetary convergence criteria.

The EU economy posted moderate GDP growth for 2014 through 2017, capping five years of sustained growth since the 2008-09 global economic crisis and the ensuing sovereign debt crisis in the euro zone in 2011. However, the bloc's recovery was uneven. Some EU member states (Czechia, Ireland, Malta, Romania, Sweden, and Spain) recorded strong growth, others (Italy) experienced modest expansion, and Greece finally ended its EU rescue program in August 2018. Overall, the EU's recovery was buoyed by lower commodities prices and accommodative monetary policy, which lowered interest rates and stimulated demand. The euro zone, which makes up about 70% of the total EU economy, performed well, achieving a growth rate not seen in a decade. In October 2017 the European Central Bank (ECB) announced it would extend its bond-buying program through September 2018, and possibly beyond that date, to keep the euro zone recovery on track. The ECB's efforts to spur more lending and investment through its asset-buying program, negative interest rates, and long-term loan refinancing programs have not yet raised inflation in line with the ECB's statutory target of just under 2%.

Despite its performance, high unemployment in some member states, high levels of public and private debt, muted productivity, an incomplete single market in services, and an aging population remain sources of potential drag on the EU's future growth. Moreover, the EU economy remains vulnerable to a slowdown of global trade and bouts of political and financial turmoil. In June 2016, the UK voted to withdraw from the EU, the first member country ever to attempt to secede. Continued uncertainty about the implications of the UK's exit from the EU (concluded January 2020) could hurt consumer and investor confidence and dampen EU growth, particularly if trade and cross-border investment significantly declines. Political disagreements between EU member states on reforms to fiscal and economic policy also may impair the EU's ability to bolster its crisis-prevention and resolution mechanisms. International investors' fears of a broad dissolution of the single currency area have largely dissipated, but these concerns could resurface if elected leaders implement policies that contravene euro-zone budget or banking rules. State interventions in ailing banks, including rescue of banks in Italy and resolution of banks in Spain, have eased financial vulnerabilities in the European banking sector even though some banks are struggling with low profitability and a large stock of bad loans, fragilities that could precipitate localized crises. Externally, the EU has continued to pursue comprehensive free trade agreements to expand EU external market share, particularly with Asian countries; EU and Japanese leaders reached a political-level agreement on a free trade agreement in July 2017, and agreement with Mexico in April 2018 on updates to an existing free trade agreement.

Real GDP (purchasing power parity): $19,885,625,000,000 (2019 est.)
$19,551,328,000,000 (2018 est.)
$19,115,988,000,000 (2017 est.)
note: data are in 2017 dollars

Real GDP growth rate: 2.3% (2017 est.)
2% (2016 est.)
2.3% (2015 est.)

Real GDP per capita: $44,436 (2019 est.)
$43,761 (2018 est.)
$42,848 (2017 est.)
note: data are in 2017 dollars

GDP (official exchange rate): $17.11 trillion (2017 est.)

Inflation rate (consumer prices): 1.1% (2019 est.)
1.7% (2018 est.)
1.5% (2017 est.)

Credit ratings:

Fitch rating: AAA (2010)

Moody's rating: Aaa (2014)

Standard & Poors rating: AA (2016)
note: The year refers to the year in which the current credit rating was first obtained.

GDP - composition, by sector of origin: *agriculture:* 1.6% (2017 est.)
industry: 25.1% (2017 est.)
services: 70.9% (2017 est.)

GDP - composition, by end use: *household consumption:* 54.4% (2016 est.)
government consumption: 20.4% (2016 est.)
investment in fixed capital: 19.8% (2016 est.)
investment in inventories: 0.4% (2016 est.)
exports of goods and services: 43.9% (2016 est.)
imports of goods and services: -40.5% (2016 est.)

Agricultural products: wheat, barley, oilseeds, sugar beets, wine, grapes, dairy products, cattle, sheep, pigs, poultry, fish

Industries: *among the world's largest and most technologically advanced regions, the EU industrial base includes:* ferrous and non-ferrous metal production and processing, metal products, petroleum, coal, cement, chemicals, pharmaceuticals, aerospace, rail transportation equipment, passenger and commercial vehicles, construction equipment, industrial equipment, shipbuilding, electrical power equipment, machine tools and automated manufacturing systems, electronics and telecommunications equipment, fishing, food and beverages, furniture, paper, textiles

Industrial production growth rate: 3.5% (2017 est.)

Labor force: 238.9 million (2016 est.)

Labor force - by occupation: *agriculture:* 5%
industry: 21.9%
services: 73.1% (2014 est.)

Unemployment rate: 8.6% (2016 est.)
9.4% (2015 est.)

Unemployment, youth ages 15-24: *total:* 18.7%
male: 18.5%
female: 19.2% (2020 est.)

Population below poverty line: 9.8% (2013 est.)
note: see individual country entries of member states

Gini Index coefficient - distribution of family income: 30.8 (2016 est.)
31 (2015 est.)

Household income or consumption by percentage share: *lowest 10%:* 2.8%
highest 10%: 23.8% (2016 est.)

Budget surplus (+) or deficit (-): -3% (of GDP) (2014)

Public debt: 86.8% of GDP (2014)
85.5% of GDP (2013)

Taxes and other revenues: 45.2% (of GDP) (2014)

Fiscal year: NA

Current account balance: $404.9 billion (2017 est.)
$359.7 billion (2016 est.)

Exports: $7,102,345,000,000 (2019 est.)
$6,929,845,000,000 (2018 est.)
$6,690,764,000,000 (2017 est.)
note: external exports, excluding intra-EU trade

Exports - partners: U.S. 20.7%, China 9.6%, Switzerland 8.1%, Turkey 4.4%, Russia 4.1% (2016 est.)

Exports - commodities: machinery, motor vehicles, pharmaceuticals and other chemicals, fuels, aircraft, plastics, iron and steel, wood pulp and paper products, alcoholic beverages, furniture

Imports: $6,649,513,000,000 (2019 est.)
$6,400,412,000,000 (2018 est.)
$6,177,446,000,000 (2017 est.)
note: external imports, excluding intra-EU trade

Imports - partners: China 20.1%, United States 14.5%, Switzerland 7.1%, Russia 6.3% (2016 est.)

Imports - commodities: fuels and crude oil, machinery, vehicles, pharmaceuticals and other chemicals, precious gemstones, textiles, aircraft, plastics, metals, ships

Reserves of foreign exchange and gold: $740.9 billion (31 December 2014 est.)
$746.9 billion (31 December 2013)
note: data are for the European Central Bank

Debt - external: $29.27 trillion (31 December 2016 est.)
$28.68 trillion (31 December 2015 est.)

Exchange rates: euros per US dollar -
0.885 (2017 est.)
0.903 (2016 est.)
0.9214 (2015 est.)
0.885 (2014 est.)
0.7634 (2013 est.)

ENERGY

Refined petroleum products - production: 11.66 million bbl/day (2016 est.)

Refined petroleum products - exports: 2.196 million bbl/day (2017 est.)

Refined petroleum products - imports: 8.613 million bbl/day (2017 est.)

Carbon dioxide emissions: 3.475 billion metric tonnes of CO2 (2015 est.)

COMMUNICATIONS

Telephones - fixed lines: *total subscriptions:* 160,149,025 (2020 est.)
subscriptions per 100 inhabitants: 36 (2020 est.)

Telephones - mobile cellular: *total subscriptions:* 540,557,924 (2020 est.)
subscriptions per 100 inhabitants: 121 (2020 est.)

Telecommunication systems: note - see individual country entries of member states

Internet country code: .eu; note - see country entries of member states for individual country codes

Internet users: *total:* 380,357,569 (2020 est.)
percent of population: 85% (2020 est.)

Broadband - fixed subscriptions: *total:* 163,772,540 (2020 est.)
subscriptions per 100 inhabitants: 37 (2020 est.)

TRANSPORTATION

National air transport system: *annual passenger traffic on registered air carriers:* 636,860,155 (2018)
annual freight traffic on registered air carriers: 31,730,660,000 (2018)

Airports - with paved runways: *total:* 1,882
over 3,047 m: 120
2,438 to 3,047 m: 341
1,524 to 2,437 m: 507
914 to 1,523 m: 425
under 914 m: 489 (2017)

Airports - with unpaved runways: *total:* 1,244
over 3,047 m: 1
2,438 to 3,047 m: 1
1,524 to 2,437 m: 15
914 to 1,523 m: 245
under 914 m: 982 (2013)

Heliports: (2021) 90

Railways: *total:* (2013) 230,548 km

Roadways: *total:* (2013) 10,582,653 km

Waterways: (2013) 53,384 km

Ports and terminals: *major port(s):* Antwerp (Belgium), Barcelona (Spain), Braila (Romania), Bremen (Germany), Burgas (Bulgaria), Constanta (Romania), Copenhagen (Denmark), Galati (Romania), Gdansk (Poland), Hamburg (Germany), Helsinki (Finland), Las Palmas (Canary Islands, Spain), Le Havre (France), Lisbon (Portugal), Marseille (France), Naples (Italy), Peiraiefs or Piraeus (Greece), Riga (Latvia), Rotterdam (Netherlands), Split (Croatia), Stockholm (Sweden), Talinn (Estonia), Tulcea (Romania), Varna (Bulgaria)

MILITARY AND SECURITY

Military and security forces: the EU's Common Security and Defense Policy (CSDP) provides the civilian, military, and political structures for EU crisis management and security issues; the highest bodies are:

the **Political and Security Committee (PSC)**, which meets at the ambassadorial level as a preparatory body for the Council of the EU; it assists with defining policies and preparing a crisis response

the **European Union Military Committee (EUMC)** is the EU's highest military body; it is composed of the chiefs of defense (CHODs) of the Member States, who are regularly represented by their permanent Military Representatives; the EUMC provides the PSC with advice and recommendations on all military matters within the EU

the **Committee for Civilian Aspects of Crisis Management (CIVCOM)** provides advice and recommendations to the PSC in parallel with the EUMC on civilian aspects of crisis management

the **Politico-Military Group (PMG)** provides advice and recommendations to the PSC on political aspects of EU military and civil-military issues, including concepts, capabilities and operations and missions, and monitors implementation

other bodies set up under the CSDP include; the Security and Defense Policy Directorate (SECDEFPOL), the Integrated approach for Security and Peace Directorate (ISP), the EU Military Staff (EUMS), the Civilian Planning and Conduct Capability (CPCC), the Military Planning and Conduct Capability (MPCC), the European Defense Agency, the European Security and Defense College (ESDC), the EU Institute for Security Studies, and the EU Satellite Center (2022)
note: in 2017, the EU set up the Permanent Structured Cooperation on Defense (PESCO), a mechanism for deepening defense cooperation amongst member states through binding commitments and collaborative programs on a variety of military-related capabilities such as cyber, maritime surveillance, medical support, operational readiness, procurement, and training; similar efforts to promote collaboration and cooperation that same year amongst members included the Military Planning and Conduct Capability (MPCC), the Coordinated Annual Review on Defense (CARD), and the European Defense Fund (EDF)

Military expenditures: 1.6% of GDP (2021 est.)
1.6% of GDP (2020)
1.4% of GDP (2019)
1.4% of GDP (2018)
1.35% of GDP (2017)
note: the European Defense Fund (EDF) has a budget of approximately $8 billion for 2021-2027; about $2.7 billion is devoted to funding collaborative defense research while about $5.3 billion is allocated for collaborative capability development projects that complement national contributions; EDF "categories for action" include areas such as information air and missile defense, cyber and information security, digital transformation, force protection, medical services, space, training, and air, ground, and naval combat capabilities (2022)

Military and security service personnel strengths: the 27 EU countries have a cumulative total of approximately 1.34 million active duty troops; the largest EU country military forces belong to France, Germany, and Italy (2021)
note: the combined forces of NATO have approximately 3.3 million active duty personnel

Military deployments: since 2003, the EU has launched more than 30 civilian and military crisis-management, advisory, and training missions in Africa, Asia, Europe, and the Middle East, as well as counter-piracy operations off the coast of Somalia and a naval operation in the Mediterranean to disrupt human smuggling and trafficking networks and prevent the loss of life at sea (2022)
note: in response to the 2022 Russian invasion of Ukraine, the EU announced that it would develop a rapid deployment force consisting of up to 5,000 troops by 2025

Military - note: the EU partners with the North Atlantic Treaty Organization (NATO); NATO is an alliance of 30 countries from North America and Europe; its role is to safeguard the security of its member countries by political and military means; NATO conducts crisis management and peacekeeping missions; member countries that participate in the military aspect of the Alliance contribute forces and equipment, which remain under national command and control until a time when they are required by NATO for a specific purpose (i.e., conflict or crisis, peacekeeping); NATO, however, does possess some common capabilities owned and operated by the Alliance, such as some early warning radar aircraft; relations between NATO and the EU were institutionalized in the early 2000s, building on steps taken during the 1990s to promote greater European responsibility in defense matters; cooperation and coordination covers a broad array of issues, including crisis management, defense and political consultations, civil preparedness, capacity building, military capabilities, maritime security, planning, cyber defense, countering hybrid threats, information sharing, logistics, defense industry, counterterrorism, etc.; since Russia's invasion of Ukraine in February 2022, the EU and NATO, EU Member States and NATO allies have intensified their work and cooperation; NATO and the EU have 21 member countries in common

there are no permanent standing EU forces, but Europe has a variety of multinational military organizations that may be deployed through the EU, in a NATO environment, upon the mandate of the participating countries, or upon the mandate of other international organizations, such as the UN or OSCE including:

EU Battlegroups (BGs) are rapid reaction multinational army units that form a key part of the EU's capacity to respond to crises and conflicts; their deployment is subject to a unanimous decision by the EU Council; BGs typically consists of 1,500-2,000 troops organized around an infantry battalion depending on the mission; the troops and equipment are drawn from EU member states and under the direction of a lead nation; two BGs are always on standby for a period of 6 months; the BGs were declared operational in 2007, but have never been used operationally due to political and financial obstacles

the **European Corps (Eurocorps)** is an independent multinational land force corps headquarters composed of personnel from six framework nations and five associated nations; the corps has no standing operational units; during a crisis, units would be drawn from participating states, and the corps would be placed at the service of the EU and NATO; Eurocorps was established in 1992 by France and Germany; Belgium (1993), Spain (1994), and Luxembourg (1996) joined over the next few years; Greece and Turkey (since 2002), Italy, Romania, and Austria (since 2009, 2016, and 2021 respectively) participate as associated nations; Poland joined in 2022; Eurocorps is headquartered in France

the **European Gendarmerie Force (EURGENDFOR)** is an operational, pre-organized, and rapidly deployable European gendarmerie/police force; it is not established at the EU level, but is capable of performing police tasks, including law enforcement, stability operations, and training in support of the EU, the UN, OSCE, NATO, and other international organizations or ad hoc coalitions; member state gendarmeries include those of France, Italy, the Netherlands, Poland, Portugal, Romania, and Spain; the Lithuanian Public Security Service is a partner, while Turkey's Gendarmerie is an observer force

the **European Medical Corps (EMC)** was set up in the aftermath of the Ebola crisis in West Africa in 2014 to enable the deployment of teams and equipment from EU member states to provide medical assistance and public health expertise in response to emergencies inside and outside the EU; as of 2022, Belgium, Czechia, Denmark, Estonia, Finland, Germany, Italy, the Netherlands, Norway, Spain, and Sweden had committed teams and equipment to the EMC

the **European Medical Command (EMC)** was formed to provide a standing EU medical capability, increase medical operational readiness, and improve interoperability amongst the 18 participating EU members; it operates closely with the NATO Framework Nations Concept's Multinational Medical Coordination Center (MMCC) under a single administrative and infrastructural framework (MMCC/EMC); the EMC was declared operational in May 2022

the **European Air Transport Command (EATC)** is a single multinational command for more than 150 military air mobility assets from seven member states, including transport, air-to-air refueling, and aeromedical evacuation; the EATC headquarters is located in the Netherlands, but the air assets remain located at member national air bases; the EATC was established in 2010

the **European Air Group (EAG)** is an independent organization formed by the air forces of its seven member nations (Belgium, France, Germany, Italy, Netherlands, Spain, and the UK) that is focused on improving interoperability between the air forces of EAG members and its 14 partner and associate nations; it was established in the late 1990s and is headquartered in the UK

the **European Maritime Force (EUROMARFOR or EMF)** is a four-nation (France, Italy, Portugal, and Spain), non-standing naval force with the ability to carry out naval, air, and amphibious operations; EUROMARFOR was formed in 1995 to conduct missions such as crisis response, humanitarian missions, peacekeeping, peace enforcement, and sea control; it can deploy under EU, NATO, or UN mandate, but also as long as the four partner nations agree

the **Combined Joint Expeditionary Force (CJEF)** is a deployable, combined French-UK military force of up to 10,000 personnel for use in a wide range of crisis scenarios, up to and including high intensity combat operations; the CJEF has no standing forces, but would be available at short notice for French-UK bilateral, NATO, EU, UN, or other operations; it was established in 2010 and declared operational in 2020

the **1st German/Netherlands (Dutch) Corps** is a combined army corps headquarters that has the ability to conduct operations under the command and control of Germany and the Netherlands, NATO, or the EU; in peacetime, approximately 1,100 Dutch and German soldiers are assigned, but during a crisis up to 80,000 troops may be assigned; it was formed in 1995 and is headquartered in Germany

the **Lithuanian-Polish-Ukrainian Brigade (LITPOLUKRBRIG)** is comprised of an international staff, three battalions, and specialized units; units affiliated with the multinational brigade remain within the structures of the armed forces of their respective countries until the brigade is activated for participation in an international operation; it was formed in 2014 and is headquartered in Poland

in 2022, the EU approved a new defense strategy designed to increase the bloc's capacity to act, including setting up a **Rapid Deployment Capacity (EU RDC)** consisting of up to 5,000 troops by 2025 (2022)

TERRORISM

Terrorist group(s): see individual EU member states

TRANSNATIONAL ISSUES

Disputes - international: as a political union, the EU has no border disputes with neighboring countries, but Estonia has no land boundary agreements with Russia, Slovenia disputes its land and maritime boundaries with Croatia, and Spain has territorial and maritime disputes with Morocco and with the UK over Gibraltar; the EU has set up a Schengen area - consisting of 22 EU member states that have signed the convention implementing the Schengen agreements or "acquis" (1985 and 1990) on the free movement of persons and the harmonization of border controls in Europe; these agreements became incorporated into EU law with the implementation of the 1997 Treaty of Amsterdam on 1 May 1999; in addition, non-EU states Iceland and Norway (as part of the Nordic Union) have been included in the Schengen area since 1996 (full members in 2001), Switzerland since 2008, and Liechtenstein since 2011 bringing the total current membership to 26; the UK (since 2000) and Ireland (since 2002) take part in only some aspects of the Schengen area, especially with respect to police and criminal matters; nine of the 13 new member states that joined the EU since 2004 joined Schengen on 21 December 2007; of the four remaining EU states, Romania, Bulgaria, and Croatia are obligated to eventually join, while Cyprus' entry is held up by the ongoing Cyprus dispute

FALKLAND ISLANDS (ISLAS MALVINAS)

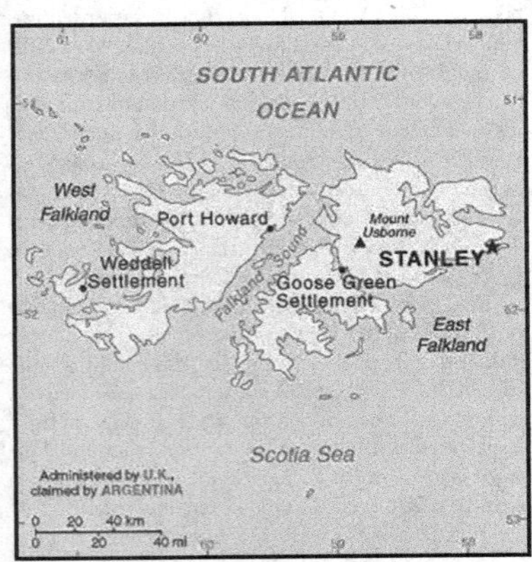

INTRODUCTION

Background: Although first sighted by an English navigator in 1592, the first landing (English) did not occur until almost a century later in 1690, and the first settlement (French) was not established until 1764. The colony was turned over to Spain two years later and the islands have since been the subject of a territorial dispute, first between Britain and Spain, then between Britain and Argentina. The UK asserted its claim to the islands by establishing a naval garrison there in 1833. Argentina invaded the islands on 2 April 1982. The British responded with an expeditionary force that landed seven weeks later and after fierce fighting forced an Argentine surrender on 14 June 1982. With hostilities ended and Argentine forces withdrawn, UK administration resumed. In response to renewed calls from Argentina for Britain to relinquish control of the islands, a referendum was held in March 2013, which resulted in 99.8% of the population voting to remain a part of the UK.

GEOGRAPHY

Location: Southern South America, islands in the South Atlantic Ocean, about 500 km east of southern Argentina

Geographic coordinates: 51 45 S, 59 00 W

Map references: South America

Area: *total:* 12,173 sq km
land: 12,173 sq km
water: 0 sq km
note: includes the two main islands of East and West Falkland and about 200 small islands
country comparison to the world: 163

Area - comparative: slightly smaller than Connecticut

Land boundaries: *total:* 0 km

Coastline: 1,288 km

Maritime claims: *territorial sea:* 12 nm
continental shelf: 200 nm
exclusive fishing zone: 200 nm

Climate: cold marine; strong westerly winds, cloudy, humid; rain occurs on more than half of days in year; average annual rainfall is 60 cm in Stanley; occasional snow all year, except in January and February, but typically does not accumulate

Terrain: rocky, hilly, mountainous with some boggy, undulating plains

Elevation: *highest point:* Mount Usborne 705 m
lowest point: Atlantic Ocean 0 m

Natural resources: fish, squid, wildlife, calcified seaweed, sphagnum moss

Land use: *agricultural land:* 92.4% (2018 est.)
arable land: 0% (2018 est.)
permanent crops: 0% (2018 est.)
permanent pasture: 92.4% (2018 est.)
forest: 0% (2018 est.)
other: 7.6% (2018 est.)

Population distribution: a very small population, with most residents living in and around Stanley

Natural hazards: strong winds persist throughout the year

Geography - note: deeply indented coast provides good natural harbors; short growing season

PEOPLE AND SOCIETY

Population: 3,198 (2016 est.)
note: data include all persons usually resident in the islands at the time of the 2016 census
country comparison to the world: 228

Nationality: *noun:* Falkland Islander(s)
adjective: Falkland Island

Ethnic groups: Falkland Islander 48.3%, British 23.1%, St. Helenian 7.5%, Chilean 4.6%, mixed 6%, other 8.5%, unspecified 2% (2016 est.)
note: data represent population by national identity

Languages: English 89%, Spanish 7.7%, other 3.3% (2006 est.)

Religions: Christian 57.1%, other 1.6%, none 35.4%, unspecified 6% (2016 est.)

Population growth rate: 0.01% (2014 est.)
country comparison to the world: 194

Birth rate: 10.9 births/1,000 population (2012 est.)
country comparison to the world: 172

Death rate: 4.9 deaths/1,000 population (2012 est.)
country comparison to the world: 200

Population distribution: a very small population, with most residents living in and around Stanley

Urbanization: *urban population:* 79.3% of total population (2022)
rate of urbanization: 0.53% annual rate of change (2020-25 est.)

Major urban areas - population: 2,000 STANLEY (capital) (2018)

Sex ratio: *total population:* 1.12 male(s)/female (2016 est.)
note: sex ratio is somewhat skewed by the high proportion of males at the Royal Air Force station, Mount Pleasant Airport (MPA); excluding MPA, the sex ratio of the total population would be 1.04

Life expectancy at birth: *total population:* 77.9
male: 75.6
female: (2017 est.) 79.6

Drinking water source: *improved: urban:* 100% of population
rural: 78.2% of population
total: 95.3% of population
unimproved: urban: 0% of population
rural: 21.8% of population
total: 4.7% of population (2020)

Sanitation facility access: *improved: urban:* 100% of population
rural: 100% of population
total: 100% of population

ENVIRONMENT

Environment - current issues: overfishing by unlicensed vessels is a problem; reindeer - introduced to the islands in 2001 from South Georgia - are part of a farming effort to produce specialty meat and diversify the islands' economy; this is the only commercial reindeer herd in the world unaffected by the 1986 Chornobyl disaster; grazing threatens important habitats including tussac grass and its ecosystem with penguins and sea lions; soil erosion from fires

Climate: cold marine; strong westerly winds, cloudy, humid; rain occurs on more than half of days in year; average annual rainfall is 60 cm in Stanley; occasional snow all year, except in January and February, but typically does not accumulate

Land use: *agricultural land:* 92.4% (2018 est.)
arable land: 0% (2018 est.)
permanent crops: 0% (2018 est.)
permanent pasture: 92.4% (2018 est.)
forest: 0% (2018 est.)
other: 7.6% (2018 est.)

Urbanization: *urban population:* 79.3% of total population (2022)
rate of urbanization: 0.53% annual rate of change (2020-25 est.)

GOVERNMENT

Country name: *conventional long form:* none
conventional short form: Falkland Islands (Islas Malvinas)
etymology: the archipelago takes its name from the Falkland Sound, the strait separating the two main islands; the channel itself was named after the Viscount of FALKLAND, who sponsored an expedition to the islands in 1690; the Spanish name for the archipelago derives from the French "Iles Malouines," the name applied to the islands by French explorer Louis-Antoine de BOUGAINVILLE in 1764

Government type: parliamentary democracy (Legislative Assembly); self-governing overseas territory of the UK

Dependency status: overseas territory of the UK; also claimed by Argentina

Capital: *name:* Stanley
geographic coordinates: 51 42 S, 57 51 W
time difference: UTC-4 (1 hour ahead of Washington, DC, during Standard Time)
etymology: named after Edward SMITH-STANLEY (1799-1869), the 14th Earl of Derby, a British statesman and three-time prime minister of the UK who never visited the islands

Administrative divisions: none (overseas territory of the UK; also claimed by Argentina)

Independence: none (overseas territory of the UK; also claimed by Argentina)

National holiday: Liberation Day, 14 June (1982)

Constitution: *history:* previous 1985; latest entered into force 1 January 2009 (The Falkland Islands Constitution Order 2008)

Legal system: English common law and local statutes

Citizenship: see United Kingdom

Suffrage: 18 years of age; universal

Executive branch: *chief of state:* King CHARLES III (since 8 September 2022); represented by Governor Alison BLAKE (since 23 July 2022)
head of government: Chief Executive Andy KEELING (since April 2021)
cabinet: Executive Council elected by the Legislative Council
elections/appointments: the monarchy is hereditary; governor appointed by the monarch; chief executive appointed by the governor

Legislative branch: *description:* unicameral Legislative Assembly, formerly the Legislative Council (10 seats; 5 members directly elected in the Stanley constituency and 3 members in the Camp constituency by simple majority vote, 2 appointed non-voting ex-officio members - the chief executive, appointed by the governor, and the financial secretary; members serve 4-year terms); note - several previous referendums - the latest in September 2020 - on whether to merge the Stanley and Camp constituencies into a single islands wide constituency, failed
elections: last held on 4 November 2021 (next to be held in November 2025)
election results: percent of vote - NA; seats - independent 8; composition of elected members -men 6, women 2, percent of women 25%

Judicial branch: *highest court(s):* Court of Appeal (consists of the court president, the chief justice as an ex officio non-resident member, and 2 justices of appeal); Supreme Court (consists of the chief justice); note - appeals beyond the Court of Appeal are referred to the Judicial Committee of the Privy Council (in London)
judge selection and term of office: chief justice, court of appeal president, and justices appointed by the governor; tenure specified in each justice's instrument of appointment
subordinate courts: Magistrate's Court (senior magistrate presides over civil and criminal divisions); Court of Summary Jurisdiction

Political parties and leaders: none; all independents

International organization participation: UPU

Diplomatic representation in the US: none (overseas territory of the UK)

Diplomatic representation from the US: *embassy:* none (overseas territory of the UK; also claimed by Argentina)

Flag description: blue with the flag of the UK in the upper hoist-side quadrant and the Falkland Island coat of arms centered on the outer half of the flag; the coat of arms contains a white ram (sheep raising was once the major economic activity) above the sailing ship Desire (whose crew discovered the islands) with a scroll at the bottom bearing the motto DESIRE THE RIGHT

National symbol(s): ram

National anthem: *name:* "Song of the Falklands"
lyrics/music: Christopher LANHAM
note: adopted 1930s; the song is the local unofficial anthem; as a territory of the United Kingdom, "God Save the King" is official (see United Kingdom)

ECONOMY

Economic overview: The economy was formerly based on agriculture, mainly sheep farming, but fishing and tourism currently comprise the bulk of economic activity. In 1987, the government began selling fishing licenses to foreign trawlers operating within the Falkland Islands' exclusive fishing zone. These license fees net more than $40 million per year, which help support the island's health, education, and welfare system. The waters around the Falkland Islands are known for their squid, which account for around 75% of the annual 200,000-ton catch.

Dairy farming supports domestic consumption; crops furnish winter fodder. Foreign exchange earnings come from shipments of high-grade wool to the UK and from the sale of postage stamps and coins.

Tourism, especially ecotourism, is increasing rapidly, with about 69,000 visitors in 2009 and adds approximately $5.5 million to the Falkland's annual GDP. The British military presence also provides a sizable economic boost. The islands are now self-financing except for defense.

In 1993, the British Geological Survey announced a 200-mile oil exploration zone around the islands, and early seismic surveys suggest substantial reserves capable of producing 500,000 barrels per day. Political tensions between the UK and Argentina remain high following the start of oil drilling activities in the waters. In May 2010 the first commercial oil discovery was made, signaling the potential for the development of a long term hydrocarbon industry in the Falkland Islands.

Real GDP (purchasing power parity): $206.4 million (2015 est.)
$164.5 million (2014 est.)
$167.5 million (2013 est.)
country comparison to the world: 220

Real GDP growth rate: 25.5% (2015 est.)
-1.8% (2014 est.)
-20.4% (2013 est.)
country comparison to the world: 3

Real GDP per capita: $70,800 (2015 est.)
$63,000 (2014 est.)
country comparison to the world: 10

GDP (official exchange rate): $206.4 million (2015 est.)

Inflation rate (consumer prices): 1.4% (2014 est.)
country comparison to the world: 83

GDP - composition, by sector of origin: *agriculture:* 41% (2015 est.)
industry: 20.6% (2015 est.)
services: 38.4% (2015 est.)

Agricultural products: fodder and vegetable crops; venison, sheep, dairy products; fish, squid

Industries: fish and wool processing; tourism

Labor force: 1,850 (2016 est.)
country comparison to the world: 226

Labor force - by occupation: *agriculture:* 41%
industry: 24.5%
services: 34.5% (2015 est.)

Unemployment rate: 1% (2016 est.)
country comparison to the world: 9

Gini Index coefficient - distribution of family income: 36 (2015)
country comparison to the world: 94

Budget: *revenues:* 67.1 million (FY09/10)
expenditures: 75.3 million (FY09/10)

Budget surplus (+) or deficit (-): -4% (of GDP) (FY09/10)
country comparison to the world: 156

Public debt: 0% of GDP (2015 est.)
country comparison to the world: 209

Taxes and other revenues: 32.5% (of GDP) (FY09/10)
country comparison to the world: 66

Fiscal year: 1 April - 31 March

Exports: $257.3 million (2015 est.)
$125 million (2004 est.)
country comparison to the world: 202

Exports - partners: Spain 78%, United States 6% (2019)

Exports - commodities: mollusks, fish, wool, sheep/goat meats, engine parts (2019)

Imports: $90 million (2004 est.)
country comparison to the world: 218

Imports - partners: United Kingdom 79%, Netherlands 16% (2019)

Imports - commodities: refined petroleum, spark-ignition engines, stone processing machinery, construction vehicles, cars (2019)

Debt - external: $0 (2017 est.)
$0 (2016 est.)
country comparison to the world: 205

Exchange rates: Falkland pounds (FKP) per US dollar -
0.7836 (2017 est.)
0.6542 (2016 est.)
0.6542 (2015)
0.6542 (2014 est.)
0.6391 (2013 est.)

ENERGY

Electricity: *installed generating capacity:* 11,000 kW (2020 est.)
consumption: 19.133 million kWh (2019 est.)
exports: 0 kWh (2020 est.)
imports: 0 kWh (2020 est.)
transmission/distribution losses: 1 million kWh (2019 est.)

Electricity generation sources: *fossil fuels:* 66.7% of total installed capacity (2020 est.)
wind: 33.3% of total installed capacity (2020 est.)

Petroleum: *total petroleum production:* 0 bbl/day (2021 est.)
refined petroleum consumption: 300 bbl/day (2019 est.)

Refined petroleum products - imports: 286 bbl/day (2015 est.)
country comparison to the world: 208

Carbon dioxide emissions: 46,000 metric tonnes of CO_2 (2019 est.)
from petroleum and other liquids: 46,000 metric tonnes of CO_2 (2019 est.)
country comparison to the world: 212

Energy consumption per capita: 0 Btu/person (2019 est.)
country comparison to the world: 198

COMMUNICATIONS

Telephones - fixed lines: *total subscriptions:* 2,000 (2018 est.)
subscriptions per 100 inhabitants: 65 (2018 est.)
country comparison to the world: 215

Telephones - mobile cellular: *total subscriptions:* 5,000 (2018 est.)
subscriptions per 100 inhabitants: 163 (2018 est.)
country comparison to the world: 220

Telecommunication systems: *general assessment:* the replacement of the rural internet and phone system was delayed due to COVID; upgrades started at the end of 2019, this included the replacement of all Multi Service Access Nodes (MSANs), the technology used to connect larger settlements; in early 2020 a new system to replace the WiMAX system (the technology used to connect smaller settlements and households) had been delayed as well due to COVID-19; once the equipment is received it will be installed in the largest base stations on East Falklands: Malo, Bombilla, and Mt Pleasant peak

"We also have MSAN equipment and radio links due to arrive towards the end of this month, and these and will be installed at Chartres, New Island, Sea Lion Island, Onion Range, Sand Bay, and Mare Harbour enabling us to migrate additional customers from the existing WiMAX network and also releasing equipment for spares." (2020)

domestic: fixed-line subscriptions approximately 65 per 100, 163 per 100 for mobile-cellular (2019)
international: country code - 500; satellite earth station - 1 Intelsat (Atlantic Ocean) with links through London to other countries (2015)

Broadcast media: TV service provided by a multi-channel service provider; radio services provided by the public broadcaster, Falkland Islands Radio Service, broadcasting on both AM and FM frequencies, and by the British Forces Broadcasting Service (BFBS) (2007)

Internet country code: .fk

Internet users: *total:* 3,343 (2019 est.)
percent of population: 99% (2019 est.)
country comparison to the world: 223

Broadband - fixed subscriptions: *total:* 1,000 (2020 est.)
subscriptions per 100 inhabitants: 33 (2020 est.)
country comparison to the world: 204

TRANSPORTATION

National air transport system: *number of registered air carriers:* 1 (2020)
inventory of registered aircraft operated by air carriers: 5

Civil aircraft registration country code prefix: VP-F

Airports: *total:* 7 (2021)
country comparison to the world: 168

Airports - with paved runways: *total:* 2
2,438 to 3,047 m: 1
914 to 1,523 m: 1 (2021)

Airports - with unpaved runways: *total:* 5
under 914 m: 5 (2021)

Roadways: *total:* 440 km (2008)
paved: 50 km (2008)
unpaved: 390 km (2008)
country comparison to the world: 198

Merchant marine: *total:* 2
by type: general cargo 1, other 1 (2021)
country comparison to the world: 175

Ports and terminals: *major seaport(s):* Stanley

MILITARY AND SECURITY

Military and security forces: no regular military forces

Military - note: defense is the responsibility of the UK, which maintains about 1,200 troops on the islands

TRANSNATIONAL ISSUES

Disputes - international: Argentina, which claims the islands in its constitution and briefly occupied them by force in 1982, agreed in 1995 to no longer seek settlement by force; UK continues to reject Argentine requests for sovereignty talks

FAROE ISLANDS

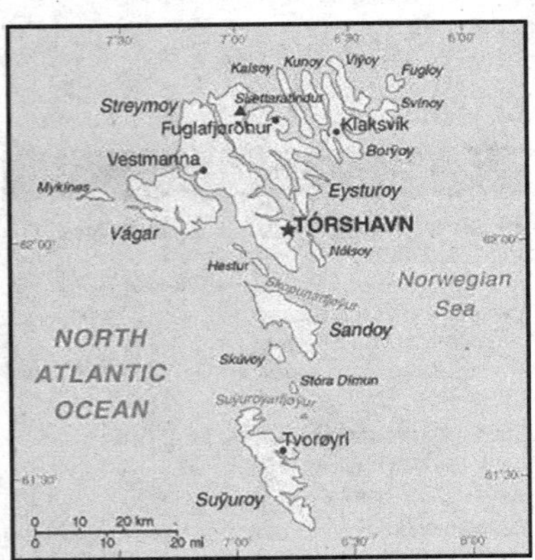

INTRODUCTION

Background: The population of the Faroe Islands, a self-governing dependency of Denmark, is largely descended from Viking settlers who arrived in the 9th century. The islands have been connected politically to Denmark since the 14th century. The Home Rule Act of 1948 granted a high degree of self-Government to the Faroese, who have autonomy over most internal affairs and external trade, while Denmark is responsible for justice, defense, and some foreign affairs. The Faroe Islands are not part of the European Union.

GEOGRAPHY

Location: Northern Europe, island group between the Norwegian Sea and the North Atlantic Ocean, about halfway between Iceland and Norway

Geographic coordinates: 62 00 N, 7 00 W

Map references: Europe

Area: *total:* 1,393 sq km
land: 1,393 sq km
water: 0 sq km (some lakes and streams)
country comparison to the world: 182

Area - comparative: eight times the size of Washington, DC

Land boundaries: *total:* 0 km

Coastline: 1,117 km

Maritime claims: *territorial sea:* 12 nm
continental shelf: 200 nm or agreed boundaries or median line
exclusive fishing zone: 200 nm or agreed boundaries or median line

Climate: mild winters, cool summers; usually overcast; foggy, windy

Terrain: rugged, rocky, some low peaks; cliffs along most of coast

Elevation: *highest point:* Slaettaratindur 882 m
lowest point: Atlantic Ocean 0 m

Natural resources: fish, whales, hydropower, possible oil and gas

Land use: *agricultural land:* 2.1% (2018 est.)
arable land: 2.1% (2018 est.)
permanent crops: 0% (2018 est.)
permanent pasture: 0% (2018 est.)
forest: 0.1% (2018 est.)
other: 97.8% (2018 est.)

Population distribution: the island of Streymoy is by far the most populous with over 40% of the population; it has approximately twice as many inhabitants as Eysturoy, the second most populous island; seven of the inhabited islands have fewer than 100 people

Natural hazards: strong winds and heavy rains can occur throughout the year

Geography - note: archipelago of 17 inhabited islands and one uninhabited island, and a few uninhabited islets; strategically located along important sea lanes in northeastern Atlantic; precipitous terrain limits habitation to small coastal lowlands

PEOPLE AND SOCIETY

Population: 52,269 (2022 est.)
country comparison to the world: 208

Nationality: *noun:* Faroese (singular and plural)
adjective: Faroese

Ethnic groups: Faroese 85.3% (Scandinavian and Anglo-Saxon descent), Danish 8.3%, other Nordic 1.4%, other 4.5% (includes Filipino, Poland, Romanian) (2022 est.)
note: data represent respondents by country of birth

Languages: Faroese 93.8% (derived from Old Norse), Danish 3.2%, other 3% (2011 est.)
note: data represent population by primary language

Religions: Christian 89.3% (predominantly Evangelical Lutheran), other 1%, none 3.8%, unspecified 6% (2011 est.)

Age structure: *0-14 years:* 19.69% (male 5,247/female 4,920)
15-24 years: 13.89% (male 3,708/female 3,465)
25-54 years: 37.01% (male 10,277/female 8,828)
55-64 years: 12% (male 3,199/female 2,996)
65 years and over: 17.41% (male 4,352/female 4,636) (2020 est.)

Median age: *total:* 37.2 years
male: 36.9 years
female: 37.7 years (2020 est.)
country comparison to the world: 72

Population growth rate: 0.63% (2022 est.)
country comparison to the world: 140

Birth rate: 14.94 births/1,000 population (2022 est.)
country comparison to the world: 116

Death rate: 8.63 deaths/1,000 population (2022 est.)
country comparison to the world: 71

Net migration rate: 0 migrant(s)/1,000 population (2022 est.)
country comparison to the world: 88

Population distribution: the island of Streymoy is by far the most populous with over 40% of the population; it has approximately twice as many inhabitants as Eysturoy, the second most populous island; seven of the inhabited islands have fewer than 100 people

Urbanization: *urban population:* 42.8% of total population (2022)
rate of urbanization: 0.89% annual rate of change (2020-25 est.)

Major urban areas - population: 21,000 TORSHAVN (capital) (2018)

Sex ratio: *at birth:* 1.07 male(s)/female
0-14 years: 1.07 male(s)/female
15-24 years: 1.09 male(s)/female
25-54 years: 1.17 male(s)/female
55-64 years: 1.09 male(s)/female
65 years and over: 0.77 male(s)/female
total population: 1.08 male(s)/female (2022 est.)

Infant mortality rate: *total:* 5.99 deaths/1,000 live births
male: 6.61 deaths/1,000 live births
female: 5.32 deaths/1,000 live births (2022 est.)
country comparison to the world: 171

Life expectancy at birth: *total population:* 81.26 years
male: 78.73 years
female: 83.97 years (2022 est.)
country comparison to the world: 42

Total fertility rate: 2.29 children born/woman (2022 est.)
country comparison to the world: 78

Drinking water source: *improved: total:* 100% of population
unimproved: total: 0% of population (2020)

Physicians density: 2.62 physicians/1,000 population (2016)

Hospital bed density: 4.2 beds/1,000 population (2016)

Education expenditures: 8.2% of GDP (2017 est.)
country comparison to the world: 9

ENVIRONMENT

Environment - current issues: coastal erosion, landslides and rockfalls, flash flooding, wind storms; oil spills

Air pollutants: *carbon dioxide emissions:* 0.63 megatons (2016 est.)

Climate: mild winters, cool summers; usually overcast; foggy, windy

Land use: *agricultural land:* 2.1% (2018 est.)
arable land: 2.1% (2018 est.)
permanent crops: 0% (2018 est.)
permanent pasture: 0% (2018 est.)
forest: 0.1% (2018 est.)
other: 97.8% (2018 est.)

Urbanization: *urban population:* 42.8% of total population (2022)
rate of urbanization: 0.89% annual rate of change (2020-25 est.)

Revenue from forest resources: *forest revenues:* 0% of GDP (2017 est.)
country comparison to the world: 167

Waste and recycling: *municipal solid waste generated annually:* 61,000 tons (2014 est.)
municipal solid waste recycled annually: 40,870 tons (2012 est.)
percent of municipal solid waste recycled: 67% (2012 est.)

Total renewable water resources: 0 cubic meters (2017 est.)

GOVERNMENT

Country name: *conventional long form:* none
conventional short form: Faroe Islands
local long form: none
local short form: Foroyar
etymology: the archipelago's name may derive from the Old Norse word "faer," meaning sheep

Government type: parliamentary democracy (Faroese Parliament); part of the Kingdom of Denmark

Dependency status: part of the Kingdom of Denmark; self-governing overseas administrative division of Denmark since 1948

Capital: *name:* Torshavn
geographic coordinates: 62 00 N, 6 46 W
time difference: UTC 0 (5 hours ahead of Washington, DC, during Standard Time)
daylight saving time: +1hr, begins last Sunday in March; ends last Sunday in October
etymology: the meaning in Danish is "Thor's harbor"

Administrative divisions: part of the Kingdom of Denmark; self-governing overseas administrative division of Denmark; there are 29 first-order municipalities (kommunur, singular - kommuna) Eidhi, Eystur, Famjin, Fuglafjordhur, Fugloy, Hov, Husavik, Hvalba, Hvannasund, Klaksvik, Kunoy, Kvivik, Nes, Porkeri, Runavik, Sandur, Sjovar, Skalavik, Skopun, Skuvoy, Sorvagur, Sumba, Sunda, Torshavn, Tvoroyri, Vagar, Vagur, Vestmanna, Vidhareidhi

Independence: none (part of the Kingdom of Denmark; self-governing overseas administrative division of Denmark)

National holiday: Olaifest (Olavsoka) (commemorates the death in battle of King OLAF II of Norway, later St. OLAF), 29 July (1030)

Constitution: *history:* 5 June 1953 (Danish Constitution), 23 March 1948 (Home Rule Act), and 24 June 2005 (Takeover Act) serve as the Faroe Islands' constitutional position in the Unity of the Realm
amendments: see entry for Denmark

Legal system: the laws of Denmark apply where applicable

Citizenship: see Denmark

Suffrage: 18 years of age; universal

Executive branch: *chief of state:* Queen MARGRETHE II of Denmark (since 14 January 1972), represented by High Commissioner Lene Moyell JOHANSEN, chief administrative officer (since 15 May 2017)
head of government: Prime Minister Bardur A STEIG NIELSEN (since 16 September 2019)
cabinet: Landsstyri appointed by the prime minister
elections/appointments: the monarchy is hereditary; high commissioner appointed by the monarch; following legislative elections, the leader of the majority party or majority coalition usually elected prime minister by the Faroese Parliament; election last held on 31 August 2019 (next to be held in 2023)
election results: *2019:* Bardur A STEIGNIELSEN elected prime minister; Parliament vote - NA
2015: Aksel V. JOHANNESEN elected prime minister; Parliament vote - NA

Legislative branch: *description:* unicameral Faroese Parliament or Logting (33 seats; members directly elected in a single nationwide constituency by proportional representation vote; members serve 4-year terms)
the Faroe Islands elect 2 members to the Danish Parliament to serve 4-year terms
elections: Faroese Parliament - last held on 31 August 2019 (next to be held in 2023)
Faroese seats in the Danish Parliament last held on 5 June 2019 (next to be held no later than June 2023)
election results: Faroese Parliament percent of vote by party - People's Party 24.2%, JF 21.2%, Union Party 21.2%, Republic 18.2%, Center Party 6%, Progress Party 6%, Self-Government Party 3%, seats by party - People's Party 8, JF 7, Union Party 7, Republic 6, Center Party 2, Progress Party 2, Self-Government Party 1, composition - men 25, women 8; percent of women 24.2%
Faroese seats in Danish Parliament - percent of vote by party - NA; seats by party - JF 1, Republic 1; composition - men 2

Judicial branch: *highest court(s):* Faroese Court or Raett (Rett - Danish) decides both civil and criminal cases; the Court is part of the Danish legal system
subordinate courts: Court of the First Instance or Tribunal de Premiere Instance; Court of Administrative Law or Tribunal Administratif; Mixed Commercial Court; Land Court

Political parties and leaders: Center Party (Midflokkurin) [Jenis av RANA]
People's Party (Folkaflokkurin) [Jorgen NICLASEN]
Progress Party (Framsokn) [Ruth VANG]
Republic (Tjodveldi) [Hogni HOYDAL] (formerly the Republican Party)
Self-Government Party (Sjalvstyri or Sjalvstyrisflokkurin) [Jogvan SKORHEIM]
Social Democratic Party (Javnadarflokkurin) or JF [Aksel V. JOHANNESEN]
Union Party (Sambandsflokkurin) [Bardur A STEIG NIELSEN]

International organization participation: Arctic Council, IMO (associate), NC, NIB, UNESCO (associate), UPU

Diplomatic representation in the US: none (self-governing overseas administrative division of Denmark)

Diplomatic representation from the US: *embassy:* none (self-governing overseas administrative division of Denmark)

Flag description: white with a red cross outlined in blue extending to the edges of the flag; the vertical part of the cross is shifted toward the hoist side in the style of the Dannebrog (Danish flag); referred to as Merkid, meaning "the banner" or "the mark," the flag resembles those of neighboring Iceland and Norway, and uses the same three colors - but in a different sequence; white represents the clear Faroese sky, as well as the foam of the waves; red and blue are traditional Faroese colors
note: the blue on the flag is a lighter blue (azure) than that found on the flags of Iceland or Norway

National symbol(s): ram; national colors: red, white, blue

National anthem: *name:* "Mitt alfagra land" (My Fairest Land)
lyrics/music: Simun av SKAROI/Peter ALBERG
note: adopted 1948; the anthem is also known as "Tu alfagra land mitt" (Thou Fairest Land of Mine); as a self-governing overseas administrative division of Denmark, the Faroe Islands are permitted their own national anthem

ECONOMY

Economic overview: The Faroese economy has experienced a period of significant growth since 2011, due to higher fish prices and increased salmon farming and catches in the pelagic fisheries. Fishing has been the main source of income for the Faroe Islands since the late 19th century, but dependence on fishing makes the economy vulnerable to price fluctuations. Nominal GDP, measured in current prices, grew 5.6% in 2015 and 6.8% in 2016. GDP growth was forecast at 6.2% in 2017, slowing to 0.5% in 2018, due to lower fisheries quotas, higher oil prices and fewer farmed salmon combined with lower salmon prices. The fisheries sector accounts for about 97% of exports, and half of GDP. Unemployment is low, estimated at 2.1% in early 2018. Aided by an annual subsidy from Denmark, which amounts to about 11% of Faroese GDP , Faroese have a standard of living equal to that of Denmark. The Faroe Islands have bilateral free trade agreements with the EU, Iceland, Norway, Switzerland, and Turkey.

For the first time in 8 years, the Faroe Islands managed to generate a public budget surplus in 2016, a trend which continued in 2017. The local government intends to use this to reduce public debt, which reached 38% of GDP in 2015. A fiscal sustainability analysis of the Faroese economy shows that a long-term tightening of fiscal policy of 5% of GDP is required for fiscal sustainability.

Increasing public infrastructure investments are likely to lead to continued growth in the short term, and the Faroese economy is becoming somewhat more diversified. Growing industries include financial services, petroleum-related businesses, shipping, maritime manufacturing services, civil aviation, IT, telecommunications, and tourism.

Real GDP (purchasing power parity): $2.001 billion (2014 est.)
$1.89 billion (2013 est.)
$1.608 billion (2012 est.)
country comparison to the world: 197

Real GDP growth rate: 5.9% (2017 est.)
7.5% (2016 est.)
2.4% (2015 est.)
country comparison to the world: 30

Real GDP per capita: $40,000 (2014 est.)
country comparison to the world: 43

GDP (official exchange rate): $2.765 billion (2014 est.)

Inflation rate (consumer prices): -0.3% (2016)
-1.7% (2015)
country comparison to the world: 15

GDP - composition, by sector of origin: *agriculture:* 18% (2013 est.)
industry: 39% (2013 est.)
services: 43% (2013 est.)

GDP - composition, by end use: *household consumption:* 52% (2013)
government consumption: 29.6% (2013)
investment in fixed capital: 18.4% (2013)

Agricultural products: potatoes, mutton, sheep skins, sheep offals, beef, sheep fat, cattle offals, cattle hides, cattle fat

Industries: fishing, fish processing, tourism, small ship repair and refurbishment, handicrafts

Industrial production growth rate: 3.4% (2009 est.)
country comparison to the world: 91

Labor force: 27,540 (2017 est.)
country comparison to the world: 205

Labor force - by occupation: *agriculture:* 15%
industry: 15%
services: 70% (December 2016 est.)

Unemployment rate: 2.2% (2017 est.)
3.4% (2016 est.)
country comparison to the world: 22

Population below poverty line: 10% (2015 est.)

Gini Index coefficient - distribution of family income: 22.7 (2013 est.)
21.6 (2011 est.)
country comparison to the world: 173

Budget: *revenues:* 835.6 million (2014 est.)
expenditures: 883.8 million (2014)
note: Denmark supplies the Faroe Islands with almost one-third of its public funds

Budget surplus (+) or deficit (-): -1.7% (of GDP) (2014 est.)
country comparison to the world: 95

Public debt: 35% of GDP (2014 est.)
country comparison to the world: 152

Taxes and other revenues: 30.2% (of GDP) (2014 est.)
country comparison to the world: 76

Fiscal year: calendar year

Exports: $1.184 billion (2016 est.)
$1.019 billion (2015 est.)
country comparison to the world: 172

Exports - partners: Russia 26.4%, UK 14.1%, Germany 8.4%, China 7.9%, Spain 6.8%, Denmark 6.2%, US 4.7%, Poland 4.4%, Norway 4.1% (2017)

Exports - commodities: fish and fish products (97%) (2017 est.)

Imports: $978.4 million (2016 est.)
$906.1 million (2015 est.)
country comparison to the world: 190

Imports - partners: Denmark 33%, China 10.7%, Germany 7.6%, Poland 6.8%, Norway 6.7%, Ireland 5%, Chile 4.3% (2017)

Imports - commodities: goods for household consumption, machinery and transport equipment, fuels, raw materials and semi-manufactures, cars

Debt - external: $387.6 million (2012)
$274.5 million (2010)
country comparison to the world: 181

Exchange rates: Danish kroner (DKK) per US dollar -
6.586 (2017 est.)
6.7269 (2016 est.)
6.7269 (2015 est.)
6.7236 (2014 est.)
5.6125 (2013 est.)

ENERGY

Electricity access: *electrification - total population:* 100% (2020)

Electricity: *installed generating capacity:* 128,000 kW (2020 est.)
consumption: 358.64 million kWh (2019 est.)
exports: 0 kWh (2020 est.)
imports: 0 kWh (2020 est.)
transmission/distribution losses: 23.16 million kWh (2019 est.)

Electricity generation sources: *fossil fuels:* 58.9% of total installed capacity (2020 est.)
wind: 15.1% of total installed capacity (2020 est.)
hydroelectricity: 26% of total installed capacity (2020 est.)

Petroleum: *total petroleum production:* 0 bbl/day (2021 est.)
refined petroleum consumption: 5,500 bbl/day (2019 est.)

Refined petroleum products - imports: 4,555 bbl/day (2015 est.)
country comparison to the world: 174

Carbon dioxide emissions: 870,000 metric tonnes of CO_2 (2019 est.)
from petroleum and other liquids: 870,000 metric tonnes of CO_2 (2019 est.)
country comparison to the world: 177

Energy consumption per capita: 0 Btu/person (2019 est.)
country comparison to the world: 199

COMMUNICATIONS

Telephones - fixed lines: *total subscriptions:* 15,341 (2020 est.)
subscriptions per 100 inhabitants: 31 (2020 est.)
country comparison to the world: 182

Telephones - mobile cellular: *total subscriptions:* 59,213 (2020 est.)
subscriptions per 100 inhabitants: 121 (2020 est.)
country comparison to the world: 203

Telecommunication systems: *general assessment:* the Faroe Islands have a highly developed communication network, which covers the whole country; from telecommunication and mobile phones to the internet and media, the Faroe Islands are at the forefront of modern communications technology; working within the special geographic circumstances of the Faroe Islands; companies have become world experts in providing digital communication solutions to remote and sparsely populated areas (2022)

domestic: roughly 31 per 100 teledensity for fixed-line and nearly 121 per 100 for mobile-cellular; both NMT (analog) and GSM (digital) mobile telephone systems are installed (2020)
international: country code - 298; landing points for the SHEFA-2, FARICE-1, and CANTAT-3 fiber-optic submarine cables from the Faroe Islands, to Denmark, Germany, UK and Iceland; satellite earth stations - 1 Orion; (2019)

Broadcast media: publicly owned TV station; the Faroese telecommunications company distributes local and international channels through its digital terrestrial network; publicly owned radio station supplemented by 3 privately owned stations broadcasting over multiple frequencies

Internet country code: .fo

Internet users: *total:* 47,703 (2019 est.)
percent of population: 98% (2019 est.)
country comparison to the world: 197

Broadband - fixed subscriptions: *total:* 18,443 (2020 est.)
subscriptions per 100 inhabitants: 38 (2020 est.)
country comparison to the world: 169

TRANSPORTATION

National air transport system: *number of registered air carriers:* 1 (2020) (registered in Denmark)
inventory of registered aircraft operated by air carriers: 3 (registered in Denmark)

Civil aircraft registration country code prefix: OY-H

Airports: *total:* 1 (2021)
country comparison to the world: 219

Airports - with paved runways: *total:* 1
1,524 to 2,437 m: 1 (2021)

Roadways: *total:* 960 km (2017)
paved: 500 km (2017)
unpaved: 460 km (2017)
note: those islands not connected by roads (bridges or tunnels) are connected by seven different ferry links operated by the nationally owned company SSL; 28 km of tunnels
country comparison to the world: 187

Merchant marine: *total:* 101
by type: container ships 6, general cargo 48, oil tanker 1, other 46 (2021)
country comparison to the world: 88

Ports and terminals: *major seaport(s):* Fuglafjordur, Torshavn, Vagur

MILITARY AND SECURITY

Military and security forces: no regular military forces or conscription

Military - note: the Government of Denmark has responsibility for defense; as such, the Danish military's Joint Arctic Command in Nuuk, Greenland is responsible for territorial defense of the Faroe Islands; the Joint Arctic Command has a contact element in the capital of Torshavn

TRANSNATIONAL ISSUES

Disputes - international: because anticipated offshore hydrocarbon resources have not been realized, earlier Faroese proposals for full independence have been deferred; Iceland, the UK, and Ireland dispute Denmark's claim to UNCLOS that the Faroe Islands' continental shelf extends beyond 200 nm

FIJI

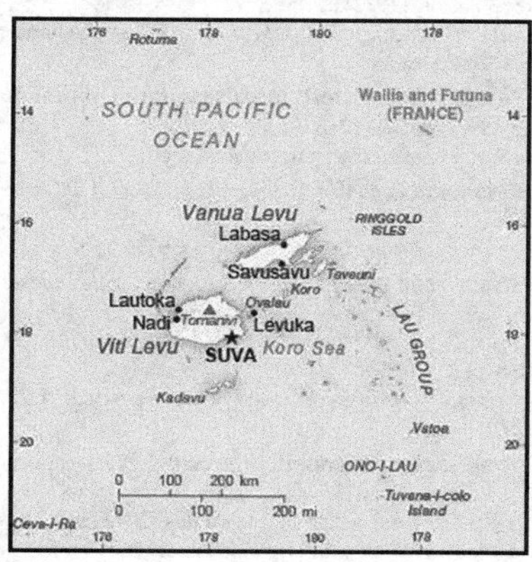

INTRODUCTION

Background: Austronesians settled Fiji around 1000 B.C., followed by successive waves of Melanesians starting around the first century A.D. Fijians traded with Polynesian groups in Samoa and Tonga, and by about 900, much of Fiji was in the Tu'i Tongan Empire's sphere of influence. The Tongan influence declined significantly by 1200, while Melanesian seafarers continued to periodically arrive in Fiji, further mixing Melanesian and Polynesian cultural traditions. Dutch explorer Abel TASMAN was the first European to spot Fiji in 1643, followed by British explorer James COOK in 1774. Captain William BLIGH plotted the islands in 1789. In the 1800s, merchants, traders, and whalers frequented the islands and the first missionaries arrived in 1835. Rival kings and chiefs competed for power, at times aided by Europeans and their weapons, and in 1865, Seru Epenisa CAKOBAU united many groups into the Confederacy of Independent Kingdoms of Viti. The arrangement proved weak and in 1871 CAKOBAU formed the Kingdom of Fiji in an attempt to centralize power. Fearing a hostile takeover by a foreign power as the kingdom's economy began to falter, CAKOBAU ceded Fiji to the UK in 1874.

The first British governor set up a plantation-style economy and brought in more than 60,000 Indians as indentured laborers, most of whom chose to stay in Fiji rather than return to India when their contracts expired. In the early 1900s, society was divided along ethnic lines, with iTaukei (indigenous Fijians), Europeans, and Indo-Fijians living in separate areas and maintaining their own languages and traditions. ITaukei fears of an Indo-Fijian takeover of government delayed independence through the 1960s; Fiji achieved independence in 1970 with agreements in place to allocate parliamentary seats by ethnic groups. Long-serving Prime Minister Kamisese MARA largely balanced these ethnic divisions, but concerns about growing Indo-Fijian political influence led to two coups in 1987. A new constitution in 1990 cemented iTaukei control of politics, leading thousands of Indo-Fijians to leave. A reformed constitution in 1997 was more equitable and led to the election of an Indo-Fijian prime minister in 1999, who was ousted in a coup the following year. In 2005, the new prime minister put forward a bill that would grant pardons to the coup perpetrators, leading Commodore Josaia BAINIMARAMA to launch a coup in 2006. BAINIMARAMA appointed himself prime minister in 2007 and continues to hold the position after elections in 2014 and 2018 that international observers deemed credible.

With well-developed infrastructure, Fiji has become a hub for the Pacific, hosting the secretariat for the Pacific Islands Forum and the main campus of the University of the South Pacific. In addition, Fiji is a center for Pacific tourism, and Nadi International Airport is by far the busiest airport in a Pacific island country.

GEOGRAPHY

Location: Oceania, island group in the South Pacific Ocean, about two-thirds of the way from Hawaii to New Zealand

Geographic coordinates: 18 00 S, 175 00 E

Map references: Oceania

Area: *total:* 18,274 sq km
land: 18,274 sq km
water: 0 sq km
country comparison to the world: 156

Area - comparative: slightly smaller than New Jersey

Land boundaries: *total:* 0 km

Coastline: 1,129 km

Maritime claims: *territorial sea:* 12 nm
contiguous zone: 24 nm
exclusive economic zone: 200 nm
continental shelf: 200-m depth or to the depth of exploitation
measured from claimed archipelagic straight baselines

Climate: tropical marine; only slight seasonal temperature variation

Terrain: mostly mountains of volcanic origin

Elevation: *highest point:* Tomanivi 1,324 m
lowest point: Pacific Ocean 0 m

Natural resources: timber, fish, gold, copper, offshore oil potential, hydropower

Land use: *agricultural land:* 23.3% (2018 est.)
arable land: 9% (2018 est.)
permanent crops: 4.7% (2018 est.)
permanent pasture: 9.6% (2018 est.)
forest: 55.7% (2018 est.)
other: 21% (2018 est.)

Irrigated land: 40 sq km (2012)

Population distribution: approximately 70% of the population lives on the island of Viti Levu; roughly half of the population lives in urban areas

Natural hazards: cyclonic storms can occur from November to January

Geography - note: consists of 332 islands, approximately 110 of which are inhabited, and more than 500 islets

PEOPLE AND SOCIETY

Population: 943,737 (2022 est.)
country comparison to the world: 163

Nationality: *noun:* Fijian(s)
adjective: Fijian

Ethnic groups: iTaukei 56.8% (predominantly Melanesian with a Polynesian admixture), Indo-Fijian 37.5%, Rotuman 1.2%, other 4.5% (European, part European, other Pacific Islanders, Chinese) (2007 est.)
note: a 2010 law replaces 'Fijian' with 'iTaukei' when referring to the original and native settlers of Fiji

Languages: English (official), iTaukei (official), Fiji Hindi (official)

Religions: Protestant 45% (Methodist 34.6%, Assembly of God 5.7%, Seventh Day Adventist 3.9%, and Anglican 0.8%), Hindu 27.9%, other Christian 10.4%, Roman Catholic 9.1%, Muslim 6.3%, Sikh 0.3%, other 0.3%, none 0.8% (2007 est.)

Age structure: *0-14 years:* 26.86% (male 128,499/female 122,873)
15-24 years: 15.51% (male 73,993/female 71,139)
25-54 years: 41.05% (male 196,932/female 187,270)
55-64 years: 9.25% (male 43,813/female 42,763)
65 years and over: 7.34% (male 31,556/female 37,136) (2020 est.)

Dependency ratios: *total dependency ratio:* 53.4
youth dependency ratio: 44.5
elderly dependency ratio: 8.9
potential support ratio: 11.2 (2020 est.)

Median age: *total:* 29.9 years
male: 29.7 years
female: 30.1 years (2020 est.)
country comparison to the world: 125

Population growth rate: 0.44% (2022 est.)
country comparison to the world: 159

Birth rate: 16.56 births/1,000 population (2022 est.)
country comparison to the world: 96

Death rate: 6.37 deaths/1,000 population (2022 est.)
country comparison to the world: 141

Net migration rate: -5.84 migrant(s)/1,000 population (2022 est.)
country comparison to the world: 208

Population distribution: approximately 70% of the population lives on the island of Viti Levu; roughly half of the population lives in urban areas

Urbanization: *urban population:* 58.2% of total population (2022)
rate of urbanization: 1.37% annual rate of change (2020-25 est.)

Major urban areas - population: 178,000 SUVA (capital) (2018)

Sex ratio: *at birth:* 1.05 male(s)/female
0-14 years: 1.04 male(s)/female
15-24 years: 1.04 male(s)/female
25-54 years: 1.06 male(s)/female
55-64 years: 1.02 male(s)/female
65 years and over: 0.6 male(s)/female
total population: 1.03 male(s)/female (2022 est.)

Maternal mortality ratio: 34 deaths/100,000 live births (2017 est.)
country comparison to the world: 107

Infant mortality rate: *total:* 10.06 deaths/1,000 live births
male: 11.59 deaths/1,000 live births
female: 8.45 deaths/1,000 live births (2022 est.)
country comparison to the world: 138

Life expectancy at birth: *total population:* 74.27 years
male: 71.6 years
female: 77.07 years (2022 est.)
country comparison to the world: 140

Total fertility rate: 2.26 children born/woman (2022 est.)
country comparison to the world: 80

Contraceptive prevalence rate: 35.5% (2021)

Drinking water source: *improved: urban:* 98.2% of population
rural: 89.1% of population
total: 94.3% of population
unimproved: urban: 1.8% of population
rural: 10.9% of population
total: 5.7% of population (2020 est.)

Current health expenditure: 3.8% of GDP (2019)

Physicians density: 0.86 physicians/1,000 population (2015)

Hospital bed density: 2 beds/1,000 population (2016)

Sanitation facility access: *improved: urban:* 100% of population
rural: 100% of population
total: 100% of population

HIV/AIDS - adult prevalence rate: 0.2% (2020 est.)
country comparison to the world: 97

Major infectious diseases: *degree of risk:* high (2020)
food or waterborne diseases: bacterial diarrhea
vectorborne diseases: malaria

Obesity - adult prevalence rate: 30.2% (2016)
country comparison to the world: 24

Alcohol consumption per capita: *total:* 2.71 liters of pure alcohol (2019 est.)
beer: 1.64 liters of pure alcohol (2019 est.)
wine: 0.29 liters of pure alcohol (2019 est.)
spirits: 0.79 liters of pure alcohol (2019 est.)
other alcohols: 0 liters of pure alcohol (2019 est.)
country comparison to the world: 120

Tobacco use: *total:* 23.1% (2020 est.)
male: 35.6% (2020 est.)
female: 10.5% (2020 est.)
country comparison to the world: 64

Education expenditures: 5.1% of GDP (2019 est.)
country comparison to the world: 59

Literacy: *total population:* 99.1%
male: 99.1%
female: 99.1% (2018)

Unemployment, youth ages 15-24: *total:* 15.4%
male: 11.9%
female: 22.4% (2016 est.)

ENVIRONMENT

Environment - current issues: the widespread practice of waste incineration is a major contributor to air pollution in the country, as are vehicle emissions in urban areas; deforestation and soil erosion are significant problems; a contributory factor to erosion is clearing of land by bush burning, a widespread practice that threatens biodiversity

Environment - international agreements: *party to:* Biodiversity, Climate Change, Climate Change-Kyoto Protocol, Climate Change-Paris Agreement, Comprehensive Nuclear Test Ban, Desertification, Endangered Species, Law of the Sea, Marine Life Conservation, Nuclear Test Ban, Ozone Layer Protection, Ship Pollution, Tropical Timber 2006, Wetlands
signed, but not ratified: none of the selected agreements

Air pollutants: *particulate matter emissions:* 10.19 micrograms per cubic meter (2016 est.)
carbon dioxide emissions: 2.05 megatons (2016 est.)
methane emissions: 0.95 megatons (2020 est.)

Climate: tropical marine; only slight seasonal temperature variation

Land use: *agricultural land:* 23.3% (2018 est.)
arable land: 9% (2018 est.)
permanent crops: 4.7% (2018 est.)
permanent pasture: 9.6% (2018 est.)
forest: 55.7% (2018 est.)
other: 21% (2018 est.)

Urbanization: *urban population:* 58.2% of total population (2022)
rate of urbanization: 1.37% annual rate of change (2020-25 est.)

Revenue from forest resources: *forest revenues:* 0.59% of GDP (2018 est.)
country comparison to the world: 63

Revenue from coal: *coal revenues:* 0% of GDP (2018 est.)
country comparison to the world: 97

Waste and recycling: *municipal solid waste generated annually:* 189,390 tons (2011 est.)
municipal solid waste recycled annually: 10,322 tons (2013 est.)
percent of municipal solid waste recycled: 5.5% (2013 est.)

Total water withdrawal: *municipal:* 25.3 million cubic meters (2017 est.)
industrial: 9.6 million cubic meters (2017 est.)
agricultural: 50 million cubic meters (2017 est.)

Total renewable water resources: 28.55 billion cubic meters (2017 est.)

GOVERNMENT

Country name: *conventional long form:* Republic of Fiji
conventional short form: Fiji
local long form: Republic of Fiji (English)/ Matanitu ko Viti (Fijian)
local short form: Fiji (English)/ Viti (Fijian)
etymology: the Fijians called their home Viti, but the neighboring Tongans called it Fisi, and in the Anglicized spelling of the Tongan pronunciation - promulgated by explorer Captain James COOK - the designation became Fiji

Government type: parliamentary republic

Capital: *name:* Suva (on Viti Levu)
geographic coordinates: 18 08 S, 178 25 E
time difference: UTC+12 (17 hours ahead of Washington, DC, during Standard Time)

etymology: the name means "little hill" in the native Fijian (iTaukei) language and refers to a mound where a temple once stood

Administrative divisions: 14 provinces and 1 dependency*; Ba, Bua, Cakaudrove, Kadavu, Lau, Lomaiviti, Macuata, Nadroga and Navosa, Naitasiri, Namosi, Ra, Rewa, Rotuma*, Serua, Tailevu

Independence: 10 October 1970 (from the UK)

National holiday: Fiji (Independence) Day, 10 October (1970)

Constitution: *history:* several previous; latest signed into law 6 September 2013
amendments: proposed as a bill by Parliament and supported by at least three quarters of its members, followed by referral to the president and then to the Electoral Commission, which conducts a referendum; passage requires approval by at least three-quarters of registered voters and assent by the president

Legal system: common law system based on the English model

International law organization participation: has not submitted an ICJ jurisdiction declaration; accepts ICCt jurisdiction

Citizenship: *citizenship by birth:* no
citizenship by descent only: at least one parent must be a citizen of Fiji
dual citizenship recognized: yes
residency requirement for naturalization: at least 5 years residency out of the 10 years preceding application

Suffrage: 18 years of age; universal

Executive branch: *chief of state:* President Ratu Wiliame KATONIVERE (since 12 November 2021)
head of government: Prime Minister Voreqe "Frank" BAINIMARAMA (since 22 September 2014)
cabinet: Cabinet appointed by the prime minister from among members of Parliament and is responsible to Parliament
elections/appointments: president elected by Parliament for a 3-year term (eligible for a second term); election last held on 22 October 2021 (next to be held in 2024); prime minister endorsed by the president
election results: Ratu Wiliame KATONIVERE elected president with 28 votes against 23 votes for Teimumu KEPA

Legislative branch: *description:* unicameral Parliament (51 seats; members directly elected in a nationwide, multi-seat constituency by open-list proportional representation vote to serve 4-year terms)
elections: last held on 14 November 2018 (next to be held in 2022)
election results: percent of vote by party - FijiFirst 50%, SODELPA 39.6%, NFP 7.4%; seats by party - FijiFirst 27, SODELPA 21, NFP 3; composition - men 41, women 10, percent of women 19.6%

Judicial branch: *highest court(s):* Supreme Court (consists of the chief justice, all justices of the Court of Appeal, and judges appointed specifically as Supreme Court judges); Court of Appeal (consists of the court president, all puisne judges of the High Court, and judges specifically appointed to the Court of Appeal); High Court (chaired by the chief justice and includes a minimum of 10 puisne judges; High Court organized into civil, criminal, family, employment, and tax divisions)
judge selection and term of office: chief justice appointed by the president of Fiji on the advice of the prime minister following consultation with the parliamentary leader of the opposition; judges of the Supreme Court, the president of the Court of Appeal, the justices of the Court of Appeal, and puisne judges of the High Court appointed by the president of Fiji upon the nomination of the Judicial Service Commission after consulting with the cabinet minister and the committee of the House of Representatives responsible for the administration of justice; the chief justice, Supreme Court judges and justices of Appeal generally required to retire at age 70, but this requirement may be waived for one or more sessions of the court; puisne judges appointed for not less than 4 years nor more than 7 years, with mandatory retirement at age 65
subordinate courts: Magistrates' Court (organized into civil, criminal, juvenile, and small claims divisions)

Political parties and leaders: FijiFirst [Veroqe "Frank" BAINIMARAMA]
Fiji Labor Party or FLP [Mahendra CHAUDHRY]
Freedom Alliance [Jagath KARUNARATNE] (formerly Fiji United Freedom Party or FUFP)
National Federation Party or NFP [Biman PRASAD] (primarily Indian)
Peoples Democratic Party or PDP [Lynda TABUYA]
Social Democratic Liberal Party or SODELPA [Viliame Rogoibulu GAVOKA]
Unity Fiji [Savenaca NARUBE]

International organization participation: ACP, ADB, AOSIS, C, CP, FAO, G-77, IAEA, IBRD, ICAO, ICCt, ICRM, IDA, IFAD, IFC, IFRCS, IHO, ILO, IMF, IMO, Interpol, IOC, IOM, ISO, ITSO, ITU, ITUC (NGOs), MIGA, OPCW, PCA, PIF, Sparteca (suspended), SPC, UN, UNCTAD, UNDOF, UNESCO, UNIDO, UNISFA, UNMISS, UNWTO, UPU, WCO, WFTU (NGOs), WHO, WIPO, WMO, WTO

Diplomatic representation in the US: *chief of mission:* Ambassador (vacant); Charge d'Affaires Akuila VUIRA
chancery: 1707 L Street NW, Suite 200, Washington, DC 20036
telephone: [1] (202) 466-8320
FAX: [1] (202) 466-8325
email address and website:
info@FijiEmbassyDC.com
https://www.fijiembassydc.com/

Diplomatic representation from the US: *chief of mission:* Ambassador (vacant); Charge d'Affaires Tony GREUBEL (since 20 January 2021); note - also accredited to Kiribati, Nauru, Tonga, and Tuvalu
embassy: 158 Princes Road, Tamavua, Suva
mailing address: 4290 Suva Place, Washington DC 20521-4290
telephone: [679] 331-4466
FAX: [679] 330-2267
email address and website:
SuvaACS@state.gov
https://fj.usembassy.gov/

Flag description: light blue with the flag of the UK in the upper hoist-side quadrant and the Fijian shield centered on the outer half of the flag; the blue symbolizes the Pacific Ocean and the Union Jack reflects the links with Great Britain; the shield - taken from Fiji's coat of arms - depicts a yellow lion, holding a coconut pod between its paws, above a white field quartered by the cross of Saint George; the four quarters depict stalks of sugarcane, a palm tree, a banana bunch, and a white dove of peace

National symbol(s): Fijian canoe; national color: light blue

National anthem: *name:* "God Bless Fiji"
lyrics/music: Michael Francis Alexander PRESCOTT/C. Austin MILES (adapted by Michael Francis Alexander PRESCOTT)
note: adopted 1970; known in Fijian as "Meda Dau Doka" (Let Us Show Pride); adapted from the hymn, "Dwelling in Beulah Land," the anthem's English lyrics are generally sung, although they differ in meaning from the official Fijian lyrics

National heritage: *total World Heritage Sites:* 1 (cultural)
selected World Heritage Site locales: Levuka Historical Port Town

ECONOMY

Economic overview: Fiji, endowed with forest, mineral, and fish resources, is one of the most developed and connected of the Pacific island economies. Earnings from the tourism industry, with an estimated 842,884 tourists visiting in 2017, and remittances from Fijian's working abroad are the country's largest foreign exchange earners.

Bottled water exports to the US is Fiji's largest domestic export. Fiji's sugar sector remains a significant industry and a major export, but crops and one of the sugar mills suffered damage during Cyclone Winston in 2016. Fiji's trade imbalance continues to widen with increased imports and sluggish performance of domestic exports.

The return to parliamentary democracy and successful elections in September 2014 improved investor confidence, but increasing bureaucratic regulation, new taxes, and lack of consultation with relevant stakeholders brought four consecutive years of decline for Fiji on the World Bank Ease of Doing Business index. Private sector investment in 2017 approached 20% of GDP, compared to 13% in 2013.

Real GDP (purchasing power parity): $9.86 billion (2020 est.)
$12.18 billion (2019 est.)
$12.23 billion (2018 est.)
note: data are in 2017 dollars
country comparison to the world: 161

Real GDP growth rate: 3% (2017 est.)
0.7% (2016 est.)
3.8% (2015 est.)
country comparison to the world: 98

Real GDP per capita: $11,000 (2020 est.)
$13,700 (2019 est.)
$13,800 (2018 est.)
note: data are in 2017 dollars
country comparison to the world: 135

GDP (official exchange rate): $4.891 billion (2017 est.)

Inflation rate (consumer prices): 3.4% (2017 est.)
3.9% (2016 est.)
country comparison to the world: 151

Credit ratings:

Moody's rating: Ba3 (2017)

Standard & Poors rating: BB- (2019)
note: The year refers to the year in which the current credit rating was first obtained.

GDP - composition, by sector of origin: *agriculture:* 13.5% (2017 est.)
industry: 17.4% (2017 est.)

services: 69.1% (2017 est.)

GDP - composition, by end use: *household consumption:* 81.3% (2017 est.)
government consumption: 24.4% (2017 est.)
investment in fixed capital: 16.9% (2017 est.)
investment in inventories: 0% (2017 est.)
exports of goods and services: 29% (2017 est.)
imports of goods and services: -51.6% (2017 est.)

Agricultural products: sugar cane, cassava, taro, poultry, vegetables, coconuts, eggs, milk, ginger, sweet potatoes

Industries: tourism, sugar processing, clothing, copra, gold, silver, lumber

Industrial production growth rate: 2.8% (2017 est.)
country comparison to the world: 108

Labor force: 353,100 (2017 est.)
country comparison to the world: 161

Labor force - by occupation: *agriculture:* 44.2%
industry: 14.3%
services: 41.6% (2011)

Unemployment rate: 4.5% (2017 est.)
5.5% (2016 est.)
country comparison to the world: 67

Unemployment, youth ages 15-24: *total:* 15.4%
male: 11.9%
female: 22.4% (2016 est.)
country comparison to the world: 104

Population below poverty line: 29.9% (2019 est.)

Gini Index coefficient - distribution of family income: 36.7 (2013 est.)
country comparison to the world: 87

Household income or consumption by percentage share: *lowest 10%:* 2.6%
highest 10%: 34.9% (2009 est.)

Budget: *revenues:* 1.454 billion (2017 est.)
expenditures: 1.648 billion (2017 est.)

Budget surplus (+) or deficit (-): -4% (of GDP) (2017 est.)
country comparison to the world: 157

Public debt: 48.9% of GDP (2017 est.)
47.5% of GDP (2016 est.)
country comparison to the world: 106

Taxes and other revenues: 29.7% (of GDP) (2017 est.)
country comparison to the world: 80

Fiscal year: calendar year

Current account balance: -$277 million (2017 est.)
-$131 million (2016 est.)
country comparison to the world: 104

Exports: $1.23 billion (2020 est.) note: data are in current year dollars
$2.64 billion (2019 est.) note: data are in current year dollars
$2.67 billion (2018 est.) note: data are in current year dollars
country comparison to the world: 170

Exports - partners: United States 29%, Australia 14%, New Zealand 7%, Japan 6%, Tonga 6% (2019)

Exports - commodities: water, refined petroleum, fish, raw sugar, gold (2019)

Imports: $1.97 billion (2020 est.) note: data are in current year dollars
$3.21 billion (2019 est.) note: data are in current year dollars
$3.1 billion (2018 est.) note: data are in current year dollars
country comparison to the world: 174

Imports - partners: Singapore 18%, Australia 13%, China 13.8%, New Zealand 11%, France 11%, South Korea 8% (2017)

Imports - commodities: refined petroleum, aircraft, cars, wheat, broadcasting equipment (2019)

Reserves of foreign exchange and gold: $1.116 billion (31 December 2017 est.)
$908.6 million (31 December 2016 est.)
country comparison to the world: 130

Debt - external: $1.022 billion (31 December 2017 est.)
$696.4 million (31 December 2016 est.)
country comparison to the world: 165

Exchange rates: Fijian dollars (FJD) per US dollar -
2.05955 (2020 est.)
2.17345 (2019 est.)
2.1104 (2018 est.)
2.0976 (2014 est.)
1.8874 (2013 est.)

ENERGY

Electricity access: *electrification - total population:* 99.6% (2018)
electrification - urban areas: 100% (2018)
electrification - rural areas: 99.2% (2018)

Electricity: *installed generating capacity:* 393,000 kW (2020 est.)
consumption: 1,022,955,000 kWh (2019 est.)
exports: 0 kWh (2020 est.)
imports: 0 kWh (2020 est.)
transmission/distribution losses: 90 million kWh (2019 est.)

Electricity generation sources: *fossil fuels:* 41.9% of total installed capacity (2020 est.)
solar: 1.6% of total installed capacity (2020 est.)
wind: 0.3% of total installed capacity (2020 est.)
hydroelectricity: 50.2% of total installed capacity (2020 est.)
biomass and waste: 6% of total installed capacity (2020 est.)

Petroleum: *total petroleum production:* 0 bbl/day (2021 est.)
refined petroleum consumption: 11,500 bbl/day (2019 est.)

Refined petroleum products - imports: 17,460 bbl/day (2015 est.)
country comparison to the world: 131

Carbon dioxide emissions: 1.691 million metric tonnes of CO2 (2019 est.)
from petroleum and other liquids: 1.691 million metric tonnes of CO2 (2019 est.)
country comparison to the world: 164

Energy consumption per capita: 32.901 million Btu/person (2019 est.)
country comparison to the world: 118

COMMUNICATIONS

Telephones - fixed lines: *total subscriptions:* 48,510 (2020 est.)
subscriptions per 100 inhabitants: 5 (2020 est.)
country comparison to the world: 157

Telephones - mobile cellular: *total subscriptions:* 991,500 (2020 est.)
subscriptions per 100 inhabitants: 111 (2020 est.)
country comparison to the world: 162

Telecommunication systems: *general assessment:* Fiji is the leading market to watch in terms of both LTE and 5G development in the region; the market boasts relatively sophisticated, advanced digital infrastructure, with telcos' heavy investment resulting in the country having the highest mobile and internet subscriptions in the Pacific Islands region; LTE, LTE-A, and fiber technologies have received the most investment by the Fijian mobile operators, LTE now accounts for the largest share of connections in the mobile segment; concentrating on the more highly populated areas, the operators are preparing for the next growth area of high-speed data; they also have 5G in mind, and are preparing their networks to be 5G-ready, anticipating an easier migration to the technology based on the relatively high LTE subscription rate; Fiji presents a challenging geographic environment for infrastructure development due to its population being spread across more than 100 islands; the majority of Fijians live on the two main islands of Viti Levu and Vanua Levu; in July 2018, the two islands were linked by the Savusavu submarine cable system, which provides a more secure link in times of emergency weather events such as the regular tropical cyclones that often cause massive destruction to the area, including destroying essential infrastructure such as electricity and telecommunications equipment; notably, the December 2021 eruption of the Hunga Tonga–Hunga Ha'apai submarine volcano in Tonga damaged the Tonga Cable which connects Fiji, and Tonga blocking the latter off from internet services; cable theft and damage of critical communications infrastructure has also become a concern in Fiji, prompting authorities to establish a joint task force to tackle the issue (2022)
domestic: fixed-line nearly 5 per 100 persons and mobile-cellular teledensity roughly 111 per 100 persons (2020)
international: country code - 679; landing points for the ICN1, SCCN, Southern Cross NEXT, Tonga Cable and Tui- Samoa submarine cable links to US, NZ, Australia and Pacific islands of Fiji, Vanuatu, Kiribati, Samoa, Tokelau, Tonga, Fallis & Futuna, and American Samoa; satellite earth stations - 2 Inmarsat (Pacific Ocean) (2019)

Broadcast media: Fiji TV, a publicly traded company, operates a free-to-air channel; Digicel Fiji operates the Sky Fiji and Sky Pacific multi-channel pay-TV services; state-owned commercial company, Fiji Broadcasting Corporation, Ltd, operates 6 radio stations - 2 public broadcasters and 4 commercial broadcasters with multiple repeaters; 5 radio stations with repeaters operated by Communications Fiji, Ltd; transmissions of multiple international broadcasters are available

Internet country code: .fj

Internet users: *total:* 444,978 (2019 est.)
percent of population: 50% (2019 est.)
country comparison to the world: 161

Broadband - fixed subscriptions: *total:* 23,062 (2020 est.)
subscriptions per 100 inhabitants: 3 (2020 est.)
country comparison to the world: 162

TRANSPORTATION

National air transport system: *number of registered air carriers:* 2 (2020)
inventory of registered aircraft operated by air carriers: 16

annual passenger traffic on registered air carriers: 1,670,216 (2018)
annual freight traffic on registered air carriers: 106.83 million (2018) mt-km

Civil aircraft registration country code prefix: DQ

Airports: *total:* 28 (2021)
country comparison to the world: 120

Airports - with paved runways: *total:* 4
over 3,047 m: 1
1,524 to 2,437 m: 1
914 to 1,523 m: 2 (2021)

Airports - with unpaved runways: *total:* 24
914 to 1,523 m: 5
under 914 m: 19 (2021)

Railways: *total:* 597 km (2008)
narrow gauge: 597 km (2008) 0.600-m gauge
note: belongs to the government-owned Fiji Sugar Corporation; used to haul sugarcane during the harvest season, which runs from May to December
country comparison to the world: 109

Roadways: *total:* 3,440 km (2011)
paved: 1,686 km (2011)
unpaved: 1,754 km (2011)
country comparison to the world: 159

Waterways: 203 km (2012) (122 km are navigable by motorized craft and 200-metric-ton barges)
country comparison to the world: 107

Merchant marine: *total:* 73
by type: general cargo 20, oil tanker 4, other 49 (2021)
country comparison to the world: 100

Ports and terminals: *major seaport(s):* Lautoka, Levuka, Suva

MILITARY AND SECURITY

Military and security forces: Republic of Fiji Military Force (RFMF): Land Force Command, Maritime Command; Fiji Police Force (2022)
note: the RFMF is subordinate to the president as the commander-in-chief, while the Fiji Police Force reports to the the Ministry of Defense, National Security, and Policing

Military expenditures: 1.5% of GDP (2021 est.)
1.4% of GDP (2020 est.)
1.6% of GDP (2019 est.) (approximately $160 million)
1.6% of GDP (2018 est.) (approximately $160 million)
1.5% of GDP (2017 est.) (approximately $150 million)
country comparison to the world: 89

Military and security service personnel strengths: approximately 4,000 active personnel (2022)

Military equipment inventories and acquisitions: the RFMF is lightly armed and equipped; Australia has provided patrol boats and a few armored personnel carriers; it also provides logistical support for RFMF regional or UN operations; in recent years, China has provided construction equipment and military vehicles (2021)

Military service age and obligation: 18-25 years of age for voluntary military service; mandatory retirement at age 55 (2022)

Military deployments: 170 Egypt (MFO); 165 Iraq (UNAMI); 150 Golan Heights (UNDOF) (2022)

Military - note: the RFMF was established in 1920; it has a history of intervening in the country's politics since the late 1980s, including coups in 1987 and 2006, and a mutiny in 2000

the RFMF also has a long tradition of participating in UN peacekeeping operations; since its first deployment of troops to South Lebanon in 1978 under the United Nations Interim Force in Lebanon (UNIFIL), it has deployed troops on nearly 20 additional UN missions

Fiji has a "shiprider" agreement with the US, which allows local maritime law enforcement officers to embark on US Coast Guard (USCG) and US Navy (USN) vessels, including to board and search vessels suspected of violating laws or regulations within Fiji's designated exclusive economic zone (EEZ) or on the high seas; "shiprider" agreements also enable USCG personnel and USN vessels with embarked USCG law enforcement personnel to work with host nations to protect critical regional resources

(2022)

TRANSNATIONAL ISSUES

Disputes - international: *Fiji-Tonga:* Fiji does not recognize Tonga's 1972 claim to the Minerva Reefs and their surrounding waters; the Minerva Reefs' 200-mile exclusive economic zone includes valuable fishing grounds

FINLAND

INTRODUCTION

Background: Finland was a province and then a grand duchy under Sweden from the 12th to the 19th centuries, and an autonomous grand duchy of Russia after 1809. It gained complete independence in 1917. During World War II, Finland successfully defended its independence through cooperation with Germany and resisted subsequent invasions by the Soviet Union - albeit with some loss of territory. In the subsequent half century, Finland transformed from a farm/forest economy to a diversified modern industrial economy; per capita income is among the highest in Western Europe. A member of the EU since 1995, Finland was the only Nordic state to join the euro single currency at its initiation in January 1999. In the 21st century, the key features of Finland's modern welfare state are high quality education, promotion of equality, and a national social welfare system - currently challenged by an aging population and the fluctuations of an export-driven economy.

GEOGRAPHY

Location: Northern Europe, bordering the Baltic Sea, Gulf of Bothnia, and Gulf of Finland, between Sweden and Russia

Geographic coordinates: 64 00 N, 26 00 E

Map references: Europe

Area: *total:* 338,145 sq km
land: 303,815 sq km
water: 34,330 sq km
country comparison to the world: 66

Area - comparative: slightly more than two times the size of Georgia; slightly smaller than Montana

Land boundaries: *total:* 2,563 km
border countries (3): Norway 709 km; Sweden 545 km; Russia 1,309 km

Coastline: 1,250 km

Maritime claims: *territorial sea:* 12 nm (in the Gulf of Finland - 3 nm)
contiguous zone: 24 nm
continental shelf: 200 m depth or to the depth of exploitation
exclusive fishing zone: 12 nm; extends to continental shelf boundary with Sweden, Estonia, and Russia

Climate: cold temperate; potentially subarctic but comparatively mild because of moderating influence of the North Atlantic Current, Baltic Sea, and more than 60,000 lakes

Terrain: mostly low, flat to rolling plains interspersed with lakes and low hills

Elevation: *highest point:* Halti (alternatively Haltia, Haltitunturi, Haltiatunturi) 1,328 m
lowest point: Baltic Sea 0 m
mean elevation: 164 m

Natural resources: timber, iron ore, copper, lead, zinc, chromite, nickel, gold, silver, limestone

Land use: *agricultural land:* 7.5% (2018 est.)
arable land: 7.4% (2018 est.)
permanent crops: 0% (2018 est.)
permanent pasture: 0.1% (2018 est.)
forest: 72.9% (2018 est.)
other: 19.6% (2018 est.)

Irrigated land: 690 sq km (2012)

Major lakes (area sq km): *fresh water lake(s):* Saimaa - 1,760 sq km; Paijanne - 1,090 sq km; Inarijarvi - 1,000 sq km; Oulujarvi - 900 sq km; Pielinen - 850 sq km

Population distribution: the vast majority of people are found in the south; the northern interior areas remain sparsely poplulated

Natural hazards: severe winters in the north

Geography - note: long boundary with Russia; Helsinki is northernmost national capital on European continent; population concentrated on small southwestern coastal plain

PEOPLE AND SOCIETY

Population: 5,601,547 (2022 est.)
country comparison to the world: 116

Nationality: *noun:* Finn(s)
adjective: Finnish

Ethnic groups: Finnish, Swedish, Russian, Estonian, Romani, Sami
note: 91.5% of the population has a Finnish background

Languages: Finnish (official) 86.5%, Swedish (official) 5.2%, Russian 1.6%, other 6.7% (2021 est.)
major-language sample(s):
World Factbook, korvaamaton perustietolähde. (Finnish)

Religions: Lutheran 66.6%, Greek Orthodox 1.1%, other 1.7%, none 30.6% (2021 est.)

Age structure: *0-14 years:* 16.41% (male 467,220/female 447,005)
15-24 years: 10.95% (male 312,179/female 297,717)
25-54 years: 37.37% (male 1,064,326/female 1,017,545)
55-64 years: 13.02% (male 357,687/female 367,610)
65 years and over: 22.26% (male 543,331/female 697,045) (2020 est.)

Dependency ratios: *total dependency ratio:* 62.4
youth dependency ratio: 25.8
elderly dependency ratio: 36.6
potential support ratio: 2.7 (2020 est.)

Median age: *total:* 42.8 years
male: 41.3 years
female: 44.4 years (2020 est.)
country comparison to the world: 31

Population growth rate: 0.24% (2022 est.)
country comparison to the world: 174

Birth rate: 10.42 births/1,000 population (2022 est.)
country comparison to the world: 182

Death rate: 10.35 deaths/1,000 population (2022 est.)
country comparison to the world: 29

Net migration rate: 2.35 migrant(s)/1,000 population (2022 est.)
country comparison to the world: 46

Population distribution: the vast majority of people are found in the south; the northern interior areas remain sparsely poplulated

Urbanization: *urban population:* 85.7% of total population (2022)
rate of urbanization: 0.42% annual rate of change (2020-25 est.)

Major urban areas - population: 1.328 million HELSINKI (capital) (2022)

Sex ratio: *at birth:* 1.05 male(s)/female
0-14 years: 1.05 male(s)/female
15-24 years: 1.05 male(s)/female
25-54 years: 1.05 male(s)/female
55-64 years: 0.97 male(s)/female
65 years and over: 0.63 male(s)/female
total population: 0.97 male(s)/female (2022 est.)

Mother's mean age at first birth: 29.5 years (2020 est.)

Maternal mortality ratio: 3 deaths/100,000 live births (2017 est.)
country comparison to the world: 177

Infant mortality rate: *total:* 2.13 deaths/1,000 live births
male: 2.31 deaths/1,000 live births
female: 1.94 deaths/1,000 live births (2022 est.)
country comparison to the world: 222

Life expectancy at birth: *total population:* 81.76 years
male: 78.86 years
female: 84.79 years (2022 est.)
country comparison to the world: 34

Total fertility rate: 1.74 children born/woman (2022 est.)
country comparison to the world: 158

Contraceptive prevalence rate: 85.5% (2015)
note: percent of women aged 18-49

Drinking water source: *improved: urban:* 100% of population
rural: 100% of population
total: 100% of population

Current health expenditure: 9.2% of GDP (2019)

Physicians density: 4.64 physicians/1,000 population (2018)

Hospital bed density: 3.6 beds/1,000 population (2018)

Sanitation facility access: *improved: urban:* 100% of population
rural: 100% of population
total: 100% of population

HIV/AIDS - adult prevalence rate: 0.1% (2018 est.)
country comparison to the world: 123

Obesity - adult prevalence rate: 22.2% (2016)
country comparison to the world: 80

Alcohol consumption per capita: *total:* 8.23 liters of pure alcohol (2019 est.)
beer: 3.76 liters of pure alcohol (2019 est.)
wine: 1.59 liters of pure alcohol (2019 est.)
spirits: 1.96 liters of pure alcohol (2019 est.)
other alcohols: 0.91 liters of pure alcohol (2019 est.)
country comparison to the world: 40

Tobacco use: *total:* 21.6% (2020 est.)
male: 26.9% (2020 est.)
female: 16.3% (2020 est.)
country comparison to the world: 75

Child marriage: *women married by age 18:* 0% (2017 est.)

Education expenditures: 6.3% of GDP (2018 est.)
country comparison to the world: 27

School life expectancy (primary to tertiary education): *total:* 19 years
male: 18 years
female: 20 years (2019)

Unemployment, youth ages 15-24: *total:* 21.4%
male: 23.2%
female: 19.4% (2020 est.)

ENVIRONMENT

Environment - current issues: limited air pollution in urban centers; some water pollution from industrial wastes, agricultural chemicals; habitat loss threatens wildlife populations

Environment - international agreements: *party to:* Air Pollution, Air Pollution-Heavy Metals, Air Pollution-Multi-effect Protocol, Air Pollution-Nitrogen Oxides, Air Pollution-Persistent Organic Pollutants, Air Pollution-Sulphur 85, Air Pollution-Sulphur 94, Air Pollution-Volatile Organic Compounds, Antarctic-Environmental Protection, Antarctic-Marine Living Resources, Antarctic Treaty, Biodiversity, Climate Change, Climate Change-Kyoto Protocol, Climate Change-Paris Agreement, Comprehensive Nuclear Test Ban, Desertification, Endangered Species, Environmental Modification, Hazardous Wastes, Law of the Sea, Marine Dumping-London Convention, Marine Dumping-London Protocol, Marine Life Conservation, Nuclear Test Ban, Ozone Layer Protection, Ship Pollution, Tropical Timber 2006, Wetlands, Whaling
signed, but not ratified: none of the selected agreements

Air pollutants: *particulate matter emissions:* 5.88 micrograms per cubic meter (2016 est.)
carbon dioxide emissions: 45.87 megatons (2016 est.)
methane emissions: 4.46 megatons (2020 est.)

Climate: cold temperate; potentially subarctic but comparatively mild because of moderating influence of the North Atlantic Current, Baltic Sea, and more than 60,000 lakes

Land use: *agricultural land:* 7.5% (2018 est.)
arable land: 7.4% (2018 est.)
permanent crops: 0% (2018 est.)
permanent pasture: 0.1% (2018 est.)
forest: 72.9% (2018 est.)
other: 19.6% (2018 est.)

Urbanization: *urban population:* 85.7% of total population (2022)
rate of urbanization: 0.42% annual rate of change (2020-25 est.)

Revenue from forest resources: *forest revenues:* 0.36% of GDP (2018 est.)
country comparison to the world: 75

Revenue from coal: *coal revenues:* 0% of GDP (2018 est.)
country comparison to the world: 98

Waste and recycling: *municipal solid waste generated annually:* 2.738 million tons (2015 est.)
municipal solid waste recycled annually: 769,926 tons (2015 est.)
percent of municipal solid waste recycled: 28.1% (2015 est.)

Major lakes (area sq km): *fresh water lake(s):* Saimaa - 1,760 sq km; Paijanne - 1,090 sq km;

Inarijarvi - 1,000 sq km; Oulujarvi - 900 sq km; Pielinen - 850 sq km

Total water withdrawal: *municipal:* 400 million cubic meters (2017 est.)
industrial: 1.417 billion cubic meters (2017 est.)
agricultural: 50 million cubic meters (2017 est.)

Total renewable water resources: 110 billion cubic meters (2017 est.)

GOVERNMENT

Country name: *conventional long form:* Republic of Finland
conventional short form: Finland
local long form: Suomen tasavalta (Finnish)/ Republiken Finland (Swedish)
local short form: Suomi (Finnish)/ Finland (Swedish)
etymology: name may derive from the ancient Fenni peoples who are first described as living in northeastern Europe in the first centuries A.D.

Government type: parliamentary republic

Capital: *name:* Helsinki
geographic coordinates: 60 10 N, 24 56 E
time difference: UTC+2 (7 hours ahead of Washington, DC, during Standard Time)
daylight saving time: +1hr, begins last Sunday in March; ends last Sunday in October
etymology: the name may derive from the Swedish *helsing*, an archaic name for "neck" (*hals*), and which may refer to a narrowing of the Vantaa River that flows into the Gulf of Finland at Helsinki; *fors* refers to "rapids," so *helsing fors* meaning becomes "the narrows' rapids"

Administrative divisions: 19 regions (maakunnat, singular - maakunta (Finnish); landskapen, singular - landskapet (Swedish)); Aland (Swedish), Ahvenanmaa (Finnish); Etela-Karjala (Finnish), Sodra Karelen (Swedish) [South Karelia]; Etela-Pohjanmaa (Finnish), Sodra Osterbotten (Swedish) [South Ostrobothnia]; Etela-Savo (Finnish), Sodra Savolax (Swedish) [South Savo]; Kanta- Hame (Finnish), Egentliga Tavastland (Swedish); Kainuu (Finnish), Kajanaland (Swedish); Keski-Pohjanmaa (Finnish), Mellersta Osterbotten (Swedish) [Central Ostrobothnia]; Keski-Suomi (Finnish), Mellersta Finland (Swedish) [Central Finland]; Kymenlaakso (Finnish), Kymmenedalen (Swedish); Lappi (Finnish), Lappland (Swedish); Paijat-Hame (Finnish), Paijanne-Tavastland (Swedish); Pirkanmaa (Finnish), Birkaland (Swedish) [Tampere]; Pohjanmaa (Finnish), Osterbotten (Swedish) [Ostrobothnia]; Pohjois-Karjala (Finnish), Norra Karelen (Swedish) [North Karelia]; Pohjois-Pohjanmaa (Finnish), Norra Osterbotten (Swedish) [North Ostrobothnia]; Pohjois-Savo (Finnish), Norra Savolax (Swedish) [North Savo]; Satakunta (Finnish and Swedish); Uusimaa (Finnish), Nyland (Swedish) [Newland]; Varsinais- Suomi (Finnish), Egentliga Finland (Swedish) [Southwest Finland]

Independence: 6 December 1917 (from Russia)

National holiday: Independence Day, 6 December (1917)

Constitution: *history:* previous 1906, 1919; latest drafted 17 June 1997, approved by Parliament 11 June 1999, entered into force 1 March 2000
amendments: proposed by Parliament; passage normally requires simple majority vote in two readings in the first parliamentary session and at least two-thirds majority vote in a single reading by the newly elected Parliament; proposals declared "urgent" by five-sixths of Parliament members can be passed by at least two-thirds majority vote in the first parliamentary session only; amended several times, last in 2018

Legal system: civil law system based on the Swedish model

International law organization participation: accepts compulsory ICJ jurisdiction with reservations; accepts ICCt jurisdiction

Citizenship: *citizenship by birth:* no
citizenship by descent only: at least one parent must be a citizen of Finland
dual citizenship recognized: yes
residency requirement for naturalization: 6 years

Suffrage: 18 years of age; universal

Executive branch: *chief of state:* President Sauli NIINISTO (since 1 March 2012)
head of government: Prime Minister Sanna MARIN (since 10 December 2019)
cabinet: Council of State or Valtioneuvosto appointed by the president, responsible to Parliament
elections/appointments: president directly elected by absolute majority popular vote in 2 rounds if needed for a 6-year term (eligible for a second term); election last held on 28 January 2018 (next to be held in January 2024); prime minister appointed by Parliament
election results: 2018: Sauli NIINISTO reelected president; percent of vote - Sauli NIINISTO (independent) 62.7%, Pekka HAAVISTO (Vihr) 12.4%, Laura HUHTASAARI (PS) 6.9%, Paavo VAYRYNEN (independent) 6.2%, Matti VANHANEN (Kesk) 4.1%, other 7.7%
2012: Sauli NIINISTO elected president; percent of vote - Sauli NIINISTO (National Coalition Party) 62.6%, Pekka HAAVISTO (Vihr) 37.4%

Legislative branch: *description:* unicameral Parliament or Eduskunta (200 seats; 199 members directly elected in single- and multi-seat constituencies by proportional representation vote and 1 member in the province of Aland directly elected by simple majority vote; members serve 4-year terms)
elections: last held on 14 April 2019 (next to be held in April 2023)
election results: percent of vote by party/coalition - SDP 20%, PS 19.5%, Kok 19.0%. Center Party 15.5%, Vihr 10%, Vas 8%, SFP 4.5%, KD 2.5%, Aland .5%; other .5%; seats by party/coalition - SDP 40, PS 39, Kok 38, Centre Party 31, Vihr 20, Vas 16, SFP 9, KD 5; Aland 1; other 1; composition men 109, women 91, percent of women 45.5%

Judicial branch: *highest court(s):* Supreme Court or Korkein Oikeus (consists of the court president and 18 judges); Supreme Administrative Court (consists of 21 judges, including the court president and organized into 3 chambers); note - Finland has a dual judicial system - courts with civil and criminal jurisdiction and administrative courts with jurisdiction for litigation between individuals and administrative organs of the state and communities
judge selection and term of office: Supreme Court and Supreme Administrative Court judges appointed by the president of the republic; judges serve until mandatory retirement at age 68
subordinate courts: 6 Courts of Appeal; 8 regional administrative courts; 27 district courts; special courts for issues relating to markets, labor, insurance, impeachment, land, tenancy, and water rights

Political parties and leaders: Aland Coalition (a coalition of several political parties on the Aland Islands)
Center Party or Kesk [Annika SAARIKKO]
Christian Democrats or KD [Sari ESSAYAH]
Finns Party or PS [Riikka PURRA]
Green League or Vihr [Maria OHISALO]
Left Alliance or Vas [Li ANDERSSON]
National Coalition Party or Kok [Petteri ORPO]
Social Democratic Party or SDP [Sanna MARIN]
Swedish People's Party or RKP or SFP [Anna-Maja HENRIKSSON]

International organization participation: ADB (nonregional member), AfDB (nonregional member), Arctic Council, Australia Group, BIS, CBSS, CD, CE, CERN, EAPC, EBRD, ECB, EIB, EITI (implementing country), EMU, ESA, EU, FAO, FATF, G-9, IADB, IAEA, IBRD, ICAO, ICC (national committees), ICCt, ICRM, IDA, IEA, IFAD, IFC, IFRCS, IHO, ILO, IMF, IMO, IMSO, Interpol, IOC, IOM, IPU, ISO, ITSO, ITU, ITUC (NGOs), MIGA, MINUSMA, NC, NEA, NIB, NSG, OAS (observer), OECD, OPCW, OSCE, Pacific Alliance (observer), Paris Club, PCA, PFP, Schengen Convention, UN, UNCTAD, UNESCO, UNHCR, UNHRC, UNIDO, UNIFIL, UNMIL, UNMOGIP, UNRWA, UNSOM, UNTSO, UPU, Wassenaar Arrangement, WCO, WFTU (NGOs), WHO, WIPO, WMO, WTO, ZC

Diplomatic representation in the US: *chief of mission:* Ambassador Mikko Tapani HAUTALA (since 17 September 2020)
chancery: 3301 Massachusetts Avenue NW, Washington, DC 20008
telephone: [1] (202) 298-5800
FAX: [1] (202) 298-6030
email address and website:
sanomat.was@formin.fi
https://finlandabroad.fi/web/usa/mission
consulate(s) general: Los Angeles, New York

Diplomatic representation from the US: *chief of mission:* Ambassador Douglas HICKEY (since 11 May 2022)
embassy: Itainen Puistotie 14 B, 00140 Helsinki
mailing address: 5310 Helsinki Place, Washington DC 20521-5310
telephone: [358] (9) 616-250
FAX: [358] (9) 174-681
email address and website:
HelsinkiACS@state.gov
https://fi.usembassy.gov/

Flag description: white with a blue cross extending to the edges of the flag; the vertical part of the cross is shifted to the hoist side in the style of the Dannebrog (Danish flag); the blue represents the thousands of lakes scattered across the country, while the white is for the snow that covers the land in winter

National symbol(s): lion; national colors: blue, white

National anthem: *name:* "Maamme" (Our Land)
lyrics/music: Johan Ludvig RUNEBERG/Fredrik PACIUS
note: in use since 1848; although never officially adopted by law, the anthem has been popular since it was first sung by a student group in 1848; Estonia's anthem uses the same melody as that of Finland

National heritage: *total World Heritage Sites:* 7 (6 cultural, 1 natural)
selected World Heritage Site locales: Fortress of Suomenlinna (c); Old Rauma (c); Petäjävesi Old Church (c); Verla Groundwood and Board Mill (c); Bronze Age Burial Site of Sammallahdenmäki

(c); High Coast / Kvarken Archipelago (n); Struve Geodetic Arc (c)

ECONOMY

Economic overview: Finland has a highly industrialized, largely free-market economy with per capita GDP almost as high as that of Austria and the Netherlands and slightly above that of Germany and Belgium. Trade is important, with exports accounting for over one-third of GDP in recent years. The government is open to, and actively takes steps to attract, foreign direct investment.

Finland is historically competitive in manufacturing, particularly in the wood, metals, engineering, telecommunications, and electronics industries. Finland excels in export of technology as well as promotion of startups in the information and communications technology, gaming, cleantech, and biotechnology sectors. Except for timber and several minerals, Finland depends on imports of raw materials, energy, and some components for manufactured goods. Because of the cold climate, agricultural development is limited to maintaining self-sufficiency in basic products. Forestry, an important export industry, provides a secondary occupation for the rural population.

Finland had been one of the best performing economies within the EU before 2009 and its banks and financial markets avoided the worst of global financial crisis. However, the world slowdown hit exports and domestic demand hard in that year, causing Finland's economy to contract from 2012 to 2014. The recession affected general government finances and the debt ratio. The economy returned to growth in 2016, posting a 1.9% GDP increase before growing an estimated 3.3% in 2017, supported by a strong increase in investment, private consumption, and net exports. Finnish economists expect GDP to grow a rate of 2-3% in the next few years.

Finland's main challenges will be reducing high labor costs and boosting demand for its exports. In June 2016, the government enacted a Competitiveness Pact aimed at reducing labor costs, increasing hours worked, and introducing more flexibility into the wage bargaining system. As a result, wage growth was nearly flat in 2017. The Government was also seeking to reform the health care system and social services. In the long term, Finland must address a rapidly aging population and decreasing productivity in traditional industries that threaten competitiveness, fiscal sustainability, and economic growth.

Real GDP (purchasing power parity): $261.39 billion (2020 est.)
$268.84 billion (2019 est.)
$265.46 billion (2018 est.)
note: data are in 2017 dollars
country comparison to the world: 59

Real GDP growth rate: 1.15% (2019 est.)
1.52% (2018 est.)
3.27% (2017 est.)
country comparison to the world: 167

Real GDP per capita: $47,300 (2020 est.)
$48,700 (2019 est.)
$48,100 (2018 est.)
note: data are in 2017 dollars
country comparison to the world: 32

GDP (official exchange rate): $269.259 billion (2019 est.)

Inflation rate (consumer prices): 1% (2019 est.)
1% (2018 est.)
0.7% (2017 est.)
country comparison to the world: 64

Credit ratings:

Fitch rating: AA+ (2016)

Moody's rating: Aa1 (2016)

Standard & Poors rating: AA+ (2014)
note: The year refers to the year in which the current credit rating was first obtained.

GDP - composition, by sector of origin: *agriculture:* 2.7% (2017 est.)
industry: 28.2% (2017 est.)
services: 69.1% (2017 est.)

GDP - composition, by end use: *household consumption:* 54.4% (2017 est.)
government consumption: 22.9% (2017 est.)
investment in fixed capital: 22.1% (2017 est.)
investment in inventories: 0.4% (2017 est.)
exports of goods and services: 38.5% (2017 est.)
imports of goods and services: -38.2% (2017 est.)

Agricultural products: milk, barley, oats, wheat, potatoes, sugar beet, rye, pork, poultry, beef

Industries: metals and metal products, electronics, machinery and scientific instruments, shipbuilding, pulp and paper, foodstuffs, chemicals, textiles, clothing

Industrial production growth rate: 6.2% (2017 est.)
country comparison to the world: 39

Labor force: 2.52 million (2020 est.)
country comparison to the world: 113

Labor force - by occupation: *agriculture:* 4%
industry: 20.7%
services: 75.3% (2017 est.)

Unemployment rate: 6.63% (2019 est.)
7.38% (2018 est.)
country comparison to the world: 106

Unemployment, youth ages 15-24: *total:* 21.4%
male: 23.2%
female: 19.4% (2020 est.)
country comparison to the world: 67

Population below poverty line: 12.2% (2019 est.)

Gini Index coefficient - distribution of family income: 27.4 (2017 est.)
22.2 (1995)
country comparison to the world: 164

Household income or consumption by percentage share: *lowest 10%:* 6.7%
highest 10%: 45.2% (2013)

Budget: *revenues:* 134.2 billion (2017 est.)
expenditures: 135.6 billion (2017 est.)
note: Central Government Budget data; these numbers represent a significant reduction from previous official reporting

Budget surplus (+) or deficit (-): -0.6% (of GDP) (2017 est.)
country comparison to the world: 64

Public debt: 61.3% of GDP (2017 est.)
62.9% of GDP (2016 est.)
note: data cover general government debt and include debt instruments issued (or owned) by government entities other than the treasury; the data include treasury debt held by foreign entities; the data include debt issued by subnational entities, as well as intragovernmental debt; intragovernmental debt consists of treasury borrowings from surpluses in the social funds, such as for retirement, medical care, and unemployment; debt instruments for the social funds are not sold at public auctions
country comparison to the world: 73

Taxes and other revenues: 53.1% (of GDP) (2017 est.)
country comparison to the world: 11

Fiscal year: calendar year

Current account balance: -$603 million (2019 est.)
-$4.908 billion (2018 est.)
country comparison to the world: 127

Exports: $108.22 billion (2019 est.) note: data are in current year dollars
$106.01 billion (2018 est.) note: data are in current year dollars
$109.513 billion (2017 est.)
country comparison to the world: 39

Exports - partners: Germany 14%, Sweden 10%, United States 8%, Netherlands 6%, China 6%, Russia 5% (2019)

Exports - commodities: refined petroleum, paper and wood pulp products, cars, stainless steel, lumber (2019)

Imports: $107.39 billion (2019 est.) note: data are in current year dollars
$109.45 billion (2018 est.) note: data are in current year dollars
$110.701 billion (2017 est.)
country comparison to the world: 38

Imports - partners: Germany 16%, Sweden 14%, Russia 13%, China 6%, Netherlands 6% (2019)

Imports - commodities: crude petroleum, cars and vehicle parts, refined petroleum, broadcasting equipment, packaged medicines (2019)

Reserves of foreign exchange and gold: $10.51 billion (31 December 2017 est.)
$11.2 billion (31 December 2016 est.)
country comparison to the world: 73

Debt - external: $631.549 billion (2019 est.)
$536.301 billion (2018 est.)
country comparison to the world: 22

Exchange rates: euros (EUR) per US dollar -
0.82771 (2020 est.)
0.90338 (2019 est.)
0.87789 (2018 est.)
0.885 (2014 est.)
0.7634 (2013 est.)

ENERGY

Electricity access: *electrification - total population:* 100% (2020)

Electricity: *installed generating capacity:* 20.418 million kW (2020 est.)
consumption: 79.356 billion kWh (2020 est.)
exports: 6.666 billion kWh (2020 est.)
imports: 21.615 billion kWh (2020 est.)
transmission/distribution losses: 2.574 billion kWh (2020 est.)

Electricity generation sources: *fossil fuels:* 13.4% of total installed capacity (2020 est.)
nuclear: 33.4% of total installed capacity (2020 est.)
solar: 0.4% of total installed capacity (2020 est.)
wind: 11.9% of total installed capacity (2020 est.)
hydroelectricity: 23.2% of total installed capacity (2020 est.)
biomass and waste: 17.8% of total installed capacity (2020 est.)

Coal: *production:* 762,000 metric tons (2020 est.)

consumption: 3.552 million metric tons (2020 est.)
exports: 101,000 metric tons (2020 est.)
imports: 2.661 million metric tons (2020 est.)
proven reserves: 0 metric tons (2019 est.)

Petroleum: *total petroleum production:* 8,300 bbl/day (2021 est.)
refined petroleum consumption: 207,400 bbl/day (2019 est.)
crude oil and lease condensate exports: 0 bbl/day (2018 est.)
crude oil and lease condensate imports: 232,400 bbl/day (2018 est.)
crude oil estimated reserves: 0 barrels (2021 est.)

Refined petroleum products - production: 310,600 bbl/day (2017 est.)
country comparison to the world: 40

Refined petroleum products - exports: 166,200 bbl/day (2017 est.)
country comparison to the world: 34

Refined petroleum products - imports: 122,200 bbl/day (2017 est.)
country comparison to the world: 48

Natural gas: *production:* 0 cubic meters (2021 est.)
consumption: 2,392,826,000 cubic meters (2020 est.)
exports: 181.143 million cubic meters (2020 est.)
imports: 2,568,532,000 cubic meters (2020 est.)
proven reserves: 0 cubic meters (2021 est.)

Carbon dioxide emissions: 41.996 million metric tonnes of CO_2 (2019 est.)
from coal and metallurgical coke: 9.377 million metric tonnes of CO_2 (2019 est.)
from petroleum and other liquids: 27.737 million metric tonnes of CO_2 (2019 est.)
from consumed natural gas: 4.882 million metric tonnes of CO_2 (2019 est.)
country comparison to the world: 62

Energy consumption per capita: 216.571 million Btu/person (2019 est.)
country comparison to the world: 20

COMMUNICATIONS

Telephones - fixed lines: *total subscriptions:* 225,000 (2020 est.)
subscriptions per 100 inhabitants: 4 (2020 est.)
country comparison to the world: 119

Telephones - mobile cellular: *total subscriptions:* 7.12 million (2020 est.)
subscriptions per 100 inhabitants: 129 (2020 est.)
country comparison to the world: 104

Telecommunication systems: *general assessment:* Finland's telecom market is among the more progressive in Europe, with operators having been at the forefront in deploying technologies and with the regulator being among the first to auction spectrum for 5G use; these efforts have been supported by the government which is working towards its target of providing a broadband service of at least 100Mb/s by 2025; 5G services were available to more than 40% of the population by early 2021, and take-up among subscribers has been strong although most will remain with LTE in the short term; the country enjoys one of the highest broadband and mobile subscription rates in the region, with customers able to make use of the latest iterations of technologies including DOCSIS3.1, LTE-A, 5G, and GPON fiber infrastructure; Finland has emerged as one of the pioneers in 5G; the auction of spectrum in the 700MHz and 3.5GHh bands has enabled network operators to extend the availability of LTE services nationally and to prepare for 5G services; Spectrum in the 2.5GHz band was auctioned in mid-2020 and has since enabled the MNOs to widen their 5G footprint considerably; there is an ongoing shift away from DSL to fiber and mobile networks (2021)
domestic: fixed-line 4 per 100 subscriptions and nearly 129 per 100 mobile-cellular (2020)
international: country code - 358; landing points for Botnia, BCS North-1 & 2, SFL, SFS-4, C-Lion1, Eastern Lights, Baltic Sea Submarine Cable, FEC, and EESF-2 & 3 submarine cables that provide links to many Finland points, Estonia, Sweden, Germany, and Russia; satellite earth stations - access to Intelsat transmission service via a Swedish satellite earth station, 1 Inmarsat (Atlantic and Indian Ocean regions); note - Finland shares the Inmarsat earth station with the other Nordic countries (Denmark, Iceland, Norway, and Sweden) (2019)

Broadcast media: a mix of 3 publicly operated TV stations and numerous privately owned TV stations; several free and special-interest pay-TV channels; cable and satellite multi-channel subscription services are available; all TV signals are broadcast digitally; Internet television, such as Netflix and others, is available; public broadcasting maintains a network of 13 national and 25 regional radio stations; a large number of private radio broadcasters and access to Internet radio

Internet country code: .fi
note - Aland Islands assigned .ax

Internet users: *total:* 5,087,180 (2020 est.)
percent of population: 92% (2020 est.)
country comparison to the world: 89

Broadband - fixed subscriptions: *total:* 1.846 million (2020 est.)
subscriptions per 100 inhabitants: 33 (2020 est.)
country comparison to the world: 59

TRANSPORTATION

National air transport system: *number of registered air carriers:* 3 (2020)
inventory of registered aircraft operated by air carriers: 77
annual passenger traffic on registered air carriers: 13,364,839 (2018)
annual freight traffic on registered air carriers: 957.64 million (2018) mt-km

Civil aircraft registration country code prefix: OH

Airports: *total:* 148 (2021)
country comparison to the world: 37

Airports - with paved runways: *total:* 74
over 3,047 m: 3
2,438 to 3,047 m: 26
1,524 to 2,437 m: 10
914 to 1,523 m: 21
under 914 m: 14 (2021)

Airports - with unpaved runways: *total:* 74
914 to 1,523 m: 3
under 914 m: 71 (2021)

Pipelines: 1,288 km gas transmission pipes, 1,976 km distribution pipes (2016)

Railways: *total:* 5,926 km (2016)
broad gauge: 5,926 km (2016) 1.524-m gauge (3,270 km electrified)
country comparison to the world: 32

Roadways: *total:* 454,000 km (2012)
highways: 78,000 km (2012) (50,000 paved, including 700 km of expressways; 28,000 unpaved)
private and forest roads: 350,000 km (2012)
urban: 26,000 km (2012)
country comparison to the world: 17

Waterways: 8,000 km (2013) (includes Saimaa Canal system of 3,577 km; southern part leased from Russia; water transport used frequently in the summer and widely replaced with sledges on the ice in winter; there are 187,888 lakes in Finland that cover 31,500 km); Finland also maintains 8,200 km of coastal fairways
country comparison to the world: 19

Merchant marine: *total:* 272
by type: bulk carrier 9, container ship 1, general cargo 74, oil tanker 4, other 184 (2021)
country comparison to the world: 57

Ports and terminals: *major seaport(s):* Helsinki, Kotka, Naantali, Porvoo, Raahe, Rauma

LNG terminal(s) (import): Pori, Tornio Manga; note - an additional terminal at Hamina is under construction and due to come online in October 2022

MILITARY AND SECURITY

Military and security forces: Finnish Defense Forces (FDF): Army (Maavoimat), Navy (Merivoimat), Air Force (Ilmavoimat); Ministry of the Interior: Border Guard (Rajavartiolaitos) (2022)
note: the Border Guard becomes part of the FDF in wartime

Military expenditures: 2% of GDP (2021 est.)
1.5% of GDP (2020)
1.4% of GDP (2019) (approximately $4.18 billion)
1.4% of GDP (2018) (approximately $4.02 billion)
1.3% of GDP (2017) (approximately $3.8 billion)
country comparison to the world: 61

Military and security service personnel strengths: approximately 22,000 active duty personnel (15,000 Army; 4,000 Navy; 3,000 Air Force) (2022)

Military equipment inventories and acquisitions: the military's inventory consists of a wide mix of mostly modern US, European, and domestically-produced weapons systems; since 2010, the US has been the leading supplier; the Finnish defense industry produces a variety of military equipment, including wheeled armored vehicles and naval vessels (2022)

Military service age and obligation: at age 18, all Finnish men are obligated to serve 5.5-12 months of service within a branch of the military or the Border Guard (length of service depends on the type of duty), and women 18-29 may volunteer for service; there is also an option to perform non-military service which lasts for 8.5 or 11.5 months; after completing their initial conscript obligation, individuals enter the reserves and remain eligible for mobilization until the age of 50 for rank-and-file and 60 for non-commissioned and commissioned officers (2022)
note 1: the military trains approximately 21,000 (20,000 Army) conscripts each year; as of 2019, women made up about 4% of the military's full-time personnel
note 2: Finland has had conscription since 1951

Military deployments: 160 Lebanon (UNIFIL) (May 2022)

Military - note: Finland is not a member of NATO, but Finland and NATO have actively cooperated in peace-support operations, exercised together, and exchanged analysis and information; Finland joined NATO's Partnership for Peace program in 1994; Finnish Armed Forces participated in NATO-led military operations and missions in the Balkans, Afghanistan, and Iraq; Finland applied for NATO membership in May 2022

Finland is a signatory of the EU's Common Security and Defense Policy (CSDP) and actively participates in CSDP crisis management missions and operations

the Finnish Armed Forces closely cooperate with the militaries of other Nordic countries through the Nordic Defense Cooperation (NORDEFCO), which consists of Denmark, Finland, Iceland, Norway, and Sweden; areas of cooperation include armaments, education, human resources, training and exercises, and operations; NORDEFCO was established in 2009 (2022)

TRANSNATIONAL ISSUES

Disputes - international: various groups in Finland advocate restoration of Karelia and other areas ceded to the former Soviet Union, but the Finnish Government asserts no territorial demands

Refugees and internally displaced persons: *refugees (country of origin):* 9,053 (Iraq) (mid-year 2021); 38,588 (Ukraine) (as of 15 November 2022)
stateless persons: 3,416 (mid-year 2021)

FRANCE

INTRODUCTION

Background: France today is one of the most modern countries in the world and is a leader among European nations. It plays an influential global role as a permanent member of the United Nations Security Council, NATO, the G-7, the G-20, the EU, and other multilateral organizations. France rejoined NATO's integrated military command structure in 2009, reversing DE GAULLE's 1966 decision to withdraw French forces from NATO. Since 1958, it has constructed a hybrid presidential-parliamentary governing system resistant to the instabilities experienced in earlier, more purely parliamentary administrations. In recent decades, its reconciliation and cooperation with Germany have proved central to the economic integration of Europe, including the introduction of a common currency, the euro, in January 1999. In the early 21st century, five French overseas entities - French Guiana, Guadeloupe, Martinique, Mayotte, and Reunion - became French regions and were made part of France proper.

GEOGRAPHY

Location: *metropolitan France:* Western Europe, bordering the Bay of Biscay and English Channel, between Belgium and Spain, southeast of the UK; bordering the Mediterranean Sea, between Italy and Spain;

French Guiana: Northern South America, bordering the North Atlantic Ocean, between Brazil and Suriname;

Guadeloupe: Caribbean, islands between the Caribbean Sea and the North Atlantic Ocean, southeast of Puerto Rico;

Martinique: Caribbean, island between the Caribbean Sea and North Atlantic Ocean, north of Trinidad and Tobago;

Mayotte: Southern Indian Ocean, island in the Mozambique Channel, about halfway between northern Madagascar and northern Mozambique;

Reunion: Southern Africa, island in the Indian Ocean, east of Madagascar

Geographic coordinates: *metropolitan France:* 46 00 N, 2 00 E;

French Guiana: 4 00 N, 53 00 W;

Guadeloupe: 16 15 N, 61 35 W;

Martinique: 14 40 N, 61 00 W;

Mayotte: 12 50 S, 45 10 E;

Reunion: 21 06 S, 55 36 E

Map references: *metropolitan France:* Europe;

French Guiana: South America;

Guadeloupe: Central America and the Caribbean;

Martinique: Central America and the Caribbean;

Mayotte: Africa;

Reunion: World

Area: *total:* 643,801 sq km; 551,500 sq km (metropolitan France)
land: 640,427 sq km; 549,970 sq km (metropolitan France)
water: 3,374 sq km; 1,530 sq km (metropolitan France)
note: the first numbers include the overseas regions of French Guiana, Guadeloupe, Martinique, Mayotte, and Reunion
country comparison to the world: 45

Area - comparative: slightly more than four times the size of Georgia; slightly less than the size of Texas

Land boundaries: *total:* 3,956 km
border countries (8): Andorra 55 km; Belgium 556 km; Germany 418 k; Italy 476 km; Luxembourg 69 km; Monaco 6 km; Spain 646 km; Switzerland 525 km
metropolitan France - total: 2751
French Guiana - *total:* 1205

Coastline: 4,853 km
metropolitan France: 3,427 km

Maritime claims: *territorial sea:* 12 nm
contiguous zone: 24 nm
exclusive economic zone: 200 nm (does not apply to the Mediterranean Sea)
continental shelf: 200-m depth or to the depth of exploitation

Climate: *metropolitan France:* generally cool winters and mild summers, but mild winters and hot summers along the Mediterranean; occasional strong, cold, dry, north-to-northwesterly wind known as the mistral;

French Guiana: tropical; hot, humid; little seasonal temperature variation;

Guadeloupe and Martinique: subtropical tempered by trade winds; moderately high humidity; rainy season (June to October); vulnerable to devastating cyclones (hurricanes) every eight years on average;

Mayotte: tropical; marine; hot, humid, rainy season during northeastern monsoon (November to May); dry season is cooler (May to November);

Reunion: tropical, but temperature moderates with elevation; cool and dry (May to November), hot and rainy (November to April)

Terrain: *metropolitan France:* mostly flat plains or gently rolling hills in north and west; remainder is mountainous, especially Pyrenees in south, Alps in east;

French Guiana: low-lying coastal plains rising to hills and small mountains;

Guadeloupe: Basse-Terre is volcanic in origin with interior mountains; Grande-Terre is low limestone formation; most of the seven other islands are volcanic in origin;

Martinique: mountainous with indented coastline; dormant volcano;

Mayotte: generally undulating, with deep ravines and ancient volcanic peaks;

Reunion: mostly rugged and mountainous; fertile lowlands along coast

Elevation: *highest point:* Mont Blanc 4,810
lowest point: Rhone River delta -2 m
mean elevation: 375 m
note: to assess the possible effects of climate change on the ice and snow cap of Mont Blanc, its surface and peak have been extensively measured in recent years; these new peak measurements have exceeded the traditional height of 4,807 m and have varied between 4,808 m and 4,811 m; the actual rock summit is 4,792 m and is 40 m away from the ice-covered summit

Natural resources: *metropolitan France:* coal, iron ore, bauxite, zinc, uranium, antimony, arsenic, potash, feldspar, fluorspar, gypsum, timber, arable land, fish, French Guiana, gold deposits, petroleum, kaolin, niobium, tantalum, clay

Land use: *agricultural land:* 52.7% (2018 est.)
arable land: 33.4% (2018 est.)
permanent crops: 1.8% (2018 est.)
permanent pasture: 17.5% (2018 est.)
forest: 29.2% (2018 est.)
other: 18.1% (2018 est.)

Irrigated land: 26,420 sq km (2012) 26,950 sq km
metropolitan France: 26,000 sq km (2012)

Major lakes (area sq km): *fresh water lake(s):* Lake Geneva (shared with Switzerland) - 580 sq km

Major rivers (by length in km): Rhine (shared with Switzerland [s], Germany, and Netherlands [m]) - 1,233 km; Loire - 1,012 km
note – [s] after country name indicates river source; [m] after country name indicates river mouth

Major watersheds (area sq km): Atlantic Ocean drainage: Loire (115,282 sq km), Seine 78,919 sq km), Rhine-Maas (198,735 sq km), *(Adriatic Sea)* Po (76,997 sq km), *(Mediterranean Sea)* Rhone (100,543 sq km)

Major aquifers: Paris Basin

Population distribution: much of the population is concentrated in the north and southeast; although there are many urban agglomerations throughout the country, Paris is by far the largest city, with Lyon ranked a distant second

Natural hazards: *metropolitan France:* flooding; avalanches; midwinter windstorms; drought; forest fires in south near the Mediterranean;
overseas departments: hurricanes (cyclones); flooding;
volcanism: Montagne Pelee (1,394 m) on the island of Martinique in the Caribbean is the most active volcano of the Lesser Antilles arc, it last erupted in 1932; a catastrophic eruption in May 1902 destroyed the city of St. Pierre, killing an estimated 30,000 people; La Soufriere (1,467 m) on the island of Guadeloupe in the Caribbean last erupted from July 1976 to March 1977; these volcanoes are part of the volcanic island arc of the Lesser Antilles that extends from Saba in the north to Grenada in the south

Geography - note: largest West European nation; most major French rivers - the Meuse, Seine, Loire, Charente, Dordogne, and Garonne - flow northward or westward into the Atlantic Ocean, only the Rhone flows southward into the Mediterranean Sea

PEOPLE AND SOCIETY

Population: 68,305,148 (2022 est.)
note: the above figure is for metropolitan France and five overseas regions; the metropolitan France population is 62,814,233
country comparison to the world: 21

Nationality: *noun:* Frenchman(men), Frenchwoman(women)
adjective: French

Ethnic groups: Celtic and Latin with Teutonic, Slavic, North African (Algerian, Moroccan, Tunisian), Indochinese, Basque minorities
note: overseas departments: Black, White, Mulatto, East Indian, Chinese, Amerindian

Languages: French (official) 100%, declining regional dialects and languages (Provencal, Breton, Alsatian, Corsican, Catalan, Basque, Flemish, Occitan, Picard); note - overseas departments: French, Creole patois, Mahorian (a Swahili dialect)
major-language sample(s):
The World Factbook, une source indispensable d'informations de base. (French)

Religions: Roman Catholic 47%, Muslim 4%, Protestant 2%, Buddhist 2%, Orthodox 1%, Jewish 1%, other 1%, none 33%, unspecified 9%
note: France maintains a tradition of secularism and has not officially collected data on religious affiliation since the 1872 national census, which complicates assessments of France's religious composition; an 1872 law prohibiting state authorities from collecting data on individuals' ethnicity or religious beliefs was reaffirmed by a 1978 law emphasizing the prohibition of the collection or exploitation of personal data revealing an individual's race, ethnicity, or political, philosophical, or religious opinions; a 1905 law codified France's separation of church and state

Age structure: *0-14 years:* 18.36% (male 6,368,767/female 6,085,318)
15-24 years: 11.88% (male 4,122,981/female 3,938,938)
25-54 years: 36.83% (male 12,619,649/female 12,366,120)
55-64 years: 12.47% (male 4,085,564/female 4,376,272)
65 years and over: 20.46% (male 6,029,303/female 7,855,244) (2020 est.)

Dependency ratios: *total dependency ratio:* 62.4
youth dependency ratio: 28.7
elderly dependency ratio: 33.7
potential support ratio: 3 (2020 est.)

Median age: *total:* 41.7 years
male: 40 years
female: 43.4 years (2020 est.)
country comparison to the world: 43

Population growth rate: 0.32% (2022 est.)
country comparison to the world: 168

Birth rate: 11.66 births/1,000 population (2022 est.)
country comparison to the world: 160

Death rate: 9.54 deaths/1,000 population (2022 est.)
country comparison to the world: 43

Net migration rate: 1.06 migrant(s)/1,000 population (2022 est.)
country comparison to the world: 64

Population distribution: much of the population is concentrated in the north and southeast; although there are many urban agglomerations throughout the country, Paris is by far the largest city, with Lyon ranked a distant second

Urbanization: *urban population:* 81.5% of total population (2022)
rate of urbanization: 0.67% annual rate of change (2020-25 est.)

Major urban areas - population: 11.142 million PARIS (capital), 1.748 million Lyon, 1.620 million Marseille-Aix-en-Provence, 1.073 million Lille, 1.049 million Toulouse, 991,000 Bordeaux (2022)

Sex ratio: *at birth:* 1.05 male(s)/female
0-14 years: 1.05 male(s)/female
15-24 years: 1.05 male(s)/female
25-54 years: 1.02 male(s)/female
55-64 years: 0.94 male(s)/female
65 years and over: 0.64 male(s)/female
total population: 0.96 male(s)/female (2022 est.)

Mother's mean age at first birth: 28.9 years (2020 est.)

Maternal mortality ratio: 8 deaths/100,000 live births (2017 est.)
country comparison to the world: 151

Infant mortality rate: *total:* 3.15 deaths/1,000 live births
male: 3.53 deaths/1,000 live births
female: 2.74 deaths/1,000 live births (2022 est.)
country comparison to the world: 210

Life expectancy at birth: *total population:* 82.59 years
male: 79.53 years
female: 85.79 years (2022 est.)
country comparison to the world: 19

Total fertility rate: 2.03 children born/woman (2022 est.)
country comparison to the world: 102

Drinking water source: *improved: urban:* 100% of population
rural: 100% of population
total: 100% of population

Current health expenditure: 11.1% of GDP (2019)

Physicians density: 3.27 physicians/1,000 population (2019)

Hospital bed density: 5.9 beds/1,000 population (2018)

Sanitation facility access: *improved: urban:* 100% of population
rural: 100% of population
total: 100% of population

HIV/AIDS - adult prevalence rate: 0.3% (2019 est.)
country comparison to the world: 81

Major infectious diseases: *note:* widespread ongoing transmission of a respiratory illness caused by the novel coronavirus (COVID-19) is occurring throughout France; as of 18 August 2022, France has reported a total of 33,275,006 cases of COVID-19 or 51,161.33 cumulative cases of COVID-19 per 100,000 population with a total of 149,848 cumulative deaths or a rate 230.39 cumulative deaths per 100,000 population; as of 16 August 2022, 80.89% of the population has received at least one dose of COVID-19 vaccine

Obesity - adult prevalence rate: 21.6% (2016)
country comparison to the world: 87

Alcohol consumption per capita: *total:* 11.44 liters of pure alcohol (2019 est.)
beer: 2.52 liters of pure alcohol (2019 est.)
wine: 6.44 liters of pure alcohol (2019 est.)
spirits: 2.3 liters of pure alcohol (2019 est.)
other alcohols: 0.18 liters of pure alcohol (2019 est.)
country comparison to the world: 8

Tobacco use: *total:* 33.4% (2020 est.)
male: 34.9% (2020 est.)
female: 31.9% (2020 est.)
country comparison to the world: 19

Education expenditures: 5.4% of GDP (2018 est.)
country comparison to the world: 42

School life expectancy (primary to tertiary education): *total:* 16 years
male: 15 years
female: 16 years (2019)

Unemployment, youth ages 15-24: *total:* 20.2%
male: 20.3%
female: 19.9% (2020 est.)

ENVIRONMENT

Environment - current issues: some forest damage from acid rain; air pollution from industrial and vehicle emissions; water pollution from urban wastes, agricultural runoff

Environment - international agreements: *party to:* Air Pollution, Air Pollution-Heavy Metals, Air Pollution-Multi-effect Protocol, Air Pollution-Nitrogen Oxides, Air Pollution-Persistent Organic Pollutants, Air Pollution-Sulphur 85, Air Pollution-Sulphur 94, Air Pollution-Volatile Organic Compounds, Antarctic-Environmental Protection, Antarctic-Marine Living Resources, Antarctic Seals, Antarctic Treaty, Biodiversity, Climate Change, Climate Change-Kyoto Protocol, Climate Change-Paris Agreement, Comprehensive Nuclear Test Ban, Desertification, Endangered Species, Hazardous Wastes, Law of the Sea, Marine Dumping-London Convention, Marine Dumping-London Protocol, Marine Life Conservation, Ozone Layer Protection, Ship Pollution, Tropical Timber 2006, Wetlands, Whaling
signed, but not ratified: none of the selected agreements

Air pollutants: *particulate matter emissions:* 11.64 micrograms per cubic meter (2016 est.)
methane emissions: 55.99 megatons (2020 est.)

Climate: *metropolitan France:* generally cool winters and mild summers, but mild winters and hot summers along the Mediterranean; occasional strong, cold, dry, north-to-northwesterly wind known as the mistral;

French Guiana: tropical; hot, humid; little seasonal temperature variation;

Guadeloupe and Martinique: subtropical tempered by trade winds; moderately high humidity; rainy season (June to October); vulnerable to devastating cyclones (hurricanes) every eight years on average;

Mayotte: tropical; marine; hot, humid, rainy season during northeastern monsoon (November to May); dry season is cooler (May to November);

Reunion: tropical, but temperature moderates with elevation; cool and dry (May to November), hot and rainy (November to April)

Land use: *agricultural land:* 52.7% (2018 est.)
arable land: 33.4% (2018 est.)
permanent crops: 1.8% (2018 est.)
permanent pasture: 17.5% (2018 est.)
forest: 29.2% (2018 est.)
other: 18.1% (2018 est.)

Urbanization: *urban population:* 81.5% of total population (2022)
rate of urbanization: 0.67% annual rate of change (2020-25 est.)

Revenue from forest resources: *forest revenues:* 0.03% of GDP (2018 est.)
country comparison to the world: 135

Revenue from coal: *coal revenues:* 0% of GDP (2018 est.)
country comparison to the world: 99

Waste and recycling: *municipal solid waste generated annually:* 33.399 million tons (2015 est.)
municipal solid waste recycled annually: 7,434,617 tons (2015 est.)
percent of municipal solid waste recycled: 22.3% (2015 est.)

Major lakes (area sq km): *fresh water lake(s):* Lake Geneva (shared with Switzerland) - 580 sq km

Major rivers (by length in km): Rhine (shared with Switzerland [s], Germany, and Netherlands [m]) - 1,233 km; Loire - 1,012 km
note – [s] after country name indicates river source; [m] after country name indicates river mouth

Major watersheds (area sq km): Atlantic Ocean drainage: Loire (115,282 sq km), Seine 78,919 sq km), Rhine-Maas (198,735 sq km), *(Adriatic Sea)* Po (76,997 sq km), *(Mediterranean Sea)* Rhone (100,543 sq km)

Major aquifers: Paris Basin

Total water withdrawal: *municipal:* 5.175 billion cubic meters (2017 est.)
industrial: 18.15 billion cubic meters (2017 est.)
agricultural: 3.113 billion cubic meters (2017 est.)

Total renewable water resources: 211 billion cubic meters (2017 est.)

GOVERNMENT

Country name: *conventional long form:* French Republic
conventional short form: France
local long form: Republique francaise
local short form: France
etymology: name derives from the Latin "Francia" meaning "Land of the Franks"; the Franks were a group of Germanic tribes located along the middle and lower Rhine River in the 3rd century A.D. who merged with Gallic-Roman populations in succeeding centuries and to whom they passed on their name

Government type: semi-presidential republic

Capital: *name:* Paris
geographic coordinates: 48 52 N, 2 20 E
time difference: UTC+1 (6 hours ahead of Washington, DC, during Standard Time)
daylight saving time: +1hr, begins last Sunday in March; ends last Sunday in October
time zone note: applies to metropolitan France only; for its overseas regions the time difference is UTC-4 for Guadeloupe and Martinique, UTC-3 for French Guiana, UTC+3 for Mayotte, and UTC+4 for Reunion
etymology: name derives from the Parisii, a Celtic tribe that inhabited the area from the 3rd century B.C., but who were conquered by the Romans in the 1st century B.C.; the Celtic settlement became the Roman town of Lutetia Parisiorum (Lutetia of the Parisii); over subsequent centuries it became Parisium and then just Paris

Administrative divisions: 18 regions (regions, singular - region); Auvergne-Rhone-Alpes, Bourgogne-Franche-Comte (Burgundy-Free County), Bretagne (Brittany), Centre-Val de Loire (Center-Loire Valley), Corse (Corsica), Grand Est (Grand East), Guadeloupe, Guyane (French Guiana), Hauts-de-France (Upper France), Ile-de-France, Martinique, Mayotte, Normandie (Normandy), Nouvelle-Aquitaine (New Aquitaine), Occitanie (Occitania), Pays de la Loire (Lands of the Loire), Provence-Alpes-Cote d'Azur, Reunion
note: France is divided into 13 metropolitan regions (including the "collectivity" of Corse or Corsica) and 5 overseas regions (French Guiana, Guadeloupe, Martinique, Mayotte, and Reunion) and is subdivided into 96 metropolitan departments and 5 overseas departments (which are the same as the overseas regions)

Dependent areas: Clipperton Island, French Polynesia, French Southern and Antarctic Lands, New Caledonia, Saint Barthelemy, Saint Martin, Saint Pierre and Miquelon, Wallis and Futuna
note: the US Government does not recognize claims to Antarctica; New Caledonia has been considered a "sui generis" collectivity of France since 1998, a unique status falling between that of an independent country and a French overseas department

Independence: *no official date of independence:* 486 (Frankish tribes unified under Merovingian kingship); 10 August 843 (Western Francia established from the division of the Carolingian Empire); 14 July 1789 (French monarchy overthrown); 22 September 1792 (First French Republic founded); 4 October 1958 (Fifth French Republic established)

National holiday: Fete de la Federation, 14 July (1790); note - although often incorrectly referred to as Bastille Day, the celebration actually commemorates the holiday held on the first anniversary of the storming of the Bastille (on 14 July 1789) and the establishment of a constitutional monarchy; other names for the holiday are Fete Nationale (National Holiday) and quatorze juillet (14th of July)

Constitution: *history:* many previous; latest effective 4 October 1958
amendments: proposed by the president of the republic (upon recommendation of the prime minister and Parliament) or by Parliament; proposals submitted by Parliament members require passage by both houses followed by approval in a referendum; passage of proposals submitted by the government can bypass a referendum if submitted by the president to Parliament and passed by at least three-fifths majority vote by Parliament's National Assembly; amended many times, last in 2008

Legal system: civil law; review of administrative but not legislative acts

International law organization participation: has not submitted an ICJ jurisdiction declaration; accepts ICCt jurisdiction

Citizenship: *citizenship by birth:* no
citizenship by descent only: at least one parent must be a citizen of France
dual citizenship recognized: yes
residency requirement for naturalization: 5 years

Suffrage: 18 years of age; universal

Executive branch: *chief of state:* President Emmanuel MACRON (since 14 May 2017)
head of government: Prime Minister Élisabeth BORNE (since 16 May 2022)
cabinet: Council of Ministers appointed by the president at the suggestion of the prime minister
elections/appointments: president directly elected by absolute majority popular vote in 2 rounds if needed for a 5-year term (eligible for a second term); election last held on 10 April 2022 with a runoff held on 24 April 2022 (next to be held in April 2027); prime minister appointed by the president
election results: *2022:* Emmanuel MACRON reelected in second round; percent of vote in first round - Emmanuel MACRON (LREM) 27.8%, Marine LE PEN (RN) 23.2%, Jean-Luc MELENCHON (LFI) 22%, Eric ZEMMOUR (Reconquete) 7.1%, Valerie PECRESSE (LR) 4.8%, Yannick JADOT (EELV) 4.6%, Jean LASSALLE (Resistons!) 3.1%, Fabien ROUSSEL (PCF) 2.3%, Nicolas DUPONT-AIGNAN (DLF) 2.1%, Anne HIDALGO 1.8%, other 1.2%; percent of vote in second round - MACRON 58.5%, LE PEN 41.5%

2017: Emmanuel MACRON elected president in second round; percent of vote in first round - Emmanuel MACRON (EM) 24%, Marine LE PEN (FN) 21.3%, Francois FILLON (LR) 20%, Jean-Luc MELENCHON (FI) 19.6%, Benoit HAMON (PS) 6.4%, other 8.7%; percent of vote in second round - MACRON 66.1%, LE PEN 33.9%

Legislative branch: *description:* bicameral Parliament or Parlement consists of:
Senate or Senat (348 seats - 328 for metropolitan France and overseas departments and regions of Guadeloupe, Martinique, French Guiana, Reunion, and Mayotte, 2 for New Caledonia, 2 for French Polynesia, 1 for Saint-Pierre and Miquelon, 1 for Saint-Barthelemy, 1 for Saint-Martin, 1 for Wallis and Futuna, and 12 for French nationals abroad; members indirectly elected by departmental electoral colleges using absolute majority vote in 2 rounds if needed for departments with 1-3 members, and proportional representation vote in departments with 4 or more members; members serve 6-year terms with one-half of the membership renewed every 3 years)
National Assembly or Assemblee Nationale (577 seats - 556 for metropolitan France, 10 for overseas departments, and 11 for citizens abroad; members directly elected by absolute majority vote in 2 rounds if needed to serve 5-year terms)
elections:
Senate - last held on 24 and 27 September 2020 (next to be held in September 2023)
National Assembly - last held on 12 and 19 June 2022 (next to be held in June 2027)
election results:
Senate - percent of vote by party - NA; seats by political caucus (party or group of parties) - NA ; composition - men 226, women 122, percent of women 35.1%
National Assembly - percent of vote by party/coalition in the first round - ENS 25.8%, NUPES 25.7%, RN 18.7%, UDC 11.3%, other 18.5%; seats by party/coalition in the first round - NUPES 4, ENS 1; percent of vote in the second round - ENS 38.6%, NUPES 31.6%, RN 17.3%, UDC 7.3%, other 5.2%, seats by party/coalition in the second round - ENS 244, NUPES 127, RN 89, UDC 64, other 48

Judicial branch: *highest court(s):* Court of Cassation or Cour de Cassation (consists of the court president, 6 divisional presiding judges, 120 trial judges, and 70 deputy judges organized into 6 divisions - 3 civil, 1 commercial, 1 labor, and 1 criminal); Constitutional Council (consists of 9 members)
judge selection and term of office: Court of Cassation judges appointed by the president of the republic from nominations from the High Council of the Judiciary, presided over by the Court of Cassation and 15 appointed members; judges appointed for life; Constitutional Council members - 3 appointed by the president of the republic and 3 each by the National Assembly and Senate presidents; members serve 9-year, non-renewable terms with one-third of the membership renewed every 3 years
subordinate courts: appellate courts or Cour d'Appel; regional courts or Tribunal de Grande Instance; first instance courts or Tribunal d'instance; administrative courts
note: in April 2021, the French Government submitted a bill on judicial reform to Parliament

Political parties and leaders: Citizen and Republican Movement or MRC [Jean-Luc LAURENT]
Debout la France or DLF [Nicolas DUPONT-AIGNAN]
Democratic Movement or MoDem [Francois BAYROU]
Ecologist Pole or PE
Europe Ecology - the Greens or EELV [vacant]
French Communist Party or PCF [Fabien ROUSSEL]
Horizons [Hubert VALADE]
La France Insoumise or FI [Jean-Luc MELENCHON]
La Republique en Marche! or LREM [Stanislas GUERINI]
Movement of Progressives or MDP [Robert HUE]
National Rally or RN [Jordan BARDELLA, acting president] (formerly National Front or FN)
New Democrats or LND [Aurelien TACHE, Emilie CARIOU] (formerly Ecology Democracy Solidarity or EDS)
New Ecological and Social People's Union or NUPES [collective leadership] (electoral coalition including FI, PE, PS, PCF)
Radical Party of the Left or PRV [Laurent HENART]
Reconquete [Eric ZEMMOUR]
Resistons! [Jean LASSALLE]
Socialist Party or PS [Olivier FAURE]
The Patriots or LP [Florian PHILIPPOT]
The Republicans or LR [Christian JACOB]
Together or ENS [Richard Ferrand] (electoral coalition including LREM, MoDem, Horizons, PRV)
Union of Democrats and Independents or UDI [Jean-Christophe LAGARDE]
Union of Right and Center or UDC [Christian JACOB] (electoral coalition including LR, UDI)

International organization participation: ADB (nonregional member), AfDB (nonregional member), Arctic Council (observer), Australia Group, BDEAC, BIS, BSEC (observer), CBSS (observer), CE, CERN, EAPC, EBRD, ECB, EIB, EITI (implementing country), EMU, ESA, EU, FAO, FATF, FZ, G-5, G-7, G-8, G-10, G-20, IADB, IAEA, IBRD, ICAO, ICC (national committees), ICCt, ICRM, IDA, IEA, IFAD, IFC, IFRCS, IGAD (partners), IHO, ILO, IMF, IMO, IMSO, InOC, Interpol, IOC, IOM, IPU, ISO, ITSO, ITU, ITUC (NGOs), MIGA, MINURSO, MINUSMA, MINUSTAH, MONUSCO, NATO, NEA, NSG, OAS (observer), OECD, OIF, OPCW, OSCE, Pacific Alliance (observer), Paris Club, PCA, PIF (partner), Schengen Convention, SELEC (observer), SPC, UN, UNCTAD, UNESCO, UNHCR, UNHRC, UNIDO, UNIFIL, Union Latina, UNMIL, UNOCI, UNRWA, UN Security Council (permanent), UNTSO, UNWTO, UPU, Wassenaar Arrangement, WCO, WFTU (NGOs), WHO, WIPO, WMO, WTO, ZC

Diplomatic representation in the US: *chief of mission:* Ambassador Philippe Noel Marie Marc ETIENNE (since 8 July 2019)
chancery: 4101 Reservoir Road NW, Washington, DC 20007
telephone: [1] (202) 944-6000
FAX: [1] (202) 944-6166
email address and website:
info@ambafrance-us.org
https://franceintheus.org/
consulate(s) general: Atlanta, Boston, Chicago, Houston, Los Angeles, Miami, New Orleans, New York, San Francisco, Washington, DC

Diplomatic representation from the US: *chief of mission:* Ambassador Denise Campbell BAUER (since 5 February 2022); note - also accredited to Monaco
embassy: 2 avenue Gabriel, 75008 Paris
mailing address: 9200 Paris Place, Washington DC 20521-9200
telephone: [33] (1) 43-12-22-22, [33] (1) 42-66-97-83
FAX: [33] (1) 42-66-97-83
email address and website:
Citizeninfo@state.gov
https://fr.usembassy.gov/
consulate(s) general: Marseille, Strasbourg
consulate(s): Bordeaux, Lyon, Rennes

Flag description: three equal vertical bands of blue (hoist side), white, and red; known as the "Le drapeau tricolore" (French Tricolor), the origin of the flag dates to 1790 and the French Revolution when the "ancient French color" of white was combined with the blue and red colors of the Parisian militia; the official flag for all French dependent areas
note: for the first four years, 1790-94, the order of colors was reversed, red-white-blue, instead of the current blue-white- red; the design and/or colors are similar to a number of other flags, including those of Belgium, Chad, Cote d'Ivoire, Ireland, Italy, Luxembourg, and Netherlands

National symbol(s): Gallic rooster, fleur-de-lis, Marianne (female personification); national colors: blue, white, red

National anthem: *name:* "La Marseillaise" (The Song of Marseille)
lyrics/music: Claude-Joseph ROUGET de Lisle
note: adopted 1795, restored 1870; originally known as "Chant de Guerre pour l'Armee du Rhin" (War Song for the Army of the Rhine), the National Guard of Marseille made the song famous by singing it while marching into Paris in 1792 during the French Revolutionary Wars

National heritage: *total World Heritage Sites:* 49 (43 cultural, 5 natural, 1 mixed); note - includes one site in New Caledonia and one site in French Polynesia
selected World Heritage Site locales: Chartres Cathedral (c); Palace and Park of Versailles (c); Prehistoric Sites and Decorated Caves of the Vézère Valley (c); Pyrénées - Mont Perdu (m); Cistercian Abbey of Fontenay (c); Paris, Banks of the Seine (c); The Loire Valley between Sully-sur-Loire and Chalonnes (c); Pont du Gard (Roman Aqueduct) (c); Amiens Cathedral (c); Palace and Park of Fontainebleau (c); Historic Fortified City of Carcassonne (c); Gulf of Porto: Calanche of Piana, Gulf of Girolata, Scandola Reserve (n)

ECONOMY

Economic overview: The French economy is diversified across all sectors. The government has partially or fully privatized many large companies, including Air France, France Telecom, Renault, and Thales. However, the government maintains a strong presence in some sectors, particularly power, public transport, and defense industries. France is the most visited country in the world with 89 million foreign tourists in 2017. France's leaders remain committed to a capitalism in which they maintain social equity by means of laws, tax policies, and social spending that mitigate economic inequality.

France's real GDP grew by 1.9% in 2017, up from 1.2% the year before. The unemployment rate (including overseas territories) increased from 7.8% in 2008 to 10.2% in 2015, before falling to 9.0% in 2017. Youth unemployment in metropolitan France decreased from 24.6% in the fourth quarter of 2014 to 20.6% in the fourth quarter of 2017.

France's public finances have historically been strained by high spending and low growth. In 2017, the budget deficit improved to 2.7% of GDP, bringing it in compliance with the EU-mandated 3% deficit target. Meanwhile, France's public debt rose from 89.5% of GDP in 2012 to 97% in 2017.

Since entering office in May 2017, President Emmanuel MACRON launched a series of economic reforms to improve competitiveness and boost economic growth. President MACRON campaigned on reforming France's labor code and in late 2017 implemented a range of reforms to increase flexibility in the labor market by making it easier for firms to hire and fire and simplifying negotiations between employers and employees. In addition to labor reforms, President MACRON's 2018 budget cuts public spending, taxes, and social security contributions to spur private investment and increase purchasing power. The government plans to gradually reduce corporate tax rate for businesses from 33.3% to 25% by 2022.

Real GDP (purchasing power parity): $2,832,170,000,000 (2020 est.)
$3,082,300,000,000 (2019 est.)
$3,036,490,000,000 (2018 est.)
note: data are in 2017 dollars
country comparison to the world: 9

Real GDP growth rate: 1.49% (2019 est.)
1.81% (2018 est.)
2.42% (2017 est.)
country comparison to the world: 154

Real GDP per capita: $42,000 (2020 est.)
$45,800 (2019 est.)
$45,300 (2018 est.)
note: data are in 2017 dollars
country comparison to the world: 38

GDP (official exchange rate): $2,715,574,000,000 (2019 est.)

Inflation rate (consumer prices): 1.1% (2019 est.)
1.8% (2018 est.)
1% (2017 est.)
country comparison to the world: 71

Credit ratings:

Fitch rating: AA (2014)

Moody's rating: Aa2 (2015)

Standard & Poors rating: AA (2013)
note: The year refers to the year in which the current credit rating was first obtained.

GDP - composition, by sector of origin: *agriculture:* 1.7% (2017 est.)
industry: 19.5% (2017 est.)
services: 78.8% (2017 est.)

GDP - composition, by end use: *household consumption:* 54.1% (2017 est.)
government consumption: 23.6% (2017 est.)
investment in fixed capital: 22.5% (2017 est.)
investment in inventories: 0.9% (2017 est.)
exports of goods and services: 30.9% (2017 est.)
imports of goods and services: -32% (2017 est.)

Agricultural products: wheat, sugar beet, milk, barley, maize, potatoes, grapes, rapeseed, pork, apples

Industries: machinery, chemicals, automobiles, metallurgy, aircraft, electronics; textiles, food processing; tourism

Industrial production growth rate: 2% (2017 est.)
country comparison to the world: 130

Labor force: 27.742 million (2020 est.)
country comparison to the world: 19

Labor force - by occupation: *agriculture:* 2.8% (2016 est.)
industry: 20% (2016 est.)
services: 77.2% (2016 est.)

Unemployment rate: 8.12% (2019 est.)
8.69% (2018 est.)
note: includes overseas territories
country comparison to the world: 129

Unemployment, youth ages 15-24: *total:* 20.2%
male: 20.3%
female: 19.9% (2020 est.)
country comparison to the world: 77

Population below poverty line: 13.6% (2018 est.)

Gini Index coefficient - distribution of family income: 31.6 (2017 est.)
29.2 (2015)
country comparison to the world: 142

Household income or consumption by percentage share: *lowest 10%:* 3.6%
highest 10%: 25.4% (2013)

Budget: *revenues:* 1.392 trillion (2017 est.)
expenditures: 1.459 trillion (2017 est.)

Budget surplus (+) or deficit (-): -2.6% (of GDP) (2017 est.)
country comparison to the world: 116

Public debt: 96.8% of GDP (2017 est.)
96.6% of GDP (2016 est.)
note: data cover general government debt and include debt instruments issued (or owned) by government entities other than the treasury; the data include treasury debt held by foreign entities; the data include debt issued by subnational entities, as well as intragovernmental debt; intragovernmental debt consists of treasury borrowings from surpluses in the social funds, such as for retirement, medical care, and unemployment; debt instruments for the social funds are not sold at public auctions
country comparison to the world: 20

Taxes and other revenues: 53.8% (of GDP) (2017 est.)
country comparison to the world: 10

Fiscal year: calendar year

Current account balance: -$18.102 billion (2019 est.)
-$16.02 billion (2018 est.)
country comparison to the world: 197

Exports: $746.91 billion (2020 est.) note: data are in current year dollars
$891.18 billion (2019 est.) note: data are in current year dollars
$918.97 billion (2018 est.) note: data are in current year dollars
country comparison to the world: 5

Exports - partners: Germany 14%, United States 8%, Italy 7%, Spain 7%, Belgium 7%, United Kingdom 7% (2019)

Exports - commodities: aircraft, packaged medicines, cars and vehicle parts, gas turbines, wine (2019)

Imports: $803.66 billion (2020 est.) note: data are in current year dollars
$919.63 billion (2019 est.) note: data are in current year dollars
$947.31 billion (2018 est.) note: data are in current year dollars
country comparison to the world: 4

Imports - partners: Germany 18%, Belgium 9%, Italy 9%, Spain 7%, China 7%, Netherlands 6%, United Kingdom 5% (2019)

Imports - commodities: cars, crude petroleum, refined petroleum, packaged medicines, aircraft machinery (2019)

Reserves of foreign exchange and gold: $156.4 billion (31 December 2017 est.)
$138.2 billion (31 December 2015 est.)
country comparison to the world: 16

Debt - external: $6,356,459,000,000 (2019 est.)
$6,058,438,000,000 (2018 est.)
country comparison to the world: 3

Exchange rates: euros (EUR) per US dollar -
0.82771 (2020 est.)
0.90338 (2019 est.)
0.87789 (2018 est.)
0.885 (2014 est.)
0.7634 (2013 est.)

ENERGY

Electricity access: *electrification - total population:* 100% (2020)

Electricity: *installed generating capacity:* 138.611 million kW (2020 est.)
consumption: 472.699 billion kWh (2020 est.)
exports: 64.425 billion kWh (2020 est.)
imports: 19.613 billion kWh (2020 est.)
transmission/distribution losses: 36.203 billion kWh (2020 est.)

Electricity generation sources: *fossil fuels:* 8% of total installed capacity (2020 est.)
nuclear: 68.4% of total installed capacity (2020 est.)
solar: 2.5% of total installed capacity (2020 est.)
wind: 7.3% of total installed capacity (2020 est.)
hydroelectricity: 11.7% of total installed capacity (2020 est.)
tide and wave: 0.2% of total installed capacity (2020 est.)
biomass and waste: 2% of total installed capacity (2020 est.)

Coal: *production:* 2.312 million metric tons (2020 est.)
consumption: 10.712 million metric tons (2020 est.)
exports: 35,000 metric tons (2020 est.)
imports: 7.891 million metric tons (2020 est.)
proven reserves: 0 metric tons (2019 est.)

Petroleum: *total petroleum production:* 81,500 bbl/day (2021 est.)
refined petroleum consumption: 1,688,500 bbl/day (2019 est.)
crude oil and lease condensate exports: 0 bbl/day (2018 est.)
crude oil and lease condensate imports: 1,064,700 bbl/day (2018 est.)
crude oil estimated reserves: 61.7 million barrels (2021 est.)

Refined petroleum products - production: 1.311 million bbl/day (2017 est.)
country comparison to the world: 15

Refined petroleum products - exports: 440,600 bbl/day (2017 est.)

country comparison to the world: 19

Refined petroleum products - imports: 886,800 bbl/day (2017 est.)
country comparison to the world: 8

Natural gas: *production:* 16.226 million cubic meters (2019 est.)
consumption: 38,192,256,000 cubic meters (2020 est.)
exports: 9,103,795,000 cubic meters (2020 est.)
imports: 46,105,385,000 cubic meters (2020 est.)
proven reserves: 7.787 billion cubic meters (2021 est.)

Carbon dioxide emissions: 338.425 million metric tonnes of CO2 (2019 est.)
from coal and metallurgical coke: 26.971 million metric tonnes of CO2 (2019 est.)
from petroleum and other liquids: 225.865 million metric tonnes of CO2 (2019 est.)
from consumed natural gas: 85.589 million metric tonnes of CO2 (2019 est.)
country comparison to the world: 18

Energy consumption per capita: 151.053 million Btu/person (2019 est.)
country comparison to the world: 34

COMMUNICATIONS

Telephones - fixed lines: *total subscriptions:* 37.759 million (2020 est.)
subscriptions per 100 inhabitants: 58 (2020 est.)
country comparison to the world: 5

Telephones - mobile cellular: *total subscriptions:* 72.751 million (2020 est.)
subscriptions per 100 inhabitants: 111 (2020 est.)
country comparison to the world: 23

Telecommunication systems: *general assessment:* France's telecom market is one of the largest in Europe; there is a multi-year Engage 2025 plan which is focused on growth in the developing markets, and on the greater use of artificial intelligence and data; there are many MVNOs in the market; LTE networks provide near universal coverage, and carry about 95% of mobile data traffic; operators have launched 5G services, and these have been supported by the late-2020 auction of spectrum in the 3.5GHz range; France's fixed broadband market is increasingly focused on fiber, which accounted for 71% of all fixed lines at the beginning of 2021; growth in the fiber sector has been stimulated by households securing faster data packages during the pandemic; the number of DSL lines has fallen sharply as customers migrate to fiber infrastructure (2021)
domestic: nearly 58 per 100 persons for fixed-line and over 111 per 100 for mobile-cellular subscriptions (2020)
international: country code - 33; landing points for Circe South, TAT-14, INGRID, FLAG Atlantic-1, Apollo, HUGO, IFC-1, ACE, SeaMeWe-3 & 4, Dunant, Africa-1, AAE-1, Atlas Offshore, Hawk, IMEWE, Med Cable, PEACE Cable, and TE North/TGN-Eurasia/SEACOM/Alexandros/Medex submarine cables providing links throughout Europe, Asia, Australia, the Middle East, Southeast Asia, Africa and US; satellite earth stations - more than 3 (2 Intelsat (with total of 5 antennas - 2 for Indian Ocean and 3 for Atlantic Ocean), NA Eutelsat, 1 Inmarsat - Atlantic Ocean region); HF radiotelephone communications with more than 20 countries (2019)
overseas departments: country codes: French Guiana - 594; landing points for Ella Link, Kanawa, Americas II to South America, Europe, Caribbean and US; Guadeloupe - 590; landing points for GCN, Southern Caribbean Fiber, and ECFS around the Caribbean and US; Martinique - 596; landing points for Americas II, ECFS, and Southern Caribbean Fiber to South America, US and around the Caribbean; Mayotte - 262; landing points for FLY-LION3 and LION2 to East Africa and East African Islands in Indian Ocean; Reunion - 262; landing points for SAFE, METISS, and LION submarine cables to Asia, South and East Africa, Southeast Asia and nearby Indian Ocean Island countries of Mauritius, and Madagascar (2019)

Broadcast media: a mix of both publicly operated and privately owned TV stations; state-owned France television stations operate 4 networks, one of which is a network of regional stations, and has part-interest in several thematic cable/satellite channels and international channels; a large number of privately owned regional and local TV stations; multi-channel satellite and cable services provide a large number of channels; public broadcaster Radio France operates 7 national networks, a series of regional networks, and operates services for overseas territories and foreign audiences; Radio France Internationale, under the Ministry of Foreign Affairs, is a leading international broadcaster; a large number of commercial FM stations, with many of them consolidating into commercial networks

Internet country code: metropolitan France - .fr; French Guiana - .gf; Guadeloupe - .gp; Martinique - .mq; Mayotte - .yt; Reunion - .re

Internet users: *total:* 57,272,921 (2020 est.)
percent of population: 85% (2020 est.)
country comparison to the world: 16

Broadband - fixed subscriptions: *total:* 30.627 million (2020 est.)
subscriptions per 100 inhabitants: 47 (2020 est.)
country comparison to the world: 7

TRANSPORTATION

National air transport system: *number of registered air carriers:* 19 (2020)
inventory of registered aircraft operated by air carriers: 553
annual passenger traffic on registered air carriers: 70,188,028 (2018)
annual freight traffic on registered air carriers: 4,443,790,000 (2018) mt-km

Civil aircraft registration country code prefix: F

Airports: *total:* 464 (2021)
country comparison to the world: 15

Airports - with paved runways: *total:* 294
over 3,047 m: 14
2,438 to 3,047 m: 25
1,524 to 2,437 m: 97
914 to 1,523 m: 83
under 914 m: 75 (2021)

Airports - with unpaved runways: *total:* 170
1,524 to 2,437 m: 1
914 to 1,523 m: 64
under 914 m: 105 (2021)

Heliports: 1 (2021)

Pipelines: 15,322 km gas, 2,939 km oil, 5,084 km refined products (2013)

Railways: *total:* 29,640 km (2014)
standard gauge: 29,473 km (2014) 1.435-m gauge (15,561 km electrified)
narrow gauge: 167 km (2014) 1.000-m gauge (63 km electrified)
country comparison to the world: 10

Roadways: *total:* 1,053,215 km (2011)
urban: 654,201 km (2011)
non-urban: 399,014 km (2011)
country comparison to the world: 7

Waterways: *metropolitan France:* 8,501 km (1,621 km navigable by craft up to 3,000 metric tons) (2010)

Merchant marine: *total:* 548
by type: container ship 29, general cargo 50, oil tanker 28, other 441 (2021)
note: includes Monaco
country comparison to the world: 41

Ports and terminals: *major seaport(s):*
Atlantic Ocean: Brest, Calais, Dunkerque, Le Havre, Nantes
Mediterranean Sea: Marseille
container port(s) (TEUs): Le Havre (2,822,910) (2019)

LNG terminal(s) (import): Dunkerque, Fos Cavaou, Fos Tonkin, Montoir de Bretagne
river port(s): Bordeaux (Garronne); Nantes - Saint Nazaire (Loire); Paris, Rouen (Seine); Strasbourg (Rhine)
cruise/ferry port(s): Calais, Cherbourg, Le Havre

Transportation - note: begun in 1988 and completed in 1994, the Channel Tunnel (nicknamed the Chunnel) is a 50.5-km (31.4-mi) rail tunnel beneath the English Channel at the Strait of Dover that runs from Folkestone, Kent, England to Coquelles, Pas-de-Calais in northern France; it is the only fixed link between the island of Great Britain and mainland Europe

MILITARY AND SECURITY

Military and security forces: French Armed Forces (Forces Armées Françaises): Army (l'Armee de Terre; includes Foreign Legion), Navy (Marine Nationale), Air and Space Force (l'Armee de l'Air et de l'Espace); includes Air Defense), National Guard (Reserves), National Gendarmerie (2022)
note: the National Gendarmerie is a paramilitary police force that is a branch of the Armed Forces and therefore part of the Ministry of Defense but under the jurisdiction of the Ministry of the Interior; it also has additional duties to the Ministry of Justice

Military expenditures: 1.9% of GDP (2022 est.)
1.9% of GDP (2021)
2% of GDP (2020)
1.8% of GDP (2019) (approximately $59.1 billion)
1.8% of GDP (2018) (approximately $57 billion)
country comparison to the world: 65

Military and security service personnel strengths: approximately 205,000 active-duty troops (115,000 Army; 35,000 Navy; 40,000 Air Force; 15,000 other, such as joint staffs, administration, logistics, procurement, medical service, etc.); approximately 100,000 National Gendarmerie; approximately 75,000 National Guard (2022)

Military equipment inventories and acquisitions: the French military's inventory consists mostly of domestically produced weapons systems, including

some jointly produced with other European countries; there is a limited mix of armaments from other Western countries, particularly the US; France has a defense industry capable of manufacturing the full spectrum of air, land, and naval military weapons systems (2022)
note: as of 2022, two major future acquisition programs for the French military included the Franco-German-Spanish Future Combat Air System, or FCAS (known in France as the système combat aérien du futur, or SCAF) and a next-generation tank development project with Germany known as the Main Ground Combat System, or MGCS

Military service age and obligation: 18-25 years of age for voluntary military service for men and women; no conscription (abolished 2001); 12-month service obligation; women serve in noncombat posts (2022)
note 1: in 2019, women comprised approximately approximately 16% of the uniformed armed forces
note 2: men between the ages of 17.5 and 39.5 years of age, of any nationality, may join the French Foreign Legion; those volunteers selected for service sign five-year contracts
note 3: in 2018, Parliament passed a law that would require military service for all genders beginning in 2024; Prime Minister MACRON included the measure in his platform hoping that it would reinvigorate a sense of civic duty; the service would include two components: the first would take place around age 16 and include one month of training and civic service, while the second component would last between three months and a year and be more geared towards defense and security duties; France began a pilot for the program in 2019

Military deployments: approximately 3,000 Burkina Faso/Chad/Niger (Operation Barkhane, Operation Sabre); approximately 300 Central African Republic; 300 Comoros; approximately 900 Cote D'Ivoire; approximately 1,450 Djibouti; 220 Estonia (NATO); approximately 2,000 French Guyana; approximately 900 French Polynesia; approximately 1,000 French West Indies; 350 Gabon; approximately 500 Middle East (Iraq/Jordan/Syria); 600 Lebanon (UNIFIL); approximately 1,400 New Caledonia; approximately 1,700 Reunion Island; approximately 800 Romania (NATO); approximately 350 Senegal; approximately 650 United Arab Emirates (2022)
note 1: France has been a contributing member of the EuroCorps since 1992
note 2: in response to Russia's 2022 invasion of Ukraine, some NATO countries, including France, have sent additional troops to the battlegroups deployed in NATO territory in eastern Europe

Military - note: France was one of the original 12 countries to sign the North Atlantic Treaty (also known as the Washington Treaty), which created NATO in 1949; in 1966, President Charles DE GAULLE decided to withdraw France from NATO's integrated military structure, reflecting his desire for greater military independence, particularly vis-à-vis the US, and the refusal to integrate France's nuclear deterrent or accept any form of control over its armed forces; it did, however, sign agreements with NATO setting out procedures in the event of Soviet aggression; beginning with the fall of the Berlin Wall in 1989, France distanced itself from the 1966 decision and has regularly contributed troops to NATO's military operations, being one of the largest troop-contributing states; in 2009 it officially announced its decision to fully participate in NATO structures

in 2010, France and the UK signed a declaration on defense and security cooperation that included greater military interoperability and a Combined Joint Expeditionary Force (CJEF), a deployable, combined Anglo-French military force for use in a wide range of crisis scenarios, up to and including high intensity combat operations; the CJEF has no standing forces, but would be available at short notice for French-UK bilateral, NATO, EU, UN, or other operations; combined training exercises began in 2011; as of 2020, the CJEF was assessed as having full operating capacity with the ability to rapidly deploy over 10,000 personnel capable of high intensity operations, peacekeeping, disaster relief, and humanitarian assistance

the French Foreign Legion, established in 1831, is a military force that is open to foreign recruits willing to serve in the French Armed Forces for service in France and abroad; the Foreign Legion is an integrated part of the French Army and is comprised of approximately 8,000 personnel in eight regiments, a regiment-sized demi-brigade, a battalion-sized overseas detachment, a battalion-sized recruiting group, and a command staff; the combat units are a mix of armored cavalry and airborne, light, mechanized, and motorized infantry (2022)

TERRORISM

Terrorist group(s): Islamic Revolutionary Guard Corps/Qods Force; Islamic State of Iraq and ash-Sham (ISIS); al-Qa'ida

TRANSNATIONAL ISSUES

Disputes - international: Madagascar claims the French territories of Bassas da India, Europa Island, Glorioso Islands, and Juan de Nova Island; Comoros claims Mayotte; Mauritius claims Tromelin Island; territorial dispute between Suriname and the French overseas department of French Guiana; France asserts a territorial claim in Antarctica (Adelie Land); France and Vanuatu claim Matthew and Hunter Islands, east of New Caledonia

Refugees and internally displaced persons: *refugees (country of origin):* 37,744 (Afghanistan), 23,980 (Sri Lanka), 23,510 (Syria), 21,070 (Sudan), 19,007 (Democratic Republic of the Congo), 16,995 (Russia), 15,090 (Guinea), 14,296 (Serbia and Kosovo), 13,180 (Turkey), 10,849 (Cambodia), 9,328 (Iraq) 8,519 (China), 8,338 (Cote d'Ivoire), 8,218 (Eritrea), 7,628 (Vietnam), 6,947 (Bangladesh), 6,649 (Somalia), 6,642 (Albania), 6,371 (Laos), 6,074 (Mauritania), 5,908 (Mali) (mid-year 2021); 118,994 (Ukraine) (as of 31 October 2022)
stateless persons: 2,094 (mid-year 2021)

Illicit drugs: *metropolitan France:* transshipment point for South American cocaine, Southwest Asian heroin, and European synthetics;

French Guiana: small amount of marijuana grown for local consumption; minor transshipment point to Europe;

Martinique: transshipment point for cocaine and marijuana bound for the US and Europe

FRENCH POLYNESIA

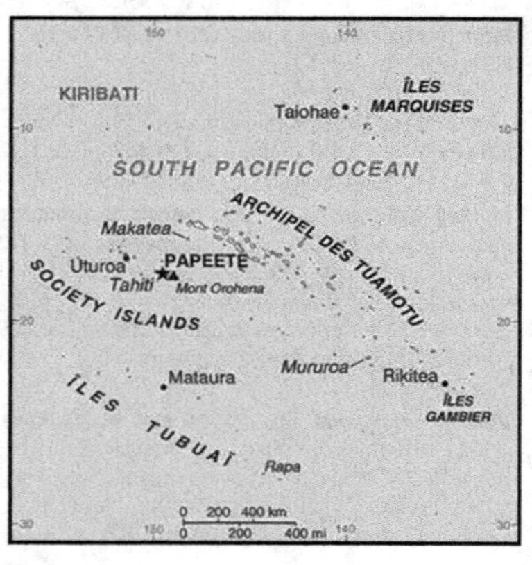

INTRODUCTION

Background: French Polynesia consists of five archipelagos - the Austral Islands, the Gambier Islands, the Marquesas Islands, the Society Islands, and the Tuamotu Archipelago. The Marquesas were first settled around 200 B.C. and the Society Islands around A.D. 300. Raiatea in the Society Islands became a center for religion and culture. Exploration of the other islands emanated from Raiatea and by 1000, there were small permanent settlements in all the island groups. Ferdinand MAGELLAN was the first European to see the islands of French Polynesia in 1520, and successive European voyagers traveled through them over the next two centuries. In 1767, British explorer Samuel WALLIS was the first European to visit Tahiti, followed by French navigator Louis Antoine de BOUGAINVILLE in 1768, and British explorer James COOK in 1769. King POMARE I united Tahiti and surrounding islands into the Kingdom of Tahiti in 1788. Protestant missionaries arrived in 1797 and POMARE I's successor converted in the 1810s, along with most Tahitians. In the 1830s, Queen POMARE IV refused to allow French Catholic missionaries to operate, leading France to declare a protectorate over Tahiti and fight the French-Tahitian War of the 1840s in an attempt to annex the islands. POMARE IV requested British assistance to fight France, and while the UK did not provide material support, it did diplomatically pressure France to simply maintain its protectorate status.

In 1880, King POMARE V ceded Tahiti and its possessions to France, changing its status into a colony. France then claimed the Gambier Islands and Tuamotu Archipelago and by 1901 had incorporated all five island groups into its establishments in Oceania. A Tahitian nationalist movement formed in 1940, leading France to grant French citizenship to the islanders in 1946 and change it to an overseas territory. In 1957, the islands' name was changed to French Polynesia and the following year, 64% of voters chose to stay part of France when they approved a new constitution. Uninhabited Mururoa Atoll was established as a French nuclear test site in 1962 and tests were conducted between 1966 and 1992 (underground beginning in 1975). France also conducted tests at Fangataufa Atoll, including its last nuclear test in 1996.

France granted French Polynesia partial internal autonomy in 1977 and expanded autonomy in 1984. French Polynesia was converted into an overseas collectivity in 2003 and renamed an overseas country inside the Republic in 2004. Proindependence politicians won a surprise majority in local elections that same year but in subsequent elections have been relegated to a vocal minority. In 2013, French Polynesia was relisted on the UN List of Non-Self Governing Territories.

GEOGRAPHY

Location: Oceania, five archipelagoes (Archipel des Tuamotu, Iles Gambier, Iles Marquises, Iles Tubuai, Society Islands) in the South Pacific Ocean about halfway between South America and Australia

Geographic coordinates: 15 00 S, 140 00 W

Map references: Oceania

Area: *total:* 4,167 sq km (118 islands and atolls; 67 are inhabited)
land: 3,827 sq km
water: 340 sq km
country comparison to the world: 174

Area - comparative: slightly less than one-third the size of Connecticut

Land boundaries: *total:* 0 km

Coastline: 2,525 km

Maritime claims: *territorial sea:* 12 nm
exclusive economic zone: 200 nm

Climate: tropical, but moderate

Terrain: mixture of rugged high islands and low islands with reefs

Elevation: *highest point:* Mont Orohena 2,241 m
lowest point: Pacific Ocean 0 m

Natural resources: timber, fish, cobalt, hydropower

Land use: *agricultural land:* 12.5% (2018 est.)
arable land: 0.7% (2018 est.)
permanent crops: 6.3% (2018 est.)
permanent pasture: 5.5% (2018 est.)
forest: 43.7% (2018 est.)
other: 43.8% (2018 est.)

Irrigated land: 10 sq km (2012)

Population distribution: the majority of the population lives in the Society Islands, one of five archipelagos that includes the most populous island - Tahiti - with approximately 70% of the nation's population

Natural hazards: occasional cyclonic storms in January

Geography - note: *includes five archipelagoes:* four volcanic (Iles Gambier, Iles Marquises, Iles Tubuai, Society Islands) and one coral (Archipel des Tuamotu); the Tuamotu Archipelago forms the largest group of atolls in the world - 78 in total, 48 inhabited; Makatea in the Tuamotu Archipelago is one of the three great phosphate rock islands in the Pacific Ocean - the others are Banaba (Ocean Island) in Kiribati and Nauru

PEOPLE AND SOCIETY

Population: 299,356 (2022 est.)
country comparison to the world: 181

Nationality: *noun:* French Polynesian(s)
adjective: French Polynesian

Ethnic groups: Polynesian 78%, Chinese 12%, local French 6%, metropolitan French 4%

Languages: French (official) 73.5%, Tahitian 20.1%, Marquesan 2.6%, Austral languages 1.2%, Paumotu 1%, other 1.6% (2017 est.)
major-language sample(s):
The World Factbook, une source indispensable d'informations de base. (French)

Religions: Protestant 54%, Roman Catholic 30%, other 10%, no religion 6%

Age structure: *0-14 years:* 21.69% (male 32,920/female 31,100)
15-24 years: 14.72% (male 22,640/female 20,793)
25-54 years: 44.24% (male 66,921/female 63,636)
55-64 years: 10.31% (male 15,610/female 14,823)
65 years and over: 9.04% (male 12,854/female 13,824) (2020 est.)

Dependency ratios: *total dependency ratio:* 45.5
youth dependency ratio: 32.3
elderly dependency ratio: 13.2
potential support ratio: 7.6 (2020 est.)

Median age: *total:* 33.3 years
male: 33 years
female: 33.5 years (2020 est.)
country comparison to the world: 98

Population growth rate: 0.73% (2022 est.)
country comparison to the world: 126

Birth rate: 13.47 births/1,000 population (2022 est.)
country comparison to the world: 136

Death rate: 5.59 deaths/1,000 population (2022 est.)
country comparison to the world: 179

Net migration rate: -0.63 migrant(s)/1,000 population (2022 est.)
country comparison to the world: 128

Population distribution: the majority of the population lives in the Society Islands, one of five archipelagos that includes the most populous island - Tahiti - with approximately 70% of the nation's population

Urbanization: *urban population:* 62.2% of total population (2022)
rate of urbanization: 0.65% annual rate of change (2020-25 est.)

Major urban areas - population: 136,000 PAPEETE (capital) (2018)

Sex ratio: *at birth:* 1.05 male(s)/female
0-14 years: 1.06 male(s)/female
15-24 years: 1.09 male(s)/female
25-54 years: 1.05 male(s)/female
55-64 years: 1.05 male(s)/female
65 years and over: 0.79 male(s)/female
total population: 1.05 male(s)/female (2022 est.)

Infant mortality rate: *total:* 4.4 deaths/1,000 live births
male: 5.3 deaths/1,000 live births
female: 3.46 deaths/1,000 live births (2022 est.)
country comparison to the world: 183

Life expectancy at birth: *total population:* 78.43 years
male: 76.11 years
female: 80.86 years (2022 est.)
country comparison to the world: 70

Total fertility rate: 1.81 children born/woman (2022 est.)
country comparison to the world: 142

Drinking water source: *improved: total:* 100% of population
unimproved: total: 0% of population (2020 est.)

Sanitation facility access: *improved: total:* 97% of population
unimproved: total: 3% of population (2020 est.)

Major infectious diseases: *degree of risk:* high (2020)
food or waterborne diseases: bacterial diarrhea
vectorborne diseases: malaria

Unemployment, youth ages 15-24: *total:* 56.7%
male: 54.5%
female: 59.7% (2012 est.)

ENVIRONMENT

Environment - current issues: sea level rise; extreme weather events (cyclones, storms, and tsunamis producing floods, landslides, erosion, and reef damage); droughts; fresh water scarcity

Air pollutants: *carbon dioxide emissions:* 0.77 megatons (2016 est.)

Climate: tropical, but moderate

Land use: *agricultural land:* 12.5% (2018 est.)
arable land: 0.7% (2018 est.)
permanent crops: 6.3% (2018 est.)
permanent pasture: 5.5% (2018 est.)
forest: 43.7% (2018 est.)
other: 43.8% (2018 est.)

Urbanization: *urban population:* 62.2% of total population (2022)
rate of urbanization: 0.65% annual rate of change (2020-25 est.)

Waste and recycling: *municipal solid waste generated annually:* 147,000 tons (2013 est.)
municipal solid waste recycled annually: 57,330 tons (2013 est.)
percent of municipal solid waste recycled: 39% (2013 est.)

GOVERNMENT

Country name: *conventional long form:* Overseas Lands of French Polynesia
conventional short form: French Polynesia
local long form: Pays d'outre-mer de la Polynesie Francaise
local short form: Polynesie Francaise
former: Establishments in Oceania, French Establishments in Oceania
etymology: the term "Polynesia" is an 18th-century construct composed of two Greek words, "poly" (many) and "nesoi" (islands), and refers to the more than 1,000 islands scattered over the central and southern Pacific Ocean

Government type: parliamentary democracy (Assembly of French Polynesia); an overseas collectivity of France

Dependency status: overseas country of France; note - overseas territory of France from 1946-2003; overseas collectivity of France since 2003, though it is often referred to as an overseas country due to its degree of autonomy

Capital: *name:* Papeete (located on Tahiti)
geographic coordinates: 17 32 S, 149 34 W

time difference: UTC-10 (5 hours behind Washington, DC, during Standard Time)
etymology: the name means "water basket" and refers to the fact that the islanders originally used calabashes enclosed in baskets to fetch water at a spring in the area

Administrative divisions: 5 administrative subdivisions (subdivisions administratives, singular - subdivision administrative): Iles Australes (Austral Islands), Iles du Vent (Windward Islands), Iles Marquises (Marquesas Islands), Iles Sous-le-Vent (Leeward Islands), Iles Tuamotu-Gambier; note - the Leeward Islands and the Windward Islands together make up the Society Islands (Iles de la Societe)

Independence: none (overseas land of France)

National holiday: Fete de la Federation, 14 July (1790); note - the local holiday is Internal Autonomy Day, 29 June (1880)

Constitution: *history:* 4 October 1958 (French Constitution)
amendments: French constitution amendment procedures apply

Legal system: the laws of France, where applicable, apply

Citizenship: see France

Suffrage: 18 years of age; universal

Executive branch: *chief of state:* President Emmanuel MACRON (since 14 May 2017), represented by High Commissioner of the Republic Dominique SORAIN (since 10 July 2019)
head of government: President of French Polynesia Edouard FRITCH (since 12 September 2014)
cabinet: Council of Ministers approved by the Assembly from a list of its members submitted by the president
elections/appointments: French president directly elected by absolute majority popular vote in 2 rounds if needed for a 5-year term (eligible for a second term); high commissioner appointed by the French president on the advice of the French Ministry of Interior; French Polynesia president indirectly elected by Assembly of French Polynesia for a 5-year term (no term limits)

Legislative branch: *description:* unicameral Assembly of French Polynesia or Assemblée de la Polynésie française (57 seats; elections held in 2 rounds; in the second round, 38 members directly elected in multi-seat constituencies by a closed-list proportional representation vote; the party receiving the most votes gets an additional 19 seats; members serve 5-year terms; French Polynesia indirectly elects 2 senators to the French Senate via an electoral college by absolute majority vote for 6-year terms with one-half the membership renewed every 3 years and directly elects 3 deputies to the French National Assembly by absolute majority vote in 2 rounds if needed for 5-year terms

French Polynesia indirectly elects 2 senators to the French Senate via an electoral college by absolute majority vote for 6-year terms with one-half the membership renewed every 3 years and directly elects 3 deputies to the French National Assembly by absolute majority vote in 2 rounds if needed for 5-year terms
elections: Assembly of French Polynesia - last held on 22 April 2018 and 6 May 2018 (next to be held in 2023) French Senate - last held on 28 September 2020 (next to be held on 30 September 2023)

French National Assembly - last held in 2 rounds on 12 and 19 June 2017 (next to be held in 2027)
election results: Assembly of French Polynesia - percent of vote by party - Tapura Huiraatira 45.1%, Popular Rally 29.3%, Tavini Huiraatira 25.6%; seats by party - Tapura Huiraatira 38, Popular Rally 11, Tavini Huiraatira 8; composition - men 27, women 30, percent of women 52.6%

French Senate - percent of vote by party - NA; seats by party - Popular Rally 1, People's Servant Party 1; composition - NA

French National Assembly - percent of vote by party - NA; seats by party - Tavini Huiraatura 3; composition - NA

Judicial branch: *highest court(s):* Court of Appeal or Cour d'Appel (composition NA); note - appeals beyond the French Polynesia Court of Appeal are heard by the Court of Cassation (in Paris)
judge selection and term of office: judges assigned from France normally for 3 years
subordinate courts: Court of the First Instance or Tribunal de Premiere Instance; Court of Administrative Law or Tribunal Administratif

Political parties and leaders: A Tia Porinetia [Teva ROHFRITSCH]
Alliance for a New Democracy or ADN (includes The New Star [Philip SCHYLE], This Country is Yours [Nicole BOUTEAU])
List of the People (Tapura Huiraatira) [Edouard FRITICH]
New Fatherland Party (Ai'a Api) [Emile VERNAUDON]
Our Home alliance
People's Servant Party (Tavini Huiraatira) [Oscar TEMARU]
Rally of the Maohi People (Amuitahira'a o te Nuna'a Maohi) [Gaston FLOSSE] (formerly known as Popular Rally (Tahoeraa Huiraatira))
Union for Democracy alliance or UPD [Oscar TEMARU]

International organization participation: ITUC (NGOs), PIF (associate member), SPC, UPU, WMO

Diplomatic representation in the US: none (overseas lands of France)

Diplomatic representation from the US: *embassy:* none (overseas lands of France)

Flag description: *two red horizontal bands encase a wide white band in a 1:2:*1 ratio; centered on the white band is a disk with a blue and white wave pattern depicting the sea on the lower half and a gold and white ray pattern depicting the sun on the upper half; a Polynesian canoe rides on the wave pattern; the canoe has a crew of five represented by five stars that symbolize the five island groups; red and white are traditional Polynesian colors
note: identical to the red-white-red flag of Tahiti, the largest and most populous of the islands in French Polynesia, but which has no emblem in the white band; the flag of France is used for official occasions

National symbol(s): outrigger canoe, Tahitian gardenia (Gardenia taitensis) flower; national colors: red, white

National anthem: *name:* "Ia Ora 'O Tahiti Nui" (Long Live Tahiti Nui)
lyrics/music: Maeva BOUGES, Irmine TEHEI, Angele TEROROTUA, Johanna NOUVEAU, Patrick AMARU, Louis MAMATUI, and Jean-Pierre CELESTIN (the compositional group created both the lyrics and music)
note: adopted 1993; serves as a local anthem; as a territory of France, "La Marseillaise" is official (see France)

National heritage: *total World Heritage Sites:* 1 (cultural); note - excerpted from the France entry
selected World Heritage Site locales: Taputapuātea

Government - note: under certain acts of France, French Polynesia has acquired autonomy in all areas except those relating to police, monetary policy, tertiary education, immigration, and defense and foreign affairs; the duties of its president are fashioned after those of the French prime minister

ECONOMY

Economic overview: Since 1962, when France stationed military personnel in the region, French Polynesia has changed from a subsistence agricultural economy to one in which a high proportion of the work force is either employed by the military or supports the tourist industry. With the halt of French nuclear testing in 1996, the military contribution to the economy fell sharply.

After growing at an average yearly rate of 4.2% from 1997-2007, the economic and financial crisis in 2008 marked French Polynesia's entry into recession. However, since 2014, French Polynesia has shown signs of recovery. Business turnover reached 1.8% year-on-year in September 2016, tourism increased 1.8% in 2015, and GDP grew 2.0% in 2015.

French Polynesia's tourism-dominated service sector accounted for 85% of total value added for the economy in 2012. Tourism employs 17% of the workforce. Pearl farming is the second biggest industry, accounting for 54% of exports in 2015; however, the output has decreased to 12.5 tons – the lowest level since 2008. A small manufacturing sector predominantly processes commodities from French Polynesia's primary sector - 8% of total economy in 2012 - including agriculture and fishing.

France has agreed to finance infrastructure, marine businesses, and cultural and ecological sites at roughly $80 million per year between 2015 and 2020. Japan, the US, and China are French Polynesia's three largest trade partners.

Real GDP (purchasing power parity): $5.49 billion (2017 est.)
$5.383 billion (2016 est.)
$6.963 billion (2015 est.)
country comparison to the world: 173

Real GDP growth rate: 2% (2015 est.)
-2.7% (2014 est.)
-2.5% (2010 est.)
country comparison to the world: 135

Real GDP per capita: $17,000 (2015 est.)
$20,100 (2014 est.)
$22,700 (2010)
country comparison to the world: 100

GDP (official exchange rate): $4.795 billion (2015 est.)

Inflation rate (consumer prices): 0% (2015 est.)
0.3% (2014 est.)
country comparison to the world: 20

GDP - composition, by sector of origin: *agriculture:* 2.5% (2009)
industry: 13% (2009)
services: 84.5% (2009)

GDP - composition, by end use: *household consumption:* 66.9% (2014 est.)
government consumption: 33.6% (2014 est.)
investment in fixed capital: 19.4% (2014 est.)
investment in inventories: 0.1% (2014 est.)
exports of goods and services: 17.5% (2014 est.)
imports of goods and services: -37.5% (2014 est.)

Agricultural products: coconuts, fruit, roots/tubers nes, pineapples, cassava, sugar cane, eggs, tropical fruit, tomatoes

Industries: tourism, pearls, agricultural processing, handicrafts, phosphates

Labor force: 126,300 (2016 est.)
country comparison to the world: 178

Labor force - by occupation: *agriculture:* 13%
industry: 19%
services: 68% (2013 est.)

Unemployment rate: 21.8% (2012)
11.7% (2010)
country comparison to the world: 192

Unemployment, youth ages 15-24: *total:* 56.7%
male: 54.5%
female: 59.7% (2012 est.)
country comparison to the world: 3

Population below poverty line: 19.7% (2009 est.)

Budget: *revenues:* 1.891 billion (2012)
expenditures: 1.833 billion (2011)

Budget surplus (+) or deficit (-): 1.2% (of GDP) (2012)
country comparison to the world: 28

Taxes and other revenues: 39.4% (of GDP) (2012)
country comparison to the world: 46

Fiscal year: calendar year

Current account balance: $207.7 million (2014 est.)
$158.8 million (2013 est.)
country comparison to the world: 57

Exports: $1.245 billion (2014 est.)
$1.168 billion (2013 est.)
country comparison to the world: 168

Exports - partners: Japan 23.1%, Hong Kong 21.5%, Kyrgyzstan 15.9%, US 15.9%, France 12.4% (2017)

Exports - commodities: cultured pearls, coconut products, mother-of-pearl, vanilla, shark meat

Imports: $2.235 billion (2014 est.)
$2.271 billion (2013 est.)
country comparison to the world: 170

Imports - partners: France 27.9%, South Korea 12.1%, US 10.1%, China 7.3%, NZ 6.7%, Singapore 4.2% (2017)

Imports - commodities: fuels, foodstuffs, machinery and equipment

Exchange rates: Comptoirs Francais du Pacifique francs (XPF) per US dollar -
110.2 (2017 est.)
107.84 (2016 est.)
107.84 (2015 est.)
89.85 (2014 est.)
90.56 (2013 est.)

ENERGY

Electricity access: *electrification - total population:* 100% (2020)

Electricity: *installed generating capacity:* 272,000 kW (2020 est.)
consumption: 639.7 million kWh (2019 est.)
exports: 0 kWh (2019 est.)
imports: 0 kWh (2019 est.)
transmission/distribution losses: 41 million kWh (2019 est.)

Electricity generation sources: *fossil fuels:* 66.5% of total installed capacity (2020 est.)
solar: 6.1% of total installed capacity (2020 est.)
hydroelectricity: 27.4% of total installed capacity (2020 est.)

Petroleum: *total petroleum production:* 0 bbl/day (2021 est.)
refined petroleum consumption: 6,700 bbl/day (2019 est.)

Refined petroleum products - imports: 6,785 bbl/day (2015 est.)
country comparison to the world: 160

Carbon dioxide emissions: 1.03 million metric tonnes of CO_2 (2019 est.)
from petroleum and other liquids: 1.03 million metric tonnes of CO_2 (2019 est.)
country comparison to the world: 172

Energy consumption per capita: 0 Btu/person (2019 est.)
country comparison to the world: 200

COMMUNICATIONS

Telephones - fixed lines: *total subscriptions:* 94,000 (2020 est.)
subscriptions per 100 inhabitants: 33 (2020 est.)
country comparison to the world: 138

Telephones - mobile cellular: *total subscriptions:* 335,000 (2020 est.)
subscriptions per 100 inhabitants: 119 (2020 est.)
country comparison to the world: 178

Telecommunication systems: *general assessment:* French Polynesia has one of the most advanced telecoms infrastructures in the Pacific Islands region; the remoteness of the country with its scattering of 130 islands and atolls has made connectivity vital for its inhabitants; the first submarine cable was deployed in 2010 and since then additional cables have been connected to the islands, vastly improving French Polynesia's international connectivity; an additional domestic submarine cable, the Natitua Sud, will connect more remote islands by the end of 2022; French Polynesia is also a hub for satellite communications in the region; a considerable number of consumers access FttP-based services; with the first data center in French Polynesia on the cards, the quality and price of broadband services is expected to improve as content will be able to be cached locally, reducing costs for consumers; for 2022, fixed broadband subscriptions reached an estimated 22%; about 43% of the country's mobile connections are on 3G networks, while LTE accounts for 12%; by 2025, LTE is expected to account for more than half of all connections; it is also estimated that 77% of mobile subscribers will have smart phones by 2025 (2022)
domestic: fixed-line subscriptions nearly 33 per 100 persons and mobile-cellular density is roughly 119 per 100 persons (2020)
international: country code - 689; landing points for the NATITUA, Manatua, and Honotua submarine cables to other French Polynesian Islands, Cook Islands, Niue, Samoa and US; satellite earth station - 1 Intelsat (Pacific Ocean) (2019)

Broadcast media: French public overseas broadcaster Reseau Outre-Mer provides 2 TV channels and 1 radio station; 1 government-owned TV station; a small number of privately owned radio stations (2019)

Internet country code: .pf

Internet users: *total:* 203,878 (2019 est.)
percent of population: 73% (2019 est.)
country comparison to the world: 175

Broadband - fixed subscriptions: *total:* 64,000 (2020 est.)
subscriptions per 100 inhabitants: 23 (2020 est.)
country comparison to the world: 138

TRANSPORTATION

National air transport system: *number of registered air carriers:* 2 (2020) (registered in France)
inventory of registered aircraft operated by air carriers: 19 (registered in France)

Civil aircraft registration country code prefix: F-OH

Airports: *total:* 54 (2021)
country comparison to the world: 86

Airports - with paved runways: *total:* 45
over 3,047 m: 2
1,524 to 2,437 m: 5
914 to 1,523 m: 33
under 914 m: 5 (2021)

Airports - with unpaved runways: *total:* 9
914 to 1,523 m: 4
under 914 m: 5 (2021)

Heliports: 1 (2021)

Roadways: *total:* 2,590 km (1999)
paved: 1,735 km (1999)
unpaved: 855 km (1999)
country comparison to the world: 168

Merchant marine: *total:* 24
by type: general cargo 14, other 10 (2021)
country comparison to the world: 142

Ports and terminals: *major seaport(s):* Papeete

MILITARY AND SECURITY

Military and security forces: no regular military forces

Military - note: defense is the responsibility of France; France maintains forces (about 900 troops) in French Polynesia

TRANSNATIONAL ISSUES

Disputes - international: none

FRENCH SOUTHERN AND ANTARCTIC LANDS

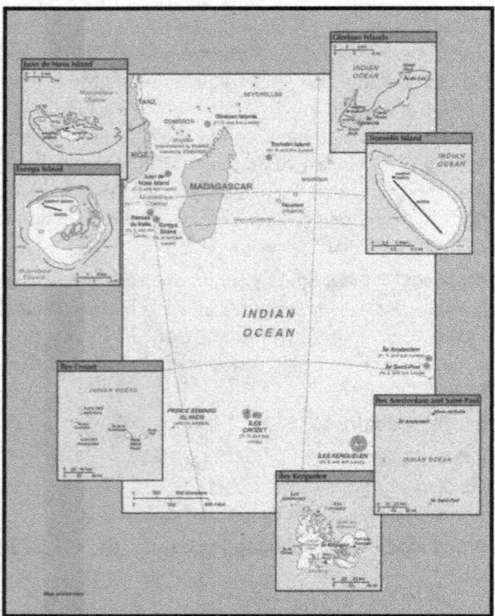

INTRODUCTION

Background: In February 2007, the Iles Eparses became an integral part of the French Southern and Antarctic Lands (TAAF). The Southern Lands are now divided into five administrative districts, two of which are archipelagos, Iles Crozet and Iles Kerguelen; the third is a district composed of two volcanic islands, Ile Saint-Paul and Ile Amsterdam; the fourth, Iles Eparses, consists of five scattered tropical islands around Madagascar. They contain no permanent inhabitants and are visited only by researchers studying the native fauna, scientists at the various scientific stations, fishermen, and military personnel. The fifth district is the Antarctic portion, which consists of "Adelie Land," a thin slice of the Antarctic continent discovered and claimed by the French in 1840.

Ile Amsterdam: Discovered but not named in 1522 by the Spanish, the island subsequently received the appellation of Nieuw Amsterdam from a Dutchman; it was claimed by France in 1843. A short-lived attempt at cattle farming began in 1871. A French meteorological station established on the island in 1949 is still in use.

Ile Saint Paul: Claimed by France since 1893, the island was a fishing industry center from 1843 to 1914. In 1928, a spiny lobster cannery was established, but when the company went bankrupt in 1931, seven workers were abandoned. Only two survived until 1934 when rescue finally arrived.

Iles Crozet: A large archipelago formed from the Crozet Plateau, Iles Crozet is divided into two main groups: L'Occidental (the West), which includes Ile aux Cochons, Ilots des Apotres, Ile des Pingouins, and the reefs Brisants de l'Heroine; and L'Oriental (the East), which includes Ile d'Est and Ile de la Possession (the largest island of the Crozets). Discovered and claimed by France in 1772, the islands were used for seal hunting and as a base for whaling. Originally administered as a dependency of Madagascar, they became part of the TAAF in 1955.

Iles Kerguelen: This island group, discovered in 1772, consists of one large island (Ile Kerguelen) and about 300 smaller islands. A permanent group of 50 to 100 scientists resides at the main base at Port-aux-Francais.

Adelie Land: The only non-insular district of the TAAF is the Antarctic claim known as "Adelie Land." The US Government does not recognize it as a French dependency.

Bassas da India: A French possession since 1897, this atoll is a volcanic rock surrounded by reefs and is awash at high tide.

Europa Island: This heavily wooded island has been a French possession since 1897; it is the site of a small military garrison that staffs a weather station.

Glorioso Islands: A French possession since 1892, the Glorioso Islands are composed of two lushly vegetated coral islands (Ile Glorieuse and Ile du Lys) and three rock islets. A military garrison operates a weather and radio station on Ile Glorieuse.

Juan de Nova Island: Named after a famous 15th-century Spanish navigator and explorer, the island has been a French possession since 1897. It has been exploited for its guano and phosphate. Presently a small military garrison oversees a meteorological station.

Tromelin Island: First explored by the French in 1776, the island came under the jurisdiction of Reunion in 1814. At present, it serves as a sea turtle sanctuary and is the site of an important meteorological station.

GEOGRAPHY

Location: southeast and east of Africa, islands in the southern Indian Ocean, some near Madagascar and others about equidistant between Africa, Antarctica, and Australia; note - French Southern and Antarctic Lands include Ile Amsterdam, Ile Saint- Paul, Iles Crozet, Iles Kerguelen, Bassas da India, Europa Island, Glorioso Islands, Juan de Nova Island, and Tromelin Island in the southern Indian Ocean, along with the French-claimed sector of Antarctica, "Adelie Land"; the US does not recognize the French claim to "Adelie Land"

Geographic coordinates:

Ile Amsterdam (Ile Amsterdam et Ile Saint-Paul): 37 50 S, 77 32 E;

Ile Saint-Paul (Ile Amsterdam et Ile Saint-Paul): 38 72 S, 77 53 E;

Iles Crozet: 46 25 S, 51 00 E;

Iles Kerguelen: 49 15 S, 69 35 E;

Bassas da India (Iles Eparses): 21 30 S, 39 50 E;

Europa Island (Iles Eparses): 22 20 S, 40 22 E;

Glorioso Islands (Iles Eparses): 11 30 S, 47 20 E;

Juan de Nova Island (Iles Eparses): 17 03 S, 42 45 E;

Tromelin Island (Iles Eparses): 15 52 S, 54 25 E

Map references: Antarctic RegionAfrica

Area:

Ile Amsterdam (Ile Amsterdam et Ile Saint-Paul): total - 55 sq km; land - 55 sq km; water - 0 sq km

Ile Saint-Paul (Ile Amsterdam et Ile Saint-Paul): total - 7 sq km; land - 7 sq km; water - 0 sq km

Iles Crozet: total - 352 sq km; land - 352 sq km; water - 0 sq km

Iles Kerguelen: total - 7,215 sq km; land - 7,215 sq km; water - 0 sq km

Bassas da India (Iles Eparses): total - 80 sq km; land - 0.2 sq km; water - 79.8 sq km (lagoon)

Europa Island (Iles Eparses): total - 28 sq km; land - 28 sq km; water - 0 sq km

Glorioso Islands (Iles Eparses): total - 5 sq km; land - 5 sq km; water - 0 sq km

Juan de Nova Island (Iles Eparses): total - 4.4 sq km; land - 4.4 sq km; water - 0 sq km

Tromelin Island (Iles Eparses): total - 1 sq km; land - 1 sq km; water - 0 sq km
note: excludes "Adelie Land" claim of about 500,000 sq km in Antarctica that is not recognized by the US

Area - comparative:

Ile Amsterdam (Ile Amsterdam et Ile Saint-Paul): less than one-half the size of Washington, DC;

Ile Saint-Paul (Ile Amsterdam et Ile Saint-Paul): more than 10 times the size of the National Mall in Washington, DC;

Iles Crozet: about twice the size of Washington, DC;

Iles Kerguelen: slightly larger than Delaware;

Bassas da India (Iles Eparses): land area about one-third the size of the National Mall in Washington, DC;

Europa Island (Iles Eparses): about one-sixth the size of Washington, DC;

Glorioso Islands (Iles Eparses): about eight times the size of the National Mall in Washington, DC;

Juan de Nova Island (Iles Eparses): about seven times the size of the National Mall in Washington, DC;

Tromelin Island (Iles Eparses): about 1.7 times the size of the National Mall in Washington, DC

Land boundaries: *total:* 0 km

Coastline:

Ile Amsterdam (Ile Amsterdam et Ile Saint-Paul): 28 km

Ile Saint-Paul (Ile Amsterdam et Ile Saint-Paul):

Iles Kerguelen: 2,800 km

Bassas da India (Iles Eparses): 35.2 km

Europa Island (Iles Eparses): 22.2 km

Glorioso Islands (Iles Eparses): 35.2 km

Juan de Nova Island (Iles Eparses): 24.1 km

Tromelin Island (Iles Eparses): 3.7 km

Maritime claims: *territorial sea:* 12 nm
exclusive economic zone: 200 nm from Iles Kerguelen and Iles Eparses (does not include the rest of French Southern and Antarctic Lands); Juan de Nova Island and Tromelin Island claim a continental shelf of 200-m depth or to the depth of exploitation

Climate:

Ile Amsterdam et Ile Saint-Paul: oceanic with persistent westerly winds and high humidity;

Iles Crozet: windy, cold, wet, and cloudy;

Iles Kerguelen: oceanic, cold, overcast, windy;

Iles Eparses: tropical

Terrain:

Ile Amsterdam (Ile Amsterdam et Ile Saint-Paul): a volcanic island with steep coastal cliffs; the center floor of the volcano is a large plateau;

Ile Saint-Paul (Ile Amsterdam et Ile Saint-Paul): triangular in shape, the island is the top of a volcano, rocky with steep cliffs on the eastern side; has active thermal springs;

Iles Crozet: a large archipelago formed from the Crozet Plateau is divided into two groups of islands;

Iles Kerguelen: the interior of the large island of Ile Kerguelen is composed of high mountains, hills, valleys, and plains with peninsulas stretching off its coasts;

Bassas da India (Iles Eparses): atoll, awash at high tide; shallow (15 m) lagoon;

Europa Island, Glorioso Islands, Juan de Nova Island: low, flat, and sandy;

Tromelin Island (Iles Eparses): low, flat, sandy; likely volcanic seamount

Elevation: *highest point:* Mont de la Dives on Ile Amsterdam (Ile Amsterdam et Ile Saint-Paul) 867 m
lowest point: Indian Ocean 0 m
highest points throughout the French Southern and Antarctic Lands: unnamed location on Ile Saint-Paul (Ile Amsterdam et Ile Saint-Paul) 272 m; Pic Marion-Dufresne in Iles Crozet 1090 m; Mont Ross in Iles Kerguelen 1850 m; unnamed location on Bassas de India (Iles Eparses) 2.4 m;24 unnamed location on Europa Island (Iles Eparses) 24 m; unnamed location on Glorioso Islands (Iles Eparses) 12 m; unnamed location on Juan de Nova Island (Iles Eparses) 10 m; unnamed location on Tromelin Island (Iles Eparses) 7 m

Natural resources: fish, crayfish, note, Glorioso Islands and Tromelin Island (Iles Eparses) have guano, phosphates, and coconuts
note: in the 1950's and 1960's, several species of trout were introduced to Iles Kerguelen of which two, Brown trout and Brook trout, survived to establish wild populations; reindeer were also introduced to Iles Kerguelen in 1956 as a source of fresh meat for whaling crews, the herd today, one of two in the Southern Hemisphere, is estimated to number around 4,000

Natural hazards: Ile Amsterdam and Ile Saint-Paul are inactive volcanoes; Iles Eparses subject to periodic cyclones; Bassas da India is a maritime hazard since it is under water for a period of three hours prior to and following the high tide and surrounded by reefs
volcanism: Reunion Island - Piton de la Fournaise (2,632 m), which has erupted many times in recent years including 2010, 2015, and 2017, is one of the world's most active volcanoes; although rare, eruptions outside the volcano's caldera could threaten nearby cities

Geography - note: islands' component is widely scattered across remote locations in the southern Indian Ocean

Bassas da India (Iles Eparses): atoll is a circular reef atop a long-extinct, submerged volcano;

Europa Island and Juan de Nova Island (Iles Eparses): wildlife sanctuary for seabirds and sea turtles;

Glorioso Island (Iles Eparses): islands and rocks are surrounded by an extensive reef system;

Tromelin Island (Iles Eparses): climatologically important location for forecasting cyclones in the western Indian Ocean; wildlife sanctuary (seabirds, tortoises)

PEOPLE AND SOCIETY

Population: no indigenous inhabitants

Ile Amsterdam (Ile Amsterdam et Ile Saint-Paul): uninhabited but has a meteorological station

Ile Saint-Paul (Ile Amsterdam et Ile Saint-Paul): uninhabited but is frequently visited by fishermen and has a scientific research cabin for short stays

Iles Crozet: uninhabited except for 18 to 30 people staffing the Alfred Faure research station on Ile del la Possession

Iles Kerguelen: 50 to 100 scientists are located at the main base at Port-aux-Francais on Ile Kerguelen

Bassas da India (Iles Eparses): uninhabitable

Europa Island, Glorioso Islands, Juan de Nova Island (Iles Eparses): a small French military garrison and a few meteorologists on each possession; visited by scientists

Tromelin Island (Iles Eparses): uninhabited, except for visits by scientists

ENVIRONMENT

Environment - current issues: introduction of foreign species on Iles Crozet has caused severe damage to the original ecosystem; overfishing of Patagonian toothfish around Iles Crozet and Iles Kerguelen

Climate:

Ile Amsterdam et Ile Saint-Paul: oceanic with persistent westerly winds and high humidity;

Iles Crozet: windy, cold, wet, and cloudy;

Iles Kerguelen: oceanic, cold, overcast, windy;

Iles Eparses: tropical

GOVERNMENT

Country name: *conventional long form:* Territory of the French Southern and Antarctic Lands
conventional short form: French Southern and Antarctic Lands
local long form: Territoire des Terres Australes et Antarctiques Francaises
local short form: Terres Australes et Antarctiques Francaises
abbreviation: TAAF
etymology: self-descriptive name specifying the territories' affiliation and location in the Southern Hemisphere

Dependency status: overseas territory of France since 1955

Administrative divisions: none (overseas territory of France); there are no first-order administrative divisions as defined by the US Government, but there are 5 administrative districts named Iles Crozet, Iles Eparses, Iles Kerguelen, Ile Saint-Paul et Ile Amsterdam; the fifth district is the "Adelie Land" claim in Antarctica that is not recognized by the US

Legal system: the laws of France, where applicable, apply

Citizenship: see France

Executive branch: *chief of state:* President Emmanuel MACRON (since 14 May 2017), represented by Prefect Florence JEANBLANC- RISLER (since 5 October 2022)

International organization participation: UPU

Diplomatic representation in the US: none (overseas territory of France)

Diplomatic representation from the US: *embassy:* none (overseas territory of France)

Flag description: the flag of France is used

National anthem: *note:* as a territory of France, "La Marseillaise" is official (see France)

ECONOMY

Economic overview: Economic activity is limited to servicing meteorological and geophysical research stations, military bases, and French and other fishing fleets. The fish catches landed on Iles Kerguelen by foreign ships are exported to France and Reunion.

COMMUNICATIONS

Internet country code: .tf

Communications - note: has one or more meteorological stations on each possession

TRANSPORTATION

Airports: *total:* 4 (2021)
country comparison to the world: 186

Airports - with unpaved runways: *total:* 4
914 to 1,523 m: 4 (2022)

Note: 1 - Europa Island, 1 - Glorioso Islands, 1 - Juan de Nova Island, 1 - Tromelin Island

Heliports: 3 (2022)

Note: 1 - Ile Amsterdam, 1 - Ile Kerguelen, 1 - Ile de la Possession

Merchant marine: *total:* 2
by type: other 2 (2021)
country comparison to the world: 176

Ports and terminals: none; offshore anchorage only

MILITARY AND SECURITY

Military - note: defense is the responsibility of France; French forces on Mayotte, the Détachement de Légion Étrangère de Mayotte (DLEM), regularly deploys small elements for periodic rotations to Europa Island, Glorioso Islands, Juan de Nova Island, and Tromelin Island

TRANSNATIONAL ISSUES

Disputes - international: French claim to "Adelie Land" in Antarctica is not recognized by the US;

Bassas da India, Europa Island, Glorioso Islands, Juan de Nova Island (Iles Eparses): ; claimed by Madagascar; the vegetated drying cays of Banc du Geyser, which were claimed by Madagascar in 1976, also fall within the EEZ claims of the Comoros and France (Glorioso Islands); ;

Tromelin Island (Iles Eparses):; claimed by Mauritius

G

GABON

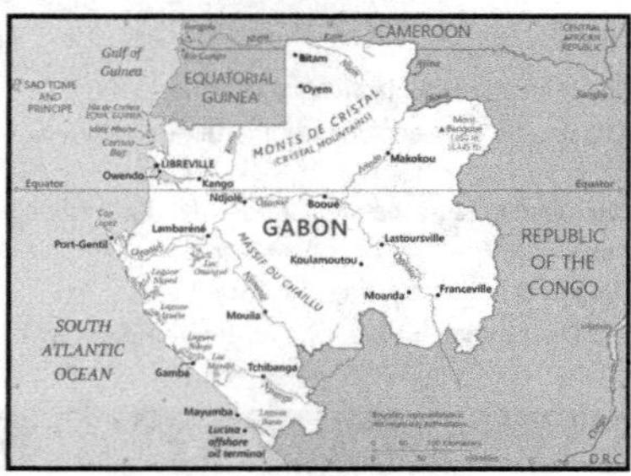

INTRODUCTION

Background: Gabon, a sparsely populated country known for its dense rainforests and vast petroleum reserves, is one of the most prosperous and stable countries in central Africa. Approximately 40 ethnic groups are represented, the largest of which is the Fang, a group that covers the northern third of Gabon and expands north into Equatorial Guinea and Cameroon. From about the early 1300s, various kingdoms emerged in and surrounding present-day Gabon, including the Kingdoms of Loango and Orungu. Because most early Bantu languages spoken in these kingdoms did not have a written form, historical traditions were passed on orally, resulting in much of Gabon's early history being lost over time. Portuguese traders who arrived in the mid-1400s gave the area its name of Gabon. At that time, indigenous trade networks began to engage with European traders, exchanging goods such as ivory and wood. For a century beginning in the 1760s, trade came to focus mostly on enslaved people. While many groups in Gabon participated in the slave trade, the Fang were a notable exception. As the slave trade declined in the late 1800s, France colonized the country and directed a widespread extraction of Gabonese resources. Anti-colonial rhetoric by Gabon's educated elites increased significantly in the early 1900s, but no widespread rebellion materialized. French decolonization following World War II led to the country's independence in 1960.

Within a year of independence, the government changed from a parliamentary to a presidential system, and Leon M'BA won the first presidential election in 1961. El Hadj Omar BONGO Ondimba - one of the longest ruling heads of state in history - was M'BA's vice president and assumed the presidency after M'BA's death in 1967. BONGO went on to dominate the country's political scene for four decades (1967-2009). In 1968, he declared Gabon a single-party state and created the Parti Democratique Gabonais (PDG), which remains the predominant party in Gabonese politics today. In the early 1990s, he reintroduced a multiparty system under a new constitution after he was confronted with growing political opposition. He was reelected by wide margins in 1995, 1998, 2002, and 2005 against a divided opposition and amidst allegations of fraud. Following President BONGO's death in 2009, a new election brought his son, Ali BONGO Ondimba, to power. President Ali BONGO Ondimba was reelected in 2016 in a close election against a united opposition. Gabon's Constitutional Court reviewed the contested election results and ruled in his favor.

GEOGRAPHY

Location: Central Africa, bordering the Atlantic Ocean at the Equator, between Republic of the Congo and Equatorial Guinea

Geographic coordinates: 1 00 S, 11 45 E

Map references: Africa

Area: *total:* 267,667 sq km
land: 257,667 sq km
water: 10,000 sq km
country comparison to the world: 78

Area - comparative: slightly smaller than Colorado

Land boundaries: *total:* 3,261 km
border countries (3): Cameroon 349 km; Republic of the Congo 2,567 km; Equatorial Guinea 345 km

Coastline: 885 km

Maritime claims: *territorial sea:* 12 nm
contiguous zone: 24 nm
exclusive economic zone: 200 nm

Climate: tropical; always hot, humid

Terrain: narrow coastal plain; hilly interior; savanna in east and south

Elevation: *highest point:* Mont Bengoue 1,050 m
lowest point: Atlantic Ocean 0 m
mean elevation: 377 m

Natural resources: petroleum, natural gas, diamond, niobium, manganese, uranium, gold, timber, iron ore, hydropower

Land use: *agricultural land:* 19% (2018 est.)
arable land: 1.2% (2018 est.)
permanent crops: 0.6% (2018 est.)
permanent pasture: 17.2% (2018 est.)
forest: 81% (2018 est.)
other: 0% (2018 est.)

Irrigated land: 40 sq km (2012)

Major watersheds (area sq km): Atlantic Ocean drainage: Congo (3,730,881 sq km)

Major aquifers: Congo Basin

Population distribution: the relatively small population is spread in pockets throughout the country; the largest urban center is the capital of Libreville, located along the Atlantic coast in the northwest as shown in this population distribution map

Natural hazards: none

Geography - note: a small population and oil and mineral reserves have helped Gabon become one of Africa's wealthier countries; in general, these circumstances have allowed the country to maintain and conserve its pristine rain forest and rich biodiversity

PEOPLE AND SOCIETY

Population: 2,340,613 (2022 est.)
country comparison to the world: 146

Nationality: *noun:* Gabonese (singular and plural)
adjective: Gabonese

Ethnic groups: Gabonese-born 80.1% (includes Fang 23.2%, Shira-Punu/Vili 18.9%, Nzabi-Duma 11.3%, Mbede-Teke 6.9%, Myene 5%, Kota-Kele 4.9%, Okande-Tsogo 2.1%, Pygmy .3%, other 7.5%), Cameroonian 4.6%, Malian 2.4%, Beninese 2.1%, acquired Gabonese nationality 1.6%, Togolese 1.6%, Senegalese 1.1%, Congolese (Brazzaville) 1%, other 5.5% (includes Congolese (Kinshasa), Equatorial Guinean, Nigerian) (2012 est.)

Languages: French (official), Fang, Myene, Nzebi, Bapounou/Eschira, Bandjabi

Religions: Roman Catholic 42.3%, Protestant 12.3%, other Christian 27.4%, Muslim 9.8%, animist 0.6%, other 0.5%, none/no answer 7.1% (2012 est.)

Demographic profile: Gabon's oil revenues have given it one of the highest per capita income levels in Sub-Saharan Africa, but the wealth is not evenly distributed and poverty is widespread. Unemployment is especially prevalent among the large youth population; more than 60% of the population is under the age of 25. With a fertility rate still averaging more than 4 children per woman, the youth population will continue to grow and further strain the mismatch between Gabon's supply of jobs and the skills of its labor force.

Gabon has been a magnet to migrants from neighboring countries since the 1960s because of the discovery of oil, as well as the country's political stability and timber, mineral, and natural gas resources. Nonetheless, income inequality and high unemployment have created slums in Libreville full of migrant workers from Senegal, Nigeria, Cameroon, Benin, Togo, and elsewhere in West Africa. In 2011, Gabon declared an end to refugee status for 9,500 remaining Congolese nationals to whom it had granted asylum during the Republic of the Congo's civil war between 1997 and 2003. About 5,400 of these refugees received permits to reside in Gabon.

Age structure: *0-14 years:* 36.45% (male 413,883/female 399,374)
15-24 years: 21.9% (male 254,749/female 233,770)
25-54 years: 32.48% (male 386,903/female 337,776)
55-64 years: 5.19% (male 58,861/female 56,843)
65 years and over: 3.98% (male 44,368/female 44,381) (2020 est.)

Dependency ratios: *total dependency ratio:* 68.9
youth dependency ratio: 62.9
elderly dependency ratio: 6
potential support ratio: 16.8 (2020 est.)

Median age: *total:* 21 years
male: 21.4 years
female: 20.6 years (2020 est.)
country comparison to the world: 186

Population growth rate: 2.4% (2022 est.)
country comparison to the world: 28

Birth rate: 26.03 births/1,000 population (2022 est.)
country comparison to the world: 44

Death rate: 5.67 deaths/1,000 population (2022 est.)
country comparison to the world: 175

Net migration rate: 3.67 migrant(s)/1,000 population (2022 est.)
country comparison to the world: 31

Population distribution: the relatively small population is spread in pockets throughout the country; the largest urban center is the capital of Libreville, located along the Atlantic coast in the northwest as shown in this population distribution map

Urbanization: *urban population:* 90.7% of total population (2022)

rate of urbanization: 2.27% annual rate of change (2020-25 est.)

Major urban areas - population: 857,000 LIBREVILLE (capital) (2022)

Sex ratio: *at birth:* 1.03 male(s)/female
0-14 years: 1.03 male(s)/female
15-24 years: 1.08 male(s)/female
25-54 years: 1.12 male(s)/female
55-64 years: 1 male(s)/female
65 years and over: 0.78 male(s)/female
total population: 1.08 male(s)/female (2022 est.)

Mother's mean age at first birth: 19.6 years (2012 est.)
note: data represents median age at first birth among women 20-49

Maternal mortality ratio: 252 deaths/100,000 live births (2017 est.)
country comparison to the world: 41

Infant mortality rate: *total:* 28.56 deaths/1,000 live births
male: 31.58 deaths/1,000 live births
female: 25.46 deaths/1,000 live births (2022 est.)
country comparison to the world: 57

Life expectancy at birth: *total population:* 69.7 years
male: 67.98 years
female: 71.48 years (2022 est.)
country comparison to the world: 174

Total fertility rate: 3.31 children born/woman (2022 est.)
country comparison to the world: 43

Contraceptive prevalence rate: 31.1% (2012)

Drinking water source: *improved: urban:* 97.2% of population
rural: 55.3% of population
total: 93.1% of population
unimproved: urban: 2.8% of population
rural: 44.7% of population
total: 6.9% of population (2020 est.)

Current health expenditure: 2.8% of GDP (2019)

Physicians density: 0.65 physicians/1,000 population (2018)

Hospital bed density: 6.3 beds/1,000 population

Sanitation facility access: *improved: urban:* 81.3% of population
rural: 55.1% of population
total: 78.7% of population
unimproved: urban: 18.7% of population
rural: 44.9% of population
total: 21.3% of population (2020 est.)

HIV/AIDS - adult prevalence rate: 3% (2020 est.)
country comparison to the world: 16

Major infectious diseases: *degree of risk:* very high (2020)
food or waterborne diseases: bacterial diarrhea, hepatitis A, and typhoid fever
vectorborne diseases: malaria and dengue fever
water contact diseases: schistosomiasis
animal contact diseases: rabies

Obesity - adult prevalence rate: 15% (2016)
country comparison to the world: 127

Alcohol consumption per capita: *total:* 6.47 liters of pure alcohol (2019 est.)
beer: 5.31 liters of pure alcohol (2019 est.)
wine: 0.62 liters of pure alcohol (2019 est.)
spirits: 0.5 liters of pure alcohol (2019 est.)
other alcohols: 0.04 liters of pure alcohol (2019 est.)
country comparison to the world: 64

Children under the age of 5 years underweight: 6.4% (2012)
country comparison to the world: 71

Education expenditures: 2.8% of GDP (2019 est.)
country comparison to the world: 160

Literacy: *definition:* age 15 and over can read and write
total population: 84.7%
male: 85.9%
female: 83.4% (2018)

ENVIRONMENT

Environment - current issues: deforestation (the forests that cover three-quarters of the country are threatened by excessive logging); burgeoning population exacerbating disposal of solid waste; oil industry contributing to water pollution; wildlife poaching

Environment - international agreements: *party to:* Biodiversity, Climate Change, Climate Change-Kyoto Protocol, Climate Change-Paris Agreement, Comprehensive Nuclear Test Ban, Desertification, Endangered Species, Hazardous Wastes, Law of the Sea, Marine Dumping-London Convention, Nuclear Test Ban, Ozone Layer Protection, Ship Pollution, Tropical Timber 2006, Wetlands, Whaling
signed, but not ratified: none of the selected agreements

Air pollutants: *particulate matter emissions:* 38.51 micrograms per cubic meter (2016 est.)
carbon dioxide emissions: 5.32 megatons (2016 est.)
methane emissions: 1.13 megatons (2020 est.)

Climate: tropical; always hot, humid

Land use: *agricultural land:* 19% (2018 est.)
arable land: 1.2% (2018 est.)
permanent crops: 0.6% (2018 est.)
permanent pasture: 17.2% (2018 est.)
forest: 81% (2018 est.)
other: 0% (2018 est.)

Urbanization: *urban population:* 90.7% of total population (2022)
rate of urbanization: 2.27% annual rate of change (2020-25 est.)

Revenue from forest resources: *forest revenues:* 2.6% of GDP (2018 est.)
country comparison to the world: 26

Revenue from coal: *coal revenues:* 0% of GDP (2018 est.)
country comparison to the world: 100

Waste and recycling: *municipal solid waste generated annually:* 238,102 tons (1995 est.)

Major watersheds (area sq km): Atlantic Ocean drainage: Congo (3,730,881 sq km)

Major aquifers: Congo Basin

Total water withdrawal: *municipal:* 84.7 million cubic meters (2017 est.)
industrial: 14.1 million cubic meters (2017 est.)
agricultural: 40.3 million cubic meters (2017 est.)

Total renewable water resources: 166 billion cubic meters (2017 est.)

GOVERNMENT

Country name: *conventional long form:* Gabonese Republic
conventional short form: Gabon
local long form: Republique Gabonaise
local short form: Gabon
etymology: name originates from the Portuguese word "gabao" meaning "cloak," which is roughly the shape that the early explorers gave to the estuary of the Komo River by the capital of Libreville

Government type: presidential republic

Capital: *name:* Libreville
Geographic coordinates: 0 23 N, 9 27 E
time difference: UTC+1 (6 hours ahead of Washington, DC, during Standard Time)
etymology: original site settled by freed slaves and the name means "free town" in French; named in imitation of Freetown, the capital of Sierra Leone

Administrative divisions: 9 provinces; Estuaire, Haut-Ogooue, Moyen-Ogooue, Ngounie, Nyanga, Ogooue-Ivindo, Ogooue-Lolo, Ogooue- Maritime, Woleu-Ntem

Independence: 17 August 1960 (from France)

National holiday: Independence Day, 17 August (1960)

Constitution: *history:* previous 1961; latest drafted May 1990, adopted 15 March 1991, promulgated 26 March 1991
amendments: proposed by the president of the republic, by the Council of Ministers, or by one third of either house of Parliament; passage requires Constitutional Court evaluation, at least two-thirds majority vote of two thirds of the Parliament membership convened in joint session, and approval in a referendum; constitutional articles on Gabon's democratic form of government cannot be amended; amended several times, last in 2020

Legal system: mixed legal system of French civil law and customary law

International law organization participation: has not submitted an ICJ jurisdiction declaration; accepts ICCt jurisdiction

Citizenship: *citizenship by birth:* no
citizenship by descent only: at least one parent must be a citizen of Gabon
dual citizenship recognized: no
residency requirement for naturalization: 10 years

Suffrage: 18 years of age; universal

Executive branch: *chief of state:* President Ali BONGO Ondimba (since 16 October 2009)
head of government: Prime Minister Rose Christiane Ossouka RAPONDA (since 16 July 2020)
cabinet: Council of Ministers appointed by the prime minister in consultation with the president
elections/appointments: president directly elected by simple majority popular vote for a 7-year term (no term limits); election last held on 27 August 2016 (next to be held in August 2023); prime minister appointed by the president
election results: Ali BONGO Ondimba reelected president; percent of vote - Ali BONGO Ondimba (PDG) 49.8%, Jean PING (UFC) 48.2%, other 2.0% (2016)

Legislative branch: *description:* bicameral Parliament or Parlement consists of:
Senate or Senat (102 seats; members indirectly elected by municipal councils and departmental assemblies by absolute majority vote in 2 rounds if needed; members serve 6-year terms)
National Assembly or Assemblee Nationale (143 seats; members elected in single-seat constituencies by absolute majority vote in 2 rounds if needed; members serve 5-year terms)
elections: Senate - last held on 30 January and 6 February 2021 (next to be held in December 2026)

National Assembly - held in 2 rounds on 6 and 27 October 2018 (next to be held in 2023)
election results: Senate - percent of vote by party - NA; seats by party - PDG 81, CLR 7, PSD 2, ADERE-UPG 1, UPG 1, PGCI 1, independent 7; composition - NA
National Assembly - percent of vote by party - NA; seats by party - PDG 98, The Democrats or LD 11, RV 8, Social Democrats of Gabon 5, RH&M 4, other 9, independent 8; composition - men 121, women 22, percent of women 15.4%; note - total Parliament percent of women NA

Judicial branch: *highest court(s):* Supreme Court (consists of 4 permanent specialized supreme courts - Supreme Court or Cour de Cassation, Administrative Supreme Court or Conseil d'Etat, Accounting Supreme Court or Cour des Comptes, Constitutional Court or Cour Constitutionnelle, and the non-permanent Court of State Security, initiated only for cases of high treason by the president and criminal activity by executive branch officials)
judge selection and term of office: appointment and tenure of Supreme, Administrative, Accounting, and State Security courts NA; Constitutional Court judges appointed - 3 by the national president, 3 by the president of the Senate, and 3 by the president of the National Assembly; judges serve single renewable 7-year terms
subordinate courts: Courts of Appeal; county courts; military courts

Political parties and leaders: Circle of Liberal Reformers or CLR [Gen. Jean-Boniface ASSELE]
Democratic and Republican Alliance or ADERE [DIDJOB Divungui di Ndinge]
Gabonese Democratic Party or PDG [Ali BONGO Ondimba]
Independent Center Party of Gabon or PGCI [Luccheri GAHILA]
Legacy and Modernity Party or RH&M
National Woodcutters' Rally - Rally for Gabon or RNB-RPG [Paul Mba ABESSOLE]
Restoration of Republican Values or RV
Social Democratic Party or PSD [Pierre Claver MAGANGA-MOUSSAVOU]
Social Democrats of Gabon
The Democrats or LD [Guy NZOUBA-NDAMA]
Union for the New Republic or UPRN [Louis Gaston MAYILA]
Union of Forces for Change or UFC [Jean PING]
Union of Gabonese People or UPG [Richard MOULOMBA]
Paul Mba Abessole

International organization participation: ACP, AfDB, AU, BDEAC, CEMAC, FAO, FZ, G-24, G-77, IAEA, IBRD, ICAO, ICCt, ICRM, IDA, IDB, IFAD, IFC, IFRCS, ILO, IMF, IMO, IMSO, Interpol, IOC, IOM, IPU, ISO, ITSO, ITU, ITUC (NGOs), MIGA, NAM, OIC, OIF, OPCW, UN, UNCTAD, UNESCO, UNHRC, UNIDO, UNWTO, UPU, WCO, WHO, WIPO, WMO, WTO

Diplomatic representation in the US: *chief of mission:* Charge D'Affaires Rod Ciangillan REMBENDAMBYA, Counselor (17 March 2021)
chancery: 2034 20th Street NW, Suite 200, Washington, DC 20009
telephone: [1] (202) 797-1000
FAX: [1] (301) 332-0668
email address and website:
info@gaboneembassyusa.org
https://gabonembassyusa.org/en/

Diplomatic representation from the US: *chief of mission:* Ambassador (vacant); Charge d'Affaires Samuel R. WATSON; note - also accredited to Sao Tome and Principe
embassy: Sabliere, B.P. 4000, Libreville
mailing address: 2270 Libreville Place, Washington, DC 20521-2270
telephone: [241] 011-45-71-00
FAX: [241] 011-45-71-05
email address and website:
ACSLibreville@state.gov
https://ga.usembassy.gov/

Flag description: three equal horizontal bands of green (top), yellow, and blue; green represents the country's forests and natural resources, gold represents the equator (which transects Gabon) as well as the sun, blue represents the sea

National symbol(s): *black panther; national colors:* green, yellow, blue

National anthem: *name:* "La Concorde" (The Concorde)
lyrics/music: Georges Aleka DAMAS
note: adopted 1960

National heritage: *total World Heritage Sites:* 2 (1 natural, 1 mixed)
selected World Heritage Site locales: Ecosystem and Relict Cultural Landscape of Lopé-Okanda (m); Ivindo National Park (n)

ECONOMY

Economic overview: Gabon enjoys a per capita income four times that of most Sub-Saharan African nations, but because of high income inequality, a large proportion of the population remains poor. Gabon relied on timber and manganese exports until oil was discovered offshore in the early 1970s. From 2010 to 2016, oil accounted for approximately 80% of Gabon's exports, 45% of its GDP, and 60% of its state budget revenues.

Gabon faces fluctuating international prices for its oil, timber, and manganese exports. A rebound of oil prices from 2001 to 2013 helped growth, but declining production, as some fields passed their peak production, has hampered Gabon from fully realizing potential gains. GDP grew nearly 6% per year over the 2010-14 period, but slowed significantly from 2014 to just 1% in 2017 as oil prices declined. Low oil prices also weakened government revenue and negatively affected the trade and current account balances. In the wake of lower revenue, Gabon signed a 3-year agreement with the IMF in June 2017.

Despite an abundance of natural wealth, poor fiscal management and over-reliance on oil has stifled the economy. Power cuts and water shortages are frequent. Gabon is reliant on imports and the government heavily subsidizes commodities, including food, but will be hard pressed to tamp down public frustration with unemployment and corruption.

Real GDP (purchasing power parity): $32.05 billion (2020 est.)
$32.48 billion (2019 est.)
$31.25 billion (2018 est.)
note: data are in 2017 dollars
country comparison to the world: 135

Real GDP growth rate: 0.5% (2017 est.)
2.1% (2016 est.)
3.9% (2015 est.)
country comparison to the world: 184

Real GDP per capita: $14,400 (2020 est.)
$15,000 (2019 est.)
$14,700 (2018 est.)
note: data are in 2017 dollars
country comparison to the world: 108

GDP (official exchange rate): $16.064 billion (2019 est.)

Inflation rate (consumer prices): 2.4% (2019 est.)
4.7% (2018 est.)
2.6% (2017 est.)
country comparison to the world: 124

Credit ratings:

Fitch rating: CCC (2020)

Moody's rating: Caa1 (2018)

Standard & Poors rating: N/A (2016)
note: The year refers to the year in which the current credit rating was first obtained.

GDP - composition, by sector of origin: *agriculture:* 5% (2017 est.)
industry: 44.7% (2017 est.)
services: 50.4% (2017 est.)

GDP - composition, by end use: *household consumption:* 37.6% (2017 est.)
government consumption: 14.1% (2017 est.)
investment in fixed capital: 29% (2017 est.)
investment in inventories: -0.6% (2016 est.)
exports of goods and services: 46.7% (2017 est.)
imports of goods and services: -26.8% (2017 est.)

Agricultural products: plantains, cassava, sugar cane, yams, taro, vegetables, maize, groundnuts, game meat, rubber

Industries: petroleum extraction and refining; manganese, gold; chemicals, ship repair, food and beverages, textiles, lumbering and plywood, cement

Industrial production growth rate: 1.8% (2017 est.)
country comparison to the world: 135

Labor force: 557,800 (2017 est.)
country comparison to the world: 153

Labor force - by occupation: *agriculture:* 64%
industry: 12%
services: 24% (2005 est.)

Unemployment rate: 28% (2015 est.)
20.4% (2014 est.)
country comparison to the world: 203

Population below poverty line: 33.4% (2017 est.)

Gini Index coefficient - distribution of family income: 38 (2017 est.)
country comparison to the world: 74

Household income or consumption by percentage share: *lowest 10%:* 2.5%
highest 10%: 32.7% (2005)

Budget: *revenues:* 2.634 billion (2017 est.)
expenditures: 2.914 billion (2017 est.)

Budget surplus (+) or deficit (-): -1.9% (of GDP) (2017 est.)
country comparison to the world: 101

Public debt: 62.7% of GDP (2017 est.)
64.2% of GDP (2016 est.)
country comparison to the world: 69

Taxes and other revenues: 17.6% (of GDP) (2017 est.)
country comparison to the world: 167

Fiscal year: calendar year

Current account balance: -$725 million (2017 est.)
-$1.389 billion (2016 est.)
country comparison to the world: 135

Exports: $10.8 billion (2019 est.)
$9.533 billion (2018 est.)
$9.145 billion (2017 est.)
country comparison to the world: 100

Exports - partners: China 63%, Singapore 5% (2019)

Exports - commodities: crude petroleum, manganese, lumber, veneer sheeting, refined petroleum (2019)

Imports: $5.02 billion (2019 est.)
$4.722 billion (2018 est.)
$4.749 billion (2017 est.)
country comparison to the world: 137

Imports - partners: France 22%, China 17%, Belgium 6%, United States 6%, United Arab Emirates 5% (2019)

Imports - commodities: poultry meats, excavation machinery, packaged medicines, cars, rice (2019)

Reserves of foreign exchange and gold: $981.6 million (31 December 2017 est.)
$804.1 million (31 December 2016 est.)
country comparison to the world: 133

Debt - external: $6.49 billion (31 December 2017 est.)
$5.321 billion (31 December 2016 est.)
country comparison to the world: 127

Exchange rates: Cooperation Financiere en Afrique Centrale francs (XAF) per US dollar -
605.3 (2017 est.)
593.01 (2016 est.)
593.01 (2015 est.)
591.45 (2014 est.)
494.42 (2013 est.)

ENERGY

Electricity access: *electrification - total population:* 92% (2019)
electrification - urban areas: 99% (2019)
electrification - rural areas: 39% (2019)

Electricity: *installed generating capacity:* 784,000 kW (2020 est.)
consumption: 3.134 billion kWh (2019 est.)
exports: 0 kWh (2019 est.)
imports: 511 million kWh (2019 est.)
transmission/distribution losses: 389 million kWh (2019 est.)

Electricity generation sources: *fossil fuels:* 40.6% of total installed capacity (2020 est.)
solar: 0.1% of total installed capacity (2020 est.)
hydroelectricity: 59% of total installed capacity (2020 est.)
biomass and waste: 0.3% of total installed capacity (2020 est.)

Petroleum: *total petroleum production:* 175,000 bbl/day (2021 est.)
refined petroleum consumption: 14,400 bbl/day (2019 est.)
crude oil and lease condensate exports: 178,400 bbl/day (2018 est.)
crude oil and lease condensate imports: 0 bbl/day (2018 est.)
crude oil estimated reserves: 2 billion barrels (2021 est.)

Refined petroleum products - production: 16,580 bbl/day (2017 est.)
country comparison to the world: 91

Refined petroleum products - exports: 4,662 bbl/day (2015 est.)
country comparison to the world: 91

Refined petroleum products - imports: 10,680 bbl/day (2015 est.)
country comparison to the world: 146

Natural gas: *production:* 319.102 million cubic meters (2019 est.)
consumption: 319.102 million cubic meters (2019 est.)
exports: 0 cubic meters (2021 est.)
imports: 0 cubic meters (2021 est.)
proven reserves: 25.995 billion cubic meters (2021 est.)

Carbon dioxide emissions: 2.651 million metric tonnes of CO2 (2019 est.)
from petroleum and other liquids: 2.025 million metric tonnes of CO2 (2019 est.)
from consumed natural gas: 626,000 metric tonnes of CO2 (2019 est.)
country comparison to the world: 152

Energy consumption per capita: 26.786 million Btu/person (2019 est.)
country comparison to the world: 127

COMMUNICATIONS

Telephones - fixed lines: *total subscriptions:* 25,428 (2020 est.)
subscriptions per 100 inhabitants: 1 (2020 est.)
country comparison to the world: 171

Telephones - mobile cellular: *total subscriptions:* 3,049,530 (2020 est.)
subscriptions per 100 inhabitants: 137 (2020 est.)
country comparison to the world: 138

Telecommunication systems: *general assessment:* the telecom market was liberalized in 1999 when the government awarded three mobile telephony licenses and two ISP licenses and established an independent regulatory authority; in contrast with the mobile market, Gabon's fixed-line and internet sectors have remained underdeveloped due to a lack of competition and high prices; the country has sufficient international bandwidth on the SAT-3/WASC/SAFE submarine cable; the arrival of the ACE submarine cable, combined with progressing work on the CAB cable, has increased back haul capacity supporting mobile data traffic (2022)
domestic: fixed-line is a little over 1 per 100 subscriptions; a growing mobile cellular network with multiple providers is making telephone service more widely available with mobile cellular teledensity at nearly 139 per 100 persons (2020)
international: country code - 241; landing points for the SAT-3/WASC, ACE and Libreville-Port Gentil Cable fiber-optic submarine cable that provides connectivity to Europe and West Africa; satellite earth stations - 3 Intelsat (Atlantic Ocean) (2019)

Broadcast media: state owns and operates 2 TV stations and 2 radio broadcast stations; a few private radio and TV stations; transmissions of at least 2 international broadcasters are accessible; satellite service subscriptions are available

Internet country code: .ga

Internet users: *total:* 1,379,951 (2020 est.)
percent of population: 62% (2020 est.)
country comparison to the world: 139

Broadband - fixed subscriptions: *total:* 44,607 (2020 est.)
subscriptions per 100 inhabitants: 2 (2020 est.)
country comparison to the world: 144

TRANSPORTATION

National air transport system: *number of registered air carriers:* 3 (2020)
inventory of registered aircraft operated by air carriers: 8

Civil aircraft registration country code prefix: TR

Airports: *total:* 44 (2021)
country comparison to the world: 97

Airports - with paved runways: *total:* 14
over 3,047 m: 1
2,438 to 3,047 m: 2
1,524 to 2,437 m: 9
914 to 1,523 m: 1
under 914 m: 1 (2021)

Airports - with unpaved runways: *total:* 30
1,524 to 2,437 m: 7
914 to 1,523 m: 9 (2013)
under 914 m: 14 (2021)

Pipelines: 807 km gas, 1,639 km oil, 3 km water (2013)

Railways: *total:* 649 km (2014)
standard gauge: 649 km (2014) 1.435-m gauge
country comparison to the world: 106

Roadways: *total:* 14,300 km (2001)
paved: 900 km (2001)
unpaved: 13,400 km (2001)
country comparison to the world: 126

Waterways: 1,600 km (2010) (310 km on Ogooue River)
country comparison to the world: 50

Merchant marine: *total:* 62
by type: bulk carrier 1, general cargo 17, oil tanker 17, other 27 (2021)
country comparison to the world: 111

Ports and terminals: *major seaport(s):* Libreville, Owendo, Port-Gentil
oil terminal(s): Gamba, Lucina

MILITARY AND SECURITY

Military and security forces: Gabonese Armed Forces (Force Armées Gabonaise or FAG; aka Gabonese Defense and Security Forces): Land Forces (Army), National Navy, Air Force, National Gendarmerie (includes Coast Guard), Corps of Firemen; Republican Guard (2022)
note: the National Police Forces, under the Ministry of Interior, and the National Gendarmerie, under the Ministry of Defense, are responsible for law enforcement and public security; elements of the armed forces and the Republican Guard, an elite unit that protects the president under his direct authority, sometimes performed internal security functions

Military expenditures: 1.7% of GDP (2021 est.)
1.8% of GDP (2020 est.)
1.6% of GDP (2019 est.) (approximately $450 million)
1.6% of GDP (2018 est.) (approximately $440 million)
1.8% of GDP (2017 est.) (approximately $480 million)
country comparison to the world: 78

Military and security service personnel strengths: approximately 6,500 active duty troops including the Republican Guard and Gendarmerie (2022)

Military equipment inventories and acquisitions: the Gabonese military is lightly armed with a mixed inventory from a variety of suppliers; since 2010, providers have included Brazil, China, France, Germany, and South Africa (2021)

Military service age and obligation: 20 years of age for voluntary military service; no conscription (2021)

Military - note: members of the Gabonese Defense Forces attempted a failed coup in January 2019

Maritime threats: the International Maritime Bureau reports the territorial and offshore waters in the Niger Delta and Gulf of Guinea remain a very high risk for piracy and armed robbery of ships; in 2021, there were 34 reported incidents of piracy and armed robbery at sea in the Gulf of Guinea region; although a significant decrease from the total number of 81 incidents in 2020, it included the one hijacking and three of five ships fired upon worldwide; while boarding and attempted boarding to steal valuables from ships and crews are the most common types of incidents, almost a third of all incidents involve a hijacking and/or kidnapping; in 2021, 57 crew members were kidnapped in seven separate incidents in the Gulf of Guinea, representing 100% of kidnappings worldwide; Nigerian pirates in particular are well armed and very aggressive, operating as far as 200 nm offshore; the Maritime Administration of the US Department of Transportation has issued a Maritime Advisory (2022-001 - Gulf of Guinea-Piracy/Armed Robbery/Kidnapping for Ransom) effective 4 January 2022, which states in part, "Piracy, armed robbery, and kidnapping for ransom continue to serve as significant threats to US-flagged vessels transiting or operating in the Gulf of Guinea"

TRANSNATIONAL ISSUES

Disputes - international: UN urges Equatorial Guinea and Gabon to resolve the sovereignty dispute over Gabon-occupied Mbane Island and lesser islands and to establish a maritime boundary in hydrocarbon-rich Corisco Bay

GAMBIA, THE

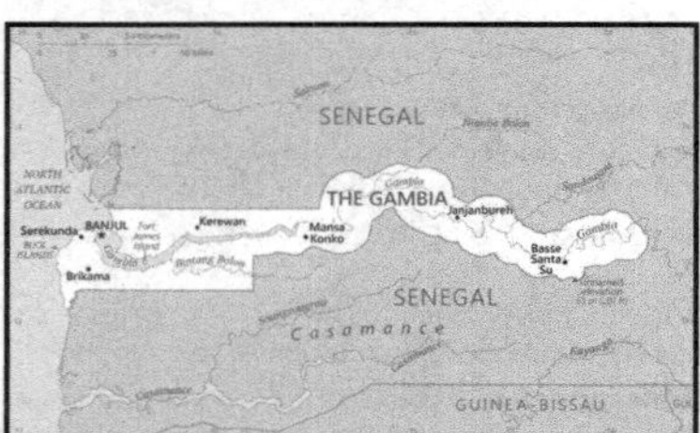

INTRODUCTION

Background: In the 10th century, Muslim merchants established some of The Gambia's earliest large settlements as trans-Saharan trade hubs. These settlements eventually grew into major export centers sending slaves, gold, and ivory across the Sahara. Between the 16th and 17th centuries, European colonial powers began establishing trade with The Gambia. In 1664, the United Kingdom established a colony in The Gambia focused on exporting enslaved people across the Atlantic. During the roughly 300 years of the trans-Atlantic slave trade, the UK and other European powers may have exported as many as 3 million people from The Gambia.

The Gambia gained its independence from the UK in 1965. Geographically surrounded by Senegal, it formed the short-lived confederation of Senegambia between 1982 and 1989. In 1994, Yahya JAMMEH led a military coup overthrowing the president and banning political activity. He subsequently won every presidential election until 2016, when he lost to Adama BARROW, who headed an opposition coalition during free and fair elections. BARROW won reelection in December 2021. The Gambia is the only member of the Economic Community of West African States that does not have presidential term limits. Since the 2016 election, The Gambia and the US have enjoyed improved relations. US assistance to the country has supported military education and training programs, capacity building, and democracy-strengthening activities.

GEOGRAPHY

Location: Western Africa, bordering the North Atlantic Ocean and Senegal

Geographic coordinates: 13 28 N, 16 34 W

Map references: Africa

Area: *total:* 11,300 sq km
land: 10,120 sq km
water: 1,180 sq km
country comparison to the world: 165

Area - comparative: slightly less than twice the size of Delaware

Land boundaries: *total:* 749 km
border countries (1): Senegal 749 km

Coastline: 80 km

Maritime claims: *territorial sea:* 12 nm
contiguous zone: 18 nm
continental shelf: extent not specified
exclusive fishing zone: 200 nm

Climate: tropical; hot, rainy season (June to November); cooler, dry season (November to May)

Terrain: flood plain of the Gambia River flanked by some low hills

Elevation: *highest point:* unnamed elevation 63 m; 3 km southeast of the town of Sabi
lowest point: Atlantic Ocean 0 m
mean elevation: 34 m

Natural resources: fish, clay, silica sand, titanium (rutile and ilmenite), tin, zircon

Land use: *agricultural land:* 56.1% (2018 est.)
arable land: 41% (2018 est.)
permanent crops: 0.5% (2018 est.)
permanent pasture: 14.6% (2018 est.)
forest: 43.9% (2018 est.)
other: 0% (2018 est.)

Irrigated land: 50 sq km (2012)

Major rivers (by length in km): Gambia river mouth (shared with Senegal and Guinea [s]) - 1,094 km
note – [s] after country name indicates river source; [m] after country name indicates river mouth

Major aquifers: Senegalo-Mauritanian Basin

Population distribution: settlements are found scattered along the Gambia River; the largest communities, including the capital of Banjul, and the country's largest city, Serekunda, are found at the mouth of the Gambia River along the Atlantic coast as shown in this population distribution map

Natural hazards: droughts

Geography - note: almost an enclave of Senegal; smallest country on the African mainland

PEOPLE AND SOCIETY

Population: 2,413,403 (2022 est.)
country comparison to the world: 144

Nationality: *noun:* Gambian(s)
adjective: Gambian

Ethnic groups: Mandinka/Jahanka 33.3%, Fulani/Tukulur/Lorobo 18.2%, Wolof 12.9%, Jola/Karoninka 11%, Serahuleh 7.2%, Serer 3.5%, other 4%, non-Gambian 9.9% (2019-20 est.)

Languages: English (official), Mandinka, Wolof, Fula, other indigenous vernaculars

Religions: Muslim 96.4%, Christian 3.5%, other or none 0.1% (2019-20 est.)

Demographic profile: The Gambia's youthful age structure – almost 60% of the population is under the age of 25 – is likely to persist because the country's total fertility rate remains strong at nearly 4 children per woman. The overall literacy rate is around 55%, and is significantly lower for women than for men. At least 70% of the populace are farmers who are reliant on rain-fed agriculture and cannot afford improved seeds and fertilizers. Crop failures caused by droughts between 2011 and 2013 have increased poverty, food shortages, and malnutrition.

The Gambia is a source country for migrants and a transit and destination country for migrants and refugees. Since the 1980s, economic deterioration, drought, and high unemployment, especially among youths, have driven both domestic migration (largely urban) and migration abroad (legal and illegal). Emigrants are largely skilled workers, including doctors and nurses, and provide a significant amount of remittances. The top receiving countries for Gambian emigrants are Spain, the US, Nigeria, Senegal, and the UK. While the Gambia and Spain do not share historic, cultural, or trade ties, rural Gambians have migrated to Spain in large numbers because of its proximity and the availability of jobs in its underground economy (this flow slowed following the onset of Spain's late 2007 economic crisis).

The Gambia's role as a host country to refugees is a result of wars in several of its neighboring West African countries. Since 2006, refugees from the Casamance conflict in Senegal have replaced their pattern of flight and return with permanent settlement in The Gambia, often moving in with relatives along the Senegal-Gambia border. The strain of providing for about 7,400 Casamance refugees has increased poverty among Gambian villagers.

Age structure: *0-14 years:* 35.15% (male 391,993/female 388,816)
15-24 years: 20.12% (male 221,519/female 225,414)
25-54 years: 36.39% (male 396,261/female 412,122)
55-64 years: 4.53% (male 48,032/female 52,538)
65 years and over: 3.81% (male 38,805/female 45,801) (2021 est.)

Dependency ratios: *total dependency ratio:* 86.9
youth dependency ratio: 82.1
elderly dependency ratio: 4.7
potential support ratio: 21.1 (2020 est.)

Median age: *total:* 21.8 years
male: 21.5 years
female: 22.2 years (2020 est.)
country comparison to the world: 182

Population growth rate: 2.29% (2022 est.)
country comparison to the world: 33

Birth rate: 28.78 births/1,000 population (2022 est.)
country comparison to the world: 32

Death rate: 5.81 deaths/1,000 population (2022 est.)
country comparison to the world: 167

Net migration rate: -0.04 migrant(s)/1,000 population (2022 est.)
country comparison to the world: 99

Population distribution: settlements are found scattered along the Gambia River; the largest communities, including the capital of Banjul, and the country's largest city, Serekunda, are found at the mouth of the Gambia River along the Atlantic coast as shown in this population distribution map

Urbanization: *urban population:* 63.9% of total population (2022)
rate of urbanization: 3.75% annual rate of change (2020-25 est.)

Major urban areas - population: 470,000 BANJUL (capital) (2022)
note: includes the local government areas of Banjul and Kanifing

Sex ratio: *at birth:* 1.03 male(s)/female
0-14 years: 1.02 male(s)/female
15-24 years: 1.01 male(s)/female
25-54 years: 0.96 male(s)/female
55-64 years: 0.76 male(s)/female
65 years and over: 0.88 male(s)/female
total population: 0.98 male(s)/female (2022 est.)

Mother's mean age at first birth: 20.7 years (2019/20 est.)
note: data represents median age at first birth among women 25-49

Maternal mortality ratio: 597 deaths/100,000 live births (2017 est.)
country comparison to the world: 13

Infant mortality rate: *total:* 37.19 deaths/1,000 live births
male: 40.75 deaths/1,000 live births
female: 33.53 deaths/1,000 live births (2022 est.)
country comparison to the world: 38

Life expectancy at birth: *total population:* 67.6 years
male: 65.83 years
female: 69.41 years (2022 est.)
country comparison to the world: 188

Total fertility rate: 3.79 children born/woman (2022 est.)
country comparison to the world: 32

Contraceptive prevalence rate: 18.9% (2019/20)

Drinking water source: *improved: urban:* 91.8% of population
rural: 85.7% of population
total: 89.5% of population
unimproved: urban: 8.2% of population
rural: 14.3% of population
total: 10.5% of population (2020 est.)

Current health expenditure: 3.8% of GDP (2019)

Physicians density: 0.08 physicians/1,000 population (2020)

Hospital bed density: 1.1 beds/1,000 population (2011)

Sanitation facility access: *improved: urban:* 75.8% of population
rural: 33.6% of population
total: 60% of population
unimproved: urban: 24.2% of population
rural: 66.4% of population
total: 40% of population (2020 est.)

HIV/AIDS - adult prevalence rate: 1.8% (2020 est.)
country comparison to the world: 25

Major infectious diseases: *degree of risk:* very high (2020)
food or waterborne diseases: bacterial and protozoal diarrhea, hepatitis A, and typhoid fever
vectorborne diseases: malaria and dengue fever
water contact diseases: schistosomiasis
animal contact diseases: rabies
respiratory diseases: meningococcal meningitis
note: on 21 March 2022, the US Centers for Disease Control and Prevention (CDC) issued a Travel Alert for polio in Africa; The Gambia is currently considered a high risk to travelers for circulating vaccine-derived polioviruses (cVDPV); vaccine-derived poliovirus (VDPV) is a strain of the weakened poliovirus that was initially included in oral polio vaccine (OPV) and *that has changed over time and behaves more like the wild or naturally occurring virus;* this means it can be spread more easily to people who are unvaccinated against polio and who come in contact with the stool or respiratory secretions, such as from a sneeze, of an "infected" person who received oral polio vaccine; the CDC recommends that before any international travel, anyone unvaccinated, incompletely vaccinated, or with an unknown polio vaccination status should complete the routine polio vaccine series; before travel to any high-risk destination, CDC recommends that adults who previously completed the full, routine polio vaccine series receive a single, lifetime booster dose of polio vaccine

Obesity - adult prevalence rate: 10.3% (2016)
country comparison to the world: 139

Alcohol consumption per capita: *total:* 2.67 liters of pure alcohol (2019 est.)
beer: 0.21 liters of pure alcohol (2019 est.)
wine: 0 liters of pure alcohol (2019 est.)
spirits: 0.02 liters of pure alcohol (2019 est.)
other alcohols: 2.44 liters of pure alcohol (2019 est.)
country comparison to the world: 121

Tobacco use: *total:* 11.1% (2020 est.)
male: 21.4% (2020 est.)
female: 0.8% (2020 est.)
country comparison to the world: 129

Children under the age of 5 years underweight: 11.6% (2019/20)
country comparison to the world: 52

Child marriage: *women married by age 15:* 7.5%
women married by age 18: 25.7%
men married by age 18: 0.2% (2020 est.)

Education expenditures: 2.9% of GDP (2019 est.)
country comparison to the world: 154

Literacy: *definition:* age 15 and over can read and write
total population: 50.8%
male: 61.8%
female: 41.6% (2015)

Unemployment, youth ages 15-24: *total:* 25.8%
male: 21%
female: 32.3% (2018 est.)

ENVIRONMENT

Environment - current issues: deforestation due to slash-and-burn agriculture; desertification; water pollution; water-borne diseases

Environment - international agreements: *party to:* Biodiversity, Climate Change, Climate Change-Kyoto Protocol, Climate Change-Paris Agreement, Desertification, Endangered Species, Hazardous Wastes, Law of the Sea, Nuclear Test Ban, Ozone Layer Protection, Ship Pollution, Wetlands, Whaling
signed, but not ratified: Comprehensive Nuclear Test Ban

Air pollutants: *particulate matter emissions:* 32.2 micrograms per cubic meter (2016 est.)
carbon dioxide emissions: 0.53 megatons (2016 est.)
methane emissions: 1.96 megatons (2020 est.)

Climate: tropical; hot, rainy season (June to November); cooler, dry season (November to May)

Land use: *agricultural land:* 56.1% (2018 est.)
arable land: 41% (2018 est.)
permanent crops: 0.5% (2018 est.)
permanent pasture: 14.6% (2018 est.)
forest: 43.9% (2018 est.)
other: 0% (2018 est.)

Urbanization: *urban population:* 63.9% of total population (2022)
rate of urbanization: 3.75% annual rate of change (2020-25 est.)

Revenue from forest resources: *forest revenues:* 2.47% of GDP (2018 est.)
country comparison to the world: 28

Revenue from coal: *coal revenues:* 0% of GDP (2018 est.)
country comparison to the world: 101

Waste and recycling: *municipal solid waste generated annually:* 193,441 tons (2002 est.)

Major rivers (by length in km): Gambia river mouth (shared with Senegal and Guinea [s]) - 1,094 km
note – [s] after country name indicates river source; [m] after country name indicates river mouth

Major aquifers: Senegalo-Mauritanian Basin

Total water withdrawal: *municipal:* 41.2 million cubic meters (2017 est.)
industrial: 21.2 million cubic meters (2017 est.)
agricultural: 39.2 million cubic meters (2017 est.)

Total renewable water resources: 8 billion cubic meters (2017 est.)

GOVERNMENT

Country name: *conventional long form:* Republic of The Gambia
conventional short form: The Gambia
etymology: named for the Gambia River that flows through the heart of the country

Government type: presidential republic

Capital: *name:* Banjul
Geographic coordinates: 13 27 N, 16 34 W
time difference: UTC 0 (5 hours ahead of Washington, DC, during Standard Time)
etymology: Banjul is located on Saint Mary's Island at the mouth of the Gambia River; the Mandinka used to gather fibrous plants on the island for the manufacture of ropes; "bang julo" is Mandinka for "rope fiber"; mispronunciation over time caused the term became the word Banjul

Administrative divisions: 5 regions, 1 city*, and 1 municipality**; Banjul*, Central River, Kanifing**, Lower River, North Bank, Upper River, West Coast

Independence: 18 February 1965 (from the UK)

National holiday: Independence Day, 18 February (1965)

Constitution: *history:* previous 1965 (Independence Act), 1970; latest adopted 8 April 1996, approved by referendum 8 August 1996, effective 16 January 1997; note - in early 2018, the "Constitutional Review Commission," was established to draft and assist in instituting a new constitution; a second draft completed in March 2020 was rejected by the National Assembly in September; the president announced in January 2022 government plans to draft a new constitution
amendments: proposed by the National Assembly; passage requires at least three-fourths majority vote by the Assembly membership in each of several readings and approval by the president of the republic; a referendum is required for amendments affecting national sovereignty, fundamental rights and freedoms, government structures and authorities, taxation, and public funding; passage by referendum requires participation of at least 50% of eligible voters and approval by at least 75% of votes cast; amended 2001, 2004, 2018

Legal system: mixed legal system of English common law, Islamic law, and customary law

International law organization participation: accepts compulsory ICJ jurisdiction with reservations; accepts ICCt jurisdiction

Citizenship: *citizenship by birth:* yes
citizenship by descent only: yes
dual citizenship recognized: no
residency requirement for naturalization: 5 years

Suffrage: 18 years of age; universal

Executive branch: *chief of state:* President Adama BARROW (since 19 January 2022); Vice President Isatou TOURAY (since 15 March 2019); note - the president is both chief of state and head of government
head of government: President Adama BARROW (since 19 January 2022); Vice President Isatou TOURAY (since 15 March 2019)
cabinet: Cabinet appointed by the president
elections/appointments: president directly elected by simple majority popular vote for a 5-year term (no term limits); election last held on 4 December 2021 (next to be held in 2026); vice president appointed by the president
election results: Adama BARROW reelected president; percent of vote - Adama BARROW (National People's Party) 53.2%, Ousainou DARBOE (United Democratic Party) 27.7%, Mamma KANDEH (GDC)12.3%, Halifa SALLAH (PDOIS) 3.8%, Essa M. FAAL (Independent) 2%, Abdoulie Ebrima JAMMEH (NUP) 1% (2021)

Legislative branch: *description:* unicameral National Assembly (58 seats; 53 members directly elected in single-seat constituencies by simple majority vote and 5 appointed by the president; members serve 5-year terms)
elections: last held on 9 April 2022 (next to be held in 2027)
election results: percent of vote by party - NPP 33.9%, UDP 28.3%, independent 22.6%, NRP 7.5%, PDOIS 3.7%, APRL 3.7%; seats by party - NPP 18, UDP 15, independent 12,NRP 4, APRL 2, PDOIS 2; composition - men 52, women 6, percent of women 10.3%

Judicial branch: *highest court(s):* Supreme Court of The Gambia (consists of the chief justice and 6 justices; court sessions held with 5 justices)
judge selection and term of office: justices appointed by the president after consultation with the Judicial Service Commission, a 6-member independent body of high-level judicial officials, a presidential appointee, and a National Assembly appointee; justices appointed for life or until mandatory retirement at age 75
subordinate courts: Court of Appeal; High Court; Special Criminal Court; Khadis or Muslim courts; district tribunals; magistrates courts; cadi courts

Political parties and leaders: Alliance for Patriotic Reorientation and Construction or APRC [Fabakary JATTA]
Coalition 2016 [collective leadership] (electoral coalition includes UDP, PDOIS, NRP, GMC, GDC, PPP, and GPDP)
Gambia Democratic Congress or GDC [Mama KANDEH]
Gambia Moral Congress or GMC [Mai FATTY]
Gambia Party for Democracy and Progress or GPDP [Sarja JARJOU]
National Convention Party or NCP [Yaya SANYANG and Majanko SAMUSA (both claiming leadership)]
National Democratic Action Movement or NDAM [Lamin Yaa JUARA]
National People's Party or NPP [Adama BARROW]
National Reconciliation Party or NRP [Hamat BAH]
People's Democratic Organization for Independence and Socialism or PDOIS [Halifa SALLAH]
People's Progressive Party or PPP [Yaya CEESAY)]
United Democratic Party or UDP [Ousainou DARBOE]

International organization participation: ACP, AfDB, AU, ECOWAS, FAO, G-77, IBRD, ICAO, ICCt, ICRM, IDA, IDB, IFAD, IFC, IFRCS, ILO, IMF, IMO, Interpol, IOC, IOM, IPU, ISO (correspondent), ITSO, ITU, ITUC (NGOs), MIGA, MINUSMA, NAM, OIC, OPCW, UN, UNAMID, UNCTAD, UNESCO, UNHRC, UNIDO, UNISFA, UNMIL, UNOCI, UNWTO, UPU, WCO, WFTU (NGOs), WHO, WIPO, WMO, WTO

Diplomatic representation in the US: *chief of mission:* Ambassador (vacant); Charge d'Affaires Mustapha SOSSEH (16 March 2022)
chancery: 5630 16th Street NW, Washington, DC 20011
telephone: [1] (202) 785-1399; [1] (202) 785-1428
FAX: [1] (202) 785-1430
email address and website:
info@gambiaembassy.us
https://www.gambiaembassydc.us/home

Diplomatic representation from the US: *chief of mission:* Ambassador Sharon L. CROMER (since 18 March 2022)
embassy: Kairaba Avenue, Fajara, P.M.B. 19, Banjul
mailing address: 2070 Banjul Place, Washington DC 20521-2070
telephone: [220] 439-2856
FAX: [220] 439-2475
email address and website:
ConsularBanjul@state.gov
https://gm.usembassy.gov/

Flag description: three equal horizontal bands of red (top), blue with white edges, and green; red stands for the sun and the savannah, blue represents the Gambia River, and green symbolizes forests and agriculture; the white stripes denote unity and peace

National symbol(s): lion; national colors: red, blue, green, white

National anthem: *name:* "For The Gambia, Our Homeland"
lyrics/music: Virginia Julie HOWE/adapted by Jeremy Frederick HOWE
note: adopted 1965; the music is an adaptation of the traditional Mandinka song "Foday Kaba Dumbuya"

National heritage: *total World Heritage Sites:* 2 (both cultural)
selected World Heritage Site locales: Kunta Kinteh Island and Related Sites; Stone Circles of Senegambia

ECONOMY

Economic overview: The government has invested in the agriculture sector because three-quarters of the population depends on the sector for its livelihood and agriculture provides for about one-third of GDP, making The Gambia largely reliant on sufficient rainfall. The agricultural sector has untapped potential - less than half of arable land is cultivated and agricultural productivity is low. Small-scale manufacturing activity features the processing of cashews, groundnuts, fish, and hides. The Gambia's reexport trade accounts for almost 80% of goods exports and China has been its largest trade partner for both exports and imports for several years.

The Gambia has sparse natural resource deposits. It relies heavily on remittances from workers overseas and tourist receipts. Remittance inflows to The Gambia amount to about one-fifth of the country's GDP. The Gambia's location on the ocean and proximity to Europe has made it one of the most frequented tourist destinations in West Africa, boosted by private sector investments in eco-tourism and facilities. Tourism normally brings in about 20% of GDP, but it suffered in 2014 from tourists' fears of Ebola virus in neighboring West African countries. Unemployment and underemployment remain high.

Economic progress depends on sustained bilateral and multilateral aid, on responsible government economic management, and on continued technical assistance from multilateral and bilateral donors. International donors and lenders were concerned about the quality of fiscal management under the administration of former President Yahya JAMMEH, who reportedly stole hundreds of millions of dollars of the country's funds during his 22 years in power, but anticipate significant improvements under the new administration of President Adama BARROW, who assumed power in early 2017. As of April 2017, the IMF, the World Bank, the European Union, and the African Development Bank were all negotiating with the new government of The Gambia to provide financial support in the coming months to ease the country's financial crisis.

The country faces a limited availability of foreign exchange, weak agricultural output, a border closure with Senegal, a slowdown in tourism, high inflation, a large fiscal deficit, and a high domestic debt burden that has crowded out private sector investment and driven interest rates to new highs. The government has committed to taking steps to reduce the deficit, including through expenditure caps, debt consolidation, and reform of state-owned enterprises.

Real GDP (purchasing power parity): $5.22 billion (2020 est.)
$5.22 billion (2019 est.)
$4.92 billion (2018 est.)
note: data are in 2017 dollars
country comparison to the world: 176

Real GDP growth rate: 4.6% (2017 est.)
0.4% (2016 est.)
5.9% (2015 est.)
country comparison to the world: 58

Real GDP per capita: $2,200 (2020 est.)
$2,200 (2019 est.)
$2,200 (2018 est.)
note: data are in 2017 dollars
country comparison to the world: 209

GDP (official exchange rate): $1.746 billion (2019 est.)

Inflation rate (consumer prices): 7.1% (2019 est.)
6.5% (2018 est.)
8% (2017 est.)
country comparison to the world: 194

GDP - composition, by sector of origin: *agriculture:* 20.4% (2017 est.)
industry: 14.2% (2017 est.)
services: 65.4% (2017 est.)

GDP - composition, by end use: *household consumption:* 90.7% (2017 est.)
government consumption: 12% (2017 est.)
investment in fixed capital: 19.2% (2017 est.)
investment in inventories: -2.7% (2017 est.)
exports of goods and services: 20.8% (2017 est.)
imports of goods and services: -40% (2017 est.)

Agricultural products: groundnuts, milk, oil palm fruit, millet, sorghum, rice, maize, vegetables, cassava, fruit

Industries: peanuts, fish, hides, tourism, beverages, agricultural machinery assembly, woodworking, metalworking, clothing

Industrial production growth rate: -0.8% (2017 est.)
country comparison to the world: 175

Labor force: 777,100 (2007 est.)
country comparison to the world: 147

Labor force - by occupation: *agriculture:* 75%
industry: 19%
services: 6% (1996 est.)

Unemployment, youth ages 15-24: *total:* 25.8%
male: 21%
female: 32.3% (2018 est.)
country comparison to the world: 53

Population below poverty line: 48.6% (2015 est.)

Gini Index coefficient - distribution of family income: 35.9 (2015 est.)
country comparison to the world: 96

Household income or consumption by percentage share: *lowest 10%:* 2%
highest 10%: 36.9% (2003)

Budget: *revenues:* 300.4 million (2017 est.)
expenditures: 339 million (2017 est.)

Budget surplus (+) or deficit (-): -2.6% (of GDP) (2017 est.)
country comparison to the world: 117

Public debt: 88% of GDP (2017 est.)
82.3% of GDP (2016 est.)
country comparison to the world: 28

Taxes and other revenues: 20.3% (of GDP) (2017 est.)
country comparison to the world: 148

Fiscal year: calendar year

Current account balance: -$194 million (2017 est.)
-$85 million (2016 est.)
country comparison to the world: 98

Exports: $350 million (2018 est.) note: data are in current year dollars
$448 million (2018 est.)
$435 million (2017 est.)
country comparison to the world: 197

Exports - partners: China 38%, India 22%, Mali 7%, Chile 5% (2017)

Exports - commodities: lumber, cashews, refined petroleum, fish oil, ground nut oil (2019)

Imports: $620 million (2018 est.) note: data are in current year dollars
$851 million (2018 est.)
$754 million (2017 est.)
country comparison to the world: 197

Imports - partners: China 33%, India 10%, Senegal 5%, Brazil 5% (2019)

Imports - commodities: clothing and apparel, refined petroleum, rice, raw sugar, palm oil (2019)

Reserves of foreign exchange and gold: $170 million (31 December 2017 est.)
$87.64 million (31 December 2016 est.)
country comparison to the world: 179

Debt - external: $586.8 million (31 December 2017 est.)
$571.2 million (31 December 2016 est.)
country comparison to the world: 175

Exchange rates: dalasis (GMD) per US dollar -
51.75 (2020 est.)
51.4 (2019 est.)
49.515 (2018 est.)
41.89 (2014 est.)
41.733 (2013 est.)

ENERGY

Electricity access: *electrification - total population:* 49% (2019)
electrification - urban areas: 69% (2019)
electrification - rural areas: 16% (2019)

Electricity: *installed generating capacity:* 137,000 kW (2020 est.)
consumption: 235.035 million kWh (2019 est.)
exports: 0 kWh (2019 est.)
imports: 0 kWh (2019 est.)
transmission/distribution losses: 69.8 million kWh (2019 est.)

Electricity generation sources: *fossil fuels:* 98.9% of total installed capacity (2020 est.)
solar: 1% of total installed capacity (2020 est.)

Petroleum: *total petroleum production:* 0 bbl/day (2021 est.)
refined petroleum consumption: 3,900 bbl/day (2019 est.)

Refined petroleum products - exports: 42 bbl/day (2015 est.)
country comparison to the world: 122

Refined petroleum products - imports: 3,738 bbl/day (2015 est.)
country comparison to the world: 181

Carbon dioxide emissions: 606,000 metric tonnes of CO_2 (2019 est.)
from petroleum and other liquids: 606,000 metric tonnes of CO_2 (2019 est.)
country comparison to the world: 186

Energy consumption per capita: 3.547 million Btu/person (2019 est.)
country comparison to the world: 177

COMMUNICATIONS

Telephones - fixed lines: *total subscriptions:* 60,000 (2020 est.)
subscriptions per 100 inhabitants: 2 (2020 est.)
country comparison to the world: 152

Telephones - mobile cellular: *total subscriptions:* 2,677,954 (2020 est.)
subscriptions per 100 inhabitants: 111 (2020 est.)
country comparison to the world: 143

Telecommunication systems: *general assessment:* Gambia's telecom market has five mobile networks providing effective competition; mobile subscriptions are well above the African average, itself a testament to the poor condition of the fixed-line infrastructure and the lack of availability of fixed services in many rural areas of the country; there are only four licensed ISPs, which are small networks serving local areas, and so competition is minimal; their limited services are complemented by the fixed-wireless offerings of three of the MNOs; the government has embarked on a National Broadband Network program aimed at closing the digital divide affecting many parts of the country; despite efforts to improve internet connectivity, the country ranks among the lowest globally in terms of digital readiness. (2022)
domestic: fixed-line subscriptions nearly 2 per 100 with one dominant company and mobile-cellular teledensity nearly 111 per 100 persons (2020)
international: country code - 220; landing point for the ACE submarine cable to West Africa and Europe; microwave radio relay links to Senegal and Guinea-Bissau; satellite earth station - 1 Intelsat (Atlantic Ocean) (2019)

Broadcast media: 1 state-run TV-channel; one privately-owned TV-station; 1 Online TV-station; three state-owned radio station and 31 privately owned radio stations; eight community radio stations; transmissions of multiple international broadcasters are available, some via shortwave radio; cable and satellite TV subscription services are obtainable in some parts of the country
(2019)

Internet country code: .gm

Internet users: *total:* 894,166 (2020 est.)
percent of population: 37% (2020 est.)
country comparison to the world: 149

Broadband - fixed subscriptions: *total:* 5,000 (2020 est.)
subscriptions per 100 inhabitants: 0.2 (2020 est.)
country comparison to the world: 188

TRANSPORTATION

National air transport system: *number of registered air carriers:* 2 (2020)

inventory of registered aircraft operated by air carriers: 6
annual passenger traffic on registered air carriers: 53,735 (2018)

Civil aircraft registration country code prefix: C5

Airports: *total:* 1 (2021)
country comparison to the world: 220

Airports - with paved runways : *total:* 1
over 3,047 m: 1 (2021)

Roadways: *total:* 2,977 km (2011)
paved: 518 km (2011)
unpaved: 2,459 km (2011)
country comparison to the world: 162

Waterways: 390 km (2010) (on River Gambia; small oceangoing vessels can reach 190 km)
country comparison to the world: 97

Merchant marine: *total:* 8
by type: other 8 (2021)
country comparison to the world: 160

Ports and terminals: *major seaport(s):* Banjul

MILITARY AND SECURITY

Military and security forces: Gambian Armed Forces (GAF): the Gambian National Army (GNA), Gambia Navy, Gambia Air Force, Republican National Guard (2022)
note: the National Guard is responsible for VIP protection, riot control, and presidential security

Military expenditures: 0.8% of GDP (2021 est.)
0.8% of GDP (2020 est.)
0.8% of GDP (2019 est.) (approximately $25 million)
0.7% of GDP (2018 est.) (approximately $20 million)
0.7% of GDP (2017 est.) (approximately $20 million)
country comparison to the world: 142

Military and security service personnel strengths: information varies; approximately 3,000 active troops (2022)

Military equipment inventories and acquisitions: the GAF has a limited equipment inventory; since 2000, it has received only a few second-hand items from Georgia and Taiwan (2021)

Military service age and obligation: 18-25 years of age for male and female voluntary military service (18-22 for officers); no conscription; service obligation 6 months (2021)

Military - note: in 2017, several members of the Economic Community of West African States (ECOWAS) sent security forces to The Gambia to conduct stability operations and provide assistance and training following the 2016 election; as of 2022, the ECOWAS Mission in the Gambia (ECOMIG) was comprised of about 1,000 military and gendarmerie personnel from Ghana, Nigeria, and Senegal

as of 2022, the Gambian Armed Forces' (GAF) principal responsibilities included aiding civil authorities in emergencies and providing natural disaster relief the GAF traces its origins to the Gambia Regiment of the British Army; established in 1901, the Gambia Regiment was part of the West African Frontier Force (WAFF, later Royal West African Frontier Force or RWAFF) and served in both World Wars, including the British 1944-45 military campaign in Burma; the Gambia Regiment was disbanded in 1958 and replaced by the Field Force, a police paramilitary unit; the Field Force was responsible for The Gambia's security until the establishment of the Gambian Armed Forces in 1985; in addition, a defense agreement signed in 1965 between The Gambia and Senegal provided mutual assistance in the face of an external threat; from 1981-1989, The Gambia and Senegal formed a Confederal Army that was made up of troops from both countries

the military in Gambia, including the Field Force, has a history of heavy involvement in the country's politics, including multiple coups or coup attempts and mutinies; as of 2022, the Gambia Armed Forces' principal responsibilities included aiding civil authorities in emergencies and providing natural disaster relief (2022)

TRANSNATIONAL ISSUES

Disputes - international: attempts to stem refugees, cross-border raids, arms smuggling, and other illegal activities by separatists from southern Senegal's Casamance region, as well as from conflicts in other west African states

GAZA STRIP

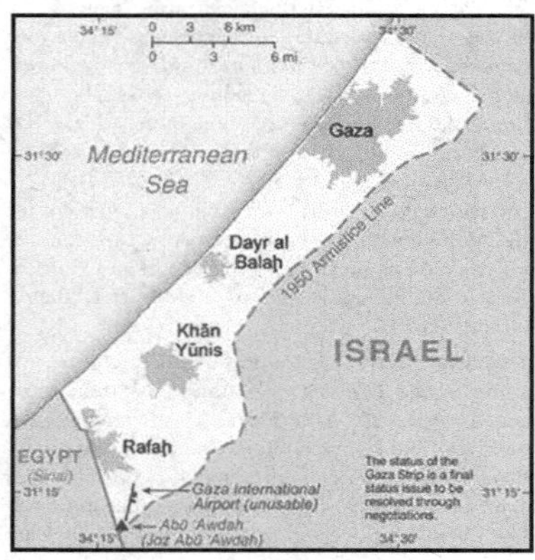

INTRODUCTION

Background: The Gaza Strip has been under the de facto governing authority of the Islamic Resistance Movement (HAMAS) since 2007, and has faced years of conflict, poverty, and humanitarian crises. Inhabited since at least the 15th century B.C., the Gaza Strip area has been dominated by many different peoples and empires throughout its history; it was incorporated into the Ottoman Empire in the early 16th century. The Gaza Strip fell to British forces during World War I, becoming a part of the British Mandate of Palestine. Following the 1948 Arab-Israeli War, Egypt administered the newly formed Gaza Strip; Israel captured it in the Six-Day War in 1967. Under a series of agreements known as the Oslo accords signed between 1993 and 1999, Israel transferred to the newly-created Palestinian Authority (PA) security and civilian responsibility for many Palestinian-populated areas of the Gaza Strip as well as the West Bank.

In 2000, a violent intifada or uprising began, and in 2001 negotiations to determine the permanent status of the West bank and Gaza Strip stalled. Subsequent attempts to re-start negotiations have not resulted in progress toward determining final status of the Israeli- Palestinian conflict. Israel in late 2005 unilaterally withdrew all of its settlers and soldiers and dismantled its military facilities in the Gaza Strip, but it continues to control the Gaza Strip's land and maritime borders and airspace. In early 2006, HAMAS won a majority in the Palestinian Legislative Council election. Fatah, the dominant Palestinian political faction in the West Bank, and HAMAS failed to maintain a unity government, leading to violent clashes between their respective supporters and HAMAS's violent seizure of all PA military and governmental institutions in the Gaza Strip in June 2007. Since HAMAS's takeover, Israel and Egypt have enforced tight restrictions on movement and access of goods and individuals into and out of the territory. Fatah and HAMAS have since reached a series of agreements aimed at restoring political unity between the Gaza Strip and the West Bank but have struggled to enact them.

Palestinian militants in the Gaza Strip and the Israel Defense Forces periodically exchange projectiles and air strikes, respectively, threatening broader conflict. In May 2021, HAMAS launched rockets at Israel, sparking an 11-day conflict that also involved other Gaza-based militant groups. Egypt, Qatar, and the UN Special Coordinator for the Middle East Peace Process have negotiated ceasefires to avert a broader conflict. Since 2018, HAMAS has also coordinated demonstrations along the Gaza-Israel security fence. Many of these protests have turned violent, resulting in several Israeli soldiers' deaths and injuries as well as more than 200 Palestinian deaths and thousands of injuries, most of which occurred during weekly March of Return protests from 2018 to the end of 2019.

GEOGRAPHY

Location: Middle East, bordering the Mediterranean Sea, between Egypt and Israel

Geographic coordinates: 31 25 N, 34 20 E

Map references: Middle East

Area: *total:* 360 sq km
land: 360 sq km
water: 0 sq km

Area - comparative: slightly more than twice the size of Washington, DC

Land boundaries: *total:* 72 km
border countries (2): Egypt 13 km; Israel 59 km

Coastline: 40 km

Maritime claims: see entry for Israel
note: effective 3 January 2009, the Gaza maritime area is closed to all maritime traffic and is under blockade imposed by Israeli Navy until further notice

Climate: temperate, mild winters, dry and warm to hot summers

Terrain: flat to rolling, sand- and dune-covered coastal plain

Elevation: *highest point:* Abu 'Awdah (Joz Abu 'Awdah) 105 m
lowest point: Mediterranean Sea 0 m

Natural resources: arable land, natural gas

Irrigated land: (2012) 240 sq km; note - includes the West Bank

Population distribution: population concentrated in major cities, particularly Gaza City in the north

Natural hazards: droughts

Geography - note: once a strategic strip of land along Mideast-North African trade routes that has experienced an incredibly turbulent history; the town of Gaza itself has been besieged countless times in its history; Israel evacuated its civilian settlements and soldiers from the Gaza Strip in 2005

PEOPLE AND SOCIETY

Population: 1,997,328 (2022 est.)

Ethnic groups: Palestinian Arab

Languages: Arabic, Hebrew (spoken by many Palestinians), English (widely understood)
major-language sample(s):
يمكن الاستغناء عنه للمعلومات الأساسية
كتاب حقائق العالم، المصدر الذي لا
(Arabic)

Religions: Muslim 98.0 - 99.0% (predominantly Sunni), Christian <1.0%, other, unaffiliated, unspecified <1.0% (2012 est.)
note: Israel dismantled its settlements in September 2005; Gaza has had no Jewish population since then

Age structure: *0-14 years:* 42.53% (male 418,751/female 397,013)
15-24 years: 21.67% (male 210,240/female 205,385)
25-54 years: 29.47% (male 275,976/female 289,277)
55-64 years: 3.66% (male 36,409/female 33,731)
65 years and over: 2.68% (male 27,248/female 24,191) (2020 est.)

Dependency ratios: *total dependency ratio:* 71.2
youth dependency ratio: 65.7
elderly dependency ratio: 5.5
potential support ratio: 18.2 (2020 est.)
note: data represent Gaza Strip and the West Bank

Median age: *total:* 18 years
male: 17.7 years
female: 18.4 years (2020 est.)

Population growth rate: 2.02% (2022 est.)

Birth rate: 27.67 births/1,000 population (2022 est.)

Death rate: 2.91 deaths/1,000 population (2022 est.)

Net migration rate: -4.55 migrant(s)/1,000 population (2022 est.)

Population distribution: population concentrated in major cities, particularly Gaza City in the north

Urbanization: *urban population:* 77.3% of total population (2022)
rate of urbanization: 2.85% annual rate of change (2020-25 est.)
note: data represent Gaza Strip and the West Bank

Major urban areas - population: 756,000 Gaza (2022)

Sex ratio: *at birth:* 1.06 male(s)/female
0-14 years: 1.05 male(s)/female
15-24 years: 1.03 male(s)/female
25-54 years: 0.94 male(s)/female
55-64 years: 1.07 male(s)/female
65 years and over: 0.94 male(s)/female
total population: 1.02 male(s)/female (2022 est.)

Maternal mortality ratio: 27 deaths/100,000 live births (2017 est.)
note: data represent Gaza Strip and the West Bank

Infant mortality rate: *total:* 15.23 deaths/1,000 live births
male: 16.4 deaths/1,000 live births
female: 13.99 deaths/1,000 live births (2022 est.)

Life expectancy at birth: *total population:* 75.4 years
male: 73.65 years
female: 77.25 years (2022 est.)

Total fertility rate: 3.44 children born/woman (2022 est.)

Contraceptive prevalence rate: 57.3% (2019/20)
note: includes Gaza Strip and West Bank

Drinking water source: *improved: urban:* 98.9% of population
rural: 99% of population
total: 98.9% of population
unimproved: urban: 1.1% of population
rural: 1% of population
total: 1.1% of population (2020 est.)
note: includes Gaza Strip and the West Bank

Physicians density: 2.71 physicians/1,000 population (2020)

Hospital bed density: 1.3 beds/1,000 population (2019)

Sanitation facility access: *improved: urban:* 99.9% of population
rural: 98.6% of population
total: 99.6% of population
unimproved: urban: 0.1% of population
rural: 1.4% of population
total: 0.4% of population (2020 est.)
note: note includes Gaza Strip and the West Bank

Major infectious diseases: *note:* on 21 March 2022, the US Centers for Disease Control and Prevention (CDC) issued a Travel Alert for polio in Asia; the Gaza Strip is currently considered a high risk to travelers for polio; the CDC recommends that before any international travel, anyone unvaccinated, incompletely vaccinated, or with an unknown polio vaccination status should complete the routine polio vaccine series; before travel to any high-risk destination, the CDC recommends that adults who previously completed the full, routine polio vaccine series receive a single, lifetime booster dose of polio vaccine

Children under the age of 5 years underweight: 2.1% (2019/20)
note: estimate is for Gaza Strip and the West Bank

Child marriage: *women married by age 15:* 0.7%
women married by age 18: 13.4% (2020 est.)
note: includes both the Gaza Strip and the West Bank

Education expenditures: 5.3% of GDP (2018 est.)
note: includes Gaza Strip and the West Bank

Literacy: *definition:* age 15 and over can read and write
total population: 97.5%
male: 98.8%
female: 96.2% (2020)
note: estimates are for Gaza Strip and the West Bank

School life expectancy (primary to tertiary education): *total:* 13 years
male: 12 years
female: 14 years (2020)
note: data represent Gaza Strip and the West Bank

Unemployment, youth ages 15-24: *total:* 42.1%
male: 36.6%
female: 70% (2020 est.)
note: includes the West Bank

ENVIRONMENT

Environment - current issues: soil degradation; desertification; water pollution from chemicals and pesticides; salination of fresh water; improper sewage treatment; water-borne disease; depletion and contamination of underground water resources

Air pollutants: *carbon dioxide emissions:* 3.23 megatons (2016 est.)
note: data represent combined total from the Gaza Strip and the West Bank.

Climate: temperate, mild winters, dry and warm to hot summers

Urbanization: *urban population:* 77.3% of total population (2022)
rate of urbanization: 2.85% annual rate of change (2020-25 est.)
note: data represent Gaza Strip and the West Bank

Revenue from forest resources: *forest revenues:* 0% of GDP (2018 est.)

Waste and recycling: *municipal solid waste generated annually:* 1.387 million tons (2016 est.)
municipal solid waste recycled annually: 6,935 tons (2013 est.)
percent of municipal solid waste recycled: 0.5% (2013 est.)
note: data represent combined total from the Gaza Strip and the West Bank.

Total water withdrawal: *municipal:* 181.2 million cubic meters (2017 est.)
industrial: 32 million cubic meters (2017 est.)
agricultural: 162 million cubic meters (2017 est.)
note: data represent combined total from the Gaza Strip and the West Bank.

Total renewable water resources: 837 million cubic meters (2017 est.)
note: data represent combined total from the Gaza Strip and the West Bank.

GOVERNMENT

Country name: *conventional long form:* none
conventional short form: Gaza Strip
local long form: none
local short form: Qita' Ghazzah
etymology: named for the largest city in the enclave, Gaza, whose settlement can be traced back to at least the 15th century B.C. (as "Ghazzat")

ECONOMY

Economic overview: Movement and access restrictions, violent attacks, and the slow pace of post-conflict reconstruction continue to degrade economic conditions in the Gaza Strip, the smaller of the two areas comprising the Palestinian territories. Israeli controls became more restrictive after HAMAS seized control of the territory in June 2007. Under Hamas control, Gaza has suffered from rising unemployment, elevated poverty rates, and a sharp contraction of the private sector, which had relied primarily on export markets.

Since April 2017, the Palestinian Authority has reduced payments for electricity supplied to Gaza and cut salaries for its employees there, exacerbating poor economic conditions. Since 2014, Egypt's crackdown on the Gaza Strip's extensive tunnel-based smuggling network has exacerbated fuel, construction material, and consumer goods shortages in the territory. Donor support for reconstruction following the 51-day conflict in 2014 between Israel and HAMAS and other Gaza-based militant groups has fallen short of post-conflict needs.

Real GDP (purchasing power parity): see entry for the West Bank

Real GDP growth rate: -15.2% (2014 est.)
5.6% (2013 est.)
7% (2012 est.)
note: excludes the West Bank

Real GDP per capita: $6,220 (2019 est.)
$6,318 (2018 est.)
$6,402 (2017 est.)
see entry for the the West Bank

GDP (official exchange rate): $2.938 billion (2014 est.)
note: excludes the West Bank

Inflation rate (consumer prices): 0.2% (2017 est.)
-0.2% (2016 est.)
note: excludes the West Bank

GDP - composition, by sector of origin: *agriculture:* 3% (2017 est.)
industry: 21.1% (2017 est.)
services: 75% (2017 est.)
note: data exclude the West Bank

GDP - composition, by end use: *household consumption:* 88.6% (2017 est.)
government consumption: 26.3% (2017 est.)
investment in fixed capital: 22.4% (2017 est.)
investment in inventories: 0% (2017 est.)
exports of goods and services: 18.6% (2017 est.)
imports of goods and services: -55.6% (2017 est.)
note: data exclude the West Bank

Agricultural products: tomatoes, cucumbers, olives, poultry, milk, potatoes, sheep milk, eggplants, gourds

Industries: textiles, food processing, furniture

Industrial production growth rate: 2.2% (2017 est.)
note: see entry for the West Bank

Labor force: 1.24 million (2017 est.)
note: excludes the West Bank

Labor force - by occupation: *agriculture:* 5.2%
industry: 10%
services: 84.8% (2015 est.)
note: data exclude the West Bank

Unemployment rate: 27.9% (2017 est.)
27% (2016 est.)
note: data exclude the West Bank

Unemployment, youth ages 15-24: *total:* 42.1%
male: 36.6%
female: 70% (2020 est.)
note: includes the West Bank

Population below poverty line: 30% (2011 est.)
note: data exclude the West Bank

Gini Index coefficient - distribution of family income: 33.7 (2016 est.)

Budget: see entry for the West Bank

Fiscal year: calendar year

Current account balance: -$1.444 billion (2017 est.)
-$1.348 billion (2016 est.)
note: excludes the West Bank

Exports: $1.955 billion (2017 est.)
$1.827 billion (2016 est.)

Exports - commodities: strawberries, carnations, vegetables, fish (small and irregular shipments, as permitted to transit the Israeli-controlled Kerem Shalom crossing)

Imports: $8.59 billion (2018 est.)
$7.852 billion (2017 est.)
see entry for the West Bank

Imports - commodities: food, consumer goods, fuel

Reserves of foreign exchange and gold: $446.3 million (31 December 2017 est.)
$583 million (31 December 2015 est.)

Debt - external: see entry for the West Bank

Exchange rates: see entry for the West Bank

ENERGY

Electricity access: *electrification - total population:* 100% (2018)
note: data for Gaza Strip and West Bank combined

Electricity: *installed generating capacity:* 215,000 kW (2020 est.) Data represented includes both the Gaza Strip and West Bank
consumption: 5,702,816,000 kWh (2019 est.) Data represented includes both the Gaza Strip and West Bank
exports: 0 kWh (2019 est.) Data represented includes both the Gaza Strip and West Bank
imports: 5.9 billion kWh (2019 est.) Data represented includes both the Gaza Strip and West Bank
transmission/distribution losses: 847 million kWh (2019 est.) Data represented includes both the Gaza Strip and West Bank

Electricity generation sources: *fossil fuels:* 100% of total installed capacity (2020 est.) Data represented includes both the Gaza Strip and West Bank

Petroleum: *total petroleum production:* 0 bbl/day (2021 est.) Data represented includes both the Gaza Strip and West Bank
refined petroleum consumption: 24,600 bbl/day (2019 est.) Data represented includes both the Gaza Strip and West Bank

Carbon dioxide emissions: 3.341 million metric tonnes of CO_2 (2019 est.) Data represented includes both the Gaza Strip and West Bank
from petroleum and other liquids: 3.341 million metric tonnes of CO_2 (2019 est.) Data includes both the Gaza Strip and West Bank

Energy consumption per capita: 13.604 million Btu/person (2019 est.) Data represented includes both the Gaza Strip and West Bank

COMMUNICATIONS

Telephones - fixed lines: *total subscriptions:* 466,283 (2020 est.)
subscriptions per 100 inhabitants: 9 (2020 est.)
includes the West Bank

Telephones - mobile cellular: *total subscriptions:* 4,274,119 (2020 est.)
subscriptions per 100 inhabitants: 84 (2020 est.)
includes the West Bank

Telecommunication systems: *general assessment:* Israel, which controls Palestinian frequencies and telecom infrastructure, limits mobile internet speeds in the Palestinian territories to levels that are significantly lower than in Israel and Jewish West Bank settlements; the World Bank urged Israel to let Palestinian cellular companies set up more advanced networks, and to ease restrictions on the import of equipment needed to build and operate them; Israel is rolling out fifth generation technology for its citizens, while the West Bank operates on 3G and Gaza, 2G; Israeli mobile operators don't officially service Palestinian areas, but many Palestinians use the faster Israeli networks with SIM cards; the Times of Israel reported in November that Israel tentatively agreed to let Palestinian operators launch 4G services (2022)
domestic: Israeli company BEZEQ and the Palestinian company PALTEL are responsible for fixed-line services; the Palestinian JAWWAL company provides cellular services; a slow 2G network allows calls and limited data transmission; fixed-line 9 per 100 and mobile-cellular 84 per 100 (includes West Bank) (2020)
international: country code 970 or 972 (2018)

Broadcast media: 1 TV station and about 10 radio stations; satellite TV accessible

Internet country code: .ps; note - IANA has designated .ps for the Gaza Strip, same as the West Bank

Internet users: *total:* 3,602,452 (2020 est.)
percent of population: 75% (2020 est.)
note: includes the West Bank

Broadband - fixed subscriptions: *total:* 376,911 (2020 est.)
subscriptions per 100 inhabitants: 7 (2020 est.)
note: includes the West Bank

TRANSPORTATION

Airports: *total:* 1 (2021)

Airports - with paved runways: *total:* 1
under 914 m: 1 (2021)
note - non-operational

Heliports: 1 (2021)

Roadways: *note:* see entry for the West Bank

Ports and terminals: *major seaport(s):* Gaza

MILITARY AND SECURITY

Military and security forces: HAMAS does not have a conventional military in the Gaza Strip but maintains security forces in addition to its military wing, the 'Izz al-Din al-Qassam Brigades; the military wing reports to the HAMAS Political Bureau; there are several other militant groups operating in the Gaza Strip, most notably the Al-Quds Brigades of Palestine Islamic Jihad, which are usually but not always beholden to HAMAS's authority (2022)

Military expenditures: not available

Military and security service personnel strengths: the military wing of HAMAS has an estimated 20-25,000 fighters (2022)

Military equipment inventories and acquisitions: the military wing of HAMAS is armed with light weapons, including an inventory of improvised rocket, anti-tank missile, and mortar capabilities; HAMAS acquires its weapons through smuggling or local construction and receives some military support from Iran (2021)

Military - note: since seizing control of the Gaza Strip in 2007, HAMAS has claimed responsibility for numerous rocket attacks into Israel and organized protests at the border between Gaza and Israel, resulting in violent clashes, casualties, and reprisal military actions by the Israel Defense Forces (IDF); HAMAS and Israel fought an 11-day conflict in May of 2021, which ended in an informal truce; sporadic clashes continued into 2022, including incendiary balloon attacks from Gaza and retaliatory IDF strikes; Palestine Islamic Jihad (PIJ) has conducted numerous attacks on Israel since the 1980s, including a barrage of mortar and rocket strikes in 2020, also prompting IDF counter-strikes; see Appendix T for more details on HAMAS and PIJ

in 2017, HAMAS and PIJ announced the formation of a "joint operations room" to coordinate the activities of their armed wings; by late 2020, the formation consisted of 12 militant groups operating in Gaza and had conducted its first joint training exercise (2022)

TERRORISM

Terrorist group(s): Army of Islam; Abdallah Azzam Brigades; al-Aqsa Martyrs Brigade; HAMAS; Islamic Revolutionary Guard Corps/Qods Force; Islamic State of Iraq and ash-Sham - Sinai Province (ISIS-SP); Mujahidin Shura Council in the Environs of Jerusalem; Palestine Islamic Jihad (PIJ); Palestine Liberation Front; Popular Front for the Liberation of Palestine (PFLP); PFLP-General Command

TRANSNATIONAL ISSUES

Disputes - international: according to the Oslo Accords, the status of the Gaza Strip is a final status issue to be resolved through negotiations; Israel removed settlers and military personnel from Gaza Strip in September 2005

Refugees and internally displaced persons: *refugees (country of origin):* 1,476,706 (Palestinian refugees) (2020)
IDPs: 131,000 (includes persons displaced within the Gaza Strip due to the intensification of the Israeli-Palestinian conflict since June 2014 and other Palestinian IDPs in the Gaza Strip and West Bank who fled as long ago as 1967, although confirmed cumulative data do not go back beyond 2006) (2020); note - data represent Gaza Strip and West Bank

GEORGIA

INTRODUCTION

Background: The region of present day Georgia contained the ancient kingdoms of Colchis and Kartli-Iberia. The area came under Roman influence in the first centuries A.D., and Christianity became the state religion in the 330s. Domination by Persians, Arabs, and Turks was followed by a Georgian golden age (11th-13th centuries) that was cut short by the Mongol invasion of 1236. Subsequently, the Ottoman and Persian empires competed for influence in the region. Georgia was absorbed into the Russian Empire in the 19th century. Independent for three years (1918-1921) following the Russian revolution, it was forcibly incorporated into the USSR in 1921 and regained its independence when the Soviet Union dissolved in 1991.

Mounting public discontent over rampant corruption and ineffective government services, followed by an attempt by the incumbent Georgian Government to manipulate parliamentary elections in November 2003, touched off widespread protests that led to the resignation of Eduard SHEVARDNADZE, president since 1995. In the aftermath of that popular movement, which became known as the "Rose Revolution," new elections in early 2004 swept Mikheil SAAKASHVILI into power along with his United National Movement (UNM) party. SAAKASHVILI made progress on market reforms and good governance during his time in power, but also faced accusations of abuse of office. Progress was also complicated by Russian assistance and support to the separatist regions of Abkhazia and South Ossetia that led to periodic flare-ups in tension and violence and that culminated in a five-day conflict in August 2008 between Russia and Georgia, including the invasion of large portions of Georgian territory. Russian troops pledged to pull back from most occupied Georgian territory, but in late August 2008 Russia unilaterally recognized the independence of Abkhazia and South Ossetia, and Russian military forces remain in those regions.

Billionaire Bidzina IVANISHVILI's unexpected entry into politics in October 2011 brought the divided opposition together under his Georgian Dream coalition, which won a majority of seats in the October 2012 parliamentary elections and removed UNM from power. Conceding defeat, SAAKASHVILI named IVANISHVILI as prime minister and allowed Georgian Dream to create a new government. Giorgi MARGVELASHVILI became president in November 2013, ending a tense year of power-sharing between SAAKASHVILI and IVANISHVILI and SAAKASHVILI then left the country. At the time, these changes in leadership represented unique examples of a former Soviet state that emerged to conduct democratic and peaceful government transitions of power. IVANISHVILI voluntarily resigned from office after the presidential succession, and in the following years, the prime minister position has seen frequent turnover. Most recently, Irakli GARIBASHVILI became prime minister in February 2021, replacing Giorgi GAKHARIA, who later in the year formed his own opposition party. In October 2021, SAAKASHVILI returned to Georgia, where he was immediately arrested to serve six years in prison on outstanding abuse of office convictions. Popular and government support for integration with the West is high in Georgia. Joining the EU and NATO are among the country's top foreign policy goals.

GEOGRAPHY

Location: Southwestern Asia, bordering the Black Sea, between Turkey and Russia, with a sliver of land north of the Caucasus extending into Europe; note - Georgia views itself as part of Europe; geopolitically, it can be classified as falling within Europe, the Middle East, or both

Geographic coordinates: 42 00 N, 43 30 E

Map references: Asia

Area: *total:* 69,700 sq km
land: 69,700 sq km
water: 0 sq km
note: approximately 12,560 sq km, or about 18% of Georgia's area, is Russian occupied; the seized area includes all of Abkhazia and the breakaway region of South Ossetia, which consists of the northern part of Shida Kartli, eastern slivers of the Imereti region and Racha-Lechkhumi and Kvemo Svaneti, and part of western Mtskheta-Mtianeti
country comparison to the world: 121

Area - comparative: slightly smaller than South Carolina; slightly larger than West Virginia

Land boundaries: *total:* 1,814 km
border countries (4): Armenia 219 km; Azerbaijan 428 km; Russia 894 km; Turkey 273 km

Coastline: 310 km

Maritime claims: *territorial sea:* 12 nm
exclusive economic zone: 200 nm

Climate: warm and pleasant; Mediterranean-like on Black Sea coast

Terrain: largely mountainous with Great Caucasus Mountains in the north and Lesser Caucasus Mountains in the south; Kolkhet'is Dablobi (Kolkhida Lowland) opens to the Black Sea in the west; Mtkvari River Basin in the east; fertile soils in river valley flood plains and foothills of Kolkhida Lowland

Elevation: *highest point:* Mt'a Shkhara 5,193 m
lowest point: Black Sea 0 m
mean elevation: 1,432 m

Natural resources: timber, hydropower, manganese deposits, iron ore, copper, minor coal and oil deposits; coastal climate and soils allow for important tea and citrus growth

Land use: *agricultural land:* 35.5% (2018 est.)
arable land: 5.8% (2018 est.)
permanent crops: 1.8% (2018 est.)
permanent pasture: 27.9% (2018 est.)
forest: 39.4% (2018 est.)
other: 25.1% (2018 est.)

Irrigated land: 4,330 sq km (2012)

Population distribution: settlement concentrated in the central valley, particularly in the capital city of

Tbilisi in the east; smaller urban agglomerations dot the Black Sea coast, with Bat'umi being the largest

Natural hazards: earthquakes

Geography - note: *note 1:* strategically located east of the Black Sea; Georgia controls much of the Caucasus Mountains and the routes through them
note 2: the world's four deepest caves are all in Georgia, including two that are the only known caves on earth deeper than 2,000 m: Krubera Cave at -2,197 m (-7,208 ft; reached in 2012) and Veryovkina Cave at -2,212 (-7,257 ft; reached in 2018)

PEOPLE AND SOCIETY

Population: 4,935,518 (2022 est.)
country comparison to the world: 126

Nationality: *noun:* Georgian(s)
adjective: Georgian

Ethnic groups: Georgian 86.8%, Azeri 6.3%, Armenian 4.5%, other 2.3% (includes Russian, Ossetian, Yazidi, Ukrainian, Kist, Greek) (2014 est.)

Languages: Georgian (official) 87.6%, Azeri 6.2%, Armenian 3.9%, Russian 1.2%, other 1%; note - Abkhaz is the official language in Abkhazia (2014 est.)
major-language sample(s):
მსოფლიო ფაქტების წიგნი, ძირითადი ინფორმაციის აუცილებელი წყარო.
(Georgian)

Religions: Orthodox (official) 83.4%, Muslim 10.7%, Armenian Apostolic 2.9%, other 1.2% (includes Catholic, Jehovah's Witness, Yazidi, Protestant, Jewish), none 0.5%, unspecified/no answer 1.2% (2014 est.)

Age structure: *0-14 years:* 18.42% (male 472,731/ female 435,174)
15-24 years: 10.9% (male 286,518/female 250,882)
25-54 years: 40.59% (male 984,942/female 1,016,353)
55-64 years: 13.24% (male 288,650/female 364,117)
65 years and over: 16.85% (male 326,219/female 504,444) (2020 est.)

Dependency ratios: *total dependency ratio:* 55
youth dependency ratio: 31.3
elderly dependency ratio: 23.6
potential support ratio: 4.2 (2020 est.)

Median age: *total:* 38.6 years
male: 35.9 years
female: 41.4 years (2020 est.)
country comparison to the world: 60

Population growth rate: 0.03% (2022 est.)
country comparison to the world: 192

Birth rate: 11 births/1,000 population (2022 est.)
country comparison to the world: 168

Death rate: 10.8 deaths/1,000 population (2022 est.)
country comparison to the world: 24

Net migration rate: 0.06 migrant(s)/1,000 population (2022 est.)
country comparison to the world: 81

Population distribution: settlement concentrated in the central valley, particularly in the capital city of Tbilisi in the east; smaller urban agglomerations dot the Black Sea coast, with Bat'umi being the largest

Urbanization: *urban population:* 60.3% of total population (2022)
rate of urbanization: 0.35% annual rate of change (2020-25 est.)
note: data include Abkhazia and South Ossetia

Major urban areas - population: 1.080 million TBILISI (capital) (2022)

Sex ratio: *at birth:* 1.05 male(s)/female
0-14 years: 1.07 male(s)/female
15-24 years: 1.14 male(s)/female
25-54 years: 0.98 male(s)/female
55-64 years: 0.78 male(s)/female
65 years and over: 0.54 male(s)/female
total population: 0.92 male(s)/female (2022 est.)

Mother's mean age at first birth: 25.9 years (2019 est.)
note: data does not cover Abkhazia and South Ossetia

Maternal mortality ratio: 25 deaths/100,000 live births (2017 est.)
country comparison to the world: 121

Infant mortality rate: *total:* 14.77 deaths/1,000 live births
male: 16.9 deaths/1,000 live births
female: 12.53 deaths/1,000 live births (2022 est.)
country comparison to the world: 102

Life expectancy at birth: *total population:* 77.5 years
male: 73.45 years
female: 81.74 years (2022 est.)
country comparison to the world: 89

Total fertility rate: 1.75 children born/woman (2022 est.)
country comparison to the world: 154

Contraceptive prevalence rate: 40.6% (2018)

Drinking water source: *improved: urban:* 99.4% of population
rural: 94.3% of population
total: 97.3% of population
unimproved: urban: 0.6% of population
rural: 5.7% of population
total: 2.7% of population (2020 est.)

Current health expenditure: 6.7% of GDP (2019)

Physicians density: 5.11 physicians/1,000 population (2020)

Hospital bed density: 2.9 beds/1,000 population (2014)

Sanitation facility access: *improved: urban:* 96.3% of population
rural: 72.7% of population
total: 86.7% of population
unimproved: urban: 3.7% of population
rural: 27.3% of population
total: 13.3% of population (2020 est.)

HIV/AIDS - adult prevalence rate: 0.3% (2020 est.)
country comparison to the world: 82

Obesity - adult prevalence rate: 21.7% (2016)
country comparison to the world: 86

Alcohol consumption per capita: *total:* 7.45 liters of pure alcohol (2019 est.)
beer: 1.71 liters of pure alcohol (2019 est.)
wine: 3.19 liters of pure alcohol (2019 est.)
spirits: 2.52 liters of pure alcohol (2019 est.)
other alcohols: 0.02 liters of pure alcohol (2019 est.)
country comparison to the world: 53

Tobacco use: *total:* 31.7% (2020 est.)
male: 56.3% (2020 est.)
female: 7.1% (2020 est.)
country comparison to the world: 24

Children under the age of 5 years underweight: 2.1% (2018)
country comparison to the world: 108

Child marriage: *women married by age 15:* 0.3%
women married by age 18: 13.9%
men married by age 18: 0.5% (2018 est.)

Education expenditures: 3.8% of GDP (2020 est.)
country comparison to the world: 111

Literacy: *definition:* age 15 and over can read and write
total population: 99.6%
male: 99.7%
female: 99.5% (2019)

School life expectancy (primary to tertiary education): *total:* 16 years
male: 15 years
female: 16 years (2020)

Unemployment, youth ages 15-24: *total:* 39.4%
male: 40.1%
female: 38.3% (2020 est.)

ENVIRONMENT

Environment - current issues: air pollution, particularly in Rust'avi; heavy water pollution of Mtkvari River and the Black Sea; inadequate supplies of potable water; soil pollution from toxic chemicals; land and forest degradation; biodiversity loss; waste management

Environment - international agreements: *party to:* Air Pollution, Biodiversity, Climate Change, Climate Change-Kyoto Protocol, Climate Change-Paris Agreement, Comprehensive Nuclear Test Ban, Desertification, Endangered Species, Hazardous Wastes, Law of the Sea, Marine Dumping-London Protocol, Ozone Layer Protection, Ship Pollution, Wetlands
signed, but not ratified: none of the selected agreements

Air pollutants: *particulate matter emissions:* 21.2 micrograms per cubic meter (2016 est.)
carbon dioxide emissions: 10.13 megatons (2016 est.)
methane emissions: 6.05 megatons (2020 est.)

Climate: warm and pleasant; Mediterranean-like on Black Sea coast

Land use: *agricultural land:* 35.5% (2018 est.)
arable land: 5.8% (2018 est.)
permanent crops: 1.8% (2018 est.)
permanent pasture: 27.9% (2018 est.)
forest: 39.4% (2018 est.)
other: 25.1% (2018 est.)

Urbanization: *urban population:* 60.3% of total population (2022)
rate of urbanization: 0.35% annual rate of change (2020-25 est.)
note: data include Abkhazia and South Ossetia

Revenue from forest resources: *forest revenues:* 0.07% of GDP (2018 est.)
country comparison to the world: 123

Revenue from coal: *coal revenues:* 0.01% of GDP (2018 est.)
country comparison to the world: 49

Waste and recycling: *municipal solid waste generated annually:* 800,000 tons (2015 est.)

Total water withdrawal: *municipal:* 359,974,627.7 cubic meters (2017 est.)
industrial: 402,206,287.9 cubic meters (2017 est.)

agricultural: 1,060,819,084.4 cubic meters (2017 est.)

Total renewable water resources: 63.33 billion cubic meters (2017 est.)

GOVERNMENT

Country name: *conventional long form:* none
conventional short form: Georgia
local long form: none
local short form: Sak'art'velo
former: Georgian Soviet Socialist Republic
etymology: the Western name may derive from the Persian designation "gurgan" meaning "Land of the Wolves"; the native name "Sak'art'velo" means "Land of the Kartvelians" and refers to the core central Georgian region of Kartli

Government type: semi-presidential republic

Capital: *name:* Tbilisi
geographic coordinates: 41 41 N, 44 50 E
time difference: UTC+4 (9 hours ahead of Washington, DC, during Standard Time)
etymology: the name in Georgian means "warm place," referring to the numerous sulfuric hot springs in the area

Administrative divisions: 9 regions (mkharebi, singular - mkhare), 1 city (kalaki), and 2 autonomous republics (avtomnoy respubliki, singular - avtom respublika)
regions: Guria, Imereti, Kakheti, Kvemo Kartli, Mtskheta Mtianeti, Racha-Lechkhumi and Kvemo Svaneti, Samegrelo and Zemo Svaneti, Samtskhe-Javakheti, Shida Kartli; note - the breakaway region of South Ossetia consists of the northern part of Shida Kartli, eastern slivers of the Imereti region and Racha-Lechkhumi and Kvemo Svaneti, and part of western Mtskheta-Mtianeti
city: Tbilisi
autonomous republics: Abkhazia or Ap'khazet'is Avtonomiuri Respublika (Sokhumi), Ajaria or Acharis Avtonomiuri Respublika (Bat'umi)
note 1: the administrative centers of the two autonomous republics are shown in parentheses
note 2: the United States recognizes the breakaway regions of Abkhazia and South Ossetia to be part of Georgia

Independence: 9 April 1991 (from the Soviet Union); notable earlier date: A.D. 1008 (Georgia unified under King BAGRAT III)

National holiday: Independence Day, 26 May (1918); note - 26 May 1918 was the date of independence from Soviet Russia, 9 April 1991 was the date of independence from the Soviet Union

Constitution: *history:* previous 1921, 1978 (based on 1977 Soviet Union constitution); latest approved 24 August 1995, effective 17 October 1995
amendments: proposed as a draft law supported by more than one half of the Parliament membership or by petition of at least 200,000 voters; passage requires support by at least three fourths of the Parliament membership in two successive sessions three months apart and the signature and promulgation by the president of Georgia; amended several times, last in 2020 (legislative electoral system revised)

Legal system: civil law system

International law organization participation: accepts compulsory ICJ jurisdiction; accepts ICCt jurisdiction

Citizenship: *citizenship by birth:* no
citizenship by descent only: at least one parent must be a citizen of Georgia
dual citizenship recognized: no
residency requirement for naturalization: 10 years

Suffrage: 18 years of age; universal

Executive branch: *chief of state:* President Salome ZOURABICHVILI (since 16 December 2018)
head of government: Prime Minister Irakli GARIBASHVILI (since 22 February 2021)
cabinet: Cabinet of Ministers
elections/appointments: president directly elected by absolute majority popular vote in 2 rounds if needed for a 5-year term (eligible for a second term); election last held on 28 November 2018 (next to be held in 2024); prime minister nominated by Parliament, appointed by the president
note - 2017 constitutional amendments made the 2018 election the last where the president was directly elected; future presidents will be elected by a 300-member College of Electors; in light of these changes, ZOURABICHVILI was allowed a six-year term
election results: 2018 Salome ZOURABICHVILI elected president in runoff; percent of vote - Salome ZOURABICHVILI (independent, backed by Georgian Dream) 59.5%, Grigol VASHADZE (UNM) 40.5%; Irakli GARIBASHVILI approved as prime minister by Parliamentary vote 89-2
2013 Giorgi MARGVELASHVILI is sworn in as president (Georgian Dream) 62.1%, David BAKRADZE (ENM) 21.7%, Nino BURJANADZE (DM-UG) 10.2%, other 6%

Legislative branch: *description:* unicameral Parliament or Sakartvelos Parlamenti (150 seats statutory, 144 current; 120 members directly elected in a single nationwide constituency by closed, party-list proportional representation vote and 30 directly elected in single-seat constituencies by at least 50% majority vote, with a runoff if needed; no party earning less than 40% of total votes may claim a majority; members serve 4-year terms)
elections: last held on 31 October and 21 November 2020 (next to be held in October 2024)
election results: percent of vote by party - Georgian Dream 48.2%, UNM 27.2%, European Georgia 3.8%, Lelo 3.2%, Strategy 3.2%, Alliance of Patriots 3.1%, Girchi 2.9%, Citizens 1.3%, Labor 1%; seats by party - Georgian Dream 90, UNM 36, European Georgia 5, Lelo 4, Strategy 4, Alliance of Patriots 4, Girchi 4, Citizens 2, Labor 1; composition (as of October 2021) - men 117, women 27, percent of women 18.8%

Judicial branch: *highest court(s):* Supreme Court (consists of 28 judges organized into several specialized judicial chambers; number of judges determined by the president of Georgia); Constitutional Court (consists of 9 judges); note - the Abkhazian and Ajarian Autonomous republics each have a supreme court and a hierarchy of lower courts
judge selection and term of office: Supreme Court judges nominated by the High Council of Justice (a 14-member body consisting of the Supreme Court chairperson, common court judges, and appointees of the president of Georgia) and appointed by Parliament; judges appointed for life; Constitutional Court judges appointed 3 each by the president, by Parliament, and by the Supreme Court judges; judges appointed for 10- year terms
subordinate courts: Courts of Appeal; regional (town) and district courts

Political parties and leaders: Alliance of Patriots [Irma INASHVILI]
Citizens Party [Aleko ELISASHVILI]
European Georgia-Movement for Liberty [Giga BOKERIA]
European Socialists [Fridon INJIA]
For Georgia [Giorgi GAKHARIA]
Georgian Dream-Democratic Georgia [Irakli KOBAKHIDZE]
Girchi-More Freedom [Zurab JAPARIDZE]
Labor Party [Shalva NATELASHVILI]
Lelo for Georgia [Mamuka KHAZARADZE]
New Political Centre-Girchi [Iago KHVICHIA]
Republican Party [Khatuna SAMNIDZE]
Strategy Aghmashenebeli [Giorgi VASHADZE]
United National Movement or UNM [Nikanor "Nika" MELIA]

International organization participation: ADB, BSEC, CD, CE, CPLP (associate), EAPC, EBRD, FAO, G-11, GCTU, GUAM, IAEA, IBRD, ICAO, ICC (national committees), ICCt, ICRM, IDA, IFAD, IFC, IFRCS, ILO, IMF, IMO, Interpol, IOC, IOM, IPU, ISO (correspondent), ITSO, ITU, ITUC (NGOs), MIGA, OAS (observer), OIF (observer), OPCW, OSCE, PFP, SELEC (observer), UN, UNCTAD, UNESCO, UNIDO, UNWTO, UPU, WCO, WHO, WIPO, WMO, WTO

Diplomatic representation in the US: *chief of mission:* Ambassador David ZALKALIANI (since 7 June 2022)
chancery: 1824 R Street NW, Washington, DC 20009
telephone: [1] (202) 387-2390
FAX: [1] (202) 387-0864
email address and website:
embgeo.usa@mfa.gov.ge
https://georgiaembassyusa.org/contact/
consulate(s) general: New York

Diplomatic representation from the US: *chief of mission:* Ambassador Kelly C. DEGNAN (since 31 January 2020)
embassy: 11 Georgian-American Friendship Avenue, Didi Dighomi, Tbilisi, 0131
mailing address: 7060 Tbilisi Place, Washington, DC 20521-7060
telephone: [995] (32) 227-70-00
FAX: [995] (32) 253-23-10
email address and website:
askconsultbilisi@state.gov
https://ge.usembassy.gov/

Flag description: white rectangle with a central red cross extending to all four sides of the flag; each of the four quadrants displays a small red bolnur-katskhuri cross; sometimes referred to as the Five-Cross Flag; although adopted as the official Georgian flag in 2004, the five-cross design is based on a 14th century banner of the Kingdom of Georgia

National symbol(s): Saint George, lion; national colors: red, white

National anthem: *name:* "Tavisupleba" (Liberty)
lyrics/music: Davit MAGRADSE/ Zakaria PALIASHVILI (adapted by Joseb KETSCHAKMADSE)
note: adopted 2004; after the Rose Revolution, a new anthem with music based on the operas "Abesalom da Eteri" and "Daisi" was adopted

National heritage: *total World Heritage Sites:* 4 (3 cultural, 1 natural)

selected World Heritage Site locales: Gelati Monastery (c); Historical Monuments of Mtskheta (c); Upper Svaneti (c); Colchic Rainforests and Wetlands (n)

ECONOMY

Economic overview: Georgia's main economic activities include cultivation of agricultural products such as grapes, citrus fruits, and hazelnuts; mining of manganese, copper, and gold; and producing alcoholic and nonalcoholic beverages, metals, machinery, and chemicals in small-scale industries. The country imports nearly all of its needed supplies of natural gas and oil products. It has sizeable hydropower capacity that now provides most of its electricity needs.

Georgia has overcome the chronic energy shortages and gas supply interruptions of the past by renovating hydropower plants and by increasingly relying on natural gas imports from Azerbaijan instead of from Russia. Construction of the Baku-Tbilisi-Ceyhan oil pipeline, the South Caucasus gas pipeline, and the Baku-Tbilisi-Kars railroad are part of a strategy to capitalize on Georgia's strategic location between Europe and Asia and develop its role as a transit hub for gas, oil, and other goods.

Georgia's economy sustained GDP growth of more than 10% in 2006-07, based on strong inflows of foreign investment, remittances, and robust government spending. However, GDP growth slowed following the August 2008 conflict with Russia, and sank to negative 4% in 2009 as foreign direct investment and workers' remittances declined in the wake of the global financial crisis. The economy rebounded in the period 2010-17, but FDI inflows, the engine of Georgian economic growth prior to the 2008 conflict, have not recovered fully. Unemployment remains persistently high.

The country is pinning its hopes for faster growth on a continued effort to build up infrastructure, enhance support for entrepreneurship, simplify regulations, and improve professional education, in order to attract foreign investment and boost employment, with a focus on transportation projects, tourism, hydropower, and agriculture. Georgia had historically suffered from a chronic failure to collect tax revenues; however, since 2004 the government has simplified the tax code, increased tax enforcement, and cracked down on petty corruption, leading to higher revenues. The government has received high marks from the World Bank for improvements in business transparency. Since 2012, the Georgian Dream-led government has continued the previous administration's low-regulation, low-tax, free market policies, while modestly increasing social spending and amending the labor code to comply with International Labor Standards. In mid-2014, Georgia concluded an association agreement with the EU, paving the way to free trade and visa-free travel. In 2017, Georgia signed Free Trade Agreement (FTA) with China as part of Tbilisi's efforts to diversify its economic ties. Georgia is seeking to develop its Black Sea ports to further facilitate East-West trade.

Real GDP (purchasing power parity): $52.33 billion (2020 est.)
$55.76 billion (2019 est.)
$53.12 billion (2018 est.)
note: data are in 2017 dollars
country comparison to the world: 109

Real GDP growth rate: 5% (2017 est.)
2.8% (2016 est.)
2.9% (2015 est.)
country comparison to the world: 47

Real GDP per capita: $14,100 (2020 est.)
$15,000 (2019 est.)
$14,300 (2018 est.)
note: data are in 2017 dollars
country comparison to the world: 111

GDP (official exchange rate): $17.694 billion (2019 est.)

Inflation rate (consumer prices): 4.8% (2019 est.)
2.6% (2018 est.)
6% (2017 est.)
country comparison to the world: 178

Credit ratings:

Fitch rating: BB (2019)

Moody's rating: Ba2 (2017)

Standard & Poors rating: BB (2019)
note: The year refers to the year in which the current credit rating was first obtained.

GDP - composition, by sector of origin: *agriculture:* 8.2% (2017 est.)
industry: 23.7% (2017 est.)
services: 67.9% (2017 est.)

GDP - composition, by end use: *household consumption:* 62.8% (2017 est.)
government consumption: 17.1% (2017 est.)
investment in fixed capital: 29.5% (2017 est.)
investment in inventories: 2.4% (2017 est.)
exports of goods and services: 50.4% (2017 est.)
imports of goods and services: -62.2% (2017 est.)

Agricultural products: milk, grapes, maize, potatoes, wheat, watermelons, tomatoes, tangerines/mandarins, barley, apples

Industries: steel, machine tools, electrical appliances, mining (manganese, copper, gold), chemicals, wood products, wine

Industrial production growth rate: 6.7% (2017 est.)
country comparison to the world: 34

Labor force: 686,000 (2019 est.)
country comparison to the world: 150

Labor force - by occupation: *agriculture:* 55.6%
industry: 8.9%
services: 35.5% (2006 est.)

Unemployment rate: 11.8% (2016 est.)
country comparison to the world: 161

Unemployment, youth ages 15-24: *total:* 39.4%
male: 40.1%
female: 38.3% (2020 est.)
country comparison to the world: 13

Population below poverty line: 19.5% (2019 est.)

Gini Index coefficient - distribution of family income: 36.4 (2018 est.)
46 (2011)
country comparison to the world: 89

Household income or consumption by percentage share: *lowest 10%:* 2%
highest 10%: 31.3% (2008)

Budget: *revenues:* 4.352 billion (2017 est.)
expenditures: 4.925 billion (2017 est.)

Budget surplus (+) or deficit (-): -3.8% (of GDP) (2017 est.)
country comparison to the world: 153

Public debt: 44.9% of GDP (2017 est.)
44.4% of GDP (2016 est.)
note: data cover general government debt and include debt instruments issued (or owned) by government entities other than the treasury; the data include treasury debt held by foreign entities; the data include debt issued by subnational entities; Georgia does not maintain intragovernmental debt or social funds
country comparison to the world: 116

Taxes and other revenues: 28.7% (of GDP) (2017 est.)
country comparison to the world: 91

Fiscal year: calendar year

Current account balance: -$1.348 billion (2017 est.)
-$1.84 billion (2016 est.)
country comparison to the world: 156

Exports: $5.94 billion (2020 est.) note: data are in current year dollars
$9.54 billion (2019 est.) note: data are in current year dollars
$8.9 billion (2018 est.) note: data are in current year dollars
country comparison to the world: 120

Exports - partners: Russia 12%, Azerbaijan 12%, Armenia 9%, Bulgaria 8%, China 6%, Turkey 6%, Ukraine 6% (2019)

Exports - commodities: copper, cars, iron alloys, wine, packaged medicines (2019)

Imports: $8.94 billion (2020 est.) note: data are in current year dollars
$11.11 billion (2019 est.) note: data are in current year dollars
$10.77 billion (2018 est.) note: data are in current year dollars
country comparison to the world: 112

Imports - partners: Turkey 17%, China 11%, Russia 9%, Azerbaijan 6%, United States 6%, Germany 5% (2019)

Imports - commodities: cars, refined petroleum, copper, packaged medicines, natural gas (2019)

Reserves of foreign exchange and gold: $3.039 billion (31 December 2017 est.)
$2.756 billion (31 December 2016 est.)
country comparison to the world: 108

Debt - external: $18.149 billion (2019 est.)
$17.608 billion (2018 est.)
country comparison to the world: 96

Exchange rates: laris (GEL) per US dollar -
2.535 (2017 est.)
2.3668 (2016 est.)
2.3668 (2015 est.)
2.2694 (2014 est.)
1.7657 (2013 est.)

ENERGY

Electricity access: *electrification - total population:* 100% (2020)

Electricity: *installed generating capacity:* 4.579 million kW (2020 est.)
consumption: 12,062,080,000 kWh (2019 est.)
exports: 256 million kWh (2020 est.)
imports: 1.712 billion kWh (2020 est.)
transmission/distribution losses: 918.2 million kWh (2019 est.)

Electricity generation sources: *fossil fuels:* 25.3% of total installed capacity (2020 est.)
wind: 0.8% of total installed capacity (2020 est.)

hydroelectricity: 73.9% of total installed capacity (2020 est.)

Coal: *production:* 99,000 metric tons (2020 est.)
consumption: 362,000 metric tons (2020 est.)
exports: 1,000 metric tons (2020 est.)
imports: 277,000 metric tons (2020 est.)
proven reserves: 201 million metric tons (2019 est.)

Petroleum: *total petroleum production:* 300 bbl/day (2021 est.)
refined petroleum consumption: 32,400 bbl/day (2019 est.)
crude oil and lease condensate exports: 100 bbl/day (2018 est.)
crude oil and lease condensate imports: 0 bbl/day (2018 est.)
crude oil estimated reserves: 35 million barrels (2021 est.)

Refined petroleum products - production: 247 bbl/day (2017 est.)
country comparison to the world: 106

Refined petroleum products - exports: 2,052 bbl/day (2015 est.)
country comparison to the world: 104

Refined petroleum products - imports: 28,490 bbl/day (2015 est.)
country comparison to the world: 101

Natural gas: *production:* 6.088 million cubic meters (2020 est.)
consumption: 2,539,649,000 cubic meters (2020 est.)
exports: 0 cubic meters (2021 est.)
imports: 2,534,892,000 cubic meters (2020 est.)
proven reserves: 8.495 billion cubic meters (2021 est.)

Carbon dioxide emissions: 10.299 million metric tonnes of CO2 (2019 est.)
from coal and metallurgical coke: 1.063 million metric tonnes of CO2 (2019 est.)
from petroleum and other liquids: 4.245 million metric tonnes of CO2 (2019 est.)
from consumed natural gas: 4.992 million metric tonnes of CO2 (2019 est.)
country comparison to the world: 104

Energy consumption per capita: 63.286 million Btu/person (2019 est.)
country comparison to the world: 87

COMMUNICATIONS

Telephones - fixed lines: *total subscriptions:* 387,698 (2020 est.)
subscriptions per 100 inhabitants: 10 (2020 est.)
country comparison to the world: 102

Telephones - mobile cellular: *total subscriptions:* 5,100,101 (2020 est.)
subscriptions per 100 inhabitants: 128 (2020 est.)
country comparison to the world: 120

Telecommunication systems: *general assessment:* the telecom sector has been attempting for many years to overcome the decades of under-investment in its fixed-line infrastructure during the Soviet era; concerted efforts to privatize state-owned enterprises and open up the telecom market have been mostly successful, with a large number of networks now competing in both the fixed-line and the mobile segments; more needs to be done, however, to give investors the confidence to enter a market that has barely moved in terms of revenue growth over the last decade, and where regulatory overreach has sometimes come perilously close to arresting further development; Georgia's government moved fast following the collapse of the Soviet Union to liberalize the country's telecom market; this resulted in a relatively high number of networks competing in the under-developed fixed-line segment as well as in the emerging mobile market; both segments remain dominated by just a few companies (2022)
domestic: fixed-line subscriptions over 9 per 100, cellular telephone networks cover the entire country; mobile-cellular teledensity roughly 128 per 100 persons; intercity facilities include a fiber-optic line between T'bilisi and K'ut'aisi; the mobile and mobile broadband segments have both demonstrated solid growth in 2021, (2020)
international: country code - 995; landing points for the Georgia-Russia, Diamond Link Global, and Caucasus Cable System fiber-optic submarine cable that provides connectivity to Russia, Romania and Bulgaria; international service is available by microwave, landline, and satellite through the Moscow switch; international electronic mail and telex service are available (2019)

Broadcast media: The Tbilisi-based Georgian Public Broadcaster (GPB) includes Channel 1, Channel 2, and the Batumi-based Adjara TV, and the State Budget funds all three; there are also a number of independent commercial television broadcasters, such as Imedi, Rustavi 2, Pirveli TV, Maestro, Kavkasia, Georgian Dream Studios (GDS), Obiektivi, Mtavari Arkhi, and a small Russian language operator TOK TV; Tabula and Post TV are web-based television outlets; all of these broadcasters and web-based television outlets, except GDS, carry the news; the Georgian Orthodox Church also operates a satellite-based television station called Unanimity; there are 26 regional television broadcasters across Georgia that are members of the Georgian Association of Regional Broadcasters and/or the Alliance of Georgian Broadcasters; the broadcaster organizations seek to strengthen the regional media's capacities and distribution of regional products: a nationwide digital switchover occurred in 2015; there are several dozen private radio stations; GPB operates 2 radio stations (2019)

Internet country code: .ge

Internet users: *total:* 3,628,500 (July 2022 est.)
percent of population: 91.2% (July 2022 est.)
country comparison to the world: 104

Broadband - fixed subscriptions: *total:* 972,162 (2020 est.)
subscriptions per 100 inhabitants: 24 (2020 est.)
country comparison to the world: 75

TRANSPORTATION

National air transport system: *number of registered air carriers:* 4 (2020)
inventory of registered aircraft operated by air carriers: 12
annual passenger traffic on registered air carriers: 516,034 (2018)
annual freight traffic on registered air carriers: 750,000 (2018) mt-km

Civil aircraft registration country code prefix: 4L

Airports: *total:* 22 (2021)
country comparison to the world: 134

Airports - with paved runways : *total:* 18
over 3,047 m: 1
2,438 to 3,047 m: 7
1,524 to 2,437 m: 3
914 to 1,523 m: 5
under 914 m: 2 (2021)

Airports - with unpaved runways: *total:* 4
1,524 to 2,437 m: 1
914 to 1,523 m: 2
under 914 m: 1 (2021)

Heliports: 2 (2021)

Pipelines: 1,596 km gas, 1,175 km oil (2013)

Railways: *total:* 1,363 km (2014)
narrow gauge: 37 km (2014) 0.912-m gauge (37 km electrified)
broad gauge: 1,326 km (2014) 1.520-m gauge (1,251 km electrified)
country comparison to the world: 84

Roadways: *total:* 20,295 km (2018)
country comparison to the world: 112

Merchant marine: *total:* 25
by type: bulk carrier 2, general cargo 3, other 20 (2021)
country comparison to the world: 141

Ports and terminals: *major seaport(s):* Black Sea - Batumi, Poti

MILITARY AND SECURITY

Military and security forces: Georgian Defense Forces: Land Forces (includes Aviation and Air Defense Forces), Special Operations Forces, National Guard; Ministry of Internal Affairs: Border Police, Coast Guard (includes Georgian naval forces, which were merged with the Coast Guard in 2009) (2022)

Military expenditures: 1.7% of GDP (2021 est.)
1.8% of GDP (2020 est.)
1.8% of GDP (2019) (approximately $780 million)
1.9% of GDP (2018) (approximately $760 million)
1.9% of GDP (2017) (approximately $750 million)
country comparison to the world: 79

Military and security service personnel strengths: information varies; approximately 30,000 troops, including active National Guard forces (2022)
note: in December 2020, the Parliament of Georgia adopted a resolution determining that the Georgian Defense Forces would have maximum peacetime strength of 37,000 troops

Military equipment inventories and acquisitions: the Georgian Defense Forces are equipped mostly with older Russian and Soviet-era weapons; since 2010, it has received limited quantities of equipment from European countries and the US (2021)

Military service age and obligation: 18-27 years of age for voluntary active duty military service; conscription abolished in 2016, but reinstated in 2017 for men 18 to 27 years of age; conscript service obligation is 12 months (2022)
note 1: approximately 6-7,000 individuals are called up annually for conscription for service; approximately 25% enter the Defense Forces, while the remainder serve in the Ministry of Internal Affairs or as prison guards in the Ministry of Corrections
note 2: as of 2019, women made up about 6% of the military's full-time personnel

Military - note: as of 2022, up to 10,000 Russian troops continued to occupy the breakaway regions of Abkhazia and South Ossetia

TRANSNATIONAL ISSUES

Disputes - international: Russia's military support and subsequent recognition of Abkhazia and South Ossetia independence in 2008 continue to sour relations with Georgia

Refugees and internally displaced persons: *refugees (country of origin):* 25,204 (Ukraine) (as of 15 November 2022)
IDPs: 305,000 (displaced in the 1990s as a result of armed conflict in the breakaway republics of Abkhazia and South Ossetia; displaced in 2008 by fighting between Georgia and Russia over South Ossetia) (2021)
stateless persons: 534 (mid-year 2021)

Illicit drugs: located on a major drug trafficking route where Southwest Asian opium, heroin and precursor chemicals are transported; marijuana trafficking increased

GERMANY

INTRODUCTION

Background: As Europe's largest economy and second most populous nation (after Russia), Germany is a key member of the continent's economic, political, and defense organizations. European power struggles immersed Germany in two devastating world wars in the first half of the 20th century and left the country occupied by the victorious Allied powers of the US, UK, France, and the Soviet Union in 1945. With the advent of the Cold War, two German states were formed in 1949: the western Federal Republic of Germany (FRG) and the eastern German Democratic Republic (GDR). The democratic FRG embedded itself in key western economic and security organizations, the EC (now the EU) and NATO, while the communist GDR was on the front line of the Soviet-led Warsaw Pact. The decline of the USSR and the end of the Cold War allowed for German reunification in 1990. Since then, Germany has expended considerable funds to bring eastern productivity and wages up to western standards. In January 1999, Germany and 10 other EU countries introduced a common European exchange currency, the euro.

GEOGRAPHY

Location: Central Europe, bordering the Baltic Sea and the North Sea, between the Netherlands and Poland, south of Denmark

geographic coordinates: 51 00 N, 9 00 E

Map references: Europe

Area: *total:* 357,022 sq km
land: 348,672 sq km
water: 8,350 sq km
country comparison to the world: 64

Area - comparative: three times the size of Pennsylvania; slightly smaller than Montana

Land boundaries: *total:* 3,694 km
border countries (9): Austria 801 km; Belgium 133 km; Czechia 704 km; Denmark 140 km; France 418 km; Luxembourg 128 km; Netherlands 575 km; Poland 447 km; Switzerland 348 km

Coastline: 2,389 km

Maritime claims: *territorial sea:* 12 nm
exclusive economic zone: 200 nm
continental shelf: 200-m depth or to the depth of exploitation

Climate: temperate and marine; cool, cloudy, wet winters and summers; occasional warm mountain (foehn) wind

Terrain: lowlands in north, uplands in center, Bavarian Alps in south

Elevation: *highest point:* Zugspitze 2,963 m
lowest point: Neuendorf bei Wilster -3.5 m
mean elevation: 263 m

Natural resources: coal, lignite, natural gas, iron ore, copper, nickel, uranium, potash, salt, construction materials, timber, arable land

Land use: *agricultural land:* 48% (2018 est.)
arable land: 34.1% (2018 est.)
permanent crops: 0.6% (2018 est.)
permanent pasture: 13.3% (2018 est.)
forest: 31.8% (2018 est.)
other: 20.2% (2018 est.)

Irrigated land: 6,500 sq km (2012)

Major lakes (area sq km): *fresh water lake(s):* Lake Constance (shared with Switzerland and Austria) - 540 sq km
salt water lake(s): Stettiner Haff/Zalew Szczecinski (shared with Poland) - 900 sq km

Major rivers (by length in km): Danube river source (shared with Austria, Slovakia, Czechia, Hungary, Croatia, Serbia, Bulgaria, Ukraine, Moldova, and Romania [m]) - 2,888 km; Elbe river mouth (shared with Czechia [s]) - 1,252 km; Rhine (shared with Switzerland [s], France, and Netherlands [m]) - 1,233 km
note – [s] after country name indicates river source; [m] after country name indicates river mouth

Major watersheds (area sq km): Atlantic Ocean drainage: Rhine-Maas (198,735 sq km), *(Black Sea)* Danube (795,656 sq km)

Population distribution: most populous country in Europe; a fairly even distribution throughout most of the country, with urban areas attracting larger and denser populations, particularly in the far western part of the industrial state of North Rhine-Westphalia

Natural hazards: flooding

Geography - note: strategic location on North European Plain and along the entrance to the Baltic Sea; most major rivers in Germany - the Rhine, Weser, Oder, Elbe - flow northward; the Danube, which originates in the Black Forest, flows eastward

PEOPLE AND SOCIETY

Population: 84,316,622 (2022 est.)
country comparison to the world: 18

Nationality: *noun:* German(s)
adjective: German

Ethnic groups: German 86.3%, Turkish 1.8%, Polish 1%, Syrian 1%, Romanian 1%, other/stateless/unspecified 8.9% (2020 est.)
note: data represent population by nationality

Languages: German (official); note - Danish, Frisian, Sorbian, and Romani are official minority languages; Low German, Danish, North Frisian, Sater Frisian, Lower Sorbian, Upper Sorbian, and Romani are recognized as regional languages under the European Charter for Regional or Minority Languages
major-language sample(s): Das World Factbook, die unverzichtbare Quelle für grundlegende Informationen. (German)

Religions: Roman Catholic 26.7%, Protestant 24.3%, Muslim 3.5%, other 4.8%, none 40.7% (2020 est.)

Age structure: *0-14 years:* 12.89% (male 5,302,850/female 5,025,863)
15-24 years: 9.81% (male 4,012,412/female 3,854,471)
25-54 years: 38.58% (male 15,553,328/female 15,370,417)
55-64 years: 15.74% (male 6,297,886/female 6,316,024)
65 years and over: 22.99% (male 8,148,873/female 10,277,538) (2020 est.)

Dependency ratios: *total dependency ratio:* 55.4
youth dependency ratio: 21.7
elderly dependency ratio: 33.7
potential support ratio: 3 (2020 est.)

Median age: *total:* 47.8 years
male: 46.5 years
female: 49.1 years (2020 est.)
country comparison to the world: 4

Population growth rate: -0.11% (2022 est.)
country comparison to the world: 205

Birth rate: 9.08 births/1,000 population (2022 est.)
country comparison to the world: 201

Death rate: 11.98 deaths/1,000 population (2022 est.)
country comparison to the world: 15

Net migration rate: 1.78 migrant(s)/1,000 population (2022 est.)
country comparison to the world: 53

Population distribution: most populous country in Europe; a fairly even distribution throughout most of the country, with urban areas attracting larger and denser populations, particularly in the far western part of the industrial state of North Rhine-Westphalia

Urbanization: *urban population:* 77.6% of total population (2022)
rate of urbanization: 0.13% annual rate of change (2020-25 est.)

Major urban areas - population: 3.571 million BERLIN (capital), 1.788 million Hamburg, 1.566 million Munich, 1.137 million Cologne, 791,000 Frankfurt (2022)

Sex ratio: *at birth:* 1.05 male(s)/female
0-14 years: 1.04 male(s)/female
15-24 years: 1.03 male(s)/female
25-54 years: 1.05 male(s)/female
55-64 years: 1 male(s)/female
65 years and over: 0.7 male(s)/female
total population: 0.98 male(s)/female (2022 est.)

Mother's mean age at first birth: 29.9 years (2020 est.)

Maternal mortality ratio: 7 deaths/100,000 live births (2017 est.)
country comparison to the world: 154

Infant mortality rate: *total:* 3.19 deaths/1,000 live births
male: 3.56 deaths/1,000 live births
female: 2.8 deaths/1,000 live births (2022 est.)
country comparison to the world: 208

Life expectancy at birth: *total population:* 81.51 years
male: 79.15 years
female: 84 years (2022 est.)
country comparison to the world: 38

Total fertility rate: 1.57 children born/woman (2022 est.)
country comparison to the world: 192

Contraceptive prevalence rate: 67% (2018)
note: percent of women aged 18-49

Drinking water source: *improved: urban:* 100% of population
rural: 100% of population
total: 100% of population

Current health expenditure: 11.7% of GDP (2019)

Physicians density: 4.44 physicians/1,000 population (2020)

Hospital bed density: 8 beds/1,000 population (2017)

Sanitation facility access: *improved: urban:* 100% of population
rural: 100% of population
total: 100% of population

HIV/AIDS - adult prevalence rate: 0.1% (2020 est.)
country comparison to the world: 124

Obesity - adult prevalence rate: 22.3% (2016)
country comparison to the world: 79

Alcohol consumption per capita: *total:* 10.56 liters of pure alcohol (2019 est.)
beer: 5.57 liters of pure alcohol (2019 est.)
wine: 3.02 liters of pure alcohol (2019 est.)
spirits: 1.97 liters of pure alcohol (2019 est.)
other alcohols: 0 liters of pure alcohol (2019 est.)
country comparison to the world: 19

Tobacco use: *total:* 22% (2020 est.)
male: 24.1% (2020 est.)
female: 19.9% (2020 est.)
country comparison to the world: 72

Children under the age of 5 years underweight: 0.5% (2014/17)
country comparison to the world: 127

Education expenditures: 5% of GDP (2018 est.)
country comparison to the world: 64

Literacy: School life expectancy (primary to tertiary education): *total:* 17 years
male: 17 years
female: 17 years (2019)

Unemployment, youth ages 15-24: *total:* 7.2%
male: 7.9%
female: 6.4% (2020 est.)

ENVIRONMENT

Environment - current issues: emissions from coal-burning utilities and industries contribute to air pollution; acid rain, resulting from sulfur dioxide emissions, is damaging forests; pollution in the Baltic Sea from raw sewage and industrial effluents from rivers in eastern Germany; hazardous waste disposal; government established a mechanism for ending the use of nuclear power by 2022; government working to meet EU commitment to identify nature preservation areas in line with the EU's Flora, Fauna, and Habitat directive

Environment - international agreements: *party to:* Air Pollution, Air Pollution-Heavy Metals, Air Pollution-Multi-effect Protocol, Air Pollution-Nitrogen Oxides, Air Pollution-Persistent Organic Pollutants, Air Pollution-Sulphur 85, Air Pollution-Sulphur 94, Air Pollution-Volatile Organic Compounds, Antarctic-Environmental Protection, Antarctic-Marine Living Resources, Antarctic Seals, Antarctic Treaty, Biodiversity, Climate Change, Climate Change-Kyoto Protocol, Climate Change-Paris Agreement, Comprehensive Nuclear Test Ban, Desertification, Endangered Species, Environmental Modification, Hazardous Wastes, Law of the Sea, Marine Dumping-London Convention, Marine Dumping-London Protocol, Nuclear Test Ban, Ozone Layer Protection, Ship Pollution, Tropical Timber 2006, Wetlands, Whaling
signed, but not ratified: none of the selected agreements

Air pollutants: *particulate matter emissions:* 11.71 micrograms per cubic meter (2016 est.)
carbon dioxide emissions: 727.97 megatons (2016 est.)
methane emissions: 49.92 megatons (2020 est.)

Climate: temperate and marine; cool, cloudy, wet winters and summers; occasional warm mountain (foehn) wind

Land use: *agricultural land:* 48% (2018 est.)
arable land: 34.1% (2018 est.)
permanent crops: 0.6% (2018 est.)
permanent pasture: 13.3% (2018 est.)
forest: 31.8% (2018 est.)
other: 20.2% (2018 est.)

Urbanization: *urban population:* 77.6% of total population (2022)
rate of urbanization: 0.13% annual rate of change (2020-25 est.)

Revenue from forest resources: *forest revenues:* 0.03% of GDP (2018 est.)
country comparison to the world: 136

Revenue from coal: *coal revenues:* 0.02% of GDP (2018 est.)
country comparison to the world: 43

Waste and recycling: *municipal solid waste generated annually:* 51.046 million tons (2015 est.)
municipal solid waste recycled annually: 24,415,302 tons (2015 est.)
percent of municipal solid waste recycled: 47.8% (2015 est.)

Major lakes (area sq km): *fresh water lake(s):* Lake Constance (shared with Switzerland and Austria) - 540 sq km
salt water lake(s): Stettiner Haff/Zalew Szczecinski (shared with Poland) - 900 sq km

Major rivers (by length in km): Danube river source (shared with Austria, Slovakia, Czechia, Hungary, Croatia, Serbia, Bulgaria, Ukraine, Moldova, and Romania [m]) - 2,888 km; Elbe river mouth (shared with Czechia [s]) - 1,252 km; Rhine (shared with Switzerland [s], France, and Netherlands [m]) - 1,233 km
note – [s] after country name indicates river source; [m] after country name indicates river mouth

Major watersheds (area sq km): Atlantic Ocean drainage: Rhine-Maas (198,735 sq km), *(Black Sea)* Danube (795,656 sq km)

Total water withdrawal: *municipal:* 4.388 billion cubic meters (2017 est.)
industrial: 19.75 billion cubic meters (2017 est.)
agricultural: 299.7 million cubic meters (2017 est.)

Total renewable water resources: 154 billion cubic meters (2017 est.)

GOVERNMENT

Country name: *conventional long form:* Federal Republic of Germany
conventional short form: Germany
local long form: Bundesrepublik Deutschland
local short form: Deutschland
former: German Reich
etymology: the Gauls (Celts) of Western Europe may have referred to the newly arriving Germanic tribes who settled in neighboring areas east of the Rhine during the first centuries B.C. as "Germani," a term the Romans adopted as "Germania"; the native designation "Deutsch" comes from the Old High German "diutisc" meaning "of the people"

Government type: federal parliamentary republic

Capital: *name:* Berlin
Geographic coordinates: 52 31 N, 13 24 E
time difference: UTC+1 (6 hours ahead of Washington, DC, during Standard Time)
daylight saving time: +1hr, begins last Sunday in March; ends last Sunday in October
etymology: the origin of the name is unclear but may be related to the old West Slavic (Polabian) word "berl" or "birl," meaning "swamp"

Administrative divisions: 16 states (Laender, singular - Land); Baden-Wuerttemberg, Bayern (Bavaria), Berlin, Brandenburg, Bremen, Hamburg, Hessen (Hesse), Mecklenburg-Vorpommern (Mecklenburg-Western Pomerania), Niedersachsen (Lower Saxony), Nordrhein-Westfalen (North Rhine-Westphalia), Rheinland-Pfalz (Rhineland-Palatinate), Saarland,

Sachsen (Saxony), Sachsen-Anhalt (Saxony-Anhalt), Schleswig-Holstein, Thueringen (Thuringia); note - Bayern, Sachsen, and Thueringen refer to themselves as free states (Freistaaten, singular - Freistaat), while Bremen calls itself a Free Hanseatic City (Freie Hansestadt) and Hamburg considers itself a Free and Hanseatic City (Freie und Hansestadt)

Independence: 18 January 1871 (establishment of the German Empire); divided into four zones of occupation (UK, US, USSR, and France) in 1945 following World War II; Federal Republic of Germany (FRG or West Germany) proclaimed on 23 May 1949 and included the former UK, US, and French zones; German Democratic Republic (GDR or East Germany) proclaimed on 7 October 1949 and included the former USSR zone; West Germany and East Germany unified on 3 October 1990; all four powers formally relinquished rights on 15 March 1991; notable earlier dates: 10 August 843 (Eastern Francia established from the division of the Carolingian Empire); 2 February 962 (crowning of OTTO I, recognized as the first Holy Roman Emperor)

National holiday: German Unity Day, 3 October (1990)

Constitution: *history:* previous 1919 (Weimar Constitution); latest drafted 10-23 August 1948, approved 12 May 1949, promulgated 23 May 1949, entered into force 24 May 1949
amendments: proposed by Parliament; passage and enactment into law require two-thirds majority vote by both the Bundesrat (upper house) and the Bundestag (lower house) of Parliament; articles including those on basic human rights and freedoms cannot be amended; amended many times, last in 2020; note - in early 2021, the German federal government introduced a bill to incorporate children's rights into the constitution

Legal system: civil law system

International law organization participation: accepts compulsory ICJ jurisdiction with reservations; accepts ICCt jurisdiction

Citizenship: *citizenship by birth:* no
citizenship by descent only: at least one parent must be a German citizen or a resident alien who has lived in Germany at least 8 years
dual citizenship recognized: yes, but requires prior permission from government
residency requirement for naturalization: 8 years

Suffrage: 18 years of age; universal; age 16 for some state and municipal elections

Executive branch: *chief of state:* President Frank-Walter STEINMEIER (since 19 March 2017)
head of government: Chancellor Olaf SCHOLZ (since 8 December 2021)
cabinet: Cabinet or Bundesminister (Federal Ministers) recommended by the chancellor, appointed by the president
elections/appointments: president indirectly elected by a Federal Convention consisting of all members of the Federal Parliament (Bundestag) and an equivalent number of delegates indirectly elected by the state parliaments; president serves a 5-year term (eligible for a second term); election last held on 13 February 2022 (next to be held in February 2027); following the most recent Federal Parliament election, the party or coalition with the most representatives usually elects the chancellor who is appointed by the president to serve a renewable 4-year term; Federal Parliament vote for chancellor last held on 8 December 2021 (next to be held after the Bundestag election in 2025)
election results: *2017:* Frank-Walter STEINMEIER reelected president; Federal Convention vote count - Frank-Walter STEINMEIER (SPD) 1,045, Max OTTE 140, Gerhard TRABERT (The Left) 96, Stefanie GEBAUER (Free Voters) 58, abstentions 86; Olaf SCHOLZ (SPD) elected chancellor; Federal Parliament vote - 395 to 303
2012: Joachim GAUCK elected president; Federal Convention vote count - Joachim GAUCK 911, Beate KLARSFELD 126, Olaf ROSE 3

Legislative branch: *description:* bicameral Parliament or Parlament consists of:
Federal Council or Bundesrat (69 seats statutory, 71 current; members appointed by each of the 16 state governments) Federal Diet or Bundestag (736 seats statutory, 736 for the 2021-25 term - total seats can vary each electoral term; currently includes 4 seats for independent members; approximately one-half of members directly elected in multi-seat constituencies by proportional representation vote and approximately one-half directly elected in single-seat constituencies by simple majority vote; members' terms depend upon the states they represent)
elections: Bundesrat - none; determined by the composition of the state-level governments; the composition of the Bundesrat has the potential to change any time one of the 16 states holds an election
Bundestag - last held on 26 September 2021 (next to be held in September 2025 at the latest); almost all postwar German governments have been coalitions
election results: Bundesrat - composition - men 46, women 23, percent of women 33.3%
Bundestag - percent of vote by party - SPD 28%, CDU/CSU 26.8%, Alliance '90/Greens 16%, FDP 12.5%, AfD 11%, The Left 5.3%, other .4%; seats by party - SPD 206, CDU/CSU 197, Alliance '90/Greens 118, FDP 92, AfD 81, The Left 39, other 3; composition - men 479, women 257, percent of women 34.9%; note - total Parliament percent of women 34.8%

note - due to Germany's recognition of the concepts of "overhang" (when a party's share of the nationwide votes would entitle it to fewer seats than the number of individual constituency seats won in an election under Germany's mixed member proportional system) and "leveling" (whereby additional seats are elected to supplement the members directly elected by each constituency in order to ensure that each party's share of the total seats is roughly proportional to the party's overall shares of votes at the national level), the 20th Bundestag is the largest to date

Judicial branch: *highest court(s):* Federal Court of Justice (court consists of 127 judges, including the court president, vice presidents, presiding judges, other judges and organized into 25 Senates subdivided into 12 civil panels, 5 criminal panels, and 8 special panels); Federal Constitutional Court or Bundesverfassungsgericht (consists of 2 Senates each subdivided into 3 chambers, each with a chairman and 8 members)
judge selection and term of office: Federal Court of Justice judges selected by the Judges Election Committee, which consists of the Secretaries of Justice from each of the 16 federated states and 16 members appointed by the Federal Parliament; judges appointed by the president; judges serve until mandatory retirement at age 65; Federal Constitutional Court judges - one-half elected by the House of Representatives and one-half by the Senate; judges appointed for 12- year terms with mandatory retirement at age 68
subordinate courts: Federal Administrative Court; Federal Finance Court; Federal Labor Court; Federal Social Court; each of the 16 federated states or Land has its own constitutional court and a hierarchy of ordinary (civil, criminal, family) and specialized (administrative, finance, labor, social) courts; two English-speaking commercial courts opened in late 2020 in the state of Baden-Wuerttemberg - English-speaking Stuttgart Commercial Court and English-speaking Mannheim Commercial Court

Political parties and leaders: Alliance '90/Greens [Ricarda LANG and Omid NOURIPOUR]
Alternative for Germany or AfD [Alice WEIDEL and Tino CHRUPALLA]
Christian Democratic Union or CDU [Friedrich MERZ]
Christian Social Union or CSU [Markus SOEDER]
Free Democratic Party or FDP [Christian LINDNER]
Free Voters [Hubert AIWANGER]
The Left or Die Linke [Janine WISSLER and Martin SCHIRDEWAN]
Social Democratic Party or SPD [Saskia ESKEN and Lars KLINGBEIL]

International organization participation: ADB (nonregional member), AfDB (nonregional member), Arctic Council (observer), Australia Group, BIS, BSEC (observer), CBSS, CD, CDB, CE, CERN, EAPC, EBRD, ECB, EIB, EITI (implementing country), EMU, ESA, EU, FAO, FATF, G-5, G-7, G-8, G-10, G-20, IADB, IAEA, IBRD, ICAO, ICC (national committees), ICCt, ICRM, IDA, IEA, IFAD, IFC, IFRCS, IGAD (partners), IHO, ILO, IMF, IMO, IMSO, Interpol, IOC, IOM, IPU, ISO, ITSO, ITU, ITUC (NGOs), MIGA, MINURSO, MINUSMA, NATO, NEA, NSG, OAS (observer), OECD, OPCW, OSCE, Pacific Alliance (observer), Paris Club, PCA, Schengen Convention, SELEC (observer), SICA (observer), UN, UNAMID, UNCTAD, UNESCO, UNHCR, UNHRC, UNIDO, UNIFIL, UNMISS, UNRWA, UNSOM, UNWTO, UPU, Wassenaar Arrangement, WCO, WHO, WIPO, WMO, WTO, ZC

Diplomatic representation in the US: *chief of mission:* Ambassador Emily Margarethe HABER (since 22 June 2018)
chancery: 4645 Reservoir Road NW, Washington, DC 20007
telephone: [1] (202) 298-4000
FAX: [1] (202) 298-4261
email address and website:
info@washington.diplo.de
https://www.germany.info/us-en
consulate(s) general: Atlanta, Boston, Chicago, Houston, Los Angeles, Miami, New York, San Francisco

Diplomatic representation from the US: *chief of mission:* Ambassador Amy GUTMANN (since 17 February 2022)
embassy: Pariser Platz 2, 10117 Berlin
Clayallee 170, 14191 Berlin (administrative services)
mailing address: 5090 Berlin Place, Washington DC 20521-5090
telephone: [49] (30) 8305-0
FAX: [49] (30) 8305-1215
email address and website:
BerlinPCO@state.gov

https://de.usembassy.gov/
consulate(s) general: Dusseldorf, Frankfurt am Main, Hamburg, Leipzig, Munich

Flag description: three equal horizontal bands of black (top), red, and gold; these colors have played an important role in German history and can be traced back to the medieval banner of the Holy Roman Emperor - a black eagle with red claws and beak on a gold field

National symbol(s): eagle; national colors: black, red, yellow

National anthem: *name:* "Das Lied der Deutschen" (Song of the Germans)
lyrics/music: August Heinrich HOFFMANN VON FALLERSLEBEN/Franz Joseph HAYDN
note: adopted 1922; the anthem, also known as "Deutschlandlied" (Song of Germany), was originally adopted for its connection to the March 1848 liberal revolution; following appropriation by the Nazis of the first verse, specifically the phrase, "Deutschland, Deutschland ueber alles" (Germany, Germany above all) to promote nationalism, it was banned after 1945; in 1952, its third verse was adopted by West Germany as its national anthem; in 1990, it became the national anthem for the reunited Germany

National heritage: *total World Heritage Sites:* 51 (48 cultural, 3 natural)
selected World Heritage Site locales: Museumsinsel (Museum Island), Berlin (c); Palaces and Parks of Potsdam and Berlin (c); Speyer Cathedral (c); Upper Middle Rhine Valley (c); Aachen Cathedral (c); Bauhaus and its Sites in Weimar, Dessau, and Bernau (c); Caves and Ice Age Art in the Swabian Jura (c); Mines of Rammelsberg, Historic Town of Goslar, and Upper Harz Water Management System (c); Roman Monuments, Cathedral of St. Peter, and Church of Our Lady in Trier (c); Hanseatic City of Lübeck (c); Old Town of Regensburg (c); Messel Pit Fossil Site (n)

ECONOMY

Economic overview: The German economy - the fifth largest economy in the world in PPP terms and Europe's largest - is a leading exporter of machinery, vehicles, chemicals, and household equipment. Germany benefits from a highly skilled labor force, but, like its Western European neighbors, faces significant demographic challenges to sustained long-term growth. Low fertility rates and a large increase in net immigration are increasing pressure on the country's social welfare system and necessitate structural reforms.

Reforms launched by the government of Chancellor Gerhard SCHROEDER (1998-2005), deemed necessary to address chronically high unemployment and low average growth, contributed to strong economic growth and falling unemployment. These advances, as well as a government subsidized, reduced working hour scheme, help explain the relatively modest increase in unemployment during the 2008-09 recession - the deepest since World War II. The German Government introduced a minimum wage in 2015 that increased to $9.79 (8.84 euros) in January 2017.

Stimulus and stabilization efforts initiated in 2008 and 2009 and tax cuts introduced in Chancellor Angela MERKEL's second term increased Germany's total budget deficit - including federal, state, and municipal - to 4.1% in 2010, but slower spending and higher tax revenues reduced the deficit to 0.8% in 2011 and in 2017 Germany reached a budget surplus of 0.7%. A constitutional amendment approved in 2009 limits the federal government to structural deficits of no more than 0.35% of GDP per annum as of 2016, though the target was already reached in 2012.

Following the March 2011 Fukushima nuclear disaster, Chancellor Angela MERKEL announced in May 2011 that eight of the country's 17 nuclear reactors would be shut down immediately and the remaining plants would close by 2022. Germany plans to replace nuclear power largely with renewable energy, which accounted for 29.5% of gross electricity consumption in 2016, up from 9% in 2000. Before the shutdown of the eight reactors, Germany relied on nuclear power for 23% of its electricity generating capacity and 46% of its base-load electricity production.

The German economy suffers from low levels of investment, and a government plan to invest 15 billion euros during 2016-18, largely in infrastructure, is intended to spur needed private investment. Domestic consumption, investment, and exports are likely to drive German GDP growth in 2018, and the country's budget and trade surpluses are likely to remain high.

Real GDP (purchasing power parity): $4,238,800,000,000 (2020 est.)
$4,457,050,000,000 (2019 est.)
$4,432,430,000,000 (2018 est.)
note: data are in 2017 dollars
country comparison to the world: 5

Real GDP growth rate: 0.59% (2019 est.)
1.3% (2018 est.)
2.91% (2017 est.)
country comparison to the world: 183

Real GDP per capita: $50,900 (2020 est.)
$53,600 (2019 est.)
$53,500 (2018 est.)
note: data are in 2017 dollars
country comparison to the world: 26

GDP (official exchange rate): $3,860,923,000,000 (2019 est.)

Inflation rate (consumer prices): 1.4% (2019 est.)
1.7% (2018 est.)
1.5% (2017 est.)
country comparison to the world: 84

Credit ratings:

Fitch rating: AAA (1994)

Moody's rating: Aaa (1986)

Standard & Poors rating: AAA (1983)
note: The year refers to the year in which the current credit rating was first obtained. Credit ratings prior to 1989 refer to West Germany.

GDP - composition, by sector of origin: *agriculture:* 0.7% (2017 est.)
industry: 30.7% (2017 est.)
services: 68.6% (2017 est.)

GDP - composition, by end use: *household consumption:* 53.1% (2017 est.)
government consumption: 19.5% (2017 est.)
investment in fixed capital: 20.4% (2017 est.)
investment in inventories: -0.5% (2017 est.)
exports of goods and services: 47.3% (2017 est.)
imports of goods and services: -39.7% (2017 est.)

Agricultural products: milk, sugar beet, wheat, barley, potatoes, pork, maize, rye, rapeseed, triticale

Industries: among the world's largest and most technologically advanced producers of iron, steel, coal, cement, chemicals, machinery, vehicles, machine tools, electronics, automobiles, food and beverages, shipbuilding, textiles

Industrial production growth rate: 3.3% (2017 est.)
country comparison to the world: 95

Labor force: 44.585 million (2020 est.)
country comparison to the world: 14

Labor force - by occupation: *agriculture:* 1.4%
industry: 24.2%
services: 74.3% (2016)

Unemployment rate: 4.98% (2019 est.)
5.19% (2018 est.)
country comparison to the world: 76

Unemployment, youth ages 15-24: *total:* 7.2%
male: 7.9%
female: 6.4% (2020 est.)
country comparison to the world: 160

Population below poverty line: 14.8% (2018 est.)

Gini Index coefficient - distribution of family income: 31.9 (2016 est.)
30 (1994)
country comparison to the world: 140

Household income or consumption by percentage share: *lowest 10%:* 3.6%
highest 10%: 24% (2000)

Budget: *revenues:* 1.665 trillion (2017 est.)
expenditures: 1.619 trillion (2017 est.)

Budget surplus (+) or deficit (-): 1.3% (of GDP) (2017 est.)
country comparison to the world: 25

Public debt: 63.9% of GDP (2017 est.)
67.9% of GDP (2016 est.)
note: general government gross debt is defined in the Maastricht Treaty as consolidated general government gross debt at nominal value, outstanding at the end of the year in the following categories of government liabilities (as defined in ESA95): currency and deposits (AF.2), securities other than shares excluding financial derivatives (AF.3, excluding AF.34), and loans (AF.4); the general government sector comprises the sub-sectors of central government, state government, local government and social security funds; the series are presented as a percentage of GDP and in millions of euros; GDP used as a denominator is the gross domestic product at current market prices; data expressed in national currency are converted into euro using end-of-year exchange rates provided by the European Central Bank
country comparison to the world: 62

Taxes and other revenues: 45% (of GDP) (2017 est.)
country comparison to the world: 22

Fiscal year: calendar year

Current account balance: $280.238 billion (2019 est.)
$297.434 billion (2018 est.)
country comparison to the world: 1

Exports: $1,671,650,000,000 (2020 est.) note: data are in current year dollars
$1,813,190,000,000 (2019 est.) note: data are in current year dollars
$1,881,510,000,000 (2018 est.) note: data are in current year dollars
country comparison to the world: 3

Exports - partners: United States 9%, France 8%, China 7%, Netherlands 6%, United Kingdom 6%, Italy 5%, Poland 5%, Austria 5% (2019)

Exports - commodities: cars and vehicle parts, packaged medicines, aircraft, medical cultures/vaccines, industrial machinery (2019)

Imports: $1,452,560,000,000 (2020 est.) note: data are in current year dollars
$1,593,720,000,000 (2019 est.) note: data are in current year dollars
$1,635,580,000,000 (2018 est.) note: data are in current year dollars
country comparison to the world: 3

Imports - partners: Netherlands 9%, China 8%, France 7%, Belgium 6%, Poland 6%, Italy 6%, Czechia 5%, United States 5% (2019)

Imports - commodities: cars and vehicle parts, packaged medicines, crude petroleum, refined petroleum, medical cultures/vaccines (2019)

Reserves of foreign exchange and gold: $200.1 billion (31 December 2017 est.)
$173.7 billion (31 December 2015 est.)
country comparison to the world: 13

Debt - external: $5,671,463,000,000 (2019 est.)
$5,751,408,000,000 (2018 est.)
country comparison to the world: 4

Exchange rates: euros (EUR) per US dollar -
0.82771 (2020 est.)
0.90338 (2019 est.)
0.87789 (2018 est.)
0.885 (2014 est.)
0.7634 (2013 est.)

ENERGY

Electricity access: *electrification - total population:* 100% (2020)

Electricity: *installed generating capacity:* 248.265 million kW (2020 est.)
consumption: 500,350,034,000 kWh (2020 est.)
exports: 66.931 billion kWh (2020 est.)
imports: 48.047 billion kWh (2020 est.)
transmission/distribution losses: 25,970,966,000 kWh (2020 est.)

Electricity generation sources: *fossil fuels:* 40.5% of total installed capacity (2020 est.)
nuclear: 11.1% of total installed capacity (2020 est.)
solar: 9.2% of total installed capacity (2020 est.)
wind: 23.9% of total installed capacity (2020 est.)
hydroelectricity: 4.5% of total installed capacity (2020 est.)
tide and wave: 0.2% of total installed capacity (2020 est.)
biomass and waste: 10.4% of total installed capacity (2020 est.)

Coal: *production:* 114.86 million metric tons (2020 est.)
consumption: 145.379 million metric tons (2020 est.)
exports: 2.317 million metric tons (2020 est.)
imports: 31.503 million metric tons (2020 est.)
proven reserves: 35.9 billion metric tons (2019 est.)

Petroleum: *total petroleum production:* 135,000 bbl/day (2021 est.)
refined petroleum consumption: 2,346,500 bbl/day (2019 est.)
crude oil and lease condensate exports: 0 bbl/day (2018 est.)
crude oil and lease condensate imports: 1,720,600 bbl/day (2018 est.)
crude oil estimated reserves: 115.2 million barrels (2021 est.)

Refined petroleum products - production: 2.158 million bbl/day (2017 est.)
country comparison to the world: 9

Refined petroleum products - exports: 494,000 bbl/day (2017 est.)
country comparison to the world: 17

Refined petroleum products - imports: 883,800 bbl/day (2017 est.)
country comparison to the world: 9

Natural gas: *production:* 5,128,909,000 cubic meters (2020 est.)
consumption: 87,546,767,000 cubic meters (2020 est.)
exports: 0 cubic meters (2020 est.)
imports: 83,121,531,000 cubic meters (2020 est.)
proven reserves: 23.39 billion cubic meters (2021 est.)

Carbon dioxide emissions: 726.881 million metric tonnes of CO_2 (2019 est.)
from coal and metallurgical coke: 218.636 million metric tonnes of CO_2 (2019 est.)
from petroleum and other liquids: 316.064 million metric tonnes of CO_2 (2019 est.)
from consumed natural gas: 192.181 million metric tonnes of CO_2 (2019 est.)
country comparison to the world: 6

Energy consumption per capita: 161.174 million Btu/person (2019 est.)
country comparison to the world: 31

COMMUNICATIONS

Telephones - fixed lines: *total subscriptions:* 38.3 million (2020 est.)
subscriptions per 100 inhabitants: 46 (2020 est.)
country comparison to the world: 4

Telephones - mobile cellular: *total subscriptions:* 107.4 million (2020 est.)
subscriptions per 100 inhabitants: 128 (2020 est.)
country comparison to the world: 16

Telecommunication systems: *general assessment:* with one of Europe's largest telecom markets, Germany hosts a number of significant operators which offer effective competition in the mobile and broadband sectors; the German mobile market is driven by mobile data, with the number of mobile broadband subscribers having increased rapidly in recent years; with LTE now effectively universally available, considerable progress has recently been made in building out 5G networks (2022)
domestic: extensive system of automatic telephone exchanges connected by modern networks of fiber-optic cable, coaxial cable, microwave radio relay, and a domestic satellite system; cellular telephone service is widely available, expanding rapidly, and includes roaming service to many foreign countries; approximately 46 per 100 for fixed-line and 128 per 100 for mobile-cellular (2020)
international: country code - 49; landing points for SeaMeWe-3, TAT-14, AC-1, CONTACT-3, Fehmarn Balt, C-Lion1, GC1, GlobalConnect-KPN, and Germany-Denmark 2 & 3 - submarine cables to Europe, Africa, the Middle East, Asia, Southeast Asia and Australia; as well as earth stations in the Inmarsat, Intelsat, Eutelsat, and Intersputnik satellite systems (2019)

Broadcast media: a mixture of publicly operated and privately owned TV and radio stations; 70 national and regional public broadcasters compete with nearly 400 privately owned national and regional TV stations; more than 90% of households have cable or satellite TV; hundreds of radio stations including multiple national radio networks, regional radio networks, and a large number of local radio stations

Internet country code: .de

Internet users: *total:* 74,844,784 (2020 est.)
percent of population: 90% (2020 est.)
country comparison to the world: 10

Broadband - fixed subscriptions: *total:* 36,215,303 (2020 est.)
subscriptions per 100 inhabitants: 43 (2020 est.)
country comparison to the world: 5

TRANSPORTATION

National air transport system: *number of registered air carriers:* 20 (2020)
inventory of registered aircraft operated by air carriers: 1,113
annual passenger traffic on registered air carriers: 109,796,202 (2018)
annual freight traffic on registered air carriers: 7,969,860,000 (2018) mt-km

Civil aircraft registration country code prefix: D

Airports: *total:* 539 (2021)
country comparison to the world: 12

Airports - with paved runways: *total:* 318
over 3,047 m: 14
2,438 to 3,047 m: 49
1,524 to 2,437 m: 60
914 to 1,523 m: 70
under 914 m: 125 (2021)

Airports - with unpaved runways: *total:* 221
1,524 to 2,437 m: 1
914 to 1,523 m: 35
under 914 m: 185 (2021)

Heliports: 23 (2021)

Pipelines: 37 km condensate, 26,985 km gas, 2,400 km oil, 4,479 km refined products, 8 km water (2013)

Railways: *total:* 33,590 km (2017)
standard gauge: 33,331 km (2015) 1.435-m gauge (19,973 km electrified)
narrow gauge: 220 km 1.000-m gauge (79 km electrified)
15 km 0.900-mm gauge, 24 km 0.750-mm gauge (2015)
country comparison to the world: 7

Roadways: *total:* 625,000 km (2017)
paved: 625,000 km (2017) (includes 12,996 km of expressways)
note: includes local roads
country comparison to the world: 13

Waterways: 7,467 km (2012) (Rhine River carries most goods; Main-Danube Canal links North Sea and Black Sea)
country comparison to the world: 20

Merchant marine: *total:* 599
by type: container ship 77, general cargo 85, oil tanker 36, other 401 (2021)
country comparison to the world: 38

Ports and terminals: *major seaport(s):*
Baltic Sea: Kiel, Rostock
North Sea: Bremerhaven, Brunsbuttel, Emden, Hamburg, Wilhelmshaven
oil terminal(s): Brunsbuttel Canal terminals
container port(s) (TEUs): Bremen/Bremerhaven (4,856,900), Hamburg (9,274,215) (2019)

LNG terminal(s) (import): Hamburg
river port(s): Bremen (Weser); Bremerhaven (Geeste); Duisburg, Karlsruhe, Neuss-Dusseldorf (Rhine); Lubeck (Wakenitz); Brunsbuttel, Hamburg (Elbe)

MILITARY AND SECURITY

Military and security forces: Federal Armed Forces (Bundeswehr): Army (Heer), Navy (Deutsche Marine, includes naval air arm), Air Force (Luftwaffe, includes air defense), Joint Support Service (Streitkraeftebasis, SKB), Central Medical Service (Zentraler Sanitaetsdienst, ZSanDstBw), Cyber and Information Space Command (Kommando Cyber und Informationsraum, Kdo CIR) (2022)

Military expenditures: 1.5% of GDP (2022 est.)
1.5% of GDP (2021)
1.5% of GDP (2020)
1.4% of GDP (2019) (approximately $60.1 billion)
1.3% of GDP (2018) (approximately $55.4 billion)
country comparison to the world: 90

Military and security service personnel strengths: approximately 184,000 active duty personnel (63,000 Army; 16,000 Navy; 27,000 Air Force; 27,000 Joint Support Service; 20,000 Medical Service, 16,000 Cyber and Information Space Command; 15,000 other, including central staff, support, etc.) (2022)
note: Germany in 2020 announced it planned to increase the size of the military to about 200,000 troops by 2025

Military equipment inventories and acquisitions: the German Federal Armed Forces inventory is comprised of weapons systems produced domestically or jointly with other European countries and Western imports, particularly from the US; since 2010, the US has been the leading foreign supplier; Germany's defense industry is capable of manufacturing the full spectrum of air, land, and naval military weapons systems, and is one of the world's leading arms exporters (2022)

Military service age and obligation: 17-23 years of age for male and female voluntary military service (must have completed compulsory full-time education and have German citizenship); conscription ended July 2011; service obligation 7-23 months or 12 years; women have been eligible for voluntary service in all military branches and positions since 2001 (2022)
note: in 2021, women accounted for about 12% of the German military

Military deployments: up to 500 Iraq (NATO); 1,030 Lithuania (NATO); up to 1,400 Mali (MINUSMA/EUTM); 280 Slovakia (NATO) (2022)
note 1: in November 2022, Germany pledged to withdraw its troops from Mali by Spring 2024
note 2: in response to Russia's 2022 invasion of Ukraine, some NATO countries, including Germany, have sent additional troops and equipment to the battlegroups deployed in NATO territory in eastern Europe

Military - note: the Federal Republic of Germany joined NATO in May 1955; with the reunification of Germany in October 1990, the states of the former German Democratic Republic joined the Federal Republic of Germany in its membership of NATO

the German Army has incorporated a joint Franco-German mechanized infantry brigade since 1989, a Dutch airmobile infantry brigade since 2014, and a Dutch mechanized infantry brigade since 2016; in addition, the German Navy's Sea Battalion (includes marine infantry, naval divers, reconnaissance, and security forces) has worked closely with the Dutch Marine Corps since 2016, including as a binational amphibious landing group (2022)

TERRORISM

Terrorist group(s): Islamic Revolutionary Guard Corps/Qods Force; Islamic State of Iraq and ash-Sham (ISIS); al-Qa'ida

TRANSNATIONAL ISSUES

Disputes - international: none

Refugees and internally displaced persons: *refugees (country of origin):* 616,325 (Syria), 152,677 (Afghanistan), 147,400 (Iraq), 62,152 (Eritrea), 45,704 (Iran), 34,465 (Turkey), 29,137 (Somalia), 9,329 (Russia), 9,323 (Nigeria), 8,600 (Pakistan), 7,503 (Serbia and Kosovo), 6,057 (Ethiopia) (mid-year 2021); 1,021,667 (Ukraine) (as of 22 November 2022)
stateless persons: 26,980 (mid-year 2021)

Illicit drugs: maritime transshipment point for cocaine heading to Europe

GHANA

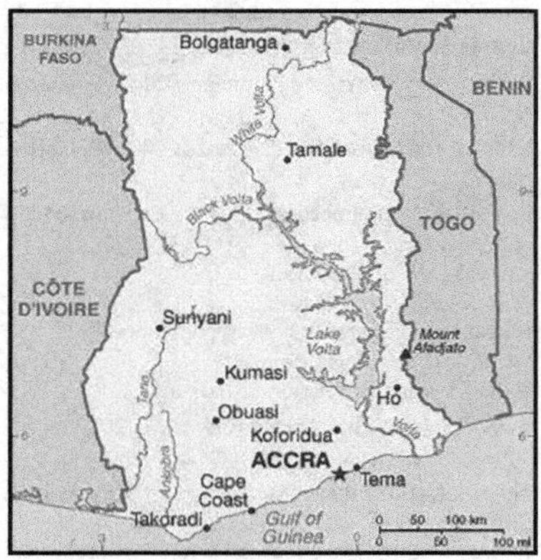

INTRODUCTION

Background: Ghana is a multiethnic country rich in natural resources and is one of the most stable and democratic countries in West Africa. Ghana has been inhabited for at least several thousand years, however, little is known about its early inhabitants. By the 12th century, the gold trade started to boom in Bono (Bonoman) state in what is today southern Ghana, and it became the genesis of Akan power and wealth in the region. Beginning in the 15th century, the Portuguese, followed by other European powers, arrived and contested for trading rights. Numerous kingdoms and empires emerged in the area, among the most powerful were the Kingdom of Dagbon in the north and the Asante (Ashanti) Empire in the south. By the mid-18th century, Asante was a highly organized state with immense wealth; it provided enslaved people for the Atlantic slave trade, and in return received firearms that facilitated its territorial expansion. The Asante resisted increasing British influence in the coastal areas, engaging in a series of wars during the 19th century before ultimately falling under British control. Formed from the merger of the British colony of the Gold Coast and the Togoland trust territory, Ghana in 1957 became the first Sub-Saharan country in colonial Africa to gain its independence, with Kwame NKRUMAH as its first leader.

Ghana endured a series of coups before Lt. Jerry RAWLINGS took power in 1981 and banned political parties. After approving a new constitution and restoring multiparty politics in 1992, RAWLINGS won presidential elections in 1992 and 1996 but was constitutionally prevented from running for a third term in 2000. John KUFUOR of the opposition New Patriotic Party (NPP) succeeded him and was reelected in 2004. John Atta MILLS of the National Democratic Congress won the 2008 presidential election and took over as head of state. MILLS died in July 2012 and was constitutionally succeeded by his vice president, John Dramani MAHAMA, who subsequently won the December 2012 presidential election. In 2016, Nana Addo Dankwa AKUFO-ADDO of the NPP defeated MAHAMA, marking the third time that Ghana's presidency had changed parties since the return to democracy. AKUFO-ADDO was reelected in 2020. In recent years, Ghana has taken an active role in promoting regional stability and is highly integrated in international affairs.

GEOGRAPHY

Location: Western Africa, bordering the Gulf of Guinea, between Cote d'Ivoire and Togo

Geographic coordinates: 8 00 N, 2 00 W

Map references: Africa

Area: *total:* 238,533 sq km
land: 227,533 sq km
water: 11,000 sq km
country comparison to the world: 82

Area - comparative: slightly smaller than Oregon

Land boundaries: *total:* 2,420 km
border countries (3): Burkina Faso 602 km; Cote d'Ivoire 720 km; Togo 1098 km

Coastline: 539 km

Maritime claims: *territorial sea:* 12 nm
contiguous zone: 24 nm
exclusive economic zone: 200 nm
continental shelf: 200 nm

Climate: tropical; warm and comparatively dry along southeast coast; hot and humid in southwest; hot and dry in north

Terrain: mostly low plains with dissected plateau in south-central area

Elevation: *highest point:* Mount Afadjato 885 m
lowest point: Atlantic Ocean 0 m
mean elevation: 190 m

Natural resources: gold, timber, industrial diamonds, bauxite, manganese, fish, rubber, hydropower, petroleum, silver, salt, limestone

Land use: *agricultural land:* 69.1% (2018 est.)
arable land: 20.7% (2018 est.)
permanent crops: 11.9% (2018 est.)
permanent pasture: 36.5% (2018 est.)
forest: 21.2% (2018 est.)
other: 9.7% (2018 est.)

Irrigated land: 340 sq km (2012)

Major rivers (by length in km): Volta river mouth (shared with Burkina Faso [s]) - 1,600 km
note – [s] after country name indicates river source; [m] after country name indicates river mouth

Major watersheds (area sq km): Atlantic Ocean drainage: Volta (410,991 sq km)

Population distribution: population is concentrated in the southern half of the country, with the highest concentrations being on or near the Atlantic coast as shown in this population distribution map

Natural hazards: dry, dusty, northeastern harmattan winds from January to March; droughts

Geography - note: Lake Volta is the world's largest artificial lake (manmade reservoir) by surface area (8,482 sq km; 3,275 sq mi); the lake was created following the completion of the Akosombo Dam in 1965, which holds back the White Volta and Black Volta Rivers

PEOPLE AND SOCIETY

Population: 33,107,275 (2022 est.)
country comparison to the world: 44

Nationality: *noun:* Ghanaian(s)
adjective: Ghanaian

Ethnic groups: Akan 45.7%, Mole-Dagbani 18.5%, Ewe 12.8%, Ga-Dangme 7.1%, Gurma 6.4%, Guan 3.2%, Grusi 2.7%, Mande 2%, other 1.6% (2021 est.)

Languages: Asante 16%, Ewe 14%, Fante 11.6%, Boron (Brong) 4.9%, Dagomba 4.4%, Dangme 4.2%, Dagarte (Dagaba) 3.9%, Kokomba 3.5%, Akyem 3.2%, Ga 3.1%, other 31.2% (2010 est.)
note: English is the official language

Religions: Christian 71.3% (Pentecostal/Charismatic 31.6%, Protestant 17.4%, Catholic 10%, other 12.3%), Muslim 19.9%, traditionalist 3.2%, other 4.5%, none 1.1% (2021 est.)

Demographic profile: Ghana has a young age structure, with approximately 57% of the population under the age of 25. Its total fertility rate fell significantly during the 1980s and 1990s but has stalled at around four children per woman for the last few years. Fertility remains higher in the northern region than the Greater Accra region. On average, desired fertility has remained stable for several years; urban dwellers want fewer children than rural residents. Increased life expectancy, due to better health care, nutrition, and hygiene, and reduced fertility have increased Ghana's share of elderly persons; Ghana's proportion of persons aged 60+ is among the highest in Sub-Saharan Africa. Poverty has declined in Ghana, but it remains pervasive in the northern region, which is susceptible to droughts and floods and has less access to transportation infrastructure, markets, fertile farming land, and industrial centers. The northern region also has lower school enrollment, higher illiteracy, and fewer opportunities for women.

Ghana was a country of immigration in the early years after its 1957 independence, attracting labor migrants largely from Nigeria and other neighboring countries to mine minerals and harvest cocoa – immigrants composed about 12% of Ghana's population in 1960. In the late 1960s, worsening economic and social conditions discouraged immigration, and hundreds of thousands of immigrants, mostly Nigerians, were expelled.

During the 1970s, severe drought and an economic downturn transformed Ghana into a country of emigration; neighboring Cote d'Ivoire was the initial destination. Later, hundreds of thousands of Ghanaians migrated to Nigeria to work in its booming oil industry, but most were deported in 1983 and 1985 as oil prices plummeted. Many Ghanaians then turned to more distant destinations, including other parts of Africa, Europe, and North America, but the majority continued to migrate within West Africa. Since the 1990s, increased emigration of skilled Ghanaians, especially to the US and the UK, drained the country of its health care and education professionals. Internally, poverty and other developmental disparities continue to drive Ghanaians from the north to the south, particularly to its urban centers.

Age structure: *0-14 years:* 37.44% (male 5,524,932/female 5,460,943)
15-24 years: 18.64% (male 2,717,481/female 2,752,601)
25-54 years: 34.27% (male 4,875,985/female 5,177,959)
55-64 years: 5.21% (male 743,757/female 784,517)
65 years and over: 4.44% (male 598,387/female 703,686) (2020 est.)

Dependency ratios: *total dependency ratio:* 67.4
youth dependency ratio: 62.2
elderly dependency ratio: 5.3
potential support ratio: 17.1 (2020 est.)

Median age: *total:* 21.4 years
male: 21 years
female: 21.9 years (2020 est.)
country comparison to the world: 184

Population growth rate: 2.23% (2022 est.)
country comparison to the world: 35

Birth rate: 28.55 births/1,000 population (2022 est.)
country comparison to the world: 34

Death rate: 6.14 deaths/1,000 population (2022 est.)
country comparison to the world: 150

Net migration rate: -0.16 migrant(s)/1,000 population (2022 est.)
country comparison to the world: 107

Population distribution: population is concentrated in the southern half of the country, with the highest concentrations being on or near the Atlantic coast as shown in this population distribution map

Urbanization: *urban population:* 58.6% of total population (2022)
rate of urbanization: 3.06% annual rate of change (2020-25 est.)

Major urban areas - population: 3.630 million Kumasi, 2.605 million ACCRA (capital), 1.035 million Sekondi Takoradi (2022)

Sex ratio: *at birth:* 1.03 male(s)/female
0-14 years: 1.02 male(s)/female
15-24 years: 0.99 male(s)/female
25-54 years: 0.89 male(s)/female
55-64 years: 0.88 male(s)/female
65 years and over: 0.72 male(s)/female
total population: 0.95 male(s)/female (2022 est.)

Mother's mean age at first birth: 20.7 years (2014 est.)
note: data represents median age at first birth among women 25-49

Maternal mortality ratio: 308 deaths/100,000 live births (2017 est.)
country comparison to the world: 36

Infant mortality rate: *total:* 32.59 deaths/1,000 live births
male: 36.05 deaths/1,000 live births
female: 29.03 deaths/1,000 live births (2022 est.)
country comparison to the world: 46

Life expectancy at birth: *total population:* 69.37 years
male: 67.7 years
female: 71.09 years (2022 est.)
country comparison to the world: 178

Total fertility rate: 3.66 children born/woman (2022 est.)
country comparison to the world: 33

Contraceptive prevalence rate: 27.2% (2017/18)

Drinking water source: *improved: urban:* 98.7% of population
rural: 83.8% of population
total: 92.4% of population
unimproved: urban: 1.3% of population
rural: 16.2% of population
total: 7.6% of population (2020 est.)

Current health expenditure: 3.4% of GDP (2019)

Physicians density: 0.17 physicians/1,000 population (2020)

Hospital bed density: 0.9 beds/1,000 population (2011)

Sanitation facility access: *improved: urban:* 84.8% of population
rural: 52.8% of population
total: 71.1% of population
unimproved: urban: 15.2% of population
rural: 47.2% of population
total: 28.9% of population (2020 est.)

HIV/AIDS - adult prevalence rate: 1.7% (2020 est.)
country comparison to the world: 26

Major infectious diseases: *degree of risk:* very high (2020)
food or waterborne diseases: bacterial and protozoal diarrhea, hepatitis A, and typhoid fever
vectorborne diseases: malaria, dengue fever, and yellow fever
water contact diseases: schistosomiasis
animal contact diseases: rabies
respiratory diseases: meningococcal meningitis
note: since October 2021, there has been a yellow fever outbreak in Ghana with numerous cases, including some deaths, in the following regions: Savannah, Upper West, Bono, and Oti; the CDC recommends travelers going to Ghana should receive vaccination against yellow fever at least 10 days before travel and

should take steps to prevent mosquito bites while there; those never vaccinated against yellow fever should avoid travel to Nigeria during the outbreak; there are no medications to treat or cure yellow fever

Obesity - adult prevalence rate: 10.9% (2016)
country comparison to the world: 136

Alcohol consumption per capita: *total:* 1.59 liters of pure alcohol (2019 est.)
beer: 0.53 liters of pure alcohol (2019 est.)
wine: 0.05 liters of pure alcohol (2019 est.)
spirits: 0.39 liters of pure alcohol (2019 est.)
other alcohols: 0.61 liters of pure alcohol (2019 est.)
country comparison to the world: 137

Tobacco use: *total:* 3.5% (2020 est.)
male: 6.6% (2020 est.)
female: 0.3% (2020 est.)
country comparison to the world: 164

Children under the age of 5 years underweight: 12.6% (2017/18)
country comparison to the world: 45

Child marriage: *women married by age 15:* 5%
women married by age 18: 19.3%
men married by age 18: 3.9% (2018 est.)

Education expenditures: 4% of GDP (2018 est.)
country comparison to the world: 103

Literacy: *definition:* age 15 and over can read and write
total population: 79%
male: 83.5%
female: 74.5% (2018)

School life expectancy (primary to tertiary education): *total:* 12 years
male: 12 years
female: 12 years (2020)

Unemployment, youth ages 15-24: *total:* 9.1%
male: 9.4%
female: 8.7% (2017 est.)

ENVIRONMENT

Environment - current issues: recurrent drought in north severely affects agricultural activities; deforestation; overgrazing; soil erosion; poaching and habitat destruction threaten wildlife populations; water pollution; inadequate supplies of potable water

Environment - international agreements: *party to:* Biodiversity, Climate Change, Climate Change-Kyoto Protocol, Climate Change-Paris Agreement, Comprehensive Nuclear Test Ban, Desertification, Endangered Species, Environmental Modification, Hazardous Wastes, Law of the Sea, Marine Dumping-London Protocol, Nuclear Test Ban, Ozone Layer Protection, Ship Pollution, Tropical Timber 2006, Wetlands, Whaling
signed, but not ratified: Marine Life Conservation

Air pollutants: *particulate matter emissions:* 31.95 micrograms per cubic meter (2016 est.)
carbon dioxide emissions: 16.67 megatons (2016 est.)
methane emissions: 22.75 megatons (2020 est.)

Climate: tropical; warm and comparatively dry along southeast coast; hot and humid in southwest; hot and dry in north

Land use: *agricultural land:* 69.1% (2018 est.)
arable land: 20.7% (2018 est.)
permanent crops: 11.9% (2018 est.)
permanent pasture: 36.5% (2018 est.)
forest: 21.2% (2018 est.)
other: 9.7% (2018 est.)

Urbanization: *urban population:* 58.6% of total population (2022)
rate of urbanization: 3.06% annual rate of change (2020-25 est.)

Revenue from forest resources: *forest revenues:* 3.51% of GDP (2018 est.)
country comparison to the world: 21

Revenue from coal: *coal revenues:* 0% of GDP (2018 est.)
country comparison to the world: 102

Waste and recycling: *municipal solid waste generated annually:* 3,538,275 tons (2005 est.)

Major rivers (by length in km): Volta river mouth (shared with Burkina Faso [s]) - 1,600 km
note – [s] after country name indicates river source; [m] after country name indicates river mouth

Major watersheds (area sq km): Atlantic Ocean drainage: Volta (410,991 sq km)

Total water withdrawal: *municipal:* 299.6 million cubic meters (2017 est.)
industrial: 95 million cubic meters (2017 est.)
agricultural: 1.07 billion cubic meters (2017 est.)

Total renewable water resources: 56.2 billion cubic meters (2017 est.)

GOVERNMENT

Country name: *conventional long form:* Republic of Ghana
conventional short form: Ghana
former: Gold Coast
etymology: named for the medieval West African kingdom of the same name but whose location was actually further north than the modern country

Government type: presidential republic

Capital: *name:* Accra
Geographic coordinates: 5 33 N, 0 13 W
time difference: UTC 0 (5 hours ahead of Washington, DC, during Standard Time)
etymology: the name derives from the Akan word "nkran" meaning "ants," and refers to the numerous anthills in the area around the capital

Administrative divisions: 16 regions; Ahafo, Ashanti, Bono, Bono East, Central, Eastern, Greater Accra, North East, Northern, Oti, Savannah, Upper East, Upper West, Volta, Western, Western North

Independence: 6 March 1957 (from the UK)

National holiday: Independence Day, 6 March (1957)

Constitution: *history:* several previous; latest drafted 31 March 1992, approved and promulgated 28 April 1992, entered into force 7 January 1993
amendments: proposed by Parliament; consideration requires prior referral to the Council of State, a body of prominent citizens who advise the president of the republic; passage of amendments to "entrenched" constitutional articles (including those on national sovereignty, fundamental rights and freedoms, the structure and authorities of the branches of government, and amendment procedures) requires approval in a referendum by at least 40% participation of eligible voters and at least 75% of votes cast, followed by at least two-thirds majority vote in Parliament, and assent of the president; amendments to non-entrenched articles do not require referenda; amended 1996

Legal system: mixed system of English common law and customary law

International law organization participation: has not submitted an ICJ jurisdiction declaration; accepts ICCt jurisdiction

Citizenship: *citizenship by birth:* no
citizenship by descent only: at least one parent or grandparent must be a citizen of Ghana
dual citizenship recognized: yes
residency requirement for naturalization: 5 years

Suffrage: 18 years of age; universal

Executive branch: *chief of state:* President Nana Addo Dankwa AKUFO-ADDO (since 7 January 2017); Vice President Mahamudu BAWUMIA (since 7 January 2017); the president is both chief of state and head of government
head of government: President Nana Addo Dankwa AKUFO-ADDO (since 7 January 2017); Vice President Mahamudu BAWUMIA (since 7 January 2017)
cabinet: Council of Ministers; nominated by the president, approved by Parliament
elections/appointments: president and vice president directly elected on the same ballot by absolute majority popular vote in 2 rounds if needed for a 4-year term (eligible for a second term); election last held on 7 December 2020 (next to be held in December 2024)
election results: Nana Addo Dankwa AKUFO-ADDO reelected president in the first round; percent of vote - Nana Addo Dankwa AKUFO-ADDO (NPP) 51.3%, John Dramani MAHAMA (NDC) 47.4%, other 1.3% (2020)

Legislative branch: *description:* unicameral Parliament (275 seats; members directly elected in single-seat constituencies by simple majority vote to serve 4-year terms)
elections: last held on 7 December 2020 (next to be held in December 2024)
election results: percent of vote by party - NA; seats by party (preliminary) - NPP 137, NDC 137, independent 1; composition - men 235, women 40, percent of women 14.5%

Judicial branch: *highest court(s):* Supreme Court (consists of the chief justice and 13 justices)
judge selection and term of office: chief justice appointed by the president in consultation with the Council of State (a small advisory body of prominent citizens) and with the approval of Parliament; other justices appointed by the president upon the advice of the Judicial Council (an 18-member independent body of judicial, military and police officials, and presidential nominees) and on the advice of the Council of State; justices can retire at age 60, with compulsory retirement at age 70
subordinate courts: Court of Appeal; High Court; Circuit Court; District Court; regional tribunals

Political parties and leaders: All Peoples Congress or APC [Hassan AYARIGA]
Convention People's Party or CPP [Onsy Kwame NKRUMAH, acting]
Ghana Freedom Party or GFP [Akua DONKOR]
Ghana Union Movement or GUM [Christian Kwabena ANDREWS]
Great Consolidated Popular Party or GCPP [Henry Herbert LARTEY]
Liberal Party of Ghana or LPG [Kofi AKPALOO]

National Democratic Congress or NDC [John Dramani MAHAMA]
National Democratic Party or NDP [Nana Konadu Agyeman RAWLINGS]
New Patriotic Party or NPP [Nana Addo Dankwa AKUFO-ADDO]
People's National Convention or PNC [David APASERA]
Progressive People's Party or PPP [Paa Kwesi NDUOM]
United Front Party or UFP [Dr. Nana A. BOATENG]
United Progressive Party or UPP [Akwasi Addai ODIKE]
note: Ghana has more than 20 registered parties; included are those which participated in the 2020 general election

International organization participation: ACP, AfDB, ATMIS, AU, C, ECOWAS, EITI (compliant country), FAO, G-24, G-77, IAEA, IBRD, ICAO, ICC (national committees), ICCt, ICRM, IDA, IFAD, IFC, IFRCS, ILO, IMF, IMO, IMSO, Interpol, IOC, IOM, IPU, ISO, ITSO, ITU, ITUC (NGOs), MIGA, MINURSO, MINUSMA, MONUSCO, NAM, OAS (observer), OIF, OPCW, UN, UNAMID, UNCTAD, UNESCO, UNHCR, UNIDO, UNIFIL, UNISFA, UNMIL, UNMISS, UNOCI, UNSOM, UNWTO, UPU, WCO, WFTU (NGOs), WHO, WIPO, WMO, WTO

Diplomatic representation in the US: *chief of mission:* Ambassador Alima MAHAMA (since 7 July 2021)
chancery: 3512 International Drive NW, Washington, DC 20008
telephone: [1] (202) 686-4520
FAX: [1] (202) 686-4527
email address and website:
info@ghanaembassydc.org
https://ghanaembassydc.org/
consulate(s) general: New York

Diplomatic representation from the US: *chief of mission:* Ambassador Virginia E. PALMER (since 16 June 2022)
embassy: No. 24, Fourth Circular Road, Cantonments, Accra, P.O. Box 2288, Accra
mailing address: 2020 Accra Place, Washington DC 20521-2020
telephone: [233] (0) 30-274-1000
email address and website:
ACSAccra@state.gov
https://gh.usembassy.gov/

Flag description: three equal horizontal bands of red (top), yellow, and green, with a large black five-pointed star centered in the yellow band; red symbolizes the blood shed for independence, yellow represents the country's mineral wealth, while green stands for its forests and natural wealth; the black star is said to be the lodestar of African freedom
note: uses the popular Pan-African colors of Ethiopia; similar to the flag of Bolivia, which has a coat of arms centered in the yellow band

National symbol(s): black star, golden eagle; national colors: red, yellow, green, black

National anthem: *name:* "God Bless Our Homeland Ghana"
lyrics/music: unknown/Philip GBEHO
note: music adopted 1957, lyrics adopted 1966; the lyrics were changed twice, in 1960 when a republic was declared and after a 1966 coup

National heritage: *total World Heritage Sites:* 2 (both cultural)
selected World Heritage Site locales: Forts and Castles, Volta, Greater Accra, Central and Western Regions; Asante Traditional Buildings

ECONOMY

Economic overview: Ghana has a market-based economy with relatively few policy barriers to trade and investment in comparison with other countries in the region, and Ghana is endowed with natural resources. Ghana's economy was strengthened by a quarter century of relatively sound management, a competitive business environment, and sustained reductions in poverty levels, but in recent years has suffered the consequences of loose fiscal policy, high budget and current account deficits, and a depreciating currency.

Agriculture accounts for about 20% of GDP and employs more than half of the workforce, mainly small landholders. Gold, oil, and cocoa exports, and individual remittances, are major sources of foreign exchange. Expansion of Ghana's nascent oil industry has boosted economic growth, but the fall in oil prices since 2015 reduced by half Ghana's oil revenue. Production at Jubilee, Ghana's first commercial offshore oilfield, began in mid-December 2010. Production from two more fields, TEN and Sankofa, started in 2016 and 2017 respectively. The country's first gas processing plant at Atuabo is also producing natural gas from the Jubilee field, providing power to several of Ghana's thermal power plants.

As of 2018, key economic concerns facing the government include the lack of affordable electricity, lack of a solid domestic revenue base, and the high debt burden. The AKUFO-ADDO administration has made some progress by committing to fiscal consolidation, but much work is still to be done. Ghana signed a $920 million extended credit facility with the IMF in April 2015 to help it address its growing economic crisis. The IMF fiscal targets require Ghana to reduce the deficit by cutting subsidies, decreasing the bloated public sector wage bill, strengthening revenue administration, boosting tax revenues, and improving the health of Ghana's banking sector. Priorities for the new administration include rescheduling some of Ghana's $31 billion debt, stimulating economic growth, reducing inflation, and stabilizing the currency. Prospects for new oil and gas production and follow through on tighter fiscal management are likely to help Ghana's economy in 2018.

Real GDP (purchasing power parity): $164.84 billion (2020 est.)
$164.16 billion (2019 est.)
$154.13 billion (2018 est.)
note: data are in 2017 dollars
country comparison to the world: 73

Real GDP growth rate: 8.4% (2017 est.)
3.7% (2016 est.)
3.8% (2015 est.)
country comparison to the world: 6

Real GDP per capita: $5,300 (2020 est.)
$5,400 (2019 est.)
$5,200 (2018 est.)
note: data are in 2017 dollars
country comparison to the world: 169

GDP (official exchange rate): $65.363 billion (2019 est.)

Inflation rate (consumer prices): 8.4% (2019 est.)
9.8% (2018 est.)
12.3% (2017 est.)
country comparison to the world: 201

Credit ratings:

Fitch rating: B (2013)

Moody's rating: B3 (2015)

Standard & Poors rating: B- (2020)
note: The year refers to the year in which the current credit rating was first obtained.

GDP - composition, by sector of origin: *agriculture:* 18.3% (2017 est.)
industry: 24.5% (2017 est.)
services: 57.2% (2017 est.)

GDP - composition, by end use: *household consumption:* 80.1% (2017 est.)
government consumption: 8.6% (2017 est.)
investment in fixed capital: 13.7% (2017 est.)
investment in inventories: 1.1% (2017 est.)
exports of goods and services: 43% (2017 est.)
imports of goods and services: -46.5% (2017 est.)

Agricultural products: cassava, yams, plantains, maize, oil palm fruit, taro, rice, cocoa, oranges, pineapples

Industries: mining, lumbering, light manufacturing, aluminum smelting, food processing, cement, small commercial ship building, petroleum

Industrial production growth rate: 16.7% (2017 est.)
country comparison to the world: 2

Labor force: 12.49 million (2017 est.)
country comparison to the world: 45

Labor force - by occupation: *agriculture:* 44.7%
industry: 14.4%
services: 40.9% (2013 est.)

Unemployment rate: 11.9% (2015 est.)
5.2% (2013 est.)
country comparison to the world: 163

Unemployment, youth ages 15-24: *total:* 9.1%
male: 9.4%
female: 8.7% (2017 est.)
country comparison to the world: 144

Population below poverty line: 23.4% (2016 est.)

Gini Index coefficient - distribution of family income:
43.5 (2016 est.)
42.3 (2012-13)
41.9 (2005-06)
country comparison to the world: 39

Household income or consumption by percentage share: *lowest 10%:* 2%
highest 10%: 32.8% (2006)

Budget: *revenues:* 9.544 billion (2017 est.)
expenditures: 12.36 billion (2017 est.)

Budget surplus (+) or deficit (-): -6% (of GDP) (2017 est.)
country comparison to the world: 183

Public debt: 71.8% of GDP (2017 est.)
73.4% of GDP (2016 est.)
country comparison to the world: 47

Taxes and other revenues: 20.3% (of GDP) (2017 est.)
country comparison to the world: 149

Fiscal year: calendar year

Current account balance: -$2.131 billion (2017 est.)
-$2.86 billion (2016 est.)
country comparison to the world: 169

Exports: $25.59 billion (2019 est.) note: data are in current year dollars

$22.51 billion (2018 est.) note: data are in current year dollars
country comparison to the world: 73

Exports - partners: Switzerland 23%, India 17%, China 12%, United Arab Emirates 8%, South Africa 8% (2019)

Exports - commodities: gold, crude petroleum, cocoa products, manganese, cashews (2019)

Imports: $26.91 billion (2019 est.) note: data are in current year dollars
$23.22 billion (2018 est.) note: data are in current year dollars
country comparison to the world: 74

Imports - partners: China 24%, Nigeria 22%, United States 5% (2019)

Imports - commodities: metal tubing, ships, cars, refined petroleum, rice (2019)

Reserves of foreign exchange and gold: $7.555 billion (31 December 2017 est.)
$6.162 billion (31 December 2016 est.)
country comparison to the world: 81

Debt - external: $20.467 billion (2019 est.)
$17.885 billion (2018 est.)
country comparison to the world: 93

Exchange rates: cedis (GHC) per US dollar -
5.86 (2020 est.)
5.68 (2019 est.)
4.9 (2018 est.)
3.712 (2014 est.)
2.895 (2013 est.)

ENERGY

Electricity access: *electrification - total population:* 85% (2019)
electrification - urban areas: 93% (2019)
electrification - rural areas: 75% (2019)

Electricity: *installed generating capacity:* 5.312 million kW (2020 est.)
consumption: 13,107,757,000 kWh (2019 est.)
exports: 1.801 billion kWh (2020 est.)
imports: 58 million kWh (2020 est.)
transmission/distribution losses: 2.474 billion kWh (2019 est.)

Electricity generation sources: *fossil fuels:* 63.8% of total installed capacity (2020 est.)
solar: 0.3% of total installed capacity (2020 est.)
hydroelectricity: 35.9% of total installed capacity (2020 est.)
biomass and waste: 0.1% of total installed capacity (2020 est.)

Coal: *production:* 0 metric tons (2020 est.)
consumption: 48,000 metric tons (2020 est.)
exports: 0 metric tons (2020 est.)
imports: 48,000 metric tons (2020 est.)
proven reserves: 0 metric tons (2019 est.)

Petroleum: *total petroleum production:* 185,700 bbl/day (2021 est.)
refined petroleum consumption: 98,000 bbl/day (2019 est.)
crude oil and lease condensate exports: 176,800 bbl/day (2018 est.)
crude oil and lease condensate imports: 3,900 bbl/day (2018 est.)
crude oil estimated reserves: 660 million barrels (2021 est.)

Refined petroleum products - production: 2,073 bbl/day (2015 est.)
country comparison to the world: 104

Refined petroleum products - exports: 2,654 bbl/day (2015 est.)
country comparison to the world: 100

Refined petroleum products - imports: 85,110 bbl/day (2015 est.)
country comparison to the world: 59

Natural gas: *production:* 1,598,653,000 cubic meters (2019 est.)
consumption: 2,224,568,000 cubic meters (2019 est.)
exports: 0 cubic meters (2021 est.)
imports: 625.915 million cubic meters (2019 est.)
proven reserves: 22.653 billion cubic meters (2021 est.)

Carbon dioxide emissions: 18.093 million metric tonnes of CO2 (2019 est.)
from coal and metallurgical coke: 160,000 metric tonnes of CO2 (2019 est.)
from petroleum and other liquids: 13.569 million metric tonnes of CO2 (2019 est.)
from consumed natural gas: 4.364 million metric tonnes of CO2 (2019 est.)
country comparison to the world: 88

Energy consumption per capita: 11.239 million Btu/person (2019 est.)
country comparison to the world: 152

COMMUNICATIONS

Telephones - fixed lines: *total subscriptions:* 307,668 (2020 est.)
subscriptions per 100 inhabitants: 1 (2020 est.)
country comparison to the world: 108

Telephones - mobile cellular: *total subscriptions:* 40,461,609 (2020 est.)
subscriptions per 100 inhabitants: 130 (2020 est.)
country comparison to the world: 39

Telecommunication systems: *general assessment:* challenged by unreliable electricity and shortage of skilled labor, Ghana seeks to extend telecom services nationally; investment in fiber infrastructure and off-grid solutions provide data coverage to over 23 million people; launch of LTE has improved mobile data services, including m-commerce and banking; moderately competitive Internet market, most through mobile networks; international submarine cables, and terrestrial cables have improved Internet capacity; LTE services are widely available; the relatively high cost of 5G-compatible devices also inhibits most subscribers from migrating from 3G and LTE platforms (2022)
domestic: fixed-line data less than 1 per 100 subscriptions; competition among multiple mobile-cellular providers has spurred growth with a voice subscribership of more than 130 per 100 persons (2020)
international: country code - 233; landing points for the SAT-3/WASC, MainOne, ACE, WACS and GLO-1 fiber-optic submarine cables that provide connectivity to South and West Africa, and Europe; satellite earth stations - 4 Intelsat (Atlantic Ocean); microwave radio relay link to Panaftel system connects Ghana to its neighbors; GhanaSat-1 nanosatellite launched in 2017 (2017)

Broadcast media: state-owned TV station, 2 state-owned radio networks; several privately owned TV stations and a large number of privately owned radio stations; transmissions of multiple international broadcasters are accessible; several cable and satellite TV subscription services are obtainable

Internet country code: .gh

Internet users: *total:* 18,022,308 (2020 est.)
percent of population: 58% (2020 est.)
country comparison to the world: 41

Broadband - fixed subscriptions: *total:* 78,371 (2020 est.)
subscriptions per 100 inhabitants: 0.3 (2020 est.)
country comparison to the world: 132

TRANSPORTATION

National air transport system: *number of registered air carriers:* 3 (2020)
inventory of registered aircraft operated by air carriers: 21
annual passenger traffic on registered air carriers: 467,438 (2018)

Civil aircraft registration country code prefix: 9G

Airports: *total:* 10 (2021)
country comparison to the world: 154

Airports - with paved runways: *total:* 7
over 3,047 m: 1
2,438 to 3,047 m: 1
1,524 to 2,437 m: 3
914 to 1,523 m: 2 (2021)

Airports - with unpaved runways: *total:* 3
914 to 1,523 m: 3 (2021)

Pipelines: 681.3 km gas, 11.4 km oil, 435 km refined products (2022)

Railways: *total:* 947 km (2022)
narrow gauge: 947 km (2022) 1.067-m gauge
country comparison to the world: 92

Roadways: *total:* 65,725 km (2021)
paved: 14,948 km (2021)
unpaved: 50,777 km (2021)
urban: 28,480 km 27% total paved 73% total unpaved
country comparison to the world: 72

Waterways: 1,293 km (2011) (168 km for launches and lighters on Volta, Ankobra, and Tano Rivers; 1,125 km of arterial and feeder waterways on Lake Volta)
country comparison to the world: 60

Merchant marine: *total:* 51
by type: general cargo 7, oil tanker 3, other 41 (2021)
country comparison to the world: 118

Ports and terminals: *major seaport(s):* Takoradi, Tema

MILITARY AND SECURITY

Military and security forces: Ghana Armed Forces: Army, Navy, Air Force (2022)

Military expenditures: 0.5% of GDP (2021 est.)
0.4% of GDP (2020 est.)
0.4% of GDP (2019 est.) (approximately $360 million)
0.3% of GDP (2018 est.) (approximately $330 million)
0.3% of GDP (2017 est.) (approximately $300 million)
country comparison to the world: 159

Military and security service personnel strengths: approximately 14,000 active personnel (10,000 Army; 2,000 Navy; 2,000 Air Force) (2022)

Military equipment inventories and acquisitions: the inventory of the Ghana Armed Forces is a mix of Russian, Chinese, and Western equipment; since 2010, China has been the leading supplier of arms (2022)

Military service age and obligation: 18-26 years of age for voluntary military service, with basic education certificate; no conscription (2022)

Military deployments: 140 Mali (MINUSMA); 875 Lebanon (UNIFIL); 725 (plus about 275 police) South Sudan (UNMISS); 650 Sudan (UNISFA) (May 2022)
note: since sending a contingent of troops to the Congo in 1960, the military has been a regular contributor to African- and UN-sponsored peacekeeping missions

Military - note: the military of Ghana traces its origins to the Gold Coast Constabulary that was established in 1879 and renamed the Gold Coast Regiment in 1901; the Gold Coast Regiment was part of the West African Frontier Force (WAFF), a multi-regiment force formed by the British colonial office in 1900 to garrison the West African colonies of Gold Coast (Ghana), Nigeria (Lagos and the protectorates of Northern and Southern Nigeria), Sierra Leone, and Gambia; the WAFF served with distinction in both East and West Africa during World War I; in 1928, it received royal recognition and was re-named the Royal West African Frontier Force (RWAFF); the RWAFF went on to serve in World War II as part of the British 81st and 82nd (West African) divisions in the East Africa and Burma campaigns; following independence in 1957, the Gold Coast Regiment formed the basis for the new Ghanaian Army
as of 2022, the primary missions for the Ghanaian military included assisting other security services with internal security and patrolling the country's economic exclusion zone, which has led to efforts to expand the Navy's capabilities in recent years; in 2022, Ghana beefed up its military presence in the north of the country against threats from the terrorist organization Jama'at Nasr al-Islam wal Muslimin (JNIM), a coalition of al-Qa'ida linked militant groups, which has conducted attacks in the neighboring countries of Burkina Faso, Cote d'Ivoire, and Togo

Maritime threats: the International Maritime Bureau reports the territorial and offshore waters in the Niger Delta and Gulf of Guinea remain a very high risk for piracy and armed robbery of ships; in 2021, there were 34 reported incidents of piracy and armed robbery at sea in the Gulf of Guinea region; although a significant decrease from the total number of 81 incidents in 2020, it included the one hijacking and three of five ships fired upon worldwide; while boarding and attempted boarding to steal valuables from ships and crews are the most common types of incidents, almost a third of all incidents involve a hijacking and/or kidnapping; in 2021, 57 crew members were kidnapped in seven separate incidents in the Gulf of Guinea, representing 100% of kidnappings worldwide; Nigerian pirates in particular are well armed and very aggressive, operating as far as 200 nm offshore; the Maritime Administration of the US Department of Transportation has issued a Maritime Advisory (2022-001 - Gulf of Guinea-Piracy/Armed Robbery/Kidnapping for Ransom) effective 4 January 2022, which states in part, "Piracy, armed robbery, and kidnapping for ransom continue to serve as significant threats to US-flagged vessels transiting or operating in the Gulf of Guinea"

TRANSNATIONAL ISSUES

Disputes - international: disputed maritime border between Ghana and Cote d'Ivoire

Illicit drugs: a transit and destination point for illicit drugs trafficked from Asia and South America to other African nations and Europe, and to a lesser extent the United States; cultivation of cannabis for domestic use and is trafficked to regional markets or to Europe

GIBRALTAR

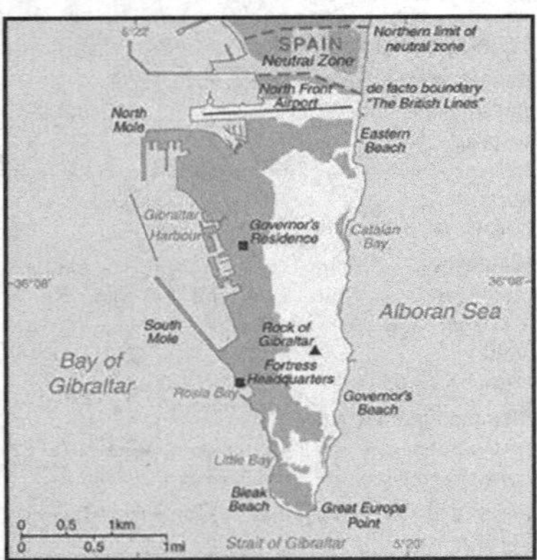

INTRODUCTION

Background: Strategically important, Gibraltar was reluctantly ceded to Great Britain by Spain in the 1713 Treaty of Utrecht; the British garrison was formally declared a colony in 1830. In a referendum held in 1967, Gibraltarians voted overwhelmingly to remain a British dependency. The subsequent granting of autonomy in 1969 by the UK led Spain to close the border and sever all communication links. Between 1997 and 2002, the UK and Spain held a series of talks on establishing temporary joint sovereignty over Gibraltar. In response to these talks, the Gibraltar Government called a referendum in late 2002 in which the majority of citizens voted overwhelmingly against any sharing of sovereignty with Spain. Since late 2004, Spain, the UK, and Gibraltar have held tripartite talks with the aim of cooperatively resolving problems that affect the local population, and work continues on cooperation agreements in areas such as taxation and financial services; communications and maritime security; policy; legal and customs services; environmental protection; and education and visa services. A new noncolonial constitution came into force in 2007, and the European Court of First Instance recognized Gibraltar's right to regulate its own tax regime in December 2008. The UK retains responsibility for defense, foreign relations, internal security, and financial stability.
Spain and the UK continue to spar over the territory. Throughout 2009, a dispute over Gibraltar's claim to territorial waters extending out three miles gave rise to periodic non-violent maritime confrontations between Spanish and UK naval patrols, and in 2013, the British reported a record number of entries by Spanish vessels into waters claimed by Gibraltar following a dispute over Gibraltar's creation of an artificial reef in those waters. Spain renewed its demands for an eventual return of Gibraltar to Spanish control after the UK's June 2016 vote to leave the EU, but London has dismissed any connection between the vote and its continued sovereignty over Gibraltar.

GEOGRAPHY

Location: Southwestern Europe, bordering the Strait of Gibraltar, which links the Mediterranean Sea and the North Atlantic Ocean, on the southern coast of Spain

Geographic coordinates: 36 08 N, 5 21 W

Map references: Europe

Area: *total:* 7 sq km
land: 6.5 sq km
water: 0 sq km
country comparison to the world: 244

Area - comparative: more than 10 times the size of The National Mall in Washington, D.C.

Land boundaries: *total:* 1.2 km
border countries (1): Spain 1.2 km

Coastline: 12 km

Maritime claims: *territorial sea:* 3 nm

Climate: Mediterranean with mild winters and warm summers

Terrain: a narrow coastal lowland borders the Rock of Gibraltar

Elevation: *highest point:* Rock of Gibraltar 426 m
lowest point: Mediterranean Sea 0 m

Natural resources: none

Land use: *agricultural land:* 0% (2011 est.)
other: 100% (2018 est.)

Natural hazards: occasional droughts; no streams or large bodies of water on the peninsula (all potable water comes from desalination)

Geography - note: *note 1:* strategic location on Strait of Gibraltar that links the North Atlantic Ocean and Mediterranean Sea
note 2: one of only two British territories where traffic drives on the right, the other being the

island of Diego Garcia in the British Indian Ocean Territory

PEOPLE AND SOCIETY

Population: 29,573 (2022 est.)
country comparison to the world: 217

Nationality: *noun:* Gibraltarian(s)
adjective: Gibraltar

Ethnic groups: Gibraltarian 79%, other British 13.2%, Spanish 2.1%, Moroccan 1.6%, other EU 2.4%, other 1.6% (2012 est.)
note: data represent population by nationality

Languages: English (used in schools and for official purposes), Spanish, Italian, Portuguese

Religions: Roman Catholic 72.1%, Church of England 7.7%, other Christian 3.8%, Muslim 3.6%, Jewish 2.4%, Hindu 2%, other 1.1%, none 7.1%, unspecified 0.1% (2012 est.)

Age structure: *0-14 years:* 20.24% (male 3,080/female 2,907)
15-24 years: 13.07% (male 2,000/female 1,866)
25-54 years: 41.28% (male 6,289/female 5,922)
55-64 years: 8.71% (male 1,082/female 1,495)
65 years and over: 16.7% (male 2,378/female 2,562) (2020 est.)

Median age: *total:* 35.5 years
male: 34.4 years
female: 36.6 years (2020 est.)
country comparison to the world: 84

Population growth rate: 0.19% (2022 est.)
country comparison to the world: 181

Birth rate: 13.93 births/1,000 population (2022 est.)
country comparison to the world: 129

Death rate: 8.76 deaths/1,000 population (2022 est.)
country comparison to the world: 67

Net migration rate: -3.25 migrant(s)/1,000 population (2022 est.)
country comparison to the world: 185

Urbanization: *urban population:* 100% of total population (2022)
rate of urbanization: 0.45% annual rate of change (2015-20 est.)

Major urban areas - population: 35,000 GIBRALTAR (capital) (2018)

Sex ratio: *at birth:* 1.05 male(s)/female
0-14 years: 1.05 male(s)/female
15-24 years: 1.06 male(s)/female
25-54 years: 1.05 male(s)/female
55-64 years: 0.79 male(s)/female
65 years and over: 0.95 male(s)/female
total population: 1.02 male(s)/female (2022 est.)

Infant mortality rate: *total:* 6.25 deaths/1,000 live births
male: 7.06 deaths/1,000 live births
female: 5.41 deaths/1,000 live births (2022 est.)
country comparison to the world: 169

Life expectancy at birth: *total population:* 80.42 years
male: 77.58 years
female: 83.41 years (2022 est.)
country comparison to the world: 50

Total fertility rate: 1.9 children born/woman (2022 est.)
country comparison to the world: 126

Drinking water source: *improved: total:* 100% of population
unimproved: total: 0% of population (2020)

Sanitation facility access: *improved: total:* 100% of population
unimproved: total: 0% of population (2020)

ENVIRONMENT

Environment - current issues: *limited natural freshwater resources:* more than 90% of drinking water supplied by desalination, the remainder from stored rainwater; a separate supply of saltwater used for sanitary services

Air pollutants: *carbon dioxide emissions:* 0.63 megatons (2016 est.)

Climate: Mediterranean with mild winters and warm summers

Land use: *agricultural land:* 0% (2011 est.)
other: 100% (2018 est.)

Urbanization: *urban population:* 100% of total population (2022)
rate of urbanization: 0.45% annual rate of change (2015-20 est.)

Waste and recycling: *municipal solid waste generated annually:* 16,954 tons (2012 est.)

GOVERNMENT

Country name: *conventional long form:* none
conventional short form: Gibraltar
etymology: from the Spanish derivation of the Arabic "Jabal Tariq," which means "Mountain of Tariq" and which refers to the Rock of Gibraltar

Government type: parliamentary democracy (Parliament); self-governing overseas territory of the UK

Dependency status: overseas territory of the UK

Capital: *name:* Gibraltar
Geographic coordinates: 36 08 N, 5 21 W
time difference: UTC+1 (6 hours ahead of Washington, DC, during Standard Time)
daylight saving time: +1hr, begins last Sunday in March; ends last Sunday in October
etymology: from the Spanish derivation of the Arabic "Jabal Tariq," which means "Mountain of Tariq" and which refers to the Rock of Gibraltar

Administrative divisions: none (overseas territory of the UK)

Independence: none (overseas territory of the UK)

National holiday: National Day, 10 September (1967); note - day of the national referendum to decide whether to remain with the UK or join Spain

Constitution: *history:* previous 1969; latest passed by referendum 30 November 2006, entered into effect 14 December 2006, entered into force 2 January 2007
amendments: proposed by Parliament and requires prior consent of the British monarch (through the Secretary of State); passage requires at least three-fourths majority vote in Parliament followed by simple majority vote in a referendum; note – only sections 1 through 15 in Chapter 1 (Protection of Fundamental Rights and Freedoms) can be amended by Parliament

Legal system: the laws of the UK, where applicable, apply

Citizenship: see United Kingdom

Suffrage: 18 years of age; universal; and British citizens with six months residence or more

Executive branch: *chief of state:* King CHARLES III (since 8 September 2022); represented by Governor Sir David STEEL (since 11 June 2020)
head of government: Chief Minister Fabian PICARDO (since 9 December 2011)
cabinet: Council of Ministers appointed from among the 17 elected members of Parliament by the governor in consultation with the chief minister
elections/appointments: the monarchy is hereditary; governor appointed by the monarch; following legislative elections, the leader of the majority party or majority coalition usually appointed chief minister by the governor

Legislative branch: *description:* unicameral Parliament (18 seats; 17 members directly elected in a single nationwide constituency by majority vote and 1 appointed by Parliament as speaker; members serve 4-year terms)
elections: last held on 17 October 2019 (next to be held in 2023)
election results: percent of vote by party - GSLP-Liberal Alliance 58.8% (GSLP 41.2%, LPG 17.6%), GSD 35.3%, TG 5.8%, independent 1.4%; seats by party - GSLP-Liberal Alliance 10 (GSLP 7, LPG 3), GSD 6, TG 1; composition including Parliament speaker - men 16, women 2, percent of women 11.1%

Judicial branch: *highest court(s):* Court of Appeal (consists of at least 3 judges, including the court president); Supreme Court of Gibraltar (consists of the chief justice and 3 judges); note - appeals beyond the Court of Appeal are heard by the Judicial Committee of the Privy Council (in London)
judge selection and term of office: Court of Appeal and Supreme Court judges appointed by the governor upon the advice of the Judicial Service Commission, a 7-member body of judges and appointees of the governor; tenure of the Court of Appeal president based on terms of appointment; Supreme Court chief justice and judges normally appointed until retirement at age 67 but tenure can be extended 3 years
subordinate courts: Court of First Instance; Magistrates' Court; specialized tribunals for issues relating to social security, taxes, and employment

Political parties and leaders: Gibraltar Liberal Party or Liberal Party of Gibraltar or LPG [Joseph GARCIA]
Gibraltar Social Democrats or GSD [Keith AZOPARDI]
Gibraltar Socialist Labor Party or GSLP [Fabian PICARDO]
GSLP-Liberal Alliance (includes GSLP and LPG)
Together Gibraltar or TG [Marlene HASSAN-NAHON]

International organization participation: ICC (NGOs), Interpol (subbureau), UPU

Diplomatic representation in the US: none (overseas territory of the UK)

Diplomatic representation from the US: *embassy:* none (overseas territory of the UK)

Flag description: two horizontal bands of white (top, double width) and red with a three-towered red castle in the center of the white band; hanging from the castle gate is a gold key centered in the red band; the design is that of Gibraltar's coat of arms granted on 10 July 1502 by King Ferdinand and Queen Isabella of Spain; the castle symbolizes Gibraltar as a fortress, while the key represents Gibraltar's strategic importance - the key to the Mediterranean

National symbol(s): Barbary macaque; national colors: red, white, yellow

National anthem: *name:* "Gibraltar Anthem"
lyrics/music: Peter EMBERLEY
note: adopted 1994; serves as a local anthem; as an overseas territory of the United Kingdom, "God Save the King" is official (see United Kingdom)

ECONOMY

Economic overview: Self-sufficient Gibraltar benefits from an extensive shipping trade, offshore banking, and its position as an international conference center. Tax rates are low to attract foreign investment. The British military presence has been sharply reduced and now contributes about 7% to the local economy, compared with 60% in 1984. In recent years, Gibraltar has seen major structural change from a public to a private sector economy, but changes in government spending still have a major impact on the level of employment.

The financial sector, tourism (over 11 million visitors in 2012), gaming revenues, shipping services fees, and duties on consumer goods also generate revenue. The financial sector, tourism, and the shipping sector contribute 30%, 30%, and 25%, respectively, of GDP. Telecommunications, e-commerce, and e-gaming account for the remaining 15%.

Real GDP (purchasing power parity): $2.044 billion (2014 est.)
$1.85 billion (2013 est.)
$2 billion (2012 est.)
note: data are in 2014 dollars
country comparison to the world: 196

Real GDP per capita: $61,700 (2014 est.)
$43,000 (2008 est.)
$41,200 (2007 est.)
country comparison to the world: 15

GDP (official exchange rate): $2.044 billion (2014 est.)

Inflation rate (consumer prices): 2.5% (2013 est.)
2.2% (2012 est.)
country comparison to the world: 127

GDP - composition, by sector of origin: *agriculture:* 0% (2016 est.)
industry: 0% (2008 est.)
services: 100% (2016 est.)

Agricultural products: none

Industries: tourism, banking and finance, ship repairing, tobacco

Industrial production growth rate: NA

Labor force: 24,420 (2014 est.)
country comparison to the world: 208

Labor force - by occupation: *agriculture:* NEGL
industry: 1.8%
services: 98.2% (2014 est.)

Unemployment rate: 1% (2016 est.)
country comparison to the world: 10

Population below poverty line: NA

Household income or consumption by percentage share: *lowest 10%:* NA
highest 10%: NA

Budget: *revenues:* 475.8 million (2008 est.)
expenditures: 452.3 million (2008 est.)

Budget surplus (+) or deficit (-): 1.1% (of GDP) (2008 est.)
country comparison to the world: 31

Public debt: 7.5% of GDP (2008 est.)
8.4% of GDP (2006 est.)
country comparison to the world: 200

Taxes and other revenues: 23.3% (of GDP) (2008 est.)
country comparison to the world: 127

Fiscal year: 1 July - 30 June

Exports: $202.3 million (2014 est.)
$271 million (2004 est.)
country comparison to the world: 204

Exports - partners: Poland 31%, Netherlands 27%, France 11%, Germany 8%, United States 6% (2019)

Exports - commodities: cars, ships, refined petroleum, fish, recreational boats (2019)

Imports: $2.967 billion (2004 est.)
country comparison to the world: 158

Imports - partners: Spain 19%, US 12%, India 12%, Italy 12%, Netherlands 11%, United Kingdom 7%, Greece 6% (2019)

Imports - commodities: refined petroleum, recreational boats, cars, coal tar oil, crude petroleum (2019)

Debt - external: NA

Exchange rates: Gibraltar pounds (GIP) per US dollar -
0.885 (2017 est.)
0.903 (2016 est.)
0.9214 (2015 est.)
0.885 (2014 est.)
0.7634 (2013 est.)

ENERGY

Electricity access: *electrification - total population:* 100% (2020)

Electricity: *installed generating capacity:* 43,000 kW (2020 est.)
consumption: 198.86 million kWh (2019 est.)
exports: 0 kWh (2019 est.)
imports: 0 kWh (2019 est.)
transmission/distribution losses: 7 million kWh (2019 est.)

Electricity generation sources: *fossil fuels:* 100% of total installed capacity (2020 est.)

Petroleum: *total petroleum production:* 0 bbl/day (2021 est.)
refined petroleum consumption: 83,700 bbl/day (2019 est.)

Refined petroleum products - imports: 74,200 bbl/day (2015 est.)
country comparison to the world: 66

Natural gas: *production:* 0 cubic meters (2021 est.)
consumption: 74.756 million cubic meters (2020 est.)
exports: 0 cubic meters (2021 est.)
imports: 56.719 million cubic meters (2019 est.)
proven reserves: 0 cubic meters (2021 est.)

Carbon dioxide emissions: 14.256 million metric tonnes of CO2 (2019 est.)
from petroleum and other liquids: 14.146 million metric tonnes of CO2 (2019 est.)
from consumed natural gas: 111,000 metric tonnes of CO2 (2019 est.)
country comparison to the world: 97

Energy consumption per capita: 0 Btu/person (2019 est.)
country comparison to the world: 201

COMMUNICATIONS

Telephones - fixed lines: *total subscriptions:* 17,041 (2020 est.)
subscriptions per 100 inhabitants: 51 (2020 est.)
country comparison to the world: 178

Telephones - mobile cellular: *total subscriptions:* 35,438 (2020 est.)
subscriptions per 100 inhabitants: 105 (2020 est.)
country comparison to the world: 210

Telecommunication systems: *general assessment:* Gibraltar's population is urban based, served by a digital telephone exchange supported by a fiber optic and copper infrastructure; near universal mobile and Internet use (2019)
domestic: automatic exchange facilities; over 51 per 100 fixed-line and 105 per 100 mobile-cellular (2020)
international: country code - 350; landing point for the EIG to Europe, Asia, Africa and the Middle East via submarine cables; radiotelephone; microwave radio relay; satellite earth station - 1 Intelsat (Atlantic Ocean) (2019)

Broadcast media: Gibraltar Broadcasting Corporation (GBC) provides TV and radio broadcasting services via 1 TV station and 4 radio stations; British Forces Broadcasting Service (BFBS) operates 1 radio station; broadcasts from Spanish radio and TV stations are accessible

Internet country code: .gi

Internet users: *total:* 31,684 (2019 est.)
percent of population: 94% (2019 est.)
country comparison to the world: 207

Broadband - fixed subscriptions: *total:* 21,009 (2020 est.)
subscriptions per 100 inhabitants: 62 (2020 est.)
country comparison to the world: 164

TRANSPORTATION

Civil aircraft registration country code prefix: VP-G

Airports: *total:* 1 (2021)
country comparison to the world: 222

Airports - with paved runways: *total:* 1
1,524 to 2,437 m: 1 (2021)

Roadways: *total:* 29 km (2007)
paved: 29 km (2007)
country comparison to the world: 220

Merchant marine: *total:* 202
by type: bulk carrier 8, container ship 19, general cargo 55, oil tanker 20, other 100 (2021)
country comparison to the world: 67

Ports and terminals: *major seaport(s):* Gibraltar

MILITARY AND SECURITY

Military and security forces: Royal Gibraltar Regiment (2022)

Military - note: defense is the responsibility of the UK

TRANSNATIONAL ISSUES

Disputes - international: in 2002, Gibraltar residents voted overwhelmingly by referendum to reject any "shared sovereignty" arrangement; the Government of Gibraltar insists on equal participation in talks between the UK and Spain; Spain disapproves of UK plans to grant Gibraltar even greater autonomy

GREECE

INTRODUCTION

Background: Greece achieved independence from the Ottoman Empire in 1830. During the second half of the 19th century and the first half of the 20th century, it gradually added neighboring islands and territories, most with Greek-speaking populations. In World War II, Greece was first invaded by Italy (1940) and subsequently occupied by Germany (1941-44); fighting endured in a protracted civil war between supporters of the king and other anti-communist and communist rebels. Following the latter's defeat in 1949, Greece joined NATO in 1952. In 1967, a group of military officers seized power, establishing a military dictatorship that suspended many political liberties and forced the king to flee the country. In 1974 following the collapse of the dictatorship, democratic elections and a referendum created a parliamentary republic and abolished the monarchy. In 1981, Greece joined the EC (now the EU); it became the 12th member of the European Economic and Monetary Union in 2001. Greece has suffered a severe economic crisis since late 2009, due to nearly a decade of chronic overspending and structural rigidities. Beginning in 2010, Greece entered three bailout agreements - the first two with the European Commission, the European Central Bank, and the IMF; and the third in 2015 with the European Stability Mechanism - worth in total about $300 billion. The Greek Government formally exited the third bailout in August 2018.

GEOGRAPHY

Location: Southern Europe, bordering the Aegean Sea, Ionian Sea, and the Mediterranean Sea, between Albania and Turkey

Geographic coordinates: 39 00 N, 22 00 E

Map references: Europe

Area: *total:* 131,957 sq km
land: 130,647 sq km
water: 1,310 sq km
country comparison to the world: 97

Area - comparative: slightly smaller than Alabama

Land boundaries: *total:* 1,110 km
border countries (4): Albania 212 km; Bulgaria 472 km; North Macedonia 234 km; Turkey 192 km

Coastline: 13,676 km

Maritime claims: *territorial sea:* 6 nm
continental shelf: 200-m depth or to the depth of exploitation

Climate: temperate; mild, wet winters; hot, dry summers

Terrain: mountainous with ranges extending into the sea as peninsulas or chains of islands

Elevation: *highest point:* Mount Olympus 2,917
lowest point: Mediterranean Sea 0 m
mean elevation: 498 m
note: Mount Olympus actually has 52 peaks but its highest point, Mytikas (meaning "nose"), rises to 2,917 meters; in Greek mythology, Olympus' Mytikas peak was the home of the Greek gods

Natural resources: lignite, petroleum, iron ore, bauxite, lead, zinc, nickel, magnesite, marble, salt, hydropower potential

Land use: *agricultural land:* 63.4% (2018 est.)
arable land: 19.7% (2018 est.)
permanent crops: 8.9% (2018 est.)
permanent pasture: 34.8% (2018 est.)
forest: 30.5% (2018 est.)
other: 6.1% (2018 est.)

Irrigated land: 15,550 sq km (2012)

Population distribution: one-third of the population lives in and around metropolitan Athens; the remainder of the country has moderate population density mixed with sizeable urban clusters

Natural hazards: severe earthquakes
volcanism: Santorini (367 m) has been deemed a Decade Volcano by the International Association of Volcanology and Chemistry of the Earth's Interior, worthy of study due to its explosive history and close proximity to human populations; although there have been very few eruptions in recent centuries, Methana and Nisyros in the Aegean are classified as historically active

Geography - note: strategic location dominating the Aegean Sea and southern approach to Turkish Straits; a peninsular country, possessing an archipelago of about 2,000 islands

PEOPLE AND SOCIETY

Population: 10,533,871 (2022 est.)
country comparison to the world: 88

Nationality: *noun:* Greek(s)
adjective: Greek

Ethnic groups: Greek 91.6%, Albanian 4.4%, other 4% (2011 est.)
note: data represent citizenship; Greece does not collect data on ethnicity

Languages: Greek (official) 99%, other (includes English and French) 1%
major-language sample(s):
Παγκόσμιο Βιβλίο Δεδομένων, η απαραίτητη πηγή βασικών πληροφοριών. (Greek)

Religions: Greek Orthodox 81-90%, Muslim 2%, other 3%, none 4-15%, unspecified 1% (2015 est.)

Age structure: *0-14 years:* 14.53% (male 794,918/female 745,909)
15-24 years: 10.34% (male 577,134/female 519,819)
25-54 years: 39.6% (male 2,080,443/female 2,119,995)
55-64 years: 13.1% (male 656,404/female 732,936)
65 years and over: 22.43% (male 1,057,317/female 1,322,176) (2020 est.)

Dependency ratios: *total dependency ratio:* 56.1
youth dependency ratio: 21.3
elderly dependency ratio: 34.8
potential support ratio: 2.9 (2020 est.)

Median age: *total:* 45.3 years
male: 43.7 years
female: 46.8 years (2020 est.)
country comparison to the world: 9

Population growth rate: -0.34% (2022 est.)
country comparison to the world: 218

Birth rate: 7.61 births/1,000 population (2022 est.)
country comparison to the world: 220

Death rate: 12.04 deaths/1,000 population (2022 est.)
country comparison to the world: 14

Net migration rate: 1 migrant(s)/1,000 population (2022 est.)
country comparison to the world: 65

Population distribution: one-third of the population lives in and around metropolitan Athens; the remainder of the country has moderate population density mixed with sizeable urban clusters

Urbanization: *urban population:* 80.4% of total population (2022)
rate of urbanization: 0.11% annual rate of change (2020-25 est.)

Major urban areas - population: 3.154 million ATHENS (capital), 814,000 Thessaloniki (2022)

Sex ratio: *at birth:* 1.07 male(s)/female
0-14 years: 1.06 male(s)/female
15-24 years: 1.14 male(s)/female
25-54 years: 1 male(s)/female
55-64 years: 0.89 male(s)/female
65 years and over: 0.71 male(s)/female
total population: 0.95 male(s)/female (2022 est.)

Mother's mean age at first birth: 30.7 years (2020 est.)

Maternal mortality ratio: 3 deaths/100,000 live births (2017 est.)
country comparison to the world: 178

Infant mortality rate: *total:* 3.55 deaths/1,000 live births
male: 3.94 deaths/1,000 live births
female: 3.13 deaths/1,000 live births (2022 est.)
country comparison to the world: 196

Life expectancy at birth: *total population:* 81.49 years
male: 78.96 years
female: 84.2 years (2022 est.)
country comparison to the world: 40

Total fertility rate: 1.4 children born/woman (2022 est.)
country comparison to the world: 213

Drinking water source: *improved: urban:* 100% of population
rural: 100% of population

total: 100% of population

Current health expenditure: 7.8% of GDP (2019)

Physicians density: 6.31 physicians/1,000 population (2019)

Hospital bed density: 4.2 beds/1,000 population (2018)

Sanitation facility access: *improved: urban:* 100% of population
rural: 100% of population
total: 100% of population

HIV/AIDS - adult prevalence rate: 0.2% (2020 est.)
country comparison to the world: 98

Obesity - adult prevalence rate: 24.9% (2016)
country comparison to the world: 54

Alcohol consumption per capita: *total:* 6.33 liters of pure alcohol (2019 est.)
beer: 2.13 liters of pure alcohol (2019 est.)
wine: 2.66 liters of pure alcohol (2019 est.)
spirits: 1.45 liters of pure alcohol (2019 est.)
other alcohols: 0.08 liters of pure alcohol (2019 est.)
country comparison to the world: 66

Tobacco use: *total:* 33.5% (2020 est.)
male: 36.5% (2020 est.)
female: 30.5% (2020 est.)
country comparison to the world: 18

Education expenditures: 3.6% of GDP (2018 est.)
country comparison to the world: 117

Literacy: *definition:* age 15 and over can read and write
total population: 97.9%
male: 98.5%
female: 97.4% (2018)

School life expectancy (primary to tertiary education): *total:* 20 years
male: 20 years
female: 20 years (2019)

Unemployment, youth ages 15-24: *total:* 35%
male: 31.4%
female: 39.3% (2020 est.)

ENVIRONMENT

Environment - current issues: air pollution; air emissions from transport and electricity power stations; water pollution; degradation of coastal zones; loss of biodiversity in terrestrial and marine ecosystems; increasing municipal and industrial waste

Environment - international agreements: *party to:* Air Pollution, Air Pollution-Nitrogen Oxides, Air Pollution-Sulphur 94, Antarctic-Environmental Protection, Antarctic-Marine Living Resources, Antarctic Treaty, Biodiversity, Climate Change, Climate Change-Kyoto Protocol, Climate Change-Paris Agreement, Comprehensive Nuclear Test Ban, Desertification, Endangered Species, Environmental Modification, Hazardous Wastes, Law of the Sea, Marine Dumping-London Convention, Nuclear Test Ban, Ozone Layer Protection, Ship Pollution, Tropical Timber 2006, Wetlands
signed, but not ratified: Air Pollution-Heavy Metals, Air Pollution-Multi-effect Protocol, Air Pollution-Persistent Organic Pollutants, Air Pollution-Volatile Organic Compounds

Air pollutants: *particulate matter emissions:* 15.69 micrograms per cubic meter (2016 est.)
carbon dioxide emissions: 62.43 megatons (2016 est.)
methane emissions: 9.8 megatons (2020 est.)

Climate: temperate; mild, wet winters; hot, dry summers

Land use: *agricultural land:* 63.4% (2018 est.)
arable land: 19.7% (2018 est.)
permanent crops: 8.9% (2018 est.)
permanent pasture: 34.8% (2018 est.)
forest: 30.5% (2018 est.)
other: 6.1% (2018 est.)

Urbanization: *urban population:* 80.4% of total population (2022)
rate of urbanization: 0.11% annual rate of change (2020-25 est.)

Revenue from forest resources: *forest revenues:* 0.01% of GDP (2018 est.)
country comparison to the world: 148

Revenue from coal: *coal revenues:* 0.04% of GDP (2018 est.)
country comparison to the world: 32

Waste and recycling: *municipal solid waste generated annually:* 5,477,424 tons (2014 est.)
municipal solid waste recycled annually: 1,040,711 tons (2014 est.)
percent of municipal solid waste recycled: 19% (2014 est.)

Total water withdrawal: *municipal:* 1.991 billion cubic meters (2017 est.)
industrial: 208.3 million cubic meters (2017 est.)
agricultural: 9.041 billion cubic meters (2017 est.)

Total renewable water resources: 68.4 billion cubic meters (2017 est.)

GOVERNMENT

Country name: *conventional long form:* Hellenic Republic
conventional short form: Greece
local long form: Elliniki Dimokratia
local short form: Ellas or Ellada
former: Hellenic State, Kingdom of Greece
etymology: the English name derives from the Roman (Latin) designation "Graecia," meaning "Land of the Greeks"; the Greeks call their country "Hellas" or "Ellada"

Government type: parliamentary republic

Capital: *name:* Athens
geographic coordinates: 37 59 N, 23 44 E
time difference: UTC+2 (7 hours ahead of Washington, DC, during Standard Time)
daylight saving time: +1hr, begins last Sunday in March; ends last Sunday in October
etymology: Athens is the oldest European capital city; according to tradition, the city is named after Athena, the Greek goddess of wisdom; in actuality, the appellation probably derives from a lost name in a pre-Hellenic language

Administrative divisions: 13 regions (perifereies, singular - perifereia) and 1 autonomous monastic state* (aftonomi monastiki politeia); Agion Oros* (Mount Athos), Anatoliki Makedonia kai Thraki (East Macedonia and Thrace), Attiki (Attica), Dytiki Ellada (West Greece), Dytiki Makedonia (West Macedonia), Ionia Nisia (Ionian Islands), Ipeiros (Epirus), Kentriki Makedonia (Central Macedonia), Kriti (Crete), Notio Aigaio (South Aegean), Peloponnisos (Peloponnese), Sterea Ellada (Central Greece), Thessalia (Thessaly), Voreio Aigaio (North Aegean)

Independence: 3 February 1830 (from the Ottoman Empire); note - 25 March 1821, outbreak of the national revolt against the Ottomans; 3 February 1830, signing of the London Protocol recognizing Greek independence by Great Britain, France, and Russia

National holiday: Independence Day, 25 March (1821)

Constitution: *history:* many previous; latest entered into force 11 June 1975
amendments: proposed by at least 50 members of Parliament and agreed by three-fifths majority vote in two separate ballots at least 30 days apart; passage requires absolute majority vote by the next elected Parliament; entry into force finalized through a "special parliamentary resolution"; articles on human rights and freedoms and the form of government cannot be amended; amended 1986, 2001, 2008, 2019

Legal system: civil legal system based on Roman law

International law organization participation: accepts compulsory ICJ jurisdiction with reservations; accepts ICCt jurisdiction

Citizenship: *citizenship by birth:* no
citizenship by descent only: at least one parent must be a citizen of Greece
dual citizenship recognized: yes
residency requirement for naturalization: 10 years

Suffrage: 17 years of age; universal and compulsory

Executive branch: *chief of state:* President Ekaterini SAKELLAROPOULOU (since 13 March 2020)
head of government: Prime Minister Kyriakos MITSOTAKIS (since 8 July 2019)
cabinet: Cabinet appointed by the president on the recommendation of the prime minister
elections/appointments: president elected by Hellenic Parliament for a 5-year term (eligible for a second term); election last held on 22 January 2020 (next to be held by February 2025); president appoints as prime minister the leader of the majority party or coalition in the Hellenic Parliament
election results:
2020: Katerina SAKELLAROPOULOU (independent) elected president by Parliament - 261 of 300 votes; note - SAKELLAROPOULOU is Greece's first woman president
2015: Prokopis PAVLOPOULOS (ND) elected president by Parliament - 233 of 300 votes

Legislative branch: *description:* unicameral Hellenic Parliament or Vouli ton Ellinon (300 seats; 280 members in multi-seat constituencies and 12 members in a single nationwide constituency directly elected by open party-list proportional representation vote; 8 members in single-seat constituencies elected by simple majority vote; members serve up to 4 years); note - only parties surpassing a 3% threshold are entitled to parliamentary seats; parties need 10 seats to become formal parliamentary groups but can retain that status if the party participated in the last election and received the minimum 3% threshold
elections: last held on 7 July 2019 (next to be held by July 2023)
election results: percent of vote by party - ND 39.9%, SYRIZA 31.5%, KINAL 8.1%, KKE 5.3%, Greek Solution 3.7%, MeRA25 3.4%, other 8.1%; seats by party - ND 158, SYRIZA 86, KINAL 22, KKE 15, Greek Solution 10, MeRA25 9; composition - men 244, women 56, percent of women 18.7%

Judicial branch: *highest court(s):* Supreme Civil and Criminal Court or Areios Pagos (consists of 56

judges, including the court presidents); Council of State (supreme administrative court) (consists of the president, 7 vice presidents, 42 privy councilors, 48 associate councilors and 50 reporting judges, organized into six 5- and 7-member chambers; Court of Audit (government audit and enforcement) consists of the president, 5 vice presidents, 20 councilors, and 90 associate and reporting judges
judge selection and term of office: Supreme Court judges appointed by presidential decree on the advice of the Supreme Judicial Council (SJC), which includes the president of the Supreme Court, other judges, and the prosecutor of the Supreme Court; judges appointed for life following a 2-year probationary period; Council of State president appointed by the Greek Cabinet to serve a 4-year term; other judge appointments and tenure NA; Court of Audit president appointed by decree of the president of the republic on the advice of the SJC; court president serves a 4-year term or until age 67; tenure of vice presidents, councilors, and judges NA
subordinate courts: Courts of Appeal and Courts of First Instance (district courts)

Political parties and leaders: Anticapitalist Left Cooperation for the Overthrow or ANTARSYA [collective leadership]
Coalition of the Radical Left or SYRIZA [Alexios (Alexis) TSIPRAS]
Communist Party of Greece or KKE [Dimitrios KOUTSOUMBAS]
Democratic Left or DIMAR [Athanasios (Thanasis) THEOCHAROPOULOS]
European Realistic Disobedience Front or MeRA25 [Ioannis (Yanis) VAROUFAKIS]
Greek Solution [Kyriakos VELOPOULOS]
Independent Greeks or ANEL [Panagiotis (Panos) KAMMENOS]
New Democracy or ND [Kyriakos MITSOTAKIS]
PASOK - Movement for Change or PASOK-KINAL [Nikos ANDROULAKIS]
Popular Unity or LAE [Nikolaos CHOUNTIS]
Union of Centrists or EK [Vasileios (Vasilis) LEVENTIS]

International organization participation: Australia Group, BIS, BSEC, CD, CE, CERN, EAPC, EBRD, ECB, EIB, EMU, ESA, EU, FAO, FATF, IAEA, IBRD, ICAO, ICC (national committees), ICCt, ICRM, IDA, IEA, IFAD, IFC, IFRCS, IGAD (partners), IHO, ILO, IMF, IMO, IMSO, Interpol, IOC, IOM, IPU, ISO, ITSO, ITU, ITUC (NGOs), MIGA, NATO, NEA, NSG, OAS (observer), OECD, OIF, OPCW, OSCE, PCA, Schengen Convention, SELEC, UN, UNCTAD, UNESCO, UNHCR, UNIDO, UNIFIL, UNWTO, UPU, Wassenaar Arrangement, WCO, WFTU (NGOs), WHO, WIPO, WMO, WTO, ZC

Diplomatic representation in the US: *chief of mission:* Ambassador Alexandra PAPADOPOULOU (since 6 February 2021)
chancery: 2217 Massachusetts Avenue NW, Washington, DC 20008
telephone: [1] (202) 939-1300
FAX: [1] (202) 939-1324
email address and website:
gremb.was@mfa.gr
https://www.mfa.gr/usa/en/the-embassy/
consulate(s) general: Boston, Chicago, Los Angeles, New York, Tampa (FL), San Francisco
consulate(s): Atlanta, Houston

Diplomatic representation from the US: *chief of mission:* Ambassador George James TSUNIS (since 10 May 2022)
embassy: 91 Vasillisis Sophias Avenue, 10160 Athens
mailing address: 7100 Athens Place, Washington DC 20521-7100
telephone: [30] (210) 721-2951
FAX: [30] (210) 724-5313
email address and website:
athensamericancitizenservices@state.gov
https://gr.usembassy.gov/
consulate(s) general: Thessaloniki

Flag description: nine equal horizontal stripes of blue alternating with white; a blue square bearing a white cross appears in the upper hoist-side corner; the cross symbolizes Greek Orthodoxy, the established religion of the country; there is no agreed upon meaning for the nine stripes or for the colors
note: Greek legislation states that the flag colors are cyan and white, but cyan can mean "blue" in Greek, so the exact shade of blue has never been set and has varied from a light to a dark blue over time; in general, the hue of blue normally encountered is a form of azure

National symbol(s): Greek cross (white cross on blue field, arms equal length); national colors: blue, white

National anthem: *name:* "Ymnos eis tin Eleftherian" (Hymn to Liberty)
lyrics/music: Dionysios SOLOMOS/Nikolaos MANTZAROS
note: adopted 1864; the anthem is based on a 158-stanza poem by the same name, which was inspired by the Greek Revolution of 1821 against the Ottomans (only the first two stanzas are used); Cyprus also uses "Hymn to Liberty" as its anthem

National heritage: *total World Heritage Sites:* 18 (16 cultural, 2 mixed)
selected World Heritage Site locales: Acropolis, Athens (c); Archaeological site of Delphi (c); Meteora (m); Medieval City of Rhodes (c); Archaeological site of Olympia (c); Archaeological site of Mycenae and Tiryns (c); Old Town of Corfu (c); Mount Athos (m); Delos (c); Archaeological Site of Philippi (c)

ECONOMY

Economic overview: Greece has a capitalist economy with a public sector accounting for about 40% of GDP and with per capita GDP about two-thirds that of the leading euro-zone economies. Tourism provides 18% of GDP. Immigrants make up nearly one-fifth of the work force, mainly in agricultural and unskilled jobs. Greece is a major beneficiary of EU aid, equal to about 3.3% of annual GDP.

The Greek economy averaged growth of about 4% per year between 2003 and 2007, but the economy went into recession in 2009 as a result of the world financial crisis, tightening credit conditions, and Athens' failure to address a growing budget deficit. By 2013, the economy had contracted 26%, compared with the pre-crisis level of 2007. Greece met the EU's Growth and Stability Pact budget deficit criterion of no more than 3% of GDP in 2007-08, but violated it in 2009, when the deficit reached 15% of GDP. Deteriorating public finances, inaccurate and misreported statistics, and consistent underperformance on reforms prompted major credit rating agencies to downgrade Greece's international debt rating in late 2009 and led the country into a financial crisis. Under intense pressure from the EU and international market participants, the government accepted a bailout program that called on Athens to cut government spending, decrease tax evasion, overhaul the civil-service, health-care, and pension systems, and reform the labor and product markets. Austerity measures reduced the deficit to 1.3% in 2017. Successive Greek governments, however, failed to push through many of the most unpopular reforms in the face of widespread political opposition, including from the country's powerful labor unions and the general public.

In April 2010, a leading credit agency assigned Greek debt its lowest possible credit rating, and in May 2010, the IMF and euro-zone governments provided Greece emergency short- and medium-term loans worth $147 billion so that the country could make debt repayments to creditors. Greece, however, struggled to meet the targets set by the EU and the IMF, especially after Eurostat - the EU's statistical office - revised upward Greece's deficit and debt numbers for 2009 and 2010. European leaders and the IMF agreed in October 2011 to provide Athens a second bailout package of $169 billion. The second deal called for holders of Greek government bonds to write down a significant portion of their holdings to try to alleviate Greece's government debt burden. However, Greek banks, saddled with a significant portion of sovereign debt, were adversely affected by the write down and $60 billion of the second bailout package was set aside to ensure the banking system was adequately capitalized.

In 2014, the Greek economy began to turn the corner on the recession. Greece achieved three significant milestones: balancing the budget - not including debt repayments; issuing government debt in financial markets for the first time since 2010; and generating 0.7% GDP growth — the first economic expansion since 2007.

Despite the nascent recovery, widespread discontent with austerity measures helped propel the far-left Coalition of the Radical Left (SYRIZA) party into government in national legislative elections in January 2015. Between January and July 2015, frustrations grew between the SYRIZA-led government and Greece's EU and IMF creditors over the implementation of bailout measures and disbursement of funds. The Greek government began running up significant arrears to suppliers, while Greek banks relied on emergency lending, and Greece's future in the euro zone was called into question. To stave off a collapse of the banking system, Greece imposed capital controls in June 2015, then became the first developed nation to miss a loan payment to the IMF, rattling international financial markets. Unable to reach an agreement with creditors, Prime Minister Alexios TSIPRAS held a nationwide referendum on 5 July on whether to accept the terms of Greece's bailout, campaigning for the ultimately successful "no" vote. The TSIPRAS government subsequently agreed, however, to a new $96 billion bailout in order to avert Greece's exit from the monetary bloc. On 20 August 2015, Greece signed its third bailout, allowing it to cover significant debt payments to its EU and IMF creditors and to ensure the banking sector retained access to emergency liquidity. The TSIPRAS government — which retook office on 20 September 2015 after calling new elections in late August — successfully secured disbursal of two delayed tranches of bailout funds. Despite the economic turmoil, Greek GDP did not contract as sharply as feared, boosted in part by a strong tourist season.

In 2017, Greece saw improvements in GDP and unemployment. Unfinished economic reforms, a massive non-performing loan problem, and ongoing uncertainty regarding the political direction of the country hold the economy back. Some estimates put Greece's black market at 20- to 25% of GDP, as more people have stopped reporting their income to avoid paying taxes that, in some cases, have risen to 70% of an individual's gross income.

Real GDP (purchasing power parity): $292.4 billion (2020 est.)
$318.68 billion (2019 est.)
$312.87 billion (2018 est.)
note: data are in 2017 dollars
country comparison to the world: 55

Real GDP growth rate: 1.87% (2019 est.)
1.91% (2018 est.)
1.44% (2017 est.)
country comparison to the world: 144

Real GDP per capita: $27,300 (2020 est.)
$29,700 (2019 est.)
$29,200 (2018 est.)
note: data are in 2017 dollars
country comparison to the world: 69

GDP (official exchange rate): $209.79 billion (2019 est.)

Inflation rate (consumer prices): 0.2% (2019 est.)
0.6% (2018 est.)
1.1% (2017 est.)
country comparison to the world: 28

Credit ratings:

Fitch rating: BB (2020)

Moody's rating: Ba3 (2020)

Standard & Poors rating: BB- (2019)
note: The year refers to the year in which the current credit rating was first obtained.

GDP - composition, by sector of origin: *agriculture:* 4.1% (2017 est.)
industry: 16.9% (2017 est.)
services: 79.1% (2017 est.)

GDP - composition, by end use: *household consumption:* 69.6% (2017 est.)
government consumption: 20.1% (2017 est.)
investment in fixed capital: 12.5% (2017 est.)
investment in inventories: -1% (2017 est.)
exports of goods and services: 33.4% (2017 est.)
imports of goods and services: -34.7% (2017 est.)

Agricultural products: maize, olives, wheat, milk, peaches/nectarines, oranges, tomatoes, grapes, milk, potatoes

Industries: tourism, food and tobacco processing, textiles, chemicals, metal products; mining, petroleum

Industrial production growth rate: 3.5% (2017 est.)
country comparison to the world: 85

Labor force: 4 million (2020 est.)
country comparison to the world: 90

Labor force - by occupation: *agriculture:* 12.6%
industry: 15%
services: 72.4% (30 October 2015 est.)

Unemployment rate: 17.3% (2019 est.)
19.34% (2018 est.)
country comparison to the world: 183

Unemployment, youth ages 15-24: *total:* 35%
male: 31.4%
female: 39.3% (2020 est.)
country comparison to the world: 26

Population below poverty line: 17.9% (2018 est.)

Gini Index coefficient - distribution of family income: 34.4 (2017 est.)
35.7 (2011)
country comparison to the world: 114

Household income or consumption by percentage share: *lowest 10%:* 1.7%
highest 10%: 26.7% (2015 est.)

Budget: *revenues:* 97.99 billion (2017 est.)
expenditures: 96.35 billion (2017 est.)

Budget surplus (+) or deficit (-): 0.8% (of GDP) (2017 est.)
country comparison to the world: 36

Public debt: 181.8% of GDP (2017 est.)
183.5% of GDP (2016 est.)
country comparison to the world: 2

Taxes and other revenues: 48.8% (of GDP) (2017 est.)
country comparison to the world: 17

Fiscal year: calendar year

Current account balance: -$3.114 billion (2019 est.)
-$6.245 billion (2018 est.)
country comparison to the world: 175

Exports: $59.02 billion (2020 est.) note: data are in current year dollars
$81.18 billion (2019 est.) note: data are in current year dollars
$81.87 billion (2018 est.) note: data are in current year dollars
country comparison to the world: 53

Exports - partners: Italy 10%, Germany 7%, Turkey 5%, Cyprus 5%, Bulgaria 5% (2019)

Exports - commodities: refined petroleum, packaged medicines, aluminum plating, computers, cotton (2019)

Imports: $71.76 billion (2020 est.) note: data are in current year dollars
$83.19 billion (2019 est.) note: data are in current year dollars
$85.8 billion (2018 est.) note: data are in current year dollars
country comparison to the world: 49

Imports - partners: Germany 11%, China 9%, Italy 8%, Iraq 7%, Russia 6%, Netherlands 5% (2019)

Imports - commodities: crude petroleum, refined petroleum, packaged medicines, cars, ships (2019)

Reserves of foreign exchange and gold: $7.807 billion (31 December 2017 est.)
$6.026 billion (31 December 2015 est.)
country comparison to the world: 80

Debt - external: $484.888 billion (2019 est.)
$478.646 billion (2018 est.)
country comparison to the world: 25

Exchange rates: euros (EUR) per US dollar -
0.82771 (2020 est.)
0.90338 (2019 est.)
0.87789 (2018 est.)
0.885 (2014 est.)
0.7634 (2013 est.)

ENERGY

Electricity access: *electrification - total population:* 100% (2020)

Electricity: *installed generating capacity:* 21.545 million kW (2020 est.)
consumption: 46.18 billion kWh (2020 est.)
exports: 967 million kWh (2020 est.)
imports: 9.831 billion kWh (2020 est.)
transmission/distribution losses: 3.256 billion kWh (2020 est.)

Electricity generation sources: *fossil fuels:* 56.5% of total installed capacity (2020 est.)
solar: 10.7% of total installed capacity (2020 est.)
wind: 23% of total installed capacity (2020 est.)
hydroelectricity: 8.5% of total installed capacity (2020 est.)
biomass and waste: 1.4% of total installed capacity (2020 est.)

Coal: *production:* 13.851 million metric tons (2020 est.)
consumption: 13.828 million metric tons (2020 est.)
exports: 7,000 metric tons (2020 est.)
imports: 305,000 metric tons (2020 est.)
proven reserves: 2.876 billion metric tons (2019 est.)

Petroleum: *total petroleum production:* 4,800 bbl/day (2021 est.)
refined petroleum consumption: 309,600 bbl/day (2019 est.)
crude oil and lease condensate exports: 4,100 bbl/day (2018 est.)
crude oil and lease condensate imports: 491,300 bbl/day (2018 est.)
crude oil estimated reserves: 10 million barrels (2021 est.)

Refined petroleum products - production: 655,400 bbl/day (2017 est.)
country comparison to the world: 28

Refined petroleum products - exports: 371,900 bbl/day (2017 est.)
country comparison to the world: 22

Refined petroleum products - imports: 192,200 bbl/day (2017 est.)
country comparison to the world: 35

Natural gas: *production:* 5.748 million cubic meters (2019 est.)
consumption: 5,831,987,000 cubic meters (2020 est.)
exports: 33.244 million cubic meters (2020 est.)
imports: 5,219,409,000 cubic meters (2019 est.)
proven reserves: 991 million cubic meters (2021 est.)

Carbon dioxide emissions: 70.163 million metric tonnes of CO_2 (2019 est.)
from coal and metallurgical coke: 13.404 million metric tonnes of CO_2 (2019 est.)
from petroleum and other liquids: 46.401 million metric tonnes of CO_2 (2019 est.)
from consumed natural gas: 10.358 million metric tonnes of CO_2 (2019 est.)
country comparison to the world: 50

Energy consumption per capita: 108.022 million Btu/person (2019 est.)
country comparison to the world: 51

COMMUNICATIONS

Telephones - fixed lines: *total subscriptions:* 5,028,332 (2020 est.)
subscriptions per 100 inhabitants: 48 (2020 est.)
country comparison to the world: 28

Telephones - mobile cellular: *total subscriptions:* 11,412,995 (2020 est.)

subscriptions per 100 inhabitants: 109 (2020 est.)
country comparison to the world: 82

Telecommunication systems: *general assessment:* Greece's telecom market is susceptible to the country's volatile economy, and as a result revenue among the key networks has been variable; broadband subscriptions in Greece are developing steadily despite the difficult economic conditions; the main networks are concentrating investment on fiber-based next generation networks, enabling them to reach the European broadband targets for 2025; their work is also supported by government ultra-fast broadband projects, largely funded by the EC and aimed at delivering a service of at least 100Mb/s to under served areas; Greece's well-developed mobile market is dominated by the three MNOs; Networks continue to invest in LTE infrastructure and technologies to provide networks capable of meeting customer demand for data services; after extensive trials of 5G, the MNOs were able to launch commercial services in early 2021 following the December 2020 allocation of frequencies in a range of bands; the rapid rollout of 5G encouraged the shut down of the 3G network (a process expected to be completed by the end of 2021) and reallocate for LTE and 5G. (2022)
domestic: microwave radio relay trunk system; extensive open-wire connections; submarine cable to offshore islands; nearly 46 per 100 subscribers for fixed-line and 110 per 100 for mobile-cellular (2020)
international: country code - 30; landing points for the SEA-ME-WE-3, Adria-1, Italy-Greece 1, OTEGLOBE, MedNautilus Submarine System, Aphrodite 2, AAE-1 and Silphium optical telecommunications submarine cable that provides links to Europe, the Middle East, Africa, Southeast Asia, Asia and Australia; tropospheric scatter; satellite earth stations - 4 (2 Intelsat - 1 Atlantic Ocean and 1 Indian Ocean, 1 Eutelsat, and 1 Inmarsat - Indian Ocean region) (2019)

Broadcast media: broadcast media dominated by the private sector; roughly 150 private TV channels, about 10 of which broadcast nationwide; 1 government-owned terrestrial TV channel with national coverage; 3 privately owned satellite channels; multi-channel satellite and cable TV services available; upwards of 1,500 radio stations, all of them privately owned; government-owned broadcaster has 2 national radio stations

Internet country code: .gr

Internet users: *total:* 8,346,434 (2020 est.)
percent of population: 78% (2020 est.)
country comparison to the world: 67

Broadband - fixed subscriptions: *total:* 4,257,026 (2020 est.)
subscriptions per 100 inhabitants: 41 (2020 est.)
country comparison to the world: 35

TRANSPORTATION

National air transport system: *number of registered air carriers:* 11 (2020)
inventory of registered aircraft operated by air carriers: 97
annual passenger traffic on registered air carriers: 15,125,933 (2018)
annual freight traffic on registered air carriers: 21.91 million (2018) mt-km

Civil aircraft registration country code prefix: SX

Airports: *total:* 77 (2021)
country comparison to the world: 69

Airports - with paved runways: *total:* 68
over 3,047 m: 6
2,438 to 3,047 m: 15
1,524 to 2,437 m: 19
914 to 1,523 m: 18
under 914 m: 10 (2021)

Airports - with unpaved runways: *total:* 9
914 to 1,523 m: 2
under 914 m: 7 (2021)

Heliports: 9 (2021)

Pipelines: 1,466 km gas, 94 km oil (2013)

Railways: *total:* 2,548 km (2014)
standard gauge: 1,565 km (2014) 1.435-m gauge (764 km electrified)
narrow gauge: 961 km (2014) 1.000-m gauge 220.750 km-mm gauge
country comparison to the world: 67

Roadways: *total:* 117,000 km (2018)
country comparison to the world: 42

Waterways: 6 km (2012) (the 6-km-long Corinth Canal crosses the Isthmus of Corinth; it shortens a sea voyage by 325 km)
country comparison to the world: 117

Merchant marine: *total:* 1,236
by type: bulk carrier 158, container ship 5, general cargo 89, oil tanker 337, other 647 (2021)
country comparison to the world: 22

Ports and terminals: *major seaport(s):* Aspropyrgos, Pachi, Piraeus, Thessaloniki
oil terminal(s): Agioi Theodoroi
container port(s) (TEUs): Piraeus (5,648,000) (2019)
LNG terminal(s) (import): Revithoussa

MILITARY AND SECURITY

Military and security forces: Hellenic Armed Forces: Hellenic Army (Ellinikos Stratos, ES; includes National Guard reserves), Hellenic Navy (Elliniko Polemiko Navtiko, EPN), Hellenic Air Force (Elliniki Polemiki Aeroporia, EPA; includes air defense); Ministry of Shipping Affairs and Island Policy: Coast Guard (2022)
note: the police (under the Ministry of Citizen Protection) and the armed forces (Ministry of National Defense) share law enforcement duties in certain border areas; border protection is coordinated by a deputy minister for national defense

Military expenditures: 3.8% of GDP (2022 est.)
3.6% of GDP (2021)
2.9% of GDP (2020)
2.3% of GDP (2019) (approximately $7.95 billion)
2.5% of GDP (2018) (approximately $8.31 billion)
country comparison to the world: 20

Military and security service personnel strengths: approximately 125,000 active duty personnel (90,000 Army; 15,000 Navy; 20,000 Air Force); approximately 35,000 National Guard (2022)

Military equipment inventories and acquisitions: the inventory of the Hellenic Armed Forces consists of a mix of imported weapons from Europe and the US, as well as a limited number of domestically produced systems, particularly naval vessels; Germany has been the leading supplier of weapons systems to Greece since 2010; Greece's defense industry is capable of producing a range of military hardware, including naval vessels and associated subsystems (2021)
note: in addition to finalizing an update to the Mutual Defense Cooperation Agreement with the US, Greece also entered into a security agreement with France in 2021 that included the sale of frigates and fighter aircraft to augment its aging weapons systems

Military service age and obligation: 19-45 years of age for compulsory military service for men; 12-month obligation for all services (note - as an exception, the duration of the full military service is 9 instead of 12 months if conscripts, after the initial training, serve the entire remaining time in certain areas of the eastern borders, in Cyprus, or in certain military units); 18 years of age for voluntary military service for men and women (2022)
note 1: compulsory service applies to any individual whom the Greek authorities consider to be Greek, regardless of whether the individual considers himself Greek, has a foreign citizenship and passport, or was born or lives outside of Greece; Greek citizens living permanently outside of Greece have the right to postpone their conscription; they are permanently exempted from their military obligations when they reach the age of 45 years old
note 2: up to 50% of the Greek military is comprised of conscripts
note 3: as of 2019, women comprised approximately 19% of the military's full-time personnel

Military deployments: approximately 1,000 Cyprus; 100 Kosovo (NATO); 100 Lebanon (UNIFIL) (2022)

Military - note: Greece joined NATO in 1952

TERRORISM

Terrorist group(s): Islamic State of Iraq and ash-Sham (ISIS); Revolutionary Struggle; Revolutionary People's Liberation Party/Front (DHKP/C)

TRANSNATIONAL ISSUES

Disputes - international: Greece and Turkey continue discussions to resolve their complex maritime, air, territorial, and boundary disputes in the Aegean Sea; the mass migration of unemployed Albanians still remains a problem for developed countries, chiefly Greece and Italy

Refugees and internally displaced persons: *refugees (country of origin):* 38,496 (Syria), 25,188 (Afghanistan), 12,657 (Iraq), 5,002 (West Bank and Gaza) (mid-year 2021); 19,997 (Ukraine) (as of 8 November 2022)
stateless persons: 5,552 (mid-year 2021)
note: 1,228,228 estimated refugee and migrant arrivals (January 2015-November 2022); as of the end of February 2022, Greece hosted an estimated 161,419 refugees and asylum seekers

Illicit drugs: a gateway to Europe for traffickers smuggling cannabis products and heroin from the Middle East and Southwest Asia to the West and precursor chemicals to the East; some South American cocaine transits or is consumed in Greece; money laundering related to drug trafficking and organized crime

GREENLAND

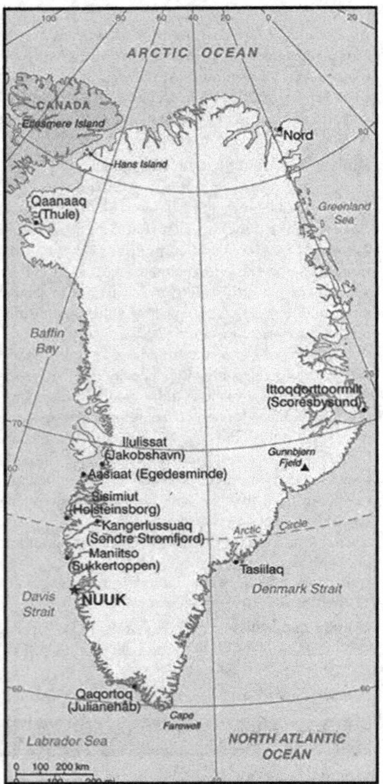

INTRODUCTION

Background: Greenland, the world's largest island, is about 80% ice-capped. Vikings reached the island in the 10th century from Iceland; Danish colonization began in the 18th century, and Greenland became an integral part of the Danish Realm in 1953. It joined the European Community (now the EU) with Denmark in 1973 but withdrew in 1985 over a dispute centered on stringent fishing quotas. Greenland remains a member of the Overseas Countries and Territories Association of the EU. Greenland was granted self-government in 1979 by the Danish parliament; the law went into effect the following year. Greenland voted in favor of increased self-rule in November 2008 and acquired greater responsibility for internal affairs when the Act on Greenland Self-Government was signed into law in June 2009. Denmark, however, continues to exercise control over several policy areas on behalf of Greenland, including foreign affairs, security, and financial policy in consultation with Greenland's Self-Rule Government.

GEOGRAPHY

Location: Northern North America, island between the Arctic Ocean and the North Atlantic Ocean, northeast of Canada

Geographic coordinates: 72 00 N, 40 00 W

Map references: Arctic Region

Area: *total:* 2,166,086 sq km
land: 2,166,086 sq km (approximately 1,710,000 sq km ice-covered)
country comparison to the world: 13

Area - comparative: slightly more than three times the size of Texas

Land boundaries: *total:* 0 km

Coastline: 44,087 km

Maritime claims: *territorial sea:* 3 nm
continental shelf: 200 nm or agreed boundaries or median line
exclusive fishing zone: 200 nm or agreed boundaries or median line

Climate: arctic to subarctic; cool summers, cold winters

Terrain: flat to gradually sloping icecap covers all but a narrow, mountainous, barren, rocky coast

Elevation: *highest point:* Gunnbjorn Fjeld 3,694 m
lowest point: Atlantic Ocean 0 m
mean elevation: 1,792 m

Natural resources: coal, iron ore, lead, zinc, molybdenum, diamonds, gold, platinum, niobium, tantalite, uranium, fish, seals, whales, hydropower, possible oil and gas

Land use: *agricultural land:* 0.6% (2018 est.)
arable land: 0% (2018 est.)
permanent crops: 0% (2018 est.)
permanent pasture: 0.6% (2018 est.)
forest: 0% (2018 est.)
other: 99.4% (2018 est.)

Population distribution: settlement concentrated on the southwest shoreline, with limited settlements scattered along the remaining coast; interior is uninhabited

Natural hazards: continuous permafrost over northern two-thirds of the island

Geography - note: dominates North Atlantic Ocean between North America and Europe; sparse population confined to small settlements along coast; close to one-quarter of the population lives in the capital, Nuuk; world's second largest ice sheet after that of Antarctica covering an area of 1.71 million sq km (660,000 sq mi) or about 79% of the island, and containing 2.85 million cu km (684 thousand cu mi) of ice (this is almost 7% of all of the world's fresh water); if all this ice were converted to liquid water, one estimate is that it would be sufficient to raise the height of the world's oceans by 7.2 m (24 ft)

PEOPLE AND SOCIETY

Population: 57,792 (2022 est.)
country comparison to the world: 206

Nationality: *noun:* Greenlander(s)
adjective: Greenlandic

Ethnic groups: Greenlandic 89.1%, Danish 7.5%, other Nordic peoples 0.9%, and other 2.5% (2022 est.)
note: data represent population by country of birth

Languages: Greenlandic (West Greenlandic or Kalaallisut is the official language), Danish, English

Religions: Evangelical Lutheran, traditional Inuit spiritual beliefs

Age structure: *0-14 years:* 20.82% (male 6,079/female 5,916)
15-24 years: 14.45% (male 4,186/female 4,137)
25-54 years: 39.72% (male 11,962/female 10,921)
55-64 years: 14.66% (male 4,561/female 3,886)
65 years and over: 10.36% (male 3,170/female 2,798) (2020 est.)

Median age: *total:* 34.3 years
male: 35.1 years
female: 33.4 years (2020 est.)
country comparison to the world: 92

Population growth rate: -0.02% (2022 est.)
country comparison to the world: 199

Birth rate: 13.79 births/1,000 population (2022 est.)
country comparison to the world: 132

Death rate: 8.96 deaths/1,000 population (2022 est.)
country comparison to the world: 61

Net migration rate: -5 migrant(s)/1,000 population (2022 est.)
country comparison to the world: 203

Population distribution: settlement concentrated on the southwest shoreline, with limited settlements scattered along the remaining coast; interior is uninhabited

Urbanization: *urban population:* 87.7% of total population (2022)
rate of urbanization: 0.41% annual rate of change (2020-25 est.)

Major urban areas - population: 18,000 NUUK (capital) (2018)

Sex ratio: *at birth:* 1.05 male(s)/female
0-14 years: 1.03 male(s)/female
15-24 years: 1.01 male(s)/female
25-54 years: 1.08 male(s)/female
55-64 years: 1.19 male(s)/female
65 years and over: 0.84 male(s)/female
total population: 1.08 male(s)/female (2022 est.)

Infant mortality rate: *total:* 8.75 deaths/1,000 live births
male: 10.25 deaths/1,000 live births
female: 7.16 deaths/1,000 live births (2022 est.)
country comparison to the world: 142

Life expectancy at birth: *total population:* 73.98 years
male: 71.28 years
female: 76.82 years (2022 est.)
country comparison to the world: 143

Total fertility rate: 1.91 children born/woman (2022 est.)
country comparison to the world: 123

Drinking water source: *improved: urban:* 100% of population
rural: 100% of population
total: 100% of population

Physicians density: 1.87 physicians/1,000 population (2016)

Hospital bed density: 14 beds/1,000 population (2016)

Sanitation facility access: *improved: urban:* 100% of population
rural: 100% of population
total: 100% of population

Education expenditures: 10.6% of GDP (2018 est.)
country comparison to the world: 2

Literacy: *definition:* age 15 and over can read and write
total population: 100%
male: 100%
female: 100% (2015)

ENVIRONMENT

Environment - current issues: especially vulnerable to climate change and disruption of the Arctic environment; preservation of the Inuit traditional way of life, including whaling and seal hunting

Air pollutants: *carbon dioxide emissions:* 0.51 megatons (2016 est.)

Climate: arctic to subarctic; cool summers, cold winters

Land use: *agricultural land:* 0.6% (2018 est.)
arable land: 0% (2018 est.)
permanent crops: 0% (2018 est.)
permanent pasture: 0.6% (2018 est.)
forest: 0% (2018 est.)
other: 99.4% (2018 est.)

Urbanization: *urban population:* 87.7% of total population (2022)
rate of urbanization: 0.41% annual rate of change (2020-25 est.)

Revenue from forest resources: *forest revenues:* 0% of GDP (2018 est.)
country comparison to the world: 169

Revenue from coal: *coal revenues:* 0% of GDP (2018 est.)
country comparison to the world: 103

Waste and recycling: *municipal solid waste generated annually:* 50,000 tons (2010 est.)

GOVERNMENT

Country name: *conventional long form:* none
conventional short form: Greenland
local long form: none
local short form: Kalaallit Nunaat
etymology: named by Norwegian adventurer Erik THORVALDSSON (Erik the Red) in A.D. 985 in order to entice settlers to the island

Government type: parliamentary democracy (Parliament of Greenland or Inatsisartut)

Dependency status: part of the Kingdom of Denmark; self-governing overseas administrative division of Denmark since 1979

Capital: *name:* Nuuk (Godthaab)
geographic coordinates: 64 11 N, 51 45 W
time difference: UTC-3 (2 hours ahead of Washington, DC, during Standard Time)
daylight saving time: +1hr, begins last Sunday in March; ends last Sunday in October
time zone note: Greenland has four time zones
etymology: "nuuk" is the Inuit word for "cape" and refers to the city's position at the end of the Nuup Kangerlua fjord

Administrative divisions: 5 municipalities (kommuner, singular kommune); Avannaata, Kujalleq, Qeqertalik, Qeqqata, Sermersooq
note: Northeast Greenland National Park (Kalaallit Nunaanni Nuna Eqqissisimatitaq) and the Thule Air Base in Pituffik (in northwest Greenland) are two unincorporated areas; the national park's 972,000 sq km - about 46% of the island - makes it the largest national park in the world and also the most northerly

Independence: none (extensive self-rule as part of the Kingdom of Denmark; foreign affairs is the responsibility of Denmark, but Greenland actively participates in international agreements relating to Greenland)

National holiday: National Day, June 21; note - marks the summer solstice and the longest day of the year in the Northern Hemisphere

Constitution: *history:* previous 1953 (Greenland established as a constituency in the Danish constitution), 1979 (Greenland Home Rule Act); latest 21 June 2009 (Greenland Self-Government Act)

Legal system: the laws of Denmark apply where applicable and Greenlandic law applies to other areas

Citizenship: see Denmark

Suffrage: 18 years of age; universal

Executive branch: *chief of state:* Queen MARGRETHE II of Denmark (since 14 January 1972), represented by High Commissioner Mikaela ENGELL (since April 2011)
head of government: Premier Mute B. EGEDE (since 23 April 2021)
cabinet: Self-rule Government (Naalakkersuisut) elected by the Parliament (Inatsisartut)
elections/appointments: the monarchy is hereditary; high commissioner appointed by the monarch; premier indirectly elected by Parliament for a 4-year term
election results:
2021: Mute B. EGEDE elected premier; Parliament vote - Mute B. EGEDE 20-0
2014: Kim KIELSEN elected premier; Parliament vote - Kim KIELSEN (S) 27.2%, Sara OLSVIG (IA) 25.5%, Randi Vestergaard EVALDSEN (D) 19.5%, other 27.8%

Legislative branch: *description:* unicameral Parliament or Inatsisartut (31 seats; members directly elected in multi-seat constituencies by party-list proportional representation vote - using the d'Hondt method - to serve 4-year terms)
Greenland elects 2 members to the Danish Parliament to serve 4-year terms
elections:
Greenland Parliament - last held on 6 April 2021 (next to be held in 2025)
Greenland members to Danish Parliament - last held on 5 June 2019 (next to be held by 4 June 2023)
election results:
Greenland Parliament - percent of vote by party - IA 38.7%, S 32.2%, N 12.9%, D 9.7%, A 6.5%; seats by party - IA 12, S 10, N 4, D 3, A 2; composition - men 21, women 10, percent of women 32.2%
Greenland members in Danish Parliament - percent of vote by party - NA; seats by party - IA 1, S 1; composition - 2 women

Judicial branch: *highest court(s):* High Court of Greenland (consists of the presiding professional judge and 2 lay assessors); note - appeals beyond the High Court of Greenland can be heard by the Supreme Court (in Copenhagen)
judge selection and term of office: judges appointed by the monarch upon the recommendation of the Judicial Appointments Council, a 6-member independent body of judges and lawyers; judges appointed for life with retirement at age 70
subordinate courts: Court of Greenland; 18 district or magistrates' courts

Political parties and leaders: Democrats Party (Demokraatit) or D [Jens Frederik NIELSEN]
Fellowship Party (Atassut) or A [Aqqalu JERIMIASSEN]
Forward Party (Siumut) or S [Erik JENSEN]
Inuit Community (Inuit Ataqatigiit) or IA [Mute Bourup EGEDE]
Signpost Party (Naleraq) or N [Pele BROBERG] (formerly Partii Naleraq)

International organization participation: Arctic Council, ICC, NC, NIB, UPU

Diplomatic representation in the US: *chief of mission:* Kenneth HOEGH, Head of Representation; note - Greenland also has offices in the Danish consulates in Chicago and New York
chancery: Greenland Representation
3200 Whitehaven Street, NW
Washington, DC 20008
telephone: 202-797-5392
email address and website:
washington@nanoq.gl
https://naalakkersuisut.gl/en/Naalakkersuisut/Groenlands-repraesentation-Washington

Diplomatic representation from the US: *chief of mission:* Consul Joanie SIMON (since June 2021)
embassy: Aalisartut Aqqutaa 47
Nuuk 3900
Greenland
telephone: (+299) 384100
email address and website:
https://dk.usembassy.gov/embassy-consulate/nuuk/

Flag description: two equal horizontal bands of white (top) and red with a large disk slightly to the hoist side of center - the top half of the disk is red, the bottom half is white; the design represents the sun reflecting off a field of ice; the colors are the same as those of the Danish flag and symbolize Greenland's links to the Kingdom of Denmark

National symbol(s): polar bear; national colors: red, white

National anthem: *name:* "Nunarput utoqqarsuanngoravit" (Our Country, Who's Become So Old also translated as You Our Ancient Land)
lyrics/music: Henrik LUND/Jonathan PETERSEN
note: adopted 1916; the government also recognizes "Nuna asiilasooq" as a secondary anthem

National heritage: *total World Heritage Sites:* 3 (2 cultural, 1 natural); note - excerpted from the Denmark entry
selected World Heritage Site locales: Ilulissat Icefjord (n); Kujataa, Norse and Inuit Farming (c); Aasivissuit–Nipisat, Inuit Hunting Ground (c)

ECONOMY

Economic overview: Greenland's economy depends on exports of shrimp and fish, and on a substantial subsidy from the Danish Government. Fish account for over 90% of its exports, subjecting the economy to price fluctuations. The subsidy from the Danish Government is budgeted to be about $535 million in 2017, more than 50% of government revenues, and 25% of GDP.

The economy is expanding after a period of decline. The economy contracted between 2012 and 2014, grew by 1.7% in 2015 and by 7.7%in 2016. The expansion has been driven by larger quotas for shrimp, the predominant Greenlandic export, and also by increased activity in the construction sector, especially in Nuuk, the capital. Private consumption and tourism also are contributing to GDP growth more than in previous years. Tourism in Greenland grew annually around 20% in 2015 and 2016, largely a result of increasing numbers of cruise lines now operating in Greenland's western and southern waters during the peak summer tourism season.

The public sector, including publicly owned enterprises and the municipalities, plays a dominant role in Greenland's economy. During the last decade the Greenland Self Rule Government pursued conservative fiscal and monetary policies, but public pressure has increased for better schools, health care, and retirement systems. The budget was in deficit in 2014 and 2016, but public debt remains low at about 5% of GDP. The government plans a balanced budget for the 2017–20 period.

Significant challenges face the island, including low levels of qualified labor, geographic dispersion, lack of industry diversification, the long-term sustainability of the public budget, and a declining population due to emigration. Hydrocarbon exploration has ceased with declining oil prices. The island has potential for natural resource exploitation with rare-earth, uranium, and iron ore mineral projects proposed, but a lack of infrastructure hinders development.

Real GDP (purchasing power parity): $2.413 billion (2015 est.)
$2.24 billion (2014 est.)
$2.203 billion (2013 est.)
note: data are in 2015 US dollars
country comparison to the world: 192

Real GDP growth rate: 7.7% (2016 est.)
1.7% (2015 est.)
-0.8% (2014 est.)
country comparison to the world: 10

Real GDP per capita: $41,800 (2015 est.)
$38,800 (2014 est.)
$38,500 (2013 est.)
country comparison to the world: 39

GDP (official exchange rate): $2.221 billion (2015 est.)

Inflation rate (consumer prices): 0.3% (January 2017 est.)
1.2% (January 2016 est.)
country comparison to the world: 32

GDP - composition, by sector of origin: *agriculture:* 15.9% (2015 est.)
industry: 10.1% (2015 est.)
services: 73.9% (2015)

GDP - composition, by end use: *household consumption:* 68.1% (2015 est.)
government consumption: 28% (2015 est.)
investment in fixed capital: 14.3% (2015 est.)
investment in inventories: -13.9% (2015 est.)
exports of goods and services: 18.2% (2015 est.)
imports of goods and services: -28.6% (2015 est.)

Agricultural products: sheep, cattle, reindeer, fish, shellfish

Industries: fish processing (mainly shrimp and Greenland halibut); anorthosite and ruby mining; handicrafts, hides and skins, small shipyards

Labor force: 26,840 (2015 est.)
country comparison to the world: 206

Labor force - by occupation: *agriculture:* 15.9%
industry: 10.1%
services: 73.9% (2015 est.)

Unemployment rate: 9.1% (2015 est.)
10.3% (2014 est.)
country comparison to the world: 140

Population below poverty line: 16.2% (2015 est.)

Gini Index coefficient - distribution of family income: 33.9 (2015 est.)
34.3 (2014 est.)
country comparison to the world: 119

Budget: *revenues:* 1.719 billion (2016 est.)
expenditures: 1.594 billion (2016 est.)

Budget surplus (+) or deficit (-): 5.6% (of GDP) (2016 est.)
country comparison to the world: 5

Public debt: 13% of GDP (2015 est.)
country comparison to the world: 196

Taxes and other revenues: 77.4% (of GDP) (2016 est.)
country comparison to the world: 3

Fiscal year: calendar year

Exports: $407.1 million (2015 est.)
$599.7 million (2014 est.)
country comparison to the world: 194

Exports - partners: Denmark 55%, China 22%, Japan 6% (2019)

Exports - commodities: fish, crustaceans, fishing ships (2019)

Imports: $783.5 million (2015 est.)
$866.1 million (2014 est.)
country comparison to the world: 195

Imports - partners: Denmark 51%, Spain 23%, Sweden 12%, Iceland 7% (2019)

Imports - commodities: fishing ships, refined petroleum, construction vehicles, crustaceans, delivery trucks (2019)

Debt - external: $36.4 million (2010)
$58 million (2009)
country comparison to the world: 197

Exchange rates: Danish kroner (DKK) per US dollar -
6.586 (2017 est.)
6.7309 (2016 est.)
6.7309 (2015 est.)
6.7326 (2014 est.)
5.6125 (2013 est.)

ENERGY

Electricity access: *electrification - total population:* 100% (2020)

Electricity: *installed generating capacity:* 187,000 kW (2020 est.)
consumption: 481.7 million kWh (2019 est.)
exports: 0 kWh (2020 est.)
imports: 0 kWh (2020 est.)
transmission/distribution losses: 17 million kWh (2019 est.)

Electricity generation sources: *fossil fuels:* 15.8% of total installed capacity (2020 est.)
hydroelectricity: 84.2% of total installed capacity (2020 est.)

Coal: *proven reserves:* 183 million metric tons (2019 est.)

Petroleum: *total petroleum production:* 0 bbl/day (2021 est.)
refined petroleum consumption: 4,000 bbl/day (2019 est.)

Refined petroleum products - imports: 3,973 bbl/day (2015 est.)
country comparison to the world: 177

Natural gas: *production:* 0 cubic meters (2021 est.)
consumption: 0 cubic meters (2021 est.)
exports: 0 cubic meters (2021 est.)
imports: 0 cubic meters (2021 est.)
proven reserves: 0 cubic meters (2021 est.)

Carbon dioxide emissions: 605,000 metric tonnes of CO2 (2019 est.)
from petroleum and other liquids: 605,000 metric tonnes of CO2 (2019 est.)
country comparison to the world: 187

COMMUNICATIONS

Telephones - fixed lines: *total subscriptions:* 6,352 (2020 est.)
subscriptions per 100 inhabitants: 11 (2020 est.)
country comparison to the world: 199

Telephones - mobile cellular: *total subscriptions:* 65,958 (2020 est.)
subscriptions per 100 inhabitants: 116 (2020 est.)
country comparison to the world: 201

Telecommunication systems: *general assessment:* adequate domestic and international service provided by satellite, cables, and microwave radio relay; the fundamental telecommunications infrastructure consists of a digital radio link from Nanortalik in south Greenland to Uummannaq in north Greenland; satellites cover north and east Greenland for domestic and foreign telecommunications; a marine cable connects south and west Greenland to the rest of the world, extending from Nuuk and Qaqortoq to Canada and Iceland; a contract has been awarded to build a 5G network in Greenland, initially covering three towns, with 10 towns, including Greenland's capital Nuuk to follow (2022)
domestic: nearly 11 per 100 for fixed-line subscriptions and 116 per 100 for mobile-cellular (2020)
international: country code - 299; landing points for Greenland Connect, Greenland Connect North, Nunavut Undersea Fiber System submarine cables to Greenland, Iceland, and Canada; satellite earth stations - 15 (12 Intelsat, 1 Eutelsat, 2 Americom GE-2 (all Atlantic Ocean)) (2019)

Broadcast media: the Greenland Broadcasting Company provides public radio and TV services throughout the island with a broadcast station and a series of repeaters; a few private local TV and radio stations; Danish public radio rebroadcasts are available (2019)

Internet country code: .gl

Internet users: *total:* 39,358 (2019 est.)
percent of population: 70% (2019 est.)
country comparison to the world: 203

Broadband - fixed subscriptions: *total:* 15,649 (2020 est.)
subscriptions per 100 inhabitants: 28 (2020 est.)
country comparison to the world: 173

TRANSPORTATION

National air transport system: *number of registered air carriers:* 1 (2020) (registered in Denmark)
inventory of registered aircraft operated by air carriers: 8 (registered in Denmark)

Civil aircraft registration country code prefix: OY-H

Airports: *total:* 15 (2021)
country comparison to the world: 146

Airports - with paved runways: *total:* 10
2,438 to 3,047 m: 2
1,524 to 2,437 m: 1
914 to 1,523 m: 1
under 914 m: 6 (2021)

Airports - with unpaved runways: *total:* 5
1,524 to 2,437 m: 1
914 to 1,523 m: 2
under 914 m: 2 (2021)

Roadways: *note:* although there are short roads in towns, there are no roads between towns; inter-urban transport is either by sea or by air

Merchant marine: *total:* 8
by type: other 8 (2021)
country comparison to the world: 161

Ports and terminals: *major seaport(s):* Sisimiut

MILITARY AND SECURITY

Military and security forces: no regular military forces or conscription

Military - note: the Danish military's Joint Arctic Command in Nuuk is responsible for the defense of Greenland

TRANSNATIONAL ISSUES

Disputes - international: managed dispute between Canada and Denmark over Hans Island in the Kennedy Channel between Canada's Ellesmere Island and Greenland; Denmark (Greenland) and Norway have made submissions to the Commission on the Limits of the Continental Shelf (CLCS) and Russia is collecting additional data to augment its 2001 CLCS submission

GRENADA

INTRODUCTION

Background: Carib Indians inhabited Grenada when Christopher COLUMBUS landed on the island in 1498, but it remained uncolonized for more than a century. The French settled Grenada in the 17th century, established sugar estates, and imported large numbers of African slaves. Britain took the island in 1762 and vigorously expanded sugar production. In the 19th century, cacao eventually surpassed sugar as the main export crop; in the 20th century, nutmeg became the leading export. In 1967, Britain gave Grenada autonomy over its internal affairs. Full independence was attained in 1974, making Grenada one of the smallest independent countries in the Western Hemisphere. In 1979, a leftist New Jewel Movement seized power under Maurice BISHOP, ushering in the Grenada Revolution. On 19 October 1983, factions within the revolutionary government overthrew and killed BISHOP and members of his party. Six days later, the island was invaded by US forces and those of six other Caribbean nations, which quickly captured the ringleaders and their hundreds of Cuban advisers. The rule of law was restored, and democratic elections were reinstituted the following year and have continued since then.

GEOGRAPHY

Location: Caribbean, island between the Caribbean Sea and Atlantic Ocean, north of Trinidad and Tobago

Geographic coordinates: 12 07 N, 61 40 W

Map references: Central America and the Caribbean

Area: *total:* 344 sq km
land: 344 sq km
water: 0 sq km
country comparison to the world: 207

Area - comparative: twice the size of Washington, DC

Land boundaries: *total:* 0 km

Coastline: 121 km

Maritime claims: *territorial sea:* 12 nm
exclusive economic zone: 200 nm

Climate: tropical; tempered by northeast trade winds

Terrain: volcanic in origin with central mountains

Elevation: *highest point:* Mount Saint Catherine 840 m
lowest point: Caribbean Sea 0 m

Natural resources: timber, tropical fruit

Land use: *agricultural land:* 32.3% (2018 est.)
arable land: 8.8% (2018 est.)
permanent crops: 20.6% (2018 est.)
permanent pasture: 2.9% (2018 est.)
forest: 50% (2018 est.)
other: 17.7% (2018 est.)

Irrigated land: 20 sq km (2012)

Population distribution: approximately one-third of the population is found in the capital of St. George's; the island's population is concentrated along the coast

Natural hazards: lies on edge of hurricane belt; hurricane season lasts from June to November
volcanism: Mount Saint Catherine (840 m) lies on the island of Grenada; Kick 'em Jenny, an active submarine volcano (seamount) on the Caribbean Sea floor, lies about 8 km north of the island of Grenada; these two volcanoes are at the southern end of the volcanic island arc of the Lesser Antilles that extends up to the Netherlands dependency of Saba in the north

Geography - note: the administration of the islands of the Grenadines group is divided between Saint Vincent and the Grenadines and Grenada

PEOPLE AND SOCIETY

Population: 113,949 (2022 est.)
country comparison to the world: 190

Nationality: *noun:* Grenadian(s)
adjective: Grenadian

Ethnic groups: African descent 82.4%, mixed 13.3%, East Indian 2.2%, other 1.3%, unspecified 0.9% (2011 est.)

Languages: English (official), French patois

Religions: Protestant 49.2% (includes Pentecostal 17.2%, Seventh Day Adventist 13.2%, Anglican 8.5%, Baptist 3.2%, Church of God 2.4%, Evangelical 1.9%, Methodist 1.6%, other 1.2%), Roman Catholic 36%, Jehovah's Witness 1.2%, Rastafarian 1.2%, other 5.5%, none 5.7%, unspecified 1.3% (2011 est.)

Age structure: *0-14 years:* 23.23% (male 13,709/female 12,564)
15-24 years: 14.14% (male 8,034/female 7,959)
25-54 years: 40.05% (male 23,104/female 22,187)
55-64 years: 11.69% (male 6,734/female 6,490)
65 years and over: 10.89% (male 5,774/female 6,539) (2020 est.)

Dependency ratios: *total dependency ratio:* 50.5
youth dependency ratio: 35.8
elderly dependency ratio: 14.7
potential support ratio: 6.8 (2020 est.)

Median age: *total:* 33.3 years
male: 33.1 years
female: 33.4 years (2020 est.)
country comparison to the world: 99

Population growth rate: 0.32% (2022 est.)
country comparison to the world: 169

Birth rate: 13.94 births/1,000 population (2022 est.)
country comparison to the world: 128

Death rate: 8.31 deaths/1,000 population (2022 est.)
country comparison to the world: 79

Net migration rate: -2.43 migrant(s)/1,000 population (2022 est.)
country comparison to the world: 173

Population distribution: approximately one-third of the population is found in the capital of St. George's; the island's population is concentrated along the coast

Urbanization: *urban population:* 36.9% of total population (2022)

rate of urbanization: 0.86% annual rate of change (2020-25 est.)

Major urban areas - population: 39,000 SAINT GEORGE'S (capital) (2018)

Sex ratio: *at birth:* 1.1 male(s)/female
0-14 years: 1.09 male(s)/female
15-24 years: 1.02 male(s)/female
25-54 years: 1.05 male(s)/female
55-64 years: 1.04 male(s)/female
65 years and over: 0.69 male(s)/female
total population: 1.03 male(s)/female (2022 est.)

Maternal mortality ratio: 25 deaths/100,000 live births (2017 est.)
country comparison to the world: 122

Infant mortality rate: *total:* 9.4 deaths/1,000 live births
male: 8.94 deaths/1,000 live births
female: 9.9 deaths/1,000 live births (2022 est.)
country comparison to the world: 140

Life expectancy at birth: *total population:* 75.74 years
male: 73.13 years
female: 78.6 years (2022 est.)
country comparison to the world: 118

Total fertility rate: 1.93 children born/woman (2022 est.)
country comparison to the world: 117

Drinking water source: *improved: total:* 96.8% of population
unimproved: total: 3.2% of population (2017 est.)

Current health expenditure: 5% of GDP (2019)

Physicians density: 1.44 physicians/1,000 population (2018)

Hospital bed density: 3.6 beds/1,000 population (2017)

Sanitation facility access: *improved: total:* 93.7% of population
unimproved: total: 6.3% of population (2020 est.)

HIV/AIDS - adult prevalence rate: 0.5% (2018 est.)
country comparison to the world: 67

Obesity - adult prevalence rate: 21.3% (2016)
country comparison to the world: 90

Alcohol consumption per capita: *total:* 8.62 liters of pure alcohol (2019 est.)
beer: 3.54 liters of pure alcohol (2019 est.)
wine: 0.56 liters of pure alcohol (2019 est.)
spirits: 4.21 liters of pure alcohol (2019 est.)
other alcohols: 0.31 liters of pure alcohol (2019 est.)
country comparison to the world: 37

Education expenditures: 3.6% of GDP (2018 est.)
country comparison to the world: 118

Literacy: *definition:* age 15 and over can read and write
total population: 98.6%
male: 98.6%
female: 98.6% (2014 est.)

School life expectancy (primary to tertiary education): *total:* 19 years
male: 18 years
female: 19 years (2018)

ENVIRONMENT

Environment - current issues: deforestation causing habitat destruction and species loss; coastal erosion and contamination; pollution and sedimentation; inadequate solid waste management

Environment - international agreements: *party to:* Biodiversity, Climate Change, Climate Change-Kyoto Protocol, Climate Change-Paris Agreement, Comprehensive Nuclear Test Ban, Desertification, Endangered Species, Law of the Sea, Ozone Layer Protection, Ship Pollution, Wetlands, Whaling
signed, but not ratified: none of the selected agreements

Air pollutants: *particulate matter emissions:* 21.56 micrograms per cubic meter (2016 est.)
carbon dioxide emissions: 0.27 megatons (2016 est.)
methane emissions: 2.04 megatons (2020 est.)

Climate: tropical; tempered by northeast trade winds

Land use: *agricultural land:* 32.3% (2018 est.)
arable land: 8.8% (2018 est.)
permanent crops: 20.6% (2018 est.)
permanent pasture: 2.9% (2018 est.)
forest: 50% (2018 est.)
other: 17.7% (2018 est.)

Urbanization: *urban population:* 36.9% of total population (2022)
rate of urbanization: 0.86% annual rate of change (2020-25 est.)

Revenue from forest resources: *forest revenues:* 0% of GDP (2018 est.)
country comparison to the world: 170

Revenue from coal: *coal revenues:* 0% of GDP (2018 est.)
country comparison to the world: 104

Waste and recycling: *municipal solid waste generated annually:* 29,536 tons (2012 est.)

Total water withdrawal: *municipal:* 12 million cubic meters (2017 est.)
industrial: 0 cubic meters (2017 est.)
agricultural: 2.1 million cubic meters (2017 est.)

Total renewable water resources: 200 million cubic meters (2017 est.)

GOVERNMENT

Country name: *conventional long form:* none
conventional short form: Grenada
etymology: derivation of the name remains obscure; some sources attribute the designation to Spanish influence (most likely named for the Spanish city of Granada), with subsequent French and English interpretations resulting in the present-day Grenada; in Spanish "granada" means "pomegranate"

Government type: parliamentary democracy under a constitutional monarchy; a Commonwealth realm

Capital: *name:* Saint George's
geographic coordinates: 12 03 N, 61 45 W
time difference: UTC-4 (1 hour ahead of Washington, DC, during Standard Time)
etymology: the 1763 Treaty of Paris transferred possession of Grenada from France to Great Britain; the new administration renamed Ville de Fort Royal (Fort Royal Town) to Saint George's Town, after the patron saint of England; eventually the name became simply Saint George's

Administrative divisions: 6 parishes and 1 dependency*; Carriacou and Petite Martinique*, Saint Andrew, Saint David, Saint George, Saint John, Saint Mark, Saint Patrick

Independence: 7 February 1974 (from the UK)

National holiday: Independence Day, 7 February (1974)

Constitution: *history:* previous 1967; latest presented 19 December 1973, effective 7 February 1974, suspended 1979 following a revolution but restored in 1983
amendments: proposed by either house of Parliament; passage requires two-thirds majority vote by the membership in both houses and assent of the governor general; passage of amendments to constitutional sections, such as personal rights and freedoms, the structure, authorities, and procedures of the branches of government, the delimitation of electoral constituencies, or the procedure for amending the constitution, also requires two-thirds majority approval in a referendum; amended 1991, 1992

Legal system: common law based on English model

International law organization participation: has not submitted an ICJ jurisdiction declaration; accepts ICCt jurisdiction

Citizenship: *citizenship by birth:* yes
citizenship by descent only: yes
dual citizenship recognized: yes
residency requirement for naturalization: 7 years for persons from a non-Caribbean state and 4 years for a person from a Caribbean state

Suffrage: 18 years of age; universal

Executive branch: *chief of state:* King CHARLES III (since 8 September 2022); represented by Governor General Cecile LA GRENADE (since 7 May 2013)
head of government: Prime Minister Keith MITCHELL (since 20 February 2013)
cabinet: Cabinet appointed by the governor general on the advice of the prime minister
elections/appointments: the monarchy is hereditary; governor general appointed by the monarch; following legislative elections, the leader of the majority party or majority coalition usually appointed prime minister by the governor general

Legislative branch: *description:* bicameral Parliament consists of:
Senate (13 seats; members appointed by the governor general - 10 on the advice of the prime minister and 3 on the advice of the leader of the opposition party; members serve 5-year terms)
House of Representatives (15 seats; members directly elected in single-seat constituencies by simple majority vote to serve 5-year terms)
elections: Senate - last appointments on 27 April 2018 (next no later than 2023)
House of Representatives - last held on 13 March 2018 (next no later than 2023)
election results: Senate - percent by party - NA; seats by party - NA; composition - men 11, women 2 percent of women 15.4%
House of Representatives - percent of vote by party - NNP 58.9%, NDC 40.5%; other 0.6% seats by party - NNP 15; composition - men 8, women 7, percent of women 46.7%; note - total Parliament percent of women 32.1%

Judicial branch: *highest court(s):* regionally, the Eastern Caribbean Supreme Court (ECSC) is the superior court of the Organization of Eastern Caribbean States; the ECSC - headquartered on St. Lucia - consists of the Court of Appeal - headed by the chief justice and 4 judges - and the High Court with 18 judges; the Court of Appeal is itinerant,

traveling to member states on a schedule to hear appeals from the High Court and subordinate courts; High Court judges reside in the member states, with 2 in Grenada; appeals beyond the ECSC in civil and criminal matters are heard by the Judicial Committee of the Privy Council (in London)
judge selection and term of office: chief justice of Eastern Caribbean Supreme Court appointed by Her Majesty, Queen ELIZABETH II; other justices and judges appointed by the Judicial and Legal Services Commission, and independent body of judicial officials; Court of Appeal justices appointed for life with mandatory retirement at age 65; High Court judges appointed for life with mandatory retirement at age 62
subordinate courts: magistrates' courts; Court of Magisterial Appeals

Political parties and leaders: National Democratic Congress or NDC [Dickon MITCHELL]
New National Party or NNP [Keith MITCHELL]

International organization participation: ACP, AOSIS, CARIFORUM, CARIBCAN, Caricom, CBI, CDB, CELAC, CSME, ECCU, EPA, FAO, G-77, IBRD, ICAO, ICCt (signatory), ICRM, IDA, IFAD, IFC, IFRCS, ILO, IMF, IMO, Interpol, IOC, ITU, ITUC, LAES, MIGA, NAM, OAS, OECS, OPANAL, OPCW, Petrocaribe, UN, UNCTAD, UNESCO, UNIDO, UPU, WHO, WIPO, WTO

Diplomatic representation in the US: *chief of mission:* Ambassador Yolande Yvonne SMITH (since 8 April 2019)
chancery: 1701 New Hampshire Avenue NW, Washington, DC 20009
telephone: [1] (202) 265-2561
FAX: [1] (202) 265-2468
email address and website:
embassy@grenadaembassyusa.org
https://grenadaembassyusa.org/
consulate(s) general: Miami, New York

Diplomatic representation from the US: *chief of mission:* the US does not have an official embassy in Grenada; the US Ambassador to Barbados is accredited to Grenada
embassy: Lance-aux-Epines, Saint George's
mailing address: 3180 Grenada Place, Washington DC 20521-3180
telephone: [1] (473) 444-1173
FAX: [1] (473) 444-4820
email address and website:
StgeorgesACS@state.gov
https://bb.usembassy.gov/embassy/grenada/

Flag description: a rectangle divided diagonally into yellow triangles (top and bottom) and green triangles (hoist side and outer side), with a red border around the flag; there are seven yellow, five-pointed stars with three centered in the top red border, three centered in the bottom red border, and one on a red disk superimposed at the center of the flag; there is also a symbolic nutmeg pod on the hoist-side triangle (Grenada is a leading nutmeg producer); the seven stars stand for the seven administrative divisions, with the central star denoting the capital, St. George's; yellow represents the sun and the warmth of the people, green stands for vegetation and agriculture, and red symbolizes harmony, unity, and courage

National symbol(s): Grenada dove, bougainvillea flower; national colors: red, yellow, green

National anthem: *name:* "Hail Grenada"
lyrics/music: Irva Merle BAPTISTE/Louis Arnold MASANTO
note: adopted 1974

ECONOMY

Economic overview: Grenada relies on tourism and revenue generated by St. George's University - a private university offering degrees in medicine, veterinary medicine, public health, the health sciences, nursing, arts and sciences, and business - as its main source of foreign exchange. In the past two years the country expanded its sources of revenue, including from selling passports under its citizenship by investment program. These projects produced a resurgence in the construction and manufacturing sectors of the economy.

In 2017, Grenada experienced its fifth consecutive year of growth and the government successfully marked the completion of its five-year structural adjustment program that included among other things austerity measures, increased tax revenue and debt restructuring. Public debt-to-GDP was reduced from 100% of GDP in 2013 to 71.8% in 2017.

Real GDP (purchasing power parity): $1.7 billion (2020 est.)
$1.91 billion (2019 est.)
$1.87 billion (2018 est.)
note: data are in 2017 dollars
country comparison to the world: 200

Real GDP growth rate: 5.1% (2017 est.)
3.7% (2016 est.)
6.4% (2015 est.)
country comparison to the world: 43

Real GDP per capita: $15,100 (2020 est.)
$17,100 (2019 est.)
$16,800 (2018 est.)
note: data are in 2017 dollars
country comparison to the world: 107

GDP (official exchange rate): $1.119 billion (2017 est.)

Inflation rate (consumer prices): 0.9% (2017 est.)
1.7% (2016 est.)
country comparison to the world: 58

Credit ratings:

Standard & Poors rating: SD (2013)
note: The year refers to the year in which the current credit rating was first obtained.

GDP - composition, by sector of origin: *agriculture:* 6.8% (2017 est.)
industry: 15.5% (2017 est.)
services: 77.7% (2017 est.)

GDP - composition, by end use: *household consumption:* 63% (2017 est.)
government consumption: 12% (2017 est.)
investment in fixed capital: 20% (2017 est.)
investment in inventories: -0.1% (2017 est.)
exports of goods and services: 60% (2017 est.)
imports of goods and services: -55% (2017 est.)

Agricultural products: bananas, watermelons, sweet potatoes, sugar cane, tomatoes, plantains, coconuts, melons, cucumbers, cabbages

Industries: food and beverages, textiles, light assembly operations, tourism, construction, education, call-center operations

Industrial production growth rate: 10% (2017 est.)
country comparison to the world: 16

Labor force: 55,270 (2017 est.)
country comparison to the world: 188

Labor force - by occupation: *agriculture:* 11%
industry: 20%
services: 69% (2008 est.)

Unemployment rate: 24% (2017 est.)
28.2% (2016 est.)
country comparison to the world: 196

Population below poverty line: 38% (2008 est.)

Budget: *revenues:* 288.4 million (2017 est.)
expenditures: 252.3 million (2017 est.)

Budget surplus (+) or deficit (-): 3.2% (of GDP) (2017 est.)
country comparison to the world: 12

Public debt: 70.4% of GDP (2017 est.)
82% of GDP (2016 est.)
country comparison to the world: 51

Taxes and other revenues: 25.8% (of GDP) (2017 est.)
country comparison to the world: 116

Fiscal year: calendar year

Current account balance: -$77 million (2017 est.)
-$34 million (2016 est.)
country comparison to the world: 84

Exports: $650 million (2018 est.) note: data are in current year dollars
$44.2 million (2016 est.)
country comparison to the world: 186

Exports - partners: United States 40%, Saint Vincent and the Grenadines 7%, Saint Lucia 7%, France 6%, Netherlands 5%, Germany 5%, Ireland 5%, Antigua and Barbuda 5% (2019)

Exports - commodities: fish, nutmeg, cocoa beans, fruits, wheat, toilet paper (2019)

Imports: $640 million (2018 est.) note: data are in current year dollars
$314.7 million (2016 est.)
country comparison to the world: 196

Imports - partners: United States 35%, Canada 24%, China 5% (2019)

Imports - commodities: aircraft, poultry meat, cars, refined petroleum, food preparation materials (2019)

Reserves of foreign exchange and gold: $199.1 million (31 December 2017 est.)
$198 million (31 December 2015 est.)
country comparison to the world: 175

Debt - external: $793.5 million (2017 est.)
$682.3 million (2016 est.)
country comparison to the world: 169

Exchange rates: East Caribbean dollars (XCD) per US dollar -
2.7 (2017 est.)
2.7 (2016 est.)
2.7 (2015 est.)
2.7 (2014 est.)
2.7 (2013 est.)

ENERGY

Electricity access: *electrification - total population:* 95.3% (2018)

Electricity: *installed generating capacity:* 55,000 kW (2020 est.)
consumption: 194.495 million kWh (2019 est.)

exports: 0 kWh (2020 est.)
imports: 0 kWh (2020 est.)
transmission/distribution losses: 19 million kWh (2019 est.)

Electricity generation sources: *fossil fuels:* 98.3% of total installed capacity (2020 est.)
solar: 1.6% of total installed capacity (2020 est.)
wind: 0.1% of total installed capacity (2020 est.)

Petroleum: *total petroleum production:* 0 bbl/day (2021 est.)
refined petroleum consumption: 2,200 bbl/day (2019 est.)

Refined petroleum products - imports: 1,886 bbl/day (2015 est.)
country comparison to the world: 191

Carbon dioxide emissions: 316,000 metric tonnes of CO2 (2019 est.)
from petroleum and other liquids: 316,000 metric tonnes of CO2 (2019 est.)
country comparison to the world: 196

Energy consumption per capita: 39.799 million Btu/person (2019 est.)
country comparison to the world: 107

COMMUNICATIONS

Telephones - fixed lines: *total subscriptions:* 16,000 (2020 est.)
subscriptions per 100 inhabitants: 14 (2020 est.)
country comparison to the world: 180

Telephones - mobile cellular: *total subscriptions:* 122,000 (2020 est.)
subscriptions per 100 inhabitants: 108 (2020 est.)
country comparison to the world: 189

Telecommunication systems: *general assessment:* the telecom sector has seen a decline in subscriber numbers (particularly for prepaid mobile services the mainstay of short term visitors) and revenue; fixed and mobile broadband services are two areas that have benefited from the crisis as employees and students have resorted to working from home; one area of the telecom market that is not prepared for growth is 5G mobile; governments, regulators, and even the mobile network operators have shown that they have not been investing in 5G opportunities at the present time; network expansion and enhancements remain concentrated around improving LTE coverage (2021)
domestic: 14 per 100 for fixed-line and 108 per 100 for mobile-cellular (2020)
international: country code - 1-473; landing points for the ECFS, Southern Caribbean Fiber and CARCIP submarine cables with links to 13 Caribbean islands extending from the British Virgin Islands to Trinidad & Tobago including Puerto Rico and Barbados; SHF radiotelephone links to Trinidad and Tobago and Saint Vincent; VHF and UHF radio links to Trinidad (2019)

Broadcast media: multiple publicly and privately owned television and radio stations; Grenada Information Service (GIS) is government-owned and provides television and radio services; the Grenada Broadcasting Network, jointly owned by the government and the Caribbean Communications Network of Trinidad and Tobago, operates a TV station and 2 radio stations; Meaningful Television (MTV) broadcasts island-wide and is part of a locally-owned media house, Moving Target Company, that also includes an FM radio station and a weekly newspaper; multi-channel cable TV subscription service is provided by Columbus Communications Grenada (FLOW GRENADA) and is available island wide; approximately 25 private radio stations also broadcast throughout the country (2019)

Internet country code: .gd

Internet users: *total:* 64,136 (2020 est.)
percent of population: 57% (2020 est.)
country comparison to the world: 191

Broadband - fixed subscriptions: *total:* 32,000 (2020 est.)
subscriptions per 100 inhabitants: 28 (2020 est.)
country comparison to the world: 150

TRANSPORTATION

Civil aircraft registration country code prefix: J3

Airports: *total:* 3 (2021)
country comparison to the world: 194

Airports - with paved runways: *total:* 3
2,438 to 3,047 m: 1
1,524 to 2,437 m: 1
under 914 m: 1 (2021)

Roadways: *total:* 1,127 km (2017)
paved: 902 km (2017)
unpaved: 225 km (2017)
country comparison to the world: 182

Merchant marine: *total:* 6
by type: general cargo 3, other 3 (2021)
country comparison to the world: 164

Ports and terminals: *major seaport(s):* Saint George's

MILITARY AND SECURITY

Military and security forces: no regular military forces; the Royal Grenada Police Force (under the Ministry of National Security) includes a Coast Guard and a paramilitary Special Services Unit (2022)

Military - note: Grenada joined the Caribbean Regional Security System (RSS) in 1985; RSS signatories (Antigua and Barbuda, Barbados, Dominica, Saint Kitts, Saint Lucia, and Saint Vincent and the Grenadines) agreed to prepare contingency plans and assist one another, on request, in national emergencies, prevention of smuggling, search and rescue, immigration control, fishery protection, customs and excise control, maritime policing duties, protection of off-shore installations, pollution control, national and other disasters, and threats to national security (2022)

TRANSNATIONAL ISSUES

Disputes - international: none

Illicit drugs: a transit point for cocaine and marijuana destined for North America, Europe, and elsewhere in the Caribbean

GUAM

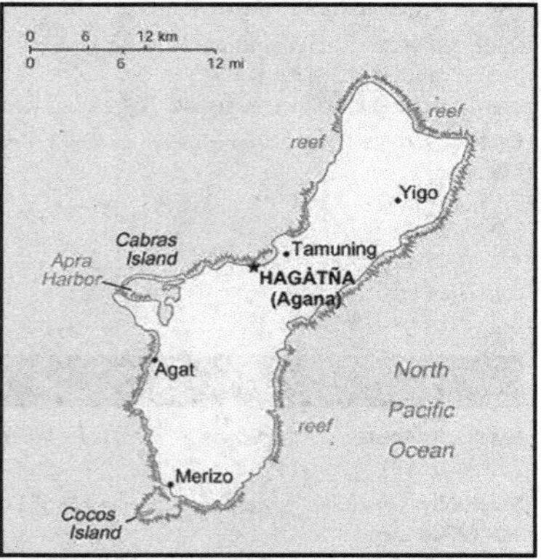

INTRODUCTION

Background: Guam was settled by Austronesian people around 1500 B.C. These people became the indigenous Chamorro and were influenced by later migrations, including the Micronesians in the first millennium A.D., and island Southeast Asians around 900. Society was stratified with higher classes living along the coast and lower classes living inland. Spanish explorer Ferdinand MAGELLAN was the first European to see Guam in 1521 and Spain claimed the island in 1565 as it served as a refueling stop for ships between Mexico and the Philippines. Spain formally colonized Guam in 1668. Spain's brutal repression of the Chamorro, along with new diseases and intermittent warfare, reduced the indigenous population from more than 100,000 to less than 5,000 by the 1700s. Spain tried to repopulate the island by forcing people from nearby islands to settle on Guam and preventing them from escaping.

Guam became a hub for whalers and traders in the western Pacific in the early 1800s. During the 1898 Spanish-American War, the US Navy occupied Guam and set up a military administration. The US Navy opposed local control of government despite repeated petitions by the Chamorro. Japan invaded Guam in 1941 and instituted a repressive regime. During the US recapture of Guam in 1944, the island's two largest villages were destroyed. After World War II, political pressure from local Chamorro leaders led to Guam being established as an unincorporated organized territory in 1950 with US citizenship granted to all Chamorro. In a referendum in 1982, more than 75% of voters chose closer relations with the US over independence, although no change in status was made because of disagreements on the future right of Chamorro self-determination. The US military holds about 29% of Guam's land and stations several thousand troops on the island. The installations are some of the most strategically important US bases in the Pacific; they also constitute the island's most important source of income and economic stability.

GEOGRAPHY

Location: Oceania, island in the North Pacific Ocean, about three-quarters of the way from Hawaii to the Philippines

Geographic coordinates: 13 28 N, 144 47 E

Map references: Oceania

Area: *total:* 544 sq km
land: 544 sq km
water: 0 sq km
country comparison to the world: 194

Area - comparative: three times the size of Washington, DC

Land boundaries: *total:* 0 km

Coastline: 125.5 km

Maritime claims: *territorial sea:* 12 nm
exclusive economic zone: 200 nm

Climate: tropical marine; generally warm and humid, moderated by northeast trade winds; dry season (January to June), rainy season (July to December); little seasonal temperature variation

Terrain: volcanic origin, surrounded by coral reefs; relatively flat coralline limestone plateau (source of most fresh water), with steep coastal cliffs and narrow coastal plains in north, low hills in center, mountains in south

Elevation: *highest point:* Mount Lamlam 406 m
lowest point: Pacific Ocean 0 m

Natural resources: aquatic wildlife (supporting tourism), fishing (largely undeveloped)

Land use: *agricultural land:* 33.4% (2018 est.)
arable land: 1.9% (2018 est.)
permanent crops: 16.7% (2018 est.)
permanent pasture: 14.8% (2018 est.)
forest: 47.9% (2018 est.)
other: 18.7% (2018 est.)

Irrigated land: 2 sq km (2012)

Population distribution: no large cities exist on the island, though large villages (municipalities) attract much of the population; the largest of these is Dededo

Natural hazards: frequent squalls during rainy season; relatively rare but potentially destructive typhoons (June to December)

Geography - note: largest and southernmost island in the Mariana Islands archipelago and the largest island in Micronesia; strategic location in western North Pacific Ocean

PEOPLE AND SOCIETY

Population: 169,086 (2022 est.)
country comparison to the world: 185

Nationality: *noun:* Guamanian(s) (US citizens)
adjective: Guamanian

Ethnic groups: Chamorro 37.3%, Filipino 26.3%, White 7.1%, Chuukese 7%, Korean 2.2%, other Pacific Islander 2%, other Asian 2%, Chinese 1.6%, Palauan 1.6%, Japanese 1.5%, Pohnpeian 1.4%, mixed 9.4%, other 0.6% (2010 est.)

Languages: English 43.6%, Filipino 21.2%, Chamorro 17.8%, other Pacific island languages 10%, Asian languages 6.3%, other 1.1% (2010 est.)

Religions: Christian (predominantly Roman Catholic) 94.2%, folk religions 1.5%, Buddhist 1.1%, other 1.6%, unaffiliated 1.7% (2020 est.)

Age structure: *0-14 years:* 27.22% (male 23,748/female 22,122)
15-24 years: 16.08% (male 14,522/female 12,572)
25-54 years: 36.65% (male 31,880/female 29,871)
55-64 years: 10.5% (male 9,079/female 8,610)
65 years and over: 9.54% (male 7,504/female 8,577) (2020 est.)

Dependency ratios: *total dependency ratio:* 52.4
youth dependency ratio: 36.4
elderly dependency ratio: 16.1
potential support ratio: 6.2 (2020 est.)

Median age: *total:* 29.4 years
male: 28.7 years
female: 30.2 years (2020 est.)
country comparison to the world: 130

Population growth rate: 0.16% (2022 est.)
country comparison to the world: 183

Birth rate: 18.56 births/1,000 population (2022 est.)
country comparison to the world: 76

Death rate: 6.03 deaths/1,000 population (2022 est.)
country comparison to the world: 157

Net migration rate: -10.96 migrant(s)/1,000 population (2022 est.)
country comparison to the world: 223

Population distribution: no large cities exist on the island, though large villages (municipalities) attract much of the population; the largest of these is Dededo

Urbanization: *urban population:* 95.1% of total population (2022)
rate of urbanization: 0.84% annual rate of change (2020-25 est.)

Major urban areas - population: 147,000 HAGATNA (capital) (2018)

Sex ratio: *at birth:* 1.07 male(s)/female
0-14 years: 1.07 male(s)/female
15-24 years: 1.16 male(s)/female
25-54 years: 1.07 male(s)/female
55-64 years: 1.07 male(s)/female
65 years and over: 0.71 male(s)/female
total population: 1.06 male(s)/female (2022 est.)

Infant mortality rate: *total:* 11.46 deaths/1,000 live births
male: 11.49 deaths/1,000 live births
female: 11.44 deaths/1,000 live births (2022 est.)
country comparison to the world: 125

Life expectancy at birth: *total population:* 77.5 years
male: 75.07 years
female: 80.08 years (2022 est.)
country comparison to the world: 90

Total fertility rate: 2.78 children born/woman (2022 est.)
country comparison to the world: 57

Drinking water source: *improved: total:* 99.7% of population
unimproved: total: 0.3% of population (2020 est.)

Sanitation facility access: *improved: urban:* 89.8% of population (2015 est.)
rural: 89.8% of population (2015 est.)
total: 89.8% of population (2015 est.)
unimproved: urban: 10.2% of population (2015 est.)
rural: 10.2% of population (2015 est.)
total: 10.2% of population (2015 est.)

Unemployment, youth ages 15-24: *total:* 29.4%
male: 29.7%
female: 28.9% (2011 est.)

ENVIRONMENT

Environment - current issues: fresh water scarcity; reef damage; inadequate sewage treatment; extermination of native bird populations by the rapid proliferation of the brown tree snake, an exotic, invasive species

Climate: tropical marine; generally warm and humid, moderated by northeast trade winds; dry season (January to June), rainy season (July to December); little seasonal temperature variation

Land use: *agricultural land:* 33.4% (2018 est.)
arable land: 1.9% (2018 est.)
permanent crops: 16.7% (2018 est.)
permanent pasture: 14.8% (2018 est.)
forest: 47.9% (2018 est.)
other: 18.7% (2018 est.)

Urbanization: *urban population:* 95.1% of total population (2022)
rate of urbanization: 0.84% annual rate of change (2020-25 est.)

Revenue from forest resources: *forest revenues:* 0% of GDP (2018 est.)
country comparison to the world: 171

Revenue from coal: *coal revenues:* 0% of GDP (2018 est.)
country comparison to the world: 105

Waste and recycling: *municipal solid waste generated annually:* 141,500 tons (2012 est.)
municipal solid waste recycled annually: 25,258 tons (2011 est.)
percent of municipal solid waste recycled: 17.9% (2011 est.)

GOVERNMENT

Country name: *conventional long form:* none
conventional short form: Guam
local long form: none
local short form: Guahan
abbreviation: GU
etymology: the native Chamorro name for the island "Guahan" (meaning "we have" or "ours") was changed to Guam in the 1898 Treaty of Paris, whereby Spain relinquished Guam, Cuba, Puerto Rico, and the Philippines to the US

Government type: unincorporated organized territory of the US with local self-government; republican form of territorial government with separate executive, legislative, and judicial branches

Dependency status: unincorporated organized territory of the US with policy relations between Guam and the Federal Government under the jurisdiction of the Office of Insular Affairs, US Department of the Interior, Washington, DC

Capital: *name:* Hagatna (Agana)
geographic coordinates: 13 28 N, 144 44 E
time difference: UTC+10 (15 hours ahead of Washington, DC, during Standard Time)
etymology: the name is derived from the Chamoru word "haga," meaning "blood", and may refer to the bloodlines of the various families that established the original settlement

Administrative divisions: none (territory of the US)

Independence: none (territory of the US)

National holiday: Discovery Day (or Magellan Day), first Monday in March (1521)

Constitution: *history:* effective 1 July 1950 (Guam Act of 1950 serves as a constitution)
amendments: amended many times, last in 2015

Legal system: common law modeled on US system; US federal laws apply

Citizenship: see United States

Suffrage: 18 years of age; universal; note - Guamanians are US citizens but do not vote in US presidential elections

Executive branch: *chief of state:* President Joseph R. BIDEN Jr. (since 20 January 2021); Vice President Kamala D. HARRIS (since 20 January 2021)
head of government: Governor Lourdes LEON GUERRERO (since 7 January 2019); Lieutenant Governor Josh TENORIO (since 7 January 2019)
cabinet: Cabinet appointed by the governor with the consent of the Legislature
elections/appointments: president and vice president indirectly elected on the same ballot by an Electoral College of 'electors' chosen from each state to serve a 4-year term (eligible for a second term); under the US Constitution, residents of unincorporated territories, such as Guam, do not vote in elections for US president and vice president; however, they may vote in Democratic and Republican presidential primary elections; governor and lieutenant governor elected on the same ballot by absolute majority vote in 2 rounds if needed for a 4-year term (eligible for 2 consecutive terms); election last held on 8 November 2022 (next to be held in November 2026)
election results: Lourdes LEON GUERRERO reelected governor; percent of vote - Lourdes LEON GUERRERO (Democratic Party) 55%, Felix CAMACHO (Republican Party) 44%; Josh TENORIO (Democratic Party) elected lieutenant governor

Legislative branch: *description:* unicameral Legislature of Guam or Liheslaturan Guahan (15 seats; members elected in a single countrywide constituency by simple majority vote to serve 2-year terms)

Guam directly elects 1 member by simple majority vote to serve a 2-year term as the delegate to the US House of Representatives; note - the delegate can vote when serving on a committee and when the House meets as the Committee of the Whole House, but not when legislation is submitted for a "full floor" House vote
elections: Guam Legislature - last held on 3 November 2020 (next to be held on 5 November 2022) delegate to the US House of Representatives - last held on 3 November 2020 with runoff on 17 November (next to be held on 5 November 2022)
election results: Guam Legislature - percent of vote by party - NA; seats by party - Democratic Party 10, Republican Party 5; composition - men 5, women 10, percent of women 66.7%

Guam delegate to the US House of Representatives - Democratic Party 1 (man)

Judicial branch: *highest court(s):* Supreme Court of Guam (consists of 3 justices); note - appeals beyond the Supreme Court of Guam are referred to the US Supreme Court
judge selection and term of office: justices appointed by the governor and confirmed by the Guam legislature; justices appointed for life subject to retention election every 10 years
subordinate courts: Superior Court of Guam - includes several divisions; US Federal District Court for the District of Guam (a US territorial court; appeals beyond this court are heard before the US Court of Appeals for the Ninth Circuit)

Political parties and leaders: Democratic Party [Anthony "Tony" M. BABAUTA]
Republican Party [Juan Carlos BENITEZ]

International organization participation: AOSIS (observer), IOC, PIF (observer), SPC, UPU

Diplomatic representation in the US: none (territory of the US)

Diplomatic representation from the US: *embassy:* none (territory of the US)

Flag description: territorial flag is dark blue with a narrow red border on all four sides; centered is a red-bordered, pointed, vertical ellipse containing a beach scene, a proa or outrigger canoe with sail, and a palm tree with the word GUAM superimposed in bold red letters; the proa is sailing in Agana Bay with the promontory of Punta Dos Amantes, near the capital, in the background; the shape of the central emblem is that of a Chamorro sling stone, used as a weapon for defense or hunting; blue represents the sea and red the blood shed in the struggle against oppression
note: the US flag is the national flag

National symbol(s): coconut tree; national colors: deep blue, red

National anthem: *name:* "Fanohge Chamoru" (Stand Ye Guamanians)
lyrics/music: Ramon Manalisay SABLAN [English], Lagrimas UNTALAN [Chamoru]/Ramon Manalisay SABLAN
note: adopted 1919; the local anthem is also known as "Guam Hymn"; as a territory of the United States, "The Star- Spangled Banner," which generally follows the playing of "Stand Ye Guamanians," is official (see United States)

ECONOMY

Economic overview: US national defense spending is the main driver of Guam's economy, followed closely by tourism and other services. Guam serves as a forward US base for the Western Pacific and is home to thousands of American military personnel. Total federal spending (defense and non-defense) amounted to $1.988 billion in 2016, or 34.2 of Guam's GDP. Of that total, federal grants and cover-over payments amounted to $3444.1 million in 2016, or 35.8% of Guam's total revenues for the fiscal year. In 2016, Guam's economy grew 0.3%. Despite slow growth, Guam's economy has been stable over the last decade. National defense spending cushions the island's economy against fluctuations in tourism. Service exports, mainly spending by foreign tourists in Guam, amounted to over $1 billion for the first time in 2016, or 17.8% of GDP.

Real GDP (purchasing power parity): $5.793 billion (2016 est.)
$5.697 billion (2015 est.)
$5.531 billion (2014 est.)
country comparison to the world: 171

Real GDP growth rate: 0.4% (2016 est.)
0.5% (2015 est.)
1.6% (2014 est.)
country comparison to the world: 185

Real GDP per capita: $35,600 (2016 est.)
$35,200 (2015 est.)
$34,400 (2014 est.)
country comparison to the world: 55

GDP (official exchange rate): $5.793 billion (2016 est.)

Inflation rate (consumer prices): 1% (2017 est.)
0% (2016 est.)
country comparison to the world: 65

GDP - composition, by sector of origin: *services:* 58.4% (2015 est.)

GDP - composition, by end use: *household consumption:* 56.2% (2016 est.)
government consumption: 55% (2016 est.)
investment in fixed capital: 20.6% (2016 est.)
exports of goods and services: 19.4% (2016 est.)
imports of goods and services: -51.2% (2016 est.)

Agricultural products: fruits, copra, vegetables; eggs, pork, poultry, beef

Industries: national defense, tourism, construction, transshipment services, concrete products, printing and publishing, food processing, textiles

Labor force: 73,210 (2016 est.)
note: includes only the civilian labor force
country comparison to the world: 183

Labor force - by occupation: *agriculture:* 0.3%
industry: 21.6%
services: 78.1% (2013 est.)

Unemployment rate: 4.5% (2017 est.)
3.9% (2016 est.)
country comparison to the world: 68

Unemployment, youth ages 15-24: *total:* 29.4%
male: 29.7%
female: 28.9% (2011 est.)
country comparison to the world: 35

Population below poverty line: 23% (2001 est.)

Budget: *revenues:* 1.24 billion (2016 est.)
expenditures: 1.299 billion (2016 est.)

Budget surplus (+) or deficit (-): -1% (of GDP) (2016 est.)
country comparison to the world: 78

Public debt: 22.1% of GDP (2016 est.)
32.1% of GDP (2013)
country comparison to the world: 184

Taxes and other revenues: 21.4% (of GDP) (2016 est.)
country comparison to the world: 139

Fiscal year: 1 October - 30 September

Exports: $1.124 billion (2016 est.)
$1.046 billion (2015 est.)
country comparison to the world: 175

Exports - partners: South Korea 31%, Hong Kong 27%, Taiwan 18%, Philippines 7% (2019)

Exports - commodities: scrap iron, electric batteries, gas turbines, scrap copper, beauty products (2019)

Imports: $2.964 billion (2016 est.)
$3.054 billion (2015 est.)
country comparison to the world: 159

Imports - partners: Singapore 33%, Japan 21%, South Korea 18%, Hong Kong 9%, Malaysia 6% (2019)

Imports - commodities: refined petroleum, trunks/cases, cars, insulated wire, broadcasting equipment (2019)

Exchange rates: the US dollar is used

ENERGY

Electricity access: *electrification - total population:* 100% (2020)

Electricity: *installed generating capacity:* 455,000 kW (2020 est.)
consumption: 1.683 billion kWh (2019 est.)
exports: 0 kWh (2020 est.)
imports: 0 kWh (2020 est.)
transmission/distribution losses: 85 million kWh (2019 est.)

Electricity generation sources: *fossil fuels:* 96% of total installed capacity (2020 est.)
solar: 4% of total installed capacity (2020 est.)

Petroleum: *total petroleum production:* 0 bbl/day (2021 est.) Data represented includes both Guam and Northern Mariana Islands
refined petroleum consumption: 2,100 bbl/day (2019 est.) Data represented includes both Guam and Northern Mariana Islands

Refined petroleum products - imports: 13,500 bbl/day (2015 est.)
country comparison to the world: 141

Carbon dioxide emissions: 1.828 million metric tonnes of CO_2 (2019 est.)
from petroleum and other liquids: 1.828 million metric tonnes of CO_2 (2019 est.)
country comparison to the world: 160

Energy consumption per capita: 152.767 million Btu/person (2019 est.)
country comparison to the world: 33

COMMUNICATIONS

Telephones - fixed lines: *total subscriptions:* 70,000 (2020 est.)
subscriptions per 100 inhabitants: 41 (2020 est.)
country comparison to the world: 147

Telephones - mobile cellular: *total subscriptions:* 98,000 (2009 est.)
subscriptions per 100 inhabitants: 62 (2009 est.)
country comparison to the world: 191

Telecommunication systems: *general assessment:* Guam's telecommunications companies provide important services that allow other businesses on island to operate; Guam plays a larger, and growing role, in global telecommunications infrastructure, the submarine fiber optic cables that land on Guam benefit island residents and the local economy; in the Asia-Pacific region the demand for 4G, 5G, and broadband access is rapidly increasing; the 11 submarine cables that currently land on Guam, connecting the U.S. to the Asia-Pacific region, are some of the more than 400 cables that are the backbone of global telecommunications, providing nearly all of the world's internet and phone service (2021)
domestic: fixed-line subscriptions 41 per 100 and 62 per 100 mobile-cellular subscriptions in 2004 (2020)
international: country code - 1-671; major landing points for Atisa, HANTRU1, HK-G, JGA-N, JGA-S, PIPE-1, SEA-US, SxS, Tata TGN-Pacific, AJC, GOKI, AAG, AJC and Mariana-Guam Cable submarine cables between Asia, Australia, and the US (Guam is a transpacific communications hub for major carriers linking the US and Asia); satellite earth stations - 2 Intelsat (Pacific Ocean) (2019)

Broadcast media: about a dozen TV channels, including digital channels; multi-channel cable TV services are available; roughly 20 radio stations

Internet country code: .gu

Internet users: *total:* 135,509 (2019 est.)
percent of population: 81% (2019 est.)

Broadband - fixed subscriptions: *total:* 3,000 (2020 est.)
subscriptions per 100 inhabitants: 2 (2020 est.)
country comparison to the world: 193

TRANSPORTATION

Civil aircraft registration country code prefix: N

Airports: *total:* 5 (2021)
country comparison to the world: 179

Airports - with paved runways: *total:* 4
over 3,047 m: 2
2,438 to 3,047 m: 1
914 to 1,523 m: 1 (2021)

Airports - with unpaved runways: *total:* 1
under 914 m: 1 (2021)

Roadways: *total:* 1,045 km (2008)
country comparison to the world: 185

Merchant marine: *total:* 3
by type: other 3 (2021)
country comparison to the world: 170

Ports and terminals: *major seaport(s):* Apra Harbor

MILITARY AND SECURITY

Military and security forces: Guam (US Army) National Guard

Military - note: defense is the responsibility of the US; the US military maintains over 6,000 personnel on Guam, including an air base, an air wing, and a naval installation command (2022)

TRANSNATIONAL ISSUES

Disputes - international: none

GUATEMALA

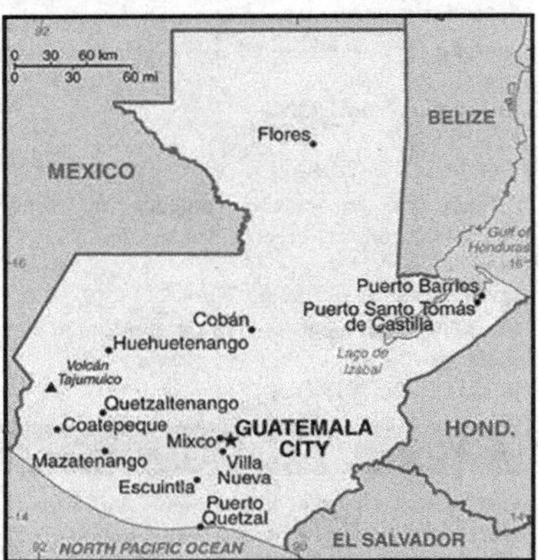

INTRODUCTION

Background: The Maya civilization flourished in Guatemala and surrounding regions during the first millennium A.D. After almost three centuries as a Spanish colony, Guatemala won its independence in 1821. During the second half of the 20th century, it experienced a variety of military and civilian governments, as well as a 36-year guerrilla war. In 1996, the government signed a peace agreement formally ending the internal conflict.

GEOGRAPHY

Location: Central America, bordering the North Pacific Ocean, between El Salvador and Mexico, and bordering the Gulf of Honduras (Caribbean Sea) between Honduras and Belize

Geographic coordinates: 15 30 N, 90 15 W

Map references: Central America and the Caribbean

Area: *total:* 108,889 sq km
land: 107,159 sq km
water: 1,730 sq km

Area - comparative: slightly smaller than Pennsylvania

Land boundaries: *total:* 1,667 km
border countries (4): Belize 266 km; El Salvador 199 km; Honduras 244 km; Mexico 958 km

Coastline: 400 km

Maritime claims: *territorial sea:* 12 nm
exclusive economic zone: 200 nm
continental shelf: 200-m depth or to the depth of exploitation

Climate: tropical; hot, humid in lowlands; cooler in highlands

Terrain: *two east-west trending mountain chains divide the country into three regions:* the mountainous highlands, the Pacific coast south of mountains, and the vast northern Peten lowlands

Elevation: *highest point:* Volcan Tajumulco (highest point in Central America) 4,220 m
lowest point: Pacific Ocean 0 m
mean elevation: 759 m

Natural resources: petroleum, nickel, rare woods, fish, chicle, hydropower

Land use: *agricultural land:* 41.2% (2018 est.)
arable land: 14.2% (2018 est.)
permanent crops: 8.8% (2018 est.)
permanent pasture: 18.2% (2018 est.)
forest: 33.6% (2018 est.)
other: 25.2% (2018 est.)

Irrigated land: 3,375 sq km (2012)

Major lakes (area sq km): *fresh water lake(s):* Lago de Izabal - 590 sq km

Population distribution: the vast majority of the populace resides in the southern half of the country, particularly in the mountainous regions; more than half of the population lives in rural areas

Natural hazards: numerous volcanoes in mountains, with occasional violent earthquakes; Caribbean coast extremely susceptible to hurricanes and other tropical storms
volcanism: significant volcanic activity in the Sierra Madre range; Santa Maria (3,772 m) has been deemed a Decade Volcano by the International Association of Volcanology and Chemistry of the Earth's Interior, worthy of study due to its explosive history and close proximity to human populations; Pacaya (2,552 m), which erupted in May 2010 causing an ashfall on Guatemala City and prompting evacuations, is one of the country's most active volcanoes with frequent eruptions since 1965; other historically active volcanoes include Acatenango, Almolonga, Atitlan, Fuego, and Tacana; see note 2 under "Geography - note"

Geography - note: *note 1:* despite having both eastern and western coastlines (Caribbean Sea and Pacific Ocean respectively), there are no natural harbors on the west coast
note 2: Guatemala is one of the countries along the Ring of Fire, a belt of active volcanoes and earthquake epicenters bordering the Pacific Ocean; up to 90% of the world's earthquakes and some 75% of the world's volcanoes occur within the Ring of Fire

PEOPLE AND SOCIETY

Population: 17,703,190 (2022 est.)

Nationality: *noun:* Guatemalan(s)
adjective: Guatemalan

Ethnic groups: Mestizo (mixed Amerindian-Spanish - in local Spanish called Ladino) 56%, Maya 41.7%, Xinca (Indigenous, non-Maya) 1.8%, African descent 0.2%, Garifuna (mixed West and Central African, Island Carib, and Arawak) 0.1%, foreign 0.2% (2018 est.)

Languages: Spanish (official) 69.9%, Maya languages 29.7% (Q'eqchi' 8.3%, K'iche 7.8%, Mam 4.4%, Kaqchikel 3%, Q'anjob'al 1.2%, Poqomchi' 1%, other 4%), other 0.4% (includes Xinca and Garifuna); note - the 2003 Law of National Languages officially recognized 23 indigenous languages, including 21 Maya languages, Xinca, and Garifuna (2018 est.)
major-language sample(s): La Libreta Informativa del Mundo, la fuente indispensable de información básica. (Spanish)

Religions: Roman Catholic 41.7%, Evangelical 38.8%, other 2.7%, atheist 0.1%, none 13.8%, unspecified 2.9% (2018 est.)

Demographic profile: Guatemala is a predominantly poor country that struggles in several areas of health and development, including infant, child, and maternal mortality, malnutrition, literacy, and contraceptive awareness and use. The country's large indigenous population is disproportionately affected. Guatemala is the most populous country in Central America and has the highest fertility rate in Latin America. It also has the highest population growth rate in Latin America, which is likely to continue because of its large reproductive-age population and high birth rate. Almost half of Guatemala's population is under age 19, making it the youngest population in Latin America. Guatemala's total fertility rate has slowly declined during the last few decades due in part to limited government-funded health programs. However, the birth rate is still more close to three children per woman and is markedly higher among its rural and indigenous populations.

Guatemalans have a history of emigrating legally and illegally to Mexico, the United States, and Canada because of a lack of economic opportunity, political instability, and natural disasters. Emigration, primarily to the United States, escalated during the 1960 to 1996 civil war and accelerated after a peace agreement was signed. Thousands of Guatemalans who fled to Mexico returned after the war, but labor migration to southern Mexico continues.

Age structure: *0-14 years:* 33.68% (male 2,944,145/female 2,833,432)
15-24 years: 19.76% (male 1,705,730/female 1,683,546)
25-54 years: 36.45% (male 3,065,933/female 3,186,816)
55-64 years: 5.41% (male 431,417/female 496,743)
65 years and over: 4.7% (male 363,460/female 442,066) (2020 est.)

Dependency ratios: *total dependency ratio:* 62.3
youth dependency ratio: 54.1
elderly dependency ratio: 8.2
potential support ratio: 12.2 (2020 est.)

Median age: *total:* 23.2 years
male: 22.6 years
female: 23.8 years (2020 est.)

Population growth rate: 1.58% (2022 est.)

Birth rate: 22.34 births/1,000 population (2022 est.)

Death rate: 4.91 deaths/1,000 population (2022 est.)

Net migration rate: -1.66 migrant(s)/1,000 population (2022 est.)

Population distribution: the vast majority of the populace resides in the southern half of the country, particularly in the mountainous regions; more than half of the population lives in rural areas

Urbanization: *urban population:* 52.7% of total population (2022)
rate of urbanization: 2.59% annual rate of change (2020-25 est.)

Major urban areas - population: 3.036 million GUATEMALA CITY (capital) (2022)

Sex ratio: *at birth:* 1.05 male(s)/female
0-14 years: 1.04 male(s)/female
15-24 years: 1.01 male(s)/female
25-54 years: 0.96 male(s)/female
55-64 years: 0.87 male(s)/female
65 years and over: 0.68 male(s)/female
total population: 0.98 male(s)/female (2022 est.)

Mother's mean age at first birth: 20.6 years (2014/15 est.)
note: data represents median age at first birth among women 25-49

Maternal mortality ratio: 95 deaths/100,000 live births (2017 est.)

Infant mortality rate: *total:* 26.18 deaths/1,000 live births
male: 29.51 deaths/1,000 live births
female: 22.69 deaths/1,000 live births (2022 est.)

Life expectancy at birth: *total population:* 72.91 years
male: 70.88 years
female: 75.04 years (2022 est.)

Total fertility rate: 2.62 children born/woman (2022 est.)

Contraceptive prevalence rate: 60.6% (2014/15)

Drinking water source: *improved: urban:* 97.9% of population
rural: 92.2% of population
total: 95% of population
unimproved: urban: 2.1% of population
rural: 8% of population
total: 5% of population (2020 est.)

Current health expenditure: 6.2% of GDP (2019)

Physicians density: 1.24 physicians/1,000 population (2020)

Hospital bed density: 0.4 beds/1,000 population (2017)

Sanitation facility access: *improved: urban:* 90.4% of population
rural: 66.3% of population
total: 78.8% of population
unimproved: urban: 9.6% of population
rural: 33.7% of population
total: 21.2% of population (2020 est.)

HIV/AIDS - adult prevalence rate: 0.2% (2020 est.)

Major infectious diseases: *degree of risk:* high (2020)
food or waterborne diseases: bacterial diarrhea, hepatitis A, and typhoid fever
vectorborne diseases: dengue fever and malaria

Obesity - adult prevalence rate: 21.2% (2016)

Alcohol consumption per capita: *total:* 1.63 liters of pure alcohol (2019 est.)
beer: 0.9 liters of pure alcohol (2019 est.)
wine: 0.05 liters of pure alcohol (2019 est.)
spirits: 0.68 liters of pure alcohol (2019 est.)
other alcohols: 0.01 liters of pure alcohol (2019 est.)

Tobacco use: *total:* 10.9% (2020 est.)
male: 20.1% (2020 est.)
female: 1.6% (2020 est.)

Children under the age of 5 years underweight: 12.4% (2014/15)

Education expenditures: 3.3% of GDP (2020 est.)

Literacy: *definition:* age 15 and over can read and write
total population: 80.8%
male: 85.3%
female: 76.7% (2018)

School life expectancy (primary to tertiary education): *total:* 11 years
male: 11 years
female: 10 years (2019)

Unemployment, youth ages 15-24: *total:* 4.6%
male: 4%
female: 5.7% (2019 est.)

ENVIRONMENT

Environment - current issues: deforestation in the Peten rainforest; soil erosion; water pollution

Environment - international agreements: *party to:* Antarctic Treaty, Biodiversity, Climate Change, Climate Change-Kyoto Protocol, Climate Change-Paris Agreement, Comprehensive Nuclear Test Ban, Desertification, Endangered Species, Environmental Modification, Hazardous Wastes, Law of the Sea,

Marine Dumping-London Convention, Marine Dumping-London Protocol, Nuclear Test Ban, Ozone Layer Protection, Ship Pollution, Tropical Timber 2006, Wetlands
signed, but not ratified: none of the selected agreements

Air pollutants: *particulate matter emissions:* 23.59 micrograms per cubic meter (2016 est.)
carbon dioxide emissions: 16.78 megatons (2016 est.)
methane emissions: 10.7 megatons (2020 est.)

Climate: tropical; hot, humid in lowlands; cooler in highlands

Land use: *agricultural land:* 41.2% (2018 est.)
arable land: 14.2% (2018 est.)
permanent crops: 8.8% (2018 est.)
permanent pasture: 18.2% (2018 est.)
forest: 33.6% (2018 est.)
other: 25.2% (2018 est.)

Urbanization: *urban population:* 52.7% of total population (2022)
rate of urbanization: 2.59% annual rate of change (2020-25 est.)

Revenue from forest resources: *forest revenues:* 0.78% of GDP (2018 est.)

Revenue from coal: *coal revenues:* 0% of GDP (2018 est.)

Waste and recycling: *municipal solid waste generated annually:* 2,756,741 tons (2015 est.)

Major lakes (area sq km): *fresh water lake(s):* Lago de Izabal - 590 sq km

Total water withdrawal: *municipal:* 835 million cubic meters (2017 est.)
industrial: 603.1 million cubic meters (2017 est.)
agricultural: 1.886 billion cubic meters (2017 est.)

Total renewable water resources: 127.91 billion cubic meters (2017 est.)

GOVERNMENT

Country name: *conventional long form:* Republic of Guatemala
conventional short form: Guatemala
local long form: Republica de Guatemala
local short form: Guatemala
etymology: the Spanish conquistadors used many native Americans as allies in their conquest of Guatemala; the site of their first capital (established in 1524), a former Maya settlement, was called "Quauhtemallan" by their Nahuatl-speaking Mexican allies, a name that means "land of trees" or "forested land", but which the Spanish pronounced "Guatemala"; the Spanish applied that name to a re-founded capital city three years later and eventually it became the name of the country

Government type: presidential republic

Capital: *name:* Guatemala City
geographic coordinates: 14 37 N, 90 31 W
time difference: UTC-6 (1 hour behind Washington, DC, during Standard Time)
etymology: the Spanish conquistadors used many native Americans as allies in their conquest of Guatemala; the site of their first capital (established in 1524), a former Maya settlement, was called "Quauhtemallan" by their Nahuatl-speaking Mexican allies, a name that means "land of trees" or "forested land", but which the Spanish pronounced "Guatemala"; the Spanish applied that name to a re-founded capital city three years later and eventually it became the name of the country

Administrative divisions: 22 departments (departamentos, singular - departamento); Alta Verapaz, Baja Verapaz, Chimaltenango, Chiquimula, El Progreso, Escuintla, Guatemala, Huehuetenango, Izabal, Jalapa, Jutiapa, Peten, Quetzaltenango, Quiche, Retalhuleu, Sacatepequez, San Marcos, Santa Rosa, Solola, Suchitepequez, Totonicapan, Zacapa

Independence: 15 September 1821 (from Spain)

National holiday: Independence Day, 15 September (1821)

Constitution: *history:* several previous; latest adopted 31 May 1985, effective 14 January 1986; suspended and reinstated in 1994
amendments: proposed by the president of the republic, by agreement of 10 or more deputies of Congress, by the Constitutional Court, or by public petition of at least 5,000 citizens; passage requires at least two-thirds majority vote by the Congress membership and approval by public referendum, referred to as "popular consultation"; constitutional articles such as national sovereignty, the republican form of government, limitations on those seeking the presidency, or presidential tenure cannot be amended; amended 1993

Legal system: civil law system; judicial review of legislative acts

International law organization participation: has not submitted an ICJ jurisdiction declaration; accepts ICCt jurisdiction

Citizenship: *citizenship by birth:* yes
citizenship by descent only: yes
dual citizenship recognized: yes
residency requirement for naturalization: 5 years with no absences of six consecutive months or longer or absences totaling more than a year

Suffrage: 18 years of age; universal; note - active duty members of the armed forces and police by law cannot vote and are restricted to their barracks on election day

Executive branch: *chief of state:* President Alejandro GIAMMATTEI (since 14 January 2020); Vice President Cesar Guillermo CASTILLO Reyes (since 14 January 2020); note - the president is both chief of state and head of government
head of government: President Alejandro GIAMMATTEI (since 14 January 2020); Vice President Cesar Guillermo CASTILLO Reyes (since 14 January 2020)
cabinet: Council of Ministers appointed by the president
elections/appointments: president and vice president directly elected on the same ballot by absolute majority popular vote in 2 rounds if needed for a 4-year term (not eligible for consecutive terms); election last held on 16 June 2019 with a runoff on 11 August 2019 (next to be held in June 2023)
election results: 2019: Alejandro GIAMMATTEI elected president; percent of vote in first round - Sandra TORRES (UNE) 25.5%, Alejandro GIAMMATTEI (VAMOS) 14%, Edmond MULET (PHG) 11.2%, Thelma CABRERA (MLP) 10.4%, Roberto ARZU (PAN-PODEMOS) 6.1%, other 32.8%; percent of vote in second round - Alejandro GIAMMATTEI (VAMOS) 58%, Sandra TORRES (UNE) 42%
2015: Jimmy Ernesto MORALES Cabrera elected president in second round; percent of vote in first round - Jimmy Ernesto MORALES Cabrera (FNC) 23.9%, Sandra TORRES (UNE) 19.8%, Manuel BALDIZON (LIDER) 19.6%, other 36.7%; percent of vote in second round - Jimmy Ernesto MORALES Cabrera 67.4%, Sandra TORRES 32.6%

Legislative branch: *description:* unicameral Congress of the Republic or Congreso de la Republica (160 seats; 128 members directly elected in multi-seat constituencies in the country's 22 departments and 32 directly elected in a single nationwide constituency by closed party-list proportional representation vote, using the D'Hondt method; members serve 4-year terms)
elections: last held on 16 June 2019 (next to be held on June 2023)
election results: percent of vote by party - NA; seats by party - UNE 52, VAMOS 17, UCN 12, VALOR 9, BIEN 8, FCN-NACION 8, SEMILLA 7, TODOS 7, VIVA 7, CREO 6, PHG 6, VICTORIA 4, Winaq 4, PC 3, PU 3, URNG 3, PAN 2, MLP 1, PODEMOS 1; composition - men 129, women 31, percent of women 19.4%

Judicial branch: *highest court(s):* Supreme Court of Justice or Corte Suprema de Justicia (consists of 13 magistrates, including the court president and organized into 3 chambers); note - the court president also supervises trial judges countrywide; note - the Constitutional Court or Corte de Constitucionalidad of Guatemala resides outside the country's judicial system; its sole purpose is the interpretation of the constitution and to see that the laws and regulations are not superior to the constitution (consists of 5 titular magistrates and 5 substitute magistrates)
judge selection and term of office: Supreme Court magistrates elected by the Congress of the Republic from candidates proposed by the Postulation Committee, an independent body of deans of the country's university law schools, representatives of the country's law associations, and representatives of the Courts of Appeal; magistrates elected for concurrent, renewable 5-year terms; Constitutional Court judges - 1 elected by the Congress of the Republic, 1 by the Supreme Court, 1 by the president of the republic, 1 by the (public) University of San Carlos, and 1 by the Assembly of the College of Attorneys and Notaries; judges elected for renewable, consecutive 5-year terms; the presidency of the court rotates among the magistrates for a single 1-year term
subordinate courts: Appellate Courts of Accounts, Contentious Administrative Tribunal, courts of appeal, first instance courts, child and adolescence courts, minor or peace courts

Political parties and leaders: Bienestar Nacional or BIEN [Fidel REYES LEE]
Citizen Prosperity or PC [Hernan MEJIA and Jorge GARCIA SILVA]
Commitment, Renewal, and Order or CREO [Rodolfo NEUTZE]
Everyone Together for Guatemala or TODOS [Felipe ALEJOS]
Guatemalan National Revolutionary Unity or URNG-MAIZ or URNG [Walter FELIX]
Humanist Party of Guatemala or PHG [Rudio MERIDA]
Movement for the Liberation of Peoples or MLP [Thelma CABRERA and Vincenta JERONIMO]
Movimiento Semilla or SEMILLA [Samuel PEREZ Alvarez]
National Advancement Party or PAN [Manuel CONDE]

National Convergence Front or FCN-NACION [Javier HERNANDEZ]
National Unity for Hope or UNE [Sandra TORRES and Jorge VARGAS]
Nationalist Change Union or UCN [Carlos ROJAS and Sofia HERNANDEZ] (dissolved 16 December 2021)
PODEMOS [Jose LEON]
Political Movement Winaq or Winaq [Sonia GUTIERREZ Raguay]
Value or VALOR [Zury RIOS and Lucrecia MARROQUIN]
Vamos por una Guatemala Diferente or VAMOS [Alejandro GIAMMATTEI]
Victory or VICTORIA [Abraham RIVERA and his four sons Amilcar, Juan, Manuel, and Edgar]
Vision with Values or VIVA [Armando Damian CASTILLO Alvarado]

International organization participation: BCIE, CACM, CD, CELAC, EITI (compliant country), FAO, G-24, G-77, IADB, IAEA, IBRD, ICAO, ICC (national committees), ICCt (signatory), ICRM, IDA, IFAD, IFC, IFRCS, IHO, ILO, IMF, IMO, Interpol, IOC, IOM, IPU, ISO (correspondent), ITSO, ITU, ITUC (NGOs), LAES, LAIA (observer), MIGA, MINUSTAH, MONUSCO, NAM, OAS, OPANAL, OPCW, Pacific Alliance (observer), PCA, Petrocaribe, SICA, UN, UNCTAD, UNESCO, UNIDO, UNIFIL, Union Latina, UNISFA, UNITAR, UNMISS, UNOCI, UNWTO, UPU, WCO, WFTU (NGOs), WHO, WIPO, WMO, WTO

Diplomatic representation in the US: *chief of mission:* Ambassador Alfonso Jose QUINONEZ LEMUS (since 17 July 2020)
chancery: 2220 R Street NW, Washington, DC 20008
telephone: [1] (202) 745-4953
FAX: [1] (202) 745-1908
email address and website:
infoembaguateeuu@minex.gob.gt
consulate(s) general: Atlanta, Chicago, Del Rio (TX), Denver, Houston, Los Angeles, McAllen (TX), Miami, New York, Oklahoma City, Philadelphia, Phoenix, Providence (RI), Raleigh (NC), San Bernardino (CA), San Francisco, Seattle
consulate(s): Lake Worth (FL), Silver Spring (MD), Tucson (AZ)

Diplomatic representation from the US: *chief of mission:* Ambassador William W. POPP (since 13 August 2020)
embassy: Avenida Reforma 7-01, Zone 10, Guatemala City
mailing address: 3190 Guatemala Place, Washington DC 20521-3190
telephone: [502] 2326-4000
FAX: [502] 2326-4654
email address and website:
AmCitsGuatemala@state.gov
https://gt.usembassy.gov/

Flag description: three equal vertical bands of light blue (hoist side), white, and light blue, with the coat of arms centered in the white band; the coat of arms includes a green and red quetzal (the national bird) representing liberty and a scroll bearing the inscription LIBERTAD 15 DE SEPTIEMBRE DE 1821 (the original date of independence from Spain) all superimposed on a pair of crossed rifles signifying Guatemala's willingness to defend itself and a pair of crossed swords representing honor and framed by a laurel wreath symbolizing victory; the blue bands represent the Pacific Ocean and Caribbean Sea; the white band denotes peace and purity
note: one of only two national flags featuring a firearm, the other is Mozambique

National symbol(s): quetzal (bird); national colors: blue, white

National anthem: *name:* "Himno Nacional de Guatemala" (National Anthem of Guatemala)
lyrics/music: Jose Joaquin PALMA/Rafael Alvarez OVALLE
note: adopted 1897, modified lyrics adopted 1934; Cuban poet Jose Joaquin PALMA anonymously submitted lyrics to a public contest calling for a national anthem; his authorship was not discovered until 1911

National heritage: *total World Heritage Sites:* 3 (2 cultural, 1 mixed)
selected World Heritage Site locales: Antigua Guatemala (c); Tikal National Park (m); Archaeological Park and Ruins of Quirigua (c)

ECONOMY

Economic overview: Guatemala is the most populous country in Central America with a GDP per capita roughly half the average for Latin America and the Caribbean. The agricultural sector accounts for 13.5% of GDP and 31% of the labor force; key agricultural exports include sugar, coffee, bananas, and vegetables. Guatemala is the top remittance recipient in Central America as a result of Guatemala's large expatriate community in the US. These inflows are a primary source of foreign income, equivalent to two-thirds of the country's exports and about a tenth of its GDP.

The 1996 peace accords, which ended 36 years of civil war, removed a major obstacle to foreign investment, and Guatemala has since pursued important reforms and macroeconomic stabilization. The Dominican Republic-Central America Free Trade Agreement (CAFTA-DR) entered into force in July 2006, spurring increased investment and diversification of exports, with the largest increases in ethanol and non-traditional agricultural exports. While CAFTA-DR has helped improve the investment climate, concerns over security, the lack of skilled workers, and poor infrastructure continue to hamper foreign direct investment.

The distribution of income remains highly unequal with the richest 20% of the population accounting for more than 51% of Guatemala's overall consumption. More than half of the population is below the national poverty line, and 23% of the population lives in extreme poverty. Poverty among indigenous groups, which make up more than 40% of the population, averages 79%, with 40% of the indigenous population living in extreme poverty. Nearly one-half of Guatemala's children under age five are chronically malnourished, one of the highest malnutrition rates in the world.

Real GDP (purchasing power parity): $141.5 billion (2020 est.)
$143.68 billion (2019 est.)
$138.33 billion (2018 est.)
note: data are in 2017 dollars

Real GDP growth rate: 2.8% (2017 est.)
3.1% (2016 est.)
4.1% (2015 est.)

Real GDP per capita: $8,400 (2020 est.)
$8,700 (2019 est.)
$8,500 (2018 est.)
note: data are in 2017 dollars

GDP (official exchange rate): $76.678 billion (2019 est.)

Inflation rate (consumer prices): 3.7% (2019 est.)
3.7% (2018 est.)
4.4% (2017 est.)

Credit ratings:

Fitch rating: BB- (2020)

Moody's rating: Ba1 (2010)

Standard & Poors rating: BB- (2017)
note: The year refers to the year in which the current credit rating was first obtained.

GDP - composition, by sector of origin: *agriculture:* 13.3% (2017 est.)
industry: 23.4% (2017 est.)
services: 63.2% (2017 est.)

GDP - composition, by end use: *household consumption:* 86.3% (2017 est.)
government consumption: 9.7% (2017 est.)
investment in fixed capital: 12.3% (2017 est.)
investment in inventories: -0.2% (2017 est.)
exports of goods and services: 18.8% (2017 est.)
imports of goods and services: -26.9% (2017 est.)

Agricultural products: sugar cane, bananas, oil palm fruit, maize, melons, potatoes, milk, plantains, pineapples, rubber

Industries: sugar, textiles and clothing, furniture, chemicals, petroleum, metals, rubber, tourism

Industrial production growth rate: 1.8% (2017 est.)

Labor force: 6.664 million (2017 est.)

Labor force - by occupation: *agriculture:* 31.4%
industry: 12.8%
services: 55.8% (2017 est.)

Unemployment rate: 2.3% (2017 est.)
2.4% (2016 est.)

Unemployment, youth ages 15-24: *total:* 4.6%
male: 4%
female: 5.7% (2019 est.)

Population below poverty line: 59.3% (2014 est.)

Gini Index coefficient - distribution of family income: 48.3 (2014 est.)
56 (2011)

Household income or consumption by percentage share: *lowest 10%:* 1.6%
highest 10%: 38.4% (2014)

Budget: *revenues:* 8.164 billion (2017 est.)
expenditures: 9.156 billion (2017 est.)

Budget surplus (+) or deficit (-): -1.3% (of GDP) (2017 est.)

Public debt: 24.7% of GDP (2017 est.)
24.5% of GDP (2016 est.)

Taxes and other revenues: 10.8% (of GDP) (2017 est.)

Fiscal year: calendar year

Current account balance: $1.134 billion (2017 est.)
$1.023 billion (2016 est.)

Exports: $13.12 billion (2020 est.) note: data are in current year dollars
$13.6 billion (2019 est.) note: data are in current year dollars
$13.35 billion (2018 est.) note: data are in current year dollars

Exports - partners: United States 33%, El Salvador 12%, Honduras 8%, Mexico 5%, Nicaragua 5% (2019)

Exports - commodities: bananas, raw sugar, coffee, cardamom, palm oil (2019)

Imports: $19.3 billion (2020 est.) note: data are in current year dollars
$21.52 billion (2019 est.) note: data are in current year dollars
$21.17 billion (2018 est.) note: data are in current year dollars

Imports - partners: United States 36%, China 12%, Mexico 11%, El Salvador 5% (2019)

Imports - commodities: refined petroleum, broadcasting equipment, packaged medicines, cars, delivery trucks (2019)

Reserves of foreign exchange and gold: $11.77 billion (31 December 2017 est.)
$9.156 billion (31 December 2016 est.)

Debt - external: $22.92 billion (31 December 2017 est.)
$21.45 billion (31 December 2016 est.)

Exchange rates: quetzales (GTQ) per US dollar -
7.323 (2017 est.)
7.5999 (2016 est.)
7.5999 (2015 est.)
7.6548 (2014 est.)
7.7322 (2013 est.)

ENERGY

Electricity access: *electrification - total population:* 92% (2019)
electrification - urban areas: 99% (2019)
electrification - rural areas: 85% (2019)

Electricity: *installed generating capacity:* 5.185 million kW (2020 est.)
consumption: 10,793,650,000 kWh (2019 est.)
exports: 2.19 billion kWh (2019 est.)
imports: 1.141 billion kWh (2019 est.)
transmission/distribution losses: 1.587 billion kWh (2019 est.)

Electricity generation sources: *fossil fuels:* 39.4% of total installed capacity (2020 est.)
solar: 1.5% of total installed capacity (2020 est.)
wind: 2.1% of total installed capacity (2020 est.)
hydroelectricity: 38% of total installed capacity (2020 est.)
geothermal: 2.2% of total installed capacity (2020 est.)
biomass and waste: 17% of total installed capacity (2020 est.)

Coal: *production:* 0 metric tons (2020 est.)
consumption: 2.28 million metric tons (2020 est.)
exports: 0 metric tons (2020 est.)
imports: 2.376 million metric tons (2020 est.)
proven reserves: 0 metric tons (2019 est.)

Petroleum: *total petroleum production:* 10,300 bbl/day (2021 est.)
refined petroleum consumption: 112,600 bbl/day (2019 est.)
crude oil and lease condensate exports: 6,700 bbl/day (2018 est.)
crude oil and lease condensate imports: 0 bbl/day (2018 est.)
crude oil estimated reserves: 86.1 million barrels (2021 est.)

Refined petroleum products - production: 1,162 bbl/day (2015 est.)

Refined petroleum products - exports: 10,810 bbl/day (2015 est.)

Refined petroleum products - imports: 97,900 bbl/day (2015 est.)

Carbon dioxide emissions: 19.041 million metric tonnes of CO2 (2019 est.)
from coal and metallurgical coke: 5.037 million metric tonnes of CO2 (2019 est.)
from petroleum and other liquids: 14.004 million metric tonnes of CO2 (2019 est.)

Energy consumption per capita: 19.411 million Btu/person (2019 est.)

COMMUNICATIONS

Telephones - fixed lines: *total subscriptions:* 2,272,467 (2020 est.)
subscriptions per 100 inhabitants: 13 (2020 est.)

Telephones - mobile cellular: *total subscriptions:* 20,390,671 (2020 est.)
subscriptions per 100 inhabitants: 114 (2020 est.)

Telecommunication systems: *general assessment:* Guatemala's telecom infrastructure has suffered from years of under investment from state and provincial government; the poor state of fixed-line infrastructure has led to Guatemala having one of the lowest fixed-line teledensities in the region; in many rural regions of the country there is no fixed-line access available, and so mobile services are adopted by necessity; private investment has been supported by government and regulatory efforts, resulting in a steady growth in the number of fixed lines which has supported growth in the fixed broadband segment; delays in launching LTE services left the country lagging behind in the development of mobile broadband and the benefits which it can bring to the country's social and economic growth; two new submarine cables are due for completion by 2022; improved international connectivity should drive further uptake of both fixed and mobile broadband services; intense competition among the networks has helped to improve services and lower prices for end-users; given the commercial impetus of networks, insufficient government financial investment has resulted in many regional areas remaining with poor or non-existent services; the country benefits from one of the most open regulatory frameworks, with all telecom sectors having been open to competition since 1996; mobile subscriptions are on par with the regional average, though the slower growth in the mobile subscriber base suggests a level of market saturation, with the emphasis among networks being on generating revenue via mobile data services (2021)
domestic: fixed-line teledensity roughly 13 per 100 persons; fixed-line investments are concentrating on improving rural connectivity; mobile-cellular teledensity about 114 per 100 persons (2020)
international: country code - 502; landing points for the ARCOS, AMX-1, American Movil-Texius West Coast Cable and the SAm-1 fiber-optic submarine cable system that, together, provide connectivity to South and Central America, parts of the Caribbean, and the US; connected to Central American Microwave System; satellite earth station - 1 Intelsat (Atlantic Ocean) (2019)

Broadcast media: 4 privately owned national terrestrial TV channels dominate TV broadcasting; multi-channel satellite and cable services are available; 1 government-owned radio station and hundreds of privately owned radio stations (2019)

Internet country code: .gt

Internet users: *total:* 8,429,167 (2020 est.)
percent of population: 50% (2020 est.)

Broadband - fixed subscriptions: *total:* 612,000 (2020 est.)
subscriptions per 100 inhabitants: 3 (2020 est.)

TRANSPORTATION

National air transport system: *number of registered air carriers:* 3 (2020)
inventory of registered aircraft operated by air carriers: 5
annual passenger traffic on registered air carriers: 145,795 (2018)
annual freight traffic on registered air carriers: 110,000 (2018) mt-km

Civil aircraft registration country code prefix: TG

Airports: *total:* 291 (2021)

Airports - with paved runways: *total:* 16
2,438 to 3,047 m: 2
1,524 to 2,437 m: 4
914 to 1,523 m: 6
under 914 m: 4 (2021)

Airports - with unpaved runways: *total:* 275
2,438 to 3,047 m: 1
1,524 to 2,437 m: 2
914 to 1,523 m: 77
under 914 m: 195 (2021)

Heliports: 1 (2021)

Pipelines: 480 km oil (2013)

Railways: *total:* 800 km (2018)
narrow gauge: 800 km (2018) 0.914-m gauge
note: despite the existence of a railway network, all rail service was suspended in 2007 and no passenger or freight train currently runs in the country (2018)

Roadways: *total:* 17,440 km (2020)
paved: 7,458 km (2020)
unpaved: 9,982 km (2020) (includes 4,548 km of rural roads)

Waterways: 990 km (2012) (260 km navigable year round; additional 730 km navigable during high-water season)

Merchant marine: *total:* 9
by type: oil tanker 1, other 8 (2021)

Ports and terminals: *major seaport(s):* Puerto Quetzal, Santo Tomas de Castilla

MILITARY AND SECURITY

Military and security forces: Army of Guatemala (Ejercito de Guatemala): Land Forces (Fuerzas de Tierra), Naval Forces (Fuerzas de Mar), and Air Force (Fuerza de Aire); Ministry of Government (Interior): National Civil Police (Policia Nacional Civil; includes paramilitary units) (2022)

Military expenditures: 0.4% of GDP (2022 est.)
0.4% of GDP (2021)
0.4% of GDP (2020)
0.4% of GDP (2019) (approximately $530 million)
0.4% of GDP (2018) (approximately $470 million)

Military and security service personnel strengths: information varies; approximately 20,000 active military personnel (18,000 Land Forces; 1,000 Naval Forces; 1,000 Air Forces); approximately 30,000 National Civil Police (2022)

Military equipment inventories and acquisitions: the Guatemalan military inventory is small and mostly comprised of older US equipment; since 2010, Guatemala has received small amounts of equipment from several countries, including the US (2022)

Military service age and obligation: all male citizens between the ages of 18 and 50 are eligible for military service; in practice, most of the force is volunteer, however, a selective draft system is employed, resulting in a small portion of 17-21 year-olds being conscripted; conscript service obligation varies from 1 to 2 years; women may volunteer (2022)
note: as of 2017, women comprised up to 10% of the active military

Military deployments: 155 Democratic Republic of the Congo (MONUSCO) (May 2022)

Military - note: since the 2000s, the Guatemalan Government has used the Army to support the National Civil Police in internal security operations (as permitted by the constitution) to combat organized crime, gang violence, and narco-trafficking

the military held power during most of Guatemala's 36-year civil war (1960-1996) and conducted a campaign of widespread violence and repression, particularly against the country's majority indigenous population; more than 200,000 people were estimated to have been killed or disappeared during the conflict (2022)

TRANSNATIONAL ISSUES

Disputes - international: *Guatemala-Belize:* Demarcated but insecure boundary due to Guatemala's claims to more than half of Belizean territory. Line of Adjacency operates in lieu of an international boundary to control influx of Guatemalan squatters onto Belizean territory. Smuggling, narcotics trafficking, and human trafficking for sexual exploitation and debt bondage are all problems. Belize lacks resources to detect and extradite impoverished Guatemalan peasants squatting in Belizean rain forests in the remote border areas. Both countries agreed in April 2012 to hold simultaneous referenda, scheduled for 6 October 2013, to decide whether to refer the dispute to the ICJ for binding resolution, but this vote was suspended indefinitely. At present, Belize and Honduras 12-nm territorial sea claims close off Guatemalan access to Caribbean in the Bahia de Amatique. Maritime boundary remains unresolved pending further negotiation.
Guatemala-Mexico: Mexico must deal with thousands of impoverished Guatemalans and other Central Americans who cross the porous border looking for work in Mexico and the US.

Refugees and internally displaced persons: *IDPs:* 243,000 (more than three decades of internal conflict that ended in 1996 displaced mainly the indigenous Maya population and rural peasants; ongoing drug cartel and gang violence) (2021)

Illicit drugs: a major transit country for illegal drugs destined for the United States with increasing cultivation originating from Guatemala; farmers cultivate opium poppy and cannabis

GUERNSEY

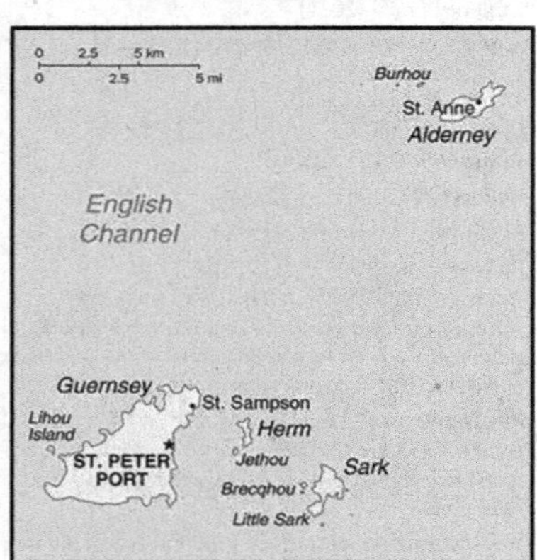

INTRODUCTION

Background: Guernsey and the other Channel Islands represent the last remnants of the medieval Duchy of Normandy, which held sway in both France and England. The islands were the only British soil occupied by German troops in World War II. The Bailiwick of Guernsey consists of the main island of Guernsey and a number of smaller islands including Alderney, Sark, Herm, Jethou, Brecqhou, and Lihou. The Bailiwick is a self-governing British Crown dependency that is not part of the UK. However, the UK Government is constitutionally responsible for its defense and international representation.

GEOGRAPHY

Location: Western Europe, islands in the English Channel, northwest of France

Geographic coordinates: 49 28 N, 2 35 W

Map references: Europe

Area: *total:* 78 sq km
land: 78 sq km
water: 0 sq km
note: includes Alderney, Guernsey, Herm, Sark, and some other smaller islands
country comparison to the world: 227

Area - comparative: about one-half the size of Washington, DC

Land boundaries: *total:* 0 km

Coastline: 50 km

Maritime claims: *territorial sea:* 12 nm
exclusive fishing zone: 12 nm

Climate: temperate with mild winters and cool summers; about 50% of days are overcast

Terrain: mostly flat with low hills in southwest

Elevation: *highest point:* Le Moulin on Sark 114 m
lowest point: English Channel 0 m

Natural resources: cropland

Natural hazards: very large tidal variation and fast currents can make local waters dangerous

Geography - note: large, deepwater harbor at Saint Peter Port

PEOPLE AND SOCIETY

Population: 67,491 (2022 est.)
country comparison to the world: 203

Nationality: *noun:* Channel Islander(s)
adjective: Channel Islander

Ethnic groups: Guernsey 53.1%, UK and Ireland 23.9%, Portugal 2.2%, Latvia 1.5%, other Europe 2.8%, other 4.4%, unspecified 11.4% (2020 est.)
note: data represent population by country of birth; the native population is of British and Norman-French descent

Languages: English, French, Norman-French dialect spoken in country districts

Religions: Protestant (Anglican, Presbyterian, Baptist, Congregational, Methodist), Roman Catholic

Age structure: *0-14 years:* 14.5% (male 5,008/female 4,712)
15-24 years: 10.58% (male 3,616/female 3,476)
25-54 years: 40.73% (male 13,821/female 13,492)
55-64 years: 13.96% (male 4,635/female 4,728)
65 years and over: 20.23% (male 6,229/female 7,335) (2020 est.)

Dependency ratios: *total dependency ratio:* 49
youth dependency ratio: 22.3
elderly dependency ratio: 26.7
potential support ratio: 3.7 (2020 est.)
note: data represent Guernsey and Jersey

Median age: *total:* 44.3 years
male: 43 years
female: 45.6 years (2020 est.)
country comparison to the world: 17

Population growth rate: 0.23% (2022 est.)
country comparison to the world: 177

Birth rate: 9.75 births/1,000 population (2022 est.)
country comparison to the world: 191

Death rate: 9.17 deaths/1,000 population (2022 est.)
country comparison to the world: 55

Net migration rate: 1.7 migrant(s)/1,000 population (2022 est.)
country comparison to the world: 55

Urbanization: *urban population:* 31.1% of total population (2022)
rate of urbanization: 0.68% annual rate of change (2020-25 est.)
note: data include Guernsey and Jersey

Major urban areas - population: 16,000 SAINT PETER PORT (capital) (2018)

Sex ratio: *at birth:* 1.05 male(s)/female
0-14 years: 1.06 male(s)/female
15-24 years: 1.04 male(s)/female
25-54 years: 1.03 male(s)/female
55-64 years: 0.98 male(s)/female
65 years and over: 0.73 male(s)/female
total population: 0.99 male(s)/female (2022 est.)

Infant mortality rate: *total:* 3.36 deaths/1,000 live births
male: 3.85 deaths/1,000 live births
female: 2.83 deaths/1,000 live births (2022 est.)
country comparison to the world: 202

Life expectancy at birth: *total population:* 83.23 years
male: 80.52 years
female: 86.07 years (2022 est.)
country comparison to the world: 11

Total fertility rate: 1.58 children born/woman (2022 est.)
country comparison to the world: 189

Drinking water source: *improved: total:* 94.2% of population
unimproved: total: 5.9% of population (2017 est.)
note: includes data for Jersey

Sanitation facility access: *improved: total:* 98% of population
unimproved: total: 1.2% of population (2017)
note: data represent Guernsey and Jersey

ENVIRONMENT

Environment - current issues: coastal erosion, coastal flooding; declining biodiversity due to land abandonment and succession to scrub or woodland

Climate: temperate with mild winters and cool summers; about 50% of days are overcast

Urbanization: *urban population:* 31.1% of total population (2022)
rate of urbanization: 0.68% annual rate of change (2020-25 est.)
note: data include Guernsey and Jersey

Waste and recycling: *municipal solid waste generated annually:* 178,933 tons (2016 est.)
municipal solid waste recycled annually: 50,871 tons (2016 est.)
percent of municipal solid waste recycled: 28.4% (2016 est.)
note: data include combined totals for Guernsey and Jersey.

GOVERNMENT

Country name: *conventional long form:* Bailiwick of Guernsey
conventional short form: Guernsey
former: Norman Isles
etymology: the name is of Old Norse origin, but the meaning of the root "Guern(s)" is uncertain; the "-ey" ending means "island"

Government type: parliamentary democracy (States of Deliberation)

Dependency status: British crown dependency

Capital: *name:* Saint Peter Port
geographic coordinates: 49 27 N, 2 32 W
time difference: UTC 0 (5 hours ahead of Washington, DC, during Standard Time)
daylight saving time: +1hr, begins last Sunday in March; ends last Sunday in October
etymology: Saint Peter Port is the name of the town and its surrounding parish; the "port" distinguishes this parish from that of Saint Peter on the other side of the island

Administrative divisions: none (British Crown dependency); there are no first-order administrative divisions as defined by the US Government, but there are 10 parishes: Castel, Forest, Saint Andrew, Saint Martin, Saint Peter Port, Saint Pierre du Bois, Saint Sampson, Saint Saviour, Torteval, Vale
note: two additional parishes for Guernsey are sometimes listed - Saint Anne on the island of Alderney and Saint Peter on the island of Sark - but they are generally not included in the enumeration of parishes

Independence: none (British Crown dependency)

National holiday: Liberation Day, 9 May (1945)

Constitution: *history:* unwritten; includes royal charters, statutes, and common law and practice
amendments: new laws or changes to existing laws are initiated by the States of Deliberation; passage requires majority vote; many laws have been passed; in 2019, 60 laws were passed

Legal system: customary legal system based on Norman customary law; includes elements of the French civil code and English common law

Citizenship: see United Kingdom

Suffrage: 16 years of age; universal

Executive branch: *chief of state:* King CHARLES III (since 8 September 2022); represented by Lieutenant-Governor Vice Admiral Ian CORDER (since 14 March 2016)
head of government: Chief Minister Peter FERBRACHE (since 16 October 2020); Bailiff Richard McMAHON (since 11 May 2020); note - the chief minister is the president of the Policy and Resources Committee and is the de facto head of government; the Policy and Resources Committee, elected by the States of Deliberation, functions as the executive; the 5 members all have equal voting rights
cabinet: none
elections/appointments: the monarchy is hereditary; lieutenant governor and bailiff appointed by the monarch; chief minister, who is the president of the Policy and Resources Committee indirectly elected by the States of Deliberation for a 4-year term; last held on 6 May 2016 (next to be held in June 2020)
election results: 2020: Peter FERBRACHE (independent) elected president of the Policy and Resources Committee and chief minister: percent of States of Guernsey vote - 57.5%
2016: Gavin ST. PIER (independent) elected president of the Policy and Resources Committee and chief minister

Legislative branch: *description:* unicameral States of Deliberation (40 seats; 38 People's Deputies and 2 representatives of the States of Alderney; members directly elected by majority vote to serve 4-year terms); note - non-voting members include the bailiff (presiding officer), attorney-general, and solicitor-general
elections: last held on 7 October 2020 (next to be held in June 2025)
election results: percent of vote - NA; seats - independent 38; composition - men 32, women 8, percent of women 20%

Judicial branch: *highest court(s):* Guernsey Court of Appeal (consists of the Bailiff of Guernsey, who is the ex-officio president of the Guernsey Court of Appeal, and at least 12 judges); Royal Court (organized into 3 divisions - Full Court sits with 1 judge and 7 to 12 jurats acting as judges of fact, Ordinary Court sits with 1 judge and normally 3 jurats, and Matrimonial Causes Division sits with 1 judge and 4 jurats); note - appeals beyond Guernsey courts are heard by the Judicial Committee of the Privy Council (in London)
judge selection and term of office: Royal Court Bailiff, Deputy Bailiff, and Court of Appeal justices appointed by the British Crown and hold office at Her Majesty's pleasure; jurats elected by the States of Election, a body chaired by the Bailiff and a number of jurats
subordinate courts: Court of Alderney; Court of the Seneschal of Sark; Magistrates' Court (includes Juvenile Court); Contracts Court; Ecclesiastical Court; Court of Chief Pleas

Political parties and leaders: none; all independents

International organization participation: UPU

Diplomatic representation in the US: none (British crown dependency)

Diplomatic representation from the US: *embassy:* none (British crown dependency)

Flag description: white with the red cross of Saint George (patron saint of England) extending to the edges of the flag and a yellow equal-armed cross of William the Conqueror superimposed on the Saint George cross; the red cross represents the old ties with England and the fact that Guernsey is a British Crown dependency; the gold cross is a replica of the one used by Duke William of Normandy at the Battle of Hastings in 1066

National symbol(s): Guernsey cow, donkey; national colors: red, white, yellow

National anthem: *name:* "Sarnia Cherie" (Guernsey Dear)
lyrics/music: George DEIGHTON/Domencio SANTANGELO
note: adopted 1911; serves as a local anthem; as a British crown dependency, "God Save the King" is official (see United Kingdom)

ECONOMY

Economic overview: Financial services accounted for about 21% of employment and about 32% of total income in 2016 in this tiny, prosperous Channel Island economy. Construction, manufacturing, and horticulture, mainly tomatoes and cut flowers, have been declining. Financial services, professional services, tourism, retail, and the public sector have been growing. Light tax and death duties make Guernsey a popular offshore financial center.

Real GDP (purchasing power parity): $3.465 billion (2015 est.)
$3.451 billion (2014 est.)
$3.42 billion (2013 est.)
note: data are in 2015 dollars
country comparison to the world: 187

Real GDP growth rate: 0.4% (2015 est.)
1.2% (2014 est.)
4.2% (2012 est.)
country comparison to the world: 186

Real GDP per capita: $52,500 (2014 est.)
country comparison to the world: 23

GDP (official exchange rate): $2.742 billion (2005 est.)

Inflation rate (consumer prices): 3.4% (June 2006 est.)
country comparison to the world: 152

GDP - composition, by sector of origin: *agriculture:* 3% (2000)
industry: 10% (2000)
services: 87% (2000)

Agricultural products: tomatoes, greenhouse flowers, sweet peppers, eggplant, fruit; Guernsey cattle

Industries: tourism, banking

Labor force: 31,470 (March 2006)
country comparison to the world: 202

Unemployment rate: 1.2% (2016 est.)
country comparison to the world: 14

Budget: *revenues:* 563.6 million (2005)
expenditures: 530.9 million (2005 est.)

Budget surplus (+) or deficit (-): 1.2% (of GDP) (2005)
country comparison to the world: 29

Taxes and other revenues: 20.6% (of GDP) (2005)
country comparison to the world: 146

Fiscal year: calendar year

Exports - commodities: tomatoes, flowers and ferns, sweet peppers, eggplant, other vegetables

Imports - commodities: coal, gasoline, oil, machinery, and equipment

Exchange rates: Guernsey pound per US dollar
0.7836 (2017 est.)
0.738 (2016 est.)
0.738 (2015)
0.6542 (2014)
0.607 (2013)

ENERGY

Electricity access: *electrification - total population:* 100% (2020)

COMMUNICATIONS

Telephones - fixed lines: *total subscriptions:* 33,940 (2020 est.)
subscriptions per 100 inhabitants: 54 (2020 est.)
country comparison to the world: 168

Telephones - mobile cellular: *total subscriptions:* 43,824 (2009 est.)
subscriptions per 100 inhabitants: 79 (2009 est.)
country comparison to the world: 207

Telecommunication systems: *general assessment:* fixed network broadband services are those delivered over physical copper connections, fiber connections and fixed wireless communications links (e.g. WiMax); they do not include services delivered over 2G, 3G and 4G mobile networks (2021)
domestic: fixed-line 47 per 100 and mobile-cellular 112 per 100 persons (2021)
international: country code - 44; landing points for Guernsey-Jersey, HUGO, INGRID, Channel Islands -9 Liberty and UK-Channel Islands-7 submarine cable to UK and France (2019)

Broadcast media: multiple UK terrestrial TV broadcasts are received via a transmitter in Jersey with relays in Jersey, Guernsey, and Alderney; satellite packages are available; BBC Radio Guernsey and 1 other radio station operating

Internet country code: .gg

Internet users: *total:* 54,726 (2019 est.)
percent of population: 84% (2019 est.)
country comparison to the world: 193

Broadband - fixed subscriptions: *total:* 25,336 (2020 est.)
subscriptions per 100 inhabitants: 40 (2020 est.)
country comparison to the world: 158

TRANSPORTATION

National air transport system: *number of registered air carriers:* 1 (2020) (registered in UK)
inventory of registered aircraft operated by air carriers: 9 (registered in UK)

Civil aircraft registration country code prefix: 2

Airports: *total:* 2 (2021)
country comparison to the world: 198

Airports - with paved runways: *total:* 2
1,524 to 2,437 m: 1
under 914 m: 1 (2021)

Roadways: *total:* 260 km (2017)
country comparison to the world: 204

Ports and terminals: *major seaport(s):* Braye Bay, Saint Peter Port

MILITARY AND SECURITY

Military - note: defense is the responsibility of the UK

TRANSNATIONAL ISSUES

Disputes - international: none

Illicit drugs: NA

GUINEA

INTRODUCTION

Background: Guinea's deep Muslim heritage arrived via the neighboring Almoravid Empire in the 11th century. Following Almoravid decline, Guinea existed on the fringe of several African kingdoms, all competing for regional dominance. In the 13th century, the Mali Empire took control of Guinea, encouraging its already growing Muslim faith. After the fall of the West African empires, various smaller kingdoms controlled Guinea. In the 18th century, Fulani Muslims established an Islamic state in central Guinea that represents one of the earliest examples of a written constitution and alternating leadership. While European traders first arrived in the 16th century, it was the French who secured colonial rule in the 19th century.

In 1958, Guinea achieved independence from France. Sekou TOURE became Guinea's first post-independence president; he established a dictatorial regime and ruled until his death in 1984, after which General Lansana CONTE staged a coup and seized the government. He too established an authoritarian regime and manipulated presidential elections until his death in December 2008, when Captain Moussa Dadis CAMARA led a military coup, seized power, and suspended the constitution. In September 2009, presidential guards opened fire on an opposition rally, killing more than 150 people in Conakry, the capital. In early December 2009, CAMARA was wounded in an assassination attempt and exiled to Burkina Faso. In 2010 and 2013 respectively, the country held its first free and fair presidential and legislative elections. Alpha CONDE won the 2010 and 2015 presidential elections. CONDE's first cabinet was the first all-civilian government in Guinean history. In March 2020, Guinea passed a new constitution in a national referendum that changed presidential term limit rules. CONDE argued that, given this change, he was allowed to run for a third term, which he then won in October 2020. On 5 September 2021, Col Mamady DOUMBOUYA led special forces troops in a successful military coup, ousting and detaining CONDE and establishing the National Committee for Reconciliation and Development (CNRD). DOUMBOUYA and the CNRD suspended the constitution and dissolved the government and the legislature. DOUMBOUYA was sworn in as transition president on 1 October 2021, and appointed Mohamed BEAVOGUI as transition prime minister a week later. BEAVOGUI subsequently formed a largely technocratic cabinet. The National Transition Council (CNT), which acts as the legislative body for the transition, was formed on 22 January 2022. The 81-member CNT is led by Dr. Dansa KOUROUMA and consists of appointed members representing a broad swath of Guinean society.

GEOGRAPHY

Location: Western Africa, bordering the North Atlantic Ocean, between Guinea-Bissau and Sierra Leone

Geographic coordinates: 11 00 N, 10 00 W

Map references: Africa

Area: *total:* 245,857 sq km
land: 245,717 sq km
water: 140 sq km

Area - comparative: slightly smaller than Oregon; slightly larger than twice the size of Pennsylvania

Land boundaries: *total:* 4,046 km
border countries (6): Cote d'Ivoire 816 km; Guinea-Bissau 421 km; Liberia 590 km; Mali 1062 km; Senegal 363 km; Sierra Leone 794 km

Coastline: 320 km

Maritime claims: *territorial sea:* 12 nm
exclusive economic zone: 200 nm

Climate: generally hot and humid; monsoonal-type rainy season (June to November) with southwesterly winds; dry season (December to May) with northeasterly harmattan winds

Terrain: generally flat coastal plain, hilly to mountainous interior

Elevation: *highest point:* Mont Nimba 1,752 m
lowest point: Atlantic Ocean 0 m
mean elevation: 472 m

Natural resources: bauxite, iron ore, diamonds, gold, uranium, hydropower, fish, salt

Land use: *agricultural land:* 58.1% (2018 est.)
arable land: 11.8% (2018 est.)
permanent crops: 2.8% (2018 est.)
permanent pasture: 43.5% (2018 est.)
forest: 26.5% (2018 est.)
other: 15.4% (2018 est.)

Irrigated land: 950 sq km (2012)

Major rivers (by length in km): Niger river source (shared with Mali, and Nigeria [m]) - 4,200 km; Gambia river source (shared with Senegal and The Gambia [m]) - 1,094 km
note – [s] after country name indicates river source; [m] after country name indicates river mouth

Major watersheds (area sq km): Atlantic Ocean drainage: Niger (2,261,741 sq km), Senegal (456,397 sq km)

Population distribution: areas of highest density are in the west and south; interior is sparsely populated as shown in this population distribution map

Natural hazards: hot, dry, dusty harmattan haze may reduce visibility during dry season

Geography - note: the Niger and its important tributary the Milo River have their sources in the Guinean highlands

PEOPLE AND SOCIETY

Population: 13,237,832 (2022 est.)

Nationality: *noun:* Guinean(s)
adjective: Guinean

Ethnic groups: Fulani (Peuhl) 33.4%, Malinke 29.4%, Susu 21.2%, Guerze 7.8%, Kissi 6.2%, Toma 1.6%, other/foreign 0.4% (2018 est.)

Languages: French (official), Pular, Maninka, Susu, other native languages
note: about 40 languages are spoken; each ethnic group has its own language

Religions: Muslim 89.1%, Christian 6.8%, animist 1.6%, other 0.1%, none 2.4% (2014 est.)

Demographic profile: Guinea's strong population growth is a result of declining mortality rates and sustained elevated fertility. The population growth rate was somewhat tempered in the 2000s because of a period of net outmigration. Although life expectancy and mortality rates have improved over the last two decades, the nearly universal practice of female genital cutting continues to contribute to high infant and maternal mortality rates. Guinea's total fertility remains high at about 5 children per woman because of the ongoing preference for larger families, low contraceptive usage and availability, a lack of educational attainment and empowerment among women, and poverty. A lack of literacy and vocational training programs limit job prospects for youths, but even those with university degrees often have no option but to work in the informal sector. About 60% of the country's large youth population is unemployed.

Tensions and refugees have spilled over Guinea's borders with Sierra Leone, Liberia, and Cote d'Ivoire. During the 1990s Guinea harbored as many as half a million refugees from Sierra Leone and Liberia, more refugees than any other African country for much of that decade. About half sought refuge in the volatile "Parrot's Beak" region of southwest Guinea, a wedge of land jutting into Sierra Leone near the Liberian border. Many were relocated within Guinea in the early 2000s because the area suffered repeated cross-border attacks from various government and rebel forces, as well as anti-refugee violence.

Age structure: *0-14 years:* 41.2% (male 2,601,221/female 2,559,918)
15-24 years: 19.32% (male 1,215,654/female 1,204,366)
25-54 years: 30.85% (male 1,933,141/female 1,930,977)
55-64 years: 4.73% (male 287,448/female 305,420)
65 years and over: 3.91% (male 218,803/female 270,492) (2020 est.)

Dependency ratios: *total dependency ratio:* 85.2
youth dependency ratio: 79.7
elderly dependency ratio: 5.5
potential support ratio: 18.3 (2020 est.)

Median age: *total:* 19.1 years
male: 18.9 years
female: 19.4 years (2020 est.)

Population growth rate: 2.76% (2022 est.)

Birth rate: 35.67 births/1,000 population (2022 est.)

Death rate: 8.12 deaths/1,000 population (2022 est.)

Net migration rate: 0 migrant(s)/1,000 population (2022 est.)

Population distribution: areas of highest density are in the west and south; interior is sparsely populated as shown in this population distribution map

Urbanization: *urban population:* 37.7% of total population (2022)
rate of urbanization: 3.64% annual rate of change (2020-25 est.)

Major urban areas - population: 2.049 million CONAKRY (capital) (2022)

Sex ratio: *at birth:* 1.03 male(s)/female
0-14 years: 1.02 male(s)/female
15-24 years: 1.01 male(s)/female
25-54 years: 1 male(s)/female
55-64 years: 0.94 male(s)/female
65 years and over: 0.68 male(s)/female
total population: 1 male(s)/female (2022 est.)

Mother's mean age at first birth: 19.9 years (2018 est.)
note: data represents median age at first birth among women 20-49

Maternal mortality ratio: 576 deaths/100,000 live births (2017 est.)

Infant mortality rate: *total:* 49.63 deaths/1,000 live births
male: 54.39 deaths/1,000 live births
female: 44.74 deaths/1,000 live births (2022 est.)

Life expectancy at birth: *total population:* 63.9 years
male: 62.04 years
female: 65.82 years (2022 est.)

Total fertility rate: 4.85 children born/woman (2022 est.)

Contraceptive prevalence rate: 10.9% (2018)

Drinking water source: *improved: urban:* 99.5% of population
rural: 76.9% of population
total: 85.2% of population
unimproved: urban: 0.5% of population
rural: 23.1% of population
total: 14.8% of population (2020 est.)

Current health expenditure: 4% of GDP (2019)

Physicians density: 0.23 physicians/1,000 population (2018)

Hospital bed density: 0.3 beds/1,000 population (2011)

Sanitation facility access: *improved: urban:* 90.9% of population
rural: 38.7% of population
total: 58% of population
unimproved: urban: 9.1% of population
rural: 61.3% of population
total: 42% of population (2020 est.)

HIV/AIDS - adult prevalence rate: 1.4% (2020 est.)

Major infectious diseases: *degree of risk:* very high (2020)
food or waterborne diseases: bacterial and protozoal diarrhea, hepatitis A, and typhoid fever
vectorborne diseases: malaria, dengue fever, and yellow fever
water contact diseases: schistosomiasis
animal contact diseases: rabies
aerosolized dust or soil contact diseases: Lassa fever (2016)
note: on 21 March 2022, the US Centers for Disease Control and Prevention (CDC) issued a Travel Alert for polio in Africa; Guinea is currently considered a high risk to travelers for circulating vaccine-derived polioviruses (cVDPV); vaccine-derived poliovirus (VDPV) is a strain of the weakened poliovirus that was initially included in oral polio vaccine (OPV) and *that has changed over time and behaves more like the wild or naturally occurring virus;* this means it can be spread more easily to people who are unvaccinated against polio and who come in contact with the stool or respiratory secretions, such as from a sneeze, of an "infected" person who received oral polio vaccine; the CDC recommends that before any international travel, anyone unvaccinated, incompletely vaccinated, or with an unknown polio vaccination status should complete the routine polio vaccine series; before travel to any high-risk destination, the CDC recommends that adults who previously completed the full, routine polio vaccine series receive a single, lifetime booster dose of polio vaccine

Obesity - adult prevalence rate: 7.7% (2016)

Alcohol consumption per capita: *total:* 0.33 liters of pure alcohol (2019 est.)
beer: 0.29 liters of pure alcohol (2019 est.)
wine: 0.01 liters of pure alcohol (2019 est.)

spirits: 0.03 liters of pure alcohol (2019 est.)
other alcohols: 0 liters of pure alcohol (2019 est.)

Children under the age of 5 years underweight: 16.3% (2018)

Child marriage: *women married by age 15:* 17%
women married by age 18: 46.5%
men married by age 18: 1.9% (2018 est.)

Education expenditures: 2.2% of GDP (2020 est.)

Literacy: *definition:* age 15 and over can read and write
total population: 39.6%
male: 54.4%
female: 27.7% (2018)

School life expectancy (primary to tertiary education): *total:* 9 years
male: 10 years
female: 8 years (2014)

Unemployment, youth ages 15-24: *total:* 7.1%
male: 6.1%
female: 7.9% (2019 est.)

ENVIRONMENT

Environment - current issues: deforestation; inadequate potable water; desertification; soil contamination and erosion; overfishing, overpopulation in forest region; poor mining practices lead to environmental damage; water pollution; improper waste disposal

Environment - international agreements: *party to:* Biodiversity, Climate Change, Climate Change-Kyoto Protocol, Climate Change-Paris Agreement, Comprehensive Nuclear Test Ban, Desertification, Endangered Species, Hazardous Wastes, Law of the Sea, Ozone Layer Protection, Ship Pollution, Wetlands, Whaling
signed, but not ratified: none of the selected agreements

Air pollutants: *particulate matter emissions:* 22.43 micrograms per cubic meter (2016 est.)
carbon dioxide emissions: 3 megatons (2016 est.)
methane emissions: 11.13 megatons (2020 est.)

Climate: generally hot and humid; monsoonal-type rainy season (June to November) with southwesterly winds; dry season (December to May) with northeasterly harmattan winds

Land use: *agricultural land:* 58.1% (2018 est.)
arable land: 11.8% (2018 est.)
permanent crops: 2.8% (2018 est.)
permanent pasture: 43.5% (2018 est.)
forest: 26.5% (2018 est.)
other: 15.4% (2018 est.)

Urbanization: *urban population:* 37.7% of total population (2022)
rate of urbanization: 3.64% annual rate of change (2020-25 est.)

Revenue from forest resources: *forest revenues:* 4.81% of GDP (2018 est.)

Revenue from coal: *coal revenues:* 0% of GDP (2018 est.)

Food insecurity: *severe localized food insecurity: due to reduced incomes* - about 1.22 million people are projected to be in need of food assistance between June and August 2022, primarily due to food access constraints on account of the economic effects of the COVID-19 pandemic (2022)

Waste and recycling: *municipal solid waste generated annually:* 596,911 tons (1996 est.)
municipal solid waste recycled annually: 29,846 tons (2005 est.)
percent of municipal solid waste recycled: 5% (2005 est.)

Major rivers (by length in km): Niger river source (shared with Mali, and Nigeria [m]) - 4,200 km; Gambia river source (shared with Senegal and The Gambia [m]) - 1,094 km
note – [s] after country name indicates river source; [m] after country name indicates river mouth

Major watersheds (area sq km): Atlantic Ocean drainage: Niger (2,261,741 sq km), Senegal (456,397 sq km)

Total water withdrawal: *municipal:* 224.8 million cubic meters (2017 est.)
industrial: 56.2 million cubic meters (2017 est.)
agricultural: 292.9 million cubic meters (2017 est.)

Total renewable water resources: 226 billion cubic meters (2017 est.)

GOVERNMENT

Country name: *conventional long form:* Republic of Guinea
conventional short form: Guinea
local long form: Republique de Guinee
local short form: Guinee
former: French Guinea
etymology: the country is named after the Guinea region of West Africa that lies along the Gulf of Guinea and stretches north to the Sahel

Government type: presidential republic

Capital: *name:* Conakry
geographic coordinates: 9 30 N, 13 42 W
time difference: UTC 0 (5 hours ahead of Washington, DC, during Standard Time)
etymology: according to tradition, the name derives from the fusion of the name *Cona*, a Baga wine and cheese producer who lived on Tombo Island (the original site of the present-day capital), and the word *nakiri*, which in Susu means "the other bank" or "the other side"; supposedly, Baga's palm grove produced the best wine on the island and people traveling to sample his vintage, would say: "I am going to Cona, on the other bank (*Cona-nakiri*)," which over time became Conakry

Administrative divisions: 7 regions administrative (administrative regions) and 1 gouvenorat (governorate)*; Boke, Conakry*, Faranah, Kankan, Kindia, Labe, Mamou, N'Zerekore

Independence: 2 October 1958 (from France)

National holiday: Independence Day, 2 October (1958)

Constitution: *history:* previous 1958, 1990; latest 2010, which was suspended on 5 September 2021 via a coup d'etat; on 27 September, the Transitional Charter was released, which supersedes the constitution until a new constitution is promulgated
amendments: proposed by the National Assembly or by the president of the republic; consideration of proposals requires approval by simple majority vote by the Assembly; passage requires approval in referendum; the president can opt to submit amendments directly to the Assembly, in which case approval requires at least two-thirds majority vote; revised in 2020

Legal system: civil law system based on the French model

International law organization participation: accepts compulsory ICJ jurisdiction with reservations; accepts ICCt jurisdiction

Citizenship: *citizenship by birth:* no
citizenship by descent only: at least one parent must be a citizen of Guinea
dual citizenship recognized: no
residency requirement for naturalization: na

Suffrage: 18 years of age; universal

Executive branch: *chief of state:* President Col. Mamady DOUMBOUYA (since 1 October 2021); note - on 5 September 2021, Col. Mamady DOUMBOUYA led a military coup in which President CONDE was arrested and detained, the constitution suspended, and the government and People's National Assembly dissolved; on 1 October 2021, DOUMBOUYA was sworn in as transitional president
head of government: Prime Minister Bernard GOMOU (since 20 August 2022); note - GOMOU had been acting prime minister since 16 July 2022 replacing Mohamed BEAVOGUI who stepped down due to health reasons
cabinet: formerly, the Council of Ministers appointed by the president; note - the 5 September 2021 military coup arrested and detained the president, suspended the constitution, and dissolved the government and legislature
elections/appointments: formerly, the president was directly elected by absolute majority popular vote in 2 rounds if needed for a 5-year term (eligible for a second term) and the prime minister appointed by the president; election last held on 18 October 2020; note - a new election time table has not been announced by the transitional government
election results: in the election of 18 October 2020, Alpha CONDE reelected president in the first round; percent of vote - Alpha CONDE (RPG) 59.5%, Cellou Dalein DIALLO (UFDG) 33.5%, other 7%; note - following the military coup of 5 September 2021, coup leader Col. Mamady DOUMBOUYA was sworn in as transitional president on 1 October 2021

Legislative branch: *description:* formerly the People's National Assembly; note - on 5 September 2021, Col. Mamady DOUMBOUYA led a military coup in which President CONDE was arrested and detained, the constitution suspended, and the government and People's National Assembly dissolved; on 22 January 2022, an 81-member Transitional National Council was installed
elections: 81 members to the Transitional National Council were appointed by the transitional president Col. Mamady DOUMBOUYA on 22 January 2022; elections for a permanent legislature had not been announced as of late January 2022
election results: 81 members of the National Transitional Council appointed on 22 January 2022 by the transitional president; the members represent all of the country's socio-professional organizations and political parties

Judicial branch: *highest court(s):* Supreme Court or Cour Supreme (organized into Administrative Chamber and Civil, Penal, and Social Chamber; court consists of the first president, 2 chamber presidents, 10 councilors, the solicitor general, and NA deputies); Constitutional Court - suspended on 5 September 2021
judge selection and term of office: Supreme Court first president appointed by the national president after consultation with the National Assembly; other

members appointed by presidential decree; members serve 9-year terms until age 65
subordinate courts: Court of Appeal or Cour d'Appel; High Court of Justice or Cour d'Assises; Court of Account (Court of Auditors); Courts of First Instance (Tribunal de Premiere Instance); labor court; military tribunal; justices of the peace; specialized courts

Political parties and leaders: African Congress for Democracy and Renewal or CADRE [Daniel KOLIE]
Alliance for National Renewal or ARN [Pepe Koulemou KOULEMOU]
Alliance for National Renewal or ARENA [Sekou Koureissy CONDE]
Bloc Liberal or BL [Faya MILLIMONO]
Citizen Generation or GECI [Mohamed SOUMAH]
Citizen Party for the Defense of Collective Interests or PCDIC [Hamidou BARRY]
Democratic Alliance for Renewal or ADR [Alpha Oumar Taran DIALLO]
Democratic National Movement or MND [Ousmane DORE]
Democratic Union for Renewal and Progress or UDRP [Edouard Zoutomou KPOGHOMOU]
Democratic Union of Guinea or UDG [Mamadou SYLLA]
Democratic People's Movement of Guinea or MPDG [Siaka BARRY]
Democratic Workers' Party of Guinea or PDTG [Talibi Dos CAMARA]
Front for the National Alliance or FAN [Makale CAMARA]
Generation for Reconciliation Union and Prosperity or GRUP [Papa Koly KOUROUMA]
Guinea for Democracy and Balance or GDE [Aboubacar SOUMAH]
Guinean Party for Peaceful Coexistence and Development or PGCD [Nene Moussa Maleya CAMARA]
Guinean Party for Solidarity and Democracy or PGSD [Elie KAMANO]
Guinean Union for Democracy and Development or UGDD [Francis HABA]
Guinean Rally for Development or RGD [Abdoul Kabele CAMARA]
Guinean Rally for Unity and Development or RGUD [Abraham BOURE]
Guinean Renaissance Party or PGR [Ibrahima Sory CONDE]
Modern Guinea [Thierno Yaya DIALLO]
Movement for Solidarity and Development or MSD [Abdoulaye DIALLO]
National Committee for Reconciliation and Development [Colonel Mamady DOUMBOUYA]
National Front for Development or FND [Alhousseine Makanera KAKE]
National Union for Prosperity or UNP [Alpha Mady SOUMAH]
National Party for Hope and Development or PEDN [Lansana KOUYATE]
New Democratic Forces or NFD [Mouctar DIALLO]
New Generation for the Republic or NGR [Abbe SYLLA]
New Guinea or NG [Mohamed CISSE]
New Political Generation or NGP [Badra KONE]
Party for Progress and Change or PPC [Aboubacar Biro SOUMAH]
Party of Citizen Action through Labor or PACT [Makale TRAORE]
Party of Democrats for Hope or PADES [Ousmane KABA]
Party of Freedom and Progress or PLP [Laye Souleymane DIALLO]
Party of Hope for National Development or PEDN [Lansana KOUYATE]
Rally for Renaissance and Development or RRD [Abdoulaye KOUROUMA]
Rally for the Guinean People or RPG [vacant]
Rally for the Integrated Development of Guinea or RDIG [Jean Marc TELIANO]
Rally for the Republic or RPR [Diabaty DORE]
Union for Progress and Renewal or UPR [Ousmane BAH]
Union for the Defense of Republican Interests or UDIR [Bouya KONATE]
Union for the Progress of Guinea or UPG [Jacques GBONIMY]
Union of Democratic Forces or UFD [Mamadou Baadiko BAH]
Union of Democratic Forces of Guinea or UFDG [Cellou Dalein DIALLO]
Union of Democrats for the Renaissance of Guinea or UDRG [Amadou Oury BAH]
Union of Republican Forces or UFR [Sidya TOURE]
Unity and Progress Party or PUP [Fode BANGOURA]

International organization participation: ACP, AfDB, EITI (compliant country), FAO, G-77, IBRD, ICAO, ICCt, ICRM, IDA, IDB, IFAD, IFC, IFRCS, ILO, IMF, IMO, Interpol, IOC, IOM, IPU, ISO (correspondent), ITSO, ITU, ITUC (NGOs), MIGA, MINURSO, MINUSMA, MONUSCO, NAM, OIC, OIF, OPCW, UN, UNCTAD, UNESCO, UNHCR, UNIDO, UNISFA, UNMISS, UNOCI, UNWTO, UPU, WCO, WFTU (NGOs), WHO, WIPO, WMO, WTO

Diplomatic representation in the US: *chief of mission:* Ambassador Kerfalla YANSANE (since 24 January 2018)
chancery: 2112 Leroy Place NW, Washington, DC 20008
telephone: [1] (202) 986-4300
FAX: [1] (202) 986-3800
email address and website:
http://guineaembassyusa.org/en/welcome-to-the-embassy-of-guinea-washington-usa/

Diplomatic representation from the US: *chief of mission:* Ambassador Troy FITRELL (since January 2022)
embassy: Transversale No. 2, Centre Administratif de Koloma, Commune de Ratoma, Conakry
mailing address: 2110 Conakry Place, Washington DC 20521-2110
telephone: [224] 65-10-40-00
FAX: [224] 65-10-42-97
email address and website:
ConakryACS@state.gov
https://gn.usembassy.gov/

Flag description: three equal vertical bands of red (hoist side), yellow, and green; red represents the people's sacrifice for liberation and work; yellow stands for the sun, for the riches of the earth, and for justice; green symbolizes the country's vegetation and unity
note: uses the popular Pan-African colors of Ethiopia; the colors from left to right are the reverse of those on the flags of neighboring Mali and Senegal

National symbol(s): elephant; national colors: red, yellow, green

National anthem: *name:* "Liberte" (Liberty)
lyrics/music: unknown/Fodeba KEITA
note: adopted 1958

National heritage: *total World Heritage Sites:* 1 (natural)
selected World Heritage Site locales: Mount Nimba Strict Nature Reserve

ECONOMY

Economic overview: Guinea is a poor country of approximately 12.9 million people in 2016 that possesses the world's largest reserves of bauxite and largest untapped high-grade iron ore reserves, as well as gold and diamonds. In addition, Guinea has fertile soil, ample rainfall, and is the source of several West African rivers, including the Senegal, Niger, and Gambia. Guinea's hydro potential is enormous and the country could be a major exporter of electricity. The country also has tremendous agriculture potential. Gold, bauxite, and diamonds are Guinea's main exports. International investors have shown interest in Guinea's unexplored mineral reserves, which have the potential to propel Guinea's future growth.

Following the death of long-term President Lansana CONTE in 2008 and the coup that followed, international donors, including the G-8, the IMF, and the World Bank, significantly curtailed their development programs in Guinea. However, the IMF approved a 3-year Extended Credit Facility arrangement in 2012, following the December 2010 presidential elections. In September 2012, Guinea achieved Heavily Indebted Poor Countries completion point status. Future access to international assistance and investment will depend on the government's ability to be transparent, combat corruption, reform its banking system, improve its business environment, and build infrastructure. In April 2013, the government amended its mining code to reduce taxes and royalties. In 2014, Guinea complied with requirements of the Extractive Industries Transparency Initiative by publishing its mining contracts. Guinea completed its program with the IMF in October 2016 even though some targeted reforms have been delayed. Currently Guinea is negotiating a new IMF program which will be based on Guinea's new five-year economic plan, focusing on the development of higher value-added products, including from the agro-business sector and development of the rural economy.

Political instability, a reintroduction of the Ebola virus epidemic, low international commodity prices, and an enduring legacy of corruption, inefficiency, and lack of government transparency are factors that could impact Guinea's future growth. Economic recovery will be a long process while the government adjusts to lower inflows of international donor aid following the surge of Ebola-related emergency support. Ebola stalled promising economic growth in the 2014-15 period and impeded several projects, such as offshore oil exploration and the Simandou iron ore project. The economy, however, grew by 6.6% in 2016 and 6.7% in 2017, mainly due to growth from bauxite mining and thermal energy generation as well as the resiliency of the agricultural sector. The 240-megawatt Kaleta Dam, inaugurated in September 2015, has expanded access to electricity for residents of Conakry. An combined with fears of Ebola virus, continue to undermine Guinea's economic viability.

Guinea's iron ore industry took a hit in 2016 when investors in the Simandou iron ore project announced plans to divest from the project. In 2017, agriculture output and public investment boosted economic growth, while the mining sector continued to play a prominent role in economic performance.

Successive governments have failed to address the country's crumbling infrastructure. Guinea suffers from chronic electricity shortages; poor roads, rail lines and bridges; and a lack of access to clean water - all of which continue to plague economic development. The present government, led by President Alpha CONDE, is working to create an environment to attract foreign investment and hopes to have greater participation from western countries and firms in Guinea's economic development.

Real GDP (purchasing power parity): $35.08 billion (2020 est.)
$32.78 billion (2019 est.)
$31.03 billion (2018 est.)
note: data are in 2017 dollars

Real GDP growth rate: 8.2% (2017 est.)
10.5% (2016 est.)
3.8% (2015 est.)

Real GDP per capita: $2,700 (2020 est.)
$2,600 (2019 est.)
$2,500 (2018 est.)
note: data are in 2017 dollars

GDP (official exchange rate): $13.55 billion (2019 est.)

Inflation rate (consumer prices): 9.4% (2019 est.)
9.8% (2018 est.)
8.9% (2017 est.)

GDP - composition, by sector of origin: *agriculture:* 19.8% (2017 est.)
industry: 32.1% (2017 est.)
services: 48.1% (2017 est.)

GDP - composition, by end use: *household consumption:* 80.8% (2017 est.)
government consumption: 6.6% (2017 est.)
investment in fixed capital: 9.1% (2017 est.)
investment in inventories: 18.5% (2017 est.)
exports of goods and services: 21.9% (2017 est.)
imports of goods and services: -36.9% (2017 est.)

Agricultural products: rice, cassava, groundnuts, maize, oil palm fruit, fonio, plantains, sugar cane, sweet potatoes, vegetables

Industries: bauxite, gold, diamonds, iron ore; light manufacturing, agricultural processing

Industrial production growth rate: 11% (2017 est.)

Labor force: 5.558 million (2017 est.)

Labor force - by occupation: *agriculture:* 76%
industry: 24% (2006 est.)

Unemployment rate: 2.7% (2017 est.)
2.8% (2016 est.)

Unemployment, youth ages 15-24: *total:* 7.1%
male: 6.1%
female: 7.9% (2019 est.)

Population below poverty line: 43.7% (2018 est.)

Gini Index coefficient - distribution of family income: 33.7 (2012 est.)
40.3 (1994)

Household income or consumption by percentage share: *lowest 10%:* 2.7%
highest 10%: 30.3% (2007)

Budget: *revenues:* 1.7 billion (2017 est.)
expenditures: 1.748 billion (2017 est.)

Budget surplus (+) or deficit (-): -0.5% (of GDP) (2017 est.)

Public debt: 37.9% of GDP (2017 est.)
41.8% of GDP (2016 est.)

Taxes and other revenues: 16.6% (of GDP) (2017 est.)

Fiscal year: calendar year

Current account balance: -$705 million (2017 est.)
-$2.705 billion (2016 est.)

Exports: $4.04 billion (2019 est.) note: data are in current year dollars
$4.08 billion (2018 est.) note: data are in current year dollars
$4.733 billion (2017 est.)

Exports - partners: United Arab Emirates 39%, China 36%, India 6% (2019)

Exports - commodities: aluminum, gold, bauxite, diamonds, fish, cashews (2019)

Imports: $4.32 billion (2019 est.) note: data are in current year dollars
$4.18 billion (2018 est.) note: data are in current year dollars
$7.317 billion (2017 est.)

Imports - partners: China 39%, India 8%, Netherlands 6%, Belgium 5%, United Arab Emirates 5% (2019)

Imports - commodities: rice, refined petroleum, packaged medicines, delivery trucks, cars (2019)

Reserves of foreign exchange and gold: $331.8 million (31 December 2017 est.)
$383.4 million (31 December 2016 est.)

Debt - external: $1.458 billion (31 December 2017 est.)
$1.462 billion (31 December 2016 est.)

Exchange rates: Guinean francs (GNF) per US dollar -
9,953 (2020 est.)
9,542.5 (2019 est.)
9,092 (2018 est.)
7,485.5 (2014 est.)
7,014.1 (2013 est.)

ENERGY

Electricity access: *electrification - total population:* 46% (2019)
electrification - urban areas: 84% (2019)
electrification - rural areas: 24% (2019)

Electricity: *installed generating capacity:* 992,000 kW (2020 est.)
consumption: 1.781 billion kWh (2019 est.)
exports: 0 kWh (2019 est.)
imports: 0 kWh (2019 est.)
transmission/distribution losses: 280 million kWh (2019 est.)

Electricity generation sources: *fossil fuels:* 22.2% of total installed capacity (2020 est.)
solar: 0.7% of total installed capacity (2020 est.)
hydroelectricity: 77.1% of total installed capacity (2020 est.)

Petroleum: *total petroleum production:* 0 bbl/day (2021 est.)
refined petroleum consumption: 19,800 bbl/day (2019 est.)

Refined petroleum products - imports: 18,460 bbl/day (2015 est.)

Carbon dioxide emissions: 2.981 million metric tonnes of CO2 (2019 est.)
from petroleum and other liquids: 2.981 million metric tonnes of CO2 (2019 est.)

Energy consumption per capita: 4.133 million Btu/person (2019 est.)

COMMUNICATIONS

Telephones - fixed lines: *total subscriptions:* 0 (2018 est.)
subscriptions per 100 inhabitants: 0 (2018 est.)

Telephones - mobile cellular: *total subscriptions:* 13.795 million (2020 est.)
subscriptions per 100 inhabitants: 105 (2020 est.)

Telecommunication systems: *general assessment:* the number of mobile subscribers grew strongly while revenue also increased steadily; fixed broadband services are still very limited and expensive, though there have been some positive developments in recent years; the landing of the first international submarine cable in 2012, and the setting up of an IXP in mid-2013, increased the bandwidth available to the ISPs, and helped reduce the cost of internet services for end-users; a National Backbone Network was completed in mid-2020, connecting administrative centers across the country; almost all internet connections are made via mobile networks; GSM services account for a dwindling proportion of connections, in line with the greater reach of services based on 3G and LTE (2022)
domestic: fixed-line teledensity is less than 1 per 100 persons; mobile-cellular subscribership is just over 105 per 100 persons (2020)
international: country code - 224; ACE submarine cable connecting Guinea with 20 landing points in Western and South Africa and Europe; satellite earth station - 1 Intelsat (Atlantic Ocean (2019)

Broadcast media: Government maintains marginal control over broadcast media; single state-run TV station; state-run radio broadcast station also operates several stations in rural areas; a dozen private television stations; a steadily increasing number of privately owned radio stations, nearly all in Conakry, and about a dozen community radio stations; foreign TV programming available via satellite and cable subscription services
(2022)

Internet country code: .gn

Internet users: *total:* 3,414,526 (2020 est.)
percent of population: 26% (2020 est.)

Broadband - fixed subscriptions: *total:* 1,000 (2020 est.)
subscriptions per 100 inhabitants: 0.01 (2020 est.)

TRANSPORTATION

Civil aircraft registration country code prefix: 3X

Airports: *total:* 16 (2021)

Airports - with paved runways: *total:* 4
over 3,047 m: 1
1,524 to 2,437 m: 3 (2021)

Airports - with unpaved runways: *total:* 12
1,524 to 2,437 m: 7
914 to 1,523 m: 3
under 914 m: 2 (2021)

Railways: *total:* 1,086 km (2017)
standard gauge: 279 km (2017) 1.435-m gauge
narrow gauge: 807 km (2017) 1.000-m gauge

Roadways: *total:* 44,301 km (2018)

paved: 3,346 km (2018)
unpaved: 40,955 km (2018)

Waterways: 1,300 km (2011) (navigable by shallow-draft native craft in the northern part of the Niger River system)

Merchant marine: *total:* 2
by type: other 2 (2021)

Ports and terminals: *major seaport(s):* Conakry, Kamsar

MILITARY AND SECURITY

Military and security forces: National Armed Forces: Army, Guinean Navy (Armee de Mer or Marine Guineenne), Guinean Air Force (Force Aerienne de Guinee), Presidential Security Battalion (Battailon Autonome de la Sécurité Presidentielle, BASP), Gendarmerie (2022)
note: the National Gendarmerie is overseen by the Ministry of Defense, while the National Police is under the Ministry of Security; the Gendarmerie and National Police share responsibility for internal security, but only the Gendarmerie can arrest police or military officials

Military expenditures: 1.5% of GDP (2021 est.)
1.4% of GDP (2020 est.)
1.6% of GDP (2019 est.) (approximately $270 million)
1.8% of GDP (2018 est.) (approximately $280 million)
1.8% of GDP (2017 est.) (approximately $260 million)

Military and security service personnel strengths: approximately 12,000 active personnel (9,000 Army; 400 Navy; 800 Air Force; 300 BASP; 1,500 Gendarmerie) (2022)

Military equipment inventories and acquisitions: the inventory of the Guinean military consists largely of aging and outdated (mostly Soviet-era) equipment; since 2010, it has received small amounts of equipment from China, France, Russia, and South Africa (2022)

Military service age and obligation: Voluntary and selective conscripted service, 9-24 mos (2022)

Military deployments: 670 Mali (MINUSMA) (May 2022)

Military - note: the Army is responsible for external defense, but also has some domestic security responsibilities; piracy and natural resource protection in the Gulf of Guinea are key areas of concern for the small Navy, which possesses only a few patrol boats (2022)

Maritime threats: the International Maritime Bureau reports the territorial and offshore waters in the Niger Delta and Gulf of Guinea remain a very high risk for piracy and armed robbery of ships; in 2021, there were 34 reported incidents of piracy and armed robbery at sea in the Gulf of Guinea region; although a significant decrease from the total number of 81 incidents in 2020, it included the one hijacking and three of five ships fired upon worldwide; while boarding and attempted boarding to steal valuables from ships and crews are the most common types of incidents, almost a third of all incidents involve a hijacking and/or kidnapping; in 2021, 57 crew members were kidnapped in seven separate incidents in the Gulf of Guinea, representing 100% of kidnappings worldwide; Nigerian pirates in particular are well armed and very aggressive, operating as far as 200 nm offshore; the Maritime Administration of the US Department of Transportation has issued a Maritime Advisory (2022-001 - Gulf of Guinea-Piracy/Armed Robbery/Kidnapping for Ransom) effective 4 January 2022, which states in part, "Piracy, armed robbery, and kidnapping for ransom continue to serve as significant threats to US-flagged vessels transiting or operating in the Gulf of Guinea"

TRANSNATIONAL ISSUES

Disputes - international: Sierra Leone considers Guinea's definition of the flood plain limits to define the left bank boundary of the Makona and Moa Rivers excessive and protests Guinea's continued occupation of these lands, including the hamlet of Yenga, occupied since 1998

Trafficking in persons: *current situation:* Guinea is a source, transit, and, to a lesser extent, a destination country for men, women, and children subjected to forced labor and sex trafficking; the majority of trafficking victims are Guinean children; Guinean girls are subjected to domestic servitude and commercial sexual exploitation, while boys are forced to beg, work as street vendors, shoe shiners, or miners; some Guinean children are forced to mine in Senegal, Mali, and possibly other West African countries; Guinean women and girls are subjected to domestic servitude and sex trafficking in Nigeria, Cote d'Ivoire, Benin, Senegal, Greece, and Spain, while Chinese and Vietnamese women are reportedly forced into prostitution in Guinea
tier rating: Tier 2 Watch List — Guinea does not fully meet the minimum standards for the elimination of trafficking; however it is making significant efforts to do so; the government drafted a new anti-trafficking action plan, provided support to eight victims exploited in the Middle East, and incorporated anti-trafficking training into the law enforcement curriculum; however, the government did not overall increase efforts compared to the last rating period; investigations and prosecutions of trafficking crimes decreased, victim identification was inadequate, and NGO's providing victim services did not receive government support; for the fourth year, resources for the anti-trafficking committee or the Office for the Protection of Gender, Children and Morals were inadequate; a Quranic teacher was not prosecuted for allegedly forcing child begging; Guinea was downgraded to Tier 2 Watch List (2020)

Illicit drugs: NA

GUINEA-BISSAU

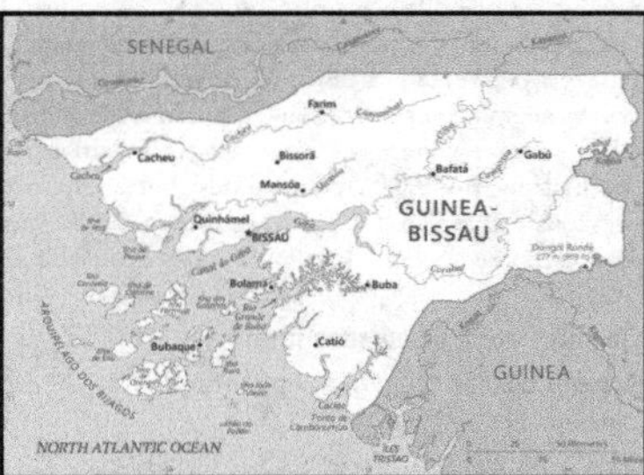

INTRODUCTION

Background: For much of its history, Guinea-Bissau was under the control of the Mali Empire and the Kaabu Kingdom. In the 16th century, Portugal began establishing trading posts along Guinea-Bissau's shoreline. Initially, the Portuguese were restricted to the coastline and islands. However, the slave and gold trades were lucrative to local African leaders, and the Portuguese were slowly able to expand their power and influence inland. Starting in the 18th century, the Mali Empire and Kingdom of Kaabu slowly disintegrated into smaller local entities. By the 19th century, Portugal had fully incorporated Guinea-Bissau into its empire.

Since gaining independence in 1974, Guinea-Bissau has experienced considerable political and military upheaval. In 1980, a military coup established General Joao Bernardo 'Nino' VIEIRA as president. VIEIRA's regime suppressed political opposition and purged political rivals. Several coup attempts through the 1980s and early 1990s failed to unseat him. In May 1999, a military mutiny and civil war led to VIEIRA's ouster. In February 2000, a transitional government turned over power to opposition leader Kumba YALA. In September 2003, a bloodless military coup overthrew YALA and installed businessman Henrique ROSA as interim president. In 2005, former President VIEIRA was reelected, pledging to pursue economic development and national reconciliation; he was assassinated in March 2009. In June 2009, Malam Bacai SANHA was elected president, but he passed away in January 2012 from a long-term illness. In April 2012, a military coup prevented the second-round of the presidential election from taking place. Following mediation from the Economic Community of Western African States, a civilian transitional government assumed power. In 2014, Jose Mario VAZ was elected president after a free and fair election. In June 2019, VAZ became the first president in Guinea-Bissau's history to complete a full presidential term. Umaro Sissoco EMBALO was elected president in December 2019, but he did not take office until February 2020 because of a prolonged challenge to the election results.

GEOGRAPHY

Location: Western Africa, bordering the North Atlantic Ocean, between Guinea and Senegal

Geographic coordinates: 12 00 N, 15 00 W

Map references: Africa

Area: *total:* 36,125 sq km
land: 28,120 sq km
water: 8,005 sq km

Area - comparative: slightly less than three times the size of Connecticut

Land boundaries: *total:* 762 km
border countries (2): Guinea 421 km; Senegal 341 km

Coastline: 350 km

Maritime claims: *territorial sea:* 12 nm
exclusive economic zone: 200 nm

Climate: tropical; generally hot and humid; monsoonal-type rainy season (June to November) with southwesterly winds; dry season (December to May) with northeasterly harmattan winds

Terrain: mostly low-lying coastal plain with a deeply indented estuarine coastline rising to savanna in east; numerous off-shore islands including the Arquipelago Dos Bijagos consisting of 18 main islands and many small islets

Elevation: *highest point:* Dongol Ronde 277 m
lowest point: Atlantic Ocean 0 m
mean elevation: 70 m

Natural resources: fish, timber, phosphates, bauxite, clay, granite, limestone, unexploited deposits of petroleum

Land use: *agricultural land:* 44.8% (2018 est.)
arable land: 8.2% (2018 est.)
permanent crops: 6.9% (2018 est.)
permanent pasture: 29.7% (2018 est.)
forest: 55.2% (2018 est.)
other: 0% (2018 est.)

Irrigated land: 250 sq km (2012)

Major aquifers: Senegalo-Mauritanian Basin

Population distribution: approximately one-fifth of the population lives in the capital city of Bissau along the Atlantic coast; the remainder is distributed among the eight other, mainly rural, regions as shown in this population distribution map

Natural hazards: hot, dry, dusty harmattan haze may reduce visibility during dry season; brush fires

Geography - note: this small country is swampy along its western coast and low-lying inland

PEOPLE AND SOCIETY

Population: 2,026,778 (2022 est.)

Nationality: *noun:* Bissau-Guinean(s)
adjective: Bissau-Guinean

Ethnic groups: Balanta 30%, Fulani 30%, Manjaco 14%, Mandinga 13%, Papel 7%, unspecified smaller ethnic groups 6% (2015 est.)

Languages: Portuguese-based Creole, Portuguese (official; largely used as a second or third language), Pular (a Fula language), Mandingo

Religions: Muslim 46.1%, folk religions 30.6%, Christian 18.9%, other or unaffiliated 4.4% (2020 est.)

Demographic profile: Guinea-Bissau's young and growing population is sustained by high fertility; approximately 60% of the population is under the age of 25. Its large reproductive-age population and total fertility rate of more than 4 children per woman offsets the country's high infant and maternal mortality rates. The latter is among the world's highest because of the prevalence of early childbearing, a lack of birth spacing, the high percentage of births outside of health care facilities, and a shortage of medicines and supplies.

Guinea-Bissau's history of political instability, a civil war, and several coups (the latest in 2012) have resulted in a fragile state with a weak economy, high unemployment, rampant corruption, widespread poverty, and thriving drug and child trafficking. With the country lacking educational infrastructure, school funding and materials, and qualified teachers, and with the cultural emphasis placed on religious education, parents frequently send boys to study in residential Koranic schools (daaras) in Senegal and The Gambia. They often are extremely deprived and are forced into street begging or agricultural work by marabouts (Muslim religious teachers), who enrich themselves at the expense of the children. Boys who leave their marabouts often end up on the streets of Dakar or other large Senegalese towns and are vulnerable to even worse abuse.

Some young men lacking in education and job prospects become involved in the flourishing international drug trade. Local drug use and associated violent crime are growing.

Age structure: *0-14 years:* 43.17% (male 417,810/female 414,105)
15-24 years: 20.38% (male 192,451/female 200,370)
25-54 years: 30.24% (male 275,416/female 307,387)
55-64 years: 3.12% (male 29,549/female 30,661)
65 years and over: 3.08% (male 25,291/female 34,064) (2020 est.)

Dependency ratios: *total dependency ratio:* 81.2
youth dependency ratio: 76
elderly dependency ratio: 5.2
potential support ratio: 19.1 (2020 est.)

Median age: *total:* 18 years
male: 17.4 years
female: 18.6 years (2020 est.)

Population growth rate: 2.53% (2022 est.)

Birth rate: 36.45 births/1,000 population (2022 est.)

Death rate: 7.5 deaths/1,000 population (2022 est.)

Net migration rate: -3.63 migrant(s)/1,000 population (2022 est.)

Population distribution: approximately one-fifth of the population lives in the capital city of Bissau along the Atlantic coast; the remainder is distributed among the eight other, mainly rural, regions as shown in this population distribution map

Urbanization: *urban population:* 45% of total population (2022)
rate of urbanization: 3.22% annual rate of change (2020-25 est.)

Major urban areas - population: 643,000 BISSAU (capital) (2022)

Sex ratio: *at birth:* 1.03 male(s)/female
0-14 years: 1.01 male(s)/female
15-24 years: 0.96 male(s)/female
25-54 years: 0.91 male(s)/female
55-64 years: 1.1 male(s)/female
65 years and over: 0.7 male(s)/female
total population: 0.96 male(s)/female (2022 est.)

Maternal mortality ratio: 667 deaths/100,000 live births (2017 est.)

Infant mortality rate: *total:* 49.05 deaths/1,000 live births
male: 54.84 deaths/1,000 live births
female: 43.08 deaths/1,000 live births (2022 est.)

Life expectancy at birth: *total population:* 63.68 years
male: 61.45 years
female: 65.99 years (2022 est.)

Total fertility rate: 4.69 children born/woman (2022 est.)

Contraceptive prevalence rate: 20.6% (2018/19)

Drinking water source: *improved: urban:* 90.6% of population
rural: 59.1% of population
total: 73.1% of population
unimproved: urban: 9.4% of population
rural: 40.9% of population
total: 26.9% of population (2020 est.)

Current health expenditure: 8.4% of GDP (2019)

Physicians density: 0.2 physicians/1,000 population (2020)

Sanitation facility access: *improved: urban:* 62.4% of population
rural: 7.6% of population
total: 31.8% of population
unimproved: urban: 37.6% of population
rural: 92.4% of population
total: 68.2% of population (2020 est.)

HIV/AIDS - adult prevalence rate: 3% (2020 est.)

Major infectious diseases: *degree of risk:* very high (2020)
food or waterborne diseases: bacterial and protozoal diarrhea, hepatitis A, and typhoid fever
vectorborne diseases: malaria, dengue fever, and yellow fever
water contact diseases: schistosomiasis
animal contact diseases: rabies
note: on 21 March 2022, the US Centers for Disease Control and Prevention (CDC) issued a Travel Alert for polio in Africa; Guinea-Bissau is currently considered a high risk to travelers for circulating vaccine-derived polioviruses (cVDPV); vaccine-derived poliovirus (VDPV) is a strain of the weakened poliovirus that was initially included in oral polio vaccine (OPV) and *that has changed over time and behaves more like the wild or naturally occurring virus;* this means it can be spread more easily to people who are unvaccinated against polio and who come in contact with the stool or respiratory secretions, such as from a sneeze, of an "infected" person who received oral polio vaccine; the CDC recommends that before any international travel, anyone unvaccinated, incompletely vaccinated, or with an unknown polio vaccination status should complete the routine polio vaccine series; before travel to any high-risk destination, the CDC recommends that adults who previously completed the full, routine polio vaccine series receive a single, lifetime booster dose of polio vaccine

Obesity - adult prevalence rate: 9.5% (2016)

Alcohol consumption per capita: *total:* 3.21 liters of pure alcohol (2019 est.)
beer: 0.41 liters of pure alcohol (2019 est.)
wine: 0.98 liters of pure alcohol (2019 est.)
spirits: 0.54 liters of pure alcohol (2019 est.)
other alcohols: 1.28 liters of pure alcohol (2019 est.)

Tobacco use: *total:* 9% (2020 est.)
male: 17% (2020 est.)
female: 0.9% (2020 est.)

Children under the age of 5 years underweight: 18.8% (2019)

Child marriage: *women married by age 15:* 8.1%
women married by age 18: 25.7%
men married by age 18: 2.2% (2019 est.)

Education expenditures: 2.9% of GDP (2019 est.)

Literacy: *definition:* age 15 and over can read and write
total population: 59.9%
male: 71.8%
female: 48.3% (2015)

ENVIRONMENT

Environment - current issues: deforestation (rampant felling of trees for timber and agricultural purposes); soil erosion; overgrazing; overfishing

Environment - international agreements: *party to:* Biodiversity, Climate Change, Climate Change-Kyoto Protocol, Climate Change-Paris Agreement, Comprehensive Nuclear Test Ban, Desertification, Endangered Species, Hazardous Wastes, Law of the Sea, Nuclear Test Ban, Ozone Layer Protection, Ship Pollution, Wetlands, Whaling
signed, but not ratified: none of the selected agreements

Air pollutants: *particulate matter emissions:* 27.12 micrograms per cubic meter (2016 est.)
carbon dioxide emissions: 0.29 megatons (2016 est.)
methane emissions: 1.46 megatons (2020 est.)

Climate: tropical; generally hot and humid; monsoonal-type rainy season (June to November) with southwesterly winds; dry season (December to May) with northeasterly harmattan winds

Land use: *agricultural land:* 44.8% (2018 est.)
arable land: 8.2% (2018 est.)
permanent crops: 6.9% (2018 est.)
permanent pasture: 29.7% (2018 est.)
forest: 55.2% (2018 est.)
other: 0% (2018 est.)

Urbanization: *urban population:* 45% of total population (2022)
rate of urbanization: 3.22% annual rate of change (2020-25 est.)

Revenue from forest resources: *forest revenues:* 9.24% of GDP (2018 est.)

Revenue from coal: *coal revenues:* 0% of GDP (2018 est.)

Waste and recycling: *municipal solid waste generated annually:* 289,514 tons (2015 est.)

Major aquifers: Senegalo-Mauritanian Basin

Total water withdrawal: *municipal:* 34.1 million cubic meters (2017 est.)
industrial: 11.9 million cubic meters (2017 est.)
agricultural: 144 million cubic meters (2017 est.)

Total renewable water resources: 31.4 billion cubic meters (2017 est.)

GOVERNMENT

Country name: *conventional long form:* Republic of Guinea-Bissau
conventional short form: Guinea-Bissau
local long form: Republica da Guine-Bissau
local short form: Guine-Bissau
former: Portuguese Guinea
etymology: the country is named after the Guinea region of West Africa that lies along the Gulf of Guinea and stretches north to the Sahel; "Bissau," the name of the capital city, distinguishes the country from neighboring Guinea

Government type: semi-presidential republic

Capital: *name:* Bissau
geographic coordinates: 11 51 N, 15 35 W
time difference: UTC 0 (5 hours ahead of Washington, DC, during Standard Time)
etymology: the meaning of Bissau is uncertain, it might be an alternative name for the Papel people who live in the area of the city of Bissau

Administrative divisions: 9 regions (regioes, singular - regiao); Bafata, Biombo, Bissau, Bolama/Bijagos, Cacheu, Gabu, Oio, Quinara, Tombali

Independence: 24 September 1973 (declared); 10 September 1974 (from Portugal)

National holiday: Independence Day, 24 September (1973)

Constitution: *history:* promulgated 16 May 1984; note - constitution suspended following military coup April 2012, restored 2014; note - in May 2020, President EMBALO established a commission to draft a revised constitution
amendments: proposed by the National People's Assembly if supported by at least one third of its members, by the Council of State (a presidential consultant body), or by the government; passage requires approval by at least two-thirds majority vote of the Assembly; constitutional articles on the republican and secular form of government and national sovereignty cannot be amended; amended 1991, 1993, 1996

Legal system: mixed legal system of civil law, which incorporated Portuguese law at independence and influenced by Economic Community of West African States (ECOWAS), West African Economic and Monetary Union (UEMOA), African Francophone Public Law, and customary law

International law organization participation: accepts compulsory ICJ jurisdiction; non-party state to the ICCt

Citizenship: *citizenship by birth:* yes
citizenship by descent only: yes
dual citizenship recognized: no
residency requirement for naturalization: 5 years

Suffrage: 18 years of age; universal

Executive branch: *chief of state:* President Umaro Sissoko EMBALO (since 27 February 2020); note - President EMBALO was declared winner of the 29 December 2019 runoff presidential election by the electoral commission, in late February 2020, EMBALO inaugurated himself with only military leadership present, even though the Supreme Court of Justice had yet to rule on an electoral litigation appeal lodged by his political rival Domingos Simoes PEREIRA
head of government: Prime Minister Nuno NABIAM (since 27 February 2020)
cabinet: Cabinet nominated by the prime minister, appointed by the president
elections/appointments: president directly elected by absolute majority popular vote in 2 rounds if needed for up to 2 consecutive 5-year terms; election last held on 24 November 2019 with a runoff on 29 December 2019 (next to be held in 2024); prime minister appointed by the president after consultation with party leaders in the National People's Assembly; note - the president cannot apply for a third consecutive term
election results: Umaro Sissoco EMBALO elected president in second round; percent of vote in first round - Domingos Simoes PEREIRA (PAIGC) 40.1%, Umaro Sissoco EMBALO (Madem G15) 27.7%, Nuno Gomez NABIAM (APU-PDGB) 13.2%, Jose Mario VAZ (independent) 12.4%, other 6.6%; percent of vote in second round - Umaro Sissoco EMBALO 53.6%, Domingos Simoes PEREIRA 46.5% (2019)

Legislative branch: *description:* unicameral National People's Assembly or Assembleia Nacional Popular (102 seats; 100 members directly elected in 27 multi-seat constituencies by closed party-list proportional representation vote and 2 elected in single-seat constituencies for citizens living abroad (Africa 1, Europe 1); all members serve 4-year terms)
elections: note: President dissolved parliament on 16 May 2022 and decreed new elections for 18 December 2022
last held on 10 March 2019 (next to be held in March 2023)
election results: percent of vote by party - PAIGC 35.2%, Madem G-15 21.1%, PRS 21.1%, other 22.6%; seats by party - PAIGC 47, Madem G-15 27, PRS 21, other 7; composition - men 88, women 14, percent of women 13.7%

Judicial branch: *highest court(s):* Supreme Court or Supremo Tribunal de Justica (consists of 9 judges and organized into Civil, Criminal, and Social and Administrative Disputes Chambers); note - the Supreme Court has both appellate and constitutional jurisdiction
judge selection and term of office: judges nominated by the Higher Council of the Magistrate, a major government organ responsible for judge appointments, dismissals, and judiciary discipline; judges appointed by the president for life
subordinate courts: Appeals Court; regional (first instance) courts; military court

Political parties and leaders: African Party for the Independence of Guinea and Cabo Verde or PAIGC [Domingos SIMOES PEREIRA]
Democratic Convergence Party or PCD [Vicente FERNANDES]
Movement for Democratic Alternation Group of 15 or MADEM-G15 [Braima CAMARA]
National People's Assembly – Democratic Party of Guinea Bissau or APU-PDGB [Nuno Gomes NABIAM]
New Democracy Party or PND [Mamadu Iaia DJALO]
Party for Social Renewal or PRS [Alberto NAMBEIA]
Republican Party for Independence and Development or PRID [Aristides GOMES]
Union for Change or UM [Agnelo REGALA]

International organization participation: ACP, AfDB, AOSIS, AU, CPLP, ECOWAS, FAO, FZ, G-77, IBRD, ICAO, ICRM, IDA, IDB, IFAD, IFC, IFRCS, ILO, IMF, IMO, Interpol, IOC, IOM, IPU, ITSO, ITU, ITUC (NGOs), MIGA, MINUSMA, NAM, OIC, OIF, OPCW, UN, UNCTAD, UNESCO, UNIDO, UNWTO, UPU, WADB (regional), WAEMU, WCO, WFTU (NGOs), WHO, WIPO, WMO, WTO

Diplomatic representation in the US: *chief of mission:* none; note - Guinea-Bissau does not have official representation in Washington, DC

Diplomatic representation from the US: *embassy:* the US Embassy suspended operations on 14 June 1998; the US Ambassador to Senegal is accredited to Guinea-Bissau; US diplomatic representation in Guinea-Bissau is conducted through the US Embassy in Dakar and the Guinea-Bissau Liaison Office located in Bissau
mailing address: 2080 Bissau Place, Washington DC 20521-2080
email address and website:
dakarACS@state.gov
https://gw.usmission.gov/

Flag description: two equal horizontal bands of yellow (top) and green with a vertical red band on the hoist side; there is a black five-pointed star centered in the red band; yellow symbolizes the sun; green denotes hope; red represents blood shed during the struggle for independence; the black star stands for African unity
note: uses the popular Pan-African colors of Ethiopia; the flag design was heavily influenced by the Ghanaian flag

National symbol(s): black star; national colors: red, yellow, green, black

National anthem: *name:* "Esta e a Nossa Patria Bem Amada" (This Is Our Beloved Country)
lyrics/music: Amilcar Lopes CABRAL/XIAO He
note: adopted 1974; a delegation from then Portuguese Guinea visited China in 1963 and heard music by XIAO He; Amilcar Lopes CABRAL, the leader of Guinea-Bissau's independence movement, asked the composer to create a piece that would inspire his people to struggle for independence

ECONOMY

Economic overview: Guinea-Bissau is highly dependent on subsistence agriculture, cashew nut exports, and foreign assistance. Two out of three Bissau-Guineans remain below the absolute poverty line. The legal economy is based on cashews and fishing. Illegal logging and trafficking in narcotics also play significant roles. The combination of limited economic prospects, weak institutions, and favorable geography have made this West African country a way station for drugs bound for Europe.

Guinea-Bissau has substantial potential for development of mineral resources, including phosphates, bauxite, and mineral sands. Offshore oil and gas exploration has begun. The country's climate and soil make it feasible to grow a wide range of cash crops, fruit, vegetables, and tubers; however, cashews generate more than 80% of export receipts and are the main source of income for many rural communities.

The government was deposed in August 2015, and since then, a political stalemate has resulted in weak governance and reduced donor support.

The country is participating in a three-year, IMF extended credit facility program that was suspended because of a planned bank bailout. The program was renewed in 2017, but the major donors of direct budget support (the EU, World Bank, and African Development Bank) have halted their programs indefinitely. Diversification of the economy remains a key policy goal, but Guinea- Bissau's poor infrastructure and business climate will constrain this effort.

Real GDP (purchasing power parity): $3.64 billion (2020 est.)
$3.73 billion (2019 est.)
$3.56 billion (2018 est.)
note: data are in 2017 dollars

Real GDP growth rate: 5.9% (2017 est.)
6.3% (2016 est.)
6.1% (2015 est.)

Real GDP per capita: $1,800 (2020 est.)
$1,900 (2019 est.)
$1,900 (2018 est.)
note: data are in 2017 dollars

GDP (official exchange rate): $1.339 billion (2019 est.)

Inflation rate (consumer prices): 0.2% (2019 est.)
0.3% (2018 est.)
1.6% (2017 est.)

GDP - composition, by sector of origin: *agriculture:* 50% (2017 est.)
industry: 13.1% (2017 est.)
services: 36.9% (2017 est.)

GDP - composition, by end use: *household consumption:* 83.9% (2017 est.)
government consumption: 12% (2017 est.)
investment in fixed capital: 4.1% (2017 est.)
investment in inventories: 0.2% (2017 est.)
exports of goods and services: 26.4% (2017 est.)
imports of goods and services: -26.5% (2017 est.)

Agricultural products: rice, cashew nuts, roots/tubers nes, oil palm fruit, plantains, cassava, groundnuts, vegetables, coconuts, fruit

Industries: agricultural products processing, beer, soft drinks

Industrial production growth rate: 2.5% (2017 est.)

Labor force: 731,300 (2013 est.)

Labor force - by occupation: *agriculture:* 82%
industry and services: 18% (2000 est.)

Population below poverty line: 67% (2015 est.)

Gini Index coefficient - distribution of family income: 50.7 (2010 est.)

Household income or consumption by percentage share: *lowest 10%:* 2.9%
highest 10%: 28% (2002)

Budget: *revenues:* 246.2 million (2017 est.)
expenditures: 263.5 million (2017 est.)

Budget surplus (+) or deficit (-): -1.3% (of GDP) (2017 est.)

Public debt: 53.9% of GDP (2017 est.)
57.9% of GDP (2016 est.)

Taxes and other revenues: 18.2% (of GDP) (2017 est.)

Fiscal year: calendar year

Current account balance: -$27 million (2017 est.)
$16 million (2016 est.)

Exports: $290 million (2019 est.) note: data are in current year dollars
$380 million (2018 est.) note: data are in current year dollars

Exports - partners: India 50%, Belgium 28%, Cote d'Ivoire 8% (2019)

Exports - commodities: cashews, gold, fish, lumber, aluminum ores (2019)

Imports: $500 million (2019 est.) note: data are in current year dollars
$460 million (2018 est.) note: data are in current year dollars

Imports - partners: Portugal 31%, Senegal 20%, China 10%, Netherlands 7%, Pakistan 7% (2019)

Imports - commodities: refined petroleum, rice, wheat products, soups/broths, malt extract (2019)

Reserves of foreign exchange and gold: $356.4 million (31 December 2017 est.)
$349.4 million (31 December 2016 est.)

Debt - external: $1.095 billion (31 December 2010 est.)
$941.5 million (31 December 2000 est.)

Exchange rates: Communaute Financiere Africaine francs (XOF) per US dollar -
605.3 (2017 est.)
593.01 (2016 est.)
593.01 (2015 est.)
591.45 (2014 est.)
494.42 (2013 est.)

ENERGY

Electricity access: *electrification - total population:* 28% (2019)
electrification - urban areas: 56% (2019)
electrification - rural areas: 7% (2019)

Electricity: *installed generating capacity:* 28,000 kW (2020 est.)
consumption: 76.458 million kWh (2019 est.)
exports: 0 kWh (2019 est.)
imports: 0 kWh (2019 est.)
transmission/distribution losses: 6 million kWh (2019 est.)

Electricity generation sources: *fossil fuels:* 97.6% of total installed capacity (2020 est.)
solar: 2.4% of total installed capacity (2020 est.)

Petroleum: *total petroleum production:* 0 bbl/day (2021 est.)
refined petroleum consumption: 2,200 bbl/day (2019 est.)

Refined petroleum products - imports: 2,625 bbl/day (2015 est.)

Carbon dioxide emissions: 342,000 metric tonnes of CO2 (2019 est.)
from petroleum and other liquids: 342,000 metric tonnes of CO2 (2019 est.)

Energy consumption per capita: 2.46 million Btu/person (2019 est.)

COMMUNICATIONS

Telephones - mobile cellular: *total subscriptions:* 1,913,858 (2020 est.)
subscriptions per 100 inhabitants: 97 (2020 est.)

Telecommunication systems: *general assessment:* small system including a combination of microwave radio relay, open-wire lines, radiotelephone, and mobile cellular communications; 2 mobile network operators; one of the poorest countries in the world and this is reflected in the country's telecommunications development; radio is the most important source of information for the public (2020)
domestic: fixed-line teledensity less than 1 per 100 persons; mobile cellular teledensity is just over 97 per 100 persons (2020)
international: country code - 245; ACE submarine cable connecting Guinea-Bissau with 20 landing points in Western and South Africa and Europe (2019)

Broadcast media: 1 state-owned TV station, Televisao da Guine-Bissau (TGB) and a second station, Radio e Televisao de Portugal (RTP) Africa, is operated by Portuguese public broadcaster (RTP); 1

state-owned radio station, several private radio stations, and some community radio stations; multiple international broadcasters are available (2019)

Internet country code: .gw

Internet users: *total:* 452,640 (2020 est.)
percent of population: 23% (2020 est.)

Broadband - fixed subscriptions: *total:* 2,383 (2020 est.)
subscriptions per 100 inhabitants: 0.1 (2020 est.)

TRANSPORTATION

Civil aircraft registration country code prefix: J5

Airports: *total:* 8 (2021)

Airports - with paved runways: *total:* 2
over 3,047 m: 1
1,524 to 2,437 m: 1 (2021)

Airports - with unpaved runways: *total:* 6
1,524 to 2,437 m: 1
914 to 1,523 m: 2
under 914 m: 3 (2021)

Roadways: *total:* 4,400 km (2018)
paved: 453 km (2018)
unpaved: 3,947 km (2018)

Waterways: 1,367 km (2022) major rivers Geba-550km, Corubal 560 km, Cacheu 257 km (rivers are partially navigable; many inlets and creeks provide shallow-water access to much of interior)

Merchant marine: *total:* 8
by type: general cargo 5, other 3 (2021)

Ports and terminals: *major seaport(s):* Bissau, Buba, Cacheu, Farim

MILITARY AND SECURITY

Military and security forces: People's Revolutionary Armed Force (FARP): Army, Navy, Air Force; Ministry of Internal Administration: Guard Nacional (a gendarmerie force), Public Order Police, Border Police, Rapid Intervention Police, Maritime Police (2022)
note: the Public Order Police is responsible for maintaining law and order, while the Judicial Police, under the Ministry of Justice, has primary responsibility for investigating drug trafficking, terrorism, and other transnational crimes

Military expenditures: 1.8% of GDP (2021 est.)
1.7% of GDP (2020 est.)
1.9% of GDP (2019 est.) (approximately $50 million)
1.7% of GDP (2018 est.) (approximately $45 million)
1.7% of GDP (2017 est.) (approximately $45 million)

Military and security service personnel strengths: approximately 4,000 total active troops, including a few hundred air and naval personnel (2022)

Military equipment inventories and acquisitions: the FARP is poorly armed with an inventory consisting of Soviet-era equipment, much of which is reportedly unserviceable; the only reported deliveries of military equipment since 2015 were patrol boats from Spain in 2017 and non-lethal equipment from China in 2015; Guinea-Bissau has also discussed acquiring military equipment with Indonesia (2022)

Military service age and obligation: 18-25 years of age for selective compulsory military service (Air Force service is voluntary); 16 years of age or younger, with parental consent, for voluntary service (2022)

Military - note: from 2012-2020, the Economic Community of West Africa (ECOWAS) deployed a security force to Guinea-Bissau to manage the post-coup transition, including protecting key political figures and public buildings, restoring civil institutions, and re-establishing the rule of law; at the height of the deployment, the force, known as the ECOWAS Mission in Guinea- Bissau (ECOMIB), deployed nearly 700 military and police personnel from Burkina Faso, Nigeria, and Senegal (2022)

TRANSNATIONAL ISSUES

Disputes - international: a longstanding low-grade conflict continues in parts of Casamance, in Senegal across the border; some rebels use Guinea-Bissau as a safe haven

Refugees and internally displaced persons: *refugees (country of origin):* 7,757 (Senegal) (2022)

Trafficking in persons: *current situation:* Guinea-Bissau is a country of origin and destination for children subjected to forced labor and sex trafficking; the scope of the problem of trafficking women or men for forced labor or forced prostitution is unknown; boys reportedly were transported to southern Senegal for forced manual and agricultural labor; girls may be subjected to forced domestic service and child prostitution in Senegal and Guinea; both boys and girls are forced to work as street vendors in cities in Guinea-Bissau and Senegal
tier rating: Tier 2 Watch List — Guinea-Bissau does not fully meet the minimum standards for the elimination of trafficking but is making significant efforts to do so; efforts include identifying forced child begging victims, cooperating with Moroccan authorities on international crime investigations, and approving a new action plan; yet, the government has not convicted a trafficker, identified fewer trafficking victims, and lacked resources or the political will to fight trafficking or to enact its action plan, which would meet minimum standards; Guinea-Bissau was granted a waiver under the Trafficking Victims Protection Act from downgrade to Tier 3 (2020)

Illicit drugs: important transit country for South American cocaine en route to Europe; enabling environment for trafficker operations due to pervasive corruption; archipelago-like geography near the capital facilitates drug smuggling

GUYANA

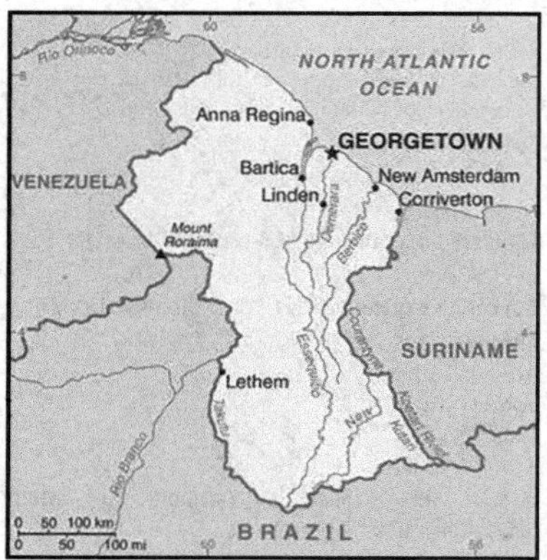

INTRODUCTION

Background: Originally a Dutch colony in the 17th century, by 1815 Guyana had become a British possession. The abolition of slavery led to settlement of urban areas by former slaves and the importation of indentured servants from India to work the sugar plantations. The resulting ethnocultural divide has persisted and has led to turbulent politics. Guyana achieved independence from the UK in 1966, and since then it has been ruled mostly by socialist-oriented governments. In 1992, Cheddi JAGAN was elected president in what is considered the country's first free and fair election since independence. After his death five years later, his wife, Janet JAGAN, became president but resigned in 1999 due to poor health. Her successor, Bharrat JAGDEO, was elected in 2001 and again in 2006. Early elections held in May 2015 resulted in the first change in governing party and the replacement of President Donald RAMOTAR by current President David GRANGER. After a December 2018 no-confidence vote against the GRANGER government, national elections were constitutionally required to take place within three months. After over a year of extra-constitutional rule by the GRANGER administration, elections were held, though voting irregularities led to a nationwide recount. The current Irfaan ALI administration was sworn in to office in August 2020. The discovery of oil in 2015 has been the primary economic and political focus, with many hoping the significant reserves will transform one of the poorest countries in the region.

GEOGRAPHY

Location: Northern South America, bordering the North Atlantic Ocean, between Suriname and Venezuela

Geographic coordinates: 5 00 N, 59 00 W

Map references: South America

Area: *total:* 214,969 sq km
land: 196,849 sq km
water: 18,120 sq km

Area - comparative: slightly smaller than Idaho; almost twice the size of Tennessee

Land boundaries: *total:* 2,933 km
border countries (3): Brazil 1,308 km; Suriname 836 km; Venezuela 789 km

Coastline: 459 km

Maritime claims: *territorial sea:* 12 nm
exclusive economic zone: 200 nm
continental shelf: 200 nm or to the outer edge of the continental margin

Climate: tropical; hot, humid, moderated by northeast trade winds; two rainy seasons (May to August, November to January)

Terrain: mostly rolling highlands; low coastal plain; savanna in south

Elevation: *highest point:* Laberintos del Norte on Mount Roraima 2,775 m
lowest point: Atlantic Ocean 0 m
mean elevation: 207 m

Natural resources: bauxite, gold, diamonds, hardwood timber, shrimp, fish

Land use: *agricultural land:* 8.4% (2018 est.)
arable land: 2.1% (2018 est.)
permanent crops: 0.1% (2018 est.)
permanent pasture: 6.2% (2018 est.)
forest: 77.4% (2018 est.)
other: 14.2% (2018 est.)

Irrigated land: 1,430 sq km (2012)

Major watersheds (area sq km): Atlantic Ocean drainage: Amazon (6,145,186 sq km), Orinoco (953,675 sq km)

Population distribution: population is heavily concentrated in the northeast in and around Georgetown, with noteable concentrations along the Berbice River to the east; the remainder of the country is sparsely populated

Natural hazards: flash flood threat during rainy seasons

Geography - note: the third-smallest country in South America after Suriname and Uruguay; substantial portions of its western and eastern territories are claimed by Venezuela and Suriname respectively; contains some of the largest unspoiled rainforests on the continent

PEOPLE AND SOCIETY

Population: 789,683 (2022 est.)

Nationality: *noun:* Guyanese (singular and plural)
adjective: Guyanese

Ethnic groups: East Indian 39.8%, African descent 29.3%, mixed 19.9%, Amerindian 10.5%, other 0.5% (includes Portuguese, Chinese, White) (2012 est.)

Languages: English (official), Guyanese Creole, Amerindian languages (including Caribbean and Arawak languages), Indian languages (including Caribbean Hindustani, a dialect of Hindi), Chinese (2014 est.)

Religions: Protestant 34.8% (Pentecostal 22.8%, Seventh Day Adventist 5.4%, Anglican 5.2%, Methodist 1.4%), Hindu 24.8%, Roman Catholic 7.1%, Muslim 6.8%, Jehovah's Witness 1.3%, Rastafarian 0.5%, other Christian 20.8%, other 0.9%, none 3.1% (2012 est.)

Demographic profile: Guyana is the only English-speaking country in South America and shares cultural and historical bonds with the Anglophone Caribbean. Guyana's two largest ethnic groups are the Afro-Guyanese (descendants of African slaves) and the Indo-Guyanese (descendants of Indian indentured laborers), which together comprise about three quarters of Guyana's population. Tensions periodically have boiled over between the two groups, which back ethnically based political parties and vote along ethnic lines. Poverty reduction has stagnated since the late 1990s. About one-third of the Guyanese population lives below the poverty line; indigenous people are disproportionately affected. Although Guyana's literacy rate is reported to be among the highest in the Western Hemisphere, the level of functional literacy is considerably lower, which has been attributed to poor education quality, teacher training, and infrastructure.

Guyana's emigration rate is among the highest in the world - more than 55% of its citizens reside abroad - and it is one of the largest recipients of remittances relative to GDP among Latin American and Caribbean counties. Although remittances are a vital source of income for most citizens, the pervasive emigration of skilled workers deprives Guyana of professionals in healthcare and other key sectors. More than 80% of Guyanese nationals with tertiary level educations have emigrated. Brain drain and the concentration of limited medical resources in Georgetown hamper Guyana's ability to meet the health needs of its predominantly rural population. Guyana has one of the highest HIV prevalence rates in the region and continues to rely on international support for its HIV treatment and prevention programs.

Age structure: *0-14 years:* 23.91% (male 91,317/female 88,025)
15-24 years: 21.23% (male 81,294/female 77,987)
25-54 years: 39.48% (male 154,825/female 141,385)
55-64 years: 8.37% (male 29,385/female 33,386)
65 years and over: 7.01% (male 21,325/female 31,275) (2020 est.)

Dependency ratios: *total dependency ratio:* 53.2
youth dependency ratio: 42.5
elderly dependency ratio: 10.7
potential support ratio: 9.3 (2020 est.)

Median age: *total:* 27.5 years
male: 27.2 years
female: 27.9 years (2020 est.)

Population growth rate: 0.24% (2022 est.)

Birth rate: 16.72 births/1,000 population (2022 est.)

Death rate: 6.91 deaths/1,000 population (2022 est.)

Net migration rate: -7.42 migrant(s)/1,000 population (2022 est.)

Population distribution: population is heavily concentrated in the northeast in and around Georgetown, with noteable concentrations along the Berbice River to the east; the remainder of the country is sparsely populated

Urbanization: *urban population:* 27% of total population (2022)
rate of urbanization: 1.01% annual rate of change (2020-25 est.)

Major urban areas - population: 110,000 GEORGETOWN (capital) (2018)

Sex ratio: *at birth:* 1.05 male(s)/female
0-14 years: 1.04 male(s)/female
15-24 years: 1.05 male(s)/female
25-54 years: 1.11 male(s)/female
55-64 years: 0.98 male(s)/female
65 years and over: 0.69 male(s)/female
total population: 1.04 male(s)/female (2022 est.)

Mother's mean age at first birth: 20.8 years (2009 est.)
note: data represents median age at first birth among women 25-29

Maternal mortality ratio: 667 deaths/100,000 live births (2017 est.)

Infant mortality rate: *total:* 22.15 deaths/1,000 live births
male: 25.05 deaths/1,000 live births
female: 19.1 deaths/1,000 live births (2022 est.)

Life expectancy at birth: *total population:* 71.87 years
male: 70.03 years
female: 73.8 years (2022 est.)

Total fertility rate: 2.06 children born/woman (2022 est.)

Contraceptive prevalence rate: 29.9% (2019/20)

Drinking water source: *improved: urban:* 100% of population
rural: 95.6% of population
total: 96.8% of population
unimproved: urban: 0% of population
rural: 4.4% of population
total: 3.2% of population (2020 est.)

Current health expenditure: 4.9% of GDP (2019)

Physicians density: 1.42 physicians/1,000 population (2020)

Hospital bed density: 1.7 beds/1,000 population (2016)

Sanitation facility access: *improved: urban:* 97.8% of population
rural: 95.4% of population
total: 96% of population
unimproved: urban: 2.2% of population
rural: 4.6% of population
total: 4% of population (2020 est.)

HIV/AIDS - adult prevalence rate: 1.3% (2020 est.)

Major infectious diseases: *degree of risk:* very high (2020)
food or waterborne diseases: bacterial and protozoal diarrhea, hepatitis A, and typhoid fever
vectorborne diseases: dengue fever and malaria

Obesity - adult prevalence rate: 20.2% (2016)

Alcohol consumption per capita: *total:* 5.11 liters of pure alcohol (2019 est.)
beer: 2.75 liters of pure alcohol (2019 est.)
wine: 0.04 liters of pure alcohol (2019 est.)
spirits: 2.3 liters of pure alcohol (2019 est.)
other alcohols: 0.02 liters of pure alcohol (2019 est.)

Tobacco use: *total:* 12.1% (2020 est.)
male: 21.7% (2020 est.)
female: 2.4% (2020 est.)

Children under the age of 5 years underweight: 8.2% (2014)

Education expenditures: 4.5% of GDP (2018 est.)

Literacy: *definition:* age 15 and over has ever attended school
total population: 88.5%
male: 87.2%
female: 89.8% (2015)

School life expectancy (primary to tertiary education): *total:* 11 years
male: 11 years
female: 12 years (2012)

Unemployment, youth ages 15-24: *total:* 26.5%
male: 20.7%
female: 34.6% (2018 est.)

ENVIRONMENT

Environment - current issues: water pollution from sewage and agricultural and industrial chemicals; deforestation

Environment - international agreements: *party to:* Biodiversity, Climate Change, Climate Change-Kyoto Protocol, Climate Change-Paris Agreement, Comprehensive Nuclear Test Ban, Desertification, Endangered Species, Hazardous Wastes, Law of the Sea, Marine Dumping-London Protocol, Ozone Layer Protection, Ship Pollution, Tropical Timber 2006
signed, but not ratified: none of the selected agreements

Air pollutants: *particulate matter emissions:* 20.46 micrograms per cubic meter (2016 est.)
carbon dioxide emissions: 2.38 megatons (2016 est.)
methane emissions: 1.81 megatons (2020 est.)

Climate: tropical; hot, humid, moderated by northeast trade winds; two rainy seasons (May to August, November to January)

Land use: *agricultural land:* 8.4% (2018 est.)
arable land: 2.1% (2018 est.)
permanent crops: 0.1% (2018 est.)
permanent pasture: 6.2% (2018 est.)
forest: 77.4% (2018 est.)
other: 14.2% (2018 est.)

Urbanization: *urban population:* 27% of total population (2022)
rate of urbanization: 1.01% annual rate of change (2020-25 est.)

Revenue from forest resources: *forest revenues:* 4.56% of GDP (2018 est.)

Revenue from coal: *coal revenues:* 0% of GDP (2018 est.)

Waste and recycling: *municipal solid waste generated annually:* 179,252 tons (2010 est.)
municipal solid waste recycled annually: 968 tons (2010 est.)
percent of municipal solid waste recycled: 0.5% (2010 est.)

Major watersheds (area sq km): Atlantic Ocean drainage: Amazon (6,145,186 sq km), Orinoco (953,675 sq km)

Total water withdrawal: *municipal:* 61.3 million cubic meters (2017 est.)
industrial: 20.4 million cubic meters (2017 est.)
agricultural: 1.363 billion cubic meters (2017 est.)

Total renewable water resources: 271 billion cubic meters (2017 est.)

GOVERNMENT

Country name: *conventional long form:* Cooperative Republic of Guyana
conventional short form: Guyana
former: British Guiana
etymology: the name is derived from Guiana, the original name for the region that included British Guiana, Dutch Guiana, and French Guiana; ultimately the word is derived from an indigenous Amerindian language and means "Land of Many Waters" (referring to the area's multitude of rivers and streams)

Government type: parliamentary republic

Capital: *name:* Georgetown
geographic coordinates: 6 48 N, 58 09 W
time difference: UTC-4 (1 hour ahead of Washington, DC, during Standard Time)
etymology: when the British took possession of the town from the Dutch in 1812, they renamed it Georgetown in honor of King GEORGE III (1738-1820)

Administrative divisions: 10 regions; Barima-Waini, Cuyuni-Mazaruni, Demerara-Mahaica, East Berbice-Corentyne, Essequibo Islands-West Demerara, Mahaica-Berbice, Pomeroon-Supenaam, Potaro-Siparuni, Upper Demerara-Berbice, Upper Takutu-Upper Essequibo

Independence: 26 May 1966 (from the UK)

National holiday: Republic Day, 23 February (1970)

Constitution: *history:* several previous; latest promulgated 6 October 1980
amendments: proposed by the National Assembly; passage of amendments affecting constitutional articles, such as national sovereignty, government structure and powers, and constitutional amendment procedures, requires approval by the Assembly membership, approval in a referendum, and assent of the president; other amendments only require Assembly approval; amended many times, last in 2016

Legal system: common law system, based on the English model, with some Roman-Dutch civil law influence

International law organization participation: has not submitted an ICJ jurisdiction declaration; accepts ICCt jurisdiction

Citizenship: *citizenship by birth:* yes
citizenship by descent only: yes
dual citizenship recognized: no
residency requirement for naturalization: na

Suffrage: 18 years of age; universal

Executive branch: *chief of state:* President Mohammed Irfaan ALI (since 2 August 2020); First Vice President Mark PHILLIPS (since 2 August 2020); Vice President Bharrat JAGDEO (since 2 August 2020); Prime Minister Mark PHILLIPS (since 2 August 2020); note - the president is both chief of state and head of government
head of government: President Mohammed Irfaan ALI (since 2 August 2020); First Vice President Mark PHILLIPS (since 2 August 2020); Vice President Bharrat JAGDEO (since 2 August 2020)
cabinet: Cabinet of Ministers appointed by the president, responsible to the National Assembly
elections/appointments: the predesignated candidate of the winning party in the last National Assembly election becomes president for a 5-year term (no term limits); election last held on 2 March 2020 (next to be held in 2025); prime minister appointed by the president
election results: *2020:* Mohammed Irfaan ALI (PPP/C) designated president by the majority party in the National Assembly
2015: David GRANGER (APNU-AFC) designated president by the majority party in the National Assembly

Legislative branch: *description:* unicameral National Assembly (70 seats; 40 members directly elected in a single nationwide constituencies, 25 directly elected in multi-seat constituencies - all by closed-list proportional representation vote, 2 non-elected ministers, 2 non-elected parliamentary secretaries, and the speaker; members serve 5-year terms)
elections: last held on 2 March 2020 (next to be held in 2025)
election results: percent of vote by party - PPP/C 50.69%, APNU-AFC 47.34%, LJP 0.58%, ANUG 0.5%, TNM 0.05%, other 0.84%; seats by party - PPP/C 33, APNU-AFC 31, LJP-ANUG-TNM 1; composition (elected and non-elected) - men 45, women 25, percent of women 35.7%; note - the initial results were declared invalid and a partial recount was conducted from 6 May to 8 June 2020, in which PPP/C was declared the winner

Judicial branch: *highest court(s):* Supreme Court of Judicature (consists of the Court of Appeal with a chief justice and 3 justices, and the High Court with a chief justice and 10 justices organized into 3- or 5-judge panels); note - in 2009, Guyana acceded to the Caribbean Court of Justice as the final court of appeal in civil and criminal cases, replacing that of the Judicial Committee of the Privy Council (in London)
judge selection and term of office: Court of Appeal and High Court chief justices appointed by the president; other judges of both courts appointed by the Judicial Service Commission, a body appointed by the president; judges appointed for life with retirement at age 65
subordinate courts: Land Court; magistrates' courts

Political parties and leaders: A New and United Guyana or ANUG [Ralph RAMKARRAN]
A Partnership for National Unity or APNU [Joseph HARMON]
Alliance for Change or AFC [Khemraj RAMJATTAN]
Justice for All Party [Chandra Narine SHARMA]
Liberty and Justice Party or LJP [Lenox SHUMAN]
National Independent Party or NIP [Saphier Husain SUBEDAR]
People's Progressive Party/Civic or PPP/C [Dr. Bharrat JAGDEO]
The New Movement or TNM [Dr. Asha KISSOON]
The United Force or TUF [Marissa NADIR]
United Republican Party or URP [Vishnu BANDHU]

International organization participation: ACP, AOSIS, C, Caricom, CD, CDB, CELAC, FAO, G-77, IADB, IBRD, ICAO, ICCt, ICRM, IDA, IFAD, IFC, IFRCS, ILO, IMF, IMO, Interpol, IOC, IOM, ISO (correspondent), ITU, LAES, MIGA, NAM, OAS, OIC, OPANAL, OPCW, PCA, Petrocaribe, PROSUR, UN, UNASUR, UNCTAD, UNESCO, UNIDO, UPU, WCO, WFTU (NGOs), WHO, WIPO, WMO, WTO

Diplomatic representation in the US: *chief of mission:* Ambassador Samuel Archibald HINDS (since 7 July 2021)
chancery: 2490 Tracy Place NW, Washington, DC 20008
telephone: [1] (202) 265-6900
FAX: [1] (202) 232-1297
email address and website:
guyanaembassydc@verizon.net
http://www.guyanaembassyusa.org/
consulate(s) general: New York

Diplomatic representation from the US: *chief of mission:* Ambassador Sarah-Ann LYNCH (since 13 March 2019)
embassy: 100 Young and Duke Streets, Kingston, Georgetown
mailing address: 3170 Georgetown Place, Washington DC 20521-3170

telephone: [592] 225-4900 through 4909
FAX: [592] 225-8497
email address and website:
acsgeorge@state.gov
https://gy.usembassy.gov/

Flag description: green with a red isosceles triangle (based on the hoist side) superimposed on a long, yellow arrowhead; there is a narrow, black border between the red and yellow, and a narrow, white border between the yellow and the green; green represents forest and foliage; yellow stands for mineral resources and a bright future; white symbolizes Guyana's rivers; red signifies zeal and the sacrifice of the people; black indicates perseverance; also referred to by its nickname The Golden Arrowhead

National symbol(s): Canje pheasant (hoatzin), jaguar, Victoria Regia water lily; national colors: red, yellow, green, black, white

National anthem: *name:* "Dear Land of Guyana, of Rivers and Plains"
lyrics/music: Archibald Leonard LUKERL/Robert Cyril Gladstone POTTER
note: adopted 1966

ECONOMY

Economic overview: The Guyanese economy exhibited moderate economic growth in recent years and is based largely on agriculture and extractive industries. The economy is heavily dependent upon the export of six commodities - sugar, gold, bauxite, shrimp, timber, and rice - which represent nearly 60% of the country's GDP and are highly susceptible to adverse weather conditions and fluctuations in commodity prices. Guyana closed or consolidated several sugar estates in 2017, reducing production of sugar to a forecasted 147,000 tons in 2018, less than half of 2017 production. Much of Guyana's growth in recent years has come from a surge in gold production. With a record-breaking 700,000 ounces of gold produced in 2016, Gold production in Guyana has offset the economic effects of declining sugar production. In January 2018, estimated 3.2 billion barrels of oil were found offshore and Guyana is scheduled to become a petroleum producer by March 2020.

Guyana's entrance into the Caricom Single Market and Economy in January 2006 broadened the country's export market, primarily in the raw materials sector. Guyana has experienced positive growth almost every year over the past decade. Inflation has been kept under control. Recent years have seen the government's stock of debt reduced significantly - with external debt now less than half of what it was in the early 1990s. Despite these improvements, the government is still juggling a sizable external debt against the urgent need for expanded public investment. In March 2007, the Inter-American Development Bank, Guyana's principal donor, canceled Guyana's nearly $470 million debt, equivalent to 21% of GDP, which along with other Highly Indebted Poor Country debt forgiveness, brought the debt-to-GDP ratio down from 183% in 2006 to 52% in 2017. Guyana had become heavily indebted as a result of the inward-looking, state-led development model pursued in the 1970s and 1980s. Chronic problems include a shortage of skilled labor and a deficient infrastructure.

Real GDP (purchasing power parity): $14.69 billion (2020 est.)
$10.24 billion (2019 est.)
$9.72 billion (2018 est.)
note: data are in 2017 dollars

Real GDP growth rate: 2.1% (2017 est.)
3.4% (2016 est.)
3.1% (2015 est.)

Real GDP per capita: $18,700 (2020 est.)
$13,100 (2019 est.)
$12,500 (2018 est.)
note: data are in 2017 dollars

GDP (official exchange rate): $3.561 billion (2017 est.)

Inflation rate (consumer prices): 2% (2017 est.)
0.8% (2016 est.)

GDP - composition, by sector of origin: *agriculture:* 15.4% (2017 est.)
industry: 15.3% (2017 est.)
services: 69.3% (2017 est.)

GDP - composition, by end use: *household consumption:* 71.1% (2017 est.)
government consumption: 18.2% (2017 est.)
investment in fixed capital: 25.4% (2017 est.)
investment in inventories: 0% (2017 est.)
exports of goods and services: 47.8% (2017 est.)
imports of goods and services: -63% (2017 est.)

Agricultural products: rice, sugar cane, coconuts, pumpkins, squash, gourds, milk, eggplants, green chillies/peppers, poultry

Industries: bauxite, sugar, rice milling, timber, textiles, gold mining

Industrial production growth rate: -5% (2017 est.)

Labor force: 313,800 (2013 est.)

Unemployment rate: 11.1% (2013)
11.3% (2012)

Unemployment, youth ages 15-24: *total:* 26.5%
male: 20.7%
female: 34.6% (2018 est.)

Population below poverty line: 35% (2006 est.)

Gini Index coefficient - distribution of family income: 44.6 (2007)
43.2 (1999)

Household income or consumption by percentage share: *lowest 10%:* 1.3%
highest 10%: 33.8% (1999)

Budget: *revenues:* 1.002 billion (2017 est.)
expenditures: 1.164 billion (2017 est.)

Budget surplus (+) or deficit (-): -4.5% (of GDP) (2017 est.)

Public debt: 52.2% of GDP (2017 est.)
50.7% of GDP (2016 est.)

Taxes and other revenues: 28.1% (of GDP) (2017 est.)

Fiscal year: calendar year

Current account balance: -$237 million (2017 est.)
$13 million (2016 est.)

Exports: $1.8 billion (2019 est.) note: data are in current year dollars
$1.58 billion (2018 est.) note: data are in current year dollars

Exports - partners: Trinidad and Tobago 31%, Canada 11%, Portugal 11%, Ghana 8%, Norway 6%, United Arab Emirates 5% (2019)

Exports - commodities: ships, gold, shipping containers, excavation machinery, aluminum ores, rice (2019)

Imports: $4 billion (2019 est.) note: data are in current year dollars
$3.12 billion (2018 est.) note: data are in current year dollars

Imports - partners: United States 26%, Singapore 18%, Trinidad and Tobago 16%, Liberia 11%, China 5%, Norway 5% (2019)

Imports - commodities: ships, refined petroleum, excavation machinery, shipping containers, aircraft (2019)

Reserves of foreign exchange and gold: $565.4 million (31 December 2017 est.)
$581 million (31 December 2016 est.)

Debt - external: $1.69 billion (31 December 2017 est.)
$1.542 billion (31 December 2016 est.)

Exchange rates: Guyanese dollars (GYD) per US dollar -
207 (2017 est.)
206.5 (2016 est.)
206.5 (2015 est.)
206.5 (2014 est.)
206.45 (2013 est.)

ENERGY

Electricity access: *electrification - total population:* 91.8% (2018)
electrification - urban areas: 96.9% (2018)
electrification - rural areas: 90% (2018)

Electricity: *installed generating capacity:* 380,000 kW (2020 est.)
consumption: 905.4 million kWh (2019 est.)
exports: 0 kWh (2019 est.)
imports: 0 kWh (2019 est.)
transmission/distribution losses: 247 million kWh (2019 est.)

Electricity generation sources: *fossil fuels:* 97.4% of total installed capacity (2020 est.)
solar: 1.6% of total installed capacity (2020 est.)
biomass and waste: 0.9% of total installed capacity (2020 est.)

Petroleum: *total petroleum production:* 110,200 bbl/day (2021 est.)
refined petroleum consumption: 18,100 bbl/day (2019 est.)

Refined petroleum products - imports: 13,720 bbl/day (2015 est.)

Carbon dioxide emissions: 2.743 million metric tonnes of CO2 (2019 est.)
from petroleum and other liquids: 2.743 million metric tonnes of CO2 (2019 est.)

Energy consumption per capita: 48.608 million Btu/person (2019 est.)

COMMUNICATIONS

Telephones - fixed lines: *total subscriptions:* 125,000 (2020 est.)
subscriptions per 100 inhabitants: 16 (2020 est.)

Telephones - mobile cellular: *total subscriptions:* 856,000 (2020 est.)
subscriptions per 100 inhabitants: 109 (2020 est.)

Telecommunication systems: *general assessment:* after many years of delays and legal challenges, the 2016 Telecommunications Act was brought into force in October 2020 by the newly elected government of the People's Party Progressive (PPP);

the Telecommunications Act sets out a framework for enabling competition across all segments of the telecommunications sector in Guyana; the mobile market has been open to competition since 2001; the Telecommunications Act presents the country with the potential to benefit from a more level playing field that may attract new players, but nevertheless Guyana's relatively small size and low GDP may restrict it from reaching its full potential for some more years to come (2021)
domestic: fixed-line teledensity is about 16 per 100 persons; mobile-cellular teledensity about 83 per 109 persons (2020)
international: country code - 592; landing point for the SG-SCS submarine cable to Suriname, and the Caribbean; satellite earth station - 1 Intelsat (Atlantic Ocean) (2019)

Broadcast media: government-dominated broadcast media; the National Communications Network (NCN) TV is state-owned; a few private TV stations relay satellite services; the state owns and operates 2 radio stations broadcasting on multiple frequencies capable of reaching the entire country; government limits on licensing of new private radio stations has constrained competition in broadcast media

Internet country code: .gy

Internet users: *total:* 289,627 (2019 est.)
percent of population: 37% (2019 est.)

Broadband - fixed subscriptions: *total:* 95,000 (2020 est.)
subscriptions per 100 inhabitants: 12 (2020 est.)

TRANSPORTATION

Civil aircraft registration country code prefix: 8R

Airports: *total:* 117 (2021)

Airports - with paved runways: *total:* 11
1,524 to 2,437 m: 2
914 to 1,523 m: 1
under 914 m: 8 (2021)

Airports - with unpaved runways: *total:* 106
1,524 to 2,437 m: 1
914 to 1,523 m: 16
under 914 m: 89 (2021)

Roadways: *total:* 3,995 km (2019)
paved: 799 km (2019)
unpaved: 3,196 km (2019)

Waterways: 330 km (2012) (the Berbice, Demerara, and Essequibo Rivers are navigable by oceangoing vessels for 150 km, 100 km, and 80 km respectively)

Merchant marine: *total:* 56
by type: general cargo 26, oil tanker 7, other 23 (2021)

Ports and terminals: *major seaport(s):* Georgetown

MILITARY AND SECURITY

Military and security forces: the Guyana Defense Force is a unified force with ground, air, and coast guard components, as well as a militia (Guyana People's Militia) (2022)

Military expenditures: 1% of GDP (2021 est.)
1.2% of GDP (2020 est.)
1.3% of GDP (2019 est.) (approximately $95 million)
1.3% of GDP (2018 est.) (approximately $85 million)
1.2% of GDP (2017 est.) (approximately $80 million)

Military and security service personnel strengths: approximately 4,000 active duty military personnel (2022)

Military equipment inventories and acquisitions: the Guyana Defense Force's limited inventory is mostly comprised of second-hand platforms from a variety of foreign suppliers, including Brazil, China, the former Soviet Union, the UK, and the US (2022)

Military service age and obligation: 18 years of age or older for voluntary military service; no conscription (2022)

Military - note: the Guyana Defense Force was established in 1965; its primary missions are defense of the country, assisting civil authorities with law and order as needed, and contributing to the economic development of the country; the GDF's ground force officers are trained at the British Royal Military Academy at Sandhurst, while coast guard officers receive training at the British Royal Naval College (2022)

TRANSNATIONAL ISSUES

Disputes - international: all of the area west of the Essequibo River is claimed by Venezuela preventing any discussion of a maritime boundary; Guyana has expressed its intention to join Barbados in asserting claims before UN Convention on the Law of the Sea (UNCLOS) that Trinidad and Tobago's maritime boundary with Venezuela extends into their waters; Suriname claims a triangle of land between the New and Kutari/Koetari Rivers in a historic dispute over the headwaters of the Courantyne

Refugees and internally displaced persons: *refugees (country of origin):* 24,500 (Venezuela) (economic and political crisis; includes Venezuelans who have claimed asylum, are recognized as refugees, or received alternative legal stay) (2021)

Illicit drugs: transshipment point for cocaine destined for the United States, Canada, the Caribbean, Europe, and West Africa; growing domestic drug consumption problem

HAITI

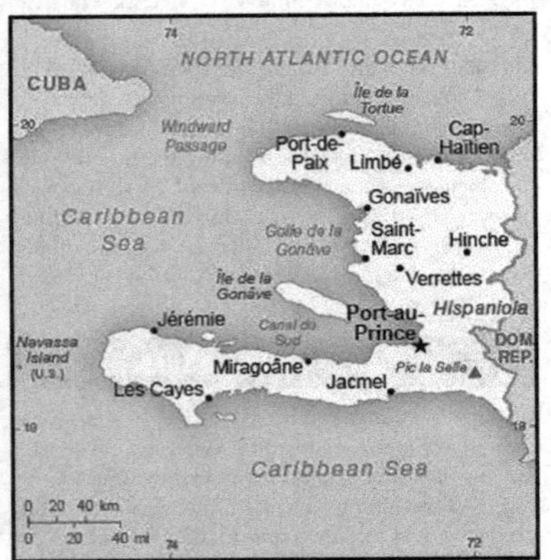

INTRODUCTION

Background: The native Taino - who inhabited the island of Hispaniola when Christopher COLUMBUS first landed on it in 1492 - were virtually wiped out by Spanish settlers within 25 years. In the early 17th century, the French established a presence on Hispaniola. In 1697, Spain ceded to the French the western third of the island, which later became Haiti. The French colony, based on forestry and sugar-related industries, became one of the wealthiest in the Caribbean but relied heavily on the forced labor of enslaved Africans and environmentally degrading practices. In the late 18th century, Toussaint L'OUVERTURE led a revolution of Haiti's nearly half a million slaves that ended France's rule on the island. After a prolonged struggle, and under the leadership of Jean-Jacques DESSALINES, Haiti became the first country in the world led by former slaves after declaring its independence in 1804, but it was forced to pay an indemnity of 100 million francs (equivalent to $21 billion USD in March 2022) to France for more than a century and was shunned by other countries for nearly 40 years. On 12 July 1862, the US officially recognized Haiti, but foreign economic influence and internal political instability induced the US to occupy Haiti from 1915-1934. Subsequently, Francois "Papa Doc" DUVALIER and then his son Jean-Claude "Baby Doc" DUVALIER led repressive and corrupt regimes that ruled Haiti in 1957-1971 and 1971-1986, respectively. President Jovenel MOISE was assassinated on 7 July 2021, leading the country further into an extra-constitutional governance structure and contributing to the country's growing fragility. President MOISE's five-year term would have ended on 7 February 2022; his assassination plunged Haiti deeper into a political crisis that was not anticipated in its constitution. Thus, on 20 July 2021, the Government of Haiti installed Ariel HENRY - whom President MOISE had nominated - as prime minister. As of March 2022, Haiti had no president, no parliamentary quorum, and a dysfunctional high court due to a lack of judges. Haiti has long been plagued by natural disasters. In January 2010, a major 7.0 magnitude earthquake struck Haiti with an epicenter about 25 km (15 mi) west of the capital, Port-au-Prince. Estimates are that over 300,000 people were killed and some 1.5 million left homeless. The earthquake was assessed as the worst in this region over the last 200 years. A 7.2 magnitude earthquake hit Haiti's southern peninsula in August 2021, causing well over 2,000 deaths; an estimated 500,000 required emergency humanitarian aid. Haiti is the poorest country in the Western Hemisphere, as well as one of the most unequal in wealth distribution.

GEOGRAPHY

Location: Caribbean, western one-third of the island of Hispaniola, between the Caribbean Sea and the North Atlantic Ocean, west of the Dominican Republic

Geographic coordinates: 19 00 N, 72 25 W

Map references: Central America and the Caribbean

Area: *total:* 27,750 sq km
land: 27,560 sq km
water: 190 sq km

Area - comparative: slightly smaller than Maryland

Land boundaries: *total:* 376 km
border countries (1): Dominican Republic 376 km

Coastline: 1,771 km

Maritime claims: *territorial sea:* 12 nm
contiguous zone: 24 nm
exclusive economic zone: 200 nm
continental shelf: to depth of exploitation

Climate: tropical; semiarid where mountains in east cut off trade winds

Terrain: mostly rough and mountainous

Elevation: *highest point:* Pic la Selle 2,674 m
lowest point: Caribbean Sea 0 m
mean elevation: 470 m

Natural resources: bauxite, copper, calcium carbonate, gold, marble, hydropower, arable land

Land use: *agricultural land:* 66.4% (2018 est.)
arable land: 38.5% (2018 est.)
permanent crops: 10.2% (2018 est.)
permanent pasture: 17.7% (2018 est.)
forest: 3.6% (2018 est.)
other: 30% (2018 est.)

Irrigated land: 970 sq km (2012)

Population distribution: fairly even distribution; largest concentrations located near coastal areas

Natural hazards: lies in the middle of the hurricane belt and subject to severe storms from June to October; occasional flooding and earthquakes; periodic droughts

Geography - note: shares island of Hispaniola with Dominican Republic (western one-third is Haiti, eastern two-thirds is the Dominican Republic); it is the most mountainous nation in the Caribbean

PEOPLE AND SOCIETY

Population: 11,334,637 (2022 est.)

Nationality: *noun:* Haitian(s)
adjective: Haitian

Ethnic groups: Black 95%, mixed and White 5%

Languages: French (official), Creole (official)
major-language sample(s): The World Factbook, une source indispensable d'informations de base. (French)

Religions: Catholic 55%, Protestant 29%, Vodou 2.1%, other 4.6%, none 10% (2018 est.)
note: 50-80% of Haitians incorporate some elements of Vodou culture or practice in addition to another religion, most often Roman Catholicism; Vodou was recognized as an official religion in 2003

Age structure: *0-14 years:* 31.21% (male 1,719,961/female 1,734,566)
15-24 years: 20.71% (male 1,145,113/female 1,146,741)
25-54 years: 38.45% (male 2,110,294/female 2,145,209)
55-64 years: 5.3% (male 280,630/female 305,584)
65 years and over: 4.33% (male 210,451/female 269,228) (2020 est.)

Dependency ratios: *total dependency ratio:* 60.4
youth dependency ratio: 52.1
elderly dependency ratio: 8.3
potential support ratio: 13.3 (2020 est.)

Median age: *total:* 24.1 years
male: 23.8 years
female: 24.3 years (2020 est.)

Population growth rate: 1.2% (2022 est.)

Birth rate: 21.12 births/1,000 population (2022 est.)

Death rate: 7.23 deaths/1,000 population (2022 est.)

Net migration rate: -1.88 migrant(s)/1,000 population (2022 est.)

Population distribution: fairly even distribution; largest concentrations located near coastal areas

Urbanization: *urban population:* 58.8% of total population (2022)
rate of urbanization: 2.47% annual rate of change (2020-25 est.)

Major urban areas - population: 2.915 million PORT-AU-PRINCE (capital) (2022)

Sex ratio: *at birth:* 1.01 male(s)/female
0-14 years: 0.99 male(s)/female
15-24 years: 0.99 male(s)/female
25-54 years: 0.98 male(s)/female
55-64 years: 0.92 male(s)/female
65 years and over: 0.62 male(s)/female
total population: 0.97 male(s)/female (2022 est.)

Mother's mean age at first birth: 22.4 years (2016/7 est.)
note: data represents median age at first birth among women 25-49

Maternal mortality ratio: 480 deaths/100,000 live births (2017 est.)

Infant mortality rate: *total:* 40.02 deaths/1,000 live births
male: 45.71 deaths/1,000 live births
female: 34.26 deaths/1,000 live births (2022 est.)

Life expectancy at birth: *total population:* 65.95 years
male: 63.26 years
female: 68.67 years (2022 est.)

Total fertility rate: 2.43 children born/woman (2022 est.)

Contraceptive prevalence rate: 34.3% (2016/17)

Drinking water source: *improved: urban:* 91.9% of population
rural: 56.1% of population
total: 76.5% of population
unimproved: urban: 8.1% of population
rural: 43.9% of population
total: 23.5% of population (2020 est.)

Current health expenditure: 4.7% of GDP (2019)

Physicians density: 0.23 physicians/1,000 population (2018)

Hospital bed density: 0.7 beds/1,000 population (2013)

Sanitation facility access: *improved: urban:* 82.9% of population
rural: 42.6% of population
total: 65.6% of population
unimproved: urban: 17.1% of population
rural: 57.4% of population
total: 34.4% of population (2020 est.)

HIV/AIDS - adult prevalence rate: 1.9% (2020 est.)

Major infectious diseases: *degree of risk:* very high (2020)
food or waterborne diseases: bacterial and protozoal diarrhea, hepatitis A and E, and typhoid fever
vectorborne diseases: dengue fever and malaria

Obesity - adult prevalence rate: 22.7% (2016)

Alcohol consumption per capita: *total:* 2.85 liters of pure alcohol (2019 est.)
beer: 0.55 liters of pure alcohol (2019 est.)
wine: 0.03 liters of pure alcohol (2019 est.)
spirits: 2.26 liters of pure alcohol (2019 est.)
other alcohols: 0 liters of pure alcohol (2019 est.)

Tobacco use: *total:* 7.7% (2020 est.)
male: 12.2% (2020 est.)
female: 3.1% (2020 est.)

Children under the age of 5 years underweight: 9.5% (2016/17)

Child marriage: *women married by age 15:* 2.1%
women married by age 18: 14.9%
men married by age 18: 1.6% (2017 est.)

Education expenditures: 1.7% of GDP (2018 est.)

Literacy: *definition:* age 15 and over can read and write
total population: 61.7%
male: 65.3%
female: 58.3% (2016)

ENVIRONMENT

Environment - current issues: extensive deforestation (much of the remaining forested land is being cleared for agriculture and used as fuel); soil erosion; overpopulation leads to inadequate supplies of potable water and a lack of sanitation; natural disasters

Environment - international agreements: *party to:* Biodiversity, Climate Change, Climate Change-Kyoto Protocol, Climate Change-Paris Agreement, Desertification, Hazardous Wastes, Law of the Sea, Marine Dumping-London Convention, Marine Life Conservation, Ozone Layer Protection
signed, but not ratified: Nuclear Test Ban

Air pollutants: *particulate matter emissions:* 14.63 micrograms per cubic meter (2016 est.)
carbon dioxide emissions: 2.98 megatons (2016 est.)
methane emissions: 6.12 megatons (2020 est.)

Climate: tropical; semiarid where mountains in east cut off trade winds

Land use: *agricultural land:* 66.4% (2018 est.)
arable land: 38.5% (2018 est.)
permanent crops: 10.2% (2018 est.)
permanent pasture: 17.7% (2018 est.)
forest: 3.6% (2018 est.)
other: 30% (2018 est.)

Urbanization: *urban population:* 58.8% of total population (2022)
rate of urbanization: 2.47% annual rate of change (2020-25 est.)

Revenue from forest resources: *forest revenues:* 0.68% of GDP (2018 est.)

Revenue from coal: *coal revenues:* 0% of GDP (2018 est.)

Food insecurity: severe localized food insecurity: due to reduced agricultural production, sociopolitical turmoil, natural disasters - about 4.56 million people are estimated to be facing severe acute food insecurity and in need of urgent food assistance between March and June 2022; the high levels of food insecurity are the result of consecutive reduced cereal harvests between 2018 and 2021, and elevated food prices, exacerbated by socio-political turmoil and worsening insecurity; the lack of income-earning opportunities, amid worsening insecurity and difficult macroeconomic conditions, is likely to heighten food insecurity in 2022 (2022)

Waste and recycling: *municipal solid waste generated annually:* 2,309,852 tons (2015 est.)

Total water withdrawal: *municipal:* 190 million cubic meters (2017 est.)
industrial: 51 million cubic meters (2017 est.)
agricultural: 1.209 billion cubic meters (2017 est.)

Total renewable water resources: 14.022 billion cubic meters (2017 est.)

GOVERNMENT

Country name: *conventional long form:* Republic of Haiti
conventional short form: Haiti
local long form: Republique d'Haiti (French)/ Repiblik d Ayiti (Haitian Creole)
local short form: Haiti (French)/ Ayiti (Haitian Creole)
etymology: the native Taino name means "Land of High Mountains" and was originally applied to the entire island of Hispaniola

Government type: semi-presidential republic

Capital: *name:* Port-au-Prince
geographic coordinates: 18 32 N, 72 20 W
time difference: UTC-5 (same time as Washington, DC, during Standard Time)
daylight saving time: +1hr, begins second Sunday in March; ends first Sunday in November
etymology: according to tradition, in 1706, a Captain de Saint-Andre named the bay and its surrounding area after his ship Le Prince; the name of the town that grew there means, "the Port of The Prince"

Administrative divisions: 10 departments (departements, singular - departement); Artibonite, Centre, Grand'Anse, Nippes, Nord, Nord-Est, Nord- Ouest, Ouest, Sud, Sud-Est

Independence: 1 January 1804 (from France)

National holiday: Independence Day, 1 January (1804)

Constitution: *history:* many previous; latest adopted 10 March 1987, with substantial revisions in June 2012; note – the constitution is commonly referred to as the "amended 1987 constitution"
amendments: proposed by the executive branch or by either the Senate or the Chamber of Deputies; consideration of proposed amendments requires support by at least two-thirds majority of both houses; passage requires at least twothirds majority of the membership present and at least two-thirds majority of the votes cast; approved amendments enter into force after installation of the next president of the republic; constitutional articles on the democratic and republican form of government cannot be amended; amended many times, last in 2012

Legal system: civil law system strongly influenced by Napoleonic Code

International law organization participation: accepts compulsory ICJ jurisdiction; non-party state to the ICCt

Citizenship: *citizenship by birth:* no
citizenship by descent only: at least one parent must be a native-born citizen of Haiti
dual citizenship recognized: yes
residency requirement for naturalization: 5 years

Suffrage: 18 years of age; universal

Executive branch: *chief of state:* President (vacant); note - Prime Minister Ariel HENRY assumed executive responsibilities, including naming Cabinet members, following the assassination of President MOISE on 7 July 2021; new elections have not yet been scheduled
head of government: Prime Minister Ariel HENRY (since 20 July 2021)
cabinet: Cabinet chosen by the prime minister in consultation with the president; parliament must ratify the Cabinet and Prime Minister's governing policy
elections/appointments: president directly elected by absolute majority popular vote in 2 rounds if needed for a 5-year term (eligible for a single non-consecutive term); last election had been originally scheduled for 9 October 2016 but was postponed until 20 November 2016 due to Hurricane Matthew
election results: 2016: Jovenel MOISE elected president in first round; percent of vote - Jovenel MOISE (PHTK) 55.6%, Jude CELESTIN (LAPEH) 19.6%, Jean-Charles MOISE (PPD) 11%, Maryse NARCISSE (FL) 9%; other 4.8%
2011: Michel MARTELLY elected president in runoff; percent of vote - Michel MARTELLY (Peasant's Response) 68%, Mirlande MANIGAT (RDNP) 32%

Legislative branch: *description:* bicameral legislature or le Corps legislatif ou le Parlement consists of:
le Sénat de la République or Senate (30 seats; 10 filled as of March 2022); members directly elected in multi-seat constituencies by absolute majority vote in 2 rounds if needed; members serve 6-year terms (2-term limit) with one-third of the membership renewed every 2 years)
la Chambre des députés or Chamber of Deputies (119 seats; 0 filled as of March 2022; members directly elected in single-seat constituencies by absolute majority vote in 2 rounds if needed; members serve 4-year terms; no term limits); note - when the 2 chambers meet collectively it is known as L'Assemblée nationale or the National Assembly and is convened for specific purposes spelled out in the constitution
elections: Senate - last held on 20 November 2016 with runoff on 29 January 2017 (next originally

scheduled for 27 October 2019 but postponed until political and civil society actors agree to a consensual process)
Chamber of Deputies - last held on 9 August 2015 with runoff on 25 October 2015 and 20 November 2016 (next originally scheduled for 27 October 2019 but postponed until political and civil society actors agree to a consensual process)
election results: Senate - percent of vote by party - NA; seats by party - NA; composition - men 10, women 0, percent of women 0%
Chamber of Deputies - percent of vote by party - NA; seats by party - NA; composition - NA
note: the Chamber of Deputies is currently defunct, and the Senate is only one-third filled (not enough seats for a quorum)

Judicial branch: *highest court(s):* Supreme Court or Cour de cassation (consists of a chief judge and other judges); note 1 - the Cour de cassation currently has no chief judge and only 3 sitting members and is not functional; note 2 - Haiti is a member of the Caribbean Court of Justice; Constitutional Court, called for in the 1987 constitution but not yet established; High Court of Justice, for trying high government officials - currently not functional
judge selection and term of office: judges appointed by the president from candidate lists submitted by the Senate of the National Assembly; note - Article 174 of Haiti's constitution states that judges of the Supreme Court are appointed for 10 years, whereas Article 177 states that judges of the Supreme Court are appointed for life
subordinate courts: Courts of Appeal; Courts of First Instance; magistrate's courts; land, labor, and children's courts
note: the Superior Council of the Judiciary or Conseil Superieur du Pouvoir Judiciaire is a 9-member body charged with the administration and oversight of the judicial branch of government

Political parties and leaders: Alternative League for Haitian Progress and Emancipation (Ligue Alternative pour le Progres et l'Emancipation Haitienne) or LAPEH [Jude CELESTIN]
Christian Movement for a New Haiti or MCNH or Mochrenha [Luc MESADIEU]
Christian National Movement for the Reconstruction of Haiti or UNCRH [Jean Chavannes JEUNE]
Combat of Peasant Workers to Liberate Haiti (Konbit Travaye Peyizan Pou Libere Ayiti) or Kontra Pep La [Jean William JEANTY]
Convention for Democratic Unity or KID [Evans PAUL]
Cooperative Action to Rebuild Haiti or KONBA [Jean William JEANTY]
December 16 Platform or Platfom 16 Desanm [Dr. Gerard BLOT]
Democratic Alliance Party or ALYANS [Evans PAUL] (coalition includes KID and PPRH)
Democratic Centers' National Council or CONACED [Osner FEVRY]
Democratic and Popular Sector (Secteur Democratique et Populaire) or SDP [Nenel CASSY, Andre MICHEL, and Marjorie MICHEL]
Democratic Unity Convention (Konvansyon Inite Demokratik) or KID [Enold JOSEPH]
Dessalinian Patriotic and Popular Movement or MOPOD [Jean Andre VICTOR]
Effort and Solidarity to Create an Alternative for the People or ESKAMP [Joseph JASME]
Fanmi Lavalas or FL [Maryse NARCISSE and former President Jean Bertrand ARISTIDE]
Forward (En Avant) [Jerry TARDIEU]
Fusion of Haitian Social Democrats (Fusion Des Sociaux-Démocrates Haïtiens) or FHSD [Edmonde Supplice BEAUZILE]
G18 Policy Platform (Plateforme Politique G18) [Joseph WUILSON]
Haiti in Action (Ayiti An Aksyon Haiti's Action) or AAA [Youri LATORTUE]
Haitian Tet Kale Party (Parti Haitien Tet Kale) or PHTK [Line Sainphaar BALTHAZAR]
Independent Movement for National Reconciliation or MIRN [Luc FLEURINORD]
Lavni Organization or LAVNI [Yves CRISTALIN]
Lod Demokratik [Jean Renel SENATUS]
Love Haiti (Renmen Ayiti) or RA [Jean Henry CEANT]
MTV Ayiti [Reginald BOULOS]
National Consortium of Haitian Political Parties (Consortium National des Partis Politiques Haitiens) or CNPPH [Jeantel JOSEPH]
National Shield Network (Reseau Bouclier National) [Victor PROPHANE and Garry BODEAU]
Organization of the People's Struggle (Oganizasyon Pep Kap Lite) or OPL [Edgard LEBLANC]
Patriotic Unity (Inite Patriyotik) or Inite [Sorel YACINTHE and Levaillant Louis JEUNE]
Platform Pitit Desalin (Politik Pitit Dessalines) or PPD [Jean-Charles MOISE]
Political Party for Us All or Bridge (Pont) or Pou Nou Tout [Jean Marie CHERESTAL]
Popular Patriotic Dessalinien Movement (Mouvement Patriotique Populaire Dessalinien) or MOPOD [Jean Andre VICTOR]
Rally of Progressive National Democrats (Rassemblement des Democrates Nationaux Progressistes) or RDNP [Eric JEAN-BAPTISTE]
Respe (Respect) [Charles Henry BAKER]
Women and Families Political Parties (Defile Pati Politik Fanm Ak Fanmi) [Marie Rebecca GUILLAUME]

International organization participation: ACP, AOSIS, Caricom, CD, CDB, CELAC, FAO, G-77, IADB, IAEA, IBRD, ICAO, ICC (NGOs), ICRM, IDA, IFAD, IFC, IFRCS, ILO, IMF, IMO, Interpol, IOC, IOM, IPU, ITSO, ITU, ITUC (NGOs), LAES, MIGA, NAM, OAS, OIF, OPANAL, OPCW, PCA, Petrocaribe, UN, UNCTAD, UNESCO, UNIDO, Union Latina, UNWTO, UPU, WCO, WFTU (NGOs), WHO, WIPO, WMO, WTO

Diplomatic representation in the US: *chief of mission:* Ambassador Bocchit EDMOND (since 23 December 2020)
chancery: 2311 Massachusetts Avenue NW, Washington, DC 20008
telephone: [1] (202) 332-4090
FAX: [1] (202) 745-7215
email address and website:
amb.washington@diplomatie.ht
https://www.haiti.org/
consulate(s) general: Atlanta, Boston, Chicago, Miami, Orlando (FL), New York, San Juan (Puerto Rico)

Diplomatic representation from the US: *chief of mission:* Ambassador (vacant); Charge d'Affaires Nicole D. THERIOT
embassy: Tabarre 41, Route de Tabarre, Port-au-Prince
mailing address: 3400 Port-au-Prince Place, Washington, DC 20521-3400
telephone: [011] (509) 2229-8000
FAX: [011] (509) 2229-8027
email address and website:
acspap@state.gov
https://ht.usembassy.gov/

Flag description: two equal horizontal bands of blue (top) and red with a centered white rectangle bearing the coat of arms, which contains a palm tree flanked by flags and two cannons above a scroll bearing the motto L'UNION FAIT LA FORCE (Union Makes Strength); the colors are taken from the French Tricolor and represent the union of blacks and mulattoes

National symbol(s): Hispaniolan trogon (bird), hibiscus flower; national colors: blue, red

National anthem: *name:* "La Dessalinienne" (The Dessalines Song)
lyrics/music: Justin LHERISSON/Nicolas GEFFRARD
note: adopted 1904; named for Jean-Jacques DESSALINES, a leader in the Haitian Revolution and first ruler of an independent Haiti

National heritage: *total World Heritage Sites:* 1 (cultural)
selected World Heritage Site locales: National History Park – Citadel, Sans Souci, Ramiers

ECONOMY

Economic overview: Haiti is a free market economy with low labor costs and tariff-free access to the US for many of its exports. Two-fifths of all Haitians depend on the agricultural sector, mainly small-scale subsistence farming, which remains vulnerable to damage from frequent natural disasters. Poverty, corruption, vulnerability to natural disasters, and low levels of education for much of the population represent some of the most serious impediments to Haiti's economic growth. Remittances are the primary source of foreign exchange, equivalent to more than a quarter of GDP, and nearly double the combined value of Haitian exports and foreign direct investment.

Currently the poorest country in the Western Hemisphere, with close to 60% of the population living under the national poverty line, Haiti's GDP growth rose to 5.5% in 2011 as the Haitian economy began recovering from the devastating January 2010 earthquake that destroyed much of its capital city, Port-au-Prince, and neighboring areas. However, growth slowed to below 2% in 2015 and 2016 as political uncertainty, drought conditions, decreasing foreign aid, and the depreciation of the national currency took a toll on investment and economic growth. Hurricane Matthew, the fiercest Caribbean storm in nearly a decade, made landfall in Haiti on 4 October 2016, with 140 mile-per-hour winds, creating a new humanitarian emergency. An estimated 2.1 million people were affected by the category 4 storm, which caused extensive damage to crops, houses, livestock, and infrastructure across Haiti's southern peninsula.

US economic engagement under the Caribbean Basin Trade Partnership Act (CBTPA) and the 2008 Haitian Hemispheric Opportunity through Partnership Encouragement Act (HOPE II) have contributed to an increase in apparel exports and investment by providing duty-free access to the US. The Haiti Economic Lift Program (HELP) Act of 2010 extended the CBTPA and HOPE II until 2020, while the Trade Preferences Extension Act of 2015 extended trade benefits provided to Haiti in the HOPE and HELP Acts through September 2025. Apparel sector exports in 2016 reached approximately $850 million and account for over 90% of Haitian exports and more than 10% of the GDP.

Investment in Haiti is hampered by the difficulty of doing business and weak infrastructure, including access to electricity. Haiti's outstanding external debt was cancelled by donor countries following the 2010 earthquake, but has since risen to $2.6 billion as of December 2017, the majority of which is owed to Venezuela under the PetroCaribe program. Although the government has increased its revenue collection, it continues to rely on formal international economic assistance for fiscal sustainability, with over 20% of its annual budget coming from foreign aid or direct budget support.

Real GDP (purchasing power parity): $31.62 billion (2020 est.)
$32.72 billion (2019 est.)
$33.28 billion (2018 est.)
note: data are in 2017 dollars

Real GDP growth rate: 1.2% (2017 est.)
1.5% (2016 est.)
1.2% (2015 est.)

Real GDP per capita: $2,800 (2020 est.)
$2,900 (2019 est.)
$3,000 (2018 est.)
note: data are in 2017 dollars

GDP (official exchange rate): $8.608 billion (2017 est.)

Inflation rate (consumer prices): 14.7% (2017 est.)
13.4% (2016 est.)

GDP - composition, by sector of origin: *agriculture:* 22.1% (2017 est.)
industry: 20.3% (2017 est.)
services: 57.6% (2017 est.)

GDP - composition, by end use: *household consumption:* 99.1% (2017 est.)
government consumption: 10% (2016 est.)
investment in fixed capital: 32.6% (2016 est.)
investment in inventories: -1.4% (2017 est.)
exports of goods and services: 20% (2017 est.)
imports of goods and services: -60.3% (2017 est.)
note: figure for household consumption also includes government consumption

Agricultural products: sugar cane, cassava, mangoes/guavas, plantains, bananas, yams, avocados, maize, rice, vegetables

Industries: textiles, sugar refining, flour milling, cement, light assembly using imported parts

Industrial production growth rate: 0.9% (2017 est.)

Labor force: 4.594 million (2014 est.)
note: shortage of skilled labor; unskilled labor abundant

Labor force - by occupation: *agriculture:* 38.1%
industry: 11.5%
services: 50.4% (2010)

Unemployment rate: 40.6% (2010 est.)
note: widespread unemployment and underemployment; more than two-thirds of the labor force do not have formal jobs

Population below poverty line: 58.5% (2012 est.)

Gini Index coefficient - distribution of family income: 41.1 (2012 est.)
59.2 (2001)

Household income or consumption by percentage share: *lowest 10%:* 0.7%
highest 10%: 47.7% (2001)

Budget: *revenues:* 1.567 billion (2017 est.)
expenditures: 1.65 billion (2017 est.)

Budget surplus (+) or deficit (-): -1% (of GDP) (2017 est.)

Public debt: 31.1% of GDP (2017 est.)
33.9% of GDP (2016 est.)

Taxes and other revenues: 18.2% (of GDP) (2017 est.)

Fiscal year: 1 October - 30 September

Current account balance: -$348 million (2017 est.)
-$83 million (2016 est.)

Exports: $1.73 billion (2019 est.) note: data are in current year dollars
$1.78 billion (2018 est.) note: data are in current year dollars

Exports - partners: United States 81%, Canada 7% (2019)

Exports - commodities: clothing and apparel, eels, essential oils, perfumes, mangoes, cocoa beans (2019)

Imports: $5.21 billion (2019 est.) note: data are in current year dollars
$5.67 billion (2018 est.) note: data are in current year dollars

Imports - partners: United States 39%, China 22%, Turkey 5% (2019)

Imports - commodities: refined petroleum, rice, clothing and apparel, palm oil, poultry meats (2019)

Reserves of foreign exchange and gold: $2.361 billion (31 December 2017 est.)
$2.11 billion (31 December 2016 est.)

Debt - external: $2.762 billion (31 December 2017 est.)
$2.17 billion (31 December 2016 est.)

Exchange rates: gourdes (HTG) per US dollar -
65.21 (2017 est.)
63.34 (2016 est.)
63.34 (2015 est.)
50.71 (2014 est.)
45.22 (2013 est.)

ENERGY

Electricity access: *electrification - total population:* 39% (2019)
electrification - urban areas: 60% (2019)
electrification - rural areas: 12% (2019)

Electricity: *installed generating capacity:* 3.453 million kW (2020 est.)
consumption: 339 million kWh (2019 est.)
exports: 0 kWh (2019 est.)
imports: 0 kWh (2019 est.)
transmission/distribution losses: 643 million kWh (2019 est.)

Electricity generation sources: *fossil fuels:* 85.8% of total installed capacity (2020 est.)
solar: 0.3% of total installed capacity (2020 est.)
hydroelectricity: 13.9% of total installed capacity (2020 est.)

Petroleum: *total petroleum production:* 0 bbl/day (2021 est.)
refined petroleum consumption: 21,100 bbl/day (2019 est.)

Refined petroleum products - imports: 20,030 bbl/day (2015 est.)

Natural gas: *production:* 0 cubic meters (2021 est.)
consumption: 3.341 million cubic meters (2020 est.)
exports: 0 cubic meters (2021 est.)
imports: 3.341 million cubic meters (2020 est.)
proven reserves: 0 cubic meters (2021 est.)

Carbon dioxide emissions: 3.139 million metric tonnes of CO2 (2019 est.)
from petroleum and other liquids: 3.137 million metric tonnes of CO2 (2019 est.)
from consumed natural gas: 2,000 metric tonnes of CO2 (2019 est.)

Energy consumption per capita: 3.97 million Btu/person (2019 est.)

COMMUNICATIONS

Telephones - fixed lines: *total subscriptions:* 6,000 (2020 est.)

Telephones - mobile cellular: *total subscriptions:* 7.319 million (2020 est.)
subscriptions per 100 inhabitants: 64 (2020 est.)

Telecommunication systems: *general assessment:* Haiti is in desperate need of maintaining effective communication services to enable it to keep going through the countless natural disasters, the country's telecoms sector is really only surviving on the back of international goodwill to repair and replace the systems destroyed in the latest upheaval; Haiti's fixed-line infrastructure is now practically non-existent, having been torn apart by Hurricane Matthew in 2016; what aid and additional investment has been forthcoming has been directed towards mobile solutions; over half of the country can afford a mobile handset or the cost of a monthly subscription; and mobile broadband subscriptions is half of that again – an estimated 28% in 2022; international aid continues to flow in to try and help the country's telecoms sector recover – the World Bank has released a further $120 million to go on top of the $60 million grant provided after the last major 7.2 earthquake in August 2021 (2022)
domestic: fixed-line is less than 1 per 100; mobile-cellular teledensity is nearly 64 per 100 persons (2020)
international: country code - 509; landing points for the BDSNi and Fibralink submarine cables to 14 points in the Bahamas and Dominican Republic; satellite earth station - 1 Intelsat (Atlantic Ocean) (2019)

Broadcast media: per 2019 data released by Haitian telecommunications regulator CONATEL (Conseil National des Télécommunications), there are 398 legal sound broadcasting stations on the territory, including about 60 community radio stations, and 7 radio stations on the AM band; the FM band in Haiti is oversaturated by 158 percent; most radio stations broadcast 17 to 19 hours a day; there are 105 television stations operating in Haiti, including 36 TV stations in Port- au- Prince, 41 others in the provinces, and more than 40 radio-television stations; a large number of broadcasting stations operate irregularly and some stations operate with technical parameters that do not comply with established standards, thus causing harmful interference to existing telecommunications systems; VOA Creole Service broadcasts daily on 30 affiliate stations
(2019)

Internet country code: .ht

Internet users: *total:* 3,990,887 (2020 est.)
percent of population: 35% (2020 est.)

Broadband - fixed subscriptions: *total:* 31,000 (2020 est.)
subscriptions per 100 inhabitants: 0.3 (2020 est.)

TRANSPORTATION

National air transport system: *number of registered air carriers:* 1 (2020)
inventory of registered aircraft operated by air carriers: 1

Civil aircraft registration country code prefix: HH

Airports: *total:* 14 (2021)

Airports - with paved runways: *total:* 4
2,438 to 3,047 m: 2
914 to 1,523 m: 2 (2021)

Airports - with unpaved runways: *total:* 10
914 to 1,523 m: 2
under 914 m: 8 (2021)

Roadways: *total:* 4,102 km (2011)
paved: 600 km (2011)
unpaved: 3,502 km (2011)

Merchant marine: *total:* 4
by type: general cargo 3, other 1 (2021)

Ports and terminals: *major seaport(s):* Cap-Haitien, Gonaives, Jacmel, Port-au-Prince

MILITARY AND SECURITY

Military and security forces: the Haitian Armed Forces (FAdH), disbanded in 1995, began to be reconstituted in 2017 to assist with natural disaster relief, border security, and combating transnational crime; it established an Army command in 2018 (2022)

note: the Haitian National Police (under the Ministry of Justice and Public Security) has a number of specialized units, including a coast guard, a presidential guard, and a paramilitary rapid-response Motorized Intervention Unit or BIM

Military expenditures: not available

Military and security service personnel strengths: approximately 1,200 active military troops (the force is planned to eventually have around 5,000 personnel); approximately 16,000 National Police (2022)

Military service age and obligation: not available

Military - note: according to the Haitian Government, the mission of the reconstituted armed forces will focus on patrolling the border with the Dominican Republic, combating smuggling, and executing recovery efforts after natural disasters

the UN Stabilization Mission in Haiti (MINUSTAH) operated in Haiti from 2004 until 2017; its mission was to help restore stability after President Bertrand ARISTIDE fled the country, including assisting with the political process, strengthening government institutions, and promoting and protecting human rights; following the completion of MINUSTAH's mandate in 2017, a smaller peacekeeping mission, the UN Mission for Justice Support in Haiti (MINUJUSTH), operated until 2019; its mission was to assist with the further development and strengthening of the national police, as well as Haiti's justice and prison systems, and to promote and protect human rights; in 2019, the UN established the UN Integrated Office in Haiti (BINUH) with the political mission of advising the Haiti Government in elections, governance, and security; BINUH's current mandate last until July 2023 (2022)

Maritime threats: the International Maritime Bureau reports the territorial waters of Haiti are a risk for armed robbery against ships; in 2021, four attacks against commercial vessels were reported, a slight decrease from the five attacks reported in 2020; most of these occurred in the main port of Port-au-Prince while ships were berthed or at anchor

TRANSNATIONAL ISSUES

Disputes - international: since 2004, peacekeepers from the UN Stabilization Mission in Haiti have assisted in maintaining civil order in Haiti; the mission currently includes 6,685 military, 2,607 police, and 443 civilian personnel; despite efforts to control illegal migration, Haitians cross into the Dominican Republic and sail to neighboring countries; Haiti claims US-administered Navassa Island

Refugees and internally displaced persons: *IDPs:* 17,000 (violence among armed gangs in the metropolitan area os Port-au-Prince) (2021)
stateless persons: 2,992 (2018); note - individuals without a nationality who were born in the Dominican Republic prior to January 2010

Illicit drugs: a transit point for cocaine from South America and marijuana from Jamaica en route to the United States; not a producer or large consumer of illicit drugs; some cultivation of cannabis for local consumption

HEARD ISLAND AND MCDONALD ISLANDS

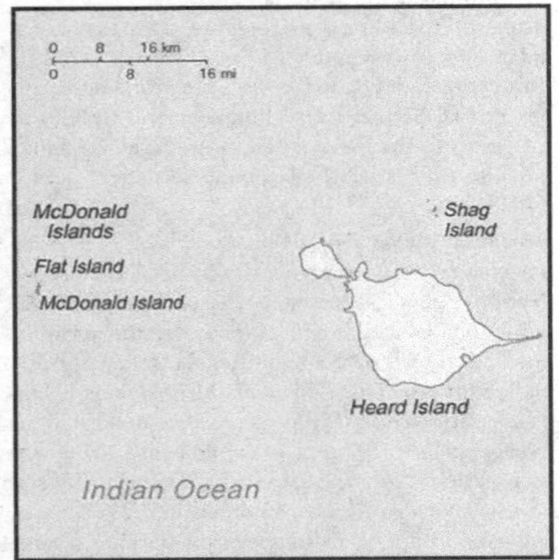

INTRODUCTION

Background: American sailor John HEARD discovered Heard Island in 1853 and thought it was a glacier that had broken away from Antarctica. Fellow American William MCDONALD discovered the McDonald Islands the following year. Starting in 1855, sealers lived on the islands harvesting elephant seal oil; by the time the practice was ended in 1877, most of the islands' seals were killed. The UK formally claimed the islands in 1910 and Australian explorer Douglas MAWSON visited Heard Island in 1929. In 1947, the UK transferred the islands to Australia for its Antarctica research, but Australia closed the research station on Heard Island in 1954 when it opened a new research station on the Antarctic continent. McDonald Island has been an active volcano since it emerged from dormancy in 1992, and the island doubled in size after an eruption in 1996. In 1997, the islands were named a UNESCO World Heritage Site. Populated by a large number of bird species, seals, and penguins, the islands are primarily used for research with limited fishing being permitted in the surrounding waters.

GEOGRAPHY

Location: islands in the Indian Ocean, about two-thirds of the way from Madagascar to Antarctica

Geographic coordinates: 53 06 S, 72 31 E

Map references: Antarctic Region

Area: *total:* 412 sq km
land: 412 sq km
water: 0 sq km

Area - comparative: slightly more than two times the size of Washington, DC

Land boundaries: *total:* 0 km

Coastline: 101.9 km

Maritime claims: *territorial sea:* 12 nm
exclusive fishing zone: 200 nm

Climate: antarctic

Terrain: Heard Island - 80% ice-covered, bleak and mountainous, dominated by a large massif (Big Ben) and an active volcano (Mawson Peak); McDonald Islands - small and rocky

Elevation: *highest point:* Mawson Peak on Big Ben volcano 2,745 m
lowest point: Indian Ocean 0 m

Natural resources: fish

Land use: *agricultural land:* 0% (2011 est.)
other: 100% (2018 est.)

Natural hazards: Mawson Peak, an active volcano, is on Heard Island

Geography - note: Mawson Peak on Heard Island is the highest Australian mountain (at 2,745 meters, it is taller than Mt. Kosciuszko in Australia proper), and one of only two active volcanoes located in Australian territory, the other being McDonald Island; in 1992, McDonald Island broke its dormancy and began erupting; it has erupted several times since, most recently in 2005

PEOPLE AND SOCIETY

Population: uninhabited

ENVIRONMENT

Environment - current issues: none; uninhabited and mostly ice covered

Climate: antarctic

Land use: *agricultural land:* 0% (2011 est.)
other: 100% (2018 est.)

GOVERNMENT

Country name: *conventional long form:* Territory of Heard Island and McDonald Islands
conventional short form: Heard Island and McDonald Islands
abbreviation: HIMI
etymology: named after American Captain John HEARD, who sighted the island on 25 November 1853, and American Captain William McDONALD, who discovered the islands on 4 January 1854

Dependency status: territory of Australia; administered from Canberra by the Department of Agriculture, Water and the Environment (Australian Antarctic Division)

Legal system: the laws of Australia apply where applicable

Diplomatic representation in the US: none (territory of Australia)

Diplomatic representation from the US: *embassy:* none (territory of Australia)

Flag description: the flag of Australia is used

National heritage: *total World Heritage Sites:* 1 (natural); note - excerpted from the Australia entry
selected World Heritage Site locales: Heard Island and McDonald Islands

ECONOMY

Economic overview: The islands have no indigenous economic activity, but the Australian Government allows limited fishing in the surrounding waters. Visits to Heard Island typically focus on terrestrial and marine research and infrequent private expeditions.

COMMUNICATIONS

Internet country code: .hm

TRANSPORTATION

Ports and terminals: none; offshore anchorage only

MILITARY AND SECURITY

Military - note: defense is the responsibility of Australia; Australia conducts fisheries patrols

TRANSNATIONAL ISSUES

Disputes - international: none

Illicit drugs: NA

HOLY SEE (VATICAN CITY)

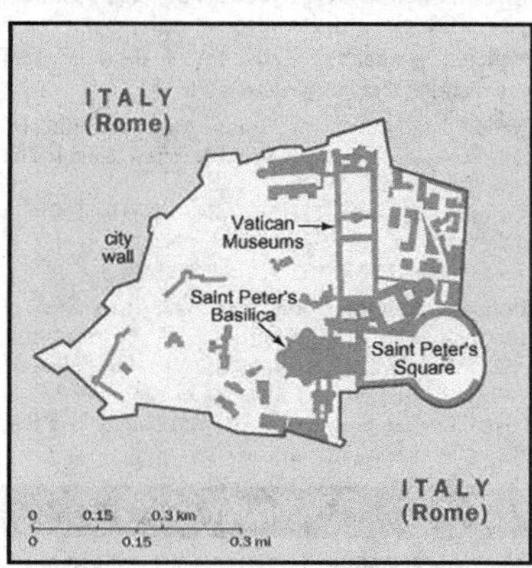

INTRODUCTION

Background: Popes in their secular role ruled portions of the Italian peninsula for more than a thousand years until the mid-19th century, when many of the Papal States were seized by the newly united Kingdom of Italy. In 1870, the pope's holdings were further circumscribed when Rome itself was annexed. Disputes between a series of "prisoner" popes and Italy were resolved in 1929 by three Lateran Treaties, which established the independent state of Vatican City and granted Roman Catholicism special status in Italy. In 1984, a concordat between the Holy See and Italy modified certain of the earlier treaty provisions, including the primacy of Roman Catholicism as the Italian state religion. Present concerns of the Holy See include religious freedom, threats against minority Christian communities in Africa and the Middle East, the plight of refugees and migrants, sexual misconduct by clergy, international development, interreligious dialogue and reconciliation, and the application of church doctrine in an era of rapid change and globalization. About 1.3 billion people worldwide profess Catholicism - the world's largest Christian faith.

GEOGRAPHY

Location: Southern Europe, an enclave of Rome (Italy)

Geographic coordinates: 41 54 N, 12 27 E

Map references: Europe

Area: *total:* 0 sq km
land: 0.44 sq km
water: 0 sq km

Area - comparative: about 0.7 times the size of the National Mall in Washington, DC

Land boundaries: *total:* 3.4 km
border countries (1): Italy 3.4 km

Coastline: 0 km (landlocked)

Maritime claims: none (landlocked)

Climate: temperate; mild, rainy winters (September to May) with hot, dry summers (May to September)

Terrain: urban; low hill

Elevation: *highest point:* Vatican Gardens (Vatican Hill) 78 m
lowest point: Saint Peter's Square 19 m

Natural resources: none

Land use: *agricultural land:* 0% (2018 est.)
other: 100% (2018 est.)

Natural hazards: occasional earthquakes

Geography - note: landlocked; an enclave in Rome, Italy; world's smallest state; beyond the territorial boundary of Vatican City, the Lateran Treaty of 1929 grants the Holy See extraterritorial authority over 23 sites in Rome and five outside of Rome, including the Pontifical Palace at Castel Gandolfo (the Pope's summer residence)

PEOPLE AND SOCIETY

Population: 1,000 (2022 est.)

Nationality: *noun:* none
adjective: none

Ethnic groups: Italian, Swiss, Argentinian, and other nationalities from around the world (2017)

Languages: Italian, Latin, French, various other languages
major-language sample(s): L'Almanacco dei fatti del mondo, l'indispensabile fonte per le informazioni di base. (Italian)

Religions: Roman Catholic

Population growth rate: 0% (2014 est.)

Urbanization: *urban population:* 100% of total population (2022)
rate of urbanization: 0% annual rate of change (2020-25 est.)

Major urban areas - population: 1,000 VATICAN CITY (capital) (2018)

Drinking water source: *improved: total:* 100% of population
unimproved: total: 0% of population (2017 est.)

ENVIRONMENT

Environment - current issues: some air pollution from the surrounding city of Rome

Environment - international agreements: *party to:* Comprehensive Nuclear Test Ban, Ozone Layer Protection
signed, but not ratified: Air Pollution, Environmental Modification

Air pollutants: *methane emissions:* 0 megatons (2020 est.)

Climate: temperate; mild, rainy winters (September to May) with hot, dry summers (May to September)

Land use: *agricultural land:* 0% (2018 est.)
other: 100% (2018 est.)

Urbanization: *urban population:* 100% of total population (2022)
rate of urbanization: 0% annual rate of change (2020-25 est.)

Total renewable water resources: 0 cubic meters (2017 est.)

GOVERNMENT

Country name: *conventional long form:* The Holy See (Vatican City State)
conventional short form: Holy See (Vatican City)
local long form: La Santa Sede (Stato della Citta del Vaticano)
local short form: Santa Sede (Citta del Vaticano)
etymology: "holy" comes from the Greek word "hera" meaning "sacred"; "see" comes from the Latin word "sedes" meaning "seat," and refers to the episcopal chair; the term "Vatican" derives from the hill Mons Vaticanus on which the Vatican is located and which comes from the Latin "vaticinari" (to prophesy), referring to the fortune tellers and soothsayers who frequented the area in Roman times

Government type: ecclesiastical elective monarchy; self-described as an "absolute monarchy"

Capital: *name:* Vatican City
geographic coordinates: 41 54 N, 12 27 E
time difference: UTC+1 (6 hours ahead of Washington, DC, during Standard Time)
daylight saving time: +1hr, begins last Sunday in March; ends last Sunday in October
etymology: the term "Vatican" derives from the hill Mons Vaticanus on which the Vatican is located and which comes from the Latin "vaticinari" (to prophesy), referring to the fortune tellers and soothsayers who frequented the area in Roman times

Administrative divisions: none

Independence: 11 February 1929; note - the three treaties signed with Italy on 11 February 1929 acknowledged, among other things, the full sovereignty of the Holy See and established its territorial extent; however, the origin of the Papal States, which over centuries varied considerably in extent, may be traced back to A.D. 754

National holiday: Election Day of Pope FRANCIS, 13 March (2013)

Constitution: *history:* previous 1929, 1963; latest promulgated November 2000, effective 22 February 2001 (Fundamental Law of Vatican City State, the main governing document of the Vatican's civil entities); the Roman Curia is the administrative apparatus – the departments and ministries – used by the pontiff in governing the church; note - Pope Francis in October 2013, instituted a 9-member Council of Cardinal Advisers to reform the Roman Curia to include writing a new constitution; in June 2018, Pope Francis approved the Council of Cardinals' first draft of the new constitution, *Predicatae Evangelium* (Preach the Gospel); it became effective 5 June 2022, replacing *Pastor Bonus*, the previous governing document of the Roman Curia
amendments: note - although the Fundamental Law of Vatican City State makes no mention of amendments, Article Four (drafting laws), states that this legislative responsibility resides with the Pontifical Commission for Vatican City State; draft legislation is submitted through the Secretariat of State and considered by the pope

Legal system: religious legal system based on canon (religious) law

International law organization participation: has not submitted an ICJ jurisdiction declaration; non-party state to the ICCt

Citizenship: *citizenship by birth:* no
citizenship by descent only: no
dual citizenship recognized: no
residency requirement for naturalization: not applicable
note: in the Holy See, citizenship is acquired by law, ex iure, or by adminstrative decision; in the first instance, citizenship is a function of holding office within the Holy See as in the case of cardinals resident in Vatican City or diplomats of the Holy See; in the second instance, citizenship may be requested in a limited set of circumstances for those who reside within Vatican City under papal authorization, as a function of their office or service, or as the spouses and children of current citizens; citizenship is lost once an individual no longer permanently resides in Vatican City, normally reverting to the citizenship previously held

Suffrage: election of the pope is limited to cardinals less than 80 years old

Executive branch: *chief of state:* Pope FRANCIS (since 13 March 2013)
head of government: President of the Pontifical Commission for the State of Vatican City and President of the Governorate of the Vatican City State is Fernando Vergez Alzaga (since 1 October 2021)
cabinet: Pontifical Commission for the State of Vatican City appointed by the pope
elections/appointments: pope elected by the College of Cardinals, usually for life or until voluntary resignation; election last held on 13 March 2013 (next to be held after the death or resignation of the current pope); Secretary of State appointed by the pope
election results:
2013: Jorge Mario BERGOGLIO, former Archbishop of Buenos Aires, elected Pope FRANCIS

Legislative branch: *description:* unicameral Pontifical Commission for the State of Vatican City or Pontificia Commissione per lo Stato della Citta del Vaticano (7 seats; the president of the Governorate of Vatican City State and 6 cardinals appointed by the pope to serve 5-year terms)
elections: last held on 11 July 2018
election results: composition - men 7, women 0

Judicial branch: *highest court(s):* Supreme Court or Supreme Tribunal of the Apostolic Signatura (consists of the cardinal prefect, who serves as ex-officio president of the court, and 2 other cardinals of the Prefect Signatura); note - judicial duties were established by the Motu Proprio, papal directive, of Pope PIUS XII on 1 May 1946; most Vatican City criminal matters are handled by the Republic of Italy courts
judge selection and term of office: cardinal prefect appointed by the pope; the other 2 cardinals of the court appointed by the cardinal prefect on a yearly basis
subordinate courts: Appellate Court of Vatican City; Tribunal of Vatican City

Political parties and leaders: none

International organization participation: CE (observer), IAEA, Interpol, IOM, ITSO, ITU, ITUC (NGOs), OAS (observer), OPCW, OSCE, Schengen Convention (de facto member), SICA (observer), UN (observer), UNCTAD, UNHCR, Union Latina (observer), UNWTO (observer), UPU, WIPO, WTO (observer)

Diplomatic representation in the US: *chief of mission:* Apostolic Nuncio Archbishop Christophe PIERRE (since 27 June 2016)
chancery: 3339 Massachusetts Avenue NW, Washington, DC 20008
telephone: [1] (202) 333-7121
FAX: [1] (202) 337-4036
email address and website:
nuntiususa@nuntiususa.org
http://www.nuntiususa.org/

Diplomatic representation from the US: *chief of mission:* Ambassador Joe DONNELLY (since 11 April 2022)
embassy: Via Sallustiana, 49, 00187 Rome
mailing address: 5660 Holy See Place, Washington DC 20521-5660
telephone: [39] (06) 4674-1
FAX: [39] (06) 4674-3411
email address and website:
https://va.usembassy.gov/

Flag description: two vertical bands of yellow (hoist side) and white with the arms of the Holy See, consisting of the crossed keys of Saint Peter surmounted by the three-tiered papal tiara, centered in the white band; the yellow color represents the pope's spiritual power, the white his worldly power

National symbol(s): crossed keys beneath a papal tiara; national colors: yellow, white

National anthem: *name:* "Inno e Marcia Pontificale" (Hymn and Pontifical March); often called The Pontifical Hymn
lyrics/music: Raffaello LAVAGNA/Charles-Francois GOUNOD
note: adopted 1950

National heritage: *total World Heritage Sites:* 2 (both cultural)
selected World Heritage Site locales: Historic Center of Rome, the Properties of the Holy See in that City Enjoying Extraterritorial Rights and San Paolo Fuori le Mura; Vatican City

ECONOMY

Economic overview: The Holy See is supported financially by a variety of sources, including investments, real estate income, and donations from Catholic individuals, dioceses, and institutions; these help fund the Roman Curia (Vatican bureaucracy), diplomatic missions, and media outlets. Moreover, an annual collection taken up in dioceses and from direct donations go to a non-budgetary fund, known as Peter's Pence, which is used directly by the pope for charity, disaster relief, and aid to churches in developing nations.

The separate Vatican City State budget includes the Vatican museums and post office and is supported financially by the sale of stamps, coins, medals, and tourist mementos as well as fees for admission to museums and publication sales. Revenues increased between 2010 and 2011 because of expanded operating hours and a growing number of visitors. However, the Holy See did not escape the financial difficulties experienced by other European countries; in 2012, it started a spending review to determine where to cut costs to reverse its 2011 budget deficit of $20 million. The Holy See generated a modest surplus in 2012 before recording a $32 million deficit in 2013, driven primarily by the decreasing value of gold. The incomes and living standards of lay workers are comparable to those of counterparts who work in the city of Rome so most public expenditures go to wages and other personnel costs;. In February 2014, Pope FRANCIS created the Secretariat of the Economy to oversee financial and administrative operations of the Holy See, part of a broader campaign to reform the Holy See's finances.

Industries: printing; production of coins, medals, postage stamps; mosaics, staff uniforms; worldwide banking and financial activities

Labor force: 4,822 (2016)

Labor force - by occupation: *note:* essentially services with a small amount of industry; nearly all dignitaries, priests, nuns, guards, and the approximately 3,000 lay workers live outside the Vatican

Budget: *revenues:* 315 million (2013)
expenditures: 348 million (2013)

Fiscal year: calendar year

Exchange rates: euros (EUR) per US dollar -
0.885 (2017 est.)
0.903 (2016 est.)
0.9214 (2015 est.)
0.885 (2014 est.)
0.7634 (2013 est.)

ENERGY

Electricity access: *electrification - total population:* 100% (2020)

COMMUNICATIONS

Telecommunication systems: *general assessment:* the Vatican's interior telecommunication system is composed of two strongly integrated subsystem: fixed infrastructure and mobile infrastructure; it is important to note that the mobile communication system has been designed to be capable of using satellite connections so that it is possible to ensure the telecommunication services whenever needed, following the Pastoral travels of the Pope; the telephone system operates through an automatic digital exchange (2020)
domestic: the telephone system operates through an automatic digital exchange (2020)
international: country code - 39; uses Italian system

Broadcast media: the Vatican Television Center (CTV) transmits live broadcasts of the Pope's Sunday and Wednesday audiences, as well as the Pope's public celebrations; CTV also produces documentaries; Vatican Radio is the Holy See's official broadcasting service broadcasting via shortwave, AM and FM frequencies, and via satellite and Internet connections; Vatican News website partners with Vatican Radio and provides Catholic news provided by the Vatican (2021)

Internet country code: .va

Communications - note: the Vatican Apostolic Library is one of the world's oldest libraries, formally established in 1475, but actually much older; it holds a significant collection of historic texts including 1.1 million printed books and 75,000 codices (manuscript books with handwritten contents); it serves as a research library for history, law, philosophy, science, and theology; the library's collections have been described as "the world's greatest treasure house of the writings at the core of Western tradition"

MILITARY AND SECURITY

Military and security forces: the Pontifical Swiss Guard Corps (Corpo della Guardia Svizzera Pontificia) serves as the de facto military force of Vatican City; the Gendarmerie Corps of Vatican City (Corpo della Gendarmeriais) is a police force that helps augment the Pontifical Swiss Guard Corps during the Pope's appearances, as well as providing general security, traffic direction, and investigative duties for the Vatican City State (2022)
note: the Swiss Guard Corps has protected the Pope and his residence since 1506

Military service age and obligation: Pontifical Swiss Guard Corps: 19-30 years of age for voluntary military service; no conscription; must be a single Roman Catholic male with Swiss citizenship who has completed basic training with the Swiss military and can obtain a certificate of good conduct; qualified candidates must apply to serve; the service contract is between 2 and 25 years (2022)

Military - note: defense is the responsibility of Italy

TRANSNATIONAL ISSUES

Disputes - international: none

Illicit drugs: NA

HONDURAS

INTRODUCTION

Background: Once part of Spain's vast empire in the New World, Honduras became an independent nation in 1821. After two and a half decades of mostly military rule, a freely elected civilian government came to power in 1982. During the 1980s, Honduras proved a haven for anti-Sandinista contras fighting the Marxist Nicaraguan Government and an ally to Salvadoran Government forces fighting leftist guerrillas. The country was devastated by Hurricane Mitch in 1998, which killed about 5,600 people and caused approximately $2 billion in damage. Since then, the economy has slowly rebounded, despite COVID and severe storm-related setbacks in 2020 and 2021.

GEOGRAPHY

Location: Central America, bordering the Caribbean Sea, between Guatemala and Nicaragua and bordering the Gulf of Fonseca (North Pacific Ocean), between El Salvador and Nicaragua

Geographic coordinates: 15 00 N, 86 30 W

Map references: Central America and the Caribbean

Area: *total:* 112,090 sq km
land: 111,890 sq km
water: 200 sq km

Area - comparative: slightly larger than Tennessee

Land boundaries: *total:* 1,575 km
border countries (3): Guatemala 244 km; El Salvador 391 km; Nicaragua 940 km

Coastline: 823 km (Caribbean Sea 669 km, Gulf of Fonseca 163 km)

Maritime claims: *territorial sea:* 12 nm
contiguous zone: 24 nm
exclusive economic zone: 200 nm
continental shelf: natural extension of territory or to 200 nm

Climate: subtropical in lowlands, temperate in mountains

Terrain: mostly mountains in interior, narrow coastal plains

Elevation: *highest point:* Cerro Las Minas 2,870 m
lowest point: Caribbean Sea 0 m
mean elevation: 684 m

Natural resources: timber, gold, silver, copper, lead, zinc, iron ore, antimony, coal, fish, hydropower

Land use: *agricultural land:* 28.8% (2018 est.)
arable land: 9.1% (2018 est.)
permanent crops: 4% (2018 est.)
permanent pasture: 15.7% (2018 est.)
forest: 45.3% (2018 est.)
other: 25.9% (2018 est.)

Irrigated land: 900 sq km (2012)

Major lakes (area sq km): *salt water lake(s):* Laguna de Caratasca - 1,110 sq km

Population distribution: most residents live in the mountainous western half of the country; unlike other Central American nations, Honduras is the only one with an urban population that is distributed between two large centers - the capital of Tegucigalpa and the city of San Pedro Sula; the Rio Ulua valley in the north is the only densely populated lowland area

Natural hazards: frequent, but generally mild, earthquakes; extremely susceptible to damaging hurricanes and floods along the Caribbean coast

Geography - note: has only a short Pacific coast but a long Caribbean shoreline, including the virtually uninhabited eastern Mosquito Coast

PEOPLE AND SOCIETY

Population: 9,459,440 (2022 est.)

Nationality: *noun:* Honduran(s)
adjective: Honduran

Ethnic groups: Mestizo (mixed Amerindian and European) 90%, Amerindian 7%, African descent 2%, White 1%

Languages: Spanish (official), Amerindian dialects
major-language sample(s): La Libreta Informativa del Mundo, la fuente indispensable de información básica. (Spanish)

Religions: Evangelical/Protestant 48%, Roman Catholic 34%, other 1%, none 17% (2020 est.)

Demographic profile: Honduras is one of the poorest countries in Latin America and has one of the world's highest murder rates. More than half of the population lives in poverty and per capita income is one of the lowest in the region. Poverty rates are higher among rural and indigenous people and in the south, west, and along the eastern border than in the north and central areas where most of Honduras' industries and infrastructure are concentrated. The increased productivity needed to break Honduras' persistent high poverty rate depends, in part, on further improvements in educational attainment. Although primary-school enrollment is near 100%, educational quality is poor, the drop-out rate and grade repetition remain high, and teacher and school accountability is low.

Honduras' population growth rate has slowed since the 1990s and is now 1.2% annually with a birth rate that averages 2.1 children per woman and more among rural, indigenous, and poor women. Honduras' young adult population - ages 15 to 29 - is projected to continue growing rapidly for the next three decades and then stabilize or slowly shrink. Population growth and limited job prospects outside of agriculture will continue to drive emigration. Remittances represent about a fifth of GDP.

Age structure: *0-14 years:* 30.2% (male 1,411,537/female 1,377,319)
15-24 years: 21.03% (male 969,302/female 972,843)
25-54 years: 37.79% (male 1,657,260/female 1,832,780)
55-64 years: 5.58% (male 233,735/female 281,525)
65 years and over: 5.4% (male 221,779/female 277,260) (2020 est.)

Dependency ratios: *total dependency ratio:* 55.2
youth dependency ratio: 47.5
elderly dependency ratio: 7.7
potential support ratio: 13 (2020 est.)

Median age: *total:* 24.4 years
male: 23.5 years
female: 25.2 years (2020 est.)

Population growth rate: 1.19% (2022 est.)

Birth rate: 17.92 births/1,000 population (2022 est.)

Death rate: 4.68 deaths/1,000 population (2022 est.)

Net migration rate: -1.34 migrant(s)/1,000 population (2022 est.)

Population distribution: most residents live in the mountainous western half of the country; unlike other Central American nations, Honduras is the only one with an urban population that is distributed between two large centers - the capital of Tegucigalpa and the city of San Pedro Sula; the Rio Ulua valley in the north is the only densely populated lowland area

Urbanization: *urban population:* 59.6% of total population (2022)
rate of urbanization: 2.48% annual rate of change (2020-25 est.)

Major urban areas - population: 1.527 million TEGUCIGALPA (capital), 956,000 San Pedro Sula (2022)

Sex ratio: *at birth:* 1.03 male(s)/female
0-14 years: 1.03 male(s)/female
15-24 years: 1 male(s)/female
25-54 years: 0.9 male(s)/female
55-64 years: 0.83 male(s)/female
65 years and over: 0.71 male(s)/female
total population: 0.95 male(s)/female (2022 est.)

Mother's mean age at first birth: 20.3 years (2011/12 est.)
note: data represents median age a first birth among women 25-49

Maternal mortality ratio: 65 deaths/100,000 live births (2017 est.)

Infant mortality rate: *total:* 15.08 deaths/1,000 live births
male: 17.2 deaths/1,000 live births
female: 12.89 deaths/1,000 live births (2022 est.)

Life expectancy at birth: *total population:* 75.17 years
male: 71.63 years
female: 78.82 years (2022 est.)

Total fertility rate: 2.01 children born/woman (2022 est.)

Contraceptive prevalence rate: 69.4% (2019)

Drinking water source: *improved: urban:* 100% of population
rural: 90.7% of population
total: 96.1% of population
unimproved: urban: 0% of population
rural: 9.3% of population
total: 3.9% of population (2020 est.)

Current health expenditure: 7.3% of GDP (2019)

Physicians density: 0.5 physicians/1,000 population (2020)

Hospital bed density: 0.6 beds/1,000 population (2017)

Sanitation facility access: *improved: urban:* 96.7% of population
rural: 87.9% of population
total: 93% of population
unimproved: urban: 3.3% of population
rural: 12.1% of population
total: 7% of population (2020 est.)

HIV/AIDS - adult prevalence rate: 0.2% (2020 est.)

Major infectious diseases: *degree of risk:* high (2020)
food or waterborne diseases: bacterial diarrhea, hepatitis A, and typhoid fever
vectorborne diseases: dengue fever and malaria

Obesity - adult prevalence rate: 21.4% (2016)

Alcohol consumption per capita: *total:* 2.73 liters of pure alcohol (2019 est.)
beer: 1.6 liters of pure alcohol (2019 est.)
wine: 0.04 liters of pure alcohol (2019 est.)
spirits: 1.09 liters of pure alcohol (2019 est.)
other alcohols: 0 liters of pure alcohol (2019 est.)

Children under the age of 5 years underweight: 7.1% (2011/12)

Education expenditures: 4.9% of GDP (2019 est.)

Literacy: *definition:* age 15 and over can read and write
total population: 88.5%
male: 88.2%
female: 88.7% (2019)

School life expectancy (primary to tertiary education): *total:* 10 years
male: 10 years
female: 11 years (2019)

Unemployment, youth ages 15-24: *total:* 17.8%
male: 11.1%
female: 27.7% (2020 est.)

ENVIRONMENT

Environment - current issues: urban population expanding; deforestation results from logging and the clearing of land for agricultural purposes; further land degradation and soil erosion hastened by uncontrolled development and improper land use practices such as farming of marginal lands; mining activities polluting Lago de Yojoa (the country's largest source of fresh water), as well as several rivers and streams, with heavy metals

Environment - international agreements: *party to:* Biodiversity, Climate Change, Climate Change-Kyoto Protocol, Climate Change-Paris Agreement, Comprehensive Nuclear Test Ban, Desertification, Endangered Species, Environmental Modification, Hazardous Wastes, Law of the Sea, Marine Dumping-London Convention, Nuclear Test Ban, Ozone Layer Protection, Ship Pollution, Tropical Timber 2006, Wetlands
signed, but not ratified: none of the selected agreements

Air pollutants: *particulate matter emissions:* 20.12 micrograms per cubic meter (2016 est.)
carbon dioxide emissions: 9.81 megatons (2016 est.)
methane emissions: 7.72 megatons (2020 est.)

Climate: subtropical in lowlands, temperate in mountains

Land use: *agricultural land:* 28.8% (2018 est.)
arable land: 9.1% (2018 est.)
permanent crops: 4% (2018 est.)
permanent pasture: 15.7% (2018 est.)
forest: 45.3% (2018 est.)
other: 25.9% (2018 est.)

Urbanization: *urban population:* 59.6% of total population (2022)
rate of urbanization: 2.48% annual rate of change (2020-25 est.)

Revenue from forest resources: *forest revenues:* 0.91% of GDP (2018 est.)

Revenue from coal: *coal revenues:* 0% of GDP (2018 est.)

Waste and recycling: *municipal solid waste generated annually:* 2,162,028 tons (2016 est.)

Major lakes (area sq km): *salt water lake(s):* Laguna de Caratasca - 1,110 sq km

Total water withdrawal: *municipal:* 315 million cubic meters (2017 est.)
industrial: 114 million cubic meters (2017 est.)
agricultural: 1.178 billion cubic meters (2017 est.)

Total renewable water resources: 92.164 billion cubic meters (2017 est.)

GOVERNMENT

Country name: *conventional long form:* Republic of Honduras
conventional short form: Honduras
local long form: Republica de Honduras
local short form: Honduras
etymology: the name means "depths" in Spanish and refers to the deep anchorage in the northern Bay of Trujillo

Government type: presidential republic

Capital: *name:* Tegucigalpa; note - article eight of the Honduran constitution states that the twin cities of Tegucigalpa and Comayaguela, jointly, constitute the capital of the Republic of Honduras; however, virtually all governmental institutions are on the Tegucigalpa side, which in practical terms makes Tegucigalpa the capital
geographic coordinates: 14 06 N, 87 13 W
time difference: UTC-6 (1 hour behind Washington, DC during Standard Time)
etymology: while most sources agree that Tegucigalpa is of Nahuatl derivation, there is no consensus on its original meaning

Administrative divisions: 18 departments (departamentos, singular - departamento); Atlantida, Choluteca, Colon, Comayagua, Copan, Cortes, El Paraiso, Francisco Morazan, Gracias a Dios, Intibuca, Islas de la Bahia, La Paz, Lempira, Ocotepeque, Olancho, Santa Barbara, Valle, Yoro

Independence: 15 September 1821 (from Spain)

National holiday: Independence Day, 15 September (1821)

Constitution: *history:* several previous; latest approved 11 January 1982, effective 20 January 1982
amendments: proposed by the National Congress with at least two-thirds majority vote of the membership; passage requires at least two-thirds majority vote of Congress in its next annual session; constitutional articles, such as the form of government, national sovereignty, the presidential term, and the procedure for amending the constitution, cannot be amended; amended several times, last in 2021

Legal system: civil law system

International law organization participation: accepts compulsory ICJ jurisdiction with reservations; accepts ICCt jurisdiction

Citizenship: *citizenship by birth:* yes
citizenship by descent only: yes
dual citizenship recognized: yes
residency requirement for naturalization: 1 to 3 years

Suffrage: 18 years of age; universal and compulsory

Executive branch: *chief of state:* President Iris Xiomara CASTRO de Zelaya (since 27 January 2022); Vice Presidents Salvador NASRALLA, Doris GUTIERREZ, and Renato FLORENTINO (since 27 January 2022); note - the president is both chief of state and head of government; CASTRO is Honduras' first female president
head of government: President Iris Xiomara CASTRO de Zelaya (since 27 January 2022); Vice Presidents Salvador NASRALLA, Doris GUTIERREZ, and Renato FLORENTINO (since 27 January 2022)
cabinet: Cabinet appointed by president
elections/appointments: president directly elected by simple majority popular vote for a 4-year term; election last held on 28 November 2021 (next to be held in 30 November 2025); note - in 2015, the Constitutional Chamber of the Honduran Supreme Court struck down the constitutional provisions on presidential term limits
election results: *2021:* Iris Xiomara CASTRO de Zelaya elected president; percent of vote - Iris Xiomara CASTRO de Zelaya (LIBRE) 51.1%, Nasry Juan ASFURA Zablah (PNH) 36.9%, Yani Benjamin ROSENTHAL Hidalgo (PL) 10%, other 2%
2017: Juan Orlando HERNANDEZ Alvarado reelected president; percent of vote - Juan Orlando HERNANDEZ Alvarado (PNH) 43%, Salvador NASRALLA (Alianza de Oposicion contra la Dictadura) 41.4%, Luis Orlando ZELAYA Medrano (PL) 14.7%, other 0.9%

Legislative branch: *description:* unicameral National Congress or Congreso Nacional (128 seats; members directly elected in 18 multi-seat constituencies by closed party-list proportional representation vote; members serve 4-year terms)
elections: last held on 28 November 2021 (next to be held on 30 November 2025)
election results: percent of vote by party - LIBRE 39.8%, PNH 31.3%, PL 16.4%, PSH 10.9%, DC 0.8%, PAC 0.8%; seats by bloc or party - LIBRE 51, PNH 40, PL 21, PSH 14, DC 1, PAC 1; composition - men 93, women 35, percent of women 27.3%
note: seats by bloc or party as of 1 May 2022 - LIBRE 50, PNH 44, PL 22, PSH 10, DC 1, PAC 1

Judicial branch: *highest court(s):* Supreme Court of Justice or Corte Suprema de Justicia (15 principal judges, including the court president, and 7 alternates; court organized into civil, criminal, constitutional, and labor chambers); note - the court has both judicial and constitutional jurisdiction
judge selection and term of office: court president elected by his peers; judges elected by the National Congress from candidates proposed by the Nominating Board, a diverse 7-member group of judicial officials and other government and non-government officials nominated by each of their organizations; judges elected by Congress for renewable, 7-year terms
subordinate courts: courts of appeal; courts of first instance; justices of the peace

Political parties and leaders: Anti-Corruption Party or PAC [Marlene ALVARENGA]
Christian Democratic Party or DC [Carlos PORTILLO]
Democratic Liberation of Honduras or Liderh [Lempira VIANA]
Democratic Unification Party or UD [Alfonso DIAZ Narvaez]
The Front or El Frente [Kelin PEREZ]
Honduran Patriotic Alliance or AP [Romeo VASQUEZ Velasquez]
Innovation and Unity Party or PINU [Guillermo VALLE]
Liberal Party or PL [Yani Benjamin ROSENTHAL Hidalgo]
Liberty and Refoundation Party or LIBRE [Jose Manuel ZELAYA Rosales]
National Party of Honduras or PNH [Juan Nasry ASFURA]
New Route or NR [Esdras Amado LOPEZ]
Opposition Alliance against the Dictatorship or Alianza de Oposicion contra la Dictadura [Salvador NASRALLA] (electoral coalition)
Savior Party of Honduras or PSH [Salvador Alejandro Cesar NASRALLA Salum]
Vamos or Let's Go [Jose COTO]
We Are All Honduras (Todos Somos Honduras) or TSH [Marlon Oniel ESCOTO Valerio]

International organization participation: BCIE, CACM, CD, CELAC, EITI (candidate country), FAO, G-11, G-77, IADB, IAEA, IBRD, ICAO, ICCt, ICRM, IDA, IFAD, IFC, IFRCS, ILO, IMF, IMO, Interpol, IOC (suspended), IOM, IPU, ISO (subscriber), ITSO, ITU, ITUC (NGOs), LAES, LAIA (observer), MIGA, MINURSO, MINUSTAH, NAM, OAS, OPANAL, OPCW, Pacific Alliance (observer), PCA, Petrocaribe, SICA, UN, UNCTAD, UNHRC, UNESCO, UNIDO, Union Latina, UNWTO, UPU, WCO (suspended), WFTU (NGOs), WHO, WIPO, WMO, WTO

Diplomatic representation in the US: *chief of mission:* Ambassador (vacant)
chancery: 1220 19th Street NW, Suite #320, Washington, DC 20036
telephone: [1] (202) 966-7702
FAX: [1] (202) 966-9751
email address and website:
https://hondurasembusa.org/
consulate(s) general: Atlanta, Chicago, Houston, Los Angeles, Miami, New Orleans, New York, San Francisco
consulate(s): Dallas, McAllen (TX)

Diplomatic representation from the US: *chief of mission:* Ambassador Laura F. DOGU (since 12 April 2022)
embassy: Avenida La Paz, Tegucigalpa M.D.C.
mailing address: 3480 Tegucigalpa Place, Washington DC 20521-3480
telephone: [504] 2236-9320,
FAX: [504] 2236-9037
email address and website:
usahonduras@state.gov
https://hn.usembassy.gov/

Flag description: three equal horizontal bands of cerulean blue (top), white, and cerulean blue, with five cerulean, five-pointed stars arranged in an X pattern centered in the white band; the stars represent the members of the former Federal Republic of Central America: Costa Rica, El Salvador, Guatemala, Honduras, and Nicaragua; the blue bands symbolize the Pacific Ocean and the Caribbean Sea; the white band represents the land between the two bodies of water and the peace and prosperity of its people
note: similar to the flag of El Salvador, which features a round emblem encircled by the words REPUBLICA DE EL SALVADOR EN LA AMERICA CENTRAL centered in the white band; also similar to the flag of Nicaragua, which features a triangle encircled by the words REPUBLICA DE NICARAGUA on top and AMERICA CENTRAL on the bottom, centered in the white band

National symbol(s): scarlet macaw, white-tailed deer; national colors: blue, white

National anthem: *name:* "Himno Nacional de Honduras" (National Anthem of Honduras)
lyrics/music: Augusto Constancio COELLO/Carlos HARTLING
note: adopted 1915; the anthem's seven verses chronicle Honduran history; on official occasions, only the chorus and last verse are sung

National heritage: *total World Heritage Sites:* 2 (1 cultural, 1 natural)
selected World Heritage Site locales: Maya Site of Copan (c); Río Plátano Biosphere Reserve (n)

ECONOMY

Economic overview: Honduras, the second poorest country in Central America, suffers from extraordinarily unequal distribution of income, as well as high underemployment. While historically dependent on the export of bananas and coffee, Honduras has diversified its export base to include apparel and automobile wire harnessing.

Honduras's economy depends heavily on US trade and remittances. The US-Central America-Dominican Republic Free Trade Agreement came into force in 2006 and has helped foster foreign direct investment, but physical and political insecurity, as well as crime and perceptions of corruption, may deter potential investors; about 15% of foreign direct investment is from US firms.

The economy registered modest economic growth of 3.1%-4.0% from 2010 to 2017, insufficient to improve living standards for the nearly 65% of the population in poverty. In 2017, Honduras faced rising public debt, but its economy has performed better than expected due to low oil prices and improved investor confidence. Honduras signed a three-year standby arrangement with the IMF in December 2014, aimed at easing Honduras's poor fiscal position.

Real GDP (purchasing power parity): $50.89 billion (2020 est.)
$55.91 billion (2019 est.)
$54.46 billion (2018 est.)
note: data are in 2017 dollars

Real GDP growth rate: 4.8% (2017 est.)
3.8% (2016 est.)
3.8% (2015 est.)

Real GDP per capita: $5,100 (2020 est.)
$5,700 (2019 est.)
$5,700 (2018 est.)
note: data are in 2017 dollars

GDP (official exchange rate): $25.145 billion (2019 est.)

Inflation rate (consumer prices): 4.3% (2019 est.)
4.3% (2018 est.)
3.9% (2017 est.)

Credit ratings:

Moody's rating: B1 (2017)

Standard & Poors rating: BB- (2017)
note: The year refers to the year in which the current credit rating was first obtained.

GDP - composition, by sector of origin: *agriculture:* 14.2% (2017 est.)
industry: 28.8% (2017 est.)
services: 57% (2017 est.)

GDP - composition, by end use: *household consumption:* 77.7% (2017 est.)
government consumption: 13.8% (2017 est.)
investment in fixed capital: 23.1% (2017 est.)
investment in inventories: 0.7% (2017 est.)
exports of goods and services: 43.6% (2017 est.)
imports of goods and services: -58.9% (2017 est.)

Agricultural products: sugarcane, oil palm fruit, milk, bananas, maize, coffee, melons, oranges, poultry, beans

Industries: sugar processing, coffee, woven and knit apparel, wood products, cigars

Industrial production growth rate: 4.5% (2017 est.)

Labor force: 3.735 million (2017 est.)

Labor force - by occupation: *agriculture:* 39.2%
industry: 20.9%
services: 39.8% (2005 est.)

Unemployment rate: 5.6% (2017 est.)
6.3% (2016 est.)
note: about one-third of the people are underemployed

Unemployment, youth ages 15-24: *total:* 17.8%
male: 11.1%
female: 27.7% (2020 est.)

Population below poverty line: 48.3% (2018 est.)

Gini Index coefficient - distribution of family income: 52.1 (2018 est.)
45.7 (2009)

Household income or consumption by percentage share: *lowest 10%:* 1.2%
highest 10%: 38.4% (2014)

Budget: *revenues:* 4.658 billion (2017 est.)
expenditures: 5.283 billion (2017 est.)

Budget surplus (+) or deficit (-): -2.7% (of GDP) (2017 est.)

Public debt: 39.5% of GDP (2017 est.)
38.5% of GDP (2016 est.)

Taxes and other revenues: 20.3% (of GDP) (2017 est.)

Fiscal year: calendar year

Current account balance: -$380 million (2017 est.)
-$587 million (2016 est.)

Exports: $7.16 billion (2019 est.) note: data are in current year dollars
$7.14 billion (2018 est.) note: data are in current year dollars

Exports - partners: United States 53%, El Salvador 8%, Guatemala 5%, Nicaragua 5% (2019)

Exports - commodities: clothing and apparel, coffee, insulated wiring, bananas, palm oil (2019)

Imports: $11.5 billion (2019 est.) note: data are in current year dollars
$11.78 billion (2018 est.) note: data are in current year dollars

Imports - partners: United States 42%, China 10%, Guatemala 8%, El Salvador 8%, Mexico 6% (2019)

Imports - commodities: refined petroleum, clothing and apparel, packaged medicines, broadcasting equipment, insulated wiring (2019)

Reserves of foreign exchange and gold: $4.708 billion (31 December 2017 est.)
$3.814 billion (31 December 2016 est.)

Debt - external: $9.137 billion (2019 est.)
$8.722 billion (2018 est.)

Exchange rates: lempiras (HNL) per US dollar -
23.74 (2017 est.)
22.995 (2016 est.)
22.995 (2015 est.)
22.098 (2014 est.)
21.137 (2013 est.)

ENERGY

Electricity access: *electrification - total population:* 81% (2019)
electrification - urban areas: 91% (2019)
electrification - rural areas: 68% (2019)

Electricity: *installed generating capacity:* 3.991 million kW (2020 est.)
consumption: 8,140,480,000 kWh (2019 est.)
exports: 540 million kWh (2019 est.)
imports: 787 million kWh (2019 est.)
transmission/distribution losses: 3.16 billion kWh (2019 est.)

Electricity generation sources: *fossil fuels:* 46.7% of total installed capacity (2020 est.)
solar: 10.3% of total installed capacity (2020 est.)
wind: 7.5% of total installed capacity (2020 est.)
hydroelectricity: 24.7% of total installed capacity (2020 est.)
geothermal: 2.7% of total installed capacity (2020 est.)
biomass and waste: 8.1% of total installed capacity (2020 est.)

Coal: *production:* 0 metric tons (2020 est.)
consumption: 25,000 metric tons (2020 est.)
exports: 0 metric tons (2020 est.)
imports: 25,000 metric tons (2020 est.)
proven reserves: 0 metric tons (2019 est.)

Petroleum: *total petroleum production:* 0 bbl/day (2021 est.)
refined petroleum consumption: 66,800 bbl/day (2019 est.)

Refined petroleum products - exports: 12,870 bbl/day (2015 est.)

Refined petroleum products - imports: 56,120 bbl/day (2015 est.)

Carbon dioxide emissions: 8.523 million metric tonnes of CO2 (2019 est.)
from coal and metallurgical coke: 61,000 metric tonnes of CO2 (2019 est.)
from petroleum and other liquids: 8.462 million metric tonnes of CO2 (2019 est.)

Energy consumption per capita: 19.8 million Btu/person (2019 est.)

COMMUNICATIONS

Telephones - fixed lines: *total subscriptions:* 531,763 (2020 est.)
subscriptions per 100 inhabitants: 5 (2020 est.)

Telephones - mobile cellular: *total subscriptions:* 6,960,654 (2020 est.)
subscriptions per 100 inhabitants: 70 (2020 est.)

Telecommunication systems: *general assessment:* Honduras is among the poorest countries in Central America and has long been plagued by an unstable political framework which has rendered telecom sector reform difficult; this has created real difficulties for telcos as well as consumers; fixed-line teledensity, at only 4.9%, is significantly lower than the Latin American and Caribbean average; poor fixed-line infrastructure has been exacerbated by low investment and topographical difficulties which have made investment in rural areas unattractive or uneconomical; the internet has been slow to develop; DSL and cable modem technologies are available but are relatively expensive, while higher speed services are largely restricted to the major urban centers; the demand for broadband is steadily increasing and there has been some investment in network upgrades to fiber-based infrastructure
(2022)
domestic: private sub-operators allowed to provide fixed lines in order to expand telephone coverage contributing to a fixed-line teledensity of slightly

over 5 per 100; mobile-cellular subscribership is roughly 70 per 100 persons (2020)
international: country code - 504; landing points for both the ARCOS and the MAYA-1 fiber-optic submarine cable systems that together provide connectivity to South and Central America, parts of the Caribbean, and the US; satellite earth stations - 2 Intelsat (Atlantic Ocean); connected to Central American Microwave System (2019)

Broadcast media: multiple privately owned terrestrial TV networks, supplemented by multiple cable TV networks; Radio Honduras is the lone government-owned radio network; roughly 300 privately owned radio stations (2019)

Internet country code: .hn

Internet users: *total:* 4,159,935 (2020 est.)
percent of population: 42% (2020 est.)

Broadband - fixed subscriptions: *total:* 396,916 (2020)
subscriptions per 100 inhabitants: 4 (2020 est.)

TRANSPORTATION

National air transport system: *number of registered air carriers:* 4 (2020)
inventory of registered aircraft operated by air carriers: 26
annual passenger traffic on registered air carriers: 251,149 (2018)
annual freight traffic on registered air carriers: 450,000 (2018) mt-km

Civil aircraft registration country code prefix: HR

Airports: *total:* 103 (2021)

Airports - with paved runways: *total:* 13
2,438 to 3,047 m: 3
1,524 to 2,437 m: 3
914 to 1,523 m: 4
under 914 m: 3 (2021)

Airports - with unpaved runways: *total:* 90
1,524 to 2,437 m: 1
914 to 1,523 m: 16
under 914 m: 73 (2021)

Railways: *total:* 699 km (2014)
narrow gauge: 164 km (2014) 1.067-m gauge
115 km 1.057-mm gauge
420 km 0.914-mm gauge

Roadways: *total:* 14,742 km (2012)
paved: 3,367 km (2012)
unpaved: 11,375 km (2012) (1,543 km summer only)
note: an additional 8,951 km of non-official roads used by the coffee industry

Waterways: 465 km (2012) (most navigable only by small craft)

Merchant marine: *total:* 505
by type: bulk carrier 1, general cargo 244, oil tanker 82, other 178 (2021)

Ports and terminals: *major seaport(s):* La Ceiba, Puerto Cortes, San Lorenzo, Tela

MILITARY AND SECURITY

Military and security forces: Honduran Armed Forces (Fuerzas Armadas de Honduras, FFAA): Army (Ejercito), Honduran Naval Force (FNH; includes marines), Honduran Air Force (Fuerza Aerea Hondurena, FAH), Honduran Military Police of Public Order (PMOP); Security Secretariat: Public Security Forces (includes Honduran National Police paramilitary units) (2022)
note: the PMOP was created in 2013 to support the Honduran National Police (HNP) against narcotics trafficking and organized crime; as of 2022, the PMOP had approximately 5,000 troops; it reported to military authorities but conducted operations sanctioned by both civilian security officials and military leaders

Military expenditures: 1.6% of GDP (2021 est.)
1.6% of GDP (2020 est.)
1.6% of GDP (2019 est.) (approximately $510 million)
1.6% of GDP (2018 est.) (approximately $500 million)
1.7% of GDP (2017 est.) (approximately $510 million)

Military and security service personnel strengths: approximately 16,000 active personnel (7,500 Army; 1,500 Navy, including about 1,000 marines; 2,000 Air Force; 5,000 Military Police of Public Order); approximately 18,000 National Police (2022)

Military equipment inventories and acquisitions: the FFAA's inventory is comprised of mostly older imported equipment from Israel, the UK, and the US; since 2010, Honduras has received limited amounts of military equipment from several countries, including Colombia, Israel, and the Netherlands (2022)

Military service age and obligation: 18 years of age for voluntary 2- to 3-year military service (men and women); no conscription (2022)
note: as of 2017, women made up over 4% of the active duty military

Military - note: the armed forces, including the PMOP, are subordinate to the Secretariat of Defense, while the HNP reports to the Secretariat of Security; the National Interinstitutional Security Force is an interagency command that coordinates the overlapping responsibilities of the HNP, PMOP, National Intelligence Directorate, and Public Ministry (public prosecutor) but exercises coordination, command, and control responsibilities only during interagency operations involving those forces (2022)

TRANSNATIONAL ISSUES

Disputes - international: *Honduras-El Salvador:* International Court of Justice (ICJ) ruled on the delimitation of "bolsones" (disputed areas) along the El Salvador-Honduras border in 1992 with final settlement by the parties in 2006 after an Organization of American States survey and a further ICJ ruling in 2003; the 1992 ICJ ruling advised a tripartite resolution to a maritime boundary in the Gulf of Fonseca with consideration of Honduran access to the Pacific; El Salvador continues to claim tiny Conejo Island, not mentioned in the ICJ ruling, off Honduras in the Gulf of Fonseca.
Honduras-Belize: Honduras claims the Belizean-administered Sapodilla Cays off the coast of Belize in its constitution, but agreed to a joint ecological park around the cays should Guatemala consent to a maritime corridor in the Caribbean under the OAS-sponsored 2002 Belize-Guatemala Differendum

Refugees and internally displaced persons: IDPs: 247,000 (violence, extortion, threats, forced recruitment by urban gangs between 2004 and 2018) (2021)

Illicit drugs: transshipment point for cocaine destined for the United States and precursor chemicals used to produce illicit drugs; some experimental coca cultivation

HONG KONG

INTRODUCTION

Background: Seized by the UK in 1841, Hong Kong was formally ceded by China the following year at the end of the First Opium War; the Kowloon Peninsula was added in 1860 at the end of the Second Opium War, and was further extended when Britain obtained a 99-year lease of the New Territories in 1898. Pursuant to an agreement signed by China and the UK on 19 December 1984, Hong Kong became the Hong Kong Special Administrative Region (HKSAR) of the People's Republic of China on 1 July 1997. In this agreement, China promised that, under its "one country, two systems" formula, China's socialist economic and strict political system would not be imposed on Hong Kong and that Hong Kong would enjoy a "high degree of autonomy" in all matters except foreign and defense affairs for the subsequent 50 years.

Since the turnover, Hong Kong has continued to enjoy success as an international financial center. However, dissatisfaction with the Hong Kong Government and growing Chinese political influence has been a central issue and led to considerable civil unrest, including large-scale pro-democracy demonstrations in 2019 after the HKSAR attempted to revise a local ordinance to allow extraditions to mainland China. In response, the governments of the HKSAR and China took several actions that reduced the city's autonomy and placed new restrictions on the rights of Hong Kong residents, moves that were widely criticized to be in direct contravention of obligations under the Hong Kong Basic Law and the Sino-British Joint Declaration. Chief among these actions was a sweeping national security law for Hong Kong imposed by the Chinese Government in June 2020 that criminalized acts such as those interpreted as secession, subversion, terrorism, and collusion with foreign or external forces. The law ushered in a widespread crackdown on public protests, criticism of authorities, and freedom of speech, and was used by authorities to target pro-democracy activists, organizations, and media companies. Democratic lawmakers and political figures were arrested, while others fled abroad. At the

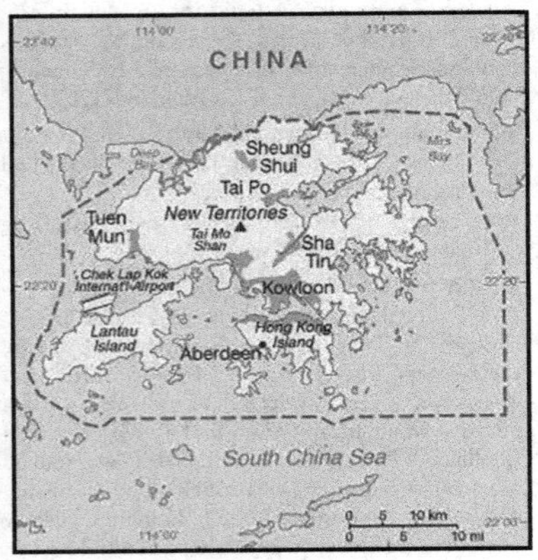

same time, dozens of civil society groups and several independent media outlets were closed or have disbanded. In March 2021, Beijing imposed a more restrictive electoral system, including restructuring the Legislative Council (LegCo) and allowing only government-approved candidates to run for office, claiming it was to ensure a system of "patriots" governed Hong Kong. The changes ensured that virtually all seats in the December 2021 LegCo election were won by pro-establishment candidates and effectively ended political opposition to Beijing in the territory.

GEOGRAPHY

Location: Eastern Asia, bordering the South China Sea and China

Geographic coordinates: 22 15 N, 114 10 E

Map references: Southeast Asia

Area: *total:* 1,108 sq km
land: 1,073 sq km
water: 35 sq km

Area - comparative: six times the size of Washington, DC

Land boundaries: *total:* 33 km
regional borders (1): China 33 km

Coastline: 733 km

Maritime claims: *territorial sea:* 12 nm

Climate: subtropical monsoon; cool and humid in winter, hot and rainy from spring through summer, warm and sunny in fall

Terrain: hilly to mountainous with steep slopes; lowlands in north

Elevation: *highest point:* Tai Mo Shan 958 m
lowest point: South China Sea 0 m

Natural resources: outstanding deepwater harbor, feldspar

Land use: *agricultural land:* 5% (2018 est.)
arable land: 3.2% (2018 est.)
permanent crops: 0.9% (2018 est.)
permanent pasture: 0.9% (2018 est.)
forest: 0% (2018 est.)
other: 95% (2018 est.)

Irrigated land: 10 sq km (2012)

Population distribution: population fairly evenly distributed

Natural hazards: occasional typhoons

Geography - note: consists of a mainland area (the New Territories) and more than 200 islands

PEOPLE AND SOCIETY

Population: 7,276,588 (2022 est.)

Nationality: *noun:* Chinese/Hong Konger
adjective: Chinese/Hong Kong

Ethnic groups: Chinese 92%, Filipino 2.5%, Indonesian 2.1%, other 3.4% (2016 est.)

Languages: Cantonese (official) 88.9%, English (official) 4.3%, Mandarin (official) 1.9%, other Chinese dialects 3.1%, other 1.9% (2016 est.)
major-language sample(s):
世界概况, 必須擁有的基本資料参考书 (Cantonese)

Religions: Buddhist or Taoist 27.9%, Protestant 6.7%, Roman Catholic 5.3%, Muslim 4.2%, Hindu 1.4%, Sikh 0.2%, other or none 54.3% (2016 est.)
note: many people practice Confucianism, regardless of their religion or not having a religious affiliation

Age structure: *0-14 years:* 12.81% (male 490,477/female 437,971)
15-24 years: 8.81% (male 334,836/female 303,897)
25-54 years: 42.66% (male 1,328,529/female 1,763,970)
55-64 years: 17.24% (male 582,047/female 668,051)
65 years and over: 18.48% (male 625,453/female 714,676) (2020 est.)

Dependency ratios: *total dependency ratio:* 44.7
youth dependency ratio: 18.3
elderly dependency ratio: 26.3
potential support ratio: 3.8 (2020 est.)

Median age: *total:* 45.6 years
male: 44.2 years
female: 46.5 years (2020 est.)

Population growth rate: 0.17% (2022 est.)

Birth rate: 8.04 births/1,000 population (2022 est.)

Death rate: 7.98 deaths/1,000 population (2022 est.)

Net migration rate: 1.65 migrant(s)/1,000 population (2022 est.)

Population distribution: population fairly evenly distributed

Urbanization: *urban population:* 100% of total population (2022)
rate of urbanization: 0.58% annual rate of change (2020-25 est.)

Major urban areas - population: 7.643 million Hong Kong (2022)

Sex ratio: *at birth:* 1.06 male(s)/female
0-14 years: 1.09 male(s)/female
15-24 years: 1.13 male(s)/female
25-54 years: 0.78 male(s)/female
55-64 years: 0.82 male(s)/female
65 years and over: 0.71 male(s)/female
total population: 0.86 male(s)/female (2022 est.)

Mother's mean age at first birth: 29.8 years (2008 est.)

Infant mortality rate: *total:* 2.55 deaths/1,000 live births
male: 2.82 deaths/1,000 live births
female: 2.26 deaths/1,000 live births (2022 est.)

Life expectancy at birth: *total population:* 83.61 years
male: 80.91 years
female: 86.46 years (2022 est.)

Total fertility rate: 1.22 children born/woman (2022 est.)

Contraceptive prevalence rate: 66.7% (2017)

Drinking water source: *improved: urban:* 100% of population
total: 100% of population

Physicians density: 2.04 physicians/1,000 population (2020)

Hospital bed density: 4.9 beds/1,000 population (2020)

Sanitation facility access: *improved: urban:* 96.4% of population
total: 96.4% of population
unimproved: urban: 3.6% of population
total: 3.6% of population (2017)

Education expenditures: 4.4% of GDP (2020 est.)

School life expectancy (primary to tertiary education): *total:* 17 years
male: 17 years
female: 18 years (2020)

Unemployment, youth ages 15-24: *total:* 15.5%
male: 17.3%
female: 13.6% (2020 est.)

ENVIRONMENT

Environment - current issues: air and water pollution from rapid urbanization; urban waste pollution; industrial pollution

Air pollutants: *carbon dioxide emissions:* 43.64 megatons (2016 est.)

Climate: subtropical monsoon; cool and humid in winter, hot and rainy from spring through summer, warm and sunny in fall

Land use: *agricultural land:* 5% (2018 est.)
arable land: 3.2% (2018 est.)
permanent crops: 0.9% (2018 est.)
permanent pasture: 0.9% (2018 est.)
forest: 0% (2018 est.)
other: 95% (2018 est.)

Urbanization: *urban population:* 100% of total population (2022)
rate of urbanization: 0.58% annual rate of change (2020-25 est.)

Revenue from forest resources: *forest revenues:* 0% of GDP (2018 est.)

Revenue from coal: *coal revenues:* 0% of GDP (2018 est.)

Waste and recycling: *municipal solid waste generated annually:* 5,679,816 tons (2015 est.)
municipal solid waste recycled annually: 1,931,138 tons (2016 est.)
percent of municipal solid waste recycled: 34% (2016 est.)

GOVERNMENT

Country name: *conventional long form:* Hong Kong Special Administrative Region
conventional short form: Hong Kong
local long form: Heung Kong Takpit Hangching Ku (Eitel/Dyer-Ball)
local short form: Heung Kong (Eitel/Dyer-Ball)
abbreviation: HK
etymology: probably an imprecise phonetic rendering of the Cantonese name meaning "fragrant harbor"

Government type: presidential limited democracy; a special administrative region of the People's Republic of China

Dependency status: special administrative region of the People's Republic of China

Administrative divisions: none (special administrative region of the People's Republic of China)

Independence: none (special administrative region of China)

National holiday: National Day (Anniversary of the Founding of the People's Republic of China), 1 October (1949); note - 1 July (1997) is celebrated as Hong Kong Special Administrative Region Establishment Day

Constitution: *history:* several previous (governance documents while under British authority); latest drafted April 1988 to February 1989, approved March 1990, effective 1 July 1997 (Basic Law of the Hong Kong Special Administrative Region of the People's Republic of China serves as the constitution); note - since 1990, China's National People's Congress has interpreted specific articles of the Basic Law
amendments: proposed by the Standing Committee of the National People's Congress (NPC), the People's Republic of China State Council, or the Special Administrative Region of Hong Kong; submittal of proposals to the NPC requires two-thirds majority vote by the Legislative Council of Hong Kong, approval by two thirds of Hong Kong's deputies to the NPC, and approval by the Hong Kong chief executive; final passage requires approval by the NPC

Legal system: mixed legal system of common law based on the English model and Chinese customary law (in matters of family and land tenure); PRC imposition of National Security Law incorporates elements of Chinese civil law

Citizenship: see China

Suffrage: 18 years of age in direct elections for 20 of the 90 Legislative Council seats and all of the seats in 18 district councils; universal for permanent residents living in the territory of Hong Kong for the past 7 years; note - in indirect elections, suffrage is limited to about 220,000 members of functional constituencies for the other 70 legislature seats and a 1,500- member election committee for the chief executive drawn from broad sectoral groupings, central government bodies, municipal organizations, and elected Hong Kong officials

Executive branch: *chief of state:* President of China XI Jinping (since 14 March 2013)
head of government: Chief Executive John LEE Ka-chieu (since 1 July 2022)
cabinet: Executive Council or ExCo appointed by the chief executive
elections/appointments: president indirectly elected by National People's Congress for a 5-year term (eligible for a second term); election last held on 17 March 2018 (next to be held in March 2023); chief executive indirectly elected by the Election Committee and appointed by the PRC Government for a 5-year term (eligible for a second term); election last held on 8 May 2022 (next to be held in 2027)
election results: 2022: John LEE was the only candidate and won with over 99% of the vote by the Election Committee
2017: Election Committee vote - Carrie LAM (non-partisan) 777, John TSANG (non-partisan) 365, WOO Kwok-hing (nonpartisan) 21, 23 ballots rejected (1,186 votes cast)
note: electoral changes that Beijing imposed in March 2021 expanded the Election Committee to 1,500 members

Legislative branch: *description:* unicameral Legislative Council or LegCo (90 seats); 20 members directly elected in 2-seat constituencies, 30 indirectly elected by the approximately 220,000 members of various functional constituencies based on a variety of methods, and 50 indirectly elected by the 1,500-member Election Committee; members serve 4-year terms; note - in March 2021, China's National People's Congress amended the electoral rules and system for the LegCo; the total number of seats increased from 70 to 90, directly elected geographical constituencies were reduced from 35 to 20 seats, while trade-based indirectly elected functional constituencies remained at 30; an additional 40 seats were elected by the 1,500-member Election Commission; all political candidates are evaluated by the Candidate Eligibility Review Committee (CERC), established in April 2022; the CERC consists of the chairperson, 2-4 official members, and 1-3 non-official members, all appointed by the chief executive
elections: last held on 19 Dec 2021 (next scheduled for 2025)
election results: percent of vote by bloc: pro-Beijing 93%, non-establishment 7%; seats by block/party - pro-Beijing 89 (DAB 19, FTU 8, BPA 7, NPP 5, Liberal Party 4, FEW 2, FLU 2, other 46), non-establishment 1 (Third Side); composition - men 73, women 17, percent of women 18.9%; voter turnout 30.2%; note - Hong Kong's leading pro-democracy political parties boycotted the 2021 election

Judicial branch: *highest court(s):* Court of Final Appeal (consists of the chief justice, 3 permanent judges, and 20 non-permanent judges); note - a sitting bench consists of the chief justice, 3 permanent judges, and 1 non-permanent judge
judge selection and term of office: all judges appointed by the Hong Kong Chief Executive upon the recommendation of the Judicial Officers Recommendation Commission, an independent body consisting of the Secretary for Justice, other judges, and judicial and legal professionals; permanent judges serve until normal retirement at age 65, but term can be extended; non-permanent judges appointed for renewable 3-year terms without age limit
subordinate courts: High Court (consists of the Court of Appeal and Court of First Instance); District Courts (includes Family and Land Courts); magistrates' courts; specialized tribunals

Political parties and leaders: *parties:* Bauhinia Party or BP [WONG Chau-chi and LI Shan]
Business and Professionals Alliance for Hong Kong or BPA [LO Wai-kwok]
Civic Party [vacant]
Democratic Alliance for the Betterment and Progress of Hong Kong or DAB [Starry LEE Wai-king]
Democratic Party [LO Kin-hei]
Hong Kong Association for Democracy and People's Livelihood of ADPL [Bruce LIU]
Labor Party [Steven KWOK Wing-kin; arrested in 2020]
League of Social Democrats or LSD [CHAN Po-ying]
Liberal Party or LP [led by Tommy CHEUNG; chaired by Peter SHIU]
Neighborhood and Workers Service Center or NWSC [LEUNG Yui-chung]
New People's Party or NPP [Regina IP]
People Power or PP [LEUNG Ka-shing]
Third Side [TIK Chi-yeun]
other: Hong Kong Federation of Trade Unions or HKFTU [labor and political group presided over by NG Chau-pei and chaired by WONG Kwok]
Hong Kong Federation of Education Workers or HKFEW [WONG Kwan-yu]
Federation of Hong Kong and Kowloon Labour Unions or HKFLU [represented by POON Siu-Ping]
Roundtable [Michael TIEN Puk-sun]
Professional Power [Christine FONG Kwok Shan]
Kowloon West New Dynamic or KWND [Priscilla LEUNG]
New Prospect for Hong Kong [Gary ZHANG Xinyu]
New Century Forum [MA Fung-kwak]
Path of Democracy [Ronny TONG] (think tank)
note(s) - pro-democracy - Civic Party, Democratic Party, Labor Party, LSD, PP, Professional Commons; pro-Beijing - DAB, FTU, Liberal Party, NPP, BPA, BP; non-establishment - Third Side, Path of Democracy; there is no political party ordinance, so there are no registered political parties; politically active groups register as societies or companies
by the end of 2021, the leading pro-democracy figures in Hong Kong had been effectively removed from the political arena under the provisions of Beijing's 2021 electoral changes or via charges under the 2020 national security law; in addition, dozens of pro-democracy organizations, including political parties, unions, churches, civil rights groups, and media organizations have disbanded or closed

International organization participation: ADB, APEC, BIS, FATF, ICC (national committees), IHO, IMF, IMO (associate), Interpol (subbureau), IOC, ISO (correspondent), ITUC (NGOs), UNWTO (associate), UPU, WCO, WMO, WTO

Diplomatic representation in the US: *chief of mission:* none (Special Administrative Region of China); Hong Kong Economic and Trade Office (HKETO) carries out normal liaison activities and communication with the US Government and other US entities; Eddie MAK, JP (since 3 July 2018) is the Hong Kong Commissioner to the US Government of the Hong Kong Special Administrative Region; *address:* 1520 18th Street NW, Washington, DC 20036; *telephone:* [1] (202) 331-8947; *FAX:* [1] (202) 331-8958; hketo@hketowashington.gov.hk
HKETO offices: New York, San Francisco

Diplomatic representation from the US: *chief of mission:* Consul General Hanscom SMITH (since July 2019); note - also accredited to Macau
embassy: 26 Garden Road, Central, Hong Kong
mailing address: 8000 Hong Kong Place, Washington DC 20521-8000
telephone: [852] 2523-9011
FAX: [852] 2845-1598
email address and website:
acshk@state.gov
https://hk.usconsulate.gov/

Flag description: red with a stylized, white, five-petal Bauhinia flower in the center; each petal contains a small, red, five-pointed star in its middle; the red color is the same as that on the Chinese flag and represents the motherland; the fragrant Bauhinia - developed in Hong Kong the late 19th century - has come to symbolize the region; the five stars echo those on the flag of China

National symbol(s): orchid tree flower; national colors: red, white

National anthem: *note:* as a Special Administrative Region of China, "Yiyongjun Jinxingqu" is the official anthem (see China)

ECONOMY

Economic overview: Hong Kong has a free market economy, highly dependent on international trade and finance - the value of goods and services trade, including the sizable share of reexports, is about four times GDP. Hong Kong has no tariffs on imported goods, and it levies excise duties on only four commodities, whether imported or produced locally: hard alcohol, tobacco, oil, and methyl alcohol. There are no quotas or dumping laws. Hong Kong continues to link its currency closely to the US dollar, maintaining an arrangement established in 1983.

Excess liquidity, low interest rates and a tight housing supply have caused Hong Kong property prices to rise rapidly. The lower and middle-income segments of the population increasingly find housing unaffordable.

Hong Kong's open economy has left it exposed to the global economic situation. Its continued reliance on foreign trade and investment makes it vulnerable to renewed global financial market volatility or a slowdown in the global economy.

Mainland China has long been Hong Kong's largest trading partner, accounting for about half of Hong Kong's total trade by value. Hong Kong's natural resources are limited, and food and raw materials must be imported. As a result of China's easing of travel restrictions, the number of mainland tourists to the territory surged from 4.5 million in 2001 to 47.3 million in 2014, outnumbering visitors from all other countries combined. After peaking in 2014, overall tourist arrivals dropped 2.5% in 2015 and 4.5% in 2016. The tourism sector rebounded in 2017, with visitor arrivals rising 3.2% to 58.47 million. Travelers from Mainland China totaled 44.45 million, accounting for 76% of the total.

The Hong Kong Government is promoting the Special Administrative Region (SAR) as the preferred business hub for renminbi (RMB) internationalization. Hong Kong residents are allowed to establish RMB-denominated savings accounts, RMB-denominated corporate and Chinese government bonds have been issued in Hong Kong, RMB trade settlement is allowed, and investment schemes such as the Renminbi Qualified Foreign Institutional Investor (RQFII) Program was first launched in Hong Kong. Offshore RMB activities experienced a setback, however, after the People's Bank of China changed the way it set the central parity rate in August 2015. RMB deposits in Hong Kong fell from 1.0 trillion RMB at the end of 2014 to 559 billion RMB at the end of 2017, while RMB trade settlement handled by banks in Hong Kong also shrank from 6.8 trillion RMB in 2015 to 3.9 trillion RMB in 2017.

Hong Kong has also established itself as the premier stock market for Chinese firms seeking to list abroad. In 2015, mainland Chinese companies constituted about 50% of the firms listed on the Hong Kong Stock Exchange and accounted for about 66% of the exchange's market capitalization.

During the past decade, as Hong Kong's manufacturing industry moved to the mainland, its service industry has grown rapidly. In 2014, Hong Kong and China signed a new agreement on achieving basic liberalization of trade in services in Guangdong Province under the Closer Economic Partnership Agreement (CEPA), adopted in 2003 to forge closer ties between Hong Kong and the mainland. The new measures, which took effect in March 2015, cover a negative list and a most-favored treatment provision. On the basis of the Guangdong Agreement, the Agreement on Trade in Services signed in November 2015 further enhanced liberalization, including extending the implementation of the majority of Guangdong pilot liberalization measures to the whole Mainland, reducing the restrictive measures in the negative list, and adding measures in the positive lists for cross-border services as well as cultural and telecommunications services. In June 2017, the Investment Agreement and the Agreement on Economic and Technical Cooperation (Ecotech Agreement) were signed under the framework of CEPA.

Hong Kong's economic integration with the mainland continues to be most evident in the banking and finance sector. Initiatives like the Hong Kong-Shanghai Stock Connect, the Hong Kong-Shenzhen Stock Connect the Mutual Recognition of Funds, and the Bond Connect scheme are all important steps towards opening up the Mainland's capital markets and have reinforced Hong Kong's role as China's leading offshore RMB market. Additional connect schemes such as ETF Connect (for exchange-traded fund products) are also under exploration by Hong Kong authorities. In 2017, Chief Executive Carrie LAM announced plans to increase government spending on research and development, education, and technological innovation with the aim of spurring continued economic growth through greater sector diversification.

Real GDP (purchasing power parity): $420.13 billion (2020 est.)
$447.34 billion (2019 est.)
$454.98 billion (2018 est.)
note: data are in 2017 dollars

Real GDP growth rate: -1.25% (2019 est.)
2.86% (2018 est.)
3.8% (2017 est.)

Real GDP per capita: $56,200 (2020 est.)
$59,600 (2019 est.)
$61,100 (2018 est.)
note: data are in 2017 dollars

GDP (official exchange rate): $365.753 billion (2019 est.)

Inflation rate (consumer prices): 2.8% (2019 est.)
2.4% (2018 est.)
1.4% (2017 est.)

Credit ratings:

Fitch rating: AA- (2020)

Moody's rating: Aa3 (2020)

Standard & Poors rating: AA+ (2017)
note: The year refers to the year in which the current credit rating was first obtained.

GDP - composition, by sector of origin: *agriculture:* 0.1% (2017 est.)
industry: 7.6% (2017 est.)
services: 92.3% (2017 est.)

GDP - composition, by end use: *household consumption:* 67% (2017 est.)
government consumption: 9.9% (2017 est.)
investment in fixed capital: 21.8% (2017 est.)
investment in inventories: 0.4% (2017 est.)
exports of goods and services: 188% (2017 est.)
imports of goods and services: -187.1% (2017 est.)

Agricultural products: pork, poultry, spinach, vegetables, pork offals, game meat, fruit, lettuce, green onions, pig fat

Industries: trading and logistics, financial services, professional services, tourism, cultural and creative, clothing and textiles, shipping, electronics, toys, clocks and watches

Industrial production growth rate: 1.7% (2017 est.)

Labor force: 3.627 million (2020 est.)

Labor force - by occupation: *agriculture:* 3.8% (2013 est.)
industry: 2% (2016 est.)
services: 54.5% (2016 est.)
industry and services: 12.5% (2013 est.)
agriculture/fishing/forestry/mining: 10.1% (2013)
manufacturing: 17.1% (2013 est.)
note: above data exclude public sector

Unemployment rate: 2.93% (2019 est.)
2.83% (2018 est.)

Unemployment, youth ages 15-24: *total:* 15.5%
male: 17.3%
female: 13.6% (2020 est.)

Population below poverty line: 19.9% (2016 est.)

Gini Index coefficient - distribution of family income: 53.9 (2016)
53.7 (2011 est.)

Budget: *revenues:* 79.34 billion (2017 est.)
expenditures: 61.64 billion (2017 est.)

Budget surplus (+) or deficit (-): 5.2% (of GDP) (2017 est.)

Public debt: 0.1% of GDP (2017 est.)
0.1% of GDP (2016 est.)

Taxes and other revenues: 23.2% (of GDP) (2017 est.)

Fiscal year: 1 April - 31 March

Current account balance: $22.469 billion (2019 est.)
$13.516 billion (2018 est.)

Exports: $615.88 billion (2020 est.) note: data are in current year dollars
$649.02 billion (2019 est.) note: data are in current year dollars
$681.28 billion (2018 est.) note: data are in current year dollars

Exports - partners: China 23%, India 14%, Netherlands 6%, United Kingdom 5% (2019)

Exports - commodities: gold, broadcasting equipment, integrated circuits, diamonds, telephones (2019)

Imports: $609.13 billion (2020 est.) note: data are in current year dollars
$642.8 billion (2019 est.) note: data are in current year dollars
$682.05 billion (2018 est.) note: data are in current year dollars

Imports - partners: China 46%, Taiwan 7%, Singapore 7%, South Korea 5%, United States 5%, Japan 5% (2019)

Imports - commodities: integrated circuits, broadcasting equipment, office machinery, telephones, diamonds (2019)

Reserves of foreign exchange and gold: $431.4 billion (31 December 2017 est.)
$386.2 billion (31 December 2016 est.)

Debt - external: $1,648,409,000,000 (2019 est.)
$1,670,919,000,000 (2018 est.)

Exchange rates: Hong Kong dollars (HKD) per US dollar -
7.75225 (2020 est.)
7.8285 (2019 est.)
7.8133 (2018 est.)
7.752 (2014 est.)
7.754 (2013 est.)

ENERGY

Electricity access: *electrification - total population:* 100% (2020)

Electricity: *installed generating capacity:* 14.168 million kW (2020 est.)
consumption: 44,183,900,000 kWh (2020 est.)
exports: 0 kWh (2020 est.)
imports: 12.7 billion kWh (2020 est.)
transmission/distribution losses: 1.622 billion kWh (2020 est.)

Electricity generation sources: *fossil fuels:* 99.6% of total installed capacity (2020 est.)
biomass and waste: 0.4% of total installed capacity (2020 est.)

Coal: *production:* 0 metric tons (2020 est.)
consumption: 5.485 million metric tons (2020 est.)
exports: 0 metric tons (2020 est.)
imports: 5.485 million metric tons (2020 est.)
proven reserves: 0 metric tons (2019 est.)

Petroleum: *total petroleum production:* 100 bbl/day (2021 est.)
refined petroleum consumption: 404,600 bbl/day (2019 est.)
crude oil and lease condensate exports: 0 bbl/day (2018 est.)
crude oil and lease condensate imports: 0 bbl/day (2018 est.)
crude oil estimated reserves: 0 barrels (2021 est.)

Refined petroleum products - production: 0 bbl/day (2015 est.)

Refined petroleum products - exports: 13,570 bbl/day (2015 est.)

Refined petroleum products - imports: 402,100 bbl/day (2015 est.)

Natural gas: *production:* 0 cubic meters (2021 est.)
consumption: 4,913,021,000 cubic meters (2020 est.)
exports: 0 cubic meters (2021 est.)
imports: 4,913,021,000 cubic meters (2020 est.)
proven reserves: 0 cubic meters (2021 est.)

Carbon dioxide emissions: 92.493 million metric tonnes of CO_2 (2019 est.)
from coal and metallurgical coke: 23.557 million metric tonnes of CO_2 (2019 est.)
from petroleum and other liquids: 62.451 million metric tonnes of CO_2 (2019 est.)
from consumed natural gas: 6.484 million metric tonnes of CO_2 (2019 est.)

Energy consumption per capita: 172.009 million Btu/person (2019 est.)

COMMUNICATIONS

Telephones - fixed lines: *total subscriptions:* 3,900,599 (2020 est.)
subscriptions per 100 inhabitants: 52 (2020 est.)

Telephones - mobile cellular: *total subscriptions:* 21,865,215 (2020 est.)
subscriptions per 100 inhabitants: 292 (2020 est.)

Telecommunication systems: *general assessment:* Hong Kong's telecommunications sector continues to stay near the top of world rankings for the industry; it has kept its #1 spot in the Asian region in terms of the maturity of its telecom market – a reflection of the high penetration rates across mobile, mobile broadband, and fixed broadband; even fixed-line teledensity in Hong Kong is impressive at over 50%, although it too has started a gradual decline in keeping with most other telecom markets around the world, as consumers slowly transition over to the mobile platform for all of their communication needs (2022)
domestic: microwave radio relay links and extensive fiber-optic network; fixed-line is over 52 per 100 and mobile-cellular is nearly 292 subscriptions per 100 (2020)
international: country code - 852; landing points for the AAE-1, AAG, APCN-2, APG, ASE, FEA, FNAL, RNAL, H2HE, SeaMeWe-3, SJC and TGN-IA submarine cables that provide connections to Asia, US, Australia, the Middle East, and Europe; satellite earth stations - 3 Intelsat (1 Pacific Ocean and 2 Indian Ocean); coaxial cable to Guangzhou, China (2022)

Broadcast media: 34 commercial terrestrial TV networks each with multiple stations; multi-channel satellite and cable TV systems available; 3 licensed broadcasters of terrestrial radio, one of which is government funded, operate about 12 radio stations; note - 4 digital radio broadcasters operated in Hong Kong from 2010 to 2017, but all digital radio services were terminated in September 2017 due to weak market demand (2019)

Internet country code: .hk

Internet users: *total:* 6,883,256 (2020 est.)
percent of population: 92% (2020 est.)

Broadband - fixed subscriptions: *total:* 2,885,586 (2020 est.)
subscriptions per 100 inhabitants: 39 (2020 est.)

TRANSPORTATION

National air transport system: *number of registered air carriers:* 12 (2020) (registered in China)
inventory of registered aircraft operated by air carriers: 275 (registered in China)
annual passenger traffic on registered air carriers: 47,101,822 (2018)
annual freight traffic on registered air carriers: 12,676,720,000 (2018) mt-km

Civil aircraft registration country code prefix: B-H

Airports: *total:* 2 (2021)

Airports - with paved runways: *total:* 2
over 3,047 m: 1
1,524 to 2,437 m: 1 (2021)

Heliports: 9 (2021)

Roadways: *total:* 2,193 km (2021)
paved: 2,193 km (2021)

Merchant marine: *total:* 2,718
by type: bulk carrier 1,158, container ship 558, general cargo 184, oil tanker 388, other 430 (2021)

Ports and terminals: *major seaport(s):* Hong Kong
container port(s) (TEUs): Hong Kong (18,361,000) (2019)

MILITARY AND SECURITY

Military and security forces: no regular indigenous military forces; Hong Kong Police Force (specialized units include the Police Counterterrorism Response Unit, the Explosive Ordnance Disposal Bureau, the Special Duties Unit, the Airport Security Unit, and the VIP Protection Unit) (2022)
note: the Hong Kong garrison of China's People's Liberation Army (PLA) includes elements of the PLA Army, PLA Navy, and PLA Air Force; these forces are under the direct leadership of the Central Military Commission in Beijing and under administrative control of the adjacent Southern Theater Command

Military - note: defense is the responsibility of China

TRANSNATIONAL ISSUES

Disputes - international: Hong Kong plans to reduce its 2,800-hectare Frontier Closed Area (FCA) to 400 hectares by 2015; the FCA was established in 1951 as a buffer zone between Hong Kong and mainland China to prevent illegal migration from and the smuggling of goods

Trafficking in persons: *current situation:* human traffickers exploit domestic and foreign victims in Hong Kong, and traffickers also exploit victims from Hong Kong abroad; traffickers exploit women from Eastern Europe, Africa, and Southeast Asia in sex trafficking; some women in Hong Kong – often with the assistance of their families – deceive Indian and Pakistani men into arranged marriages involving forced domestic service, bonded labor in construction and other physically demanding industries, and other forms of abuse via exploitative contracts; drug trafficking syndicates coerced South American women to carry drugs into Hong Kong; employment agencies hired foreign domestic workers under false pretenses and forced them into commercial sex, sometimes through debt-based coercion
tier rating: Tier 2 Watch List — Hong Kong does not fully meet the minimum standards for the elimination of trafficking but is making significant efforts to do so; Hong Kong is hiring and training 98 new employees within the immigration, customs, labor, and justice departments dedicated to trafficking issues; authorities screened more than 7,000 vulnerable individuals for trafficking; the labor department introduced a victim identification mechanism to its division offices; the government provided anti-trafficking training to various officials; the government did not investigate, prosecute, or convict any cases of labor trafficking, investigated fewer sex trafficking cases, and did not provide victims any governmentfunded services; the government continued to penalize victims for unlawful acts traffickers compelled them to commit; no legislation was enacted to fully criminalize all forms of trafficking (2020)

Illicit drugs: modern banking system provides conduit for money laundering; groups involved in money laundering range from local street organizations to sophisticated international syndicates involved in assorted criminal activities, including drug trafficking; major source of precursor chemicals used in the production of illicit narcotics

HUNGARY

INTRODUCTION

Background: Hungary became a Christian kingdom in A.D. 1000 and for many centuries served as a bulwark against Ottoman Turkish expansion in Europe. The kingdom eventually became part of the polyglot Austro-Hungarian Empire, which collapsed during World War I. The country fell under communist rule following World War II. In 1956, a revolt and an announced withdrawal from the Warsaw Pact were met with a massive military intervention by Moscow. Under the leadership of Janos KADAR in 1968, Hungary began liberalizing its economy, introducing so-called "Goulash Communism." Hungary held its first multiparty elections in 1990 and initiated a free market economy. It joined NATO in 1999 and the EU five years later.

GEOGRAPHY

Location: Central Europe, northwest of Romania

Geographic coordinates: 47 00 N, 20 00 E

Map references: Europe

Area: *total:* 93,028 sq km
land: 89,608 sq km
water: 3,420 sq km

Area - comparative: slightly smaller than Virginia; about the same size as Indiana

Land boundaries: *total:* 2,106 km
border countries (7): Austria 321 km; Croatia 348 km; Romania 424 km; Serbia 164 km; Slovakia 627 km; Slovenia 94 km; Ukraine 128 km

Coastline: 0 km (landlocked)

Maritime claims: none (landlocked)

Climate: temperate; cold, cloudy, humid winters; warm summers

Terrain: mostly flat to rolling plains; hills and low mountains on the Slovakian border

Elevation: *highest point:* Kekes 1,014 m
lowest point: Tisza River 78 m
mean elevation: 143 m

Natural resources: bauxite, coal, natural gas, fertile soils, arable land

Land use: *agricultural land:* 58.9% (2018 est.)
arable land: 48.5% (2018 est.)
permanent crops: 2% (2018 est.)
permanent pasture: 8.4% (2018 est.)
forest: 22.5% (2018 est.)
other: 18.6% (2018 est.)

Irrigated land: 1,721 sq km (2012)

Major lakes (area sq km): *fresh water lake(s):* Lake Balaton - 590 sq km

Major rivers (by length in km): Danube (shared with Germany [s], Austria, Slovakia, Croatia, Serbia, Bulgaria, Ukraine, Moldova, and Romania [m]) - 2,888 km
note – [s] after country name indicates river source; [m] after country name indicates river mouth

Major watersheds (area sq km): Atlantic Ocean drainage: *(Black Sea)* Danube (795,656 sq km)

Population distribution: a fairly even distribution throughout most of the country, with urban areas attracting larger and denser populations

Geography - note: landlocked; strategic location astride main land routes between Western Europe and Balkan Peninsula as well as between Ukraine and Mediterranean basin; the north-south flowing Duna (Danube) and Tisza Rivers divide the country into three large regions

PEOPLE AND SOCIETY

Population: 9,699,577 (2022 est.)

Nationality: *noun:* Hungarian(s)
adjective: Hungarian

Ethnic groups: Hungarian 85.6%, Romani 3.2%, German 1.9%, other 2.6%, unspecified 14.1% (2011 est.)
note: percentages add up to more than 100% because respondents were able to identify more than one ethnic group; Romani populations are usually underestimated in official statistics and may represent 5–10% of Hungary's population

Languages: Hungarian (official) 99.6%, English 16%, German 11.2%, Russian 1.6%, Romanian 1.3%, French 1.2%, other 4.2%; note - shares sum to more than 100% because some respondents gave more than one answer on the census; Hungarian is the mother tongue of 98.9% of Hungarian speakers (2011 est.)
major-language sample(s): A World Factbook nélkülözhetetlen forrása az alapvető információnak. (Hungarian)

Religions: Roman Catholic 37.2%, Calvinist 11.6%, Lutheran 2.2%, Greek Catholic 1.8%, other 1.9%, none 18.2%, no response 27.2% (2011 est.)

Age structure: *0-14 years:* 14.54% (male 731,542/female 689,739)
15-24 years: 10.43% (male 526,933/female 492,388)
25-54 years: 42.17% (male 2,075,763/female 2,044,664)
55-64 years: 12.17% (male 552,876/female 636,107)
65 years and over: 20.69% (male 773,157/female 1,248,658) (2020 est.)

Dependency ratios: *total dependency ratio:* 46.9
youth dependency ratio: 22
elderly dependency ratio: 30.8
potential support ratio: 3.2 (2020 est.)

Median age: *total:* 43.6 years
male: 41.5 years
female: 45.5 years (2020 est.)

Population growth rate: -0.3% (2022 est.)

Birth rate: 8.65 births/1,000 population (2022 est.)

Death rate: 12.88 deaths/1,000 population (2022 est.)

Net migration rate: 1.23 migrant(s)/1,000 population (2022 est.)

Population distribution: a fairly even distribution throughout most of the country, with urban areas attracting larger and denser populations

Urbanization: *urban population:* 72.6% of total population (2022)
rate of urbanization: 0.05% annual rate of change (2020-25 est.)

Major urban areas - population: 1.775 million BUDAPEST (capital) (2022)

Sex ratio: *at birth:* 1.06 male(s)/female
0-14 years: 1.06 male(s)/female
15-24 years: 1.07 male(s)/female
25-54 years: 1.02 male(s)/female
55-64 years: 0.88 male(s)/female
65 years and over: 0.51 male(s)/female
total population: 0.91 male(s)/female (2022 est.)

Mother's mean age at first birth: 28.4 years (2020 est.)

Maternal mortality ratio: 12 deaths/100,000 live births (2017 est.)

Infant mortality rate: *total:* 4.62 deaths/1,000 live births
male: 4.95 deaths/1,000 live births
female: 4.27 deaths/1,000 live births (2022 est.)

Life expectancy at birth: *total population:* 77.2 years
male: 73.55 years
female: 81.06 years (2022 est.)

Total fertility rate: 1.48 children born/woman (2022 est.)

Drinking water source: *improved:* *urban:* 100% of population
rural: 100% of population
total: 100% of population

Current health expenditure: 6.4% of GDP (2019)

Physicians density: 6.06 physicians/1,000 population (2020)

Hospital bed density: 7 beds/1,000 population (2018)

Sanitation facility access: *improved:* *urban:* 100% of population
rural: 100% of population
total: 100% of population

HIV/AIDS - adult prevalence rate: (2018 est.) <.1%

Major infectious diseases: *degree of risk:* intermediate (2016)
vectorborne diseases: tickborne encephalitis (2016)

Obesity - adult prevalence rate: 26.4% (2016)

Alcohol consumption per capita: *total:* 10.79 liters of pure alcohol (2019 est.)
beer: 3.96 liters of pure alcohol (2019 est.)
wine: 3.33 liters of pure alcohol (2019 est.)
spirits: 3.5 liters of pure alcohol (2019 est.)
other alcohols: 0 liters of pure alcohol (2019 est.)

Tobacco use: *total:* 31.8% (2020 est.)
male: 35.8% (2020 est.)
female: 27.8% (2020 est.)

Education expenditures: 4.6% of GDP (2018 est.)

Literacy: *definition:* age 15 and over can read and write
total population: 99.1%
male: 99.1%

female: 99% (2015)

School life expectancy (primary to tertiary education): *total:* 13 years
male: 12 years
female: 14 years (2019)

Unemployment, youth ages 15-24: *total:* 12.8%
male: 11.9%
female: 14% (2020 est.)

ENVIRONMENT

Environment - current issues: air and water pollution are some of Hungary's most serious environmental problems; water quality in the Hungarian part of the Danube has improved but is still plagued by pollutants from industry and large-scale agriculture; soil pollution

Environment - international agreements: *party to:* Air Pollution, Air Pollution-Heavy Metals, Air Pollution-Multi-effect Protocol, Air Pollution-Nitrogen Oxides, Air Pollution-Persistent Organic Pollutants, Air Pollution-Sulphur 85, Air Pollution-Sulphur 94, Air Pollution-Volatile Organic Compounds, Antarctic Treaty, Biodiversity, Climate Change, Climate Change-Kyoto Protocol, Climate Change-Paris Agreement, Comprehensive Nuclear Test Ban, Desertification, Endangered Species, Environmental Modification, Hazardous Wastes, Law of the Sea, Marine Dumping-London Convention, Nuclear Test Ban, Ozone Layer Protection, Ship Pollution, Tropical Timber 2006, Wetlands, Whaling
signed, but not ratified: Antarctic-Environmental Protection

Air pollutants: *particulate matter emissions:* 15.62 micrograms per cubic meter (2016 est.)
carbon dioxide emissions: 45.54 megatons (2016 est.)
methane emissions: 7.25 megatons (2020 est.)

Climate: temperate; cold, cloudy, humid winters; warm summers

Land use: *agricultural land:* 58.9% (2018 est.)
arable land: 48.5% (2018 est.)
permanent crops: 2% (2018 est.)
permanent pasture: 8.4% (2018 est.)
forest: 22.5% (2018 est.)
other: 18.6% (2018 est.)

Urbanization: *urban population:* 72.6% of total population (2022)
rate of urbanization: 0.05% annual rate of change (2020-25 est.)

Revenue from forest resources: *forest revenues:* 0.1% of GDP (2018 est.)

Revenue from coal: *coal revenues:* 0.01% of GDP (2018 est.)

Waste and recycling: *municipal solid waste generated annually:* 3.712 million tons (2015 est.)
municipal solid waste recycled annually: 962,893 tons (2015 est.)
percent of municipal solid waste recycled: 25.9% (2015 est.)

Major lakes (area sq km): *fresh water lake(s):* Lake Balaton - 590 sq km

Major rivers (by length in km): Danube (shared with Germany [s], Austria, Slovakia, Croatia, Serbia, Bulgaria, Ukraine, Moldova, and Romania [m]) - 2,888 km
note – [s] after country name indicates river source; [m] after country name indicates river mouth

Major watersheds (area sq km): Atlantic Ocean drainage: *(Black Sea)* Danube (795,656 sq km)

Total water withdrawal: *municipal:* 624.5 million cubic meters (2017 est.)
industrial: 3.358 billion cubic meters (2017 est.)
agricultural: 518.6 million cubic meters (2017 est.)

Total renewable water resources: 104 billion cubic meters (2017 est.)

GOVERNMENT

Country name: *conventional long form:* none
conventional short form: Hungary
local long form: none
local short form: Magyarorszag
former: Kingdom of Hungary, Hungarian People's Republic, Hungarian Soviet Republic, Hungarian Republic
etymology: the Byzantine Greeks refered to the tribes that arrived on the steppes of Eastern Europe in the 9th century as the "Oungroi," a name that was later Latinized to "Ungri" and which became "Hungari"; the name originally meant an "[alliance of] ten tribes"; the Hungarian name "Magyarorszag" means "Country of the Magyars"; the term may derive from the most prominent of the Hungarian tribes, the Megyer

Government type: parliamentary republic

Capital: *name:* Budapest
geographic coordinates: 47 30 N, 19 05 E
time difference: UTC+1 (6 hours ahead of Washington, DC, during Standard Time)
daylight saving time: +1hr, begins last Sunday in March; ends last Sunday in October
etymology: the Hungarian capital city was formed in 1873 from the merger of three cities on opposite banks of the Danube: Buda and Obuda (Old Buda) on the western shore and Pest on the eastern; the origins of the original names are obscure, but according to the second century A.D. geographer, Ptolemy, the settlement that would become Pest was called "Pession" in ancient times; "Buda" may derive from either a Slavic or Turkic personal name

Administrative divisions: 19 counties (megyek, singular - megye), 23 cities with county rights (megyei jogu varosok, singular - megyei jogu varos), and 1 capital city (fovaros)
counties: Bacs-Kiskun, Baranya, Bekes, Borsod-Abauj-Zemplen, Csongrad-Csanad, Fejer, Gyor-Moson-Sopron, Hajdu-Bihar, Heves, Jasz-Nagykun-Szolnok, Komarom-Esztergom, Nograd, Pest, Somogy, Szabolcs-Szatmar-Bereg, Tolna, Vas, Veszprem, Zala
cities with county rights: Bekescsaba, Debrecen, Dunaujvaros, Eger, Erd, Gyor, Hodmezovasarhely, Kaposvar, Kecskemet, Miskolc, Nagykanizsa, Nyiregyhaza, Pecs, Salgotarjan, Sopron, Szeged, Szekesfehervar, Szekszard, Szolnok, Szombathely, Tatabanya, Veszprem, Zalaegerszeg
capital city: Budapest

Independence: 16 November 1918 (republic proclaimed); notable earlier dates: 25 December 1000 (crowning of King STEPHEN I, traditional founding date); 30 March 1867 (Austro-Hungarian dual monarchy established)

National holiday: Saint Stephen's Day, 20 August (1083); note - commemorates his canonization and the transfer of his remains to Buda (now Budapest) in 1083

Constitution: *history:* previous 1949 (heavily amended in 1989 following the collapse of communism); latest approved 18 April 2011, signed 25 April 2011, effective 1 January 2012
amendments: proposed by the president of the republic, by the government, by parliamentary committee, or by Parliament members; passage requires two-thirds majority vote of Parliament members and approval by the president; amended several times, last in 2018

Legal system: civil legal system influenced by the German model

International law organization participation: accepts compulsory ICJ jurisdiction with reservations; accepts ICC jurisdiction

Citizenship: *citizenship by birth:* no
citizenship by descent only: at least one parent must be a citizen of Hungary
dual citizenship recognized: yes
residency requirement for naturalization: 8 years

Suffrage: 18 years of age, 16 if married and marriage is registered in Hungary; universal

Executive branch: *chief of state:* President Katalin NOVAK (since 10 May 2022)
head of government: Prime Minister Viktor ORBAN (since 29 May 2010)
cabinet: Cabinet of Ministers proposed by the prime minister and appointed by the president
elections/appointments: president indirectly elected by the National Assembly with two-thirds majority vote in first round or simple majority vote in second round for a 5-year term (eligible for a second term); election last held on 11 March 2022 (next to be held spring 2027); prime minister elected by the National Assembly on the recommendation of the president; election last held on 3 April 2022 (next to be held April or May 2027)
election results: *2022:* Katalin NOVAK (Fidesz) elected president; National Assembly vote - 137 to 51
2017: Janos ADER (Fidesz) reelected president; National Assembly vote - 131 to 39
2010: Viktor ORBAN (Fidesz) reelected prime minister

Legislative branch: *description:* unicameral National Assembly or Orszaggyules (199 seats; 106 members directly elected in single-member constituencies by simple majority vote and 93 members directly elected in a single nationwide constituency by party-list proportional representation vote, using the d'Hondt method; members serve 4-year terms)
elections: last held on 3 April 2022 (next to be held in April 2026)
election results: percent of vote by party list - Fidesz-KDNP 54.1%, United for Hungary 34.5%, Mi Hazank 5.9%, other 5.5%; seats by party - Fidesz-KDNP 135, United for Hungary 57, Mi Hazank 6, independent 1; composition - men 175, women 24, percent of women 12.1%

Judicial branch: *highest court(s):* Curia or Supreme Judicial Court (consists of the president, vice president, department heads, and has a maximum of 113 judges, and is organized into civil, criminal, and administrative-labor departments; Constitutional Court (consists of 15 judges, including the court president and vice president)
judge selection and term of office: Curia president elected by the National Assembly on the recommendation of the president of the republic; other Curia

judges appointed by the president upon the recommendation of the National Judicial Council, a separate 15-member administrative body; judge tenure based on interim evaluations until normal retirement at age 62; Constitutional Court judges, including the president of the court, elected by the National Assembly; court vice president elected by the court itself; members serve 12-year terms with mandatory retirement at age 62
subordinate courts: 5 regional courts of appeal; 19 regional or county courts (including Budapest Metropolitan Court); 20 administrative-labor courts; 111 district or local courts

Political parties and leaders: Christian Democratic People's Party or KDNP [Zsolt SEMJEN]
Democratic Coalition or DK [Ferenc GYURCSANY]
Dialogue for Hungary (Parbeszed) or PM [Bence TORDAI, Rebeka SZABO]
Fidesz-Hungarian Civic Alliance or Fidesz [Viktor ORBAN]
Hungarian Socialist Party or MSZP [Bertalan TOTH, Agnes KUNHALMI]
LMP-Hungary's Green Party [Peter UNGAR, Erzsebet SCHMUCK]
Mi Hazank (Our Homeland Movement) or MHM [Laszlo TOROCZKAI]
Momentum Movement (Momentum Mozgalom) [Ferenc GELENCSER]
Movement for a Better Hungary or Jobbik [Marton GYONGYOSI]
National Self-Government of Germans in Hungary or LdU [Ibolya HOCK-ENGLENDER]
United for Hungary (a coalition of Jobbik, MSZP, Dialogue, DK, LMP, and Momentum)

International organization participation: Australia Group, BIS, CD, CE, CEI, CERN, EAPC, EBRD, ECB, EIB, ESA (cooperating state), EU, FAO, G-9, IAEA, IBRD, ICAO, ICC (national committees), ICCt, ICRM, IDA, IEA, IFAD, IFC, IFRCS, ILO, IMF, IMO, IMSO, Interpol, IOC, IOM, IPU, ISO, ITSO, ITU, ITUC (NGOs), MIGA, MINURSO, NATO, NEA, NSG, OAS (observer), OECD, OIF (observer), OPCW, OSCE, PCA, Schengen Convention, SELEC, UN, UNCTAD, UNESCO, UNFICYP, UNHCR, UNIDO, UNIFIL, UNWTO, UPU, Wassenaar Arrangement, WCO, WFTU (NGOs), WHO, WIPO, WMO, WTO, ZC

Diplomatic representation in the US: *chief of mission:* Ambassador Szabolcs Ferenc TAKACS (since 23 December 2020)
chancery: 3910 Shoemaker Street NW, Washington, DC 20008
telephone: [1] (202) 362-6730
FAX: [1] (202) 966-8135
email address and website:
info@mfa.gov.hu
https://washington.mfa.gov.hu/eng
consulate(s) general: Chicago, Los Angeles, New York

Diplomatic representation from the US: *chief of mission:* Ambassador (vacant); Charge d'Affaires Marc DILLARD (since 30 October 2020)
embassy: Szabadsag ter 12, H-1054 Budapest
mailing address: 5270 Budapest Place, US Department of State, Washington, DC 20521-5270
telephone: [36] (1) 475-4400
FAX: [36] (1) 475-4248
email address and website:
acs.budapest@state.gov
https://hu.usembassy.gov/

Flag description: three equal horizontal bands of red (top), white, and green; the flag dates to the national movement of the 18th and 19th centuries, and fuses the medieval colors of the Hungarian coat of arms with the revolutionary tricolor form of the French flag; folklore attributes virtues to the colors: red for strength, white for faithfulness, and green for hope; alternatively, the red is seen as being for the blood spilled in defense of the land, white for freedom, and green for the pasturelands that make up so much of the country

National symbol(s): Holy Crown of Hungary (Crown of Saint Stephen); national colors: red, white, green

National anthem: *name:* "Himnusz" (Hymn)
lyrics/music: Ferenc KOLCSEY/Ferenc ERKEL
note: adopted 1844

National heritage: *total World Heritage Sites:* 8 (7 cultural, 1 natural)
selected World Heritage Site locales: Budapest, including the Banks of the Danube, the Buda Castle Quarter, and Andrássy Avenue (c); Old Village of Hollókő and its Surroundings (c); Caves of Aggtelek Karst and Slovak Karst (n); Millenary Benedictine Abbey of Pannonhalma and its Natural Environment (c); Hortobágy National Park - the Puszta (c); Early Christian Necropolis of Pécs (Sopianae) (c); Fertö / Neusiedlersee Cultural Landscape (c); Tokaj Wine Region Historic Cultural Landscape (c)

ECONOMY

Economic overview: Hungary has transitioned from a centrally planned to a market-driven economy with a per capita income approximately two thirds of the EU-28 average; however, in recent years the government has become more involved in managing the economy. Budapest has implemented unorthodox economic policies to boost household consumption and has relied on EU-funded development projects to generate growth.

Following the fall of communism in 1990, Hungary experienced a drop-off in exports and financial assistance from the former Soviet Union. Hungary embarked on a series of economic reforms, including privatization of state-owned enterprises and reduction of social spending programs, to shift from a centrally planned to a market-driven economy, and to reorient its economy towards trade with the West. These efforts helped to spur growth, attract investment, and reduce Hungary's debt burden and fiscal deficits. Despite these reforms, living conditions for the average Hungarian initially deteriorated as inflation increased and unemployment reached double digits. Conditions slowly improved over the 1990s as the reforms came to fruition and export growth accelerated. Economic policies instituted during that decade helped position Hungary to join the European Union in 2004. Hungary has not yet joined the euro-zone. Hungary suffered a historic economic contraction as a result of the global economic slowdown in 2008-09 as export demand and domestic consumption dropped, prompting it to take an IMF-EU financial assistance package.

Since 2010, the government has backpedaled on many economic reforms and taken a more populist approach towards economic management. The government has favored national industries and government-linked businesses through legislation, regulation, and public procurements. In 2011 and 2014, Hungary nationalized private pension funds, which squeezed financial service providers out of the system, but also helped Hungary curb its public debt and lower its budget deficit to below 3% of GDP, as subsequent pension contributions have been channeled into the state-managed pension fund. Hungary's public debt (at 74.5% of GDP) is still high compared to EU peers in Central Europe. Real GDP growth has been robust in the past few years due to increased EU funding, higher EU demand for Hungarian exports, and a rebound in domestic household consumption. To further boost household consumption ahead of the 2018 election, the government embarked on a six-year phased increase to minimum wages and public sector salaries, decreased taxes on foodstuffs and services, cut the personal income tax from 16% to 15%, and implemented a uniform 9% business tax for small and medium-sized enterprises and large companies. Real GDP growth slowed in 2016 due to a cyclical decrease in EU funding, but increased to 3.8% in 2017 as the government pre-financed EU funded projects ahead of the 2018 election.

Systemic economic challenges include pervasive corruption, labor shortages driven by demographic declines and migration, widespread poverty in rural areas, vulnerabilities to changes in demand for exports, and a heavy reliance on Russian energy imports.

Real GDP (purchasing power parity): $302.32 billion (2020 est.)
$318.09 billion (2019 est.)
$303.98 billion (2018 est.)
note: data are in 2017 dollars

Real GDP growth rate: 4.58% (2019 est.)
5.44% (2018 est.)
4.45% (2017 est.)

Real GDP per capita: $31,000 (2020 est.)
$32,600 (2019 est.)
$31,100 (2018 est.)
note: data are in 2017 dollars

GDP (official exchange rate): $163.251 billion (2019 est.)

Inflation rate (consumer prices): 3.3% (2019 est.)
2.8% (2018 est.)
2.3% (2017 est.)

Credit ratings:

Fitch rating: BBB (2019)

Moody's rating: Baa3 (2016)

Standard & Poors rating: BBB (2019)
note: The year refers to the year in which the current credit rating was first obtained.

GDP - composition, by sector of origin: *agriculture:* 3.9% (2017 est.)
industry: 31.3% (2017 est.)
services: 64.8% (2017 est.)

GDP - composition, by end use: *household consumption:* 49.6% (2017 est.)
government consumption: 20% (2017 est.)
investment in fixed capital: 21.6% (2017 est.)
investment in inventories: 1% (2017 est.)
exports of goods and services: 90.2% (2017 est.)
imports of goods and services: -82.4% (2017 est.)

Agricultural products: maize, wheat, milk, sunflower seed, barley, rapeseed, sugar beet, apples, pork, grapes

Industries: mining, metallurgy, construction materials, processed foods, textiles, chemicals (especially pharmaceuticals), motor vehicles

Industrial production growth rate: 7.4% (2017 est.)

Labor force: 4.414 million (2020 est.)

Labor force - by occupation: *agriculture:* 4.9%
industry: 30.3%
services: 64.5% (2015 est.)

Unemployment rate: 3.45% (2019 est.)
3.71% (2018 est.)

Unemployment, youth ages 15-24: *total:* 12.8%
male: 11.9%
female: 14% (2020 est.)

Population below poverty line: 12.3% (2018 est.)

Gini Index coefficient - distribution of family income: 30.6 (2017 est.)
28.6 (2014)

Household income or consumption by percentage share: *lowest 10%:* 3.3%
highest 10%: 22.4% (2015)

Budget: *revenues:* 61.98 billion (2017 est.)
expenditures: 64.7 billion (2017 est.)

Budget surplus (+) or deficit (-): -2% (of GDP) (2017 est.)
note: Hungary has been under the EU Excessive Deficit Procedure since it joined the EU in 2004; in March 2012, the EU elevated its Excessive Deficit Procedure against Hungary and proposed freezing 30% of the country's Cohesion Funds because 2011 deficit reductions were not achieved in a sustainable manner; in June 2012, the EU lifted the freeze, recognizing that steps had been taken to reduce the deficit; the Hungarian deficit increased above 3% both in 2013 and in 2014 due to sluggish growth and the government's fiscal tightening

Public debt: 73.6% of GDP (2017 est.)
76% of GDP (2016 est.)
note: general government gross debt is defined in the Maastricht Treaty as consolidated general government gross debt at nominal value, outstanding at the end of the year in the following categories of government liabilities: currency and deposits, securities other than shares excluding financial derivatives, and national, state, and local government and social security funds.

Taxes and other revenues: 44.5% (of GDP) (2017 est.)

Fiscal year: calendar year

Current account balance: -$392 million (2019 est.)
$510 million (2018 est.)

Exports: $123.83 billion (2020 est.) note: data are in current year dollars
$134.55 billion (2019 est.) note: data are in current year dollars
$134.66 billion (2018 est.) note: data are in current year dollars

Exports - partners: Germany 27%, Romania 5%, Italy 5%, Slovakia 5% (2019)

Exports - commodities: cars and vehicle parts, packaged medicines, spark-ignition engines, video displays, broadcasting equipment (2019)

Imports: $120.25 billion (2020 est.) note: data are in current year dollars
$129.9 billion (2019 est.) note: data are in current year dollars
$127.52 billion (2018 est.) note: data are in current year dollars

Imports - partners: Germany 25%, China 6%, Poland 6%, Austria 6%, Czechia 5%, Slovakia 5%, Italy 5%, Netherlands 5% (2019)

Imports - commodities: cars and vehicle parts, integrated circuits, packaged medicines, broadcasting equipment, crude petroleum (2019)

Reserves of foreign exchange and gold: $28 billion (31 December 2017 est.)
$25.82 billion (31 December 2016 est.)

Debt - external: $123.256 billion (2019 est.)
$125.29 billion (2018 est.)

Exchange rates: forints (HUF) per US dollar -
295.3276 (2020 est.)
299.4939 (2019 est.)
283.5923 (2018 est.)
279.33 (2014 est.)
232.6 (2013 est.)

ENERGY

Electricity access: *electrification - total population:* 100% (2020)

Electricity: *installed generating capacity:* 10.873 million kW (2020 est.)
consumption: 41.533 billion kWh (2020 est.)
exports: 7.498 billion kWh (2020 est.)
imports: 19.176 billion kWh (2020 est.)
transmission/distribution losses: 3.139 billion kWh (2020 est.)

Electricity generation sources: *fossil fuels:* 36.1% of total installed capacity (2020 est.)
nuclear: 46% of total installed capacity (2020 est.)
solar: 7.4% of total installed capacity (2020 est.)
wind: 2% of total installed capacity (2020 est.)
hydroelectricity: 0.7% of total installed capacity (2020 est.)
tide and wave: 0.5% of total installed capacity (2020 est.)
geothermal: 0.1% of total installed capacity (2020 est.)
biomass and waste: 7.3% of total installed capacity (2020 est.)

Coal: *production:* 6.956 million metric tons (2020 est.)
consumption: 8.079 million metric tons (2020 est.)
exports: 230,000 metric tons (2020 est.)
imports: 1.395 million metric tons (2020 est.)
proven reserves: 2.909 billion metric tons (2019 est.)

Petroleum: *total petroleum production:* 35,200 bbl/day (2021 est.)
refined petroleum consumption: 180,600 bbl/day (2019 est.)
crude oil and lease condensate exports: 8,000 bbl/day (2018 est.)
crude oil and lease condensate imports: 134,800 bbl/day (2018 est.)
crude oil estimated reserves: 12.1 million barrels (2021 est.)

Refined petroleum products - production: 152,400 bbl/day (2017 est.)

Refined petroleum products - exports: 58,720 bbl/day (2017 est.)

Refined petroleum products - imports: 82,110 bbl/day (2017 est.)

Natural gas: *production:* 1,685,020,000 cubic meters (2020 est.)
consumption: 10,545,459,000 cubic meters (2020 est.)
exports: 3,757,583,000 cubic meters (2020 est.)
imports: 11,677,990,000 cubic meters (2020 est.)
proven reserves: 3.738 billion cubic meters (2021 est.)

Carbon dioxide emissions: 48.589 million metric tonnes of CO2 (2019 est.)
from coal and metallurgical coke: 7.501 million metric tonnes of CO2 (2019 est.)
from petroleum and other liquids: 21.568 million metric tonnes of CO2 (2019 est.)
from consumed natural gas: 19.52 million metric tonnes of CO2 (2019 est.)

Energy consumption per capita: 108.212 million Btu/person (2019 est.)

COMMUNICATIONS

Telephones - fixed lines: *total subscriptions:* 2,970,347 (2020 est.)
subscriptions per 100 inhabitants: 31 (2020 est.)

Telephones - mobile cellular: *total subscriptions:* 10,332,660 (2020 est.)
subscriptions per 100 inhabitants: 107 (2020 est.)

Telecommunication systems: *general assessment:* Hungary benefits from having a developed telecom infrastructure, with a focus among operators to develop the 5G sector and upgrade fixed networks to provide a 1Gb/s service; services based on 5G have been supported by the January 2021 multi-spectrum auction for spectrum in the 900MHz and 1800MHz bands; the number of fixed-lines continues to fall as subscribers migrate to the mobile platform for voice and data services; operators have looked to bundled packages to boost revenue and retain subscribers; the broadband market has effective infrastructure based competition, with an extensive cable network competing against DSL services and a vibrant and rapidly expanding fiber sector; the regulator has also introduced a number of measures aimed at promoting market competition, which is pushing the drive for higher speed platforms and encouraging operators to invest in technology upgrades; as a result, Hungary now has the highest fixed broadband penetration rate in Eastern Europe; the number of super fast broadband connections (above 30Mb/s) accounted for 78% of all fixed broadband connections (2022)
domestic: competition among mobile-cellular service providers has led to a sharp increase in the use of mobile-cellular phones, and a decrease in the number of fixed-line connections, with just under 31 fixed per 100 persons and 107 mobile-cellular subscriptions per 100 (2020)
international: country code - 36; Hungary has fiber-optic cable connections with all neighboring countries; the international switch is in Budapest; satellite earth stations - 2 Intelsat (Atlantic Ocean and Indian Ocean regions), 1 Inmarsat, 1 (very small aperture terminal) VSAT system of ground terminals

Broadcast media: mixed system of state-supported public service broadcast media and private broadcasters; the 5 publicly owned TV channels and the 2 main privately owned TV stations are the major national broadcasters; a large number of special interest channels; highly developed market for satellite and cable TV services with about two-thirds of viewers utilizing their services; 4 state-supported public-service radio networks; a large number of local stations including commercial, public service, nonprofit, and community radio stations; digital transition completed at the end of 2013; governmentlinked businesses have greatly consolidated ownership in broadcast and print media (2019)

Internet country code: .hu

Internet users: *total:* 8,588,776 (July 2022 est.)
percent of population: 89.3% (July 2022 est.)

Broadband - fixed subscriptions: *total:* 3,265,308 (2020 est.)
subscriptions per 100 inhabitants: 34 (2020 est.)

TRANSPORTATION

National air transport system: *number of registered air carriers:* 5 (2020)
inventory of registered aircraft operated by air carriers: 145
annual passenger traffic on registered air carriers: 31,226,848 (2018)

Civil aircraft registration country code prefix: HA

Airports: *total:* 41 (2021)

Airports - with paved runways: *total:* 20
over 3,047 m: 2
2,438 to 3,047 m: 6
1,524 to 2,437 m: 6
914 to 1,523 m: 5
under 914 m: 1 (2021)

Airports - with unpaved runways: *total:* 21
1,524 to 2,437 m: 2
914 to 1,523 m: 8
under 914 m: 11 (2021)

Heliports: 3 (2021)

Pipelines: 5,874 km gas (high-pressure transmission system), 83,732 km gas (low-pressure distribution network), 850 km oil, 1,200 km refined products (2018)

Railways: *total:* 8,049 km (2014)
standard gauge: 7,794 km (2014) 1.435-m gauge (2,889 km electrified)
narrow gauge: 219 km (2014) 0.760-m gauge
broad gauge: 36 km (2014) 1.524-m gauge

Roadways: *total:* 203,601 km (2014)
paved: 77,087 km (2014) (includes 1,582 km of expressways)
unpaved: 126,514 km (2014)

Waterways: 1,622 km (2011) (most on Danube River)

Merchant marine: *total:* 1
by type: other 1 (2021)

Ports and terminals: *river port(s):* Baja, Csepel (Budapest), Dunaujvaros, Gyor-Gonyu, Mohacs (Danube)

MILITARY AND SECURITY

Military and security forces: the Hungarian Defense Forces (HDF) are a unified force (Joint Force Command) with Land Forces, Air Forces, and Logistics components (2022)

Military expenditures: 1.7% of GDP (2022 est.)
1.8% of GDP (2021)
1.8% of GDP (2020)
1.3% of GDP (2019) (approximately $3.02 billion)
1% of GDP (2018) (approximately $2.4 billion)

Military and security service personnel strengths: approximately 21,000 active duty troops (16,000 Army; 5,000 Air Force) (2022)
note: in 2017, Hungary announced plans to increase the number of active soldiers to around 37,000, but did not give a timeline

Military equipment inventories and acquisitions: the military's inventory consists largely of Soviet-era weapons, with a smaller mix of more modern European and US equipment; since 2010, Hungary has received limited quantities of equipment from several European countries and the US (2021)

Military service age and obligation: 18-25 years of age for voluntary military service; no conscription (abolished 2005); 6-month service obligation (2022)
note: as of 2019, women comprised approximately 20% of Hungary's full-time military personnel

Military deployments: 160 Bosnia-Herzegovina (EUFOR stabilization force); 150 Iraq (NATO); 470 Kosovo (NATO/KFOR) (2022)

Military - note: Hungary joined NATO in 1999; Czechia, Hungary, and Poland were invited to begin accession talks at NATO's Madrid Summit in 1997 and in March 1999 they became the first former members of the Warsaw Pact to join the Alliance (2022)

TERRORISM

Terrorist group(s): Islamic State of Iraq and ash-Sham (ISIS)

TRANSNATIONAL ISSUES

Disputes - international: bilateral government, legal, technical and economic working group negotiations continue in 2006 with Slovakia over Hungary's failure to complete its portion of the Gabcikovo-Nagymaros hydroelectric dam project along the Danube; as a member state that forms part of the EU's external border, Hungary has implemented the strict Schengen border rules

Refugees and internally displaced persons: *refugees (country of origin):* 32,271 (Ukraine) (as of 22 November 2022)
stateless persons: 130 (mid-year 2021)

Illicit drugs: transshipment point for Southwest Asian heroin and cannabis and for South American cocaine destined for Western Europe; limited producer of precursor chemicals, particularly for amphetamine and methamphetamine; efforts to counter money laundering, related to organized crime and drug trafficking are improving but remain vulnerable; significant consumer of ecstasy

ICELAND

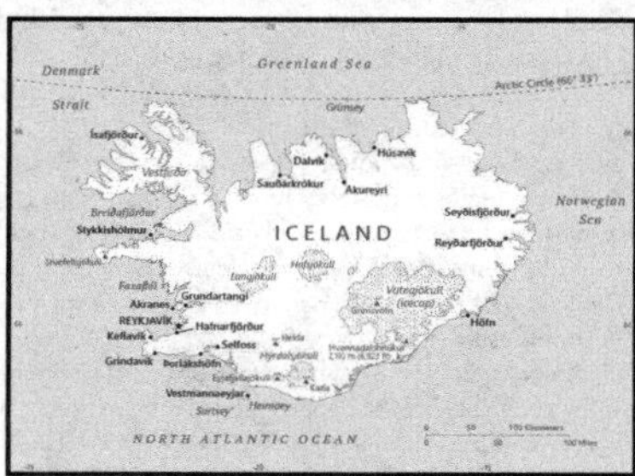

INTRODUCTION

Background: Settled by Norwegian and Celtic (Scottish and Irish) immigrants during the late 9th and 10th centuries A.D., Iceland boasts the world's oldest functioning legislative assembly, the Althingi, established in 930. Independent for over 300 years, Iceland was subsequently ruled by Norway and Denmark. Fallout from the Askja volcano of 1875 devastated the Icelandic economy and caused widespread famine. Over the next quarter century, 20% of the island's population emigrated, mostly to Canada and the US. Denmark granted limited home rule in 1874 and complete independence in 1944. The second half of the 20th century saw substantial economic growth driven primarily by the fishing industry. The economy diversified greatly after the country joined the European Economic Area in 1994, but Iceland was especially hard hit by the global financial crisis in the years following 2008. The economy is now on an upward trajectory, fueled primarily by a tourism and construction boom. Literacy, longevity, and social cohesion are first rate by world standards.

GEOGRAPHY

Location: Northern Europe, island between the Greenland Sea and the North Atlantic Ocean, northwest of the United Kingdom

Geographic coordinates: 65 00 N, 18 00 W

Map references: Arctic Region

Area: *total:* 103,000 sq km
land: 100,250 sq km
water: 2,750 sq km

Area - comparative: slightly smaller than Pennsylvania; about the same size as Kentucky

Land boundaries: *total:* 0 km

Coastline: 4,970 km

Maritime claims: *territorial sea:* 12 nm
exclusive economic zone: 200 nm
continental shelf: 200 nm or to the edge of the continental margin

Climate: temperate; moderated by North Atlantic Current; mild, windy winters; damp, cool summers

Terrain: mostly plateau interspersed with mountain peaks, icefields; coast deeply indented by bays and fiords

Elevation: *highest point:* Hvannadalshnukur (at Vatnajokull Glacier) 2,110 m
lowest point: Atlantic Ocean 0 m
mean elevation: 557 m

Natural resources: fish, hydropower, geothermal power, diatomite

Land use: *agricultural land:* 18.7% (2018 est.)
arable land: 1.2% (2018 est.)
permanent crops: 0% (2018 est.)
permanent pasture: 17.5% (2018 est.)
forest: 0.3% (2018 est.)
other: 81% (2018 est.)

Population distribution: Iceland is almost entirely urban with half of the population located in and around the capital of Reykjavik; smaller clusters are primarily found along the coast in the north and west

Natural hazards: earthquakes and volcanic activity
volcanism: Iceland, situated on top of a hotspot, experiences severe volcanic activity; Eyjafjallajokull (1,666 m) erupted in 2010, sending ash high into the atmosphere and seriously disrupting European air traffic; scientists continue to monitor nearby Katla (1,512 m), which has a high probability of eruption in the very near future, potentially disrupting air traffic; Grimsvoetn and Hekla are Iceland's most active volcanoes; other historically active volcanoes include Askja, Bardarbunga, Brennisteinsfjoll, Esjufjoll, Hengill, Krafla, Krisuvik, Kverkfjoll, Oraefajokull, Reykjanes, Torfajokull, and Vestmannaeyjar

Geography - note: strategic location between Greenland and Europe; westernmost European country; Reykjavik is the northernmost national capital in the world; more land covered by glaciers than in all of continental Europe

PEOPLE AND SOCIETY

Population: 357,603 (2022 est.)

Nationality: *noun:* Icelander(s)
adjective: Icelandic

Ethnic groups: Icelandic 81.3%, Polish 5.6%, Danish 1%, other 12.1% (2021 est.)
note: data represent population by country of birth

Languages: Icelandic, English, Nordic languages, German

Religions: Evangelical Lutheran Church of Iceland (official) 62.3%, Roman Catholic 4%, Independent Congregation of Reykjavik 2.7%, Independent Congregation of Hafnarfjordur 2%, pagan worship 1.4%, Icelandic Ethical Humanist Association 1.1%, other (includes Zuist and Pentecostal) or unspecified 19%, none 7.6% (2021 est.)

Age structure: *0-14 years:* 20.31% (male 36,394/female 34,837)
15-24 years: 12.85% (male 22,748/female 22,317)
25-54 years: 39.44% (male 70,227/female 68,095)
55-64 years: 11.94% (male 20,762/female 21,111)
65 years and over: 15.47% (male 25,546/female 28,697) (2020 est.)

Dependency ratios: *total dependency ratio:* 54
youth dependency ratio: 29.9
elderly dependency ratio: 24.1
potential support ratio: 4.2 (2020 est.)

Median age: *total:* 37.1 years
male: 36.6 years
female: 37.7 years (2020 est.)

Population growth rate: 0.93% (2022 est.)

Birth rate: 12.96 births/1,000 population (2022 est.)

Death rate: 6.56 deaths/1,000 population (2022 est.)

Net migration rate: 2.89 migrant(s)/1,000 population (2022 est.)

Population distribution: Iceland is almost entirely urban with half of the population located in and around the capital of Reykjavik; smaller clusters are primarily found along the coast in the north and west

Urbanization: *urban population:* 94% of total population (2022)
rate of urbanization: 0.74% annual rate of change (2020-25 est.)

Major urban areas - population: 216,000 REYKJAVIK (capital) (2018)

Sex ratio: *at birth:* 1.05 male(s)/female
0-14 years: 1.04 male(s)/female
15-24 years: 1.02 male(s)/female
25-54 years: 1.03 male(s)/female
55-64 years: 0.98 male(s)/female
65 years and over: 0.76 male(s)/female
total population: 1 male(s)/female (2022 est.)

Mother's mean age at first birth: 28.7 years (2020 est.)

Maternal mortality ratio: 4 deaths/100,000 live births (2017 est.)

Infant mortality rate: *total:* 1.65 deaths/1,000 live births
male: 1.83 deaths/1,000 live births
female: 1.46 deaths/1,000 live births (2022 est.)

Life expectancy at birth: *total population:* 83.64 years
male: 81.41 years
female: 85.97 years (2022 est.)

Total fertility rate: 1.95 children born/woman (2022 est.)

Drinking water source: *improved: urban:* 100% of population
rural: 100% of population
total: 100% of population

Current health expenditure: 8.6% of GDP (2019)

Physicians density: 4.14 physicians/1,000 population (2019)

Hospital bed density: 2.8 beds/1,000 population (2019)

Sanitation facility access: *improved: urban:* 100% of population
rural: 100% of population
total: 100% of population

HIV/AIDS - adult prevalence rate: 0.1% (2020)

Obesity - adult prevalence rate: 21.9% (2016)

Alcohol consumption per capita: *total:* 7.72 liters of pure alcohol (2019 est.)
beer: 4.39 liters of pure alcohol (2019 est.)
wine: 2.11 liters of pure alcohol (2019 est.)
spirits: 1.22 liters of pure alcohol (2019 est.)
other alcohols: 0 liters of pure alcohol (2019 est.)

Tobacco use: *total:* 12% (2020 est.)
male: 11.9% (2020 est.)
female: 12% (2020 est.)

Education expenditures: 7.6% of GDP (2018 est.)

School life expectancy (primary to tertiary education): *total:* 19 years
male: 18 years
female: 20 years (2019)

Unemployment, youth ages 15-24: *total:* 10%
male: 11.1%
female: 9% (2020 est.)

ENVIRONMENT

Environment - current issues: water pollution from fertilizer runoff

Environment - international agreements: *party to:* Air Pollution, Air Pollution-Persistent Organic Pollutants, Antarctic Treaty, Biodiversity, Climate Change, Climate Change-Kyoto Protocol, Climate Change-Paris Agreement, Comprehensive Nuclear Test Ban, Desertification, Endangered Species, Hazardous Wastes, Law of the Sea, Marine Dumping-London Convention, Marine Dumping-London Protocol, Nuclear Test Ban, Ozone Layer Protection, Ship Pollution, Wetlands, Whaling
signed, but not ratified: Air Pollution-Heavy Metals, Environmental Modification, Marine Life Conservation

Air pollutants: *particulate matter emissions:* 5.94 micrograms per cubic meter (2016 est.)
carbon dioxide emissions: 2.06 megatons (2016 est.)
methane emissions: 0.59 megatons (2020 est.)

Climate: temperate; moderated by North Atlantic Current; mild, windy winters; damp, cool summers

Land use: *agricultural land:* 18.7% (2018 est.)
arable land: 1.2% (2018 est.)
permanent crops: 0% (2018 est.)
permanent pasture: 17.5% (2018 est.)
forest: 0.3% (2018 est.)
other: 81% (2018 est.)

Urbanization: *urban population:* 94% of total population (2022)
rate of urbanization: 0.74% annual rate of change (2020-25 est.)

Revenue from forest resources: *forest revenues:* 0% of GDP (2018 est.)

Revenue from coal: *coal revenues:* 0% of GDP (2018 est.)

Waste and recycling: *municipal solid waste generated annually:* 525,000 tons (2015 est.)
municipal solid waste recycled annually: 293,003 tons (2013 est.)
percent of municipal solid waste recycled: 55.8% (2013 est.)

Total water withdrawal: *municipal:* 80 million cubic meters (2017 est.)
industrial: 198 million cubic meters (2017 est.)
agricultural: 300,000 cubic meters (2017 est.)

Total renewable water resources: 170 billion cubic meters (2017 est.)

GOVERNMENT

Country name: *conventional long form:* Republic of Iceland
conventional short form: Iceland
local long form: Lydveldid Island
local short form: Island
etymology: Floki VILGERDARSON, an early Norse explorer of the island (9th century), applied the name "Land of Ice" after spotting a fjord full of drift ice to the north and spending a bitter winter on the island; he eventually settled on the island, however, after he saw how it greened up in the summer and that it was, in fact, habitable

Government type: unitary parliamentary republic

Capital: *name:* Reykjavik
geographic coordinates: 64 09 N, 21 57 W
time difference: UTC 0 (5 hours ahead of Washington, DC, during Standard Time)
etymology: the name means "smoky bay" in Icelandic and refers to the steamy, smoke-like vapors discharged by hot springs in the area

Administrative divisions: 64 municipalities (sveitarfelog, singular - sveitarfelagidh); Akranes, Akureyri, Arneshreppur, Asahreppur, Blaskogabyggdh, Bolungarvik, Borgarbyggdh, Dalabyggdh, Dalvikurbyggdh, Eyjafjardharsveit, Eyja-og Miklaholtshreppur, Fjallabyggdh, Fjardhabyggdh, Fljotsdalshreppur, Floahreppur, Gardhabaer, Grimsnes-og Grafningshreppur, Grindavikurbaer, Grundarfjardharbaer, Grytubakkahreppur, Hafnarfjordhur, Horgarsveit, Hrunamannahreppur, Hunathing Vestra, Hunabyggdh, Hvalfjardharsveit, Hveragerdhi, Isafjardharbaer, Kaldrananeshreppur, Kjosarhreppur, Kopavogur, Langanesbyggdh, Mosfellsbaer, Mulathing, Myrdalshreppur, Nordhurthing, Rangarthing Eystra, Rangarthing Ytra, Reykholahreppur, Reykjanesbaer, Reykjavik, Seltjarnarnes, Skaftarhreppur, Skagabyggdh, Skagafjordhur, Skeidha-og Gnupverjahreppur, Skorradalshreppur, Snaefellsbaer, Strandabyggdh, Stykkisholmur, Sudhavikurhreppur, Sudhurnesjabaer, Svalbardhsstrandarhreppur, Sveitarfelagidh Arborg, Sveitarfelagidh Hornafjordhur, Sveitarfelagidh Olfus, Sveitarfelagidh Skagastrond, Sveitarfelagidh Vogar, Talknafjardharhreppur, Thingeyjarsveit, Tjorneshreppur, Vestmannaeyjar, Vesturbyggdh, Vopnafjardharhreppur

Independence: 1 December 1918 (became a sovereign state under the Danish Crown); 17 June 1944 (from Denmark; birthday of Jon SIGURDSSON, leader of Iceland's 19th Century independence movement)

National holiday: Independence Day, 17 June (1944)

Constitution: *history:* several previous; latest ratified 16 June 1944, effective 17 June 1944 (at independence)
amendments: proposed by the Althingi; passage requires approval by the Althingi and by the next elected Althingi, and confirmation by the president of the republic; proposed amendments to Article 62 of the constitution – that the Evangelical Lutheran Church shall be the state church of Iceland – also require passage by referendum; amended many times, last in 2013

Legal system: civil law system influenced by the Danish model

International law organization participation: has not submitted an ICJ jurisdiction declaration; accepts ICCt jurisdiction

Citizenship: *citizenship by birth:* no
citizenship by descent only: at least one parent must be a citizen of Iceland
dual citizenship recognized: yes
residency requirement for naturalization: 3 to 7 years

Suffrage: 18 years of age; universal

Executive branch: *chief of state:* President Gudni Thorlacius JOHANNESSON (since 1 August 2016)
head of government: Prime Minister Katrin JAKOBSDOTTIR (since 30 November 2017)
cabinet: Cabinet appointed by the president upon the recommendation of the prime minister
elections/appointments: president directly elected by simple majority popular vote for a 4-year term (no term limits); election last held on 27 June 2020 (next to be held in 2024); following legislative elections, the leader of the majority party or majority coalition becomes prime minister
election results: *2020:* Gudni Thorlacius JOHANNESSON reelected president; percent of vote - Gudni Thorlacius JOHANNESSON (independent) 92.2%, Gudmundur Franklin JONSSON (independent) 7.8%
2016: Gudni Thorlacius JOHANNESSON elected president; Gudni Thorlacius JOHANNESSON (independent) 39.1%, Halla TOMASDOTTIR (independent) 27.9%, Andri Snær MAGNASON (Democracy Movement) 14.3%, Davíd ODDSSON (independent) 13.7%, other 5%

Legislative branch: *description:* unicameral Althingi or Parliament (63 seats; members directly elected in multi-seat constituencies by closed-list proportional representation vote using the D'Hondt method; members serve 4-year terms)
elections: last held on 25 September 2021 (next to be held in 2025)
election results: percent of vote by party - IP 25.4%, PP 20.6%, LGM 12.7%, SDA 9.5%, People's Party 9.5%, Pirate Party 9.5%, Reform Party 7.9%. CP 4.8%; seats by party - IP 16, PP 13, LGM 8, SDA 6, People's Party 6, Pirate Party 6, Reform Party 5, CP 3; composition - men 33, women 30; percent of women 47.6%

Judicial branch: *highest court(s):* Supreme Court or Haestirettur (consists of 9 judges)
judge selection and term of office: judges proposed by Ministry of Interior selection committee and appointed by the president; judges appointed for an indefinite period
subordinate courts: Appellate Court or Landsrettur; 8 district courts; Labor Court

Political parties and leaders: Centrist Party (Midflokkurinn) or CP [Sigmundur David GUNNLAUGSSON]
Independence Party (Sjalfstaedisflokkurinn) or IP [Bjarni BENEDIKTSSON]
Left-Green Movement (Vinstrihreyfingin-graent frambod) or LGM [Katrin JAKOBSDOTTIR]
People's Party (Flokkur Folksins) [Inga SAELAND]
Pirate Party (Piratar) [Halldora MOGENSEN]
Progressive Party (Framsoknarflokkurinn) or PP [Sigurdur Ingi JOHANNSSON]
Reform Party (Vidreisn) [Thorgerdur Katrin GUNNARSDOTTIR]
Social Democratic Alliance (Samfylkingin) or SDA [Logi Mar EINARSSON]

International organization participation: Arctic Council, Australia Group, BIS, CBSS, CD, CE, EAPC, EBRD, EFTA, FAO, FATF, IAEA, IBRD, ICAO, ICC (national committees), ICCt, ICRM, IDA, IFAD, IFC, IFRCS, IHO, ILO, IMF, IMO, IMSO, Interpol, IOC, IOM, IPU, ISO, ITSO, ITU, ITUC (NGOs), MIGA, NATO, NC, NEA, NIB, NSG, OAS (observer), OECD, OPCW, OSCE, PCA,

Schengen Convention, UN, UNCTAD, UNESCO, UPU, WCO, WHO, WIPO, WMO, WTO

Diplomatic representation in the US: *chief of mission:* Ambassador Bergdis ELLERTSDOTTIR (since 16 September 2019)
chancery: House of Sweden, 2900 K Street NW, #509, Washington, DC 20007
telephone: [1] (202) 265-6653
FAX: [1] (202) 265-6656
email address and website:
washington@mfa.is
https://www.government.is/diplomatic-missions/embassy-of-iceland-in-washington-d.c/
consulate(s) general: New York

Diplomatic representation from the US: *chief of mission:* Ambassador Carrin F. PATMAN (since 6 October 2022)
embassy: Engjateigur 7, 105 Reykjavik
mailing address: 5640 Reykjavik Place, Washington, D.C. 20521-5640
telephone: [354] 595-2200
FAX: [354] 562-9118
email address and website:
ReykjavikConsular@state.gov
https://is.usembassy.gov/

Flag description: blue with a red cross outlined in white extending to the edges of the flag; the vertical part of the cross is shifted to the hoist side in the style of the Dannebrog (Danish flag); the colors represent three of the elements that make up the island: red is for the island's volcanic fires, white recalls the snow and ice fields of the island, and blue is for the surrounding ocean

National symbol(s): gyrfalcon; national colors: blue, white, red

National anthem: *name:* "Lofsongur" (Song of Praise)
lyrics/music: Matthias JOCHUMSSON/Sveinbjorn SVEINBJORNSSON
note: adopted 1944; also known as "O, Gud vors lands" (O, God of Our Land), the anthem was originally written and performed in 1874

National heritage: *total World Heritage Sites:* 3 (1 cultural, 2 natural)
selected World Heritage Site locales: Thingvellir National Park (c); Surtsey (n); Vatnajökull National Park - Dynamic Nature of Fire and Ice (n)

ECONOMY

Economic overview: Iceland's economy combines a capitalist structure and free-market principles with an extensive welfare system. Except for a brief period during the 2008 crisis, Iceland has in recent years achieved high growth, low unemployment, and a remarkably even distribution of income. Iceland's economy has been diversifying into manufacturing and service industries in the last decade, particularly within the fields of tourism, software production, and biotechnology. Abundant geothermal and hydropower sources have attracted substantial foreign investment in the aluminum sector, boosted economic growth, and sparked some interest from high-tech firms looking to establish data centers using cheap green energy.

Tourism, aluminum smelting, and fishing are the pillars of the economy. For decades the Icelandic economy depended heavily on fisheries, but tourism has now surpassed fishing and aluminum as Iceland's main export industry. Tourism accounted for 8.6% of Iceland's GDP in 2016, and 39% of total exports of merchandise and services. From 2010 to 2017, the number of tourists visiting Iceland increased by nearly 400%. Since 2010, tourism has become a main driver of Icelandic economic growth, with the number of tourists reaching 4.5 times the Icelandic population in 2016. Iceland remains sensitive to fluctuations in world prices for its main exports, and to fluctuations in the exchange rate of the Icelandic Krona.

Following the privatization of the banking sector in the early 2000s, domestic banks expanded aggressively in foreign markets, and consumers and businesses borrowed heavily in foreign currencies. Worsening global financial conditions throughout 2008 resulted in a sharp depreciation of the krona vis-a-vis other major currencies. The foreign exposure of Icelandic banks, whose loans and other assets totaled nearly nine times the country's GDP, became unsustainable. Iceland's three largest banks collapsed in late 2008. GDP fell 6.8% in 2009, and unemployment peaked at 9.4% in February 2009. Three new banks were established to take over the domestic assets of the collapsed banks. Two of them have majority ownership by the state, which intends to re-privatize them.

Since the collapse of Iceland's financial sector, government economic priorities have included stabilizing the krona, implementing capital controls, reducing Iceland's high budget deficit, containing inflation, addressing high household debt, restructuring the financial sector, and diversifying the economy. Capital controls were lifted in March 2017, but some financial protections, such as reserve requirements for specified investments connected to new inflows of foreign currency, remain in place.

Real GDP (purchasing power parity): $19.16 billion (2020 est.)
$20.52 billion (2019 est.)
$20.01 billion (2018 est.)
note: data are in 2017 dollars

Real GDP growth rate: 1.94% (2019 est.)
3.88% (2018 est.)
4.57% (2017 est.)

Real GDP per capita: $52,300 (2020 est.)
$56,900 (2019 est.)
$56,700 (2018 est.)
note: data are in 2017 dollars

GDP (official exchange rate): $24.614 billion (2019 est.)

Inflation rate (consumer prices): 3% (2019 est.)
2.6% (2018 est.)
1.7% (2017 est.)

Credit ratings:

Fitch rating: A (2017)

Moody's rating: A2 (2019)

Standard & Poors rating: A (2017)
note: The year refers to the year in which the current credit rating was first obtained.

GDP - composition, by sector of origin: *agriculture:* 5.8% (2017 est.)
industry: 19.7% (2017 est.)
services: 74.6% (2017 est.)

GDP - composition, by end use: *household consumption:* 50.4% (2017 est.)
government consumption: 23.3% (2017 est.)
investment in fixed capital: 22.1% (2017 est.)
investment in inventories: 0% (2017 est.)
exports of goods and services: 47% (2017 est.)
imports of goods and services: -42.8% (2017 est.)

Agricultural products: milk, mutton, poultry, potatoes, barley, pork, eggs, beef, other meat, sheep skins

Industries: tourism, fish processing; aluminum smelting; geothermal power, hydropower; medical/pharmaceutical products

Industrial production growth rate: 2.4% (2017 est.)

Labor force: 200,000 (2020 est.)

Labor force - by occupation: *agriculture:* 4.8%
industry: 22.2%
services: 73% (2008)

Unemployment rate: 3.62% (2019 est.)
2.73% (2018 est.)

Unemployment, youth ages 15-24: *total:* 10%
male: 11.1%
female: 9% (2020 est.)

Population below poverty line: 8.8% (2017 est.)

Gini Index coefficient - distribution of family income: 26.8 (2015 est.)
25 (2005)

Budget: *revenues:* 10.39 billion (2017 est.)
expenditures: 10.02 billion (2017 est.)

Budget surplus (+) or deficit (-): 1.5% (of GDP) (2017 est.)

Public debt: 40% of GDP (2017 est.)
51.7% of GDP (2016 est.)

Taxes and other revenues: 42.4% (of GDP) (2017 est.)

Fiscal year: calendar year

Current account balance: $1.496 billion (2019 est.)
$814 million (2018 est.)

Exports: $7.43 billion (2020 est.) note: data are in current year dollars
$11.01 billion (2019 est.) note: data are in current year dollars
$12.26 billion (2018 est.) note: data are in current year dollars

Exports - partners: Netherlands 23%, United Kingdom 9%, Germany 9%, Spain 8%, United States 7%, France 7%, Canada 5% (2019)

Exports - commodities: aluminum and aluminum products, fish products, aircraft, iron alloys, animal meal (2019)

Imports: $7.55 billion (2020 est.) note: data are in current year dollars
$9.76 billion (2019 est.) note: data are in current year dollars
$11.34 billion (2018 est.) note: data are in current year dollars

Imports - partners: Norway 11%, Netherlands 10%, Germany 8%, Denmark 8%, United States 7%, United Kingdom 6%, China 6%, Sweden 5% (2019)

Imports - commodities: refined petroleum, aluminum oxide, carbon/graphite electronics, cars, packaged medicines (2019)

Reserves of foreign exchange and gold: $6.567 billion (31 December 2017 est.)
$7.226 billion (31 December 2016 est.)

Debt - external: $19.422 billion (2019 est.)
$22.055 billion (2018 est.)

Exchange rates: Icelandic kronur (ISK) per US dollar -
127.05 (2020 est.)

121.68 (2019 est.)
121.86 (2018 est.)
131.92 (2014 est.)
116.77 (2013 est.)

ENERGY

Electricity access: *electrification - total population:* 100% (2020)

Electricity: *installed generating capacity:* 2.967 million kW (2020 est.)
consumption: 17,912,066,000 kWh (2020 est.)
exports: 0 kWh (2020 est.)
imports: 0 kWh (2020 est.)
transmission/distribution losses: 519 million kWh (2020 est.)

Electricity generation sources: *hydroelectricity:* 67.6% of total installed capacity (2020 est.)
geothermal: 32.3% of total installed capacity (2020 est.)

Coal: *production:* 0 metric tons (2020 est.)
consumption: 142,000 metric tons (2020 est.)
exports: 0 metric tons (2020 est.)
imports: 136,000 metric tons (2020 est.)
proven reserves: 0 metric tons (2019 est.)

Petroleum: *total petroleum production:* 0 bbl/day (2021 est.)
refined petroleum consumption: 19,700 bbl/day (2019 est.)

Refined petroleum products - exports: 2,530 bbl/day (2017 est.)

Refined petroleum products - imports: 20,220 bbl/day (2017 est.)

Carbon dioxide emissions: 3.337 million metric tonnes of CO2 (2019 est.)
from coal and metallurgical coke: 459,000 metric tonnes of CO2 (2019 est.)
from petroleum and other liquids: 2.879 million metric tonnes of CO2 (2019 est.)

COMMUNICATIONS

Telephones - fixed lines: *total subscriptions:* 107,032 (2020 est.)
subscriptions per 100 inhabitants: 31 (2020 est.)

Telephones - mobile cellular: *total subscriptions:* 421,384 (2020 est.)
subscriptions per 100 inhabitants: 123 (2020 est.)

Telecommunication systems: *general assessment:* Iceland has one of the smallest yet most progressive telecom markets in Europe; the country in 2020 became the top in Europe for fiber penetration; it aims to provide a fixed broadband service of at least 100Mb/s to 99.9% of the population by the end of 2021, an ambitious target by international standards and one which it is likely to achieve given the progress which operators have made in extending the reach of fiber networks; there is effective competition in the mobile and broadband markets, with a number of players having emerged to challenge the dominance of the two leading operators which have interests across the telecom sectors; the telecom market has shown some resilience in recent years following the significant economic downturn a decade ago, supported by continuing investment in mobile and fixed-line broadband infrastructure by operators and well as by the government's Telecommunications Fund which is supporting Next Generation Access networks, particularly in rural areas (2022)
domestic: 31 per 100 for fixed line and nearing 123 per 100 for mobile-cellular subscriptions (2020)
international: country code - 354; landing points for the CANTAT-3, FARICE-1, Greenland Connect and DANICE submarine cable system that provides connectivity to Canada, the Faroe Islands, Greenland, UK, Denmark, and Germany; satellite earth stations - 2 Intelsat (Atlantic Ocean), 1 Inmarsat (Atlantic and Indian Ocean regions); note - Iceland shares the Inmarsat earth station with the other Nordic countries (Denmark, Finland, Norway, and Sweden) (2019)

Broadcast media: state-owned public TV broadcaster (RUV) operates 21 TV channels nationally (RUV and RUV 2, though RUV 2 is used less frequently); RUV broadcasts nationally, every household in Iceland is required to have RUV as it doubles as the emergency broadcast network; RUV also operates stringer offices in the north (Akureyri) and the east (Egilsstadir) but operations are all run out of RUV headquarters in Reykjavik; there are 3 privately owned TV stations; Stod 2 (Channel 2) is owned by Syn, following 365 Media and Vodafone merger, and is headquartered in Reykjavik; Syn also operates 4 sports channels under Stod 2; N4 is the only television station headquartered outside of Reykjavik, in Akureyri, with local programming for the north, south, and east of Iceland; Hringbraut is the newest station and is headquartered in Reykjavik; all of these television stations have nationwide penetration as 100% of households have multi-channel services though digital and/or fiber-optic connections

RUV operates 3 radio stations (RAS 1, RAS2, and Rondo) as well as 4 regional stations (but they mostly act as range extenders for RUV radio broadcasts nationwide); there is 1 privately owned radio conglomerate, Syn (4 stations), that broadcasts nationwide, and 3 other radio stations that broadcast to the most densely populated regions of the country. In addition there are upwards of 20 radio stations that operate regionally
(2019)

Internet country code: .is

Internet users: *total:* 362,798 (2020 est.)
percent of population: 99% (2020 est.)

Broadband - fixed subscriptions: *total:* 141,816 (2020 est.)
subscriptions per 100 inhabitants: 42 (2020 est.)

TRANSPORTATION

National air transport system: *number of registered air carriers:* 6 (2020)
inventory of registered aircraft operated by air carriers: 63
annual passenger traffic on registered air carriers: 7,819,740 (2018)
annual freight traffic on registered air carriers: 163.65 million (2018) mt-km

Civil aircraft registration country code prefix: TF

Airports: *total:* 96 (2021)

Airports - with paved runways: *total:* 7
over 3,047 m: 1
1,524 to 2,437 m: 3
914 to 1,523 m: 3 (2021)

Airports - with unpaved runways: *total:* 89
1,524 to 2,437 m: 3
914 to 1,523 m: 26
under 914 m: 60 (2021)

Roadways: *total:* 12,898 km (2012)
paved/oiled gravel: 5,647 km (2012) (excludes urban roads)
unpaved: 7,251 km (2012)

Merchant marine: *total:* 41
by type: general cargo 5, oil tanker 2, other 34 (2021)

Ports and terminals: *major seaport(s):* Grundartangi, Hafnarfjordur, Reykjavik

MILITARY AND SECURITY

Military and security forces: no regular military forces; Ministry of Interior: Icelandic Coast Guard (includes both air and maritime elements); Icelandic National Police (2022)

Military and security service personnel strengths: the Icelandic Coast Guard has approximately 250 personnel (2022)

Military equipment inventories and acquisitions: the Icelandic Coast Guard's inventory consists of equipment from mostly European suppliers (2022)

Military - note: Iceland was one of the original 12 countries to sign the North Atlantic Treaty (also known as the Washington Treaty) in 1949; Iceland is the only NATO member that has no standing military force; defense of Iceland remains a NATO commitment and NATO maintains an air policing presence in Icelandic airspace; Iceland participates in international peacekeeping missions with the civilian-manned Icelandic Crisis Response Unit (ICRU)

Iceland cooperates with the militaries of other Nordic countries through the Nordic Defense Cooperation (NORDEFCO), which consists of Denmark, Finland, Iceland, Norway, and Sweden; areas of cooperation include armaments, education, human resources, training and exercises, and operations; NORDEFCO was established in 2009

in 1951, Iceland and the US concluded an agreement to make arrangements regarding the defense of Iceland and for the use of facilities in Iceland to that end; the agreement, along with NATO membership, is one of the two pillars of Iceland's security policy; since 2007 Iceland has concluded cooperation agreements with Canada, Denmark, Norway, and the UK; it also has regular consultations with Germany and France on security and defense (2022)

TRANSNATIONAL ISSUES

Disputes - international: Iceland, the UK, and Ireland dispute Denmark's claim that the Faroe Islands' continental shelf extends beyond 200 nm; the European Free Trade Association Surveillance Authority filed a suit against Iceland, claiming the country violated the Agreement on the European Economic Area in failing to pay minimum compensation to Icesave depositors

Refugees and internally displaced persons: *stateless persons:* 73 (mid-year 2021)

INDIA

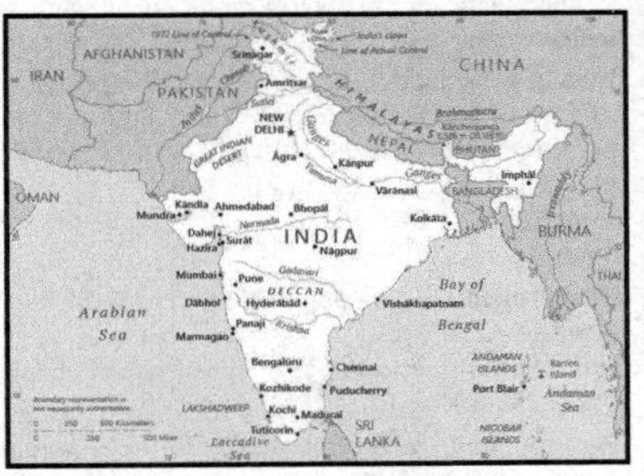

INTRODUCTION

Background: The Indus Valley civilization, one of the world's oldest, flourished during the 3rd and 2nd millennia B.C. and extended into northwestern India. Aryan tribes from the northwest infiltrated the Indian subcontinent about 1500 B.C.; their merger with the earlier Dravidian inhabitants created the classical Indian culture. The Maurya Empire of the 4th and 3rd centuries B.C. - which reached its zenith under ASHOKA - united much of South Asia. The Golden Age ushered in by the Gupta dynasty (4th to 6th centuries A.D.) saw a flowering of Indian science, art, and culture. Islam spread across the subcontinent over a period of 700 years. In the 10th and 11th centuries, Turks and Afghans invaded India and established the Delhi Sultanate. In the early 16th century, the Emperor BABUR established the Mughal Dynasty, which ruled India for more than three centuries. European explorers began establishing footholds in India during the 16th century.

By the 19th century, Great Britain had become the dominant political power on the subcontinent and India was seen as the "Jewel in the Crown" of the British Empire. The British Indian Army played a vital role in both World Wars. Years of nonviolent resistance to British rule, led by Mohandas GANDHI and Jawaharlal NEHRU, eventually resulted in Indian independence in 1947. Large-scale communal violence took place before and after the subcontinent partition into two separate states - India and Pakistan. The neighboring countries have fought three wars since independence, the last of which was in 1971 and resulted in East Pakistan becoming the separate nation of Bangladesh. India's nuclear weapons tests in 1998 emboldened Pakistan to conduct its own tests that same year. In November 2008, terrorists originating from Pakistan conducted a series of coordinated attacks in Mumbai, India's financial capital. India's economic growth following the launch of economic reforms in 1991, a massive youthful population, and a strategic geographic location have contributed to India's emergence as a regional and global power. However, India still faces pressing problems such as environmental degradation, extensive poverty, and widespread corruption, and its restrictive business climate challenges economic growth expectations.

GEOGRAPHY

Location: Southern Asia, bordering the Arabian Sea and the Bay of Bengal, between Burma and Pakistan

Geographic coordinates: 20 00 N, 77 00 E

Map references: Asia

Area: *total:* 3,287,263 sq km
land: 2,973,193 sq km
water: 314,070 sq km

Area - comparative: slightly more than one-third the size of the US

Land boundaries: *total:* 13,888 km
border countries (6): Bangladesh 4,142 km; Bhutan 659 km; Burma 1,468 km; China 2,659 km; Nepal 1,770 km; Pakistan 3,190 km

Coastline: 7,000 km

Maritime claims: *territorial sea:* 12 nm
contiguous zone: 24 nm
exclusive economic zone: 200 nm
continental shelf: 200 nm or to the edge of the continental margin

Climate: varies from tropical monsoon in south to temperate in north

Terrain: upland plain (Deccan Plateau) in south, flat to rolling plain along the Ganges, deserts in west, Himalayas in north

Elevation: *highest point:* Kanchenjunga 8,586 m
lowest point: Indian Ocean 0 m
mean elevation: 160 m

Natural resources: coal (fourth-largest reserves in the world), antimony, iron ore, lead, manganese, mica, bauxite, rare earth elements, titanium ore, chromite, natural gas, diamonds, petroleum, limestone, arable land

Land use: *agricultural land:* 60.5% (2018 est.)
arable land: 52.8% (2018 est.)
permanent crops: 4.2% (2018 est.)
permanent pasture: 3.5% (2018 est.)
forest: 23.1% (2018 est.)
other: 16.4% (2018 est.)

Irrigated land: 667,000 sq km (2012)

Major lakes (area sq km): *salt water lake(s):* Chilika Lake - 1,170 sq km

Major rivers (by length in km): Brahmaputra (shared with China [s] and Bangladesh [m]) - 3,969 km; Indus (shared with China [s] and Pakistan [m]) - 3,610 km; Ganges river source (shared with Bangladesh [m]) - 2,704 km; Godavari - 1,465 km; Sutlej (shared with China [s] and Pakistan [m]) - 1,372 km; Yamuna - 1,370 km; Narmada - 1,289 km; Chenab river source (shared with Pakistan [m]) - 1,086 km; Ghaghara river mouth (shared with China [s] and Nepal) - 1,080 km

note – [s] after country name indicates river source; [m] after country name indicates river mouth

Major watersheds (area sq km): Indian Ocean drainage: Brahmaputra (651,335 sq km), Ganges (1,016,124 sq km), Indus (1,081,718 sq km), Irrawaddy (413,710 sq km)

Major aquifers: Indus-Ganges-Brahmaputra Basin

Population distribution: with the notable exception of the deserts in the northwest, including the Thar Desert, and the mountain fringe in the north, a very high population density exists throughout most of the country; the core of the population is in the north along the banks of the Ganges, with other river valleys and southern coastal areas also having large population concentrations

Natural hazards: droughts; flash floods, as well as widespread and destructive flooding from monsoonal rains; severe thunderstorms; earthquakes
volcanism: Barren Island (354 m) in the Andaman Sea has been active in recent years

Geography - note: dominates South Asian subcontinent; near important Indian Ocean trade routes; Kanchenjunga, third tallest mountain in the world, lies on the border with Nepal

PEOPLE AND SOCIETY

Population: 1,389,637,446 (2022 est.)

Nationality: *noun:* Indian(s)
adjective: Indian

Ethnic groups: Indo-Aryan 72%, Dravidian 25%, and other 3% (2000)

Languages: Hindi 43.6%, Bengali 8%, Marathi 6.9%, Telugu 6.7%, Tamil 5.7%, Gujarati 4.6%, Urdu 4.2%, Kannada 3.6%, Odia 3.1%, Malayalam 2.9%, Punjabi 2.7%, Assamese 1.3%, Maithili 1.1%, other 5.6%; note - English enjoys the status of subsidiary official language but is the most important language for national, political, and commercial communication; there are 22 other officially recognized languages: Assamese, Bengali, Bodo, Dogri, Gujarati, Hindi, Kannada, Kashmiri, Konkani, Maithili, Malayalam, Manipuri, Marathi, Nepali, Odia, Punjabi, Sanskrit, Santali, Sindhi, Tamil, Telugu, Urdu; Hindustani is a popular variant of Hindi/Urdu spoken widely throughout northern India but is not an official language (2011 est.)
major-language sample(s):
विश्व फेसबुक, आधारभूत जानकारी का एक अपरिहार्य स्रोत
(Hindi)

Religions: Hindu 79.8%, Muslim 14.2%, Christian 2.3%, Sikh 1.7%, other and unspecified 2% (2011 est.)

Age structure: *0-14 years:* 26.31% (male 185,017,089/female 163,844,572)
15-24 years: 17.51% (male 123,423,531/female 108,739,780)
25-54 years: 41.56% (male 285,275,667/female 265,842,319)
55-64 years: 7.91% (male 52,444,817/female 52,447,038)
65 years and over: 6.72% (male 42,054,459/female 47,003,975) (2020 est.)

Dependency ratios: *total dependency ratio:* 48.7
youth dependency ratio: 38.9
elderly dependency ratio: 9.8
potential support ratio: 10.2 (2020 est.)

Median age: *total:* 28.7 years
male: 28 years
female: 29.5 years (2020 est.)

Population growth rate: 0.67% (2022 est.)

Birth rate: 16.82 births/1,000 population (2022 est.)

Death rate: 10.3 deaths/1,000 population (2022 est.)

Net migration rate: 0.16 migrant(s)/1,000 population (2022 est.)

Population distribution: with the notable exception of the deserts in the northwest, including the Thar Desert, and the mountain fringe in the north, a very high population density exists throughout most of the country; the core of the population is in the north along the banks of the Ganges, with other river valleys and southern coastal areas also having large population concentrations

Urbanization: *urban population:* 35.9% of total population (2022)
rate of urbanization: 2.33% annual rate of change (2020-25 est.)

Major urban areas - population: 32.066 million NEW DELHI (capital), 20.961 million Mumbai, 15.134 million Kolkata, 13.193 million Bangalore, 11.503 million Chennai, 10.534 million Hyderabad (2022)

Sex ratio: *at birth:* 1.1 male(s)/female
0-14 years: 1.11 male(s)/female
15-24 years: 1.12 male(s)/female
25-54 years: 1.07 male(s)/female
55-64 years: 0.95 male(s)/female
65 years and over: 0.71 male(s)/female
total population: 1.06 male(s)/female (2022 est.)

Mother's mean age at first birth: 21.2 years (2019/21)
note: data represents median age at first birth among women 25-49

Maternal mortality ratio: 145 deaths/100,000 live births (2017 est.)

Infant mortality rate: *total:* 30.31 deaths/1,000 live births
male: 29.95 deaths/1,000 live births
female: 30.7 deaths/1,000 live births (2022 est.)

Life expectancy at birth: *total population:* 67.22 years
male: 65.46 years
female: 69.16 years (2022 est.)

Total fertility rate: 2.1 children born/woman (2022 est.)

Contraceptive prevalence rate: 66.7% (2019/20)

Drinking water source: *improved: urban:* 96.9% of population
rural: 94.7% of population
total: 95.5% of population
unimproved: urban: 3.1% of population
rural: 5.3% of population
total: 4.5% of population (2020 est.)

Current health expenditure: 3% of GDP (2019)

Physicians density: 0.74 physicians/1,000 population (2020)

Hospital bed density: 0.5 beds/1,000 population (2017)

Sanitation facility access: *improved: urban:* 98.6% of population
rural: 75.2% of population
total: 83.4% of population
unimproved: urban: 1.4% of population
rural: 24.8% of population
total: 16.6% of population (2020 est.)

HIV/AIDS - adult prevalence rate: 0.2% (2017 est.)

Major infectious diseases: *degree of risk:* very high (2020)
food or waterborne diseases: bacterial diarrhea, hepatitis A and E, and typhoid fever
vectorborne diseases: dengue fever, Crimean-Congo hemorrhagic fever, Japanese encephalitis, and malaria
water contact diseases: leptospirosis
animal contact diseases: rabies
note: clusters of cases of a respiratory illness caused by the novel coronavirus (COVID-19) are being reported across 27 States and Union Territories in India; as of 18 August 2022, India has reported a total of 44,298,864 cases of COVID-19 or 3,210.05 cumulative cases of COVID-19 per 100,000 population with a total of 527,206 cumulative deaths or a rate 38.20 cumulative deaths per 100,000 population; as of 17 August 2022, 72.69% of the population has received at least one dose of COVID-19 vaccine

Obesity - adult prevalence rate: 3.9% (2016)

Alcohol consumption per capita: *total:* 3.09 liters of pure alcohol (2019 est.)
beer: 0.23 liters of pure alcohol (2019 est.)
wine: 0 liters of pure alcohol (2019 est.)
spirits: 2.85 liters of pure alcohol (2019 est.)
other alcohols: 0 liters of pure alcohol (2019 est.)

Tobacco use: *total:* 27.2% (2020 est.)
male: 41.3% (2020 est.)
female: 13% (2020 est.)

Children under the age of 5 years underweight: 33.4% (2016/18)

Child marriage: *women married by age 15:* 6.8%
women married by age 18: 27.3%
men married by age 18: 4.2% (2016 est.)

Education expenditures: 3.5% of GDP (2016 est.)

Literacy: *definition:* age 15 and over can read and write
total population: 74.4%
male: 82.4%
female: 65.8% (2018)

School life expectancy (primary to tertiary education): *total:* 12 years
male: 12 years
female: 12 years (2020)

Unemployment, youth ages 15-24: *total:* 19.8%
male: 19.5%
female: 21% (2020 est.)

ENVIRONMENT

Environment - current issues: deforestation; soil erosion; overgrazing; desertification; air pollution from industrial effluents and vehicle emissions; water pollution from raw sewage and runoff of agricultural pesticides; tap water is not potable throughout the country; huge and growing population is overstraining natural resources; preservation and quality of forests; biodiversity loss

Environment - international agreements: *party to:* Antarctic-Environmental Protection, Antarctic-Marine Living Resources, Antarctic Treaty, Biodiversity, Climate Change, Climate Change-Kyoto Protocol, Climate Change-Paris Agreement, Desertification, Endangered Species, Environmental Modification, Hazardous Wastes, Law of the Sea, Nuclear Test Ban, Ozone Layer Protection, Ship Pollution, Tropical Timber 2006, Wetlands, Whaling
signed, but not ratified: none of the selected agreements

Air pollutants: *particulate matter emissions:* 65.2 micrograms per cubic meter (2016 est.)
carbon dioxide emissions: 2,407.67 megatons (2016 est.)
methane emissions: 559.11 megatons (2020 est.)

Climate: varies from tropical monsoon in south to temperate in north

Land use: *agricultural land:* 60.5% (2018 est.)
arable land: 52.8% (2018 est.)
permanent crops: 4.2% (2018 est.)
permanent pasture: 3.5% (2018 est.)
forest: 23.1% (2018 est.)
other: 16.4% (2018 est.)

Urbanization: *urban population:* 35.9% of total population (2022)
rate of urbanization: 2.33% annual rate of change (2020-25 est.)

Revenue from forest resources: *forest revenues:* 0.14% of GDP (2018 est.)

Revenue from coal: *coal revenues:* 1.15% of GDP (2018 est.)

Waste and recycling: *municipal solid waste generated annually:* 168,403,240 tons (2001 est.)
municipal solid waste recycled annually: 8,420,162 tons (2013 est.)
percent of municipal solid waste recycled: 5% (2013 est.)

Major lakes (area sq km): *salt water lake(s):* Chilika Lake - 1,170 sq km

Major rivers (by length in km): Brahmaputra (shared with China [s] and Bangladesh [m]) - 3,969 km; Indus (shared with China [s] and Pakistan [m]) - 3,610 km; Ganges river source (shared with Bangladesh [m]) - 2,704 km; Godavari - 1,465 km; Sutlej (shared with China [s] and Pakistan [m]) - 1,372 km; Yamuna - 1,370 km; Narmada - 1,289 km; Chenab river source (shared with Pakistan [m]) - 1,086 km; Ghaghara river mouth (shared with China [s] and Nepal) - 1,080 km
note – [s] after country name indicates river source; [m] after country name indicates river mouth

Major watersheds (area sq km): Indian Ocean drainage: Brahmaputra (651,335 sq km), Ganges (1,016,124 sq km), Indus (1,081,718 sq km), Irrawaddy (413,710 sq km)

Major aquifers: Indus-Ganges-Brahmaputra Basin

Total water withdrawal: *municipal:* 56 billion cubic meters (2017 est.)
industrial: 17 billion cubic meters (2017 est.)
agricultural: 688 billion cubic meters (2017 est.)

Total renewable water resources: 1.911 trillion cubic meters (2017 est.)

GOVERNMENT

Country name: *conventional long form:* Republic of India
conventional short form: India
local long form: Republic of India (English)/ Bharatiya Ganarajya (Hindi)
local short form: India (English)/ Bharat (Hindi)
etymology: the English name derives from the Indus River; the Indian name "Bharat" may derive from the "Bharatas" tribe mentioned in the Vedas of the second millennium B.C.; the name is also associated with Emperor Bharata, the legendary conqueror of all of India

Government type: federal parliamentary republic

Capital: *name:* New Delhi
geographic coordinates: 28 36 N, 77 12 E

time difference: UTC+5.5 (10.5 hours ahead of Washington, DC, during Standard Time)
etymology: the city's name is associated with various myths and legends; the original name for the city may have been Dhilli or Dhillika; alternatively, the name could be a corruption of the Hindustani words "dehleez" or "dehali" - both terms meaning "threshold" or "gateway" - and indicative of the city as a gateway to the Gangetic Plain; after the British decided to move the capital of their Indian Empire from Calcutta to Delhi in 1911, they created a new governmental district south of the latter designated as New Delhi; the new capital was not formally inaugurated until 1931

Administrative divisions: 28 states and 8 union territories*; Andaman and Nicobar Islands*, Andhra Pradesh, Arunachal Pradesh, Assam, Bihar, Chandigarh*, Chhattisgarh, Dadra and Nagar Haveli and Daman and Diu*, Delhi*, Goa, Gujarat, Haryana, Himachal Pradesh, Jammu and Kashmir*, Jharkhand, Karnataka, Kerala, Ladakh*, Lakshadweep*, Madhya Pradesh, Maharashtra, Manipur, Meghalaya, Mizoram, Nagaland, Odisha, Puducherry*, Punjab, Rajasthan, Sikkim, Tamil Nadu, Telangana, Tripura, Uttar Pradesh, Uttarakhand, West Bengal
note: although its status is that of a union territory, the official name of Delhi is National Capital Territory of Delhi

Independence: 15 August 1947 (from the UK)

National holiday: Republic Day, 26 January (1950)

Constitution: *history:* previous 1935 (preindependence); latest draft completed 4 November 1949, adopted 26 November 1949, effective 26 January 1950
amendments: proposed by either the Council of States or the House of the People; passage requires majority participation of the total membership in each house and at least two-thirds majority of voting members of each house, followed by assent of the president of India; proposed amendments to the constitutional amendment procedures also must be ratified by at least one half of the India state legislatures before presidential assent; amended many times, last in 2020

Legal system: common law system based on the English model; separate personal law codes apply to Muslims, Christians, and Hindus; judicial review of legislative acts

International law organization participation: accepts compulsory ICJ jurisdiction with reservations; non-party state to the ICCt

Citizenship: *citizenship by birth:* no
citizenship by descent only: at least one parent must be a citizen of India
dual citizenship recognized: no
residency requirement for naturalization: 5 years

Suffrage: 18 years of age; universal

Executive branch: *chief of state:* President Ram Nath KOVIND (since 25 July 2017); Vice President M. Venkaiah NAIDU (since 11 August 2017)
head of government: Prime Minister Narendra MODI (since 26 May 2014)
cabinet: Union Council of Ministers recommended by the prime minister, appointed by the president
elections/appointments: president indirectly elected by an electoral college consisting of elected members of both houses of Parliament for a 5-year term (no term limits); election last held on 17 July 2017 (next to be held in July 2022); vice president indirectly elected by an electoral college consisting of elected members of both houses of Parliament for a 5-year term (no term limits); election last held on 5 August 2017 (next to be held in August 2022); following legislative elections, the prime minister is elected by Lok Sabha members of the majority party
election results: Ram Nath KOVIND elected president; percent of electoral college vote - Ram Nath KOVIND (BJP) 65.7% Meira KUMAR (INC) 34.3%; M. Venkaiah NAIDU elected vice president; electoral college vote - M. Venkaiah NAIDU (BJP) 516, Gopalkrishna GANDHI (independent) 244

Legislative branch: *description:* bicameral Parliament or Sansad consists of:
Council of States or Rajya Sabha (245 seats; 233 members indirectly elected by state and territorial assemblies by proportional representation vote and 12 members appointed by the president; members serve 6-year terms with one-third of the membership renewed every 2 years at various dates)
House of the People or Lok Sabha (545 seats; 543 members directly elected in single-seat constituencies by simple majority vote and 2 appointed by the president; members serve 5-year terms)
elections: Council of States - last held by state and territorial assemblies at various dates in 2019 (in progress March through July 2022 to fill 70 expiry seats)
House of the People - last held April-May 2019 in 7 phases (next to be held in 2024)
election results: Council of States - percent of vote by party - NA; seats by party - BJP 97, INC 34, AITC 13, DMK 10, other 2, independent 2; composition - men 209, women 29, percent of women 13.8%
House of the People - percent of vote by party - BJP 55.8%, INC 9.6%, AITC 4.4%, YSRCP 4.4%, DMK 4.2%, SS 3.3%, JDU 2.9%, BJD 2.2%, BSP 1.8%, TRS 1.7%, LJP 1.1%, NCP 0.9%, SP 0.9%, other 6.4%, independent 0.7%; seats by party - BJP 303, INC 52, DMK 24, AITC 22, YSRCP 22, SS 18, JDU 16, BJD 12, BSP 10, TRS 9, LJP 6, NCP 5, SP 5, other 35, independent 4, vacant 2; composition - men 465, women 78, percent of women 14.3%; note - total Parliament percent of women 11.3%

Judicial branch: *highest court(s):* Supreme Court (consists of 28 judges, including the chief justice)
judge selection and term of office: justices appointed by the president to serve until age 65
subordinate courts: High Courts; District Courts; Labour Court
note: in mid-2011, India's Cabinet approved the "National Mission for Justice Delivery and Legal Reform" to eliminate judicial corruption and reduce the backlog of cases

Political parties and leaders: Aam Aadmi Party or AAP [Arvind KEJRIWAL]
All India Trinamool Congress or AITC [Mamata BANERJEE]
Bahujan Samaj Party or BSP [MAYAWATI]
Bharatiya Janata Party or BJP [Jagat Prakash NADDA]
Biju Janata Dal or BJD [Naveen PATNAIK]
Communist Party of India-Marxist or CPI(M) [Sitaram YECHURY]
Dravida Munnetra Khazhagam [Muthuvel Karunanidhi STALIN]
Indian National Congress or INC [Mallikarjun KHARGE]
Nationalist Congress Party or NCP [Sharad PAWAR]
Rashtriya Janata Dal or RJD [Lalu Prasad YADAV]
Samajwadi Party or SP [Akhilesh YADAV]
Shiromani Akali Dal or SAD [Sukhbir Singh BADAL]
Shiv Sena or SS [Uddhav THACKERAY]
Telegana Rashtra Samithi or TRS [K. Chandrashekar RAO]
Telugu Desam Party or TDP [N. Chandrababu NAIDU]
YSR Congress or YSRCP or YCP [Y.S. Jaganmohan REDDY]
note: India has dozens of national and regional political parties

International organization participation: ADB, AfDB (nonregional member), Arctic Council (observer), ARF, ASEAN (dialogue partner), BIMSTEC, BIS, BRICS, C, CD, CERN (observer), CICA, CP, EAS, FAO, FATF, G-15, G-20, G-24, G-5, G-77, IAEA, IBRD, ICAO, ICC (national committees), ICRM, IDA, IFAD, IFC, IFRCS, IHO, ILO, IMF, IMO, IMSO, Interpol, IOC, IOM, IPU, ISO, ITSO, ITU, ITUC (NGOs), LAS (observer), MIGA, MINURSO, MONUSCO, NAM, OAS (observer), OECD, OPCW, Pacific Alliance (observer), PCA, PIF (partner), Quad, SAARC, SACEP, SCO (observer), UN, UNCTAD, UNDOF, UNESCO, UNHCR, UNHRC, UNIDO, UNIFIL, UNISFA, UNITAR, UNMISS, UNOCI, UNSOM, UNWTO, UPU, Wassenaar Arrangement, WCO, WFTU (NGOs), WHO, WIPO, WMO, WTO

Diplomatic representation in the US: *chief of mission:* Ambassador Taranjit Singh SANDHU (since 6 February 2020)
chancery: 2107 Massachusetts Avenue NW, Washington, DC 20008; Consular Wing located at 2536 Massachusetts Avenue NW, Washington, DC 20008
telephone: [1] (202) 939-7000
FAX: [1] (202) 265-4351
email address and website:
minca.washington@mea.gov.in (community affairs)
https://www.indianembassyusa.gov.in/
consulate(s) general: Atlanta, Chicago, Houston, New York, San Francisco

Diplomatic representation from the US: *chief of mission:* Ambassador (vacant); Charge d'Affaires Patricia A. LACINA (since 9 September 2021)
embassy: Shantipath, Chanakyapuri, New Delhi - 110021
mailing address: 9000 New Delhi Place, Washington DC 20521-9000
telephone: [91] (11) 2419-8000
FAX: [91] (11) 2419-0017
email address and website:
acsnd@state.gov
https://in.usembassy.gov/
consulate(s) general: Chennai (Madras), Hyderabad, Kolkata (Calcutta), Mumbai (Bombay)

Flag description: three equal horizontal bands of saffron (subdued orange) (top), white, and green, with a blue chakra (24-spoked wheel) centered in the white band; saffron represents courage, sacrifice, and the spirit of renunciation; white signifies purity and truth; green stands for faith and fertility; the blue chakra symbolizes the wheel of life in movement and death in stagnation
note: similar to the flag of Niger, which has a small orange disk centered in the white band

National symbol(s): the Lion Capital of Ashoka, which depicts four Asiatic lions standing back to back mounted on a circular abacus, is the official emblem; Bengal tiger; lotus flower; national colors: saffron, white, green

National anthem: *name:* "Jana-Gana-Mana" (Thou Art the Ruler of the Minds of All People)
lyrics/music: Rabindranath TAGORE
note: adopted 1950; Rabindranath TAGORE, a Nobel laureate, also wrote Bangladesh's national anthem

National heritage: *total World Heritage Sites:* 40 (32 cultural, 7 natural, 1 mixed)
selected World Heritage Site locales: Taj Mahal (c); Red Fort Complex (c); Ellora Caves (c); Hill Forts of Rajasthan (c); Sundarbans National Park (n); Rock Shelters of Bhimbetka (c); Champaner-Pavagadh Archaeological Park (c); Dholavira: A Harappan City (c); Jaipur (c); Mahabodhi Temple Complex at Bodh Gaya (c); Manas Wildlife Sanctuary (n); Nanda Devi and Valley of Flowers National Parks (n); Khangchendzonga National Park (m)

ECONOMY

Economic overview: India's diverse economy encompasses traditional village farming, modern agriculture, handicrafts, a wide range of modern industries, and a multitude of services. Slightly less than half of the workforce is in agriculture, but services are the major source of economic growth, accounting for nearly two-thirds of India's output but employing less than one-third of its labor force. India has capitalized on its large educated English-speaking population to become a major exporter of information technology services, business outsourcing services, and software workers. Nevertheless, per capita income remains below the world average. India is developing into an openmarket economy, yet traces of its past autarkic policies remain. Economic liberalization measures, including industrial deregulation, privatization of state-owned enterprises, and reduced controls on foreign trade and investment, began in the early 1990s and served to accelerate the country's growth, which averaged nearly 7% per year from 1997 to 2017.

India's economic growth slowed in 2011 because of a decline in investment caused by high interest rates, rising inflation, and investor pessimism about the government's commitment to further economic reforms and about slow world growth. Investors' perceptions of India improved in early 2014, due to a reduction of the current account deficit and expectations of post-election economic reform, resulting in a surge of inbound capital flows and stabilization of the rupee. Growth rebounded in 2014 through 2016. Despite a high growth rate compared to the rest of the world, India's government-owned banks faced mounting bad debt, resulting in low credit growth. Rising macroeconomic imbalances in India and improving economic conditions in Western countries led investors to shift capital away from India, prompting a sharp depreciation of the rupee through 2016.

The economy slowed again in 2017, due to shocks of "demonetizaton" in 2016 and introduction of GST in 2017. Since the election, the government has passed an important goods and services tax bill and raised foreign direct investment caps in some sectors, but most economic reforms have focused on administrative and governance changes, largely because the ruling party remains a minority in India's upper house of Parliament, which must approve most bills.

India has a young population and corresponding low dependency ratio, healthy savings and investment rates, and is increasing integration into the global economy. However, long-term challenges remain significant, including: India's discrimination against women and girls, an inefficient power generation and distribution system, ineffective enforcement of intellectual property rights, decades-long civil litigation dockets, inadequate transport and agricultural infrastructure, limited non-agricultural employment opportunities, high spending and poorly targeted subsidies, inadequate availability of quality basic and higher education, and accommodating rural-tourban migration.

Real GDP (purchasing power parity): $8,443,360,000,000 (2020 est.)
$9,174,040,000,000 (2019 est.)
$8,817,670,000,000 (2018 est.)
note: data are in 2017 dollars

Real GDP growth rate: 4.86% (2019 est.)
6.78% (2018 est.)
6.55% (2017 est.)

Real GDP per capita: $6,100 (2020 est.)
$6,700 (2019 est.)
$6,500 (2018 est.)
note: data are in 2017 dollars

GDP (official exchange rate): $2,835,927,000,000 (2019 est.)

Inflation rate (consumer prices): 3.7% (2019 est.)
3.9% (2018 est.)
3.3% (2017 est.)

Credit ratings:
Fitch rating: BBB- (2006)
Moody's rating: Baa3 (2020)
Standard & Poors rating: BBB- (2007)
note: The year refers to the year in which the current credit rating was first obtained.

GDP - composition, by sector of origin: *agriculture:* 15.4% (2016 est.)
industry: 23% (2016 est.)
services: 61.5% (2016 est.)

GDP - composition, by end use: *household consumption:* 59.1% (2017 est.)
government consumption: 11.5% (2017 est.)
investment in fixed capital: 28.5% (2017 est.)
investment in inventories: 3.9% (2017 est.)
exports of goods and services: 19.1% (2017 est.)
imports of goods and services: -22% (2017 est.)

Agricultural products: sugar cane, rice, wheat, buffalo milk, milk, potatoes, vegetables, bananas, maize, mangoes/guavas

Industries: textiles, chemicals, food processing, steel, transportation equipment, cement, mining, petroleum, machinery, software, pharmaceuticals

Industrial production growth rate: 5.5% (2017 est.)

Labor force: 521.9 million (2017 est.)

Labor force - by occupation: *agriculture:* 47%
industry: 22%
services: 31% (FY 2014 est.)

Unemployment rate: 8.5% (2017 est.)
8.5% (2016 est.)

Unemployment, youth ages 15-24: *total:* 19.8%
male: 19.5%
female: 21% (2020 est.)

Population below poverty line: 21.9% (2011 est.)

Gini Index coefficient - distribution of family income: 35.7 (2011 est.)
37.8 (1997)

Household income or consumption by percentage share: *lowest 10%:* 3.6%
highest 10%: 29.8% (2011)

Budget: *revenues:* 238.2 billion (2017 est.)
expenditures: 329 billion (2017 est.)

Budget surplus (+) or deficit (-): -3.5% (of GDP) (2017 est.)

Public debt: 71.2% of GDP (2017 est.)
69.5% of GDP (2016 est.)
note: data cover central government debt, and exclude debt instruments issued (or owned) by government entities other than the treasury; the data include treasury debt held by foreign entities; the data exclude debt issued by subnational entities, as well as intragovernmental debt; intragovernmental debt consists of treasury borrowings from surpluses in the social funds, such as for retirement, medical care, and unemployment; debt instruments for the social funds are not sold at public auctions

Taxes and other revenues: 9.2% (of GDP) (2017 est.)

Fiscal year: 1 April - 31 March

Current account balance: -$29.748 billion (2019 est.)
-$65.939 billion (2018 est.)

Exports: $484.95 billion (2020 est.) note: data are in current year dollars
$546.03 billion (2019 est.) note: data are in current year dollars
$537.04 billion (2018 est.) note: data are in current year dollars

Exports - partners: United States 17%, United Arab Emirates 9%, China 5% (2019)

Exports - commodities: refined petroleum, diamonds, packaged medicines, jewelry, cars (2019)

Imports: $493.18 billion (2020 est.) note: data are in current year dollars
$619.48 billion (2019 est.) note: data are in current year dollars
$642.96 billion (2018 est.) note: data are in current year dollars

Imports - partners: China 15%, United States 7%, United Arab Emirates 6%, Saudi Arabia 5% (2019)

Imports - commodities: crude petroleum, gold, coal, diamonds, natural gas (2019)

Reserves of foreign exchange and gold: $409.8 billion (31 December 2017 est.)
$359.7 billion (31 December 2016 est.)

Debt - external: $555.388 billion (2019 est.)
$518.34 billion (2018 est.)

Exchange rates: Indian rupees (INR) per US dollar -
73.565 (2020 est.)
71.05 (2019 est.)
70.7675 (2018 est.)
64.152 (2014 est.)
61.03 (2013 est.)

ENERGY

Electricity access: *electrification - total population:* 99% (2019)
electrification - urban areas: 99% (2019)
electrification - rural areas: 99% (2019)

Electricity: *installed generating capacity:* 432.768 million kW (2020 est.)
consumption: 1,229,387,712,000 kWh (2019 est.)
exports: 9.491 billion kWh (2019 est.)
imports: 5.794 billion kWh (2019 est.)
transmission/distribution losses: 270.701 billion kWh (2019 est.)

Electricity generation sources: *fossil fuels:* 75.5% of total installed capacity (2020 est.)
nuclear: 2.8% of total installed capacity (2020 est.)
solar: 4.2% of total installed capacity (2020 est.)
wind: 4.6% of total installed capacity (2020 est.)
hydroelectricity: 10.7% of total installed capacity (2020 est.)
biomass and waste: 2.3% of total installed capacity (2020 est.)

Coal: *production:* 743.214 million metric tons (2020 est.)
consumption: 883.979 million metric tons (2020 est.)
exports: 1.029 million metric tons (2020 est.)
imports: 219.212 million metric tons (2020 est.)
proven reserves: 105.931 billion metric tons (2019 est.)

Petroleum: *total petroleum production:* 771,400 bbl/day (2021 est.)
refined petroleum consumption: 4,920,100 bbl/day (2019 est.)
crude oil and lease condensate exports: 0 bbl/day (2018 est.)
crude oil and lease condensate imports: 4.53 million bbl/day (2018 est.)
crude oil estimated reserves: 4,604,900,000 barrels (2021 est.)

Refined petroleum products - production: 4.897 million bbl/day (2015 est.)

Refined petroleum products - exports: 1.305 million bbl/day (2015 est.)

Refined petroleum products - imports: 653,300 bbl/day (2015 est.)

Natural gas: *production:* 27,734,833,000 cubic meters (2020 est.)
consumption: 61,646,806,000 cubic meters (2020 est.)
exports: 91.916 million cubic meters (2019 est.)
imports: 33,911,973,000 cubic meters (2020 est.)
proven reserves: 1,380,614,000,000 cubic meters (2021 est.)

Carbon dioxide emissions: 2,314,738,000 metric tonnes of CO2 (2019 est.)
from coal and metallurgical coke: 1,574,331,000 metric tonnes of CO2 (2019 est.)
from petroleum and other liquids: 615.903 million metric tonnes of CO2 (2019 est.)
from consumed natural gas: 124.505 million metric tonnes of CO2 (2019 est.)

Energy consumption per capita: 23.231 million Btu/person (2019 est.)

COMMUNICATIONS

Telephones - fixed lines: *total subscriptions:* 20,052,162 (2020 est.)
subscriptions per 100 inhabitants: 1 (2020 est.)

Telephones - mobile cellular: *total subscriptions:* 1.15 billion (2020 est.)
subscriptions per 100 inhabitants: 84 (2020 est.)

Telecommunication systems: *general assessment:* India's telecommunications sector has struggled for growth over the last five years; the sector's lackluster performance has been in spite of concerted efforts by the government to bolster the underlying infrastructure in a bid to achieve universal coverage; instead, the country's relatively liberal regulatory environment has encouraged fierce competition and price wars among the operators; State-owned as well as private operators have been forced to seek redress from the government in order to avoid bankruptcy; one particular area of contention has been the billions owed by the operators to the government in the form of Adjusted Gross Revenue (AGR) dues – usage and licensing fees charged by the Department of Telecommunications (DoT) – that have been the subject of long-standing court battles over what should be counted as revenue; the government won that battle in the Supreme Court in 2019, but the financial impairment of that decision has pushed a number of telcos to the brink; add the impact of the Covid-19 crisis in 2020 and 2021 to the mix, and the government had to come to the industry's rescue by introducing a major reform package in September 2021; along with changes to the definition of AGR with regard to non-telecom revenue, the package includes a four-year moratorium on AGR dues and spectrum instalments; the government has also deferred the spectrum auctions for 5G until later in 2022; mobile spectrum in India is already in short supply in terms of providing the necessary capacity to reach universal coverage, but the cash-strapped MNOs may not yet be in a sufficiently strong financial position for which to make the 5G spectrum auction viable (2022)
domestic: fixed-line subscriptions stands at roughly 1 per 100 and mobile-cellular at nearly 84 per 100 (2020)
international: country code - 91; a number of major international submarine cable systems, including SEA-ME-WE-3 & 4, AAE-1, BBG, EIG, FALCON, FEA, GBICS, MENA, IMEWE, SEACOM/ Tata TGN-Eurasia, SAFE, WARF, Bharat Lanka Cable System, IOX, Chennai-Andaman & Nicobar Island Cable, SAEx2, Tata TGN-Tata Indicom and i2icn that provide connectivity to Europe, Africa, Asia, the Middle East, South East Asia, numerous Indian Ocean islands including Australia ; satellite earth stations - 8 Intelsat (Indian Ocean) and 1 Inmarsat; Indian Ocean region (2022)

Broadcast media: Doordarshan, India's public TV network, has a monopoly on terrestrial broadcasting and operates about 20 national, regional, and local services; a large and increasing number of privately owned TV stations are distributed by cable and satellite service providers; in 2020, 130 million households paid for cable and satellite television across India and as of 2018, cable and satellite TV offered over 850 TV channels; government controls AM radio with All India Radio operating domestic and external networks; news broadcasts via radio are limited to the All India Radio Network; since 2000, privately owned FM stations have been permitted and their numbers have increased rapidly (2020)

Internet country code: .in

Internet users: *total:* 593.4 million (2020 est.)
percent of population: 43% (2020 est.)

Broadband - fixed subscriptions: *total:* 22.95 million (2020 est.)
subscriptions per 100 inhabitants: 2 (2020 est.)

TRANSPORTATION

National air transport system: *number of registered air carriers:* 14 (2020)
inventory of registered aircraft operated by air carriers: 485
annual passenger traffic on registered air carriers: 164,035,637 (2018)
annual freight traffic on registered air carriers: 2,703,960,000 (2018) mt-km

Civil aircraft registration country code prefix: VT

Airports: *total:* 346 (2021)

Airports - with paved runways: *total:* 253
over 3,047 m: 22
2,438 to 3,047 m: 59
1,524 to 2,437 m: 76
914 to 1,523 m: 82
under 914 m: 14 (2021)

Airports - with unpaved runways: *total:* 93
over 3,047 m: 1
2,438 to 3,047 m: 3
1,524 to 2,437 m: 6
914 to 1,523 m: 38
under 914 m: 45 (2021)

Heliports: 45 (2021)

Pipelines: 17,389 km natural gas, 10, 419 km crude oil, 3,544 liquid petroleum gas, 14,729 km refined products (2020) 9 km condensate/gas, 20 km oil/gas/water (2013) (2020)

Railways: *total:* 65,554 km (2014)
narrow gauge: 1,604 km (2014) 1.000-m gauge
broad gauge: 63,950 km (2014) (39, 329 km electrified)

Roadways: *total:* 6,371,847 km (2021) note: includes 140,995 km of national highways and expressways, 171.039 km of state highways , and 6,059,813 km of other roads
note: includes 96,214 km of national highways and expressways, 147,800 km of state highways, and 4,455,010 km of other roads

Waterways: 14,500 km (2012) (5,200 km on major rivers and 485 km on canals suitable for mechanized vessels)

Merchant marine: *total:* 1,801
by type: bulk carrier 63, container ship 22, general cargo 587, oil tanker 136, other 993 (2021)

Ports and terminals: *major seaport(s):* Chennai, Jawaharal Nehru Port, Kandla, Kolkata (Calcutta), Mumbai (Bombay), Sikka, Vishakhapatnam
container port(s) (TEUs): Jawaharal Nehru Port (5,100,891), Mundra (4,732,699) (2019)

LNG terminal(s) (import): Dabhol, Dahej, Hazira, Kochi

MILITARY AND SECURITY

Military and security forces: Indian Armed Forces: Army, Navy, Air Force, Coast Guard; Frontier Corps; Defense Security Corps; Ministry of Home Affairs: Central Armed Police Forces (includes Assam Rifles, Border Security Force, Central Industrial Security Force, Central Reserve Police Force, Indo-Tibetan Border Police, National Security Guards, Sashastra Seema Bal) (2022)
note 1: the Defense Security Corps provides security for Ministry of Defense sites
note 2: the Border Security Force (BSF) is responsible for the Indo-Pakistan and Indo-Bangladesh borders; the Sashastra Seema Bal (SSB or Armed Border Force) guards the Indo-Nepal and Indo-Bhutan borders
note 3: the Central Reserve Police Force (CRPF) includes a Rapid Reaction Force (RAF) for riot control and the Commando Battalion for Resolute Action (COBRA) for counter-insurgency operations
note 4: the Assam Rifles are under the administrative control of the Ministry of Home Affairs, while

operational control falls under the Ministry of Defense (specifically the Indian Army)

Military expenditures: 2.2% of GDP (2021 est.)
2.6% of GDP (2020 est.)
2.4% of GDP (2019) (approximately $93.9 billion)
2.4% of GDP (2018) (approximately $88.2 billion)
2.4% of GDP (2017) (approximately $83.8 billion)

Military and security service personnel strengths: information varies; approximately 1.45 million active personnel (estimated 1.25 million Army; 65,000 Navy; 140,000 Air Force; 12,000 Coast Guard) (2022)

Military equipment inventories and acquisitions: the military's inventory consists mostly of Russian- and Soviet-origin equipment along with a smaller mix of Western and domestically-produced arms; since 2010, Russia has been the leading supplier of arms to India; other key suppliers included France, Israel, and the US; India's defense industry is capable of producing a range of air, land, missile, and naval weapons systems for both domestic use and export; it also produces weapons systems under license (2022)

Military service age and obligation: ages vary by service, but generally 16.5-27 years of age for voluntary military service for men and women; no conscription (2022)
note 1: in 2022, the Indian Government announced that it would begin recruiting 46,000 men aged 17.5-21 annually to serve on 4-year contracts under a process called the Agnipath scheme; at the end of their tenure, 25% would be retained for longer terms of service, while the remainder would be forced to leave the military, although some of those leaving would be eligible to serve in the Coast Guard, the Merchant Navy, civilian positions in the Ministry of Defense, and in the paramilitary forces of the Ministry of Home Affairs, such as the Central Armed Police Forces and Assam Rifles
note 2: as of 2022, women made up about .59% of the Army, 1.1% of the Air Force, and 6% of the Navy
note 3: the Indian military accepts citizens of Nepal and Bhutan; descendants of refugees from Tibet who arrived before 1962 and have resided permanently in India; peoples of Indian origin from nations such as Burma, the Democratic Republic of the Congo, Ethiopia, Kenya, Malawi, Pakistan, Sri Lanka, Tanzania, Uganda, and Vietnam with the intention of permanently settling in India; eligible candidates from "friendly foreign nations" may apply to the Armed Forces Medical Services
note 4: the British began to recruit Nepalese citizens (Gurkhas) into the East India Company Army during the Anglo- Nepalese War (1814-1816), and the Gurkhas subsequently were brought into the British Indian Army; following the partition of India in 1947, an agreement between Nepal, India, and Great Britain allowed for the transfer of the 10 regiments from the British Indian Army to the separate British and Indian armies; six regiments of Gurkhas (aka Gorkhas in India) regiments went to the new Indian Army; a seventh regiment was later added

Military deployments: 1,900 Democratic Republic of the Congo (MONUSCO); 110 Golan Heights (UNDOF); 900 Lebanon (UNIFIL); 2,350 South Sudan (UNMISS); 310 Sudan (UNISFA) (May 2022)

Military - note: as of 2022, the Indian Armed Forces were chiefly focused on China and Pakistan; the short 1962 Sino-India War left in place one of the world's longest disputed international borders, resulting in occasional standoffs between Indian and Chinese security forces, including lethal clashes in 1975 and 2020; meanwhile, India and Pakistan have fought several conflicts since 1947, including the Indo-Pakistan War of 1965 and the Indo-Pakistan and Bangladesh War of Independence of 1971, as well as two clashes over the disputed region of Kashmir (the First Kashmir War of 1947 and the 1999 Kargil Conflict); a fragile cease-fire in Kashmir was reached in 2003, revised in 2018, and reaffirmed in 2021, although the Line of Control remained contested as of 2022, and India has accused Pakistan of backing armed separatists and terrorist organizations in Jammu and Kashmir where Indian forces have conducted counterinsurgency operations since the 1980s; in addition, India and Pakistan have battled over the Siachen Glacier of Kashmir, which was seized by India in 1984 with Pakistan attempting to retake the area at least three times between 1985 and 1995; despite a cease-fire, as of 2022 both sides continued to maintain a permanent military presence there with outposts at altitudes above 20,000 feet (over 6,000 meters) where most casualties were due to extreme weather and the hazards of operating in the high mountain terrain of the world's highest conflict, including avalanches, exposure, and altitude sickness (2022)

TERRORISM

Terrorist group(s): Harakat ul-Mujahidin; Harakat ul-Jihad-i-Islami; Hizbul Mujahideen; Indian Mujahedeen; Islamic State of Iraq and ash- Sham – India; Jaish-e-Mohammed; Lashkar-e Tayyiba; al-Qa'ida; al-Qa'ida in the Indian Subcontinent; Islamic Revolutionary Guard Corps (IRGC)/Qods Force

TRANSNATIONAL ISSUES

Disputes - international: *India-China:* since China and India launched a security and foreign policy dialogue in 2005, consolidated discussions related to the dispute over most of their rugged, militarized boundary, regional nuclear proliferation, Indian claims that China transferred missiles to Pakistan, and other matters continue; Kashmir remains the site of the world's largest and most militarized territorial dispute with portions under the de facto administration of China (Aksai Chin), India (Jammu and Kashmir), and Pakistan (Azad Kashmir and Northern Areas)
India-Pakistan: India and Pakistan resumed bilateral dialogue in February 2011 after a two-year hiatus, have maintained the 2003 cease-fire in Kashmir, and continue to have disputes over water sharing of the Indus River and its tributaries; UN Military Observer Group in India and Pakistan has maintained a small group of peacekeepers since 1949; India does not recognize Pakistan's ceding historic Kashmir lands to China in 1964; to defuse tensions and prepare for discussions on a maritime boundary, India and Pakistan seek technical resolution of the disputed boundary in Sir Creek estuary at the mouth of the Rann of Kutch in the Arabian Sea; Pakistani maps continue to show its Junagadh claim in Indian Gujarat State
India-Bangladesh: Prime Minister SINGH's September 2011 visit to Bangladesh resulted in the signing of a Protocol to the 1974 Land Boundary Agreement between India and Bangladesh, which had called for the settlement of longstanding boundary disputes over undemarcated areas and the exchange of territorial enclaves, but which had never been implemented; Bangladesh referred its maritime boundary claims with Burma and India to the International Tribunal on the Law of the Sea
India-Nepal: the Joint Border Committee with Nepal continues to examine contested boundary sections, including the 400 sq km dispute over the source of the Kalapani River; India maintains a strict border regime to keep out Maoist insurgents and control illegal cross-border activities from Nepal

Refugees and internally displaced persons: *refugees (country of origin):* 92,885 (Sri Lanka), 73,407 (Tibet/China), 20,325 (Burma), 8,537 (Afghanistan) (mid-year 2021)
IDPs: 506,000 (armed conflict and intercommunal violence) (2021)
stateless persons: 19,677 (mid-year 2021)

Illicit drugs: source and transit point for illicit narcotics and precursor chemicals bound for Europe, Africa, Southeast Asia, and North America; in 2020 India exported over $19 billion of illegal pharmaceutical drugs; illegal opium poppy growing in the Northeast; traffickers retool commercial chemical factories to produce large volumes of ephedrine, methamphetamine, and other drugs illicitly

INDIAN OCEAN

INTRODUCTION

Background: The Indian Ocean is the third largest of the world's five oceans (after the Pacific Ocean and Atlantic Ocean, but larger than the Southern Ocean and Arctic Ocean). Four critically important access waterways are the Suez Canal (Egypt), Bab el Mandeb (Djibouti-Yemen), Strait of Hormuz (Iran-Oman), and Strait of Malacca (Indonesia-Malaysia).The decision by the International Hydrographic Organization in the spring of 2000 to delimit a fifth ocean, the Southern Ocean, removed the portion of the Indian Ocean south of 60 degrees south latitude.

GEOGRAPHY

Location: body of water between Africa, the Southern Ocean, Asia, and Australia

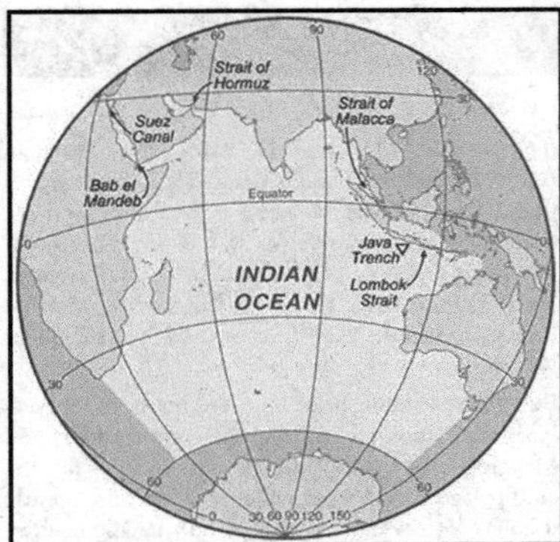

Geographic coordinates: 20 00 S, 80 00 E

Map references: Political Map of the World

Area: *total:* 70.56 million sq km
note: includes Andaman Sea, Arabian Sea, Bay of Bengal, Great Australian Bight, Gulf of Aden, Gulf of Oman, Mozambique Channel, Persian Gulf, Red Sea, Savu Sea, Strait of Malacca, Timor Sea, and other tributary water bodies

Area - comparative: almost 7 times the size of the US

Coastline: 66,526 km

Climate: northeast monsoon (December to April), southwest monsoon (June to October); tropical cyclones occur during May/June and October/November in the northern Indian Ocean and January/February in the southern Indian Ocean

Ocean volume: *ocean volume:* 264 million cu km
percent of World Ocean total volume: 19.8%

Major ocean currents: the counterclockwise Indian Ocean Gyre comprised of the southward flowing warm Agulhas and East Madagascar Currents in the west, the eastward flowing South Indian Current in the south, the northward flowing cold West Australian Current in the east, and the westward flowing South Equatorial Current in the north; a distinctive annual reversal of surface currents occurs in the northern Indian Ocean; low atmospheric pressure over southwest Asia from hot, rising, summer air results in the southwest monsoon and southwest-to-northeast winds and clockwise currents, while high pressure over northern Asia from cold, falling, winter air results in the northeast monsoon and northeast-to-southwest winds and counterclockwise currents

Elevation: *highest point:* sea level
lowest point: Java Trench -7,192 m unnamed deep
mean depth: -3,741 m

Natural resources: oil and gas fields, fish, shrimp, sand and gravel aggregates, placer deposits, polymetallic nodules

Natural hazards: occasional icebergs pose navigational hazard in southern reaches

Geography - note: major chokepoints include Bab el Mandeb, Strait of Hormuz, Strait of Malacca, southern access to the Suez Canal, and the Lombok Strait

ENVIRONMENT

Environment - current issues: marine pollution caused by ocean dumping, waste disposal, and oil spills; deep sea mining; oil pollution in Arabian Sea, Persian Gulf, and Red Sea; coral reefs threatened due to climate change, direct human pressures, and inadequate governance, awareness, and political will; loss of biodiversity; endangered marine species include the dugong, seals, turtles, and whales

Marine fisheries: the Indian Ocean fisheries are the third most important in the world accounting for 15.3%, or 12,248,064 mt of the global catch in 2019; tuna, small pelagic fish, and shrimp are important species in these regions; the Food and Agriculture Organization delineated two fishing regions in the Indian Ocean:
Eastern Indian Ocean region (Region 57) is the most important region and the fifth largest producing region in the world with 8.5%, or 6,784,778 mt, of the global catch in 2019; the region encompasses the waters north of 55° South latitude and east of 80° East longitude including the Bay of Bengal and Andaman Sea with the major producers including India (2,362,481 mt), Indonesia (1,940,558 mt), Burma (1,114,777 mt), Bangladesh (877,837 mt), and Sri Lanka (373,369 mt); the principal catches include shad, Skipjack tuna, mackerel, shrimp, and sardinellas
Western Indian Ocean region (Region 51) is the world's sixth largest producing region with more than 6.8% or 5,463,286 mt of the global catch in 2019; this region encompasses the waters north of 40° South latitude and west of 80° East longitude including the western Indian Ocean, Arabian Sea, Persian Gulf, and Red Sea as well as the waters along the east coast of Africa and Madagascar, the south coast of the Arabian Peninsula, and the west coast of India with major producers including India (2,207,125 mt), Oman (580,048 mt), Pakistan (341,730 mt), and Mozambique (274,791 mt); the principal catches include Skipjack and Yellowfin tuna, mackerel, sardines, shrimp, and cephalopods

Regional fisheries bodies: Indian Ocean Tuna Commission, Commission for the Conservation of Southern Bluefin Tuna, Regional Commission for Fisheries (Persian Gulf/Gulf of Oman), Southeast Asia Fisheries Development Center, Southwest Indian Ocean Fisheries Commission, South Indian Ocean Fisheries Agreement

Climate: northeast monsoon (December to April), southwest monsoon (June to October); tropical cyclones occur during May/June and October/November in the northern Indian Ocean and January/February in the southern Indian Ocean

GOVERNMENT

Country name: *etymology:* named for the country of India, which makes up much of its northern border

ECONOMY

Economic overview: The Indian Ocean provides major sea routes connecting the Middle East, Africa, and East Asia with Europe and the Americas. It carries a particularly heavy traffic of petroleum and petroleum products from the oilfields of the Persian Gulf and Indonesia. Its fish are of great and growing importance to the bordering countries for domestic consumption and export. Fishing fleets from Russia, Japan, South Korea, and Taiwan also exploit the Indian Ocean, mainly for shrimp and tuna. Large reserves of hydrocarbons are being tapped in the offshore areas of Saudi Arabia, Iran, India, and western Australia. An estimated 40% of the world's offshore oil production comes from the Indian Ocean. Beach sands rich in heavy minerals and offshore placer deposits are actively exploited by bordering countries, particularly India, South Africa, Indonesia, Sri Lanka, and Thailand.

TRANSPORTATION

Ports and terminals: *major seaport(s):* Chennai (Madras, India); Colombo (Sri Lanka); Durban (South Africa); Jakarta (Indonesia); Kolkata (Calcutta, India); Melbourne (Australia); Mumbai (Bombay, India); Richards Bay (South Africa)

MILITARY AND SECURITY

Maritime threats: the International Maritime Bureau continues to report the territorial waters of littoral states and offshore waters as high risk for piracy and armed robbery against ships, particularly in the Gulf of Aden, along the east coast of Africa, the Bay of Bengal, and the Strait of Malacca; the presence of several naval task forces in the Gulf of Aden and additional antipiracy measures on the part of ship operators, including the use of on-board armed security teams, have reduced incidents of piracy; 2021 saw one incident in the region of the Horn of Africa; the EU naval mission, Operation ATALANTA, continues its operations in the Gulf of Aden and Indian Ocean through 2022; naval units from Japan, India, and China also operate in conjunction with EU forces; China has established a logistical base in Djibouti to support its deployed naval units in the Horn of Africa

the Maritime Administration of the US Department of Transportation has issued a Maritime Advisory (2022-003 Persian Gulf, Strait of Hormuz, Gulf of Oman, Arabian Sea, Red Sea-Threats to US and International Shipping from Iran) effective 28 February 2022, which states in part that "heightened military activities and increased political tensions in this region continue to present risk to commercial shipping...there is a continued possibility that Iran and/or its regional proxies could take actions against US and partner interests in the region;" Coalition Task Force (CTF) Sentinel has been established to provide escorts for commercial shipping transiting the Persian Gulf, Strait of Hormuz, and Gulf of Oman

TRANSNATIONAL ISSUES

Disputes - international: some maritime disputes (see littoral states)

INDONESIA

INTRODUCTION

Background: The archipelago was once largely under the control of Buddhist and Hindu rulers. By around the 7th century, a Buddhist kingdom arose on Sumatra and expanded into Java and the Malay Peninsula until it was conquered in the late 13th century by the Hindu Majapahit Empire from Java. Majapahit (1290-1527) united most of modern-day Indonesia and Malaysia. Traders introduced Islam in the trade ports around the 11th century, and Indonesians gradually adopted Islam over the next 500 years. The Portuguese conquered parts of Indonesia in the 16th century, but they were ousted by the Dutch (except in East Timor), who began colonizing the islands in the early 17th century. It would be the early 20th century before Dutch colonial rule was established across the entirety of what would become the boundaries of the modern Indonesian state.

Japan occupied the islands from 1942 to 1945. Indonesia declared its independence shortly before Japan's surrender, but it required four years of sometimes brutal fighting, intermittent negotiations, and UN mediation before the Netherlands agreed to transfer sovereignty in 1949. A period of sometimes unruly parliamentary democracy ended in 1957 when President SOEKARNO declared martial law and instituted "Guided Democracy." After an abortive coup in 1965 by alleged communist sympathizers, SOEKARNO was gradually eased from power. From 1967 until 1998, President SUHARTO ruled Indonesia with his "New Order" government. After street protests toppled SUHARTO in 1998, free and fair legislative elections took place in 1999. Indonesia is now the world's third most populous democracy, the world's largest archipelagic state, and the world's largest Muslim-majority nation. Current issues include: alleviating poverty, improving education, preventing terrorism, consolidating democracy after four decades of authoritarianism, implementing economic and financial reforms, stemming corruption, reforming the criminal justice system, addressing climate change, and controlling infectious diseases, particularly those of global and regional importance. In 2005, Indonesia reached a historic peace agreement with armed separatists in Aceh. Indonesia continues to face low intensity armed resistance in Papua by the separatist Free Papua Movement.

GEOGRAPHY

Location: Southeastern Asia, archipelago between the Indian Ocean and the Pacific Ocean

Geographic coordinates: 5 00 S, 120 00 E

Map references: Southeast Asia

Area: *total:* 1,904,569 sq km
land: 1,811,569 sq km
water: 93,000 sq km

Area - comparative: slightly less than three times the size of Texas

Land boundaries: *total:* 2,958 km
border countries (3): Malaysia 1,881 km; Papua New Guinea 824 km; Timor-Leste 253 km

Coastline: 54,716 km

Maritime claims: *territorial sea:* 12 nm
exclusive economic zone: 200 nm
measured from claimed archipelagic straight baselines

Climate: tropical; hot, humid; more moderate in highlands

Terrain: mostly coastal lowlands; larger islands have interior mountains

Elevation: *highest point:* Puncak Jaya 4,884 m
lowest point: Indian Ocean 0 m
mean elevation: 367 m

Natural resources: petroleum, tin, natural gas, nickel, timber, bauxite, copper, fertile soils, coal, gold, silver

Land use: *agricultural land:* 31.2% (2018 est.)
arable land: 13% (2018 est.)
permanent crops: 12.1% (2018 est.)
permanent pasture: 6.1% (2018 est.)
forest: 51.7% (2018 est.)
other: 17.1% (2018 est.)

Irrigated land: 67,220 sq km (2012)

Major lakes (area sq km): *fresh water lake(s):* Danau Toba - 1,150 sq km
note - located in the caldera of a super volcano that erupted more than 70,000 years ago; it is the largest volcanic lake in the World

Major rivers (by length in km): Sepik (shared with Papua New Guinea [s]) - 1,126 km; Fly (shared with Papua New Guinea [s]) - 1,050 km
note – [s] after country name indicates river source; [m] after country name indicates river mouth

Population distribution: major concentration on the island of Java, which is considered one of the most densely populated places on earth; of the outer islands (those surrounding Java and Bali), Sumatra contains some of the most significant clusters, particularly in the south near the Selat Sunda, and along the northeastern coast near Medan; the cities of Makasar (Sulawesi), Banjarmasin (Kalimantan) are also heavily populated

Natural hazards: occasional floods; severe droughts; tsunamis; earthquakes; volcanoes; forest fires
volcanism: Indonesia contains the most volcanoes of any country in the world - some 76 are historically active; significant volcanic activity occurs on Java, Sumatra, the Sunda Islands, Halmahera Island, Sulawesi Island, Sangihe Island, and in the Banda Sea; Merapi (2,968 m), Indonesia's most active volcano and in eruption since 2010, has been deemed a Decade Volcano by the International Association of Volcanology and Chemistry of the Earth's Interior, worthy of study due to its explosive history and close proximity to human populations; on 22 December 2018, a large explosion and flank collapse destroyed most of the 338 m high island of Anak Krakatau (Child of Krakatau) and generated a deadly tsunami inundating portions of western Java and southern Sumatra leaving more than 400 dead; other notable historically active volcanoes include Agung, Awu, Karangetang, Krakatau (Krakatoa), Makian, Raung, Sinabung, and Tambora; see note 2 under "Geography - note"

Geography - note: *note 1:* according to Indonesia's National Coordinating Agency for Survey and Mapping, the total number of islands in the archipelago is 13,466, of which 922 are permanently inhabited (Indonesia is the world's largest country comprised solely of islands); the country straddles the equator and occupies a strategic location astride or along major sea lanes from the Indian Ocean to the Pacific Ocean
note 2: Indonesia is one of the countries along the Ring of Fire, a belt of active volcanoes and earthquake epicenters bordering the Pacific Ocean; up to 90% of the world's earthquakes and some 75% of the world's volcanoes occur within the Ring of Fire; 80% of tsunamis, caused by volcanic or seismic events, occur within the "Pacific Ring of Fire"
note 3: despite having the fourth largest population in the world, Indonesia is the most heavily forested region on earth after the Amazon
note 4: two major food crops apparently developed on the island of New Guinea: bananas and sugarcane

PEOPLE AND SOCIETY

Population: 277,329,163 (2022 est.)

Nationality: *noun:* Indonesian(s)
adjective: Indonesian

Ethnic groups: Javanese 40.1%, Sundanese 15.5%, Malay 3.7%, Batak 3.6%, Madurese 3%, Betawi 2.9%, Minangkabau 2.7%, Buginese 2.7%, Bantenese 2%, Banjarese 1.7%, Balinese 1.7%, Acehnese 1.4%, Dayak 1.4%, Sasak 1.3%, Chinese 1.2%, other 15% (2010 est.)

Languages: Bahasa Indonesia (official, modified form of Malay), English, Dutch, local dialects (of which the most widely spoken is Javanese); note - more than 700 languages are used in Indonesia
major-language sample(s): Fakta Dunia, sumber informasi dasar yang sangat diperlukan. (Indonesian)

Religions: Muslim 87.2%, Protestant 7%, Roman Catholic 2.9%, Hindu 1.7%, other 0.9% (includes Buddhist and Confucian), unspecified 0.4% (2010 est.)

Demographic profile: Indonesia has the world's fourth-largest population. It is predominantly Muslim and has the largest Muslim population of any country in the world. The population is projected to increase to as much as 320 million by 2045. A government-supported family planning program. The total fertility rate (TFR) – the average number of births per woman – from 5.6 in the mid-1960s to 2.7 in the mid-1990s. The success of the program was also due to the social acceptance of family planning, which received backing from influential Muslim leaders and organizations.

The fertility decline slowed in the late 1990's when responsibility for family planning programs shifted to the district level, where the programs were not prioritized. Since 2012 the national government revitalized the national family planning program, and Indonesia's TFR has slowly decreased to 2.3 in 2020. The government may reach its goal of achieving replacement level fertility – 2.1 children per woman – but the large number of women of childbearing age ensures significant population growth for many years.

Indonesia is a source country for labor migrants, a transit country for asylum seekers, and a destination mainly for highly skilled migrant workers. International labor migration, both legal and illegal, from Indonesia to other parts of Asia (most commonly Malaysia) and the Middle East has taken place for decades because of high unemployment and underemployment, poverty, and low wages domestically. Increasing numbers of migrant workers are drawn to Australia, Canada, New Zealand, and the US. The majority of Indonesian labor migration is temporary and consists predominantly of low-skilled workers, mainly women working as domestics.

Indonesia's strategic location between Asia and Australia and between the Pacific and Indian Oceans – and its relatively easy accessibility via boat – appeal to asylum seekers. It is also an attractive transit location because of its easy entry requirements and the ability to continue on to Australia. Recent asylum seekers have come from Afghanistan, Burma (Rohingyas), Iraq, Somalia, and Sri Lanka. Since 2013, when Australia tightening its immigration policy, thousands of migrants and asylum seekers have been stranded in Indonesia, where they live in precarious conditions and receive only limited support from international organizations. The situation for refugees in Indonesia has also worsened because Australia and the US, which had resettled the majority of refugees in Indonesia, have significantly lowered their intake.

Age structure: *0-14 years:* 23.87% (male 32,473,246/female 31,264,034)
15-24 years: 16.76% (male 22,786,920/female 21,960,130)
25-54 years: 42.56% (male 58,249,570/female 55,409,579)
55-64 years: 8.99% (male 11,033,838/female 12,968,005)
65 years and over: 7.82% (male 9,099,773/female 11,781,271) (2020 est.)

Dependency ratios: *total dependency ratio:* 47.5
youth dependency ratio: 38.3
elderly dependency ratio: 9.2
potential support ratio: 10.8 (2020 est.)

Median age: *total:* 31.1 years
male: 30.5 years
female: 31.8 years (2020 est.)

Population growth rate: 0.79% (2022 est.)

Birth rate: 15.32 births/1,000 population (2022 est.)

Death rate: 6.75 deaths/1,000 population (2022 est.)

Net migration rate: -0.71 migrant(s)/1,000 population (2022 est.)

Population distribution: major concentration on the island of Java, which is considered one of the most densely populated places on earth; of the outer islands (those surrounding Java and Bali), Sumatra contains some of the most significant clusters, particularly in the south near the Selat Sunda, and along the northeastern coast near Medan; the cities of Makasar (Sulawesi), Banjarmasin (Kalimantan) are also heavily populated

Urbanization: *urban population:* 57.9% of total population (2022)
rate of urbanization: 1.99% annual rate of change (2020-25 est.)

Major urban areas - population: 11.075 million JAKARTA (capital), 3.622 million Bekasi, 3.005 million Surabaya, 2.942 million Depok, 2.638 million Bandung, 2.456 million Tangerang (2022)

Sex ratio: *at birth:* 1.05 male(s)/female
0-14 years: 1.05 male(s)/female
15-24 years: 1.05 male(s)/female
25-54 years: 0.99 male(s)/female
55-64 years: 0.98 male(s)/female
65 years and over: 0.66 male(s)/female
total population: 1 male(s)/female (2022 est.)

Mother's mean age at first birth: 22.4 years (2017 est.)
note: data represents median age at first birth among women 25-49

Maternal mortality ratio: 177 deaths/100,000 live births (2017 est.)

Infant mortality rate: *total:* 19.73 deaths/1,000 live births
male: 22.15 deaths/1,000 live births
female: 17.18 deaths/1,000 live births (2022 est.)

Life expectancy at birth: *total population:* 73.08 years
male: 70.86 years
female: 75.4 years (2022 est.)

Total fertility rate: 2.01 children born/woman (2022 est.)

Contraceptive prevalence rate: 55.5% (2018)

Drinking water source: *improved: urban:* 98.2% of population
rural: 86.8% of population
total: 93.3% of population
unimproved: urban: 1.8% of population
rural: 13.2% of population
total: 6.7% of population (2020 est.)

Current health expenditure: 2.9% of GDP (2019)

Physicians density: 0.62 physicians/1,000 population (2020)

Hospital bed density: 1 beds/1,000 population (2017)

Sanitation facility access: *improved: urban:* 97.2% of population
rural: 86.5% of population
total: 92.5% of population
unimproved: urban: 2.8% of population
rural: 13.5% of population
total: 7.5% of population (2020 est.)

HIV/AIDS - adult prevalence rate: 0.4% (2020 est.)

Major infectious diseases: *degree of risk:* very high (2020)
food or waterborne diseases: bacterial diarrhea, hepatitis A, and typhoid fever
vectorborne diseases: dengue fever and malaria
note: a new coronavirus is causing sustained community spread of respiratory illness (COVID-19) in Indonesia; as of 18 August 2022, Indonesia has reported a total of 6,301,523 cases of COVID-19 or 2,303.83 cumulative cases of COVID-19 per 100,000 population with a total of 157,317 cumulative deaths or a rate 57.51 cumulative deaths per 100,000 population; as of 9 August 2022, 74.09% of the population has received at least one dose of COVID-19 vaccine

Obesity - adult prevalence rate: 6.9% (2016)

Alcohol consumption per capita: *total:* 0.08 liters of pure alcohol (2019 est.)
beer: 0.06 liters of pure alcohol (2019 est.)
wine: 0.01 liters of pure alcohol (2019 est.)
spirits: 0.02 liters of pure alcohol (2019 est.)
other alcohols: 0 liters of pure alcohol (2019 est.)

Tobacco use: *total:* 37.6% (2020 est.)
male: 71.4% (2020 est.)
female: 3.7% (2020 est.)

Children under the age of 5 years underweight: 17.7% (2018)

Child marriage: *women married by age 15:* 2%
women married by age 18: 16.3% (2017 est.)

Education expenditures: 2.8% of GDP (2019 est.)

Literacy: *definition:* age 15 and over can read and write
total population: 96%
male: 97.4%
female: 94.6% (2020)

School life expectancy (primary to tertiary education): *total:* 14 years
male: 14 years
female: 14 years (2018)

Unemployment, youth ages 15-24: *total:* 14.8%
male: 15.1%
female: 14.3% (2020 est.)

People - note: Indonesia is the fourth most populous nation in the World after China, India, and the United States; more than half of the Indonesian population - roughly 150 million people or 55% - live on the island of Java (about the size of California) making it the most crowded island on earth

ENVIRONMENT

Environment - current issues: large-scale deforestation (much of it illegal) and related wildfires cause heavy smog; over-exploitation of marine resources; environmental problems associated with rapid urbanization and economic development, including air pollution, traffic congestion, garbage management, and reliable water and waste water services; water pollution from industrial wastes, sewage

Environment - international agreements: *party to:* Biodiversity, Climate Change, Climate Change-Kyoto Protocol, Climate Change-Paris Agreement, Comprehensive Nuclear Test Ban, Desertification, Endangered Species, Hazardous Wastes, Law of the Sea, Nuclear Test Ban, Ozone Layer Protection, Ship Pollution, Tropical Timber 2006, Wetlands
signed, but not ratified: Marine Life Conservation

Air pollutants: *particulate matter emissions:* 15.58 micrograms per cubic meter (2016 est.)
carbon dioxide emissions: 563.32 megatons (2016 est.)
methane emissions: 244.5 megatons (2020 est.)

Climate: tropical; hot, humid; more moderate in highlands

Land use: *agricultural land:* 31.2% (2018 est.)
arable land: 13% (2018 est.)
permanent crops: 12.1% (2018 est.)
permanent pasture: 6.1% (2018 est.)
forest: 51.7% (2018 est.)
other: 17.1% (2018 est.)

Urbanization: *urban population:* 57.9% of total population (2022)
rate of urbanization: 1.99% annual rate of change (2020-25 est.)

Revenue from forest resources: *forest revenues:* 0.39% of GDP (2018 est.)

Revenue from coal: *coal revenues:* 1.06% of GDP (2018 est.)

Waste and recycling: *municipal solid waste generated annually:* 65.2 million tons (2016 est.)
municipal solid waste recycled annually: 4.564 million tons (2016 est.)
percent of municipal solid waste recycled: 7% (2016 est.)

Major lakes (area sq km): *fresh water lake(s):* Danau Toba - 1,150 sq km
note - located in the caldera of a super volcano that erupted more than 70,000 years ago; it is the largest volcanic lake in the World

Major rivers (by length in km): Sepik (shared with Papua New Guinea [s]) - 1,126 km; Fly (shared with Papua New Guinea [s]) - 1,050 km
note – [s] after country name indicates river source; [m] after country name indicates river mouth

Total water withdrawal: *municipal:* 23.8 billion cubic meters (2017 est.)
industrial: 9.135 billion cubic meters (2017 est.)
agricultural: 189.7 billion cubic meters (2017 est.)

Total renewable water resources: 2.019 trillion cubic meters (2017 est.)

GOVERNMENT

Country name: *conventional long form:* Republic of Indonesia
conventional short form: Indonesia
local long form: Republik Indonesia
local short form: Indonesia
former: Netherlands East Indies (Dutch East Indies), Netherlands New Guinea
etymology: the name is an 18th-century construct of two Greek words, "Indos" (India) and "nesoi" (islands), meaning "Indian islands"

Government type: presidential republic

Capital: *name:* Jakarta; note - Indonesian lawmakers on 18 January 2022 approved the relocation of the country's capital from Jakarta to a site in East Kalimantan, a jungle area of Borneo; the move to Nusantara, the name of the new capital, will take several years
geographic coordinates: 6 10 S, 106 49 E
time difference: UTC+7 (12 hours ahead of Washington, DC, during Standard Time)
time zone note: Indonesia has three time zones
etymology: "Jakarta" derives from the Sanscrit "Jayakarta" meaning "victorious city" and refers to a successful defeat and expulsion of the Portuguese in 1527; previously the port had been named "Sunda Kelapa"

Administrative divisions: 34 provinces (provinsi-provinsi, singular - provinsi), 1 autonomous province*, 1 special region** (daerah-daerah istimewa, singular - daerah istimewa), and 1 national capital district*** (daerah khusus ibukota); Aceh*, Bali, Banten, Bengkulu, Gorontalo, Jakarta***, Jambi, Jawa Barat (West Java), Jawa Tengah (Central Java), Jawa Timur (East Java), Kalimantan Barat (West Kalimantan), Kalimantan Selatan (South Kalimantan), Kalimantan Tengah (Central Kalimantan), Kalimantan Timur (East Kalimantan), Kalimantan Utara (North Kalimantan), Kepulauan Bangka Belitung (Bangka Belitung Islands), Kepulauan Riau (Riau Islands), Lampung, Maluku, Maluku Utara (North Maluku), Nusa Tenggara Barat (West Nusa Tenggara), Nusa Tenggara Timur (East Nusa Tenggara), Papua, Papua Barat (West Papua), Papua Pegunungan (Papua Highlands), Papua Selatan (South Papua), Papua Tengah (Central Papua), Riau, Sulawesi Barat (West Sulawesi), Sulawesi Selatan (South Sulawesi), Sulawesi Tengah (Central Sulawesi), Sulawesi Tenggara (Southeast Sulawesi), Sulawesi Utara (North Sulawesi), Sumatera Barat (West Sumatra), Sumatera Selatan (South Sumatra), Sumatera Utara (North Sumatra), Yogyakarta**
note: following the implementation of decentralization beginning on 1 January 2001, regencies and municipalities have become the key administrative units responsible for providing most government services

Independence: 17 August 1945 (declared independence from the Netherlands)

National holiday: Independence Day, 17 August (1945)

Constitution: *history:* drafted July to August 1945, effective 18 August 1945, abrogated by 1949 and 1950 constitutions; 1945 constitution restored 5 July 1959
amendments: proposed by the People's Consultative Assembly, with at least two thirds of its members present; passage requires simple majority vote by the Assembly membership; constitutional articles on the unitary form of the state cannot be amended; amended several times, last in 2002

Legal system: civil law system based on the Roman-Dutch model and influenced by customary law

International law organization participation: has not submitted an ICJ jurisdiction declaration; non-party state to the ICCt

Citizenship: *citizenship by birth:* no
citizenship by descent only: at least one parent must be a citizen of Indonesia
dual citizenship recognized: no
residency requirement for naturalization: 5 continuous years

Suffrage: 17 years of age; universal; married persons regardless of age

Executive branch: *chief of state:* President Joko "Jokowi" WIDODO (since 20 October 2014); Vice President Ma'ruf AMIN (since 20 October 2019); note - the president is both chief of state and head of government
head of government: President Joko "Jokowi" WIDODO (since 20 October 2014); Vice President Ma'ruf AMIN (since 20 October 2019)
cabinet: Cabinet appointed by the president
elections/appointments: president and vice president directly elected by absolute majority popular vote for a 5-year term (eligible for a second term); election last held on 17 April 2019 (next election 2024)
election results:
2019: Joko WIDODO elected president; percent of vote - Joko WIDODO (PDI-P) 55.5%, PRABOWO Subianto Djojohadikusumo (GERINDRA) 44.5%
2014: Joko WIDODO elected president; percent of vote - Joko WIDODO (PDI-P) 53.15%, PRABOWO Subianto Djojohadikusumo (GERINDRA) 46.85%

Legislative branch: *description:* bicameral People's Consultative Assembly or Majelis Permusyawaratan Rakyat (MPR) consists of:
Regional Representative Council or Dewan Perwakilan Daerah (136 seats; non-partisan members directly elected in multi-seat constituencies - 4 each from the country's 34 electoral districts - by proportional representation vote to serve 5-year terms); note - the Regional Representative Council has no legislative authority
House of Representatives or Dewan Perwakilan Rakyat (DPR) (575 seats; members directly elected in multi-seat constituencies by single non-transferable vote to serve 5-year terms) (2019)
elections: Regional Representative Council - last held on 17 April 2019 (next to be held 2024)
House of Representatives - last held on 17 April 2019 (next to be held 2024) (2019)
election results: Regional Representative Council - all seats elected on a non-partisan basis; composition - men 102, women 34, percent of women 25%
House of Representatives - percent of vote by party - PDI-P 19.3%, Gerindra 12.6%, Golkar 12.3%, PKB 9.7%, Nasdem 9.1%, PKS 8.2%, PD 7.8%, PAN 6.8%, PPP 4.5%, other 9.6%; seats by party - PDI-P 128, Golkar 85, Gerindra 78, Nasdem 59, PKB 58, PD 54, PKS 50, PAN 44, PPP 19; composition - men 449, women 126, percent of women 21.9%; total People's Consultative Assembly percent of women 22.5% (2019)

Judicial branch: *highest court(s):* Supreme Court or Mahkamah Agung (51 judges divided into 8 chambers); Constitutional Court or Mahkamah Konstitusi (consists of 9 judges)
judge selection and term of office: Supreme Court judges nominated by Judicial Commission, appointed by president with concurrence of parliament; judges serve until retirement at age 65; Constitutional Court judges - 3 nominated by president, 3 by Supreme Court, and 3 by parliament; judges appointed by the president; judges serve until mandatory retirement at age 70
subordinate courts: High Courts of Appeal, district courts, religious courts

Political parties and leaders: Berkarya Party [Muchdi PURWOPRANJONO]
Crescent Star Party or PBB [Yusril Ihza MAHENDRA]
Democrat Party or PD [Agus Harimurti YUDHOYONO]
Functional Groups Party or GOLKAR [Airlangga HARTARTO]
Great Indonesia Movement Party or GERINDRA [PRABOWO Subianto Djojohadikusumo]
Garuda Party or Change Indonesia Movement Party [Ahmad Ridha SABANA]
Indonesia Democratic Party-Struggle or PDI-P [MEGAWATI Sukarnoputri]
Indonesian Justice and Unity Party or PKPI [Yussuf SOLICHIEN]
Indonesian Solidarity Party or PSI [GIRING GANESHA]
National Awakening Party or PKB [Muhaiman ISKANDAR]
National Democratic Party or NasDem [Surya PALOH]
National Mandate Party or PAN [Zulkifli HASAN]
People's Conscience Party or Hanura [Oesman Sapta ODANG]
Perindo Party [Hary TANOESOEDIBJO]
Prosperous Justice Party or PKS [Ahmad SYAIKHU]
United Development Party or PPP [Muhamad MARDIONO]

International organization participation: ADB, APEC, ARF, ASEAN, BIS, CD, CICA (observer), CP, D-8, EAS, EITI (compliant country), FAO, G-11, G-15, G-20, G-77, IAEA, IBRD, ICAO, ICC (national committees), ICRM, IDA, IDB, IFAD, IFC, IFRCS, IHO, ILO, IMF, IMO, IMSO, Interpol, IOC, IOM (observer), IORA, IPU, ISO, ITSO, ITU, ITUC (NGOs), MIGA, MINURSO, MINUSTAH, MONUSCO, MSG (associate member), NAM, OECD (enhanced engagement), OIC, OPCW, PIF (partner), UN, UNAMID, UNCTAD, UNESCO, UNHRC, UNIDO, UNIFIL, UNISFA, UNMIL, UNWTO, UPU, WCO, WFTU (NGOs), WHO, WIPO, WMO, WTO

Diplomatic representation in the US: *chief of mission:* Ambassador Rosan Perkasa ROESLANI (since 13 January 2022)
chancery: 2020 Massachusetts Avenue NW, Washington, DC 20036
telephone: [1] (202) 775-5200
FAX: [1] (202) 775-5365
email address and website:
http://www.embassyofindonesia.org/
consulate(s) general: Chicago, Houston, Los Angeles, New York, San Francisco

Diplomatic representation from the US: *chief of mission:* Ambassador Sung Y. KIM (since 21 October 2020)
embassy: Jl. Medan Merdeka Selatan No. 3-5, Jakarta 10110
mailing address: 8200 Jakarta Place, Washington DC 20521-8200
telephone: [62] (21) 5083-1000
FAX: [62] (21) 385-7189
email address and website:
jakartaacs@state.gov
https://id.usembassy.gov/
consulate(s) general: Surabaya
consulate(s): Medan

Flag description: two equal horizontal bands of red (top) and white; the colors derive from the banner of the Majapahit Empire of the 13th-15th centuries; red symbolizes courage, white represents purity
note: similar to the flag of Monaco, which is shorter; also similar to the flag of Poland, which is white (top) and red

National symbol(s): garuda (mythical bird); national colors: red, white

National anthem: *name:* "Indonesia Raya" (Great Indonesia)
lyrics/music: Wage Rudolf SOEPRATMAN
note: adopted 1945

National heritage: *total World Heritage Sites:* 9 (5 cultural, 4 natural)
selected World Heritage Site locales: Borobudur Temple Compounds (c); Komodo National Park (n); Prambanan Temple Compounds (c); Ujung Kulon National Park (n); Sangiran Early Man Site (c); Lorentz National Park (n); Tropical Rainforest Heritage of Sumatra (n); Cultural Landscape of Bali Province (c); Ombilin Coal Mining Heritage of Sawahlunto (c)

ECONOMY

Economic overview: Indonesia, the largest economy in Southeast Asia, has seen a slowdown in growth since 2012, mostly due to the end of the commodities export boom. During the global financial crisis, Indonesia outperformed its regional neighbors and joined China and India as the only G20 members posting growth. Indonesia's annual budget deficit is capped at 3% of GDP, and the Government of Indonesia lowered its debt-to-GDP ratio from a peak of 100% shortly after the Asian financial crisis in 1999 to 34% today. In May 2017 Standard & Poor's became the last major ratings agency to upgrade Indonesia's sovereign credit rating to investment grade.

Poverty and unemployment, inadequate infrastructure, corruption, a complex regulatory environment, and unequal resource distribution among its regions are still part of Indonesia's economic landscape. President Joko WIDODO - elected in July 2014 – seeks to develop Indonesia's maritime resources and pursue other infrastructure development, including significantly increasing its electrical power generation capacity. Fuel subsidies were significantly reduced in early 2015, a move which has helped the government redirect its spending to development priorities. Indonesia, with the nine other ASEAN members, will continue to move towards participation in the ASEAN Economic Community, though full implementation of economic integration has not yet materialized.

Real GDP (purchasing power parity): $3,130,470,000,000 (2020 est.)
$3,196,620,000,000 (2019 est.)
$3,043,880,000,000 (2018 est.)
note: data are in 2017 dollars

Real GDP growth rate: 5.03% (2019 est.)
5.17% (2018 est.)
5.07% (2017 est.)

Real GDP per capita: $11,400 (2020 est.)
$11,800 (2019 est.)
$11,400 (2018 est.)
note: data are in 2017 dollars

GDP (official exchange rate): $1,119,720,000,000 (2019 est.)

Inflation rate (consumer prices): 2.8% (2019 est.)
3.2% (2018 est.)
3.8% (2017 est.)

Credit ratings:

Fitch rating: BBB (2017)

Moody's rating: Baa2 (2018)

Standard & Poors rating: BBB (2019)
note: The year refers to the year in which the current credit rating was first obtained.

GDP - composition, by sector of origin: *agriculture:* 13.7% (2017 est.)
industry: 41% (2017 est.)
services: 45.4% (2017 est.)

GDP - composition, by end use: *household consumption:* 57.3% (2017 est.)
government consumption: 9.1% (2017 est.)
investment in fixed capital: 32.1% (2017 est.)
investment in inventories: 0.3% (2017 est.)
exports of goods and services: 20.4% (2017 est.)
imports of goods and services: -19.2% (2017 est.)

Agricultural products: oil palm fruit, rice, maize, sugar cane, coconuts, cassava, bananas, eggs, poultry, rubber

Industries: petroleum and natural gas, textiles, automotive, electrical appliances, apparel, footwear, mining, cement, medical instruments and appliances, handicrafts, chemical fertilizers, plywood, rubber, processed food, jewelry, and tourism

Industrial production growth rate: 4.1% (2017 est.)

Labor force: 129.366 million (2019 est.)

Labor force - by occupation: *agriculture:* 32%
industry: 21%
services: 47% (2016 est.)

Unemployment rate: 5.31% (2018 est.)
5.4% (2017 est.)

Unemployment, youth ages 15-24: *total:* 14.8%
male: 15.1%
female: 14.3% (2020 est.)

Population below poverty line: 9.4% (2019 est.)

Gini Index coefficient - distribution of family income: 37.8 (2018 est.)
39.4 (2005)

Household income or consumption by percentage share: *lowest 10%:* 3.4%
highest 10%: 28.2% (2010)

Budget: *revenues:* 131.7 billion (2017 est.)
expenditures: 159.6 billion (2017 est.)

Budget surplus (+) or deficit (-): -2.7% (of GDP) (2017 est.)

Public debt: 28.8% of GDP (2017 est.)
28.3% of GDP (2016 est.)

Taxes and other revenues: 13% (of GDP) (2017 est.)

Fiscal year: calendar year

Current account balance: -$30.359 billion (2019 est.)
-$30.633 billion (2018 est.)

Exports: $178.26 billion (2020 est.) note: data are in current year dollars
$200.1 billion (2019 est.) note: data are in current year dollars
$211.93 billion (2018 est.) note: data are in current year dollars

Exports - partners: China 15%, United States 10%, Japan 9%, Singapore 8%, India 7%, Malaysia 5% (2019)

Exports - commodities: coal, palm oil, natural gas, cars, gold (2019)

Imports: $159.64 billion (2020 est.) note: data are in current year dollars
$204.23 billion (2019 est.) note: data are in current year dollars
$218.65 billion (2018 est.) note: data are in current year dollars

Imports - partners: China 27%, Singapore 12%, Japan 8%, Thailand 5%, United States 5%, South Korea 5%, Malaysia 5% (2019)

Imports - commodities: refined petroleum, crude petroleum, vehicle parts, telephones, natural gas (2019)

Reserves of foreign exchange and gold: $130.2 billion (31 December 2017 est.)

Debt - external: $393.252 billion (2019 est.)
$360.945 billion (2018 est.)

Exchange rates: Indonesian rupiah (IDR) per US dollar -
14,110 (2020 est.)
14,015 (2019 est.)
14,470 (2018 est.)
13,389.4 (2014 est.)
11,865.2 (2013 est.)

ENERGY

Electricity access: *electrification - total population:* 99% (2019)
electrification - urban areas: 100% (2019)

electrification - rural areas: 99% (2019)

Electricity: *installed generating capacity:* 69.065 million kW (2020 est.)
consumption: 256,742,190,000 kWh (2019 est.)
exports: 0 kWh (2020 est.)
imports: 1.553 billion kWh (2020 est.)
transmission/distribution losses: 25.08 billion kWh (2019 est.)

Electricity generation sources: *fossil fuels:* 82.3% of total installed capacity (2020 est.)
wind: 0.2% of total installed capacity (2020 est.)
hydroelectricity: 6.8% of total installed capacity (2020 est.)
geothermal: 5.7% of total installed capacity (2020 est.)
biomass and waste: 5% of total installed capacity (2020 est.)

Coal: *production:* 563.728 million metric tons (2020 est.)
consumption: 132.548 million metric tons (2020 est.)
exports: 409.892 million metric tons (2020 est.)
imports: 8.95 million metric tons (2020 est.)
proven reserves: 39.891 billion metric tons (2019 est.)

Petroleum: *total petroleum production:* 842,300 bbl/day (2021 est.)
refined petroleum consumption: 1.649 million bbl/day (2019 est.)
crude oil and lease condensate exports: 204,000 bbl/day (2018 est.)
crude oil and lease condensate imports: 309,700 bbl/day (2018 est.)
crude oil estimated reserves: 2.48 billion barrels (2021 est.)

Refined petroleum products - production: 950,000 bbl/day (2015 est.)

Refined petroleum products - exports: 79,930 bbl/day (2015 est.)

Refined petroleum products - imports: 591,500 bbl/day (2015 est.)

Natural gas: *production:* 62,612,013,000 cubic meters (2020 est.)
consumption: 38,673,953,000 cubic meters (2020 est.)
exports: 23,938,060,000 cubic meters (2020 est.)
imports: 0 cubic meters (2021 est.)
proven reserves: 1,408,478,000,000 cubic meters (2021 est.)

Carbon dioxide emissions: 563.543 million metric tonnes of CO_2 (2019 est.)
from coal and metallurgical coke: 267.326 million metric tonnes of CO_2 (2019 est.)
from petroleum and other liquids: 209.279 million metric tonnes of CO_2 (2019 est.)
from consumed natural gas: 86.938 million metric tonnes of CO_2 (2019 est.)

Energy consumption per capita: 29.68 million Btu/person (2019 est.)

COMMUNICATIONS

Telephones - fixed lines: *total subscriptions:* 9,662,135 (2020 est.)
subscriptions per 100 inhabitants: 4 (2020 est.)

Telephones - mobile cellular: *total subscriptions:* 355,620,388 (2020 est.)
subscriptions per 100 inhabitants: 130 (2020 est.)

Telecommunication systems: *general assessment:* Indonesia faces more than the usual number of obstacles in terms of enabling widespread access to quality telecommunications services for its population of more than 270 million; the geographical challenges have been further compounded by a variety of social, political, and economic problems over the years that have kept the country's wealth distributed very thinly; the fixed-line (fiber) and mobile operators have continued to expand and upgrade their networks across the country; Indonesia's 18,000 islands (many of which, however, are sparsely populated) makes the deployment of fixed-line infrastructure on a broad scale difficult; there has been renewed activity in fiber optic cable, but the bundling of fixed-line telephony with TV and internet services will see the country's teledensity stabilize; mobile subscriptions have reached more than 130% and is projected to exceed 150% by 2026; with 4G LTE universally available, the major mobile companies have been busy launching 5G services in selected areas; the rollout of 5G will be hampered by the lack of availability of suitable frequencies; the 4G had to be reallocated from broadcasting services, and indications are that the same process is going to have to be followed in order to allow the expansion of 5G into its core frequency bands (3.3 to 4.2GHz) (2022)
domestic: fixed-line subscribership roughly 4 per 100 and mobile-cellular 130 per 100 persons (2020)
international: country code - 62; landing points for the SEA-ME-WE-3 & 5, DAMAI, JASUKA, BDM, Dumai-Melaka Cable System, IGG, JIBA, Link 1, 3, 4, & 5, PGASCOM, B3J2, Tanjung Pandam-Sungai Kakap Cable System, JAKABARE, JAYABAYA, INDIGO-West, Matrix Cable System, ASC, SJJK, Jaka2LaDeMa, S-U-B Cable System, JBCS, MKCS, BALOK, Palapa Ring East, West and Middle, SMPCS Packet-1 and 2, LTCS, TSCS, SEA-US and Kamal Domestic Submarine Cable System, 35 submarine cable networks that provide links throughout Asia, the Middle East, Australia, Southeast Asia, Africa and Europe; satellite earth stations - 2 Intelsat (1 Indian Ocean and 1 Pacific Ocean) (2019)

Broadcast media: mixture of about a dozen national TV networks - 1 public broadcaster, the remainder private broadcasters - each with multiple transmitters; more than 100 local TV stations; widespread use of satellite and cable TV systems; public radio broadcaster operates 6 national networks, as well as regional and local stations; overall, more than 700 radio stations with more than 650 privately operated (2019)

Internet country code: .id

Internet users: *total:* 147,702,755 (2020 est.)
percent of population: 54% (2020 est.)

Broadband - fixed subscriptions: *total:* 11,722,218 (2020 est.)
subscriptions per 100 inhabitants: 4 (2020 est.)

TRANSPORTATION

National air transport system: *number of registered air carriers:* 25 (2020)
inventory of registered aircraft operated by air carriers: 611
annual passenger traffic on registered air carriers: 115,154,100 (2018)
annual freight traffic on registered air carriers: 1,131,910,000 (2018) mt-km

Civil aircraft registration country code prefix: PK

Airports: *total:* 673 (2021)

Airports - with paved runways: *total:* 186
over 3,047 m: 5
2,438 to 3,047 m: 21
1,524 to 2,437 m: 51
914 to 1,523 m: 72
under 914 m: 37 (2021)

Airports - with unpaved runways: *total:* 487
1,524 to 2,437 m: 4
914 to 1,523 m: 23
under 914 m: 460 (2021)

Heliports: 76 (2021)

Pipelines: 1,064 km condensate, 150 km condensate/gas, 11,702 km gas, 119 km liquid petroleum gas, 7,767 km oil, 77 km oil/gas/water, 728 km refined products, 53 km unknown, 44 km water (2013)

Railways: *total:* 8,159 km (2014)
narrow gauge: 8,159 km (2014) 1.067-m gauge (565 km electrified)
note: 4,816 km operational

Roadways: *total:* 496,607 km (2011)
paved: 283,102 km (2011)
unpaved: 213,505 km (2011)

Waterways: 21,579 km (2011)

Merchant marine: *total:* 10,427
by type: bulk carrier 148, container ship 226, general cargo 2,238, oil tanker 676, other 7,139 (2021)

Ports and terminals: *major seaport(s):* Banjarmasin, Belawan, Kotabaru, Krueg Geukueh, Palembang, Panjang, Sungai Pakning, Tanjung Perak, Tanjung Priok
container port(s) (TEUs): Tanjung Perak (3,900,000), Tanjung Priok (7,600,000) (2019)

LNG terminal(s) (export): Bontang, Tangguh

LNG terminal(s) (import): Arun, Lampung, West Java

MILITARY AND SECURITY

Military and security forces: Indonesian National Armed Forces (Tentara Nasional Indonesia, TNI): Army (TNI-Angkatan Darat (TNI-AD)), Navy (TNI-Angkatan Laut (TNI-AL); includes Marine Corps (Korps Marinir or KorMar)), Air Force (TNI-Angkatan Udara (TNI-AU)) (2022)
note 1: in 2014, Indonesia created a Maritime Security Agency (Bakamla) to coordinate the actions of all maritime security agencies, including the Navy, the Indonesian Sea and Coast Guard (Kesatuan Penjagaan Laut dan Pantai, KPLP), the Water Police (Polair), Customs (Bea Cukai), and Ministry of Marine Affairs and Fisheries
note 2: the Indonesian National Police includes a paramilitary Mobile Brigade Corps (BRIMOB); following the Bali terror bombing in 2002, the National Police formed a special counterterrorism force called Detachment 88 (Densus or Detasemen Khusus 88 Antiteror); Detachment 88 often works with the TNI's Joint Special Operations Command, which has counterterrorism and counterinsurgency units

Military expenditures: 0.8% of GDP (2021 est.)
0.8% of GDP (2020)
0.8% of GDP (2019) (approximately $15.5 billion)
0.7% of GDP (2018) (approximately $14.5 billion)
0.9% of GDP (2017) (approximately $15.5 billion)

Military and security service personnel strengths: approximately 400,000 active duty troops (300,000

Army; 60,000 Navy, including about 20,000 marines; 30,000 Air Force) (2022)

Military equipment inventories and acquisitions: the Indonesian military inventory comes from a wide variety of sources; since 2010, the top suppliers have included China, France, Germany, the Netherlands, Russia, South Korea, the UK, and the US; the TNI has been engaged in a long-term modernization program since 2010 with uneven success; Indonesia has a growing defense industry fueled by technology transfers and cooperation agreements with several countries; in 2019, the Indonesian Government said that growing its domestic defense industry was a national priority over the following 10 years (2022)

Military service age and obligation: 18-45 years of age for voluntary military service, with selective conscription authorized (males, age 18), but not utilized; 2-year service obligation, with reserve obligation to age 45 (officers) (2021)

Military deployments: 225 (plus about 140 police) Central African Republic (MINUSCA); 1,025 Democratic Republic of the Congo (MONUSCO); 1,225 Lebanon (UNIFIL) (May 2022)

Military - note: as of 2022, Indonesian military and police forces were engaged in counter-insurgency operations in Papua against the West Papua Liberation Army, the military wing of the Free Papua Organization, which has been fighting a low-level insurgency since the 1960s when Indonesia annexed the former Dutch colony; since 2019, there has been an increase in militant activity in Papua and a larger Indonesian military presence; Papua was formally incorporated into Indonesia in 1969; in addition, the Indonesian military has been assisting police in Sulawesi in countering the Mujahideen Indonesia Timur (MIT; aka East Indonesia Mujahideen), a local militant group affiliated with the Islamic State of Iraq and ash-Sham (ISIS)

Indonesia is not a formal claimant in the South China Sea, although some of its waters lie within China's "nine-dash line" maritime claims, resulting in some stand offs in recent years; since 2016, the Indonesian military has bolstered its presence on Great Natuna Island (aka Pulau Natuna Besar), the main island of the Middle Natuna Archipelago, which is part of the Riau Islands Province, held military exercises in surrounding waters, and increased security cooperation (2022)

Maritime threats: the International Maritime Bureau continues to report the territorial and offshore waters in the Strait of Malacca and South China Sea as high risk for piracy and armed robbery against ships; the number of attacks decreased from 26 incidents in 2020 to nine in 2021 due to aggressive maritime patrolling by regional authorities; vessels continue to be boarded while anchored or berthed at Indonesian ports with seven vessels attacked; hijacked vessels are often disguised and cargo diverted to ports in East Asia

TERRORISM

Terrorist group(s): Islamic State of Iraq and ash-Sham (aka Jemaah Anshorut Daulah); Jemaah Islamiyah

TRANSNATIONAL ISSUES

Disputes - international: Indonesia has a stated foreign policy objective of establishing stable fixed land and maritime boundaries with all of its neighbors; three stretches of land borders with Timor-Leste have yet to be delimited, two of which are in the Oecussi exclave area, and no maritime or Exclusive Economic Zone (EEZ) boundaries have been established between the countries; all borders between Indonesia and Australia have been agreed upon bilaterally, but a 1997 treaty that would settle the last of their maritime and EEZ boundary has yet to be ratified by Indonesia's legislature; Indonesian groups challenge Australia's claim to Ashmore Reef; Australia has closed parts of the Ashmore and Cartier Reserve to Indonesian traditional fishing and placed restrictions on certain catches; land and maritime negotiations with Malaysia are ongoing, and disputed areas include the controversial Tanjung Datu and Camar Wulan border area in Borneo and the maritime boundary in the Ambalat oil block in the Celebes Sea; Indonesia and Singapore continue to work on finalizing their 1973 maritime boundary agreement by defining unresolved areas north of Indonesia's Batam Island; Indonesian secessionists, squatters, and illegal migrants create repatriation problems for Papua New Guinea; maritime delimitation talks continue with Palau; EEZ negotiations with Vietnam are ongoing, and the two countries in Fall 2011 agreed to work together to reduce illegal fishing along their maritime boundary

Refugees and internally displaced persons: *refugees (country of origin):* 5,792 (Afghanistan) (mid-year 2021)
IDPs: 73,000 (inter-communal, inter-faith, and separatist violence between 1998 and 2004 in Aceh and Papua; religious attacks and land conflicts in 2007 and 2013; most IDPs in Aceh, Maluku, East Nusa Tengarra) (2021)
stateless persons: 668 (mid-year 2021)

Illicit drugs: a transit and destination point for illicit narcotics; consumer of crystal methamphetamine trafficked in Burma and Pakistan and also transit to Australia and New Zealand; significant consumer of ecstasy from China and the Netherlands and domestically grown cannabis

IRAN

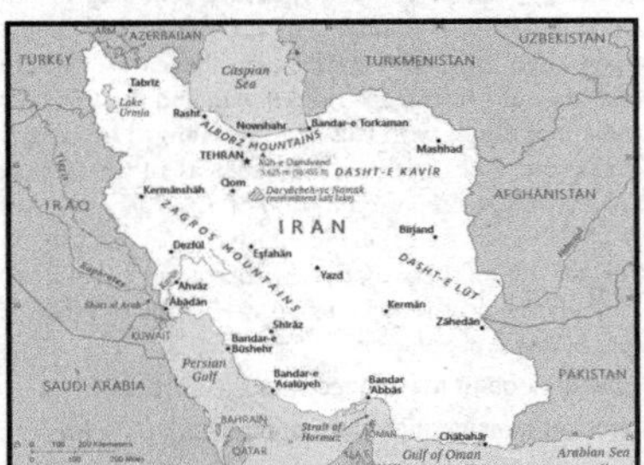

INTRODUCTION

Background: Known as Persia until 1935, Iran became an Islamic republic in 1979 after the ruling monarchy was overthrown and Shah Mohammad Reza PAHLAVI was forced into exile. Conservative clerical forces led by Ayatollah Ruhollah KHOMEINI established a theocratic system of government with ultimate political authority vested in a learned religious scholar referred to commonly as the Supreme Leader who, according to the constitution, is accountable only to the Assembly of Experts - a popularly elected 88-member body of clerics. US-Iranian relations became strained when a group of Iranian students seized the US Embassy in Tehran in November 1979 and held embassy personnel hostage until mid-January 1981. The US cut off diplomatic relations with Iran in April 1980. During the period 1980-88, Iran fought a bloody, indecisive war with Iraq that eventually expanded into the Persian Gulf and led to clashes between US Navy and Iranian military forces. Iran has been designated a state sponsor of terrorism and was subject to US, UN, and EU economic sanctions and export controls because of its continued involvement in terrorism and concerns over possible military dimensions of its nuclear program until Joint Comprehensive Plan of Action (JCPOA) Implementation Day in 2016. The US began gradually re-imposing sanctions on Iran after the US withdrawal from JCPOA in May 2018.

Following the election of reformer Hojjat ol-Eslam Mohammad KHATAMI as president in 1997 and a reformist Majles (legislature) in 2000, a campaign to foster political reform in response to popular dissatisfaction was initiated. The movement floundered as conservative politicians, supported by the Supreme Leader, unelected institutions of authority like the Council of Guardians, and the security services reversed and blocked reform measures while increasing security repression. Starting with nationwide municipal elections in 2003 and continuing through Majles elections in 2004, conservatives reestablished control over Iran's elected government institutions, which culminated with the August 2005 inauguration of hardliner Mahmud AHMADI-NEJAD as president. His controversial reelection in June 2009 sparked nationwide protests over allegations of electoral fraud, but the protests were quickly suppressed. Deteriorating economic conditions due primarily to government mismanagement and international sanctions prompted at least two major economically based protests in July and October 2012, but Iran's internal security situation remained stable. President AHMADI-NEJAD's independent streak angered regime establishment figures, including the Supreme Leader, leading to conservative opposition to his agenda for the last year of his presidency, and an alienation of his political supporters. In June 2013, Iranians elected a centrist cleric Dr. Hasan Fereidun RUHANI to the presidency. A longtime senior member in the regime, he made promises of reforming society and Iran's foreign policy. In July 2015, Iran and the five permanent members, plus Germany

(P5+1) signed the JCPOA under which Iran agreed to restrictions on its nuclear program in exchange for sanctions relief; however, the US reimposed sanctions in 2018 dealing a blow to RUHANI's legacy and the Iranian economy. Negotiations to restore the deal started in 2021 and are ongoing. Iran held elections in February 2020 for the Majles and the president in June 2021, resulting in a hardline and conservative monopoly across the regime's elected and unelected institutions. President Ebrahim RAISI is a hardline cleric with a decades-long career in Iran's judiciary and has had limited foreign policy and economic experience.

GEOGRAPHY

Location: Middle East, bordering the Gulf of Oman, the Persian Gulf, and the Caspian Sea, between Iraq and Pakistan

Geographic coordinates: 32 00 N, 53 00 E

Map references: Middle East

Area: *total:* 1,648,195 sq km
land: 1,531,595 sq km
water: 116,600 sq km

Area - comparative: almost 2.5 times the size of Texas; slightly smaller than Alaska

Land boundaries: *total:* 5,894 km
border countries (7): Afghanistan 921 km; Armenia 44 km; Azerbaijan 689 km; Iraq 1,599 km; Pakistan 959 km; Turkey 534 km; Turkmenistan 1,148 km

Coastline: 2,440 km - note: Iran also borders the Caspian Sea (740 km)

Maritime claims: *territorial sea:* 12 nm
contiguous zone: 24 nm
exclusive economic zone: bilateral agreements or median lines in the Persian Gulf
continental shelf: natural prolongation

Climate: mostly arid or semiarid, subtropical along Caspian coast

Terrain: rugged, mountainous rim; high, central basin with deserts, mountains; small, discontinuous plains along both coasts

Elevation: *highest point:* Kuh-e Damavand 5,625 m
lowest point: Caspian Sea -28 m
mean elevation: 1,305 m

Natural resources: petroleum, natural gas, coal, chromium, copper, iron ore, lead, manganese, zinc, sulfur

Land use: *agricultural land:* 30.1% (2018 est.)
arable land: 10.8% (2018 est.)
permanent crops: 1.2% (2018 est.)
permanent pasture: 18.1% (2018 est.)
forest: 6.8% (2018 est.)
other: 63.1% (2018 est.)

Irrigated land: 95,530 sq km (2012)

Major lakes (area sq km): *salt water lake(s):* Caspian Sea (shared with Russia, Azerbaijan, Turkmenistan, and Kazakhstan) - 374,000 sq km; Lake Urmia - 5,200 sq km; Lake Namak - 750 sq km

Major rivers (by length in km): Euphrates (shared with Turkey [s], Syria, and Iraq [m]) - 3,596 km; Tigris (shared with Turkey, Syria, and Iraq [m]) - 1,950 km; Helmand (shared with Afghanistan [s]) - 1,130 km
note – [s] after country name indicates river source; [m] after country name indicates river mouth

Major watersheds (area sq km): Indian Ocean drainage: *(Persian Gulf)* Tigris and Euphrates (918,044 sq km)

Population distribution: population is concentrated in the north, northwest, and west, reflecting the position of the Zagros and Elburz Mountains; the vast dry areas in the center and eastern parts of the country, around the deserts of the Dasht-e Kavir and Dasht-e Lut, have a much lower population density

Natural hazards: periodic droughts, floods; dust storms, sandstorms; earthquakes

Geography - note: strategic location on the Persian Gulf and Strait of Hormuz, which are vital maritime pathways for crude oil transport

PEOPLE AND SOCIETY

Population: 86,758,304 (2022 est.)

Nationality: *noun:* Iranian(s)
adjective: Iranian

Ethnic groups: Persian, Azeri, Kurd, Lur, Baloch, Arab, Turkmen, and Turkic tribes

Languages: Persian Farsi (official), Azeri and other Turkic dialects, Kurdish, Gilaki and Mazandarani, Luri, Balochi, Arabic
major-language sample(s):
ی برای کسب اطلاعات کلی جهان
چکیده نامه جهان، منبعی ضرور
(Persian)

Religions: Muslim (official) 99.6% (Shia 90-95%, Sunni 5-10%), other (includes Zoroastrian, Jewish, and Christian) 0.3%, unspecified 0.2% (2016 est.)

Age structure: *0-14 years:* 24.11% (male 10,472,844/female 10,000,028)
15-24 years: 13.36% (male 5,806,034/female 5,537,561)
25-54 years: 48.94% (male 21,235,038/female 20,327,384)
55-64 years: 7.72% (male 3,220,074/female 3,337,420)
65 years and over: 5.87% (male 2,316,677/female 2,670,254) (2020 est.)

Dependency ratios: *total dependency ratio:* 45.6
youth dependency ratio: 36
elderly dependency ratio: 9.6
potential support ratio: 14.2 (2020 est.)

Median age: *total:* 31.7 years
male: 31.5 years
female: 32 years (2020 est.)

Population growth rate: 0.98% (2022 est.)

Birth rate: 15.27 births/1,000 population (2022 est.)

Death rate: 5.17 deaths/1,000 population (2022 est.)

Net migration rate: -0.3 migrant(s)/1,000 population (2022 est.)

Population distribution: population is concentrated in the north, northwest, and west, reflecting the position of the Zagros and Elburz Mountains; the vast dry areas in the center and eastern parts of the country, around the deserts of the Dasht-e Kavir and Dasht-e Lut, have a much lower population density

Urbanization: *urban population:* 76.8% of total population (2022)
rate of urbanization: 1.32% annual rate of change (2020-25 est.)

Major urban areas - population: 9.382 million TEHRAN (capital), 3.318 million Mashhad, 2.219 million Esfahan, 1.699 million Shiraz, 1.644 million Tabriz, 1.587 million Karaj (2022)

Sex ratio: *at birth:* 1.05 male(s)/female
0-14 years: 1.05 male(s)/female
15-24 years: 1.05 male(s)/female
25-54 years: 1.05 male(s)/female
55-64 years: 0.96 male(s)/female
65 years and over: 0.77 male(s)/female
total population: 1.03 male(s)/female (2022 est.)

Maternal mortality ratio: 16 deaths/100,000 live births (2017 est.)

Infant mortality rate: *total:* 14.84 deaths/1,000 live births
male: 15.97 deaths/1,000 live births
female: 13.65 deaths/1,000 live births (2022 est.)

Life expectancy at birth: *total population:* 75.25 years
male: 73.89 years
female: 76.67 years (2022 est.)

Total fertility rate: 1.93 children born/woman (2022 est.)

Drinking water source: *improved: urban:* 99.8% of population
rural: 98.1% of population
total: 99.4% of population
unimproved: urban: 0.2% of population
rural: 1.9% of population
total: 0.6% of population (2020 est.)

Current health expenditure: 6.7% of GDP (2019)

Physicians density: 1.58 physicians/1,000 population (2018)

Hospital bed density: 1.6 beds/1,000 population (2017)

Sanitation facility access: *improved: urban:* 100% of population
rural: 100% of population
total: 100% of population

HIV/AIDS - adult prevalence rate: (2020 est.) <.1%

Major infectious diseases: *degree of risk:* intermediate (2020)
food or waterborne diseases: bacterial diarrhea
vectorborne diseases: Crimean-Congo hemorrhagic fever
note: a new coronavirus is causing sustained community spread of respiratory illness (COVID-19) in Iran; sustained community spread means that people have been infected with the virus, but how or where they became infected is not known, and the spread is ongoing; illness with this virus has ranged from mild to severe with fatalities reported; as of 18 August 2022, Iran has reported a total of 7,493,317 cases of COVID-19 or 8,921.36 cumulative cases of COVID-19 per 100,000 population with a total of 143,160 cumulative deaths or a rate 170.44 cumulative deaths per 100,000 population

Obesity - adult prevalence rate: 25.8% (2016)

Alcohol consumption per capita: *total:* 0.02 liters of pure alcohol (2019 est.)
beer: 0 liters of pure alcohol (2019 est.)
wine: 0 liters of pure alcohol (2019 est.)
spirits: 0.02 liters of pure alcohol (2019 est.)
other alcohols: 0 liters of pure alcohol (2019 est.)

Tobacco use: *total:* 13.6% (2020 est.)
male: 24.1% (2020 est.)
female: 3.1% (2020 est.)

Children under the age of 5 years underweight: 4.1% (2010/11)

Education expenditures: 3.7% of GDP (2019 est.)

Literacy: *definition:* age 15 and over can read and write
total population: 85.5%

male: 90.4%
female: 80.8% (2016)

School life expectancy (primary to tertiary education): *total:* 15 years
male: 15 years
female: 15 years (2017)

Unemployment, youth ages 15-24: *total:* 23.7%
male: 21.2%
female: 36% (2020 est.)

ENVIRONMENT

Environment - current issues: air pollution, especially in urban areas, from vehicle emissions, refinery operations, and industrial effluents; deforestation; overgrazing; desertification; oil pollution in the Persian Gulf; wetland losses from drought; soil degradation (salination); inadequate supplies of potable water; water pollution from raw sewage and industrial waste; urbanization

Environment - international agreements: *party to:* Biodiversity, Climate Change, Climate Change-Kyoto Protocol, Desertification, Endangered Species, Hazardous Wastes, Marine Dumping-London Convention, Marine Dumping-London Protocol, Nuclear Test Ban, Ozone Layer Protection, Ship Pollution, Wetlands
signed, but not ratified: Climate Change-Paris Agreement, Comprehensive Nuclear Test Ban, Environmental
Modification, Law of the Sea, Marine Life Conservation

Air pollutants: *particulate matter emissions:* 35.09 micrograms per cubic meter (2016 est.)
carbon dioxide emissions: 661.71 megatons (2016 est.)
methane emissions: 158.71 megatons (2020 est.)

Climate: mostly arid or semiarid, subtropical along Caspian coast

Land use: *agricultural land:* 30.1% (2018 est.)
arable land: 10.8% (2018 est.)
permanent crops: 1.2% (2018 est.)
permanent pasture: 18.1% (2018 est.)
forest: 6.8% (2018 est.)
other: 63.1% (2018 est.)

Urbanization: *urban population:* 76.8% of total population (2022)
rate of urbanization: 1.32% annual rate of change (2020-25 est.)

Revenue from forest resources: *forest revenues:* 0.01% of GDP (2017 est.)

Revenue from coal: *coal revenues:* 0.01% of GDP (2017 est.)

Waste and recycling: *municipal solid waste generated annually:* 17.885 million tons (2017 est.)
municipal solid waste recycled annually: 894,250 tons (2017 est.)
percent of municipal solid waste recycled: 5% (2017 est.)

Major lakes (area sq km): *salt water lake(s):* Caspian Sea (shared with Russia, Azerbaijan, Turkmenistan, and Kazakhstan) - 374,000 sq km; Lake Urmia - 5,200 sq km; Lake Namak - 750 sq km

Major rivers (by length in km): Euphrates (shared with Turkey [s], Syria, and Iraq [m]) - 3,596 km; Tigris (shared with Turkey, Syria, and Iraq [m]) - 1,950 km; Helmand (shared with Afghanistan [s]) - 1,130 km

note – [s] after country name indicates river source; [m] after country name indicates river mouth

Major watersheds (area sq km): Indian Ocean drainage: *(Persian Gulf)* Tigris and Euphrates (918,044 sq km)

Total water withdrawal: *municipal:* 6.2 billion cubic meters (2017 est.)
industrial: 1.1 billion cubic meters (2017 est.)
agricultural: 86 billion cubic meters (2017 est.)

Total renewable water resources: 137.045 billion cubic meters (2017 est.)

GOVERNMENT

Country name: *conventional long form:* Islamic Republic of Iran
conventional short form: Iran
local long form: Jomhuri-ye Eslami-ye Iran
local short form: Iran
former: Persia
etymology: name derives from the Avestan term "aryanam" meaning "Land of the Noble [Ones]"

Government type: theocratic republic

Capital: *name:* Tehran
geographic coordinates: 35 42 N, 51 25 E
time difference: UTC+3.5 (8.5 hours ahead of Washington, DC, during Standard Time)
daylight saving time: +1hr, begins fourth Wednesday in March; ends fourth Friday in September
etymology: various explanations of the city's name have been proffered, but the most plausible states that it derives from the Persian words *tah* meaning "end or bottom" and *ran* meaning "[mountain] slope" to signify "bottom of the mountain slope"; Tehran lies at the bottom slope of the Elburz Mountains

Administrative divisions: 31 provinces (ostanha, singular - ostan); Alborz, Ardabil, Azarbayjan-e Gharbi (West Azerbaijan), Azarbayjan-e Sharqi (East Azerbaijan), Bushehr, Chahar Mahal va Bakhtiari, Esfahan, Fars, Gilan, Golestan, Hamadan, Hormozgan, Ilam, Kerman, Kermanshah, Khorasan-e Jonubi (South Khorasan), Khorasan-e Razavi (Razavi Khorasan), Khorasan-e Shomali (North Khorasan), Khuzestan, Kohgiluyeh va Bowyer Ahmad, Kordestan, Lorestan, Markazi, Mazandaran, Qazvin, Qom, Semnan, Sistan va Baluchestan, Tehran, Yazd, Zanjan

Independence: 1 April 1979 (Islamic Republic of Iran proclaimed); notable earlier dates: ca. 550 B.C. (Achaemenid (Persian) Empire established); A.D. 1501 (Iran reunified under the Safavid Dynasty); 1794 (beginning of Qajar Dynasty); 12 December 1925 (modern Iran established under the PAHLAVI Dynasty)

National holiday: Republic Day, 1 April (1979)

Constitution: *history:* previous 1906; latest adopted 24 October 1979, effective 3 December 1979
amendments: proposed by the supreme leader – after consultation with the Exigency Council – and submitted as an edict to the "Council for Revision of the Constitution," a body consisting of various executive, legislative, judicial, and academic leaders and members; passage requires absolute majority vote in a referendum and approval of the supreme leader; articles including Iran's political system, its religious basis, and its form of government cannot be amended; amended 1989

Legal system: religious legal system based on secular and Islamic law

International law organization participation: has not submitted an ICJ jurisdiction declaration; non-party state to the ICCt

Citizenship: *citizenship by birth:* no
citizenship by descent only: the father must be a citizen of Iran
dual citizenship recognized: no
residency requirement for naturalization: 5 years

Suffrage: 18 years of age; universal

Executive branch: *chief of state:* Supreme Leader Ali Hoseini-KHAMENEI (since 4 June 1989)
head of government: President Ebrahim RAISI (since 18 June 2021); First Vice President Mohammad MOKHBER (since 8 August 2021)
cabinet: Council of Ministers selected by the president with legislative approval; the supreme leader has some control over appointments to several ministries
elections/appointments: supreme leader appointed for life by Assembly of Experts; president directly elected by absolute majority popular vote in 2 rounds if needed for a 4-year term (eligible for a second term and an additional nonconsecutive term); election last held on 18 June 2021 (next to be held in June 2025)
election results: 2021: Ebrahim RAISI elected president; percent of vote - Ebrahim RAISI (CCA) 72.4%, Mohsen REZAI (RFII) 13.8%, Abbdolnaser HEMATI (ECP) 9.8%, Amir-Hosein Qazizadeh-HASHEMI (Islamic Law Party) 4%
2017: Hasan Fereidun RUHANI reelected president; percent of vote - Hasan Fereidun RUHANI (Moderation and Development Party) 58.8%, Ebrahim RAISI (Combat Clergy Association) 39.4% , Mostafa Mir-SALIM Islamic Coalition Party) 1.2%, Mostafa HASHEMI-TABA (Executives of Construction Party) 0.5%
note: 3 oversight bodies are also considered part of the executive branch of government

Legislative branch: *description:* unicameral Islamic Consultative Assembly or Majles-e Shura-ye Eslami or Majles (290 seats; 285 members directly elected in single- and multi-seat constituencies by 2-round vote, and 1 seat each for Zoroastrians, Jews, Assyrian and Chaldean Christians, Armenians in the north of the country and Armenians in the south; members serve 4-year terms); note - all candidates to the Majles must be approved by the Council of Guardians, a 12-member group of which 6 are appointed by the supreme leader and 6 are jurists nominated by the judiciary and elected by the Majles
elections: first round held on 21 February 2020 and second round for 11 remaining seats held on 11 September 2020 (next full Majles election to be held in 2024)
election results: percent of vote by coalition (first round) - NA; seats by coalition (first round) - conservatives and hardliners 226, reformists 19, independents 40, religious minorities 5; as of June 2021 by-elections; composition - men 274, women 16, percent of women 5.6%

Judicial branch: *highest court(s):* Supreme Court (consists of the chief justice and organized into 42 two-bench branches, each with a justice and a judge)
judge selection and term of office: Supreme Court president appointed by the head of the High Judicial Council (HJC), a 5-member body to include the Supreme Court chief justice, the prosecutor general, and 3 clergy, in consultation with judges of the Supreme Court; president appointed for a single, renewable 5-year term; other judges appointed by the HJC; judge tenure NA

subordinate courts: Penal Courts I and II; Islamic Revolutionary Courts; Courts of Peace; Special Clerical Court (functions outside the judicial system and handles cases involving clerics); military courts

Political parties and leaders: Combatant Clergy Association [Mostafa POURMOHAMMADI] (an active political group)
Executives of Construction Party [Hossein MARASHI]
Followers of the Guardianship of the Jurisprudent [Ali LARIJANI]
Front of Islamic Revolutionary Stability [Sadegh MAHSOULI, secretary general]
Islamic Coalition Party [Asadollah BADAMCHIAN]
Islamic Iran Participation Front [associated with former President Mohammed KHATAMI]
Islamic Law Party
Militant Clerics Society (Majma-e Ruhaniyoun-e Mobarez) or MRM [Mohammad Mousavi KHOEINIHA]
Moderation and Development Party [Hassan ROUHANI]
National Trust Party (Hezb-e E'temad-eMelli) or HEM [Elias HAZRATI]
National Unity Party
Pervasive Coalition of Reformists [Ali SUFI, chairman] (includes Council for Coordinating the Reforms Front, National
Trust Party, Union of Islamic Iran People Party, Moderation and Development Party)
Principlists Grand Coalition (includes Combatant Clergy Association and Islamic Coalition Party, Society of Devotees and Pathseekers of the Islamic Revolution, Front of Islamic Revolution Stability)
Progress, Welfare, and Justice Front [Mohammad Saeed AHADIAN]
Progress and Justice Population of Islamic Iran or PJP [Hosein GHORBANZADEH, general secretary]
Resistance Front of Islamic Iran [Yadollah HABIBI, general secretary]
The Society of the Militant Clergy of Tehran (Jame'eh-ye Ruhaniyyat-e Mobarez-e Tehran) or JRM)
Union of Islamic Iran People's Party (Hezb-e Ettehad-e Iran-e Eslami) [Azar MANSOURI]
Wayfarers of the Islamic Revolution

International organization participation: CICA, CP, D-8, ECO, FAO, G-15, G-24, G-77, IAEA, IBRD, ICAO, ICC (national committees), ICRM, IDA, IDB, IFAD, IFC, IFRCS, IHO, ILO, IMF, IMO, IMSO, Interpol, IOC, IOM, IPU, ISO, ITSO, ITU, MIGA, NAM, OIC, OPCW, OPEC, PCA, SAARC (observer), SCO (observer), UN, UNAMID, UNCTAD, UNESCO, UNHCR, UNIDO, UNITAR, UNWTO, UPU, WCO, WFTU (NGOs), WHO, WIPO, WMO, WTO (observer)

Diplomatic representation in the US: *chief of mission:* none; Iran has an Interests Section in the Pakistani Embassy; address: Iranian Interests Section, Embassy of Pakistan, 1250 23rd Street NW, Washington, DC 20037; telephone: [1] (202) 965-4990; FAX [1] (202) 965-1073; info@daftar.org

Diplomatic representation from the US: *embassy:* none; the US Interests Section is located in the Embassy of Switzerland; US Foreign Interests Section, Embassy of Switzerland, Pasdaran, Shahid Mousavi Street (Golestan 5th), Corner of Paydarfard Street, No. 55, Tehran

Flag description: three equal horizontal bands of green (top), white, and red; the national emblem (a stylized representation of the word Allah in the shape of a tulip, a symbol of martyrdom) in red is centered in the white band; ALLAH AKBAR (God is Great) in white Arabic script is repeated 11 times along the bottom edge of the green band and 11 times along the top edge of the red band; green is the color of Islam and also represents growth, white symbolizes honesty and peace, red stands for bravery and martyrdom

National symbol(s): lion; national colors: green, white, red

National anthem: *name:* "Soroud-e Melli-ye Jomhouri-ye Eslami-ye Iran" (National Anthem of the Islamic Republic of Iran)
lyrics/music: multiple authors/Hassan RIAHI
note 1: adopted 1990; Iran has had six national anthems; the first, entitled "Salam-e Shah" (Royal Salute) was in use from 1873-1909; next came "Salamati-ye Dowlat-e Elliye-ye Iran" (Salute of the Sublime State of Persia, 1909-1933); it was followed by "Sorud-e melli" (The Imperial Anthem of Iran; 1933-1979), which chronicled the exploits of the Pahlavi Dynasty; "Ey Iran" (Oh Iran) functioned unofficially as the national anthem for a brief period between the ouster of the Shah in 1979 and the early days of the Islamic Republic in 1980; "Payandeh Bada Iran" (Long Live Iran) was used between 1980 and 1990 during the time of Ayatollah KHOMEINI
note 2: a recording of the current Iranian national anthem is unavailable since the US Navy Band does not record anthems for countries from which the US does not anticipate official visits; the US does not have diplomatic relations with Iran

National heritage: *total World Heritage Sites:* 26 (24 cultural, 2 natural)
selected World Heritage Site locales: Persepolis (c); Tchogha Zanbil (c); Bam and its Cultural Landscape (c); Golestan Palace (c); Shushtar Historical Hydraulic System (c); Pasargadae (c); Hyrcanian Forests (n); Tabriz Historic Bazaar Complex (c); Meidan Emam, Esfahan (c); Bisotun (c)

ECONOMY

Economic overview: Iran's economy is marked by statist policies, inefficiencies, and reliance on oil and gas exports, but Iran also possesses significant agricultural, industrial, and service sectors. The Iranian government directly owns and operates hundreds of state-owned enterprises and indirectly controls many companies affiliated with the country's security forces. Distortions - including corruption, price controls, subsidies, and a banking system holding billions of dollars of non-performing loans - weigh down the economy, undermining the potential for private-sector-led growth.

Private sector activity includes small-scale workshops, farming, some manufacturing, and services, in addition to medium-scale construction, cement production, mining, and metalworking. Significant informal market activity flourishes and corruption is widespread.

The lifting of most nuclear-related sanctions under the Joint Comprehensive Plan of Action (JCPOA) in January 2016 sparked a restoration of Iran's oil production and revenue that drove rapid GDP growth, but economic growth declined in 2017 as oil production plateaued. The economy continues to suffer from low levels of investment and declines in productivity since before the JCPOA, and from high levels of unemployment, especially among women and college-educated Iranian youth.

In May 2017, the re-election of President Hasan RUHANI generated widespread public expectations that the economic benefits of the JCPOA would expand and reach all levels of society. RUHANI will need to implement structural reforms that strengthen the banking sector and improve Iran's business climate to attract foreign investment and encourage the growth of the private sector. Sanctions that are not related to Iran's nuclear program remain in effect, and these—plus fears over the possible re-imposition of nuclear-related sanctions—will continue to deter foreign investors from engaging with Iran.

Real GDP (purchasing power parity): $1,044,310,000,000 (2020 est.)
$1,027,240,000,000 (2019 est.)
$1.102 trillion (2018 est.)
note: data are in 2017 dollars

Real GDP growth rate: 3.7% (2017 est.)
12.5% (2016 est.)
-1.6% (2015 est.)

Real GDP per capita: $12,400 (2020 est.)
$12,400 (2019 est.)
$13,500 (2018 est.)
note: data are in 2017 dollars

GDP (official exchange rate): $581.252 billion (2019 est.)

Inflation rate (consumer prices): 10% (2017 est.)
9.6% (2017 est.)
9.1% (2016 est.)
note: official Iranian estimate

GDP - composition, by sector of origin: *agriculture:* 9.6% (2016 est.)
industry: 35.3% (2016 est.)
services: 55% (2017 est.)

GDP - composition, by end use: *household consumption:* 49.7% (2017 est.)
government consumption: 14% (2017 est.)
investment in fixed capital: 20.6% (2017 est.)
investment in inventories: 14.5% (2017 est.)
exports of goods and services: 26% (2017 est.)
imports of goods and services: -24.9% (2017 est.)

Agricultural products: wheat, sugar cane, milk, sugar beet, tomatoes, barley, potatoes, oranges, poultry, apples

Industries: petroleum, petrochemicals, gas, fertilizer, caustic soda, textiles, cement and other construction materials, food processing (particularly sugar refining and vegetable oil production), ferrous and nonferrous metal fabrication, armaments

Industrial production growth rate: 3% (2017 est.)

Labor force: 30.5 million (2017 est.)
note: shortage of skilled labor

Labor force - by occupation: *agriculture:* 16.3%
industry: 35.1%
services: 48.6% (2013 est.)

Unemployment rate: 11.8% (2017 est.)
12.4% (2016 est.)
note: data are Iranian Government numbers

Unemployment, youth ages 15-24: *total:* 23.7%
male: 21.2%
female: 36% (2020 est.)

Population below poverty line: 18.7% (2007 est.)

Gini Index coefficient - distribution of family income: 40.8 (2017 est.)

Household income or consumption by percentage share: *lowest 10%:* 2.6%
highest 10%: 29.6% (2005)

Budget: *revenues:* 74.4 billion (2017 est.)

expenditures: 84.45 billion (2017 est.)

Budget surplus (+) or deficit (-): -2.3% (of GDP) (2017 est.)

Public debt: 39.5% of GDP (2017 est.)
47.5% of GDP (2016 est.)
note: includes publicly guaranteed debt

Taxes and other revenues: 17.3% (of GDP) (2017 est.)

Fiscal year: 21 March - 20 March

Current account balance: $9.491 billion (2017 est.)
$16.28 billion (2016 est.)

Exports: $101.4 billion (2017 est.)
$83.98 billion (2016 est.)

Exports - partners: China 48%, India 12%, South Korea 8%, Turkey 6%, United Arab Emirates 5% (2019)

Exports - commodities: crude petroleum, polymers, industrial alcohols, iron, pistachios (2019)

Imports: $76.39 billion (2017 est.)
$63.14 billion (2016 est.)

Imports - partners: China 28%, United Arab Emirates 20%, India 11%, Turkey 7%, Brazil 6%, Germany 5% (2019)

Imports - commodities: rice, corn, broadcasting equipment, soybean products, beef (2019)

Reserves of foreign exchange and gold: $120.6 billion (31 December 2017 est.)
$133.7 billion (31 December 2016 est.)

Debt - external: $7.995 billion (31 December 2017 est.)
$8.196 billion (31 December 2016 est.)

Exchange rates: Iranian rials (IRR) per US dollar -
32,769.7 (2017 est.)
30,914.9 (2016 est.)
30,914.9 (2015 est.)
29,011.5 (2014 est.)
25,912 (2013 est.)

ENERGY

Electricity access: *electrification - total population:* 100% (2020)

Electricity: *installed generating capacity:* 80.553 million kW (2020 est.)
consumption: 279,826,390,000 kWh (2019 est.)
exports: 6.365 billion kWh (2019 est.)
imports: 2.738 billion kWh (2019 est.)
transmission/distribution losses: 34.303 billion kWh (2019 est.)

Electricity generation sources: *fossil fuels:* 88.7% of total installed capacity (2020 est.)
nuclear: 1.9% of total installed capacity (2020 est.)
solar: 0.1% of total installed capacity (2020 est.)
wind: 0.2% of total installed capacity (2020 est.)
hydroelectricity: 9.1% of total installed capacity (2020 est.)

Coal: *production:* 2.783 million metric tons (2020 est.)
consumption: 2.794 million metric tons (2020 est.)
exports: 76,000 metric tons (2020 est.)
imports: 87,000 metric tons (2020 est.)
proven reserves: 1.203 billion metric tons (2019 est.)

Petroleum: *total petroleum production:* 3,450,300 bbl/day (2021 est.)
refined petroleum consumption: 1.934 million bbl/day (2019 est.)
crude oil and lease condensate exports: 2,230,900 bbl/day (2018 est.)
crude oil and lease condensate imports: 33,500 bbl/day (2018 est.)
crude oil estimated reserves: 208.6 billion barrels (2021 est.)

Refined petroleum products - production: 1.764 million bbl/day (2015 est.)

Refined petroleum products - exports: 397,200 bbl/day (2015 est.)

Refined petroleum products - imports: 64,160 bbl/day (2015 est.)

Natural gas: *production:* 237,561,415,000 cubic meters (2019 est.)
consumption: 220,704,282,000 cubic meters (2019 est.)
exports: 17,607,046,000 cubic meters (2019 est.)
imports: 1,153,457,000 cubic meters (2019 est.)
proven reserves: 33,987,296,000,000 cubic meters (2021 est.)

Carbon dioxide emissions: 646.038 million metric tonnes of CO_2 (2019 est.)
from coal and metallurgical coke: 5.142 million metric tonnes of CO_2 (2019 est.)
from petroleum and other liquids: 204.21 million metric tonnes of CO_2 (2019 est.)
from consumed natural gas: 436.687 million metric tonnes of CO_2 (2019 est.)

Energy consumption per capita: 145.54 million Btu/person (2019 est.)

COMMUNICATIONS

Telephones - fixed lines: *total subscriptions:* 29,093,587 (2020 est.)
subscriptions per 100 inhabitants: 35 (2020 est.)

Telephones - mobile cellular: *total subscriptions:* 127,624,951 (2020 est.)
subscriptions per 100 inhabitants: 152 (2020 est.)

Telecommunication systems: *general assessment:* Iran's telecom infrastructure has suffered from sanctions in recent years, which prevented the import of equipment and devices and encouraged widespread smuggling, with a consequent loss of tax revenue; to address this, the government introduced a device registration scheme, and bolstered the capacity for domestically manufactured mobile phones; companies have invested in broadening the reach of their LTE networks, which has increased network capacity and improved the quality of mobile broadband services; the country is also looking to 5G; the sector is still limited by low frequency bands; the government is addressing this with plans to reallocate the 3.5GHz band for 5G use; Iran is keen to grow its digital economy; Iran offers significant opportunities for growth in the telecoms sector; the country has one of the largest populations in the Middle East, and there is a high proportion of youthful, tech savvy users having considerable demand for both fixed and mobile telecom services; companies are offering national roaming to improve services in rural areas (2022)
domestic: approximately 35 per 100 for fixed-line and 152 per 100 for mobile-cellular subscriptions (2020)
international: country code - 98; landing points for Kuwait-Iran, GBICS & MENA, FALCON, OMRAN/3PEG Cable System, POI and UAE-Iran submarine fiber-optic cable to the Middle East, Africa and India; (TAE) fiber-optic line runs from Azerbaijan through the northern portion of Iran to Turkmenistan with expansion to Georgia and Azerbaijan; HF radio and microwave radio relay to Turkey, Azerbaijan, Pakistan, Afghanistan, Turkmenistan, Syria, Kuwait, Tajikistan, and Uzbekistan; satellite earth stations - 13 (9 Intelsat and 4 Inmarsat) (2019)

Broadcast media: state-run broadcast media with no private, independent broadcasters; Islamic Republic of Iran Broadcasting (IRIB), the state-run TV broadcaster, operates 19 nationwide channels including a news channel, about 34 provincial channels, and several international channels; about 20 foreign Persian-language TV stations broadcasting on satellite TV are capable of being seen in Iran; satellite dishes are illegal and, while their use is subjectively tolerated, authorities confiscate satellite dishes from time to time; IRIB operates 16 nationwide radio networks, a number of provincial stations, and an external service; most major international broadcasters transmit to Iran (2019)

Internet country code: .ir

Internet users: *total:* 75,594,081 (2020 est.)
percent of population: 84% (2020 est.)

Broadband - fixed subscriptions: *total:* 9,564,195 (2020 est.)
subscriptions per 100 inhabitants: 11 (2020 est.)

TRANSPORTATION

National air transport system: *number of registered air carriers:* 22 (2020)
inventory of registered aircraft operated by air carriers: 237
annual passenger traffic on registered air carriers: 25,604,871 (2018)
annual freight traffic on registered air carriers: 290.74 million (2018) mt-km

Civil aircraft registration country code prefix: EP

Airports: *total:* 319 (2021)

Airports - with paved runways: *total:* 140
over 3,047 m: 42
2,438 to 3,047 m: 29
1,524 to 2,437 m: 26
914 to 1,523 m: 36
under 914 m: 7 (2021)

Airports - with unpaved runways: *total:* 179
over 3,047 m: 1
2,438 to 3,047 m: 2
1,524 to 2,437 m: 9
914 to 1,523 m: 135
under 914 m: 32 (2021)

Heliports: 26 (2021)

Pipelines: 7 km condensate, 973 km condensate/gas, 20,794 km gas, 570 km liquid petroleum gas, 8,625 km oil, 7,937 km refined products (2013)

Railways: *total:* 8,483.5 km (2014)
standard gauge: 8,389.5 km (2014) 1.435-m gauge (189.5 km electrified)
broad gauge: 94 km (2014) 1.676-m gauge

Roadways: *total:* 223,485 km (2018)
paved: 195,485 km (2018)
unpaved: 28,000 km (2018)

Waterways: 850 km (2012) (on Karun River; some navigation on Lake Urmia)

Merchant marine: *total:* 893
by type: bulk carrier 32, container ship 31, general cargo 371, oil tanker 84, other 375 (2021)

Ports and terminals: *major seaport(s):* Bandar-e Asaluyeh, Bandar Abbas, Bandar-e Emam Khomeyni
container port(s) (TEUs): Bandar Abbas

MILITARY AND SECURITY

Military and security forces: the military forces of Iran are divided between the Islamic Republic of Iran Regular Forces (Artesh) and the Islamic Revolutionary Guard Corps (Sepah)

Islamic Republic of Iran Regular Forces or Islamic Republic of Iran Army (Artesh): Ground Forces, Navy (includes marines), Air Force, Air Defense Forces; Islamic Revolutionary Guard Corps (IRGC or Sepah): Ground Forces, Navy (includes marines), Aerospace Force (controls strategic missile force), Qods Force (aka Quds Force; special operations), Cyber Electronic Command, Basij Paramilitary Forces; Law Enforcement Forces (2022)

note 1: the Artesh Navy operates Iran's larger warships and operates in the Gulf of Oman, the Caspian Sea, and deep waters in the region and beyond; the IRGC Navy has responsibility for the closer-in Persian Gulf and Strait of Hormuz

note 2: the Basij is a volunteer paramilitary group under the IRGC with local organizations across the country, which sometimes acts as an auxiliary law enforcement unit; it is formally known as the Organization for the Mobilization of the Oppressed; it is also known as the Popular Mobilization Army

note 3: Law Enforcement Forces include border and security troops

Military expenditures: 2.3% of GDP (2021 est.)
2.1% of GDP (2020 est.)
2.5% of GDP (2019 est.) (approximately $22.8 billion)
3.4% of GDP (2018 est.) (approximately $29.1 billion)
3.4% of GDP (2017 est.) (approximately $31.2 billion)

Military and security service personnel strengths: information varies; approximately 550-600,000 active armed forces personnel; approximately 400,000 Islamic Republic of Iran Regular Forces (350,000 Ground Forces; 18,000 Navy; 40,000 Air Force/Air Defense Forces); approximately 150-190,000 Islamic Revolutionary Guard Corps (100-150,000 Ground Forces; 20,000 Navy; 15,000 Aerospace Force; 5-15,000 Qods Force); estimated 90,000 active Basij Paramilitary Forces (2022)

Military equipment inventories and acquisitions: the Iranian military's inventory includes a mix of domestically-produced and mostly older foreign equipment largely of Chinese, Russian, Soviet, and US origin (US equipment acquired prior to the Islamic Revolution in 1979); Iran has also received some military equipment from North Korea, including midget submarines and ballistic missiles; Iran has a defense industry with the capacity to develop, produce, support, and sustain air, land, missile, and naval weapons programs (2021)

Military service age and obligation: 18 years of age for men for compulsory military service; 16 years of age for volunteers; 17 years of age for Law Enforcement Forces; 15 years of age for Basij Forces (Popular Mobilization Army); conscript military service obligation is 18-24 months, depending on the location of service (soldiers serving in places of high security risk and deprived areas serve shorter terms); women exempt from military service (2021)

note: as of 2019, approximately 80% of Artesh ground forces personnel were conscripts, while Navy and Air/Air Defense Force personnel were primarily volunteers; conscripts reportedly comprised more than 50% of the IRGC

Military deployments: estimated to have up to 3,000 military personnel in Syria (2022)
note: Iran has recruited, trained, and funded thousands of Syrian and foreign fighters to support the ASAD regime during the Syrian civil war

Military - note: the Islamic Revolutionary Guard Corps (IRGC) was formed in May 1979 in the immediate aftermath of Shah Mohammad Reza PAHLAVI's fall, as leftists, nationalists, and Islamists jockeyed for power; while the interim prime minister controlled the government and state institutions, such as the Army, followers of Ayatollah Ruhollah KHOMEINI organized counterweights, including the IRGC, to protect the Islamic revolution; the IRGC's command structure bypassed the elected president and went directly to KHOMEINI; the Iran-Iraq War (1980–88) transformed the IRGC into more of a conventional fighting force with its own ground, air, naval, and special forces, plus control over Iran's strategic missile and rocket forces; as of 2022, the IRGC was a highly institutionalized and parallel military force to Iran's regular armed forces (Artesh); it was heavily involved in internal security and had significant influence in the political and economic spheres of Iranian society, as well as Iran's foreign policy; on the economic front, it owned factories and corporations and subsidiaries in banking, infrastructure, housing, airlines, tourism and other sectors; its special operations forces, known as the Qods/Quds Force, specialized in foreign missions and has provided advice, funding, guidance, material support, training, and weapons to militants in countries such as Afghanistan, Iraq, Syria, and Yemen, as well as extremist groups, including HAMAS, Hizballah, Kata'ib Hizballah, and Palestine Islamic Jihad (see Appendix T for additional details on the IRGC and Qods Force); the Qods Force also conducts intelligence and reconnaissance operations

the Supreme Council for National Security (SCNS) is the senior-most body for formulating Iran's foreign and security policy; it is formally chaired by the president, who also appoints the SCNS secretary; its members include the speaker of the Majles, the head of the judiciary, the chief of the Armed Forces General Staff (chief of defense or CHOD), the commanders of the Artesh (regular forces) and IRGC, and the ministers of defense, foreign affairs, interior, and intelligence; the SCNS reports to the supreme leader; the supreme leader is the commander-in-chief of the armed forces (2022)

Maritime threats: the Maritime Administration of the US Department of Transportation has issued a Maritime Advisory (2022-003 Persian Gulf, Strait of Hormuz, Gulf of Oman, Arabian Sea, Red Sea-Threats to US and International Shipping from Iran) effective 28 February 2022, which states in part that "heightened military activities and increased political tensions in this region continue to present risk to commercial shipping...there is a continued possibility that Iran and/or its regional proxies could take actions against US and partner interests in the region;" Coalition Task Force (CTF) Sentinel has been established to provide escorts for commercial shipping transiting the Persian Gulf, Strait of Hormuz, and Gulf of Oman

TERRORISM

Terrorist group(s): Islamic Revolutionary Guard Corps (IRGC)/Qods Force; Islamic State of Iraq and ash-Sham (ISIS); Jaysh al Adl (Jundallah); Kurdistan Workers' Party (PKK); al-Qa'ida

TRANSNATIONAL ISSUES

Disputes - international: *Iran-Afghanistan*: Iran protests Afghanistan's limiting flow of dammed Helmand River tributaries during drought; Afghan and Iranian commissioners have discussed boundary monument densification and resurvey
Iran-Azerbaijan-Kazakhstan-Russia: Azerbaijan, Kazakhstan, and Russia ratified a Caspian seabed delimitation treaty in 2018 based on equidistance, while Iran continues to insist on a one-fifth slice of the sea
Iran-Iraq: Iraq's lack of a maritime boundary with Iran prompts jurisdiction disputes beyond the mouth of the Shatt al Arab in the Persian Gulf
Iran-UAE: Iran and UAE dispute Tunb Islands and Abu Musa Island, which are occupied by Iran; the dispute was rehashed at the September 2021 UN General Assembly meeting; Iran's Islamic Revolution Guards Corp opened an airport on Greater Tunb in February 2022

Refugees and internally displaced persons: *refugees (country of origin):* 2.6 million undocumented Afghans, 780,000 Afghan refugee card holders, 20,000 Iraqi refugee card holders (2020)
stateless persons: 34 (mid-year 2021)

Trafficking in persons: *current situation:* Iran is a presumed source, transit, and destination country for men, women, and children subjected to sex trafficking and forced labor; Iranian and Afghan boys and girls are forced into prostitution domestically; Iranian women are subjected to sex trafficking in Iran, Pakistan, the Persian Gulf, and Europe; Azerbaijani women and children are also sexually exploited in Iran; Afghan migrants and refugees and Pakistani men and women are subjected to conditions of forced labor in Iran; NGO reports indicate that criminal organizations play a significant role in human trafficking in Iran
tier rating: Tier 3 — Iran does not fully meet the minimum standards for the elimination of trafficking and is not making significant efforts to do so; therefore, Iran remained in Tier 3; the government continued a policy of recruiting and using child soldiers, government officials perpetrated sex trafficking of adults and children and continued trafficking both in Iran and overseas; the government continued to force or coerce children and adults to fight for Iranian-led militias operating in Syria and provided financial support to militias fighting in armed conflicts in the region using child soldiers; authorities failed to identify and protect trafficking victims among vulnerable populations; law enforcement treated trafficking victims as criminals, facing severe punishment or death for unlawful acts traffickers compelled them to commit (2020)

Illicit drugs: significant transit and destination country for opiates and cannabis products mainly from Afghanistan; produces and consumes methamphetamine and traffics it to international markets; one of the primary transshipment routes for Southwest Asian heroin to Europe

IRAQ

INTRODUCTION

Background: Formerly part of the Ottoman Empire, Iraq was occupied by the United Kingdom during World War I and was declared a League of Nations mandate under UK administration in 1920. Iraq attained its independence as a kingdom in 1932. It was proclaimed a "republic" in 1958 after a coup overthrew the monarchy, but in actuality, a series of strongmen ruled the country until 2003. The last was SADDAM Husayn from 1979 to 2003. Territorial disputes with Iran led to an inconclusive and costly eight-year war (1980-88). In August 1990, Iraq seized Kuwait but was expelled by US-led UN coalition forces during the Gulf War of January-February 1991. After Iraq's expulsion, the UN Security Council (UNSC) required Iraq to scrap all weapons of mass destruction and long-range missiles and to allow UN verification inspections. Continued Iraqi noncompliance with UNSC resolutions led to the Second Gulf War in March 2003 and the ouster of the SADDAM Husayn regime by US-led forces.

In October 2005, Iraqis approved a constitution in a national referendum and, pursuant to this document, elected a 275-member Council of Representatives (COR) in December 2005. The COR approved most cabinet ministers in May 2006, marking the transition to Iraq's first constitutional government in nearly a half century. Iraq held elections for provincial councils in all governorates - except for Iraq's Kurdistan Region and Kirkuk - in January 2009 and in April and June 2013, and has repeatedly postponed the next provincial elections, originally planned for April 2017. Iraq has held four national legislative elections since 2006, most recently in October 2021 when 329 legislators were elected to the COR. The acting Iraqi National Intelligence Service Director General Mustafa al-KADHIMI became prime minister in May 2020 after the previous prime minister resigned in late 2019 because of widespread protests demanding more employment opportunities and an end to corruption. His mandate as prime minister was to guide Iraq toward an early national legislative election, which was held in October 2021.

Between 2014 and 2017, Iraq was engaged in a military campaign against the Islamic State of Iraq and ash-Sham (ISIS) to recapture territory lost in the western and northern portion of the country. Iraqi and allied forces recaptured Mosul, the country's second-largest city, in 2017 and drove ISIS out of its other urban strongholds. In December 2017, then-Prime Minister Haydar al-ABADI publicly declared victory against ISIS while continuing operations against the group's residual presence in rural areas. Also in late 2017, ABADI responded to an independence referendum held by the Kurdistan Regional Government by ordering Iraqi forces to take control of disputed territories across central and northern Iraq that were previously occupied and governed by Kurdish forces.

GEOGRAPHY

Location: Middle East, bordering the Persian Gulf, between Iran and Kuwait

Geographic coordinates: 33 00 N, 44 00 E

Map references: Middle East

Area: *total:* 438,317 sq km
land: 437,367 sq km
water: 950 sq km

Area - comparative: slightly more than three times the size of New York state

Land boundaries: *total:* 3,809 km
border countries (6): Iran 1,599 km; Jordan 179 km; Kuwait 254 km; Saudi Arabia 811 km; Syria 599 km; Turkey 367 km

Coastline: 58 km

Maritime claims: *territorial sea:* 12 nm
continental shelf: not specified

Climate: mostly desert; mild to cool winters with dry, hot, cloudless summers; northern mountainous regions along Iranian and Turkish borders experience cold winters with occasionally heavy snows that melt in early spring, sometimes causing extensive flooding in central and southern Iraq

Terrain: mostly broad plains; reedy marshes along Iranian border in south with large flooded areas; mountains along borders with Iran and Turkey

Elevation: *highest point:* Cheekha Dar (Kurdish for "Black Tent") 3,611 m
lowest point: Persian Gulf 0 m
mean elevation: 312 m

Natural resources: petroleum, natural gas, phosphates, sulfur

Land use: *agricultural land:* 18.1% (2018 est.)
arable land: 8.4% (2018 est.)
permanent crops: 0.5% (2018 est.)
permanent pasture: 9.2% (2018 est.)
forest: 1.9% (2018 est.)
other: 80% (2018 est.)

Irrigated land: 35,250 sq km (2012)

Major lakes (area sq km): *fresh water lake(s):* Lake Hammar - 1,940 sq km

Major rivers (by length in km): Euphrates river mouth (shared with Turkey[s], Syria, and Iran) - 3,596 km; Tigris river mouth (shared with Turkey[s], Syria, and Iran) - 1,950 km; the Tigris and Euphrates join to form the Shatt al Arab
note – [s] after country name indicates river source; [m] after country name indicates river mouth

Major watersheds (area sq km): Indian Ocean drainage: *(Persian Gulf)* Tigris and Euphrates (918,044 sq km)

Major aquifers: Arabian Aquifer System

Population distribution: population is concentrated in the north, center, and eastern parts of the country, with many of the larger urban agglomerations found along extensive parts of the Tigris and Euphrates Rivers; much of the western and southern areas are either lightly populated or uninhabited

Natural hazards: dust storms; sandstorms; floods

Geography - note: strategic location on Shatt al Arab waterway and at the head of the Persian Gulf

PEOPLE AND SOCIETY

Population: 40,462,701 (2022 est.)

Nationality: *noun:* Iraqi(s)
adjective: Iraqi

Ethnic groups: Arab 75-80%, Kurdish 15-20%, other 5% (includes Turkmen, Yezidi, Shabak, Kaka'i, Bedouin, Romani, Assyrian, Circassian, Sabaean-Mandaean, Persian)
note: data is a 1987 government estimate; no more recent reliable numbers are available

Languages: Arabic (official), Kurdish (official), Turkmen (a Turkish dialect), Syriac (Neo-Aramaic), and Armenian are official in areas where native speakers of these languages constitute a majority of the population
major-language sample(s):
كتاب حقائق العالم، أحسن مصدر للمعلومات الأساسية
(Arabic)

Religions: Muslim (official) 95-98% (Shia 61-64%, Sunni 29-34%), Christian 1% (includes Catholic, Orthodox, Protestant, Assyrian Church of the East), other 1-4% (2015 est.)
note: the last census in Iraq was in 1997; while there has been voluntary relocation of many Christian families to northern Iraq, the overall Christian population has decreased at least 50% and perhaps as high as 90% since the fall of the SADDAM Husayn regime in 2003, according to US Embassy estimates, with many fleeing to Syria, Jordan, and Lebanon

Age structure: *0-14 years:* 37.02% (male 7,349,868/female 7,041,405)
15-24 years: 19.83% (male 3,918,433/female 3,788,157)
25-54 years: 35.59% (male 6,919,569/female 6,914,856)
55-64 years: 4.23% (male 805,397/female 839,137)
65 years and over: 3.33% (male 576,593/female 719,240) (2020 est.)

Dependency ratios: *total dependency ratio:* 69.9
youth dependency ratio: 64.1
elderly dependency ratio: 5.9
potential support ratio: 17.1 (2020 est.)

Median age: *total:* 21.2 years
male: 20.8 years
female: 21.6 years (2020 est.)

Population growth rate: 2% (2022 est.)

Birth rate: 24.7 births/1,000 population (2022 est.)

Death rate: 3.9 deaths/1,000 population (2022 est.)

Net migration rate: -0.83 migrant(s)/1,000 population (2022 est.)

Population distribution: population is concentrated in the north, center, and eastern parts of the country, with many of the larger urban agglomerations found along extensive parts of the Tigris and Euphrates Rivers; much of the western and southern areas are either lightly populated or uninhabited

Urbanization: *urban population:* 71.4% of total population (2022)
rate of urbanization: 2.91% annual rate of change (2020-25 est.)

Major urban areas - population: 7.512 million BAGHDAD (capital), 1.737 million Mosul, 1.414 million Basra, 1.052 million Kirkuk, 930,000 Najaf, 878,000 Erbil (2022)

Sex ratio: *at birth:* 1.05 male(s)/female
0-14 years: 1.04 male(s)/female
15-24 years: 1.04 male(s)/female
25-54 years: 1 male(s)/female
55-64 years: 0.97 male(s)/female
65 years and over: 0.65 male(s)/female
total population: 1.01 male(s)/female (2022 est.)

Maternal mortality ratio: 79 deaths/100,000 live births (2017 est.)

Infant mortality rate: *total:* 19.62 deaths/1,000 live births
male: 21.34 deaths/1,000 live births
female: 17.83 deaths/1,000 live births (2022 est.)

Life expectancy at birth: *total population:* 73.18 years
male: 71.3 years
female: 75.15 years (2022 est.)

Total fertility rate: 3.25 children born/woman (2022 est.)

Contraceptive prevalence rate: 52.8% (2018)

Drinking water source: *improved: urban:* 100% of population
rural: 97.4% of population
total: 99.3% of population
unimproved: urban: 0% of population
rural: 2.6% of population
total: 0.7% of population (2020 est.)

Current health expenditure: 4.5% of GDP (2019)

Physicians density: 0.97 physicians/1,000 population (2020)

Hospital bed density: 1.3 beds/1,000 population (2017)

Sanitation facility access: *improved: urban:* 100% of population
rural: 100% of population *total:* 100% of population

Major infectious diseases: *degree of risk:* intermediate (2020)
food or waterborne diseases: bacterial diarrhea, hepatitis A, and typhoid fever
note: widespread ongoing transmission of a respiratory illness caused by the novel coronavirus (COVID-19) is occurring throughout Iraq; as of 18 August 2022, Iraq has reported a total of 2,454,213 cases of COVID-19 or 6,101.59 cumulative cases of COVID-19 per 100,000 population with a total of 25,338 cumulative deaths or a rate of 62.99 cumulative deaths per 100,000 population; as of 7 August 2022, 25.30% of the population has received at least one dose of COVID-19 vaccine

Obesity - adult prevalence rate: 30.4% (2016)

Alcohol consumption per capita: *total:* 0.16 liters of pure alcohol (2019 est.)
beer: 0.11 liters of pure alcohol (2019 est.)
wine: 0 liters of pure alcohol (2019 est.)
spirits: 0.04 liters of pure alcohol (2019 est.)
other alcohols: 0 liters of pure alcohol (2019 est.)

Tobacco use: *total:* 18.5% (2020 est.)
male: 35.1% (2020 est.)
female: 1.8% (2020 est.)

Children under the age of 5 years underweight: 3.9% (2018)

Child marriage: *women married by age 15:* 7.2%
women married by age 18: 27.9% (2018 est.)

Literacy: *definition:* age 15 and over can read and write
total population: 85.6%
male: 91.2%
female: 79.9% (2017)

Unemployment, youth ages 15-24: *total:* 25.6%
male: 22%
female: 63.3% (2017)

ENVIRONMENT

Environment - current issues: government water control projects drained most of the inhabited marsh areas east of An Nasiriyah by drying up or diverting the feeder streams and rivers; a once sizable population of Marsh Arabs, who inhabited these areas for thousands of years, has been displaced; furthermore, the destruction of the natural habitat poses serious threats to the area's wildlife populations; inadequate supplies of potable water; soil degradation (salination) and erosion; desertification; military and industrial infrastructure has released heavy metals and other hazardous substances into the air, soil, and groundwater; major sources of environmental damage are effluents from oil refineries, factory and sewage discharges into rivers, fertilizer and chemical contamination of the soil, and industrial air pollution in urban areas

Environment - international agreements: *party to:* Biodiversity, Climate Change, Climate Change-Kyoto Protocol, Comprehensive Nuclear Test Ban, Desertification, Endangered Species, Hazardous Wastes, Law of the Sea, Nuclear Test Ban, Ozone Layer Protection, Ship Pollution, Wetlands
signed, but not ratified: Climate Change-Paris Agreement, Environmental Modification

Air pollutants: *particulate matter emissions:* 57.73 micrograms per cubic meter (2016 est.)
carbon dioxide emissions: 190.06 megatons (2016 est.)
methane emissions: 17.44 megatons (2020 est.)

Climate: mostly desert; mild to cool winters with dry, hot, cloudless summers; northern mountainous regions along Iranian and Turkish borders experience cold winters with occasionally heavy snows that melt in early spring, sometimes causing extensive flooding in central and southern Iraq

Land use: *agricultural land:* 18.1% (2018 est.)
arable land: 8.4% (2018 est.)
permanent crops: 0.5% (2018 est.)
permanent pasture: 9.2% (2018 est.)
forest: 1.9% (2018 est.)
other: 80% (2018 est.)

Urbanization: *urban population:* 71.4% of total population (2022)
rate of urbanization: 2.91% annual rate of change (2020-25 est.)

Revenue from forest resources: *forest revenues:* 0% of GDP (2018 est.)

Revenue from coal: *coal revenues:* 0% of GDP (2018 est.)

Food insecurity: *severe localized food insecurity: due to civil conflict and economic slowdown* - the 2022 Humanitarian Needs Overview identified 2.5 million people in need of humanitarian assistance, of which 960,000 have acute humanitarian needs; while the number of people in need remained similar to the previous year, the severity of those needs increased, largely due to the impact of the COVID-19 pandemic on top of an existing humanitarian crisis, leading to a 35% increase in the number of people in acute need; more than half of these are concentrated in the governorates of Nineveh and Anbar; the number of severely food insecure people is estimated at about 435,000, while 731,000 are vulnerable to food insecurity (2022)

Waste and recycling: *municipal solid waste generated annually:* 13.14 million tons (2015 est.)

Major lakes (area sq km): *fresh water lake(s):* Lake Hammar - 1,940 sq km

Major rivers (by length in km): Euphrates river mouth (shared with Turkey[s], Syria, and Iran) - 3,596 km; Tigris river mouth (shared with Turkey[s], Syria, and Iran) - 1,950 km; the Tigris and Euphrates join to form the Shatt al Arab
note – [s] after country name indicates river source; [m] after country name indicates river mouth

Major watersheds (area sq km): Indian Ocean drainage: *(Persian Gulf)* Tigris and Euphrates (918,044 sq km)

Major aquifers: Arabian Aquifer System

Total water withdrawal: *municipal:* 1.23 billion cubic meters (2017 est.)
industrial: 2.05 billion cubic meters (2017 est.)
agricultural: 35.27 billion cubic meters (2017 est.)

Total renewable water resources: 89.86 billion cubic meters (2017 est.)

GOVERNMENT

Country name: *conventional long form:* Republic of Iraq
conventional short form: Iraq
local long form: Jumhuriyat al-Iraq/Komar-i Eraq
local short form: Al Iraq/Eraq
former: Mesopotamia, Mandatory Iraq, Hashemite Kingdom of Iraq
etymology: the name probably derives from "Uruk" (Biblical "Erech"), the ancient Sumerian and Babylonian city on the Euphrates River

Government type: federal parliamentary republic

Capital: *name:* Baghdad
geographic coordinates: 33 20 N, 44 24 E
time difference: UTC+3 (8 hours ahead of Washington, DC, during Standard Time)
etymology: although the origin of the name is disputed, it likely has compound Persian roots with *bagh* and *dad* meaning "god" and "given" respectively to create the meaning of "bestowed by God"

Administrative divisions: 18 governorates (muhafazat, singular - muhafazah (Arabic); parezgakan,

singular - parezga (Kurdish)); 'Al Anbar; Al Basrah; Al Muthanna; Al Qadisiyah (Ad Diwaniyah); An Najaf; Arbil (Erbil) (Arabic), Hewler (Kurdish); As Sulaymaniyah (Arabic), Slemani (Kurdish); Babil; Baghdad; Dahuk (Arabic), Dihok (Kurdish); Dhi Qar; Diyala; Karbala'; Kirkuk; Maysan; Ninawa; Salah ad Din; Wasit
note: Iraq's Kurdistan Regional Government administers Arbil, Dahuk, and As Sulaymaniyah (as Hewler, Dihok, and Slemani respectively)

Independence: 3 October 1932 (from League of Nations mandate under British administration); note - on 28 June 2004 the Coalition Provisional Authority transferred sovereignty to the Iraqi Interim Government

National holiday: Independence Day, 3 October (1932); Republic Day, 14 July (1958)

Constitution: *history:* several previous; latest adopted by referendum 15 October 2005
amendments: proposed by the president of the republic and the Council of Minsters collectively, or by one fifth of the Council of Representatives members; passage requires at least two-thirds majority vote by the Council of Representatives, approval by referendum, and ratification by the president; passage of amendments to articles on citizen rights and liberties requires two-thirds majority vote of Council of Representatives members after two successive electoral terms, approval in a referendum, and ratification by the president

Legal system: mixed legal system of civil and Islamic law

International law organization participation: has not submitted an ICJ jurisdiction declaration; non-party state to the ICCt

Citizenship: *citizenship by birth:* no
citizenship by descent only: at least one parent must be a citizen of Iraq
dual citizenship recognized: yes
residency requirement for naturalization: 10 years

Suffrage: 18 years of age; universal

Executive branch: *chief of state:* President Abdul Latif RASHID (since 13 October 2022; vice presidents (vacant)
head of government: Prime Minister-Designate Mohammed Shia al-SUDANI (since 13 October 2022)
cabinet: Council of Ministers proposed by the prime minister, approved by Council of Representatives
elections/appointments: president indirectly elected by Council of Representatives (COR) to serve a 4-year term (eligible for a second term); COR parliamentary election for president last held on 13 October 2022 (next to be held in 2026)
election results:
2022: COR vote in first round - Abdul Latif RASHID (PUK) 157, Barham SALIH (PUK) 99; Abdul Latif RASHID elected president in second round - Abdul latif RASHID 167, Barham SALIH 99
2018: COR vote in first round - Barham SALIH (PUK) 165, Fuad HUSAYN (KDP) 90; Barham SALIH elected president in second round - Barham SALIH 219, Fuad HUSAYN 22; note - the COR vote on 1 October 2018 failed due to a lack of quorum, and a new session was held on 2 October 2018
2014: Fuad MASUM elected president in first round; COR vote - Fuad MASUM (PUK) 211, Barham SALIH (PUK) 17; Haydar al-ABADI (Da'wa Party) approved as prime minister

Legislative branch: *description:* unicameral Council of Representatives of Iraq (COR) or Majlis an-Nuwwab al-Iraqiyy (329 seats; 320 members directly elected in 83 multi-seat constituencies by single nontransferable vote, 9 seats reserved for minorities - 5 for Christians, 1 each for Sabaean-Mandaeans, Yazidis, Shabaks, Fayli Kurds, and 25% of seats allocated to women; members serve 4-year terms); note - in late 2020, the COR approved an electoral law, replacing the proportional representation voting system with the single non-transferable system
elections: last held on 10 October 2021 (next to be held in October 2025)
election results: percent of vote by party/coalition - NA; seats by party/coalition - Sadrist Bloc 73, National Progress Alliance 37, State of Law Coalition 33, Kurdish Democratic Party 31, Al Fatah Alliance 17, Kurdistan Alliance 17, Al Iraq Alliance 14, New Generation Movement 14, Ishraqet Konoon 6, Tasmin Alliance 5, Babylon Movement 4, National Contract Alliance 4, National State Forces Alliance 4, other 22, independent 43; composition - men 234, women 95, percent of women 28.9%

Judicial branch: *highest court(s):* Federal Supreme Court or FSC (consists of 9 judges); note - court jurisdiction limited to constitutional issues, application of federal laws, ratification of election results for the COR, judicial competency disputes, and disputes between regions or governorates and the central government; Court of Cassation (consists of a court president, 5 vice presidents, and at least 24 judges)
judge selection and term of office: Federal Supreme Court judges nominated by the HJC President, the FSC Chief Justice, the Public Prosecutor's Office chief, and the head of the Judicial Oversight Commission; FSC members required to retire at age 72; Court of Cassation judges appointed by the HJC and confirmed by the Council of Representatives to serve until retirement nominally at age 63, but can be extended to age 66 by the HJC
subordinate courts: Courts of Appeal (governorate level); civil courts, including first instance, personal status, labor, and customs; criminal courts including felony, misdemeanor, investigative, major crimes, juvenile, and traffic courts

Political parties and leaders: Al Fatah Alliance [Hadi al-AMIRI]
Azm Alliance [Khamis al-KHANJAR]
Babylon Movement [Rayan al-KILDANI]
Imtidad
Ishraqet Konoon [Jaafar AZIZ]
Kurdistan Democratic Party or KDP [Masoud BARZANI]
National Contract Alliance [Falih al-FAYYADH]
National State Forces Alliance [Ammar al-HAKIM]
National Wisdom Trend [Ammar al-HAKIM]
New Generation Movement or Naway Nwe [SHASWAR Abd al-Wahid Qadir]
Patriotic Union of Kurdistan or PUK [Bafel TALABANI]
Sadrist Movement [Muqtada al-SADR]
State of Law Coalition [Nuri al-MALIKI]
Taqadum or Progress Party [Muhammad al-HALBUSI]
Tasmin Alliance [Sarah al-SALIHI]
numerous smaller independent, religious, local, tribal, and minority parties

International organization participation: ABEDA, AFESD, AMF, CAEU, CICA, EITI (compliant country), FAO, G-77, IAEA, IBRD, ICAO, ICRM, IDA, IDB, IFAD, IFC, IFRCS, ILO, IMF, IMO, IMSO, Interpol, IOC, IPU, ISO, ITSO, ITU, LAS, MIGA, NAM, OAPEC, OIC, OPCW, OPEC, PCA, UN, UNCTAD, UNESCO, UNIDO, UNWTO, UPU, WCO, WFTU (NGOs), WHO, WIPO, WMO, WTO (observer)

Diplomatic representation in the US: *chief of mission:* Ambassador (vacant); Charge d'Affaires Mohammed Husham Malik AL FITYAN (since 22 March 2022)
chancery: 3421 Massachusetts Avenue NW, Washington, DC 20007
telephone: [1] (202) 742-1600
FAX: [1] (202) 333-1129
email address and website:
http://www.iraqiembassy.us/
consulate(s) general: Detroit, Los Angeles

Diplomatic representation from the US: *chief of mission:* Ambassador Alina L. ROMANOWSKI (since 2 June 2022)
embassy: Al-Kindi Street, International Zone, Baghdad; note - consulate in Al Basrah closed as of 28 September 2018
mailing address: 6060 Baghdad Place, Washington DC 20521-6060
telephone: 0760-030-3000
email address and website:
BaghdadACS@state.gov
https://iq.usembassy.gov/

Flag description: three equal horizontal bands of red (top), white, and black; the Takbir (Arabic expression meaning "God is great") in green Arabic script is centered in the white band; the band colors derive from the Arab Liberation flag and represent oppression (black), overcome through bloody struggle (red), to be replaced by a bright future (white); the Council of Representatives approved this flag in 2008 as a compromise replacement for the Ba'thist SADDAM-era flag
note: similar to the flag of Syria, which has two stars but no script; Yemen, which has a plain white band; and that of Egypt, which has a golden Eagle of Saladin centered in the white band

National symbol(s): golden eagle; national colors: red, white, black

National anthem: *name:* "Mawtini" (My Homeland)
lyrics/music: Ibrahim TOUQAN/Mohammad FLAYFEL
note: adopted 2004; following the ouster of SADDAM Husayn, Iraq adopted "Mawtini," a popular folk song throughout the Arab world; also serves as an unofficial anthem of the Palestinian people

National heritage: *total World Heritage Sites:* 6 (5 cultural, 1 mixed)
selected World Heritage Site locales: Ashur (Qal'at Sherqat) (c); Babylon (c); Erbil Citadel (c); Hatra (c); Samarra Archaeological City (c); The Ahwar (Marshland) of Southern Iraq: Refuge of Biodiversity and the Relict Landscape of the Mesopotamian Cities (m)

ECONOMY

Economic overview: Iraq's GDP growth slowed to 1.1% in 2017, a marked decline compared to the previous two years as domestic consumption and investment fell because of civil violence and a sluggish oil market. The Iraqi Government received its third tranche of funding from its 2016 Stand-By

Arrangement (SBA) with the IMF in August 2017, which is intended to stabilize its finances by encouraging improved fiscal management, needed economic reform, and expenditure reduction. Additionally, in late 2017 Iraq received more than $1.4 billion in financing from international lenders, part of which was generated by issuing a $1 billion bond for reconstruction and rehabilitation in areas liberated from ISIL. Investment and key sector diversification are crucial components to Iraq's long-term economic development and require a strengthened business climate with enhanced legal and regulatory oversight to bolster private-sector engagement. The overall standard of living depends on global oil prices, the central government passage of major policy reforms, a stable security environment post-ISIS, and the resolution of civil discord with the Kurdish Regional Government (KRG).

Iraq's largely state-run economy is dominated by the oil sector, which provides roughly 85% of government revenue and 80% of foreign exchange earnings, and is a major determinant of the economy's fortunes. Iraq's contracts with major oil companies have the potential to further expand oil exports and revenues, but Iraq will need to make significant upgrades to its oil processing, pipeline, and export infrastructure to enable these deals to reach their economic potential.

In 2017, Iraqi oil exports from northern fields were disrupted following a KRG referendum that resulted in the Iraqi Government reasserting federal control over disputed oil fields and energy infrastructure in Kirkuk. The Iraqi government and the KRG dispute the role of federal and regional authorities in the development and export of natural resources. In 2007, the KRG passed an oil law to develop IKR oil and gas reserves independent of the federal government. The KRG has signed about 50 contracts with foreign energy companies to develop its reserves, some of which lie in territories taken by Baghdad in October 2017. The KRG is able to unilaterally export oil from the fields it retains control of through its own pipeline to Turkey, which Baghdad claims is illegal. In the absence of a national hydrocarbons law, the two sides have entered into five provisional oil- and revenue-sharing deals since 2009, all of which collapsed.

Iraq is making slow progress enacting laws and developing the institutions needed to implement economic policy, and political reforms are still needed to assuage investors' concerns regarding the uncertain business climate. The Government of Iraq is eager to attract additional foreign direct investment, but it faces a number of obstacles, including a tenuous political system and concerns about security and societal stability. Rampant corruption, outdated infrastructure, insufficient essential services, skilled labor shortages, and antiquated commercial laws stifle investment and continue to constrain growth of private, nonoil sectors. Under the Iraqi constitution, some competencies relevant to the overall investment climate are either shared by the federal government and the regions or are devolved entirely to local governments. Investment in the IKR operates within the framework of the Kurdistan Region Investment Law (Law 4 of 2006) and the Kurdistan Board of Investment, which is designed to provide incentives to help economic development in areas under the authority of the KRG.

Inflation has remained under control since 2006. However, Iraqi leaders remain hard-pressed to translate macroeconomic gains into an improved standard of living for the Iraqi populace. Unemployment remains a problem throughout the country despite a bloated public sector. Overregulation has made it difficult for Iraqi citizens and foreign investors to start new businesses. Corruption and lack of economic reforms - such as restructuring banks and developing the private sector – have inhibited the growth of the private sector.

Real GDP (purchasing power parity): $372.27 billion (2020 est.)
$415.32 billion (2019 est.)
$397.64 billion (2018 est.)
note: data are in 2017 dollars

Real GDP growth rate: -2.1% (2017 est.)
13.1% (2016 est.)
2.5% (2015 est.)

Real GDP per capita: $9,300 (2020 est.)
$10,600 (2019 est.)
$10,300 (2018 est.)
note: data are in 2017 dollars

GDP (official exchange rate): $231.994 billion (2019 est.)

Inflation rate (consumer prices): -0.1% (2019 est.)
0.3% (2018 est.)
0.2% (2017 est.)

Credit ratings:

Fitch rating: B- (2015)

Moody's rating: Caa1 (2017)

Standard & Poors rating: B- (2015)
note: The year refers to the year in which the current credit rating was first obtained.

GDP - composition, by sector of origin: *agriculture:* 3.3% (2017 est.)
industry: 51% (2017 est.)
services: 45.8% (2017 est.)

GDP - composition, by end use: *household consumption:* 50.4% (2013 est.)
government consumption: 22.9% (2016 est.)
investment in fixed capital: 20.6% (2016 est.)
investment in inventories: 0% (2016 est.)
exports of goods and services: 32.5% (2016 est.)
imports of goods and services: -40.9% (2016 est.)

Agricultural products: wheat, barley, dates, tomatoes, rice, maize, grapes, potatoes, rice, watermelons

Industries: petroleum, chemicals, textiles, leather, construction materials, food processing, fertilizer, metal fabrication/processing

Industrial production growth rate: 0.7% (2017 est.)

Labor force: 8.9 million (2010 est.)

Labor force - by occupation: *agriculture:* 21.6%
industry: 18.7%
services: 59.8% (2008 est.)

Unemployment rate: 16% (2012 est.)
15% (2010 est.)

Unemployment, youth ages 15-24: *total:* 25.6%
male: 22%
female: 63.3% (2017)

Population below poverty line: 23% (2014 est.)

Gini Index coefficient - distribution of family income: 29.5 (2012 est.)

Household income or consumption by percentage share: *lowest 10%:* 3.6%
highest 10%: 25.7% (2007 est.)

Budget: *revenues:* 68.71 billion (2017 est.)
expenditures: 76.82 billion (2017 est.)

Budget surplus (+) or deficit (-): -4.2% (of GDP) (2017 est.)

Public debt: 59.7% of GDP (2017 est.)
66% of GDP (2016 est.)

Taxes and other revenues: 35.7% (of GDP) (2017 est.)

Fiscal year: calendar year

Current account balance: $4.344 billion (2017 est.)
-$13.38 billion (2016 est.)

Exports: $50.61 billion (2020 est.) note: data are in current year dollars
$88.9 billion (2019 est.) note: data are in current year dollars
$91.93 billion (2018 est.) note: data are in current year dollars

Exports - partners: China 26%, India 24%, South Korea 9%, United States 8%, Italy 6%, Greece 6% (2019)

Exports - commodities: crude petroleum, refined petroleum, gold, dates, petroleum coke (2019)

Imports: $54.72 billion (2020 est.) note: data are in current year dollars
$72.28 billion (2019 est.) note: data are in current year dollars
$56.88 billion (2018 est.) note: data are in current year dollars

Imports - partners: United Arab Emirates 28%, Turkey 21%, China 19% (2019)

Imports - commodities: refined petroleum, broadcasting equipment, cars, jewelry, cigarettes (2019)

Reserves of foreign exchange and gold: $48.88 billion (31 December 2017 est.)
$45.36 billion (31 December 2016 est.)

Debt - external: $73.02 billion (31 December 2017 est.)
$64.16 billion (31 December 2016 est.)

Exchange rates: Iraqi dinars (IQD) per US dollar -
1,184 (2017 est.)
1,182 (2016 est.)
1,182 (2015 est.)
1,167.63 (2014 est.)
1,213.72 (2013 est.)

ENERGY

Electricity access: *electrification - total population:* 100% (2020)

Electricity: *installed generating capacity:* 28.369 million kW (2020 est.)
consumption: 46,492,540,000 kWh (2019 est.)
exports: 0 kWh (2019 est.)
imports: 14.18 billion kWh (2019 est.)
transmission/distribution losses: 58.502 billion kWh (2019 est.)

Electricity generation sources: *fossil fuels:* 97.8% of total installed capacity (2020 est.)
solar: 0.1% of total installed capacity (2020 est.)
hydroelectricity: 2.1% of total installed capacity (2020 est.)

Petroleum: *total petroleum production:* 4,161,500 bbl/day (2021 est.)
refined petroleum consumption: 863,300 bbl/day (2019 est.)
crude oil and lease condensate exports: 3,975,800 bbl/day (2018 est.)
crude oil and lease condensate imports: 0 bbl/day (2018 est.)

crude oil estimated reserves: 145.019 billion barrels (2021 est.)

Refined petroleum products - production: 398,000 bbl/day (2015 est.)

Refined petroleum products - exports: 8,284 bbl/day (2015 est.)

Refined petroleum products - imports: 255,100 bbl/day (2015 est.)

Natural gas: *production:* 10,710,773,000 cubic meters (2019 est.)
consumption: 18,014,129,000 cubic meters (2019 est.)
exports: 0 cubic meters (2021 est.)
imports: 7,303,356,000 cubic meters (2019 est.)
proven reserves: 3,728,926,000,000 cubic meters (2021 est.)

Carbon dioxide emissions: 143.479 million metric tonnes of CO2 (2019 est.)
from petroleum and other liquids: 108.14 million metric tonnes of CO2 (2019 est.)
from consumed natural gas: 35.339 million metric tonnes of CO2 (2019 est.)

Energy consumption per capita: 63.174 million Btu/person (2019 est.)

COMMUNICATIONS

Telephones - fixed lines: *total subscriptions:* 2,699,758 (2020 est.)
subscriptions per 100 inhabitants: 7 (2020 est.)

Telephones - mobile cellular: *total subscriptions:* 37,475,325 (2020 est.)
subscriptions per 100 inhabitants: 93 (2020 est.)

Telecommunication systems: *general assessment:* Iraq continues to face a number of political and economic challenges, though increasing civil stability has made it easier for mobile and fixed-line operators to rebuild telecom services and infrastructure damaged during the last few years; the government extended the licenses held by the MNOs for an additional three years to compensate for the chaos and destruction caused between 2014 and 2017 when Islamic State held sway in many areas of the country; the companies have struggled to develop LTE services; most services are still based on GSM and 3G, except in the Kurdish region where LTE is more widely available (2022)
domestic: about 7 per 100 for fixed-line and 93 per 100 for mobile-cellular subscriptions (2020)
international: country code - 964; landing points for FALCON, and GBICS/MENA submarine cables providing connections to the Middle East, Africa and India; satellite earth stations - 4 (2 Intelsat - 1 Atlantic Ocean and 1 Indian Ocean, 1 Intersputnik - Atlantic Ocean region, and 1 Arabsat (inoperative)); local microwave radio relay connects border regions to Jordan, Kuwait, Syria, and Turkey (2019)

Broadcast media: the number of private radio and TV stations has increased rapidly since 2003; government-owned TV and radio stations are operated by the publicly funded Iraqi Media Network; private broadcast media are mostly linked to political, ethnic, or religious groups; satellite TV is available to an estimated 70% of viewers and many of the broadcasters are based abroad; transmissions of multiple international radio broadcasters are accessible (2019)

Internet country code: .iq

Internet users: *total:* 24,133,502 (2020 est.)
percent of population: 60% (2020 est.)

Broadband - fixed subscriptions: *total:* 6,254,099 (2020 est.)
subscriptions per 100 inhabitants: 16 (2020 est.)

TRANSPORTATION

National air transport system: *number of registered air carriers:* 4 (2020)
inventory of registered aircraft operated by air carriers: 34
annual passenger traffic on registered air carriers: 2,075,065 (2018)
annual freight traffic on registered air carriers: 16.2 million (2018) mt-km

Civil aircraft registration country code prefix: YI

Airports: *total:* 102 (2021)

Airports - with paved runways: *total:* 72
over 3,047 m: 20
2,438 to 3,047 m: 34
1,524 to 2,437 m: 4
914 to 1,523 m: 7
under 914 m: 7 (2021)

Airports - with unpaved runways: *total:* 30
over 3,047 m: 3
2,438 to 3,047 m: 5
1,524 to 2,437 m: 3
914 to 1,523 m: 13
under 914 m: 6 (2021)

Heliports: 16 (2021)

Pipelines: 2,455 km gas, 913 km liquid petroleum gas, 5,432 km oil, 1,637 km refined products (2013)

Railways: *total:* 2,272 km (2014)
standard gauge: 2,272 km (2014) 1.435-m gauge

Roadways: *total:* 59,623 km (2012)
paved: 59,623 km (2012) (includes Kurdistan region)

Waterways: 5,279 km (2012) (the Euphrates River (2,815 km), Tigris River (1,899 km), and Third River (565 km) are the principal waterways)

Merchant marine: *total:* 68
by type: general cargo 1, oil tanker 6, other 61 (2021)

Ports and terminals: *river port(s):* Al Basrah (Shatt al Arab); Khawr az Zubayr, Umm Qasr (Khawr az Zubayr waterway)

MILITARY AND SECURITY

Military and security forces: Ministry of Defense: Iraqi Army, Army Aviation Command, Iraqi Navy, Iraqi Air Force, Iraqi Air Defense Command, Special Forces Command, Special Security Division (Green Zone protection)
National-Level Security Forces: Iraqi Counterterrorism Service (CTS), Prime Minister's Special Forces Division, Presidential Brigades
Ministry of Interior: Federal Police Forces Command, Border Guard Forces Command, Federal Intelligence and Investigations Agency, Emergency Response Division, Facilities Protection Directorate, and Provincial Police
Ministry of Oil: Energy Police Directorate
Kurdistan Regional Government Ministry of Peshmerga: Regional Guard Brigades, Unit (or Division) 70 Forces, Unit (or Division) 80 Forces, special operations/counter-terrorism forces (Counter Terrorism Group, CTG and Counter Terrorism Directorate, CTD); note - Unit 70 and the CTG are associated with the Patriotic Union of Kurdistan (PUK) political party, while Unit 80 and the CTD are associated with the Kurdistan Democratic Party (KDP); Kurdistan Regional Government Ministry of Interior: Zeravani and Emergency Response Forces (paramilitary internal security forces)
Popular Mobilization Committee (PMC): Popular Mobilization Forces (PMF), Tribal Mobilization Forces (TMF); the PMF and TMF are a collection of approximately 60 militias of widely varied sizes and political interests (2022)

Military expenditures: 3.7% of GDP (2021 est.)
4.1% of GDP (2020 est.)
3.8% of GDP (2019 est.) (approximately $14.6 billion)
4.5% of GDP (2018 est.) (approximately $16 billion)
6% of GDP (2017 est.) (approximately $20.4 billion)

Military and security service personnel strengths: information varies; approximately 200,000 personnel under the Ministry of Defense (190,000 Army/Aviation Command/Special Forces; 5,000 Navy; 5,000 Air/Air Defense Forces); approximately 25,000 National-Level Security Forces; Ministry of Peshmerga: approximately 150,000-plus (45-50,000 Regional Guard Brigades; 40-45,000 Unit 70 Forces; 65-70,000 Unit 80 Forces); estimated 100-160,000 Popular Mobilization Forces (2022)

Military equipment inventories and acquisitions: the Iraqi military's inventory includes a mix of equipment from a wide variety of sources, including Europe, South Africa, South Korea, Russia, and the US; since 2010, Russia and the US have been the leading suppliers of military hardware to Iraq (2022)

Military service age and obligation: 18-40 years of age for voluntary military service; no conscription (2022)
note: service in the armed forces was mandatory in Iraq from 1935 up until 2003

Military - note: as of 2022, Iraqi security forces (ISF) continued to conduct counterinsurgency and counterterrorism operations against the Islamic State of Iraq and ash-Sham (ISIS) terrorist group, particularly in northern and western Iraq; Kurdish Security Forces (KSF, aka Peshmerga) also conducted operations against ISIS

the KSF were formally recognized as a legitimate Iraqi military force under the country's constitution and have operated jointly with the Iraqi military against ISIS militants, but they also operate outside of Iraqi military command structure; since 2021, the ISF and the KSF have conducted joint counter-ISIS operations in an area known as the Kurdish Coordination Line (KCL), a swath of disputed territory in northern Iraq claimed by both the Kurdistan Regional Government and the central Iraqi Government; the KSF/Peshmerga report to the Kurdistan Regional Government or Kurdistan Democratic Party and Patriotic Union of Kurdistan parties instead of the Iraqi Ministry of Defense

Popular Mobilization Commission and Affiliated Forces (PMF or PMC), also known as Popular Mobilization Units (PMU, or al-Hashd al-Sha'abi in Arabic), tribal militia units have fought alongside the Iraqi military against ISIS since 2014, but the majority of these forces continue to largely ignore the 2016 Law of the Popular Mobilization Authority, which mandated that armed militias must be regulated in a fashion similar to Iraq's other security forces and act under the Iraqi Government's direct control; the Iraqi Government funds the PMF, and the prime minister legally commands it, but many of the militia units take orders from associated political parties and/or other government officials, including some with ties to the Iranian Revolutionary Guard Corps (IRGC) and some that have been designated as terrorist organizations by the US; the PMF/PMU is an umbrella organization comprised of many different militias, the majority of which are Shia:

--Shia militias backed by Iran; they are considered the most active and capable, and include such groups as the Badr Organization (Saraya al-Sala), Asaib Ahl al-Haq, and Kataib Hizballah

--Shia militias affiliated with Shia political parties, but not aligned with Iran, such as the Peace Brigades (Saray al-Salam)

--Shia militias not connected with political parties, but affiliated with the Najaf-based Grand Ayatollah Ali al-SISTANI (Iraq's supreme Shia cleric), such as the Hawza militias

--other PMF/PMU militias include Sunni Tribal Mobilization militias, or Hashd al-Asha'iri; some of these militias take orders from the ISF and local authorities while others respond to orders from the larger Shia PMU militias; still other militias include Yazidi and Christian militias and the Turkmen brigades; the links of these forces to the PMU is not always clear-cut and may be loosely based on financial, legal, or political incentives

at the request of the Iraqi government, NATO agreed to establish an advisory, training and capacity-building mission for the Iraqi military in October 2018; as of 2022, the NATO Mission Iraq (NMI) had about 500 troops; in December 2021, the task force that leads the defeat ISIS mission in Iraq, Combined Joint Task Force – Operation Inherent Resolve (CJTFOIR), transitioned from a combat role to an advise, assist, and enable role (2022)

TERRORISM

Terrorist group(s): Ansar al-Islam; Asa'ib Ahl al-Haq; Islamic Revolutionary Guard Corps (IRGC)/Qods Force; Islamic State of Iraq and ash- Sham (ISIS); Jaysh Rijal al-Tariq al-Naqshabandi; Kata'ib Hizballah; Kurdistan Workers' Party (PKK)

TRANSNATIONAL ISSUES

Disputes - international: *Iraq-Iran*: Iraq's lack of a maritime boundary with Iran prompts jurisdiction disputes beyond the mouth of the Shatt al Arab in the Persian Gulf
Iraq-Turkey: Turkey has expressed concern over the autonomous status of Kurds in Iraq

Refugees and internally displaced persons: *refugees (country of origin):* 15,272 (Turkey), 7,881 (West Bank and Gaza Strip) (mid-year 2021); 261,046 (Syria) (2022)
IDPs: 1,184,818 (displacement in central and northern Iraq since January 2014) (2022)
stateless persons: 47,253 (mid-year 2021); note - in the 1970s and 1980s under SADDAM Husayn's regime, thousands of Iraq's Faili Kurds, followers of Shia Islam, were stripped of their Iraqi citizenship, had their property seized by the government, and many were deported; some Faili Kurds had their citizenship reinstated under the 2006 Iraqi Nationality Law, but others lack the documentation to prove their Iraqi origins; some Palestinian refugees persecuted by the SADDAM regime remain stateless

IRELAND

INTRODUCTION

Background: Celtic tribes arrived on the island between 600 and 150 B.C. Invasions by Norsemen that began in the late 8th century were finally ended when King Brian BORU defeated the Danes in 1014. Norman invasions began in the 12th century and set off more than seven centuries of Anglo-Irish struggle marked by fierce rebellions and harsh repressions. The Irish famine of the mid-19th century was responsible for a drop in the island's population by more than one quarter through starvation, disease, and emigration. For more than a century afterward, the population of the island continued to fall only to begin growing again in the 1960s. Over the last 50 years, Ireland's high birthrate has made it demographically one of the youngest populations in the EU.

The modern Irish state traces its origins to the failed 1916 Easter Monday Uprising that galvanized nationalist sentiment and fostered a guerrilla war resulting in independence from the UK in 1921 with the signing of the Anglo-Irish Treaty and the creation of the Irish Free State. The treaty was deeply controversial in Ireland in part because it helped solidify the partition of Ireland, with six of the island's 32 counties remaining in the UK as Northern Ireland. The split between pro-Treaty and anti-Treaty partisans led to the Irish Civil War (1922-23). The traditionally dominant political parties in Ireland, Fine Gael and Fianna Fail, are de facto descendants of the opposing sides of the treaty debate. Ireland formally left the British Dominion in 1949 when Ireland declared itself a republic.

Deep sectarian divides between the Catholic and Protestant populations and systemic discrimination in Northern Ireland erupted into years of violence known as the "Troubles" that began in the 1960s. In 1998, the governments of Ireland and the UK, along with most political parties in Northern Ireland, reached the Belfast/Good Friday Agreement with the support of the US. This agreement helped end the Troubles and initiated a new phase of cooperation between the Irish and British Governments.

Ireland was neutral in World War II and continues its policy of military neutrality. Ireland joined the European Community in 1973 and the euro-zone currency union in 1999. The economic boom years of the Celtic Tiger (1995-2007) saw rapid economic growth, which came to an abrupt end in 2008 with the meltdown of the Irish banking system. As a small, open economy, Ireland has excelled at courting foreign direct investment, especially from US multi-nationals, which helped the economy recover from the financial crisis and insolated it from the economic shocks of the COVID-19 pandemic.

GEOGRAPHY

Location: Western Europe, occupying five-sixths of the island of Ireland in the North Atlantic Ocean, west of Great Britain

Geographic coordinates: 53 00 N, 8 00 W

Map references: Europe

Area: *total:* 70,273 sq km
land: 68,883 sq km
water: 1,390 sq km
country comparison to the world: 120

Area - comparative: slightly larger than West Virginia

Land boundaries: *total:* 490 km
border countries (1): UK 490 km

Coastline: 1,448 km

Maritime claims: *territorial sea:* 12 nm
exclusive fishing zone: 200 nm

Climate: temperate maritime; modified by North Atlantic Current; mild winters, cool summers; consistently humid; overcast about half the time

Terrain: mostly flat to rolling interior plain surrounded by rugged hills and low mountains; sea cliffs on west coast

Elevation: *highest point:* Carrauntoohil 1,041 m
lowest point: Atlantic Ocean 0 m
mean elevation: 118 m

Natural resources: natural gas, peat, copper, lead, zinc, silver, barite, gypsum, limestone, dolomite

Land use: *agricultural land:* 66.1% (2018 est.)
arable land: 15.4% (2018 est.)
permanent crops: 0% (2018 est.)
permanent pasture: 50.7% (2018 est.)
forest: 10.9% (2018 est.)
other: 23% (2018 est.)

Irrigated land: 0 sq km (2012)

Population distribution: population distribution is weighted to the eastern side of the island, with the largest concentration being in and around Dublin; populations in the west are small due to mountainous land, poorer soil, lack of good transport routes, and fewer job opportunities

Natural hazards: rare extreme weather events

Geography - note: strategic location on major air and sea routes between North America and northern Europe; over 40% of the population resides within 100 km of Dublin

PEOPLE AND SOCIETY

Population: 5,275,004 (2022 est.)
country comparison to the world: 123

Nationality: *noun:* Irishman(men), Irishwoman(women), Irish (collective plural)
adjective: Irish

Ethnic groups: Irish 82.2%, Irish travelers 0.7%, other White 9.5%, Asian 2.1%, Black 1.4%, other 1.5%, unspecified 2.6% (2016 est.)

Languages: English (official, the language generally used), Irish (Gaelic or Gaeilge) (official, spoken by approximately 39.8% of the population as of 2016; mainly spoken in areas along Ireland's western coast known as gaeltachtai, which are officially recognized regions where Irish is the predominant language)

Religions: Roman Catholic 78.3%, Church of Ireland 2.7%, other Christian 1.6%, Orthodox 1.3%, Muslim 1.3%, other 2.4%, none 9.8%, unspecified 2.6% (2016 est.)

Age structure: *0-14 years:* 21.15% (male 560,338/female 534,570)
15-24 years: 12.08% (male 316,239/female 308,872)
25-54 years: 42.19% (male 1,098,058/female 1,085,794)
55-64 years: 10.77% (male 278,836/female 278,498)
65 years and over: 13.82% (male 331,772/female 383,592) (2020 est.)

Dependency ratios: *total dependency ratio:* 54.8
youth dependency ratio: 32.3
elderly dependency ratio: 22.6
potential support ratio: 4.4 (2020 est.)

Median age: *total:* 37.8 years
male: 37.4 years
female: 38.2 years (2020 est.)
country comparison to the world: 66

Population growth rate: 0.94% (2022 est.)
country comparison to the world: 100

Birth rate: 12.32 births/1,000 population (2022 est.)
country comparison to the world: 149

Death rate: 6.73 deaths/1,000 population (2022 est.)
country comparison to the world: 129

Net migration rate: 3.79 migrant(s)/1,000 population (2022 est.)
country comparison to the world: 30

Population distribution: population distribution is weighted to the eastern side of the island, with the largest concentration being in and around Dublin; populations in the west are small due to mountainous land, poorer soil, lack of good transport routes, and fewer job opportunities

Urbanization: *urban population:* 64.2% of total population (2022)
rate of urbanization: 1.15% annual rate of change (2020-25 est.)

Major urban areas - population: 1.256 million DUBLIN (capital) (2022)

Sex ratio: *at birth:* 1.06 male(s)/female
0-14 years: 1.05 male(s)/female
15-24 years: 1.02 male(s)/female
25-54 years: 1.01 male(s)/female
55-64 years: 1.01 male(s)/female
65 years and over: 0.71 male(s)/female
total population: 1 male(s)/female (2022 est.)

Mother's mean age at first birth: 30.9 years (2020 est.)

Maternal mortality ratio: 5 deaths/100,000 live births (2017 est.)
country comparison to the world: 165

Infant mortality rate: *total:* 3.47 deaths/1,000 live births
male: 3.9 deaths/1,000 live births
female: 3.01 deaths/1,000 live births (2022 est.)
country comparison to the world: 197

Life expectancy at birth: *total population:* 81.66 years
male: 79.35 years
female: 84.1 years (2022 est.)
country comparison to the world: 37

Total fertility rate: 1.92 children born/woman (2022 est.)
country comparison to the world: 120

Drinking water source: *improved: urban:* 97% of population
rural: 98.1% of population
total: 97.4% of population
unimproved: urban: 3% of population
rural: 1.9% of population
total: 2.6% of population (2020 est.)

Current health expenditure: 6.7% of GDP (2019)

Physicians density: 3.49 physicians/1,000 population (2020)

Hospital bed density: 3 beds/1,000 population (2018)

Sanitation facility access: *improved: urban:* 97.8% of population
rural: 99.1% of population
total: 98.3% of population
unimproved: urban: 2.2% of population
rural: 0.9% of population
total: 1.7% of population (2020 est.)

HIV/AIDS - adult prevalence rate: 0.2% (2020 est.)
country comparison to the world: 102

Obesity - adult prevalence rate: 25.3% (2016)
country comparison to the world: 51

Alcohol consumption per capita: *total:* 10.91 liters of pure alcohol (2019 est.)
beer: 4.92 liters of pure alcohol (2019 est.)
wine: 2.88 liters of pure alcohol (2019 est.)
spirits: 2.29 liters of pure alcohol (2019 est.)
other alcohols: 0.82 liters of pure alcohol (2019 est.)
country comparison to the world: 15

Tobacco use: *total:* 20.8% (2020 est.)
male: 22.5% (2020 est.)
female: 19% (2020 est.)
country comparison to the world: 81

Education expenditures: 3.4% of GDP (2018 est.)
country comparison to the world: 130

School life expectancy (primary to tertiary education): *total:* 19 years
male: 19 years
female: 19 years (2019)

Unemployment, youth ages 15-24: *total:* 15.3%
male: 15.3%
female: 15.3% (2020 est.)

ENVIRONMENT

Environment - current issues: water pollution, especially of lakes, from agricultural runoff; acid rain kills plants, destroys soil fertility, and contributes to deforestation

Environment - international agreements: *party to:* Air Pollution, Air Pollution-Nitrogen Oxides, Air Pollution-Persistent Organic Pollutants, Air Pollution-Sulphur 94, Biodiversity, Climate Change, Climate Change-Kyoto Protocol, Climate Change-Paris Agreement, Comprehensive Nuclear Test Ban, Desertification, Endangered Species, Environmental Modification, Hazardous Wastes, Law of the Sea, Marine Dumping-London Convention, Marine Dumping-London Protocol, Nuclear Test Ban, Ozone Layer Protection, Ship Pollution, Tropical Timber 2006, Wetlands, Whaling
signed, but not ratified: Air Pollution-Heavy Metals, Air Pollution-Multi-effect Protocol, Marine Life Conservation

Air pollutants: *particulate matter emissions:* 8.26 micrograms per cubic meter (2016 est.)
carbon dioxide emissions: 37.71 megatons (2016 est.)
methane emissions: 13.67 megatons (2020 est.)

Climate: temperate maritime; modified by North Atlantic Current; mild winters, cool summers; consistently humid; overcast about half the time

Land use: *agricultural land:* 66.1% (2018 est.)
arable land: 15.4% (2018 est.)
permanent crops: 0% (2018 est.)
permanent pasture: 50.7% (2018 est.)
forest: 10.9% (2018 est.)
other: 23% (2018 est.)

Urbanization: *urban population:* 64.2% of total population (2022)
rate of urbanization: 1.15% annual rate of change (2020-25 est.)

Revenue from forest resources: *forest revenues:* 0.01% of GDP (2018 est.)
country comparison to the world: 150

Revenue from coal: *coal revenues:* 0% of GDP (2018 est.)
country comparison to the world: 115

Waste and recycling: *municipal solid waste generated annually:* 2,692,537 tons (2012 est.)
municipal solid waste recycled annually: 888,537 tons (2012 est.)
percent of municipal solid waste recycled: 33% (2012 est.)

Total water withdrawal: *municipal:* 631 million cubic meters (2017 est.)
industrial: 51 million cubic meters (2017 est.)
agricultural: 179 million cubic meters (2017 est.)

Total renewable water resources: 52 billion cubic meters (2017 est.)

GOVERNMENT

Country name: *conventional long form:* none
conventional short form: Ireland
local long form: none
local short form: Eire

etymology: the modern Irish name "Eire" evolved from the Gaelic "Eriu," the name of the matron goddess of Ireland (goddess of the land); the names "Ireland" in English and "Eire" in Irish are direct translations of each other

Government type: parliamentary republic

Capital: *name:* Dublin
geographic coordinates: 53 19 N, 6 14 W
time difference: UTC 0 (5 hours ahead of Washington, DC, during Standard Time)
daylight saving time: +1hr, begins last Sunday in March; ends last Sunday in October
etymology: derived from Irish *dubh* and *lind* meaning respectively "black, dark" and "pool" and which referred to the dark tidal pool where the River Poddle entered the River Liffey; today the area is the site of the castle gardens behind Dublin Castle

Administrative divisions: 28 counties and 3 cities*; Carlow, Cavan, Clare, Cork, Cork*, Donegal, Dublin*, Dun Laoghaire-Rathdown, Fingal, Galway, Galway*, Kerry, Kildare, Kilkenny, Laois, Leitrim, Limerick, Longford, Louth, Mayo, Meath, Monaghan, Offaly, Roscommon, Sligo, South Dublin, Tipperary, Waterford, Westmeath, Wexford, Wicklow

Independence: 6 December 1921 (from the UK by the Anglo-Irish Treaty, which ended British rule); 6 December 1922 (Irish Free State established); 18 April 1949 (Republic of Ireland Act enabled)

National holiday: Saint Patrick's Day, 17 March; note - marks the traditional death date of Saint Patrick, patron saint of Ireland, during the latter half of the fifth century A.D. (most commonly cited years are c. 461 and c. 493); although Saint Patrick's feast day was celebrated in Ireland as early as the ninth century, it only became an official public holiday in Ireland in 1903

Constitution: *history:* previous 1922; latest drafted 14 June 1937, adopted by plebiscite 1 July 1937, effective 29 December 1937
amendments: proposed as bills by Parliament; passage requires majority vote by both the Senate and House of Representatives, majority vote in a referendum, and presidential signature; amended many times, last in 2019

Legal system: common law system based on the English model but substantially modified by customary law; judicial review of legislative acts by Supreme Court

International law organization participation: accepts compulsory ICJ jurisdiction with reservations; accepts ICCt jurisdiction

Citizenship: *citizenship by birth:* no, unless a parent of a child born in Ireland has been legally resident in Ireland for at least three of the four years prior to the birth of the child
citizenship by descent only: yes
dual citizenship recognized: yes
residency requirement for naturalization: 4 of the previous 8 years

Suffrage: 18 years of age; universal

Executive branch: *chief of state:* President Michael D. HIGGINS (since 11 November 2011)
head of government: Taoiseach (Prime Minister) Micheál MARTIN (since 27 June 2020); note - MARTIN will serve through December 2022 and will then be succeeded by Leo VARADKAR
cabinet: Cabinet nominated by the prime minister, appointed by the president, approved by the Dali Eireann (lower house of Parliament)
elections/appointments: president directly elected by majority popular vote for a 7-year term (eligible for a second term); election last held on 26 October 2018 (next to be held no later than November 2025); taoiseach (prime minister) nominated by the House of Representatives (Dail Eireann), appointed by the president
election results: *2018:* Michael D. HIGGINS reelected president; percent of vote - Michael D. HIGGINS (independent) 55.8%, Peter CASEY (independent) 23.3%, Sean GALLAGHER (independent) 6.4%, Liadh NI RIADA (Sinn Fein) 6.4%, Joan FREEMAN (independent) 6%, Gavin DUFFY (independent) 2.2%
2011: Michael D. HIGGINS elected president in second round; percent of vote in first round - Michael D. HIGGINS (Labor) 39.6%, Sean GALLAGHER (independent) 28.5%, Martin McGuinness (Sinn Féin) 13.7%, Gay Mitchell (Fine Gael) 6.4%, David Norris (independent) 6.2%, Mary DAVIS (independent) 2.7%; percent of vote in second round - Michael D. HIGGINS 56.8%, Sean GALLAGHER 35.5%

Legislative branch: *description:* bicameral Parliament or Oireachtas consists of:
Senate or Seanad Eireann (60 seats; 49 members indirectly elected from 5 vocational panels of nominees by an electoral college, 11 appointed by the prime minister
House of Representatives or Dail Eireann (160 seats; members directly elected in multi-seat constituencies by proportional representation vote; all Parliament members serve 5-year terms)
elections: Senate - last held early on 21-30 May 2020 (next to be held in March 2025)
House of Representatives - last held on 8 February 2020 (next to be held no later than 2025)
election results: Senate - percent of vote by party - Fianna Fail 35%, Fine Gael 26.7%, Labor Party 6.7%, Sinn Fein 6.7%, Green Party 6.7%, Human Dignity Alliance 1.6%, independent 16.7%; seats by party - Fianna Fail 21, Fine Gael 16, Labor Party 4, Sinn Fein 4, Green Party 4, Human Dignity Alliance 1, independent 10; composition - men 36, women 24, percent of women 40%
House of Representatives - percent of vote by party - Sinn Fein 22.6%, Fianna Fail 22.6%, Fine Gael 20.7%, Green Party 6.3%, Labor Party 4.5%, Social Democrats 3.8%, PBPS 3.2%, Aontu 0.6%, Right to Change 0.6%, independent 15%; seats by party - Sinn Fein 36, Fianna Fail 36, Fine Gael 33, Green Party 10, Labor Party 7, Social Democrats 6, PBPS 5, Aontu 1, Right to Change 1, Independents 24; composition as of March 2022 - men 123, women 37, percent of women 23.1%; note - total Parliament percent of women 27.7%

Judicial branch: *highest court(s):* Supreme Court of Ireland (consists of the chief justice, 9 judges, 2 ex-officio members - the presidents of the High Court and Court of Appeal - and organized in 3-, 5-, or 7-judge panels, depending on the importance or complexity of an issue of law)
judge selection and term of office: judges nominated by the prime minister and Cabinet and appointed by the president; chief justice serves in the position for 7 years; judges can serve until age 70
subordinate courts: High Court, Court of Appeal; circuit and district courts; criminal courts

Political parties and leaders: Aontu [Peadar TOIBIN]
Solidarity-People Before Profit or PBPS [collective leadership]
Fianna Fail [Micheal MARTIN]
Fine Gael [Leo VARADKAR]
Green Party [Eamon RYAN]
Human Dignity Alliance [Ronan MULLEN]
Labor (Labour) Party Ivana BACIK]
Renua Ireland (vacant)
Right to Change or RTC [Joan COLLINS]
Sinn Fein [Mary Lou McDONALD]
Social Democrats [Catherine MURPHY, Roisin SHORTALL]
Socialist Party [collective leadership]
The Workers' Party [collective leadership]

International organization participation: ADB (nonregional member), Australia Group, BIS, CD, CE, EAPC, EBRD, ECB, EIB, EMU, ESA, EU, FAO, FATF, IAEA, IBRD, ICAO, ICC (national committees), ICCt, ICRM, IDA, IEA, IFAD, IFC, IFRCS, IGAD (partners), IHO, ILO, IMF, IMO, Interpol, IOC, IOM, IPU, ISO, ITSO, ITU, ITUC (NGOs), MIGA, MINURSO, MONUSCO, NEA, NSG, OAS (observer), OECD, OPCW, OSCE, Paris Club, PCA, PFP, UN, UNCTAD, UNDOF, UNESCO, UNHCR, UNIDO, UNIFIL, UNOCI, UNRWA, UNTSO, UPU, Wassenaar Arrangement, WCO, WHO, WIPO, WMO, WTO, ZC

Diplomatic representation in the US: *chief of mission:* Ambassador Geraldine Byrne NASON (since 16 September 2022)
chancery: 2234 Massachusetts Avenue NW, Washington, DC 20008
telephone: [1] (202) 462-3939
FAX: [1] (202) 232-5993
email address and website:
https://www.dfa.ie/irish-embassy/usa/
consulate(s) general: Atlanta, Austin (TX), Boston, Chicago, New York, San Francisco

Diplomatic representation from the US: *chief of mission:* Ambassador Claire D. CRONIN (since 10 February 2022)
embassy: 42 Elgin Road, Ballsbridge, Dublin 4
mailing address: 5290 Dublin Place, Washington DC 20521-5290
telephone: [353] (1) 668-8777
FAX: [353] (1) 688-8056
email address and website:
ACSDublin@state.gov
https://ie.usembassy.gov/

Flag description: three equal vertical bands of green (hoist side), white, and orange; officially the flag colors have no meaning, but a common interpretation is that the green represents the Irish nationalist (Gaelic) tradition of Ireland; orange represents the Orange tradition (minority supporters of William of Orange); white symbolizes peace (or a lasting truce) between the green and the orange
note: similar to the flag of Cote d'Ivoire, which is shorter and has the colors reversed - orange (hoist side), white, and green; also similar to the flag of Italy, which is shorter and has colors of green (hoist side), white, and red

National symbol(s): harp, shamrock (trefoil); national colors: blue, green

National anthem: *name:* "Amhran na bhFiánn" (The Soldier's Song)
lyrics/music: Peadar KEARNEY [English], Liam O RINN [Irish]/Patrick HEENEY and Peadar KEARNEY

note: adopted 1926; instead of "Amhran na bhFiann," the song "Ireland's Call" is often used at athletic events where citizens of Ireland and Northern Ireland compete as a unified team

National heritage: *total World Heritage Sites:* 2 (both cultural)
selected World Heritage Site locales: Brú na Bóinne - Archaeological Ensemble of the Bend of the Boyne; Sceilg Mhichíl

ECONOMY

Economic overview: Ireland is a small, modern, trade-dependent economy. It was among the initial group of 12 EU nations that began circulating the euro on 1 January 2002. GDP growth averaged 6% in 1995-2007, but economic activity dropped sharply during the world financial crisis and the subsequent collapse of its domestic property market and construction industry during 2008-11. Faced with sharply reduced revenues and a burgeoning budget deficit from efforts to stabilize its fragile banking sector, the Irish Government introduced the first in a series of draconian budgets in 2009. These measures were not sufficient to stabilize Ireland's public finances. In 2010, the budget deficit reached 32.4% of GDP - the world's largest deficit, as a percentage of GDP. In late 2010, the former COWEN government agreed to a $92 billion loan package from the EU and IMF to help Dublin recapitalize Ireland's banking sector and avoid defaulting on its sovereign debt. In March 2011, the KENNY government intensified austerity measures to meet the deficit targets under Ireland's EU-IMF bailout program.

In late 2013, Ireland formally exited its EU-IMF bailout program, benefiting from its strict adherence to deficit-reduction targets and success in refinancing a large amount of banking-related debt. In 2014, the economy rapidly picked up. In late 2014, the government introduced a fiscally neutral budget, marking the end of the austerity program. Continued growth of tax receipts has allowed the government to lower some taxes and increase public spending while keeping to its deficit-reduction targets. In 2015, GDP growth exceeded 26%. The magnitude of the increase reflected one-off statistical revisions, multinational corporate restructurings in intellectual property, and the aircraft leasing sector, rather than real gains in the domestic economy, which was still growing. Growth moderated to around 4.1% in 2017, but the recovering economy assisted lowering the deficit to 0.6% of GDP.

In the wake of the collapse of the construction sector and the downturn in consumer spending and business investment during the 2008-11 economic crisis, the export sector, dominated by foreign multinationals, has become an even more important component of Ireland's economy. Ireland's low corporation tax of 12.5% and a talented pool of high-tech laborers have been some of the key factors in encouraging business investment. Loose tax residency requirements made Ireland a common destination for international firms seeking to pay less tax or, in the case of U.S. multinationals, defer taxation owed to the United States. In 2014, amid growing international pressure, the Irish government announced it would phase in more stringent tax laws, effectively closing a commonly used loophole. The Irish economy continued to grow in 2017 and is forecast to do so through 2019, supported by a strong export sector, robust job growth, and low inflation, to the point that the Government must now address concerns about overheating and potential loss of competitiveness. The greatest risks to the economy are the UK's scheduled departure from the European Union ("Brexit") in March 2019, possible changes to international taxation policies that could affect Ireland's revenues, and global trade pressures.

Real GDP (purchasing power parity): $447.97 billion (2020 est.)
$433.17 billion (2019 est.)
$410.33 billion (2018 est.)
note: data are in 2017 dollars
country comparison to the world: 44

Real GDP growth rate: 5.86% (2019 est.)
9.42% (2018 est.)
9.49% (2017 est.)
country comparison to the world: 32

Real GDP per capita: $89,700 (2020 est.)
$87,800 (2019 est.)
$84,300 (2018 est.)
note: data are in 2017 dollars
country comparison to the world: 5

GDP (official exchange rate): $398.476 billion (2019 est.)

Inflation rate (consumer prices): 0.9% (2019 est.)
0.4% (2018 est.)
0.3% (2017 est.)
country comparison to the world: 59

Credit ratings:

Fitch rating: A+ (2017)

Moody's rating: A2 (2017)

Standard & Poors rating: AA- (2019)
note: The year refers to the year in which the current credit rating was first obtained.

GDP - composition, by sector of origin: *agriculture:* 1.2% (2017 est.)
industry: 38.6% (2017 est.)
services: 60.2% (2017 est.)

GDP - composition, by end use: *household consumption:* 34% (2017 est.)
government consumption: 10.1% (2017 est.)
investment in fixed capital: 23.4% (2017 est.)
investment in inventories: 1.2% (2017 est.)
exports of goods and services: 119.9% (2017 est.)
imports of goods and services: -89.7% (2017 est.)

Agricultural products: milk, barley, beef, wheat, potatoes, pork, oats, poultry, mushrooms/truffles, mutton

Industries: pharmaceuticals, chemicals, computer hardware and software, food products, beverages and brewing; medical devices

Industrial production growth rate: 7.8% (2017 est.)
country comparison to the world: 25

Labor force: 2.289 million (2020 est.)
country comparison to the world: 117

Labor force - by occupation: *agriculture:* 5%
industry: 11%
services: 84% (2015 est.)

Unemployment rate: 4.98% (2019 est.)
5.78% (2018 est.)
country comparison to the world: 75

Unemployment, youth ages 15-24: *total:* 15.3%
male: 15.3%
female: 15.3% (2020 est.)
country comparison to the world: 107

Population below poverty line: 13.1% (2018 est.)

Gini Index coefficient - distribution of family income: 32.8 (2016 est.)
35.9 (1987 est.)
country comparison to the world: 132

Household income or consumption by percentage share: *lowest 10%:* 2.9%
highest 10%: 27.2% (2000)

Budget: *revenues:* 86.04 billion (2017 est.)
expenditures: 87.19 billion (2017 est.)

Budget surplus (+) or deficit (-): -0.3% (of GDP) (2017 est.)
country comparison to the world: 53

Public debt: 68.6% of GDP (2017 est.)
73.6% of GDP (2016 est.)
note: data cover general government debt and include debt instruments issued (or owned) by government entities other than the treasury; the data include treasury debt held by foreign entities; the data include debt issued by subnational entities, as well as intragovernmental debt; intragovernmental debt consists of treasury borrowings from surpluses in the social funds, such as for retirement, medical care, and unemployment; debt instruments for the social funds are not sold at public auctions
country comparison to the world: 54

Taxes and other revenues: 26% (of GDP) (2017 est.)
country comparison to the world: 115

Fiscal year: calendar year

Current account balance: -$44.954 billion (2019 est.)
$24.154 billion (2018 est.)
country comparison to the world: 202

Exports: $502.31 billion (2019 est.) note: data are in current year dollars
$471.6 billion (2018 est.) note: data are in current year dollars
$440.693 billion (2017 est.)
country comparison to the world: 12

Exports - partners: United States 28%, Belgium 10%, Germany 10%, UK 9%, China 5%, Netherlands 5% (2019)

Exports - commodities: medical cultures/vaccines, nitrogen compounds, packaged medicines, integrated circuits, scented mixtures (2019)

Imports: $452.98 billion (2019 est.) note: data are in current year dollars
$361.12 billion (2018 est.) note: data are in current year dollars
$359.725 billion (2017 est.)
country comparison to the world: 14

Imports - partners: United Kingdom 31%, United States 16%, Germany 10%, Netherlands 5%, France 5% (2019)

Imports - commodities: aircraft, computers, packaged medicines, refined petroleum, medical cultures/vaccines (2019)

Reserves of foreign exchange and gold: $4.412 billion (31 December 2017 est.)
$2.203 billion (31 December 2015 est.)
country comparison to the world: 99

Debt - external: $2,829,303,000,000 (2019 est.)
$2,758,949,000,000 (2018 est.)
country comparison to the world: 9

Exchange rates: euros (EUR) per US dollar -
0.82771 (2020 est.)
0.90338 (2019 est.)
0.87789 (2018 est.)
0.885 (2014 est.)
0.7634 (2013 est.)

ENERGY

Electricity access: *electrification - total population:* 100% (2020)

Electricity: *installed generating capacity:* 11.43 million kW (2020 est.)
consumption: 30.627 billion kWh (2020 est.)
exports: 1.913 billion kWh (2020 est.)
imports: 1.761 billion kWh (2020 est.)
transmission/distribution losses: 2.309 billion kWh (2020 est.)

Electricity generation sources: *fossil fuels:* 57.8% of total installed capacity (2020 est.)
solar: 0.2% of total installed capacity (2020 est.)
wind: 34.8% of total installed capacity (2020 est.)
hydroelectricity: 3.7% of total installed capacity (2020 est.)
biomass and waste: 3.6% of total installed capacity (2020 est.)

Coal: *production:* 0 metric tons (2020 est.)
consumption: 351,000 metric tons (2020 est.)
exports: 132,000 metric tons (2020 est.)
imports: 408,000 metric tons (2020 est.)
proven reserves: 14 million metric tons (2019 est.)

Petroleum: *total petroleum production:* 600 bbl/day (2021 est.)
refined petroleum consumption: 159,100 bbl/day (2019 est.)
crude oil and lease condensate exports: 0 bbl/day (2018 est.)
crude oil and lease condensate imports: 60,300 bbl/day (2018 est.)
crude oil estimated reserves: 0 barrels (2021 est.)

Refined petroleum products - production: 64,970 bbl/day (2017 est.)
country comparison to the world: 76

Refined petroleum products - exports: 37,040 bbl/day (2017 est.)
country comparison to the world: 59

Refined petroleum products - imports: 126,600 bbl/day (2017 est.)
country comparison to the world: 47

Natural gas: *production:* 2,652,180,000 cubic meters (2019 est.)
consumption: 5,491,562,000 cubic meters (2019 est.)
exports: 0 cubic meters (2021 est.)
imports: 2,846,971,000 cubic meters (2019 est.)
proven reserves: 9.911 billion cubic meters (2021 est.)

Carbon dioxide emissions: 35.475 million metric tonnes of CO_2 (2019 est.)
from coal and metallurgical coke: 1.43 million metric tonnes of CO_2 (2019 est.)
from petroleum and other liquids: 23.08 million metric tonnes of CO_2 (2019 est.)
from consumed natural gas: 10.965 million metric tonnes of CO_2 (2019 est.)
country comparison to the world: 71

Energy consumption per capita: 133.674 million Btu/person (2019 est.)
country comparison to the world: 41

COMMUNICATIONS

Telephones - fixed lines: *total subscriptions:* 1,678,651 (2020 est.)
subscriptions per 100 inhabitants: 34 (2020 est.)
country comparison to the world: 58

Telephones - mobile cellular: *total subscriptions:* 5,234,027 (2020 est.)
subscriptions per 100 inhabitants: 106 (2020 est.)
country comparison to the world: 119

Telecommunication systems: *general assessment:* Ireland's telecom market has rebounded from a long period in which fiscal constraints inhibited investment in the sector; significant infrastructure projects are underway, including the NBN which aims to deliver a fiberbased service of at least 150Mb/s nationally by the end of 2022; the renewed optimism has been seen in company investment in extending fiber-based networks providing 1Gb/s services; the mobile sector is preparing for a multifrequency availability later in 2021 which will greatly increase the amount of frequencies available, and provide a boost for 5G services; the MNOs are rapidly expanding the reach of 5G (2021)
domestic: increasing levels of broadband access particularly in urban areas; fixed-line 34 per 100 and mobile-cellular 106 per 100 subscriptions; digital system using cable and microwave radio relay (2020)
international: country code - 353; landing point for the AEConnect -1, Celtic-Norse, Havfrue/AEC-2, GTT Express, Celtic, ESAT-1, IFC-1, Solas, Pan European Crossing, ESAT-2, CeltixConnect -1 & 2, GTT Atlantic, Sirius South, Emerald Bridge Fibres and Geo Eirgrid submarine cable with links to the US, Canada, Norway, Isle of Man and UK; satellite earth stations - 81 (2019)

Broadcast media: publicly owned broadcaster Radio Telefis Eireann (RTE) operates 4 TV stations; commercial TV stations are available; about 75% of households utilize multi-channel satellite and TV services that provide access to a wide range of stations; RTE operates 4 national radio stations and has launched digital audio broadcasts on several stations; a number of commercial broadcast stations operate at the national, regional, and local levels (2019)

Internet country code: .ie

Internet users: *total:* 4,586,820 (2020 est.)
percent of population: 92% (2020 est.)
country comparison to the world: 96

Broadband - fixed subscriptions: *total:* 1,516,473 (2020 est.)
subscriptions per 100 inhabitants: 31 (2020 est.)
country comparison to the world: 65

TRANSPORTATION

National air transport system: *number of registered air carriers:* 9 (2020)
inventory of registered aircraft operated by air carriers: 450
annual passenger traffic on registered air carriers: 167,598,633 (2018)
annual freight traffic on registered air carriers: 168.71 million (2018) mt-km

Civil aircraft registration country code prefix: EI

Airports: *total:* 40 (2021)
country comparison to the world: 105

Airports - with paved runways: *total:* 16
over 3,047 m: 1
2,438 to 3,047 m: 1
1,524 to 2,437 m: 4
914 to 1,523 m: 5
under 914 m: 5 (2021)

Airports - with unpaved runways: *total:* 24
2,438 to 3,047 m: 1
914 to 1,523 m: 2
under 914 m: 21 (2021)

Pipelines: 2,427 km gas (2017)

Railways: *total:* 4,301 km (2018)
narrow gauge: 1,930 km (2018) 0.914-m gauge (operated by the Irish Peat Board to transport peat to power stations and briquetting plants)
broad gauge: 2,371 km (2018) 1.600-m gauge (53 km electrified)
country comparison to the world: 43

Roadways: *total:* 99,830 km (2018)
paved: 99,830 km (2018) (includes 2,717 km of expressways)
country comparison to the world: 47

Waterways: 956 km (2010) (pleasure craft only)
country comparison to the world: 73

Merchant marine: *total:* 96
by type: bulk carrier 12, general cargo 36, oil tanker 1, other 47 (2021)
country comparison to the world: 91

Ports and terminals: *major seaport(s):* Dublin, Shannon Foynes
cruise port(s): Cork (250,000), Dublin (359,966) (2020)
container port(s) (TEUs): Dublin (529,563) (2016)
river port(s): Cork (Lee), Waterford (Suir)

MILITARY AND SECURITY

Military and security forces: Irish Defense Forces (Oglaigh na h-Eireannn): Army, Air Corps, Naval Service, Reserve Defense Forces (2022)

Military expenditures: 0.3% of GDP (2021)
0.3% of GDP (2020)
0.3% of GDP (2019) (approximately $1.27 billion)
0.3% of GDP (2018) (approximately $1.25 billion
0.3% of GDP (2017) (approximately $1.21 billion)
country comparison to the world: 164

Military and security service personnel strengths: approximately 8,500 active duty personnel (6,800 Army; 900 Naval Service; 800 Air Corps) (2022)

Military equipment inventories and acquisitions: the Irish Defense Forces have a small inventory of imported weapons systems from a variety of mostly European countries; the UK is the leading supplier of military hardware to Ireland since 2010 (2021)

Military service age and obligation: 18-25 years of age for male and female voluntary military service recruits to the Defence Forces (18-27 years of age for the Naval Service); 18-26 for cadetship (officer) applicants; 12-year service (5 active, 7 reserves) (2022)
note: as of 2021, women made up about 7% of the military's full-time personnel
note 2: the Defense Forces are open to refugees under the Refugee Act of 1996 and nationals of the European Economic Area, which include EU member states, Iceland, Liechtenstein, and Norway

Military deployments: 130 Golan Heights (UNDOF); 320 Lebanon (UNIFIL) (May 2022)

Military - note: the Irish Defense Forces trace their origins back to the Irish Volunteers, a unit established in 1913; the Irish Volunteers took part in the 1916 Easter Rising and the Irish War of Independence, 1919-1921

Ireland has a long-standing policy of military neutrality; however, it participates in international peacekeeping and humanitarian operations, as well as crisis management; Ireland is a signatory of the EU's Common Security and Defense Policy and has committed a battalion of troops to the EU's Rapid Reaction Force; Ireland is not a member of NATO, but has a relationship going back to 1997 when it deployed personnel in support of the NATO-led peacekeeping operations in Bosnia and Herzegovina; Ireland joined NATO's Partnership for Peace program in 1999; Ireland has been an active participate in UN peacekeeping operations since the 1950s

TERRORISM

Terrorist group(s): Continuity Irish Republican Army; New Irish Republican Army; Islamic State of Iraq and ash-Sham (ISIS)

TRANSNATIONAL ISSUES

Disputes - international: *Ireland-Denmark*: Ireland, Iceland, and the UK dispute Denmark's claim that the Faroe Islands' continental shelf extends beyond 200 nm; Iceland, Norway, and the Faroe Islands signed an agreement in 2019 extending the Faroe Islands' northern continental shelf area

Refugees and internally displaced persons: *refugees (country of origin)*: 58,511 (Ukraine) (as of 22 November 2022)
stateless persons: 107 (mid-year 2021)

Illicit drugs: transshipment point for and consumer of hashish from North Africa to the UK and Netherlands and of Europeanproduced synthetic drugs; increasing consumption of South American cocaine; minor transshipment point for heroin and cocaine destined for Western Europe; despite recent legislation, narcotics-related money laundering - using bureaux de change, trusts, and shell companies involving the offshore financial community - remains a concern

ISLE OF MAN

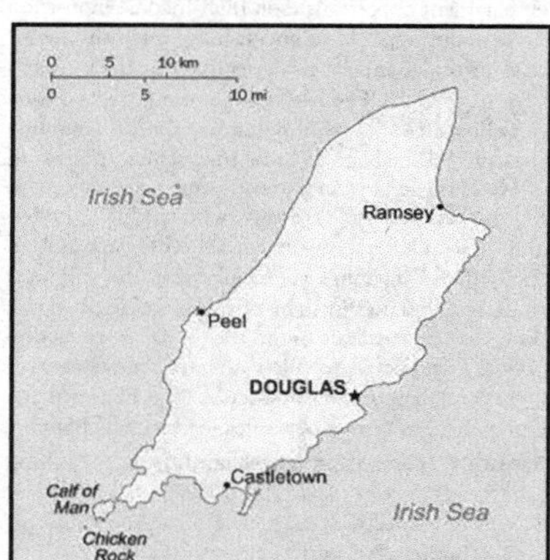

INTRODUCTION

Background: Part of the Norwegian Kingdom of the Hebrides until the 13th century when it was ceded to Scotland, the isle came under the British crown in 1765. Current concerns include reviving the almost extinct Manx Gaelic language. The Isle of Man is a British Crown dependency, which makes it a self-governing possession of the British Crown that is not part of the UK. The UK Government, however, remains constitutionally responsible for its defense and international representation.

GEOGRAPHY

Location: Western Europe, island in the Irish Sea, between Great Britain and Ireland

Geographic coordinates: 54 15 N, 4 30 W

Map references: Europe

Area: *total:* 572 sq km
land: 572 sq km
water: 0 sq km

Area - comparative: slightly more than three times the size of Washington, DC

Land boundaries: *total:* 0 km

Coastline: 160 km

Maritime claims: *territorial sea:* 12 nm
exclusive fishing zone: 12 nm

Climate: temperate; cool summers and mild winters; overcast about a third of the time

Terrain: hills in north and south bisected by central valley

Elevation: *highest point:* Snaefell 621 m
lowest point: Irish Sea 0 m

Natural resources: none

Land use: *agricultural land:* 74.7% (2018 est.)
arable land: 43.8% (2018 est.)
permanent crops: 0% (2018 est.)
permanent pasture: 30.9% (2018 est.)
forest: 6.1% (2018 est.)
other: 19.2% (2018 est.)

Irrigated land: 0 sq km (2012)

Population distribution: most people concentrated in cities and large towns of which Douglas, in the southeast, is the largest

Natural hazards: occasional high winds and rough seas

Geography - note: one small islet, the Calf of Man, lies to the southwest and is a bird sanctuary

PEOPLE AND SOCIETY

Population: 91,382 (2022 est.)

Nationality: *noun:* Manxman(men), Manxwoman(women)
adjective: Manx

Ethnic groups: White 94.7%, Asian 3.1%, Mixed 1%, Black 0.6%, other 0.4% (2021 est.)
note: data represent population by nationality

Languages: English, Manx Gaelic (about 2% of the population has some knowledge)

Religions: Christian 54.7%, Muslim 0.5%, Buddhist 0.5%, Hindu 0.4%, Jewish 0.2%, none 43.8% (2021 est.)

Age structure: *0-14 years:* 16.28% (male 7,688/female 7,046)
15-24 years: 11.02% (male 5,328/female 4,642)
25-54 years: 37.8% (male 17,080/female 17,131)
55-64 years: 13.82% (male 6,284/female 6,219)
65 years and over: 21.08% (male 9,023/female 10,058) (2020 est.)

Median age: *total:* 44.6 years
male: 43.6 years
female: 45.6 years (2020 est.)

Population growth rate: 0.52% (2022 est.)

Birth rate: 10.58 births/1,000 population (2022 est.)

Death rate: 10.18 deaths/1,000 population (2022 est.)

Net migration rate: 4.76 migrant(s)/1,000 population (2022 est.)

Population distribution: most people concentrated in cities and large towns of which Douglas, in the southeast, is the largest

Urbanization: *urban population:* 53.3% of total population (2022)
rate of urbanization: 0.97% annual rate of change (2020-25 est.)

Major urban areas - population: 27,000 DOUGLAS (capital) (2018)

Sex ratio: *at birth:* 1.08 male(s)/female
0-14 years: 1.08 male(s)/female
15-24 years: 1.18 male(s)/female
25-54 years: 1 male(s)/female
55-64 years: 1.02 male(s)/female
65 years and over: 0.75 male(s)/female
total population: 1.01 male(s)/female (2022 est.)

Infant mortality rate: *total:* 4.24 deaths/1,000 live births
male: 4.59 deaths/1,000 live births
female: 3.85 deaths/1,000 live births (2022 est.)

Life expectancy at birth: *total population:* 82.04 years
male: 80.23 years
female: 84 years (2022 est.)

Total fertility rate: 1.89 children born/woman (2022 est.)

Drinking water source: *improved: total:* 99.1% of population
unimproved: total: 0.9% of population (2020)

Unemployment, youth ages 15-24: *total:* 10.1%
male: 11.8%
female: 8.2% (2011 est.)

ENVIRONMENT

Environment - current issues: air pollution, marine pollution; waste disposal (both household and industrial)

Climate: temperate; cool summers and mild winters; overcast about a third of the time

Land use: *agricultural land:* 74.7% (2018 est.)
arable land: 43.8% (2018 est.)
permanent crops: 0% (2018 est.)
permanent pasture: 30.9% (2018 est.)

forest: 6.1% (2018 est.)
other: 19.2% (2018 est.)

Urbanization: *urban population:* 53.3% of total population (2022)
rate of urbanization: 0.97% annual rate of change (2020-25 est.)

Revenue from forest resources: *forest revenues:* 0% of GDP (2017 est.)

Waste and recycling: *municipal solid waste generated annually:* 50,551 tons (2011 est.)
municipal solid waste recycled annually: 25,276 tons (2011 est.)
percent of municipal solid waste recycled: 50% (2011 est.)

GOVERNMENT

Country name: *conventional long form:* none
conventional short form: Isle of Man
abbreviation: I.O.M.
etymology: the name "man" may be derived from the Celtic word for "mountain"

Government type: parliamentary democracy (Tynwald)

Dependency status: British crown dependency

Capital: *name:* Douglas
geographic coordinates: 54 09 N, 4 29 W
time difference: UTC 0 (5 hours ahead of Washington, DC, during Standard Time)
daylight saving time: +1hr, begins last Sunday in March; ends last Sunday in October
etymology: name derives from the Dhoo and Glass Rivers, which flow through the valley in which the town is located and which in Manx mean the "dark" and the "light" rivers respectively

Administrative divisions: none; there are no first-order administrative divisions as defined by the US Government, but there are 24 local authorities each with its own elections

Independence: none (British Crown dependency)

National holiday: Tynwald Day, 5 July (1417); date Tynwald Day was first recorded

Constitution: *history:* development of the Isle of Man constitution dates to at least the 14th century
amendments: proposed as a bill in the House of Keys, by the "Government," by a "Member of the House," or through petition to the House or Legislative Council; passage normally requires three separate readings and approval of at least 13 House members; following both House and Council agreement, assent is required by the lieutenant governor on behalf of the Crown; the constitution has been expanded and amended many times, last in 2020

Legal system: the laws of the UK apply where applicable and include Manx statutes

Citizenship: see United Kingdom

Suffrage: 16 years of age; universal

Executive branch: *chief of state:* Lord of Mann King CHARLES III (since 8 September 2022); represented by Lieutenant Governor Sir John LORIMER (since 29 September 2021)
head of government: Chief Minister Alfred CANNAN (since 12 October 2021)
cabinet: Council of Ministers appointed by the lieutenant governor
elections/appointments: the monarchy is hereditary; lieutenant governor appointed by the monarch; chief minister indirectly elected by the Tynwald for a 5-year term (eligible for second term); election last held on 23 September 2021 (next to be held in 2026)
election results: 2021: Alfred CANNAN (independent) elected chief minister; Tynwald House of Keys vote - 21 of 24
2016: Howard QUAYLE elected chief minister; Tynwald House of Keys vote - 21 of 33

Legislative branch: *description:* bicameral Tynwald or the High Court of Tynwald consists of:
Legislative Council (11 seats; includes the President of Tynwald, 2 ex-officio members - the Lord Bishop of Sodor and Man and the attorney general (non-voting) - and 8 members indirectly elected by the House of Keys with renewal of 4 members every 2 years; elected members serve 4-year terms)
House of Keys (24 seats; 2 members directly elected by simple majority vote from 12 constituencies to serve 5-year terms)
elections: Legislative Council - last held 29 February 2020 (next to be held on 28 February 2022)
House of Keys - last held on 23 September 2021 (next to be held in September 2026)
election results: Legislative Council - composition (as of 2021) - men 6, women 4, 1 vacancies; percent of women 36.4%
House of Keys - percent of vote by party - Liberal Vannin 5.3%, Manx Labour Prty 5.1%, Green Party 3.3% independent 86.3%; seats by party - independent 21; Manx Labour Party 2, Liberal Vannin 1, Green Party 0; composition – men 14, women 10, percent of women 41.7%; note - total Tynwald percent of women 37.1%

Judicial branch: *highest court(s):* Isle of Man High Court of Justice (consists of 3 permanent judges or "deemsters" and 1 judge of appeal; organized into the Staff of Government Division or Court of Appeal and the Civil Division); the Court of General Gaol Delivery is not formally part of the High Court but is administered as though part of the High Court and deals with serious criminal cases; note - appeals beyond the Court of Appeal are referred to the Judicial Committee of the Privy Council (in London)
judge selection and term of office: deemsters appointed by the Lord Chancellor of England on the nomination of the lieutenant governor; deemsters can serve until age 70
subordinate courts: High Court; Court of Summary Gaol Delivery; Summary Courts; Magistrate's Court; specialized courts

Political parties and leaders: Green Party [Andrew LANGAN-NEWTON]
Liberal Vannin Party or LVP [Lawrie HOOPER]
Manx Labor Party [Joney FARAGHER]
Mec Vannin [Mark KERMODE] (sometimes referred to as the Manx Nationalist Party)
note: most members sit as independents

International organization participation: UPU

Diplomatic representation in the US: none (British crown dependency)

Diplomatic representation from the US: *embassy:* none (British crown dependency)

Flag description: red with the Three Legs of Man emblem (triskelion), in the center; the three legs are joined at the thigh and bent at the knee; in order to have the toes pointing clockwise on both sides of the flag, a two-sided emblem is used; the flag is based on the coat of arms of the last recognized Norse King of Mann, Magnus III (r. 1252-65); the triskelion has its roots in an early Celtic sun symbol

National symbol(s): triskelion (a motif of three legs); national colors: red, white

National anthem: *name:* "Arrane Ashoonagh dy Vannin" (O Land of Our Birth)
lyrics/music: William Henry GILL [English], John J. KNEEN [Manx]/traditional
note: adopted 2003, in use since 1907; serves as a local anthem; as a British Crown dependency, "God Save the King" is official (see United Kingdom) and is played when the sovereign, members of the royal family, or the lieutenant governor are present

ECONOMY

Economic overview: Financial services, manufacturing, and tourism are key sectors of the economy. The government offers low taxes and other incentives to high-technology companies and financial institutions to locate on the island; this has paid off in expanding employment opportunities in high-income industries. As a result, agriculture and fishing, once the mainstays of the economy, have declined in their contributions to GDP. The Isle of Man also attracts online gambling sites and the film industry. Online gambling sites provided about 10% of the islands income in 2014. The Isle of Man currently enjoys free access to EU markets and trade is mostly with the UK. The Isle of Man's trade relationship with the EU derives from the United Kingdom's EU membership and will need to be renegotiated in light of the United Kingdom's decision to withdraw from the bloc. A transition period is expected to allow the free movement of goods and agricultural products to the EU until the end of 2020 or until a new settlement is negotiated.

Real GDP (purchasing power parity): $6.792 billion (2015 est.)
$7.428 billion (2014 est.)
$6.298 billion (2013 est.)
note: data are in 2014 US dollars

Real GDP growth rate: -8.6% (2015 est.)
17.9% (2014 est.)
2.1% (2010 est.)

Real GDP per capita: $84,600 (2014 est.)
$86,200 (2013 est.)
$73,700 (2012 est.)

GDP (official exchange rate): $6.792 billion (2015 est.)

Inflation rate (consumer prices): 4.1% (2017 est.)
1% (2016 est.)

Credit ratings:

Moody's rating: Aa3 (2020)

Standard & Poors rating: N/A (2014)
note: The year refers to the year in which the current credit rating was first obtained.

GDP - composition, by sector of origin: *agriculture:* 1% (FY12/13 est.)
industry: 13% (FY12/13 est.)
services: 86% (FY12/13 est.)

Agricultural products: cereals, vegetables; cattle, sheep, pigs, poultry

Industries: financial services, light manufacturing, tourism

Labor force: 41,790 (2006)

Labor force - by occupation: *manufacturing:* 5% (2006 est.)
construction: 8% (2006 est.)
tourism: 1% (2006 est.)
transport and communications: 9% (2006 est.)

agriculture, forestry, and fishing: 2% (2006 est.)
gas, electricity, and water: 1% (2006 est.)
wholesale and retail distribution: 11% (2006 est.)
professional and scientific services: 20% (2006 est.)
public administration: 7% (2006 est.)
banking and finance: 23% (2006 est.)
entertainment and catering: 5% (2006 est.)
miscellaneous services: 8% (2006 est.)

Unemployment rate: 1.1% (2017 est.)
2% (April 2011 est.)

Unemployment, youth ages 15-24: *total:* 10.1%
male: 11.8%
female: 8.2% (2011 est.)

Budget: *revenues:* 965 million (FY05/06 est.)
expenditures: 943 million (FY05/06 est.)

Budget surplus (+) or deficit (-): 0.3% (of GDP) (FY05/06 est.)

Taxes and other revenues: 14.2% (of GDP) (FY05/06 est.)

Fiscal year: 1 April - 31 March

Exports - commodities: tweeds, herring, processed shellfish, beef, lamb

Imports - commodities: timber, fertilizers, fish

Exchange rates: Manx pounds (IMP) per US dollar -
0.7836 (2017 est.)
0.738 (2016 est.)
0.738 (2015)
0.6542 (2014)
0.6472 (2013 est.)

ENERGY

Electricity access: *electrification - total population:* 100% (2020)

COMMUNICATIONS

Telecommunication systems: *general assessment:* the Isle of Man has an extensive communications infrastructure consisting of telephone cables, submarine cables, and an array of television and mobile phone transmitters and towers (2022)
domestic: landline, telefax, mobile cellular telephone system
international: country code - 44; fiber-optic cable, microwave radio relay, satellite earth station, submarine cable

Broadcast media: national public radio broadcasts over 3 FM stations and 1 AM station; 2 commercial broadcasters operating with 1 having multiple FM stations; receives radio and TV services via relays from British TV and radio broadcasters

Internet country code: .im

TRANSPORTATION

Civil aircraft registration country code prefix: M

Airports: *total:* 1 (2021)

Airports - with paved runways: *total:* 1
1,524 to 2,437 m: 1 (2021)

Railways: *total:* 63 km (2008)
narrow gauge: 6 km (2008) 1.076-m gauge (6 km electrified)
57 0.914-mm gauge (29 km electrified) **note:** primarily summer tourist attractions

Roadways: *total:* 1,107 km (2022)
paved: 1,107 km

Ports and terminals: *major seaport(s):* Douglas, Ramsey

MILITARY AND SECURITY

Military - note: defense is the responsibility of the UK

TRANSNATIONAL ISSUES

Disputes - international: none identified

ISRAEL

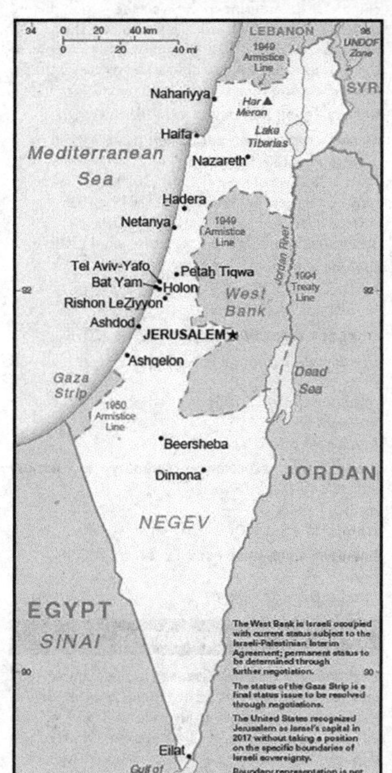

INTRODUCTION

Background: Israel has emerged as a regional economic and military powerhouse, leveraging its booming high-tech sector, massive defense industry, and concerns about Iran to foster partnerships around the world. The State of Israel was established in 1948. The UN General Assembly had proposed to partition the British Mandate for Palestine into an Arab and Jewish state. Arab states rejected the UN plan and were subsequently defeated militarily in the 1948 war that followed the withdrawal of the British on 14 May 1948. Israel was admitted as a member of the UN in 1949 and saw rapid population growth, primarily due to migration from Europe and the Middle East, over the following years. Israel and its Arab neighbors fought wars in 1967 and 1973 and Israel signed peace treaties with Egypt in 1979 and Jordan in 1994. Israel took control of the West Bank and Gaza Strip in the course of the 1967 war, and subsequently administered those territories through military authorities. Israel and Palestinian officials signed interim agreements in the 1990s that created an interim period of Palestinian self-rule in parts of the West Bank and Gaza. Israel withdrew from Gaza in 2005. While the most recent formal efforts between Israel and the Palestinian Authority to negotiate final status issues occurred in 2013-2014, the US continues its efforts to advance peace. Immigration to Israel continues, with more than 20,000 new immigrants, mostly Jewish, in 2020.

The Israeli economy has undergone a dramatic transformation in the last 25 years, led by cutting-edge, high-tech sectors. Offshore gas discoveries in the Mediterranean, most notably in the Tamar and Leviathan gasfields, place Israel at the center of a potential regional natural gas market. However, longer-term structural issues such as low labor force participation among minority populations, low workforce productivity, high costs for housing and consumer staples, and a lack of competition, remain a concern for many Israelis and an important consideration for Israeli politicians. Former Prime Minister Benjamin NETANYAHU dominated Israel's political landscape from 2009 to June 2021, becoming Israel's longest serving prime minister before he was unseated by Naftali BENNETT, after Israel's fourth election in two years.

BENNETT formed the most ideologically diverse coalition in Israel's history, including the participation of an Arab-Israeli party. He only served as prime minister for a year before stepping down on 1 July 2022 in favor of Yair LAPID. Israel signed normalization agreements – brokered by the US – with Bahrain, the United Arab Emirates, and Morocco in late 2020 and reached an agreement with Sudan in early 2021.

GEOGRAPHY

Location: Middle East, bordering the Mediterranean Sea, between Egypt and Lebanon

Geographic coordinates: 31 30 N, 34 45 E

Map references: Middle East

Area: *total:* 21,937 sq km
land: 21,497 sq km
water: 440 sq km

Area - comparative: slightly larger than New Jersey

Land boundaries: *total:* 1,068 km
border countries (6): Egypt 208 km; Gaza Strip 59 km; Jordan 327 km (20 km are within the Dead Sea); Lebanon 81 km; Syria 83 km; West Bank 330 km

Coastline: 273 km

Maritime claims: *territorial sea:* 12 nm
continental shelf: to depth of exploitation

Climate: temperate; hot and dry in southern and eastern desert areas

Terrain: Negev desert in the south; low coastal plain; central mountains; Jordan Rift Valley

Elevation: *highest point:* Mitspe Shlagim 2,224 m; note - this is the highest named point, the actual highest point is an unnamed dome slightly to the west of Mitspe Shlagim at 2,236 m; both points are on the northeastern border of Israel, along the southern end of the Anti-Lebanon mountain range
lowest point: Dead Sea -431 m
mean elevation: 508 m note - does not include elevation data from the Golan Heights

Natural resources: timber, potash, copper ore, natural gas, phosphate rock, magnesium bromide, clays, sand

Land use: *agricultural land:* 23.8% (2018 est.)
arable land: 13.7% (2018 est.)
permanent crops: 3.8% (2018 est.)
permanent pasture: 6.3% (2018 est.)
forest: 7.1% (2018 est.)
other: 69.1% (2018 est.)

Irrigated land: 2,250 sq km (2012)

Major lakes (area sq km): *salt water lake(s):* Dead Sea (shared with Jordan and West Bank) - 1,020 sq km
note - endorheic hypersaline lake; 9.6 times saltier than the ocean; lake shore is 431 meters below sea level

Population distribution: population concentrated in and around Tel-Aviv, as well as around the Sea of Galilee; the south remains sparsely populated with the exception of the shore of the Gulf of Aqaba

Natural hazards: sandstorms may occur during spring and summer; droughts; periodic earthquakes

Geography - note: *note 1:* Lake Tiberias (Sea of Galilee) is an important freshwater source; the Dead Sea is the second saltiest body of water in the world (after Lake Assal in Djibouti)
note 2: the Malham Cave in Mount Sodom is the world's longest salt cave at 10 km (6 mi); its survey is not complete and its length will undoubtedly increase; Mount Sodom is actually a hill some 220 m (722 ft) high that is 80% salt (multiple salt layers covered by a veneer of rock)
note 3: in March 2019, there were 380 Israeli settlements,to include 213 settlements and 132 outposts in the West Bank, and 35 settlements in East Jerusalem; there are no Israeli settlements in the Gaza Strip, as all were evacuated in 2005 (2019)

PEOPLE AND SOCIETY

Population: 8,914,885 (2022 est.) (includes populations of the Golan Heights or Golan Sub-District and also East Jerusalem, which was annexed by Israel after 1967)
note: approximately 227,100 Israeli settlers live in East Jerusalem (2019); following the March 2019 US recognition of the Golan Heights as being part of Israel, *The World Factbook* no longer includes Israeli settler population of the Golan Heights (estimated at 23,400 in 2019) in its overall Israeli settler total

Nationality: *noun:* Israeli(s)
adjective: Israeli

Ethnic groups: Jewish 74% (of which Israel-born 78.7%, Europe/America/Oceania-born 14.8%, Africa-born 4.2%, Asia-born 2.3%), Arab 21.1%, other 4.9% (2020 est.)

Languages: Hebrew (official), Arabic (special status under Israeli law), English (most commonly used foreign language)
major-language sample(s):
העולם, המקור החיוני למידע בסיסי ספר עובדות
(Hebrew)

Religions: Jewish 74%, Muslim 18%, Christian 1.9%, Druze 1.6%, other 4.5% (2020 est.)

Age structure: *0-14 years:* 26.76% (male 1,187,819/female 1,133,365)
15-24 years: 15.67% (male 694,142/female 665,721)
25-54 years: 37.2% (male 1,648,262/female 1,579,399)
55-64 years: 8.4% (male 363,262/female 365,709)
65 years and over: 11.96% (male 467,980/female 569,816) (2020 est.)

Dependency ratios: *total dependency ratio:* 67.3
youth dependency ratio: 46.6
elderly dependency ratio: 20.8
potential support ratio: 4.8 (2020 est.)

Median age: *total:* 30.4 years
male: 29.8 years
female: 31 years (2020 est.)

Population growth rate: 1.44% (2022 est.)

Birth rate: 17.41 births/1,000 population (2022 est.)

Death rate: 5.05 deaths/1,000 population (2022 est.)

Net migration rate: 2.02 migrant(s)/1,000 population (2022 est.)

Population distribution: population concentrated in and around Tel-Aviv, as well as around the Sea of Galilee; the south remains sparsely populated with the exception of the shore of the Gulf of Aqaba

Urbanization: *urban population:* 92.8% of total population (2022)
rate of urbanization: 1.51% annual rate of change (2020-25 est.)

Major urban areas - population: 4.344 million Tel Aviv-Yafo, 1.164 million Haifa, 957,000 JERUSALEM (capital) (2022)

Sex ratio: *at birth:* 1.05 male(s)/female
0-14 years: 1.05 male(s)/female
15-24 years: 1.04 male(s)/female
25-54 years: 1.04 male(s)/female
55-64 years: 1.01 male(s)/female
65 years and over: 0.7 male(s)/female
total population: 1.01 male(s)/female (2022 est.)

Mother's mean age at first birth: 27.7 years (2019 est.)

Maternal mortality ratio: 3 deaths/100,000 live births (2017 est.)

Infant mortality rate: *total:* 3.56 deaths/1,000 live births
male: 3.82 deaths/1,000 live births
female: 3.28 deaths/1,000 live births (2022 est.)

Life expectancy at birth total population: 83.35 years
male: 81.45 years
female: 85.34 years (2022 est.)

Total fertility rate: 2.56 children born/woman (2022 est.)

Drinking water source: *improved: urban:* 100% of population
rural: 100% of population
total: 100% of population

Current health expenditure: 7.5% of GDP (2019)

Physicians density: 3.63 physicians/1,000 population (2020)

Hospital bed density: 3 beds/1,000 population (2018)

Sanitation facility access: *improved: urban:* 100% of population
rural: 99.3% of population
total: 99.9% of population
unimproved: urban: 0% of population
rural: 0.7% of population
total: 0.1% of population (2020 est.)

HIV/AIDS - adult prevalence rate: 0.2% (2018 est.)

Major infectious diseases: *note:* on 21 March 2022, the US Centers for Disease Control and Prevention (CDC) issued a Travel Alert for polio in Asia; Israel is currently considered a high risk to travelers for circulating vaccine-derived polioviruses (cVDPV); vaccine-derived poliovirus (VDPV) is a strain of the weakened poliovirus that was initially included in oral polio vaccine (OPV) and *that has changed over time and behaves more like the wild or naturally occurring virus;* this means it can be spread more easily to people who are unvaccinated against polio and who come in contact with the stool or respiratory secretions, such as from a sneeze, of an "infected" person who received oral polio vaccine; the CDC recommends that before any international travel, anyone unvaccinated, incompletely vaccinated, or with an unknown polio vaccination status should complete the routine polio vaccine series; before travel to any high-risk destination, the CDC recommends that adults who previously completed the full, routine polio vaccine series receive a single, lifetime booster dose of polio vaccine

Obesity - adult prevalence rate: 26.1% (2016)

Alcohol consumption per capita: *total:* 3.07 liters of pure alcohol (2019 est.)
beer: 1.78 liters of pure alcohol (2019 est.)
wine: 0.08 liters of pure alcohol (2019 est.)
spirits: 1.16 liters of pure alcohol (2019 est.)
other alcohols: 0.04 liters of pure alcohol (2019 est.)

Tobacco use: *total:* 21.2% (2020 est.)
male: 28.9% (2020 est.)
female: 13.5% (2020 est.)

Education expenditures: 6.2% of GDP (2018 est.)

Literacy: *definition:* age 15 and over can read and write
total population: 97.8%
male: 98.7%
female: 96.8% (2011)

School life expectancy (primary to tertiary education): *total:* 16 years
male: 15 years
female: 17 years (2019)

Unemployment, youth ages 15-24: *total:* 7.9%
male: 7.6%
female: 8.2% (2020 est.)

ENVIRONMENT

Environment - current issues: limited arable land and restricted natural freshwater resources; desertification; air pollution from industrial and vehicle emissions; groundwater pollution from industrial and domestic waste, chemical fertilizers, and pesticides

Environment - international agreements: *party to:* Biodiversity, Climate Change, Climate

Change-Kyoto Protocol, Climate Change-Paris Agreement, Desertification, Endangered Species, Hazardous Wastes, Nuclear Test Ban, Ozone Layer Protection, Ship Pollution, Wetlands, Whaling
signed, but not ratified: Comprehensive Nuclear Test Ban, Marine Life Conservation

Air pollutants: *particulate matter emissions:* 19.46 micrograms per cubic meter (2016 est.)
carbon dioxide emissions: 65.17 megatons (2016 est.)
methane emissions: 13.02 megatons (2020 est.)

Climate: temperate; hot and dry in southern and eastern desert areas

Land use: *agricultural land:* 23.8% (2018 est.)
arable land: 13.7% (2018 est.)
permanent crops: 3.8% (2018 est.)
permanent pasture: 6.3% (2018 est.)
forest: 7.1% (2018 est.)
other: 69.1% (2018 est.)

Urbanization: *urban population:* 92.8% of total population (2022)
rate of urbanization: 1.51% annual rate of change (2020-25 est.)

Revenue from forest resources: *forest revenues:* 0% of GDP (2018 est.)

Revenue from coal: *coal revenues:* 0% of GDP (2018 est.)

Waste and recycling: *municipal solid waste generated annually:* 5.4 million tons (2015 est.)
municipal solid waste recycled annually: 1.35 million tons (2017 est.)
percent of municipal solid waste recycled: 25% (2017 est.)

Major lakes (area sq km): *salt water lake(s):* Dead Sea (shared with Jordan and West Bank) - 1,020 sq km
note - endorheic hypersaline lake; 9.6 times saltier than the ocean; lake shore is 431 meters below sea level

Total water withdrawal: *municipal:* 983 million cubic meters (2017 est.)
industrial: 72 million cubic meters (2017 est.)
agricultural: 1.249 billion cubic meters (2017 est.)

Total renewable water resources: 1.78 billion cubic meters (2017 est.)

GOVERNMENT

Country name: *conventional long form:* State of Israel
conventional short form: Israel
local long form: Medinat Yisra'el
local short form: Yisra'el
former: Mandatory Palestine
etymology: named after the ancient Kingdom of Israel; according to Biblical tradition, the Jewish patriarch Jacob received the name "Israel" ("He who struggles with God") after he wrestled an entire night with an angel of the Lord; Jacob's 12 sons became the ancestors of the Israelites, also known as the Twelve Tribes of Israel, who formed the Kingdom of Israel

Government type: parliamentary democracy

Capital: *name:* Jerusalem; note - the US recognized Jerusalem as Israel's capital in December 2017 without taking a position on the specific boundaries of Israeli sovereignty
geographic coordinates: 31 46 N, 35 14 E
time difference: UTC+2 (7 hours ahead of Washington, DC, during Standard Time)
daylight saving time: +1hr, Friday before the last Sunday in March; ends the last Sunday in October
etymology: Jerusalem's settlement may date back to 2800 B.C.; it is named Urushalim in Egyptian texts of the 14th century B.C.; *uru-shalim* likely means "foundation of [by] the god Shalim", and derives from Hebrew/Semitic *yry*, "to found or lay a cornerstone", and *Shalim*, the Canaanite god of dusk and the nether world; Shalim was associated with sunset and peace and the name is based on the same S-L-M root from which Semitic words for "peace" are derived (Salam or Shalom in modern Arabic and Hebrew); this confluence has thus led to naming interpretations such as "The City of Peace" or "The Abode of Peace"

Administrative divisions: 6 districts (mehozot, singular - mehoz); Central, Haifa, Jerusalem, Northern, Southern, Tel Aviv

Independence: 14 May 1948 (following League of Nations mandate under British administration)

National holiday: Independence Day, 14 May (1948); note - Israel declared independence on 14 May 1948, but the Jewish calendar is lunar and the holiday may occur in April or May

Constitution: *history:* no formal constitution; some functions of a constitution are filled by the Declaration of Establishment (1948), the Basic Laws, and the Law of Return (as amended)
amendments: proposed by Government of Israel ministers or by the Knesset; passage requires a majority vote of Knesset members and subject to Supreme Court judicial review; 11 of the 13 Basic Laws have been amended at least once, latest in 2020 (Basic Law: the Knesset)

Legal system: mixed legal system of English common law, British Mandate regulations, and Jewish, Christian, and Muslim religious laws

International law organization participation: has not submitted an ICJ jurisdiction declaration; withdrew acceptance of ICCt jurisdiction in 2002

Citizenship: *citizenship by birth:* no
citizenship by descent only: at least one parent must be a citizen of Israel
dual citizenship recognized: yes, but naturalized citizens are not allowed to maintain dual citizenship
residency requirement for naturalization: 3 out of the 5 years preceding the application for naturalization
note: Israeli law (Law of Return, 5 July 1950) provides for the granting of citizenship to any Jew - defined as a person being born to a Jewish mother or having converted to Judaism while renouncing any other religion - who immigrates to and expresses a desire to settle in Israel on the basis of the Right of aliyah; the 1970 amendment of this act extended the right to family members including the spouse of a Jew, any child or grandchild, and the spouses of children and grandchildren

Suffrage: 18 years of age; universal; 17 years of age for municipal elections

Executive branch: *chief of state:* President Isaac HERZOG (since 7 July 2021)
head of government: on 13 November 2022, President HERZOG tasked Benjamin NETANYHU with forming a new government
cabinet: Cabinet selected by prime minister and approved by the Knesset
elections/appointments: president indirectly elected by the Knesset for a single 7-year term; election last held on 2 June 2021 (next to be held in June 2028); following legislative elections, the president, in consultation with party leaders, tasks a Knesset member (usually the member of the largest party) with forming a new government
election results:
2021: Issac HERZOG elected president; Knesset vote - Issac HERZOG (independent) 87, Miriam PERETZ (independent) 26, invalid/blank 7

Legislative branch: *description:* unicameral Knesset (120 seats; members directly elected in a single nationwide constituency by closed-list proportional representation vote, with a 3.25% vote threshold to gain representation; members serve 4-year terms)
elections: last held on 1 November 2022 (next scheduled for November 2026)
election results: percent by party - Likud 23.4%, Yesh Atid 17.8%, Religious Zionist Party 10.8%, National Unity 9.1%, Shas 8.2%, UTJ 5.9%, Yisrael Beiteinu 4.5%, United Arab List 4.1%, Hadash-Ta'al 3.8%, Labor 3.7%, Meretz 3.2%, other 1.6%; seats by party - Likud 32, Yesh Atid 24, Religious Zionist Party 14, National Unity 12, Shas 11, UTJ 7, Yisrael Beiteinu 6, Hadash-Ta'al 5, United Arab List 5, Labor 4; composition - men 91, women 29, percentage of women 24.2%

Judicial branch: *highest court(s):* Supreme Court (consists of the president, deputy president, 13 justices, and 2 registrars) and normally sits in panels of 3 justices; in special cases, the panel is expanded with an uneven number of justices
judge selection and term of office: judges selected by the 9-member Judicial Selection Committee, consisting of the Minister of Justice (chair), the president of the Supreme Court, two other Supreme Court justices, 1 other Cabinet minister, 2 Knesset members, and 2 representatives of the Israel Bar Association; judges can serve up to mandatory retirement at age 70
subordinate courts: district and magistrate courts; national and regional labor courts; family and juvenile courts; special and Rabbinical courts

Political parties and leaders: Blue and White [Benny GANTZ]
Joint Arab List [Ayman ODEH] (alliance includes Hadash, Ta'al, Balad)
Labor Party or HaAvoda [Merav MICHAELI]
Likud [Binyamin NETANYAHU]
Meretz [Zehava GAL-ON]
National Unity [alliance includes Blue and White and New Hope]
New Hope [Gideon SA'AR]
Religious Zionist Party [Bezalel SMOTRICH, chairperson]
SHAS [Aryeh DERI]
United Arab List [Mansour ABBAS]
United Torah Judaism or UTJ [Moshe GAFNI] (alliance includes Agudat Israel and Degel HaTorah)
Yamina [Ayelet SHAKED]
Yesh Atid [Yair LAPID]
Yisrael Beiteinu [Avigdor LIEBERMAN]

International organization participation: BIS, BSEC (observer), CE (observer), CERN, CICA, EBRD, FAO, IADB, IAEA, IBRD, ICAO, ICC (national committees), ICRM, IDA, IFAD, IFC, IFRCS, ILO, IMF, IMO, IMSO, Interpol, IOC, IOM, IPU, ISO, ITSO, ITU, ITUC (NGOs), MIGA, OAS (observer), OECD, OPCW (signatory), OSCE (partner), Pacific Alliance (observer), Paris Club, PCA, SELEC (observer), UN, UNCTAD, UNESCO, UNHCR, UNIDO, UNWTO, UPU, WCO, WHO, WIPO, WMO, WTO

Diplomatic representation in the US: *chief of mission:* Ambassador Michael HERZOG (since 5 September 2021)
chancery: 3514 International Drive NW, Washington, DC 20008
telephone: [1] (202) 364-5500
FAX: [1] (202) 364-5607
email address and website:
consular@washington.mfa.gov.il
https://embassies.gov.il/washington/Pages/default.aspx
consulate(s) general: Atlanta, Boston, Chicago, Houston, Los Angeles, Miami, New York, San Francisco

Diplomatic representation from the US: *chief of mission:* ambassador Thomas NIDES (since 5 December 2021)
embassy: 14 David Flusser Street, Jerusalem, 9378322
mailing address: 6350 Jerusalem Place, Washington DC 20521-6350
telephone: [972] (2) 630-4000
FAX: [972] (2) 630-4070
email address and website:
JerusalemACS@state.gov
https://il.usembassy.gov/
branch office(s): Tel Aviv
note: on 14 May 2018, the US Embassy relocated to Jerusalem from Tel Aviv; on 4 March 2019, Consulate General Jerusalem merged into US Embassy Jerusalem to form a single diplomatic mission

Flag description: white with a blue hexagram (six-pointed linear star) known as the Magen David (Star of David or Shield of David) centered between two equal horizontal blue bands near the top and bottom edges of the flag; the basic design resembles a traditional Jewish prayer shawl (tallit), which is white with blue stripes; the hexagram as a Jewish symbol dates back to medieval times
note: the Israeli flag proclamation states that the flag colors are sky blue and white, but the exact shade of blue has never been set and can vary from a light to a dark blue

National symbol(s): Star of David (Magen David), menorah (seven-branched lampstand); national colors: blue, white

National anthem: *name:* "Hatikvah" (The Hope)
lyrics/music: Naftali Herz IMBER/traditional, arranged by Samuel COHEN
note: adopted 2004, unofficial since 1948; used as the anthem of the Zionist movement since 1897; the 1888 arrangement by Samuel COHEN is thought to be based on the Romanian folk song "Carul cu boi" (The Ox Driven Cart)

National heritage: *total World Heritage Sites:* 9 (all cultural)
selected World Heritage Site locales: Masada; Old City of Acre; White City of Tel-Aviv - the Modern Movement; Biblical Tels - Megiddo, Hazor, Beer Sheba; Incense Route - Desert Cities in the Negev; Bahá'i Holy Places; Sites of Human Evolution at Mount Carmel; Caves of Maresha and Bet-Guvrin; Necropolis of Bet She'arim

ECONOMY

Economic overview: Israel has a technologically advanced free market economy. Cut diamonds, high-technology equipment, and pharmaceuticals are among its leading exports. Its major imports include crude oil, grains, raw materials, and military equipment. Israel usually posts sizable trade deficits, which are offset by tourism and other service exports, as well as significant foreign investment inflows.

Since March 2020, economic growth has slowed compared to recent historical averages, but Israel's slump has been less severe than in other Middle Eastern countries because of its swift vaccine roll-out and diversified economic base. Between 2016 and 2019, growth averaged 3.6% per year, led by exports. Israel's new government is hoping to pass the country's first budget in two years, which, combined with prudent fiscal policy and strong global trade ties would probably enable Israel to recover from economic challenges caused by the COVID-19 pandemic.

Natural gas fields discovered off Israel's coast since 2009 have brightened Israel's energy security outlook. The Tamar and Leviathan fields were some of the world's largest offshore natural gas finds in the last decade. In 2020, Israel began exporting gas to Egypt and Jordan.

Income inequality and high housing and commodity prices continue to be a concern for many Israelis. Israel's income inequality and poverty rates are among the highest of OECD countries, and there is a broad perception among the public that a small number of "tycoons" have a cartel-like grip over the major parts of the economy. Government officials have called for reforms to boost the housing supply and to increase competition in the banking sector to address these public grievances. Despite calls for reforms, the restricted housing supply continues to impact younger Israelis seeking to purchase homes. Tariffs and non-tariff barriers, coupled with guaranteed prices and customs tariffs for farmers kept food prices high. Private consumption is expected to drive growth through 2021, with consumers benefitting from low inflation and a strong currency.

In the long term, Israel faces structural issues including low labor participation rates for its fastest growing social segments - the ultraorthodox and Arab-Israeli communities. Also, Israel's progressive, globally competitive, knowledge-based technology sector employs only about 8% of the workforce, with the rest mostly employed in manufacturing and services - sectors which face downward wage pressures from global competition. Expenditures on educational institutions remain low compared to most other OECD countries with similar GDP per capita.

Real GDP (purchasing power parity): $353.39 billion (2020 est.)
$362.23 billion (2019 est.)
$350.15 billion (2018 est.)
note: data are in 2017 dollars

Real GDP growth rate: -2.6% (2020 est.)
3.28% (2019 est.)
3.69% (2018 est.)

Real GDP per capita: $38,300 (2020 est.)
$40,000 (2019 est.)
$39,400 (2018 est.)
note: data are in 2017 dollars

GDP (official exchange rate): $394.93 billion (2019 est.)

Inflation rate (consumer prices): 1.8% (2020 est.)
0.8% (2019 est.)
0.8% (2018 est.)

Credit ratings:

Fitch rating: A+ (2016)

Moody's rating: A1 (2008)

Standard & Poors rating: AA- (2018)
note: the year refers to the year in which the current credit rating was first obtained.

GDP - composition, by sector of origin: *agriculture:* 2.4% (2017 est.)
industry: 26.5% (2017 est.)
services: 69.5% (2017 est.)

GDP - composition, by end use: *household consumption:* 55.1% (2017 est.)
government consumption: 22.8% (2017 est.)
investment in fixed capital: 20.1% (2017 est.)
investment in inventories: 0.7% (2017 est.)
exports of goods and services: 28.9% (2017 est.)
imports of goods and services: -27.5% (2017 est.)

Agricultural products: milk, potatoes, poultry, tomatoes, carrots, turnips, tangerines/mandarins, green chillies/peppers, eggs, vegetables

Industries: high-technology products (including aviation, communications, computer-aided design and manufactures, medical electronics, fiber optics), wood and paper products, potash and phosphates, food, beverages, and tobacco, caustic soda, cement, pharmaceuticals, construction, metal products, chemical products, plastics, cut diamonds, textiles, footwear

Industrial production growth rate: 3.5% (2017 est.)

Labor force: 3.893 million (2020 est.)

Labor force - by occupation: *agriculture:* 1.1%
industry: 17.3%
services: 81.6% (2015 est.)

Unemployment rate: 4.4% (2020 est.)
3.81% (2019 est.)
4% (2018 est.)

Unemployment, youth ages 15-24: *total:* 7.9%
male: 7.6%
female: 8.2% (2020 est.)

Population below poverty line: 22% (2014 est.)
note: Israel's poverty line is $7.30 per person per day

Gini Index coefficient - distribution of family income:
37 (2018 est.)
39 (2016 est.)
39.2 (2008)

Household income or consumption by percentage share: *lowest 10%:* 1.7%
highest 10%: 31.3% (2010)

Budget: *revenues:* 93.11 billion (2017 est.)
expenditures: 100.2 billion (2017 est.)

Budget surplus (+) or deficit (-): -2% (of GDP) (2017 est.)

Public debt: 72.6% of GDP (2020 est.)
59.6% of GDP (2019 est.)
60.4% of GDP (2018 est.)

Taxes and other revenues: 26.5% (of GDP) (2017 est.)

Fiscal year: calendar year

Current account balance: $20.642 billion (2020 est.)
$13.411 billion (2019 est.)
$7.888 billion (2018 est.)

Exports: $113.87 billion (2020 est.) note: data are in current year dollars
$115.57 billion (2019 est.) note: data are in current year dollars
$110.05 billion (2018 est.) note: data are in current year dollars

Exports - partners: United States 26%, China 9%, United Kingdom 7% (2020)

Exports - commodities: diamonds, packaged medicines, medical instruments, integrated circuits, refined petroleum (2019)

Imports: $96.53 billion (2020 est.) note: data are in current year dollars
$108.26 billion (2019 est.) note: data are in current year dollars
$107.74 billion (2018 est.) note: data are in current year dollars

Imports - partners: United States 12%, China 11%, Germany 7.5%, Switzerland 7%, Turkey 6% (2020)

Imports - commodities: diamonds, cars, crude petroleum, refined petroleum, broadcasting equipment (2019)

Reserves of foreign exchange and gold: $173.292 billion (2020 est.)
$113 billion (31 December 2017 est.)
$95.45 billion (31 December 2016 est.)

Debt - external: $132.5 billion (31 December 2020 est.)
$99.886 billion (2019 est.)
$94.247 billion (2018 est.)

Exchange rates: new Israeli shekels (ILS) per US dollar -
3.44 (2020 est.)
3.4684 (2019 est.)
3.7332 (2018 est.)
3.8869 (2014 est.)
3.5779 (2013 est.)

ENERGY

Electricity access: *electrification - total population:* 100% (2020)

Electricity: *installed generating capacity:* 18.993 million kW (2020 est.)
consumption: 59,192,500,000 kWh (2019 est.)
exports: 6.243 billion kWh (2020 est.)
imports: 0 kWh (2020 est.)
transmission/distribution losses: 2.642 billion kWh (2019 est.)

Electricity generation sources: *fossil fuels:* 93.7% of total installed capacity (2020 est.)
solar: 5.9% of total installed capacity (2020 est.)
wind: 0.3% of total installed capacity (2020 est.)

Coal: *production:* 0 metric tons (2020 est.)
consumption: 5.089 million metric tons (2020 est.)
exports: 0 metric tons (2020 est.)
imports: 5.565 million metric tons (2020 est.)
proven reserves: 0 metric tons (2019 est.)

Petroleum: *total petroleum production:* 0 bbl/day (2021 est.)
refined petroleum consumption: 232,400 bbl/day (2019 est.)
crude oil and lease condensate exports: 0 bbl/day (2018 est.)
crude oil and lease condensate imports: 232,900 bbl/day (2018 est.)
crude oil estimated reserves: 12.7 million barrels (2021 est.)

Refined petroleum products - production: 294,300 bbl/day (2017 est.)

Refined petroleum products - exports: 111,700 bbl/day (2017 est.)

Refined petroleum products - imports: 98,860 bbl/day (2017 est.)

Natural gas: *production:* 10,474,299,000 cubic meters (2019 est.)
consumption: 9,442,435,000 cubic meters (2019 est.)
exports: 0 cubic meters (2021 est.)
imports: 820.508 million cubic meters (2019 est.)
proven reserves: 176.017 billion cubic meters (2021 est.)

Carbon dioxide emissions: 61.092 million metric tonnes of CO2 (2019 est.)
from coal and metallurgical coke: 13.653 million metric tonnes of CO2 (2019 est.)
from petroleum and other liquids: 29.416 million metric tonnes of CO2 (2019 est.)
from consumed natural gas: 18.023 million metric tonnes of CO2 (2019 est.)

Energy consumption per capita: 113.273 million Btu/person (2019 est.)

COMMUNICATIONS

Telephones - fixed lines: *total subscriptions:* 3.37 million (2020 est.)
subscriptions per 100 inhabitants: 39 (2020 est.)

Telephones - mobile cellular: *total subscriptions:* 12.27 million (2020 est.)
subscriptions per 100 inhabitants: 142 (2020 est.)

Telecommunication systems: *general assessment:* Israel's developed economy largely revolves around high technology products, primarily used in the medical, biotechnology, agricultural, materials, and military industries; the country also attracts investment in its cyber-security industry, and has established itself as a hub for thousands of start-up companies; to underpin these developments, Israel has developed a robust telecoms sector; household broadband subscriptions is high, with a focus on fiber-network deployment; LTE services are almost universally available, while the August 2020 multi-frequency bands also enabled the MNOs to provide services based on 5G; 5G will be supported by moves to close down GSM and 3G networks in stages through to the end of 2025, with the physical assets and frequencies to be repurposed for LTE and 5G use (2022)
domestic: good system of coaxial cable and microwave radio relay; all systems are digital; competition among both fixed-line and mobile cellular providers results in good coverage countrywide; fixed-line nearly 39 per 100 and nearly 142 per 100 for mobile-cellular subscriptions (2020)
international: country code - 972; landing points for the MedNautilus Submarine System, Tameres North, Jonah and Lev Submarine System, submarine cables that provide links to Europe, Cyprus, and parts of the Middle East; satellite earth stations - 3 Intelsat (2 Atlantic Ocean and 1 Indian Ocean) (2019)

Broadcast media: the Israel Broadcasting Corporation (est 2015) broadcasts on 3 channels, two in Hebrew and the other in Arabic; multi- channel satellite and cable TV packages provide access to foreign channels; the Israeli Broadcasting Corporation broadcasts on 8 radio networks with multiple repeaters and Israel Defense Forces Radio broadcasts over multiple stations; about 15 privately owned radio stations; overall more than 100 stations and repeater stations (2019)

Internet country code: .il

Internet users: *total:* 8,293,590 (2020 est.)
percent of population: 90% (2020 est.)

Broadband - fixed subscriptions: *total:* 2,602,079 (2020 est.)
subscriptions per 100 inhabitants: 30 (2020 est.)

TRANSPORTATION

National air transport system: *number of registered air carriers:* 6 (2020)
inventory of registered aircraft operated by air carriers: 64
annual passenger traffic on registered air carriers: 7,404,373 (2018)
annual freight traffic on registered air carriers: 994.54 million (2018) mt-km

Civil aircraft registration country code prefix: 4X

Airports: *total:* 42 (2021)

Airports - with paved runways: *total:* 33
over 3,047 m: 3
2,438 to 3,047 m: 5
1,524 to 2,437 m: 5
914 to 1,523 m: 12
under 914 m: 8 (2021)

Airports - with unpaved runways: *total:* 9
914 to 1,523 m: 3
under 914 m: 6 (2021)

Heliports: 3 (2021)

Pipelines: 763 km gas, 442 km oil, 261 km refined products (2013)

Railways: *total:* 1,384 km (2019) (2019)
standard gauge: 1,384 km (2014) 1.435-m gauge

Roadways: *total:* 19,555 km (2017)
paved: 19,555 km (2017) (includes 449 km of expressways)

Merchant marine: *total:* 41
by type: container ship 6, general cargo 2, oil tanker 4, other 29 (2021)

Ports and terminals: *major seaport(s):* Ashdod, Elat (Eilat), Hadera, Haifa
container port(s) (TEUs): Ashdod (1,584,000) (2019)

LNG terminal(s) (import): Hadera

MILITARY AND SECURITY

Military and security forces: Israel Defense Forces (IDF): Ground Forces, Israel Naval Force (IN, includes commandos), Israel Air Force (IAF, includes air defense); Ministry of Public Security: Border Police (2022)
note: the Border Police is a unit within the Israel Police with its own organizational and command structure; it works both independently as well as in cooperation with or in support of the Israel Police and the IDF

Military expenditures: 5% of GDP (2021 est.)
5% of GDP (2020 est.)
5.2% of GDP (2019 est.) (approximately $20 billion)
5.3% of GDP (2018 est.) (approximately $19.9 billion)
5.5% of GDP (2017 est.) (approximately $19.7 billion)

Military and security service personnel strengths: approximately 173,000 active duty personnel (130,000 Ground Forces; 9,000 Naval; 34,000 Air Force) (2022)

Military equipment inventories and acquisitions: the majority of the IDF's inventory is comprised of weapons that are domestically-produced or imported from Europe and the US; since 2010, the US has been the leading supplier of arms to Israel; Israel has a broad defense industrial base that can develop, produce, support, and sustain a wide variety of weapons systems for both domestic use and export, particularly armored vehicles, unmanned aerial systems, air defense, and guided missiles (2022)

Military service age and obligation: 18 years of age for compulsory military service; 17 years of age for voluntary military service; Jews and Druze can be conscripted; Christians, Circassians, and Muslims may volunteer; both sexes are obligated to military service; conscript service obligation is 32 months for enlisted men and about 24 months for enlisted women (varies based on military occupation); officers serve 48 months; pilots commit to 9 years of service; reserve obligation to age 41-51 (men), age 24 (women) (2022)
note 1: women have served in the Israeli military since its establishment in 1948; as of 2021, women made up about 35% of IDF personnel; more than 90% of military specialties, including combat specialties, were open to women and more than 3,000 women were serving in combat units; the IDF's first mixed-gender infantry unit, the Caracal Battalion, was established in 2004
note 2: as of 2021, conscripts comprised about 70% of the IDF ground forces
note 3: the IDF recruits non-Israeli Jews and non-Jews with a minimum of one Jewish grandparent, as well as converts to Judaism; each year the IDF brings in about 800-1,000 foreign recruits from around the world

Military - note: the United Nations Disengagement Observer Force (UNDOF) has operated in the Golan between Israel and Syria since 1974 to monitor the ceasefire following the 1973 Arab-Israeli War and supervise the areas of separation between the two countries; as of mid-2022, UNDOF consisted of about 1,000 personnel

since the outbreak of the Syrian civil war in 2011, Israel has routinely carried out air strikes in Syria targeting Iranian, Iranian-backed militia and Hizballah forces, and some Syrian Government military positions; over the same period, the IDF has carried out numerous strikes against Hizballah in Lebanon in response to attacks on Israeli territory; Israel fought a month-long war in Lebanon with Hizballah in 2006 (see Appendix T for details on Hizballah)

as of 2022, the IDF also conducted frequent operations against the HAMAS and Palestine Islamic Jihad (PIJ) terrorist groups operating out of the Gaza Strip; since seizing control of the Gaza Strip in 2007, HAMAS has claimed responsibility for numerous rocket attacks into Israel and organized protests at the border between Gaza and Israel, resulting in violent clashes, casualties, and reprisal military actions by the IDF; HAMAS and Israel fought an 11-day conflict in May of 2021, which ended in an informal truce; sporadic clashes continued into 2022, including incendiary balloon attacks from Palestinian territory and retaliatory IDF strikes; PIJ has conducted numerous attacks on Israel since the 1980s, including a barrage of mortar and rocket strikes in February 2020 (see Appendix-T for more details on HAMAS and Palestine Islamic Jihad)

Israel has Major Non-NATO Ally (MNNA) status with the US; MNNA is a designation under US law that provides foreign partners with certain benefits in the areas of defense trade and security cooperation; while MNNA status provides military and economic privileges, it does not entail any security commitments (2022)

TERRORISM

Terrorist group(s): Islamic State of Iraq and ash-Sham (ISIS); Popular Front for the Liberation of Palestine; Palestinian Islamic Jihad

TRANSNATIONAL ISSUES

Disputes - international: *Israel-Gaza Strip:* Israel withdrew its settlers and military from the Gaza Strip and from four settlements in the West Bank in August 2005
Israel-Syria: Golan Heights is Israeli-controlled (Lebanon claims the Shab'a Farms area of Golan Heights); in March 2019, the US Government recognized Israel's sovereignty over the Golan Heights; since 1948, about 350 peacekeepers from the UN Truce Supervision Organization headquartered in Jerusalem monitor ceasefires, supervise armistice agreements, prevent isolated incidents from escalating, and assist other UN personnel in the region
Israel-West Bank: West Bank is Israeli-occupied with current status subject to the Israeli-Palestinian Interim Agreement - permanent status to be determined through further negotiation; in 2002, Israel began construction of a "seam line" separation barrier along parts of the Green Line and within the West Bank; as of mid-2020, plans were to continue barrier construction

Refugees and internally displaced persons: *refugees (country of origin):* 12,181 (Eritrea), 5,061 (Ukraine) (2019)
stateless persons: 42 (mid-year 2021)

Illicit drugs: increasingly concerned about ecstasy, cocaine, and heroin abuse; drugs arrive in country from Lebanon and, increasingly, from Jordan; money-laundering center

ITALY

INTRODUCTION

Background: Italy became a nation-state in 1861 when the regional states of the peninsula, along with Sardinia and Sicily, were united under King Victor EMMANUEL II. An era of parliamentary government came to a close in the early 1920s when Benito MUSSOLINI established a Fascist dictatorship. His alliance with Nazi Germany led to Italy's defeat in World War II. A democratic republic replaced the monarchy in 1946 and economic revival followed. Italy is a charter member of NATO and the European Economic Community (EEC) and its subsequent successors the EC and the EU. It has been at the forefront of European economic and political unification, joining the Economic and Monetary Union in 1999. Persistent problems include sluggish economic growth, high youth and female unemployment, organized crime, corruption, and economic disparities between southern Italy and the more prosperous north.

GEOGRAPHY

Location: Southern Europe, a peninsula extending into the central Mediterranean Sea, northeast of Tunisia

Geographic coordinates: 42 50 N, 12 50 E

Map references: Europe

Area: *total:* 301,340 sq km
land: 294,140 sq km
water: 7,200 sq km
note: includes Sardinia and Sicily

Area - comparative: almost twice the size of Georgia; slightly larger than Arizona

Land boundaries: *total:* 1,836.4 km
border countries (6): Austria 404 km; France 476 km; Holy See (Vatican City) 3.4 km; San Marino 37 km; Slovenia 218 km; Switzerland 698 km

Coastline: 7,600 km

Maritime claims: *territorial sea:* 12 nm
continental shelf: 200-m depth or to the depth of exploitation

Climate: predominantly Mediterranean; alpine in far north; hot, dry in south

Terrain: mostly rugged and mountainous; some plains, coastal lowlands

Elevation: *highest point:* Mont Blanc (Monte Bianco) de Courmayeur (a secondary peak of Mont Blanc) 4,748 m
lowest point: Mediterranean Sea 0 m

mean elevation: 538 m

Natural resources: coal, antimony, mercury, zinc, potash, marble, barite, asbestos, pumice, fluorspar, feldspar, pyrite (sulfur), natural gas and crude oil reserves, fish, arable land

Land use: *agricultural land:* 47.1% (2018 est.)
arable land: 22.8% (2018 est.)
permanent crops: 8.6% (2018 est.)
permanent pasture: 15.7% (2018 est.)
forest: 31.4% (2018 est.)
other: 21.5% (2018 est.)

Irrigated land: 39,500 sq km (2012)

Major watersheds (area sq km): Atlantic Ocean drainage: Rhine-Maas (198,735 sq km), *(Black Sea)* Danube (795,656 sq km), *(Adriatic Sea)* Po (76,997 sq km), *(Mediterranean Sea)* Rhone (100,543 sq km)

Population distribution: despite a distinctive pattern with an industrial north and an agrarian south, a fairly even population distribution exists throughout most of the country, with coastal areas, the Po River Valley, and urban centers (particularly Milan, Rome, and Naples), attracting larger and denser populations

Natural hazards: regional risks include landslides, mudflows, avalanches, earthquakes, volcanic eruptions, flooding; land subsidence in Venice
volcanism: significant volcanic activity; Etna (3,330 m), which is in eruption as of 2010, is Europe's most active volcano; flank eruptions pose a threat to nearby Sicilian villages; Etna, along with the famous Vesuvius, which remains a threat to the millions of nearby residents in the Bay of Naples area, have both been deemed Decade Volcanoes by the International Association of Volcanology and Chemistry of the Earth's Interior, worthy of study due to their explosive history and close proximity to human populations; Stromboli, on its namesake island, has also been continuously active with moderate volcanic activity; other historically active volcanoes include Campi Flegrei, Ischia, Larderello, Pantelleria, Vulcano, and Vulsini

Geography - note: strategic location dominating central Mediterranean as well as southern sea and air approaches to Western Europe

PEOPLE AND SOCIETY

Population: 61,095,551 (2022 est.)

Nationality: *noun:* Italian(s)
adjective: Italian

Ethnic groups: Italian (includes small clusters of German-, French-, and Slovene-Italians in the north and Albanian-Italians and Greek- Italians in the south)

Languages: Italian (official), German (parts of Trentino-Alto Adige region are predominantly German-speaking), French (small French-speaking minority in Valle d'Aosta region), Slovene (Slovene-speaking minority in the Trieste-Gorizia area)
major-language sample(s): L'Almanacco dei fatti del mondo, l'indispensabile fonte per le informazioni di base. (Italian)

Religions: Christian 80.8% (overwhelmingly Roman Catholic with very small groups of Jehovah's Witnesses and Protestants), Muslim 4.9%, unaffiliated 13.4%, other 0.9% (2020 est.)

Age structure: *0-14 years:* 13.45% (male 4,292,431/ female 4,097,732)
15-24 years: 9.61% (male 3,005,402/female 2,989,764)
25-54 years: 40.86% (male 12,577,764/female 12,921,614)
55-64 years: 14% (male 4,243,735/female 4,493,581)
65 years and over: 22.08% (male 5,949,560/female 7,831,076) (2020 est.)

Dependency ratios: *total dependency ratio:* 57
youth dependency ratio: 20.4
elderly dependency ratio: 36.6
potential support ratio: 2.7 (2020 est.)

Median age: *total:* 46.5 years
male: 45.4 years
female: 47.5 years (2020 est.)

Population growth rate: -0.13% (2022 est.)

Birth rate: 6.95 births/1,000 population (2022 est.)

Death rate: 11.31 deaths/1,000 population (2022 est.)

Net migration rate: 3.02 migrant(s)/1,000 population (2022 est.)

Population distribution: despite a distinctive pattern with an industrial north and an agrarian south, a fairly even population distribution exists throughout most of the country, with coastal areas, the Po River Valley, and urban centers (particularly Milan, Rome, and Naples), attracting larger and denser populations

Urbanization: *urban population:* 71.7% of total population (2022)
rate of urbanization: 0.27% annual rate of change (2020-25 est.)

Major urban areas - population: 4.298 million ROME (capital), 3.149 million Milan, 2.180 million Naples, 1.798 million Turin, 907,000 Bergamo, 850,000 Palermo (2022)

Sex ratio: *at birth:* 1.06 male(s)/female
0-14 years: 1.05 male(s)/female
15-24 years: 1.01 male(s)/female
25-54 years: 0.97 male(s)/female
55-64 years: 0.95 male(s)/female
65 years and over: 0.67 male(s)/female
total population: 0.93 male(s)/female (2022 est.)

Mother's mean age at first birth: 31.4 years (2020 est.)

Maternal mortality ratio: 2 deaths/100,000 live births (2017 est.)

Infant mortality rate: *total:* 3.16 deaths/1,000 live births
male: 3.32 deaths/1,000 live births
female: 2.99 deaths/1,000 live births (2022 est.)

Life expectancy at birth: *total population:* 82.59 years
male: 80.25 years
female: 85.08 years (2022 est.)

Total fertility rate: 1.22 children born/woman (2022 est.)

Contraceptive prevalence rate: 65.1% (2013)
note: percent of women aged 18-49

Drinking water source: *improved: total:* 99.9% of population
unimproved: total: 0.1% of population (2020 est.)

Current health expenditure: 8.7% of GDP (2019)

Physicians density: 3.95 physicians/1,000 population (2020)

Hospital bed density: 3.1 beds/1,000 population (2018)

Sanitation facility access: *improved: urban:* 100% of population
rural: 100% of population
total: 100% of population

HIV/AIDS - adult prevalence rate: 0.2% (2020 est.)

Major infectious diseases: *note:* a new coronavirus is causing respiratory illness (COVID-19) in Italy; illness with this virus has ranged from mild to severe with fatalities reported; as of 6 June 2022, Italy has reported a total of 17,505,973 cases of COVID-19 or 29,352 cumulative cases of COVID-19 per 100,000 population with a total of 166,949 cumulative deaths or a rate of 279.9 cumulative deaths per 100,000 population; as of 6 June 2022, 84.1% of the population has received at least one dose of COVID-19 vaccine; the US Department of Homeland Security has issued instructions requiring US passengers who have been in Italy to travel through select airports where the US Government has implemented enhanced screening procedures

Obesity - adult prevalence rate: 19.9% (2016)

Alcohol consumption per capita: *total:* 7.65 liters of pure alcohol (2019 est.)
beer: 1.99 liters of pure alcohol (2019 est.)
wine: 4.83 liters of pure alcohol (2019 est.)
spirits: 0.83 liters of pure alcohol (2019 est.)
other alcohols: 0 liters of pure alcohol (2019 est.)

Tobacco use: *total:* 23.1% (2020 est.)
male: 26.6% (2020 est.)
female: 19.5% (2020 est.)

Education expenditures: 4.3% of GDP (2018 est.)

Literacy: *definition:* age 15 and over can read and write
total population: 99.2%
male: 99.4%
female: 99% (2018)

School life expectancy (primary to tertiary education): *total:* 16 years
male: 16 years
female: 17 years (2019)

Unemployment, youth ages 15-24: *total:* 29.4%
male: 27.9%
female: 31.8% (2020 est.)

ENVIRONMENT

Environment - current issues: air pollution from industrial emissions such as sulfur dioxide; coastal and inland rivers polluted from industrial and agricultural effluents; acid rain damaging lakes; inadequate industrial waste treatment and disposal facilities

Environment - international agreements: *party to:* Air Pollution, Air Pollution-Nitrogen Oxides, Air Pollution-Persistent Organic Pollutants, Air Pollution-Sulphur 85, Air Pollution-Sulphur 94, Air Pollution-Volatile Organic Compounds, Antarctic-Environmental Protection, Antarctic-Marine Living Resources, Antarctic Seals, Antarctic Treaty, Biodiversity, Climate Change, Climate Change-Kyoto Protocol, Climate Change-Paris Agreement, Comprehensive Nuclear Test Ban, Desertification, Endangered Species, Environmental Modification, Hazardous Wastes, Law of the Sea, Marine Dumping-London Convention, Marine Dumping- London Protocol, Nuclear Test Ban, Ozone Layer Protection, Ship Pollution, Tropical Timber 2006, Wetlands, Whaling
signed, but not ratified: Air Pollution-Heavy Metals, Air Pollution-Multi-effect Protocol

Air pollutants: *particulate matter emissions:* 15.28 micrograms per cubic meter (2016 est.)
methane emissions: 41.3 megatons (2020 est.)

Climate: predominantly Mediterranean; alpine in far north; hot, dry in south

Land use: *agricultural land:* 47.1% (2018 est.)
arable land: 22.8% (2018 est.)
permanent crops: 8.6% (2018 est.)
permanent pasture: 15.7% (2018 est.)
forest: 31.4% (2018 est.)
other: 21.5% (2018 est.)

Urbanization: *urban population:* 71.7% of total population (2022)
rate of urbanization: 0.27% annual rate of change (2020-25 est.)

Revenue from forest resources: *forest revenues:* 0.01% of GDP (2018 est.)

Revenue from coal: *coal revenues:* 0% of GDP (2018 est.)

Waste and recycling: *municipal solid waste generated annually:* 29.524 million tons (2015 est.)
municipal solid waste recycled annually: 7,646,716 tons (2015 est.)
percent of municipal solid waste recycled: 25.9% (2015 est.)

Major watersheds (area sq km): Atlantic Ocean drainage: Rhine-Maas (198,735 sq km), *(Black Sea)* Danube (795,656 sq km), *(Adriatic Sea)* Po (76,997 sq km), *(Mediterranean Sea)* Rhone (100,543 sq km)

Total water withdrawal: *municipal:* 9.488 billion cubic meters (2017 est.)
industrial: 7.7 billion cubic meters (2017 est.)
agricultural: 17 billion cubic meters (2017 est.)

Total renewable water resources: 191.3 billion cubic meters (2017 est.)

GOVERNMENT

Country name: *conventional long form:* Italian Republic
conventional short form: Italy
local long form: Repubblica Italiana
local short form: Italia
former: Kingdom of Italy
etymology: derivation is unclear, but the Latin "Italia" may come from the Oscan "Viteliu" meaning "[Land] of Young Cattle" (the bull was a symbol of southern Italic tribes)

Government type: parliamentary republic

Capital: *name:* Rome
geographic coordinates: 41 54 N, 12 29 E
time difference: UTC+1 (6 hours ahead of Washington, DC, during Standard Time)
daylight saving time: +1hr, begins last Sunday in March; ends last Sunday in October
etymology: by tradition, named after Romulus, one of the legendary founders of the city and its first king

Administrative divisions: 15 regions (regioni, singular - regione) and 5 autonomous regions (regioni autonome, singular - regione autonoma)
regions: Abruzzo, Basilicata, Calabria, Campania, Emilia-Romagna, Lazio (Latium), Liguria, Lombardia, Marche, Molise, Piemonte (Piedmont), Puglia (Apulia), Toscana (Tuscany), Umbria, Veneto
autonomous regions: Friuli Venezia Giulia, Sardegna (Sardinia), Sicilia (Sicily), Trentino-Alto Adige (Trentino-South Tyrol) or Trentino-Suedtirol (German), Valle d'Aosta (Aosta Valley) or Vallee d'Aoste (French)

Independence: 17 March 1861 (Kingdom of Italy proclaimed; Italy was not finally unified until 1871)

National holiday: Republic Day, 2 June (1946)

Constitution: *history:* previous 1848 (originally for the Kingdom of Sardinia and adopted by the Kingdom of Italy in 1861); latest enacted 22 December 1947, adopted 27 December 1947, entered into force 1 January 1948
amendments: proposed by both houses of Parliament; passage requires two successive debates and approval by absolute majority of each house on the second vote; a referendum is only required when requested by one fifth of the members of either house, by voter petition, or by 5 Regional Councils (elected legislative assemblies of the 15 first-level administrative regions and 5 autonomous regions of Italy); referendum not required if an amendment has been approved by a two-thirds majority in each house in the second vote; amended many times, last in 2020

Legal system: civil law system; judicial review of legislation under certain conditions in Constitutional Court

International law organization participation: accepts compulsory ICJ jurisdiction with reservations; accepts ICCt jurisdiction

Citizenship: *citizenship by birth:* no
citizenship by descent only: at least one parent must be a citizen of Italy
dual citizenship recognized: yes
residency requirement for naturalization: 4 years for EU nationals, 5 years for refugees and specified exceptions, 10 years for all others

Suffrage: 18 years of age; universal except in senatorial elections, where minimum age is 25

Executive branch: *chief of state:* President Sergio MATTARELLA (since 3 February 2015)
head of government: Prime Minister Giorgia MELONI (since 22 October 2022); the prime minister's official title is President of the Council of Ministers
cabinet: Council of Ministers proposed by the prime minister, known officially as the President of the Council of Ministers and locally as the Premier; nominated by the president; the current deputy prime ministers, known officially as vice presidents of the Council of Ministers, are Matteo SALVINI (L) and Luigi Di MAIO (M5S) (since 1 June 2018)
elections/appointments: president indirectly elected by an electoral college consisting of both houses of Parliament and 58 regional representatives for a 7-year term (no term limits); election last held on 24-29 January 2022 (eight rounds) (next to be held in 2029); prime minister appointed by the president, confirmed by parliament
election results: 2022: Sergio MATTARELLA (independent) reelected president; electoral college vote count in eighth round - 759 out of 1,009 (505 vote threshold)
2015: Sergio MATTARELLA (independent) elected president; electoral college vote count in fourth round - 665 out of 995 (505 vote threshold)

Legislative branch: *description:* bicameral Parliament or Parlamento consists of:
Senate or Senato della Repubblica (320 seats; 116 members directly elected in single-seat constituencies by simple majority vote, 193 members in multi-seat constituencies and 6 members in multi-seat constituencies abroad directly elected by party-list proportional representation vote to serve 5-year terms and 5 ex-officio members appointed by the president of the Republic to serve for life)
Chamber of Deputies or Camera dei Deputati (630 seats; 629 members directly elected in single- and multi-seat constituencies by proportional representation vote and 1 member from Valle d'Aosta elected by simple majority vote; members serve 5-year terms)
elections: Senate - last held on 25 September 2022
Chamber of Deputies - last held on 25 September 2022; note - snap elections were called when Prime Minister DRAGHI resigned and the parliament was dissolved on 21 July 2022 (next to be held 30 September 2027)
election results: Senate - percent of vote by party - NA; seats by party - center-right coalition (FdI 65, Lega 30, FI 18), center-left coalition (PD 40, AVS 3), M5S 28, Action-Italia Viva 9, SVP 2, MAIE 1, ScN 1; composition (as of September 2022) - men 131, women 69, percent of women 34.5%
Chamber of Deputies - percent of vote by party - NA; seats by party - center-right coalition (FdI 119, Lega 66, FI 45), center-left coalition (PD 69, AVS 12), M5S 52, Action-Italia Viva 21, SVP 3, MAIE 1, ScN 1; composition (as of September 2022) - men 271, women 129, percent of women 32.3%; note - total Parliament percent of women 33%
note: in October 2019, Italy's Parliament voted to reduce the number of Senate seats from 315 to 200 and the number of Chamber of Deputies seats from 630 to 400; a referendum to reduce the membership of Parliament held on 20-21 September 2020 was approved, effective for the September 2022 snap election

Judicial branch: *highest court(s):* Supreme Court of Cassation or Corte Suprema di Cassazione (consists of the first president (chief justice), deputy president, 54 justices presiding over 6 civil and 7 criminal divisions, and 288 judges; an additional 30 judges of lower courts serve as supporting judges; cases normally heard by 5-judge panels; more complex cases heard by 9-judge panels); Constitutional Court or Corte Costituzionale (consists of the court president and 14 judges)
judge selection and term of office: Supreme Court judges appointed by the High Council of the Judiciary, headed by the president of the republic; judges may serve for life; Constitutional Court judges - 5 appointed by the president, 5 elected by Parliament, 5 elected by select higher courts; judges serve up to 9 years
subordinate courts: various lower civil and criminal courts (primary and secondary tribunals and courts of appeal)

Political parties and leaders: Action-Italia Viva [Carlo CALENDA and Matteo RENZI]
Associative Movement of Italians Abroad or MAIE [Ricardo Antonio MERIO]
Brothers of Italy or FdI [Giorgia MELONI]
Democratic Party or PD [Enrico LETTA]
Five Star Movement or M5S [Giuseppe CONTE]
Forza Italia or FI [Silvio BERLUSCONI]
Free and Equal (Liberi e Uguali) or LeU [Pietro GRASSO]
Greens and Left Alliance or AVS [Angelo BONELLI]
Italexit [Gianluigi PARAGONE]]
League or Lega [Matteo SALVINI]

More Europe or +EU [Emma BONINO]
Popular Union or PU [Luigi DE MAGISTRIS]
South calls North or ScN [Cateno DE LUCA]
South Tyrolean Peoples Party or SVP [Philipp ACHAMMER]
other minor parties

International organization participation: ADB (nonregional member), AfDB (nonregional member), Arctic Council (observer), Australia Group, BIS, BSEC (observer), CBSS (observer), CD, CDB, CE, CEI, CERN, EAPC, EBRD, ECB, EIB, EITI (implementing country), EMU, ESA, EU, FAO, FATF, G-7, G-8, G-10, G-20, IADB, IAEA, IBRD, ICAO, ICC (national committees), ICCt, ICRM, IDA, IEA, IFAD, IFC, IFRCS, IGAD (partners), IHO, ILO, IMF, IMO, IMSO, Interpol, IOC, IOM, IPU, ISO, ITSO, ITU, ITUC (NGOs), LAIA (observer), MIGA, MINURSO, MINUSMA, NATO, NEA, NSG, OAS (observer), OECD, OPCW, OSCE, Pacific Alliance (observer), Paris Club, PCA, PIF (partner), Schengen Convention, SELEC (observer), SICA (observer), UN, UNCTAD, UNESCO, UNHCR, UNIDO, UNIFIL, Union Latina, UNMOGIP, UNRWA, UNTSO, UNWTO, UPU, Wassenaar Arrangement, WCO, WHO, WIPO, WMO, WTO, ZC

Diplomatic representation in the US: *chief of mission:* Ambassador Maria Angela ZAPPIA (since 15 September 2021)
chancery: 3000 Whitehaven Street NW, Washington, DC 20008
telephone: [1] (202) 612-4400
FAX: [1] (202) 518-2154
email address and website:
amb.washington@cert.esteri.it
https://ambwashingtondc.esteri.it/ambasciata_washington/en/
consulate(s) general: Boston, Chicago, Detroit, Houston, Miami, New York, Los Angeles, Philadelphia, San Francisco
consulate(s): Charlotte (NC), Cleveland (OH), Detroit (MI), Hattiesburg (MS), Honolulu (HI), New Orleans, Newark (NJ), Norfolk (VA), Pittsburgh (PA), Portland (OR), Seattle

Diplomatic representation from the US: *chief of mission:* Ambassador (vacant); Charge d'Affaires Thomas D. SMITHAM (since 4 January 2021); note - also accredited to San Marino
embassy: via Vittorio Veneto 121, 00187 Roma
mailing address: 9500 Rome Place, Washington DC 20521-9500
telephone: [39] 06-46741
FAX: [39] 06-4674-2244
email address and website:
uscitizenrome@state.gov
https://it.usembassy.gov/
consulate(s) general: Florence, Milan, Naples

Flag description: three equal vertical bands of green (hoist side), white, and red; design inspired by the French flag brought to Italy by Napoleon in 1797; colors are those of Milan (red and white) combined with the green uniform color of the Milanese civic guard
note: similar to the flag of Mexico, which is longer, uses darker shades of green and red, and has its coat of arms centered on the white band; Ireland, which is longer and is green (hoist side), white, and orange; also similar to the flag of the Cote d'Ivoire, which has the colors reversed - orange (hoist side), white, and green

National symbol(s): white, five-pointed star (Stella d'Italia); national colors: red, white, green

National anthem: *name:* "Il Canto degli Italiani" (The Song of the Italians)
lyrics/music: Goffredo MAMELI/Michele NOVARO
note: adopted 1946; the anthem, originally written in 1847, is also known as "L'Inno di Mameli" (Mameli's Hymn), and "Fratelli D'Italia" (Brothers of Italy)

National heritage: *total World Heritage Sites:* 58 (53 cultural, 5 natural)
selected World Heritage Site locales: Historic Center of Rome (c); Archaeological Areas of Pompeii, Herculaneum, and Torre Annunziata (c); Venice and its Lagoon (c); Historic Center of Florence (c); Piazza del Duomo, Pisa (c); Historic Centre of Naples (c); Portovenere, Cinque Terre, and the Islands (c); Villa d'Este, Tivoli (c); Mount Etna (n); Rock Drawings in Valcamonica (c); Historic Siena (c)

ECONOMY

Economic overview: Italy's economy comprises a developed industrial north, dominated by private companies, and a less-developed, highly subsidized, agricultural south, with a legacy of unemployment and underdevelopment. The Italian economy is driven in large part by the manufacture of high-quality consumer goods produced by small and medium-sized enterprises, many of them family-owned. Italy also has a sizable underground economy, which by some estimates accounts for as much as 17% of GDP. These activities are most common within the agriculture, construction, and service sectors.

Italy is the third-largest economy in the euro zone, but its exceptionally high public debt and structural impediments to growth have rendered it vulnerable to scrutiny by financial markets. Public debt has increased steadily since 2007, reaching 131% of GDP in 2017. Investor concerns about Italy and the broader euro-zone crisis eased in 2013, bringing down Italy's borrowing costs on sovereign government debt from euro-era records. The government still faces pressure from investors and European partners to sustain its efforts to address Italy's longstanding structural economic problems, including labor market inefficiencies, a sluggish judicial system, and a weak banking sector. Italy's economy returned to modest growth in late 2014 for the first time since 2011. In 2015-16, Italy's economy grew at about 1% each year, and in 2017 growth accelerated to 1.5% of GDP. In 2017, overall unemployment was 11.4%, but youth unemployment remained high at 37.1%. GDP growth is projected to slow slightly in 2018.

Real GDP (purchasing power parity): $2,322,140,000,000 (2020 est.)
$2,548,190,000,000 (2019 est.)
$2,540,890,000,000 (2018 est.)
note: data are in 2017 dollars

Real GDP growth rate: 0.34% (2019 est.)
0.83% (2018 est.)
1.73% (2017 est.)

Real GDP per capita: $39,000 (2020 est.)
$42,700 (2019 est.)
$42,100 (2018 est.)
note: data are in 2017 dollars

GDP (official exchange rate): $2,002,763,000,000 (2019 est.)

Inflation rate (consumer prices): 0.6% (2019 est.)
1.1% (2018 est.)
1.2% (2017 est.)

Credit ratings:

Fitch rating: BBB- (2020)

Moody's rating: Baa3 (2018)

Standard & Poors rating: BBB (2017)
note: The year refers to the year in which the current credit rating was first obtained.

GDP - composition, by sector of origin: *agriculture:* 2.1% (2017 est.)
industry: 23.9% (2017 est.)
services: 73.9% (2017 est.)

GDP - composition, by end use: *household consumption:* 61% (2017 est.)
government consumption: 18.6% (2017 est.)
investment in fixed capital: 17.5% (2017 est.)
investment in inventories: -0.2% (2017 est.)
exports of goods and services: 31.4% (2017 est.)
imports of goods and services: -28.3% (2017 est.)

Agricultural products: milk, grapes, wheat, maize, tomatoes, apples, olives, sugar beet, oranges, rice

Industries: tourism, machinery, iron and steel, chemicals, food processing, textiles, motor vehicles, clothing, footwear, ceramics

Industrial production growth rate: 2.1% (2017 est.)

Labor force: 22.92 million (2020 est.)

Labor force - by occupation: *agriculture:* 3.9%
industry: 28.3%
services: 67.8% (2011)

Unemployment rate: 9.88% (2019 est.)
10.63% (2018 est.)

Unemployment, youth ages 15-24: *total:* 29.4%
male: 27.9%
female: 31.8% (2020 est.)

Population below poverty line: 20.1% (2018 est.)

Gini Index coefficient - distribution of family income: 35.9 (2017 est.)
27.3 (1995)

Household income or consumption by percentage share: *lowest 10%:* 2.3%
highest 10%: 26.8% (2000)

Budget: *revenues:* 903.3 billion (2017 est.)
expenditures: 948.1 billion (2017 est.)

Budget surplus (+) or deficit (-): -2.3% (of GDP) (2017 est.)

Public debt: 131.8% of GDP (2017 est.)
132% of GDP (2016 est.)
note: Italy reports its data on public debt according to guidelines set out in the Maastricht Treaty; general government gross debt is defined in the Maastricht Treaty as consolidated general government gross debt at nominal value, outstanding at the end of the year, in the following categories of government liabilities (as defined in ESA95): currency and deposits (AF.2), securities other than shares excluding financial derivatives (AF.3, excluding AF.34), and loans (AF.4); the general government sector comprises central, state, and local government and social security funds

Taxes and other revenues: 46.6% (of GDP) (2017 est.)

Fiscal year: calendar year

Current account balance: $59.517 billion (2019 est.)

$51.735 billion (2018 est.)

Exports: $558.26 billion (2020 est.) note: data are in current year dollars
$636.01 billion (2019 est.) note: data are in current year dollars
$656.06 billion (2018 est.) note: data are in current year dollars

Exports - partners: Germany 12%, France 11%, United States 10%, United Kingdom 5%, Spain 5%, Switzerland 5% (2019)

Exports - commodities: packaged medicines, cars and vehicle parts, refined petroleum, valves, trunks/cases, wine (2019)

Imports: $486.35 billion (2020 est.) note: data are in current year dollars
$569.7 billion (2019 est.) note: data are in current year dollars
$605.44 billion (2018 est.) note: data are in current year dollars

Imports - partners: Germany 16%, France 9%, China 7%, Spain 5%, Netherlands 5%, Belgium 5% (2019)

Imports - commodities: crude petroleum, cars, packaged medicines, natural gas, refined petroleum (2019)

Reserves of foreign exchange and gold: $151.2 billion (31 December 2017 est.)
$130.6 billion (31 December 2015 est.)

Debt - external: $2,463,208,000,000 (2019 est.)
$2,533,153,000,000 (2018 est.)

Exchange rates: euros (EUR) per US dollar -
0.82771 (2020 est.)
0.90338 (2019 est.)
0.87789 (2018 est.)
0.885 (2014 est.)
0.7634 (2013 est.)

ENERGY

Electricity access: *electrification - total population:* 100% (2020)

Electricity: *installed generating capacity:* 121.442 million kW (2020 est.)
consumption: 286.375 billion kWh (2020 est.)
exports: 7.587 billion kWh (2020 est.)
imports: 39.787 billion kWh (2020 est.)
transmission/distribution losses: 17.702 billion kWh (2020 est.)

Electricity generation sources: *fossil fuels:* 55.9% of total installed capacity (2020 est.)
solar: 9.2% of total installed capacity (2020 est.)
wind: 6.9% of total installed capacity (2020 est.)
hydroelectricity: 17.5% of total installed capacity (2020 est.)
tide and wave: 0.2% of total installed capacity (2020 est.)
geothermal: 2.2% of total installed capacity (2020 est.)
biomass and waste: 8.1% of total installed capacity (2020 est.)

Coal: *production:* 1.456 million metric tons (2020 est.)
consumption: 9.335 million metric tons (2020 est.)
exports: 368,000 metric tons (2020 est.)
imports: 8.235 million metric tons (2020 est.)
proven reserves: 17 million metric tons (2019 est.)

Petroleum: *total petroleum production:* 107,700 bbl/day (2021 est.)
refined petroleum consumption: 1,255,100 bbl/day (2019 est.)
crude oil and lease condensate exports: 10,100 bbl/day (2018 est.)
crude oil and lease condensate imports: 1.253 million bbl/day (2018 est.)
crude oil estimated reserves: 497.9 million barrels (2021 est.)

Refined petroleum products - production: 1.607 million bbl/day (2017 est.)

Refined petroleum products - exports: 615,900 bbl/day (2017 est.)

Refined petroleum products - imports: 422,500 bbl/day (2017 est.)

Natural gas: *production:* 3,888,491,000 cubic meters (2020 est.)
consumption: 74,313,109,000 cubic meters (2019 est.)
exports: 314.656 million cubic meters (2020 est.)
imports: 70,908,014,000 cubic meters (2019 est.)
proven reserves: 45.76 billion cubic meters (2021 est.)

Carbon dioxide emissions: 332.041 million metric tonnes of CO2 (2019 est.)
from coal and metallurgical coke: 27.194 million metric tonnes of CO2 (2019 est.)
from petroleum and other liquids: 162.472 million metric tonnes of CO2 (2019 est.)
from consumed natural gas: 142.375 million metric tonnes of CO2 (2019 est.)

Energy consumption per capita: 112.606 million Btu/person (2019 est.)

COMMUNICATIONS

Telephones - fixed lines: *total subscriptions:* 19,607,341 (2020 est.)
subscriptions per 100 inhabitants: 32 (2020 est.)

Telephones - mobile cellular: *total subscriptions:* 77,581,048 (2020 est.)
subscriptions per 100 inhabitants: 128 (2020 est.)

Telecommunication systems: *general assessment:* Italy's large telecom market has one of the most progressive fiber sectors in Europe, with regulatory measures encouraging network sharing; regulatory measures have also been introduced to facilitate access to next generation networks (NGNs), and a number of deals have been brokered which enable the main telcoms to provide bundled services to large numbers of the population; Italy's vibrant mobile market has one of the highest subscription rates in Europe, though the number of subscribers has fallen in recent years as customers respond to attractive off-net pricing which has reduced the financial benefit of having SIM cards from different providers; network companies were among the first in Europe to trial services based on 5G; the high cost also encouraged the regulator in early 2021 to consider extending the licenses by an additional six years (2021)
domestic: high-capacity cable and microwave radio relay trunks; 32 per 100 for fixed-line and nearly 128 per 100 for mobile-cellular subscriptions (2020)
international: country code - 39; landing points for Italy-Monaco, Italy-Libya, Italy-Malta, Italy-Greece-1, Italy-Croatia, BlueMed, Janna, FEA, SeaMeWe-3 & 4 & 5, Trapani-Kelibia, Columbus-III, Didon, GO-1, HANNIBAL System, MENA, Bridge International, Malta-Italy Interconnector, Melita1, IMEWE, VMSCS, AAE-1, and OTEGLOBE, submarine cables that provide links to Asia, the Middle East, Europe, North Africa, Southeast Asia, Australia and US; satellite earth stations - 3 Intelsat (with a total of 5 antennas - 3 for Atlantic Ocean and 2 for Indian Ocean) (2019)

Broadcast media: two Italian media giants dominate with 3 national terrestrial stations and privately owned companies with 3 national terrestrial stations; a large number of private stations, a satellite TV network; 3 AM/FM nationwide radio stations; about 1,300 commercial radio stations

Internet country code: .it

Internet users: *total:* 41,614,669 (2020 est.)
percent of population: 70% (2020 est.)

Broadband - fixed subscriptions: *total:* 18,128,787 (2020 est.)
subscriptions per 100 inhabitants: 30 (2020 est.)

TRANSPORTATION

National air transport system: *number of registered air carriers:* 9 (2020)
inventory of registered aircraft operated by air carriers: 180
annual passenger traffic on registered air carriers: 27,630,435 (2018)
annual freight traffic on registered air carriers: 1.418 billion (2018) mt-km

Civil aircraft registration country code prefix: I

Airports: *total:* 129 (2021)

Airports - with paved runways: *total:* 98
over 3,047 m: 9
2,438 to 3,047 m: 31
1,524 to 2,437 m: 18
914 to 1,523 m: 29
under 914 m: 11 (2021)

Airports - with unpaved runways: *total:* 31
1,524 to 2,437 m: 1
914 to 1,523 m: 10
under 914 m: 20 (2021)

Heliports: 5 (2021)

Pipelines: 20,223 km gas, 1,393 km oil, 1,574 km refined products (2013)

Railways: *total:* 18,892.4 km (2014)
standard gauge: 18,770.1 km (2014) 1.435-m gauge (12,893.6 km electrified)
narrow gauge: 122.3 km (2014) 1.000-m gauge (122.3 km electrified)
1289.3 0.950-mm gauge (151.3 km electrified)

Roadways: *total:* 487,700 km (2007)
paved: 487,700 km (2007) (includes 6,700 km of expressways)

Waterways: 2,400 km (2012) (used for commercial traffic; of limited overall value compared to road and rail)

Merchant marine: *total:* 1,296
by type: bulk carrier 36, container ship 7, general cargo 111, oil tanker 103, other 1,039 (2021)

Ports and terminals: *major seaport(s):* Augusta, Cagliari, Genoa, Livorno, Taranto, Trieste, Venice
oil terminal(s): Melilli (Santa Panagia) oil terminal, Sarroch oil terminal
container port(s) (TEUs): Genoa (2,621,472), Gioia Tauro (2,523,000) (2019)

LNG terminal(s) (import): Panigaglia (La Spezia), Adriatic (Porto Levante), Oristano (Sardinia), Ravenna, Toscana (Livorno)

MILITARY AND SECURITY

Military and security forces: Italian Armed Forces: Army (Esercito Italiano, EI), Navy (Marina Militare Italiana, MMI; includes aviation, marines), Italian Air Force (Aeronautica Militare Italiana, AMI); Carabinieri Corps (Arma dei Carabinieri, CC) (2022)
note 1: the Carabinieri is the national gendarmerie; for its civil police functions, the Carabinieri falls under the control of the Ministry of the Interior
note 2: the Financial Guard (Guardia di Finanza) under the Ministry of Economy and Finance is a force with military status and nationwide remit for financial crime investigations, including narcotics trafficking, smuggling, and illegal immigration

Military expenditures: 1.55% of GDP (2022)
1.5% of GDP (2021)
1.6% of GDP (2020)
1.2% of GDP (2019) (approximately $30.1 billion)
1.2% of GDP (2018) (approximately $31 billion)

Military and security service personnel strengths: approximately 170,000 active personnel (100,000 Army; 30,000 Navy; 40,000 Air Force); approximately 108,000 Carabinieri (2022)

Military equipment inventories and acquisitions: the military's inventory includes a mix of domestically-produced, jointly-produced, and imported weapons systems, mostly from Europe and the US; the US has been the leading supplier of weapons to Italy since 2010; the Italian defense industry is capable of producing equipment across all the military domains with particular strengths in naval vessels and aircraft; it also participates in joint development and production of advanced weapons systems with other European countries and the US (2022)

Military service age and obligation: 17-25 years of age for voluntary military service for men and women (some variations on age depending on the military branch); voluntary service is a minimum of 12 months with the option to extend in the Armed Forces or compete for positions in the Military Corps of the Italian Red Cross, the State Police, the Carabinieri, the Guardia di Finanza, the Penitentiary Police, or the National Fire Brigade; recruits can also volunteer for 4 years military service; conscription abolished 2004 (2022)
note: women may serve in any military branch; as of 2019, women made up about 6% of the military's full-time personnel

Military deployments: 120 Djibouti; 900 Middle East/Iraq/Kuwait (NATO, European Assistance Mission Iraq); 640 Kosovo (NATO/KFOR); 250 Latvia (NATO); 875 Lebanon (UNIFIL); 400 Libya; 290 Niger; 250 Romania (NATO); 150 Somalia (EUTM) (2022)
note: in response to Russia's invasion of Ukraine, some NATO countries, including Italy, have sent additional troops and equipment to the battlegroups deployed in NATO territory in eastern Europe

Military - note: Italy is a member of NATO and was one of the original 12 countries to sign the North Atlantic Treaty (also known as the Washington Treaty) in 1949

Italy is an active participant in EU, NATO, UN, and other multinational military, security, and humanitarian operations abroad; as of 2022, it hosted the headquarters for the EU's Mediterranean naval operations force (EUNAVFOR-MED) in Rome and the US Navy's 6th Fleet in Naples; Italy was admitted to the UN in 1955 and in 1960 participated in its first UN peacekeeping mission, the UN Operation in Congo (ONUC); since 1960, it has committed more than 60,000 troops to UN missions; since 2006, Italy has hosted a training center in Vicenza for police personnel destined for peacekeeping missions

TERRORISM

Terrorist group(s): Islamic State of Iraq and ash-Sham (ISIS)

TRANSNATIONAL ISSUES

Disputes - international: Italy's long coastline and developed economy entices tens of thousands of illegal immigrants from southeastern Europe and northern Africa
Italy-Austria-Switzerland: borders are shifting because glacier peaks that had served as a natural boundary are melting

Refugees and internally displaced persons: *refugees (country of origin):* 19,441 (Nigeria), 15,337 (Pakistan), 12,962 (Afghanistan), 10,609 (Mali), 7,901 (Somalia), 5,845 (Gambia), 5,079 (Iraq) (mid-year 2021); 173,231 (Ukraine) (as of 22 November 2022)
stateless persons: 3,000 (mid-year 2021)
note: 685,463 estimated refugee and migrant arrivals (January 2015-November 2022)

Illicit drugs: important gateway for drug trafficking; organized crime groups allied with Colombian and Spanish groups trafficking cocaine to Europe

J

JAMAICA

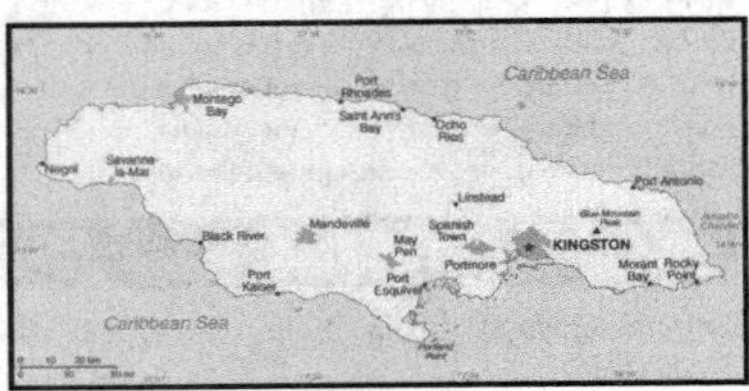

INTRODUCTION

Background: The island - "discovered" by Christopher COLUMBUS in 1494 - was settled by the Spanish early in the 16th century. The Native Taino, who had inhabited Jamaica for centuries, were gradually exterminated and replaced by African slaves. England seized the island in 1655 and established a plantation economy based on sugar, cocoa, and coffee. The abolition of slavery in 1834 freed a quarter million slaves, many of whom became small farmers. Jamaica gradually increased its independence from Britain. In 1958, it joined other British Caribbean colonies in forming the Federation of the West Indies. Jamaica withdrew from the Federation in 1961 and gained full independence in 1962. Deteriorating economic conditions during the 1970s led to recurrent violence as rival gangs affiliated with the major political parties evolved into powerful organized crime networks involved in international drug smuggling and money laundering. Violent crime, drug trafficking, corruption, the COVID-19 pandemic, and poverty pose significant challenges to the government today. Nonetheless, many rural and resort areas remain relatively safe and contribute substantially to the economy.

GEOGRAPHY

Location: Caribbean, island in the Caribbean Sea, south of Cuba

Geographic coordinates: 18 15 N, 77 30 W

Map references: Central America and the Caribbean

Area: *total:* 10,991 sq km
land: 10,831 sq km
water: 160 sq km

Area - comparative: about half the size of New Jersey; slightly smaller than Connecticut

Land boundaries: *total:* 0 km

Coastline: 1,022 km

Maritime claims: *territorial sea:* 12 nm
contiguous zone: 24 nm
exclusive economic zone: 200 nm
continental shelf: 200 nm or to edge of the continental margin
measured from claimed archipelagic straight baselines

Climate: tropical; hot, humid; temperate interior

Terrain: mostly mountains, with narrow, discontinuous coastal plain

Elevation: *highest point:* Blue Mountain Peak 2,256 m
lowest point: Caribbean Sea 0 m
mean elevation: 18 m

Natural resources: bauxite, alumina, gypsum, limestone

Land use: *agricultural land:* 41.4% (2018 est.)
arable land: 11.1% (2018 est.)
permanent crops: 9.2% (2018 est.)
permanent pasture: 21.1% (2018 est.)
forest: 31.1% (2018 est.)
other: 27.5% (2018 est.)

Irrigated land: 250 sq km (2012)

Population distribution: population density is high throughout, but increases in and around Kingston, Montego Bay, and Port Esquivel

Natural hazards: hurricanes (especially July to November)

Geography - note: third largest island in the Caribbean (after Cuba and Hispaniola); strategic location between Cayman Trench and Jamaica Channel, the main sea lanes for the Panama Canal

PEOPLE AND SOCIETY

Population: 2,818,596 (2022 est.)

Nationality: *noun:* Jamaican(s)
adjective: Jamaican

Ethnic groups: Black 92.1%, mixed 6.1%, East Indian 0.8%, other 0.4%, unspecified 0.7% (2011 est.)

Languages: English, English patois

Religions: Protestant 64.8% (includes Seventh Day Adventist 12.0%, Pentecostal 11.0%, Other Church of God 9.2%, New Testament Church of God 7.2%, Baptist 6.7%, Church of God in Jamaica 4.8%, Church of God of Prophecy 4.5%, Anglican 2.8%, United Church 2.1%, Methodist 1.6%, Revived 1.4%, Brethren 0.9%, and Moravian 0.7%), Roman Catholic 2.2%, Jehovah's Witness 1.9%, Rastafarian 1.1%, other 6.5%, none 21.3%, unspecified 2.3% (2011 est.)

Age structure: *0-14 years:* 25.2% (male 360,199/female 347,436)
15-24 years: 17.95% (male 255,102/female 248,927)
25-54 years: 38.06% (male 518,583/female 550,410)
55-64 years: 9.63% (male 133,890/female 136,442)
65 years and over: 9.17% (male 121,969/female 135,612) (2020 est.)

Dependency ratios: *total dependency ratio:* 48
youth dependency ratio: 34.6
elderly dependency ratio: 13.4
potential support ratio: 7.4 (2020 est.)

Median age: *total:* 29.4 years
male: 28.6 years
female: 30.1 years (2020 est.)

Population growth rate: 0.08% (2022 est.)

Birth rate: 15.91 births/1,000 population (2022 est.)

Death rate: 7.43 deaths/1,000 population (2022 est.)

Net migration rate: -7.7 migrant(s)/1,000 population (2022 est.)

Population distribution: population density is high throughout, but increases in and around Kingston, Montego Bay, and Port Esquivel

Urbanization: *urban population:* 57% of total population (2022)
rate of urbanization: 0.79% annual rate of change (2020-25 est.)

Major urban areas - population: 595,000 KINGSTON (capital) (2022)

Sex ratio: *at birth:* 1.05 male(s)/female
0-14 years: 1.04 male(s)/female
15-24 years: 1.03 male(s)/female
25-54 years: 0.94 male(s)/female
55-64 years: 0.98 male(s)/female
65 years and over: 0.75 male(s)/female
total population: 0.98 male(s)/female (2022 est.)

Mother's mean age at first birth: 21.2 years (2008 est.)
note: data represents median age at first birth among women 25-29

Maternal mortality ratio: 80 deaths/100,000 live births (2017 est.)

Infant mortality rate: *total:* 11.17 deaths/1,000 live births
male: 12.43 deaths/1,000 live births
female: 9.84 deaths/1,000 live births (2022 est.)

Life expectancy at birth: *total population:* 75.75 years
male: 73.98 years
female: 77.6 years (2022 est.)

Total fertility rate: 2.06 children born/woman (2022 est.)

Drinking water source: *improved: urban:* 98.3% of population
rural: 93.9% of population
total: 96.4% of population
unimproved: urban: 1.7% of population
rural: 6.1% of population
total: 3.6% of population (2020 est.)

Current health expenditure: 6.1% of GDP (2019)

Physicians density: 0.53 physicians/1,000 population (2018)

Hospital bed density: 1.7 beds/1,000 population (2017)

Sanitation facility access: *improved: urban:* 98.6% of population
rural: 99.4% of population
total: 98.9% of population
unimproved: urban: 1.4% of population
rural: 0.6% of population
total: 1.1% of population (2020 est.)

HIV/AIDS - adult prevalence rate: 1.4% (2020 est.)

Obesity - adult prevalence rate: 24.7% (2016)

Alcohol consumption per capita: *total:* 3.46 liters of pure alcohol (2019 est.)
beer: 1.19 liters of pure alcohol (2019 est.)
wine: 0.25 liters of pure alcohol (2019 est.)
spirits: 1.66 liters of pure alcohol (2019 est.)
other alcohols: 0.35 liters of pure alcohol (2019 est.)

Tobacco use: *total:* 9.4% (2020 est.)
male: 15% (2020 est.)
female: 3.8% (2020 est.)

Children under the age of 5 years underweight: 4.4% (2016)

Education expenditures: 5.4% of GDP (2020 est.)

Literacy: *definition:* age 15 and over has ever attended school

total population: 88.7%
male: 84%
female: 93.1% (2015)

School life expectancy (primary to tertiary education): *total:* 12 years
male: 11 years
female: 13 years (2015)

Unemployment, youth ages 15-24: *total:* 20.6%
male: 16.8%
female: 25.4% (2019 est.)

ENVIRONMENT

Environment - current issues: heavy rates of deforestation; coastal waters polluted by industrial waste, sewage, and oil spills; damage to coral reefs; air pollution in Kingston from vehicle emissions; land erosion

Environment - international agreements: *party to:* Biodiversity, Climate Change, Climate Change-Kyoto Protocol, Climate Change-Paris Agreement, Comprehensive Nuclear Test Ban, Desertification, Endangered Species, Hazardous Wastes, Law of the Sea, Marine Dumping-London Convention, Marine Life Conservation, Nuclear Test Ban, Ozone Layer Protection, Ship Pollution, Wetlands
signed, but not ratified: none of the selected agreements

Air pollutants: *particulate matter emissions:* 13.25 micrograms per cubic meter (2016 est.)
carbon dioxide emissions: 8.23 megatons (2016 est.)
methane emissions: 1.08 megatons (2020 est.)

Climate: tropical; hot, humid; temperate interior

Land use: *agricultural land:* 41.4% (2018 est.)
arable land: 11.1% (2018 est.)
permanent crops: 9.2% (2018 est.)
permanent pasture: 21.1% (2018 est.)
forest: 31.1% (2018 est.)
other: 27.5% (2018 est.)

Urbanization: *urban population:* 57% of total population (2022)
rate of urbanization: 0.79% annual rate of change (2020-25 est.)

Revenue from forest resources: *forest revenues:* 0.15% of GDP (2018 est.)

Revenue from coal: *coal revenues:* 0% of GDP (2018 est.)

Waste and recycling: *municipal solid waste generated annually:* 1,051,695 tons (2016 est.)

Total water withdrawal: *municipal:* 140 million cubic meters (2017 est.)
industrial: 1.1 billion cubic meters (2017 est.)
agricultural: 114 million cubic meters (2017 est.)

Total renewable water resources: 10.823 billion cubic meters (2017 est.)

GOVERNMENT

Country name: *conventional long form:* none
conventional short form: Jamaica
etymology: from the native Taino word "haymaca" meaning "Land of Wood and Water" or possibly "Land of Springs"

Government type: parliamentary democracy (Parliament) under a constitutional monarchy; a Commonwealth realm

Capital: *name:* Kingston
geographic coordinates: 18 00 N, 76 48 W
time difference: UTC-5 (same time as Washington, DC, during Standard Time)
etymology: the name is a blending of the words "king's" and "town"; the English king at the time of the city's founding in 1692 was WILLIAM III (r. 1689-1702)

Administrative divisions: 14 parishes; Clarendon, Hanover, Kingston, Manchester, Portland, Saint Andrew, Saint Ann, Saint Catherine, Saint Elizabeth, Saint James, Saint Mary, Saint Thomas, Trelawny, Westmoreland
note: for local government purposes, Kingston and Saint Andrew were amalgamated in 1923 into the present single corporate body known as the Kingston and Saint Andrew Corporation

Independence: 6 August 1962 (from the UK)

National holiday: Independence Day, 6 August (1962)

Constitution: *history:* several previous (preindependence); latest drafted 1961-62, submitted to British Parliament 24 July 1962, entered into force 6 August 1962 (at independence)
amendments: proposed by Parliament; passage of amendments to "non-entrenched" constitutional sections, such as lowering the voting age, requires majority vote by the Parliament membership; passage of amendments to "entrenched" sections, such as fundamental rights and freedoms, requires two-thirds majority vote of Parliament; passage of amendments to "specially entrenched" sections such as the dissolution of Parliament or the executive authority of the monarch requires two-thirds approval by Parliament and approval in a referendum; amended many times, last in 2017

Legal system: common law system based on the English model

International law organization participation: has not submitted an ICJ jurisdiction declaration; non-party state to the ICCt

Citizenship: *citizenship by birth:* yes
citizenship by descent only: yes
dual citizenship recognized: yes
residency requirement for naturalization: 4 out of the previous 5 years

Suffrage: 18 years of age; universal

Executive branch: *chief of state:* King CHARLES III (since 8 September 2022); represented by Governor General Sir Patrick L. ALLEN (since 26 February 2009)
head of government: Prime Minister Andrew HOLNESS (since 3 March 2016)
cabinet: Cabinet appointed by the governor general on the advice of the prime minister
elections/appointments: the monarchy is hereditary; governor general appointed by the monarch on the recommendation of the prime minister; following legislative elections, the leader of the majority party or majority coalition in the House of Representatives is appointed prime minister by the governor general

Legislative branch: *description:* bicameral Parliament consists of:
Senate (21 seats; 13 members appointed by the governor general on the advice of the prime minister and 8 members appointed by the governor general on the advice of the opposition party leader; members serve 5-year terms (no term limits) or until Parliament is dissolved)
House of Representatives (63 seats; members directly elected in single-seat constituencies by simple majority vote to serve 5-year terms (no term limits) or until Parliament is dissolved)
elections: Senate - last full slate of appointments early on 3 September 2020 (next full slate in 2025)
House of Representatives - last held on 3 September 2020 (next to be held in 2025)
election results: Senate - percent by party - NA; seats by party - NA; composition (as of June 2021) - men 13, women 8, percent of women 38.1%
House of Representatives - percent of vote by party - JLP 57%, PNP 42.8%, independent 0.2%; seats by party - JLP 48, PNP 15; composition (as of June 2021) - men 45, women 18; percent of women 28.6%; note - total Parliament percent of women 31%

Judicial branch: *highest court(s):* Court of Appeal (consists of president of the court and a minimum of 4 judges); Supreme Court (40 judges organized in specialized divisions); note - appeals beyond Jamaica's highest courts are referred to the Judicial Committee of the Privy Council (in London) rather than to the Caribbean Court of Justice (the appellate court for member states of the Caribbean Community)
judge selection and term of office: chief justice of the Supreme Court and president of the Court of Appeal appointed by the governor-general on the advice of the prime minister; other judges of both courts appointed by the governorgeneral on the advice of the Judicial Service Commission; judges of both courts serve till age 70
subordinate courts: resident magistrate courts, district courts, and petty sessions courts

Political parties and leaders: Jamaica Labor Party or JLP [Andrew Michael HOLNESS]
Jamaica Progressive Party or JPP [Gilbert Alexander EDWARDS]
People's National Party or PNP [Mark GOLDING]
United Independents' Congress or UIC [Joseph L. PATTERSON]

International organization participation: ACP, AOSIS, C, Caricom, CDB, CELAC, FAO, G-15, G-77, IADB, IAEA, IBRD, ICAO, ICC (NGOs), ICRM, IDA, IFAD, IFC, IFRCS, IHO, ILO, IMF, IMO, Interpol, IOC, IOM, ISO, ITSO, ITU, LAES, MIGA, NAM, OAS, OPANAL, OPCW, Petrocaribe, UN, UNCTAD, UNESCO, UNIDO, UNITAR, UNWTO, UPU, WCO, WFTU (NGOs), WHO, WIPO, WMO, WTO

Diplomatic representation in the US: *chief of mission:* Ambassador Audrey Patrice MARKS (since 18 January 2017)
chancery: 1520 New Hampshire Avenue NW, Washington, DC 20036
telephone: [1] (202) 452-0660
FAX: [1] (202) 452-0036
email address and website:
firstsec@jamaicaembassy.org
http://www.embassyofjamaica.org/
consulate(s) general: Miami, New York
consulate(s): Atlanta, Boston, Chicago, Concord (MA), Houston, Los Angeles, Philadelphia, Richmond (VA), San Francisco, Seattle

Diplomatic representation from the US: *chief of mission:* Ambassador N. Nickolas PERRY (since 13 May 2022)
embassy: 142 Old Hope Road, Kingston 6

mailing address: 3210 Kingston Place, Washington DC 20521-3210
telephone: (876) 702-6000 (2018)
FAX: (876) 702-6348 (2018)
email address and website:
KingstonACS@state.gov
https://jm.usembassy.gov/

Flag description: diagonal yellow cross divides the flag into four triangles - green (top and bottom) and black (hoist side and fly side); green represents hope, vegetation, and agriculture, black reflects hardships overcome and to be faced, and yellow recalls golden sunshine and the island's natural resources

National symbol(s): green-and-black streamertail (bird), Guaiacum officinale (Guaiacwood); national colors: green, yellow, black

National anthem: *name:* "Jamaica, Land We Love"
lyrics/music: Hugh Braham SHERLOCK/Robert Charles LIGHTBOURNE
note: adopted 1962

National heritage: *total World Heritage Sites:* 1 (mixed)
selected World Heritage Site locales: Blue and John Crow Mountains

ECONOMY

Economic overview: The Jamaican economy is heavily dependent on services, which accounts for more than 70% of GDP. The country derives most of its foreign exchange from tourism, remittances, and bauxite/alumina. Earnings from remittances and tourism each account for 14% and 20% of GDP, while bauxite/alumina exports have declined to less than 5% of GDP.

Jamaica's economy has grown on average less than 1% a year for the last three decades and many impediments remain to growth: a bloated public sector which crowds out spending on important projects; high crime and corruption; red-tape; and a high debt-to-GDP ratio. Jamaica, however, has made steady progress in reducing its debt-to-GDP ratio from a high of almost 150% in 2012 to less than 110% in 2017, in close collaboration with the International Monetary Fund (IMF). The current IMF Stand-By Agreement requires Jamaica to produce an annual primary surplus of 7%, in an attempt to reduce its debt burden below 60% by 2025.

Economic growth reached 1.6% in 2016, but declined to 0.9% in 2017 after intense rainfall, demonstrating the vulnerability of the economy to weather-related events. The HOLNESS administration therefore faces the difficult prospect of maintaining fiscal discipline to reduce the debt load while simultaneously implementing growth inducing policies and attacking a serious crime problem. High unemployment exacerbates the crime problem, including gang violence fueled by advanced fee fraud (lottery scamming) and the drug trade.

Real GDP (purchasing power parity): $25.89 billion (2020 est.)
$28.83 billion (2019 est.)
$28.57 billion (2018 est.)
note: data are in 2017 dollars

Real GDP growth rate: 0.7% (2017 est.)
1.5% (2016 est.)
0.9% (2015 est.)

Real GDP per capita: $8,700 (2020 est.)
$9,800 (2019 est.)
$9,700 (2018 est.)
note: data are in 2017 dollars

GDP (official exchange rate): $15.847 billion (2019 est.)

Inflation rate (consumer prices): 3.9% (2019 est.)
3.7% (2018 est.)
4.3% (2017 est.)

Credit ratings:

Fitch rating: B+ (2019)

Moody's rating: B2 (2019)

Standard & Poors rating: B+ (2019)
note: The year refers to the year in which the current credit rating was first obtained.

GDP - composition, by sector of origin: *agriculture:* 7% (2017 est.)
industry: 21.1% (2017 est.)
services: 71.9% (2017 est.)

GDP - composition, by end use: *household consumption:* 81.9% (2017 est.)
government consumption: 13.7% (2017 est.)
investment in fixed capital: 21.3% (2017 est.)
investment in inventories: 0.1% (2017 est.)
exports of goods and services: 30.1% (2017 est.)
imports of goods and services: -47.1% (2017 est.)

Agricultural products: sugar cane, goat milk, yams, poultry, coconuts, oranges, bananas, gourds, plantains, grapefruit

Industries: agriculture, mining, manufacture, construction, financial and insurance services, tourism, telecommunications

Industrial production growth rate: 0.9% (2017 est.)

Labor force: 1.113 million (2020 est.)

Labor force - by occupation: *agriculture:* 16.1%
industry: 16%
services: 67.9% (2017)

Unemployment rate: 7.72% (2019 est.)
9.13% (2018 est.)

Unemployment, youth ages 15-24: *total:* 20.6%
male: 16.8%
female: 25.4% (2019 est.)

Population below poverty line: 17.1% (2016 est.)

Gini Index coefficient - distribution of family income: 35 (2016)
38 (2015)

Household income or consumption by percentage share: *lowest 10%:* 2.6%
highest 10%: 29.3% (2015)

Budget: *revenues:* 4.382 billion (2017 est.)
expenditures: 4.314 billion (2017 est.)

Budget surplus (+) or deficit (-): 0.5% (of GDP) (2017 est.)

Public debt: 101% of GDP (2017 est.)
113.6% of GDP (2016 est.)

Taxes and other revenues: 29.7% (of GDP) (2017 est.)

Fiscal year: 1 April - 31 March

Current account balance: -$298 million (2019 est.)
-$288 million (2018 est.)

Exports: $5.92 billion (2019 est.) note: data are in current year dollars
$5.79 billion (2018 est.) note: data are in current year dollars

Exports - partners: United States 32%, Netherlands 11%, Germany 9%, Canada 7%, Iceland 7% (2019)

Exports - commodities: bauxite, refined petroleum, aluminum, rum, fruits, nuts (2019)

Imports: $8.25 billion (2019 est.) note: data are in current year dollars
$7.89 billion (2018 est.) note: data are in current year dollars

Imports - partners: United States 43%, China 11% (2019)

Imports - commodities: refined petroleum, cars, crude petroleum, natural gas, packaged medicines (2019)

Reserves of foreign exchange and gold: $3.781 billion (31 December 2017 est.)
$2.719 billion (31 December 2016 est.)

Debt - external: $13.876 billion (2019 est.)
$13.912 billion (2018 est.)

Exchange rates: Jamaican dollars (JMD) per US dollar -
128.36 (2017 est.)
125.14 (2016 est.)
125.126 (2015 est.)
116.898 (2014 est.)
110.935 (2013 est.)

ENERGY

Electricity access: *electrification - total population:* 99% (2019)
electrification - urban areas: 100% (2019)
electrification - rural areas: 97% (2019)

Electricity: *installed generating capacity:* 1.216 million kW (2020 est.)
consumption: 3,050,780,000 kWh (2019 est.)
exports: 0 kWh (2020 est.)
imports: 0 kWh (2020 est.)
transmission/distribution losses: 1.149 billion kWh (2019 est.)

Electricity generation sources: *fossil fuels:* 87.5% of total installed capacity (2020 est.)
solar: 1.2% of total installed capacity (2020 est.)
wind: 6.8% of total installed capacity (2020 est.)
hydroelectricity: 4% of total installed capacity (2020 est.)
biomass and waste: 0.6% of total installed capacity (2020 est.)

Coal: *production:* 0 metric tons (2020 est.)
consumption: 61,000 metric tons (2020 est.)
exports: 0 metric tons (2020 est.)
imports: 82,000 metric tons (2020 est.)
proven reserves: 0 metric tons (2019 est.)

Petroleum: *total petroleum production:* 3,000 bbl/day (2021 est.)
refined petroleum consumption: 61,100 bbl/day (2019 est.)
crude oil and lease condensate exports: 0 bbl/day (2018 est.)
crude oil and lease condensate imports: 20,100 bbl/day (2018 est.)
crude oil estimated reserves: 0 barrels (2021 est.)

Refined petroleum products - production: 24,250 bbl/day (2017 est.)

Refined petroleum products - exports: 823 bbl/day (2015 est.)

Refined petroleum products - imports: 30,580 bbl/day (2015 est.)

Natural gas: *production:* 0 cubic meters (2021 est.)

consumption: 693.422 million cubic meters (2020 est.)
exports: 0 cubic meters (2021 est.)
imports: 667.115 million cubic meters (2020 est.)
proven reserves: 0 cubic meters (2021 est.)

Carbon dioxide emissions: 10.002 million metric tonnes of CO2 (2019 est.)
from coal and metallurgical coke: 177,000 metric tonnes of CO2 (2019 est.)
from petroleum and other liquids: 9.276 million metric tonnes of CO2 (2019 est.)
from consumed natural gas: 549,000 metric tonnes of CO2 (2019 est.)

Energy consumption per capita: 49.7 million Btu/person (2019 est.)

COMMUNICATIONS

Telephones - fixed lines: *total subscriptions:* 436,249 (2020 est.)
subscriptions per 100 inhabitants: 15 (2020 est.)

Telephones - mobile cellular: *total subscriptions:* 2,873,259 (2020 est.)
subscriptions per 100 inhabitants: 97 (2020 est.)

Telecommunication systems: *general assessment:* Jamaica's telecom sector has for many years been propped up by the mobile sector, which accounts for the vast majority of internet connections and voice lines; it also accounts for just over half of telecom sector revenue; in December 2020, the government announced the rollout of a national broadband network costing up to $237 million; the funding will be spent on improving connectivity in under served areas, improving access to education, and deploying networks to public locations such as hospitals, municipal institutions, and police stations; to aid in this national broadband effort, the government received a donation of 650km of fiber cabling from local cable TV providers and the two main toll road operators; to encourage the use of digital channels as the country deals with the Covid-19 pandemic (2021)
domestic: fixed-line subscriptions nearly 15 per 100, cellular-mobile roughly 97 per 100 subscriptions (2020)
international: country code - 1-876 and 1-658; landing points for the ALBA-1, CFX-1, Fibralink, East-West, and Cayman-Jamaican Fiber System submarine cables providing connections to South America, parts of the Caribbean, Central America and the US; satellite earth stations - 2 Intelsat (Atlantic Ocean) (2019)

Broadcast media: 3 free-to-air TV stations, subscription cable services, and roughly 30 radio stations (2019)

Internet country code: .jm

Internet users: *total:* 1,621,552 (2019 est.)
percent of population: 55% (2019 est.)

Broadband - fixed subscriptions: *total:* 385,603 (2020 est.)
subscriptions per 100 inhabitants: 13 (2020 est.)

TRANSPORTATION

National air transport system: *number of registered air carriers:* 0 (2020)

Civil aircraft registration country code prefix: 6Y

Airports: *total:* 28 (2021)

Airports - with paved runways: *total:* 11
2,438 to 3,047 m: 2
914 to 1,523 m: 4
under 914 m: 5 (2021)

Airports - with unpaved runways: *total:* 17
914 to 1,523 m: 1
under 914 m: 16 (2021)

Roadways: *total:* 22,121 km (2011) (includes 44 km of expressways)
paved: 16,148 km (2011)
unpaved: 5,973 km (2011)

Merchant marine: *total:* 43
by type: bulk carrier 1, container ship 5, general cargo 9, oil tanker 1, other 27 (2021)

Ports and terminals: *major seaport(s):* Discovery Bay (Port Rhoades), Kingston, Montego Bay, Port Antonio, Port Esquivel, Port Kaiser, Rocky Point
container port(s) (TEUs): Kingston (1,647,609) (2019)

MILITARY AND SECURITY

Military and security forces: Jamaica Defense Force (JDF): Jamaica Regiment (Ground Forces), Maritime-Air-Cyber Command (includes Coast Guard, Air Wing, Military Intelligence Unit, Special Activities Regiment, and Military Cyber Corps), Support Brigade (logistics, engineers, health service, and military police); Jamaica National Service Corps (JNSC); Jamaica Constabulary Force (JCF) (2022)
note: the JNSC is a third category of service that military recruits can join as a preparatory phase for future careers; JNSC soldiers receive basic military, vocational, and life skills training; upon completion of 12 months of service, soldiers can continue on with the JDF or the JDF reserves or seek opportunities in other public sector entities such as the JCF, the Department of Correctional Services, the Jamaica Fire Brigade, the Jamaica Customs Agency, or the Passport Immigration and Citizenship Agency

Military expenditures: 1.4% of GDP (2021 est.)
1.7% of GDP (2020 est.)
1.6% of GDP (2019 est.) (approximately $300 million)
1.4% of GDP (2018 est.) (approximately $260 million)
1% of GDP (2017 est.) (approximately $190 million)

Military and security service personnel strengths: approximately 4,000 active duty personnel (2022)

Military equipment inventories and acquisitions: the JDF is lightly armed with a limited inventory featuring equipment mostly from Europe and the US (2022)

Military service age and obligation: no conscription; 18-23 for voluntary military service (17 with parental consent); 18-28 for the reserves; since 2017, the JDF's standard mode of recruitment is to enroll recruits ages 18-23 through the Jamaica National Service Corps (JNSC); in the JNSC, soldiers receive basic military, vocational, and life skills training; upon completion of 12 months of service, soldiers can continue on with the JDF or seek other opportunities with other government agencies (2022)

Military - note: as of 2022, the JDF's primary missions were maritime/border and internal security, including support to police operations in combating crime and violence

TRANSNATIONAL ISSUES

Disputes - international: none identified

Illicit drugs: the largest Caribbean source of marijuana which is trafficked to other Caribbean countries for illegal weapons and other contraband; transit point for cocaine trafficked from South America to North America and other international markets

JAN MAYEN

INTRODUCTION

Background: This desolate, arctic, mountainous island was named after a Dutch whaling captain who indisputably discovered it in 1614 (earlier claims are inconclusive). Visited only occasionally by seal hunters and trappers over the following centuries, the island came under Norwegian sovereignty in 1929. The long dormant Beerenberg volcano, the northernmost active volcano on earth, resumed activity in 1970 and the most recent eruption occurred in 1985.

GEOGRAPHY

Location: Northern Europe, island between the Greenland Sea and the Norwegian Sea, northeast of Iceland

Geographic coordinates: 71 00 N, 8 00 W

Map references: Arctic Region

Area: *total:* 377 sq km
land: 377 sq km
water: 0 sq km

Area - comparative: slightly more than twice the size of Washington, DC

Land boundaries: *total:* 0 km

Coastline: 124.1 km

Maritime claims: *territorial sea:* 12 nm
contiguous zone: 24 nm
exclusive economic zone: 200 nm
continental shelf: 200-m depth or to the depth of exploitation

Climate: arctic maritime with frequent storms and persistent fog

Terrain: volcanic island, partly covered by glaciers

Elevation: *highest point:* Haakon VII Toppen on Beerenberg 2,277

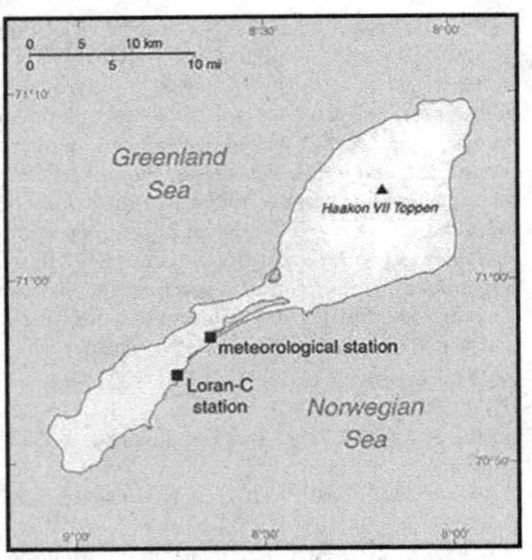

lowest point: Norwegian Sea 0 m
note: Beerenberg volcano has numerous peaks; the highest point on the volcano rim is named Haakon VII Toppen, after Norway's first king following the reestablishment of Norwegian independence in 1905

Natural resources: none

Land use: *agricultural land:* 0% (2011 est.)
other: 100% (2018 est.)

Irrigated land: 0 sq km (2012)

Natural hazards: dominated by the volcano Beerenberg
volcanism: Beerenberg (2,227 m) is Norway's only active volcano; volcanic activity resumed in 1970; the most recent eruption occurred in 1985

Geography - note: barren volcanic spoon-shaped island with some moss and grass flora; island consists of two parts: a larger northeast Nord-Jan (the spoon "bowl") and the smaller Sor-Jan (the "handle"), linked by a 2.5 km-wide isthmus (the "stem") with two large lakes, Sorlaguna (South Lagoon) and Nordlaguna (North Lagoon)

PEOPLE AND SOCIETY

Population: no indigenous inhabitants
note: military personnel operate the the weather and coastal services radio station

ENVIRONMENT

Environment - current issues: pollutants transported from southerly latitudes by winds, ocean currents, and rivers accumulate in the food chains of native animals; climate change

Climate: arctic maritime with frequent storms and persistent fog

Land use: *agricultural land:* 0% (2011 est.)
other: 100% (2018 est.)

GOVERNMENT

Country name: *conventional long form:* none
conventional short form: Jan Mayen
etymology: named after Dutch Captain Jan Jacobszoon MAY, one of the first explorers to reach the island in 1614

Dependency status: territory of Norway; since August 1994, administered from Oslo through the county governor (fylkesmann) of Nordland; however, authority has been delegated to a station commander of the Norwegian Defense Communication Service; in 2010, Norway designated the majority of Jan Mayen as a nature reserve

Legal system: the laws of Norway apply where applicable

Flag description: the flag of Norway is used

ECONOMY

Economic overview: Jan Mayen is a volcanic island with no exploitable natural resources, although surrounding waters contain substantial fish stocks and potential untapped petroleum resources. Economic activity is limited to providing services for employees of Norway's radio and meteorological stations on the island.

COMMUNICATIONS

Broadcast media: a coastal radio station has been remotely operated since 1994

TRANSPORTATION

Airports: *total:* 1 (2021)

Airports - with unpaved runways: *total:* 1
1,524 to 2,437 m: 1 (2021)

Ports and terminals: none; offshore anchorage only

MILITARY AND SECURITY

Military - note: defense is the responsibility of Norway

TRANSNATIONAL ISSUES

Disputes - international: none identified

JAPAN

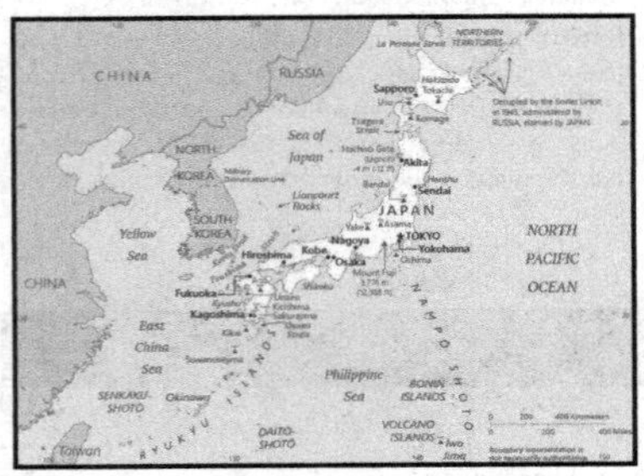

INTRODUCTION

Background: In 1603, after decades of civil warfare, the Tokugawa shogunate (a military-led, dynastic government) ushered in a long period of relative political stability and isolation from foreign influence. For more than two centuries this policy enabled Japan to enjoy a flowering of its indigenous culture. Japan opened its ports after signing the Treaty of Kanagawa with the US in 1854 and began to intensively modernize and industrialize. During the late 19th and early 20th centuries, Japan became a regional power that was able to defeat the forces of both China and Russia. It occupied Korea, Formosa (Taiwan), and southern Sakhalin Island. In 1931-32 Japan occupied Manchuria, and in 1937 it launched a full-scale invasion of China. Japan attacked US forces in 1941 - triggering America's entry into World War II - and soon occupied much of East and Southeast Asia. After its defeat in World War II, Japan recovered to become an economic power and an ally of the US. While the emperor retains his throne as a symbol of national unity, elected politicians hold actual decision-making power. Following three decades of unprecedented growth, Japan's economy experienced a major slowdown starting in the 1990s, but the country remains an economic power. In March 2011, Japan's strongest-ever earthquake, and an accompanying tsunami, devastated the northeast part of Honshu island, killed thousands, and damaged several nuclear power plants. Prime Minister Shinzo ABE was reelected to office in December 2012, and embarked on ambitious economic and security reforms to improve Japan's economy and bolster the country's international standing. In November 2019, ABE became Japan's longest-serving post-war prime minister; he resigned in September 2020 and was succeeded by Yoshihide SUGA. Fumio KISHIDA became prime minister in October 2021.

GEOGRAPHY

Location: Eastern Asia, island chain between the North Pacific Ocean and the Sea of Japan, east of the Korean Peninsula

Geographic coordinates: 36 00 N, 138 00 E

Map references: Asia

Area: *total:* 377,915 sq km
land: 364,485 sq km
water: 13,430 sq km
note: includes Bonin Islands (Ogasawara-gunto), Daito-shoto, Minami-jima, Okino-tori-shima, Ryukyu Islands (Nanseishoto), and Volcano Islands (Kazan-retto)

Area - comparative: slightly smaller than California

Land boundaries: *total:* 0 km

Coastline: 29,751 km

Maritime claims: *territorial sea:* 12 nm; between 3 nm and 12 nm in the international straits - La Perouse or Soya, Tsugaru, Osumi, and the Korea and Tsushima Straits
contiguous zone: 24 nm
exclusive economic zone: 200 nm

Climate: varies from tropical in south to cool temperate in north

Terrain: mostly rugged and mountainous

Elevation: *highest point:* Mount Fuji 3,776 m
lowest point: Hachiro-gata -4 m
mean elevation: 438 m

Natural resources: negligible mineral resources, fish; note - with virtually no natural energy resources, Japan is the world's largest importer of coal and liquefied natural gas, as well as the second largest importer of oil

Land use: *agricultural land:* 12.5% (2018 est.)
arable land: 11.7% (2018 est.)
permanent crops: 0.8% (2018 est.)
permanent pasture: 0% (2018 est.)
forest: 68.5% (2018 est.)
other: 19% (2018 est.)

Irrigated land: 24,690 sq km (2012)

Major lakes (area sq km): *fresh water lake(s):* Biwa-ko 688 sq km

Population distribution: all primary and secondary regions of high population density lie on the coast; one-third of the population resides in and around Tokyo on the central plain (Kanto Plain)

Natural hazards: many dormant and some active volcanoes; about 1,500 seismic occurrences (mostly tremors but occasional severe earthquakes) every year; tsunamis; typhoons
volcanism: both Unzen (1,500 m) and Sakura-jima (1,117 m), which lies near the densely populated city of Kagoshima, have been deemed Decade Volcanoes by the International Association of Volcanology and Chemistry of the Earth's Interior, worthy of study due to their explosive history and close proximity to human populations; other notable historically active volcanoes include Asama, Honshu Island's most active volcano, Aso, Bandai, Fuji, Iwo-Jima, Kikai, Kirishima, Komaga-take, Oshima, Suwanosejima, Tokachi, Yake-dake, and Usu; see note 2 under "Geography - note"

Geography - note: *note 1:* strategic location in northeast Asia; composed of four main islands - from north: Hokkaido, Honshu (the largest and most populous), Shikoku, and Kyushu (the "Home Islands") - and 6,848 smaller islands and islets
note 2: Japan annually records the most earthquakes in the world; it is one of the countries along the Ring of Fire, a belt of active volcanoes and earthquake epicenters bordering the Pacific Ocean; up to 90% of the world's earthquakes and some 75% of the world's volcanoes occur within the Ring of Fire

PEOPLE AND SOCIETY

Population: 124,214,766 (2022 est.)

Nationality: *noun:* Japanese (singular and plural)
adjective: Japanese

Ethnic groups: Japanese 97.9%, Chinese 0.6%, Korean 0.4%, other 1.1% (includes Vietnamese, Filipino, and Brazilian) (2017 est.)
note: data represent population by nationality; up to 230,000 Brazilians of Japanese origin migrated to Japan in the 1990s to work in industries; some have returned to Brazil

Languages: Japanese
major-language sample(s):
必要不可欠な基本情報の源、ワールド・ファクトブック
(Japanese)

Religions: Shintoism 70.5%, Buddhism 67.2%, Christianity 1.5%, other 5.9% (2019 est.)
note: total adherents exceeds 100% because many people practice both Shintoism and Buddhism

Age structure: *0-14 years:* 12.49% (male 8,047,183/female 7,623,767)
15-24 years: 9.47% (male 6,254,352/female 5,635,377)
25-54 years: 36.8% (male 22,867,385/female 23,317,140)
55-64 years: 12.06% (male 7,564,067/female 7,570,732)
65 years and over: 29.18% (male 16,034,973/female 20,592,496) (2020 est.)

Dependency ratios: *total dependency ratio:* 69
youth dependency ratio: 21
elderly dependency ratio: 48
potential support ratio: 2.1 (2020 est.)

Median age: *total:* 48.6 years
male: 47.2 years
female: 50 years (2020 est.)

Population growth rate: -0.39% (2022 est.)

Birth rate: 6.95 births/1,000 population (2022 est.)

Death rate: 11.59 deaths/1,000 population (2022 est.)

Net migration rate: 0.74 migrant(s)/1,000 population (2022 est.)

Population distribution: all primary and secondary regions of high population density lie on the coast; one-third of the population resides in and around Tokyo on the central plain (Kanto Plain)

Urbanization: *urban population:* 92% of total population (2022)
rate of urbanization: -0.25% annual rate of change (2020-25 est.)

Major urban areas - population: 37.274 million TOKYO (capital), 19.060 million Osaka, 9.572 million Nagoya, 5.503 million Kitakyushu-Fukuoka, 2.935 million Shizuoka-Hamamatsu, 2.669 million Sapporo (2022)

Sex ratio: *at birth:* 1.06 male(s)/female
0-14 years: 1.06 male(s)/female
15-24 years: 1.09 male(s)/female
25-54 years: 1 male(s)/female
55-64 years: 1 male(s)/female
65 years and over: 0.65 male(s)/female
total population: 0.95 male(s)/female (2022 est.)

Mother's mean age at first birth: 30.7 years (2018 est.)

Maternal mortality ratio: 5 deaths/100,000 live births (2017 est.)

Infant mortality rate: *total:* 1.9 deaths/1,000 live births
male: 2 deaths/1,000 live births
female: 1.79 deaths/1,000 live births (2022 est.)

Life expectancy at birth: *total population:* 84.83 years
male: 81.92 years
female: 87.9 years (2022 est.)

Total fertility rate: 1.38 children born/woman (2022 est.)

Contraceptive prevalence rate: 39.8% (2015)
note: percent of women aged 20-49

Drinking water source: *improved: total:* 99.1% of population
unimproved: total: 0.1% of population (2020 est.)

Current health expenditure: 10.7% of GDP (2019)

Physicians density: 2.48 physicians/1,000 population (2018)

Hospital bed density: 13 beds/1,000 population (2018)

Sanitation facility access: *improved: total:* 99.9% of population
unimproved: total: 0.1% of population (2020 est.)

HIV/AIDS - adult prevalence rate: (2020 est.) <.1%

Major infectious diseases: *respiratory diseases:* Covid-19 (see note) (2020)
note: clusters of cases of respiratory illness caused by a new coronavirus (COVID-19) in Japan; illness with this virus has ranged from mild to severe with fatalities reported; as of 18 August 2022, Japan has reported a total of 16,161,801 cases of COVID-19 or 12,778.50 cumulative cases of COVID-19 per 100,000 population with a total of 35,955 cumulative deaths or a rate of 28.42 cumulative deaths per 100,000 population; as of 17 August 2022, 83.48% of the population has received at least one dose of COVID-19 vaccine

Obesity - adult prevalence rate: 4.3% (2016)

Alcohol consumption per capita: *total:* 8.36 liters of pure alcohol (2019 est.)
beer: 1.35 liters of pure alcohol (2019 est.)
wine: 0.29 liters of pure alcohol (2019 est.)
spirits: 1.63 liters of pure alcohol (2019 est.)
other alcohols: 5.09 liters of pure alcohol (2019 est.)

Tobacco use: *total:* 20.1% (2020 est.)
male: 30.1% (2020 est.)
female: 10% (2020 est.)

Education expenditures: 3.2% of GDP (2017 est.)

School life expectancy (primary to tertiary education): *total:* 15 years
male: 15 years
female: 15 years (2018)

Unemployment, youth ages 15-24: *total:* 4.6%
male: 5%
female: 4.2% (2020 est.)

ENVIRONMENT

Environment - current issues: air pollution from power plant emissions results in acid rain; acidification of lakes and reservoirs degrading water quality and threatening aquatic life; Japan is one of the largest consumers of fish and tropical timber, contributing to the depletion of these resources in Asia and elsewhere; following the 2011 Fukushima nuclear disaster, Japan originally planned to phase out nuclear power, but it has now implemented a new policy of seeking to restart nuclear power plants that meet strict new safety standards; waste management is an ongoing issue; Japanese municipal facilities used to burn high volumes of trash, but air pollution issues forced the government to adopt an aggressive recycling policy

Environment - international agreements: *party to:* Antarctic-Environmental Protection, Antarctic-Marine Living Resources, Antarctic Seals, Antarctic Treaty, Biodiversity, Climate Change, Climate Change-Kyoto Protocol, Climate Change-Paris Agreement, Comprehensive Nuclear Test Ban, Desertification, Endangered Species, Environmental Modification, Hazardous Wastes, Law of the Sea, Marine Dumping-London Convention, Marine Dumping-London Protocol, Nuclear Test Ban, Ozone Layer Protection, Ship Pollution, Tropical Timber 2006, Wetlands

signed, but not ratified: none of the selected agreements

Air pollutants: *particulate matter emissions:* 11.45 micrograms per cubic meter (2016 est.)
carbon dioxide emissions: 1,135.89 megatons (2016 est.)
methane emissions: 29.99 megatons (2020 est.)

Climate: varies from tropical in south to cool temperate in north

Land use: *agricultural land:* 12.5% (2018 est.)
arable land: 11.7% (2018 est.)
permanent crops: 0.8% (2018 est.)
permanent pasture: 0% (2018 est.)
forest: 68.5% (2018 est.)
other: 19% (2018 est.)

Urbanization: *urban population:* 92% of total population (2022)
rate of urbanization: -0.25% annual rate of change (2020-25 est.)

Revenue from forest resources: *forest revenues:* 0.02% of GDP (2018 est.)

Revenue from coal: *coal revenues:* 0% of GDP (2018 est.)

Waste and recycling: *municipal solid waste generated annually:* 43.981 million tons (2015 est.)
municipal solid waste recycled annually: 2,155,069 tons (2015 est.)
percent of municipal solid waste recycled: 4.9% (2015 est.)

Major lakes (area sq km): *fresh water lake(s):* Biwa-ko 688 sq km

Total water withdrawal: *municipal:* 15.41 billion cubic meters (2017 est.)
industrial: 11.61 billion cubic meters (2017 est.)
agricultural: 54.43 billion cubic meters (2017 est.)

Total renewable water resources: 430 billion cubic meters (2017 est.)

GOVERNMENT

Country name: *conventional long form:* none
conventional short form: Japan
local long form: Nihon-koku/Nippon-koku
local short form: Nihon/Nippon
etymology: the English word for Japan comes via the Chinese name for the country "Cipangu"; both Nihon and Nippon mean "where the sun originates" and are frequently translated as "Land of the Rising Sun"

Government type: parliamentary constitutional monarchy

Capital: *name:* Tokyo
geographic coordinates: 35 41 N, 139 45 E
time difference: UTC+9 (14 hours ahead of Washington, DC, during Standard Time)
etymology: originally known as Edo, meaning "estuary" in Japanese, the name was changed to Tokyo, meaning "eastern capital," in 1868

Administrative divisions: 47 prefectures; Aichi, Akita, Aomori, Chiba, Ehime, Fukui, Fukuoka, Fukushima, Gifu, Gunma, Hiroshima, Hokkaido, Hyogo, Ibaraki, Ishikawa, Iwate, Kagawa, Kagoshima, Kanagawa, Kochi, Kumamoto, Kyoto, Mie, Miyagi, Miyazaki, Nagano, Nagasaki, Nara, Niigata, Oita, Okayama, Okinawa, Osaka, Saga, Saitama, Shiga, Shimane, Shizuoka, Tochigi, Tokushima, Tokyo, Tottori, Toyama, Wakayama, Yamagata, Yamaguchi, Yamanashi

Independence: 3 May 1947 (current constitution adopted as amendment to Meiji Constitution); notable earlier dates: 11 February 660 B.C. (mythological date of the founding of the nation by Emperor JIMMU); 29 November 1890 (Meiji Constitution provides for constitutional monarchy)

National holiday: Birthday of Emperor NARUHITO, 23 February (1960); note - celebrates the birthday of the current emperor

Constitution: *history:* previous 1890; latest approved 6 October 1946, adopted 3 November 1946, effective 3 May 1947
amendments: proposed by the Diet; passage requires approval by at least two-thirds majority of both houses of the Diet and approval by majority in a referendum; note - the constitution has not been amended since its enactment in 1947

Legal system: civil law system based on German model; system also reflects Anglo-American influence and Japanese traditions; judicial review of legislative acts in the Supreme Court

International law organization participation: accepts compulsory ICJ jurisdiction with reservations; accepts ICCt jurisdiction

Citizenship: *citizenship by birth:* no
citizenship by descent only: at least one parent must be a citizen of Japan
dual citizenship recognized: no
residency requirement for naturalization: 5 years

Suffrage: 18 years of age; universal

Executive branch: *chief of state:* Emperor NARUHITO (since 1 May 2019); note - succeeds his father who abdicated on 30 April 2019
head of government: Prime Minister Fumio KISHIDA (since 4 October 2021)
cabinet: Cabinet appointed by the prime minister
elections/appointments: the monarchy is hereditary; the leader of the majority party or majority coalition in the House of Representatives usually becomes prime minister
election results: Fumio KISHIDA relected prime minister on 10 November 2021 by the lower house with 297 votes against 108 for Yukio EDANO and in the upper houese 141 for KISHIDA and 60 for EDANO

Legislative branch: *description:* bicameral Diet or Kokkai consists of:
House of Councillors or Sangi-in (245 seats, currently 242; 146 members directly elected in multi-seat districts by simple majority vote and 96 directly elected in a single national constituency by proportional representation vote; members serve 6-year terms with half the membership renewed every 3 years); note - the number of seats increases to 248 at the July 2022 election for renewal of half the membership
House of Representatives or Shugi-in (465 seats; 289 members directly elected in single-seat districts by simple majority vote and 176 directly elected in multi-seat districts by party-list proportional representation vote; members serve 4-year terms)
elections: House of Councillors - last held on 21 July 2019 (next to be held in July 2022)
House of Representatives - last held on 31 October 2021 (next to be held by October 2025)
election results: House of Councillors - percent of vote by party - NA; seats by party - LDP 55, DP 32, Komeito 14, JCP 6, Osaka Ishin no Kai (Initiatives from Osaka) 7, PLPTYF 1, SDP 1, independent 5; composition - men 186, women 56, percent of women 21.3%
House of Representatives - percent of vote by party - NA; seats by party - LDP 261, CDP 96, Ishin 41, Komeito 32, DPFP 11, JCP 10, Reiwa 3, SDP 1, independent 10; composition - men 420, women 45, percent of women 9.7%; note - total Diet percent of women 14.7%
note: the Diet in June 2017 redrew Japan's electoral district boundaries and reduced from 475 to 465 seats in the House of Representatives; the amended electoral law, which cuts 6 seats in single-seat districts and 4 in multi-seat districts, was reportedly intended to reduce voting disparities between densely and sparsely populated voting districts

Judicial branch: *highest court(s):* Supreme Court or Saiko saibansho (consists of the chief justice and 14 associate justices); note - the Supreme Court has jurisdiction in constitutional issues
judge selection and term of office: Supreme Court chief justice designated by the Cabinet and appointed by the monarch; associate justices appointed by the Cabinet and confirmed by the monarch; all justices are reviewed in a popular referendum at the first general election of the House of Representatives following each judge's appointment and every 10 years afterward
subordinate courts: 8 High Courts (Koto-saiban-sho), each with a Family Court (Katei-saiban-sho); 50 District Courts (Chiho saibansho), with 203 additional branches; 438 Summary Courts (Kani saibansho)

Political parties and leaders: Constitutional Democratic Party of Japan or CDP [Kenta IZUMI]
Democratic Party for the People Japan or DPFP [Yuichiro TAMAKI]
Group of Reformists [Sakihito OZAWA]
Japan Communist Party or JCP [Kazuo SHII]
Japan Innovation Party or Nippon Ishin no kai or Ishin [Ichiro MATSUI]
Komeito [Natsuo YAMAGUCHI]
Liberal Democratic Party or LDP [Fumio KISHIDA]
Liberal Party [Ichiro OZAWA] (formerly People's Life Party & Taro Yamamoto and Friends or PLPTYF)
Party of Hope or Kibo no To [Nariaki NAKAYAMA]
Reiwa Shinsengumi [Taro YAMAMOTO]
Social Democratic Party or SDP [Mizuho FUKUSHIMA]

International organization participation: ADB, AfDB (nonregional member), APEC, Arctic Council (observer), ARF, ASEAN (dialogue partner), Australia Group, BIS, CD, CE (observer), CERN (observer), CICA (observer), CP, CPLP (associate), EAS, EBRD, EITI (implementing country), FAO, FATF, G-5, G-7, G-8, G-10, G-20, IADB, IAEA, IBRD, ICAO, ICC (national committees), ICCt, ICRM, IDA, IEA, IFAD, IFC, IFRCS, IGAD (partners), IHO, ILO, IMF, IMO, IMSO, Interpol, IOC, IOM, IPU, ISO, ITSO, ITU, ITUC (NGOs), LAIA (observer), MIGA, NEA, NSG, OAS (observer), OECD, OPCW, OSCE (partner), Pacific Alliance (observer), Paris Club, PCA, PIF (partner), Quad, SAARC (observer), SELEC (observer), SICA (observer), UN, UNCTAD, UNESCO, UNHCR, UNHRC, UNIDO, UNMISS, UNRWA, UNWTO, UPU, Wassenaar Arrangement, WCO, WFTU (NGOs), WHO, WIPO, WMO, WTO, ZC

Diplomatic representation in the US: *chief of mission:* Ambassador TOMITA Koji (since 17 February 2021)

chancery: 2520 Massachusetts Avenue NW, Washington, DC 20008
telephone: [1] (202) 238-6700
FAX: [1] (202) 328-2187
email address and website:
https://www.us.emb-japan.go.jp/itprtop_en/index.html
consulate(s) general: Anchorage (AK), Atlanta, Boston, Chicago, Denver (CO), Detroit (MI), Hagatna (Guam), Honolulu, Houston, Los Angeles, Miami, Nashville (TN), New York, Portland (OR), San Francisco, Saipan (Northern Mariana Islands), Seattle (WA)

Diplomatic representation from the US: *chief of mission:* Ambassador Rahm EMANUEL (since 25 March 2022)
embassy: 1-10-5 Akasaka, Minato-ku, Tokyo 107-8420
mailing address: 9800 Tokyo Place, Washington DC 20521-9800
telephone: [81] (03) 3224-5000
FAX: [81] (03) 3224-5856
email address and website:
TokyoACS@state.gov
https://jp.usembassy.gov/
consulate(s) general: Naha (Okinawa), Osaka-Kobe, Sapporo
consulate(s): Fukuoka, Nagoya

Flag description: white with a large red disk (representing the sun without rays) in the center

National symbol(s): red sun disc, chrysanthemum; national colors: red, white

Kikumon – the Japanese Family Coat of Arms of the emperor:

National anthem: *name:* "Kimigayo" (The Emperor's Reign)
lyrics/music: unknown/Hiromori HAYASHI
note: adopted 1999; unofficial national anthem since 1883; oldest anthem lyrics in the world, dating to the 10th century or earlier; there is some opposition to the anthem because of its association with militarism and worship of the emperor

National heritage: *total World Heritage Sites:* 25 (20 cultural, 5 natural)
selected World Heritage Site locales: Buddhist Monuments in the Horyu-ji Area (c); Historic Monuments of Ancient Nara (c); Himeji-jo (c); Shiretoko (n); Mozu-Furuichi Kofun Group: Mounded Tombs of Ancient Japan (c); Iwami Ginzan Silver Mine and its Cultural Landscape (c); Jomon Prehistoric Sites in Northern Japan (c); Yakushima (n); Historic Monuments of Ancient Kyoto (c); Hiroshima Peace Memorial (Genbaku Dome) (c)

ECONOMY

Economic overview: Over the past 70 years, government-industry cooperation, a strong work ethic, mastery of high technology, and a comparatively small defense allocation (slightly less than 1% of GDP) have helped Japan develop an advanced economy. Two notable characteristics of the post-World War II economy were the close interlocking structures of manufacturers, suppliers, and distributors, known as keiretsu, and the guarantee of lifetime employment for a substantial portion of the urban labor force. Both features have significantly eroded under the dual pressures of global competition and domestic demographic change.

Measured on a purchasing power parity basis that adjusts for price differences, Japan in 2017 stood as the fourth-largest economy in the world after first-place China, which surpassed Japan in 2001, and third-place India, which edged out Japan in 2012. For three postwar decades, overall real economic growth was impressive - averaging 10% in the 1960s, 5% in the 1970s, and 4% in the 1980s. Growth slowed markedly in the 1990s, averaging just 1.7%, largely because of the aftereffects of inefficient investment and the collapse of an asset price bubble in the late 1980s, which resulted in several years of economic stagnation as firms sought to reduce excess debt, capital, and labor. Modest economic growth continued after 2000, but the economy has fallen into recession four times since 2008.

Japan enjoyed an uptick in growth since 2013, supported by Prime Minister Shinzo ABE's "Three Arrows" economic revitalization agenda - dubbed "Abenomics" - of monetary easing, "flexible" fiscal policy, and structural reform. Led by the Bank of Japan's aggressive monetary easing, Japan is making modest progress in ending deflation, but demographic decline – a low birthrate and an aging, shrinking population – poses a major long-term challenge for the economy. The government currently faces the quandary of balancing its efforts to stimulate growth and institute economic reforms with the need to address its sizable public debt, which stands at 235% of GDP. To help raise government revenue, Japan adopted legislation in 2012 to gradually raise the consumption tax rate. However, the first such increase, in April 2014, led to a sharp contraction, so Prime Minister ABE has twice postponed the next increase, which is now scheduled for October 2019. Structural reforms to unlock productivity are seen as central to strengthening the economy in the long-run.

Scarce in critical natural resources, Japan has long been dependent on imported energy and raw materials. After the complete shutdown of Japan's nuclear reactors following the earthquake and tsunami disaster in 2011, Japan's industrial sector has become even more dependent than before on imported fossil fuels. However, ABE's government is seeking to restart nuclear power plants that meet strict new safety standards and is emphasizing nuclear energy's importance as a base-load electricity source. In August 2015, Japan successfully restarted one nuclear reactor at the Sendai Nuclear Power Plant in Kagoshima prefecture, and several other reactors around the country have since resumed operations; however, opposition from local governments has delayed several more restarts that remain pending. Reforms of the electricity and gas sectors, including full liberalization of Japan's energy market in April 2016 and gas market in April 2017, constitute an important part of Prime Minister Abe's economic program.

Under the Abe Administration, Japan's government sought to open the country's economy to greater foreign competition and create new export opportunities for Japanese businesses, including by joining 11 trading partners in the Trans-Pacific Partnership (TPP). Japan became the first country to ratify the TPP in December 2016, but the United States signaled its withdrawal from the agreement in January 2017. In November 2017 the remaining 11 countries agreed on the core elements of a modified agreement, which they renamed the Comprehensive and Progressive Agreement for Trans-Pacific Partnership (CPTPP). Japan also reached agreement with the European Union on an Economic Partnership Agreement in July 2017, and is likely seek to ratify both agreements in the Diet this year.

Real GDP (purchasing power parity): $5,224,850,000,000 (2019 est.) note: data are in 2017 dollars
$5,210,770,000,000 (2018 est.) note: data are in 2017 dollars
$5,180,326,000,000 (2017 est.)

Real GDP growth rate: 0.7% (2019 est.)
0.29% (2018 est.)
2.19% (2017 est.)

Real GDP per capita: $41,400 (2019 est.) note: data are in 2017 dollars
$41,200 (2018 est.) note: data are in 2017 dollars
$40,859 (2017 est.)

GDP (official exchange rate): $5,078,679,000,000 (2019 est.)

Inflation rate (consumer prices): 0.4% (2019 est.)
0.9% (2018 est.)
0.4% (2017 est.)

Credit ratings:

Fitch rating: A (2015)

Moody's rating: A1 (2014)

Standard & Poors rating: A+ (2015)
note: The year refers to the year in which the current credit rating was first obtained.

GDP - composition, by sector of origin: *agriculture:* 1.1% (2017 est.)
industry: 30.1% (2017 est.)
services: 68.7% (2017 est.)

GDP - composition, by end use: *household consumption:* 55.5% (2017 est.)
government consumption: 19.6% (2017 est.)
investment in fixed capital: 24% (2017 est.)
investment in inventories: 0% (2017 est.)
exports of goods and services: 17.7% (2017 est.)
imports of goods and services: -16.8% (2017 est.)

Agricultural products: rice, milk, sugar beet, vegetables, eggs, poultry, potatoes, cabbages, onions, pork

Industries: among world's largest and most technologically advanced producers of motor vehicles, electronic equipment, machine tools, steel and nonferrous metals, ships, chemicals, textiles, processed foods

Industrial production growth rate: 1.4% (2017 est.)

Labor force: 66.54 million (2020 est.)

Labor force - by occupation: *agriculture:* 2.9%
industry: 26.2%
services: 70.9% (February 2015 est.)

Unemployment rate: 2.36% (2019 est.)
2.44% (2018 est.)

Unemployment, youth ages 15-24: *total:* 4.6%
male: 5%
female: 4.2% (2020 est.)

Population below poverty line: 16.1% (2013 est.)

Gini Index coefficient - distribution of family income: 32.9 (2013 est.)
24.9 (1993)

Household income or consumption by percentage share: *lowest 10%:* 2.7%
highest 10%: 24.8% (2008)

Budget: *revenues:* 1.714 trillion (2017 est.)
expenditures: 1.885 trillion (2017 est.)

Budget surplus (+) or deficit (-): -3.5% (of GDP) (2017 est.)

Public debt: 237.6% of GDP (2017 est.)
235.6% of GDP (2016 est.)

Taxes and other revenues: 35.2% (of GDP) (2017 est.)

Fiscal year: 1 April - 31 March

Current account balance: $185.644 billion (2019 est.)
$177.08 billion (2018 est.)

Exports: $793.32 billion (2020 est.) note: data are in current year dollars
$904.63 billion (2019 est.) note: data are in current year dollars
$929.83 billion (2018 est.) note: data are in current year dollars

Exports - partners: United States 19%, China 18%, South Korea 6%, Taiwan 6% (2019)

Exports - commodities: cars and vehicle parts, integrated circuits, personal appliances, ships (2019)

Imports: $799.52 billion (2020 est.) note: data are in current year dollars
$913.25 billion (2019 est.) note: data are in current year dollars
$928.42 billion (2018 est.) note: data are in current year dollars

Imports - partners: China 23%, United States 11%, Australia 6% (2019)

Imports - commodities: crude petroleum, natural gas, coal, integrated circuits, broadcasting equipment (2019)

Reserves of foreign exchange and gold: $1.264 trillion (31 December 2017 est.)
$1.233 trillion (31 December 2015 est.)

Debt - external: $4,254,271,000,000 (2019 est.)
$3,944,898,000,000 (2018 est.)

Exchange rates: yen (JPY) per US dollar -
104.205 (2020 est.)
108.605 (2019 est.)
112.7 (2018 est.)
121.02 (2014 est.)
97.44 (2013 est.)

ENERGY

Electricity access: *electrification - total population:* 100% (2020)

Electricity: *installed generating capacity:* 348.666 million kW (2020 est.)
consumption: 903,698,740,000 kWh (2019 est.)
exports: 0 kWh (2020 est.)
imports: 0 kWh (2020 est.)
transmission/distribution losses: 44.094 billion kWh (2019 est.)

Electricity generation sources: *fossil fuels:* 73.5% of total installed capacity (2020 est.)
nuclear: 4.8% of total installed capacity (2020 est.)
solar: 8.8% of total installed capacity (2020 est.)
wind: 1% of total installed capacity (2020 est.)
hydroelectricity: 10% of total installed capacity (2020 est.)
geothermal: 0.3% of total installed capacity (2020 est.)
biomass and waste: 1.6% of total installed capacity (2020 est.)

Coal: *production:* 29.84 million metric tons (2020 est.)
consumption: 210.882 million metric tons (2020 est.)
exports: 3.201 million metric tons (2020 est.)
imports: 174.486 million metric tons (2020 est.)
proven reserves: 350 million metric tons (2019 est.)

Petroleum: *total petroleum production:* 10,200 bbl/day (2021 est.)
refined petroleum consumption: 3,739,300 bbl/day (2019 est.)
crude oil and lease condensate exports: 0 bbl/day (2018 est.)
crude oil and lease condensate imports: 3,012,800 bbl/day (2018 est.)
crude oil estimated reserves: 44.1 million barrels (2021 est.)

Refined petroleum products - production: 3.467 million bbl/day (2017 est.)

Refined petroleum products - exports: 370,900 bbl/day (2017 est.)

Refined petroleum products - imports: 1.1 million bbl/day (2017 est.)

Natural gas: *production:* 1,928,431,000 cubic meters (2020 est.)
consumption: 102,108,738,000 cubic meters (2019 est.)
exports: 28,000 cubic meters (2019 est.)
imports: 105,255,103,000 cubic meters (2019 est.)
proven reserves: 20.898 billion cubic meters (2021 est.)

Carbon dioxide emissions: 1,103,234,000 metric tonnes of CO_2 (2019 est.)
from coal and metallurgical coke: 439.243 million metric tonnes of CO_2 (2019 est.)
from petroleum and other liquids: 444.271 million metric tonnes of CO_2 (2019 est.)
from consumed natural gas: 219.72 million metric tonnes of CO_2 (2019 est.)

Energy consumption per capita: 147.107 million Btu/person (2019 est.)

COMMUNICATIONS

Telephones - fixed lines: *total subscriptions:* 61,978,594 (2020 est.)
subscriptions per 100 inhabitants: 49 (2020 est.)

Telephones - mobile cellular: *total subscriptions:* 195,054,893 (2020 est.)
subscriptions per 100 inhabitants: 154 (2020 est.)

Telecommunication systems: *general assessment:* Japan has one of the best developed telecom markets globally, the fixed-line segment remains stagnant and the focus for growth is in the mobile sector; the MNOs have shifted their investment from LTE to 5G, and growth in 5G showed early promise although there have been recent setbacks; these have partly been attributed to the economic difficulties, the impact of restrictions imposed during the pandemic, and unfavourable investment climate (not helped by the delay of the Tokyo Olympics from 2020 to 2021), and to restrictions in the supply of 5G-enabled devices; the fixed broadband market is dominated by fiber, with a strong cable platform also evident; fiber will continue to increase its share of the fixed broadband market, largely at the expense of DSL; the mobile market is dominated by three MNOs, mobile broadband subscriber growth is expected to be relatively low over the next five years, partly due to the high existing subscriptions though growth has been stimulated by measures which have encouraged people to school and work from home; there has also been a boost in accessing entertainment via mobile devices since 2020; plans to provide 55% population coverage with 5G by March 2022 and nationwide 5G coverage by 2023 (2021)
domestic: high level of modern technology and excellent service of every kind; 49 per 100 for fixed-line and 152 per 100 for mobile-cellular subscriptions (2020)
international: country code - 81; numerous submarine cables with landing points for HSCS, JIH, RJCN, APCN-2, JUS, EAC-C2C, PC-1, Tata TGN-Pacific, FLAG North Asia Loop/REACH North Asia Loop, APCN-2, FASTER, SJC, SJC2, Unity/EAC-Pacific, JGA-N, APG, ASE, AJC, JUPITER, MOC, Okinawa Cellular Cable, KJCN, GOKI, KJCN, and SeaMeWE-3, submarine cables provide links throughout Asia, Australia, the Middle East, Europe, Southeast Asia, Africa and US; satellite earth stations - 7 Intelsat (Pacific and Indian Oceans), 1 Intersputnik (Indian Ocean region), 2 Inmarsat (Pacific and Indian Ocean regions), and 8 SkyPerfect JSAT (2019)

Broadcast media: a mixture of public and commercial broadcast TV and radio stations; 6 national terrestrial TV networks including 1 public broadcaster; the large number of radio and TV stations available provide a wide range of choices; satellite and cable services provide access to international channels (2019)

Internet country code: .jp

Internet users: *total:* 113,252,419 (2020 est.)
percent of population: 90% (2020 est.)

Broadband - fixed subscriptions: *total:* 44,000,791 (2020 est.)
subscriptions per 100 inhabitants: 35 (2020 est.)

TRANSPORTATION

National air transport system: *number of registered air carriers:* 22 (2020)
inventory of registered aircraft operated by air carriers: 673
annual passenger traffic on registered air carriers: 126,387,527 (2018)
annual freight traffic on registered air carriers: 9,420,660,000 (2018) mt-km

Civil aircraft registration country code prefix: JA

Airports: *total:* 175 (2021)

Airports - with paved runways: *total:* 142
over 3,047 m: 6
2,438 to 3,047 m: 45
1,524 to 2,437 m: 38
914 to 1,523 m: 28
under 914 m: 25 (2021)

Airports - with unpaved runways: *total:* 33
914 to 1,523 m: 5
under 914 m: 28 (2021)

Heliports: 16 (2021)

Pipelines: 4,456 km gas, 174 km oil, 104 km oil/gas/water (2013)

Railways: *total:* 27,311 km (2015)
standard gauge: 4,800 km (2015) 1.435-m gauge (4,800 km electrified)
narrow gauge: 124 km (2015) 1.372-m gauge (124 km electrified)
dual gauge: 132 km (2015) 1.435-1.067-m gauge (132 km electrified)
22,207 km 1.067-mm gauge (15,430 km electrified)

48 km 0.762-m gauge (48 km electrified)

Roadways: *total:* 1,218,772 km (2015)
paved: 992,835 km (2015) (includes 8,428 km of expressways)
unpaved: 225,937 km (2015)

Waterways: 1,770 km (2010) (seagoing vessels use inland seas)

Merchant marine: *total:* 5,201
by type: bulk carrier 148, container ship 45, general cargo 1,900, oil tanker 666, other 2,442 (2021)

Ports and terminals: *major seaport(s):* Chiba, Kawasaki, Kobe, Mizushima, Moji, Nagoya, Osaka, Tokyo, Tomakomai, Yokohama
container port(s) (TEUs): Kobe (2,871,642), Nagoya (2,844,004), Osaka (2,456,028), Tokyo (4,510,000), Yokohama (2,990,000) (2019)

LNG terminal(s) (import): Chita, Fukwoke, Futtsu, Hachinone, Hakodate, Hatsukaichi, Higashi Ohgishima, Higashi Niigata, Himeiji, Joetsu, Kagoshima, Kawagoe, Kita Kyushu, Mizushima, Nagasaki, Naoetsu, Negishi, Ohgishima, Oita, Sakai, Sakaide, Senboku, Shimizu, Shin Minato, Sodegaura, Tobata, Yanai, Yokkaichi
Okinawa - Nakagusuku

MILITARY AND SECURITY

Military and security forces: Japan Self-Defense Force (JSDF): Ground Self-Defense Force (Rikujou Jieitai, GSDF; includes aviation), Maritime Self-Defense Force (Kaijou Jieitai, MSDF; includes naval aviation), Air Self-Defense Force (Koukuu Jieitai, ASDF); Japan Coast Guard (Ministry of Land, Transport, Infrastructure and Tourism) (2022)

Military expenditures: 1% of GDP (2022 est.)
1% of GDP (2021)
1% of GDP (2020)
0.9% of GDP (2019) (approximately $53.4 billion)
0.9% of GDP (2018) (approximately $53.5 billion)
note: the Japanese Government in 2022 pledged to "substantially" increase defense spending in the next few years to counter what Tokyo sees as a growing security threat posed by China

Military and security service personnel strengths: approximately 240,000 active personnel (150,000 Ground; 45,000 Maritime; 45,000 Air); 14,000 Coast Guard (2022)

Military equipment inventories and acquisitions: the JSDF is equipped with a mix of imported and domestically-produced equipment; Japan has a robust defense industry and is capable of producing a wide range of air, ground, and naval weapons systems; the majority of its weapons imports are from the US and some domestically-produced weapons are US-origin and manufactured under license (2022)

Military service age and obligation: 18 years of age for voluntary military service for men and women (maximum enlistment age 32); no conscription (2022)
note: as of 2020, women made up about 7% of the military's full-time personnel

Military deployments: approximately 180 Djibouti (2022)

Military - note: Japan was disarmed after its defeat in World War II; shortly after the Korean War began in 1950, US occupation forces in Japan created a 75,000-member lightly armed force called the National Police Reserve; the current Self Defense Force was founded in 1954

in addition to having one of the region's largest and best equipped militaries, Japan's alliance with the US (signed in 1951) is one of the cornerstones of the country's security, as well as a large part of the US security role in Asia; as of 2022, approximately 55,000 US troops and other military assets, including aircraft and naval ships, were stationed in Japan and had exclusive use of more than 80 bases and facilities; in exchange for their use, the US guarantees Japan's security; the Japanese Government provides about $2 billion per year to offset the cost of stationing US forces in Japan; in addition, it pays compensation to localities hosting US troops, rent for bases, and costs for new facilities to support the US presence

Japan has Major Non-NATO Ally (MNNA) status with the US; MNNA is a designation under US law that provides foreign partners with certain benefits in the areas of defense trade and security cooperation; while MNNA status provides military and economic privileges, it does not entail any security commitments (2022)

TRANSNATIONAL ISSUES

Disputes - international: *Japan-China-Taiwan:* the Japanese-administered Senkaku Islands (Diaoyu Tai) are also claimed by China and Taiwan; Senkaku-shoto is situated near key shipping lanes, rich fishing grounds, and possibly significant oil and natural gas reserves
Japan-Russia: the sovereignty dispute over the islands of Etorofu, Kunashiri, and Shikotan, and the Habomai group, known in Japan as the "Northern Territories" and in Russia as the "Southern Kuril Islands," occupied by the Soviet Union in 1945, now administered by Russia and claimed by Japan, remains the primary sticking point to signing a peace treaty formally ending World War II hostilities
Japan-South Korea: Japan and South Korea claim Liancourt Rocks (Take-shima/Tok-do) occupied by South Korea since 1954

Refugees and internally displaced persons: *stateless persons:* 707 (mid-year 2021)

JERSEY

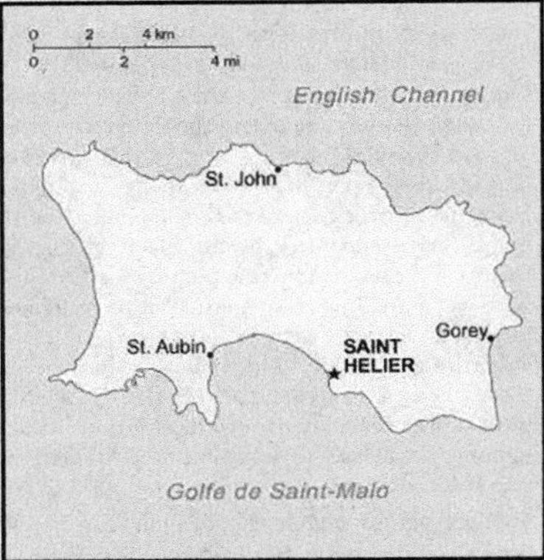

INTRODUCTION

Background: Jersey and the other Channel Islands represent the last remnants of the medieval Duchy of Normandy that held sway in both France and England. These islands were the only British soil occupied by German troops in World War II. The Bailiwick of Jersey is a British Crown dependency, which means that it is not part of the UK but is rather a self-governing possession of the British Crown. However, the UK Government is constitutionally responsible for its defense and international representation.

GEOGRAPHY

Location: Western Europe, island in the English Channel, northwest of France

Geographic coordinates: 49 15 N, 2 10 W

Map references: Europe

Area: *total:* 116 sq km
land: 116 sq km
water: 0 sq km

Area - comparative: about two-thirds the size of Washington, DC

Land boundaries: *total:* 0 km

Coastline: 70 km

Maritime claims: *territorial sea:* 12 nm
exclusive fishing zone: 12 nm

Climate: temperate; mild winters and cool summers

Terrain: gently rolling plain with low, rugged hills along north coast

Elevation: *highest point:* Les Platons 136 m
lowest point: English Channel 0 m

Natural resources: arable land

Land use: *agricultural land:* 66% (2018 est.)
arable land: 66% (2018 est.)
permanent crops: 0% (2018 est.)
permanent pasture: 0% (2018 est.)
forest: 0% (2018 est.)
other: 34% (2018 est.)

Population distribution: fairly even distribution; no notable trends

Natural hazards: very large tidal variation can be hazardous to navigation

Geography - note: largest and southernmost of Channel Islands; about 30% of population concentrated in Saint Helier

PEOPLE AND SOCIETY

Population: 102,146 (2022 est.)

Nationality: *noun:* Channel Islander(s)
adjective: Channel Islander

Ethnic groups: Jersey 44.4%, British 30.5%, Portuguese/Madeiran 9.4%, Polish 3%, Irish 2.1%, other 10.6% (2021 est.)

Languages: English (official) 94.5%, Portuguese 4.6%, other 0.9% (includes French (official) and Jerriais) (2001 est.)
note: data represent main spoken language; the traditional language of Jersey is Jerriais or Jersey French (a Norman language), which was spoken by fewer than 3,000 people as of 2001; two thirds of Jerriais speakers are aged 60 and over

Religions: Protestant (Anglican, Baptist, Congregational New Church, Methodist, Presbyterian), Roman Catholic

Age structure: *0-14 years:* 16.63% (male 8,689/ female 8,124)
15-24 years: 12.98% (male 6,764/female 6,354)
25-54 years: 40.12% (male 20,499/female 20,054)
55-64 years: 13.22% (male 6,515/female 6,844)
65 years and over: 17.05% (male 7,324/female 9,906) (2020 est.)

Dependency ratios: *total dependency ratio:* 49
youth dependency ratio: 22.3
elderly dependency ratio: 26.7
potential support ratio: 3.7 (2020 est.)
note: data represent Guernsey and Jersey

Median age: *total:* 37.5 years
male: 36 years
female: 39.5 years (2020 est.)

Population growth rate: 0.64% (2022 est.)

Birth rate: 12.41 births/1,000 population (2022 est.)

Death rate: 7.75 deaths/1,000 population (2022 est.)

Net migration rate: 1.76 migrant(s)/1,000 population (2022 est.)

Population distribution: fairly even distribution; no notable trends

Urbanization: *urban population:* 31.1% of total population (2022)
rate of urbanization: 0.68% annual rate of change (2020-25 est.)
note: data include Guernsey and Jersey

Major urban areas - population: 34,000 SAINT HELIER (capital) (2018)

Sex ratio: *at birth:* 1.06 male(s)/female
0-14 years: 1.07 male(s)/female
15-24 years: 1.07 male(s)/female
25-54 years: 1.04 male(s)/female
55-64 years: 0.95 male(s)/female
65 years and over: 0.61 male(s)/female
total population: 0.97 male(s)/female (2022 est.)

Infant mortality rate: *total:* 3.87 deaths/1,000 live births
male: 4.32 deaths/1,000 live births
female: 3.4 deaths/1,000 live births (2022 est.)

Life expectancy at birth: *total population:* 82.63 years
male: 80.13 years
female: 85.28 years (2022 est.)

Total fertility rate: 1.66 children born/woman (2022 est.)

Drinking water source: *improved: total:* 94.2% of population
unimproved: total: 5.9% of population (2017 est.)
note: includes data for Guernsey

Sanitation facility access: *improved: total:* 98.5% of population
unimproved: total: 1.5% of population (2017)

ENVIRONMENT

Environment - current issues: habitat and species depletion due to human encroachment; water pollution; improper solid waste disposal

Climate: temperate; mild winters and cool summers

Land use: *agricultural land:* 66% (2018 est.)
arable land: 66% (2018 est.)
permanent crops: 0% (2018 est.)
permanent pasture: 0% (2018 est.)
forest: 0% (2018 est.)
other: 34% (2018 est.)

Urbanization: *urban population:* 31.1% of total population (2022)
rate of urbanization: 0.68% annual rate of change (2020-25 est.)
note: data include Guernsey and Jersey

Waste and recycling: *municipal solid waste generated annually:* 178,933 tons (2016 est.)
municipal solid waste recycled annually: 50,871 tons (2016 est.)
percent of municipal solid waste recycled: 28.4% (2016 est.)
note: data include combined totals for Guernsey and Jersey.

GOVERNMENT

Country name: *conventional long form:* Bailiwick of Jersey
conventional short form: Jersey
former: Norman Isles
etymology: the name is of Old Norse origin, but the meaning of the root "Jer(s)" is uncertain; the "-ey" ending means "island"

Government type: parliamentary democracy (Assembly of the States of Jersey)

Dependency status: British crown dependency

Capital: *name:* Saint Helier
geographic coordinates: 49 11 N, 2 06 W
time difference: UTC 0 (5 hours ahead of Washington, DC, during Standard Time)
daylight saving time: +1hr, begins last Sunday in March; ends last Sunday in October
etymology: named after Saint HELIER, the patron saint of Jersey, who was reputedly martyred on the island in A.D. 555

Administrative divisions: none (British crown dependency); there are no first-order administrative divisions as defined by the US Government, but there are 12 parishes; Grouville, Saint Brelade, Saint Clement, Saint Helier, Saint John, Saint Lawrence, Saint Martin, Saint Mary, Saint Ouen, Saint Peter, Saint Saviour, Trinity

Independence: none (British Crown dependency)

National holiday: Liberation Day, 9 May (1945)

Constitution: *history:* unwritten; partly statutes, partly common law and practice
amendments: proposed by a government minister to the Assembly of the States of Jersey, by an Assembly member, or by an elected parish head; passage requires several Assembly readings, a majority vote by the Assembly, review by the UK Ministry of Justice, and approval of the British monarch (Royal Assent)

Legal system: the laws of the UK apply where applicable; includes local statutes

Citizenship: see United Kingdom

Suffrage: 16 years of age; universal

Executive branch: *chief of state:* King CHARLES III (since 8 September 2022); represented by Lieutenant Governor Sir Stephen DALTON (since 13 March 2017)
head of government: Chief Minister John LE FONDRE (since 8 June 2018); Bailiff Timothy Le COCQ (since 17 October 2019)
cabinet: Council of Ministers appointed individually by the states
elections/appointments: the monarchy is hereditary; Council of Ministers, including the chief minister, indirectly elected by the Assembly of States; lieutenant governor and bailiff appointed by the monarch

Legislative branch: *description:* unicameral Assembly of the States of Jersey (49 elected members; 8 senators to serve 4-year terms, and 29 deputies and 12 connetables, or heads of parishes, to serve 4-year terms; 5 non-voting members appointed by the monarch include the bailiff, lieutenant governor, dean of Jersey, attorney general, and the solicitor general)
elections: last held on 22 June 2022 (next to be held in 2026)
election results: percent of vote - BW 71.4%, RJ 20.4%, JA 2%, PP 2%, JLC 4.1%; seats by party - BW 35, RJ 10, JA 1, PP 1, JLC 2; composition - men NA, women NA, percent of women NA%

Judicial branch: *highest court(s):* Jersey Court of Appeal (consists of the bailiff, deputy bailiff, and 12 judges); Royal Court (consists of the bailiff, deputy bailiff, 6 commissioners and lay people referred to as jurats, and is organized into Heritage, Family, Probate, and Samedi Divisions); appeals beyond the Court of Appeal are heard by the Judicial Committee of the Privy Council (in London)
judge selection and term of office: Jersey Court of Appeal bailiffs and judges appointed by the Crown upon the advice of the Secretary of State for Justice; bailiffs and judges appointed for "extent of good behavior;" Royal Court bailiffs appointed by the Crown upon the advice of the Secretary of State for Justice; commissioners appointed by the bailiff; jurats appointed by the Electoral College; bailiffs and commissioners appointed for "extent of good behavior;" jurats appointed until retirement at age 72
subordinate courts: Magistrate's Court; Youth Court; Petty Debts Court; Parish Hall Enquires (a process of preliminary investigation into youth and minor adult offenses to determine need for presentation before a court)

Political parties and leaders: Better Way or BW (group of independent candidates)
Jersey Alliance or JA [Mark BOLEAT]
Jersey Liberal Conservatives or JLC [Sir Philip BAILHACHE]
Progress Party or PP [Steve PALLETT]
Reform Jersey or RJ [Sam MEZEC]
note: most deputies sit as independents

International organization participation: UPU

Diplomatic representation in the US: *chief of mission:* none (British Crown dependency)

Diplomatic representation from the US: *embassy:* none (British Crown dependency)

Flag description: white with a diagonal red cross extending to the corners of the flag; in the upper quadrant, surmounted by a yellow crown, a red shield with three lions in yellow; according to tradition, the ships of Jersey - in an attempt to differentiate themselves from English ships flying the horizontal cross of St. George - rotated the cross to the "X" (saltire) configuration; because this arrangement still resembled the Irish cross of St. Patrick, the yellow Plantagenet crown and Jersey coat of arms were added

National symbol(s): Jersey cow; national colors: red, white

National anthem: *name:* "Isle de Siez Nous" (Island Home)
lyrics/music: Gerard LE FEUVRE
note: adopted 2008; serves as a local anthem; as a British Crown dependency, "God Save the King" is official (see United Kingdom)

ECONOMY

Economic overview: Jersey's economy is based on international financial services, agriculture, and tourism. In 2016, the financial services sector accounted for about 41% of the island's output. Agriculture represented about 1% of Jersey's economy in 2016.

Potatoes are an important export crop, shipped mostly to the UK. The Jersey breed of dairy cattle originated on the island and is known worldwide. The dairy industry remains important to the island with approximately $8.8 million gallons of milk produced in 2015. Tourism accounts for a significant portion of Jersey's economy, with more than 700,000 total visitors in 2015. Living standards come close to those of the UK. All raw material and energy requirements are imported as well as a large share of Jersey's food needs. Light taxes and death duties make the island a popular offshore financial center. Jersey maintains its relationship with the EU through the UK. Therefore, in light of the UK's decision to leave the EU, Jersey will also need to renegotiate its ties to the EU.

Real GDP (purchasing power parity): $5.569 billion (2016 est.)
$5.514 billion (2015 est.)
$4.98 billion (2014 est.)
note: data are in 2015 US dollars

Real GDP growth rate: 1% (2016 est.)
10.7% (2015 est.)

Real GDP per capita: $56,600 (2016 est.)
$49,500 (2015 est.)

GDP (official exchange rate): $5.004 billion (2015 est.)

Inflation rate (consumer prices): 3.7% (2006)

GDP - composition, by sector of origin: *agriculture:* 2% (2010)
industry: 2% (2010)
services: 96% (2010)

Agricultural products: potatoes, cauliflower, tomatoes; beef, dairy products

Industries: tourism, banking and finance, dairy, electronics

Labor force: 59,950 (2017 est.)

Labor force - by occupation: *agriculture:* 3%
industry: 12%
services: 85% (2014 est.)

Unemployment rate: 4% (2015 est.)
4.6% (2014 est.)

Gini Index coefficient - distribution of family income: 0.3 (2014 est.)
0.3 (2013 est.)

Budget: *revenues:* 829 million (2005)
expenditures: 851 million (2005)

Budget surplus (+) or deficit (-): -0.4% (of GDP) (2005)

Taxes and other revenues: 16.6% (of GDP) (2005)

Fiscal year: 1 April - 31 March

Exports - commodities: light industrial and electrical goods, dairy cattle, foodstuffs, textiles, flowers

Imports - commodities: machinery and transport equipment, manufactured goods, foodstuffs, mineral fuels, chemicals

Exchange rates: Jersey pounds (JEP) per US dollar
0.7836 (2017 est.)
0.738 (2016 est.)
0.738 (2015)
0.6542 (2012)
0.6391 (2011 est.)

ENERGY

Electricity access: *electrification - total population:* 100% (2020)

Carbon dioxide emissions: 450,000 metric tonnes of CO2 (2012 est.)

COMMUNICATIONS

Telephones - fixed lines: *total subscriptions:* 48,310 (2019 est.)
subscriptions per 100 inhabitants: 44 (2019 est.)

Telephones - mobile cellular: *total subscriptions:* 83,900 (2009 est.)
subscriptions per 100 inhabitants: 95 (2009 est.)

Telecommunication systems: *general assessment:* the telecommunication services comprise of Internet, telephone, broadcasting and postal services, which allow islanders to contact people and receive information; Internet connectivity to the rest of the world is provided by undersea cables linked to Guernsey, the UK and France; (2021)
domestic: fixed-line 47 per 100 and mobile-cellular 120 per 100 subscriptions (2021)
international: country code - 44; landing points for the INGRID, UK-Channel Islands-8, and Guernsey-Jersey-4, submarine cable connectivity to Guernsey, the UK, and France (2019)

Broadcast media: multiple UK terrestrial TV broadcasts are received via a transmitter in Jersey; satellite packages available; BBC Radio Jersey and 1 other radio station operating

Internet country code: .je

Internet users: *total:* 44,198 (2019 est.)
percent of population: 41% (2019 est.)

Broadband - fixed subscriptions: *total:* 39,699 (2020 est.)
subscriptions per 100 inhabitants: 37 (2020 est.)

TRANSPORTATION

National air transport system: *number of registered air carriers:* 1 (2020) (registered in UK)
inventory of registered aircraft operated by air carriers: 4 (registered in UK)

Airports: *total:* 1 (2021)

Airports - with paved runways: *total:* 1
1,524 to 2,437 m: 1 (2021)

Roadways: *total:* 576 km (2010)

Ports and terminals: *major seaport(s):* Gorey, Saint Aubin, Saint Helier

MILITARY AND SECURITY

Military - note: defense is the responsibility of the UK

TRANSNATIONAL ISSUES

Disputes - international: none identified

JORDAN

INTRODUCTION

Background: Following World War I and the dissolution of the Ottoman Empire, the League of Nations awarded Britain the mandate to govern much of the Middle East. Britain demarcated a semi-autonomous region of Transjordan from Palestine in 1921 and recognized ABDALLAH I from the Hashemite family as the country's first leader. The Hashemites also controlled Hijaz, or the western coastal area of modern day Saudi Arabia until 1925, when they were pushed out by Ibn SAUD and Wahhabi tribes. The country gained its independence in 1946 and thereafter became The Hashemite Kingdom of Jordan.

The country has had four kings. Jordan's long-time ruler, King HUSSEIN (1953-99), successfully navigated competing pressures from the major powers (US, USSR, and UK), various Arab states, Israel, and Palestinian militants, which led to a brief civil war in 1970 referred to as "Black September" and ended in King HUSSEIN's ouster of the militants from Jordan. Jordan's borders also have changed. In 1948, Jordan took control of the West Bank and East Jerusalem, eventually annexing those territories in 1950 and granting its new Palestinian residents Jordanian citizenship. In 1967, Jordan lost the West Bank and East Jerusalem to Israel in the Six-Day

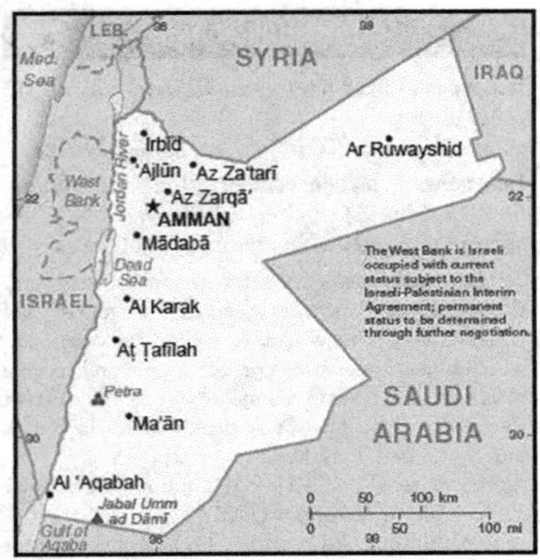

War but retained administrative claims until 1988 when King HUSSEIN permanently relinquished Jordanian claims to the West Bank in favor of the Palestinian Liberation Organization (PLO). King HUSSEIN signed a peace treaty with Israel in 1994, after Israel and the PLO signed the Oslo Accords in 1993.

Jordanian kings continue to claim custodianship of the holy sites in Jerusalem by virtue of their Hashemite heritage as descendants of the Prophet Mohammad and agreements with Israel and Jerusalem-based religious and Palestinian leaders. After Israel captured East Jerusalem in the 1967 War, it authorized the Jordanian-controlled Islamic Trust, or Waqf, to continue administering affairs in the Al Haram ash Sharif/Temple Mount holy compound, and the Jordan-Israel peace treaty reaffirmed Jordan's "special role" in administering the Muslim holy shrines in Jerusalem.

King HUSSEIN died in 1999 and was succeeded by his eldest son, ABDALLAH II, who remains the current king. In 2009, King ABDALLAH II designated his son HUSSEIN as the Crown Prince. During his reign, ABDALLAH II has contended with a series of challenges, including the Arab Spring influx of refugees from neighboring states and a perennially weak economy.

GEOGRAPHY

Location: Middle East, northwest of Saudi Arabia, between Israel (to the west) and Iraq

Geographic coordinates: 31 00 N, 36 00 E

Map references: Middle East

Area: *total:* 89,342 sq km
land: 88,802 sq km
water: 540 sq km

Area - comparative: about three-quarters the size of Pennsylvania; slightly smaller than Indiana

Land boundaries: *total:* 1,744 km
border countries (5): Iraq 179 km; Israel 307 km; Saudi Arabia 731 km; Syria 379 km; West Bank 148 km

Coastline: 26 km

Maritime claims: *territorial sea:* 3 nm

Climate: mostly arid desert; rainy season in west (November to April)

Terrain: mostly arid desert plateau; a great north-south geological rift along the west of the country is the dominant topographical feature and includes the Jordan River Valley, the Dead Sea, and the Jordanian Highlands

Elevation: *highest point:* Jabal Umm ad Dami 1,854 m
lowest point: Dead Sea -431 m
mean elevation: 812 m

Natural resources: phosphates, potash, shale oil

Land use: *agricultural land:* 11.4% (2018 est.)
arable land: 2% (2018 est.)
permanent crops: 1% (2018 est.)
permanent pasture: 8.4% (2018 est.)
forest: 1.1% (2018 est.)
other: 87.5% (2018 est.)

Irrigated land: 964 sq km (2012)

Major lakes (area sq km): *salt water lake(s):* Dead Sea (shared with Israel and West Bank) - 1,020 sq km
note - endorheic hypersaline lake; 9.6 times saltier than the ocean; lake shore is 431 meters below sea level

Major watersheds (area sq km): Indian Ocean drainage: *(Persian Gulf)* Tigris and Euphrates (918,044 sq km)

Major aquifers: Arabian Aquifer System

Population distribution: population heavily concentrated in the west, and particularly the northwest, in and around the capital of Amman; a sizeable, but smaller population is located in the southwest along the shore of the Gulf of Aqaba

Natural hazards: droughts; periodic earthquakes; flash floods

Geography - note: strategic location at the head of the Gulf of Aqaba and as the Arab country that shares the longest border with Israel and the occupied West Bank; the Dead Sea, the lowest point in Asia and the second saltiest body of water in the world (after Lac Assal in Djibouti), lies on Jordan's western border with Israel and the West Bank; Jordan is almost landlocked but does have a 26 km southwestern coastline with a single port, Al 'Aqabah (Aqaba)

PEOPLE AND SOCIETY

Population: 10,998,531 (2022 est.)
note: increased estimate reflects revised assumptions about the net migration rate due to the increased flow of Syrian refugees

Nationality: *noun:* Jordanian(s)
adjective: Jordanian

Ethnic groups: Jordanian 69.3%, Syrian 13.3%, Palestinian 6.7%, Egyptian 6.7%, Iraqi 1.4%, other 2.6% (includes Armenian, Circassian) (2015 est.)
note: data represent population by self-identified nationality

Languages: Arabic (official), English (widely understood among upper and middle classes)
major-language sample(s):
يمكن الاستغناء عنه للمعلومات الأساسية
كتاب حقائق العالم، المصدر الذي لا
(Arabic)

Religions: Muslim 97.1% (official; predominantly Sunni), Christian 2.1% (majority Greek Orthodox, but some Greek and Roman Catholics, Syrian Orthodox, Coptic Orthodox, Armenian Orthodox, and Protestant denominations), Buddhist 0.4%, Hindu 0.1%, Jewish <0.1%, folk <0.1%, other <0.1%, unaffiliated <0.1% (2020 est.)

Age structure: *0-14 years:* 33.05% (male 1,837,696/female 1,738,935)
15-24 years: 19.77% (male 1,126,567/female 1,012,812)
25-54 years: 38.39% (male 2,250,328/female 1,903,996)
55-64 years: 5.11% (male 290,633/female 262,827)
65 years and over: 3.67% (male 194,464/female 202,386) (2020 est.)

Dependency ratios: *total dependency ratio:* 58.2
youth dependency ratio: 52
elderly dependency ratio: 6.3
potential support ratio: 16 (2020 est.)

Median age: *total:* 23.5 years
male: 23.9 years
female: 22.9 years (2020 est.)

Population growth rate: 0.81% (2022 est.)

Birth rate: 22.58 births/1,000 population (2022 est.)

Death rate: 3.45 deaths/1,000 population (2022 est.)

Net migration rate: -11.08 migrant(s)/1,000 population (2022 est.)

Population distribution: population heavily concentrated in the west, and particularly the northwest, in and around the capital of Amman; a sizeable, but smaller population is located in the southwest along the shore of the Gulf of Aqaba

Urbanization: *urban population:* 91.8% of total population (2022)
rate of urbanization: 0.98% annual rate of change (2020-25 est.)

Major urban areas - population: 2.210 million AMMAN (capital) (2022)

Sex ratio: *at birth:* 1.06 male(s)/female
0-14 years: 1.06 male(s)/female
15-24 years: 1.08 male(s)/female
25-54 years: 1.17 male(s)/female
55-64 years: 1.12 male(s)/female
65 years and over: 0.84 male(s)/female
total population: 1.1 male(s)/female (2022 est.)

Mother's mean age at first birth: 24.6 years (2017/18 est.)
note: data represents median age at first birth among women 25-49

Maternal mortality ratio: 46 deaths/100,000 live births (2017 est.)

Infant mortality rate: *total:* 13.9 deaths/1,000 live births
male: 15.04 deaths/1,000 live births
female: 12.69 deaths/1,000 live births (2022 est.)

Life expectancy at birth: *total population:* 76.01 years
male: 74.51 years
female: 77.6 years (2022 est.)

Total fertility rate: 2.96 children born/woman (2022 est.)

Contraceptive prevalence rate: 51.8% (2017/18)

Drinking water source: *improved: urban:* 99.2% of population
rural: 97.9% of population
total: 99.1% of population
unimproved: urban: 0.8% of population
rural: 2.1% of population
total: 0.9% of population (2020 est.)

Current health expenditure: 7.6% of GDP (2019)

Physicians density: 2.66 physicians/1,000 population (2019)

Hospital bed density: 1.5 beds/1,000 population (2017)

Sanitation facility access: *improved: urban:* 98.8% of population
rural: 97.8% of population
total: 98.7% of population
unimproved: urban: 1.2% of population
rural: 2.2% of population
total: 1.3% of population (2020 est.)

HIV/AIDS - adult prevalence rate: (2020 est.) <.1%

Major infectious diseases: *note:* widespread ongoing transmission of a respiratory illness caused by the novel coronavirus (COVID-19) is occurring throughout Jordan; as of 18 August 2022, Jordan has reported a total of 1,726,717 cases of COVID-19 or 16,923.39 cumulative cases of COVID-19 per 100,000 population with a total of 14,095 cumulative deaths or a rate of 138.14 cumulative deaths per 100,000 population; as of 7 August 2022, 43.21% of the population has received at least one dose of COVID-19 vaccine

Obesity - adult prevalence rate: 35.5% (2016)

Alcohol consumption per capita: *total:* 0.25 liters of pure alcohol (2019 est.)
beer: 0.06 liters of pure alcohol (2019 est.)
wine: 0 liters of pure alcohol (2019 est.)
spirits: 0.19 liters of pure alcohol (2019 est.)
other alcohols: 0 liters of pure alcohol (2019 est.)

Tobacco use: *total:* 34.8% (2020 est.)
male: 56.8% (2020 est.)
female: 12.8% (2020 est.)

Children under the age of 5 years underweight: 3% (2012)

Child marriage: *women married by age 15:* 1.5%
women married by age 18: 9.7%
men married by age 18: 0.1% (2018 est.)

Education expenditures: 3% of GDP (2019 est.)

Literacy: *definition:* age 15 and over can read and write
total population: 98.2%
male: 98.6%
female: 97.8% (2018)

School life expectancy (primary to tertiary education): *total:* 11 years
male: 10 years
female: 11 years (2020)

Unemployment, youth ages 15-24: *total:* 37.3%
male: 34.8%
female: 49.4% (2019 est.)

ENVIRONMENT

Environment - current issues: limited natural freshwater resources; declining water table; salinity; deforestation; overgrazing; soil erosion; desertification; biodiversity and ecosystem damage/loss

Environment - international agreements: *party to:* Biodiversity, Climate Change, Climate Change-Kyoto Protocol, Climate Change-Paris Agreement, Comprehensive Nuclear Test Ban, Desertification, Endangered Species, Hazardous Wastes, Law of the Sea, Marine Dumping-London Convention, Nuclear Test Ban, Ozone Layer Protection, Ship Pollution, Wetlands
signed, but not ratified: none of the selected agreements

Air pollutants: *particulate matter emissions:* 32.09 micrograms per cubic meter (2016 est.)
carbon dioxide emissions: 25.11 megatons (2016 est.)
methane emissions: 6.04 megatons (2020 est.)

Climate: mostly arid desert; rainy season in west (November to April)

Land use: *agricultural land:* 11.4% (2018 est.)
arable land: 2% (2018 est.)
permanent crops: 1% (2018 est.)
permanent pasture: 8.4% (2018 est.)
forest: 1.1% (2018 est.)
other: 87.5% (2018 est.)

Urbanization: *urban population:* 91.8% of total population (2022)
rate of urbanization: 0.98% annual rate of change (2020-25 est.)

Revenue from forest resources: *forest revenues:* 0.02% of GDP (2018 est.)

Revenue from coal: *coal revenues:* 0% of GDP (2018 est.)

Waste and recycling: *municipal solid waste generated annually:* 2,529,997 tons (2013 est.)
municipal solid waste recycled annually: 177,100 tons (2014 est.)
percent of municipal solid waste recycled: 7% (2014 est.)

Major lakes (area sq km): *salt water lake(s):* Dead Sea (shared with Israel and West Bank) - 1,020 sq km
note - endorheic hypersaline lake; 9.6 times saltier than the ocean; lake shore is 431 meters below sea level

Major watersheds (area sq km): Indian Ocean drainage: *(Persian Gulf)* Tigris and Euphrates (918,044 sq km)

Major aquifers: Arabian Aquifer System

Total water withdrawal: *municipal:* 456.9 million cubic meters (2017 est.)
industrial: 32.5 million cubic meters (2017 est.)
agricultural: 554.7 million cubic meters (2017 est.)

Total renewable water resources: 937 million cubic meters (2017 est.)

GOVERNMENT

Country name: *conventional long form:* Hashemite Kingdom of Jordan
conventional short form: Jordan
local long form: Al Mamlakah al Urduniyah al Hashimiyah
local short form: Al Urdun
former: Transjordan
etymology: named for the Jordan River, which makes up part of Jordan's northwest border

Government type: parliamentary constitutional monarchy

Capital: *name:* Amman
geographic coordinates: 31 57 N, 35 56 E
time difference: UTC+2 (7 hours ahead of Washington, DC, during Standard Time)
daylight saving time: +1hr, begins last Friday in February; ends last Friday in October
etymology: in the 13th century B.C., the Ammonites named their main city "Rabbath Ammon"; "rabbath" designated "capital," so the name meant "The Capital of [the] Ammon[ites]"; over time, the "Rabbath" came to be dropped and the city became known simply as "Ammon" and then "Amman"

Administrative divisions: 12 governorates (muhafazat, singular - muhafazah); 'Ajlun, Al 'Aqabah, Al Balqa', Al Karak, Al Mafraq, Al 'Asimah (Amman), At Tafilah, Az Zarqa', Irbid, Jarash, Ma'an, Madaba

Independence: 25 May 1946 (from League of Nations mandate under British administration)

National holiday: Independence Day, 25 May (1946)

Constitution: *history:* previous 1928 (preindependence); latest initially adopted 28 November 1947, revised and ratified 1 January 1952
amendments: constitutional amendments require at least a two-thirds majority vote of both the Senate and the House and ratification by the king; no amendment of the constitution affecting the rights of the king and the succession to the throne is permitted during the king's reign; amended several times, last in 2016

Legal system: mixed system developed from codes instituted by the Ottoman Empire (based on French law), British common law, and Islamic law

International law organization participation: has not submitted an ICJ jurisdiction declaration; accepts ICCt jurisdiction

Citizenship: *citizenship by birth:* no
citizenship by descent only: the father must be a citizen of Jordan
dual citizenship recognized: yes
residency requirement for naturalization: 15 years

Suffrage: 18 years of age; universal

Executive branch: *chief of state:* King ABDALLAH II (since 7 February 1999); Heir Apparent Crown Prince HUSSEIN (eldest son of the monarch, born on 28 June 1994)
head of government: Prime Minister Bisher AL-KHASAWNEH (since 7 October 2020)
cabinet: Cabinet appointed by the monarch prime minister in consultation with the prime minister
elections/appointments: the monarchy is hereditary; prime minister appointed by the monarch

Legislative branch: *description:* bicameral National Assembly or Majlis al-'Umma consists of:
Senate or the House of Notables or Majlis al-Ayan (65 seats; members appointed by the monarch to serve 4-year terms) Chamber of Deputies or House of Representatives or Majlis al-Nuwaab (130 seats; 115 members directly elected in 23 multi-seat constituencies by open-list proportional representation vote and 15 seats for women; 12 of the 115 seats reserved for Christian, Chechen, and Circassian candidates; members serve 4-year terms)
elections: Senate - last appointments on 27 Sep 2020 (next appointments in 2024)
Chamber of Deputies - last held on 10 November 2020 (next to be held in November 2024)
election results: Senate - composition men 58, women 7, percent of women 10.8%
Chamber of Deputies - note - tribal, centrist, and pro-government candidates dominated in the 130-seat election; the Islamic Action Front, the political wing of the Muslim Brotherhood, garnered only 10 seats, down from 15 in the previous election; women, who are guaranteed 15 seats by Jordan's legislative quota system, won 16 seats, down from 20 seats won in the previous election; composition - men 114, women 16, percent of women 12.3%; note - total National Assembly percent of women 11.8%

Judicial branch: *highest court(s):* Court of Cassation or Supreme Court (consists of 15 members, including the chief justice); Constitutional Court (consists of 9 members)

judge selection and term of office: Supreme Court chief justice appointed by the king; other judges nominated by the Judicial Council, an 11-member judicial policymaking body consisting of high-level judicial officials and judges, and approved by the king; judge tenure generally not limited; Constitutional Court members appointed by the king for 6-year non-renewable terms with one-third of the membership renewed every 2 years
subordinate courts: Courts of Appeal; Great Felonies Court; religious courts; military courts; juvenile courts; Land Settlement Courts; Income Tax Court; Higher Administrative Court; Customs Court; special courts including the State Security Court

Political parties and leaders: Jordan has 54 registered political parties, four of which currently have seats in the elected Chamber of Deputies - the Islamic Action Front, the Islamic Centrist Party, the United Jordanian Front Party, and the National Loyalty Party

International organization participation: ABEDA, AFESD, AMF, CAEU, CD, CICA, EBRD, FAO, G-11, G-77, IAEA, IBRD, ICAO, ICC (national committees), ICCt, ICRM, IDA, IDB, IFAD, IFC, IFRCS, ILO, IMF, IMO, IMSO, Interpol, IOC, IOM, IPU, ISO, ITSO, ITU, ITUC (NGOs), LAS, MIGA, MINUSTAH, MINUSMA, MONUSCO, NAM, NATO (partner), OIC, OPCW, OSCE (partner), PCA, UN, UNAMID, UNCTAD, UNESCO, UNHCR, UNIDO, UNISFA, UNMIL, UNMISS, UNOCI, UNRWA, UNWTO, UPU, WCO, WFTU (NGOs), WHO, WIPO, WMO, WTO

Diplomatic representation in the US: *chief of mission:* Ambassador Dina Khalil Tawfiq KAWAR (since 27 June 2016)
chancery: 3504 International Drive NW, Washington, DC 20008
telephone: [1] (202) 966-2664
FAX: [1] (202) 966-3110
email address and website:
hkjconsular@jordanembassyus.org
http://www.jordanembassyus.org/

Diplomatic representation from the US: *chief of mission:* Ambassador Henry T. WOOSTER (since 8 October 2020)
embassy: Abdoun, Al-Umawyeen St., Amman
mailing address: 6050 Amman Place, Washington DC 20521-6050
telephone: [962] (6) 590-6000
FAX: [962] (6) 592-0163
email address and website:
Amman-ACS@state.gov
https://jo.usembassy.gov/

Flag description: three equal horizontal bands of black (top), representing the Abbassid Caliphate, white, representing the Ummayyad Caliphate, and green, representing the Fatimid Caliphate; a red isosceles triangle on the hoist side, representing the Great Arab Revolt of 1916, and bearing a small white seven-pointed star symbolizing the seven verses of the opening Sura (Al-Fatiha) of the Holy Koran; the seven points on the star represent faith in One God, humanity, national spirit, humility, social justice, virtue, and aspirations; design is based on the Arab Revolt flag of World War I

National symbol(s): eagle; national colors: black, white, green, red

National anthem: *name:* "As-salam al-malaki al-urdoni" (Long Live the King of Jordan)
lyrics/music: Abdul-Mone'm al-RIFAI'/Abdul-Qader al-TANEER
note: adopted 1946; the shortened version of the anthem is used most commonly, while the full version is reserved for special occasions

National heritage: *total World Heritage Sites:* 6 (5 cultural, 1 mixed)
selected World Heritage Site locales: Petra (c); Quseir Amra (c); Um er-Rasas (Kastrom Mefa'a) (c); Wadi Rum Protected Area (m); Baptism Site "Bethany Beyond the Jordan" (Al-Maghtas) (c); As-Salt - The Place of Tolerance and Urban Hospitality (c)

ECONOMY

Economic overview: Jordan's economy is among the smallest in the Middle East, with insufficient supplies of water, oil, and other natural resources, underlying the government's heavy reliance on foreign assistance. Other economic challenges for the government include chronic high rates of unemployment and underemployment, budget and current account deficits, and government debt.

King ABDALLAH, during the first decade of the 2000s, implemented significant economic reforms, such as expanding foreign trade and privatizing state-owned companies that attracted foreign investment and contributed to average annual economic growth of 8% for 2004 through 2008. The global economic slowdown and regional turmoil contributed to slower growth from 2010 to 2017 - with growth averaging about 2.5% per year - and hurt export-oriented sectors, construction/real estate, and tourism. Since the onset of the civil war in Syria and resulting refugee crisis, one of Jordan's most pressing socioeconomic challenges has been managing the influx of approximately 660,000 UN-registered refugees, more than 80% of whom live in Jordan's urban areas. Jordan's own official census estimated the refugee number at 1.3 million Syrians as of early 2016.

Jordan is nearly completely dependent on imported energy—mostly natural gas—and energy consistently makes up 25-30% of Jordan's imports. To diversify its energy mix, Jordan has secured several contracts for liquefied and pipeline natural gas, developed several major renewables projects, and is currently exploring nuclear power generation and exploitation of abundant oil shale reserves. In August 2016, Jordan and the IMF agreed to a $723 million Extended Fund Facility that aims to build on the three-year, $2.1 billion IMF program that ended in August 2015 with the goal of helping Jordan correct budgetary and balance of payments imbalances.

Real GDP (purchasing power parity): $100.16 billion (2020 est.)
$101.74 billion (2019 est.)
$99.79 billion (2018 est.)
note: data are in 2017 dollars

Real GDP growth rate: 2% (2019 est.)
1.94% (2018 est.)
2.12% (2017 est.)

Real GDP per capita: $9,800 (2020 est.)
$10,100 (2019 est.)
$10,000 (2018 est.)
note: data are in 2017 dollars

GDP (official exchange rate): $44.568 billion (2019 est.)

Inflation rate (consumer prices): 0.3% (2019 est.)
4.4% (2018 est.)
3.3% (2017 est.)

Credit ratings:

Fitch rating: BB- (2019)

Moody's rating: B1 (2013)

Standard & Poors rating: B+ (2017)
note: The year refers to the year in which the current credit rating was first obtained.

GDP - composition, by sector of origin: *agriculture:* 4.5% (2017 est.)
industry: 28.8% (2017 est.)
services: 66.6% (2017 est.)

GDP - composition, by end use: *household consumption:* 80.5% (2017 est.)
government consumption: 19.8% (2017 est.)
investment in fixed capital: 22.8% (2017 est.)
investment in inventories: 0.7% (2017 est.)
exports of goods and services: 34.2% (2017 est.)
imports of goods and services: -58% (2017 est.)

Agricultural products: tomatoes, poultry, olives, milk, potatoes, cucumbers, vegetables, watermelons, green chillies/peppers, peaches/nectarines

Industries: tourism, information technology, clothing, fertilizer, potash, phosphate mining, pharmaceuticals, petroleum refining, cement, inorganic chemicals, light manufacturing

Industrial production growth rate: 1.4% (2017 est.)

Labor force: 731,000 (2020 est.)

Labor force - by occupation: *agriculture:* 2%
industry: 20%
services: 78% (2013 est.)

Unemployment rate: 19.1% (2019 est.)
18.61% (2018 est.)
note: official rate; unofficial rate is approximately 30%

Unemployment, youth ages 15-24: *total:* 37.3%
male: 34.8%
female: 49.4% (2019 est.)

Population below poverty line: 15.7% (2018 est.)

Gini Index coefficient - distribution of family income: 33.7 (2010 est.)
36.4 (1997)

Household income or consumption by percentage share: *lowest 10%:* 3.4%
highest 10%: 28.7% (2010 est.)

Budget: *revenues:* 9.462 billion (2017 est.)
expenditures: 11.51 billion (2017 est.)

Budget surplus (+) or deficit (-): -5.1% (of GDP) (2017 est.)

Public debt: 95.9% of GDP (2017 est.)
95.1% of GDP (2016 est.)
note: data cover central government debt and include debt instruments issued (or owned) by government entities other than the treasury; the data include treasury debt held by foreign entities; the data exclude debt issued by subnational entities, as well as intragovernmental debt; intragovernmental debt consists of treasury borrowings from surpluses in the social funds, such as for retirement, medical care, and unemployment; debt instruments for the social funds are not sold at public auctions

Taxes and other revenues: 23.6% (of GDP) (2017 est.)

Fiscal year: calendar year

Current account balance: -$1.222 billion (2019 est.)
-$2.964 billion (2018 est.)

Exports: $16.29 billion (2019 est.) note: data are in current year dollars
$15.09 billion (2018 est.) note: data are in current year dollars

Exports - partners: United States 21%, Saudi Arabia 13%, India 8%, Iraq 7%, United Arab Emirates 5%, China 5% (2019)

Exports - commodities: fertilizers, calcium phosphates, packaged medicines, clothing and apparel, phosphoric acid (2019)

Imports: $22.04 billion (2019 est.) note: data are in current year dollars
$22.92 billion (2018 est.) note: data are in current year dollars

Imports - partners: China 17%, Saudi Arabia 15%, United States 6%, United Arab Emirates 6%, Egypt 5%, India 5% (2019)

Imports - commodities: cars, refined petroleum, natural gas, crude petroleum, clothing and apparel (2019)

Reserves of foreign exchange and gold: $15.56 billion (31 December 2017 est.)
$15.54 billion (31 December 2016 est.)

Debt - external: $32.088 billion (2019 est.)
$29.916 billion (2018 est.)

Exchange rates: Jordanian dinars (JOD) per US dollar -
0.709 (2020 est.)
0.709 (2019 est.)
0.70925 (2018 est.)
0.71 (2014 est.)
0.71 (2013 est.)

ENERGY

Electricity access: *electrification - total population:* 100% (2020)

Electricity: *installed generating capacity:* 5.644 million kW (2020 est.)
consumption: 17,366,400,000 kWh (2019 est.)
exports: 98 million kWh (2019 est.)
imports: 239 million kWh (2019 est.)
transmission/distribution losses: 2.249 billion kWh (2019 est.)

Electricity generation sources: *fossil fuels:* 83.5% of total installed capacity (2020 est.)
solar: 11.7% of total installed capacity (2020 est.)
wind: 4.6% of total installed capacity (2020 est.)
hydroelectricity: 0.2% of total installed capacity (2020 est.)

Coal: *production:* 0 metric tons (2020 est.)
consumption: 219,000 metric tons (2020 est.)
exports: 0 metric tons (2020 est.)
imports: 219,000 metric tons (2020 est.)
proven reserves: 0 metric tons (2019 est.)

Petroleum: *total petroleum production:* 0 bbl/day (2021 est.)
refined petroleum consumption: 114,800 bbl/day (2019 est.)
crude oil and lease condensate exports: 0 bbl/day (2018 est.)
crude oil and lease condensate imports: 47,400 bbl/day (2018 est.)
crude oil estimated reserves: 1 million barrels (2021 est.)

Refined petroleum products - production: 67,240 bbl/day (2015 est.)

Refined petroleum products - exports: 0 bbl/day (2015 est.)

Refined petroleum products - imports: 68,460 bbl/day (2015 est.)

Natural gas: *production:* 115.872 million cubic meters (2019 est.)
consumption: 4,650,978,000 cubic meters (2019 est.)
exports: 375.849 million cubic meters (2019 est.)
imports: 4,910,954,000 cubic meters (2019 est.)
proven reserves: 6.031 billion cubic meters (2021 est.)

Carbon dioxide emissions: 23.47 million metric tonnes of CO_2 (2019 est.)
from coal and metallurgical coke: 381,000 metric tonnes of CO_2 (2019 est.)
from petroleum and other liquids: 15.786 million metric tonnes of CO_2 (2019 est.)
from consumed natural gas: 7.303 million metric tonnes of CO_2 (2019 est.)

Energy consumption per capita: 39.331 million Btu/person (2019 est.)

COMMUNICATIONS

Telephones - fixed lines: *total subscriptions:* 391,486 (2020 est.)
subscriptions per 100 inhabitants: 4 (2020 est.)

Telephones - mobile cellular: *total subscriptions:* 6,987,891 (2020 est.)
subscriptions per 100 inhabitants: 68 (2020 est.)

Telecommunication systems: *general assessment:* Jordan's government has focused on the use of ICT in a range of sectors, aimed at transforming the relatively small economy through the use of digital services; this policy has helped the country rise in the league tables for digital connectivity and internet readiness, and it has also attracted investment from foreign companies; during the ongoing global pandemic, the start-up sector has been further encouraged to develop solutions to combat the crisis, while other efforts have facilitated e-government services and encouraged businesses to adapt to new methods of working through their own digital transformation; these developments have been supported by the highly developed mobile sector, led by three major regional players which have near-comprehensive LTE network coverage (2022)
domestic: a 1995 telecommunications law opened all non-fixed-line services to private competition; in 2005, the monopoly over fixed-line services terminated and the entire telecommunications sector was opened to competition; currently fixed-line stands at nearly 4 per 100 persons and multiple mobile-cellular providers with subscribership over 68 per 100 persons (2020)
international: country code - 962; landing point for the FEA and Taba-Aqaba submarine cable networks providing connectivity to Europe, the Middle East, Southeast Asia and Asia; satellite earth stations - 33 (3 Intelsat, 1 Arabsat, and 29 land and maritime Inmarsat terminals (2019)

Broadcast media: radio and TV dominated by the government-owned Jordan Radio and Television Corporation (JRTV) that operates a main network, a sports network, a film network, and a satellite channel; first independent TV broadcaster aired in 2007; international satellite TV and Israeli and Syrian TV broadcasts are available; roughly 30 radio stations with JRTV operating the main government-owned station; transmissions of multiple international radio broadcasters are available

Internet country code: .jo

Internet users: *total:* 6,768,137 (2019 est.)
percent of population: 67% (2019 est.)

Broadband - fixed subscriptions: *total:* 630,545 (2020 est.)
subscriptions per 100 inhabitants: 6 (2020 est.)

TRANSPORTATION

National air transport system: *number of registered air carriers:* 4 (2020)
inventory of registered aircraft operated by air carriers: 54
annual passenger traffic on registered air carriers: 3,383,805 (2018)
annual freight traffic on registered air carriers: 175.84 million (2018) mt-km

Civil aircraft registration country code prefix: JY

Airports: *total:* 18 (2021)

Airports - with paved runways: *total:* 16
over 3,047 m: 8
2,438 to 3,047 m: 5
1,524 to 2,437 m: 2
914 to 1,523 m: 1 (2021)

Airports - with unpaved runways: *total:* 2
under 914 m: 2 (2021)

Heliports: 1 (2021)

Pipelines: 473 km gas, 49 km oil (2013)

Railways: *total:* 509 km (2020)
narrow gauge: 509 km (2014) 1.050-m gauge

Roadways: *total:* 7,203 km (2011)
paved: 7,203 km (2011)

Merchant marine: *total:* 35
by type: general cargo 6, oil tanker 1, other 28 (2021)

Ports and terminals: *major seaport(s):* Al 'Aqabah

MILITARY AND SECURITY

Military and security forces: Jordanian Armed Forces (JAF): Royal Jordanian Army (includes Special Operations Forces, Border Guards, Royal Guard), Royal Jordanian Air Force, Royal Jordanian Coast Guard; Ministry of Interior: Public Security Directorate (includes national police, the Gendarmerie, and the Civil Defense Directorate) (2022)
note: the armed forces report administratively to the minister of defense and have a support role for internal security; the prime minister serves as defense minister, but there is no separate ministry of defense

Military expenditures: 5% of GDP (2021 est.)
5% of GDP (2020 est.)
5.6% of GDP (2019 est.) (approximately $5.18 billion)
5.6% of GDP (2018 est.) (approximately $5.14 billion)
5.7% of GDP (2017 est.) (approximately $5.18 billion)

Military and security service personnel strengths: approximately 94,500 active duty armed forces personnel (80,000 Army; 14,000 Air Force; 500 Coast Guard); approximately 15,000 Gendarmerie Forces (2022)

Military equipment inventories and acquisitions: the JAF inventory is comprised of a wide mix of imported equipment from Europe, some Gulf States, Russia, and the US; since 2010, the Netherlands and the US have been the leading suppliers (2022)

Military service age and obligation: 17 years of age for voluntary military service for men (women can volunteer to serve in noncombat military positions in the Royal Jordanian Arab Army Women's Corps and RJAF); initial service term 2 years, with option to reenlist for up to 18 years; conscription was abolished in 1991, but in 2020 Jordan announced the reinstatement of compulsory military service for jobless men aged between 25 and 29 with 12 months of service, made up of 3 months of military training and 9 months of professional and technical training; in 2019, Jordan announced a voluntary 4-month National Military Service program for men and women aged between 18-25 years who have been unemployed for at least 6 months; service would include 1 month for military training with the remaining 3 months dedicated to vocational training in the sectors of construction and tourism (2022)
note: most women serve in the medical service; outside the medical service, women comprised about 1.5% of the military as of 2019

Military deployments: 330 Mali (MINUSMA) (May 2022)

Military - note: the Jordanian military traces its origins back to the Arab Legion, which was formed under the British protectorate of Transjordan in the 1920s

due largely to its proximity to regional conflicts in Iraq and Syria, the presence of major terrorist organizations in both of those countries, and the Israeli-Palestinian conflict, the highest priorities of Jordan's military and security services in 2022 included securing its borders and the potential for domestic terrorist attacks; the terrorist group Hizballah and Iranianbacked militia forces were operating in southwestern Syria near Jordan's border while fighters from the Islamic State of Iraq and ash-Sham (ISIS) terrorist group continued operating in both Iraq and Syria; ISIS fighters included Jordanian nationals, some of whom have returned to Jordan; meanwhile, individuals and groups sympathetic to Palestine have planned and conducted terrorist attacks in Jordan

Jordan has Major Non-NATO Ally (MNNA) status with the US; MNNA is a designation under US law that provides foreign partners with certain benefits in the areas of defense trade and security cooperation; while MNNA status provides military and economic privileges, it does not entail any security commitments

Jordan signed a peace treaty with Israel in 1994 (2022)

TERRORISM

Terrorist group(s): Islamic State of Iraq and ash-Sham (ISIS)

TRANSNATIONAL ISSUES

Disputes - international: *Jordan-Iraq:* the two countries signed a border agreement in 1984; Jordan has ratified the treaty, but it has not been confirmed that Iraq has ratified it; as of 2010, the agreement had not been registered with the UN
Jordan-Israel: none identified
Jordan-Saudi Arabia: Jordan and Saudi Arabia signed an agreement to demarcate their maritime borders in 2007
Jordan-Syria: the two countries signed an agreement in 2005 to settle the border dispute based on a 1931 demarcation accord; the two countries began demarcation in 2006
Jordan-West Bank: none identified

Refugees and internally displaced persons: *refugees (country of origin):* 2,307,011 (Palestinian refugees) (2020); 66,665 (Iraq), 12,866 (Yemen), 6,013 Sudan (2021); 676,621 (Syria) (2022)
stateless persons: 63 (mid-year 2021)

Illicit drugs: primarily a transshipment country for amphetamine tablets originating in Lebanon and Syria and destined for Saudi Arabia, Israel, and Gulf countries; the government is increasingly concerned about domestic consumption of illicit drugs

KAZAKHSTAN

INTRODUCTION

Background: Ethnic Kazakhs derive from a mix of Turkic nomadic tribes that migrated to the region in the 15th century. The Kazakh steppe was conquered by the Russian Empire in the 18th and 19th centuries, and Kazakhstan became a Soviet Republic in 1925. Repression and starvation caused by forced agricultural collectivization led to more than a million deaths in the early 1930s. During the 1950s and 1960s, the agricultural "Virgin Lands" program led to an influx of settlers (mostly ethnic Russians, but also other nationalities) and at the time of Kazakhstan's independence in 1991, ethnic Kazakhs were a minority. Non-Muslim ethnic minorities departed Kazakhstan in large numbers from the mid-1990s through the mid-2000s and a national program has repatriated about a million ethnic Kazakhs (from Uzbekistan, Tajikistan, Mongolia, and the Xinjiang region of China) back to Kazakhstan. As a result of this shift, the ethnic Kazakh share of the population now exceeds two thirds.

Kazakhstan's economy is the largest in Central Asia, mainly due to the country's vast natural resources. Current issues include: diversifying the economy, attracting foreign direct investment, enhancing Kazakhstan's economic competitiveness, and strengthening economic relations with neighboring states and foreign powers.

GEOGRAPHY

Location: Central Asia, northwest of China; a small portion west of the Ural (Oral) River in easternmost Europe

Geographic coordinates: 48 00 N, 68 00 E

Map references: Asia

Area: *total:* 2,724,900 sq km
land: 2,699,700 sq km
water: 25,200 sq km

Area - comparative: slightly less than four times the size of Texas

Land boundaries: *total:* 13,364 km
border countries (5): China 1,765 km; Kyrgyzstan 1,212 km; Russia 7,644 km; Turkmenistan 413 km; Uzbekistan 2,330 km

Coastline: 0 km (landlocked); note - Kazakhstan borders the Aral Sea, now split into two bodies of water (1,070 km), and the Caspian Sea (1,894 km)

Maritime claims: none (landlocked)

Climate: continental, cold winters and hot summers, arid and semiarid

Terrain: vast flat steppe extending from the Volga in the west to the Altai Mountains in the east and from the plains of western Siberia in the north to oases and deserts of Central Asia in the south

Elevation: *highest point:* Pik Khan-Tengri 7,010 m
note - the northern most 7,000 meter peak in the World
lowest point: Qauyndy Oysy -132 m
mean elevation: 387 m

Natural resources: major deposits of petroleum, natural gas, coal, iron ore, manganese, chrome ore, nickel, cobalt, copper, molybdenum, lead, zinc, bauxite, gold, uranium

Land use: *agricultural land:* 77.4% (2018 est.)
arable land: 8.9% (2018 est.)
permanent crops: 0% (2018 est.)
permanent pasture: 68.5% (2018 est.)
forest: 1.2% (2018 est.)
other: 21.4% (2018 est.)

Irrigated land: 20,660 sq km (2012)

Major lakes (area sq km): *fresh water lake(s):* Ozero Balkhash - 22,000 sq km; Ozero Zaysan - 1,800 sq km
salt water lake(s): Caspian Sea (shared with Iran, Azerbaijan, Turkmenistan, and Russia) - 374,000 sq km; Aral Sea (north) - 3,300 sq km; Ozero Alakol - 2,650 sq km; Ozero Teniz 1,590 sq km; Ozero Seletytenzi - 780 sq km; Ozero Sasykkol - 740 sq km

Major rivers (by length in km): Syr Darya river mouth (shared with Kyrgyzstan [s], Uzbekistan, and Tajikistan) - 3,078 km
note – [s] after country name indicates river source; [m] after country name indicates river mouth

Major watersheds (area sq km): Internal *(endorheic basin)* drainage: Tarim Basin (1,152,448 sq km), Amu Darya (534,739 sq km), Syr Darya (782,617 sq km), Lake Balkash (510,015 sq km)

Population distribution: most of the country displays a low population density, particularly the interior; population clusters appear in urban agglomerations in the far northern and southern portions of the country

Natural hazards: earthquakes in the south; mudslides around Almaty

Geography - note: world's largest landlocked country and one of only two landlocked countries in the world that extends into two continents (the other is Azerbaijan); Russia leases approximately 6,000 sq km of territory enclosing the Baikonur Cosmodrome; in January 2004, Kazakhstan and Russia extended the lease to 2050

PEOPLE AND SOCIETY

Population: 19,398,331 (2022 est.)

Nationality: *noun:* Kazakhstani(s)
adjective: Kazakhstani

Ethnic groups: Kazakh (Qazaq) 68%, Russian 19.3%, Uzbek 3.2%, Ukrainian 1.5%, Uighur 1.5%, Tatar 1.1%, German 1%, other 4.4% (2019 est.)

Languages: Kazakh (official, Qazaq) 83.1% (understand spoken language) and trilingual (Kazakh, Russian, English) 22.3% (2017 est.); Russian (official, used in everyday business, designated the "language of interethnic communication") 94.4% (understand spoken language) (2009 est.)
major-language sample(s):

Әлемдік деректер кітабы, негізгі ақпараттың таптырмайтын көзі.
(Kazakh)

Книга фактов о мире – незаменимый источник базовой информации.
(Russian)

Religions: Muslim 70.2%, Christian 26.2% (mainly Russian Orthodox), other 0.2%, atheist 2.8%, unspecified 0.5% (2009 est.)

Demographic profile: Nearly 40% of Kazakhstan's population is under the age of 25. Like many former Soviet states, Kazakhstan's total fertility rate (TFR) – the average number of births per woman – decreased after independence amidst economic problems and fell below replacement level, 2.1. However, in the late 2000s, as the economy improved and incomes rose, Kazakhstan experienced a small baby boom and TFR reached 2.5. TFR has since fallen and is now just over 2.1. Mortality rates are also decreasing and life expectancy is rising, signs that Kazakhstan's demographic transition is progressing.

Kazakhstan has a diverse population consisting of Asian ethnic groups (predominantly Kazakhs, as well as Uzbeks, Uighurs, and Tatars) and ethnic Europeans (mainly Russians but also Ukrainians and Germans). Approximately two thirds of Kazakhstan's population today is Kazakh. During the mid-20th century, as Kazakhstan industrialized, waves of ethnic Russians and deportees from other parts of the Soviet Union arrived. Eventually, the ethnic Russian population outnumbered the Kazakhs. In the 1990s, following Kazakhstan's independence, Russian and other ethnic Europeans began emigrating, while some ethnic Kazakhs (referred to as Oralmans) returned to their homeland from neighboring countries, China, and Mongolia. As a result, the country's ethnic make-up changed, and a Kazakh majority was reestablished.

In recent years, Kazakhstan has shifted from being mainly a migrant-sending country to a migrant-receiving country. Due to its oildriven economic boom, Kazakhstan has become a more popular destination. The country needs highly skilled workers in the industrial, business, and education sectors and low-skilled labor in agriculture, markets, services, and construction. Kazakhstan is increasingly reliant on migrant workers, primarily from Kyrgyzstan, Tajikistan, and Uzbekistan, to fill its labor shortage. At the same time, highly skilled Kazakhs continue to emigrate, mostly to Russia, seeking higher salaries or further education.

Age structure: *0-14 years:* 26.13% (male 2,438,148/female 2,550,535)
15-24 years: 12.97% (male 1,262,766/female 1,212,645)
25-54 years: 42.23% (male 3,960,188/female 4,102,845)
55-64 years: 10.25% (male 856,180/female 1,099,923)
65 years and over: 8.43% (male 567,269/female 1,041,450) (2020 est.)

Dependency ratios: *total dependency ratio:* 58.8
youth dependency ratio: 46.3

elderly dependency ratio: 12.6
potential support ratio: 8 (2020 est.)

Median age: *total:* 31.6 years
male: 30.3 years
female: 32.8 years (2020 est.)

Population growth rate: 0.77% (2022 est.)

Birth rate: 15.38 births/1,000 population (2022 est.)

Death rate: 8.11 deaths/1,000 population (2022 est.)

Net migration rate: 0.39 migrant(s)/1,000 population (2022 est.)

Population distribution: most of the country displays a low population density, particularly the interior; population clusters appear in urban agglomerations in the far northern and southern portions of the country

Urbanization: *urban population:* 58% of total population (2022)
rate of urbanization: 1.19% annual rate of change (2020-25 est.)

Major urban areas - population: 1.958 million Almaty, 1.254 million NUR-SULTAN (capital), 1.126 million Shimkent (2022)

Sex ratio: *at birth:* 0.94 male(s)/female
0-14 years: 0.94 male(s)/female
15-24 years: 1.04 male(s)/female
25-54 years: 0.96 male(s)/female
55-64 years: 0.78 male(s)/female
65 years and over: 0.35 male(s)/female
total population: 0.9 male(s)/female (2022 est.)

Mother's mean age at first birth: 28.9 years (2019 est.)

Maternal mortality ratio: 10 deaths/100,000 live births (2017 est.)

Infant mortality rate: *total:* 19.18 deaths/1,000 live births
male: 21.73 deaths/1,000 live births
female: 16.79 deaths/1,000 live births (2022 est.)

Life expectancy at birth: *total population:* 72.53 years
male: 67.43 years
female: 77.31 years (2022 est.)

Total fertility rate: 2.11 children born/woman (2022 est.)

Contraceptive prevalence rate: 53% (2018)
note: percent of women aged 18-49

Drinking water source: *improved: urban:* 100% of population
rural: 93.8% of population
total: 97.4% of population
unimproved: urban: 0% of population
rural: 6.2% of population
total: 2.6% of population (2020 est.)

Current health expenditure: 2.8% of GDP (2019)

Physicians density: 3.98 physicians/1,000 population (2020)

Hospital bed density: 6.1 beds/1,000 population (2014)

Sanitation facility access: *improved: urban:* 99.9% of population
rural: 99.9% of population
total: 99.9% of population
unimproved: urban: 0.1% of population
rural: 0.1% of population
total: 0.1% of population (2020 est.)

HIV/AIDS - adult prevalence rate: 0.3% (2020 est.)

Obesity - adult prevalence rate: 21% (2016)

Alcohol consumption per capita: *total:* 3.73 liters of pure alcohol (2019 est.)
beer: 2.52 liters of pure alcohol (2019 est.)
wine: 0.16 liters of pure alcohol (2019 est.)
spirits: 1.05 liters of pure alcohol (2019 est.)
other alcohols: 0 liters of pure alcohol (2019 est.)

Tobacco use: *total:* 23.2% (2020 est.)
male: 39.6% (2020 est.)
female: 6.7% (2020 est.)

Children under the age of 5 years underweight: 2% (2015)

Education expenditures: 2.9% of GDP (2019 est.)

Literacy: *definition:* age 15 and over can read and write
total population: 99.8%
male: 99.8%
female: 99.7% (2018)

School life expectancy (primary to tertiary education): *total:* 16 years
male: 15 years
female: 16 years (2020)

Unemployment, youth ages 15-24: *total:* 3.8%
male: 3.4%
female: 4.2% (2020 est.)

ENVIRONMENT

Environment - current issues: radioactive or toxic chemical sites associated with former defense industries and test ranges scattered throughout the country pose health risks for humans and animals; industrial pollution is severe in some cities; because the two main rivers that flowed into the Aral Sea have been diverted for irrigation, it is drying up and leaving behind a harmful layer of chemical pesticides and natural salts; these substances are then picked up by the wind and blown into noxious dust storms; pollution in the Caspian Sea; desertification; soil pollution from overuse of agricultural chemicals and salination from poor infrastructure and wasteful irrigation practices

Environment - international agreements: *party to:* Air Pollution, Antarctic Treaty, Biodiversity, Climate Change, Climate Change-Kyoto Protocol, Climate Change- Paris Agreement, Comprehensive Nuclear Test Ban, Desertification, Endangered Species, Environmental Modification, Hazardous Wastes, Ozone Layer Protection, Ship Pollution, Wetlands
signed, but not ratified: none of the selected agreements

Air pollutants: *particulate matter emissions:* 11.32 micrograms per cubic meter (2016 est.)
carbon dioxide emissions: 247.21 megatons (2016 est.)
methane emissions: 45.03 megatons (2020 est.)

Climate: continental, cold winters and hot summers, arid and semiarid

Land use: *agricultural land:* 77.4% (2018 est.)
arable land: 8.9% (2018 est.)
permanent crops: 0% (2018 est.)
permanent pasture: 68.5% (2018 est.)
forest: 1.2% (2018 est.)
other: 21.4% (2018 est.)

Urbanization: *urban population:* 58% of total population (2022)
rate of urbanization: 1.19% annual rate of change (2020-25 est.)

Revenue from forest resources: *forest revenues:* 0% of GDP (2018 est.)

Revenue from coal: *coal revenues:* 0.99% of GDP (2018 est.)

Waste and recycling: *municipal solid waste generated annually:* 4,659,740 tons (2012 est.)
municipal solid waste recycled annually: 136,064 tons (2012 est.)
percent of municipal solid waste recycled: 2.9% (2012 est.)

Major lakes (area sq km): *fresh water lake(s):* Ozero Balkhash - 22,000 sq km; Ozero Zaysan - 1,800 sq km
salt water lake(s): Caspian Sea (shared with Iran, Azerbaijan, Turkmenistan, and Russia) - 374,000 sq km; Aral Sea (north) - 3,300 sq km; Ozero Alakol - 2,650 sq km; Ozero Teniz 1,590 sq km; Ozero Seletytenzi - 780 sq km; Ozero Sasykkol - 740 sq km

Major rivers (by length in km): Syr Darya river mouth (shared with Kyrgyzstan [s], Uzbekistan, and Tajikistan) - 3,078 km
note – [s] after country name indicates river source; [m] after country name indicates river mouth

Major watersheds (area sq km): Internal *(endorheic basin)* drainage: Tarim Basin (1,152,448 sq km), Amu Darya (534,739 sq km), Syr Darya (782,617 sq km), Lake Balkash (510,015 sq km)

Total water withdrawal: *municipal:* 2.347 billion cubic meters (2017 est.)
industrial: 6.984 billion cubic meters (2017 est.)
agricultural: 15.12 billion cubic meters (2017 est.)

Total renewable water resources: 108.41 billion cubic meters (2017 est.)

GOVERNMENT

Country name: *conventional long form:* Republic of Kazakhstan
conventional short form: Kazakhstan
local long form: Qazaqstan Respublikasy
local short form: Qazaqstan
former: Kazakh Soviet Socialist Republic
etymology: the name "Kazakh" may derive from the Turkic word "kaz" meaning "to wander," recalling the Kazakh's nomadic lifestyle; the Persian suffix "-stan" means "place of" or "country," so the word Kazakhstan literally means "Land of the Wanderers"

Government type: presidential republic

Capital: *name:* Astana
geographic coordinates: 51 10 N, 71 25 E
time difference: UTC+6 (11 hours ahead of Washington, DC, during Standard Time)
time zone note: Kazakhstan has two time zones
etymology: the name means "capital city" in Kazakh
note: on 17 September 2022, Kazakhstan changed the name of its capital city from Nur-Sultan back to Astana; this was not the first time the city had its name changed; founded in 1830 as Akmoly, it became Akmolinsk in 1832, Tselinograd in 1961, Akmola (Aqmola) in 1992, Astana in 1998, and Nur-Sultan in 2019; the latest name change occurred just three and a half years after the city was renamed to honor a long-serving (28-year) former president, who subsequently fell out of favor

Administrative divisions: 17 provinces (oblystar, singular - oblys) and 4 cities* (qalalar, singular - qala); Abay (Semey), Almaty (Qonaev), Almaty*, Aqmola (Kokshetau), Aqtobe, Astana*, Atyrau, Batys Qazaqstan [West Kazakhstan] (Oral), Bayqongyr*, Mangghystau (Aqtau), Pavlodar, Qaraghandy,

Qostanay, Qyzylorda, Shyghys Qazaqstan [East Kazakhstan] (Oskemen), Shymkent*, Soltustik Qazaqstan [North Kazakhstan] (Petropavl), Turkistan, Ulytau (Zhezqazghan), Zhambyl (Taraz), Zhetisu (Taldyqorghan)
note: administrative divisions have the same names as their administrative centers (exceptions have the administrative center name following in parentheses); in 1995, the Governments of Kazakhstan and Russia entered into an agreement whereby Russia would lease for a period of 20 years an area of 6,000 sq km enclosing the Baikonur space launch facilities and the city of Bayqongyr (Baikonur, formerly Leninsk); in 2004, a new agreement extended the lease to 2050

Independence: 16 December 1991 (from the Soviet Union)

National holiday: Independence Day, 16 December (1991)

Constitution: *history:* previous 1937, 1978 (preindependence), 1993; latest approved by referendum 30 August 1995, effective 5 September 1995
amendments: introduced by a referendum initiated by the president of the republic, on the recommendation of Parliament, or by the government; the president has the option of submitting draft amendments to Parliament or directly to a referendum; passage of amendments by Parliament requires four-fifths majority vote of both houses and the signature of the president; passage by referendum requires absolute majority vote by more than one half of the voters in at least two thirds of the oblasts, major cities, and the capital, followed by the signature of the president; amended several times, last in 2019

Legal system: civil law system influenced by Roman-Germanic law and by the theory and practice of the Russian Federation

International law organization participation: has not submitted an ICJ jurisdiction declaration; non-party state to the ICCt

Citizenship: *citizenship by birth:* no
citizenship by descent only: at least one parent must be a citizen of Kazakhstan
dual citizenship recognized: no
residency requirement for naturalization: 5 years

Suffrage: 18 years of age; universal

Executive branch: *chief of state:* President Kasym-Zhomart TOKAYEV (since 20 March 2019)
head of government: Prime Minister Alikhan SMAILOV (since 11 January 2022); note - Prime Minister Askar MAMIN resigned on 5 January 2022 in the wake of massive protests of his government that began 2 January 2022 following a sudden, steep rise in gasoline prices
cabinet: the president appoints ministers after consultations with the Chair of the Security Council; the president has veto power over all appointments except for the ministers of defense, internal affairs, and foreign affairs; however, the president is required to discuss these three offices with the National Security Committee
elections/appointments: president directly elected by simple majority popular vote for a 7-year term (prior to September 2022, the president of Kazakhstan could serve up to two terms of five years each; the legislation was changed in September 2022, reducing the maximum number of terms to one term of seven years); election last held on 20 November 2022 (next to be held in 2029); prime minister and deputy prime ministers appointed by the president, approved by the Mazhilis
election results: 2022: Kasym-Zhomart TOKAYEV elected president; percent of vote - Kasym-Zhomart TOKAYEV (Nur Otan) 81.3%, Jiguli DAIRABAEV 3.4%, Qaraqat ABDEN 2.6%, Meiram QAJYKEN 2.5%, Nurian AUESBAEV 2.2%, Saltanat TURSYNBEKOVA 2.1%, other 5.8%
2019: Kasym-Zhomart TOKAYEV elected president; percent of vote - Kasym-Zhomart TOKAYEV (Nur Otan) 71%, Amirzhan KOSANOV (Ult Tagdyry) 16.2%, Daniya YESPAYEVA (Ak Zhol) 5.1%, other 7.7%
1991: Nursultan NAZARBAYEV elected the first president of Kazakhstan; percent of vote 98.8%, other 1.2%

Legislative branch: *description:* bicameral Parliament consists of:
Senate (49 seats statutory, 48 as of October 2021); 34 members indirectly elected by 2-round majority vote by the oblastlevel assemblies and 15 members appointed by decree of the president; members serve 6-year terms, with one-half of the membership renewed every 3 years)
Mazhilis (107 seats; 98 members directly elected in a single national constituency by proportional representation vote to serve 5-year terms and 9 indirectly elected by the Assembly of People of Kazakhstan, a 351-member, presidentially appointed advisory body designed to represent the country's ethnic minorities)
elections: Senate - last held on 12 August 2020 (next to be held in August 2023)
Mazhilis - last held on 10 January 2021 (next to be held in 2026)
election results: Senate - percent of vote by party - NA; seats by party - NA; composition (as of October 2021) - men 39, women 9, percent of women 18.4%
Mazhilis - percent of vote by party - Nur Otan 71.1%, Ak Zhol 11%, QHP 9.1%, other 8.8%; seats by party - Nur Otan 76, Ak Zhol 12, QHP 10; composition (as of October 2021) - men 78, women 29, percent of women 27.1%; note - total Parliament percent of women 24.4%

Judicial branch: *highest court(s):* Supreme Court of the Republic (consists of 44 members); Constitutional Council (consists of the chairperson and 6 members)
judge selection and term of office: Supreme Court judges proposed by the president of the republic on recommendation of the Supreme Judicial Council and confirmed by the Senate; judges normally serve until age 65 but can be extended to age 70; Constitutional Council - the president of the republic, the Senate chairperson, and the Mazhilis chairperson each appoints 2 members for a 6-year term; chairperson of the Constitutional Council appointed by the president for a 6-year term
subordinate courts: regional and local courts

Political parties and leaders: Adal [Serik SULTANGALI] (formerly Birlik (Unity) Party)
Ak Zhol (Bright Path) Party or Democratic Party of Kazakhstan Ak Zhol [Azat PERUASHEV]
Amanat [Erlan QOSANOV] (formerly Nur Otan (Radiant Fatherland))
National Social Democratic Party or NSDP [Ashat Nurmagambetuly RAHYMJANOV]
People's Democratic (Patriotic) Party or Auyl or AHDPP [Ali BEKTAYEV]
People's Party of Kazakhstan or QHP [Eruhamet ERTISBAEV]

International organization participation: ADB, CICA, CIS, CSTO, EAEU, EAPC, EBRD, ECO, EITI (compliant country), FAO, GCTU, IAEA, IBRD, ICAO, ICC (NGOs), ICRM, IDA, IDB, IFAD, IFC, IFRCS, ILO, IMF, IMO, Interpol, IOC, IOM, IPU, ISO, ITSO, ITU, MIGA, MINURSO, NAM (observer), NSG, OAS (observer), OIC, OPCW, OSCE, PFP, SCO, UN, UNCTAD, UNESCO, UNHRC, UNIDO, UN Security Council (temporary), UNWTO, UPU, WCO, WFTU (NGOs), WHO, WIPO, WMO, WTO, ZC

Diplomatic representation in the US: *chief of mission:* Ambassador Yerzhan ASHIKBAYEV (since 7 July 2021)
chancery: 1401 16th Street NW, Washington, DC 20036
telephone: [1] (202) 232-5488
FAX: [1] (202) 232-5845
email address and website:
washington@mfa.kz
https://www.gov.kz/memleket/entities/mfa-washington?lang=en
consulate(s) general: New York

Diplomatic representation from the US: *chief of mission:* Ambassador (vacant); Charge d'Affaires Judy KUO (since October 2021)
embassy: Rakhymzhan Koshkarbayev Avenue, No. 3, Nur-Sultan 010010
mailing address: 2230 Nur-Sultan Place, Washington DC 20521-2230
telephone: [7] (7172) 70-21-00
FAX: [7] (7172) 54-09-14
email address and website:
USAKZ@state.gov
https://kz.usembassy.gov/
consulate(s) general: Almaty

Flag description: a gold sun with 32 rays above a soaring golden steppe eagle, both centered on a sky blue background; the hoist side displays a national ornamental pattern "koshkar-muiz" (the horns of the ram) in gold; the blue color is of religious significance to the Turkic peoples of the country, and so symbolizes cultural and ethnic unity; it also represents the endless sky as well as water; the sun, a source of life and energy, exemplifies wealth and plenitude; the sun's rays are shaped like grain, which is the basis of abundance and prosperity; the eagle has appeared on the flags of Kazakh tribes for centuries and represents freedom, power, and the flight to the future

National symbol(s): golden eagle; national colors: blue, yellow

National anthem: *name:* "Menin Qazaqstanim" (My Kazakhstan)
lyrics/music: Zhumeken NAZHIMEDENOV and Nursultan NAZARBAYEV/Shamshi KALDAYAKOV
note: adopted 2006; President Nursultan NAZARBAYEV played a role in revising the lyrics

National heritage: *total World Heritage Sites:* 5 (3 cultural, 2 natural)
selected World Heritage Site locales: Mausoleum of Khoja Ahmed Yasawi (c); Petroglyphs at Tanbaly (c); Saryarka - Steppe and Lakes of Northern Kazakhstan (n); Silk Roads: the Chang'an-Tianshan Corridor (c); Western Tien-Shan (n)

ECONOMY

Economic overview: Kazakhstan's vast hydrocarbon and mineral reserves form the backbone of its economy. Geographically the largest of the former Soviet republics, excluding Russia, Kazakhstan, g possesses substantial fossil fuel reserves and other minerals and metals, such as uranium, copper, and zinc. It also has a large agricultural sector featuring livestock and grain. The government realizes that its economy suffers from an overreliance on oil and extractive industries and has made initial attempts to diversify its economy by targeting sectors like transport, pharmaceuticals, telecommunications, petrochemicals and food processing for greater development and investment. It also adopted a Subsoil Code in December 2017 with the aim of increasing exploration and investment in the hydrocarbon, and particularly mining, sectors.

Kazakhstan's oil production and potential is expanding rapidly. A $36.8 billion expansion of Kazakhstan's premiere Tengiz oil field by Chevron-led Tengizchevroil should be complete in 2022. Meanwhile, the super-giant Kashagan field finally launched production in October 2016 after years of delay and an estimated $55 billion in development costs. Kazakhstan's total oil production in 2017 climbed 10.5%.

Kazakhstan is landlocked and depends on Russia to export its oil to Europe. It also exports oil directly to China. In 2010, Kazakhstan joined Russia and Belarus to establish a Customs Union in an effort to boost foreign investment and improve trade. The Customs Union evolved into a Single Economic Space in 2012 and the Eurasian Economic Union (EAEU) in January 2015. Supported by rising commodity prices, Kazakhstan's exports to EAEU countries increased 30.2% in 2017. Imports from EAEU countries grew by 24.1%.

The economic downturn of its EAEU partner, Russia, and the decline in global commodity prices from 2014 to 2016 contributed to an economic slowdown in Kazakhstan. In 2014, Kazakhstan devalued its currency, the tenge, and announced a stimulus package to cope with its economic challenges. In the face of further decline in the ruble, oil prices, and the regional economy, Kazakhstan announced in 2015 it would replace its currency band with a floating exchange rate, leading to a sharp fall in the value of the tenge. Since reaching a low of 391 to the dollar in January 2016, the tenge has modestly appreciated, helped by somewhat higher oil prices. While growth slowed to about 1% in both 2015 and 2016, a moderate recovery in oil prices, relatively stable inflation and foreign exchange rates, and the start of production at Kashagan helped push 2017 GDP growth to 4%.

Despite some positive institutional and legislative changes in the last several years, investors remain concerned about corruption, bureaucracy, and arbitrary law enforcement, especially at the regional and municipal levels. An additional concern is the condition of the country's banking sector, which suffers from poor asset quality and a lack of transparency. Investors also question the potentially negative effects on the economy of a contested presidential succession as Kazakhstan's first president, Nursultan NAZARBAYEV, turned 77 in 2017.

Real GDP (purchasing power parity): $475.18 billion (2020 est.)
$487.87 billion (2019 est.)
$466.86 billion (2018 est.)
note: data are in 2017 dollars

Real GDP growth rate: 6.13% (2019 est.)
4.41% (2018 est.)
4.38% (2017 est.)

Real GDP per capita: $25,300 (2020 est.)
$26,400 (2019 est.)
$25,500 (2018 est.)
note: data are in 2017 dollars

GDP (official exchange rate): $181.194 billion (2019 est.)

Inflation rate (consumer prices): 5.2% (2019 est.)
6% (2018 est.)
7.3% (2017 est.)

Credit ratings:

Fitch rating: BBB (2016)

Moody's rating: Baa3 (2016)

Standard & Poors rating: BBB- (2016)
note: The year refers to the year in which the current credit rating was first obtained.

GDP - composition, by sector of origin: *agriculture:* 4.7% (2017 est.)
industry: 34.1% (2017 est.)
services: 61.2% (2017 est.)

GDP - composition, by end use: *household consumption:* 53.2% (2017 est.)
government consumption: 11.1% (2017 est.)
investment in fixed capital: 22.5% (2017 est.)
investment in inventories: 4.8% (2017 est.)
exports of goods and services: 35.4% (2017 est.)
imports of goods and services: -27.1% (2017 est.)

Agricultural products: wheat, milk, potatoes, barley, watermelons, melons, linseed, onions, maize, sunflower seed

Industries: oil, coal, iron ore, manganese, chromite, lead, zinc, copper, titanium, bauxite, gold, silver, phosphates, sulfur, uranium, iron and steel; tractors and other agricultural machinery, electric motors, construction materials

Industrial production growth rate: 5.8% (2017 est.)

Labor force: 8.685 million (2020 est.)

Labor force - by occupation: *agriculture:* 18.1%
industry: 20.4%
services: 61.6% (2017 est.)

Unemployment rate: 4.8% (2019 est.)
4.85% (2018 est.)

Unemployment, youth ages 15-24: *total:* 3.8%
male: 3.4%
female: 4.2% (2020 est.)

Population below poverty line: 4.3% (2018 est.)

Gini Index coefficient - distribution of family income: 27.5 (2017 est.)
31.5 (2003)

Household income or consumption by percentage share: *lowest 10%:* 4.2%
highest 10%: 23.3% (2016)

Budget: *revenues:* 35.48 billion (2017 est.)
expenditures: 38.3 billion (2017 est.)

Budget surplus (+) or deficit (-): -1.8% (of GDP) (2017 est.)

Public debt: 20.8% of GDP (2017 est.)
19.7% of GDP (2016 est.)

Taxes and other revenues: 22.3% (of GDP) (2017 est.)

Fiscal year: calendar year

Current account balance: -$7.206 billion (2019 est.)
-$138 million (2018 est.)

Exports: $51.75 billion (2020 est.) note: data are in current year dollars
$65.91 billion (2019 est.) note: data are in current year dollars
$67.15 billion (2018 est.) note: data are in current year dollars

Exports - partners: China 13%, Italy 12%, Russia 10%, Netherlands 7%, France 6%, South Korea 5% (2019)

Exports - commodities: crude petroleum, natural gas, copper, iron alloys, radioactive chemicals (2019)

Imports: $44.3 billion (2020 est.) note: data are in current year dollars
$51.5 billion (2019 est.) note: data are in current year dollars
$46.23 billion (2018 est.) note: data are in current year dollars

Imports - partners: Russia 34%, China 24% (2019)

Imports - commodities: packaged medicines, natural gas, cars, broadcasting equipment, aircraft (2019)

Reserves of foreign exchange and gold: $30.75 billion (31 December 2017 est.)
$29.53 billion (31 December 2016 est.)

Debt - external: $159.351 billion (2019 est.)
$163.73 billion (2018 est.)

Exchange rates: tenge (KZT) per US dollar -
420.0049 (2020 est.)
385.9248 (2019 est.)
370.4648 (2018 est.)
221.73 (2014 est.)
179.19 (2013 est.)

ENERGY

Electricity access: *electrification - total population:* 100% (2020)

Electricity: *installed generating capacity:* 25.022 million kW (2020 est.)
consumption: 92,133,960,000 kWh (2019 est.)
exports: 2.419 billion kWh (2019 est.)
imports: 1.935 billion kWh (2019 est.)
transmission/distribution losses: 9.689 billion kWh (2019 est.)

Electricity generation sources: *fossil fuels:* 88.2% of total installed capacity (2020 est.)
solar: 0.9% of total installed capacity (2020 est.)
wind: 0.7% of total installed capacity (2020 est.)
hydroelectricity: 10.1% of total installed capacity (2020 est.)

Coal: *production:* 102.338 million metric tons (2020 est.)
consumption: 74.819 million metric tons (2020 est.)
exports: 3.002 million metric tons (2020 est.)
imports: 993,000 metric tons (2020 est.)
proven reserves: 25.605 billion metric tons (2019 est.)

Petroleum: *total petroleum production:* 1,864,900 bbl/day (2021 est.)
refined petroleum consumption: 320,600 bbl/day (2019 est.)
crude oil and lease condensate exports: 1,531,600 bbl/day (2018 est.)
crude oil and lease condensate imports: 500 bbl/day (2018 est.)
crude oil estimated reserves: 30 billion barrels (2021 est.)

Refined petroleum products - production: 290,700 bbl/day (2015 est.)

Refined petroleum products - exports: 105,900 bbl/day (2015 est.)

Refined petroleum products - imports: 39,120 bbl/day (2015 est.)

Natural gas: *production:* 25,785,505,000 cubic meters (2019 est.)
consumption: 14,557,101,000 cubic meters (2019 est.)
exports: 16,418,081,000 cubic meters (2019 est.)
imports: 7,713,978,000 cubic meters (2019 est.)
proven reserves: 2,406,928,000,000 cubic meters (2021 est.)

Carbon dioxide emissions: 263.689 million metric tonnes of CO2 (2019 est.)
from coal and metallurgical coke: 195.926 million metric tonnes of CO2 (2019 est.)
from petroleum and other liquids: 39.205 million metric tonnes of CO2 (2019 est.)
from consumed natural gas: 28.557 million metric tonnes of CO2 (2019 est.)

Energy consumption per capita: 180.726 million Btu/person (2019 est.)

COMMUNICATIONS

Telephones - fixed lines: *total subscriptions:* 3.091 million (2020 est.)
subscriptions per 100 inhabitants: 16 (2020 est.)

Telephones - mobile cellular: *total subscriptions:* 24,293,900 (2020 est.)
subscriptions per 100 inhabitants: 129 (2020 est.)

Telecommunication systems: *general assessment:* Kazakhstan has one of the most developed telecommunications sectors in the Central Asian region; this is especially true of the mobile segment, where widespread network coverage has enabled very high penetration rates reaching 180% as far back as 2012; the mobile and fixed-line segments have both pared back their subscriber numbers to more modest levels; the telcos have still been successful in terms of improving their margins and revenues by growing value-added services along with exploiting the capabilities of their higher speed networks (4G LTE as well as fiber) to drive significant increases in data usage; Kazakhstan has enjoyed a high fixed-line teledensity thanks to concerted efforts to invest in the fixed-line infrastructure as well as next-generation networks; demand for traditional voice services is on the wane as customers take a preference for the flexibility and ubiquity of the mobile platform for voice as well as data services; mobile clearly dominates the telecom sector in Kazakhstan, yet 2020 saw a sharp drop in subscriber numbers for both mobile voice and mobile broadband services as the Covid-19 crisis took hold; with the exception of fixed-line voice services, Kazakhstan's telecom market is expected to return to moderate growth from 2022 onward; the extensive deployment of LTE networks across the country (along with the prospect of 5G services being added to the mix in 2023) points towards an even greater uptake of lucrative mobile broadband services, in particular (2021)
domestic: intercity by landline and microwave radio relay; number of fixed-line connections is approximately 16 per 100 persons; mobile-cellular subscriber base 129 per 100 persons (2020)
international: country code - 7; international traffic with other former Soviet republics and China carried by landline and microwave radio relay and with other countries by satellite and by the TAE fiber-optic cable; satellite earth stations - 2 Intelsat

Broadcast media: the state owns nearly all radio and TV transmission facilities and operates national TV and radio networks; there are 96 TV channels, many of which are owned by the government, and 4 state-run radio stations; some former state-owned media outlets have been privatized; households with satellite dishes have access to foreign media; a small number of commercial radio stations operate along with state-run radio stations; recent legislation requires all media outlets to register with the government and all TV providers to broadcast in digital format by 2018; broadcasts reach some 99% of the population as well as neighboring countries (2018)

Internet country code: .kz

Internet users: *total:* 16,465,777 (July 2022 est.)
percent of population: 86% (July 2022 est.)

Broadband - fixed subscriptions: *total:* 2,620,400 (2020 est.)
subscriptions per 100 inhabitants: 14 (2020 est.)

TRANSPORTATION

National air transport system: *number of registered air carriers:* 12 (2020)
inventory of registered aircraft operated by air carriers: 84
annual passenger traffic on registered air carriers: 7,143,797 (2018)
annual freight traffic on registered air carriers: 50.22 million (2018) mt-km

Civil aircraft registration country code prefix: UP

Airports: *total:* 96 (2021)

Airports - with paved runways: *total:* 63
over 3,047 m: 10
2,438 to 3,047 m: 25
1,524 to 2,437 m: 15
914 to 1,523 m: 5
under 914 m: 8 (2021)

Airports - with unpaved runways: *total:* 33
over 3,047 m: 5
2,438 to 3,047 m: 7
1,524 to 2,437 m: 3
914 to 1,523 m: 5
under 914 m: 13 (2021)

Heliports: 3 (2021)

Pipelines: 658 km condensate, 15,429 km gas (2020), 8,020 km oil (2020), 1,095 km refined products, 1,975 km water (2017)
(2020)

Railways: *total:* 16,636 km (2020)
broad gauge: 16,636 km (2020) 1.520-m gauge (4,237 km electrified)

Roadways: *total:* 96,167 km (2021)
paved: 83,813 km (2021)
unpaved: 12,354 km (2021)

Waterways: 43,983 km (2020) (on the Ertis (Irtysh) River (80%) and Syr Darya (Syrdariya) River)

Merchant marine: *total:* 119
by type: general cargo 3, oil tanker 7, other 109 (2021)

Ports and terminals: *major seaport(s):* Caspian Sea - Aqtau (Shevchenko), Atyrau (Gur'yev)
river port(s): Oskemen (Ust-Kamenogorsk), Pavlodar, Semey (Semipalatinsk) (Irtysh River)

MILITARY AND SECURITY

Military and security forces: Armed Forces of the Republic of Kazakhstan: Land Forces, Naval Forces, Air and Air Defense Forces; Ministry of Internal Affairs: National Police; Committee for National Security: Border Service (2022)

Military expenditures: 1% of GDP (2021 est.)
1.1% of GDP (2020 est.)
1.1% of GDP (2019 est.) (approximately $3.6 billion)
0.9% of GDP (2018 est.) (approximately $3.06 billion)
0.8% of GDP (2017 est.) (approximately $2.85 billion)

Military and security service personnel strengths: information varies; approximately 40,000 active duty personnel (25,000 Land Forces; 3,000 Naval Forces; 12,000 Air and Air Defense Forces) (2022)

Military equipment inventories and acquisitions: the Kazakh military's inventory is comprised of mostly older Russian and Soviet-era equipment; since 2010, Russia has been the leading supplier of weapons systems (2022)

Military service age and obligation: all men 18-27 are required to serve in the military for 12-24 months (2022)

Military - note: Kazakhstan has been a member of the Collective Security Treaty Organization (CSTO) since 1994 and contributes troops to CSTO's rapid reaction force (2022)

TRANSNATIONAL ISSUES

Disputes - international: *Kazakhstan-China:* in 1998, Kazakhstan and China agreed to split two disputed border areas nearly evenly; demarcation with China completed in 2002
Kazakhstan-Kyrgyzstan: in January 2019, Kyrgyzstan ratified the 2017 agreement on the demarcation of the Kyrgyzstan-Kazakhstan border
Kazakhstan-Russia: Russia boundary delimitation was ratified on November 2005; field demarcation commenced in 2007 and was expected to be completed by 2013
Kazakhstan-Turkmenistan: Kazakhstan and Turkmenistan signed a treaty on the delimitation and demarcation process in 2001; field demarcation of the boundaries with Kazakhstan commenced in 2005; Turkmenistan and Kazakhstan agreed to their border in the Caspian Sea in 2014
Kazakhstan-Uzbekistan: field demarcation of the boundaries with Kazakhstan commenced in 2004; disputed territory is held by Uzbekistan but the overwhelming majority of residents are ethnic Kazakhs; the two countries agreed on draft final demarcation documents in March 2022 and planned to hold another meeting in April 2022

Refugees and internally displaced persons: *stateless persons:* 7,915 (mid-year 2021)

Illicit drugs: synthetic drugs dominate the local illicit drug market, smuggled from Southeast Asia, China, Russia and Europe; however the number of domestic clandestine laboratories producing synthetic drugs continues to increase; remains a transit country for Afghan heroin destined for Russia and Europe.

KENYA

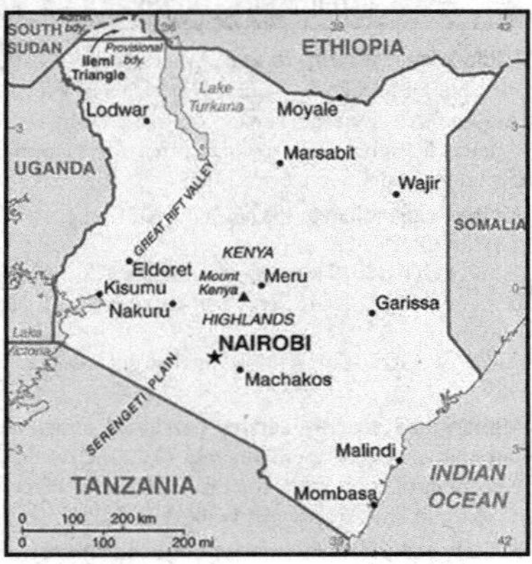

INTRODUCTION

Background: Trade centers such as Mombasa have existed along the Kenyan and Tanzanian coastlines, known as the Land of Zanj, since at least the 2nd century. These centers traded with the outside world, including China, India, Indonesia, the Middle East, North Africa, and Persia. By around the 9th century, the mix of Africans, Arabs, and Persians who lived and traded there became known as Swahili ("people of the coast") with a distinct language (KiSwahili) and culture. The Portuguese arrived in the 1490s and, using Mombasa as a base, sought to monopolize trade in the Indian Ocean. The Portuguese were pushed out in the late 1600s by the combined forces of Oman and Pate, an island off the coast. In 1890, Germany and the UK divided up the region, with the UK taking the north and the Germans the south, including present-day Tanzania, Burundi, and Rwanda. The British established the East Africa Protectorate in 1895, which in 1920 was converted into a colony and named Kenya after its highest mountain. Numerous political disputes between the colony and the UK subsequently led to the violent Mau Mau Uprising, which began in 1952, and the eventual declaration of independence in 1963.

Jomo KENYATTA, the founding president and an icon of the liberation struggle, led Kenya from independence in 1963 until his death in 1978, when Vice President Daniel Arap MOI took power in a constitutional succession. The country was a de facto one-party state from 1969 until 1982, after which time the ruling Kenya African National Union (KANU) changed the constitution to make itself the sole legal political party in Kenya. MOI acceded to internal and external pressure for political liberalization in late 1991. The ethnically fractured opposition failed to dislodge KANU from power in elections in 1992 and 1997, which were marred by violence and fraud. President MOI stepped down in December 2002 following fair and peaceful elections. Mwai KIBAKI, running as the candidate of the multiethnic, united opposition group, the National Rainbow Coalition (NARC), defeated KANU candidate Uhuru KENYATTA, the son of founding president Jomo KENYATTA, and assumed the presidency following a campaign centered on an anticorruption platform.

KIBAKI's reelection in 2007 resulted in two months of post-election ethnic violence that caused the death of more than 1,100 people and the dislocation of hundreds of thousands. Opposition candidate, Raila ODINGA, accused the government of widespread vote rigging. African Union-sponsored mediation led by former UN Secretary General Kofi ANNAN resulted in a power-sharing accord that brought ODINGA into the government in the restored position of prime minister. The power sharing accord included a broad reform agenda, the centerpiece of which was constitutional reform. In 2010, Kenyans overwhelmingly adopted a new constitution in a national referendum. The new constitution introduced additional checks and balances to executive power and devolved power and resources to 47 newly created counties. It also eliminated the position of prime minister. Uhuru KENYATTA won the first presidential election under the new constitution in March 2013. KENYATTA won a second and final term in office in November 2017 following a contentious, repeat election. In August 2022, William RUTO won a close presidential election; he assumed the office the following month after the Kenyan Supreme Court upheld the victory.

GEOGRAPHY

Location: Eastern Africa, bordering the Indian Ocean, between Somalia and Tanzania

Geographic coordinates: 1 00 N, 38 00 E

Map references: Africa

Area: *total:* 580,367 sq km
land: 569,140 sq km
water: 11,227 sq km

Area - comparative: five times the size of Ohio; slightly more than twice the size of Nevada

Land boundaries: *total:* 3,457 km
border countries (5): Ethiopia 867 km; Somalia 684 km; South Sudan 317 km; Tanzania 775 km; Uganda 814 km

Coastline: 536 km

Maritime claims: *territorial sea:* 12 nm
exclusive economic zone: 200 nm
continental shelf: 200-m depth or to the depth of exploitation

Climate: varies from tropical along coast to arid in interior

Terrain: low plains rise to central highlands bisected by Great Rift Valley; fertile plateau in west

Elevation: *highest point:* Mount Kenya 5,199 m
lowest point: Indian Ocean 0 m
mean elevation: 762 m

Natural resources: limestone, soda ash, salt, gemstones, fluorspar, zinc, diatomite, gypsum, wildlife, hydropower

Land use: *agricultural land:* 48.1% (2018 est.)
arable land: 9.8% (2018 est.)
permanent crops: 0.9% (2018 est.)
permanent pasture: 37.4% (2018 est.)
forest: 6.1% (2018 est.)
other: 45.8% (2018 est.)

Irrigated land: 1,030 sq km (2012)

Major lakes (area sq km): *fresh water lake(s):* Lake Victoria (shared with Tanzania and Uganda) - 62,940 sq km
salt water lake(s): Lake Turkana (shared with Ethiopia) - 6,400 sq km

Major watersheds (area sq km): Atlantic Ocean drainage: *(Mediterranean Sea)* Nile (3,254,853 sq km)

Major aquifers: Ogaden-Juba Basin

Population distribution: population heavily concentrated in the west along the shore of Lake Victoria; other areas of high density include the capital of Nairobi, and in the southeast along the Indian Ocean coast as shown in this population distribution map

Natural hazards: recurring drought; flooding during rainy seasons
volcanism: limited volcanic activity; the Barrier (1,032 m) last erupted in 1921; South Island is the only other historically active volcano

Geography - note: the Kenyan Highlands comprise one of the most successful agricultural production regions in Africa; glaciers are found on Mount Kenya, Africa's second highest peak; unique physiography supports abundant and varied wildlife of scientific and economic value; Lake Victoria, the world's largest tropical lake and the second largest fresh water lake, is shared among three countries: Kenya, Tanzania, and Uganda

PEOPLE AND SOCIETY

Population: 55,864,655 (2022 est.)

Nationality: *noun:* Kenyan(s)
adjective: Kenyan

Ethnic groups: Kikuyu 17.1%, Luhya 14.3%, Kalenjin 13.4%, Luo 10.7%, Kamba 9.8%, Somali 5.8%, Kisii 5.7%, Mijikenda 5.2%, Meru 4.2%, Maasai 2.5%, Turkana 2.1%, non-Kenyan 1%, other 8.2% (2019 est.)

Languages: English (official), Kiswahili (official), numerous indigenous languages
major-language sample(s): The World Factbook, the indispensable source for basic information. (English)
The World Factbook, Chanzo cha Lazima Kuhusu Habari ya Msingi. (Kiswahili)

Religions: Christian 85.5% (Protestant 33.4%, Catholic 20.6%, Evangelical 20.4%, African Instituted Churches 7%, other Christian 4.1%), Muslim 10.9%, other 1.8%, none 1.6%, don't know/no answer 0.2% (2019 est.)

Demographic profile: Kenya has experienced dramatic population growth since the mid-20th century as a result of its high birth rate and its declining mortality rate. Almost 40% of Kenyans are under the age of 15 as of 2022 because of sustained high fertility, early marriage and childbearing, and an unmet need for family planning. Kenya's persistent rapid population growth strains the labor market, social services, arable land, and natural resources. Although Kenya in 1967 was the first Sub-Saharan country to launch a nationwide family planning program, progress in reducing the birth rate has largely stalled since the late 1990s, when the government decreased its support for family planning to focus on the HIV epidemic. Government commitment and international technical support spurred Kenyan contraceptive use, decreasing the fertility rate (children per woman) from about 8 in the late 1970s to less than 5 children twenty years later, but it has plateaued at 3 children as of 2022.

Kenya is a source of emigrants and a host country for refugees. In the 1960s and 1970s, Kenyans pursued higher education in the UK because of colonial ties, but as British immigration rules tightened, the US, the then Soviet Union, and Canada became attractive study destinations. Kenya's stagnant economy and political problems during the 1980s and 1990s led to an outpouring of Kenyan students and professionals seeking permanent opportunities in the West and southern Africa. Nevertheless, Kenya's relative stability since its independence in 1963 has attracted hundreds of thousands of refugees escaping violent conflicts in neighboring countries; Kenya was sheltering nearly 280,000 Somali refugees as of 2022.

Age structure: *0-14 years:* 38.71% (male 10,412,321/female 10,310,908)
15-24 years: 20.45% (male 5,486,641/female 5,460,372)
25-54 years: 33.75% (male 9,046,946/female 9,021,207)
55-64 years: 4.01% (male 1,053,202/female 1,093,305)
65 years and over: 3.07% (male 750,988/female 892,046) (2020 est.)

Dependency ratios: *total dependency ratio:* 69.8
youth dependency ratio: 65.5
elderly dependency ratio: 4.3
potential support ratio: 23.5 (2020 est.)

Median age: *total:* 20 years
male: 19.9 years
female: 20.1 years (2020 est.)

Population growth rate: 2.12% (2022 est.)

Birth rate: 26.39 births/1,000 population (2022 est.)

Death rate: 5.01 deaths/1,000 population (2022 est.)

Net migration rate: -0.19 migrant(s)/1,000 population (2022 est.)

Population distribution: population heavily concentrated in the west along the shore of Lake Victoria; other areas of high density include the capital of Nairobi, and in the southeast along the Indian Ocean coast as shown in this population distribution map

Urbanization: *urban population:* 29% of total population (2022)
rate of urbanization: 4.09% annual rate of change (2020-25 est.)

Major urban areas - population: 5.119 million NAIROBI (capital), 1.389 million Mombassa (2022)

Sex ratio: *at birth:* 1.02 male(s)/female
0-14 years: 1.01 male(s)/female
15-24 years: 1.01 male(s)/female
25-54 years: 1.01 male(s)/female
55-64 years: 0.98 male(s)/female
65 years and over: 0.75 male(s)/female
total population: 1 male(s)/female (2022 est.)

Mother's mean age at first birth: 20.3 years (2014 est.)
note: data represents median age at first birth among women 25-49

Maternal mortality ratio: 342 deaths/100,000 live births (2017 est.)

Infant mortality rate: *total:* 27.86 deaths/1,000 live births
male: 30.92 deaths/1,000 live births
female: 24.74 deaths/1,000 live births (2022 est.)

Life expectancy at birth: *total population:* 69.69 years
male: 67.98 years
female: 71.43 years (2022 est.)

Total fertility rate: 3.29 children born/woman (2022 est.)

Contraceptive prevalence rate: 64.6% (2020)

Drinking water source: *improved: urban:* 91.3% of population
rural: 63.3% of population
total: 71.2% of population
unimproved: urban: 8.7% of population
rural: 36.7% of population
total: 28.8% of population (2020 est.)

Current health expenditure: 4.6% of GDP (2019)

Physicians density: 0.16 physicians/1,000 population (2018)

Sanitation facility access: *improved: urban:* 84% of population
rural: 48.1% of population
total: 58.2% of population
unimproved: urban: 16% of population
rural: 51.9% of population
total: 41.8% of population (2020 est.)

HIV/AIDS - adult prevalence rate: 4.2% (2020 est.)

Major infectious diseases: *degree of risk:* very high (2020)
food or waterborne diseases: bacterial and protozoal diarrhea, hepatitis A, and typhoid fever
vectorborne diseases: malaria, dengue fever, and Rift Valley fever
water contact diseases: schistosomiasis
animal contact diseases: rabies

Obesity - adult prevalence rate: 7.1% (2016)

Alcohol consumption per capita: *total:* 1.68 liters of pure alcohol (2019 est.)
beer: 0.81 liters of pure alcohol (2019 est.)
wine: 0.04 liters of pure alcohol (2019 est.)
spirits: 0.81 liters of pure alcohol (2019 est.)
other alcohols: 0.03 liters of pure alcohol (2019 est.)

Tobacco use: *total:* 11.1% (2020 est.)
male: 19.5% (2020 est.)
female: 2.7% (2020 est.)

Children under the age of 5 years underweight: 11.2% (2014)

Education expenditures: 5.1% of GDP (2020 est.)

Literacy: *definition:* age 15 and over can read and write
total population: 81.5%
male: 85%
female: 78.2% (2018)

Unemployment, youth ages 15-24: *total:* 12.9%
male: 12%
female: 13.8% (2019)

ENVIRONMENT

Environment - current issues: water pollution from urban and industrial wastes; water shortage and degraded water quality from increased use of pesticides and fertilizers; flooding; water hyacinth infestation in Lake Victoria; deforestation; soil erosion; desertification; poaching

Environment - international agreements: *party to:* Biodiversity, Climate Change, Climate Change-Kyoto Protocol, Climate Change-Paris Agreement, Comprehensive Nuclear Test Ban, Desertification, Endangered Species, Hazardous Wastes, Law of the Sea, Marine Dumping-London Convention, Marine Dumping-London Protocol, Marine Life Conservation, Nuclear Test Ban, Ozone Layer Protection, Ship Pollution, Wetlands, Whaling
signed, but not ratified: none of the selected agreements

Air pollutants: *particulate matter emissions:* 25.85 micrograms per cubic meter (2016 est.)
carbon dioxide emissions: 17.91 megatons (2016 est.)
methane emissions: 37.65 megatons (2020 est.)

Climate: varies from tropical along coast to arid in interior

Land use: *agricultural land:* 48.1% (2018 est.)
arable land: 9.8% (2018 est.)
permanent crops: 0.9% (2018 est.)
permanent pasture: 37.4% (2018 est.)
forest: 6.1% (2018 est.)
other: 45.8% (2018 est.)

Urbanization: *urban population:* 29% of total population (2022)
rate of urbanization: 4.09% annual rate of change (2020-25 est.)

Revenue from forest resources: *forest revenues:* 1.3% of GDP (2018 est.)

Revenue from coal: *coal revenues:* 0% of GDP (2018 est.)

Food insecurity: *exceptional shortfall in aggregate food production/supplies: due to drought conditions* - in the March to June 2022 period, about 4.1 million people were estimated to be severely food insecure; this figure is about 40% higher than the same time last year; severe rainfall deficits during the March-May 2022 rainy season have impaired pasture regeneration in several central, northern and eastern pastoral and agro-pastoral areas; as of late July 2022, between 25% and more than 85% of the grassland was affected by severe drought reflecting consecutive poor rainy seasons since late 2020 affecting both crop and livestock production; prices of maize are at high levels across the country due to reduced availability and high fuel prices inflating production and transportation costs; as the June–September 2022 dry season has started and forecasts point to a poor October–December 2022 "short-rains" season, food insecurity conditions are expected to further deteriorate (2022)

Waste and recycling: *municipal solid waste generated annually:* 5,595,099 tons (2010 est.)
municipal solid waste recycled annually: 447,608 tons (2009 est.)
percent of municipal solid waste recycled: 8% (2009 est.)

Major lakes (area sq km): *fresh water lake(s):* Lake Victoria (shared with Tanzania and Uganda) - 62,940 sq km
salt water lake(s): Lake Turkana (shared with Ethiopia) - 6,400 sq km

Major watersheds (area sq km): Atlantic Ocean drainage: *(Mediterranean Sea)* Nile (3,254,853 sq km)

Major aquifers: Ogaden-Juba Basin

Total water withdrawal: *municipal:* 495 million cubic meters (2017 est.)
industrial: 303 million cubic meters (2017 est.)
agricultural: 3.234 billion cubic meters (2017 est.)

Total renewable water resources: 30.7 billion cubic meters (2017 est.)

GOVERNMENT

Country name: *conventional long form:* Republic of Kenya
conventional short form: Kenya
local long form: Republic of Kenya (English)/ Jamhuri ya Kenya (Swahili)
local short form: Kenya
former: British East Africa
etymology: named for Mount Kenya; the meaning of the name is unclear but may derive from the Kikuyu, Embu, and Kamba words "kirinyaga," "kirenyaa," and "kiinyaa" - all of which mean "God's resting place"

Government type: presidential republic

Capital: *name:* Nairobi
geographic coordinates: 1 17 S, 36 49 E
time difference: UTC+3 (8 hours ahead of Washington, DC, during Standard Time)
etymology: the name derives from the Maasai expression meaning "cool waters" and refers to a cold water stream that flowed through the area in the late 19th century

Administrative divisions: 47 counties; Baringo, Bomet, Bungoma, Busia, Elgeyo/Marakwet, Embu, Garissa, Homa Bay, Isiolo, Kajiado, Kakamega, Kericho, Kiambu, Kilifi, Kirinyaga, Kisii, Kisumu, Kitui, Kwale, Laikipia, Lamu, Machakos, Makueni, Mandera, Marsabit, Meru, Migori, Mombasa, Murang'a, Nairobi City, Nakuru, Nandi, Narok, Nyamira, Nyandarua, Nyeri, Samburu, Siaya, Taita/ Taveta, Tana River, Tharaka-Nithi, Trans Nzoia, Turkana, Uasin Gishu, Vihiga, Wajir, West Pokot

Independence: 12 December 1963 (from the UK)

National holiday: Jamhuri Day (Independence Day), 12 December (1963); note - Madaraka Day, 1 June (1963) marks the day Kenya attained internal self-rule

Constitution: *history:* current constitution passed by referendum on 4 August 2010
amendments: amendments can be proposed by either house of Parliament or by petition of at least one million eligible voters; passage of amendments by Parliament requires approval by at least two-thirds majority vote of both houses in each of two readings, approval in a referendum by majority of votes cast by at least 20% of eligible voters in at least one half of Kenya's counties, and approval by the president; passage of amendments introduced by petition requires approval by a majority of county assemblies, approval by majority vote of both houses, and approval by the president

Legal system: mixed legal system of English common law, Islamic law, and customary law; judicial review in the new Supreme Court established by the new constitution

International law organization participation: accepts compulsory ICJ jurisdiction with reservations; accepts ICCt jurisdiction

Citizenship: *citizenship by birth:* no
citizenship by descent only: at least one parent must be a citizen of Kenya
dual citizenship recognized: yes
residency requirement for naturalization: 4 out of the previous 7 years

Suffrage: 18 years of age; universal

Executive branch: *chief of state:* President William RUTO (since 13 September 2022); note - the president is both chief of state and head of government
head of government: President William RUTO (since 13 September 2022)
cabinet: Cabinet appointed by the president, subject to confirmation by the National Assembly
elections/appointments: president and deputy president directly elected on the same ballot by qualified majority popular vote for a 5-year term (eligible for a second term); in addition to receiving an absolute majority popular vote, the presidential candidate must also win at least 25% of the votes cast in at least 24 of the 47 counties to avoid a run-off; election last held on 9 August 2022 (next to be held in 2027)
election results: 2017: Uhuru KENYATTA reelected president; percent of vote - Uhuru KENYATTA (Jubilee Party) 98.3%, Raila ODINGA (ODM) 1%, other 0.7%; note - Kenya held a previous presidential election on 8 August 2017, but Kenya's Supreme Court on 1 September 2017 nullified the results, citing irregularities; the political opposition boycotted the October vote
2013: Uhuru KENYATTA elected president in first round; percent of vote - Uhuru KENYATTA (TNA) 50.1%, Raila ODINGA (ODM) 43.7%, Musalia MUDAVADI (UDF) 4.0%, other 2.2%

Legislative branch: *description:* bicameral Parliament consists of:
Senate (68 seats; 47 members directly elected in single-seat constituencies by simple majority vote and 20 directly elected by proportional representation vote - 16 women, 2 representing youth, 2 representing the disabled, and one Senate speaker; members serve 5-year terms)
National Assembly (350 seats; 290 members directly elected in single-seat constituencies by simple majority vote, 47 women in single-seat constituencies elected by simple majority vote, and 12 members nominated by the National Assembly - 6 representing youth and 6 representing the disabled, and one Assembly speaker; members serve 5-year terms)
elections: Senate - last held on 9 August 2022 (next to be held in August 2027)
National Assembly - last held on 9 August 2022 (next to be held in August 2027)
election results: Senate - percent of vote by party/ coalition - NA; seats by party/coalition - Kenya Kwanza 34; Azimio La Umoja 33; composition - men 47, women 21, percent of women is 31%
National Assembly - percent of vote by party/coalition - NA; seats by party/coalition - Azimio La Umoja 173, Kenya Kwanza 161, independent 12, other 3; composition - men 275, women 75, percent of women 21.4%; note - total Parliament percent of women 23%

Judicial branch: *highest court(s):* Supreme Court (consists of chief and deputy chief justices and 5 judges)
judge selection and term of office: chief and deputy chief justices nominated by Judicial Service Commission (JSC) and appointed by the president with approval of the National Assembly; other judges nominated by the JSC and appointed by president; chief justice serves a nonrenewable 10-year term or until age 70, whichever comes first; other judges serve until age 70
subordinate courts: High Court; Court of Appeal; military courts; magistrates' courts; religious courts

Political parties and leaders: Azimio La Umoja–One Kenya Coalition Party [Raila ODINGA] (includes DAP-K, JP, KANU, KUP, MCC, MDG, ODM, PAA, UDM, UDP, UPA, UPIA, and WDM-K)
Amani National Congress or ANC [Musalia MUDAVADI]
Chama Cha Kazi or CCK [Moses KURIA]
Democratic Action Party or DAP-K [Wafula WAMUNYINYI]
Democratic Party or DP [Joseph MUNYAO, Chairman]
Forum for the Restoration of Democracy–Kenya or FORD-Kenya [Moses WETANGULA]
Grand Dream Development Party or GDDP [Fabian KYULE]
Independents
Jubilee Party or JP [Uhuru KENYATTA]
Kenya African National Union or KANU [Gideon MOI]
Kenya Kwanza coalition [William RUTO] (includes ANC, CCK, DP, FORD-Kenya, TSP, and UDA)
Kenya Union Party or KUP [John LONYANGAPUO]
Maendeleo Chap Chap Party or MCC [Alfred MUTUA]
Movement for Democracy and Growth or MDG [David OCHIENG]
National Agenda Party or NAP-K [Alfayo AGUFANA]
National Ordinary People Empowerment Union or NOPEU [Rodgers MPURU, Secretary General]
Orange Democratic Movement or ODM [Raila ODINGA]
Pamoja African Alliance or PAA [Amason KINGI]
The Service Party or TSP [Mwangi KIUNJURI]
United Democratic Alliance or UDA [William RUTO]
United Democratic Movement or UDM [Philip MURGOR]
United Democratic Party or UDP [Cyrus Jirongo]
United Party of Independent Alliance or UPIA [Ukur YATANI]
United Progressive Alliance or UPA [Kenneth NYAMWAMU]
Wiper Democratic Movement-Kenya or WDM-K [Kalonzo MUSYOKA]
note: only parties with seats in the National Assembly and Senate included

International organization participation: ACP, AfDB, ATMIS, AU, C, CD, COMESA, EAC, EADB, FAO, G-15, G-77, IAEA, IBRD, ICAO, ICCT, ICRM, IDA, IFAD, IFC, IFRCS, IGAD, ILO, IMF, IMO, IMSO, Interpol, IOC, IOM, IPU, ISO, ITSO, ITU, ITUC (NGOs), MIGA, MINUSMA, MONUSCO, NAM, OPCW, PCA, UN, UNAMID, UNCTAD, UNESCO, UNHCR, UNIDO, UNIFIL, UNISFA, UNMIL, UNMISS, UNSOM, UNWTO, UPU, WCO, WHO, WMO, WTO

Diplomatic representation in the US: *chief of mission:* Ambassador Lazarus Ombai AMAYO (since 17 July 2020)
chancery: 1616 P Street NW, Suite 340, Washington, DC 20036
telephone: [1] (202) 387-6101
FAX: [1] (202) 462-3829
email address and website:
information@kenyaembassydc.org
https://kenyaembassydc.org/#
consulate(s) general: Los Angeles
consulate(s): New York

Diplomatic representation from the US: *chief of mission:* Ambassador (vacant); Charge d'Affaires Eric W. KNEEDLER (since 20 January 2021)
embassy: P.O. Box 606 Village Market, 00621 Nairobi

mailing address: 8900 Nairobi Place, Washington, DC 20521-8900
telephone: [254] (20) 363-6000
FAX: [254] (20) 363-6157
email address and website:
kenya_acs@state.gov
https://ke.usembassy.gov/

Flag description: three equal horizontal bands of black (top), red, and green; the red band is edged in white; a large Maasai warrior's shield covering crossed spears is superimposed at the center; black symbolizes the majority population, red the blood shed in the struggle for freedom, green stands for natural wealth, and white for peace; the shield and crossed spears symbolize the defense of freedom

National symbol(s): lion; national colors: black, red, green, white

National anthem: *name:* "Ee Mungu Nguvu Yetu" (Oh God of All Creation)
lyrics/music: Graham HYSLOP, Thomas KALUME, Peter KIBUKOSYA, Washington OMONDI, and George W. SENOGA-ZAKE/traditional, adapted by Graham HYSLOP, Thomas KALUME, Peter KIBUKOSYA, Washington OMONDI, and George W. SENOGA-ZAKE
note: adopted 1963; based on a traditional Kenyan folk song

National heritage: *total World Heritage Sites:* 7 (4 cultural, 3 natural)
selected World Heritage Site locales: Lake Turkana National Parks (n); Mount Kenya National Park (n); Lamu Old Town (c); Sacred Mijikenda Kaya Forests (c); Fort Jesus, Mombasa (c); Kenya Lake System in the Great Rift Valley (n); Thimlich Ohinga Archaeological Site (c)

ECONOMY

Economic overview: Kenya is the economic, financial, and transport hub of East Africa. Kenya's real GDP growth has averaged over 5% for the last decade. Since 2014, Kenya has been ranked as a lower middle income country because its per capita GDP crossed a World Bank threshold. While Kenya has a growing entrepreneurial middle class and steady growth, its economic development has been impaired by weak governance and corruption. Although reliable numbers are hard to find, unemployment and under-employment are extremely high, and could be near 40% of the population. In 2013, the country adopted a devolved system of government with the creation of 47 counties, and is in the process of devolving state revenues and responsibilities to the counties.

Agriculture remains the backbone of the Kenyan economy, contributing one-third of GDP. About 75% of Kenya's population of roughly 48.5 million work at least part-time in the agricultural sector, including livestock and pastoral activities. Over 75% of agricultural output is from small-scale, rain-fed farming or livestock production. Tourism also holds a significant place in Kenya's economy. In spite of political turmoil throughout the second half of 2017, tourism was up 20%, showcasing the strength of this sector. Kenya has long been a target of terrorist activity and has struggled with instability along its northeastern borders. Some high visibility terrorist attacks during 2013-2015 (e.g., at Nairobi's Westgate Mall and Garissa University) affected the tourism industry severely, but the sector rebounded strongly in 2016-2017 and appears poised to continue growing.

Inadequate infrastructure continues to hamper Kenya's efforts to improve its annual growth so that it can meaningfully address poverty and unemployment. The KENYATTA administration has been successful in courting external investment for infrastructure development. International financial institutions and donors remain important to Kenya's growth and development, but Kenya has also successfully raised capital in the global bond market issuing its first sovereign bond offering in mid-2014, with a second occurring in February 2018. The first phase of a Chinese-financed and constructed standard gauge railway connecting Mombasa and Nairobi opened in May 2017.

In 2016 the government was forced to take over three small and undercapitalized banks when underlying weaknesses were exposed. The government also enacted legislation that limits interest rates banks can charge on loans and set a rate that banks must pay their depositors. This measure led to a sharp shrinkage of credit in the economy. A prolonged election cycle in 2017 hurt the economy, drained government resources, and slowed GDP growth. Drought-like conditions in parts of the country pushed 2017 inflation above 8%, but the rate had fallen to 4.5% in February 2018.

The economy, however, is well placed to resume its decade-long 5%-6% growth rate. While fiscal deficits continue to pose risks in the medium term, other economic indicators, including foreign exchange reserves, interest rates, current account deficits, remittances and FDI are positive. The credit and drought-related impediments were temporary. Now In his second term, President KENYATTA has pledged to make economic growth and development a centerpiece of his second administration, focusing on his "Big Four" initiatives of universal healthcare, food security, affordable housing, and expansion of manufacturing.

Real GDP (purchasing power parity): $226.94 billion (2020 est.)
$227.64 billion (2019 est.)
$216.05 billion (2018 est.)
note: data are in 2017 dollars

Real GDP growth rate: 5.39% (2019 est.)
6.32% (2018 est.)
4.79% (2017 est.)

Real GDP per capita: $4,200 (2020 est.)
$4,300 (2019 est.)
$4,200 (2018 est.)
note: data are in 2017 dollars

GDP (official exchange rate): $95.52 billion (2019 est.)

Inflation rate (consumer prices): 5.1% (2019 est.)
4.6% (2018 est.)
8% (2017 est.)

Credit ratings:

Fitch rating: B+ (2007)

Moody's rating: B2 (2018)

Standard & Poors rating: B+ (2010)
note: The year refers to the year in which the current credit rating was first obtained.

GDP - composition, by sector of origin: *agriculture:* 34.5% (2017 est.)
industry: 17.8% (2017 est.)
services: 47.5% (2017 est.)

GDP - composition, by end use: *household consumption:* 79.5% (2017 est.)
government consumption: 14.3% (2017 est.)
investment in fixed capital: 18.9% (2017 est.)
investment in inventories: -1% (2017 est.)
exports of goods and services: 13.9% (2017 est.)
imports of goods and services: -25.5% (2017 est.)

Agricultural products: sugar cane, milk, maize, potatoes, bananas, camel milk, cassava, sweet potatoes, mangoes/guavas, cabbages

Industries: small-scale consumer goods (plastic, furniture, batteries, textiles, clothing, soap, cigarettes, flour), agricultural products, horticulture, oil refining; aluminum, steel, lead; cement, commercial ship repair, tourism, information technology

Industrial production growth rate: 3.6% (2017 est.)

Labor force: 19.6 million (2017 est.)

Labor force - by occupation: *agriculture:* 61.1%
industry: 6.7%
services: 32.2% (2005 est.)

Unemployment rate: 40% (2013 est.)
40% (2001 est.)

Unemployment, youth ages 15-24: *total:* 12.9%
male: 12%
female: 13.8% (2019)

Population below poverty line: 36.1% (2015 est.)

Gini Index coefficient - distribution of family income:
40.8 (2015 est.)
42.5 (2008 est.)

Household income or consumption by percentage share: *lowest 10%:* 1.8%
highest 10%: 37.8% (2005)

Budget: *revenues:* 13.95 billion (2017 est.)
expenditures: 19.24 billion (2017 est.)

Budget surplus (+) or deficit (-): -6.7% (of GDP) (2017 est.)

Public debt: 54.2% of GDP (2017 est.)
53.2% of GDP (2016 est.)

Taxes and other revenues: 17.6% (of GDP) (2017 est.)

Fiscal year: 1 July - 30 June

Current account balance: -$57.594 billion (2019 est.)
-$56.194 billion (2018 est.)

Exports: $11.49 billion (2019 est.) note: data are in current year dollars
$11.56 billion (2018 est.) note: data are in current year dollars
$9.723 billion (2017 est.)

Exports - partners: Uganda 10%, United States 9%, Netherlands 8%, Pakistan 7%, United Kingdom 6%, United Arab Emirates 6%, Tanzania 5% (2019)

Exports - commodities: tea, cut flowers, refined petroleum, coffee, titanium (2019)

Imports: $20.41 billion (2019 est.) note: data are in current year dollars
$20.17 billion (2018 est.) note: data are in current year dollars
$18.653 billion (2017 est.)

Imports - partners: China 24%, United Arab Emirates 10%, India 10%, Saudi Arabia 7%, Japan 5% (2019)

Imports - commodities: refined petroleum, cars, packaged medicines, wheat, iron products (2019)

Reserves of foreign exchange and gold: $7.354 billion (31 December 2017 est.)
$7.256 billion (31 December 2016 est.)

Debt - external: $29.289 billion (2019 est.)
$25.706 billion (2018 est.)

Exchange rates: Kenyan shillings (KES) per US dollar -
111.45 (2020 est.)
101.4 (2019 est.)
102.4 (2018 est.)
98.179 (2014 est.)
87.921 (2013 est.)

ENERGY

Electricity access: *electrification - total population:* 85% (2019)
electrification - urban areas: 99% (2019)
electrification - rural areas: 79% (2019)

Electricity: *installed generating capacity:* 3.304 million kW (2020 est.)
consumption: 8.243 billion kWh (2019 est.)
exports: 16 million kWh (2019 est.)
imports: 277 million kWh (2019 est.)
transmission/distribution losses: 2.724 billion kWh (2019 est.)

Electricity generation sources: *fossil fuels:* 8.3% of total installed capacity (2020 est.)
solar: 1% of total installed capacity (2020 est.)
wind: 10.7% of total installed capacity (2020 est.)
hydroelectricity: 32.6% of total installed capacity (2020 est.)
geothermal: 46.2% of total installed capacity (2020 est.)
biomass and waste: 1.2% of total installed capacity (2020 est.)

Coal: *production:* 0 metric tons (2020 est.)
consumption: 821,000 metric tons (2020 est.)
exports: 0 metric tons (2020 est.)
imports: 822,000 metric tons (2020 est.)
proven reserves: 0 metric tons (2019 est.)

Petroleum: *total petroleum production:* 0 bbl/day (2021 est.)
refined petroleum consumption: 116,400 bbl/day (2019 est.)
crude oil and lease condensate exports: 0 bbl/day (2018 est.)
crude oil and lease condensate imports: 0 bbl/day (2018 est.)
crude oil estimated reserves: 0 barrels (2021 est.)

Refined petroleum products - production: 13,960 bbl/day (2015 est.)

Refined petroleum products - exports: 173 bbl/day (2015 est.)

Refined petroleum products - imports: 90,620 bbl/day (2015 est.)

Carbon dioxide emissions: 17.709 million metric tonnes of CO2 (2019 est.)
from coal and metallurgical coke: 1.25 million metric tonnes of CO2 (2019 est.)
from petroleum and other liquids: 16.459 million metric tonnes of CO2 (2019 est.)

Energy consumption per capita: 6.31 million Btu/person (2019 est.)

COMMUNICATIONS

Telephones - fixed lines: *total subscriptions:* 66,646 (2020 est.)
subscriptions per 100 inhabitants: (2020 est.) less than 1

Telephones - mobile cellular: *total subscriptions:* 61,408,904 (2020 est.)
subscriptions per 100 inhabitants: 114 (2020 est.)

Telecommunication systems: *general assessment:* Kenya's telecom market continues to undergo considerable changes in the wake of increased competition, improved international connectivity, and rapid developments in the mobile market; the country is directly connected to a number of submarine cables, and with Mombasa through a terrestrial network, the country serves as a key junction for onward connectivity to the Arabian states and the Far East; numerous competitors are rolling out national and metropolitan backbone networks and wireless access networks to deliver services to population centers across the country; several fiber infrastructure sharing agreements have been forged, and as a result the number of fiber broadband connections has increased sharply in recent years; much of the progress in the broadband segment is due to the government's revised national broadband strategy, which has been updated with goals through to 2030, and which are largely dependent on mobile broadband platforms based on LTE and 5G (2022)
domestic: fixed-line subscriptions stand at less than 1 per 100 persons; multiple providers in the mobile-cellular segment of the market fostering a boom in mobile-cellular telephone usage with teledensity reaching 114 per 100 persons (2020)
international: country code - 254; landing point for the EASSy, TEAMS, LION2, DARE1, PEACE Cable, and SEACOM fiber-optic submarine cable systems covering East, North and South Africa, Europe, the Middle East, and Asia; satellite earth stations - 4 Intelsat; launched first micro satellites in 2018 (2019)

Broadcast media: about a half-dozen large-scale privately owned media companies with TV and radio stations, as well as a state-owned TV broadcaster, provide service nationwide; satellite and cable TV subscription services available; state-owned radio broadcaster operates 2 national radio channels and provides regional and local radio services in multiple languages; many private radio stations broadcast on a national level along with over 100 private and non-profit regional stations broadcasting in local languages; TV transmissions of all major international broadcasters available, mostly via paid subscriptions; direct radio frequency modulation transmissions available for several foreign government-owned broadcasters (2019)

Internet country code: .ke

Internet users: *total:* 16,131,390 (2020 est.)

Broadband - fixed subscriptions: *total:* 674,191 (2020 est.)
subscriptions per 100 inhabitants: 1 (2020 est.)

TRANSPORTATION

National air transport system: *number of registered air carriers:* 25 (2020)
inventory of registered aircraft operated by air carriers: 188
annual passenger traffic on registered air carriers: 5,935,831 (2018)
annual freight traffic on registered air carriers: 294.97 million (2018) mt-km

Civil aircraft registration country code prefix: 5Y

Airports: *total:* 197 (2021)

Airports - with paved runways: *total:* 16
over 3,047 m: 5
2,438 to 3,047 m: 2
1,524 to 2,437 m: 2
914 to 1,523 m: 6
under 914 m: 1 (2021)

Airports - with unpaved runways: *total:* 181
1,524 to 2,437 m: 14
914 to 1,523 m: 107
under 914 m: 60 (2021)

Pipelines: 4 km oil, 1,432 km refined products (2018)

Railways: *total:* 3,819 km (2018)
standard gauge: 485 km (2018) 1.435-m gauge
narrow gauge: 3,334 km (2018) 1.000-m gauge

Roadways: *total:* 161,452 km (2018)
paved: 14,420 km (2017) (8,500 km highways, 1,872 urban roads, and 4,048 rural roads)
unpaved: 147,032 km (2017)

Waterways: (2011) none specifically; the only significant inland waterway is the part of Lake Victoria within the boundaries of Kenya; Kisumu is the main port and has ferry connections to Uganda and Tanzania

Merchant marine: *total:* 26
by type: oil tanker 3, other 23 (2021)

Ports and terminals: *major seaport(s):* Kisumu, Mombasa

LNG terminal(s) (import): Mombasa

MILITARY AND SECURITY

Military and security forces: Kenya Defense Forces (KDF): Kenya Army, Kenya Navy, Kenya Air Force (2022)
note 1: the National Police Service maintains internal security and reports to the Ministry of Interior and Coordination of National Government; it includes a paramilitary General Service Unit and Rapid Deployment Unit
note 2: the Kenya Coast Guard Service (established 2018) is under the Ministry of Interior but led by a military officer and comprised of personnel from the military, as well as the National Police Service, intelligence services, and other government agencies

Military expenditures: 1.2% of GDP (2021 est.)
1.2% of GDP (2020)
1.2% of GDP (2019) (approximately $1.21 billion)
1.3% of GDP (2018) (approximately $1.24 billion)
1.4% of GDP (2017) (approximately $1.19 billion)

Military and security service personnel strengths: approximately 24,000 personnel (20,000 Army; 1,500 Navy; 2,500 Air Force) (2022)

Military equipment inventories and acquisitions: the KDF's inventory traditionally carried mostly older or second-hand Western weapons systems, particularly from France, the UK, and the US; however, since the 2000s it has sought to modernize and diversify its imports, and suppliers have included more than a dozen countries including China, Italy, Jordan, and the US (2022)

Military service age and obligation: no conscription; 18-26 years of age for male and female voluntary service (under 18 with parental consent; upper limit 30 years of age for specialists, tradesmen, or women with a diploma; 39 years of age for chaplains/imams); 9-year service obligation (7 years for Kenyan Navy) and subsequent 3-year re-enlistments; applicants must be Kenyan citizens (2022)

Military deployments: 260 Democratic Republic of the Congo (MONUSCO); 3,650 Somalia (ATMIS) (2022)

note: in November 2022, Kenya sent approximately 900 troops to the eastern part of the Democratic Republic of the Congo (DRC) as part of a newly-formed East Africa Community Regional Force (EACRF) to assist the DRC military against the rebel group M23; the force is led by Kenya

Military - note: Kenyan military forces intervened in Somalia in October 2011 to combat the al Qaida-affiliated al-Shabaab terrorist group, which had conducted numerous cross-border attacks into Kenya; in November 2011, the UN and the African Union invited Kenya to incorporate its forces into the African Union Mission in Somalia (AMISOM); Kenyan forces were formally integrated into AMISOM in February 2012; as of 2022, they consisted of approximately 3,600 troops and were responsible for AMISOM's Sector 2 comprising Lower and Middle Jubba (see Appendix T for additional details on al- Shabaab; note - as of May 2022, AMISOM was renamed the AU Transition Mission in Somalia or ATMIS)

the Kenya Military Forces were created following independence in 1963; the current Kenya Defense Forces (KDF) were established, and its composition laid out, in the 2010 constitution; the KDF is governed by the Kenya Defense Forces Act of 2012; the Kenya Army traces its origins back to the Kings African Rifles (KAR); the KAR was a British colonial regiment raised from Britain's various possessions in East Africa from 1902 until independence in the 1960s; it conducted both military and internal security functions within the colonial territories, and served outside the territories during the World Wars (2022)

Maritime threats: the International Maritime Bureau reports that shipping in territorial and offshore waters in the Indian Ocean remain at risk for piracy and armed robbery against ships

TERRORISM

Terrorist group(s): al-Shabaab; Islamic Revolutionary Guard Corps (IRGC)/Qods Force

TRANSNATIONAL ISSUES

Disputes - international: *Kenya-Ethiopia:* their border was demarcated in the 1950s and approved in 1970; in 2012, Kenya and Ethiopia agreed to redemarcate their boundary following disputes over beacons and cross-border crime

Kenya-Somalia: Kenya works hard to prevent the clan and militia fighting in Somalia from spreading across the border, which has long been open to nomadic pastoralists; in 2021, the International Court of Justice (ICJ) gave Somalia control over a disputed ocean area where the seabeds are believed to hold vasts oil and gas deposits; the ICJ ruling gave Somalia the rights to several offshore oil exploration blocks previously claimed by Kenya; Kenya did not recognize the court's decision

Kenya-South Sudan: two thirds of the boundary that separates Kenya and South Sudan's sovereignty known as the Ilemi Triangle has been unclear since British colonial times; Kenya has administered the area since colonial times; officials from Kenya and South Sudan signed a memorandum of understanding on boundary delimitation and demarcation and agreed to set up a joint committee; as of July 2019, the demarcation process was to begin in 90 days, but was delayed due to a lack of funding

Kenya-Sudan: Kenya served as an important mediator in brokering Sudan's north-south separation in February 2005

Kenya-Tanzania: Kenya and Tanzania were conducting a joint reaffirmation process in November 2021 to ensure the border was visibly marked with pillars

Kenya-Uganda: Kenya and Uganda began a joint demarcation of the boundary in 2021

Refugees and internally displaced persons: *refugees (country of origin):* 279,625 (Somalia), 151,087 (South Sudan), 52,312 (Democratic Republic of the Congo), 21,066 (Ethiopia), 7,697 (Burundi), 5,022 (Sudan) (2022)

IDPs: 190,000 (election-related violence, intercommunal violence, resource conflicts, al-Shabaab attacks in 2017 and 2018) (2021)

stateless persons: 16,820 (mid-year 2021); note - the stateless population consists of Nubians, Kenyan Somalis, and coastal Arabs; the Nubians are descendants of Sudanese soldiers recruited by the British to fight for them in East Africa more than a century ago; Nubians did not receive Kenyan citizenship when the country became independent in 1963; only recently have Nubians become a formally recognized tribe and had less trouble obtaining national IDs; Galjeel and other Somalis who have lived in Kenya for decades are included with more recent Somali refugees and denied ID cards

Illicit drugs: a transit country for a variety of illicit drugs, including heroin and cocaine; transit location for precursor chemicals used to produce methamphetamine and other drugs; transshipment country for heroin from Southwest Asia destined for international markets, mainly Europe, and cocaine transits shipped through Ethiopia from South America; cultivates cannabis and miraa (khat) for both local use and export

KIRIBATI

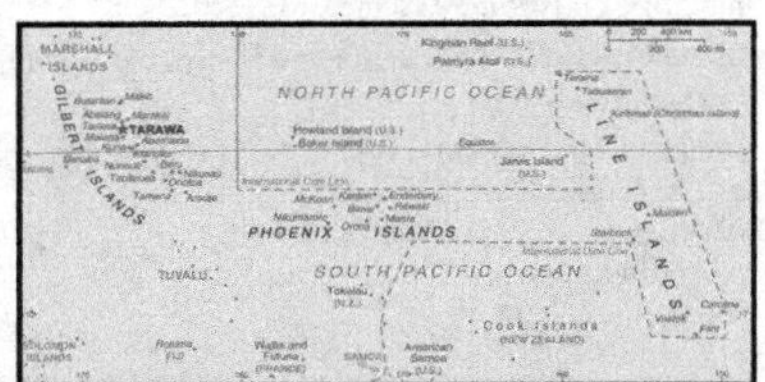

INTRODUCTION

Background: Kiribati is made up of three distinct island groups - the Gilbert Islands, the Line Islands, and the Phoenix Islands. The first Austronesian voyagers arrived in the Gilbert Islands as early as 3000 B.C., but these islands were not widely settled until about A.D. 200 by Micronesians. Around 1300, Samoans and Tongans invaded the southern Gilbert Islands, bringing Polynesian cultural elements with them. Later arrivals by Fijians brought Melanesian elements to the Gilbert Islands, and extensive intermarriage between the Micronesian, Polynesian, and Melanesian people led to the creation of what would become Gilbertese cultural traditions by the time Europeans spotted the islands in the 1600s. The Phoenix Islands and Line Islands were both visited by various Melanesian and Polynesian peoples, but their isolation and lack of natural resources meant that long-term settlements were not possible and both island groups were uninhabited by the time of European contact.

Kiribati experienced sustained European contact by the 1760s; all three island groups were named and charted by 1826. American whaling ships frequently passed through the islands, and the UK declared a protectorate over the Gilbert and nearby Ellice Islands in 1892 to block growing US influence. Phosphate-rich Banaba Island was annexed to the protectorate in 1900. In 1916, the protectorate became a colony, and some Line Islands were added in 1916 and 1919, with the final ones added in 1972. The Phoenix Islands were added to the colony in 1937, and the UK agreed to share jurisdiction of some of them with the US because of their strategic location for aviation. Japan occupied the northern Gilbert Islands in 1941; the islands of Makin and Tarawa were the sites of major US amphibious victories over entrenched Japanese garrisons in 1943. The UK continued to rule the colony after World War II. The Ellice Islands became its own colony in 1974. The Gilbert Islands became fully self-governing in 1977 and independent in 1979 as Kiribati, the Gilbertese spelling of Gilberts. The US relinquished all claims to the sparsely inhabited Phoenix and Line Islands in a 1979 treaty of friendship.

In 1994, Kiribati adjusted the international date line to the east of the Line Islands, bringing all islands in the country to the same day and giving Kiribati the earliest time zone in the world. Kiribati is a leading climate change and marine protection advocate. The Phoenix Islands Protected Area was established in 2008; in 2010, it became the world's largest (and deepest) UNESCO World Heritage site. In 2012, Kiribati purchased a 22 sq km (8.5 sq mi) plot of land in Fiji for potential eventual resettlement of its population because of climate change.

GEOGRAPHY

Location: Oceania, group of 32 coral atolls and one raised coral island in the Pacific Ocean, straddling the Equator; the capital Tarawa is about halfway between Hawaii and Australia

Geographic coordinates: 1 25 N, 173 00 E

Map references: Oceania

Area: *total:* 811 sq km

land: 811 sq km

water: 0 sq km

note: includes three island groups - Gilbert Islands, Line Islands, and Phoenix Islands - dispersed over about 3.5 million sq km (1.35 million sq mi)

Area - comparative: four times the size of Washington, DC

Land boundaries: *total:* 0 km

Coastline: 1,143 km

Maritime claims: *territorial sea:* 12 nm
exclusive economic zone: 200 nm

Climate: tropical; marine, hot and humid, moderated by trade winds

Terrain: mostly low-lying coral atolls surrounded by extensive reefs

Elevation: *highest point:* unnamed elevation on Banaba 81 m
lowest point: Pacific Ocean 0 m
mean elevation: 2 m

Natural resources: phosphate (production discontinued in 1979), coconuts (copra), fish

Land use: *agricultural land:* 42% (2018 est.)
arable land: 2.5% (2018 est.)
permanent crops: 39.5% (2018 est.)
permanent pasture: 0% (2018 est.)
forest: 15% (2018 est.)
other: 43% (2018 est.)

Irrigated land: 0 sq km (2012)

Population distribution: consists of three achipelagos spread out over an area roughly the size of India; the eastern Line Islands and central Phoenix Islands are sparsely populated, but the western Gilbert Islands are some of the most densely settled places on earth, with the main island of South Tarawa boasting a population density similar to Tokyo or Hong Kong

Natural hazards: typhoons can occur any time, but usually November to March; occasional tornadoes; low level of some of the islands make them sensitive to changes in sea level

Geography - note: 21 of the 33 islands are inhabited; Banaba (Ocean Island) in Kiribati is one of the three great phosphate rock islands in the Pacific Ocean - the others are Makatea in French Polynesia, and Nauru; Kiribati is the only country in the world to fall into all four hemispheres (northern, southern, eastern, and western)

PEOPLE AND SOCIETY

Population: 114,189 (2022 est.)

Nationality: *noun:* I-Kiribati (singular and plural)
adjective: Kiribati

Ethnic groups: I-Kiribati 95.78%, I-Kiribati/mixed 3.8%, Tuvaluan 0.2%, other 1.7% (2020 est.)

Languages: Gilbertese, English (official)

Religions: Roman Catholic 58.9%, Kiribati Uniting Church 21.2%, Kiribati Protestant Church 8.4%, Church of Jesus Christ 5.6%, Seventh Day Adventist 2.1%, Baha'i 2.1%, other 1.7% (2020 est.)

Age structure: *0-14 years:* 28.47% (male 16,223/female 15,604)
15-24 years: 20.24% (male 11,171/female 11,459)
25-54 years: 40.05% (male 21,530/female 23,249)
55-64 years: 6.65% (male 3,350/female 4,084)
65 years and over: 4.59% (male 2,004/female 3,122) (2020 est.)

Dependency ratios: *total dependency ratio:* 67
youth dependency ratio: 60
elderly dependency ratio: 7
potential support ratio: 14.2 (2020 est.)

Median age: *total:* 25.7 years
male: 24.8 years
female: 26.6 years (2020 est.)

Population growth rate: 1.04% (2022 est.)

Birth rate: 20.12 births/1,000 population (2022 est.)

Death rate: 6.92 deaths/1,000 population (2022 est.)

Net migration rate: -2.8 migrant(s)/1,000 population (2022 est.)

Population distribution: consists of three achipelagos spread out over an area roughly the size of India; the eastern Line Islands and central Phoenix Islands are sparsely populated, but the western Gilbert Islands are some of the most densely settled places on earth, with the main island of South Tarawa boasting a population density similar to Tokyo or Hong Kong

Urbanization: *urban population:* 57.1% of total population (2022)
rate of urbanization: 2.77% annual rate of change (2020-25 est.)

Major urban areas - population: 64,000 TARAWA (capital) (2018)

Sex ratio: *at birth:* 1.05 male(s)/female
0-14 years: 1.04 male(s)/female
15-24 years: 0.98 male(s)/female
25-54 years: 0.92 male(s)/female
55-64 years: 0.82 male(s)/female
65 years and over: 0.46 male(s)/female
total population: 0.94 male(s)/female (2022 est.)

Mother's mean age at first birth: 23.1 years (2009 est.)
note: data represents median age at first birth among women 25-29

Maternal mortality ratio: 92 deaths/100,000 live births (2017 est.)

Infant mortality rate: *total:* 32.93 deaths/1,000 live births
male: 34.88 deaths/1,000 live births
female: 30.87 deaths/1,000 live births (2022 est.)

Life expectancy at birth: *total population:* 67.9 years
male: 65.3 years
female: 70.64 years (2022 est.)

Total fertility rate: 2.2 children born/woman (2022 est.)

Contraceptive prevalence rate: 33.5% (2018/19)

Drinking water source: *improved: urban:* 97.2% of population
rural: 63.1% of population
total: 82% of population
unimproved: urban: 2.8% of population
rural: 36.9% of population
total: 18% of population (2020 est.)

Current health expenditure: 10.3% of GDP (2019)

Physicians density: 0.2 physicians/1,000 population (2013)

Hospital bed density: 1.9 beds/1,000 population (2016)

Sanitation facility access: *improved: urban:* 75.4% of population
rural: 45.4% of population
total: 62.1% of population
unimproved: urban: 24.6% of population
rural: 54.6% of population
total: 37.9% of population (2020 est.)

Major infectious diseases: *degree of risk:* high (2020)
food or waterborne diseases: bacterial diarrhea
vectorborne diseases: malaria

Obesity - adult prevalence rate: 46% (2016)

Alcohol consumption per capita: *total:* 0.43 liters of pure alcohol (2019 est.)
beer: 0.26 liters of pure alcohol (2019 est.)
wine: 0 liters of pure alcohol (2019 est.)
spirits: 0.17 liters of pure alcohol (2019 est.)
other alcohols: 0 liters of pure alcohol (2019 est.)

Tobacco use: *total:* 40.6% (2020 est.)
male: 53.9% (2020 est.)
female: 27.3% (2020 est.)

Children under the age of 5 years underweight: 6.9% (2018/19)

Child marriage: *women married by age 15:* 2.4%
women married by age 18: 18.4%
men married by age 18: 8.6% (2019 est.)

Education expenditures: 12.4% of GDP (2019 est.)

Unemployment, youth ages 15-24: *total:* 22.5%
male: 21.2%
female: 24.6% (2019 est.)

ENVIRONMENT

Environment - current issues: heavy pollution in lagoon of south Tarawa atoll due to overcrowding mixed with traditional practices such as lagoon latrines and open-pit dumping; ground water at risk; potential for water shortages, disease; coastal erosion

Environment - international agreements: *party to:* Biodiversity, Climate Change, Climate Change-Kyoto Protocol, Climate Change-Paris Agreement, Comprehensive Nuclear Test Ban, Desertification, Hazardous Wastes, Law of the Sea, Marine Dumping-London Convention, Ozone Layer Protection, Ship Pollution, Wetlands, Whaling
signed, but not ratified: none of the selected agreements

Air pollutants: *particulate matter emissions:* 10.45 micrograms per cubic meter (2016 est.)
carbon dioxide emissions: 0.07 megatons (2016 est.)
methane emissions: 0.02 megatons (2020 est.)

Climate: tropical; marine, hot and humid, moderated by trade winds

Land use: *agricultural land:* 42% (2018 est.)
arable land: 2.5% (2018 est.)
permanent crops: 39.5% (2018 est.)
permanent pasture: 0% (2018 est.)
forest: 15% (2018 est.)
other: 43% (2018 est.)

Urbanization: *urban population:* 57.1% of total population (2022)
rate of urbanization: 2.77% annual rate of change (2020-25 est.)

Revenue from forest resources: *forest revenues:* 0.04% of GDP (2018 est.)

Revenue from coal: *coal revenues:* 0% of GDP (2018 est.)

Waste and recycling: *municipal solid waste generated annually:* 35,724 tons (2016 est.)

Total renewable water resources: 0 cubic meters (2017 est.)

GOVERNMENT

Country name: *conventional long form:* Republic of Kiribati
conventional short form: Kiribati

local long form: Republic of Kiribati
local short form: Kiribati
former: Gilbert Islands
etymology: the name is the local pronunciation of "Gilberts," the former designation of the islands; originally named after explorer Thomas GILBERT, who mapped many of the islands in 1788
note: pronounced keer-ree-bahss

Government type: presidential republic

Capital: *name:* Tarawa
geographic coordinates: 1 21 N, 173 02 E
time difference: UTC+12 (17 hours ahead of Washington, DC, during Standard Time)
time zone note: Kiribati has three time zones: the Gilbert Islands group at UTC+12, the Phoenix Islands at UTC+13, and the Line Islands at UTC+14
etymology: in Kiribati creation mythology, "tarawa" was what the spider Nareau named the land to distinguish it from "karawa" (the sky) and "marawa" (the ocean)

Administrative divisions: 3 geographical units: Gilbert Islands, Line Islands, Phoenix Islands; note - there are no first-order administrative divisions, but there are 6 districts (Banaba, Central Gilberts, Line Islands, Northern Gilberts, Southern Gilberts, Tarawa) and 21 island councils - one for each of the inhabited islands (Abaiang, Abemama, Aranuka, Arorae, Banaba, Beru, Butaritari, Kanton, Kiritimati, Kuria, Maiana, Makin, Marakei, Nikunau, Nonouti, Onotoa, Tabiteuea, Tabuaeran, Tamana, Tarawa, Teraina)

Independence: 12 July 1979 (from the UK)

National holiday: Independence Day, 12 July (1979)

Constitution: *history:* The Gilbert and Ellice Islands Order in Council 1915, The Gilbert Islands Order in Council 1975 (preindependence); latest promulgated 12 July 1979 (at independence)
amendments: proposed by the House of Assembly; passage requires two-thirds majority vote by the Assembly membership; passage of amendments affecting the constitutional section on amendment procedures and parts of the constitutional chapter on citizenship requires deferral of the proposal to the next Assembly meeting where approval is required by at least two-thirds majority vote of the Assembly membership and support of the nominated or elected Banaban member of the Assembly; amendments affecting the protection of fundamental rights and freedoms also requires approval by at least two-thirds majority in a referendum; amended several times, last in 2018

Legal system: English common law supplemented by customary law

International law organization participation: has not submitted an ICJ jurisdiction declaration; non-party state to the ICCt

Citizenship: *citizenship by birth:* no
citizenship by descent only: at least one parent must be a native-born citizen of Kiribati
dual citizenship recognized: no
residency requirement for naturalization: 7 years

Suffrage: 18 years of age; universal

Executive branch: *chief of state:* President Taneti MAAMAU (since 11 March 2016); Vice President Teuea TOATU (since 19 June 2019); note - the president is both chief of state and head of government
head of government: President Taneti MAAMAU (since 11 March 2016); Vice President Teuea TOATU (since 19 June 2019)
cabinet: Cabinet appointed by the president from among House of Assembly members
elections/appointments: president directly elected by simple majority popular vote following nomination of candidates from among House of Assembly members; term is 4 years (eligible for 2 additional terms); election last held on 22 June 2020 (next to be held in 2024); vice president appointed by the president
election results: Taneti MAAMAU reelected president; percent of vote - Taneti MAAMAU (TKB) 59.3%, Banuera BERINA (BKM) 40.7%.

Legislative branch: *description:* unicameral House of Assembly or Maneaba Ni Maungatabu (46 seats; 44 members directly elected in single- and multi-seat constituencies by absolute majority vote in two-rounds if needed; 1 member appointed by the Rabi Council of Leaders - representing Banaba Island, and 1 ex officio member - the attorney general; members serve 4-year terms)
elections: legislative elections originally scheduled to be held in two rounds on 7 and 15 April 2020 but rescheduled for 14 and 21 April (next to be held in 2024)
election results: percent of vote by party (second round) - NA; seats by party (second round) - TKB 22, BKM 22, 1 independent

Judicial branch: *highest court(s):* High Court (consists of a chief justice and other judges as prescribed by the president); note - the High Court has jurisdiction on constitutional issues
judge selection and term of office: chief justice appointed by the president on the advice of the cabinet in consultation with the Public Service Commission (PSC); other judges appointed by the president on the advice of the chief justice along with the PSC
subordinate courts: Court of Appeal; magistrates' courts

Political parties and leaders: Boutokaan Kiribati Moa Party or BKM [Tessie LAMBOURNE]
Tobwaan Kiribati Party or TKP [Taneti MAAMAU]

International organization participation: ABEDA, ACP, ADB, AOSIS, C, FAO, IBRD, ICAO, ICRM, IDA, IFAD, IFC, IFRCS, ILO, IMF, IMO, IOC, ITU, ITUC (NGOs), OPCW, PIF, Sparteca, SPC, UN, UNCTAD, UNESCO, UPU, WHO, WIPO, WMO

Diplomatic representation in the US: *chief of mission:* Ambassador Teburoro TITO (since 24 January 2018)
chancery: 685 Third Avenue, Suite 1109, New York, NY 10017
telephone: [1] (212) 867-3310
FAX: [1] (212) 867-3320
email address and website:
Kimission.newyork@mfa.gov.ki
note - the Kiribati Permanent Mission to the UN serves as the embassy

Diplomatic representation from the US: *embassy:* the US does not have an embassy in Kiribati; the US Ambassador to Fiji is accredited to Kiribati

Flag description: the upper half is red with a yellow frigatebird flying over a yellow rising sun, and the lower half is blue with three horizontal wavy white stripes to represent the Pacific ocean; the white stripes represent the three island groups - the Gilbert, Line, and Phoenix Islands; the 17 rays of the sun represent the 16 Gilbert Islands and Banaba (formerly Ocean Island); the frigatebird symbolizes authority and freedom

National symbol(s): frigatebird; national colors: red, white, blue, yellow

National anthem: *name:* "Teirake kaini Kiribati" (Stand Up, Kiribati)
lyrics/music: Urium Tamuera IOTEBA
note: adopted 1979

National heritage: *total World Heritage Sites:* 1 (natural)
selected World Heritage Site locales: Phoenix Islands Protected Area

ECONOMY

Economic overview: A remote country of 33 scattered coral atolls, Kiribati has few natural resources and is one of the least developed Pacific Island countries. Commercially viable phosphate deposits were exhausted by the time of independence from the United Kingdom in 1979. Earnings from fishing licenses and seafarer remittances are important sources of income. Although the number of seafarers employed declined due to changes in global shipping demands, remittances are expected to improve with more overseas temporary and seasonal work opportunities for Kiribati nationals.

Economic development is constrained by a shortage of skilled workers, weak infrastructure, and remoteness from international markets. The public sector dominates economic activity, with ongoing capital projects in infrastructure including road rehabilitation, water and sanitation projects, and renovations to the international airport, spurring some growth. Public debt increased from 23% of GDP at the end of 2015 to 25.8% in 2016.

Kiribati is dependent on foreign aid, which was estimated to have contributed over 32.7% in 2016 to the government's finances. The country's sovereign fund, the Revenue Equalization Reserve Fund (RERF), which is held offshore, had an estimated balance of $855.5 million in late July 2016. The RERF seeks to avoid exchange rate risk by holding investments in more than 20 currencies, including the Australian dollar, US dollar, the Japanese yen, and the Euro. Drawdowns from the RERF helped finance the government's annual budget.

Real GDP (purchasing power parity): $270 million (2020 est.)
$270 million (2019 est.)
$260 million (2018 est.)
note: data are in 2017 dollars

Real GDP growth rate: 3.1% (2017 est.)
1.1% (2016 est.)
10.3% (2015 est.)

Real GDP per capita: $2,300 (2020 est.)
$2,300 (2019 est.)
$2,300 (2018 est.)
note: data are in 2017 dollars

GDP (official exchange rate): $197 million (2017 est.)

Inflation rate (consumer prices): 0.4% (2017 est.)
1.9% (2016 est.)

GDP - composition, by sector of origin: *agriculture:* 23% (2016 est.)
industry: 7% (2016 est.)
services: 70% (2016 est.)

Agricultural products: coconuts, roots/tubers nes, bananas, vegetables, taro, tropical fruit, poultry, pork, nuts, eggs

Industries: fishing, handicrafts

Industrial production growth rate: 1.1% (2012 est.)

Labor force: 39,000 (2010 est.)
note: economically active, not including subsistence farmers

Labor force - by occupation: *agriculture:* 15%
industry: 10%
services: 75% (2010)

Unemployment rate: 30.6% (2010 est.)
6.1% (2005)

Unemployment, youth ages 15-24: *total:* 22.5%
male: 21.2%
female: 24.6% (2019 est.)

Budget: *revenues:* 151.2 million (2017 est.)
expenditures: 277.5 million (2017 est.)

Budget surplus (+) or deficit (-): -64.1% (of GDP) (2017 est.)

Public debt: 26.3% of GDP (2017 est.)
22.9% of GDP (2016 est.)

Taxes and other revenues: 76.8% (of GDP) (2017 est.)

Current account balance: $18 million (2017 est.)
$35 million (2016 est.)

Exports: $30 million (2019 est.) note: data are in current year dollars
$20 million (2018 est.) note: data are in current year dollars

Exports - partners: Thailand 53%, Philippines 17%, South Korea 10%, Japan 9% (2019)

Exports - commodities: fish and fish produces, ships, coconut oil, copra (2019)

Imports: $180 million (2019 est.) note: data are in current year dollars
$170 million (2018 est.) note: data are in current year dollars

Imports - partners: China 20%, Fiji 19%, Australia 12%, Taiwan 11%, South Korea 11%, New Zealand 7%, Japan 5% (2019)

Imports - commodities: refined petroleum, netting, raw sugar, rice, poultry meats (2019)

Reserves of foreign exchange and gold: $0 (31 December 2017 est.)
$8.37 million (31 December 2010 est.)

Debt - external: $40.9 million (2016 est.)
$32.3 million (2015 est.)

Exchange rates: Australian dollars (AUD) per US dollar -
1.31 (2017 est.)
1.34 (2016 est.)
1.34 (2015 est.)
1.33 (2014 est.)
1.11 (2013 est.)
note: the Australian dollar circulates as legal tender

ENERGY

Electricity access: *electrification - total population:* 100% (2020)

Electricity: *installed generating capacity:* 11,000 kW (2020 est.)
consumption: 25.137 million kWh (2019 est.)
exports: 0 kWh (2020 est.)
imports: 0 kWh (2020 est.)
transmission/distribution losses: 4.7 million kWh (2019 est.)

Electricity generation sources: *fossil fuels:* 84.9% of total installed capacity (2020 est.)
solar: 15.1% of total installed capacity (2020 est.)

Petroleum: *total petroleum production:* 0 bbl/day (2021 est.)
refined petroleum consumption: 500 bbl/day (2019 est.)

Refined petroleum products - imports: 420 bbl/day (2015 est.)

Carbon dioxide emissions: 76,000 metric tonnes of CO_2 (2019 est.)
from petroleum and other liquids: 76,000 metric tonnes of CO_2 (2019 est.)

Energy consumption per capita: 9.335 million Btu/person (2019 est.)

COMMUNICATIONS

Telephones - fixed lines: *total subscriptions:* 33 (2020 est.)
subscriptions per 100 inhabitants: (2020 est.) less than 1

Telephones - mobile cellular: *total subscriptions:* 54,661 (2020 est.)
subscriptions per 100 inhabitants: 46 (2020 est.)

Telecommunication systems: *general assessment:* generally good national and international service; wireline service available on Tarawa and Kiritimati (Christmas Island); connections to outer islands by HF/VHF radiotelephone; recently formed (mobile network operator) MNO is implementing the first phase of improvements with 3G and 4G upgrades on some islands; islands are connected to each other and the rest of the world via satellite; launch of Kacific-1 in December 2019 will improve telecommunication for Kiribati (2020)
domestic: fixed-line less than 1 per 100 and mobile-cellular approximately 46 per 100 subscriptions (2020)
international: country code - 686; landing point for the Southern Cross NEXT submarine cable system from Australia, 7 Pacific Ocean island countries to the US; satellite earth station - 1 Intelsat (Pacific Ocean) (2019)

Broadcast media: multi-channel TV packages provide access to Australian and US stations; 1 government-operated radio station broadcasts on AM, FM, and shortwave (2017)

Internet country code: .ki

Internet users: *total:* 45,390 (2020 est.)
percent of population: 38% (2020 est.)

Broadband - fixed subscriptions: *total:* 185 (2020 est.)
subscriptions per 100 inhabitants: 0.2 (2020 est.)

TRANSPORTATION

National air transport system: *number of registered air carriers:* 2 (2020)
inventory of registered aircraft operated by air carriers: 8
annual passenger traffic on registered air carriers: 66,567 (2018)

Civil aircraft registration country code prefix: T3

Airports: *total:* 19 (2021)

Airports - with paved runways: *total:* 4
1,524 to 2,437 m: 4 (2021)

Airports - with unpaved runways: *total:* 15
914 to 1,523 m: 10
under 914 m: 5 (2021)

Roadways: *total:* 670 km (2017)

Waterways: 5 km (2012) (small network of canals in Line Islands)

Merchant marine: *total:* 88
by type: bulk carrier 3, general cargo 35, oil tanker 12, other 38 (2021)

Ports and terminals: *major seaport(s):* Betio (Tarawa Atoll), Canton Island, English Harbor

MILITARY AND SECURITY

Military and security forces: no regular military forces; Kiribati Police and Prison Service (Ministry of Justice)

Military - note: defense assistance is provided by Australia and NZ
Kiribati has a "shiprider" agreement with the US, which allows local maritime law enforcement officers to embark on US Coast Guard (USCG) and US Navy (USN) vessels, including to board and search vessels suspected of violating laws or regulations within Kiribati's designated exclusive economic zone (EEZ) or on the high seas; "shiprider" agreements also enable USCG personnel and USN vessels with embarked USCG law enforcement personnel to work with host nations to protect critical regional resources (2022)

TRANSNATIONAL ISSUES

Disputes - international: none identified

KOREA, NORTH

INTRODUCTION

Background: The first recorded kingdom (Choson) on the Korean Peninsula dates from approximately 2300 B.C. Over the subsequent centuries, three main kingdoms - Kogoryo, Paekche, and Silla - were established on the Peninsula. By the 5th century A.D., Kogoryo emerged as the most powerful, with control over much of the Peninsula, as well as part of Manchuria (modern-day northeast China). However, Silla allied with the Chinese to create the first unified Korean state in the late 7th century (688). Following the

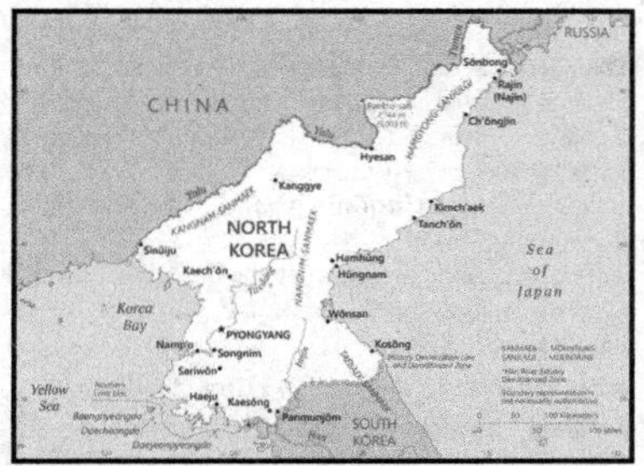

collapse of Silla in the 9th century, Korea was unified under the Koryo (Goryeo; 918-1392) and the Chosen (Joseon; 1392-1910) dynasties.

Korea became the object of intense imperialistic rivalry between the Chinese (its traditional benefactor), Japanese, and Russian empires in the latter half of the 19th and early 20th centuries. Following the Sino-Japanese War (1894-95) and the Russo-Japanese War (1904-1905), Korea was occupied by Imperial Japan. In 1910, Japan formally annexed the entire peninsula. After World War II, Korea was split with the northern half coming under Soviet-sponsored communist control. After the Korean War (1950-53), during which North Korea failed to conquer UN-backed South Korea (Republic of Korea, ROK), North Korea (Democratic People's Republic of Korea, DPRK), under its founder President KIM Il Sung, adopted a policy of *juche* ("self-reliance") as a check against outside influence. North Korea demonized the US as the ultimate threat to its social system through state-funded propaganda, and molded political, economic, and military policies around the core ideological objective of eventual unification of Korea under Pyongyang's control. KIM Il Sung's son, KIM Jong Il, was officially designated as his father's successor in 1980, assuming a growing political and managerial role until the elder KIM's death in 1994. Under KIM Jong Il's reign, North Korea continued developing nuclear weapons and ballistic missiles. KIM Jong Un was publicly unveiled as his father's successor in 2010. Following KIM Jong Il's death in 2011, KIM Jong Un quickly assumed power and has since occupied the regime's highest political and military posts.

After decades of economic mismanagement and resource misallocation, the North since the mid-1990s has faced chronic food shortages and economic stagnation. In recent years, the North's domestic agricultural production has increased, but still falls far short of producing sufficient food to provide for its entire population. Starting in 2002, North Korea began to ease restrictions to allow semi-private markets, but has made few other efforts to meet its goal of improving the overall standard of living. New economic development plans in the 2010s failed to meet government-mandated goals for key industrial sectors, food production, or overall economic performance. In response, the North Korean leader in early 2021 admitted these failures, but vowed to continue "self-reliant" policies.

North Korea has a history of provocative regional military actions and posturing that are of major concern to the international community and have limited North Korea's international engagement, particularly economically. These include proliferation of military-related items; long-range missile development; WMD programs including tests of nuclear devices in 2006, 2009, 2013, 2016, and 2017; and large conventional armed forces. In 2013, North Korea declared a policy of simultaneous development of its nuclear weapons program and economy. In late 2017, KIM Jong Un declared the North's nuclear weapons development complete. In 2018, KIM announced a pivot towards diplomacy, including a re-prioritization of economic development, a pause in missile testing beginning in late 2017, and a refrain from anti-US rhetoric starting in June 2018. Since 2018, KIM has participated in four meetings with Chinese President XI Jinping, three with South Korean President MOON Jae-in, and three with US President TRUMP. Since 2019, North Korea has continued developing its ballistic missile program and issued statements condemning the US, and vowing to further strengthen its military capabilities, including long range missiles and nuclear weapons. North Korea remains one of the world's most isolated and one of Asia's poorest countries.

GEOGRAPHY

Location: Eastern Asia, northern half of the Korean Peninsula bordering the Korea Bay and the Sea of Japan, between China and South Korea

Geographic coordinates: 40 00 N, 127 00 E

Map references: Asia

Area: *total:* 120,538 sq km
land: 120,408 sq km
water: 130 sq km

Area - comparative: slightly larger than Virginia; slightly smaller than Mississippi

Land boundaries: *total:* 1,607 km
border countries (3): China 1,352 km; South Korea 237 km; Russia 18 km

Coastline: 2,495 km

Maritime claims: *territorial sea:* 12 nm
exclusive economic zone: 200 nm
note: military boundary line 50 nm in the Sea of Japan and the exclusive economic zone limit in the Yellow Sea where all foreign vessels and aircraft without permission are banned

Climate: temperate, with rainfall concentrated in summer; long, bitter winters

Terrain: mostly hills and mountains separated by deep, narrow valleys; wide coastal plains in west, discontinuous in east

Elevation: *highest point:* Paektu-san 2,744 m
lowest point: Sea of Japan 0 m
mean elevation: 600 m

Natural resources: coal, iron ore, limestone, magnesite, graphite, copper, zinc, lead, precious metals, hydropower

Land use: *agricultural land:* 21.8% (2018 est.)
arable land: 19.5% (2018 est.)
permanent crops: 1.9% (2018 est.)
permanent pasture: 0.4% (2018 est.)
forest: 46% (2018 est.)
other: 32.2% (2018 est.)

Irrigated land: 14,600 sq km (2012)

Population distribution: population concentrated in the plains and lowlands; least populated regions are the mountainous provinces adjacent to the Chinese border; largest concentrations are in the western provinces, particularly the municipal district of Pyongyang, and around Hungnam and Wonsan in the east

Natural hazards: late spring droughts often followed by severe flooding; occasional typhoons during the early fall
volcanism: P'aektu-san (2,744 m) (also known as Baitoushan, Baegdu, or Changbaishan), on the Chinese border, is considered historically active

Geography - note: strategic location bordering China, South Korea, and Russia; mountainous interior is isolated and sparsely populated

PEOPLE AND SOCIETY

Population: 25,955,138 (2022 est.)

Nationality: *noun:* Korean(s)
adjective: Korean

Ethnic groups: racially homogeneous; there is a small Chinese community and a few ethnic Japanese

Languages: Korean
major-language sample(s):
월드 팩트북, 필수적인 기본 정보 제공처
(Korean)

Religions: traditionally Buddhist and Confucian, some Christian and syncretic Chondogyo (Religion of the Heavenly Way)
note: autonomous religious activities now almost nonexistent; government-sponsored religious groups exist to provide illusion of religious freedom

Age structure: *0-14 years:* 20.33% (male 2,680,145/female 2,571,334)
15-24 years: 14.39% (male 1,873,814/female 1,842,269)
25-54 years: 43.77% (male 5,671,900/female 5,633,861)
55-64 years: 11.77% (male 1,454,000/female 1,585,830)
65 years and over: 9.75% (male 878,176/female 1,640,031) (2021 est.)

Dependency ratios: *total dependency ratio:* 41.2
youth dependency ratio: 28
elderly dependency ratio: 13.2
potential support ratio: 7.6 (2020 est.)

Median age: *total:* 34.6 years
male: 33.2 years
female: 36.2 years (2020 est.)

Population growth rate: 0.46% (2022 est.)

Birth rate: 14.21 births/1,000 population (2022 est.)

Death rate: 9.53 deaths/1,000 population (2022 est.)

Net migration rate: -0.04 migrant(s)/1,000 population (2022 est.)

Population distribution: population concentrated in the plains and lowlands; least populated regions are the mountainous provinces adjacent to the Chinese border; largest concentrations are in the western provinces, particularly the municipal district of Pyongyang, and around Hungnam and Wonsan in the east

Urbanization: *urban population:* 62.9% of total population (2022)
rate of urbanization: 0.85% annual rate of change (2020-25 est.)

Major urban areas - population: 3.133 million PYONGYANG (capital) (2022)

Sex ratio: *at birth:* 1.06 male(s)/female
0-14 years: 1.04 male(s)/female

15-24 years: 1.02 male(s)/female
25-54 years: 1.01 male(s)/female
55-64 years: 0.92 male(s)/female
65 years and over: 0.33 male(s)/female
total population: 0.95 male(s)/female (2022 est.)

Maternal mortality ratio: 89 deaths/100,000 live births (2017 est.)

Infant mortality rate: *total:* 22.21 deaths/1,000 live births
male: 25.03 deaths/1,000 live births
female: 19.23 deaths/1,000 live births (2022 est.)

Life expectancy at birth: *total population:* 71.77 years
male: 67.88 years
female: 75.88 years (2022 est.)

Total fertility rate: 1.9 children born/woman (2022 est.)

Contraceptive prevalence rate: 70.2% (2017)

Drinking water source: *improved: urban:* 97.8% of population
rural: 89.1% of population
total: 94.5% of population
unimproved: urban: 2.2% of population
rural: 10.9% of population
total: 5.5% of population (2020 est.)

Physicians density: 3.68 physicians/1,000 population (2017)

Sanitation facility access: *improved: urban:* 92.7% of population
rural: 73.1% of population
total: 85.3% of population
unimproved: urban: 7.3% of population
rural: 26.9% of population
total: 14.7% of population (2020 est.)

Obesity - adult prevalence rate: 6.8% (2016)

Alcohol consumption per capita: *total:* 3.61 liters of pure alcohol (2019 est.)
beer: 0.12 liters of pure alcohol (2019 est.)
wine: 0 liters of pure alcohol (2019 est.)
spirits: 3.48 liters of pure alcohol (2019 est.)
other alcohols: 0 liters of pure alcohol (2019 est.)

Tobacco use: *total:* 17.4% (2020 est.)
male: 34.8% (2020 est.)
female: 0% (2020 est.)

Children under the age of 5 years underweight: 9.3% (2017)

Literacy: *definition:* age 15 and over can read and write
total population: 100%
male: 100%
female: 100% (2015)

School life expectancy (primary to tertiary education): *total:* 11 years
male: 11 years
female: 11 years (2015)

ENVIRONMENT

Environment - current issues: water pollution; inadequate supplies of potable water; waterborne disease; deforestation; soil erosion and degradation

Environment - international agreements: *party to:* Antarctic Treaty, Biodiversity, Climate Change, Climate Change-Kyoto Protocol, Climate Change-Paris Agreement, Desertification, Environmental Modification, Hazardous Wastes, Ozone Layer Protection, Ship Pollution, Wetlands
signed, but not ratified: Antarctic-Environmental Protection, Law of the Sea

Air pollutants: *particulate matter emissions:* 30.4 micrograms per cubic meter (2016 est.)
carbon dioxide emissions: 28.28 megatons (2016 est.)
methane emissions: 18.68 megatons (2020 est.)

Climate: temperate, with rainfall concentrated in summer; long, bitter winters

Land use: *agricultural land:* 21.8% (2018 est.)
arable land: 19.5% (2018 est.)
permanent crops: 1.9% (2018 est.)
permanent pasture: 0.4% (2018 est.)
forest: 46% (2018 est.)
other: 32.2% (2018 est.)

Urbanization: *urban population:* 62.9% of total population (2022)
rate of urbanization: 0.85% annual rate of change (2020-25 est.)

Food insecurity: *widespread lack of access: due to low food consumption levels, poor dietary diversity, and economic downturn* - a large portion of the population suffers from low levels of food consumption and very poor dietary diversity; the economic constraints, particularly resulting from the global impact of the COVID-19 pandemic, have increased the population's vulnerability to food insecurity; the food gap is estimated at about 860,000 mt, equivalent to approximately 2-3 months of food use, if this gap is not adequately covered through commercial imports and/or food aid, households could experience a harsh lean period (2022)

Total water withdrawal: *municipal:* 902.8 million cubic meters (2017 est.)
industrial: 1.145 billion cubic meters (2017 est.)
agricultural: 6.61 billion cubic meters (2017 est.)

Total renewable water resources: 77.15 billion cubic meters (2017 est.)

GOVERNMENT

Country name: *conventional long form:* Democratic People's Republic of Korea
conventional short form: North Korea
local long form: Choson-minjujuui-inmin-konghwaguk
local short form: Choson
abbreviation: DPRK
etymology: derived from the Chinese name for Goryeo, which was the Korean dynasty that united the peninsula in the 10th century A.D.; the North Korean name "Choson" means "[Land of the] Morning Calm"

Government type: dictatorship, single-party state; official state ideology of "Juche" or "national self-reliance"

Capital: *name:* Pyongyang
geographic coordinates: 39 01 N, 125 45 E
time difference: UTC+9 (14 hours ahead of Washington, DC, during Standard Time)
time zone note: on 5 May 2018, North Korea reverted to UTC+9, the same time zone as South Korea
etymology: the name translates as "flat land" in Korean

Administrative divisions: 9 provinces (do, singular and plural) and 4 special administration cities (si, singular and plural)
provinces: Chagang, Hambuk (North Hamgyong), Hamnam (South Hamgyong), Hwangbuk (North Hwanghae), Hwangnam (South Hwanghae), Kangwon, P'yongbuk (North Pyongan), P'yongnam (South Pyongan), Ryanggang
special administration cities: Kaesong, Nampo, P'yongyang, Rason
note: P'yongyang is identified as a directly controlled city, while Kaesong, Nampo, and Rason are designated as special cities

Independence: 15 August 1945 (from Japan)

National holiday: Founding of the Democratic People's Republic of Korea (DPRK), 9 September (1948)

Constitution: *history:* previous 1948, 1972; latest adopted 1998 (during KIM Jong-il era)
amendments: proposed by the Supreme People's Assembly (SPA); passage requires more than two-thirds majority vote of the total SPA membership; revised several times, last in 2019

Legal system: civil law system based on the Prussian model; system influenced by Japanese traditions and Communist legal theory

International law organization participation: has not submitted an ICJ jurisdiction declaration; non-party state to the ICCt

Citizenship: *citizenship by birth:* no
citizenship by descent only: at least one parent must be a citizen of North Korea
dual citizenship recognized: no
residency requirement for naturalization: unknown

Suffrage: 17 years of age; universal and compulsory

Executive branch: *chief of state:* State Affairs Commission President KIM Jong Un (since 17 December 2011); note - North Korea revised its constitution in 2019 to define "the Chairman of the State Affairs Commission" as "the supreme leader who represents the state"; functions as the commander-in-chief and chief executive; the specific titles associated with this office have changed multiple times under KIM's tenure, however, KIM Jong Un has been supreme leader since his father's death in 2011
head of government: Supreme People's Assembly President CHOE Ryong Hae (since 11 April 2019); note - functions as the technical head of state and performs related duties, such as receiving ambassadors' credentials (2021)
cabinet: Cabinet or Naegak members appointed by the Supreme People's Assembly except the Minister of People's Armed Forces
elections/appointments: chief of state and premier indirectly elected by the Supreme People's Assembly; election last held on 10 March 2019 (next to be held in March 2024)
election results:
KIM Jong Un reelected unopposed
note: the Korean Workers' Party continues to list deceased leaders KIM Il Sung and KIM Jong Il as Eternal President and Eternal General Secretary respectively

Legislative branch: *description:* unicameral Supreme People's Assembly or Ch'oego Inmin Hoeui (687 seats; members directly elected by majority vote in 2 rounds if needed to serve 5-year terms); note - the Korean Workers' Party selects all candidates
elections: last held on 10 March 2019 (next to be held March 2024)

election results: percent of vote by party - NA; seats by party - KWP 607, KSDP 50, Chondoist Chongu Party 22, General Association of Korean Residents in Japan (Chongryon) 5, religious associations 3; ruling party approves a list of candidates who are elected without opposition; composition as of March 2022 - men 566, women 121, percent of women 17.6%
note: KWP, KSDP, Chondoist Chongu Party, and Chongryon are under the KWP's control; a token number of seats reserved for minor parties

Judicial branch: *highest court(s):* Supreme Court or Central Court (consists of one judge and 2 "People's Assessors" or, for some cases, 3 judges)
judge selection and term of office: judges elected by the Supreme People's Assembly for 5-year terms
subordinate courts: lower provincial courts as determined by the Supreme People's Assembly

Political parties and leaders: *major parties:* Korean Workers' Party or KWP [KIM Jong Un, general secretary]
General Association of Korean Residents in Japan (Chongryon) [HO Chong Man]
minor parties: Chondoist Chongu Party [RI Myong Chol] (under KWP control)
Social Democratic Party or KSDP [PAK Yong Il] (under KWP control)

International organization participation: ARF, FAO, G-77, ICAO, ICRM, IFAD, IFRCS, IHO, IMO, IMSO, IOC, IPU, ISO, ITSO, ITU, NAM, UN, UNCTAD, UNESCO, UNIDO, UNWTO, UPU, WFTU (NGOs), WHO, WIPO, WMO

Diplomatic representation in the US: *chief of mission:* none; North Korea has a Permanent Mission to the UN in New York

Diplomatic representation from the US: *embassy:* none; the Swedish Embassy in Pyongyang represents the US as consular protecting power

Flag description: three horizontal bands of blue (top), red (triple width), and blue; the red band is edged in white; on the hoist side of the red band is a white disk with a red five-pointed star; the broad red band symbolizes revolutionary traditions; the narrow white bands stand for purity, strength, and dignity; the blue bands signify sovereignty, peace, and friendship; the red star represents socialism

National symbol(s): red star, chollima (winged horse); national colors: red, white, blue

National anthem: *name:* "Aegukka" (Patriotic Song)
lyrics/music: PAK Se Yong/KIM Won Gyun
note: adopted 1947; both North Korea's and South Korea's anthems share the same name and have a vaguely similar melody but have different lyrics; the North Korean anthem is also known as "Ach'imun pinnara" (Let Morning Shine)

National heritage: *total World Heritage Sites:* 2 (both cultural)
selected World Heritage Site locales: Koguryo Tombs Complex; Historic Monuments and Sites in Kaesong

ECONOMY

Economic overview: North Korea, one of the world's most centrally directed and least open economies, faces chronic economic problems. Industrial capital stock is nearly beyond repair as a result of decades of mismanagement, underinvestment, shortages of spare parts, and poor maintenance. Corruption and resource misallocation, including show projects, large-scale military spending, and development of its ballistic missile and nuclear programs, severely draws off resources needed for investment and civilian consumption. Industrial and power outputs have stagnated for years at a fraction of pre-1990 levels. Frequent weather-related crop failures aggravated chronic food shortages caused by on-going systemic problems, including a lack of arable land, collective farming practices, poor soil quality, insufficient fertilization, and persistent shortages of tractors and fuel.

The mid 1990s through mid-2000s were marked by severe famine and widespread starvation. Significant food aid was provided by the international community through 2009. Since that time, food assistance has declined significantly. In the last few years, domestic corn and rice production has improved, although domestic production does not fully satisfy demand. A large portion of the population continues to suffer from prolonged malnutrition and poor living conditions. Since 2002, the government has allowed semi-private markets to begin selling a wider range of goods, allowing North Koreans to partially make up for diminished public distribution system rations. It also implemented changes in the management process of communal farms in an effort to boost agricultural output.

In December 2009, North Korea carried out a redenomination of its currency, capping the amount of North Korean won that could be exchanged for the new notes, and limiting the exchange to a one-week window. A concurrent crackdown on markets and foreign currency use yielded severe shortages and inflation, forcing Pyongyang to ease the restrictions by February 2010. In response to the sinking of the South Korean warship Cheonan and the shelling of Yeonpyeong Island in 2010, South Korea's government cut off most aid, trade, and bilateral cooperation activities. In February 2016, South Korea ceased its remaining bilateral economic activity by closing the Kaesong Industrial Complex in response to North Korea's fourth nuclear test a month earlier. This nuclear test and another in September 2016 resulted in two United Nations Security Council Resolutions that targeted North Korea's foreign currency earnings, particularly coal and other mineral exports. Throughout 2017, North Korea's continued nuclear and missile tests led to a tightening of UN sanctions, resulting in full sectoral bans on DPRK exports and drastically limited key imports. Over the last decade, China has been North Korea's primary trading partner.

The North Korean Government continues to stress its goal of improving the overall standard of living, but has taken few steps to make that goal a reality for its populace. In 2016, the regime used two mass mobilizations — one totaling 70 days and another 200 days — to spur the population to increase production and complete construction projects quickly. The regime released a five-year economic development strategy in May 2016 that outlined plans for promoting growth across sectors. Firm political control remains the government's overriding concern, which likely will inhibit formal changes to North Korea's current economic system.

Real GDP (purchasing power parity): $40 billion (2015 est.)
$40 billion (2014 est.)
$40 billion (2013 est.)
note: data are in 2015 US dollars
North Korea does not publish reliable National Income Accounts data; the data shown are derived from purchasing power parity (PPP) GDP estimates that were made by Angus MADDISON in a study conducted for the OECD; his figure for 1999 was extrapolated to 2015 using estimated real growth rates for North Korea's GDP and an inflation factor based on the US GDP deflator; the results were rounded to the nearest $10 billion.

Real GDP growth rate: -1.1% (2015 est.)
1% (2014 est.)
1.1% (2013 est.)

Real GDP per capita: $1,700 (2015 est.)
$1,800 (2014 est.)
$1,800 (2013 est.)
note: data are in 2015 US dollars

GDP (official exchange rate): $28 billion (2013 est.)

Inflation rate (consumer prices): NA

GDP - composition, by sector of origin: *agriculture:* 22.5% (2017 est.)
industry: 47.6% (2017 est.)
services: 29.9% (2017 est.)

GDP - composition, by end use: *exports of goods and services:* 5.9% (2016 est.)
imports of goods and services: -11.1% (2016 est.)

Agricultural products: rice, maize, vegetables, apples, potatoes, cabbages, fruit, sweet potatoes, beans, soybeans

Industries: military products; machine building, electric power, chemicals; mining (coal, iron ore, limestone, magnesite, graphite, copper, zinc, lead, and precious metals), metallurgy; textiles, food processing; tourism

Industrial production growth rate: 1% (2017 est.)

Labor force: 14 million (2014 est.)
note: estimates vary widely

Labor force - by occupation: *agriculture:* 37%
industry: 63% (2008 est.)

Unemployment rate: 25.6% (2013 est.)
25.5% (2012 est.)

Budget: *revenues:* 3.2 billion (2007 est.)
expenditures: 3.3 billion (2007 est.)

Budget surplus (+) or deficit (-): -0.4% (of GDP) (2007 est.)

Taxes and other revenues: 11.4% (of GDP) (2007 est.)
note: excludes earnings from state-operated enterprises

Fiscal year: calendar year

Exports: $222 million (2018)
$4.582 billion (2017 est.)
$2.908 billion (2015 est.)

Exports - partners: China 67%, Suriname 6% (2019)

Exports - commodities: watch components, fake hair, iron alloys, instructional models, tungsten (2019)

Imports: $2.32 billion (2018 est.)
$3.86 billion (2016 est.)

Imports - partners: China 96% (2019)

Imports - commodities: clothing and apparel, soybean oil, rice, wheat products, clocks/watches (2019)

Debt - external: $5 billion (2013 est.)

Exchange rates: North Korean won (KPW) per US dollar (average market rate)
135 (2017 est.)
130 (2016 est.)
130 (2015 est.)
98.5 (2013 est.)
155.5 (2012 est.)

ENERGY

Electricity access: *electrification - total population:* 26% (2019)
electrification - urban areas: 36% (2019)
electrification - rural areas: 11% (2019)

Electricity: *installed generating capacity:* 8.413 million kW (2020 est.)
consumption: 13,930,320,000 kWh (2019 est.)
exports: 0 kWh (2020 est.)
imports: 0 kWh (2020 est.)
transmission/distribution losses: 2.146 billion kWh (2019 est.)

Electricity generation sources: *fossil fuels:* 15.8% of total installed capacity (2020 est.)
solar: 0.1% of total installed capacity (2020 est.)
hydroelectricity: 84.1% of total installed capacity (2020 est.)

Coal: *production:* 16.376 million metric tons (2020 est.)
consumption: 6.698 million metric tons (2020 est.)
exports: 0 metric tons (2020 est.)
imports: 22,000 metric tons (2020 est.)
proven reserves: 600 million metric tons (2019 est.)

Petroleum: *total petroleum production:* 0 bbl/day (2021 est.)
refined petroleum consumption: 20,300 bbl/day (2019 est.)
crude oil and lease condensate exports: 0 bbl/day (2018 est.)
crude oil and lease condensate imports: 10,600 bbl/day (2018 est.)
crude oil estimated reserves: 0 barrels (2021 est.)

Refined petroleum products - production: 11,270 bbl/day (2015 est.)

Refined petroleum products - exports: 0 bbl/day (2015 est.)

Refined petroleum products - imports: 8,260 bbl/day (2015 est.)

Carbon dioxide emissions: 18.465 million metric tonnes of CO2 (2019 est.)
from coal and metallurgical coke: 15.252 million metric tonnes of CO2 (2019 est.)
from petroleum and other liquids: 3.213 million metric tonnes of CO2 (2019 est.)

Energy consumption per capita: 12.61 million Btu/person (2019 est.)

COMMUNICATIONS

Telephones - fixed lines: *total subscriptions:* 1.18 million (2020 est.)
subscriptions per 100 inhabitants: 5 (2020 est.)

Telephones - mobile cellular: *total subscriptions:* 6 million (2020 est.)
subscriptions per 100 inhabitants: 23 (2020 est.)

Telecommunication systems: *general assessment:* following years of isolationism and economic under-achievement, North Korea languishes near the bottom of the world's telecom maturity index alongside Afghanistan and Turkmenistan (who also happen to be struggling under repressive political regimes); the obstacles to building a functioning telecom network are so numerous that a fixed-line segment barely exists; mobile communication is estimated to have eased up slightly to reach 19% in 2021, yet the high cost of ownership coupled with strict censorship makes mobile communications the exclusive domain of senior government officials and diplomats; for those citizens living close to China, it has been possible to obtain Chinese handsets and SIM cards, and to connect to towers (illegally) located just across the border; while this offers access to the outside world and at much lower prices than the state-controlled offerings, the risks are high including steep fines and the possibility of jail time; North Korea has been slightly more effective in building an IT sector and a nascent digital economy on the back of a concerted effort to grow a sizeable, well-trained IT workforce; but even here, its capabilities have been directed more towards nefarious activities such as cyber crime and hacking into Western countries' computer systems; North Korea's determination to put itself offside with the rest of the world in pursuit of its ideology can only lead to tighter controls on communications inside and outside of the country (2022)
domestic: fixed-lines are approximately 5 per 100 and mobile-cellular 23 per 100 persons (2020)
international: country code - 850; satellite earth stations - 2 (1 Intelsat - Indian Ocean, 1 Russian - Indian Ocean region); other international connections through Moscow and Beijing

Broadcast media: no independent media; radios and TVs are pre-tuned to government stations; 4 government-owned TV stations; the Korean Workers' Party owns and operates the Korean Central Broadcasting Station, and the state-run Voice of Korea operates an external broadcast service; the government prohibits listening to and jams foreign broadcasts (2019)

Internet country code: .kp

TRANSPORTATION

National air transport system: *number of registered air carriers:* 1 (2020)
inventory of registered aircraft operated by air carriers: 4
annual passenger traffic on registered air carriers: 103,560 (2018)
annual freight traffic on registered air carriers: 250,000 (2018) mt-km

Civil aircraft registration country code prefix: P

Airports: *total:* 82 (2021)

Airports - with paved runways: *total:* 39
over 3,047 m: 3
2,438 to 3,047 m: 22
1,524 to 2,437 m: 8
914 to 1,523 m: 2
under 914 m: 4 (2021)

Airports - with unpaved runways: *total:* 43
2,438 to 3,047 m: 3
1,524 to 2,437 m: 17
914 to 1,523 m: 15
under 914 m: 8 (2021)

Heliports: 23 (2021)

Pipelines: 6 km oil (2013)

Railways: *total:* 7,435 km (2014)
standard gauge: 7,435 km (2014) 1.435-m gauge (5,400 km electrified)
note: figures are approximate; some narrow-gauge railway also exists

Roadways: *total:* 25,554 km (2006)
paved: 724 km (2006)
unpaved: 24,830 km (2006)

Waterways: 2,250 km (2011) (most navigable only by small craft)

Merchant marine: *total:* 264
by type: bulk carrier 8, container ship 5, general cargo 189, oil tanker 33, other 29 (2021)

Ports and terminals: *major seaport(s):* Ch'ongjin, Haeju, Hungnam, Namp'o, Songnim, Sonbong (formerly Unggi), Wonsan

MILITARY AND SECURITY

Military and security forces: Korean People's Army (KPA): KPA Ground Forces, KPA Navy, KPA Air Force and Air Defense Forces, KPA Strategic Forces (missile forces), KPA Special Forces (special operations forces); Security Guard Command (aka Bodyguard Command); Ministry of Social Security (formerly Ministry of Public Security): Border Guards, civil security forces; Ministry of State Security: internal security, investigations (2021)
note 1: the Security Guard Command protects the Kim family, other senior leadership figures, and government facilities
note 2: the North also has a large paramilitary/militia force organized into the Worker Peasant Red Guard and Red Youth Guard; these organizations are present at all levels of government (province, county, ward) and are under the control of the Korean Workers' Party in peacetime, but revert to KPA control in crisis or war; they are often mobilized for domestic projects, such as road building and agricultural support

Military expenditures: between 2010 and 2019, military expenditures accounted for an estimated 20-25% of North Korea's GDP annually; North Korea in the 2010s and 2020s has increasingly relied on illicit activities — including cybercrime — to generate revenue for its weapons of mass destruction and ballistic missile programs to evade US and UN sanctions

Military and security service personnel strengths: information varies widely; estimated 1.15 million active troops (950,000 Army; 120,000 Air Force; 60,000 Navy; 10,000 Strategic Missile Forces); estimated 200,000 internal security forces (2022)

Military equipment inventories and acquisitions: the KPA is equipped with older weapon systems originally acquired from the former Soviet Union, Russia, and China, as well as some domestically-produced equipment; North Korea manufactures copies and provides some upgrades to the older foreign weapon systems; it also produces a diverse array of military hardware, including small arms, munitions, light armored vehicles, tanks, naval vessels and submarines, and some advanced weapons systems, such as ballistic missiles (2021)
note: since 2006, the UN Security Council has passed nearly a dozen resolutions sanctioning North Korea for developing nuclear weapons and related activities, starting with Resolution 1718, which condemned the North's first nuclear test and placed sanctions on the supply of heavy weaponry (including tanks, armored combat vehicles, large calibre artillery, combat aircraft, attack helicopters, warships, and missiles and missile launchers), missile technology and material, and select luxury goods; additional resolutions have expanded to include all arms, including small arms and light weapons; the US and other countries have also imposed unilateral sanctions

Military service age and obligation: 17 years of age for compulsory military service for men and women;

service obligation 10 years for men, 5 years for women (some information indicates service for men was reduced in 2021 to 7-8 years) (2022)
note: the bulk of the KPA is made up of conscripts; as many as 20% of North Korean males between the ages of 16 and 54 are in the military at a given time and possibly up to 30 percent of males between the ages of 18 and 27, not counting the reserves or paramilitary units

Military - note: in addition to the invasion of South Korea and the subsequent Korean War (1950-53), North Korea from the 1960s to the 1980s launched a considerable number of limited military and subversive actions against South Korea using special forces and terrorist tactics; including aggressive skirmishes along the DMZ, overt attempts to assassinate South Korean leaders, kidnappings, the bombing of an airliner, and a failed effort in 1968 to foment an insurrection and conduct a guerrilla war in the South with more than 100 seaborne commandos; from the 1990s until 2010, the North lost two submarines and a semi-submersible boat attempting to insert infiltrators into the South (1996, 1998) and provoked several engagements in the Northwest Islands area along the disputed Northern Limit Line (NLL), including naval skirmishes between patrol boats in 1999 and 2002, the torpedoing and sinking of a South Korean Navy corvette in 2010, and the bombardment of a South Korean Marine Corps installation on Yeonpyeong Island, also in 2010; since 2010, further minor incidents continue to occur periodically along the DMZ, where both the KPA and the South Korean military maintain large numbers of troops

in 2018, North Korea and South Korea signed a tension reduction agreement known as the Comprehensive Military Agreement (CMA), which established land, sea, and air buffer zones along the DMZ and the NLL; implementation of the CMA required the removal of some land mines and guard posts; the efforts led to a reduction of tension in the DMZ, but as of 2022 North Korea had failed to uphold much of its side of the agreement

the KPA was founded in 1948; Kim Jong Un is the KPA supreme commander, while operational control of the armed forces resides in the General Staff Department (GSD), which reports directly to Kim; the GSD maintains overall control of all military forces and is charged with turning Kim's directives into operational military orders; the Ministry of National Defense (MND) is responsible for administrative control of the military and external relations with foreign militaries

as of 2022, North Korea's growing ballistic missile program included close- (CRBM), short- (SRBM), medium- (MRBM), intermediate- (IRBM), and intercontinental- (ICBM) range ballistic missiles; the North received its first ballistic missiles, short-range FROGs (free rocket over ground), from the Soviet Union in the 1960s, but its modern ballistic missile program is generally thought to date back to the mid-1970s when it received a Soviet Scud-class missile, likely from Egypt; the North reverse-engineered the missile and developed an indigenously built version in 1984; it flight-tested its first Scud-based medium-range Nodong missile in 1990, and probably began development of the multi-stage Taepodong missiles around this time as well; the North revealed its first road-mobile ICBM in 2012 and conducted the first test of an ICBM-class system in 2017; it conducted additional ICBM tests in 2022 (2022)

TRANSNATIONAL ISSUES

Disputes - international: *North Korea-China:* risking arrest, imprisonment, and deportation, tens of thousands of North Koreans cross into China to escape famine, economic privation, and political oppression; North Korea and China dispute the sovereignty of certain islands in Yalu and Tumen Rivers

North Korea-Japan: North Korea supports South Korea in rejecting Japan's claim to Liancourt Rocks (Tok-do/Take-shima)

North Korea-South Korea: Military Demarcation Line within the 4-km-wide Demilitarized Zone has separated North from South Korea since 1953; periodic incidents in the Yellow Sea with South Korea which claims the Northern Limiting Line as a maritime boundary

Refugees and internally displaced persons: *IDPs:* undetermined (2021)

Trafficking in persons: *current situation:* North Korea is a source country for men, women, and children who are subjected to forced labor, forced marriage, and sex trafficking; in the recent past, many North Korean women and girls lured by promises of food, jobs, and freedom migrated to China illegally to escape poor social and economic conditions only to be forced into prostitution, marriage, or exploitative labor arrangements; North Koreans do not have a choice in the work the government assigns them and are not free to change jobs at will; many North Korean workers recruited to work abroad under bilateral contracts with foreign governments are subjected to forced labor and reportedly face government reprisals if they try to escape or complain to outsiders; thousands of North Koreans, including children, are subjected to forced labor in prison camps
tier rating: Tier 3 — the government of North Korea does not fully meet the minimum standards for the elimination of trafficking and is not making significant efforts to do so; during this reporting period there was a government policy or pattern of forced labor of adults and children in prison camps, labor training centers, and through its imposition of forced labor conditions on North Korean overseas contract workers; proceeds from state-sponsored forced labor fund government functions and illicit activities; the government has made no effort to address human trafficking (2020)

Illicit drugs: at present there is insufficient information to determine the current level of involvement of government officials in the production or trafficking of illicit drugs, but for years, from the 1970s into the 2000s, citizens of North Korea, many of them diplomatic employees of the government, were apprehended abroad while trafficking in narcotics; police investigations in Taiwan, Japan and Australia during that period have linked North Korea to large illicit shipments of heroin and methamphetamine

KOREA, SOUTH

INTRODUCTION

Background: The first recorded kingdom (Choson) on the Korean Peninsula dates from approximately 2300 B.C. Over the subsequent centuries, three main kingdoms - Kogoryo, Paekche, and Silla - were established on the Peninsula. By the 5th century A.D., Kogoryo emerged as the most powerful, with control over much of the Peninsula, as well as part of Manchuria (modern-day northeast China). However, Silla allied with the Chinese to create the first unified Korean state in the late 7th century (688). Following the collapse of Silla in the 9th century, Korea was unified under the Koryo (Goryeo; 918-1392) and the Chosen (Joseon; 1392-1910) dynasties.

Korea became the object of intense imperialistic rivalry between the Chinese (its traditional benefactor), Japanese, and Russian empires in the latter half of the 19th and early 20th centuries. Following the Sino-Japanese War (1894-95) and the Russo-Japanese War (1904-1905), Korea was occupied by Imperial Japan. In 1910, Tokyo formally annexed the entire Peninsula. Korea regained its independence following Japan's surrender to the US and its allies in 1945. After World War II, a democratic government (Republic of Korea, ROK) was set up in the southern half of the Korean Peninsula while a communist-style government was installed in the north (North Korea; aka Democratic People's Republic of Korea, DPRK). During the Korean War (1950-53), US troops and UN forces fought alongside ROK soldiers to defend South Korea from a North Korean invasion supported by communist China and the Soviet Union. A 1953 armistice split the Peninsula along a demilitarized zone at about the 38th parallel. PARK Chung-hee took over leadership of the country in a 1961 coup. During his regime from 1961 to 1979, South Korea achieved rapid economic growth, with per capita income rising to roughly 17 times the level of North Korea in 1979.

PARK was assassinated in 1979, and subsequent years were marked by political turmoil and continued authoritarian rule as the country's pro-democracy movement grew. South Korea held its first free presidential election under a revised democratic constitution in 1987, with former South Korean Army general ROH Tae-woo winning a close race. In 1993, KIM Young-sam (1993-98) became the first civilian president of South Korea's new democratic era. President KIM Dae-jung (1998-2003) won the Nobel Peace Prize in 2000 for his contributions to South Korean democracy and his "Sunshine Policy" of engagement with North Korea. President PARK Geun-hye, daughter of former South Korean President PARK Chung-hee, took office in February 2013 as South Korea's first female leader. In December 2016, the National Assembly passed an impeachment motion against President PARK over her alleged involvement in a corruption and influence-peddling scandal, immediately suspending her presidential authorities. The impeachment was upheld in March 2017, triggering an early presidential election in May 2017 won by MOON Jae-in.

South Korea hosted the Winter Olympic and Paralympic Games in February 2018, in which North Korea also participated. Discord with North Korea has permeated inter-Korean relations for much of the past decade, highlighted by North Korea's attacks on a South Korean ship and island in 2010, the exchange of artillery fire across the DMZ in 2015, and multiple nuclear and missile tests in 2016 and 2017. North Korea's participation in the Winter Olympics, dispatch of a senior delegation to Seoul, and three inter-Korean summits in 2018 appear to have ushered in a temporary period of respite, buoyed by the historic US-North Korea summits in 2018 and 2019. Nevertheless, relations were stagnant into early 2022.

GEOGRAPHY

Location: Eastern Asia, southern half of the Korean Peninsula bordering the Sea of Japan and the Yellow Sea

Geographic coordinates: 37 00 N, 127 30 E

Map references: Asia

Area: *total:* 99,720 sq km
land: 96,920 sq km
water: 2,800 sq km

Area - comparative: slightly smaller than Pennsylvania; slightly larger than Indiana

Land boundaries: *total:* 237 km
border countries (1): North Korea 237 km

Coastline: 2,413 km

Maritime claims: *territorial sea:* 12 nm; between 3 nm and 12 nm in the Korea Strait
contiguous zone: 24 nm
exclusive economic zone: 200 nm
continental shelf: not specified

Climate: temperate, with rainfall heavier in summer than winter; cold winters

Terrain: mostly hills and mountains; wide coastal plains in west and south

Elevation: *highest point:* Halla-san 1,950 m
lowest point: Sea of Japan 0 m
mean elevation: 282 m

Natural resources: coal, tungsten, graphite, molybdenum, lead, hydropower potential

Land use: *agricultural land:* 18.1% (2018 est.)
arable land: 15.3% (2018 est.)
permanent crops: 2.2% (2018 est.)
permanent pasture: 0.6% (2018 est.)
forest: 63.9% (2018 est.)
other: 18% (2018 est.)

Irrigated land: 7,780 sq km (2012)

Population distribution: with approximately 70% of the country considered mountainous, the country's population is primarily concentrated in the lowland areas, where density is quite high; Gyeonggi Province in the northwest, which surrounds the capital of Seoul and contains the port of Incheon, is the most densely populated province; Gangwon in the northeast is the least populated

Natural hazards: occasional typhoons bring high winds and floods; low-level seismic activity common in southwest
volcanism: Halla (1,950 m) is considered historically active although it has not erupted in many centuries

Geography - note: strategic location on Korea Strait; about 3,000 mostly small and uninhabited islands lie off the western and southern coasts

PEOPLE AND SOCIETY

Population: 51,844,834 (2022 est.)

Nationality: *noun:* Korean(s)
adjective: Korean

Ethnic groups: homogeneous

Languages: Korean, English (widely taught in elementary, junior high, and high school)
major-language sample(s):
월드 팩트북, 필수적인 기본 정보 제공처
(Korean)

Religions: Protestant 19.7%, Buddhist 15.5%, Catholic 7.9%, none 56.9% (2015 est.)
note: many people also carry on at least some Confucian traditions and practices

Age structure: *0-14 years:* 12.02% (male 3,191,584/female 3,025,029)
15-24 years: 10.75% (male 2,900,013/female 2,658,057)
25-54 years: 44.83% (male 12,106,860/female 11,077,642)
55-64 years: 15.66% (male 3,958,718/female 4,142,322)
65 years and over: 16.74% (male 3,766,138/female 4,888,799) (2020 est.)

Dependency ratios: *total dependency ratio:* 39.5
youth dependency ratio: 17.5
elderly dependency ratio: 22
potential support ratio: 4.5 (2020 est.)

Median age: *total:* 43.2 years
male: 41.6 years
female: 45 years (2020 est.)

Population growth rate: 0.24% (2022 est.)

Birth rate: 6.92 births/1,000 population (2022 est.)

Death rate: 7.12 deaths/1,000 population (2022 est.)

Net migration rate: 2.63 migrant(s)/1,000 population (2022 est.)

Population distribution: with approximately 70% of the country considered mountainous, the country's population is primarily concentrated in the lowland areas, where density is quite high; Gyeonggi Province in the northwest, which surrounds the capital of Seoul and contains the port of Incheon, is the most densely populated province; Gangwon in the northeast is the least populated

Urbanization: *urban population:* 81.4% of total population (2022)
rate of urbanization: 0.31% annual rate of change (2020-25 est.)

Major urban areas - population: 9.976 million SEOUL (capital), 3.468 million Busan, 2.834 million Incheon, 2.185 million Daegu (Taegu), 1.573 million Daejon (Taejon), 1.526 million Gwangju (Kwangju) (2022)

Sex ratio: *at birth:* 1.05 male(s)/female
0-14 years: 1.05 male(s)/female
15-24 years: 1.09 male(s)/female
25-54 years: 1.11 male(s)/female
55-64 years: 0.95 male(s)/female
65 years and over: 0.6 male(s)/female
total population: 1.01 male(s)/female (2022 est.)

Mother's mean age at first birth: 32.2 years (2019 est.)

Maternal mortality ratio: 11 deaths/100,000 live births (2017 est.)

Infant mortality rate: *total:* 2.87 deaths/1,000 live births
male: 3.08 deaths/1,000 live births
female: 2.64 deaths/1,000 live births (2022 est.)

Life expectancy at birth: *total population:* 82.97 years
male: 79.88 years
female: 86.24 years (2022 est.)

Total fertility rate: 1.1 children born/woman (2022 est.)

Contraceptive prevalence rate: 82.3% (2018)
note: percent of women aged 20-49

Drinking water source: *improved: total:* 99.9% of population
unimproved: total: 0.1% of population (2020 est.)

Current health expenditure: 8.2% of GDP (2019)

Physicians density: 2.48 physicians/1,000 population (2019)

Hospital bed density: 12.4 beds/1,000 population (2018)

Sanitation facility access: *improved: total:* 99.9% of population
unimproved: total: 0.1% of population (2020 est.)

Major infectious diseases: *respiratory diseases:* Covid-19 (see note) (2020)
note: a novel coronavirus is causing an outbreak of respiratory illness (COVID-19) in South Korea; as of 18 August 2022, South Korea has reported a total of 21,861,296 cases of COVID-19 or 42,640.22 cumulative cases of COVID-19 per 100,000 population with a total of 25,813 cumulative deaths or a rate of 50.34 cumulative deaths per 100,000 population; as of 17 August 2022, 87.01% of the population has received at least one dose of COVID-19 vaccine

Obesity - adult prevalence rate: 4.7% (2016)

Alcohol consumption per capita: *total:* 7.74 liters of pure alcohol (2019 est.)
beer: 1.72 liters of pure alcohol (2019 est.)
wine: 0.15 liters of pure alcohol (2019 est.)

spirits: 0.22 liters of pure alcohol (2019 est.)
other alcohols: 5.66 liters of pure alcohol (2019 est.)

Tobacco use: *total:* 20.8% (2020 est.)
male: 35.7% (2020 est.)
female: 5.9% (2020 est.)

Education expenditures: 4.5% of GDP (2018 est.)

School life expectancy (primary to tertiary education): *total:* 17 years
male: 17 years
female: 16 years (2019)

Unemployment, youth ages 15-24: *total:* 10.3%
male: 11%
female: 9.7% (2020 est.)

ENVIRONMENT

Environment - current issues: air pollution in large cities; acid rain; water pollution from the discharge of sewage and industrial effluents; drift net fishing; solid waste disposal; transboundary air pollution from China

Environment - international agreements: *party to:* Antarctic-Environmental Protection, Antarctic-Marine Living Resources, Antarctic Treaty, Biodiversity, Climate Change, Climate Change-Kyoto Protocol, Climate Change-Paris Agreement, Comprehensive Nuclear Test Ban, Desertification, Endangered Species, Environmental Modification, Hazardous Wastes, Law of the Sea, Marine Dumping-London Convention, Marine Dumping-London Protocol, Nuclear Test Ban, Ozone Layer Protection, Ship Pollution, Tropical Timber 2006, Wetlands, Whaling
signed, but not ratified: none of the selected agreements

Air pollutants: *particulate matter emissions:* 24.57 micrograms per cubic meter (2016 est.)
carbon dioxide emissions: 620.3 megatons (2016 est.)
methane emissions: 30.28 megatons (2020 est.)

Climate: temperate, with rainfall heavier in summer than winter; cold winters

Land use: *agricultural land:* 18.1% (2018 est.)
arable land: 15.3% (2018 est.)
permanent crops: 2.2% (2018 est.)
permanent pasture: 0.6% (2018 est.)
forest: 63.9% (2018 est.)
other: 18% (2018 est.)

Urbanization: *urban population:* 81.4% of total population (2022)
rate of urbanization: 0.31% annual rate of change (2020-25 est.)

Revenue from forest resources: *forest revenues:* 0.01% of GDP (2018 est.)

Revenue from coal: *coal revenues:* 0% of GDP (2018 est.)

Waste and recycling: *municipal solid waste generated annually:* 18,218,975 tons (2014 est.)
municipal solid waste recycled annually: 10,567,006 tons (2014 est.)
percent of municipal solid waste recycled: 58% (2014 est.)

Total water withdrawal: *municipal:* 6.672 billion cubic meters (2017 est.)
industrial: 4.45 billion cubic meters (2017 est.)
agricultural: 15.96 billion cubic meters (2017 est.)

Total renewable water resources: 69.7 billion cubic meters (2017 est.)

GOVERNMENT

Country name: *conventional long form:* Republic of Korea
conventional short form: South Korea
local long form: Taehan-min'guk
local short form: Han'guk
abbreviation: ROK
etymology: derived from the Chinese name for Goryeo, which was the Korean dynasty that united the peninsula in the 10th century A.D.; the South Korean name "Han'guk" derives from the long form, "Taehan-min'guk," which is itself a derivation from "Daehan-je'guk," which means "the Great Empire of the Han"; "Han" refers to the "Sam'han" or the "Three Han Kingdoms" (Goguryeo, Baekje, and Silla from the Three Kingdoms Era, 1st-7th centuries A.D.)

Government type: presidential republic

Capital: *name:* Seoul; note - Sejong, located some 120 km (75 mi) south of Seoul, serves as an administrative capital for segments of the South Korean Government
geographic coordinates: 37 33 N, 126 59 E
time difference: UTC+9 (14 hours ahead of Washington, DC, during Standard Time)
etymology: the name originates from the Korean word meaning "capital city" and which is believed to be derived from Seorabeol, the name of the capital of the ancient Korean Kingdom of Silla

Administrative divisions: 9 provinces (do, singular and plural), 6 metropolitan cities (gwangyeoksi, singular and plural), 1 special city (teugbyeolsi), and 1 special self-governing city (teukbyeoljachisi)
provinces: Chungcheongbuk-do (North Chungcheong), Chungcheongnam-do (South Chungcheong), Gangwon-do, Gyeongsangbuk-do (North Gyeongsang), Gyeonggi-do, Gyeongsangnam-do (South Gyeongsang), Jeju-do (Jeju), Jeollabuk-do (North Jeolla), Jeollanam-do (South Jeolla)
metropolitan cities: Busan (Pusan), Daegu (Taegu), Daejeon (Taejon), Gwangju (Kwangju), Incheon (Inch'on), Ulsan
special city: Seoul
special self-governing city: Sejong

Independence: 15 August 1945 (from Japan)

National holiday: Liberation Day, 15 August (1945)

Constitution: *history:* several previous; latest passed by National Assembly 12 October 1987, approved in referendum 28 October 1987, effective 25 February 1988
amendments: proposed by the president or by majority support of the National Assembly membership; passage requires at least two-thirds majority vote by the Assembly membership, approval in a referendum by more than one half of the votes by more than one half of eligible voters, and promulgation by the president; amended several times, last in 1987

Legal system: mixed legal system combining European civil law, Anglo-American law, and Chinese classical thought

International law organization participation: has not submitted an ICJ jurisdiction declaration; accepts ICCt jurisdiction

Citizenship: *citizenship by birth:* no
citizenship by descent only: at least one parent must be a citizen of South Korea
dual citizenship recognized: no
residency requirement for naturalization: 5 years

Suffrage: 18 years of age; universal; note - the voting age was lowered from 19 to 18 beginning with the 2020 national election

Executive branch: *chief of state:* President YOON Suk Yeol (since 10 May 2022); the president is both chief of state and head of government; Prime Minister HAN Deok-Soo (since 21 May 2022) serves as the principal executive assistant to the president, similar to the role of a vice president
head of government: President YOON Suk Yeol (since 10 May 2022)
cabinet: State Council appointed by the president on the prime minister's recommendation
elections/appointments: president directly elected by simple majority popular vote for a single 5-year term; election last held on 9 March 2022 (next to be held March 2027); prime minister appointed by president with consent of National Assembly
election results: *2022:* YOON Suk-yeol (PPP) 48.56%, LEE Jae-myung (DP) 47.83% (note - voter turnout 77.1%)
2017: MOON Jae-in (DP) 41.09%, HONG joon-pyo (Liberty Korea Party) 24.04%, AHN Cheol-soo (PP) 21.42%

Legislative branch: *description:* unicameral National Assembly or Kuk Hoe (300 seats statutory, current 295; 253 members directly elected in single-seat constituencies by simple majority vote and 47 directly elected in a single national constituency by proportional representation vote; members serve 4-year terms)
elections: last held on 15 April 2020 (next to be held on 10 April 2024)
election results: percent of vote by party - NA; seats by party - DP/Together Citizens Party 180, United Future Party (now PPP) 103, JP 6, ODP 3, PP 3, independent 5; composition as of April 2022 - men 240, women 55, percent of women 18.6%

Judicial branch: *highest court(s):* Supreme Court (consists of a chief justice and 13 justices); Constitutional Court (consists of a court head and 8 justices)
judge selection and term of office: Supreme Court chief justice appointed by the president with the consent of the National Assembly; other justices appointed by the president upon the recommendation of the chief justice and consent of the National Assembly; position of the chief justice is a 6-year nonrenewable term; other justices serve 6-year renewable terms; Constitutional Court justices appointed - 3 by the president, 3 by the National Assembly, and 3 by the Supreme Court chief justice; court head serves until retirement at age 70, while other justices serve 6-year renewable terms with mandatory retirement at age 65
subordinate courts: High Courts; District Courts; Branch Courts (organized under the District Courts); specialized courts for family and administrative issues

Political parties and leaders: Basic Income Party [SHIN Ji-hye]
Democratic Party of Korea or DPK [LEE Jae-myung] (renamed from Minjoo Party of Korea or MPK in October 2016; formerly New Politics Alliance for

Democracy or NPAD, which was a merger of the Democratic Party or DP (formerly DUP) [KIM Han-gil] and the New Political Vision Party or NPVP [AHN Cheol-soo] in March 2014; includes the former Open Democratic Party [CHOI Kong-wook], which merged with the DP in January 2022; also includes the Together Citizens' Party or Platform Party [WOO Hee-jong, CHOI Bae-geun], which merged with the DP in May 2022)
Justice Party or JP [YEO Young-kug]
People Power Party or PPP [LEE Jun-seok] (renamed from United Future Party in September 2020, formerly Liberty Korea Party)
People's Party or PP [AHN Cheol-soo]
Transition Korea [CHO Jung-hun]
note: the Democratic (Minjoo) Party is South Korea's largest party and its main progressive party; the People Power Party (PPP) is a conservative grouping and is South Korea's second-largest party; the PPP and its predecessor parties have controlled the National Assembly for all but nine of the 33 years since the 1987 Constitution went into effect

International organization participation: ADB, AfDB (nonregional member), APEC, Arctic Council (observer), ARF, ASEAN (dialogue partner), Australia Group, BIS, CD, CICA, CP, EAS, EBRD, FAO, FATF, G-20, IADB, IAEA, IBRD, ICAO, ICC (national committees), ICCt, ICRM, IDA, IEA, IFAD, IFC, IFRCS, IHO, ILO, IMF, IMO, IMSO, Interpol, IOC, IOM, IPU, ISO, ITSO, ITU, ITUC (NGOs), LAIA (observer), MIGA, MINURSO, MINUSTAH, NEA, NSG, OAS (observer), OECD, OPCW, OSCE (partner), Pacific Alliance (observer), Paris Club (associate), PCA, PIF (partner), SAARC (observer), SICA (observer), UN, UNAMID, UNCTAD, UNESCO, UNHCR, UNHRC, UNIDO, UNIFIL, UNISFA, UNMIL, UNMISS, UNMOGIP, UNOCI, UNWTO, UPU, Wassenaar Arrangement, WCO, WHO, WIPO, WMO, WTO, ZC

Diplomatic representation in the US: *chief of mission:* Ambassador (Appointed) CHO Tae-yong (since 11 June 2022)
chancery: 2450 Massachusetts Avenue NW, Washington, DC 20008
telephone: [1] (202) 939-5600
FAX: [1] (202) 797-0595
email address and website:
generalusa@mofa.go.kr
https://overseas.mofa.go.kr/us-en/index.do
consulate(s) general: Anchorage (AK), Atlanta, Boston, Chicago, Dallas (TX), Hagatna (Guam), Honolulu, Houston, Los Angeles, New York, San Francisco, Seattle, Washington DC

Diplomatic representation from the US: *chief of mission:* Ambassador Philip S. GOLDBERG (since 29 July 2022)
embassy: 188 Sejong-daero, Jongno-gu, Seoul
mailing address: 9600 Seoul Place, Washington, DC 20521-9600
telephone: [82] (2) 397-4114
FAX: [82] (2) 397-4101
email address and website:
seoulinfoACS@state.gov
https://kr.usembassy.gov/
consulate(s): Busan

Flag description: white with a red (top) and blue yin-yang symbol in the center; there is a different black trigram from the ancient I Ching (Book of Changes) in each corner of the white field; the South Korean national flag is called Taegukki; white is a traditional Korean color and represents peace and purity; the blue section represents the negative cosmic forces of the yin, while the red symbolizes the opposite positive forces of the yang; each trigram (kwae) denotes one of the four universal elements, which together express the principle of movement and harmony

National symbol(s): taegeuk (yin yang symbol), Hibiscus syriacus (Rose of Sharon), Siberian tiger; national colors: red, white, blue, black

National anthem: *name:* "Aegukga" (Patriotic Song)
lyrics/music: YUN Ch'i-Ho or AN Ch'ang-Ho/ AHN Eaktay
note: adopted 1948, well-known by 1910; both North Korea's and South Korea's anthems share the same name and have a vaguely similar melody but have different lyrics

National heritage: *total World Heritage Sites:* 15 (13 cultural, 2 natural)
selected World Heritage Site locales: Jeju Volcanic Island and Lava Tubes (n); Changdeokgung Palace Complex (c); Jongmyo Shrine (c); Seokguram Grotto and Bulguksa Temple (c); Gochang, Hwasun, and Ganghwa Dolmen Sites (c); Gyeongju Historic Areas (c); Namhansanseong (c); Baekje Historic Areas (c); Sansa, Buddhist Mountain Monasteries in Korea (c); Royal Tombs of the Joseon Dynasty (c)

ECONOMY

Economic overview: After emerging from the 1950-53 war with North Korea, South Korea emerged as one of the 20th century's most remarkable economic success stories, becoming a developed, globally connected, high-technology society within decades. In the 1960s, GDP per capita was comparable with levels in the poorest countries in the world. In 2004, South Korea's GDP surpassed one trillion dollars.

Beginning in the 1960s under President PARK Chung-hee, the government promoted the import of raw materials and technology, encouraged saving and investment over consumption, kept wages low, and directed resources to export-oriented industries that remain important to the economy to this day. Growth surged under these policies, and frequently reached double-digits in the 1960s and 1970s. Growth gradually moderated in the 1990s as the economy matured, but remained strong enough to propel South Korea into the ranks of the advanced economies of the OECD by 1997. These policies also led to the emergence of family-owned chaebol conglomerates such as Daewoo, Hyundai, and Samsung, which retained their dominant positions even as the government loosened its grip on the economy amid the political changes of the 1980s and 1990s.

The Asian financial crisis of 1997-98 hit South Korea's companies hard because of their excessive reliance on short-term borrowing, and GDP ultimately plunged by 7% in 1998. South Korea tackled difficult economic reforms following the crisis, including restructuring some chaebols, increasing labor market flexibility, and opening up to more foreign investment and imports. These steps lead to a relatively rapid economic recovery. South Korea also began expanding its network of free trade agreements to help bolster exports, and has since implemented 16 free trade agreements covering 58 countries—including the United State and China—that collectively cover more than three-quarters of global GDP.

In 2017, the election of President MOON Jae-in brought a surge in consumer confidence, in part, because of his successful efforts to increase wages and government spending. These factors combined with an uptick in export growth to drive real GDP growth to more than 3%, despite disruptions in South Korea's trade with China over the deployment of a US missile defense system in South Korea.

In 2018 and beyond, South Korea will contend with gradually slowing economic growth - in the 2-3% range - not uncommon for advanced economies. This could be partially offset by efforts to address challenges arising from its rapidly aging population, inflexible labor market, continued dominance of the chaebols, and heavy reliance on exports rather than domestic consumption. Socioeconomic problems also persist, and include rising inequality, poverty among the elderly, high youth unemployment, long working hours, low worker productivity, and corruption.

Real GDP (purchasing power parity): $2,187,800,000,000 (2020 est.)
$2,208,960,000,000 (2019 est.)
$2,164,810,000,000 (2018 est.)
note: data are in 2017 dollars

Real GDP growth rate: 2.04% (2019 est.)
2.91% (2018 est.)
3.16% (2017 est.)

Real GDP per capita: $42,300 (2020 est.)
$42,700 (2019 est.)
$41,900 (2018 est.)
note: data are in 2017 dollars

GDP (official exchange rate): $1,646,604,000,000 (2019 est.)

Inflation rate (consumer prices): 0.3% (2019 est.)
1.4% (2018 est.)
1.9% (2017 est.)

Credit ratings:

Fitch rating: AA- (2012)

Moody's rating: Aa2 (2015)

Standard & Poors rating: AA (2016)
note: The year refers to the year in which the current credit rating was first obtained.

GDP - composition, by sector of origin: *agriculture:* 2.2% (2017 est.)
industry: 39.3% (2017 est.)
services: 58.3% (2017 est.)

GDP - composition, by end use: *household consumption:* 48.1% (2017 est.)
government consumption: 15.3% (2017 est.)
investment in fixed capital: 31.1% (2017 est.)
investment in inventories: 0% (2017 est.)
exports of goods and services: 43.1% (2017 est.)
imports of goods and services: -37.7% (2017 est.)

Agricultural products: rice, vegetables, cabbages, milk, onions, pork, poultry, eggs, tangerines/mandarins, potatoes

Industries: electronics, telecommunications, automobile production, chemicals, shipbuilding, steel

Industrial production growth rate: 4.6% (2017 est.)

Labor force: 26.839 million (2020 est.)

Labor force - by occupation: *agriculture:* 4.8%
industry: 24.6%
services: 70.6% (2017 est.)

Unemployment rate: 3.76% (2019 est.)
3.85% (2018 est.)

Unemployment, youth ages 15-24: *total:* 10.3%
male: 11%
female: 9.7% (2020 est.)

Population below poverty line: 14.4% (2016 est.)

Gini Index coefficient - distribution of family income: 35.4 (2015 est.)
31.6 (2012 est.)

Household income or consumption by percentage share: *lowest 10%:* 6.8%
highest 10%: 48.5% (2015 est.)

Budget: *revenues:* 357.1 billion (2017 est.)
expenditures: 335.8 billion (2017 est.)

Budget surplus (+) or deficit (-): 1.4% (of GDP) (2017 est.)

Public debt: 39.5% of GDP (2017 est.)
39.9% of GDP (2016 est.)

Taxes and other revenues: 23.2% (of GDP) (2017 est.)

Fiscal year: calendar year

Current account balance: $59.971 billion (2019 est.)
$77.467 billion (2018 est.)

Exports: $606.71 billion (2020 est.) note: data are in current year dollars
$660.51 billion (2019 est.) note: data are in current year dollars
$729.94 billion (2018 est.) note: data are in current year dollars

Exports - partners: China 25%, United States 14%, Vietnam 9%, Hong Kong 6%, Japan 5% (2019)

Exports - commodities: integrated circuits, cars and vehicle parts, refined petroleum, ships, office machinery (2019)

Imports: $540.96 billion (2020 est.) note: data are in current year dollars
$607.54 billion (2019 est.) note: data are in current year dollars
$649.23 billion (2018 est.) note: data are in current year dollars

Imports - partners: China 22%, United States 12%, Japan 9% (2019)

Imports - commodities: crude petroleum, integrated circuits, natural gas, refined petroleum, coal (2019)

Reserves of foreign exchange and gold: $389.2 billion (31 December 2017 est.)
$371.1 billion (31 December 2016 est.)

Debt - external: $457.745 billion (2019 est.)
$435.98 billion (2018 est.)

Exchange rates: South Korean won (KRW) per US dollar -
1,084.65 (2020 est.)
1,189.9 (2019 est.)
1,119.8 (2018 est.)
1,130.95 (2014 est.)
1,052.96 (2013 est.)

ENERGY

Electricity access: *electrification - total population:* 100% (2020)

Electricity: *installed generating capacity:* 135.789 million kW (2020 est.)
consumption: 531.258 billion kWh (2020 est.)
exports: 0 kWh (2020 est.)
imports: 0 kWh (2020 est.)
transmission/distribution losses: 18.61 billion kWh (2020 est.)

Electricity generation sources: *fossil fuels:* 64.8% of total installed capacity (2020 est.)
nuclear: 27.7% of total installed capacity (2020 est.)
solar: 3.3% of total installed capacity (2020 est.)
wind: 0.6% of total installed capacity (2020 est.)
hydroelectricity: 1.3% of total installed capacity (2020 est.)
tide and wave: 0.7% of total installed capacity (2020 est.)
geothermal: 0% of total installed capacity (2020 est.)
biomass and waste: 1.7% of total installed capacity (2020 est.)

Coal: *production:* 16.364 million metric tons (2020 est.)
consumption: 140.579 million metric tons (2020 est.)
exports: 16,000 metric tons (2020 est.)
imports: 123.784 million metric tons (2020 est.)
proven reserves: 326 million metric tons (2019 est.)

Petroleum: *total petroleum production:* 37,400 bbl/day (2021 est.)
refined petroleum consumption: 2,598,700 bbl/day (2019 est.)
crude oil and lease condensate exports: 0 bbl/day (2018 est.)
crude oil and lease condensate imports: 3,034,400 bbl/day (2018 est.)

Refined petroleum products - production: 3.302 million bbl/day (2017 est.)

Refined petroleum products - exports: 1.396 million bbl/day (2017 est.)

Refined petroleum products - imports: 908,800 bbl/day (2017 est.)

Natural gas: *production:* 240.042 million cubic meters (2019 est.)
consumption: 53,419,105,000 cubic meters (2019 est.)
exports: 0 cubic meters (2019 est.)
imports: 55,417,677,000 cubic meters (2019 est.)
proven reserves: 7.079 billion cubic meters (2021 est.)

Carbon dioxide emissions: 686.954 million metric tonnes of CO2 (2019 est.)
from coal and metallurgical coke: 319.383 million metric tonnes of CO2 (2019 est.)
from petroleum and other liquids: 255.518 million metric tonnes of CO2 (2019 est.)
from consumed natural gas: 112.052 million metric tonnes of CO2 (2019 est.)

Energy consumption per capita: 242.346 million Btu/person (2019 est.)

COMMUNICATIONS

Telephones - fixed lines: *total subscriptions:* 23,858,239 (2020 est.)
subscriptions per 100 inhabitants: 47 (2020 est.)

Telephones - mobile cellular: *total subscriptions:* 70,513,676 (2020 est.)
subscriptions per 100 inhabitants: 138 (2020 est.)

Telecommunication systems: *general assessment:* South Korea is second only to Hong Kong in the world rankings of telecom market maturity; it is also on the leading edge of the latest telecom technology developments, including around 6G; with its highly urbanized, tech-savvy population, South Korea also enjoys very high communication levels across all segments – fixed-line telephony (44% at the start of 2022), fixed broadband (46%), mobile voice and data (144%), and mobile broadband (120%); the performance of the mobile sector is on a par with other developed markets around the region, but it's the wire line segment that allows South Korea to stand out from the crowd; this is partly a reflection of the large proportion of its population who live in apartment buildings (around 60%), making fiber and apartment LAN connections relatively easy and cost-effective to deploy; the government's Ultra Broadband convergence Network (UBcN) had aimed to reach 50% adoption by the end of 2022, but that target may be a few more years away; fixed-line teledensity is also at a very high level compared to most of the rest of the world, but it has been on a sharp decline from a rate of 60% ten years ago; on the mobile front, users have enthusiastically migrated from one generation of mobile platform to the next as each iteration becomes available; there also doesn't appear to be any great concern about there being a lack of demand for 5G in South Korea (when the country is already well supported by 4G networks), with 30% of all subscribers having already made the switch; part of the reason behind the rapid transition may be the subsidized handsets on offer from each of the MNOs and the MVNOs (2022)
domestic: fixed-line approximately 47 per 100 and mobile-cellular services 134 per 100 persons; rapid assimilation of a full range of telecommunications technologies leading to a boom in e-commerce (2020)
international: country code - 82; landing points for EAC-C2C, FEA, SeaMeWe-3, TPE, APCN-2, APG, FLAG North Asia Loop/REACH North Asia Loop, KJCN, NCP, and SJC2 submarine cables providing links throughout Asia, Australia, the Middle East, Africa, Europe, Southeast Asia and US; satellite earth stations - 66 (2019)

Broadcast media: multiple national TV networks with 2 of the 3 largest networks publicly operated; the largest privately owned network, Seoul Broadcasting Service (SBS), has ties with other commercial TV networks; cable and satellite TV subscription services available; publicly operated radio broadcast networks and many privately owned radio broadcasting networks, each with multiple affiliates, and independent local stations

Internet country code: .kr

Internet users: *total:* 50,281,152 (2020 est.)
percent of population: 97% (2020 est.)

Broadband - fixed subscriptions: *total:* 22,327,182 (2020 est.)
subscriptions per 100 inhabitants: 44 (2020 est.)

TRANSPORTATION

National air transport system: *number of registered air carriers:* 14 (2020)
inventory of registered aircraft operated by air carriers: 424
annual passenger traffic on registered air carriers: 88,157,579 (2018)
annual freight traffic on registered air carriers: 11,929,560,000 (2018) mt-km

Civil aircraft registration country code prefix: HL

Airports: *total:* 111 (2021)

Airports - with paved runways: *total:* 71
over 3,047 m: 4
2,438 to 3,047 m: 19
1,524 to 2,437 m: 12

914 to 1,523 m: 13
under 914 m: 23 (2021)

Airports - with unpaved runways: *total:* 40
914 to 1,523 m: 2
under 914 m: 38 (2021)

Heliports: 466 (2021)

Pipelines: 3,790 km gas, 16 km oil, 889 km refined products (2018)

Railways: *total:* 3,979 km (2016)
standard gauge: 3,979 km (2016) 1.435-m gauge (2,727 km electrified)

Roadways: *total:* 100,428 km (2016)
paved: 92,795 km (2016) (includes 4,193 km of expressways)
unpaved: 7,633 km (2016)

Waterways: 1,600 km (2011) (most navigable only by small craft)

Merchant marine: *total:* 1,904
by type: bulk carrier 78, container ship 91, general cargo 360, oil tanker 184, other 1,191 (2021)

Ports and terminals: *major seaport(s):* Busan, Incheon, Gunsan, Kwangyang, Mokpo, Pohang, Ulsan, Yeosu
container port(s) (TEUs): Busan (21,992,001), Incheon (3,091,955), Kwangyang (2,378,337) (2019)

LNG terminal(s) (import): Incheon, Kwangyang, Pyeongtaek, Samcheok, Tongyeong, Yeosu

MILITARY AND SECURITY

Military and security forces: Armed Forces of the Republic of Korea: Republic of Korea Army (ROKA), Navy (ROKN, includes Marine Corps, ROKMC), Air Force (ROKAF); Military reserves include Mobilization Reserve Forces (First Combat Forces) and Homeland Defense Forces (Regional Combat Forces); Ministry of Maritime Affairs and Fisheries: Korea Coast Guard (2022)
note: in January 2022, the South Korean military announced the formation of a space branch under its Joint Chiefs of Staff to coordinate the development of space and space-enabled capabilities across the Army, Navy and Air Force

Military expenditures: 2.6% of GDP (2022 est.)
2.6% of GDP (2021)
2.6% of GDP (2020)
2.7% of GDP (2019) (approximately $58.1 billion)
2.5% of GDP (2018) (approximately $55.8 billion)

Military and security service personnel strengths: approximately 555,000 active duty personnel (420,000 Army; 70,000 Navy, including about 30,000 Marines; 65,000 Air Force) (2022)

Military equipment inventories and acquisitions: the South Korean military is equipped with a mix of domestically-produced and imported weapons systems; South Korea has a robust defense industry and production includes armored fighting vehicles, artillery, aircraft, and naval ships; since 2010, the top foreign weapons supplier has been the US, and some domestically-produced systems are built under US license (2022)

Military service age and obligation: 18-35 years of age for compulsory military service for all men; minimum conscript service obligation varies by service - 18 months (Army, Marines), 20 months (Navy), 21 months (Air Force); 18-26 years of age for voluntary military service for men and women (2022)
note 1: women, in service since 1950, are able to serve in all branches, including as officers, and in 2020 comprised about 7.5% of the active duty military
note 2: in 2022, about 330,000 of the military's active personnel were conscripts; the military brings on over 200,000 conscripts each year

Military deployments: 250 Lebanon (UNIFIL); 280 South Sudan (UNMISS); 170 United Arab Emirates; note - since 2009, South Korea has kept a naval flotilla with approximately 300 personnel in the waters off of the Horn of Africa and the Arabian Peninsula (2022)

Military - note: the 1953 US-South Korea Mutual Defense Treaty is a cornerstone of South Korea's security; the Treaty committed the US to provide assistance in the event of an attack, particularly from North Korea; in addition, the Treaty gave the US permission to station land, air, and sea forces in and about the territory of South Korea as determined by mutual agreement; as of 2022, the US maintained approximately 28,000 military personnel in the country

the South Korean military has assisted the US in conflicts in Afghanistan (5,000 troops; 2001-2014), Iraq (20,000 troops; 2003-2008), and Vietnam (325,000 troops; 1964-1973)

South Korea has Major Non-NATO Ally (MNNA) status with the US; MNNA is a designation under US law that provides foreign partners with certain benefits in the areas of defense trade and security cooperation; while MNNA status provides military and economic privileges, it does not entail any security commitments

in 2016, South Korea concluded an agreement with the EU for participation in EU Common Security and Defense Policy (CSDP) missions and operations, such as the EU Naval Force Somalia – Operation Atalanta, which protects maritime shipping and conducts counter-piracy operations off the coast of East Africa

South Korea has been engaged with NATO through dialogue and security cooperation since 2005 and is considered by NATO to be a global partner; it has participated in NATO-led missions and exercises, including leading an integrated civilian-military reconstruction team in Afghanistan as part of the NATO-led International Security Assistance Force, 2010-2013; it has also cooperated with NATO in countering the threat of piracy in the Gulf of Aden by providing naval vessels as escorts

in addition to the invasion of South Korea and the subsequent Korean War (1950-53), North Korea from the 1960s to the 1980s launched a considerable number of limited military and subversive actions against South Korea using special forces and terrorist tactics; including aggressive skirmishes along the DMZ, overt attempts to assassinate South Korean leaders, kidnappings, the bombing of an airliner, and a failed effort in 1968 to foment an insurrection and conduct a guerrilla war in the South with more than 100 seaborne commandos; from the 1990s until 2010, the North lost two submarines and a semi-submersible boat attempting to insert infiltrators into the South (1996, 1998) and provoked several engagements in the Northwest Islands area along the disputed Northern Limit Line (NLL), including naval skirmishes between patrol boats in 1999 and 2002, the torpedoing and sinking of a South Korean corvette, the *Cheonan*, in 2010, and the bombardment of a South Korean Marine Corps installation on Yeonpyeong Island, also in 2010; since 2010, further minor incidents continue to occur periodically along the DMZ, where both the North and the South Korean militaries maintain large numbers of troops

in 2018, North Korea and South Korea signed a tension reduction agreement known as the Comprehensive Military Agreement (CMA), which established land, sea, and air buffer zones along the DMZ and the NLL; implementation of the CMA required the removal of some land mines and guard posts; the efforts led to a reduction of tension in the DMZ, but as of 2022 North Korea had failed to uphold much of its side of the agreement

TRANSNATIONAL ISSUES

Disputes - international: *South Korea-Japan:* South Korea and Japan claim Liancourt Rocks (Tok-do/Take-shima), occupied by South Korea since 1954

South Korea-North Korea: Military Demarcation Line within the 4-km-wide Demilitarized Zone has separated North from South Korea since 1953; periodic incidents with North Korea in the Yellow Sea over the Northern Limit Line, which South Korea claims as a maritime boundary

Refugees and internally displaced persons: *stateless persons:* 204 (mid-year 2021)

Illicit drugs: precursor chemicals used for illicit drugs, such as acetic anhydride, pseudoephedrine, and ephedrine, imported from the United States, Japan, India, and China and then either resold within South Korea or smuggled into other countries

KOSOVO

INTRODUCTION

Background: The central Balkans were part of the Roman and Byzantine Empires before ethnic Serbs migrated to the territories of modern Kosovo in the 7th century. During the medieval period, Kosovo became the center of a Serbian Empire and saw the construction of many important Serb religious sites, including many architecturally significant Serbian Orthodox monasteries. The defeat of Serbian forces at the Battle of Kosovo in 1389 led to five centuries of Ottoman rule during which large numbers of Turks and Albanians moved to Kosovo. By the end of the 19th century, Albanians replaced Serbs as the dominant ethnic group in Kosovo. Serbia reacquired control over the region from the Ottoman Empire during the First Balkan War of 1912. After World War II, Kosovo's present-day boundaries were established

when Kosovo became an autonomous province of Serbia in the Socialist Federal Republic of Yugoslavia (S.F.R.Y.). Despite legislative concessions, Albanian nationalism increased in the 1980s, which led to riots and calls for Kosovo's independence. The Serbs - many of whom viewed Kosovo as their cultural heartland - instituted a new constitution in 1989 revoking Kosovo's autonomous status. Kosovo's Albanian leaders responded in 1991 by organizing a referendum declaring Kosovo independent. Serbia undertook repressive measures against the Kosovar Albanians in the 1990s, provoking a Kosovar Albanian insurgency.

Beginning in 1998, Serbia conducted a brutal counterinsurgency campaign that resulted in massacres and massive expulsions of ethnic Albanians (some 800,000 ethnic Albanians were forced from their homes in Kosovo). After international attempts to mediate the conflict failed, a three-month NATO military operation against Serbia beginning in March 1999 forced the Serbs to agree to withdraw their military and police forces from Kosovo. UN Security Council Resolution 1244 (1999) placed Kosovo under a transitional administration, the UN Interim Administration Mission in Kosovo, pending a determination of Kosovo's future status. A UN-led process began in late 2005 to determine Kosovo's final status. The 2006-07 negotiations ended without agreement between Belgrade and Pristina, though the UN issued a comprehensive report on Kosovo's final status that endorsed independence. On 17 February 2008, the Kosovo Assembly declared Kosovo independent. Since then, close to 100 countries have recognized Kosovo, and it has joined numerous international organizations. In October 2008, Serbia sought an advisory opinion from the International Court of Justice (ICJ) on the legality under international law of Kosovo's declaration of independence. The ICJ released the advisory opinion in July 2010 affirming that Kosovo's declaration of independence did not violate general principles of international law, UN Security Council Resolution 1244, or the Constitutive Framework. The opinion was closely tailored to Kosovo's unique history and circumstances.

Demonstrating Kosovo's development into a sovereign, multi-ethnic, democratic country, the international community ended the period of Supervised Independence in 2012. Kosovo held its most recent national and municipal elections in 2021, ushering in a government led by the Self-Determination Movement's (VV) Albin KURTI, a former political prisoner who did not fight in the 1998-99 war. Serbia continues to reject Kosovo's independence, but the two countries agreed in April 2013 to normalize their relations through EU-facilitated talks, which produced several subsequent agreements the parties are implementing to varying degrees, though they have not yet reached a comprehensive normalization of relations. Kosovo has pursued bilateral recognitions and memberships in international organizations, moves that Serbia strongly opposes. Kosovo signed a Stabilization and Association Agreement with the EU in 2015, and the EU named Kosovo as among the six Western Balkan countries that will be able to join the organization once it meets the criteria to accede. Kosovo also seeks memberships in the UN and in NATO.

GEOGRAPHY

Location: Southeastern Europe, between Serbia and Macedonia

Geographic coordinates: 42 35 N, 21 00 E

Map references: Europe

Area: *total:* 10,887 sq km
land: 10,887 sq km
water: 0 sq km

Area - comparative: slightly larger than Delaware

Land boundaries: *total:* 714 km
border countries (4): Albania 112 km; North Macedonia 160 km; Montenegro 76 km; Serbia 366 km

Coastline: 0 km (landlocked)

Maritime claims: none (landlocked)

Climate: influenced by continental air masses resulting in relatively cold winters with heavy snowfall and hot, dry summers and autumns; Mediterranean and alpine influences create regional variation; maximum rainfall between October and December

Terrain: flat fluvial basin at an elevation of 400-700 m above sea level surrounded by several high mountain ranges with elevations of 2,000 to 2,500 m

Elevation: *highest point:* Gjeravica/Deravica 2,656 m
lowest point: Drini i Bardhe/Beli Drim (located on the border with Albania) 297 m
mean elevation: 450 m

Natural resources: nickel, lead, zinc, magnesium, lignite, kaolin, chrome, bauxite

Land use: *agricultural land:* 52.8% (2018 est.)
arable land: 27.4% (2018 est.)
permanent crops: 1.9% (2018 est.)
permanent pasture: 23.5% (2018 est.)
forest: 41.7% (2018 est.)
other: 5.5% (2018 est.)

Major watersheds (area sq km): Atlantic Ocean drainage: *(Black Sea)* Danube (795,656 sq km)

Population distribution: population clusters exist throughout the country, the largest being in the east in and around the capital of Pristina

Geography - note: the 41-km long Nerodimka River divides into two branches each of which flows into a different sea: the northern branch flows into the Sitnica River, which via the Ibar, Morava, and Danube Rivers ultimately flows into the Black Sea; the southern branch flows via the Lepenac and Vardar Rivers into the Aegean Sea

PEOPLE AND SOCIETY

Population: 1,952,701 (2022 est.)

Nationality: *noun:* Kosovan
adjective: Kosovan
note: Kosovo, a neutral term, is sometimes also used as a noun or adjective as in Kosovo Albanian, Kosovo Serb, Kosovo minority, or Kosovo citizen

Ethnic groups: Albanians 92.9%, Bosniaks 1.6%, Serbs 1.5%, Turk 1.1%, Ashkali 0.9%, Egyptian 0.7%, Gorani 0.6%, Romani 0.5%, other/unspecified 0.2% (2011 est.)
note: these estimates may under-represent Serb, Romani, and some other ethnic minorities because they are based on the 2011 Kosovo national census, which excluded northern Kosovo (a largely Serb-inhabited region) and was partially boycotted by Serb and Romani communities in southern Kosovo

Languages: Albanian (official) 94.5%, Bosnian 1.7%, Serbian (official) 1.6%, Turkish 1.1%, other 0.9% (includes Romani), unspecified 0.1%; note - in municipalities where a community's mother tongue is not one of Kosovo's official languages, the language of that community may be given official status according to the 2006 Law on the Use of Languages (2011 est.)
major-language sample(s): Libri i Fakteve Boterore, burimi vital per informacione elementare. (Albanian)

Religions: Muslim 95.6%, Roman Catholic 2.2%, Orthodox 1.5%, other 0.1%, none 0.1%, unspecified 0.6% (2011 est.)

Age structure: *0-14 years:* 24.07% (male 241,563/female 223,568)
15-24 years: 16.95% (male 170,566/female 157,063)
25-54 years: 42.56% (male 433,914/female 388,595)
55-64 years: 8.67% (male 85,840/female 81,782)
65 years and over: 7.75% (male 63,943/female 85,940) (2020 est.)

Median age: *total:* 30.5 years
male: 30.2 years
female: 30.8 years (2020 est.)

Population growth rate: 0.57% (2022 est.)

Birth rate: 14.85 births/1,000 population (2022 est.)

Death rate: 8.12 deaths/1,000 population (2022 est.)

Net migration rate: -1.07 migrant(s)/1,000 population (2022 est.)

Population distribution: population clusters exist throughout the country, the largest being in the east in and around the capital of Pristina

Major urban areas - population: 216,870 PRISTINA (capital) (2019)

Sex ratio: *at birth:* 1.08 male(s)/female
0-14 years: 1.08 male(s)/female
15-24 years: 1.08 male(s)/female
25-54 years: 1.11 male(s)/female
55-64 years: 1.05 male(s)/female
65 years and over: 0.6 male(s)/female
total population: 1.06 male(s)/female (2022 est.)

Infant mortality rate: *total:* 27.12 deaths/1,000 live births
male: 28.74 deaths/1,000 live births
female: 25.38 deaths/1,000 live births (2022 est.)

Life expectancy at birth: *total population:* 71.12 years
male: 68.83 years
female: 73.58 years (2022 est.)

Total fertility rate: 1.9 children born/woman (2022 est.)

Unemployment, youth ages 15-24: *total:* 49.7%
male: 45.9%
female: 57.6% (2020 est.)

ENVIRONMENT

Environment - current issues: air pollution (pollution from power plants and nearby lignite mines take a toll on people's health); water scarcity and pollution; land degradation

Air pollutants: *carbon dioxide emissions:* 8.94 megatons (2016 est.)
methane emissions: 0.54 megatons (2020 est.)

Climate: influenced by continental air masses resulting in relatively cold winters with heavy snowfall and hot, dry summers and autumns; Mediterranean and alpine influences create regional variation; maximum rainfall between October and December

Land use: *agricultural land:* 52.8% (2018 est.)
arable land: 27.4% (2018 est.)
permanent crops: 1.9% (2018 est.)
permanent pasture: 23.5% (2018 est.)
forest: 41.7% (2018 est.)
other: 5.5% (2018 est.)

Revenue from forest resources: *forest revenues:* 0% of GDP (2018 est.)

Revenue from coal: *coal revenues:* 0.31% of GDP (2018 est.)

Waste and recycling: *municipal solid waste generated annually:* 319,000 tons (2015 est.)

Major watersheds (area sq km): Atlantic Ocean drainage: *(Black Sea)* Danube (795,656 sq km)

GOVERNMENT

Country name: *conventional long form:* Republic of Kosovo
conventional short form: Kosovo
local long form: Republika e Kosoves (Albanian)/ Republika Kosovo (Serbian)
local short form: Kosove (Albanian)/ Kosovo (Serbian)
etymology: name derives from the Serbian "kos" meaning "blackbird," an ellipsis (linguistic omission) for "kosove polje" or "field of the blackbirds"

Government type: parliamentary republic

Capital: *name:* Pristina (Prishtine, Prishtina)
geographic coordinates: 42 40 N, 21 10 E
time difference: UTC+1 (6 hours ahead of Washington, DC, during Standard Time)
daylight saving time: +1hr, begins last Sunday in March; ends last Sunday in October
etymology: the name may derive from a Proto-Slavic word reconstructed as "pryshchina," meaning "spring (of water)"

Administrative divisions: 38 municipalities (komunat, singular - komuna (Albanian); opstine, singular - opstina (Serbian)); Decan (Decani), Dragash (Dragas), Ferizaj (Urosevac), Fushe Kosove (Kosovo Polje), Gjakove (Dakovica), Gjilan (Gnjilane), Gllogovc (Glogovac), Gracanice (Gracanica), Hani i Elezit (Deneral Jankovic), Istog (Istok), Junik, Kacanik, Kamenice (Kamenica), Kline (Klina), Kllokot (Klokot), Leposaviq (Leposavic), Lipjan (Lipljan), Malisheve (Malisevo), Mamushe (Mamusa), Mitrovice e Jugut (Juzna Mitrovica) [South Mitrovica], Mitrovice e Veriut (Severna Mitrovica) [North Mitrovica], Novoberde (Novo Brdo), Obiliq (Obilic), Partesh (Partes), Peje (Pec), Podujeve (Podujevo), Prishtine (Pristina), Prizren, Rahovec (Orahovac), Ranillug (Ranilug), Shterpce (Strpce), Shtime (Stimlje), Skenderaj (Srbica), Suhareke (Suva Reka), Viti (Vitina), Vushtrri (Vucitrn), Zubin Potok, Zvecan

Independence: 17 February 2008 (from Serbia)

National holiday: Independence Day, 17 February (2008)

Constitution: *history:* previous 1974, 1990; latest (postindependence) draft finalized 2 April 2008, signed 7 April 2008, ratified 9 April 2008, entered into force 15 June 2008; note - amendment 24, passed by the Assembly in August 2015, established the Kosovo Relocated Specialist Institution, referred to as the Kosovo Specialist Chamber or "Specialist Court," to try war crimes allegedly committed by members of the Kosovo Liberation Army in the late 1990s
amendments: proposed by the government, by the president of the republic, or by one fourth of Assembly deputies; passage requires two-thirds majority vote of the Assembly, including two-thirds majority vote of deputies representing non-majority communities, followed by a favorable Constitutional Court assessment; amended several times, last in 2020

Legal system: civil law system; note - the European Union Rule of Law Mission (EULEX) retained limited executive powers within the Kosovo judiciary for complex cases from 2008 to 2018

International law organization participation: has not submitted an ICJ jurisdiction declaration; non-party state to the ICCt

Citizenship: *citizenship by birth:* no
citizenship by descent only: at least one parent must be a citizen of Kosovo
dual citizenship recognized: yes
residency requirement for naturalization: 5 years

Suffrage: 18 years of age; universal

Executive branch: *chief of state:* President Vjosa OSMANI-Sadriu (since 4 April 2021)
head of government: Prime Minister Albin KURTI (since 22 March 2021)
cabinet: Cabinet elected by the Assembly
elections/appointments: president indirectly elected by at least two-thirds majority vote of the Assembly for a 5-year term; if a candidate does not attain a two-thirds threshold in the first two ballots, the candidate winning a simple majority vote in the third ballot is elected (eligible for a second term); election last held on 3-4 April 2021 (next to be held in 2026); prime minister indirectly elected by the Assembly
election results: *2021:* Vjosa OSMANI-Sadriu elected president in the third ballot; Assembly vote - Vjosa OSMANI-Sadriu (Guxo!) 71 votes; Albin KURTI (LVV) elected prime minister; Assembly vote - 67-30
2016: Hashim THACI elected president in third ballot; Assembly vote - Hashim THACI (PDK) 71 votes; Ramush HARADINAJ (AAK) elected prime minister; Assembly vote - 61 votes

Legislative branch: *description:* unicameral Assembly or Kuvendi i Kosoves/Skupstina Kosova (120 seats; 100 members directly elected by open-list proportional representation vote with 20 seats reserved for ethnic minorities - 10 for Serbs and 10 for other ethnic minorities; members serve 4-year terms)
elections: last held on 14 February 2021 (next to be held in 2025)
election results: percent of vote by party - LVV 50%, PDK 16.9%, LDK 12.7%, AAK 7.1%, Serb List 5.1%, other 8.2%; seats by party - LVV 58, PDK 19, LDK 15, Serb List 10, AAK 8, other 10; composition as of December 2021 - men 79, women 41, percent of women 34.2%

Judicial branch: *highest court(s):* Supreme Court (consists of the court president and 18 judges and organized into Appeals Panel of the Kosovo Property Agency and Special Chamber); Constitutional Court (consists of the court president, vice president, and 7 judges)
judge selection and term of office: Supreme Court judges nominated by the Kosovo Judicial Council, a 13-member independent body staffed by judges and lay members, and also responsible for overall administration of Kosovo's judicial system; judges appointed by the president of the Republic of Kosovo; judges appointed until mandatory retirement age; Constitutional Court judges nominated by the Kosovo Assembly and appointed by the president of the republic to serve single, 9-year terms
subordinate courts: Court of Appeals (organized into 4 departments: General, Serious Crime, Commercial Matters, and Administrative Matters); Basic Court (located in 7 municipalities, each with several branches)
note: in August 2015, the Kosovo Assembly approved a constitutional amendment that establishes the Kosovo Relocated Specialist Judicial Institution, also referred to as the Kosovo Specialist Chambers or "Special Court"; the court, located at the Hague in the Netherlands, began operating in late 2016 and has jurisdiction to try crimes against humanity, war crimes, and other crimes under Kosovo law that occurred in the 1998-2000 period

Political parties and leaders: Alliance for the Future of Kosovo or AAK [Ramush HARADINAJ]
Alternativa [Mimoza KUSARI-LILA]
Ashkali Party for Integration or PAI [Bekim ARIFI]
Democratic League of Kosovo or LDK [Lumir ABDIXHIKU]
Democratic Party of Kosovo or PDK [Memli KRASNIQI]
Guxo! [Donika GERVALLA-SCHWARZ]
Independent Liberal Party or SLS [Slobodan PETROVIC]
New Democratic Initiative of Kosovo or IRDK [Elbert KRASNIQI]
New Democratic Party or NDS [Emilja REDXEPI]
New Kosovo Alliance or AKR [Behgjet PACOLLI]
Progressive Movement of Kosovar Roma or LPRK [Erxhan GALUSHI]
Romani Initiative [Gazmend SALIJEVCI]
Self-Determination Movement (Lëvizja Vetevendosje) or LVV [Albin KURTI]
Serb List or SL [Goran RAKIC]
Social Democratic Initiative or NISMA [Fatmir LIMAJ] (formerly Initiative for Kosovo)
Social Democratic Party of Kosovo or PSD [Dardan MOLLIQAJ]
Social Democratic Union or SDU [Duda BALJE]
Turkish Democratic Party of Kosovo or KDTP [Fikrim DAMKA]
Unique Gorani Party JGP [Adem HODZA]
Vakat Coalition or VAKAT [Rasim DEMIRI]

International organization participation: IBRD, IDA, IFC, IMF, ITUC (NGOs), MIGA, OIF (observer)

Diplomatic representation in the US: *chief of mission:* Ambassador Ilir DUGOLLI (since 13 January 2022)
chancery: 2175 K Street NW, Suite 300, Washington, DC 20037
telephone: [1] (202) 450-2130
FAX: [1] (202) 735-0609
email address and website:
https://www.ambasada-ks.net/us/?page=2,1
consulate(s) general: New York
consulate(s): Des Moines (IA)

Diplomatic representation from the US: *chief of mission:* Ambassador Jeffrey M. HOVENIER (since 10 January 2022)
embassy: Arberia/Dragodan, Rr. 4 KORRIKU Nr. 25, Pristina
mailing address: 9520 Pristina Place, Washington DC 20521-9520
telephone: [383] 38-59-59-3000
FAX: [383] 38-604-890
email address and website:
PristinaACS@state.gov
https://xk.usembassy.gov/

Flag description: centered on a dark blue field is a gold-colored silhouette of Kosovo surmounted by six white, five-pointed stars arrayed in a slight arc; each star represents one of the major ethnic groups of Kosovo: Albanians, Serbs, Turks, Gorani, Roma, and Bosniaks
note: one of only two national flags that uses a map as a design element; the flag of Cyprus is the other

National symbol(s): six, five-pointed, white stars; national colors: blue, gold, white

National anthem: *name:* Europe
lyrics/music: no lyrics/Mendi MENGJIQI
note: adopted 2008; Kosovo chose to exclude lyrics in its anthem so as not to offend the country's minority ethnic groups

National heritage: *total World Heritage Sites:* 1 (cultural)
selected World Heritage Site locales: Medieval Monuments in Kosovo

ECONOMY

Economic overview: Kosovo's economy has shown progress in transitioning to a market-based system and maintaining macroeconomic stability, but it is still highly dependent on the international community and the diaspora for financial and technical assistance. Remittances from the diaspora - located mainly in Germany, Switzerland, and the Nordic countries - are estimated to account for about 17% of GDP and international donor assistance accounts for approximately 10% of GDP. With international assistance, Kosovo has been able to privatize a majority of its state-owned enterprises.

Kosovo's citizens are the second poorest in Europe, after Moldova, with a per capita GDP (PPP) of $10,400 in 2017. An unemployment rate of 33%, and a youth unemployment rate near 60%, in a country where the average age is 26, encourages emigration and fuels a significant informal, unreported economy. Most of Kosovo's population lives in rural towns outside of the capital, Pristina. Inefficient, near-subsistence farming is common - the result of small plots, limited mechanization, and a lack of technical expertise. Kosovo enjoys lower labor costs than the rest of the region. However, high levels of corruption, little contract enforcement, and unreliable electricity supply have discouraged potential investors. The official currency of Kosovo is the euro, but the Serbian dinar is also used illegally in Serb majority communities. Kosovo's tie to the euro has helped keep core inflation low.

Minerals and metals production - including lignite, lead, zinc, nickel, chrome, aluminum, magnesium, and a wide variety of construction materials - once the backbone of industry, has declined because of aging equipment and insufficient investment, problems exacerbated by competing and unresolved ownership claims of Kosovo's largest mines. A limited and unreliable electricity supply is a major impediment to economic development. The US Government is cooperating with the Ministry of Economic Development (MED) and the World Bank to conclude a commercial tender for the construction of Kosovo C, a new lignite-fired power plant that would leverage Kosovo's large lignite reserves. MED also has plans for the rehabilitation of an older bituminous-fired power plant, Kosovo B, and the development of a coal mine that could supply both plants.

In June 2009, Kosovo joined the World Bank and International Monetary Fund, the Central Europe Free Trade Area (CEFTA) in 2006, the European Bank for Reconstruction and Development in 2012, and the Council of Europe Development Bank in 2013. In 2016, Kosovo implemented the Stabilization and Association Agreement (SAA) negotiations with the EU, focused on trade liberalization. In 2014, nearly 60% of customs duty-eligible imports into Kosovo were EU goods. In August 2015, as part of its EU-facilitated normalization process with Serbia, Kosovo signed agreements on telecommunications and energy distribution, but disagreements over who owns economic assets, such as the Trepca mining conglomerate, within Kosovo continue.

Kosovo experienced its first federal budget deficit in 2012, when government expenditures climbed sharply. In May 2014, the government introduced a 25% salary increase for public sector employees and an equal increase in certain social benefits. Central revenues could not sustain these increases, and the government was forced to reduce its planned capital investments. The government, led by Prime Minister MUSTAFA - a trained economist - recently made several changes to its fiscal policy, expanding the list of duty-free imports, decreasing the Value Added Tax (VAT) for basic food items and public utilities, and increasing the VAT for all other goods.

While Kosovo's economy continued to make progress, unemployment has not been reduced, nor living standards raised, due to lack of economic reforms and investment.

Real GDP (purchasing power parity): $19.13 billion (2020 est.)
$20.55 billion (2019 est.)
$19.58 billion (2018 est.)
note: data are in 2017 dollars

Real GDP growth rate: 3.7% (2017 est.)
4.1% (2016 est.)
4.1% (2015 est.)

Real GDP per capita: $10,800 (2020 est.)
$11,500 (2019 est.)
$10,900 (2018 est.)
note: data are in 2017 dollars

GDP (official exchange rate): $7.926 billion (2019 est.)

Inflation rate (consumer prices): 2.6% (2019 est.)
1% (2018 est.)
1.4% (2017 est.)

GDP - composition, by sector of origin: *agriculture:* 11.9% (2017 est.)
industry: 17.7% (2017 est.)
services: 70.4% (2017 est.)

GDP - composition, by end use: *household consumption:* 84.3% (2017 est.)
government consumption: 13.6% (2017 est.)
investment in fixed capital: 29% (2017 est.)
investment in inventories: 0% (2016 est.)
exports of goods and services: 27% (2017 est.)
imports of goods and services: -53.8% (2017 est.)

Agricultural products: wheat, corn, berries, potatoes, peppers, fruit; dairy, livestock; fish

Industries: mineral mining, construction materials, base metals, leather, machinery, appliances, foodstuffs and beverages, textiles

Industrial production growth rate: 1.2% (2016 est.)

Labor force: 500,300 (2017 est.)
note: includes those estimated to be employed in the gray economy

Labor force - by occupation: *agriculture:* 4.4%
industry: 17.4%
services: 78.2% (2017 est.)

Unemployment rate: 30.5% (2017 est.)
27.5% (2016 est.)
note: Kosovo has a large informal sector that may not be reflected in these data

Unemployment, youth ages 15-24: *total:* 49.7%
male: 45.9%
female: 57.6% (2020 est.)

Population below poverty line: 17.6% (2015 est.)

Gini Index coefficient - distribution of family income: 29 (2017 est.)
24.1 (2014 est.)

Household income or consumption by percentage share: *lowest 10%:* 3.8%
highest 10%: 22% (2015 est.)

Budget: *revenues:* 2.054 billion (2017 est.)
expenditures: 2.203 billion (2017 est.)

Budget surplus (+) or deficit (-): -2.1% (of GDP) (2017 est.)

Public debt: 21.2% of GDP (2017 est.)
19.4% of GDP (2016 est.)

Taxes and other revenues: 29% (of GDP) (2017 est.)

Current account balance: -$467 million (2017 est.)
-$533 million (2016 est.)

Exports: $1.69 billion (2020 est.) note: data are in current year dollars
$2.31 billion (2019 est.) note: data are in current year dollars
$2.28 billion (2018 est.) note: data are in current year dollars

Exports - partners: Albania 16%, India 14%, North Macedonia 12.1%, Serbia 10.6%, Switzerland 5.6%, Germany 5.4% (2017)

Exports - commodities: mining and processed metal products, scrap metals, leather products, machinery, appliances, prepared foodstuffs, beverages and tobacco, vegetable products, textiles and apparel

Imports: $4.19 billion (2020 est.) note: data are in current year dollars
$4.45 billion (2019 est.) note: data are in current year dollars

$4.5 billion (2018 est.) note: data are in current year dollars

Imports - partners: Germany 12.4%, Serbia 12.3%, Turkey 9.6%, China 9.1%, Italy 6.4%, North Macedonia 5.1%, Albania 5%, Greece 4.4% (2017)

Imports - commodities: foodstuffs, livestock, wood, petroleum, chemicals, machinery, minerals, textiles, stone, ceramic and glass products, electrical equipment

Reserves of foreign exchange and gold: $683.9 million (31 December 2016 est.)
$708.7 million (31 December 2015 est.)

Debt - external: $2.388 billion (2019 est.)
$2.409 billion (2018 est.)

Exchange rates: euros (EUR) per US dollar -
0.885 (2017 est.)
0.903 (2016 est.)
0.9214 (2015 est.)
0.885 (2014 est.)
0.7634 (2013 est.)

ENERGY

Electricity access: *electrification - total population:* 100% (2020)

Electricity: *installed generating capacity:* 1.424 million kW (2020 est.)
consumption: 4,860,740,000 kWh (2019 est.)
exports: 2.715 billion kWh (2020 est.)
imports: 2.572 billion kWh (2020 est.)
transmission/distribution losses: 1.145 billion kWh (2019 est.)

Electricity generation sources: *fossil fuels:* 95.6% of total installed capacity (2020 est.)
solar: 0.1% of total installed capacity (2020 est.)
wind: 1.1% of total installed capacity (2020 est.)
hydroelectricity: 3.2% of total installed capacity (2020 est.)

Coal: *production:* 8.538 million metric tons (2020 est.)
consumption: 8.549 million metric tons (2020 est.)
exports: 9,000 metric tons (2020 est.)
imports: 20,000 metric tons (2020 est.)
proven reserves: 1.564 billion metric tons (2019 est.)

Petroleum: *refined petroleum consumption:* 12,800 bbl/day (2019 est.)

Refined petroleum products - exports: 192 bbl/day (2015 est.)

Refined petroleum products - imports: 14,040 bbl/day (2015 est.)

Carbon dioxide emissions: 8.009 million metric tonnes of CO_2 (2019 est.)
from coal and metallurgical coke: 6.1 million metric tonnes of CO_2 (2019 est.)
from petroleum and other liquids: 1.909 million metric tonnes of CO_2 (2019 est.)

Energy consumption per capita: 51.462 million Btu/person (2019 est.)

COMMUNICATIONS

Telephones - fixed lines: *total subscriptions:* 383,763 (2020 est.)
subscriptions per 100 inhabitants: 6 (2019 est.)

Telephones - mobile cellular: *total subscriptions:* 562,000 (2015 est.)
subscriptions per 100 inhabitants: 32 (2015 est.)

Telecommunication systems: *general assessment:* Kosovo has benefited from financial and regulatory assistance as part of the EU pre-accession process; the telecom sector has been liberalized, and legislation has aligned the sector with the EU's revised regulatory framework; poor telecom infrastructure has meant that fixed-line communication remains low by European standards; unlike most markets, the fixed-line broadband sector is dominated by new players; there is effective competition between the main cable and DSL operators, though as yet there is little progress with the expansion of fiber networks; the mobile sector accounts for most telecom lines for voice services, as well as the greater part of telecom revenue; two MNOs dominate the sector (2022)
domestic: fixed-line roughly 6 per 100 and mobile-cellular 32 per 100 persons (2019)
international: country code - 383

Internet country code: .xk; note - assigned as a temporary code under UN Security Council resolution 1244/99

Internet users: *total:* 1,502,658 (2019 est.)
percent of population: 84% (2019 est.)

TRANSPORTATION

National air transport system: *number of registered air carriers:* 0 (2020)

Civil aircraft registration country code prefix: Z6

Airports: *total:* 6 (2021)

Airports - with paved runways: *total:* 3
2,438 to 3,047 m: 1
1,524 to 2,437 m: 1
under 914 m: 1 (2021)

Airports - with unpaved runways: *total:* 3
under 914 m: 3 (2021)

Heliports: 2 (2021)

Railways: *total:* 333 km (2015)
standard gauge: 333 km (2015) 1.435-m gauge

Roadways: *total:* 2,012 km (2015)
paved: 1,921 km (2015) (includes 78 km of expressways)
unpaved: 91 km (2015)

MILITARY AND SECURITY

Military and security forces: Kosovo Security Force (KSF; Forca e Sigurisë së Kosovës or FSK): Land Force Command; Logistics Command; Doctrine and Training Command; National Guard Command (2022)
note: as of 2022, the Kosovo Government continued the process of transitioning the KSF into a multi-ethnic territorial defense force, in accordance with a 10-year plan which began in 2019

Military expenditures: 1% of GDP (2021 est.)
1.1% of GDP (2020 est.)
0.8% of GDP (2019 est.) (approximately $160 million)
0.8% of GDP (2018 est.) (approximately $150 million)
0.7% of GDP (2017 est.) (approximately $130 million)

Military and security service personnel strengths: approximately 3,300 KSF personnel, including reserves (2022)

Military equipment inventories and acquisitions: the KSF is equipped with small arms and light vehicles only; it relies on donations, and since 2013 has received donated equipment from Turkey and the US (2021)

Military service age and obligation: service is voluntary; must be over the age of 18 and a citizen of Kosovo; upper age for enlisting is 30 for officers, 25 for other ranks, although these may be waived for recruits with key skills considered essential for the KSF
(2021)

Military - note: the NATO-led Kosovo Force (KFOR) has operated in the country as a peace support force since 1999; KFOR is responsible for providing a safe and secure environment and ensuring freedom of movement for all citizens, as well as assisting in developing the Kosovo Security Force; as of 2022, it numbered about 3,700 troops from 28 countries

TERRORISM

Terrorist group(s): Islamic State of Iraq and ash-Sham (ISIS)

TRANSNATIONAL ISSUES

Disputes - international: NATO-led Kosovo Force peacekeepers under UN Interim Administration Mission in Kosovo authority continue to ensure a safe and secure environment and freedom of movement for all Kosovo citizens

Kosovo-Albania: none identified

Kosovo-Montenegro: their 2015 demarcation agreement was ratified by Montenegro in December 2015 and by Kosovo in March 2018, but the actual demarcation has not been completed; as of March 2021, Kosovo Prime Minister Albin KURTI said that after the new Montenegrin government is formed, he would broach the subject of reopening the agreement

Kosovo-North Macedonia: Kosovo and North Macedonia completed demarcation of their boundary in September 2008; both countries ratified the demarcation documents on October 17, 2009, after high-level consultations resolved the disputed section of border around Debelde/Tanusevci

Kosovo-Serbia: Serbia with several other states protest the US's and other countries' recognition of Kosovo's declaration of its status as a sovereign and independent state in February 2008; ethnic Serbian municipalities along Kosovo's northern border challenge final status of Kosovo-Serbia boundary; Kosovo's and Serbia's temporary agreement on license plates expired on 21 April 2022; the two countries are meeting on 13 May to reach a permanent agreement

Refugees and internally displaced persons: *IDPs:* 16,000 (primarily ethnic Serbs displaced during the 1998-1999 war fearing reprisals from the majority ethnic- Albanian population; a smaller number of ethnic Serbs, Roma, Ashkali, and Egyptians fled their homes in 2004 as a result of violence) (2021)
note: 8,372 estimated refugee and migrant arrivals (January 2015-October 2022)

KUWAIT

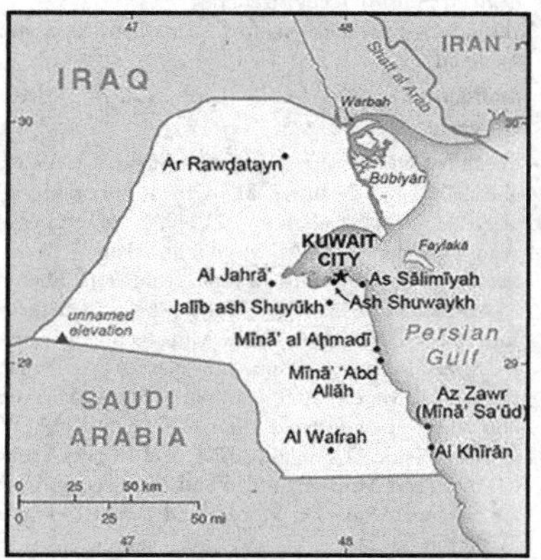

INTRODUCTION

Background: Kuwait has been ruled by the AL-SABAH dynasty since the 18th century. The threat of Ottoman invasion in 1899 prompted Amir Mubarak AL-SABAH to seek protection from Britain, ceding foreign and defense responsibility to Britain until 1961, when the country attained its independence. Kuwait was attacked and overrun by Iraq in August 1990. Following several weeks of aerial bombardment, a US-led UN coalition began a ground assault in February 1991 that liberated Kuwait in four days. In 1992, the Amir reconstituted the parliament that he had dissolved in 1986. Amid the 2010-11 uprisings and protests across the Arab world, stateless Arabs, known as Bidoon, staged small protests in early 2011 demanding citizenship, jobs, and other benefits available to Kuwaiti nationals. Other demographic groups, notably Islamists and Kuwaitis from tribal backgrounds, soon joined the growing protest movements, which culminated in late 2011 with the resignation of the prime minister amidst allegations of corruption. Demonstrations renewed in late 2012 in response to an amiri decree amending the electoral law that lessened the voting power of the tribal blocs.

An opposition coalition of Sunni Islamists, tribal populists, and some liberals, largely boycotted legislative elections in 2012 and 2013, which ushered in a legislature more amenable to the government's agenda. Faced with the prospect of painful subsidy cuts, oppositionists and independents actively participated in the November 2016 election, winning nearly half of the seats, but a cohesive opposition alliance largely ceased to exist with the 2016 election and the opposition became increasingly factionalized. Since coming to power in 2006, the Amir has dissolved the National Assembly on seven occasions (the Constitutional Court annulled the Assembly elections in June 2012 and again in June 2013) and shuffled the cabinet over a dozen times, usually citing political stagnation and gridlock between the legislature and the government.

The current Amir, who assumed his role in 2020, launched a "National Dialogue" in September 2021 meant to resolve political gridlock. As part of the "National Dialogue," the Amir pardoned several opposition figures who had been living in exile, and they returned to Kuwait. Legislative challenges remain, and the cabinet was reshuffled in March 2022.

GEOGRAPHY

Location: Middle East, bordering the Persian Gulf, between Iraq and Saudi Arabia

Geographic coordinates: 29 30 N, 45 45 E

Map references: Middle East

Area: *total:* 17,818 sq km
land: 17,818 sq km
water: 0 sq km

Area - comparative: slightly smaller than New Jersey

Land boundaries: *total:* 475 km
border countries (2): Iraq 254 km; Saudi Arabia 221 km

Coastline: 499 km

Maritime claims: *territorial sea:* 12 nm

Climate: dry desert; intensely hot summers; short, cool winters

Terrain: flat to slightly undulating desert plain

Elevation: *highest point:* 3.6 km W. of Al-Salmi Border Post 300 m
lowest point: Persian Gulf 0 m
mean elevation: 108 m

Natural resources: petroleum, fish, shrimp, natural gas

Land use: *agricultural land:* 8.5% (2018 est.)
arable land: 0.6% (2018 est.)
permanent crops: 0.3% (2018 est.)
permanent pasture: 7.6% (2018 est.)
forest: 0.4% (2018 est.)
other: 91.1% (2018 est.)

Irrigated land: 105 sq km (2012)

Major watersheds (area sq km): Indian Ocean drainage: *(Persian Gulf)* Tigris and Euphrates (918,044 sq km)

Major aquifers: Arabian Aquifer System

Population distribution: densest settlement is along the Persian Gulf, particularly in Kuwait City and on Bubiyan Island; significant population threads extend south and west along highways that radiate from the capital, particularly in the southern half of the country

Natural hazards: sudden cloudbursts are common from October to April and bring heavy rain, which can damage roads and houses; sandstorms and dust storms occur throughout the year but are most common between March and August

Geography - note: strategic location at head of Persian Gulf

PEOPLE AND SOCIETY

Population: 3,068,155 (2022 est.)
note: Kuwait's Public Authority for Civil Information estimates the country's total population to be 4,420,110 for 2019, with non-Kuwaitis accounting for nearly 70% of the population

Nationality: *noun:* Kuwaiti(s)
adjective: Kuwaiti

Ethnic groups: Kuwaiti 30.4%, other Arab 27.4%, Asian 40.3%, African 1%, other 0.9% (includes European, North American, South American, and Australian) (2018 est.)

Languages: Arabic (official), English widely spoken
major-language sample(s):
يمكن الاستغناء عنه للمعلومات الأساسية
كتاب حقائق العالم، المصدر الذي لا
(Arabic)

Religions: Muslim (official) 74.6%, Christian 18.2%, other and unspecified 7.2% (2013 est.)
note: data represent the total population; about 72% of the population consists of immigrants

Age structure: *0-14 years:* 24.29% (male 378,778/female 348,512)
15-24 years: 14.96% (male 245,354/female 202,642)
25-54 years: 52.39% (male 984,813/female 583,632)
55-64 years: 5.43% (male 90,583/female 72,026)
65 years and over: 2.92% (male 38,614/female 48,752) (2020 est.)

Dependency ratios: *total dependency ratio:* 32.4
youth dependency ratio: 28.4
elderly dependency ratio: 4
potential support ratio: 24.9 (2020 est.)

Median age: *total:* 29.7 years
male: 30.7 years
female: 27.9 years (2020 est.)

Population growth rate: 1.17% (2022 est.)

Birth rate: 17.78 births/1,000 population (2022 est.)

Death rate: 2.25 deaths/1,000 population (2022 est.)

Net migration rate: -3.87 migrant(s)/1,000 population (2022 est.)

Population distribution: densest settlement is along the Persian Gulf, particularly in Kuwait City and on Bubiyan Island; significant population threads extend south and west along highways that radiate from the capital, particularly in the southern half of the country

Urbanization: *urban population:* 100% of total population (2022)
rate of urbanization: 1.35% annual rate of change (2020-25 est.)

Major urban areas - population: 3.239 million KUWAIT (capital) (2022)

Sex ratio: *at birth:* 1.05 male(s)/female
0-14 years: 1.09 male(s)/female
15-24 years: 1.19 male(s)/female
25-54 years: 1.66 male(s)/female
55-64 years: 1.21 male(s)/female
65 years and over: 0.66 male(s)/female
total population: 1.37 male(s)/female (2022 est.)

Maternal mortality ratio: 12 deaths/100,000 live births (2017 est.)

Infant mortality rate: *total:* 7.43 deaths/1,000 live births
male: 7.75 deaths/1,000 live births
female: 7.1 deaths/1,000 live births (2022 est.)

Life expectancy at birth: *total population:* 79.13 years

male: 77.67 years
female: 80.65 years (2022 est.)

Total fertility rate: 2.24 children born/woman (2022 est.)

Drinking water source: *improved: total:* 100% of population
unimproved: total: 0% of population (2020 est.)

Current health expenditure: 5.5% of GDP (2019)

Physicians density: 2.34 physicians/1,000 population (2020)

Hospital bed density: 2 beds/1,000 population (2017)

Sanitation facility access: *improved: total:* 100% of population
unimproved: total: 0% of population (2020 est.)

HIV/AIDS - adult prevalence rate: (2018 est.) <.1%

Obesity - adult prevalence rate: 37.9% (2016)

Alcohol consumption per capita: *total:* 0 liters of pure alcohol (2019 est.)
beer: 0 liters of pure alcohol (2019 est.)
wine: 0 liters of pure alcohol (2019 est.)
spirits: 0 liters of pure alcohol (2019 est.)
other alcohols: 0 liters of pure alcohol (2019 est.)

Tobacco use: *total:* 17.9% (2020 est.)
male: 33.5% (2020 est.)
female: 2.2% (2020 est.)

Children under the age of 5 years underweight: 3% (2014)

Education expenditures: 6.6% of GDP (2020 est.)

Literacy: *definition:* age 15 and over can read and write
total population: 96.5%
male: 97.1%
female: 95.4% (2020)

School life expectancy (primary to tertiary education): *total:* 15 years
male: 13 years
female: 16 years (2015)

Unemployment, youth ages 15-24: *total:* 15.4%
male: 9.4%
female: 30% (2016 est.)

ENVIRONMENT

Environment - current issues: limited natural freshwater resources; some of world's largest and most sophisticated desalination facilities provide much of the water; air and water pollution; desertification; loss of biodiversity

Environment - international agreements: *party to:* Biodiversity, Climate Change, Climate Change-Kyoto Protocol, Climate Change-Paris Agreement, Comprehensive Nuclear Test Ban, Desertification, Endangered Species, Environmental Modification, Hazardous Wastes, Law of the Sea, Nuclear Test Ban, Ozone Layer Protection, Ship Pollution, Wetlands
signed, but not ratified: Marine Dumping-London Convention

Air pollutants: *particulate matter emissions:* 57.17 micrograms per cubic meter (2016 est.)
carbon dioxide emissions: 98.73 megatons (2016 est.)
methane emissions: 6.21 megatons (2020 est.)

Climate: dry desert; intensely hot summers; short, cool winters

Land use: *agricultural land:* 8.5% (2018 est.)
arable land: 0.6% (2018 est.)
permanent crops: 0.3% (2018 est.)
permanent pasture: 7.6% (2018 est.)
forest: 0.4% (2018 est.)
other: 91.1% (2018 est.)

Urbanization: *urban population:* 100% of total population (2022)
rate of urbanization: 1.35% annual rate of change (2020-25 est.)

Revenue from forest resources: *forest revenues:* 0% of GDP (2018 est.)

Revenue from coal: *coal revenues:* 0% of GDP (2018 est.)

Waste and recycling: *municipal solid waste generated annually:* 1.75 million tons (2010 est.)

Major watersheds (area sq km): Indian Ocean drainage: *(Persian Gulf)* Tigris and Euphrates (918,044 sq km)

Major aquifers: Arabian Aquifer System

Total water withdrawal: *municipal:* 448.3 million cubic meters (2017 est.)
industrial: 23.3 million cubic meters (2017 est.)
agricultural: 778.4 million cubic meters (2017 est.)

Total renewable water resources: 20 million cubic meters (2017 est.)

GOVERNMENT

Country name: *conventional long form:* State of Kuwait
conventional short form: Kuwait
local long form: Dawlat al Kuwayt
local short form: Al Kuwayt
etymology: the name derives from the capital city, which is from Arabic "al-Kuwayt" a diminutive of "kut" meaning "fortress," possibly a reference to a small castle built on the current location of Kuwait City by the Beni Khaled tribe in the 17th century

Government type: constitutional monarchy (emirate)

Capital: *name:* Kuwait City
geographic coordinates: 29 22 N, 47 58 E
time difference: UTC+3 (8 hours ahead of Washington, DC, during Standard Time)
etymology: the name derives from Arabic "al-Kuwayt" a diminutive of "kut" meaning "fortress," possibly a reference to a small castle built on the current location of Kuwait City by the Beni Khaled tribe in the 17th century

Administrative divisions: 6 governorates (muhafazat, singular - muhafazah); Al Ahmadi, Al 'Asimah, Al Farwaniyah, Al Jahra', Hawalli, Mubarak al Kabir

Independence: 19 June 1961 (from the UK)

National holiday: National Day, 25 February (1950)

Constitution: *history:* approved and promulgated 11 November 1962; suspended 1976 to 1981 (4 articles); 1986 to 1991; May to July 1999
amendments: proposed by the amir or supported by at least one third of the National Assembly; passage requires two-thirds consent of the Assembly membership and promulgation by the amir; constitutional articles on the initiation, approval, and promulgation of general legislation cannot be amended

Legal system: mixed legal system consisting of English common law, French civil law, and Islamic sharia law

International law organization participation: has not submitted an ICJ jurisdiction declaration; non-party state to the ICCt

Citizenship: *citizenship by birth:* no
citizenship by descent only: at least one parent must be a citizen of Kuwait
dual citizenship recognized: no
residency requirement for naturalization: not specified

Suffrage: 21 years of age and at least 20-year citizenship

Executive branch: *chief of state:* Ahmad al-NAWAF al-Sabah (since 24 July 2022); Crown Prince Mishal al-AHMAD al-Sabah, born in 1940, is the brother of Amir Nawaf al-AHMAD al-Jabir al-Sabah
head of government: Prime Minister Sheikh Muhammad al-Sabah al-SALIM al-Sabah (since 19 July 2022); First Deputy Prime Minister and Minister of Interior Sheikh Ahmed al-NAWAF al-Sabah (since 22 March 2022), Deputy Prime Minister and Minister of Defense Sheikh Talal al-KHALID al-Sabah (since 1 August 2022), and Deputy Prime Minister and Minister of Oil and Minister of State for Cabinet Affairs Dr. Mohammed al-FARIS (since 22 March 2022)
cabinet: Council of Ministers appointed by the prime minister, approved by the amir
elections/appointments: amir chosen from within the ruling family, confirmed by the National Assembly; prime minister and deputy prime ministers appointed by the amir; crown prince appointed by the amir and approved by the National Assembly

Legislative branch: *description:* unicameral National Assembly or Majlis al-Umma (65 seats; 50 members directly elected from 5 multi-seat constituencies by simple majority vote and 15 ex-officio members (cabinet ministers) appointed by the amir; members serve 4-year terms)
elections: last held on 29 September 2022 (next to be held in 2026)
election results: 50 nonpartisans elected, of which 28 were opposition candidates; composition - men 48, women 2, percent of women 4%

Judicial branch: *highest court(s):* Constitutional Court (consists of 5 judges); Supreme Court or Court of Cassation (organized into several circuits, each with 5 judges)
judge selection and term of office: all Kuwaiti judges appointed by the Amir upon recommendation of the Supreme Judicial Council, a consultative body comprised of Kuwaiti judges and Ministry of Justice officials
subordinate courts: High Court of Appeal; Court of First Instance; Summary Court

Political parties and leaders: none; the government does not recognize any political parties or allow their formation, although no formal law bans political parties

International organization participation: ABEDA, AfDB (nonregional member), AFESD, AMF, BDEAC, CAEU, CD, FAO, G-77, GCC, IAEA, IBRD, ICAO, ICC (national committees), ICRM, IDA, IDB, IFAD, IFC, IFRCS, IHO, ILO, IMF, IMO, IMSO, Interpol, IOC, IPU, ISO, ITSO, ITU, ITUC (NGOs), LAS, MIGA, NAM, OAPEC, OIC, OPCW, OPEC, Paris Club (associate), PCA, UN, UNCTAD, UNESCO, UNIDO, UNRWA, UN Security Council (temporary), UNWTO, UPU, WCO, WFTU (NGOs), WHO, WIPO, WMO, WTO

Diplomatic representation in the US: *chief of mission:* Ambassador SALEM Abdallah al-Jaber al-Sabah (since 10 October 2021)
chancery: 2940 Tilden Street NW, Washington, DC 20008
telephone: [1] (202) 966-0702
FAX: [1] (202) 966-8468
email address and website:
https://www.kuwaitembassy.us/
consulate(s) general: Beverly Hills (CA), New York

Diplomatic representation from the US: *chief of mission:* Ambassador (vacant); Chargé d'Affaires James HOLTSNIDER (since July 2021)
embassy: P.O. Box 77, Safat 13001
mailing address: 6200 Kuwait Place, Washington DC 20521-6200
telephone: [00] (965) 2259-1001
FAX: [00] (965) 2538-0282
email address and website:
KuwaitACS@state.gov
https://kw.usembassy.gov/

Flag description: three equal horizontal bands of green (top), white, and red with a black trapezoid based on the hoist side; colors and design are based on the Arab Revolt flag of World War I; green represents fertile fields, white stands for purity, red denotes blood on Kuwaiti swords, black signifies the defeat of the enemy

National symbol(s): golden falcon; national colors: green, white, red, black

National anthem: *name:* "Al-Nasheed Al-Watani" (National Anthem)
lyrics/music: Ahmad MUSHARI al-Adwani/ Ibrahim Nasir al-SOULA
note: adopted 1978; the anthem is only used on formal occasions

ECONOMY

Economic overview: Kuwait has a geographically small, but wealthy, relatively open economy with crude oil reserves of about 102 billion barrels - more than 6% of world reserves. Kuwaiti officials plan to increase production to 4 million barrels of oil equivalent per day by 2020. Petroleum accounts for over half of GDP, 92% of export revenues, and 90% of government income.

With world oil prices declining, Kuwait realized a budget deficit in 2015 for the first time more than a decade; in 2016, the deficit grew to 16.5% of GDP. Kuwaiti authorities announced cuts to fuel subsidies in August 2016, provoking outrage among the public and National Assembly, and the Amir dissolved the government for the seventh time in ten years. In 2017 the deficit was reduced to 7.2% of GDP, and the government raised $8 billion by issuing international bonds. Despite Kuwait's dependence on oil, the government has cushioned itself against the impact of lower oil prices, by saving annually at least 10% of government revenue in the Fund for Future Generations.

Kuwait has failed to diversify its economy or bolster the private sector, because of a poor business climate, a large public sector that employs about 74% of citizens, and an acrimonious relationship between the National Assembly and the executive branch that has stymied most economic reforms. The Kuwaiti Government has made little progress on its long-term economic development plan first passed in 2010. While the government planned to spend up to $104 billion over four years to diversify the economy, attract more investment, and boost private sector participation in the economy, many of the projects did not materialize because of an uncertain political situation or delays in awarding contracts. To increase non-oil revenues, the Kuwaiti Government in August 2017 approved draft bills supporting a Gulf Cooperation Council-wide value added tax scheduled to take effect in 2018.

Real GDP (purchasing power parity): $209.74 billion (2019 est.)
$208.85 billion (2018 est.)
$206.274 billion (2017 est.)
note: data are in 2017 dollars

Real GDP growth rate: -3.3% (2017 est.)
2.2% (2016 est.)
-1% (2015 est.)

Real GDP per capita: $49,900 (2019 est.) note: data are in 2017 dollars
$50,500 (2018 est.) note: data are in 2017 dollars
$50,856 (2017 est.)

GDP (official exchange rate): $134.638 billion (2019 est.)

Inflation rate (consumer prices): 1.5% (2017 est.)
3.5% (2016 est.)

Credit ratings:

Fitch rating: AA (2008)

Moody's rating: A1 (2020)

Standard & Poors rating: AA- (2020)
note: The year refers to the year in which the current credit rating was first obtained.

GDP - composition, by sector of origin: *agriculture:* 0.4% (2017 est.)
industry: 58.7% (2017 est.)
services: 40.9% (2017 est.)

GDP - composition, by end use: *household consumption:* 43.1% (2017 est.)
government consumption: 24.5% (2017 est.)
investment in fixed capital: 26.5% (2017 est.)
investment in inventories: 3.5% (2017 est.)
exports of goods and services: 49.4% (2017 est.)
imports of goods and services: -47% (2017 est.)

Agricultural products: eggs, dates, tomatoes, cucumbers, poultry, milk, mutton, potatoes, vegetables, eggplants

Industries: petroleum, petrochemicals, cement, shipbuilding and repair, water desalination, food processing, construction materials

Industrial production growth rate: 2.8% (2017 est.)

Labor force: 2.695 million (2017 est.)
note: non-Kuwaitis represent about 60% of the labor force

Unemployment rate: 1.1% (2017 est.)
1.1% (2016 est.)

Unemployment, youth ages 15-24: *total:* 15.4%
male: 9.4%
female: 30% (2016 est.)

Budget: *revenues:* 50.5 billion (2017 est.)
expenditures: 62.6 billion (2017 est.)

Budget surplus (+) or deficit (-): -10% (of GDP) (2017 est.)

Public debt: 20.6% of GDP (2017 est.)
9.9% of GDP (2016 est.)

Taxes and other revenues: 41.8% (of GDP) (2017 est.)

Fiscal year: 1 April - 31 March

Current account balance: $7.127 billion (2017 est.)
-$5.056 billion (2016 est.)

Exports: $72.83 billion (2019 est.) note: data are in current year dollars
$85.2 billion (2018 est.) note: data are in current year dollars

Exports - partners: China 20%, South Korea 16%, India 15%, Japan 10%, Taiwan 6%, Vietnam 5% (2019)

Exports - commodities: crude petroleum, refined petroleum, aircraft, natural gas, industrial hydrocarbon products (2019)

Imports: $59.65 billion (2019 est.) note: data are in current year dollars
$68.2 billion (2018 est.) note: data are in current year dollars

Imports - partners: China 14%, United Arab Emirates 12%, United States 10%, Saudi Arabia 6%, Japan 6%, Germany 5%, India 5% (2019)

Imports - commodities: cars, broadcasting equipment, natural gas, packaged medicines, jewelry (2019)

Reserves of foreign exchange and gold: $33.7 billion (31 December 2017 est.)
$31.13 billion (31 December 2016 est.)

Debt - external: $47.24 billion (31 December 2017 est.)
$38.34 billion (31 December 2016 est.)

Exchange rates: Kuwaiti dinars (KD) per US dollar -
0.3049 (2020 est.)
0.3037 (2019 est.)
0.304 (2018 est.)
0.3009 (2014 est.)
0.2845 (2013 est.)

ENERGY

Electricity access: *electrification - total population:* 100% (2020)

Electricity: *installed generating capacity:* 19.371 million kW (2020 est.)
consumption: 63,802,360,000 kWh (2019 est.)
exports: 0 kWh (2019 est.)
imports: 0 kWh (2019 est.)
transmission/distribution losses: 6.701 billion kWh (2019 est.)

Electricity generation sources: *fossil fuels:* 99.9% of total installed capacity (2020 est.)
wind: 0.1% of total installed capacity (2020 est.)

Coal: *production:* 0 metric tons (2020 est.)
consumption: 68,000 metric tons (2020 est.)
exports: 0 metric tons (2020 est.)
imports: 68,000 metric tons (2020 est.)
proven reserves: 0 metric tons (2019 est.)

Petroleum: *total petroleum production:* 2,720,500 bbl/day (2021 est.)
refined petroleum consumption: 342,000 bbl/day (2019 est.)
crude oil and lease condensate exports: 1,837,900 bbl/day (2018 est.)
crude oil and lease condensate imports: 0 bbl/day (2018 est.)
crude oil estimated reserves: 101.5 billion barrels (2021 est.)

Refined petroleum products - production: 915,800 bbl/day (2015 est.)

Refined petroleum products - exports: 705,500 bbl/day (2015 est.)

Refined petroleum products - imports: 0 bbl/day (2015 est.)

Natural gas: *production:* 19,509,907,000 cubic meters (2019 est.)
consumption: 24,322,970,000 cubic meters (2019 est.)
exports: 0 cubic meters (2021 est.)
imports: 4,805,531,000 cubic meters (2019 est.)
proven reserves: 1,783,958,000,000 cubic meters (2021 est.)

Carbon dioxide emissions: 92.582 million metric tonnes of CO2 (2019 est.)
from coal and metallurgical coke: 578,000 metric tonnes of CO2 (2019 est.)
from petroleum and other liquids: 44.288 million metric tonnes of CO2 (2019 est.)
from consumed natural gas: 47.715 million metric tonnes of CO2 (2019 est.)

Energy consumption per capita: 381.985 million Btu/person (2019 est.)

COMMUNICATIONS

Telephones - fixed lines: *total subscriptions:* 583,463 (2020 est.)
subscriptions per 100 inhabitants: 14 (2020 est.)

Telephones - mobile cellular: *total subscriptions:* 6,770,346 (2020 est.)
subscriptions per 100 inhabitants: 159 (2020 est.)

Telecommunication systems: *general assessment:* Kuwait's telecom infrastructure is well developed, with a focus on mobile infrastructure and services; the telecom sector is important to the country's economy, and this will become more pronounced in coming years as the economy is purposefully transitioned away from a dependence on oil and gas to one which is increasingly knowledge-based and focused on ICT and related services; the MNOs have focused investment on 5G networks, which support and promote the growth of data traffic; this in turn has been a catalyst for revenue growth in recent quarters; while Kuwait's mobile sector shows considerable progress; the country's fixed broadband system is the lowest in the region; the government has stepped up efforts to build up fixed broadband networks, and ultimately this sector offers a potential future growth opportunity; improvements to the fixed broadband infrastructure will help develop sectors such as e-commerce, along with smart infrastructure developments, and tech start-ups (2022)
domestic: fixed-line subscriptions are nearly 14 per 100 and mobile-cellular stands at nearly 159 per 100 subscriptions (2020)
international: country code - 965; landing points for the FOG, GBICS, MENA, Kuwait-Iran, and FALCON submarine cables linking Africa, the Middle East, and Asia; microwave radio relay to Saudi Arabia; satellite earth stations - 6 (3 Intelsat - 1 Atlantic Ocean and 2 Indian Ocean, 1 Inmarsat - Atlantic Ocean, and 2 Arabsat) (2019)

Broadcast media: state-owned TV broadcaster operates 4 networks and a satellite channel; several private TV broadcasters have emerged; satellite TV available and pan-Arab TV stations are especially popular; state-owned Radio Kuwait broadcasts on a number of channels in Arabic and English; first private radio station emerged in 2005; transmissions of at least 2 international radio broadcasters are available (2019)

Internet country code: .kw

Internet users: *total:* 4,227,857 (2020 est.)
percent of population: 99% (2020 est.)

Broadband - fixed subscriptions: *total:* 73,948 (2020 est.)
subscriptions per 100 inhabitants: 2 (2020 est.)

TRANSPORTATION

National air transport system: *number of registered air carriers:* 2 (2020)
inventory of registered aircraft operated by air carriers: 44
annual passenger traffic on registered air carriers: 6,464,847 (2018)
annual freight traffic on registered air carriers: 392.36 million (2018) mt-km

Civil aircraft registration country code prefix: 9K

Airports: *total:* 7 (2021)

Airports - with paved runways: *total:* 4
over 3,047 m: 1
2,438 to 3,047 m: 2
914 to 1,523 m: 1 (2021)

Airports - with unpaved runways: *total:* 3
1,524 to 2,437 m: 1
under 914 m: 2 (2021)

Heliports: 4 (2021)

Pipelines: 261 km gas, 540 km oil, 57 km refined products (2013)

Roadways: *total:* 5,749 km (2018)
paved: 4,887 km (2018)
unpaved: 862 km (2018)

Merchant marine: *total:* 165
by type: general cargo 15, oil tanker 28, other 122 (2021)

Ports and terminals: *major seaport(s):* Ash Shu'aybah, Ash Shuwaykh, Az Zawr (Mina' Sa'ud), Mina' 'Abd Allah, Mina' al Ahmadi

MILITARY AND SECURITY

Military and security forces: Kuwaiti Armed Forces (KAF): Kuwaiti Land Forces (KLF), Kuwaiti Navy, Kuwaiti Air Force (Al-Quwwat al-Jawwiya al-Kuwaitiya; includes Kuwaiti Air Defense Force, KADF), 25th Commando Brigade, and the Kuwait Emiri Guard Brigade; Kuwaiti National Guard (KNG); Coast Guard (Ministry of Interior) (2022)
note 1: the Kuwait Amiri Guard Authority and the 25th Commando Brigade exercise independent command authority within the Kuwaiti Armed Forces, although activities such as training and equipment procurement are often coordinated with the other services
note 2: the Kuwaiti National Guard reports directly to the prime minister and the amir and possesses an independent command structure, equipment inventory, and logistics corps separate from the Ministry of Defense, the regular armed services, and the Ministry of Interior; it is responsible for protecting critical infrastructure and providing support for the Ministries of Interior and Defense as required

Military expenditures: 6.8% of GDP (2021 est.)
6.3% of GDP (2020 est.)
5.6% of GDP (2019) (approximately $10.2 billion)
5.1% of GDP (2018) (approximately $9.25 billion)
5.6% of GDP (2017) (approximately $10 billion)

Military and security service personnel strengths: approximately 17,000 active duty armed forces personnel (12,500 Army, including the Amiri Guard and 25th Commando Brigade; 2,000 Navy; 2,500 Air Force); approximately 6,500 National Guard (2022)

Military equipment inventories and acquisitions: the military's inventory consists of weapons from a wide variety of sources, including Western Europe, Russia, the United Arab Emirates, and the US; the US has been the leading supplier of arms to Kuwait since 2010 (2022)

Military service age and obligation: 18-26 years of age for voluntary military service; Kuwait reintroduced 12-month mandatory service for men aged 18-35 in May 2017 after having suspended conscription in 2001; mandatory service is divided in two phases – 4 months for training and 8 months for military service; women were allowed to volunteer in 2021 (2022)
note: the National Guard is restricted to citizens, but in 2018, the Army began allowing non-Kuwaitis to join on contract or as non-commissioned officers; that same year, it also began allowing stateless people (Bidoon) to join

Military - note: as of 2022, the US had approximately 13,000 military personnel based in Kuwait as part of a 1991 Defense Cooperation Agreement and a 2013 Acquisition and Cross-Servicing Agreement

Kuwait has Major Non-NATO Ally (MNNA) status with the US; MNNA is a designation under US law that provides foreign partners with certain benefits in the areas of defense trade and security cooperation; while MNNA status provides military and economic privileges, it does not entail any security commitments (2022)

TRANSNATIONAL ISSUES

Disputes - international: *Kuwait-Iraq:* no maritime boundary exists with Iraq in the Persian Gulf

Kuwait-Saudi Arabia: their maritime boundary was established in 2000 and has a neutral zone but its extension to Iran's maritime boundary has not been negotiated

Refugees and internally displaced persons: *stateless persons:* 92,020 (mid-year 2021); note - Kuwait's 1959 Nationality Law defined citizens as persons who settled in the country before 1920 and who had maintained normal residence since then; one-third of the population, descendants of Bedouin tribes, missed the window of opportunity to register for nationality rights after Kuwait became independent in 1961 and were classified as bidun (meaning "without"); since the 1980s Kuwait's bidun have progressively lost their rights, including opportunities for employment and education, amid official claims that they are nationals of other countries who have destroyed their identification documents in hopes of gaining Kuwaiti citizenship; Kuwaiti authorities have delayed processing citizenship applications and labeled biduns as "illegal residents," denying them access to civil documentation, such as birth and marriage certificates

KYRGYZSTAN

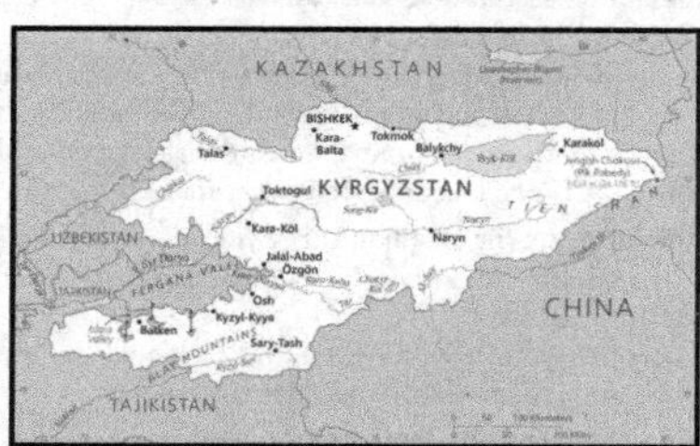

INTRODUCTION

Background: A Central Asian country of incredible natural beauty and proud nomadic traditions, most of the territory of present-day Kyrgyzstan was formally annexed by the Russian Empire in 1876. The Kyrgyz staged a major revolt against the Tsarist Empire in 1916 in which almost one-sixth of the Kyrgyz population was killed. Kyrgyzstan became a Soviet republic in 1926 and achieved independence in 1991 when the USSR dissolved. Nationwide demonstrations in 2005 and 2010 resulted in the ouster of the country's first two presidents, Askar AKAEV and Kurmanbek BAKIEV. Interim President Roza OTUNBAEVA led a transitional government and following a nationwide election, President Almazbek ATAMBAEV was sworn in as president in 2011. In 2017, ATAMBAEV became the first Kyrgyzstani president to step down after serving one full six-year term as required in the country's constitution. Former prime minister and ruling Social-Democratic Party of Kyrgyzstan member, Sooronbay JEENBEKOV, replaced him after winning the 2017 presidential election, which was the most competitive in the country's history, although international and local election observers noted cases of vote buying and abuse of public resources. In October 2020, protests against legislative election results spread across Kyrgyzstan, leading to JEENBEKOV's resignation from the presidency, and catapulting previously imprisoned Sadyr JAPAROV to acting president. In January 2021, Kyrgyzstanis formerly elected JAPAROV as president and approved a referendum to move Kyrgyzstan from a parliamentary to a presidential system. In April 2021, Kyrgyzstanis voted in favor of draft constitutional changes that consolidated power in the presidency. Pro-government parties won a majority in the Jogorku Kenesh (Kyrgyzstan's legislature) in November 2021 elections. Continuing concerns for Kyrgyzstan include the trajectory of democratization, endemic corruption, a history of tense, and at times violent, interethnic relations, border security vulnerabilities, and potential terrorist threats.

GEOGRAPHY

Location: Central Asia, west of China, south of Kazakhstan

Geographic coordinates: 41 00 N, 75 00 E

Map references: Asia

Area: *total:* 199,951 sq km
land: 191,801 sq km
water: 8,150 sq km

Area - comparative: slightly smaller than South Dakota

Land boundaries: *total:* 4,573 km
border countries (4): China 1,063 km; Kazakhstan 1,212 km; Tajikistan 984 km; Uzbekistan 1,314 km

Coastline: 0 km (landlocked)

Maritime claims: none (landlocked)

Climate: dry continental to polar in high Tien Shan Mountains; subtropical in southwest (Fergana Valley); temperate in northern foothill zone

Terrain: peaks of the Tien Shan mountain range and associated valleys and basins encompass the entire country

Elevation: *highest point:* Jengish Chokusu (Pik Pobedy) 7,439 m
lowest point: Kara-Daryya (Karadar'ya) 132 m
mean elevation: 2,988 m

Natural resources: abundant hydropower; gold, rare earth metals; locally exploitable coal, oil, and natural gas; other deposits of nepheline, mercury, bismuth, lead, and zinc

Land use: *agricultural land:* 55.4% (2018 est.)
arable land: 6.7% (2018 est.)
permanent crops: 0.4% (2018 est.)
permanent pasture: 48.3% (2018 est.)
forest: 5.1% (2018 est.)
other: 39.5% (2018 est.)

Irrigated land: 10,233 sq km (2012)

Major lakes (area sq km): *salt water lake(s):* Ozero Issyk-Kul 6,240 sq km
note - second largest saline lake after the Caspian Sea; second highest mountain lake after Lake Titicaca; it is an endorheic mountain basin; although surrounded by snow capped mountains it never freezes

Major rivers (by length in km): Syr Darya river source (shared with Tajikistan, Uzbekistan, and Kazakhstan [m]) - 3,078 km
note – [s] after country name indicates river source; [m] after country name indicates river mouth

Major watersheds (area sq km): Internal *(endorheic basin)* drainage: Tarim Basin (1,152,448 sq km), *(Aral Sea basin)* Amu Darya (534,739 sq km), Syr Darya (782,617 sq km)

Population distribution: the vast majority of Kyrgyzstanis live in rural areas; densest population settlement is to the north in and around the capital, Bishkek, followed by Osh in the west; the least densely populated area is the east, southeast in the Tien Shan mountains

Natural hazards: major flooding during snow melt; prone to earthquakes

Geography - note: landlocked; entirely mountainous, dominated by the Tien Shan range; 94% of the country is 1,000 m above sea level with an average elevation of 2,750 m; many tall peaks, glaciers, and high-altitude lakes

PEOPLE AND SOCIETY

Population: 6,071,750 (2022 est.)

Nationality: *noun:* Kyrgyzstani(s)
adjective: Kyrgyzstani

Ethnic groups: Kyrgyz 73.8%, Uzbek 14.8%, Russian 5.1%, Dungan 1.1%, other 5.2% (includes Uyghur, Tajik, Turk, Kazakh, Tatar, Ukrainian, Korean, German) (2021 est.)

Languages: Kyrgyz (official) 71.4%, Uzbek 14.4%, Russian (official) 9%, other 5.2% (2009 est.)
major-language sample(s):
Дүйнөлүк фактылар китеби, негизги маалыматтын маанилүү булагы.
(Kyrgyz)

Religions: Muslim 90% (majority Sunni), Christian 7% (Russian Orthodox 3%), other 3% (includes Jewish, Buddhist, Baha'i) (2017 est.)

Demographic profile: Kyrgyzstan is a sparsely populated country whose population is unevenly distributed. More than 50% of the population lives in or around the two cities of Bishkek and Osh and their surrounding districts, which together account for about 12% of the country's area. Kyrgyzstan's population continues to grow rapidly owing to its high fertility rate and the traditional preference for larger families, a low mortality rate, a growing share of women of reproductive age, and measures to support families with children. The country has a youthful age structure; over 45% of the population is under the age of 25 as of 2022. Nevertheless, Kyrgyzstan is transitioning from an agricultural society with high fertility and mortality rates to an industrial society with lower fertility and mortality rates.

As part of the USSR, Kyrgyzstan's rapid population growth was not problematic because its needs were redistributed among the Soviet States. As an independent state, however, population growth became burdensome. International labor migration continues to serve as a safety valve that decreases pressure on the labor market and resources (healthcare, education, and pensions), while also reducing poverty through much-needed remittances. The main destinations for labor migrants are Russia and Kazakhstan, where wages are higher; almost a third of Kyrgyzstan's working-age population migrates to Russia alone. Outmigration was most pronounced in the 1990s, after the collapse of the USSR, when ethnic Russians, Ukrainians, and Germans left Kyrgyzstan, changing the proportion of ethnic Kyrgyz in the country from barely 50% in 1992 to almost three-quarters today.

While Kyrgyzstan is a net emigration country, it does receive immigrants. The majority of immigrants are from the Commonwealth of Independent States – particularly Kazakhstan, Russia, and Uzbekistan – but more recent arrivals also include persons from China, Turkey, and Turkmenistan. Chinese immigrants work primarily in construction and gold mining, while Turkish immigrants mainly work in construction, trade, education, and services. Border areas between Kyrgyzstan, Tajikistan, and Uzbekistan experience irregular migration, but many of these migrants plan to move on to Europe.

Age structure: *0-14 years:* 30.39% (male 930,455/female 882,137)
15-24 years: 15.7% (male 475,915/female 460,604)
25-54 years: 40.02% (male 1,172,719/female 1,214,624)

55-64 years: 8.09% (male 210,994/female 271,480)
65 years and over: 5.8% (male 132,134/female 213,835) (2020 est.)

Dependency ratios: *total dependency ratio:* 59.7
youth dependency ratio: 52.1
elderly dependency ratio: 7.5
potential support ratio: 13.2 (2020 est.)

Median age: *total:* 27.3 years
male: 26.1 years
female: 28.5 years (2020 est.)

Population growth rate: 0.86% (2022 est.)

Birth rate: 19.54 births/1,000 population (2022 est.)

Death rate: 6.12 deaths/1,000 population (2022 est.)

Net migration rate: -4.87 migrant(s)/1,000 population (2022 est.)

Population distribution: the vast majority of Kyrgyzstanis live in rural areas; densest population settlement is to the north in and around the capital, Bishkek, followed by Osh in the west; the least densely populated area is the east, southeast in the Tien Shan mountains

Urbanization: *urban population:* 37.5% of total population (2022)
rate of urbanization: 2.05% annual rate of change (2020-25 est.)

Major urban areas - population: 1.082 million BISHKEK (capital) (2022)

Sex ratio: *at birth:* 1.07 male(s)/female
0-14 years: 1.06 male(s)/female
15-24 years: 1.03 male(s)/female
25-54 years: 0.96 male(s)/female
55-64 years: 0.78 male(s)/female
65 years and over: 0.5 male(s)/female
total population: 0.96 male(s)/female (2022 est.)

Mother's mean age at first birth: 22.6 years (2019 est.)

Maternal mortality ratio: 60 deaths/100,000 live births (2017 est.)

Infant mortality rate: *total:* 25.66 deaths/1,000 live births
male: 29.83 deaths/1,000 live births
female: 21.22 deaths/1,000 live births (2022 est.)

Life expectancy at birth: *total population:* 72.35 years
male: 68.27 years
female: 76.71 years (2022 est.)

Total fertility rate: 2.5 children born/woman (2022 est.)

Contraceptive prevalence rate: 39.4% (2018)

Drinking water source: *improved: urban:* 100% of population
rural: 89.9% of population
total: 93.6% of population
unimproved: urban: 0% of population
rural: 10.1% of population
total: 6.4% of population (2020 est.)

Current health expenditure: 4.5% of GDP (2019)

Physicians density: 2.21 physicians/1,000 population (2014)

Hospital bed density: 4.4 beds/1,000 population (2014)

Sanitation facility access: *improved: urban:* 100% of population
rural: 100% of population
total: 100% of population

HIV/AIDS - adult prevalence rate: 0.2% (2020 est.)

Obesity - adult prevalence rate: 16.6% (2016)

Alcohol consumption per capita: *total:* 4.02 liters of pure alcohol (2019 est.)
beer: 0.43 liters of pure alcohol (2019 est.)
wine: 0.23 liters of pure alcohol (2019 est.)
spirits: 3.35 liters of pure alcohol (2019 est.)
other alcohols: 0 liters of pure alcohol (2019 est.)

Tobacco use: *total:* 25.4% (2020 est.)
male: 48% (2020 est.)
female: 2.8% (2020 est.)

Children under the age of 5 years underweight: 1.8% (2018)

Child marriage: *women married by age 15:* 0.3%
women married by age 18: 12.9% (2018 est.)

Education expenditures: 5.4% of GDP (2019 est.)

Literacy: *definition:* age 15 and over can read and write
total population: 99.6%
male: 99.7%
female: 99.5% (2018)

School life expectancy (primary to tertiary education): *total:* 13 years
male: 13 years
female: 13 years (2020)

Unemployment, youth ages 15-24: *total:* 9.6%
male: 7.8%
female: 13.4% (2018 est.)

ENVIRONMENT

Environment - current issues: water pollution; many people get their water directly from contaminated streams and wells; as a result, water-borne diseases are prevalent; increasing soil salinity from faulty irrigation practices; air pollution due to rapid increase of traffic

Environment - international agreements: *party to:* Air Pollution, Biodiversity, Climate Change, Climate Change-Kyoto Protocol, Climate Change-Paris Agreement, Comprehensive Nuclear Test Ban, Desertification, Endangered Species, Environmental Modification, Hazardous Wastes, Ozone Layer Protection, Wetlands
signed, but not ratified: none of the selected agreements

Air pollutants: *particulate matter emissions:* 18.12 micrograms per cubic meter (2016 est.)
carbon dioxide emissions: 9.79 megatons (2016 est.)
methane emissions: 4.47 megatons (2020 est.)

Climate: dry continental to polar in high Tien Shan Mountains; subtropical in southwest (Fergana Valley); temperate in northern foothill zone

Land use: *agricultural land:* 55.4% (2018 est.)
arable land: 6.7% (2018 est.)
permanent crops: 0.4% (2018 est.)
permanent pasture: 48.3% (2018 est.)
forest: 5.1% (2018 est.)
other: 39.5% (2018 est.)

Urbanization: *urban population:* 37.5% of total population (2022)
rate of urbanization: 2.05% annual rate of change (2020-25 est.)

Revenue from forest resources: *forest revenues:* 0.01% of GDP (2018 est.)

Revenue from coal: *coal revenues:* 0.21% of GDP (2018 est.)

Waste and recycling: *municipal solid waste generated annually:* 1,113,300 tons (2015 est.)

Major lakes (area sq km): *salt water lake(s):* Ozero Issyk-Kul 6,240 sq km
note - second largest saline lake after the Caspian Sea; second highest mountain lake after Lake Titicaca; it is an endorheic mountain basin; although surrounded by snow capped mountains it never freezes

Major rivers (by length in km): Syr Darya river source (shared with Tajikistan, Uzbekistan, and Kazakhstan [m]) - 3,078 km
note – [s] after country name indicates river source; [m] after country name indicates river mouth

Major watersheds (area sq km): Internal *(endorheic basin)* drainage: Tarim Basin (1,152,448 sq km), *(Aral Sea basin)* Amu Darya (534,739 sq km), Syr Darya (782,617 sq km)

Total water withdrawal: *municipal:* 224 million cubic meters (2017 est.)
industrial: 336 million cubic meters (2017 est.)
agricultural: 7.1 billion cubic meters (2017 est.)

Total renewable water resources: 23.618 billion cubic meters (2017 est.)

GOVERNMENT

Country name: *conventional long form:* Kyrgyz Republic
conventional short form: Kyrgyzstan
local long form: Kyrgyz Respublikasy
local short form: Kyrgyzstan
former: Kirghiz Soviet Socialist Republic
etymology: a combination of the Turkic words "kyrg" (forty) and "-yz" (tribes) with the Persian suffix "-stan" (country) creating the meaning "Land of the Forty Tribes"; the name refers to the 40 clans united by the mythic Kyrgyz hero, MANAS

Government type: parliamentary republic

Capital: *name:* Bishkek
geographic coordinates: 42 52 N, 74 36 E
time difference: UTC+6 (11 hours ahead of Washington, DC, during Standard Time)
etymology: founded in 1868 as a Russian settlement on the site of a previously destroyed fortress named "Pishpek"; the name was retained and overtime became "Bishkek"

Administrative divisions: 7 provinces (oblustar, singular - oblus) and 2 cities* (shaarlar, singular - shaar); Batken Oblusu, Bishkek Shaary*, Chuy Oblusu (Bishkek), Jalal-Abad Oblusu, Naryn Oblusu, Osh Oblusu, Osh Shaary*, Talas Oblusu, Ysyk-Kol Oblusu (Karakol)
note: administrative divisions have the same names as their administrative centers (exceptions have the administrative center name following in parentheses)

Independence: 31 August 1991 (from the Soviet Union)

National holiday: Independence Day, 31 August (1991)

Constitution: *history:* previous 1993, 2007, 2010; latest approved by referendum in April 2021 that transitioned Kyrgyzstan from a parliamentary to a presidential system, and implemented changes that allow the president to serve for two 5-year terms rather that one 6-year term, reduced the number of seats in Kyrgyzstan's legislature from 120 to 90, and established a Kurultay - a public advisory council *amendments:* proposed as a draft law by the majority of the Supreme Council membership or by petition of 300,000 voters; passage requires at least two-thirds majority vote of the Council membership in each of at least three readings of the draft two months apart; the draft may be submitted to a referendum if approved by two thirds of the Council membership; adoption requires the signature of the president

Legal system: civil law system, which includes features of French civil law and Russian Federation laws

International law organization participation: has not submitted an ICJ jurisdiction declaration; non-party state to the ICCt

Citizenship: *citizenship by birth:* no
citizenship by descent only: at least one parent must be a citizen of Kyrgyzstan
dual citizenship recognized: yes, but only if a mutual treaty on dual citizenship is in force
residency requirement for naturalization: 5 years

Suffrage: 18 years of age; universal

Executive branch: *chief of state:* President Sadyr JAPAROV (since 28 January 2021)
head of government: President Sadyr JAPAROV (since 28 January 2021)
cabinet: Cabinet of Ministers appointed by the president
elections/appointments: president directly elected by absolute majority popular vote in 2 rounds if needed for a five-year term (eligible for a second term); election last held on 10 January 2021 (next to be held in 2027)
election results: 2021: Sadyr JAPAROV elected president in first round; percent of vote - Sadyr JAPAROV (Mekenchil) 79.2%, Adakhan MADUMAROV (United Kyrgyzstan) 6.8%, other 14%
2017: Sooronbay JEENBEKOV elected president; Sooronbay JEENBEKOV (Social Democratic Party of Kosovo) 54.7%, Omurbek BABANOV (independent) 33.8%, Adakhan MADUMAROV (United Kyrgyzstan) 6.6%, and other 4.9%
note: the President is both Chief of State and Head of Government.

Legislative branch: *description:* unicameral Supreme Council or Jogorku Kenesh (90 seats statutory, current 88; 54 seats allocated for proportional division among political party lists from the national vote and 36 seats allocated for candidates running in single-seat constituencies; members serve 5-year terms; parties must receive 5% of the vote to win seats in the Council)
elections: last held on 28 November 2021 (next to be held in 2026)
election results: percent of vote by party - AJK 19.1%, Ishenim 15%, Yntymak 12.1%, Alliance 9.2%, Butun Kyrgyzstan 7.8%, Yiman Nuru 6.8%, other 30%; seats by party - AJK 15, Ishenim 12, Yntymak 9, Alliance 7, Butun Kyrgyzstan 6, Yiman Nuru 5, other 36; composition - men 70, women 18, percent of women 20.5%

Judicial branch: *highest court(s):* Supreme Court (consists of 25 judges); Constitutional Chamber of the Supreme Court (consists of the chairperson, deputy chairperson, and 9 judges)
judge selection and term of office: Supreme Court and Constitutional Court judges appointed by the Supreme Council on the recommendation of the president; Supreme Court judges serve for 10 years, Constitutional Court judges serve for 15 years; mandatory retirement at age 70 for judges of both courts
subordinate courts: Higher Court of Arbitration; oblast (provincial) and city courts

Political parties and leaders: Alliance [Mirlan JEENCHOROEV]
Ata-Jurt Kyrgyzstan (Homeland) or AJK [Aybek MATKERIMOV]
Butun Kyrgyzstan (All Kyrgyzstan) [Adakhan MADUMAROV]
Ishenim (Trust in Kyrgyz) [Rysbat AMATOV]
Mekenchil (Patriotic Party) [Sadyr JAPAROV]
Social Democratic Party of Kosovo or SDPK (dissolved in 2020)
Social Democrats or SDK [Temirlan SULTANBEKOV]
United Kyrgyzstan [Adakhan Kumsanbayevich MADUMAROV]
Yntymak (Unity) [Marlen MAMATALIEV]
Yyman Nuru (Light of Faith) [Nurjigit KADYRBEKOV]

International organization participation: ADB, CICA, CIS, CSTO, EAEC, EAEU, EAPC, EBRD, ECO, EITI (compliant country), FAO, GCTU, IAEA, IBRD, ICAO, ICC (NGOs), ICRM, IDA, IDB, IFAD, IFC, IFRCS, ILO, IMF, Interpol, IOC, IOM, IPU, ISO (correspondent), ITSO, ITU, MIGA, NAM (observer), OIC, OPCW, OSCE, PCA, PFP, SCO, UN, UNAMID, UNCTAD, UNESCO, UNIDO, UNISFA, UNMIL, UNMISS, UNWTO, UPU, WCO, WFTU (NGOs), WHO, WIPO, WMO, WTO

Diplomatic representation in the US: *chief of mission:* Ambassador Baktybek AMANBAYEV (since 7 July 2021)
chancery: 2360 Massachusetts Avenue NW, Washington, DC 20008
telephone: [1] (202) 449-9822
FAX: [1] (202) 449-8275
email address and website:
kgembassy.usa@mfa.gov.kg; kgconsulate.washington@mfa.gov.kg

Diplomatic representation from the US: *chief of mission:* Ambassador (vacant); Charge d'Affaires Sonata COULTER (since September 2021)
embassy: 171 Prospect Mira, Bishkek 720016
mailing address: 7040 Bishkek Place, Washington DC 20521-7040
telephone: [996] (312) 597-000
FAX: [996] (312) 597-744
email address and website:
ConsularBishkek@state.gov
https://kg.usembassy.gov/

Flag description: red field with a yellow sun in the center having 40 rays representing the 40 Kyrgyz tribes; on the obverse side the rays run counterclockwise, on the reverse, clockwise; in the center of the sun is a red ring crossed by two sets of three lines, a stylized representation of a "tunduk" - the crown of a traditional Kyrgyz yurt; red symbolizes bravery and valor, the sun evinces peace and wealth

National symbol(s): white falcon; national colors: red, yellow

National anthem: *name:* "Kyrgyz Respublikasynyn Mamlekettik Gimni" (National Anthem of the Kyrgyz Republic)
lyrics/music: Djamil SADYKOV and Eshmambet KULUEV/Nasyr DAVLESOV and Kalyi MOLDOBASANOV
note: adopted 1992

National heritage: *total World Heritage Sites:* 3 (2 cultural, 1 natural)
selected World Heritage Site locales: Sulaiman-Too Sacred Mountain (c); Silk Roads: the Chang'an-Tianshan Corridor (c); Western Tien Shan (n)

ECONOMY

Economic overview: Kyrgyzstan is a landlocked, mountainous, lower middle income country with an economy dominated by minerals extraction, agriculture, and reliance on remittances from citizens working abroad. Cotton, wool, and meat are the main agricultural products, although only cotton is exported in any quantity. Other exports include gold, mercury, uranium, natural gas, and - in some years - electricity. The country has sought to attract foreign investment to expand its export base, including construction of hydroelectric dams, but a difficult investment climate and an ongoing legal battle with a Canadian firm over the joint ownership structure of the nation's largest gold mine deter potential investors. Remittances from Kyrgyz migrant workers, predominantly in Russia and Kazakhstan, are equivalent to more than one-quarter of Kyrgyzstan's GDP.

Following independence, Kyrgyzstan rapidly implemented market reforms, such as improving the regulatory system and instituting land reform. In 1998, Kyrgyzstan was the first Commonwealth of Independent States country to be accepted into the World Trade Organization. The government has privatized much of its ownership shares in public enterprises. Despite these reforms, the country suffered a severe drop in production in the early 1990s and has again faced slow growth in recent years as the global financial crisis and declining oil prices have dampened economies across Central Asia. The Kyrgyz government remains dependent on foreign donor support to finance its annual budget deficit of approximately 3 to 5% of GDP.

Kyrgyz leaders hope the country's August 2015 accession to the Eurasian Economic Union (EAEU) will bolster trade and investment, but slowing economies in Russia and China and low commodity prices continue to hamper economic growth. Large-scale trade and investment pledged by Kyrgyz leaders has been slow to develop. Many Kyrgyz entrepreneurs and politicians complain that non-tariff measures imposed by other EAEU member states are hurting certain sectors of the Kyrgyz economy, such as meat and dairy production, in which they have comparative advantage. Since acceding to the EAEU, the Kyrgyz Republic has continued harmonizing its laws and regulations to meet EAEU standards, though many local entrepreneurs believe this process as disjointed and incomplete. Kyrgyzstan's economic development continues to be hampered by corruption, lack of administrative transparency, lack of diversity in domestic industries, and difficulty attracting foreign aid and investment.

Real GDP (purchasing power parity): $31.02 billion (2020 est.)
$33.95 billion (2019 est.)
$32.46 billion (2018 est.)
note: data are in 2017 dollars

Real GDP growth rate: 4.6% (2017 est.)
4.3% (2016 est.)
3.9% (2015 est.)

Real GDP per capita: $4,700 (2020 est.)
$5,300 (2019 est.)

$5,100 (2018 est.)
note: data are in 2017 dollars

GDP (official exchange rate): $8.442 billion (2019 est.)

Inflation rate (consumer prices): 1.1% (2019 est.)
1.5% (2018 est.)
3.1% (2017 est.)

Credit ratings:

Moody's rating: B2 (2015)

Standard & Poors rating: NR (2016)
note: The year refers to the year in which the current credit rating was first obtained.

GDP - composition, by sector of origin: *agriculture:* 14.6% (2017 est.)
industry: 31.2% (2017 est.)
services: 54.2% (2017 est.)

GDP - composition, by end use: *household consumption:* 85.4% (2017 est.)
government consumption: 18.9% (2017 est.)
investment in fixed capital: 33.2% (2017 est.)
investment in inventories: 1.8% (2017 est.)
exports of goods and services: 39.7% (2017 est.)
imports of goods and services: -79% (2017 est.)

Agricultural products: milk, potatoes, sugar beet, maize, wheat, barley, tomatoes, watermelons, onions, carrots/turnips

Industries: small machinery, textiles, food processing, cement, shoes, lumber, refrigerators, furniture, electric motors, gold, rare earth metals

Industrial production growth rate: 10.9% (2017 est.)

Labor force: 2.841 million (2017 est.)

Labor force - by occupation: *agriculture:* 48%
industry: 12.5%
services: 39.5% (2005 est.)

Unemployment rate: 3.18% (2019 est.)
2.59% (2018 est.)

Unemployment, youth ages 15-24: *total:* 9.6%
male: 7.8%
female: 13.4% (2018 est.)

Population below poverty line: 20.1% (2019 est.)

Gini Index coefficient - distribution of family income: 27.7 (2018 est.)
29 (2001)

Household income or consumption by percentage share: *lowest 10%:* 4.4%
highest 10%: 22.9% (2014 est.)

Budget: *revenues:* 2.169 billion (2017 est.)
expenditures: 2.409 billion (2017 est.)

Budget surplus (+) or deficit (-): -3.2% (of GDP) (2017 est.)

Public debt: 56% of GDP (2017 est.)
55.9% of GDP (2016 est.)

Taxes and other revenues: 28.7% (of GDP) (2017 est.)

Fiscal year: calendar year

Current account balance: -$306 million (2017 est.)
-$792 million (2016 est.)

Exports: $3.11 billion (2019 est.) note: data are in current year dollars
$2.73 billion (2018 est.) note: data are in current year dollars
$2.352 billion (2017 est.)

Exports - partners: United Kingdom 56%, Kazakhstan 13%, Russia 13%, Uzbekistan 5% (2019)

Exports - commodities: gold, precious metals, various beans, refined petroleum, scrap copper (2019)

Imports: $5.67 billion (2019 est.) note: data are in current year dollars
$5.86 billion (2018 est.) note: data are in current year dollars
$4.953 billion (2017 est.)

Imports - partners: China 53%, Russia 17%, Kazakhstan 7%, Uzbekistan 7%, Turkey 5% (2019)

Imports - commodities: refined petroleum, footwear, clothing and apparel, broadcasting equipment, walnuts (2019)

Reserves of foreign exchange and gold: $2.177 billion (31 December 2017 est.)
$1.97 billion (31 December 2016 est.)

Debt - external: $8.372 billion (2019 est.)
$8.066 billion (2018 est.)

Exchange rates: soms (KGS) per US dollar -
68.35 (2017 est.)
69.914 (2016 est.)
69.914 (2015 est.)
64.462 (2014 est.)
53.654 (2013 est.)

ENERGY

Electricity access: *electrification - total population:* 100% (2020)

Electricity: *installed generating capacity:* 4.626 million kW (2020 est.)
consumption: 12,324,140,000 kWh (2019 est.)
exports: 271 million kWh (2019 est.)
imports: 269 million kWh (2019 est.)
transmission/distribution losses: 2.514 billion kWh (2019 est.)

Electricity generation sources: *fossil fuels:* 8.5% of total installed capacity (2020 est.)
hydroelectricity: 91.5% of total installed capacity (2020 est.)

Coal: *production:* 2.287 million metric tons (2020 est.)
consumption: 1.717 million metric tons (2020 est.)
exports: 984,000 metric tons (2020 est.)
imports: 481,000 metric tons (2020 est.)
proven reserves: 971 million metric tons (2019 est.)

Petroleum: *total petroleum production:* 700 bbl/day (2021 est.)
refined petroleum consumption: 32,100 bbl/day (2019 est.)
crude oil and lease condensate exports: 1,400 bbl/day (2018 est.)
crude oil and lease condensate imports: 8,200 bbl/day (2018 est.)
crude oil estimated reserves: 40 million barrels (2021 est.)

Refined petroleum products - production: 6,996 bbl/day (2015 est.)

Refined petroleum products - exports: 2,290 bbl/day (2015 est.)

Refined petroleum products - imports: 34,280 bbl/day (2015 est.)

Natural gas: *production:* 25.542 million cubic meters (2019 est.)
consumption: 207.845 million cubic meters (2019 est.)
exports: 0 cubic meters (2021 est.)
imports: 191.478 million cubic meters (2019 est.)
proven reserves: 5.663 billion cubic meters (2021 est.)

Carbon dioxide emissions: 7.88 million metric tonnes of CO2 (2019 est.)
from coal and metallurgical coke: 2.967 million metric tonnes of CO2 (2019 est.)
from petroleum and other liquids: 4.505 million metric tonnes of CO2 (2019 est.)
from consumed natural gas: 408,000 metric tonnes of CO2 (2019 est.)

Energy consumption per capita: 35.059 million Btu/person (2019 est.)

COMMUNICATIONS

Telephones - fixed lines: *total subscriptions:* 299,000 (2020 est.)
subscriptions per 100 inhabitants: 5 (2020 est.)

Telephones - mobile cellular: *total subscriptions:* 8.511 million (2020 est.)
subscriptions per 100 inhabitants: 130 (2020 est.)

Telecommunication systems: *general assessment:* the country's telecom sector (specifically the mobile segment) has likewise been able to prosper; ongoing political tension, increasing repression of the media and information, and continuing problems with corporate governance may be putting a strain on further growth by reducing the country's appeal to much-needed foreign investors; Kyrgyzstan has been reasonably successful in its attempts to liberalize its economy and open up its telecom market to competition; the mobile market has achieved high levels of penetration (140% in 2021) along with a fairly competitive operating environment with four major players; mobile broadband has come along strongly, reaching over 125% penetration in 2019 before falling back slightly during the Covid-19 crisis; slow-to-moderate growth is expected for both segments in coming years, supported by the anticipated rollout of 5G services starting from late 2022 (2022)
domestic: fixed-line penetration at nearly 5 per 100 persons remains low and concentrated in urban areas; mobile-cellular subscribership up to over 130 per 100 persons (2020)
international: country code - 996; connections with other CIS (Commonwealth of Independent States, 9 members post- Soviet Republics in EU) countries by landline or microwave radio relay and with other countries by leased connections with Moscow international gateway switch and by satellite; satellite earth stations - 2 (1 Intersputnik, 1 Intelsat) (2019)

Broadcast media: state-funded public TV broadcaster KTRK has nationwide coverage; also operates Ala-Too 24 news channel which broadcasts 24/7 and 4 other educational, cultural, and sports channels; ELTR and Channel 5 are state-owned stations with national reach; the switchover to digital TV in 2017 resulted in private TV station growth; approximately 20 stations are struggling to increase their own content up to 50% of airtime, as required by law, instead of rebroadcasting primarily programs from Russian channels or airing unlicensed movies and music; 3 Russian TV stations also broadcast; state-funded radio stations and about 10 significant private radio stations also exist (2019)

Internet country code: .kg

Internet users: *total:* 3,683,700 (July 2022 est.)
percent of population: 55% (July 2022 est.)

Broadband - fixed subscriptions: *total:* 289,000 (2020 est.)
subscriptions per 100 inhabitants: 4 (2020 est.)

TRANSPORTATION

National air transport system: *number of registered air carriers:* 5 (2020)
inventory of registered aircraft operated by air carriers: 17
annual passenger traffic on registered air carriers: 709,198 (2018)

Civil aircraft registration country code prefix: EX

Airports: *total:* 28 (2021)

Airports - with paved runways: *total:* 18
over 3,047 m: 1
2,438 to 3,047 m: 3
1,524 to 2,437 m: 11
under 914 m: 3 (2021)

Airports - with unpaved runways: *total:* 10
1,524 to 2,437 m: 1
914 to 1,523 m: 1
under 914 m: 8 (2021)

Pipelines: 4,195 km gas (2022), 16 km oil (2022) (2022)

Railways: *total:* 424 km (2022)
broad gauge: 424 km (2018) 1.520-m gauge

Roadways: *total:* 34,000 km (2022)

Waterways: 576 km (2022)

Ports and terminals: *lake port(s):* Balykchy (Ysyk-Kol or Rybach'ye)(Lake Ysyk-Kol)

MILITARY AND SECURITY

Military and security forces: Armed Forces of the Kyrgyz Republic: Land Forces, Air Defense Forces, National Guard; Internal Troops; State Committee for National Security (GKNB): Border Service (2022)

Military expenditures: 1.7% of GDP (2021 est.)
1.8% of GDP (2020 est.)
2.3% of GDP (2019 est.) (approximately $410 million)
2.3% of GDP (2018 est.) (approximately $400 million)
2.3% of GDP (2017 est.) (approximately $390 million)

Military and security service personnel strengths: approximately 12,000 active duty troops (8,500 Land Forces; 2,500 Air Force/Air Defense; 1,000 National Guard) (2022)

Military equipment inventories and acquisitions: the Kyrgyz military inventory is comprised of mostly older Russian and Soviet-era equipment; Kyrgyzstan relies on donations of military equipment, which come mostly from Russia under a 2013 agreement between Bishkek and Moscow (2022)

Military service age and obligation: 18-27 years of age for compulsory or voluntary male military service in the Armed Forces or Interior Ministry; 12-month service obligation (9 months for university graduates), with optional fee-based 3-year service in the call-up mobilization reserve; women may volunteer at age 19; 16-17 years of age for military cadets, who cannot take part in military operations (2022)

Military - note: Kyrgyzstan has been a member of the Collective Security Treaty Organization (CSTO) since 1994 and contributes troops to CSTO's rapid reaction force (2022)

TRANSNATIONAL ISSUES

Disputes - international: *Kyrgyzstan-China:* a 2009 treaty settled a border dispute, with Kyrgyzstan receiving the Khan Tengri Peak and Kyrgyzstan ceding to China the Uzengi-Kush area

Kyrgyzstan-Kazakhstan: in January 2019, Kyrgyzstan ratified the 2017 agreement on the demarcation of the Kyrgyzstan-Kazakhstan border

Kyrgyzstan-Tajikistan: as the last major Central Asian boundary dispute with lengthy undelimited sections, the lowland (NE part) of the Kyrgz-Tajik line seems intractable despite recent Kyrgyz-Uzbek compromises and agreements on delimitation and demarcation

Kyrgyzstan-Uzbekistan: delimitation of approximately 15% or 200 km of border with Uzbekistan is hampered by serious disputes over enclaves and other areas; Kyrgyz and Uzbek officials signed an agreement in March 2021 on the final delimitation and demarcation of the Kyrgyzstan-Uzbekistan border; the accord included several land swaps that gave Kyrgyzstan more territory but was offset by Uzbekistan retaining use of reservoirs on Kyrgyz land; although a Kyrgyz official returned from the March 2021 meetings and said the decades-old border dispute was 100% resolved, his talks with residents in some affected areas showed that agreement had not been reached on all border segments

Refugees and internally displaced persons: *stateless persons:* 16 (mid-year 2021)

Illicit drugs: a prime transshipment location; illegal drugs move from Afghanistan to Russia, and sometimes into Europe

LAOS

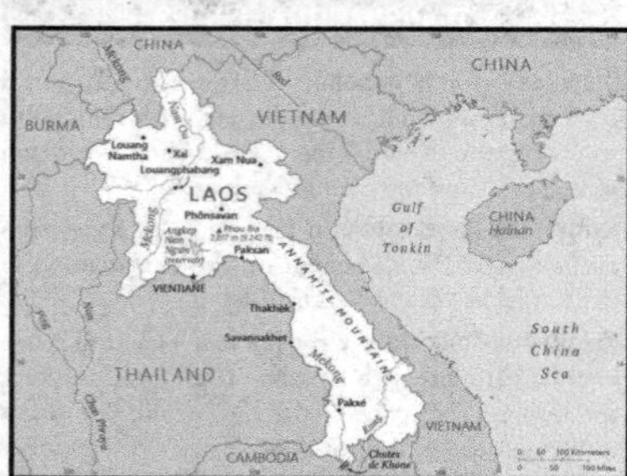

INTRODUCTION

Background: Modern-day Laos has its roots in the ancient Lao kingdom of Lan Xang, established in the 14th century under King FA NGUM. For 300 years Lan Xang had influence reaching into present-day Cambodia and Thailand, as well as over all of what is now Laos. After centuries of gradual decline, Laos came under the domination of Siam (Thailand) from the late 18th century until the late 19th century, when it became part of French Indochina. The Franco-Siamese Treaty of 1907 defined the current Lao border with Thailand. In 1975, the communist Pathet Lao took control of the government, ending a six-century-old monarchy and instituting a strict socialist regime closely aligned to Vietnam. A gradual, limited return to private enterprise and the liberalization of foreign investment laws began in 1988. Laos became a member of ASEAN in 1997 and the WTO in 2013.

In the 2010s, the country benefited from direct foreign investment, particularly in the natural resource and industry sectors. Construction of a number of large hydropower dams and expanding mining activities have also boosted the economy. Laos has retained its official commitment to communism and maintains close ties with its two communist neighbors, Vietnam and China, both of which continue to exert substantial political and economic influence on the country. China, for example, provided 70% of the funding for a $5.9 billion, 400-km railway line between the Chinese border and the capital Vientiane, which opened for operations in December 2021. Laos financed the remaining 30% with loans from China. At the same time, Laos has expanded its economic reliance on the West and other Asian countries, such as Japan, Malaysia, Singapore, Taiwan, and Thailand.

GEOGRAPHY

Location: Southeastern Asia, northeast of Thailand, west of Vietnam

Geographic coordinates: 18 00 N, 105 00 E

Map references: Southeast Asia

Area: *total:* 236,800 sq km
land: 230,800 sq km
water: 6,000 sq km

Area - comparative: about twice the size of Pennsylvania; slightly larger than Utah

Land boundaries: *total:* 5,274 km
border countries (5): Burma 238 km; Cambodia 555 km; China 475 km; Thailand 1,845 km; Vietnam 2,161 km

Coastline: 0 km (landlocked)

Maritime claims: none (landlocked)

Climate: tropical monsoon; rainy season (May to November); dry season (December to April)

Terrain: mostly rugged mountains; some plains and plateaus

Elevation: *highest point:* Phu Bia 2,817 m
lowest point: Mekong River 70 m
mean elevation: 710 m

Natural resources: timber, hydropower, gypsum, tin, gold, gemstones

Land use: *agricultural land:* 10.6% (2018 est.)
arable land: 6.2% (2018 est.)
permanent crops: 0.7% (2018 est.)
permanent pasture: 3.7% (2018 est.)
forest: 67.9% (2018 est.)
other: 21.5% (2018 est.)

Irrigated land: 3,100 sq km (2012)

Major rivers (by length in km): Mekong (shared with China [s], Burma, Thailand, Cambodia, and Vietnam [m]) - 4,350 km
note – [s] after country name indicates river source; [m] after country name indicates river mouth

Major watersheds (area sq km): Pacific Ocean drainage: Mekong (805,604 sq km)

Population distribution: most densely populated area is in and around the capital city of Vientiane; large communities are primarily found along the Mekong River along the southwestern border; overall density is considered one of the lowest in Southeast Asia

Natural hazards: floods, droughts

Geography - note: landlocked; most of the country is mountainous and thickly forested; the Mekong River forms a large part of the western boundary with Thailand

PEOPLE AND SOCIETY

Population: 7,749,595 (2022 est.)

Nationality: *noun:* Lao(s) or Laotian(s)
adjective: Lao or Laotian

Ethnic groups: Lao 53.2%, Khmou 11%, Hmong 9.2%, Phouthay 3.4%, Tai 3.1%, Makong 2.5%, Katong 2.2%, Lue 2%, Akha 1.8%, other 11.6% (2015 est.)
note: the Laos Government officially recognizes 49 ethnic groups, but the total number of ethnic groups is estimated to be well over 200

Languages: Lao (official), French, English, various ethnic languages
major-language sample(s):

ແຫລ່ງທີ່ຂາດບໍ່ໄດ້ສໍາລັບຂໍ້ມູນຕົ້ນຕໍ"

(Lao)

Religions: Buddhist 64.7%, Christian 1.7%, none 31.4%, other/not stated 2.1% (2015 est.)

Demographic profile: Laos is a predominantly rural country with a youthful population – almost 55% of the population is under the age of 25. Its progress on health and development issues has been uneven geographically, among ethnic groups, and socioeconomically. Laos has made headway in poverty reduction, with the poverty rate almost halving from 46% in 1992/93 to 22% in 2012/13. Nevertheless, pronounced rural-urban disparities persist, and income inequality is rising. Poverty most affects populations in rural and highland areas, particularly ethnic minority groups.

The total fertility rate (TFR) has decreased markedly from around 6 births per woman on average in 1990 to approximately 2.8 in 2016, but it is still one of the highest in Southeast Asia. TFR is higher in rural and remote areas, among ethnic minority groups, the less-educated, and the poor; it is lower in urban areas and among the more educated and those with higher incomes. Although Laos' mortality rates have improved substantially over the last few decades, the maternal mortality rate and childhood malnutrition remain at high levels. As fertility and mortality rates continue to decline, the proportion of Laos' working-age population will increase, and its share of dependents will shrink. The age structure shift will provide Laos with the potential to realize a demographic dividend during the next few decades, if it can improve educational access and quality and gainfully employ its growing working-age population in productive sectors. Currently, Laos primary school enrollment is nearly universal, but the drop-out rate remains problematic. Secondary school enrollment has also increased but remains low, especially for girls.

Laos has historically been a country of emigration and internal displacement due to conflict and a weak economy. The Laos civil war (1953 – 1975) mainly caused internal displacement (numbering in the hundreds of thousands). Following the end of the Vietnam War in 1975, indigenous people in remote, war-struck areas were resettled and more than 300,000 people fled to Thailand to escape the communist regime that took power. The majority of those who sought refuge in Thailand ultimately were resettled in the US (mainly Hmong who fought with US forces), and lesser numbers went to France, Canada, and Australia.

The Laos Government carried out resettlement programs between the mid-1980s and mid-1990s to relocate ethnic minority groups from the rural northern highlands to development areas in the lowlands ostensibly to alleviate poverty, make basic services more accessible, eliminate slash-and-burn agriculture and opium production, integrate ethnic minorities, and control rebel groups (including Hmong insurgents). For many, however, resettlement has exacerbated poverty, led to the loss of livelihoods, and increased food insecurity and mortality rates. As the resettlement programs started to wane in the second half of the 1990s, migration from the northern highlands to urban centers – chiefly the capital Vientiane – to pursue better jobs in the growing manufacturing and service sectors became the main type of relocation. Migration of villagers from the south seeking work in neighboring Thailand also increased. Thailand is the main international migration destination for Laotians because of the greater availability of jobs and higher pay than at home; nearly a million Laotian migrants were estimated to live in Thailand as of 2015.

Age structure: *0-14 years:* 31.25% (male 1,177,297/female 1,149,727)
15-24 years: 20.6% (male 763,757/female 770,497)
25-54 years: 38.29% (male 1,407,823/female 1,443,774)
55-64 years: 5.73% (male 206,977/female 219,833)
65 years and over: 4.13% (male 139,665/female 168,046) (2020 est.)

Dependency ratios: *total dependency ratio:* 56.8
youth dependency ratio: 50.1
elderly dependency ratio: 6.7
potential support ratio: 15 (2020 est.)

Median age: *total:* 24 years
male: 23.7 years
female: 24.4 years (2020 est.)

Population growth rate: 1.34% (2022 est.)

Birth rate: 20.9 births/1,000 population (2022 est.)

Death rate: 6.37 deaths/1,000 population (2022 est.)

Net migration rate: -1.17 migrant(s)/1,000 population (2022 est.)

Population distribution: most densely populated area is in and around the capital city of Vientiane; large communities are primarily found along the Mekong River along the southwestern border; overall density is considered one of the lowest in Southeast Asia

Urbanization: *urban population:* 37.6% of total population (2022)
rate of urbanization: 2.99% annual rate of change (2020-25 est.)

Major urban areas - population: 706,000 VIENTIANE (capital) (2022)

Sex ratio: *at birth:* 1.04 male(s)/female
0-14 years: 1.03 male(s)/female
15-24 years: 1 male(s)/female
25-54 years: 0.99 male(s)/female
55-64 years: 0.94 male(s)/female
65 years and over: 0.71 male(s)/female
total population: 0.99 male(s)/female (2022 est.)

Maternal mortality ratio: 185 deaths/100,000 live births (2017 est.)

Infant mortality rate: *total:* 37.78 deaths/1,000 live births
male: 41.76 deaths/1,000 live births
female: 33.63 deaths/1,000 live births (2022 est.)

Life expectancy at birth: *total population:* 68.15 years
male: 66.49 years
female: 69.88 years (2022 est.)

Total fertility rate: 2.35 children born/woman (2022 est.)

Contraceptive prevalence rate: 54.1% (2017)

Drinking water source: *improved: urban:* 97.1% of population
rural: 84.1% of population
total: 88.8% of population
unimproved: urban: 2.9% of population
rural: 15.9% of population
total: 11.2% of population (2020 est.)

Current health expenditure: 2.6% of GDP (2019)

Physicians density: 0.35 physicians/1,000 population (2020)

Hospital bed density: 1.5 beds/1,000 population (2012)

Sanitation facility access: *improved: urban:* 100% of population
rural: 72% of population
total: 82.2% of population
unimproved: urban: 0% of population
rural: 28% of population
total: 17.8% of population (2020 est.)

HIV/AIDS - adult prevalence rate: 0.3% (2020 est.)

Major infectious diseases: *degree of risk:* very high (2020)
food or waterborne diseases: bacterial and protozoal diarrhea, hepatitis A, and typhoid fever
vectorborne diseases: dengue fever and malaria

Obesity - adult prevalence rate: 5.3% (2016)

Alcohol consumption per capita: *total:* 8.15 liters of pure alcohol (2019 est.)
beer: 3.62 liters of pure alcohol (2019 est.)
wine: 0.07 liters of pure alcohol (2019 est.)
spirits: 4.46 liters of pure alcohol (2019 est.)
other alcohols: 0 liters of pure alcohol (2019 est.)

Tobacco use: *total:* 31.8% (2020 est.)
male: 53.3% (2020 est.)
female: 10.3% (2020 est.)

Children under the age of 5 years underweight: 21.1% (2017)

Child marriage: *women married by age 15:* 7.1%
women married by age 18: 32.7%
men married by age 18: 10.8% (2017 est.)

Education expenditures: 2.9% of GDP (2014 est.)

Literacy: *definition:* age 15 and over can read and write
total population: 84.7%
male: 90%
female: 79.4% (2015)

School life expectancy (primary to tertiary education): *total:* 10 years
male: 10 years
female: 10 years (2020)

Unemployment, youth ages 15-24: *total:* 18.2%
male: 20.8%
female: 15.5% (2017 est.)

ENVIRONMENT

Environment - current issues: unexploded ordnance; deforestation; soil erosion; loss of biodiversity; water pollution, most of the population does not have access to potable water

Environment - international agreements: *party to:* Biodiversity, Climate Change, Climate Change-Kyoto Protocol, Climate Change-Paris Agreement, Comprehensive Nuclear Test Ban, Desertification, Endangered Species, Environmental Modification, Hazardous Wastes, Law of the Sea, Nuclear Test Ban, Ozone Layer Protection, Wetlands, Whaling
signed, but not ratified: none of the selected agreements

Air pollutants: *particulate matter emissions:* 24.49 micrograms per cubic meter (2016 est.)
carbon dioxide emissions: 17.76 megatons (2016 est.)
methane emissions: 9 megatons (2020 est.)

Climate: tropical monsoon; rainy season (May to November); dry season (December to April)

Land use: *agricultural land:* 10.6% (2018 est.)
arable land: 6.2% (2018 est.)
permanent crops: 0.7% (2018 est.)
permanent pasture: 3.7% (2018 est.)
forest: 67.9% (2018 est.)
other: 21.5% (2018 est.)

Urbanization: *urban population:* 37.6% of total population (2022)
rate of urbanization: 2.99% annual rate of change (2020-25 est.)

Revenue from forest resources: *forest revenues:* 1.48% of GDP (2018 est.)

Waste and recycling: *municipal solid waste generated annually:* 351,900 tons (2015 est.)
municipal solid waste recycled annually: 35,190 tons (2015 est.)
percent of municipal solid waste recycled: 10% (2015 est.)

Major rivers (by length in km): Mekong (shared with China [s], Burma, Thailand, Cambodia, and Vietnam [m]) - 4,350 km
note – [s] after country name indicates river source; [m] after country name indicates river mouth

Major watersheds (area sq km): Pacific Ocean drainage: Mekong (805,604 sq km)

Total water withdrawal: *municipal:* 130 million cubic meters (2017 est.)
industrial: 170 million cubic meters (2017 est.)
agricultural: 7.02 billion cubic meters (2017 est.)

Total renewable water resources: 333.5 billion cubic meters (2017 est.)

GOVERNMENT

Country name: *conventional long form:* Lao People's Democratic Republic
conventional short form: Laos
local long form: Sathalanalat Paxathipatai Paxaxon Lao
local short form: Mueang Lao (unofficial)
etymology: name means "Land of the Lao [people]"

Government type: communist state

Capital: *name:* Vientiane (Viangchan)
geographic coordinates: 17 58 N, 102 36 E
time difference: UTC+7 (12 hours ahead of Washington, DC, during Standard Time)
etymology: the meaning in Pali, a Buddhist liturgical language, is "city of sandalwood"

Administrative divisions: 17 provinces (khoueng, singular and plural) and 1 prefecture* (kampheng nakhon); Attapu, Bokeo, Bolikhamxai, Champasak, Houaphan, Khammouan, Louangnamtha, Louangphabang, Oudomxai, Phongsali, Salavan, Savannakhet, Viangchan (Vientiane)*, Viangchan, Xaignabouli, Xaisomboun, Xekong, Xiangkhouang

Independence: 19 July 1949 (from France by the Franco-Lao General Convention); 22 October 1953 (Franco-Lao Treaty recognizes full independence)

National holiday: Republic Day (National Day), 2 December (1975)

Constitution: *history:* previous 1947 (preindependence); latest promulgated 13-15 August 1991
amendments: proposed by the National Assembly; passage requires at least two-thirds majority vote of the Assembly membership and promulgation by the president of the republic; amended 2003, 2015

Legal system: civil law system similar in form to the French system

International law organization participation: has not submitted an ICJ jurisdiction declaration; non-party state to the ICCt

Citizenship: *citizenship by birth:* no

citizenship by descent only: at least one parent must be a citizen of Laos
dual citizenship recognized: no
residency requirement for naturalization: 10 years

Suffrage: 18 years of age; universal

Executive branch: *chief of state:* President THONGLOUN Sisoulit (since 22 March 2021); Vice Presidents PANI Yathotou and BOUNTHONG Chitmani (since 22 March 2021)
head of government: Prime Minister PHANKHAM Viphavan (since 22 March 2021); Deputy Prime Ministers CHANSAMON Chan-gnalat, SONXAI Siphandon, KIKEO Khaikhamphithoun (since 22 March 2021); VILAI Lakhamfong, SALEUMXAI Kommasit (since June 2022)
cabinet: Council of Ministers appointed by the president, approved by the National Assembly
elections/appointments: president and vice president indirectly elected by the National Assembly for a 5-year term (no term limits); election last held on 22 March 2021 (next to be held in March 2026); prime minister nominated by the president, elected by the National Assembly for 5-year term
election results:
2021: THONGLOUN Sisoulit (LPRP) elected president; National Assembly vote: 161-1; PANI Yathotou and BOUNTHONG Chitmani (LPRP) elected vice presidents; National Assembly vote NA; PHANKHAM Viphavan (LPRP) elected prime minister; National Assembly vote: 158-3
2016: BOUNNYANG Vorachit (LPRP) elected president; PHANKHAM Viphavan (LPRP) elected vice president; percent of National Assembly vote - NA; THONGLOUN Sisoulit (LPRP) elected prime minister; percent of National Assembly vote - NA

Legislative branch: *description:* unicameral National Assembly or Sapha Heng Xat (164 seats; members directly elected in multi-seat constituencies by simple majority vote from candidate lists provided by the Lao People's Revolutionary Party; members serve 5-year terms)
elections:
last held on 21 February 2021 (next to be held in 2026)
election results:
percent of vote by party - NA; seats by party - LPRP 158, independent 6; composition - men 128, women 36, percent of women 21.9%

Judicial branch: *highest court(s):* People's Supreme Court (consists of the court president and organized into criminal, civil, administrative, commercial, family, and juvenile chambers, each with a vice president and several judges)
judge selection and term of office: president of People's Supreme Court appointed by the National Assembly upon the recommendation of the president of the republic for a 5-year term; vice presidents of the People's Supreme Court appointed by the president of the republic upon the recommendation of the National Assembly; appointment of chamber judges NA; tenure of court vice presidents and chamber judges NA
subordinate courts: appellate courts; provincial, municipal, district, and military courts

Political parties and leaders: Lao People's Revolutionary Party or LPRP [THONGLOUN Sisoulit]
note: other parties proscribed

International organization participation: ADB, ARF, ASEAN, CP, EAS, FAO, G-77, IAEA, IBRD, ICAO, ICRM, IDA, IFAD, IFC, IFRCS, ILO, IMF, Interpol, IOC, IPU, ISO (subscriber), ITU, MIGA, NAM, OIF, OPCW, PCA, UN, UNCTAD, UNESCO, UNIDO, UNWTO, UPU, WCO, WFTU (NGOs), WHO, WIPO, WMO, WTO

Diplomatic representation in the US: *chief of mission:* Ambassador Sisavath INPHACHANH (since 7 June 2022)
chancery: 2222 S Street NW, Washington, DC 20008
telephone: [1] (202) 328-9148; [1] (202) 332-6416
FAX: [1] (202) 332-4923
email address and website:
embasslao@gmail.com; laoemb@verizon.net
https://laoembassy.com/
consulate(s): New York

Diplomatic representation from the US: *chief of mission:* Ambassador Peter HAYMOND (since 7 February 2020)
embassy: Ban Somvang Tai, Thadeua Road, Km 9, Hatsayfong District, Vientiane
mailing address: 4350 Vientiane Place, Washington DC 20521-4350
telephone: [856] 21-48-7000
FAX: [856] 21-48-7040
email address and website:
CONSLAO@state.gov
https://la.usembassy.gov/

Flag description: three horizontal bands of red (top), blue (double width), and red with a large white disk centered in the blue band; the red bands recall the blood shed for liberation; the blue band represents the Mekong River and prosperity; the white disk symbolizes the full moon against the Mekong River, but also signifies the unity of the people under the Lao People's Revolutionary Party, as well as the country's bright future

National symbol(s): elephant; national colors: red, white, blue

National anthem: *name:* "Pheng Xat Lao" (Hymn of the Lao People)
lyrics/music: SISANA Sisane/THONGDY Sounthonevichit
note: music adopted 1945, lyrics adopted 1975; the anthem's lyrics were changed following the 1975 Communist revolution that overthrew the monarchy

National heritage: *total World Heritage Sites:* 3 (all cultural)
selected World Heritage Site locales: Town of Luangphrabang; Vat Phou and Associated Ancient Settlements; Megalithic Jar Sites in Xiengkhuang - Plain of Jars

ECONOMY

Economic overview: The government of Laos, one of the few remaining one-party communist states, began decentralizing control and encouraging private enterprise in 1986. Economic growth averaged more than 6% per year in the period 1988-2008, and Laos' growth has more recently been amongst the fastest in Asia, averaging more than 7% per year for most of the last decade.

Nevertheless, Laos remains a country with an underdeveloped infrastructure, particularly in rural areas. It has a basic, but improving, road system, and limited external and internal land-line telecommunications. Electricity is available to 83% of the population. Agriculture, dominated by rice cultivation in lowland areas, accounts for about 20% of GDP and 73% of total employment. Recently, the country has faced a persistent current account deficit, falling foreign currency reserves, and growing public debt.

Laos' economy is heavily dependent on capital-intensive natural resource exports. The economy has benefited from high-profile foreign direct investment in hydropower dams along the Mekong River, copper and gold mining, logging, and construction, although some projects in these industries have drawn criticism for their environmental impacts.

Laos gained Normal Trade Relations status with the US in 2004 and applied for Generalized System of Preferences trade benefits in 2013 after being admitted to the World Trade Organization earlier in the year. Laos held the chairmanship of ASEAN in 2016. Laos is in the process of implementing a value-added tax system. The government appears committed to raising the country's profile among foreign investors and has developed special economic zones replete with generous tax incentives, but a limited labor pool, a small domestic market, and corruption remain impediments to investment. Laos also has ongoing problems with the business environment, including onerous registration requirements, a gap between legislation and implementation, and unclear or conflicting regulations.

Real GDP (purchasing power parity): $56.79 billion (2020 est.)
$56.54 billion (2019 est.)
$53.62 billion (2018 est.)
note: data are in 2017 dollars

Real GDP growth rate: 6.9% (2017 est.)
7% (2016 est.)
7.3% (2015 est.)

Real GDP per capita: $7,800 (2020 est.)
$7,900 (2019 est.)
$7,600 (2018 est.)
note: data are in 2017 dollars

GDP (official exchange rate): $16.97 billion (2017 est.)

Inflation rate (consumer prices): 0.8% (2017 est.)
1.6% (2016 est.)

Credit ratings:

Fitch rating: CCC (2020)

Moody's rating: Caa2 (2020)
note: The year refers to the year in which the current credit rating was first obtained.

GDP - composition, by sector of origin: *agriculture:* 20.9% (2017 est.)
industry: 33.2% (2017 est.)
services: 45.9% (2017 est.)

GDP - composition, by end use: *household consumption:* 63.7% (2017 est.)
government consumption: 14.1% (2017 est.)
investment in fixed capital: 30.9% (2017 est.)
investment in inventories: 3.1% (2017 est.)
exports of goods and services: 34.6% (2017 est.)
imports of goods and services: -43.2% (2017 est.)

Agricultural products: rice, roots/tubers nes, cassava, sugar cane, vegetables, bananas, maize, watermelons, coffee, taro

Industries: mining (copper, tin, gold, gypsum); timber, electric power, agricultural processing, rubber, construction, garments, cement, tourism

Industrial production growth rate: 8% (2017 est.)

Labor force: 3.582 million (2017 est.)

Labor force - by occupation: *agriculture:* 73.1%
industry: 6.1%

services: 20.6% (2012 est.)

Unemployment rate: 0.7% (2017 est.)
0.7% (2016 est.)

Unemployment, youth ages 15-24: *total:* 18.2%
male: 20.8%
female: 15.5% (2017 est.)

Population below poverty line: 18.3% (2018 est.)

Gini Index coefficient - distribution of family income: 36.4 (2012 est.)
34.6 (2002)

Household income or consumption by percentage share: *lowest 10%:* 3.3%
highest 10%: 30.3% (2008)

Budget: *revenues:* 3.099 billion (2017 est.)
expenditures: 4.038 billion (2017 est.)

Budget surplus (+) or deficit (-): -5.5% (of GDP) (2017 est.)

Public debt: 63.6% of GDP (2017 est.)
58.4% of GDP (2016 est.)

Taxes and other revenues: 18.3% (of GDP) (2017 est.)

Fiscal year: 1 October - 30 September

Current account balance: -$2.057 billion (2017 est.)
-$2.07 billion (2016 est.)

Exports: $6.99 billion (2019 est.) note: data are in current year dollars
$6.39 billion (2018 est.) note: data are in current year dollars

Exports - partners: Thailand 36%, China 28%, Vietnam 16% (2019)

Exports - commodities: electricity, copper, rubber, gold, flavored water (2019)

Imports: $7.52 billion (2019 est.) note: data are in current year dollars
$7.56 billion (2018 est.) note: data are in current year dollars

Imports - partners: Thailand 53%, China 26%, Vietnam 10% (2019)

Imports - commodities: refined petroleum, cars, cattle, iron structures, steel products (2019)

Reserves of foreign exchange and gold: $1.27 billion (31 December 2017 est.)
$940.1 million (31 December 2016 est.)

Debt - external: $14.9 billion (31 December 2017 est.)
$12.9 billion (31 December 2016 est.)

Exchange rates: kips (LAK) per US dollar -
8,231.1 (2017 est.)
8,129.1 (2016 est.)
8,129.1 (2015 est.)
8,147.9 (2014 est.)
8,049 (2013 est.)

ENERGY

Electricity access: *electrification - total population:* 95% (2019)
electrification - urban areas: 98% (2019)
electrification - rural areas: 93% (2019)

Electricity: *installed generating capacity:* 9.346 million kW (2020 est.)
consumption: 5,108,640,000 kWh (2019 est.)
exports: 24.114 billion kWh (2019 est.)
imports: 1.345 billion kWh (2019 est.)
transmission/distribution losses: 2.262 billion kWh (2019 est.)

Electricity generation sources: *fossil fuels:* 35.6% of total installed capacity (2020 est.)
solar: 0.1% of total installed capacity (2020 est.)
hydroelectricity: 64.1% of total installed capacity (2020 est.)
biomass and waste: 0.2% of total installed capacity (2020 est.)

Coal: *production:* 16.04 million metric tons (2020 est.)
consumption: 15.823 million metric tons (2020 est.)
exports: 235,000 metric tons (2020 est.)
imports: 18,000 metric tons (2020 est.)
proven reserves: 503 million metric tons (2019 est.)

Petroleum: *total petroleum production:* 0 bbl/day (2021 est.)
refined petroleum consumption: 19,300 bbl/day (2019 est.)

Refined petroleum products - imports: 17,460 bbl/day (2015 est.)

Carbon dioxide emissions: 40.726 million metric tonnes of CO2 (2019 est.)
from coal and metallurgical coke: 37.871 million metric tonnes of CO2 (2019 est.)
from petroleum and other liquids: 2.855 million metric tonnes of CO2 (2019 est.)

Energy consumption per capita: 73.187 million Btu/person (2019 est.)

COMMUNICATIONS

Telephones - fixed lines: *total subscriptions:* 1.491 million (2020 est.)
subscriptions per 100 inhabitants: 20 (2020 est.)

Telephones - mobile cellular: *total subscriptions:* 4.1 million (2020 est.)
subscriptions per 100 inhabitants: 56 (2020 est.)

Telecommunication systems: *general assessment:* Laos joined the World Trade Organization (WTO) in 2013; one of the conditions of admittance was to establish an independent regulator for its telecom sector within two years; the government had committed to do so by February 2015 as part of the accession agreement; there still has been no sign of any firm plans being made to create an independent regulatory body; the Ministry of Posts and Telecommunications (MPT) retains the primary role in regulating the country's telecom market; with the government also having a financial stake (in part or in whole) in every one of the major fixed-line and mobile operators, the MPT's position and decision-making is far from what could be considered independent; sufficient returns on investment cannot be guaranteed with such strict pricing controls as well as the potential for political interference; fixed-line and mobile penetration levels have, as a result, remained much lower than what's seen in neighboring South East Asian markets; there are signs of growth in the mobile broadband segment as LTE network coverage slowly widens and, more recently, the country's first 5G services start to come on stream; residents in the capital will at least be able to enjoy high-speed services in the near future, while the rest of the country waits patiently to catch up with the rest of the world. (2022)
domestic: fixed-line nearly 20 per 100 and 56 per 100 for mobile-cellular subscriptions (2020)
international: country code - 856; satellite earth station - 1 Intersputnik (Indian Ocean region) and a second to be developed by China

Broadcast media: 6 TV stations operating out of Vientiane - 3 government-operated and the others commercial; 17 provincial stations operating with nearly all programming relayed via satellite from the government-operated stations in Vientiane; Chinese and Vietnamese programming relayed via satellite from Lao National TV; broadcasts available from stations in Thailand and Vietnam in border areas; multi-channel satellite and cable TV systems provide access to a wide range of foreign stations; state-controlled radio with state-operated Lao National Radio (LNR) broadcasting on 5 frequencies - 1 AM, 1 SW, and 3 FM; LNR's AM and FM programs are relayed via satellite constituting a large part of the programming schedules of the provincial radio stations; Thai radio broadcasts available in border areas and transmissions of multiple international broadcasters are also accessible

Internet country code: .la

Internet users: *total:* 2,473,689 (2020 est.)
percent of population: 34% (2020 est.)

Broadband - fixed subscriptions: *total:* 128,000 (2020 est.)
subscriptions per 100 inhabitants: 2 (2020 est.)

TRANSPORTATION

National air transport system: *number of registered air carriers:* 1 (2020)
inventory of registered aircraft operated by air carriers: 12
annual passenger traffic on registered air carriers: 1,251,961 (2018)
annual freight traffic on registered air carriers: 1.53 million (2018) mt-km

Civil aircraft registration country code prefix: RDPL

Airports: *total:* 41 (2021)

Airports - with paved runways: *total:* 8
2,438 to 3,047 m: 3
1,524 to 2,437 m: 4
914 to 1,523 m: 1 (2021)

Airports - with unpaved runways: *total:* 33
1,524 to 2,437 m: 2
914 to 1,523 m: 9
under 914 m: 22 (2021)

Pipelines: 540 km refined products (2013)

Roadways: *total:* 39,586 km (2009)
paved: 5,415 km (2009)
unpaved: 34,171 km (2009)

Waterways: 4,600 km (2012) (primarily on the Mekong River and its tributaries; 2,900 additional km are intermittently navigable by craft drawing less than 0.5 m)

Merchant marine: *total:* 1
by type: general cargo 1 (2021)

MILITARY AND SECURITY

Military and security forces: Lao People's Armed Forces (LPAF): Lao People's Army (LPA, includes Riverine Force), Air Force, Self-Defense Militia Forces (2022)

Military expenditures: 0.2% of GDP (2019 est.) (approximately $120 million)
0.2% of GDP (2018 est.) (approximately $110 million)
0.2% of GDP (2017 est.) (approximately $100 million)
0.2% of GDP (2016 est.) (approximately $95 million)

0.2% of GDP (2015 est.) (approximately $85 million)

Military and security service personnel strengths: information is limited and estimates vary; approximately 30,000 active duty troops (26,000 Army; 4,000 Air Force) (2022)

Military equipment inventories and acquisitions: the LPAF is armed largely with Soviet-era weapons acquired from the former Soviet Union, Russia, and Vietnam; since 2010, China and Russia have been the leading suppliers of military equipment to Laos (2022)

Military service age and obligation: 18 years of age for compulsory or voluntary military service; minimum 18-month service obligation (2022)

Military - note: the LPAF's primary missions are border and internal security, including counterinsurgency and counterterrorism

Vietnam is the Laotian military's primary security partner, although in recent years, Laos has expanded defense ties with China (2022)

TRANSNATIONAL ISSUES

Disputes - international: *Laos-Burma:* none identified
Laos-Cambodia: in 2021, the two countries agreed to increase efforts to combat drug trafficking and other transnational crimes and to complete the last 14% of their border demarcation
Laos-Cambodia-Vietnam: Cambodia and Vietnam are concerned about Laos' extensive plans for upstream dam construction and the potential harm it poses to fisheries and farming downstream
Laos-China: concern among Mekong River Commission members that China's construction of eight dams on the Upper Mekong River and construction of more dams on its tributaries will affect water levels, sediment flows, and fisheries
Laos-Thailand: talks continue as of 2018 on completion of demarcation with Thailand but disputes remain over islands in the Mekong River
Laos-Vietnam: Laos and Vietnam completed border demarcation in 2016

Illicit drugs: Bokeo Province part of the "Golden Triangle," a notorious drug production and transit area; remains a poppy cultivator and source of illicit opium and a transit hub for other illicit drugs such as amphetamine-type stimulants (ATS) and chemical precursors; estimate of 4,925 ha of opium poppy cultivated in Laos in 2018

LATVIA

INTRODUCTION

Background: Several eastern Baltic tribes merged in medieval times to form the ethnic core of the Latvian people (ca. 8th-12th centuries A.D.). The region subsequently came under the control of Germans, Poles, Swedes, and finally, Russians. A Latvian republic emerged following World War I, but it was annexed by the USSR in 1940 - an action never recognized by the US and many other countries. Latvia reestablished its independence in 1991 following the breakup of the Soviet Union. Although the last Russian troops left in 1994, the status of the Russian minority (some 25% of the population) remains of concern to Moscow. Latvia acceded to both NATO and the EU in the spring of 2004; it joined the euro zone in 2014 and the OECD in 2016. A dual citizenship law was adopted in 2013, easing naturalization for non-citizen children.

GEOGRAPHY

Location: Eastern Europe, bordering the Baltic Sea, between Estonia and Lithuania

Geographic coordinates: 57 00 N, 25 00 E

Map references: Europe

Area: *total:* 64,589 sq km
land: 62,249 sq km
water: 2,340 sq km

Area - comparative: slightly larger than West Virginia

Land boundaries: *total:* 1,370 km
border countries (4): Belarus 161 km; Estonia 333 km; Lithuania 544 km; Russia 332 km

Coastline: 498 km

Maritime claims: *territorial sea:* 12 nm
exclusive economic zone: limits as agreed to by Estonia, Finland, Latvia, Sweden, and Russia
continental shelf: 200 m depth or to the depth of exploitation

Climate: maritime; wet, moderate winters

Terrain: low plain

Elevation: *highest point:* Gaizina Kalns 312 m
lowest point: Baltic Sea 0 m
mean elevation: 87 m

Natural resources: peat, limestone, dolomite, amber, hydropower, timber, arable land

Land use: *agricultural land:* 29.2% (2018 est.)
arable land: 18.6% (2018 est.)
permanent crops: 0.1% (2018 est.)
permanent pasture: 10.5% (2018 est.)
forest: 54.1% (2018 est.)
other: 16.7% (2018 est.)

Irrigated land: 12 sq km (2012)
note: land in Latvia is often too wet and in need of drainage not irrigation; approximately 16,000 sq km or 85% of agricultural land has been improved by drainage

Population distribution: largest concentration of people is found in and around the port and capital city of Riga; small agglomerations are scattered throughout the country

Natural hazards: large percentage of agricultural fields can become waterlogged and require drainage

Geography - note: most of the country is composed of fertile low-lying plains with some hills in the east

PEOPLE AND SOCIETY

Population: 1,842,226 (2022 est.)

Nationality: *noun:* Latvian(s)
adjective: Latvian

Ethnic groups: Latvian 62.7%, Russian 24.5%, Belarusian 3.1%, Ukrainian 2.2%, Polish 2%, Lithuanian 1.1%, other 1.8%, unspecified 2.6% (2021 est.)

Languages: Latvian (official) 56.3%, Russian 33.8%, other 0.6% (includes Polish, Ukrainian, and Belarusian), unspecified 9.4%; note - data represent language usually spoken at home (2011 est.)
major-language sample(s): World Factbook, neaizstājams avots pamata informāciju. (Latvian)

Religions: Lutheran 36.2%, Roman Catholic 19.5%, Orthodox 19.1%, other Christian 1.6%, other 0.1%, unspecified/none 23.5% (2017 est.)

Age structure: *0-14 years:* 15.32% (male 148,120/female 140,028)
15-24 years: 9% (male 87,372/female 81,965)
25-54 years: 40.41% (male 380,817/female 379,359)
55-64 years: 14.77% (male 125,401/female 152,548)
65 years and over: 20.5% (male 128,151/female 257,471) (2020 est.)

Dependency ratios: *total dependency ratio:* 59
youth dependency ratio: 26.1
elderly dependency ratio: 32.9
potential support ratio: 3 (2020 est.)

Median age: *total:* 44.4 years
male: 40.5 years
female: 48 years (2020 est.)

Population growth rate: -1.11% (2022 est.)

Birth rate: 8.73 births/1,000 population (2022 est.)

Death rate: 14.65 deaths/1,000 population (2022 est.)

Net migration rate: -5.19 migrant(s)/1,000 population (2022 est.)

Population distribution: largest concentration of people is found in and around the port and capital city of Riga; small agglomerations are scattered throughout the country

Urbanization: *urban population:* 68.5% of total population (2022)

rate of urbanization: -0.68% annual rate of change (2020-25 est.)

Major urban areas - population: 625,000 RIGA (capital) (2022)

Sex ratio: *at birth:* 1.05 male(s)/female
0-14 years: 1.06 male(s)/female
15-24 years: 1.06 male(s)/female
25-54 years: 1.02 male(s)/female
55-64 years: 0.84 male(s)/female
65 years and over: 0.36 male(s)/female
total population: 0.86 male(s)/female (2022 est.)

Mother's mean age at first birth: 27.3 years (2020 est.)

Maternal mortality ratio: 19 deaths/100,000 live births (2017 est.)

Infant mortality rate: *total:* 4.85 deaths/1,000 live births
male: 5.27 deaths/1,000 live births
female: 4.42 deaths/1,000 live births (2022 est.)

Life expectancy at birth: *total population:* 75.91 years
male: 71.47 years
female: 80.56 years (2022 est.)

Total fertility rate: 1.54 children born/woman (2022 est.)

Drinking water source: *improved: urban:* 99.9% of population
rural: 98.6% of population
total: 99.5% of population
unimproved: urban: 0.1% of population
rural: 1.4% of population
total: 0.5% of population (2020 est.)

Current health expenditure: 6.6% of GDP (2019)

Physicians density: 3.4 physicians/1,000 population (2020)

Hospital bed density: 5.5 beds/1,000 population (2018)

Sanitation facility access: *improved: urban:* 98.9% of population
rural: 85.3% of population
total: 94.6% of population
unimproved: urban: 1.1% of population
rural: 14.7% of population
total: 5.4% of population (2020 est.)

HIV/AIDS - adult prevalence rate: 0.3% (2019 est.)

Major infectious diseases: *degree of risk:* intermediate (2020)
vectorborne diseases: tickborne encephalitis

Obesity - adult prevalence rate: 23.6% (2016)

Alcohol consumption per capita: *total:* 12.9 liters of pure alcohol (2019 est.)
beer: 4.9 liters of pure alcohol (2019 est.)
wine: 1.7 liters of pure alcohol (2019 est.)
spirits: 5.3 liters of pure alcohol (2019 est.)
other alcohols: 1 liters of pure alcohol (2019 est.)

Tobacco use: *total:* 37% (2020 est.)
male: 50.3% (2020 est.)
female: 23.7% (2020 est.)

Education expenditures: 4.2% of GDP (2018 est.)

Literacy: *definition:* age 15 and over can read and write
total population: 99.9%
male: 99.9%
female: 99.9% (2018)

School life expectancy (primary to tertiary education): *total:* 16 years
male: 16 years
female: 17 years (2019)

Unemployment, youth ages 15-24: *total:* 14.9%
male: 14.4%
female: 15.5% (2020 est.)

ENVIRONMENT

Environment - current issues: while land, water, and air pollution are evident, Latvia's environment has benefited from a shift to service industries after the country regained independence; improvements have occurred in drinking water quality, sewage treatment, household and hazardous waste management, as well as reduction of air pollution; concerns include nature protection and the management of water resources and the protection of the Baltic Sea

Environment - international agreements: *party to:* Air Pollution, Air Pollution-Heavy Metals, Air Pollution-Multi-effect Protocol, Air Pollution-Persistent Organic Pollutants, Biodiversity, Climate Change, Climate Change-Kyoto Protocol, Climate Change-Paris Agreement, Comprehensive Nuclear Test Ban, Desertification, Endangered Species, Hazardous Wastes, Law of the Sea, Ozone Layer Protection, Ship Pollution, Tropical Timber 2006, Wetlands
signed, but not ratified: none of the selected agreements

Air pollutants: *particulate matter emissions:* 12.72 micrograms per cubic meter (2016 est.)
carbon dioxide emissions: 7 megatons (2016 est.)
methane emissions: 1.85 megatons (2020 est.)

Climate: maritime; wet, moderate winters

Land use: *agricultural land:* 29.2% (2018 est.)
arable land: 18.6% (2018 est.)
permanent crops: 0.1% (2018 est.)
permanent pasture: 10.5% (2018 est.)
forest: 54.1% (2018 est.)
other: 16.7% (2018 est.)

Urbanization: *urban population:* 68.5% of total population (2022)
rate of urbanization: -0.68% annual rate of change (2020-25 est.)

Revenue from forest resources: *forest revenues:* 0.85% of GDP (2018 est.)

Revenue from coal: *coal revenues:* 0% of GDP (2018 est.)

Waste and recycling: *municipal solid waste generated annually:* 857,000 tons (2015 est.)
municipal solid waste recycled annually: 181,941 tons (2015 est.)
percent of municipal solid waste recycled: 21.2% (2015 est.)

Total water withdrawal: *municipal:* 94.4 million cubic meters (2017 est.)
industrial: 25.2 million cubic meters (2017 est.)
agricultural: 61.5 million cubic meters (2017 est.)

Total renewable water resources: 34.94 billion cubic meters (2017 est.)

GOVERNMENT

Country name: *conventional long form:* Republic of Latvia
conventional short form: Latvia
local long form: Latvijas Republika
local short form: Latvija
former: Latvian Soviet Socialist Republic (while occupied by the USSR)
etymology: the name "Latvia" originates from the ancient Latgalians, one of four eastern Baltic tribes that formed the ethnic core of the Latvian people (ca. 8th-12th centuries A.D.)

Government type: parliamentary republic

Capital: *name:* Riga
geographic coordinates: 56 57 N, 24 06 E
time difference: UTC+2 (7 hours ahead of Washington, DC, during Standard Time)
daylight saving time: +1hr, begins last Sunday in March; ends last Sunday in October
etymology: of the several theories explaining the name's origin, the one relating to the city's role in Baltic and North Sea commerce is the most probable; the name is likely related to the Latvian word "rija," meaning "warehouse," where the 'j' became a 'g' under the heavy German influence in the city from the late Middle Ages to the early 20th century

Administrative divisions: 36 municipalities (novadi, singular - novads) and 7 state cities (valstpilsetu pasvaldibas, singular valstspilsetas pasvaldiba)
municipalities: Adazi, Aizkraukle, Aluksne, Augsdaugava, Balvi, Bauska, Cesis, Dienvidkurzeme, Dobele, Gulbene, Jekabpils, Jelgava, Kekava, Kraslava, Kuldiga, Limbazi, Livani, Ludza, Madona, Marupe, Ogre, Olaine, Preili, Rezekne, Ropazi, Salaspils, Saldus, Saulkrasti, Sigulda, Smiltene, Talsi, Tukums, Valka, Valmiera, Varaklani, Ventspils
cities: Daugavpils, Jelgava, Jurmala, Liepaja, Rezekne, Riga, Ventspils

Independence: 18 November 1918 (from Soviet Russia); 4 May 1990 (declared from the Soviet Union); 6 September 1991 (recognized by the Soviet Union)

National holiday: Independence Day (Republic of Latvia Proclamation Day), 18 November (1918); note - 18 November 1918 was the date Latvia established its statehood and its concomitant independence from Soviet Russia; 4 May 1990 was the date it declared the restoration of Latvian statehood and its concomitant independence from the Soviet Union

Constitution: *history:* several previous (pre-1991 independence); note - following the restoration of independence in 1991, parts of the 1922 constitution were reintroduced 4 May 1990 and fully reintroduced 6 July 1993
amendments: proposed by two thirds of Parliament members or by petition of one tenth of qualified voters submitted through the president; passage requires at least two-thirds majority vote of Parliament in each of three readings; amendment of constitutional articles, including national sovereignty, language, the parliamentary electoral system, and constitutional amendment procedures, requires passage in a referendum by majority vote of at least one half of the electorate; amended several times, last in 2019

Legal system: civil law system with traces of socialist legal traditions and practices

International law organization participation: has not submitted an ICJ jurisdiction declaration; accepts ICCt jurisdiction

Citizenship: *citizenship by birth:* no
citizenship by descent only: at least one parent must be a citizen of Latvia
dual citizenship recognized: no
residency requirement for naturalization: 5 years

Suffrage: 18 years of age; universal

Executive branch: *chief of state:* President Egils LEVITS (since 8 July 2019)
head of government: Prime Minister Krisjanis KARINS (since 23 January 2019)
cabinet: Cabinet of Ministers nominated by the prime minister, appointed by Parliament
elections/appointments: president indirectly elected by Parliament for a 4-year term (eligible for a second term); election last held on 29 May 2019 (next to be held in 2023); prime minister appointed by the president, confirmed by Parliament
election results:
2019: Egils LEVITS elected president; Parliament vote - Egils LEVITS 61 votes, Didzis SMITS 24 votes, Juris JANSONS 8 votes; Krisjanis KARINS confirmed prime minister 61-39
2015: Raimonds VEJONIS elected president; Raimonds VEJOONIS 55 votes, Egils LEVITS 42 votes

Legislative branch: *description:* unicameral Parliament or Saeima (100 seats; members directly elected in multi-seat constituencies by party-list proportional representation vote; members serve 4-year terms)
elections:
last held on 6 October 2018 (next to be held in October 2022)
election results:
percent of vote by party - S 19.8%, KPV LV 14.3%, JKP 13.6%, AP! 12%, NA 11%, ZZS 9.9%, JV 6.7%, other 12.7%; seats by party - S 23, KPV LV 16, JKP 16, AP! 13, NA 13, ZZS 11, JV 8; composition as of April 2022 - men 73, women 27, percent of women 27%

Judicial branch: *highest court(s):* Supreme Court (consists of the Senate with 36 judges); Constitutional Court (consists of 7 judges)
judge selection and term of office: Supreme Court judges nominated by chief justice and confirmed by the Saeima; judges serve until age 70, but term can be extended 2 years; Constitutional Court judges - 3 nominated by Saeima members, 2 by Cabinet ministers, and 2 by plenum of Supreme Court; all judges confirmed by Saeima majority vote; Constitutional Court president and vice president serve in their positions for 3 years; all judges serve 10-year terms; mandatory retirement at age 70
subordinate courts: district (city) and regional courts

Political parties and leaders: Development/For! or AP! [Daniels PAVLUTS, Juris PUCE]
For a Humane Latvia or PCL [Maris MOZVILLO] (formerly known as Who Owns the State?)
National Alliance "All For Latvia!"-"For Fatherland and Freedom/LNNK" or NA [Raivis DZINTARS]
New Unity or JV [Arturs Krišjānis KARINS]
Social Democratic Party "Harmony" or S [Janis URBANOVICS]
The Conservatives or K [Janis BORDANS] (formerly known as New Conservative Party or JKP)
Union of Greens and Farmers or ZZS [Aivars LEMBERGS]
United List or AS [Uldis PILENS] (electoral coalition including the Latvian Green Party or LZP, Latvian Association of Regions or LRA, Liepaja Party)

International organization participation: Australia Group, BA, BIS, CBSS, CD, CE, EAPC, EBRD, ECB, EIB, EMU, ESA (cooperating state), EU, FAO, IAEA, IBRD, ICAO, ICC (NGOs), ICCt, ICRM, IDA, IFC, IFRCS, IHO, ILO, IMF, IMO, IMSO, Interpol, IOC, IOM, IPU, ISO (correspondent), ITU, ITUC (NGOs), MIGA, NATO, NIB, NSG, OAS (observer), OIF (observer), OPCW, OSCE, PCA, Schengen Convention, UN, UNCTAD, UNESCO, UNHCR, UNWTO, UPU, Wassenaar Arrangement, WCO, WHO, WIPO, WMO, WTO

Diplomatic representation in the US: *chief of mission:* Ambassador Maris SELGA (since 16 September 2019)
chancery: 2306 Massachusetts Avenue NW, Washington, DC 20008
telephone: [1] (202) 328-2840
FAX: [1] (202) 328-2860
email address and website:
embassy.usa@mfa.gov.lv
https://www2.mfa.gov.lv/en/usa

Diplomatic representation from the US: *chief of mission:* Ambassador John Leslie CARWILE (since 5 November 2019)
embassy: 1 Samnera Velsa Street (former Remtes), Riga LV-1510
mailing address: 4520 Riga Place, Washington DC 20521-4520
telephone: [371] 6710-7000
FAX: [371] 6710-7050
email address and website:
askconsular-riga@state.gov
https://lv.usembassy.gov/

Flag description: three horizontal bands of maroon (top), white (half-width), and maroon; the flag is one of the older banners in the world; a medieval chronicle mentions a red standard with a white stripe being used by Latvian tribes in about 1280

National symbol(s): white wagtail (bird); national colors: maroon, white

National anthem: *name:* "Dievs, sveti Latviju!" (God Bless Latvia)
lyrics/music: Karlis BAUMANIS
note: adopted 1920, restored 1990; first performed in 1873 while Latvia was a part of Russia; banned during the Soviet occupation from 1940 to 1990

National heritage: *total World Heritage Sites:* 2 (both cultural)
selected World Heritage Site locales: Historic Center of Riga; Struve Geodetic Arc

ECONOMY

Economic overview: Latvia is a small, open economy with exports contributing more than half of GDP. Due to its geographical location, transit services are highly-developed, along with timber and wood-processing, agriculture and food products, and manufacturing of machinery and electronics industries. Corruption continues to be an impediment to attracting foreign direct investment and Latvia's low birth rate and decreasing population are major challenges to its long-term economic vitality.

Latvia's economy experienced GDP growth of more than 10% per year during 2006-07, but entered a severe recession in 2008 as a result of an unsustainable current account deficit and large debt exposure amid the slowing world economy. Triggered by the collapse of the second largest bank, GDP plunged by more than 14% in 2009 and, despite strong growth since 2011, the economy took until 2017 return to pre-crisis levels in real terms. Strong investment and consumption, the latter stoked by rising wages, helped the economy grow by more than 4% in 2017, while inflation rose to 3%. Continued gains in competitiveness and investment will be key to maintaining economic growth, especially in light of unfavorable demographic trends, including the emigration of skilled workers, and one of the highest levels of income inequality in the EU.

In the wake of the 2008-09 crisis, the IMF, EU, and other international donors provided substantial financial assistance to Latvia as part of an agreement to defend the currency's peg to the euro in exchange for the government's commitment to stringent austerity measures. The IMF/EU program successfully concluded in December 2011, although, the austerity measures imposed large social costs. The majority of companies, banks, and real estate have been privatized, although the state still holds sizable stakes in a few large enterprises, including 80% ownership of the Latvian national airline. Latvia officially joined the World Trade Organization in February 1999 and the EU in May 2004. Latvia also joined the euro zone in 2014 and the OECD in 2016.

Real GDP (purchasing power parity): $56.92 billion (2020 est.)
$59.06 billion (2019 est.)
$57.88 billion (2018 est.)
note: data are in 2017 dollars

Real GDP growth rate: 2.08% (2019 est.)
4.2% (2018 est.)
3.23% (2017 est.)

Real GDP per capita: $29,900 (2020 est.)
$30,900 (2019 est.)
$30,000 (2018 est.)
note: data are in 2017 dollars

GDP (official exchange rate): $34.084 billion (2019 est.)

Inflation rate (consumer prices): 2.8% (2019 est.)
2.5% (2018 est.)
2.9% (2017 est.)

Credit ratings:

Fitch rating: A- (2014)

Moody's rating: A3 (2015)

Standard & Poors rating: A+ (2020)
note: The year refers to the year in which the current credit rating was first obtained.

GDP - composition, by sector of origin: *agriculture:* 3.9% (2017 est.)
industry: 22.4% (2017 est.)
services: 73.7% (2017 est.)

GDP - composition, by end use: *household consumption:* 61.8% (2017 est.)
government consumption: 18.2% (2017 est.)
investment in fixed capital: 19.9% (2017 est.)
investment in inventories: 1.5% (2017 est.)
exports of goods and services: 60.6% (2017 est.)
imports of goods and services: -61.9% (2017 est.)

Agricultural products: wheat, milk, rapeseed, barley, oats, potatoes, rye, beans, pork, poultry

Industries: processed foods, processed wood products, textiles, processed metals, pharmaceuticals, railroad cars, synthetic fibers, electronics

Industrial production growth rate: 10.6% (2017 est.)

Labor force: 885,000 (2020 est.)

Labor force - by occupation: *agriculture:* 7.7%
industry: 24.1%
services: 68.1% (2016 est.)

Unemployment rate: 6.14% (2019 est.)

6.51% (2018 est.)

Unemployment, youth ages 15-24: *total:* 14.9%
male: 14.4%
female: 15.5% (2020 est.)

Population below poverty line: 22.9% (2018 est.)

Gini Index coefficient - distribution of family income: 35.6 (2017 est.)
35.4 (2014)

Household income or consumption by percentage share: *lowest 10%:* 2.2%
highest 10%: 26.3% (2015)

Budget: *revenues:* 11.39 billion (2017 est.)
expenditures: 11.53 billion (2017 est.)

Budget surplus (+) or deficit (-): -0.5% (of GDP) (2017 est.)

Public debt: 36.3% of GDP (2017 est.)
37.4% of GDP (2016 est.)
note: data cover general government debt, and includes debt instruments issued (or owned) by government entities, including sub-sectors of central government, state government, local government, and social security funds

Taxes and other revenues: 37.5% (of GDP) (2017 est.)

Fiscal year: calendar year

Current account balance: -$222 million (2019 est.)
-$99 million (2018 est.)

Exports: $20.23 billion (2020 est.) note: data are in current year dollars
$20.5 billion (2019 est.) note: data are in current year dollars
$21.12 billion (2018 est.) note: data are in current year dollars

Exports - partners: Lithuania 16%, Estonia 10%, Russia 9%, Germany 7%, Sweden 6%, United Kingdom 6% (2019)

Exports - commodities: lumber, broadcasting equipment, whiskey and other hard liquors, wheat, packaged medicines (2019)

Imports: $19.84 billion (2020 est.) note: data are in current year dollars
$20.79 billion (2019 est.) note: data are in current year dollars
$21.38 billion (2018 est.) note: data are in current year dollars

Imports - partners: Russia 21%, Lithuania 14%, Germany 9%, Poland 7%, Estonia 7% (2019)

Imports - commodities: refined petroleum, broadcasting equipment, cars, packaged medicines, aircraft (2019)

Reserves of foreign exchange and gold: $4.614 billion (31 December 2017 est.)
$3.514 billion (31 December 2016 est.)

Debt - external: $40.164 billion (2019 est.)
$42.488 billion (2018 est.)

Exchange rates: euros (EUR) per US dollar -
0.82771 (2020 est.)
0.90338 (2019 est.)
0.87789 (2018 est.)
0.885 (2014 est.)
0.7634 (2013 est.)

ENERGY

Electricity access: *electrification - total population:* 100% (2020)

Electricity: *installed generating capacity:* 3.089 million kW (2020 est.)
consumption: 6.706 billion kWh (2020 est.)
exports: 2.548 billion kWh (2020 est.)
imports: 4.173 billion kWh (2020 est.)
transmission/distribution losses: 377 million kWh (2020 est.)

Electricity generation sources: *fossil fuels:* 33.4% of total installed capacity (2020 est.)
solar: 0.1% of total installed capacity (2020 est.)
wind: 3.2% of total installed capacity (2020 est.)
hydroelectricity: 47.5% of total installed capacity (2020 est.)
biomass and waste: 15.9% of total installed capacity (2020 est.)

Coal: *production:* 0 metric tons (2020 est.)
consumption: 39,000 metric tons (2020 est.)
exports: 3,000 metric tons (2020 est.)
imports: 40,000 metric tons (2020 est.)
proven reserves: 0 metric tons (2019 est.)

Petroleum: *total petroleum production:* 1,600 bbl/day (2021 est.)
refined petroleum consumption: 39,900 bbl/day (2019 est.)
crude oil and lease condensate exports: 0 bbl/day (2018 est.)
crude oil and lease condensate imports: 0 bbl/day (2018 est.)
crude oil estimated reserves: 0 barrels (2021 est.)

Refined petroleum products - production: 0 bbl/day (2017 est.)

Refined petroleum products - exports: 16,180 bbl/day (2017 est.)

Refined petroleum products - imports: 54,370 bbl/day (2017 est.)

Natural gas: *production:* 0 cubic meters (2021 est.)
consumption: 1,067,798,000 cubic meters (2020 est.)
exports: 0 cubic meters (2021 est.)
imports: 1,067,798,000 cubic meters (2020 est.)
proven reserves: 0 cubic meters (2021 est.)

Carbon dioxide emissions: 8.45 million metric tonnes of CO_2 (2019 est.)
from coal and metallurgical coke: 149,000 metric tonnes of CO_2 (2019 est.)
from petroleum and other liquids: 5.693 million metric tonnes of CO_2 (2019 est.)
from consumed natural gas: 2.608 million metric tonnes of CO_2 (2019 est.)

Energy consumption per capita: 86.645 million Btu/person (2019 est.)

COMMUNICATIONS

Telephones - fixed lines: *total subscriptions:* 211,849 (2020 est.)
subscriptions per 100 inhabitants: 11 (2020 est.)

Telephones - mobile cellular: *total subscriptions:* 2,051,359 (2020 est.)
subscriptions per 100 inhabitants: 109 (2020 est.)

Telecommunication systems: *general assessment:* the telecom market continues to benefit from investment and from regulatory measures aimed at developing 5G and fiber based infrastructure; there is effective competition in the mobile market, with extensive services based on LTE-A technologies to boost data speeds; a large scale 5G deployment is not expected until 2023; in the fixed-line broadband sector, the country is ranked second highest in Europe (after Iceland) for fiber coverage and take-up, closely followed by Lithuania; with this infrastructure in place, the country has also developed a sophisticated digital economy, with e-commerce and e-government services widely available (2021)
domestic: fixed-line roughly 11 per 100 and mobile-cellular nearly 109 per 100 subscriptions (2020)
international: country code - 371; the Latvian network is now connected via fiber-optic cable to Estonia, Finland, and Sweden

Broadcast media: several national and regional commercial TV stations are foreign-owned, 2 national TV stations are publicly owned; system supplemented by privately owned regional and local TV stations; cable and satellite multi-channel TV services with domestic and foreign broadcasts available; publicly owned broadcaster operates 4 radio networks with dozens of stations throughout the country; dozens of private broadcasters also operate radio stations

Internet country code: .lv

Internet users: *total:* 1,663,739 (July 2022 est.)
percent of population: 89.8% (July 2022 est.)

Broadband - fixed subscriptions: *total:* 490,569 (2020 est.)
subscriptions per 100 inhabitants: 26 (2020 est.)

TRANSPORTATION

National air transport system: *number of registered air carriers:* 3 (2020)
inventory of registered aircraft operated by air carriers: 53
annual passenger traffic on registered air carriers: 4,058,762 (2018)
annual freight traffic on registered air carriers: 4.01 million (2018) mt-km

Civil aircraft registration country code prefix: YL

Airports: *total:* 42 (2021)

Airports - with paved runways: *total:* 18
over 3,047 m: 1
2,438 to 3,047 m: 3
1,524 to 2,437 m: 4
914 to 1,523 m: 3
under 914 m: 7 (2021)

Airports - with unpaved runways: *total:* 24
under 914 m: 24 (2021)

Heliports: 1 (2021)

Pipelines: 1,213 km gas, 417 km refined products (2018)

Railways: *total:* 1,860 km (2018)
narrow gauge: 34 km (2018) 0.750-m gauge
broad gauge: 1,826 km (2018) 1.520-m gauge

Roadways: *total:* 70,244 km (2018)
paved: 15,158 km (2018)
unpaved: 55,086 km (2018)

Waterways: 300 km (2010) (navigable year-round)

Merchant marine: *total:* 70
by type: general cargo 22, oil tanker 9, other 39 (2021)

Ports and terminals: *major seaport(s):* Riga, Ventspils

MILITARY AND SECURITY

Military and security forces: National Armed Forces (Nacionalie Brunotie Speki): Land Forces (Latvijas

Sauszemes Speki), Naval Force (Latvijas Juras Speki, includes Coast Guard (Latvijas Kara Flote)), Air Force (Latvijas Gaisa Speki), National Guard (2022)

Military expenditures: 2.1% of GDP (2022 est.)
2.2% of GDP (2021)
2.2% of GDP (2020)
2% of GDP (2019) (approximately $920 million)
2.1% of GDP (2018) (approximately $900 million)

Military and security service personnel strengths: approximately 7,500 active duty troops (6,500 Land Forces; 500 Naval Force/Coast Guard; 500 Air Force; note - some Land Forces are considered joint forces); 8,200 National Guard (2022)

Military equipment inventories and acquisitions: the Latvian military's inventory is limited and consists of a mixture of Soviet-era and more modern--mostly second-hand-- European and US equipment; since 2010, it has received limited amounts of equipment from several European countries, Israel, and the US (2021)

Military service age and obligation: 18 years of age for voluntary male and female military service; no conscription (abolished 2007) (2022)
note 1: in July 2022, the Latvian Government announced that it was reinstating mandatory military service for men aged 18-27 (women voluntarily) beginning in July 2023; service would be for one year in the Land Forces or alternatively in internal affairs, health, or welfare structures
note 2: as of 2019, women comprised about 16% of the military's full-time personnel

Military deployments: 130 Kosovo (KFOR/NATO) (2022)

Military - note: Latvia became a member of NATO in 2004
since 2017, Latvia has hosted a Canadian-led multi-national NATO ground force battlegroup as part of the Alliance's Enhanced Forward Presence initiative; in addition, Latvia hosts a NATO-led divisional headquarters (Multinational Division North; activated 2020), which coordinates training and preparation activities of its respective subordinate NATO battlegroups in Estonia and Latvia

NATO also has provided air protection for Latvia since 2004 through its Air Policing mission; NATO member countries that possess air combat capabilities voluntarily contribute to the mission on 4-month rotations (2022)

TRANSNATIONAL ISSUES

Disputes - international: *Latvia-Belarus:* Belarus and Latvia signed joint demarcation map in September 2008
Latvia-Estonia: demarcation reportedly completed in 1998
Latvia-Lithuania: boundary demarcation was completed by the end of 1998; the Latvian parliament has not ratified its 1998 maritime boundary treaty with Lithuania, primarily due to concerns over oil exploration rights
Latvia-Russia: Russia demands better Latvian treatment of ethnic Russians in Latvia; in March 2007, Latvia and Russia signed a border treaty, which includes Latvia withdrawing claims to a district now in Russia that was part of Latvia before WWII; the permanent demarcation of the boundary between Latvia and Russia was completed and came into force in April 2018; as a member state that forms part of the EU's external border, Latvia has implemented the strict Schengen border rules with Russia

Refugees and internally displaced persons: *refugees (country of origin):* 35,283 (Ukraine) (as of 15 November 2022)
stateless persons: 209,168 (mid-year 2021); note - individuals who were Latvian citizens prior to the 1940 Soviet occupation and their descendants were recognized as Latvian citizens when the country's independence was restored in 1991; citizens of the former Soviet Union residing in Latvia who have neither Latvian nor other citizenship are considered non-citizens (officially there is no statelessness in Latvia) and are entitled to non-citizen passports; children born after Latvian independence to stateless parents are entitled to Latvian citizenship upon their parents' request; non-citizens cannot vote or hold certain government jobs and are exempt from military service but can travel visa-free in the EU under the Schengen accord like Latvian citizens; non-citizens can obtain naturalization if they have been permanent residents of Latvia for at least five years, pass tests in Latvian language and history, and know the words of the Latvian national anthem

Illicit drugs: transshipment and destination point for cocaine, synthetic drugs, opiates, and cannabis from Southwest Asia, Western Europe, Latin America, and neighboring Baltic countries; despite improved legislation, vulnerable to money laundering due to nascent enforcement capabilities and comparatively weak regulation of offshore companies and the gaming industry; CIS organized crime (including counterfeiting, corruption, extortion, stolen cars, and prostitution) accounts for most laundered proceeds

LEBANON

INTRODUCTION

Background: As a result of its location at the crossroads of three continents, the area that is modern-day Lebanon is rich in cultural and religious diversity. This region was subject to various foreign conquests for much of its history, including by the Romans, Arabs, and Ottomans. Following World War I, France acquired a mandate over the northern portion of the former Ottoman Empire province of Syria. From it the French demarcated the region of Lebanon in 1920, and it gained independence in 1943. Since then, Lebanon has experienced periods of political turmoil interspersed with prosperity built on its historical position as a regional center for finance and trade, although that status has significantly diminished since the beginning of Lebanon's economic crisis in 2019, which includes simultaneous currency, debt, and banking crises. The country's 1975-90 civil war, which resulted in an estimated 120,000 fatalities, was followed by years of social and political instability. Sectarianism is a key element of Lebanese political life. Neighboring Syria has historically influenced Lebanon's foreign and domestic policies, and its military occupied Lebanon from 1976 until 2005. Hizballah - a major Lebanese political party, militia, and US-designated foreign terrorist organization - and Israel continued attacks and counterattacks against each other after Syria's withdrawal, and fought a brief war in 2006. Lebanon's borders with Syria and Israel remain unresolved.

GEOGRAPHY

Location: Middle East, bordering the Mediterranean Sea, between Israel and Syria

Geographic coordinates: 33 50 N, 35 50 E

Map references: Middle East

Area: *total:* 10,400 sq km
land: 10,230 sq km
water: 170 sq km

Area - comparative: about one-third the size of Maryland

Land boundaries: *total:* 484 km
border countries (2): Israel 81 km; Syria 403 km

Coastline: 225 km

Maritime claims: *territorial sea:* 12 nm

Climate: Mediterranean; mild to cool, wet winters with hot, dry summers; the Lebanon Mountains experience heavy winter snows

Terrain: narrow coastal plain; El Beqaa (Bekaa Valley) separates Lebanon and Anti-Lebanon Mountains

Elevation: *highest point:* Qornet es Saouda 3,088 m
lowest point: Mediterranean Sea 0 m
mean elevation: 1,250 m

Natural resources: limestone, iron ore, salt, water-surplus state in a water-deficit region, arable land

Land use: *agricultural land:* 63.3% (2018 est.)
arable land: 11.9% (2018 est.)
permanent crops: 12.3% (2018 est.)
permanent pasture: 39.1% (2018 est.)
forest: 13.4% (2018 est.)

other: 23.3% (2018 est.)

Irrigated land: 1,040 sq km (2012)

Population distribution: the majority of the people live on or near the Mediterranean coast, and of these most live in and around the capital, Beirut; favorable growing conditions in the Bekaa Valley, on the southeastern side of the Lebanon Mountains, have attracted farmers and thus the area exhibits a smaller population density

Natural hazards: earthquakes; dust storms, sandstorms

Geography - note: smallest country in continental Asia; Nahr el Litani is the only major river in Near East not crossing an international boundary; rugged terrain historically helped isolate, protect, and develop numerous factional groups based on religion, clan, and ethnicity

PEOPLE AND SOCIETY

Population: 5,296,814 (2022 est.)

Nationality: *noun:* Lebanese (singular and plural)
adjective: Lebanese

Ethnic groups: Arab 95%, Armenian 4%, other 1%
note: many Christian Lebanese do not identify themselves as Arab but rather as descendants of the ancient Canaanites and prefer to be called Phoenicians

Languages: Arabic (official), French, English, Armenian
major-language sample(s):

يمكن الاستغناء عنه للمعلومات الأساسية

كتاب حقائق العالم، المصدر الذي لا

(Arabic)

Religions: Muslim 67.8% (31.9% Sunni, 31.2% Shia, smaller percentages of Alawites and Ismailis), Christian 32.4% (Maronite Catholics are the largest Christian group), Druze 4.5%, very small numbers of Jews, Baha'is, Buddhists, and Hindus (2020 est.)
note: data represent the religious affiliation of the citizen population (data do not include Lebanon's sizable Syrian and Palestinian refugee populations); 18 religious sects recognized

Age structure: *0-14 years:* 20.75% (male 581,015/female 554,175)
15-24 years: 14.98% (male 417,739/female 401,357)
25-54 years: 46.69% (male 1,296,250/female 1,257,273)
55-64 years: 9.62% (male 250,653/female 275,670)
65 years and over: 7.96% (male 187,001/female 248,479) (2020 est.)

Dependency ratios: *total dependency ratio:* 48.4
youth dependency ratio: 37.2
elderly dependency ratio: 11.2
potential support ratio: 8.9 (2020 est.)

Median age: *total:* 33.7 years
male: 33.1 years
female: 34.4 years (2020 est.)

Population growth rate: 0.66% (2022 est.)

Birth rate: 13.1 births/1,000 population (2022 est.)

Death rate: 5.57 deaths/1,000 population (2022 est.)

Net migration rate: -0.94 migrant(s)/1,000 population (2022 est.)

Population distribution: the majority of the people live on or near the Mediterranean coast, and of these most live in and around the capital, Beirut; favorable growing conditions in the Bekaa Valley, on the southeastern side of the Lebanon Mountains, have attracted farmers and thus the area exhibits a smaller population density

Urbanization: *urban population:* 89.3% of total population (2022)
rate of urbanization: -1.23% annual rate of change (2020-25 est.)

Major urban areas - population: 2.433 million BEIRUT (capital) (2022)

Sex ratio: *at birth:* 1.05 male(s)/female
0-14 years: 1.05 male(s)/female
15-24 years: 1.04 male(s)/female
25-54 years: 1.03 male(s)/female
55-64 years: 0.93 male(s)/female
65 years and over: 0.67 male(s)/female
total population: 1 male(s)/female (2022 est.)

Maternal mortality ratio: 29 deaths/100,000 live births (2017 est.)

Infant mortality rate: *total:* 7.04 deaths/1,000 live births
male: 7.6 deaths/1,000 live births
female: 6.45 deaths/1,000 live births (2022 est.)

Life expectancy at birth: *total population:* 78.76 years
male: 77.36 years
female: 80.23 years (2022 est.)

Total fertility rate: 1.71 children born/woman (2022 est.)

Drinking water source: *improved: total:* 100% of population
unimproved: total: 0% of population (2020 est.)

Current health expenditure: 8.7% of GDP (2019)

Physicians density: 2.21 physicians/1,000 population (2019)

Hospital bed density: 2.7 beds/1,000 population (2017)

Sanitation facility access: *improved: total:* 100% of population
unimproved: total: 0% of population (2020 est.)

HIV/AIDS - adult prevalence rate: (2020 est.) <.1%

Major infectious diseases: *note:* widespread ongoing transmission of a respiratory illness caused by the novel coronavirus (COVID-19) is occurring throughout Lebanon; as of 18 August 2022, Lebanon has reported a total of 1,200,111 cases of COVID-19 or 17,582.89 cumulative cases of COVID-19 per 100,000 population with a total of 10,589 cumulative deaths or a rate of 155.14 cumulative deaths per 100,000 population; as of 7 August 2022, 48.5% of the population has received at least one dose of COVID-19 vaccine

Obesity - adult prevalence rate: 32% (2016)

Alcohol consumption per capita: *total:* 1.14 liters of pure alcohol (2019 est.)
beer: 0.38 liters of pure alcohol (2019 est.)
wine: 0.21 liters of pure alcohol (2019 est.)
spirits: 0.53 liters of pure alcohol (2019 est.)
other alcohols: 0.02 liters of pure alcohol (2019 est.)

Tobacco use: *total:* 38.2% (2020 est.)
male: 47.5% (2020 est.)
female: 28.9% (2020 est.)

Child marriage: *women married by age 15:* 1.4%
women married by age 18: 6% (2016 est.)

Education expenditures: 2.6% of GDP (2019 est.)

Literacy: *definition:* age 15 and over can read and write
total population: 95.1%
male: 96.9%
female: 93.3% (2018)

School life expectancy (primary to tertiary education): *total:* 11 years
male: 12 years
female: 11 years (2014)

Unemployment, youth ages 15-24: *total:* 23.4%
male: 24.5%
female: 21.4% (2019)

ENVIRONMENT

Environment - current issues: deforestation; soil deterioration, erosion; desertification; species loss; air pollution in Beirut from vehicular traffic and the burning of industrial wastes; pollution of coastal waters from raw sewage and oil spills; waste-water management

Environment - international agreements: *party to:* Biodiversity, Climate Change, Climate Change-Kyoto Protocol, Climate Change-Paris Agreement, Comprehensive Nuclear Test Ban, Desertification, Endangered Species, Hazardous Wastes, Law of the Sea, Nuclear Test Ban, Ozone Layer Protection, Ship Pollution, Wetlands
signed, but not ratified: Environmental Modification, Marine Life Conservation

Air pollutants: *particulate matter emissions:* 30.67 micrograms per cubic meter (2016 est.)
carbon dioxide emissions: 24.8 megatons (2016 est.)
methane emissions: 3.37 megatons (2020 est.)

Climate: Mediterranean; mild to cool, wet winters with hot, dry summers; the Lebanon Mountains experience heavy winter snows

Land use: *agricultural land:* 63.3% (2018 est.)
arable land: 11.9% (2018 est.)
permanent crops: 12.3% (2018 est.)
permanent pasture: 39.1% (2018 est.)
forest: 13.4% (2018 est.)
other: 23.3% (2018 est.)

Urbanization: *urban population:* 89.3% of total population (2022)
rate of urbanization: -1.23% annual rate of change (2020-25 est.)

Revenue from forest resources: *forest revenues:* 0% of GDP (2018 est.)

Revenue from coal: *coal revenues:* 0% of GDP (2018 est.)

Food insecurity: *widespread lack of access: due to the ongoing financial and economic crisis* - in September 2021, the United Nations estimated that, taking into account multiple factors other than income, such as access to health, education and public utilities, 82% of the population lives in multidimensional poverty in 2021, up from 42% in 2019 (2022)

Waste and recycling: *municipal solid waste generated annually:* 2.04 million tons (2014 est.)
municipal solid waste recycled annually: 163,200 tons (2014 est.)
percent of municipal solid waste recycled: 8% (2014 est.)

Total water withdrawal: *municipal:* 240 million cubic meters (2017 est.)
industrial: 900 million cubic meters (2017 est.)

agricultural: 700 million cubic meters (2017 est.)

Total renewable water resources: 4.503 billion cubic meters (2017 est.)

GOVERNMENT

Country name: *conventional long form:* Lebanese Republic
conventional short form: Lebanon
local long form: Al Jumhuriyah al Lubnaniyah
local short form: Lubnan
former: Greater Lebanon
etymology: derives from the Semitic root "lbn" meaning "white" and refers to snow-capped Mount Lebanon

Government type: parliamentary republic

Capital: *name:* Beirut
geographic coordinates: 33 52 N, 35 30 E
time difference: UTC+2 (7 hours ahead of Washington, DC, during Standard Time)
daylight saving time: +1hr, begins last Sunday in March; ends last Sunday in October
etymology: derived from the Canaanite or Phoenician word "ber'ot," meaning "the wells" or "fountain," which referred to the site's accessible water table

Administrative divisions: 8 governorates (mohafazat, singular - mohafazah); Aakkar, Baalbek-Hermel, Beqaa (Bekaa), Beyrouth (Beirut), Liban- Nord (North Lebanon), Liban-Sud (South Lebanon), Mont-Liban (Mount Lebanon), Nabatiye

Independence: 22 November 1943 (from League of Nations mandate under French administration)

National holiday: Independence Day, 22 November (1943)

Constitution: *history:* drafted 15 May 1926, adopted 23 May 1926
amendments: proposed by the president of the republic and introduced as a government bill to the National Assembly or proposed by at least 10 members of the Assembly and agreed upon by two thirds of its members; if proposed by the National Assembly, review and approval by two-thirds majority of the Cabinet is required; if approved, the proposal is next submitted to the Cabinet for drafting as an amendment; Cabinet approval requires at least two-thirds majority, followed by submission to the National Assembly for discussion and vote; passage requires at least two-thirds majority vote of a required two-thirds quorum of the Assembly membership and promulgation by the president; amended several times, last in 2004

Legal system: mixed legal system of civil law based on the French civil code, Ottoman legal tradition, and religious laws covering personal status, marriage, divorce, and other family relations of the Jewish, Islamic, and Christian communities

International law organization participation: has not submitted an ICJ jurisdiction declaration; non-party state to the ICCt

Citizenship: *citizenship by birth:* no
citizenship by descent only: the father must be a citizen of Lebanon
dual citizenship recognized: yes
residency requirement for naturalization: unknown

Suffrage: 21 years of age; authorized for all men and women regardless of religion; excludes persons convicted of felonies and other crimes or those imprisoned; excludes all military and security service personnel regardless of rank

Executive branch: *chief of state:* President Michel AWN (since 31 October 2016)
head of government: Prime Minister Najib MIQATI (since 20 September 2021)
cabinet: Cabinet chosen by the prime minister in consultation with the president and Parliament
elections/appointments: president indirectly elected by Parliament with two-thirds majority vote in the first round and if needed absolute majority vote in a second round for a 6-year term (eligible for non-consecutive terms); last held on 31 October 2016 (next to be held in 2022); prime minister appointed by the president in consultation with Parliament; deputy prime minister determined during cabinet formation
election results:
2022: on 10 November 2022, Parliament in its fifth session failed to elect a president; next session is called for November 17
2016: Michel AWN elected president in second round; National Assembly vote - Michel AWN (FPM) 83 votes; note - in the initial election held on 23 April 2014, no candidate received the required two-thirds vote, and subsequent attempts failed because Parliament lacked the necessary quorum of 86 members to hold a vote; the president was finally elected in its 46th attempt on 31 October 2016

Legislative branch: *description:* unicameral Lebanese Parliament or Majlis al-Nuwab in Arabic, Chambre des députés in French (128 seats; members directly elected in multi-member constituencies by open list proportional representation vote, apportioned evenly between Christian and Muslims; members serve 4-year terms)
elections:
last held on 15 May 2022 (next to be held in May 2026)
election results:
percent of vote by coalition/party – NA; seats by party/coalition – FPM 16, LF 14, Amal Movement 13, Hezbollah 13, PSP 9, FM (candidates did not run in 2022; members ran as independents) 8, Kata'ib Party 4, other 30, independent 21; composition - men 120, women 8, percent of women 6.3%
note: Lebanon's constitution states the Lebanese Parliament cannot conduct regular business until it elects a president when the position is vacant

Judicial branch: *highest court(s):* Court of Cassation or Supreme Court (organized into 8 chambers, each with a presiding judge and 2 associate judges); Constitutional Council (consists of 10 members)
judge selection and term of office: Court of Cassation judges appointed by Supreme Judicial Council, a 10-member body headed by the chief justice, and includes other judicial officials; judge tenure NA; Constitutional Council members appointed - 5 by the Council of Ministers and 5 by parliament; members serve 5-year terms
subordinate courts: Courts of Appeal; Courts of First Instance; specialized tribunals, religious courts; military courts

Political parties and leaders: Al-Ahbash or Association of Islamic Charitable Projects or AICP [Shaykh Hussam QARAQIRA]
Amal Movement ("Hope Movement") [Nabih BERRI]
Azm Movement [Najib MIQATI]
Ba'th Arab Socialist Party of Lebanon [leader disputed]
Free Patriotic Movement or FPM [Gibran BASSIL]
Future Movement Bloc or FM [Sa'ad al-HARIRI]
Hizballah [Hassan NASRALLAH]
Islamic Action Front or IAF [Sheikh Zuhayr al-JU'AYD]
Kata'ib Party [Sami GEMAYEL]
Lebanese Democratic Party [Talal ARSLAN]
Lebanese Forces or LF [Samir JA'JA]
Marada Movement [Sulayman FRANJIEH]
Progressive Socialist Party or PSP [Walid JUNBLATT]
Social Democrat Hunshaqian Party [Sabuh KALPAKIAN]
Syrian Social Nationalist Party or SSNP [Rabi BANAT]
Tashnaq or Armenian Revolutionary Federation [Hagop PAKRADOUNIAN]

International organization participation: ABEDA, AFESD, AMF, CAEU, FAO, G-24, G-77, IAEA, IBRD, ICAO, ICC (national committees), ICRM, IDA, IDB, IFAD, IFC, IFRCS, ILO, IMF, IMO, IMSO, Interpol, IOC, IPU, ISO, ITSO, ITU, LAS, MIGA, NAM, OAS (observer), OIC, OIF, OPCW, PCA, UN, UNCTAD, UNESCO, UNHCR, UNIDO, UNRWA, UNWTO, UPU, WCO, WFTU (NGOs), WHO, WIPO, WMO, WTO (observer)

Diplomatic representation in the US: *chief of mission:* Ambassador (vacant); Charge d'Affaires Wael HACHEM, Counselor (since 15 March 2021)
chancery: 2560 28th Street NW, Washington, DC 20008
telephone: [1] (202) 939-6300
FAX: [1] (202) 939-6324
email address and website:
info@lebanonembassyus.org
http://www.lebanonembassyus.org/
consulate(s) general: Detroit, New York, Los Angeles

Diplomatic representation from the US: *chief of mission:* Ambassador Dorothy C. SHEA (since 11 March 2020)
embassy: Awkar-Facing the Municipality, Main Street, Beirut
mailing address: 6070 Beirut Place, Washington DC 20521-6070
telephone: [961] (04) 543-600
FAX: [961] (4) 544-019
email address and website:
BeirutACS@state.gov
https://lb.usembassy.gov/

Flag description: three horizontal bands consisting of red (top), white (middle, double width), and red (bottom) with a green cedar tree centered in the white band; the red bands symbolize blood shed for liberation, the white band denotes peace, the snow of the mountains, and purity; the green cedar tree is the symbol of Lebanon and represents eternity, steadiness, happiness, and prosperity

National symbol(s): cedar tree; national colors: red, white, green

National anthem: *name:* "Kulluna lil-watan" (All Of Us, For Our Country!)
lyrics/music: Rachid NAKHLE/Wadih SABRA
note: adopted 1927; chosen following a nationwide competition

National heritage: *total World Heritage Sites:* 5 (all cultural)

selected World Heritage Site locales: Anjar; Baalbek; Byblos; Tyre; Ouadi Qadisha (the Holy Valley) and the Forest of the Cedars of God (Horsh Arz el-Rab)

ECONOMY

Economic overview: Lebanon has a free-market economy and a strong laissez-faire commercial tradition. The government does not restrict foreign investment; however, the investment climate suffers from red tape, corruption, arbitrary licensing decisions, complex customs procedures, high taxes, tariffs, and fees, archaic legislation, and inadequate intellectual property rights protection. The Lebanese economy is service-oriented; main growth sectors include banking and tourism.

The 1975-90 civil war seriously damaged Lebanon's economic infrastructure, cut national output by half, and derailed Lebanon's position as a Middle Eastern banking hub. Following the civil war, Lebanon rebuilt much of its war-torn physical and financial infrastructure by borrowing heavily, mostly from domestic banks, which saddled the government with a huge debt burden. Pledges of economic and financial reforms made at separate international donor conferences during the 2000s have mostly gone unfulfilled, including those made during the Paris III Donor Conference in 2007, following the July 2006 war. The "CEDRE" investment event hosted by France in April 2018 again rallied the international community to assist Lebanon with concessional financing and some grants for capital infrastructure improvements, conditioned upon long-delayed structural economic reforms in fiscal management, electricity tariffs, and transparent public procurement, among many others.

The Syria conflict cut off one of Lebanon's major markets and a transport corridor through the Levant. The influx of nearly one million registered and an estimated 300,000 unregistered Syrian refugees has increased social tensions and heightened competition for low-skill jobs and public services. Lebanon continues to face several long-term structural weaknesses that predate the Syria crisis, notably, weak infrastructure, poor service delivery, institutionalized corruption, and bureaucratic over-regulation. Chronic fiscal deficits have increased Lebanon's debt-to-GDP ratio, the third highest in the world; most of the debt is held internally by Lebanese banks. These factors combined to slow economic growth to the 1-2% range in 2011-17, after four years of averaging 8% growth. Weak economic growth limits tax revenues, while the largest government expenditures remain debt servicing, salaries for government workers, and transfers to the electricity sector. These limitations constrain other government spending, limiting its ability to invest in necessary infrastructure improvements, such as water, electricity, and transportation. In early 2018, the Lebanese government signed long-awaited contract agreements with an international consortium for petroleum exploration and production as part of the country's first offshore licensing round. Exploration is expected to begin in 2019.

Real GDP (purchasing power parity): $79.51 billion (2020 est.)
$99.76 billion (2019 est.)
$106.93 billion (2018 est.)
note: data are in 2017 dollars

Real GDP growth rate: 1.5% (2017 est.)
1.7% (2016 est.)
0.2% (2015 est.)

Real GDP per capita: $11,600 (2020 est.)
$14,600 (2019 est.)
$15,600 (2018 est.)
note: data are in 2017 dollars

GDP (official exchange rate): $53.253 billion (2019 est.)

Inflation rate (consumer prices): 2.8% (2019 est.)
6% (2018 est.)
4.4% (2017 est.)

Credit ratings:

Fitch rating: RD (2020)

Moody's rating: C (2020)

Standard & Poors rating: D (2020)
note: The year refers to the year in which the current credit rating was first obtained.

GDP - composition, by sector of origin: *agriculture:* 3.9% (2017 est.)
industry: 13.1% (2017 est.)
services: 83% (2017 est.)

GDP - composition, by end use: *household consumption:* 87.6% (2017 est.)
government consumption: 13.3% (2017 est.)
investment in fixed capital: 21.8% (2017 est.)
investment in inventories: 0.5% (2017 est.)
exports of goods and services: 23.6% (2017 est.)
imports of goods and services: -46.4% (2017 est.)

Agricultural products: potatoes, milk, tomatoes, apples, oranges, olives, wheat, cucumbers, poultry, lemons

Industries: banking, tourism, real estate and construction, food processing, wine, jewelry, cement, textiles, mineral and chemical products, wood and furniture products, oil refining, metal fabricating

Industrial production growth rate: -21.1% (2017 est.)

Labor force: 2.166 million (2016 est.)
note: excludes as many as 1 million foreign workers and refugees

Labor force - by occupation: *agriculture:* 39% (2009 est.)

Unemployment rate: 9.7% (2007)

Unemployment, youth ages 15-24: *total:* 23.4%
male: 24.5%
female: 21.4% (2019)

Population below poverty line: 27.4% (2011 est.)

Gini Index coefficient - distribution of family income: 31.8 (2011 est.)

Budget: *revenues:* 11.62 billion (2017 est.)
expenditures: 15.38 billion (2017 est.)

Budget surplus (+) or deficit (-): -6.9% (of GDP) (2017 est.)

Public debt: 146.8% of GDP (2017 est.)
145.5% of GDP (2016 est.)
note: data cover central government debt and exclude debt instruments issued (or owned) by government entities other than the treasury; the data include treasury debt held by foreign entities; the data include debt issued by subnational entities, as well as intragovernmental debt; intragovernmental debt consists of treasury borrowings from surpluses in the social funds, such as for retirement, medical care, and unemployment

Taxes and other revenues: 21.5% (of GDP) (2017 est.)

Fiscal year: calendar year

Current account balance: -$12.37 billion (2017 est.)
-$11.18 billion (2016 est.)

Exports: $18.17 billion (2019 est.) note: data are in current year dollars
$19.16 billion (2018 est.) note: data are in current year dollars

Exports - partners: Switzerland 27%, United Arab Emirates 15%, South Korea 11%, Saudi Arabia 7%, Kuwait 6% (2019)

Exports - commodities: gold, jewelry, shotguns, diamonds, scrap copper (2019)

Imports: $31.34 billion (2019 est.) note: data are in current year dollars
$32.78 billion (2018 est.) note: data are in current year dollars

Imports - partners: United Arab Emirates 11%, China 10%, Italy 8%, Greece 8%, Turkey 7%, United States 6% (2019)

Imports - commodities: refined petroleum, cars, packaged medicines, jewelry, gold (2019)

Reserves of foreign exchange and gold: $55.42 billion (31 December 2017 est.)
$54.04 billion (31 December 2016 est.)

Debt - external: $33.077 billion (2019 est.)
$33.655 billion (2018 est.)

Exchange rates: Lebanese pounds (LBP) per US dollar -
1,517.5 (2020 est.)
1,513 (2019 est.)
1,506.5 (2018 est.)
1,507.5 (2014 est.)
1,507.5 (2013 est.)

ENERGY

Electricity access: *electrification - total population:* 100% (2020)

Electricity: *installed generating capacity:* 3.768 million kW (2020 est.)
consumption: 18,715,620,000 kWh (2019 est.)
exports: 0 kWh (2019 est.)
imports: 900 million kWh (2019 est.)
transmission/distribution losses: 2.219 billion kWh (2019 est.)

Electricity generation sources: *fossil fuels:* 94.3% of total installed capacity (2020 est.)
solar: 0.5% of total installed capacity (2020 est.)
hydroelectricity: 5% of total installed capacity (2020 est.)
biomass and waste: 0.2% of total installed capacity (2020 est.)

Coal: *production:* 0 metric tons (2020 est.)
consumption: 268,000 metric tons (2020 est.)
exports: 0 metric tons (2020 est.)
imports: 268,000 metric tons (2020 est.)
proven reserves: 0 metric tons (2019 est.)

Petroleum: *total petroleum production:* 0 bbl/day (2021 est.)
refined petroleum consumption: 168,500 bbl/day (2019 est.)

Refined petroleum products - imports: 151,100 bbl/day (2015 est.)

Carbon dioxide emissions: 25.838 million metric tonnes of CO_2 (2019 est.)

from coal and metallurgical coke: 563,000 metric tonnes of CO2 (2019 est.)
from petroleum and other liquids: 25.275 million metric tonnes of CO2 (2019 est.)

Energy consumption per capita: 53.528 million Btu/person (2019 est.)

COMMUNICATIONS

Telephones - fixed lines: *total subscriptions:* 875,480 (2020 est.)
subscriptions per 100 inhabitants: 13 (2020 est.)

Telephones - mobile cellular: *total subscriptions:* 4,288,221 (2020 est.)
subscriptions per 100 inhabitants: 63 (2020 est.)

Telecommunication systems: *general assessment:* Lebanon's economic crisis has had a dire effect on the country's telecom services; although some progress has been made with developing 5G, the poor economic conditions have contributed to an erratic electricity supply and a lack of fuel to maintain generators; this has meant that internet services to areas of the country are not available on a regular basis, frustrating all those who depend on stable connectivity, and stalling business growth; adding to the difficulties are the combined stresses of the pandemic and the political crisis; a caretaker cabinet in September 2021 made way for a new government though there is little confidence on the ground that sectarian-based political horse-trading will give way to responsible governing to improve the lot of the stressed populace (2022)
domestic: fixed-line nearly 13 per 100 and nearly 63 per 100 for mobile-cellular subscriptions (2020)
international: country code - 961; landing points for the IMEWE, BERYTAR AND CADMOS submarine cable links to Europe, Africa, the Middle East and Asia; satellite earth stations - 2 Intelsat (1 Indian Ocean and 1 Atlantic Ocean) (2019)

Broadcast media: 7 TV stations, 1 of which is state owned; more than 30 radio stations, 1 of which is state owned; satellite and cable TV services available; transmissions of at least 2 international broadcasters are accessible through partner stations (2019)

Internet country code: .lb

Internet users: *total:* 6,825,442 (2020 est.)
percent of population: 84% (2020 est.)

Broadband - fixed subscriptions: *total:* 432,070 (2020 est.)
subscriptions per 100 inhabitants: 6 (2020 est.)

TRANSPORTATION

National air transport system: *number of registered air carriers:* 1 (2020)
inventory of registered aircraft operated by air carriers: 21
annual passenger traffic on registered air carriers: 2,981,937 (2018)
annual freight traffic on registered air carriers: 56.57 million (2018) mt-km

Civil aircraft registration country code prefix: OD

Airports: *total:* 8 (2021)

Airports - with paved runways: *total:* 5
over 3,047 m: 1
2,438 to 3,047 m: 2
1,524 to 2,437 m: 1
under 914 m: 1 (2021)

Airports - with unpaved runways: *total:* 3
914 to 1,523 m: 2
under 914 m: 1 (2021)

Heliports: 1 (2021)

Pipelines: 88 km gas (2013)

Railways: *total:* 401 km (2017)
standard gauge: 319 km (2017) 1.435-m gauge
narrow gauge: 82 km (2017) 1.050-m gauge
note: rail system is still unusable due to damage sustained from fighting in the 1980s and in 2006

Roadways: *total:* 21,705 km (2017)

Merchant marine: *total:* 48
by type: bulk carrier 2, general cargo 31, oil tanker 1, other 14 (2021)

Ports and terminals: *major seaport(s):* Beirut, Tripoli
container port(s) (TEUs): Beirut (1,229,100) (2019)

MILITARY AND SECURITY

Military and security forces: Lebanese Armed Forces (LAF): Army Command (includes Presidential Guard Brigade, Land Border Regiments), Naval Forces, Air Forces; Ministry of Interior: Internal Security Forces Directorate (law enforcement; includes Mobile Gendarmerie), Directorate for General Security (DGS; border control, some domestic security duties) (2022)
note: the commander of the LAF is also the commander of the Army; the LAF patrols external borders, while official border checkpoints are under the authority of Directorate for General Security

Military expenditures: 3.2% of GDP (2021 est.)
3% of GDP (2020 est.)
4.7% of GDP (2019 est.) (approximately $3.6 billion)
5.1% of GDP (2018 est.) (approximately $4.1 billion)
4.6% of GDP (2017 est.) (approximately $3.95 billion)

Military and security service personnel strengths: approximately 80,000 active troops (77,000 Army; 1,500 Navy; 1,500 Air Force) (2022)

Military equipment inventories and acquisitions: the LAF inventory includes a wide mix of mostly older equipment from a diverse array of countries; since 2010, the US has been the leading supplier of armaments (mostly second-hand equipment) to Lebanon (2022)

Military service age and obligation: 17-25 years of age for men and women for voluntary military service; no conscription (2022)
note: as of 2020, women comprised about 5% of the active duty military

Military - note: as of 2022, the Lebanese military faced multiple challenges, including securing parts of the border with war-torn Syria from infiltrations of militants linked to the Islamic State of Iraq and ash-Sham (ISIS) and al-Qa'ida terrorist groups and maintaining stability along its volatile border with Israel, where the Iranian-backed and Lebanon-based terrorist group Hizballah conducted a war with Israel in 2006 and tensions remained high, including occasional armed skirmishes; the military also faced a financial crisis as government debt and national economic difficulties undercut its ability to fully pay and supply personnel, which has sparked domestic and international fears that the armed forces may disintegrate

the United Nations Interim Force In Lebanon (UNIFIL) has operated in the country since 1978, originally under UNSCRs 425 and 426 to confirm Israeli withdrawal from Lebanon, restore international peace and security, and assist the Lebanese Government in restoring its effective authority in the area; following the July-August 2006 war, the UN Security Council adopted resolution 1701 enhancing UNIFIL and deciding that in addition to the original mandate, it would, among other things, monitor the cessation of hostilities, support the Lebanese Armed Forces as they deployed throughout the south of Lebanon, and provide assistance for humanitarian access for civilians and the return of displaced persons; UNIFIL had approximately 9,500 personnel deployed in the country as of mid-2022 (2022)

TERRORISM

Terrorist group(s): Abdallah Azzam Brigades; al-Aqsa Martyrs Brigade; Asbat al-Ansar; HAMAS; Hizballah; Islamic Revolutionary Guard Corps/Qods Force; Islamic State of Iraq and ash-Sham (ISIS); al-Nusrah Front (Hay'at Tahrir al-Sham); Palestine Liberation Front; Popular Front for the Liberation of Palestine (PFLP); PFLP-General Command

TRANSNATIONAL ISSUES

Disputes - international: *Lebanon-Syria:* lacking a treaty or other documentation describing the boundary, portions of the Lebanon-Syria boundary are unclear with several sections in dispute; in March 2021, Syria signed a contract with a Russian company for oil and gas exploration in a maritime area Lebanon claims as its own based on a 2011 map sent to the UN
Lebanon-Israel: Lebanon has claimed Shab'a Farms area in the Israeli-controlled Golan Heights; Lebanon and Israel resumed negotiations over their maritime border in 2020, but their efforts were derailed when Lebanon argued that the map the UN was using needed modifications

Refugees and internally displaced persons: *refugees (country of origin):* 479,537 (Palestinian refugees) (2020); 825,081 (Syria) (2022)
IDPs: 7,000 (2020)
stateless persons: undetermined (2016); note - tens of thousands of persons are stateless in Lebanon, including many Palestinian refugees and their descendants, Syrian Kurds denaturalized in Syria in 1962, children born to Lebanese women married to foreign or stateless men; most babies born to Syrian refugees, and Lebanese children whose births are unregistered

Illicit drugs: source country for amphetamine tablets destined for Saudi Arabia, Qatar, United Arab Emirates, Libya and Sudan; in 2021 authorities in various Near Eastern countries seized millions of captagon tablets that originated in or transited to Lebanon, prompting Lebanese authorities to conduct raids on captagon production facilities and trafficking rings within the country

LESOTHO

INTRODUCTION

Background: Paramount chief MOSHOESHOE I consolidated what would become Basutoland in the early 19th century and made himself king in 1822. Continuing encroachments by Dutch settlers from the neighboring Orange Free State caused the king to enter into an 1868 agreement with the UK by which Basutoland became a British protectorate, and after 1884, a crown colony. Upon independence in 1966, the country was renamed the Kingdom of Lesotho. The Basotho National Party ruled the country during its first two decades. King MOSHOESHOE II was exiled in 1990, but returned to Lesotho in 1992 and was reinstated in 1995 and subsequently succeeded by his son, King LETSIE III, in 1996. Constitutional government was restored in 1993 after seven years of military rule. In 1998, violent protests and a military mutiny following a contentious election prompted a brief but bloody intervention by South African and Batswana military forces under the aegis of the Southern African Development Community. Subsequent constitutional reforms restored relative political stability. Peaceful parliamentary elections were held in 2002, but the National Assembly elections in 2007 were hotly contested and aggrieved parties disputed how the electoral law was applied to award proportional seats in the Assembly. In 2012, competitive elections involving 18 parties saw Prime Minister Motsoahae Thomas THABANE form a coalition government - the first in the country's history - that ousted the 14-year incumbent, Pakalitha MOSISILI, who peacefully transferred power the following month. MOSISILI returned to power in snap elections in February 2015 after the collapse of THABANE's coalition government and an alleged attempted military coup. In June 2017, THABANE returned to become prime minister.

GEOGRAPHY

Location: Southern Africa, an enclave of South Africa

Geographic coordinates: 29 30 S, 28 30 E

Map references: Africa

Area: *total:* 30,355 sq km
land: 30,355 sq km
water: 0 sq km

Area - comparative: slightly smaller than Maryland

Land boundaries: *total:* 1,106 km
border countries (1): South Africa 1,106 km

Coastline: 0 km (landlocked)

Maritime claims: none (landlocked)

Climate: temperate; cool to cold, dry winters; hot, wet summers

Terrain: mostly highland with plateaus, hills, and mountains

Elevation: *highest point:* Thabana Ntlenyana 3,482 m
lowest point: junction of the Orange and Makhaleng Rivers 1,400 m
mean elevation: 2,161 m

Natural resources: water, agricultural and grazing land, diamonds, sand, clay, building stone

Land use: *agricultural land:* 76.1% (2018 est.)
arable land: 10.1% (2018 est.)
permanent crops: 0.1% (2018 est.)
permanent pasture: 65.9% (2018 est.)
forest: 1.5% (2018 est.)
other: 22.4% (2018 est.)

Irrigated land: 30 sq km (2012)

Major rivers (by length in km): Orange river source (shared with South Africa and Namibia [m]) - 2,092 km

note – [s] after country name indicates river source; [m] after country name indicates river mouth

Major watersheds (area sq km): Atlantic Ocean drainage: Orange (941,351 sq km)

Population distribution: relatively higher population density in the western half of the nation, with the capital of Maseru, and the smaller cities of Mafeteng, Teyateyaneng, and Leribe attracting the most people as shown in this population distribution map

Natural hazards: periodic droughts

Geography - note: landlocked, an enclave of (completely surrounded by) South Africa; mountainous, more than 80% of the country is 1,800 m above sea level

PEOPLE AND SOCIETY

Population: 2,193,970 (2022 est.)

Nationality: *noun:* Mosotho (singular), Basotho (plural)
adjective: Basotho

Ethnic groups: Sotho 99.7%, Europeans, Asians, and other 0.3%

Languages: Sesotho (official) (southern Sotho), English (official), Zulu, Xhosa

Religions: Protestant 47.8% (Pentecostal 23.1%, Lesotho Evangelical 17.3%, Anglican 7.4%), Roman Catholic 39.3%, other Christian 9.1%, non-Christian 1.4%, none 2.3% (2014 est.)

Demographic profile: Lesotho faces great socioeconomic challenges. More than half of its population lives below the poverty line, and the country's HIV/AIDS prevalence rate is the second highest in the world. In addition, Lesotho is a small, mountainous, landlocked country with little arable land, leaving its population vulnerable to food shortages and reliant on remittances. Lesotho's persistently high infant, child, and maternal mortality rates have been increasing during the last decade, according to the last two Demographic and Health Surveys. Despite these significant shortcomings, Lesotho has made good progress in education; it is on-track to achieve universal primary education and has one of the highest adult literacy rates in Africa.

Lesotho's migration history is linked to its unique geography; it is surrounded by South Africa with which it shares linguistic and cultural traits. Lesotho at one time had more of its workforce employed outside its borders than any other country. Today remittances equal about 17% of its GDP. With few job options at home, a high rate of poverty, and higher wages available across the border, labor migration to South Africa replaced agriculture as the prevailing Basotho source of income decades ago. The majority of Basotho migrants were single men contracted to work as gold miners in South Africa. However, migration trends changed in the 1990s, and fewer men found mining jobs in South Africa because of declining gold prices, stricter immigration policies, and a preference for South African workers.

Although men still dominate cross-border labor migration, more women are working in South Africa, mostly as domestics, because they are widows or their husbands are unemployed. Internal rural-urban flows have also become more frequent, with more women migrating within the country to take up jobs in the garment industry or moving to care for loved ones with HIV/AIDS. Lesotho's small population of immigrants is increasingly composed of Taiwanese and Chinese migrants who are involved in the textile industry and small retail businesses.

Age structure: *0-14 years:* 31.3% (male 309,991/female 306,321)
15-24 years: 19.26% (male 181,874/female 197,452)
25-54 years: 38.86% (male 373,323/female 391,901)
55-64 years: 4.98% (male 52,441/female 45,726)
65 years and over: 5.6% (male 57,030/female 53,275) (2020 est.)

Dependency ratios: *total dependency ratio:* 59.2
youth dependency ratio: 51.3
elderly dependency ratio: 7.9
potential support ratio: 12.7 (2020 est.)

Median age: *total:* 24.7 years
male: 24.7 years
female: 24.7 years (2020 est.)

Population growth rate: 0.76% (2022 est.)

Birth rate: 23.15 births/1,000 population (2022 est.)

Death rate: 11.05 deaths/1,000 population (2022 est.)

Net migration rate: -4.55 migrant(s)/1,000 population (2022 est.)

Population distribution: relatively higher population density in the western half of the nation, with the capital of Maseru, and the smaller cities of Mafeteng, Teyateyaneng, and Leribe attracting the most people as shown in this population distribution map

Urbanization: *urban population:* 29.9% of total population (2022)
rate of urbanization: 2.77% annual rate of change (2020-25 est.)

Major urban areas - population: 202,000 MASERU (capital) (2018)

Sex ratio: *at birth:* 1.03 male(s)/female
0-14 years: 1.01 male(s)/female
15-24 years: 1.01 male(s)/female
25-54 years: 1.02 male(s)/female
55-64 years: 0.74 male(s)/female
65 years and over: 0.48 male(s)/female
total population: 0.98 male(s)/female (2022 est.)

Mother's mean age at first birth: 20.9 years (2014 est.)
note: data represents median age at first birth among women 25-49

Maternal mortality ratio: 544 deaths/100,000 live births (2017 est.)

Infant mortality rate: *total:* 48.44 deaths/1,000 live births
male: 54 deaths/1,000 live births
female: 42.72 deaths/1,000 live births (2022 est.)

Life expectancy at birth: *total population:* 59.57 years
male: 57.57 years
female: 61.64 years (2022 est.)

Total fertility rate: 2.92 children born/woman (2022 est.)

Contraceptive prevalence rate: 64.9% (2018)

Drinking water source: *improved: urban:* 95.7% of population
rural: 77.2% of population
total: 82.6% of population
unimproved: urban: 4.3% of population
rural: 22.8% of population
total: 17.4% of population (2020 est.)

Current health expenditure: 11.3% of GDP (2019)

Physicians density: 0.47 physicians/1,000 population (2018)

Sanitation facility access: *improved: urban:* 93.6% of
population rural: 62.4% of population
total: 71.4% of population
unimproved: urban: 6.4% of population
rural: 37.6% of population
total: 28.6% of population (2020 est.)

HIV/AIDS - adult prevalence rate: 21.1% (2020 est.)

Major infectious diseases: *degree of risk:* intermediate (2020)
food or waterborne diseases: bacterial diarrhea, hepatitis A, and typhoid fever

Obesity - adult prevalence rate: 16.6% (2016)

Alcohol consumption per capita: *total:* 3.56 liters of pure alcohol (2019 est.)
beer: 1.98 liters of pure alcohol (2019 est.)
wine: 0.44 liters of pure alcohol (2019 est.)
spirits: 0.31 liters of pure alcohol (2019 est.)
other alcohols: 0.82 liters of pure alcohol (2019 est.)

Tobacco use: *total:* 24.3% (2020 est.)
male: 43.1% (2020 est.)
female: 5.4% (2020 est.)

Children under the age of 5 years underweight: 10.5% (2018)

Child marriage: *women married by age 15:* 1%
women married by age 18: 16.4%
men married by age 18: 1.9% (2018 est.)

Education expenditures: 7.4% of GDP (2020 est.)

Literacy: *definition:* age 15 and over can read and write
total population: 79.4%
male: 70.1%
female: 88.3% (2015)

School life expectancy (primary to tertiary education): *total:* 12 years
male: 12 years
female: 13 years (2017)

Unemployment, youth ages 15-24: *total:* 35.5%
male: 31.2%
female: 41.5% (2019 est.)

ENVIRONMENT

Environment - current issues: population pressure forcing settlement in marginal areas results in overgrazing, severe soil erosion, and soil exhaustion; desertification; Highlands Water Project controls, stores, and redirects water to South Africa

Environment - international agreements: *party to:* Biodiversity, Climate Change, Climate Change-Kyoto Protocol, Climate Change-Paris Agreement, Comprehensive Nuclear Test Ban, Desertification, Endangered Species, Hazardous Wastes, Law of the Sea, Marine Life Conservation, Ozone Layer Protection, Wetlands
signed, but not ratified: none of the selected agreements

Air pollutants: *particulate matter emissions:* 27.78 micrograms per cubic meter (2016 est.)
carbon dioxide emissions: 2.51 megatons (2016 est.)
methane emissions: 2.56 megatons (2020 est.)

Climate: temperate; cool to cold, dry winters; hot, wet summers

Land use: *agricultural land:* 76.1% (2018 est.)
arable land: 10.1% (2018 est.)
permanent crops: 0.1% (2018 est.)
permanent pasture: 65.9% (2018 est.)
forest: 1.5% (2018 est.)
other: 22.4% (2018 est.)

Urbanization: *urban population:* 29.9% of total population (2022)
rate of urbanization: 2.77% annual rate of change (2020-25 est.)

Revenue from forest resources: *forest revenues:* 3.34% of GDP (2018 est.)

Revenue from coal: *coal revenues:* 0% of GDP (2018 est.)

Food insecurity: *severe localized food insecurity: due to poor harvests and increased food prices -* according to the latest national food security assessment, 22% of the rural population are expected to face acute food insecurity between October 2022 and March 2023, compared to 15% between July and September 2022; the forecasted proportion translates into 320,000 people in rural areas, while an additional 201,000 people in urban areas are foreseen to also need assistance; the foreseen increase of acute food insecurity levels is primarily due to the reduced harvest, high food prices in basic food and non-food commodities and a slow recovery of households' income reflecting a downturn in economic growth; harvesting of the 2022 main-season summer cereal crops, mostly maize and sorghum, is complete; production of maize, the main cereal staple, is about one-third of the average, while the sorghum output is almost negligible; the poor harvest was primarily due to torrential rainfalls during January and February 2022, which caused localized flooding and resulted in crop losses (2022)

Waste and recycling: *municipal solid waste generated annually:* 73,457 tons (2006 est.)

Major rivers (by length in km): Orange river source (shared with South Africa and Namibia [m]) - 2,092 km
note – [s] after country name indicates river source; [m] after country name indicates river mouth

Major watersheds (area sq km): Atlantic Ocean drainage: Orange (941,351 sq km)

Total water withdrawal: *municipal:* 20 million cubic meters (2017 est.)
industrial: 20 million cubic meters (2017 est.)
agricultural: 3.8 million cubic meters (2017 est.)

Total renewable water resources: 3.022 billion cubic meters (2017 est.)

GOVERNMENT

Country name: *conventional long form:* Kingdom of Lesotho
conventional short form: Lesotho
local long form: Kingdom of Lesotho
local short form: Lesotho
former: Basutoland
etymology: the name translates as "Land of the Sesotho Speakers"

Government type: parliamentary constitutional monarchy

Capital: *name:* Maseru
geographic coordinates: 29 19 S, 27 29 E
time difference: UTC+2 (7 hours ahead of Washington, DC, during Standard Time)
etymology: in the Sesotho language the name means "[place of] red sandstones"

Administrative divisions: 10 districts; Berea, Butha-Buthe, Leribe, Mafeteng, Maseru, Mohale's Hoek, Mokhotlong, Qacha's Nek, Quthing, Thaba- Tseka

Independence: 4 October 1966 (from the UK)

National holiday: Independence Day, 4 October (1966)

Constitution: *history:* previous 1959, 1967; latest adopted 2 April 1993 (effectively restoring the 1967 version)
amendments: proposed by Parliament; passage of amendments affecting constitutional provisions, including fundamental rights and freedoms, sovereignty of the kingdom, the office of the king, and powers of Parliament, requires a majority vote by the National Assembly, approval by the Senate, approval in a referendum by a majority of qualified voters, and assent of the king; passage of amendments other than those specified provisions requires at least a two-thirds majority vote in both houses of Parliament; amended several times, last in 2011

Legal system: mixed legal system of English common law and Roman-Dutch law; judicial review of legislative acts in High Court and Court of Appeal

International law organization participation: accepts compulsory ICJ jurisdiction with reservations; accepts ICCt jurisdiction

Citizenship: *citizenship by birth:* yes
citizenship by descent only: yes
dual citizenship recognized: no
residency requirement for naturalization: 5 years

Suffrage: 18 years of age; universal

Executive branch: *chief of state:* King LETSIE III (since 7 February 1996); note - King LETSIE III

formerly occupied the throne from November 1990 to February 1995 while his father was in exile
head of government: Prime Minister Ntsokoane Samuel MATEKANE (4 November 2022)
cabinet: consists of the prime minister, appointed by the King on the advice of the Council of State, the deputy prime minister, and 26 other ministers
elections/appointments: the monarchy is hereditary, but under the terms of the constitution that came into effect after the March 1993 election, the monarch is a "living symbol of national unity" with no executive or legislative powers; under traditional law, the College of Chiefs has the power to depose the monarch, to determine next in line of succession, or to serve as regent in the event that a successor is not of mature age; following legislative elections, the leader of the majority party or majority coalition in the Assembly automatically becomes prime minister

Legislative branch: *description:* bicameral Parliament consists of:
Senate (33 seats; 22 principal chiefs and 11 other senators nominated by the king with the advice of the Council of State, a 13-member body of key government and non-government officials; members serve 5-year terms)
National Assembly (120 seats; 80 members directly elected in single-seat constituencies by simple majority vote and 40 elected through proportional representation; members serve 5-year terms)
elections:
Senate - last nominated by the king on July 2022 (next in late July 2027)
National Assembly - last held on 7 October 2022 (next to be held on October 2027)
election results:
Senate - percent of votes by party - NA, seats by party - NA; composition - men 26, women 7, percent of women 21.2%
National Assembly - percent of votes by party - RFP 38.9%, DC 24.7%, ABC 7.1%, BAP 5.4%, AD 4.0%, MEC 3.2%, LCD 2.3%, SR 2.1%, BNP 1.4%, PFD 0.9%, BCM 0.8%, MPS 0.8%, MIP 0.7%; seats by party - RFP 56, DC 29, ABC 8, BAP 6, AD 5, MEC 4, LCD 3, SR 2, BNP 1, PFD 1,BCM 1, MPS 1, NIP 1, HOPE 1, TBD 1; composition - men 87, women 28, percent of women 23.3%; note - total Parliament percent of women 22.9%

Judicial branch: *highest court(s):* Court of Appeal (consists of the court president, such number of justices of appeal as set by Parliament, and the Chief Justice and the puisne judges of the High Court ex officio); High Court (consists of the chief justice and such number of puisne judges as set by Parliament); note - both the Court of Appeal and the High Court have jurisdiction in constitutional issues
judge selection and term of office: Court of Appeal president and High Court chief justice appointed by the monarch on the advice of the prime minister; puisne judges appointed by the monarch on advice of the Judicial Service Commission, an independent body of judicial officers and officials designated by the monarch; judges of both courts can serve until age 75
subordinate courts: Magistrate Courts; customary or traditional courts; military courts

Political parties and leaders: All Basotho Convention or ABC [Nkaku KABI]
Alliance of Democrats or AD [Monyane MOLELEKI]
Basotho Action Party or BAP [Nqosa MAHAO]
Basotho National Party or BNP [Thesele MASERIBANE]
Democratic Congress or DC [Mathibeli MOKHOTHU]
Democratic Party of Lesotho or DPL [Limpho TAU]
Lesotho Congress for Democracy or LCD [Mothetjoa METSING]
Movement of Economic Change or MEC [Selibe MOCHOBOROANE]
National Independent Party or NIP [Kimetso MATHABA]
Popular Front for Democracy of PFD [Lekhetho RAKUOANE]
Reformed Congress of Lesotho or RCL [Keketso RANTSO]

International organization participation: ACP, AfDB, AU, C, CD, FAO, G-77, IAEA, IBRD, ICAO, ICCt, ICRM, IDA, IFAD, IFC, IFRCS, ILO, IMF, Interpol, IOC, IOM, IPU, ISO (correspondent), ITU, MIGA, NAM, OPCW, SACU, SADC, UN, UNAMID, UNCTAD, UNESCO, UNHCR, UNIDO, UNWTO, UPU, WCO, WFTU (NGOs), WHO, WIPO, WMO, WTO

Diplomatic representation in the US: *chief of mission:* Ambassador (vacant); Charge d'Affaires Masopha Phoofolo Moses KAO, Counselor (28 May 2021)
chancery: 2511 Massachusetts Avenue NW, Washington, DC 20008
telephone: [1] (202) 797-5533
FAX: [1] (202) 234-6815
email address and website: lesothoembassy@verizon.net
https://www.gov.ls/

Diplomatic representation from the US: *chief of mission:* Ambassador Maria E. BREWER (since 10 March 2022)
embassy: 254 Kingsway Avenue, Maseru
mailing address: 2340 Maseru Place, Washington DC 20521-2340
telephone: [266] 22312666
FAX: [266] 22310116
email address and website:
USConsularMaseru@state.gov
https://ls.usembassy.gov/

Flag description: three horizontal stripes of blue (top), white, and green in the proportions of 3:4:3; the colors represent rain, peace, and prosperity respectively; centered in the white stripe is a black Basotho hat representing the indigenous people; the flag was unfurled in October 2006 to celebrate 40 years of independence

National symbol(s): mokorotio (Basotho hat); national colors: blue, white, green, black

National anthem: *name:* "Lesotho fatse la bo ntat'a rona" (Lesotho, Land of Our Fathers)
lyrics/music: Francois COILLARD/Ferdinand-Samuel LAUR
note: adopted 1967; music derives from an 1823 Swiss songbook

National heritage: *total World Heritage Sites:* 1 (mixed)
selected World Heritage Site locales: Maloti-Drakensberg Park

ECONOMY

Economic overview: Small, mountainous, and completely landlocked by South Africa, Lesotho depends on a narrow economic base of textile manufacturing, agriculture, remittances, and regional customs revenue. About three-fourths of the people live in rural areas and engage in animal herding and subsistence agriculture, although Lesotho produces less than 20% of the nation's demand for food. Agriculture is vulnerable to weather and climate variability.

Lesotho relies on South Africa for much of its economic activity; Lesotho imports 85% of the goods it consumes from South Africa, including most agricultural inputs. Households depend heavily on remittances from family members working in South Africa in mines, on farms, and as domestic workers, though mining employment has declined substantially since the 1990s. Lesotho is a member of the Southern Africa Customs Union (SACU), and revenues from SACU accounted for roughly 26% of total GDP in 2016; however, SACU revenues are volatile and expected to decline over the next 5 years. Lesotho also gains royalties from the South African Government for water transferred to South Africa from a dam and reservoir system in Lesotho. However, the government continues to strengthen its tax system to reduce dependency on customs duties and other transfers.

The government maintains a large presence in the economy - government consumption accounted for about 26% of GDP in 2017. The government remains Lesotho's largest employer; in 2016, the government wage bill rose to 23% of GDP – the largest in Sub-Saharan Africa. Lesotho's largest private employer is the textile and garment industry - approximately 36,000 Basotho, mainly women, work in factories producing garments for export to South Africa and the US. Diamond mining in Lesotho has grown in recent years and accounted for nearly 35% of total exports in 2015. Lesotho managed steady GDP growth at an average of 4.5% from 2010 to 2014, dropping to about 2.5% in 2015-16, but poverty remains widespread around 57% of the total population.

Real GDP (purchasing power parity): $4.88 billion (2020 est.)
$5.49 billion (2019 est.)
$5.51 billion (2018 est.)
note: data are in 2017 dollars

Real GDP growth rate: -1.6% (2017 est.)
3.1% (2016 est.)
2.5% (2015 est.)

Real GDP per capita: $2,300 (2020 est.)
$2,600 (2019 est.)
$2,600 (2018 est.)
note: data are in 2017 dollars

GDP (official exchange rate): $2.462 billion (2019 est.)

Inflation rate (consumer prices): 5.3% (2019 est.)
3.8% (2018 est.)
5.1% (2017 est.)

Credit ratings:

Fitch rating: B (2019)
note: The year refers to the year in which the current credit rating was first obtained.

GDP - composition, by sector of origin: *agriculture:* 5.8% (2016 est.)
industry: 39.2% (2016 est.)
services: 54.9% (2017 est.)

GDP - composition, by end use: *household consumption:* 69.2% (2017 est.)
government consumption: 26.4% (2017 est.)
investment in fixed capital: 31.4% (2017 est.)
investment in inventories: -13.4% (2017 est.)
exports of goods and services: 40.8% (2017 est.)
imports of goods and services: -54.4% (2017 est.)

Agricultural products: milk, potatoes, maize, vegetables, fruit, beef, game meat, mutton, beans, wool

Industries: food, beverages, textiles, apparel assembly, handicrafts, construction, tourism

Industrial production growth rate: 12.5% (2017 est.)

Labor force: 930,800 (2017 est.)

Labor force - by occupation: *agriculture:* 86%
industry and services: 14% (2002 est.)
note: most of the resident population is engaged in subsistence agriculture; roughly 35% of the active male wage earners work in South Africa

Unemployment rate: 28.1% (2014 est.)
25% (2008 est.)

Unemployment, youth ages 15-24: *total:* 35.5%
male: 31.2%
female: 41.5% (2019 est.)

Population below poverty line: 49.7% (2017 est.)

Gini Index coefficient - distribution of family income: 44.9 (2017 est.)
56 (1986-87)

Household income or consumption by percentage share: *lowest 10%:* 1%
highest 10%: 39.4% (2003)

Budget: *revenues:* 1.09 billion (2017 est.)
expenditures: 1.255 billion (2017 est.)

Budget surplus (+) or deficit (-): -6% (of GDP) (2017 est.)

Public debt: 33.7% of GDP (2017 est.)
36.2% of GDP (2016 est.)

Taxes and other revenues: 39.7% (of GDP) (2017 est.)

Fiscal year: 1 April - 31 March

Current account balance: -$102 million (2017 est.)
-$201 million (2016 est.)

Exports: $900 million (2020 est.) note: data are in current year dollars
$1.09 billion (2019 est.) note: data are in current year dollars
$1.25 billion (2018 est.) note: data are in current year dollars

Exports - partners: United States 29%, Belgium 26%, South Africa 25%, Switzerland 6% (2019)

Exports - commodities: diamonds, clothing and apparel, low-voltage protection equipment, wheat products, footwear (2019)

Imports: $1.96 billion (2020 est.) note: data are in current year dollars
$2.2 billion (2019 est.) note: data are in current year dollars
$2.39 billion (2018 est.) note: data are in current year dollars

Imports - partners: South Africa 85%, China 5% (2019)

Imports - commodities: refined petroleum, clothing and apparel, packaged medicines, delivery trucks, poultry meats (2019)

Reserves of foreign exchange and gold: $657.7 million (31 December 2017 est.)
$925.2 million (31 December 2016 est.)

Debt - external: $868 million (2019 est.)
$834 million (2018 est.)

Exchange rates: maloti (LSL) per US dollar -
14.48 (2017 est.)
14.71 (2016 est.)
14.71 (2015 est.)
12.76 (2014 est.)
10.85 (2013 est.)

ENERGY

Electricity access: *electrification - total population:* 36% (2019)
electrification - urban areas: 63% (2019)
electrification - rural areas: 26% (2019)

Electricity: *installed generating capacity:* 74,000 kW (2020 est.)
consumption: 912.8 million kWh (2019 est.)
exports: 0 kWh (2019 est.)
imports: 541.7 million kWh (2019 est.)
transmission/distribution losses: 129.9 million kWh (2019 est.)

Electricity generation sources: *solar:* 0.2% of total installed capacity (2020 est.)
hydroelectricity: 99.8% of total installed capacity (2020 est.)

Petroleum: *total petroleum production:* 0 bbl/day (2021 est.)
refined petroleum consumption: 5,100 bbl/day (2019 est.)

Refined petroleum products - imports: 5,118 bbl/day (2015 est.)

Carbon dioxide emissions: 736,000 metric tonnes of CO2 (2019 est.)
from petroleum and other liquids: 736,000 metric tonnes of CO2 (2019 est.)

Energy consumption per capita: 7.823 million Btu/person (2019 est.)

COMMUNICATIONS

Telephones - fixed lines: *total subscriptions:* 11,574 (2020 est.)
subscriptions per 100 inhabitants: 1 (2020 est.)

Telephones - mobile cellular: *total subscriptions:* 1,562,648 (2020 est.)
subscriptions per 100 inhabitants: 73 (2020 est.)

Telecommunication systems: *general assessment:* until late 2020, Lesotho's telecom regulator maintained a market duopoly which is focused on fixed-line services; competition was insufficient to promote effective price reductions for consumers, while the regulator had no mechanisms in place to monitor the telcos to ensure quality of service and fair pricing for consumers; the small size of the country's population provided little incentive for new players to enter the market; a positive outcome for consumers was the deployment in early 2021 of a service to monitor traffic and billing; this ended the practice whereby the regulator was dependent on telcos submitting data about their performance, billing, and other matters; the regulator has also turned its attention to addressing multiple SIM ownership and stem incidences of crimes committed using unregistered SIMs; in May 2022, it instructed the country's MNOs to begin registering SIM cards on their networks from the following month; fixed-wireless 5G trials began in early 2019 (2022)
domestic: fixed-line is less than 1 per 100 subscriptions; mobile-cellular service subscribership nearly 73 per 100 persons; rudimentary system consisting of a modest number of landlines, a small microwave radio relay system, and a small radiotelephone communication system (2020)
international: country code - 266; Internet accessibility has improved with several submarine fiber optic cables that land on African east and west coasts, but the country's land locked position makes access prices expensive; satellite earth station - 1 Intelsat (Atlantic Ocean) (2019)

Broadcast media: 1 state-owned TV station and 2 state-owned radio stations; government controls most private broadcast media; satellite TV subscription service available; transmissions of multiple international broadcasters obtainable (2019)

Internet country code: .ls

Internet users: *total:* 921,168 (2020 est.)
percent of population: 43% (2020 est.)

Broadband - fixed subscriptions: *total:* 5,060 (2020 est.)
subscriptions per 100 inhabitants: 0.2 (2020 est.)

TRANSPORTATION

Civil aircraft registration country code prefix: 7P

Airports: *total:* 24 (2021)

Airports - with paved runways: *total:* 3
over 3,047 m: 1
914 to 1,523 m: 1
under 914 m: 1 (2021)

Airports - with unpaved runways: *total:* 21
914 to 1,523 m: 5
under 914 m: 16 (2021)

Roadways: *total:* 5,940 km (2011)
paved: 1,069 km (2011)
unpaved: 4,871 km (2011)

MILITARY AND SECURITY

Military and security forces: Lesotho Defense Force (LDF): Army (includes Air Wing) (2022)
note: the Lesotho Mounted Police Service is responsible for internal security and reports to the Minister of Police and Public Safety

Military expenditures: 1.5% of GDP (2021 est.)
1.5% of GDP (2020 est.)
1.8% of GDP (2019 est.) (approximately $60 million)
2.1% of GDP (2018 est.) (approximately $65 million)
2.2% of GDP (2017 est.) (approximately $70 million)

Military and security service personnel strengths: approximately 2,000 personnel (2022)

Military equipment inventories and acquisitions: the LDF has a small inventory of older and second-hand equipment from a variety of countries (2021)

Military service age and obligation: 20-30 years of age for voluntary military service; no conscription (2022)

Military - note: Lesotho's declared policy for its military is the maintenance of the country's sovereignty and the preservation of internal security; in practice, external security is guaranteed by South Africa

the LDF began in 1964 as the Police Mobile Unit (PMU); the PMU was designated as the Lesotho Paramilitary Force in 1980 and became the Royal Lesotho Defense Force in 1986; it was subsequently renamed the Lesotho Defense Force in 1993 (2022)

TRANSNATIONAL ISSUES

Disputes - international: *Lesotho-South Africa:* South Africa has placed military units to assist police operations along the border of Lesotho, Zimbabwe, and Mozambique to control smuggling, poaching, and illegal migration

LIBERIA

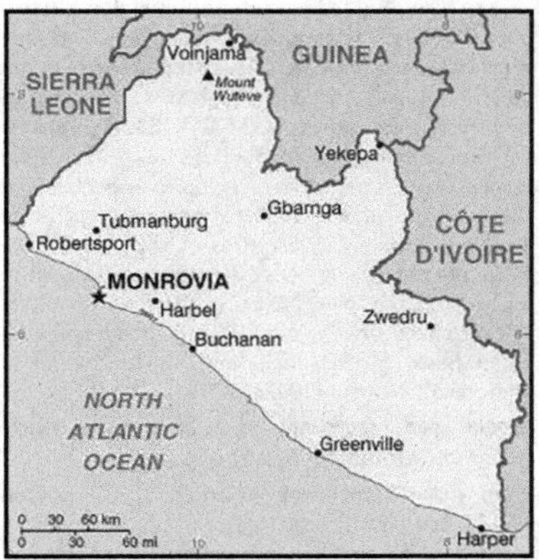

INTRODUCTION

Background: With 28 ethnic groups and languages, Liberia is one of the most ethnically diverse countries in the world. For hundreds of years, the Mali and Songhai Empires claimed most of Liberia. Beginning in the 15th century, European traders began establishing outposts along the Liberian coast. Unlike its neighbors, however, Liberia did not fall under European colonial rule. In the early 19th century, the US began sending freed enslaved people and other people of color to Liberia to establish settlements. In 1847, these settlers declared independence from the US, writing their own constitution and establishing Africa's first republic.

Early in Liberia's history, tensions arose between the Americo-Liberian settlers and the indigenous population. In 1980, Samuel DOE, who was from the indigenous population, led a military coup and ushered in a decade of authoritarian rule. In December 1989, Charles TAYLOR launched a rebellion against DOE's regime that led to a prolonged civil war in which DOE was killed. A period of relative peace in 1997 permitted an election that brought TAYLOR to power. In 2000, fighting resumed. An August 2003 peace agreement ended the war and prompted President TAYLOR's resignation. TAYLOR was later convicted by the UN-backed Special Court for Sierra Leone in The Hague for his involvement in Sierra Leone's civil war. In late 2005, President Ellen JOHNSON SIRLEAF became president after two years of transitional governments; she was the first female head of state in Africa. In 2011, JOHNSON SIRLEAF won reelection but struggled to rebuild Liberia's economy, particularly following the 2014-15 Ebola epidemic, and to reconcile a nation still recovering from 14 years of fighting. In 2017, former soccer star George WEAH won the presidential runoff election, marking the first successful transfer of power from one democratically elected government to another since the end of Liberia's civil wars. Like his predecessor, WEAH has struggled to improve the country's economy. The next presidential election is scheduled for 2023.

GEOGRAPHY

Location: Western Africa, bordering the North Atlantic Ocean, between Cote d'Ivoire and Sierra Leone

Geographic coordinates: 6 30 N, 9 30 W

Map references: Africa

Area: *total:* 111,369 sq km
land: 96,320 sq km
water: 15,049 sq km

Area - comparative: slightly larger than Virginia

Land boundaries: *total:* 1,667 km
border countries (3): Guinea 590 km; Cote d'Ivoire 778 km; Sierra Leone 299 km

Coastline: 579 km

Maritime claims: *territorial sea:* 12 nm
contiguous zone: 24 nm
exclusive economic zone: 200 nm
continental shelf: 200 nm

Climate: tropical; hot, humid; dry winters with hot days and cool to cold nights; wet, cloudy summers with frequent heavy showers

Terrain: mostly flat to rolling coastal plains rising to rolling plateau and low mountains in northeast

Elevation: *highest point:* Mount Wuteve 1,447 m
lowest point: Atlantic Ocean 0 m
mean elevation: 243 m

Natural resources: iron ore, timber, diamonds, gold, hydropower

Land use: *agricultural land:* 28.1% (2018 est.)
arable land: 5.2% (2018 est.)
permanent crops: 2.1% (2018 est.)
permanent pasture: 20.8% (2018 est.)
forest: 44.6% (2018 est.)
other: 27.3% (2018 est.)

Irrigated land: 30 sq km (2012)

Population distribution: more than half of the population lives in urban areas, with approximately one-third living within an 80-km radius of Monrovia as shown in this population distribution map

Natural hazards: dust-laden harmattan winds blow from the Sahara (December to March)

Geography - note: facing the Atlantic Ocean, the coastline is characterized by lagoons, mangrove swamps, and river-deposited sandbars; the inland grassy plateau supports limited agriculture

PEOPLE AND SOCIETY

Population: 5,358,483 (2022 est.)

Nationality noun: Liberian(s)
adjective: Liberian

Ethnic groups: Kpelle 20.3%, Bassa 13.4%, Grebo 10%, Gio 8%, Mano 7.9%, Kru 6%, Lorma 5.1%, Kissi 4.8%, Gola 4.4%, Krahn 4%, Vai 4%, Mandingo 3.2%, Gbandi 3%, Mende 1.3%, Sapo 1.3%, other Liberian 1.7%, other African 1.4%, non-African .1% (2008 est.)

Languages: English 20% (official), some 20 ethnic group languages few of which can be written or used in correspondence

Religions: Christian 85.6%, Muslim 12.2%, Traditional 0.6%, other 0.2%, none 1.5% (2008 est.)

Demographic profile: Liberia's high fertility rate of nearly 5 children per woman and large youth cohort – more than 60% of the population is under the age of 25 – will sustain a high dependency ratio for many years to come. Significant progress has been made in preventing child deaths, despite a lack of health care workers and infrastructure. Infant and child mortality have dropped nearly 70% since 1990; the annual reduction rate of about 5.4% is the highest in Africa.

Nevertheless, Liberia's high maternal mortality rate remains among the world's worst; it reflects a high unmet need for family planning services, frequency of early childbearing, lack of quality obstetric care, high adolescent fertility, and a low proportion of births attended by a medical professional. Female mortality is also increased by the prevalence of female genital cutting (FGC), which is practiced by 10 of Liberia's 16 tribes and affects more than two-thirds of women and girls. FGC is an initiation ritual performed in rural bush schools, which teach traditional beliefs on marriage and motherhood and are an obstacle to formal classroom education for Liberian girls.

Liberia has been both a source and a destination for refugees. During Liberia's 14-year civil war (1989-2003), more than 250,000 people became refugees and another half million were internally displaced. Between 2004 and the cessation of refugee status for Liberians in June 2012, the UNHCR helped more than 155,000 Liberians to voluntarily repatriate, while others returned home on their own. Some Liberian refugees spent more than two decades living in other West African countries. Liberia hosted more than 125,000 Ivoirian refugees escaping post-election violence in 2010-11; as of mid-2017, about 12,000 Ivoirian refugees were still living in Liberia as of October 2017 because of instability.

Age structure: *0-14 years:* 43.35% (male 1,111,479/female 1,087,871)
15-24 years: 20.35% (male 516,136/female 516,137)
25-54 years: 30.01% (male 747,983/female 774,615)
55-64 years: 3.46% (male 89,150/female 86,231)
65 years and over: 2.83% (male 70,252/female 73,442) (2020 est.)

Dependency ratios: *total dependency ratio:* 77.6
youth dependency ratio: 71.7
elderly dependency ratio: 5.9
potential support ratio: 17 (2020 est.)

Median age: *total:* 18 years
male: 17.7 years
female: 18.2 years (2020 est.)

Population growth rate: 2.73% (2022 est.)

Birth rate: 36.64 births/1,000 population (2022 est.)

Death rate: 6.62 deaths/1,000 population (2022 est.)

Net migration rate: -2.74 migrant(s)/1,000 population (2022 est.)

Population distribution: more than half of the population lives in urban areas, with approximately one-third living within an 80-km radius of Monrovia as shown in this population distribution map

Urbanization: *urban population:* 53.1% of total population (2022)

rate of urbanization: 3.41% annual rate of change (2015-20 est.)

Major urban areas - population: 1.623 million MONROVIA (capital) (2022)

Sex ratio: *at birth:* 1.03 male(s)/female
0-14 years: 1.02 male(s)/female
15-24 years: 1 male(s)/female
25-54 years: 0.97 male(s)/female
55-64 years: 1.02 male(s)/female
65 years and over: 0.77 male(s)/female
total population: 1 male(s)/female (2022 est.)

Mother's mean age at first birth: 19.1 years (2019/20 est.)
note: data represents median age at first birth among women 25-49

Maternal mortality ratio: 661 deaths/100,000 live births (2017 est.)

Infant mortality rate: *total:* 44.57 deaths/1,000 live births
male: 48.68 deaths/1,000 live births
female: 40.34 deaths/1,000 live births (2022 est.)

Life expectancy at birth: *total population:* 65.45 years
male: 63.19 years
female: 67.78 years (2022 est.)

Total fertility rate: 4.79 children born/woman (2022 est.)

Contraceptive prevalence rate: 24.9% (2019/20)

Drinking water source: *improved: urban:* 96.2% of population
rural: 70.6% of population
total: 84% of population
unimproved: urban: 3.8% of population
rural: 29.4% of population
total: 16% of population (2020 est.)

Current health expenditure: 8.5% of GDP (2019)

Physicians density: 0.05 physicians/1,000 population (2018)

Sanitation facility access: *improved: urban:* 68% of population
rural: 25.2% of population
total: 47.5% of population
unimproved: urban: 32% of population
rural: 74.8% of population
total: 52.5% of population (2020 est.)

HIV/AIDS - adult prevalence rate: 1.1% (2020 est.)

Major infectious diseases: *degree of risk:* very high (2020)
food or waterborne diseases: bacterial and protozoal diarrhea, hepatitis A, and typhoid fever
vectorborne diseases: malaria, dengue fever, and yellow fever
water contact diseases: schistosomiasis
animal contact diseases: rabies
aerosolized dust or soil contact diseases: Lassa fever
note: on 21 March 2022, the US Centers for Disease Control and Prevention (CDC) issued a Travel Alert for polio in Africa; Liberia is currently considered a high risk to travelers for circulating vaccine-derived polioviruses (cVDPV); vaccine-derived poliovirus (VDPV) is a strain of the weakened poliovirus that was initially included in oral polio vaccine (OPV) and *that has changed over time and behaves more like the wild or naturally occurring virus*; this means it can be spread more easily to people who are unvaccinated against polio and who come in contact with the stool or respiratory secretions, such as from a sneeze, of an "infected" person who received oral polio vaccine; the CDC recommends that before any international travel, anyone unvaccinated, incompletely vaccinated, or with an unknown polio vaccination status should complete the routine polio vaccine series; before travel to any high-risk destination, the CDC recommends that adults who previously completed the full, routine polio vaccine series receive a single, lifetime booster dose of polio vaccine

Obesity - adult prevalence rate: 9.9% (2016)

Alcohol consumption per capita: *total:* 3.12 liters of pure alcohol (2019 est.)
beer: 0.38 liters of pure alcohol (2019 est.)
wine: 0.44 liters of pure alcohol (2019 est.)
spirits: 2.28 liters of pure alcohol (2019 est.)
other alcohols: 0.02 liters of pure alcohol (2019 est.)

Tobacco use: *total:* 8.2% (2020 est.)
male: 14.3% (2020 est.)
female: 2% (2020 est.)

Children under the age of 5 years underweight: 10.9% (2019/20)

Child marriage: *women married by age 15:* NA
women married by age 18: NA
men married by age 18: 8.4% (2020 est.)

Education expenditures: 2.3% of GDP (2020 est.)

Literacy: *definition:* age 15 and over can read and write
total population: 48.3%
male: 62.7%
female: 34.1% (2017)

Unemployment, youth ages 15-24: *total:* 2.3%
male: 2.4%
female: 2.2% (2016 est.)

ENVIRONMENT

Environment - current issues: tropical rain forest deforestation; soil erosion; loss of biodiversity; hunting of endangered species for bushmeat; pollution of coastal waters from oil residue and raw sewage; pollution of rivers from industrial run-off; burning and dumping of household waste

Environment - international agreements: *party to:* Biodiversity, Climate Change, Climate Change-Kyoto Protocol, Climate Change-Paris Agreement, Comprehensive Nuclear Test Ban, Desertification, Endangered Species, Hazardous Wastes, Law of the Sea, Nuclear Test Ban, Ozone Layer Protection, Ship Pollution, Tropical Timber 2006, Wetlands, Whaling
signed, but not ratified: Environmental Modification, Marine Life Conservation

Air pollutants: *particulate matter emissions:* 17.19 micrograms per cubic meter (2016 est.)
carbon dioxide emissions: 1.39 megatons (2016 est.)
methane emissions: 6.56 megatons (2020 est.)

Climate: tropical; hot, humid; dry winters with hot days and cool to cold nights; wet, cloudy summers with frequent heavy showers

Land use: *agricultural land:* 28.1% (2018 est.)
arable land: 5.2% (2018 est.)
permanent crops: 2.1% (2018 est.)
permanent pasture: 20.8% (2018 est.)
forest: 44.6% (2018 est.)
other: 27.3% (2018 est.)

Urbanization: *urban population:* 53.1% of total population (2022)
rate of urbanization: 3.41% annual rate of change (2015-20 est.)

Revenue from forest resources: *forest revenues:* 13.27% of GDP (2018 est.)

Revenue from coal: *coal revenues:* 0% of GDP (2018 est.)

Food insecurity: *severe localized food insecurity: due to high food prices and economic downturn* - according to the latest analysis, about 940,000 people were estimated to be in "Crisis" and above between June and August 2021 due to high food inflation rates and the negative effects of the COVID-19 pandemic on the economy; production of rice, a main food staple, was estimated at a below-average level in 2021, a factor that is expected to further aggravate food insecurity in 2022; prices of staple food have been on the rise in most domestic markets since early 2021; the main drivers of the food insecurity are the effects on crop production of floods and high infestations of pests, including Fall Armyworm in some localized areas (2022)

Waste and recycling: *municipal solid waste generated annually:* 564,467 tons (2007 est.)

Total water withdrawal: *municipal:* 80.2 million cubic meters (2017 est.)
industrial: 53.4 million cubic meters (2017 est.)
agricultural: 12.3 million cubic meters (2017 est.)

Total renewable water resources: 232 billion cubic meters (2017 est.)

GOVERNMENT

Country name: *conventional long form:* Republic of Liberia
conventional short form: Liberia
etymology: name derives from the Latin word "liber" meaning "free"; so named because the nation was created as a homeland for liberated African-American slaves

Government type: presidential republic

Capital: *name:* Monrovia
geographic coordinates: 6 18 N, 10 48 W
time difference: UTC 0 (5 hours ahead of Washington, DC, during Standard Time)
etymology: named after James MONROE (1758-1831), the fifth president of the United States and supporter of the colonization of Liberia by freed slaves; one of two national capitals named for a US president, the other is Washington, D.C.

Administrative divisions: 15 counties; Bomi, Bong, Gbarpolu, Grand Bassa, Grand Cape Mount, Grand Gedeh, Grand Kru, Lofa, Margibi, Maryland, Montserrado, Nimba, River Cess, River Gee, Sinoe

Independence: 26 July 1847

National holiday: Independence Day, 26 July (1847)

Constitution: *history:* previous 1847 (at independence); latest drafted 19 October 1983, revision adopted by referendum 3 July 1984, effective 6 January 1986
amendments: proposed by agreement of at least two thirds of both National Assembly houses or by petition of at least 10,000 citizens; passage requires at least two-thirds majority approval of both houses and approval in a referendum by at least two-thirds majority of registered voters; amended 2011, 2020

Legal system: mixed legal system of common law, based on Anglo-American law, and customary law

International law organization participation: accepts compulsory ICJ jurisdiction with reservations; accepts ICCt jurisdiction

Citizenship: *citizenship by birth:* no
citizenship by descent only: at least one parent must be a citizen of Liberia

dual citizenship recognized: no
residency requirement for naturalization: 2 years

Suffrage: 18 years of age; universal

Executive branch: *chief of state:* President George WEAH (since 22 January 2018); Vice President Jewel HOWARD-TAYLOR (since 22 January 2018); note - the president is both chief of state and head of government
head of government: President George WEAH (since 22 January 2018); Vice President Jewel HOWARD-TAYLOR (since 22 January 2018)
cabinet: Cabinet appointed by the president, confirmed by the Senate
elections/appointments: president directly elected by absolute majority popular vote in 2 rounds if needed for a 6-year term (eligible for a second term); election last held on 10 October 2017 with a runoff on 26 December 2017 (next to be held on 10 October 2023); the runoff originally scheduled for 7 November 2017 was delayed due to allegations of fraud in the first round, which the Supreme Court dismissed (2017)
election results:
George WEAH elected president in second round; percent of vote in first round - George WEAH (Coalition for Democratic Change) 38.4%, Joseph BOAKAI (UP) 28.8%, Charles BRUMSKINE (LP) 9.6%, Prince JOHNSON (MDR) 8.2%, Alexander B. CUMMINGS (ANC) 7.2%, other 7.8%; percentage of vote in second round - George WEAH 61.5%, Joseph BOAKAI 38.5%

Legislative branch: *description:* bicameral National Assembly consists of:
The Liberian Senate (30 seats; members directly elected in 15 2-seat districts by simple majority vote to serve 9-year staggered terms; each district elects 1 senator and elects the second senator 3 years later, followed by a 6-year hiatus, after which the first Senate seat is up for election)

House of Representatives (73 seats; members directly elected in single-seat districts by simple majority vote to serve 6-year terms; eligible for a second term)
elections:
Senate - general election held on 8 December 2020 with half the seats up for election (next to be held on 10 October 2023)
House of Representatives - last held on 10 October 2017 (next to be held 10 October 2023)
election results:
Senate - percent of vote by party - Collaborating Political Parties 40.3%, Congress for Democratic Change 28%, People's Unification Party 6.4%, Movement for Democracy and Reconstructions 4.3%, All Liberia Coalition 1.0%, Rainbow Alliance 1.1%, Liberia Restoration Party 0.82%, Liberia National Union 0.77%, Movement for Progressive Change 0.74%, United People's Party 0.66%, Liberia Transformation Party 0.16%, National Democratic Coalition 0.07%, Movement for One Liberia 0.01; seats by coalition/party- CPP 13, CDC 5, PUP 2, MDR 1, NDC 1; composition - men 28, women 2, percent of women 6.7%

House of Representatives - percent of vote by party/coalition - Coalition for Democratic Change 15.6%, UP 14%, LP 8.7%, ANC 6.1%, PUP 5.9%, ALP 5.1%, MDR 3.4%, other 41.2%; seats by coalition/party - Coalition for Democratic Change 21, UP 20, PUP 5, LP 3, ALP 3, MDR 2, independent 13, other 6; composition - men 65, women 8, percent of women 11%; total Parliament percent of women 9.7%

Judicial branch: *highest court(s):* Supreme Court (consists of a chief justice and 4 associate justices); note - the Supreme Court has jurisdiction for all constitutional cases
judge selection and term of office: chief justice and associate justices appointed by the president of Liberia with consent of the Senate; judges can serve until age 70
subordinate courts: judicial circuit courts; special courts, including criminal, civil, labor, traffic; magistrate and traditional or customary courts

Political parties and leaders: All Liberian Party or ALP [Benoi UREY]
Alliance for Peace and Democracy or APD [Marcus S. G. DAHN]
Alternative National Congress or ANC [Orishil GOULD]
Coalition for Democratic Change [George WEAH] (includes CDC, NPP, and LPDP) Congress for Democratic Change or CDC [Mulbah MORLU]
Liberia Destiny Party or LDP [Nathaniel BARNES]
Liberia National Union or LINU [Nathaniel BLAMA]
Liberia Transformation Party or LTP [Julius SUKU]
Liberian People Democratic Party or LPDP [Alex J. TYLER]
Liberian People's Party or LPP [Yanqui ZAZA]
Liberty Party or LP [Musa Hassan BILITY]
Movement for Democracy and Reconstruction or MDR [Prince Y. JOHNSON]
Movement for Economic Empowerment [Dr. J. Mill JONES]
Movement for Progressive Change or MPC [Simeon FREEMAN]
National Democratic Coalition or NDC [Dew MAYSON]
National Democratic Party of Liberia or NDPL [D. Nyandeh SIEH]
National Patriotic Party or NPP [Jewel HOWARD TAYLOR]
National Reformist Party or NRP [Maximillian T. W. DIABE]
National Union for Democratic Progress or NUDP [Victor BARNEY]
People's Unification Party or PUP [Isobe GBORKORKOLLIE]
Unity Party or UP [Rev. J. Luther TARPEH]
United People's Party [MacDonald WENTO]
Victory for Change Party or VCP [Marcus R. JONES]

International organization participation: ACP, AfDB, AU, ECOWAS, EITI (compliant country), FAO, G-77, IAEA, IBRD, ICAO, ICC (NGOs), ICCt, ICRM, IDA, IFAD, IFC, IFRCS, ILO, IMF, IMO, IMSO, Interpol, IOC, IOM, ISO (correspondent), ITU, ITUC (NGOs), MIGA, MINUSMA, NAM, OPCW, UN, UNCTAD, UNESCO, UNIDO, UNISFA, UNWTO, UPU, WCO, WFTU (NGOs), WHO, WIPO, WMO, WTO (observer)

Diplomatic representation in the US: *chief of mission:* Ambassador George S.W. PATTEN, Sr. (since 11 January 2019)
chancery: 5201 16th Street NW, Washington, DC 20011
telephone: [1] (202) 723-0437
FAX: [1] (202) 723-0436
email address and website:
info@liberiaemb.org
http://www.liberianembassyus.org/
consulate(s) general: New York

Diplomatic representation from the US: *chief of mission:* Ambassador Michael A. MCCARTHY (since 22 January 2021)
embassy: 502 Benson Street, Monrovia
mailing address: 8800 Monrovia Place, Washington DC 20521-8800
telephone: [231] 77-677-7000
FAX: [231] 77-677-7370
email address and website:
ACSMonrovia@state.gov
https://lr.usembassy.gov/

Flag description: 11 equal horizontal stripes of red (top and bottom) alternating with white; a white five-pointed star appears on a blue square in the upper hoist-side corner; the stripes symbolize the signatories of the Liberian Declaration of Independence; the blue square represents the African mainland, and the star represents the freedom granted to the ex-slaves; according to the constitution, the blue color signifies liberty, justice, and fidelity, the white color purity, cleanliness, and guilelessness, and the red color steadfastness, valor, and fervor
note: the design is based on the US flag

National symbol(s): white star; national colors: red, white, blue

National anthem: *name:* "All Hail, Liberia Hail!"
lyrics/music: Daniel Bashiel WARNER/Olmstead LUCA
note: lyrics adopted 1847, music adopted 1860; the anthem's author later became the third president of Liberia

ECONOMY

Economic overview: Liberia is a low-income country that relies heavily on foreign assistance and remittances from the diaspora. It is richly endowed with water, mineral resources, forests, and a climate favorable to agriculture. Its principal exports are iron ore, rubber, diamonds, and gold. Palm oil and cocoa are emerging as new export products. The government has attempted to revive raw timber extraction and is encouraging oil exploration.

In the 1990s and early 2000s, civil war and government mismanagement destroyed much of Liberia's economy, especially infrastructure in and around the capital. Much of the conflict was fueled by control over Liberia's natural resources. With the conclusion of fighting and the installation of a democratically elected government in 2006, businesses that had fled the country began to return. The country achieved high growth during the period 2010-13 due to favorable world prices for its commodities. However, during the 2014-2015 Ebola crisis, the economy declined and many foreign-owned businesses departed with their capital and expertise. The epidemic forced the government to divert scarce resources to combat the spread of the virus, reducing funds available for needed public investment. The cost of addressing the Ebola epidemic coincided with decreased economic activity reducing government revenue, although higher donor support significantly offset this loss. During the same period, global commodities prices for key exports fell and have yet to recover to pre-Ebola levels.

In 2017, gold was a key driver of growth, as a new mining project began its first full year of production; iron ore exports are also increased as Arcelor Mittal opened new mines at Mount Gangra. The completion of the rehabilitation of the Mount Coffee Hydroelectric Dam increased electricity production to support ongoing and future economic activity, although electricity tariffs remain high relative to other countries in the region and transmission infrastructure is limited. Presidential and legislative elections in October 2017 generated election-related spending pressures.

Revitalizing the economy in the future will depend on economic diversification, increasing investment and trade, higher global commodity prices, sustained foreign aid and remittances, development of infrastructure and institutions, combating corruption, and maintaining political stability and security.

Real GDP (purchasing power parity): $6.85 billion (2020 est.)
$7.05 billion (2019 est.)
$7.21 billion (2018 est.)
note: data are in 2017 dollars

Real GDP growth rate: 2.5% (2017 est.)
-1.6% (2016 est.)
0% (2015 est.)

Real GDP per capita: $1,400 (2020 est.)
$1,400 (2019 est.)
$1,500 (2018 est.)
note: data are in 2017 dollars

GDP (official exchange rate): $3.071 billion (2019 est.)

Inflation rate (consumer prices): 12.4% (2017 est.)
8.8% (2016 est.)

GDP - composition, by sector of origin: *agriculture:* 34% (2017 est.)
industry: 13.8% (2017 est.)
services: 52.2% (2017 est.)

GDP - composition, by end use: *household consumption:* 128.8% (2016 est.)
government consumption: 16.7% (2016 est.)
investment in fixed capital: 19.5% (2016 est.)
investment in inventories: 6.7% (2016 est.)
exports of goods and services: 17.5% (2016 est.)
imports of goods and services: -89.2% (2016 est.)

Agricultural products: cassava, sugar cane, oil palm fruit, rice, bananas, vegetables, plantains, rubber, taro, maize

Industries: mining (iron ore and gold), rubber processing, palm oil processing, diamonds

Industrial production growth rate: 9% (2017 est.)

Labor force: 1.677 million (2017 est.)

Labor force - by occupation: *agriculture:* 70%
industry: 8%
services: 22% (2000 est.)

Unemployment rate: 2.8% (2014 est.)

Unemployment, youth ages 15-24: *total:* 2.3%
male: 2.4%
female: 2.2% (2016 est.)

Population below poverty line: 50.9% (2016 est.)

Gini Index coefficient - distribution of family income: 35.3 (2016 est.)
38.2 (2007)

Household income or consumption by percentage share: *lowest 10%:* 2.4%
highest 10%: 30.1% (2007)

Budget: *revenues:* 553.6 million (2017 est.)
expenditures: 693.8 million (2017 est.)

Budget surplus (+) or deficit (-): -4.3% (of GDP) (2017 est.)

Public debt: 34.4% of GDP (2017 est.)
28.3% of GDP (2016 est.)

Taxes and other revenues: 16.9% (of GDP) (2017 est.)

Fiscal year: calendar year

Current account balance: -$627 million (2017 est.)
-$464 million (2016 est.)

Exports: $550 million (2019 est.) note: data are in current year dollars
$530 million (2018 est.) note: data are in current year dollars
$359 million (2017 est.)

Exports - partners: Guyana 32%, Poland 10%, Switzerland 8%, Japan 7%, China 5% (2019)

Exports - commodities: ships, iron, gold, rubber, crude petroleum (2019)

Imports: $1.24 billion (2019 est.) note: data are in current year dollars
$1.25 billion (2018 est.) note: data are in current year dollars
$2.118 billion (2017 est.)

Imports - partners: China 41%, Japan 21%, South Korea 18% (2019)

Imports - commodities: ships, refined petroleum, iron structures, boat propellers, centrifuges (2019)

Reserves of foreign exchange and gold: $459.8 million (31 December 2017 est.)
$528.7 million (31 December 2016 est.)

Debt - external: $826 million (2019 est.)
$679 million (2018 est.)

Exchange rates: Liberian dollars (LRD) per US dollar -
109.4 (2017 est.)
93.4 (2016 est.)
93.4 (2015 est.)
85.3 (2014 est.)
83.893 (2013 est.)

ENERGY

Electricity access: *electrification - total population:* 12% (2019)
electrification - urban areas: 18% (2019)
electrification - rural areas: 6% (2019)

Electricity: *installed generating capacity:* 196,000 kW (2020 est.)
consumption: 292 million kWh (2019 est.)
exports: 0 kWh (2019 est.)
imports: 0 kWh (2019 est.)
transmission/distribution losses: 26 million kWh (2019 est.)

Electricity generation sources: *fossil fuels:* 40.5% of total installed capacity (2020 est.)
solar: 0.5% of total installed capacity (2020 est.)
hydroelectricity: 59.1% of total installed capacity (2020 est.)

Petroleum: *total petroleum production:* 0 bbl/day (2021 est.)
refined petroleum consumption: 9,200 bbl/day (2019 est.)

Refined petroleum products - imports: 8,181 bbl/day (2015 est.)

Carbon dioxide emissions: 1.346 million metric tonnes of CO2 (2019 est.)
from petroleum and other liquids: 1.346 million metric tonnes of CO2 (2019 est.)

Energy consumption per capita: 3.79 million Btu/person (2019 est.)

COMMUNICATIONS

Telephones - fixed lines: *total subscriptions:* 6,000 (2020 est.)
subscriptions per 100 inhabitants: 0 (2020 est.)

Telephones - mobile cellular: *total subscriptions:* 1.653 million (2020 est.)
subscriptions per 100 inhabitants: 33 (2020 est.)

Telecommunication systems: *general assessment:* Liberia has a telecom market which is mainly based on mobile networks; this is due to the civil war which destroyed much of the fixed-line infrastructure; to facilitate LTC Mobile's market entry, the government in January 2022 set in train amendments to telecom legislation; internet services are available from a number of wireless ISPs as well as the mobile operators; the high cost and limited bandwidth of connections means that internet access is expensive and rates are very low; additional bandwidth is available from an international submarine cable but considerable investment is still needed in domestic fixed-line infrastructure before end-users can make full use of the cable (2022)
domestic: fixed-line less than 1 per 100; mobile-cellular subscription base growing and teledensity approached 33 per 100 persons (2020)
international: country code - 231; landing point for the ACE submarine cable linking 20 West African countries and Europe; satellite earth station - 1 Intelsat (Atlantic Ocean) (2019)

Broadcast media: 8 private and 1 government-owned TV station; satellite TV service available; 1 state-owned radio station; approximately 20 independent radio stations broadcasting in Monrovia, with approximately 80 more local stations operating in other areas; transmissions of 4 international (including the British Broadcasting Corporation and Radio France Internationale) broadcasters are available (2019)

Internet country code: .lr

Internet users: *total:* 1,314,996 (2020 est.)
percent of population: 26% (2020 est.)

Broadband - fixed subscriptions: *total:* 13,000 (2020 est.)
subscriptions per 100 inhabitants: 0.3 (2020 est.)

TRANSPORTATION

Civil aircraft registration country code prefix: A8

Airports: *total:* 29 (2021)

Airports - with paved runways: *total:* 2
over 3,047 m: 1
1,524 to 2,437 m: 1 (2021)

Airports - with unpaved runways: *total:* 27
1,524 to 2,437 m: 5
914 to 1,523 m: 8
under 914 m: 14 (2021)

Pipelines: 4 km oil (2013)

Railways: *total:* 429 km (2008)
standard gauge: 345 km (2008) 1.435-m gauge
narrow gauge: 84 km (2008) 1.067-m gauge
note: most sections of the railways inoperable due to damage sustained during the civil wars from 1980 to 2003, but many are being rebuilt

Roadways: *total:* 10,600 km (2018)
paved: 657 km (2018)
unpaved: 9,943 km (2018)

Merchant marine: *total:* 3,942

by type: bulk carrier 1,487, container ship 878, general cargo 131, oil tanker 851, other 595 (2021)

Ports and terminals: *major seaport(s):* Buchanan, Monrovia

MILITARY AND SECURITY

Military and security forces: Armed Forces of Liberia (AFL): Army, Liberian Coast Guard, Air Wing (2022)
note: the AFL Air Wing was previously disbanded in 2005 and has been under redevelopment since 2019; the Liberian National Police and the Liberian Drug Enforcement Agency are under the Ministry of Justice

Military expenditures: 0.7% of GDP (2021 est.)
0.5% of GDP (2020 est.)
0.6% of GDP (2019 est.) (approximately $25 million)
0.5% of GDP (2018 est.) (approximately $20 million)
0.4% of GDP (2017 est.) (approximately $19 million)

Military and security service personnel strengths: approximately 2,000 active personnel (2022)

Military equipment inventories and acquisitions: the military has a limited inventory; since 2010, it has received small quantities of equipment, including donations, from countries such as China and the US (2021)

Military service age and obligation: 18-35 years of age for men and women for voluntary military service; no conscription (2022)
note: as of 2020, women made up less than 1% of the active military

Military deployments: 160 Mali (MINUSMA) (May 2022)

Military - note: the first militia unit established for defense of the colony was raised in 1832; the Armed Forces of Liberia (AFL) traces its origins to the 1908 establishment of the Liberia Frontier Force, which became the Liberian National Guard in 1965; the AFL was established in 1970; at the end of the second civil war in 2003, military and police forces were disbanded and approximately 100,000 military, police, and rebel combatants were disarmed; the AFL began to rebuild in 2003 with US assistance and the first infantry battalion of the restructured AFL was re-activated in late 2007; a second battalion was added in 2008

the UN Mission in Liberia (UNMIL) was established in 2003 as a peacekeeping force; at its height, UNMIL was comprised of about 15,000 personnel, including more than 3,000 troops absorbed from the Economic Community of West African States (ECOWAS) peacekeeping mission; Liberian forces reassumed full control of the country's security in June of 2016, and the UNMIL mission was ended in 2018

Maritime threats: the International Maritime Bureau reports the territorial and offshore waters in the Niger Delta and Gulf of Guinea remain a very high risk for piracy and armed robbery of ships; in 2021, there were 34 reported incidents of piracy and armed robbery at sea in the Gulf of Guinea region; although a significant decrease from the total number of 81 incidents in 2020, it included the one hijacking and three of five ships fired upon worldwide; while boarding and attempted boarding to steal valuables from ships and crews are the most common types of incidents, almost a third of all incidents involve a hijacking and/or kidnapping; in 2021, 57 crew members were kidnapped in seven separate incidents in the Gulf of Guinea, representing 100% of kidnappings worldwide; Nigerian pirates in particular are well armed and very aggressive, operating as far as 200 nm offshore; the Maritime Administration of the US Department of Transportation has issued a Maritime Advisory (2022-001 - Gulf of Guinea-Piracy/Armed Robbery/Kidnapping for Ransom) effective 4 January 2022, which states in part, "Piracy, armed robbery, and kidnapping for ransom continue to serve as significant threats to US-flagged vessels transiting or operating in the Gulf of Guinea"

TRANSNATIONAL ISSUES

Disputes - international: *Liberia-Guinea:* none identified
Liberia-Sierra Leone: none identified

Illicit drugs: not a significant transit country for illicit narcotics but proximity to major drug routes contribute to trafficking; not a significant producer of illicit narcotics; local drug use involves marijuana, heroin, cocaine, the synthetic opioid tramadol, and amphetamine-type stimulants

LIBYA

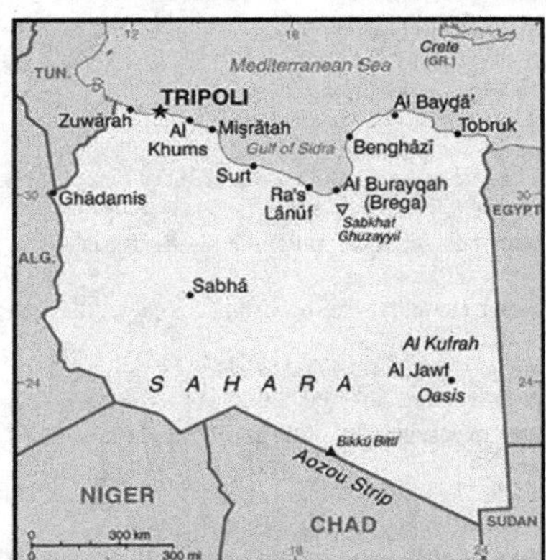

INTRODUCTION

Background: Berbers have inhabited central north Africa since ancient times, but the region has been settled and ruled by Phoenicians, Greeks, Carthaginians, Persians, Egyptians, Greeks, Romans, and Vandals. In the the 7th century, Islam spread through the region; in the mid-16th century, Ottoman rule began. The Italians supplanted the Ottoman Turks in the area around Tripoli in 1911 and did not relinquish their hold until 1943 when they were defeated in World War II. Libya then passed to UN administration and achieved independence in 1951. Following a 1969 military coup, Col. Muammar al-QADHAFI assumed leadership and began to espouse his political system at home, which was a combination of socialism and Islam. During the 1970s, QADHAFI used oil revenues to promote his ideology outside Libya, supporting subversive and terrorist activities that included the downing of two airliners - one over Scotland, another in Northern Africa - and a discotheque bombing in Berlin. UN sanctions in 1992 isolated QADHAFI politically and economically following the attacks; sanctions were lifted in 2003 following Libyan acceptance of responsibility for the bombings and agreement to claimant compensation. QADHAFI also agreed to end Libya's program to develop weapons of mass destruction, and he made significant strides in normalizing relations with Western nations.

Unrest that began in several Middle Eastern and North African countries in late 2010 erupted in Libyan cities in early 2011. QADHAFI's brutal crackdown on protesters spawned an eight-month civil war that saw the emergence of a National Transitional Council (NTC), UN authorization of air and naval intervention by the international community, and the toppling of the QADHAFI regime. In 2012, the NTC handed power to an elected parliament, the General National Congress (GNC). Voters chose a new parliament to replace the GNC in June 2014 - the House of Representatives (HoR) - which relocated to the eastern city of Tobruk after fighting broke out in Tripoli and Benghazi in July 2014.

In December 2015, the UN brokered an agreement among a broad array of Libyan political parties and social groups - known as the Libyan Political Agreement (LPA) - establishing an interim executive body, the Government of National Accord (GNA). However, the HoR and defunct-GNC-affiliated political hardliners continued to oppose the GNA and hamper the LPA's implementation, leaving Libya with eastern and western-based rival governments. In September 2017, UN Special Representative Ghassan SALAME announced a new roadmap for national political reconciliation. In November 2018, the international community supported SALAME's recalibrated Action Plan for Libya that aimed to break the political deadlock by holding a National Conference in early 2019. These plans, however, were derailed when the eastern-based self-described Libyan National Army (LNA) launched an offensive to seize Tripoli in April 2019. Several countries sent armed personnel and advanced military equipment into Libya. The LNA's offensive collapsed in June 2020, and a subsequent UN-sponsored cease-fire in October 2020 helped formalize the pause in fighting between rival camps, although foreign forces, fighters, and mercenaries that aided eastern and western factions during the fighting remain in Libya.

In early 2021, the UN-facilitated Libyan Political Dialogue Forum selected a new prime minister for an interim government, the Government of National Unity (GNU), and a new presidential council charged with preparing for presidential and parliamentary elections in December 2021 and uniting the country's state institutions. The HoR approved the GNU and its cabinet in March 2021, providing Libya with its first unified government since 2014. On 22 December 2021, Libya's parliament postponed the first round of the presidential election to an undetermined date in the future. Talks in June 2022 failed to reach agreement on eligibility requirements for presidential candidates.

GEOGRAPHY

Location: Northern Africa, bordering the Mediterranean Sea, between Egypt, Tunisia, and Algeria

Geographic coordinates: 25 00 N, 17 00 E

Map references: Africa

Area: *total:* 1,759,540 sq km
land: 1,759,540 sq km
water: 0 sq km

Area - comparative: about 2.5 times the size of Texas; slightly larger than Alaska

Land boundaries: *total:* 4,339 km
border countries (6): Algeria 989 km; Chad 1,050 km; Egypt 1,115 km; Niger 342 km; Sudan 382 km; Tunisia 461 km

Coastline: 1,770 km

Maritime claims: *territorial sea:* 12 nm
exclusive fishing zone: 62 nm
note: Gulf of Sidra closing line - 32 degrees, 30 minutes north

Climate: Mediterranean along coast; dry, extreme desert interior

Terrain: mostly barren, flat to undulating plains, plateaus, depressions

Elevation: *highest point:* Bikku Bitti 2,267 m
lowest point: Sabkhat Ghuzayyil -47 m
mean elevation: 423 m

Natural resources: petroleum, natural gas, gypsum

Land use: *agricultural land:* 8.8% (2018 est.)
arable land: 1% (2018 est.)
permanent crops: 0.2% (2018 est.)
permanent pasture: 7.6% (2018 est.)
forest: 0.1% (2018 est.)
other: 91.1% (2018 est.)

Irrigated land: 4,700 sq km (2012)

Major watersheds (area sq km): Internal *(endorheic basin)* drainage: Lake Chad (2,497,738 sq km)

Major aquifers: Nubian Aquifer System, North Western Sahara Aquifer System, Murzuk-Djado Basin

Population distribution: well over 90% of the population lives along the Mediterranean coast in and between Tripoli to the west and Al Bayda to the east; the interior remains vastly underpopulated due to the Sahara and lack of surface water as shown in this population distribution map

Natural hazards: hot, dry, dust-laden ghibli is a southern wind lasting one to four days in spring and fall; dust storms, sandstorms

Geography - note: *note 1:* more than 90% of the country is desert or semidesert
note 2: the volcano Waw an Namus lies in south central Libya in the middle of the Sahara; the caldera is an oasis - the name means "oasis of mosquitoes" - containing several small lakes surrounded by vegetation and hosting various insects and a large diversity of birds

PEOPLE AND SOCIETY

Population: 7,137,931 (2022 est.)
note: immigrants make up just over 12% of the total population, according to UN data (2019)

Nationality: *noun:* Libyan(s)
adjective: Libyan

Ethnic groups: Berber and Arab 97%, other 3% (includes Egyptian, Greek, Indian, Italian, Maltese, Pakistani, Tunisian, and Turkish)

Languages: Arabic (official), Italian, English (all widely understood in the major cities); Berber (Nafusi, Ghadamis, Suknah, Awjilah, Tamasheq)
major-language sample(s):

يمكن الاستغناء عنه للمعلومات الأساسية

كتاب حقائق العالم، المصدر الذي لا

(Arabic)

Religions: Muslim (official; virtually all Sunni) 96.6%, Christian 2.7%, Buddhist <1%, Hindu <1%, Jewish <1%, folk religion <1%, other <1%, unaffiliated <1% (2020 est.)
note: non-Sunni Muslims include native Ibadhi Muslims (<1% of the population) and foreign Muslims

Demographic profile: Despite continuing unrest, Libya remains a destination country for economic migrants. It is also a hub for transit migration to Europe because of its proximity to southern Europe and its lax border controls. Labor migrants have been drawn to Libya since the development of its oil sector in the 1960s. Until the latter part of the 1990s, most migrants to Libya were Arab (primarily Egyptians and Sudanese). However, international isolation stemming from Libya's involvement in international terrorism and a perceived lack of support from Arab countries led QADHAFI in 1998 to adopt a decade-long pan-African policy that enabled large numbers of Sub- Saharan migrants to enter Libya without visas to work in the construction and agricultural industries. Although Sub-Saharan Africans provided a cheap labor source, they were poorly treated and were subjected to periodic mass expulsions.

By the mid-2000s, domestic animosity toward African migrants and a desire to reintegrate into the international community motivated QADHAFI to impose entry visas on Arab and African immigrants and to agree to joint maritime patrols and migrant repatriations with Italy, the main recipient of illegal migrants departing Libya. As his regime neared collapse in 2011, QADHAFI reversed his policy of cooperating with Italy to curb illegal migration and sent boats loaded with migrants and asylum seekers to strain European resources. Libya's 2011 revolution decreased immigration drastically and prompted nearly 800,000 migrants to flee to third countries, mainly Tunisia and Egypt, or to their countries of origin. The inflow of migrants declined in 2012 but returned to normal levels by 2013, despite continued hostility toward Sub-Saharan Africans and a less-inviting job market.

While Libya is not an appealing destination for migrants, since 2014, transiting migrants – primarily from East and West Africa – continue to exploit its political instability and weak border controls and use it as a primary departure area to migrate across the central Mediterranean to Europe in growing numbers. In addition, more than 200,000 people were displaced internally as of August 2017 by fighting between armed groups in eastern and western Libya and, to a lesser extent, by inter-tribal clashes in the country's south.

Age structure: *0-14 years:* 33.65% (male 1,184,755/female 1,134,084)
15-24 years: 15.21% (male 534,245/female 513,728)
25-54 years: 41.57% (male 1,491,461/female 1,373,086)
55-64 years: 5.52% (male 186,913/female 193,560)
65 years and over: 4.04% (male 129,177/female 149,526) (2020 est.)

Dependency ratios: *total dependency ratio:* 47.7
youth dependency ratio: 41
elderly dependency ratio: 6.7
potential support ratio: 15 (2020 est.)

Median age: *total:* 25.8 years
male: 25.9 years
female: 25.7 years (2020 est.)

Population growth rate: 1.65% (2022 est.)

Birth rate: 21.56 births/1,000 population (2022 est.)

Death rate: 3.45 deaths/1,000 population (2022 est.)

Net migration rate: -1.61 migrant(s)/1,000 population (2022 est.)

Population distribution: well over 90% of the population lives along the Mediterranean coast in and between Tripoli to the west and Al Bayda to the east; the interior remains vastly underpopulated due to the Sahara and lack of surface water as shown in this population distribution map

Urbanization: *urban population:* 81.3% of total population (2022)
rate of urbanization: 1.45% annual rate of change (2020-25 est.)

Major urban areas - population: 1.176 million TRIPOLI (capital), 953,000 Misratah, 848,000 Benghazi (2022)

Sex ratio: *at birth:* 1.05 male(s)/female
0-14 years: 1.04 male(s)/female
15-24 years: 1.04 male(s)/female
25-54 years: 1.08 male(s)/female
55-64 years: 0.97 male(s)/female
65 years and over: 0.73 male(s)/female
total population: 1.04 male(s)/female (2022 est.)

Maternal mortality ratio: 72 deaths/100,000 live births (2017 est.)

Infant mortality rate: *total:* 11.22 deaths/1,000 live births
male: 12.66 deaths/1,000 live births
female: 9.7 deaths/1,000 live births (2022 est.)

Life expectancy at birth: *total population:* 77.18 years
male: 74.94 years
female: 79.53 years (2022 est.)

Total fertility rate: 3.09 children born/woman (2022 est.)

Contraceptive prevalence rate: 27.7% (2014)

Drinking water source: *improved: total:* 99.9% of population
unimproved: total: 0.1% of population (2020 est.)

Physicians density: 2.09 physicians/1,000 population (2017)

Hospital bed density: 3.2 beds/1,000 population (2017)

Sanitation facility access: *improved: total:* 99.3% of population
unimproved: total: 0.7% of population (2020 est.)

HIV/AIDS - adult prevalence rate: 0.1% (2020 est.)

Obesity - adult prevalence rate: 32.5% (2016)

Alcohol consumption per capita: *total:* 0.01 liters of pure alcohol (2019 est.)
beer: 0 liters of pure alcohol (2019 est.)
wine: 0.01 liters of pure alcohol (2019 est.)
spirits: 0 liters of pure alcohol (2019 est.)
other alcohols: 0 liters of pure alcohol (2019 est.)

Children under the age of 5 years underweight: 11.7% (2014)

Literacy: *definition:* age 15 and over can read and write
total population: 91%
male: 96.7%
female: 85.6% (2015)

Unemployment, youth ages 15-24: *total:* 48.7%
male: 40.8%
female: 67.8% (2012 est.)

ENVIRONMENT

Environment - current issues: desertification; limited natural freshwater resources; the Great Manmade River Project, the largest water development scheme in the world, brings water from large aquifers under the Sahara to coastal cities; water pollution is a significant problem; the combined impact of sewage, oil byproducts, and industrial waste threatens Libya's coast and the Mediterranean Sea

Environment - international agreements: *party to:* Biodiversity, Climate Change, Climate Change-Kyoto Protocol, Comprehensive Nuclear Test Ban, Desertification, Endangered Species, Hazardous Wastes, Marine Dumping-London Convention, Nuclear Test Ban, Ozone Layer Protection, Ship Pollution, Wetlands
signed, but not ratified: Climate Change-Paris Agreement, Law of the Sea

Air pollutants: *particulate matter emissions:* 44.17 micrograms per cubic meter (2016 est.)
carbon dioxide emissions: 50.56 megatons (2016 est.)
methane emissions: 45.76 megatons (2020 est.)

Climate: Mediterranean along coast; dry, extreme desert interior

Land use: *agricultural land:* 8.8% (2018 est.)
arable land: 1% (2018 est.)
permanent crops: 0.2% (2018 est.)
permanent pasture: 7.6% (2018 est.)
forest: 0.1% (2018 est.)
other: 91.1% (2018 est.)

Urbanization: *urban population:* 81.3% of total population (2022)
rate of urbanization: 1.45% annual rate of change (2020-25 est.)

Revenue from forest resources: *forest revenues:* 0.06% of GDP (2018 est.)

Revenue from coal: *coal revenues:* 0% of GDP (2018 est.)

Food insecurity: *severe localized food insecurity: due to civil insecurity, economic and political instability, and high food prices* - an estimated 800,000 people, 10% of the population, need humanitarian assistance, of which 500,000 require food assistance; the country relies heavily on imports (up to 90%) to cover its cereal consumption requirements (mostly wheat for human consumption and barley for feed); between 2016 and 2020, the country sourced over 30% of its wheat imports from Ukraine, and 20% from the Russian Federation; almost 65% of total maize imports of 650,000 mt, and 50% of total barley imports of 1 million mt originated from Ukraine, making the Libya vulnerable to disruptions in shipments from the Black Sea region (2022)

Waste and recycling: *municipal solid waste generated annually:* 2,147,596 tons (2011 est.)

Major watersheds (area sq km): Internal *(endorheic basin)* drainage: Lake Chad (2,497,738 sq km)

Major aquifers: Nubian Aquifer System, North Western Sahara Aquifer System, Murzuk-Djado Basin

Total water withdrawal: *municipal:* 700 million cubic meters (2017 est.)
industrial: 280 million cubic meters (2017 est.)
agricultural: 4.85 billion cubic meters (2017 est.)

Total renewable water resources: 700 million cubic meters (2017 est.)

GOVERNMENT

Country name: *conventional long form:* State of Libya
conventional short form: Libya
local long form: Dawiat Libiya
local short form: Libiya
etymology: name derives from the Libu, an ancient Libyan tribe first mentioned in texts from the 13th century B.C.

Government type: in transition

Capital: *name:* Tripoli (Tarabulus)
geographic coordinates: 32 53 N, 13 10 E
time difference: UTC+2 (7 hours ahead of Washington, DC, during Standard Time)
etymology: originally founded by the Phoenicians as Oea in the 7th century B.C., the city changed rulers many times over the successive centuries; by the beginning of the 3rd century A.D. the region around the city was referred to as Regio Tripolitana by the Romans, meaning "region of the three cities" - namely Oea (i.e., modern Tripoli), Sabratha (to the west), and Leptis Magna (to the east); over time, the shortened name of "Tripoli" came to refer to just Oea, which derives from the Greek words *tria* and *polis* meaning "three cities"

Administrative divisions: 22 governorates (muhafazah, singular - muhafazat); Al Butnan, Al Jabal al Akhdar, Al Jabal al Gharbi, Al Jafarah, Al Jufrah, Al Kufrah, Al Marj, Al Marqab, Al Wahat, An Nuqat al Khams, Az Zawiyah, Banghazi (Benghazi), Darnah, Ghat, Misratah, Murzuq, Nalut, Sabha, Surt, Tarabulus (Tripoli), Wadi al Hayat, Wadi ash Shati

Independence: 24 December 1951 (from UN trusteeship)

National holiday: Liberation Day, 23 October (2011)

Constitution: *history:* previous 1951, 1977; in July 2017, the Constitutional Assembly completed and approved a draft of a new permanent constitution; in September 2018, the House of Representatives passed a constitutional referendum law in a session with contested reports of the quorum needed to pass the vote, and submitted it to the High National Elections Commission in December to begin preparations for a constitutional referendum; the referendum is planned in 2022, following the presidential election

Legal system: Libya's post-revolution legal system is in flux and driven by state and non-state entities

International law organization participation: has not submitted an ICJ jurisdiction declaration; non-party state to the ICCt

Citizenship: *citizenship by birth:* no
citizenship by descent only: at least one parent or grandparent must be a citizen of Libya
dual citizenship recognized: no
residency requirement for naturalization: varies from 3 to 5 years

Suffrage: 18 years of age, universal

Executive branch: *chief of state:* Chairman, Presidential Council, Mohammed Al MENFI (since 5 February 2021)
head of government: Interim Prime Minister Abdul Hamid DUBAYBAH (since 5 February 2021)
elections/appointments:
Libya's first direct presidential election, scheduled for 24 December 2021, was not held

Legislative branch: *description:* unicameral House of Representatives (Majlis Al Nuwab) or HoR (200 seats including 32 reserved for women; members directly elected by majority vote; member term NA); note - the High State Council serves as an advisory group for the HoR
elections:
last held on 25 June 2014
election results:
25 June 2014 - percent of vote by party - NA; seats by party - NA; composition; note - only 188 of the 200 seats were filled in the June 2014 election because of boycotts and lack of security at some polling stations; some elected members of the HoR also boycotted the election

Judicial branch: *highest court(s):* Libya's judicial system consists of a supreme court, central high courts (in Tripoli, Benghazi, and Sabha), and a series of lower courts; the judicial system is factious given the ongoing tension between Libya's eastern and western regions; since 2011, Libyan political factions and armed groups have targeted judges and courthouses

Political parties and leaders: NA

International organization participation: ABEDA, AfDB, AFESD, AMF, AMU, AU, BDEAC, CAEU, COMESA, FAO, G-77, IAEA, IBRD, ICAO, ICC (NGOs), ICRM, IDA, IDB, IFAD, IFC, IFRCS, ILO, IMF, IMO, IMSO, Interpol, IOC, IOM, IPU, ISO, ITSO, ITU, LAS, LCBC, MIGA, NAM, OAPEC, OIC, OPCW, OPEC, PCA, UN, UNCTAD, UNESCO, UNHRC, UNIDO, UNSMIL, UNWTO, UPU, WCO, WFTU (NGOs), WHO, WIPO, WMO, WTO (observer)

Diplomatic representation in the US: *chief of mission:* Ambassador (vacant); Charge d'Affaires Khaled DAIEF (since 27 August 2021)
chancery: 1460 Dahlia Street NW, Washington, DC 20012
telephone: [1] (202) 944-9601
FAX: [1] (202) 944-9606
email address and website:
info@embassyoflibyadc.com
https://www.embassyoflibyadc.org/

Diplomatic representation from the US: *chief of mission:* Ambassador Richard B. NORLAND (since 22 August 2019)
embassy: operations suspended

mailing address: 8850 Tripoli Place, Washington, DC 20521-8850
telephone: [216] 71-107-000
email address and website:
LibyaACS@state.gov
https://ly.usembassy.gov/
note: the US Embassy in Tripoli closed in July 2014 due to fighting near the embassy related to Libyan civil unrest; embassy staff and operations temporarily first relocated to Valetta, Malta and currently are temporarily relocated to Tunis, Tunisia

Flag description: three horizontal bands of red (top), black (double width), and green with a white crescent and star centered on the black stripe; the National Transitional Council reintroduced this flag design of the former Kingdom of Libya (1951-1969) on 27 February 2011; it replaced the former all-green banner promulgated by the QADHAFI regime in 1977; the colors represent the three major regions of the country: red stands for Fezzan, black symbolizes Cyrenaica, and green denotes Tripolitania; the crescent and star represent Islam, the main religion of the country

National symbol(s): star and crescent, hawk; national colors: red, black, green

National anthem: *name:* "Libya, Libya, Libya"
lyrics/music: Al Bashir AL AREBI/Mohamad Abdel WAHAB
note: also known as "Ya Beladi" or "Oh, My Country!"; adopted 1951; readopted 2011 with some modification to the lyrics; during the QADHAFI years between 1969 and 2011, the anthem was "Allahu Akbar," (God is Great) a marching song of the Egyptian Army in the 1956 Suez War

National heritage: *total World Heritage Sites:* 5 (all cultural)
selected World Heritage Site locales: Archaeological Site of Cyrene; Archaeological Site of Leptis Magna, Archaeological Site of Sabratha; Rock-Art Sites of Tadrart Acacus; Old Town of Ghadamès

ECONOMY

Economic overview: Libya's economy, almost entirely dependent on oil and gas exports, has struggled since 2014 given security and political instability, disruptions in oil production, and decline in global oil prices. The Libyan dinar has lost much of its value since 2014 and the resulting gap between official and black market exchange rates has spurred the growth of a shadow economy and contributed to inflation. The country suffers from widespread power outages, caused by shortages of fuel for power generation. Living conditions, including access to clean drinking water, medical services, and safe housing have all declined since 2011. Oil production in 2017 reached a five-year high, driving GDP growth, with daily average production rising to 879,000 barrels per day. However, oil production levels remain below the average pre-Revolution highs of 1.6 million barrels per day.

The Central Bank of Libya continued to pay government salaries to a majority of the Libyan workforce and to fund subsidies for fuel and food, resulting in an estimated budget deficit of about 17% of GDP in 2017. Low consumer confidence in the banking sector and the economy as a whole has driven a severe liquidity shortage.

Real GDP (purchasing power parity): $70.65 billion (2020 est.)
$102.84 billion (2019 est.)
$100.3 billion (2018 est.)
note: data are in 2017 dollars

Real GDP growth rate: 64% (2017 est.)
-7.4% (2016 est.)
-13% (2015 est.)

Real GDP per capita: $10,300 (2020 est.)
$15,200 (2019 est.)
$15,000 (2018 est.)
note: data are in 2017 dollars

GDP (official exchange rate): $52.259 billion (2019 est.)

Inflation rate (consumer prices): 28.5% (2017 est.)
25.9% (2016 est.)

GDP - composition, by sector of origin: *agriculture:* 1.3% (2017 est.)
industry: 52.3% (2017 est.)
services: 46.4% (2017 est.)

GDP - composition, by end use: *household consumption:* 71.6% (2017 est.)
government consumption: 19.4% (2017 est.)
investment in fixed capital: 2.7% (2017 est.)
investment in inventories: 1.3% (2016 est.)
exports of goods and services: 38.8% (2017 est.)
imports of goods and services: -33.8% (2017 est.)

Agricultural products: potatoes, watermelons, tomatoes, onions, dates, milk, olives, wheat, poultry, vegetables

Industries: petroleum, petrochemicals, aluminum, iron and steel, food processing, textiles, handicrafts, cement

Industrial production growth rate: 60.3% (2017 est.)

Labor force: 1.114 million (2017 est.)

Labor force - by occupation: *agriculture:* 17%
industry: 23%
services: 59% (2004 est.)

Unemployment rate: 30% (2004 est.)

Unemployment, youth ages 15-24: *total:* 48.7%
male: 40.8%
female: 67.8% (2012 est.)

Population below poverty line: *note:* about one-third of Libyans live at or below the national poverty line

Budget: *revenues:* 15.78 billion (2017 est.)
expenditures: 23.46 billion (2017 est.)

Budget surplus (+) or deficit (-): -25.1% (of GDP) (2017 est.)

Public debt: 4.7% of GDP (2017 est.)
7.5% of GDP (2016 est.)

Taxes and other revenues: 51.6% (of GDP) (2017 est.)

Fiscal year: calendar year

Current account balance: $2.574 billion (2017 est.)
-$4.575 billion (2016 est.)

Exports: $29.96 billion (2018 est.) note: data are in current year dollars
$11.99 billion (2016 est.)

Exports - partners: Italy 18%, China 16%, Germany 15%, Spain 15%, United Arab Emirates 6%, France 6%, United States 5% (2019)

Exports - commodities: crude petroleum, natural gas, gold, refined petroleum, scrap iron (2019)

Imports: $18.85 billion (2018 est.) note: data are in current year dollars
$8.667 billion (2016 est.)

Imports - partners: China 16%, Turkey 14%, Italy 9%, United Arab Emirates 9%, Egypt 5% (2019)

Imports - commodities: refined petroleum, cars, broadcasting equipment, cigarettes, jewelry (2019)

Reserves of foreign exchange and gold: $74.71 billion (31 December 2017 est.)
$66.05 billion (31 December 2016 est.)

Debt - external: $3.02 billion (31 December 2017 est.)
$3.116 billion (31 December 2016 est.)

Exchange rates: Libyan dinars (LYD) per US dollar -
1.413 (2017 est.)
1.3904 (2016 est.)
1.3904 (2015 est.)
1.379 (2014 est.)
1.2724 (2013 est.)

ENERGY

Electricity access: *electrification - total population:* 100% (2019)

Electricity: *installed generating capacity:* 10.516 million kW (2020 est.)
consumption: 25,360,340,000 kWh (2019 est.)
exports: 0 kWh (2019 est.)
imports: 465 million kWh (2019 est.)
transmission/distribution losses: 6.801 billion kWh (2019 est.)

Electricity generation sources: *fossil fuels:* 100% of total installed capacity (2020 est.)

Petroleum: *total petroleum production:* 1,252,800 bbl/day (2021 est.)
refined petroleum consumption: 219,700 bbl/day (2019 est.)
crude oil and lease condensate exports: 1,067,400 bbl/day (2018 est.)
crude oil and lease condensate imports: 0 bbl/day (2018 est.)
crude oil estimated reserves: 48.363 billion barrels (2021 est.)

Refined petroleum products - production: 89,620 bbl/day (2015 est.)

Refined petroleum products - exports: 16,880 bbl/day (2015 est.)

Refined petroleum products - imports: 168,200 bbl/day (2015 est.)

Natural gas: *production:* 12,414,736,000 cubic meters (2020 est.)
consumption: 7,669,690,000 cubic meters (2019 est.)
exports: 4,441,150,000 cubic meters (2020 est.)
imports: 0 cubic meters (2021 est.)
proven reserves: 1,504,868,000,000 cubic meters (2021 est.)

Carbon dioxide emissions: 38.297 million metric tonnes of CO_2 (2019 est.)
from petroleum and other liquids: 30.018 million metric tonnes of CO_2 (2019 est.)
from consumed natural gas: 8.279 million metric tonnes of CO_2 (2019 est.)

Energy consumption per capita: 107.118 million Btu/person (2019 est.)

COMMUNICATIONS

Telephones - fixed lines: *total subscriptions:* 1.576 million (2020 est.)
subscriptions per 100 inhabitants: 23 (2020 est.)

Telephones - mobile cellular: *total subscriptions:* 2.922 million (2020 est.)
subscriptions per 100 inhabitants: 43 (2020 est.)

Telecommunication systems: *general assessment:* political and security instability in Libya has disrupted its telecom sector; much of its infrastructure remains superior to that in most other African countries; rival operators fight for control; investment in fiber backbone and upgrades to international cables; limited LTE and 5G service; some satellite broadband; in 2021 Libya signed deals and projects with US firms to upgrade portions of its infrastructure, increasing the diversity of its telecommunications networks (2022)
domestic: nearly 23 per 100 fixed-line and over 43 per 100 mobile-cellular subscriptions; service generally adequate (2020)
international: country code - 218; landing points for LFON, EIG, Italy-Libya, Silphium and Tobrok-Emasaed submarine cable system connecting Europe, Africa, the Middle East and Asia; satellite earth stations - 4 Intelsat, Arabsat, and Intersputnik; microwave radio relay to Tunisia and Egypt; tropospheric scatter to Greece; participant in Medarabtel (2019)

Broadcast media: state-funded and private TV stations; some provinces operate local TV stations; pan-Arab satellite TV stations are available; state-funded radio (2019)

Internet country code: .ly

Internet users: *total:* 1,491,040 (2019 est.)
percent of population: 22% (2019 est.)

Broadband - fixed subscriptions: *total:* 332,000 (2020 est.)
subscriptions per 100 inhabitants: 5 (2020 est.)

TRANSPORTATION

National air transport system: *number of registered air carriers:* 9 (2020)
inventory of registered aircraft operated by air carriers: 55
annual passenger traffic on registered air carriers: 927,153 (2018)

Civil aircraft registration country code prefix: 5A

Airports: *total:* 146 (2021)

Airports - with paved runways: *total:* 68
over 3,047 m: 23
2,438 to 3,047 m: 7
1,524 to 2,437 m: 30
914 to 1,523 m: 7
under 914 m: 1 (2021)

Airports - with unpaved runways: *total:* 78
over 3,047 m: 2
2,438 to 3,047 m: 5
1,524 to 2,437 m: 14
914 to 1,523 m: 37
under 914 m: 20 (2021)

Heliports: 2 (2021)

Pipelines: 882 km condensate, 3,743 km gas, 7,005 km oil (2013)

Roadways: *total:* 37,000 km (2010)
paved: 34,000 km (2010)
unpaved: 3,000 km (2010)

Merchant marine: *total:* 94
by type: general cargo 2, oil tanker 12, other 80 (2021)

Ports and terminals: *major seaport(s):* Marsa al Burayqah (Marsa el Brega), Tripoli
oil terminal(s): Az Zawiyah, Ra's Lanuf

LNG terminal(s) (export): Marsa el Brega

MILITARY AND SECURITY

Military and security forces: Libya lacks a nationwide military and the interim government, the Government of National Unity (GNU), relies on its cooperation with disparate militias that it cannot entirely control for security; the GNU has a ministry of defense and access to various ground, air, and naval/coast guard forces comprised of a mix of semi-regular military units, militias, civilian volunteers, and foreign troops and mercenaries

the Libyan National Army (LNA), under de facto LNA commander Khalifa HAFTER, also includes various ground, air, and naval units comprised of semi-regular military personnel, militias, and foreign troops and mercenaries; as of 2022, the LNA operated independently from the GNU and exerted influence throughout eastern, central, and southern Libya (2022)
note 1: the Stabilization Support Authority (SSA) is a state-funded militia established in January 2021 by the GNU; it is tasked with securing government buildings and officials, participating in combat operations, apprehending those suspected of national security crimes, and cooperating with other security bodies
note 2: the national police force under the Ministry of Interior oversees internal security (with support from military forces under the Ministry of Defense), but much of Libya's security-related police work generally falls to informal armed groups, which received government salaries but lacked formal training, supervision, or consistent accountability

Military expenditures: not available

Military and security service personnel strengths: estimates not available

Military equipment inventories and acquisitions: both the forces aligned with the GNU and the LNA are largely equipped with weapons of Russian or Soviet origin; as of 2021, Turkey was the top provider of arms and equipment to the forces supporting the GNU, while the United Arab Emirates was the main supporter of the LNA (2021)

Military service age and obligation: not available

Military - note: Turkey has been the primary backer of the GNU/GNA; Turkish military advisers have trained and assisted western/GNU Libyan forces in accordance with a 2019 Turkey-GNA security agreement; Turkey has also provided thousands of Syrian mercenaries to Libya, as well as ammunition, weapons and aerial drones; Russia, the United Arab Emirates, and Egypt have been the main supporters of the LNA; the LNA has used fighters from other countries, including Chad, Sudan, and Syria

as of 2022, ISIS continued to maintain a relatively weak presence in Libya with small bands of fighters operating out of ungoverned spaces and conducting small-scale attacks throughout the country (2022)

TERRORISM

Terrorist group(s): Ansar al-Sharia groups; Islamic State of Iraq and ash-Sham - Libya (ISIS-L); al-Mulathamun Battalion (al-Mourabitoun); al-Qa'ida in the Islamic Maghreb (AQIM)

TRANSNATIONAL ISSUES

Disputes - international: *Libya-Algeria:* dormant disputes include Libyan claims of about 32,000 sq km still reflected on its maps of southeastern Algeria
Libya-Chad: various Chadian rebels from the Aozou region reside in southern Libya; Libyan forces clashed with Chadian rebels in September 2021
Libya-Egypt: none identified
Libya-Niger: the boundary is poorly defined but has never been disputed by either country
Libya-Sudan: none identified
Libya-Tunisia: none identified

Refugees and internally displaced persons: *refugees (country of origin):* 18,322 (Sudan) (refugees and asylum seekers), 15,325 (Syria) (refugees and asylum seekers), 5,004 (Eritrea) (2022)
IDPs: 159,996 (conflict between pro-QADHAFI and anti-QADHAFI forces in 2011; post-QADHAFI tribal clashes 2014) (2022)

LIECHTENSTEIN

INTRODUCTION

Background: The Principality of Liechtenstein was established within the Holy Roman Empire in 1719. Occupied by both French and Russian troops during the Napoleonic Wars, it became a sovereign state in 1806 and joined the German Confederation in 1815. Liechtenstein became fully independent in 1866 when the Confederation dissolved. Until the end of World War I, it was closely tied to Austria, but the economic devastation caused by that conflict forced Liechtenstein to enter into a customs and monetary union with Switzerland. Since World War II (in which Liechtenstein remained neutral), the country's low taxes have spurred outstanding economic growth. In 2000, shortcomings in banking regulatory oversight resulted in concerns about the use of financial institutions for money laundering. However, Liechtenstein implemented anti-money laundering legislation and a Mutual Legal Assistance Treaty with the US that went into effect in 2003.

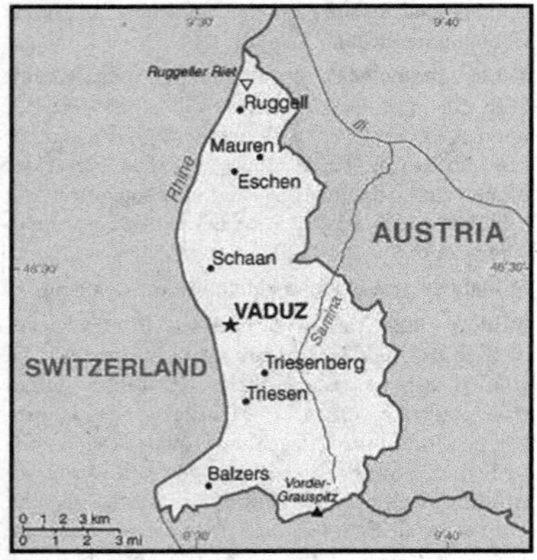

GEOGRAPHY

Location: Central Europe, between Austria and Switzerland

Geographic coordinates: 47 16 N, 9 32 E

Map references: Europe

Area: *total:* 160 sq km
land: 160 sq km
water: 0 sq km

Area - comparative: about 0.9 times the size of Washington, DC

Land boundaries: *total:* 75 km
border countries (2): Austria 34 km; Switzerland 41 km

Coastline: 0 km (doubly landlocked)

Maritime claims: none (landlocked)

Climate: continental; cold, cloudy winters with frequent snow or rain; cool to moderately warm, cloudy, humid summers

Terrain: mostly mountainous (Alps) with Rhine Valley in western third

Elevation: *highest point:* Vorder-Grauspitz 2,599 m
lowest point: Ruggeller Riet 430 m

Natural resources: hydroelectric potential, arable land

Land use: *agricultural land:* 37.6% (2018 est.)
arable land: 18.8% (2018 est.)
permanent crops: 0% (2018 est.)
permanent pasture: 18.8% (2018 est.)
forest: 43.1% (2018 est.)
other: 19.3% (2018 est.)

Irrigated land: 0 sq km (2012)

Major watersheds (area sq km): Atlantic Ocean drainage: Rhine-Maas (198,735 sq km)

Population distribution: most of the population is found in the western half of the country along the Rhine River

Natural hazards: avalanches, landslides

Geography - note: along with Uzbekistan, one of only two doubly landlocked countries in the world; variety of microclimatic variations based on elevation

PEOPLE AND SOCIETY

Population: 39,711 (2022 est.)
note: immigrants make up 67% of the total population, according to UN data (2019)

Nationality: *noun:* Liechtensteiner(s)
adjective: Liechtenstein

Ethnic groups: Liechtensteiner 65.5%, Swiss 9.6%, Austrian 6%, German 4.5%, Italian 3.1%, other 11.4% (2020 est.)
note: data represent population by nationality

Languages: German 91.5% (official) (Alemannic is the main dialect), Italian 1.5%, Turkish 1.3%, Portuguese 1.1%, other 4.6% (2015 est.)
major-language sample(s): Das World Factbook, die unverzichtbare Quelle für grundlegende Informationen. (German)

Religions: Roman Catholic (official) 73.4%, Protestant Reformed 6.3%, Muslim 5.9%, Christian Orthodox 1.3%, Lutheran 1.2%, other Protestant 0.7%, other Christian 0.3%, other 0.8%, none 7%, unspecified 3.3% (2015 est.)

Age structure: *0-14 years:* 15.2% (male 3,259/female 2,688)
15-24 years: 11.29% (male 2,238/female 2,181)
25-54 years: 40.22% (male 7,869/female 7,872)
55-64 years: 14.41% (male 2,711/female 2,930)
65 years and over: 18.88% (male 3,403/female 3,986) (2020 est.)

Median age: *total:* 43.7 years
male: 42 years
female: 45.3 years (2020 est.)

Population growth rate: 0.72% (2022 est.)

Birth rate: 10.32 births/1,000 population (2022 est.)

Death rate: 7.98 deaths/1,000 population (2022 est.)

Net migration rate: 4.81 migrant(s)/1,000 population (2022 est.)

Population distribution: most of the population is found in the western half of the country along the Rhine River

Urbanization: *urban population:* 14.5% of total population (2022)
rate of urbanization: 1.15% annual rate of change (2020-25 est.)

Major urban areas - population: 5,000 VADUZ (capital) (2018)

Sex ratio: *at birth:* 1.25 male(s)/female
0-14 years: 1.24 male(s)/female
15-24 years: 1.04 male(s)/female
25-54 years: 1 male(s)/female
55-64 years: 0.92 male(s)/female
65 years and over: 0.69 male(s)/female
total population: 0.99 male(s)/female (2022 est.)

Mother's mean age at first birth: 31.3 years (2017)

Infant mortality rate: *total:* 4.05 deaths/1,000 live births
male: 4.41 deaths/1,000 live births
female: 3.59 deaths/1,000 live births (2022 est.)

Life expectancy at birth: *total population:* 82.56 years
male: 80.33 years
female: 85.38 years (2022 est.)

Total fertility rate: 1.69 children born/woman (2022 est.)

Education expenditures: 2.6% of GDP (2011 est.)

School life expectancy (primary to tertiary education): *total:* 15 years
male: 16 years
female: 14 years (2019)

ENVIRONMENT

Environment - current issues: some air pollution generated locally, some carried over from surrounding countries

Environment - international agreements: *party to:* Air Pollution, Air Pollution-Heavy Metals, Air Pollution-Nitrogen Oxides, Air Pollution-Persistent Organic Pollutants, Air Pollution-Sulphur 85, Air Pollution-Sulphur 94, Air Pollution-Volatile Organic Compounds, Biodiversity, Climate Change, Climate Change-Kyoto Protocol, Climate Change-Paris Agreement, Comprehensive Nuclear Test Ban, Desertification, Endangered Species, Hazardous Wastes, Ozone Layer Protection, Wetlands
signed, but not ratified: Air Pollution-Multi-effect Protocol, Law of the Sea

Air pollutants: *carbon dioxide emissions:* 0.05 megatons (2016 est.)
methane emissions: 0.02 megatons (2020 est.)

Climate: continental; cold, cloudy winters with frequent snow or rain; cool to moderately warm, cloudy, humid summers

Land use: *agricultural land:* 37.6% (2018 est.)
arable land: 18.8% (2018 est.)
permanent crops: 0% (2018 est.)
permanent pasture: 18.8% (2018 est.)
forest: 43.1% (2018 est.)
other: 19.3% (2018 est.)

Urbanization: *urban population:* 14.5% of total population (2022)
rate of urbanization: 1.15% annual rate of change (2020-25 est.)

Revenue from forest resources: *forest revenues:* 0% of GDP (2017 est.)

Waste and recycling: *municipal solid waste generated annually:* 32,382 tons (2015 est.)
municipal solid waste recycled annually: 20,919 tons (2015 est.)
percent of municipal solid waste recycled: 64.6% (2015 est.)

Major watersheds (area sq km): Atlantic Ocean drainage: Rhine-Maas (198,735 sq km)

Total water withdrawal: *municipal:* 7.9 million cubic meters (2017 est.)

Total renewable water resources: 0 cubic meters (2017 est.)

GOVERNMENT

Country name: *conventional long form:* Principality of Liechtenstein
conventional short form: Liechtenstein
local long form: Fuerstentum Liechtenstein
local short form: Liechtenstein
etymology: named after the Liechtenstein dynasty that purchased and united the counties of Schellenburg and Vaduz and that was allowed by the Holy Roman Emperor in 1719 to rename the new property after their family; the name in German means "light (bright) stone"

Government type: constitutional monarchy

Capital: *name:* Vaduz
geographic coordinates: 47 08 N, 9 31 E
time difference: UTC+1 (6 hours ahead of Washington, DC, during Standard Time)
daylight saving time: +1hr, begins last Sunday in March; ends last Sunday in October

etymology: may be a conflation from the Latin *vallis* (valley) and the High German *diutisk* (meaning "German") to produce *Valdutsch* ("German valley"), which over time simplified and came to refer specifically to Vaduz, the town

Administrative divisions: 11 communes (Gemeinden, singular - Gemeinde); Balzers, Eschen, Gamprin, Mauren, Planken, Ruggell, Schaan, Schellenberg, Triesen, Triesenberg, Vaduz

Independence: 23 January 1719 (Principality of Liechtenstein established); 12 July 1806 (independence from the Holy Roman Empire); 24 August 1866 (independence from the German Confederation)

National holiday: National Day, 15 August (1940); note - a National Day was originally established in 1940 to combine celebrations for the Feast of the Assumption (15 August) with those honoring the birthday of former Prince FRANZ JOSEF II (1906-1989) whose birth fell on 16 August; after the prince's death, National Day became the official national holiday by law in 1990

Constitution: *history:* previous 1862; latest adopted 5 October 1921
amendments: proposed by Parliament, by the reigning prince (in the form of "Government" proposals), by petition of at least 1,500 qualified voters, or by at least four communes; passage requires unanimous approval of Parliament members in one sitting or three-quarters majority vote in two successive sittings; referendum required only if petitioned by at least 1,500 voters or by at least four communes; passage by referendum requires absolute majority of votes cast; amended many times, last in 2020

Legal system: civil law system influenced by Swiss, Austrian, and German law

International law organization participation: accepts compulsory ICJ jurisdiction with reservations; accepts ICCt jurisdiction

Citizenship: *citizenship by birth:* no
citizenship by descent only: the father must be a citizen of Liechtenstein; in the case of a child born out of wedlock, the mother must be a citizen
dual citizenship recognized: no
residency requirement for naturalization: 5 years

Suffrage: 18 years of age; universal

Executive branch: *chief of state:* Prince HANS-ADAM II (since 13 November 1989, assumed executive powers on 26 August 1984); Heir Apparent and Regent of Liechtenstein Prince ALOIS (son of the monarch, born 11 June 1968); note - 15 August 2004, HANS-ADAM II transferred the official duties of the ruling prince to ALOIS, but HANS-ADAM II retains status of chief of state
head of government: Prime Minister Daniel RISCH; Deputy Prime Minister Sabine MONAUNI (both since 25 March 2021)
cabinet: Cabinet elected by the Parliament, confirmed by the monarch
elections/appointments: the monarchy is hereditary; following legislative elections, the leader of the majority party in the Parliament usually appointed the head of government by the monarch, and the leader of the largest minority party in the Landtag usually appointed the deputy head of government by the monarch if there is a coalition government

Legislative branch: *description:* unicameral Parliament or Landtag (25 seats; members directly elected in 2 multi-seat constituencies by open-list proportional representation vote to serve 4-year terms)
elections:
last held on 7 February 2021 (next to be held on 7 February 2025)
election results:
percent of vote by party - FBP 40%, VU 40%, FL 12%, DpL 8%; seats by party - FBP 10, VU 10, FL 3, DpL 2; composition - men 18, women 7, percent of women 28%

Judicial branch: *highest court(s):* Supreme Court or Oberster Gerichtshof (consists of 5 judges); Constitutional Court or Verfassungsgericht (consists of 5 judges and 5 alternates)
judge selection and term of office: judges of both courts elected by the Landtag and appointed by the monarch; Supreme Court judges serve 4-year renewable terms; Constitutional Court judges appointed for renewable 5-year terms
subordinate courts: Court of Appeal or Obergericht (second instance), Court of Justice (first instance), Administrative Court, county courts

Political parties and leaders: Democrats for Liechtenstein (Demokraten pro Liechtenstein) or DpL [Thomas REHAK]
Fatherland Union (Vaterlaendische Union) or VU [Guenther FRITZ]
Progressive Citizens' Party (Fortschrittliche Buergerpartei) or FBP [Thomas BANZER]
The Free List (Die Freie Liste) or FL [Pepo FRICK and Conny BUECHEL BRUEHWILER]
The Independents (Die Unabhaengigen) or DU [Harald "Harry" QUADERER]

International organization participation: CD, CE, EBRD, EFTA, IAEA, ICCt, ICRM, IFRCS, Interpol, IOC, IPU, ITSO, ITU, ITUC (NGOs), OAS (observer), OPCW, OSCE, PCA, Schengen Convention, UN, UNCTAD, UPU, WIPO, WTO

Diplomatic representation in the US: *chief of mission:* Ambassador Georg SPARBER (since 1 December 2021)
chancery: 2900 K Street NW, Suite 602B, Washington, DC 20007
telephone: [1] (202) 331-0590
FAX: [1] (202) 331-3221
email address and website:
info@embassyli.org
https://www.liechtensteinusa.org/

Diplomatic representation from the US: *embassy:* the US does not have an embassy in Liechtenstein; the US Ambassador to Switzerland is accredited to Liechtenstein

Flag description: two equal horizontal bands of blue (top) and red with a gold crown on the hoist side of the blue band; the colors may derive from the blue and red livery design used in the principality's household in the 18th century; the prince's crown was introduced in 1937 to distinguish the flag from that of Haiti

National symbol(s): princely hat (crown); national colors: blue, red

National anthem: *name:* "Oben am jungen Rhein" (High Above the Young Rhine)
lyrics/music: Jakob Joseph JAUCH/Josef FROMMELT
note: adopted 1850, revised 1963; uses the tune of "God Save the King"

ECONOMY

Economic overview: Despite its small size and lack of natural resources, Liechtenstein has developed into a prosperous, highly industrialized, free-enterprise economy with a vital financial services sector and one of the highest per capita income levels in the world. The Liechtenstein economy is widely diversified with a large number of small and medium-sized businesses, particularly in the services sector. Low business taxes - a flat tax of 12.5% on income is applied - and easy incorporation rules have induced many holding companies to establish nominal offices in Liechtenstein, providing 30% of state revenues.

The country participates in a customs union with Switzerland and uses the Swiss franc as its national currency. It imports more than 90% of its energy requirements. Liechtenstein has been a member of the European Economic Area (an organization serving as a bridge between the European Free Trade Association and the EU) since May 1995. The government is working to harmonize its economic policies with those of an integrated EU. As of 2015, 54% of Liechtenstein's workforce consisted of cross-border commuters, largely from Austria, Germany, and Switzerland.

Since 2008, Liechtenstein has faced renewed international pressure - particularly from Germany and the US - to improve transparency in its banking and tax systems. In December 2008, Liechtenstein signed a Tax Information Exchange Agreement with the US. Upon Liechtenstein's conclusion of 12 bilateral information-sharing agreements, the OECD in October 2009 removed the principality from its "grey list" of countries that had yet to implement the organization's Model Tax Convention. By the end of 2010, Liechtenstein had signed 25 Tax Information Exchange Agreements or Double Tax Agreements. In 2011, Liechtenstein joined the Schengen area, which allows passport-free travel across 26 European countries. In 2015, Liechtenstein and the EU agreed to clamp down on tax fraud and evasion and in 2018 will start automatically exchanging information on the bank accounts of each other's residents.

Real GDP (purchasing power parity): $4.978 billion (2014 est.)
$3.2 billion (2009 est.)
$3.216 billion (2008 est.)

Real GDP growth rate: 1.8% (2012 est.)
-0.5% (2011 est.)
3.1% (2007 est.)

Real GDP per capita: $139,100 (2009 est.)
$90,100 (2008 est.)
$91,300 (2007 est.)

GDP (official exchange rate): $6.672 billion (2014 est.)

Inflation rate (consumer prices): -0.4% (2016 est.)
-0.2% (2013)

Credit ratings:

Standard & Poors rating: AAA (1996)
note: The year refers to the year in which the current credit rating was first obtained.

GDP - composition, by sector of origin: *agriculture:* 7% (2014)
industry: 41% (2014)
services: 52% (2014)

Agricultural products: wheat, barley, corn, potatoes; livestock, dairy products

Industries: electronics, metal manufacturing, dental products, ceramics, pharmaceuticals, food products, precision instruments, tourism, optical instruments

Labor force: 38,520 (2015 est.) (2012)
note: 51% of the labor force in Liechtenstein commute daily from Austria, Switzerland, and Germany

Labor force - by occupation: *agriculture:* 0.8%
industry: 36.9%
services: 62.3% (2015)

Unemployment rate: 2.4% (2015)
2.4% (2014)

Budget: *revenues:* 995.3 million (2012 est.)
expenditures: 890.4 million (2011 est.)

Budget surplus (+) or deficit (-): 1.6% (of GDP) (2012 est.)

Taxes and other revenues: 14.9% (of GDP) (2012 est.)

Fiscal year: calendar year

Exports: $3.217 billion (2015 est.)
$3.774 billion (2014 est.)
note: trade data exclude trade with Switzerland

Exports - commodities: small specialty machinery, connectors for audio and video, parts for motor vehicles, dental products, hardware, prepared foodstuffs, electronic equipment, optical products

Imports: $2.23 billion (2014 est.)
note: trade data exclude trade with Switzerland

Imports - commodities: agricultural products, raw materials, energy products, machinery, metal goods, textiles, foodstuffs, motor vehicles

Debt - external: $0 (2015 est.)
note: public external debt only; private external debt unavailable

Exchange rates: Swiss francs (CHF) per US dollar -
0.9875 (2017 est.)
0.9852 (2016 est.)
0.9852 (2015 est.)
0.9627 (2014 est.)
0.9152 (2013 est.)

ENERGY

Electricity access: *electrification - total population:* 100% (2020)

COMMUNICATIONS

Telephones - fixed lines: *total subscriptions:* 12,607 (2020 est.)
subscriptions per 100 inhabitants: 33 (2020 est.)

Telephones - mobile cellular: *total subscriptions:* 48,887 (2020 est.)
subscriptions per 100 inhabitants: 128 (2020 est.)

Telecommunication systems: *general assessment:* automatic telephone system; 44 Internet service providers in Liechtenstein and Switzerland combined; FttP (fiber to the home) penetration marketed 3rd highest in EU; fiber network reaches 3/4 of the population (2020)
domestic: fixed-line roughly 33 per 100 and mobile-cellular services 128 per 100 (2020)
international: country code - 423; linked to Swiss networks by cable and microwave radio relay

Broadcast media: relies on foreign terrestrial and satellite broadcasters for most broadcast media services; first Liechtenstein-based TV station established August 2008; Radio Liechtenstein operates multiple radio stations; a Swiss-based broadcaster operates one radio station in Liechtenstein

Internet country code: .li

Internet users: *total:* 37,260 (2019 est.)
percent of population: 98% (2019 est.)

Broadband - fixed subscriptions: *total:* 18,050 (2020 est.)
subscriptions per 100 inhabitants: 47 (2020 est.)

TRANSPORTATION

Civil aircraft registration country code prefix: HB

Pipelines: 434.5 km gas (2018)

Railways: *total:* 9 km (2018)
standard gauge: 9 km (2018) 1.435-m gauge (electrified)
note: belongs to the Austrian Railway System connecting Austria and Switzerland

Roadways: *total:* 630 km (2019)

Waterways: 28 km (2010)

Merchant marine: *total:* 20
by type: bulk carrier 16, general cargo 1, other 3 (includes Switzerland) (2021)

MILITARY AND SECURITY

Military and security forces: no regular military forces; the National Police is responsible for all matters relating to the safety and security of Liechtenstein

TRANSNATIONAL ISSUES

Disputes - international: none

Illicit drugs: has strengthened money laundering controls, but money laundering remains a concern due to Liechtenstein's sophisticated offshore financial services sector

LITHUANIA

INTRODUCTION

Background: Lithuanian lands were united under MINDAUGAS in 1236; over the next century, through alliances and conquest, Lithuania extended its territory to include most of present-day Belarus and Ukraine. By the end of the 14th century Lithuania was the largest state in Europe. An alliance with Poland in 1386 led the two countries into a union through the person of a common ruler. In 1569, Lithuania and Poland formally united into a single dual state, the Polish-Lithuanian Commonwealth. This entity survived until 1795 when its remnants were partitioned by surrounding countries. Lithuania regained its independence following World War I but was annexed by the USSR in 1940 - an action never recognized by the US and many other countries. On 11 March 1990, Lithuania became the first of the Soviet republics to declare its independence, but Moscow did not recognize this proclamation until September of 1991 (following the abortive coup in Moscow). The last Russian troops withdrew in 1993. Lithuania subsequently restructured its economy for integration into Western European institutions; it joined both NATO and the EU in the spring of 2004. In 2015, Lithuania joined the euro zone, and it joined the Organization for Economic Cooperation and Development in 2018.

GEOGRAPHY

Location: Eastern Europe, bordering the Baltic Sea, between Latvia and Russia, west of Belarus

Geographic coordinates: 56 00 N, 24 00 E

Map references: Europe

Area: *total:* 65,300 sq km
land: 62,680 sq km
water: 2,620 sq km

Area - comparative: slightly larger than West Virginia

Land boundaries: *total:* 1,545 km
border countries (4): Belarus 640 km; Latvia 544 km; Poland 100 km; Russia (Kaliningrad) 261 km

Coastline: 90 km

Maritime claims: *territorial sea:* 12 nm

Climate: transitional, between maritime and continental; wet, moderate winters and summers

Terrain: lowland, many scattered small lakes, fertile soil

Elevation: *highest point:* Aukstojas 294 m
lowest point: Baltic Sea 0 m
mean elevation: 110 m

Natural resources: peat, arable land, amber

Land use: *agricultural land:* 44.8% (2018 est.)
arable land: 34.9% (2018 est.)
permanent crops: 0.5% (2018 est.)
permanent pasture: 9.4% (2018 est.)
forest: 34.6% (2018 est.)
other: 20.6% (2018 est.)

Irrigated land: 44 sq km (2012)

Major lakes (area sq km): *salt water lake(s):* Curonian Lagoon (shared with Russia) - 1,620 sq km

Population distribution: fairly even population distribution throughout the country, but somewhat greater concentrations in the southern cities of Vilnius and Kaunas, and the western port of Klaipeda

Natural hazards: occasional floods, droughts

Geography - note: fertile central plains are separated by hilly uplands that are ancient glacial deposits

PEOPLE AND SOCIETY

Population: 2,683,546 (2022 est.)

Nationality: *noun:* Lithuanian(s)
adjective: Lithuanian

Ethnic groups: Lithuanian 84.6%, Polish 6.5%, Russian 5%, Belarusian 1%, other 1.1%, unspecified 1.8% (2021 est.)

Languages: Lithuanian (official) 85.3%, Russian 6.8%, Polish 5.1%, other 1.1%, two mother tongues 1.7% (2021 est.)
major-language sample(s): Pasaulio enciklopedija – naudingas bendrosios informacijos šaltinis. (Lithuanian)

Religions: Roman Catholic 74.2%, Russian Orthodox 3.7%, Old Believer 0.6%, Evangelical Lutheran 0.6%, Evangelical Reformist 0.2%, other (including Sunni Muslim, Jewish, Greek Catholic, and Karaite) 0.9%, none 6.1%, unspecified 13.7% (2021 est.)

Age structure: *0-14 years:* 15.26% (male 213,802/female 202,948)
15-24 years: 10.23% (male 144,679/female 134,822)
25-54 years: 38.96% (male 528,706/female 535,485)
55-64 years: 15.1% (male 183,854/female 228,585)
65 years and over: 20.45% (male 190,025/female 368,558) (2020 est.)

Dependency ratios: *total dependency ratio:* 56.5
youth dependency ratio: 24.2
elderly dependency ratio: 32.3
potential support ratio: 3.1 (2020 est.)

Median age: *total:* 44.5 years
male: 40.2 years
female: 48.2 years (2020 est.)

Population growth rate: -1.04% (2022 est.)

Birth rate: 9.26 births/1,000 population (2022 est.)

Death rate: 15.12 deaths/1,000 population (2022 est.)

Net migration rate: -4.54 migrant(s)/1,000 population (2022 est.)

Population distribution: fairly even population distribution throughout the country, but somewhat greater concentrations in the southern cities of Vilnius and Kaunas, and the western port of Klaipeda

Urbanization: *urban population:* 68.5% of total population (2022)
rate of urbanization: -0.12% annual rate of change (2020-25 est.)

Major urban areas - population: 541,000 VILNIUS (capital) (2022)

Sex ratio: *at birth:* 1.06 male(s)/female
0-14 years: 1.05 male(s)/female
15-24 years: 1.07 male(s)/female
25-54 years: 1 male(s)/female
55-64 years: 0.81 male(s)/female
65 years and over: 0.45 male(s)/female
total population: 0.86 male(s)/female (2022 est.)

Mother's mean age at first birth: 28.2 years (2020 est.)

Maternal mortality ratio: 5 deaths/100,000 live births (2017 est.)

Infant mortality rate: *total:* 3.63 deaths/1,000 live births
male: 4.09 deaths/1,000 live births
female: 3.15 deaths/1,000 live births (2022 est.)

Life expectancy at birth: *total population:* 75.78 years
male: 70.42 years
female: 81.44 years (2022 est.)

Total fertility rate: 1.61 children born/woman (2022 est.)

Drinking water source: *improved: urban:* 100% of population
rural: 93.8% of population
total: 98% of population
unimproved: urban: 0% of population
rural: 6.2% of population
total: 2% of population (2020 est.)

Current health expenditure: 7% of GDP (2019)

Physicians density: 5.08 physicians/1,000 population (2020)

Hospital bed density: 6.4 beds/1,000 population (2018)

Sanitation facility access: *improved: urban:* 99.5% of population
rural: 88.7% of population
total: 96% of population
unimproved: urban: 0.5% of population
rural: 11.3% of population
total: 4% of population (2020 est.)

HIV/AIDS - adult prevalence rate: 0.1% (2019 est.)

Major infectious diseases: *degree of risk:* intermediate (2020)
vectorborne diseases: tickborne encephalitis

Obesity - adult prevalence rate: 26.3% (2016)

Alcohol consumption per capita: *total:* 11.93 liters of pure alcohol (2019 est.)
beer: 4.61 liters of pure alcohol (2019 est.)
wine: 0.88 liters of pure alcohol (2019 est.)
spirits: 4.96 liters of pure alcohol (2019 est.)
other alcohols: 1.48 liters of pure alcohol (2019 est.)

Tobacco use: *total:* 32% (2020 est.)
male: 42.1% (2020 est.)
female: 21.8% (2020 est.)

Education expenditures: 3.9% of GDP (2018 est.)

Literacy: *definition:* age 15 and over can read and write
total population: 99.8%
male: 99.8%
female: 99.8% (2015)

School life expectancy (primary to tertiary education): *total:* 16 years
male: 16 years
female: 17 years (2019)

Unemployment, youth ages 15-24: *total:* 19.6%
male: 21.5%
female: 17.3% (2020 est.)

ENVIRONMENT

Environment - current issues: water pollution; air pollution; deforestation; threatened animal and plant species; chemicals and waste materials released into the environment contaminate soil and groundwater; soil degradation and erosion

Environment - international agreements: *party to:* Air Pollution, Air Pollution-Heavy Metals, Air Pollution-Multi-effect Protocol, Air Pollution-Nitrogen Oxides, Air Pollution-Persistent Organic Pollutants, Air Pollution-Sulphur 85, Air Pollution-Sulphur 94, Air Pollution-Volatile Organic Compounds, Biodiversity, Climate Change, Climate Change-Kyoto Protocol, Climate Change-Paris Agreement, Comprehensive Nuclear Test Ban, Desertification, Endangered Species, Environmental Modification, Hazardous Wastes, Law of the Sea, Ozone Layer Protection, Ship Pollution, Tropical Timber 2006, Wetlands, Whaling
signed, but not ratified: none of the selected agreements

Air pollutants: *particulate matter emissions:* 11.49 micrograms per cubic meter (2016 est.)
carbon dioxide emissions: 12.96 megatons (2016 est.)
methane emissions: 3.15 megatons (2020 est.)

Climate: transitional, between maritime and continental; wet, moderate winters and summers

Land use: *agricultural land:* 44.8% (2018 est.)
arable land: 34.9% (2018 est.)
permanent crops: 0.5% (2018 est.)
permanent pasture: 9.4% (2018 est.)
forest: 34.6% (2018 est.)
other: 20.6% (2018 est.)

Urbanization: *urban population:* 68.5% of total population (2022)
rate of urbanization: -0.12% annual rate of change (2020-25 est.)

Revenue from forest resources: *forest revenues:* 0.31% of GDP (2018 est.)

Revenue from coal: *coal revenues:* 0% of GDP (2018 est.)

Waste and recycling: *municipal solid waste generated annually:* 1.3 million tons (2015 est.)
municipal solid waste recycled annually: 297,960 tons (2015 est.)
percent of municipal solid waste recycled: 22.9% (2015 est.)

Major lakes (area sq km): *salt water lake(s):* Curonian Lagoon (shared with Russia) - 1,620 sq km

Total water withdrawal: *municipal:* 130.4 million cubic meters (2017 est.)
industrial: 69.7 million cubic meters (2017 est.)
agricultural: 58.9 million cubic meters (2017 est.)

Total renewable water resources: 24.5 billion cubic meters (2017 est.)

GOVERNMENT

Country name: *conventional long form:* Republic of Lithuania
conventional short form: Lithuania
local long form: Lietuvos Respublika
local short form: Lietuva
former: Lithuanian Soviet Socialist Republic (while occupied by the USSR)
etymology: meaning of the name "Lietuva" remains unclear and is debated by scholars; it may derive from the Lietava, a stream in east central Lithuania

Government type: semi-presidential republic

Capital: *name:* Vilnius
geographic coordinates: 54 41 N, 25 19 E

time difference: UTC+2 (7 hours ahead of Washington, DC, during Standard Time)
daylight saving time: +1hr, begins last Sunday in March; ends last Sunday in October
etymology: named after the Vilnia River, which flows into the Neris River at Vilnius; the river name derives from the Lithuanian word "vilnis" meaning "a surge"

Administrative divisions: 60 municipalities (savivaldybe, singular - savivaldybe); Akmene, Alytaus Miestas, Alytus, Anksciai, Birstonas, Birzai, Druskininkai, Elektrenai, Ignalina, Jonava, Joniskis, Jurbarkas, Kaisiadorys, Kalvarija, Kauno Miestas, Kaunas, Kazlu Rudos, Kedainiai, Kelme, Klaipedos Miestas, Klaipeda, Kretinga, Kupiskis, Lazdijai, Marijampole, Mazeikiai, Moletai, Neringa, Pagegiai, Pakruojis, Palangos Miestas, Panevezio Miestas, Panevezys, Pasvalys, Plunge, Prienai, Radviliskis, Raseiniai, Rietavas, Rokiskis, Sakiai, Salcininkai, Siauliu Miestas, Siauliai, Silale, Silute, Sirvintos, Skuodas, Svencionys, Taurage, Telsiai, Trakai, Ukmerge, Utena, Varena, Vilkaviskis, Vilniaus Miestas, Vilnius, Visaginas, Zarasai

Independence: 16 February 1918 (from Soviet Russia and Germany); 11 March 1990 (declared from the Soviet Union); 6 September 1991 (recognized by the Soviet Union); notable earlier dates: 6 July 1253 (coronation of MINDAUGAS, traditional founding date); 1 July 1569 (Polish-Lithuanian Commonwealth created)

National holiday: Independence Day (or National Day), 16 February (1918); note - 16 February 1918 was the date Lithuania established its statehood and its concomitant independence from Soviet Russia and Germany; 11 March 1990 was the date it declared the restoration of Lithuanian statehood and its concomitant independence from the Soviet Union

Constitution: *history:* several previous; latest adopted by referendum 25 October 1992, entered into force 2 November 1992
amendments: proposed by at least one fourth of all Parliament members or by petition of at least 300,000 voters; passage requires two-thirds majority vote of Parliament in each of two readings three months apart and a presidential signature; amendments to constitutional articles on national sovereignty and constitutional amendment procedure also require three-fourths voter approval in a referendum; amended many times, last in 2019

Legal system: civil law system; legislative acts can be appealed to the Constitutional Court

International law organization participation: accepts compulsory ICJ jurisdiction with reservations; accepts ICCt jurisdiction

Citizenship: *citizenship by birth:* no
citizenship by descent only: at least one parent must be a citizen of Lithuania
dual citizenship recognized: no
residency requirement for naturalization: 10 years

Suffrage: 18 years of age; universal

Executive branch: *chief of state:* President Gitanas NAUSEDA (since 12 July 2019)
head of government: Prime Minister Ingrida SIMONYTE (since 24 November 2020)
cabinet: Council of Ministers nominated by the prime minister, appointed by the president, and approved by Parliament
elections/appointments: president directly elected by absolute majority popular vote in 2 rounds if needed for a 5-year term (eligible for a second term); election last held on 12 and 26 May 2019 (next to be held in May 2024); prime minister appointed by the president, approved by Parliament
election results:
2019: Gitanas NAUSEDA elected president in second round; percent of vote - Gitanas NAUSEDA (independent) 66.7%, Ingrida SIMONYTE (independent) 33.3%; Saulius SKVERNELIS (LVZS) approved as prime minister by Parliament vote - 62 to 10
2009: Dalia GRYBAUSKAITE elected president; Dalia GRYBAUSKAITE 69.1%, Algirdas BUTKEVICIUS 11.8%, Valentinas MAZURONIS 6.2%, Valdemar TOMASEVSKI 4.7%, and other 8.2%

Legislative branch: *description:* unicameral Parliament or Seimas (141 seats; 71 members directly elected in single-seat constituencies by absolute majority vote and 70 directly elected in a single nationwide constituency by proportional representation vote; members serve 4-year terms)
elections:
last held on 11 and 25 October 2020 (next to be held in October 2024)
election results:
percent of vote by party - NA; seats by party - TS-LKD 50, LVZS 32, LSDP 13, LRLS 13, Freedom 11, DP 10, AWPL 3, LSDDP 3, LT 1, Greens 1, independent 4; composition as of July 2022 - men 101, women 40, percent of women 28.4%

Judicial branch: *highest court(s):* Supreme Court (consists of 37 judges); Constitutional Court (consists of 9 judges)
judge selection and term of office: Supreme Court judges nominated by the president and appointed by the Seimas; judges serve 5-year renewable terms; Constitutional Court judges appointed by the Seimas from nominations - 3 each by the president of the republic, the Seimas chairperson, and the Supreme Court president; judges serve 9-year, nonrenewable terms; one-third of membership reconstituted every 3 years
subordinate courts: Court of Appeals; district and local courts

Political parties and leaders: Electoral Action of Lithuanian Poles or LLRA [Valdemar TOMASEVSKI]
Freedom and Justice Party or LT [Remigijus ZEMAITAITIS] (formerly Lithuanian Freedom Union (Liberals))
Freedom Party or LP [Ausrine ARMONAITE]
Homeland Union-Lithuanian Christian Democrats or TS-LKD [Gabrielius LANDSBERGIS]
Labor Party or DP [Andrius MAZURONIS]
Lithuanian Center Party or LCP [Naglis PUTEIKIS]
Lithuanian Farmers and Greens Union or LVZS [Ramunas KARBAUSKIS]
Lithuanian Green Party or LZP [Remigijus LAPINSKAS]
Lithuanian Liberal Movement or LS or LRLS [Viktorija CMILYTE-NIELSEN]
Lithuanian List or LL [Darius KUOLYS]
Lithuanian Regions Party or LRP [Jonas PINSKUS] (formerly Lithuanian Social Democratic Labor Party or LSDDP)
Lithuanian Social Democratic Party or LSDP [Vilija BLINKEVICIUTE]

International organization participation: Australia Group, BA, BIS, CBSS, CD, CE, EAPC, EBRD, ECB, EIB, EU, FAO, IAEA, IBRD, ICAO, ICC (national committees), ICCt, ICRM, IDA, IFC, IFRCS, ILO, IMF, IMO, Interpol, IOC, IOM, IPU, ISO, ITU, ITUC (NGOs), MIGA, NATO, NIB, NSG, OAS (observer), OECD, OIF (observer), OPCW, OSCE, PCA, Schengen Convention, UN, UNCTAD, UNESCO, UNHRC, UNIDO, UNWTO, UPU, Wassenaar Arrangement, WCO, WHO, WIPO, WMO, WTO

Diplomatic representation in the US: *chief of mission:* Ambassador Audra PLEPYTE (since 7 July 2021)
chancery: 2622 16th Street NW, Washington, DC 20009
telephone: [1] (202) 234-5860
FAX: [1] (202) 328-0466
email address and website:
info@usa.mfa.lt
https://usa.mfa.lt/usa/en/
consulate(s) general: Chicago, Los Angeles, New York

Diplomatic representation from the US: *chief of mission:* Ambassador Robert S. GILCHRIST (since 4 February 2020)
embassy: Akmenu gatve 6, Vilnius, LT-03106
mailing address: 4510 Vilnius Place, Washington DC 20521-4510
telephone: [370] (5) 266-5500
FAX: [370] (5) 266-5510
email address and website:
consec@state.gov
https://lt.usembassy.gov/

Flag description: three equal horizontal bands of yellow (top), green, and red; yellow symbolizes golden fields, as well as the sun, light, and goodness; green represents the forests of the countryside, in addition to nature, freedom, and hope; red stands for courage and the blood spilled in defense of the homeland

National symbol(s): mounted knight known as Vytis (the Chaser), white stork; national colors: yellow, green, red

National anthem: *name:* "Tautiska giesme" (The National Song)
lyrics/music: Vincas KUDIRKA
note: adopted 1918, restored 1990; written in 1898 while Lithuania was a part of Russia; banned during the Soviet occupation from 1940 to 1990

National heritage: *total World Heritage Sites:* 4 (all cultural)
selected World Heritage Site locales: Vilnius Historic Center; Curonian Spit; Kernavė Archaeological Site; Struve Geodetic Arc

ECONOMY

Economic overview: After the country declared independence from the Soviet Union in 1990, Lithuania faced an initial dislocation that is typical during transitions from a planned economy to a free-market economy. Macroeconomic stabilization policies, including privatization of most state-owned enterprises, and a strong commitment to a currency board arrangement led to an open and rapidly growing economy and rising consumer demand. Foreign investment and EU funding aided in the transition. Lithuania joined the WTO in May 2001, the EU in May 2004, and the euro zone in January 2015, and is now working to complete the OECD accession roadmap it received in July 2015. In 2017, joined the OECD Working Group on Bribery, an important step in the OECD accession process.

The Lithuanian economy was severely hit by the 2008-09 global financial crisis, but it has rebounded and become one of the fastest growing in the EU. Increases in exports, investment, and wage growth that supported consumption helped the economy grow by 3.6% in 2017. In 2015, Russia was Lithuania's largest trading partner, followed by Poland, Germany, and Latvia; goods and services trade between the US and Lithuania totaled $2.2 billion. Lithuania opened a self-financed liquefied natural gas terminal in January 2015, providing the first non-Russian supply of natural gas to the Baltic States and reducing Lithuania's dependence on Russian gas from 100% to approximately 30% in 2016.

Lithuania's ongoing recovery hinges on improving the business environment, especially by liberalizing labor laws, and improving competitiveness and export growth, the latter hampered by economic slowdowns in the EU and Russia. In addition, a steady outflow of young and highly educated people is causing a shortage of skilled labor, which, combined with a rapidly aging population, could stress public finances and constrain long-term growth.

Real GDP (purchasing power parity): $102.66 billion (2020 est.)
$103.56 billion (2019 est.)
$99.25 billion (2018 est.)
note: data are in 2017 dollars

Real GDP growth rate: 4.33% (2019 est.)
3.99% (2018 est.)
4.37% (2017 est.)

Real GDP per capita: $36,700 (2020 est.)
$37,100 (2019 est.)
$35,400 (2018 est.)
note: data are in 2017 dollars

GDP (official exchange rate): $54.597 billion (2019 est.)

Inflation rate (consumer prices): 2.3% (2019 est.)
2.7% (2018 est.)
3.7% (2017 est.)

Credit ratings:

Fitch rating: A (2020)

Moody's rating: A3 (2015)

Standard & Poors rating: A+ (2020)
note: The year refers to the year in which the current credit rating was first obtained.

GDP - composition, by sector of origin: *agriculture:* 3.5% (2017 est.)
industry: 29.4% (2017 est.)
services: 67.2% (2017 est.)

GDP - composition, by end use: *household consumption:* 63.9% (2017 est.)
government consumption: 16.6% (2017 est.)
investment in fixed capital: 18.8% (2017 est.)
investment in inventories: -1.3% (2017 est.)
exports of goods and services: 81.6% (2017 est.)
imports of goods and services: -79.3% (2017 est.)

Agricultural products: wheat, milk, sugar beet, rapeseed, barley, triticale, potatoes, oats, peas, beans

Industries: metal-cutting machine tools, electric motors, televisions, refrigerators and freezers, petroleum refining, shipbuilding (small ships), furniture, textiles, food processing, fertilizer, agricultural machinery, optical equipment, lasers, electronic components, computers, amber jewelry, information technology, video game development, app/software development, biotechnology

Industrial production growth rate: 5.9% (2017 est.)

Labor force: 1.333 million (2020 est.)

Labor force - by occupation: *agriculture:* 9.1%
industry: 25.2%
services: 65.8% (2015 est.)

Unemployment rate: 8.4% (2019 est.)
8.5% (2018 est.)

Unemployment, youth ages 15-24: *total:* 19.6%
male: 21.5%
female: 17.3% (2020 est.)

Population below poverty line: 20.6% (2018 est.)

Gini Index coefficient - distribution of family income: 37.3 (2017 est.)
35 (2014)

Household income or consumption by percentage share: *lowest 10%:* 2.2%
highest 10%: 28.8% (2015)

Budget: *revenues:* 15.92 billion (2017 est.)
expenditures: 15.7 billion (2017 est.)

Budget surplus (+) or deficit (-): 0.5% (of GDP) (2017 est.)

Public debt: 39.7% of GDP (2017 est.)
40.1% of GDP (2016 est.)
note: official data; data cover general government debt and include debt instruments issued (or owned) by government entities other than the treasury; the data include treasury debt held by foreign entities, debt issued by subnational entities, as well as intragovernmental debt; intragovernmental debt consists of treasury borrowings from surpluses in the social funds, such as for retirement, medical care, and unemployment; debt instruments for the social funds are sold at public auctions

Taxes and other revenues: 33.7% (of GDP) (2017 est.)

Fiscal year: calendar year

Current account balance: $1.817 billion (2019 est.)
$131 million (2018 est.)

Exports: $41.48 billion (2020 est.) note: data are in current year dollars
$42.3 billion (2019 est.) note: data are in current year dollars
$40.36 billion (2018 est.) note: data are in current year dollars

Exports - partners: Russia 13%, Latvia 9%, Poland 8%, Germany 7%, Estonia 5% (2019)

Exports - commodities: refined petroleum, furniture, cigarettes, wheat, polyethylene (2019)

Imports: $36.06 billion (2020 est.) note: data are in current year dollars
$39.46 billion (2019 est.) note: data are in current year dollars
$39.38 billion (2018 est.) note: data are in current year dollars

Imports - partners: Poland 12%, Russia 12%, Germany 12%, Latvia 7%, Netherlands 5% (2019)

Imports - commodities: crude petroleum, cars, packaged medicines, refined petroleum, electricity (2019)

Reserves of foreign exchange and gold: $4.45 billion (31 December 2017 est.)
$1.697 billion (31 December 2015 est.)

Debt - external: $37.859 billion (2019 est.)
$41.999 billion (2018 est.)

Exchange rates: litai (LTL) per US dollar -
0.82771 (2020 est.)
0.90338 (2019 est.)
0.87789 (2018 est.)
0.9012 (2014 est.)
0.7525 (2013 est.)

ENERGY

Electricity access: *electrification - total population:* 100% (2020)

Electricity: *installed generating capacity:* 3.512 million kW (2020 est.)
consumption: 11.063 billion kWh (2020 est.)
exports: 4.105 billion kWh (2020 est.)
imports: 12.013 billion kWh (2020 est.)
transmission/distribution losses: 951 million kWh (2020 est.)

Electricity generation sources: *fossil fuels:* 38% of total installed capacity (2020 est.)
solar: 3% of total installed capacity (2020 est.)
wind: 35.5% of total installed capacity (2020 est.)
hydroelectricity: 6.9% of total installed capacity (2020 est.)
biomass and waste: 16.7% of total installed capacity (2020 est.)

Coal: *production:* 0 metric tons (2020 est.)
consumption: 221,000 metric tons (2020 est.)
exports: 75,000 metric tons (2020 est.)
imports: 268,000 metric tons (2020 est.)
proven reserves: 0 metric tons (2019 est.)

Petroleum: *total petroleum production:* 4,000 bbl/day (2021 est.)
refined petroleum consumption: 68,000 bbl/day (2019 est.)
crude oil and lease condensate exports: 900 bbl/day (2018 est.)
crude oil and lease condensate imports: 194,900 bbl/day (2018 est.)
crude oil estimated reserves: 12 million barrels (2021 est.)

Refined petroleum products - production: 196,500 bbl/day (2015 est.)

Refined petroleum products - exports: 174,800 bbl/day (2015 est.)

Refined petroleum products - imports: 42,490 bbl/day (2015 est.)

Natural gas: *production:* 0 cubic meters (2021 est.)
consumption: 2,230,854,000 cubic meters (2019 est.)
exports: 497.923 million cubic meters (2020 est.)
imports: 2,818,513,000 cubic meters (2020 est.)
proven reserves: 0 cubic meters (2021 est.)

Carbon dioxide emissions: 14.503 million metric tonnes of CO2 (2019 est.)
from coal and metallurgical coke: 693,000 metric tonnes of CO2 (2019 est.)
from petroleum and other liquids: 9.488 million metric tonnes of CO2 (2019 est.)
from consumed natural gas: 4.322 million metric tonnes of CO2 (2019 est.)

Energy consumption per capita: 101.651 million Btu/person (2019 est.)

COMMUNICATIONS

Telephones - fixed lines: *total subscriptions:* 322,108 (2020 est.)
subscriptions per 100 inhabitants: 12 (2020 est.)

Telephones - mobile cellular: *total subscriptions:* 3,671,995 (2020 est.)
subscriptions per 100 inhabitants: 135 (2020 est.)

Telecommunication systems: *general assessment:* Lithuania's small telecoms market is among the more advanced in Europe, particularly given the universal access to LTE infrastructure and the extensive fiber footprint; in line with the country's Digital Agenda, the focus among telcos has been to invest in fiber, with an emphasis on delivering gigabyte data speeds; SIM card penetration is relatively high for the region and most subscribers are higher ARPU postpaid subscribers; network operators continue to market mobile broadband services, made possible from investments in LTE technologies; LTE services are available nationally, and although there have been some initial trials of 5G commercial services are not expected to be launched until mid to late 2021; the regulator has consulted on the release of spectrum for 5G in a range of bands, and the auction is tentatively scheduled for the first quarter of 2021; according to regulator data, the total revenue of the electronic communications sector in the third quarter of 2020 was the highest it has been since the fourth quarter of 2010; revenue growth in the mobile sector was driven mainly mobile internet services (2021)
domestic: nearly 12 per 100 for fixed-line subscriptions; rapid expansion of mobile-cellular services has resulted in a steady decline in the number of fixed-line connections; mobile-cellular teledensity stands at about 174 per 100 persons (2020)
international: country code - 370; landing points for the BCS East, BCS East-West Interlink and NordBalt connecting Lithuania to Sweden, and Latvia ; further transmission by satellite; landline connections to Latvia and Poland (2019)

Broadcast media: public broadcaster operates 3 channels with the third channel - a satellite channel - introduced in 2007; various privately owned commercial TV broadcasters operate national and multiple regional channels; many privately owned local TV stations; multi-channel cable and satellite TV services available; publicly owned broadcaster operates 3 radio networks; many privately owned commercial broadcasters, with repeater stations in various regions throughout the country

Internet country code: .lt

Internet users: *total:* 2,603,900 (July 2022 est.)
percent of population: 97.8% (July 2022 est.)

Broadband - fixed subscriptions: *total:* 796,814 (2020 est.)
subscriptions per 100 inhabitants: 29 (2020 est.)

TRANSPORTATION

National air transport system: *number of registered air carriers:* 3 (2020)
inventory of registered aircraft operated by air carriers: 50
annual passenger traffic on registered air carriers: 26,031 (2018)

Civil aircraft registration country code prefix: LY

Airports: *total:* 61 (2021)

Airports - with paved runways: *total:* 22
over 3,047 m: 3
2,438 to 3,047 m: 1
1,524 to 2,437 m: 7
914 to 1,523 m: 2
under 914 m: 9 (2021)

Airports - with unpaved runways: *total:* 39
over 3,047 m: 1
914 to 1,523 m: 2
under 914 m: 36 (2021)

Pipelines: 1,921 km gas, 121 km refined products (2013)

Railways: *total:* 1,768 km (2014)
standard gauge: 22 km (2014) 1.435-m gauge
broad gauge: 1,746 km (2014) 1.520-m gauge (122 km electrified)

Roadways: *total:* 84,166 km (2012)
paved: 72,297 km (2012) (includes 312 km of expressways)
unpaved: 11,869 km (2012)

Waterways: 441 km (2007) (navigable year-round)

Merchant marine: *total:* 64
by type: container ship 4, general cargo 24, oil tanker 2, other 34 (2021)

Ports and terminals: *major seaport(s):* Klaipeda
oil terminal(s): Butinge oil terminal

LNG terminal(s) (import): Klaipeda

MILITARY AND SECURITY

Military and security forces: Lithuanian Armed Forces (Lietuvos Ginkluotosios Pajegos): Land Forces (Sausumos Pajegos), Naval Forces (Karines Juru Pajegos), Air Forces (Karines Oro Pajegos), Special Operations Forces (Specialiuju Operaciju Pajegos); National Defense Volunteer Forces (Savanoriu Pajegos); National Riflemen's Union (2022)
note: the National Rifleman's Union is a paramilitary force that acts as an additional reserve force

Military expenditures: 2.5% of GDP (2022 est.)
2% of GDP (2021 est.)
2.1% of GDP (2020)
2% of GDP (2019) (approximately $1.7 billion)
2% of GDP (2018) (approximately $1.59 billion)

Military and security service personnel strengths: approximately 17,000 active duty personnel (13,500 Army, including about 5,000 National Defense Voluntary Forces; 500 Navy; 1,000 Air Force; 2,000 other, including special operations forces, logistics support, training, etc); estimated 11,000 Riflemen Union (2022)

Military equipment inventories and acquisitions: the Lithuanian Armed Forces' inventory is mostly a mix of Western weapons systems and Soviet-era equipment (primarily aircraft and helicopters); as of 2021, Germany was the leading supplier of armaments to Lithuania (2021)

Military service age and obligation: 19-26 years of age for conscripted military service for men; 9-month service obligation; in 2015, Lithuania reinstated conscription after having converted to a professional military in 2008; 18-38 for voluntary service for men and women (2022)
note 1: Lithuania conscripts up to 4,000 males each year; conscripts are selected using an automated lottery system
note 2: as of 2019, women comprised about 12% of the military's full-time personnel

Military deployments: *note:* contributes about 350-550 troops to the Lithuania, Poland, and Ukraine joint military brigade (LITPOLUKRBRIG), which was established in 2014; the brigade is headquartered in Poland and is comprised of an international staff, three battalions, and specialized units; units affiliated with the multinational brigade remain within the structures of the armed forces of their respective countries until the brigade is activated for participation in an international operation

Military - note: Lithuania became a member of NATO in 2004

since 2017, Lithuania has hosted a German-led multi-national NATO ground force battlegroup as part of the Alliance's Enhanced Forward Presence initiative; NATO also has provided air protection for Lithuania since 2004 through its Air Policing mission; NATO member countries that possess air combat capabilities voluntarily contribute to the mission on 4-month rotations; NATO fighter aircraft are hosted at Lithuania's Šiauliai Air Base (2022)

TRANSNATIONAL ISSUES

Disputes - international: *Lithuania-Belarus:* as of January 2007, ground demarcation of the boundary with Belarus was complete and mapped with final ratification documents in preparation
Lithuania-Lativa: boundary demarcated with Latvia was completed in 1998
Lithuania-Russia: Lithuania and Russia committed to demarcating their boundary in 2006 in accordance with the land and maritime treaty ratified by Russia in May 2003 and by Lithuania in 1999; Lithuania operates a simplified transit regime for Russian nationals traveling from the Kaliningrad coastal exclave into Russia, while still conforming, as a EU member state having an external border with a non-EU member, to strict Schengen border rules; in January 2018, demarcation of the Lithuania-Russia border was completed

Refugees and internally displaced persons: *refugees (country of origin):* 70,667 (Ukraine) (as of 22 November 2022)
stateless persons: 2,721 (mid-year 2021)

Illicit drugs: source country for amphetamine tablets

LUXEMBOURG

INTRODUCTION

Background: Founded in 963, Luxembourg became a grand duchy in 1815 and an independent state under the Netherlands. It lost more than half of its territory to Belgium in 1839 but gained a larger measure of autonomy. In 1867, Luxembourg attained full independence under the condition that it promise perpetual neutrality. Overrun by Germany in both world wars, it ended its neutrality in 1948 when it entered into the Benelux Customs Union and when it joined NATO the

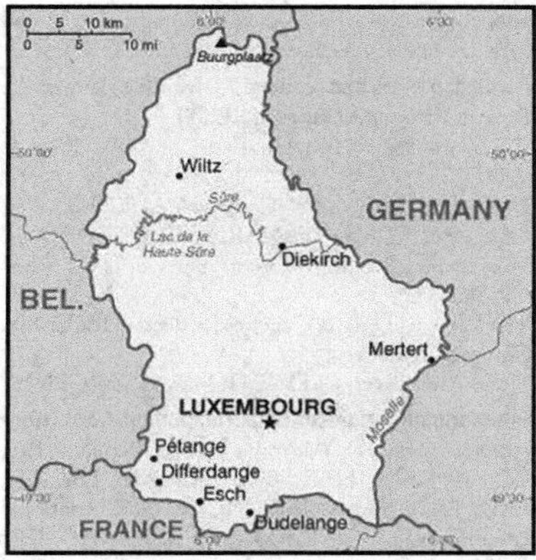

following year. In 1957, Luxembourg became one of the six founding countries of the EEC (later the EU), and in 1999 it joined the euro currency zone.

GEOGRAPHY

Location: Western Europe, between France and Germany

Geographic coordinates: 49 45 N, 6 10 E

Map references: Europe

Area: *total:* 2,586 sq km
land: 2,586 sq km
water: 0 sq km

Area - comparative: slightly smaller than Rhode Island; about half the size of Delaware

Land boundaries: *total:* 327 km
border countries (3): Belgium 130 km; France 69 km; Germany 128 km

Coastline: 0 km (landlocked)

Maritime claims: none (landlocked)

Climate: modified continental with mild winters, cool summers

Terrain: mostly gently rolling uplands with broad, shallow valleys; uplands to slightly mountainous in the north; steep slope down to Moselle flood plain in the southeast

Elevation: *highest point:* Buurgplaatz 559 m
lowest point: Moselle River 133 m
mean elevation: 325 m

Natural resources: iron ore (no longer exploited), arable land

Land use: *agricultural land:* 50.7% (2018 est.)
arable land: 24% (2018 est.)
permanent crops: 0.6% (2018 est.)
permanent pasture: 26.1% (2018 est.)
forest: 33.5% (2018 est.)
other: 15.8% (2018 est.)

Irrigated land: 0 sq km (2012)

Major watersheds (area sq km): Atlantic Ocean drainage: Rhine-Maas (198,735 sq km)

Population distribution: most people live in the south, on or near the border with France

Natural hazards: occasional flooding

Geography - note: landlocked; the only grand duchy in the world

PEOPLE AND SOCIETY

Population: 650,364 (2022 est.)

Nationality: *noun:* Luxembourger(s)
adjective: Luxembourg

Ethnic groups: Luxembourger 52.9%, Portuguese 14.5%, French 7.6%, Italian 3.7%, Belgian 3%, German 2%, Spanish 1.3%, Romania 1%, other 14% (2022 est.)
note: data represent population by nationality

Languages: Luxembourgish (official administrative and judicial language and national language (spoken vernacular)) 55.8%, Portuguese 15.7%, French (official administrative, judicial, and legislative language) 12.1%, German (official administrative and judicial language) 3.1%, Italian 2.9%, English 2.1%, other 8.4% (2011 est.)

Religions: Christian (predominantly Roman Catholic) 70.6%, Muslim 2.3%, other (includes Buddhist, folk religions, Hindu, Jewish) 0.4%, unaffiliated 26.7% (2020 est.)

Age structure: *0-14 years:* 16.73% (male 54,099/female 51,004)
15-24 years: 11.78% (male 37,946/female 36,061)
25-54 years: 43.93% (male 141,535/female 134,531)
55-64 years: 12.19% (male 39,289/female 37,337)
65 years and over: 15.37% (male 43,595/female 52,984) (2020 est.)

Dependency ratios: *total dependency ratio:* 42.8
youth dependency ratio: 22.2
elderly dependency ratio: 20.5
potential support ratio: 4.9 (2020 est.)

Median age: *total:* 39.5 years
male: 38.9 years
female: 40 years (2020 est.)

Population growth rate: 1.64% (2022 est.)

Birth rate: 11.61 births/1,000 population (2022 est.)

Death rate: 7.21 deaths/1,000 population (2022 est.)

Net migration rate: 12.01 migrant(s)/1,000 population (2022 est.)

Population distribution: most people live in the south, on or near the border with France

Urbanization: *urban population:* 91.9% of total population (2022)
rate of urbanization: 1.43% annual rate of change (2020-25 est.)

Major urban areas - population: 120,000 LUXEMBOURG (capital) (2018)

Sex ratio: *at birth:* 1.06 male(s)/female
0-14 years: 1.06 male(s)/female
15-24 years: 1.05 male(s)/female
25-54 years: 1.05 male(s)/female
55-64 years: 1.06 male(s)/female
65 years and over: 0.7 male(s)/female
total population: 1.02 male(s)/female (2022 est.)

Mother's mean age at first birth: 31 years (2020 est.)

Maternal mortality ratio: 5 deaths/100,000 live births (2017 est.)

Infant mortality rate: *total:* 3.25 deaths/1,000 live births
male: 3.65 deaths/1,000 live births
female: 2.83 deaths/1,000 live births (2022 est.)

Life expectancy at birth: *total population:* 82.98 years
male: 80.52 years
female: 85.58 years (2022 est.)

Total fertility rate: 1.63 children born/woman (2022 est.)

Drinking water source: *improved:* *urban:* 100% of population
rural: 98.6% of population
total: 99.9% of population
unimproved: *urban:* 0% of population
rural: 1.4% of population
total: 0.1% of population (2020 est.)

Current health expenditure: 5.4% of GDP (2019)

Physicians density: 3.01 physicians/1,000 population (2017)

Hospital bed density: 4.3 beds/1,000 population (2019)

Sanitation facility access: *improved:* *urban:* 100% of population
rural: 99.9% of population
total: 100% of population
unimproved: *urban:* 0% of population
rural: 0.1% of population
total: 0% of population (2020 est.)

HIV/AIDS - adult prevalence rate: 0.3% (2018 est.)

Obesity - adult prevalence rate: 22.6% (2016)

Alcohol consumption per capita: *total:* 11 liters of pure alcohol (2019 est.)
beer: 4.04 liters of pure alcohol (2019 est.)
wine: 4.73 liters of pure alcohol (2019 est.)
spirits: 2.14 liters of pure alcohol (2019 est.)
other alcohols: 0 liters of pure alcohol (2019 est.)

Tobacco use: *total:* 21.1% (2020 est.)
male: 22.4% (2020 est.)
female: 19.8% (2020 est.)

Education expenditures: 3.7% of GDP (2018 est.)

School life expectancy (primary to tertiary education): *total:* 14 years
male: 14 years
female: 14 years (2019)

Unemployment, youth ages 15-24: *total:* 23.2%
male: 24.8%
female: 21.3% (2020 est.)

ENVIRONMENT

Environment - current issues: air and water pollution in urban areas, soil pollution of farmland; unsustainable patterns of consumption (transport, energy, recreation, space) threaten biodiversity and landscapes

Environment - international agreements: *party to:* Air Pollution, Air Pollution-Heavy Metals, Air Pollution-Multi-effect Protocol, Air Pollution-Nitrogen Oxides, Air Pollution-Persistent Organic Pollutants, Air Pollution-Sulphur 85, Air Pollution-Sulphur 94, Air Pollution-Volatile Organic Compounds, Biodiversity, Climate Change, Climate Change-Kyoto Protocol, Climate Change-Paris Agreement, Comprehensive Nuclear Test Ban, Desertification, Endangered Species, Hazardous Wastes, Law of the Sea, Marine Dumping-London Convention, Marine Dumping-London Protocol, Nuclear Test Ban, Ozone Layer Protection, Ship Pollution, Tropical Timber 2006, Wetlands, Whaling
signed, but not ratified: Environmental Modification

Air pollutants: *particulate matter emissions:* 10.21 micrograms per cubic meter (2016 est.)
carbon dioxide emissions: 8.99 megatons (2016 est.)
methane emissions: 0.61 megatons (2020 est.)

Climate: modified continental with mild winters, cool summers

Land use: *agricultural land:* 50.7% (2018 est.)
arable land: 24% (2018 est.)
permanent crops: 0.6% (2018 est.)
permanent pasture: 26.1% (2018 est.)
forest: 33.5% (2018 est.)
other: 15.8% (2018 est.)

Urbanization: *urban population:* 91.9% of total population (2022)
rate of urbanization: 1.43% annual rate of change (2020-25 est.)

Revenue from forest resources: *forest revenues:* 0.01% of GDP (2018 est.)

Revenue from coal: *coal revenues:* 0% of GDP (2018 est.)

Waste and recycling: *municipal solid waste generated annually:* 356,000 tons (2015 est.)
municipal solid waste recycled annually: 100,997 tons (2015 est.)
percent of municipal solid waste recycled: 28.4% (2015 est.)

Major watersheds (area sq km): Atlantic Ocean drainage: Rhine-Maas (198,735 sq km)

Total water withdrawal: *municipal:* 43.6 million cubic meters (2017 est.)
industrial: 1.6 million cubic meters (2017 est.)
agricultural: 400,000 cubic meters (2017 est.)

Total renewable water resources: 3.5 billion cubic meters (2017 est.)

GOVERNMENT

Country name: *conventional long form:* Grand Duchy of Luxembourg
conventional short form: Luxembourg
local long form: Grand Duche de Luxembourg
local short form: Luxembourg
etymology: the name derives from the Celtic "lucilem" (little) and the German "burg" (castle or fortress) to produce the meaning of the "little castle"; the name is actually ironic, since for centuries the Fortress of Luxembourg was one of Europe's most formidable fortifications; the name passed to the surrounding city and then to the country itself

Government type: constitutional monarchy

Capital: *name:* Luxembourg
geographic coordinates: 49 36 N, 6 07 E
time difference: UTC+1 (6 hours ahead of Washington, DC, during Standard Time)
daylight saving time: +1hr, begins last Sunday in March; ends last Sunday in October
etymology: the name derives from the Celtic *lucilem* (little) and the German *burg* (castle or fortress) to produce the meaning of the "little castle"; the name is actually ironic, since for centuries the Fortress of Luxembourg was one of Europe's most formidable fortifications; the name passed to the city that grew around the fortress

Administrative divisions: 12 cantons (cantons, singular - canton); Capellen, Clervaux, Diekirch, Echternach, Esch-sur-Alzette, Grevenmacher, Luxembourg, Mersch, Redange, Remich, Vianden, Wiltz

Independence: 1839 (from the Netherlands)

National holiday: National Day (birthday of Grand Duke HENRI), 23 June; note - this date of birth is not the true date of birth for any of the Royals, but the national festivities were shifted in 1962 to allow observance during a more favorable time of year

Constitution: *history:* previous 1842 (heavily amended 1848, 1856); latest effective 17 October 1868
amendments: proposed by the Chamber of Deputies or by the monarch to the Chamber; passage requires at least two-thirds majority vote by the Chamber in two successive readings three months apart; a referendum can be substituted for the second reading if approved by more than a quarter of the Chamber members or by 25,000 valid voters; adoption by referendum requires a majority of all valid voters; amended many times, last in 2020

Legal system: civil law system

International law organization participation: accepts compulsory ICJ jurisdiction; accepts ICCt jurisdiction

Citizenship: *citizenship by birth:* limited to situations where the parents are either unknown, stateless, or when the nationality law of the parents' state of origin does not permit acquisition of citizenship by descent when the birth occurs outside of national territory
citizenship by descent only: at least one parent must be a citizen of Luxembourg
dual citizenship recognized: yes
residency requirement for naturalization: 7 years

Suffrage: 18 years of age; universal and compulsory

Executive branch: *chief of state:* Grand Duke HENRI (since 7 October 2000); Heir Apparent Prince GUILLAUME (son of the monarch, born 11 November 1981)
head of government: Prime Minister Xavier BETTEL (since 4 December 2013); Deputy Prime Minister Francois BAUSCH (since 11 October 2019); Deputy Prime Minister Daniel KERSCH (since 4 February 2020)
cabinet: Council of Ministers recommended by the prime minister, appointed by the monarch
elections/appointments: the monarchy is hereditary; following elections to the Chamber of Deputies, the leader of the majority party or majority coalition usually appointed prime minister by the monarch; deputy prime minister appointed by the monarch; prime minister and deputy prime minister are responsible to the Chamber of Deputies

Legislative branch: *description:* unicameral Chamber of Deputies or Chambre des Deputes (60 seats; members directly elected in multi-seat constituencies by party-list proportional representation vote; members serve 5-year terms); note - a 21-member Council of State appointed by the Grand Duke on the advice of the prime minister serves as an advisory body to the Chamber of Deputies
elections:
last held on 14 October 2018 (next to be held by 31 October 2023)
election results:
percent of vote by party - CSV 35%, LSAP 16.7%, DP 20%, Green Party 9%, ADR 6.7%, Pirate Party 3.3%, The Left 3.3%; seats by party - CSV 21, DP 12, LSAP 10, Green Party 9, ADR 4, Pirate Party 2, The Left 2; composition (as of September 2021) - men 40, women 20, percent of women 33.3%

Judicial branch: *highest court(s):* Supreme Court of Justice includes Court of Appeal and Court of Cassation (consists of 27 judges on 9 benches); Constitutional Court (consists of 9 members)
judge selection and term of office: judges of both courts appointed by the monarch for life
subordinate courts: Court of Accounts; district and local tribunals and courts

Political parties and leaders: Alternative Democratic Reform Party or ADR [Fred KEUP]
Christian Social People's Party or CSV [Claude WISELER]
Democratic Party or DP [Corinne CAHEN]
Green Party [Djuna BERNARD, Meris SEHOVIC]
Luxembourg Socialist Workers' Party or LSAP [Yves CRUCHTEN]
The Left (dei Lenk/la Gauche) [collective leadership, Central Committee]
Pirate Party [Sven CLEMENT, Marc GOERGEN]

International organization participation: ADB (nonregional member), Australia Group, Benelux, BIS, CD, CE, EAPC, EBRD, ECB, EIB, EMU, ESA, EU, FAO, FATF, IAEA, IBRD, ICAO, ICC (national committees), ICCt, ICRM, IDA, IEA, IFAD, IFC, IFRCS, ILO, IMF, IMO, Interpol, IOC, IOM, IPU, ISO, ITSO, ITU, ITUC (NGOs), MIGA, NATO, NEA, NSG, OAS (observer), OECD, OIF, OPCW, OSCE, PCA, Schengen Convention, UN, UNCTAD, UNESCO, UNHCR, UNHRC, UNIDO, UNRWA, UPU, Wassenaar Arrangement, WCO, WHO, WIPO, WMO, WTO, ZC

Diplomatic representation in the US: *chief of mission:* Ambassador Nicole BINTNER-BAKSHIAN (since 19 August 2021)
chancery: 2200 Massachusetts Avenue NW, Washington, DC 20008
telephone: [1] (202) 265-4171
FAX: [1] (202) 328-8270
email address and website:
washington.amb@mae.etat.lu
https://washington.mae.lu/en.html
consulate(s) general: New York, San Francisco

Diplomatic representation from the US: *chief of mission:* Ambassador Thomas M. BARRETT (since 10 February 2022)
embassy: 22 Boulevard Emmanuel Servais, L-2535 Luxembourg City
mailing address: 5380 Luxembourg Place, Washington DC 20521-5380
telephone: [352] 46-01-23-00
FAX: [352] 46-14-01
email address and website:
Luxembourgconsular@state.gov
https://lu.usembassy.gov/

Flag description: three equal horizontal bands of red (top), white, and light blue; similar to the flag of the Netherlands, which uses a darker blue and is shorter; the coloring is derived from the Grand Duke's coat of arms (a red lion on a white and blue striped field)

National symbol(s): red, rampant lion; national colors: red, white, light blue

National anthem: *name:* "Ons Heemecht" (Our Motherland); "De Wilhelmus" (The William)
lyrics/music: Michel LENTZ/Jean-Antoine ZINNEN; Nikolaus WELTER/unknown
note: "Ons Heemecht," adopted 1864, is the national anthem, while "De Wilhelmus," adopted 1919, serves as a royal anthem for use when members of the grand ducal family enter or exit a ceremony in Luxembourg

National heritage: *total World Heritage Sites:* 1 (cultural)
selected World Heritage Site locales: Luxembourg City Old Quarters and Fortifications

ECONOMY

Economic overview: This small, stable, high-income economy has historically featured solid growth, low inflation, and low unemployment. Luxembourg, the only Grand Duchy in the world, is a landlocked country in northwestern Europe surrounded by Belgium, France, and Germany. Despite its small landmass and small population, Luxembourg is the fifth-wealthiest country in the world when measured on a gross domestic product (PPP) per capita basis. Luxembourg has one of the highest current account surpluses as a share of GDP in the euro zone, and it maintains a healthy budgetary position, with a 2017 surplus of 0.5% of GDP, and the lowest public debt level in the region.

Since 2002, Luxembourg's government has proactively implemented policies and programs to support economic diversification and to attract foreign direct investment. The government focused on key innovative industries that showed promise for supporting economic growth: logistics, information and communications technology (ICT); health technologies, including biotechnology and biomedical research; clean energy technologies, and more recently, space technology and financial services technologies. The economy has evolved and flourished, posting strong GDP growth of 3.4% in 2017, far outpacing the European average of 1.8%.

Luxembourg remains a financial powerhouse – the financial sector accounts for more than 35% of GDP - because of the exponential growth of the investment fund sector through the launch and development of cross-border funds (UCITS) in the 1990s. Luxembourg is the world's second-largest investment fund asset domicile, after the US, with $4 trillion of assets in custody in financial institutions.

Luxembourg has lost some of its advantage as a favorable tax location because of OECD and EU pressure, as well as the "LuxLeaks" scandal, which revealed advantageous tax treatments offered to foreign corporations. In 2015, the government's compliance with EU requirements to implement automatic exchange of tax information on savings accounts - thus ending banking secrecy - has constricted banking activity. Likewise, changes to the way EU members collect taxes from e-commerce has cut Luxembourg's sales tax revenues, requiring the government to raise additional levies and to reduce some direct social benefits as part of the tax reform package of 2017. The tax reform package also included reductions in the corporate tax rate and increases in deductions for families, both intended to increase purchasing power and increase competitiveness.

Real GDP (purchasing power parity): $69.72 billion (2020 est.)
$70.64 billion (2019 est.)
$69.06 billion (2018 est.)
note: data are in 2017 dollars

Real GDP growth rate: 2.31% (2019 est.)
3.14% (2018 est.)
1.81% (2017 est.)

Real GDP per capita: $110,300 (2020 est.)
$113,900 (2019 est.)
$113,600 (2018 est.)
note: data are in 2017 dollars

GDP (official exchange rate): $71.089 billion (2019 est.)

Inflation rate (consumer prices): 1.7% (2019 est.)
1.5% (2018 est.)
1.7% (2017 est.)

Credit ratings:

Fitch rating: AAA (1994)

Moody's rating: Aaa (1989)

Standard & Poors rating: AAA (1994)
note: The year refers to the year in which the current credit rating was first obtained.

GDP - composition, by sector of origin: *agriculture:* 0.3% (2017 est.)
industry: 12.8% (2017 est.)
services: 86.9% (2017 est.)

GDP - composition, by end use: *household consumption:* 30.2% (2017 est.)
government consumption: 16.5% (2017 est.)
investment in fixed capital: 16.2% (2017 est.)
investment in inventories: 1.1% (2017 est.)
exports of goods and services: 230% (2017 est.)
imports of goods and services: -194% (2017 est.)

Agricultural products: milk, wheat, barley, triticale, potatoes, pork, beef, grapes, rapeseed, oats

Industries: banking and financial services, construction, real estate services, iron, metals, and steel, information technology, telecommunications, cargo transportation and logistics, chemicals, engineering, tires, glass, aluminum, tourism, biotechnology

Industrial production growth rate: 1.9% (2017 est.)

Labor force: 476,000 (2020 est.)
note: data exclude foreign workers; in addition to the figure for domestic labor force, about 150,000 workers commute daily from France, Belgium, and Germany

Labor force - by occupation: *agriculture:* 1.1%
industry: 20%
services: 78.9% (2013 est.)

Unemployment rate: 5.36% (2019 est.)
5.46% (2018 est.)

Unemployment, youth ages 15-24: *total:* 23.2%
male: 24.8%
female: 21.3% (2020 est.)

Population below poverty line: 17.5% (2018 est.)

Gini Index coefficient - distribution of family income: 34.9 (2017 est.)
26 (2005 est.)

Household income or consumption by percentage share: *lowest 10%:* 3.5%
highest 10%: 23.8% (2000)

Budget: *revenues:* 27.75 billion (2017 est.)
expenditures: 26.8 billion (2017 est.)

Budget surplus (+) or deficit (-): 1.5% (of GDP) (2017 est.)

Public debt: 23% of GDP (2017 est.)
20.8% of GDP (2016 est.)
note: data cover general government debt and include debt instruments issued (or owned) by government entities other than the treasury; the data include treasury debt held by foreign entities; the data include debt issued by subnational entities, as well as intragovernmental debt; intragovernmental debt consists of treasury borrowings from surpluses in the social funds, such as for retirement, medical care, and unemployment; debt instruments for the social funds are not sold at public auctions

Taxes and other revenues: 44.4% (of GDP) (2017 est.)

Fiscal year: calendar year

Current account balance: $3.254 billion (2019 est.)
$3.296 billion (2018 est.)

Exports: $137.09 billion (2020 est.) note: data are in current year dollars
$133.59 billion (2019 est.) note: data are in current year dollars
$136.11 billion (2018 est.) note: data are in current year dollars

Exports - partners: Germany 23%, France 13%, Belgium 12%, Netherlands 6%, Italy 5% (2019)

Exports - commodities: iron and iron products, tires, cars, broadcasting equipment, clothing and apparel (2019)

Imports: $110.1 billion (2020 est.) note: data are in current year dollars
$108.29 billion (2019 est.) note: data are in current year dollars
$110.28 billion (2018 est.) note: data are in current year dollars

Imports - partners: Belgium 27%, Germany 24%, France 11%, Netherlands 5% (2019)

Imports - commodities: cars, refined petroleum, broadcasting equipment, scrap iron, aircraft (2019)

Reserves of foreign exchange and gold: $878 million (31 December 2017 est.)
$974 million (31 December 2016 est.)

Debt - external: $4,266,792,000,000 (2019 est.)
$4,581,617,000,000 (2018 est.)

Exchange rates: euros (EUR) per US dollar -
0.82771 (2020 est.)
0.90338 (2019 est.)
0.87789 (2018 est.)
0.885 (2014 est.)
0.7634 (2013 est.)

ENERGY

Electricity access: *electrification - total population:* 100% (2020)

Electricity: *installed generating capacity:* 1.899 million kW (2020 est.)
consumption: 6.188 billion kWh (2020 est.)
exports: 1.079 billion kWh (2020 est.)
imports: 6.543 billion kWh (2020 est.)
transmission/distribution losses: 156 million kWh (2020 est.)

Electricity generation sources: *fossil fuels:* 13.8% of total installed capacity (2020 est.)
solar: 14.6% of total installed capacity (2020 est.)
wind: 27.7% of total installed capacity (2020 est.)
hydroelectricity: 7.5% of total installed capacity (2020 est.)
biomass and waste: 36.4% of total installed capacity (2020 est.)

Coal: *production:* 0 metric tons (2020 est.)
consumption: 65,000 metric tons (2020 est.)
exports: 0 metric tons (2020 est.)
imports: 74,000 metric tons (2020 est.)
proven reserves: 0 metric tons (2019 est.)

Petroleum: *total petroleum production:* 0 bbl/day (2021 est.)
refined petroleum consumption: 63,900 bbl/day (2019 est.)

Refined petroleum products - imports: 59,020 bbl/day (2017 est.)

Natural gas: *production:* 0 cubic meters (2021 est.)

consumption: 776.022 million cubic meters (2019 est.)
exports: 0 cubic meters (2021 est.)
imports: 772.624 million cubic meters (2019 est.)
proven reserves: 0 cubic meters (2021 est.)

Carbon dioxide emissions: 11.308 million metric tonnes of CO2 (2019 est.)
from coal and metallurgical coke: 149,000 metric tonnes of CO2 (2019 est.)
from petroleum and other liquids: 9.564 million metric tonnes of CO2 (2019 est.)
from consumed natural gas: 1.594 million metric tonnes of CO2 (2019 est.)

Energy consumption per capita: 310.068 million Btu/person (2019 est.)

COMMUNICATIONS

Telephones - fixed lines: *total subscriptions:* 268,090 (2020 est.)
subscriptions per 100 inhabitants: 43 (2020 est.)

Telephones - mobile cellular: *total subscriptions:* 890,000 (2020 est.)
subscriptions per 100 inhabitants: 142 (2020 est.)

Telecommunication systems: *general assessment:* Luxembourg has a small telecom sector; there remains some pressure from regulatory measures, though no further reductions to fixed and mobile interconnection tariffs have been imposed through to 2024; high mobile penetration has slowed subscriber growth in the mobile market since 2005, though a recent law requiring SIM card registration has not had an adverse effect on the number of mobile subscribers despite network operators deactivating unregistered cards (2021)
domestic: fixed-line teledensity about 43 per 100 persons; nationwide mobile-cellular telephone system with market for mobile-cellular phones virtually saturated with about 142 per 100 mobile-cellular (2020)
international: country code - 352

Broadcast media: Luxembourg has a long tradition of operating radio and TV services for pan-European audiences and is home to Europe's largest privately owned broadcast media group, the RTL Group, which operates 46 TV stations and 29 radio stations in Europe; also home to Europe's largest satellite operator, Societe Europeenne des Satellites (SES); domestically, the RTL Group operates TV and radio networks; other domestic private radio and TV operators and French and German stations available; satellite and cable TV services available

Internet country code: .lu

Internet users: *total:* 624,115 (2020 est.)
percent of population: 99% (2020 est.)

Broadband - fixed subscriptions: *total:* 235,155 (2020 est.)
subscriptions per 100 inhabitants: 38 (2020 est.)

TRANSPORTATION

National air transport system: *number of registered air carriers:* 4 (2020)
inventory of registered aircraft operated by air carriers: 66
annual passenger traffic on registered air carriers: 2,099,102 (2018)
annual freight traffic on registered air carriers: 7,323,040,000 (2018) mt-km

Civil aircraft registration country code prefix: LX

Airports: *total:* 2 (2021)

Airports - with paved runways: *total:* 1
over 3,047 m: 1 (2021)

Airports - with unpaved runways: *total:* 1
under 914 m: 1 (2021)

Heliports: 1 (2021)

Pipelines: 142 km gas, 27 km refined products (2013)

Railways: *total:* 275 km (2014)
standard gauge: 275 km (2014) 1.435-m gauge (275 km electrified)

Roadways: *total:* 2,875 km (2019)

Waterways: 37 km (2010) (on Moselle River)

Merchant marine: *total:* 153
by type: bulk carrier 4, container ship 1, general cargo 23, oil tanker 3, other 122 (2021)

Ports and terminals: *river port(s):* Mertert (Moselle)

MILITARY AND SECURITY

Military and security forces: Luxembourg Army (l'Armée Luxembourgeoise) (2022)

Military expenditures: 0.6% of GDP (2022 est.)
0.5% of GDP (2021)
0.6% of GDP (2020)
0.5% of GDP (2019) (approximately $420 million)
0.5% of GDP (2018) (approximately $380 million)

Military and security service personnel strengths: approximately 900 active personnel (2022)

Military equipment inventories and acquisitions: the inventory of Luxembourg's Army is a small mix of Western-origin equipment; since 2010, it has received equipment from several European countries (2021)

Military service age and obligation: 18-26 years of age for voluntary military service for men and women; no conscription (abolished 1969) (2022)
note 1: since 2003, the Army has allowed EU citizens 18-24 years of age who have been a resident in the country for at least 36 months to volunteer
note 2: as of 2019, women made up about 8% of the military's full-time personnel

Military - note: Luxembourg is a member of NATO and was one of the original 12 countries to sign the North Atlantic Treaty (also known as the Washington Treaty) in 1949

in 2015, Belgium, the Netherlands, and Luxembourg signed an agreement to conduct joint air policing of their territories; under the agreement, which went into effect in January of 2017, the Belgian and Dutch Air Forces trade responsibility for patrolling the skies over the three countries (2022)

TRANSNATIONAL ISSUES

Disputes - international: none identified

Refugees and internally displaced persons: *refugees (country of origin):* 6,756 (Ukraine) (as of 25 October 2022)
stateless persons: 194 (mid-year 2021)

MACAU

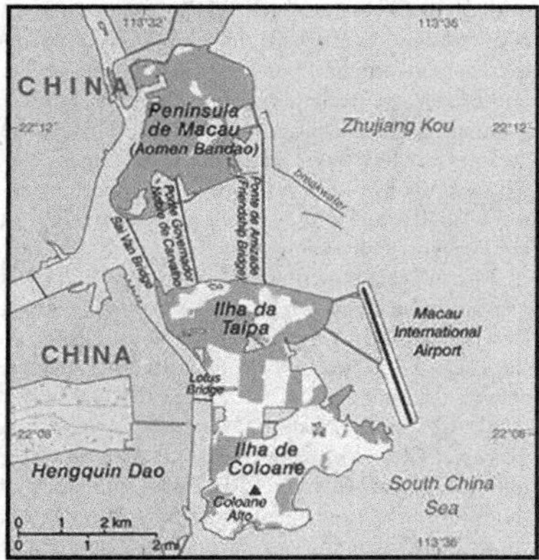

INTRODUCTION

Background: Colonized by the Portuguese in the 16th century, Macau was the first European settlement in the Far East. Pursuant to an agreement signed by China and Portugal on 13 April 1987, Macau became the Macau Special Administrative Region of the People's Republic of China on 20 December 1999. In this agreement, China promised that, under its "one country, two systems" formula, China's political and economic system would not be imposed on Macau, and that Macau would enjoy a "high degree of autonomy" in all matters except foreign affairs and defense for the subsequent 50 years.

GEOGRAPHY

Location: Eastern Asia, bordering the South China Sea and China

Geographic coordinates: 22 10 N, 113 33 E

Map references: Southeast Asia

Area: *total:* 28 sq km
land: 28.2 sq km
water: 0 sq km

Area - comparative: less than one-sixth the size of Washington, DC

Land boundaries: *total:* 3 km
regional borders (1): China 3 km

Coastline: 41 km

Maritime claims: not specified

Climate: subtropical; marine with cool winters, warm summers

Terrain: generally flat

Elevation: *highest point:* Alto Coloane 172 m
lowest point: South China Sea 0 m

Natural resources: NEGL

Land use: *agricultural land:* 0% (2018 est.)
other: 100% (2018 est.)

Irrigated land: 0 sq km (2012)

Population distribution: population fairly equally distributed

Natural hazards: typhoons

Geography - note: essentially urban; an area of land reclaimed from the sea measuring 5.2 sq km and known as Cotai now connects the islands of Coloane and Taipa; the island area is connected to the mainland peninsula by three bridges

PEOPLE AND SOCIETY

Population: 635,293 (2022 est.)

Nationality: *noun:* Chinese
adjective: Chinese

Ethnic groups: Chinese 88.7%, Portuguese 1.1%, mixed 1.1%, other 9.2% (includes Macanese - mixed Portuguese and Asian ancestry) (2016 est.)

Languages: Cantonese 80.1%, Mandarin 5.5%, other Chinese dialects 5.3%, Tagalog 3%, English 2.8%, Portuguese 0.6%, other 2.8%; note - Chinese and Portuguese are official languages; Macanese, a Portuguese-based Creole, is also spoken (2016 est.)
major-language sample(s):
世界概况, 必須擁有的基本資料参考书 (Cantonese)

Religions: folk religion 58.9%, Buddhist 17.3%, Christian 7.2%, other 1.2%, none 15.4% (2020 est.)

Age structure: *0-14 years:* 13.43% (male 42,449/female 40,051)
15-24 years: 10.45% (male 33,845/female 30,354)
25-54 years: 49% (male 134,302/female 166,762)
55-64 years: 14.57% (male 44,512/female 45,007)
65 years and over: 12.56% (male 36,223/female 40,953) (2020 est.)

Dependency ratios: *total dependency ratio:* 35.7
youth dependency ratio: 19.5
elderly dependency ratio: 16.2
potential support ratio: 6.2 (2020 est.)

Median age: *total:* 40.8 years
male: 40.7 years
female: 40.9 years (2020 est.)

Population growth rate: 0.75% (2022 est.)

Birth rate: 9.11 births/1,000 population (2022 est.)

Death rate: 4.72 deaths/1,000 population (2022 est.)

Net migration rate: 3.15 migrant(s)/1,000 population (2022 est.)

Population distribution: population fairly equally distributed

Urbanization: *urban population:* 100% of total population (2022)
rate of urbanization: 1.46% annual rate of change (2020-25 est.)

Major urban areas - population: 672,000 Macau (2022)

Sex ratio: *at birth:* 1.05 male(s)/female
0-14 years: 1.05 male(s)/female
15-24 years: 1.11 male(s)/female
25-54 years: 0.83 male(s)/female
55-64 years: 0.97 male(s)/female
65 years and over: 0.74 male(s)/female
total population: 0.9 male(s)/female (2022 est.)

Infant mortality rate: *total:* 4.59 deaths/1,000 live births
male: 4.68 deaths/1,000 live births
female: 4.5 deaths/1,000 live births (2022 est.)

Life expectancy at birth: *total population:* 84.98 years
male: 82.09 years
female: 88.02 years (2022 est.)

Total fertility rate: 1.22 children born/woman (2022 est.)

Drinking water source:

Improved: 100% of population
unimproved: 0% of population (2020)

Education expenditures: 3.1% of GDP (2019 est.)

Literacy: *definition:* age 15 and over can read and write
total population: 96.5%
male: 98.2%
female: 95% (2016)

School life expectancy (primary to tertiary education): *total:* 17 years
male: 16 years
female: 18 years (2020)

Unemployment, youth ages 15-24: *total:* 8.1%
male: 9.9%
female: 6.4% (2020 est.)

ENVIRONMENT

Environment - current issues: air pollution; coastal waters pollution; insufficient policies in reducing and recycling solid wastes; increasing population density worsening noise pollution

Air pollutants: *carbon dioxide emissions:* 2.07 megatons (2016 est.)

Climate: subtropical; marine with cool winters, warm summers

Land use: *agricultural land:* 0% (2018 est.)
other: 100% (2018 est.)

Urbanization: *urban population:* 100% of total population (2022)
rate of urbanization: 1.46% annual rate of change (2020-25 est.)

Revenue from forest resources: *forest revenues:* 0% of GDP (2018 est.)

Revenue from coal: *coal revenues:* 0% of GDP (2018 est.)

Waste and recycling: *municipal solid waste generated annually:* 377,942 tons (2016 est.)
municipal solid waste recycled annually: 75,588 tons (2014 est.)
percent of municipal solid waste recycled: 20% (2014 est.)

GOVERNMENT

Country name: *conventional long form:* Macau Special Administrative Region
conventional short form: Macau
official long form: Aomen Tebie Xingzhengqu (Chinese)/ Regiao Administrativa Especial de Macau (Portuguese)
official short form: Aomen (Chinese)/ Macau (Portuguese)
etymology: name is thought to derive from the A-Ma Temple - built in 1488 and dedicated to Mazu, the goddess of seafarers and fishermen - which is referred to locally as "Maa Gok" - and in Portuguese became

"Macau"; the Chinese name Aomen means "inlet gates"

Government type: executive-led limited democracy; a special administrative region of the People's Republic of China

Dependency status: special administrative region of the People's Republic of China

Administrative divisions: none (special administrative region of the People's Republic of China)

Independence: none (special administrative region of China)

National holiday: National Day (anniversary of the Founding of the People's Republic of China), 1 October (1949); note - 20 December (1999) is celebrated as Macau Special Administrative Region Establishment Day

Constitution: *history:* previous 1976 (Organic Statute of Macau, under Portuguese authority); latest adopted 31 March 1993, effective 20 December 1999 (Basic Law of the Macau Special Administrative Region of the People's Republic of China serves as Macau's constitution)
amendments: proposed by the Standing Committee of the National People's Congress (NPC), the People's Republic of China State Council, and the Macau Special Administrative Region; submittal of proposals to the NPC requires two-thirds majority vote by the Legislative Assembly of Macau, approval by two thirds of Macau's deputies to the NPC, and consent of the Macau chief executive; final passage requires approval by the NPC; amended 2005, 2012

Legal system: civil law system based on the Portuguese model

Citizenship: see China

Suffrage: 18 years of age in direct elections for some legislative positions, universal for permanent residents living in Macau for the past 7 years; note - indirect elections are limited to organizations registered as "corporate voters" and an election committee for the chief executive drawn from broad regional groupings, municipal organizations, central government bodies, and elected Macau officials

Executive branch: *chief of state:* President of China XI Jinping (since 14 March 2013)
head of government: Chief Executive HO lat Seng (since 20 December 2019)
cabinet: Executive Council appointed by the chief executive
elections/appointments: president indirectly elected by National People's Congress for a 5-year term (eligible for a second term); election last held on 17 March 2018 (next to be held in March 2023); chief executive chosen by a 400-member Election Committee for a 5-year term (eligible for a second term); election last held on 24 August 2019 (next to be held in 2024)
election results:
2019: HO Iat Seng (unopposed; received 392 out of 400 votes)
2014: Fernando CHUI Sai (unopposed; received 380 of 396 votes)

Legislative branch: *description:* unicameral Legislative Assembly or Regiao Administrativa Especial de Macau (33 seats; 14 members directly elected by proportional representation vote, 12 indirectly elected by an electoral college of professional and commercial interest groups, and 7 appointed by the chief executive; members serve 4-year terms)
elections:
last held on 12 September 2021 (next to be held in September 2025)
election results:
percent of vote - ACUM 20.1%, UPD 18%, NE 13.8%, UMG 12.7%, UPP 11.4%, ABL 10.8%, PS 6.6%, other 6.6%; seats by political group - ACUM 3, UPD 2, UMG 2, UPP 2, ABL 2, NE 2, PS 1; composition NA

Judicial branch: *highest court(s):* Court of Final Appeal of Macau Special Administrative Region (consists of the court president and 2 associate justices)
judge selection and term of office: justices appointed by the Macau chief executive upon the recommendation of an independent commission of judges, lawyers, and "eminent" persons; judge tenure NA
subordinate courts: Court of Second Instance; Court of First instance; Lower Court; Administrative Court

Political parties and leaders: Alliance for Change or APM [Melinda CHAN Mei-yi]
Alliance for a Happy Home or ABL [WONG Kit-cheng] (an electoral list of UPP)
Macau Civic Power [Agnes LAM Iok-fong]
Macau-Guangdong Union or UMG [MAK Soi-kun]
Macau Citizens' Development Association or ACDM [Becky SONG Pek-kei]
New Democratic Macau Association or ANMD [AU Kam-san]
New Hope or NE [Jose Maria Pereira COUTINHO]
New Macau Association (New Macau Progressives) or AMN or ANPM [Sulu SOU Ka-hou]
New Union for Macau's Development or NUDM [Angela LEONG On-kei]
Progress Promotion Union
Prosperous Democratic Macau Association or APMD (an electoral list of AMN)
Union for Development or UPD [HO Sut Heng]
Union for Promoting Progress or UPP [HO Ion-sang]
United Citizens Association of Macau or ACUM [CHAN Meng-kam]
note: there is no political party ordinance, so there are no registered political parties; politically active groups register as societies or companies

International organization participation: ICC (national committees), IHO, IMF, IMO (associate), Interpol (subbureau), ISO (correspondent), UNESCO (associate), UNWTO (associate), UPU, WCO, WMO, WTO

Diplomatic representation in the US: none (Special Administrative Region of China)

Diplomatic representation from the US: *embassy:* the US has no offices in Macau; US Consulate General in Hong Kong is accredited to Macau

Flag description: green with a lotus flower above a stylized bridge and water in white, beneath an arc of five gold, five-pointed stars: one large in the center of the arc and two smaller on either side; the lotus is the floral emblem of Macau, the three petals represent the peninsula and two islands that make up Macau; the five stars echo those on the flag of China

National symbol(s): lotus blossom; national colors: green, white, yellow

National anthem: *note:* as a Special Administrative Region of China, "Yiyongjun Jinxingqu" is the official anthem (see China)

ECONOMY

Economic overview: Since opening up its locally-controlled casino industry to foreign competition in 2001, Macau has attracted tens of billions of dollars in foreign investment, transforming the territory into one of the world's largest gaming centers. Macau's gaming and tourism businesses were fueled by China's decision to relax travel restrictions on Chinese citizens wishing to visit Macau. In 2016, Macau's gaming-related taxes accounted for more than 76% of total government revenue.

Macau's economy slowed dramatically in 2009 as a result of the global economic slowdown, but strong growth resumed in the 2010-13 period, largely on the back of tourism from mainland China and the gaming sectors. In 2015, this city of 646,800 hosted nearly 30.7 million visitors. Almost 67% came from mainland China. Macau's traditional manufacturing industry has slowed greatly since the termination of the Multi-Fiber Agreement in 2005. Services export — primarily gaming — increasingly has driven Macau's economic performance. Mainland China's anti-corruption campaign brought Macau's gambling boom to a halt in 2014, with spending in casinos contracting 34.3% in 2015. As a result, Macau's inflation-adjusted GDP contracted 21.5% in 2015 and another 2.1% in 2016 - down from double-digit expansion rates in the period 2010-13 - but the economy recovered handsomely in 2017.

Macau continues to face the challenges of managing its growing casino industry, risks from money-laundering activities, and the need to diversify the economy away from heavy dependence on gaming revenues. Macau's currency, the pataca, is closely tied to the Hong Kong dollar, which is also freely accepted in the territory.

Real GDP (purchasing power parity): $35.58 billion (2020 est.)
$81.44 billion (2019 est.)
$83.64 billion (2018 est.)
note: data are in 2017 dollars

Real GDP growth rate: 9.1% (2017 est.)
-0.9% (2016 est.)
-21.6% (2015 est.)

Real GDP per capita: $54,800 (2020 est.)
$127,200 (2019 est.)
$132,400 (2018 est.)
note: data are in 2017 dollars

GDP (official exchange rate): $53.841 billion (2019 est.)

Inflation rate (consumer prices): 2.7% (2019 est.)
3% (2018 est.)
1.2% (2017 est.)

Credit ratings:

Fitch rating: AA (2018)

Moody's rating: Aa3 (2016)
note: The year refers to the year in which the current credit rating was first obtained.

GDP - composition, by sector of origin: *agriculture:* 0% (2016 est.)
industry: 6.3% (2017 est.)
services: 93.7% (2017 est.)

GDP - composition, by end use: *household consumption:* 24.2% (2017 est.)
government consumption: 9.9% (2017 est.)
investment in fixed capital: 18.5% (2017 est.)
investment in inventories: 0.8% (2017 est.)
exports of goods and services: 79.4% (2017 est.)

imports of goods and services: -32% (2017 est.)

Agricultural products: pork, poultry, beef, pig fat, pig offals, eggs, pepper, cattle offals, cattle hides, goose/guinea fowl meat

Industries: tourism, gambling, clothing, textiles, electronics, footwear, toys

Industrial production growth rate: 2% (2017 est.)

Labor force: 392,000 (2020 est.)

Labor force - by occupation: *agriculture:* 2.5%
industry: 9.8%
services: 4.4%
industry and services: 12.4%
agriculture/fishing/forestry/mining: 15%
manufacturing: 25.9%
construction: 7.1%
transportation and utilities: 2.6%
commerce: 20.3% (2013 est.)

Unemployment rate: 2% (2017 est.)
1.9% (2016 est.)

Unemployment, youth ages 15-24: *total:* 8.1%
male: 9.9%
female: 6.4% (2020 est.)

Gini Index coefficient - distribution of family income: 35 (2013)
38 (2008)

Budget: *revenues:* 14.71 billion (2017 est.)
expenditures: 9.684 billion (2017 est.)

Budget surplus (+) or deficit (-): 10% (of GDP) (2017 est.)

Public debt: 0% of GDP (2017 est.)
0% of GDP (2016 est.)

Taxes and other revenues: 29.2% (of GDP) (2017 est.)

Fiscal year: calendar year

Current account balance: $16.75 billion (2017 est.)
$12.22 billion (2016 est.)

Exports: $45.35 billion (2019 est.) note: data are in current year dollars
$45.62 billion (2018 est.) note: data are in current year dollars
note: includes reexports

Exports - partners: Hong Kong 66%, China 9% (2019)

Exports - commodities: broadcasting equipment, jewelry, watches, trunks/cases, telephones (2019)

Imports: $17.35 billion (2019 est.) note: data are in current year dollars
$18.28 billion (2018 est.) note: data are in current year dollars

Imports - partners: China 33%, Hong Kong 31%, France 5% (2019)

Imports - commodities: jewelry, watches, electricity, aircraft, cars (2019)

Reserves of foreign exchange and gold: $20.17 billion (31 December 2017 est.)
$18.89 billion (31 December 2015 est.)
note: the Fiscal Reserves Act that came into force on 1 January 2012 requires the fiscal reserves to be separated from the foreign exchange reserves and to be managed separately; the transfer of assets took place in February 2012

Debt - external: $0 (31 December 2013)
$0 (31 December 2012)

Exchange rates: patacas (MOP) per US dollar -
8 (2017 est.)
7.9951 (2016 est.)
7.9951 (2015 est.)
7.985 (2014 est.)
7.9871 (2013 est.)

ENERGY

Electricity access: *electrification - total population:* 100% (2020)

Electricity: *installed generating capacity:* 478,000 kW (2020 est.)
consumption: 5,278,600,000 kWh (2020 est.)
exports: 0 kWh (2020 est.)
imports: 4,852,600,000 kWh (2020 est.)
transmission/distribution losses: 136 million kWh (2020 est.)

Electricity generation sources: *fossil fuels:* 66.4% of total installed capacity (2020 est.)
biomass and waste: 33.6% of total installed capacity (2020 est.)

Petroleum: *total petroleum production:* 0 bbl/day (2021 est.)
refined petroleum consumption: 14,300 bbl/day (2019 est.)

Refined petroleum products - imports: 14,180 bbl/day (2015 est.)

Natural gas: *production:* 0 cubic meters (2021 est.)
consumption: 136.714 million cubic meters (2019 est.)
exports: 0 cubic meters (2021 est.)
imports: 133.712 million cubic meters (2019 est.)
proven reserves: 0 cubic meters (2021 est.)

Carbon dioxide emissions: 2.012 million metric tonnes of CO2 (2019 est.)
from coal and metallurgical coke: 0 metric tonnes of CO2 (2019 est.)
from petroleum and other liquids: 1.744 million metric tonnes of CO2 (2019 est.)
from consumed natural gas: 268,000 metric tonnes of CO2 (2019 est.)

Energy consumption per capita: 81.407 million Btu/person (2019 est.)

COMMUNICATIONS

Telephones - fixed lines: *total subscriptions:* 110,000 (2020 est.)
subscriptions per 100 inhabitants: 17 (2020 est.)

Telephones - mobile cellular: *total subscriptions:* 2.793 million (2020 est.)
subscriptions per 100 inhabitants: 430 (2020 est.)

Telecommunication systems: *general assessment:* Macau's economy and GDP have been on a roller coaster ride since the start of the Covid-19 pandemic in 2020; the Special Administrative Region (SAR) of China is heavily dependent on tourists coming from the mainland and Hong Kong to play in Macau's many casinos, but the ensuing lock downs contributed to a dramatic fall in visitor numbers as well as income; this too, has had a major effect on the telecom sector (particularly in the mobile segment) with short-stay visitors as well as foreign workers on temporary-stay visas being forced to stay away.; total mobile subscription numbers are estimated to have dropped from a high of 2.8 million in 2019 (representing a whopping 442% penetration rate in a region with a population of just 700,000) to less than half that by the end of 2021: 1.3 million subscribers; Macau had almost the highest mobile penetration rate in the world; it is now sitting at a more 'reasonable' level of 200%; a significant bounce back can be expected to follow the easing of travel restrictions, although perhaps not up to the same lofty heights achieved in 2019; asecond factor behind the steep fall in 2020 was the introduction of a Cyber Security Law that required all prepaid SIM cards to become registered or face being deactivated in October 2020; the combined effect of the pandemic and the new restrictions meant that prepaid subscriber numbers fell by more than 80%; postpaid accounts, largely the domain of Macau's permanent residents, were barely affected by the external upheaval; they continued to increase in number, year-on-year, and provided better returns to the operators thanks to substantially increased data usage during the lock downs; the mobile broadband market has experienced the same dramatic fluctuations as the broader mobile segment over the last two years, at least in terms of subscriber numbers; but this is largely because mobile broadband uptake is inextricably tied to the base mobile offering in Macau; with total mobile broadband data traffic going up, not down, between 2019 and 2021, that again points to the strength of the contract segment helping to drive future growth in Macau's telecom sector (2022)
domestic: fixed-line nearly 17 per 100 and mobile-cellular roughly 430 per 100 persons (2020)
international: country code - 853; landing point for the SEA-ME-WE-3 submarine cable network that provides links to Asia, Africa, Australia, the Middle East, and Europe; HF radiotelephone communication facility; satellite earth station - 1 Intelsat (Indian Ocean) (2019)

Broadcast media: local government dominates broadcast media; 2 television stations operated by the government with one broadcasting in Portuguese and the other in Cantonese and Mandarin; 1 cable TV and 4 satellite TV services available; 3 radio stations broadcasting, of which 2 are government-operated (2019)

Internet country code: .mo

Internet users: *total:* 571,421 (2020 est.)
percent of population: 88% (2020 est.)

Broadband - fixed subscriptions: *total:* 208,000 (2020 est.)
subscriptions per 100 inhabitants: 32 (2020 est.)

TRANSPORTATION

National air transport system: *number of registered air carriers:* 1 (2020) (registered in China)
inventory of registered aircraft operated by air carriers: 21 (registered in China)
annual passenger traffic on registered air carriers: 3,157,724 (2018)
annual freight traffic on registered air carriers: 31.84 million (2018) mt-km

Civil aircraft registration country code prefix: B-M

Airports: *total:* 1 (2021)

Airports - with paved runways: *total:* 1
over 3,047 m: 1 (2021)

Heliports: 2 (2021)

Roadways: *total:* 428 km (2017)
*paved:*428 km (2017)

Merchant marine: *total:* 1
by type: other 1 (2021)

Ports and terminals: *major seaport(s):* Macau

MILITARY AND SECURITY

Military and security forces: no regular indigenous military forces; Macau Public Security Police Force (includes the Police Intervention Tactical Unit or UTIP for counterterrorism operations)

Military - note: defense is the responsibility of China; the Chinese People's Liberation Army (PLA) maintains a garrison in Macau

TRANSNATIONAL ISSUES

Disputes - international: none identified

Trafficking in persons: *current situation:* Macau is a destination and, to a much lesser extent, source for women and children subjected to sex trafficking and possibly forced labor; most victims come from the Chinese mainland, but others are trafficked from China, Russia, and Southeast Asia; victims are lured in by false job offers and forced into prostitution, often being confined to massage parlors and illegal brothels where their identity documents are confiscated and they are threatened with violence; Chinese, Russian, and Thai criminal organizations are believed to be involved in recruiting women for Macau's commercial sex industry
tier rating: Tier 2 Watch List — Macau does not fully meet the minimum standards for the elimination of trafficking but is making significant efforts to do so; the government trained police, customs, and social welfare officials on human trafficking, funded an awareness campaign, and provided services to victims; authorities convicted three sex traffickers but did not sentence anyone to significant prison terms; authorities investigated only one potential trafficking case and made no prosecutions; the government provided no assistance to any victims, and officials did not initiate any prosecutions or sentence convicted traffickers to significant terms of imprisonment; Macau was downgraded to Tier 2 Watch List (2020)

Illicit drugs: asian organized crime groups involved in drug trafficking and money laundering

MADAGASCAR

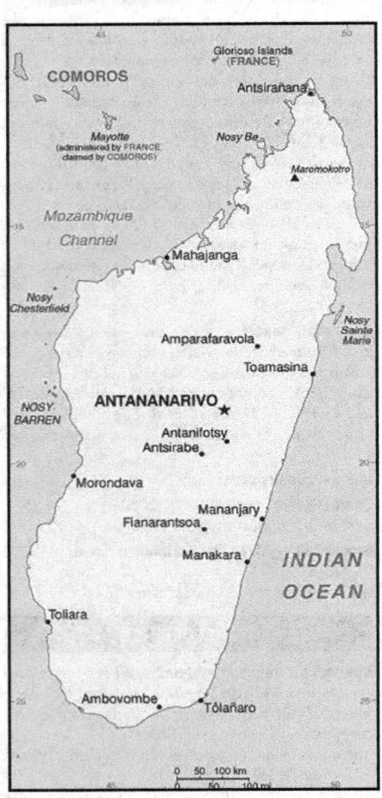

INTRODUCTION

Background: Madagascar was one of the last major habitable landmasses on earth settled by humans. While there is some evidence of human presence on the island in the millennia B.C., large-scale settlement began between A.D. 350 and 550 with settlers from present-day Indonesia. The island attracted Arab and Persian traders as early as the 7th century, and migrants from Africa arrived around A.D. 1000. Madagascar was a pirate stronghold during the late 17th and early 18th centuries, and served as a slave trading center into the 19th century. From the 16th to the late 19th century, a native Merina Kingdom dominated much of Madagascar. The island was conquered by the French in 1896 who made it a colony; independence was regained in 1960.

During 1992-93, free presidential and National Assembly elections were held ending 17 years of single-party rule. In 1997, in the second presidential race, Didier RATSIRAKA, the leader during the 1970s and 1980s, returned to the presidency. The 2001 presidential election was contested between the followers of Didier RATSIRAKA and Marc RAVALOMANANA, nearly causing secession of half of the country. In 2002, the High Constitutional Court announced RAVALOMANANA the winner. RAVALOMANANA won a second term in 2006 but, following protests in 2009, handed over power to the military, which then conferred the presidency on the mayor of Antananarivo, Andry RAJOELINA, in what amounted to a coup d'etat. Following a lengthy mediation process led by the Southern African Development Community, Madagascar held UN-supported presidential and parliamentary elections in 2013. Former de facto finance minister Hery RAJAONARIMAMPIANINA won a runoff election in December 2013 and was inaugurated in January 2014. In January 2019, RAJOELINA was declared the winner of a runoff election against RAVALOMANANA; both RATSIRAKA and RAJAONARIMAMPIANINA also ran in the first round of the election, which took place in November 2018.

GEOGRAPHY

Location: Southern Africa, island in the Indian Ocean, east of Mozambique

Geographic coordinates: 20 00 S, 47 00 E

Map references: Africa

Area: *total:* 587,041 sq km
land: 581,540 sq km
water: 5,501 sq km

Area - comparative: almost four times the size of Georgia; slightly less than twice the size of Arizona

Land boundaries: *total:* 0 km

Coastline: 4,828 km

Maritime claims: *territorial sea:* 12 nm
contiguous zone: 24 nm
exclusive economic zone: 200 nm
continental shelf: 200 nm or 100 nm from the 2,500-m isobath

Climate: tropical along coast, temperate inland, arid in south

Terrain: narrow coastal plain, high plateau and mountains in center

Elevation: *highest point:* Maromokotro 2,876 m
lowest point: Indian Ocean 0 m
mean elevation: 615 m

Natural resources: graphite, chromite, coal, bauxite, rare earth elements, salt, quartz, tar sands, semiprecious stones, mica, fish, hydropower

Land use: *agricultural land:* 71.1% (2018 est.)
arable land: 6% (2018 est.)
permanent crops: 1% (2018 est.)
permanent pasture: 64.1% (2018 est.)
forest: 21.5% (2018 est.)
other: 7.4% (2018 est.)

Irrigated land: 10,860 sq km (2012)

Population distribution: most of population lives on the eastern half of the island; significant clustering is found in the central highlands and eastern coastline as shown in this population distribution map

Natural hazards: periodic cyclones; drought; and locust infestation
volcanism: Madagascar's volcanoes have not erupted in historical times

Geography - note: world's fourth-largest island; strategic location along Mozambique Channel; despite Madagascar's close proximity to the African continent, ocean currents isolate the island resulting in high rates of endemic plant and animal species; approximately 90% of the flora and fauna on the island are found nowhere else

PEOPLE AND SOCIETY

Population: 28,172,462 (2022 est.)

Nationality: *noun:* Malagasy (singular and plural)
adjective: Malagasy

Ethnic groups: Malayo-Indonesian (Merina and related Betsileo), Cotiers (mixed African, Malayo-Indonesian, and Arab ancestry -Betsimisaraka, Tsimihety, Antaisaka, Sakalava), French, Indian, Creole, Comoran

Languages: Malagasy (official) 99.9%, French (official) 23.6%, English 8.2%, other 0.6% (2018 est.)
note: shares sum to more than 100% because some respondents gave more than one answer on the census

Religions: Church of Jesus Christ in Madagascar/Malagasy Lutheran Church/Anglican Church 34%, Roman Catholic 32.3%, other Christian 8.1%, traditional/Animist 1.7%, Muslim 1.4%, other 0.6%, none 21.9% (2021 est.)

Demographic profile: Madagascar's youthful population – just over 60% are under the age of 25 – and high total fertility rate of more than 4 children per women ensures that the Malagasy population will continue its rapid growth trajectory for the foreseeable future. The population is predominantly rural and poor; chronic malnutrition is prevalent, and large families are the norm. Many young Malagasy girls are withdrawn from school, marry early (often pressured to do so by their parents), and soon begin having children. Early childbearing, coupled with Madagascar's widespread poverty and lack of access to skilled health care providers during delivery, increases the risk of death and serious health problems for young mothers and their babies.

Child marriage perpetuates gender inequality and is prevalent among the poor, the uneducated, and rural households – as of 2013, of Malagasy women aged 20 to 24, more than 40% were married and more than a third had given birth by the age of 18. Although the legal age for marriage is 18, parental consent is often given for earlier marriages or the law is flouted, especially in rural areas that make up nearly 65% of the country. Forms of arranged marriage whereby young girls are married to older men in exchange for oxen or money are traditional. If a union does not work out, a girl can be placed in another marriage, but the dowry paid to her family diminishes with each unsuccessful marriage.

Madagascar's population consists of 18 main ethnic groups, all of whom speak the same Malagasy language. Most Malagasy are multi-ethnic, however, reflecting the island's diversity of settlers and historical contacts (see Background). Madagascar's legacy of hierarchical societies practicing domestic slavery (most notably the Merina Kingdom of the 16th to the 19th century) is evident today in persistent class tension, with some ethnic groups maintaining a caste system. Slave descendants are vulnerable to unequal access to education and jobs, despite Madagascar's constitutional guarantee of free compulsory primary education and its being party to several international conventions on human rights. Historical distinctions also remain between central highlanders and coastal people.

Age structure: *0-14 years:* 38.86% (male 5,278,838/female 5,196,036)
15-24 years: 20.06% (male 2,717,399/female 2,689,874)
25-54 years: 33.02% (male 4,443,147/female 4,456,691)
55-64 years: 4.6% (male 611,364/female 627,315)
65 years and over: 3.47% (male 425,122/female 509,951) (2020 est.)

Dependency ratios: *total dependency ratio:* 75.9
youth dependency ratio: 70.5
elderly dependency ratio: 5.5
potential support ratio: 18.3 (2020 est.)

Median age: *total:* 20.3 years
male: 20.1 years
female: 20.5 years (2020 est.)

Population growth rate: 2.27% (2022 est.)

Birth rate: 28.68 births/1,000 population (2022 est.)

Death rate: 6 deaths/1,000 population (2022 est.)

Net migration rate: 0 migrant(s)/1,000 population (2022 est.)

Population distribution: most of population lives on the eastern half of the island; significant clustering is found in the central highlands and eastern coastline as shown in this population distribution map

Urbanization: *urban population:* 39.9% of total population (2022)
rate of urbanization: 4.26% annual rate of change (2020-25 est.)

Major urban areas - population: 3.700 million ANTANANARIVO (capital) (2022)

Sex ratio: *at birth:* 1.03 male(s)/female
0-14 years: 1.02 male(s)/female
15-24 years: 1.02 male(s)/female
25-54 years: 1 male(s)/female
55-64 years: 0.98 male(s)/female
65 years and over: 0.78 male(s)/female
total population: 1 male(s)/female (2022 est.)

Mother's mean age at first birth: 19.5 years (2021 est.)
note: data represents median age at first birth among women 25-29

Maternal mortality ratio: 335 deaths/100,000 live births (2017 est.)

Infant mortality rate: *total:* 39.04 deaths/1,000 live births
male: 42.33 deaths/1,000 live births
female: 35.65 deaths/1,000 live births (2022 est.)

Life expectancy at birth: *total population:* 68.17 years
male: 66.8 years
female: 69.57 years (2022 est.)

Total fertility rate: 3.62 children born/woman (2022 est.)

Contraceptive prevalence rate: 49.7% (2020)

Drinking water source: *improved: urban:* 85% of population
rural: 38% of population
total: 56.1% of population
unimproved: urban: 15% of population
rural: 62% of population
total: 43.9% of population (2020 est.)

Current health expenditure: 3.7% of GDP (2019)

Physicians density: 0.2 physicians/1,000 population (2018)

Hospital bed density: 0.2 beds/1,000 population

Sanitation facility access: *improved: urban:* 49.2% of population
rural: 22.1% of population
total: 32.6% of population
unimproved: urban: 50.8% of population
rural: 77.9% of population
total: 67.4% of population (2020 est.)

HIV/AIDS - adult prevalence rate: 0.3% (2020 est.)

Major infectious diseases: *degree of risk:* very high (2020)
food or waterborne diseases: bacterial diarrhea, hepatitis A, and typhoid fever
vectorborne diseases: malaria and dengue fever
water contact diseases: schistosomiasis
animal contact diseases: rabies
note: on 21 March 2022, the US Centers for Disease Control and Prevention (CDC) issued a Travel Alert for polio in Africa; Madagascar is currently considered a high risk to travelers for circulating vaccine-derived polioviruses (cVDPV); vaccine-derived poliovirus (VDPV) is a strain of the weakened poliovirus that was initially included in oral polio vaccine (OPV) and *that has changed over time and behaves more like the wild or naturally occurring virus*; this means it can be spread more easily to people who are unvaccinated against polio and who come in contact with the stool or respiratory secretions, such as from a sneeze, of an "infected" person who received oral polio vaccine; the CDC recommends that before any international travel, anyone unvaccinated, incompletely vaccinated, or with an unknown polio vaccination status should complete the routine polio vaccine series; before travel to any high-risk destination, the CDC recommends that adults who previously completed the full, routine polio vaccine series receive a single, lifetime booster dose of polio vaccine

Obesity - adult prevalence rate: 5.3% (2016)

Alcohol consumption per capita: *total:* 0.89 liters of pure alcohol (2019 est.)
beer: 0.5 liters of pure alcohol (2019 est.)
wine: 0.07 liters of pure alcohol (2019 est.)
spirits: 0.32 liters of pure alcohol (2019 est.)
other alcohols: 0 liters of pure alcohol (2019 est.)

Tobacco use: *total:* 27.8% (2020 est.)
male: 42.7% (2020 est.)
female: 12.8% (2020 est.)

Children under the age of 5 years underweight: 26.4% (2018)

Child marriage: *women married by age 15:* 12.7%
women married by age 18: 40.3%
men married by age 18: 11.8% (2018 est.)

Education expenditures: 2.9% of GDP (2019 est.)

Literacy: *definition:* age 15 and over can read and write
total population: 76.7%
male: 78.4%
female: 75.1% (2018)

School life expectancy (primary to tertiary education): *total:* 10 years
male: 10 years
female: 10 years (2018)

Unemployment, youth ages 15-24: *total:* 3.4%
male: 3.9%
female: 3% (2015 est.)

ENVIRONMENT

Environment - current issues: erosion and soil degredation results from deforestation and overgrazing; desertification; agricultural fires; surface water contaminated with raw sewage and other organic wastes; wildlife preservation (endangered species of flora and fauna unique to the island)

Environment - international agreements: *party to:* Biodiversity, Climate Change, Climate Change-Kyoto Protocol, Climate Change-Paris Agreement, Comprehensive Nuclear Test Ban, Desertification, Endangered Species, Hazardous Wastes, Law of the Sea, Marine Dumping-London Protocol, Marine

Life Conservation, Nuclear Test Ban, Ozone Layer Protection, Ship Pollution, Tropical Timber 2006, Wetlands
signed, but not ratified: none of the selected agreements

Air pollutants: *particulate matter emissions:* 21.44 micrograms per cubic meter (2016 est.)
carbon dioxide emissions: 3.91 megatons (2016 est.)
methane emissions: 10.14 megatons (2020 est.)

Climate: tropical along coast, temperate inland, arid in south

Land use: *agricultural land:* 71.1% (2018 est.)
arable land: 6% (2018 est.)
permanent crops: 1% (2018 est.)
permanent pasture: 64.1% (2018 est.)
forest: 21.5% (2018 est.)
other: 7.4% (2018 est.)

Urbanization: *urban population:* 39.9% of total population (2022)
rate of urbanization: 4.26% annual rate of change (2020-25 est.)

Revenue from forest resources: *forest revenues:* 4.34% of GDP (2018 est.)

Revenue from coal: *coal revenues:* 0% of GDP (2018 est.)

Food insecurity: *severe localized food insecurity: due to the effects of extreme weather events and slow economic recovery* - according to the latest May 2022 analysis, the prevalence of food insecurity in the southern regions is projected to peak at 2.1 million people by December 2022 until at least March 2023; overall, the number of people requiring humanitarian assistance by the end of 2022 is expected to be about 30 percent higher compared to the peak number in 2021; the poor food security situation is mainly the consequence of six consecutive poor agricultural seasons that culminated in very tight food supplies for rural households and curbed incomes from crop sales; high rates of poverty and increased prices of essential food commodities, combined with a high reliance on market supplies due to low harvests for own consumption, are also contributing to the high rates of food insecurity across the southern regions (2022)

Waste and recycling: *municipal solid waste generated annually:* 3,768,759 tons (2016 est.)

Total water withdrawal: *municipal:* 395 million cubic meters (2017 est.)
industrial: 161.9 million cubic meters (2017 est.)
agricultural: 13 billion cubic meters (2017 est.)

Total renewable water resources: 337 billion cubic meters (2017 est.)

GOVERNMENT

Country name: *conventional long form:* Republic of Madagascar
conventional short form: Madagascar
local long form: Republique de Madagascar/Repoblikan'i Madagasikara
local short form: Madagascar/Madagasikara
former: Malagasy Republic
etymology: the name "Madageiscar" was first used by the 13th-century Venetian explorer Marco POLO, as a corrupted transliteration of Mogadishu, the Somali port with which POLO confused the island

Government type: semi-presidential republic

Capital: *name:* Antananarivo
geographic coordinates: 18 55 S, 47 31 E
time difference: UTC+3 (8 hours ahead of Washington, DC, during Standard Time)
etymology: the name, which means "City of the Thousand," was bestowed by 17th century King ADRIANJAKAKING to honor the soldiers assigned to guard the city

Administrative divisions: 6 provinces (faritany); Antananarivo, Antsiranana, Fianarantsoa, Mahajanga, Toamasina, Toliara

Independence: 26 June 1960 (from France)

National holiday: Independence Day, 26 June (1960)

Constitution: *history:* previous 1992; latest passed by referendum 17 November 2010, promulgated 11 December 2010
amendments: proposed by the president of the republic in consultation with the cabinet or supported by a least two thirds of both the Senate and National Assembly membership; passage requires at least three-fourths approval of both the Senate and National Assembly and approval in a referendum; constitutional articles, including the form and powers of government, the sovereignty of the state, and the autonomy of Madagascar's collectivities, cannot be amended

Legal system: civil law system based on the old French civil code and customary law in matters of marriage, family, and obligation

International law organization participation: accepts compulsory ICJ jurisdiction with reservations; accepts ICCt jurisdiction

Citizenship: *citizenship by birth:* no
citizenship by descent only: the father must be a citizen of Madagascar; in the case of a child born out of wedlock, the mother must be a citizen
dual citizenship recognized: no
residency requirement for naturalization: unknown

Suffrage: 18 years of age; universal

Executive branch: *chief of state:* President Andry RAJOELINA (since 21 January 2019)
head of government: Prime Minister Christian NTSAY (since 6 June 2018)
cabinet: Council of Ministers appointed by the prime minister
elections/appointments: president directly elected by absolute majority popular vote in 2 rounds if needed for a 5-year term (eligible for a second term); election last held on 7 November and 19 December 2018 (next to be held in 2023); prime minister nominated by the National Assembly, appointed by the president
election results:
2018: Andry RAJOELINA elected President in second round; percent of vote in first round - Andry RAJOELINA (TGV) 39.2%, Marc RAVALOMANANA (TIM) 35.4%, other 25.4%; percent of vote in second round - Andry RAJOELINA (TGV) 55.7%, Marc RAVALOMANANA (TIM) 44.3%
2013: Hery Martial RAJAONARIMAMPIANINA elected president in second round; percent of vote in first round - Hery Martial RAJAONARIMAMPIANINA (HVM) 15.9%, Jean Louis ROBINSON (AVANA) 21.1%, other 63%; percent of vote in second round - Hery Martial RAJAONARIMAMPIANINA (HVM) 53.5%, Jean Louis ROBINSON (AVANA) 46.5%

Legislative branch: *description:* bicameral Parliament consists of:
Senate or Antenimieran-Doholona (18 seats; 12 members indirectly elected by an electoral college of municipal, communal, regional, and provincial leaders and 6 appointed by the president; members serve 5-year terms)
National Assembly or Antenimierampirenena (151 seats; 87 members directly elected in single-seat constituencies by simple majority vote and 64 directly elected in multi-seat constituencies by closed-list proportional representation vote; members serve 5-year terms)
elections:
Senate - last held on 11 December 2020 (next to be held in December 2025)
National Assembly - last held on 27 May 2019 (next to be held in May 2024)
election results:
2020: Senate - percent of vote by party - NA; elected seats by party - Irmar 10, Malagasy Miara Miainga 2; composition - men 16, women 2, percent of women 11%
2019: National Assembly - percent of vote by party -Independent Pro-HVM 18%, MAPAR 17%, MAPAR pro-HVM 16%, TIM 13%' VPM-MMM 10%, GPS/ARD 7%, HIARAKA ISIKA 3%, LEADER FANILO 3%, VERTS 3%, TAMBATRA 1%, independent 9%; composition - men 123, women 28, percent of women 18.5%; note - total Parliament percent of women 17.8%

Judicial branch: *highest court(s):* Supreme Court or Cour Supreme (consists of 11 members; addresses judicial administration issues only); High Constitutional Court or Haute Cour Constitutionnelle (consists of 9 members); note - the judiciary includes a High Court of Justice responsible for adjudicating crimes and misdemeanors by government officials, including the president
judge selection and term of office: Supreme Court heads elected by the president and judiciary officials to serve 3-year, single renewable terms; High Constitutional Court members appointed - 3 each by the president, by both legislative bodies, and by the Council of Magistrates; members serve single, 7-year terms
subordinate courts: Courts of Appeal; Courts of First Instance

Political parties and leaders: Economic Liberalism and Democratic Action for National Recovery or LEADER FANILO [Jean Max RAKOTOMAMONJY]
FOMBA [Ny Rado RAFALIMANANA]
Gideons Fighting Against Poverty in Madagascar (Gedeona Miady amin'ny Fahantrana eto Madagascar) or GFFM [Andre Christian Dieu Donne MAILHOL]
Green Party or VERTS (Antoko Maintso) [Alexandre GEORGET]
I Love Madagascar (Tiako I Madagasikara) or TIM [Marc RAVALOMANANA]
Irmar
Malagasy Aware (Malagasy Tonga Saina) or MTS [Roland RATSIRAKA]
Malagasy Raising Together (Malagasy Miara-Miainga) or MMM [Hajo ANDRIANAINARIVELO]
New Force for Madagascar (Hery Vaovao ho an'ny Madagasikara) or HVM [Hery Martial RAJAONARIMAMPIANINA Rakotoarimanana]
Total Refoundation of Madagascar (Refondation Totale de Madagascar) or RTM [Joseph Martin RANDRIAMAMPIONONA]
Vanguard for the Renovation of Madagascar (Avant-Garde pour la renovation de Madagascar) or AREMA [Didier RATSIRAKA]

Young Malagasies Determined (Malagasy: Tanora malaGasy Vonona) or TGV [Andry RAJOELINA] and MAPAR [Andry RAJOELINA], and IRD (We are all with Andry Rajoelina) [Andry RAJOELINA]

International organization participation: ACP, AfDB, AU, CD, COMESA, EITI (candidate country), FAO, G-77, IAEA, IBRD, ICAO, ICC (NGOs), ICCt, ICRM, IDA, IFAD, IFC, IFRCS, ILO, IMF, IMO, InOC, Interpol, IOC, IOM, IPU, ISO (correspondent), ITSO, ITU, ITUC (NGOs), MIGA, NAM, OIF, OPCW, PCA, SADC, UN, UNCTAD, UNESCO, UNHCR, UNIDO, UNWTO, UPU, WCO, WFTU (NGOs), WHO, WIPO, WMO, WTO

Diplomatic representation in the US: *chief of mission:*
Ambassador (vacant); Charge d'Affaires Amielle Pelenne NIRINIAVISOA MARCEDA (since 31 October 2019)
chancery: 2374 Massachusetts Avenue NW, Washington, DC 20008
telephone: [1] (202) 265-5525
FAX: [1] (202) 265-3034
email address and website:
contact@us-madagascar-embassy.org
https://us-madagascar-embassy.org/
consulate(s) general: New York

Diplomatic representation from the US: *chief of mission:* Ambassador (vacant); Charge d'Affaires Tobias H. GLUCKSMAN
embassy: Lot 207A, Andranoro, Antehiroka, 105 Antananarivo
mailing address: 2040 Antananarivo Place, Washington DC 20521-2040
telephone: [261] 20-23-480-00
FAX: [261] 20-23-480-35
email address and website:
antanACS@state.gov
https://mg.usembassy.gov/

Flag description: two equal horizontal bands of red (top) and green with a vertical white band of the same width on hoist side; by tradition, red stands for sovereignty, green for hope, white for purity

National symbol(s): traveller's palm, zebu; national colors: red, green, white

National anthem: *name:* "Ry Tanindraza nay malala o" (Oh, Our Beloved Fatherland)
lyrics/music: Pasteur RAHAJASON/Norbert RAHARISOA
note: adopted 1959

National heritage: *total World Heritage Sites:* 3 (1 cultural, 2 natural)
selected World Heritage Site locales: Tsingy de Bemaraha Strict Nature Reserve (n); Ambohimanga Royal Hill (c); Atsinanana Rainforests (n)

ECONOMY

Economic overview: Madagascar is a mostly unregulated economy with many untapped natural resources, but no capital markets, a weak judicial system, poorly enforced contracts, and rampant government corruption. The country faces challenges to improve education, healthcare, and the environment to boost long-term economic growth. Agriculture, including fishing and forestry, is a mainstay of the economy, accounting for more than one-fourth of GDP and employing roughly 80% of the population. Deforestation and erosion, aggravated by bushfires, slash-and-burn clearing techniques, and the use of firewood as the primary source of fuel, are serious concerns to the agriculture dependent economy.

After discarding socialist economic policies in the mid-1990s, Madagascar followed a World Bank- and IMF-led policy of privatization and liberalization until a 2009 coup d'état led many nations, including the United States, to suspend non-humanitarian aid until a democratically-elected president was inaugurated in 2014. The pre-coup strategy had placed the country on a slow and steady growth path from an extremely low starting point. Exports of apparel boomed after gaining duty-free access to the US market in 2000 under the African Growth and Opportunity Act (AGOA); however, Madagascar's failure to comply with the requirements of the AGOA led to the termination of the country's duty-free access in January 2010, a sharp fall in textile production, a loss of more than 100,000 jobs, and a GDP drop of nearly 11%.

Madagascar regained AGOA access in January 2015 and ensuing growth has been slow and fragile. Madagascar produces around 80% of the world's vanilla and its reliance on this commodity for most of its foreign exchange is a significant source of vulnerability. Economic reforms have been modest and the country's financial sector remains weak, limiting the use of monetary policy to control inflation. An ongoing IMF program aims to strengthen financial and investment management capacity.

Real GDP (purchasing power parity): $41.82 billion (2020 est.)
$43.65 billion (2019 est.)
$41.81 billion (2018 est.)
note: data are in 2017 dollars

Real GDP growth rate: 4.2% (2017 est.)
4.2% (2016 est.)
3.1% (2015 est.)

Real GDP per capita: $1,500 (2020 est.)
$1,600 (2019 est.)
$1,600 (2018 est.)
note: data are in 2017 dollars

GDP (official exchange rate): $13.964 billion (2019 est.)

Inflation rate (consumer prices): 5.6% (2019 est.)
8.6% (2018 est.)
8.5% (2017 est.)

GDP - composition, by sector of origin: *agriculture:* 24% (2017 est.)
industry: 19.5% (2017 est.)
services: 56.4% (2017 est.)

GDP - composition, by end use: *household consumption:* 67.1% (2017 est.)
government consumption: 11.2% (2017 est.)
investment in fixed capital: 15.1% (2017 est.)
investment in inventories: 8.8% (2017 est.)
exports of goods and services: 31.5% (2017 est.)
imports of goods and services: -33.7% (2017 est.)

Agricultural products: rice, sugar cane, cassava, sweet potatoes, milk, vegetables, bananas, mangoes/guavas, tropical fruit, potatoes

Industries: meat processing, seafood, soap, beer, leather, sugar, textiles, glassware, cement, automobile assembly plant, paper, petroleum, tourism, mining

Industrial production growth rate: 5.2% (2017 est.)

Labor force: 13.4 million (2017 est.)

Unemployment rate: 1.8% (2017 est.)
1.8% (2016 est.)

Unemployment, youth ages 15-24: *total:* 3.4%
male: 3.9%
female: 3% (2015 est.)

Population below poverty line: 70.7% (2012 est.)

Gini Index coefficient - distribution of family income: 42.6 (2012 est.)
42.7 (2010)

Household income or consumption by percentage share: *lowest 10%:* 2.2%
highest 10%: 34.7% (2010 est.)

Budget: *revenues:* 1.828 billion (2017 est.)
expenditures: 2.136 billion (2017 est.)

Budget surplus (+) or deficit (-): -2.7% (of GDP) (2017 est.)

Public debt: 36% of GDP (2017 est.)
38.4% of GDP (2016 est.)

Taxes and other revenues: 15.9% (of GDP) (2017 est.)

Fiscal year: calendar year

Current account balance: -$35 million (2017 est.)
$57 million (2016 est.)

Exports: $4.09 billion (2019 est.) note: data are in current year dollars
$4.41 billion (2018 est.) note: data are in current year dollars
$4.839 billion (2017 est.)

Exports - partners: United States 19%, France 18%, United Arab Emirates 7%, China 6%, Japan 6%, Germany 5%, India 5% (2019)

Exports - commodities: vanilla, nickel, gold, clothing and apparel, gemstones (2019)

Imports: $4.7 billion (2019 est.) note: data are in current year dollars
$4.82 billion (2018 est.) note: data are in current year dollars
$5.796 billion (2017 est.)

Imports - partners: China 24%, France 11%, United Arab Emirates 9%, India 7%, South Africa 5% (2019)

Imports - commodities: refined petroleum, rice, cars, packaged medicines, clothing and apparel (2019)

Reserves of foreign exchange and gold: $1.6 billion (31 December 2017 est.)
$1.076 billion (31 December 2016 est.)

Debt - external: $3.085 billion (2019 est.)
$4.107 billion (2018 est.)

Exchange rates: Malagasy ariary (MGA) per US dollar -
3,116.1 (2017 est.)
3,176.5 (2016 est.)
3,176.5 (2015 est.)
2,933.5 (2014 est.)
2,414.8 (2013 est.)

ENERGY

Electricity access: *electrification - total population:* 39% (2019)
electrification - urban areas: 64% (2019)
electrification - rural areas: 23% (2019)

Electricity: *installed generating capacity:* 587,000 kW (2020 est.)
consumption: 1,720,140,000 kWh (2019 est.)
exports: 0 kWh (2020 est.)
imports: 0 kWh (2020 est.)
transmission/distribution losses: 131 million kWh (2019 est.)

Electricity generation sources: *fossil fuels:* 59.8% of total installed capacity (2020 est.)

solar: 1.1% of total installed capacity (2020 est.)
hydroelectricity: 38.2% of total installed capacity (2020 est.)
biomass and waste: 1% of total installed capacity (2020 est.)

Coal: *production:* 0 metric tons (2020 est.)
consumption: 107,000 metric tons (2020 est.)
exports: 0 metric tons (2020 est.)
imports: 115,000 metric tons (2020 est.)
proven reserves: 0 metric tons (2019 est.)

Petroleum: *total petroleum production:* 0 bbl/day (2021 est.)
refined petroleum consumption: 21,100 bbl/day (2019 est.)

Refined petroleum products - imports: 18,880 bbl/day (2015 est.)

Carbon dioxide emissions: 4.218 million metric tonnes of CO2 (2019 est.)
from coal and metallurgical coke: 1.044 million metric tonnes of CO2 (2019 est.)
from petroleum and other liquids: 3.175 million metric tonnes of CO2 (2019 est.)

Energy consumption per capita: 2.307 million Btu/person (2019 est.)

COMMUNICATIONS

Telephones - fixed lines: *total subscriptions:* 69,000 (2020 est.)

Telephones - mobile cellular: *total subscriptions:* 15.869 million (2020 est.)
subscriptions per 100 inhabitants: 57 (2020 est.)

Telecommunication systems: *general assessment:* Telecom services in Madagascar have benefited from intensifying competition between the main operators; there have been positive developments with the country's link to international submarine cables, particularly the METISS cable connecting to South Africa and Mauritius; in addition, the country's connection to the Africa-1 cable, expected in late 2023, will provide it with links to Kenya, Djibouti, countries in north and south Africa, as well Pakistan, the UAE, Saudi Arabia, and France; a national fiber backbone has been implemented connecting the major cities; in addition, the government has progressed with its five-year plan to develop a digital platform running to 2024; various schemes within the program have been managed by a unit within the President's office; penetration rates in all market sectors remain below the average for the African region, and so there remains considerable growth potential; much progress was made in 2020, stimulated by the particular conditions related to the pandemic, which encouraged greater use of voice and data services (2022)
domestic: less than 1 per 100 for fixed-line and mobile-cellular teledensity about 57 per 100 persons (2020)
international: country code - 261; landing points for the EASSy, METISS, and LION fiber-optic submarine cable systems connecting to numerous Indian Ocean Islands, South Africa, and Eastern African countries; satellite earth stations - 2 (1 Intelsat - Indian Ocean, 1 Intersputnik - Atlantic Ocean region) (2019)

Broadcast media: state-owned Radio Nationale Malagasy (RNM) and Television Malagasy (TVM) have an extensive national network reach; privately owned radio and TV broadcasters in cities and major towns; state-run radio dominates in rural areas; relays of 2 international broadcasters are available in Antananarivo (2019)

Internet country code: .mg

Internet users: *total:* 2,696,931 (2019 est.)
percent of population: 10% (2019 est.)

Broadband - fixed subscriptions: *total:* 32,000 (2020 est.)
subscriptions per 100 inhabitants: 0.1 (2020 est.)

TRANSPORTATION

National air transport system: *number of registered air carriers:* 4 (2020)
inventory of registered aircraft operated by air carriers: 18
annual passenger traffic on registered air carriers: 541,290 (2018)
annual freight traffic on registered air carriers: 16.25 million (2018) mt-km

Civil aircraft registration country code prefix: 5R

Airports: *total:* 83 (2021)

Airports - with paved runways: *total:* 26
over 3,047 m: 1
2,438 to 3,047 m: 2
1,524 to 2,437 m: 6
914 to 1,523 m: 16
under 914 m: 1 (2021)

Airports - with unpaved runways: *total:* 57
1,524 to 2,437 m: 1
914 to 1,523 m: 38
under 914 m: 18 (2021)

Railways: *total:* 836 km (2018)
narrow gauge: 836 km (2018) 1.000-m gauge

Roadways: *total:* 31,640 km (2018)

Waterways: 600 km (2011) (432 km navigable)

Merchant marine: *total:* 27
by type: general cargo 14, oil tanker 2, other 11 (2021)

Ports and terminals: *major seaport(s):* Antsiranana (Diego Suarez), Mahajanga, Toamasina, Toliara (Tulear)

MILITARY AND SECURITY

Military and security forces: Madagascar People's Armed Forces (PAF): Army, Navy, Air Force; Ministry of Defense: National Gendarmerie; Ministry of Public Security: National Police (2022)
note: the National Gendarmerie is separate from the PAF and is responsible for maintaining law and order in rural areas at the village level, protecting government facilities, and operating a maritime police contingent; the National Police is responsible for maintaining law and order in urban areas

Military expenditures: 0.7% of GDP (2021 est.)
0.7% of GDP (2020 est.)
0.5% of GDP (2019 est.) (approximately $130 million)
0.5% of GDP (2018 est.) (approximately $130 million)
0.5% of GDP (2017 est.) (approximately $120 million)

Military and security service personnel strengths: approximately 13,000 personnel (12,000 Army; 500 Navy; 500 Air Force); estimated 10,000 Gendarmerie (2022)

Military equipment inventories and acquisitions: the PAF's inventory consists mostly of aging Soviet-era equipment; since 2010, it has received limited amounts of second-hand equipment from France, South Africa, and the UAE (2022)

Military service age and obligation: 18-25 years of age for men and women; service obligation 18 months; no conscription; women are permitted to serve in all branches (2022)

Military - note: one of the military's duties is assisting the gendarmerie with maintaining law and order in rural areas, particularly in areas affected by banditry, cattle rustling (cattle thieves are known as dahalo), and criminal groups (2022)

TRANSNATIONAL ISSUES

Disputes - international: *Madagascar-France:* claims Bassas da India, Europa Island, Glorioso Islands, and Juan de Nova Island (all administered by France); the vegetated drying cays of Banc du Geyser, which were claimed by Madagascar in 1976, also fall within the EEZ claim of France
Madagascar-Comoros: the vegetated drying cays of Banc du Geyser, which were claimed by Madagascar in 1976, also fall within the EEZ claim of the Comoros

Illicit drugs: illicit producer of cannabis (cultivated and wild varieties) used mostly for domestic consumption; transshipment point for Southwest Asian heroin

MALAWI

INTRODUCTION

Background: Malawi shares its name with the Chewa word for flames and is linked to the Maravi people from whom the Chewa language originated. The Maravi settled in what is now Malawi around 1400 during one of the later waves of Bantu migration across central and southern Africa. Several of Malawi's ethnic groups trace their origins to different Maravi lineages. A powerful Maravi kingdom, established around 1500, reached its zenith around 1700, when it controlled what is now southern and central Malawi as well as portions of neighboring Mozambique and Zambia before beginning to decline because of destabilization from the escalating global trade in enslaved people. In the early 1800s, widespread conflict in southern Africa displaced various ethnic Ngoni groups, some of which moved

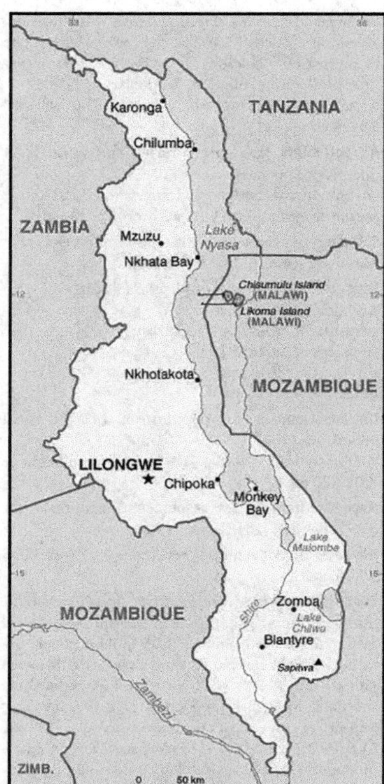

into Malawi and further undermined the Maravi. Members of the Yao ethnic group - which had long traded with Malawi from Mozambique - introduced Islam and began to settle in Malawi in significant numbers in the mid-1800s; in the late 1800s, members of the Lomwe ethnic group also moved into southern Malawi from Mozambique. British missionary and trading activity increased in the area around Lake Nyasa in the mid-1800s, and Britain declared a protectorate, called British Central Africa, over what is now Malawi in 1891 and eliminated various political entities that sought to retain their autonomy over the subsequent decade. The British renamed the territory Nyasaland in 1907 and it was part of the colonial Federation of Rhodesia and Nyasaland - including present-day Zambia and Zimbabwe - from 1953 to 1963 before gaining independence as Malawi in 1964.

Hastings Kamuzu BANDA served as prime minister at independence and, when the country became a republic in 1966, he became president. He later instituted one-party rule under his Malawi Congress Party (MCP) and was declared president for life. After three decades of one-party rule, the country held multiparty presidential and parliamentary elections in 1994 under a provisional constitution that came into full effect the following year. Bakili MULUZI of the United Democratic Front party became the first freely elected president of Malawi when he defeated BANDA at the polls in 1994; he won reelection in 1999. President Bingu wa MUTHARIKA was elected in 2004 and subsequently started his own party, the Democratic Progressive Party, in 2005. MUTHARIKA was reelected to a second term in 2009. He died abruptly in 2012 and was succeeded by Vice President Joyce BANDA, who had earlier started her own party, the People's Party. MUTHARIKA's brother, Peter MUTHARIKA, defeated BANDA in the election in 2014. Peter MUTHARIKA was reelected in a disputed election in 2019 that resulted in countrywide protests. The courts ordered a new the election, and in 2020 Lazarus CHAKWERA of the MCP was elected president after defeating MUTHARIKA as head of a coalition of opposition parties. Population growth, increasing pressure on agricultural lands, corruption, and the scourge of HIV/AIDS pose major problems for Malawi.

GEOGRAPHY

Location: Southern Africa, east of Zambia, west and north of Mozambique

Geographic coordinates: 13 30 S, 34 00 E

Map references: Africa

Area: *total:* 118,484 sq km
land: 94,080 sq km
water: 24,404 sq km

Area - comparative: slightly smaller than Pennsylvania

Land boundaries: *total:* 2,857 km
border countries (3): Mozambique 1,498 km; Tanzania 512 km; Zambia 847 km

Coastline: 0 km (landlocked)

Maritime claims: none (landlocked)

Climate: sub-tropical; rainy season (November to May); dry season (May to November)

Terrain: narrow elongated plateau with rolling plains, rounded hills, some mountains

Elevation: *highest point:* Sapitwa (Mount Mlanje) 3,002 m
lowest point: junction of the Shire River and international boundary with Mozambique 37 m
mean elevation: 779 m

Natural resources: limestone, arable land, hydropower, unexploited deposits of uranium, coal, and bauxite

Land use: *agricultural land:* 59.2% (2018 est.)
arable land: 38.2% (2018 est.)
permanent crops: 1.4% (2018 est.)
permanent pasture: 19.6% (2018 est.)
forest: 34% (2018 est.)
other: 6.8% (2018 est.)

Irrigated land: 740 sq km (2012)

Major lakes (area sq km): *fresh water lake(s):* Lake Malawi (shared with Mozambique and Tanzania) - 22,490
salt water lake(s): Lake Chilwa - 1,040 sq km

Major rivers (by length in km): Zambezi (shared with Zambia [s], Angola, Zimbabwe, Namibia, Tanzania, and Mozambique [m]) - 2,740 km
note – [s] after country name indicates river source; [m] after country name indicates river mouth

Major watersheds (area sq km): Atlantic Ocean drainage: Congo (3,730,881 sq km)
Indian Ocean drainage: Zambezi (1,332,412 sq km)

Population distribution: population density is highest south of Lake Nyasa as shown in this population distribution map

Natural hazards: flooding; droughts; earthquakes

Geography - note: landlocked; Lake Nyasa, some 580 km long, is the country's most prominent physical feature; it contains more fish species than any other lake on earth

PEOPLE AND SOCIETY

Population: 20,794,353 (2022 est.)

Nationality: *noun:* Malawian(s)
adjective: Malawian

Ethnic groups: Chewa 34.3%, Lomwe 18.8%, Yao 13.2%, Ngoni 10.4%, Tumbuka 9.2%, Sena 3.8%, Mang'anja 3.2%, Tonga 1.8%, Nyanja 1.8%, Nkhonde 1%, other 2.2%, foreign 0.3% (2018 est.)

Languages: English (official), Chewa (common), Lambya, Lomwe, Ngoni, Nkhonde, Nyakyusa, Nyanja, Sena, Tonga, Tumbuka, Yao
note: Chewa and Nyanja are mutually intelligible dialects; Nkhonde and Nyakyusa are mutually intelligible dialects

Religions: Protestant 33.5% (includes Church of Central Africa Presbyterian 14.2%, Seventh Day Adventist/Baptist 9.4%, Pentecostal 7.6%, Anglican 2.3%), Roman Catholic 17.2%, other Christian 26.6%, Muslim 13.8%, traditionalist 1.1%, other 5.6%, none 2.1% (2018 est.)

Demographic profile: Malawi has made great improvements in maternal and child health, but has made less progress in reducing its high fertility rate. In both rural and urban areas, very high proportions of mothers are receiving prenatal care and skilled birth assistance, and most children are being vaccinated. Malawi's fertility rate, however, has only declined slowly, decreasing from more than 7 children per woman in the 1980s to about 5.5 today. Nonetheless, Malawians prefer smaller families than in the past, and women are increasingly using contraceptives to prevent or space pregnancies. Rapid population growth and high population density is putting pressure on Malawi's land, water, and forest resources. Reduced plot sizes and increasing vulnerability to climate change, further threaten the sustainability of Malawi's agriculturally based economy and will worsen food shortages. About 80% of the population is employed in agriculture.

Historically, Malawians migrated abroad in search of work, primarily to South Africa and present-day Zimbabwe, but international migration became uncommon after the 1970s, and most migration in recent years has been internal. During the colonial period, Malawians regularly migrated to southern Africa as contract farm laborers, miners, and domestic servants. In the decade and a half after independence in 1964, the Malawian Government sought to transform its economy from one dependent on small-scale farms to one based on estate agriculture. The resulting demand for wage labor induced more than 300,000 Malawians to return home between the mid-1960s and the mid-1970s. In recent times, internal migration has generally been local, motivated more by marriage than economic reasons.

Age structure: *0-14 years:* 45.87% (male 4,843,107/female 4,878,983)
15-24 years: 20.51% (male 2,151,417/female 2,195,939)
25-54 years: 27.96% (male 2,944,936/female 2,982,195)
55-64 years: 2.98% (male 303,803/female 328,092)

65 years and over: 2.68% (male 249,219/female 318,938) (2020 est.)

Dependency ratios: *total dependency ratio:* 83.9
youth dependency ratio: 79.1
elderly dependency ratio: 4.9
potential support ratio: 20.6 (2020 est.)

Median age: *total:* 16.8 years
male: 16.7 years
female: 16.9 years (2020 est.)

Population growth rate: 2.34% (2022 est.)

Birth rate: 27.94 births/1,000 population (2022 est.)

Death rate: 4.58 deaths/1,000 population (2022 est.)

Net migration rate: 0 migrant(s)/1,000 population (2022 est.)

Population distribution: population density is highest south of Lake Nyasa as shown in this population distribution map

Urbanization: *urban population:* 18% of total population (2022)
rate of urbanization: 4.41% annual rate of change (2020-25 est.)

Major urban areas - population: 1.222 million LILONGWE (capital), 995,000 Blantyre-Limbe (2022)

Sex ratio: *at birth:* 1.02 male(s)/female
0-14 years: 0.99 male(s)/female
15-24 years: 0.97 male(s)/female
25-54 years: 0.95 male(s)/female
55-64 years: 0.9 male(s)/female
65 years and over: 0.64 male(s)/female
total population: 0.96 male(s)/female (2022 est.)

Mother's mean age at first birth: 19.1 years (2015/16 est.)
note: data represents median age at first birth among women 20-49

Maternal mortality ratio: 349 deaths/100,000 live births (2017 est.)

Infant mortality rate: *total:* 33.43 deaths/1,000 live births
male: 37.86 deaths/1,000 live births
female: 28.93 deaths/1,000 live births (2022 est.)

Life expectancy at birth: *total population:* 72.44 years
male: 69.33 years
female: 75.59 years (2022 est.)

Total fertility rate: 3.4 children born/woman (2022 est.)

Contraceptive prevalence rate: 65.6% (2019/20)

Drinking water source: *improved: urban:* 96.7% of population
rural: 91% of population
total: 92% of population
unimproved: urban: 3.3% of population
rural: 9% of population
total: 8% of population (2020 est.)

Current health expenditure: 7.4% of GDP (2019)

Physicians density: 0.05 physicians/1,000 population (2020)

Hospital bed density: 1.3 beds/1,000 population (2011)

Sanitation facility access: *improved: urban:* 59.9% of population
rural: 35.9% of population
total: 40% of population
unimproved: urban: 40.1% of population
rural: 64.1% of population
total: 60% of population (2020 est.)

HIV/AIDS - adult prevalence rate: 8.1% (2020 est.)

Major infectious diseases: *degree of risk:* very high (2020)
food or waterborne diseases: bacterial and protozoal diarrhea, hepatitis A, and typhoid fever
vectorborne diseases: malaria and dengue fever
water contact diseases: schistosomiasis
animal contact diseases: rabies
note: on 21 March 2022, the US Centers for Disease Control and Prevention (CDC) issued a Travel Alert for polio in Africa; Malawi is currently considered a high risk to travelers for circulating vaccine-derived polioviruses (cVDPV); vaccine-derived poliovirus (VDPV) is a strain of the weakened poliovirus that was initially included in oral polio vaccine (OPV) and *that has changed over time and behaves more like the wild or naturally occurring virus;* this means it can be spread more easily to people who are unvaccinated against polio and who come in contact with the stool or respiratory secretions, such as from a sneeze, of an "infected" person who received oral polio vaccine; the CDC recommends that before any international travel, anyone unvaccinated, incompletely vaccinated, or with an unknown polio vaccination status should complete the routine polio vaccine series; before travel to any high-risk destination, the CDC recommends that adults who previously completed the full, routine polio vaccine series receive a single, lifetime booster dose of polio vaccine

Obesity - adult prevalence rate: 5.8% (2016)

Alcohol consumption per capita: *total:* 2.04 liters of pure alcohol (2019 est.)
beer: 0.08 liters of pure alcohol (2019 est.)
wine: 0 liters of pure alcohol (2019 est.)
spirits: 0.25 liters of pure alcohol (2019 est.)
other alcohols: 1.7 liters of pure alcohol (2019 est.)

Tobacco use: *total:* 10.8% (2020 est.)
male: 17.5% (2020 est.)
female: 4.1% (2020 est.)

Children under the age of 5 years underweight: 9% (2019)

Education expenditures: 2.9% of GDP (2020 est.)

Literacy: *definition:* age 15 and over can read and write
total population: 62.1%
male: 69.8%
female: 55.2% (2015)

School life expectancy (primary to tertiary education): *total:* 11 years
male: 11 years
female: 11 years (2011)

Unemployment, youth ages 15-24: *total:* 8.5%
male: 6.7%
female: 10.6% (2017 est.)

ENVIRONMENT

Environment - current issues: deforestation; land degradation; water pollution from agricultural runoff, sewage, industrial wastes; siltation of spawning grounds endangers fish populations; negative effects of climate change (extreme high temperatures, changing precipitation patterns)

Environment - international agreements: *party to:* Biodiversity, Climate Change, Climate Change-Kyoto Protocol, Climate Change-Paris Agreement, Comprehensive Nuclear Test Ban, Desertification, Endangered Species, Environmental Modification, Hazardous Wastes, Law of the Sea, Marine Life Conservation, Nuclear Test Ban, Ozone Layer Protection, Ship Pollution, Wetlands
signed, but not ratified: none of the selected agreements

Air pollutants: *particulate matter emissions:* 22.14 micrograms per cubic meter (2016 est.)
carbon dioxide emissions: 1.3 megatons (2016 est.)
methane emissions: 11.12 megatons (2020 est.)

Climate: sub-tropical; rainy season (November to May); dry season (May to November)

Land use: *agricultural land:* 59.2% (2018 est.)
arable land: 38.2% (2018 est.)
permanent crops: 1.4% (2018 est.)
permanent pasture: 19.6% (2018 est.)
forest: 34% (2018 est.)
other: 6.8% (2018 est.)

Urbanization: *urban population:* 18% of total population (2022)
rate of urbanization: 4.41% annual rate of change (2020-25 est.)

Revenue from forest resources: *forest revenues:* 6.19% of GDP (2018 est.)

Revenue from coal: *coal revenues:* 0.03% of GDP (2018 est.)

Food insecurity: *severe localized food insecurity: due to reduced incomes and shortfalls in cereal production* - an estimated 1.65 million people are facing "Crisis" levels of food insecurity between January and March 2022, underpinned by localized shortfalls in cereal production and the lingering impact of an economic downturn due to the COVID-19 pandemic; a moderate decline in cereal production in 2022, particularly in southern districts, and increasing food prices are expected to lead to an increased prevalence of food insecurity in the last quarter of 2022; the prevalence of food insecurity is likely to increase in the second half of 2022 and early 2023 mainly due to the high food prices and low cereal production in southern districts; in addition to the adverse impacts of the low cereal harvest in the south and high food prices across the country, a third factor that is foreseen to contribute to a worsening of food insecurity conditions is the forecasted slow economic growth in 2022, underpinned by the lingering effects of the COVID-19 pandemic and the country's elevated debt levels (2022)

Waste and recycling: *municipal solid waste generated annually:* 1,297,844 tons (2013 est.)

Major lakes (area sq km): *fresh water lake(s):* Lake Malawi (shared with Mozambique and Tanzania) - 22,490
salt water lake(s): Lake Chilwa - 1,040 sq km

Major rivers (by length in km): Zambezi (shared with Zambia [s], Angola, Zimbabwe, Namibia, Tanzania, and Mozambique [m]) - 2,740 km
note – [s] after country name indicates river source; [m] after country name indicates river mouth

Major watersheds (area sq km): Atlantic Ocean drainage: Congo (3,730,881 sq km)
Indian Ocean drainage: Zambezi (1,332,412 sq km)

Total water withdrawal: *municipal:* 143.1 million cubic meters (2017 est.)
industrial: 47.7 million cubic meters (2017 est.)
agricultural: 1.166 billion cubic meters (2017 est.)

Total renewable water resources: 17.28 billion cubic meters (2017 est.)

GOVERNMENT

Country name: *conventional long form:* Republic of Malawi
conventional short form: Malawi
local long form: Dziko la Malawi
local short form: Malawi
former: British Central African Protectorate, Nyasaland Protectorate, Nyasaland
etymology: named for the East African Maravi Kingdom of the 16th century; the word "maravi" means "fire flames"

Government type: presidential republic

Capital: *name:* Lilongwe
geographic coordinates: 13 58 S, 33 47 E
time difference: UTC+2 (7 hours ahead of Washington, DC, during Standard Time)
etymology: named after the Lilongwe River that flows through the city

Administrative divisions: 28 districts; Balaka, Blantyre, Chikwawa, Chiradzulu, Chitipa, Dedza, Dowa, Karonga, Kasungu, Likoma, Lilongwe, Machinga, Mangochi, Mchinji, Mulanje, Mwanza, Mzimba, Neno, Ntcheu, Nkhata Bay, Nkhotakota, Nsanje, Ntchisi, Phalombe, Rumphi, Salima, Thyolo, Zomba

Independence: 6 July 1964 (from the UK)

National holiday: Independence Day, 6 July (1964); note - also called Republic Day since 6 July 1966

Constitution: *history:* previous 1953 (preindependence), 1964, 1966; latest drafted January to May 1994, approved 16 May 1994, entered into force 18 May 1995
amendments: proposed by the National Assembly; passage of amendments affecting constitutional articles, including the sovereignty and territory of the state, fundamental constitutional principles, human rights, voting rights, and the judiciary, requires majority approval in a referendum and majority approval by the Assembly; passage of other amendments requires at least two-thirds majority vote of the Assembly; amended several times, last in 2017

Legal system: mixed legal system of English common law and customary law; judicial review of legislative acts in the Supreme Court of Appeal

International law organization participation: accepts compulsory ICJ jurisdiction with reservations; accepts ICCt jurisdiction

Citizenship: *citizenship by birth:* no
citizenship by descent only: at least one parent must be a citizen of Malawi
dual citizenship recognized: no
residency requirement for naturalization: 7 years

Suffrage: 18 years of age; universal

Executive branch: *chief of state:* President Lazarus CHAKWERA (since 28 June 2020); Vice President Saulos CHILIMA (since 3 February 2020); note - the president is both chief of state and head of government
head of government: President Lazarus CHAKWERA (since 28 June 2020); Vice President Saulos CHILIMA (since 3 February 2020)
cabinet: Cabinet named by the president
elections/appointments: president directly elected by simple majority popular vote for a 5-year term (eligible for a second term); election last held on 23 June 2020 (next to be held in 2025)
election results:
Lazarus CHAKWERA elected president; Lazarus CHAKWERA (MCP) 59.3%, Peter Mutharika (DPP) 39.9%, other 0.8% (2020)

Legislative branch: *description:* unicameral National Assembly (193 seats; members directly elected in single-seat constituencies by simple majority vote to serve 5-year terms)
elections:
last held on 21 May 2019 (next to be held in May 2024)
election results:
percent of vote by party - n/a; seats by party - DPP 62, MCP 55, UDF 10, PP 5, other 5, independent 55, vacant 1; composition - men 161, women 32, percent of women 16.6%

Judicial branch: *highest court(s):* Supreme Court of Appeal (consists of the chief justice and at least 3 judges)
judge selection and term of office: Supreme Court chief justice appointed by the president and confirmed by the National Assembly; other judges appointed by the president upon the recommendation of the Judicial Service Commission, which regulates judicial officers; judges serve until age 65
subordinate courts: High Court; magistrate courts; Industrial Relations Court; district and city traditional or local courts

Political parties and leaders: Democratic Progressive Party or DPP [Peter MUTHARIKA]
Malawi Congress Party or MCP [Lazarus CHAKWERA]
People's Party or PP [Joyce BANDA]
United Democratic Front or UDF
United Transformation Movement or UTM [Saulos CHILIMA]

International organization participation: ACP, AfDB, AU, C, CD, COMESA, FAO, G-77, IAEA, IBRD, ICAO, ICCt, ICRM, IDA, IFAD, IFC, IFRCS, ILO, IMF, IMO, Interpol, IOC, IOM, IPU, ISO (correspondent), ITSO, ITU, ITUC (NGOs), MIGA, MINURSO, MONUSCO, NAM, OPCW, SADC, UN, UNCTAD, UNESCO, UNHRC, UNIDO, UNISFA, UNOCI, UNWTO, UPU, WCO, WFTU (NGOs), WHO, WIPO, WMO, WTO

Diplomatic representation in the US: *chief of mission:* Ambassador Esme Jynet CHOMBO (since 19 April 2022)
chancery: 2408 Massachusetts Avenue NW, Washington, DC 20008
telephone: [1] (202) 721-0270
FAX: [1] (202) 721-0288
email address and website:
malawiembassy-dc.org
http://www.malawiembassy-dc.org/

Diplomatic representation from the US: *chief of mission:* Ambassador David YOUNG (since 5 May 2022)
embassy: 16 Jomo Kenyatta Road, Lilongwe 3
mailing address: 2280 Lilongwe Place, Washington DC 20521-2280
telephone: [265] (0) 177-3166
FAX: [265] (0) 177-0471
email address and website:
LilongweConsular@state.gov
https://mw.usembassy.gov/

Flag description: three equal horizontal bands of black (top), red, and green with a radiant, rising, red sun centered on the black band; black represents the native peoples, red the blood shed in their struggle for freedom, and green the color of nature; the rising sun represents the hope of freedom for the continent of Africa

National symbol(s): lion; national colors: black, red, green

National anthem: *name:* "Mulungu dalitsa Malawi" (Oh God Bless Our Land of Malawi)
lyrics/music: Michael-Fredrick Paul SAUKA
note: adopted 1964

National heritage: *total World Heritage Sites:* 2 (1 cultural, 1 natural)
selected World Heritage Site locales: Lake Malawi National Park (n); Chongoni Rock-Art Area (c)

ECONOMY

Economic overview: Landlocked Malawi ranks among the world's least developed countries. The country's economic performance has historically been constrained by policy inconsistency, macroeconomic instability, poor infrastructure, rampant corruption, high population growth, and poor health and education outcomes that limit labor productivity. The economy is predominately agricultural with about 80% of the population living in rural areas. Agriculture accounts for about one-third of GDP and 80% of export revenues. The performance of the tobacco sector is key to short-term growth as tobacco accounts for more than half of exports, although Malawi is looking to diversify away from tobacco to other cash crops.

The economy depends on substantial inflows of economic assistance from the IMF, the World Bank, and individual donor nations. Donors halted direct budget support from 2013 to 2016 because of concerns about corruption and fiscal carelessness, but the World Bank resumed budget support in May 2017. In 2006, Malawi was approved for relief under the Heavily Indebted Poor Countries (HIPC) program but recent increases in domestic borrowing mean that debt servicing in 2016 exceeded the levels prior to HIPC debt relief.

Heavily dependent on rain-fed agriculture, with corn being the staple crop, Malawi's economy was hit hard by the El Nino-driven drought in 2015 and 2016, and now faces threat from the fall armyworm. The drought also slowed economic activity, led to two consecutive years of declining economic growth, and contributed to high inflation rates. Depressed food prices over 2017 led to a significant drop in inflation (from an average of 21.7% in 2016 to 12.3% in 2017), with a similar drop in interest rates.

Real GDP (purchasing power parity): $28.44 billion (2020 est.)
$28.22 billion (2019 est.)
$26.69 billion (2018 est.)
note: data are in 2017 dollars

Real GDP growth rate: 4% (2017 est.)
2.3% (2016 est.)
3% (2015 est.)

Real GDP per capita: $1,500 (2020 est.)
$1,500 (2019 est.)
$1,500 (2018 est.)
note: data are in 2017 dollars

GDP (official exchange rate): $7.766 billion (2019 est.)

Inflation rate (consumer prices): 9.3% (2019 est.)
12.4% (2018 est.)
11.7% (2017 est.)

GDP - composition, by sector of origin: *agriculture:* 28.6% (2017 est.)
industry: 15.4% (2017 est.)
services: 56% (2017 est.)

GDP - composition, by end use: *household consumption:* 84.3% (2017 est.)
government consumption: 16.3% (2017 est.)
investment in fixed capital: 15.3% (2017 est.)
investment in inventories: 0% (2017 est.)
exports of goods and services: 27.9% (2017 est.)
imports of goods and services: -43.8% (2017 est.)

Agricultural products: sweet potatoes, cassava, sugar cane, maize, mangoes/guavas, potatoes, tomatoes, pigeon peas, bananas, plantains

Industries: tobacco, tea, sugar, sawmill products, cement, consumer goods

Industrial production growth rate: 1.2% (2017 est.)

Labor force: 7 million (2013 est.)

Labor force - by occupation: *agriculture:* 76.9%
industry: 4.1%
services: 19% (2013 est.)

Unemployment rate: 20.4% (2013 est.)

Unemployment, youth ages 15-24: *total:* 8.5%
male: 6.7%
female: 10.6% (2017 est.)

Population below poverty line: 51.5% (2016 est.)

Gini Index coefficient - distribution of family income: 44.7 (2016 est.)
39 (2004)

Household income or consumption by percentage share: *lowest 10%:* 2.2%
highest 10%: 37.5% (2010 est.)

Budget: *revenues:* 1.356 billion (2017 est.)
expenditures: 1.567 billion (2017 est.)

Budget surplus (+) or deficit (-): -3.4% (of GDP) (2017 est.)

Public debt: 59.2% of GDP (2017 est.)
60.3% of GDP (2016 est.)

Taxes and other revenues: 21.7% (of GDP) (2017 est.)

Fiscal year: 1 July - 30 June

Current account balance: -$591 million (2017 est.)
-$744 million (2016 est.)

Exports: $1.16 billion (2019 est.) note: data are in current year dollars
$1.11 billion (2018 est.) note: data are in current year dollars
$9.658 billion (2017 est.)

Exports - partners: Belgium 16%, United States 8%, Egypt 7%, South Africa 6%, Germany 6%, Kenya 5%, United Arab Emirates 5% (2019)

Exports - commodities: tobacco, tea, raw sugar, beans, soybean products, clothing and apparel (2019)

Imports: $3.2 billion (2019 est.) note: data are in current year dollars
$2.92 billion (2018 est.) note: data are in current year dollars
$11.631 billion (2017 est.)

Imports - partners: South Africa 17%, China 16%, United Arab Emirates 9%, India 9%, United Kingdom 8% (2019)

Imports - commodities: postage stamps, refined petroleum, packaged medicines, fertilizers, office machinery/parts (2019)

Reserves of foreign exchange and gold: $780.2 million (31 December 2017 est.)
$585.7 million (31 December 2016 est.)

Debt - external: $2.102 billion (31 December 2017 est.)
$1.5 billion (31 December 2016 est.)

Exchange rates: Malawian kwachas (MWK) per US dollar -
762.4951 (2020 est.)
736.6548 (2019 est.)
732.335 (2018 est.)
499.6 (2014 est.)
424.9 (2013 est.)

ENERGY

Electricity access: *electrification - total population:* 13% (2019)
electrification - urban areas: 55% (2019)
electrification - rural areas: 5% (2019)

Electricity: *installed generating capacity:* 618,000 kW (2020 est.)
consumption: 1,117,378,000 kWh (2019 est.)
exports: 0 kWh (2019 est.)
imports: 0 kWh (2019 est.)
transmission/distribution losses: 460 million kWh (2019 est.)

Electricity generation sources: *fossil fuels:* 11.8% of total installed capacity (2020 est.)
solar: 3.2% of total installed capacity (2020 est.)
hydroelectricity: 81.9% of total installed capacity (2020 est.)
biomass and waste: 3.2% of total installed capacity (2020 est.)

Coal: *production:* 48,000 metric tons (2020 est.)
consumption: 47,000 metric tons (2020 est.)
exports: 0 metric tons (2020 est.)
imports: 0 metric tons (2020 est.)
proven reserves: 2 million metric tons (2019 est.)

Petroleum: *total petroleum production:* 0 bbl/day (2021 est.)
refined petroleum consumption: 9,400 bbl/day (2019 est.)
crude oil and lease condensate exports: 0 bbl/day (2018 est.)
crude oil and lease condensate imports: 0 bbl/day (2018 est.)
crude oil estimated reserves: 0 barrels (2021 est.)

Refined petroleum products - imports: 4,769 bbl/day (2015 est.)
proven reserves: 0 cubic meters (2021 est.)

Carbon dioxide emissions: 1.542 million metric tonnes of CO_2 (2019 est.)
from coal and metallurgical coke: 203,000 metric tonnes of CO_2 (2019 est.)
from petroleum and other liquids: 1.339 million metric tonnes of CO_2 (2019 est.)

Energy consumption per capita: 1.809 million Btu/person (2019 est.)

COMMUNICATIONS

Telephones - fixed lines: *total subscriptions:* 12,465 (2020 est.)

Telephones - mobile cellular: *total subscriptions:* 10,004,680 (2020 est.)
subscriptions per 100 inhabitants: 52 (2020 est.)

Telecommunication systems: *general assessment:* with few resources, Malawi is one of the world's least developed countries; there has been little investment in fixed-line telecom infrastructure, and as a result, the country's two mobile networks Airtel Malawi and TMN provide the vast majority of connections for voice and data services; both operators have invested in LTE technologies to improve the quality of data services; the lack of market competition, together with limited international internet bandwidth, has also resulted in some of the highest prices for telecom services in the region; the government in late 2020 secured an average 80% reduction in the cost of data bundles offered by the MNOs; following continuing customer complaints, the regulator in mid-2021 ensured that costs were again reduced, this time by about a third; mobile penetration remains low in comparison to the regional average and so there are considerable opportunities for further growth, particularly in the mobile broadband sector; low penetration is partly attributed to the lack of competition, though there is the possibility that a new play come launch services by the end of 2022; the internet sector is reasonably competitive, with about 50 licensed ISPs, though the limited availability and high cost of international bandwidth has held back growth and kept broadband access prices among the highest in the region; these limitations are being addressed, with the second phase of the national fiber backbone having started in mid-2021 (2022)
domestic: limited fixed-line subscribership less than 1 per 100 households; mobile-cellular services are expanding but network coverage is limited and is based around the main urban areas; mobile-cellular subscribership roughly 52 per 100 households (2020)
international: country code - 265; satellite earth stations - 2 Intelsat (1 Indian Ocean, 1 Atlantic Ocean) (2019)

Broadcast media: radio is the main broadcast medium; privately owned Zodiak radio has the widest national broadcasting reach, followed by state-run radio; numerous private and community radio stations broadcast in cities and towns around the country; the largest TV network is government-owned, but at least 4 private TV networks broadcast in urban areas; relays of multiple international broadcasters are available (2019)

Internet country code: .mw

Internet users: *total:* 2,608,025 (2019 est.)
percent of population: 14% (2019 est.)

Broadband - fixed subscriptions: *total:* 12,255 (2020 est.)
subscriptions per 100 inhabitants: 0.1 (2020 est.)

TRANSPORTATION

National air transport system: *number of registered air carriers:* 2 (2020)
inventory of registered aircraft operated by air carriers: 9
annual passenger traffic on registered air carriers: 10,545 (2018)
annual freight traffic on registered air carriers: 10,000 (2018) mt-km

Civil aircraft registration country code prefix: 7Q

Airports: *total:* 32 (2021)

Airports - with paved runways: *total:* 7
over 3,047 m: 1
1,524 to 2,437 m: 2
914 to 1,523 m: 4 (2021)

Airports - with unpaved runways: *total:* 25 (2013)

1,524 to 2,437 m: 1
914 to 1,523 m: 11
under 914 m: 13 (2021)

Railways: *total:* 767 km (2014)
narrow gauge: 767 km (2014) 1.067-m gauge

Roadways: *total:* 15,452 km (2015)
paved: 4,074 km (2015)
unpaved: 11,378 km (2015)

Waterways: 700 km (2010) (on Lake Nyasa [Lake Malawi] and Shire River)

Ports and terminals: *lake port(s):* Chipoka, Monkey Bay, Nkhata Bay, Nkhotakota, Chilumba (Lake Nyasa)

MILITARY AND SECURITY

Military and security forces: Malawi Defense Force (MDF): Army (includes marine unit), Air Force (established as a separate service August 2019; previously was an air wing under the Army); Ministry of Homeland Security: Malawi Police Service (2022)
note: the MDF reports directly to the president as commander in chief; the Malawi Ministry of Defense was abolished in 2011

Military expenditures: 0.9% of GDP (2021 est.)
0.9% of GDP (2020 est.)
1.1% of GDP (2019 est.) (approximately $90 million)
0.8% of GDP (2018 est.) (approximately $70 million)
0.7% of GDP (2017 est.) (approximately $60 million)

Military and security service personnel strengths: information varies; approximately 8,000 active duty troops (including about 500 air and marine forces personnel) (2022)

Military equipment inventories and acquisitions: the MDF's inventory is comprised of mostly obsolescent or second-hand equipment from China, a few European countries, and South Africa (2021)

Military service age and obligation: 18 years of age for men and women for voluntary military service; high school equivalent required for enlisted recruits and college equivalent for officer recruits; initial engagement is 7 years for enlisted personnel and 10 years for officers (2022)

Military deployments: 750 Democratic Republic of the Congo (MONUSCO) (May 2022)

Military - note: the MDF's primary responsibility is external security; it is also tasked as necessary with carrying out policing or other domestic activities, such as disaster relief; Malawi contributes regularly to African Union and UN peace support operations
the MDF was established in 1964 from elements of the Kings African Rifles (KAR), a British colonial regiment raised from Great Britain's various possessions in East Africa from 1902 until independence in the 1960s; the KAR conducted both military and internal security functions within the colonial territories, and served outside the territories during the World Wars (2022)

TRANSNATIONAL ISSUES

Disputes - international: *Malawi-Mozambique:* the two countries have held exercises to reaffirm boundaries a number of times
Malawi-Tanzania: dispute with Tanzania over the boundary in Lake Nyasa (Lake Malawi) and the meandering Songwe River; Malawi contends that the entire lake up to the Tanzanian shoreline is its territory, while Tanzania claims the border is in the center of the lake; the conflict was reignited in 2012 when Malawi awarded a license to a British company for oil exploration in the lake
Malawi-Zambia: border demarcation was completed in 2011; in 2018, the redemarcation exercise determined that some parts of Malawi actually belonged to Zambia

Refugees and internally displaced persons: *refugees (country of origin):* 34,643 (Democratic Republic of the Congo) (refugees and asylum seekers), 12,959 (Burundi) (refugees and asylum seekers), 7,738 (Rwanda) (refugees and asylum seekers) (2022)

Illicit drugs: NA

MALAYSIA

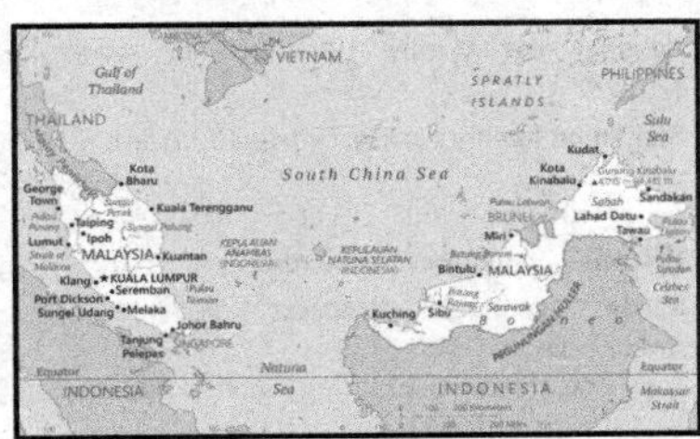

INTRODUCTION

Background: Malaysia's location has long made it an important cultural, economic, historical, social, and trade link between the islands of Southeast Asia and the mainland. Through the Strait of Malacca, which separates the Malay Peninsula from the archipelago, flowed maritime trade and with it influences from China, India, the Middle East, and the east coast of Africa. Prior to the 14th century, several powerful maritime empires existed in what is modern-day Malaysia, including the Srivijayan, which controlled much of the southern part of the peninsula between the 7th and 13th centuries, and the Majapahit Empire, which took control over most of the peninsula and the Malay Archipelago between the 13th and 14th centuries. The adoption of Islam between the 13th and 17th centuries also saw the rise of a number of powerful maritime states and sultanates on the Malay Peninsula and the island of Borneo, such as the port city of Malacca (Melaka), which at its height in the 15th century had a navy and hosted thousands of Chinese, Arab, Persian, and Indian merchants.

The Portuguese in the 16th century and the Dutch in the 17th century were the first European colonial powers to establish themselves on the Malay Peninsula and Southeast Asia. However, it was the British who ultimately secured their hegemony across the territory and during the late 18th and 19th centuries established colonies and protectorates in the area that is now Malaysia. These holdings were occupied by Japan from 1942 to 1945. In 1948, the British-ruled territories on the Malay Peninsula except Singapore formed the Federation of Malaya, which became independent in 1957. Malaysia was formed in 1963 when the former British colonies of Singapore, as well as Sabah and Sarawak on the northern coast of Borneo, joined the Federation. The first several years of the country's independence were marred by a communist insurgency, Indonesian confrontation with Malaysia, Philippine claims to Sabah, and Singapore's expulsion in 1965. During the 22-year term of Prime Minister MAHATHIR Mohamad (1981-2003), Malaysia was successful in diversifying its economy from dependence on exports of raw materials to the development of manufacturing, services, and tourism. Prime Minister MAHATHIR and a newly-formed coalition of opposition parties defeated Prime Minister Mohamed NAJIB bin Abdul Razak's United Malays National Organization (UMNO) in May 2018, ending over 60 years of uninterrupted rule by UMNO. MAHATHIR resigned in February 2020 amid a political dispute. King ABDULLAH then selected Tan Sri MUHYIDDIN Yassin as the new prime minister. MUHYIDDIN resigned in August 2021 after losing a majority of support in parliament. King ABDULLAH next selected ISMAIL SABRI Yakoob as the successor prime minister.

GEOGRAPHY

Location: Southeastern Asia, peninsula bordering Thailand and northern one-third of the island of Borneo, bordering Indonesia, Brunei, and the South China Sea, south of Vietnam

Geographic coordinates: 2 30 N, 112 30 E

Map references: Southeast Asia

Area: *total:* 329,847 sq km
land: 328,657 sq km
water: 1,190 sq km

Area - comparative: slightly larger than New Mexico

Land boundaries: *total:* 2,742 km
border countries (3): Brunei 266 km; Indonesia 1,881 km; Thailand 595 km

Coastline: 4,675 km (Peninsular Malaysia 2,068 km, East Malaysia 2,607 km)

Maritime claims: *territorial sea:* 12 nm
exclusive economic zone: 200 nm
continental shelf: 200-m depth or to the depth of exploitation; specified boundary in the South China Sea

Climate: tropical; annual southwest (April to October) and northeast (October to February) monsoons

Terrain: coastal plains rising to hills and mountains

Elevation: *highest point:* Gunung Kinabalu 4,095 m
lowest point: Indian Ocean 0 m
mean elevation: 419 m

Natural resources: tin, petroleum, timber, copper, iron ore, natural gas, bauxite

Land use: *agricultural land:* 23.2% (2018 est.)
arable land: 2.9% (2018 est.)

permanent crops: 19.4% (2018 est.)
permanent pasture: 0.9% (2018 est.)
forest: 62% (2018 est.)
other: 14.8% (2018 est.)

Irrigated land: 3,800 sq km (2012)

Population distribution: a highly uneven distribution with over 80% of the population residing on the Malay Peninsula

Natural hazards: flooding; landslides; forest fires

Geography - note: strategic location along Strait of Malacca and southern South China Sea

PEOPLE AND SOCIETY

Population: 33,871,431 (2022 est.)

Nationality: *noun:* Malaysian(s)
adjective: Malaysian

Ethnic groups: Bumiputera 62.5% (Malays and indigenous peoples, including Orang Asli, Dayak, Anak Negeri), Chinese 20.6%, Indian 6.2%, other 0.9%, non-citizens 9.8% (2019 est.)

Languages: Bahasa Malaysia (official), English, Chinese (Cantonese, Mandarin, Hokkien, Hakka, Hainan, Foochow), Tamil, Telugu, Malayalam, Panjabi, Thai; note - Malaysia has 134 living languages - 112 indigenous languages and 22 non-indigenous languages; in East Malaysia, there are several indigenous languages; the most widely spoken are Iban and Kadazan
major-language sample(s): Buku Fakta Dunia, sumber yang diperlukan untuk maklumat asas. (Bahasa Malaysia)

Religions: Muslim (official) 61.3%, Buddhist 19.8%, Christian 9.2%, Hindu 6.3%, Confucianism, Taoism, other traditional Chinese religions 1.3%, other 0.4%, none 0.8%, unspecified 1% (2010 est.)

Demographic profile: Malaysia's multi-ethnic population consists of the bumiputera – Malays and other indigenous peoples – (62%), ethnic Chinese (21%), ethnic Indians (6%), and foreigners (10%). The majority of Malaysia's ethnic Chinese and Indians trace their roots to the British colonialists' recruitment of hundreds of thousands of Chinese and Indians as mine and plantation workers between the early-19th century and the 1930s. Most Malays have maintained their rural lifestyle, while the entrepreneurial Chinese have achieved greater wealth and economic dominance. In order to eradicate Malay poverty, the Malaysian Government in 1971 adopted policies that gave preference to the bumiputera in public university admissions, government jobs and contracts, and property ownership. Affirmative action continues to benefit well-off urban bumiputera but has done little to alleviate poverty for their more numerous rural counterparts. The policies have pushed ethnic Chinese and Indians to study at private or foreign universities (many do not return) and have created and sustained one of the world's largest civil services, which is 85-90% Malay.

The country's age structure has changed significantly since the 1960s, as fertility and mortality rates have declined. Malaysia's total fertility rate (TFR) has dropped from 5 children per woman in 1970, to 3 in 1998, to 2.1 in 2015 as a result of increased educational attainment and labor participation among women, later marriages, increased use of contraception, and changes in family size preference related to urbanization. The TFR is higher among Malays, rural residents (who are mainly Malay), the poor, and the less-educated. Despite the reduced fertility rate, Malaysia's population will continue to grow, albeit at a decreasing rate, for the next few decades because of its large number of reproductive-age women. The youth population has been shrinking, and the working-age population (15-64 year olds) has been growing steadily. Malaysia's labor market has successfully absorbed the increasing number of job seekers, leading to sustained economic growth. However, the favorable age structure is changing, and around 2020, Malaysia will start to become a rapidly aging society. As the population ages, Malaysia will need to better educate and train its labor force, raise productivity, and continue to increase the number of women workers in order to further develop its economy.

More than 1.8 million Malaysians lived abroad as of 2015, including anywhere from 350,000 to 785,000 workers, more than half of whom have an advanced level of education. The vast majority of emigrants are ethnic Chinese, seeking better educational and job opportunities abroad because of institutionalized ethnic discrimination favoring the Malays. The primary destination country is nearby Singapore, followed by Bangladesh and Australia. Hundreds of thousands of Malaysians also commute across the causeway to Singapore daily for work.

Brain drain is an impediment to Malaysia's goal of becoming a high-income country. The situation is compounded by a migrant inflow that is composed almost entirely of low-skilled laborers who work mainly in manufacturing, agriculture, and construction. Officially, Malaysia had about 1.8 million legal foreign workers as of mid-year 2017 – largely from Indonesia, Nepal, the Philippines, and Bangladesh – but as many as 3 to 4 million are estimated to be in the country illegally. Immigrants outnumber ethnic Indians and could supplant the ethnic Chinese as Malaysia's second largest population group around 2035.

Age structure: *0-14 years:* 26.8% (male 4,504,562/female 4,246,681)
15-24 years: 16.63% (male 2,760,244/female 2,670,186)
25-54 years: 40.86% (male 6,737,826/female 6,604,776)
55-64 years: 8.81% (male 1,458,038/female 1,418,280)
65 years and over: 6.9% (male 1,066,627/female 1,184,863) (2020 est.)

Dependency ratios: *total dependency ratio:* 44.2
youth dependency ratio: 33.8
elderly dependency ratio: 10.4
potential support ratio: 9.7 (2020 est.)

Median age: *total:* 29.2 years
male: 28.9 years
female: 29.6 years (2020 est.)

Population growth rate: 1.03% (2022 est.)

Birth rate: 14.55 births/1,000 population (2022 est.)

Death rate: 5.69 deaths/1,000 population (2022 est.)

Net migration rate: 1.48 migrant(s)/1,000 population (2022 est.)

Population distribution: a highly uneven distribution with over 80% of the population residing on the Malay Peninsula

Urbanization: *urban population:* 78.2% of total population (2022)
rate of urbanization: 1.87% annual rate of change (2020-25 est.)

Major urban areas - population: 8.420 million KUALA LUMPUR (capital), 1.065 million Johor Bahru, 842,000 Ipoh (2022)

Sex ratio: *at birth:* 1.07 male(s)/female
0-14 years: 1.06 male(s)/female
15-24 years: 1.05 male(s)/female
25-54 years: 1.07 male(s)/female
55-64 years: 1 male(s)/female
65 years and over: 1.14 male(s)/female
total population: 1.05 male(s)/female (2022 est.)

Maternal mortality ratio: 29 deaths/100,000 live births (2017 est.)

Infant mortality rate: *total:* 6.59 deaths/1,000 live births
male: 6.97 deaths/1,000 live births
female: 6.19 deaths/1,000 live births (2022 est.)

Life expectancy at birth: *total population:* 76.13 years
male: 74.5 years
female: 77.87 years (2022 est.)

Total fertility rate: 1.75 children born/woman (2022 est.)

Contraceptive prevalence rate: 52.2% (2014)

Drinking water source: *improved: urban:* 99.4% of population
rural: 90.7% of population
total: 97.5% of population
unimproved: urban: 0.6% of population
rural: 9.3% of population
total: 2.5% of population (2020 est.)

Current health expenditure: 3.8% of GDP (2019)

Physicians density: 1.54 physicians/1,000 population (2020)

Hospital bed density: 1.9 beds/1,000 population (2017)

Sanitation facility access: *improved: urban:* 99% of population
unimproved: urban: 0.1% of population

HIV/AIDS - adult prevalence rate: 0.4% (2020 est.)

Major infectious diseases: *degree of risk:* intermediate (2020)
food or waterborne diseases: bacterial diarrhea
vectorborne diseases: dengue fever
water contact diseases: leptospirosis

Obesity - adult prevalence rate: 15.6% (2016)

Alcohol consumption per capita: *total:* 0.64 liters of pure alcohol (2019 est.)
beer: 0.48 liters of pure alcohol (2019 est.)
wine: 0.04 liters of pure alcohol (2019 est.)
spirits: 0.11 liters of pure alcohol (2019 est.)
other alcohols: 0.01 liters of pure alcohol (2019 est.)

Tobacco use: *total:* 22.5% (2020 est.)
male: 43.8% (2020 est.)
female: 1.1% (2020 est.)

Children under the age of 5 years underweight: 14.1% (2019)

Education expenditures: 4.2% of GDP (2019 est.)

Literacy: *definition:* age 15 and over can read and write
total population: 95%
male: 96.2%
female: 93.6% (2019)

School life expectancy (primary to tertiary education): *total:* 13 years
male: 13 years
female: 14 years (2019)

Unemployment, youth ages 15-24: *total:* 12%
male: 11.4%
female: 13% (2020 est.)

ENVIRONMENT

Environment - current issues: air pollution from industrial and vehicular emissions; water pollution from raw sewage; deforestation; smoke/haze from Indonesian forest fires; endangered species; coastal reclamation damaging mangroves and turtle nesting sites

Environment - international agreements: *party to:* Antarctic-Environmental Protection, Antarctic Treaty, Biodiversity, Climate Change, Climate Change-Kyoto Protocol, Climate Change-Paris Agreement, Comprehensive Nuclear Test Ban, Desertification, Endangered Species, Hazardous Wastes, Law of the Sea, Marine Life Conservation, Nuclear Test Ban, Ozone Layer Protection, Ship Pollution, Tropical Timber 2006, Wetlands
signed, but not ratified: none of the selected agreements

Air pollutants: *particulate matter emissions:* 16.04 micrograms per cubic meter (2016 est.)
carbon dioxide emissions: 248.29 megatons (2016 est.)
methane emissions: 51.51 megatons (2020 est.)

Climate: tropical; annual southwest (April to October) and northeast (October to February) monsoons

Land use: *agricultural land:* 23.2% (2018 est.)
arable land: 2.9% (2018 est.)
permanent crops: 19.4% (2018 est.)
permanent pasture: 0.9% (2018 est.)
forest: 62% (2018 est.)
other: 14.8% (2018 est.)

Urbanization: *urban population:* 78.2% of total population (2022)
rate of urbanization: 1.87% annual rate of change (2020-25 est.)

Revenue from forest resources: *forest revenues:* 1.57% of GDP (2018 est.)

Revenue from coal: *coal revenues:* 0.02% of GDP (2018 est.)

Waste and recycling: *municipal solid waste generated annually:* 12,982,685 tons (2014 est.)
municipal solid waste recycled annually: 2,271,970 tons (2016 est.)
percent of municipal solid waste recycled: 17.5% (2016 est.)

Total water withdrawal: *municipal:* 1.342 billion cubic meters (2017 est.)
industrial: 1.641 billion cubic meters (2017 est.)
agricultural: 2.505 billion cubic meters (2017 est.)

Total renewable water resources: 580 billion cubic meters (2017 est.)

GOVERNMENT

Country name: *conventional long form:* none
conventional short form: Malaysia
local long form: none
local short form: Malaysia
former: British Malaya, Malayan Union, Federation of Malaya
etymology: the name means "Land of the Malays"

Government type: federal parliamentary constitutional monarchy
note: all Peninsular Malaysian states have hereditary rulers (commonly referred to as sultans) except Melaka (Malacca) and Pulau Pinang (Penang); those two states along with Sabah and Sarawak in East Malaysia have governors appointed by government; powers of state governments are limited by the federal constitution; under terms of federation, Sabah and Sarawak retain certain constitutional prerogatives (e.g., right to maintain their own immigration controls)

Capital: *name:* Kuala Lumpur; note - nearby Putrajaya is referred to as a federal government administrative center but not the capital; Parliament meets in Kuala Lumpur
geographic coordinates: 3 10 N, 101 42 E
time difference: UTC+8 (13 hours ahead of Washington, DC, during Standard Time)
etymology: the Malay word for "river junction or estuary" is *kuala* and *lumpur* means "mud"; together the words render the meaning of "muddy confluence"

Administrative divisions: 13 states (negeri-negeri, singular - negeri); Johor, Kedah, Kelantan, Melaka, Negeri Sembilan, Pahang, Perak, Perlis, Pulau Pinang, Sabah, Sarawak, Selangor, Terengganu; and 1 federal territory (Wilayah Persekutuan) with 3 components, Kuala Lumpur, Labuan, and Putrajaya

Independence: 31 August 1957 (from the UK)

National holiday: Independence Day (or Merdeka Day), 31 August (1957) (independence of Malaya); Malaysia Day, 16 September (1963) (formation of Malaysia)

Constitution: *history:* previous 1948; latest drafted 21 February 1957, effective 27 August 1957
amendments: proposed as a bill by Parliament; passage requires at least two-thirds majority vote by the Parliament membership in the bill's second and third readings; a number of constitutional sections are excluded from amendment or repeal; amended many times, last in 2019

Legal system: mixed legal system of English common law, Islamic (sharia) law, and customary law; judicial review of legislative acts in the Federal Court at request of supreme head of the federation

International law organization participation: has not submitted an ICJ jurisdiction declaration; non-party state to the ICCt

Citizenship: *citizenship by birth:* no
citizenship by descent only: at least one parent must be a citizen of Malaysia
dual citizenship recognized: no
residency requirement for naturalization: 10 out 12 years preceding application

Suffrage: 18 years of age; universal (2019)

Executive branch: *chief of state:* King Sultan ABDULLAH Sultan Ahmad Shah (since 24 January 2019); note - King MUHAMMAD V (formerly known as TUANKU Muhammad FARIS Petra) (selected on 14 October 2016; installed on 13 December 2016) resigned on 6 January 2019; the position of the king is primarily ceremonial, but he is the final arbiter on the appointment of the prime minister
head of government: Prime Minister ANWAR Ibrahim (since 25 November 2022)
cabinet: Cabinet appointed by the prime minister from among members of Parliament with the consent of the king
elections/appointments: king elected by and from the hereditary rulers of 9 states for a 5-year term; election is on a rotational basis among rulers of the 9 states; election last held on 24 January 2019 (next to be held in 2024); prime minister designated from among members of the House of Representatives; following legislative elections, the leader who commands support of the majority of members in the House becomes prime minister

Legislative branch: *description:* bicameral Parliament of Malaysia or Parlimen Malaysia consists of:
Senate or Dewan Negara (70 seats; 44 members appointed by the king and 26 indirectly elected by 13 state legislatures; members serve 3-year terms)
House of Representatives or Dewan Rakyat (222 seats; members directly elected in single-seat constituencies by simple majority vote to serve 5-year terms) (2019)
elections:
Senate - appointed
House of Representatives - last held on 19 Nov 2022 (next national elections scheduled for 2027)
election results:
Senate - appointed; composition - men 54, women 14, percent of women 20.6%
2022: House of Representatives - percent of vote by party/coalition - PH 37.5%, PN 30.4%, BN 22.4%, GPS 4%, WARISAN 1.8%, GRS 1.3%, other 2.6%; seats by party/coalition - PH 81, PN 73, BN 30, GPS 23, GRS 6, WARISAN 3, PBM 1, KDM 1, MUDA 1, independents/unaffiliated 3
2018: House of Representatives - percent of vote by party/coalition - PH 45.6%, BN 33.8%, PAS 16.9%, WARISAN 2.3%, other 1.4%; seats by party/coalition - PH 113, BN 79, PAS 18, WARISAN 8, USA 1, independent 3; composition -men 199, women 23, percent of women 10.4%; note - total Parliament percent of women 12.8%
note: as of May 2022, seats by party/coalition - PH 90, PN 50, BN 42, GPS 18, WARISAN 7, PEJUANG 4, PBM 3, PSB 1, MUDA 1, independent 4, vacant 2

Judicial branch: *highest court(s):* Federal Court (consists of the chief justice, president of the Court of Appeal, chief justice of the High Court of Malaya, chief judge of the High Court of Sabah and Sarawak, 8 judges, and 1 "additional" judge); note -Malaysia has a dual judicial hierarchy of civil and religious (sharia) courts
judge selection and term of office: Federal Court justices appointed by the monarch on advice of the prime minister; judges serve until mandatory retirement at age 66 with the possibility of a single 6-month extension
subordinate courts: Court of Appeal; High Court; Sessions Court; Magistrates' Court

Political parties and leaders: National Front (Barisan Nasional) or BN:
All Malaysian Indian Progressive Front or IPF [Loganathan THORAISAMY]
Love Malaysia Party or PCM [Huan Cheng GUAN]
Malaysian Chinese Association (Persatuan Cina Malaysia) or MCA [Wee Ka SIONG]
Malaysian Indian Congress (Kongres India Malaysia) or MIC [Vigneswaran SANASEE]
Malaysian Indian Muslim Congress or KIMMA [Datuk Seri Haji SYED]
Malaysia Makkal Sakti Party or MMSP [R.S. THANENTHIRAN]
United Malays National Organization (Pertubuhan Kebansaan Melayu Bersatu) or UNMO [Ahmad Zahid HAMIDI]

United Sabah People's Party (Parti Bersatu Rakyat Sabah) or PBRS [Joseph KURUP]

Coalition of Hope (Pakatan Harapan) or PH:
Democratic Action Party (Parti Tindakan Demokratik) or DAP [LIM Guan Eng]
National Trust Party (Parti Amanah Negara) or AMANAH [Mohamad SABU]
People's Justice Party (Parti Keadilan Rakyat) or PKR [ANWAR Ibrahim]
United Progressive Kinabalu Organization or UPKO [Wilfred Madius TANGAU]

Coalition Perikatan Nasional (National Alliance) or PN: Homeland Solidarity Party (Parti Solidariti Tanah Airku) or STAR [Datuk Seri Jeffrey Kitingan]
Malaysian People's Movement Party (Parti Gerakan Rakyat Malaysia) or GERAKAN or PGRM [Dominic Lau Hoe CHAI]
Malaysian United Indigenous Party (Parti Pribumi Bersatu Malaysia) or PPBM or BERSATU [Tan Sri MUHYIDDIN Yassin]
Pan-Malaysian Islamic Party (Parti Islam se Malaysia) or PAS [Abdul HADI Awang]
Parti Gerakan Rakyat Malaysia or GERAKAN [Dominic Lau Hoe CHAI]

Sarawak Parties Alliance (Gabungan Parti Sarawak) or GPS [ABANG JOHARI Openg]: Progressive Democratic Party or PDP [TIONG King Sing]
Sarawak People's Party (Parti Rakyat Sarawak) or PRS [James MASING]
Sarawak United People's Party (Parti Bersatu Rakyat Sarawak) or SUPP [Dr. SIM Kui Hian]
United Traditional Bumiputera Party (Parti Pesaka Bumiputera Bersata) or PBB [Abang Abdul Rahman Johari Abang Openg or "Abang Jo"]

Gabungan Rakya Sabah or GRS:
Homeland Solidarity Party or STAR [Jeffrey KITINGAN]
Malaysian United Indigenous Party (Parti Pribumi Bersatu Malaysia) or PPBM [Tan Sri MUHYIDDIN Yassin]
Sabah Progressive Party or SAPP [Yong Teck LEE]
United Sabah Party (Parti Bersatu Sabah) or PBS [Maximus ONGKILI]

Others receiving votes in 2022 general election:
Gerakan Tanah Air or GTA Party [Hajiji NOOR] (a coalition of parties in Sabah)
Malaysian Nation Party (Parti Bangsa Malaysia) or PBM [Larry Sng Wei SHIEN] (formerly Sarawak Workers Party)
Malaysian United Democratic Alliance or MUDA [Syed SADDIQ bin Syed Abdul Rahman]
Perikatan Rakyat Bersatu Sarawak or PERKASA (coalition of Sarawak parties)
Sabah Heritage Party (Parti Warisan Sabah) or WARISAN [SHAFIE Apdal]
Social Democratic Harmony Party or KDM [Peter ANTHONY]
Socialist Party of Malaysia or PSM [Michael Jeyakumar DEVARA]

International organization participation: ADB, APEC, ARF, ASEAN, BIS, C, CICA (observer), CP, D-8, EAS, FAO, G-15, G-77, IAEA, IBRD, ICAO, ICC (national committees), ICRM, IDA, IDB, IFAD, IFC, IFRCS, IHO, ILO, IMF, IMO, IMSO, Interpol, IOC, IPU, ISO, ITSO, ITU, ITUC (NGOs), MIGA, MINURSO, MONUSCO, NAM, OIC, OPCW, PCA, PIF (partner), UN, UNAMID, UNCTAD, UNESCO, UNHRC, UNIDO, UNIFIL, UNISFA, UNMIL, UNWTO, UPU, WCO, WFTU (NGOs), WHO, WIPO, WMO, WTO

Diplomatic representation in the US: *chief of mission:* ambassador (vacant); Charge d'Affaires Fairuz Adli Mohd ROZALI (since 28 August 2021)
chancery: 3516 International Court NW, Washington, DC 20008
telephone: [1] (202) 572-9700
FAX: [1] (202) 572-9882
email address and website:
mwwashington@kln.gov.my
https://www.kln.gov.my/web/usa_washington/home
consulate(s) general: Los Angeles, New York

Diplomatic representation from the US: *chief of mission:* Ambassador Brian D. McFEETERS (since 26 February 2021)
embassy: 376 Jalan Tun Razak, 50400 Kuala Lumpur
mailing address: 4210 Kuala Lumpur, Washington DC 20521-4210
telephone: [60] (3) 2168-5000
FAX: [60] (3) 2142-2207
email address and website:
KLACS@state.gov
https://my.usembassy.gov/

Flag description: 14 equal horizontal stripes of red (top) alternating with white (bottom); there is a dark blue rectangle in the upper hoist-side corner bearing a yellow crescent and a yellow 14-pointed star; the flag is often referred to as Jalur Gemilang (Stripes of Glory); the 14 stripes stand for the equal status in the federation of the 13 member states and the federal government; the 14 points on the star represent the unity between these entities; the crescent is a traditional symbol of Islam; blue symbolizes the unity of the Malay people and yellow is the royal color of Malay rulers
note: the design is based on the flag of the US

National symbol(s): tiger, hibiscus; national colors: gold, black

National anthem: *name:* "Negaraku" (My Country)
lyrics/music: collective, led by Tunku ABDUL RAHMAN/Pierre Jean DE BERANGER
note: adopted 1957; full version only performed in the presence of the king; the tune, which was adopted from a popular French melody titled "La Rosalie," was originally the anthem of Perak, one of Malaysia's 13 states

National heritage: *total World Heritage Sites:* 4 (2 cultural, 2 natural)
selected World Heritage Site locales: Gunung Mulu National Park (n); Kinabalu Park (n); Malacca and George Town, Historic Cities of the Straits of Malacca (c); Archaeological Heritage of the Lenggong Valley (c)

ECONOMY

Economic overview: Malaysia, an upper middle-income country, has transformed itself since the 1970s from a producer of raw materials into a multi-sector economy. Under current Prime Minister NAJIB, Malaysia is attempting to achieve high-income status by 2020 and to move further up the value-added production chain by attracting investments in high technology, knowledge-based industries and services. NAJIB's Economic Transformation Program is a series of projects and policy measures intended to accelerate the country's economic growth. The government has also taken steps to liberalize some services sub-sectors. Malaysia is vulnerable to a fall in world commodity prices or a general slowdown in global economic activity.

The NAJIB administration is continuing efforts to boost domestic demand and reduce the economy's dependence on exports. Domestic demand continues to anchor economic growth, supported mainly by private consumption, which accounts for 53% of GDP. Nevertheless, exports - particularly of electronics, oil and gas, and palm oil - remain a significant driver of the economy. In 2015, gross exports of goods and services were equivalent to 73% of GDP. The oil and gas sector supplied about 22% of government revenue in 2015, down significantly from prior years amid a decline in commodity prices and diversification of government revenues. Malaysia has embarked on a fiscal reform program aimed at achieving a balanced budget by 2020, including rationalization of subsidies and the 2015 introduction of a 6% value added tax. Sustained low commodity prices throughout the period not only strained government finances, but also shrunk Malaysia's current account surplus and weighed heavily on the Malaysian ringgit, which was among the region's worst performing currencies during 2013-17. The ringgit hit new lows following the US presidential election amid a broader selloff of emerging market assets.

Bank Negara Malaysia (the central bank) maintains adequate foreign exchange reserves; a well-developed regulatory regime has limited Malaysia's exposure to riskier financial instruments, although it remains vulnerable to volatile global capital flows. In order to increase Malaysia's competitiveness, Prime Minister NAJIB raised possible revisions to the special economic and social preferences accorded to ethnic Malays under the New Economic Policy of 1970, but retreated in 2013 after he encountered significant opposition from Malay nationalists and other vested interests. In September 2013 NAJIB launched the new Bumiputra Economic Empowerment Program, policies that favor and advance the economic condition of ethnic Malays.

Malaysia signed the 12-nation Trans-Pacific Partnership (TPP) free trade agreement in February 2016, although the future of the TPP remains unclear following the US withdrawal from the agreement. Along with nine other ASEAN members, Malaysia established the ASEAN Economic Community in 2015, which aims to advance regional economic integration.

Real GDP (purchasing power parity): $855.6 billion (2020 est.)
$906.24 billion (2019 est.)
$868.85 billion (2018 est.)
note: data are in 2017 dollars

Real GDP growth rate: 4.31% (2019 est.)
4.77% (2018 est.)
5.81% (2017 est.)

Real GDP per capita: $26,400 (2020 est.)
$28,400 (2019 est.)
$27,600 (2018 est.)
note: data are in 2017 dollars

GDP (official exchange rate): $364.631 billion (2019 est.)

Inflation rate (consumer prices): 0.6% (2019 est.)
0.9% (2018 est.)
3.8% (2017 est.)
note: approximately 30% of goods are price-controlled

Credit ratings:

Fitch rating: BBB+ (2020)

Moody's rating: A3 (2004)

Standard & Poors rating: A- *(2003)*
note: The year refers to the year in which the current credit rating was first obtained.

GDP - composition, by sector of origin: *agriculture:* 8.8% (2017 est.)
industry: 37.6% (2017 est.)
services: 53.6% (2017 est.)

GDP - composition, by end use: *household consumption:* 55.3% (2017 est.)
government consumption: 12.2% (2017 est.)
investment in fixed capital: 25.3% (2017 est.)
investment in inventories: 0.3% (2017 est.)
exports of goods and services: 71.4% (2017 est.)
imports of goods and services: -64.4% (2017 est.)

Agricultural products: oil palm fruit, rice, poultry, eggs, vegetables, rubber, coconuts, bananas, pineapples, pork

Industries: Peninsular Malaysia - rubber and oil palm processing and manufacturing, petroleum and natural gas, light manufacturing, pharmaceuticals, medical technology, electronics and semiconductors, timber processing; Sabah -logging, petroleum and natural gas production; Sarawak - agriculture processing, petroleum and natural gas production, logging

Industrial production growth rate: 5% (2017 est.)

Labor force: 15.139 million (2020 est.)

Labor force - by occupation: *agriculture:* 11%
industry: 36%
services: 53% (2012 est.)

Unemployment rate: 3.3% (2019 est.)
3.33% (2018 est.)

Unemployment, youth ages 15-24: *total:* 12%
male: 11.4%
female: 13% (2020 est.)

Population below poverty line: 5.6% (2018 est.)

Gini Index coefficient - distribution of family income: 41 (2015 est.)
49.2 (1997)

Household income or consumption by percentage share: *lowest 10%:* 1.8%
highest 10%: 34.7% (2009 est.)

Budget: *revenues:* 51.25 billion (2017 est.)
expenditures: 60.63 billion (2017 est.)

Budget surplus (+) or deficit (-): -3% (of GDP) (2017 est.)

Public debt: 54.1% of GDP (2017 est.)
56.2% of GDP (2016 est.)
note: this figure is based on the amount of federal government debt, RM501.6 billion ($167.2 billion) in 2012; this includes Malaysian Treasury bills and other government securities, as well as loans raised externally and bonds and notes issued overseas; this figure excludes debt issued by non-financial public enterprises and guaranteed by the federal government, which was an additional $47.7 billion in 2012

Taxes and other revenues: 16.4% (of GDP) (2017 est.)

Fiscal year: calendar year

Current account balance: $12.295 billion (2019 est.)
$8.027 billion (2018 est.)

Exports: $207.37 billion (2020 est.) note: data are in current year dollars
$237.83 billion (2019 est.) note: data are in current year dollars
$245.89 billion (2018 est.) note: data are in current year dollars

Exports - partners: Singapore 13%, China 13%, United States 11%, Hong Kong 6%, Japan 6%, Thailand 5% (2019)

Exports - commodities: integrated circuits, refined petroleum, natural gas, semiconductors, palm oil (2019)

Imports: $185.59 billion (2020 est.) note: data are in current year dollars
$210.68 billion (2019 est.) note: data are in current year dollars
$221.83 billion (2018 est.) note: data are in current year dollars

Imports - partners: China 24%, Singapore 14%, Japan 6%, United States 6%, Taiwan 5%, Thailand 5% (2019)

Imports - commodities: integrated circuits, refined petroleum, crude petroleum, broadcasting equipment, coal (2019)

Reserves of foreign exchange and gold: $102.4 billion (31 December 2017 est.)
$94.5 billion (31 December 2016 est.)

Debt - external: $224.596 billion (2019 est.)
$226.901 billion (2018 est.)

Exchange rates: ringgits (MYR) per US dollar -
4.064 (2020 est.)
4.161 (2019 est.)
4.166 (2018 est.)
3.91 (2014 est.)
3.27 (2013 est.)

ENERGY

Electricity access: *electrification - total population:* 100% (2020)

Electricity: *installed generating capacity:* 34.959 million kW (2020 est.)
consumption: 150.062 billion kWh (2019 est.)
exports: 669 million kWh (2019 est.)
imports: 19 million kWh (2019 est.)
transmission/distribution losses: 12.124 billion kWh (2019 est.)

Electricity generation sources: *fossil fuels:* 87.5% of total installed capacity (2020 est.)
solar: 0.7% of total installed capacity (2020 est.)
hydroelectricity: 10.9% of total installed capacity (2020 est.)
biomass and waste: 1% of total installed capacity (2020 est.)

Coal: *production:* 2.977 million metric tons (2020 est.)
consumption: 35.268 million metric tons (2020 est.)
exports: 17,000 metric tons (2020 est.)
imports: 37.295 million metric tons (2020 est.)
proven reserves: 226 million metric tons (2019 est.)

Petroleum: *total petroleum production:* 593,800 bbl/day (2021 est.)
refined petroleum consumption: 718,600 bbl/day (2019 est.)
crude oil and lease condensate exports: 303,600 bbl/day (2018 est.)
crude oil and lease condensate imports: 182,300 bbl/day (2018 est.)
crude oil estimated reserves: 3.6 billion barrels (2021 est.)

Refined petroleum products - production: 528,300 bbl/day (2015 est.)

Refined petroleum products - exports: 208,400 bbl/day (2015 est.)

Refined petroleum products - imports: 304,600 bbl/day (2015 est.)

Natural gas: *production:* 74,985,350,000 cubic meters (2019 est.)
consumption: 39,586,915,000 cubic meters (2019 est.)
exports: 34,197,548,000 cubic meters (2020 est.)
imports: 4,008,073,000 cubic meters (2020 est.)
proven reserves: 1,189,306,000,000 cubic meters (2021 est.)

Carbon dioxide emissions: 254.764 million metric tonnes of CO_2 (2019 est.)
from coal and metallurgical coke: 81.726 million metric tonnes of CO_2 (2019 est.)
from petroleum and other liquids: 94.934 million metric tonnes of CO_2 (2019 est.)
from consumed natural gas: 78.104 million metric tonnes of CO_2 (2019 est.)

Energy consumption per capita: 123.755 million Btu/person (2019 est.)

COMMUNICATIONS

Telephones - fixed lines: *total subscriptions:* 7,467,900 (2020 est.)
subscriptions per 100 inhabitants: 23 (2020 est.)

Telephones - mobile cellular: *total subscriptions:* 43,723,600 (2020 est.)
subscriptions per 100 inhabitants: 135 (2020 est.)

Telecommunication systems: *general assessment:* as part of a diverse range of initiatives designed to move the country from developing to developed status by 2025, Malaysia has enabled and encouraged open competition in its telecommunications market; the result is very high penetration levels in both the mobile (147%) and mobile broadband (127%) segments, and near-universal coverage of 4G LTE networks; steady growth is occurring as more fiber optic cable networks are being deployed around the country; consumers are the main beneficiaries of the highly competitive market; they enjoy widespread access to high-speed mobile services as well as attractive offers on bundles to keep data use up but prices low; the downside is that most of Malaysia's MNOs and MVNOs have struggled to increase revenue in line with growth in subscriber numbers as well as demand for broadband data; while the operators have been very successful in moving a significant proportion (now over 30%) of customers from prepaid over to higher-value postpaid accounts, ARPU continues to fall year after year as a result of competitive pricing pressures; the mobile market, in particular, has become overcrowded and the government is keen to see further rationalization and consolidation with the operators; while customers will no doubt continue to enjoy high quality services at competitive rates, the new entity will be hopeful of squeezing better margins through improved economies of scale; the government's next move is to encourage the private mobile operators to sign up to the country's wholesale 5G network; this will develop and deploy the 5G infrastructure across the country; the government's stated intent was to avoid duplication of networks and infrastructure, and thus reduce investment costs for the operators; to date, no MNO has agreed to the deal and are instead demanding the development of a dual wholesale network model (one that no doubt offers more flexible terms, at least in the eyes of the

MNOs); Malaysia's 5G rollout has, in effect, come to a standstill while the government tries to find a way to restart negotiations (2022)
domestic: fixed-line roughly 23 per 100 and mobile-cellular teledensity roughly 135 per 100 persons; domestic satellite system with 2 earth stations (2020)
international: country code - 60; landing points for BBG, FEA, SAFE, SeaMeWe-3 & 4 & 5, AAE-1, JASUKA, BDM, Dumai-Melaka Cable System, BRCS, ACE, AAG, East-West Submarine Cable System, SEAX-1, SKR1M, APCN-2, APG, BtoBe, BaSICS, and Labuan-Brunei Submarine and MCT submarine cables providing connectivity to Asia, the Middle East, Southeast Asia, Australia and Europe; satellite earth stations - 2 Intelsat (1 Indian Ocean, 1 Pacific Ocean); launch of Kacific-1 satellite in 2019 (2019)

Broadcast media: state-owned TV broadcaster operates 2 TV networks with relays throughout the country, and the leading private commercial media group operates 4 TV stations with numerous relays throughout the country; satellite TV subscription service is available; state-owned radio broadcaster operates multiple national networks, as well as regional and local stations; many private commercial radio broadcasters and some subscription satellite radio services are available; about 55 radio stations overall (2019)

Internet country code: .my

Internet users: *total:* 29,129,398 (2020 est.)
percent of population: 90% (2020 est.)

Broadband - fixed subscriptions: *total:* 3,358,800 (2020 est.)
subscriptions per 100 inhabitants: 10 (2020 est.)

TRANSPORTATION

National air transport system: *number of registered air carriers:* 13 (2020)
inventory of registered aircraft operated by air carriers: 270
annual passenger traffic on registered air carriers: 60,481,772 (2018)
annual freight traffic on registered air carriers: 1,404,410,000 (2018) mt-km

Civil aircraft registration country code prefix: 9M

Airports: *total:* 114 (2021)

Airports - with paved runways: *total:* 39
over 3,047 m: 8
2,438 to 3,047 m: 8
1,524 to 2,437 m: 7
914 to 1,523 m: 8
under 914 m: 8 (2021)

Airports - with unpaved runways: *total:* 75
914 to 1,523 m: 6
under 914 m: 69 (2021)

Heliports: 4 (2021)

Pipelines: 354 km condensate, 6,439 km gas, 155 km liquid petroleum gas, 1,937 km oil, 43 km oil/gas/water, 114 km refined products, 26 km water (2013)

Railways: *total:* 1,851 km (2014)
standard gauge: 59 km (2014) 1.435-m gauge (59 km electrified)
narrow gauge: 1,792 km (2014) 1.000-m gauge (339 km electrified)

Roadways: *total:* 144,403 km (2010) (excludes local roads)
paved: 116,169 km (2010) (includes 1,821 km of expressways)
unpaved: 28,234 km (2010)

Waterways: 7,200 km (2011) (Peninsular Malaysia 3,200 km; Sabah 1,500 km; Sarawak 2,500 km)

Merchant marine: *total:* 1,769
by type: bulk carrier 16, container ship 28, general cargo 174, oil tanker 153, other 1,398 (2021)

Ports and terminals: *major seaport(s):* Bintulu, Johor Bahru, George Town (Penang), Pelabuhan Klang (Port Klang), Tanjung Pelepas
container port(s) (TEUs): Port Kelang (Port Klang) (13,580,717), Tanjung Pelepas (9,100,000) (2019)

LNG terminal(s) (export): Bintulu (Sarawak)

LNG terminal(s) (import): Sungei Udang

MILITARY AND SECURITY

Military and security forces: Malaysian Armed Forces (Angkatan Tentera Malaysia, ATM): Malaysian Army (Tentera Darat Malaysia), Royal Malaysian Navy (Tentera Laut Diraja Malaysia, TLDM), Royal Malaysian Air Force (Tentera Udara Diraja Malaysia, TUDM); Ministry of Home Affairs: Royal Malaysian Police (PRMD), Malaysian Maritime Enforcement Agency (MMEA; aka Malaysian Coast Guard) (2022)
note 1: the PRMD includes the General Operations Force, a paramilitary force with a variety of roles, including patrolling borders, counter-terrorism, maritime security, and counterinsurgency
note 2: Malaysia created a National Special Operations Force in 2016 for combating terrorism threats; the force is comprised of personnel from the Armed Forces, the Royal Malaysian Police, and the Malaysian Maritime Enforcement Agency

Military expenditures: 1% of GDP (2022 est.)
1% of GDP (2021)
1.1% of GDP (2020)
1% of GDP (2019) (approximately $7.84 billion)
1% of GDP (2018) (approximately $7.63 billion)

Military and security service personnel strengths: approximately 115,000 active duty troops (80,000 Army; 18,000 Navy; 17,000 Air Force) (2022)

Military equipment inventories and acquisitions: the military fields a diverse mix of mostly older imported weapons systems; since 2010, it has received military equipment from approximately 20 countries, with Germany and Spain being the leading suppliers (2021)

Military service age and obligation: 17 years 6 months of age for voluntary military service for men and women (younger with parental consent and proof of age); mandatory retirement age 60; no conscription (2021)
note - in 2020, the military announced a goal of having 10% of the active force comprised of women

Military deployments: 830 Lebanon (UNIFIL) (May 2022)

Military - note: maritime security has long been a top priority for the Malaysian Armed Forces, but it has received even greater emphasis in the 2000s, particularly anti-piracy operations in the Strait of Malacca and countering Chinese naval incursions in Malaysia's Economic Exclusion Zone, as well as addressing identified shortfalls in maritime capabilities; as such, it has undertaken modest efforts to procure more modern ships, improve air and maritime surveillance, expand the Navy's support infrastructure (particularly bases/ports) and domestic ship-building capacities, restructure naval command and control, and increase naval cooperation with regional and international partners; as of 2022, for example, the Navy had 6 frigates fitting out or under construction and scheduled for completion by 2023, which will increase the number of operational frigates from 2 to 8; in addition, it began tri-lateral air and naval patrols with Indonesia and the Philippines in 2017; Malaysia also cooperates closely with the US military, including on maritime surveillance and participating regularly in bilateral and multilateral training exercises

Malaysia is a member of the Five Powers Defense Arrangements (FPDA), a series of mutual assistance agreements reached in 1971 embracing Australia, Malaysia, New Zealand, Singapore, and the UK; the FPDA commits the members to consult with one another in the event or threat of an armed attack on any of the members and to mutually decide what measures should be taken, jointly or separately; there is no specific obligation to intervene militarily (2022)

Maritime threats: the International Maritime Bureau reports the territorial and offshore waters in the South China Sea as high risk for piracy and armed robbery against ships; numerous commercial vessels have been attacked and hijacked both at anchor and while underway; hijacked vessels are often disguised and cargo diverted to ports in East Asia; crews have been murdered or cast adrift; the Singapore Straits saw 35 attacks against commercial vessels in 2021, a 50% increase over 2020 and the highest number of incidents reported since 1992; vessels were boarded in 33 of the 35 incidents, one crew was injured, another assaulted and two threatened during these incidents

TERRORISM

Terrorist group(s): Islamic State of Iraq and ash-Sham (ISIS); Jemaah Islamiyah (JI); Abu Sayyaf Group (ASG)

TRANSNATIONAL ISSUES

Disputes - international: piracy remains a problem in the Malacca Strait
Malaysia-Brunei: per Letters of Exchange signed in 2009, Malaysia in 2010 ceded two hydrocarbon concession blocks to Brunei; in 2009, the media reported that Brunei had dropped its claims to the Limbang corridor, but Brunei responded that the subject had never been discussed during recent talks between the two countries
Malaysia-China-Philippines-Vietnam: while the 2002 "Declaration on the Conduct of Parties in the South China Sea" has eased tensions over the Spratly Islands, it is not the legally binding "code of conduct" sought by some parties, which is currently being negotiated between China and ASEAN; Malaysia was not party to the March 2005 joint accord among the national oil companies of China, the Philippines, and Vietnam on conducting marine seismic activities in the Spratly Islands
Malaysia-Indonesia: land and maritime negotiations with Indonesia are ongoing, and disputed areas include the controversial Tanjung Datu and Camar Wulan border area in Borneo and the maritime boundary in the Ambalat oil block in the Celebes Sea

Malaysia-Philippines: Philippines retains a dormant claim to the eastern part of Malaysia's Sabah State in northern Borneo
Malaysia-Singapore: disputes continue over deliveries of fresh water to Singapore, Singapore's land reclamation, bridge construction, and maritime boundaries in the Johor and Singapore Straits; in 2008, the International Court of Justice awarded sovereignty of Pedra Branca (Pulau Batu Puteh/Horsburgh Island) to Singapore, and Middle Rocks to Malaysia but did not rule on maritime regimes, boundaries, or disposition of South Ledge
Malaysia-Thailand: in 2008, separatist violence in Thailand's predominantly Muslim southern provinces prompts Malaysia to take measures to close and to monitor the border with Thailand to stem terrorist activities

Refugees and internally displaced persons: *refugees (country of origin)*: 120,126 (Burma) (mid-year 2021)
stateless persons: 112,003 (mid-year 2021); note - Malaysia's stateless population consists of Rohingya refugees from Burma, ethnic Indians, and the children of Filipino and Indonesian illegal migrants; Burma stripped the Rohingya of their nationality in 1982; Filipino and Indonesian children who have not been registered for birth certificates by their parents or who received birth certificates stamped "foreigner" are not eligible to attend government schools; these children are vulnerable to statelessness should they not be able to apply to their parents' country of origin for passports

Trafficking in persons: *current situation:* Malaysia is a destination and, to a lesser extent, a source and transit country for women and children subjected to conditions of forced labor and women and children subjected to sex trafficking; Malaysia is mainly a destination country for foreign workers who migrate willingly from countries including Indonesia, Nepal, India, Thailand, China, the Philippines, Burma, Cambodia, Laos, Bangladesh, Pakistan, and Vietnam, but subsequently they encounter forced labor or debt bondage at the hands of their employers in the domestic, agricultural, construction, plantation, and industrial sectors; a small number of Malaysian citizens were reportedly trafficked internally and to Singapore, China, and Japan for commercial sexual exploitation; refugees are also vulnerable to trafficking; some officials are reportedly complicit in facilitating trafficking; traffickers lure Rohingya women and girls residing in refugee camps in Bangladesh to Malaysia, where they are coerced to engage in commercial sex
tier rating: Tier 2 Watch List — Malaysia does not fully meet the minimum standards for the elimination of trafficking but is making significant efforts to do so; the government identified more victims, increased the number of trafficking-specialist prosecutors, drafted victim identification standard operating procedures, identified two volunteer victim assistance specialists that worked with more than 100 victims, and co-hosted the first national conference on anti-trafficking; however, authorities prosecuted and convicted fewer traffickers and investigated few trafficking cases; despite the issue of corruption, insufficient efforts were made to prosecute officials' complicity in trafficking-related crimes or to report the results of investigations into such crimes; insufficient interagency coordination and victim services discouraged foreign victims from participating in criminal proceedings; no resources were devoted to a written plan that, if implemented, would constitute significant efforts to meet the minimum standards; Malaysia was granted a waiver per the Trafficking Victims Protection Act from an otherwise required downgrade to Tier 3 (2020)

Illicit drugs: methamphetamine is the most used and trafficked drug controlled by criminal organizations that produce it; crystal methamphetamine, MDMA (ecstasy), cannabis products, heroin, ketamine, and Erimin 5 (nimetazepam) are smuggled into the country; a transit point for trafficking cocaine and other drugs to the Australian market

MALDIVES

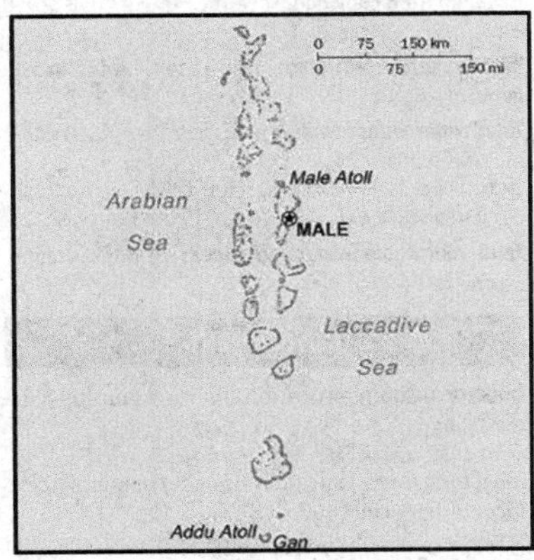

INTRODUCTION

Background: A sultanate since the 12th century, the Maldives became a British protectorate in 1887. The islands became a republic in 1968, three years after independence. President Maumoon Abdul GAYOOM dominated Maldives' political scene for 30 years, elected to six successive terms by single-party referendums. Following political demonstrations in the capital Male in August 2003, GAYOOM and his government pledged to embark upon a process of liberalization and democratic reforms, including a more representative political system and expanded political freedoms. Political parties were legalized in 2005.
In June 2008, a constituent assembly - termed the "Special Majlis" - finalized a new constitution ratified by GAYOOM in August 2008. The first-ever presidential elections under a multi-candidate, multi-party system were held in October 2008. GAYOOM was defeated in a runoff poll by Mohamed NASHEED, a political activist who had been jailed several years earlier by the GAYOOM regime. In early February 2012, after several weeks of street protests in response to his ordering the arrest of a top judge, NASHEED purportedly resigned the presidency and handed over power to Vice President Mohammed WAHEED Hassan Maniku. A government-appointed Commission of National Inquiry concluded there was no evidence of a coup, but NASHEED contends that police and military personnel forced him to resign. NASHEED, WAHEED, and Abdulla YAMEEN Abdul Gayoom ran in the 2013 elections with YAMEEN ultimately winning the presidency after three rounds of voting. As president, YAMEEN weakened democratic institutions, curtailed civil liberties, jailed his political opponents, restricted the press, and exerted control over the judiciary to strengthen his hold on power and limit dissent. In September 2018, YAMEEN lost his reelection bid to Ibrahim Mohamed SOLIH, a parliamentarian of the Maldivian Democratic Party (MDP), who had the support of a coalition of four parties that came together to defeat YAMEEN and restore democratic norms to Maldives. In April 2019, SOLIH's MDP won 65 of 87 seats in parliament.

GEOGRAPHY

Location: Southern Asia, group of atolls in the Indian Ocean, south-southwest of India

Geographic coordinates: 3 15 N, 73 00 E

Map references: Asia

Area: *total:* 298 sq km
land: 298 sq km
water: 0 sq km

Area - comparative: about 1.7 times the size of Washington, DC

Land boundaries: *total:* 0 km

Coastline: 644 km

Maritime claims: *territorial sea:* 12 nm
contiguous zone: 24 nm
exclusive economic zone: 200 nm
measured from claimed archipelagic straight baselines

Climate: tropical; hot, humid; dry, northeast monsoon (November to March); rainy, southwest monsoon (June to August)

Terrain: flat coral atolls, with white sandy beaches; sits atop the submarine volcanic Chagos-Laccadive Ridge

Elevation: *highest point:* 8th tee, golf course, Villingi Island 5 m
lowest point: Indian Ocean 0 m
mean elevation: 2 m

Natural resources: fish

Land use: *agricultural land:* 23.3% (2018 est.)
arable land: 10% (2018 est.)
permanent crops: 10% (2018 est.)
permanent pasture: 3.3% (2018 est.)

forest: 3% (2018 est.)
other: 73.7% (2018 est.)

Irrigated land: 0 sq km (2012)

Population distribution: about a third of the population lives in the centrally located capital city of Male and almost a tenth in southern Addu City; the remainder of the populace is spread over the 200 or so populated islands of the archipelago

Natural hazards: tsunamis; low elevation of islands makes them sensitive to sea level rise

Geography - note: smallest Asian country; archipelago of 1,190 coral islands grouped into 26 atolls (200 inhabited islands, plus 80 islands with tourist resorts); strategic location astride and along major sea lanes in Indian Ocean

PEOPLE AND SOCIETY

Population: 390,164 (2022 est.)

Nationality: *noun:* Maldivian(s)
adjective: Maldivian

Ethnic groups: homogeneous mixture of Sinhalese, Dravidian, Arab, Australasian, and African resulting from historical changes in regional hegemony over marine trade routes

Languages: Dhivehi (official, dialect of Sinhala, script derived from Arabic), English (spoken by most government officials)

Religions: Sunni Muslim (official)

Age structure: *0-14 years:* 22.13% (male 44,260/female 42,477)
15-24 years: 17.24% (male 37,826/female 29,745)
25-54 years: 48.91% (male 104,217/female 87,465)
55-64 years: 6.91% (male 12,942/female 14,123)
65 years and over: 4.81% (male 8,417/female 10,432) (2020 est.)

Dependency ratios: *total dependency ratio:* 30.2
youth dependency ratio: 25.5
elderly dependency ratio: 4.7
potential support ratio: 21.4 (2020 est.)

Median age: *total:* 29.5 years
male: 29.2 years
female: 30 years (2020 est.)

Population growth rate: -0.14% (2022 est.)

Birth rate: 15.54 births/1,000 population (2022 est.)

Death rate: 4.15 deaths/1,000 population (2022 est.)

Net migration rate: -12.78 migrant(s)/1,000 population (2022 est.)

Population distribution: about a third of the population lives in the centrally located capital city of Male and almost a tenth in southern Addu City; the remainder of the populace is spread over the 200 or so populated islands of the archipelago

Urbanization: *urban population:* 41.5% of total population (2022)
rate of urbanization: 2.34% annual rate of change (2020-25 est.)

Major urban areas - population: 177,000 MALE (capital) (2018)

Sex ratio: *at birth:* 1.05 male(s)/female
0-14 years: 1.04 male(s)/female
15-24 years: 1.2 male(s)/female
25-54 years: 1.11 male(s)/female
55-64 years: 0.89 male(s)/female
65 years and over: 0.75 male(s)/female
total population: 1.08 male(s)/female (2022 est.)

Mother's mean age at first birth: 23.2 years (2016/17 est.)
note: data represents median age at first birth among women 25-49

Maternal mortality ratio: 53 deaths/100,000 live births (2017 est.)

Infant mortality rate: *total:* 25.7 deaths/1,000 live births
male: 28.76 deaths/1,000 live births
female: 22.49 deaths/1,000 live births (2022 est.)

Life expectancy at birth: *total population:* 76.94 years
male: 74.57 years
female: 79.42 years (2022 est.)

Total fertility rate: 1.71 children born/woman (2022 est.)

Contraceptive prevalence rate: 18.8% (2016/17)

Drinking water source: *improved: urban:* 99% of population
rural: 100% of population
total: 99.6% of population
unimproved: urban: 1% of population
rural: 0% of population
total: 0.4% of population (2020 est.)

Current health expenditure: 8% of GDP (2019)

Physicians density: 2.05 physicians/1,000 population (2019)

Hospital bed density: 4.3 beds/1,000 population

Sanitation facility access: *improved: urban:* 100% of population
rural: 99.1% of population
total: 99.5% of population
unimproved: urban: 0% of population
rural: 0.9% of population
total: 0.5% of population (2020 est.)

Obesity - adult prevalence rate: 8.6% (2016)

Alcohol consumption per capita: *total:* 1.38 liters of pure alcohol (2019 est.)
beer: 0.33 liters of pure alcohol (2019 est.)
wine: 0.59 liters of pure alcohol (2019 est.)
spirits: 0.45 liters of pure alcohol (2019 est.)
other alcohols: 0 liters of pure alcohol (2019 est.)

Tobacco use: *total:* 25.2% (2020 est.)
male: 44.4% (2020 est.)
female: 6% (2020 est.)

Children under the age of 5 years underweight: 14.8% (2016/17)

Child marriage: *women married by age 15:* 0%
women married by age 18: 2.2%
men married by age 18: 2.2% (2017 est.)

Education expenditures: 4.1% of GDP (2019 est.)

Literacy: *definition:* age 15 and over can read and write
total population: 97.7%
male: 97.3%
female: 98.1% (2016)

School life expectancy (primary to tertiary education): *total:* 13 years
male: 12 years
female: 14 years (2019)

Unemployment, youth ages 15-24: *total:* 15.5%
male: 18.5%
female: 11.7% (2019 est.)

ENVIRONMENT

Environment - current issues: rising sea levels threaten land; depletion of freshwater aquifers threatens water supplies; inadequate sewage treatment; coral reef bleaching

Environment - international agreements: *party to:* Biodiversity, Climate Change, Climate Change-Kyoto Protocol, Climate Change-Paris Agreement, Comprehensive Nuclear Test Ban, Desertification, Endangered Species, Hazardous Wastes, Law of the Sea, Ozone Layer Protection, Ship Pollution
signed, but not ratified: none of the selected agreements

Air pollutants: *particulate matter emissions:* 7.63 micrograms per cubic meter (2016 est.)
carbon dioxide emissions: 1.44 megatons (2016 est.)
methane emissions: 0.14 megatons (2020 est.)

Climate: tropical; hot, humid; dry, northeast monsoon (November to March); rainy, southwest monsoon (June to August)

Land use: *agricultural land:* 23.3% (2018 est.)
arable land: 10% (2018 est.)
permanent crops: 10% (2018 est.)
permanent pasture: 3.3% (2018 est.)
forest: 3% (2018 est.)
other: 73.7% (2018 est.)

Urbanization: *urban population:* 41.5% of total population (2022)
rate of urbanization: 2.34% annual rate of change (2020-25 est.)

Revenue from forest resources: *forest revenues:* 0% of GDP (2018 est.)

Revenue from coal: *coal revenues:* 0% of GDP (2018 est.)

Waste and recycling: *municipal solid waste generated annually:* 211,506 tons (2015 est.)

Total water withdrawal: *municipal:* 5.6 million cubic meters (2017 est.)
industrial: 300,000 cubic meters (2017 est.)
agricultural: 0 cubic meters (2017 est.)

Total renewable water resources: 30 million cubic meters (2017 est.)

GOVERNMENT

Country name: *conventional long form:* Republic of Maldives
conventional short form: Maldives
local long form: Dhivehi Raajjeyge Jumhooriyyaa
local short form: Dhivehi Raajje
etymology: archipelago apparently named after the main island (and capital) of Male; the word "Maldives" means "the islands (dives) of Male"; alternatively, the name may derive from the Sanskrit word "maladvipa" meaning "garland of islands"; Dhivehi Raajje in Dhivehi means "Kingdom of the Dhivehi people"

Government type: presidential republic

Capital: *name:* Male
geographic coordinates: 4 10 N, 73 30 E
time difference: UTC+5 (10 hours ahead of Washington, DC, during Standard Time)
etymology: derived from the Sanskrit word "mahaalay" meaning "big house"

Administrative divisions: 21 administrative atolls (atholhuthah, singular - atholhu); Addu (Addu City), Ariatholhu Dhekunuburi (South Ari

Atoll), Ariatholhu Uthuruburi (North Ari Atoll), Faadhippolhu, Felidhuatholhu (Felidhu Atoll), Fuvammulah, Hahdhunmathi, Huvadhuatholhu Dhekunuburi (South Huvadhu Atoll), Huvadhuatholhu Uthuruburi (North Huvadhu Atoll), Kolhumadulu, Maale (Male), Maaleatholhu (Male Atoll), Maalhosmadulu Dhekunuburi (South Maalhosmadulu), Maalhosmadulu Uthuruburi (North Maalhosmadulu), Miladhunmadulu Dhekunuburi (South Miladhunmadulu), Miladhunmadulu Uthuruburi (North Miladhunmadulu), Mulakatholhu (Mulaku Atoll), Nilandheatholhu Dhekunuburi (South Nilandhe Atoll), Nilandheatholhu Uthuruburi (North Nilandhe Atoll), Thiladhunmathee Dhekunuburi (South Thiladhunmathi), Thiladhunmathee Uthuruburi (North Thiladhunmathi)

Independence: 26 July 1965 (from the UK)

National holiday: Independence Day, 26 July (1965)

Constitution: *history:* many previous; latest ratified 7 August 2008
amendments: proposed by Parliament; passage requires at least three-quarters majority vote by its membership and the signature of the president of the republic; passage of amendments to constitutional articles on rights and freedoms and the terms of office of Parliament and of the president also requires a majority vote in a referendum; amended 2015

Legal system: Islamic (sharia) legal system with English common law influences, primarily in commercial matters

International law organization participation: has not submitted an ICJ jurisdiction declaration; accepts ICCt jurisdiction

Citizenship: *citizenship by birth:* no
citizenship by descent only: at least one parent must be a citizen of Maldives
dual citizenship recognized: yes
residency requirement for naturalization: unknown

Suffrage: 18 years of age; universal

Executive branch: *chief of state:* President Ibrahim "Ibu" Mohamed SOLIH (since 17 November 2018); Vice President Faisal NASEEM (since 17 November 2018); the president is both chief of state and head of government
head of government: President Ibrahim "Ibu" Mohamed SOLIH (since 17 November 2018); Vice President Faisal NASEEM (since 17 November 2018)
cabinet: Cabinet of Ministers appointed by the president, approved by Parliament
elections/appointments: president directly elected by absolute majority popular vote in 2 rounds if needed for a 5-year term (eligible for a second term); election last held on 23 September 2018 (next to be held in 2023)
election results:
2018: Ibrahim Mohamed SOLIH elected president (in the first round); Ibrahim Mohamed SOLIH (MDP) 58.3%, Abdulla YAMEEN Abdul Gayoom (PPM) 41.7%

Legislative branch: *description:* unicameral Parliament or People's Majlis (87 seats - includes 2 seats added by the Elections Commission in late 2018; members directly elected in single-seat constituencies by simple majority vote to serve 5-year terms)
elections:
last held on 6 April 2019 (next to be held in 2023)
election results:
percent of vote - MDP 44.7%, JP 10.8%, PPM 8.7%, PNC 6.4%, MDA 2.8%, other 5.6%, independent 21%; seats by party - MDP 65, JP 5, PPM 5, PNC 3, MDA 2, independent 7; composition - men 83, women 4, percent of women 4.6%

Judicial branch: *highest court(s):* Supreme Court (consists of the chief justice and 6 justices
judge selection and term of office: Supreme Court judges appointed by the president in consultation with the Judicial Service Commission - a 10-member body of selected high government officials and the public - and upon confirmation by voting members of the People's Majlis; judges serve until mandatory retirement at age 70
subordinate courts: High Court; Criminal, Civil, Family, Juvenile, and Drug Courts; Magistrate Courts (on each of the inhabited islands)

Political parties and leaders: Adhaalath (Justice) Party or AP [Sheikh Imran ABDULLA]
Dhivehi Rayyithunge Party or DRP [Abdulla JABIR]
Maldives Development Alliance or MDA [Ahmed Shiyam MOHAMED]
Maldivian Democratic Party or MDP [Mohamed NASHEED]
Maldives Labor and Social Democratic Party or MLSDP [Ahmed SHIHAM]
Maldives Third Way Democrats or MTD [Ahmed ADEEB]
Maumoon/Maldives Reform Movement or MRM [Ahmed Faris MAUMOON]
National Democratic Congress [Yousuf Maaniu]
People's National Congress or PNC [Abdul Raheem ABDULLA]
Progressive Party of Maldives or PPM [Abdulla YAMEEN]
Republican (Jumhooree) Party or JP [Qasim IBRAHIM]
(2020)

International organization participation: ADB, AOSIS, C, CP, FAO, G-77, IBRD, ICAO, ICC (NGOs), ICCt, IDA, IDB, IFAD, IFC, IFRCS, ILO, IMF, IMO, Interpol, IOC, IOM, IPU, ITU, MIGA, NAM, OIC, OPCW, SAARC, SACEP, UN, UNCTAD, UNESCO, UNIDO, UNWTO, UPU, WCO, WHO, WIPO, WMO, WTO

Diplomatic representation in the US: *chief of mission:*
Maldives has no embassy in the US, but its Permanent Representative to the UN in New York, Thilmeeza HUSSAIN (since 8 July 2019), is accredited to the US and serves as ambassador
chancery: 801 Second Avenue, Suite 202E, New York, NY 10017
telephone: [1] (212) 599-6194; [1] (212) 599-6195
FAX: [1] (212) 661-6405
email address and website:
info@maldivesmission.com
http://www. maldivesmission.com/

Diplomatic representation from the US: *embassy:* the US does not have an embassy in Maldives; the US is in the process of opening an embassy in Maldives; as of March 2022, there is no US Ambassador to Maldives; until late 2021, the US Ambassador to Sri Lanka was also accredited to the Maldives

Flag description: red with a large green rectangle in the center bearing a vertical white crescent moon; the closed side of the crescent is on the hoist side of the flag; red recalls those who have sacrificed their lives in defense of their country, the green rectangle represents peace and prosperity, and the white crescent signifies Islam

National symbol(s): coconut palm, yellowfin tuna; national colors: red, green, white

National anthem: *name:* "Gaumee Salaam" (National Salute)
lyrics/music: Mohamed Jameel DIDI/ Wannakuwattawaduge DON AMARADEVA
note: lyrics adopted 1948, music adopted 1972; between 1948 and 1972, the lyrics were sung to the tune of "Auld Lang Syne"

ECONOMY

Economic overview: Maldives has quickly become a middle-income country, driven by the rapid growth of its tourism and fisheries sectors, but the country still contends with a large and growing fiscal deficit. Infrastructure projects, largely funded by China, could add significantly to debt levels. Political turmoil and the declaration of a state of emergency in February 2018 led to the issuance of travel warnings by several countries whose citizens visit Maldives in significant numbers, but the overall impact on tourism revenue was unclear.
In 2015, Maldives' Parliament passed a constitutional amendment legalizing foreign ownership of land; foreign land-buyers must reclaim at least 70% of the desired land from the ocean and invest at least $1 billion in a construction project approved by Parliament. Diversifying the economy beyond tourism and fishing, reforming public finance, increasing employment opportunities, and combating corruption, cronyism, and a growing drug problem are near-term challenges facing the government. Over the longer term, Maldivian authorities worry about the impact of erosion and possible global warming on their low-lying country; 80% of the area is 1 meter or less above sea level.

Real GDP (purchasing power parity): $7.05 billion (2020 est.)
$10.37 billion (2019 est.)
$9.69 billion (2018 est.)
note: data are in 2017 dollars

Real GDP growth rate: 4.8% (2017 est.)
4.5% (2016 est.)
2.2% (2015 est.)

Real GDP per capita: $13,000 (2020 est.)
$19,500 (2019 est.)
$18,800 (2018 est.)
note: data are in 2017 dollars

GDP (official exchange rate): $4.505 billion (2017 est.)

Inflation rate (consumer prices): 2.3% (2017 est.)
0.8% (2016 est.)

Credit ratings:

Fitch rating: CCC (2020)

Moody's rating: B3 (2020)
note: The year refers to the year in which the current credit rating was first obtained.

GDP - composition, by sector of origin: *agriculture:* 3% (2015 est.)
industry: 16% (2015 est.)
services: 81% (2015 est.)

GDP - composition, by end use: *exports of goods and services:* 93.6% (2016 est.)
imports of goods and services: 89% (2016 est.)

Agricultural products: papayas, vegetables, roots/ tubers nes, nuts, fruit, other meat, tomatoes, coconuts, bananas, maize

Industries: tourism, fish processing, shipping, boat building, coconut processing, woven mats, rope, handicrafts, coral and sand mining

Industrial production growth rate: 14% (2012 est.)

Labor force: 222,200 (2017 est.)

Labor force - by occupation: *agriculture:* 7.7%
industry: 22.8%
services: 69.5% (2017 est.)

Unemployment rate: 2.9% (2017 est.)
3.2% (2016 est.)

Unemployment, youth ages 15-24: *total:* 15.5%
male: 18.5%
female: 11.7% (2019 est.)

Population below poverty line: 8.2% (2016 est.)

Gini Index coefficient - distribution of family income: 31.3 (2016 est.)
37.4 (2004 est.)

Household income or consumption by percentage share: *lowest 10%:* 1.2%
highest 10%: 33.3% (FY09/10)

Budget: *revenues:* 1.19 billion (2016 est.)
expenditures: 1.643 billion (2016 est.)

Budget surplus (+) or deficit (-): -10.1% (of GDP) (2016 est.)

Public debt: 63.9% of GDP (2017 est.)
61.7% of GDP (2016 est.)

Taxes and other revenues: 26.4% (of GDP) (2016 est.)

Fiscal year: calendar year

Current account balance: -$876 million (2017 est.)
-$1.033 billion (2016 est.)

Exports: $3.72 billion (2019 est.) note: data are in current year dollars
$3.58 billion (2018 est.) note: data are in current year dollars

Exports - partners: Thailand 24%, United States 13%, China 12%, France 11%, Germany 11%, Italy 5%, United Kingdom 5% (2019)

Exports - commodities: fish products, natural gas, scrap iron, jewelry, liquid pumps (2019)

Imports: $4.09 billion (2019 est.) note: data are in current year dollars
$4.1 billion (2018 est.) note: data are in current year dollars

Imports - partners: United Arab Emirates 24%, China 16%, Singapore 14%, India 11%, Malaysia 6%, Thailand 5% (2019)

Imports - commodities: refined petroleum, fruits, furniture, broadcasting equipment, lumber (2019)

Reserves of foreign exchange and gold: $477.9 million (31 December 2016 est.)
$575.8 million (31 December 2015 est.)

Debt - external: $848.8 million (31 December 2016 est.)
$696.2 million (31 December 2015 est.)

Exchange rates: rufiyaa (MVR) per US dollar -
15.42 (2017 est.)
15.35 (2016 est.)

ENERGY

Electricity access: *electrification - total population:* 100% (2020)

Electricity: *installed generating capacity:* 545,000 kW (2020 est.)
consumption: 586.5 million kWh (2019 est.)
exports: 0 kWh (2020 est.)
imports: 0 kWh (2020 est.)
transmission/distribution losses: 21 million kWh (2019 est.)

Electricity generation sources: *fossil fuels:* 99.6% of total installed capacity (2020 est.)
wind: 0.4% of total installed capacity (2020 est.)

Petroleum: *total petroleum production:* 0 bbl/day (2021 est.)
refined petroleum consumption: 15,300 bbl/day (2019 est.)

Refined petroleum products - imports: 10,840 bbl/day (2015 est.)

Carbon dioxide emissions: 2.286 million metric tonnes of CO2 (2019 est.)
from petroleum and other liquids: 2.286 million metric tonnes of CO2 (2019 est.)

Energy consumption per capita: 59.69 million Btu/person (2019 est.)

COMMUNICATIONS

Telephones - fixed lines: *total subscriptions:* 14,508 (2020 est.)
subscriptions per 100 inhabitants: 3 (2020 est.)

Telephones - mobile cellular: *total subscriptions:* 717,708 (2020 est.)
subscriptions per 100 inhabitants: 133 (2020 est.)

Telecommunication systems: *general assessment:* with its economy so heavily dependent on tourism, the Maldives has suffered heavy economic as well as health casualties during the pandemic; the country had a relatively short period of lock down and was willing to welcome visitors back as early as July 2020; but the effective shutdown of international air travel for most of the year resulted in the bottom falling out of the Maldives' tourism industry, taking GDP down 32% in the process; the economy fared better in 2021, with a return to growth, yet it may still be a few years before the country's key industries can return to the same level of prosperity that they previously enjoyed; the country's high number of tourists and expatriate workers has inflated the penetration rate for mobile services, making it one of the highest in the world; that rate crashed in 2020 as demand for SIM cards (primarily prepaid) dried up; however, the number of contract subscribers increased as locals took advantage of competitive pricing offers from operators; everything now rests on a fast return to normality, with tourists helping to boost the nation's coffers as well as buying up those prepaid SIM cards; with commercial 5G services already launched and fiber networks rapidly expanding around the country, the Maldives is primed to deliver world-class telecommunications services to its domestic and international customers (2021)
domestic: fixed-line is at nearly 3 per 100 persons and mobile-cellular subscriptions stands at nearly 133 per 100 persons (2020)
international: country code - 960; landing points for Dhiraagu Cable Network, NaSCOM, Dhiraagu-SLT Submarine Cable Networks and WARF submarine cables providing connections to 8 points in Maldives, India, and Sri Lanka; satellite earth station - 3 Intelsat (Indian Ocean) (2019)

Broadcast media: state-owned radio and TV monopoly until recently; 4 state-operated and 7 privately owned TV stations and 4 state-operated and 7 privately owned radio stations (2019)

Internet country code: .mv

Internet users: *total:* 340,542 (2020 est.)
percent of population: 63% (2020 est.)

Broadband - fixed subscriptions: *total:* 63,685 (2020 est.)
subscriptions per 100 inhabitants: 12 (2020 est.)

TRANSPORTATION

National air transport system: *number of registered air carriers:* 3 (2020)
inventory of registered aircraft operated by air carriers: 36
annual passenger traffic on registered air carriers: 1,147,247 (2018)
annual freight traffic on registered air carriers: 7.75 million (2018)

Civil aircraft registration country code prefix: 8Q

Airports: *total:* 9 (2021)

Airports - with paved runways: *total:* 7
over 3,047 m: 1
2,438 to 3,047 m: 1
1,524 to 2,437 m: 1
914 to 1,523 m: 4 (2021)

Airports - with unpaved runways: *total:* 2
914 to 1,523 m: 2 (2021)

Roadways: *total:* 93 km (2018)
paved: 93 km (2018) - 60 km in Malée; 16 km on Addu Atolis; 17 km on Laamu
note: island roads are mainly compacted coral

Merchant marine: *total:* 68
by type: general cargo 21, oil tanker 19, other 28 (2021)

Ports and terminals: *major seaport(s):* Male

MILITARY AND SECURITY

Military and security forces: the Republic of Maldives has no distinct army, navy, or air force but a single security unit called the Maldives National Defense Force (MNDF) comprised of ground forces, an air element, a coastguard, a presidential security division, and a special protection group (2022)
note: the Maldives Police Service is responsible for internal security and reports to the Ministry of Home Affairs

Military expenditures: not available

Military and security service personnel strengths: approximately 2,500 personnel (2022)

Military equipment inventories and acquisitions: India has provided most of the equipment in the MNDF's inventory (2022)

Military service age and obligation: 18-28 years of age for voluntary service; no conscription; 10th grade or equivalent education required; must not be a member of a political party (2022)

Military - note: the MNDF is primarily tasked to reinforce the Maldives Police Service and ensure security in the country's exclusive economic zone (2022)

TERRORISM

Terrorist group(s): Islamic State of Iraq and ash-Sham (ISIS)

TRANSNATIONAL ISSUES

Disputes - international: none identified

Illicit drugs: NA

MALI

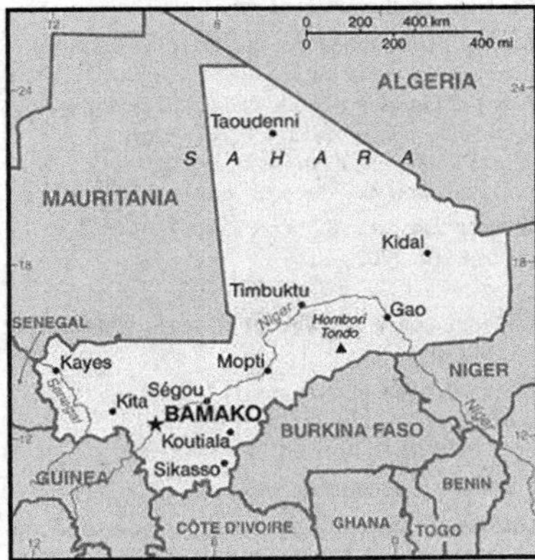

INTRODUCTION

Background: Present-day Mali is named after the Mali Empire that ruled the region between the 13th and 16th centuries. At its peak in the 14th century, it was the largest and wealthiest empire in West Africa and controlled an area about twice the size of modern-day France. Primarily a trading empire, Mali derived its wealth from gold and maintained several goldfields and trade routes in the Sahel. The empire also influenced West African culture through the spread of its language, laws, and customs, but by the 16th century it fragmented into mostly small chiefdoms. The Songhai Empire, previously a Mali dependency centered in Timbuktu, gained prominence in the 15th and 16th centuries. Under Songhai rule, Timbuktu became a large commercial center and well-known for its scholarship and religious teaching. Timbuktu remains a center of culture in West Africa today. In the late 16th century, the Songhai Empire fell to Moroccan invaders and disintegrated into independent sultanates and kingdoms.

France, expanding from Senegal, seized control of the area in the 1890s and incorporated it into French West Africa as French Sudan. In 1960, French Sudan gained independence from France and became the Mali Federation. When Senegal withdrew after only a few months, the remaining area was renamed the Republic of Mali. Mali saw 31 years of dictatorship until 1991, when a military coup led by Amadou Toumani TOURE ousted the government, established a new constitution, and instituted a multiparty democracy. President Alpha Oumar KONARE won Mali's first two democratic presidential elections in 1992 and 1997. In keeping with Mali's two-term constitutional limit, he stepped down in 2002 and was succeeded by Amadou Toumani TOURE, who won a second term in 2007.

In 2012, rising ethnic tensions and an influx of fighters - some linked to Al-Qa'ida - from Libya led to a rebellion and military coup. Following the coup, rebels expelled the military from the country's three northern regions, allowing terrorist organizations to develop strongholds in the area. With French military intervention, the Malian Government managed to retake most of the north. However, the government's grasp in the region remains weak with local militias, terrorists, and insurgent groups continuously trying to expand control. In 2015, the Malian Government and northern rebels signed an internationally mediated peace accord. Despite a June 2017 target for implementation of the agreement, the signatories have made little progress. Extremist groups were left out of the peace process, and terrorist attacks remain common.

Ibrahim Boubacar KEITA won the Malian presidential elections in 2013 and 2018. Aside from security and logistic shortfalls, international observers deemed these elections credible. Terrorism, banditry, ethnic-based violence, and extra-judicial military killings plagued the country during KEITA's second term. In August 2020, the military arrested KEITA, his prime minister, and other senior members of the government and established a military junta called the National Committee for the Salvation of the People (CNSP). In September 2020, the junta established a transition government and appointed Bah N'DAW, a retired army officer and former defense minister, as interim president and Colonel Assimi GOITA, the coup leader and chairman of the CNSP, as interim vice president. The transition government's charter allowed it to rule for up to 18 months before calling a general election.

In May 2021, Colonel Assimi GOITA led a military takeover, arresting the interim president after a Cabinet shake up removed GOITA's key allies. GOITA was sworn in as transition president in June 2021 and Choguel Kokalla MAIGA was sworn in as prime minister. In January 2022, the Economic Community of West African States (ECOWAS) imposed sanctions against the transition government and member states closed their borders after the transition government presented a five-year extension to the electoral calendar. ECOWAS and the transition government continue to work to negotiate an acceptable electoral calendar.

GEOGRAPHY

Location: interior Western Africa, southwest of Algeria, north of Guinea, Cote d'Ivoire, and Burkina Faso, west of Niger

Geographic coordinates: 17 00 N, 4 00 W

Map references: Africa

Area: *total:* 1,240,192 sq km
land: 1,220,190 sq km
water: 20,002 sq km

Area - comparative: slightly less than twice the size of Texas

Land boundaries: *total:* 7,908 km
border countries (6): Algeria 1,359 km; Burkina Faso 1,325 km; Cote d'Ivoire 599 km; Guinea 1,062 km; Mauritania 2,236 km; Niger 838 km, Senegal 489 km

Coastline: 0 km (landlocked)

Maritime claims: none (landlocked)

Climate: subtropical to arid; hot and dry (February to June); rainy, humid, and mild (June to November); cool and dry (November to February)

Terrain: mostly flat to rolling northern plains covered by sand; savanna in south, rugged hills in northeast

Elevation: *highest point:* Hombori Tondo 1,155 m
lowest point: Senegal River 23 m
mean elevation: 343 m

Natural resources: gold, phosphates, kaolin, salt, limestone, uranium, gypsum, granite, hydropower, note, bauxite, iron ore, manganese, tin, and copper deposits are known but not exploited

Land use: *agricultural land:* 34.1% (2018 est.)
arable land: 5.6% (2018 est.)
permanent crops: 0.1% (2018 est.)
permanent pasture: 28.4% (2018 est.)
forest: 10.2% (2018 est.)
other: 55.7% (2018 est.)

Irrigated land: 3,780 sq km (2012)

Major lakes (area sq km): *fresh water lake(s):* Lac Faguibine - 590 sq km
note - the Niger River is the only source of water for the lake; in recent years the lake is dry

Major rivers (by length in km): Niger (shared with Guinea [s], Niger, and Nigeria [m]) - 4,200 km; Senegal (shared with Guinea [s], Senegal, and Mauritania [m]) - 1,641 km
note – [s] after country name indicates river source; [m] after country name indicates river mouth

Major watersheds (area sq km): Atlantic Ocean drainage: Niger (2,261,741 sq km), Senegal (456,397 sq km), Volta (410,991 sq km)

Major aquifers: Lullemeden-Irhazer Basin, Taodeni-Tanezrouft Basin

Population distribution: the overwhelming majority of the population lives in the southern half of the country, with greater density along the border with Burkina Faso as shown in this population distribution map

Natural hazards: hot, dust-laden harmattan haze common during dry seasons; recurring droughts; occasional Niger River flooding

Geography - note: landlocked; divided into three natural zones: the southern, cultivated Sudanese; the central, semiarid Sahelian; and the northern, arid Saharan

PEOPLE AND SOCIETY

Population: 20,741,769 (2022 est.)

Nationality: *noun:* Malian(s)
adjective: Malian

Ethnic groups: Bambara 33.3%, Fulani (Peuhl) 13.3%, Sarakole/Soninke/Marka 9.8%, Senufo/Manianka 9.6%, Malinke 8.8%, Dogon 8.7%, Sonrai 5.9%, Bobo 2.1%, Tuareg/Bella 1.7%, other Malian 6%, from members of Economic Community of West Africa 0.4%, other 0.3% (2018 est.)

Languages: French (official), Bambara 46.3%, Peuhl/Foulfoulbe 9.4%, Dogon 7.2%, Maraka/Soninke 6.4%, Malinke 5.6%, Sonrhai/Djerma 5.6%, Minianka 4.3%, Tamacheq 3.5%, Senoufo 2.6%, Bobo 2.1%, other 6.3%, unspecified 0.7% (2009 est.)
note: Mali has 13 national languages in addition to its official language

Religions: Muslim 93.9%, Christian 2.8%, animist 0.7%, none 2.5% (2018 est.)

Demographic profile: Mali's total population is expected to double by 2035; its capital Bamako is one of the fastest-growing cities in Africa. A young age structure, a declining mortality rate, and a sustained high total fertility rate of 5.5 children per woman – the fourth highest in the world, as of 2022 – ensure continued rapid population growth for the foreseeable future. Significant outmigration only marginally tempers this growth. Despite decreases, Mali's infant, child, and maternal mortality rates remain among the highest in Sub-Saharan Africa because of limited access to and adoption of family planning, early childbearing, short birth intervals, the prevalence of female genital cutting, infrequent use of skilled birth attendants, and a lack of emergency obstetrical and neonatal care.

Mali's high total fertility rate has been virtually unchanged for decades, as a result of the ongoing preference for large families, early childbearing, the lack of female education and empowerment, poverty, and extremely low contraceptive use. Slowing Mali's population growth by lowering its birth rate will be essential for poverty reduction, improving food security, and developing human capital and the economy.

Mali has a long history of seasonal migration and emigration driven by poverty, conflict, demographic pressure, unemployment, food insecurity, and droughts. Many Malians from rural areas migrate during the dry period to nearby villages and towns to do odd jobs or to adjoining countries to work in agriculture or mining. Pastoralists and nomads move seasonally to southern Mali or nearby coastal states. Others migrate long term to Mali's urban areas, Cote d'Ivoire, other neighboring countries, and in smaller numbers to France, Mali's former colonial ruler. Since the early 1990s, Mali's role has grown as a transit country for regional migration flows and illegal migration to Europe. Human smugglers and traffickers exploit the same regional routes used for moving contraband drugs, arms, and cigarettes.

Between early 2012 and 2013, renewed fighting in northern Mali between government forces and Tuareg secessionists and their Islamist allies, a French-led international military intervention, as well as chronic food shortages, caused the displacement of hundreds of thousands of Malians. Most of those displaced domestically sought shelter in urban areas of southern Mali, except for pastoralist and nomadic groups, who abandoned their traditional routes, gave away or sold their livestock, and dispersed into the deserts of northern Mali or crossed into neighboring countries. Almost all Malians who took refuge abroad (mostly Tuareg and Maure pastoralists) stayed in the region, largely in Mauritania, Niger, and Burkina Faso.

Age structure: *0-14 years:* 47.69% (male 4,689,121/female 4,636,685)
15-24 years: 19% (male 1,768,772/female 1,945,582)
25-54 years: 26.61% (male 2,395,566/female 2,806,830)
55-64 years: 3.68% (male 367,710/female 352,170)
65 years and over: 3.02% (male 293,560/female 297,401) (2020 est.)

Dependency ratios: *total dependency ratio:* 98
youth dependency ratio: 93.1
elderly dependency ratio: 4.9
potential support ratio: 20.4 (2020 est.)

Median age: *total:* 16 years
male: 15.3 years
female: 16.7 years (2020 est.)

Population growth rate: 2.95% (2022 est.)

Birth rate: 41.07 births/1,000 population (2022 est.)

Death rate: 8.53 deaths/1,000 population (2022 est.)

Net migration rate: -3.08 migrant(s)/1,000 population (2022 est.)

Population distribution: the overwhelming majority of the population lives in the southern half of the country, with greater density along the border with Burkina Faso as shown in this population distribution map

Urbanization: *urban population:* 45.4% of total population (2022)
rate of urbanization: 4.57% annual rate of change (2020-25 est.)

Major urban areas - population: 2.817 million BAMAKO (capital) (2022)

Sex ratio: *at birth:* 1.03 male(s)/female
0-14 years: 1.01 male(s)/female
15-24 years: 0.91 male(s)/female
25-54 years: 0.87 male(s)/female
55-64 years: 1.05 male(s)/female
65 years and over: 0.84 male(s)/female
total population: 0.95 male(s)/female (2022 est.)

Mother's mean age at first birth: 19.2 years (2018 est.)
note: data represents median age at first birth among women 20-49

Maternal mortality ratio: 562 deaths/100,000 live births (2017 est.)

Infant mortality rate: *total:* 60.64 deaths/1,000 live births
male: 66.04 deaths/1,000 live births
female: 55.08 deaths/1,000 live births (2022 est.)

Life expectancy at birth: *total population:* 62.41 years
male: 60.19 years
female: 64.7 years (2022 est.)

Total fertility rate: 5.54 children born/woman (2022 est.)

Contraceptive prevalence rate: 17.2% (2018)

Drinking water source: *improved: urban:* 99.9% of population
rural: 75.9% of population
total: 86.4% of population
unimproved: urban: 0.1% of population
rural: 24.1% of population
total: 13.6% of population (2020 est.)

Current health expenditure: 3.9% of GDP (2019)

Physicians density: 0.13 physicians/1,000 population (2018)

Hospital bed density: 0.1 beds/1,000 population

Sanitation facility access: *improved: urban:* 85.7% of population
rural: 44.7% of population
total: 62.7% of population
unimproved: urban: 14.3% of population
rural: 55.3% of population
total: 37.3% of population (2020 est.)

HIV/AIDS - adult prevalence rate: 0.9% (2020 est.)

Major infectious diseases: *degree of risk:* very high (2020)
food or waterborne diseases: bacterial and protozoal diarrhea, hepatitis A, and typhoid fever
vectorborne diseases: malaria and dengue fever
water contact diseases: schistosomiasis
animal contact diseases: rabies
respiratory diseases: meningococcal meningitis

Obesity - adult prevalence rate: 8.6% (2016)

Alcohol consumption per capita: *total:* 0.6 liters of pure alcohol (2019 est.)
beer: 0.09 liters of pure alcohol (2019 est.)
wine: 0 liters of pure alcohol (2019 est.)
spirits: 0.02 liters of pure alcohol (2019 est.)
other alcohols: 0.49 liters of pure alcohol (2019 est.)

Tobacco use: *total:* 8.3% (2020 est.)
male: 15.6% (2020 est.)
female: 1% (2020 est.)

Children under the age of 5 years underweight: 18.1% (2019)

Child marriage: *women married by age 15:* 15.9%
women married by age 18: 53.7%
men married by age 18: 2.1% (2018 est.)

Education expenditures: 3.4% of GDP (2019 est.)

Literacy: *definition:* age 15 and over can read and write
total population: 35.5%
male: 46.2%
female: 25.7% (2018)

School life expectancy (primary to tertiary education): *total:* 7 years
male: 8 years
female: 7 years (2017)

Unemployment, youth ages 15-24: *total:* 2.4%
male: 2.6%
female: 2.3% (2018 est.)

ENVIRONMENT

Environment - current issues: deforestation; soil erosion; desertification; loss of pasture land; inadequate supplies of potable water

Environment - international agreements: *party to:* Biodiversity, Climate Change, Climate Change-Kyoto Protocol, Climate Change-Paris Agreement, Comprehensive Nuclear Test Ban, Desertification, Endangered Species, Hazardous Wastes, Law of the Sea, Ozone Layer Protection, Tropical Timber 2006, Wetlands, Whaling
signed, but not ratified: Nuclear Test Ban

Air pollutants: *particulate matter emissions:* 31.17 micrograms per cubic meter (2016 est.)
carbon dioxide emissions: 3.18 megatons (2016 est.)
methane emissions: 19.16 megatons (2020 est.)

Climate: subtropical to arid; hot and dry (February to June); rainy, humid, and mild (June to November); cool and dry (November to February)

Land use: *agricultural land:* 34.1% (2018 est.)
arable land: 5.6% (2018 est.)
permanent crops: 0.1% (2018 est.)
permanent pasture: 28.4% (2018 est.)
forest: 10.2% (2018 est.)
other: 55.7% (2018 est.)

Urbanization: *urban population:* 45.4% of total population (2022)
rate of urbanization: 4.57% annual rate of change (2020-25 est.)

Revenue from forest resources: *forest revenues:* 2.02% of GDP (2018 est.)

Revenue from coal: *coal revenues:* 0% of GDP (2018 est.)

Food insecurity: *severe localized food insecurity:*

due to civil insecurity and high food prices - the food security situation deteriorated in 2021, particularly in conflict-affected central and northern areas; according to the latest analysis, about 1.84 million people are estimated to be in "Crisis" and above between June and August 2022, as a result of worsening conflicts, weather shocks, reduced cereal production in 2021 and high food prices
(2022)

Waste and recycling: *municipal solid waste generated annually:* 1,937,354 tons (2012 est.)

Major lakes (area sq km): *fresh water lake(s):* Lac Faguibine - 590 sq km
note - the Niger River is the only source of water for the lake; in recent years the lake is dry

Major rivers (by length in km): Niger (shared with Guinea [s], Niger, and Nigeria [m]) - 4,200 km; Senegal (shared with Guinea [s], Senegal, and Mauritania [m]) - 1,641 km
note – [s] after country name indicates river source; [m] after country name indicates river mouth

Major watersheds (area sq km): Atlantic Ocean drainage: Niger (2,261,741 sq km), Senegal (456,397 sq km), Volta (410,991 sq km)

Major aquifers: Lullemeden-Irhazer Basin, Taodeni-Tanezrouft Basin

Total water withdrawal: *municipal:* 107 million cubic meters (2017 est.)
industrial: 4 million cubic meters (2017 est.)
agricultural: 5.075 billion cubic meters (2017 est.)

Total renewable water resources: 120 billion cubic meters (2017 est.)

GOVERNMENT

Country name: *conventional long form:* Republic of Mali
conventional short form: Mali
local long form: Republique de Mali
local short form: Mali
former: French Sudan, Sudanese Republic, Mali Federation
etymology: name derives from the West African Mali Empire of the 13th to 16th centuries A.D.

Government type: semi-presidential republic

Capital: *name:* Bamako
geographic coordinates: 12 39 N, 8 00 W
time difference: UTC 0 (5 hours ahead of Washington, DC, during Standard Time)
etymology: the name in the Bambara language can mean either "crocodile tail" or "crocodile river" and three crocodiles appear on the city seal

Administrative divisions: 10 regions (regions, singular - region), 1 district*; District de Bamako*, Gao, Kayes, Kidal, Koulikoro, Menaka, Mopti, Segou, Sikasso, Taoudenni, Tombouctou (Timbuktu); note - Menaka and Taoudenni were legislated in 2016, but implementation has not been confirmed by the US Board on Geographic Names

Independence: 22 September 1960 (from France)

National holiday: Independence Day, 22 September (1960)

Constitution: *history:* several previous; latest drafted August 1991, approved by referendum 12 January 1992, effective 25 February 1992, suspended briefly in 2012
amendments: proposed by the president of the republic or by members of the National Assembly; passage requires two-thirds majority vote by the Assembly and approval in a referendum; constitutional sections on the integrity of the state, its republican and secular form of government, and its multiparty system cannot be amended; note - the transition government in June 2022 announced the formation of a commission which will draft a new constitution by August

Legal system: civil law system based on the French civil law model and influenced by customary law; judicial review of legislative acts in the Constitutional Court

International law organization participation: has not submitted an ICJ jurisdiction declaration; accepts ICCt jurisdiction

Citizenship: *citizenship by birth:* no
citizenship by descent only: at least one parent must be a citizen of Mali
dual citizenship recognized: yes
residency requirement for naturalization: 5 years

Suffrage: 18 years of age; universal

Executive branch: *chief of state:* Transition President Assimi GOITA (since 7 June 2021); note - an August 2020 coup d'etat deposed President Ibrahim Boubacar KEITA; on 21 September 2020, a group of 17 electors chosen by the Malian military junta, known as the National Committee for the Salvation of the People (CNSP) and led by Colonel Assimi GOITA, selected Bah NDAW as transition president; GOITA served as vice president of the transitional government which was inaugurated on 25 September 2020; Vice President GOITA seized power on 25 May 2021; NDAW resigned on 26 May 2021; on 6 June 2022, GOITA's government announced a transition period of 24 months with a return to civilian rule effective March 2024
head of government: Transition Prime Minister Choguel MAIGA (appointed by Transitional President Assimi GOITA on 7 June 2021)
note: former transition Prime Minister Moctar OUANE was arrested and detained by the military on 24 May 2021 and resigned on 26 May 2021
cabinet: Council of Ministers appointed by the prime minister
elections/appointments: president directly elected by absolute majority popular vote in 2 rounds if needed for a 5-year term (eligible for a second term); election last held on 29 July 2018 with runoff on 12 August 2018; prime minister appointed by the president; note - on 21 February 2022, the transition government adopted a charter allowing transition authorities to rule for up to 5 years; thereafter transition President GOITA is barred from being a candidate in presidential elections.
election results:
2018: Ibrahim Boubacar KEITA elected president in second round; percent of vote in first round -Ibrahim Boubacar KEITA (RPM) 41.7%, Soumaila CISSE (URD) 17.8%, other 40.5%; percent of vote in second round -Ibrahim Boubacar KEITA (RPM) 67.2%, Soumaila CISSE (URD) 32.8%
2013: Ibrahim Boubacar KEITA elected president in second round; percent of vote in first round - Ibrahim Boubacar KEITA (RPM) 39.8%, Soumaila CISSE (URD) 19.7%, other 40.5%; percent of vote in second round - Ibrahim Boubacar KEITA (RPM) 77.6%, Soumaila CISSE (URD) 22.4%

Legislative branch: *description:* unicameral National Assembly or Assemblee Nationale (147 seats; members directly elected in single and multi-seat constituencies by absolute majority vote in 2 rounds if needed; 13 seats reserved for citizens living abroad; members serve 5-year terms)
note - the National Assembly was dissolved on 18 August 2020 following a military coup and the resignation of President KEITA; the transition government created a National Transition Council (CNT) whose 121 members were selected by then-transition vice president Assimi GOITA; the CNT acts as the transition government's legislative body with Malick DIAW serving as the president; in February 2022 the CNT increased the number of seats to 147 but the additional seats have not yet been filled
elections:
last held on 30 March and 19 April 2020
election results:
percent of vote by party - NA; seats by party - NA
composition - NA

Judicial branch: *highest court(s):* Supreme Court or Cour Supreme (consists of 19 judges organized into judicial, administrative, and accounting sections); Constitutional Court (consists of 9 judges)
judge selection and term of office: Supreme Court judges appointed by the Ministry of Justice to serve 5-year terms; Constitutional Court judges selected - 3 each by the president, the National Assembly, and the Supreme Council of the Magistracy; members serve single renewable 7-year terms
subordinate courts: Court of Appeal; High Court of Justice (jurisdiction limited to cases of high treason or criminal offenses by the president or ministers while in office); administrative courts (first instance and appeal); commercial courts; magistrate courts; labor courts; juvenile courts; special court of state security

Political parties and leaders: African Solidarity for Democracy and Independence or SADI [Oumar MARIKO]
Alliance for Democracy and Progress or ADP-Maliba [Amadou THIAM]
Alliance for Democracy in Mali-Pan-African Party for Liberty, Solidarity, and Justice or ADEMA-PASJ [Tiemoko SANGARE]
Alliance for the Solidarity of Mali-Convergence of Patriotic Forces or ASMA-CFP [Amadou CISSE, vice-president, acting]
Convergence for the Development of Mali or CODEM [Housseyni Amion GUINDO]
Democratic Alliance for Peace or ADP-Maliba [Aliou Boubacar DIALLO]
Movement for Mali or MPM [Brahima DIANESSY deputy]
Party for National Renewal (also Rebirth or Renaissance or PARENA) [Tiebile DRAME]
Rally for Mali or RPM [Boucary TRETA]
Social Democratic Convention or CDS [Mamadou Bakary "Blaise" SANGARE]
Union for Democracy and Development or UDD [Hassane BARRY]
Union for Republic and Democracy or URD [Soumaïla CISSE]
Yéléma [Moussa MARA]
note 1: only parties with 2 or more seats in the last National Assembly parliamentary elections (30 March and 19 April 2020) listed
note 2: the National Assembly was dissolved on 18 August 2020 following a military coup and replaced with a National Transition Council; currently 121 members, party affiliations unknown

International organization participation: ACP, AfDB, AU (suspended), CD, ECOWAS (suspended), EITI (compliant country), FAO, FZ, G-77, IAEA, IBRD, ICAO, ICCt, ICRM, IDA, IDB, IFAD, IFC, IFRCS, ILO, IMF, Interpol, IOC, IOM, IPU, ISO, ITSO, ITU, ITUC (NGOs), MIGA, MONUSCO, NAM, OIC, OIF, OPCW, UN, UNAMID, UNCTAD, UNDP, UNESCO, UNFPA, UNHCR, UNIDO, UNISFA, UNMISS, UNOPS, UN Women, UNWTO, UPU, WADB (regional), WAEMU, World Bank Group, WCO, WFTU (NGOs), WHO, WIPO, WMO, WTO

Diplomatic representation in the US: *chief of mission:* Ambassador Sékou BERTHE (since 16 September 2022)
chancery: 2130 R Street NW, Washington, DC 20008
telephone: [1] (202) 332-2249
FAX: [1] (202) 332-6603
email address and website:
infos@mali.embassy.us
https://www.maliembassy.us/

Diplomatic representation from the US: *chief of mission:* Ambassador Dennis B. HANKINS (since 15 March 2019)
embassy: ACI 2000, Rue 243, (located off the Roi Bin Fahad Aziz Bridge west of the Bamako central district), Porte 297, Bamako
mailing address: 2050 Bamako Place, Washington DC 20521-2050
telephone: [223] 20-70-23-00
FAX: [223] 20-70-24-79
email address and website:
ACSBamako@state.gov
https://ml.usembassy.gov/

Flag description: three equal vertical bands of green (hoist side), yellow, and red
note: uses the popular Pan-African colors of Ethiopia; the colors from left to right are the same as those of neighboring Senegal (which has an additional green central star) and the reverse of those on the flag of neighboring Guinea

National symbol(s): Great Mosque of Djenne; national colors: green, yellow, red

National anthem: *name:* "Le Mali" (Mali)
lyrics/music: Seydou Badian KOUYATE/ Banzoumana SISSOKO
note: adopted 1962; also known as "Pour L'Afrique et pour toi, Mali" (For Africa and for You, Mali) and "A ton appel Mali" (At Your Call, Mali)

National heritage: *total World Heritage Sites:* 4 (3 cultural, 1 mixed)
selected World Heritage Site locales: Old Towns of Djenné (c); Timbuktu (c); Cliff of Bandiagara (Land of the Dogons) (m); Tomb of Askia (c)

ECONOMY

Economic overview: Among the 25 poorest countries in the world, landlocked Mali depends on gold mining and agricultural exports for revenue. The country's fiscal status fluctuates with gold and agricultural commodity prices and the harvest; cotton and gold exports make up around 80% of export earnings. Mali remains dependent on foreign aid.

Economic activity is largely confined to the riverine area irrigated by the Niger River; about 65% of Mali's land area is desert or semidesert. About 10% of the population is nomadic and about 80% of the labor force is engaged in farming and fishing. Industrial activity is concentrated on processing farm commodities. The government subsidizes the production of cereals to decrease the country's dependence on imported foodstuffs and to reduce its vulnerability to food price shocks.

Mali is developing its iron ore extraction industry to diversify foreign exchange earnings away from gold, but the pace will depend on global price trends. Although the political coup in 2012 slowed Mali's growth, the economy has since bounced back, with GDP growth above 5% in 2014-17, although physical insecurity, high population growth, corruption, weak infrastructure, and low levels of human capital continue to constrain economic development. Higher rainfall helped to boost cotton output in 2017, and the country's 2017 budget increased spending more than 10%, much of which was devoted to infrastructure and agriculture. Corruption and political turmoil are strong downside risks in 2018 and beyond.

Real GDP (purchasing power parity): $44.89 billion (2020 est.)
$45.64 billion (2019 est.)
$43.57 billion (2018 est.)
note: data are in 2017 dollars

Real GDP growth rate: 5.4% (2017 est.)
5.8% (2016 est.)
6.2% (2015 est.)

Real GDP per capita: $2,200 (2020 est.)
$2,300 (2019 est.)
$2,300 (2018 est.)
note: data are in 2017 dollars

GDP (official exchange rate): $17.508 billion (2019 est.)

Inflation rate (consumer prices): 1.9% (2018 est.)
1.8% (2017 est.)
1.7% (2017 est.)

Credit ratings:

Moody's rating: Caa1 (2020)
note: The year refers to the year in which the current credit rating was first obtained.

GDP - composition, by sector of origin: *agriculture:* 41.8% (2017 est.)
industry: 18.1% (2017 est.)
services: 40.5% (2017 est.)

GDP - composition, by end use: *household consumption:* 82.9% (2017 est.)
government consumption: 17.4% (2017 est.)
investment in fixed capital: 19.3% (2017 est.)
investment in inventories: -0.7% (2017 est.)
exports of goods and services: 22.1% (2017 est.)
imports of goods and services: -41.1% (2017 est.)

Agricultural products: maize, rice, millet, sorghum, mangoes/guavas, cotton, watermelons, green onions/shallots, okra, sugar cane

Industries: food processing; construction; phosphate and gold mining

Industrial production growth rate: 6.3% (2017 est.)

Labor force: 6.447 million (2017 est.)

Labor force - by occupation: *agriculture:* 80%
industry and services: 20% (2005 est.)

Unemployment rate: 7.9% (2017 est.)
7.8% (2016 est.)

Unemployment, youth ages 15-24: *total:* 2.4%
male: 2.6%
female: 2.3% (2018 est.)

Population below poverty line: 42.1% (2019 est.)

Gini Index coefficient - distribution of family income:
40.1 (2001)
50.5 (1994)

Household income or consumption by percentage share: *lowest 10%:* 3.5%
highest 10%: 25.8% (2010 est.)

Budget: *revenues:* 3.075 billion (2017 est.)
expenditures: 3.513 billion (2017 est.)

Budget surplus (+) or deficit (-): -2.9% (of GDP) (2017 est.)

Public debt: 35.4% of GDP (2017 est.)
36% of GDP (2016 est.)

Taxes and other revenues: 20% (of GDP) (2017 est.)

Fiscal year: calendar year

Current account balance: -$886 million (2017 est.)
-$1.015 billion (2016 est.)

Exports: $4.18 billion (2018 est.) note: data are in current year dollars
$2.803 billion (2016 est.)

Exports - partners: United Arab Emirates 66%, Switzerland 26% (2019)

Exports - commodities: gold, cotton, sesame seeds, lumber, vegetable oils/residues (2019)

Imports: $6.08 billion (2018 est.) note: data are in current year dollars
$3.403 billion (2016 est.)

Imports - partners: Senegal 23%, Cote d'Ivoire 15%, China 11%, France 9% (2019)

Imports - commodities: refined petroleum, clothing and apparel, packaged medicines, cement, broadcasting equipment (2019)

Reserves of foreign exchange and gold: $647.8 million (31 December 2017 est.)
$395.7 million (31 December 2016 est.)

Debt - external: $4.192 billion (31 December 2017 est.)
$3.981 billion (31 December 2016 est.)

Exchange rates: Communaute Financiere Africaine francs (XOF) per US dollar -
605.3 (2017 est.)
593.01 (2016 est.)
593.01 (2015 est.)
591.45 (2014 est.)
494.42 (2013 est.)

ENERGY

Electricity access: *electrification - total population:* 50% (2019)
electrification - urban areas: 78% (2019)
electrification - rural areas: 28% (2019)

Electricity: *installed generating capacity:* 890,000 kW (2020 est.)
consumption: 2,620,980,000 kWh (2019 est.)
exports: 550 million kWh (2019 est.)
imports: 200 million kWh (2019 est.)
transmission/distribution losses: 346 million kWh (2019 est.)

Electricity generation sources: *fossil fuels:* 67.4% of total installed capacity (2020 est.)
solar: 1% of total installed capacity (2020 est.)
hydroelectricity: 29.7% of total installed capacity (2020 est.)
biomass and waste: 1.9% of total installed capacity (2020 est.)

Petroleum: *total petroleum production:* 0 bbl/day (2021 est.)
refined petroleum consumption: 37,600 bbl/day (2019 est.)

Refined petroleum products - imports: 20,610 bbl/day (2015 est.)

Carbon dioxide emissions: 5.679 million metric tonnes of CO2 (2019 est.)
from petroleum and other liquids: 5.679 million metric tonnes of CO2 (2019 est.)

Energy consumption per capita: 4.396 million Btu/person (2019 est.)

COMMUNICATIONS

Telephones - fixed lines: *total subscriptions:* 281,638 (2020 est.)
subscriptions per 100 inhabitants: 1 (2020 est.)

Telephones - mobile cellular: *total subscriptions:* 25,315,598 (2020 est.)
subscriptions per 100 inhabitants: 125 (2020 est.)

Telecommunication systems: *general assessment:* Mali's telecom systems are challenged by recent conflict, geography, areas of low population, poverty, security issues, and high illiteracy; telecom infrastructure is barely adequate in urban areas and not available in most of the country with underinvestment in fixed-line networks; high mobile penetration and potential for mobile broadband service; local plans for IXP; dependent on neighboring countries for international bandwidth and access to submarine cables (2022)
domestic: fixed-line subscribership is over 1 per 100 persons; mobile-cellular subscribership has increased sharply to 125 per 100 persons; increasing use of local radio loops to extend network coverage to remote areas (2020)
international: country code - 223; satellite communications center and fiber-optic links to neighboring countries; satellite earth stations - 2 Intelsat (1 Atlantic Ocean, 1 Indian Ocean) (2020)

Broadcast media: national public TV broadcaster; 2 privately owned companies provide subscription services to foreign multi-channel TV packages; national public radio broadcaster supplemented by a large number of privately owned and community broadcast stations; transmissions of multiple international broadcasters are available (2019)

Internet country code: .ml

Internet users: *total:* 5,467,725 (2020 est.)
percent of population: 27% (2020 est.)

Broadband - fixed subscriptions: *total:* 243,806 (2020 est.)
subscriptions per 100 inhabitants: 1 (2020 est.)

TRANSPORTATION

National air transport system: *number of registered air carriers:* 0 (2020)

Civil aircraft registration country code prefix: TZ, TT

Airports: *total:* 25 (2021)

Airports - with paved runways: *total:* 8
over 3,047 m: 1
2,438 to 3,047 m: 4
1,524 to 2,437 m: 2
914 to 1,523 m: 1 (2021)

Airports - with unpaved runways: *total:* 17
1,524 to 2,437 m: 3
914 to 1,523 m: 9
under 914 m: 5 (2021)

Heliports: 2 (2021)

Railways: *total:* 593 km (2014)
narrow gauge: 593 km (2014) 1.000-m gauge

Roadways: *total:* 139,107 km (2018)

Waterways: 1,800 km (2011) (downstream of Koulikoro; low water levels on the River Niger cause problems in dry years; in the months before the rainy season the river is not navigable by commercial vessels)

Ports and terminals: *river port(s):* Koulikoro (Niger)

MILITARY AND SECURITY

Military and security forces: Malian Armed Forces (Forces Armées Maliennes or FAMA): Army (includes a riverine patrol force), Republic of Mali Air Force; National Gendarmerie; National Guard (2022)
note 1: the Gendarmerie and the National Guard are under the authority of the Ministry of Defense and Veterans Affairs (Ministere De La Defense Et Des Anciens Combattants, MDAC), but operational control is shared with the Ministry of Internal Security and Civil Protection
note 2: the Gendarmerie's primary mission is internal security and public order; its duties also include territorial defense, humanitarian operations, intelligence gathering, and protecting private property, mainly in rural areas; it also has a specialized border security unit
note 3: the National Guard is a military force responsible for providing security to government facilities and institutions, prison service, public order, humanitarian operations, some border security, and intelligence gathering; its forces include a camel corps for patrolling the deserts and borders of northern Mali
note 4: there are also pro-government militias operating in Mali, such as the Imghad Tuareg Self-Defense Group and Allies (GATIA); the leader of GATIA is also a general in the national army

Military expenditures: 3.5% of GDP (2021 est.)
3.4% of GDP (2020 est.)
3.1% of GDP (2019 est.) (approximately $630 million)
3.1% of GDP (2018 est.) (approximately $600 million)
3.2% of GDP (2017 est.) (approximately $600 million)

Military and security service personnel strengths: information varies; approximately 20,000 active FAMA personnel (includes up to 2,000 Air Force); approximately 5,000 Gendarmerie; approximately 10,000 National Guard (2022)

Military equipment inventories and acquisitions: the FAMA's inventory consists primarily of Soviet-era equipment, although in recent years it has received limited quantities of mostly second-hand armaments from more than a dozen countries, including Russia (2022)

Military service age and obligation: 18 years of age for men and women for selective compulsory and voluntary military service; 2-year conscript service obligation (2022)

Military deployments: *note:* until announcing its withdrawal in May of 2022, Mali was part of a five-nation anti-jihadist task force known as the G5 Sahel Group, set up in 2014 with Burkina Faso, Chad, Mauritania, and Niger; Mali had committed 1,100 troops and 200 gendarmes to the force

Military - note: prior to the coup in August 2020 and military takeover in May 2021, the Malian military had intervened in the political arena at least five times since the country gained independence in 1960; two attempts failed (1976 and 1978), while three succeeded in overturning civilian rule (1968, 1991, and 2012); the military collapsed in 2012 during the fighting against Tuareg rebels and Islamic militants; it has been since rebuilt, but continues to have limited capabilities and is heavily reliant on external assistance

as of 2022, Malian security forces were actively engaged in operations against several insurgent terrorist groups affiliated with al-Qa'ida and the Islamic State of Iraq and ash-Sham (ISIS), as well as other rebel groups, communal militias, and criminal bands spread across the central, northern, and southern regions of the country; the government was reportedly in control of only an estimated 10-20% of the country's central and northern territories, and terror attacks were increasing in the more heavily populated south, including around the capital Bamako; the Macina Liberation Front (FLM), part of the Jama'at Nusrat al Islam wal Muslimin (JNIM) coalition of al-Qa'ida-linked terror groups, has played a large role in a surge in violence in Mali's central and southern regions; in the north, the Islamic State of Iraq and ash-Sham in the Greater Sahara (ISIS-GS) has been able to reassert itself in 2022

the United Nations Multidimensional Integrated Stabilization Mission in Mali (MINUSMA) has operated in the country since 2013; the Mission's responsibilities include providing security, rebuilding Malian security forces, protecting civilians, supporting national political dialogue, and assisting in the reestablishment of Malian government authority; as of mid-2022, MINUSMA had around 15,000 personnel deployed; in June 2022, the UN extended its mission another 12 months

the European Union Training Mission in Mali (EUTM-M) and the French military (under a separate, bi-lateral mission) have also operated in the country since 2013; the EUTM-M provides advice and training to the Malian Armed Forces and military assistance to the G5 Sahel Joint Force; as of May 2022, the mission included about 1,100 personnel from more than 20 European countries; in April of 2022, the EU said it would suspend its training program in Mali, citing issues with the ruling military government, including human rights abuses and the presence of Russian private military contractors; in August 2022, France completed withdrawing the last of its forces from Mali, also citing obstructions from the military government; prior to the withdrawal, more than 2,000 French troops had provided military assistance and conducted counter-terrorism/counter-insurgency operations

in December 2021, the Malian military government contracted with a Russian private military company to provide training for local armed forces and security to senior Malian officials; as of mid-2022, there were an estimated 1,000 Russian military contractors in Mali (2022)

TERRORISM

Terrorist group(s): Ansar al-Dine; Islamic State of Iraq and ash-Sham in the Greater Sahara (ISIS-GS); Jama'at Nusrat al-Islam wal-Muslimin (JNIM); al-Mulathamun Battalion (al-Mourabitoun)

TRANSNATIONAL ISSUES

Disputes - international: *Mali-Burkina Faso:* demarcation is underway with Burkina Faso

Refugees and internally displaced persons: *refugees (country of origin):* 24,519 (Burkina Faso) (refugees and asylum seekers), 15,229 (Niger) (refugees and asylum seekers), 14,950 (Mauritania) (refugees and asylum seekers) (2022)
IDPs: 422,620 (Tuareg rebellion since 2012) (2022)

Trafficking in persons: *current situation:* Mali is a source, transit, and destination country for men, women, and children subjected to forced labor and sex trafficking; women and girls are forced into domestic servitude, agricultural labor, and support roles in gold mines, as well as subjected to sex trafficking; Malian boys are found in conditions of forced labor in agricultural settings, gold mines, and the informal commercial sector, as well as forced begging in Mali and neighboring countries; Malians and other Africans who travel through Mali to Mauritania, Algeria, or Libya in hopes of reaching Europe are particularly at risk of becoming victims of human trafficking; men and boys, primarily of Songhai ethnicity, are subjected to debt bondage in the salt mines of Taoudenni in northern Mali; some members of Mali's Tuareg community are subjected to traditional slavery-related practices, and this involuntary servitude reportedly has extended to their children; reports indicate that non-governmental armed groups operating in northern Mali recruited children as combatants, cooks, porters, guards, spies, and sex slaves; slaveholders use some members of the Tuareg community in hereditary servitude where communities rather than individuals or families exploit the enslaved
tier rating: Tier 2 Watch List — Mali does not fully meet the minimum standards for the elimination of trafficking but is making significant efforts to do so; government efforts included prosecuting hereditary slavery cases, increasing convictions, continuing training and awareness raising activities, releasing all children associated with the Malian armed forces (FAMa) to an international organization for care, training law enforcement officials on protection of children in armed conflict, identifying 215 children used by armed groups and referring them to international organizations for care; however, the government did not stop all use of children in the FAMa; the government continued to provide support to and collaborate with the Imghad Tuareg and the Allies Self-Defense Group, which recruited and used child soldiers; authorities did not investigate any suspects for child soldier offenses or make efforts to prevent it; law enforcement lacked resources and training about human trafficking; services for victims remained insufficient; therefore, Mali was downgraded to Tier 2 Watch List (2020)

Illicit drugs: a transit point for illicit drugs trafficked to Europe; trafficking controlled by armed groups, criminal organizations, terrorist groups and government officials that facilitate, protect and profit from the activity

MALTA

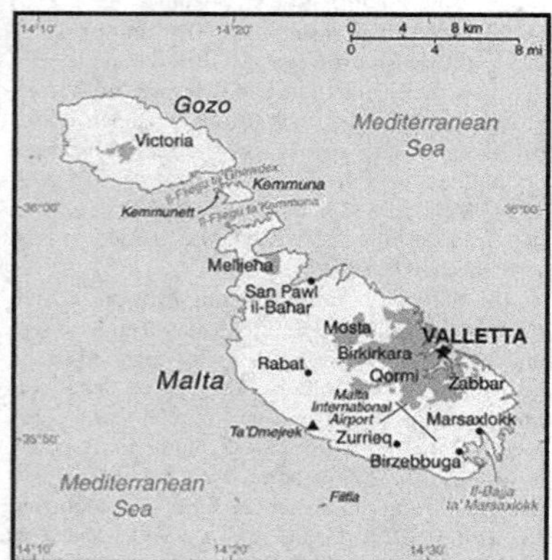

INTRODUCTION

Background: With a civilization that dates back thousands of years, Malta boasts some of the oldest megalithic sites in the world. Situated in the center of the Mediterranean, Malta's islands have long served as a strategic military asset, with the islands at various times having come under control of the Phoenicians, Carthaginians, Greeks, Romans, Byzantines, Moors, Normans, Sicilians, Spanish, Knights of St. John, and the French. Most recently a British colony (since 1814), Malta gained its independence in 1964 and declared itself a republic 10 years later. While under British rule, the island staunchly supported the UK through both world wars. Since about the mid-1980s, the island has transformed itself into a freight transshipment point, a financial center, and a tourist destination while its key industries moved toward more service-oriented activities. Malta became an EU member in May 2004 and began using the euro as currency in 2008.

GEOGRAPHY

Location: Southern Europe, islands in the Mediterranean Sea, south of Sicily (Italy)

Geographic coordinates: 35 50 N, 14 35 E

Map references: Europe

Area: *total:* 316 sq km
land: 316 sq km
water: 0 sq km

Area - comparative: slightly less than twice the size of Washington, DC

Land boundaries: *total:* 0 km

Coastline: 196.8 km (excludes 56 km for the island of Gozo)

Maritime claims: *territorial sea:* 12 nm
contiguous zone: 24 nm
continental shelf: 200-m depth or to the depth of exploitation
exclusive fishing zone: 25 nm

Climate: Mediterranean; mild, rainy winters; hot, dry summers

Terrain: mostly low, rocky, flat to dissected plains; many coastal cliffs

Elevation: *highest point:* Ta'Dmejrek on Dingli Cliffs 253 m
lowest point: Mediterranean Sea 0 m

Natural resources: limestone, salt, arable land

Land use: *agricultural land:* 32.3% (2018 est.)
arable land: 28.4% (2018 est.)
permanent crops: 3.9% (2018 est.)
permanent pasture: 0% (2018 est.)
forest: 0.9% (2018 est.)
other: 66.8% (2018 est.)

Irrigated land: 35 sq km (2012)

Population distribution: most of the population lives on the eastern half of Malta, the largest of the three inhabited islands

Natural hazards: occasional droughts

Geography - note: the country comprises an archipelago, with only the three largest islands (Malta, Ghawdex or Gozo, and Kemmuna or Comino) inhabited; numerous bays provide good harbors; Malta and Tunisia are discussing oil exploration on the continental shelf between their countries, although no commercially viable reserves have been found as of 2017

PEOPLE AND SOCIETY

Population: 464,186 (2022 est.)

Nationality: *noun:* Maltese (singular and plural)
adjective: Maltese

Ethnic groups: Maltese (descendants of ancient Carthaginians and Phoenicians with strong elements of Italian and other Mediterranean stock)

Languages: Maltese (official) 90.1%, English (official) 6%, multilingual 3%, other 0.9% (2005 est.)

Religions: Roman Catholic (official) more than 90% (2006 est.)

Age structure: *0-14 years:* 14.38% (male 33,934/female 31,823)
15-24 years: 10.33% (male 24,445/female 22,811)
25-54 years: 41.1% (male 97,685/female 90,264)
55-64 years: 12.88% (male 29,533/female 29,353)
65 years and over: 21.3% (male 44,644/female 52,775) (2020 est.)

Dependency ratios: *total dependency ratio:* 55.5
youth dependency ratio: 22.4
elderly dependency ratio: 33.2
potential support ratio: 3 (2020 est.)

Median age: *total:* 42.3 years
male: 41.2 years
female: 43.5 years (2020 est.)

Population growth rate: 0.67% (2022 est.)

Birth rate: 9.73 births/1,000 population (2022 est.)

Death rate: 8.48 deaths/1,000 population (2022 est.)

Net migration rate: 5.49 migrant(s)/1,000 population (2022 est.)

Population distribution: most of the population lives on the eastern half of Malta, the largest of the three inhabited islands

Urbanization: *urban population:* 94.9% of total population (2022)
rate of urbanization: 0.28% annual rate of change (2020-25 est.)

Major urban areas - population: 213,000 VALLETTA (capital) (2018)

Sex ratio: *at birth:* 1.04 male(s)/female
0-14 years: 1.06 male(s)/female
15-24 years: 1.07 male(s)/female
25-54 years: 1.09 male(s)/female
55-64 years: 1.01 male(s)/female
65 years and over: 0.7 male(s)/female
total population: 1.02 male(s)/female (2022 est.)

Mother's mean age at first birth: 29.3 years (2020 est.)
note: data refers to the average of the different child-bearing ages of first-order births

Maternal mortality ratio: 6 deaths/100,000 live births (2017 est.)

Infant mortality rate: *total:* 4.53 deaths/1,000 live births
male: 4.43 deaths/1,000 live births
female: 4.64 deaths/1,000 live births (2022 est.)

Life expectancy at birth: *total population:* 83.2 years
male: 81.11 years
female: 85.38 years (2022 est.)

Total fertility rate: 1.5 children born/woman (2022 est.)

Drinking water source: *improved: urban:* 100% of population
rural: 100% of population
total: 100% of population

Current health expenditure: 8.2% of GDP (2019)

Physicians density: 2.86 physicians/1,000 population (2015)

Hospital bed density: 4.5 beds/1,000 population (2017)

Sanitation facility access: *improved: urban:* 100% of population
rural: 100% of population
total: 100% of population

HIV/AIDS - adult prevalence rate: 0.1% (2016 est.)

Obesity - adult prevalence rate: 28.9% (2016)

Alcohol consumption per capita: *total:* 8.07 liters of pure alcohol (2019 est.)
beer: 2.8 liters of pure alcohol (2019 est.)
wine: 2.34 liters of pure alcohol (2019 est.)
spirits: 2.51 liters of pure alcohol (2019 est.)
other alcohols: 0.42 liters of pure alcohol (2019 est.)

Tobacco use: *total:* 24% (2020 est.)
male: 26.4% (2020 est.)
female: 21.6% (2020 est.)

Education expenditures: 4.7% of GDP (2017 est.)

Literacy: *definition:* age 15 and over can read and write
total population: 94.5%
male: 93%
female: 96% (2018)

School life expectancy (primary to tertiary education): *total:* 17 years
male: 16 years
female: 17 years (2019)

Unemployment, youth ages 15-24: *total:* 10.7%
male: 13.1%
female: 8% (2020 est.)

ENVIRONMENT

Environment - current issues: limited natural freshwater resources; increasing reliance on desalination; deforestation; wildlife preservation

Environment - international agreements: *party to:* Air Pollution, Biodiversity, Climate Change, Climate Change-Kyoto Protocol, Climate Change-Paris Agreement, Comprehensive Nuclear Test Ban, Desertification, Endangered Species, Hazardous Wastes, Law of the Sea, Marine Dumping-London Convention, Nuclear Test Ban, Ozone Layer Protection, Ship Pollution, Tropical Timber 2006, Wetlands
signed, but not ratified: none of the selected agreements

Air pollutants: *particulate matter emissions:* 13.97 micrograms per cubic meter (2016 est.)
carbon dioxide emissions: 1.34 megatons (2016 est.)
methane emissions: 0.2 megatons (2020 est.)

Climate: Mediterranean; mild, rainy winters; hot, dry summers

Land use: *agricultural land:* 32.3% (2018 est.)
arable land: 28.4% (2018 est.)
permanent crops: 3.9% (2018 est.)
permanent pasture: 0% (2018 est.)
forest: 0.9% (2018 est.)
other: 66.8% (2018 est.)

Urbanization: *urban population:* 94.9% of total population (2022)
rate of urbanization: 0.28% annual rate of change (2020-25 est.)

Revenue from forest resources: *forest revenues:* 0% of GDP (2018 est.)

Revenue from coal: *coal revenues:* 0% of GDP (2018 est.)

Waste and recycling: *municipal solid waste generated annually:* 269,000 tons (2015 est.)
municipal solid waste recycled annually: 17,996 tons (2015 est.)
percent of municipal solid waste recycled: 6.7% (2015 est.)

Total water withdrawal: *municipal:* 37.4 million cubic meters (2017 est.)
industrial: 1 million cubic meters (2017 est.)
agricultural: 25.4 million cubic meters (2017 est.)

Total renewable water resources: 50.5 million cubic meters (2017 est.)

GOVERNMENT

Country name: *conventional long form:* Republic of Malta
conventional short form: Malta
local long form: Repubblika ta' Malta
local short form: Malta
etymology: the ancient Greeks called the island "Melite" meaning "honey-sweet" from the Greek word "meli" meaning "honey" and referring to the island's honey production

Government type: parliamentary republic

Capital: *name:* Valletta
geographic coordinates: 35 53 N, 14 30 E
time difference: UTC+1 (6 hours ahead of Washington, DC, during Standard Time)
daylight saving time: +1hr, begins last Sunday in March; ends last Sunday in October
etymology: named in honor of Jean de VALETTE, the Grand Master of the Order of Saint John (crusader knights), who successfully led a defense of the island from an Ottoman invasion in 1565

Administrative divisions: 68 localities (Il-lokalita); Attard, Balzan, Birgu, Birkirkara, Birzebbuga, Bormla, Dingli, Fgura, Floriana, Fontana, Ghajnsielem, Gharb, Gharghur, Ghasri, Ghaxaq, Gudja, Gzira, Hamrun, Iklin, Imdina, Imgarr, Imqabba, Imsida, Imtarfa, Isla, Kalkara, Kercem, Kirkop, Lija, Luqa, Marsa, Marsaskala, Marsaxlokk, Mellieha, Mosta, Munxar, Nadur, Naxxar, Paola, Pembroke, Pieta, Qala, Qormi, Qrendi, Rabat, Rabat (Ghawdex), Safi, San Giljan/Saint Julian, San Gwann/Saint John, San Lawrenz/Saint Lawrence, Sannat, San Pawl il-Bahar/Saint Paul's Bay, Santa Lucija/Saint Lucia, Santa Venera/Saint Venera, Siggiewi, Sliema, Swieqi, Tarxien, Ta' Xbiex, Valletta, Xaghra, Xewkija, Xghajra, Zabbar, Zebbug, Zebbug (Ghawdex), Zejtun, Zurrieq

Independence: 21 September 1964 (from the UK)

National holiday: Independence Day, 21 September (1964); Republic Day, 13 December (1974)

Constitution: *history:* many previous; latest adopted 21 September 1964
amendments: proposals (Acts of Parliament) require at least two-thirds majority vote by the House of Representatives; passage of Acts requires majority vote by referendum, followed by final majority vote by the House and assent of the president of the republic; amended many times, last in 2020

Legal system: mixed legal system of English common law and civil law based on the Roman and Napoleonic civil codes; subject to European Union law

International law organization participation: accepts compulsory ICJ jurisdiction with reservations; accepts ICCt jurisdiction

Citizenship: *citizenship by birth:* no
citizenship by descent only: at least one parent must be a citizen of Malta
dual citizenship recognized: no
residency requirement for naturalization: 5 years

Suffrage: 18 years of age (16 in local council elections); universal

Executive branch: *chief of state:* President George VELLA (since 4 April 2019)
head of government: Prime Minister Robert ABELA (13 January 2020)
cabinet: Cabinet appointed by the president on the advice of the prime minister
elections/appointments: president indirectly elected by the House of Representatives for a single 5-year term; election last held on 2 April 2019 (next to be held by April 2024); following legislative elections, the leader of the majority party or majority coalition usually appointed prime minister by the president for a 5-year term; deputy prime minister appointed by the president on the advice of the prime minister
election results:
2019: George VELLA (PL) elected president; House of Representatives vote - unanimous; *2020:* Robert ABELA (PL) appointed prime minister

2014: Maria Louise Coleiro PRECO elected president; House of Representatives vote - unanimous

Legislative branch: *description:* unicameral House of Representatives or Il-Kamra Tad-Deputati, a component of the Parliament of Malta (65 seats statutory, 79 for 2022-2027 term; members directly elected in 5 multi-seat constituencies by proportional representation vote; members serve 5-year terms)
elections:
last held on 26 March 2022 (next to be held in 2027)
election results:
percent of vote by party - PL 55.1%, PN 41.7%, other 3.2%; seats by party - PL 38, PN 29; composition - men 57, women 22, percent of women 27.8%; note - due to underrepresentation by women in the combined general on 26 March and two casual elections on 7 and 12 April (10 seats or 14.9%), an additional 12 seats were awarded because their percentage did not meet the 40% threshold required by the Malta Constitution or the General Elections Amendment Act 2021

Judicial branch: *highest court(s)*: Court of Appeal (consists of either 1 or 3 judges); Constitutional Court (consists of 3 judges); Court of Criminal Appeal (consists of either 1 or 3 judges)
judge selection and term of office: Court of Appeal and Constitutional Court judges appointed by the president, usually upon the advice of the prime minister; judges of both courts serve until age 65
subordinate courts: Civil Court (divided into the General Jurisdiction Section, Family Section, and Voluntary Section); Criminal Court; Court of Magistrates; Gozo Courts (for the islands of Gozo and Comino)

Political parties and leaders: AD+PD or ADPD [Carmel CACOPARDO] (formed from the merger of Democratic Alternative or AD and Democratic Party (Partit Demokratiku) or PD)
Labor Party (Partit Laburista) or PL [Robert ABELA]
Nationalist Party (Partit Nazzjonalista) or PN [Bernard GRECH]

International organization participation: Australia Group, C, CD, CE, EAPC, EBRD, ECB, EIB, EMU, EU, FAO, IAEA, IBRD, ICAO, ICC (NGOs), ICCt, ICRM, IDA, IFAD, IFC, IFRCS, ILO, IMF, IMO, IMSO, Interpol, IOC, IOM, IPU, ISO, ITSO, ITU, ITUC (NGOs), MIGA, NSG, OAS (observer), OPCW, OSCE, PCA, PFP, Schengen Convention, UN, UNCTAD, UNESCO, UNIDO, Union Latina (observer), UNWTO, UPU, Wassenaar Arrangement, WCO, WHO, WIPO, WMO, WTO

Diplomatic representation in the US: *chief of mission:* Ambassador Keith AZZOPARDI (since 17 September 2018)
chancery: 2017 Connecticut Avenue NW, Washington, DC 20008
telephone: [1] (202) 462-3611; [1] (202) 462-3612
FAX: [1] (202) 387-5470
email address and website:
maltaembassy.washington@gov.mt
https://foreignandeu.gov.mt/en/Embassies/ME_United_States/Pages/ME_United_States.aspx

Diplomatic representation from the US: *chief of mission:* Ambassador (vacant); Charge d'Affaires Gwendolyn "Wendy" GREEN (since August 2020)
embassy: Ta' Qali National Park, Attard, ATD 4000
mailing address: 5800 Valletta Place, Washington DC 20521-5800
telephone: [356] 2561-4000
email address and website:
ACSMalta@state.gov
https://mt.usembassy.gov/

Flag description: two equal vertical bands of white (hoist side) and red; in the upper hoist-side corner is a representation of the George Cross, edged in red; according to legend, the colors are taken from the red and white checkered banner of Count Roger of Sicily who removed a bi-colored corner and granted it to Malta in 1091; an uncontested explanation is that the colors are those of the Knights of Saint John who ruled Malta from 1530 to 1798; in 1942, King George VI of the UK awarded the George Cross to the islanders for their exceptional bravery and gallantry in World War II; since independence in 1964, the George Cross bordered in red has appeared directly on the white field

National symbol(s): Maltese eight-pointed cross; national colors: red, white

National anthem: *name:* "L-Innu Malti" (The Maltese Anthem)
lyrics/music: Dun Karm PSAILA/Robert SAMMUT
note: adopted 1945; written in the form of a prayer

National heritage: *total World Heritage Sites:* 3 (all cultural)
selected World Heritage Site locales: City of Valletta; Hal Saflieni Hypogeum; Megalithic Temples of Malta

ECONOMY

Economic overview: Malta's free market economy – the smallest economy in the euro-zone – relies heavily on trade in both goods and services, principally with Europe. Malta produces less than a quarter of its food needs, has limited fresh water supplies, and has few domestic energy sources. Malta's economy is dependent on foreign trade, manufacturing, and tourism. Malta joined the EU in 2004 and adopted the euro on 1 January 2008.

Malta has weathered the euro-zone crisis better than most EU member states due to a low debt-to-GDP ratio and financially sound banking sector. It maintains one of the lowest unemployment rates in Europe, and growth has fully recovered since the 2009 recession. In 2014 through 2016, Malta led the euro zone in growth, expanding more than 4.5% per year.

Malta's services sector continues to grow, with sustained growth in the financial services and online gaming sectors. Advantageous tax schemes remained attractive to foreign investors, though EU discussions of anti-tax avoidance measures have raised concerns among Malta's financial services and insurance providers, as the measures could have a significant impact on those sectors. The tourism sector also continued to grow, with 2016 showing record-breaking numbers of both air and cruise passenger arrivals.

Malta's GDP growth remains strong and is supported by a strong labor market. The government has implemented new programs, including free childcare, to encourage increased labor participation. The high cost of borrowing and small labor market remain potential constraints to future economic growth. Increasingly, other EU and European migrants are relocating to Malta for employment, though wages have remained low compared to other European countries. Inflation remains low.

Real GDP (purchasing power parity): $20.6 billion (2020 est.)
$22.15 billion (2019 est.)
$20.99 billion (2018 est.)
note: data are in 2017 dollars

Real GDP growth rate: 4.94% (2019 est.)
5.17% (2018 est.)
8.03% (2017 est.)

Real GDP per capita: $39,200 (2020 est.)
$44,000 (2019 est.)
$43,300 (2018 est.)
note: data are in 2017 dollars

GDP (official exchange rate): $14.986 billion (2019 est.)

Inflation rate (consumer prices): 1.6% (2019 est.)
1.1% (2018 est.)
1.3% (2017 est.)

Credit ratings:

Fitch rating: A+ (2017)

Moody's rating: A2 (2019)

Standard & Poors rating: A- (2016)
note: The year refers to the year in which the current credit rating was first obtained.

GDP - composition, by sector of origin: *agriculture:* 1.1% (2017 est.)
industry: 10.2% (2017 est.)
services: 88.7% (2017 est.)

GDP - composition, by end use: *household consumption:* 45.2% (2017 est.)
government consumption: 15.3% (2017 est.)
investment in fixed capital: 21.1% (2017 est.)
investment in inventories: 0.3% (2017 est.)
exports of goods and services: 136.1% (2017 est.)
imports of goods and services: -117.9% (2017 est.)

Agricultural products: milk, tomatoes, potatoes, onions, cauliflowers, broccoli, eggplants, pork, cabbages, poultry

Industries: tourism, electronics, ship building and repair, construction, food and beverages, pharmaceuticals, footwear, clothing, tobacco, aviation services, financial services, information technology services

Industrial production growth rate: -3.3% (2016 est.)

Labor force: 223,000 (2019 est.)

Labor force - by occupation: *agriculture:* 1.6%
industry: 20.7%
services: 77.7% (2016 est.)

Unemployment rate: 0.78% (2019 est.)
0.89% (2018 est.)

Unemployment, youth ages 15-24: *total:* 10.7%
male: 13.1%
female: 8% (2020 est.)

Population below poverty line: 17.1% (2018 est.)

Gini Index coefficient - distribution of family income: 29.2 (2017 est.)
27.7 (2014)

Budget: *revenues:* 5.076 billion (2017 est.)
expenditures: 4.583 billion (2017 est.)

Budget surplus (+) or deficit (-): 3.9% (of GDP) (2017 est.)

Public debt: 50.7% of GDP (2017 est.)
56.3% of GDP (2016 est.)
note: Malta reports public debt at nominal value outstanding at the end of the year, according to guidelines set out in the Maastricht Treaty for general government gross debt; the data include the following categories of government liabilities (as defined in ESA95): currency and deposits (AF.2), securities other than shares excluding financial derivatives (AF.3, excluding AF.34), and loans (AF.4); general government comprises the central, state, and local governments, and social security funds

Taxes and other revenues: 40.4% (of GDP) (2017 est.)

Fiscal year: calendar year

Current account balance: $1.561 billion (2019 est.)
$1.55 billion (2018 est.)

Exports: $19.04 billion (2020 est.) note: data are in current year dollars
$20.76 billion (2019 est.) note: data are in current year dollars
$20.19 billion (2018 est.) note: data are in current year dollars

Exports - partners: Germany 12%, France 9%, Italy 9% (2019)

Exports - commodities: integrated circuits, refined petroleum, packaged medicines, children's toys and stuffed animals, postage stamps (2019)

Imports: $18.01 billion (2020 est.) note: data are in current year dollars
$18.45 billion (2019 est.) note: data are in current year dollars
$17.87 billion (2018 est.) note: data are in current year dollars

Imports - partners: Russia 22%, Italy 12%, United Kingdom 11%, Germany 6%, Turkey 5%, France 5%, China 5%, South Korea 5% (2019)

Imports - commodities: refined petroleum, recreational boats, ships, aircraft, coal tar oil (2019)

Reserves of foreign exchange and gold: $833 million (31 December 2017 est.)
$677.1 million (31 December 2016 est.)

Debt - external: $98.179 billion (2019 est.)
$104.467 billion (2018 est.)

Exchange rates: euros (EUR) per US dollar -
0.82771 (2020 est.)
0.90338 (2019 est.)
0.87789 (2018 est.)
0.885 (2014 est.)
0.7634 (2013 est.)

ENERGY

Electricity access: *electrification - total population:* 100% (2020)

Electricity: *installed generating capacity:* 784,000 kW (2020 est.)
consumption: 2,497,143,000 kWh (2019 est.)
exports: 4 million kWh (2020 est.)
imports: 420 million kWh (2020 est.)
transmission/distribution losses: 158 million kWh (2019 est.)

Electricity generation sources: *fossil fuels:* 88.5% of total installed capacity (2020 est.)
solar: 11.2% of total installed capacity (2020 est.)
biomass and waste: 0.3% of total installed capacity (2020 est.)

Petroleum: *total petroleum production:* 0 bbl/day (2021 est.)
refined petroleum consumption: 54,000 bbl/day (2019 est.)

Refined petroleum products - exports: 10,400 bbl/day (2015 est.)

Refined petroleum products - imports: 52,290 bbl/day (2015 est.)

Natural gas: *production:* 0 cubic meters (2021 est.)
consumption: 415.606 million cubic meters (2020 est.)
exports: 0 cubic meters (2021 est.)
imports: 415.606 million cubic meters (2020 est.)
proven reserves: 0 cubic meters (2021 est.)

Carbon dioxide emissions: 9.576 million metric tonnes of CO2 (2019 est.)
from petroleum and other liquids: 8.831 million metric tonnes of CO2 (2019 est.)
from consumed natural gas: 745,000 metric tonnes of CO2 (2019 est.)

Energy consumption per capita: 267.739 million Btu/person (2019 est.)

COMMUNICATIONS

Telephones - fixed lines: *total subscriptions:* 259,456 (2020 est.)
subscriptions per 100 inhabitants: 59 (2020 est.)

Telephones - mobile cellular: *total subscriptions:* 633,123 (2020 est.)
subscriptions per 100 inhabitants: 143 (2020 est.)

Telecommunication systems: *general assessment:* Malta's small telecom sector is among the most advanced in Europe; this has been helped by the topography, which has made it relatively easy for operators to expand the reach of their fiber infrastructure; with high mobile and broadband penetration rates, the government and regulator have effective strategies in place to capitalize on these infrastructure developments to ensure that the population has among the fastest data rates in Europe, and is well positioned to take advantage of emerging e-commerce opportunities; the sector has also been stimulated by regulatory measures designed to reduce consumer prices; the incumbent telco is investing in a sub sea cable to connect the islands to France and Egypt; expected to be ready for service in 2022, the cable will further enhance Malta's internet bandwidth and lead to reduced prices for end-users; there has also been some encouragement to increase market competition (2021)
domestic: fixed-line approximately 59 per 100 persons and mobile-cellular subscribership 143 per 100 persons; automatic system featuring submarine cable and microwave radio relay between islands (2020)
international: country code - 356; landing points for the Malta-Gozo Cable, VMSCS, GO-1 Mediterranean Cable System, Malta Italy Interconnector, Melita-1, and the Italy-Malta submarine cable connections to Italy; satellite earth station - 1 Intelsat (Atlantic Ocean) (2019)

Broadcast media: 2 publicly owned TV stations, Television Malta broadcasting nationally plus an educational channel; several privately owned national television stations, 2 of which are owned by political parties; Italian and British broadcast programs are available; multi-channel cable and satellite TV services are available; publicly owned radio broadcaster operates 3 stations; roughly 20 commercial radio stations (2019)

Internet country code: .mt

Internet users: *total:* 448,339 (2020 est.)
percent of population: 87% (2020 est.)

Broadband - fixed subscriptions: *total:* 213,419 (2020 est.)
subscriptions per 100 inhabitants: 48 (2020 est.)

TRANSPORTATION

National air transport system: *number of registered air carriers:* 13 (2020)
inventory of registered aircraft operated by air carriers: 180
annual passenger traffic on registered air carriers: 2,576,898 (2018)
annual freight traffic on registered air carriers: 5.14 million (2018) mt-km

Civil aircraft registration country code prefix: 9H

Airports: *total:* 1 (2021)

Airports - with paved runways: *total:* 1
over 3,047 m: 1 (2021)

Heliports: 2 (2021)

Roadways: *total:* 3,096 km (2008)
paved: 2,704 km (2008)
unpaved: 392 km (2008)
urban: 1,422 km (2001)
non-urban: 832 km (2001)

Merchant marine: *total:* 2,137
by type: bulk carrier 601, container ship 310, general cargo 218, oil tanker 412, other 596 (2021)

Ports and terminals: *major seaport(s):* Marsaxlokk (Malta Freeport), Valletta
container port(s) (TEUs): Marsaxlokk (2,722,889) (2019)

LNG terminal(s) (import): Delimara

MILITARY AND SECURITY

Military and security forces: the Armed Forces of Malta (AFM) is a joint force with land, maritime, and air elements, plus a Volunteer Reserve Force (2022)
note: the AFM and the Malta Police Force are both under the Ministry of Home Affairs, National Security, and Law Enforcement

Military expenditures: 0.5% of GDP (2021 est.)
0.6% of GDP (2020)
0.5% of GDP (2019) (approximately $110 million)
0.5% of GDP (2018) (approximately $110 million)
0.5% of GDP (2017) (approximately $110 million)

Military and security service personnel strengths: approximately 2,000 active duty personnel (2021)

Military equipment inventories and acquisitions: the military has a small inventory that consists of equipment from a mix of European countries, particularly Italy, and the US (2021)

Military service age and obligation: 18-30 years of age for men and women for voluntary military service; no conscription (2022)

Military - note: Malta maintains a security policy of neutrality, but contributes to EU and UN military missions and joined NATO's Partnership for Peace program in 1995 (suspended in 1996, but reactivated in 2008); it also participates in various bilateral and multinational military exercises; Malta cooperates closely with Italy on defense matters; in 1973, Italy established a military mission in Malta to provide advice, training, and search and rescue assistance

TRANSNATIONAL ISSUES

Disputes - international: none identified

Refugees and internally displaced persons: *stateless persons:* 11 (mid-year 2021)
note: 8,440 estimated refugee and migrant arrivals by sea (January 2015-October 2022)

Illicit drugs: minor transshipment point for hashish from North Africa to Western Europe

MARSHALL ISLANDS

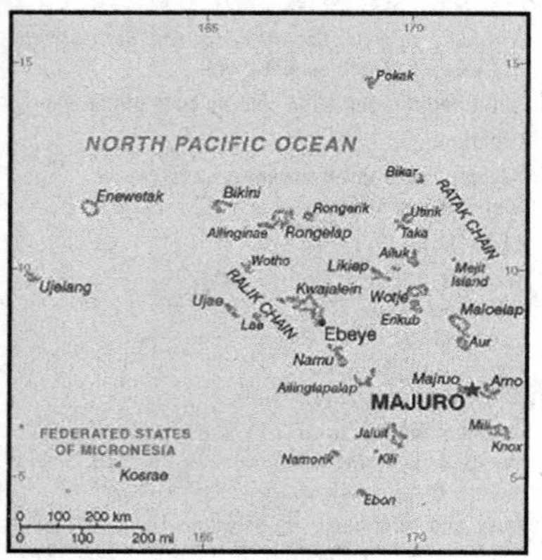

INTRODUCTION

Background: Humans arrived in the Marshall Islands in the first millennium B.C. and gradually created permanent settlements on the various atolls. The early inhabitants were skilled navigators who frequently traveled between atolls using stick charts to map the islands. Society became organized under two paramount chiefs, one each for the Ratak (Sunrise) Chain and the Ralik (Sunset) Chain. The traditional hierarchy continued even after contact with Europeans in the early 1500s. Spain formally claimed the islands in 1592, but few other Europeans passed by the islands in the next two centuries. In 1788, British sea captain John MARSHALL undertook an exploratory voyage, and the islands were mapped in the early 1800s by Russian explorers. In the 1850s, US Protestant missionaries began arriving on the islands. Germany established a supply station on Jaluit Atoll and bought the islands from Spain in 1884, although paramount chiefs continued to rule.

Japan seized the Marshall Islands in 1914 and was granted a League of Nations Mandate to administer the islands in 1920. Japan built large military bases throughout the Marshall Islands, and during World War II, the US captured the bases on Kwajalein, Enewetak, and Majuro Atolls in Operations Flintlock and Catchpole. The Marshall Islands came under US administration as part of the Trust Territory of the Pacific Islands (TTPI) in 1947. Between 1946 and 1958, the US resettled populations from Bikini and Enewetak Atolls and conducted 67 nuclear tests; people from Ailinginae and Rongelap Atolls were also evacuated because of nuclear fallout, and all four atolls remain largely uninhabited. In 1979, the Marshall Islands drafted a constitution separate from the rest of the TTPI and declared independence under President Amata KABUA, a paramount chief. In 2000, Kessai NOTE became the first commoner elected president. In 2016, Hilda HEINE was the first woman elected president.

In 1982, the Marshall Islands signed a Compact of Free Association (COFA) with the US, which granted the Marshall Islands financial assistance and access to many US domestic programs in exchange for exclusive US military access and defense responsibilities; the COFA entered into force in 1986 and its funding was renewed in 2003. The Marshall Islands hosts the US Army Kwajalein Atoll Reagan Missile Test Site, a key installation in the US missile defense network. Kwajalein also hosts one of four dedicated ground antennas that assist in the operation of the Global Positioning System (GPS) navigation system (the others are at Cape Canaveral, Florida (US), on Ascension (Saint Helena, Ascension, and Tristan da Cunha), and at Diego Garcia (British Indian Ocean Territory)).

GEOGRAPHY

Location: Oceania, consists of 29 atolls and five isolated islands in the North Pacific Ocean, about halfway between Hawaii and Australia; the atolls and islands are situated in two, almost-parallel island chains - the Ratak (Sunrise) group and the Ralik (Sunset) group; the total number of islands and islets is about 1,225; 22 of the atolls and four of the islands are uninhabited

Geographic coordinates: 9 00 N, 168 00 E

Map references: Oceania

Area: *total:* 181 sq km
land: 181 sq km
water: 0 sq km
note: the archipelago includes 11,673 sq km of lagoon waters and encompasses the atolls of Bikini, Enewetak, Kwajalein, Majuro, Rongelap, and Utirik

Area - comparative: about the size of Washington, DC

Land boundaries: *total:* 0 km

Coastline: 370.4 km

Maritime claims: *territorial sea:* 12 nm
contiguous zone: 24 nm
exclusive economic zone: 200 nm

Climate: tropical; hot and humid; wet season May to November; islands border typhoon belt

Terrain: low coral limestone and sand islands

Elevation: *highest point:* East-central Airik Island, Maloelap Atoll 14 m
lowest point: Pacific Ocean 0 m
mean elevation: 2 m

Natural resources: coconut products, marine products, deep seabed minerals

Land use: *agricultural land:* 50.7% (2018 est.)
arable land: 7.8% (2018 est.)
permanent crops: 31.2% (2018 est.)
permanent pasture: 11.7% (2018 est.)
forest: 49.3% (2018 est.)
other: 0% (2018 est.)

Irrigated land: 0 sq km (2012)

Population distribution: most people live in urban clusters found on many of the country's islands; more than two-thirds of the population lives on the atolls of Majuro and Ebeye

Natural hazards: infrequent typhoons

Geography - note: the islands of Bikini and Enewetak are former US nuclear test sites; Kwajalein atoll, famous as a World War II battleground, surrounds the world's largest lagoon and is used as a US missile test range; the island city of Ebeye is the second largest settlement in the Marshall Islands, after the capital of Majuro, and one of the most densely populated locations in the Pacific

PEOPLE AND SOCIETY

Population: 79,906 (2022 est.)

Nationality: *noun:* Marshallese (singular and plural)
adjective: Marshallese

Ethnic groups: Marshallese 92.1%, mixed Marshallese 5.9%, other 2% (2006 est.)

Languages: Marshallese (official) 98.2%, other languages 1.8% (1999 est.)
major-language sample(s): Bok eo an Lalin kin Melele ko Rejimwe ej jikin ebōk melele ko raurōk. (Marshallese)
note: English (official), widely spoken as a second language

Religions: Protestant 80.5% (United Church of Christ 47%, Assembly of God 16.2%, Bukot Nan Jesus 5.4%, Full Gospel 3.3%, Reformed Congressional Church 3%, Salvation Army 1.9%, Seventh Day Adventist 1.4%, Meram in Jesus 1.2%, other Protestant 1.1%), Roman Catholic 8.5%, Church of Jesus Christ 7%, Jehovah's Witness 1.7%, other 1.2%, none 1.1% (2011 est.)

Age structure: *0-14 years:* 32.94% (male 13,090/female 12,575)
15-24 years: 19.09% (male 7,568/female 7,308)
25-54 years: 37.35% (male 14,834/female 14,270)
55-64 years: 5.92% (male 2,269/female 2,341)
65 years and over: 4.7% (male 1,805/female 1,857) (2020 est.)

Median age: *total:* 23.8 years
male: 23.6 years
female: 23.9 years (2020 est.)

Population growth rate: 1.34% (2022 est.)

Birth rate: 22 births/1,000 population (2022 est.)

Death rate: 4.28 deaths/1,000 population (2022 est.)

Net migration rate: -4.37 migrant(s)/1,000 population (2022 est.)

Population distribution: most people live in urban clusters found on many of the country's islands; more than two-thirds of the population lives on the atolls of Majuro and Ebeye

Urbanization: *urban population:* 78.5% of total population (2022)
rate of urbanization: 0.61% annual rate of change (2020-25 est.)

Major urban areas - population: 31,000 MAJURO (capital) (2018)

Sex ratio: *at birth:* 1.05 male(s)/female
0-14 years: 1.04 male(s)/female
15-24 years: 1.03 male(s)/female
25-54 years: 1.05 male(s)/female
55-64 years: 0.95 male(s)/female
65 years and over: 0.77 male(s)/female
total population: 1.03 male(s)/female (2022 est.)

Infant mortality rate: *total:* 21.66 deaths/1,000 live births
male: 25.19 deaths/1,000 live births
female: 17.96 deaths/1,000 live births (2022 est.)

Life expectancy at birth: *total population:* 74.65 years
male: 72.4 years
female: 77.01 years (2022 est.)

Total fertility rate: 2.76 children born/woman (2022 est.)

Drinking water source: *improved: urban:* 100% of population
rural: 99.8% of population
total: 100% of population
unimproved: urban: 0% of population
rural: 0.2% of population
total: 0% of population (2020 est.)

Current health expenditure: 16.3% of GDP (2019)

Physicians density: 0.42 physicians/1,000 population (2012)

Hospital bed density: 2.7 beds/1,000 population

Sanitation facility access: *improved: urban:* 96.6% of population
rural: 65.4% of population
total: 89.7% of population
unimproved: urban: 3.4% of population
rural: 34.6% of population
total: 10.3% of population (2020 est.)

Major infectious diseases: *degree of risk:* high (2020)
food or waterborne diseases: bacterial diarrhea
vectorborne diseases: malaria

Obesity - adult prevalence rate: 52.9% (2016)

Tobacco use: *total:* 28.5% (2020 est.)
male: 48.7% (2020 est.)
female: 8.3% (2020 est.)

Children under the age of 5 years underweight: 11.9% (2017)

Education expenditures: 9.6% of GDP (2019 est.)

Literacy: *definition:* age 15 and over can read and write
total population: 98.3%
male: 98.3%
female: 98.2% (2011)

School life expectancy (primary to tertiary education): *total:* 10 years
male: 10 years
female: 10 years (2019)

Unemployment, youth ages 15-24: *total:* 26%
male: 31%
female: 14.2% (2019 est.)

ENVIRONMENT

Environment - current issues: inadequate supplies of potable water; pollution of Majuro lagoon from household waste and discharges from fishing vessels; sea level rise

Environment - international agreements: *party to:* Biodiversity, Climate Change, Climate Change-Kyoto Protocol, Climate Change-Paris Agreement, Comprehensive Nuclear Test Ban, Desertification, Hazardous Wastes, Law of the Sea, Marine Dumping-London Protocol, Ozone Layer Protection, Ship Pollution, Wetlands, Whaling
signed, but not ratified: none of the selected agreements

Air pollutants: *particulate matter emissions:* 9.43 micrograms per cubic meter (2016 est.)
carbon dioxide emissions: 0.14 megatons (2016 est.)
methane emissions: 0.03 megatons (2020 est.)

Climate: tropical; hot and humid; wet season May to November; islands border typhoon belt

Land use: *agricultural land:* 50.7% (2018 est.)
arable land: 7.8% (2018 est.)
permanent crops: 31.2% (2018 est.)
permanent pasture: 11.7% (2018 est.)
forest: 49.3% (2018 est.)
other: 0% (2018 est.)

Urbanization: *urban population:* 78.5% of total population (2022)
rate of urbanization: 0.61% annual rate of change (2020-25 est.)

Revenue from forest resources: *forest revenues:* 0% of GDP (2018 est.)
vectorborne diseases: malaria

Waste and recycling: *municipal solid waste generated annually:* 8,614 tons (2013 est.)
municipal solid waste recycled annually: 2,653 tons (2007 est.)
percent of municipal solid waste recycled: 30.8% (2007 est.)

Total renewable water resources: 0 cubic meters (2017 est.)

GOVERNMENT

Country name: *conventional long form:* Republic of the Marshall Islands
conventional short form: Marshall Islands
local long form: Republic of the Marshall Islands
local short form: Marshall Islands
former: Trust Territory of the Pacific Islands, Marshall Islands District
abbreviation: RMI
etymology: named after British Captain John MARSHALL, who charted many of the islands in 1788

Government type: mixed presidential-parliamentary system in free association with the US

Capital: *name:* Majuro; note - the capital is an atoll of 64 islands; governmental buildings are housed on three fused islands on the eastern side of the atoll: Djarrit, Uliga, and Delap
geographic coordinates: 7 06 N, 171 23 E
time difference: UTC+12 (17 hours ahead of Washington, DC, during Standard Time)
etymology: Majuro means "two openings" or "two eyes" and refers to the two major northern passages through the atoll into the Majuro lagoon

Administrative divisions: 24 municipalities; Ailinglaplap, Ailuk, Arno, Aur, Bikini & Kili, Ebon, Enewetak & Ujelang, Jabat, Jaluit, Kwajalein, Lae, Lib, Likiep, Majuro, Maloelap, Mejit, Mili, Namorik, Namu, Rongelap, Ujae, Utrik, Wotho, Wotje

Independence: 21 October 1986 (from the US-administered UN trusteeship)

National holiday: Constitution Day, 1 May (1979)

Constitution: *history:* effective 1 May 1979
amendments: proposed by the National Parliament or by a constitutional convention; passage by Parliament requires at least two-thirds majority vote of the total membership in each of two readings and approval by a majority of votes in a referendum; amendments submitted by a constitutional convention require approval of at least two thirds of votes in a referendum; amended several times, last in 2018

Legal system: mixed legal system of US and English common law, customary law, and local statutes

International law organization participation: accepts compulsory ICJ jurisdiction with reservations; accepts ICCt jurisdiction

Citizenship: *citizenship by birth:* no
citizenship by descent only: at least one parent must be a citizen of the Marshall Islands
dual citizenship recognized: no
residency requirement for naturalization: 5 years

Suffrage: 18 years of age; universal

Executive branch: *chief of state:* President David KABUA (since 13 January 2020); note - the president is both chief of state and head of government
head of government: President David KABUA (since 13 January 2020)
cabinet: Cabinet nominated by the president from among members of the Nitijela, appointed by Nitijela speaker
elections/appointments: president indirectly elected by the Nitijela from among its members for a 4-year term (no term limits); election last held on 6 January 2020 (next to be held in 2024)
election results:
David KABUA elected president; Parliament vote - David KABUA 20, Hilda C. HEINE 12

Legislative branch: *description:* unicameral National Parliament consists of:
Nitijela (33 seats; members in 19 single- and 5 multi-seat constituencies directly elected by simple majority vote to serve 4-year terms); note - the Council of Iroij, a 12-member group of tribal leaders advises the Presidential Cabinet and reviews legislation affecting customary law or any traditional practice); members appointed to serve 1-year terms
elections:
last held on 18 November 2019 (next to be held by November 2023)
election results:
percent of vote by party - NA; seats by party - independent 33; composition - men 31, women 2, percent of women 6.1%

Judicial branch: *highest court(s):* Supreme Court (consists of the chief justice and 2 associate justices)
judge selection and term of office: judges appointed by the Cabinet upon the recommendation of the Judicial Service Commission (consists of the chief justice of the High Court, the attorney general and a private citizen selected by the Cabinet) and upon approval of the Nitijela; the current chief justice, appointed in 2013, serves for 10 years; Marshallese citizens appointed as justices serve until retirement at age 72
subordinate courts: High Court; District Courts; Traditional Rights Court; Community Courts

Political parties and leaders: traditionally there have been no formally organized political parties; what has existed more closely resembles factions or interest groups because they do not have party headquarters, formal platforms, or party structures

International organization participation: ACP, ADB, AOSIS, FAO, G-77, IAEA, IBRD, ICAO, ICCt, IDA, IFAD, IFC, ILO, IMF, IMO, IMSO, Interpol, IOC, IOM, ITU, OPCW, PIF, Sparteca, SPC, UN, UNCTAD, UNESCO, UNHRC, WHO

Diplomatic representation in the US: *chief of mission:* Ambassador Gerald M. ZACKIOS (since 16 September 2016)
chancery: 2433 Massachusetts Avenue NW, Washington, DC 20008
telephone: [1] (202) 234-5414

FAX: [1] (202) 232-3236
email address and website:
info@rmiembassyus.org
https://www.rmiembassyus.org/
consulate(s) general: Honolulu, Springdale (AR)

Diplomatic representation from the US: *chief of mission:* Ambassador Roxanne CABRAL (since 6 February 2020)
embassy: Mejen Weto, Ocean Side, Majuro
mailing address: 4380 Majuro Place, Washington DC 20521-4380
telephone: [692] 247-4011
FAX: [692] 247-4012
email address and website:
MAJConsular@state.gov
https://mh.usembassy.gov/

Flag description: blue with two stripes radiating from the lower hoist-side corner - orange (top) and white; a white star with four large rays and 20 small rays appears on the hoist side above the two stripes; blue represents the Pacific Ocean, the orange stripe signifies the Ralik Chain or sunset and courage, while the white stripe signifies the Ratak Chain or sunrise and peace; the star symbolizes the cross of Christianity, each of the 24 rays designates one of the electoral districts in the country and the four larger rays highlight the principal cultural centers of Majuro, Jaluit, Wotje, and Ebeye; the rising diagonal band can also be interpreted as representing the equator, with the star showing the archipelago's position just to the north

National symbol(s): a 24-rayed star; national colors: blue, white, orange

National anthem: *name:* "Forever Marshall Islands"
lyrics/music: Amata KABUA
note: adopted 1981

National heritage: *total World Heritage Sites:* 1 (cultural)
selected World Heritage Site locales: Bikini Atoll Nuclear Test Site

ECONOMY

Economic overview: US assistance and lease payments for the use of Kwajalein Atoll as a US military base are the mainstay of this small island country. Agricultural production, primarily subsistence, is concentrated on small farms; the most important commercial crops are coconuts and breadfruit. Industry is limited to handicrafts, tuna processing, and copra. Tourism holds some potential. The islands and atolls have few natural resources, and imports exceed exports.

The Marshall Islands received roughly $1 billion in aid from the US during the period 1986-2001 under the original Compact of Free Association (Compact). In 2002 and 2003, the US and the Marshall Islands renegotiated the Compact's financial package for a 20-year period, 2004 to 2024. Under the amended Compact, the Marshall Islands will receive roughly $1.5 billion in direct US assistance. Under the amended Compact, the US and Marshall Islands are also jointly funding a Trust Fund for the people of the Marshall Islands that will provide an income stream beyond 2024, when direct Compact aid ends.

Real GDP (purchasing power parity): $240 million (2019 est.)
$220 million (2018 est.)
$219 million (2017 est.)
note: data are in 2017 dollars

Real GDP growth rate: 2.5% (2017 est.)
3.6% (2016 est.)
2% (2015 est.)

Real GDP per capita: $4,000 (2019 est.) note: data are in 2017 dollars
$3,800 (2018 est.) note: data are in 2017 dollars
$3,776 (2017 est.)

GDP (official exchange rate): $222 million (2017 est.)

Inflation rate (consumer prices): 0% (2017 est.)
-1.5% (2016 est.)

GDP - composition, by sector of origin: *agriculture:* 4.4% (2013 est.)
industry: 9.9% (2013 est.)
services: 85.7% (2013 est.)

GDP - composition, by end use: *government consumption:* 50% (2016 est.)
investment in fixed capital: 17.8% (2016 est.)
investment in inventories: 0.2% (2016 est.)
exports of goods and services: 52.9% (2016 est.)
imports of goods and services: -102.3% (2016 est.)

Agricultural products: coconuts

Industries: copra, tuna processing, tourism, craft items (from seashells, wood, and pearls)

Labor force: 10,670 (2013 est.)

Labor force - by occupation: *agriculture:* 11%
industry: 16.3%
services: 72.7% (2011 est.)

Unemployment rate: 36% (2006 est.)
30.9% (2000 est.)

Unemployment, youth ages 15-24: *total:* 26%
male: 31%
female: 14.2% (2019 est.)

Budget: *revenues:* 116.7 million (2013 est.)
expenditures: 113.9 million (2013 est.)

Budget surplus (+) or deficit (-): 1.3% (of GDP) (2013 est.)

Public debt: 25.5% of GDP (2017 est.)
30% of GDP (2016 est.)

Taxes and other revenues: 52.6% (of GDP) (2013 est.)

Fiscal year: 1 October - 30 September

Current account balance: -$1 million (2017 est.)
$15 million (2016 est.)

Exports: $130 million (2018 est.) note: data are in current year dollars

Exports - partners: Poland 28%, Denmark 19%, South Korea 13%, Indonesia 10%, Cyprus 6% (2019)

Exports - commodities: ships, fish, recreational boats, broadcasting equipment, coal tar oil (2019)

Imports: $170 million (2018 est.) note: data are in current year dollars
$103.8 million (2016 est.)

Imports - partners: South Korea 39%, China 27%, Japan 15% (2019)

Imports - commodities: ships, refined petroleum, centrifuges, recreational boats, boat propellers (2019)

Debt - external: $97.96 million (2013 est.)
$87 million (2008 est.)

Exchange rates: the US dollar is used

ENERGY

Electricity access: *electrification - total population:* 96.3% (2018)
electrification - urban areas: 95.7% (2018)
electrification - rural areas: 98.4% (2018)

Refined petroleum products - production: 0 bbl/day (2015 est.)

Refined petroleum products - exports: 0 bbl/day (2015 est.)

Refined petroleum products - imports: 2,060 bbl/day (2015 est.)

Carbon dioxide emissions: 293,700 metric tonnes of CO_2 (2017 est.)

COMMUNICATIONS

Telephones - fixed lines: *total subscriptions:* 2,361 (2018 est.)
subscriptions per 100 inhabitants: 4 (2018 est.)

Telephones - mobile cellular: *total subscriptions:* 16,000 (2020 est.)
subscriptions per 100 inhabitants: 27 (2020 est.)

Telecommunication systems: *general assessment:* the National Telecommunications Act, through Bill No. 66, ushered in a new era in telecommunications in the Marshall Islands; this will enable an open, competitive market for telecommunications that is regulated by a Telecommunications Commissioner; telecom officials announced that they would be able to offer satellite internet services beginning in mid-2023; the World Bank has been promoting telecommunications reform here for a decade and has a multi-million-dollar telecommunications reform grant program in progress (2022)
domestic: Majuro Atoll and Ebeye and Kwajalein islands have regular, seven-digit, direct-dial telephones; other islands interconnected by high frequency radiotelephone (used mostly for government purposes) and mini-satellite telephones; fixed-line roughly 4 per 100 persons and mobile-cellular is nearly 27 per 100 persons (2020)
international: country code - 692; satellite earth stations - 2 Intelsat (Pacific Ocean); US Government satellite communications system on Kwajalein

Broadcast media: no TV broadcast station; a cable network is available on Majuro with programming via videotape replay and satellite relays; 4 radio broadcast stations; American Armed Forces Radio and Television Service (AFRTS) provides satellite radio and television service to Kwajalein Atoll (2019)

Internet country code: .mh

Internet users: *total:* 22,929 (2019 est.)
percent of population: 39% (2019 est.)

Broadband - fixed subscriptions: *total:* 1,000 (2020 est.)
subscriptions per 100 inhabitants: 2 (2020 est.)

Communications - note: Kwajalein hosts one of four dedicated ground antennas that assist in the operation of the Global Positioning System (GPS) navigation system (the others are at Cape Canaveral, Florida (US), on Ascension (Saint Helena, Ascension, and Tristan da Cunha), and at Diego Garcia (British Indian Ocean Territory))

TRANSPORTATION

National air transport system: *number of registered air carriers:* 1 (2020)
inventory of registered aircraft operated by air carriers: 3

annual passenger traffic on registered air carriers: 24,313 (2018)
annual freight traffic on registered air carriers: 130,000 (2018) mt-km

Civil aircraft registration country code prefix: V7

Airports: *total:* 15 (2021)

Airports - with paved runways: *total:* 4
1,524 to 2,437 m: 3
914 to 1,523 m: 1 (2021)

Airports - with unpaved runways: *total:* 11
914 to 1,523 m: 10
under 914 m: 1 (2021)

Roadways: *total:* 2,028 km (2007)
*paved:*75 km (2007)
unpaved: 1,953 km

Merchant marine: *total:* 3,817
by type: bulk carrier 1,733, container ship 248, general cargo 66, oil tanker 970, other 800 (2021)

Ports and terminals: *major seaport(s):* Enitwetak Island, Kwajalein, Majuro

MILITARY AND SECURITY

Military and security forces: no regular military forces; the national police (Marshall Islands Police Department, MIPD), local police forces, and the Sea Patrol (maritime police) maintain internal security; the MIPD and Sea Patrol report to the Ministry of Justice; local police report to their respective local government councils

Military - note: defense is the responsibility of the US the Marshall Islands have a "shiprider" agreement with the US, which allows local maritime law enforcement officers to embark on US Coast Guard (USCG) and US Navy (USN) vessels, including to board and search vessels suspected of violating laws or regulations within its designated exclusive economic zone (EEZ) or on the high seas; "shiprider" agreements also enable USCG personnel and USN vessels with embarked USCG law enforcement personnel to work with host nations to protect critical regional resources (2022)

TRANSNATIONAL ISSUES

Disputes - international: *Marshall Islands-US:* claims US territory of Wake Island; the Marshall Islands put its claim on record with the UN in 2016

MAURITANIA

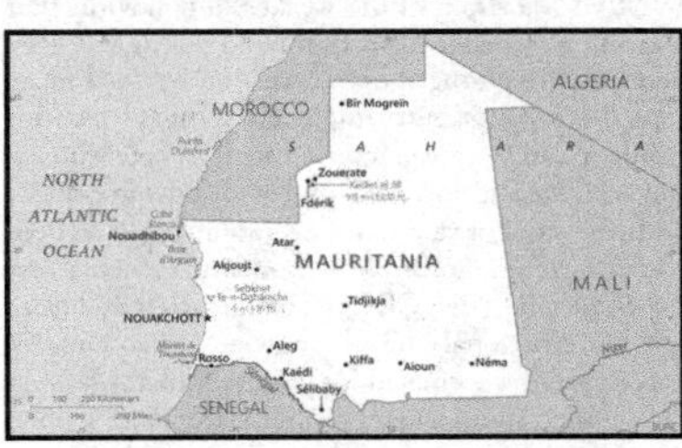

INTRODUCTION

Background: The Berber and Bafour people were among the first to settle in what is now Mauritania. Originally a nomadic people, they were among the first in recorded history to convert from a nomadic to agricultural lifestyle. These groups account for roughly one third of Mauritania's ethnic makeup. The remainder of Mauritania's ethnic groups derive from former enslaved peoples and Sub-Saharan ethnic groups originating mainly from the Senegal River Valley. These three groups are organized according to a strict caste system with deep ethnic divides that still exist today.

A former French colony, Mauritania achieved independence from France in 1960. Mauritania initially began as a single-party, authoritarian regime and saw 49 years of dictatorships, flawed elections, failed attempts at democracy, and military coups. Ould Abdel AZIZ led the last coup in 2008, and was elected president in 2009 and reelected in 2014. Mohamed Ould Cheikh GHAZOUANI was elected president in 2019, and his inauguration marked the first peaceful transition of power from one democratically elected president to another, solidifying Mauritania's status as an emerging democracy. International observers recognized the elections as relatively free and fair.

The country is working to address a continuing practice of slavery and its vestiges. Mauritania officially abolished slavery in 1981, but the practice was not criminalized until 2007. Between 2005 and 2011, Al-Qaeda in the Islamic Maghreb (AQIM) launched a series of attacks killing American and foreign tourists and aid workers, attacking diplomatic and government facilities, and ambushing Mauritanian soldiers and gendarmes. Although Mauritania has not seen an attack since 2011, AQIM and similar groups remain active in the Sahel region.

GEOGRAPHY

Location: Western Africa, bordering the North Atlantic Ocean, between Senegal and Western Sahara

Geographic coordinates: 20 00 N, 12 00 W

Map references: Africa

Area: *total:* 1,030,700 sq km
land: 1,030,700 sq km
water: 0 sq km

Area - comparative: slightly larger than three times the size of New Mexico; about six times the size of Florida

Land boundaries: *total:* 5,002 km
border countries (4): Algeria 460 km; Mali 2,236 km; Morocco 1,564 km; Senegal 742 km

Coastline: 754 km

Maritime claims: *territorial sea:* 12 nm
contiguous zone: 24 nm
exclusive economic zone: 200 nm
continental shelf: 200 nm or to the edge of the continental margin

Climate: desert; constantly hot, dry, dusty

Terrain: mostly barren, flat plains of the Sahara; some central hills

Elevation: *highest point:* Kediet Ijill 915 m
lowest point: Sebkhet Te-n-Dghamcha -5 m
mean elevation: 276 m

Natural resources: iron ore, gypsum, copper, phosphate, diamonds, gold, oil, fish

Land use: *agricultural land:* 38.5% (2018 est.)
arable land: 0.4% (2018 est.)
permanent crops: 0% (2018 est.)
permanent pasture: 38.1% (2018 est.)
forest: 0.2% (2018 est.)
other: 61.3% (2018 est.)

Irrigated land: 450 sq km (2012)

Major rivers (by length in km): Senegal river mouth (shared with Guinea [s], Senegal and Mali) - 1,641 km
note – [s] after country name indicates river source; [m] after country name indicates river mouth

Major watersheds (area sq km): Atlantic Ocean drainage: Niger (2,261,741 sq km), Senegal (456,397 sq km)

Major aquifers: Senegalo-Mauritanian Basin, Taodeni-Tanzerouft Basin

Population distribution: with most of the country being a desert, vast areas of the country, particularly in the central, northern, and eastern areas, are without sizeable population clusters; half the population lives in or around the coastal capital of Nouakchott; smaller clusters are found near the southern border with Mali and Senegal as shown in this population distribution map

Natural hazards: hot, dry, dust/sand-laden sirocco wind primarily in March and April; periodic droughts

Geography - note: Mauritania is considered both a part of North Africa's Maghreb region and West Africa's Sahel region; most of the population is concentrated in the cities of Nouakchott and Nouadhibou and along the Senegal River in the southern part of the country

PEOPLE AND SOCIETY

Population: 4,161,925 (2022 est.)

Nationality: *noun:* Mauritanian(s)
adjective: Mauritanian

Ethnic groups: Black Moors (Haratines - Arabic-speaking descendants of African origin who are or were enslaved by White Moors) 40%, White Moors (of Arab-Berber descent, known as Beydane) 30%, Sub-Saharan Mauritanians (non-Arabic speaking, largely resident in or originating from the Senegal River Valley, including Halpulaar, Fulani, Soninke, Wolof, and Bambara ethnic groups) 30%

Languages: Arabic (official and national), Pular, Soninke, Wolof (all national languages), French; note - the spoken Arabic in Mauritania differs considerably from the Modern Standard Arabic used for official written purposes or in the media;

the Mauritanian dialect, which incorporates many Berber words, is referred to as Hassaniya
major-language sample(s):
يمكن الاستغناء عنه للمعلومات الأساسية
كتاب حقائق العالم، المصدر الذي لا
(Arabic)

Religions: Muslim (official) 100%

Demographic profile: With a sustained total fertility rate of about 4 children per woman and almost 60% of the population under the age of 25, Mauritania's population is likely to continue growing for the foreseeable future. Mauritania's large youth cohort is vital to its development prospects, but available schooling does not adequately prepare students for the workplace. Girls continue to be underrepresented in the classroom, educational quality remains poor, and the dropout rate is high. The literacy rate is only about 50%, even though access to primary education has improved since the mid-2000s. Women's restricted access to education and discriminatory laws maintain gender inequality - worsened by early and forced marriages and female genital cutting.

The denial of education to black Moors also helps to perpetuate slavery. Although Mauritania abolished slavery in 1981 (the last country in the world to do so) and made it a criminal offense in 2007, the millenniums-old practice persists largely because anti-slavery laws are rarely enforced and the custom is so ingrained. According to a 2018 nongovernmental organization's report, a little more than 2% of Mauritania's population is enslaved, which includes individuals sujbected to forced labor and forced marriage, although many thousands of individuals who are legally free contend with discrimination, poor education, and a lack of identity papers and, therefore, live in de facto slavery. The UN and international press outlets have claimed that up to 20% of Mauritania's population is enslaved, which would be the highest rate worldwide.

Drought, poverty, and unemployment have driven outmigration from Mauritania since the 1970s. Early flows were directed toward other West African countries, including Senegal, Mali, Cote d'Ivoire, and Gambia. The 1989 Mauritania-Senegal conflict forced thousands of black Mauritanians to take refuge in Senegal and pushed labor migrants toward the Gulf, Libya, and Europe in the late 1980s and early 1990s. Mauritania has accepted migrants from neighboring countries to fill labor shortages since its independence in 1960 and more recently has received refugees escaping civil wars, including tens of thousands of Tuaregs who fled Mali in 2012.

Mauritania was an important transit point for Sub-Saharan migrants moving illegally to North Africa and Europe. In the mid-2000s, as border patrols increased in the Strait of Gibraltar, security increased around Spain's North African enclaves (Ceuta and Melilla), and Moroccan border controls intensified, illegal migration flows shifted from the Western Mediterranean to Spain's Canary Islands. In 2006, departure points moved southward along the West African coast from Morocco and then Western Sahara to Mauritania's two key ports (Nouadhibou and the capital Nouakchott), and illegal migration to the Canaries peaked at almost 32,000. The numbers fell dramatically in the following years because of joint patrolling off the West African coast by Frontex (the EU's border protection agency), Spain, Mauritania, and Senegal; the expansion of Spain's border surveillance system; and the 2008 European economic downturn.

Age structure: *0-14 years:* 37.56% (male 755,788/female 748,671)
15-24 years: 19.71% (male 387,140/female 402,462)
25-54 years: 33.91% (male 630,693/female 727,518)
55-64 years: 4.9% (male 88,888/female 107,201)
65 years and over: 3.92% (male 66,407/female 90,707) (2020 est.)

Dependency ratios: *total dependency ratio:* 75
youth dependency ratio: 69.5
elderly dependency ratio: 5.6
potential support ratio: 18 (2020 est.)

Median age: *total:* 21 years
male: 20.1 years
female: 22 years (2020 est.)

Population growth rate: 1.99% (2022 est.)

Birth rate: 28.06 births/1,000 population (2022 est.)

Death rate: 7.43 deaths/1,000 population (2022 est.)

Net migration rate: -0.72 migrant(s)/1,000 population (2022 est.)

Population distribution: with most of the country being a desert, vast areas of the country, particularly in the central, northern, and eastern areas, are without sizeable population clusters; half the population lives in or around the coastal capital of Nouakchott; smaller clusters are found near the southern border with Mali and Senegal as shown in this population distribution map

Urbanization: *urban population:* 56.9% of total population (2022)
rate of urbanization: 3.84% annual rate of change (2020-25 est.)

Major urban areas - population: 1.432 million NOUAKCHOTT (capital) (2022)

Sex ratio: *at birth:* 1.03 male(s)/female
0-14 years: 1.01 male(s)/female
15-24 years: 0.96 male(s)/female
25-54 years: 0.86 male(s)/female
55-64 years: 0.83 male(s)/female
65 years and over: 0.61 male(s)/female
total population: 0.93 male(s)/female (2022 est.)

Mother's mean age at first birth: 21.8 years (2019/21)
note: data represents median age at first birth among women 25-49

Maternal mortality ratio: 766 deaths/100,000 live births (2017 est.)

Infant mortality rate: *total:* 50.99 deaths/1,000 live births
male: 56.89 deaths/1,000 live births
female: 44.91 deaths/1,000 live births (2022 est.)

Life expectancy at birth: *total population:* 65.22 years
male: 62.77 years
female: 67.75 years (2022 est.)

Total fertility rate: 3.53 children born/woman (2022 est.)

Contraceptive prevalence rate: 11.5% (2019/20)

Drinking water source: *improved: urban:* 98.7% of population
rural: 68.4% of population
total: 85.2% of population
unimproved: urban: 1.3% of population
rural: 31.6% of population
total: 14.8% of population (2020 est.)

Current health expenditure: 3.3% of GDP (2019)

Physicians density: 0.19 physicians/1,000 population (2018)

Sanitation facility access: *improved: urban:* 83.5% of population
rural: 25.2% of population
total: 57.5% of population
unimproved: urban: 16.5% of population
rural: 74.8% of population
total: 42.5% of population (2020 est.)

HIV/AIDS - adult prevalence rate: 0.3% (2020 est.)

Major infectious diseases: *degree of risk:* very high (2020)
food or waterborne diseases: bacterial and protozoal diarrhea, hepatitis A, and typhoid fever
vectorborne diseases: malaria and dengue fever
animal contact diseases: rabies
respiratory diseases: meningococcal meningitis
note: on 21 March 2022, the US Centers for Disease Control and Prevention (CDC) issued a Travel Alert for polio in Africa; Mauritania is currently considered a high risk to travelers for circulating vaccine-derived polioviruses (cVDPV); vaccine-derived poliovirus (VDPV) is a strain of the weakened poliovirus that was initially included in oral polio vaccine (OPV) and *that has changed over time and behaves more like the wild or naturally occurring virus*; this means it can be spread more easily to people who are unvaccinated against polio and who come in contact with the stool or respiratory secretions, such as from a sneeze, of an "infected" person who received oral polio vaccine; the CDC recommends that before any international travel, anyone unvaccinated, incompletely vaccinated, or with an unknown polio vaccination status should complete the routine polio vaccine series; before travel to any high-risk destination, the CDC recommends that adults who previously completed the full, routine polio vaccine series receive a single, lifetime booster dose of polio vaccine

Obesity - adult prevalence rate: 12.7% (2016)

Alcohol consumption per capita: *total:* 0 liters of pure alcohol (2019 est.)
beer: 0 liters of pure alcohol (2019 est.)
wine: 0 liters of pure alcohol (2019 est.)
spirits: 0 liters of pure alcohol (2019 est.)
other alcohols: 0 liters of pure alcohol (2019 est.)

Tobacco use: *total:* 10.7% (2020 est.)
male: 19.3% (2020 est.)
female: 2.1% (2020 est.)

Children under the age of 5 years underweight: 19.2% (2018)

Education expenditures: 1.9% of GDP (2020 est.)

Literacy: *definition:* age 15 and over can read and write
total population: 53.5%
male: 63.7%
female: 43.4% (2017)

School life expectancy (primary to tertiary education): *total:* 9 years
male: 9 years
female: 10 years (2019)

Unemployment, youth ages 15-24: *total:* 21.1%
male: 18.8%
female: 24.9% (2017 est.)

ENVIRONMENT

Environment - current issues: overgrazing, deforestation, and soil erosion aggravated by drought are contributing to desertification; limited natural freshwater resources away from the Senegal, which is the only perennial river; locust infestation

Environment - international agreements: *party to:* Biodiversity, Climate Change, Climate Change-Kyoto Protocol, Climate Change-Paris Agreement, Comprehensive Nuclear Test Ban, Desertification, Endangered Species, Hazardous Wastes, Law of the Sea, Nuclear Test Ban, Ozone Layer Protection, Ship Pollution, Wetlands, Whaling
signed, but not ratified: none of the selected agreements

Air pollutants: *particulate matter emissions:* 40.82 micrograms per cubic meter (2016 est.)
carbon dioxide emissions: 2.74 megatons (2016 est.)
methane emissions: 6.16 megatons (2020 est.)

Climate: desert; constantly hot, dry, dusty

Land use: *agricultural land:* 38.5% (2018 est.)
arable land: 0.4% (2018 est.)
permanent crops: 0% (2018 est.)
permanent pasture: 38.1% (2018 est.)
forest: 0.2% (2018 est.)
other: 61.3% (2018 est.)

Urbanization: *urban population:* 56.9% of total population (2022)
rate of urbanization: 3.84% annual rate of change (2020-25 est.)

Revenue from forest resources: *forest revenues:* 1.3% of GDP (2018 est.)

Revenue from coal: *coal revenues:* 0% of GDP (2018 est.)

Food insecurity: *severe localized food insecurity: due to shortfall in agricultural production and economic downturn* - according to the latest analysis, about 878,000 people are assessed to be in need of humanitarian assistance between June and August 2022 as a result of shortfalls in cereal and livestock production in 2021 and reduced incomes owing to the negative effects of the COVID-19 pandemic on the economy (2022)

Waste and recycling: *municipal solid waste generated annually:* 454,000 tons (2009 est.)
municipal solid waste recycled annually: 36,320 tons (2009 est.)
percent of municipal solid waste recycled: 8% (2009 est.)

Major rivers (by length in km): Senegal river mouth (shared with Guinea [s], Senegal and Mali) - 1,641 km
note – [s] after country name indicates river source; [m] after country name indicates river mouth

Major watersheds (area sq km): Atlantic Ocean drainage: Niger (2,261,741 sq km), Senegal (456,397 sq km)

Major aquifers: Senegalo-Mauritanian Basin, Taodeni-Tanzerouft Basin

Total water withdrawal: *municipal:* 95.4 million cubic meters (2017 est.)
industrial: 31.8 million cubic meters (2017 est.)
agricultural: 1.223 billion cubic meters (2017 est.)

Total renewable water resources: 11.4 billion cubic meters (2017 est.)

GOVERNMENT

Country name: *conventional long form:* Islamic Republic of Mauritania
conventional short form: Mauritania
local long form: Al Jumhuriyah al Islamiyah al Muritaniyah
local short form: Muritaniyah
etymology: named for the ancient kingdom of Mauretania (3rd century B.C. to 1st century A.D.) and the subsequent Roman province (1st-7th centuries A.D.), which existed further north in present-day Morocco; the name derives from the Mauri (Moors), the Berber-speaking peoples of northwest Africa

Government type: presidential republic

Capital: *name:* Nouakchott
geographic coordinates: 18 04 N, 15 58 W
time difference: UTC 0 (5 hours ahead of Washington, DC, during Standard Time)
etymology: may derive from the Berber "nawakshut" meaning "place of the winds"

Administrative divisions: 15 regions (wilayas, singular - wilaya); Adrar, Assaba, Brakna, Dakhlet Nouadhibou, Gorgol, Guidimaka, Hodh ech Chargui, Hodh El Gharbi, Inchiri, Nouakchott Nord, Nouakchott Ouest, Nouakchott Sud, Tagant, Tiris Zemmour, Trarza

Independence: 28 November 1960 (from France)

National holiday: Independence Day, 28 November (1960)

Constitution: *history:* previous 1964; latest adopted 12 July 1991
amendments: proposed by the president of the republic or by Parliament; consideration of amendments by Parliament requires approval of at least one third of the membership; a referendum is held only if the amendment is approved by two-thirds majority vote; passage by referendum requires simple majority vote by eligible voters; passage of amendments proposed by the president can bypass a referendum if approved by at least three-fifths majority vote by Parliament; amended 2006, 2012, 2017

Legal system: mixed legal system of Islamic and French civil law

International law organization participation: has not submitted an ICJ jurisdiction declaration; non-party state to the ICCt

Citizenship: *citizenship by birth:* no
citizenship by descent only: at least one parent must be a citizen of Mauritania
dual citizenship recognized: no
residency requirement for naturalization: 5 years

Suffrage: 18 years of age; universal

Executive branch: *chief of state:* President Mohamed Ould Cheikh el GHAZOUANI (since 1 August 2019)
head of government: Prime Minister Mohamed Ould BILAL (since 6 August 2020)
cabinet: Council of Ministers - nominees suggested by the prime minister, appointed by the president
elections/appointments: president directly elected by absolute majority popular vote in 2 rounds if needed for a 5-year term (eligible for a second term); election last held on 22 June 2019 (next to be held on 22 June 2024); prime minister appointed by the president
election results:
2019: Mohamed Ould Cheikh El GHAZOUANI elected president in first round; percent of vote -Mahamed Ould Cheikh El GHAZOUANI (UPR) 52%, Biram Dah Ould ABEID (independent) 18.6%, Sidi Mohamed Ould BOUBACAR (independent) 17.9%, other 11.5%
2014: Mohamed Ould Abdel AZIZ elected president in first round; percent of vote - Mohamed Ould Abdel AZIZ (UPR) 81.9%, Biram Dah ABEID (IRA) 8.7%, Boidiel Ould HOUMEIT (El Wiam) 4.5%, Ibrahima Moctar SARR (SJD/MR) 4.4%, other 0.5%

Legislative branch: *description:* unicameral Parliament or Barlamane consists of the National Assembly or Al Jamiya Al Wataniya (157 seats statutory, 153 current term; 113 members in single- and multi-seat constituencies directly elected by a combination of plurality and proportional representation voting systems, 40 members in a single, nationwide constituency directly elected by proportional representation vote (20 seats are reserved for women candidates in the nationwide constituency) , and 4 members directly elected by the diaspora; all members serve 5-year terms)
elections:
first held as the unicameral National Assembly in 2 rounds on 1 and 15 September 2018 (next to be held in 2023)
election results:
National Assembly - percent of vote by party - NA; seats by party - UPR 95, Tawassoul 14, UDP 6, El Karama 6, AND 4, PUCM 4, RFD 3, UFP 3, Shura Party for Development 3, Burst of Youth for the Nation 3, SAWAB 3, APP 3, DIL 2, El Wiam 2, AJD/MR 2, Coalition of Wava Mauritanian Party 1, El Ghad 1, National Democratic Union 1, Ravah Party 1, Party of Peace and Democratic Progress 1, El Islah 1; composition - men, 122, women 31, percent of women 20.3%
note: a referendum held in August 2017 approved a constitutional amendment to change the Parliament structure from bicameral to unicameral by abolishing the Senate and creating Regional Councils for local development

Judicial branch: *highest court(s):* Supreme Court or Cour Supreme (subdivided into 7 chambers: 2 civil, 2 labor, 1 commercial, 1 administrative, and 1 criminal, each with a chamber president and 2 councilors); Constitutional Council (consists of 9 members); High Court of Justice (consists of 9 members)
judge selection and term of office: Supreme Court president appointed by the president of the republic to serve a 5-year renewable term; Constitutional Council members appointed - 3 by the president of the republic, 2 by the president of the National Assembly, 1 by the prime minister, 1 by the leader of the democratic opposition, 1 by the largest opposition party in the National Assembly, and 1 by the second largest party in the National Assembly; members serve single, 9-year terms with one-third of membership renewed every 3 years; High Court of Justice members appointed by Parliament - 6 by the ruling Coalition of Majority Parties and 3 by opposition parties
subordinate courts: Courts of Appeal; courts of first instance or wilya courts are established in the regions' headquarters and include commercial and labor courts, criminal courts, Moughataa (district) Courts, and informal/customary courts

Political parties and leaders: Alliance for Justice and Democracy/Movement for Renewal or AJD/MR [Ibrahima Moctar SARR]
Burst of Youth for the Nation or Sursaut or PSJN [Lalla Mint CHERIF]
El Insaf or Equity Party [Mohamed Melainine Ould EYIH]
El Islah Party [Mohamed Ould TALEBNA]

El Karama Party [Cheikhna Ould Mohamed Ould HAJBOU]
Initiative for the Resurgence of the Abolitionist Movement or IRA [Biram Dah ABEID]
National Democratic Alliance or AND [Yacoub Ould MOINE]
National Rally for Reform and Development or RNRD or TAWASSOUL [Mohamed Mahmoud Ould SEYIDI]
Party for Conciliation and Prosperity or HIWAR [Valle Mint Mini]
Popular (or People's) Progressive Alliance or APP [Messaoud Ould BOULKHEIR]
Rally (or Assembly) of Democratic Forces or RFD [Ahmed Ould DADDAH]
Sawab Party [Ahmed Salem Ould HORMA]
Union for Democracy and Progress or UDP [Naha Mint MOUKNASS]
Union of the Forces of Progress or UFP [Mohamed Ould MAOULOUD]

International organization participation: ABEDA, ACP, AfDB, AFESD, AMF, AMU, AU, CAEU, EITI (compliant country), FAO, G-77, IAEA, IBRD, ICAO, ICC (NGOs), ICRM, IDA, IDB, IFAD, IFC, IFRCS, IHO (pending member), ILO, IMF, IMO, Interpol, IOC, IOM, IPU, ISO (correspondent), ITSO, ITU, ITUC (NGOs), LAS, MIGA, MIUSMA, NAM, OIC, OIF, OPCW, UN, UNCTAD, UNESCO, UNHRC, UNIDO, UNWTO, UPU, WCO, WHO, WIPO, WMO, WTO

Diplomatic representation in the US: *chief of mission:* Ambassador BOIDE Cisse (since 15 September 2021)
chancery: 2129 Leroy Place NW, Washington, DC 20008
telephone: [1] (202) 232-5700
FAX: [1] (202) 319-2623
email address and website:
office@mauritaniaembassyus.com
http://mauritaniaembassyus.com/

Diplomatic representation from the US: *chief of mission:* Ambassador Cynthia KIERSCHT (since 29 March 2021)
embassy: Nouadhibou Road, Avenue Al Quds, NOT PRTZ, Nouakchott
mailing address: 2430 Nouakchott Place, Washington DC 20521-2430
telephone: [222] 4525-2660
FAX: [222] 4525-1592
email address and website:
consularnkc@state.gov
https://mr.usembassy.gov/

Flag description: green with a yellow, five-pointed star between the horns of a yellow, upward-pointing crescent moon; red stripes along the top and bottom edges; the crescent, star, and color green are traditional symbols of Islam; green also represents hope for a bright future; the yellow color stands for the sands of the Sahara; red symbolizes the blood shed in the struggle for independence

National symbol(s): five-pointed star between the horns of a horizontal crescent moon; national colors: green, yellow

National anthem: *name:* "Bilāda l-'ubāti l- hudāti l-kirām" (Land of the Proud, Guided by Noblemen)
lyrics/music: unknown/traditional, Rageh DAOUD
note: adopted 16 November 2017

National heritage: *total World Heritage Sites:* 2 (1 cultural, 1 natural)
selected World Heritage Site locales: Ancient Ksour (Fortified Villages) of Ouadane, Chinguetti, Tichitt, and Oualata (c); Banc d'Arguin National Park (n)

ECONOMY

Economic overview: Mauritania's economy is dominated by extractive industries (oil and mines), fisheries, livestock, agriculture, and services. Half the population still depends on farming and raising livestock, even though many nomads and subsistence farmers were forced into the cities by recurrent droughts in the 1970s, 1980s, 2000s, and 2017. Recently, GDP growth has been driven largely by foreign investment in the mining and oil sectors.

Mauritania's extensive mineral resources include iron ore, gold, copper, gypsum, and phosphate rock, and exploration is ongoing for tantalum, uranium, crude oil, and natural gas. Extractive commodities make up about three-quarters of Mauritania's total exports, subjecting the economy to price swings in world commodity markets. Mining is also a growing source of government revenue, rising from 13% to 30% of total revenue from 2006 to 2014. The nation's coastal waters are among the richest fishing areas in the world, and fishing accounts for about 15% of budget revenues, 45% of foreign currency earnings. Mauritania processes a total of 1,800,000 tons of fish per year, but overexploitation by foreign and national fleets threaten the sustainability of this key source of revenue.

The economy is highly sensitive to international food and extractive commodity prices. Other risks to Mauritania's economy include its recurring droughts, dependence on foreign aid and investment, and insecurity in neighboring Mali, as well as significant shortages of infrastructure, institutional capacity, and human capital. In December 2017, Mauritania and the IMF agreed to a three year agreement under the Extended Credit Facility to foster economic growth, maintain macroeconomic stability, and reduce poverty. Investment in agriculture and infrastructure are the largest components of the country's public expenditures.

Real GDP (purchasing power parity): $23.17 billion (2020 est.)
$23.52 billion (2019 est.)
$22.2 billion (2018 est.)
note: data are in 2017 dollars

Real GDP growth rate: 3.5% (2017 est.)
1.8% (2016 est.)
0.4% (2015 est.)

Real GDP per capita: $5,000 (2020 est.)
$5,200 (2019 est.)
$5,000 (2018 est.)
note: data are in 2017 dollars

GDP (official exchange rate): $706 million (2018 est.)

Inflation rate (consumer prices): 2.2% (2019 est.)
3.1% (2018 est.)
2.2% (2017 est.)

GDP - composition, by sector of origin: *agriculture:* 27.8% (2017 est.)
industry: 29.3% (2017 est.)
services: 42.9% (2017 est.)

GDP - composition, by end use: *household consumption:* 64.9% (2017 est.)
government consumption: 21.8% (2017 est.)
investment in fixed capital: 56.1% (2017 est.)
investment in inventories: -3.2% (2017 est.)
exports of goods and services: 39% (2017 est.)
imports of goods and services: -78.6% (2017 est.)

Agricultural products: rice, milk, goat milk, sheep milk, sorghum, mutton, beef, camel milk, camel meat, dates

Industries: fish processing, oil production, mining (iron ore, gold, copper)
note: gypsum deposits have never been exploited

Industrial production growth rate: 1% (2017 est.)

Labor force: 1.437 million (2017 est.)

Labor force - by occupation: *agriculture:* 50%
industry: 1.9%
services: 48.1% (2014 est.)

Unemployment rate: 10.2% (2017 est.)
10.1% (2016 est.)

Unemployment, youth ages 15-24: *total:* 21.1%
male: 18.8%
female: 24.9% (2017 est.)

Population below poverty line: 31% (2014 est.)

Gini Index coefficient - distribution of family income: 32.6 (2014 est.)
39 (2006 est.)

Household income or consumption by percentage share: *lowest 10%:* 2.5%
highest 10%: 29.5% (2000)

Budget: *revenues:* 1.354 billion (2017 est.)
expenditures: 1.396 billion (2017 est.)

Budget surplus (+) or deficit (-): -0.8% (of GDP) (2017 est.)

Public debt: 96.6% of GDP (2017 est.)
100% of GDP (2016 est.)

Taxes and other revenues: 27.4% (of GDP) (2017 est.)

Fiscal year: calendar year

Current account balance: -$711 million (2017 est.)
-$707 million (2016 est.)

Exports: $2.52 billion (2019 est.) note: data are in current year dollars
$2.06 billion (2018 est.) note: data are in current year dollars
$302 million (2017 est.)

Exports - partners: China 32%, Switzerland 13%, Spain 9%, Japan 9%, Italy 5% (2019)

Exports - commodities: iron ore, fish products, gold, mollusks, processed crustaceans (2019)

Imports: $3.68 billion (2019 est.) note: data are in current year dollars
$3.28 billion (2018 est.) note: data are in current year dollars
$319 million (2017 est.)

Imports - partners: China 26%, France 6%, Spain 6%, Morocco 6%, United Arab Emirates 5% (2019)

Imports - commodities: ships, aircraft, wheat, raw sugar, refined petroleum (2019)

Reserves of foreign exchange and gold: $875 million (31 December 2017 est.)
$849.3 million (31 December 2016 est.)

Debt - external: $4.15 billion (31 December 2017 est.)
$3.899 billion (31 December 2016 est.)

Exchange rates: ouguiyas (MRO) per US dollar -
363.6 (2017 est.)
352.37 (2016 est.)
352.37 (2015 est.)
319.7 (2014 est.)
299.5 (2013 est.)

ENERGY

Electricity access: *electrification - total population:* 32% (2019)
electrification - urban areas: 56% (2019)
electrification - rural areas: 4% (2019)

Electricity: *installed generating capacity:* 656,000 kW (2020 est.)
consumption: 1.577 billion kWh (2019 est.)
exports: 0 kWh (2019 est.)
imports: 0 kWh (2019 est.)
transmission/distribution losses: 245 million kWh (2019 est.)

Electricity generation sources: *fossil fuels:* 73.2% of total installed capacity (2020 est.)
solar: 8.1% of total installed capacity (2020 est.)
wind: 6.8% of total installed capacity (2020 est.)
hydroelectricity: 11.9% of total installed capacity (2020 est.)

Petroleum: *total petroleum production:* 0 bbl/day (2021 est.)
refined petroleum consumption: 27,500 bbl/day (2019 est.)
crude oil and lease condensate exports: 4,800 bbl/day (2018 est.)
crude oil and lease condensate imports: 0 bbl/day (2018 est.)
crude oil estimated reserves: 20 million barrels (2021 est.)

Refined petroleum products - imports: 17,290 bbl/day (2015 est.)

Natural gas: *proven reserves:* 28.317 billion cubic meters (2021 est.)

Carbon dioxide emissions: 4.041 million metric tonnes of CO2 (2019 est.)
from petroleum and other liquids: 4.041 million metric tonnes of CO2 (2019 est.)

Energy consumption per capita: 13.558 million Btu/person (2019 est.)

COMMUNICATIONS

Telephones - fixed lines: *total subscriptions:* 62,099 (2020 est.)
subscriptions per 100 inhabitants: 1 (2020 est.)

Telephones - mobile cellular: *total subscriptions:* 4,932,571 (2020 est.)
subscriptions per 100 inhabitants: 106 (2020 est.)

Telecommunication systems: *general assessment:* Mauritania's small population and low economic output has limited the country's ability to develop sustained growth in the telecom sector; low disposable income has restricted growth in the use of services, and thus of revenue which telcos can hope to gain from subscribers; this has impacted on their ability to invest in network upgrades and improvements to service offerings; this has been reflected in the repeated fines imposed against them by the regulator for failing to ensure a good quality of service; there are also practical challenges relating to transparency and tax burdens which have hindered foreign investment; financial support has been forthcoming from the government as well as the World Bank and European Investment Bank; their efforts have focused on implementing appropriate regulatory measures and promoting the further penetration of fixed-line broadband services by improving the national backbone network, ensuring connectivity to international telecom cables, and facilitating operator access to infrastructure; progress has been made to improve internet bandwidth capacity, including the completion of a cable link at the border with Algeria, and the connection to the EllaLink submarine cable; the final stage of the national backbone network was completed in December 2021, which now runs to some 4,000km; penetration of fixed telephony and broadband service is very low and is expected to remain so in coming years, though growth is anticipated following improvements to backbone infrastructure and the reduction in access pricing; most voice and data services are carried over the mobile networks (2022)
domestic: fixed-line teledensity roughly 1 per 100 persons; mobile-cellular network coverage extends mainly to urban areas with a teledensity of roughly 106 per 100 persons; mostly cable and open-wire lines; a domestic satellite telecommunications system links Nouakchott with regional capitals (2020)
international: country code - 222; landing point for the ACE submarine cable for connectivity to 19 West African countries and 2 European countries; satellite earth stations - 3 (1 Intelsat - Atlantic Ocean, 2 Arabsat) (2019)

Broadcast media: 12 TV stations: 6 government-owned and 6 private (the 6th was started in early 2022, owed by the President of Mauritanian Businessmen); in October 2017, the government suspended most private TV stations due to non-payment of broadcasting fees, but they later negotiated payment options with the government and are back since 2019. There are 19 radio broadcasters: 15 government-owned, 4 (Radio Nouakchott Libre, Radio Tenwir, Radio Kobeni and Mauritanid) private; all 4 private radio stations broadcast from Nouakchott; of the 15 government stations, 4 broadcast from Nouakchott (Radio Mauritanie, Radio Jeunesse, Radio Koran and Mauritanid) and the other 12 broadcast from each of the 12 regions outside Nouakchott; Radio Jeunesse and Radio Koran are now also being re-broadcast in all the regions. (2022)

Internet country code: .mr

Internet users: *total:* 1,906,360 (2020 est.)
percent of population: 41% (2020 est.)

Broadband - fixed subscriptions: *total:* 18,457 (2020 est.)
subscriptions per 100 inhabitants: 0.4 (2020 est.)

TRANSPORTATION

National air transport system: *number of registered air carriers:* 1 (2020)
inventory of registered aircraft operated by air carriers: 6
annual passenger traffic on registered air carriers: 454,435 (2018)

Civil aircraft registration country code prefix: 5T

Airports: *total:* 30 (2021)

Airports - with paved runways: *total:* 9
2,438 to 3,047 m: 5
1,524 to 2,437 m: 4 (2021)

Airports - with unpaved runways: *total:* 21
2,438 to 3,047 m: 1
1,524 to 2,437 m: 10
914 to 1,523 m: 8
under 914 m: 2 (2021)

Railways: *total:* 728 km (2014)
standard gauge: 728 km (2014) 1.435-m gauge

Roadways: *total:* 12,253 km (2018)
paved: 3,988 km (2018)
unpaved: 8,265 km (2018)

Waterways: 1,086 km (2022) (some navigation possible on the Senegal River)

Merchant marine: *total:* 5
by type: general cargo 2, other 3 (2021)

Ports and terminals: *major seaport(s):* Nouadhibou, Nouakchott

MILITARY AND SECURITY

Military and security forces: Mauritanian Armed Forces: National Army, Mauritanian Navy (Marine Mauritanienne), Islamic Republic of Mauritania Air Group (Groupement Aerienne Islamique de Mauritanie, GAIM); Gendarmerie (Ministry of Defense); Ministry of Interior and Decentralization: National Police, National Guard, General Group for Road Safety (2022)
note 1: the National Police is responsible for enforcing the law and maintaining order in urban areas, while the Gendarmerie is responsible for maintaining civil order around metropolitan areas and providing law enforcement services in rural areas
note 2: the National Guard performs a limited police function in keeping with its peacetime role of providing security at government facilities, to include prisons; regional authorities may call upon the National Guard to restore civil order during riots and other large-scale disturbances
note 3: the General Group for Road Safety maintains security on roads and operates checkpoints throughout the country

Military expenditures: 2.5% of GDP (2022 est.)
2.4% of GDP (2021 est.)
2.5% of GDP (2020 est.)
2.1% of GDP (2019 est.) (approximately $440 million)
2.3% of GDP (2018 est.) (approximately $430 million)

Military and security service personnel strengths: approximately 16,000 active armed forces personnel (15,000 Army; 700 Navy; 300 Air Force); estimated 3,000 Gendarmerie; estimated 2,000 National Guard (2022)

Military equipment inventories and acquisitions: the Mauritanian Armed Forces' inventory is limited and made up largely of older French and Soviet-era equipment; since 2010, Mauritania has received a limited amount of mostly second-hand military equipment from a variety of suppliers, with China as the leading provider (2022)

Military service age and obligation: 18 is the legal minimum age for voluntary military service; no conscription (2022)

Military deployments: 470 (plus about 320 police) Central African Republic (MINUSCA) (May 2022)
note: Mauritania is part of a four (formerly five)-nation anti-jihadist task force known as the G4 Sahel Group, set up in 2014 with Burkina Faso, Chad, Mali (withdrew in 2022), and Niger; it has committed 550 troops and 100 gendarmes to the force; as of 2020, defense forces from each of the participating states were allowed to pursue terrorist fighters up to 100 km into neighboring countries; the force is backed by France, the UN, and the US

Military - note: since a spate of terrorist attacks in the 2000s, including a 2008 attack on a military base in the country's north that resulted in the deaths of 12 soldiers, the Mauritanian Government has increased the defense budget and military equipment acquisitions, enhanced military training, heightened security cooperation with its neighbors and the international community, and built up the military's special operations and civil-military affairs forces (2022)

TERRORISM

Terrorist group(s): Al-Qa'ida in the Islamic Maghreb (AQIM)

TRANSNATIONAL ISSUES

Disputes - international: *Mauritania-Algeria:* none identified
Mauritania-Mali: there are no border disputes, but the border has not been demarcated; talks on demarcation were reportedly being held in February 2022
Mauritania-Morocco: Mauritanian claims to Western Sahara remain dormant; tensions arose in 2016 when Mauritanian soldiers were deployed to Lagouira, a city in the southernmost part of Morocco, and raised their flag
Mauritania-Senegal: none identified

Refugees and internally displaced persons: *refugees (country of origin):* 26,001 (Sahrawis) (mid-year 2021); 97,127 (Mali) (2022)

Trafficking in persons: *current situation:* Mauritania is a source, transit, and destination country for men, women, and children subjected to conditions of forced labor and sex trafficking; adults and children from traditional slave castes are subjected to slavery-related practices rooted in ancestral master-slave relationships; Mauritanian boys are trafficked within the country by religious teachers for forced begging; Mauritanian girls, as well as girls from Mali, Senegal, The Gambia, and other West African countries, are forced into domestic servitude; Mauritanian women and girls are forced into prostitution in the country or transported to countries in the Middle East for the same purpose
tier rating: Tier 2 Watch List — Mauritania does not fully meet the minimum standards for the elimination of trafficking but is making significant efforts to do so and was upgraded to Tier 2 Watch List; the government convicted five hereditary slaveholders, drafted new anti-trafficking legislation and a national action plan, raised awareness on child forced begging in Quranic schools with imams and religious leaders by establishing an inter-ministerial committee, published a child protection guide, and operated a cash transfer program; however, the government rarely imprisoned convicted slaveholders and did not identify any victims; government agencies lacked resources; government officials refuse to investigate or prosecute political offenders (2020)

Illicit drugs: NA

MAURITIUS

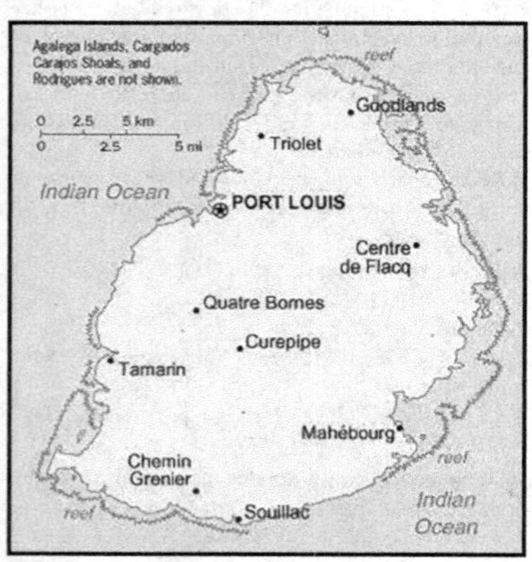

INTRODUCTION

Background: Although known to Arab and European sailors since at least the early 1500s, the island of Mauritius was uninhabited until 1638 when the Dutch established a settlement named in honor of Prince Maurits van NASSAU. Their presence led to the rapid disappearance of the flightless dodo bird that has since become one of the most well-known examples of extinction in modern times. The Dutch abandoned their financially distressed settlement in 1710, although a number of formerly enslaved people remained. In 1722, the French established what would become a highly profitable settlement focused on sugar cane plantations that were reliant on the labor of enslaved people brought to Mauritius from other parts of Africa. In the 1790s, the island had a brief period of autonomous rule when plantation owners rejected French control because of laws ending slavery that were temporarily in effect during the French Revolution. Britain captured the Island in 1810 as part of the Napoleonic Wars but kept most of the French administrative structure, which remains to this day in the form of the country's legal codes and widespread use of the French Creole language. The abolition of slavery in 1835 - later than most other British colonies - led to increased reliance on contracted laborers from the Indian subcontinent to work on plantations. Today their descendants form the majority of the population. Mauritius remained a strategically important British naval base, and later an air station, playing a role during World War II for anti-submarine and convoy operations, as well as for the collection of signals intelligence.

Mauritius gained independence from the UK in 1968 as a Parliamentary Republic and has remained a stable democracy with regular free elections and a positive human rights record. The country also attracted considerable foreign investment and now has one of Africa's highest per capita incomes. Mauritius' often fractious coalition politics has been dominated by two prominent families each of which has had father-son pairs who have been prime minister over multiple, often nonconsecutive, terms. Seewoosagur RAMGOOLAM (1968-76) was Mauritius' first prime minister and he was succeeded by Anerood JUGNAUTH (1982-95, 2000-03, 2014-17); his son Navin RAMGOOLAM (1995-2000, 2005-14); and Paul Raymond BERENGER (2003-05), the only non-Hindu prime minister of post-independence Mauritius. In 2017, Pravind JUGNAUTH became prime minister after his father stepped down short of completing his term, and he was elected in his own right in 2019. Mauritius claims the French island of Tromelin and the British Chagos Archipelago (British Indian Ocean Territory). Since 2017, Mauritius has secured favorable UN General Assembly resolutions and an International Court of Justice advisory opinion relating to its sovereignty dispute with the UK.

GEOGRAPHY

Location: Southern Africa, island in the Indian Ocean, about 800 km (500 mi) east of Madagascar

Geographic coordinates: 20 17 S, 57 33 E

Map references: Africa

Area: *total:* 2,040 sq km
land: 2,030 sq km
water: 10 sq km
note: includes Agalega Islands, Cargados Carajos Shoals (Saint Brandon), and Rodrigues

Area - comparative: almost 11 times the size of Washington, DC

Land boundaries: *total:* 0 km

Coastline: 177 km

Maritime claims: *territorial sea:* 12 nm
exclusive economic zone: 200 nm
continental shelf: 200 nm or to the edge of the continental margin
measured from claimed archipelagic straight baselines

Climate: tropical, modified by southeast trade winds; warm, dry winter (May to November); hot, wet, humid summer (November to May)

Terrain: small coastal plain rising to discontinuous mountains encircling central plateau

Elevation: *highest point:* Mont Piton 828 m
lowest point: Indian Ocean 0 m

Natural resources: arable land, fish

Land use: *agricultural land:* 43.8% (2018 est.)
arable land: 38.4% (2018 est.)
permanent crops: 2% (2018 est.)
permanent pasture: 3.4% (2018 est.)
forest: 17.3% (2018 est.)
other: 38.9% (2018 est.)

Irrigated land: 190 sq km (2012)

Population distribution: population density is one of the highest in the world; urban cluster are found throught the main island, with a greater density in and around Port Luis; population on Rodrigues Island is spread across the island with a slightly denser cluster on the north coast as shown in this population distribution map

Natural hazards: cyclones (November to April); almost completely surrounded by reefs that may pose maritime hazards

Geography - note: the main island, from which the country derives its name, is of volcanic origin and is almost entirely surrounded by coral reefs; former home of the dodo, a large flightless bird related to pigeons, driven to extinction by the end of the 17th century through a combination of hunting and the introduction of predatory species

PEOPLE AND SOCIETY

Population: 1,308,222 (2022 est.)

Nationality: *noun:* Mauritian(s)
adjective: Mauritian

Ethnic groups: Indo-Mauritian (compose approximately two thirds of the total population), Creole, Sino-Mauritian, Franco-Mauritian
note: Mauritius has not had a question on ethnicity on its national census since 1972

Languages: Creole 86.5%, Bhojpuri 5.3%, French 4.1%, two languages 1.4%, other 2.6% (includes English, one of the two official languages of the National Assembly, which is spoken by less than 1% of the population), unspecified 0.1% (2011 est.)

Religions: Hindu 48.5%, Roman Catholic 26.3%, Muslim 17.3%, other Christian 6.4%, other 0.6%, none 0.7%, unspecified 0.1% (2011 est.)

Demographic profile: Mauritius has transitioned from a country of high fertility and high mortality rates in the 1950s and mid-1960s to one with among the lowest population growth rates in the developing world today. After World War II, Mauritius' population began to expand quickly due to increased fertility and a dramatic drop in mortality rates as a result of improved health care and the eradication of malaria. This period of heightened population growth – reaching about 3% a year – was followed by one of the world's most rapid birth rate declines.

The total fertility rate fell from 6.2 children per women in 1963 to 3.2 in 1972 – largely the result of improved educational attainment, especially among young women, accompanied by later marriage and the adoption of family planning methods. The family planning programs' success was due to support from the government and eventually the traditionally pronatalist religious communities, which both recognized that controlling population growth was necessary because of Mauritius' small size and limited resources. Mauritius' fertility rate has consistently been below replacement level since the late 1990s, a rate that is substantially lower than nearby countries in southern Africa.

With no indigenous population, Mauritius' ethnic mix is a product of more than two centuries of European colonialism and continued international labor migration. Sugar production relied on slave labor mainly from Madagascar, Mozambique, and East Africa from the early 18th century until its abolition in 1835, when slaves were replaced with indentured Indians. Most of the influx of indentured labor – peaking between the late 1830s and early 1860s – settled permanently creating massive population growth of more than 7% a year and reshaping the island's social and cultural composition. While Indians represented about 12% of Mauritius' population in 1837, they and their descendants accounted for roughly two-thirds by the end of the 19th century. Most were Hindus, but the majority of the free Indian traders were Muslims.

Mauritius again turned to overseas labor when its success in clothing and textile exports led to a labor shortage in the mid-1980s. Clothing manufacturers brought in contract workers (increasingly women) from China, India, and, to a lesser extent Bangladesh and Madagascar, who worked longer hours for lower wages under poor conditions and were viewed as more productive than locals. Downturns in the sugar and textile industries in the mid-2000s and a lack of highly qualified domestic workers for Mauritius' growing services sector led to the emigration of low-skilled workers and a reliance on skilled foreign labor. Since 2007, Mauritius has pursued a circular migration program to enable citizens to acquire new skills and savings abroad and then return home to start businesses and to invest in the country's development.

Age structure: *0-14 years:* 19.44% (male 137,010/female 131,113)
15-24 years: 14.06% (male 98,480/female 95,472)
25-54 years: 43.11% (male 297,527/female 297,158)
55-64 years: 12.31% (male 80,952/female 88,785)
65 years and over: 11.08% (male 63,230/female 89,638) (2020 est.)

Dependency ratios: *total dependency ratio:* 41.5
youth dependency ratio: 23.7
elderly dependency ratio: 17.7
potential support ratio: 5.6 (2020 est.)

Median age: *total:* 36.3 years
male: 35 years
female: 37.6 years (2020 est.)

Population growth rate: 0.1% (2022 est.)

Birth rate: 9.86 births/1,000 population (2022 est.)

Death rate: 8.86 deaths/1,000 population (2022 est.)

Net migration rate: 0 migrant(s)/1,000 population (2022 est.)

Population distribution: population density is one of the highest in the world; urban cluster are found throught the main island, with a greater density in and around Port Luis; population on Rodrigues Island is spread across the island with a slightly denser cluster on the north coast as shown in this population distribution map

Urbanization: *urban population:* 40.8% of total population (2022)
rate of urbanization: 0.28% annual rate of change (2020-25 est.)

Major urban areas - population: 149,000 PORT LOUIS (capital) (2018)

Sex ratio: *at birth:* 1.07 male(s)/female
0-14 years: 1.05 male(s)/female
15-24 years: 1.03 male(s)/female
25-54 years: 1 male(s)/female
55-64 years: 0.9 male(s)/female
65 years and over: 0.47 male(s)/female
total population: 0.95 male(s)/female (2022 est.)

Maternal mortality ratio: 61 deaths/100,000 live births (2017 est.)

Infant mortality rate: *total:* 12.08 deaths/1,000 live births
male: 13.63 deaths/1,000 live births
female: 10.43 deaths/1,000 live births (2022 est.)

Life expectancy at birth: *total population:* 74.86 years
male: 72.04 years
female: 77.88 years (2022 est.)

Total fertility rate: 1.35 children born/woman (2022 est.)

Contraceptive prevalence rate: 63.8% (2014)

Drinking water source: *improved: urban:* 99.9% of population
rural: 99.8% of population
total: 99.9% of population
unimproved: urban: 0.1% of population
rural: 0.2% of population
total: 0.1% of population (2020 est.)

Current health expenditure: 6.2% of GDP (2019)

Physicians density: 2.71 physicians/1,000 population (2020)

Hospital bed density: 3.7 beds/1,000 population (2020)

Sanitation facility access: *improved: urban:* 99.9% of population
unimproved: urban: 0.1% of population

HIV/AIDS - adult prevalence rate: 1.7% (2020 est.)

Obesity - adult prevalence rate: 10.8% (2016)

Alcohol consumption per capita: *total:* 3.39 liters of pure alcohol (2019 est.)
beer: 1.94 liters of pure alcohol (2019 est.)
wine: 0.23 liters of pure alcohol (2019 est.)
spirits: 0.88 liters of pure alcohol (2019 est.)
other alcohols: 0.03 liters of pure alcohol (2019 est.)

Tobacco use: *total:* 20.2% (2020 est.)
male: 37.3% (2020 est.)
female: 3% (2020 est.)

Education expenditures: 4.6% of GDP (2020 est.)

Literacy: *definition:* age 15 and over can read and write
total population: 91.3%
male: 93.4%
female: 89.4% (2018)

School life expectancy (primary to tertiary education): *total:* 15 years
male: 14 years
female: 16 years (2017)

Unemployment, youth ages 15-24: *total:* 21.8%
male: 16.8%
female: 28.4% (2019 est.)

ENVIRONMENT

Environment - current issues: water pollution, degradation of coral reefs; soil erosion; wildlife preservation; solid waste disposal

Environment - international agreements: *party to:* Antarctic-Marine Living Resources, Biodiversity, Climate Change, Climate Change-Kyoto Protocol, Climate Change-Paris Agreement, Desertification, Endangered Species, Environmental Modification, Hazardous Wastes, Law of the Sea, Marine Life Conservation, Nuclear Test Ban, Ozone Layer Protection, Ship Pollution, Wetlands
signed, but not ratified: none of the selected agreements

Air pollutants: *particulate matter emissions:* 13.54 micrograms per cubic meter (2016 est.)
carbon dioxide emissions: 4.35 megatons (2016 est.)
methane emissions: 2.06 megatons (2020 est.)

Climate: tropical, modified by southeast trade winds; warm, dry winter (May to November); hot, wet, humid summer (November to May)

Land use: *agricultural land:* 43.8% (2018 est.)
arable land: 38.4% (2018 est.)
permanent crops: 2% (2018 est.)
permanent pasture: 3.4% (2018 est.)
forest: 17.3% (2018 est.)

other: 38.9% (2018 est.)

Urbanization: *urban population:* 40.8% of total population (2022)
rate of urbanization: 0.28% annual rate of change (2020-25 est.)

Revenue from forest resources: *forest revenues:* 0% of GDP (2018 est.)

Revenue from coal: *coal revenues:* 0% of GDP (2018 est.)

Waste and recycling: *municipal solid waste generated annually:* 438,000 tons (2016 est.)

Total water withdrawal: *municipal:* 260 million cubic meters (2017 est.)
industrial: 12 million cubic meters (2017 est.)
agricultural: 344 million cubic meters (2017 est.)

Total renewable water resources: 2.751 billion cubic meters (2017 est.)

GOVERNMENT

Country name: *conventional long form:* Republic of Mauritius
conventional short form: Mauritius
local long form: Republic of Mauritius
local short form: Mauritius
etymology: island named after Prince Maurice VAN NASSAU, stadtholder of the Dutch Republic, in 1598
note: pronounced mah-rish-us

Government type: parliamentary republic

Capital: *name:* Port Louis
geographic coordinates: 20 09 S, 57 29 E
time difference: UTC+4 (9 hours ahead of Washington, DC, during Standard Time)
etymology: named after LOUIS XV, who was king of France in 1736 when the port became the administrative center of Mauritius and a major reprovisioning stop for French ships traveling between Europe and Asia

Administrative divisions: 9 districts and 3 dependencies*; Agalega Islands*, Black River, Cargados Carajos Shoals*, Flacq, Grand Port, Moka, Pamplemousses, Plaines Wilhems, Port Louis, Riviere du Rempart, Rodrigues*, Savanne

Independence: 12 March 1968 (from the UK)

National holiday: Independence and Republic Day, 12 March (1968 & 1992); note - became independent and a republic on the same date in 1968 and 1992 respectively

Constitution: *history:* several previous; latest adopted 12 March 1968
amendments: proposed by the National Assembly; passage of amendments affecting constitutional articles, including the sovereignty of the state, fundamental rights and freedoms, citizenship, or the branches of government, requires approval in a referendum by at least three-fourths majority of voters followed by a unanimous vote by the Assembly; passage of other amendments requires only two-thirds majority vote by the Assembly; amended many times, last in 2016

Legal system: civil legal system based on French civil law with some elements of English common law

International law organization participation: accepts compulsory ICJ jurisdiction with reservations; accepts ICCt jurisdiction

Citizenship: *citizenship by birth:* yes
citizenship by descent only: yes
dual citizenship recognized: yes
residency requirement for naturalization: 5 out of the previous 7 years including the last 12 months

Suffrage: 18 years of age; universal

Executive branch: *chief of state:* President Pritivirajsing ROOPUN (since 2 December 2019); Vice President Marie Cyril EDDY Boissézon (since 2 December 2019); note - President Ameenah GURIB-FAKIM, the country's first female president, resigned on 23 March 2018 amid a credit card scandal; Acting Presidents served from March 2018 until ROOPUN's appointment in 2019
head of government: Prime Minister Pravind JUGNAUTH (since 23 January 2017); note - Prime Minister Sir Anerood JUGNAUTH stepped down on 23 January 2017 in favor of his son, Pravind Kumar JUGNAUTH, who was then appointed prime minister; following 7 November 2019 parliamentary elections, Pravind JUGNAUTH remained prime minister and home affairs minister and also became defense minister
cabinet: Cabinet of Ministers (Council of Ministers) appointed by the president on the recommendation of the prime minister
elections/appointments: president and vice president indirectly elected by the National Assembly for 5-year renewable terms; election last held on 7 November 2019 (next to be held in 2024); the president appoints the prime minister and deputy prime minister who have the majority support in the National Assembly
election results:
2019: Pritivirajsing ROOPUN (MSM) elected president by the National Assembly - unanimous vote; note - GURIB-FAKIM resigned on 23 March 2018
2015: Ameenah GURIB-FAKIM (independent) elected president by the National Assembly - unanimous vote; note -GURIB-FAKIM was Mauritius' first female president

Legislative branch: *description:* unicameral National Assembly or Assemblee Nationale (70 seats maximum; 62 members directly elected multi-seat constituencies by simple majority vote and up to 8 seats allocated to non-elected party candidates by the Office of Electoral Commissioner; members serve a 5-year term)
elections:
last held on 7 November 2019 (next to be held by late 2024)
election results:
percent of vote by party - MSM 61%, Mauritius Labour Party 23%, MMM 13%, OPR 3%; elected seats by party as of - the Militant Socialist Movement (MSM) wins 38 seats, the Mauritius Labour Party (PTR) or (MLP) 14, Mauritian Militant Movement (MMM) 8 and the Rodrigues People's Organization (OPR) 2; composition as of July 2022 -men 56, women 14, percent of women 20% (2019)

Judicial branch: *highest court(s):* Supreme Court of Mauritius (consists of the chief justice, a senior puisne judge, and 24 puisne judges); note - the Judicial Committee of the Privy Council (in London) serves as the final court of appeal
judge selection and term of office: chief justice appointed by the president after consultation with the prime minister; senior puisne judge appointed by the president with the advice of the chief justice; other puisne judges appointed by the president with the advice of the Judicial and Legal Commission, a 4-member body of judicial officials including the chief justice; all judges serve until retirement at age 67
subordinate courts: lower regional courts known as District Courts, Court of Civil Appeal; Court of Criminal Appeal; Public Bodies Appeal Tribunal

Political parties and leaders: Alliance Morisien (Mauritian Alliance 2019; coalition includes PM, MSM, ML, and MAG) [Pravind JUGNAUTH]
Mauritian Militant Movement (Mouvement Militant Mauricien) or MMM [Paul BERENGER]
Mauritian Social Democratic Party (Parti Mauricien Social Democrate) or PMSD [Xavier Luc DUVAL]
Mauritius Labor Party (Parti Travailliste) or PTR or MLP [Navinchandra RAMGOOLAM]
Militant Platform or PM (Plateforme Militante) [Steven OBEEGADOO]
Militant Socialist Movement (Mouvement Socialist Mauricien) or MSM [Pravind JUGNAUTH]
Muvman Liberater or ML [Ivan COLLENDAVELLOO]
National Alliance (coalition includes PTR and PMSD) [Navinchandra RAMGOOLAM]
Patriotic Movement (Mouvement Patriotique) or MAG [Alan GANOO]
Rodrigues Peoples Organization (Organisation du Peuple Rodriguais) or OPR [Serge CLAIR]
note: only parties with seats in the National Assembly listed

International organization participation: ACP, AfDB, AOSIS, AU, C, CD, COMESA, CPLP (associate), FAO, G-77, IAEA, IBRD, ICAO, ICC (NGOs), ICCt, ICRM, IDA, IFAD, IFC, IFRCS, IHO, ILO, IMF, IMO, IMSO, InOC, Interpol, IOC, IOM, IPU, ISO, ITSO, ITU, ITUC (NGOs), MIGA, NAM, OIF, OPCW, PCA, SAARC (observer), SADC, UN, UNCTAD, UNESCO, UNIDO, UNWTO, UPU, WCO, WFTU (NGOs), WHO, WIPO, WMO, WTO

Diplomatic representation in the US: *chief of mission:* Ambassador Purmanund JHUGROO (since 7 July 2021)
chancery: 1709 N Street NW, Washington, DC 20036; administrative offices at 3201 Connecticut Avenue NW, Suite 441, Washington, DC 20036
telephone: [1] (202) 244-1491; [1] (202) 244-1492
FAX: [1] (202) 966-0983
email address and website:
mauritius.embassy@verizon.net; washingtonemb@govmu.org
https://mauritius-washington.govmu.org/Pages/index.aspx

Diplomatic representation from the US: *chief of mission:* Ambassador (vacant); Charge d'Affaires Judes E. DEBAERE (since June 2019); note - also accredited to Seychelles
embassy: 4th Floor, Rogers House, John Kennedy Avenue, Port Louis
mailing address: 2450 Port Louis Place, Washington, DC 20521-2450
telephone: [230] 202-4400
FAX: [230] 208-9534
email address and website:
PTLConsular@state.gov
https://mu.usembassy.gov/

Flag description: four equal horizontal bands of red (top), blue, yellow, and green; red represents self-determination and independence, blue the Indian Ocean surrounding the island, yellow has been interpreted as the new light of independence,

golden sunshine, or the bright future, and green can symbolize either agriculture or the lush vegetation of the island
note: while many national flags consist of three - and in some cases five - horizontal bands of color, the flag of Mauritius is the world's only national flag to consist of four horizontal color bands

National symbol(s): dodo bird, Trochetia Boutoniana flower; national colors: red, blue, yellow, green

National anthem: *name:* "Motherland"
lyrics/music: Jean Georges PROSPER/Philippe GENTIL
note: adopted 1968

National heritage: *total World Heritage Sites:* 2 (both cultural)
selected World Heritage Site locales: Aapravasi Ghat; Le Morne Cultural Landscape

ECONOMY

Economic overview: Since independence in 1968, Mauritius has undergone a remarkable economic transformation from a low-income, agriculturally based economy to a diversified, upper middle-income economy with growing industrial, financial, and tourist sectors. Mauritius has achieved steady growth over the last several decades, resulting in more equitable income distribution, increased life expectancy, lowered infant mortality, and a much-improved infrastructure.

The economy currently depends on sugar, tourism, textiles and apparel, and financial services, but is expanding into fish processing, information and communications technology, education, and hospitality and property development. Sugarcane is grown on about 90% of the cultivated land area but sugar makes up only around 3-4% of national GDP. Authorities plan to emphasize services and innovation in the coming years. After several years of slow growth, government policies now seek to stimulate economic growth in five areas: serving as a gateway for international investment into Africa; increasing the use of renewable energy; developing smart cities; growing the ocean economy; and upgrading and modernizing infrastructure, including public transportation, the port, and the airport.

Mauritius has attracted more than 32,000 offshore entities, many aimed at commerce in India, South Africa, and China. The Mauritius International Financial Center is under scrutiny by international bodies promoting fair tax competition and Mauritius has been cooperating with the European Union and the United states in the automatic exchange of account information. Mauritius is also a member of the OECD/G20's Inclusive Framework on Base Erosion and Profit Shifting and is under pressure to review its Double Taxation Avoidance Agreements. The offshore sector is vulnerable to changes in the tax framework and authorities have been working on a Financial Services Sector Blueprint to enable Mauritius to transition to a jurisdiction of higher value added. Mauritius' textile sector has taken advantage of the Africa Growth and Opportunity Act, a preferential trade program that allows duty free access to the US market, with Mauritian exports to the US growing by 35.6 % from 2000 to 2014. However, lack of local labor as well as rising labor costs eroding the competitiveness of textile firms in Mauritius.

Mauritius' sound economic policies and prudent banking practices helped mitigate negative effects of the global financial crisis in 2008-09. GDP grew in the 3-4% per year range in 2010-17, and the country continues to expand its trade and investment outreach around the globe. Growth in the US and Europe fostered goods and services exports, including tourism, while lower oil prices kept inflation low. Mauritius continues to rank as one of the most business-friendly environments on the continent and passed a Business Facilitation Act to improve competitiveness and long-term growth prospects. A new National Economic Development Board was set up in 2017-2018 to spearhead efforts to promote exports and attract inward investment.

Real GDP (purchasing power parity): $24.64 billion (2020 est.)
$28.95 billion (2019 est.)
$28.1 billion (2018 est.)
note: data are in 2017 dollars

Real GDP growth rate: 3.8% (2017 est.)
3.8% (2016 est.)
3.6% (2015 est.)

Real GDP per capita: $19,500 (2020 est.)
$22,900 (2019 est.)
$22,200 (2018 est.)
note: data are in 2017 dollars

GDP (official exchange rate): $14.004 billion (2019 est.)

Inflation rate (consumer prices): 0.4% (2019 est.)
3.2% (2018 est.)
3.6% (2017 est.)

Credit ratings:

Moody's rating: Baa1 (2012)
note: The year refers to the year in which the current credit rating was first obtained.

GDP - composition, by sector of origin: *agriculture:* 4% (2017 est.)
industry: 21.8% (2017 est.)
services: 74.1% (2017 est.)

GDP - composition, by end use: *household consumption:* 81% (2017 est.)
government consumption: 15.1% (2017 est.)
investment in fixed capital: 17.3% (2017 est.)
investment in inventories: -0.4% (2017 est.)
exports of goods and services: 42.1% (2017 est.)
imports of goods and services: -55.1% (2017 est.)

Agricultural products: sugar cane, poultry, pumpkins, gourds, potatoes, eggs, tomatoes, pineapples, bananas, fruit

Industries: food processing (largely sugar milling), textiles, clothing, mining, chemicals, metal products, transport equipment, nonelectrical machinery, tourism

Industrial production growth rate: 3.2% (2017 est.)

Labor force: 554,000 (2020 est.)

Labor force - by occupation: *agriculture:* 8%
industry: 29.8%
services: 62.2% (2014 est.)

Unemployment rate: 6.65% (2019 est.)
6.84% (2018 est.)

Unemployment, youth ages 15-24: *total:* 21.8%
male: 16.8%
female: 28.4% (2019 est.)

Population below poverty line: 10.3% (2017 est.)

Gini Index coefficient - distribution of family income: 36.8 (2017 est.)
39 (2006 est.)

Budget: *revenues:* 2.994 billion (2017 est.)
expenditures: 3.038 billion (2017 est.)

Budget surplus (+) or deficit (-): -0.3% (of GDP) (2017 est.)

Public debt: 64% of GDP (2017 est.)
66.1% of GDP (2016 est.)

Taxes and other revenues: 22.5% (of GDP) (2017 est.)

Fiscal year: 1 July - 30 June

Current account balance: -$875 million (2017 est.)
-$531 million (2016 est.)

Exports: $5.17 billion (2019 est.) note: data are in current year dollars
$5.59 billion (2018 est.) note: data are in current year dollars

Exports - partners: France 10%, South Africa 10%, United States 10%, United Kingdom 8%, Zambia 7%, Madagascar 6% (2019)

Exports - commodities: fish products, raw sugar, clothing and apparel, diamonds, refined petroleum (2019)

Imports: $7.41 billion (2019 est.) note: data are in current year dollars
$7.53 billion (2018 est.) note: data are in current year dollars

Imports - partners: China 15%, India 13%, France 10%, South Africa 8%, United Arab Emirates 7% (2019)

Imports - commodities: refined petroleum, cars, fish products, aircraft, packaged medicines (2019)

Reserves of foreign exchange and gold: $5.984 billion (31 December 2017 est.)
$4.967 billion (31 December 2016 est.)

Debt - external: $226.799 billion (2019 est.)
$232.17 billion (2018 est.)

Exchange rates: Mauritian rupees (MUR) per US dollar -
39.65 (2020 est.)
36.51 (2019 est.)
34.4 (2018 est.)
35.057 (2014 est.)
30.622 (2013 est.)

ENERGY

Electricity access: *electrification - total population:* 100% (2020)

Electricity: *installed generating capacity:* 936,000 kW (2020 est.)
consumption: 2,904,500,000 kWh (2019 est.)
exports: 0 kWh (2019 est.)
imports: 0 kWh (2019 est.)
transmission/distribution losses: 182.4 million kWh (2019 est.)

Electricity generation sources: *fossil fuels:* 75.4% of total installed capacity (2020 est.)
solar: 5.3% of total installed capacity (2020 est.)
wind: 0.7% of total installed capacity (2020 est.)
hydroelectricity: 3.7% of total installed capacity (2020 est.)
biomass and waste: 15% of total installed capacity (2020 est.)

Coal: *production:* 0 metric tons (2020 est.)
consumption: 661,000 metric tons (2020 est.)
exports: 0 metric tons (2020 est.)
imports: 1.189 million metric tons (2020 est.)

proven reserves: 0 metric tons (2019 est.)

Petroleum: *total petroleum production:* 0 bbl/day (2021 est.)
refined petroleum consumption: 36,700 bbl/day (2019 est.)

Refined petroleum products - imports: 26,960 bbl/day (2015 est.)

Carbon dioxide emissions: 7.191 million metric tonnes of CO_2 (2019 est.)
from coal and metallurgical coke: 1.595 million metric tonnes of CO_2 (2019 est.)
from petroleum and other liquids: 5.596 million metric tonnes of CO_2 (2019 est.)

Energy consumption per capita: 79.448 million Btu/person (2019 est.)

COMMUNICATIONS

Telephones - fixed lines: *total subscriptions:* 478,700 (2020 est.)
subscriptions per 100 inhabitants: 38 (2020 est.)

Telephones - mobile cellular: *total subscriptions:* 1,912,900 (2020 est.)
subscriptions per 100 inhabitants: 150 (2020 est.)

Telecommunication systems: *general assessment:* the telecom sector in Mauritius has long been supported by the varied needs of tourists; this has stimulated the mobile market, leading to a particularly high penetration rate; the response of the country's telcos to tourist requirements also contributed to the country being among the first in the region to provide services based on 3G and WiMAX technologies; the country has seen improved international internet capacity in recent years, with direct cables linking to India, Madagascar, and South Africa, as well as other connections to Rodrigues and Reunion; despite these advantages, some services remain slow; at the end of 2021, the median mobile data rate available was only 21Mb/s, ranking the country 84th of 138 monitored; the median fixed broadband data rate was about 19.8Mb/s, with a rank of 117th of 178 countries; mobile subscribers in Mauritius secured 5G services in mid-2021; this followed the regulator's award of spectrum in two bands to the MNOs; the award was made directly, rather than via an auction, since the regulator was keen to see services made available as soon as possible; this will help the government's ambition to make telecommunications a pillar of economic growth, and to have a fully digital-based infrastructure; such infrastructure will also contribute to a revival of tourism, the mainstay of the economy; although GDP growth returned in 2021, the number of tourist arrivals remains a fraction of the pre-pandemic level (2022)
domestic: fixed-line teledensity over 37 per 100 persons and mobile-cellular services teledensity roughly 150 per 100 persons (2020)
international: country code - 230; landing points for the SAFE, MARS, IOX Cable System, METISS and LION submarine cable system that provides links to Asia, Africa, Southeast Asia, Indian Ocean Islands of Reunion, Madagascar, and Mauritius; satellite earth station - 1 Intelsat (Indian Ocean); new microwave link to Reunion; HF radiotelephone links to several countries (2019)

Broadcast media: the government maintains control over TV broadcasting through the Mauritius Broadcasting Corporation (MBC), which only operates digital TV stations since June 2015; MBC is a shareholder in a local company that operates 2 pay-TV stations; the state retains the largest radio broadcast network with multiple stations; several private radio broadcasters have entered the market since 2001; transmissions of at least 2 international broadcasters are available (2019)

Internet country code: .mu

Internet users: *total:* 822,731 (2020 est.)
percent of population: 65% (2020 est.)

Broadband - fixed subscriptions: *total:* 323,200 (2020 est.)
subscriptions per 100 inhabitants: 25 (2020 est.)

TRANSPORTATION

National air transport system: *number of registered air carriers:* 1 (2020)
inventory of registered aircraft operated by air carriers: 13
annual passenger traffic on registered air carriers: 1,745,291 (2018)
annual freight traffic on registered air carriers: 233.72 million (2018) mt-km

Civil aircraft registration country code prefix: 3B

Airports: *total:* 5 (2021)

Airports - with paved runways: *total:* 2
over 3,047 m: 1
914 to 1,523 m: 1 (2021)

Airports - with unpaved runways: *total:* 3
914 to 1,523 m: 2
under 914 m: 1 (2021)

Roadways: *total:* 2,428 km (2015)
paved: 2,379 km (2015) (includes 99 km of expressways)
*unpaved:*49 km (2015)

Merchant marine: *total:* 29
by type: general cargo 1, oil tanker 4, other 24 (2021)

Ports and terminals: *major seaport(s):* Port Louis

MILITARY AND SECURITY

Military and security forces: no regular military forces; the Mauritius Police Force (MPF) under the Ministry of Defense includes a paramilitary unit known as the Special Mobile Force, which includes some motorized infantry and light armored units; the MPF also has a Police Helicopter Squadron, a Special Support Unit (riot police), and the National Coast Guard (also includes an air squadron) (2022)

Military expenditures: 0.2% of GDP (2021 est.)
0.2% of GDP (2020 est.)
0.3% of GDP (2019 est.) (approximately $80 million)
0.3% of GDP (2018 est.) (approximately $80 million)
0.3% of GDP (2017 est.) (approximately $80 million)

Military and security service personnel strengths: approximately 1,700 Special Mobile Force; approximately 800 National Coast Guard (2022)

Military equipment inventories and acquisitions: the MPF's inventory is comprised of mostly second-hand equipment from Western European countries and India; since 2010, India has been the primary supplier (2022)

Military service age and obligation: service is voluntary (2022)

Military - note: as of 2022, the country's primary security partner was India, and Indian naval vessels often patrol Mauritian waters; the MPF has also received assistance and training from France, the UK, and the US; the MPF's chief security concerns were piracy and narcotics trafficking
the Special Mobile Force was created in 1960 following the withdrawal of the British garrison (2022)

TRANSNATIONAL ISSUES

Disputes - international: Mauritius and Seychelles claim the Chagos Islands (UK-administered British Indian Ocean Territory); claims French-administered Tromelin Island
Mauritius-France: Mauritius has claimed French-administered Tromelin Island (part of the French Southern and Antarctic Lands) since 1976
Mauritius-UK: Mauritius and Seychelles claim the Chagos Islands (UK-administered British Indian Ocean Territory)

Illicit drugs: consumer and transshipment point for heroin from South Asia; small amounts of cannabis produced and consumed locally; significant offshore financial industry creates potential for money laundering

MEXICO

INTRODUCTION

Background: The site of several advanced Amerindian civilizations - including the Olmec, Toltec, Teotihuacan, Zapotec, Maya, and Aztec - Mexico was conquered and colonized by Spain in the early 16th century. Administered as the Viceroyalty of New Spain for three centuries, it achieved independence early in the 19th century. Elections held in 2000 marked the first time since the 1910 Mexican Revolution that an opposition candidate - Vicente FOX of the National Action Party (PAN) - defeated the party in government, the Institutional Revolutionary Party (PRI). He was succeeded in 2006 by another PAN candidate Felipe CALDERON, but Enrique PENA NIETO regained the presidency for the PRI in 2012. Left-leaning anti-establishment politician and former mayor of Mexico City (2000-05) Andres Manuel LOPEZ OBRADOR, from the National Regeneration Movement (MORENA), became president in December 2018.

The global financial crisis in late 2008 caused a massive economic downturn in Mexico the following

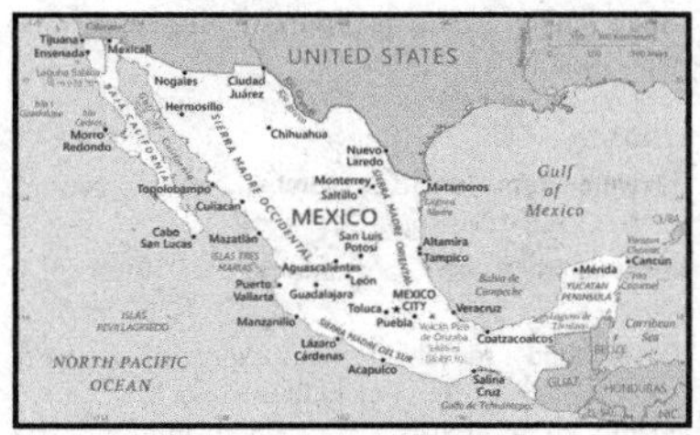

year. Growth rebounded to about 5% in 2010, but then averaged roughly half that for the rest of the decade. Notwithstanding this challenge, Mexico is currently the largest goods trading partner of the US – with $614.5 billion in two-way goods trade during 2019. US exports of goods and services to Mexico supported 1.2 million jobs in the US in 2015 (the latest data available) according to estimates from the Department of Commerce. Mexico's GDP contracted by 8.2% in 2020 due to pandemic-induced closures, its lowest level since the Great Depression, but Mexico's economy rebounded in 2021 when it grew by 4.8%, driven largely by increased remittances, despite supply chain and pandemic-related challenges.

The US-Mexico-Canada Agreement (USMCA, or T-MEC by its Spanish acronym) entered into force on 1 July 2020 and replaced its predecessor, the North American Free Trade Agreement (NAFTA). Mexico amended its constitution on 1 May 2019 to facilitate the implementation of the labor components of USMCA.

Ongoing economic and social concerns include low real wages, high underemployment, inequitable income distribution, and few advancement opportunities for the largely indigenous population in the impoverished southern states. Since 2007, Mexico's powerful transnational criminal organizations have engaged in a struggle to control criminal markets, resulting in tens of thousands of drug-related homicides and forced disappearances.

GEOGRAPHY

Location: North America, bordering the Caribbean Sea and the Gulf of Mexico, between Belize and the United States and bordering the North Pacific Ocean, between Guatemala and the United States

Geographic coordinates: 23 00 N, 102 00 W

Map references: North America

Area: *total:* 1,964,375 sq km
land: 1,943,945 sq km
water: 20,430 sq km

Area - comparative: slightly less than three times the size of Texas

Land boundaries: *total:* 4,389 km
border countries (3): Belize 276 km; Guatemala 958 km; US 3,155 km

Coastline: 9,330 km

Maritime claims: *territorial sea:* 12 nm
contiguous zone: 24 nm
exclusive economic zone: 200 nm
continental shelf: 200 nm or to the edge of the continental margin

Climate: varies from tropical to desert

Terrain: high, rugged mountains; low coastal plains; high plateaus; desert

Elevation: *highest point:* Volcan Pico de Orizaba 5,636 m
lowest point: Laguna Salada -10 m
mean elevation: 1,111 m

Natural resources: petroleum, silver, antimony, copper, gold, lead, zinc, natural gas, timber

Land use: *agricultural land:* 54.9% (2018 est.)
arable land: 11.8% (2018 est.)
permanent crops: 1.4% (2018 est.)
permanent pasture: 41.7% (2018 est.)
forest: 33.3% (2018 est.)
other: 11.8% (2018 est.)

Irrigated land: 65,000 sq km (2012)

Major lakes (area sq km): *fresh water lake(s):* Laguna de Chapala - 1,140 sq km
salt water lake(s): Laguna de Terminos - 1,550 sq km

Major rivers (by length in km): Rio Grande river mouth (shared with US [s]) - 3,057 km; Colorado river mouth (shared with US [s]) - 2,333 km
note – [s] after country name indicates river source; [m] after country name indicates river mouth

Major watersheds (area sq km): Atlantic Ocean drainage: *(Gulf of Mexico)* Rio Grande/Bravo (607,965 sq km)
Pacific Ocean drainage: *(Gulf of California)* Colorado (703,148 sq km)

Major aquifers: Atlantic and Gulf Coastal Plains Aquifer

Population distribution: most of the population is found in the middle of the country between the states of Jalisco and Veracruz; approximately a quarter of the population lives in and around Mexico City

Natural hazards: tsunamis along the Pacific coast, volcanoes and destructive earthquakes in the center and south, and hurricanes on the Pacific, Gulf of Mexico, and Caribbean coasts
volcanism: volcanic activity in the central-southern part of the country; the volcanoes in Baja California are mostly dormant; Colima (3,850 m), which erupted in 2010, is Mexico's most active volcano and is responsible for causing periodic evacuations of nearby villagers; it has been deemed a Decade Volcano by the International Association of Volcanology and Chemistry of the Earth's Interior, worthy of study due to its explosive history and close proximity to human populations; Popocatepetl (5,426 m) poses a threat to Mexico City; other historically active volcanoes include Barcena, Ceboruco, El Chichon, Michoacan-Guanajuato, Pico de Orizaba, San Martin, Socorro, and Tacana; see note 2 under "Geography - note"

Geography - note: *note 1:* strategic location on southern border of the US; Mexico is one of the countries along the Ring of Fire, a belt of active volcanoes and earthquake epicenters bordering the Pacific Ocean; up to 90% of the world's earthquakes and some 75% of the world's volcanoes occur within the Ring of Fire
note 2: some of the world's most important food crops were first domesticated in Mexico; the "Three Sisters" companion plants -winter squash, maize (corn), and climbing beans - served as the main agricultural crops for various North American Indian groups; all three apparently originated in Mexico but then were widely disseminated through much of North America; avocado, amaranth, and chili peppers also emanate from Mexico, as does vanilla, the world's most popular aroma and flavor spice; although cherry tomatoes originated in Ecuador, their domestication in Mexico transformed them into the larger modern tomato
note 3: the Sac Actun cave system at 348 km (216 mi) is the longest underwater cave in the world and the second longest cave worldwide, after Mammoth Cave in the United States (see "Geography - note" under United States)
note 4: the prominent Yucatan Peninsula that divides the Gulf of Mexico from the Caribbean Sea is shared by Mexico, Guatemala, and Belize; just on the northern coast of Yucatan, near the town of Chicxulub (pronounce cheek-sha-loob), lie the remnants of a massive crater (some 150 km in diameter and extending well out into the Gulf of Mexico); formed by an asteroid or comet when it struck the earth 66 million years ago, the impact is now widely accepted as initiating a worldwide climate disruption that caused a mass extinction of 75% of all the earth's plant and animal species - including the non-avian dinosaurs

PEOPLE AND SOCIETY

Population: 129,150,971 (2022 est.)

Nationality: *noun:* Mexican(s)
adjective: Mexican

Ethnic groups: Mestizo (Amerindian-Spanish) 62%, predominantly Amerindian 21%, Amerindian 7%, other 10% (mostly European) (2012 est.)
note: Mexico does not collect census data on ethnicity

Languages: Spanish only 93.8%, Spanish and indigenous languages 5.4%, indigenous only 0.6%, unspecified 0.2%; note -indigenous languages include various Mayan, Nahuatl, and other regional languages (2020 est.)
major-language sample(s): La Libreta Informativa del Mundo, la fuente indispensable de información básica. (Spanish)

Religions: Roman Catholic 78%, Protestant/evangelical Christian 11.2%, other 0.002%, unaffiliated (includes atheism) 10.6% (2020 est.)

Age structure: *0-14 years:* 26.01% (male 17,111,199/female 16,349,767)
15-24 years: 16.97% (male 11,069,260/female 10,762,784)
25-54 years: 41.06% (male 25,604,223/female 27,223,720)
55-64 years: 8.29% (male 4,879,048/female 5,784,176)
65 years and over: 7.67% (male 4,373,807/female 5,491,581) (2020 est.)
elderly dependency ratio: 11.4
potential support ratio: 8.7 (2020 est.)

Median age: *total:* 29.3 years
male: 28.2 years
female: 30.4 years (2020 est.)

Population growth rate: 0.51% (2022 est.)

Birth rate: 13.55 births/1,000 population (2022 est.)

Death rate: 7.71 deaths/1,000 population (2022 est.)

Net migration rate: -0.76 migrant(s)/1,000 population (2022 est.)

Population distribution: most of the population is found in the middle of the country between the states of Jalisco and Veracruz; approximately a quarter of the population lives in and around Mexico City

Urbanization: *urban population:* 81.3% of total population (2022)

rate of urbanization: 1.4% annual rate of change (2020-25 est.)

Major urban areas - population: 22.085 million MEXICO CITY (capital), 5.340 million Guadalajara, 5.037 million Monterrey, 3.295 million Puebla, 2.576 million Toluca de Lerdo, 2.221 million Tijuana (2022)

Sex ratio: *at birth:* 1.05 male(s)/female
0-14 years: 1.05 male(s)/female
15-24 years: 1.09 male(s)/female
25-54 years: 0.91 male(s)/female
55-64 years: 0.84 male(s)/female
65 years and over: 0.75 male(s)/female
total population: 0.96 male(s)/female (2022 est.)

Mother's mean age at first birth: 21.3 years (2008 est.)

Maternal mortality ratio: 33 deaths/100,000 live births (2017 est.)

Infant mortality rate: *total:* 11.86 deaths/1,000 live births
male: 13.11 deaths/1,000 live births
female: 10.55 deaths/1,000 live births (2022 est.)

Life expectancy at birth: *total population:* 72.32 years
male: 68.93 years
female: 75.88 years (2022 est.)

Total fertility rate: 1.68 children born/woman (2022 est.)

Contraceptive prevalence rate: 73.1% (2018)

Drinking water source: *improved: urban:* 100% of population
rural: 98.3% of population
total: 99.7% of population
unimproved: urban: 0% of population
rural: 1.7% of population
total: 0.3% of population (2020 est.)

Current health expenditure: 5.4% of GDP (2019)

Physicians density: 2.43 physicians/1,000 population (2019)

Hospital bed density: 1 beds/1,000 population (2018)

Sanitation facility access: *improved: urban:* 99.9% of population
rural: 96.4% of population
total: 99.2% of population
unimproved: urban: 0.1% of population
rural: 3.6% of population
total: 0.8% of population (2020 est.)

HIV/AIDS - adult prevalence rate: 0.4% (2020 est.)

Major infectious diseases: *degree of risk:* intermediate (2020)
food or waterborne diseases: bacterial diarrhea and hepatitis A
vectorborne diseases: dengue fever
note: a new coronavirus is causing sustained community spread of respiratory illness (COVID-19) in Mexico; sustained community spread means that people have been infected with the virus, but how or where they became infected is not known, and the spread is ongoing; illness with this virus has ranged from mild to severe with fatalities reported; as of 18 August 2022, Mexico has reported a total of 6,939,755 cases of COVID-19 or 5,382.46 cumulative cases of COVID-19 per 100,000 population with a total of 328,798 cumulative deaths or a rate of 255.01 cumulative deaths per 100,000 population; as of 5 August 2022, 74.23% of the population has received at least one dose of COVID-19 vaccine

Obesity - adult prevalence rate: 28.9% (2016)

Alcohol consumption per capita: *total:* 4.25 liters of pure alcohol (2019 est.)
beer: 3.72 liters of pure alcohol (2019 est.)
wine: 0.19 liters of pure alcohol (2019 est.)
spirits: 0.19 liters of pure alcohol (2019 est.)
other alcohols: 0.15 liters of pure alcohol (2019 est.)

Tobacco use: *total:* 13.1% (2020 est.)
male: 19.9% (2020 est.)
female: 6.2% (2020 est.)

Children under the age of 5 years underweight: 4.7% (2018/19)

Child marriage: *women married by age 15:* 3.6%
women married by age 18: 20.7% (2018 est.)

Education expenditures: 4.3% of GDP (2018 est.)

Literacy: *definition:* age 15 and over can read and write
total population: 95.2%
male: 96.1%
female: 94.5% (2020)

School life expectancy (primary to tertiary education): *total:* 15 years
male: 15 years
female: 15 years (2019)

Unemployment, youth ages 15-24: *total:* 8.1%
male: 7.8%
female: 8.7% (2020 est.)

ENVIRONMENT

Environment - current issues: scarcity of hazardous waste disposal facilities; rural to urban migration; natural freshwater resources scarce and polluted in north, inaccessible and poor quality in center and extreme southeast; raw sewage and industrial effluents polluting rivers in urban areas; deforestation; widespread erosion; desertification; deteriorating agricultural lands; serious air and water pollution in the national capital and urban centers along US-Mexico border; land subsidence in Valley of Mexico caused by groundwater depletion
note: the government considers the lack of clean water and deforestation national security issues

Environment - international agreements: *party to:* Biodiversity, Climate Change, Climate Change-Kyoto Protocol, Climate Change-Paris Agreement, Comprehensive Nuclear Test Ban, Desertification, Endangered Species, Hazardous Wastes, Law of the Sea, Marine Dumping-London Convention, Marine Dumping-London Protocol, Marine Life Conservation, Nuclear Test Ban, Ozone Layer Protection, Ship Pollution, Tropical Timber 2006, Wetlands, Whaling
signed, but not ratified: none of the selected agreements

Air pollutants: *particulate matter emissions:* 20.08 micrograms per cubic meter (2016 est.)
carbon dioxide emissions: 486.41 megatons (2016 est.)
methane emissions: 135.77 megatons (2020 est.)

Climate: varies from tropical to desert

Land use: *agricultural land:* 54.9% (2018 est.)
arable land: 11.8% (2018 est.)
permanent crops: 1.4% (2018 est.)
permanent pasture: 41.7% (2018 est.)
forest: 33.3% (2018 est.)
other: 11.8% (2018 est.)

Urbanization: *urban population:* 81.3% of total population (2022)
rate of urbanization: 1.4% annual rate of change (2020-25 est.)

Revenue from forest resources: *forest revenues:* 0.1% of GDP (2018 est.)

Revenue from coal: *coal revenues:* 0.03% of GDP (2018 est.)

Waste and recycling: *municipal solid waste generated annually:* 53.1 million tons (2015 est.)
municipal solid waste recycled annually: 2.655 million tons (2013 est.)
percent of municipal solid waste recycled: 5% (2013 est.)

Major lakes (area sq km): *fresh water lake(s):* Laguna de Chapala - 1,140 sq km
salt water lake(s): Laguna de Terminos - 1,550 sq km

Major rivers (by length in km): Rio Grande river mouth (shared with US [s]) - 3,057 km; Colorado river mouth (shared with US [s]) - 2,333 km
note – [s] after country name indicates river source; [m] after country name indicates river mouth

Major watersheds (area sq km): Atlantic Ocean drainage: *(Gulf of Mexico)* Rio Grande/Bravo (607,965 sq km)
Pacific Ocean drainage: *(Gulf of California)* Colorado (703,148 sq km)

Major aquifers: Atlantic and Gulf Coastal Plains Aquifer

Total water withdrawal: *municipal:* 14.23 billion cubic meters (2017 est.)
industrial: 6.814 billion cubic meters (2017 est.)
agricultural: 66.8 billion cubic meters (2017 est.)

Total renewable water resources: 461.888 billion cubic meters (2017 est.)

GOVERNMENT

Country name: *conventional long form:* United Mexican States
conventional short form: Mexico
local long form: Estados Unidos Mexicanos
local short form: Mexico
former: Mexican Republic, Mexican Empire
etymology: named after the capital city, whose name stems from the Mexica, the largest and most powerful branch of the Aztecs; the meaning of the name is uncertain

Government type: federal presidential republic

Capital: *name:* Mexico City (Ciudad de Mexico)
geographic coordinates: 19 26 N, 99 08 W
time difference: UTC-6 (1 hour behind Washington, DC, during Standard Time)
daylight saving time: +1hr, begins first Sunday in April; ends last Sunday in October
time zone note: Mexico has four time zones
etymology: named after the Mexica, the largest and most powerful branch of the Aztecs; the meaning of the name is uncertain

Administrative divisions: 32 states (estados, singular - estado); Aguascalientes, Baja California, Baja California Sur, Campeche, Chiapas, Chihuahua, Coahuila, Colima, Cuidad de Mexico, Durango, Guanajuato, Guerrero, Hidalgo, Jalisco, Mexico, Michoacan, Morelos, Nayarit, Nuevo Leon, Oaxaca, Puebla, Queretaro, Quintana Roo, San Luis Potosi, Sinaloa, Sonora, Tabasco, Tamaulipas, Tlaxcala, Veracruz, Yucatan, Zacatecas

Independence: 16 September 1810 (declared independence from Spain); 27 September 1821 (recognized by Spain)

National holiday: Independence Day, 16 September (1810)

Constitution: *history:* several previous; latest approved 5 February 1917
amendments: proposed by the Congress of the Union; passage requires approval by at least two thirds of the members present and approval by a majority of the state legislatures; amended many times, last in 2020

Legal system: civil law system with US constitutional law influence; judicial review of legislative acts

International law organization participation: accepts compulsory ICJ jurisdiction with reservations; accepts ICCt jurisdiction

Citizenship: *citizenship by birth:* yes
citizenship by descent only: yes
dual citizenship recognized: not specified
residency requirement for naturalization: 5 years

Suffrage: 18 years of age; universal and compulsory

Executive branch: *chief of state:* President Andres Manuel LOPEZ OBRADOR (since 1 December 2018); note - the president is both chief of state and head of government
head of government: President Andres Manuel LOPEZ OBRADOR (since 1 December 2018)
cabinet: Cabinet appointed by the president; note - appointment of attorney general, the head of the Bank of Mexico, and senior treasury officials require consent of the Senate
elections/appointments: president directly elected by simple majority popular vote for a single 6-year term; election last held on 1 July 2018 (next to be held in July 2024)
election results:
2018: Andres Manuel LOPEZ OBRADOR elected president; percent of vote - Andres Manuel LOPEZ OBRADOR (MORENA) 53.2%, Ricardo ANAYA (PAN) 22.3%, Jose Antonio MEADE Kuribrena (PRI) 16.4%, Jaime RODRIGUEZ Calderon 5.2% (independent), other 2.9%
2012: Enrique PENA NIETO elected president; percent of vote - Enrique PENA NIETO (PRI) 38.2%, Andres Manuel LOPEZ OBRADOR (PRD) 31.6%, Josefina Eugenia VAZQUEZ Mota (PAN) 25.4%, other 4.8%

Legislative branch: *description:* bicameral National Congress or Congreso de la Union consists of:
Senate or Camara de Senadores (128 seats; 96 members directly elected in multi-seat constituencies by simple majority vote and 32 directly elected in a single, nationwide constituency by proportional representation vote; members serve 6-year terms)

Chamber of Deputies or Camara de Diputados (500 seats; 300 members directly elected in single-seat constituencies by simple majority vote and 200 directly elected in a single, nationwide constituency by proportional representation vote; members serve 3-year terms)
elections:
Senate - last held on 1 July 2018 (next to be held in July 2024)
Chamber of Deputies - last held on 6 June 2021 (next to be held in July 2024)
election results:
Senate - percent of vote by party - percent of vote by party - NA; seats by party - MORENA 58, PAN 22, PRI 14, PRD 9, MC 7, PT 7, PES 5, PVEM 5, PNA/PANAL 1; composition (as of July 2018) - men 65, women 63, percent of women 49.2%
Chamber of Deputies - percent of vote by party - NA; seats by party - MORENA 197, PAN 111, PRI 69, PVEM 44, PT 38, MC 25, PRD 16; composition - men 250, women 250, percent of women 50%; note - overall percent of women in National Congress 49.8%
note: as of the 2018 election, senators will be eligible for a second term and deputies up to 4 consecutive terms

Judicial branch: *highest court(s):* Supreme Court of Justice or Suprema Corte de Justicia de la Nacion (consists of the chief justice and 11 justices and organized into civil, criminal, administrative, and labor panels) and the Electoral Tribunal of the Federal Judiciary (organized into the superior court, with 7 judges including the court president, and 5 regional courts, each with 3 judges)
judge selection and term of office: Supreme Court justices nominated by the president of the republic and approved by two-thirds vote of the members present in the Senate; justices serve 15-year terms; Electoral Tribunal superior and regional court judges nominated by the Supreme Court and elected by two-thirds vote of members present in the Senate; superior court president elected from among its members to hold office for a 4-year term; other judges of the superior and regional courts serve staggered, 9-year terms
subordinate courts: federal level includes circuit, collegiate, and unitary courts; state and district level courts
note: in April 2021, the Mexican congress passed a judicial reform which changed 7 articles of the constitution and preceded a new Organic Law on the Judicial Branch of the Federation

Political parties and leaders: Citizen's Movement (Movimiento Ciudadano) or MC [Clemente CASTANEDA Hoeflich]
Institutional Revolutionary Party (Partido Revolucionario Institucional) or PRI [Claudia RUIZ Massieu]
Labor Party (Partido del Trabajo) or PT [Alberto ANAYA Gutierrez]
Mexican Green Ecological Party (Partido Verde Ecologista de Mexico) or PVEM [Karen CASTREJON Trujillo]
Movement for National Regeneration (Movimiento Regeneracion Nacional) or MORENA [Mario DELGADO Carillo]
National Action Party (Partido Accion Nacional) or PAN [Antonio CORTES Mendoza]
Party of the Democratic Revolution (Partido de la Revolucion Democratica) or PRD [Jesus ZAMBRANO Grijalva]
This Is For Mexico (Va Por Mexico) (alliance that includes PAN, PRI, and PRD)
Together We Make History (Juntos Hacemos Historia) (alliance that included MORENA, PT, PVEM) (dissolved 23 December 2020)

International organization participation: APEC, Australia Group, BCIE, BIS, CAN (observer), Caricom (observer), CD, CDB, CE (observer), CELAC, CSN (observer), EBRD, FAO, FATF, G-3, G-15, G-20, G-24, G-5, IADB, IAEA, IBRD, ICAO, ICC (national committees), ICCt, ICRM, IDA, IFAD, IFC, IFRCS, IHO, ILO, IMF, IMO, IMSO, Interpol, IOC, IOM, IPU, ISO, ITSO, ITU, ITUC (NGOs), LAES, LAIA, MIGA, NAFTA, NAM (observer), NEA, NSG, OAS, OECD, OPANAL, OPCW, Pacific Alliance, Paris Club (associate), PCA, SICA (observer), UN, UNASUR (observer), UNCTAD, UNESCO, UNHCR, UNHRC, UNIDO, Union Latina (observer), UNWTO, UPU, USMCA, Wassenaar Arrangement, WCO, WFTU (NGOs), WHO, WIPO, WMO, WTO

Diplomatic representation in the US: *chief of mission:* Ambassador Esteban MOCTEZUMA Barragan (since 20 April 2021)
chancery: 1911 Pennsylvania Avenue NW, Washington, DC 20006
telephone: [1] (202) 728-1600
FAX: [1] (202) 728-1698
email address and website:
mexembussa@sre.gob.mx
https://embamex.sre.gob.mx/eua/index.php/en/
consulate(s) general: Atlanta (GA), Austin (TX), Boston (MA), Chicago (IL), Dallas (TX), Denver (GA), El Paso (TX), Houston (TX), Laredo (TX), Miami (FL), New York (NY), Nogales (AZ), Phoenix (AZ), Raleigh (NC), Sacramento (CA), San Antonio (TX), San Diego (CA), San Francisco (CA), San Jose (CA), San Juan (Puerto Rico)
consulate(s): Albuquerque (NM), Boise (ID), Brownsville (TX), Calexico (CA), Del Rio (TX), Detroit (MI), Douglas (AZ), Eagle Pass (TX), Fresno (CA), Indianapolis (IN), Kansas City (MO), Las Vegas (NV), Little Rock (AR), Los Angeles (CA), McAllen (TX), Milwaukee (WI), New Orleans (LA), Omaha (NE), Orlando (FL), Oxnard (CA), Philadelphia (PA), Portland (OR), Presidio (TX), Salt Lake City (UT), San Bernardino (CA), Santa Ana (CA), Seattle (WA), St. Paul (MN), Tucson (AZ), Yuma (AZ)

Diplomatic representation from the US: *chief of mission:* Ambassador Ken SALAZAR (since 14 September 2021)
embassy: Paseo de la Reforma 305, Colonia Cuauhtemoc, 06500 Mexico, CDMX
mailing address: 8700 Mexico City Place, Washington DC 20521-8700
telephone: (011) [52]-55-5080-2000
FAX: (011) 52-55-5080-2005
email address and website:
ACSMexicoCity@state.gov
https://mx.usembassy.gov/
consulate(s) general: Ciudad Juarez, Guadalajara, Hermosillo, Matamoros, Merida, Monterrey, Nogales, Nuevo Laredo, Tijuana

Flag description: three equal vertical bands of green (hoist side), white, and red; Mexico's coat of arms (an eagle with a snake in its beak perched on a cactus) is centered in the white band; green signifies hope, joy, and love; white represents peace and honesty; red stands for hardiness, bravery, strength, and valor; the coat of arms is derived from a legend that the wandering Aztec people were to settle at a location where they would see an eagle on a cactus eating a snake; the city they founded, Tenochtitlan, is now Mexico City
note: similar to the flag of Italy, which is shorter, uses lighter shades of green and red, and does not display anything in its white band

National symbol(s): golden eagle; national colors: green, white, red

National anthem: *name:* "Himno Nacional Mexicano" (National Anthem of Mexico)
lyrics/music: Francisco Gonzalez BOCANEGRA/Jaime Nuno ROCA

note: adopted 1943, in use since 1854; also known as "Mexicanos, al grito de Guerra" (Mexicans, to the War Cry); according to tradition, Francisco Gonzalez BOCANEGRA, an accomplished poet, was uninterested in submitting lyrics to a national anthem contest; his fiancee locked him in a room and refused to release him until the lyrics were completed

National heritage: *total World Heritage Sites:* 35 (27 cultural, 6 natural, 2 mixed)
selected World Heritage Site locales: Historic Mexico City (c); Earliest 16th-Century Monasteries on the Slopes of Popocatepetl (c); Teotihuacan (c); Whale Sanctuary of El Vizcaino (n); Monarch Butterfly Biosphere Reserve (n); Tehuacán-Cuicatlán Valley (m); Historic Puebla (c); El Tajin (c); Historic Tlacotalpan (c); Historic Oaxaca and Monte Albán (c); Palenque (c); Chichen-Itza (c); Uxmal (c)

ECONOMY

Economic overview: Mexico's $2.4 trillion economy – 11th largest in the world - has become increasingly oriented toward manufacturing since the North American Free Trade Agreement (NAFTA) entered into force in 1994. Per capita income is roughly one-third that of the US; income distribution remains highly unequal.

Mexico has become the US' second-largest export market and third-largest source of imports. In 2017, two-way trade in goods and services exceeded $623 billion. Mexico has free trade agreements with 46 countries, putting more than 90% of its trade under free trade agreements. In 2012, Mexico formed the Pacific Alliance with Peru, Colombia, and Chile.

Mexico's current government, led by President Enrique PENA NIETO, has emphasized economic reforms, passing and implementing sweeping energy, financial, fiscal, and telecommunications reform legislation, among others, with the long-term aim to improve competitiveness and economic growth across the Mexican economy. Since 2015, Mexico has held public auctions of oil and gas exploration and development rights and for long-term electric power generation contracts. Mexico has also issued permits for private sector import, distribution, and retail sales of refined petroleum products in an effort to attract private investment into the energy sector and boost production.

Since 2013, Mexico's economic growth has averaged 2% annually, falling short of private-sector expectations that President PENA NIETO's sweeping reforms would bolster economic prospects. Growth is predicted to remain below potential given falling oil production, weak oil prices, structural issues such as low productivity, high inequality, a large informal sector employing over half of the workforce, weak rule of law, and corruption. Mexico's economy remains vulnerable to uncertainty surrounding the future of NAFTA — because the United States is its top trading partner and the two countries share integrated supply chains — and to potential shifts in domestic policies following the inauguration of a new a president in December 2018.

Real GDP (purchasing power parity): $2,306,320,000,000 (2020 est.)
$2,513,410,000,000 (2019 est.)
$2,514,780,000,000 (2018 est.)
note: data are in 2017 dollars

Real GDP growth rate: -0.3% (2019 est.)
2.19% (2018 est.)
2.34% (2017 est.)

Real GDP per capita: $17,900 (2020 est.)
$19,700 (2019 est.)
$19,900 (2018 est.)
note: data are in 2017 dollars

GDP (official exchange rate): $1,269,956,000,000 (2019 est.)

Inflation rate (consumer prices): 3.6% (2019 est.)
4.9% (2018 est.)
6% (2017 est.)

Credit ratings:

Fitch rating: BBB- (2020)

Moody's rating: Baa1 (2020)

Standard & Poors rating: *BBB (2020)*
note: The year refers to the year in which the current credit rating was first obtained.

GDP - composition, by sector of origin: *agriculture:* 3.6% (2017 est.)
industry: 31.9% (2017 est.)
services: 64.5% (2017 est.)

GDP - composition, by end use: *household consumption:* 67% (2017 est.)
government consumption: 11.8% (2017 est.)
investment in fixed capital: 22.3% (2017 est.)
investment in inventories: 0.8% (2017 est.)
exports of goods and services: 37.8% (2017 est.)
imports of goods and services: -39.7% (2017 est.)

Agricultural products: sugarcane, maize, milk, oranges, sorghum, tomatoes, poultry, wheat, green chillies/peppers, eggs

Industries: food and beverages, tobacco, chemicals, iron and steel, petroleum, mining, textiles, clothing, motor vehicles, consumer durables, tourism

Industrial production growth rate: -0.6% (2017 est.)

Labor force: 50.914 million (2020 est.)

Labor force - by occupation: *agriculture:* 13.4%
industry: 24.1%
services: 61.9% (2011)

Unemployment rate: 3.49% (2019 est.)
3.33% (2018 est.)
note: underemployment may be as high as 25%

Unemployment, youth ages 15-24: *total:* 8.1%
male: 7.8%
female: 8.7% (2020 est.)

Population below poverty line: 41.9% (2018 est.)

Gini Index coefficient - distribution of family income: 36.8 (2018 est.)
48.3 (2008)

Household income or consumption by percentage share: *lowest 10%:* 2%
highest 10%: 40% (2014)

Budget: *revenues:* 261.4 billion (2017 est.)
expenditures: 273.8 billion (2017 est.)

Budget surplus (+) or deficit (-): -1.1% (of GDP) (2017 est.)

Public debt: 54.3% of GDP (2017 est.)
56.8% of GDP (2016 est.)

Taxes and other revenues: 22.7% (of GDP) (2017 est.)

Fiscal year: calendar year

Current account balance: -$4.351 billion (2019 est.)
-$25.415 billion (2018 est.)

Exports: $434.93 billion (2020 est.) note: data are in current year dollars
$492.73 billion (2019 est.) note: data are in current year dollars
$480.1 billion (2018 est.) note: data are in current year dollars

Exports - partners: United States 75% (2019)

Exports - commodities: cars and vehicle parts, computers, delivery trucks, crude petroleum, insulated wiring (2019)

Imports: $410.66 billion (2020 est.) note: data are in current year dollars
$495.79 billion (2019 est.) note: data are in current year dollars
$505.05 billion (2018 est.) note: data are in current year dollars

Imports - partners: United States 54%, China 14% (2019)

Imports - commodities: integrated circuits, refined petroleum, cars and vehicle parts, office machinery/parts, telephones (2019)

Reserves of foreign exchange and gold: $175.3 billion (31 December 2017 est.)
$178.4 billion (31 December 2016 est.)
note: Mexico also maintains access to an $88 million Flexible Credit Line with the IMF

Debt - external: $456.713 billion (2019 est.)
$448.268 billion (2018 est.)

Exchange rates: Mexican pesos (MXN) per US dollar -
19.8 (2020 est.)
19.22824 (2019 est.)
20.21674 (2018 est.)
15.848 (2014 est.)
13.292 (2013 est.)

ENERGY

Electricity access: *electrification - total population:* 100% (2020)

Electricity: *installed generating capacity:* 93.43 million kW (2020 est.)
consumption: 267.34 billion kWh (2020 est.)
exports: 5.954 billion kWh (2020 est.)
imports: 9.965 billion kWh (2020 est.)
transmission/distribution losses: 42.121 billion kWh (2020 est.)

Electricity generation sources: *fossil fuels:* 75.7% of total installed capacity (2020 est.)
nuclear: 3.6% of total installed capacity (2020 est.)
solar: 4.4% of total installed capacity (2020 est.)
wind: 6.5% of total installed capacity (2020 est.)
hydroelectricity: 7.6% of total installed capacity (2020 est.)
geothermal: 1.5% of total installed capacity (2020 est.)
biomass and waste: 0.8% of total installed capacity (2020 est.)

Coal: *production:* 9.886 million metric tons (2020 est.)
consumption: 10.241 million metric tons (2020 est.)
exports: 3,000 metric tons (2020 est.)
imports: 5.182 million metric tons (2020 est.)
proven reserves: 1.211 billion metric tons (2019 est.)

Petroleum: *total petroleum production:* 1,905,500 bbl/day (2021 est.)
refined petroleum consumption: 1,928,800 bbl/day (2019 est.)
crude oil and lease condensate exports: 1,283,300 bbl/day (2018 est.)

crude oil and lease condensate imports: 3,900 bbl/day (2018 est.)
crude oil estimated reserves: 5,786,100,000 barrels (2021 est.)

Refined petroleum products - production: 844,600 bbl/day (2017 est.)

Refined petroleum products - exports: 155,800 bbl/day (2017 est.)

Refined petroleum products - imports: 867,500 bbl/day (2017 est.)

Natural gas: *production:* 27,037,730,000 cubic meters (2019 est.)
consumption: 86,101,223,000 cubic meters (2019 est.)
exports: 53.037 million cubic meters (2019 est.)
imports: 59,119,362,000 cubic meters (2019 est.)
proven reserves: 180.321 billion cubic meters (2021 est.)

Carbon dioxide emissions: 463.739 million metric tonnes of CO2 (2019 est.)
from coal and metallurgical coke: 43.24 million metric tonnes of CO2 (2019 est.)
from petroleum and other liquids: 260.311 million metric tonnes of CO2 (2019 est.)
from consumed natural gas: 160.188 million metric tonnes of CO2 (2019 est.)

Energy consumption per capita: 61.597 million Btu/person (2019 est.)

COMMUNICATIONS

Telephones - fixed lines: *total subscriptions:* 24,500,456 (2020 est.)
subscriptions per 100 inhabitants: 19 (2020 est.)

Telephones - mobile cellular: *total subscriptions:* 122,898,392 (2020 est.)
subscriptions per 100 inhabitants: 95 (2020 est.)

Telecommunication systems: *general assessment:* with a large population and relatively low broadband and mobile penetration, (86 lines for mobile broadband for every 100 habitants in June 2021) Mexico's telecom sector has potential for growth; adequate telephone service for business and government; improving quality and increasing mobile cellular availability, with mobile subscribers far outnumbering fixed-line subscribers (24.6 million fixed line subscribers and 125 million mobile line subscribers in June 2021); relatively low broadband and mobile penetration, potential for growth and international investment; extensive microwave radio relay network; considerable use of fiber-optic cable and coaxial cable; 5G development slow in part due to high costs (2021)
domestic: fixed-line teledensity exceeds 65 lines per every 100 households; mobile-cellular teledensity is about 99 per 100 persons; domestic satellite system with 120 earth stations (2021)
international: country code - 52; Columbus-2 fiber-optic submarine cable with access to the US, Virgin Islands, Canary Islands, Spain, and Italy; the ARCOS-1 and the MAYA-1 submarine cable system together provide access to Central America, parts of South America and the Caribbean, and the U.S.; Pan-American Crossing (PAC) submarine cable system provides access to Panama, California, U.S., and Costa Rica; Lazaro Cardenas-Manzanillo Santiago submarines cable system (LCMSSCS) provides access to Michoacan, Guerrero, and Colima, Mexico; AMX-1 submarine cable system with access to Colombia, Brazil, Puerto Rico, Gulf of California Cable submarine cable systems that connects La Paz, Baja California Sur and Topolobambo, Sinaloa; and Aurora submarine cable system provides access to Guatemala, Panama, Ecuador, Colombia, Mexico, and the U.S. satellite earth stations - 124 (36 Intelsat, 1 Solidaridad (giving Mexico improved access to South America, Central America, and much of the US as well as enhancing domestic communications), 9 Panamsat, numerous Inmarsat mobile earth stations); linked to Central American Microwave System of trunk connections (2022)

Broadcast media: telecom reform in 2013 enabled the creation of new broadcast television channels after decades of a quasi-monopoly; Mexico has 885 TV stations and 1,841 radio stations and most are privately owned; the Televisa group once had a virtual monopoly in TV broadcasting, but new broadcasting groups and foreign satellite and cable operators are now available; in 2016, Mexico became the first country in Latin America to complete the transition from analog to digital transmissions, allowing for better image and audio quality and a wider selection of programming from networks (2022)

Internet country code: .mx

Internet users: *total:* 92,831,582 (2020 est.)
percent of population: 72% (2020 est.)

Broadband - fixed subscriptions: *total:* 21,936,131 (2020 est.)
subscriptions per 100 inhabitants: 17 (2020 est.)

TRANSPORTATION

National air transport system: *number of registered air carriers:* 16 (2020)
inventory of registered aircraft operated by air carriers: 370
annual passenger traffic on registered air carriers: 64,569,640 (2018)
annual freight traffic on registered air carriers: 1,090,380,000 (2018) mt-km

Civil aircraft registration country code prefix: XA

Airports: *total:* 1,714 (2021)

Airports - with paved runways: *total:* 243
over 3,047 m: 12
2,438 to 3,047 m: 32
1,524 to 2,437 m: 80
914 to 1,523 m: 86
under 914 m: 33 (2021)

Airports - with unpaved runways: *total:* 1,471
over 3,047 m: 1
2,438 to 3,047 m: 1
1,524 to 2,437 m: 42
914 to 1,523 m: 281
under 914 m: 1,146 (2021)

Heliports: 1 (2021)

Pipelines: 17,210 km natural gas (2022), 9,757 km oil (2017), 10,237 km refined products (2020)

Railways: *total:* 23,389 km (2017)
standard gauge: 23,389 km (2017) 1.435-m gauge (27 km electrified)

Roadways: *total:* 704,884 km (2017)
paved: 175,526 km (2017) (includes 10,845 km of expressways)
unpaved: 529,358 km (2017)

Waterways: 2,900 km (2012) (navigable rivers and coastal canals mostly connected with ports on the country's east coast)

Merchant marine: *total:* 671
by type: container ship 1, bulk carrier 4, general cargo 11, oil tanker 31, other 624 (2021)

Ports and terminals: *major seaport(s):* Altamira, Coatzacoalcos, Lazaro Cardenas, Manzanillo, Veracruz
oil terminal(s): Cayo Arcas terminal, Dos Bocas terminal
cruise port(s): Cancun, Cozumel, Ensenada
container port(s) (TEUs): Lazaro Cardenas (1,318,732), Manzanillo (3,069,189), Veracruz (1,144,156) (2019)

LNG terminal(s) (import): Altamira, Ensenada

MILITARY AND SECURITY

Military and security forces: the Mexican Armed Forces are divided between the Secretariat of National Defense and the Secretariat of the Navy: Secretariat of National Defense (Secretaria de Defensa Nacional, SEDENA): Army (Ejercito), Mexican Air Force (Fuerza Aerea Mexicana, FAM), National Guard; Secretariat of the Navy (Secretaria de Marina, SEMAR): Mexican Navy (Armada de Mexico (ARM), includes Naval Air Force (FAN), Mexican Naval Infantry Corps (Cuerpo de Infanteria de Marina, Mexmar or CIM)); Secretariat of Public Security and Civilian Protection (Secretaria de Seguridad y Proteccion Ciudadana) (2022)
note: the National Guard was formed in 2019 of personnel from the former Federal Police (disbanded in December 2019) and military police units of the Army and Navy; up until September 2022, the Guard was under the civilian-led Secretariat of Security and Civilian Protection, while the SEDENA had day-to-day operational control and provided the commanders and the training; in September 2022, complete control of the Guard was handed over to the SEDENA/Mexican Army; the Guard, along with state and municipal police, is responsible for enforcing the law and maintaining order; the regular military also actively supports police operations

Military expenditures: 0.8% of GDP (2022 est.)
0.8% of GDP (2021)
0.6% of GDP (2020)
0.5% of GDP (2019) (approximately $13.4 billion)
0.5% of GDP (2018) (approximately $12.5 billion)

Military and security service personnel strengths: information varies; approximately 218,000 armed forces personnel (160,000 Army; 8,000 Air Force; 50,000 Navy, including about 20,000 marines); approximately 110,000 National Guard personnel (2022)

Military equipment inventories and acquisitions: the Mexican military inventory includes a mix of domestically-produced and imported equipment from a variety of mostly Western suppliers; since 2010, the US has been the leading supplier of military hardware to Mexico; Mexico's defense industry produces naval vessels and light armored vehicles, as well as small arms and other miscellaneous equipment (2022)

Military service age and obligation: 18 years of age for compulsory military service for males (selection for service determined by lottery); conscript service obligation is 12 months; those selected serve on Saturdays in a Batallón del Servicio Militar Nacional (National Military Service Battalion) composed entirely of 1-year Servicio Militar Nacional (SMN) conscripts; conscripts remain in reserve status until the age of 40; 16 years of age with consent for

voluntary enlistment; cadets enrolled in military schools from the age of 15 are considered members of the armed forces; women are eligible for voluntary military service (2022)
note: as of 2022, women comprised about 15% of the active duty military

Military - note: the constitution was amended in 2019 to grant the president the authority to use the armed forces to protect internal and national security, and courts have upheld the legality of the armed forces' role in law enforcement activities in support of civilian authorities through 2028; as of 2022, Mexican military operations were heavily focused on internal security duties, particularly in countering drug cartels and organized crime groups, as well as border control and immigration enforcement; the armed forces also administered most of the country's land and sea ports and customs services, and it built and ran approximately 2,700 branches of a state-owned development bank; in addition, President LOPEZ OBRADOR has placed the military in charge of a growing number of infrastructure projects, such as building a new airport for Mexico City and sections of a train line in the country's southeast (2022)

TRANSNATIONAL ISSUES

Disputes - international: *Mexico-Belize:* Mexico and Belize are working to solve minor border demarcation discrepancies arising from inaccuracies in the 1898 border treaty
Mexico-Guatemala: Mexico must deal with thousands of impoverished Guatemalans and other Central Americans who cross the porous border looking for work in Mexico and the US
Mexico-US: the US has intensified security measures to monitor and control legal and illegal persons, transport, and commodities across its border with Mexico

Refugees and internally displaced persons: *refugees (country of origin):* 22,254 (Honduras), 10,662 (El Salvador) (mid-year 2021); 82,976 (Venezuela) (economic and political crisis; includes Venezuelans who have claimed asylum, are recognized as refugees, or have received alternative legal stay) (2021)
IDPs: 379,000 (government's quashing of Zapatista uprising in 1994 in eastern Chiapas Region; drug cartel violence and government's military response since 2007; violence between and within indigenous groups) (2021)
stateless persons: 13 (mid-year 2021)

Illicit drugs: major source and transit country for heroin, marijuana, methamphetamine, and illicit synthetic drugs including fentanyl and counterfeit pills destined for the United States; main transit country for cocaine from South America, a transit route and destination for fentanyl and associated precursors originating from China

MICRONESIA, FEDERATED STATES OF

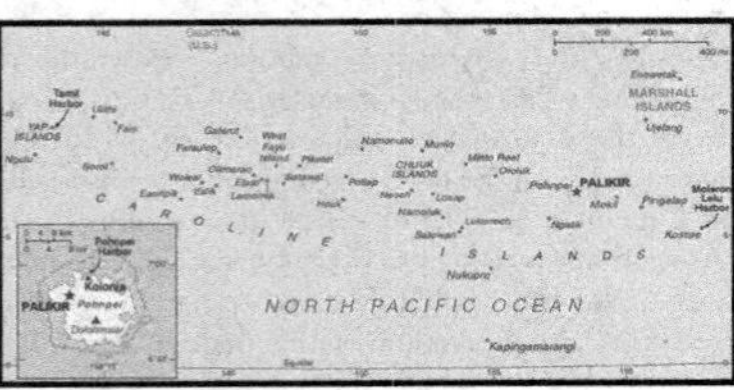

INTRODUCTION

Background: Each of the four states that compose the Federated States of Micronesia (FSM) - Chuuk, Kosrae, Pohnpei, and Yap - has its own unique history and cultural traditions. The first humans arrived in what is now the FSM in the second millennium B.C. In the 800s A.D., construction of the artificial islets at the Nan Madol complex in Pohnpei began, with the main architecture being built around 1200. At its height, Nan Madol united the approximately 25,000 people of Pohnpei under the Saudeleur Dynasty. Around the same time, Kosrae was united in a kingdom centered in Leluh by 1250. Yap's society became strictly hierarchical, with chiefs receiving tributes from islands up to 1,100 km (700 mi) away. Widespread human settlement in Chuuk began in the 1300s, and the different islands in the Chuuk Lagoon were frequently at war with one another.

Portuguese and Spanish explorers visited a few of the islands in the 1500s and Spain began exerting nominal, but not day-to-day, control over some of the islands - which they named the Caroline Islands - in the 1600s. Christian missionaries arrived in the 1800s, in particular to Chuuk and Kosrae. By the 1870s, nearly every Kosraean had converted to Christianity and religion continues to play an important role in daily life on the island. In 1899, Spain sold all of the FSM to Germany. Japan seized the islands in 1914 and was granted a League of Nations mandate to administer them in 1920. The Japanese navy built bases across most of the islands and headquartered their Pacific naval operations in Chuuk. The US bombed Chuuk in 1944 during Operation Hailstone in World War II, destroying 250 Japanese planes and 40 ships. The US military largely bypassed the other islands in its leapfrog campaign across the Pacific.

The FSM came under US administration as part of the Trust Territory of the Pacific Islands in 1947, which comprised six districts: Chuuk, the Marshall Islands, the Northern Mariana Islands, Palau, Pohnpei, and Yap; Kosrae was separated from Pohnpei into a separate district in 1977. In 1979, Chuuk, Kosrae, Pohnpei, and Yap ratified the FSM Constitution and declared independence while the other three districts opted to pursue separate political statuses. In 1982, the FSM signed a Compact of Free Association (COFA) with the US, which granted the FSM financial assistance and access to many US domestic programs in exchange for exclusive US military access and defense responsibilities; the COFA entered into force in 1986 and its funding was renewed in 2003. There are significant inter-island rivalries stemming from their different histories and cultures. Chuuk, the most populous but poorest state, has pushed for secession, but an independence referendum has been repeatedly postponed and may not be held.

Eligible Micronesians can live, work, and study in any part of the US and its territories without a visa - this privilege reduces stresses on the island economy and the environment. Micronesians serve in the US armed forces and military recruiting from the FSM, per capita, is higher than many US states.

GEOGRAPHY

Location: Oceania, island group in the North Pacific Ocean, about three-quarters of the way from Hawaii to Indonesia

Geographic coordinates: 6 55 N, 158 15 E

Map references: Oceania

Area: *total:* 702 sq km
land: 702 sq km
water: 0 sq km (fresh water only)
note: includes Pohnpei (Ponape), Chuuk (Truk) Islands, Yap Islands, and Kosrae (Kosaie)
country comparison to the world: 191

Area - comparative: four times the size of Washington, DC (land area only)

Land boundaries: *total:* 0 km

Coastline: 6,112 km

Maritime claims: *territorial sea:* 12 nm
exclusive economic zone: 200 nm

Climate: tropical; heavy year-round rainfall, especially in the eastern islands; located on southern edge of the typhoon belt with occasionally severe damage

Terrain: islands vary geologically from high mountainous islands to low, coral atolls; volcanic outcroppings on Pohnpei, Kosrae, and Chuuk

Elevation: *highest point:* Nanlaud on Pohnpei 782 m
lowest point: Pacific Ocean 0 m

Natural resources: timber, marine products, deep-seabed minerals, phosphate

Land use: *agricultural land:* 25.5% (2018 est.)
arable land: 2.3% (2018 est.)
permanent crops: 19.7% (2018 est.)
permanent pasture: 3.5% (2018 est.)
forest: 74.5% (2018 est.)
other: 0% (2018 est.)

Irrigated land: 0 sq km (2012)

Population distribution: the majority of the populaton lives in the coastal areas of the high islands; the mountainous interior is largely uninhabited; less than half of the population lives in urban areas

Natural hazards: typhoons (June to December)

Geography - note: composed of four major island groups totaling 607 islands

PEOPLE AND SOCIETY

Population: 101,009 (2022 est.)
country comparison to the world: 194

Nationality: *noun:* Micronesian(s)
adjective: Micronesian; Chuukese, Kosraen(s), Pohnpeian(s), Yapese

Ethnic groups: Chuukese/Mortlockese 49.3%, Pohnpeian 29.8%, Kosraean 6.3%, Yapese 5.7%, Yap outer islanders 5.1%, Polynesian 1.6%, Asian 1.4%, other 0.8% (2010 est.)

Languages: English (official and common language), Chuukese, Kosrean, Pohnpeian, Yapese, Ulithian, Woleaian, Nukuoro, Kapingamarangi

Religions: Roman Catholic 54.7%, Protestant 41.1% (includes Congregational 38.5%, Baptist 1.1%, Seventh Day Adventist 0.8%, Assembly of God 0.7%), Church of Jesus Christ 1.5%, other 1.9%, none 0.7%, unspecified 0.1% (2010 est.)

Age structure: *0-14 years:* 28.24% (male 14,585/female 14,129)
15-24 years: 18.62% (male 9,473/female 9,461)
25-54 years: 40.81% (male 19,998/female 21,493)
55-64 years: 7.38% (male 3,602/female 3,898)
65 years and over: 4.95% (male 2,260/female 2,776) (2021 est.)

Dependency ratios: *total dependency ratio:* 55.2
youth dependency ratio: 48.4
elderly dependency ratio: 6.8
potential support ratio: 14.7 (2020 est.)

Median age: *total:* 26.3 years
male: 25.5 years
female: 27.1 years (2020 est.)
country comparison to the world: 154

Population growth rate: -0.67% (2022 est.)
country comparison to the world: 227

Birth rate: 18.39 births/1,000 population (2022 est.)
country comparison to the world: 80

Death rate: 4.19 deaths/1,000 population (2022 est.)
country comparison to the world: 211

Net migration rate: -20.91 migrant(s)/1,000 population (2022 est.)
country comparison to the world: 229

Population distribution: the majority of the population lives in the coastal areas of the high islands; the mountainous interior is largely uninhabited; less than half of the population lives in urban areas

Urbanization: *urban population:* 23.2% of total population (2022)
rate of urbanization: 1.52% annual rate of change (2020-25 est.)

Major urban areas - population: 7,000 PALIKIR (capital) (2018)

Sex ratio: *at birth:* 1.05 male(s)/female
0-14 years: 1.03 male(s)/female
15-24 years: 1 male(s)/female
25-54 years: 0.92 male(s)/female
55-64 years: 0.92 male(s)/female
65 years and over: 0.57 male(s)/female
total population: 0.96 male(s)/female (2022 est.)

Maternal mortality ratio: 88 deaths/100,000 live births (2017 est.)
country comparison to the world: 75

Infant mortality rate: *total:* 21.9 deaths/1,000 live births
male: 25.02 deaths/1,000 live births
female: 18.63 deaths/1,000 live births (2022 est.)
country comparison to the world: 76

Life expectancy at birth: *total population:* 74.44 years
male: 72.34 years
female: 76.66 years (2022 est.)
country comparison to the world: 137

Total fertility rate: 2.24 children born/woman (2022 est.)
country comparison to the world: 83

Drinking water source: *improved: total:* 78.6% of population
unimproved: total: 21.4% of population (2017 est.)

Current health expenditure: 11.4% of GDP (2019)

Hospital bed density: 3.2 beds/1,000 population

Sanitation facility access: *improved: total:* 88.3% of population
unimproved: total: 11.7% of population (2017 est.)

Major infectious diseases: *degree of risk:* high (2020)
food or waterborne diseases: bacterial diarrhea
vectorborne diseases: malaria

Obesity - adult prevalence rate: 45.8% (2016)
country comparison to the world: 10

Alcohol consumption per capita: *total:* 1.59 liters of pure alcohol (2019 est.)
beer: 0.92 liters of pure alcohol (2019 est.)
wine: 0.13 liters of pure alcohol (2019 est.)
spirits: 0.52 liters of pure alcohol (2019 est.)
other alcohols: 0.01 liters of pure alcohol (2019 est.)
country comparison to the world: 138

Education expenditures: 9.7% of GDP (2018 est.)
country comparison to the world: 4

Unemployment, youth ages 15-24: *total:* 18.9%
male: 10.4%
female: 29.9% (2014)

ENVIRONMENT

Environment - current issues: overfishing; sea level rise due to climate change threatens land; water pollution, toxic pollution from mining; solid waste disposal

Environment - international agreements: *party to:* Biodiversity, Climate Change, Climate Change-Kyoto Protocol, Climate Change-Paris Agreement, Comprehensive Nuclear Test Ban, Desertification, Hazardous Wastes, Law of the Sea, Ozone Layer Protection
signed, but not ratified: none of the selected agreements

Air pollutants: *particulate matter emissions:* 10.23 micrograms per cubic meter (2016 est.)
carbon dioxide emissions: 0.14 megatons (2016 est.)
methane emissions: 0.02 megatons (2020 est.)

Climate: tropical; heavy year-round rainfall, especially in the eastern islands; located on southern edge of the typhoon belt with occasionally severe damage

Land use: *agricultural land:* 25.5% (2018 est.)
arable land: 2.3% (2018 est.)
permanent crops: 19.7% (2018 est.)
permanent pasture: 3.5% (2018 est.)
forest: 74.5% (2018 est.)
other: 0% (2018 est.)

Urbanization: *urban population:* 23.2% of total population (2022)
rate of urbanization: 1.52% annual rate of change (2020-25 est.)

Revenue from forest resources: *forest revenues:* 0.02% of GDP (2018 est.)
country comparison to the world: 143

Waste and recycling: *municipal solid waste generated annually:* 26,040 tons (2016 est.)

Total renewable water resources: 0 cubic meters (2017 est.)

GOVERNMENT

Country name: *conventional long form:* Federated States of Micronesia
conventional short form: none
local long form: Federated States of Micronesia
local short form: none
former: New Philippines; Caroline Islands; Trust Territory of the Pacific Islands, Ponape, Truk, and Yap Districts
abbreviation: FSM
etymology: the term "Micronesia" is a 19th-century construct of two Greek words, "micro" (small) and "nesoi" (islands), and refers to thousands of small islands in the western Pacific Ocean

Government type: federal republic in free association with the US

Capital: *name:* Palikir
geographic coordinates: 6 55 N, 158 09 E
time difference: UTC+11 (16 hours ahead of Washington, DC, during Standard Time)
time zone note: Micronesia has two time zones
note: Palikir became the new capital of the country in 1989, three years after independence; Kolonia, the former capital, remains the site for many foreign embassies; it also serves as the Pohnpei state capital

Administrative divisions: 4 states; Chuuk (Truk), Kosrae (Kosaie), Pohnpei (Ponape), Yap

Independence: 3 November 1986 (from the US-administered UN trusteeship)

National holiday: Constitution Day, 10 May (1979)

Constitution: *history:* drafted June 1975, ratified 1 October 1978, entered into force 10 May 1979
amendments: proposed by Congress, by a constitutional convention, or by public petition; passage requires approval by at least three-fourths majority vote in at least three fourths of the states; amended 1990; note – at least every 10 years as part of a general or special election, voters are asked whether to hold a constitution convention; a majority of affirmative votes is required to proceed; amended many times, last in 2019 (approval by referendum to hold a constitutional convention)

Legal system: mixed legal system of common and customary law

International law organization participation: has not submitted an ICJ jurisdiction declaration; non-party state to the ICCt

Citizenship: *citizenship by birth:* no
citizenship by descent only: at least one parent must be a citizen of FSM
dual citizenship recognized: no
residency requirement for naturalization: 5 years

Suffrage: 18 years of age; universal

Executive branch: *chief of state:* President David W. PANUELO (since 11 May 2019); Vice President Yosiwo P. GEORGE (since 11 May 2015); note - the president is both chief of state and head of government
head of government: President David W. PANUELO (since 11 May 2019); Vice President Yosiwo P. GEORGE (since 11 May 2015)
cabinet: Cabinet includes the vice president and the heads of the 8 executive departments

elections/appointments: president and vice president indirectly elected by Congress from among the 4 'at large' senators for a 4-year term (eligible for a second term); election last held on 11 May 2019 (next to be held in 2023)
election results:
David W. PANUELO elected president by Congress; Yosiwo P GEORGE reelected vice president

Legislative branch: *description:* unicameral Congress (14 seats; 10 members directly elected in single-seat constituencies by simple majority vote to serve 2-year terms and 4 at- large members directly elected from each of the 4 states by proportional representation vote to serve 4-year terms)
elections:
last held on 2 March 2021 (next to be held on March 2023)
election results:
percent of vote - NA; seats - independent 14; composition as of July 2022 - men 13, women 1, percent of women 7.1%

Judicial branch: *highest court(s):* Federated States of Micronesia (FSM) Supreme Court (consists of the chief justice and not more than 5 associate justices and organized into appellate and criminal divisions)
judge selection and term of office: justices appointed by the FSM president with the approval of two-thirds of Congress; justices appointed for life
subordinate courts: the highest state-level courts are: Chuuk Supreme Court; Korsae State Court; Pohnpei State Court; Yap State Court

Political parties and leaders: no formal parties

International organization participation: ACP, ADB, AOSIS, FAO, G-77, IBRD, ICAO, ICRM, IDA, IFC, IFRCS, IMF, IOC, IOM, IPU, ITSO, ITU, MIGA, OPCW, PIF, Sparteca, SPC, UN, UNCTAD, UNESCO, WHO, WMO

Diplomatic representation in the US: *chief of mission:* Ambassador Akillino Harris SUSAIA (since 24 April 2017)
chancery: 1725 N Street NW, Washington, DC 20036
telephone: [1] (202) 223-4383
FAX: [1] (202) 223-4391
email address and website:
dcmission@fsmembassy.fm
https://fsmembassy.fm/
consulate(s) general: Honolulu, Portland (OR), Tamuning (Guam)

Diplomatic representation from the US: *chief of mission:* Ambassador Carmen G. CANTOR (since 31 January 2020)
embassy: 1286 US Embassy Place, Kolonia, Pohnpei, FM 96941
mailing address: 4120 Kolonia Place, Washington, D.C. 20521-4120
telephone: [691] 320-2187
FAX: [691] 320-2186
email address and website:
koloniaacs@state.gov
https://fm.usembassy.gov/

Flag description: light blue with four white five-pointed stars centered; the stars are arranged in a diamond pattern; blue symbolizes the Pacific Ocean, the stars represent the four island groups of Chuuk, Kosrae, Pohnpei, and Yap

National symbol(s): four, five-pointed, white stars on a light blue field, hibiscus flower; national colors: light blue, white

National anthem: *name:* "Patriots of Micronesia"
lyrics/music: unknown/August Daniel BINZER
note: adopted 1991; also known as "Across All Micronesia"; the music is based on the 1820 German patriotic song "Ich hab mich ergeben", which was the West German national anthem from 1949-1950; variants of this tune are used in Johannes BRAHMS' "Festival Overture" and Gustav MAHLER's "Third Symphony"

National heritage: *total World Heritage Sites:* 1 (cultural)
selected World Heritage Site locales: Nan Madol: Ceremonial Center of Eastern Micronesia

ECONOMY

Economic overview: Economic activity consists largely of subsistence farming and fishing, and government, which employs two-thirds of the adult working population and receives funding largely - 58% in 2013 – from Compact of Free Association assistance provided by the US. The islands have few commercially valuable mineral deposits. The potential for tourism is limited by isolation, lack of adequate facilities, and limited internal air and water transportation.

Under the terms of the original Compact, the US provided $1.3 billion in grants and aid from 1986 to 2001. The US and the Federated States of Micronesia (FSM) negotiated a second (amended) Compact agreement in 2002-03 that took effect in 2004. The amended Compact runs for a 20-year period to 2023; during which the US will provide roughly $2.1 billion to the FSM. The amended Compact also develops a trust fund for the FSM that will provide a comparable income stream beyond 2024 when Compact grants end.

The country's medium-term economic outlook appears fragile because of dependence on US assistance and lackluster performance of its small and stagnant private sector.

Real GDP (purchasing power parity): $390 million (2019 est.)
$390 million (2018 est.)
$389 million (2017 est.)
note: data are in 2017 dollars
country comparison to the world: 214

Real GDP growth rate: 2% (2017 est.)
2.9% (2016 est.)
3.9% (2015 est.)
country comparison to the world: 137

Real GDP per capita: $3,500 (2019 est.) note: data are in 2017 dollars
$3,500 (2018 est.) note: data are in 2017 dollars
$3,200 (2015 est.)
country comparison to the world: 190

GDP (official exchange rate): $328 million (2017 est.)

Inflation rate (consumer prices): 0.5% (2017 est.)
0.5% (2016 est.)
country comparison to the world: 42

GDP - composition, by sector of origin: *agriculture:* 26.3% (2013 est.)
industry: 18.9% (2013 est.)
services: 54.8% (2013 est.)

GDP - composition, by end use: *household consumption:* 83.5% (2013 est.)
government consumption: 48.4% (2016 est.)
investment in fixed capital: 29.5% (2016 est.)
investment in inventories: 1.9% (2016 est.)
exports of goods and services: 27.5% (2016 est.)
imports of goods and services: -77% (2016 est.)

Agricultural products: coconuts, cassava, vegetables, sweet potatoes, bananas, pork, plantains, fruit, eggs, beef

Industries: tourism, construction; specialized aquaculture, craft items (shell and wood)

Labor force: 37,920 (2010 est.)
country comparison to the world: 199

Labor force - by occupation: *agriculture:* 0.9%
industry: 5.2%
services: 93.9% (2013 est.)
note: two-thirds of the labor force are government employees

Unemployment rate: 16.2% (2010 est.)
country comparison to the world: 180

Unemployment, youth ages 15-24: *total:* 18.9%
male: 10.4%
female: 29.9% (2014)
country comparison to the world: 85

Population below poverty line: 41.2% (2013 est.)

Gini Index coefficient - distribution of family income: 40.1 (2013 est.)
country comparison to the world: 63

Budget: *revenues:* 213.8 million (FY12/13 est.)
expenditures: 192.1 million (FY12/13 est.)

Budget surplus (+) or deficit (-): 6.6% (of GDP) (FY12/13 est.)
country comparison to the world: 4

Public debt: 24.5% of GDP (2017 est.)
25.3% of GDP (2016 est.)
country comparison to the world: 176

Taxes and other revenues: 65.2% (of GDP) (FY12/13 est.)
country comparison to the world: 7

Fiscal year: 1 October - 30 September

Current account balance: $12 million (2017 est.)
$11 million (2016 est.)
country comparison to the world: 62

Exports: $88.3 million (2013 est.)
country comparison to the world: 210

Exports - partners: Thailand 73%, Japan 10%, China 9% (2019)

Exports - commodities: fish and fish products, coral/shells, scrap metals, mollusks, office machinery/parts (2019)

Imports: $167.8 million (2015 est.)
$258.5 million (2013 est.)
country comparison to the world: 214

Imports - partners: United States 32%, China 16%, Japan 14%, Taiwan 9%, Philippines 6%, South Korea 6% (2019)

Imports - commodities: poultry meats, netting, broadcasting equipment, various meats, fish products (2019)

Reserves of foreign exchange and gold: $203.7 million (31 December 2017 est.)
$135.1 million (31 December 2015 est.)
country comparison to the world: 174

Debt - external: $93.6 million (2013 est.)
$93.5 million (2012 est.)
country comparison to the world: 194

Exchange rates: the US dollar is used

ENERGY

Electricity access: *electrification - total population:* 82% (2018)
electrification - urban areas: 93.5% (2018)
electrification - rural areas: 78.7% (2018)

Coal: *production:* 0 metric tons (2020 est.)
consumption: 0 metric tons (2020 est.)
exports: 0 metric tons (2020 est.)
imports: 0 metric tons (2020 est.)

Petroleum: *refined petroleum consumption:* 1,200 bbl/day (2019 est.)

Refined petroleum products - production: 0 bbl/day (2014)
country comparison to the world: 177

Refined petroleum products - exports: 0 bbl/day
country comparison to the world: 182

Natural gas: *production:* 0 cubic meters (2021 est.)
consumption: 0 cubic meters (2021 est.)
exports: 0 cubic meters (2021 est.)
imports: 0 cubic meters (2021 est.)
proven reserves: 0 cubic meters (2021 est.)

Carbon dioxide emissions: 177,000 metric tonnes of CO_2 (2019 est.)
from coal and metallurgical coke: 0 metric tonnes of CO_2 (2019 est.)
from petroleum and other liquids: 177,000 metric tonnes of CO_2 (2019 est.)
from consumed natural gas: 0 metric tonnes of CO_2 (2019 est.)
country comparison to the world: 204

Energy consumption per capita: 0 Btu/person (2019 est.)
country comparison to the world: 202

COMMUNICATIONS

Telephones - fixed lines: *total subscriptions:* 7,000 (2020 est.)
subscriptions per 100 inhabitants: 6 (2020 est.)
country comparison to the world: 195

Telephones - mobile cellular: *total subscriptions:* 22,000 (2020 est.)
subscriptions per 100 inhabitants: 19 (2020 est.)
country comparison to the world: 214

Telecommunication systems: *general assessment:* adequate system, the demand for mobile broadband is increasing due to mobile services being the primary and most wide-spread source for Internet access across the region (2020)
domestic: islands interconnected by shortwave radiotelephone, satellite (Intelsat) ground stations, and some coaxial and fiber-optic cable; mobile-cellular service available on the major islands; fixed line teledensity roughly 6 per 100 and mobile-cellular nearly 19 per 100 (2020)
international: country code - 691; landing points for the Chuukk-Pohnpei Cable and HANTRU-1 submarine cable system linking the Federated States of Micronesia and the US; satellite earth stations - 5 Intelsat (Pacific Ocean) (2019)

Broadcast media: no TV broadcast stations; each state has a multi-channel cable service with TV transmissions carrying roughly 95% imported programming and 5% local programming; about a half-dozen radio stations (2009)

Internet country code: .fm

Internet users: *total:* 39,834 (2019 est.)
percent of population: 35% (2019 est.)
country comparison to the world: 202

Broadband - fixed subscriptions: *total:* 6,000 (2020 est.)
subscriptions per 100 inhabitants: 5 (2020 est.)
country comparison to the world: 183

TRANSPORTATION

Civil aircraft registration country code prefix: V6

Airports: *total:* 6 (2021)
country comparison to the world: 174

Airports - with paved runways: *total:* 6
1,524 to 2,437 m: 4
914 to 1,523 m: 2 (2021)

Roadways: note - paved and unpaved circumferential roads, most interior roads are unpaved

Merchant marine: *total:* 38
by type: general cargo 19, oil tanker 4, other 15 (2021)
country comparison to the world: 127

Ports and terminals: *major seaport(s):* Colonia (Tamil Harbor), Molsron Lele Harbor, Pohnepi Harbor

MILITARY AND SECURITY

Military and security forces: no military forces; Federated States of Micronesia National Police (includes a maritime wing)

Military - note: defense is the responsibility of the US Micronesia has a "shiprider" agreement with the US, which allows local maritime law enforcement officers to embark on US Coast Guard (USCG) and US Navy (USN) vessels, including to board and search vessels suspected of violating laws or regulations within Micronesia's designated exclusive economic zone (EEZ) or on the high seas; "shiprider" agreements also enable USCG personnel and USN vessels with embarked USCG law enforcement personnel to work with host nations to protect critical regional resources (2022)

TRANSNATIONAL ISSUES

Disputes - international: none identified

Illicit drugs: major consumer of cannabis

MOLDOVA

INTRODUCTION

Background: A large portion of present day Moldovan territory became a province of the Russian Empire in 1812 and then unified with Romania in 1918 in the aftermath of World War I. This territory was then incorporated into the Soviet Union at the close of World War II. Although Moldova has been independent from the Soviet Union since 1991, Russian forces have remained on Moldovan territory east of the Nistru River in the breakaway region of Transnistria.

Years of Communist Party rule in Moldova from 2001-09 ultimately ended with election-related violent protests and a rerun of parliamentary elections in 2009. A series of pro-Europe ruling coalitions governed Moldova from 2010-19, but pro-Russia Igor DODON won the presidency in 2016 and his Socialist Party of the Republic of Moldova won a plurality in the legislative election in 2019. Pro-EU reformist candidate Maia SANDU defeated DODON in his reelection bid in November 2020 and the Party of Action and Solidarity, which SANDU founded in 2015, won a parliamentary majority in an early legislative election in July 2021. Prime Minister Natalia GAVRILITA and her cabinet took office in August 2021.

GEOGRAPHY

Location: Eastern Europe, northeast of Romania

Geographic coordinates: 47 00 N, 29 00 E

Map references: Europe

Area: *total:* 33,851 sq km
land: 32,891 sq km
water: 960 sq km

Area - comparative: slightly larger than Maryland

Land boundaries: *total:* 1,885 km
border countries (2): Romania 683 km; Ukraine 1202 km

Coastline: 0 km (landlocked)

Maritime claims: none (landlocked)

Climate: moderate winters, warm summers

Terrain: rolling steppe, gradual slope south to Black Sea

Elevation: *highest point:* Dealul Balanesti 430 m
lowest point: Dniester (Nistru) 2 m

mean elevation: 139 m

Natural resources: lignite, phosphorites, gypsum, limestone, arable land

Land use: *agricultural land:* 74.9% (2018 est.)
arable land: 55.1% (2018 est.)
permanent crops: 9.1% (2018 est.)
permanent pasture: 10.7% (2018 est.)
forest: 11.9% (2018 est.)
other: 13.2% (2018 est.)

Irrigated land: 2,283 sq km (2012)

Major rivers (by length in km): Danube (shared with Germany [s], Austria, Slovakia, Czechia, Hungary, Croatia, Serbia, Bulgaria, Ukraine, and Romania [m]) - 2,888 km; Dniester (shared with Ukraine [s/m]) - 1,411 km
note – [s] after country name indicates river source; [m] after country name indicates river mouth

Major watersheds (area sq km): Atlantic Ocean drainage: *(Black Sea)* Danube (795,656 sq km)

Population distribution: pockets of agglomeration exist throughout the country, the largest being in the center of the country around the capital of Chisinau, followed by Tiraspol and Balti

Natural hazards: landslides

Geography - note: landlocked; well endowed with various sedimentary rocks and minerals including sand, gravel, gypsum, and limestone

PEOPLE AND SOCIETY

Population: 3,287,326 (2022 est.)

Nationality: *noun:* Moldovan(s)
adjective: Moldovan

Ethnic groups: Moldovan 75.1%, Romanian 7%, Ukrainian 6.6%, Gagauz 4.6%, Russian 4.1%, Bulgarian 1.9%, other 0.8% (2014 est.)

Languages: Moldovan/Romanian 80.2% (official) (56.7% identify their mother tongue as Moldovan, which is virtually the same as Romanian; 23.5% identify Romanian as their mother tongue), Russian 9.7%, Gagauz 4.2% (a Turkish language), Ukrainian 3.9%, Bulgarian 1.5%, Romani 0.3%, other 0.2% (2014 est.); note - data represent mother tongue
major-language sample(s): Cartea informativa a lumii, sursa indispensabila pentru informatii de baza. (Moldovan/Romanian)

Religions: Orthodox 90.1%, other Christian 2.6%, other 0.1%, agnostic <0.1%, atheist 0.2%, unspecified 6.9% (2014 est.)

Age structure: *0-14 years:* 18.31% (male 317,243/female 298,673)
15-24 years: 11.27% (male 196,874/female 182,456)
25-54 years: 43.13% (male 738,103/female 712,892)
55-64 years: 13.26% (male 205,693/female 240,555)
65 years and over: 14.03% (male 186,949/female 285,058) (2020 est.)

Dependency ratios: *total dependency ratio:* 39.6
youth dependency ratio: **22.2**
elderly dependency ratio: 17.4
potential support ratio: 5.7 (2020 est.)

Median age: *total:* 37.7 years
male: 36.2 years
female: 39.5 years (2020 est.)

Population growth rate: -1.12% (2022 est.)

Birth rate: 10.19 births/1,000 population (2022 est.)

Death rate: 12.47 deaths/1,000 population (2022 est.)

Net migration rate: -8.87 migrant(s)/1,000 population (2022 est.)

Population distribution: pockets of agglomeration exist throughout the country, the largest being in the center of the country around the capital of Chisinau, followed by Tiraspol and Balti

Urbanization: *urban population:* 43.2% of total population (2022)
rate of urbanization: 0.09% annual rate of change (2020-25 est.)

Major urban areas - population: 491,000 CHISINAU (capital) (2022)

Sex ratio: *at birth:* 1.06 male(s)/female
0-14 years: 1.06 male(s)/female
15-24 years: 1.08 male(s)/female
25-54 years: 1.04 male(s)/female
55-64 years: 0.86 male(s)/female
65 years and over: 0.46 male(s)/female
total population: 0.96 male(s)/female (2022 est.)

Mother's mean age at first birth: 25.2 years (2019 est.)

Maternal mortality ratio: 19 deaths/100,000 live births (2017 est.)

Infant mortality rate: *total:* 11.6 deaths/1,000 live births
male: 13.55 deaths/1,000 live births
female: 9.54 deaths/1,000 live births (2022 est.)

Life expectancy at birth: *total population:* 72.44 years
male: 68.6 years
female: 76.52 years (2022 est.)

Total fertility rate: 1.59 children born/woman (2022 est.)

Contraceptive prevalence rate: 56% (2020)

Drinking water source: *improved: urban:* 98.9% of population
rural: 87% of population
total: 92.1% of population
unimproved: urban: 1.1% of population
rural: 13% of population
total: 7.9% of population (2020 est.)

Current health expenditure: 6.4% of GDP (2019)

Physicians density: 3.1 physicians/1,000 population (2020)

Hospital bed density: 5.7 beds/1,000 population (2014)

Sanitation facility access: *improved: urban:* 99% of population
rural: 83.1% of population
total: 89.9% of population
unimproved: urban: 1% of population
rural: 16.9% of population
total: 10.1% of population (2020 est.)

HIV/AIDS - adult prevalence rate: 0.8% (2020 est.)

Obesity - adult prevalence rate: 18.9% (2016)

Alcohol consumption per capita: *total:* 7.45 liters of pure alcohol (2019 est.)
beer: 1.53 liters of pure alcohol (2019 est.)
wine: 3.57 liters of pure alcohol (2019 est.)
spirits: 2.25 liters of pure alcohol (2019 est.)
other alcohols: 0.1 liters of pure alcohol (2019 est.)

Tobacco use: *total:* 29% (2020 est.)
male: 51.7% (2020 est.)
female: 6.2% (2020 est.)

Children under the age of 5 years underweight: 2.2% (2012)

Education expenditures: 6.1% of GDP (2019 est.)

Literacy: *definition:* age 15 and over can read and write
total population: 99.4%
male: 99.7%
female: 99.1% (2015)

School life expectancy (primary to tertiary education): *total:* 14 years
male: 14 years
female: 15 years (2020)

Unemployment, youth ages 15-24: *total:* 10.9%
male: 9.9%
female: 12.3% (2020 est.)

ENVIRONMENT

Environment - current issues: heavy use of agricultural chemicals has contaminated soil and groundwater; extensive soil erosion and declining soil fertility from poor farming methods

Environment - international agreements: *party to:* Air Pollution, Air Pollution-Heavy Metals, Air Pollution-Persistent Organic Pollutants, Biodiversity, Climate Change, Climate Change-Kyoto Protocol, Climate Change-Paris Agreement, Comprehensive Nuclear Test Ban, Desertification, Endangered Species, Hazardous Wastes, Law of the Sea, Ozone Layer Protection, Ship Pollution, Wetlands
signed, but not ratified: Air Pollution-Multi-effect Protocol

Air pollutants: *particulate matter emissions:* 15.97 micrograms per cubic meter (2016 est.)
carbon dioxide emissions: 5.12 megatons (2016 est.)
methane emissions: 3.29 megatons (2020 est.)

Climate: moderate winters, warm summers

Land use: *agricultural land:* 74.9% (2018 est.)
arable land: 55.1% (2018 est.)
permanent crops: 9.1% (2018 est.)
permanent pasture: 10.7% (2018 est.)
forest: 11.9% (2018 est.)
other: 13.2% (2018 est.)

Urbanization: *urban population:* 43.2% of total population (2022)
rate of urbanization: 0.09% annual rate of change (2020-25 est.)

Revenue from forest resources: *forest revenues:* 0.26% of GDP (2018 est.)

Revenue from coal: *coal revenues:* 0% of GDP (2018 est.)

Waste and recycling: *municipal solid waste generated annually:* 3,981,200 tons (2015 est.)
municipal solid waste recycled annually: 609,920 tons (2015 est.)
percent of municipal solid waste recycled: 15.3% (2015 est.)

Major rivers (by length in km): Danube (shared with Germany [s], Austria, Slovakia, Czechia, Hungary, Croatia, Serbia, Bulgaria, Ukraine, and Romania [m]) - 2,888 km; Dniester (shared with Ukraine [s/m]) - 1,411 km
note – [s] after country name indicates river source; [m] after country name indicates river mouth

Major watersheds (area sq km): Atlantic Ocean drainage: *(Black Sea)* Danube (795,656 sq km)

Total water withdrawal: *municipal:* 148 million cubic meters (2017 est.)
industrial: 650 million cubic meters (2017 est.)
agricultural: 42 million cubic meters (2017 est.)

Total renewable water resources: 12.27 billion cubic meters (2017 est.)

GOVERNMENT

Country name: *conventional long form:* Republic of Moldova
conventional short form: Moldova
local long form: Republica Moldova
local short form: Moldova
former: Moldavian Soviet Socialist Republic, Moldovan Soviet Socialist Republic
etymology: named for the Moldova River in neighboring eastern Romania

Government type: parliamentary republic

Capital: *name:* Chisinau in Moldovan (Kishinev in Russian)
geographic coordinates: 47 00 N, 28 51 E
time difference: UTC+2 (7 hours ahead of Washington, DC, during Standard Time)
daylight saving time: +1hr, begins last Sunday in March; ends last Sunday in October
etymology: origin unclear but may derive from the archaic Romanian word *chisla* ("spring" or "water source") and *noua* ("new") because the original settlement was built at the site of a small spring
note: pronounced KEE-shee-now (KIH-shi-nyov)

Administrative divisions: 32 raions (raioane, singular - raion), 3 municipalities (municipii, singular - municipiul), 1 autonomous territorial unit (unitatea teritoriala autonoma), and 1 territorial unit (unitatea teritoriala)
raions: Anenii Noi, Basarabeasca, Briceni, Cahul, Cantemir, Calarasi, Causeni, Cimislia, Criuleni, Donduseni, Drochia, Dubasari, Edinet, Falesti, Floresti, Glodeni, Hincesti, Ialoveni, Leova, Nisporeni, Ocnita, Orhei, Rezina, Riscani, Singerei, Soldanesti, Soroca, Stefan Voda, Straseni, Taraclia, Telenesti, Ungheni
municipalities: Balti, Bender, Chisinau
autonomous territorial unit: Gagauzia
territorial unit: Stinga Nistrului (Transnistria)

Independence: 27 August 1991 (from the Soviet Union)

National holiday: Independence Day, 27 August (1991)

Constitution: *history:* previous 1978; latest adopted 29 July 1994, effective 27 August 1994
amendments: proposed by voter petition (at least 200,000 eligible voters), by at least one third of Parliament members, or by the government; passage requires two-thirds majority vote of Parliament within one year of initial proposal; revisions to constitutional articles on sovereignty, independence, and neutrality require majority vote by referendum; articles on fundamental rights and freedoms cannot be amended; amended many times, last in 2018

Legal system: civil law system with Germanic law influences; Constitutional Court review of legislative acts

International law organization participation: has not submitted an ICJ jurisdiction declaration; accepts ICCt jurisdiction

Citizenship: *citizenship by birth:* no
citizenship by descent only: at least one parent must be a citizen of Moldova
dual citizenship recognized: no
residency requirement for naturalization: 10 years

Suffrage: 18 years of age; universal

Executive branch: *chief of state:* President Maia SANDU (since 24 December 2020)
head of government: Prime Minister Natalia GAVRILITA (since 6 August 2021)
cabinet: Cabinet proposed by the prime minister-designate, nominated by the president, approved through a vote of confidence in Parliament
elections/appointments: president directly elected for a 4-year term (eligible for a second term); election last held on 15 November 2020 (next to be held in fall 2024); prime minister designated by the president upon consultation with Parliament; within 15 days from designation, the prime minister-designate must request a vote of confidence for his/her proposed work program from the Parliament
election results:
2020: Maia SANDU elected president; percent of vote (second round results) - Maia SANDU (PAS) 57.7%, Igor DODON (PSRM) 42.3%
2016: Igor DODON elected president; percent of vote 52.1%, and Maia SANDU 47.9%

Legislative branch: *description:* unicameral Parliament (101 seats; 51 members directly elected in single-seat constituencies by simple majority vote and 50 members directly elected in a single, nationwide constituency by closed party-list proportional representation vote; all members serve 4-year terms
elections:
last held on 11 July 2021 (next scheduled in July 2025)
election results:
percent of vote by party - PAS 52.8%, BECS (PSRM+PCRM) 27.1%, SHOR 5.7%; seats by party - PAS 63, BECS 32, SHOR 6; composition as of July 2022 - men 60, women 41, percent of women 40.6%

Judicial branch: *highest court(s):* Supreme Court of Justice (consists of the chief judge, 3 deputy-chief judges, 45 judges, and 7 assistant judges); Constitutional Court (consists of the court president and 6 judges); note - the Constitutional Court is autonomous to the other branches of government; the Court interprets the Constitution and reviews the constitutionality of parliamentary laws and decisions, decrees of the president, and acts of the government
judge selection and term of office: Supreme Court of Justice judges appointed by the president upon the recommendation of the Superior Council of Magistracy, an 11-member body of judicial officials; all judges serve 4-year renewable terms; Constitutional Court judges appointed 2 each by Parliament, the president, and the Higher Council of Magistracy for 6-year terms; court president elected by other court judges for a 3-year term
subordinate courts: Courts of Appeal; Court of Business Audit; municipal courts

Political parties and leaders: Party of Action and Solidarity or PAS [Igor GROSU]
Electoral Bloc of Communists and Socialists or BCS [Vlad BATRINCEA, PSRM and Vladimir VORONIN, PCRM]
Party of Communists of the Republic of Moldova or PCRM [Vladimir VORONIN]
Party of Socialists of the Republic of Moldova or PSRM [Vlad BATRINCEA]
SOR Party or PS [Ilan SHOR]

International organization participation: BSEC, CD, CE, CEI, CIS, EAEU (observer), EAPC, EBRD, FAO, GCTU, GUAM, IAEA, IBRD, ICAO, ICC (NGOs), ICCt, ICRM, IDA, IFAD, IFC, IFRCS, ILO, IMF, IMO, Interpol, IOC, IOM, IPU, ISO (correspondent), ITU, ITUC (NGOs), MIGA, OIF, OPCW, OSCE, PFP, SELEC, UN, UNCTAD, UNESCO, UNHCR, UNIDO, Union Latina, UNMIL, UNMISS, UNOCI, UNWTO, UPU, WCO, WHO, WIPO, WMO, WTO

Diplomatic representation in the US: *chief of mission:* Ambassador (vacant); Charge d'Affaires Carolina PEREBINOS (since 27 July 2022)
chancery: 2101 S Street NW, Washington, DC 20008
telephone: [1] (202) 667-1130
FAX: [1] (202) 667-2624
email address and website:
washington@mfa.gov.md
https://sua.mfa.gov.md/en

Diplomatic representation from the US: *chief of mission:* Ambassador Kent D. LOGSDON (since 16 February 2022)
embassy: 103 Mateevici Street, Chisinau MD-2009
mailing address: 7080 Chisinau Place, Washington DC 20521-7080
telephone: [373] (22) 408-300
FAX: [373] (22) 233-044
email address and website:
ChisinauACS@state.gov
https://md.usembassy.gov/

Flag description: three equal vertical bands of Prussian blue (hoist side), chrome yellow, and vermilion red; emblem in center of flag is of a Roman eagle of dark gold (brown) outlined in black with a red beak and talons carrying a yellow cross in its beak and a green olive branch in its right talons and a yellow scepter in its left talons; on its breast is a shield divided horizontally red over blue with a stylized aurochs head, star, rose, and crescent all in black-outlined yellow; based on the color scheme of the flag of Romania - with which Moldova shares a history and culture - but Moldova's blue band is lighter; the reverse of the flag displays a mirrored image of the coat of arms
note: one of only three national flags that differ on their obverse and reverse sides - the others are Paraguay and Saudi Arabia

National symbol(s): aurochs (a type of wild cattle); national colors: blue, yellow, red

National anthem: *name:* "Limba noastra" (Our Language)
lyrics/music: Alexei MATEEVICI/Alexandru CRISTEA
note: adopted 1994

National heritage: *total World Heritage Sites:* 1 (cultural)
selected World Heritage Site locales: Struve Geodetic Arc

ECONOMY

Economic overview: Despite recent progress, Moldova remains one of the poorest countries in

Europe. With a moderate climate and productive farmland, Moldova's economy relies heavily on its agriculture sector, featuring fruits, vegetables, wine, wheat, and tobacco. Moldova also depends on annual remittances of about $1.2 billion - almost 15% of GDP - from the roughly one million Moldovans working in Europe, Israel, Russia, and elsewhere.

With few natural energy resources, Moldova imports almost all of its energy supplies from Russia and Ukraine. Moldova's dependence on Russian energy is underscored by a more than $6 billion debt to Russian natural gas supplier Gazprom, largely the result of unreimbursed natural gas consumption in the breakaway region of Transnistria. Moldova and Romania inaugurated the Ungheni-Iasi natural gas interconnector project in August 2014. The 43-kilometer pipeline between Moldova and Romania, allows for both the import and export of natural gas. Several technical and regulatory delays kept gas from flowing into Moldova until March 2015. Romanian gas exports to Moldova are largely symbolic. In 2018, Moldova awarded a tender to Romanian Transgaz to construct a pipeline connecting Ungheni to Chisinau, bringing the gas to Moldovan population centers. Moldova also seeks to connect with the European power grid by 2022.

The government's stated goal of EU integration has resulted in some market-oriented progress. Moldova experienced better than expected economic growth in 2017, largely driven by increased consumption, increased revenue from agricultural exports, and improved tax collection. During fall 2014, Moldova signed an Association Agreement and a Deep and Comprehensive Free Trade Agreement with the EU (AA/DCFTA), connecting Moldovan products to the world's largest market. The EU AA/DCFTA has contributed to significant growth in Moldova's exports to the EU. In 2017, the EU purchased over 65% of Moldova's exports, a major change from 20 years previously when the Commonwealth of Independent States (CIS) received over 69% of Moldova's exports. A $1 billion assetstripping heist of Moldovan banks in late 2014 delivered a significant shock to the economy in 2015; the subsequent bank bailout increased inflationary pressures and contributed to the depreciation of the leu and a minor recession. Moldova's growth has also been hampered by endemic corruption, which limits business growth and deters foreign investment, and Russian restrictions on imports of Moldova's agricultural products. The government's push to restore stability and implement meaningful reform led to the approval in 2016 of a $179 million three-year IMF program focused on improving the banking and fiscal environments, along with additional assistance programs from the EU, World Bank, and Romania. Moldova received two IMF tranches in 2017, totaling over $42.5 million.

Over the longer term, Moldova's economy remains vulnerable to corruption, political uncertainty, weak administrative capacity, vested bureaucratic interests, energy import dependence, Russian political and economic pressure, heavy dependence on agricultural exports, and unresolved separatism in Moldova's Transnistria region.

Real GDP (purchasing power parity): $32.26 billion (2020 est.)
$34.68 billion (2019 est.)
$33.48 billion (2018 est.)
note: data are in 2017 dollars

Real GDP growth rate: 4.5% (2017 est.)
4.3% (2016 est.)
-0.4% (2015 est.)

Real GDP per capita: $12,300 (2020 est.)
$13,000 (2019 est.)
$12,400 (2018 est.)
note: data are in 2017 dollars

GDP (official exchange rate): $11.982 billion (2019 est.)

Inflation rate (consumer prices): 4.8% (2019 est.)
3% (2018 est.)
6.5% (2017 est.)

Credit ratings:

Moody's rating: B3 (2010)
note: The year refers to the year in which the current credit rating was first obtained.

GDP - composition, by sector of origin: *agriculture:* 17.7% (2017 est.)
industry: 20.3% (2017 est.)
services: 62% (2017 est.)

GDP - composition, by end use: *household consumption:* 85.8% (2017 est.)
government consumption: 19% (2017 est.)
investment in fixed capital: 21.9% (2017 est.)
investment in inventories: 1.4% (2017 est.)
exports of goods and services: 42.5% (2017 est.)
imports of goods and services: -70.7% (2017 est.)

Agricultural products: maize, wheat, sunflower seed, grapes, apples, sugar beet, milk, potatoes, barley, plums/sloes

Industries: sugar processing, vegetable oil, food processing, agricultural machinery; foundry equipment, refrigerators and freezers, washing machines; hosiery, shoes, textiles

Industrial production growth rate: 3% (2017 est.)

Labor force: 1.295 million (2017 est.)

Labor force - by occupation: *agriculture:* 32.3%
industry: 12%
services: 55.7% (2017 est.)

Unemployment rate: 4.99% (2019 est.)
3.16% (2018 est.)

Unemployment, youth ages 15-24: *total:* 10.9%
male: 9.9%
female: 12.3% (2020 est.)

Population below poverty line: 7.3% (2018 est.)

Gini Index coefficient - distribution of family income: 25.7 (2018 est.)
26.8 (2014 est.)

Household income or consumption by percentage share: *lowest 10%:* 4.2%
highest 10%: 22.1% (2014 est.)

Budget: *revenues:* 2.886 billion (2017 est.)
expenditures: 2.947 billion (2017 est.)
note: National Public Budget

Budget surplus (+) or deficit (-): -0.6% (of GDP) (2017 est.)

Public debt: 31.5% of GDP (2017 est.)
35.8% of GDP (2016 est.)

Taxes and other revenues: 30.2% (of GDP) (2017 est.)

Fiscal year: calendar year

Current account balance: -$602 million (2017 est.)
-$268 million (2016 est.)

Exports: $3.24 billion (2020 est.) note: data are in current year dollars
$3.66 billion (2019 est.) note: data are in current year dollars
$3.45 billion (2018 est.) note: data are in current year dollars

Exports - partners: Romania 27%, Russia 9%, Italy 9%, Germany 9%, Turkey 6%, Poland 5% (2019)

Exports - commodities: insulated wiring, sunflower seeds, wine, corn, seats (2019)

Imports: $5.93 billion (2020 est.) note: data are in current year dollars
$6.62 billion (2019 est.) note: data are in current year dollars
$6.39 billion (2018 est.) note: data are in current year dollars

Imports - partners: Romania 20%, Russia 10%, Ukraine 9%, Germany 8%, China 7%, Turkey 6%, Italy 6% (2019)

Imports - commodities: refined petroleum, cars, insulated wiring, packaged medicines, broadcasting equipment (2019)

Reserves of foreign exchange and gold: $2.803 billion (31 December 2017 est.)
$2.206 billion (31 December 2016 est.)

Debt - external: $7.232 billion (2019 est.)
$7.16 billion (2018 est.)

Exchange rates: Moldovan lei (MDL) per US dollar -
18.49 (2017 est.)
19.924 (2016 est.)
19.924 (2015 est.)
19.83 (2014 est.)
14.036 (2013 est.)

ENERGY

Electricity access: *electrification - total population:* 100% (2020)

Electricity: *installed generating capacity:* 594,000 kW (2020 est.)
consumption: 4,591,230,000 kWh (2019 est.)
exports: 0 kWh (2020 est.)
imports: 629 million kWh (2020 est.)
transmission/distribution losses: 571 million kWh (2019 est.)

Electricity generation sources: *fossil fuels:* 93.6% of total installed capacity (2020 est.)
solar: 0.1% of total installed capacity (2020 est.)
wind: 1.2% of total installed capacity (2020 est.)
hydroelectricity: 4.5% of total installed capacity (2020 est.)
biomass and waste: 0.6% of total installed capacity (2020 est.)

Coal: *production:* 0 metric tons (2020 est.)
consumption: 133,000 metric tons (2020 est.)
exports: 0 metric tons (2020 est.)
imports: 133,000 metric tons (2020 est.)
proven reserves: 0 metric tons (2019 est.)

Petroleum: *total petroleum production:* 0 bbl/day (2021 est.)
refined petroleum consumption: 22,000 bbl/day (2019 est.)

Refined petroleum products - production: 232 bbl/day (2015 est.)

Refined petroleum products - exports: 275 bbl/day (2015 est.)

Refined petroleum products - imports: 18,160 bbl/day (2015 est.)

Natural gas: *production:* 57,000 cubic meters (2019 est.)
consumption: 2,802,400,000 cubic meters (2019 est.)
exports: 0 cubic meters (2021 est.)
imports: 2,802,344,000 cubic meters (2019 est.)
proven reserves: 0 cubic meters (2021 est.)

Carbon dioxide emissions: 8.114 million metric tonnes of CO_2 (2019 est.)
from coal and metallurgical coke: 374,000 metric tonnes of CO_2 (2019 est.)
from petroleum and other liquids: 2.968 million metric tonnes of CO_2 (2019 est.)
from consumed natural gas: 4.773 million metric tonnes of CO_2 (2019 est.)

Energy consumption per capita: 40.398 million Btu/person (2019 est.)

COMMUNICATIONS

Telephones - fixed lines: *total subscriptions:* 1,027,689 (2020 est.)
subscriptions per 100 inhabitants: 25 (2020 est.)

Telephones - mobile cellular: *total subscriptions:* 3,420,383 (2020 est.)
subscriptions per 100 inhabitants: 85 (2020 est.)

Telecommunication systems: *general assessment:* the telecom market has been affected by a combination of high unemployment and economic difficulties which have led to constraints on consumer spending; this has resulted in telecom revenue having fallen steadily in recent years; this decline continued into 2020, with a 6.3% in revenue from the important mobile sector alone, year-on-year; Moldova's aspirations to join the EU have encouraged the government and regulator to adopt a range of measures to bring the country's telecoms sector into line with EU principles and standards; in July 2017 the Electronic Communications Act was amended to accommodate the 2009 European regulatory framework, while further amendments were adopted in December 2017 and additional changes were proposed in 2019; Moldova is also part of the Eastern Partnership group of countries, and as such has set in train a glide path to reducing roaming charges, effective between 2022 and 2026; the country's broadband strategy through to 2025 has been supported by the ITU and industry counterparts from Korea; the internet market is developing rapidly, and though the penetration rate is well below the average for most European countries there are many opportunities for further development; the market is highly competitive, with 101 active ISPs as of early 2021; the number of cable broadband subscribers is increasing steadily, though fiber is now by far the strongest sector; by the end of 2020 fiber accounted for about 72.3% of all fixed broadband connections; the mobile market has also grown rapidly, and the sector accounts for the majority of total telecoms revenue; the near comprehensive geographical reach of their mobile networks, market brand recognition and existing customer relationships will make for steady subscriber growth in coming years (2022)
domestic: competition among mobile telephone providers has spurred subscriptions; little interest in expanding fixed-line service which is roughly 25 per 100; mobile-cellular teledensity nearly 85 per 100 persons (2020)
international: country code - 373; service through Romania and Russia via landline; satellite earth stations - at least 3 -Intelsat, Eutelsat, and Intersputnik

Broadcast media: state-owned national radio-TV broadcaster operates 1 TV and 1 radio station; a total of nearly 70 terrestrial TV channels and some 50 radio stations are in operation; Russian and Romanian channels also are available (2019)

Internet country code: .md

Internet users: *total:* 3,067,466 (July 2022 est.)
percent of population: 76.3% (July 2022 est.)

Broadband - fixed subscriptions: *total:* 719,001 (2020 est.)
subscriptions per 100 inhabitants: 18 (2020 est.)

TRANSPORTATION

National air transport system: *number of registered air carriers:* 6 (2020)
inventory of registered aircraft operated by air carriers: 21
annual passenger traffic on registered air carriers: 1,135,999 (2018)
annual freight traffic on registered air carriers: 640,000 (2018) mt-km

Civil aircraft registration country code prefix: ER

Airports: *total:* 7 (2021)

Airports - with paved runways: *total:* 5
over 3,047 m: 1
2,438 to 3,047 m: 2
1,524 to 2,437 m: 2 (2021)

Airports - with unpaved runways: *total:* 2
1,524 to 2,437 m: 1
under 914 m: 1 (2021)

Pipelines: 2,026 km gas (2021) (2021)

Railways: *total:* 1,171 km (2014)
standard gauge: 14 km (2014) 1.435-m gauge
broad gauge: 1,157 km (2014) 1.520-m gauge

Roadways: *total:* 9,352 km (2012)
paved: 8,835 km (2012)
unpaved: 517 km (2012)

Waterways: 558 km (2011) (in public use on Danube, Dniester and Prut Rivers)

Merchant marine: *total:* 147
by type: bulk carrier 5, container ship 5, general cargo 97, oil tanker 7, other 33 (2021)

MILITARY AND SECURITY

Military and security forces: National Army: Land Forces (Fortele Terestre ale Republicii Moldova, FTRM); Air Forces (Forţele Aeriene ale Republicii Moldova, FARM); Ministry of Internal Affairs: Carabinieri Troops (2022)
note: the Carabinieri is a quasi-militarized gendarmerie responsible for protecting public buildings, maintaining public order, and other national security functions

Military expenditures: 0.4% of GDP (2021 est.)
0.4% of GDP (2020 est.)
0.4% of GDP (2019 est.) (approximately $160 million)
0.4% of GDP (2018 est.) (approximately $130 million)
0.4% of GDP (2017 est.) (approximately $120 million)

Military and security service personnel strengths: approximately 6,500 active troops (2022)

Military equipment inventories and acquisitions: the Moldovan military's inventory is limited and almost entirely comprised of older Russian and Soviet-era equipment; since 2000, it has received small amounts of donated material from other nations, including the US (2021)

Military service age and obligation: 18-27 years of age for compulsory or voluntary military service; male registration required at age 16; 12-month service obligation (2022)
note: as of 2019, women made up about 20% of the military's full-time personnel

Military - note: Moldova is constitutionally neutral, but has maintained a relationship with NATO since 1992; bilateral cooperation started when Moldova joined NATO's Partnership for Peace program in 1994; Moldova has contributed small numbers of troops to NATO's Kosovo Force (KFOR) since 2014, and a civilian NATO liaison office was established in Moldova in 2017 at the request of the Moldovan Government to promote practical cooperation and facilitate support

the 1992 war between Moldovan forces and Transnistrian separatists backed by Russian troops ended with a cease-fire; as of 2022, Russia maintained approximately 1,500 troops in Transnistria, some of which served under the authority of a peacekeeping force known as a Joint Control Commission that also included Moldovan and separatist personnel; the remainder of the Russian contingent (the Operative Group of the Russian Troops or OGRT) guarded a depot of Soviet-era ammunition and trained Transnistrian separatist paramilitary troops (2022)

TRANSNATIONAL ISSUES

Disputes - international: *Moldova-Romania:* none identified
Moldova-Ukraine: Ukraine and Moldova signed an agreement officially delimiting their border in 1999, but the border has not been demarcated due to Moldova's difficulties with the break-away region of Transnistria; Moldova and Ukraine operate joint customs posts to monitor the transit of people and commodities through Moldova's break-away Transnistria region, which remains under the auspices of an Organization for Security and Cooperation in Europe-mandated peacekeeping mission comprised of Moldovan, Transnistrian, Russian, and Ukrainian troops

Refugees and internally displaced persons: *refugees (country of origin):* 96,646 (Ukraine) (as of 22 November 2022)
stateless persons: 3,372 (mid-year 2021)

Illicit drugs: limited cultivation of opium poppy and cannabis, mostly for CIS consumption; transshipment point for illicit drugs from Southwest Asia via Central Asia to Russia, Western Europe, and possibly the US; widespread crime and underground economic activity

MONACO

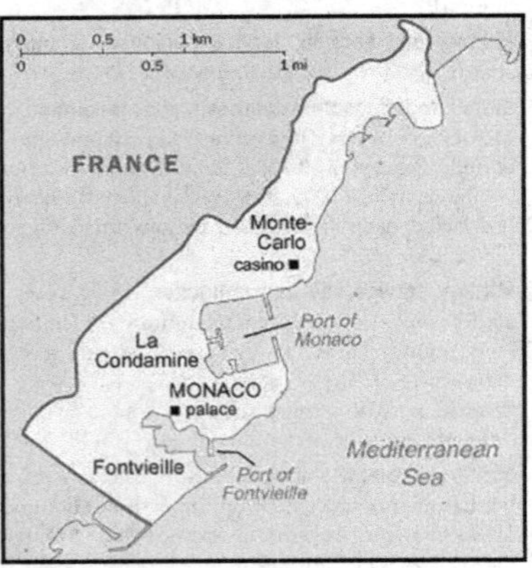

INTRODUCTION

Background: The Genoese built a fortress on the site of present day Monaco in 1215. The current ruling GRIMALDI family first seized control in 1297 but was not able to permanently secure its holding until 1419. Economic development was spurred in the late 19th century with a railroad linkup to France and the opening of a casino. Since then, the principality's mild climate, splendid scenery, and gambling facilities have made Monaco world famous as a tourist and recreation center.

GEOGRAPHY

Location: Western Europe, bordering the Mediterranean Sea on the southern coast of France, near the border with Italy

Geographic coordinates: 43 44 N, 7 24 E

Map references: Europe

Area: *total:* 2 sq km
land: 2 sq km
water: 0 sq km

Area - comparative: about three times the size of the National Mall in Washington, DC

Land boundaries: *total:* 6 km
border countries (1): France 6 km

Coastline: 4.1 km

Maritime claims: *territorial sea:* 12 nm
exclusive economic zone: 12 nm

Climate: Mediterranean with mild, wet winters and hot, dry summers

Terrain: hilly, rugged, rocky

Elevation: *highest point:* Chemin des Revoires on Mont Agel 162 m
lowest point: Mediterranean Sea 0 m

Natural resources: none

Land use: *agricultural land:* 1% (2018 est.)
arable land: 0% (2018 est.)
permanent crops: 1% (2018 est.)
permanent pasture: 0% (2018 est.)
forest: 0% (2018 est.)
other: 99% (2018 est.)

Irrigated land: 0 sq km (2012)

Population distribution: the second most densely populated country in the world (after Macau); its entire population living on 2 square km

Natural hazards: none

Geography - note: second-smallest independent state in the world (after the Holy See); smallest country with a coastline; almost entirely urban

PEOPLE AND SOCIETY

Population: 31,400 (2022 est.)
note: immigrants make up almost 68% of the total population, according to UN data (2019)

Nationality: *noun:* Monegasque(s) or Monacan(s)
adjective: Monegasque or Monacan

Ethnic groups: Monegasque 32.1%, French 19.9%, Italian 15.3%, British 5%, Belgian 2.3%, Swiss 2%, German 1.9%, Russian 1.8%, American 1.1%, Dutch 1.1%, Moroccan 1%, other 16.6% (2016 est.)
note: data represent population by country of birth

Languages: French (official), English, Italian, Monegasque
major-language sample(s): The World Factbook, une source indispensable d'informations de base. (French)

Religions: Roman Catholic 90% (official), other 10%

Age structure: *0-14 years:* 9.41% (male 1,497/female 1,415)
15-24 years: 9.52% (male 1,538/female 1,406)
25-54 years: 30.46% (male 4,779/female 4,644)
55-64 years: 15.47% (male 2,370/female 2,417)
65 years and over: 35.15% (male 4,817/female 6,057) (2020 est.)

Median age: *total:* 55.4 years
male: 53.7 years
female: 57 years (2020 est.)

Population growth rate: 0.6% (2022 est.)

Birth rate: 6.66 births/1,000 population (2022 est.)

Death rate: 10.7 deaths/1,000 population (2022 est.)

Net migration rate: 10.03 migrant(s)/1,000 population (2022 est.)

Population distribution: the second most densely populated country in the world (after Macau); its entire population living on 2 square km

Urbanization: *urban population:* 100% of total population (2022)
rate of urbanization: 0.5% annual rate of change (2020-25 est.)

Major urban areas - population: 39,000 MONACO (capital) (2018)

Sex ratio: *at birth:* 1.04 male(s)/female
0-14 years: 1.05 male(s)/female
15-24 years: 1.07 male(s)/female
25-54 years: 1.03 male(s)/female
55-64 years: 0.97 male(s)/female
65 years and over: 0.76 male(s)/female
total population: 0.94 male(s)/female (2022 est.)

Infant mortality rate: *total:* 1.76 deaths/1,000 live births
male: 2.07 deaths/1,000 live births
female: 1.45 deaths/1,000 live births (2022 est.)

Life expectancy at birth: *total population:* 89.52 years
male: 85.7 years
female: 93.49 years (2022 est.)

Total fertility rate: 1.53 children born/woman (2022 est.)

Drinking water source: *improved: urban:* 100% of population
total: 100% of population

Current health expenditure: 1.5% of GDP (2019)

Physicians density: 7.51 physicians/1,000 population (2014)

Hospital bed density: 13.8 beds/1,000 population (2012)

Sanitation facility access: *improved: urban:* 100% of population
total: 100% of population

Education expenditures: 1.2% of GDP (2019 est.)

Unemployment, youth ages 15-24: *total:* 26.7%
male: 25.7%
female: 27.9% (2016 est.)

ENVIRONMENT

Environment - current issues: no serious issues; actively monitors pollution levels in air and water

Environment - international agreements: *party to:* Air Pollution, Air Pollution-Heavy Metals, Air Pollution-Sulphur 94, Air Pollution-Volatile Organic Compounds, Antarctic-Environmental Protection, Antarctic Treaty, Biodiversity, Climate Change, Climate Change-Kyoto Protocol, Climate Change-Paris Agreement, Comprehensive Nuclear Test Ban, Desertification, Endangered Species, Hazardous Wastes, Law of the Sea, Marine Dumping-London Convention, Ozone Layer Protection, Ship Pollution, Wetlands, Whaling
signed, but not ratified: none of the selected agreements

Air pollutants: *particulate matter emissions:* 12.2 micrograms per cubic meter (2016 est.)
methane emissions: 0.05 megatons (2020 est.)

Climate: Mediterranean with mild, wet winters and hot, dry summers

Land use: *agricultural land:* 1% (2018 est.)
arable land: 0% (2018 est.)
permanent crops: 1% (2018 est.)
permanent pasture: 0% (2018 est.)
forest: 0% (2018 est.)
other: 99% (2018 est.)

Urbanization: *urban population:* 100% of total population (2022)
rate of urbanization: 0.5% annual rate of change (2020-25 est.)

Revenue from forest resources: *forest revenues:* 0% of GDP (2018 est.)

Waste and recycling: *municipal solid waste generated annually:* 46,000 tons (2012 est.)
municipal solid waste recycled annually: 2,484 tons (2012 est.)
percent of municipal solid waste recycled: 5.4% (2012 est.)

Total water withdrawal: *municipal:* 5 million cubic meters (2017 est.)
industrial: 0 cubic meters (2017 est.)
agricultural: 0 cubic meters (2017 est.)

GOVERNMENT

Country name: *conventional long form:* Principality of Monaco
conventional short form: Monaco
local long form: Principaute de Monaco
local short form: Monaco
etymology: founded as a Greek colony in the 6th century B.C., the name derives from two Greek words "monos" (single, alone) and "oikos" (house) to convey the sense of a people "living apart" or in a "single habitation"

Government type: constitutional monarchy

Capital: *name:* Monaco
geographic coordinates: 43 44 N, 7 25 E
time difference: UTC+1 (6 hours ahead of Washington, DC, during Standard Time)
daylight saving time: +1hr, begins last Sunday in March; ends last Sunday in October
etymology: founded as a Greek colony in the 6th century B.C., the name derives from two Greek words *monos* (single, alone) and *oikos* (house) to convey the sense of a people "living apart" or in a "single habitation"

Administrative divisions: none; there are no first-order administrative divisions as defined by the US Government, but there are 4 quarters (quartiers, singular - quartier); Fontvieille, La Condamine, Monaco-Ville, Monte-Carlo; note - Moneghetti, a part of La Condamine, is sometimes called the 5th quarter of Monaco

Independence: 1419 (beginning of permanent rule by the House of GRIMALDI)

National holiday: National Day (Saint Rainier's Day), 19 November (1857)

Constitution: *history:* previous 1911 (suspended 1959); latest adopted 17 December 1962
amendments: proposed by joint agreement of the chief of state (the prince) and the National Council; passage requires two-thirds majority vote of National Council members; amended 2002

Legal system: civil law system influenced by French legal tradition

International law organization participation: has not submitted an ICJ jurisdiction declaration; non-party state to the ICCt

Citizenship: *citizenship by birth:* no
citizenship by descent only: the father must be a citizen of Monaco; in the case of a child born out of wedlock, the mother must be a citizen and father unknown
dual citizenship recognized: no
residency requirement for naturalization: 10 years

Suffrage: 18 years of age; universal

Executive branch: *chief of state:* Prince ALBERT II (since 6 April 2005)
head of government: Minister of State Pierre DARTOUT (since 1 September 2020)
cabinet: Council of Government under the authority of the monarch
elections/appointments: the monarchy is hereditary; minister of state appointed by the monarch from a list of three French national candidates presented by the French Government

Legislative branch: *description:* unicameral National Council or Conseil National (24 seats; 16 members directly elected in multi-seat constituencies by simple majority vote and 8 directly elected by proportional representation vote; members serve 5-year terms)
elections:
last held on 11 February 2018 (next to be held on 28 February 2023)
election results:
percent of vote by party - Priorite Monaco 57.7%, Horizon Monaco 26.1%, Union Monegasque 16.2%; seats by party - Priorite Monaco 21, Horizon Monaco 2, Union Monegasque 1; composition - men 16, women 8, percent of women 33.3%

Judicial branch: *highest court(s):* Supreme Court (consists of 5 permanent members and 2 substitutes)
judge selection and term of office: Supreme Court members appointed by the monarch upon the proposals of the National Council, State Council, Crown Council, Court of Appeal, and Trial Court
subordinate courts: Court of Appeal; Civil Court of First Instance

Political parties and leaders: Horizon Monaco [Laurent NOUVION]
Priorite Monaco or Primo! [Stephane VALERI]
Union Monegasque [Jean-Francois ROBILLON]

International organization participation: CD, CE, FAO, IAEA, ICAO, ICC (national committees), ICRM, IFRCS, IHO, IMO, IMSO, Interpol, IOC, IPU, ITSO, ITU, OAS (observer), OIF, OPCW, OSCE, Schengen Convention (de facto member), UN, UNCTAD, UNESCO, UNIDO, Union Latina, UNWTO, UPU, WHO, WIPO, WMO

Diplomatic representation in the US: *chief of mission:* Ambassador Maguy MACCARIO-DOYLE (since 3 December 2013)
chancery: 888 17th Street NW, Washington, DC 20006
telephone: [1] (202) 234-1530
FAX: [1] (202) 244-7656
email address and website:
info@monacodc.org
https://monacodc.org/index.html
consulate(s) general: New York

Diplomatic representation from the US: *embassy:* US does not have an embassy in Monaco; the US Ambassador to France is accredited to Monaco; the US Consul General in Marseille (France), under the authority of the US Ambassador to France, handles diplomatic and consular matters concerning Monaco; +(33)(1) 43-12-22-22, enter zero "0" after the automated greeting; US Embassy Paris, 2 Avenue Gabriel, 75008 Paris, France

Flag description: two equal horizontal bands of red (top) and white; the colors are those of the ruling House of Grimaldi and have been in use since 1339, making the flag one of the world's oldest national banners
note: similar to the flag of Indonesia which is longer and the flag of Poland which is white (top) and red

National symbol(s): red and white lozenges (diamond shapes); national colors: red, white

National anthem: *name:* "A Marcia de Muneghu" (The March of Monaco)
lyrics/music: Louis NOTARI/Charles ALBRECHT
note: music adopted 1867, lyrics adopted 1931; although French is commonly spoken, only the Monegasque lyrics are official; the French version is known as "Hymne Monegasque" (Monegasque Anthem); the words are generally only sung on official occasions

ECONOMY

Economic overview: Monaco, bordering France on the Mediterranean coast, is a popular resort, attracting tourists to its casino and pleasant climate. The principality also is a banking center and has successfully sought to diversify into services and small, high-value-added, nonpolluting industries. The state retains monopolies in a number of sectors, including tobacco, the telephone network, and the postal service. Living standards are high, roughly comparable to those in prosperous French metropolitan areas.

The state has no income tax and low business taxes and thrives as a tax haven both for individuals who have established residence and for foreign companies that have set up businesses and offices. Monaco, however, is not a tax-free shelter; it charges nearly 20% value-added tax, collects stamp duties, and companies face a 33% tax on profits unless they can show that three-quarters of profits are generated within the principality. Monaco was formally removed from the OECD's "grey list" of uncooperative tax jurisdictions in late 2009, but continues to face international pressure to abandon its banking secrecy laws and help combat tax evasion. In October 2014, Monaco officially became the 84th jurisdiction participating in the OECD's Multilateral Convention on Mutual Administrative Assistance in Tax Matters, an effort to combat offshore tax avoidance and evasion.

Monaco's reliance on tourism and banking for its economic growth has left it vulnerable to downturns in France and other European economies which are the principality's main trade partners. In 2009, Monaco's GDP fell by 11.5% as the euro-zone crisis precipitated a sharp drop in tourism and retail activity and home sales. A modest recovery ensued in 2010 and intensified in 2013, with GDP growth of more than 9%, but Monaco's economic prospects remain uncertain.

Real GDP (purchasing power parity): $7.672 billion (2015 est.)
$7.279 billion (2014 est.)
$6.79 billion (2013 est.)
note: data are in 2015 US dollars

Real GDP growth rate: 5.4% (2015 est.)
7.2% (2014 est.)
9.6% (2013 est.)

Real GDP per capita: $115,700 (2015 est.)
$109,200 (2014 est.)
$101,900 (2013 est.)

GDP (official exchange rate): $6.006 billion (2015 est.)

Inflation rate (consumer prices): 1.5% (2010)

GDP - composition, by sector of origin: *agriculture:* 0% (2013)
industry: 14% (2013)
services: 86% (2013)

Agricultural products: none

Industries: banking, insurance, tourism, construction, small-scale industrial and consumer products

Industrial production growth rate: 6.8% (2015)

Labor force: 52,000 (2014 est.)
note: includes all foreign workers

Labor force - by occupation: *agriculture:* 0%
industry: 16.1%
services: 83.9% (2012 est.)

Unemployment rate: 2% (2012)

Unemployment, youth ages 15-24: *total:* 26.7%
male: 25.7%
female: 27.9% (2016 est.)

Budget: *revenues:* 896.3 million (2011 est.)
expenditures: 953.6 million (2011 est.)

Budget surplus (+) or deficit (-): -1% (of GDP) (2011 est.)

Taxes and other revenues: 14.9% (of GDP) (2011 est.)

Fiscal year: calendar year

Exports: $964.6 million (2017 est.)
$1.115 billion (2011)
note: full customs integration with France, which collects and rebates Monegasque trade duties; also participates in EU market system through customs union with France

Exports - partners: Italy 19%, Germany 14%, United Kingdom 9%, Switzerland 9%, Spain 8%, United States 6%, Belgium 5%
(2019)

Exports - commodities: jewelry, perfumes, watches, packaged medicines, plastic products (2019)

Imports: $1.371 billion (2017 est.)
$1.162 billion (2011 est.)
note: full customs integration with France, which collects and rebates Monegasque trade duties; also participates in EU market system through customs union with France

Imports - partners: Italy 34%, Switzerland 16%, Germany 9%, United Kingdom 7% (2019)

Imports - commodities: jewelry, recreational boats, cars and vehicle parts, watches, general wares (2019)

Exchange rates: euros (EUR) per US dollar -
0.885 (2017 est.)
0.903 (2016 est.)
0.9214 (2015 est.)
0.885 (2014 est.)
0.7634 (2013 est.)

ENERGY

Electricity access: *electrification - total population:* 100% (2020)

COMMUNICATIONS

Telephones - fixed lines: *total subscriptions:* 43,706 (2020 est.)
subscriptions per 100 inhabitants: 111 (2020 est.)

Telephones - mobile cellular: *total subscriptions:* 35,485 (2020 est.)
subscriptions per 100 inhabitants: 90 (2020 est.)

Telecommunication systems: *general assessment:* modern automatic telephone system; the country's sole fixed-line operator offers a full range of services to residential and business customers; competitive mobile telephony market; 4G LTE widely available (2020)
domestic: fixed-line a little over 111 per 100 and mobile-cellular teledensity exceeds 90 per 100 persons (2020)
international: country code - 377; landing points for the EIG and Italy-Monaco submarine cables connecting Monaco to Europe, Africa, the Middle East and Asia; no satellite earth stations; connected by cable into the French communications system (2019)

Broadcast media: TV Monte-Carlo operates a TV network; cable TV available; Radio Monte-Carlo has extensive radio networks in France and Italy with French-language broadcasts to France beginning in the 1960s and Italian-language broadcasts to Italy beginning in the 1970s; other radio stations include Riviera Radio and Radio Monaco

Internet country code: .mc

Internet users: *total:* 37,798 (2019 est.)
percent of population: 97% (2019 est.)

Broadband - fixed subscriptions: *total:* 20,877 (2020 est.)
subscriptions per 100 inhabitants: 53 (2020 est.)

TRANSPORTATION

Civil aircraft registration country code prefix: 3A

Heliports: 1 (2021)

Railways: *note:* Monaco has a single railway station but does not operate its own train service; the French operator SNCF operates rail services in Monaco

Ports and terminals: *major seaport(s):* Hercules Port

MILITARY AND SECURITY

Military and security forces: no regular military forces; Ministry of Interior: Compagnie des Carabiniers du Prince (Prince's Company of Carabiniers), Corps des Sapeurs-pompiers de Monaco (Fire and Emergency), Police Department (2022)
note: the primary responsibility for the Compagnie des Carabiniers du Prince is guarding the palace

Military service age and obligation: the Compagnie des Carabiniers du Prince is staffed by French nationals (2022)

Military - note: defense is the responsibility of France

TRANSNATIONAL ISSUES

Disputes - international: none identified

MONGOLIA

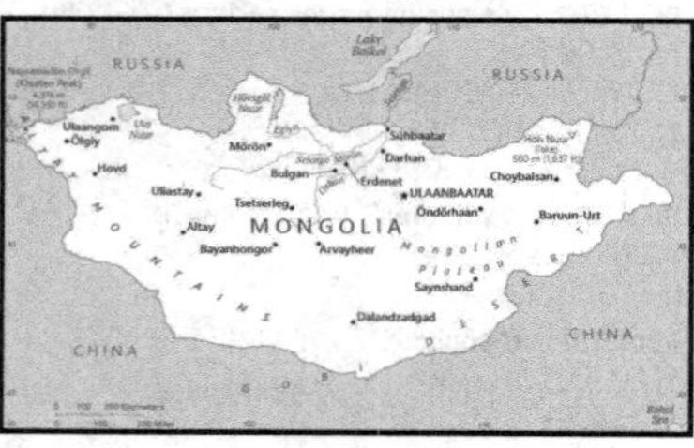

INTRODUCTION

Background: The peoples of Mongolia have a long history under a number of nomadic empires dating back to the period of the Xiongnu in the 4th century B.C. The name Mongol goes back to at least the 11th century A.D. The most famous Mongol, TEMÜÜJIN (aka Genghis Khan) emerged as the ruler of all Mongols in the early 1200s. By the time of his death in 1227, he had created through conquest a Mongol Empire that extended across much of Eurasia. His descendants, including ÖGÖDEI and KHUBILAI (aka Kublai Khan), continued military campaigns of conquest, taking control of Eastern Europe, the Middle East, and the rest of China where KHUBILAI established the Yuan Dynasty in the 1270s. The Mongols attempted to invade Japan and Java before their empire broke apart in the 14th century. In the 17th century, Mongolia fell under the rule of the Manchus of the Chinese Qing Dynasty. Following the collapse of the Manchus in 1911, Mongolia declared its independence, achieving it with help from the Soviet Union in 1921. Mongolia became a socialist state (the Mongolian People's Republic) in 1924. Following independence and until the collapse of the Soviet Union in 1989, the country was a Soviet satellite state, and heavily reliant on economic, military, and political assistance from Moscow. The period also was marked by purges, political repression, economic stagnation, and tensions with China.

Mongolia peacefully transitioned to an independent democracy in 1990. In 1992, it adopted a new constitution and established a free market economy. Since the country's transition, it has conducted eight presidential and nine legislative elections as of 2021. Throughout the period, the ex-communist Mongolian People's Revolutionary Party (MPRP) - which took the name Mongolian People's Party (MPP) in 2010 - has competed for political power with the Democratic Party (DP) and several other smaller parties, including a new party formed by former President ENKHBAYAR, which confusingly adopted for itself the MPRP name until it merged with MPP in 2021. In the 2016 parliamentary elections, the MPP won overwhelming control of the Parliament over the DP, which had overseen a sharp decline in Mongolia's economy during its control of the Parliament in the preceding years. Mongolians elected a DP member, Khaltmaa BATTULGA, as president in 2017. The June 2020 parliamentary elections left the MPP with continued dominant control of the parliament. Mongolians elected former prime minister and MPP member Ukhnaa KHURELSUKH as president in 2021. Mongolia maintains close cultural, political, and military ties with Russia while China is its largest economic partner. Mongolia's foreign relations are focused on preserving its autonomy by balancing relations with China and Russia, as well as its other major partners, Japan, South Korea, and the US.

GEOGRAPHY

Location: Northern Asia, between China and Russia

Geographic coordinates: 46 00 N, 105 00 E

Map references: Asia

Area: *total:* 1,564,116 sq km
land: 1,553,556 sq km
water: 10,560 sq km

Area - comparative: slightly smaller than Alaska; more than twice the size of Texas

Land boundaries: *total:* 8,082 km
border countries (2): China 4,630 km; Russia 3,452 km

Coastline: 0 km (landlocked)

Maritime claims: none (landlocked)

Climate: desert; continental (large daily and seasonal temperature ranges)

Terrain: vast semidesert and desert plains, grassy steppe, mountains in west and southwest; Gobi Desert in south-central

Elevation: *highest point:* Nayramadlin Orgil (Khuiten Peak) 4,374 m
lowest point: Hoh Nuur 560 m
mean elevation: 1,528 m

Natural resources: oil, coal, copper, molybdenum, tungsten, phosphates, tin, nickel, zinc, fluorspar, gold, silver, iron

Land use: *agricultural land:* 73% (2018 est.)
arable land: 0.4% (2018 est.)
permanent crops: 0% (2018 est.)
permanent pasture: 72.6% (2018 est.)
forest: 7% (2018 est.)
other: 20% (2018 est.)

Irrigated land: 840 sq km (2012)

Major lakes (area sq km): *fresh water lake(s):* Hovsgol Nuur - 2,620 sq km; Har Us Nuur - 1,760 sq km;
salt water lake(s): Uvs Nuur - 3,350 sq km; Hyargas Nuur - 1,360 sq km

Major rivers (by length in km): Amur (shared with China [s] and Russia [m]) - 4,444 km
note – [s] after country name indicates river source; [m] after country name indicates river mouth

Population distribution: sparsely distributed population throughout the country; the capital of Ulaanbaatar and the northern city of Darhan support the highest population densities

Natural hazards: dust storms; grassland and forest fires; drought; "zud," which is harsh winter conditions

Geography - note: landlocked; strategic location between China and Russia

PEOPLE AND SOCIETY

Population: 3,227,863 (2022 est.)
note: Mongolia is one of the least densely populated countries in the world (2 people per sq km); twice as many ethnic Mongols (some 6 million) live in Inner Mongolia (Nei Mongol) in neighboring China

Nationality: *noun:* Mongolian(s)
adjective: Mongolian

Ethnic groups: Khalkh 83.8%, Kazak 3.8%, Durvud 2.6%, Bayad 2%, Buriad 1.4%, Zakhchin 1.2%, Dariganga 1.1%, other 4.1% (2020 est.)

Languages: Mongolian 90% (official) (Khalkha dialect is predominant), Turkic, Russian (1999)

major-language sample(s): Дэлхийн баримтат ном, үндсэн мэдээллийн зайлшгүй эх сурвалж. (Mongolian)

Religions: Buddhist 51.7%, Muslim 3.2%, Shamanist 2.5%, Christian 1.3%, other 0.7%, none 40.6% (2020 est.)

Age structure: *0-14 years:* 26.96% (male 435,596/female 418,524)
15-24 years: 14.93% (male 239,495/female 233,459)
25-54 years: 45.29% (male 694,481/female 740,334)
55-64 years: 8.04% (male 115,560/female 139,129)
65 years and over: 4.78% (male 60,966/female 90,482) (2020 est.)

Dependency ratios: *total dependency ratio:* 54.8
youth dependency ratio: 48.1
elderly dependency ratio: 6.7
potential support ratio: 15 (2020 est.)

Median age: *total:* 29.8 years
male: 28.8 years
female: 30.7 years (2020 est.)

Population growth rate: 0.88% (2022 est.)

Birth rate: 15.84 births/1,000 population (2022 est.)

Death rate: 6.3 deaths/1,000 population (2022 est.)

Net migration rate: -0.77 migrant(s)/1,000 population (2022 est.)

Population distribution: sparsely distributed population throughout the country; the capital of Ulaanbaatar and the northern city of Darhan support the highest population densities

Urbanization: *urban population:* 68.9% of total population (2022)
rate of urbanization: 1.4% annual rate of change (2020-25 est.)

Major urban areas - population: 1.645 million ULAANBAATAR (capital) (2022)

Sex ratio: *at birth:* 1.05 male(s)/female
0-14 years: 1.04 male(s)/female
15-24 years: 1.03 male(s)/female
25-54 years: 0.93 male(s)/female
55-64 years: 0.82 male(s)/female
65 years and over: 0.51 male(s)/female
total population: 0.95 male(s)/female (2022 est.)

Mother's mean age at first birth: 20.5 years (2008 est.)
note: data represents median age at first birth among women 20-24

Maternal mortality ratio: 45 deaths/100,000 live births (2017 est.)

Infant mortality rate: *total:* 20.18 deaths/1,000 live births
male: 23.26 deaths/1,000 live births
female: 16.95 deaths/1,000 live births (2022 est.)

Life expectancy at birth: *total population:* 71.37 years
male: 67.19 years
female: 75.76 years (2022 est.)

Total fertility rate: 1.91 children born/woman (2022 est.)

Contraceptive prevalence rate: 48.1% (2018)

Drinking water source: *improved: urban:* 98.4% of population
rural: 64.2% of population
total: 87.6% of population
unimproved: urban: 1.6% of population
rural: 35.8% of population
total: 12.4% of population (2020 est.)

Current health expenditure: 3.8% of GDP (2019)

Physicians density: 3.85 physicians/1,000 population (2018)

Hospital bed density: 8 beds/1,000 population (2017)

Sanitation facility access: *improved: urban:* 97.4% of population
rural: 69.9% of population
total: 88.8% of population
unimproved: urban: 2.6% of population
rural: 30.1% of population
total: 11.2% of population (2020 est.)

HIV/AIDS - adult prevalence rate: (2020 est.) <.1%

Obesity - adult prevalence rate: 20.6% (2016)

Alcohol consumption per capita: *total:* 5.46 liters of pure alcohol (2019 est.)
beer: 2.18 liters of pure alcohol (2019 est.)
wine: 1.46 liters of pure alcohol (2019 est.)
spirits: 1.82 liters of pure alcohol (2019 est.)
other alcohols: 0 liters of pure alcohol (2019 est.)

Tobacco use: *total:* 29.4% (2020 est.)
male: 51.7% (2020 est.)
female: 7.1% (2020 est.)

Children under the age of 5 years underweight: 1.8% (2018)

Child marriage: *women married by age 15:* 0.9%
women married by age 18: 12%
men married by age 18: 2.1% (2018 est.)

Education expenditures: 4.9% of GDP (2019 est.)

Literacy: *definition:* age 15 and over can read and write
total population: 99.2%
male: 99.1%
female: 99.2% (2020)

School life expectancy (primary to tertiary education): *total:* 15 years
male: 14 years
female: 16 years (2019)

Unemployment, youth ages 15-24: *total:* 17.9%
male: 16.9%
female: 19.5% (2020 est.)

ENVIRONMENT

Environment - current issues: limited natural freshwater resources in some areas; the burning of soft coal in power plants and the lack of enforcement of environmental laws leads to air pollution in Ulaanbaatar; deforestation and overgrazing increase soil erosion from wind and rain; water pollution; desertification and mining activities have a deleterious effect on the environment

Environment - international agreements: *party to:* Antarctic Treaty, Biodiversity, Climate Change, Climate Change-Kyoto Protocol, Climate Change-Paris Agreement, Comprehensive Nuclear Test Ban, Desertification, Endangered Species, Environmental Modification, Hazardous Wastes, Law of the Sea, Nuclear Test Ban, Ozone Layer Protection, Ship Pollution, Wetlands, Whaling
signed, but not ratified: none of the selected agreements

Air pollutants: *particulate matter emissions:* 40.42 micrograms per cubic meter (2016 est.)
carbon dioxide emissions: 25.37 megatons (2016 est.)

methane emissions: 13.72 megatons (2020 est.)

Climate: desert; continental (large daily and seasonal temperature ranges)

Land use: *agricultural land:* 73% (2018 est.)
arable land: 0.4% (2018 est.)
permanent crops: 0% (2018 est.)
permanent pasture: 72.6% (2018 est.)
forest: 7% (2018 est.)
other: **20**% (2018 est.)

Urbanization: *urban population:* 68.9% of total population (2022)
rate of urbanization: 1.4% annual rate of change (2020-25 est.)

Revenue from forest resources: *forest revenues:* 0.14% of GDP (2018 est.)

Revenue from coal: *coal revenues:* 8.62% of GDP (2018 est.)

Waste and recycling: *municipal solid waste generated annually:* 2.9 million tons (2016 est.)

Major lakes (area sq km): *fresh water lake(s):* Hovsgol Nuur - 2,620 sq km; Har Us Nuur - 1,760 sq km;
salt water lake(s): Uvs Nuur - 3,350 sq km; Hyargas Nuur - 1,360 sq km

Major rivers (by length in km): Amur (shared with China [s] and Russia [m]) - 4,444 km
note – [s] after country name indicates river source; [m] after country name indicates river mouth

Total water withdrawal: *municipal:* 45.3 million cubic meters (2017 est.)
industrial: 166.2 million cubic meters (2017 est.)
agricultural: 250.9 million cubic meters (2017 est.)

Total renewable water resources: 34.8 billion cubic meters (2017 est.)

GOVERNMENT

Country name: *conventional long form:* none
conventional short form: Mongolia
local long form: none
local short form: Mongol Uls
former: Outer Mongolia, Mongolian People's Republic
etymology: the name means "Land of the Mongols" in Latin; the Mongolian name Mongol Uls translates as "Mongol State"

Government type: semi-presidential republic

Capital: *name:* Ulaanbaatar
geographic coordinates: 47 55 N, 106 55 E
time difference: UTC+8 (13 hours ahead of Washington, DC, during Standard Time)
daylight saving time: +1hr, begins last Saturday in March; ends last Saturday in September
time zone note: Mongolia has two time zones - Ulaanbaatar Time (8 hours in advance of UTC) and Hovd Time (7 hours in advance of UTC)
etymology: the name means "red hero" in Mongolian and honors national hero Damdin SUKHBAATAR, leader of the partisan army that with Soviet Red Army help, liberated Mongolia from Chinese occupation in the early 1920s

Administrative divisions: 21 provinces (aymguud, singular - aymag) and 1 municipality* (singular - hot); Arhangay, Bayanhongor, Bayan-Olgiy, Bulgan, Darhan-Uul, Dornod, Dornogovi, Dundgovi, Dzavhan (Zavkhan), Govi-Altay, Govisumber, Hentiy, Hovd, Hovsgol, Omnogovi, Orhon, Ovorhangay, Selenge, Suhbaatar, Tov, Ulaanbaatar*, Uvs

Independence: 29 December 1911 (independence declared from China; in actuality, autonomy attained); 11 July 1921 (from China)

National holiday: Naadam (games) holiday (commemorates independence from China in the 1921 Revolution), 11-15 July; Constitution Day (marks the date that the Mongolian People's Republic was created under a new constitution), 26 November (1924)

Constitution: *history:* several previous; latest adopted 13 January 1992, effective 12 February 1992
amendments: proposed by the State Great Hural, by the president of the republic, by the government, or by petition submitted to the State Great Hural by the Constitutional Court; conducting referenda on proposed amendments requires at least two-thirds majority vote of the State Great Hural; passage of amendments by the State Great Hural requires at least three-quarters majority vote; passage by referendum requires majority participation of qualified voters and a majority of votes; amended 1999, 2000, 2019

Legal system: civil law system influenced by Soviet and Romano-Germanic legal systems; constitution ambiguous on judicial review of legislative acts

International law organization participation: has not submitted an ICJ jurisdiction declaration; accepts ICCt jurisdiction

Citizenship: *citizenship by birth:* no
citizenship by descent only: both parents must be citizens of Mongolia; one parent if born within Mongolia
dual citizenship recognized: no
residency requirement for naturalization: 5 years

Suffrage: 18 years of age; universal

Executive branch: *chief of state:* President Ukhnaagiin KHURELSUKH (since 25 June 2021)
head of government: Prime Minister Luvsannamsrai OYUN-ERDENE (since 27 January 2021); Deputy Prime Minister Ulziisaikhan ENKHTUVSHIN (since 18 October 2017)
cabinet: directly appointed by the prime minister following a constitutional amendment ratified in November 2019; prior to the amendment, the cabinet was nominated by the prime minister in consultation with the president and confirmed by the State Great Hural (parliament)
elections/appointments: presidential candidates nominated by political parties represented in the State Great Hural and directly elected by simple majority popular vote for one 6-year term; election last held on 9 June 2021; following legislative elections, the leader of the majority party or majority coalition is usually elected prime minister by the State Great Hural
election results:
Ukhnaagiin KHURELSUKH elected president in first round; percent of vote - Ukhnaa KHURELSUKH (Mongolian People's Party) 67.7%, Dangaasuren ENKHBAT (HUN Coalition) 20.31%, Sodnomzundui ERDENE (Democratic Party) 5.99%

Legislative branch: *description:* unicameral State Great Hural or Ulsyn Ikh Khural (76 seats; members directly elected in single-seat constituencies by simple majority vote; each constituency requires at least 50% voter participation for the poll to be valid; members serve 4-year terms)
elections:
last held on 24 June 2020 (next to be held in 2024)
election results:
percent of vote by party - MPP 44.9%, DP 24.5%, Our Coalition 8.1%, independent 8.7%, Right Person Electorate Coalition 5.2%, other 8.5%; seats by party - MPP 62, DP 11, Our Coalition 1, Right Person Electorate Coalition 1; independent 1; composition - 63 men, 13 women; percent of women 17.1%

Judicial branch: *highest court(s):* Supreme Court (consists of the Chief Justice and 24 judges organized into civil, criminal, and administrative chambers); Constitutional Court or Tsets (consists of the chairman and 8 members)
judge selection and term of office: Supreme Court chief justice and judges appointed by the president upon recommendation by the General Council of Courts - a 14-member body of judges and judicial officials - to the State Great Hural; appointment is for life; chairman of the Constitutional Court elected from among its members; members appointed from nominations by the State Great Hural - 3 each by the president, the State Great Hural, and the Supreme Court; appointment is 6 years; chairmanship limited to a single renewable 3-year term
subordinate courts: aimag (provincial) and capital city appellate courts; soum, inter-soum, and district courts; Administrative Cases Courts

Political parties and leaders: Civil Will-Green Party or CWGP [Tserendorj GANKHUYAG]
Democratic Party or DP [Tsogtgerel ODON]
Justice Party [Batbayar NASANBILEG]
Mongolian National Democratic Party or MNDP [Bayanjargal TSOGTGEREL]
Mongolian People's Party or MPP [Luvsannamsrai OYUN-ERDENE]
Mongolian Social Democratic Party or MSDP [Adiya GANBAATAR]
Mongolian Traditionally United Party or MTUP [Batdelgeriin BATBOLD]
National Labor Party or HUN [Togmid Dorhkhand]
Our Coalition (coalition of the MPRP, Civil Will-Green Party, and Mongolian Traditionally United Party formed for the 2020 election)
Right Person Electorate Coalition of ZKEE (coalition of the National Labor Party, Mongolian Social [Badrakhyn NAIDALAA]
note: there were 35 total registered parties as of December 2021

International organization participation: ADB, ARF, CD, CICA, CP, EBRD, EITI (compliant country), FAO, G-77, IAEA, IBRD, ICAO, ICC (NGOs), ICCt, ICRM, IDA, IFAD, IFC, IFRCS, ILO, IMF, IMO, IMSO, Interpol, IOC, IOM, IPU, ISO, ITSO, ITU, ITUC, MIGA, MINURSO, MONUSCO, NAM, OPCW, OSCE, SCO (observer), UN, UNAMID, UNCTAD, UNESCO, UNIDO, UNISFA, UNMISS, UNWTO, UPU, WCO, WHO, WIPO, WMO, WTO

Diplomatic representation in the US: *chief of mission:* Ambassador BATBAYAR Ulziidelger (since 1 December 2021)
chancery: 2833 M Street NW, Washington, DC 20007
telephone: [1] (202) 333-7117
FAX: [1] (202) 298-9227
email address and website:
washington@mfa.gov.mn
http://mongolianembassy.us/
consulate(s) general: New York, San Francisco

Diplomatic representation from the US: *chief of mission:* Ambassador Michael S. KLECHESKI (since 22 February 2019)
embassy: Denver Street #3, 11th Micro-District, Ulaanbaatar 14190
mailing address: 4410 Ulaanbaatar Place, Washington DC 20521-4410
telephone: [976] 7007-6001
FAX: [976] 7007-6174
email address and website:
UlaanbaatarACS@state.gov
https://mn.usembassy.gov/

Flag description: three, equal vertical bands of red (hoist side), blue, and red; centered on the hoist-side red band in yellow is the national emblem ("soyombo" - a columnar arrangement of abstract and geometric representation for fire, sun, moon, earth, water, and the yin-yang symbol); blue represents the sky, red symbolizes progress and prosperity

National symbol(s): soyombo emblem; national colors: red, blue, yellow

National anthem: *name:* "Mongol ulsyn toriin duulal" (National Anthem of Mongolia)
lyrics/music: Tsendiin DAMDINSUREN/Bilegiin DAMDINSUREN and Luvsanjamts MURJORJ
note: music adopted 1950, lyrics adopted 2006; lyrics altered on numerous occasions

National heritage: *total World Heritage Sites:* 5 (3 cultural, 2 natural)
selected World Heritage Site locales: Uvs Nuur Basin (n); Orkhon Valley Cultural Landscape (c); Petroglyphic Complexes of the Mongolian Altai (c); Great Burkhan Khaldun Mountain and surrounding sacred landscape (c); Landscapes of Dauria (n)

ECONOMY

Economic overview: Foreign direct investment in Mongolia's extractive industries – which are based on extensive deposits of copper, gold, coal, molybdenum, fluorspar, uranium, tin, and tungsten - has transformed Mongolia's landlocked economy from its traditional dependence on herding and agriculture. Exports now account for more than 40% of GDP. Mongolia depends on China for more than 60% of its external trade - China receives some 90% of Mongolia's exports and supplies Mongolia with more than one-third of its imports. Mongolia also relies on Russia for 90% of its energy supplies, leaving it vulnerable to price increases. Remittances from Mongolians working abroad, particularly in South Korea, are significant.

Soviet assistance, at its height one-third of GDP, disappeared almost overnight in 1990 and 1991 at the time of the dismantlement of the USSR. The following decade saw Mongolia endure both deep recession, because of political inaction, and natural disasters, as well as strong economic growth, because of market reforms and extensive privatization of the formerly state-run economy. The country opened a fledgling stock exchange in 1991. Mongolia joined the WTO in 1997 and seeks to expand its participation in regional economic and trade regimes.

Growth averaged nearly 9% per year in 2004-08 largely because of high copper prices globally and new gold production. By late 2008, Mongolia was hit by the global financial crisis and Mongolia's real economy contracted 1.3% in 2009. In early 2009, the IMF reached a $236 million Stand-by Arrangement with Mongolia and it emerged from the crisis with a stronger banking sector and better fiscal management. In October 2009, Mongolia passed long-awaited legislation on an investment agreement to develop the Oyu Tolgoi (OT) mine, among the world's largest untapped copper-gold deposits. However, a dispute with foreign investors developing OT called into question the attractiveness of Mongolia as a destination for foreign investment. This caused a severe drop in FDI, and a slowing economy, leading to the dismissal of Prime Minister Norovyn ALTANKHUYAG in November 2014. The economy had grown more than 10% per year between 2011 and 2013 - largely on the strength of commodity exports and high government spending - before slowing to 7.8% in 2014, and falling to the 2% level in 2015. Growth rebounded from a brief 1.6% contraction in the third quarter of 2016 to 5.8% during the first three quarters of 2017, largely due to rising commodity prices.

The May 2015 agreement with Rio Tinto to restart the OT mine and the subsequent $4.4 billion finance package signing in December 2015 stemmed the loss of investor confidence. The current government has made restoring investor trust and reviving the economy its top priority, but has failed to invigorate the economy in the face of the large drop-off in foreign direct investment, mounting external debt, and a sizeable budget deficit. Mongolia secured a $5.5 billion financial assistance package from the IMF and a host of international creditors in May 2017, which is expected to improve Mongolia's long-term fiscal and economic stability as long as Ulaanbaatar can advance the agreement's difficult contingent reforms, such as consolidating the government's off-balance sheet liabilities and rehabilitating the Mongolian banking sector.

Real GDP (purchasing power parity): $37.6 billion (2020 est.)
$39.72 billion (2019 est.)
$37.77 billion (2018 est.)
note: data are in 2017 dollars

Real GDP growth rate: 5.1% (2017 est.)
1.2% (2016 est.)
2.4% (2015 est.)

Real GDP per capita: $11,500 (2020 est.)
$12,300 (2019 est.)
$11,900 (2018 est.)
note: data are in 2017 dollars

GDP (official exchange rate): $11.14 billion (2017 est.)

Inflation rate (consumer prices): 4.6% (2017 est.)
0.5% (2016 est.)

Credit ratings:

Fitch rating: B (2018)

Moody's rating: B3 (2018)

Standard & Poors rating: B (2018)
note: The year refers to the year in which the current credit rating was first obtained.

GDP - composition, by sector of origin: *agriculture:* 12.1% (2017 est.)
industry: 38.2% (2017 est.)
services: 49.7% (2017 est.)

GDP - composition, by end use: *household consumption:* 49.2% (2017 est.)
government consumption: 12.3% (2017 est.)
investment in fixed capital: 23.8% (2017 est.)
investment in inventories: 12.4% (2017 est.)
exports of goods and services: 59.5% (2017 est.)
imports of goods and services: -57.1% (2017 est.)

Agricultural products: milk, wheat, goat milk, potatoes, mutton, sheep milk, beef, goat meat, horse meat, carrots/turnips

Industries: construction and construction materials; mining (coal, copper, molybdenum, fluorspar, tin, tungsten, gold); oil; food and beverages; processing of animal products, cashmere and natural fiber manufacturing

Industrial production growth rate: -1% (2017 est.)

Labor force: 1.241 million (2017 est.)

Labor force - by occupation: *agriculture:* 31.1%
industry: 18.5%
services: 50.5% (2016)

Unemployment rate: 8% (2017 est.)
7.9% (2016 est.)

Unemployment, youth ages 15-24: *total:* 17.9%
male: 16.9%
female: 19.5% (2020 est.)

Population below poverty line: 28.4% (2018 est.)

Gini Index coefficient - distribution of family income: 32.7 (2018 est.)
36.5 (2008)

Household income or consumption by percentage share: *lowest 10%:* 13.7%
highest 10%: 5.7% (2017)

Budget: *revenues:* 2.967 billion (2017 est.)
expenditures: 3.681 billion (2017 est.)

Budget surplus (+) or deficit (-): -6.4% (of GDP) (2017 est.)

Public debt: 91.4% of GDP (2017 est.)
90% of GDP (2016 est.)

Taxes and other revenues: 26.6% (of GDP) (2017 est.)

Fiscal year: calendar year

Current account balance: -$1.155 billion (2017 est.)
-$700 million (2016 est.)

Exports: $7.65 billion (2020 est.) note: data are in current year dollars
$8.42 billion (2019 est.) note: data are in current year dollars
$7.71 billion (2018 est.) note: data are in current year dollars

Exports - partners: China 81%, Switzerland 9% (2019)

Exports - commodities: coal, copper, gold, iron, crude petroleum (2019)

Imports: $7.34 billion (2020 est.) note: data are in current year dollars
$9.25 billion (2019 est.) note: data are in current year dollars
$8.48 billion (2018 est.) note: data are in current year dollars

Imports - partners: China 31%, Russia 29%, Japan 10%, South Korea 5% (2019)

Imports - commodities: refined petroleum, cars, delivery trucks, construction vehicles, aircraft (2019)

Reserves of foreign exchange and gold: $3.016 billion (31 December 2017 est.)
$1.296 billion (31 December 2016 est.)

Debt - external: $29.945 billion (2019 est.)
$28.046 billion (2018 est.)

Exchange rates: togrog/tugriks (MNT) per US dollar -
2,378.1 (2017 est.)
2,140.3 (2016 est.)

2,140.3 (2015 est.)
1,970.3 (2014 est.)
1,817.9 (2013 est.)

ENERGY

Electricity access: *electrification - total population:* 91% (2019)
electrification - urban areas: 99% (2019)
electrification - rural areas: 73% (2019)

Electricity: *installed generating capacity:* 1.479 million kW (2020 est.)
consumption: 7,336,520,000 kWh (2019 est.)
exports: 24 million kWh (2019 est.)
imports: 1.723 billion kWh (2019 est.)
transmission/distribution losses: 892 million kWh (2019 est.)

Electricity generation sources: *fossil fuels:* 89.2% of total installed capacity (2020 est.)
solar: 1.3% of total installed capacity (2020 est.)
wind: 8.1% of total installed capacity (2020 est.)
hydroelectricity: 1.3% of total installed capacity (2020 est.)

Coal: *production:* 43.904 million metric tons (2020 est.)
consumption: 8.818 million metric tons (2020 est.)
exports: 28.551 million metric tons (2020 est.)
imports: 1,000 metric tons (2020 est.)
proven reserves: 2.52 billion metric tons (2019 est.)

Petroleum: *total petroleum production:* 16,700 bbl/day (2021 est.)
refined petroleum consumption: 35,800 bbl/day (2019 est.)
crude oil and lease condensate exports: 14,700 bbl/day (2018 est.)

Refined petroleum products - imports: 24,190 bbl/day (2015 est.)

Carbon dioxide emissions: 22.74 million metric tonnes of CO_2 (2019 est.)
from coal and metallurgical coke: 17.445 million metric tonnes of CO_2 (2019 est.)
from petroleum and other liquids: 5.295 million metric tonnes of CO_2 (2019 est.)

Energy consumption per capita: 83.045 million Btu/person (2019 est.)

COMMUNICATIONS

Telephones - fixed lines: *total subscriptions:* 160,153 (2020 est.)
subscriptions per 100 inhabitants: 5 (2020 est.)

Telephones - mobile cellular: *total subscriptions:* 4,363,919 (2020 est.)
subscriptions per 100 inhabitants: 133 (2020 est.)

Telecommunication systems: *general assessment:* liberalized and competitive telecoms market comprises of a number of operators; fixed-line penetration increased steadily in the years to 2018 as more people took on fixed-line access for voice calls and to access copper-based broadband services; the number of lines fell in 2019, and again and more sharply in 2020, partly through the economic consequences of the pandemic (GDP fell 5.3% in 2020, year-on-year) and partly due to the migration to the mobile platform and to VoIP; fixed broadband penetration remains low, mainly due to a limited number of fixed lines and the dominance of the mobile platform; the attraction of fixed broadband as a preferred access where it is available is waning as the mobile networks are upgraded with greater capacity and capabilities; the growing popularity of mobile broadband continues to underpin overall broadband and telecom sector growth, with Mongolia's market very much being dominated by mobile services, supported by widely available LTE; this will largely determine and shape the future direction of Mongolia's developing digital economy (2021)
domestic: very low fixed-line teledensity of less than 5 per 100; there are four mobile-cellular providers and subscribership is roughly 133 per 100 persons (2020)
international: country code - 976; satellite earth stations - 7 (2016)

Broadcast media: following a law passed in 2005, Mongolia's state-run radio and TV provider converted to a public service provider; also available are 68 radio and 160 TV stations, including multi-channel satellite and cable TV providers; transmissions of multiple international broadcasters are available (2019)

Internet country code: .mn

Internet users: *total:* 2,065,324 (2020 est.)
percent of population: 63% (2020 est.)

Broadband - fixed subscriptions: *total:* 307,166 (2020 est.)
subscriptions per 100 inhabitants: 9 (2020 est.)

TRANSPORTATION

National air transport system: *number of registered air carriers:* 4 (2020)
inventory of registered aircraft operated by air carriers: 12
annual passenger traffic on registered air carriers: 670,360 (2018)
annual freight traffic on registered air carriers: 7.82 million (2018) mt-km

Civil aircraft registration country code prefix: JU

Airports: *total:* 44 (2021)

Airports - with paved runways: *total:* 15
over 3,047 m: 2
2,438 to 3,047 m: 10
1,524 to 2,437 m: 3 (2021)

Airports - with unpaved runways: *total:* 29
over 3,047 m: 2
2,438 to 3,047 m: 2
1,524 to 2,437 m: 24
under 914 m: 1 (2021)

Heliports: 1 (2021)

Railways: *total:* 1,815 km (2017)
broad gauge: 1,815 km (2017) 1.520-m gauge
note: national operator Ulaanbaatar Railway is jointly owned by the Mongolian Government and by the Russian State Railway

Roadways: *total:* 113,200 km (2017)
paved: 10,600 km (2017)
unpaved: 102,600 km (2017)

Waterways: 580 km (2010) (the only waterway in operation is Lake Hovsgol) (135 km); Selenge River (270 km) and Orhon River (175 km) are navigable but carry little traffic; lakes and rivers ice-free from May to September)

Merchant marine: *total:* 302
by type: bulk carrier 4, container ship 7, general cargo 131, oil tanker 64, other 96 (2021)

MILITARY AND SECURITY

Military and security forces: Mongolian Armed Forces (MAF): Mongolian Ground Force (aka General Purpose Troops), Air/Air Defense Force, Cyber Security, Special Forces, Civil Engineering, Civil Defense Forces (2022)
note: the National Police Agency and the General Authority for Border Protection, which operate under the Ministry of Justice and Home Affairs, are primarily responsible for internal security; they are assisted by the General Intelligence Agency under the prime minister; the Armed Forces assist the internal security forces in providing domestic emergency assistance and disaster relief

Military expenditures: 0.8% of GDP (2021 est.)
0.8% of GDP (2020 est.)
0.7% of GDP (2019 est.) (approximately $240 million)
0.7% of GDP (2018 est.) (approximately $240 million)
0.8% of GDP (2017 est.) (approximately $110 million)

Military and security service personnel strengths: information varies; approximately 9,000 active duty troops (2022)

Military equipment inventories and acquisitions: the MAF are armed with Soviet-era equipment supplemented by deliveries of second-hand Russian weapons (2021)

Military service age and obligation: 18-27 years of age for compulsory and voluntary military service (can enter military schools at age 17); 12-month conscript service obligation for men in the army, air forces, or police (can be extended 3 months under special circumstances); conscription service can be exchanged for a 24-month stint in the civil service or a cash payment determined by the Mongolian Government; after conscription, soldiers can contract into military service for 2 or 4 years; volunteer military service for men and women is 24 months, which can be extended for another two years up to the age of 31 (2022)

Military deployments: 860 South Sudan (UNMISS) (May 2022)
note: from 2003 to July 2021, some 3,300 Mongolian troops served in Afghanistan, including about 1,300 under the NATO-led Resolute Support Mission (2015 to 2021); since 2002, Mongolia has deployed more than 19,000 peacekeepers and observers to UN operations in more than a dozen countries

Military - note: Mongolia has been engaged in dialogue and cooperation with NATO since 2005 and is considered by NATO to be a global partner; Mongolia supported the NATO-led Kosovo Force from 2005-2007 and contributed troops to the NATO-led International Security Assistance Force in Afghanistan from 2009-2014, as well as to the follow-on Resolute Support Mission that provided training, advice, and other assistance to the Afghan security forces (2015-2021)

TRANSNATIONAL ISSUES

Disputes - international: none identified

Refugees and internally displaced persons: *stateless persons:* 17 (mid-year 2021)

Illicit drugs: NA

MONTENEGRO

INTRODUCTION

Background: The use of the name Crna Gora or Black Mountain (Montenegro) began in the 13th century in reference to a highland region in the Serbian province of Zeta. The later medieval state of Zeta maintained its existence until 1496 when Montenegro finally fell under Ottoman rule. Over subsequent centuries, Montenegro managed to maintain a level of autonomy within the Ottoman Empire. From the 16th to 19th centuries, Montenegro was a theocracy ruled by a series of bishop princes; in 1852, it transformed into a secular principality. Montenegro was recognized as an independent sovereign principality at the Congress of Berlin in 1878. After World War I, during which Montenegro fought on the side of the Allies, Montenegro was absorbed by the Kingdom of Serbs, Croats, and Slovenes, which became the Kingdom of Yugoslavia in 1929. At the conclusion of World War II, it became a constituent republic of the Socialist Federal Republic of Yugoslavia. When the latter dissolved in 1992, Montenegro joined with Serbia, creating the Federal Republic of Yugoslavia and, after 2003, shifting to a looser State Union of Serbia and Montenegro. In May 2006, Montenegro invoked its right under the Constitutional Charter of Serbia and Montenegro to hold a referendum on independence from the two-state union. The vote for severing ties with Serbia barely exceeded 55% - the threshold set by the EU - allowing Montenegro to formally restore its independence on 3 June 2006. In 2017, Montenegro joined NATO and is currently completing its EU accession process, having officially applied to join the EU in December 2008.

GEOGRAPHY

Location: Southeastern Europe, between the Adriatic Sea and Serbia

Geographic coordinates: 42 30 N, 19 18 E

Map references: Europe

Area: *total:* 13,812 sq km
land: 13,452 sq km
water: 360 sq km

Area - comparative: slightly smaller than Connecticut; slightly larger than twice the size of Delaware

Land boundaries: *total:* 680 km
border countries (5): Albania 186 km; Bosnia and Herzegovina 242 km; Croatia 19 km; Kosovo 76 km; Serbia 157 km

Coastline: 293.5 km

Maritime claims: *territorial sea:* 12 nm
continental shelf: defined by treaty

Climate: Mediterranean climate, hot dry summers and autumns and relatively cold winters with heavy snowfalls inland

Terrain: highly indented coastline with narrow coastal plain backed by rugged high limestone mountains and plateaus

Elevation: *highest point:* Zia Kolata 2,534 m
lowest point: Adriatic Sea 0 m
mean elevation: 1,086 m

Natural resources: bauxite, hydroelectricity

Land use: *agricultural land:* 38.2% (2018 est.)
arable land: 12.9% (2018 est.)
permanent crops: 1.2% (2018 est.)
permanent pasture: 24.1% (2018 est.)
forest: 40.4% (2018 est.)
other: 21.4% (2018 est.)

Irrigated land: 24 sq km (2012)

Major lakes (area sq km): *fresh water lake(s):* Lake Scutari (shared with Albania) - 400 sq km
note - largest lake in the Balkans

Major watersheds (area sq km): Atlantic Ocean drainage: *(Black Sea)* Danube (795,656 sq km)

Population distribution: highest population density is concentrated in the south, southwest; the extreme eastern border is the least populated area

Natural hazards: destructive earthquakes

Geography - note: strategic location along the Adriatic coast

PEOPLE AND SOCIETY

Population: 604,966 (2022 est.)

Nationality: *noun:* Montenegrin(s)
adjective: Montenegrin

Ethnic groups: Montenegrin 45%, Serbian 28.7%, Bosniak 8.7%, Albanian 4.9%, Muslim 3.3%, Romani 1%, Croat 1%, other 2.6%, unspecified 4.9% (2011 est.)

Languages: Serbian 42.9%, Montenegrin (official) 37%, Bosnian 5.3%, Albanian 5.3%, Serbo-Croat 2%, other 3.5%, unspecified 4% (2011 est.)
major-language sample(s): Knjiga svetskih činjenica, neophodan izvor osnovnih informacija. (Serbian)
Knjiga svjetskih činjenica, neophodan izvor osnovnih informacija. (Montenegrin/Bosnian)

Religions: Orthodox 72.1%, Muslim 19.1%, Catholic 3.4%, atheist 1.2%, other 1.5%, unspecified 2.6% (2011 est.)

Age structure: *0-14 years:* 18.14% (male 57,402/female 53,217)
15-24 years: 12.78% (male 40,220/female 37,720)
25-54 years: 39.65% (male 120,374/female 121,461)
55-64 years: 13.41% (male 40,099/female 41,670)
65 years and over: 16.02% (male 42,345/female 55,351) (2020 est.)

Dependency ratios: *total dependency ratio:* 51.1
youth dependency ratio: 27.3
elderly dependency ratio: 23.8
potential support ratio: 4.2 (2020 est.)

Median age: *total:* 39.6 years
male: 38.1 years
female: 41.1 years (2020 est.)

Population growth rate: -0.41% (2022 est.)

Birth rate: 11.19 births/1,000 population (2022 est.)

Death rate: 10.33 deaths/1,000 population (2022 est.)

Net migration rate: -4.97 migrant(s)/1,000 population (2022 est.)

Population distribution: highest population density is concentrated in the south, southwest; the extreme eastern border is the least populated area

Urbanization: *urban population:* 68.2% of total population (2022)
rate of urbanization: 0.45% annual rate of change (2020-25 est.)

Major urban areas - population: 177,000 PODGORICA (capital) (2018)

Sex ratio: *at birth:* 1.04 male(s)/female
0-14 years: 1.07 male(s)/female
15-24 years: 1.07 male(s)/female
25-54 years: 0.99 male(s)/female
55-64 years: 0.96 male(s)/female
65 years and over: 0.69 male(s)/female
total population: 0.97 male(s)/female (2022 est.)

Mother's mean age at first birth: 26.3 years (2010 est.)

Maternal mortality ratio: 6 deaths/100,000 live births (2017 est.)

Infant mortality rate: *total:* 3.24 deaths/1,000 live births
male: 2.72 deaths/1,000 live births
female: 3.79 deaths/1,000 live births (2022 est.)

Life expectancy at birth: *total population:* 77.75 years
male: 75.32 years
female: 80.27 years (2022 est.)

Total fertility rate: 1.81 children born/woman (2022 est.)

Contraceptive prevalence rate: 20.7% (2018)

Drinking water source: *improved: urban:* 100% of population
rural: 98.2% of population
total: 99.4% of population
unimproved: urban: 0% of population
rural: 1.8% of population
total: 0.6% of population (2020 est.)

Current health expenditure: 8.3% of GDP (2019)

Physicians density: 2.74 physicians/1,000 population (2020)

Hospital bed density: 3.9 beds/1,000 population (2017)

Sanitation facility access: *improved: urban:* 100% of population
rural: 93.9% of population
total: 98% of population
unimproved: urban: 0% of population
rural: 6.1% of population
total: 2% of population (2020 est.)

HIV/AIDS - adult prevalence rate: (2020 est.) <.1%

Major infectious diseases: *degree of risk:* intermediate (2020)
food or waterborne diseases: bacterial diarrhea
vectorborne diseases: Crimean-Congo hemorrhagic fever

Obesity - adult prevalence rate: 23.3% (2016)

Alcohol consumption per capita: *total:* 9.91 liters of pure alcohol (2019 est.)
beer: 3.83 liters of pure alcohol (2019 est.)
wine: 2.68 liters of pure alcohol (2019 est.)
spirits: 3.22 liters of pure alcohol (2019 est.)
other alcohols: 0.16 liters of pure alcohol (2019 est.)

Tobacco use: *total:* 31.4% (2020 est.)
male: 31.6% (2020 est.)
female: 31.1% (2020 est.)

Children under the age of 5 years underweight: 3.7% (2018/19)

Child marriage: *women married by age 15:* 1.9%
women married by age 18: 5.8%
men married by age 18: 3.2% (2018 est.)

Literacy: *definition:* age 15 and over can read and write
total population: 98.8%
male: 99.5%
female: 98.3% (2018)

School life expectancy (primary to tertiary education): *total:* 15 years
male: 15 years
female: 16 years (2020)

Unemployment, youth ages 15-24: *total:* 36%
male: 33.6%
female: 39.7% (2020 est.)

ENVIRONMENT

Environment - current issues: pollution of coastal waters from sewage outlets, especially in tourist-related areas such as Kotor; serious air pollution in Podgorica, Pljevlja and Niksic; air pollution in Pljevlja is caused by the nearby lignite power plant and the domestic use of coal and wood for household heating

Environment - international agreements: *party to:* Air Pollution, Air Pollution-Heavy Metals, Air Pollution-Persistent Organic Pollutants, Biodiversity, Climate Change, Climate Change-Kyoto Protocol, Climate Change-Paris Agreement, Comprehensive Nuclear Test Ban, Desertification, Endangered Species, Hazardous Wastes, Law of the Sea, Marine Dumping-London Convention, Marine Life Conservation, Nuclear Test Ban, Ozone Layer Protection, Ship Pollution, Wetlands
signed, but not ratified: none of the selected agreements

Air pollutants: *particulate matter emissions:* 20.17 micrograms per cubic meter (2016 est.)
carbon dioxide emissions: 2.02 megatons (2016 est.)
methane emissions: 0.75 megatons (2020 est.)

Climate: Mediterranean climate, hot dry summers and autumns and relatively cold winters with heavy snowfalls inland

Land use: *agricultural land:* 38.2% (2018 est.)
arable land: 12.9% (2018 est.)
permanent crops: 1.2% (2018 est.)
permanent pasture: 24.1% (2018 est.)
forest: 40.4% (2018 est.)
other: 21.4% (2018 est.)

Urbanization: *urban population:* 68.2% of total population (2022)
rate of urbanization: 0.45% annual rate of change (2020-25 est.)

Revenue from forest resources: *forest revenues:* 0.43% of GDP (2018 est.)

Revenue from coal: *coal revenues:* 0.12% of GDP (2018 est.)

Waste and recycling: *municipal solid waste generated annually:* 332,000 tons (2015 est.)
municipal solid waste recycled annually: 17,994 tons (2015 est.)
percent of municipal solid waste recycled: 5.4% (2015 est.)

Major lakes (area sq km): *fresh water lake(s):* Lake Scutari (shared with Albania) - 400 sq km
note - largest lake in the Balkans

Major watersheds (area sq km): Atlantic Ocean drainage: *(Black Sea)* Danube (795,656 sq km)

Total water withdrawal: *municipal:* 96.4 million cubic meters (2017 est.)
industrial: 62.8 million cubic meters (2017 est.)
agricultural: 1.7 million cubic meters (2017 est.)

GOVERNMENT

Country name: *conventional long form:* none
conventional short form: Montenegro
local long form: none
local short form: Crna Gora
former: People's Republic of Montenegro, Socialist Republic of Montenegro, Republic of Montenegro
etymology: the country's name locally as well as in most Western European languages means "black mountain" and refers to the dark coniferous forests on Mount Lovcen and the surrounding area

Government type: parliamentary republic

Capital: *name:* Podgorica; note - Cetinje retains the status of "Old Royal Capital"
geographic coordinates: 42 26 N, 19 16 E
time difference: UTC+1 (6 hours ahead of Washington, DC, during Standard Time)
daylight saving time: +1 hr, begins last Sunday in March; ends last Sunday in October
etymology: the name translates as "beneath Gorica"; the meaning of Gorica is "hillock"; the reference is to the small hill named Gorica that the city is built around

Administrative divisions: 24 municipalities (opstine, singular - opstina); Andrijevica, Bar, Berane, Bijelo Polje, Budva, Cetinje, Danilovgrad, Gusinje, Herceg Novi, Kolasin, Kotor, Mojkovac, Niksic, Petnijica, Plav, Pljevlja, Pluzine, Podgorica, Rozaje, Savnik, Tivat, Tuzi, Ulcinj, Zabljak

Independence: 3 June 2006 (from the State Union of Serbia and Montenegro); notable earlier dates: 13 March 1852 (Principality of Montenegro established); 13 July 1878 (Congress of Berlin recognizes Montenegrin independence); 28 August 1910 (Kingdom of Montenegro established)

National holiday: Statehood Day, 13 July (1878, the day the Berlin Congress recognized Montenegro as the 27th independent state in the world, and 1941, the day the Montenegrins staged an uprising against fascist occupiers and sided with the partisan communist movement)

Constitution: *history:* several previous; latest adopted 22 October 2007
amendments: proposed by the president of Montenegro, by the government, or by at least 25 members of the Assembly; passage of draft proposals requires two-thirds majority vote of the Assembly, followed by a public hearing; passage of draft amendments requires two-thirds majority vote of the Assembly; changes to certain constitutional articles, such as sovereignty, state symbols, citizenship, and constitutional change procedures, require three-fifths majority vote in a referendum; amended 2013

Legal system: civil law

International law organization participation: has not submitted an ICJ jurisdiction declaration; accepts ICCt jurisdiction

Citizenship: *citizenship by birth:* no
citizenship by descent only: at least one parent must be a citizen of Montenegro
dual citizenship recognized: no
residency requirement for naturalization: 10 years

Suffrage: 18 years of age; universal

Executive branch: *chief of state:* President Milo DJUKANOVIC (since 20 May 2018)
head of government: Prime Minister Dritan ABAZOVIC (since 28 April 2022)
cabinet: Ministers act as cabinet
elections/appointments: president directly elected by absolute majority popular vote in 2 rounds if needed for a 5-year term (eligible for a second term); election last held on 15 April 2018 (next to be held in 2023); prime minister nominated by the president, approved by the Assembly
election results:
2018: Milo DJUKANOVIC elected president in the first round; percent of vote - Milo DJUKANOVIC (DPS) 53.9%, Mladen BOJANIC (independent) 33.4%, Draginja VUKSANOVIC (SDP) 8.2%, Marko MILACIC (PRAVA) 2.8%, other 1.7%
2013: Filip VUJANOVIC reelected president; percent of vote Filip VUJANOVIC (DPS) 51.2%, Miodrag LEKIC (independent) 48.8%

Legislative branch: *description:* unicameral Assembly or Skupstina (81 seats; members directly elected in a single nationwide constituency by proportional representation vote; members serve 4-year terms)
elections:
last held on 30 August 2020 (next to be held in 2024)
election results:
percent of vote by party/coalition - DPS 35.1%, ZBCG 32.6%, MNIM 12.5%, URA 5.5%, SD 4.1%, BS 3.9%, SDP 3.1%, AL 1.6%, Albanian Coalition 1.1%, other 0.4%; seats by party/coalition - DPS 30, ZBCG 27, MNIM 10, URA 4, BS 3, SD 3, SDP 2, AL 1, Albanian Coalition 1.; composition as of July 2022 - men 59, women 22, percent of women 27.2%

Judicial branch: *highest court(s):* Supreme Court or Vrhovni Sud (consists of the court president, deputy president, and 15 judges); Constitutional Court or Ustavni Sud (consists of the court president and 7 judges)
judge selection and term of office: Supreme Court president proposed by general session of the Supreme Court and elected by the Judicial Council, a 9-member body consisting of judges, lawyers designated by the Assembly, and the minister of judicial affairs; Supreme Court president elected for a single renewable, 5-year term; other judges elected by the Judicial Council for life; Constitutional Court judges - 2 proposed by the president of Montenegro and 5 by the

Assembly, and elected by the Assembly; court president elected from among the court members; court president elected for a 3-year term, other judges serve 9-year terms
subordinate courts: Administrative Courts; Appellate Court; Commercial Courts; High Courts; basic courts

Political parties and leaders: Albanian Alternative or AA [Nik DELJOSAJ]
Albanian Coalition (includes DP, DSCG, DUA for 2020 election)
Albanian Coalition Perspective or AKP
Albanian List or AL [Nik DELJOSAJ and Nazif CUNGU] (coalition includes AA, Forca, AKP, DSA)
Bosniak Party or BS [Ervin IBRAHIMOVIC]
Croatian Civic Initiative or HGI [Adrian VUKSANOVIC]
Croatian Reform Party [Marija VUCINOVIC]
Democratic Alliance or DEMOS [Miodrag LEKIC]
Democratic Front or DF [collective leadership] (coalition includes NOVA, PZP, DNP, RP)
Democratic League in Montenegro or DSCG [Mehmet BARDHI]
Democratic League of Albanians or DSA Democratic Montenegro or DCG [Aleksa BECIC]
Democratic Party or DP [Fatmir GJEKA]
Democratic Party of Socialists or DPS [Milo DJUKANOVIC]
Democratic Party of Unity or DSJ [Nebojsa JUSKOVIC]
Democratic People's Party or DNP [Milan KNEZEVIC]
Democratic Serb Party or DSS [Dragica PEROVIC]
Democratic Union of Albanians or DUA [Mehmet ZENKA]
For the Future of Montenegro or ZBCG [Zdravko KRIVOKAPIC] (electoral coalition includes SNP and 2 alliances - DF, NP)
In Black and White [Dritan ABAZOVIC] (electoral list)
Liberal Party or LP [Andrija POPOVIC]
Movement for Changes or PZP [Nebojsa MEDOJEVIC]
New Democratic Power or FORCA [Nazif CUNGU]
New Serb Democracy or NSD or NOVA [Andrija MANDIC]
Party of Pensioners, Disabled, and Restitution or PUPI [Momir JOKSIMOVIC]
Peace is Our Nation or MNIM [Aleksa BECIC] (coalition includes Democrats, DEMOS, New Left, PUPI)
Popular Movement or NP [Miodrag DAVIDOVIC] (coalition includes DEMOS, RP, UCG, and several minor parties)
Social Democratic Party or SDP [Rasko KONJEVIC]
Social Democrats or SD [Damir SEHOVIC]
Socialist People's Party or SNP [Vladimir JOKOVIC]
True Montenegro or PRAVA or PCG [Marko MILACIC]
United Montenegro or UCG [Goran DANILOVIC] (split from DEMOS)
United Reform Action or URA [Dritan ABAZOVIC]
Workers' Party or RP [Maksim VUCINIC]

International organization participation: CE, CEI, EAPC, EBRD, FAO, IAEA, IBRD, ICAO, ICC (NGOs), ICCt, ICRM, IDA, IFC, IFRCS, IHO, ILO, IMF, IMO, IMSO, Interpol, IOC, IOM, IPU, ISO (correspondent), ITSO, ITU, ITUC (NGOs), MIGA, NATO, OAS (observer), OIF (observer), OPCW, OSCE, PCA, PFP, SELEC, UN, UNCTAD, UNESCO, UNHCR, UNHRC, UNIDO, UNWTO, UPU, WCO, WHO, WIPO, WMO, WTO

Diplomatic representation in the US: *chief of mission:* Ambassador (vacant); Charge d'Affaires Marija STJEPCEVIC (since 4 February 2021)
chancery: 1610 New Hampshire Avenue NW, Washington, DC, 20009
telephone: [1] (202) 234-6108
FAX: [1] (202) 234-6109
email address and website:
usa@mfa.gov.me
consulate(s) general: New York

Diplomatic representation from the US: *chief of mission:* Ambassador Judy Rising REINKE (since 20 December 2018)
embassy: Dzona Dzeksona 2, 81000 Podgorica
mailing address: 5570 Podgorica Place, Washington DC 20521-5570
telephone: +382 (0)20-410-500
FAX: [382] (0)20-241-358
email address and website:
PodgoricaACS@state.gov
https://me.usembassy.gov/

Flag description: a red field bordered by a narrow golden-yellow stripe with the Montenegrin coat of arms centered; the arms consist of a double-headed golden eagle - symbolizing the unity of church and state - surmounted by a crown; the eagle holds a golden scepter in its right claw and a blue orb in its left; the breast shield over the eagle shows a golden lion passant on a green field in front of a blue sky; the lion is a symbol of episcopal authority and harkens back to the three and a half centuries when Montenegro was ruled as a theocracy

National symbol(s): double-headed eagle; national colors: red, gold

National anthem: *name:* "Oj, svijetla majska zoro" (Oh, Bright Dawn of May)
lyrics/music: Sekula DRLJEVIC/unknown, arranged by Zarko MIKOVIC
note: adopted 2004; music based on a Montenegrin folk song

National heritage: *total World Heritage Sites:* 4 (3 cultural, 1 natural)
selected World Heritage Site locales: Natural and Culturo-Historical Region of Kotor (c); Durmitor National Park (n); Stećci Medieval Tombstones Graveyards (c); Fortified City of Kotor Venetian Defense Works (c)

ECONOMY

Economic overview: Montenegro's economy is transitioning to a market system. Around 90% of Montenegrin state-owned companies have been privatized, including 100% of banking, telecommunications, and oil distribution. Tourism, which accounts for more than 20% of Montenegro's GDP, brings in three times as many visitors as Montenegro's total population every year. Several new luxury tourism complexes are in various stages of development along the coast, and a number are being offered in connection with nearby boating and yachting facilities. In addition to tourism, energy and agriculture are considered two distinct pillars of the economy. Only 20% of Montenegro's hydropower potential is utilized. Montenegro plans to become a net energy exporter, and the construction of an underwater cable to Italy, which will be completed by the end of 2018, will help meet its goal.

Montenegro uses the euro as its domestic currency, though it is not an official member of the euro zone. In January 2007, Montenegro joined the World Bank and IMF, and in December 2011, the WTO. Montenegro began negotiations to join the EU in 2012, having met the conditions set down by the European Council, which called on Montenegro to take steps to fight corruption and organized crime.

The government recognizes the need to remove impediments in order to remain competitive and open the economy to foreign investors. Net foreign direct investment in 2017 reached $848 million and investment per capita is one of the highest in Europe, due to a low corporate tax rate. The biggest foreign investors in Montenegro in 2017 were Norway, Russia, Italy, Azerbaijan and Hungary.

Montenegro is currently planning major overhauls of its road and rail networks, and possible expansions of its air transportation system. In 2014, the Government of Montenegro selected two Chinese companies to construct a 41 km-long section of the country's highway system, which will become part of China's Belt and Road Initiative. Cheaper borrowing costs have stimulated Montenegro's growing debt, which currently sits at 65.9% of GDP, with a forecast, absent fiscal consolidation, to increase to 80% once the repayment to China's Ex/Im Bank of a €800 million highway loan begins in 2019. Montenegro first instituted a value-added tax (VAT) in April 2003, and introduced differentiated VAT rates of 17% and 7% (for tourism) in January 2006. The Montenegrin Government increased the non-tourism Value Added Tax (VAT) rate to 21% as of January 2018, with the goal of reducing its public debt.

Real GDP (purchasing power parity): $11.36 billion (2020 est.)
$13.39 billion (2019 est.)
$12.87 billion (2018 est.)
note: data are in 2017 dollars

Real GDP growth rate: 4.3% (2017 est.)
2.9% (2016 est.)
3.4% (2015 est.)

Real GDP per capita: $18,300 (2020 est.)
$21,500 (2019 est.)
$20,700 (2018 est.)
note: data are in 2017 dollars

GDP (official exchange rate): $5.486 billion (2019 est.)

Inflation rate (consumer prices): 0.3% (2019 est.)
2.6% (2018 est.)
2.3% (2017 est.)

Credit ratings:

Moody's rating: B1 (2016)

Standard & Poors rating: B+ (2014)
note: The year refers to the year in which the current credit rating was first obtained.

GDP - composition, by sector of origin: *agriculture:* 7.5% (2016 est.)
industry: 15.9% (2016 est.)
services: 76.6% (2016 est.)

GDP - composition, by end use: *household consumption:* 76.8% (2016 est.)
government consumption: 19.6% (2016 est.)
investment in fixed capital: 23.2% (2016 est.)

investment in inventories: 2.9% (2016 est.)
exports of goods and services: 40.5% (2016 est.)
imports of goods and services: -63% (2016 est.)

Agricultural products: milk, potatoes, grapes, vegetables, tomatoes, watermelons, wheat, apples, cabbages, barley

Industries: steelmaking, aluminum, agricultural processing, consumer goods, tourism

Industrial production growth rate: -4.2% (2017 est.)

Labor force: 167,000 (2020 est.)

Labor force - by occupation: *agriculture:* 7.9%
industry: 17.1%
services: 75% (2017 est.)

Unemployment rate: 15.82% (2019 est.)
18.8% (2018 est.)

Unemployment, youth ages 15-24: *total:* 36%
male: 33.6%
female: 39.7% (2020 est.)

Population below poverty line: 24.5% (2018 est.)

Gini Index coefficient - distribution of family income: 39 (2015 est.)
32.3 (2013 est.)

Household income or consumption by percentage share: *lowest 10%:* 3.5%
highest 10%: 25.7% (2014 est.)

Budget: *revenues:* 1.78 billion (2017 est.)
expenditures: 2.05 billion (2017 est.)

Budget surplus (+) or deficit (-): -5.6% (of GDP) (2017 est.)

Public debt: 67.2% of GDP (2017 est.)
66.4% of GDP (2016 est.)
note: data cover general government debt, and includes debt instruments issued (or owned) by government entities other than the treasury; the data include treasury debt held by foreign entities; the data include debt issued by subnational entities, as well as intragovernmental debt; intragovernmental debt consists of treasury borrowings from surpluses in the social funds, such as for retirement, medical care, and unemployment; debt instruments for the social funds are not sold at public auctions

Taxes and other revenues: 37.2% (of GDP) (2017 est.)

Fiscal year: calendar year

Current account balance: -$780 million (2017 est.)
-$710 million (2016 est.)

Exports: $1.24 billion (2020 est.) note: data are in current year dollars
$2.42 billion (2019 est.) note: data are in current year dollars
$2.35 billion (2018 est.) note: data are in current year dollars

Exports - partners: Serbia 17%, Hungary 15%, China 11%, Russia 7%, Bosnia and Herzegovina 6%, Germany 6%, Italy 5%, Poland 5% (2019)

Exports - commodities: aluminum, packaged medicines, cars, zinc, wine (2019)

Imports: $2.9 billion (2020 est.) note: data are in current year dollars
$3.59 billion (2019 est.) note: data are in current year dollars
$3.67 billion (2018 est.) note: data are in current year dollars

Imports - partners: Serbia 30%, Bosnia and Herzegovina 8%, Croatia 8%, Italy 6%, Greece 6%, Germany 5% (2019)

Imports - commodities: refined petroleum, cars, packaged medicines, recreational boats, cigarettes (2019)

Reserves of foreign exchange and gold: $1.077 billion (31 December 2017 est.)
$846.5 million (31 December 2016 est.)

Debt - external: $2.516 billion (31 December 2017 est.)
$2.224 billion (31 December 2016 est.)

Exchange rates: euros (EUR) per US dollar -
0.885 (2017 est.)
0.903 (2016 est.)
0.9214 (2015 est.)
0.885 (2014 est.)
0.7634 (2013 est.)

ENERGY

Electricity access: *electrification - total population:* 100% (2020)

Electricity: *installed generating capacity:* 1.007 million kW (2020 est.)
consumption: 3,246,760,000 kWh (2019 est.)
exports: 943 million kWh (2019 est.)
imports: 1.196 billion kWh (2019 est.)
transmission/distribution losses: 493 million kWh (2019 est.)

Electricity generation sources: *fossil fuels:* 42.3% of total installed capacity (2020 est.)
wind: 10.5% of total installed capacity (2020 est.)
hydroelectricity: 47.2% of total installed capacity (2020 est.)

Coal: *production:* 1.456 million metric tons (2020 est.)
consumption: 1.351 million metric tons (2020 est.)
exports: 96,000 metric tons (2020 est.)
imports: 1,000 metric tons (2020 est.)
proven reserves: 142 million metric tons (2019 est.)

Petroleum: *total petroleum production:* 0 bbl/day (2021 est.)
refined petroleum consumption: 7,600 bbl/day (2019 est.)

Refined petroleum products - exports: 357 bbl/day (2015 est.)

Refined petroleum products - imports: 6,448 bbl/day (2015 est.)

Carbon dioxide emissions: 2.447 million metric tonnes of CO_2 (2019 est.)
from coal and metallurgical coke: 1.333 million metric tonnes of CO_2 (2019 est.)
from petroleum and other liquids: 1.114 million metric tonnes of CO_2 (2019 est.)

Energy consumption per capita: 77.286 million Btu/person (2019 est.)

COMMUNICATIONS

Telephones - fixed lines: *total subscriptions:* 191,768 (2020 est.)
subscriptions per 100 inhabitants: 31 (2020 est.)

Telephones - mobile cellular: *total subscriptions:* 1,080,089 (2020 est.)
subscriptions per 100 inhabitants: 172 (2020 est.)

Telecommunication systems: *general assessment:* a small telecom market supported by a population of only 623,000; fixed broadband services are available via a variety of technology platforms, though fiber is the dominant platform, accounting for almost 40% of connections; the growth of fiber has largely been at the expense of DSL as customers are migrated to fiber networks as these are built out progressively; mobile penetration is particularly high, though this is partly due to the significant number of tourists visiting the country seasonally, as also to the popularity of subscribers having multiple prepaid cards; in the wake of the pandemic and associated restrictions on travel, the number of mobile subscribers fell in 2020, as also in the first quarter of 2021, year-on-year; networks support a vibrant mobile broadband services sector, largely based on LTE; two of the MNOs began trialing 5G in May 2021, though commercial services will not gain traction until after the multispectrum auction is completed at the end of 2021; spectrum is available in the 694-790MHz and 3400-3800MHz ranges, as well as in the 26.5-27.5GHz range (2021)
domestic: GSM mobile-cellular service, available through multiple providers; fixed-line over 30 per 100 and mobilecellular 172 per 100 persons (2020)
international: country code - 382; 2 international switches connect the national system

Broadcast media: state-funded national radio-TV broadcaster operates 2 terrestrial TV networks, 1 satellite TV channel, and 2 radio networks; 4 local public TV stations and 14 private TV stations; 14 local public radio stations, 35 private radio stations, and several on-line media (2019)

Internet country code: .me

Internet users: *total:* 484,619 (2020 est.)
percent of population: 78% (2020 est.)

Broadband - fixed subscriptions: *total:* 184,176 (2020 est.)
subscriptions per 100 inhabitants: 29 (2020 est.)

TRANSPORTATION

National air transport system: *number of registered air carriers:* 1 (2020)
inventory of registered aircraft operated by air carriers: 4
annual passenger traffic on registered air carriers: 565,522 (2018)
annual freight traffic on registered air carriers: 130,000 (2018) mt-km

Civil aircraft registration country code prefix: 4O

Airports: *total:* 5 (2021)

Airports - with paved runways: *total:* 5
2,438 to 3,047 m: 2
1,524 to 2,437 m: 1
914 to 1,523 m: 1
under 914 m: 1 (2021)

Heliports: 1 (2021)

Railways: *total:* 250 km (2017)
standard gauge: 250 km (2017) 1.435-m gauge (224 km electrified)

Roadways: *total:* 7,762 km (2010)
paved: 7,141 km (2010)
*unpaved:*621 km (2010)

Merchant marine: *total:* 17
by type: bulk carrier 4, other 13 (2021)

Ports and terminals: *major seaport(s):* Bar

MILITARY AND SECURITY

Military and security forces: the Armed Forces of the Republic of Montenegro is a joint force with land, air, and naval elements (2022)

Military expenditures: 1.8% of GDP (2022 est.)
1.6% of GDP (2021)
1.7% of GDP (2020)
1.3% of GDP (2019) (approximately $130 million)
1.4% of GDP (2018) (approximately $120 million)

Military and security service personnel strengths: approximately 2,000 active duty troops (2022)

Military equipment inventories and acquisitions: the military's inventory is small and consists mostly of Soviet-era equipment inherited from the former Yugoslavia military, with a limited mix of other imported systems; since 2010, it has received small quantities of equipment from Austria, Turkey, and the US (2021)

Military service age and obligation: 18 is the legal minimum age for voluntary military service; conscription abolished in 2006 (2021)
note: as of 2019, women made up about 6% of the military's full-time personnel

Military - note: Montenegro became a member of NATO in 2017; as of 2022, Greece and Italy provided NATO's air policing mission for Montenegro

TRANSNATIONAL ISSUES

Disputes - international: *Montenegro-Albania:* none identified
Montenegro-Bosnia and Herzegovina: the two countries signed a border agreement in August 2015; sovereignty of the disputed Sutorina territory was given to Montenegro
Montenegro-Croartia: the two countries in 2002 reached a temporary agreement designating the Prevlaka Peninsula as part of Croatia, in October 2020, a Montenegrin official resurrected the dormant dispute over the Prevlaka Peninsula by stating that Montenegro had a good chance of winning it through international arbitration
Montenegro-Kosovo: a 2015 border agreement was ratified by Montenegro in 2015 and by Kosovo in 2018, but the actual demarcation has not been completed
Montenegro-Serbia: The former republic boundary – when the two countries were one and called the Federal Republic of Yugoslavia – serves as the boundary until a line is formally delimited and demarcated

Refugees and internally displaced persons: *refugees (country of origin):* 28,639 (Ukraine) (as of 1 November 2022)
stateless persons: 458 (mid-year 2021)
note: 28,034 estimated refugee and migrant arrivals (January 2015-November 2022)

Illicit drugs: drug trafficking groups are major players in the procurement and transportation of large quantities of cocaine destined for European markets

MONTSERRAT

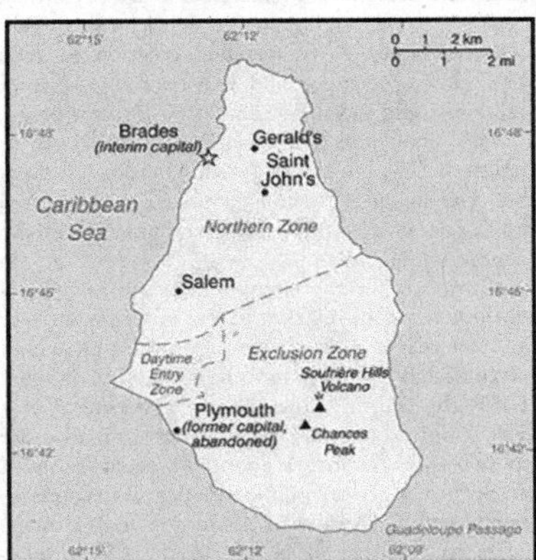

INTRODUCTION

Background: English and Irish colonists from St. Kitts first settled on Montserrat in 1632; the first African slaves arrived three decades later. The British and French fought for possession of the island for most of the 18th century, but it finally was confirmed as a British possession in 1783. The island's sugar plantation economy was converted to small farm landholdings in the mid-19th century. Much of this island was devastated and two thirds of the population fled abroad because of the eruption of the Soufriere Hills Volcano that began on 18 July 1995. Montserrat has endured volcanic activity since, with the last eruption occurring in 2013.

GEOGRAPHY

Location: Caribbean, island in the Caribbean Sea, southeast of Puerto Rico

Geographic coordinates: 16 45 N, 62 12 W

Map references: Central America and the Caribbean

Area: *total:* 102 sq km
land: 102 sq km
water: 0 sq km

Area - comparative: about 0.6 times the size of Washington, DC

Land boundaries: *total:* 0 km

Coastline: 40 km

Maritime claims: *territorial sea:* 12 nm
exclusive fishing zone: 200 nm

Climate: tropical; little daily or seasonal temperature variation

Terrain: volcanic island, mostly mountainous, with small coastal lowland

Elevation: *highest point:* Soufriere Hills volcano pre-eruption height was 915 m; current lava dome is subject to periodic build up and collapse; estimated dome height was 1,050 m in 2015
lowest point: Caribbean Sea 0 m

Natural resources: NEGL

Land use: *agricultural land:* 30% (2018 est.)
arable land: 20% (2018 est.)
permanent crops: 0% (2018 est.)
permanent pasture: 10% (2018 est.)
forest: 25% (2018 est.)
other: 45% (2018 est.)

Irrigated land: 0 sq km (2012)

Population distribution: only the northern half of the island is populated, the southern portion is uninhabitable due to volcanic activity

Natural hazards: volcanic eruptions; severe hurricanes (June to November)
volcanism: Soufriere Hills volcano (915 m), has erupted continuously since 1995; a massive eruption in 1997 destroyed most of the capital, Plymouth, and resulted in approximately half of the island becoming uninhabitable; the island of Montserrat is part of the volcanic island arc of the Lesser Antilles that extends from Saba in the north to Grenada in the south

Geography - note: the island is entirely volcanic in origin and comprised of three major volcanic centers of differing ages

PEOPLE AND SOCIETY

Population: 5,414 (2022 est.)
note: an estimated 8,000 refugees left the island following the resumption of volcanic activity in July 1995; some have returned

Nationality: *noun:* Montserratian(s)
adjective: Montserratian

Ethnic groups: African/Black 86.2%, mixed 4.8%, Hispanic/Spanish 3%, Caucasian/White 2.7%, East Indian/Indian 1.6%, other 1.8% (2018 est.)

Languages: English

Religions: Protestant 71.4% (includes Anglican 17.7%, Pentecostal/Full Gospel 16.1%, Seventh Day Adventist 15%, Methodist 13.9%, Church of God 6.7%, other Protestant 2%), Roman Catholic 11.4%, Rastafarian 1.4%, Hindu 1.2%, Jehovah's Witness 1%, Muslim 0.4%, other/not stated 5.1%, none 7.9% (2018 est.)

Age structure: *0-14 years:* 15.87% (male 442/female 417)
15-24 years: 19.67% (male 556/female 509)
25-54 years: 47.09% (male 1,217/female 1,313)
55-64 years: 10.47% (male 258/female 309)
65 years and over: 7.15% (male 209/female 178) (2022 est.)

Median age: *total:* 34.8 years
male: 34.1 years
female: 35.6 years (2020 est.)

Population growth rate: 0.5% (2022 est.)

Birth rate: 10.9 births/1,000 population (2022 est.)

Death rate: 5.91 deaths/1,000 population (2022 est.)

Net migration rate: 0 migrant(s)/1,000 population (2022 est.)

Population distribution: only the northern half of the island is populated, the southern portion is uninhabitable due to volcanic activity

Urbanization: *urban population:* 9.2% of total population (2022)
rate of urbanization: 0.94% annual rate of change (2020-25 est.)

Sex ratio: *at birth:* 1.03 male(s)/female

0-14 years: 1.06 male(s)/female
15-24 years: 1.08 male(s)/female
25-54 years: 1 male(s)/female
55-64 years: 0.92 male(s)/female
65 years and over: 1.92 male(s)/female
total population: 1 male(s)/female (2022 est.)

Infant mortality rate: *total:* 10.36 deaths/1,000 live births
male: 8.37 deaths/1,000 live births
female: 12.45 deaths/1,000 live births (2022 est.)

Life expectancy at birth: *total population:* 75.7 years
male: 76.66 years
female: 74.7 years (2022 est.)

Total fertility rate: 1.32 children born/woman (2022 est.)

Drinking water source: *improved: total:* 98.1% of population
unimproved: total: 1.9% of population (2020 est.)

Education expenditures: 9.1% of GDP (2019 est.)

School life expectancy (primary to tertiary education): *total:* 14 years
male: 13 years
female: 15 years (2019)

ENVIRONMENT

Environment - current issues: land erosion occurs on slopes that have been cleared for cultivation

Climate: tropical; little daily or seasonal temperature variation

Land use: *agricultural land:* 30% (2018 est.)
arable land: 20% (2018 est.)
permanent crops: 0% (2018 est.)
permanent pasture: 10% (2018 est.)
forest: 25% (2018 est.)
other: 45% (2018 est.)

Urbanization: *urban population:* 9.2% of total population (2022)
rate of urbanization: 0.94% annual rate of change (2020-25 est.)

GOVERNMENT

Country name: *conventional long form:* none
conventional short form: Montserrat
etymology: island named by explorer Christopher COLUMBUS in 1493 after the Benedictine abbey Santa Maria de Montserrat, near Barcelona, Spain

Government type: parliamentary democracy; self-governing overseas territory of the UK

Dependency status: overseas territory of the UK

Capital: *name:* Plymouth; note - Plymouth was abandoned in 1997 because of volcanic activity; interim government buildings have been built at Brades Estate, the de facto capital, in the Carr's Bay/Little Bay vicinity at the northwest end of Montserrat
geographic coordinates: 16 42 N, 62 13 W
time difference: UTC-4 (1 hour ahead of Washington, DC, during Standard Time)
etymology: now entirely deserted because of volcanic activity, the city was originally named after Plymouth, England; *de jure*, Plymouth remains the capital city of Montserrat; it is therefore the only ghost town that serves as the capital of a political entity

Administrative divisions: 3 parishes; Saint Anthony, Saint Georges, Saint Peter

Independence: none (overseas territory of the UK)

National holiday: Birthday of Queen ELIZABETH II, usually celebrated the Monday after the second Saturday in June (1926)

Constitution: *history:* previous 1960; latest put into force 20 October 2010 (The Montserrat Constitution Order 2010)
amendments: amended 2011, 2020

Legal system: English common law

Citizenship: see United Kingdom

Suffrage: 18 years of age; universal

Executive branch: *chief of state:* King CHARLES III (since 8 September 2022); represented by Governor Andrew PEARCE (since 1 February 2018)
head of government: Premier Easton TAYLOR-FARRELL (since 19 November 2019); note - effective with the Constitution Order 2010, October 2010, the office of premier replaced the office of chief minister
cabinet: Executive Council consists of the governor, the premier, 3 other ministers, the attorney general, and the finance secretary
elections/appointments: the monarchy is hereditary; governor appointed by the monarch; following legislative elections, the leader of the majority party usually becomes premier

Legislative branch: *description:* unicameral Legislative Assembly (12 seats; 9 members directly elected in a single constituency by absolute majority vote in 2 rounds to serve 5-year terms; the speaker, normally elected from the outside by the Assembly for a 5-year term, and 2 ex-officio members - the attorney general and financial secretary)
elections:
last held on 18 November 2019 (next scheduled for 2024)
election results:
percent of vote by party - MCAP 42.7%, PDM 29.9%, other 17.1%; seats by party - MCAP 5, PDM 3, independent 1; composition, including the speaker and 2 ex-officio members - men 8, women 4, percent of women 33.3%

Judicial branch: *highest court(s):* the Eastern Caribbean Supreme Court (ECSC) is the superior court of the Organization of Eastern Caribbean States; the ECSC - headquartered on St. Lucia - consists of the Court of Appeal - headed by the chief justice and 4 judges - and the High Court with 18 judges; the Court of Appeal is itinerant, traveling to member states on a schedule to hear appeals from the High Court and subordinate courts; High Court judges reside in the member states, with 1 assigned to Montserrat; Montserrat is also a member of the Caribbean Court of Justice
judge selection and term of office: chief justice of Eastern Caribbean Supreme Court appointed by the Her Majesty, Queen ELIZABETH II; other justices and judges appointed by the Judicial and Legal Services Commission, and independent body of judicial officials; Court of Appeal justices appointed for life with mandatory retirement at age 65; High Court judges appointed for life with mandatory retirement at age 62
subordinate courts: magistrate's court

Political parties and leaders: Movement for Change and Prosperity or MCAP [Easton Taylor FARRELL]
People's Democratic Movement or PDM [Paul LEWIS]

International organization participation: Caricom, CDB, Interpol (subbureau), OECS, UPU

Diplomatic representation in the US: none (overseas territory of the UK)

Diplomatic representation from the US: *embassy:* none (overseas territory of the UK); alternate contact is the US Embassy in Barbados [1] (246) 227-4000; US Embassy Bridgetown, Wildey Business Park, St. Michael BB 14006, Barbados, WI

Flag description: blue with the flag of the UK in the upper hoist-side quadrant and the Montserratian coat of arms centered in the outer half of the flag; the arms feature a woman in green dress, Erin, the female personification of Ireland, standing beside a yellow harp and embracing a large dark cross with her right arm; Erin and the harp are symbols of Ireland reflecting the territory's Irish ancestry; blue represents awareness, trustworthiness, determination, and righteousness

National anthem: *note:* as a territory of the UK, "God Save the King" is official (see United Kingdom)

ECONOMY

Economic overview: Severe volcanic activity, which began in July 1995, has put a damper on this small, open economy. A catastrophic eruption in June 1997 closed the airport and seaports, causing further economic and social dislocation. Two-thirds of the 12,000 inhabitants fled the island. Some began to return in 1998 but lack of housing limited the number. The agriculture sector continued to be affected by the lack of suitable land for farming and the destruction of crops.

Prospects for the economy depend largely on developments in relation to the volcanic activity and on public sector construction activity. Half of the island remains uninhabitable. In January 2013, the EU announced the disbursement of a $55.2 million aid package to Montserrat in order to boost the country's economic recovery, with a specific focus on public finance management, public sector reform, and prudent economic management. Montserrat is tied to the EU through the UK. Although the UK is leaving the EU, Montserrat's aid will not be affected as Montserrat maintains a direct agreement with the EU regarding aid.

Real GDP (purchasing power parity): $167.4 million (2011 est.)
$155.9 million (2010 est.)
$162.7 million (2009 est.)

Real GDP growth rate: 7.4% (2011 est.)
-4.2% (2010 est.)

Real GDP per capita: $34,000 (2011 est.)
$31,100 (2010 est.)
$32,300 (2009 est.)

GDP (official exchange rate): $167.4 million (2011 est.)

Inflation rate (consumer prices): 1.2% (2017 est.)
-0.2% (2016 est.)

Credit ratings:

Standard & Poors rating: BBB- (2020)
note: The year refers to the year in which the current credit rating was first obtained.

GDP - composition, by sector of origin: *agriculture:* 1.9% (2017 est.)
industry: 7.8% (2017 est.)

services: 90.3% (2017 est.)

GDP - composition, by end use: *household consumption:* 90.8% (2017 est.)
government consumption: 50.4% (2017 est.)
investment in fixed capital: 17.9% (2017 est.)
investment in inventories: -0.1% (2017 est.)
exports of goods and services: 29.5% (2017 est.)
imports of goods and services: -88.6% (2017 est.)

Agricultural products: cabbages, carrots, cucumbers, tomatoes, onions, peppers; livestock products

Industries: tourism, rum, textiles, electronic appliances

Industrial production growth rate: -21% (2017 est.)

Labor force: 4,521 (2012)

Labor force - by occupation: *agriculture:* 1.4%
industry: 12.7%
services: 85.9% (2017 est.)

Unemployment rate: 5.6% (2017 est.)
6% (1998 est.)

Budget: *revenues:* 66.67 million (2017 est.)
expenditures: 47.04 million (2017 est.)

Fiscal year: 1 April - 31 March

Current account balance: -$15.4 million (2017 est.)
-$12.2 million (2016 est.)

Exports: $4.4 million (2017 est.)
$5.2 million (2016 est.)

Exports - partners: Antigua and Barbuda 19%, United States 18%, France 17%, Singapore 14%, Belgium 9%, Netherlands 5% (2019)

Exports - commodities: sand, iron products, seats, medical instruments, fish (2019)

Imports: $39.44 million (2017 est.)
$36.1 million (2016 est.)

Imports - partners: United States 70%, United Kingdom 6% (2019)

Imports - commodities: refined petroleum, cars, oranges, electric motors, broadcasting equipment (2019)

Reserves of foreign exchange and gold: $47.58 million (31 December 2017 est.)
$51.47 million (31 December 2015 est.)

Debt - external: $8.9 million (1997)

Exchange rates: East Caribbean dollars (XCD) per US dollar -
2.7 (2017 est.)
2.7 (2016 est.)
2.7 (2015 est.)
2.7 (2014 est.)
2.7 (2013 est.)

ENERGY

Electricity: *installed generating capacity:* 5,000 kW (2020 est.)
consumption: 21.56 million kWh (2019 est.)
exports: 0 kWh (2020 est.)
imports: 0 kWh (2020 est.)
transmission/distribution losses: 1 million kWh (2019 est.)

Electricity generation sources: *fossil fuels:* 100% of total installed capacity (2020 est.)

Petroleum: *total petroleum production:* 0 bbl/day (2021 est.)
refined petroleum consumption: 200 bbl/day (2019 est.)

Refined petroleum products - imports: 406 bbl/day (2015 est.)

Carbon dioxide emissions: 33,000 metric tonnes of CO_2 (2019 est.)
from petroleum and other liquids: 33,000 metric tonnes of CO_2 (2019 est.)

Energy consumption per capita: 0 Btu/person (2019 est.)

COMMUNICATIONS

Telephones - fixed lines: *total subscriptions:* 3,000 (2018 est.)
subscriptions per 100 inhabitants: 60 (2018 est.)

Telephones - mobile cellular: *total subscriptions:* 5,000 (2018 est.)
subscriptions per 100 inhabitants: 101 (2019 est.)

Telecommunication systems: *general assessment:* telecom market one of growth in Caribbean and fully digitalized; high dependency on tourism and offshore financial services; operators expand FttP (Fiber to Home) services; LTE launches and operators invest in mobile networks; effective competition in all sectors (2020)
domestic: fixed-line roughly 60 per 100 and mobile-cellular teledensity nearly 101 per 100 persons (2019)
international: country code - 1-664; landing point for the ECFS optic submarine cable with links to 14 other islands in the eastern Caribbean extending from the British Virgin Islands to Trinidad (2019)

Broadcast media: Radio Montserrat, a public radio broadcaster, transmits on 1 station and has a repeater transmission to a second station; repeater transmissions from the GEM Radio Network of Trinidad and Tobago provide another 2 radio stations; cable and satellite TV available (2007)

Internet country code: .ms

Internet users: *total:* 2,744 (2019 est.)
percent of population: 55% (2019 est.)

Broadband - fixed subscriptions: *total:* 2,700 (2018 est.)
subscriptions per 100 inhabitants: 55 (2018 est.)

TRANSPORTATION

National air transport system: *number of registered air carriers:* 1 (2020)
inventory of registered aircraft operated by air carriers: 3

Civil aircraft registration country code prefix: VP-M

Airports: *total:* 1 (2021)

Airports - with paved runways: *total:* 1
under 914 m: 1 (2021)

Roadways: *note:* volcanic eruptions that began in 1995 destroyed most of the 227 km road system; a new road infrastructure has been built on the north end of the island

Ports and terminals: *major seaport(s):* Little Bay, Plymouth

MILITARY AND SECURITY

Military and security forces: no regular military forces; Royal Montserrat Defense Force (ceremonial, civil defense duties), Montserrat Police Force

Military - note: defense is the responsibility of the UK

TRANSNATIONAL ISSUES

Disputes - international: none identified

Illicit drugs: transshipment point for South American narcotics destined for the US and Europe

MOROCCO

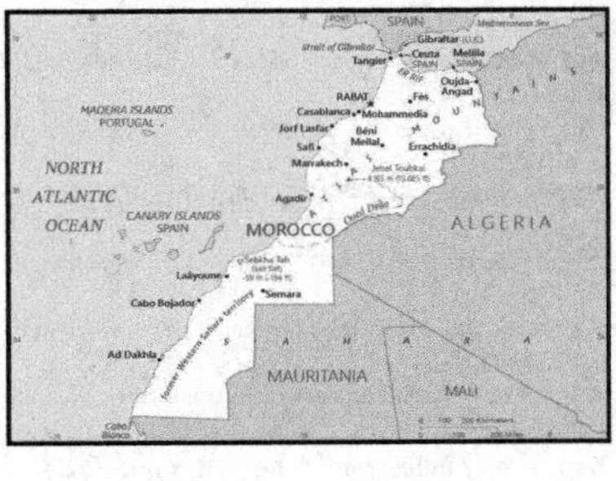

INTRODUCTION

Background: In 788, about a century after the Arab conquest of North Africa, a series of Moroccan Muslim dynasties began to rule in Morocco. In the 16th century, the Sa'adi monarchy, particularly under Ahmad al-MANSUR (1578-1603), repelled foreign invaders and inaugurated a golden age. The Alaouite Dynasty, to which the current Moroccan royal family belongs, dates from the 17th century. In 1860, Spain occupied northern Morocco and ushered in a half-century of trade rivalry among European powers that saw Morocco's sovereignty steadily erode; in 1912, the French imposed a protectorate over the country. A protracted independence struggle with France ended successfully in 1956. The internationalized city of Tangier and most Spanish possessions were turned over to the new country that same year. Sultan MOHAMMED V, the current monarch's grandfather, organized the new state as a constitutional monarchy and in 1957 assumed the title of king. Since Spain's 1976 withdrawal from Western Sahara, Morocco has extended its de facto administrative control to roughly 75% of this territory; however, the UN does not recognize Morocco as the administering power for Western Sahara. The UN since 1991 has monitored a cease-fire between Morocco and the Polisario Front - an organization advocating the territory's independence - and restarted negotiations over the status of the territory in December 2018. On 10 December 2020, the US recognized Morocco's sovereignty over all of Western Sahara.

King MOHAMMED VI in early 2011 responded to the spread of pro-democracy protests in the North Africa region by implementing a reform program that included a new constitution, passed by popular referendum in July 2011, under which some new powers were extended to parliament and the prime minister, but ultimate authority remains in the hands of the monarch. In November 2011, the Justice and Development Party (PJD) - a moderate Islamist party - won the largest number of seats in parliamentary elections, becoming the first Islamist party to lead the Moroccan Government. In September 2015, Morocco held its first direct elections for regional councils, one of the reforms included in the 2011 constitution. The PJD again won the largest number of seats in nationwide parliamentary elections in October 2016, but it lost its plurality to the pro-business National Rally of Independents (RNI) in September 2021. In December 2020, Morocco signed a normalization agreement with Israel, similar to those that Bahrain, the United Arab Emirates, and Sudan had concluded with Israel earlier in 2020.

GEOGRAPHY

Location: Northern Africa, bordering the North Atlantic Ocean and the Mediterranean Sea, between Algeria and Mauritania

Geographic coordinates: 28 30 N, 10 00 W

Map references: Africa

Area: *total:* 716,550 sq km
land: 716,300 sq km
water: 250 sq km

Area - comparative: slightly larger than twice the size of California

Land boundaries: *total:* 3,523.5 km
Spain (Melilla) 10.5 km exclave of Penon de Velez de la
border countries (3): Algeria 1,941 km; Mauritania 1,564 km; Spain (Ceuta) 8 km and Spain (Melilla) 10.5 km
note: an additional 75-meter border segment exists between Morocco and the Spanish exclave of Penon de Velez de la Gomera

Coastline: 2,945 km

Maritime claims: *territorial sea:* 12 nm
contiguous zone: 24 nm
exclusive economic zone: 200 nm
continental shelf: 200-m depth or to the depth of exploitation

Climate: Mediterranean in the north, becoming more extreme in the interior; in the south, hot, dry desert; rain is rare; cold offshore air currents produce fog and heavy dew
note: data does not include former Western Sahara

Terrain: mountainous northern coast (Rif Mountains) and interior (Atlas Mountains) bordered by large plateaus with intermontane valleys, and fertile coastal plains; the south is mostly low, flat desert with large areas of rocky or sandy surfaces

Elevation: *highest point:* Jebel Toubkal 4,165 m
lowest point: Sebkha Tah -59 m
mean elevation: 909 m

Natural resources: phosphates, iron ore, manganese, lead, zinc, fish, salt

Land use: *agricultural land:* 67.5% (2018 est.)
arable land: 17.5% (2018 est.)
permanent crops: 2.9% (2018 est.)
permanent pasture: 47.1% (2018 est.)
forest: 11.5% (2018 est.)
other: 21% (2018 est.)
note: does not include the area of the former Western Sahara, which is almost exclusively desert

Irrigated land: 14,850 sq km (2012)

Major rivers (by length in km): Draa - 1,100 km

Population distribution: the highest population density is found along the Atlantic and Mediterranean coasts; a number of densely populated agglomerations are found scattered through the Atlas Mountains as shown in this population distribution map

Natural hazards: in the north, the mountains are geologically unstable and subject to earthquakes; periodic droughts; windstorms; flash floods; landslides; in the south, a hot, dry, dust/sand-laden sirocco wind can occur during winter and spring; widespread harmattan haze exists 60% of time, often severely restricting visibility

Geography - note: strategic location along Strait of Gibraltar; the only African nation to have both Atlantic and Mediterranean coastlines; the waters off the Atlantic coast are particularly rich fishing areas

PEOPLE AND SOCIETY

Population: 36,738,229 (2022 est.)
note: includes Western Sahara

Nationality: *noun:* Moroccan(s)
adjective: Moroccan

Ethnic groups Arab-Berber 99%, other 1%
note: does not include data from the former Western Sahara

Languages: Arabic (official), Berber languages (Tamazight (official), Tachelhit, Tarifit), French (often the language of business, government, and diplomacy); note - the proportion of Berber speakers is disputed; does not include data from the former Western Sahara
major-language sample(s):
احسن مصدر متاع المعلومات الأساسية
كتاب ديال لحقائق متاع العالم،
(Arabic)

Religions: Muslim 99% (official; virtually all Sunni, <0.1% Shia), other 1% (includes Christian, Jewish, and Baha'i); note - Jewish about 3,000-3,500 (2020 est.)
note: does not include data from the former Western Sahara

Demographic profile: Morocco is undergoing a demographic transition. Its population is growing but at a declining rate, as people live longer and women have fewer children. Infant, child, and maternal mortality rates have been reduced through better health care, nutrition, hygiene, and vaccination coverage, although disparities between urban and rural and rich and poor households persist. Morocco's shrinking child cohort reflects the decline of its total fertility rate from 5 in mid-1980s to 2.2 in 2010, which is a result of increased female educational attainment, higher contraceptive use, delayed marriage, and the desire for smaller families. Young adults (persons aged 15-29) make up almost 26% of the total population and represent a potential economic asset if they can be gainfully employed. Currently, however, many youths are unemployed because Morocco's job creation rate has not kept pace with the growth of its working-age population. Most youths who have jobs work in the informal sector with little security or benefits.

During the second half of the 20th century, Morocco became one of the world's top emigration countries, creating large, widely dispersed migrant communities in Western Europe. The Moroccan Government has encouraged emigration since its independence in 1956, both to secure remittances for funding national development and as an outlet to prevent unrest in rebellious (often Berber) areas. Although Moroccan labor migrants earlier targeted Algeria and France, the flood of Moroccan "guest workers" from the mid-1960s to the early 1970s spread widely across northwestern Europe to fill unskilled jobs in the booming manufacturing, mining, construction, and agriculture industries. Host societies and most Moroccan migrants expected this migration to be temporary, but deteriorating economic conditions in Morocco related to the 1973 oil crisis and tighter European immigration policies resulted in these stays becoming permanent.

A wave of family migration followed in the 1970s and 1980s, with a growing number of second generation Moroccans opting to become naturalized citizens of their host countries. Spain and Italy emerged as new destination countries in the mid-1980s, but their introduction of visa restrictions in the early 1990s pushed Moroccans increasingly to migrate either legally by marrying Moroccans already in Europe or illegally to work in the underground economy. Women began to make up a growing share of these labor migrants. At the same time, some higher-skilled Moroccans went to the US and Quebec, Canada.

In the mid-1990s, Morocco developed into a transit country for asylum seekers from Sub-Saharan Africa and illegal labor migrants from Sub-Saharan Africa and South Asia trying to reach Europe via southern Spain, Spain's Canary Islands, or Spain's North African enclaves, Ceuta and Melilla. Forcible expulsions by Moroccan and Spanish security forces have not deterred these illegal migrants or calmed Europe's security concerns. Rabat remains unlikely to adopt an EU agreement to take back third-country nationals who have entered the EU illegally via Morocco. Thousands of other illegal migrants have chosen to stay in Morocco until they earn enough money for further travel or permanently as a "second-best" option. The launching of a regularization program in 2014 legalized the status of some migrants and granted them equal access to education, health care, and work, but xenophobia and racism remain obstacles.

Age structure: *0-14 years:* 27.04% (male 4,905,626/female 4,709,333)
15-24 years: 16.55% (male 2,953,523/female 2,930,708)
25-54 years: 40.64% (male 7,126,781/female 7,325,709)
55-64 years: 8.67% (male 1,533,771/female 1,548,315)
65 years and over: 7.11% (male 1,225,307/female 1,302,581) (2020 est.)
note: does not include data from the former Western Sahara

Dependency ratios: *total dependency ratio:* 52.4
youth dependency ratio: 40.8

elderly dependency ratio: 11.6
potential support ratio: 8.6 (2020 est.)
note: does not include data from the former Western Sahara

Median age: *total:* 29.1 years
male: 28.7 years
female: 29.6 years (2020 est.)
note: does not include data from the former Western Sahara

Population growth rate: 0.91% (2022 est.)
note: does not include data from the former Western Sahara

Birth rate: 17.42 births/1,000 population (2022 est.)
note: does not include data from the former Western Sahara

Death rate: 6.6 deaths/1,000 population (2022 est.)
note: does not include data from the former Western Sahara

Net migration rate: -1.74 migrant(s)/1,000 population (2022 est.)
note: does not include data from the former Western Sahara

Population distribution: the highest population density is found along the Atlantic and Mediterranean coasts; a number of densely populated agglomerations are found scattered through the Atlas Mountains as shown in this population distribution map

Urbanization: *urban population:* 64.6% of total population (2022)
rate of urbanization: 1.88% annual rate of change (2020-25 est.)
note: data does not include former Western Sahara

Major urban areas - population: 3.840 million Casablanca, 1.932 million RABAT (capital), 1.267 million Fes, 1.238 million Tangier, 1.277 million Marrakech, 960,000 Agadir (2022)

Sex ratio: *at birth:* 1.05 male(s)/female
0-14 years: 1.04 male(s)/female
15-24 years: 1.01 male(s)/female
25-54 years: 0.98 male(s)/female
55-64 years: 0.97 male(s)/female
65 years and over: 0.81 male(s)/female
total population: 1 male(s)/female (2022 est.)
note: does not include data from the former Western Sahara

Maternal mortality ratio: 70 deaths/100,000 live births (2017 est.)
note: does not include data from the former Western Sahara

Infant mortality rate: *total:* 19.2 deaths/1,000 live births
male: 21.47 deaths/1,000 live births
female: 16.81 deaths/1,000 live births (2022 est.)
note: does not include data from the former Western Sahara

Life expectancy at birth: *total population:* 73.68 years
male: 71.98 years
female: 75.46 years (2022 est.)
note: does not include data from the former Western Sahara

Total fertility rate: 2.29 children born/woman (2022 est.)
note: does not include data from the former Western Sahara

Contraceptive prevalence rate: 70.8% (2018)
note: does not include data from the former Western Sahara

Drinking water source: *improved: urban:* 98.3% of population
rural: 79.1% of population
total: 91% of population
unimproved: urban: 1.7% of population
rural: 20.9% of population
total: 9% of population (2017 est.)
note: does not include data from the former Western Sahara

Current health expenditure: 5.3% of GDP (2019)
note: does not include data from the former Western Sahara

Physicians density: 0.73 physicians/1,000 population (2017)
note: does not include data from the former Western Sahara

Hospital bed density: 1 beds/1,000 population (2017)
note: does not include data from the former Western Sahara

Sanitation facility access: *improved: urban:* 98.2% of population
rural: 72.4% of population
total: 88.8% of population
unimproved: urban: 1.8% of population
rural: 27.6% of population
total: 11.2% of population (2020 est.)
note: does not include data from the former Western Sahara

HIV/AIDS - adult prevalence rate: (2020 est.) <.1%
note: does not include data from the former Western Sahara

Obesity - adult prevalence rate: 26.1% (2016)
note: does not include data from the former Western Sahara

Alcohol consumption per capita: *total:* 0.51 liters of pure alcohol (2019 est.)
beer: 0.18 liters of pure alcohol (2019 est.)
wine: 0.24 liters of pure alcohol (2019 est.)
spirits: 0.09 liters of pure alcohol (2019 est.)
other alcohols: 0 liters of pure alcohol (2019 est.)

Tobacco use: *total:* 14.5% (2020 est.)
male: 28.2% (2020 est.)
female: 0.8% (2020 est.)

Children under the age of 5 years underweight: 2.6% (2017/18)
note: does not include data from the former Western Sahara

Child marriage: *women married by age 15:* 0.5%
women married by age 18: 13.7% (2018 est.)

Literacy: *definition:* age 15 and over can read and write
total population: 73.8%
male: 83.3%
female: 64.6% (2018)
note: does not include data from the former Western Sahara

School life expectancy (primary to tertiary education): *total:* 14 years
male: 14 years
female: 14 years (2020)
note: does not include data from the former Western Sahara

Unemployment, youth ages 15-24: *total:* 22.2%
male: 22%
female: 22.8% (2016 est.)
note: does not include data from the former Western Sahara

ENVIRONMENT

Environment - current issues: in the north, land degradation/desertification (soil erosion resulting from farming of marginal areas, overgrazing, destruction of vegetation); water and soil pollution due to dumping of industrial wastes into the ocean and inland water sources, and onto the land; in the south, desertification; overgrazing; sparse water and lack of arable land
note: data does not include former Western Sahara

Environment - international agreements: *party to:* Biodiversity, Climate Change, Climate Change-Kyoto Protocol, Climate Change-Paris Agreement, Comprehensive Nuclear Test Ban, Desertification, Endangered Species, Hazardous Wastes, Law of the Sea, Marine Dumping-London Convention, Marine Dumping-London Protocol, Nuclear Test Ban, Ozone Layer Protection, Ship Pollution, Wetlands, Whaling
signed, but not ratified: Environmental Modification

Air pollutants: *particulate matter emissions:* 30.99 micrograms per cubic meter (2016 est.)
carbon dioxide emissions: 61.28 megatons (2016 est.)
methane emissions: 17.16 megatons (2020 est.)
note: data does not include former Western Sahara

Climate: Mediterranean in the north, becoming more extreme in the interior; in the south, hot, dry desert; rain is rare; cold offshore air currents produce fog and heavy dew
note: data does not include former Western Sahara

Land use: *agricultural land:* 67.5% (2018 est.)
arable land: 17.5% (2018 est.)
permanent crops: 2.9% (2018 est.)
permanent pasture: 47.1% (2018 est.)
forest: 11.5% (2018 est.)
other: 21% (2018 est.)
note: does not include the area of the former Western Sahara, which is almost exclusively desert

Urbanization: *urban population:* 64.6% of total population (2022)
rate of urbanization: 1.88% annual rate of change (2020-25 est.)
note: data does not include former Western Sahara

Revenue from forest resources: *forest revenues:* 0.13% of GDP (2018 est.)

Revenue from coal: *coal revenues:* 0% of GDP (2018 est.)

Waste and recycling: *municipal solid waste generated annually:* 6.852 million tons (2014 est.)
municipal solid waste recycled annually: 548,160 tons (2014 est.)
percent of municipal solid waste recycled: 8% (2014 est.)
note: data does not include former Western Sahara

Major rivers (by length in km): Draa - 1,100 km

Total water withdrawal: *municipal:* 1.063 billion cubic meters (2017 est.)
industrial: 212 million cubic meters (2017 est.)
agricultural: 9.156 billion cubic meters (2017 est.)
note: data does not include former Western Sahara

Total renewable water resources: 29 billion cubic meters (2017 est.)
note: data does not include former Western Sahara

GOVERNMENT

Country name: *conventional long form:* Kingdom of Morocco
conventional short form: Morocco
local long form: Al Mamlakah al Maghribiyah
local short form: Al Maghrib
former: French Protectorate in Morocco, Spanish Protectorate in Morocco, Ifni, Spanish Sahara, Western Sahara
etymology: the English name "Morocco" derives from, respectively, the Spanish and Portuguese names "Marruecos" and "Marrocos," which stem from "Marrakesh" the Latin name for the former capital of ancient Morocco; the Arabic name "Al Maghrib" translates as "The West"

Government type: parliamentary constitutional monarchy

Capital: *name:* Rabat
geographic coordinates: 34 01 N, 6 49 W
time difference: UTC+1 (6 hours ahead of Washington, DC, during Standard Time)
etymology: name derives from the Arabic title "Ribat el-Fath," meaning "stronghold of victory," applied to the newly constructed citadel in 1170

Administrative divisions: 12 regions; Beni Mellal-Khenifra, Casablanca-Settat, Dakhla-Oued Ed-Dahab, Draa-Tafilalet, Fes-Meknes, Guelmim-Oued Noun, Laayoune-Sakia El Hamra, Marrakech-Safi, Oriental, Rabat-Sale-Kenitra, Souss-Massa, Tanger-Tetouan-Al Hoceima
note: effective 10 December 2020, the US Government recognizes the sovereignty of Morocco over all of the territory of former Western Sahara

Independence: 2 March 1956 (from France)

National holiday: Throne Day (accession of King MOHAMMED VI to the throne), 30 July (1999)

Constitution: *history:* several previous; latest drafted 17 June 2011, approved by referendum 1 July 2011; note - sources disagree on whether the 2011 referendum was for a new constitution or for reforms to the previous constitution
amendments: proposed by the king, by the prime minister, or by members in either chamber of Parliament; passage requires at least two-thirds majority vote by both chambers and approval in a referendum; the king can opt to submit self-initiated proposals directly to a referendum

Legal system: mixed legal system of civil law based on French civil law and Islamic (sharia) law; judicial review of legislative acts by Constitutional Court

International law organization participation: has not submitted an ICJ jurisdiction declaration; non-party state to the ICCt

Citizenship: *citizenship by birth:* no
citizenship by descent only: the father must be a citizen of Morocco; if the father is unknown or stateless, the mother must be a citizen
dual citizenship recognized: yes
residency requirement for naturalization: 5 years

Suffrage: 18 years of age; universal

Executive branch: *chief of state:* King MOHAMMED VI (since 30 July 1999)
head of government: Prime Minister Aziz AKHANNOUCH (since 7 October 2021)
cabinet: Council of Ministers chosen by the prime minister in consultation with Parliament and appointed by the monarch; the monarch chooses the ministers of Interior, Foreign Affairs, Islamic Affairs, and National Defense Administration
elections/appointments: the monarchy is hereditary; prime minister appointed by the monarch from the majority party following legislative elections

Legislative branch: *description:* bicameral Parliament consists of:
House of Councillors or Majlis al-Mustacharine (120 seats; members indirectly elected by an electoral college of local councils, professional organizations, and labor unions; members serve 6-year terms)

House of Representatives or Majlis al-Nuwab (395 seats; 305 members directly elected in multi-seat constituencies by proportional representation vote and 90 directly elected in a single nationwide constituency by proportional representation vote; members serve 5-year terms); note - 60 seats reserved for women and 30 seats for those under age 40 in regional multi-seat constituencies, with the seats divided proportionally among the 12 regions by population size of the region
elections:
House of Councillors - last held on 5 October 2021 (next to be held by 31 October 2027)
House of Representatives - last held on 8 September 2021 (next to be held by 30 September 2026)
election results:
House of Councillors - percent of vote by party - NA; seats by party - RNI 27, PAM 19, PI 17, MP 12, USFP 8, UGIM 6, CDT 3, PJD 3, UC 2, UMT 2, Amal 1, FDT 1, MDS 1, PRD 1, independent 1; composition as of October 2021) men 105, women 15, percent of women 12.5%
House of Representatives - percent of vote by party NA; seats by party - RNI 102, PAM 87, PI 81, USFP 34, MP 28, PPS 22, UC 18, PJD 13, MDS 5, other 5; composition as of July 2022 - men 305, women 90, percent of women 24.1%; note -overall percent of women in Parliament 21.4%

Judicial branch: *highest court(s):* Supreme Court or Court of Cassation (consists of 5-judge panels organized into civil, family matters, commercial, administrative, social, and criminal sections); Constitutional Court (consists of 12 members)
judge selection and term of office: Supreme Court judges appointed by the Superior Council of Judicial Power, a 20-member body presided over by the monarch, which includes the Supreme Court president, the prosecutor general, representatives of the appeals and first instance courts (among them 1 woman magistrate), the president of the National Council for Human Rights (CNDH), and 5 "notable persons" appointed by the monarch; judges appointed for life; Constitutional Court members - 6 designated by the monarch and 6 elected by Parliament; court president appointed by the monarch from among the court members; members serve 9-year nonrenewable terms
subordinate courts: courts of appeal; High Court of Justice; administrative and commercial courts; regional and Sadad courts (for religious, civil and administrative, and penal adjudication); first instance courts

Political parties and leaders: Action Party or PA [Mohammed EL IDRISSI]
Amal (hope) Party [Mohamed BANI]
An-Nahj Ad-Dimocrati or An-Nahj or Democratic Way [Mustapha BRAHMA]
Authenticity and Modernity Party or PAM [Abdellatif OUAHBI]
Constitutional Union Party or UC [Mohamed SAJID]
Democratic and Social Movement or MDS [Mahmoud ARCHANE]
Democratic Forces Front or FFD [Mustapha BENALI]
Democratic Society Party or PSD [Zhour CHAKKAFI]
Green Left Party or PGV [Mohamed FARES]
Istiqlal (Independence) Party or PI [Nizar BARAKA]
Moroccan Liberal Party or PML [Isaac CHARIA]
Moroccan Union for Democracy or UMD [Jamal MANDRI]
National Democratic Party [Abdellah KADIRI]
National Ittihadi Congress or CNI [Abdesalam EL AZIZ]
National Rally of Independents or RNI [Aziz AKHANNOUCH]
Neo-Democrats Party [Mohamed DARIF]
Party of Development Reform or PRD [Abderrahmane EL KOHEN]
Party of Justice and Development or PJD [Abdelilah BENKIRANE]
Party of Liberty and Social Justice [Miloud MOUSSAOUI]
Party of Progress and Socialism or PPS [Nabil BENABDELLAH]
Popular Movement or MP [Mohand LAENSER]
Renaissance and Virtue Party [Mohamed KHALIDI]
Renaissance Party [Said EL GHENNIOUI]
Renewal and Equity Party or PRE [Chakir ACHEHABAR]
Shoura (consultation) and Istiqlal Party [Ahmed BELGHAZI]
Socialist Union of Popular Forces or USFP [Driss LACHGAR]
Unified Socialist Party or GSU [Nabila MOUNIB]
Unity and Democracy Party [Ahmed FITRI]

International organization participation: ABEDA, AfDB, AFESD, AMF, AMU, AU, CAEU, CD, EBRD, FAO, G-11, G-77, IAEA, IBRD, ICAO, ICC (national committees), ICRM, IDA, IDB, IFAD, IFC, IFRCS, IHO, ILO, IMF, IMO, IMSO, Interpol, IOC, IOM, IPU, ISO, ITSO, ITU, ITUC (NGOs), LAS, MIGA, MONUSCO, NAM, OAS (observer), OIC, OIF, OPCW, OSCE (partner), Pacific Alliance (observer), Paris Club (associate), PCA, SICA (observer), UN, UNCTAD, UNESCO, UNHCR, UNIDO, UNOCI, UNSC (temporary), UNWTO, UPU, WCO, WHO, WIPO, WMO, WTO

Diplomatic representation in the US: *chief of mission:* Ambassador Lalla Joumala ALAOUI (since 24 April 2017)
chancery: 3508 International Drive NW, Washington, DC 20008
telephone: [1] (202) 462-7979
FAX: [1] (202) 462-7643
email address and website:
Washingtonembbmorocco@maec.gov.ma
https://www.embassyofmorocco.us/
consulate(s) general: New York

Diplomatic representation from the US: *chief of mission:* Ambassador (vacant); Charge d'Affaires Lawrence M. RANDOLPH (since 4 January 2021)
embassy: Km 5.7 Avenue Mohammed VI, Souissi, Rabat 10170
mailing address: 9400 Rabat Place, Washington DC 20521-9400
telephone: [212] 0537-637-200
FAX: [212] 0537-637-201
email address and website:

ACSCasablanca@state.gov (US Consulate General Casablanca)
https://ma.usembassy.gov/
consulate(s) general: Casablanca

Flag description: red with a green pentacle (five-pointed, linear star) known as Sulayman's (Solomon's) seal in the center of the flag; red and green are traditional colors in Arab flags, although the use of red is more commonly associated with the Arab states of the Persian Gulf; the pentacle represents the five pillars of Islam and signifies the association between God and the nation; design dates to 1912

National symbol(s): pentacle symbol, lion; national colors: red, green

National anthem: *name:* "Hymne Cherifien" (Hymn of the Sharif)
lyrics/music: Ali Squalli HOUSSAINI/Leo MORGAN
note: music adopted 1956, lyrics adopted 1970

National heritage: *total World Heritage Sites:* 9 (all cultural)
selected World Heritage Site locales: Medina of Fez; Medina of Marrakesh; Ksar of Ait-Ben-Haddou; Historic City of Meknes; Archaeological Site of Volubilis; Medina of Tétouan (formerly known as Titawin); Medina of Essaouira (formerly Mogador); Portuguese City of Mazagan (El Jadida); Historic and Modern Rabat

ECONOMY

Economic overview: Morocco has capitalized on its proximity to Europe and relatively low labor costs to work towards building a diverse, open, market-oriented economy. Key sectors of the economy include agriculture, tourism, aerospace, automotive, phosphates, textiles, apparel, and subcomponents. Morocco has increased investment in its port, transportation, and industrial infrastructure to position itself as a center and broker for business throughout Africa. Industrial development strategies and infrastructure improvements - most visibly illustrated by a new port and free trade zone near Tangier - are improving Morocco's competitiveness.

In the 1980s, Morocco was a heavily indebted country before pursuing austerity measures and pro-market reforms, overseen by the IMF. Since taking the throne in 1999, King MOHAMMED VI has presided over a stable economy marked by steady growth, low inflation, and gradually falling unemployment, although poor harvests and economic difficulties in Europe contributed to an economic slowdown. To boost exports, Morocco entered into a bilateral Free Trade Agreement with the US in 2006 and an Advanced Status agreement with the EU in 2008. In late 2014, Morocco eliminated subsidies for gasoline, diesel, and fuel oil, dramatically reducing outlays that weighed on the country's budget and current account. Subsidies on butane gas and certain food products remain in place. Morocco also seeks to expand its renewable energy capacity with a goal of making renewable more than 50% of installed electricity generation capacity by 2030.

Despite Morocco's economic progress, the country suffers from high unemployment, poverty, and illiteracy, particularly in rural areas. Key economic challenges for Morocco include reforming the education system and the judiciary.

Real GDP (purchasing power parity): $259.42 billion (2020 est.)
$279.3 billion (2019 est.)
$272.53 billion (2018 est.)
note: data are in 2017 dollars

Real GDP growth rate: 2.5% (2019 est.)
2.96% (2018 est.)
3.98% (2017 est.)

Real GDP per capita: $6,900 (2020 est.)
$7,500 (2019 est.)
$7,400 (2018 est.)
note: data are in 2017 dollars

GDP (official exchange rate): $118.858 billion (2019 est.)

Inflation rate (consumer prices): 0.2% (2019 est.)
2% (2018 est.)
0.7% (2017 est.)

Credit ratings:

Fitch rating: BB+ (2020)

Moody's rating: Ba1 (1999)

Standard & Poors rating: BBB- (2010)
note: The year refers to the year in which the current credit rating was first obtained.

GDP - composition, by sector of origin: *agriculture:* 14% (2017 est.)
industry: 29.5% (2017 est.)
services: 56.5% (2017 est.)

GDP - composition, by end use: *household consumption:* 58% (2017 est.)
government consumption: 18.9% (2017 est.)
investment in fixed capital: 28.4% (2017 est.)
investment in inventories: 4.2% (2017 est.)
exports of goods and services: 37.1% (2017 est.)
imports of goods and services: -46.6% (2017 est.)

Agricultural products: wheat, sugar beet, milk, potatoes, olives, tangerines/mandarins, tomatoes, oranges, barley, onions

Industries: automotive parts, phosphate mining and processing, aerospace, food processing, leather goods, textiles, construction, energy, tourism

Industrial production growth rate: 2.8% (2017 est.)

Labor force: 10.399 million (2020 est.)

Labor force - by occupation: *agriculture:* 39.1%
industry: 20.3%
services: 40.5% (2014 est.)

Unemployment rate: 9.23% (2019 est.)
9.65% (2018 est.)

Unemployment, youth ages 15-24: *total:* 22.2%
male: 22%
female: 22.8% (2016 est.)
note: does not include data from the former Western Sahara

Population below poverty line: 4.8% (2013 est.)

Gini Index coefficient - distribution of family income: 39.5 (2013 est.)
39.5 (1999 est.)

Household income or consumption by percentage share: *lowest 10%:* 2.7%
highest 10%: 33.2% (2007)

Budget: *revenues:* 22.81 billion (2017 est.)
expenditures: 26.75 billion (2017 est.)

Budget surplus (+) or deficit (-): -3.6% (of GDP) (2017 est.)

Public debt: 65.1% of GDP (2017 est.)
64.9% of GDP (2016 est.)

Taxes and other revenues: 20.9% (of GDP) (2017 est.)

Fiscal year: calendar year

Current account balance: -$5.075 billion (2019 est.)
-$6.758 billion (2018 est.)

Exports: $37.52 billion (2020 est.) note: data are in current year dollars
$44.05 billion (2019 est.) note: data are in current year dollars
$43.25 billion (2018 est.) note: data are in current year dollars

Exports - partners: Spain 23%, France 19% (2019)

Exports - commodities: cars, insulated wiring, fertilizers, phosphoric acid, clothing and apparel (2019)

Imports: $46.26 billion (2020 est.) note: data are in current year dollars
$54.1 billion (2019 est.) note: data are in current year dollars
$55.38 billion (2018 est.) note: data are in current year dollars

Imports - partners: Spain 19%, France 11%, China 9%, United States 7%, Germany 5%, Turkey 5%, Italy 5% (2019)

Imports - commodities: refined petroleum, cars and vehicle parts, natural gas, coal, low-voltage protection equipment (2019)

Reserves of foreign exchange and gold: $26.27 billion (31 December 2017 est.)
$25.37 billion (31 December 2016 est.)

Debt - external: $52.957 billion (2019 est.)
$51.851 billion (2018 est.)

Exchange rates: Moroccan dirhams (MAD) per US dollar -
9.0065 (2020 est.)
9.657 (2019 est.) 9.48825 (2018 est.)
9.7351 (2014 est.)
8.3798 (2013 est.)

ENERGY

Electricity access: *electrification - total population:* 100% (2020)

Electricity: *installed generating capacity:* 14.187 million kW (2020 est.)
consumption: 29,447,883,000 kWh (2019 est.)
exports: 624 million kWh (2020 est.)
imports: 856 million kWh (2020 est.)
transmission/distribution losses: 6.703 billion kWh (2019 est.)

Electricity generation sources: *fossil fuels:* 81.6% of total installed capacity (2020 est.)
solar: 1.1% of total installed capacity (2020 est.)
wind: 13% of total installed capacity (2020 est.)
hydroelectricity: 4.4% of total installed capacity (2020 est.)

Coal: *production:* 0 metric tons (2020 est.)
consumption: 9.321 million metric tons (2020 est.)
exports: 0 metric tons (2020 est.)
imports: 9.321 million metric tons (2020 est.)
proven reserves: 14 million metric tons (2019 est.)

Petroleum: *total petroleum production:* 0 bbl/day (2021 est.)
refined petroleum consumption: 307,500 bbl/day (2019 est.)
crude oil and lease condensate exports: 0 bbl/day (2018 est.)

crude oil and lease condensate imports: 0 bbl/day (2018 est.)
crude oil estimated reserves: 700,000 barrels (2021 est.)

Refined petroleum products - production: 66,230 bbl/day (2017 est.)

Refined petroleum products - exports: 9,504 bbl/day (2015 est.)

Refined petroleum products - imports: 229,300 bbl/day (2015 est.)

Natural gas: *production:* 105.678 million cubic meters (2019 est.)
consumption: 1,051,658,000 cubic meters (2019 est.)
exports: 0 cubic meters (2021 est.)
imports: 950.765 million cubic meters (2019 est.)
proven reserves: 1.444 billion cubic meters (2021 est.)

Carbon dioxide emissions: 60.2 million metric tonnes of CO2 (2019 est.)
from coal and metallurgical coke: 20.267 million metric tonnes of CO2 (2019 est.)
from petroleum and other liquids: 37.834 million metric tonnes of CO2 (2019 est.)
from consumed natural gas: 2.099 million metric tonnes of CO2 (2019 est.)

Energy consumption per capita: 24.59 million Btu/person (2019 est.)

COMMUNICATIONS

Telephones - fixed lines: *total subscriptions:* 2,357,286 (2020 est.)
subscriptions per 100 inhabitants: 6 (2020 est.)

Telephones - mobile cellular: *total subscriptions:* 49,421,023 (2020 est.)
subscriptions per 100 inhabitants: 134 (2020 est.)

Telecommunication systems: *general assessment:* despite Morocco's economic progress, the country suffers from high unemployment and illiteracy affecting telecom market, particularly in rural areas; national network nearly 100% digital using fiber-optic links; improved rural service employs microwave radio relay; one of the most state-of-the-art markets in Africa; high mobile penetration rates in the region with low cost for broadband Internet access; improvement in LTE reach and capabilities; service providers have all successfully completed 5G proofs of concept and are currently lining up 5G equipment providers for both radio and core technology; regulatory agency expects to conduct the 5G spectrum auction in 2023; mobile Internet accounts for 93% of all Internet connections; World Bank provided funds for Morocco's digital transformation; government supported digital education during pandemic; submarine cables and satellite provide connectivity to Asia, Africa, the Middle East, Europe, and Australia (2022)
domestic: fixed-line teledensity is just over 6 per 100 persons and mobile-cellular subscribership is nearly 134 per 100 persons; good system composed of open-wire lines, cables, and microwave radio relay links; principal switching centers are Casablanca and Rabat (2020)
international: country code - 212; landing point for the Atlas Offshore, Estepona-Tetouan, Canalink and SEA-ME-WE-3 fiber-optic telecommunications undersea cables that provide connectivity to Asia, Africa, the Middle East, Europe and Australia; satellite earth stations - 2 Intelsat (Atlantic Ocean) and 1 Arabsat; microwave radio relay to Gibraltar, Spain, and Western Sahara (2019)

Broadcast media: 2 TV broadcast networks with state-run Radio-Television Marocaine (RTM) operating one network and the state partially owning the other; foreign TV broadcasts are available via satellite dish; 3 radio broadcast networks with RTM operating one; the government-owned network includes 10 regional radio channels in addition to its national service (2019)

Internet country code: .ma

Internet users: *total:* 31,004,869 (2020 est.)
percent of population: 84% (2020 est.)

Broadband - fixed subscriptions: *total:* 2,102,434 (2020 est.)
subscriptions per 100 inhabitants: 6 (2020 est.)

Communications - note: the University of al-Quarawiyyin Library in Fez is recognized as the oldest existing, continually operating library in the world, dating back to A.D. 859; among its holdings are approximately 4,000 ancient Islamic manuscripts

TRANSPORTATION

National air transport system: *number of registered air carriers:* 3 (2020)
inventory of registered aircraft operated by air carriers: 76
annual passenger traffic on registered air carriers: 8,132,917 (2018)
annual freight traffic on registered air carriers: 97.71 million (2018) mt-km

Civil aircraft registration country code prefix: CN

Airports: *total:* 62 (2021)

Airports - with paved runways: *total:* 36
over 3,047 m: 13
2,438 to 3,047 m: 12
1,524 to 2,437 m: 6
914 to 1,523 m: 4
under 914 m: 1 (2021)

Airports - with unpaved runways: *total:* 26
2,438 to 3,047 m: 2
1,524 to 2,437 m: 6
914 to 1,523 m: 12
under 914 m: 6 (2021)

Heliports: 1 (2021)

Pipelines: 944 km gas, 270 km oil, 175 km refined products (2013)

Railways: *total:* 2,067 km (2014)
standard gauge: 2,067 km (2014) 1.435-m gauge (1,022 km electrified)

Roadways: *total:* 57,300 km (2018)

Merchant marine: *total:* 93
by type: container ship 6, general cargo 5, oil tanker 2, other 80 (2021)

Ports and terminals: *major seaport(s):* Ad Dakhla, Agadir, Casablanca, Jorf Lasfar, Laayoune (El Aaiun), Mohammedia, Safi, Tangier
container port(s) (TEUs): Tangier (4,801,713) (2019)

LNG terminal(s) (import): Jorf Lasfar (planned)

MILITARY AND SECURITY

Military and security forces: Royal Armed Forces: Royal Moroccan Army (includes the Moroccan Royal Guard), Royal Moroccan Navy (includes Coast Guard, marines), Royal Moroccan Air Force; Ministry of Defense (aka Administration of National Defense): Royal Moroccan Gendarmerie; Ministry of Interior: National Police, Auxiliary Forces (2022)
note 1: the National Police manages internal law enforcement in cities; the Royal Gendarmerie is responsible for law enforcement in rural regions and on national highways
note 2: the Auxiliary Forces provide support to the Gendarmerie and National Police; it includes a Mobile Intervention Corps, a motorized paramilitary security force that supplements the military and the police as needed
note 3: the Moroccan Royal Guard was established in the 11th century and is considered one of the world's oldest active units still in military service

Military expenditures: 4.5% of GDP (2021 est.)
4.5% of GDP (2020 est.)
3.4% of GDP (2019 est.) (approximately $7.46 billion)
3.3% of GDP (2018 est.) (approximately $7.12 billion)
3.4% of GDP (2017 est.) (approximately $7.08 billion)

Military and security service personnel strengths: approximately 200,000 active personnel (175,000 Army; 10,000 Navy; 15,000 Air Force); estimated 20,000 Gendarmerie; estimated 5,000 Mobile Intervention Corps (2022)

Military equipment inventories and acquisitions: the Moroccan military's inventory is comprised of mostly older French and US equipment; since 2010, it has received equipment from about a dozen countries with France and the US as the leading suppliers (2021)

Military service age and obligation: 19-25 years of age for 12-month compulsory and voluntary military service for men and women (conscription abolished 2006 and reintroduced in 2019) (2022)

Military deployments: 775 Central African Republic (MINUSCA); 925 Democratic Republic of the Congo (MONUSCO) (May 2022)

Military - note: Moroccan military forces were engaged in combat operations against the Polisario Front (aka Frente Popular para la Liberación de Saguia el-Hamra y de Río de Oro or Frente Polisario) from 1975 until a UN-brokered cease-fire in 1991; a 2,500-kilometer long sand berm, built in 1987, separates the forces of Morocco and the Polisario Front

the UN Mission for the Referendum in Western Sahara (MINURSO) was established by Security Council resolution 690 in April 1991 in accordance with settlement proposals accepted in August 1988 by Morocco and the Polisario Front; MINURSO was unable to carry out all the original settlement proposals, but as of 2022 continued to monitor the cease-fire and reduce the threat of mines and unexploded ordnance, and has provided logistic support to the Office of the UN High Commissioner for Refugees (UNHCR)-led confidence building measures with personnel and air and ground assets

Morocco has Major Non-NATO Ally (MNNA) status with the US; MNNA is a designation under

US law that provides foreign partners with certain benefits in the areas of defense trade and security cooperation; while MNNA status provides military and economic privileges, it does not entail any security commitments (2022)

TERRORISM

Terrorist group(s): Islamic State of Iraq and ash-Sham (ISIS)

TRANSNATIONAL ISSUES

Disputes - international: *Morocco-Algeria:* Algeria's border with Morocco remains an irritant to bilateral relations, each nation accusing the other of harboring militants and arms smuggling
Morocco-Mauritania: tensions arose in 2016 when Mauritanian soldiers were deployed to Lagouira, a city in the southernmost part of Morocco, and raised their flag
Morocco-Spain: Morocco protests Spain's control over the coastal enclaves of Ceuta, Melilla, and Penon de Velez de la Gomera, the islands of Penon de Alhucemas and Islas Chafarinas, and surrounding waters; both countries claim Isla Perejil (Leila Island); discussions have not progressed on a comprehensive maritime delimitation, setting limits on resource exploration and refugee interdiction, since Morocco's 2002 rejection of Spain's unilateral designation of a median line from the Canary Islands; Morocco serves as one of the primary launching areas of illegal migration into Spain from North Africa

Illicit drugs: one of the world's largest cannabis-producing countries with Europe as the main market; hashish is also smuggled to South America and the Caribbean where it is exchanged for cocaine which is distributed in Europe; MDMA (ecstasy), originating in Belgium and the Netherlands is smuggled into northern Morocco for sale on the domestic market

MOZAMBIQUE

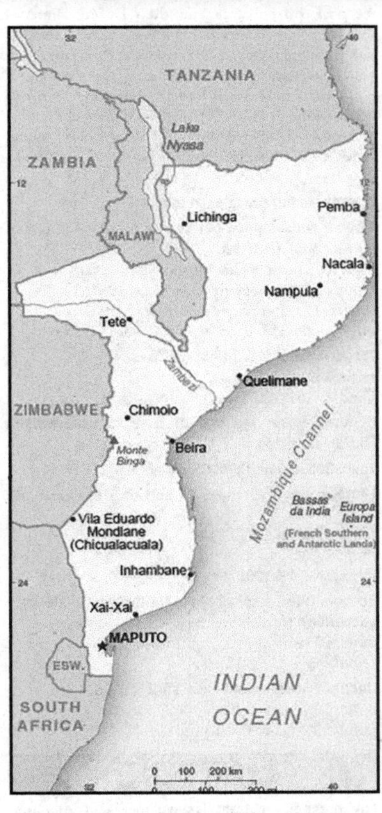

INTRODUCTION

Background: In the first half of the second millennium A.D., northern Mozambican port towns were frequented by traders from Somalia, Ethiopia, Egypt, Arabia, Persia, and India. The Portuguese were able to wrest much of the coastal trade from Arab Muslims in the centuries after 1500 and to set up their own colonies. Portugal did not relinquish Mozambique until 1975. Large-scale emigration, economic dependence on South Africa, a severe drought, and a prolonged civil war hindered the country's development until the mid-1990s. The ruling Front for the Liberation of Mozambique (FRELIMO) party formally abandoned Marxism in 1989, and a new constitution the following year provided for multiparty elections and a free market economy. A UN-negotiated peace agreement between FRELIMO and rebel Mozambique National Resistance (RENAMO) forces ended the fighting in 1992. In 2004, Mozambique underwent a delicate transition as Joaquim CHISSANO stepped down after 18 years in office. His elected successor, Armando GUEBUZA, served two terms and then passed executive power to Filipe NYUSI in 2015. RENAMO's residual armed forces intermittently engaged in a low-level insurgency after 2012, but a late December 2016 cease-fire eventually led to the two sides signing a comprehensive peace deal in August 2019. Elections in October 2019, challenged by Western observers and civil society as being problematic, resulted in resounding wins for NYUSI and FRELIMO across the country. Since October 2017, violent extremists - who an official ISIS media outlet recognized as ISIS's network in Mozambique for the first time in June 2019 - have been conducting attacks against civilians and security services in the northern province of Cabo Delgado. In 2021, Rwanda and the Southern African Development Community deployed forces to support Mozambique's efforts to counter the extremist group.

GEOGRAPHY

Location: Southeastern Africa, bordering the Mozambique Channel, between South Africa and Tanzania

Geographic coordinates: 18 15 S, 35 00 E

Map references: Africa

Area: *total:* 799,380 sq km
land: 786,380 sq km
water: 13,000 sq km

Area - comparative: slightly more than five times the size of Georgia; slightly less than twice the size of California

Land boundaries: *total:* 4,783 km
border countries (6): Malawi 1498 km; South Africa 496 km; Eswatini 108 km; Tanzania 840 km; Zambia 439 km; Zimbabwe 1,402 km

Coastline: 2,470 km

Maritime claims: *territorial sea:* 12 nm
exclusive economic zone: 200 nm

Climate: tropical to subtropical

Terrain: mostly coastal lowlands, uplands in center, high plateaus in northwest, mountains in west

Elevation: *highest point:* Monte Binga 2,436 m
lowest point: Indian Ocean 0 m
mean elevation: 345 m

Natural resources: coal, titanium, natural gas, hydropower, tantalum, graphite

Land use: *agricultural land:* 56.3% (2018 est.)
arable land: 6.4% (2018 est.)
permanent crops: 0.3% (2018 est.)
permanent pasture: 49.6% (2018 est.)
forest: 43.7% (2018 est.)
other: 0% (2018 est.)

Irrigated land: 1,180 sq km (2012)

Major lakes (area sq km): *fresh water lake(s):* Lake Malawi (shared with Malawi and Tanzania) - 22,490

Major rivers (by length in km): Zambezi river mouth (shared with Zambia [s]), Angola, Namibia, Botswana, and Zimbabwe) - 2,740 km; Limpopo river mouth (shared with South Africa [s], Botswana, and Zimbabwe) - 1,800 km
note – [s] after country name indicates river source; [m] after country name indicates river mouth

Major watersheds (area sq km): Indian Ocean drainage: Zambezi (1,332,412 sq km)

Population distribution: three large populations clusters are found along the southern coast between Maputo and Inhambane, in the central area between Beira and Chimoio along the Zambezi River, and in and around the northern cities of Nampula, Cidade de Nacala, and Pemba; the northwest and southwest are the least populated areas as shown in this population distribution map

Natural hazards: severe droughts; devastating cyclones and floods in central and southern provinces

Geography - note: the Zambezi River flows through the north-central and most fertile part of the country

PEOPLE AND SOCIETY

Population: 31,693,239 (2022 est.)

Nationality: *noun:* Mozambican(s)
adjective: Mozambican

Ethnic groups: African 99% (Makhuwa, Tsonga, Lomwe, Sena, and others), Mestizo 0.8%, other (includes European, Indian, Pakistani, Chinese) 0.2% (2017 est.)

Languages: Makhuwa 26.1%, Portuguese (official) 16.6%, Tsonga 8.6%, Nyanja 8.1, Sena 7.1%, Lomwe 7.1%, Chuwabo 4.7%, Ndau 3.8%, Tswa 3.8%, other Mozambican languages 11.8%, other 0.5%, unspecified 1.8% (2017 est.)

Religions: Roman Catholic 27.2%, Muslim 18.9%, Zionist Christian 15.6%, Evangelical/Pentecostal 15.3%, Anglican 1.7%, other 4.8%, none 13.9%, unspecified 2.5% (2017 est.)

Demographic profile: Mozambique is a poor, sparsely populated country with high fertility and mortality rates and a rapidly growing youthful population – 45% of the population is younger than 15, as of 2022. Mozambique's high poverty rate is sustained by natural disasters, disease, high population growth, low agricultural productivity, and the unequal distribution of wealth. The country's birth rate is among the world's highest, averaging around more than 5 children per woman (and higher in rural areas) for at least the last three decades. The sustained high level of fertility reflects gender inequality, low contraceptive use, early marriages and childbearing, and a lack of education, particularly among women. The high population growth rate is somewhat restrained by the country's high HIV/AIDS and overall mortality rates. Mozambique ranks among the worst in the world for HIV/AIDS prevalence, HIV/AIDS deaths, and life expectancy at birth, as of 2022.

Mozambique is predominantly a country of emigration, but internal, rural-urban migration has begun to grow. Mozambicans, primarily from the country's southern region, have been migrating to South Africa for work for more than a century. Additionally, approximately 1.7 million Mozambicans fled to Malawi, South Africa, and other neighboring countries between 1979 and 1992 to escape from civil war. Labor migrants have usually been men from rural areas whose crops have failed or who are unemployed and have headed to South Africa to work as miners; multiple generations of the same family often become miners. Since the abolition of apartheid in South Africa in 1991, other job opportunities have opened to Mozambicans, including in the informal and manufacturing sectors, but mining remains their main source of employment.

Age structure: *0-14 years:* 45.57% (male 6,950,800/female 6,766,373)
15-24 years: 19.91% (male 2,997,529/female 2,994,927)
25-54 years: 28.28% (male 3,949,085/female 4,564,031)
55-64 years: 3.31% (male 485,454/female 509,430)
65 years and over: 2.93% (male 430,797/female 449,771) (2020 est.)

Dependency ratios: *total dependency ratio:* 88.4
youth dependency ratio: 83
elderly dependency ratio: 5.4
potential support ratio: 18.5 (2020 est.)

Median age: *total:* 17 years
male: 16.3 years
female: 17.6 years (2020 est.)

Population growth rate: 2.56% (2022 est.)

Birth rate: 37.47 births/1,000 population (2022 est.)

Death rate: 10.25 deaths/1,000 population (2022 est.)

Net migration rate: -1.58 migrant(s)/1,000 population (2022 est.)

Population distribution: three large populations clusters are found along the southern coast between Maputo and Inhambane, in the central area between Beira and Chimoio along the Zambezi River, and in and around the northern cities of Nampula, Cidade de Nacala, and Pemba; the northwest and southwest are the least populated areas as shown in this population distribution map

Urbanization: *urban population:* 38.2% of total population (2022)
rate of urbanization: 4.24% annual rate of change (2020-25 est.)

Major urban areas - population: 1.797 million Matola, 1.139 million MAPUTO (capital), 927,000 Nampula (2022)

Sex ratio: *at birth:* 1.03 male(s)/female
0-14 years: 1.03 male(s)/female
15-24 years: 1 male(s)/female
25-54 years: 0.86 male(s)/female
55-64 years: 0.94 male(s)/female
65 years and over: 0.88 male(s)/female
total population: 0.97 male(s)/female (2022 est.)

Mother's mean age at first birth: 19.2 years (2011 est.)
note: data represents median age at first birth among women 20-49

Maternal mortality ratio: 289 deaths/100,000 live births (2017 est.)

Infant mortality rate: *total:* 61.38 deaths/1,000 live births
male: 63.37 deaths/1,000 live births
female: 59.33 deaths/1,000 live births (2022 est.)

Life expectancy at birth: *total population:* 57.1 years
male: 55.76 years
female: 58.49 years (2022 est.)

Total fertility rate: 4.81 children born/woman (2022 est.)

Contraceptive prevalence rate: 27.1% (2015)

Drinking water source: *improved: urban:* 93.4% of population
rural: 61.5% of population
total: 73.3% of population
unimproved: urban: 6.6% of population
rural: 38.5% of population
total: 26.7% of population (2020 est.)

Current health expenditure: 7.8% of GDP (2019)

Physicians density: 0.09 physicians/1,000 population (2020)

Hospital bed density: 0.7 beds/1,000 population (2011)

Sanitation facility access: *improved: urban:* 71.9% of population (2015 est.)
rural: 24.7% of population
total: 42.2% of population
unimproved: urban: 28.1% of population
rural: 75.3% of population
total: 57.8% of population (2020 est.)

HIV/AIDS - adult prevalence rate: 11.5% (2020 est.)

Major infectious diseases: *degree of risk:* very high (2020)
food or waterborne diseases: bacterial and protozoal diarrhea, hepatitis A, and typhoid fever
vectorborne diseases: malaria and dengue fever
water contact diseases: schistosomiasis
animal contact diseases: rabies
note: on 21 March 2022, the US Centers for Disease Control and Prevention (CDC) issued a Travel Alert for polio in Africa; Mozambique is currently considered a high risk to travelers for circulating vaccine-derived polioviruses (cVDPV); vaccine-derived poliovirus (VDPV) is a strain of the weakened poliovirus that was initially included in oral polio vaccine (OPV) and *that has changed over time and behaves more like the wild or naturally occurring virus;* this means it can be spread more easily to people who are unvaccinated against polio and who come in contact with the stool or respiratory secretions, such as from a sneeze, of an "infected" person who received oral polio vaccine; the CDC recommends that before any international travel, anyone unvaccinated, incompletely vaccinated, or with an unknown polio vaccination status should complete the routine polio vaccine series; before travel to any high-risk destination, the CDC recommends that adults who previously completed the full, routine polio vaccine series receive a single, lifetime booster dose of polio vaccine

Obesity - adult prevalence rate: 7.2% (2016)

Alcohol consumption per capita: *total:* 1.46 liters of pure alcohol (2019 est.)
beer: 1.03 liters of pure alcohol (2019 est.)
wine: 0.22 liters of pure alcohol (2019 est.)
spirits: 0.21 liters of pure alcohol (2019 est.)
other alcohols: 0 liters of pure alcohol (2019 est.)

Tobacco use: *total:* 14.3% (2020 est.)
male: 23% (2020 est.)
female: 5.6% (2020 est.)

Children under the age of 5 years underweight: 15.6% (2014/15)

Education expenditures: 6.2% of GDP (2019 est.)

Literacy: *definition:* age 15 and over can read and write
total population: 60.7%
male: 72.6%
female: 50.3% (2017)

School life expectancy (primary to tertiary education): *total:* 10 years
male: 10 years
female: 9 years (2017)

Unemployment, youth ages 15-24: *total:* 7.4%
male: 7.7%
female: 7.1% (2015 est.)

ENVIRONMENT

Environment - current issues: increased migration of the population to urban and coastal areas with adverse environmental consequences; desertification; soil erosion; deforestation; water pollution caused by artisanal mining; pollution of surface and coastal waters; wildlife preservation (elephant poaching for ivory)

Environment - international agreements: *party to:* Biodiversity, Climate Change, Climate Change-Kyoto Protocol, Climate Change-Paris Agreement, Comprehensive Nuclear Test Ban, Desertification,

Endangered Species, Hazardous Wastes, Law of the Sea, Ozone Layer Protection, Ship Pollution, Tropical Timber 2006, Wetlands
signed, but not ratified: none of the selected agreements

Air pollutants: *particulate matter emissions:* 19.44 micrograms per cubic meter (2016 est.)
carbon dioxide emissions: 7.94 megatons (2016 est.)
methane emissions: 16.26 megatons (2020 est.)

Climate: tropical to subtropical

Land use: *agricultural land:* 56.3% (2018 est.)
arable land: 6.4% (2018 est.)
permanent crops: 0.3% (2018 est.)
permanent pasture: 49.6% (2018 est.)
forest: 43.7% (2018 est.)
other: 0% (2018 est.)

Urbanization: *urban population:* 38.2% of total population (2022)
rate of urbanization: 4.24% annual rate of change (2020-25 est.)

Revenue from forest resources: *forest revenues:* 6.46% of GDP (2018 est.)

Revenue from coal: *coal revenues:* 4.17% of GDP (2018 est.)

Food insecurity: *severe localized food insecurity: due to shortfall in agricultural production and economic downturn* - the number of people in need of food assistance is expected to rise above the 1.86 million estimated in 2021-2022 because of three key factors; firstly, higher year-on-year prices of food and fuel are reducing households' purchasing power, worsening their economic access to food, particularly for low-income households; secondly, the impact of extreme weather events on agricultural production in central and southern provinces in 2022 is likely to mean that farming households in the affected areas have both low food supplies from their own production and curtailed income-earning opportunities from crop sales, impinging on their food availability and economic access to food; thirdly, there has been an increase in attacks by non-state armed groups in the northern province of Cabo Delgado in 2022
(2022)

Waste and recycling: *municipal solid waste generated annually:* 2.5 million tons (2014 est.)
municipal solid waste recycled annually: 25,000 tons (2014 est.)
percent of municipal solid waste recycled: 1% (2014 est.)

Major lakes (area sq km): *fresh water lake(s):* Lake Malawi (shared with Malawi and Tanzania) - 22,490

Major rivers (by length in km): Zambezi river mouth (shared with Zambia [s]), Angola, Namibia, Botswana, and Zimbabwe) - 2,740 km; Limpopo river mouth (shared with South Africa [s], Botswana, and Zimbabwe) - 1,800 km
note – [s] after country name indicates river source; [m] after country name indicates river mouth

Major watersheds (area sq km): Indian Ocean drainage: Zambezi (1,332,412 sq km)

Total water withdrawal: *municipal:* 372 million cubic meters (2017 est.)
industrial: 25 million cubic meters (2017 est.)
agricultural: 1.076 billion cubic meters (2017 est.)

Total renewable water resources: 217.1 billion cubic meters (2017 est.)

GOVERNMENT

Country name: *conventional long form:* Republic of Mozambique
conventional short form: Mozambique
local long form: Republica de Mocambique
local short form: Mocambique
former: Portuguese East Africa, People's Republic of Mozambique
etymology: named for the offshore island of Mozambique; the island was apparently named after Mussa al-BIK, an influential Arab slave trader who set himself up as sultan on the island in the 15th century

Government type: presidential republic

Capital: *name:* Maputo
geographic coordinates: 25 57 S, 32 35 E
time difference: UTC+2 (7 hours ahead of Washington, DC, during Standard Time)
etymology: reputedly named after the Maputo River, which drains into Maputo Bay south of the city

Administrative divisions: 10 provinces (provincias, singular - provincia), 1 city (cidade)*; Cabo Delgado, Gaza, Inhambane, Manica, Maputo, Cidade de Maputo*, Nampula, Niassa, Sofala, Tete, Zambezia

Independence: 25 June 1975 (from Portugal)

National holiday: Independence Day, 25 June (1975)

Constitution: *history:* previous 1975, 1990; latest adopted 16 November 2004, effective 21 December 2004
amendments: proposed by the president of the republic or supported by at least one third of the Assembly of the Republic membership; passage of amendments affecting constitutional provisions, including the independence and sovereignty of the state, the republican form of government, basic rights and freedoms, and universal suffrage, requires at least a two-thirds majority vote by the Assembly and approval in a referendum; referenda not required for passage of other amendments; amended 2007, 2018

Legal system: mixed legal system of Portuguese civil law and customary law; note - in rural, apply where applicable predominantly Muslim villages with no formal legal system, Islamic law may be applied

International law organization participation: has not submitted an ICJ jurisdiction declaration; non-party state to the ICCt

Citizenship: *citizenship by birth:* no
citizenship by descent only: at least one parent must be a citizen of Mozambique
dual citizenship recognized: no
residency requirement for naturalization: 5 years

Suffrage: 18 years of age; universal

Executive branch: *chief of state:* President Filipe Jacinto NYUSI (since 15 January 2015); note - the president is both chief of state and head of government
head of government: President Filipe Jacinto NYUSI (since 15 January 2015); Prime Minister Adriano Afonso MALEIANE (since 3 March 2022); note - President NYUSI removed former Prime Minister Carlos Agostinho DO ROSARIO from office on 3 March 2022 as part of a cabinet reshuffle
cabinet: Cabinet appointed by the president
elections/appointments: president elected directly by absolute majority popular vote in 2 rounds if needed for a 5-year term (eligible for 2 consecutive terms); election last held on 15 October 2019 (next to be held on 15 October 2024); prime minister appointed by the president
election results:
2019: Filipe NYUSI elected president in first round; percent of vote - Filipe NYUSI (FRELIMO) 73.0%, Ossufo MOMADE (RENAMO) 21.9%, Daviz SIMANGO (MDM) 5.1%
2014: Filipe NYUSI elected president in first round; percent of vote - Filipe NYUSI (FRELIMO) 57.0%, Afonso DHLAKAMA (RENAMO) 36.6%, Daviz SIMANGO (MDM) 6.4%

Legislative branch: *description:* unicameral Assembly of the Republic or Assembleia da Republica (250 seats; 248 members elected in multi-seat constituencies by party-list proportional representation vote and 2 members representing Mozambicans abroad directly elected by simple majority vote; members serve 5-year terms) (2019)
elections:
last held on 15 October 2019 (next to be held on 15 October 2024) (2019)
election results:
percent of vote by party - FRELIMO 71%, RENAMO 23%, MDM 4%; seats by party - FRELIMO 184, RENAMO 60, MDM 6; composition as of July 2022 - men 144, women 106, percent of women 42.4% (2019)

Judicial branch: *highest court(s):* Supreme Court (consists of the court president, vice president, and 5 judges); Constitutional Council (consists of 7 judges); note - the Higher Council of the Judiciary Magistracy is responsible for judiciary management and discipline
judge selection and term of office: Supreme Court president appointed by the president of the republic; vice president appointed by the president in consultation with the Higher Council of the Judiciary (CSMJ) and ratified by the Assembly of the Republic; other judges elected by the Assembly; judges serve 5-year renewable terms; Constitutional Council judges appointed - 1 by the president, 5 by the Assembly, and 1 by the CSMJ; judges serve 5-year nonrenewable terms
subordinate courts: Administrative Court (capital city only); provincial courts or Tribunais Judicias de Provincia; District Courts or Tribunais Judicias de Districto; customs courts; maritime courts; courts marshal; labor courts; community courts

Political parties and leaders: Democratic Movement of Mozambique (Movimento Democratico de Mocambique) or MDM [Lutero SIMANGO]
Liberation Front of Mozambique (Frente de Liberatacao de Mocambique) or FRELIMO [Filipe NYUSI]
Mozambican National Resistance (Resistencia Nacional Mocambicana) or RENAMO [Ossufo MOMADE]
note: only parties with seats in the legislature listed

International organization participation: ACP, AfDB, AU, C, CD, CPLP, EITI (compliant country), FAO, G-77, IAEA, IBRD, ICAO, ICC (NGOs), ICRM, IDA, IDB, IFAD, IFC, IFRCS, IHO, ILO, IMF, IMO, IMSO, Interpol, IOC, IOM, IPU, ISO (correspondent), ITSO, ITU, ITUC (NGOs), MIGA, NAM, OIC, OIF (observer), OPCW, SADC, UN, UNCTAD, UNESCO, UNHCR, UNIDO, Union Latina, UNISFA, UNWTO, UPU, WCO, WFTU (NGOs), WHO, WIPO, WMO, WTO

Diplomatic representation in the US: *chief of mission:* Ambassador Carlos DOS SANTOS (since 28 January 2016)
chancery: 1525 New Hampshire Avenue NW, Washington, DC 20036
telephone: [1] (202) 293-7147
FAX: [1] (202) 835-0245
email address and website:
washington.dc@embamoc.gov.mz
https://usa.embamoc.gov.mz/

Diplomatic representation from the US: *chief of mission:* Ambassador Peter Hendrick VROOMAN (since 3 March 2022)
embassy: Avenida Kenneth Kaunda, 193, Caixa Postal, 783, Maputo
mailing address: 2330 Maputo Place, Washington DC 20521-2330
telephone: [258] (21) 49-27-97
FAX: [258] (21) 49-01-14
email address and website:
consularmaputos@state.gov
https://mz.usembassy.gov/

Flag description: three equal horizontal bands of green (top), black, and yellow with a red isosceles triangle based on the hoist side; the black band is edged in white; centered in the triangle is a yellow five-pointed star bearing a crossed rifle and hoe in black superimposed on an open white book; green represents the riches of the land, white peace, black the African continent, yellow the country's minerals, and red the struggle for independence; the rifle symbolizes defense and vigilance, the hoe refers to the country's agriculture, the open book stresses the importance of education, and the star represents Marxism and internationalism
note: one of only two national flags featuring a firearm, the other is Guatemala

National symbol(s): *national colors:* green, black, yellow, white, red

National anthem: *name:* "Patria Amada" (Lovely Fatherland)
lyrics/music: Salomao J. MANHICA/unknown
note: adopted 2002

National heritage: *total World Heritage Sites:* 1 (cultural)
selected World Heritage Site locales: Island of Mozambique

ECONOMY

Economic overview: At independence in 1975, Mozambique was one of the world's poorest countries. Socialist policies, economic mismanagement, and a brutal civil war from 1977 to 1992 further impoverished the country. In 1987, the government embarked on a series of macroeconomic reforms designed to stabilize the economy. These steps, combined with donor assistance and with political stability since the multiparty elections in 1994, propelled the country's GDP, in purchasing power parity terms, from $4 billion in 1993 to about $37 billion in 2017. Fiscal reforms, including the introduction of a value-added tax and reform of the customs service, have improved the government's revenue collection abilities. In spite of these gains, about half the population remains below the poverty line and subsistence agriculture continues to employ the vast majority of the country's work force.

Mozambique's once substantial foreign debt was reduced through forgiveness and rescheduling under the IMF's Heavily Indebted Poor Countries (HIPC) and Enhanced HIPC initiatives. However, in 2016, information surfaced revealing that the Mozambican Government was responsible for over $2 billion in government-backed loans secured between 2012-14 by state-owned defense and security companies without parliamentary approval or national budget inclusion; this prompted the IMF and international donors to halt direct budget support to the Government of Mozambique. An international audit was performed on Mozambique's debt in 2016-17, but debt restructuring and resumption of donor support have yet to occur.

Mozambique grew at an average annual rate of 6%-8% in the decade leading up to 2015, one of Africa's strongest performances, but the sizable external debt burden, donor withdrawal, elevated inflation, and currency depreciation contributed to slower growth in 2016-17.

Two major International consortiums, led by American companies ExxonMobil and Anadarko, are seeking approval to develop massive natural gas deposits off the coast of Cabo Delgado province, in what has the potential to become the largest infrastructure project in Africa. . The government predicts sales of liquefied natural gas from these projects could generate several billion dollars in revenues annually sometime after 2022.

Real GDP (purchasing power parity): $38.42 billion (2020 est.)
$38.91 billion (2019 est.)
$38.04 billion (2018 est.)
note: data are in 2017 dollars

Real GDP growth rate: 3.11% (2018 est.)
3.7% (2017 est.)
4.07% (2017 est.)

Real GDP per capita: $1,200 (2020 est.)
$1,300 (2019 est.)
$1,300 (2018 est.)
note: data are in 2017 dollars

GDP (official exchange rate): $14.964 billion (2019 est.)

Inflation rate (consumer prices): 2.7% (2019 est.)
3.9% (2018 est.)
15.4% (2017 est.)

Credit ratings:

Fitch rating: CCC (2019)

Moody's rating: Caa2 (2019)

Standard & Poors rating: CCC+ (2019)
note: The year refers to the year in which the current credit rating was first obtained.

GDP - composition, by sector of origin: *agriculture:* 23.9% (2017 est.)
industry: 19.3% (2017 est.)
services: 56.8% (2017 est.)

GDP - composition, by end use: *household consumption:* 69.7% (2017 est.)
government consumption: 27.2% (2017 est.)
investment in fixed capital: 21.7% (2017 est.)
investment in inventories: 13.9% (2017 est.)
exports of goods and services: 38.3% (2017 est.)
imports of goods and services: -70.6% (2017 est.)

Agricultural products: sugar cane, cassava, maize, milk, bananas, tomatoes, sweet potatoes, rice, sorghum, potatoes

Industries: aluminum, petroleum products, chemicals (fertilizer, soap, paints), textiles, cement, glass, asbestos, tobacco, food, beverages

Industrial production growth rate: 4.9% (2017 est.)

Labor force: 12.9 million (2017 est.)

Labor force - by occupation: *agriculture:* 74.4%
industry: 3.9%
services: 21.7% (2015 est.)

Unemployment rate: 24.5% (2017 est.)
25% (2016 est.)

Unemployment, youth ages 15-24: *total:* 7.4%
male: 7.7%
female: 7.1% (2015 est.)

Population below poverty line: 46.1% (2014 est.)

Gini Index coefficient - distribution of family income: 54 (2014 est.)
47.3 (2002)

Household income or consumption by percentage share: *lowest 10%:* 1.9%
highest 10%: 36.7% (2008)

Budget: *revenues:* 3.356 billion (2017 est.)
expenditures: 4.054 billion (2017 est.)

Budget surplus (+) or deficit (-): -5.6% (of GDP) (2017 est.)

Public debt: 102.1% of GDP (2017 est.)
121.6% of GDP (2016 est.)

Taxes and other revenues: 26.7% (of GDP) (2017 est.)

Fiscal year: calendar year

Current account balance: -$3.025 billion (2019 est.)
-$4.499 billion (2018 est.)

Exports: $4.35 billion (2020 est.) note: data are in current year dollars
$5.6 billion (2019 est.) note: data are in current year dollars
$5.97 billion (2018 est.) note: data are in current year dollars

Exports - partners: South Africa 16%, India 13%, China 12%, Italy 7%, United Arab Emirates 5%, Germany 5% (2019)

Exports - commodities: coal, aluminum, natural gas, tobacco, electricity, gold, lumber (2019)

Imports: $8.38 billion (2020 est.) note: data are in current year dollars
$9.57 billion (2019 est.) note: data are in current year dollars
$10.52 billion (2018 est.) note: data are in current year dollars

Imports - partners: South Africa 31%, India 18%, China 17% (2019)

Imports - commodities: refined petroleum, chromium, iron, bauxite, electricity (2019)

Reserves of foreign exchange and gold: $3.361 billion (31 December 2017 est.)
$2.081 billion (31 December 2016 est.)

Debt - external: $10.91 billion (31 December 2017 est.)
$10.48 billion (31 December 2016 est.)

Exchange rates: meticais (MZM) per US dollar -
74.12 (2020 est.)
63.885 (2019 est.)
61.625 (2018 est.)
39.983 (2014 est.)
31.367 (2013 est.)

ENERGY

Electricity access: *electrification - total population:* 35% (2019)

electrification - urban areas: 57% (2019)
electrification - rural areas: 22% (2019)

Electricity: *installed generating capacity:* 2.765 million kW (2020 est.)
consumption: 12,724,100,000 kWh (2019 est.)
exports: 10.771 billion kWh (2019 est.)
imports: 8.276 billion kWh (2019 est.)
transmission/distribution losses: 2.768 billion kWh (2019 est.)

Electricity generation sources: *fossil fuels:* 19.6% of total installed capacity (2020 est.)
solar: 0.2% of total installed capacity (2020 est.)
hydroelectricity: 79.6% of total installed capacity (2020 est.)
biomass and waste: 0.6% of total installed capacity (2020 est.)

Coal: *production:* 7.25 million metric tons (2020 est.)
consumption: 46,000 metric tons (2020 est.)
exports: 8.355 million metric tons (2020 est.)
imports: 48,000 metric tons (2020 est.)
proven reserves: 1.792 billion metric tons (2019 est.)

Petroleum: *total petroleum production:* 0 bbl/day (2021 est.)
refined petroleum consumption: 35,400 bbl/day (2019 est.)

Refined petroleum products - imports: 25,130 bbl/day (2015 est.)

Natural gas: *production:* 5,423,828,000 cubic meters (2019 est.)
consumption: 1,397,604,000 cubic meters (2019 est.)
exports: 4,067,255,000 cubic meters (2019 est.)
imports: 0 cubic meters (2021 est.)
proven reserves: 2,831,680,000,000 cubic meters (2021 est.)

Carbon dioxide emissions: 7.753 million metric tonnes of CO_2 (2019 est.)
from coal and metallurgical coke: 109,000 metric tonnes of CO_2 (2019 est.)
from petroleum and other liquids: 4.743 million metric tonnes of CO_2 (2019 est.)
from consumed natural gas: 2.901 million metric tonnes of CO_2 (2019 est.)

Energy consumption per capita: 8.107 million Btu/person (2019 est.)

COMMUNICATIONS

Telephones - fixed lines: *total subscriptions:* 89,016 (2020 est.)

Telephones - mobile cellular: *total subscriptions:* 15,463,226 (2020 est.)
subscriptions per 100 inhabitants: 49 (2020 est.)

Telecommunication systems: *general assessment:* one of the first countries in the region to embark upon telecom reform and to open the sector to competition; the mobile segment in particular has shown strong growth; additional competition followed in late 2020; in the process, the structure of the market changed from having four operators to three; at the same time, a new licensing regime ensured that by mid-2019 all three operators had been provided with universal licenses, enabling them to offer all types of telephony and data services; mobile, fixed-line and broadband penetration rates remain far below the average for the region; in recent years the government has enforced the registration of SIM cards, but with varying success; at the end of 2016 almost five million unregistered SIM cards were deactivated but poor monitoring meant that the process was revisited in mid-2019 and again in late 2020; the high cost of international bandwidth had long hampered internet use, though the landing of two international submarine cables (SEACOM and EASSy) has reduced the cost of bandwidth and so led to drastic reductions in broadband retail prices as well as a significant jump in available bandwidth; there is some cross-platform competition, with DSL, cable, fibre, WiMAX, and mobile broadband options available, though fixed broadband options can be limited to urban areas; improvements can be expected from the ongoing rollout of a national fiber backbone networks and of upgrades to mobile infrastructure (2022)
domestic: extremely low fixed-line teledensity contrasts with rapid growth in the mobile-cellular network; operators provide coverage that includes all the main cities and key roads; fixed-line less than 1 per 100 and nearly 49 per 100 mobile-cellular teledensity (2020)
international: country code - 258; landing points for the EASSy and SEACOM/ Tata TGN-Eurasia fiber-optic submarine cable systems linking numerous east African countries, the Middle East and Asia ; satellite earth stations - 5 Intelsat (2 Atlantic Ocean and 3 Indian Ocean); TdM contracts for Itelsat for satellite broadband and bulk haul services (2020)

Broadcast media: 1 state-run TV station supplemented by private TV station; Portuguese state TV's African service, RTP Africa, and Brazilian-owned TV Miramar are available; state-run radio provides nearly 100% territorial coverage and broadcasts in multiple languages; a number of privately owned and community-operated stations; transmissions of multiple international broadcasters are available (2019):

Internet country code: .mz

Internet users: *total:* 5,313,424 (2020 est.)
percent of population: 17% (2020 est.)

Broadband - fixed subscriptions: *total:* 70,000 (2020 est.)
subscriptions per 100 inhabitants: 0.2 (2020 est.)

TRANSPORTATION

National air transport system: *number of registered air carriers:* 2 (2020)
inventory of registered aircraft operated by air carriers: 11
annual passenger traffic on registered air carriers: 540,124 (2018)
annual freight traffic on registered air carriers: 4.78 million (2018) mt-km

Civil aircraft registration country code prefix: C9

Airports: *total:* 98 (2021)

Airports - with paved runways: *total:* 21
over 3,047 m: 1
2,438 to 3,047 m: 2
1,524 to 2,437 m: 9
914 to 1,523 m: 5
under 914 m: 4 (2021)

Airports - with unpaved runways: *total:* 77
2,438 to 3,047 m: 1
1,524 to 2,437 m: 9
914 to 1,523 m: 29
under 914 m: 38 (2021)

Pipelines: 972 km gas, 278 km refined products (2013)

Railways: *total:* 4,787 km (2014)
narrow gauge: 4,787 km (2014) 1.067-m gauge

Roadways: *total:* 31,083 km (2015)
paved: 7,365 km (2015)
unpaved: 23,718 km (2015)

Waterways: 460 km (2010) (Zambezi River navigable to Tete and along Cahora Bassa Lake)

Merchant marine: *total:* 30
by type: general cargo 9, other 21 (2021)

Ports and terminals: *major seaport(s):* Beira, Maputo, Nacala

LNG terminal(s) (export): Coral Sul (FLNG)

MILITARY AND SECURITY

Military and security forces: Armed Defense Forces of Mozambique (Forcas Armadas de Defesa de Mocambique, FADM): Mozambique Army, Mozambique Navy (Marinha de Guerra de Mocambique, MGM), Mozambique Air Force (Forca Aerea de Mocambique, FAM); Ministry of Interior: Mozambique National Police (PRM), the National Criminal Investigation Service (SERNIC), Rapid Intervention Unit (UIR; police special forces), Border Security Force; other security forces include the Presidential Guard and the Force for the Protection of High-Level Individuals (2022)
note: the FADM and other security forces are referred to collectively as the Defense and Security Forces (DFS)

Military expenditures: 1.2% of GDP (2021 est.)
1.1% of GDP (2020 est.)
1.2% of GDP (2019 est.) (approximately $220 million)
1.1% of GDP (2018 est.) (approximately $210 million)
0.9% of GDP (2017 est.) (approximately $170 million)

Military and security service personnel strengths: information limited and varied; approximately 12,000 personnel (11,000 Army and about 1,000 Air Force and Navy) (2022)

Military equipment inventories and acquisitions: the FADM's inventory consists primarily of Soviet-era equipment, although since 2010 it has received limited quantities of more modern equipment from a variety of countries, mostly as aid/donations (2021)

Military service age and obligation: registration for military service is mandatory for all men and women at 18 years of age; 18-35 years of age for selective compulsory military service; 18 years of age for voluntary service for men and women; 2-year service obligation (2021)

Military - note: the Government of Mozambique is facing an insurgency driven by militants with ties to the Islamic State of Iraq and ash-Sham (ISIS) terrorist group in the northern province of Cabo Delgado, an area known for rich liquid natural gas deposits; insurgent attacks in the province began in 2017 and as of 2022, the fighting had left an estimated 4,000 dead and as many as 900,000 displaced; the FADM is widely assessed as lacking the training, equipment, and overall capabilities to address the insurgency; as of 2022, several countries from the Southern Africa Development

Community (SADC) and the European Union, as well as Rwanda and the US were providing various forms of military assistance; the SADC countries and Zambia have sent more than 3,000 military and security personnel, while the EU and the US have provided training assistance; the counterterrorism efforts of the Mozambique and allied African military and security forces have seen some success against the militants, but as of 2022 terrorist attacks had expanded into the neighboring provinces of Niassa and Nampula (2022)

TERRORISM

Terrorist group(s): Islamic State of Iraq and ash-Sham - Mozambique (ISIS-M)

TRANSNATIONAL ISSUES

Disputes - international: *Mozambique-Eswatini*: none identified
Mozambique-Malawi: the two countries have held exercises to reaffirm boundaries a number of times
Mozambique-South Africa: South Africa has placed military units to assist police operations along the border of Lesotho, Zimbabwe, and Mozambique to control smuggling, poaching, and illegal migration
Mozambique-Tanzania: none identified
Mozambique-Zambia: none identified
Mozambique-Zimbabwe: none identified

Refugees and internally displaced persons: *refugees (country of origin)*: 10,968 (Democratic Republic of Congo) (refugees and asylum seekers), 8,589 (Burundi) (refugees and asylum seekers) (2022)
IDPs: 946,508 (violence between the government and an opposition group, violence associated with extremists groups in 2018, political violence 2019) (2022)

Illicit drugs: used by transnational organized crime networks from West and East Africa and South Asia as a transit point for drug trafficking and international money laundering; heroin from Southwest Asia, cocaine from South America, precursor chemicals and controlled pharmaceuticals from India, and methamphetamine from Nigeria transit destined for Southern Africa, Northern Africa, Europe, Canada, and the United States; cannabis is cultivated in Mozambique

NAMIBIA

INTRODUCTION

Background: Various ethnic groups occupied south-western Africa prior to Germany establishing a colony over most of the territory in 1884. South Africa occupied the colony, then known as German South West Africa, in 1915 during World War I and administered it as a mandate until after World War II, when it annexed the territory. In 1966, the Marxist South-West Africa People's Organization (SWAPO) guerrilla group launched a war of independence for the area that became Namibia, but it was not until 1988 that South Africa agreed to end its administration in accordance with a UN peace plan for the entire region. Namibia gained independence in 1990 and has been governed by SWAPO since, though the party has dropped much of its Marxist ideology. President Hage GEINGOB was elected in 2014 in a landslide victory, replacing Hifikepunye POHAMBA who stepped down after serving two terms. SWAPO retained its parliamentary super majority in the 2014 elections. In 2019 elections, GEINGOB was reelected but by a substantially reduced majority and SWAPO narrowly lost its super majority in parliament.

GEOGRAPHY

Location: Southern Africa, bordering the South Atlantic Ocean, between Angola and South Africa

Geographic coordinates: 22 00 S, 17 00 E

Map references: Africa

Area: *total:* 824,292 sq km
land: 823,290 sq km
water: 1,002 sq km

Area - comparative: almost seven times the size of Pennsylvania; slightly more than half the size of Alaska

Land boundaries: *total:* 4,220 km
border countries (4): Angola 1,427 km; Botswana 1,544 km; South Africa 1,005 km; Zambia 244 km

Coastline: 1,572 km

Maritime claims: *territorial sea:* 12 nm
contiguous zone: 24 nm
exclusive economic zone: 200 nm

Climate: desert; hot, dry; rainfall sparse and erratic

Terrain: mostly high plateau; Namib Desert along coast; Kalahari Desert in east

Elevation: *highest point:* Konigstein on Brandberg 2,573 m
lowest point: Atlantic Ocean 0 m
mean elevation: 1,141 m

Natural resources: diamonds, copper, uranium, gold, silver, lead, tin, lithium, cadmium, tungsten, zinc, salt, hydropower, fish, note, suspected deposits of oil, coal, and iron ore

Land use: *agricultural land:* 47.2% (2018 est.)
arable land: 1% (2018 est.)
permanent crops: 0% (2018 est.)
permanent pasture: 46.2% (2018 est.)
forest: 8.8% (2018 est.)
other: 44% (2018 est.)

Irrigated land: 80 sq km (2012)

Major rivers (by length in km): Zambezi (shared with Zambia [s]), Angola, Botswana, Zimbabwe, and Mozambique [m]) - 2,740 km; Orange river mouth (shared with Lesotho [s], and South Africa) - 2,092 km; Okavango (shared with Angola [s], and Botswana [m]) - 1,600 km
note – [s] after country name indicates river source; [m] after country name indicates river mouth

Major watersheds (area sq km): Atlantic Ocean drainage: Orange (941,351 sq km)

Indian Ocean drainage: Zambezi (1,332,412 sq km)

Internal *(endorheic basin)* drainage: Okavango Basin (863,866 sq km)

Major aquifers: Lower Kalahari-Stampriet Basin, Upper Kalahari-Cuvelai-Upper Zambezi Basin

Population distribution: population density is very low, with the largest clustering found in the extreme north-central area along the border with Angola as shown in this population distribution map

Natural hazards: prolonged periods of drought

Geography - note: the Namib Desert, after which the country is named, is considered to be the oldest desert in the world; Namibia is the first country in the world to incorporate the protection of the environment into its constitution; some 14% of the land is protected, including virtually the entire Namib Desert coastal strip; Namib-Naukluft National Park (49,768 sq km), is the largest game park in Africa and one of the largest in the world

PEOPLE AND SOCIETY

Population: 2,727,409 (2022 est.)

Nationality: *noun:* Namibian(s)
adjective: Namibian

Ethnic groups: Ovambo 50%, Kavangos 9%, Herero 7%, Damara 7%, mixed European and African ancestry 6.5%, European 6%, Nama 5%, Caprivian 4%, San 3%, Baster 2%, Tswana .5%

Languages: Oshiwambo languages 49.7%, Nama/Damara 11%, Kavango languages 10.4%, Afrikaans 9.4% (also a common language), Herero languages 9.2%, Zambezi languages 4.9%, English (official) 2.3%, other African languages 1.5%, other European languages 0.7%, other 1% (2016 est.)
note: Namibia has 13 recognized national languages, including 10 indigenous African languages and 3 European languages

Religions: Christian 97.5%, other 0.6% (includes Muslim, Baha'i, Jewish, Buddhist), unaffiliated 1.9% (2020 est.)

Demographic profile: Planning officials view Namibia's reduced population growth rate as sustainable based on the country's economic growth over the past decade. Prior to independence in 1990, Namibia's relatively small population grew at about 3% annually, but declining fertility and the impact of HIV/AIDS slowed this growth to 1.4% by 2011, rebounding to close to 2% by 2016. Namibia's fertility rate has fallen over the last two decades – from about 4.5 children per woman in 1996 to 3.4 in 2016 – due to increased contraceptive use, higher educational attainment among women, and greater female participation in the labor force. The average age at first birth has stayed fairly constant, but the age at first marriage continues to increase, indicating a rising incidence of premarital childbearing.

The majority of Namibians are rural dwellers (about 55%) and live in the better-watered north and northeast parts of the country. Migration, historically male-dominated, generally flows from northern communal areas – non-agricultural lands where blacks were sequestered under the apartheid system – to agricultural, mining, and manufacturing centers in the center and south. After independence from South Africa, restrictions on internal movement eased, and rural-urban migration increased, bolstering urban growth.

Some Namibians – usually persons who are better-educated, more affluent, and from urban areas – continue to legally migrate to South Africa temporarily to visit family and friends and, much less frequently, to pursue tertiary education or better economic opportunities. Namibians concentrated along the country's other borders make unauthorized visits to Angola, Zambia, Zimbabwe, or Botswana, to visit family and to trade agricultural goods. Few Namibians express interest in permanently settling in other countries; they prefer the safety of their homeland, have a strong national identity, and enjoy a well-supplied retail sector. Although Namibia is receptive to foreign investment and cross-border trade, intolerance toward non-citizens is widespread.

Age structure: *0-14 years:* 35.68% (male 473,937/female 464,453)
15-24 years: 20.27% (male 267,106/female 265,882)
25-54 years: 35.47% (male 449,132/female 483,811)
55-64 years: 4.68% (male 54,589/female 68,619)
65 years and over: 3.9% (male 43,596/female 58,948) (2020 est.)

Dependency ratios: *total dependency ratio:* 67.9
youth dependency ratio: 61.8
elderly dependency ratio: 6
potential support ratio: 16.6 (2020 est.)

Median age: *total:* 21.8 years
male: 21.1 years
female: 22.6 years (2020 est.)

Population growth rate: 1.82% (2022 est.)

Birth rate: 25.01 births/1,000 population (2022 est.)

Death rate: 6.85 deaths/1,000 population (2022 est.)

Net migration rate: 0 migrant(s)/1,000 population (2022 est.)

Population distribution: population density is very low, with the largest clustering found in the extreme north-central area along the border with Angola as shown in this population distribution map

Urbanization: *urban population:* 54% of total population (2022)
rate of urbanization: 3.64% annual rate of change (2020-25 est.)

Major urban areas - population: 461,000 WINDHOEK (capital) (2022)

Sex ratio: *at birth:* 1.03 male(s)/female
0-14 years: 1.02 male(s)/female
15-24 years: 1.01 male(s)/female
25-54 years: 0.93 male(s)/female
55-64 years: 0.79 male(s)/female
65 years and over: 0.61 male(s)/female
total population: 0.96 male(s)/female (2022 est.)

Mother's mean age at first birth: 21.6 years (2013 est.)
note: data represents median age at first birth among women 25-49

Maternal mortality ratio: 195 deaths/100,000 live births (2017 est.)

Infant mortality rate: *total:* 29.42 deaths/1,000 live births
male: 31.48 deaths/1,000 live births
female: 27.3 deaths/1,000 live births (2022 est.)

Life expectancy at birth: *total population:* 66.47 years
male: 64.46 years
female: 68.53 years (2022 est.)

Total fertility rate: 2.98 children born/woman (2022 est.)

Contraceptive prevalence rate: 56.1% (2013)

Drinking water source: *improved: urban:* 98.9% of population
rural: 83.2% of population
total: 91.4% of population
unimproved: urban: 1.1% of population
rural: 16.8% of population
total: 8.6% of population (2020 est.)

Current health expenditure: 8.5% of GDP (2019)

Physicians density: 0.59 physicians/1,000 population (2018)

Hospital bed density: 2.7 beds/1,000 population

Sanitation facility access: *improved: urban:* 70.6% of population
rural: 23.6% of population
total: 48.1% of population
unimproved: urban: 29.4% of population
rural: 76.4% of population
total: 51.9% of population (2020 est.)

HIV/AIDS - adult prevalence rate: 11.6% (2020 est.)

Major infectious diseases: *degree of risk:* high (2020)
food or waterborne diseases: bacterial diarrhea, hepatitis A, and typhoid fever
vectorborne diseases: malaria
water contact diseases: schistosomiasis

Obesity - adult prevalence rate: 17.2% (2016)

Alcohol consumption per capita: *total:* 2.38 liters of pure alcohol (2019 est.)
beer: 1.37 liters of pure alcohol (2019 est.)
wine: 0.16 liters of pure alcohol (2019 est.)
spirits: 0.53 liters of pure alcohol (2019 est.)
other alcohols: 0.32 liters of pure alcohol (2019 est.)

Tobacco use: *total:* 15.1% (2020 est.)
male: 24.2% (2020 est.)
female: 6% (2020 est.)

Children under the age of 5 years underweight: 13.2% (2013)

Education expenditures: 9.4% of GDP (2020 est.)

Literacy: *definition:* age 15 and over can read and write
total population: 91.5%
male: 91.6%
female: 91.4% (2018)

Unemployment, youth ages 15-24: *total:* 38%
male: 37.5%
female: 38.5% (2018 est.)

ENVIRONMENT

Environment - current issues: depletion and degradation of water and aquatic resources; desertification; land degradation; loss of biodiversity and biotic resources; wildlife poaching

Environment - international agreements: *party to:* Antarctic-Marine Living Resources, Biodiversity, Climate Change, Climate Change-Kyoto Protocol, Climate Change-Paris Agreement, Comprehensive Nuclear Test Ban, Desertification, Endangered Species, Hazardous Wastes, Law of the Sea, Ozone Layer Protection, Ship Pollution, Wetlands
signed, but not ratified: none of the selected agreements

Air pollutants: *particulate matter emissions:* 22.59 micrograms per cubic meter (2016 est.)
carbon dioxide emissions: 4.23 megatons (2016 est.)
methane emissions: 10.4 megatons (2020 est.)

Climate: desert; hot, dry; rainfall sparse and erratic

Land use: *agricultural land:* 47.2% (2018 est.)
arable land: 1% (2018 est.)
permanent crops: 0% (2018 est.)
permanent pasture: 46.2% (2018 est.)
forest: 8.8% (2018 est.)
other: 44% (2018 est.)

Urbanization: *urban population:* 54% of total population (2022)
rate of urbanization: 3.64% annual rate of change (2020-25 est.)

Revenue from forest resources: *forest revenues:* 0.47% of GDP (2018 est.)

Revenue from coal: *coal revenues:* 0% of GDP (2018 est.)

Food insecurity: *severe localized food insecurity:* due to localized shortfalls in cereal production and rising food prices - cereal production increased in 2022 and this is expected to have a positive impact on food security, however, rising prices of basic foods is likely to limit a more substantial improvement (2022)

Waste and recycling: *municipal solid waste generated annually:* 256,729 tons (1993 est.)
municipal solid waste recycled annually: 11,553 tons (2005 est.)
percent of municipal solid waste recycled: 4.5% (2005 est.)

Major rivers (by length in km): Zambezi (shared with Zambia [s]), Angola, Botswana, Zimbabwe, and Mozambique [m]) - 2,740 km; Orange river mouth (shared with Lesotho [s], and South Africa) - 2,092 km; Okavango (shared with Angola [s], and Botswana [m]) - 1,600 km
note – [s] after country name indicates river source; [m] after country name indicates river mouth

Major watersheds (area sq km): Atlantic Ocean drainage: Orange (941,351 sq km)

Indian Ocean drainage: Zambezi (1,332,412 sq km)

Internal (*endorheic basin*) drainage: Okavango Basin (863,866 sq km)

Major aquifers: Lower Kalahari-Stampriet Basin, Upper Kalahari-Cuvelai-Upper Zambezi Basin

Total water withdrawal: *municipal:* 73 million cubic meters (2017 est.)
industrial: 14 million cubic meters (2017 est.)
agricultural: 201 million cubic meters (2017 est.)

Total renewable water resources: 39.91 billion cubic meters (2017 est.)

GOVERNMENT

Country name: *conventional long form:* Republic of Namibia
conventional short form: Namibia
local long form: Republic of Namibia
local short form: Namibia
former: German South-West Africa (Deutsch-Suedwestafrika), South-West Africa
etymology: named for the coastal Namib Desert; the name "namib" means "vast place" in the Nama/Damara language

Government type: presidential republic

Capital: *name:* Windhoek
geographic coordinates: 22 34 S, 17 05 E
time difference: UTC+1 (6 hours ahead of Washington, DC, during Standard Time)
daylight saving time: +1hr, begins first Sunday in September; ends first Sunday in April
etymology: may derive from the Afrikaans word "wind-hoek" meaning "windy corner"

Administrative divisions: 14 regions; Erongo, Hardap, //Karas, Kavango East, Kavango West, Khomas, Kunene, Ohangwena, Omaheke, Omusati, Oshana, Oshikoto, Otjozondjupa, Zambezi; note - the Karas Region was renamed //Karas in September 2013 to include the alveolar lateral click of the Khoekhoegowab language

Independence: 21 March 1990 (from South African mandate)

National holiday: Independence Day, 21 March (1990)

Constitution: *history:* adopted 9 February 1990, entered into force 21 March 1990
amendments: initiated by the Cabinet; passage requires two-thirds majority vote of the National Assembly membership and of the National Council of Parliament and assent of the president of the republic; if the National Council fails to pass an amendment, the president can call for a referendum; passage by referendum requires two-thirds majority of votes cast; amendments that detract from or repeal constitutional articles on fundamental rights and freedoms cannot be amended, and the requisite majorities needed by Parliament to amend the constitution cannot be changed; amended 1998, 2010, 2014

Legal system: mixed legal system of uncodified civil law based on Roman-Dutch law and customary law

International law organization participation: has not submitted an ICJ jurisdiction declaration; accepts ICCt jurisdiction

Citizenship: *citizenship by birth:* no
citizenship by descent only: at least one parent must be a citizen of Namibia
dual citizenship recognized: no
residency requirement for naturalization: 5 years

Suffrage: 18 years of age; universal

Executive branch: *chief of state:* President Hage GEINGOB (since 21 March 2015); Vice President Nangola MBUMBA (since 8 February 2018); note - the president is both chief of state and head of government
head of government: President Hage GEINGOB (since 21 March 2015); Vice President Nangola MBUMBA (since 8 February 2018); Prime Minister Saara KUUGONGELWA-AMADHILA (since 21 March 2015)
cabinet: Cabinet appointed by the president from among members of the National Assembly
elections/appointments: president elected by absolute majority popular vote in 2 rounds if needed for a 5-year term (eligible for a second term); election last held on 28 November 2019 (next to be held in 2024)
election results: Hage GEINGOB elected president in the first round; percent of vote - Hage GEINGOB (SWAPO) 56.3%, Panduleni ITULA (Independent) 29.4%, McHenry VENAANI (PDM) 5.3%, Bernadus SWARTBOOI (LPM) 2.7%, Apius AUCHAB (UDF) 2.7%, Esther MUINJANGUE (NUDO) 1.5%, other 2% (2019)

Legislative branch: *description:* bicameral Parliament consists of:
National Council (42 seats); members indirectly elected 3 each by the 14 regional councils to serve 5-year terms); note -the Council primarily reviews legislation passed and referred by the National Assembly
National Assembly (104 seats; 96 members directly elected in multi-seat constituencies by closed list, proportional representation vote to serve 5-year terms and 8 nonvoting members appointed by the president)
elections: National Council - elections for regional councils to determine members of the National Council held on 25 November 2020 (next to be held on 25 November 2025)
National Assembly - last held on 27 November 2019 (next to be held in 2024)
election results: National Council - percent of vote by party - NA; seats by party - SWAPO 28, LPM 6,IPC 2, PDM 2, UDF 2, NUDO 1, independent 1; composition as of July 2022 - men 36, women 6, percent of women 14.3% National Assembly - percent of vote by party - SWAPO 65.5%, PDM 16.6%, LPM 4.7%, NUDO 1.9%, APP 1.8%, UDF 1.8%, RP 1.8%, NEFF 1.7%, RDP 1.1%, CDV .7%, SWANU .6%, other 1.8%; seats by party - SWAPO 63, PDM 16, LPM 4, NUDO 2, APP 2, UDF 2, RP 2, NEFF 2, RDP 1, CDV 1, SWANU 1; composition as of July 2022 - men 58, women 46, percent of women 44.2%; note - overall percent of women in Parliament 35.6%

Judicial branch: *highest court(s):* Supreme Court (consists of the chief justice and at least 3 judges in quorum sessions)
judge selection and term of office: judges appointed by the president of Namibia upon the recommendation of the Judicial Service Commission; judges serve until age 65, but terms can be extended by the president until age 70
subordinate courts: High Court; Electoral Court, Labor Court; regional and district magistrates' courts; community courts

Political parties and leaders: All People's Party or APP [Vacant]
Christian Democratic Voice or CDV [Gothard KANDUME]
Landless People's Movement or LPM [Bernadus SWARTBOOI]
National Unity Democratic Organization or NUDO [Estes MUINJANGUE]
Namibian Economic Freedom Fighters or NEFF [Epafras MUKWIILONGO]
Popular Democratic Movement or PDM [McHenry VENAANI] (formerly Democratic Turnhalle Alliance or DTA)
Rally for Democracy and Progress or RDP [Mike KAVEKOTORA]
Republican Party or RP [Henk MUDGE]
South West Africa National Union or SWANU [Charles KATJIVIRUE]
South West Africa People's Organization or SWAPO [Hage GEINGOB]
United Democratic Front or UDF [Apius AUCHAB]
United People's Movement or UPM [Jan J. VAN WYK]

International organization participation: ACP, AfDB, AU, C, CD, CPLP (associate observer), FAO, G-77, IAEA, IBRD, ICAO, ICCt, ICRM, IDA, IFAD, IFC, IFRCS, ILO, IMF, IMO, Interpol, IOC, IOM, IPU, ISO, ITSO, ITU, ITUC (NGOs), MIGA, NAM, OPCW, SACU, SADC, UN, UNAMID, UNCTAD, UNESCO, UNHCR, UNHRC, UNIDO, UNISFA, UNMIL, UNMISS, UNOCI, UNWTO, UPU, WCO, WHO, WIPO, WMO, WTO

Diplomatic representation in the US: *chief of mission:* Ambassador Margaret Natalie MENSAH-WILLIAMS (since 18 January 2021)
chancery: 1605 New Hampshire Avenue NW, Washington, DC 20009
telephone: [1] (202) 986-0540
FAX: [1] (202) 986-0443
email address and website:
info@namibiaembassyusa.org
https://namibiaembassyusa.org/

Diplomatic representation from the US: *chief of mission:* Ambassador (vacant); Charge d'Affaires Jessica LONG (since 2 July 2021)
embassy: 14 Lossen Street, Windhoek
mailing address: 2540 Windhoek Place, Washington DC 20521-2540
telephone: [264] (061) 295-8500
FAX: [264] (061) 295-8603
email address and website:
ConsularWindhoek@state.gov
https://na.usembassy.gov/

Flag description: a wide red stripe edged by narrow white stripes divides the flag diagonally from lower hoist corner to upper fly corner; the upper hoist-side triangle is blue and charged with a golden-yellow, 12-rayed sunburst; the lower fly-side triangle is green; red signifies the heroism of the people and their determination to build a future of equal opportunity for all; white stands for peace, unity, tranquility, and harmony; blue represents the Namibian sky and the Atlantic Ocean, the country's precious water resources and rain; the golden-yellow sun denotes power and existence; green symbolizes vegetation and agricultural resources

National symbol(s): oryx (antelope); national colors: blue, red, green, white, yellow

National anthem: *name:* "Namibia, Land of the Brave" lyrics/music: Axali DOESEB
note: adopted 1991

National heritage: *total World Heritage Sites:* 2 (1 cultural, 1 natural)
selected World Heritage Site locales: Twyfelfontein or /Ui-//aes (c); Namib Sand Sea (n)

ECONOMY

Economic overview: Namibia's economy is heavily dependent on the extraction and processing of minerals for export. Mining accounts for about 12.5% of GDP, but provides more than 50% of foreign exchange earnings. Rich alluvial diamond deposits make Namibia a primary source for gem-quality diamonds. Marine diamond mining is increasingly important as the terrestrial diamond supply has dwindled. The rising cost of mining diamonds, especially from the sea, combined with increased diamond production in Russia and China, has reduced profit margins. Namibian authorities have emphasized the need to add value to raw materials, do more in-country manufacturing, and exploit the services market, especially in the logistics and transportation sectors.

Namibia is one of the world's largest producers of uranium. The Chinese-owned Husab uranium mine began producing uranium ore in 2017, and is expected to reach full production in August 2018 and produce 15 million pounds of uranium a year. Namibia also produces large quantities of zinc and is a smaller producer of gold and copper. Namibia's economy remains vulnerable to world commodity price fluctuations and drought.

Namibia normally imports about 50% of its cereal requirements; in drought years, food shortages are problematic in rural areas. A high per capita GDP, relative to the region, obscures one of the world's most unequal income distributions; the current government has prioritized exploring wealth redistribution schemes while trying to maintain a pro-business environment. GDP growth in 2017 slowed to about 1%, however, due to contractions in both the construction and mining sectors, as well as an ongoing drought. Growth is expected to recover modestly in 2018.

A five-year Millennium Challenge Corporation compact ended in September 2014. As an upper middle income country, Namibia is ineligible for a second compact. The Namibian economy is closely linked to South Africa with the Namibian dollar pegged one-to-one to the South African rand. Namibia receives 30%-40% of its revenues from the Southern African Customs Union (SACU); volatility in the size of Namibia's annual SACU allotment and global mineral prices complicates budget planning.

Real GDP (purchasing power parity): $22.6 billion (2020 est.)
$24.56 billion (2019 est.)
$24.71 billion (2018 est.)
note: data are in 2017 dollars

Real GDP growth rate: -1.56% (2019 est.)
1.13% (2018 est.)
-1.02% (2017 est.)

Real GDP per capita: $8,900 (2020 est.)
$9,800 (2019 est.)
$10,100 (2018 est.)
note: data are in 2017 dollars

GDP (official exchange rate): 12.372 billion (2019 est.)

Inflation rate (consumer prices): 3.7% (2019 est.)
4.2% (2018 est.)
6.1% (2017 est.)

Credit ratings:

Fitch rating: BB (2019)

Moody's rating: Ba3 (2020)
note: The year refers to the year in which the current credit rating was first obtained.

GDP - composition, by sector of origin Fitch rating: *BB (2019*
agriculture: 6.7% (2016 est.)
industry: 26.3% (2016 est.)
services: 67% (2017 est.)

GDP - composition, by end use: *household consumption:* 68.7% (2017 est.)
government consumption: 24.5% (2017 est.)
investment in fixed capital: 16% (2017 est.)
investment in inventories: 1.6% (2017 est.)
exports of goods and services: 36.7% (2017 est.)
imports of goods and services: -47.5% (2017 est.)

Agricultural products: roots/tubers nes, milk, maize, onions, beef, grapes, fruit, pulses nes, vegetables, millet

Industries: meatpacking, fish processing, dairy products, pasta, beverages; mining (diamonds, lead, zinc, tin, silver, tungsten, uranium, copper)

Industrial production growth rate: -0.4% (2017 est.)

Labor force: 956,800 (2017 est.)

Labor force - by occupation: *agriculture:* 31%
industry: 14%
services: 54% (2013 est.)
note: about half of Namibia's people are unemployed while about two-thirds live in rural areas; roughly two-thirds of rural dwellers rely on subsistence agriculture

Unemployment rate: 34% (2016 est.)
28.1% (2014 est.)

Unemployment, youth ages 15-24: *total:* 38%
male: 37.5%
female: 38.5% (2018 est.)

Population below poverty line: 17.4% (2015 est.)

Gini Index coefficient - distribution of family income: 59.1 (2015 est.)
70.7 (2003)

Household income or consumption by percentage share: *lowest 10%:* 2.4%
highest 10%: 42% (2010)

Budget: revenues: 4.268 billion (2017 est.)
expenditures: 5 billion (2017 est.)

Budget surplus (+) or deficit (-): -5.5% (of GDP) (2017 est.)

Public debt: 41.3% of GDP (2017 est.)
39.5% of GDP (2016 est.)

Taxes and other revenues: 32.2% (of GDP) (2017 est.)

Fiscal year: 1 April - 31 March

Current account balance: -$216 million (2019 est.)
-$465 million (2018 est.)

Exports: $3.56 billion (2020 est.) note: data are in current year dollars
$4.56 billion (2019 est.) note: data are in current year dollars
$4.95 billion (2018 est.) note: data are in current year dollars

Exports - partners: China 27%, South Africa 18%, Botswana 8%, Belgium 7% (2019)

Exports - commodities: copper, diamonds, uranium, thorium, gold, radioactive chemicals, fish (2019)

Imports: $4.54 billion (2020 est.) note: data are in current year dollars
$5.77 billion (2019 est.) note: data are in current year dollars
$6.33 billion (2018 est.) note: data are in current year dollars

Imports - partners: South Africa 47%, Zambia 16% (2019)

Imports - commodities: copper, refined petroleum, delivery trucks, diamonds, cars (2019)

Reserves of foreign exchange and gold: $2.432 billion (31 December 2017 est.)
$1.834 billion (31 December 2016 est.)

Debt - external: $7.969 billion (31 December 2017 est.)
$6.904 billion (31 December 2016 est.)

Exchange rates: Namibian dollars (NAD) per US dollar -
13.67 (2017 est.)
14.7096 (2016 est.)
14.7096 (2015 est.)
12.7589 (2014 est.)
10.8526 (2013 est.)

ENERGY

Electricity access: *electrification - total population:* 57% (2019)
electrification - urban areas: 78% (2019)
electrification - rural areas: 36% (2019)

Electricity: *installed generating capacity:* 640,000 kW (2020 est.)
consumption: 4,065,360,000 kWh (2019 est.)
exports: 119 million kWh (2019 est.)
imports: 3.417 billion kWh (2019 est.)
transmission/distribution losses: 270 million kWh (2019 est.)

Electricity generation sources: *fossil fuels:* 6.1% of total installed capacity (2020 est.)
solar: 4.7% of total installed capacity (2020 est.)
wind: 0.5% of total installed capacity (2020 est.)
hydroelectricity: 88.8% of total installed capacity (2020 est.)

Coal: *production:* 0 metric tons (2020 est.)
consumption: 38,000 metric tons (2020 est.)
exports: 0 metric tons (2020 est.)
imports: 59,000 metric tons (2020 est.)
proven reserves: 0 metric tons (2019 est.)

Petroleum: *total petroleum production:* 0 bbl/day (2021 est.)
refined petroleum consumption: 26,500 bbl/day (2019 est.)

Refined petroleum products - exports: 80 bbl/day (2015 est.)

Refined petroleum products - imports: 26,270 bbl/day (2015 est.)

Natural gas: *proven reserves:* 62.297 billion cubic meters (2021 est.)

Carbon dioxide emissions: 3.831 million metric tonnes of CO_2 (2019 est.)
from coal and metallurgical coke: 66,000 metric tonnes of CO_2 (2019 est.)
from petroleum and other liquids: 3.764 million metric tonnes of CO_2 (2019 est.)

Energy consumption per capita: 29.811 million Btu/person (2019 est.)

COMMUNICATIONS

Telephones - fixed lines: *total subscriptions:* 140,370 (2020 est.)
subscriptions per 100 inhabitants: 6 (2020 est.)

Telephones - mobile cellular: *total subscriptions:* 2,898,125 (2020 est.)
subscriptions per 100 inhabitants: 114 (2020 est.)

Telecommunication systems: *general assessment:* the government's Broadband Policy aims to provide 95% population coverage by 2024; mobile network coverage has increased sharply in recent years; by 2021, 3G infrastructure provided 89% population coverage while LTE infrastructure provided 79% coverage (compared to only 40% a year earlier); despite the relatively advanced nature of the market, progress towards 5G has been slow, partly due to unsubstantiated public concerns over health implications of the technology which caused the government to order an environmental assessment of 5G in mid-2020; the government has requested the regulator to speed up its 5G development strategy; Namibia's internet and broadband sector is reasonably competitive, its development was for many years held back by high prices for international bandwidth caused by the lack of a direct connection to international submarine cables; this market situation improved after operators invested in diversifying terrestrial access routes to adjacent countries; by the end of 2022 Namibia is expected to be connected by a 1,050km branch line of cable running between Portugal and South Africa (2022)
domestic: fixed-line subscribership is less than 6 per 100 and mobile-cellular roughly 102 per 100 persons (2020)
international: country code - 264; landing points for the ACE and WACS fiber-optic submarine cable linking southern and western African countries to Europe; satellite earth stations - 4 Intelsat (2019)

Broadcast media: 1 private and 1 state-run TV station; satellite and cable TV service available; state-run radio service broadcasts in multiple languages; about a dozen private radio stations; transmissions of multiple international broadcasters available

Internet country code: .na

Internet users: *total:* 1,041,776 (2020 est.)
percent of population: 41% (2020 est.)

Broadband - fixed subscriptions: *total:* 71,063 (2020 est.)
subscriptions per 100 inhabitants: 3 (2020 est.)

TRANSPORTATION

National air transport system: *number of registered air carriers:* 2 (2020)
inventory of registered aircraft operated by air carriers: 21
annual passenger traffic on registered air carriers: 602,893 (2018)
annual freight traffic on registered air carriers: 26.29 million (2018) mt-km

Civil aircraft registration country code prefix: V5

Airports: *total:* 112 (2021)

Airports - with paved runways: *total:* 19
over 3,047 m: 4
2,438 to 3,047 m: 2
1,524 to 2,437 m: 12
914 to 1,523 m: 1 (2021)

Airports - with unpaved runways: *total:* 93

1,524 to 2,437 m: 25
914 to 1,523 m: 52
under 914 m: 16 (2021)

Railways: *total:* 2,628 km (2014)
narrow gauge: 2,628 km (2014) 1.067-m gauge

Roadways: *total:* 48,875 km (2018)
paved: 7,893 km (2018)
unpaved: 40,982 km (2018)

Merchant marine: *total:* 14
by type: general cargo 1, other 13 (2021)

Ports and terminals: *major seaport(s):* Luderitz, Walvis Bay

MILITARY AND SECURITY

Military and security forces: Namibian Defense Force (NDF): Army, Navy, Air Force; Ministry of Home Affairs, Immigration, Safety, and Security: Namibian Police Force (includes a paramilitary Special Field Force responsible for protecting borders and government installations) (2022)

Military expenditures: 3% of GDP (2021 est.)
3.4% of GDP (2020 est.)
3.3% of GDP (2019) (approximately $620 million)
3.4% of GDP (2018) (approximately $640 million)
3.6% of GDP (2017) (approximately $670 million)

Military and security service personnel strengths: information varies; approximately 12,500 personnel (11,000 Army; 1,000 Navy; 500 Air Force) (2022)

Military equipment inventories and acquisitions: the NDF's inventory consists of a mix of Soviet-era and some more modern systems from a variety of countries, including Brazil, China, Germany, India, and South Africa; it has a small defense industry that produces items such as armored personnel carriers (2021)

Military service age and obligation: 18-25 years of age for men and women for voluntary military service; no conscription (2022) note: as of 2018, women comprised more than 20% of the active duty military

Military - note: the Namibian Defense Force (NDF) was created in 1990, largely from demobilized former members of the People's Liberation Army of Namibia (PLAN) and the South West Africa Territorial Force (SWATF); PLAN was the armed wing of the South West Africa People's Organization (SWAPO), while SWATF was an auxiliary of the South African Defense Force and comprised the armed forces of the former South West Africa, 1977-1989; from 1990-1995, the British military assisted with the forming and training the NDF (2022)

TRANSNATIONAL ISSUES

Disputes - international: Namibia-Angola-Botswana: concerns from international experts and local populations over the Okavango Delta ecology in Botswana and human displacement scuttled Namibian plans to construct a hydroelectric dam on Popa Falls along the Angola-Namibia border

Namibia-Botswana-Zambia-Zimbabwe: Namibia has supported, and in 2004 Zimbabwe dropped objections to, plans between Botswana and Zambia to build a bridge over the Zambezi River, thereby de facto recognizing a short, but not clearly delimited, Botswana-Zambia boundary in the river; the Kazungula Bridge opened to traffic in May 2021

Namibia-South Africa: the governments of South Africa and Namibia have not signed or ratified the text of the 1994 Surveyor's General agreement placing the boundary in the middle of the Orange River; Namibia claims a median line boundary, while South Africa supports the northern bank of the river

Refugees and internally displaced persons: *refugees (country of origin):* 6,096 (Democratic Republic of the Congo) (refugees and asylum seekers) (2022)

NAURU

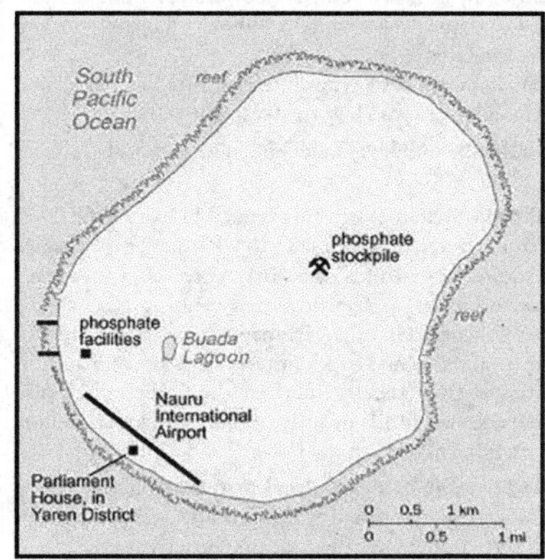

INTRODUCTION

Background: Nauru was inhabited by Micronesian and Polynesian settlers by around 1000 B.C., and the island was divided into 12 clans. Nauru developed in relative isolation because ocean currents made landfall on the island difficult. As a result, the Nauruan language does not clearly resemble any other in the Pacific region. In 1798, British sea captain John FEARN became the first European to spot the island. By 1830, European whalers used Nauru as a supply stop, trading firearms for food. In 1878, a civil war erupted on the island, reducing the population by more than a third. Germany forcibly annexed Nauru in 1888 by holding the 12 chiefs under house arrest until they consented to the annexation. Germany banned alcohol, confiscated weapons, instituted strict dress codes, and brought in Christian missionaries to convert the population. Phosphate was discovered in 1900 and heavily mined, although Nauru and Nauruans earned about one tenth of one percent of the profits from the phosphate deposits.

Australian forces captured Nauru from Germany during World War I, and in 1919, it was placed under a joint Australian-British-New Zealand mandate with Australian administration. Japan occupied Nauru during World War II and used its residents as forced labor elsewhere in the Pacific while destroying much of the infrastructure on the island. After the war, Nauru became a UN trust territory under Australian administration. Recognizing the phosphate stocks would eventually be depleted, in 1962, Australian Prime Minister Robert MENZIES offered to resettle all Nauruans on Curtis Island in Queensland, but Nauruans rejected that plan and opted for independence, which was achieved in 1968. In 1970, Nauru purchased the phosphate mining assets, and income from the mines made Nauruans among the richest people in the world. However, Nauru subsequently began a series of unwise investments in buildings, musical theater, and an airline. Nauru sued Australia in 1989 for the damage caused by mining when Australia administered the island. Widespread phosphate mining officially ceased in 2006.

Nauru went nearly bankrupt by 2000 and tried to rebrand itself as an offshore banking haven, although it ended that practice in 2005. In 2001, Australia set up the Nauru Regional Processing Center (NRPC), an offshore refugee detention facility, paying Nauru per person at the center. The NRPC was closed in 2008 but reopened in 2012. The number of refugees has steadily declined since 2014, and the remaining people were moved to a hotel in Brisbane, Australia, in 2020, effectively shuttering the NRPC. In a bid for Russian humanitarian aid, in 2008, Nauru recognized the breakaway Georgian republics of Abkhazia and South Ossetia.

GEOGRAPHY

Location: Oceania, island in the South Pacific Ocean, south of the Marshall Islands

Geographic coordinates: 0 32 S, 166 55 E

Map references: Oceania

Area: *total:* 21 sq km
land: 21 sq km
water: 0 sq km

Area - comparative: about 0.1 times the size of Washington, DC

Land boundaries: *total:* 0 km

Coastline: 30 km

Maritime claims: *territorial sea:* 12 nm
contiguous zone: 24 nm
exclusive economic zone: 200 nm Climate tropical with a monsoonal pattern; rainy season (November to February)

Terrain: sandy beach rises to fertile ring around raised coral reefs with phosphate plateau in center

Elevation: *highest point:* Command Ridge 70 m
lowest point: Pacific Ocean 0 m

Natural resources: phosphates, fish Land use
agricultural land: 20% (2018 est.)
arable land: 0% (2018 est.)
permanent crops: 20% (2018 est.)
permanent pasture: 0% (2018 est.)
forest: 0% (2018 est.)
other: 80% (2018 est.)

Irrigated land: 0 sq km (2012)

Population distribution: extensive phosphate mining made approximately 90% of the island unsuitable for farming; most people live in the fertile coastal areas, especially along the southwest coast

Natural hazards: periodic droughts

Geography - note: Nauru is the third-smallest country in the world behind the Holy See (Vatican City) and Monaco; it is the smallest country in the Pacific Ocean, the smallest country outside Europe, the world's smallest island country, and the the world's smallest independent republic; situated just 53 km south of the Equator, Nauru is one of the three great phosphate rock islands in the Pacific Ocean - the others are Banaba (Ocean Island) in Kiribati and Makatea in French Polynesia

PEOPLE AND SOCIETY

Population: 9,811 (2022 est.)

Nationality: *noun:* Nauruan(s)
adjective: Nauruan

Ethnic groups: Nauruan 88.9%, part Nauruan 6.6%, I-Kiribati 2%, other 2.5% (2007 est.)

Languages: Nauruan 93% (official, a distinct Pacific Island language), English 2% (widely understood, spoken, and used for most government and commercial purposes), other 5% (includes I-Kiribati 2% and Chinese 2%) (2011 est.)
note: data represent main language spoken at home; Nauruan is spoken by 95% of the population, English by 66%, and other languages by 12%

Religions: Protestant 60.4% (includes Nauru Congregational 35.7%, Assembly of God 13%, Nauru Independent Church 9.5%, Baptist 1.5%, and Seventh Day Adventist 0.7%), Roman Catholic 33%, other 3.7%, none 1.8%, unspecified 1.1% (2011 est.)

Age structure: *0-14 years:* 30.87% (male 1,337/female 1,684)
15-24 years: 15.68% (male 732/female 806)
25-54 years: 42.57% (male 2,115/female 2,050)
55-64 years: 6.97% (male 283/female 401)
65 years and over: 3.94% (male 133/female 254) (2022 est.)

Median age: *total:* 27 years
male: 28.2 years
female: 25.9 years (2020 est.)

Population growth rate: 0.42% (2022 est.)

Birth rate: 21.1 births/1,000 population (2022 est.)

Death rate: 6.32 deaths/1,000 population (2022 est.)

Net migration rate: -10.6 migrant(s)/1,000 population (2022 est.)

Population distribution: extensive phosphate mining made approximately 90% of the island unsuitable for farming; most people live in the fertile coastal areas, especially along the southwest coast

Urbanization: *urban population:* 100% of total population (2022)
rate of urbanization: 0.18% annual rate of change (2020-25 est.)

Sex ratio: *at birth:* 1.04 male(s)/female
0-14 years: 1.04 male(s)/female
15-24 years: 0.91 male(s)/female
25-54 years: 1.03 male(s)/female
55-64 years: 0.7 male(s)/female
65 years and over: 0.51 male(s)/female
total population: 0.96 male(s)/female (2022 est.)

Infant mortality rate: *total:* 7.84 deaths/1,000 live births
male: 10.1 deaths/1,000 live births
female: 5.5 deaths/1,000 live births (2022 est.)

Life expectancy at birth: *total population:* 67.93 years
male: 64.38 years
female: 71.62 years (2022 est.)

Total fertility rate: 2.62 children born/woman (2022 est.)

Drinking water source: *improved: urban:* 100% of population
total: 100% of population

Current health expenditure: 9.8% of GDP (2019)

Physicians density: 1.35 physicians/1,000 population (2015)

Sanitation facility access: *improved: urban:* 96.3% of population
total: 96.3% of population
unimproved: urban: 3.7% of population
total: 3.7% of population (2017 est.)

Major infectious diseases: *degree of risk:* high (2020)
food or waterborne diseases: bacterial diarrhea
vectorborne diseases: malaria

Obesity - adult prevalence rate: 61% (2016)

Alcohol consumption per capita: *total:* 2.44 liters of pure alcohol (2019 est.)
beer: 0.54 liters of pure alcohol (2019 est.)
wine: 0.09 liters of pure alcohol (2019 est.)
spirits: 1.81 liters of pure alcohol (2019 est.)
other alcohols: 0 liters of pure alcohol (2019 est.)

Tobacco use: *total:* 48.5% (2020 est.)
male: 47.8% (2020 est.)
female: 49.1% (2020 est.)

Unemployment, youth ages 15-24: *total:* 26.6%
male: 20.9%
female: 37.5% (2013)

ENVIRONMENT

Environment - current issues: limited natural freshwater resources, roof storage tanks that collect rainwater and desalination plants provide water; a century of intensive phosphate mining beginning in 1906 left the central 90% of Nauru a wasteland; cadmium residue, phosphate dust, and other contaminants have caused air and water pollution with negative impacts on health; climate change has brought on rising sea levels and inland water shortages

Environment - international agreements: *party to:* Biodiversity, Climate Change, Climate Change-Kyoto Protocol, Climate Change-Paris Agreement, Comprehensive Nuclear Test Ban, Desertification, Hazardous Wastes, Law of the Sea, Marine Dumping-London Convention, Ozone Layer Protection, Whaling
signed, but not ratified: none of the selected agreements Air pollutants
particulate matter emissions: 12.53 micrograms per cubic meter (2016 est.)
carbon dioxide emissions: 0.05 megatons (2016 est.)
methane emissions: 0.01 megatons (2020 est.)

Climate: tropical with a monsoonal pattern; rainy season (November to February)

Land use: *agricultural land:* 20% (2018 est.)
arable land: 0% (2018 est.)
permanent crops: 20% (2018 est.)
permanent pasture: 0% (2018 est.)
forest: 0% (2018 est.)
other: 80% (2018 est.)

Urbanization: *urban population:* 100% of total population (2022)
rate of urbanization: 0.18% annual rate of change (2020-25 est.)

Revenue from forest resources: *forest revenues:* 0% of GDP (2018 est.)

Waste and recycling: *municipal solid waste generated annually:* 6,192 tons (2016 est.)

Total renewable water resources: 10 million cubic meters (2017 est.)

GOVERNMENT

Country name: *conventional long form:* Republic of Nauru
conventional short form: Nauru
local long form: Republic of Nauru
local short form: Nauru
former: Pleasant Island
etymology: the island name may derive from the Nauruan word "anaoero" meaning "I go to the beach"

Government type: parliamentary republic Capital
name: no official capital; government offices in the Yaren District
time difference: UTC+12 (17 hours ahead of Washington, DC, during Standard Time)

Administrative divisions: 14 districts; Aiwo, Anabar, Anetan, Anibare, Baitsi, Boe, Buada, Denigomodu, Ewa, Ijuw, Meneng, Nibok, Uaboe, Yaren Independence
31 January 1968 (from the Australia-, NZ-, and UK-administered UN trusteeship)

National holiday: Independence Day, 31 January (1968)

Constitution: *history:* effective 29 January 1968
amendments: proposed by Parliament; passage requires two-thirds majority vote of Parliament; amendments to constitutional articles, such as the republican form of government, protection of fundamental rights and freedoms, the structure and authorities of the executive and legislative branches, also require two-thirds majority of votes in a referendum; amended several times, last in 2018

Legal system: mixed legal system of common law based on the English model and customary law International law organization participation
has not submitted an ICJ jurisdiction declaration; accepts ICCt jurisdiction

Suffrage: 20 years of age; universal and compulsory Executive branch
chief of state: President Russ KUN (since 28 September 2022); note - the president is both chief of state and head of government
head of government: President Russ KUN (since 28 September 2022) cabinet: Cabinet appointed by the president from among members of Parliament
elections/appointments: president indirectly elected by Parliament (eligible for a second term); election last held on 28 September 2022 (next to be held in 2025)
election results: Russ KUN elected president unopposed

Legislative branch: *description:* unicameral parliament (19 seats; members directly elected in multi-seat

constituencies by majority vote using the "Dowdall" counting system by which voters rank candidates on their ballots; members serve 3-year terms)
elections: last held on 24 September 2022 (next to be held in September 2025)
election results: percent of vote - NA; seats - independent 19; composition - men 17, women 2, percent of women 10.5%

Judicial branch: *highest court(s):* Supreme Court (consists of the chief justice and several justices); note - in late 2017, the Nauruan Government revoked the 1976 High Court Appeals Act, which had allowed appeals beyond the Nauruan Supreme Court, and in early 2018, the government formed its own appeals court
judge selection and term of office: judges appointed by the president to serve until age 65
subordinate courts: District Court, Family Court

Political parties and leaders: Nauru First (Naoero Amo) Party [David ADEANG]

International organization participation: ACP, ADB, AOSIS, C, FAO, G-77, ICAO, ICCt, IFAD, Interpol, IOC, IOM, ITU, OPCW, PIF, Sparteca, SPC, UN, UNCTAD, UNESCO, UPU, WHO

Diplomatic representation in the US: *chief of mission:* Ambassador Margo DEIYE (since 1 December 2021) chancery: 800 2nd Avenue, Third Floor, New York, NY 10017 telephone: [1] (212) 937-0074 FAX: [1] (212) 937-0079
email address and website:
nauru@onecommonwealth.org
https://www.un.int/nauru/

Diplomatic representation from the US: *embassy:* the US does not have an embassy in Nauru; the US Ambassador to Fiji is accredited to Nauru

Flag description: blue with a narrow, horizontal, gold stripe across the center and a large white 12-pointed star below the stripe on the hoist side; blue stands for the Pacific Ocean, the star indicates the country's location in relation to the Equator (the gold stripe) and the 12 points symbolize the 12 original tribes of Nauru; the star's white color represents phosphate, the basis of the island's wealth

National symbol(s): frigatebird, calophyllum flower; national colors: blue, yellow, white National anthem *name:* "Nauru Bwiema" (Song of Nauru) lyrics/music: Margaret HENDRIE/Laurence Henry HICKS
note: adopted 1968

ECONOMY

Economic overview: Revenues of this tiny island - a coral atoll with a land area of 21 square kilometers - traditionally have come from exports of phosphates. Few other resources exist, with most necessities being imported, mainly from Australia, its former occupier and later major source of support. Primary reserves of phosphates were exhausted and mining ceased in 2006, but mining of a deeper layer of "secondary phosphate" in the interior of the island began the following year. The secondary phosphate deposits may last another 30 years. Earnings from Nauru's export of phosphate remains an important source of income. Few comprehensive statistics on the Nauru economy exist; estimates of Nauru's GDP vary widely.

The rehabilitation of mined land and the replacement of income from phosphates are serious long-term problems. In anticipation of the exhaustion of Nauru's phosphate deposits, substantial amounts of phosphate income were invested in trust funds to help cushion the transition and provide for Nauru's economic future.

Although revenue sources for government are limited, the opening of the Australian Regional Processing Center for asylum seekers since 2012 has sparked growth in the economy. Revenue derived from fishing licenses under the "vessel day scheme" has also boosted government income. Housing, hospitals, and other capital plant are deteriorating. The cost to Australia of keeping the Nauruan government and economy afloat continues to climb.

Real GDP (purchasing power parity): $150 million (2019 est.)
$150 million (2018 est.)
$137 million (2017 est.)
note: data are in 2017 dollars Real GDP growth rate 4% (2017 est.)
10.4% (2016 est.)
2.8% (2015 est.)

Real GDP per capita: $13,500 (2019 est.) note: data are in 2017 dollars
$13,600 (2018 est.) note: data are in 2017 dollars
$10,667 (2017 est.)

GDP (official exchange rate): $114 million (2017 est.)

Inflation rate (consumer prices): 5.1% (2017 est.)
8.2% (2016 est.)

GDP - composition, by sector of origin: *agriculture:* 6.1% (2009 est.)
industry: 33% (2009 est.)
services: 60.8% (2009 est.)

GDP - composition, by end use: *household consumption:* 98% (2016 est.)
government consumption: 37.6% (2016 est.)
investment in fixed capital: 42.2% (2016 est.)
exports of goods and services: 11.2% (2016 est.)
imports of goods and services: -89.1% (2016 est.)

Agricultural products: coconuts, tropical fruit, vegetables, pork, eggs, pig offals, pig fat, poultry, papayas, cabbages

Industries: phosphate mining, offshore banking, coconut products

Labor force - by occupation: *note:* most of the labor force is employed in phosphate mining, public administration, education, and transportation

Unemployment rate: 23% (2011 est.)
90% (2004 est.)

Unemployment, youth ages 15-24: *total:* 26.6%
male: 20.9%
female: 37.5% (2013)

Budget: *revenues:* 103 million (2017 est.)
expenditures: 113.4 million (2017 est.)

Budget surplus (+) or deficit (-): -9.2% (of GDP) (2017 est.)

Public debt: 62% of GDP (2017 est.)
65% of GDP (2016 est.)

Taxes and other revenues: 90.3% (of GDP) (2017 est.)

Fiscal year: 1 July - 30 June

Current account balance: $5 million (2017 est.)
$2 million (2016 est.)

Exports: $30 million (2018 est.) note: data are in current year dollars
$110.3 million (2012 est.)

Exports - partners: Thailand 34%, Australia 16%, United States 13%, South Korea 10%, Philippines 9%, Japan 7%, France 5% (2019)

Exports - commodities: fish, calcium phosphates, low-voltage protection equipment, air conditioners, leather apparel (2019)

Imports: $90 million (2018 est.) note: data are in current year dollars
$64.9 million (2016 est.)

Imports - partners: Taiwan 52%, Australia 28% (2019)

Imports - commodities: refined petroleum, construction vehicles, tug boats, poultry meats, cars (2019)

Debt - external: $33.3 million (2004 est.)

Exchange rates: Australian dollars (AUD) per US dollar -
1.311 (2017 est.)
1.3452 (2016 est.)
1.3452 (2015 est.)
1.3291 (2014 est.)
1.1094 (2013 est.)

ENERGY

Electricity access: *electrification - total population:* 99.8% (2018)
electrification - urban areas: 99.4% (2018)
electrification - rural areas: 98.7% (2018)

Electricity: *installed generating capacity:* 15,000 kW (2020 est.)
consumption: 34.216 million kWh (2019 est.)
exports: 0 kWh (2020 est.)
imports: 0 kWh (2020 est.)
transmission/distribution losses: 0 kWh (2019 est.)

Electricity generation sources: *fossil fuels:* 100% of total installed capacity (2020 est.)

Petroleum: *total petroleum production:* 0 bbl/day (2021 est.)
refined petroleum consumption: 400 bbl/day (2019 est.)

Refined petroleum products - imports: 449 bbl/day (2015 est.)

Carbon dioxide emissions: 66,000 metric tonnes of CO2 (2019 est.)
from petroleum and other liquids: 66,000 metric tonnes of CO2 (2019 est.)

Energy consumption per capita: 0 Btu/person (2019 est.)

COMMUNICATIONS

Telephones - fixed lines: *total subscriptions:* 1,900 (2009 est.) subscriptions per 100 inhabitants: 19 (2009 est.)

Telephones - mobile cellular: *total subscriptions:* 10,000 (2020 est.)
subscriptions per 100 inhabitants: 92 (2020 est.)

Telecommunication systems: *general assessment:* relies on satellite as the primary Internet service provider and mobile operator; internet connectivity on the island is very limited and unstable due to the vulnerability of the network infrastructure to bad weather and limited network coverage, with several blind spots (2022)
domestic: fixed-line 0 per 100 and mobile-cellular subscribership approximately 92 per 100 (2020)
international: country code - 674; satellite earth station - 1 Intelsat (Pacific Ocean)

Broadcast media: 1 government-owned TV station broadcasting programs from New Zealand sent via satellite or on videotape; 1 government-owned radio station, broadcasting on AM and FM, utilizes Australian and British programs (2019)

Internet country code: .nr

Internet users: *total:* 6,136 (2019 est.)
percent of population: 57% (2019 est.)

Broadband - fixed subscriptions: *total:* 950 (2010 est.)
subscriptions per 100 inhabitants: 10 (2010 est.)

TRANSPORTATION

National air transport system: *number of registered air carriers:* 1 (2020)
inventory of registered aircraft operated by air carriers: 5
annual passenger traffic on registered air carriers: 45,457 (2018)
annual freight traffic on registered air carriers: 7.94 million (2018) mt-km

Civil aircraft registration country code prefix: C2

Airports: *total:* 1 (2021)

Airports - with paved runways: *total:* 1
1,524 to 2,437 m: 1 (2021)

Roadways: *total:* 30 km (2002)
paved: 24 km (2002)
unpaved: 6 km (2002)

Merchant marine: *total:* 3
by type: oil tanker 1, other 2 (2021)

Ports and terminals: *major seaport(s):* Nauru

MILITARY AND SECURITY

Military and security forces: no regular military forces; the police force, under the Minister for Police and Emergency Services, maintains internal security and, as necessary, external security

Military - note: Nauru maintains no defense forces; under an informal agreement, defense is the responsibility of Australia

Nauru has a "shiprider" agreement with the US, which allows local maritime law enforcement officers to embark on US Coast Guard (USCG) and US Navy (USN) vessels, including to board and search vessels suspected of violating laws or regulations within Nauru's designated exclusive economic zone (EEZ) or on the high seas; "shiprider" agreements also enable USCG personnel and USN vessels with embarked USCG law enforcement personnel to work with host nations to protect critical regional resources (2022)

TRANSNATIONAL ISSUES

Disputes - international: none identified

Refugees and internally displaced persons: *stateless persons:* 133 (mid-year 2021)

NAVASSA ISLAND

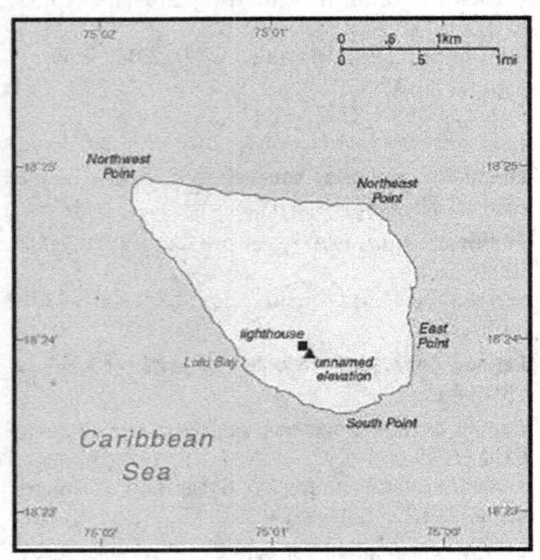

INTRODUCTION

Background: This uninhabited island was claimed by the US in 1857 for its guano. Mining took place between 1865 and 1898. The lighthouse, built in 1917, was shut down in 1996 and administration of Navassa Island transferred from the US Coast Guard to the Department of the Interior, Office of Insular Affairs. A 1998 scientific expedition to the island described it as a "unique preserve of Caribbean biodiversity." The following year it became a National Wildlife Refuge and annual scientific expeditions have continued.

GEOGRAPHY

Location: Caribbean, island in the Caribbean Sea, 30 nm west of Tiburon Peninsula of Haiti Geographic coordinates 18 25 N, 75 02 W

Map references: Central America and the Caribbean Area

total: 5 sq km
land: 5.4 sq km
water: 0 sq km
country comparison to the world: 248

Area - comparative: about nine times the size of the National Mall in Washington, DC

Land boundaries: *total:* 0 km

Coastline: 8 km

Maritime claims: *territorial sea:* 12 nm
exclusive economic zone: 200 nm

Climate: marine, tropical

Terrain: raised flat to undulating coral and limestone plateau; ringed by vertical white cliffs (9 to 15 m high)

Elevation: *highest point:* 200 m NNW of lighthouse 85 m
lowest point: Caribbean Sea 0 m

Natural resources: guano (mining discontinued in 1898)

Land use: *other:* 100% (2018 est.)

Natural hazards: hurricanes

Geography - note: strategic location 160 km south of the US Naval Base at Guantanamo Bay, Cuba; mostly exposed rock with numerous solution holes (limestone sinkholes) but with enough grassland to support goat herds; dense stands of fig trees, scattered cactus

PEOPLE AND SOCIETY

Population: uninhabited; transient Haitian fishermen and others camp on the island

ENVIRONMENT

Environment - current issues: some coral bleaching

Climate: marine, tropical

Land use: *other:* 100% (2018 est.)

GOVERNMENT

Country name: *conventional long form:* none
conventional short form: Navassa Island
etymology: the flat island was named "Navaza" by some of Christopher COLUMBUS' sailors in 1504; the name derives from the Spanish term "nava" meaning "flat land, plain, or field"

Dependency status: unorganized, unincorporated territory of the US; administered by the Fish and Wildlife Service, US Department of the Interior from the Caribbean Islands National Wildlife Refuge in Boqueron, Puerto Rico; in September 1996, the Coast Guard ceased operations and maintenance of the Navassa Island Light, a 46-meter-tall lighthouse on the southern side of the island; Haiti has claimed the island since the 19th century

Legal system: the laws of the US apply where applicable

Diplomatic representation from the US: *embassy:* none (territory of the US)

Flag description: the flag of the US is used

ECONOMY

Economic overview: Subsistence fishing and commercial trawling occur within refuge waters.

TRANSPORTATION

Ports and terminals: none; offshore anchorage only

MILITARY AND SECURITY

Military - note: defense is the responsibility of the US

TRANSNATIONAL ISSUES

Disputes - international: *Navassa Island (US)-Haiti:* claimed by Haiti and is in Haiti's constitution; the waters around Navassa island are a source of subsistence for Haitian fishermen

NEPAL

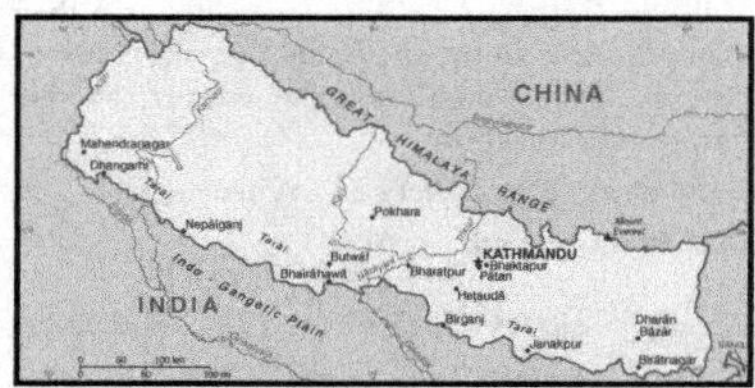

INTRODUCTION

Background: During the late 18th-early 19th centuries, the principality of Gorkha united many of the other principalities and states of the sub-Himalayan region into a Nepali Kingdom. Nepal retained its independence following the Anglo-Nepalese War of 1814-16 and the subsequent peace treaty laid the foundations for two centuries of amicable relations between Britain and Nepal. (The Brigade of Gurkhas continues to serve in the British Army to the present day.) In 1951, the Nepali monarch ended the century-old system of rule by hereditary premiers and instituted a cabinet system that brought political parties into the government. That arrangement lasted until 1960, when political parties were again banned, but was reinstated in 1990 with the establishment of a multiparty democracy within the framework of a constitutional monarchy.

An insurgency led by Maoists broke out in 1996. During the ensuing 10-year civil war between Maoist and government forces, the monarchy dissolved the cabinet and parliament and re-assumed absolute power in 2002, after the crown prince massacred the royal family in 2001. A peace accord in 2006 led to the promulgation of an interim constitution in 2007. Following a nationwide Constituent Assembly (CA) election in 2008, the newly formed CA declared Nepal a federal democratic republic, abolished the monarchy, and elected the country's first president. After the CA failed to draft a constitution by a 2012 deadline set by the Supreme Court, then-Prime Minister Baburam BHATTARAI dissolved the CA. Months of negotiations ensued until 2013 when the major political parties agreed to create an interim government headed by then-Chief Justice Khil Raj REGMI with a mandate to hold elections for a new CA. Elections were held in 2013, in which the Nepali Congress (NC) won the largest share of seats in the CA and in 2014 formed a coalition government with the second-place Communist Party of Nepal-Unified Marxist-Leninist (UML) with NC President Sushil KOIRALA serving as prime minister. Nepal's new constitution came into effect in 2015, at which point the CA became the Parliament. Khagda Prasad Sharma OLI served as the first post-constitution prime minister from 2015 to 2016. OLI resigned ahead of a no-confidence motion against him, and Parliament elected Communist Party of Nepal-Maoist (CPN-M) leader Pushpa Kamal DAHAL (aka "Prachanda") prime minister. The constitution provided for a transitional period during which three sets of elections – local, provincial, and national – needed to take place. The first local elections in 20 years occurred in three phases between May and September 2017, and state and federal elections proceeded in two phases in November and December 2017. The parties headed by OLI and DAHAL ran in coalition and swept the parliamentary elections, and OLI, who led the larger of the two parties, was sworn in as prime minister in February 2018. In May 2018, OLI and DAHAL announced the merger of their parties - the UML and CPN-M - to establish the Nepal Communist Party (NCP), which headed the government for roughly two years before infighting led the party to split. OLI from late 2020 sought to dissolve parliament and hold elections. The supreme court in July 2021 declared OLI's efforts unconstitutional and called for an appointment of the opposition-supported NC leader Sher Bahadur DEUBA as prime minister.

GEOGRAPHY

Location: Southern Asia, between China and India

Geographic coordinates: 28 00 N, 84 00 E

Map references: Asia

Area: *total:* 147,181 sq km
land: 143,351 sq km
water: 3,830 sq km

Area - comparative: slightly larger than New York state

Land boundaries: *total:* 3,159 km
border countries (2): China 1,389 km; India 1,770 km

Coastline: 0 km (landlocked)

Maritime claims: none (landlocked)

Climate: varies from cool summers and severe winters in north to subtropical summers and mild winters in south

Terrain: Tarai or flat river plain of the Ganges in south; central hill region with rugged Himalayas in north

Elevation: *highest point:* Mount Everest (highest peak in Asia and highest point on earth above sea level) 8,849 m
lowest point: Kanchan Kalan 70 m
mean elevation: 2,565 m

Natural resources: quartz, water, timber, hydropower, scenic beauty, small deposits of lignite, copper, cobalt, iron ore

Land use: *agricultural land:* 28.8% (2018 est.)
arable land: 15.1% (2018 est.)
permanent crops: 1.2% (2018 est.)
permanent pasture: 12.5% (2018 est.)
forest: 25.4% (2018 est.)
other: 45.8% (2018 est.)

Irrigated land: 13,320 sq km (2012)

Major watersheds (area sq km): Indian Ocean drainage: Brahmaputra (651,335 sq km), Ganges (1,016,124 sq km), Indus (1,081,718 sq km)

Major aquifers: Indus-Ganges-Brahmaputra Basin

Population distribution: most of the population is divided nearly equally between a concentration in the southern-most plains of the Tarai region and the central hilly region; overall density is quite low

Natural hazards: severe thunderstorms; flooding; landslides; drought and famine depending on the timing, intensity, and duration of the summer monsoons

Geography - note: landlocked; strategic location between China and India; contains eight of world's 10 highest peaks, including Mount Everest and Kanchenjunga - the world's tallest and third tallest mountains - on the borders with China and India respectively

PEOPLE AND SOCIETY

Population: 30,666,598 (2022 est.)

Nationality: *noun:* Nepali (singular and plural)
adjective: Nepali

Ethnic groups: Chhettri 16.6%, Brahman-Hill 12.2%, Magar 7.1%, Tharu 6.6%, Tamang 5.8%, Newar 5%, Kami 4.8%, Muslim 4.4%, Yadav 4%, Rai 2.3%, Gurung 2%, Damai/Dholii 1.8%, Thakuri 1.6%, Limbu 1.5%, Sarki 1.4%, Teli 1.4%, Chamar/Harijan/Ram 1.3%, Koiri/Kushwaha 1.2%, other 19% (2011 est.)
note: 125 caste/ethnic groups were reported in the 2011 national census

Languages: Nepali (official) 44.6%, Maithali 11.7%, Bhojpuri 6%, Tharu 5.8%, Tamang 5.1%, Newar 3.2%, Bajjika 3%, Magar 3%, Doteli 3%, Urdu 2.6%, Avadhi 1.9%, Limbu 1.3%, Gurung 1.2%, Baitadeli 1%, other 6.4%, unspecified 0.2%; note - 123 languages reported as mother tongue in 2011 national census; many in government and business also speak English (2011 est.)
major-language sample(s):

विश्व तथ्य पुस्तक,आधारभूत जानकारीको लागि अपरिहार्य स्रोत

(Nepali)

Religions: Hindu 81.3%, Buddhist 9%, Muslim 4.4%, Kirant 3.1%, Christian 1.4%, other 0.5%, unspecified 0.2% (2011 est.)

Age structure: *0-14 years:* 28.36% (male 4,526,786/female 4,073,642)
15-24 years: 20.93% (male 3,276,431/female 3,070,843)
25-54 years: 38.38% (male 5,251,553/female 6,387,365)
55-64 years: 6.64% (male 954,836/female 1,059,360)
65 years and over: 5.69% (male 852,969/female 874,092) (2020 est.)

Dependency ratios: *total dependency ratio:* 53
youth dependency ratio: 44.1
elderly dependency ratio: 8.9
potential support ratio: 11.2 (2020 est.)

Median age: *total:* 25.3 years
male: 23.9 years
female: 26.9 years (2020 est.)

Population growth rate: 0.78% (2022 est.)

Birth rate: 17.53 births/1,000 population (2022 est.)

Death rate: 5.58 deaths/1,000 population (2022 est.)

Net migration rate: -4.21 migrant(s)/1,000 population (2022 est.)

Population distribution: most of the population is divided nearly equally between a concentration in the southern-most plains of the Tarai region and the central hilly region; overall density is quite low

Urbanization: *urban population:* 21.5% of total population (2022)
rate of urbanization: 3.09% annual rate of change (2020-25 est.)

Major urban areas - population: 1.521 million KATHMANDU (capital) (2022)

Sex ratio: *at birth:* 1.06 male(s)/female
0-14 years: 1.06 male(s)/female
15-24 years: 1.03 male(s)/female
25-54 years: 0.87 male(s)/female
55-64 years: 0.88 male(s)/female
65 years and over: 0.91 male(s)/female
total population: 0.96 male(s)/female (2022 est.)

Mother's mean age at first birth: 20.4 years (2016 est.)
note: data represents median age at first birth among women 25-49

Maternal mortality ratio: 186 deaths/100,000 live births (2017 est.)

Infant mortality rate: *total:* 25.13 deaths/1,000 live births
male: 26.47 deaths/1,000 live births
female: 23.71 deaths/1,000 live births (2022 est.)

Life expectancy at birth: *total population:* 72.4 years
male: 71.66 years
female: 73.17 years (2022 est.)

Total fertility rate: 1.9 children born/woman (2022 est.)

Contraceptive prevalence rate: 46.7% (2019)

Drinking water source: *improved: urban:* 92.7% of population
rural: 94.4% of population
total: 94.1% of population
unimproved: urban: 7.3% of population
rural: 5.6% of population
total: 5.9% of population (2020 est.)

Current health expenditure: 4.5% of GDP (2019)

Physicians density: 0.85 physicians/1,000 population (2020)

Hospital bed density: 0.3 beds/1,000 population (2012)

Sanitation facility access: *improved: urban:* 95.1% of population
rural: 85.7% of population
total: 87.7% of population
unimproved: urban: 4.9% of population
rural: 14.3% of population
total: 12.3% of population (2020 est.)

HIV/AIDS - adult prevalence rate: 0.1% (2020 est.)

Major infectious diseases: *degree of risk:* high (2020)
food or waterborne diseases: bacterial diarrhea, hepatitis A and E, and typhoid fever
vectorborne diseases: Japanese encephalitis, malaria, and dengue fever

Obesity - adult prevalence rate: 4.1% (2016)

Alcohol consumption per capita: *total:* 0.36 liters of pure alcohol (2019 est.)
beer: 0.22 liters of pure alcohol (2019 est.)
wine: 0 liters of pure alcohol (2019 est.)
spirits: 0.13 liters of pure alcohol (2019 est.)
other alcohols: 0 liters of pure alcohol (2019 est.)

Tobacco use: *total:* 30.4% (2020 est.)
male: 47.9% (2020 est.)
female: 12.8% (2020 est.)

Children under the age of 5 years underweight: 24.4% (2019)

Child marriage: *women married by age 15:* 7.9%
women married by age 18: 32.8%
men married by age 18: 9% (2019 est.)

Education expenditures: 4.4% of GDP (2018 est.)

Literacy: *definition:* age 15 and over can read and write
total population: 67.9%
male: 78.6%
female: 59.7% (2018)

School life expectancy (primary to tertiary education): *total:* 13 years
male: 13 years
female: 13 years (2019)

Unemployment, youth ages 15-24: *total:* 21.4%
male: 19.7%
female: 23.9% (2017 est.)

ENVIRONMENT

Environment - current issues: deforestation (overuse of wood for fuel and lack of alternatives); forest degradation; soil erosion; contaminated water (with human and animal wastes, agricultural runoff, and industrial effluents); unmanaged solid-waste; wildlife conservation; vehicular emissions

Environment - international agreements: *party to:* Biodiversity, Climate Change, Climate Change-Kyoto Protocol, Climate Change-Paris Agreement, Desertification, Endangered Species, Hazardous Wastes, Law of the Sea, Nuclear Test Ban, Ozone Layer Protection, Wetlands
signed, but not ratified: Comprehensive Nuclear Test Ban, Marine Life Conservation

Air pollutants: *particulate matter emissions:* 94.33 micrograms per cubic meter (2016 est.)
carbon dioxide emissions: 9.11 megatons (2016 est.)
methane emissions: 41.15 megatons (2020 est.)

Climate: varies from cool summers and severe winters in north to subtropical summers and mild winters in south

Land use: *agricultural land:* 28.8% (2018 est.)
arable land: 15.1% (2018 est.)
permanent crops: 1.2% (2018 est.)
permanent pasture: 12.5% (2018 est.) forest: 25.4% (2018 est.) other: 45.8% (2018 est.)

Urbanization: *urban population:* 21.5% of total population (2022)
rate of urbanization: 3.09% annual rate of change (2020-25 est.)

Revenue from forest resources: *forest revenues:* 0.45% of GDP (2018 est.)

Revenue from coal: *coal revenues:* 0% of GDP (2018 est.)

Waste and recycling: *municipal solid waste generated annually:* 1,768,977 tons (2016 est.)

Major watersheds (area sq km): Indian Ocean drainage: Brahmaputra (651,335 sq km), Ganges (1,016,124 sq km), Indus (1,081,718 sq km)

Major aquifers: Indus-Ganges-Brahmaputra Basin

Total water withdrawal: *municipal:* 147.6 million cubic meters (2017 est.)
industrial: 29.5 million cubic meters (2017 est.)
agricultural: 9.32 billion cubic meters (2017 est.)

Total renewable water resources: 210.2 billion cubic meters (2017 est.)

GOVERNMENT

Country name: *conventional long form:* none
conventional short form: Nepal
local long form: none
local short form: Nepal
etymology: the Newar people of the Kathmandu Valley and surrounding areas apparently gave their name to the country; the terms "Nepal," "Newar," "Nepar," and "Newal" are phonetically different forms of the same word

Government type: federal parliamentary republic

Capital: *name:* Kathmandu
geographic coordinates: 27 43 N, 85 19 E
time difference: UTC+5.75 (10.75 hours ahead of Washington, DC, during Standard Time)
etymology: name derives from the Kasthamandap temple that stood in Durbar Square; in Sanskrit, kastha means "wood" and mandapa means "pavilion"; the three-story structure was made entirely of wood, without iron nails or supports, and dated to the late 16th century; it collapsed during a 2015 earthquake

Administrative divisions: 7 provinces (pradesh, singular - pradesh); Bagmati, Gandaki, Karnali, Lumbini, Madhesh, Province No. One, Sudurpashchim

Independence: 1768 (unified by Prithvi Narayan SHAH)

National holiday: Constitution Day, 20 September (2015); note - marks the promulgation of Nepal's constitution in 2015 and replaces the previous 28 May Republic Day as the official national day in Nepal; the Gregorian day fluctuates based on Nepal's Hindu calendar

Constitution: *history:* several previous; latest approved by the Second Constituent Assembly 16 September 2015, signed by the president and effective 20 September 2015
amendments: proposed as a bill by either house of the Federal Parliament; bills affecting a state border or powers delegated to a state must be submitted to the affected state assembly; passage of such bills requires a majority vote of that state assembly membership; bills not requiring state assembly consent require at least two-thirds majority vote by the membership of both houses of the Federal Parliament; parts of the constitution on the sovereignty, territorial integrity, independence, and sovereignty vested in the people cannot be amended; amended 2016, 2020

Legal system: English common law and Hindu legal concepts; note - new criminal and civil codes came into effect on 17 August 2018

International law organization participation: has not submitted an ICJ jurisdiction declaration; non-party state to the ICCt

Citizenship: *citizenship by birth:* yes
citizenship by descent only: yes
dual citizenship recognized: no
residency requirement for naturalization: 15 years

Suffrage: 18 years of age; universal

Executive branch: *chief of state:* President Bidhya Devi BHANDARI (since 29 October 2015); Vice President Nanda Bahadar PUN (since 31 October 2015)
head of government: Prime Minister Sher Bahadur DEUBA (since 13 July 2021); deputy prime ministers Ishwar POKHREL, Upendra YADAV (since 1 June 2018) (an)
cabinet: Council of Ministers appointed by the prime minister; cabinet dominated by the Nepal Communist Party

elections/appointments: president indirectly elected by an electoral college of the Federal Parliament and of the state assemblies for a 5-year term (eligible for a second term); election last held 13 March 2018 (next to be held in 2023); prime minister indirectly elected by the Federal Parliament
election results: Bidhya Devi BHANDARI reelected president; electoral vote - Bidhya Devi BHANDARI (CPN-UML) 39,275, Kumari Laxmi RAI (NC) 11,730

Legislative branch: *description:* bicameral Federal Parliament consists of:
National Assembly (59 seats; 56 members, including at least 3 women, 1 Dalit, 1 member with disabilities, or 1 minority indirectly elected by an electoral college of state and municipal government leaders, and 3 members, including 1 woman, nominated by the president of Nepal on the recommendation of the government; members serve 5-year terms with renewal of one-third of the membership every 2 years)
House of Representatives (275 seats statutory, current 271 with 4 vacant; 165 members directly elected in single-seat constituencies by simple majority vote and 110 members directly elected in a single nationwide constituency by closedlist proportional representation vote, with a threshold of 3% overall valid vote to be allocated a seat; members serve 5-year terms); note - the House of Representatives was dissolved on 22 May 2021, but on 13 July, the Supreme Court directed its reinstatement
elections: National Assembly - last held on 26 January 2022 (next to be held in 2024)
first election for House of Representatives held on 26 November and 7 December 2017 (next to be held on 20 November 2022)
election results: National Assembly - percent of vote by party - NA; seats by party - NCP 42, NC 13, FSFN 2, RJPN 2; composition - men 37, women 22, percent of women 37.3%
House of Representatives - percent of vote by party - NA; seats by party - NCP 174, NC 63, RJPN 17, FSFN 16, vacant 4, independent 1; composition - men 180, women 91, percent of women 33.6%; note - total Federal Parliament percent of women 33.8%

Judicial branch: *highest court(s):* Supreme Court (consists of the chief justice and up to 20 judges)
judge selection and term of office: Supreme Court chief justice appointed by the president upon the recommendation of the Constitutional Council, a 5-member, high-level advisory body headed by the prime minister; other judges appointed by the president upon the recommendation of the Judicial Council, a 5-member advisory body headed by the chief justice; the chief justice serves a 6-year term; judges serve until age 65
subordinate courts: High Court; district courts

Political parties and leaders: the Election Commission of Nepal granted ballot access under the proportional system to 88 political parties for the November-December 2017 House of Representatives election to the Federal Parliament; of these, the following 8 parties won seats:
Federal Socialist Forum, Nepal or FSFN [Upendra YADAV]
Naya Shakti Party, Nepal [Baburam BHATTARAI]
Nepal Communist Party or NCP [Khadga Prasad OLI, Pushpa Kamal DAHAL]
Nepali Congress or NC [Sher Bahadur DEUBA]
Nepal Mazdoor Kisan Party (Nepal Workers' and Peasants' Party) or NWPP [Narayan Man BIJUKCHHE]
Rastriya Janamorcha (National People's Front) [Chitra Bahadur K.C.]
Rastriya Janata Party (National People's Party, Nepal) or RJPN [Mahanta THAKUR]
Rastriya Prajatantra Party (National Democratic Party) or RPP [Rajendra Prasad LINGDEN]

International organization participation: ADB, BIMSTEC, CD, CP, FAO, G-77, IAEA, IBRD, ICAO, ICC (NGOs), ICRM, IDA, IFAD, IFC, IFRCS, ILO, IMF, IMO, Interpol, IOC, IOM, IPU, ISO, ITSO, ITU, ITUC (NGOs), MIGA, MINURSO, MINUSMA, MINUSTAH, MONUSCO, NAM, OPCW, SAARC, SACEP, UN, UNAMID, UNCTAD, UNDOF, UNESCO, UNHRC, UNIDO, UNIFIL, UNISFA, UNMIL, UNMISS, UNOCI, UNSOM, UNTSO, UNWTO, UPU, WCO, WFTU (NGOs), WHO, WIPO, WMO, WTO

Diplomatic representation in the US: *chief of mission:* Ambassador Sridhar KHATRI (since 19 April 2022)
chancery: 2730 34th Place NW, Washington, DC 20007
telephone: [1] (202) 667-4550
FAX: [1] (202) 667-5534
email address and website:
info@nepalembassyusa.org
https://us.nepalembassy.gov.np/
consulate(s) general: Chicago, New York

Diplomatic representation from the US: *chief of mission:* Ambassador Randy BERRY (since 25 October 2018)
embassy: Maharajgunj, Kathmandu
mailing address: 6190 Kathmandu Place, Washington DC 20521-6190
telephone: [977] (1) 423-4000
FAX: [977] (1) 400-7272
email address and website:
usembktm@state.gov
https://np.usembassy.gov/

Flag description: crimson red with a blue border around the unique shape of two overlapping right triangles; the smaller, upper triangle bears a white stylized moon and the larger, lower triangle displays a white 12-pointed sun; the color red represents the rhododendron (Nepal's national flower) and is a sign of victory and bravery, the blue border signifies peace and harmony; the two right triangles are a combination of two single pennons (pennants) that originally symbolized the Himalaya Mountains while their charges represented the families of the king (upper) and the prime minister, but today they are understood to denote Hinduism and Buddhism, the country's two main religions; the moon represents the serenity of the Nepalese people and the shade and cool weather in the Himalayas, while the sun depicts the heat and higher temperatures of the lower parts of Nepal; the moon and the sun are also said to express the hope that the nation will endure as long as these heavenly bodies
note: Nepal is the only country in the world whose flag is not rectangular or square

National symbol(s): rhododendron blossom; national color: red

National anthem: *name:* "Sayaun Thunga Phool Ka" (Hundreds of Flowers)
lyrics/music: Pradeep Kumar RAI/Ambar GURUNG
note: adopted 2007; after the abolition of the monarchy in 2006, a new anthem was required because of the previous anthem's praise for the king

National heritage: *total World Heritage Sites:* 4 (2 cultural, 2 natural)
selected World Heritage Site locales: Kathmandu Valley (c); Sagarmatha National Park (n); Chitwan National Park (n); Lumbini, Buddha Birthplace (c)

ECONOMY

Economic overview: Nepal is among the least developed countries in the world, with about one-quarter of its population living below the poverty line. Nepal is heavily dependent on remittances, which amount to as much as 30% of GDP. Agriculture is the mainstay of the economy, providing a livelihood for almost two-thirds of the population but accounting for less than a third of GDP. Industrial activity mainly involves the processing of agricultural products, including pulses, jute, sugarcane, tobacco, and grain.

Nepal has considerable scope for exploiting its potential in hydropower, with an estimated 42,000 MW of commercially feasible capacity. Nepal has signed trade and investment agreements with India, China, and other countries, but political uncertainty and a difficult business climate have hampered foreign investment. The United States and Nepal signed a $500 million Millennium Challenge Corporation Compact in September 2017 which will expand Nepal's electricity infrastructure and help maintain transportation infrastructure.

Massive earthquakes struck Nepal in early 2015, which damaged or destroyed infrastructure and homes and set back economic development. Although political gridlock and lack of capacity have hindered post-earthquake recovery, government-led reconstruction efforts have progressively picked up speed, although many hard hit areas still have seen little assistance. Additional challenges to Nepal's growth include its landlocked geographic location, inconsistent electricity supply, and underdeveloped transportation infrastructure.

Real GDP (purchasing power parity): $110.72 billion (2020 est.)
$113.08 billion (2019 est.)
$106.03 billion (2018 est.)
note: data are in 2017 dollars

Real GDP growth rate: 7.9% (2017 est.)
0.6% (2016 est.)
3.3% (2015 est.)

Real GDP per capita: $3,800 (2020 est.)
$4,000 (2019 est.)
$3,800 (2018 est.)
note: data are in 2017 dollars

GDP (official exchange rate): $24.88 billion (2017 est.)

Inflation rate (consumer prices): 4.5% (2017 est.)
9.9% (2016 est.)

GDP - composition, by sector of origin: *agriculture:* 27% (2017 est.)
industry: 13.5% (2017 est.)
services: 59.5% (2017 est.)

GDP - composition, by end use: *household consumption:* 78% (2017 est.)
government consumption: 11.7% (2017 est.)
investment in fixed capital: 33.8% (2017 est.)
investment in inventories: 8.7% (2017 est.)
exports of goods and services: 9.8% (2017 est.)

imports of goods and services: -42% (2017 est.)

Agricultural products: rice, vegetables, sugar cane, potatoes, maize, wheat, buffalo milk, milk, fruit, mangoes/guavas

Industries: tourism, carpets, textiles; small rice, jute, sugar, and oilseed mills; cigarettes, cement and brick production

Industrial production growth rate: 12.4% (2017 est.)

Labor force: 16.81 million (2017 est.)
note: severe lack of skilled labor

Labor force - by occupation: *agriculture:* 69%
industry: 12%
services: 19% (2015 est.)

Unemployment rate: 3% (2017 est.)
3.2% (2016 est.)

Unemployment, youth ages 15-24: *total:* 21.4%
male: 19.7%
female: 23.9% (2017 est.)

Population below poverty line: 25.2% (2011 est.)

Gini Index coefficient - distribution of family income: 32.8 (2010 est.)
47.2 (2008 est.)

Household income or consumption by percentage share: *lowest 10%:* 3.2%
highest 10%: 29.5% (2011)

Budget: *revenues:* 5.925 billion (2017 est.)
expenditures: 5.945 billion (2017 est.)

Budget surplus (+) or deficit (-): -0.1% (of GDP) (2017 est.)

Public debt: 26.4% of GDP (2017 est.)
27.9% of GDP (2016 est.)

Taxes and other revenues: 23.8% (of GDP) (2017 est.)

Fiscal year: 16 July - 15 July

Current account balance: -$93 million (2017 est.)
$1.339 billion (2016 est.)

Exports: $1.79 billion (2020 est.) note: data are in current year dollars
$2.73 billion (2019 est.) note: data are in current year dollars
$2.68 billion (2018 est.) note: data are in current year dollars Exports - partners India 68%, United States 10% (2019)

Exports - commodities: palm oil, clothing and apparel, carpets, soybean oil, flavored water (2019)

Imports: $10.68 billion (2020 est.) note: data are in current year dollars
$13.83 billion (2019 est.) note: data are in current year dollars
$14.65 billion (2018 est.) note: data are in current year dollars

Imports - partners: India 70%, China 15% (2019)

Imports - commodities: refined petroleum, iron, broadcasting equipment, natural gas, rice (2019)
Reserves of foreign exchange and gold
$9.091 billion (31 December 2017 est.)
$8.506 billion (31 December 2016 est.)

Debt - external: $5.849 billion (31 December 2017 est.)
$4.321 billion (31 December 2016 est.)

Exchange rates: Nepalese rupees (NPR) per US dollar - 104 (2017 est.)
107.38 (2016 est.)
107.38 (2015 est.)
102.41 (2014 est.)
99.53 (2013 est.)

ENERGY

Electricity access: *electrification - total population:* 93% (2019)
electrification - urban areas: 94% (2019)
electrification - rural areas: 93% (2019)

Electricity: *installed generating capacity:* 1.392 million kW (2020 est.)
consumption: 4.676 billion kWh (2019 est.)
exports: 107 million kWh (2019 est.)
imports: 1.729 billion kWh (2019 est.)
transmission/distribution losses: 1.183 billion kWh (2019 est.)

Electricity generation sources: *solar:* 2.6% of total installed capacity (2020 est.)
wind: 0.2% of total installed capacity (2020 est.)
hydroelectricity: 97.2% of total installed capacity (2020 est.)

Coal: *production:* 28,000 metric tons (2020 est.)
consumption: 839,000 metric tons (2020 est.)
exports: 0 metric tons (2020 est.)
imports: 811,000 metric tons (2020 est.)
proven reserves: 1 million metric tons (2019 est.)

Petroleum: *total petroleum production:* 0 bbl/day (2021 est.)
refined petroleum consumption: 49,400 bbl/day (2019 est.)

Refined petroleum products - imports: 26,120 bbl/day (2015 est.)

Carbon dioxide emissions: 7.708 million metric tonnes of CO2 (2019 est.)
from coal and metallurgical coke: 1.051 million metric tonnes of CO2 (2019 est.)
from petroleum and other liquids: 6.657 million metric tonnes of CO2 (2019 est.)

Energy consumption per capita: 5.219 million Btu/person (2019 est.)

COMMUNICATIONS

Telephones - fixed lines: *total subscriptions:* 726,000 (2020 est.)
subscriptions per 100 inhabitants: 2 (2020 est.)

Telephones - mobile cellular: *total subscriptions:* 38.213 million (2020 est.)
subscriptions per 100 inhabitants: 131 (2020 est.)

Telecommunication systems: *general assessment:* in relation to its telecom sector, Nepal has several topographical and economic constraints which have impeded efforts to expand network infrastructure and improve the quality of service for end-users; the fixed line market remains underdeveloped, and as a result most traffic is channeled via mobile networks; fixed broadband penetration remains very low, though to address this the government has initiated several programs as part of the Digital Nepal Framework and the wider Optical Fiber Backbone Network Expansion Project, started in 2012; supported by the Rural Telecommunications Development Fund, the programs include building out fiber backbone infrastructure and using this to provide broadband to schools and community centers nationally; telcos have also invested in fiber networks, and competition in the market is intensifying; cheap fiber-based services launched in mid-2021 prompted responses from other ISPs to provide faster and more competitively priced offers; Nepal's mobile market is relatively developed, with a focus on LTE; in 2021, the regulator considered a range of spectrum bands which could be used for 5G (2021)
domestic: fixed-line less than 2 per 100 persons and mobile-cellular nearly 131 per 100 persons (2020)
international: country code - 977; Nepal, China and Tibet connected across borders with underground and all-dielectric self-supporting (ADSS) fiber-optic cables; radiotelephone communications; microwave and fiber landlines to India; satellite earth station - 1 Intelsat (Indian Ocean) (2019)

Broadcast media: state operates 3 TV stations, as well as national and regional radio stations; 117 television channels are licensed, among those 71 are cable television channels, three are distributed through Direct-To-Home (DTH) system, and four are digital terrestrial; 736 FM radio stations are licensed and at least 314 of those radio stations are community radio stations (2019)

Internet country code: .np

Internet users: *total:* 11,071,987 (2020 est.)
percent of population: 38% (2020 est.)

Broadband - fixed subscriptions: *total:* 1.27 million (2020 est.)
subscriptions per 100 inhabitants: 4 (2020 est.)

TRANSPORTATION

National air transport system: *number of registered air carriers:* 6 (2020)
inventory of registered aircraft operated by air carriers: 39
annual passenger traffic on registered air carriers: 3,296,953 (2018)
annual freight traffic on registered air carriers: 4.66 million (2018) mt-km

Civil aircraft registration country code prefix: 9N

Airports: *total:* 47 (2021)

Airports - with paved runways: *total:* 11
over 3,047 m: 1
1,524 to 2,437 m: 3
914 to 1,523 m: 6
under 914 m: 1 (2021)

Airports - with unpaved runways: *total:* 36
1,524 to 2,437 m: 1
914 to 1,523 m: 6
under 914 m: 29 (2021)

Railways: *total:* 59 km (2018)
narrow gauge: 59 km (2018) 0.762-m gauge

Roadways: *total:* 27,990 km (2016)
paved: 11,890 km (2016)
unpaved: 16,100 km (2016)

MILITARY AND SECURITY

Military and security forces: Ministry of Defense: Nepali Army (includes Air Wing); Ministry of Home Affairs: Nepal Police, Nepal Armed Police Force (2022)
note: the Nepal Armed Police Force is paramilitary force that is responsible for border and internal security, including counter-insurgency and counter-terrorism, and assisting the Army in the event of an external invasion

Military expenditures: 1.3% of GDP (2021 est.)
1.3% of GDP (2020 est.)
2.1% of GDP (2019) (approximately $1.1 billion)
2.3% of GDP (2018) (approximately $1.11 billion)
2.6% of GDP (2017) (approximately $1.12 billion)

Military and security service personnel strengths: approximately 95,000 active troops (including a small air wing of about 500 personnel) (2022)

Military equipment inventories and acquisitions: the Army's inventory includes a mix of older equipment largely of British, Chinese, Indian, Russian, and South African origin; since 2010, Nepal has received limited amounts of newer hardware from several countries, including China, Italy, and Russia (2022)

Military service age and obligation: 18 years of age for voluntary military service (including women); no conscription (2022)
note: as of 2020, women comprised about 5% of the active duty military Military deployments
790 Central African Republic (MINUSCA); 1,150 Democratic Republic of the Congo (MONUSCO); 400 Golan Heights (UNDOF); 870 Lebanon (UNIFIL); 235 Liberia (UNSMIL); 175 Mali (MINUSMA); 1,750 (plus about 220 police) South Sudan (UNMISS) (May 2022)

Military - note: Nepal became a member of the UN in 1955 and has been an active participant in UN peacekeeping operations since, sending its first military observers to a UN peacekeeping mission in 1958 and its first peacekeeping military contingent to Egypt in 1974

the British began to recruit Nepalese citizens (Gurkhas) into the East India Company Army during the Anglo-Nepalese War (1814-1816); the Gurkhas subsequently were brought into the British Indian Army and by 1914, there were 10 Gurkha regiments, collectively known as the Gurkha Brigade; following the partition of India in 1947, an agreement between Nepal, India, and Great Britain allowed for the transfer of the 10 regiments from the British Indian Army to the separate British and Indian armies; four regiments were transferred to the British Army, where they have since served continuously as the Brigade of Gurkhas; six Gurkha (aka Gorkha in India) regiments went to the new Indian Army; a seventh regiment was later added; Gurkhas are also recruited into the Singaporean Police and a special guard in the Sultanate of Brunei known as the Gurkha Reserve Unit (2022)

TERRORISM

Terrorist group(s): Indian Mujahedeen
note: details about the history, aims, leadership, organization, areas of operation, tactics, targets, weapons, size, and sources of support of the group(s) appear(s) in Appendix-T

TRANSNATIONAL ISSUES

Disputes - international: *Nepal-China:* China may have constructed 11 buildings in Nepal's Humla region in 2021
Nepal-India: joint border commission continues to work on contested sections of boundary with India, including the 400 sq km dispute over the source of the Kalapani River; the Kalapani issue resurfaced in November 2019 when India issued a new map showing the contested area within India's borders and then built a new road in the region through Lipulekh pass, an area controlled by India but claimed by Nepal; Nepal countered by amending its constitution and issuing its own map showing the disputed area within its borders; the countries prime ministers briefly discussed the border dispute in April 2022; India has instituted a stricter border regime to restrict transit of illegal cross-border activities

Refugees and internally displaced persons: *refugees (country of origin):* 12,540 (Tibet/China), 6,365 (Bhutan) (mid-year 2021)
stateless persons: undetermined (mid-year 2021)

Illicit drugs: illicit producer of cannabis and hashish for the domestic and international drug markets; transit point for opiates from Southeast Asia to the West

NETHERLANDS

INTRODUCTION

Background: The Dutch United Provinces declared their independence from Spain in 1579; during the 17th century, they became a leading seafaring and commercial power, with settlements and colonies around the world. After a 20-year French occupation, a Kingdom of the Netherlands was formed in 1815. In 1830, Belgium seceded and formed a separate kingdom. The Netherlands remained neutral in World War I but suffered German invasion and occupation in World War II. A modern, industrialized nation, the Netherlands is also a large exporter of agricultural products. The country was a founding member of NATO and the EEC (now the EU) and participated in the introduction of the euro in 1999. In October 2010, the former Netherlands Antilles was dissolved and the three smallest islands -Bonaire, Sint Eustatius, and Saba - became special municipalities in the Netherlands administrative structure. The larger islands of Sint Maarten and Curacao joined the Netherlands and Aruba as constituent countries forming the Kingdom of the Netherlands.

In February 2018, the Sint Eustatius island council (governing body) was dissolved and replaced by a government commissioner to restore the integrity of public administration. According to the Dutch Government, the intervention will be as "short as possible and as long as needed."

GEOGRAPHY

Location: Western Europe, bordering the North Sea, between Belgium and Germany Geographic coordinates 52 31 N, 5 46 E

Map references: Europe

Area: *total:* 41,543 sq km land: 33,893 sq km water: 7,650 sq km

Area - comparative: slightly less than twice the size of New Jersey

Land boundaries: *total:* 1,053 km
border countries (2): Belgium 478 km; Germany 575 km

Coastline: 451 km

Maritime claims: *territorial sea:* 12 nm
contiguous zone: 24 nm
exclusive fishing zone: 200 nm

Climate: temperate; marine; cool summers and mild winters

Terrain: mostly coastal lowland and reclaimed land (polders); some hills in southeast

Elevation: *highest point:* Mount Scenery (on the island of Saba in the Caribbean, now considered an integral part of the Netherlands following the dissolution of the Netherlands Antilles) 862 m
lowest point: Zuidplaspolder -7 m
mean elevation: 30 m
note: the highest point on continental Netherlands is Vaalserberg at 322 m Natural resources
natural gas, petroleum, peat, limestone, salt, sand and gravel, arable land

Land use: *agricultural land:* 55.1% (2018 est.)
arable land: 29.8% (2018 est.)
permanent crops: 1.1% (2018 est.)
permanent pasture: 24.2% (2018 est.)
forest: 10.8% (2018 est.)
other: 34.1% (2018 est.)

Irrigated land: 4,860 sq km (2012)

Major rivers (by length in km): Rhine river mouth (shared with Switzerland [s], Germany, and France) - 1,233 km
note – [s] after country name indicates river source; [m] after country name indicates river mouth

Major watersheds (area sq km): Atlantic Ocean drainage: Rhine-Maas (198,735 sq km)

Population distribution: an area known as the Randstad, anchored by the cities of Amsterdam, Rotterdam, the Hague, and Utrecht, is the most densely populated region; the north tends to be less dense, though sizeable communities can be found throughout the entire country

Natural hazards: flooding
volcanism: Mount Scenery (887 m), located on the island of Saba in the Caribbean, last erupted in 1640;;

Round Hill (601 m), a dormant volcano also known as The Quill, is located on the island of St. Eustatius in the Caribbean;; these islands are at the northern end of the volcanic island arc of the Lesser Antilles that extends south to Grenada

Geography - note: located at mouths of three major European rivers (Rhine, Maas or Meuse, and Schelde); about a quarter of the country lies below sea level and only about half of the land exceeds one meter above sea level

PEOPLE AND SOCIETY

Population: 17,400,824 (2022 est.)

Nationality: *noun:* Dutchman(men), Dutchwoman(women)
adjective: Dutch

Ethnic groups: Dutch 75.4%, EU (excluding Dutch) 6.4%, Turkish 2.4%, Moroccan 2.4%, Surinamese 2.1%, Indonesian 2%, other 9.3% (2021 est.)

Languages: Dutch (official); note - Frisian is an official language in Fryslan province; Frisian, Low Saxon, Limburgish, Romani, and Yiddish have protected status under the European Charter for Regional or Minority Languages; Dutch is the official language of the three special municipalities of the Caribbean Netherlands; English is a recognized regional language on Sint Eustatius and Saba; Papiamento is a recognized regional language on Bonaire
major-language sample(s): Het Wereld Feitenboek, een onmisbare bron van informatie. (Dutch)

Religions: Roman Catholic 20.1%, Protestant 14.8% (includes Dutch Reformed, Protestant Church of The Netherlands, Calvinist), Muslim 5%, other 5.9% (includes Hindu, Buddhist, Jewish), none 54.1% (2019 est.)

Age structure: *0-14 years:* 16.11% (male 1,425,547/female 1,358,894)
15-24 years: 11.91% (male 1,049,000/female 1,008,763)
25-54 years: 38.47% (male 3,334,064/female 3,313,238)
55-64 years: 13.69% (male 1,177,657/female 1,188,613)
65 years and over: 19.82% (male 1,558,241/female 1,866,380) (2020 est.)

Dependency ratios: *total dependency ratio:* 55.6
youth dependency ratio: 24.4
elderly dependency ratio: 31.2
potential support ratio: 3.2 (2020 est.)

Median age: *total:* 42.8 years
male: 41.6 years
female: 44 years (2020 est.)

Population growth rate: 0.36% (2022 est.)

Birth rate: 10.99 births/1,000 population (2022 est.)

Death rate: 9.24 deaths/1,000 population (2022 est.)

Net migration rate: 1.9 migrant(s)/1,000 population (2022 est.)

Population distribution: an area known as the Randstad, anchored by the cities of Amsterdam, Rotterdam, the Hague, and Utrecht, is the most densely populated region; the north tends to be less dense, though sizeable communities can be found throughout the entire country

Urbanization: *urban population:* 92.9% of total population (2022)
rate of urbanization: 0.59% annual rate of change (2020-25 est.)

Major urban areas - population: 1.166 million AMSTERDAM (capital), 1.015 million Rotterdam (2022)

Sex ratio: *at birth:* 1.05 male(s)/female
0-14 years: 1.05 male(s)/female
15-24 years: 1.04 male(s)/female
25-54 years: 1.01 male(s)/female
55-64 years: 0.99 male(s)/female
65 years and over: 0.67 male(s)/female
total population: 0.98 male(s)/female (2022 est.)

Mother's mean age at first birth: 30.2 years (2020 est.)

Maternal mortality ratio: 5 deaths/100,000 live births (2017 est.)

Infant mortality rate: *total:* 3.4 deaths/1,000 live births
male: 3.76 deaths/1,000 live births
female: 3.02 deaths/1,000 live births (2022 est.)

Life expectancy at birth: *total population:* 82.16 years
male: 79.93 years
female: 84.49 years (2022 est.)

Total fertility rate: 1.78 children born/woman (2022 est.)

Contraceptive prevalence rate: 73% (2013)
note: percent of women aged 18-45

Drinking water source: *improved: urban:* 100% of population
rural: 100% of population
total: 100% of population

Current health expenditure: 10.1% of GDP (2019)

Physicians density: 4.08 physicians/1,000 population (2020)

Hospital bed density: 3.2 beds/1,000 population (2018)

Sanitation facility access: *improved: urban:* 100% of population
rural: 100% of population
total: 100% of population

HIV/AIDS - adult prevalence rate: 0.2% (2020 est.)

Obesity - adult prevalence rate: 20.4% (2016)

Alcohol consumption per capita: *total:* 8.23 liters of pure alcohol (2019 est.)
beer: 3.95 liters of pure alcohol (2019 est.)
wine: 2.92 liters of pure alcohol (2019 est.)
spirits: 1.36 liters of pure alcohol (2019 est.)
other alcohols: 0 liters of pure alcohol (2019 est.)

Tobacco use: *total:* 22.2% (2020 est.)
male: 24.4% (2020 est.)
female: 19.9% (2020 est.)

Education expenditures: 5.4% of GDP (2018 est.)

School life expectancy (primary to tertiary education): *total:* 19 years
male: 18 years
female: 19 years (2018)

Unemployment, youth ages 15-24: *total:* 9.1%
male: 9.2%
female: 9% (2020 est.)

ENVIRONMENT

Environment - current issues: water and air pollution are significant environmental problems; pollution of the country's rivers from industrial and agricultural chemicals, including heavy metals, organic compounds, nitrates, and phosphates; air pollution from vehicles and refining activities

Environment - international agreements: *party to:* Air Pollution, Air Pollution-Heavy Metals, Air Pollution-Multi-effect Protocol, Air Pollution-Nitrogen Oxides, Air Pollution-Persistent Organic Pollutants, Air Pollution-Sulphur 85, Air Pollution-Sulphur 94, Air Pollution-Volatile Organic Compounds, Antarctic-Environmental Protection, Antarctic-Marine Living Resources, Antarctic Treaty, Biodiversity, Climate Change, Climate Change-Kyoto Protocol, Climate Change-Paris Agreement, Comprehensive Nuclear Test Ban, Desertification, Endangered Species, Environmental Modification, Hazardous Wastes, Law of the Sea, Marine DumpingLondon Convention, Marine Dumping-London Protocol, Marine Life Conservation, Nuclear Test Ban, Ozone Layer Protection, Ship Pollution, Tropical Timber 2006, Wetlands, Whaling
signed, but not ratified: none of the selected agreements Air pollutants
particulate matter emissions: 12.07 micrograms per cubic meter (2016 est.)
carbon dioxide emissions: 170.78 megatons (2016 est.)
methane emissions: 17.79 megatons (2020 est.)

Climate: temperate; marine; cool summers and mild winters

Land use: *agricultural land:* 55.1% (2018 est.)
arable land: 29.8% (2018 est.)
permanent crops: 1.1% (2018 est.)
permanent pasture: 24.2% (2018 est.)
forest: 10.8% (2018 est.)
other: 34.1% (2018 est.)

Urbanization: *urban population:* 92.9% of total population (2022)
rate of urbanization: 0.59% annual rate of change (2020-25 est.)

Revenue from forest resources: *forest revenues:* 0.01% of GDP (2018 est.)

Revenue from coal: *coal revenues:* 0% of GDP (2018 est.)

Waste and recycling: *municipal solid waste generated annually:* 8.855 million tons (2015 est.)
municipal solid waste recycled annually: 2,179,216 tons (2015 est.)
percent of municipal solid waste recycled: 24.6% (2015 est.)

Major rivers (by length in km): Rhine river mouth (shared with Switzerland [s], Germany, and France) - 1,233 km
note – [s] after country name indicates river source; [m] after country name indicates river mouth

Major watersheds (area sq km): Atlantic Ocean drainage: Rhine-Maas (198,735 sq km)

Total water withdrawal: *municipal:* 1.26 billion cubic meters (2017 est.)
industrial: 14.74 billion cubic meters (2017 est.)
agricultural: 76.5 million cubic meters (2017 est.)

Total renewable water resources: 91 billion cubic meters (2017 est.)

GOVERNMENT

Country name: *conventional long form:* Kingdom of the Netherlands
conventional short form: Netherlands
local long form: Koninkrijk der Nederlanden
local short form: Nederland abbreviation: NL
etymology: the country name literally means "the lowlands" and refers to the geographic features of

the land being both flat and down river from higher areas (i.e., at the estuaries of the Scheldt, Meuse, and Rhine Rivers; only about half of the Netherlands is more than 1 meter above sea level)

Government type: parliamentary constitutional monarchy; part of the Kingdom of the Netherlands
Capital
name: Amsterdam; note - The Hague is the seat of government
geographic coordinates: 52 21 N, 4 55 E
time difference: UTC+1 (6 hours ahead of Washington, DC, during Standard Time)
daylight saving time: +1hr, begins last Sunday in March; ends last Sunday in October
time zone note: time descriptions apply to the continental Netherlands only, for the constituent countries in the Caribbean, the time difference is UTC-4
etymology: the original Dutch name, Amstellerdam, meaning "a dam on the Amstel River," dates to the 13th century; over time the name simplified to Amsterdam

Administrative divisions: 12 provinces (provincies, singular - provincie), 3 public entities* (openbare lichamen, singular - openbaar lichaam (Dutch); entidatnan publiko, singular - entidat publiko (Papiamento)); Bonaire*, Drenthe, Flevoland, Fryslan (Friesland), Gelderland, Groningen, Limburg, Noord-Brabant (North Brabant), Noord-Holland (North Holland), Overijssel, Saba*, Sint Eustatius*, Utrecht, Zeeland (Zealand), Zuid-Holland (South Holland)
note 1: the Netherlands is one of four constituent countries of the Kingdom of the Netherlands; the other three, Aruba, Curacao, and Sint Maarten, are all islands in the Caribbean; while all four parts are considered equal partners, in practice, most of the Kingdom's affairs are administered by the Netherlands, which makes up about 98% of the Kingdom's total land area and population
note 2: although Bonaire, Saba, and Sint Eustatius are officially incorporated into the country of the Netherlands under the broad designation of "public entities," Dutch Government sources regularly apply to them the more descriptive term of "special municipalities"; Bonaire, Saba, and Sint Eustatius are collectively referred to as the Caribbean Netherlands

Independence: 23 January 1579 (the northern provinces of the Low Countries conclude the Union of Utrecht breaking with Spain; on 26 July 1581, they formally declared their independence with an Act of Abjuration; however, it was not until 30 January 1648 and the Peace of Westphalia that Spain recognized this independence)

National holiday: King's Day (birthday of King WILLEM-ALEXANDER), 27 April (1967); note - King's or Queen's Day are observed on the ruling monarch's birthday; currently celebrated on 26 April if 27 April is a Sunday

Constitution: *history:* many previous to adoption of the "Basic Law of the Kingdom of the Netherlands" on 24 August 1815; revised 8 times, the latest in 1983
amendments: proposed as an Act of Parliament by or on behalf of the king or by the Second Chamber of the States General; the Second Chamber is dissolved after its first reading of the Act; passage requires a second reading by both the First Chamber and the newly elected Second Chamber, followed by at least two-thirds majority vote of both chambers, and ratification by the king; amended many times, last in 2018

Legal system: civil law system based on the French system; constitution does not permit judicial review of acts of the States General

International law organization participation: accepts compulsory ICJ jurisdiction with reservations; accepts ICCt jurisdiction

Citizenship: *citizenship by birth:* no
citizenship by descent only: at least one parent must be a citizen of the Netherlands
dual citizenship recognized: no
residency requirement for naturalization: 5 years

Suffrage: 18 years of age; universal

Executive branch: *chief of state:* King WILLEM-ALEXANDER (since 30 April 2013); Heir Apparent Princess CATHARINA-AMALIA (daughter of King WILLEM-ALEXANDER, born 7 December 2003)
head of government: Prime Minister Mark RUTTE (since 14 October 2010); Deputy Prime Ministers Sigrid KAAG and Wopke HOEKSTRA (since 10 January 2022) and Carola SCHOUTEN (since 26 October 2017); note - Mark RUTTE heads his fourth cabinet
cabinet: Council of Ministers appointed by the monarch
elections/appointments: the monarchy is hereditary; following Second Chamber elections, the leader of the majority party or majority coalition is usually appointed prime minister by the monarch; deputy prime ministers are appointed by the monarch

Legislative branch: *description:* bicameral States General or Staten Generaal consists of: Senate or Eerste Kamer (75 seats; members indirectly elected by the country's 12 provincial council members by proportional representation vote; members serve 4-year terms)
House of Representatives or Tweede Kamer (150 seats; members directly elected in multi-seat constituencies by open-list proportional representation vote to serve up to 4-year terms)
elections: First Chamber - last held on 27 May 2019 (next to be held in May 2023)
Second Chamber - last held on 15-17 March 2021 (next to be held on 31 March 2025)
election results: First Chamber - percent of vote by party - VVD 16%, CDA 12%, GL 10.7%, D66 9.3%, PvdA 8%, PVV 6.7%, SP 5.3%, CU 5.3%, PvdD 4%, SGP 2.7%, 50Plus 2.7%, FvD 1.3%, other 16%; seats by party - VVD 12, CDA 9, GL 8, D66 7, PvdA 6, PVV 5, SP 4, CU 4, PvdD 3, SGP 2, 50Plus 2, FvD 1, other 12; composition (as of September 2021) - men 52, women 23, percent of women 30.7%
Second Chamber - percent of vote by party - VVD 21.9%, D66 15%, PVV 10.8%, CDA 9.5%, SP 9.1%, PvdA 5.7%, GL 5.2%, FvD 5%, PvdD 3.8%, CU 3.4%, other 13.7%; seats by party - VVD 34, D66 24, PVV 17, CDA 15, GL 8, FvD 8, PvdD 6, PvdA 9, SP 9, CU 5, Denk 3, SGP 3, 50 Plus 1, other 6; composition (as of September 2021) - men 89, women 61, percent of women 40.7%; note - total States General percent of women 37.3%

Judicial branch: *highest court(s):* Supreme Court or Hoge Raad (consists of 41 judges: the president, 6 vice presidents, 31 justices or raadsheren, and 3 justices in exceptional service, referred to as buitengewone dienst); the court is divided into criminal, civil, tax, and ombuds chambers
judge selection and term of office: justices appointed by the monarch from a list provided by the Second Chamber of the States General; justices appointed for life or until mandatory retirement at age 70
subordinate courts: courts of appeal; district courts, each with up to 5 subdistrict courts; Netherlands Commercial Court

Political parties and leaders: Christian Democratic Appeal or CDA [Wopke HOEKSTRA]
Christian Union or CU [Gert-Jan SEGERS]
Democrats 66 or D66 [Sigrid KAAG]
Denk [Farid AZARKAN]
50Plus [Martin van ROOIJEN]
Forum for Democracy or FvD [Thierry BAUDET]
Green Left (GroenLinks) or GL [Jesse KLAVER]
Labor Party or PvdA (vacant)
Party for Freedom or PVV [Geert WILDERS]
Party for the Animals or PvdD [Esther OUWENHAND]
People's Party for Freedom and Democracy or VVD [Mark RUTTE]
Reformed Political Party or SGP [Kees VAN DER STAAIJ]
Socialist Party or SP [Lilian MARIJNISSEN]

International organization participation: ADB (nonregional member), AfDB (nonregional member), Arctic Council (observer), Australia Group, Benelux, BIS, CBSS (observer), CD, CE, CERN, EAPC, EBRD, ECB, EIB, EITI (implementing country), EMU, ESA, EU, FAO, FATF, G-10, IADB, IAEA, IBRD, ICAO, ICC (national committees), ICCt, ICRM, IDA, IEA, IFAD, IFC, IFRCS, IGAD (partners), IHO, ILO, IMF, IMO, IMSO, Interpol, IOC, IOM, IPU, ISO, ITSO, ITU, ITUC (NGOs), MIGA, MINUSMA, NATO, NEA, NSG, OAS (observer), OECD, OPCW, OSCE, Pacific Alliance (observer), Paris Club, PCA, Schengen Convention, SELEC (observer), UN, UNCTAD, UNDOF, UNESCO, UNHCR, UNHRC, UNIDO, UNMISS, UNRWA, UN Security Council (temporary), UNTSO, UNWTO, UPU, Wassenaar Arrangement, WCO, WHO, WIPO, WMO, WTO, ZC

Diplomatic representation in the US: *chief of mission:* Ambassador Andre HASPELS (since 16 September 2019)
chancery: 4200 Linnean Avenue NW, Washington, DC 20008
telephone: [1] (202) 244-5300
FAX: [1] (202) 362-3430
email address and website:
https://www.netherlandsworldwide.nl/countries/united-states/about-us/embassy-in-washington-dc
consulate(s) general: Atlanta, Chicago, Miami, New York, San Francisco

Diplomatic representation from the US: *chief of mission:* Ambassador (vacant); Charge d'Affaires Marja VERLOOP (since 17 January 2021)
embassy: John Adams Park 1, 2244 BZ Wassenaar
mailing address: 5780 Amsterdam Place, Washington DC 20521-5780
telephone: [31] (70) 310-2209
FAX: [31] (70) 310-2207
email address and website:
AmsterdamUSC@state.gov
https://nl.usembassy.gov/
consulate(s) general: Amsterdam

Flag description: three equal horizontal bands of red (bright vermilion; top), white, and blue (cobalt); similar to the flag of Luxembourg, which uses a lighter blue and is longer; the colors were derived from those of WILLIAM I, Prince of Orange, who led the Dutch Revolt against Spanish sovereignty in the latter half of the 16th century; originally the upper band was orange, but because its dye tended to turn red over time, the red shade was eventually made the permanent color; the banner is perhaps the oldest tricolor in continuous use

National symbol(s): lion, tulip; national color: orange

National anthem: *name:* "Het Wilhelmus" (The William)
lyrics/music: Philips VAN MARNIX van Sint Aldegonde (presumed)/unknown
note: adopted 1932, in use since the 17th century, making it the oldest national anthem in the world; also known as "Wilhelmus van Nassouwe" (William of Nassau), it is in the form of an acrostic, where the first letter of each stanza spells the name of the leader of the Dutch Revolt

National heritage: *total World Heritage Sites:* 12 (11 cultural, 1 natural); note - includes one site in Curacao
selected World Heritage Site locales: Schokland and Surroundings (c); Dutch Water Defense Lines (c); Van Nellefabriek (c); Mill Network at Kinderdijk-Elshout (c); Droogmakerij de Beemster (Beemster Polder) (c); Rietveld Schröderhuis (Rietveld Schröder House) (c); Wadden Sea (n); Seventeenth Century Canal Ring Area of Amsterdam inside the Singelgracht (c); Colonies of Benevolence (c); Frontiers of the Roman Empire - The Lower German Limes (c)

ECONOMY

Economic overview: The Netherlands, the sixth-largest economy in the European Union, plays an important role as a European transportation hub, with a consistently high trade surplus, stable industrial relations, and low unemployment. Industry focuses on food processing, chemicals, petroleum refining, and electrical machinery. A highly mechanized agricultural sector employs only 2% of the labor force but provides large surpluses for food-processing and underpins the country's status as the world's second largest agricultural exporter.

The Netherlands is part of the euro zone, and as such, its monetary policy is controlled by the European Central Bank. The Dutch financial sector is highly concentrated, with four commercial banks possessing over 80% of banking assets, and is four times the size of Dutch GDP.

In 2008, during the financial crisis, the government budget deficit hit 5.3% of GDP. Following a protracted recession from 2009 to 2013, during which unemployment doubled to 7.4% and household consumption contracted for four consecutive years, economic growth began inching forward in 2014. Since 2010, Prime Minister Mark RUTTE's government has implemented significant austerity measures to improve public finances and has instituted broad structural reforms in key policy areas, including the labor market, the housing sector, the energy market, and the pension system. In 2017, the government budget returned to a surplus of 0.7% of GDP, with economic growth of 3.2%, and GDP per capita finally surpassed pre-crisis levels. The fiscal policy announced by the new government in the 2018-2021 coalition plans for increases in government consumption and public investment, fueling domestic demand and household consumption and investment. The new government's policy also plans to increase demand for workers in the public and private sector, forecasting a further decline in the unemployment rate, which hit 4.8% in 2017.

Real GDP (purchasing power parity): $945.48 billion (2020 est.)
$982.22 billion (2019 est.)
$966.02 billion (2018 est.)
note: data are in 2017 dollars

Real GDP growth rate: 1.63% (2019 est.)
2.32% (2018 est.)
3.02% (2017 est.)

Real GDP per capita: $54,200 (2020 est.)
$56,600 (2019 est.)
$56,100 (2018 est.)
note: data are in 2017 dollars

GDP (official exchange rate): $907.042 billion (2019 est.)

Inflation rate (consumer prices): 2.6% (2019 est.)
1.7% (2018 est.)
1.3% (2017 est.)

Credit ratings:

Fitch rating: AAA (1994)

Moody's rating: Aaa (1986)

Standard & Poors rating: AAA (2015)
note: The year refers to the year in which the current credit rating was first obtained.

GDP - composition, by sector of origin: *agriculture:* 1.6% (2017 est.)
industry: 17.9% (2017 est.)
services: 70.2% (2017 est.)

GDP - composition, by end use: *household consumption:* 44.3% (2017 est.)
government consumption: 24.2% (2017 est.)
investment in fixed capital: 20.5% (2017 est.)
investment in inventories: 0.2% (2017 est.)
exports of goods and services: 83% (2017 est.)
imports of goods and services: -72.3% (2017 est.)

Agricultural products: milk, potatoes, sugar beet, pork, onions, wheat, poultry, tomatoes, carrots/turnips, beef

Industries: agroindustries, metal and engineering products, electrical machinery and equipment, chemicals, petroleum, construction, microelectronics, fishing

Industrial production growth rate: 3.3% (2017 est.)

Labor force: 8.907 million (2020 est.)

Labor force - by occupation: *agriculture:* 1.2%
industry: 17.2%
services: 81.6% (2015 est.)

Unemployment rate: 3.41% (2019 est.)
3.84% (2018 est.)

Unemployment, youth ages 15-24: *total:* 9.1%
male: 9.2%
female: 9% (2020 est.)

Population below poverty line: 13.6% (2019 est.)

Gini Index coefficient - distribution of family income: 28.5 (2017 est.)
25.1 (2013 est.)

Household income or consumption by percentage share: *lowest 10%:* 2.3%
highest 10%: 24.9% (2014 est.)

Budget: *revenues:* 361.4 billion (2017 est.)
expenditures: 352.4 billion (2017 est.)

Budget surplus (+) or deficit (-): 1.1% (of GDP) (2017 est.)

Public debt: 56.5% of GDP (2017 est.)
61.3% of GDP (2016 est.)
note: data cover general government debt and include debt instruments issued (or owned) by government entities other than the treasury; the data include treasury debt held by foreign entities; the data include debt issued by subnational entities, as well as intragovernmental debt; intragovernmental debt consists of treasury borrowings from surpluses in the social funds, such as for retirement, medical care, and unemployment, debt instruments for the social funds are not sold at public auctions

Taxes and other revenues: 43.4% (of GDP) (2017 est.)

Fiscal year: calendar year

Current account balance: $90.207 billion (2019 est.)
$98.981 billion (2018 est.)

Exports: $719.78 billion (2020 est.) note: data are in current year dollars
$755.77 billion (2019 est.) note: data are in current year dollars
$773.74 billion (2018 est.) note: data are in current year dollars

Exports - partners: Germany 20%, Belgium 12%, United Kingdom 9%, France 7%, United States 5% (2019)

Exports - commodities: refined petroleum, packaged medicines, broadcasting equipment, photography equipment, computers (2019)

Imports: $622.66 billion (2020 est.) note: data are in current year dollars
$661.18 billion (2019 est.) note: data are in current year dollars
$677.38 billion (2018 est.) note: data are in current year dollars

Imports - partners: Germany 15%, China 11%, Belgium 9%, United States 8%, Russia 7%, United Kingdom 5% (2019)

Imports - commodities: crude petroleum, refined petroleum, broadcasting equipment, computers, cars (2019)

Reserves of foreign exchange and gold: $38.44 billion (31 December 2017 est.)
$38.21 billion (31 December 2015 est.)

Debt - external: $4,345,413,000,000 (2019 est.)
$4,625,016,000,000 (2018 est.)

Exchange rates: euros (EUR) per US dollar -
0.82771 (2020 est.)
0.90338 (2019 est.)
0.87789 (2018 est.)
0.885 (2014 est.)
0.7634 (2013 est.)

ENERGY

Electricity access: *electrification - total population:* 100% (2020)

Electricity: *installed generating capacity:* 43.409 million kW (2020 est.)
consumption: 109.796 billion kWh (2020 est.)
exports: 22.433 billion kWh (2020 est.)
imports: 19.773 billion kWh (2020 est.)
transmission/distribution losses: 5.059 billion kWh (2020 est.)

Electricity generation sources: *fossil fuels:* 68.3% of total installed capacity (2020 est.)
nuclear: 3.3% of total installed capacity (2020 est.)
solar: 6.8% of total installed capacity (2020 est.)
wind: 13.1% of total installed capacity (2020 est.)
biomass and waste: 8.5% of total installed capacity (2020 est.)

Coal: *production:* 1.879 million metric tons (2020 est.)

consumption: 8.241 million metric tons (2020 est.)
exports: 20.164 million metric tons (2020 est.)
imports: 21.552 million metric tons (2020 est.)
proven reserves: 497 million metric tons (2019 est.)

Petroleum: *total petroleum production:* 76,100 bbl/day (2021 est.)
refined petroleum consumption: 915,200 bbl/day (2019 est.)
crude oil and lease condensate exports: 8,800 bbl/day (2018 est.)
crude oil and lease condensate imports: 1,096,500 bbl/day (2018 est.)
crude oil estimated reserves: 137.7 million barrels (2021 est.)

Refined petroleum products - production: 1.282 million bbl/day (2017 est.)

Refined petroleum products - exports: 2.406 million bbl/day (2017 est.)

Refined petroleum products - imports: 2.148 million bbl/day (2017 est.)

Natural gas: *production:* 32,857,597,000 cubic meters (2019 est.)
consumption: 44,752,918,000 cubic meters (2019 est.)
exports: 42,827,461,000 cubic meters (2019 est.)
imports: 55,767,276,000 cubic meters (2019 est.)
proven reserves: 132.608 billion cubic meters (2021 est.)

Carbon dioxide emissions: 214.416 million metric tonnes of CO2 (2019 est.)
from coal and metallurgical coke: 23.15 million metric tonnes of CO2 (2019 est.)
from petroleum and other liquids: 116.24 million metric tonnes of CO2 (2019 est.)
from consumed natural gas: 75.027 million metric tonnes of CO2 (2019 est.)

Energy consumption per capita: 219.606 million Btu/person (2019 est.)

COMMUNICATIONS

Telephones - fixed lines: *total subscriptions:* 4.937 million (2020 est.)
subscriptions per 100 inhabitants: 29 (2020 est.)

Telephones - mobile cellular: *total subscriptions:* 21.415 million (2020 est.)
subscriptions per 100 inhabitants: 125 (2020 est.)

Telecommunication systems: *general assessment:* telecom infrastructure in the Netherlands continues to be upgraded as modernization schemes undertaken by telcos make steady progress; other fiber providers have been supported by regulatory measures which have encouraged municipal governments to intervene with telcos' fiber builds, facilitating open access networks in a bid to make rollouts cheaper, and completed sooner; while the Mobile Network Operators (MNOs) are also closing down their Global System for Mobile Communication (MSM) and 3G networks and repurposing their spectrum and physical assets for LTE and 5G, the regulator has also encouraged GSM/3G roaming in the interim, thus safeguarding services such as machine to machine and other low data-use applications while individual MNOs disable their own GSM/3G networks; the country has one of the highest fixed broadband penetration rates in the world, with effective cross-platform competition between Digital Subscriber Line (DSL), Hybrid Fiber Coazial (HFC), and fiber networks; in the third quarter of 2020 the number of cable broadband connections fell for the first time, while the DSL segment has long been eclipsed by fiber; by the end of 2021, over a quarter of fixed broadband connections were on fiber infrastructure, while DSL accounted for only about 29%; almost 49% of fixed connections provided data above 100Mb/s, while an additional 43.7% provided data of at least 30Mb/s (2022)
domestic: extensive fixed-line, fiber-optic network; large cellular telephone system with five major operators utilizing the third generation of the Global System for Mobile Communications technology; one in five households now use Voice over the Internet Protocol services; fixed-line nearly 29 per 100 and mobile-cellular at 125 per 100 persons (2020)
international: country code - 31; landing points for Farland North, TAT-14, Circe North, Concerto, Ulysses 2, AC-1, UK-Netherlands 14, and COBRAcable submarine cables which provide links to the US and Europe; satellite earth stations -5 (3 Intelsat - 1 Indian Ocean and 2 Atlantic Ocean, 1 Eutelsat, and 1 Inmarsat) (2019)

Broadcast media: more than 90% of households are connected to cable or satellite TV systems that provide a wide range of domestic and foreign channels; public service broadcast system includes multiple broadcasters, 3 with a national reach and the remainder operating in regional and local markets; 2 major nationwide commercial television companies, each with 3 or more stations, and many commercial TV stations in regional and local markets; nearly 600 radio stations with a mix of public and private stations providing national or regional coverage

Internet country code: .nl

Internet users: *total:* 15,871,765 (2020 est.)
percent of population: 91% (2020 est.)

Broadband - fixed subscriptions: *total:* 7,525,016 (2020 est.)
subscriptions per 100 inhabitants: 44 (2020 est.)

TRANSPORTATION

National air transport system: *number of registered air carriers:* 8 (2020)
inventory of registered aircraft operated by air carriers: 238
annual passenger traffic on registered air carriers: 43,996,044 (2018)
annual freight traffic on registered air carriers: 5,886,510,000 (2018) mt-km

Civil aircraft registration country code prefix: PH

Airports: *total:* 29 (2021)

Airports - with paved runways: *total:* 23
over 3,047 m: 3
2,438 to 3,047 m: 11
1,524 to 2,437 m: 1
914 to 1,523 m: 6
under 914 m: 2 (2021)

Airports - with unpaved runways: *total:* 6
914 to 1,523 m: 4
under 914 m: 2 (2021)

Heliports: 1 (2021)

Pipelines: 14,000 km gas, 2,500 km oil and refined products, 3,000 km chemicals (2017)

Railways: *total:* 3,058 km (2016)
standard gauge: 3,058 km (2016) 1.435-m gauge (2,314 km electrified)

Roadways: *total:* 139,124 km (2016) (includes 3,654 km of expressways)

Waterways: 6,237 km (2012) (navigable by ships up to 50 tons)

Merchant marine: *total:* 1,199

by type: bulk carrier 10, container ship 40, general cargo 559, oil tanker 26, other 564 (2021)

Ports and terminals: *major seaport(s):* IJmuiden, Vlissingen
container port(s) (TEUs): Rotterdam (14,810,804) (2019)

LNG terminal(s) (import): Gate (Rotterdam)
river port(s): Amsterdam (Nordsee Kanaal); Moerdijk (Hollands Diep River); Rotterdam (Rhine River); Terneuzen (Western Scheldt River)

MILITARY AND SECURITY

Military and security forces: Netherlands (Dutch) Armed Forces (Nederlandse Krijgsmacht): Royal Netherlands Army, Royal Netherlands Navy (includes Naval Air Service and Marine Corps), Royal Netherlands Air Force, Royal Netherlands Marechaussee (Military Constabulary) (2022)
note: the Netherlands Coast Guard and the Dutch Caribbean Coast Guard are civilian in nature but managed by the Royal Netherlands Navy

Military expenditures: 1.7% of GDP (2022 est.)
1.5% of GDP (2021)
1.4% of GDP (2020)
1.3% of GDP (2019) (approximately $13.6 billion)
1.2% of GDP (2018) (approximately $12.3 billion)

Military and security service personnel strengths: approximately 40,000 active duty personnel (20,000 Army; 7,500 Navy; 6,500 Air Force; 6,000 Constabulary) (2022)
note: the Navy includes about 2,300 marines

Military equipment inventories and acquisitions: the military's inventory consists of a mix of domestically-produced and modern European- and US-sourced equipment; since 2010, the US has been the leading supplier of weapons systems to the Netherlands; the Netherlands has an advanced domestic defense industry that focuses on armored vehicles, naval ships, and air defense systems; it also participates with the US and other European countries on joint development and production of advanced weapons systems (2021)

Military service age and obligation: 17 years of age for voluntary service for men and women; the military is an all-volunteer force; conscription remains in place, but the requirement to show up for compulsory military service was suspended in 1997; must be a citizen of the Netherlands (2022)
note: in 2019, women made up about 11% of the military's full-time personnel Military deployments
270 Lithuania (NATO); 125 Slovakia (NATO) (2022)
note: in response to Russia's 2022 invasion of Ukraine, some NATO countries, including the Netherlands, have sent additional troops and equipment to the battlegroups deployed in NATO territory in eastern Europe

Military - note: the Netherlands is a member of NATO and was one of the original 12 countries to sign the North Atlantic Treaty (also known as the Washington Treaty) in 1949

since 1973, the Dutch Marine Corps has worked closely with the British Royal Marines, including jointly in the UK-Netherlands amphibious landing force; a Dutch Army airmobile infantry brigade and a mechanized infantry brigade have been integrated into the German Army since 2014 and 2016 respectively
in 2020, Belgium, Denmark, and the Netherlands formed a joint Composite Special Operations Component Command (C-SOCC); in 2015, Belgium, the Netherlands, and Luxembourg signed an agreement to conduct joint air policing of their territories; under the agreement, which went into effect in January of 2017, the Belgian and Dutch Air Forces trade responsibility for patrolling the skies over the three countries (2022)

TERRORISM

Terrorist group(s): Islamic State of Iraq and ash-Sham (ISIS)
note: details about the history, aims, leadership, organization, areas of operation, tactics, targets, weapons, size, and sources of support of the group(s) appear(s) in Appendix-T

TRANSNATIONAL ISSUES

Disputes - international: none identified

Refugees and internally displaced persons: *refugees (country of origin):* 37,792 (Syria), 14,787 (Eritrea), 8,368 (Somalia), 6,636 (Iraq), 5,346 (Iran) (mid-year 2021); 79,250 (Ukraine) (as of 30 September 2022)
stateless persons: 2,087 (mid-year 2021)

Illicit drugs: a significant transit country for illicit drugs, especially cocaine from South America destined for Europe; one of the largest sources of synthetic drugs for international markets; numerous methamphetamine laboratories; traffickers use postage companies to send cocaine, ecstasy or methamphetamines to global customers

NEW CALEDONIA

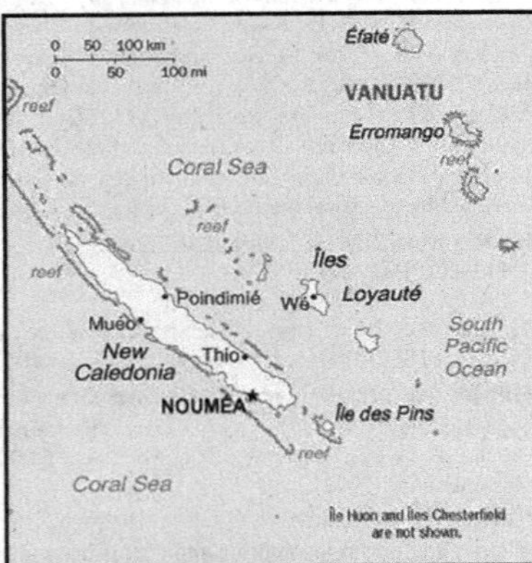

INTRODUCTION

Background: The first humans settled in New Caledonia around 1600 B.C. The Lapita were skilled navigators and evidence of their pottery around the Pacific has served as a guide for understanding human expansion in the region. Successive waves of migrants from other islands in Melanesia intermarried with the Lapita, giving rise to the Kanak ethnic group considered indigenous to New Caledonia. British explorer James COOK was the first European to visit New Caledonia in 1774, giving it the Latin name for Scotland. Missionaries first landed in New Caledonia in 1840. In 1853, France annexed New Caledonia to preclude any British attempt to claim the island. France declared it a penal colony in 1864 and sent more than 20,000 prisoners to New Caledonia in the ensuing three decades.

Nickel was discovered in 1864 and French prisoners were directed to mine it. France brought in indentured servants and enslaved labor from elsewhere in Southeast Asia to work the mines, blocking Kanaks from accessing the most profitable part of the local economy. In 1878, High Chief ATAI led a rebellion against French rule. The Kanaks were relegated to reservations, leading to periodic smaller uprisings and culminating in a large revolt in 1917 that was brutally suppressed by colonial authorities. During World War II, New Caledonia became an important base for Allied troops, and the US moved its South Pacific headquarters to the island in 1942. Following the war, New Caledonia was made an overseas territory and French citizenship was granted to all inhabitants in 1953, thereby permitting the Kanaks to move off the reservations.

The Kanak nationalist movement began in the 1950s but most voters chose to remain a territory in an independence referendum in 1958. The European population of New Caledonia boomed in the 1970s with a renewed focus on nickel mining, reigniting Kanak nationalism. Key Kanak leaders were assassinated in the early 1980s, leading to escalating violence and dozens of fatalities. The Matignon Accords of 1988 provided for a 10-year transition period. The Noumea Accord of 1998 transferred an increasing amount of governing responsibility from France to New Caledonia over a 20-year period and provided for three independence referenda. In the first held in 2018, voters rejected independence by 57 to 43 percent; in the second held in 2020, voters rejected independence 53 to 47 percent. In the third referendum held in December 2021, voters rejected independence 96 to 4 percent; however, a boycott by key Kanak groups spurred challenges about the legitimacy of the vote. In February 2021, pro-independence parties gained a majority in the New Caledonian Government for the first time.

GEOGRAPHY

Location: Oceania, islands in the South Pacific Ocean, east of Australia

Geographic coordinates: 21 30 S, 165 30 E

Map references: Oceania

Area: *total:* 18,575 sq km
land: 18,275 sq km
water: 300 sq km

Area - comparative: slightly smaller than New Jersey

Land boundaries: *total:* 0 km

Coastline: 2,254 km

Maritime claims: *territorial sea:* 12 nm
exclusive economic zone: 200 nm

Climate: tropical; modified by southeast trade winds; hot, humid

Terrain: coastal plains with interior mountains

Elevation: *highest point:* Mont Panie 1,628 m
lowest point: Pacific Ocean 0 m

Natural resources: nickel, chrome, iron, cobalt, manganese, silver, gold, lead, copper

Land use: *agricultural land:* 10.4% (2018 est.)
arable land: 0.4% (2018 est.)
permanent crops: 0.2% (2018 est.)
permanent pasture: 9.8% (2018 est.)
forest: 45.9% (2018 est.)
other: 43.7% (2018 est.)

Irrigated land: 100 sq km (2012)

Population distribution: most of the populace lives in the southern part of the main island, in and around the capital of Noumea

Natural hazards: cyclones, most frequent from November to March
volcanism: Matthew and Hunter Islands are historically active

Geography - note: consists of the main island of New Caledonia (one of the largest in the Pacific Ocean), the archipelago of Iles Loyaute, and numerous small, sparsely populated islands and atolls

PEOPLE AND SOCIETY

Population: 297,160 (2022 est.)

Nationality: *noun:* New Caledonian(s)
adjective: New Caledonian

Ethnic groups: Kanak 39.1%, European 27.1%, Wallisian, Futunian 8.2%, Tahitian 2.1%, Indonesian 1.4%, Ni-Vanuatu 1%, Vietnamese 0.9%, other 17.7%, unspecified 2.5% (2014 est.)

Languages: French (official), 33 Melanesian-Polynesian dialects
major-language sample(s): The World Factbook, une source indispensable d'informations de base. (French)

Religions: Christian 85.2%, Muslim 2.8%, other 1.6%, unaffiliated 10.4% (2020 est.)

Age structure: *0-14 years:* 21.74% (male 32,227/female 30,819)
15-24 years: 15.63% (male 23,164/female 22,163)
25-54 years: 43.73% (male 63,968/female 62,856)
55-64 years: 9.06% (male 12,700/female 13,568)
65 years and over: 9.84% (male 12,552/female 15,992) (2020 est.)

Dependency ratios: *total dependency ratio:* 46.6

youth dependency ratio: 32.4
elderly dependency ratio: 14.2
potential support ratio: 7 (2020 est.)

Median age: *total:* 32.9 years
male: 32.1 years
female: 33.7 years (2020 est.)

Population growth rate: 1.19% (2022 est.)

Birth rate: 14.13 births/1,000 population (2022 est.)

Death rate: 5.88 deaths/1,000 population (2022 est.)

Net migration rate: 3.66 migrant(s)/1,000 population (2022 est.)
note: there has been steady emigration from Wallis and Futuna to New Caledonia

Population distribution: most of the populace lives in the southern part of the main island, in and around the capital of Noumea

Urbanization: *urban population:* 72.3% of total population (2022)
rate of urbanization: 1.72% annual rate of change (2020-25 est.)

Major urban areas - population: 198,000 NOUMEA (capital) (2018)

Sex ratio: *at birth:* 1.05 male(s)/female
0-14 years: 1.04 male(s)/female
15-24 years: 1.04 male(s)/female
25-54 years: 1.02 male(s)/female
55-64 years: 0.94 male(s)/female
65 years and over: 0.59 male(s)/female
total population: 0.99 male(s)/female (2022 est.)

Infant mortality rate: *total:* 5 deaths/1,000 live births
male: 5.97 deaths/1,000 live births
female: 3.98 deaths/1,000 live births (2022 est.)

Life expectancy at birth: *total population:* 78.83 years
male: 74.93 years
female: 82.92 years (2022 est.)

Total fertility rate: 1.86 children born/woman (2022 est.)

Drinking water source: *improved: total:* 99.3% of population
unimproved: total: 0.7% of population (2020 est.)

Sanitation facility access: *improved: total:* 100% of population
unimproved: total: 0% of population (2020 est.)

Major infectious diseases: *degree of risk:* high (2020)
food or waterborne diseases: bacterial diarrhea
vectorborne diseases: malaria

Literacy: *definition:* age 15 and over can read and write
total population: 96.9%
male: 97.3%
female: 96.5% (2015)

Unemployment, youth ages 15-24: *total:* 38.4%
male: 37.1%
female: 40% (2014 est.)

ENVIRONMENT

Environment - current issues: preservation of coral reefs; prevention of invasive species; limiting erosion caused by nickel mining and forest fires

Air pollutants: *carbon dioxide emissions:* 5.33 megatons (2016 est.)

Climate: *tropical; modified by southeast trade winds; hot, humid*

Land use: *agricultural land:* 10.4% (2018 est.)
arable land: 0.4% (2018 est.)
permanent crops: 0.2% (2018 est.)
permanent pasture: 9.8% (2018 est.)
forest: 45.9% (2018 est.)
other: 43.7% (2018 est.)

Urbanization: *urban population:* 72.3% of total population (2022)
rate of urbanization: 1.72% annual rate of change (2020-25 est.)

Waste and recycling: *municipal solid waste generated annually:* 108,157 tons (2016 est.)

GOVERNMENT

Country name: *conventional long form:* Territory of New Caledonia and Dependencies
conventional short form: New Caledonia
local long form: Territoire des Nouvelle-Caledonie et Dependances
local short form: Nouvelle-Caledonie
etymology: British explorer Captain James COOK discovered and named New Caledonia in 1774; he used the appellation because the northeast of the island reminded him of Scotland (Caledonia is the Latin designation for Scotland)

Government type: parliamentary democracy (Territorial Congress); an overseas collectivity of France

Dependency status: special collectivity (or a sui generis collectivity) of France since 1998; note - independence referenda took place on 4 November 2018, 4 October 2020, and 12 December 2021 with a majority voting in each case to reject independence in favor of maintaining the status quo; an 18-month transition period is now in place (ending 30 June 2023), during which a referendum on the new status of New Caledonia within France will take place

Capital: *name:* Noumea
geographic coordinates: 22 16 S, 166 27 E
time difference: UTC+11 (16 hours ahead of Washington, DC, during Standard Time)
etymology: established in 1854 as Port-de-France, the settlement was renamed Noumea in 1866, in order to avoid any confusion with Fort-de-France in Martinique; the New Caledonian language of Ndrumbea (also spelled Ndumbea, Dubea, and Drubea) spoken in the area gave its name to the capital city, Noumea, as well as to the neighboring town (suburb) of Dumbea

Administrative divisions: 3 provinces; Province Iles (Islands Province), Province Nord (North Province), and Province Sud (South Province)

Independence: none (overseas collectivity of France); note - in three independence referenda, on 4 November 2018, 4 October 2020, and 12 December 2021, the majority voted to reject independence in favor of maintaining the status quo; an 18-month transition period is now in place (ending 30 June 2023), during which a referendum on the new status of New Caledonia within France will take place

National holiday: Fete de la Federation, 14 July (1790); note - the local holiday is New Caledonia Day, 24 September (1853)

Constitution: *history:* 4 October 1958 (French Constitution with changes as reflected in the Noumea Accord of 5 May 1998)
amendments: French constitution amendment procedures apply

Legal system: civil law system based on French civil law

Citizenship: see France

Suffrage: 18 years of age; universal

Executive branch: *chief of state:* President Emmanuel MACRON (since 14 May 2017); represented by High Commissioner Patrice FAURE (since 6 June 2021)
head of government: President of the Government Louis MAPOU (since 22 July 2021); Vice President Isabelle CHAMPMOREAU (since 22 July 2021)
cabinet: Cabinet elected from and by the Territorial Congress
elections/appointments: French president directly elected by absolute majority popular vote in 2 rounds if needed for a 5-year term (eligible for a second term); high commissioner appointed by the French president on the advice of the French Ministry of Interior; president of New Caledonia elected by Territorial Congress for a 5-year term (no term limits); election last held on 8 July 2021 (next to be held in 2026)
election results: 2021: Louis MAPOU elected president by Territorial Congress with 6 votes out of 11
2019: Thieryy SANTA elected president by Territorial Congress

Legislative branch: *description:* unicameral Territorial Congress or Congrès du Territoire (54 seats; members indirectly selected proportionally by the partisan makeup of the 3 Provincial Assemblies or Assemblés Provinciales; members of the 3 Provincial Assemblies directly elected by party-list proportional representation vote; members serve 5-year terms); note -the Customary Senate is the assembly of the various traditional councils of the Kanaks, the indigenous population, which rules on laws affecting the indigenous population
New Caledonia indirectly elects 2 members to the French Senate by an electoral colleges for a 6-year term with one seat renewed every 3 years and directly elects 2 members to the French National Assembly by absolute majority vote in 2 rounds if needed for a 5-year term
elections: Territorial Congress - last held on 12 May 2019 (next to be held in May 2024)
French Senate - election last held in September 2019 (next to be held not later than 2021)
French National Assembly - election last held on 11 and 18 June 2017 (next to be held by June 2022)
election results: Territorial Congress - percent of vote by party - N/A; seats by party - Future With Confidence 18, UNI 9, UC 9, CE 7, FLNKS 6, Oceanic Awakening 3, PT 1, LKS 1 (Anti-Independence 28, Pro-Independence 26); composition - NA
representation in French Senate - NA
representation in French National Assembly - NA
French Senate - percent of vote by party - NA; seats by party - UMP 2
French National Assembly - percent of vote by party - NA; seats by party - CE 2

Judicial branch: *highest court(s):* Court of Appeal in Noumea or Cour d'Appel; organized into civil, commercial, social, and pre-trial investigation chambers; court bench normally includes the court president and 2 counselors); Administrative Court (number of judges NA); note - final appeals beyond the Court of Appeal are referred to the Court of Cassation or Cour de Cassation (in Paris); final

appeals beyond the Administrative Court are referred to the Administrative Court of Appeal (in Paris)
judge selection and term of office: judge appointment and tenure based on France's judicial system
subordinate courts: Courts of First Instance include: civil, juvenile, commercial, labor, police, criminal, assizes, and also a pre-trial investigation chamber; Joint Commerce Tribunal; administrative courts

Political parties and leaders: Build Our Rainbow Nation
Caledonia Together or CE [Philippe GERMAIN]
Caledonian Union or UC [Daniel GOA]
Future Together (l'Avenir Ensemble) [Harold MARTIN] (dissolved 2017)
Kanak Socialist Front for National Liberation or FLNKS (alliance includes PALIKA, UNI, UC, and UPM) [Victor TUTUGORO]
Labor Party (Parti Travailliste) or PT [Louis Kotra UREGEI]
National Union for Independence (Union Nationale pour l'Independance) or UNI [Louis MAPOU]
Party of Kanak Liberation (Parti de Liberation Kanak) or PALIKA [Paul NEAOUTYINE]
Socialist Kanak Liberation or LKS [Nidoish NAISSELINE]
The Republicans (formerly The Rally or UMP) [Christian JACOB]
Union for Caledonia in France

International organization participation: ITUC (NGOs), PIF (associate member), SPC, UPU, WFTU (NGOs), WMO

Diplomatic representation in the US: none (overseas territory of France)

Diplomatic representation from the US: *embassy:* none (overseas territory of France)

Flag description: New Caledonia has two official flags; alongside the flag of France, the Kanak (indigenous Melanesian) flag has equal status; the latter consists of three equal horizontal bands of blue (top), red, and green; a large yellow disk - diameter two-thirds the height of the flag - shifted slightly to the hoist side is edged in black and displays a black fleche faitiere symbol, a native rooftop adornment

National symbol(s): fleche faitiere (native rooftop adornment), kagu bird; national colors: gray, red

National anthem: *name:* "Soyons unis, devenons freres" (Let Us Be United, Let Us Become Brothers)
lyrics/music: Chorale Melodia (a local choir)
note: adopted 2008; contains a mixture of lyrics in both French and Nengone (an indigenous language); as a self-governing territory of France, in addition to the local anthem, "La Marseillaise" is official (see France)

National heritage: *total World Heritage Sites:* 1 (natural); note - excerpted from the France entry
selected World Heritage Site locales: Lagoons of New Caledonia

ECONOMY

Economic overview: New Caledonia has 11% of the world's nickel reserves, representing the second largest reserves on the planet. Only a small amount of the land is suitable for cultivation, and food accounts for about 20% of imports. In addition to nickel, substantial financial support from France - equal to more than 15% of GDP - and tourism are keys to the health of the economy.

With the gradual increase in the production of two new nickel plants in 2015, average production of metallurgical goods stood at a record level of 94 thousand tons. However, the sector is exposed to the high volatility of nickel prices, which have been in decline since 2016. In 2017, one of the three major mining firms on the island, Vale, put its operations up for sale, triggering concerns of layoffs ahead of the 2018 independence referendum.

Real GDP (purchasing power parity): $11.11 billion (2017 est.)
$10.89 billion (2016 est.)
$10.77 billion (2015 est.)
note: data are in 2015 dollars

Real GDP growth rate: 2% (2017 est.)
1.1% (2016 est.)
3.2% (2015 est.)

Real GDP per capita: $31,100 (2015 est.)
$32,100 (2014 est.)
$29,800 (2012 est.)

GDP (official exchange rate): $9.77 billion (2017 est.)

Inflation rate (consumer prices): 1.4% (2017 est.)
0.6% (2016 est.)

GDP - composition, by sector of origin: *agriculture:* 1.4% (2017 est.)
industry: 26.4% (2017 est.)
services: 72.1% (2017 est.)

GDP - composition, by end use: *household consumption:* 64.3% (2017 est.)
government consumption: 24% (2017 est.)
investment in fixed capital: 38.4% (2017 est.)
investment in inventories: 0% (2017 est.)
exports of goods and services: 18.7% (2017 est.)
imports of goods and services: -45.5% (2017 est.)

Agricultural products: coconuts, vegetables, maize, fruit, beef, pork, potatoes, bananas, eggs, yams

Industries: nickel mining and smelting

Industrial production growth rate: 3.5% (2017 est.)

Labor force: 119,500 (2016 est.)

Labor force - by occupation: *agriculture:* 2.7%
industry: 22.4%
services: 74.9% (2010)

Unemployment rate: 14.7% (2014)
14% (2009)

Unemployment, youth ages 15-24: *total:* 38.4%
male: 37.1%
female: 40% (2014 est.)

Population below poverty line: 17% (2008)

Budget: *revenues:* 1.995 billion (2015 est.)
expenditures: 1.993 billion (2015 est.)

Budget surplus (+) or deficit (-): 0% (of GDP) (2015 est.)

Public debt: 6.5% of GDP (2015 est.)
6.5% of GDP (2014 est.)

Taxes and other revenues: 20.4% (of GDP) (2015 est.)

Fiscal year: calendar year

Current account balance: -$1.469 billion (2014 est.)
-$1.861 billion (2013 est.)

Exports: $2.207 billion (2014 est.)

Exports - partners: China 59%, South Korea 14%, Japan 11% (2019)

Exports - commodities: iron alloys, nickel, cobalt, carbonates, essential oils (2019)

Imports: $2.715 billion (2015 est.)
$4.4 billion (2014 est.)

Imports - partners: France 43%, Australia 12%, Singapore 12%, China 6% (2019)

Imports - commodities: refined petroleum, aircraft, coal, cars, packaged medicines (2019)

Debt - external: $112 million (31 December 2013 est.)
$79 million (31 December 1998 est.)

Exchange rates: Comptoirs Francais du Pacifique francs (XPF) per US dollar -
110.2 (2017 est.)
107.84 (2016 est.)
107.84 (2015 est.)
89.85 (2013 est.)
90.56 (2012 est.)

ENERGY

Electricity access: *electrification - total population:* 100% (2020)

Electricity: *installed generating capacity:* 1.071 million kW (2020 est.)
consumption: 2,940,707,000 kWh (2019 est.)
exports: 0 kWh (2020 est.)
imports: 0 kWh (2020 est.)
transmission/distribution losses: 64.293 million kWh (2019 est.)

Electricity generation sources: *fossil fuels:* 91.2% of total installed capacity (2020 est.)
wind: 1.5% of total installed capacity (2020 est.)
hydroelectricity: 7.4% of total installed capacity (2020 est.)

Coal: *production:* 0 metric tons (2020 est.)
consumption: 1.151 million metric tons (2020 est.)
exports: 0 metric tons (2020 est.)
imports: 1.151 million metric tons (2020 est.)
proven reserves: 2 million metric tons (2019 est.)

Petroleum: *total petroleum production:* 0 bbl/day (2021 est.)
refined petroleum consumption: 19,300 bbl/day (2019 est.)

Refined petroleum products - imports: 19,100 bbl/day (2015 est.)

Carbon dioxide emissions: 5.886 million metric tonnes of CO_2 (2019 est.)
from coal and metallurgical coke: 2.879 million metric tonnes of CO_2 (2019 est.)
from petroleum and other liquids: 3.007 million metric tonnes of CO_2 (2019 est.)

Energy consumption per capita: 0 Btu/person (2019 est.)

COMMUNICATIONS

Telephones - fixed lines: *total subscriptions:* 46,000 (2020 est.)
subscriptions per 100 inhabitants: 16 (2020 est.)

Telephones - mobile cellular: *total subscriptions:* 260,000 (2020 est.)
subscriptions per 100 inhabitants: 91 (2020 est.)

Telecommunication systems: *general assessment: New Caledonia's telecom sector provides fixed and mobile voice services, mobile internet, fixed broadband access, and wholesale services for other ISPs; the country is well serviced by extensive 3G and LTE networks, and is considered to have one of the highest smartphone*

adoption rates in the Pacific region; by 2025, smart phone penetration is expected to reach 71%; while DSL is still the dominant fixed broadband technology, and a nationwide FttP network; the South Pacific region has become a hub for submarine cable system developments in recent years, with further networks scheduled to come online later in 2021 and into 2022; these new cables are expected to increase competition in the region with regards to international capacity; in 2020, the government owned telco commissioned Alcatel Submarine Networks (ASN) to build the Gondwana-2 cable system to provide additional network capacity and complement the Gondwana-1 cable (2022)
domestic: fixed-line nearly 16 per 100 and mobile-cellular telephone subscribership 91 per 100 persons (2020)
international: country code - 687; landing points for the Gondwana-1 and Picot-1 providing connectivity via submarine cables around New Caledonia and to Australia; satellite earth station - 1 Intelsat (Pacific Ocean) (2019)

Broadcast media: the publicly owned French Overseas Network (RFO), which operates in France's overseas departments and territories, broadcasts over the RFO Nouvelle-Calédonie TV and radio stations; a small number of privately owned radio stations also broadcast

Internet country code: .nc

Internet users: *total:* 222,466 (2019 est.)
percent of population: 82% (2019 est.)

Broadband - fixed subscriptions: *total:* 55,000 (2020 est.)
subscriptions per 100 inhabitants: 19 (2020 est.)

TRANSPORTATION

National air transport system: *number of registered air carriers:* 3 (2020) (registered in France)
inventory of registered aircraft operated by air carriers: 15 (registered in France)

Airports: *total:* 25 (2021)

Airports - with paved runways: *total:* 12
over 3,047 m: 1
914 to 1,523 m: 10
under 914 m: 1 (2021)

Airports - with unpaved runways: *total:* 13
914 to 1,523 m: 5
under 914 m: 8 (2021)

Heliports: 8 (2021)

Roadways: *total:* 5,622 km (2006)

Merchant marine: *total:* 24
by type: general cargo 5, oil tanker 1, other 18 (2021)

Ports and terminals: *major seaport(s):* Noumea

MILITARY AND SECURITY

Military and security forces: no regular military forces; France bases land, air, and naval forces on New Caledonia (Forces Armées de la Nouvelle-Calédonie, FANC)

Military - note: defense is the responsibility of France

TRANSNATIONAL ISSUES

Disputes - international: *New Caledonia-France-Vanuatu:* Matthew and Hunter Islands east of New Caledonia claimed by France and Vanuatu

NEW ZEALAND

INTRODUCTION

Background: Polynesian settlers may have arrived in New Zealand in the late 1200s, with widespread settlement in the mid-1300s. They called the land Aotearoa, which legend holds is the name of the canoe that Kupe, the first Polynesian in New Zealand, used to sail to the country; the name Aotearoa is now in widespread use as the local Maori name for the country. Competition for land and resources led to intermittent fighting between different Maori iwi (tribes) by the 1500s as large game became extinct. Dutch explorer Abel TASMAN was the first European to see the islands in 1642 but after an encounter with local Maori, he sailed away. British captain James COOK was the next European to arrive in New Zealand in 1769, followed by whalers, sealers, and traders. The UK only nominally claimed New Zealand and included it as part of New South Wales in Australia. Concerns about increasing lawlessness led the UK to appoint its first British Resident in New Zealand in 1832, although he had few legal powers. In 1835, some Maori iwi from the North Island declared independence as the United Tribes of New Zealand. Fearing an impending French settlement and takeover, they asked the British for protection. In 1840, the British negotiated their protection in the Treaty of Waitangi, which was eventually signed by more than 500 different Maori chiefs, although many chiefs did not or were not asked to sign. In the English-language version of the treaty, the British thought the Maori ceded their land to the UK, but translations of the treaty appeared to give the British less authority, and land tenure issues stemming from the treaty are still present and being actively negotiated in New Zealand.

The UK declared New Zealand a separate colony in 1841 and gave it limited self-government in 1852. Different traditions of authority and land use led to a series of wars from the 1840s to the 1870s fought between Europeans and various Maori iwi. Along with disease, these conflicts halved the Maori population. In the 1890s, New Zealand initially expressed interest in joining independence talks with Australia but ultimately opted against it and changed its status to an independent dominion in 1907. New Zealand provided more than 100,000 troops during each World War, many of whom fought as part of the Australia and New Zealand Army Corps (ANZAC). New Zealand reaffirmed its independence in 1947, signed the Australia, New Zealand, and US (ANZUS) Treaty, and militarily supported the US in the Korean and Vietnam Wars. Beginning in 1984, New Zealand began to adopt nuclear-free policies, contributing to a dispute with the US over naval ship visits that led the US to suspend its defense obligations to New Zealand in 1986.

In recent years, New Zealand has explored reducing some of its ties to the UK. There in an active, minority movement about changing New Zealand to a republic, and in 2015-16, a referendum on changing the New Zealand flag to remove the Union Jack failed 57% to 43%.

GEOGRAPHY

Location: Oceania, islands in the South Pacific Ocean, southeast of Australia

Geographic coordinates: 41 00 S, 174 00 E

Map references: Oceania

Area: *total:* 268,838 sq km
land: 264,537 sq km
water: 4,301 sq km
note: includes Antipodes Islands, Auckland Islands, Bounty Islands, Campbell Island, Chatham Islands, and Kermadec Islands

Area - comparative: almost twice the size of North Carolina; about the size of Colorado

Land boundaries: *total:* 0 km

Coastline: 15,134 km

Maritime claims: *territorial sea:* 12 nm
contiguous zone: 24 nm
exclusive economic zone: 200 nm
continental shelf: 200 nm or to the edge of the continental margin

Climate: temperate with sharp regional contrasts

Terrain: predominately mountainous with large coastal plains

Elevation: *highest point:* Aoraki/Mount Cook 3,724 m; note - the mountain's height was 3,764 m until 14 December 1991 when it lost about 10 m in an avalanche of rock and ice; erosion of the ice cap since then has brought the height down another 30 m
lowest point: Pacific Ocean 0 m
mean elevation: 388 m

Natural resources: natural gas, iron ore, sand, coal, timber, hydropower, gold, limestone

Land use: *agricultural land:* 43.2% (2018 est.)
arable land: 1.8% (2018 est.)
permanent crops: 0.3% (2018 est.)
permanent pasture: 41.1% (2018 est.)
forest: 31.4% (2018 est.)
other: 25.4% (2018 est.)

Irrigated land: 7,210 sq km (2012)

Major lakes (area sq km): *fresh water lake(s):* Lake Taupo - 610 sq km

Population distribution: over three-quarters of New Zealanders, including the indigenous Maori, live on the North Island, primarily in urban areas

Natural hazards: earthquakes are common, though usually not severe; volcanic activity
volcanism: significant volcanism on North Island; Ruapehu (2,797 m), which last erupted in 2007, has a history of large eruptions in the past century; Taranaki has the potential to produce dangerous avalanches and lahars; other historically active volcanoes include Okataina, Raoul Island, Tongariro, and White Island; see note 2 under "Geography - note"

Geography - note: *note 1:* consists of two main islands and a number of smaller islands; South Island, the larger main island, is the 12th largest island in the world and is divided along its length by the Southern Alps; North Island is the 14th largest island in the world and is not as mountainous, but it is marked by volcanism
note 2: New Zealand lies along the Ring of Fire, a belt of active volcanoes and earthquake epicenters bordering the Pacific Ocean; up to 90% of the world's earthquakes and some 75% of the world's volcanoes occur within the Ring of Fire
note 3: almost 90% of the population lives in cities and over three-quarters on North Island; Wellington is the southernmost national capital in the world

PEOPLE AND SOCIETY

Population: 5,053,004 (2022 est.)

Nationality: *noun:* New Zealander(s)
adjective: New Zealand

Ethnic groups: European 64.1%, Maori 16.5%, Chinese 4.9%, Indian 4.7%, Samoan 3.9%, Tongan 1.8%, Cook Islands Maori 1.7%, English 1.5%, Filipino 1.5%, New Zealander 1%, other 13.7% (2018 est.)
note: based on the 2018 census of the usually resident population; percentages add up to more than 100% because respondents were able to identify more than one ethnic group

Languages: English (de facto official) 95.4%, Maori (de jure official) 4%, Samoan 2.2%, Northern Chinese 2%, Hindi 1.5%, French 1.2%, Yue 1.1%, New Zealand Sign Language (de jure official) 0.5%, other or not stated 17.2% (2018 est.)
note: shares sum to 124.1% due to multiple responses on the 2018 census Religions
Christian 37.3% (Catholic 10.1%, Anglican 6.8%, Presbyterian and Congregational 5.2%, Pentecostal 1.8%, Methodist 1.6%, Church of Jesus Christ 1.2%, other 10.7%), Hindu 2.7%, Maori 1.3%, Muslim, 1.3%, Buddhist 1.1%, other religion 1.6% (includes Judaism, Spiritualism and New Age religions, Baha'i, Asian religions other than Buddhism), no religion 48.6%, objected to answering 6.7% (2018 est.)
note: based on the 2018 census of the usually resident population; percentages add up to more than 100% because respondents were able to identify more than one religion

Age structure: *0-14 years:* 19.63% (male 496,802/female 469,853)
15-24 years: 12.92% (male 328,327/female 308,132)
25-54 years: 39.98% (male 996,857/female 972,566)
55-64 years: 11.93% (male 285,989/female 301,692)
65 years and over: 15.54% (male 358,228/female 407,031) (2020 est.)

Dependency ratios: *total dependency ratio:* 55.8
youth dependency ratio: 30.3
elderly dependency ratio: 25.5
potential support ratio: 3.9 (2020 est.)

Median age: *total:* 37.2 years
male: 36.4 years
female: 37.9 years (2020 est.)

Population growth rate: 1.17% (2022 est.)

Birth rate: 12.78 births/1,000 population (2022 est.)

Death rate: 6.89 deaths/1,000 population (2022 est.)

Net migration rate: 5.83 migrant(s)/1,000 population (2022 est.)

Population distribution: over three-quarters of New Zealanders, including the indigenous Maori, live on the North Island, primarily in urban areas

Urbanization: *urban population:* 86.9% of total population (2022)
rate of urbanization: 0.92% annual rate of change (2020-25 est.)

Major urban areas - population: 1.652 million Auckland, 419,000 WELLINGTON (capital) (2022)

Sex ratio: *at birth:* 1.05 male(s)/female
0-14 years: 1.06 male(s)/female
15-24 years: 1.06 male(s)/female
25-54 years: 1.03 male(s)/female
55-64 years: 0.95 male(s)/female
65 years and over: 0.76 male(s)/female
total population: 1 male(s)/female (2022 est.)

Mother's mean age at first birth: 27.8 years

Maternal mortality ratio: 9 deaths/100,000 live births (2017 est.)

Infant mortality rate: *total:* 3.44 deaths/1,000 live births
male: 3.64 deaths/1,000 live births
female: 3.23 deaths/1,000 live births (2022 est.)

Life expectancy at birth: *total population:* 82.54 years
male: 80.78 years
female: 84.39 years (2022 est.)

Total fertility rate: 1.86 children born/woman (2022 est.)

Contraceptive prevalence rate: 79.9% (2014/15)
note: percent of women aged 16-49

Drinking water source: *improved: urban:* 100% of population
rural: 100% of population
total: 100% of population

Current health expenditure: 9.7% of GDP (2019)

Physicians density: 3.62 physicians/1,000 population (2020)

Hospital bed density: 2.6 beds/1,000 population (2019)

Sanitation facility access: *improved: urban:* 100% of population
rural: 100% of population
total: 100% of population

HIV/AIDS - adult prevalence rate: (2020 est.) <.1%

Obesity - adult prevalence rate: 30.8% (2016)

Alcohol consumption per capita: *total:* 9.17 liters of pure alcohol (2019 est.)
beer: 3.41 liters of pure alcohol (2019 est.)
wine: 2.88 liters of pure alcohol (2019 est.)
spirits: 1.62 liters of pure alcohol (2019 est.)
other alcohols: 1.26 liters of pure alcohol (2019 est.)

Tobacco use: *total:* 13.7% (2020 est.)
male: 15% (2020 est.)
female: 12.3% (2020 est.)

Education expenditures: 6% of GDP (2018 est.)

School life expectancy (primary to tertiary education): *total:* 20 years
male: 20 years
female: 21 years (2019)

Unemployment, youth ages 15-24: *total:* 12.4%
male: 12.2%
female: 12.6% (2020 est.)

ENVIRONMENT

Environment - current issues: water quality and availability; rapid urbanization; deforestation; soil erosion and degradation; native flora and fauna hard-hit by invasive species

Environment - international agreements: *party to:* Antarctic-Environmental Protection, Antarctic-Marine Living Resources, Antarctic Treaty, Biodiversity, Climate Change, Climate Change-Kyoto Protocol, Climate Change-Paris Agreement, Comprehensive Nuclear Test Ban, Desertification, Endangered Species, Environmental Modification, Hazardous Wastes, Law of the Sea, Marine Dumping-London Convention, Marine Dumping-London Protocol, Nuclear Test Ban, Ozone Layer Protection, Ship Pollution, Tropical Timber 2006, Wetlands, Whaling
signed, but not ratified: Antarctic Seals, Marine Life Conservation

Air pollutants: *particulate matter emissions:* 5.73 micrograms per cubic meter (2016 est.)
carbon dioxide emissions: 34.38 megatons (2016 est.)
methane emissions: 34.3 megatons (2020 est.)

Climate: temperate with sharp regional contrasts

Land use: *agricultural land:* 43.2% (2018 est.)
arable land: 1.8% (2018 est.)
permanent crops: 0.3% (2018 est.)
permanent pasture: 41.1% (2018 est.)

forest: 31.4% (2018 est.)
other: 25.4% (2018 est.)

Urbanization: *urban population:* 86.9% of total population (2022)
rate of urbanization: 0.92% annual rate of change (2020-25 est.)

Revenue from forest resources: *forest revenues:* 0.5% of GDP (2018 est.)

Revenue from coal: *coal revenues:* 0.03% of GDP (2018 est.)

Waste and recycling: *municipal solid waste generated annually:* 3.405 million tons (2016 est.)

Major lakes (area sq km): *fresh water lake(s):* Lake Taupo - 610 sq km

Total water withdrawal: *municipal:* 810 million cubic meters (2017 est.)
industrial: 1.184 billion cubic meters (2017 est.)
agricultural: 3.207 billion cubic meters (2017 est.)

Total renewable water resources: 327 billion cubic meters (2017 est.)

GOVERNMENT

Country name: *conventional long form:* none
conventional short form: New Zealand
abbreviation: NZ
etymology: Dutch explorer Abel TASMAN was the first European to reach New Zealand in 1642; he named it Staten Landt, but Dutch cartographers renamed it Nova Zeelandia in 1645 after the Dutch province of Zeeland; British explorer Captain James COOK subsequently anglicized the name to New Zealand when he mapped the islands in 1769

Government type: parliamentary democracy under a constitutional monarchy; a Commonwealth realm

Capital: *name:* Wellington
geographic coordinates: 41 18 S, 174 47 E
time difference: UTC+12 (17 hours ahead of Washington, DC, during Standard Time)
daylight saving time: +1hr, begins last Sunday in September; ends first Sunday in April
time zone note: New Zealand has two time zones: New Zealand standard time (UTC+12) and Chatham Islands time (45 minutes in advance of New Zealand standard time; UTC+12:45)
etymology: named in 1840 after Arthur WELLESLEY, the first Duke of Wellington and victorious general at the Battle of Waterloo

Administrative divisions: 16 regions and 1 territory*; Auckland, Bay of Plenty, Canterbury, Chatham Islands*, Gisborne, Hawke's Bay, Manawatu-Wanganui, Marlborough, Nelson, Northland, Otago, Southland, Taranaki, Tasman, Waikato, Wellington, West Coast

Dependent areas: Cook Islands, Niue, Tokelau

Independence: 26 September 1907 (from the UK)

National holiday: Waitangi Day (Treaty of Waitangi established British sovereignty over New Zealand), 6 February (1840); Anzac Day (commemorated as the anniversary of the landing of troops of the Australian and New Zealand Army Corps during World War I at Gallipoli, Turkey), 25 April (1915)

Constitution: *history:* New Zealand has no single constitution document; the Constitution Act 1986, effective 1 January 1987, includes only part of the uncodified constitution; others include a collection of statutes or "acts of Parliament," the Treaty of Waitangi, Orders in Council, letters patent, court decisions, and unwritten conventions
amendments: proposed as bill by Parliament or by referendum called either by the government or by citizens; passage of a bill as an act normally requires two separate readings with committee reviews in between to make changes and corrections, a third reading approved by the House of Representatives membership or by the majority of votes in a referendum, and assent of the governor-general; passage of amendments to reserved constitutional provisions affecting the term of Parliament, electoral districts, and voting restrictions requires approval by 75% of the House membership or the majority of votes in a referendum; amended many times, last in 2020

Legal system: common law system, based on English model, with special legislation and land courts for the Maori

International law organization participation: accepts compulsory ICJ jurisdiction with reservations; accepts ICCt jurisdiction

Citizenship: *citizenship by birth:* no
citizenship by descent only: at least one parent must be a citizen of New Zealand
dual citizenship recognized: yes
residency requirement for naturalization: 3 years

Suffrage: 18 years of age; universal

Executive branch: *chief of state:* King CHARLES III (since 8 September 2022); represented by Governor-General Dame Cindy KIRO (since 21 October 2021)
head of government: Prime Minister Jacinda ARDERN (since 26 October 2017); Deputy Prime Minister Grant ROBERTSON (since 2 November 2020)
cabinet: Executive Council appointed by the governor-general on the recommendation of the prime minister
elections/appointments: the monarchy is hereditary; governor-general appointed by the monarch on the advice of the prime minister; following legislative elections, the leader of the majority party or majority coalition usually appointed prime minister by the governor-general; deputy prime minister appointed by the governor-general

Legislative branch: *description:* unicameral House of Representatives - commonly called Parliament (120 seats for 2020-23 term); 72 members directly elected in 65 single-seat constituencies and 7 Maori constituencies by simple majority vote and 48 directly elected by closed party-list proportional representation vote; members serve 3-year terms)
elections: last held on 17 October 2020 (next scheduled for 2023)
election results: percent of vote by party - Labor Party 49.1%, National Party 26.8%, ACT Party 8%, Green Party 6.3%, Maori Party 1%; seats by party - Labor Party 64, National Party 35, Green Party 10, ACT Party 10, Maori Party 1; composition - men 61, women 59, percent of women 49.2%

Judicial branch: *highest court(s):* Supreme Court (consists of 5 justices, including the chief justice); note - the Supreme Court in 2004 replaced the Judicial Committee of the Privy Council (in London) as the final appeals court
judge selection and term of office: justices appointed by the governor-general upon the recommendation of the attorney- general; justices appointed until compulsory retirement at age 70
subordinate courts: Court of Appeal; High Court; tribunals and authorities; district courts; specialized courts for issues related to employment, environment, family, Maori lands, youth, military; tribunals

Political parties and leaders: ACT New Zealand [David SEYMOUR]
Green Party [Marama DAVIDSON]
Mana Movement [Hone HARAWIRA] (formerly Mana Party)
Maori Party [Debbie NGAREWA-PACKER and Rawiri WAITITI]
New Zealand First Party or NZ First [Winston PETERS]
New Zealand Labor Party [Jacinda ARDERN]
New Zealand National Party [Christopher LUXON]

International organization participation: ADB, ANZUS, APEC, ARF, ASEAN (dialogue partner), Australia Group, BIS, C, CD, CP, EAS, EBRD, FAO, FATF, IAEA, IBRD, ICAO, ICC (national committees), ICCt, ICRM, IDA, IEA, IFAD, IFC, IFRCS, IHO, ILO, IMF, IMO, IMSO, Interpol, IOC, IOM, IPU, ISO, ITSO, ITU, ITUC (NGOs), MIGA, NSG, OECD, OPCW, Pacific Alliance (observer), Paris Club (associate), PCA, PIF, SICA (observer), Sparteca, SPC, UN, UNCTAD, UNESCO, UNHCR, UNIDO, UNMISS, UNTSO, UPU, Wassenaar Arrangement, WCO, WFTU (NGOs), WHO, WIPO, WMO, WTO

Diplomatic representation in the US: *chief of mission:* Ambassador Bede Gilbert CORRY (since 16 September 2022)
chancery: 37 Observatory Circle NW, Washington, DC 20008
telephone: [1] (202) 328-4800
FAX: [1] (202) 667-5277
email address and website:
wshinfo@mfat.govt.nz
https://www.mfat.govt.nz/en/countries-and-regions/americas/united-states-of-america/
consulate(s) general: Honolulu, Los Angeles, New York

Diplomatic representation from the US: *chief of mission:* Ambassador Thomas Stewart UDALL (since 1 December 2021) note - also accredited to Samoa
embassy: 29 Fitzherbert Terrace, Thorndon, Wellington 6011
mailing address: 4370 Auckland Place, Washington DC 20521-4370
telephone: [64] (4) 462-6000
FAX: [64] (4) 499-0490
email address and website:
AucklandACS@state.gov
https://nz.usembassy.gov/
consulate(s) general: Auckland

Flag description: blue with the flag of the UK in the upper hoist-side quadrant with four red five-pointed stars edged in white centered in the outer half of the flag; the stars represent the Southern Cross constellation

National symbol(s): Southern Cross constellation (four, five-pointed stars), kiwi (bird), silver fern; national colors: black, white, red (ochre)

New Zealand coat of arms:

National anthem: *name:* "God Defend New Zealand"
lyrics/music: Thomas BRACKEN [English], Thomas Henry SMITH [Maori]/John Joseph WOODS
note: adopted 1940 as national song, adopted 1977 as co-national anthem; New Zealand has two national

anthems with equal status; as a commonwealth realm, in addition to "God Defend New Zealand," "God Save the King" serves as a royal anthem (see United Kingdom); "God Save the King" normally played only when a member of the royal family or the governor-general is present; in all other cases, "God Defend New Zealand" is played

National heritage: *total World Heritage Sites:* 3 (2 natural, 1 mixed)
selected World Heritage Site locales: Te Wahipounamu – South West New Zealand (n); Tongariro National Park (m); New Zealand Sub-Antarctic Islands (n)

ECONOMY

Economic overview: Over the past 40 years, the government has transformed New Zealand from an agrarian economy, dependent on concessionary British market access, to a more industrialized, free market economy that can compete globally. This dynamic growth has boosted real incomes, but left behind some at the bottom of the ladder and broadened and deepened the technological capabilities of the industrial sector.

Per capita income rose for 10 consecutive years until 2007 in purchasing power parity terms, but fell in 2008-09. Debt-driven consumer spending drove robust growth in the first half of the decade, fueling a large balance of payments deficit that posed a challenge for policymakers. Inflationary pressures caused the central bank to raise its key rate steadily from January 2004 until it was among the highest in the OECD in 2007 and 2008. The higher rate attracted international capital inflows, which strengthened the currency and housing market while aggravating the current account deficit. Rising house prices, especially in Auckland, have become a political issue in recent years, as well as a policy challenge in 2016 and 2017, as the ability to afford housing has declined for many.

Expanding New Zealand's network of free trade agreements remains a top foreign policy priority. New Zealand was an early promoter of the Trans-Pacific Partnership (TPP) and was the second country to ratify the agreement in May 2017. Following the United States' withdrawal from the TPP in January 2017, on 10 November 2017 the remaining 11 countries agreed on the core elements of a modified agreement, which they renamed the Comprehensive and Progressive Agreement for Trans-Pacific Partnership (CPTPP). In November 2016, New Zealand opened negotiations to upgrade its FTA with China; China is one of New Zealand's most important trading partners.

Real GDP (purchasing power parity): $215.6 billion (2020 est.)
$213.5 billion (2019 est.)
$210.07 billion (2018 est.)
note: data are in 2017 dollars

Real GDP growth rate: 2.22% (2019 est.)
3.22% (2018 est.)
3.8% (2017 est.)

Real GDP per capita: $42,400 (2020 est.)
$42,900 (2019 est.)
$42,900 (2018 est.)
note: data are in 2017 dollars

GDP (official exchange rate): $205.202 billion (2019 est.)

Inflation rate (consumer prices): 1.6% (2019 est.)
1.5% (2018 est.)
1.8% (2017 est.)

Credit ratings:

Fitch rating: AA (2011)

Moody's rating: Aaa (2002)

Standard & Poors rating: AA (2011)
note: The year refers to the year in which the current credit rating was first obtained.

GDP - composition, by sector of origin: *agriculture:* 5.7% (2017 est.)
industry: 21.5% (2017 est.)
services: 72.8% (2017 est.)

GDP - composition, by end use: *household consumption:* 57.2% (2017 est.)
government consumption: 18.2% (2017 est.)
investment in fixed capital: 23.4% (2017 est.)
investment in inventories: 0.3% (2017 est.)
exports of goods and services: 27% (2017 est.)
imports of goods and services: -26.1% (2017 est.)

Agricultural products: milk, beef, kiwi fruit, apples, potatoes, mutton, grapes, wheat, barley, green onions/shallots

Industries: agriculture, forestry, fishing, logs and wood articles, manufacturing, mining, construction, financial services, real estate services, tourism

Industrial production growth rate: 1.8% (2017 est.)

Labor force: 2.709 million (2020 est.)

Labor force - by occupation: *agriculture:* 6.6%
industry: 20.7%
services: 72.7% (2017 est.)

Unemployment rate: 4.13% (2019 est.)
4.32% (2018 est.)

Unemployment, youth ages 15-24: *total:* 12.4%
male: 12.2%
female: 12.6% (2020 est.)

Gini Index coefficient - distribution of family income: 36.2 (1997)

Budget: *revenues:* 74.11 billion (2017 est.)
expenditures: 70.97 billion (2017 est.)

Budget surplus (+) or deficit (-): 1.6% (of GDP) (2017 est.)

Public debt: 31.7% of GDP (2017 est.)
33.5% of GDP (2016 est.)

Taxes and other revenues: 36.8% (of GDP) (2017 est.)

Fiscal year: 1 April - 31 March
note: this is the fiscal year for tax purposes

Current account balance: -$6.962 billion (2019 est.)
-$8.742 billion (2018 est.)

Exports: $50.43 billion (2020 est.) note: data are in current year dollars
$57.16 billion (2019 est.) note: data are in current year dollars
$57.71 billion (2018 est.) note: data are in current year dollars

Exports - partners: China 28%, Australia 14%, United States 9%, Japan 6% (2019)

Exports - commodities: dairy products, sheep/goat meats, lumber, beef products, fresh fruits (2019)

Imports: $47.86 billion (2020 est.) note: data are in current year dollars
$57.75 billion (2019 est.) note: data are in current year dollars
$58.39 billion (2018 est.) note: data are in current year dollars

Imports - partners: China 18%, Australia 15%, United States 9%, Japan 6%, Germany 5% (2019)

Imports - commodities: cars, crude petroleum, refined petroleum, delivery trucks, gas turbines (2019)

Reserves of foreign exchange and gold: $20.68 billion (31 December 2017 est.)
$17.81 billion (31 December 2016 est.)

Debt - external: $190.621 billion (2019 est.)
$192.327 billion (2018 est.)

Exchange rates: New Zealand dollars (NZD) per US dollar -
1.41794 (2020 est.)
1.52334 (2019 est.)
1.45709 (2018 est.)
1.4279 (2014 est.)
1.2039 (2013 est.)

ENERGY

Electricity access: *electrification - total population:* 100% (2020)

Electricity: *installed generating capacity:* 9.615 million kW (2020 est.)
consumption: 41,169,838,000 kWh (2019 est.)
exports: 0 kWh (2020 est.)
imports: 0 kWh (2020 est.)
transmission/distribution losses: 2,256,332,000 kWh (2019 est.)

Electricity generation sources: *fossil fuels:* 19.5% of total installed capacity (2020 est.)
nuclear: 0% of total installed capacity (2020 est.)
solar: 0.4% of total installed capacity (2020 est.)
wind: 5.3% of total installed capacity (2020 est.)
hydroelectricity: 54.8% of total installed capacity (2020 est.)
tide and wave: 0.1% of total installed capacity (2020 est.)
geothermal: 18.6% of total installed capacity (2020 est.)
biomass and waste: 1.4% of total installed capacity (2020 est.)

Coal: *production:* 3.226 million metric tons (2020 est.)
consumption: 3.001 million metric tons (2020 est.)
exports: 1.14 million metric tons (2020 est.)
imports: 1.09 million metric tons (2020 est.)
proven reserves: 7.575 billion metric tons (2019 est.)

Petroleum: *total petroleum production:* 13,400 bbl/day (2021 est.)
refined petroleum consumption: 184,600 bbl/day (2019 est.)
crude oil and lease condensate exports: 21,600 bbl/day (2018 est.)
crude oil and lease condensate imports: 99,900 bbl/day (2018 est.)
crude oil estimated reserves: 41 million barrels (2021 est.)

Refined petroleum products - production: 115,100 bbl/day (2017 est.)

Refined petroleum products - exports: 1,782 bbl/day (2017 est.)

Refined petroleum products - imports: 56,000 bbl/day (2017 est.)

Natural gas: *production:* 4,771,126,000 cubic meters (2019 est.)

consumption: 4,946,237,000 cubic meters (2019 est.)
exports: 0 cubic meters (2021 est.)
imports: 0 cubic meters (2021 est.)
proven reserves: 31.148 billion cubic meters (2021 est.)

Carbon dioxide emissions: 40.344 million metric tonnes of CO2 (2019 est.)
from coal and metallurgical coke: 5.139 million metric tonnes of CO2 (2019 est.)
from petroleum and other liquids: 25.76 million metric tonnes of CO2 (2019 est.)
from consumed natural gas: 9.445 million metric tonnes of CO2 (2019 est.)

Energy consumption per capita: 186.804 million Btu/person (2019 est.)

COMMUNICATIONS

Telephones - fixed lines: *total subscriptions:* 858,000 (2020 est.)
subscriptions per 100 inhabitants: 18 (2020 est.)

Telephones - mobile cellular: *total subscriptions:* 6.148 million (2020 est.)
subscriptions per 100 inhabitants: 127 (2020 est.)

Telecommunication systems: *general assessment:* the principal growth areas in in New Zealand's telecom market have been in mobile broadband and fiber; the UFB1 rollout was completed in November 2019 and the UFB2 rollout is scheduled to be completed by the end of 2022; Chorus noted that as of the beginning of 2022, 1Gb/s plans accounted for about 23% of all fiber connections, while 43% of business customers adopted a gigabit service; New Zealand's mobile market continues to undergo significant developments; there have been considerable gains made in LTE services, with effective competition between Spark, Vodafone NZ, and 2degrees; the widening coverage of LTE networks has been supported by the Rural Broadband Initiative rollout, which added a significant number of mobile sites to new or underserved areas; as the initiative is winding down, this has enabled the participating telcos to invest in NB-IoT and other platforms; Vodafone NZ expects to extend its NB-IoT footprint to cover at least 60% of the country by 2024; the market is undergoing additional consolidation, with approval of the merger between 2degrees and Orcon Group having been granted by regulators in May 2022; this will create the country's third-largest integrated telco, offering fixed and mobile services in competition with Spark and Vodafone NZ. The merger proposal came fast of the heels of Vocus Group and its local subsidiary Orcon having acquired 2degrees from Trilogy International in December 2021; this deal created a new company, Voyage Digital. (2020)
domestic: fixed-line roughly 18 per 100 and mobile-cellular telephone subscribership 127 per 100 persons (2020)
international: country code - 64; landing points for the Southern Cross NEXT, Aqualink, Nelson-Levin, SCCN and Hawaiki submarine cable system providing links to Australia, Fiji, American Samoa, Kiribati, Samo, Tokelau, US and around New Zealand; satellite earth stations - 8 (1 Inmarsat - Pacific Ocean, 7 other) (2019)

Broadcast media: state-owned Television New Zealand operates multiple TV networks and state-owned Radio New Zealand operates 3 radio networks and an external shortwave radio service to the South Pacific region; a small number of national commercial TV and radio stations and many regional commercial television and radio stations are available; cable and satellite TV systems are available, as are a range of streaming services (2019)

Internet country code: .nz

Internet users: *total:* 4,677,556 (2020 est.)
percent of population: 92% (2020 est.)

Broadband - fixed subscriptions: *total:* 1,764,984 (2020 est.)
subscriptions per 100 inhabitants: 37 (2020 est.)

TRANSPORTATION

National air transport system: *number of registered air carriers:* 15 (2020)
inventory of registered aircraft operated by air carriers: 199
annual passenger traffic on registered air carriers: 17,249,049 (2018)
annual freight traffic on registered air carriers: 1,349,300,000 (2018) mt-km

Civil aircraft registration country code prefix: ZK

Airports: *total:* 123 (2021)

Airports - with paved runways: *total:* 39
over 3,047 m: 2
2,438 to 3,047 m: 1
1,524 to 2,437 m: 12
914 to 1,523 m: 23
under 914 m: 1 (2021)

Airports - with unpaved runways: *total:* 84
1,524 to 2,437 m: 3
914 to 1,523 m: 33
under 914 m: 48 (2021)

Pipelines: 331 km condensate, 2,500 km gas, 172 km liquid petroleum gas, 288 km oil, 198 km refined products (2018)

Railways: *total:* 4,128 km (2018)
narrow gauge: 4,128 km (2018) 1.067-m gauge (506 km electrified)

Roadways: *total:* 94,000 km (2017)
paved: 61,600 km (2017) (includes 199 km of expressways)
unpaved: 32,400 km (2017)

Merchant marine: *total:* 115
by type: container ship 1, general cargo 12, oil tanker 4, other 98 (2021)

Ports and terminals: *major seaport(s):* Auckland, Lyttelton, Manukau Harbor, Marsden Point, Tauranga, Wellington

MILITARY AND SECURITY

Military and security forces: New Zealand Defense Force (NZDF): New Zealand Army, Royal New Zealand Navy, Royal New Zealand Air Force (2022)

Military expenditures: 1.4% of GDP (2022 est.)
1.3% of GDP (2021)
1.5% of GDP (2020)
1.4% of GDP (2019) (approximately $3.1 billion)
1.2% of GDP (2018) (approximately $2.62 billion)

Military and security service personnel strengths: approximately 9,500 active-duty troops (4,700 Army; 2,300 Navy; 2,500 Air Force) (2022)

Military equipment inventories and acquisitions: the NZDF is equipped mostly with imported weapons and equipment from Western suppliers; the US has been the leading provider since 2010 (2022)

Military service age and obligation: 17 years of age for men and women for voluntary military service; soldiers cannot be deployed until the age of 18; no conscription (2022)
note 1: New Zealand opened up all military occupations to women in 2000; in 2019, women accounted for about 18% of the uniformed full-time personnel
note 2: as of 2022, the NZDF's program for recruiting foreign volunteers had been suspended

Military deployments: up to 220 Antarctica (summer season only) (2022)

Military - note: New Zealand is a member of the Five Powers Defense Arrangements (FPDA), a series of mutual assistance agreements reached in 1971 embracing Australia, Malaysia, New Zealand, Singapore, and the UK; the FPDA commits the members to consult with one another in the event or threat of an armed attack on any of the members and to mutually decide what measures should be taken, jointly or separately; there is no specific obligation to intervene militarily

New Zealand has been part of the Australia, New Zealand, and US Security (ANZUS) Treaty since 1951; however, the US suspended its ANZUS security obligations to New Zealand in 1986 after New Zealand implemented a policy barring nuclear-armed and nuclear-powered warships from its ports; the US and New Zealand signed the Wellington Declaration in 2010, which reaffirmed close ties between the two countries, and in 2012 signed the Washington Declaration, which provided a framework for future security cooperation and defense dialogues; in 2016, a US naval ship conducted the first bilateral warship visit to New Zealand since the 1980s

New Zealand has Major Non-NATO Ally (MNNA) status with the US; MNNA is a designation under US law that provides foreign partners with certain benefits in the areas of defense trade and security cooperation; while MNNA status provides military and economic privileges, it does not entail any security commitments (2022)

TERRORISM

Terrorist group(s): Islamic State of Iraq and ash-Sham (ISIS)
note: details about the history, aims, leadership, organization, areas of operation, tactics, targets, weapons, size, and sources of support of the group(s) appear(s) in Appendix-T

TRANSNATIONAL ISSUES

Disputes - international: *New Zealand-Antarctica:* asserts a territorial claim in Antarctica (Ross Dependency)

Illicit drugs: significant consumer of amphetamines

NICARAGUA

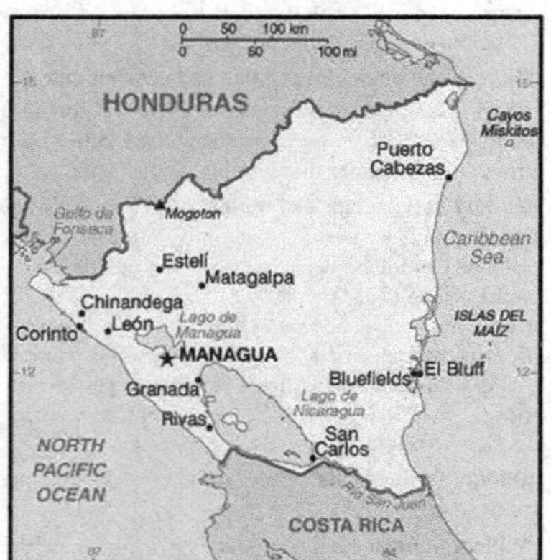

INTRODUCTION

Background: The Pacific coast of Nicaragua was settled as a Spanish colony from Panama in the early 16th century. Independence from Spain was declared in 1821 and the country became an independent republic in 1838. Britain occupied the Caribbean Coast in the first half of the 19th century, but gradually ceded control of the region in subsequent decades. Violent opposition to governmental manipulation and corruption spread to all classes by 1978 and resulted in a short-lived civil war that brought a civic-military coalition, spearheaded by the Marxist Sandinista guerrillas led by Daniel ORTEGA Saavedra to power in 1979. Nicaraguan aid to leftist rebels in El Salvador prompted the US to sponsor anti-Sandinista contra guerrillas through much of the 1980s. After losing free and fair elections in 1990, 1996, and 2001, former Sandinista President Daniel ORTEGA was elected president in 2006, 2011, 2016, and most recently in 2021. Municipal, regional, and national-level elections since 2008 have been marred by widespread irregularities. Democratic institutions have weakened under the ORTEGA regime as the president has garnered full control over all branches of government, especially after cracking down on a nationwide pro-democracy protest movement in 2018. In the lead-up to the 2021 presidential election, authorities arrested over 40 individuals linked to the political opposition, including presidential candidates, private sector leaders, NGO workers, human rights defenders, and journalists. Only five lesser-known presidential candidates of mostly small parties allied to ORTEGA's Sandinistas were allowed to run against ORTEGA in the November 2021 election.

GEOGRAPHY

Location: Central America, bordering both the Caribbean Sea and the North Pacific Ocean, between Costa Rica and Honduras

Geographic coordinates: 13 00 N, 85 00 W

Map references: Central America and the Caribbean

Area:
total: 130,370 sq km
land: 119,990 sq km
water: 10,380 sq km

Area - comparative: slightly larger than Pennsylvania; slightly smaller than New York state

Land boundaries: *total:* 1,253 km
border countries (2): Costa Rica 313 km; Honduras 940 km

Coastline: 910 km

Maritime claims: *territorial sea:* 12 nm
contiguous zone: 24 nm
continental shelf: natural prolongation

Climate: tropical in lowlands, cooler in highlands

Terrain: extensive Atlantic coastal plains rising to central interior mountains; narrow Pacific coastal plain interrupted by volcanoes

Elevation: *highest point:* Mogoton 2,085 m
lowest point: Pacific Ocean 0 m
mean elevation: 298 m

Natural resources: gold, silver, copper, tungsten, lead, zinc, timber, fish

Land use: *agricultural land:* 42.2% (2018 est.)
arable land: 12.5% (2018 est.)
permanent crops: 2.5% (2018 est.)
permanent pasture: 27.2% (2018 est.)
forest: 25.3% (2018 est.)
other: 32.5% (2018 est.)

Irrigated land: 1,990 sq km (2012)

Major lakes (area sq km): *fresh water lake(s):* Lago de Nicaragua - 8,150 sq km; Lago de Managua - 1,040 sq km

Population distribution: the overwhelming majority of the population resides in the western half of the country, with much of the urban growth centered in the capital city of Managua; coastal areas also show large population clusters

Natural hazards: destructive earthquakes; volcanoes; landslides; extremely susceptible to hurricanes
volcanism: significant volcanic activity; Cerro Negro (728 m), which last erupted in 1999, is one of Nicaragua's most active volcanoes; its lava flows and ash have been known to cause significant damage to farmland and buildings; other historically active volcanoes include Concepcion, Cosiguina, Las Pilas, Masaya, Momotombo, San Cristobal, and Telica

Geography - note: largest country in Central America; contains the largest freshwater body in Central America, Lago de Nicaragua

PEOPLE AND SOCIETY

Population: 6,301,880 (2022 est.)

Nationality: *noun:* Nicaraguan(s)
adjective: Nicaraguan

Ethnic groups: Mestizo (mixed Amerindian and White) 69%, White 17%, Black 9%, Amerindian 5%

Languages: Spanish (official) 95.3%, Miskito 2.2%, Mestizo of the Caribbean coast 2%, other 0.5%; note - English and indigenous languages found on the Caribbean coast (2005 est.)
major-language sample(s): La Libreta Informativa del Mundo, la fuente indispensable de información básica. (Spanish)

Religions: Roman Catholic 50%, Evangelical 33.2%, other 2.9%, none 0.7%, unspecified 13.2% (2017 est.)

Demographic profile: Despite being one of the poorest countries in Latin America, Nicaragua has improved its access to potable water and sanitation and has ameliorated its life expectancy, infant and child mortality, and immunization rates. However, income distribution is very uneven, and the poor, agriculturalists, and indigenous people continue to have less access to healthcare services. Nicaragua's total fertility rate has fallen from around 6 children per woman in 1980 to below replacement level today, but the high birth rate among adolescents perpetuates a cycle of poverty and low educational attainment.

Nicaraguans emigrate primarily to Costa Rica and to a lesser extent the United States. Nicaraguan men have been migrating seasonally to Costa Rica to harvest bananas and coffee since the early 20th century. Political turmoil, civil war, and natural disasters from the 1970s through the 1990s dramatically increased the flow of refugees and permanent migrants seeking jobs, higher wages, and better social and healthcare benefits. Since 2000, Nicaraguan emigration to Costa Rica has slowed and stabilized. Today roughly 300,000 Nicaraguans are permanent residents of Costa Rica - about 75% of the foreign population - and thousands more migrate seasonally for work, many illegally.

Age structure: *0-14 years:* 25.63% (male 811,731/female 777,984)
15-24 years: 19.51% (male 609,962/female 600,567)
25-54 years: 42.41% (male 1,254,683/female 1,376,052)
55-64 years: 6.63% (male 188,591/female 222,766)
65 years and over: 5.82% (male 159,140/female 201,965) (2020 est.)

Dependency ratios: *total dependency ratio:* 54.3
youth dependency ratio: 45.5
elderly dependency ratio: 8.8
potential support ratio: 11.4 (2020 est.)

Median age: *total:* 27.3 years
male: 26.4 years
female: 28.2 years (2020 est.)

Population growth rate: 0.92% (2022 est.)

Birth rate: 16.52 births/1,000 population (2022 est.)

Death rate: 5.17 deaths/1,000 population (2022 est.)

Net migration rate: -2.15 migrant(s)/1,000 population (2022 est.)

Population distribution: the overwhelming majority of the population resides in the western half of the country, with much of the urban growth centered in the capital city of Managua; coastal areas also show large population clusters

Urbanization: *urban population:* 59.6% of total population (2022)
rate of urbanization: 1.45% annual rate of change (2020-25 est.)

Major urban areas - population: 1.083 million MANAGUA (capital) (2022)

Sex ratio: *at birth:* 1.05 male(s)/female
0-14 years: 1.04 male(s)/female
15-24 years: 1.02 male(s)/female

25-54 years: 0.91 male(s)/female
55-64 years: 0.84 male(s)/female
65 years and over: 0.65 male(s)/female
total population: 0.95 male(s)/female (2022 est.)

Mother's mean age at first birth: 19.2 years (2011/12 est.)
note: data represents median age at first birth among women 25-29

Maternal mortality ratio: 198 deaths/100,000 live births (2017 est.)

Infant mortality rate: *total:* 19.09 deaths/1,000 live births
male: 22.26 deaths/1,000 live births
female: 15.77 deaths/1,000 live births (2022 est.)

Life expectancy at birth: *total population:* 74.78 years
male: 72.56 years
female: 77.11 years (2022 est.)

Total fertility rate: 1.8 children born/woman (2022 est.)

Contraceptive prevalence rate: 80.4% (2011/12)

Drinking water source: *improved: urban:* 97.5% of population
rural: 62.6% of population
total: 83.2% of population
unimproved: urban: 2.5% of population
rural: 37.4% of population
total: 16.8% of population (2020 est.)

Current health expenditure: 8.4% of GDP (2019)

Physicians density: 1.67 physicians/1,000 population (2018)

Hospital bed density: 0.9 beds/1,000 population (2017)

Sanitation facility access: *improved: urban:* 89.9% of population
rural: 66.5% of population
total: 80.3% of population
unimproved: urban: 10.1% of population
rural: 33.5% of population
total: 19.7% of population (2020 est.)

HIV/AIDS - adult prevalence rate: 0.2% (2020 est.)

Major infectious diseases: *degree of risk:* high (2020)
food or waterborne diseases: bacterial diarrhea, hepatitis A, and typhoid fever
vectorborne diseases: dengue fever and malaria

Obesity - adult prevalence rate: 23.7% (2016)

Alcohol consumption per capita: *total:* 3.69 liters of pure alcohol (2019 est.)
beer: 1.57 liters of pure alcohol (2019 est.)
wine: 0.02 liters of pure alcohol (2019 est.)
spirits: 2.1 liters of pure alcohol (2019 est.)
other alcohols: 0 liters of pure alcohol (2019 est.)

Children under the age of 5 years underweight: 4.6% (2011/12)

Education expenditures: 3.4% of GDP (2019 est.)

Literacy: *definition:* age 15 and over can read and write
total population: 82.6%
male: 82.4%
female: 82.8% (2015)

Unemployment, youth ages 15-24: *total:* 8.5%
male: 6.4%
female: 12.9% (2014 est.)

ENVIRONMENT

Environment - current issues: deforestation; soil erosion; water pollution; drought

Environment - international agreements: *party to:* Biodiversity, Climate Change, Climate Change-Kyoto Protocol, Climate Change-Paris Agreement, Comprehensive Nuclear Test Ban, Desertification, Endangered Species, Environmental Modification, Hazardous Wastes, Law of the Sea, Nuclear Test Ban, Ozone Layer Protection, Ship Pollution, Wetlands, Whaling
signed, but not ratified: none of the selected agreements

Air pollutants: *particulate matter emissions:* 16.87 micrograms per cubic meter (2016 est.)
carbon dioxide emissions: 5.59 megatons (2016 est.)
methane emissions: 6.46 megatons (2020 est.)

Climate: tropical in lowlands, cooler in highlands

Land use: *agricultural land:* 42.2% (2018 est.)
arable land: 12.5% (2018 est.)
permanent crops: 2.5% (2018 est.)
permanent pasture: 27.2% (2018 est.)
forest: 25.3% (2018 est.)
other: 32.5% (2018 est.)

Urbanization: *urban population:* 59.6% of total population (2022)
rate of urbanization: 1.45% annual rate of change (2020-25 est.)

Revenue from forest resources: *forest revenues:* 1.26% of GDP (2018 est.)

Revenue from coal: *coal revenues:* 0% of GDP (2018 est.)

Waste and recycling: *municipal solid waste generated annually:* 1,528,816 tons (2010 est.)

Major lakes (area sq km): *fresh water lake(s):* Lago de Nicaragua - 8,150 sq km; Lago de Managua - 1,040 sq km

Total water withdrawal: *municipal:* 286 million cubic meters (2017 est.)
industrial: 73.6 million cubic meters (2017 est.)
agricultural: 1.185 billion cubic meters (2017 est.)

Total renewable water resources: 164.52 billion cubic meters (2017 est.)

GOVERNMENT

Country name: *conventional long form:* Republic of Nicaragua
conventional short form: Nicaragua
local long form: Republica de Nicaragua
local short form: Nicaragua
etymology: Nicarao was the name of the largest indigenous settlement at the time of Spanish arrival; conquistador Gil GONZALEZ Davila, who explored the area (1622-23), combined the name of the community with the Spanish word "agua" (water), referring to the two large lakes in the west of the country (Lake Managua and Lake Nicaragua)

Government type: presidential republic

Capital: *name:* Managua
geographic coordinates: 12 08 N, 86 15 W
time difference: UTC-6 (1 hour behind Washington, DC, during Standard Time)
etymology: may derive from the indigenous Nahuatl term "mana-ahuac," which translates as "adjacent to the water" or a site "surrounded by water"; the city is situated on the southwestern shore of Lake Managua

Administrative divisions: 15 departments (departamentos, singular - departamento) and 2 autonomous regions* (regiones autonomistas, singular - region autonoma); Boaco, Carazo, Chinandega, Chontales, Costa Caribe Norte*, Costa Caribe Sur*, Esteli, Granada, Jinotega, Leon, Madriz, Managua, Masaya, Matagalpa, Nueva Segovia, Rio San Juan, Rivas

Independence: 15 September 1821 (from Spain)

National holiday: Independence Day, 15 September (1821)

Constitution: *history:* several previous; latest adopted 19 November 1986, effective 9 January 1987
amendments: proposed by the president of the republic or assent of at least half of the National Assembly membership; passage requires approval by 60% of the membership of the next elected Assembly and promulgation by the president of the republic; amended several times, last in 2021

Legal system: civil law system; Supreme Court may review administrative acts

International law organization participation: accepts compulsory ICJ jurisdiction with reservations; non-party state to the ICCt

Citizenship: *citizenship by birth:* yes
citizenship by descent only: yes
dual citizenship recognized: no, except in cases where bilateral agreements exist
residency requirement for naturalization: 4 years

Suffrage: 16 years of age; universal

Executive branch: *chief of state:* President Jose Daniel ORTEGA Saavedra (since 10 January 2007); Vice President Rosario MURILLO Zambrana (since 10 January 2017); note - the president is both chief of state and head of government
head of government: President Jose Daniel ORTEGA Saavedra (since 10 January 2007); Vice President Rosario MURILLO Zambrana (since 10 January 2017)
cabinet: Council of Ministers appointed by the president
elections/appointments: president and vice president directly elected on the same ballot by qualified plurality vote for a 5-year term (no term limits as of 2014); election last held on 7 November 2021 (next to be held on 1 November 2026)
election results: *2021:* Jose Daniel ORTEGA Saavedra reelected president for a fourth consecutive term; percent of vote - Jose Daniel ORTEGA Saavedra (FSLN) 75.9%, Walter ESPINOZA (PLC) 14.3%, Guillermo OSORNO (CCN) 3.3%, Marcelo MONTIEL (ALN) 3.1%, other 3.4%
2016: Jose Daniel ORTEGA Saavedra reelected president for a third consecutive term; percent of vote - Jose Daniel ORTEGA Saavedra (FSLN) 72.4%, Maximino RODRIGUEZ (PLC) 15%, Jose del Carmen ALVARADO (PLI) 4.5%, Saturnino CERRATO Hodgson (ALN) 4.3%, other 3.7%

Legislative branch: *description:* unicameral National Assembly or Asamblea Nacional (92 statutory seats, current 91; 70 members in multiseat constituencies, representing the country's 15 departments and 2 autonomous regions, and 20 members in a single nationwide constituency directly elected by party-list proportional representation vote; up to 2 seats reserved for the previous president and the runner-up candidate in the previous presidential election; members serve 5-year terms)
elections: last held on 7 November 2021 (next to be held on 1 November 2026)

election results: percent of vote by party - NA; seats by party - FSLN 75, PLC 10, ALN 2, APRE 1, PLI 2, YATAMA 1; composition - men 45, women 46, percent of women 50.6%

Judicial branch: *highest court(s):* Supreme Court or Corte Suprema de Justicia (consists of 16 judges organized into administrative, civil, criminal, and constitutional chambers)
judge selection and term of office: Supreme Court judges elected by the National Assembly to serve 5-year staggered terms
subordinate courts: Appeals Court; first instance civil, criminal, and labor courts; military courts are independent of the Supreme Court

Political parties and leaders: Alliance for the Republic or APRE [Carlos CANALES]
Alternative for Change or AC (operates in a political alliance with the FSLN) [Orlando Jose TARDENCILLA]
Autonomous Liberal Party or PAL [Rene Margarito BELLO ROMERO]
Caribbean Unity Movement or PAMUC [Armando Francisco ARISTA FLORES]
Christian Unity Party or PUC (operates in a political alliance with the FSLN) [Guillermo Daniel ORTEGA REYES]
Citizens for Liberty or CxL [Carmella ROGERS AUMBURN]; note - barred from participating in the presidential election by the Supreme Electoral Council on 6 August 2021
Conservative Party or PC [Alfredo CESAR Aguirre]
Democratic Restoration Party or PRD [Saturnino CERRATO]; note - canceled by the Supreme Electoral Council on 18 May 2021
Independent Liberal Party or PLI [Mario ASENSIO]
Liberal Constitutionalist Party or PLC [Maria Haydee OSUNA]
Moskitia Indigenous Progressive Movement or MOSKITIA PAWANKA (operates in a political alliance with the FSLN) [Wycliff Diego BLANDON]
Multiethnic Indigenous Party or PIM (operates in a political alliance with the FSLN) [Carla Elvis WHITE HODGSON]
Nationalist Liberal Party or PLN (operates in a political alliance with the FSLN) [Constantino Raul VELASQUEZ]
Nicaraguan Liberal Alliance or ALN [Alejandro MEJIA Ferreti]
Nicaraguan Party of the Christian Path or CCN [Guillermo OSORNO]
Nicaraguan Resistance Party or PRN (operates in a political alliance with the FSLN) [Julio Cesar BLANDON SANCHEZ]
Sandinista National Liberation Front or FSLN [Jose Daniel ORTEGA Saavedra]
Sandinista Renovation Movement or MRS [Suyen BARAHONA Cuan]; note - canceled by the Supreme Electoral Council on 21 June 2008; in January 2021, they rebranded and now call themselves Democratic Renovation Union or UNAMOS Sons of Mother Earth or YATAMA [Brooklyn RIVERA]
The New Sons of Mother Earth Movement or MYATAMARAN (operates in a political alliance with the FSLN) [Osorno Salomon COLEMAN]

International organization participation: BCIE, CACM, CD, CELAC, FAO, G-77, IADB, IAEA, IBRD, ICAO, ICRM, IDA, IFAD, IFC, IFRCS, ILO, IMF, IMO, Interpol, IOC, IOM, IPU, ISO (correspondent), ITSO, ITU, ITUC (NGOs), LAES, LAIA (observer), MIGA, NAM, OAS, OPANAL, OPCW, PCA, Petrocaribe, SICA, UN, UNCTAD, UNESCO, UNHCR, UNIDO, Union Latina, UNWTO, UPU, WCO, WHO, WIPO, WMO, WTO

Diplomatic representation in the US: *chief of mission:* Ambassador Francisco Obadiah CAMPBELL Hooker (since 28 June 2010)
chancery: 1627 New Hampshire Avenue NW, Washington, DC 20009
telephone: [1] (202) 939-6570; [1] (202) 939-6573
FAX: [1] (202) 939-6545
consulate(s) general: Houston, Los Angeles, Miami, New York, San Francisco

Diplomatic representation from the US: *chief of mission:* Ambassador Kevin K. SULLIVAN (since 14 November 2018)
embassy: Kilometer 5.5 Carretera Sur, Managua
mailing address: 3240 Managua Place, Washington DC 20521-3240
telephone: [505] 2252-7100,
FAX: [505] 2252-7250
email address and website:
ACS.Managua@state.gov
https://ni.usembassy.gov/

Flag description: three equal horizontal bands of blue (top), white, and blue with the national coat of arms centered in the white band; the coat of arms features a triangle encircled by the words REPUBLICA DE NICARAGUA on the top and AMERICA CENTRAL on the bottom; the banner is based on the former blue-white-blue flag of the Federal Republic of Central America; the blue bands symbolize the Pacific Ocean and the Caribbean Sea, while the white band represents the land between the two bodies of water
note: similar to the flag of El Salvador, which features a round emblem encircled by the words REPUBLICA DE EL SALVADOR EN LA AMERICA CENTRAL centered in the white band; also similar to the flag of Honduras, which has five blue stars arranged in an X pattern centered in the white band

National symbol(s): turquoise-browed motmot (bird); national colors: blue, white

National anthem: *name:* "Salve a ti, Nicaragua" (Hail to Thee, Nicaragua)
lyrics/music: Salomon Ibarra MAYORGA/traditional, arranged by Luis Abraham DELGADILLO
note: although only officially adopted in 1971, the music was approved in 1918 and the lyrics in 1939; the tune, originally from Spain, was used as an anthem for Nicaragua from the 1830s until 1876

National heritage: *total World Heritage Sites:* 2 (both cultural)
selected World Heritage Site locales: Ruins of León Viejo; León Cathedral

ECONOMY

Economic overview: Nicaragua, the poorest country in Central America and the second poorest in the Western Hemisphere, has widespread underemployment and poverty. GDP growth of 4.5% in 2017 was insufficient to make a significant difference. Textiles and agriculture combined account for nearly 50% of Nicaragua's exports. Beef, coffee, and gold are Nicaragua's top three export commodities.

The Dominican Republic-Central America-United States Free Trade Agreement has been in effect since April 2006 and has expanded export opportunities for many Nicaraguan agricultural and manufactured goods.

In 2013, the government granted a 50-year concession with the option for an additional 50 years to a newly formed Chinese-run company to finance and build an inter-oceanic canal and related projects, at an estimated cost of $50 billion. The canal construction has not started.

Real GDP (purchasing power parity): $34.98 billion (2020 est.)
$35.68 billion (2019 est.)
$37.05 billion (2018 est.)
note: data are in 2017 dollars

Real GDP growth rate: 4.9% (2017 est.)
4.7% (2016 est.)
4.8% (2015 est.)

Real GDP per capita: $5,300 (2020 est.)
$5,500 (2019 est.)
$5,700 (2018 est.)
note: data are in 2017 dollars

GDP (official exchange rate): $12.57 billion (2019 est.)

Inflation rate (consumer prices): 5.3% (2019 est.)
4.9% (2018 est.)
3.8% (2017 est.)

Credit ratings:

Fitch rating: B- (2018)

Moody's rating: B3 (2020)

Standard & Poors rating: B- (2018)
note: The year refers to the year in which the current credit rating was first obtained.

GDP - composition, by sector of origin: *agriculture:* 15.5% (2017 est.)
industry: 24.4% (2017 est.)
services: 60% (2017 est.)

GDP - composition, by end use: *household consumption:* 69.9% (2017 est.)
government consumption: 15.3% (2017 est.)
investment in fixed capital: 28.1% (2017 est.)
investment in inventories: 1.7% (2017 est.)
exports of goods and services: 41.2% (2017 est.)
imports of goods and services: -55.4% (2017 est.)

Agricultural products: sugar cane, milk, rice, maize, plantains, groundnuts, cassava, beans, coffee, poultry

Industries: food processing, chemicals, machinery and metal products, knit and woven apparel, petroleum refining and distribution, beverages, footwear, wood, electric wire harness manufacturing, mining

Industrial production growth rate: 3.5% (2017 est.)

Labor force: 3.046 million (2017 est.)

Labor force - by occupation: *agriculture:* 31%
industry: 18%
services: 50% (2011 est.)

Unemployment rate: 6.4% (2017 est.)
6.2% (2016 est.)
note: underemployment was 46.5% in 2008

Unemployment, youth ages 15-24: *total:* 8.5%
male: 6.4%
female: 12.9% (2014 est.)

Population below poverty line: 24.9% (2016 est.)

Gini Index coefficient - distribution of family income: 46.2 (2014 est.)
45.8 (2009)

Household income or consumption by percentage share: *lowest 10%:* 1.8%
highest 10%: 47.1% (2014)

Budget: *revenues:* 3.871 billion (2017 est.)
expenditures: 4.15 billion (2017 est.)

Budget surplus (+) or deficit (-): -2% (of GDP) (2017 est.)

Public debt: 33.3% of GDP (2017 est.)
31.2% of GDP (2016 est.)
note: official data; data cover general government debt and include debt instruments issued (or owned) by Government entities other than the treasury; the data include treasury debt held by foreign entities, as well as intragovernmental debt; intragovernmental debt consists of treasury borrowings from surpluses in the social funds, such as retirement, medical care, and unemployment, debt instruments for the social funds are not sold at public auctions; Nicaragua rebased its GDP figures in 2012, which reduced the figures for debt as a percentage of GDP

Taxes and other revenues: 28% (of GDP) (2017 est.)

Fiscal year: calendar year

Current account balance: -$694 million (2017 est.)
-$989 million (2016 est.)

Exports: $5.34 billion (2020 est.) note: data are in current year dollars
$5.71 billion (2019 est.) note: data are in current year dollars
$5.56 billion (2018 est.) note: data are in current year dollars

Exports - partners: United States 60%, El Salvador 5%, Mexico 5% (2019)

Exports - commodities: clothing and apparel, gold, insulated wiring, coffee, beef (2019)

Imports: $5.94 billion (2020 est.) note: data are in current year dollars
$6.25 billion (2019 est.) note: data are in current year dollars
$6.75 billion (2018 est.) note: data are in current year dollars

Imports - partners: United States 27%, Mexico 12%, China 11%, Guatemala 9%, Costa Rica 7%, El Salvador 6%, Honduras 6% (2019)

Imports - commodities: refined petroleum, clothing and apparel, crude petroleum, packaged medicines, insulated wiring (2019)

Reserves of foreign exchange and gold: $2.758 billion (31 December 2017 est.)
$2.448 billion (31 December 2016 est.)

Debt - external: $11.674 billion (2019 est.)
$11.771 billion (2018 est.)

Exchange rates: cordobas (NIO) per US dollar -
30.11 (2017 est.)
28.678 (2016 est.)
28.678 (2015 est.)
27.257 (2014 est.)
26.01 (2013 est.)

ENERGY

Electricity access: electrification - total population: 97% (2019)
electrification - urban areas: 99.2% (2019)
electrification - rural areas: 92% (2019)

Electricity: *installed generating capacity:* 1.837 million kW (2020 est.)
consumption: 3,182,620,000 kWh (2019 est.)
exports: 0 kWh (2019 est.)
imports: 434 million kWh (2019 est.)
transmission/distribution losses: 1.89 billion kWh (2019 est.)

Electricity generation sources: *fossil fuels:* 37.8% of total installed capacity (2020 est.)
solar: 0.5% of total installed capacity (2020 est.)
wind: 15.7% of total installed capacity (2020 est.)
hydroelectricity: 12.2% of total installed capacity (2020 est.)
geothermal: 16.7% of total installed capacity (2020 est.)
biomass and waste: 17.2% of total installed capacity (2020 est.)

Petroleum: *total petroleum production:* 200 bbl/day (2021 est.)
refined petroleum consumption: 35,100 bbl/day (2019 est.)
crude oil and lease condensate exports: 0 bbl/day (2018 est.)
crude oil and lease condensate imports: 13,000 bbl/day (2018 est.)
crude oil estimated reserves: 0 barrels (2021 est.)

Refined petroleum products - production: 14,720 bbl/day (2015 est.)

Refined petroleum products - exports: 460 bbl/day (2015 est.)

Refined petroleum products - imports: 20,120 bbl/day (2015 est.)

Carbon dioxide emissions: 4.851 million metric tonnes of CO2 (2019 est.)
from petroleum and other liquids: 4.851 million metric tonnes of CO2 (2019 est.)

Energy consumption per capita: 14.916 million Btu/person (2019 est.)

COMMUNICATIONS

Telephones - fixed lines: *total subscriptions:* 210,981 (2020 est.)
subscriptions per 100 inhabitants: 3 (2020 est.)

Telephones - mobile cellular: *total subscriptions:* 5,976,479 (2020 est.)
subscriptions per 100 inhabitants: 90 (2020 est.)

Telecommunication systems: *general assessment:* Nicaragua's telecoms market has mirrored the country's poor economic achievements, with fixed-line teledensity and mobile penetration also being the lowest in Central America; the fixed line broadband market remains nascent, with population penetration below 4%; most internet users are concentrated in the largest cities, given that rural and marginal areas lack access to the most basic telecom infrastructure; internet cafés provide public access to internet and email services, but these also tend to be restricted to the larger population centers; to address poor infrastructure, the World Bank has funded a project aimed at improving connectivity via a national fiber broadband network; there are separate schemes to improve broadband in eastern regions and provide links to Caribbean submarine cables; the number of mobile subscribers overtook the number of fixed lines in early 2002, and the mobile sector now accounts for most lines in service (2021)
domestic: since privatization, access to fixed-line and mobile-cellular services has improved; fixed-line teledensity roughly 3 per 100 persons; mobile-cellular telephone subscribership has increased to roughly 90 per 100 persons (2020)
international: country code - 505; landing point for the ARCOS fiber-optic submarine cable which provides connectivity to South and Central America, parts of the Caribbean, and the US; satellite earth stations - 1 Intersputnik (Atlantic Ocean region) and 1 Intelsat (Atlantic Ocean) (2019)

Broadcast media: multiple terrestrial TV stations, supplemented by cable TV in most urban areas; nearly all are government-owned or affiliated; more than 300 radio stations, both government-affiliated and privately owned (2019)

Internet country code: .ni

Internet users: *total:* 2,981,049 (2020 est.)
percent of population: 45% (2020 est.)

Broadband - fixed subscriptions: *total:* 290,351 (2020 est.)
subscriptions per 100 inhabitants: 4 (2020 est.)

TRANSPORTATION

National air transport system: *number of registered air carriers:* 1 (2020)
inventory of registered aircraft operated by air carriers: 7

Civil aircraft registration country code prefix: YN

Airports: *total:* 147 (2021)

Airports - with paved runways: *total:* 12
2,438 to 3,047 m: 3
1,524 to 2,437 m: 2
914 to 1,523 m: 3
under 914 m: 4 (2021)

Airports - with unpaved runways: *total:* 135
1,524 to 2,437 m: 1
914 to 1,523 m: 15
under 914 m: 119 (2021)

Pipelines: 54 km oil (2013)

Roadways: *total:* 23,897 km (2014)
paved: 3,346 km (2014)
unpaved: 20,551 km (2014)

Waterways: 2,220 km (2011) (navigable waterways as well as the use of the large Lake Managua and Lake Nicaragua; rivers serve only the sparsely populated eastern part of the country)

Merchant marine: *total:* 5
by type: general cargo 1, oil tanker 1, other 3 (2021)

Ports and terminals: *major seaport(s):* Bluefields, Corinto

MILITARY AND SECURITY

Military and security forces: Army of Nicaragua (Ejercito de Nicaragua, EN): Land Forces (Fuerza Terrestre); Naval Forces (Fuerza Naval); Air Forces (Fuerza Aérea); Special Operations Command (Comando de Operaciones Especiales); Nicaraguan National Police (2022)
note: both the military and the police report directly to the president

Military expenditures: 0.6% of GDP (2021 est.)
0.6% of GDP (2020 est.)
0.6% of GDP (2019) (approximately $170 million)
0.6% of GDP (2018) (approximately $180 million)
0.6% of GDP (2017) (approximately $190 million)

Military and security service personnel strengths: approximately 12,000 active personnel (10,000 Army; 800 Navy; 1,200 Air Force) (2022)

Military equipment inventories and acquisitions: the Nicaraguan military's inventory includes mostly second-hand Russian/Soviet-era equipment; since 2010, Russia has been the leading arms supplier to Nicaragua (2022)

Military service age and obligation: 18-30 years of age for voluntary military service; no conscription;

tour of duty 18-36 months; requires Nicaraguan nationality and 6th-grade education (2022)

Military - note: the modern Army of Nicaragua was created in 1979 as the Sandinista Popular Army (1979-1984); prior to 1979, the military was known as the National Guard, which was organized and trained by the US in the 1920s and 1930s; the first commander of the National Guard, Anastasio SOMOZA GARCIA, seized power in 1937 and ran the country as a military dictator until his assassination in 1956; his sons ran the country either directly or through figureheads until the Sandinistas came to power in 1979; the defeated National Guard was disbanded by the Sandinistas (2022)

TRANSNATIONAL ISSUES

Disputes - international: Nicaragua-El Salvador-Honduras: the 1992 ICJ ruling for El Salvador and Honduras advised a tripartite resolution to establish a maritime boundary in the Gulf of Fonseca, which considers Honduran access to the Pacific; the court ruled, rather, that the Gulf of Fonseca represents a condominium, with control being shared by El Salvador, Honduras, and Nicaragua; the decision allowed for the possibility that the three nations could divide the waters at a later date if they wished to do so

Nicaragua-Costa Rica: Nicaragua and Costa Rica regularly file border dispute cases with the ICJ over the delimitations of the San Juan River and the northern tip of Calero Island, virtually uninhabited areas claimed by both countries; there is an ongoing case in the ICJ to determine Pacific and Atlantic ocean maritime borders as well as land borders; in 2009, the ICJ ruled that Costa Rican vessels carrying out police activities could not use the river, but official Costa Rican vessels providing essential services to riverside inhabitants and Costa Rican tourists could travel freely on the river; in 2011, the ICJ provisionally ruled that both countries must remove personnel from the disputed area; in 2013, the ICJ rejected Nicaragua's 2012 suit to halt Costa Rica's construction of a highway paralleling the river on the grounds of irreparable environmental damage; in 2013, the ICJ, regarding the disputed territory, ordered that Nicaragua should refrain from dredging or canal construction and refill and repair damage caused by trenches connecting the river to the Caribbean and upheld its 2010 ruling that Nicaragua must remove all personnel; in early 2014, Costa Rica brought Nicaragua to the ICJ over offshore oil concessions in the disputed region; in 2018, the ICJ ruled that Nicaragua must remove a military base from a contested coastal area near the San Juan River, and that Costa Rica had sovereignty over the northern part of Isla Portillos, including the coast, but excluding Harbour Head Lagoon; additionally, Honduras was required to pay reparations for environmental damage to part of the wetlands at the mouth of the San Juan River

Nicaragua-Colombia: Nicaragua filed a case with the International Court of Justice (ICJ) against Colombia in 2013 over the delimitation of the Continental shelf beyond the 200 nautical miles from the Nicaraguan coast, as well as over the alleged violation by Colombia of Nicaraguan maritime space in the Caribbean Sea, which contains rich oil and fish resources; as of September 2021, Colombia refuses to abide by the ICJ ruling

Nicaragua-Honduras: none identified

Trafficking in persons: *current situation:* human traffickers exploit domestic and foreign victims in Nicaragua and Nicaraguans abroad; women, children, and migrants are most at risk; women and children are subject to sex trafficking within the country and its two Caribbean autonomous regions, as well as in other Central American countries, Mexico, Spain, and the United States; traffickers used social media to recruit victims with promises of high-paying jobs in restaurants, hotels, construction, and security outside of Nicaragua where they are subjected to sex or labor trafficking; traffickers exploit children through forced participation in illegal drug production and trafficking; children and persons with disabilities are subjected to forced begging; Nicaragua is also a destination for child sex tourists from the United States, Canada, and Western Europe
tier rating: Tier 3 — Nicaragua does not fully meet the minimum standards for the elimination of trafficking and is not making significant efforts to do so and was downgraded to Tier 3; the government identified slightly more victims than in the previous reporting period and prosecuted a trafficker; however, no traffickers were convicted and victim identification remained inadequate; authorities did not investigate, prosecute, or convict government employees complicit in trafficking; the government provided no victim services; prosecution, protection, and prevention efforts in the two Caribbean autonomous regions of Nicaragua continued to be much weaker than in the rest of the country (2020)

Illicit drugs: a transit route for drug traffickers smuggling cocaine from South America through Mexico into the United States via maritime and air routes

NIGER

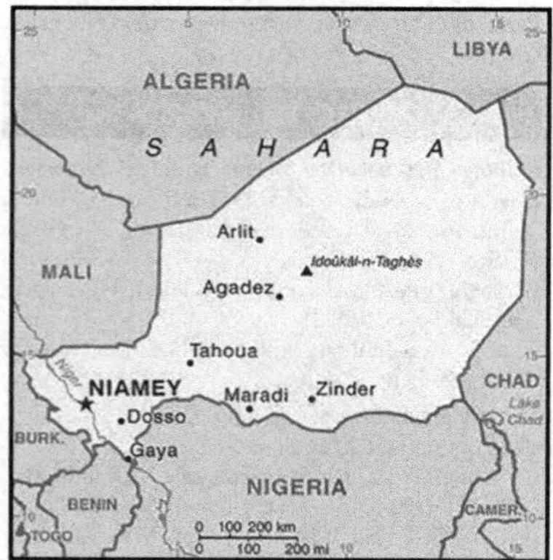

INTRODUCTION

Background: Present-day Niger originated from the nomadic peoples of the Saharan north and the agriculturalists of the south. The Taureg kingdom of Takedda was one of the largest kingdoms in the north and played a prominent role in regional trade in the 14th century. In the south, the primary ethnic groups were the Songhai-Zarma in the west, the Hausa in the center, and the Kanuri in the east. When European colonizers arrived in the 19th century, the region was an assemblage of disparate local kingdoms.

In the late 19th century, the British and French agreed to partition the middle regions of the Niger River, and France began its conquest of what would become the colony of Niger. France experienced determined local resistance - particularly during the Tuareg uprising (1916-1917) - but established a colonial administration in 1922.

After achieving independence from France in 1960, Niger experienced single-party or military rule until 1991 when political pressure forced General Ali SAIBOU to allow multiparty elections. Political infighting and democratic backsliding led to coups in 1996 and 1999. In December of that year, military officers restored democratic rule and held elections that brought Mamadou TANDJA to power. TANDJA was reelected in 2004 and spearheaded a 2009 constitutional amendment allowing him to extend his presidential term. In February 2010, military officers led another coup that deposed TANDJA. ISSOUFOU Mahamadou was elected in April 2011 and reelected in early 2016. In February 2021, BAZOUM Mohammed won the presidential election, marking Niger's first transition from one democratically elected president to another.

Niger is one of the poorest countries in the world with minimal government services and insufficient funds to develop its resource base. It is ranked last in the world on the UN Development Programme's Human Development Index. The largely agrarian and subsistence-based economy is frequently disrupted by extended droughts common to the Sahel region of Africa. The Nigerien Government continues its attempts to diversify the economy through increased oil production and mining projects. In addition, Niger is facing increased security concerns on its borders from various external threats including insecurity in Libya, spillover from the conflict and terrorism in Mali, and violent extremism in northeastern Nigeria.

GEOGRAPHY

Location: Western Africa, southeast of Algeria

Geographic coordinates: 16 00 N, 8 00 E

Map references: Africa

Area: *total:* 1.267 million sq km
land: 1,266,700 sq km
water: 300 sq km

Area - comparative: slightly less than twice the size of Texas

Land boundaries: *total:* 5,834 km
border countries (7): Algeria 951 km; Benin 277 km; Burkina Faso 622 km; Chad 1,196 km; Libya 342 km; Mali 838 km; Nigeria 1,608 km

Coastline: 0 km (landlocked)

Maritime claims: none (landlocked)

Climate: desert; mostly hot, dry, dusty; tropical in extreme south

Terrain: predominately desert plains and sand dunes; flat to rolling plains in south; hills in north

Elevation: *highest point:* Idoukal-n-Taghes 2,022 m
lowest point: Niger River 200 m
mean elevation: 474 m

Natural resources: uranium, coal, iron ore, tin, phosphates, gold, molybdenum, gypsum, salt, petroleum

Land use: *agricultural land:* 35.1% (2018 est.)
arable land: 12.3% (2018 est.)
permanent crops: 0.1% (2018 est.)
permanent pasture: 22.7% (2018 est.)
forest: 1% (2018 est.)
other: 63.9% (2018 est.)

Irrigated land: 1,000 sq km (2012)

Major lakes (area sq km): *fresh water lake(s):* Lake Chad (endorheic lake shared with Chad, Nigeria, and Cameroon) - 10,360-25,900 sq km
note - area varies by season and year to year

Major rivers (by length in km): Niger (shared with Guinea [s], Mali, Benin, and Nigeria [m]) - 4,200 km
note – [s] after country name indicates river source; [m] after country name indicates river mouth

Major watersheds (area sq km): Atlantic Ocean drainage: Niger (2,261,741 sq km)

Internal (*endorheic basin*) drainage: Lake Chad (2,497,738 sq km)

Major aquifers: Lake Chad Basin, Lullemeden-Irhazer Basin, Murzuk-Djado Basin

Population distribution: majority of the populace is located in the southernmost extreme of the country along the border with Nigeria and Benin as shown in this population distribution map

Natural hazards: recurring droughts

Geography - note: landlocked; one of the hottest countries in the world; northern four-fifths is desert, southern one-fifth is savanna, suitable for livestock and limited agriculture

PEOPLE AND SOCIETY

Population: 24,484,587 (2022 est.)

Nationality: *noun:* Nigerien(s)
adjective: Nigerien

Ethnic groups: Hausa 53.1%, Zarma/Songhai 21.2%, Tuareg 11%, Fulani (Peuhl) 6.5%, Kanuri 5.9%, Gurma 0.8%, Arab 0.4%, Tubu 0.4%, other/unavailable 0.9% (2006 est.)

Languages: French (official), Hausa, Djerma

Religions: Muslim 99.3%, Christian 0.3%, animist 0.2%, none 0.1% (2012 est.)

Demographic profile: Niger has the highest total fertility rate (TFR) of any country in the world, averaging close to 7 children per woman in 2022. A slight decline in fertility over the last few decades has stalled. This leveling off of the high fertility rate is in large part a product of the continued desire for large families. In Niger, the TFR is lower than the desired fertility rate, which makes it unlikely that contraceptive use will increase. The high TFR sustains rapid population growth and a large youth population – almost 70% of the populace is under the age of 25, as of 2022. Gender inequality, including a lack of educational opportunities for women and early marriage and childbirth, also contributes to high population growth.

Because of large family sizes, children are inheriting smaller and smaller parcels of land. The dependence of most Nigeriens on subsistence farming on increasingly small landholdings, coupled with declining rainfall and the resultant shrinkage of arable land, are all preventing food production from keeping up with population growth.

For more than half a century, Niger's lack of economic development has led to steady net out-migration. In the 1960s, Nigeriens mainly migrated to coastal West African countries to work on a seasonal basis. Some headed to Libya and Algeria in the 1970s to work in the booming oil industry until its decline in the 1980s. Since the 1990s, the principal destinations for Nigerien labor migrants have been West African countries, especially Burkina Faso and Cote d'Ivoire, while emigration to Europe and North America has remained modest. During the same period, Niger's desert trade route town Agadez became a hub for West African and other Sub-Saharan migrants crossing the Sahara to North Africa and sometimes onward to Europe.

More than 60,000 Malian refugees have fled to Niger since violence between Malian government troops and armed rebels began in early 2012. Ongoing attacks by the Boko Haram Islamist insurgency, dating to 2013 in northern Nigeria and February 2015 in southeastern Niger, pushed tens of thousands of Nigerian refugees and Nigerien returnees across the border to Niger and displaced thousands of locals in Niger's already impoverished Diffa region.

Age structure: *0-14 years:* 50.58% (male 5,805,102/female 5,713,815)
15-24 years: 19.99% (male 2,246,670/female 2,306,285)
25-54 years: 23.57% (male 2,582,123/female 2,784,464)
55-64 years: 3.17% (male 357,832/female 364,774)
65 years and over: 2.68% (male 293,430/female 317,866) (2020 est.)

Dependency ratios: *total dependency ratio:* 109.5
youth dependency ratio: 104.1
elderly dependency ratio: 5.4
potential support ratio: 18.4 (2020 est.)

Median age: *total:* 14.8 years
male: 14.5 years
female: 15.1 years (2020 est.)

Population growth rate: 3.66% (2022 est.)

Birth rate: 47.08 births/1,000 population (2022 est.)

Death rate: 9.87 deaths/1,000 population (2022 est.)

Net migration rate: -0.64 migrant(s)/1,000 population (2022 est.)

Population distribution: majority of the populace is located in the southernmost extreme of the country along the border with Nigeria and Benin as shown in this population distribution map

Urbanization: *urban population:* 16.9% of total population (2022)
rate of urbanization: 4.72% annual rate of change (2020-25 est.)

Major urban areas - population: 1.384 million NIAMEY (capital) (2022)

Sex ratio: *at birth:* 1.03 male(s)/female
0-14 years: 1.02 male(s)/female
15-24 years: 0.97 male(s)/female
25-54 years: 0.92 male(s)/female
55-64 years: 0.97 male(s)/female
65 years and over: 0.81 male(s)/female
total population: 0.98 male(s)/female (2022 est.)

Mother's mean age at first birth: 18.5 years (2012 est.)
note: data represents median age at first birth among women 20-49

Maternal mortality ratio: 509 deaths/100,000 live births (2017 est.)

Infant mortality rate: *total:* 66.81 deaths/1,000 live births
male: 71.73 deaths/1,000 live births
female: 61.75 deaths/1,000 live births (2022 est.)

Life expectancy at birth: *total population:* 60.09 years
male: 58.55 years
female: 61.68 years (2022 est.)

Total fertility rate: 6.82 children born/woman (2022 est.)

Contraceptive prevalence rate: 11% (2021)

Drinking water source: *improved: urban:* 95.8% of population
rural: 63.1% of population
total: 68.6% of population
unimproved: urban: 4.2% of population
rural: 36.9% of population
total: 31.4% of population (2020 est.)

Current health expenditure: 5.7% of GDP (2019)

Physicians density: 0.04 physicians/1,000 population (2020)

Hospital bed density: 0.4 beds/1,000 population (2017)

Sanitation facility access: *improved: urban:* 81.9% of population
rural: 13.5% of population
total: 24.8% of population
unimproved: urban: 18.1% of population
rural: 86.5% of population
total: 75.2% of population (2020 est.)

HIV/AIDS - adult prevalence rate: 0.2% (2020 est.)

Major infectious diseases: *degree of risk:* very high (2020)
food or waterborne diseases: bacterial and protozoal diarrhea, hepatitis A, and typhoid fever
vectorborne diseases: malaria and dengue fever
water contact diseases: schistosomiasis
animal contact diseases: rabies
respiratory diseases: meningococcal meningitis
note: on 21 March 2022, the US Centers for Disease Control and Prevention (CDC) issued a Travel Alert for polio in Africa; Niger is currently considered a high risk to travelers for circulating vaccine-derived polioviruses (cVDPV); vaccine-derived poliovirus (VDPV) is a strain of the weakened poliovirus that was initially included in oral polio vaccine (OPV) and that has changed over time and behaves more like the wild or naturally occurring virus; this means it can be spread more easily to people who are unvaccinated against polio and who come in contact with the stool or respiratory secretions, such as from a sneeze, of an "infected" person who received oral polio vaccine; the CDC recommends that before any international travel, anyone unvaccinated, incompletely vaccinated, or with an unknown polio vaccination status should complete the routine polio vaccine series; before travel to any high-risk destination, the CDC recommends that adults who previously completed the full, routine polio vaccine series receive a single, lifetime booster dose of polio vaccine

Obesity - adult prevalence rate: 5.5% (2016)

Alcohol consumption per capita: *total:* 0.11 liters of pure alcohol (2019 est.)
beer: 0.04 liters of pure alcohol (2019 est.)
wine: 0.01 liters of pure alcohol (2019 est.)
spirits: 0.06 liters of pure alcohol (2019 est.)
other alcohols: 0 liters of pure alcohol (2019 est.)

Tobacco use: *total:* 7.4% (2020 est.)
male: 13.7% (2020 est.)
female: 1.1% (2020 est.)

Children under the age of 5 years underweight: 31.3% (2019)

Education expenditures: 3.5% of GDP (2019 est.)

Literacy: *definition:* age 15 and over can read and write
total population: 35.1%
male: 43.6%
female: 26.7% (2018)

School life expectancy (primary to tertiary education): *total:* 6 years
male: 7 years
female: 6 years (2017)

Unemployment, youth ages 15-24: *total:* 16.6%
male: 16.1%
female: 17.5% (2017 est.)

ENVIRONMENT

Environment - current issues: overgrazing; soil erosion; deforestation; desertification; contaminated water; inadequate potable water; wildlife populations (such as elephant, hippopotamus, giraffe, and lion) threatened because of poaching and habitat destruction

Environment - international agreements: *party to:* Biodiversity, Climate Change, Climate Change-Kyoto Protocol, Climate Change-Paris Agreement, Comprehensive Nuclear Test Ban, Desertification, Endangered Species, Environmental Modification, Hazardous Wastes, Law of the Sea, Nuclear Test Ban, Ozone Layer Protection, Wetlands
signed, but not ratified: none of the selected agreements Air pollutants
particulate matter emissions: 70.8 micrograms per cubic meter (2016 est.)
carbon dioxide emissions: 2.02 megatons (2016 est.)
methane emissions: 22.99 megatons (2020 est.)

Climate: desert; mostly hot, dry, dusty; tropical in extreme south

Land use: *agricultural land:* 35.1% (2018 est.)
arable land: 12.3% (2018 est.)
permanent crops: 0.1% (2018 est.)
permanent pasture: 22.7% (2018 est.)
forest: 1% (2018 est.)
other: 63.9% (2018 est.)

Urbanization: *urban population:* 16.9% of total population (2022)
rate of urbanization: 4.72% annual rate of change (2020-25 est.)

Revenue from forest resources: *forest revenues:* 4.41% of GDP (2018 est.)

Revenue from coal: *coal revenues:* 0.03% of GDP (2018 est.)

Food insecurity: *exceptional shortfall in aggregate food production/supplies:* due to internal conflict and shortfall in cereal production - according to the latest analysis, about 4.4 million people are estimated to need humanitarian food assistance between June and August 2022, reflecting worsening conflicts and security conditions, and unfavorable weather that resulted in a sharp fall in cereal production in 2021; additionally, higher year-on-year prices of food continue to constrain access to food, aggravating conditions (2022)

Waste and recycling: *municipal solid waste generated annually:* 1,865,646 tons (1993 est.)
municipal solid waste recycled annually: 74,626 tons (2005 est.)
percent of municipal solid waste recycled: 4% (2005 est.)

Major lakes (area sq km): *fresh water lake(s):* Lake Chad (endorheic lake shared with Chad, Nigeria, and Cameroon) - 10,360-25,900 sq km
note - area varies by season and year to year

Major rivers (by length in km): Niger (shared with Guinea [s], Mali, Benin, and Nigeria [m]) - 4,200 km
note – [s] after country name indicates river source; [m] after country name indicates river mouth

Major watersheds (area sq km): Atlantic Ocean drainage: Niger (2,261,741 sq km)

Internal *(endorheic basin)* drainage: Lake Chad (2,497,738 sq km)

Major aquifers: Lake Chad Basin, Lullemeden-Irhazer Basin, Murzuk-Djado Basin

Total water withdrawal: *municipal:* 178.9 million cubic meters (2017 est.)
industrial: 36 million cubic meters (2017 est.)
agricultural: 1.536 billion cubic meters (2017 est.)

Total renewable water resources: 34.05 billion cubic meters (2017 est.)

GOVERNMENT

Country name: *conventional long form:* Republic of Niger
conventional short form: Niger
local long form: Republique du Niger
local short form: Niger
etymology: named for the Niger River that passes through the southwest of the country; from a native term "Ni Gir" meaning "River Gir"
note: pronounced nee-zhair

Government type: semi-presidential republic

Capital: *name:* Niamey
geographic coordinates: 13 31 N, 2 07 E
time difference: UTC+1 (6 hours ahead of Washington, DC, during Standard Time)
etymology: according to tradition, the site was originally a fishing village named after a prominent local tree referred to as "nia niam"

Administrative divisions: 7 regions (regions, singular - region) and 1 capital district* (communaute urbaine); Agadez, Diffa, Dosso, Maradi, Niamey*, Tahoua, Tillaberi, Zinder

Independence: 3 August 1960 (from France)

National holiday: Republic Day, 18 December (1958); note - commemorates the founding of the Republic of Niger which predated independence from France in 1960

Constitution: *history:* several previous; passed by referendum 31 October 2010, entered into force 25 November 2010
amendments: proposed by the president of the republic or by the National Assembly; consideration of amendments requires at least three-fourths majority vote by the Assembly; passage requires at least four-fifths majority vote; if disapproved, the proposed amendment is dropped or submitted to a referendum; constitutional articles on the form of government, the multiparty system, the separation of state and religion, disqualification of Assembly members, amendment procedures, and amnesty of participants in the 2010 coup cannot be amended; amended 2011,2017

Legal system: mixed legal system of civil law, based on French civil law, Islamic law, and customary law

International law organization participation: has not submitted an ICJ jurisdiction declaration; accepts ICCt jurisdiction

Citizenship: *citizenship by birth:* no
citizenship by descent only: at least one parent must be a citizen of Niger
dual citizenship recognized: yes
residency requirement for naturalization: unknown

Suffrage: 18 years of age; universal

Executive branch: *chief of state:* President Mohamed BAZOUM (since 2 April 2021)
head of government: Prime Minister Ouhoumoudou MAHAMADOU (since 3 April 2021)
cabinet: Cabinet appointed by the president
elections/appointments: president directly elected by absolute majority popular vote in 2 rounds if needed for a 5-year term (eligible for a second term); election last held on 27 December 2020 with a runoff held on 21 February 2021 (next to be held in 2025); prime minister appointed by the president, authorized by the National Assembly
election results: 2020/2021: percent of vote in first round - Mohamed BAZOUM (PNDS-Tarrayya) 39.3%, Mahamane OUSMANE (MODEN/FA Lumana Africa) 17%, Seini OUMAROU (MNSD-Nassara) 9%, Albade ABOUDA (MPR-Jamhuriya) 7.1%, other 27.6%; percent of vote in second round - Mohamed BAZOUM (PNDS-Tarrayya) 55.7%, Mahamane OUSMANE (RDR Tchanji) 44.3%
2016: ISSOUFOU Mahamadou reelected president in second round; percent of vote in first round - ISSOUFOU Mahamadou (PNDS-Tarrayya) 48.6%, Hama AMADOU (MODEN/FA Lumana Africa) 17.8%, Seini OUMAROU (MNSD-Nassara) 11.3%, other 22.3%; percent of vote in second round - ISSOUFOU Mahamadou 92%, Hama AMADOU 8%

Legislative branch: *description:* unicameral National Assembly or Assemblee Nationale (171 statutory seats - 166 currently; 158 members directly elected from 8 multi-member constituencies in 7 regions and Niamey by party-list proportional representation, 8 reserved for minorities elected in special single-seat constituencies by simple majority vote, 5 seats reserved for Nigeriens living abroad - 1 seat per continent - elected in single-seat constituencies by simple majority vote; members serve 5-year terms)
elections: last held on 27 December 2020 (next scheduled in December 2025)
election results: percent of vote by party - percent of vote by party - PNDS-Tarrayya 37.04%, MODEN/FA Lumana 8.71%, MPR-Jamhuriya 7.59%, MNSD-Nassara 6.77%, RDR-Tchanji 4.41%, CPR-Inganci 4.15%, MPN-Kishin Kassa 3.97%, PJP Generation Dubara 2.88%, ANDP Zaman Lahya 2.46%, RPP Farrilla 2.10%, ARD Adaltchi-Mutuntchi 1.74%, AMEN AMIN 1.43%, MDEN Falala 1.42%, other 15.33%; seats by party - PNDS-Tarrayya 79, MODEN/FA Lumana 19, MPR-Jamhuriya 14, MNSD-Nassara 13, CPR-Inganci 8, MPN-Kishin

Kassa 6, ANDP-Zaman Lahiya 3, RPP Farrilla 2, PJP Generation Dubara 2, ARD Adaltchi-Mutuntchi 2, AMEN AMIN 2, other 16; composition - men 123, women 43, percent of women 25.9%

Judicial branch: *highest court(s):* Constitutional Court (consists of 7 judges); High Court of Justice (consists of 7 members)
judge selection and term of office: Constitutional Court judges nominated/elected - 1 by the president of the Republic, 1 by the president of the National Assembly, 2 by peer judges, 2 by peer lawyers, 1 law professor by peers, and 1 from within Nigerien society; all appointed by the president; judges serve 6-year nonrenewable terms with one-third of membership renewed every 2 years; High Judicial Court members selected from among the legislature and judiciary; members serve 5-year terms
subordinate courts: Court of Cassation; Council of State; Court of Finances; various specialized tribunals and customary courts

Political parties and leaders: Alliance for Democracy and the Republic
Alliance for Democratic Renewal or ARD-Adaltchi-Mutuntchi [Laouan MAGAGI]
Alliance of Movements for the Emergence of Niger or AMEN AMIN [Omar Hamidou TCHIANA]
Congress for the Republic or CPR-Inganci [Maradi Kassoum MOCTAR]
Democratic Alternation for Equity in Niger
Democratic and Republican Renewal-RDR-Tchanji [Mahamane OUSMANE]
Democratic Movement for the Emergence of Niger
National Movement for the Development of Society-Nassara or MNSD-Nassara [Seini OUMAROU]
Nigerien Alliance for Democracy and Progress-Zaman Lahiya or ANDP-Zaman Lahiya [Moussa Hassane BARAZE]
Nigerien Democratic Movement for an African Federation or MODEN/FA Lumana [Hama AMADOU]
Nigerien Party for Democracy and Socialism or PNDS-Tarrayya [Mahamadou ISSOUFOU]
Nigerien Patriotic Movement or MPN-Kishin Kassa [Ibrahim YACOUBA]
Nigerien Rally for Democracy and Peace
Patriotic Movement for the Republic or MPR-Jamhuriya [Albade ABOUBA]
Peace, Justice, Progress–Generation Doubara
Rally for Democracy and Progress-Jama'a or RDP-Jama'a [Hamid ALGABID]
Rally for Peace and Progress
Social Democratic Rally or RSD-Gaskiyya [Amadou CHEIFFOU]
Social Democratic Party or PSD-Bassira [Sanoussi MAREINI]
note 1: only parties with seats in the National Assembly are listed
note 2: the SPLM and SPLM-DC are banned political parties

International organization participation: ACP, AfDB, AU, CD, ECOWAS, EITI (compliant country), Entente, FAO, FZ, G-77, IAEA, IBRD, ICAO, ICCt, ICRM, IDA, IDB, IFAD, IFC, IFRCS, ILO, IMF, Interpol, IOC, IOM, IPU, ISO (correspondent), ITSO, ITU, ITUC (NGOs), LCBC, MIGA, MINUSMA, MNJTF, MONUSCO, NAM, OIC, OIF, OPCW, UN, UNCTAD, UNESCO, UNIDO, UNMIL, UNOCI, UNWTO, UPU, WADB (regional), WAEMU, WCO, WFTU (NGOs), WHO, WIPO, WMO, WTO

Diplomatic representation in the US: *chief of mission:* Ambassador Mamadou Kiari LIMAN-TINGUIRI (since 19 April 2022)
chancery: 2204 R Street NW, Washington, DC 20008
telephone: [1] (202) 483-4224
FAX: [1] (202) 483-3169
email address and website:
communication@embassyofniger.org
http://www.embassyofniger.org/

Diplomatic representation from the US: *chief of mission:* Ambassador (vacant), Chargé d'Affaires, Susan N'GARNIM (since 23 August 2021)
embassy: BP 11201, Niamey
mailing address: 2420 Niamey Place, Washington DC 20521-2420
telephone: [227] 20-72-26-61
FAX: [227] 20-73-55-60
email address and website:
consulateniamey@state.gov
https://ne.usembassy.gov/

Flag description: three equal horizontal bands of orange (top), white, and green with a small orange disk centered in the white band; the orange band denotes the drier northern regions of the Sahara; white stands for purity and innocence; green symbolizes hope and the fertile and productive southern and western areas, as well as the Niger River; the orange disc represents the sun and the sacrifices made by the people
note: similar to the flag of India, which has a blue spoked wheel centered in the white band

National symbol(s): zebu; national colors: orange, white, green

National anthem: *name:* "La Nigerienne" (The Nigerien)
lyrics/music: Maurice Albert THIRIET/Robert JACQUET and Nicolas Abel Francois FRIONNET
note: adopted 1961 National heritage
total World Heritage Sites: 3 (1 cultural, 2 natural)
selected World Heritage Site locales: Air and Ténéré Natural Reserves (n); W-Arly-Pendjari Complex (n); Historic Agadez (c)

ECONOMY

Economic overview: Niger is a landlocked, Sub-Saharan nation, whose economy centers on subsistence crops, livestock, and some of the world's largest uranium deposits. Agriculture contributes approximately 40% of GDP and provides livelihood for over 80% of the population. The UN ranked Niger as the second least developed country in the world in 2016 due to multiple factors such as food insecurity, lack of industry, high population growth, a weak educational sector, and few prospects for work outside of subsistence farming and herding.

Since 2011 public debt has increased due to efforts to scale-up public investment, particularly that related to infrastructure, as well as due to increased security spending. The government relies on foreign donor resources for a large portion of its fiscal budget. The economy in recent years has been hurt by terrorist activity near its uranium mines and by instability in Mali and in the Diffa region of the country; concerns about security have resulted in increased support from regional and international partners on defense. Low uranium prices, demographics, and security expenditures may continue to put pressure on the government's finances.

The Government of Niger plans to exploit oil, gold, coal, and other mineral resources to sustain future growth. Although Niger has sizable reserves of oil, the prolonged drop in oil prices has reduced profitability. Food insecurity and drought remain perennial problems for Niger, and the government plans to invest more in irrigation. Niger's three-year $131 million IMF Extended Credit Facility (ECF) agreement for the years 2012-15 was extended until the end of 2016. In February 2017, the IMF approved a new 3-year $134 million ECF. In June 2017, The World Bank's International Development Association (IDA) granted Niger $1 billion over three years for IDA18, a program to boost the country's development and alleviate poverty. A $437 million Millennium Challenge Account compact for Niger, commencing in FY18, will focus on large-scale irrigation infrastructure development and community-based, climate-resilient agriculture, while promoting sustainable increases in agricultural productivity and sales.

Formal private sector investment needed for economic diversification and growth remains a challenge, given the country's limited domestic markets, access to credit, and competitiveness. Although President ISSOUFOU is courting foreign investors, including those from the US, as of April 2017, there were no US firms operating in Niger. In November 2017, the National Assembly passed the 2018 Finance Law that was geared towards raising government revenues and moving away from international support.

Real GDP (purchasing power parity): $28.97 billion (2020 est.)
$28.54 billion (2019 est.)
$26.95 billion (2018 est.)
note: data are in 2017 dollars

Real GDP growth rate: 4.9% (2017 est.)
4.9% (2016 est.)
4.3% (2015 est.)

Real GDP per capita: $1,200 (2020 est.)
$1,200 (2019 est.)
$1,200 (2018 est.)
note: data are in 2017 dollars

GDP (official exchange rate): $12.926 billion (2019 est.)

Inflation rate (consumer prices): -2.5% (2019 est.)
6.3% (2018 est.)
2.3% (2017 est.)

Credit ratings:

Moody's rating: B3 (2019)
note: The year refers to the year in which the current credit rating was first obtained.

GDP - composition, by sector of origin: *agriculture:* 41.6% (2017 est.)
industry: 19.5% (2017 est.)
services: 38.7% (2017 est.)

GDP - composition, by end use: *household consumption:* 70.2% (2017 est.)
government consumption: 9.4% (2017 est.)
investment in fixed capital: 38.6% (2017 est.)
investment in inventories: 0% (2017 est.)
exports of goods and services: 16.4% (2017 est.)
imports of goods and services: -34.6% (2017 est.)

Agricultural products: millet, cow peas, sorghum, onions, milk, groundnuts, cassava, cabbages, goat milk, fruit

Industries: uranium mining, petroleum, cement, brick, soap, textiles, food processing, chemicals, slaughterhouses

Industrial production growth rate: 6% (2017 est.)

Labor force: 6.5 million (2017 est.)

Labor force - by occupation: *agriculture:* 79.2%
industry: 3.3%
services: 17.5% (2012 est.)

Unemployment rate: 0.3% (2017 est.)
0.3% (2016 est.)

Unemployment, youth ages 15-24: *total:* 16.6%
male: 16.1%
female: 17.5% (2017 est.)

Population below poverty line: 40.8% (2018 est.)

Gini Index coefficient - distribution of family income: 34.3 (2014 est.)
50.5 (1995)

Household income or consumption by percentage share: *lowest 10%:* 3.2%
highest 10%: 26.8% (2014)

Budget: *revenues:* 1.757 billion (2017 est.)
expenditures: 2.171 billion (2017 est.)

Budget surplus (+) or deficit (-): -5% (of GDP) (2017 est.)

Public debt: 45.3% of GDP (2017 est.)
45.2% of GDP (2016 est.)

Taxes and other revenues: 21.4% (of GDP) (2017 est.)

Fiscal year: calendar year

Current account balance: -$1.16 billion (2017 est.)
-$1.181 billion (2016 est.)

Exports: $1.39 billion (2019 est.) note: data are in current year dollars
$1.45 billion (2018 est.) note: data are in current year dollars

Exports - partners: United Arab Emirates 54%, China 25%, France 7%, Pakistan 5% (2019)

Exports - commodities: gold, sesame seeds, uranium, natural gas, refined petroleum (2019)

Imports: $3.4 billion (2019 est.) note: data are in current year dollars
$3.37 billion (2018 est.) note: data are in current year dollars

Imports - partners: China 19%, France 9%, United Arab Emirates 7%, Cote d'Ivoire 6%, India 6%, Nigeria 5%, Togo 5%, Turkey 5% (2019)

Imports - commodities: rice, packaged medicines, palm oil, cars, cement (2019)

Reserves of foreign exchange and gold: $1.314 billion (31 December 2017 est.)
$1.186 billion (31 December 2016 est.)

Debt - external: $3.728 billion (31 December 2017 est.)
$2.926 billion (31 December 2016 est.)

Exchange rates: Communaute Financiere Africaine francs (XOF) per US dollar -
605.3 (2017 est.)
593.01 (2016 est.)
593.01 (2015 est.)
591.45 (2014 est.)
494.42 (2013 est.)

ENERGY

Electricity access: *electrification - total population:* 14% (2019)
electrification - urban areas: 71% (2019)
electrification - rural areas: 2% (2019)

Electricity: *installed generating capacity:* 324,000 kW (2020 est.)
consumption: 1,325,420,000 kWh (2019 est.)
exports: 0 kWh (2019 est.)
imports: 1.057 billion kWh (2019 est.)
transmission/distribution losses: 313 million kWh (2019 est.)

Electricity generation sources: *fossil fuels:* 94.1% of total installed capacity (2020 est.)
solar: 5.9% of total installed capacity (2020 est.)

Coal: *production:* 224,000 metric tons (2020 est.)
consumption: 224,000 metric tons (2020 est.)
exports: 0 metric tons (2020 est.)
imports: 0 metric tons (2020 est.)
proven reserves: 6 million metric tons (2019 est.)

Petroleum: *total petroleum production:* 8,000 bbl/day (2021 est.)
refined petroleum consumption: 13,800 bbl/day (2019 est.)
crude oil estimated reserves: 150 million barrels (2021 est.)

Refined petroleum products - production: 15,280 bbl/day (2015 est.)

Refined petroleum products - exports: 5,422 bbl/day (2015 est.)

Refined petroleum products - imports: 3,799 bbl/day (2015 est.)

Carbon dioxide emissions: 2.374 million metric tonnes of CO_2 (2019 est.)
from coal and metallurgical coke: 499,000 metric tonnes of CO_2 (2019 est.)
from petroleum and other liquids: 1.875 million metric tonnes of CO_2 (2019 est.)

Energy consumption per capita: 1.54 million Btu/person (2019 est.)

COMMUNICATIONS

Telephones - fixed lines: *total subscriptions:* 58,000 (2020)

Telephones - mobile cellular: *total subscriptions:* 14.239 million (2020 est.)
subscriptions per 100 inhabitants: 59 (2020 est.)

Telecommunication systems: *general assessment:* Niger is one of the largest countries in West Africa but also one of the poorest in the world; as with many African markets, a lack of fixed telecoms infrastructure has led to growth in mobile services; Niger's mobile penetration is modest compared to other countries in the region, while fixed broadband penetration is negligible; recent international investment to complete the Trans-Saharan Dorsal optical fibre (SDR) network has extended the reach of fiber infrastructure in the country, and also increased international capacity; new cables linking the country with Chad and Burkina Faso have extended Niger's connectivity with international cable infrastructure (2022)
domestic: fixed-line less than 1 per 100 persons and mobile-cellular at nearly 59 per 100 persons (2020)
international: country code - 227; satellite earth stations - 2 Intelsat (1 Atlantic Ocean and 1 Indian Ocean)

Broadcast media: state-run TV station; 3 private TV stations provide a mix of local and foreign programming; state-run radio has only radio station with national coverage; about 30 private radio stations operate locally; as many as 100 community radio stations broadcast; transmissions of multiple international broadcasters are available

Internet country code: .ne

Internet users: *total:* 2,331,072 (2019 est.)
percent of population: 10% (2019 est.)

Broadband - fixed subscriptions: *total:* 12,000 (2020 est.)
subscriptions per 100 inhabitants: 0.1 (2020 est.)

TRANSPORTATION

National air transport system: *number of registered air carriers:* 2 (2020)
inventory of registered aircraft operated by air carriers: 3

Civil aircraft registration country code prefix: 5U

Airports: *total:* 30 (2021)

Airports - with paved runways: *total:* 10
2,438 to 3,047 m: 3
1,524 to 2,437 m: 6
914 to 1,523 m: 1 (2021)

Airports - with unpaved runways: *total:* 20
1,524 to 2,437 m: 3
914 to 1,523 m: 15
under 914 m: 2 (2021)

Heliports: 1 (2021)

Pipelines: 464 km oil

Roadways: *total:* 18,949 km (2010)
paved: 3,912 km (2010)
unpaved: 15,037 km (2010)

Waterways: 300 km (2012) (the Niger, the only major river, is navigable to Gaya between September and March)

Merchant marine: *total:* 1
by type: general cargo 1 (2021)

MILITARY AND SECURITY

Military and security forces: Nigerien Armed Forces (Forces Armees Nigeriennes, FAN): Army, Nigerien Air Force, Niger Gendarmerie (GN); Ministry of Interior: Niger National Guard (GNN), National Police (2022)
note 1: the Gendarmerie has primary responsibility for rural security; the National Guard is responsible for domestic security and the protection of high-level officials and government buildings
note 2: the National Police includes the Directorate of Territorial Surveillance, which is charged with border management
note 3: the National Guard was formerly known as the National Forces of Intervention and Security

Military expenditures: 1.8% of GDP (2021 est.)
2% of GDP (2020 est.)
1.7% of GDP (2019 est.) (approximately $260 million)
1.9% of GDP (2018 est.) (approximately $270 million)
2% of GDP (2017 est.) (approximately $270 million)

Military and security service personnel strengths: information varies; approximately 12,000 active FAN troops (8,000 Army; 200 Air Force; 4,000 Gendarmerie); approximately 3,000 National Guard (2022)

Military equipment inventories and acquisitions: the FAN's inventory consists of a wide variety of older weapons; since 2010, the FAN has received small amounts of mostly second-hand equipment and donations from several countries with the US as the top provider (2022)

Military service age and obligation: has conscription, although it is reportedly not always enforced; 18 is the legal minimum age for compulsory or voluntary military service; enlistees must be Nigerien citizens and unmarried; 2-year service term; women may serve in health care (2022)

Military deployments: 875 Mali (MINUSMA) (May 2022)
note 1: Niger is part of a four (formerly five)-nation anti-jihadist task force known as the G5 (now G4) Sahel Group, set up in 2014 with Burkina Faso, Chad, Mali (withdrew in 2022), and Mauritania; it has committed 1,100 troops and 200 gendarmes to the force; as of 2022, defense forces from each of the participating states were allowed to pursue terrorist fighters up to 100 km into neighboring countries; the force is backed by France, the UN, and the US
note 2: Niger also has about 1,000 troops committed to the Multinational Joint Task Force (MNJTF) against Boko Haram and other terrorist groups operating in the general area of the Lake Chad Basin and along Nigeria's northeast border; national MNJTF troop contingents are deployed within their own country territories, although cross-border operations are conducted periodically

Military - note: as of 2022, the FAN was conducting counterinsurgency and counterterrorism operations against Islamic militants on at least two fronts; in the Diffa region, the Nigeria-based Boko Haram terrorist group has conducted dozens of attacks on security forces, army bases, and civilians; on Niger's western border with Mali, the Islamic State of Iraq and ash-Sham-West Africa (ISIS-WA) has conducted numerous attacks on security personnel; a series of ISIS-WA attacks on FAN forces near the Malian border in December of 2019 and January of 2020 resulted in the deaths of more than 170 soldiers; terrorist attacks continued into 2022 (2022)

TERRORISM

Terrorist group(s): Boko Haram; Islamic State of Iraq and ash-Sham in the Greater Sahara (ISIS-GS); Islamic State of Iraq and ash-Sham – West Africa (ISIS-WA); Jama'at Nusrat al-Islam wal-Muslimin (JNIM); al-Mulathamun Battalion (al-Mourabitoun)
note: details about the history, aims, leadership, organization, areas of operation, tactics, targets, weapons, size, and sources of support of the group(s) appear(s) in Appendix-T

TRANSNATIONAL ISSUES

Disputes - international: *Niger-Benin-Nigeria:* location of Niger-Benin-Nigeria tripoint is unresolved
Niger-Burkina Faso: the dispute with Burkina Faso was referred to the International Court of Justice (ICJ) in 2010; the ICJ ruled in 2013 that 786 sq km should go to Burkina Faso and 277 sq km to Niger; the ruling was implemented in 2015 and 2016, with Burkina Faso gaining 14 towns and Niger 4
Niger-Cameroon-Nigeria: only Nigeria and Cameroon have heeded the Lake Chad Commission's admonition to ratify the delimitation treaty that also includes the Chad-Niger and Niger-Nigeria boundaries
Niger-Libya: Libya claims about 25,000 sq km in a currently dormant dispute in the Tummo region

Refugees and internally displaced persons: *refugees (country of origin):* 187,136 (Nigeria), 65,621 (Mali) (refugees and asylum seekers) (2022)
IDPs: 376,809 (includes the regions of Diffa, Tillaberi, and Tahoua; unknown how many of the 11,000 people displaced by clashes between government forces and the Tuareg militant group, Niger Movement for Justice, in 2007 are still displaced; inter-communal violence; Boko Haram attacks in southern Niger, 2015) (2022)

Illicit drugs: a transit point for illicit drugs trafficked through the Sahara; drugs from South America, particularly cocaine, heroin, cannabis products, and synthetic drugs, transit en route to European and Middle Eastern markets; synthetic opioid tramadol is shipped from Nigeria through Niger to other African countries; hashish from Morocco is trafficked to Libya, Egypt, Europe, and the Middle East; traffickers are formalized networks of Arab, Tuareg, and Toubou transportation groups

NIGERIA

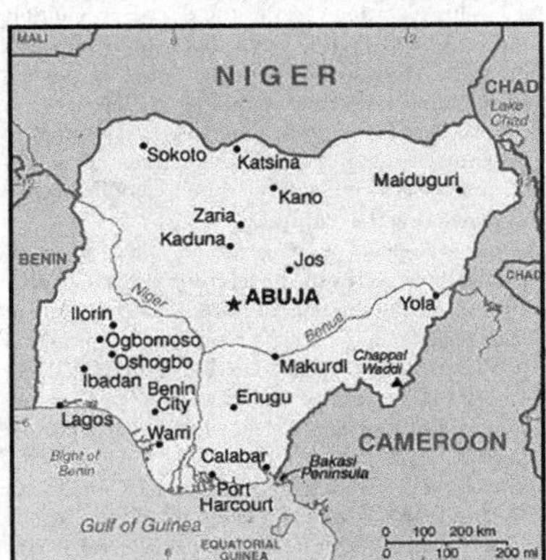

INTRODUCTION

Background: In ancient and pre-colonial times, the area of present-day Nigeria was occupied by a great diversity of ethnic groups with different languages and traditions. These included Islamic empires in northern Nigeria and smaller organized political groupings in southern Nigeria. British influence and control over what would become Nigeria and Africa's most populous country grew through the 19th century. In 1914, the British amalgamated their separately administered northern and southern territories into modern-day Nigeria. A series of constitutions after World War II granted Nigeria greater autonomy. After independence in 1960, politics were marked by coups and mostly military rule, until the death of a military head of state in 1998 allowed for a political transition. In 1999, a new constitution was adopted and a peaceful transition to civilian government was completed. The government continues to face the daunting task of institutionalizing democracy and reforming a petroleum-based economy, whose revenues have been squandered through decades of corruption and mismanagement. In addition, Nigeria continues to experience longstanding ethnic and religious tensions. Although both the 2003 and 2007 presidential elections were marred by significant irregularities and violence, Nigeria is currently experiencing its longest period of civilian rule since independence. The general elections of 2007 marked the first civilian-to-civilian transfer of power in the country's history. National and state elections in 2011 and 2015 were generally regarded as credible. The 2015 election was also heralded for the fact that the then-umbrella opposition party, the All Progressives Congress, defeated the long-ruling People's Democratic Party that had governed since 1999, and assumed the presidency, marking the first peaceful transfer of power from one party to another. Presidential and legislative elections were held in early 2019 and deemed broadly free and fair despite voting irregularities, intimidation, and violence.

GEOGRAPHY

Location: Western Africa, bordering the Gulf of Guinea, between Benin and Cameroon

Geographic coordinates: 10 00 N, 8 00 E

Map references: Africa

Area: *total:* 923,768 sq km
land: 910,768 sq km
water: 13,000 sq km

Area - comparative: about six times the size of Georgia; slightly more than twice the size of California

Land boundaries: *total:* 4,477 km
border countries (4): Benin 809 km; Cameroon 1,975 km; Chad 85 km; Niger 1,608 km

Coastline: 853 km

Maritime claims: *territorial sea:* 12 nm
exclusive economic zone: 200 nm
continental shelf: 200-m depth or to the depth of exploitation

Climate: varies; equatorial in south, tropical in center, arid in north

Terrain: southern lowlands merge into central hills and plateaus; mountains in southeast, plains in north

Elevation: *highest point:* Chappal Waddi 2,419 m
lowest point: Atlantic Ocean 0 m
mean elevation: 380 m

Natural resources: natural gas, petroleum, tin, iron ore, coal, limestone, niobium, lead, zinc, arable land

Land use: *agricultural land:* 78% (2018 est.)
arable land: 37.3% (2018 est.)
permanent crops: 7.4% (2018 est.)
permanent pasture: 33.3% (2018 est.)
forest: 9.5% (2018 est.)
other: 12.5% (2018 est.)

Irrigated land: 2,930 sq km (2012)

Major lakes (area sq km): *fresh water lake(s):* Lake Chad (endorheic lake shared with Niger, Chad, and Cameroon) - 10,360-25,900 sq km
note - area varies by season and year to year

Major rivers (by length in km): Niger river mouth (shared with Guinea [s], Mali, Benin, and Niger) - 4,200 km
note – [s] after country name indicates river source; [m] after country name indicates river mouth

Major watersheds (area sq km): Atlantic Ocean drainage: Niger (2,261,741 sq km)
Internal *(endorheic basin)* drainage: Lake Chad (2,497,738 sq km)

Major aquifers: Lake Chad Basin, Lullemeden-Irhazer Aquifer System

Population distribution: largest population of any African nation; significant population clusters are scattered throughout the country, with the highest density areas being in the south and southwest as shown in this population distribution map

Natural hazards: periodic droughts; flooding

Geography - note: the Niger River enters the country in the northwest and flows southward through tropical rain forests and swamps to its delta in the Gulf of Guinea

PEOPLE AND SOCIETY

Population: 225,082,083 (2022 est.)

Nationality: *noun:* Nigerian(s)
adjective: Nigerian

Ethnic groups: Hausa 30%, Yoruba 15.5%, Igbo (Ibo) 15.2%, Fulani 6%, Tiv 2.4%, Kanuri/Beriberi 2.4%, Ibibio 1.8%, Ijaw/Izon 1.8%, other 24.9% (2018 est.)
note: Nigeria, Africa's most populous country, is composed of more than 250 ethnic groups

Languages: English (official), Hausa, Yoruba, Igbo (Ibo), Fulani, over 500 additional indigenous languages

Religions: Muslim 53.5%, Roman Catholic 10.6%, other Christian 35.3%, other .6% (2018 est.)

Demographic profile: Nigeria's population is projected to grow from more than 186 million people in 2016 to 392 million in 2050, becoming the world's fourth most populous country. Nigeria's sustained high population growth rate will continue for the foreseeable future because of population momentum and its high birth rate. Abuja has not successfully implemented family planning programs to reduce and space births because of a lack of political will, government financing, and the availability and affordability of services and products, as well as a cultural preference for large families. Increased educational attainment, especially among women, and improvements in health care are needed to encourage and to better enable parents to opt for smaller families.

Nigeria needs to harness the potential of its burgeoning youth population in order to boost economic development, reduce widespread poverty, and channel large numbers of unemployed youth into productive activities and away from ongoing religious and ethnic violence. While most movement of Nigerians is internal, significant emigration regionally and to the West provides an outlet for Nigerians looking for economic opportunities, seeking asylum, and increasingly pursuing higher education. Immigration largely of West Africans continues to be insufficient to offset emigration and the loss of highly skilled workers. Nigeria also is a major source, transit, and destination country for forced labor and sex trafficking.

Age structure: *0-14 years:* 41.7% (male 45,571,738/female 43,674,769)
15-24 years: 20.27% (male 22,022,660/female 21,358,753)
25-54 years: 30.6% (male 32,808,913/female 32,686,474)
55-64 years: 4.13% (male 4,327,847/female 4,514,264)
65 years and over: 3.3% (male 3,329,083/female 3,733,801) (2020 est.)

Dependency ratios: *total dependency ratio:* 86
youth dependency ratio: 80.9
elderly dependency ratio: 5.1
potential support ratio: 19.6 (2020 est.)

Median age: *total:* 18.6 years
male: 18.4 years
female: 18.9 years (2020 est.)

Population growth rate: 2.53% (2022 est.)

Birth rate: 34.19 births/1,000 population (2022 est.)

Death rate: 8.7 deaths/1,000 population (2022 est.)

Net migration rate: -0.21 migrant(s)/1,000 population (2022 est.)

Population distribution: largest population of any African nation; significant population clusters are scattered throughout the country, with the highest density areas being in the south and southwest as shown in this population distribution map

Urbanization: *urban population:* 53.5% of total population (2022)
rate of urbanization: 3.92% annual rate of change (2020-25 est.)

Major urban areas - population: 15.388 million Lagos, 4.219 million Kano, 3.756 million Ibadan, 3.652 million ABUJA (capital), 3.325 million Port Harcourt, 1.841 million Benin City (2022)

Sex ratio: *at birth:* 1.06 male(s)/female
0-14 years: 1.04 male(s)/female
15-24 years: 1.03 male(s)/female
25-54 years: 1 male(s)/female
55-64 years: 0.96 male(s)/female
65 years and over: 0.77 male(s)/female
total population: 1.02 male(s)/female (2022 est.)

Mother's mean age at first birth: 20.4 years (2018 est.)
note: data represents median age at first birth among women 25-49

Maternal mortality ratio: 917 deaths/100,000 live births (2017 est.)

Infant mortality rate: *total:* 56.68 deaths/1,000 live births
male: 62.03 deaths/1,000 live births
female: 51.01 deaths/1,000 live births (2022 est.)

Life expectancy at birth: *total population:* 61.33 years
male: 59.51 years
female: 63.27 years (2022 est.)

Total fertility rate: 4.62 children born/woman (2022 est.)

Contraceptive prevalence rate: 16.6% (2018)

Drinking water source: *improved: urban:* 95.3% of population
rural: 68.8% of population
total: 82.6% of population
unimproved: urban: 4.7% of population
rural: 31.2% of population
total: 17.4% of population (2020 est.)

Current health expenditure: 3% of GDP (2019)

Physicians density: 0.38 physicians/1,000 population (2018)

Sanitation facility access: *improved: urban:* 81.6% of population
rural: 41.4% of population
total: 62.3% of population
unimproved: urban: 18.4% of population
rural: 58.6% of population
total: 37.7% of population (2020 est.)

HIV/AIDS - adult prevalence rate: 1.3% (2020 est.)

Major infectious diseases: *degree of risk:* very high (2020)
food or waterborne diseases: bacterial and protozoal diarrhea, hepatitis A and E, and typhoid fever
vectorborne diseases: malaria, dengue fever, and yellow fever
water contact diseases: leptospirosis and schistosomiasis
animal contact diseases: rabies
respiratory diseases: meningococcal meningitis
aerosolized dust or soil contact diseases: Lassa fever
note 1: on 4 May 2022, the Centers for Disease Control and Prevention issued a Travel Health Notice for a Yellow Fever outbreak in Nigeria; a large, ongoing outbreak of yellow fever in Nigeria began in September 2017; the outbreak is now spread throughout the country with the Nigerian Ministry of Health reporting cases of the disease in multiple states (Bauchi, Benue, Delta, Ebonyi, and Enugu); the CDC recommends travelers going to Nigeria should receive vaccination against yellow fever at least 10 days before travel and should take steps to prevent mosquito bites while there; those never vaccinated against yellow fever should avoid travel to Nigeria during the outbreak
note 2: widespread ongoing transmission of a respiratory illness caused by the novel coronavirus (COVID-19) is occurring throughout Nigeria; as of 18 August 2022, Nigeria has reported a total of 262,664 cases of COVID-19 or 127.42 cumulative cases of COVID-19 per 100,000 population with a total of 3,147 cumulative deaths or a rate of 1.52 cumulative death per 100,000 population
note 3: on 21 March 2022, the US Centers for Disease Control and Prevention (CDC) issued a Travel Alert for polio in Africa; Nigeria is currently considered a high risk to travelers for circulating vaccine-derived polioviruses (cVDPV); vaccine-derived poliovirus (VDPV) is a strain of the weakened poliovirus that was initially included in oral polio vaccine (OPV) and *that has changed over time and behaves more like the wild or naturally occurring virus*; this means it can be spread more easily to people who are unvaccinated against polio and who come in contact with the stool or respiratory secretions, such as from a sneeze, of an "infected" person who received oral polio vaccine; the CDC recommends that before any international travel, anyone unvaccinated, incompletely vaccinated, or with an unknown polio vaccination status should complete the routine polio vaccine

series; before travel to any high-risk destination, the CDC recommends that adults who previously completed the full, routine polio vaccine series receive a single, lifetime booster dose of polio vaccine

Obesity - adult prevalence rate: 8.9% (2016)

Alcohol consumption per capita: *total:* 4.49 liters of pure alcohol (2019 est.)
beer: 0.73 liters of pure alcohol (2019 est.)
wine: 0.09 liters of pure alcohol (2019 est.)
spirits: 0.4 liters of pure alcohol (2019 est.)
other alcohols: 3.27 liters of pure alcohol (2019 est.)

Tobacco use: *total:* 3.7% (2020 est.)
male: 6.9% (2020 est.)
female: 0.5% (2020 est.)

Children under the age of 5 years underweight: 18.4% (2019/20)

Child marriage: *women married by age 15:* 15.7%
women married by age 18: 43.4%
men married by age 18: 3.2% (2018 est.)

Literacy: *definition:* age 15 and over can read and write
total population: 62%
male: 71.3%
female: 52.7% (2018)

School life expectancy (primary to tertiary education): *total:* 9 years
male: 9 years
female: 8 years (2011)

Unemployment, youth ages 15-24: *total:* 18.3%
male: 18.4%
female: 18.2% (2019 est.)

ENVIRONMENT

Environment - current issues: serious overpopulation and rapid urbanization have led to numerous environmental problems; urban air and water pollution; rapid deforestation; soil degradation; loss of arable land; oil pollution - water, air, and soil have suffered serious damage from oil spills

Environment - international agreements: *party to:* Biodiversity, Climate Change, Climate Change-Kyoto Protocol, Climate Change-Paris Agreement, Comprehensive Nuclear Test Ban, Desertification, Endangered Species, Hazardous Wastes, Law of the Sea, Marine Dumping-London Convention, Marine Dumping-London Protocol, Marine Life Conservation, Nuclear Test Ban, Ozone Layer Protection, Ship Pollution, Wetlands
signed, but not ratified: Tropical Timber 2006

Air pollutants: *particulate matter emissions:* 48.73 micrograms per cubic meter (2016 est.)
carbon dioxide emissions: 120.37 megatons (2016 est.)
methane emissions: 143.99 megatons (2020 est.)

Climate: varies; equatorial in south, tropical in center, arid in north

Land use: *agricultural land:* 78% (2018 est.)
arable land: 37.3% (2018 est.)
permanent crops: 7.4% (2018 est.)
permanent pasture: 33.3% (2018 est.)
forest: 9.5% (2018 est.)
other: 12.5% (2018 est.)

Urbanization: *urban population:* 53.5% of total population (2022)
rate of urbanization: 3.92% annual rate of change (2020-25 est.)

Revenue from forest resources: *forest revenues:* 1.02% of GDP (2018 est.)

Revenue from coal: *coal revenues:* 0% of GDP (2018 est.)

Food insecurity: *widespread lack of access: due to persistent civil conflict in the northern areas, localized shortfalls in cereal production, and high food prices* - according to the latest analysis, about 19.45 million people are projected to be in need of humanitarian food assistance between June and August 2022, owing to the deterioration of security conditions and conflicts in northern states, localized shortfalls in staple food production, high food prices and reduced incomes (2022)

Waste and recycling: *municipal solid waste generated annually:* 27,614,830 tons (2009 est.)

Major lakes (area sq km): *fresh water lake(s):* Lake Chad (endorheic lake shared with Niger, Chad, and Cameroon) - 10,360-25,900 sq km
note - area varies by season and year to year

Major rivers (by length in km): Niger river mouth (shared with Guinea [s], Mali, Benin, and Niger) - 4,200 km
note – [s] after country name indicates river source; [m] after country name indicates river mouth

Major watersheds (area sq km): Atlantic Ocean drainage: Niger (2,261,741 sq km)
Internal *(endorheic basin)* drainage: Lake Chad (2,497,738 sq km)

Major aquifers: Lake Chad Basin, Lullemeden-Irhazer Aquifer System

Total water withdrawal: *municipal:* 5 billion cubic meters (2017 est.)
industrial: 1.965 billion cubic meters (2017 est.)
agricultural: 5.51 billion cubic meters (2017 est.)

Total renewable water resources: 286.2 billion cubic meters (2017 est.)

GOVERNMENT

Country name: *conventional long form:* Federal Republic of Nigeria
conventional short form: Nigeria
etymology: named for the Niger River that flows through the west of the country to the Atlantic Ocean; from a native term "Ni Gir" meaning "River Gir"

Government type: federal presidential republic

Capital: *name:* Abuja
geographic coordinates: 9 05 N, 7 32 E
time difference: UTC+1 (6 hours ahead of Washington, DC, during Standard Time)
etymology: Abuja is a planned capital city, it replaced Lagos in 1991; situated in the center of the country, Abuja takes its name from a nearby town, now renamed Suleja

Administrative divisions: 36 states and 1 territory*; Abia, Adamawa, Akwa Ibom, Anambra, Bauchi, Bayelsa, Benue, Borno, Cross River, Delta, Ebonyi, Edo, Ekiti, Enugu, Federal Capital Territory*, Gombe, Imo, Jigawa, Kaduna, Kano, Katsina, Kebbi, Kogi, Kwara, Lagos, Nasarawa, Niger, Ogun, Ondo, Osun, Oyo, Plateau, Rivers, Sokoto, Taraba, Yobe, Zamfara

Independence: 1 October 1960 (from the UK)

National holiday: Independence Day (National Day), 1 October (1960)

Constitution: *history:* several previous; latest adopted 5 May 1999, effective 29 May 1999
amendments: proposed by the National Assembly; passage requires at least two-thirds majority vote of both houses and approval by the Houses of Assembly of at least two thirds of the states; amendments to constitutional articles on the creation of a new state, fundamental constitutional rights, or constitution-amending procedures requires at least four-fifths majority vote by both houses of the National Assembly and approval by the Houses of Assembly in at least two thirds of the states; passage of amendments limited to the creation of a new state require at least two-thirds majority vote by the proposing National Assembly house and approval by the Houses of Assembly in two thirds of the states; amended several times, last in 2018

Legal system: mixed legal system of English common law, Islamic law (in 12 northern states), and traditional law

International law organization participation: accepts compulsory ICJ jurisdiction with reservations; accepts ICCt jurisdiction

Citizenship: *citizenship by birth:* no
citizenship by descent only: at least one parent must be a citizen of Nigeria
dual citizenship recognized: yes
residency requirement for naturalization: 15 years

Suffrage: 18 years of age; universal

Executive branch: *chief of state:* President Maj. Gen. (ret.) Muhammadu BUHARI (since 29 May 2015); Vice President Oluyemi "Yemi" OSINBAJO (since 29 May 2015); note - the president is both chief of state, head of government, and commander-inchief of the armed forces
head of government: President Maj. Gen. (ret.) Muhammadu BUHARI (since 29 May 2015); Vice President Oluyemi "Yemi" OSINBAJO (since 29 May 2015)
cabinet: Federal Executive Council appointed by the president but constrained constitutionally to include at least one member from each of the 36 states
elections/appointments: president directly elected by qualified majority popular vote and at least 25% of the votes cast in 24 of Nigeria's 36 states; president elected for a 4-year term (eligible for a second term); election last held on 23 February 2019 (next to be held on 25 February 2023)
election results:
Muhammadu BUHARI elected president; percent of vote - Muhammadu BUHARI (APC) 53%, Atiku ABUBAKAR (PDP) 39%, other 8% (2019)

Legislative branch: *description:* bicameral National Assembly consists of:
Senate (109 seats - 3 each for the 36 states and 1 for Abuja-Federal Capital Territory; members directly elected in single-seat constituencies by simple majority vote to serve 4-year terms)
House of Representatives (360 seats; members directly elected in single-seat constituencies by simple majority vote to serve 4-year terms)
elections:
Senate - last held on 23 February 2019 (next to be held on 25 February 2023)
House of Representatives - last held on 23 February 2019 (next to be held on 25 February 2023)
election results:
Senate - percent of vote by party - NA; seats by party - APC 65, PDP 39, YPP 1, TBD 3; composition - men 101, women 8, percent of women 7.3%
House of Representatives - percent of vote by party - NA; seats by party - APC 217, PDP 115, other 20, TBD 8; composition - men 347, women 13, percent

of women 3.6%; note - total National Assembly percent of women 4.5%

Judicial branch: *highest court(s):* Supreme Court (consists of the chief justice and 15 justices)
judge selection and term of office: judges appointed by the president upon the recommendation of the National Judicial Council, a 23-member independent body of federal and state judicial officials; judge appointments confirmed by the Senate; judges serve until age 70
subordinate courts: Court of Appeal; Federal High Court; High Court of the Federal Capital Territory; Sharia Court of Appeal of the Federal Capital Territory; Customary Court of Appeal of the Federal Capital Territory; state court system similar in structure to federal system

Political parties and leaders: Accord Party or ACC [Mohammad Lawal MALADO]
Africa Democratic Congress or ADC [Ralph Okey NWOSU]
All Progressives Congress or APC [Abdullahi ADAMU]
All Progressives Grand Alliance or APGA [Victor Ike OYE]
Labor Party or LP [Julius ABURE]
Peoples Democratic Party or PDP [Iyourchia AYU]
Young Progressive Party or YPP [Bishop AMAKIRI]

International organization participation: ACP, AfDB, ATMIS, AU, C, CD, D-8, ECOWAS, EITI (compliant country), FAO, G-15, G-24, G-77, IAEA, IBRD, ICAO, ICC (national committees), ICCt, ICRM, IDA, IDB, IFAD, IFC, IFRCS, IHO, ILO, IMF, IMO, IMSO, Interpol, IOC, IOM, IPU, ISO, ITSO, ITU, ITUC (NGOs), LCBC, MIGA, MINURSO, MINUSMA, MNJTF, MONUSCO, NAM, OAS (observer), OIC, OPCW, OPEC, PCA, UN, UNAMID, UNCTAD, UNESCO, UNHCR, UNIDO, UNIFIL, UNISFA, UNITAR, UNMIL, UNMISS, UNOCI, UNWTO, UPU, WCO, WFTU (NGOs), WHO, WIPO, WMO, WTO

Diplomatic representation in the US: *chief of mission:* Ambassador Uzoma Elizabeth EMENIKE (since 7 July 2021)
chancery: 3519 International Court NW, Washington, DC 20008
telephone: [1] (202) 800-7201 (ext. 100)
FAX: [1] (202) 362-6541
email address and website:
info@nigeriaembassyusa.org
https://www.nigeriaembassyusa.org/
consulate(s) general: Atlanta, New York

Diplomatic representation from the US: *chief of mission:* Ambassador Mary Beth LEONARD (since 24 December 2019)
embassy: Plot 1075 Diplomatic Drive, Central District Area, Abuja
mailing address: 8320 Abuja Place, Washington DC 20521-8320
telephone: [234] (9) 461-4000
FAX: [234] (9) 461-4036
email address and website:
AbujaACS@state.gov
https://ng.usembassy.gov/
consulate(s) general: Lagos

Flag description: three equal vertical bands of green (hoist side), white, and green; the color green represents the forests and abundant natural wealth of the country, white stands for peace and unity

National symbol(s): eagle; national colors: green, white

National anthem: *name:* "Arise Oh Compatriots, Nigeria's Call Obey"
lyrics/music: John A. ILECHUKWU, Eme Etim AKPAN, B.A. OGUNNAIKE, Sotu OMOIGUI and P.O. ADERIBIGBE/Benedict Elide ODIASE
note: adopted 1978; lyrics are a mixture of the five top entries in a national contest

National heritage: *total World Heritage Sites:* 2 (both cultural)
selected World Heritage Site locales: Sukur Cultural Landscape; Osun-Osogbo Sacred Grove

ECONOMY

Economic overview: Nigeria is Sub Saharan Africa's largest economy and relies heavily on oil as its main source of foreign exchange earnings and government revenues. Following the 2008-09 global financial crises, the banking sector was effectively recapitalized and regulation enhanced. Since then, Nigeria's economic growth has been driven by growth in agriculture, telecommunications, and services. Economic diversification and strong growth have not translated into a significant decline in poverty levels; over 62% of Nigeria's over 180 million people still live in extreme poverty.

Despite its strong fundamentals, oil-rich Nigeria has been hobbled by inadequate power supply, lack of infrastructure, delays in the passage of legislative reforms, an inefficient property registration system, restrictive trade policies, an inconsistent regulatory environment, a slow and ineffective judicial system, unreliable dispute resolution mechanisms, insecurity, and pervasive corruption. Regulatory constraints and security risks have limited new investment in oil and natural gas, and Nigeria's oil production had been contracting every year since 2012 until a slight rebound in 2017.

President BUHARI, elected in March 2015, has established a cabinet of economic ministers that includes several technocrats, and he has announced plans to increase transparency, diversify the economy away from oil, and improve fiscal management, but has taken a primarily protectionist approach that favors domestic producers at the expense of consumers. President BUHARI ran on an anti-corruption platform, and has made some headway in alleviating corruption, such as implementation of a Treasury Single Account that allows the government to better manage its resources and a more transparent government payroll and personnel system that eliminated duplicate and "ghost workers." The government also is working to develop stronger public-private partnerships for roads, agriculture, and power.

Nigeria entered recession in 2016 as a result of lower oil prices and production, exacerbated by militant attacks on oil and gas infrastructure in the Niger Delta region, coupled with detrimental economic policies, including foreign exchange restrictions. GDP growth turned positive in 2017 as oil prices recovered and output stabilized.

Real GDP (purchasing power parity): $1,013,530,000,000 (2020 est.)
$1,032,050,000,000 (2019 est.)
$1,009,750,000,000 (2018 est.)
note: data are in 2017 dollars

Real GDP growth rate: 0.8% (2017 est.)
-1.6% (2016 est.)
2.7% (2015 est.)

Real GDP per capita: $4,900 (2020 est.)
$5,100 (2019 est.)
$5,200 (2018 est.)
note: data are in 2017 dollars

GDP (official exchange rate): $475.062 billion (2019 est.)

Inflation rate (consumer prices): 11.3% (2019 est.)
12.1% (2018 est.)
16.5% (2017 est.)

Credit ratings:

Fitch rating: B (2020)

Moody's rating: B2 (2017)

Standard & Poors rating: B- (2020)
note: The year refers to the year in which the current credit rating was first obtained.

GDP - composition, by sector of origin: *agriculture:* 21.1% (2016 est.)
industry: 22.5% (2016 est.)
services: 56.4% (2017 est.)

GDP - composition, by end use: *household consumption:* 80% (2017 est.)
government consumption: 5.8% (2017 est.)
investment in fixed capital: 14.8% (2017 est.)
investment in inventories: 0.7% (2017 est.)
exports of goods and services: 11.9% (2017 est.)
imports of goods and services: -13.2% (2017 est.)

Agricultural products: cassava, yams, maize, oil palm fruit, rice, vegetables, sorghum, groundnuts, fruit, sweet potatoes

Industries: crude oil, coal, tin, columbite; rubber products, wood; hides and skins, textiles, cement and other construction materials, food products, footwear, chemicals, fertilizer, printing, ceramics, steel

Industrial production growth rate: 2.2% (2017 est.)

Labor force: 60.08 million (2017 est.)

Labor force - by occupation: *agriculture:* 70%
industry: 10%
services: 20% (1999 est.)

Unemployment rate: 16.5% (2017 est.)
13.9% (2016 est.)

Unemployment, youth ages 15-24: *total:* 18.3%
male: 18.4%
female: 18.2% (2019 est.)

Population below poverty line: 40.1% (2018 est.)

Gini Index coefficient - distribution of family income: 35.1 (2018 est.)
50.6 (1997)

Household income or consumption by percentage share: *lowest 10%:* 1.8%
highest 10%: 38.2% (2010 est.)

Budget: *revenues:* 12.92 billion (2017 est.)
expenditures: 19.54 billion (2017 est.)

Budget surplus (+) or deficit (-): -1.8% (of GDP) (2017 est.)

Public debt: 21.8% of GDP (2017 est.)
19.6% of GDP (2016 est.)

Taxes and other revenues: 3.4% (of GDP) (2017 est.)

Fiscal year: calendar year

Current account balance: $10.38 billion (2017 est.)
$2.714 billion (2016 est.)

Exports: $39.94 billion (2020 est.) note: data are in current year dollars
$69.93 billion (2019 est.) note: data are in current year dollars
$66.04 billion (2018 est.) note: data are in current year dollars

Exports - partners: India 16%, Spain 10%, United States 7%, France 7%, Netherlands 6% (2019)

Exports - commodities: crude petroleum, natural gas, scrap vessels, flexible metal tubing, cocoa beans (2019)

Imports: $72.18 billion (2020 est.) note: data are in current year dollars
$100.82 billion (2019 est.) note: data are in current year dollars
$71.64 billion (2018 est.) note: data are in current year dollars

Imports - partners: China 30%, Netherlands 11%, United States 6%, Belgium 5% (2019)

Imports - commodities: refined petroleum, cars, wheat, laboratory glassware, packaged medicines (2019)

Reserves of foreign exchange and gold: $38.77 billion (31 December 2017 est.)
$25.84 billion (31 December 2016 est.)

Debt - external: $26.847 billion (2019 est.)
$22.755 billion (2018 est.)

Exchange rates: nairas (NGN) per US dollar -
383.5 (2020 est.)
362.75 (2019 est.)
363 (2018 est.)
192.73 (2014 est.)
158.55 (2013 est.)

ENERGY

Electricity access: *electrification - total population:* 62% (2019)
electrification - urban areas: 91% (2019)
electrification - rural areas: 30% (2019)

Electricity: *installed generating capacity:* 11.691 million kW (2020 est.)
consumption: 24,611,480,000 kWh (2019 est.)
exports: 0 kWh (2019 est.)
imports: 0 kWh (2019 est.)
transmission/distribution losses: 4.713 billion kWh (2019 est.)

Electricity generation sources: *fossil fuels:* 78.1% of total installed capacity (2020 est.)
solar: 0.2% of total installed capacity (2020 est.)
hydroelectricity: 21.7% of total installed capacity (2020 est.)
biomass and waste: 0.1% of total installed capacity (2020 est.)

Coal: *production:* 44,000 metric tons (2020 est.)
consumption: 85,000 metric tons (2020 est.)
exports: 12,000 metric tons (2020 est.)
imports: 77,000 metric tons (2020 est.)
proven reserves: 344 million metric tons (2019 est.)

Petroleum: *total petroleum production:* 1,646,900 bbl/day (2021 est.)
refined petroleum consumption: 483,100 bbl/day (2019 est.)
crude oil and lease condensate exports: 1,889,100 bbl/day (2018 est.)
crude oil and lease condensate imports: 0 bbl/day (2018 est.)
crude oil estimated reserves: 36.89 billion barrels (2021 est.)

Refined petroleum products - production: 35,010 bbl/day (2017 est.)

Refined petroleum products - exports: 2,332 bbl/day (2015 est.)

Refined petroleum products - imports: 223,400 bbl/day (2015 est.)

Natural gas: *production:* 46,296,835,000 cubic meters (2019 est.)
consumption: 18,787,602,000 cubic meters (2019 est.)
exports: 27,509,177,000 cubic meters (2019 est.)
imports: 0 cubic meters (2021 est.)
proven reserves: 5,760,883,000,000 cubic meters (2021 est.)

Carbon dioxide emissions: 104.494 million metric tonnes of CO2 (2019 est.)
from coal and metallurgical coke: 231,000 metric tonnes of CO2 (2019 est.)
from petroleum and other liquids: 67.406 million metric tonnes of CO2 (2019 est.)
from consumed natural gas: 36.856 million metric tonnes of CO2 (2019 est.)

Energy consumption per capita: 8.466 million Btu/person (2019 est.)

COMMUNICATIONS

Telephones - fixed lines: *total subscriptions:* 107,031 (2020 est.)

Telephones - mobile cellular: *total subscriptions:* 204,228,678 (2020 est.)
subscriptions per 100 inhabitants: 99 (2020 est.)

Telecommunication systems: *general assessment:* one of the larger telecom markets in Africa subject to sporadic access to electricity and vandalism of infrastructure; most Internet connections are via mobile networks; market competition with affordable access; LTE technologies available but GSM is dominant; mobile penetration high due to use of multiple SIM cards and phones; government committed to expanding broadband penetration; operators to deploy fiber optic cable in six geopolitical zones and Lagos; operators invested in base stations to deplete network congestion; submarine cable break in 2020 slowed speeds and interrupted connectivity; Nigeria concluded its first 5G spectrum auction in 2021 and granted licenses to two firms; construction of 5G infrastructure has not yet been completed (2022)
domestic: fixed-line subscribership remains less than 1 per 100 persons; mobile-cellular services growing rapidly, in part responding to the shortcomings of the fixed-line network; multiple cellular providers operate nationally with subscribership base over 99 per 100 persons (2020)
international: country code - 234; landing point for the SAT-3/WASC, NCSCS, MainOne, Glo-1 & 2, ACE, and Equiano fiber-optic submarine cable that provides connectivity to Europe and South and West Africa; satellite earth stations - 3 Intelsat (2 Atlantic Ocean and 1 Indian Ocean) (2019)

Broadcast media: nearly 70 federal government-controlled national and regional TV stations; all 36 states operate TV stations; several private TV stations operational; cable and satellite TV subscription services are available; network of federal government-controlled national, regional, and state radio stations; roughly 40 state government-owned radio stations typically carry their own programs except for news broadcasts; about 20 private radio stations; transmissions of international broadcasters are available; digital broadcasting migration process completed in three states in 2018 (2019)

Internet country code: .ng

Internet users: *total:* 74,210,251 (2020 est.)
percent of population: 36% (2020 est.)

Broadband - fixed subscriptions: *total:* 65,313 (2020 est.)
subscriptions per 100 inhabitants: 0.03 (2020 est.)

TRANSPORTATION

National air transport system: *number of registered air carriers:* 13 (2020)
inventory of registered aircraft operated by air carriers: 104
annual passenger traffic on registered air carriers: 8,169,192 (2018)
annual freight traffic on registered air carriers: 19.42 million (2018) mt-km

Civil aircraft registration country code prefix: 5N

Airports: *total:* 54 (2021)

Airports - with paved runways: *total:* 40
over 3,047 m: 10
2,438 to 3,047 m: 12
1,524 to 2,437 m: 9
914 to 1,523 m: 6
under 914 m: 3 (2021)

Airports - with unpaved runways: *total:* 14
1,524 to 2,437 m: 2
914 to 1,523 m: 9
under 914 m: 3 (2021)

Heliports: 5 (2021)

Pipelines: 124 km condensate, 4,045 km gas, 164 km liquid petroleum gas, 4,441 km oil, 3,940 km refined products (2013)

Railways: *total:* 3,798 km (2014)
standard gauge: 293 km (2014) 1.435-m gauge
narrow gauge: 3,505 km (2014) 1.067-m gauge
note: as of the end of 2018, there were only six operational locomotives in Nigeria primarily used for passenger service; the majority of the rail lines are in a severe state of disrepair and need to be replaced

Roadways: *total:* 195,000 km (2017)
paved: 60,000 km (2017)
unpaved: 135,000 km (2017)

Waterways: 8,600 km (2011) (Niger and Benue Rivers and smaller rivers and creeks)

Merchant marine: *total:* 791
by type: general cargo 14, oil tanker 110, other 667 (2021)

Ports and terminals: *major seaport(s):* Bonny Inshore Terminal, Calabar, Lagos
oil terminal(s): Bonny Terminal, Brass Terminal, Escravos Terminal, Forcados Terminal, Pennington Terminal, Qua Iboe Terminal

LNG terminal(s) (export): Bonny Island

MILITARY AND SECURITY

Military and security forces: Nigerian Armed Forces: Army, Navy (includes Coast Guard), Air Force; Ministry of Interior: Nigeria Security and Civil Defense Corps (NSCDC) (2022)
note 1: the NSCDC a paramilitary agency commissioned to assist the military in the management of threats to internal security, including attacks and natural disasters
note 2: some states have created local security forces in response to increased violence, insecurity, and criminality that have exceeded the response capacity of government security forces

Military expenditures: 0.7% of GDP (2021 est.)
0.6% of GDP (2020 est.)

0.5% of GDP (2019) (approximately $3.53 billion)
0.5% of GDP (2018) (approximately $3.72 billion)
0.5% of GDP (2017) (approximately $3.42 billion)

Military and security service personnel strengths: information varies; approximately 135,000 active duty armed forces personnel (100,000 Army; 20,000 Navy/Coast Guard; 15,000 Air Force); approximately 80,000 Security and Civil Defense Corps (2022)

Military equipment inventories and acquisitions: the military's inventory consists of a wide variety of imported weapons systems of Chinese, European, Middle Eastern, Russian (including Soviet-era), and US origin; since 2010, Nigeria has undertaken a considerable military modernization program, and has received equipment from some 20 countries with China, Russia, and the US as the leading suppliers; Nigeria is also developing a defense-industry capacity, including small arms, armored personnel vehicles, and small-scale naval production (2022)

Military service age and obligation: 18-26 years of age for men and women for voluntary military service; no conscription (2022)

Military deployments: 200 Ghana (ECOMIG) (2022)
note: Nigeria has committed an Army combat brigade (approximately 3,000 troops) to the Multinational Joint Task Force (MNJTF), a regional counter-terrorism force comprised of troops from Benin, Cameroon, Chad, and Niger; MNJTF conducts operations against Boko Haram and other terrorist groups operating in the general area of the Lake Chad Basin and along Nigeria's northeast border; national MNJTF troop contingents are deployed within their own country territories, although cross-border operations are conducted periodically

Military - note: as of 2022, the Nigerian military was sub-Saharan Africa's largest and regarded as one of its most capable forces; it was focused largely on internal security and faced a number of challenges that have stretched its resources, however; the Army was deployed in all 36 of the country's states; in the northeast, it was conducting counterinsurgency/counter-terrorist operations against the Boko Haram (BH) and Islamic State of Iraq and ash-Sham in West Africa (ISIS-WA) terrorist groups, where it has deployed as many as 70,000 troops at times and jihadist-related violence has killed an estimated 35-40,000 people, mostly civilians, since 2009 (as of 2022); in the northwest, it faced growing threats from criminal gangs, bandits, and violence associated with historical and ongoing farmer-herder conflicts, as well as BH and ISIS-WA terrorists; bandits in the northwest were estimated to number in the low 10,000s and violence there has killed more than 10,000 since the mid-2010s; the military also continued to protect the oil industry in the Niger Delta region against militants and criminal activity, although the levels of violence there have decreased in recent years; beginning in May 2021, a contingent of military troops and police were deployed to eastern Nigeria to quell renewed agitation for a state of Biafra (Biafra seceded from Nigeria in the late 1960s, sparking a civil war that caused more than 1 million deaths)

as of 2022, the Navy was focused on security in the Gulf of Guinea; since 2016, it has developed a maritime strategy, boosted naval training and its naval presence in the Gulf, increased participation in regional maritime security efforts, and acquired a significant number of new naval platforms, including offshore and coastal patrol craft, fast attack boats, and air assets

the Nigerian military traces its origins to the Nigeria Regiment of the West African Frontier Force (WAFF), a multi-regiment force formed by the British colonial office in 1900 to garrison the West African colonies of Nigeria (Lagos and the protectorates of Northern and Southern Nigeria), Gold Coast, Sierra Leone, and Gambia; the WAFF served with distinction in both East and West Africa during World War I; in 1928, it received royal recognition and was re-named the Royal West African Frontier Force (RWAFF); the RWAFF went on to serve in World War II as part of the British 81st and 82nd (West African) divisions in the East Africa and Burma campaigns; in 1956, the Nigeria Regiment of the RWAFF was renamed the Nigerian Military Forces (NMF) and in 1958, the colonial government of Nigeria took over control of the NMF from the British War Office; the Nigerian Armed Forces were established following independence in 1960

Maritime threats: the International Maritime Bureau reports the territorial and offshore waters in the Niger Delta and Gulf of Guinea remain a very high risk for piracy and armed robbery of ships; in 2021, there were 34 reported incidents of piracy and armed robbery at sea in the Gulf of Guinea region; although a significant decrease from the total number of 81 incidents in 2020, it included the one hijacking and three of five ships fired upon worldwide; while boarding and attempted boarding to steal valuables from ships and crews are the most common types of incidents, almost a third of all incidents involve a hijacking and/or kidnapping; in 2021, 57 crew members were kidnapped in seven separate incidents in the Gulf of Guinea, representing 100% of kidnappings worldwide; Nigerian pirates in particular are well armed and very aggressive, operating as far as 200 nm offshore; the Maritime Administration of the US Department of Transportation has issued a Maritime Advisory (2022-001 - Gulf of Guinea-Piracy/Armed Robbery/Kidnapping for Ransom) effective 4 January 2022, which states in part, "Piracy, armed robbery, and kidnapping for ransom continue to serve as significant threats to US-flagged vessels transiting or operating in the Gulf of Guinea"

TERRORISM

Terrorist group(s): Boko Haram; Islamic State of Iraq and ash-Sham – West Africa; Jama'atu Ansarul Muslimina Fi Biladis-Sudan (Ansaru)

TRANSNATIONAL ISSUES

Disputes - international: *Nigeria-Benin:* none identified
Nigeria-Cameroon: Joint Border Commission with Cameroon reviewed 2002 ICJ ruling on the entire boundary and bilaterally resolved differences, including June 2006 Greentree Agreement that immediately ceded sovereignty of the Bakassi Peninsula to Cameroon with a phaseout of Nigerian control within two years while resolving patriation issues; demarcation of the Bakassi Peninsula and adjoining border areas should be finalized in 2022; as Lake Chad's evaporation exposed dry land, only Nigeria and Cameroon have heeded the Lake Chad Commission's admonition to ratify the delimitation treaty which also includes the Chad-Niger and Niger-Nigeria boundaries
Nigeria-Cameroon-Equatorial Guinea: the ICJ ruled on an equidistance settlement of Cameroon-Equatorial Guinea-Nigeria maritime boundary in the Gulf of Guinea, but imprecisely defined coordinates in the ICJ decision and a sovereignty dispute between Equatorial Guinea and Cameroon over an island at the mouth of the Ntem River all contribute to the delay in implementation
Nigeria-Niger: none identified

Refugees and internally displaced persons: *refugees (country of origin):* 87,054 (Cameroon) (2022)

IDPs: 3,030,544 (northeast Nigeria; Boko Haram attacks and counterinsurgency efforts in northern Nigeria; communal violence between Christians and Muslims in the middle belt region, political violence; flooding; forced evictions; cattle rustling; competition for resources) (2022)

Illicit drugs: a significant source for cannabis cultivation and methamphetamine production; a major place for transnational drug trafficking networks that supply cocaine to Asia and Europe, heroin to Europe and North America, and methamphetamine to South Africa, Southeast Asia, Australia, and New Zealand; traffickers also involved in the transportation, facilitation, and distribution of illicitly diverted tramadol

NIUE

INTRODUCTION

Background: Voyagers from Samoa first settled on Niue around A.D. 900 and a second main group of settlers came from Tonga around 1500. With only one reliable source of fresh water, conflict was high on the island. There was continued contact with both Samoa and Tonga, and customs from those islands heavily influenced Niuean culture, including the formation of an island-wide kingship system in the early 1700s. These kings, or patu-iki, were elected by Niueans. In 1774, British explorer James COOK abandoned attempts to land on the island after several unsuccessful tries, and he named it Savage Island because of the warlike appearance of the Niueans. Missionaries arrived in 1830 but were also largely unsuccessful at staying on the island until 1846, when a Niuean trained as a Samoan missionary returned to the island and provided a space from which the missionaries could work. In addition to

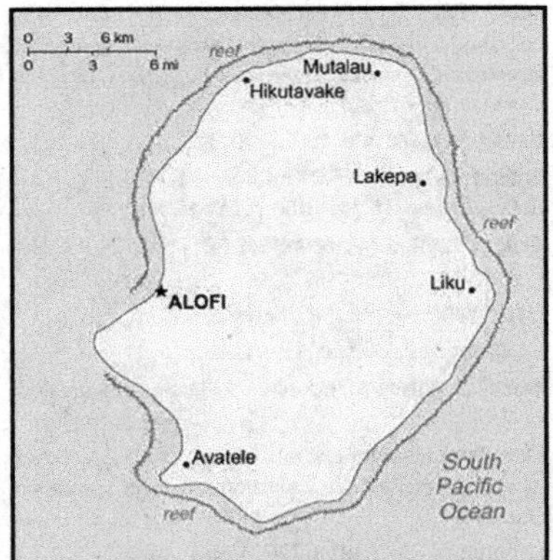

converting the population, the missionaries worked to stop the violent conflicts between Niueans and helped establish the first parliament in 1849.

In 1889, King FATAAIKI and other chiefs asked the UK for protectorate status, a request that was repeated in 1895. The UK finally agreed in 1900 and King TOGIA-PULU-TOAKI formally ceded Niue that year. In 1901, Niue was annexed to New Zealand and included as part of the Cook Islands. Niue's remoteness and cultural and linguistic differences with the Cook Islands led New Zealand to separate Niue into its own administration in 1904. The island became internally self-governing in 1974; it is an independent member of international organizations but is in free association with New Zealand, which is responsible for defense and foreign affairs.

Economic opportunities in Niue are sparse. The population has trended downwards over recent decades, with substantial emigration to New Zealand. In 2004, a cyclone destroyed much of the southern part of the capital, Alofi, and left about 15% of the population homeless. Many chose not to rebuild and instead moved to New Zealand (2,400 km to the southwest), where approximately 90% of all ethnic Niueans live.

GEOGRAPHY

Location: Oceania, island in the South Pacific Ocean, east of Tonga

Geographic coordinates: 19 02 S, 169 52 W

Map references: Oceania

Area: *total:* 260 sq km
land: 260 sq km
water: 0 sq km

Area - comparative: 1.5 times the size of Washington, DC

Land boundaries: *total:* 0 km

Coastline: 64 km

Maritime claims: *territorial sea:* 12 nm
exclusive economic zone: 200 nm

Climate: tropical; modified by southeast trade winds

Terrain: steep limestone cliffs along coast, central plateau

Elevation: *highest point:* unnamed elevation 1.4 km east of Hikutavake 80 m
lowest point: Pacific Ocean 0 m

Natural resources: arable land, fish

Land use: *agricultural land:* 19.1% (2018 est.)
arable land: 3.8% (2018 est.)
permanent crops: 11.5% (2018 est.)
permanent pasture: 3.8% (2018 est.)
forest: 71.2% (2018 est.)
other: 9.7% (2018 est.)

Irrigated land: 0 sq km (2012)

Population distribution: population distributed around the peripheral coastal areas of the island

Natural hazards: tropical cyclones

Geography - note: one of world's largest coral islands; the only major break in the surrounding coral reef occurs in the central western part of the coast

PEOPLE AND SOCIETY

Population: 2,000 (July 2022 est.)
note: because of the island's limited economic and educational opportunities, Niueans have emigrated for decades -primarily to New Zealand, but also to Australia and other Pacific island states; Niue's population peaked in 1966 at 5,194, but by 2005 had fallen to 1,508; since then it has rebounded slightly; as of 2013, 23,883 people of Niuean ancestry lived in New Zealand - with more than 20% Niue-born; this means that there are about 15 times as many persons of Niuean ancestry living in New Zealand as in Niue, possibly the most eccentric population distribution in the world

Nationality: *noun:* Niuean(s)
adjective: Niuean

Ethnic groups: Niuean 65.4%, part-Niuean 14%, non-Niuean 20.6% (2017 est.)
note: data represent the resident population

Languages: Niuean (official) 46% (a Polynesian language closely related to Tongan and Samoan), Niuean and English 32%, English (official) 11%, Niuean and others 5%, other 6% (2011 est.)

Religions: Ekalesia Niue (Congregational Christian Church of Niue - a Protestant church founded by missionaries from the London Missionary Society) 61.7%, Church of Jesus Christ 8.7%, Roman Catholic 8.4%, Jehovah's Witness 2.7%, Seventh Day Adventist 1.4%, other 8.2%, none 8.9% (2017 est.)

Population growth rate: -0.03% (2021 est.)

Population distribution: population distributed around the peripheral coastal areas of the island

Urbanization: *urban population:* 47.6% of total population (2022)
rate of urbanization: 1.43% annual rate of change (2020-25 est.)

Major urban areas - population: 1,000 ALOFI (capital) (2018)

Drinking water source: *improved: total:* 97% of population
unimproved: total: 3% of population (2020 est.)

Current health expenditure: 5.3% of GDP (2019)

Sanitation facility access: *improved: total:* 95.5% of population
unimproved: total: 4.5% of population (2020 est.)

Major infectious diseases: *degree of risk:* high (2020)
food or waterborne diseases: bacterial diarrhea
vectorborne diseases: malaria

Obesity - adult prevalence rate: 50% (2016)

Alcohol consumption per capita: *total:* 8.5 liters of pure alcohol (2019 est.)
beer: 4.28 liters of pure alcohol (2019 est.)
wine: 1.89 liters of pure alcohol (2019 est.)
spirits: 2.33 liters of pure alcohol (2019 est.)
other alcohols: 0 liters of pure alcohol (2019 est.)

ENVIRONMENT

Environment - current issues: increasing attention to conservationist practices to counter loss of soil fertility from traditional slash and burn agriculture

Environment - international agreements: *party to:* Biodiversity, Climate Change, Climate Change-Kyoto Protocol, Climate Change-Paris Agreement, Comprehensive Nuclear Test Ban, Desertification, Law of the Sea, Ozone Layer Protection, Ship Pollution
signed, but not ratified: none of the selected agreements

Air pollutants: *particulate matter emissions:* 11.47 micrograms per cubic meter (2016 est.)

Climate: tropical; modified by southeast trade winds

Land use: *agricultural land:* 19.1% (2018 est.)
arable land: 3.8% (2018 est.)
permanent crops: 11.5% (2018 est.)
permanent pasture: 3.8% (2018 est.)
forest: 71.2% (2018 est.)
other: 9.7% (2018 est.)

Urbanization: *urban population:* 47.6% of total population (2022)
rate of urbanization: 1.43% annual rate of change (2020-25 est.)

GOVERNMENT

Country name: *conventional long form:* none
conventional short form: Niue
former: Savage Island
etymology: the origin of the name is obscure; in Niuean, the word supposedly translates as "behold the coconut"
note: pronunciation falls between nyu-way and new-way, but not like new-wee

Government type: parliamentary democracy

Dependency status: self-governing in free association with New Zealand since 1974; Niue is fully responsible for internal affairs; New Zealand retains responsibility for external affairs and defense; however, these responsibilities confer no rights of control and are only exercised at the request of the Government of Niue

Capital: *name:* Alofi
geographic coordinates: 19 01 S, 169 55 W
time difference: UTC-11 (6 hours behind Washington, DC, during Standard Time)

Administrative divisions: none; there are no first-order administrative divisions as defined by the US Government, but there are 14 villages at the second order

Independence: 19 October 1974 (Niue became a self-governing state in free association with New Zealand)

National holiday: Waitangi Day (Treaty of Waitangi established British sovereignty over New Zealand), 6 February (1840)

Constitution: *history:* several previous (New Zealand colonial statutes); latest 19 October 1974 (Niue Constitution Act 1974)
amendments: proposed by the Assembly; passage requires at least two-thirds majority vote of the Assembly membership in each of three readings and approval by at least two-thirds majority votes in a referendum; passage of amendments to a number of sections, including Niue's self-governing status, British nationality and New Zealand citizenship, external affairs and defense, economic and administrative assistance by New Zealand, and amendment procedures, requires at least two-thirds majority vote by the Assembly and at least two thirds of votes in a referendum; amended 1992, 2007; note - in early 2021, the constitution review committee of the Assembly requested suggestions from the public about changes to the constitution

Legal system: English common law

Suffrage: 18 years of age; universal

Executive branch: *chief of state:* King CHARLES III (since 8 September 2022); represented by Governor-General of New Zealand Cindy KIRO (since 21 October 2021); the UK and New Zealand are represented by New Zealand High Commissioner Helen TUNNAH (since July 2020)
head of government: Premier Dalton TAGELAGI (since 10 June 2020)
cabinet: Cabinet chosen by the premier
elections/appointments: the monarchy is hereditary; premier indirectly elected by the Legislative Assembly for a 3-year term; election last held on 10 June 2020 (next to be held in 2023)
election results:
Dalton TAGELAGI elected premier; Legislative Assembly vote - Dalton TAGELAGI (independent) 13, O'Love JACOBSEN (independent) 7; Toke TALAGI lost his seat in election

Legislative branch: *description:* unicameral Assembly or Fono Ekepule (20 seats; 14 members directly elected in single-seat constituencies by simple majority vote and 6 directly elected from the National Register or "common roll" by majority vote; members serve 3-year terms)
elections:
last held on 30 May 2020 (next to be held on 2023)
election results:
percent of vote by party - NA; seats by party - independent 20; composition - men 17, women 3, percent of women 15%

Judicial branch: *highest court(s):* Court of Appeal (consists of the chief justice and up to 3 judges); note - the Judicial Committee of the Privy Council (in London) is the final appeal court beyond the Niue Court of Appeal
judge selection and term of office: Niue chief justice appointed by the governor general on the advice of the Cabinet and tendered by the premier; other judges appointed by the governor general on the advice of the Cabinet and tendered by the chief justice and the minister of justice; judges serve until age 68
subordinate courts: High Court
note: Niue is a participant in the Pacific Judicial Development Program, which is designed to build governance and the rule of law in 15 Pacific island countries

Political parties and leaders: none

International organization participation: ACP, AOSIS, FAO, IFAD, OPCW, PIF, Sparteca, SPC, UNESCO, UPU, WHO, WIPO, WMO

Diplomatic representation in the US: none (self-governing territory in free association with New Zealand)

Diplomatic representation from the US: *embassy:* none (self-governing territory in free association with New Zealand)

Flag description: yellow with the flag of the UK in the upper hoist-side quadrant; the flag of the UK bears five yellow five-pointed stars - a large star on a blue disk in the center and a smaller star on each arm of the bold red cross; the larger star stands for Niue, the smaller stars recall the Southern Cross constellation on the New Zealand flag and symbolize links with that country; yellow represents the bright sunshine of Niue and the warmth and friendship between Niue and New Zealand

National symbol(s): yellow, five-pointed star; national color: yellow

National anthem: *name:* "Ko e Iki he Lagi" (The Lord in Heaven)
lyrics/music: unknown/unknown, prepared by Sioeli FUSIKATA
note: adopted 1974

ECONOMY

Economic overview: The economy suffers from the typical Pacific island problems of geographic isolation, few resources, and a small population. The agricultural sector consists mainly of subsistence gardening, although some cash crops are grown for export. Industry consists primarily of small factories for processing passion fruit, lime oil, honey, and coconut cream. The sale of postage stamps to foreign collectors is an important source of revenue.

Government expenditures regularly exceed revenues, and the shortfall is made up by critically needed grants from New Zealand that are used to pay wages to public employees. Economic aid allocation from New Zealand in FY13/14 was US$10.1 million. Niue has cut government expenditures by reducing the public service by almost half.

The island in recent years has suffered a serious loss of population because of emigration to New Zealand. Efforts to increase GDP include the promotion of tourism and financial services, although the International Banking Repeal Act of 2002 resulted in the termination of all offshore banking licenses.

Real GDP (purchasing power parity): $10.01 million (2003 est.)

Real GDP growth rate: 6.2% (2003 est.)

Real GDP per capita: $5,800 (2003 est.)

GDP (official exchange rate): $10.01 million (2003) (2003)

Inflation rate (consumer prices): 4% (2005)

GDP - composition, by sector of origin: *agriculture:* 23.5% (2003)
industry: 26.9% (2003)
services: 49.5% (2003)

Agricultural products: coconuts, taro, fruit, sweet potatoes, tropical fruit, yams, vegetables, lemons, limes, bananas

Industries: handicrafts, food processing

Labor force: 663 (2001)

Labor force - by occupation: *note:* most work on family plantations; paid work exists only in government service, small industry, and the Niue Development Board

Unemployment rate: 12% (2001)

Budget: *revenues:* 15.07 million (FY04/05)
expenditures: 16.33 million (FY04/05)

Budget surplus (+) or deficit (-): -12.6% (of GDP) (FY04/05)

Fiscal year: 1 April - 31 March

Exports: $201,400 (2004 est.)

Exports - partners: Indonesia 92%, South Korea 5% (2019)

Exports - commodities: tanker ships, fruit juice, thermostats, textiles, measurement devices/appliances (2019)

Imports: $9.038 million (2004 est.)

Imports - partners: New Zealand 43%, United Kingdom 30%, Japan 22% (2019)

Imports - commodities: hydraulic engines, ships, refined petroleum, cars, plastics (2019)

Debt - external: $418,000 (2002 est.)

Exchange rates: New Zealand dollars (NZD) per US dollar -
1.416 (2017 est.)
1.4279 (2016 est.)
1.4279 (2015)
1.4279 (2014 est.)
1.2039 (2013 est.)

ENERGY

Electricity: *installed generating capacity:* 3,000 kW (2020 est.)
consumption: 2.6 million kWh (2019 est.)
exports: 0 kWh (2020 est.)
imports: 0 kWh (2020 est.)
transmission/distribution losses: 400,000 kWh (2019 est.)

Electricity generation sources: *fossil fuels:* 100% of total installed capacity (2020 est.)

Petroleum: *total petroleum production:* 0 bbl/day (2021 est.)
refined petroleum consumption: 100 bbl/day (2019 est.)

Refined petroleum products - imports: 54 bbl/day (2015 est.)

Carbon dioxide emissions: 8,000 metric tonnes of CO2 (2019 est.)
from petroleum and other liquids: 8,000 metric tonnes of CO2 (2019 est.)

Energy consumption per capita: 0 Btu/person (2019 est.)

COMMUNICATIONS

Telephones - fixed lines: *total subscriptions:* 1,000 (2018 est.)
subscriptions per 100 inhabitants: 62 (2018 est.)

Telecommunication systems: *general assessment:* in 2020, the Manatua One Polynesia Fiber Cable provided Niue with high speed Internet access for the first time replacing a 4 megabit satellite link with gigabit fiber connectivity; the government set out a strategy to upgrade to a new infrastructure that would be robust enough to operate reliably in

a challenging climate: 40 40°C heat, 40% humidity, salty air, frequent power outages during storms, and no air conditioning (2022)
domestic: single-line (fixed line) telephone system connects all villages on island; fixed teledensity at nearly 62 per 100 (2018)
international: country code - 683; landing point for the Manatua submarine cable linking Niue to several South Pacific Ocean Islands; expansion of satellite services (2019)

Broadcast media: 1 government-owned TV station with many of the programs supplied by Television New Zealand; 1 government-owned radio station broadcasting in AM and FM (2019)

Internet country code: .nu

Internet users: *total:* 1,292 (2019 est.)
percent of population: 80% (2019 est.)

TRANSPORTATION

Airports: *total:* 1 (2021)

Airports - with paved runways: *total:* 1
1,524 to 2,437 m: 1 (2021)

Roadways: *total:* 234 km (2017)
paved: 210 km (2017)
unpaved: 24 km

Merchant marine: *total:* 69
by type: bulk carrier 3, container ship 2, general cargo 25, oil tanker 7, other 32 (2021)

Ports and terminals: *major seaport(s):* Alofi

MILITARY AND SECURITY

Military and security forces: no regular indigenous military forces; Police Force

Military - note: defense is the responsibility of New Zealand

TRANSNATIONAL ISSUES

Disputes - international: none identified

NORFOLK ISLAND

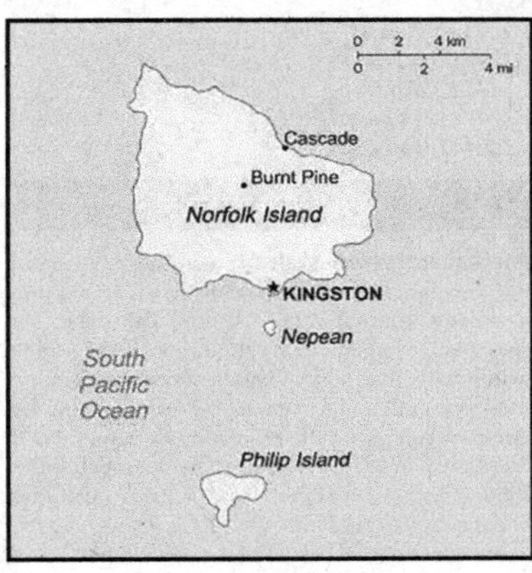

INTRODUCTION

Background: Polynesians lived on Norfolk Island between 1200 and 1500 but the remote island was uninhabited by the time British explorer James COOK landed on the island in 1774. Two British attempts at establishing the island as a penal colony (1788-1814 and 1825-55) were ultimately abandoned.

In 1856, almost 200 Pitcairn Islanders - descendants of the Bounty mutineers and their Tahitian companions - were relocated to Norfolk Island because of overcrowding on the Pitcairn Islands. Some returned to the Pitcairn Islands over the next few years but most settled permanently on Norfolk Island and recreated the land tenure and governance structures they previously had. Norfolk Island retained a great degree of local control until 1897, when it became a dependency of New South Wales. During World War II, Norfolk Island was an airbase and an important refueling stop in the South Pacific. In 1976, an Australian judge recommended Norfolk Island be incorporated fully into Australia, which Norfolk Islanders rejected. Following an appeal to the UN, Australia granted limited self-government to Norfolk Island in 1979.

With growing financial troubles during the 2000s, Australia abolished the Norfolk Island Legislative Assembly in 2015, reduced Norfolk Island's autonomy in 2016, and suspended the local council in 2020. Most services are provided by a mix of the Australian Capital Territory and the states of New South Wales and Queensland. These moves were unpopular on Norfolk Island, which has sought to have its self-government restored.

GEOGRAPHY

Location: Oceania, island in the South Pacific Ocean, east of Australia

Geographic coordinates: 29 02 S, 167 57 E

Map references: Oceania

Area: *total:* 36 sq km
land: 36 sq km
water: 0 sq km

Area - comparative: about 0.2 times the size of Washington, DC

Land boundaries: *total:* 0 km

Coastline: 32 km

Maritime claims: *territorial sea:* 12 nm
contiguous zone: 24 nm
exclusive fishing zone: 200 nm

Climate: subtropical; mild, little seasonal temperature variation

Terrain: volcanic island with mostly rolling plains

Elevation: *highest point:* Mount Bates 319 m
lowest point: Pacific Ocean 0 m

Natural resources: fish

Land use: *agricultural land:* 25% (2018 est.)
arable land: 0% (2018 est.)
permanent crops: 0% (2018 est.)
permanent pasture: 25% (2018 est.)
forest: 11.5% (2018 est.)
other: 63.5% (2018 est.)

Irrigated land: 0 sq km (2012)

Population distribution: population concentrated around the capital of Kingston

Natural hazards: tropical cyclones (especially May to July)

Geography - note: most of the 32 km coastline consists of almost inaccessible cliffs, but the land slopes down to the sea in one small southern area on Sydney Bay, where the capital of Kingston is situated

PEOPLE AND SOCIETY

Population: 1,748 (2016 est.)

Nationality: *noun:* Norfolk Islander(s)
adjective: Norfolk Islander(s)

Ethnic groups: Australian 22.8%, English 22.4%, Pitcairn Islander 20%, Scottish 6%, Irish 5.2% (2011 est.)
note: respondents were able to identify up to two ancestries; percentages represent a proportion of all responses from people in Norfolk Island, including those who did not identify an ancestry; only top responses are shown

Languages: English (official) 44.9%, Norfolk (also known as Norfuk or Norf'k, which is a mixture of 18th century English and ancient Tahitian) 40.3%, Fijian 1.8%, other 6.8%, unspecified 6.2% (2016 est.)
note: data represent language spoken at home

Religions: Protestant 46.8% (Anglican 29.2%, Uniting Church in Australia 9.8%, Presbyterian 2.9%, Seventh Day Adventist 2.7%, other 2.2%), Roman Catholic 12.6%, other Christian 2.9%, other 1.4%, none 26.7%, unspecified 9.5% (2016 est.)

Population growth rate: 0.01% (2014 est.)

Population distribution: population concentrated around the capital of Kingston

ENVIRONMENT

Environment - current issues: inadequate solid waste management; most freshwater obtained through rainwater catchment; preservation of unique ecosystem

Climate: subtropical; mild, little seasonal temperature variation

Land use: *agricultural land:* 25% (2018 est.)
arable land: 0% (2018 est.)
permanent crops: 0% (2018 est.)
permanent pasture: 25% (2018 est.)
forest: 11.5% (2018 est.)
other: 63.5% (2018 est.)

GOVERNMENT

Country name: *conventional long form:* Territory of Norfolk Island
conventional short form: Norfolk Island

etymology: named by British explorer Captain James COOK after Mary HOWARD, Duchess of Norfolk, in 1774

Government type: non-self-governing overseas territory of Australia; note - the Norfolk Island Regional Council, which began operations 1 July 2016, is responsible for planning and managing a variety of public services, including those funded by the Government of Australia

Dependency status: self-governing territory of Australia; administered from Canberra by the Department of Infrastructure, Transport, Cities & Regional Development

Capital: *name:* Kingston
geographic coordinates: 29 03 S, 167 58 E
time difference: UTC+11 (16 hours ahead of Washington, DC, during Standard Time)
daylight saving time: +1hr, begins first Sunday in October; ends first Sunday in April
etymology: the name is a blending of the words "king's" and "town"; the British king at the time of the town's settlement in the late 18th century was GEORGE III

Administrative divisions: none (territory of Australia)

Independence: none (territory of Australia)

National holiday: Bounty Day (commemorates the arrival of Pitcairn Islanders), 8 June (1856)

Constitution: *history:* previous 1913, 1957; latest effective 7 August 1979
amendments: amended many times, last in 2020

Legal system: English common law and the laws of Australia

Citizenship: see Australia

Suffrage: 18 years of age; universal

Executive branch: *chief of state:* King CHARLES III (since 8 September 2022); represented by Governor General of the Commonwealth of Australia General David HURLEY (since 1 July 2019)
head of government: Administrator Eric HUTCHINSON (since 1 April 2017)
cabinet: Executive Council consists of 4 Legislative Assembly members
elections/appointments: the monarchy is hereditary; governor general appointed by the monarch; administrator appointed by the governor general of Australia for a 2-year term and represents the monarch and Australia

Legislative branch: *description:* unicameral Norfolk Island Regional Council (5 seats; councillors directly elected by simple majority vote to serve 4-year terms); mayor elected annually by the councillors
elections:
elections last held 28 May 2016 (next rescheduled to be held in 2022)
election results:
seats by party - independent 5; composition - men 4, women 1, percent of women 20%
note: following an administrative restructuring of local government, the Legislative Assembly was dissolved on 18 June 2015 and replaced by an interim Norfolk Island Advisory Council effective 1 July 2015; the Advisory Council consisted of 5 members appointed by the Norfolk Island administrator based on nominations from the community; following elections on 28 May 2016, the new Norfolk Island Regional Council (NIRC) commenced operations on 1 July 2016; on 20 December 2020 the NIRC was suspended for three months following a public audit and this suspension was extended on 3 February 2021 for an additional three months pending the outcome of a public inquiry; the council election previously scheduled for 13 March 2021 has been postponed 12 months

Judicial branch: *highest court(s):* Supreme Court of Norfolk Island (consists of the chief justice and several justices); note - appeals beyond the Supreme Court of Norfolk Island are heard by the Federal Court and the High Court of Australia
judge selection and term of office: justices appointed by the governor general of Australia from among justices of the Federal Court of Australia; justices serve until mandatory retirement at age 70
subordinate courts: Petty Court of Sessions; specialized courts, including a Coroner's Court and the Employment Tribunal

Political parties and leaders: Norfolk Island Labor Party [Mike KELLY]
Norfolk Liberals [John BROWN]

International organization participation: UPU

Diplomatic representation in the US: none (territory of Australia)

Diplomatic representation from the US: *embassy:* none (territory of Australia)

Flag description: three vertical bands of green (hoist side), white, and green with a large green Norfolk Island pine tree centered in the slightly wider white band; green stands for the rich vegetation on the island, and the pine tree - endemic to the island - is a symbol of Norfolk Island
note: somewhat reminiscent of the flag of Canada with its use of only two colors and depiction of a prominent local floral symbol in the central white band; also resembles the green and white triband of Nigeria

National symbol(s): Norfolk Island pine

National anthem: *name:* "Come Ye Blessed"
lyrics/music: New Testament/John Prindle SCOTT
note: the local anthem, whose lyrics consist of the words from Matthew 25:34-36, 40, is also known as "The Pitcairn Anthem;" the island does not recognize "Advance Australia Fair" (which other Australian territories use); instead "God Save the King" is official (see United Kingdom)

ECONOMY

Economic overview: Norfolk Island is suffering from a severe economic downturn. Tourism, the primary economic activity, is the main driver of economic growth. The agricultural sector has become self-sufficient in the production of beef, poultry, and eggs.

Agricultural products: Norfolk Island pine seed, Kentia palm seed, cereals, vegetables, fruit; cattle, poultry

Industries: tourism, light industry, ready mixed concrete

Labor force: 978 (2006)

Labor force - by occupation: *agriculture:* 6%
industry: 14%
services: 80% (2006 est.)

Budget: *revenues:* 4.6 million (FY99/00)
expenditures: 4.8 million (FY99/00)

Fiscal year: 1 July - 30 June

Exports - partners: Philippines 29%, Singapore 21%, India 14%, Belgium 7%, Australia 5%, Canada 5% (2019)

Exports - commodities: soybean meal, Norfolk Island pine seeds, Kentia palm seeds, activated carbon, centrifuges, pesticides, postage stamps (2019)

Imports - partners: New Zealand 23%, Australia 19%, Philippines 19%, Singapore 14%, Fiji 11% (2019)

Imports - commodities: clothing and apparel, chemical analysis instruments, refined petroleum, cars, kitchen machinery (2019)

Exchange rates: Australian dollars (AUD) per US dollar -
1.311 (2017 est.)
1.3291 (2016 est.)
1.3291 (2015)
1.3291 (2014 est.)
1.1094 (2013 est.)

COMMUNICATIONS

Telecommunication systems: *general assessment:* the current infrastructure consists of fixed line telephone utilizing copper twisted pair cable and optic fiber, two Satellite Earth Station, GSM Mobile switch with five remote base stations and 2 micro cells, central public exchange which switches international as well as national calls, ADSL Broadband internet connection (Asynchronous Digital Subscriber Line), and an ISP (Internet Service Provider) (2020)
domestic: free local calls
international: country code - 672; submarine cable links with Australia and New Zealand; satellite earth station - 1

Broadcast media: 1 local radio station; broadcasts of several Australian radio and TV stations available via satellite (2009)

Internet country code: .nf

Internet users: *total:* 612 (2016 est.)
percent of population: 35% (2016 est.)

TRANSPORTATION

Airports: *total:* 1 (2021)

Airports - with paved runways: *total:* 1
1,524 to 2,437 m: 1 (2021)

Roadways: *total:* 80 km (2008)
paved: 53 km (2008)
unpaved: 27 km (2008)

Ports and terminals: *major seaport(s):* Kingston

MILITARY AND SECURITY

Military - note: defense is the responsibility of Australia

TRANSNATIONAL ISSUES

Disputes - international: none identified

NORTH MACEDONIA

INTRODUCTION

Background: North Macedonia gained its independence peacefully from Yugoslavia in 1991 under the name of "Macedonia." Greek objection to the new country's name, insisting it implied territorial pretensions to the northern Greek province of Macedonia, and democratic backsliding for several years stalled the country's movement toward Euro-Atlantic integration. Immediately after Macedonia declared independence, Greece sought to block Macedonian efforts to gain UN membership if the name "Macedonia" was used. The country was eventually admitted to the UN in 1993 as "The former Yugoslav Republic of Macedonia," and at the same time it agreed to UN-sponsored negotiations on the name dispute. In 1995, Greece lifted a 20-month trade embargo and the two countries agreed to normalize relations, but the issue of the name remained unresolved and negotiations for a solution continued. Over time, the US and over 130 other nations recognized Macedonia by its constitutional name, Republic of Macedonia. Ethnic Albanian grievances over perceived political and economic inequities escalated into a conflict in 2001 that eventually led to the internationally brokered Ohrid Framework Agreement, which ended the fighting and established guidelines for constitutional amendments and the creation of new laws that enhanced the rights of minorities. In January 2018, the government adopted a new law on languages, which elevated the Albanian language to an official language at the national level, with the Macedonian language remaining the sole official language in international relations. Relations between ethnic Macedonians and ethnic Albanians remain complicated, however.

North Macedonia's pro-Western government has used its time in office since 2017 to sign a historic deal with Greece in June 2018 to end the name dispute and revive Skopje's NATO and EU membership prospects. This followed a nearly three-year political crisis that engulfed the country but ended in June 2017 following a six-month-long government formation period after a closely contested election in December 2016. The crisis began after the 2014 legislative and presidential election, and escalated in 2015 when the opposition party began releasing wiretapped material that revealed alleged widespread government corruption and abuse. Although an EU candidate since 2005, North Macedonia has yet to open EU accession negotiations. The country still faces challenges, including fully implementing reforms to overcome years of democratic backsliding and stimulating economic growth and development. In June 2018, Macedonia and Greece signed the Prespa Accord whereby the Republic of Macedonia agreed to change its name to the Republic of North Macedonia. Following ratification by both countries, the agreement went in to force on 12 February 2019. North Macedonia signed an accession protocol to become a NATO member state in February 2019.

GEOGRAPHY

Location: Southeastern Europe, north of Greece

Geographic coordinates: 41 50 N, 22 00 E

Map references: Europe

Area: *total:* 25,713 sq km
land: 25,433 sq km
water: 280 sq km

Area - comparative: slightly larger than Vermont; almost four times the size of Delaware

Land boundaries: *total:* 838 km
border countries (5): Albania 181 km; Bulgaria 162 km; Greece 234 km; Kosovo 160 km; Serbia 101 km

Coastline: 0 km (landlocked)

Maritime claims: none (landlocked)

Climate: warm, dry summers and autumns; relatively cold winters with heavy snowfall

Terrain: mountainous with deep basins and valleys; three large lakes, each divided by a frontier line; country bisected by the Vardar River

Elevation: *highest point:* Golem Korab (Maja e Korabit) 2,764 m
lowest point: Vardar River 50 m
mean elevation: 741 m

Natural resources: low-grade iron ore, copper, lead, zinc, chromite, manganese, nickel, tungsten, gold, silver, asbestos, gypsum, timber, arable land

Land use: *agricultural land:* 44.3% (2018 est.)
arable land: 16.4% (2018 est.)
permanent crops: 1.4% (2018 est.)
permanent pasture: 26.5% (2018 est.)
forest: 39.8% (2018 est.)
other: 15.9% (2018 est.)

Irrigated land: 1,280 sq km (2012)

Major watersheds (area sq km): Atlantic Ocean drainage: *(Black Sea)* Danube (795,656 sq km)

Population distribution: a fairly even distribution throughout most of the country, with urban areas attracting larger and denser populations

Natural hazards: high seismic risks

Geography - note: landlocked; major transportation corridor from Western and Central Europe to Aegean Sea and Southern Europe to Western Europe

PEOPLE AND SOCIETY

Population: 2,130,936 (2022 est.)

Nationality: *noun:* Macedonian(s)
adjective: Macedonian

Ethnic groups: Macedonian 58.4%, Albanian 24.3%, Turkish 3.9%, Romani 2.5%, Serb 1.3%, other 2.3%, persons for whom data were taken from administrative sources and no ethnic affiliation data was available 7.2% (2021 est.)
note: Romani populations are usually underestimated in official statistics and may represent 6.5–13% of North Macedonia's population

Languages: Macedonian (official) 61.4%, Albanian (official) 24.3%, Turkish 3.4%, Romani 1.7%, other (includes Aromanian (Vlach) and Bosnian) 2%, persons for whom data were taken from administrative sources and no language data was available 7.2% (2021 est.); note - data represent mother tongue; minority languages are co-official with Macedonian in municipalities where they are spoken by at least 20% of the population; Albanian is co-official in Tetovo, Brvenica, Vrapciste, and other municipalities; Turkish is co-official in Centar Zupa and Plasnica; Romani is co-official in Suto Orizari; Aromanian is co-official in Krusevo; Serbian is co-official in Cucer Sandevo
major-language sample(s):
Книга на Светски Факти, неопходен извор на основни информации. (Macedonian)

Religions: Macedonian Orthodox 46.1%, Muslim 32.2%, other Christian 13.8%, other and non-believers 0.5%, unspecified 0.2%, persons for whom data were taken from administrative sources and no religious affiliation data was available 7.2% (2021 est.)

Age structure: *0-14 years:* 16.16% (male 177,553/female 165,992)
15-24 years: 12.65% (male 139,250/female 129,770)
25-54 years: 44.47% (male 480,191/female 465,145)
55-64 years: 12.55% (male 131,380/female 135,407)
65 years and over: 14.17% (male 131,674/female 169,609) (2020 est.)

Dependency ratios: *total dependency ratio:* 44.5
youth dependency ratio: 23.6
elderly dependency ratio: 20.9
potential support ratio: 4.8 (2020 est.)

Median age: *total:* 39 years
male: 38 years
female: 40 years (2020 est.)

Population growth rate: 0.12% (2022 est.)

Birth rate: 10.45 births/1,000 population (2022 est.)

Death rate: 9.61 deaths/1,000 population (2022 est.)

Net migration rate: 0.38 migrant(s)/1,000 population (2022 est.)

Population distribution: a fairly even distribution throughout most of the country, with urban areas attracting larger and denser populations

Urbanization: *urban population:* 59.1% of total population (2022)
rate of urbanization: 0.61% annual rate of change (2020-25 est.)

Major urban areas - population: 606,000 SKOPJE (capital) (2022)

Sex ratio: *at birth:* 1.07 male(s)/female
0-14 years: 1.07 male(s)/female
15-24 years: 1.07 male(s)/female
25-54 years: 1.04 male(s)/female
55-64 years: 0.97 male(s)/female
65 years and over: 0.55 male(s)/female
total population: 0.99 male(s)/female (2022 est.)

Mother's mean age at first birth: 26.9 years (2020 est.)

Maternal mortality ratio: 7 deaths/100,000 live births (2017 est.)

Infant mortality rate: *total:* 7.32 deaths/1,000 live births
male: 8.27 deaths/1,000 live births
female: 6.31 deaths/1,000 live births (2022 est.)

Life expectancy at birth: *total population:* 76.84 years
male: 74.73 years
female: 79.08 years (2022 est.)

Total fertility rate: 1.51 children born/woman (2022 est.)

Contraceptive prevalence rate: 59.9% (2018/19)

Drinking water source: *improved: urban:* 99.7% of population
rural: 99% of population
total: 99.4% of population
unimproved: urban: 0.3% of population
rural: 1% of population
total: 0.6% of population (2020 est.)

Current health expenditure: 7.3% of GDP (2019)

Physicians density: 2.87 physicians/1,000 population (2015)

Hospital bed density: 4.3 beds/1,000 population (2017)

Sanitation facility access: *improved: urban:* 100% of population
rural: 98% of population
total: 99.2% of population
unimproved: urban: 0% of population
rural: 2% of population
total: 0.8% of population (2020 est.)

HIV/AIDS - adult prevalence rate: (2018 est.) <.1%

Obesity - adult prevalence rate: 22.4% (2016)

Alcohol consumption per capita: *total:* 3.9 liters of pure alcohol (2019 est.)
beer: 1.93 liters of pure alcohol (2019 est.)
wine: 1.03 liters of pure alcohol (2019 est.)
spirits: 0.9 liters of pure alcohol (2019 est.)
other alcohols: 0.03 liters of pure alcohol (2019 est.)

Children under the age of 5 years underweight: 0.9% (2018/19)

Child marriage: *women married by age 15:* 0.3%
women married by age 18: 7.5% (2019 est.)

Literacy: *definition:* age 15 and over can read and write
total population: 98.4%
male: 99.1%
female: 97.6% (2020)

School life expectancy (primary to tertiary education): *total:* 14 years
male: 13 years
female: 14 years (2018)

Unemployment, youth ages 15-24: *total:* 37%
male: 35.2%
female: 40% (2020 est.)

ENVIRONMENT

Environment - current issues: air pollution from metallurgical plants; Skopje has severe air pollution problems every winter as a result of industrial emissions, smoke from wood-buring stoves, and exhaust fumes from old cars

Environment - international agreements: *party to:* Air Pollution, Air Pollution-Heavy Metals, Air Pollution-Multi-effect Protocol, Air Pollution-Nitrogen Oxides, Air Pollution-Persistent Organic Pollutants, Air Pollution-Sulphur 85, Air Pollution-Sulphur 94, Air Pollution-Volatile Organic Compounds, Biodiversity, Climate Change, Climate Change-Kyoto Protocol, Climate Change-Paris Agreement, Comprehensive Nuclear Test Ban, Desertification, Endangered Species, Hazardous Wastes, Law of the Sea, Ozone Layer Protection, Wetlands
signed, but not ratified: none of the selected agreements

Air pollutants: *particulate matter emissions:* 28.34 micrograms per cubic meter (2016 est.)
carbon dioxide emissions: 7.05 megatons (2016 est.)
methane emissions: 2.28 megatons (2020 est.)

Climate: warm, dry summers and autumns; relatively cold winters with heavy snowfall

Land use: *agricultural land:* 44.3% (2018 est.)
arable land: 16.4% (2018 est.)
permanent crops: 1.4% (2018 est.)
permanent pasture: 26.5% (2018 est.)
forest: 39.8% (2018 est.)
other: 15.9% (2018 est.)

Urbanization: *urban population:* 59.1% of total population (2022)
rate of urbanization: 0.61% annual rate of change (2020-25 est.)

Revenue from forest resources: *forest revenues:* 0.15% of GDP (2018 est.)

Revenue from coal: *coal revenues:* 0% of GDP (2018 est.)

Waste and recycling: *municipal solid waste generated annually:* 796,585 tons (2016 est.)
municipal solid waste recycled annually: 1,434 tons (2013 est.)
percent of municipal solid waste recycled: 0.2% (2013 est.)

Major watersheds (area sq km): Atlantic Ocean drainage: *(Black Sea)* Danube (795,656 sq km)

Total water withdrawal: *municipal:* 277.5 million cubic meters (2017 est.)
industrial: 225,809,581.6 cubic meters (2017 est.)
agricultural: 329,217,707.7 cubic meters (2017 est.)

Total renewable water resources: 6.4 billion cubic meters (2017 est.)

GOVERNMENT

Country name: *conventional long form:* Republic of North Macedonia
conventional short form: North Macedonia
local long form: Republika Severna Makedonija
local short form: Severna Makedonija
former: Democratic Federal Macedonia, People's Republic of Macedonia, Socialist Republic of Macedonia, Republic of Macedonia
etymology: the country name derives from the ancient kingdom of Macedon (7th to 2nd centuries B.C.)

Government type: parliamentary republic

Capital: *name:* Skopje
geographic coordinates: 42 00 N, 21 26 E
time difference: UTC+1 (6 hours ahead of Washington, DC, during Standard Time)
daylight saving time: +1hr, begins last Sunday in March; ends last Sunday in October
etymology: Skopje derives from its ancient name Scupi, the Latin designation of a classical era Greco-Roman frontier fortress town; the name may go back even further to a pre-Greek, Illyrian name

Administrative divisions: 70 municipalities (opstini, singular - opstina) and 1 city* (grad); Aracinovo, Berovo, Bitola, Bogdanci, Bogovinje, Bosilovo, Brvenica, Caska, Centar Zupa, Cesinovo-Oblesevo, Cucer Sandevo, Debar, Debarca, Delcevo, Demir Hisar, Demir Kapija, Dojran, Dolneni, Gevgelija, Gostivar, Gradsko, Ilinden, Jegunovce, Karbinci, Kavadarci, Kicevo, Kocani, Konce, Kratovo, Kriva Palanka, Krivogastani, Krusevo, Kumanovo, Lipkovo, Lozovo, Makedonska Kamenica, Makedonski Brod, Mavrovo i Rostuse, Mogila, Negotino, Novaci, Novo Selo, Ohrid, Pehcevo, Petrovec, Plasnica, Prilep, Probistip, Radovis, Rankovce, Resen, Rosoman, Skopje*, Sopiste, Staro Nagoricane, Stip, Struga, Strumica, Studenicani, Sveti Nikole, Tearce, Tetovo, Valandovo, Vasilevo, Veles, Vevcani, Vinica, Vrapciste, Zelenikovo, Zelino, Zrnovci

Independence: 8 September 1991 (referendum by registered voters endorsed independence from Yugoslavia)

National holiday: Independence Day, 8 September (1991), also known as National Day

Constitution: *history:* several previous; latest adopted 17 November 1991, effective 20 November 1991
amendments: proposed by the president of the republic, by the government, by at least 30 members of the Assembly, or by petition of at least 150,000 citizens; final approval requires a two-thirds majority vote by the Assembly; amended several times, last in 2019

Legal system: civil law system; judicial review of legislative acts

International law organization participation: has not submitted an ICJ jurisdiction declaration; accepts ICCt jurisdiction

Citizenship: *citizenship by birth:* no
citizenship by descent only: at least one parent must be a citizen of North Macedonia
dual citizenship recognized: no
residency requirement for naturalization: 8 years

Suffrage: 18 years of age; universal

Executive branch: *chief of state:* President Stevo PENDAROVSKI (since 12 May 2019)
head of government: Prime Minister Dimitar KOVACEVSKI (since 16 January 2022)
cabinet: Council of Ministers elected by the Assembly by simple majority vote
elections/appointments: president directly elected using a modified 2-round system; a candidate can only be elected in the first round with an absolute majority from all registered voters; in the second round, voter turnout must be at least 40% for the result to be deemed valid; president elected for a 5-year term (eligible for a second term); election last held on 21 April and 5 May 2019 (next to be held in 2024); following legislative elections, the leader of the majority party or majority coalition is usually elected prime minister by the Assembly; Dimitar

KOVACEVSKI elected prime minister by the Assembly on 16 January 2022; Assembly vote - NA
election results:
2019: Stevo PENDAROVSKI elected president in second round; percent of vote in first round - Stevo PENDAROVSKI (SDSM) 44.8%, Gordana SILJANOVSKA-DAVKOVA (VMRO-DPMNE) 44.2%, Blenim REKA (independent) 11.1%; percent of vote in second round - Stevo PENDAROVSKI 53.6%, Gordana SILJANOVSKA-DAVKOVA 46.4%
2014: Gjorge IVANOV reelected president in second round; percent of vote in first round - Gjorge IVANOV (VMRO-DPMNE) 53.1%, Stevo PENDAROVSKI (SDSM) 38.6%, Ilijaz HALIMI (DPA) 4.6%, Zoran POPOVSKI (GROM) 3.7%; percent of vote in second round - Gjorge IVANOV 57.3%, Stevo PENDAROVSKI (SDSM) 42.7%

Legislative branch: *description:* unicameral Assembly - Sobraine in Macedonian, Kuvend in Albanian (between 120 and 140 seats, currently 120; members directly elected in multi-seat constituencies by closed-list proportional representation vote; possibility of 3 directly elected in diaspora constituencies by simple majority vote provided there is sufficient voter turnout; members serve 4-year terms)
elections:
last held on 15 July 2020 (next to be held in 2024)
election results:
percent of vote by party/coalition - We Can 35.9%, Renewal 34.6%, BDI 11.5%, AfA-Alternative 9%, The Left 4.1%, PDSh 1.5%, other 3.4%; seats by party/coalition - We Can 46, Renewal 44, BDI 15, AfA-Alternative 12, The Left 2, PDSh 1; composition - men 70, women 50, percent of women 41.7%

Judicial branch: *highest court(s):* Supreme Court (consists of 22 judges); Constitutional Court (consists of 9 judges)
judge selection and term of office: Supreme Court judges nominated by the Judicial Council, a 7-member body of legal professionals, and appointed by the Assembly; judge tenure NA; Constitutional Court judges appointed by the Assembly for nonrenewable, 9-year terms
subordinate courts: Courts of Appeal; Basic Courts

Political parties and leaders: Alliance for Albanians or AfA [Ziadin SELA]
Alternative (Alternativa) [Afrim GASHI]
Besa Movement [Bilal KASAMI]
Democratic Party of Albanians or PDSh [Menduh THACI]
Democratic Union for Integration or BDI [Ali AHMETI]
Internal Macedonian Revolutionary Organization - Democratic Party for Macedonian National Unity or VMRO-DPMNE [Hristijan MICKOSKI]
Internal Macedonian Revolutionary Organization - People's Party or VMRO-NP [Ljubco GEORGIEVSKI]
Liberal Democratic Party or LDP [Goran MILEVSKI]
Renewal (VMRO-DPMNE coalition) [Maja MORACHANIN]
Social Democratic Union of Macedonia or SDSM [Dimitar KOVACHEVSKI]
The Left (Levica) [Dimitar APASIEV]
Turkish Democratic Party of DPT [Beycan ILYAS]
We Can (coalition includes SDSM/Besa/VMRO-NP, DPT, LDP)

International organization participation: BIS, CD, CE, CEI, EAPC, EBRD, EU (candidate country), FAO, IAEA, IBRD, ICAO, ICC (NGOs), ICCt, ICRM, IDA, IFAD, IFC, IFRCS, ILO, IMF, IMO, Interpol, IOC, IOM, IPU, ISO, ITU, ITUC (NGOs), MIGA, NATO, OAS (observer), OIF, OPCW, OSCE, PCA, PFP, SELEC, UN, UNCTAD, UNESCO, UNHCR, UNIDO, UNIFIL, UNWTO, UPU, WCO, WHO, WIPO, WMO, WTO

Diplomatic representation in the US: *chief of mission:* Ambassador Zoran POPOV (since 16 September 2022)
chancery: 2129 Wyoming Avenue NW, Washington, DC 20008
telephone: [1] (202) 667-0501
FAX: [1] (202) 667-2131
email address and website:
washington@mfa.gov.mk
consulate(s) general: Chicago, Detroit, New York

Diplomatic representation from the US: *chief of mission:* Ambassador Kate Marie BYRNES (since 12 July 2019)
embassy: Str. Samoilova, Nr. 21, 1000 Skopje
mailing address: 7120 Skopje Place, Washington, DC 20521-7120
telephone: [389] (2) 310-2000
FAX: [389] (2) 310-2499
email address and website:
SkopjeACS@state.gov
https://mk.usembassy.gov/

Flag description: a yellow sun (the Sun of Liberty) with eight broadening rays extending to the edges of the red field; the red and yellow colors have long been associated with Macedonia

National symbol(s): eight-rayed sun; national colors: red, yellow

National anthem: *name:* "Denes nad Makedonija" (Today Over Macedonia)
lyrics/music: Vlado MALESKI/Todor SKALOVSKI
note: written in 1943 and adopted in 1991, the song previously served as the anthem of the Socialist Republic of Macedonia while part of Yugoslavia

National heritage: *total World Heritage Sites:* 2 (both natural)
selected World Heritage Site locales: Natural and Cultural Heritage of the Ohrid Region; Ancient and Primeval Beech Forests of the Carpathians

ECONOMY

Economic overview: Since its independence in 1991, Macedonia has made progress in liberalizing its economy and improving its business environment. Its low tax rates and free economic zones have helped to attract foreign investment, which is still low relative to the rest of Europe. Corruption and weak rule of law remain significant problems. Some businesses complain of opaque regulations and unequal enforcement of the law.

Macedonia's economy is closely linked to Europe as a customer for exports and source of investment, and has suffered as a result of prolonged weakness in the euro zone. Unemployment has remained consistently high at about 23% but may be overstated based on the existence of an extensive gray market, estimated to be between 20% and 45% of GDP, which is not captured by official statistics.

Macedonia is working to build a country-wide natural gas pipeline and distribution network. Currently, Macedonia receives its small natural gas supplies from Russia via Bulgaria. In 2016, Macedonia signed a memorandum of understanding with Greece to build an interconnector that could connect to the Trans Adriatic Pipeline that will traverse the region once complete, or to an LNG import terminal in Greece.

Macedonia maintained macroeconomic stability through the global financial crisis by conducting prudent monetary policy, which keeps the domestic currency pegged to the euro, and inflation at a low level. However, in the last two years, the internal political crisis has hampered economic performance, with GDP growth slowing in 2016 and 2017, and both domestic private and public investments declining. Fiscal policies were lax, with unproductive public expenditures, including subsidies and pension increases, and rising guarantees for the debt of state owned enterprises, and fiscal targets were consistently missed. In 2017, public debt stabilized at about 47% of GDP, still relatively low compared to its Western Balkan neighbors and the rest of Europe.

Real GDP (purchasing power parity): $33.02 billion (2020 est.)
$34.59 billion (2019 est.)
$33.52 billion (2018 est.)
note: data are in 2017 dollars; Macedonia has a large informal sector that may not be reflected in these data

Real GDP growth rate: 0% (2017 est.)
2.9% (2016 est.)
3.9% (2015 est.)

Real GDP per capita: $15,800 (2020 est.)
$16,600 (2019 est.)
$16,100 (2018 est.)
note: data are in 2017 dollars

GDP (official exchange rate): $12.696 billion (2019 est.)

Inflation rate (consumer prices): 0.7% (2019 est.)
1.4% (2018 est.)
1.3% (2017 est.)

Credit ratings:

Fitch rating: BB+ (2019)

Standard & Poors rating: BB- (2013)
note: The year refers to the year in which the current credit rating was first obtained.

GDP - composition, by sector of origin: *agriculture:* 10.9% (2017 est.)
industry: 26.6% (2017 est.)
services: 62.5% (2017 est.)

GDP - composition, by end use: *household consumption:* 65.6% (2017 est.)
government consumption: 15.6% (2017 est.)
investment in fixed capital: 13.6% (2017 est.)
investment in inventories: 20.2% (2017 est.)
exports of goods and services: 54% (2017 est.)
imports of goods and services: -69% (2017 est.)

Agricultural products: milk, grapes, wheat, potatoes, green chillies/peppers, cabbages, tomatoes, maize, barley, watermelons

Industries: food processing, beverages, textiles, chemicals, iron, steel, cement, energy, pharmaceuticals, automotive parts

Industrial production growth rate: -7.8% (2017 est.)

Labor force: 793,000 (2020 est.)

Labor force - by occupation: *agriculture:* 16.2%
industry: 29.2%
services: 54.5% (2017 est.)

Unemployment rate: 17.29% (2019 est.)
20.7% (2018 est.)

Unemployment, youth ages 15-24: *total:* 37%
male: 35.2%

female: 40% (2020 est.)

Population below poverty line: 21.6% (2018 est.)

Gini Index coefficient - distribution of family income: 34.2 (2017 est.)
35.2 (2014)

Household income or consumption by percentage share: *lowest 10%:* 1.7%
highest 10%: 25% (2015 est.)

Budget: *revenues:* 3.295 billion (2017 est.)
expenditures: 3.605 billion (2017 est.)

Budget surplus (+) or deficit (-): -2.7% (of GDP) (2017 est.)

Public debt: 39.3% of GDP (2017 est.)
39.5% of GDP (2016 est.)
note: official data from Ministry of Finance; data cover central government debt; this data excludes debt instruments issued (or owned) by government entities other than the treasury; includes treasury debt held by foreign entitites; excludes debt issued by sub-national entities; there are no debt instruments sold for social funds

Taxes and other revenues: 29% (of GDP) (2017 est.)

Fiscal year: calendar year

Current account balance: -$151 million (2017 est.)
-$293 million (2016 est.)

Exports: $7.18 billion (2020 est.) note: data are in current year dollars
$7.78 billion (2019 est.) note: data are in current year dollars
$7.61 billion (2018 est.) note: data are in current year dollars

Exports - partners: Germany 45%, Serbia 8%, Bulgaria 5% (2019)

Exports - commodities: support catalysts, centrifuges, insulated wiring, vehicle parts, buses, seats (2019)

Imports: $8.76 billion (2020 est.) note: data are in current year dollars
$9.6 billion (2019 est.) note: data are in current year dollars
$9.23 billion (2018 est.) note: data are in current year dollars

Imports - partners: United Kingdom 14%, Germany 14%, Greece 8%, Serbia 8% (2019)

Imports - commodities: platinum, refined petroleum, laboratory ceramics, cars, insulated wiring (2019)

Reserves of foreign exchange and gold: $2.802 billion (31 December 2017 est.)
$2.755 billion (31 December 2016 est.)

Debt - external: $9.065 billion (2019 est.)
$9.398 billion (2018 est.)

Exchange rates: Macedonian denars (MKD) per US dollar -
55.8 (2017 est.)
55.733 (2016 est.)
55.733 (2015 est.)
55.537 (2014 est.)
46.437 (2013 est.)

ENERGY

Electricity access: *electrification - total population:* 100% (2020)

Electricity: *installed generating capacity:* 1.928 million kW (2020 est.)
consumption: 6,350,982,000 kWh (2019 est.)
exports: 639 million kWh (2020 est.)
imports: 2.965 billion kWh (2020 est.)
transmission/distribution losses: 979 million kWh (2019 est.)

Electricity generation sources: *fossil fuels:* 71.4% of total installed capacity (2020 est.)
solar: 0.5% of total installed capacity (2020 est.)
wind: 2.3% of total installed capacity (2020 est.)
hydroelectricity: 24.7% of total installed capacity (2020 est.)
biomass and waste: 1.1% of total installed capacity (2020 est.)

Coal: *production:* 5.026 million metric tons (2020 est.)
consumption: 5.211 million metric tons (2020 est.)
exports: 1,000 metric tons (2020 est.)
imports: 174,000 metric tons (2020 est.)
proven reserves: 332 million metric tons (2019 est.)

Petroleum: *total petroleum production:* 0 bbl/day (2021 est.)
refined petroleum consumption: 22,700 bbl/day (2019 est.)
crude oil and lease condensate exports: 0 bbl/day (2018 est.)
crude oil and lease condensate imports: 0 bbl/day (2018 est.)
crude oil estimated reserves: 0 barrels (2021 est.)

Refined petroleum products - production: 0 bbl/day (2015 est.)

Refined petroleum products - exports: 3,065 bbl/day (2015 est.)

Refined petroleum products - imports: 23,560 bbl/day (2015 est.)

Natural gas: *production:* 0 cubic meters (2021 est.)
consumption: 218.917 million cubic meters (2019 est.)
exports: 0 cubic meters (2021 est.)
imports: 218.917 million cubic meters (2019 est.)
proven reserves: 0 cubic meters (2021 est.)

Carbon dioxide emissions: 7.383 million metric tonnes of CO2 (2019 est.)
from coal and metallurgical coke: 3.866 million metric tonnes of CO2 (2019 est.)
from petroleum and other liquids: 3.094 million metric tonnes of CO2 (2019 est.)
from consumed natural gas: 423,000 metric tonnes of CO2 (2019 est.)

Energy consumption per capita: 53.572 million Btu/person (2019 est.)

COMMUNICATIONS

Telephones - fixed lines: *total subscriptions:* 415,390 (2020 est.)
subscriptions per 100 inhabitants: 20 (2020 est.)

Telephones - mobile cellular: *total subscriptions:* 1,862,138 (2020 est.)
subscriptions per 100 inhabitants: 89 (2020 est.)

Telecommunication systems: *general assessment:* as part of the EU pre-accession process, North Macedonia has built closer economic ties with the Union which accounts for 77.5% of Macedonia's exports and just over half of its imports; closer regulatory and administrative ties with European Commission (EC) institutions have done much to develop the telecom sector and prepare the market for the competitive environment encouraged in the EU; as part of EU integration legislation North Macedonia has implemented the principles of the EU's regulatory framework for communications, established an independent regulator and set out several provisions to provide for a competitive telecom market, including wholesale access to the incumbent's fixed-line network; broadband services are widely available, with effective competition between DSL and cable platforms complemented by wireless broadband and a developing fiber sector; the number of DSL subscribers has continued to fall in recent years as customers are migrated to fiber networks; the MNOs are increasingly focused on expanding their 5G networks, seeking stronger coverage across North Macedonia's high value urban areas; mobile data services are also becoming increasingly important following investments in LTE network rollouts and in upgrades to LTE-A technology (2022)
domestic: fixed-line roughly 20 per 100 and mobile-cellular 89 per 100 subscriptions (2020)
international: country code - 389

Broadcast media: public service TV broadcaster Macedonian Radio and Television operates 3 national terrestrial TV channels and 2 satellite TV channels; additionally, there are 10 regional TV stations that broadcast nationally using terrestrial transmitters, 54 TV channels with concession for cable TV, 9 regional TV stations with concessions for cable TV; 4 satellite TV channels broadcasting on a national level, 21 local commercial TV channels, and a large number of cable operators that offer domestic and international programming; the public radio broadcaster operates over 3 stations; there are 4 privately owned radio stations that broadcast nationally; 17 regional radio stations, and 49 local commercial radio stations (2019)

Internet country code: .mk

Internet users: *total:* 1,678,750 (2020 est.)
percent of population: 81% (2020 est.)

Broadband - fixed subscriptions: *total:* 475,569 (2020 est.)
subscriptions per 100 inhabitants: 23 (2020 est.)

TRANSPORTATION

Civil aircraft registration country code prefix: Z3

Airports: *total:* 10 (2021)

Airports - with paved runways: *total:* 8
2,438 to 3,047 m: 2
under 914 m: 6 (2021)

Airports - with unpaved runways: *total:* 2
914 to 1,523 m: 1
under 914 m: 1 (2021)

Pipelines: 262 km gas, 120 km oil (2017)

Railways: *total:* 925 km (2017)
standard gauge: 925 km (2017) 1.435-m gauge (313 km electrified)

Roadways: *total:* 14,182 km (2017) (includes 290 km of expressways)
paved: 9,633 km (2017)
unpaved: 4,549 km (2017)

MILITARY AND SECURITY

Military and security forces: Army of the Republic of North Macedonia (ARSM; includes a General Staff and subordinate Operations Command, Logistic Support Command, Training and Doctrine Command, Center for Electronic Reconnaissance,

Aviation Brigade, and Honor Guard Battalion) (2022)
note: the Operations Command includes air, ground, special operations, support, and reserve forces

Military expenditures: 1.8% of GDP (2022 est.)
1.5% of GDP (2021)
1.3% of GDP (2020)
1.2% of GDP (2019) (approximately $310 million)
0.9% of GDP (2018) (approximately $280 million)

Military and security service personnel strengths: approximately 6,000 active duty personnel (2022)

Military equipment inventories and acquisitions: the military's inventory consists mostly of Soviet-era equipment; since 2010, it has received small amounts of equipment from Ireland and Turkey (2021)

Military service age and obligation: 18 years of age for voluntary military service; conscription abolished in 2007 (2021)

note: as of 2022, women made up about 10% of the military's full-time personnel

Military - note: North Macedonia became the 30th member of NATO in 2020; as of 2022, Greece provided NATO's air policing mission for North Macedonia

TERRORISM

Terrorist group(s): Islamic State of Iraq and ash-Sham (ISIS)

TRANSNATIONAL ISSUES

Disputes - international: *North Macedonia-Albania:* none identified
North Macedonia-Greece: none identified
North Macedonia-Kosovo: North Macedonia and Kosovo completed demarcation of their boundary in October 2009
North Macedonia-Serbia: none identified

Refugees and internally displaced persons: *refugees (country of origin):* 6,386 (Ukraine) (as of 22 November 2022)
stateless persons: 553 (mid-year 2021)
note: 549,217 estimated refugee and migrant arrivals (January 2015-October 2022)

Illicit drugs: major transshipment point for Southwest Asian heroin and hashish; minor transit point for South American cocaine destined for Europe; although not a financial center and most criminal activity is thought to be domestic, money laundering is a problem due to a mostly cash-based economy and weak enforcement

NORTHERN MARIANA ISLANDS

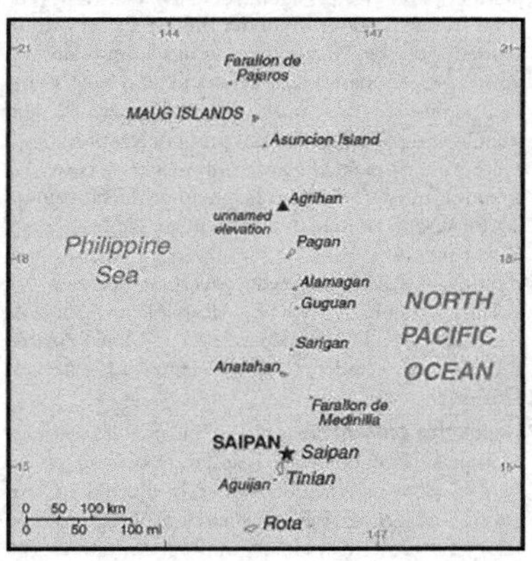

INTRODUCTION

Background: The Northern Mariana Islands were settled by Austronesian people around 1500 B.C. These people became the indigenous Chamorro and were influenced by later migrations, including of Micronesians in the first century A.D., and island Southeast Asians around 900. Spanish explorer Ferdinand MAGELLAN sailed through the Mariana Islands in 1521 and Spain claimed them in 1565. Spain formally colonized the Mariana Islands in 1668 and administered the archipelago from Guam. Spain's brutal repression of the Chamorro, along with new diseases and intermittent warfare, reduced the indigenous population by about 90% in the 1700s. With a similar dynamic occurring on Guam, Spain forced the Chamorro from the Northern Mariana Islands to resettle on Guam and prevented them from returning to their home islands. By the time the Northern Mariana Islands' Chamorro returned, many other Micronesians, including Chuukese and Yapese, had already settled on their islands.

In 1898, Spain ceded Guam to the US following the Spanish-American War but sold the Northern Mariana Islands to Germany under the German-Spanish Treaty of 1899. Germany administered the territory from German New Guinea but took a hands-off approach to day-to-day life. Following World War I, Japan administered the islands under a League of Nations mandate. Japan focused on sugar production and brought in thousands of Japanese laborers, who quickly outnumbered the Chamorro on the islands. During World War II, Japan invaded Guam from the Northern Mariana Islands and used Marianan Chamorro as translators with Guamanian Chamorro, creating friction between the two Chamorro communities that continues to this day. The US captured the Northern Mariana Islands in 1944 after the Battle of Saipan and administered them post-World War II as part of the Trust Territory of the Pacific Islands (TTPI).

On four occasions in the 1950s and 1960s, voters opted for integration with Guam, although Guam rejected it in 1969. In 1978, the Northern Mariana Islands was granted self-government separate from the rest of the TTPI and in 1986, islanders were granted US citizenship and the territory came under US sovereignty as the Commonwealth of the Northern Mariana Islands (CNMI). In 2009, the CNMI became the final US territory to elect a non-voting delegate to the US Congress.

GEOGRAPHY

Location: Oceania, islands in the North Pacific Ocean, about three-quarters of the way from Hawaii to the Philippines

Geographic coordinates: 15 12 N, 145 45 E

Map references: Oceania

Area: *total:* 464 sq km
land: 464 sq km
water: 0 sq km
note: consists of 14 islands including Saipan, Rota, and Tinian
country comparison to the world: 196

Area - comparative: 2.5 times the size of Washington, DC

Land boundaries: *total:* 0 km

Coastline: 1,482 km

Maritime claims: *territorial sea:* 12 nm
exclusive economic zone: 200 nm

Climate: tropical marine; moderated by northeast trade winds, little seasonal temperature variation; dry season December to June, rainy season July to October

Terrain: the southern islands in this north-south trending archipelago are limestone, with fringing coral reefs; the northern islands are volcanic, with active volcanoes on several islands

Elevation: *highest point:* Agrihan Volcano 965 m
lowest point: Pacific Ocean 0 m

Natural resources: arable land, fish

Land use: *agricultural land:* 6.6% (2018 est.)
arable land: 2.2% (2018 est.)
permanent crops: 2.2% (2018 est.)
permanent pasture: 2.2% (2018 est.)
forest: 65.5% (2018 est.)
other: 27.9% (2018 est.)

Irrigated land: 1 sq km (2012)

Population distribution: approximately 90% of the population lives on the island of Saipan

Natural hazards: active volcanoes on Pagan and Agrihan; typhoons (especially August to November)

Geography - note: strategic location in the North Pacific Ocean

PEOPLE AND SOCIETY

Population: 51,475 (2022 est.)
country comparison to the world: 209

Ethnic groups: Asian 50% (includes Filipino 35.3%, Chinese 6.8%, Korean 4.2%, and other Asian 3.7%), Native Hawaiian or other Pacific Islander 34.9% (includes Chamorro 23.9%, Carolinian 4.6%, and other Native Hawaiian or Pacific Islander 6.4%), other 2.5%, two or more ethnicities or races 12.7% (2010 est.)

Languages: Philippine languages 32.8%, Chamorro (official) 24.1%, English (official) 17%, other Pacific island languages 10.1% (includes Carolinian (official), Chinese 6.8%, other Asian languages 7.3%, other 1.9% (2010 est.)

Religions: Christian (Roman Catholic majority, although traditional beliefs and taboos may still be found)

Age structure: *0-14 years:* 25.02% (male 6,937/ female 5,934)
15-24 years: 16.28% (male 4,518/female 3,857)
25-54 years: 37.44% (male 9,934/female 9,325)
55-64 years: 14.01% (male 3,921/female 3,286)
65 years and over: 7.23% (male 1,988/female 1,733) (2020 est.)

Median age: *total:* 32.8 years
male: 31.8 years
female: 34.1 years (2020 est.)
country comparison to the world: 105

Population growth rate: -0.35% (2022 est.)
country comparison to the world: 219

Birth rate: 15.5 births/1,000 population (2022 est.)
country comparison to the world: 109

Death rate: 5.44 deaths/1,000 population (2022 est.)
country comparison to the world: 184

Net migration rate: -13.6 migrant(s)/1,000 population (2022 est.)
country comparison to the world: 227

Population distribution: approximately 90% of the population lives on the island of Saipan

Urbanization: *urban population:* 92% of total population (2022)
rate of urbanization: 0.36% annual rate of change (2020-25 est.)

Major urban areas - population: 51,000 SAIPAN (capital) (2018)

Sex ratio: *at birth:* 1.17 male(s)/female
0-14 years: 1.16 male(s)/female
15-24 years: 1.18 male(s)/female
25-54 years: 1.09 male(s)/female
55-64 years: 1.18 male(s)/female
65 years and over: 0.89 male(s)/female
total population: 1.13 male(s)/female (2022 est.)

Infant mortality rate: *total:* 12.48 deaths/1,000 live births
male: 15.13 deaths/1,000 live births
female: 9.38 deaths/1,000 live births (2022 est.)
country comparison to the world: 112

Life expectancy at birth: *total population:* 76.58 years
male: 74.48 years
female: 79.03 years (2022 est.)
country comparison to the world: 103

Total fertility rate: 2.63 children born/woman (2022 est.)
country comparison to the world: 63

Drinking water source: *improved: total:* 100% of population
unimproved: total: 0% of population (2020 est.)

Sanitation facility access: *improved: total:* 97.9% of population
unimproved: total: 2.1% of population (2020 est.)

ENVIRONMENT

Environment - current issues: contamination of groundwater on Saipan may contribute to disease; clean-up of landfill; protection of endangered species conflicts with development

Climate: tropical marine; moderated by northeast trade winds, little seasonal temperature variation; dry season December to June, rainy season July to October

Land use: *agricultural land:* 6.6% (2018 est.)
arable land: 2.2% (2018 est.)
permanent crops: 2.2% (2018 est.)
permanent pasture: 2.2% (2018 est.)
forest: 65.5% (2018 est.)
other: 27.9% (2018 est.)

Urbanization: *urban population:* 92% of total population (2022)
rate of urbanization: 0.36% annual rate of change (2020-25 est.)

Revenue from forest resources: *forest revenues:* 0% of GDP (2018 est.)
country comparison to the world: 189

Waste and recycling: *municipal solid waste generated annually:* 32,761 tons (2013 est.)
municipal solid waste recycled annually: 11,794 tons (2016 est.)
percent of municipal solid waste recycled: 36% (2016 est.)

GOVERNMENT

Country name: *conventional long form:* Commonwealth of the Northern Mariana Islands
conventional short form: Northern Mariana Islands
former: Trust Territory of the Pacific Islands, Mariana Islands District
abbreviation: CNMI
etymology: formally claimed and named by Spain in 1667 in honor of the Spanish Queen, MARIANA of Austria

Government type: a commonwealth in political union with and under the sovereignty of the US; republican form of government with separate executive, legislative, and judicial branches

Dependency status: commonwealth in political union with and under the sovereignty of the US; federal funds to the Commonwealth administered by the US Department of the Interior, Office of Insular Affairs, Washington, DC

Capital: *name:* Saipan
geographic coordinates: 15 12 N, 145 45 E
time difference: UTC+10 (15 hours ahead of Washington, DC, during Standard Time)
etymology: the entire island of Saipan is organized as a single municipality and serves as the capital; according to legend, when the first native voyagers arrived in their outrigger canoes they found an uninhabited island; to them it was like an empty voyage, so they named the island *saay* meaning "a voyage," and *peel* meaning "empty"; over time *Saaypeel* - "island of the empty voyage" - became Saipan

Administrative divisions: none (commonwealth in political union with the US); there are no first-order administrative divisions as defined by the US Government, but there are 4 municipalities at the second order: Northern Islands, Rota, Saipan, Tinian

Independence: none (commonwealth in political union with the US)

National holiday: Commonwealth Day, 8 January (1978)

Constitution: *history:* partially effective 9 January 1978 (Constitution of the Commonwealth of the Northern Mariana Islands); fully effective 4 November 1986 (Covenant Agreement)
amendments: proposed by constitutional convention, by public petition, or by the Legislature; ratification of proposed amendments requires approval by voters at the next general election or special election; amendments proposed by constitutional convention or by petition become effective if approved by a majority of voters and at least two-thirds majority of voters in each of two senatorial districts; amendments proposed by the Legislature are effective if approved by majority vote; amended several times, last in 2012

Legal system: the laws of the US apply, except for customs and some aspects of taxation

Citizenship: see United States

Suffrage: 18 years of age; universal; note - indigenous inhabitants are US citizens but do not vote in US presidential elections

Executive branch: *chief of state:* President Joseph R. BIDEN Jr. (since 20 January 2021); Vice President Kamala D. HARRIS (since 20 January 2021)
head of government: Governor Ralph TORRES (since 29 December 2015); Lieutenant Governor Victor HOCOG (since 29 December 2015)
cabinet: Cabinet appointed by the governor with the advice and consent of the Senate
elections/appointments: president and vice president indirectly elected on the same ballot by an Electoral College of 'electors' chosen from each state; president and vice president serve a 4-year term (eligible for a second term); under the US Constitution, residents of the Northern Mariana Islands do not vote in elections for US president and vice president; however, they may vote in Democratic and Republican party presidential primary elections; governor directly elected by absolute majority vote in 2 rounds if needed; election last held on 13 November 2018 (next to be held in 8 November 2022)
election results:
Ralph TORRES elected governor; percent of vote - Ralph TORRES (Republican) 62.2%, Juan BABAUTA (independent) 37.8%; Arnold PALACIOS (independent) elected Lieutenant Governor

Legislative branch: *description:* bicameral Northern Marianas Commonwealth Legislature consists of:
Senate (9 seats; members directly elected in single-seat constituencies by simple majority vote to serve 4-year terms) House of Representatives (20 seats; members directly elected in single-seat constituencies by simple majority vote to serve 2-year terms) the Northern Mariana Islands directly elects 1 delegate to the US House of Representatives by simple majority vote to serve a 2-year term
elections:
CNMI Senate - last held on 3 November 2020 (next to be held in November 2024)
CNMI House of Representatives - last held on 3 November 2020 (next to be held in November 2022)
Commonwealth of Northern Mariana Islands delegate to the US House of Representatives - last held on 3 November 2020 (next to be held in November 2022)
election results:
CNMI Senate - percent of vote by party - NA; seats by party - Republican Party 6, independent 3; composition - men 7, women 2, percent of women 22.2%
CNMI House of Representatives - percent of vote by party - NA; seats by party - Republican Party 9, Democrat Party 8, independent 3; composition - men 15, women 5, percent of women 25%; note - overall CNMI legislature percent of women 24.1%
delegate to US House of Representatives - seat won by independent; composition - 1 man
note: the Northern Mariana Islands delegate to the US House of Representatives can vote when serving

on a committee and when the House meets as the "Committee of the Whole House" but not when legislation is submitted for a "full floor" House vote

Judicial branch: *highest court(s):* Supreme Court of the Commonwealth of the Northern Mariana Islands (CNMI) (consists of the chief justice and 2 associate justices); US Federal District Court (consists of 1 judge); note - US Federal District Court jurisdiction limited to US federal laws; appeals beyond the CNMI Supreme Court are referred to the US Supreme Court
judge selection and term of office: CNMI Supreme Court judges appointed by the governor and confirmed by the CNMI Senate; judges appointed for 8-year terms and another term if directly elected in a popular election; US Federal District Court judges appointed by the US president and confirmed by the US Senate; judges appointed for renewable 10-year terms
subordinate courts: Superior Court

Political parties and leaders: Democratic Party [Daniel QUITUGUA]
Republican Party [James ADA]

International organization participation: PIF (observer), SPC, UPU

Diplomatic representation from the US: *embassy:* none (commonwealth in political union with the US)

Flag description: blue with a white, five-pointed star superimposed on a gray latte stone (the traditional foundation stone used in building) in the center, surrounded by a wreath; blue symbolizes the Pacific Ocean, the star represents the Commonwealth; the latte stone and the floral head wreath display elements of the native Chamorro culture

National symbol(s): latte stone; national colors: blue, white

National anthem: *name:* "Gi Talo Gi Halom Tasi" (In the Middle of the Sea)
lyrics/music: Jose S. PANGELINAN [Chamoru], David PETER [Carolinian]/Wilhelm GANZHORN
note: adopted 1996; the Carolinian version of the song is known as "Satil Matawal Pacifico;" as a commonwealth of the US, in addition to the local anthem, "The Star-Spangled Banner" is official (see United States)

ECONOMY

Economic overview: The economy of the Commonwealth of the Northern Mariana Islands(CNMI) has been on the rebound in the last few years, mainly on the strength of its tourism industry. In 2016, the CNMI's real GDP increased 28.6% over the previous year, following two years of relatively rapid growth in 2014 and 2015. Chinese and Korean tourists have supplanted Japanese tourists in the last few years. The Commonwealth is making a concerted effort to broaden its tourism by extending casino gambling from the small Islands of Tinian and Rota to the main Island of Saipan, its political and commercial center. Investment is concentrated on hotels and casinos in Saipan, the CNMI's largest island and home to about 90% of its population.
Federal grants have also contributed to economic growth and stability. In 2016, federal grants amounted to $101.4 billion which made up 26% of the CNMI government's total revenues. A small agriculture sector consists of cattle ranches and small farms producing coconuts, breadfruit, tomatoes, and melons.
Legislation is pending in the US Congress to extend the transition period to allow foreign workers to work in the CNMI on temporary visas.

Real GDP (purchasing power parity): $1.242 billion (2016 est.)
$933 million (2015 est.)
$845 million (2014 est.)
note: GDP estimate includes US subsidy; data are in 2013 dollars
country comparison to the world: 204

Real GDP growth rate: 28.6% (2016 est.)
3.8% (2015 est.)
3.5% (2014 est.)
country comparison to the world: 2

Real GDP per capita: $24,500 (2016 est.)
$18,400 (2015 est.)
$16,600 (2014 est.)
country comparison to the world: 78

GDP (official exchange rate): $1.242 billion (2016 est.)

Inflation rate (consumer prices): 0.3% (2016 est.)
0.1% (2015 est.)
country comparison to the world: 36

GDP - composition, by sector of origin: agriculture: 1.7% (2016)
industry: 58.1% (2016 est.)
services: 40.2% (2016)

GDP - composition, by end use: *household consumption:* 43.1% (2016 est.)
government consumption: 28.9% (2016 est.)
investment in fixed capital: 26.3% (2016 est.)
exports of goods and services: 73.6% (2016 est.)
imports of goods and services: -71.9% (2016 est.)

Agricultural products: vegetables and melons, fruits and nuts; ornamental plants; livestock, poultry, eggs; fish and aquaculture products

Industries: tourism, banking, construction, fishing, handicrafts, other services

Labor force: 27,970 (2010 est.)
note: includes foreign workers
country comparison to the world: 204

Labor force - by occupation: *agriculture:* 1.9%
industry: 10%
services: 88.1% (2010 est.)

Unemployment rate: 11.2% (2010 est.)
8% (2005 est.)
country comparison to the world: 158

Budget: *revenues:* 389.6 million (2016 est.)
expenditures: 344 million (2015 est.)

Budget surplus (+) or deficit (-): 3.7% (of GDP) (2016 est.)
country comparison to the world: 11

Public debt: 7.1% of GDP (2017 est.)
country comparison to the world: 201

Taxes and other revenues: 31.4% (of GDP) (2016 est.)
country comparison to the world: 72

Fiscal year: 1 October - 30 September

Exports: $914 million (2016 est.)
$520 million (2015 est.)
country comparison to the world: 179

Exports - partners: South Korea 73%, Peru 5% (2019)

Exports - commodities: scrap iron, scrap copper, scrap aluminum, computers, laboratory diagnostic equipment (2019)

Imports: $893 million (2016 est.)
$638 million (2015 est.)
country comparison to the world: 193

Imports - partners: Hong Kong 29%, Japan 29%, Singapore 16%, South Korea 9% (2019)

Imports - commodities: refined petroleum, trunks/cases, cars, watches, jewelry (2019)

Exchange rates: the US dollar is used

ENERGY

Electricity access: *electrification - total population:* 100% (2020)

Coal: *production:* 0 metric tons (2020 est.)
consumption: 0 metric tons (2020 est.)
exports: 0 metric tons (2020 est.)
imports: 0 metric tons (2020 est.)

Petroleum: *total petroleum production:* 0 bbl/day (2021 est.) Data represented includes both Guam and Northern Mariana Islands
refined petroleum consumption: 2,100 bbl/day (2019 est.) Data represented includes both Guam and Northern Mariana Islands
crude oil and lease condensate exports: 0 bbl/day (2018 est.) Data represented includes both Guam and Northern Mariana Islands
crude oil and lease condensate imports: 0 bbl/day (2018 est.) Data represented includes both Guam and Northern Mariana Islands
crude oil estimated reserves: 0 barrels (2021 est.) Data represented includes both Guam and Northern Mariana Islands

Natural gas: *production:* 0 cubic meters (2021 est.)
consumption: 0 cubic meters (2021 est.)
exports: 0 cubic meters (2021 est.)
imports: 0 cubic meters (2021 est.)
proven reserves: 0 cubic meters (2021 est.)

Carbon dioxide emissions: 0 metric tonnes of CO2 (2019 est.)
from coal and metallurgical coke: 0 metric tonnes of CO2 (2019 est.)
from consumed natural gas: 0 metric tonnes of CO2 (2019 est.)
country comparison to the world: 217

Energy consumption per capita: 0 Btu/person (2019 est.)
country comparison to the world: 207

COMMUNICATIONS

Telephones - fixed lines: *total subscriptions:* 20,000 (2020 est.)
subscriptions per 100 inhabitants: 35 (2020 est.)
country comparison to the world: 174

Telephones - mobile cellular: *total subscriptions:* 20,474 (2004 est.)
subscriptions per 100 inhabitants: 36 (2004)
country comparison to the world: 215

Telecommunication systems: *general assessment:* digital fiber-optic cables and satellites connect the islands to worldwide networks; demand for broadband growing given that mobile services are the source for Internet across region; future launch of 5G (2020)
domestic: wide variety of services available including dial-up and broadband Internet, mobile cellular, international private lines, payphones, phone cards, voicemail, and automatic call distribution systems;

fixed-line teledensity roughly 35 per 100 persons (2020)
international: country code - 1-670; landing points for the Atisa and Mariana-Guam submarine cables linking Mariana islands to Guam; satellite earth stations - 2 Intelsat (Pacific Ocean) (2019)

Broadcast media: 1 TV broadcast station on Saipan; multi-channel cable TV services are available on Saipan; 9 licensed radio broadcast stations (2009)

Internet country code: .mp

Internet users: *total:* 17,418 (2016 est.)
percent of population: 31% (2016 est.)
country comparison to the world: 213

TRANSPORTATION

Airports: *total:* 5 (2021)
country comparison to the world: 182

Airports - with paved runways: *total:* 3
2,438 to 3,047 m: 2
1,524 to 2,437 m: 1 (2021)

Airports - with unpaved runways: *total:* 2
2,438 to 3,047 m: 1
under 914 m: 1 (2021)

Heliports: 1 (2021)

Roadways: *total:* 536 km (2008)
country comparison to the world: 195

Merchant marine: *total:* 1
by type: other 1 (2019)
country comparison to the world: 185

Ports and terminals: *major seaport(s):* Saipan, Tinian, Rota

MILITARY AND SECURITY

Military - note: defense is the responsibility of the US

TRANSNATIONAL ISSUES

Disputes - international: none identified

NORWAY

INTRODUCTION

Background: Two centuries of Viking raids into Europe tapered off following the adoption of Christianity by King Olav TRYGGVASON in 994; conversion of the Norwegian kingdom occurred over the next several decades. In 1397, Norway was absorbed into a union with Denmark that lasted more than four centuries. In 1814, Norwegians resisted the cession of their country to Sweden and adopted a new constitution. Sweden then invaded Norway but agreed to let Norway keep its constitution in return for accepting the union under a Swedish king. Rising nationalism throughout the 19th century led to a 1905 referendum granting Norway independence. Although Norway remained neutral in World War I, it suffered heavy losses to its shipping. Norway proclaimed its neutrality at the outset of World War II but was nonetheless occupied for five years by Nazi Germany (1940-45). In 1949, Norway abandoned neutrality and became a member of NATO. Discovery of oil and gas in adjacent waters in the late 1960s boosted Norway's economic fortunes. In referenda held in 1972 and 1994, Norway rejected joining the EU. Key domestic issues include immigration and integration of ethnic minorities, maintaining the country's extensive social safety net with an aging population, and preserving economic competitiveness.

GEOGRAPHY

Location: Northern Europe, bordering the North Sea and the North Atlantic Ocean, west of Sweden

Geographic coordinates: 62 00 N, 10 00 E

Map references: Europe

Area: *total:* 323,802 sq km
land: 304,282 sq km
water: 19,520 sq km

Area - comparative: slightly larger than twice the size of Georgia; slightly larger than New Mexico

Land boundaries: *total:* 2,566 km
border countries (3): Finland 709 km; Sweden 1,666 km; Russia 191 km

Coastline: 25,148 km (includes mainland 2,650 km, as well as long fjords, numerous small islands, and minor indentations 22,498 km; length of island coastlines 58,133 km)

Maritime claims: *territorial sea:* 12 nm
contiguous zone: 10 nm
exclusive economic zone: 200 nm
continental shelf: 200 nm

Climate: temperate along coast, modified by North Atlantic Current; colder interior with increased precipitation and colder summers; rainy year-round on west coast

Terrain: glaciated; mostly high plateaus and rugged mountains broken by fertile valleys; small, scattered plains; coastline deeply indented by fjords; arctic tundra in north

Elevation: *highest point:* Galdhopiggen 2,469 m
lowest point: Norwegian Sea 0 m
mean elevation: 460 m

Natural resources: petroleum, natural gas, iron ore, copper, lead, zinc, titanium, pyrites, nickel, fish, timber, hydropower

Land use: *agricultural land:* 2.7% (2018 est.)
arable land: 2.2% (2018 est.)
permanent crops: 0% (2018 est.)
permanent pasture: 0.5% (2018 est.)
forest: 27.8% (2018 est.)
other: 69.5% (2018 est.)

Irrigated land: 900 sq km (2012)

Population distribution: most Norwegians live in the south where the climate is milder and there is better connectivity to mainland Europe; population clusters are found all along the North Sea coast in the southwest, and Skaggerak in the southeast; the interior areas of the north remain sparsely populated

Natural hazards: rockslides, avalanches
volcanism: Beerenberg (2,227 m) on Jan Mayen Island in the Norwegian Sea is the country's only active volcano

Geography - note: about two-thirds mountains; some 50,000 islands off its much-indented coastline; strategic location adjacent to sea lanes and air routes in North Atlantic; one of the most rugged and longest coastlines in the world

PEOPLE AND SOCIETY

Population: 5,553,840 (2022 est.)

Nationality: *noun:* Norwegian(s)
adjective: Norwegian

Ethnic groups: Norwegian 81.5% (includes about 60,000 Sami), other European 8.9%, other 9.6% (2021 est.)

Languages: Bokmal Norwegian (official), Nynorsk Norwegian (official), small Sami- and Finnish-speaking minorities; note - Sami has three dialects: Lule, North Sami, and South Sami; Sami is an official language in nine municipalities in Norway's three northernmost counties: Finnmark, Nordland, and Troms
major-language sample(s):

Verdens Faktabok, den essensielle kilden for grunnleggende informasjon. (Norwegian)

Religions: Church of Norway (Evangelical Lutheran - official) 67.5%, Muslim 3.1%, Roman Catholic 3.1%, other Christian 3.8%, other 2.6%, unspecified 19.9% (2021 est.)

Age structure: *0-14 years:* 17.96% (male 503,013/female 478,901)
15-24 years: 12.02% (male 336,597/female 320,720)
25-54 years: 40.75% (male 1,150,762/female 1,077,357)
55-64 years: 11.84% (male 328,865/female 318,398)
65 years and over: 17.43% (male 442,232/female 510,594) (2020 est.)

Dependency ratios: *total dependency ratio:* 53.3
youth dependency ratio: 26.5
elderly dependency ratio: 26.9
potential support ratio: 3.7 (2020 est.)
note: data include Svalbard and Jan Mayen Islands

Median age: *total:* 39.5 years
male: 38.8 years
female: 40.2 years (2020 est.)

Population growth rate: 0.8% (2022 est.)

Birth rate: 12 births/1,000 population (2022 est.)

Death rate: 7.96 deaths/1,000 population (2022 est.)

Net migration rate: 3.92 migrant(s)/1,000 population (2022 est.)

Population distribution: most Norwegians live in the south where the climate is milder and there is better connectivity to mainland Europe; population clusters are found all along the North Sea coast in the southwest, and Skaggerak in the southeast; the interior areas of the north remain sparsely populated

Urbanization: *urban population:* 83.7% of total population (2022)
rate of urbanization: 1.32% annual rate of change (2020-25 est.)
note: data include Svalbard and Jan Mayen Islands

Major urban areas - population: 1.071 million OSLO (capital) (2022)

Sex ratio: *at birth:* 1.05 male(s)/female
0-14 years: 1.05 male(s)/female
15-24 years: 1.05 male(s)/female
25-54 years: 1.07 male(s)/female
55-64 years: 1.04 male(s)/female
65 years and over: 0.71 male(s)/female
total population: 1.02 male(s)/female (2022 est.)

Mother's mean age at first birth: 29.8 years (2020 est.)
note: data is calculated based on actual age at first births

Maternal mortality ratio: 2 deaths/100,000 live births (2017 est.)

Infant mortality rate: *total:* 2.31 deaths/1,000 live births
male: 2.65 deaths/1,000 live births
female: 1.96 deaths/1,000 live births (2022 est.)

Life expectancy at birth: *total population:* 82.55 years
male: 80.42 years
female: 84.79 years (2022 est.)

Total fertility rate: 1.83 children born/woman (2022 est.)

Drinking water source: *improved: urban:* 100% of population
rural: 100% of population
total: 100% of population

Current health expenditure: 10.5% of GDP (2019)

Physicians density: 5.04 physicians/1,000 population (2020)

Hospital bed density: 3.5 beds/1,000 population (2018)

Sanitation facility access: *improved: urban:* 100% of population
rural: 100% of population
total: 100% of population

HIV/AIDS - adult prevalence rate: 0.1% (2018 est.)

Obesity - adult prevalence rate: 23.1% (2016)

Alcohol consumption per capita: *total:* 6.05 liters of pure alcohol (2019 est.)
beer: 2.63 liters of pure alcohol (2019 est.)
wine: 2.23 liters of pure alcohol (2019 est.)
spirits: 1 liters of pure alcohol (2019 est.)
other alcohols: 0.19 liters of pure alcohol (2019 est.)

Tobacco use: *total:* 16.2% (2020 est.)
male: 17% (2020 est.)
female: 15.4% (2020 est.)

Education expenditures: 7.6% of GDP (2018 est.)

School life expectancy (primary to tertiary education): *total:* 18 years
male: 18 years
female: 19 years (2019)

Unemployment, youth ages 15-24: *total:* 11.3%
male: 12.1%
female: 10.5% (2020 est.)

ENVIRONMENT

Environment - current issues: water pollution; acid rain damaging forests and adversely affecting lakes, threatening fish stocks; air pollution from vehicle emissions

Environment - international agreements: *party to:* Air Pollution, Air Pollution-Heavy Metals, Air Pollution-Multi-effect Protocol, Air Pollution-Nitrogen Oxides, Air Pollution-Persistent Organic Pollutants, Air Pollution-Sulphur 85, Air Pollution-Sulphur 94, Air Pollution-Volatile Organic Compounds, Antarctic-Environmental Protection, Antarctic-Marine Living Resources, Antarctic Seals, Antarctic Treaty, Biodiversity, Climate Change, Climate Change-Kyoto Protocol, Climate Change-Paris Agreement, Comprehensive Nuclear Test Ban, Desertification, Endangered Species, Environmental Modification, Hazardous Wastes, Law of the Sea, Marine Dumping-London Convention, Marine Dumping-London Protocol, Nuclear Test Ban, Ozone Layer Protection, Ship Pollution, Tropical Timber 2006, Wetlands, Whaling
signed, but not ratified: none of the selected agreements

Air pollutants: *particulate matter emissions:* 7.02 micrograms per cubic meter (2016 est.)
carbon dioxide emissions: 41.02 megatons (2016 est.)
methane emissions: 4.81 megatons (2020 est.)

Climate: temperate along coast, modified by North Atlantic Current; colder interior with increased precipitation and colder summers; rainy year-round on west coast

Land use: *agricultural land:* 2.7% (2018 est.)
arable land: 2.2% (2018 est.)
permanent crops: 0% (2018 est.)
permanent pasture: 0.5% (2018 est.)
forest: 27.8% (2018 est.)
other: 69.5% (2018 est.)

Urbanization: *urban population:* 83.7% of total population (2022)
rate of urbanization: 1.32% annual rate of change (2020-25 est.)
note: data include Svalbard and Jan Mayen Islands

Revenue from forest resources: *forest revenues:* 0.05% of GDP (2018 est.)

Revenue from coal: *coal revenues:* 0% of GDP (2018 est.)

Waste and recycling: *municipal solid waste generated annually:* 2.187 million tons (2015 est.)
municipal solid waste recycled annually: 572,119 tons (2015 est.)
percent of municipal solid waste recycled: 26.2% (2015 est.)

Total water withdrawal: *municipal:* 775.3 million cubic meters (2017 est.)
industrial: 1.071 billion cubic meters (2017 est.)
agricultural: 844.9 million cubic meters (2017 est.)

Total renewable water resources: 393 billion cubic meters (2017 est.)

GOVERNMENT

Country name: *conventional long form:* Kingdom of Norway
conventional short form: Norway
local long form: Kongeriket Norge
local short form: Norge
etymology: derives from the Old Norse words "nordr" and "vegr" meaning "northern way" and refers to the long coastline of western Norway

Government type: parliamentary constitutional monarchy

Capital: *name:* Oslo
geographic coordinates: 59 55 N, 10 45 E
time difference: UTC+1 (6 hours ahead of Washington, DC, during Standard Time)
daylight saving time: +1hr, begins last Sunday in March; ends last Sunday in October
etymology: the medieval name was spelt "Aslo"; the *as* component refered either to the Ekeberg ridge southeast of the town ("as" in modern Norwegian), or to the Aesir (Norse gods); *lo* refered to "meadow," so the most likely interpretations would have been either "the meadow beneath the ridge" or "the meadow of the gods"; both explanations are considered equally plausible

Administrative divisions: 11 counties (fylker, singular - fylke); Agder, Innlandet, More og Romsdal, Nordland, Oslo, Rogaland, Troms og Finnmark, Trondelag, Vestfold og Telemark, Vestland, Viken

Dependent areas: Bouvet Island, Jan Mayen, Svalbard

Independence: 7 June 1905 (declared the union with Sweden dissolved); 26 October 1905 (Sweden agreed to the repeal of the union); notable earlier dates: ca. 872 (traditional unification of petty Norwegian kingdoms by HARALD Fairhair); 1397 (Kalmar Union of Denmark, Norway, and Sweden); 1524 (Denmark-Norway); 17 May 1814 (Norwegian constitution adopted); 4 November 1814 (Sweden-Norway union confirmed)

National holiday: Constitution Day, 17 May (1814)

Constitution: *history:* drafted spring 1814, adopted 16 May 1814, signed by Constituent Assembly 17 May 1814

amendments: proposals submitted by members of Parliament or by the government within the first three years of Parliament's four-year term; passage requires two-thirds majority vote of a two-thirds quorum in the next elected Parliament; amended over 400 times, last in 2020

Legal system: mixed legal system of civil, common, and customary law; Supreme Court can advise on legislative acts

International law organization participation: accepts compulsory ICJ jurisdiction with reservations; accepts ICCt jurisdiction

Citizenship: *citizenship by birth:* no
citizenship by descent only: at least one parent must be a citizen of Norway
dual citizenship recognized: no
residency requirement for naturalization: 7 years

Suffrage: 18 years of age; universal

Executive branch: *chief of state:* King HARALD V (since 17 January 1991); Heir Apparent Crown Prince HAAKON MAGNUS (son of the monarch, born 20 July 1973)
head of government: Prime Minister Jonas Gahr STORE (since 14 October 2021); note - Prime Minister Erna SOLBERG resigned on 12 October 2021
cabinet: Council of State appointed by the monarch, approved by Parliament
elections/appointments: the monarchy is hereditary; following parliamentary elections, the leader of the majority party or majority coalition usually appointed prime minister by the monarch with the approval of the parliament

Legislative branch: *description:* unicameral Parliament or Storting (169 seats; members directly elected in multi-seat constituencies by list proportional representation vote; members serve 4-year terms)
elections:
last held on 13 September 2021 (next to be held on 30 September 2025)
election results:
percent of vote by party - Ap 26.3%, H 20.5%, SP 13.6%, FrP 11.7%, SV 7.6%, R 4.7%, V 4.6%, MDG 3.9%, KrF 3.8%, PF 0.2%, other 3.1%; seats by party - Ap 48, H 36, SP 28, FrP 21, SV 13, R 8, V 8, , KrF 3, MDG 3, PF 1; composition (as of October 2021) men 93, women 76, percent of women 45%

Judicial branch: *highest court(s):* Supreme Court or Hoyesterett (consists of the chief justice and 18 associate justices)
judge selection and term of office: justices appointed by the monarch (King in Council) upon the recommendation of the Judicial Appointments Board; justices can serve until mandatory retirement at age 70
subordinate courts: Courts of Appeal or Lagmennsrett; regional and district courts; Conciliation Boards; ordinary and special courts; note - in addition to professionally trained judges, elected lay judges sit on the bench with professional judges in the Courts of Appeal and district courts

Political parties and leaders: Center Party or Sp [Trygve Slagsvold VEDUM]
Christian Democratic Party or KrF [Olaug Vervik BOLLESTAD]
Conservative Party or H [Erna SOLBERG]
Green Party or MDG [Une Aina BASTHOLM]
Labor Party or Ap [Jonas Gahr STORE]
Liberal Party or V [Guri MELBY]
Patient Focus or PF [Irene OJALA]
Progress Party or FrP [Sylvi LISTHAUG]
Red Party or R [Bjonar MOXNES]
Socialist Left Party or SV [Audun LYSBAKKEN]

International organization participation: ADB (nonregional member), AfDB (nonregional member), Arctic Council, Australia Group, BIS, CBSS, CD, CE, CERN, EAPC, EBRD, EFTA, EITI (implementing country), ESA, FAO, FATF, IADB, IAEA, IBRD, ICAO, ICC (national committees), ICCt, ICRM, IDA, IEA, IFAD, IFC, IFRCS, IGAD (partners), IHO, ILO, IMF, IMO, IMSO, Interpol, IOC, IOM, IPU, ISO, ITSO, ITU, ITUC (NGOs), MIGA, MINUSMA, NATO, NC, NEA, NIB, NSG, OAS (observer), OECD, OPCW, OSCE, Paris Club, PCA, Schengen Convention, UN, UNCTAD, UNESCO, UNHCR, UNIDO, UNITAR, UNMISS, UNRWA, UNTSO, UNWTO, UPU, Wassenaar Arrangement, WCO, WHO, WIPO, WMO, WTO, ZC

Diplomatic representation in the US: *chief of mission:* Ambassador Anniken Ramberg KRUTNES (since 17 September 2020)
chancery: 2720 34th Street NW, Washington, DC 20008
telephone: [1] (202) 333-6000
FAX: [1] (202) 469-3990
email address and website:
emb.washington@mfa.no
https://www. norway. no/en/usa/
consulate(s) general: Houston, New York, San Francisco

Diplomatic representation from the US: *chief of mission:* Ambassador Marc NATHANSON (since 16 June 2022)
embassy: Morgedalsvegen 36, 0378 Oslo
mailing address: 5460 Oslo Place, Washington DC 20521-5460
telephone: [47] 21-30-85-40
FAX: [47] 22-56-27-51
email address and website:
OsloACS@state.gov
https://no.usembassy.gov/

Flag description: red with a blue cross outlined in white that extends to the edges of the flag; the vertical part of the cross is shifted to the hoist side in the style of the Dannebrog (Danish flag); the colors recall Norway's past political unions with Denmark (red and white) and Sweden (blue)

National symbol(s): lion; national colors: red, white, blue

National anthem: *name:* "Ja, vi elsker dette landet" (Yes, We Love This Country)
lyrics/music: lyrics/music: Bjornstjerne BJORNSON/ Rikard NORDRAAK
note: adopted 1864; in addition to the national anthem, "Kongesangen" (Song of the King), which uses the tune of "God Save the King," serves as the royal anthem

National heritage: *total World Heritage Sites:* 8 (7 cultural, 1 natural)
selected World Heritage Site locales: Bryggen (c); Urnes Stave Church (c); Røros Mining Town and the Circumference (c); Rock Art of Alta (c); Vegaøyan – The Vega Archipelago (c); Struve Geodetic Arc (c); West Norwegian Fjords – Geirangerfjord and Nærøyfjord (n); Rjukan-Notodden Industrial Heritage Site (c)

ECONOMY

Economic overview: Norway has a stable economy with a vibrant private sector, a large state sector, and an extensive social safety net. Norway opted out of the EU during a referendum in November 1994. However, as a member of the European Economic Area, Norway partially participates in the EU's single market and contributes sizably to the EU budget.

The country is richly endowed with natural resources such as oil and gas, fish, forests, and minerals. Norway is a leading producer and the world's second largest exporter of seafood, after China. The government manages the country's petroleum resources through extensive regulation. The petroleum sector provides about 9% of jobs, 12% of GDP, 13% of the state's revenue, and 37% of exports, according to official national estimates. Norway is one of the world's leading petroleum exporters, although oil production is close to 50% below its peak in 2000. Gas production, conversely, has more than doubled since 2000. Although oil production is historically low, it rose in 2016 for the third consecutive year due to the higher production of existing oil fields and to new fields coming on stream. Norway's domestic electricity production relies almost entirely on hydropower.

In anticipation of eventual declines in oil and gas production, Norway saves state revenue from petroleum sector activities in the world's largest sovereign wealth fund, valued at over $1 trillion at the end of 2017. To help balance the federal budget each year, the government follows a "fiscal rule," which states that spending of revenues from petroleum and fund investments shall correspond to the expected real rate of return on the fund, an amount it estimates is sustainable over time. In February 2017, the government revised the expected rate of return for the fund downward from 4% to 3%.

After solid GDP growth in the 2004-07 period, the economy slowed in 2008, and contracted in 2009, before returning to modest, positive growth from 2010 to 2017. The Norwegian economy has been adjusting to lower energy prices, as demonstrated by growth in labor force participation and employment in 2017. GDP growth was about 1.5% in 2017, driven largely by domestic demand, which has been boosted by the rebound in the labor market and supportive fiscal policies. Economic growth is expected to remain constant or improve slightly in the next few years.

Real GDP (purchasing power parity): $342.06 billion (2020 est.)
$344.69 billion (2019 est.)
$341.78 billion (2018 est.)
note: data are in 2017 dollars

Real GDP growth rate: 0.86% (2019 est.)
1.36% (2018 est.)
2.75% (2017 est.)

Real GDP per capita: $63,600 (2020 est.)
$64,500 (2019 est.)
$64,300 (2018 est.)
note: data are in 2017 dollars

GDP (official exchange rate): $405.695 billion (2019 est.)

Inflation rate (consumer prices): 2.1% (2019 est.)
2.7% (2018 est.)
1.8% (2017 est.)

Credit ratings:

Fitch rating: AAA (1995)

Moody's rating: Aaa (1997)

Standard & Poors rating: AAA (1975)
note: The year refers to the year in which the current credit rating was first obtained.

GDP - composition, by sector of origin: *agriculture:* 2.3% (2017 est.)
industry: 33.7% (2017 est.)
services: 64% (2017 est.)

GDP - composition, by end use: *household consumption:* 44.8% (2017 est.)
government consumption: 24% (2017 est.)
investment in fixed capital: 24.1% (2017 est.)
investment in inventories: 4.8% (2017 est.)
exports of goods and services: 35.5% (2017 est.)
imports of goods and services: -33.2% (2017 est.)

Agricultural products: milk, barley, wheat, potatoes, oats, pork, poultry, beef, eggs, rye

Industries: petroleum and gas, shipping, fishing, aquaculture, food processing, shipbuilding, pulp and paper products, metals, chemicals, timber, mining, textiles

Industrial production growth rate: 1.5% (2017 est.)

Labor force: 2.699 million (2020 est.)

Labor force - by occupation: *agriculture:* 2.1%
industry: 19.3%
services: 78.6% (2016 est.)

Unemployment rate: 3.72% (2019 est.)
3.89% (2018 est.)

Unemployment, youth ages 15-24: *total:* 11.3%
male: 12.1%
female: 10.5% (2020 est.)

Population below poverty line: 12.7% (2018 est.)

Gini Index coefficient - distribution of family income: 27 (2017 est.)
25.8 (1995)

Household income or consumption by percentage share: *lowest 10%:* 3.8%
highest 10%: 21.2% (2014)

Budget: *revenues:* 217.1 billion (2017 est.)
expenditures: 199.5 billion (2017 est.)

Budget surplus (+) or deficit (-): 4.4% (of GDP) (2017 est.)

Public debt: 36.5% of GDP (2017 est.)
36.4% of GDP (2016 est.)
note: data cover general government debt and include debt instruments issued (or owned) by government entities other than the treasury; the data exclude treasury debt held by foreign entities; the data exclude debt issued by subnational entities, as well as intragovernmental debt; intragovernmental debt consists of treasury borrowings from surpluses in the social funds, such as for retirement, medical care, and unemployment; debt instruments for the social funds are not sold at public auctions

Taxes and other revenues: 54.4% (of GDP) (2017 est.)

Fiscal year: calendar year

Current account balance: $16.656 billion (2019 est.)
$31.111 billion (2018 est.)

Exports: $117.06 billion (2020 est.) note: data are in current year dollars
$146.71 billion (2019 est.) note: data are in current year dollars
$165.37 billion (2018 est.) note: data are in current year dollars

Exports - partners: United Kingdom 18%, Germany 14%, Netherlands 10%, Sweden 9%, France 6%, United States 5% (2019)

Exports - commodities: crude petroleum, natural gas, fish, refined petroleum, aluminum (2019)

Imports: $119.08 billion (2020 est.) note: data are in current year dollars
$140.14 billion (2019 est.) note: data are in current year dollars
$140.3 billion (2018 est.) note: data are in current year dollars

Imports - partners: Sweden 17%, Germany 12%, China 8%, Denmark 7%, United States 6%, United Kingdom 5%, Netherlands 5% (2019)

Imports - commodities: cars, refined petroleum, broadcasting equipment, natural gas, crude petroleum (2019)

Reserves of foreign exchange and gold: $65.92 billion (31 December 2017 est.)
$57.46 billion (31 December 2015 est.)

Debt - external: $651.04 billion (2019 est.)
$648.878 billion (2018 est.)
note: Norway is a net external creditor

Exchange rates: Norwegian kroner (NOK) per US dollar -
8.81535 (2020 est.)
9.14245 (2019 est.)
8.4837 (2018 est.)
8.0646 (2014 est.)
6.3021 (2013 est.)

ENERGY

Electricity access: *electrification - total population:* 100% (2020)

Electricity: *installed generating capacity:* 38.36 million kW (2020 est.)
consumption: 124.288 billion kWh (2020 est.)
exports: 24.968 billion kWh (2020 est.)
imports: 4.496 billion kWh (2020 est.)
transmission/distribution losses: 8.909 billion kWh (2020 est.)

Electricity generation sources: *fossil fuels:* 1.2% of total installed capacity (2020 est.)
wind: 6.4% of total installed capacity (2020 est.)
hydroelectricity: 92.1% of total installed capacity (2020 est.)
biomass and waste: 0.3% of total installed capacity (2020 est.)

Coal: *production:* 69,000 metric tons (2020 est.)
consumption: 1.13 million metric tons (2020 est.)
exports: 46,000 metric tons (2020 est.)
imports: 1.172 million metric tons (2020 est.)
proven reserves: 2 million metric tons (2019 est.)

Petroleum: *total petroleum production:* 2.026 million bbl/day (2021 est.)
refined petroleum consumption: 215,900 bbl/day (2019 est.)
crude oil and lease condensate exports: 1,242,500 bbl/day (2018 est.)
crude oil and lease condensate imports: 66,300 bbl/day (2018 est.)
crude oil estimated reserves: 8,122,200,000 barrels (2021 est.)

Refined petroleum products - production: 371,600 bbl/day (2017 est.)

Refined petroleum products - exports: 432,800 bbl/day (2017 est.)

Refined petroleum products - imports: 135,300 bbl/day (2017 est.)

Natural gas: *production:* 112,052,523,000 cubic meters (2020 est.)
consumption: 3,980,351,000 cubic meters (2020 est.)
exports: 107,337,690,000 cubic meters (2020 est.)
imports: 32.196 million cubic meters (2020 est.)
proven reserves: 1,544,455,000,000 cubic meters (2021 est.)

Carbon dioxide emissions: 36.731 million metric tonnes of CO2 (2019 est.)
from coal and metallurgical coke: 3.182 million metric tonnes of CO2 (2019 est.)
from petroleum and other liquids: 25.256 million metric tonnes of CO2 (2019 est.)
from consumed natural gas: 8.294 million metric tonnes of CO2 (2019 est.)

Energy consumption per capita: 333.833 million Btu/person (2019 est.)

COMMUNICATIONS

Telephones - fixed lines: *total subscriptions:* 348,808 (2020 est.)
subscriptions per 100 inhabitants: 6 (2020 est.)

Telephones - mobile cellular: *total subscriptions:* 5,825,584 (2020 est.)
subscriptions per 100 inhabitants: 107 (2020 est.)

Telecommunication systems: *general assessment:* Norway has a sophisticated telecom market with high broadband and mobile penetration rates and a highly developed digital media sector; although not a member of the European Union, the country's telecoms sector is synchronized with relevant EC legislation; the mobile broadband sector was bolstered by the auction of spectrum in the 700MHz and 21MHz band in June 2019; additional spectrum in the 700MHz is expected to be auctioned for mobile broadband use (5G) in 2021; the broadband penetration rate is among the highest in Europe, while in recent years subscribers have been migrated to faster broadband solutions over fiber networks, VDSL and upgraded cable infrastructure; in late 2019 the government proposed making broadband of at least 20Mb/s a universal service (2021)
domestic: Norway has a domestic satellite system; the prevalence of rural areas encourages the wide use of mobile-cellular systems; fixed-line over 6 per 100 and mobile-cellular nearly 108 per 100 (2020)
international: country code - 47; landing points for the Svalbard Undersea Cable System, Polar Circle Cable, Bodo-Rost Cable, NOR5KE Viking, Celtic Norse, Tempnet Offshore FOC Network, England Cable, Denmark-Norway6, Havfrue/AEC-2, Skagerrak 4, and the Skagenfiber West & East submarine cables providing links to other Nordic countries, Europe and the US; satellite earth stations - Eutelsat, Intelsat (Atlantic Ocean), and 1 Inmarsat (Atlantic and Indian Ocean regions); note - Norway shares the Inmarsat earth station with the other Nordic countries (Denmark, Finland, Iceland, and Sweden) (2019)

Broadcast media: state-owned public radio-TV broadcaster operates 3 nationwide TV stations, 3 nationwide radio stations, and 16 regional radio stations; roughly a dozen privately owned TV stations broadcast nationally and roughly another 25 local TV stations broadcasting; nearly 75% of households have access to multi-channel cable or satellite TV; 2 privately owned radio stations broadcast nationwide and another 240 stations operate locally; Norway is the first country in the world to phase out FM radio in favor of Digital Audio Broadcasting (DAB), a process scheduled for completion in late 2017 (2019)

Internet country code: .no

Internet users: *total:* 5,218,091 (2020 est.)
percent of population: 97% (2020 est.)

Broadband - fixed subscriptions: *total:* 2,387,661 (2020 est.)
subscriptions per 100 inhabitants: 44 (2020 est.)

TRANSPORTATION

National air transport system: *number of registered air carriers:* 8 (2020)
inventory of registered aircraft operated by air carriers: 125

Civil aircraft registration country code prefix: LN

Airports: *total:* 95 (2021)

Airports - with paved runways: *total:* 67
2,438 to 3,047 m: 14
1,524 to 2,437 m: 10
914 to 1,523 m: 22
under 914 m: 21 (2021)

Airports - with unpaved runways: *total:* 28
914 to 1,523 m: 6
under 914 m: 22 (2021)

Heliports: 1 (2021)

Pipelines: 8,520 km gas, 1,304 km oil/condensate (2017)

Railways: *total:* 4,200 km (2019)
standard gauge: 4,200 km (2019) 1.435-m gauge (2,480 km electrified)

Roadways: *total:* 94,902 km (2018) (includes 455 km of expressways)

Waterways: 1,577 km (2010)

Merchant marine: *total:* 1,644
by type: bulk carrier 109, container ship 1, general cargo 242, oil tanker 96, other 1,196 (2021)

Ports and terminals: *major seaport(s):* Bergen, Haugesund, Maaloy, Mongstad, Narvik, Sture

LNG terminal(s) (export): Kamoy, Kollsnes, Melkoya Island, Tjeldbergodden

LNG terminal(s) (import): Fredrikstad, Mosjoen

MILITARY AND SECURITY

Military and security forces: Norwegian Armed Forces: Norwegian Army (Haeren), Royal Norwegian Navy (Kongelige Norske Sjoeforsvaret; includes Coastal Rangers and Coast Guard (Kystvakt)), Royal Norwegian Air Force (Kongelige Norske Luftforsvaret), Norwegian Special Forces, Norwegian Cyber Defense Force, Home Guard (Heimevernet, HV) (2022)

Military expenditures: 1.6% of GDP (2022 est.)
1.7% of GDP (2021)
2% of GDP (2020)
1.9% of GDP (2019) (approximately $8.66 billion)
1.7% of GDP (2018) (approximately $8.02 billion)

Military and security service personnel strengths: approximately 27,000 active personnel (9,000 Army; 4,300 Navy; 4,700 Air Force; 9,000 other, including special operations, cyber, joint staff, intelligence, logistics support, active Home Guard, etc.); approximately 40,000 Home Guard (2022)
note: active personnel includes about 10,000 conscripts

Military equipment inventories and acquisitions: the military's inventory includes a mix of imported European, US, and domestically-produced weapons systems and equipment; since 2010, the US has been the leading supplier of weapons systems to Norway (2021)

Military service age and obligation: 19-35 years of age for selective compulsory military service for men and women; 17 years of age for male volunteers; 18 years of age for women volunteers; 12-19 month service obligation; conscripts first serve 12 months between the ages of 19 and 28, and then up to 4-5 refresher training periods until age 35, 44, 55, or 60 depending on rank and function (2022)
note 1: Norway conscripts about 8,000 individuals annually; it has had compulsory military service since 1907
note 2: Norway was the first NATO country to allow women to serve in all combat arms branches of the military (1985); it also has an all-female special operations unit known as Jegertroppen (The Hunter Troop), which was established in 2014; as of 2021, women comprised about 20% of the military's full-time personnel
note 3: beginning in 1995, the military began offering Icelandic citizens the opportunity to apply for admission to officer schools in Norway with an associated education and service contract under special reasons and based on recommendations from Icelandic authorities; as early as 1996, Norway and Iceland entered into a cooperation agreement on the voluntary participation of Icelandic personnel in Norwegian force contributions in foreign operations

Military deployments: up to 190 Lithuania (NATO) (2022)
note: in response to Russia's 2022 invasion of Ukraine, some NATO countries, including Norway, have sent additional troops and equipment to the battlegroups deployed in NATO territory in eastern Europe

Military - note: Norway is a member of NATO and was one of the original 12 countries to sign the North Atlantic Treaty (also known as the Washington Treaty) in 1949

the Norwegian Armed Forces cooperate closely with the militaries of other Nordic countries through the Nordic Defense Cooperation (NORDEFCO), which consists of Denmark, Finland, Iceland, Norway, and Sweden; areas of cooperation include armaments, education, human resources, training and exercises, and operations; NORDEFCO was established in 2009

the first Norwegian defense organization, the leidangen, was established along the coastline in the 10th century to protect the Norwegian coast (2022)

TRANSNATIONAL ISSUES

Disputes - international: *Norway-Antarctica:* Norway asserts a territorial claim in Antarctica (Queen Maud Land and its continental shelf)
Norway-Russia: Russia amended its 2001 CLCS submission in 2015 and 2021, each time delineating the outer limits of its continental shelf further into the Arctic Ocean; Norway and Russia signed a comprehensive maritime boundary agreement in 2010, ending a dispute over an area of the Barents Sea by dividing the territory equally
Norway-Sweden: none identified

Refugees and internally displaced persons: *refugees (country of origin):* 15,542 (Syria), 11,965 (Eritrea) (mid-year 2021); 32,102 (Ukraine) (as of 15 November 2022)
stateless persons: 4,154 (mid-year 2021)

OMAN

INTRODUCTION

Background: The inhabitants of the area of Oman have long prospered from Indian Ocean trade. In the late 18th century, the nascent sultanate in Muscat signed the first in a series of friendship treaties with Britain. Over time, Oman's dependence on British political and military advisors increased, although the sultanate never became a British colony. In 1970, QABOOS bin Said Al-Said overthrew his father, and ruled as sultan for the next five decades. His extensive modernization program opened the country to the outside world. He prioritized strategic ties with the UK and US, and his moderate, independent foreign policy allowed Oman to maintain good relations with its neighbors and to avoid external entanglements.

Inspired by the popular uprisings that swept the Middle East and North Africa beginning in January 2011, some Omanis staged demonstrations, calling for more jobs and economic benefits and an end to corruption. In response to those protester demands, QABOOS in 2011 pledged to implement economic and political reforms, such as granting Oman's bicameral legislative body more power and authorizing direct elections for its lower house, which took place in November 2011. Additionally, the sultan increased unemployment benefits, and, in August 2012, issued a royal directive mandating the speedy implementation of a national job creation plan for thousands of public and private sector Omani jobs. As part of the government's efforts to decentralize authority and allow greater citizen participation in local governance, Oman successfully conducted its first municipal council elections in December 2012. Announced by the sultan in 2011, the municipal councils have the power to advise the Royal Court on the needs of local districts across Oman's 11 governorates. Sultan QABOOS, Oman's longest reigning monarch, died on 11 January 2020. His cousin, HAYTHAM bin Tariq bin Taimur Al-Said, former Minister of Heritage and Culture, was sworn in as Oman's new sultan the same day.

GEOGRAPHY

Location: Middle East, bordering the Arabian Sea, Gulf of Oman, and Persian Gulf, between Yemen and the UAE

Geographic coordinates: 21 00 N, 57 00 E

Map references: Middle East

Area: *total:* 309,500 sq km
land: 309,500 sq km
water: 0 sq km

Area - comparative: twice the size of Georgia

Land boundaries: *total:* 1,561 km
border countries (3): Saudi Arabia 658 km; UAE 609 km; Yemen 294 km

Coastline: 2,092 km

Maritime claims: *territorial sea:* 12 nm
contiguous zone: 24 nm
exclusive economic zone: 200 nm

Climate: dry desert; hot, humid along coast; hot, dry interior; strong southwest summer monsoon (May to September) in far south

Terrain: central desert plain, rugged mountains in north and south

Elevation: *highest point:* Jabal Shams 3,004 m
lowest point: Arabian Sea 0 m
mean elevation: 310 m

Natural resources: petroleum, copper, asbestos, some marble, limestone, chromium, gypsum, natural gas

Land use: *agricultural land:* 4.7% (2018 est.)
arable land: 0.1% (2018 est.)
permanent crops: 0.1% (2018 est.)
permanent pasture: 4.5% (2018 est.)
forest: 0% (2018 est.)
other: 95.3% (2018 est.)

Irrigated land: 590 sq km (2012)

Major aquifers: Arabian Aquifer System

Population distribution: the vast majority of the population is located in and around the Al Hagar Mountains in the north of the country; another smaller cluster is found around the city of Salalah in the far south; most of the country remains sparsely poplulated

Natural hazards: summer winds often raise large sandstorms and dust storms in interior; periodic droughts

Geography - note: consists of Oman proper and two northern exclaves, Musandam and Al Madhah; the former is a peninsula that occupies a strategic location adjacent to the Strait of Hormuz, a vital transit point for world crude oil

PEOPLE AND SOCIETY

Population: 3,764,348 (2022 est.)
note: immigrants make up approximately 46% of the total population (2019)

Nationality: *noun:* Omani(s)
adjective: Omani

Ethnic groups: Arab, Baluchi, South Asian (Indian, Pakistani, Sri Lankan, Bangladeshi), African

Languages: Arabic (official), English, Baluchi, Swahili, Urdu, Indian dialects
major-language sample(s):

يمكن الاستغناء عنه للمعلومات الأساسية

كتاب حقائق العالم، المصدر الذي لا

(Arabic)

Religions: Muslim 85.9%, Christian 6.4%, Hindu 5.7%, other and unaffiliated 2% (2020 est.)
note: Omani citizens represent approximately 56.4% of the population and are overwhelming Muslim (Ibadhi and Sunni sects each constitute about 45% and Shia about 5%); Christians, Hindus, and Buddhists account for roughly 5% of Omani citizens

Age structure: *0-14 years:* 30.15% (male 561,791/female 533,949)
15-24 years: 17.35% (male 331,000/female 299,516)
25-54 years: 44.81% (male 928,812/female 699,821)
55-64 years: 4.02% (male 77,558/female 68,427)
65 years and over: 3.68% (male 64,152/female 69,663) (2020 est.)

Dependency ratios: *total dependency ratio:* 33.3
youth dependency ratio: 30
elderly dependency ratio: 3.3
potential support ratio: 29.9 (2020 est.)

Median age: *total:* 26.2 years
male: 27.2 years
female: 25.1 years (2020 est.)

Population growth rate: 1.84% (2022 est.)

Birth rate: 22.11 births/1,000 population (2022 est.)

Death rate: 3.23 deaths/1,000 population (2022 est.)

Net migration rate: -0.45 migrant(s)/1,000 population (2022 est.)

Population distribution: the vast majority of the population is located in and around the Al Hagar Mountains in the north of the country; another smaller cluster is found around the city of Salalah in the far south; most of the country remains sparsely poplulated

Urbanization: *urban population:* 87.8% of total population (2022)
rate of urbanization: 2.32% annual rate of change (2020-25 est.)

Major urban areas - population: 1.623 million MUSCAT (capital) (2022)

Sex ratio: *at birth:* 1.05 male(s)/female
0-14 years: 1.05 male(s)/female
15-24 years: 1.1 male(s)/female
25-54 years: 1.32 male(s)/female
55-64 years: 1.12 male(s)/female
65 years and over: 0.79 male(s)/female
total population: 1.17 male(s)/female (2022 est.)

Maternal mortality ratio: 19 deaths/100,000 live births (2017 est.)

Infant mortality rate: *total:* 14.45 deaths/1,000 live births
male: 15.71 deaths/1,000 live births
female: 13.12 deaths/1,000 live births (2022 est.)

Life expectancy at birth: *total population:* 76.9 years
male: 74.96 years
female: 78.93 years (2022 est.)

Total fertility rate: 2.7 children born/woman (2022 est.)

Contraceptive prevalence rate: 29.7% (2014)

Drinking water source: *improved: urban:* 100% of population
rural: 97.9% of population
total: 99.7% of population
unimproved: urban: 0% of population
rural: 2.1% of population
total: 0.3% of population (2020 est.)

Current health expenditure: 4.1% of GDP (2019)

Physicians density: 1.77 physicians/1,000 population (2020)

Hospital bed density: 1.5 beds/1,000 population (2017)

Sanitation facility access: *improved: urban:* 100% of population
rural: 100% of population
total: 100% of population

HIV/AIDS - adult prevalence rate: 0.1% (2019)

Obesity - adult prevalence rate: 27% (2016)

Alcohol consumption per capita: *total:* 0.47 liters of pure alcohol (2019 est.)
beer: 0.17 liters of pure alcohol (2019 est.)
wine: 0.02 liters of pure alcohol (2019 est.)
spirits: 0.29 liters of pure alcohol (2019 est.)
other alcohols: 0 liters of pure alcohol (2019 est.)

Tobacco use: *total:* 8% (2020 est.)
male: 15.5% (2020 est.)
female: 0.4% (2020 est.)

Children under the age of 5 years underweight: 11.2% (2016/17)

Education expenditures: 5.4% of GDP (2019 est.)

Literacy: *definition:* age 15 and over can read and write
total population: 95.7%
male: 97%
female: 92.7% (2018)

School life expectancy (primary to tertiary education): *total:* 15 years
male: 14 years
female: 15 years (2020)

Unemployment, youth ages 15-24: *total:* 13.7%
male: 10.3%
female: 33.9% (2016)

ENVIRONMENT

Environment - current issues: limited natural freshwater resources; high levels of soil and water salinity in the coastal plains; beach pollution from oil spills; industrial effluents seeping into the water tables and aquifers; desertificaiton due to high winds driving desert sand into arable lands

Environment - international agreements: *party to:* Biodiversity, Climate Change, Climate Change-Kyoto Protocol, Climate Change-Paris Agreement, Comprehensive Nuclear Test Ban, Desertification, Endangered Species, Hazardous Wastes, Law of the Sea, Marine Dumping-London Convention, Ozone Layer Protection, Ship Pollution, Wetlands, Whaling
signed, but not ratified: none of the selected agreements

Air pollutants: *particulate matter emissions:* 38.25 micrograms per cubic meter (2016 est.)
carbon dioxide emissions: 63.46 megatons (2016 est.)
methane emissions: 5.6 megatons (2020 est.)

Climate: dry desert; hot, humid along coast; hot, dry interior; strong southwest summer monsoon (May to September) in far south

Land use: *agricultural land:* 4.7% (2018 est.)
arable land: 0.1% (2018 est.)
permanent crops: 0.1% (2018 est.)
permanent pasture: 4.5% (2018 est.)
forest: 0% (2018 est.)
other: 95.3% (2018 est.)

Urbanization: *urban population:* 87.8% of total population (2022)
rate of urbanization: 2.32% annual rate of change (2020-25 est.)

Revenue from forest resources: *forest revenues:* 0% of GDP (2018 est.)

Revenue from coal: *coal revenues:* 0% of GDP (2018 est.)

Waste and recycling: *municipal solid waste generated annually:* 1,734,885 tons (2014 est.)

Major aquifers: Arabian Aquifer System

Total water withdrawal: *municipal:* 130 million cubic meters (2017 est.)
industrial: 135 million cubic meters (2017 est.)
agricultural: 1.607 billion cubic meters (2017 est.)

Total renewable water resources: 1.4 billion cubic meters (2017 est.)

GOVERNMENT

Country name: *conventional long form:* Sultanate of Oman
conventional short form: Oman
local long form: Saltanat Uman
local short form: Uman
former: Sultanate of Muscat and Oman
etymology: the origin of the name is uncertain, but it apparently dates back at least 2,000 years since an "Omana" is mentioned by Pliny the Elder (1st century A.D.) and an "Omanon" by Ptolemy (2nd century A.D.)

Government type: absolute monarchy

Capital: *name:* Muscat
geographic coordinates: 23 37 N, 58 35 E
time difference: UTC+4 (9 hours ahead of Washington, DC, during Standard Time)
etymology: the name, whose meaning is uncertain, traces back almost two millennia; two 2nd century A.D. scholars, the geographer PTOLEMY and the historian ARRIAN, both mention an Arabian Sea coastal town of Moscha, which most likely referred to Muscat

Administrative divisions: 11 governorates (muhafazat, singular - muhafaza); Ad Dakhiliyah, Al Buraymi, Al Wusta, Az Zahirah, Janub al Batinah (Al Batinah South), Janub ash Sharqiyah (Ash Sharqiyah South), Masqat (Muscat), Musandam, Shamal al Batinah (Al Batinah North), Shamal ash Sharqiyah (Ash Sharqiyah North), Zufar (Dhofar)

Independence: 1650 (expulsion of the Portuguese)

National holiday: National Day, 18 November; note - celebrates Oman's independence from Portugal in 1650 and the birthday of Sultan QABOOS bin Said al Said, who reigned from 1970 to 2020

Constitution: *history:* promulgated by royal decree 6 November 1996 (the Basic Law of the Sultanate of Oman serves as the constitution); amended by royal decree in 2011
amendments: promulgated by the sultan or proposed by the Council of Oman and drafted by a technical committee as stipulated by royal decree and then promulgated through royal decree; amended by royal decree 2011, 2021

Legal system: mixed legal system of Anglo-Saxon law and Islamic law

International law organization participation: has not submitted an ICJ jurisdiction declaration; non-party state to the ICCt

Citizenship: *citizenship by birth:* no
citizenship by descent only: the father must be a citizen of Oman
dual citizenship recognized: no
residency requirement for naturalization: unknown

Suffrage: 21 years of age; universal; note - members of the military and security forces by law cannot vote

Executive branch: *chief of state:* Sultan and Prime Minister HAYTHAM bin Tariq bin Taimur Al-Said (since 11 January 2020); note - the monarch is both chief of state and head of government
head of government: Sultan and Prime Minister HAYTHAM bin Tariq bin Taimur Al-Said (since 11 January 2020)
cabinet: Cabinet appointed by the monarch

Legislative branch: *description:* bicameral Council of Oman or Majlis Oman consists of:
Council of State or Majlis al-Dawla (85 seats including the chairman; members appointed by the sultan from among former government officials and prominent educators, businessmen, and citizens)

Consultative Council or Majlis al-Shura (86 seats; members directly elected in single- and 2-seat constituencies by simple majority popular vote to serve renewable 4-year terms); note - since political reforms in 2011, legislation from the Consultative Council is submitted to the Council of State for review by the Royal Court
elections:
Council of State - last appointments on 11 July 2019 (next to be held in November 2023)
Consultative Assembly - last held on 27 October 2019 (next to be held in October 2023)
election results:
Council of State - composition - men 70, women 15, percent of women 17.6%

Consultative Council percent of vote by party - NA; seats by party - NA (organized political parties in Oman are legally banned); composition men 84, women 2, percent of women 2.3%; note - total Council of Oman percent of women 9.9%

Judicial branch: *highest court(s):* Supreme Court (consists of 5 judges)
judge selection and term of office: judges nominated by the 9-member Supreme Judicial Council (chaired by the monarch) and appointed by the monarch; judges appointed for life
subordinate courts: Courts of Appeal; Administrative Court; Courts of First Instance; sharia courts; magistrates' courts; military courts

Political parties and leaders: none; note - organized political parties are legally banned in Oman, and loyalties tend to form around tribal affiliations

International organization participation: ABEDA, AFESD, AMF, CAEU, FAO, G-77, GCC, IAEA, IBRD, ICAO, ICC (NGOs), IDA, IDB, IFAD, IFC, IHO, ILO, IMF, IMO, IMSO, Interpol, IOC, IPU, ISO, ITSO, ITU, LAS, MIGA, NAM, OIC, OPCW, UN, UNCTAD, UNESCO, UNIDO, UNWTO, UPU, WCO, WFTU (NGOs), WHO, WIPO, WMO, WTO

Diplomatic representation in the US: *chief of mission:* Ambassador Moosa Hamdan Moosa AL TAI (since 17 February 2021)
chancery: 2535 Belmont Road, NW, Washington, DC 20008
telephone: [1] (202) 387-1980

FAX: [1] (202) 745-4933
email address and website:
washington@fm.gov.om
https://www.culturaloffice.info/aboutomaniembassy

Diplomatic representation from the US: *chief of mission:* Ambassador Leslie M. TSOU (since 19 January 2020)
embassy: P.C. 115, Madinat Al Sultan Qaboos, Muscat
mailing address: 6220 Muscat Place, Washington DC 20521
telephone: [968] 2464-3400
FAX: [968] 2464-3740
email address and website:
ConsularMuscat@state.gov
https://om.usembassy.gov/

Flag description: three horizontal bands of white (top), red, and green of equal width with a broad, vertical, red band on the hoist side; the national emblem (a khanjar dagger in its sheath superimposed on two crossed swords in scabbards) in white is centered near the top of the vertical band; white represents peace and prosperity, red recalls battles against foreign invaders, and green symbolizes the Jebel al Akhdar (Green Mountains) and fertility

National symbol(s): khanjar dagger superimposed on two crossed swords; national colors: red, white, green

National anthem: *name:* "Nashid as-Salaam as-Sultani" (The Sultan's Anthem)
lyrics/music: Rashid bin Uzayyiz al KHUSAIDI/ James Frederick MILLS, arranged by Bernard EBBINGHAUS
note: adopted 1932; new lyrics written after QABOOS bin Said al Said gained power in 1970; first performed by the band of a British ship as a salute to the Sultan during a 1932 visit to Muscat; the bandmaster of the HMS Hawkins was asked to write a salutation to the Sultan on the occasion of his ship visit

National heritage: *total World Heritage Sites:* 5 (all cultural)
selected World Heritage Site locales: Bahla Fort; Archaeological Sites of Bat; Land of Frankincense; Aflaj Irrigation Systems of Oman; Ancient Qalhat

ECONOMY

Economic overview: Oman is heavily dependent on oil and gas resources, which can generate between and 68% and 85% of government revenue, depending on fluctuations in commodity prices. In 2016, low global oil prices drove Oman's budget deficit to $13.8 billion, or approximately 20% of GDP, but the budget deficit is estimated to have reduced to 12% of GDP in 2017 as Oman reduced government subsidies. As of January 2018, Oman has sufficient foreign assets to support its currency's fixed exchange rates. It is issuing debt to cover its deficit.

Oman is using enhanced oil recovery techniques to boost production, but it has simultaneously pursued a development plan that focuses on diversification, industrialization, and privatization, with the objective of reducing the oil sector's contribution to GDP. The key components of the government's diversification strategy are tourism, shipping and logistics, mining, manufacturing, and aquaculture.

Muscat also has notably focused on creating more Omani jobs to employ the rising number of nationals entering the workforce. However, high social welfare benefits - that had increased in the wake of the 2011 Arab Spring - have made it impossible for the government to balance its budget in light of current oil prices. In response, Omani officials imposed austerity measures on its gasoline and diesel subsidies in 2016. These spending cuts have had only a moderate effect on the government's budget, which is projected to again face a deficit of $7.8 billion in 2018.

Real GDP (purchasing power parity): $135.79 billion (2019 est.)
$136.92 billion (2018 est.)
$135.696 billion (2017 est.)
note: data are in 2017 dollars

Real GDP growth rate: -0.9% (2017 est.)
5% (2016 est.)
4.7% (2015 est.)

Real GDP per capita: $27,300 (2019 est.) note: data are in 2017 dollars
$28,400 (2018 est.) note: data are in 2017 dollars
$29,082 (2017 est.)

GDP (official exchange rate): $76.883 billion (2019 est.)

Inflation rate (consumer prices): 0.1% (2019 est.)
0.7% (2018 est.)
1.7% (2017 est.)

Credit ratings:

Fitch rating: BB- (2020)

Moody's rating: Ba3 (2020)

Standard & Poors rating: B+ (2020)
note: The year refers to the year in which the current credit rating was first obtained.

GDP - composition, by sector of origin: *agriculture:* 1.8% (2017 est.)
industry: 46.4% (2017 est.)
services: 51.8% (2017 est.)

GDP - composition, by end use: *household consumption:* 36.8% (2017 est.)
government consumption: 26.2% (2017 est.)
investment in fixed capital: 27.8% (2017 est.)
investment in inventories: 3% (2017 est.)
exports of goods and services: 51.5% (2017 est.)
imports of goods and services: -46.6% (2017 est.)

Agricultural products: dates, tomatoes, vegetables, goat milk, milk, cucumbers, green chillies/peppers, watermelons, sorghum, melons

Industries: crude oil production and refining, natural and liquefied natural gas production; construction, cement, copper, steel, chemicals, optic fiber

Industrial production growth rate: -3% (2017 est.)

Labor force: 2.255 million (2016 est.)
note: about 60% of the labor force is non-national

Labor force - by occupation: *agriculture:* 4.7%
industry: 49.6%
services: 45% (2016 est.)

Unemployment, youth ages 15-24: *total:* 13.7%
male: 10.3%
female: 33.9% (2016)

Budget: *revenues:* 22.14 billion (2017 est.)
expenditures: 31.92 billion (2017 est.)

Budget surplus (+) or deficit (-): -13.8% (of GDP) (2017 est.)

Public debt: 46.9% of GDP (2017 est.)
32.5% of GDP (2016 est.)
note: excludes indebtedness of state-owned enterprises

Taxes and other revenues: 31.3% (of GDP) (2017 est.)

Fiscal year: calendar year

Current account balance: -$10.76 billion (2017 est.)
-$12.32 billion (2016 est.)

Exports: $43.69 billion (2019 est.) note: data are in current year dollars
$46.32 billion (2018 est.) note: data are in current year dollars

Exports - partners: China 46%, India 8%, Japan 6%, South Korea 6%, United Arab Emirates 6%, Saudi Arabia 5% (2019)

Exports - commodities: crude petroleum, natural gas, refined petroleum, iron products, fertilizers (2019)

Imports: $32.55 billion (2019 est.) note: data are in current year dollars
$35.37 billion (2018 est.) note: data are in current year dollars

Imports - partners: United Arab Emirates 36%, China 10%, Japan 7%, India 7%, United States 5% (2019)

Imports - commodities: cars, refined petroleum, broadcasting equipment, gold, iron (2019)

Reserves of foreign exchange and gold: $16.09 billion (31 December 2017 est.)
$20.26 billion (31 December 2016 est.)

Debt - external: $46.27 billion (31 December 2017 est.)
$27.05 billion (31 December 2016 est.)

Exchange rates: Omani rials (OMR) per US dollar -
0.38505 (2020 est.)
0.38505 (2019 est.)
0.385 (2018 est.)
0.3845 (2014 est.)
0.3845 (2013 est.)

ENERGY

Electricity access: *electrification - total population:* 99% (2019)
electrification - urban areas: 100% (2019)
electrification - rural areas: 92% (2019)

Electricity: *installed generating capacity:* 8.601 million kW (2020 est.)
consumption: 32,320,020,000 kWh (2019 est.)
exports: 0 kWh (2019 est.)
imports: 0 kWh (2019 est.)
transmission/distribution losses: 3.717 billion kWh (2019 est.)

Electricity generation sources: *fossil fuels:* 100% of total installed capacity (2020 est.)

Coal: *production:* 0 metric tons (2020 est.)
consumption: 115,000 metric tons (2020 est.)
exports: 0 metric tons (2020 est.)
imports: 115,000 metric tons (2020 est.)
proven reserves: 0 metric tons (2019 est.)

Petroleum: *total petroleum production:* 978,800 bbl/day (2021 est.)
refined petroleum consumption: 234,200 bbl/day (2019 est.)
crude oil and lease condensate exports: 779,000 bbl/day (2018 est.)
crude oil and lease condensate imports: 0 bbl/day (2018 est.)
crude oil estimated reserves: 5.373 billion barrels (2021 est.)

Refined petroleum products - production: 229,600 bbl/day (2015 est.)

Refined petroleum products - exports: 33,700 bbl/day (2015 est.)

Refined petroleum products - imports: 6,041 bbl/day (2015 est.)

Natural gas: *production:* 36,596,746,000 cubic meters (2019 est.)
consumption: 24,279,419,000 cubic meters (2019 est.)
exports: 13,798,040,000 cubic meters (2019 est.)
imports: 1,605,959,000 cubic meters (2019 est.)
proven reserves: 651.286 billion cubic meters (2021 est.)

Carbon dioxide emissions: 76.321 million metric tonnes of CO2 (2019 est.)
from coal and metallurgical coke: 191,000 metric tonnes of CO2 (2019 est.)
from petroleum and other liquids: 29.682 million metric tonnes of CO2 (2019 est.)
from consumed natural gas: 46.447 million metric tonnes of CO2 (2019 est.)

Energy consumption per capita: 292.022 million Btu/person (2019 est.)

COMMUNICATIONS

Telephones - fixed lines: *total subscriptions:* 594,550 (2020 est.)
subscriptions per 100 inhabitants: 13 (2020 est.)

Telephones - mobile cellular: *total subscriptions:* 6,276,535 (2020 est.)
subscriptions per 100 inhabitants: 134 (2020 est.)

Telecommunication systems: *general assessment:* Oman has a modern mobile sector which comprises substantial coverage of both 3G and LTE networks; in February 2021 commercial 5G services were launched; the Covid-19 pandemic has caused a spike in mobile data traffic; while Oman's fixed broadband infrastructure penetration is considered low, it is being improved with the building of fiber-based networks as part of Oman's Vision 2040 program; Oman has also established itself as an important communications hub in the Middle East, with access to numerous submarine cables including the 2Africa submarine cable, which should become available during 2023-2024; the 9,800km Oman Australia Cable running from Muscat to Perth, with the potential for a branch line to Djibouti, is making progress and is expected to be completed in December 2021; this additional infrastructure will provide considerable additional bandwidth (2021)
domestic: fixed-line nearly 13 per 100 and mobile-cellular nearly 134 per 100; fixed-line phone service gradually being introduced to remote villages using wireless local loop systems (2020)
international: country code - 968; landing points for GSA, AAE-1, SeaMeWe-5, Tata TGN-Gulf, FALCON, GBICS/MENA, MENA/Guld Bridge International, TW1, BBG, EIG, OMRAN/EPEG, and POI submarine cables providing connectivity to Asia, Africa, the Middle East, Southeast Asia and Europe; satellite earth stations - 2 Intelsat (Indian Ocean) (2019)

Broadcast media: 1 state-run TV broadcaster; TV stations transmitting from Saudi Arabia, the UAE, Iran, and Yemen available via satellite TV; state-run radio operates multiple stations; first private radio station began operating in 2007 and several additional stations now operating (2019)

Internet country code: .om

Internet users: *total:* 4,851,291 (2020 est.)
percent of population: 95% (2020 est.)

Broadband - fixed subscriptions: *total:* 508,949 (2020 est.)
subscriptions per 100 inhabitants: 11 (2020 est.)

TRANSPORTATION

National air transport system: *number of registered air carriers:* 2 (2020)
inventory of registered aircraft operated by air carriers: 57
annual passenger traffic on registered air carriers: 10,438,241 (2018)
annual freight traffic on registered air carriers: 510.43 million (2018) mt-km

Civil aircraft registration country code prefix: A4O

Airports: *total:* 132 (2021)

Airports - with paved runways: *total:* 13
over 3,047 m: 7
2,438 to 3,047 m: 5
914 to 1,523 m: 1 (2021)

Airports - with unpaved runways: *total:* 119
over 3,047 m: 2
2,438 to 3,047 m: 7
1,524 to 2,437 m: 51
914 to 1,523 m: 33
under 914 m: 26 (2021)

Heliports: 3 (2021)

Pipelines: 106 km condensate, 4,224 km gas, 3,558 km oil, 33 km oil/gas/water, 264 km refined products (2013)

Roadways: *total:* 60,230 km (2012)
paved: 29,685 km (2012) (includes 1,943 km of expressways)
unpaved: 30,545 km (2012)

Merchant marine: *total:* 57
by type: general cargo 10, other 47 (2021)

Ports and terminals: *major seaport(s):* Mina' Qabus, Salalah, Suhar
container port(s) (TEUs): Salalah (4,109,000) (2019)

LNG terminal(s) (export): Qalhat

MILITARY AND SECURITY

Military and security forces: Sultan's Armed Forces (SAF): Royal Army of Oman (RAO), Royal Navy of Oman (RNO), Royal Air Force of Oman (RAFO), Royal Guard of Oman (RGO); Royal Oman Police (ROP): Civil Defense, Immigration, Customs, Royal Oman Police Coast Guard (2022)
note: in addition to its policing duties, the Royal Oman Police conducts many administrative functions similar to the responsibilities of a Ministry of Interior in other countries

Military expenditures: 8% of GDP (2021 est.)
11% of GDP (2020 est.)
11.8% of GDP (2019 est.) (approximately $12.1 billion)
11.2% of GDP (2018 est.) (approximately $11.8 billion)
12.3% of GDP (2017 est.) (approximately $12.7 billion)

Military and security service personnel strengths: approximately 40,000 active duty troops (25,000 Army, 5,000 Navy; 5,000 Air Force; 5,000 Royal Guard) (2022)

Military equipment inventories and acquisitions: the SAF's inventory includes a mix of older and some more modern weapons systems from a variety of suppliers, particularly Europe and the US; since 2010, the UK and the US have been the leading suppliers of arms to Oman (2022)

Military service age and obligation: 18-30 years of age for voluntary military service (women have been allowed to serve since 2011); no conscription (2022)

Military - note: the SAF has a longstanding security relationship with the British military going back to the 18th century; as of 2022, the SAF and the British maintained a joint training base in Oman and exercised together regularly; in 2017, Oman and the British signed an agreement allowing the British military the use of facilities at Al Duqm Port; in 2019, the US obtained access to the port (2022)

Maritime threats: the Maritime Administration of the US Department of Transportation has issued a Maritime Advisory (2022-003 Persian Gulf, Strait of Hormuz, Gulf of Oman, Arabian Sea, Red Sea-Threats to US and International Shipping from Iran) effective 28 February 2022, which states in part that "heightened military activities and increased political tensions in this region continue to present risk to commercial shipping...there is a continued possibility that Iran and/or its regional proxies could take actions against US and partner interests in the region"; Coalition Task Force (CTF) Sentinel has been established to provide escorts for commercial shipping transiting the Persian Gulf, Strait of Hormuz, and Gulf of Oman

TRANSNATIONAL ISSUES

Disputes - international: *Oman-Saudi Arabia:* none identified
Oman-UAE: boundary agreement reportedly signed and ratified with UAE in 2003 for entire border, including Oman's Musandam Peninsula and Al Madhah exclave, but details of the alignment have not been made public; Oman and UAE signed the final demarcation of their land border in 2008
Oman-Yemen: Oman and Yemen signed a border agreement in 1992; demarcation of their border was completed in 1995

Refugees and internally displaced persons: *refugees (country of origin):* 5,000 (Yemen) (2017)

PACIFIC OCEAN

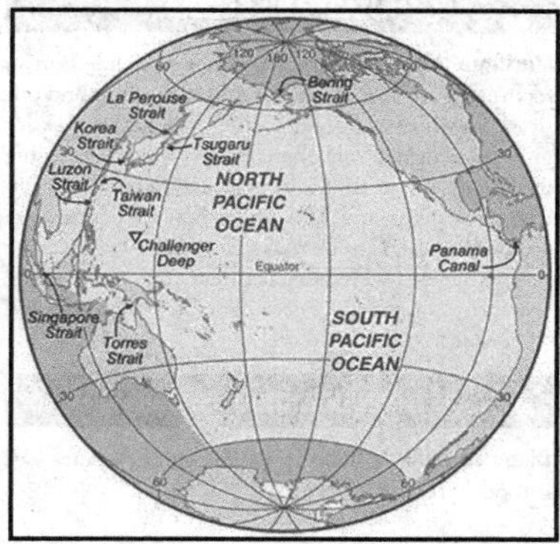

INTRODUCTION

Background: The Pacific Ocean is the largest of the world's five oceans (followed by the Atlantic Ocean, Indian Ocean, Southern Ocean, and Arctic Ocean). Strategically important access waterways include the La Perouse, Tsugaru, Tsushima, Taiwan, Singapore, and Torres Straits. The decision by the International Hydrographic Organization in the spring of 2000 to delimit a fifth ocean, the Southern Ocean, removed the portion of the Pacific Ocean south of 60 degrees south.

GEOGRAPHY

Location: body of water between the Southern Ocean, Asia, Australia, and the Western Hemisphere

Geographic coordinates: 0 00 N, 160 00 W

Map references: Political Map of the World

Area: *total:* 168.723 million sq km
note: includes Arafura Sea, Bali Sea, Banda Sea, Bering Sea, Bering Strait, Celebes Sea, Coral Sea, East China Sea, Flores Sea, Gulf of Alaska, Gulf of Thailand, Gulf of Tonkin, Java Sea, Philippine Sea, Sea of Japan, Sea of Okhotsk, Solomon Sea, South China Sea, Sulu Sea, Tasman Sea, and other tributary water bodies

Area - comparative: about 15 times the size of the US; covers about 28% of the global surface; almost equal to the total land area of the world

Coastline: 135,663 km

Climate: planetary air pressure systems and resultant wind patterns exhibit remarkable uniformity in the south and east; trade winds and westerly winds are well-developed patterns, modified by seasonal fluctuations; tropical cyclones (hurricanes) may form south of Mexico from June to October and affect Mexico and Central America; continental influences cause climatic uniformity to be much less pronounced in the eastern and western regions at the same latitude in the North Pacific Ocean; the western Pacific is monsoonal - a rainy season occurs during the summer months, when moisture-laden winds blow from the ocean over the land, and a dry season during the winter months, when dry winds blow from the Asian landmass back to the ocean; tropical cyclones (typhoons) may strike southeast and east Asia from May to December

Ocean volume: *ocean volume:* 669.88 million cu km
percent of World Ocean total volume: 50.1%

Major ocean currents: the clockwise North Pacific Gyre formed by the warm northward flowing Kuroshio Current in the west, the eastward flowing North Pacific Current in the north, the southward flowing cold California Current in the east, and the westward flowing North Equatorial Current in the south; the counterclockwise South Pacific Gyre composed of the southward flowing warm East Australian Current in the west, the eastward flowing South Pacific Current in the south, the northward flowing cold Peru (Humbolt) Current in the east, and the westward flowing South Equatorial Current in the north

Natural resources: oil and gas fields, polymetallic nodules, sand and gravel aggregates, placer deposits, fish

Natural hazards: surrounded by a zone of violent volcanic and earthquake activity sometimes referred to as the "Pacific Ring of Fire"; up to 90% of the world's earthquakes and some 75% of the world's volcanoes occur within the Ring of Fire; 80% of tsunamis, caused by volcanic or seismic events, occur within the "Pacific Ring of Fire"; subject to tropical cyclones (typhoons) in southeast and east Asia from May to December (most frequent from July to October); tropical cyclones (hurricanes) may form south of Mexico and strike Central America and Mexico from June to October (most common in August and September); cyclical El Nino/La Nina phenomenon occurs in the equatorial Pacific, influencing weather in the Western Hemisphere and the western Pacific; ships subject to superstructure icing in extreme north from October to May; persistent fog in the northern Pacific can be a maritime hazard from June to December

Geography - note: the major chokepoints are the Bering Strait, Panama Canal, Luzon Strait, and the Singapore Strait; the Equator divides the Pacific Ocean into the North Pacific Ocean and the South Pacific Ocean; dotted with low coral islands and rugged volcanic islands in the southwestern Pacific Ocean; much of the Pacific Ocean's rim lies along the Ring of Fire, a belt of active volcanoes and earthquake epicenters that accounts for up to 90% of the world's earthquakes and some 75% of the world's volcanoes; the Pacific Ocean is the deepest ocean basin averaging 4,000 m in depth

ENVIRONMENT

Environment - current issues: pollution (such as sewage, runoff from land and toxic waste); habitat destruction; over-fishing; climate change leading to sea level rise, ocean acidification, and warming; endangered marine species include the dugong, sea lion, sea otter, seals, turtles, and whales; oil pollution in Philippine Sea and South China Sea

Marine fisheries: the Pacific Ocean fisheries are the most important in the world accounting for 57.8%, or 46,144,490 mt, of the global marine capture in 2019; of the six regions delineated by the Food and Agriculture Organization in the Pacific Ocean, the following are the most important:
Northwest Pacific: region (Region 61) is the world's most important fishery producing 24% of the global catch or 19,151,516 mt in 2019; it encompasses the waters north of 20° north latitude and west of 175° west longitude with the major producers including China (29,080726 mt), Japan (3,417,871 mt), South Korea (1,403,892 mt), and Taiwan (487,739 mt); the principal catches include Alaska Pollock, Japanese anchovy, chub mackerel, and scads
Western Central Pacific: region (Region 71) is the world's second most important fishing region producing 17.3%, or 13,798,443 mt, of the global catch in 2019; tuna is the most important species in this region; the region includes the waters between 20° North and 25° South latitude and west of 175° West longitude with the major producers including Indonesia (6,907,932 mt), Vietnam (4,571,497 mt), Philippines (2,416,879 mt), Thailand (1,509,574 mt), and Malaysia (692,553 mt); the principal catches include Skipjack and Yellowfin tuna, sardinellas, and cephalopods
Southeast Pacific: region (Region 87) is the third major Pacific fishery and third largest in the world producing 9.7%, or 7,755,134 mt, of the global catch in 2019; this region includes the nutrient rich upwelling waters off the west coast of South America between 5° North and 60° South latitude and east of 120° West longitude with the major producers including Peru (4,888,730 mt), Chile (3,298,795 mt), and Ecuador (1,186,249 mt); the principal catches include Peruvian anchovy (68.5% of the catch), Jumbo flying squid, and Chilean jack mackerel
Pacific Northeast: region (Region 67) is the fourth largest Pacific Ocean fishery and seventh largest in the world producing 4% of the global catch or 3,160,372 mt in 2019; this region encompasses the waters north of 40° North latitude and east of 175° West longitude including the Gulf of Alaska and Bering Sea with the major producers including the US (3,009,568 mt), Canada (276,677 mt), and Russia (6,908 mt); the principal catches include Alaska pollock, Pacific cod, and North Pacific hake

Regional fisheries bodies: Commission for the Conservation of Southern Bluefin Tuna, Inter-American Tropical Tuna Commission, International Council for the Exploration of the Seas, North Pacific Anadromous Fish Commission, North Pacific Fisheries Commission, South Pacific Regional Fisheries Management Organization, Southeast Asian Fisheries Development Center, Western and Central Pacific Fisheries Commission

Climate: planetary air pressure systems and resultant wind patterns exhibit remarkable uniformity in the south and east; trade winds and westerly winds are well-developed patterns, modified by seasonal fluctuations; tropical cyclones (hurricanes) may form south of Mexico from June to October and affect Mexico and Central America; continental influences cause climatic uniformity to be much less pronounced in the eastern and western regions at the same latitude in the North Pacific Ocean; the western Pacific is monsoonal - a rainy season occurs during the summer months, when moisture-laden winds blow from the ocean over the land, and a dry season during the winter months, when dry winds blow from the Asian landmass back to the ocean; tropical cyclones (typhoons) may strike southeast and east Asia from May to December

GOVERNMENT

Country name: *etymology:* named by Portuguese explorer Ferdinand MAGELLAN during the Spanish circumnavigation of the world in 1521; encountering favorable winds upon reaching the ocean, he called it "Mar Pacifico," which means "peaceful sea" in both Portuguese and Spanish

ECONOMY

Economic overview: The Pacific Ocean is a major contributor to the world economy and particularly to those nations its waters directly touch. It provides low-cost sea transportation between East and West, extensive fishing grounds, offshore oil and gas fields, minerals, and sand and gravel for the construction industry. In 1996, over 60% of the world's fish catch came from the Pacific Ocean. Exploitation of offshore oil and gas reserves is playing an ever-increasing role in the energy supplies of the US, Australia, NZ, China, and Peru. The high cost of recovering offshore oil and gas, combined with the wide swings in world prices for oil since 1985, has led to fluctuations in new drillings.

TRANSPORTATION

Ports and terminals: *major seaport(s):* Bangkok (Thailand), Hong Kong (China), Kao-hsiung (Taiwan), Los Angeles (US), Manila (Philippines), Pusan (South Korea), San Francisco (US), Seattle (US), Shanghai (China), Singapore, Sydney (Australia), Vladivostok (Russia), Wellington (NZ), Yokohama (Japan)

MILITARY AND SECURITY

Maritime threats: the International Maritime Bureau reports the territorial waters of littoral states and offshore waters in the South China Sea as high risk for piracy and armed robbery against ships; an emerging threat area lies in the Celebes and Sulu Seas between the Philippines and Malaysia where 11 ships were attacked in 2021; numerous commercial vessels have been attacked and hijacked both at anchor and while underway; hijacked vessels are often disguised and cargoes stolen

TRANSNATIONAL ISSUES

Disputes - international: some maritime disputes (see littoral states)

PAKISTAN

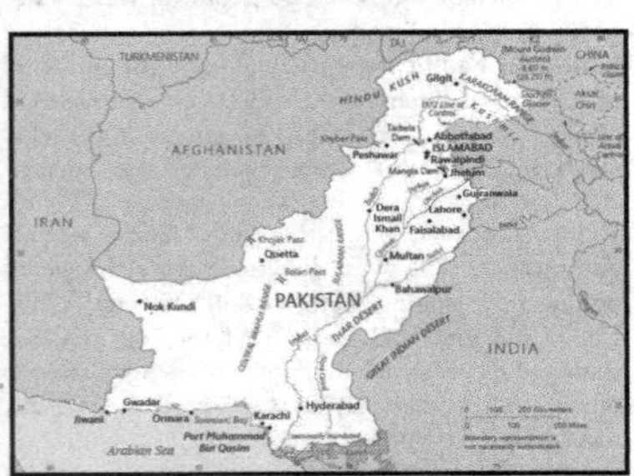

INTRODUCTION

Background: The Indus Valley civilization, one of the oldest in the world and dating back at least 5,000 years, spread over much of what is presently Pakistan. During the second millennium B.C., remnants of this culture fused with the migrating Indo-Aryan peoples. The area underwent successive invasions in subsequent centuries from the Persians, Greeks, Scythians, Arabs (who brought Islam), Afghans, and Turks. The Mughal Empire flourished in the 16th and 17th centuries; the British came to dominate the region in the 18th century. The separation in 1947 of British India into the Muslim state of Pakistan (with West and East sections) and largely Hindu India was never satisfactorily resolved, and India and Pakistan fought two wars and a limited conflict - in 1947-48, 1965, and 1999 respectively -over the disputed Kashmir territory. A third war between these countries in 1971 - in which India assisted an indigenous movement reacting to the marginalization of Bengalis in Pakistani politics - resulted in East Pakistan becoming the separate nation of Bangladesh.

In response to Indian nuclear weapons testing, Pakistan conducted its own tests in mid-1998. India-Pakistan relations improved in the mid-2000s but have been rocky since the November 2008 Mumbai attacks and have been further strained by Indian reports of cross-border militancy. Imran KHAN took office as prime minister in 2018 after the Pakistan Tehreek-e-Insaaf (PTI) party won a plurality of seats in the July 2018 general elections. Pakistan has been engaged in a decades-long armed conflict with militant groups that target government institutions and civilians, including the Tehreek-e-Taliban Pakistan (TTP) and other militant networks.

GEOGRAPHY

Location: Southern Asia, bordering the Arabian Sea, between India on the east and Iran and Afghanistan on the west and China in the north

Geographic coordinates: 30 00 N, 70 00 E

Map references: Asia

Area: *total:* 796,095 sq km
land: 770,875 sq km
water: 25,220 sq km
country comparison to the world: 37

Area - comparative: slightly more than five times the size of Georgia; slightly less than twice the size of California

Land boundaries: *total:* 7,257 km
border countries (4): Afghanistan 2,670 km; China 438 km; India 3,190 km; Iran 959 km

Coastline: 1,046 km

Maritime claims: *territorial sea:* 12 nm
contiguous zone: 24 nm
exclusive economic zone: 200 nm
continental shelf: 200 nm or to the edge of the continental margin

Climate: mostly hot, dry desert; temperate in northwest; arctic in north

Terrain: *divided into three major geographic areas:* the northern highlands, the Indus River plain in the center and east, and the Balochistan Plateau in the south and west

Elevation: *highest point:* K2 (Mt. Godwin-Austen) 8,611 m
lowest point: Arabian Sea 0 m
mean elevation: 900 m

Natural resources: arable land, extensive natural gas reserves, limited petroleum, poor quality coal, iron ore, copper, salt, limestone

Land use: *agricultural land:* 35.2% (2018 est.)
arable land: 27.6% (2018 est.)
permanent crops: 1.1% (2018 est.)
permanent pasture: 6.5% (2018 est.)
forest: 2.1% (2018 est.)
other: 62.7% (2018 est.)

Irrigated land: 202,000 sq km (2012)

Major rivers (by length in km): Indus river mouth (shared with China [s] and India) - 3,610 km; Sutlej river mouth (shared with China [s] and India) -1,372 km; Chenab river mouth (shared with India [s]) - 1,086 km
note – [s] after country name indicates river source; [m] after country name indicates river mouth

Major watersheds (area sq km): Indian Ocean drainage: Indus (1,081,718 sq km)
Internal *(endorheic basin)* drainage: Tarim Basin (1,152,448 sq km), *(Aral Sea basin)* Amu Darya (534,739 sq km)

Major aquifers: Indus Basin

Population distribution: the Indus River and its tributaries attract most of the settlement, with Punjab province the most densely populated

Natural hazards: frequent earthquakes, occasionally severe especially in north and west; flooding along the Indus after heavy rains (July and August)

Geography - note: controls Khyber Pass and Bolan Pass, traditional invasion routes between Central Asia and the Indian Subcontinent

PEOPLE AND SOCIETY

Population: 242,923,845 (2022 est.)
note: results of Pakistan's 2017 national census estimate the country's total population to be 207,684,626
country comparison to the world: 5

Nationality: *noun:* Pakistani(s)
adjective: Pakistani

Ethnic groups: Punjabi 44.7%, Pashtun (Pathan) 15.4%, Sindhi 14.1%, Saraiki 8.4%, Muhajirs 7.6%, Balochi 3.6%, other 6.3%

Languages: Punjabi 48%, Sindhi 12%, Saraiki (a Punjabi variant) 10%, Pashto (alternate name, Pashtu) 8%, Urdu (official) 8%, Balochi 3%, Hindko

2%, Brahui 1%, English (official; lingua franca of Pakistani elite and most government ministries), Burushaski, and other 8%
major-language sample(s):

ਸੰਸਾਰ ਦੀ ਤੱਥ ਕਿਤਾਬ, ਆਧਾਰੀ ਜਾਣਕਾਰੀ ਲਈ ਜ਼ਰੂਰੀ ਸਰੋਤ ਹੈ

(Punjabi)

Religions: Muslim (official) 96.5% (Sunni 85-90%, Shia 10-15%), other (includes Christian and Hindu) 3.5% (2020 est.)

Age structure: *0-14 years:* 36.01% (male 42,923,925/female 41,149,694)
15-24 years: 19.3% (male 23,119,205/female 21,952,976)
25-54 years: 34.7% (male 41,589,381/female 39,442,046)
55-64 years: 5.55% (male 6,526,656/female 6,423,993)
65 years and over: 4.44% (male 4,802,165/female 5,570,595) (2020 est.)

Dependency ratios: *total dependency ratio:* 64.4
youth dependency ratio: 57.2
elderly dependency ratio: 7.1
potential support ratio: 14 (2020 est.)

Median age: *total:* 22 years
male: 21.9 years
female: 22.1 years (2020 est.)
country comparison to the world: 180

Population growth rate: 1.95% (2022 est.)
country comparison to the world: 43

Birth rate: 26.48 births/1,000 population (2022 est.)
country comparison to the world: 41

Death rate: 6.02 deaths/1,000 population (2022 est.)
country comparison to the world: 158

Net migration rate: -0.96 migrant(s)/1,000 population (2022 est.)
country comparison to the world: 144

Population distribution: the Indus River and its tributaries attract most of the settlement, with Punjab province the most densely populated

Urbanization: *urban population:* 37.7% of total population (2022)
rate of urbanization: 2.1% annual rate of change (2020-25 est.)

Major urban areas - population: 16.840 million Karachi, 13.542 million Lahore, 3.625 million Faisalabad, 2.353 million Gujranwala, 2.343 million Peshawar, 1.198 million ISLAMABAD (capital) (2022)

Sex ratio: *at birth:* 1.05 male(s)/female
0-14 years: 1.04 male(s)/female
15-24 years: 1.05 male(s)/female
25-54 years: 1.05 male(s)/female
55-64 years: 1.02 male(s)/female
65 years and over: 0.79 male(s)/female
total population: 1.04 male(s)/female (2022 est.)

Mother's mean age at first birth: 22.8 years (2017/18 est.)
note: data represents median age at first birth among women 25-49

Maternal mortality ratio: 140 deaths/100,000 live births (2017 est.)
country comparison to the world: 61

Infant mortality rate: *total:* 53.98 deaths/1,000 live births
male: 58.34 deaths/1,000 live births
female: 49.4 deaths/1,000 live births (2022 est.)
country comparison to the world: 17

Life expectancy at birth: *total population:* 69.67 years
male: 67.62 years
female: 71.82 years (2022 est.)
country comparison to the world: 176

Total fertility rate: 3.46 children born/woman (2022 est.)
country comparison to the world: 39

Contraceptive prevalence rate: 34% (2018/19)

Drinking water source: *improved: urban:* 96.5% of population
rural: 92.5% of population
total: 94% of population
unimproved: urban: 3.5% of population
rural: 7.5% of population
total: 6% of population (2020 est.)

Current health expenditure: 3.4% of GDP (2019)

Physicians density: 1.12 physicians/1,000 population (2019)

Hospital bed density: 0.6 beds/1,000 population (2017)

Sanitation facility access: *improved: urban:* 88.6% of population
rural: 73.2% of population
total: 78.9% of population
unimproved: urban: 11.4% of population
rural: 26.8% of population
total: 21.1% of population (2020 est.)

HIV/AIDS - adult prevalence rate: 0.2% (2020 est.)
country comparison to the world: 109

HIV/AIDS - people living with HIV/AIDS: 200,000 (2020 est.)
country comparison to the world: 30

HIV/AIDS - deaths: 8,200 (2020 est.)
country comparison to the world: 21

Major infectious diseases: *degree of risk:* high (2020)
food or waterborne diseases: bacterial diarrhea, hepatitis A and E, and typhoid fever
vectorborne diseases: dengue fever and malaria
animal contact diseases: rabies
note 1: widespread ongoing transmission of a respiratory illness caused by the novel coronavirus (COVID-19) is occurring throughout Pakistan; as of 18 August 2022, Pakistan has reported a total of 1,564,231 cases of COVID-19 or 708.14 cumulative cases of COVID-19 per 100,000 population with a total of 30,542 cumulative deaths or a rate of 13.82 cumulative deaths per 100,000 population; as of 17 August 2022, 59.98% of the population has received at least one dose of COVID-19 vaccine
note 2: Pakistan is one of two countries with endemic wild polio virus (the other is Afghanistan) and considered high risk for international spread of the disease; before any international travel, anyone unvaccinated, incompletely vaccinated, or with an unknown polio vaccination status should complete the routine polio vaccine series; before travel to any high-risk destination, the US Centers for Disease Control and Prevention (CDC) recommends that adults who previously completed the full, routine polio vaccine series receive a single, lifetime booster dose of polio vaccine

Obesity - adult prevalence rate: 8.6% (2016)
country comparison to the world: 150

Alcohol consumption per capita: *total:* 0.04 liters of pure alcohol (2019 est.)
beer: 0 liters of pure alcohol (2019 est.)
wine: 0 liters of pure alcohol (2019 est.)
spirits: 0.04 liters of pure alcohol (2019 est.)
other alcohols: 0 liters of pure alcohol (2019 est.)
country comparison to the world: 180

Tobacco use: *total:* 20.2% (2020 est.)
male: 33% (2020 est.)
female: 7.3% (2020 est.)
country comparison to the world: 87

Children under the age of 5 years underweight: 23.1% (2017/18)
country comparison to the world: 14

Child marriage: *women married by age 15:* 3.6%
women married by age 18: 18.3%
men married by age 18: 4.7% (2018 est.)

Education expenditures: 2.5% of GDP (2019 est.)
country comparison to the world: 169

Literacy: *definition:* age 15 and over can read and write
total population: 58%
male: 69.3%
female: 46.5% (2019)

School life expectancy (primary to tertiary education): *total:* 9 years
male: 9 years
female: 8 years (2019)

Unemployment, youth ages 15-24: *total:* 7.9%
male: 8.2%
female: 6.8% (2018 est.)

ENVIRONMENT

Environment - current issues: water pollution from raw sewage, industrial wastes, and agricultural runoff; limited natural freshwater resources; most of the population does not have access to potable water; deforestation; soil erosion; desertification; air pollution and noise pollution in urban areas

Environment - international agreements: *party to:* Antarctic-Environmental Protection, Antarctic-Marine Living Resources, Antarctic Treaty, Biodiversity, Climate Change, Climate Change-Kyoto Protocol, Climate Change-Paris Agreement, Desertification, Endangered Species, Environmental Modification, Hazardous Wastes, Law of the Sea, Marine Dumping-London Convention, Nuclear Test Ban, Ozone Layer Protection, Ship Pollution, Wetlands
signed, but not ratified: Marine Life Conservation

Air pollutants: *particulate matter emissions:* 55.21 micrograms per cubic meter (2016 est.)
carbon dioxide emissions: 201.15 megatons (2016 est.)
methane emissions: 142.12 megatons (2020 est.)

Climate: mostly hot, dry desert; temperate in northwest; arctic in north

Land use: *agricultural land:* 35.2% (2018 est.)
arable land: 27.6% (2018 est.)
permanent crops: 1.1% (2018 est.)
permanent pasture: 6.5% (2018 est.)
forest: 2.1% (2018 est.)
other: 62.7% (2018 est.)

Urbanization: *urban population:* 37.7% of total population (2022)
rate of urbanization: 2.1% annual rate of change (2020-25 est.)

Revenue from forest resources: *forest revenues:* 0.1% of GDP (2018 est.)
country comparison to the world: 114

Revenue from coal: *coal revenues:* 0.06% of GDP (2018 est.)
country comparison to the world: 29

Food insecurity: *severe localized food insecurity: due to population displacements, economic constraints, and high prices of the main food staple* - according to the latest analysis, about 4.7 million people, 25% of the population, are estimated to be facing high levels of acute food insecurity, between April and June 2022 in 25 districts analyzed in Balochistan, Sindh and Khyber Pakhtunkhwa provinces; prices of wheat flour, the country's main staple, were at high levels in most markets in May 2022, constraining access to the staple food (2022)

Waste and recycling: *municipal solid waste generated annually:* 30.76 million tons (2017 est.)
municipal solid waste recycled annually: 2,460,800 tons (2017 est.)
percent of municipal solid waste recycled: 8% (2017 est.)

Major rivers (by length in km): Indus river mouth (shared with China [s] and India) - 3,610 km; Sutlej river mouth (shared with China [s] and India) -1,372 km; Chenab river mouth (shared with India [s]) - 1,086 km
note - [s] after country name indicates river source; [m] after country name indicates river mouth

Major watersheds (area sq km): Indian Ocean drainage: Indus (1,081,718 sq km)
Internal *(endorheic basin)* drainage: Tarim Basin (1,152,448 sq km), *(Aral Sea basin)* Amu Darya (534,739 sq km)

Major aquifers: Indus Basin

Total water withdrawal: *municipal:* 9.65 billion cubic meters (2017 est.)
industrial: 1.4 billion cubic meters (2017 est.)
agricultural: 172.4 billion cubic meters (2017 est.)

Total renewable water resources: 246.8 billion cubic meters (2017 est.)

GOVERNMENT

Country name: *conventional long form:* Islamic Republic of Pakistan
conventional short form: Pakistan
local long form: Jamhuryat Islami Pakistan
local short form: Pakistan
former: West Pakistan
etymology: the word "pak" means "pure" in Persian or Pashto, while the Persian suffix "-stan" means "place of" or "country," so the word Pakistan literally means "Land of the Pure"

Government type: federal parliamentary republic

Capital: *name:* Islamabad
geographic coordinates: 33 41 N, 73 03 E
time difference: UTC+5 (10 hours ahead of Washington, DC, during Standard Time)
etymology: derived from two words: *Islam*, an Urdu word referring to the religion of Islam, and *-abad*, a Persian suffix indicating an "inhabited place" or "city," to render the meaning "City of Islam"

Administrative divisions: 4 provinces, 2 Pakistan-administered areas*, and 1 capital territory**; Azad Kashmir*, Balochistan, Gilgit-Baltistan*, Islamabad Capital Territory**, Khyber Pakhtunkhwa, Punjab, Sindh

Independence: 14 August 1947 (from British India)

National holiday: Pakistan Day (also referred to as Pakistan Resolution Day or Republic Day), 23 March (1940); note - commemorates both the adoption of the Lahore Resolution by the All-India Muslim League during its 22-24 March 1940 session, which called for the creation of independent Muslim states, and the adoption of the first constitution of Pakistan on 23 March 1956 during the transition to the Islamic Republic of Pakistan

Constitution: *history:* several previous; latest endorsed 12 April 1973, passed 19 April 1973, entered into force 14 August 1973 (suspended and restored several times)
amendments: proposed by the Senate or by the National Assembly; passage requires at least two-thirds majority vote of both houses; amended many times, last in 2018

Legal system: common law system with Islamic law influence

International law organization participation: accepts compulsory ICJ jurisdiction with reservations; non-party state to the ICCt

Citizenship: *citizenship by birth:* yes
citizenship by descent only: at least one parent must be a citizen of Pakistan
dual citizenship recognized: yes, but limited to select countries
residency requirement for naturalization: 4 out of the previous 7 years and including the 12 months preceding application

Suffrage: 18 years of age; universal; note - there are joint electorates and reserved parliamentary seats for women and non-Muslims

Executive branch: *chief of state:* President Arif ALVI (since 9 September 2018)
head of government: Prime Minister Shehbaz SHARIF (since 11 April 2022); former Prime Minister Imran KHAN on 10 April lost a no-confidence vote in the National Assembly
cabinet: Cabinet appointed by the president upon the advice of the prime minister
elections/appointments: president indirectly elected by the Electoral College consisting of members of the Senate, National Assembly, and provincial assemblies for a 5-year term (limited to 2 consecutive terms); election last held on 4 September 2018 (next to be held in 2023); prime minister elected by the National Assembly on 17 August 2018
election results:
2018: Arif ALVI elected president; Electoral College vote - Arif ALVI (PTI) 352, Fazl-ur-REHMAN (MMA) 184, Aitzaz AHSAN (PPP) 124; Imran KHAN elected prime minister; National Assembly vote - Imran KHAN (PTI) 176, Shehbaz SHARIF (PML-N) 96

Legislative branch: *description:* bicameral Parliament or Majlis-e-Shoora consists of:
Senate (100 seats; members indirectly elected by the 4 provincial assemblies and the territories' representatives by proportional representation vote; members serve 6-year terms with one-half of the membership renewed every 3 years)
National Assembly (342 seats; 272 members directly elected in single-seat constituencies by simple majority vote and 70 members - 60 women and 10 non-Muslims - directly elected by proportional representation vote; all members serve 5-year terms)
elections:
Senate - last held on 3 March 2021 (next to be held in March 2024)
National Assembly - last held on 25 July 2018 (next to be held on 25 July 2023)
election results:
Senate - percent of vote by party - NA; seats by party - PTI 25, PPP 21, PML-N 18, BAP 13, JU-F 5, other 13, independent 5; composition - men 81, women 19, percent of women 19%
National Assembly - percent of votes by party - NA; seats by party - PTI 156, PML-N 83, PPP 55, MMA 16, MQM-P 7, BAP 5, PML-Q 5, BNP 4, GDA 3, AML 1, ANP 1, JWP 1, independent 4; composition - men 272, women 70, percent of women 20.2%; note - total Parliament percent of women 20.1%

Judicial branch: *highest court(s):* Supreme Court of Pakistan (consists of the chief justice and 16 judges)
judge selection and term of office: justices nominated by an 8-member parliamentary committee upon the recommendation of the Judicial Commission, a 9-member body of judges and other judicial professionals, and appointed by the president; justices can serve until age 65
subordinate courts: High Courts; Federal Shariat Court; provincial and district civil and criminal courts; specialized courts for issues, such as taxation, banking, and customs

Political parties and leaders: Awami National Party or ANP [Asfandyar Wali KHAN]
Awami Muslim League or AML [Sheikh Rashid AHMED]
Balochistan Awami Party or BAP [Jam Kamal KHAN]
Balochistan National Party-Awami or BNP-A [Mir Israr Ullah ZEHRI]
Balochistan National Party-Mengal or BNP-M [Sardar Akhtar Jan MENGAL]
Grand Democratic Alliance or GDA [Pir PAGARO] (includes F, NPP, PML-Q, PTI, QAT)
Jamaat-i Islami or JI [Sirajul HAQ]
Jamhoori Wattan Party or JWP [Shahzain BUGTI]
Jamiat Ulema-e-Islam or JUI-F [Maulana Fazal-ur-REHMAN]
Muttahida Majlis-e-Amal or MMA [Maulana Fazal-ur-REHMAN] (alliance of several parties)
Muttahida Qaumi Movement-London or MQM-L [Altaf HUSSAIN] (MQM split into two factions in 2016)
Muttahida Qaumi Movement-Pakistan or MQM-P [Dr. Khalid Maqbool SIDDIQUI] (MQM split into two factions in 2016)
National Party or NP [Abdul Malik BALOCH]
Pak Sarzameen Party or PSP [Mustafa KAMAL]
Pakhtunkhwa Milli Awami Party or PMAP or PkMAP [Mahmood Khan ACHAKZAI]
Pakhtunkhwa Milli Awami Party or PML-F [Pir PAGARO or Syed Shah Mardan SHAH-II]
Pakistan Muslim League-Nawaz or PML-N [Shehbaz SHARIF]
Pakistan Muslim League – Quaid-e-Azam Group or PML-Q [Chaudhry Shujaat HUSSAIN]
Pakistan Muslim League or PML-F [Pir PAGARO]
Pakistan Peoples Party or PPP [Bilawal BHUTTO ZARDARI, Asif Ali ZARDARI]
Pakistan Tehrik-e Insaaf or PTI (Pakistan Movement for Justice) [Imran KHAN]
Qaumi Awami Tehreek or AT [Sajjad Ahmed CHANDIO]
Qaumi Awami Tehreek or QAT [Ayaz Latif PALIJO]
Qaumi Watan Party or QWP [Aftab Ahmed Khan SHERPAO]
note: political alliances in Pakistan shift frequently

International organization participation: ADB, AIIB, ARF, ASEAN (sectoral dialogue partner), C,

CERN (associate member), CICA, CP, D-8, ECO, FAO, G-11, G-24, G-77, IAEA, IBRD, ICAO, ICC (national committees), ICRM, IDA, IDB, IFAD, IFC, IFRCS, IHO, ILO, IMF, IMO, IMSO, Interpol, IOC, IOM, IPU, ISO, ITSO, ITU, ITUC (NGOs), MIGA, MINURCAT, MINURSO, MINUSCA, MINUSMA, MONUSCO, NAM, OAS (observer), OIC, OPCW, PCA, SAARC, SACEP, SCO, UN, UNAMID, UNCTAD, UNESCO, UNFICYP, UNHCR, UNHRC, UNIDO, UNISFA, UNISFA, UNMISS, UNSOS, UNWTO, UPU, WCO, WFTU (NGOs), WHO, WIPO, WMO, WTO

Diplomatic representation in the US: *chief of mission:* Ambassador Sardar Masood KHAN (since 24 March 2022)
chancery: 3517 International Court NW, Washington, DC 20008
telephone: [1] (202) 243-6500
FAX: [1] (202) 686-1534
email address and website:
consularsection@embassyofpakistanusa.org
https://embassyofpakistanusa.org/
consulate(s) general: Chicago, Houston, Los Angeles, New York

Diplomatic representation from the US: *chief of mission:* Ambassador (vacant); Charge d'Affaires Angela AGGELER
embassy: Diplomatic Enclave, Ramna 5, Islamabad
mailing address: 8100 Islamabad Place, Washington, DC 20521-8100
telephone: [92] 051-201-4000
FAX: [92] 51-2338071
email address and website:
ACSIslamabad@state.gov
https://pk.usembassy.gov/
consulate(s) general: Karachi, Lahore, Peshawar

Flag description: green with a vertical white band (symbolizing the role of religious minorities) on the hoist side; a large white crescent and star are centered in the green field; the crescent, star, and color green are traditional symbols of Islam

National symbol(s): five-pointed star between the horns of a waxing crescent moon, jasmine; national colors: green, white

National anthem: *name:* "Qaumi Tarana" (National Anthem)
lyrics/music: Abu-Al-Asar Hafeez JULLANDHURI/ Ahmed Ghulamali CHAGLA
note: adopted 1954; also known as "Pak sarzamin shad bad" (Blessed Be the Sacred Land)

National heritage: *total World Heritage Sites:* 6 (all cultural)
selected World Heritage Site locales: Archaeological Ruins at Moenjodaro; Buddhist Ruins of Takht-i-Bahi; Taxila; Fort and Shalamar Gardens in Lahore; Historical Monuments at Makli, Thatta; Rohtas Fort

ECONOMY

Economic overview: Decades of internal political disputes and low levels of foreign investment have led to underdevelopment in Pakistan. Pakistan has a large English-speaking population, with English-language skills less prevalent outside urban centers. Despite some progress in recent years in both security and energy, a challenging security environment, electricity shortages, and a burdensome investment climate have traditionally deterred investors. Agriculture accounts for one-fifth of output and two-fifths of employment. Textiles and apparel account for more than half of Pakistan's export earnings; Pakistan's failure to diversify its exports has left the country vulnerable to shifts in world demand. Pakistan's GDP growth has gradually increased since 2012, and was 5.3% in 2017. Official unemployment was 6% in 2017, but this fails to capture the true picture, because much of the economy is informal and underemployment remains high. Human development continues to lag behind most of the region.

In 2013, Pakistan embarked on a $6.3 billion IMF Extended Fund Facility, which focused on reducing energy shortages, stabilizing public finances, increasing revenue collection, and improving its balance of payments position. The program concluded in September 2016. Although Pakistan missed several structural reform criteria, it restored macroeconomic stability, improved its credit rating, and boosted growth. The Pakistani rupee has remained relatively stable against the US dollar since 2015, though it declined about 10% between November 2017 and March 2018. Balance of payments concerns have reemerged, however, as a result of a significant increase in imports and weak export and remittance growth.

Pakistan must continue to address several longstanding issues, including expanding investment in education, healthcare, and sanitation; adapting to the effects of climate change and natural disasters; improving the country's business environment; and widening the country's tax base. Given demographic challenges, Pakistan's leadership will be pressed to implement economic reforms, promote further development of the energy sector, and attract foreign investment to support sufficient economic growth necessary to employ its growing and rapidly urbanizing population, much of which is under the age of 25.

In an effort to boost development, Pakistan and China are implementing the "China-Pakistan Economic Corridor" (CPEC) with $60 billion in investments targeted towards energy and other infrastructure projects. Pakistan believes CPEC investments will enable growth rates of over 6% of GDP by laying the groundwork for increased exports. CPEC-related obligations, however, have raised IMF concern about Pakistan's capital outflows and external financing needs over the medium term.

Real GDP (purchasing power parity): $1,021,130,000,000 (2020 est.)
$1,015,800,000,000 (2019 est.)
$1,005,850,000,000 (2018 est.)
note: data are in 2017 dollars
data are for fiscal years
country comparison to the world: 24

Real GDP growth rate: 5.4% (2017 est.)
4.6% (2016 est.)
4.1% (2015 est.)
note: data are for fiscal years
country comparison to the world: 36

Real GDP per capita: $4,600 (2020 est.)
$4,700 (2019 est.)
$4,700 (2018 est.)
note: data are in 2017 dollars
country comparison to the world: 177

GDP (official exchange rate): $253.183 billion (2019 est.)

Inflation rate (consumer prices): 9.3% (2019 est.)
5.2% (2018 est.)
4.2% (2017 est.)
country comparison to the world: 207

Credit ratings:

Fitch rating: B- (2018)

Moody's rating: B3 (2015)

Standard & Poors rating: B- (2019)

GDP - composition, by sector of origin: *agriculture:* 24.4% (2016 est.)
industry: 19.1% (2016 est.)
services: 56.5% (2017 est.)

GDP - composition, by end use: *household consumption:* 82% (2017 est.)
government consumption: 11.3% (2017 est.)
investment in fixed capital: 14.5% (2017 est.)
investment in inventories: 1.6% (2017 est.)
exports of goods and services: 8.2% (2017 est.)
imports of goods and services: -17.6% (2017 est.)

Agricultural products: sugar cane, buffalo milk, wheat, milk, rice, maize, potatoes, cotton, fruit, mangoes/guavas

Industries: textiles and apparel, food processing, pharmaceuticals, surgical instruments, construction materials, paper products, fertilizer, shrimp

Industrial production growth rate: 5.4% (2017 est.)
country comparison to the world: 53

Labor force: 61.71 million (2017 est.)
note: extensive export of labor, mostly to the Middle East, and use of child labor
country comparison to the world: 9

Labor force - by occupation: *agriculture:* 42.3%
industry: 22.6%
services: 35.1% (FY2015 est.)

Unemployment rate: 6% (2017 est.)
6% (2016 est.)
note: Pakistan has substantial underemployment
country comparison to the world: 97

Unemployment, youth ages 15-24: *total:* 7.9%
male: 8.2%
female: 6.8% (2018 est.)
country comparison to the world: 157

Population below poverty line: 24.3% (2015 est.)

Gini Index coefficient - distribution of family income: 33.5 (2015 est.)
30.9 (FY2011)
country comparison to the world: 127

Household income or consumption by percentage share: *lowest 10%:* 4%
highest 10%: 26.1% (FY2013)

Budget: *revenues:* 46.81 billion (2017 est.)
expenditures: 64.49 billion (2017 est.)
note: data are for fiscal years

Budget surplus (+) or deficit (-): -5.8% (of GDP) (2017 est.)
country comparison to the world: 178

Public debt: 67% of GDP (2017 est.)
67.6% of GDP (2016 est.)
country comparison to the world: 57

Taxes and other revenues: 15.4% (of GDP) (2017 est.)
country comparison to the world: 190

Fiscal year: 1 July - 30 June

Current account balance: -$7.143 billion (2019 est.)
-$19.482 billion (2018 est.)
country comparison to the world: 188

Exports: $27.3 billion (2020 est.) note: data are in current year dollars
$30.67 billion (2019 est.) note: data are in current year dollars

$30.77 billion (2018 est.) note: data are in current year dollars
country comparison to the world: 72

Exports - partners: United States 14%, China 8%, Germany 7%, United Kingdom 6% (2019)

Exports - commodities: textiles, clothing and apparel, rice, leather goods, surgical instruments (2019)

Imports: $51.07 billion (2020 est.) note: data are in current year dollars
$57.98 billion (2019 est.) note: data are in current year dollars
$68.42 billion (2018 est.) note: data are in current year dollars
country comparison to the world: 60

Imports - partners: China 28%, United Arab Emirates 11%, United States 5% (2019)

Imports - commodities: refined petroleum, crude petroleum, natural gas, palm oil, scrap iron (2019)

Reserves of foreign exchange and gold: $18.46 billion (31 December 2017 est.)
$22.05 billion (31 December 2016 est.)
country comparison to the world: 62

Debt - external: $107.527 billion (2019 est.)
$95.671 billion (2018 est.)
country comparison to the world: 54

Exchange rates: Pakistani rupees (PKR) per US dollar -
160.425 (2020 est.)
155.04 (2019 est.)
138.8 (2018 est.)
102.769 (2014 est.)
101.1 (2013 est.)

ENERGY

Electricity access: *electrification - total population:* 79% (2019)
electrification - urban areas: 91% (2019)
electrification - rural areas: 72% (2019)

Electricity: *installed generating capacity:* 39.925 million kW (2020 est.)
consumption: 103,493,520,000 kWh (2019 est.)
exports: 0 kWh (2019 est.)
imports: 487 million kWh (2019 est.)
transmission/distribution losses: 17.389 billion kWh (2019 est.)

Electricity generation sources: *fossil fuels:* 55.2% of total installed capacity (2020 est.)
nuclear: 8.2% of total installed capacity (2020 est.)
solar: 1% of total installed capacity (2020 est.)
wind: 2.8% of total installed capacity (2020 est.)
hydroelectricity: 31.9% of total installed capacity (2020 est.)
biomass and waste: 0.8% of total installed capacity (2020 est.)

Coal: *production:* 4.855 million metric tons (2020 est.)
consumption: 21.012 million metric tons (2020 est.)
exports: 1,000 metric tons (2020 est.)
imports: 17.239 million metric tons (2020 est.)
proven reserves: 3.064 billion metric tons (2019 est.)

Petroleum: *total petroleum production:* 100,700 bbl/day (2021 est.)
refined petroleum consumption: 493,400 bbl/day (2019 est.)
crude oil and lease condensate exports: 7,800 bbl/day (2018 est.)
crude oil and lease condensate imports: 198,400 bbl/day (2018 est.)
crude oil estimated reserves: 540 million barrels (2021 est.)

Refined petroleum products - production: 291,200 bbl/day (2015 est.)
country comparison to the world: 43

Refined petroleum products - exports: 25,510 bbl/day (2015 est.)
country comparison to the world: 68

Refined petroleum products - imports: 264,500 bbl/day (2015 est.)
country comparison to the world: 27

Natural gas: *production:* 38,056,250,000 cubic meters (2019 est.)
consumption: 48,391,627,000 cubic meters (2019 est.)
exports: 0 cubic meters (2021 est.)
imports: 10,743,167,000 cubic meters (2019 est.)
proven reserves: 592.218 billion cubic meters (2021 est.)

Carbon dioxide emissions: 193.869 million metric tonnes of CO2 (2019 est.)
from coal and metallurgical coke: 47.468 million metric tonnes of CO2 (2019 est.)
from petroleum and other liquids: 67.789 million metric tonnes of CO2 (2019 est.)
from consumed natural gas: 78.611 million metric tonnes of CO2 (2019 est.)
country comparison to the world: 31

Energy consumption per capita: 15.859 million Btu/person (2019 est.)
country comparison to the world: 140

COMMUNICATIONS

Telephones - fixed lines: *total subscriptions:* 2,876,794 (2020 est.)
subscriptions per 100 inhabitants: 1 (2020 est.)
country comparison to the world: 45

Telephones - mobile cellular: *total subscriptions:* 175,624,364 (2020 est.)
subscriptions per 100 inhabitants: 80 (2020 est.)
country comparison to the world: 10

Telecommunication systems: *general assessment:* Pakistan's telecom market transitioned from a regulated state-owned monopoly to a deregulated competitive structure in 2003, now aided by foreign investment; moderate growth over the last six years, supported by a young population and a rising use of mobile services; telecom infrastructure is improving, with investments in mobilecellular networks, fixed-line subscriptions declining; system consists of microwave radio relay, coaxial cable, fiber-optic cable, cellular, and satellite networks; 4G mobile services broadly available; 5G tests ongoing; data centers in major cities; mobile and broadband doing well and dominate over fixed-broadband sector; future growth (in market size as well as revenue) is likely to come from the wider availability of value-added services on top of the expansion of 4G LTE and (from 2023) 5G mobile networks; the Universal Service Fund (USF) continues to direct investment towards the development of mobile broadband (and, to a lesser extent, fiber-based networks) in under-served and even under served areas of the country, with multiple projects being approved to start in 2021 and 2022 (2021)
domestic: mobile-cellular subscribership has increased; more than 90% of Pakistanis live within areas that have cell phone coverage; fiber-optic networks are being constructed throughout the country to increase broadband access and broadband penetration in Pakistan is increasing--by the end of 2021, 50% of the population had access to broadband services; fixed-line teledensity is a little over 1 per 100 and mobile-cellular roughly 84 per 100 persons (2021)
international: country code - 92; landing points for the SEA-ME-WE-3, -4, -5, AAE-1, IMEWE, Orient Express, PEACE Cable, and TW1 submarine cable systems that provide links to Europe, Africa, the Middle East, Asia, Southeast Asia, and Australia; satellite earth stations - 3 Intelsat (1 Atlantic Ocean and 2 Indian Ocean); 3 operational international gateway exchanges (1 at Karachi and 2 at Islamabad); microwave radio relay to neighboring countries (2019)

Broadcast media: television is the most popular and dominant source of news in Pakistan with over 120 satellite tv stations licensed by the country's electronic media regulatory body, PEMRA ,and 40 media companies/channels with landing rights permission; state-run Pakistan Television Corporation (PTV) is the largest television network in the country and serves over 90% of the population with the largest terrestrial infrastructure of the country; PTV consists of nine TV Channels and PTV networks give special coverage to Kashmir; Pakistanis have access to over 100 private cable and satellite channels; 6 channels are considered the leaders for news reporting and current affairs programing in the country; state-owned Pakistan Broadcasting Corporation (PBC or Radio Pakistan) has the largest radio audience in the country, particularly in the rural areas; Radio Pakistan's AM/SW/FM stations cover 98 percent of the population and 80 percent of the total area in the country; all major newspapers have online editions and all major print publications operate websites; freedom of the press and freedom of speech in the country are fragile (2021)

Internet country code: .pk

Internet users: *total:* 55,223,083 (2020 est.)
percent of population: 25% (2020 est.)
country comparison to the world: 17

Broadband - fixed subscriptions: *total:* 2,523,027 (2020 est.)
subscriptions per 100 inhabitants: 1 (2020 est.)
country comparison to the world: 53

TRANSPORTATION

National air transport system: *number of registered air carriers:* 5 (2020)
inventory of registered aircraft operated by air carriers: 52
annual passenger traffic on registered air carriers: 6,880,637 (2018)
annual freight traffic on registered air carriers: 217.53 million (2018) mt-km

Civil aircraft registration country code prefix: AP

Airports: *total:* 151 (2021)
country comparison to the world: 35

Airports - with paved runways: *total:* 108
over 3,047 m: 15
2,438 to 3,047 m: 20
1,524 to 2,437 m: 43
914 to 1,523 m: 20
under 914 m: 10 (2021)

Airports - with unpaved runways: *total:* 43
2,438 to 3,047 m: 1

1,524 to 2,437 m: 9
914 to 1,523 m: 9
under 914 m: 24 (2021)

Heliports: 23 (2021)

Pipelines: 13,452 km gas transmission and 177,029 km gas distribution, 3,663 km oil, 1,150 km refined products (2022)

Railways: *total:* 11,881 km (2021)
narrow gauge: 389 km (2021) 1.000-m gauge
broad gauge: 11,492 km (2021) 1.676-m gauge (286 km electrified)
country comparison to the world: 21

Roadways: *total:* 264,175 km (2021)
paved: 185,463 km (2021) (includes 708 km of expressways)
unpaved: 78,712 km (2021)
country comparison to the world: 22

Merchant marine: *total:* 57
by type: bulk carrier 5, oil tanker 7, other 45 (2021)
country comparison to the world: 115

Ports and terminals: *major seaport(s):* Karachi, Port Muhammad Bin Qasim
container port(s) (TEUs): Karachi (2,097,855) (2019)

LNG terminal(s) (import): Port Qasim

MILITARY AND SECURITY

Military and security forces: Pakistan Army (includes National Guard), Pakistan Navy (includes marines, Maritime Security Agency), Pakistan Air Force (Pakistan Fizaia); Ministry of Interior: Frontier Corps, Pakistan Rangers (2022)
note 1: the National Guard is a paramilitary force and one of the Army's reserve forces, along with the Pakistan Army Reserve, the Frontier Corps, and the Pakistan Rangers
note 2: the Frontier Corps is a paramilitary force manned mostly by individuals from the tribal areas and commanded by officers from the Pakistan Army; it manages security duties in the tribal areas and on the border with Afghanistan (Balochistan and Khyber Pakhtunkhwa provinces, including the former Federally Administered Tribal Areas)
note 3: the Pakistan Rangers is a paramilitary force operating in Sindh and Punjab

Military expenditures: 4% of GDP (2022 est.)
4% of GDP (2021 est.)
4% of GDP (2020 est.)
4.1% of GDP (2019) (approximately $21.6 billion)
4.1% of GDP (2018) (approximately $21.6 billion)
country comparison to the world: 16

Military and security service personnel strengths: information varies; approximately 630,000 active duty personnel (550,000 Army; 30,000 Navy; 50,000 Air Force); approximately 150,000 Frontier Corps and Pakistan Rangers (2022)

Military equipment inventories and acquisitions: the Pakistan military inventory includes a broad mix of equipment, primarily from China, France, Russia, Turkey, Ukraine, the UK, and the US; since 2010, China has been the leading supplier of arms to Pakistan; Pakistan also has a large domestic defense industry (2022)

Military service age and obligation: 16 (or 17 depending on service) to 23 years of age for voluntary military service; soldiers cannot be deployed for combat until age 18; women serve in all three armed forces; reserve obligation to age 45 for enlisted men, age 50 for officers (2022)

Military deployments: 1,300 Central African Republic (MINUSCA); 1,970 Democratic Republic of the Congo (MONUSCO); 220 Mali (MINUSMA); 290 South Sudan (UNMISS); 220 Sudan (UNISFA) (May 2022)

Military - note: the military has carried out three coups since Pakistan's independence in 1947 and as of 2022 remained a dominant force in the country's political arena; its chief external focus was on the perceived threat from India, as well as implications of the fall of the government in Kabul, but over the past 15 years, the military also has increased its role in internal security missions, including counterinsurgency and counterterrorism; it is the lead security agency in many areas of the former Federally Administered Tribal Areas

the military establishment also has a large stake in the country's economic sector; through two large conglomerates, it is involved in a diverse array of commercial activities, including banking, construction of public projects, employment services, energy and power generation, fertilizer, food, housing, real estate, and security services

Pakistan and India have fought several conflicts since 1947, including the Indo-Pakistan War of 1965 and the Indo-Pakistan and Bangladesh War of Independence of 1971, as well as two clashes over the disputed region of Kashmir (First Kashmir War of 1947 and the Kargil Conflict of 1999); a fragile cease-fire in Kashmir was reached in 2003, revised in 2018, and reaffirmed in 2021, although the Line of Control remained contested as of 2022, and India has accused Pakistan of backing armed separatists and terrorist organizations in Jammu and Kashmir; in addition, India and Pakistan have battled over the Siachen Glacier of Kashmir, which was seized by India in 1984 with Pakistan attempting to retake the area in 1985, 1987, and 1995; despite a cease-fire, as of 2022 both sides continued to maintain a permanent military presence there with outposts at altitudes above 20,000 feet (over 6,000 meters) where most casualties were due to extreme weather or the hazards of operating in the high mountain terrain of the world's highest conflict, including avalanches, exposure, and altitude sickness

Pakistan has Major Non-NATO Ally (MNNA) status with the US; MNNA is a designation under US law that provides foreign partners with certain benefits in the areas of defense trade and security cooperation; while MNNA status provides military and economic privileges, it does not entail any security commitments (2022)

TERRORISM

Terrorist group(s): Haqqani Network; Harakat ul-Jihad-i-Islami; Harakat ul-Mujahidin; Hizbul Mujahideen; Indian Mujahedeen; Islamic State of Iraq and ash-Sham-Khorasan (ISIS-K); Islamic State of ash-Sham – India; Islamic State of ash-Sham – Pakistan; Islamic Movement of Uzbekistan; Jaish-e-Mohammed; Jaysh al Adl (Jundallah); Lashkar i Jhangvi; Lashkar-e Tayyiba; Tehrik-e-Taliban Pakistan (TTP); al-Qa'ida; al-Qa'ida in the Indian Subcontinent (AQIS)

TRANSNATIONAL ISSUES

Disputes - international: *Pakistan-Afghanistan:* since 2002, with UN assistance, Pakistan has repatriated about 5.3 million Afghan refugees, leaving about 2.74-3 million; Pakistan has sent troops across and built fences along some remote tribal areas of its treaty-defined Durand Line border with Afghanistan, which serve as bases for foreign terrorists and other illegal activities; in February 2022, amid skirmishes between Taliban and Pakistani forces, Pakistan announced its intent to finish constructing the barbed wire fence along the Durand Line and bring nearby areas under its control; Afghan, Coalition, and Pakistan military meet periodically to clarify the alignment of the boundary on the ground and on maps
Pakistan-China: none identified
Pakistan-India: Kashmir remains the site of the world's largest and most militarized territorial dispute with portions under the de facto administration of China (Aksai Chin), India (Jammu and Kashmir), and Pakistan (Azad Kashmir and Northern Areas); UN Military Observer Group in India and Pakistan has maintained a small group of peacekeepers since 1949; India does not recognize Pakistan's ceding historic Kashmir lands to China in 1964; India and Pakistan have initiated discussions on defusing the armed standoff in the Siachen glacier region; the Siachen glacier is claimed by both countries and militarily occupied by India: Pakistan opposed India's fencing the highly militarized Line of Control (completed in 2004) and the construction of the Baglihar Dam on the Chenab River (opened in 2008) in Jammu and Kashmir, which is part of the larger dispute on water sharing of the Indus River and its tributaries; to defuse tensions and prepare for discussions on a maritime boundary, India and Pakistan seek technical resolution of the disputed boundary in Sir Creek estuary at the mouth of the Rann of Kutch in the Arabian Sea; Pakistani maps continue to show Junagadh in India's Gujarat State as part of Pakistan
Pakistan-Iran: none identified

Refugees and internally displaced persons: *refugees (country of origin):* 2.62-2.88 million (1.28 million registered, 1.34-1.6 million undocumented or otherwise categorized) (Afghanistan) (2022)
IDPs: 104,000 (primarily those who remain displaced by counter-terrorism and counter-insurgency operations and violent conflict between armed non-state groups in the Federally Administered Tribal Areas and Khyber-Paktunkwa Province; more than 1 million displaced in northern Waziristan in 2014; individuals also have been displaced by repeated monsoon floods) (2021)
stateless persons: 47 (mid-year 2021)

Trafficking in persons: *current situation:* human traffickers exploit domestic and foreign victims in Pakistan and Pakistanis abroad; the largest human trafficking problem is bonded labor, where traffickers exploit a debt assumed by a worker as part of the terms of employment, entrapping sometimes generations of a family; bonded laborers are forced to work in agriculture, brick kilns, fisheries, mining, textile manufacturing, bangle- and carpet-making; traffickers buy, sell, rent, and kidnap children for forced labor in begging, domestic work, small shops, sex trafficking and stealing; some children are maimed to bring in more money for begging; Afghans, Iranians, and Pakistanis are forced into drug trafficking in border areas and Karachi; Pakistani traffickers lure women and girls away from their families with promises of marriage and exploit the women and girls in sex trafficking; militant groups kidnap, buy, or recruit children and force them to spy, fight, and conduct suicide attacks in Pakistan and Afghanistan *tier rating:* Tier 2 Watch List — Pakistan does not fully meet the minimum standards for the elimination of trafficking but is making significant efforts to do so; government efforts include convicting traffickers under the comprehensive human trafficking law, convicting more traffickers for bonded labor, and increasing registration of brick kilns nationwide for the oversight of workers traffickers target; more trafficking victims were identified; authorities initiated eight investigations against suspected traffickers of Pakistani victims overseas; authorities collaborated with international partners and foreign governments on anti-trafficking efforts; however, the government significantly decreased investigations and prosecutions of sex traffickers; bonded labor exists on farms and in brick kilns in Punjab province; no action was taken against officials involved in trafficking; several high-profile trafficking cases were dropped during the reporting period; resources were lacking for the care of identified victims; Pakistan was downgraded to Tier 2 Watch List (2020)

Illicit drugs: minor cultivator of opium poppy and cannabis with 1,400 hectares of poppy cultivated 2016; one of the world's top transit corridors for opiates and cannabis products along with Afghanistan and Iran; precursor chemicals also pass through Pakistan as a major transit point for global distribution

PALAU

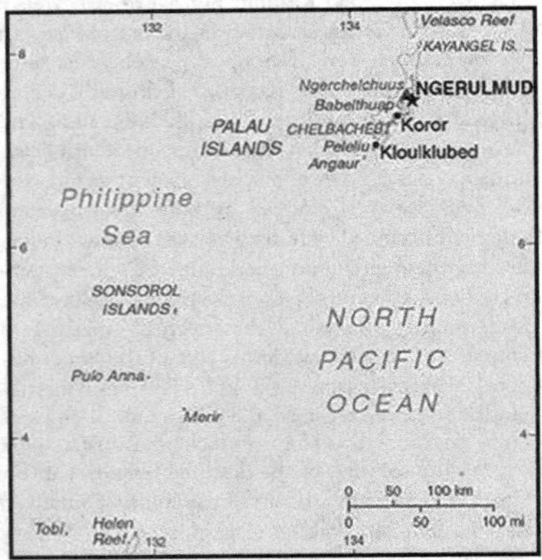

INTRODUCTION

Background: Humans arrived in the Palauan archipelago around 1000 B.C. from Southeast Asia and developed a complex, highly organized matrilineal society where high-ranking women picked the chiefs. The islands were the westernmost part of the widely scattered Pacific islands north of New Guinea that Spanish explorers named the Caroline Islands in the 17th century. There were several failed attempts by Spanish Jesuit missionaries to visit the islands in the early 1700s. Spain gained some influence in the islands and administered it from the Philippines but sold Palau to Germany in 1899 after it lost the Philippines in the Spanish-American War.

Japan seized Palau in 1914, was granted a League of Nations mandate to administer the islands in 1920, and made Koror the capital of its South Seas Mandate in 1922. By the outbreak of World War II, there were four times as many Japanese living in Koror as Palauans. In 1944, the Battle of Peleliu between US and Japanese forces resulted in more than 15,000 deaths. Following the war, Palau became part of the US-administered Trust Territory of the Pacific Islands.

Palau voted against joining the Federated States of Micronesia in 1978 and adopted its own constitution in 1981, which stated that Palau was a nuclear-free country. In 1982, Palau signed a Compact of Free Association (COFA) with the US, which granted Palau financial assistance and access to many US domestic programs in exchange for exclusive US military access and defense responsibilities. However, many Palauans saw the COFA as incompatible with the Palauan Constitution because of the US military's nuclear arsenal, and seven referenda failed to achieve ratification. Following a constitutional amendment and eighth referendum in 1993, the COFA was ratified and entered into force in 1994 when the islands gained their independence. Its funding was renewed in 2010.

Palau has been on the frontlines of combatting climate change and protecting marine resources. In 2011, Palau banned commercial shark fishing and created the world's first shark sanctuary. In 2017, Palau began stamping the Palau Pledge into passports, reminding visitors to act in ecologically and culturally responsible ways. In 2020, Palau banned coral reef-toxic sunscreens and expanded its fishing prohibition to include 80% of its exclusive economic zone.

GEOGRAPHY

Location: Oceania, group of islands in the North Pacific Ocean, southeast of the Philippines

Geographic coordinates: 7 30 N, 134 30 E

Map references: Oceania

Area: *total:* 459 sq km
land: 459 sq km
water: 0 sq km
country comparison to the world: 197

Area - comparative: slightly more than 2.5 times the size of Washington, DC

Land boundaries: *total:* 0 km

Coastline: 1,519 km

Maritime claims: *territorial sea:* 12 nm
contiguous zone: 24 nm
exclusive economic zone: 200 nm
continental shelf: 200 nm

Climate: tropical; hot and humid; wet season May to November

Terrain: varying topography from the high, mountainous main island of Babelthuap to low, coral islands usually fringed by large barrier reefs

Elevation: *highest point:* Mount Ngerchelchuus 242 m
lowest point: Pacific Ocean 0 m

Natural resources: forests, minerals (especially gold), marine products, deep-seabed minerals

Land use: *agricultural land:* 10.8% (2018 est.)
arable land: 2.2% (2018 est.)
permanent crops: 4.3% (2018 est.)
permanent pasture: 4.3% (2018 est.)
forest: 87.6% (2018 est.)
other: 1.6% (2018 est.)

Irrigated land: 0 sq km (2012)

Population distribution: most of the population is located on the southern end of the main island of Babelthuap

Natural hazards: typhoons (June to December)

Geography - note: westernmost archipelago in the Caroline chain, consists of six island groups totaling more than 300 islands; includes World War II battleground of Beliliou (Peleliu) and world-famous Rock Islands

PEOPLE AND SOCIETY

Population: 21,695 (2022 est.)
country comparison to the world: 218

Nationality: *noun:* Palauan(s)
adjective: Palauan

Ethnic groups: Palauan (Micronesian with Malayan and Melanesian admixtures) 73%, Carolinian 2%, Asian 21.7%, Caucasian 1.2%, other 2.1% (2015 est.)

Languages: Palauan (official on most islands) 65.2%, other Micronesian 1.9%, English (official) 19.1%, Filipino 9.9%, Chinese 1.2%, other 2.8% (2015 est.)
note: Sonsoralese is official in Sonsoral; Tobian is official in Tobi; Angaur and Japanese are official in Angaur

Religions: Roman Catholic 45.3%, Protestant 34.9% (includes Evangelical 26.4%, Seventh Day Adventist 6.9%, Assembly of God .9%, Baptist .7%), Modekngei 5.7% (indigenous to Palau), Muslim 3%, Church of Jesus Christ 1.5%, other 9.7% (2015 est.)

Age structure: *0-14 years:* 18.68% (male 2,090/female 1,961)
15-24 years: 15.86% (male 1,723/female 1,716)
25-54 years: 45.33% (male 6,026/female 3,804)
55-64 years: 10.68% (male 853/female 1,463)
65 years and over: 9.45% (male 501/female 1,548) (2020 est.)

Median age: *total:* 33.9 years
male: 32.9 years
female: 35.9 years (2020 est.)
country comparison to the world: 94

Population growth rate: 0.39% (2022 est.)
country comparison to the world: 161

Birth rate: 11.52 births/1,000 population (2022 est.)
country comparison to the world: 163

Death rate: 8.25 deaths/1,000 population (2022 est.)
country comparison to the world: 80

Net migration rate: 0.6 migrant(s)/1,000 population (2022 est.)
country comparison to the world: 72

Population distribution: most of the population is located on the southern end of the main island of Babelthuap

Urbanization: *urban population:* 82% of total population (2022)
rate of urbanization: 1.59% annual rate of change (2020-25 est.)

Major urban areas - population: 277 NGERULMUD (capital) (2018)

Sex ratio: *at birth:* 1.07 male(s)/female
0-14 years: 1.07 male(s)/female
15-24 years: 1.01 male(s)/female
25-54 years: 1.66 male(s)/female
55-64 years: 0.64 male(s)/female
65 years and over: 0.27 male(s)/female
total population: 1.07 male(s)/female (2022 est.)

Infant mortality rate: *total:* 11.28 deaths/1,000 live births
male: 13.26 deaths/1,000 live births
female: 9.18 deaths/1,000 live births (2022 est.)
country comparison to the world: 126

Life expectancy at birth: *total population:* 74.64 years
male: 71.48 years
female: 78 years (2022 est.)
country comparison to the world: 135

Total fertility rate: 1.7 children born/woman (2022 est.)
country comparison to the world: 168

Drinking water source: *improved: urban:* 99.6% of population
rural: 99.8% of population
total: 99.7% of population
unimproved: urban: 0.4% of population
rural: 0.2% of population
total: 0.3% of population (2020 est.)

Current health expenditure: 15.2% of GDP (2019)

Physicians density: 1.77 physicians/1,000 population (2020)

Sanitation facility access: *improved: urban:* 99.8% of population
rural: 99% of population
total: 99.6% of population
unimproved: urban: 0.2% of population
rural: 1% of population
total: 0.4% of population (2020 est.)

Major infectious diseases: *degree of risk:* high (2020)
food or waterborne diseases: bacterial diarrhea
vectorborne diseases: malaria

Obesity - adult prevalence rate: 55.3% (2016)
country comparison to the world: 3

Tobacco use: *total:* 17.6% (2020 est.)
male: 27.3% (2020 est.)
female: 7.9% (2020 est.)
country comparison to the world: 95

Literacy: *definition:* age 15 and over can read and write
total population: 96.6%
male: 96.8%
female: 96.3% (2015)

School life expectancy (primary to tertiary education): *total:* 17 years
male: 16 years
female: 17 years (2013)

Unemployment, youth ages 15-24: *total:* 5.6%

ENVIRONMENT

Environment - current issues: inadequate facilities for disposal of solid waste; threats to the marine ecosystem from sand and coral dredging, illegal and destructive fishing practices, and overfishing; climate change contributes to rising sea level and coral bleaching; drought

Environment - international agreements: *party to:* Biodiversity, Climate Change, Climate Change-Kyoto Protocol, Climate Change-Paris Agreement, Comprehensive Nuclear Test Ban, Desertification, Endangered Species, Hazardous Wastes, Law of the Sea, Ozone Layer Protection, Ship Pollution, Wetlands, Whaling
signed, but not ratified: none of the selected agreements

Air pollutants: *particulate matter emissions:* 12.18 micrograms per cubic meter (2016 est.)
carbon dioxide emissions: 0.22 megatons (2016 est.)
methane emissions: 0.06 megatons (2020 est.)

Climate: tropical; hot and humid; wet season May to November

Land use: *agricultural land:* 10.8% (2018 est.)
arable land: 2.2% (2018 est.)
permanent crops: 4.3% (2018 est.)
permanent pasture: 4.3% (2018 est.)
forest: 87.6% (2018 est.)
other: 1.6% (2018 est.)

Urbanization: *urban population:* 82% of total population (2022)
rate of urbanization: 1.59% annual rate of change (2020-25 est.)

Revenue from forest resources: *forest revenues:* 0% of GDP (2018 est.)
country comparison to the world: 191

Waste and recycling: *municipal solid waste generated annually:* 9,427 tons (2016 est.)

Total renewable water resources: 0 cubic meters (2017 est.)

GOVERNMENT

Country name: *conventional long form:* Republic of Palau
conventional short form: Palau
local long form: Beluu er a Belau
local short form: Belau
former: Trust Territory of the Pacific Islands, Palau District
etymology: from the Palauan name for the islands, Belau, which likely derives from the Palauan word "beluu" meaning "village"

Government type: presidential republic in free association with the US

Capital: *name:* Ngerulmud
geographic coordinates: 7 30 N, 134 37 E
time difference: UTC+9 (14 hours ahead of Washington, DC, during Standard Time)
etymology: the Palauan meaning is "place of fermented 'mud'" ('mud' being the native name for the keyhole angelfish); the site of the new capitol (established in 2006) had been a large hill overlooking the ocean, Ngerulmud, on which women would communally gather to offer fermented angelfish to the gods
note: Ngerulmud, on Babeldaob Island, is the smallest national capital on earth by population, with only a few hundred people; the name is pronounced en-jer-al-mud; Koror, on Koror Island, with over 11,000 residents is by far the largest settlement in Palau; it served as the country's capital from independence in 1994 to 2006

Administrative divisions: 16 states; Aimeliik, Airai, Angaur, Hatohobei, Kayangel, Koror, Melekeok, Ngaraard, Ngarchelong, Ngardmau, Ngatpang, Ngchesar, Ngeremlengui, Ngiwal, Peleliu, Sonsorol

Independence: 1 October 1994 (from the US-administered UN trusteeship)

National holiday: Constitution Day, 9 July (1981), day of a national referendum to pass the new constitution; Independence Day, 1 October (1994)

Constitution: *history:* ratified 9 July 1980, effective 1 January 1981
amendments: proposed by a constitutional convention (held at least once every 15 years with voter approval), by public petition of at least 25% of eligible voters, or by a resolution adopted by at least three fourths of National Congress members; passage requires approval by a majority of votes in at least three fourths of the states in the next regular general election; amended several times, last in 2020

Legal system: mixed legal system of civil, common, and customary law

International law organization participation: has not submitted an ICJ jurisdiction declaration; non-party state to the ICCt

Citizenship: *citizenship by birth:* no
citizenship by descent only: at least one parent must be a citizen of Palau
dual citizenship recognized: no
residency requirement for naturalization: note - no procedure for naturalization

Suffrage: 18 years of age; universal

Executive branch: *chief of state:* President Surangel WHIPPS Jr. (since 21 January 2021); Vice President Jerrlyn Uduch Sengebau SENIOR (since 21 January 2021); note - the president is both chief of state and head of government
head of government: President Surangel WHIPPS Jr. (since 21 January 2021); Vice President Jerrlyn Uduch Sengebau SENIOR (since 21 January 2021)
cabinet: Cabinet appointed by the president with the advice and consent of the Senate; also includes the vice president; the Council of Chiefs consists of chiefs from each of the states who advise the president on issues concerning traditional laws, customs, and their relationship to the constitution and laws of Palau
elections/appointments: president and vice president directly elected on separate ballots by absolute majority popular vote in 2 rounds if needed for a 4-year term (eligible for a second term); election last held on 3 November 2020 (next to be held in November 2024)
election results:
Surangel WHIPPS, Jr. elected president (in second round); percent of vote - Surangel WHIPPS, Jr. (independent) 56.7%, Raynold OILUCH (independent) 43.3%

Legislative branch: *description:* bicameral National Congress or Olbiil Era Kelulau consists of:

Senate (13 seats; members directly elected in single-seat constituencies by majority vote to serve 4-year terms)
House of Delegates (16 seats; members directly elected in single-seat constituencies by simple majority vote to serve 4-year terms)
elections:
Senate - last held on 3 November 2020 (next to be held in November 2024)
House of Delegates - last held on 3 November 2020 (next to be held in November 2024)
election results:
Senate - percent of vote - NA; seats - independent 13; composition - men 12, women 1; percent of women 7.7% House of Delegates - percent of vote - NA; seats - independent 16; composition - men 15, women 1; percent of women 6.3%; note - overall percent of women in National Congress 6.9%

Judicial branch: *highest court(s):* Supreme Court (consists of the chief justice and 3 associate justices organized into appellate trial divisions; the Supreme Court organization also includes the Common Pleas and Land Courts)
judge selection and term of office: justices nominated by a 7-member independent body consisting of judges, presidential appointees, and lawyers and appointed by the president; judges can serve until mandatory retirement at age 65
subordinate courts: National Court and other 'inferior' courts

Political parties and leaders: none

International organization participation: ACP, ADB, AOSIS, FAO, IAEA, IBRD, ICAO, ICRM, IDA, IFC, IFRCS, ILO, IMF, IMO, IMSO, IOC, IPU, MIGA, OPCW, PIF, Sparteca, SPC, UN, UNAMID, UNCTAD, UNESCO, WHO

Diplomatic representation in the US: *chief of mission:* Ambassador Hersey KYOTA (since 12 November 1997)
chancery: 1701 Pennsylvania Avenue NW, Suite 200, Washington, DC 20006
telephone: [1] (202) 349-8598
FAX: [1] (202) 452-6281
email address and website:
info@palauembassy.org
https://www.palauembassy.org/
consulate(s): Tamuning (Guam)

Diplomatic representation from the US: *chief of mission:* Ambassador John HENNESSEY-NILAND (since 6 March 2020)
embassy: Omsangel/Beklelachieb, Airai 96940
mailing address: 4260 Koror Place, Washington, DC 20521-4260
telephone: [680] 587-2920
FAX: [680] 587-2911
email address and website:
ConsularKoror@state.gov
https://pw.usembassy.gov/

Flag description: light blue with a large yellow disk shifted slightly to the hoist side; the blue color represents the ocean, the disk represents the moon; Palauans consider the full moon to be the optimum time for human activity; it is also considered a symbol of peace, love, and tranquility

National symbol(s): bai (native meeting house); national colors: blue, yellow

National anthem: *name:* "Belau rekid" (Our Palau)
lyrics/music: multiple/Ymesei O. EZEKIEL
note: adopted 1980

National heritage: *total World Heritage Sites:* 1 (mixed)
selected World Heritage Site locales: Rock Islands Southern Lagoon

ECONOMY

Economic overview: The economy is dominated by tourism, fishing, and subsistence agriculture. Government is a major employer of the work force relying on financial assistance from the US under the Compact of Free Association (Compact) with the US that took effect after the end of the UN trusteeship on 1 October 1994. The US provided Palau with roughly $700 million in aid for the first 15 years following commencement of the Compact in 1994 in return for unrestricted access to its land and waterways for strategic purposes. The population enjoys a per capita income roughly double that of the Philippines and much of Micronesia.

Business and leisure tourist arrivals reached a record 167,966 in 2015, a 14.4% increase over the previous year, but fell to 138,408 in 2016. Long-run prospects for tourism have been bolstered by the expansion of air travel in the Pacific, the rising prosperity of industrial East Asia, and the willingness of foreigners to finance infrastructure development. Proximity to Guam, the region's major destination for tourists from East Asia, and a regionally competitive tourist infrastructure enhance Palau's advantage as a destination.

Real GDP (purchasing power parity): $320 million (2019 est.)
$330 million (2018 est.)
$317 million (2017 est.)
note: data are in 2017 dollars
country comparison to the world: 215

Real GDP growth rate: -3.7% (2017 est.)
0% (2016 est.)
10.1% (2015 est.)
country comparison to the world: 215

Real GDP per capita: $17,600 (2019 est.) note: data are in 2017 dollars
$18,400 (2018 est.) note: data are in 2017 dollars
$17,841 (2017 est.)
country comparison to the world: 96

GDP (official exchange rate): $292 million (2017 est.)

Inflation rate (consumer prices): 0.9% (2017 est.)
-1% (2016 est.)
country comparison to the world: 60

GDP - composition, by sector of origin: *agriculture:* 3% (2016 est.)
industry: 19% (2016 est.)
services: 78% (2016 est.)

GDP - composition, by end use: *household consumption:* 60.5% (2016 est.)
government consumption: 27.2% (2016 est.)
investment in fixed capital: 22.7% (2016 est.)
investment in inventories: 1.9% (2016 est.)
exports of goods and services: 55.2% (2016 est.)
imports of goods and services: -67.6% (2016 est.)

Agricultural products: coconuts, cassava (manioc, tapioca), sweet potatoes; fish, pigs, chickens, eggs, bananas, papaya, breadfruit, calamansi, soursop, Polynesian chestnuts, Polynesian almonds, mangoes, taro, guava, beans, cucumbers, squash/pumpkins (various), eggplant, green onions, kangkong (watercress), cabbages (various), radishes, betel nuts, melons, peppers, noni, okra

Industries: tourism, fishing, subsistence agriculture

Labor force: 11,610 (2016)
country comparison to the world: 215

Labor force - by occupation: *agriculture:* 1.2%
industry: 12.4%
services: 86.4% (2016)

Unemployment rate: 1.7% (2015 est.)
4.1% (2012)
country comparison to the world: 16

Unemployment, youth ages 15-24: *total:* 5.6%
country comparison to the world: 165

Population below poverty line: 24.9% (2006)

Budget: *revenues:* 193 million (2012 est.)
expenditures: 167.3 million (2012 est.)

Budget surplus (+) or deficit (-): 8.8% (of GDP) (2016 est.)
country comparison to the world: 3

Public debt: 24.1% of GDP (2016 est.)
21.6% of GDP (2015)
country comparison to the world: 179

Taxes and other revenues: 66.1% (of GDP) (2016 est.)
country comparison to the world: 6

Fiscal year: 1 October - 30 September

Current account balance: -$53 million (2017 est.)
-$36 million (2016 est.)
country comparison to the world: 80

Exports: $23.17 billion (2017 est.)
$14.8 million (2015 est.)
country comparison to the world: 76

Exports - partners: Japan 70%, South Korea 15%, United States 7% (2019)

Exports - commodities: fish, computers, broadcasting equipment, office machinery/parts, scrap vessels (2019)

Imports: $4.715 billion (2018 est.)
$4.079 billion (2017 est.)
country comparison to the world: 141

Imports - partners: South Korea 19%, China 18%, Taiwan 17%, United States 17%, Japan 16% (2019)

Imports - commodities: refined petroleum, fish, cars, broadcasting equipment, modeling instruments (2019)

Reserves of foreign exchange and gold: $0 (31 December 2017 est.)
$580.9 million (31 December 2015 est.)
country comparison to the world: 193

Debt - external: $18.38 billion (31 December 2014 est.)
$16.47 billion (31 December 2013 est.)
country comparison to the world: 95

Exchange rates: the US dollar is used

ENERGY

Electricity access: *electrification - total population:* 100% (2018)

COMMUNICATIONS

Telephones - fixed lines: *total subscriptions:* 8,000 (2020 est.)
subscriptions per 100 inhabitants: 44 (2020 est.)
country comparison to the world: 192

Telephones - mobile cellular: *total subscriptions:* 24,000 (2020 est.)
subscriptions per 100 inhabitants: 133 (2020 est.)

country comparison to the world: 213

Telecommunication systems: *general assessment:* well-developed mobile sector, recently boosted by satellite network capacity upgrades; 3G services available with satellite; lack of telecom regulations; newest and most powerful commercial satellite, Kacific-1 satellite, launched in 2019 to improve telecommunications in the Asia Pacific region (2020)
domestic: fixed-line nearly 41 per 100 and mobile-cellular services roughly 134 per 100 persons (2019)
international: country code - 680; landing point for the SEA-US submarine cable linking Palau, Philippines, Micronesia, Indonesia, Hawaii (US), Guam (US) and California (US); satellite earth station - 1 Intelsat (Pacific Ocean) (2019)

Broadcast media: no broadcast TV stations; a cable TV network covers the major islands and provides access to 4 local cable stations, rebroadcasts (on a delayed basis) of a number of US stations, as well as access to a number of real-time satellite TV channels; about a half dozen radio stations (1 government-owned) (2019)

Internet country code: .pw

Internet users: *total:* 7,650 (2016 est.)
percent of population: 36% (2016 est.)
country comparison to the world: 217

Broadband - fixed subscriptions: *total:* 1,224 (2015 est.)
subscriptions per 100 inhabitants: 7 (2015 est.)
country comparison to the world: 200

TRANSPORTATION

National air transport system: *number of registered air carriers:* 1 (2020)
inventory of registered aircraft operated by air carriers: 1

Civil aircraft registration country code prefix: T8

Airports: *total:* 3 (2021)
country comparison to the world: 195

Airports - with paved runways: *total:* 1
1,524 to 2,437 m: 1 (2021)

Airports - with unpaved runways: *total:* 2
1,524 to 2,437 m: 2 (2021)

Roadways: *total:* 125 km (2018)
paved: 89 km (2018)
*unpaved:*36 km (2018)
country comparison to the world: 211

Merchant marine: *total:* 264
by type: bulk carrier 16, container ship 7, general cargo 107, oil tanker 40, other 94 (2021)
country comparison to the world: 59

Ports and terminals: *major seaport(s):* Koror

MILITARY AND SECURITY

Military and security forces: no regular military forces; the Ministry of Justice includes divisions/bureaus for public security, police functions, and maritime law enforcement

Military equipment inventories and acquisitions: since 2018, Australia and Japan have provided patrol boats to Palau's Division of Marine Law Enforcement (2021)

Military - note: under the Compact of Free Association (COFA) between Palau and the US, the US is responsible for the defense of Palau and the US military is granted access to the islands, but it has not stationed any military forces there; the COFA also allows citizens of Palau to serve in the US armed forces

Palau has a "shiprider" agreement with the US, which allows local maritime law enforcement officers to embark on US Coast Guard (USCG) and US Navy (USN) vessels, including to board and search vessels suspected of violating laws or regulations within Palau's designated exclusive economic zone (EEZ) or on the high seas; "shiprider" agreements also enable USCG personnel and USN vessels with embarked USCG law enforcement personnel to work with host nations to protect critical regional resources (2022)

TRANSNATIONAL ISSUES

Disputes - international: *Palau-Indonesia:* maritime delineation negotiations continue with Philippines, Indonesia
Palau-Philippines: maritime delineation negotiations continue with Philippines, Indonesia

PANAMA

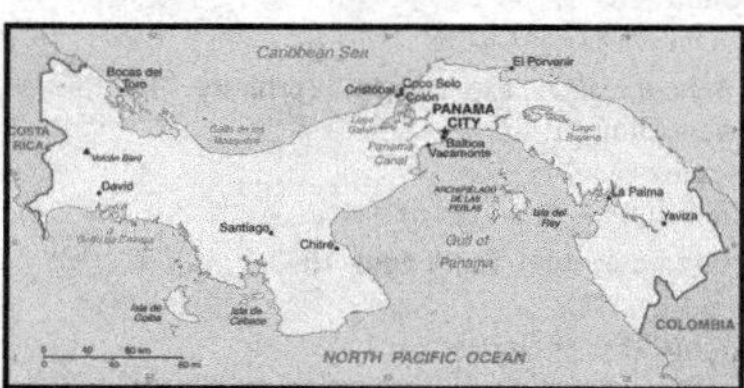

INTRODUCTION

Background: Explored and settled by the Spanish in the 16th century, Panama broke with Spain in 1821 and joined a union of Colombia, Ecuador, and Venezuela - named the Republic of Gran Colombia. When the latter dissolved in 1830, Panama remained part of Colombia. With US backing, Panama seceded from Colombia in 1903 and promptly signed a treaty with the US allowing for the construction of a canal and US sovereignty over a strip of land on either side of the structure (the Panama Canal Zone). The Panama Canal was built by the US Army Corps of Engineers between 1904 and 1914. In 1977, an agreement was signed for the complete transfer of the Canal from the US to Panama by the end of the century. Certain portions of the Zone and increasing responsibility over the Canal were turned over in the subsequent decades. With US help, dictator Manuel NORIEGA was deposed in 1989. The entire Panama Canal, the area supporting the Canal, and remaining US military bases were transferred to Panama by the end of 1999. An ambitious expansion project to more than double the Canal's capacity - by allowing for more Canal transits and larger ships - was carried out between 2007 and 2016.

GEOGRAPHY

Location: Central America, bordering both the Caribbean Sea and the North Pacific Ocean, between Colombia and Costa Rica

Geographic coordinates: 9 00 N, 80 00 W

Map references: Central America and the Caribbean

Area: *total:* 75,420 sq km
land: 74,340 sq km
water: 1,080 sq km
country comparison to the world: 118

Area - comparative: slightly smaller than South Carolina

Land boundaries: *total:* 687 km
border countries (2): Colombia 339 km; Costa Rica 348 km

Coastline: 2,490 km

Maritime claims: *territorial sea:* 12 nm
contiguous zone: 24 nm
exclusive economic zone: 200 nm or edge of continental margin

Climate: tropical maritime; hot, humid, cloudy; prolonged rainy season (May to January), short dry season (January to May)

Terrain: interior mostly steep, rugged mountains with dissected, upland plains; coastal plains with rolling hills

Elevation: *highest point:* Volcan Baru 3,475 m
lowest point: Pacific Ocean 0 m
mean elevation: 360 m

Natural resources: copper, mahogany forests, shrimp, hydropower

Land use: *agricultural land:* 30.5% (2018 est.)
arable land: 7.3% (2018 est.)
permanent crops: 2.5% (2018 est.)
permanent pasture: 20.7% (2018 est.)
forest: 43.6% (2018 est.)
other: 25.9% (2018 est.)

Irrigated land: 321 sq km (2012)

Major lakes (area sq km): *salt water lake(s):* Laguna de Chiriqui - 900 sq km

Population distribution: population is concentrated towards the center of the country, particularly around the Canal, but a sizeable segment of the populace also lives in the far west around David; the eastern third of the country is sparsely inhabited

Natural hazards: occasional severe storms and forest fires in the Darien area

Geography - note: strategic location on eastern end of isthmus forming land bridge connecting North and South America; controls Panama Canal that links North Atlantic Ocean via Caribbean Sea with North Pacific Ocean

PEOPLE AND SOCIETY

Population: 4,337,768 (2022 est.)
country comparison to the world: 127

Nationality: *noun:* Panamanian(s)
adjective: Panamanian

Ethnic groups: Mestizo (mixed Amerindian and White) 65%, Native American 12.3% (Ngabe 7.6%, Kuna 2.4%, Embera 0.9%, Bugle 0.8%, other 0.4%, unspecified 0.2%), Black or African descent 9.2%, Mulatto 6.8%, White 6.7% (2010 est.)

Languages: Spanish (official), indigenous languages (including Ngabere (or Guaymi), Buglere, Kuna, Embera, Wounaan, Naso (or Teribe), and Bri Bri), Panamanian English Creole (similar to Jamaican English Creole; a mixture of English and Spanish with elements of Ngabere; also known as Guari Guari and Colon Creole), English, Chinese (Yue and Hakka), Arabic, French Creole, other (Yiddish, Hebrew, Korean, Japanese); note - many Panamanians are bilingual
major-language sample(s): La Libreta Informativa del Mundo, la fuente indispensable de información básica. (Spanish)

Religions: Roman Catholic 48.6%, Evangelical 30.2%, other 4.7%, agnostic 0.2%, atheist 0.2%, none 12.3%, unspecified 3.7% (2018 est.)

Demographic profile: Panama is a country of demographic and economic contrasts. It is in the midst of a demographic transition, characterized by steadily declining rates of fertility, mortality, and population growth, but disparities persist based on wealth, geography, and ethnicity. Panama has one of the fastest growing economies in Latin America and dedicates substantial funding to social programs, yet poverty and inequality remain prevalent. The indigenous population accounts for a growing share of Panama's poor and extreme poor, while the non-indigenous rural poor have been more successful at rising out of poverty through rural-to-urban labor migration. The government's large expenditures on untargeted, indirect subsidies for water, electricity, and fuel have been ineffective, but its conditional cash transfer program has shown some promise in helping to decrease extreme poverty among the indigenous population.

Panama has expanded access to education and clean water, but the availability of sanitation and, to a lesser extent, electricity remains poor. The increase in secondary schooling - led by female enrollment - is spreading to rural and indigenous areas, which probably will help to alleviate poverty if educational quality and the availability of skilled jobs improve. Inadequate access to sanitation contributes to a high incidence of diarrhea in Panama's children, which is one of the main causes of Panama's elevated chronic malnutrition rate, especially among indigenous communities.

Age structure: *0-14 years:* 25.56% (male 508,131/female 487,205)
15-24 years: 16.59% (male 329,250/female 316,796)
25-54 years: 40.31% (male 794,662/female 774,905)
55-64 years: 8.54% (male 165,129/female 167,317)
65 years and over: 9.01% (male 160,516/female 190,171) (2020 est.)

Dependency ratios: *total dependency ratio:* 53.9
youth dependency ratio: 40.8
elderly dependency ratio: 13.1
potential support ratio: 7.6 (2020 est.)

Median age: *total:* 30.1 years
male: 29.6 years
female: 30.5 years (2020 est.)
country comparison to the world: 122

Population growth rate: 1.53% (2022 est.)
country comparison to the world: 64

Birth rate: 17.99 births/1,000 population (2022 est.)
country comparison to the world: 82

Death rate: 6.11 deaths/1,000 population (2022 est.)
country comparison to the world: 153

Net migration rate: 3.42 migrant(s)/1,000 population (2022 est.)
country comparison to the world: 36

Population distribution: population is concentrated towards the center of the country, particularly around the Canal, but a sizeable segment of the populace also lives in the far west around David; the eastern third of the country is sparsely inhabited

Urbanization: *urban population:* 69.1% of total population (2022)
rate of urbanization: 1.92% annual rate of change (2020-25 est.)

Major urban areas - population: 1.938 million PANAMA CITY (capital) (2022)

Sex ratio: *at birth:* 1.06 male(s)/female
0-14 years: 1.05 male(s)/female
15-24 years: 1.03 male(s)/female
25-54 years: 1.02 male(s)/female
55-64 years: 1 male(s)/female
65 years and over: 0.75 male(s)/female
total population: 1.02 male(s)/female (2022 est.)

Maternal mortality ratio: 52 deaths/100,000 live births (2017 est.)
country comparison to the world: 93

Infant mortality rate: *total:* 16.44 deaths/1,000 live births
male: 17.69 deaths/1,000 live births
female: 15.11 deaths/1,000 live births (2022 est.)
country comparison to the world: 94

Life expectancy at birth: *total population:* 77.62 years
male: 74.76 years
female: 80.66 years (2022 est.)
country comparison to the world: 87

Total fertility rate: 2.39 children born/woman (2022 est.)
country comparison to the world: 75

Contraceptive prevalence rate: 50.8% (2014/15)

Drinking water source: *improved: urban:* 100% of population
rural: 88.1% of population
total: 96.2% of population
unimproved: urban: 0% of population
rural: 11.9% of population
total: 3.8% of population (2020 est.)

Current health expenditure: 7.6% of GDP (2019)

Physicians density: 1.63 physicians/1,000 population (2019)

Hospital bed density: 2.3 beds/1,000 population (2016)

Sanitation facility access: *improved: urban:* 95.5% of population
rural: 69.1% of population
total: 87.2% of population
unimproved: urban: 4.5% of population
rural: 30.9% of population
total: 12.8% of population (2020 est.)

HIV/AIDS - adult prevalence rate: 1% (2020 est.)
country comparison to the world: 43

HIV/AIDS - people living with HIV/AIDS: 31,000 (2020 est.)
note: estimate does not include children
country comparison to the world: 73

HIV/AIDS - deaths: (2020 est.) <500
note: estimate does not include children

Major infectious diseases: *degree of risk:* intermediate (2020)
food or waterborne diseases: bacterial diarrhea
vectorborne diseases: dengue fever

Obesity - adult prevalence rate: 22.7% (2016)
country comparison to the world: 73

Alcohol consumption per capita: *total:* 6.54 liters of pure alcohol (2019 est.)
beer: 5.29 liters of pure alcohol (2019 est.)
wine: 0.02 liters of pure alcohol (2019 est.)
spirits: 1.2 liters of pure alcohol (2019 est.)
other alcohols: 0.02 liters of pure alcohol (2019 est.)
country comparison to the world: 63

Tobacco use: *total:* 5% (2020 est.)
male: 7.7% (2020 est.)
female: 2.2% (2020 est.)
country comparison to the world: 162

Children under the age of 5 years underweight: 3% (2019)
country comparison to the world: 96

Education expenditures: 3.1% of GDP (2019 est.)
country comparison to the world: 145

Literacy: *definition:* age 15 and over can read and write
total population: 95.7%
male: 98.8%
female: 95.4% (2019)

School life expectancy (primary to tertiary education): *total:* 13 years
male: 12 years
female: 13 years (2016)

Unemployment, youth ages 15-24: *total:* 40.1%
male: 30.8%
female: 51.9% (2020 est.)

ENVIRONMENT

Environment - current issues: water pollution from agricultural runoff threatens fishery resources; deforestation of tropical rain forest; land degradation and soil erosion threatens siltation of Panama Canal; air pollution in urban areas; mining threatens natural resources

Environment - international agreements: *party to:* Antarctic-Marine Living Resources, Biodiversity, Climate Change, Climate Change-Kyoto Protocol, Climate Change-Paris Agreement, Comprehensive Nuclear Test Ban, Desertification, Endangered Species, Environmental Modification, Hazardous Wastes, Law of the Sea, Marine Dumping-London Convention, Nuclear Test Ban, Ozone Layer Protection, Ship Pollution, Tropical Timber 2006, Wetlands, Whaling
signed, but not ratified: Marine Life Conservation

Air pollutants: *particulate matter emissions:* 11.18 micrograms per cubic meter (2016 est.)
carbon dioxide emissions: 10.71 megatons (2016 est.)

methane emissions: 5.97 megatons (2020 est.)

Climate: tropical maritime; hot, humid, cloudy; prolonged rainy season (May to January), short dry season (January to May)

Land use: *agricultural land:* 30.5% (2018 est.)
arable land: 7.3% (2018 est.)
permanent crops: 2.5% (2018 est.)
permanent pasture: 20.7% (2018 est.)
forest: 43.6% (2018 est.)
other: 25.9% (2018 est.)

Urbanization: *urban population:* 69.1% of total population (2022)
rate of urbanization: 1.92% annual rate of change (2020-25 est.)

Revenue from forest resources: *forest revenues:* 0.08% of GDP (2018 est.)
country comparison to the world: 120

Revenue from coal: *coal revenues:* 0% of GDP (2018 est.)
country comparison to the world: 149

Waste and recycling: *municipal solid waste generated annually:* 1,472,262 tons (2015 est.)

Major lakes (area sq km): *salt water lake(s):* Laguna de Chiriqui - 900 sq km

Total water withdrawal: *municipal:* 759.1 million cubic meters (2017 est.)
industrial: 6.2 million cubic meters (2017 est.)
agricultural: 446.1 million cubic meters (2017 est.)

Total renewable water resources: 139.3 billion cubic meters (2017 est.)

GOVERNMENT

Country name: *conventional long form:* Republic of Panama
conventional short form: Panama
local long form: Republica de Panama
local short form: Panama
etymology: named after the capital city which was itself named after a former indigenous fishing village

Government type: presidential republic

Capital: *name:* Panama City
geographic coordinates: 8 58 N, 79 32 W
time difference: UTC-5 (same time as Washington, DC, during Standard Time)
etymology: according to tradition, the name derives from a former fishing area near the present capital - an indigenous village and its adjacent beach - that were called "panama" meaning "an abundance of fish"

Administrative divisions: 10 provinces (provincias, singular - provincia) and 4 indigenous regions* (comarcas); Bocas del Toro, Chiriqui, Cocle, Colon, Darien, Embera-Wounaan*, Guna Yala*, Herrera, Los Santos, Naso Tjer Di*, Ngabe-Bugle*, Panama, Panama Oeste, Veraguas

Independence: 3 November 1903 (from Colombia; became independent from Spain on 28 November 1821)

National holiday: Independence Day (Separation Day), 3 November (1903)

Constitution: *history:* several previous; latest effective 11 October 1972
amendments: proposed by the National Assembly, by the Cabinet, or by the Supreme Court of Justice; passage requires approval by one of two procedures: 1) absolute majority vote of the Assembly membership in each of three readings and by absolute majority vote of the next elected Assembly in a single reading without textual modifications; 2) absolute majority vote of the Assembly membership in each of three readings, followed by absolute majority vote of the next elected Assembly in each of three readings with textual modifications, and approval in a referendum; amended several times, last in 2004

Legal system: civil law system; judicial review of legislative acts in the Supreme Court of Justice

International law organization participation: accepts compulsory ICJ jurisdiction with reservations; accepts ICCt jurisdiction

Citizenship: *citizenship by birth:* yes
citizenship by descent only: yes
dual citizenship recognized: no
residency requirement for naturalization: 5 years

Suffrage: 18 years of age; universal

Executive branch: *chief of state:* President Laurentino "Nito" CORTIZO Cohen (since 1 July 2019); Vice President Jose Gabriel CARRIZO Jaen (since 1 July 2019); note - the president is both chief of state and head of government
head of government: President Laurentino "Nito" CORTIZO Cohen (since 1 July 2019); Vice President Jose Gabriel CARRIZO Jaen (since 1 July 2019)
cabinet: Cabinet appointed by the president
elections/appointments: president and vice president directly elected on the same ballot by simple majority popular vote for a 5-year term; president eligible for a single non-consecutive term); election last held on 5 May 2019 (next to be held in 2024)
election results:
2019: Laurentino "Nito" CORTIZO Cohen elected president; percent of vote - Laurentino CORTIZO Cohen (PRD) 33.3%, Romulo ROUX (CD) 31%, Ricardo LOMBANA (independent) 18.8%, Jose BLANDON (Panamenista Party) 10.8%, Ana Matilde GOMEZ Ruiloba (independent) 4.8%, other 1.3%
2014: Juan Carlos VARELA elected president; percent of vote - Juan Carlos VARELA (PP) 39.1%, Jose Domingo ARIAS (CD) 31.4%, Juan Carlos NAVARRO (PRD) 28.2%, other 1.3%

Legislative branch: *description:* unicameral National Assembly or Asamblea Nacional (71 seats; 45 members directly elected in multi-seat constituencies - populous towns and cities - by open list proportional representation vote and 26 directly elected in single-seat constituencies - outlying rural districts - by simple majority vote; members serve 5-year terms)
elections:
last held on 5 May 2019 (next to be held in May 2024)
election results:
percent of vote by party - NA; seats by party - PRD 35, CD 18, Panamenista 8, MOLIRENA 5, independent 5; composition - men 55, women 16, percent of women 22.5%

Judicial branch: *highest court(s):* Supreme Court of Justice or Corte Suprema de Justicia (consists of 9 magistrates and 9 alternates and divided into civil, criminal, administrative, and general business chambers)
judge selection and term of office: magistrates appointed by the president for staggered 10-year terms
subordinate courts: appellate courts or Tribunal Superior; Labor Supreme Courts; Court of Audit; circuit courts or Tribunal Circuital (2 each in 9 of the 10 provinces); municipal courts; electoral, family, maritime, and adolescent courts

Political parties and leaders: Alliance Party or PA [Jose MUNOZ Molina]
Alternative Independent Socialist Party or PAIS [Jose ALVAREZ]
Democratic Change or CD [Romulo ROUX]
Democratic Revolutionary Party or PRD [Benicio ROBINSON]
Nationalist Republican Liberal Movement or MOLIRENA [Francisco "Pancho" ALEMAN]
Panamenista Party [Jose Isabel BLANDON Figueroa] (formerly the Arnulfista Party)
Popular Party or PP [Daniel Javier BREA Clavel] (formerly Christian Democratic Party or PDC)
Realizing Goals Party or RM [Ricardo Alberto MARTINELLI Berrocal]

International organization participation: BCIE, CAN (observer), CD, CELAC, FAO, G-77, IADB, IAEA, IBRD, ICAO, ICC (national committees), ICCt, ICRM, IDA, IFAD, IFC, IFRCS, ILO, IMF, IMO, IMSO, Interpol, IOC, IOM, IPU, ISO, ITSO, ITU, ITUC (NGOs), LAES, LAIA, MIGA, NAM, OAS, OPANAL, OPCW, Pacific Alliance (observer), PCA, SICA, UN, UNASUR (observer), UNCTAD, UNESCO, UNIDO, Union Latina, UNWTO, UPU, WCO, WFTU (NGOs), WHO, WIPO, WMO, WTO

Diplomatic representation in the US: *chief of mission:* Ambassador Ramón Eduardo MARTÍNEZ DE LA GUARDIA (since 16 September 2022)
chancery: 2862 McGill Terrace NW, Washington, DC 20007
telephone: [1] (202) 483-1407
FAX: [1] (202) 483-8413
email address and website:
info@embassyofpanama.org
https://www.embassyofpanama.org/
consulate(s) general: Houston, Miami, Los Angeles, New Orleans, New York, Philadelphia, Tampa, Washington DC

Diplomatic representation from the US: *chief of mission:* Ambassador (vacant), Charge d'Affaires Stewart TUTTLE (since August 2020)
embassy: Building 783, Demetrio Basilio Lakas Avenue, Clayton
mailing address: 9100 Panama City PL, Washington, DC 20521-9100
telephone: [507] 317-5000
FAX: [507] 317-5568
email address and website:
Panama-ACS@state.gov
https://pa.usembassy.gov/

Flag description: divided into four, equal rectangles; the top quadrants are white (hoist side) with a blue five-pointed star in the center and plain red; the bottom quadrants are plain blue (hoist side) and white with a red five-pointed star in the center; the blue and red colors are those of the main political parties (Conservatives and Liberals respectively) and the white denotes peace between them; the blue star stands for the civic virtues of purity and honesty, the red star signifies authority and law

National symbol(s): harpy eagle; national colors: blue, white, red

National anthem: *name:* "Himno Istmeno" (Isthmus Hymn)

lyrics/music: Jeronimo DE LA OSSA/Santos A. JORGE
note: adopted 1925

National heritage: *total World Heritage Sites:* 5 (2 cultural, 3 natural)
selected World Heritage Site locales: Caribbean Fortifications (c); Darien National Park (n); Talamanca Range-La Amistad National Park (n); Panamá Viejo and Historic District of Panamá (c); Coiba National Park (n)

ECONOMY

Economic overview: Panama's dollar-based economy rests primarily on a well-developed services sector that accounts for more than three-quarters of GDP. Services include operating the Panama Canal, logistics, banking, the Colon Free Trade Zone, insurance, container ports, flagship registry, and tourism and Panama is a center for offshore banking. Panama's transportation and logistics services sectors, along with infrastructure development projects, have boosted economic growth; however, public debt surpassed $37 billion in 2016 because of excessive government spending and public works projects. The US-Panama Trade Promotion Agreement was approved by Congress and signed into law in October 2011, and entered into force in October 2012.

Future growth will be bolstered by the Panama Canal expansion project that began in 2007 and was completed in 2016 at a cost of $5.3 billion - about 10-15% of current GDP. The expansion project more than doubled the Canal's capacity, enabling it to accommodate high-capacity vessels such as tankers and neopanamax vessels that are too large to traverse the existing canal. The US and China are the top users of the Canal.

Strong economic performance has not translated into broadly shared prosperity, as Panama has the second worst income distribution in Latin America. About one-fourth of the population lives in poverty; however, from 2006 to 2012 poverty was reduced by 10 percentage points.

Real GDP (purchasing power parity): $109.52 billion (2020 est.)
$133.47 billion (2019 est.)
$129.54 billion (2018 est.)
note: data are in 2017 dollars
country comparison to the world: 84

Real GDP growth rate: 5.4% (2017 est.)
5% (2016 est.)
5.8% (2015 est.)
country comparison to the world: 37

Real GDP per capita: $25,400 (2020 est.)
$31,400 (2019 est.)
$31,000 (2018 est.)
note: data are in 2017 dollars
country comparison to the world: 74

GDP (official exchange rate): $66.801 billion (2019 est.)

Inflation rate (consumer prices): 0.9% (2017 est.)
0.7% (2016 est.)
country comparison to the world: 61

Credit ratings:

Fitch rating: BBB (2011)

Moody's rating: Baa1 (2019)

Standard & Poors rating: BBB (2020)

GDP - composition, by sector of origin: *agriculture:* 2.4% (2017 est.)
industry: 15.7% (2017 est.)
services: 82% (2017 est.)

GDP - composition, by end use: *household consumption:* 45.6% (2017 est.)
government consumption: 10.7% (2017 est.)
investment in fixed capital: 42.9% (2017 est.)
investment in inventories: 3% (2017 est.)
exports of goods and services: 41.9% (2017 est.)
imports of goods and services: -44.2% (2017 est.)

Agricultural products: sugar cane, bananas, rice, poultry, milk, plantains, pineapples, maize, beef, pork

Industries: construction, brewing, cement and other construction materials, sugar milling

Industrial production growth rate: 6.3% (2017 est.)
country comparison to the world: 38

Labor force: 1.633 million (2017 est.)
note: shortage of skilled labor, but an oversupply of unskilled labor
country comparison to the world: 127

Labor force - by occupation: *agriculture:* 17%
industry: 18.6%
services: 64.4% (2009 est.)

Unemployment rate: 6.14% (2018 est.)
6% (2017 est.)
country comparison to the world: 99

Unemployment, youth ages 15-24: *total:* 40.1%
male: 30.8%
female: 51.9% (2020 est.)
country comparison to the world: 12

Population below poverty line: 22.1% (2016 est.)

Gini Index coefficient - distribution of family income: 49.2 (2018 est.)
56.1 (2003)
country comparison to the world: 16

Household income or consumption by percentage share: *lowest 10%:* 1.1%
highest 10%: 38.9% (2014 est.)

Budget: *revenues:* 12.43 billion (2017 est.)
expenditures: 13.44 billion (2017 est.)

Budget surplus (+) or deficit (-): -1.6% (of GDP) (2017 est.)
country comparison to the world: 94

Public debt: 37.8% of GDP (2017 est.)
37.4% of GDP (2016 est.)
country comparison to the world: 138

Taxes and other revenues: 20.1% (of GDP) (2017 est.)
country comparison to the world: 152

Fiscal year: calendar year

Current account balance: -$3.036 billion (2017 est.)
-$3.16 billion (2016 est.)
country comparison to the world: 174

Exports: $20.18 billion (2020 est.) note: data are in current year dollars
$28.58 billion (2019 est.) note: data are in current year dollars
$28.55 billion (2018 est.) note: data are in current year dollars
note: includes the Colon Free Zone
country comparison to the world: 82

Exports - partners: Ecuador 20%, Guatemala 14%, China 8%, United States 6%, Netherlands 6% (2019)

Exports - commodities: refined petroleum, copper, bananas, ships, coal tar oil, packaged medicines (2019)

Imports: $17.41 billion (2020 est.) note: data are in current year dollars
$27.38 billion (2019 est.) note: data are in current year dollars
$28.9 billion (2018 est.) note: data are in current year dollars
note: includes the Colon Free Zone
country comparison to the world: 92

Imports - partners: China 21%, United States 19%, Japan 16%, Colombia 6%, Ecuador 5% (2019)

Imports - commodities: ships, refined petroleum, crude petroleum, tanker ships, packaged medicines (2019)

Reserves of foreign exchange and gold: $2.703 billion (31 December 2017 est.)
$3.878 billion (31 December 2016 est.)
country comparison to the world: 114

Debt - external: $101.393 billion (2019 est.)
$94.898 billion (2018 est.)
country comparison to the world: 55

Exchange rates: balboas (PAB) per US dollar -
1 (2017 est.)
1 (2016 est.)
1 (2015 est.)
1 (2014 est.)
1 (2013 est.)

ENERGY

Electricity access: *electrification - total population:* 92% (2019)
electrification - urban areas: 99.4% (2019)
electrification - rural areas: 77% (2019)

Electricity: *installed generating capacity:* 4.106 million kW (2020 est.)
consumption: 10,808,780,000 kWh (2019 est.)
exports: 427 million kWh (2019 est.)
imports: 77 million kWh (2019 est.)
transmission/distribution losses: 1.309 billion kWh (2019 est.)

Electricity generation sources: *fossil fuels:* 24.5% of total installed capacity (2020 est.)
solar: 2.7% of total installed capacity (2020 est.)
wind: 6.4% of total installed capacity (2020 est.)
hydroelectricity: 66.2% of total installed capacity (2020 est.)
biomass and waste: 0.2% of total installed capacity (2020 est.)

Coal: *production:* 0 metric tons (2020 est.)
consumption: 1.118 million metric tons (2020 est.)
exports: 0 metric tons (2020 est.)
imports: 1.15 million metric tons (2020 est.)
proven reserves: 0 metric tons (2019 est.)

Petroleum: *total petroleum production:* 0 bbl/day (2021 est.)
refined petroleum consumption: 143,700 bbl/day (2019 est.)

Refined petroleum products - production: 0 bbl/day (2015 est.)
country comparison to the world: 188

Refined petroleum products - exports: 66 bbl/day (2015 est.)
country comparison to the world: 121

Refined petroleum products - imports: 129,200 bbl/day (2015 est.)

country comparison to the world: 45

Natural gas: *production:* 0 cubic meters (2021 est.)
consumption: 552.744 million cubic meters (2019 est.)
exports: 0 cubic meters (2021 est.)
imports: 552.744 million cubic meters (2019 est.)
proven reserves: 0 cubic meters (2021 est.)

Carbon dioxide emissions: 25.263 million metric tonnes of CO2 (2019 est.)
from coal and metallurgical coke: 1.905 million metric tonnes of CO2 (2019 est.)
from petroleum and other liquids: 22.281 million metric tonnes of CO2 (2019 est.)
from consumed natural gas: 1.077 million metric tonnes of CO2 (2019 est.)
country comparison to the world: 79

Energy consumption per capita: 98.946 million Btu/person (2019 est.)
country comparison to the world: 60

COMMUNICATIONS

Telephones - fixed lines: *total subscriptions:* 649,156 (2020 est.)
subscriptions per 100 inhabitants: 15 (2020 est.)
country comparison to the world: 85

Telephones - mobile cellular: *total subscriptions:* 5,825,677 (2020 est.)
subscriptions per 100 inhabitants: 135 (2020 est.)
country comparison to the world: 117

Telecommunication systems: *general assessment:* Panama has seen a steady increase in revenue from the telecom sector in recent years; mobile services and broadband remain the key growth sectors, with mobile connections accounting for 90% of all connections, and over half of telecom sector revenue; the mobile market has effective competition; internet services have grown in recent years as consumers responded to government fixed-line projects, improved mobile broadband connectivity and mobile applications (2021)
domestic: fixed-line about 14 per 100 and rapid subscribership of mobile-cellular telephone roughly 132 per 100 (2020)
international: country code - 507; landing points for the PAN-AM, ARCOS, SAC, AURORA, PCCS, PAC, and the MAYA-1 submarine cable systems that together provide links to the US and parts of the Caribbean, Central America, and South America; satellite earth stations - 2 Intelsat (Atlantic Ocean); connected to the Central American Microwave System (2019)

Broadcast media: multiple privately owned TV networks and a government-owned educational TV station; multi-channel cable and satellite TV subscription services are available; more than 100 commercial radio stations (2019)

Internet country code: .pa

Internet users: *total:* 2,761,452 (2020 est.)
percent of population: 64% (2020 est.)
country comparison to the world: 117

Broadband - fixed subscriptions: *total:* 562,413 (2020 est.)
subscriptions per 100 inhabitants: 13 (2020 est.)
country comparison to the world: 88

TRANSPORTATION

National air transport system: *number of registered air carriers:* 4 (2020)
inventory of registered aircraft operated by air carriers: 122
annual passenger traffic on registered air carriers: 12,939,350 (2018)
annual freight traffic on registered air carriers: 47.63 million (2018) mt-km

Civil aircraft registration country code prefix: HP

Airports: *total:* 117 (2021)
country comparison to the world: 49

Airports - with paved runways: *total:* 57
over 3,047 m: 1
2,438 to 3,047 m: 3
1,524 to 2,437 m: 3
914 to 1,523 m: 20
under 914 m: 30 (2021)

Airports - with unpaved runways: *total:* 60
1,524 to 2,437 m: 1
914 to 1,523 m: 8
under 914 m: 51 (2021)

Heliports: 3 (2021)

Pipelines: 128 km oil (2013)

Railways: *total:* 77 km (2014)
standard gauge: 77 km (2014) 1.435-m gauge
country comparison to the world: 128

Waterways: 800 km (2011) (includes the 82-km Panama Canal that is being widened)
country comparison to the world: 78

Merchant marine: *total:* 7,980
by type: bulk carrier 2,697, container ship 643, general cargo 1,381, oil tanker 771, other 2,488 (2021)
country comparison to the world: 2

Ports and terminals: *major seaport(s):* Balboa, Colon, Cristobal
container port(s) (TEUs): Balboa (2,894,654), Colon (4,379,477) (2019)

MILITARY AND SECURITY

Military and security forces: no regular military forces; Ministry of Public Security: the Panama National Police (La Policía Nacional de Panamá, PNP), National Air-Naval Service (Servicio Nacional Aeronaval, SENAN), National Border Service (Servicio Nacional de Fronteras, SENAFRONT) (2022)
note: the PNP includes paramilitary special forces units for counterterrorism and counternarcotics missions; in addition to its 3 regionally-based border security brigades, SENAFRONT includes a special forces brigade, which is comprised of special forces, counternarcotics, maritime, and rapid reaction units

Military expenditures: 1.2% of GDP (2022 est.)
1.3% of GDP (2021 est.)
1.4% of GDP (2020 est.)
1.2% of GDP (2019) (approximately $1.38 billion)
1.1% of GDP (2018) (approximately $1.33 billion)
country comparison to the world: 116

Military and security service personnel strengths: approximately 20,000 National Police; 4,000 National Border Service; 3,000 National Air-Naval Service (2022)

Military equipment inventories and acquisitions: Panama's security forces are lightly armed; Canada, Italy and the US have provided equipment to the security forces since 2010 (2022)

Military - note: the MPS's chief focuses are countering narcotics trafficking and border security; Panama's security forces have long been criticized for being ineffective and corrupt

Panama created a paramilitary National Guard (Guardia Nacional de Panamá) in the 1950s from the former National Police (established 1904); the National Guard subsequently evolved into more of a military force with some police responsibilities; it seized power in a coup in 1968 and military officers ran the country until 1989; in 1983, the National Guard was renamed the Panama Defense Force (PDF); the PDF was disbanded after the 1989 US invasion and the current national police forces were formed in 1990; the armed forces were officially abolished under the 1994 Constitution (2022)

TRANSNATIONAL ISSUES

Disputes - international: *Panama-Colombia:* organized illegal narcotics operations in Colombia operate within the remote border region with Panama
Panama-Costa Rica: none identified

Refugees and internally displaced persons: *refugees (country of origin):* 80,021 (Venezuela) (economic and political crisis; includes Venezuelans who have claimed asylum or have received alternative legal stay) (2021)

Illicit drugs: a prime sea and land passage for drugs, primarily cocaine from Colombia, from South America to North America and Europe; traffickers ship drugs in containers passing through the Panama Canal to North America and Europe

PAPUA NEW GUINEA

INTRODUCTION

Background: Papua New Guinea (PNG) was first settled between 50,000 and 60,000 years ago. PNG's harsh geography consisting of mountains, jungles, and numerous river valleys, kept many of the arriving groups isolated, giving rise to PNG's incredible ethnic and linguistic diversity. Agriculture was independently developed by some of these groups. Around 500 B.C., Austronesian voyagers settled along the coast. Spanish and Portuguese explorers periodically visited the island starting in the 1500s, but none made it into the country's interior. American and British whaling ships frequented the islands off the coast of New Guinea in the mid-1800s. In 1884, Germany declared a protectorate - and eventually a colony - over the northern part of what would become PNG and named it German

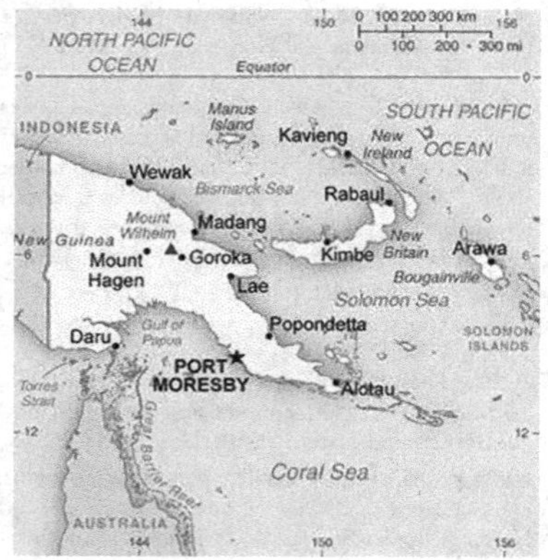

New Guinea; days later the UK followed suit on the southern part and nearby islands and called it Papua. Most of their focus was on the coastal regions, leaving the highlands largely unexplored.

The UK put its colony under Australian administration in 1902 and formalized the act in 1906. At the outbreak of World War I, Australia occupied German New Guinea and continued to rule it after the war as a League of Nations Mandate. The discovery of gold along the Bulolo River in the 1920s, led prospectors to venture into the highlands, where they found about 1 million people living in isolated communities. Japan invaded New Guinea in 1941 and reached Papua the following year. Allied victories during the New Guinea campaign pushed out the Japanese, and after the end of the war, Australia combined the two territories into one administration. Sir Michael SOMARE won elections in 1972 on the promise of achieving independence, which was realized in 1975.

A secessionist movement in Bougainville, an island well endowed in copper and gold resources, reignited in 1988 with debates about land use, profits, and an influx of outsiders at the Panguna Copper Mine. Following elections in 1992, the PNG Government took a hardline stance against Bougainville rebels and the resulting civil war led to about 20,000 deaths. In 1997, the PNG Government hired mercenaries to support its troops in Bougainville, sparking an army mutiny and forcing the prime minister to resign. PNG and Bougainville signed a truce in 1997 and a peace agreement in 2001, which granted Bougainville autonomy. An internationally-monitored nonbinding referendum asking Bougainvilleans to chose independence or greater self-rule occurred in November 2019, with 98% of voters opting for independence.

GEOGRAPHY

Location: Oceania, group of islands including the eastern half of the island of New Guinea between the Coral Sea and the South Pacific Ocean, east of Indonesia

Geographic coordinates: 6 00 S, 147 00 E

Map references: Oceania

Area: *total:* 462,840 sq km
land: 452,860 sq km
water: 9,980 sq km
country comparison to the world: 57

Area - comparative: slightly larger than California

Land boundaries: *total:* 824 km
border countries (1): Indonesia 824 km

Coastline: 5,152 km

Maritime claims: *territorial sea:* 12 nm
continental shelf: 200-m depth or to the depth of exploitation
exclusive fishing zone: 200 nm
measured from claimed archipelagic baselines

Climate: tropical; northwest monsoon (December to March), southeast monsoon (May to October); slight seasonal temperature variation

Terrain: mostly mountains with coastal lowlands and rolling foothills

Elevation: *highest point:* Mount Wilhelm 4,509 m
lowest point: Pacific Ocean 0 m
mean elevation: 667 m

Natural resources: gold, copper, silver, natural gas, timber, oil, fisheries

Land use: *agricultural land:* 2.6% (2018 est.)
arable land: 0.7% (2018 est.)
permanent crops: 1.5% (2018 est.)
permanent pasture: 0.4% (2018 est.)
forest: 63.1% (2018 est.)
other: 34.3% (2018 est.)

Irrigated land: 0 sq km (2012)

Major rivers (by length in km): Sepik river source and mouth (shared with Indonesia) - 1,126 km; Fly river source and mouth (shared with Indonesia) -1,050 km

Population distribution: population concentrated in the highlands and eastern coastal areas on the island of New Guinea; predominantly a rural distribution with only about one-fifth of the population residing in urban areas

Natural hazards: active volcanism; the country is subject to frequent and sometimes severe earthquakes; mud slides; tsunamis
volcanism: severe volcanic activity; Ulawun (2,334 m), one of Papua New Guinea's potentially most dangerous volcanoes, has been deemed a Decade Volcano by the International Association of Volcanology and Chemistry of the Earth's Interior, worthy of study due to its explosive history and close proximity to human populations; Rabaul (688 m) destroyed the city of Rabaul in 1937 and 1994; Lamington erupted in 1951 killing 3,000 people; Manam's 2004 eruption forced the island's abandonment; other historically active volcanoes include Bam, Bagana, Garbuna, Karkar, Langila, Lolobau, Long Island, Pago, St. Andrew Strait, Victory, and Waiowa; see note 2 under "Geography - note"

Geography - note: *note 1:* shares island of New Guinea with Indonesia; generally east-west trending highlands break up New Guinea into diverse ecoregions; one of world's largest swamps along southwest coast
note 2: two major food crops apparently developed on the island of New Guinea: bananas and sugarcane
note 3: Papua New Guinea is one of the countries along the Ring of Fire, a belt of active volcanoes and earthquake epicenters bordering the Pacific Ocean; up to 90% of the world's earthquakes and some 75% of the world's volcanoes occur within the Ring of Fire

PEOPLE AND SOCIETY

Population: 9,593,498 (2022 est.)
country comparison to the world: 94

Nationality: *noun:* Papua New Guinean(s)
adjective: Papua New Guinean

Ethnic groups: Melanesian, Papuan, Negrito, Micronesian, Polynesian

Languages: Tok Pisin (official), English (official), Hiri Motu (official), some 839 indigenous languages spoken (about 12% of the world's total); many languages have fewer than 1,000 speakers
note: Tok Pisin, a creole language, is widely used and understood; English is spoken by 1%-2%; Hiri Motu is spoken by less than 2%

Religions: Protestant 64.3% (Evangelical Lutheran 18.4%, Seventh Day Adventist 12.9%, Pentecostal 10.4%, United Church 10.3%, Evangelical Alliance 5.9%, Anglican 3.2%, Baptist 2.8%, Salvation Army .4%), Roman Catholic 26%, other Christian 5.3%, non-Christian 1.4%, unspecified 3.1% (2011 est.)
note: data represent only the citizen population; roughly 0.3% of the population are non-citizens, consisting of Christian 52% (predominantly Roman Catholic), other 10.7% , none 37.3%

Age structure: *0-14 years:* 31.98% (male 1,182,539/female 1,139,358)
15-24 years: 19.87% (male 731,453/female 711,164)
25-54 years: 37.68% (male 1,397,903/female 1,337,143)
55-64 years: 5.83% (male 218,529/female 204,717)
65 years and over: 4.64% (male 164,734/female 171,916) (2020 est.)

Dependency ratios: *total dependency ratio:* 63.2
youth dependency ratio: 57.4
elderly dependency ratio: 5.8
potential support ratio: 17.2 (2020 est.)

Median age: *total:* 24 years
male: 24 years
female: 24 years (2020 est.)
country comparison to the world: 171

Population growth rate: 2.35% (2022 est.)
country comparison to the world: 29

Birth rate: 29.03 births/1,000 population (2022 est.)
country comparison to the world: 31

Death rate: 5.54 deaths/1,000 population (2022 est.)
country comparison to the world: 182

Net migration rate: 0 migrant(s)/1,000 population (2022 est.)
country comparison to the world: 95

Population distribution: population concentrated in the highlands and eastern coastal areas on the island of New Guinea; predominantly a rural distribution with only about one-fifth of the population residing in urban areas

Urbanization: *urban population:* 13.6% of total population (2022)
rate of urbanization: 2.91% annual rate of change (2020-25 est.)

Major urban areas - population: 400,000 PORT MORESBY (capital) (2022)

Sex ratio: *at birth:* 1.05 male(s)/female
0-14 years: 1.04 male(s)/female
15-24 years: 1.04 male(s)/female
25-54 years: 1.02 male(s)/female
55-64 years: 0.98 male(s)/female
65 years and over: 1 male(s)/female
total population: 1.03 male(s)/female (2022 est.)

Mother's mean age at first birth: 21.9 years (2016/18)
note: data represents median age a first birth among women 25-49

Maternal mortality ratio: 145 deaths/100,000 live births (2017 est.)
country comparison to the world: 58

Infant mortality rate: *total:* 33.59 deaths/1,000 live births
male: 36.91 deaths/1,000 live births
female: 30.12 deaths/1,000 live births (2022 est.)
country comparison to the world: 41

Life expectancy at birth: *total population:* 69.43 years
male: 67.76 years
female: 71.19 years (2022 est.)
country comparison to the world: 177

Total fertility rate: 3.92 children born/woman (2022 est.)
country comparison to the world: 29

Contraceptive prevalence rate: 36.7% (2016/18)

Drinking water source: *improved: urban:* 86.2% of population
rural: 41.5% of population
total: 47.5% of population
unimproved: urban: 13.8% of population
rural: 58.5% of population
total: 52.5% of population (2020 est.)

Current health expenditure: 2.3% of GDP (2019)

Physicians density: 0.07 physicians/1,000 population (2019)

Sanitation facility access: *improved: urban:* 57.8% of population
rural: 18.2% of population
total: 23.5% of population
unimproved: urban: 42.2% of population
rural: 81.8% of population
total: 76.5% of population (2020 est.)

HIV/AIDS - adult prevalence rate: 0.9% (2020 est.)
country comparison to the world: 50

HIV/AIDS - people living with HIV/AIDS: 55,000 (2020 est.)
note: estimate does not include children
country comparison to the world: 58

HIV/AIDS - deaths: (2020 est.) <500
note: estimate does not include children

Major infectious diseases: *degree of risk:* very high (2020)
food or waterborne diseases: bacterial diarrhea, hepatitis A, and typhoid fever
vectorborne diseases: dengue fever and malaria

Obesity - adult prevalence rate: 21.3% (2016)
country comparison to the world: 91

Alcohol consumption per capita: *total:* 1.26 liters of pure alcohol (2019 est.)
beer: 0.6 liters of pure alcohol (2019 est.)
wine: 0.06 liters of pure alcohol (2019 est.)
spirits: 0.6 liters of pure alcohol (2019 est.)
other alcohols: 0 liters of pure alcohol (2019 est.)
country comparison to the world: 144

Tobacco use: *total:* 39.3% (2020 est.)
male: 53.5% (2020 est.)
female: 25.1% (2020 est.)
country comparison to the world: 5

Children under the age of 5 years underweight: 27.8% (2009/11)
country comparison to the world: 8

Child marriage: *women married by age 15:* 8%
women married by age 18: 27.3%
men married by age 18: 3.7% (2018 est.)

Education expenditures: 1.9% of GDP (2018 est.)
country comparison to the world: 180

Literacy: *definition:* age 15 and over can read and write
total population: 64.2%
male: 65.6%
female: 62.8% (2015)

People - note: the indigenous population of Papua New Guinea (PNG) is one of the most heterogeneous in the world; PNG has several thousand separate communities, most with only a few hundred people; divided by language, customs, and tradition, some of these communities have engaged in low-scale tribal conflict with their neighbors for millennia; the advent of modern weapons and modern migrants into urban areas has greatly magnified the impact of this lawlessness

ENVIRONMENT

Environment - current issues: rain forest loss as a result of growing commercial demand for tropical timber; unsustainable logging practices result in soil erosion, water quality degredation, and loss of habitat and biodiversity; large-scale mining projects cause adverse impacts on forests and water quality (discharge of heavy metals, cyanide, and acids into rivers); severe drought; inappropriate farming practices accelerate land degradion (soil erosion, siltation, loss of soil fertility); destructive fishing practices and coastal pollution due to run-off from land-based activities and oil spills

Environment - international agreements: *party to:* Antarctic Treaty, Biodiversity, Climate Change, Climate Change-Kyoto Protocol, Climate Change-Paris Agreement, Desertification, Endangered Species, Environmental Modification, Hazardous Wastes, Law of the Sea, Marine Dumping-London Convention, Nuclear Test Ban, Ozone Layer Protection, Ship Pollution, Tropical Timber 2006, Wetlands
signed, but not ratified: Comprehensive Nuclear Test Ban

Air pollutants: *particulate matter emissions:* 10.91 micrograms per cubic meter (2016 est.)
carbon dioxide emissions: 7.54 megatons (2016 est.)
methane emissions: 11.05 megatons (2020 est.)

Climate: tropical; northwest monsoon (December to March), southeast monsoon (May to October); slight seasonal temperature variation

Land use: *agricultural land:* 2.6% (2018 est.)
arable land: 0.7% (2018 est.)
permanent crops: 1.5% (2018 est.)
permanent pasture: 0.4% (2018 est.)
forest: 63.1% (2018 est.)
other: 34.3% (2018 est.)

Urbanization: *urban population:* 13.6% of total population (2022)
rate of urbanization: 2.91% annual rate of change (2020-25 est.)

Revenue from forest resources: *forest revenues:* 2.08% of GDP (2018 est.)
country comparison to the world: 33

Revenue from coal: *coal revenues:* 0% of GDP (2018 est.)
country comparison to the world: 150

Waste and recycling: *municipal solid waste generated annually:* 1 million tons (2014 est.)
municipal solid waste recycled annually: 20,000 tons (2016 est.)
percent of municipal solid waste recycled: 2% (2016 est.)

Major rivers (by length in km): Sepik river source and mouth (shared with Indonesia) - 1,126 km; Fly river source and mouth (shared with Indonesia) -1,050 km

Total water withdrawal: *municipal:* 223.5 million cubic meters (2017 est.)
industrial: 167.6 million cubic meters (2017 est.)
agricultural: 1 million cubic meters (2017 est.)

Total renewable water resources: 801 billion cubic meters (2017 est.)

GOVERNMENT

Country name: *conventional long form:* Independent State of Papua New Guinea
conventional short form: Papua New Guinea
local short form: Papuaniugini
former: German New Guinea, British New Guinea, Territory of Papua and New Guinea
abbreviation: PNG
etymology: the word "papua" derives from the Malay "papuah" describing the frizzy hair of the Melanesians; Spanish explorer Ynigo ORTIZ de RETEZ applied the term "Nueva Guinea" to the island of New Guinea in 1545 after noting the resemblance of the locals to the peoples of the Guinea coast of Africa

Government type: parliamentary democracy under a constitutional monarchy; a Commonwealth realm

Capital: *name:* Port Moresby
geographic coordinates: 9 27 S, 147 11 E
time difference: UTC+10 (15 hours ahead of Washington, DC, during Standard Time)
time zone note: Papua New Guinea has two time zones, including Bougainville (UTC+11)
etymology: named in 1873 by Captain John MORESBY (1830-1922) in honor of his father, British Admiral Sir Fairfax MORESBY (1786-1877)

Administrative divisions: 20 provinces, 1 autonomous region*, and 1 district**; Bougainville*, Central, Chimbu, Eastern Highlands, East New Britain, East Sepik, Enga, Gulf, Hela, Jiwaka, Madang, Manus, Milne Bay, Morobe, National Capital**, New Ireland, Northern, Southern Highlands, Western, Western Highlands, West New Britain, West Sepik

Independence: 16 September 1975 (from the Australia-administered UN trusteeship)

National holiday: Independence Day, 16 September (1975)

Constitution: *history:* adopted 15 August 1975, effective at independence 16 September 1975
amendments: proposed by the National Parliament; passage has prescribed majority vote requirements depending on the constitutional sections being amended – absolute majority, two-thirds majority, or three-fourths majority; amended many times, last in 2016

Legal system: mixed legal system of English common law and customary law

International law organization participation: has not submitted an ICJ jurisdiction declaration; non-party state to the ICCt

Citizenship: *citizenship by birth:* no
citizenship by descent only: at least one parent must be a citizen of Papua New Guinea
dual citizenship recognized: no
residency requirement for naturalization: 8 years

Suffrage: 18 years of age; universal

Executive branch: *chief of state:* King CHARLES III (since 8 September 2022); represented by Governor General Grand Chief Sir Bob DADAE (since 28 February 2017)
head of government: Prime Minister James MARAPE (since 30 May 2019); Deputy Prime Minister Sam BASIL (since 20 December 2020)
cabinet: National Executive Council appointed by the governor general on the recommendation of the prime minister
elections/appointments: the monarchy is hereditary; governor general nominated by the National Parliament and appointed by the chief of state; following legislative elections, the leader of the majority party or majority coalition usually appointed prime minister by the governor general pending the outcome of a National Parliament vote
election results:
James MARAPE elected prime minister; National Parliament vote - 101 to 8

Legislative branch: *description:* unicameral National Parliament (111 seats; members directly elected in single-seat constituencies - 89 local, 20 provinicial, the autonomous province of Bouganville, and the National Capital District - by majority preferential vote; members serve 5-year terms); note - the constitution allows up to 126 seats
elections:
last held from 4-22 July 2022 (next to be held in June 2027)
election results:
percent of vote by party - NA; seats by party - PANGU PATI - 38, PNC - 17, URP - 11, NAP - 5, PNC -4, SDP - 4, PFP - 3, ULP - 3, Advance PNG - 2, National Party - 2, AP - 1, Destiny Party - 1, Greens - 1, Liberal Party -1, MAP - 1, NGP - 1, ODP - 1, PLP - 1, PMC - 1, PPP - 1, PRP - 1, THE - 1, independents - 9; composition - NA

Judicial branch: *highest court(s):* Supreme Court (consists of the chief justice, deputy chief justice, 35 justices, and 5 acting justices); National Courts (consists of 13 courts located in the provincial capitals, with a total of 19 resident judges)
judge selection and term of office: Supreme Court chief justice appointed by the governor general upon advice of the National Executive Council (cabinet) after consultation with the National Justice Administration minister; deputy chief justice and other justices appointed by the Judicial and Legal Services Commission, a 5-member body that includes the Supreme Court chief and deputy chief justices, the chief ombudsman, and a member of the National Parliament; full-time citizen judges appointed for 10-year renewable terms; non-citizen judges initially appointed for 3-year renewable terms and after first renewal can serve until age 70; appointment and tenure of National Court resident judges NA
subordinate courts: district, village, and juvenile courts, military courts, taxation courts, coronial courts, mining warden courts, land courts, traffic courts, committal courts, grade five courts

Political parties and leaders: Advance PNG [Muglua DILU]
Allegiance Party or AP [Bryan KRAMER]
Destiny Party [Marsh NARAWEC]
Liberal Party [John PUNDARI]
Melanesian Alliance Party or MAP [Joseph YOPYYOPY]
National Alliance Party or NAP [Allan BIRD]
New Generation Party or NGP [Keith IDUHU]
Our Development Party or ODP [Puka TEMU]
Papua and Niugini Union Party or PANGU PATI [vacant]
Papua New Guinea Greens Party [Richard MASERE]
Papua New Guinea National Party [Kerenga KUA]
Papua New Guinea Party or PNGP [Belden NAMAH]
People's First Party or PFP [Richard MARU]
People's Labor Party or PLP [Luther WENGE]
People's Movement for Change or PMC [Gary JAFFA]
People's National Congress Party or PNC [Peter Paire O'NEILL]
People's Party or PP [Peter IPATAS]
People's Progress Party or PPP [Sir Julius CHAN]
People's Reform Party or PRP [James DONALD]
Social Democratic Party or SDP [Powes PARKOP]
Triumph Heritage Empowerment Party or THE [Don POLYE]
United Labor Party or PLP [vacant]
United Resources Party or URP [William DUMA]

International organization participation: ACP, ADB, AOSIS, APEC, ARF, ASEAN (observer), C, CD, CP, EITI (candidate country), FAO, G-77, IAEA, IBRD, ICAO, ICRM, IDA, IFAD, IFC, IFRCS, IHO, ILO, IMF, IMO, Interpol, IOC, IOM, IPU, ISO (correspondent), ITSO, ITU, MIGA, NAM, OPCW, PIF, Sparteca, SPC, UN, UNCTAD, UNESCO, UNIDO, UNMISS, UNWTO, UPU, WCO, WFTU (NGOs), WHO, WIPO, WMO, WTO

Diplomatic representation in the US: *chief of mission:* Ambassador (vacant); Charge d'Affaires Cephas KAYO, Minister (since 31 January 2018)
chancery: 1825 K Street NW, Suite 1010, Washington, DC 20006
telephone: [1] (202) 745-3680
FAX: [1] (202) 745-3679
email address and website:
info@pngembassy.org
http://www.pngembassy.org/

Diplomatic representation from the US: *chief of mission:* Ambassador (vacant); Charge d'Affaires Joe ZADROZNY (since 14 April 2022); note - also accredited to the Solomon Islands and Vanuatu
embassy: P.O. Box 1492, Port Moresby
mailing address: 4240 Port Moresby Place, Washington DC 20521-4240
telephone: [675] 308-2100
email address and website:
ConsularPortMoresby@state.gov
https://pg.usembassy.gov/

Flag description: divided diagonally from upper hoist-side corner; the upper triangle is red with a soaring yellow bird of paradise centered; the lower triangle is black with five, white, five-pointed stars of the Southern Cross constellation centered; red, black, and yellow are traditional colors of Papua New Guinea; the bird of paradise - endemic to the island of New Guinea - is an emblem of regional tribal culture and represents the emergence of Papua New Guinea as a nation; the Southern Cross, visible in the night sky, symbolizes Papua New Guinea's connection with Australia and several other countries in the South Pacific

National symbol(s): bird of paradise; national colors: red, black

National anthem: *name:* "O Arise All You Sons"
lyrics/music: Thomas SHACKLADY
note: adopted 1975

National heritage: *total World Heritage Sites:* 1 (cultural)
selected World Heritage Site locales: Kuk Early Agricultural Site

ECONOMY

Economic overview: Papua New Guinea (PNG) is richly endowed with natural resources, but exploitation has been hampered by rugged terrain, land tenure issues, and the high cost of developing infrastructure. The economy has a small formal sector, focused mainly on the export of those natural resources, and an informal sector, employing the majority of the population. Agriculture provides a subsistence livelihood for 85% of the people. The global financial crisis had little impact because of continued foreign demand for PNG's commodities.

Mineral deposits, including copper, gold, and oil, account for nearly two-thirds of export earnings. Natural gas reserves amount to an estimated 155 billion cubic meters. Following construction of a $19 billion liquefied natural gas (LNG) project, PNG LNG, a consortium led by ExxonMobil, began exporting liquefied natural gas to Asian markets in May 2014. The project was delivered on time and only slightly above budget. The success of the project has encouraged other companies to look at similar LNG projects. French supermajor Total is hopes to begin construction on the Papua LNG project by 2020. Due to lower global commodity prices, resource revenues of all types have fallen dramatically. PNG's government has recently been forced to adjust spending levels downward.

Numerous challenges still face the government of Peter O'NEILL, including providing physical security for foreign investors, regaining investor confidence, restoring integrity to state institutions, promoting economic efficiency by privatizing moribund state institutions, and maintaining good relations with Australia, its former colonial ruler. Other socio-cultural challenges could upend the economy including chronic law and order and land tenure issues. In August, 2017, PNG launched its first-ever national trade policy, PNG Trade Policy 2017-2032. The policy goal is to maximize trade and investment by increasing exports, to reduce imports, and to increase foreign direct investment (FDI).

Real GDP (purchasing power parity): $36.69 billion (2020 est.)
$38.17 billion (2019 est.)
$36.06 billion (2018 est.)
note: data are in 2017 dollars
country comparison to the world: 126

Real GDP growth rate: 2.5% (2017 est.)
1.6% (2016 est.)
5.3% (2015 est.)
country comparison to the world: 112

Real GDP per capita: $4,100 (2020 est.)
$4,300 (2019 est.)
$4,200 (2018 est.)
note: data are in 2017 dollars
country comparison to the world: 182

GDP (official exchange rate): $19.82 billion (2017 est.)

Inflation rate (consumer prices): 5.4% (2017 est.)
6.7% (2016 est.)

country comparison to the world: 186

Credit ratings:

Moody's rating: B2 (2016)

Standard & Poors rating: B- (2020)

GDP - composition, by sector of origin: *agriculture:* 22.1% (2017 est.)
industry: 42.9% (2017 est.)
services: 35% (2017 est.)

GDP - composition, by end use: *household consumption:* 43.7% (2017 est.)
government consumption: 19.7% (2017 est.)
investment in fixed capital: 10% (2017 est.)
investment in inventories: 0.4% (2017 est.)
exports of goods and services: 49.3% (2017 est.)
imports of goods and services: -22.3% (2017 est.)

Agricultural products: oil palm fruit, bananas, coconuts, fruit, sweet potatoes, game meat, yams, roots/tubers nes, vegetables, taro

Industries: copra crushing, palm oil processing, plywood production, wood chip production; mining (gold, silver, copper); crude oil and petroleum products; construction, tourism, livestock (pork, poultry, cattle), dairy products, spice products (turmeric, vanilla, ginger, cardamom, chili, pepper, citronella, and nutmeg), fisheries products

Industrial production growth rate: 3.3% (2017 est.)
country comparison to the world: 97

Labor force: 3.681 million (2017 est.)
country comparison to the world: 96

Labor force - by occupation: *agriculture:* 85%

Unemployment rate: 2.5% (2017 est.)
2.5% (2016 est.)
country comparison to the world: 29

Population below poverty line: 37% (2002 est.)

Gini Index coefficient - distribution of family income: 50.9 (1996)
country comparison to the world: 13

Household income or consumption by percentage share: *lowest 10%:* 1.7%
highest 10%: 40.5% (1996)

Budget: *revenues:* 3.638 billion (2017 est.)
expenditures: 4.591 billion (2017 est.)

Budget surplus (+) or deficit (-): -4.8% (of GDP) (2017 est.)
country comparison to the world: 168

Public debt: 36.9% of GDP (2017 est.)
36.9% of GDP (2016 est.)
country comparison to the world: 144

Taxes and other revenues: 18.4% (of GDP) (2017 est.)
country comparison to the world: 160

Fiscal year: calendar year

Current account balance: $4.859 billion (2017 est.)
$4.569 billion (2016 est.)
country comparison to the world: 30

Exports: $10.6 billion (2018 est.) note: data are in current year dollars
$9.224 billion (2016 est.)
country comparison to the world: 101

Exports - partners: Australia 26%, China 26%, Japan 22%, Taiwan 7% (2019)

Exports - commodities: natural gas, gold, copper, lumber, crude petroleum, nickel, palm oil, fish, coffee (2019)

Imports: $4.84 billion (2018 est.) note: data are in current year dollars
$2.077 billion (2016 est.)
country comparison to the world: 139

Imports - partners: Australia 33%, China 19%, Singapore 14%, Malaysia 9% (2019)

Imports - commodities: refined petroleum, excavation machinery, crude petroleum, foodstuffs, delivery trucks (2019)

Reserves of foreign exchange and gold: $1.735 billion (31 December 2017 est.)
$1.656 billion (31 December 2016 est.)
country comparison to the world: 123

Debt - external: $17.94 billion (31 December 2017 est.)
$18.28 billion (31 December 2016 est.)
country comparison to the world: 97

Exchange rates: kina (PGK) per US dollar -
3.5131 (2020 est.)
3.4042 (2019 est.)
3.36915 (2018 est.)
2.7684 (2014 est.)
2.4614 (2013 est.)

ENERGY

Electricity access: *electrification - total population:* 58.9% (2018)
electrification - urban areas: 82% (2018)
electrification - rural areas: 55.4% (2018)

Electricity: *installed generating capacity:* 1.139 million kW (2020 est.)
consumption: 3,701,693,000 kWh (2019 est.)
exports: 0 kWh (2019 est.)
imports: 0 kWh (2019 est.)
transmission/distribution losses: 340 million kWh (2019 est.)

Electricity generation sources: *fossil fuels:* 80.2% of total installed capacity (2020 est.)
hydroelectricity: 18.9% of total installed capacity (2020 est.)
biomass and waste: 1% of total installed capacity (2020 est.)

Petroleum: *total petroleum production:* 37,200 bbl/day (2021 est.)
refined petroleum consumption: 38,200 bbl/day (2019 est.)
crude oil and lease condensate exports: 60,300 bbl/day (2018 est.)
crude oil and lease condensate imports: 27,400 bbl/day (2018 est.)
crude oil estimated reserves: 159.7 million barrels (2021 est.)

Refined petroleum products - production: 22,170 bbl/day (2015 est.)
country comparison to the world: 88

Refined petroleum products - exports: 0 bbl/day (2015 est.)
country comparison to the world: 190

Refined petroleum products - imports: 17,110 bbl/day (2015 est.)
country comparison to the world: 134

Natural gas: *production:* 11,784,065,000 cubic meters (2020 est.)
consumption: 166.984 million cubic meters (2020 est.)
exports: 11,764,498,000 cubic meters (2020 est.)
imports: 0 cubic meters (2021 est.)
proven reserves: 183.125 billion cubic meters (2021 est.)

Carbon dioxide emissions: 6.491 million metric tonnes of CO2 (2019 est.)
from petroleum and other liquids: 5.965 million metric tonnes of CO2 (2019 est.)
from consumed natural gas: 526,000 metric tonnes of CO2 (2019 est.)
country comparison to the world: 128

Energy consumption per capita: 11.316 million Btu/person (2019 est.)
country comparison to the world: 151

COMMUNICATIONS

Telephones - fixed lines: *total subscriptions:* 166,000 (2020 est.)
subscriptions per 100 inhabitants: 2 (2020 est.)
country comparison to the world: 124

Telephones - mobile cellular: *total subscriptions:* 4.818 million (2020 est.)
subscriptions per 100 inhabitants: 54 (2020 est.)
country comparison to the world: 123

Telecommunication systems: *general assessment:* fixed-line teledensity in Papua New Guinea has seen little change over the past two decades; progress in the country's telecom sector has come primarily from mobile networks, where accessibility has expanded considerably in recent years, with population coverage increasing from less than 3% in 2006 to more than 90% by early 2021; the MNOs operate networks offering services based on GSM, 3G, and LTE, depending on location; GSM is prevalent in many rural and remote areas, while 3G and LTE are centered more on urban areas; MNOs' investments in 4G are growing, though GSM still represents the bulk of all mobile connections owing to the low penetration of smartphones and the concentration of high-speed data networks predominantly in high value urban areas; a lack of sufficient competition and investment in the wire line segment has driven up prices and hampered network coverage and quality; infrastructure deployment costs are high, partly due to the relatively low subscriber base, the difficult terrain, and the high proportion of the population living in rural areas; fixed telecom infrastructure is almost non-existent outside urban centers, leaving most of the population under served; PNG is the Pacific region's largest poorly developed telecom market, with only around 22% of its people connected to the internet; this falls far behind the recommended targets set in the country's National Broadband Policy drafted in 2013, which aimed to provide broadband access to 90% of the total population by 2018; the existing submarine cable infrastructure is insufficient to serve the country's needs; low international capacity has meant that internet services are expensive and slow; the cable links PNG to the Solomon Islands and Australia (landing at Sydney); despite the improvement in recent years, the country is still impacted by a connectivity infrastructure deficit, making it reliant on more expensive alternatives such as satellites, also weighing on the affordability of services for end-users (2022)
domestic: access to telephone services is not widely available; fixed-line nearly 2 per 100 and mobile-cellular nearly 48 per 100 persons (2019)
international: country code - 675; landing points for the Kumul Domestic Submarine Cable System,

PNG-LNG, APNG-2, CSCS and the PPC-1 submarine cables to Australia, Guam, PNG and Solomon Islands; satellite earth station -1 Intelsat (Pacific Ocean) (2019)

Broadcast media: 4 TV stations: 1 commercial station operating since 1987, 1 state-run station launched in 2008, 1 digital free-to-view network launched in 2014, and 1 satellite network Click TV (PNGTV) launched in 2015; the state-run National Broadcasting Corporation operates 3 radio networks with multiple repeaters and about 20 provincial stations; several commercial radio stations with multiple transmission points as well as several community stations; transmissions of several international broadcasters are accessible (2018)

Internet country code: .pg

Internet users: *total:* 965,373 (2019 est.)
percent of population: 11% (2019 est.)
country comparison to the world: 147

Broadband - fixed subscriptions: *total:* 21,000 (2020 est.)
subscriptions per 100 inhabitants: 0.2 (2020 est.)
country comparison to the world: 165

TRANSPORTATION

National air transport system: *number of registered air carriers:* 6 (2020)
inventory of registered aircraft operated by air carriers: 48
annual passenger traffic on registered air carriers: 964,713 (2018)
annual freight traffic on registered air carriers: 30.93 million (2018) mt-km

Civil aircraft registration country code prefix: P2

Airports: *total:* 561 (2021)
country comparison to the world: 11

Airports - with paved runways: *total:* 21
over 3,047 m: 1
2,438 to 3,047 m: 2
1,524 to 2,437 m: 12
914 to 1,523 m: 5
under 914 m: 1 (2021)

Airports - with unpaved runways: *total:* 540
1,524 to 2,437 m: 11
914 to 1,523 m: 53
under 914 m: 476 (2021)

Heliports: 2 (2021)

Pipelines: 264 km oil (2013)

Roadways: *total:* 9,349 km (2011)
paved: 3,000 km (2011)
unpaved: 6,349 km (2011)
country comparison to the world: 137

Waterways: 11,000 km (2011)
country comparison to the world: 14

Merchant marine: *total:* 177
by type: container ship 6, general cargo 81, oil tanker 3, other 87 (2021)
country comparison to the world: 70

Ports and terminals: *major seaport(s):* Kimbe, Lae, Madang, Rabaul, Wewak

LNG terminal(s) (export): Port Moresby

MILITARY AND SECURITY

Military and security forces: Papua New Guinea Defense Force (PNGDF; includes land, maritime, and air elements); Ministry of Police: Royal Papua New Guinea Constabulary (2022)

Military expenditures: 0.4% of GDP (2021 est.)
0.4% of GDP (2020 est.)
0.3% of GDP (2019) (approximately $100 million)
0.3% of GDP (2018) (approximately $100 million)
0.3% of GDP (2017) (approximately $110 million)
country comparison to the world: 163

Military and security service personnel strengths: approximately 3,000 active duty troops (2022)

Military equipment inventories and acquisitions: the PNGDF has a limited inventory consisting of a diverse mix of foreign-supplied weapons and equipment; Papua New Guinea has received most of its military assistance from Australia (2021)

Military service age and obligation: 18-27 for a general enlistee or 18-30 for an officer cadet; no conscription (2022)

Military - note: as of 2022, Australia and the US were assisting Papua New Guinea with expanding and improving the Defense Force naval base at Lombrum on Manus Island; the US first established a Lombrum base in 1944 during World War II

the PNGDF was established in 1973; its infantry regiment and primary unit, the Royal Pacific Islands Regiment (RPIR), is descended from Australian Army infantry battalions comprised of native soldiers and led by Australian officers and noncommissioned officers formed during World War II to help fight the Japanese; the RPIR was disbanded after the war, but reestablished in 1951 as part of the Australian Army where it continued to serve until Papua New Guinea gained its independence in 1975, when it became part of the PNGDF (2022)

TRANSNATIONAL ISSUES

Disputes - international: *Papua New Guinea-Australia:* relies on assistance from Australia to keep out illegal cross-border activities from primarily Indonesia, including goods smuggling, illegal narcotics trafficking, and squatters and secessionists

Refugees and internally displaced persons: *refugees (country of origin):* 11,601 (Indonesia) (mid-year 2021)
IDPs: 24,000 (natural disasters, tribal conflict, inter-communal violence, development projects) (2021)
stateless persons: 9 (mid-year 2021)

Trafficking in persons: *current situation:* Papua New Guinea is a source, destination, and transit country for men, women, and children subjected to sex trafficking and forced labor; women and children are subjected to sex trafficking and domestic servitude; families may sell girls into forced marriages to settle debts, leaving them vulnerable to forced domestic service; local and Chinese men are forced to labor in logging and mining camps; migrant women from Malaysia, Thailand, China, and the Philippines are subjected to sex trafficking and domestic servitude at logging and mining camps, fisheries, and entertainment sites
tier rating: Tier 3 — Papua New Guinea does not fully meet the minimum standards for the elimination of trafficking and is not making significant efforts to do so; despite remaining at Tier 3, the government continued to identify some trafficking victims and a prominent trafficking case was advanced; however, the government did not provide protective services for victims and did not systematically implement its victim identification procedures; corruption among officials in the logging sector remains a problem, and they continue to facilitate sex trafficking and forced labor; no alleged traffickers were convicted; the government dedicates little financial and human resources to combat trafficking, and awareness of trafficking is low among government officials (2020)

Illicit drugs: transit point for smuggling drugs such as methamphetamine and cocaine; major consumer of cannabis

PARACEL ISLANDS

INTRODUCTION

Background: The Paracel Islands are surrounded by productive fishing grounds and by potential oil and gas reserves. In 1932, French Indochina annexed the islands and set up a weather station on Pattle Island; maintenance was continued by its successor, Vietnam. China has occupied all the Paracel Islands since 1974, when its troops seized a South Vietnamese garrison occupying the western islands. China built a military installation on Woody Island with an airfield and artificial harbor, and has scattered garrisons on some of the other islands. The Paracel islands also are claimed by Taiwan and Vietnam.

GEOGRAPHY

Location: Southeastern Asia, group of small islands and reefs in the South China Sea, about one-third of the way from central Vietnam to the northern Philippines

Geographic coordinates: 16 30 N, 112 00 E

Map references: Southeast Asia

Area: *total:* 8 sq km ca.
land: 7.75 sq km ca.
water: 0 sq km
country comparison to the world: 243

Area - comparative: land area is about 13 times the size of the National Mall in Washington, DC

Land boundaries: *total:* 0 km

Coastline: 518 km

Maritime claims: NA

Climate: tropical

Terrain: mostly low and flat

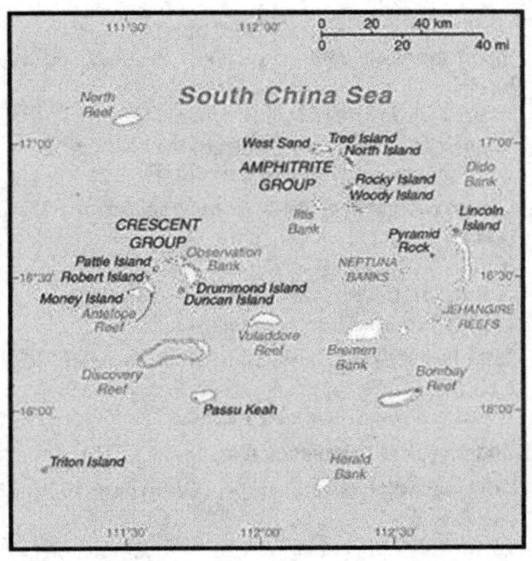

Elevation: *highest point:* unnamed location on Rocky Island 14 m
lowest point: South China Sea 0 m

Natural resources: none

Land use: *other:* 100% (2018 est.)

Irrigated land: 0 sq km (2012)

Population distribution: a population of over 1,000 Chinese resides on Woody Island, the largest of the Paracels; there are scattered Chinese garrisons on some other islands

Natural hazards: typhoons

Geography - note: composed of 130 small coral islands and reefs divided into the northeast Amphitrite Group and the western Crescent Group

PEOPLE AND SOCIETY

Population: 1,440 (July 2014 est.)
note: Chinese activity has increased in recent years, particularly on Woody Island, where the population exceeds 1,000; there are scattered Chinese garrisons on some other islands
country comparison to the world: 234

Population growth rate: 0.75% (2021 est.)
country comparison to the world: 125

Net migration rate: -0.66 migrant(s)/1,000 population (2021 est.)
country comparison to the world: 130

Population distribution: a population of over 1,000 Chinese resides on Woody Island, the largest of the Paracels; there are scattered Chinese garrisons on some other islands

ENVIRONMENT

Environment - current issues: China's use of dredged sand and coral to build artificial islands harms reef systems; ongoing human activities, including military operations, infrastructure construction, and tourism endangers local ecosystem including birds, fish, marine mammals, and marine reptiles

Climate: tropical

Land use: *other:* 100% (2018 est.)

GOVERNMENT

Country name: *conventional long form:* none
conventional short form: Paracel Islands
etymology: Portuguese navigators began to refer to the "Ilhas do Pracel" in the 16th century as a designation of low lying islets, sandbanks, and reefs scattered over a wide area; over time the name changed to "parcel" and then "paracel"

ECONOMY

Economic overview: The islands have the potential for oil and gas development. Waters around the islands support commercial fishing, but the islands themselves are not populated on a permanent basis.

TRANSPORTATION

Airports: *total:* 1 (2021)
country comparison to the world: 232

Airports - with paved runways: *total:* 1
1,524 to 2,437 m: 1 (2021)

Ports and terminals: small Chinese port facilities on Woody Island and Duncan Island

MILITARY AND SECURITY

Military - note: occupied by China, which is assessed to maintain 20 outposts in the Paracels (Antelope, Bombay, and North reefs; Drummond, Duncan, Lincoln, Middle, Money, North, Pattle, Quanfu, Robert, South, Tree, Triton, Woody, and Yagong islands; South Sand and West Sand; Observation Bank); the outposts range in size from one or two buildings to bases with significant military infrastructure; Woody Island is the main base in the Paracels and includes an airstrip with fighter aircraft hangers, naval facilities, surveillance radars, and defenses such as surface-to-air missiles and anti-ship cruise missiles; fighter aircraft have deployed to the island (2022)

TRANSNATIONAL ISSUES

Disputes - international: *Paracel Islands-China-Taiwan-Vietnam:* occupied by China, also claimed by Taiwan and Vietnam

PARAGUAY

INTRODUCTION

Background: Several Indigenous groups, principally belonging to the Guarani language family, inhabited the area of modern Paraguay before the arrival of the Spanish in the early 16th century, when the territory was incorporated into the Viceroyalty of Peru. Paraguay achieved its independence from Spain in 1811 with the help of neighboring states. In the aftermath of independence, a series of military dictators ruled the country until 1870. During the disastrous War of the Triple Alliance (1864-70) - fought against Argentina, Brazil, and Uruguay - Paraguay lost two thirds of its adult males and much of its territory. The country stagnated economically for the next half century and experienced a tumultuous series of political regimes. Following the Chaco War of 1932-35 with Bolivia, Paraguay gained a large part of the Chaco lowland region. The 35-year military dictatorship of Alfredo STROESSNER ended in 1989, and Paraguay has held relatively free and regular presidential elections since the country's return to democracy.

GEOGRAPHY

Location: Central South America, northeast of Argentina, southwest of Brazil

Geographic coordinates: 23 00 S, 58 00 W

Map references: South America

Area: *total:* 406,752 sq km
land: 397,302 sq km
water: 9,450 sq km
country comparison to the world: 61

Area - comparative: about three times the size of New York state; slightly smaller than California

Land boundaries: *total:* 4,655 km
border countries (3): Argentina 2,531 km; Bolivia 753 km; Brazil 1,371 km

Coastline: 0 km (landlocked)

Maritime claims: none (landlocked)

Climate: subtropical to temperate; substantial rainfall in the eastern portions, becoming semiarid in the far west

Terrain: grassy plains and wooded hills east of Rio Paraguay; Gran Chaco region west of Rio Paraguay mostly low, marshy plain near the river, and dry forest and thorny scrub elsewhere

Elevation: *highest point:* Cerro Pero 842 m

lowest point: junction of Rio Paraguay and Rio Parana 46 m
mean elevation: 178 m

Natural resources: hydropower, timber, iron ore, manganese, limestone

Land use: *agricultural land:* 53.8% (2018 est.)
arable land: 10.8% (2018 est.)
permanent crops: 0.2% (2018 est.)
permanent pasture: 42.8% (2018 est.)
forest: 43.8% (2018 est.)
other: 2.4% (2018 est.)

Irrigated land: 1,362 sq km (2012)

Major rivers (by length in km): Rio de la Plata/Parana (shared with Brazil [s], Argentina, and Uruguay [m]) - 4,880 km; Paraguay river mouth (shared with Brazil [s] and Argentina) - 2,549 km
note – [s] after country name indicates river source; [m] after country name indicates river mouth

Major watersheds (area sq km): Atlantic Ocean drainage: Paraná (2,582,704 sq km)

Major aquifers: Guarani Aquifer System

Population distribution: most of the population resides in the eastern half of the country; to the west lies the Gran Chaco (a semi-arid lowland plain), which accounts for 60% of the land territory, but only 2% of the overall population

Natural hazards: local flooding in southeast (early September to June); poorly drained plains may become boggy (early October to June)

Geography - note: *note 1:* landlocked; lies between Argentina, Bolivia, and Brazil; population concentrated in eastern and southern part of country
note 2: pineapples are probably indigenous to the southern Brazil-Paraguay region

PEOPLE AND SOCIETY

Population: 7,356,409 (2022 est.)
country comparison to the world: 104

Nationality: *noun:* Paraguayan(s)
adjective: Paraguayan

Ethnic groups: Mestizo (mixed Spanish and Amerindian ancestry) 95%, other 5%

Languages: Spanish (official) and Guarani (official) 46.3%, only Guarani 34%, only Spanish 15.2%, other (includes Portuguese, German, other Indigenous languages) 4.1%, no response 0.4%; note - data represent predominant household language (2012 est.)
major-language sample(s): La Libreta Informativa del Mundo, la fuente indispensable de información básica. (Spanish)

Religions: Roman Catholic 89.6%, Protestant 6.2%, other Christian 1.1%, other or unspecified 1.9%, none 1.1% (2002 est.)

Demographic profile: Paraguay falls below the Latin American average in several socioeconomic categories, including immunization rates, potable water, sanitation, and secondary school enrollment, and has greater rates of income inequality and child and maternal mortality. Paraguay's poverty rate has declined in recent years but remains high, especially in rural areas, with more than a third of the population below the poverty line. However, the well-being of the poor in many regions has improved in terms of housing quality and access to clean water, telephone service, and electricity. The fertility rate continues to drop, declining sharply from an average 4.3 births per woman in the late 1990s to about 2 in 2013, as a result of the greater educational attainment of women, increased use of contraception, and a desire for smaller families among young women.

Paraguay is a country of emigration; it has not attracted large numbers of immigrants because of political instability, civil wars, years of dictatorship, and the greater appeal of neighboring countries. Paraguay first tried to encourage immigration in 1870 in order to rebound from the heavy death toll it suffered during the War of the Triple Alliance, but it received few European and Middle Eastern immigrants. In the 20th century, limited numbers of immigrants arrived from Lebanon, Japan, South Korea, and China, as well as Mennonites from Canada, Russia, and Mexico. Large flows of Brazilian immigrants have been arriving since the 1960s, mainly to work in agriculture. Paraguayans continue to emigrate to Argentina, Brazil, Uruguay, the United States, Italy, Spain, and France.

Age structure: *0-14 years:* 23.41% (male 857,303/female 826,470)
15-24 years: 17.71% (male 640,400/female 633,525)
25-54 years: 42.63% (male 1,532,692/female 1,532,851)
55-64 years: 8.37% (male 306,100/female 295,890)
65 years and over: 7.88% (male 267,351/female 299,103) (2020 est.)

Dependency ratios: *total dependency ratio:* 55.5
youth dependency ratio: 49.9
elderly dependency ratio: 10.6
potential support ratio: 9.4 (2020 est.)

Median age: *total:* 29.7 years
male: 29.5 years
female: 29.9 years (2020 est.)
country comparison to the world: 128

Population growth rate: 1.14% (2022 est.)
country comparison to the world: 84

Birth rate: 16.32 births/1,000 population (2022 est.)
country comparison to the world: 100

Death rate: 4.87 deaths/1,000 population (2022 est.)
country comparison to the world: 201

Net migration rate: -0.07 migrant(s)/1,000 population (2022 est.)
country comparison to the world: 101

Population distribution: most of the population resides in the eastern half of the country; to the west lies the Gran Chaco (a semi-arid lowland plain), which accounts for 60% of the land territory, but only 2% of the overall population

Urbanization: *urban population:* 62.8% of total population (2022)
rate of urbanization: 1.64% annual rate of change (2020-25 est.)

Major urban areas - population: 3.452 million ASUNCION (capital) (2022)

Sex ratio: *at birth:* 1.05 male(s)/female
0-14 years: 1.03 male(s)/female
15-24 years: 1.01 male(s)/female
25-54 years: 1 male(s)/female
55-64 years: 1.03 male(s)/female
65 years and over: 0.72 male(s)/female
total population: 1.01 male(s)/female (2022 est.)

Mother's mean age at first birth: 22.9 years (2008 est.)
note: data represents median age at first birth among women 25-29

Maternal mortality ratio: 84 deaths/100,000 live births (2017 est.)
country comparison to the world: 77

Infant mortality rate: *total:* 23.21 deaths/1,000 live births
male: 27.5 deaths/1,000 live births
female: 18.7 deaths/1,000 live births (2022 est.)
country comparison to the world: 71

Life expectancy at birth: *total population:* 78.37 years
male: 75.72 years
female: 81.15 years (2022 est.)
country comparison to the world: 73

Total fertility rate: 1.89 children born/woman (2022 est.)
country comparison to the world: 132

Contraceptive prevalence rate: 68.4% (2016)

Drinking water source: *improved: urban:* 100% of population
rural: 100% of population
total: 100% of population

Current health expenditure: 7.2% of GDP (2019)

Physicians density: 1.05 physicians/1,000 population (2020)

Hospital bed density: 0.8 beds/1,000 population (2016)

Sanitation facility access: *improved: urban:* 99.6% of population
rural: 90.6% of population
total: 96.2% of population
unimproved: urban: 0.4% of population
rural: 9.4% of population
total: 3.8% of population (2020 est.)

HIV/AIDS - adult prevalence rate: 0.3% (2020 est.)
country comparison to the world: 89

HIV/AIDS - people living with HIV/AIDS: 19,000 (2020 est.)
country comparison to the world: 84

HIV/AIDS - deaths: (2020 est.) <500

Major infectious diseases: *degree of risk:* intermediate (2020)
food or waterborne diseases: bacterial diarrhea, hepatitis A, and typhoid fever
vectorborne diseases: dengue fever

Obesity - adult prevalence rate: 20.3% (2016)
country comparison to the world: 100

Alcohol consumption per capita: *total:* 5.47 liters of pure alcohol (2019 est.)
beer: 3.27 liters of pure alcohol (2019 est.)
wine: 0.59 liters of pure alcohol (2019 est.)
spirits: 1.59 liters of pure alcohol (2019 est.)
other alcohols: 0.03 liters of pure alcohol (2019 est.)
country comparison to the world: 79

Tobacco use: *total:* 11.5% (2020 est.)
male: 18.6% (2020 est.)
female: 4.4% (2020 est.)
country comparison to the world: 126

Children under the age of 5 years underweight: 1.3% (2016)
country comparison to the world: 120

Child marriage: *women married by age 15:* 3.6%
women married by age 18: 21.6% (2016 est.)

Education expenditures: 3.5% of GDP (2019 est.)
country comparison to the world: 127

Literacy: *definition:* age 15 and over can read and write
total population: 94.5%
male: 94.9%

female: 94.2% (2020)

Unemployment, youth ages 15-24: *total:* 17.1%
male: 13.1%
female: 23.3% (2020 est.)

ENVIRONMENT

Environment - current issues: deforestation; water pollution; rivers suffer from toxic dumping; tanneries release mercury and chromium into rivers and streams; loss of wetlands; inadequate means for waste disposal pose health risks for many urban residents

Environment - international agreements: *party to:* Biodiversity, Climate Change, Climate Change-Kyoto Protocol, Climate Change-Paris Agreement, Comprehensive Nuclear Test Ban, Desertification, Endangered Species, Hazardous Wastes, Law of the Sea, Ozone Layer Protection, Wetlands
signed, but not ratified: Nuclear Test Ban, Tropical Timber 2006

Air pollutants: *particulate matter emissions:* 11.16 micrograms per cubic meter (2016 est.)
carbon dioxide emissions: 7.41 megatons (2016 est.)
methane emissions: 27.65 megatons (2020 est.)

Climate: subtropical to temperate; substantial rainfall in the eastern portions, becoming semiarid in the far west

Land use: *agricultural land:* 53.8% (2018 est.)
arable land: 10.8% (2018 est.)
permanent crops: 0.2% (2018 est.)
permanent pasture: 42.8% (2018 est.)
forest: 43.8% (2018 est.)
other: 2.4% (2018 est.)

Urbanization: *urban population:* 62.8% of total population (2022)
rate of urbanization: 1.64% annual rate of change (2020-25 est.)

Revenue from forest resources: *forest revenues:* 1.21% of GDP (2018 est.)
country comparison to the world: 50

Revenue from coal: *coal revenues:* 0% of GDP (2018 est.)
country comparison to the world: 151

Waste and recycling: *municipal solid waste generated annually:* 1,818,501 tons (2015 est.)

Major rivers (by length in km): Rio de la Plata/Parana (shared with Brazil [s], Argentina, and Uruguay [m]) - 4,880 km; Paraguay river mouth (shared with Brazil [s] and Argentina) - 2,549 km
note - [s] after country name indicates river source; [m] after country name indicates river mouth

Major watersheds (area sq km): Atlantic Ocean drainage: Paraná (2,582,704 sq km)

Major aquifers: Guarani Aquifer System

Total water withdrawal: *municipal:* 362 million cubic meters (2017 est.)
industrial: 154 million cubic meters (2017 est.)
agricultural: 1.897 billion cubic meters (2017 est.)

Total renewable water resources: 387.77 billion cubic meters (2017 est.)

GOVERNMENT

Country name: *conventional long form:* Republic of Paraguay
conventional short form: Paraguay
local long form: Republica del Paraguay
local short form: Paraguay
etymology: the precise meaning of the name Paraguay is unclear, but it seems to derive from the river of the same name; one explanation has the name meaning "water of the Payagua" (an indigenous tribe that lived along the river)

Government type: presidential republic

Capital: *name:* Asuncion
geographic coordinates: 25 16 S, 57 40 W
time difference: UTC-4 (1 hour ahead of Washington, DC, during Standard Time)
daylight saving time: +1hr, begins first Sunday in October; ends last Sunday in March
etymology: the name means "assumption" and derives from the original name given to the city at its founding in 1537, Nuestra Senora Santa Maria de la Asuncion (Our Lady Saint Mary of the Assumption)

Administrative divisions: 17 departments (departamentos, singular - departamento) and 1 capital city*; Alto Paraguay, Alto Parana, Amambay, Asuncion*, Boqueron, Caaguazu, Caazapa, Canindeyu, Central, Concepcion, Cordillera, Guaira, Itapua, Misiones, Neembucu, Paraguari, Presidente Hayes, San Pedro

Independence: 14-15 May 1811 (from Spain); note - the uprising against Spanish authorities took place during the night of 14-15 May 1811 and both days are celebrated in Paraguay

National holiday: Independence Day, 14-15 May (1811) (observed 15 May); 14 May is celebrated as Flag Day

Constitution: *history:* several previous; latest approved and promulgated 20 June 1992
amendments: proposed at the initiative of at least one quarter of either chamber of the National Congress, by the president of the republic, or by petition of at least 30,000 voters; passage requires a two-thirds majority vote by both chambers and approval in a referendum; amended 2011

Legal system: civil law system with influences from Argentine, Spanish, Roman, and French civil law models; judicial review of legislative acts in Supreme Court of Justice

International law organization participation: accepts compulsory ICJ jurisdiction; accepts ICCt jurisdiction

Citizenship: *citizenship by birth:* yes
citizenship by descent only: at least one parent must be a native-born citizen of Paraguay
dual citizenship recognized: yes
residency requirement for naturalization: 3 years

Suffrage: 18 years of age; universal and compulsory until the age of 75

Executive branch: *chief of state:* President Mario ABDO BENITEZ (since 15 August 2018); Vice President Hugo Adalberto VELAZQUEZ Moreno (since 15 August 2018); note - the president is both chief of state and head of government
head of government: President Mario ABDO BENITEZ (since 15 August 2018); Vice President Hugo Adalberto VELAZQUEZ Moreno (since 15 August 2018)
cabinet: Council of Ministers appointed by the president
elections/appointments: president and vice president directly elected on the same ballot by simple majority popular vote for a single 5-year term; election last held on 22 April 2018 (next to be held in April 2023)
election results:
2018: Mario ABDO BENITEZ elected president; percent of vote - Mario ABDO BENITEZ (ANR) 49%, Efrain ALEGRE (PLRA) 45.1%, Juan Bautista YBANEZ 3.4%, other 2.5%
2013: Horacio CARTES elected president; percent of vote - Horacio CARTES (ANR) 48.5%, Efrain ALEGRE (PLRA) 39%, Mario FERREIRO (AP) 6.2%, Anibal CARRILLO (FG) 3.5%, other 2.8%

Legislative branch: *description:* bicameral National Congress or Congreso Nacional consists of:
Chamber of Senators or Camara de Senadores (45 seats; members directly elected in a single nationwide constituency by closed-list proportional representation vote to serve 5-year terms)

Chamber of Deputies or Camara de Diputados (80 seats; members directly elected in 18 multi-seat constituencies -corresponding to the country's 17 departments and capital city - by closed-list proportional representation vote to serve 5- year terms)
elections:
Chamber of Senators - last held on 22 April 2018 (next to be held in April 2023)
Chamber of Deputies - last held on 22 April 2018 (next to be held in April 2023)
election results:
Chamber of Senators - percent of vote by party/coalition - ANR 32.52%, PLRA 24.18%, FG 11.83%, PPQ 6.77%, MH 4.47%, PDP 3.66%, MCN 2.48%, UNACE 2.12%, other 11.97%; seats by party/coalition - ANR 17, PLRA 13, FG 6, PPQ 3, MH 2, PDP 2, MCN 1, UNACE 1; composition - men 38, women 7, percent of women 15.6%

Chamber of Deputies - percent of vote by party/coalition - ANR 39.1%, PLRA 17.74%, Ganar Alliance 12.08%, PPQ 4.46%, MH 3.19%; other 23.43%; seats by party/coalition - ANR 42, PLRA 17, Ganar Alliance 13, PPQ 3, MH 2, other 3; composition - men 66, women 14, percent of women 17.5%; note - total National Congress percent of women 16.8%

Judicial branch: *highest court(s):* Supreme Court of Justice or Corte Suprema de Justicia (consists of 9 justices divided 3 each into the Constitutional Court, Civil and Commercial Chamber, and Criminal Division)
judge selection and term of office: justices proposed by the Council of Magistrates or Consejo de la Magistratura, a 6- member independent body, and appointed by the Chamber of Senators with presidential concurrence; judges can serve until mandatory retirement at age 75
subordinate courts: appellate courts; first instance courts; minor courts, including justices of the peace

Political parties and leaders: Asociacion Nacional Republicana - Colorado Party or ANR [Mario ABDO BENITEZ]
Avanza Pais coalition or AP [Adolfo FERREIRO]
Broad Front coalition (Frente Guasu) or FG [Fernando Armindo LUGO Mendez]
GANAR Alliance (Great Renewed National Alliance) (alliance between PLRA and Guasu Front)
Movimiento Cruzada Nacional or MCN
Movimiento Hagamos or MH [Antonio "Tony" APURIL]
Movimiento Union Nacional de Ciudadanos Eticos or UNACE [Jorge OVIEDO MATTO]
Partido del Movimiento al Socialismo or P-MAS [Camilo Ernesto SOARES Machado]
Partido Democratica Progresista or PDP [Rafael FILIZZOLA]

Partido Encuentro Nacional or PEN [Fernando CAMACHO]
Partido Liberal Radical Autentico or PLRA [Efrain ALEGRE]
Partido Pais Solidario or PPS [Carlos Alberto FILIZZOLA Pallares]
Partido Popular Tekojoja or PPT [Sixto PEREIRA Galeano]
Patria Querida (Beloved Fatherland Party) or PPQ [Miguel CARRIZOSA]

International organization participation: CAN (associate), CD, CELAC, FAO, G-11, G-77, IADB, IAEA, IBRD, ICAO, ICC (national committees), ICCt, ICRM, IDA, IFAD, IFC, IFRCS, ILO, IMF, IMO, Interpol, IOC, IOM, IPU, ISO (correspondent), ITSO, ITU, ITUC (NGOs), LAES, LAIA, Mercosur, MIGA, MINURSO, MINUSTAH, MONUSCO, NAM (observer), OAS, OPANAL, OPCW, Pacific Alliance (observer), PCA, PROSUR, UN, UNASUR, UNCTAD, UNESCO, UNFICYP, UNHRC, UNIDO, Union Latina, UNISFA, UNMIL, UNMISS, UNOCI, UNWTO, UPU, WCO, WHO, WIPO, WMO, WTO

Diplomatic representation in the US: *chief of mission:* Ambassador Jose Antonio DOS SANTOS BEDOYA (since 15 September 2021)
chancery: 2400 Massachusetts Avenue, NW, Washington DC 20008
telephone: [1] (202) 483-6960
FAX: [1] (202) 234-4508
email address and website:
eeuuembaparsc@mre.gov.py; secretaria@embaparusa.gov.py
consulate(s) general: Los Angeles, Miami, New York

Diplomatic representation from the US: *chief of mission:* Ambassador Marc OSTFIELD (since 9 March 2022)
embassy: 1776 Mariscal Lopez Avenue, Asuncion
mailing address: 3020 Asuncion Place, Washington DC 20521-3020
telephone: [595] (21) 248-3000
FAX: [595] (21) 213-728
email address and website:
ParaguayACS@state.gov
https://py.usembassy.gov/

Flag description: three equal, horizontal bands of red (top), white, and blue with an emblem centered in the white band; unusual flag in that the emblem is different on each side; the obverse (hoist side at the left) bears the national coat of arms (a yellow five-pointed star within a green wreath capped by the words REPUBLICA DEL PARAGUAY, all within two circles); the reverse (hoist side at the right) bears a circular seal of the treasury (a yellow lion below a red Cap of Liberty and the words PAZ Y JUSTICIA (Peace and Justice)); red symbolizes bravery and patriotism, white represents integrity and peace, and blue denotes liberty and generosity
note: the three color bands resemble those on the flag of the Netherlands; one of only three national flags that differ on their obverse and reverse sides - the others are Moldova and Saudi Arabia

National symbol(s): lion; national colors: red, white, blue

National anthem: *name:* "Paraguayos, Republica o muerte!" (Paraguayans, The Republic or Death!)
lyrics/music: Francisco Esteban ACUNA de Figueroa/disputed
note: adopted 1934, in use since 1846; officially adopted following its re-arrangement in 1934

National heritage: *total World Heritage Sites:* 1 (cultural)
selected World Heritage Site locales: Jesuit Missions of La Santísima Trinidad de Paraná and Jesús de Tavarangue

ECONOMY

Economic overview: Landlocked Paraguay has a market economy distinguished by a large informal sector, featuring re-export of imported consumer goods to neighboring countries, as well as the activities of thousands of microenterprises and urban street vendors. A large percentage of the population, especially in rural areas, derives its living from agricultural activity, often on a subsistence basis. Because of the importance of the informal sector, accurate economic measures are difficult to obtain.

On a per capita basis, real income has grown steadily over the past five years as strong world demand for commodities, combined with high prices and favorable weather, supported Paraguay's commodity-based export expansion. Paraguay is the fifth largest soy producer in the world. Drought hit in 2008, reducing agricultural exports and slowing the economy even before the onset of the global recession. The economy fell 3.8% in 2009, as lower world demand and commodity prices caused exports to contract. Severe drought and outbreaks of hoof-and-mouth disease in 2012 led to a brief drop in beef and other agricultural exports. Since 2014, however, Paraguay's economy has grown at a 4% average annual rate due to strong production and high global prices, at a time when other countries in the region have contracted.

The Paraguayan Government recognizes the need to diversify its economy and has taken steps in recent years to do so. In addition to looking for new commodity markets in the Middle East and Europe, Paraguayan officials have promoted the country's low labor costs, cheap energy from its massive Itaipu Hydroelectric Dam, and single-digit tax rate on foreign firms. As a result, the number of factories operating in the country – mostly transplants from Brazil - has tripled since 2014.

Corruption, limited progress on structural reform, and deficient infrastructure are the main obstacles to long-term growth. Judicial corruption is endemic and is seen as the greatest barrier to attracting more foreign investment. Paraguay has been adverse to public debt throughout its history, but has recently sought to finance infrastructure improvements to attract foreign investment.

Real GDP (purchasing power parity): $87.98 billion (2020 est.)
$88.87 billion (2019 est.)
$89.23 billion (2018 est.)
note: data are in 2017 dollars
country comparison to the world: 95

Real GDP growth rate: 4.8% (2017 est.)
4.3% (2016 est.)
3.1% (2015 est.)
country comparison to the world: 55

Real GDP per capita: $12,300 (2020 est.)
$12,600 (2019 est.)
$12,800 (2018 est.)
note: data are in 2017 dollars
country comparison to the world: 124

GDP (official exchange rate): $38.94 billion (2017 est.)

Inflation rate (consumer prices): 3.6% (2017 est.)
4.1% (2016 est.)
country comparison to the world: 156

Credit ratings:

Fitch rating: BB+ (2018)

Moody's rating: Ba1 (2015)

Standard & Poors rating: BB (2014)

GDP - composition, by sector of origin: *agriculture:* 17.9% (2017 est.)
industry: 27.7% (2017 est.)
services: 54.5% (2017 est.)

GDP - composition, by end use: *household consumption:* 66.7% (2017 est.)
government consumption: 11.3% (2017 est.)
investment in fixed capital: 17.3% (2017 est.)
investment in inventories: 0.3% (2017 est.)
exports of goods and services: 46.6% (2017 est.)
imports of goods and services: -42.2% (2017 est.)

Agricultural products: soybeans, sugar cane, maize, cassava, wheat, rice, beef, milk, oranges, oil palm fruit

Industries: sugar processing, cement, textiles, beverages, wood products, steel, base metals, electric power

Industrial production growth rate: 2% (2017 est.)
country comparison to the world: 132

Labor force: 3.428 million (2017 est.)
country comparison to the world: 100

Labor force - by occupation: *agriculture:* 26.5%
industry: 18.5%
services: 55% (2008)

Unemployment rate: 5.7% (2017 est.)
6% (2016 est.)
country comparison to the world: 93

Unemployment, youth ages 15-24: *total:* 17.1%
male: 13.1%
female: 23.3% (2020 est.)
country comparison to the world: 95

Population below poverty line: 23.5% (2019 est.)

Gini Index coefficient - distribution of family income:
46.2 (2018 est.)
53.2 (2009)
country comparison to the world: 24

Household income or consumption by percentage share: *lowest 10%:* 1.5%
highest 10%: 37.6% (2013 est.)

Budget: *revenues:* 5.524 billion (2017 est.)
expenditures: 5.968 billion (2017 est.)

Budget surplus (+) or deficit (-): -1.1% (of GDP) (2017 est.)
country comparison to the world: 84

Public debt: 19.5% of GDP (2017 est.)
18.9% of GDP (2016 est.)
country comparison to the world: 191

Taxes and other revenues: 14.2% (of GDP) (2017 est.)
country comparison to the world: 202

Fiscal year: calendar year

Current account balance: -$298 million (2017 est.)
$416 million (2016 est.)
country comparison to the world: 108

Exports: $11.81 billion (2020 est.) note: data are in current year dollars
$13.27 billion (2019 est.) note: data are in current year dollars
$14.36 billion (2018 est.) note: data are in current year dollars
country comparison to the world: 98

Exports - partners: Brazil 32%, Argentina 22%, Chile 8%, Russia 8% (2019)

Exports - commodities: soybeans and soybean products, electricity, beef, corn, insulated wiring (2019)

Imports: $10.62 billion (2020 est.) note: data are in current year dollars
$13.15 billion (2019 est.) note: data are in current year dollars
$13.88 billion (2018 est.) note: data are in current year dollars
country comparison to the world: 104

Imports - partners: Brazil 24%, United States 22%, China 17%, Argentina 10%, Chile 5% (2019)

Imports - commodities: broadcasting equipment, cars, pesticides, refined petroleum, tires (2019)

Reserves of foreign exchange and gold: $7.877 billion (31 December 2017 est.)
$6.881 billion (31 December 2016 est.)
country comparison to the world: 79

Debt - external: $16.622 billion (2019 est.)
$16.238 billion (2018 est.)
country comparison to the world: 102

Exchange rates: guarani (PYG) per US dollar -
7,045 (2020 est.)
6,426 (2019 est.)
5,915.4 (2018 est.)
5,160.4 (2014 est.)
4,462.2 (2013 est.)

ENERGY

Electricity access: *electrification - total population:* 100% (2020)

Electricity: *installed generating capacity:* 8.831 million kW (2020 est.)
consumption: 12,718,590,000 kWh (2019 est.)
exports: 31.748 billion kWh (2019 est.)
imports: 0 kWh (2019 est.)
transmission/distribution losses: 4.47 billion kWh (2019 est.)

Electricity generation sources: *hydroelectricity:* 100% of total installed capacity (2020 est.)

Petroleum: *total petroleum production:* 2,000 bbl/day (2021 est.)
refined petroleum consumption: 56,900 bbl/day (2019 est.)

Refined petroleum products - imports: 40,760 bbl/day (2015 est.)
country comparison to the world: 89

Carbon dioxide emissions: 7.896 million metric tonnes of CO_2 (2019 est.)
from coal and metallurgical coke: 3,000 metric tonnes of CO_2 (2019 est.)
from petroleum and other liquids: 7.893 million metric tonnes of CO_2 (2019 est.)
country comparison to the world: 116

Energy consumption per capita: 62.775 million Btu/person (2019 est.)
country comparison to the world: 89

COMMUNICATIONS

Telephones - fixed lines: *total subscriptions:* 249,231 (2020 est.)
subscriptions per 100 inhabitants: 3 (2020 est.)
country comparison to the world: 117

Telephones - mobile cellular: *total subscriptions:* 7,865,050 (2020 est.)
subscriptions per 100 inhabitants: 110 (2020 est.)
country comparison to the world: 99

Telecommunication systems: *general assessment:* limited progress on structural reform and deficient infrastructure of the landlocked country are obstacles to the telecom platform; effective competition in mobile market, serving 96% of population through LTE; deployment of fiber; operator enabled 109 free Internet points across the country and is looking to expand to 430 points in 2022; dependent on neighboring countries for access to submarine cables (2022)
domestic: deficiencies in provision of fixed-line service have resulted in expansion of mobile-cellular services fostered by competition among multiple providers; Internet market also open to competition; fixed-line just over 3 per 100 and mobile-cellular just over 105 per 100 of the population (2020)
international: country code - 595; Paraguay's landlocked position means they must depend on neighbors for interconnection with submarine cable networks, making it cost more for broadband services; satellite earth station - 1 Intelsat (Atlantic Ocean) (2019)

Broadcast media: 6 privately owned TV stations; about 75 commercial and community radio stations; 1 state-owned radio network (2019)

Internet country code: .py

Internet users: *total:* 4.92 million (2021 est.)
percent of population: 64% (2021 est.)
country comparison to the world: 90

Broadband - fixed subscriptions: *total:* 562,369 (2020 est.)
subscriptions per 100 inhabitants: 8 (2020 est.)
country comparison to the world: 89

TRANSPORTATION

National air transport system: *number of registered air carriers:* 2 (2020)
inventory of registered aircraft operated by air carriers: 8
annual passenger traffic on registered air carriers: 560,631 (2018)
annual freight traffic on registered air carriers: 1.97 million (2018) mt-km

Civil aircraft registration country code prefix: ZP

Airports: *total:* 799 (2021)
country comparison to the world: 9

Airports - with paved runways: *total:* 15
over 3,047 m: 3
1,524 to 2,437 m: 7
914 to 1,523 m: 5 (2021)

Airports - with unpaved runways: *total:* 784
1,524 to 2,437 m: 23
914 to 1,523 m: 290
*under 914 m:*471 (2021)

Railways: *total:* 30 km (2014)
standard gauge: 30 km (2014) 1.435-m gauge
country comparison to the world: 133

Roadways: *total:* 78,811 km (2020)
paved: 8,573 km (2020)
unpaved: 70,238 km (2020)
country comparison to the world: 61

Waterways: 3,100 km (2012) (primarily on the Paraguay and Paraná River systems)
country comparison to the world: 34

Merchant marine: *total:* 110
by type: container ship 3, general cargo 25, oil tanker 5, other 77 (2021)
note: as of 2017, Paraguay registered 2,012 fluvial vessels of which 1,741 were commercial barges
country comparison to the world: 85

Ports and terminals: *river port(s):* Asuncion, Villeta, San Antonio, Encarnacion (Parana)

MILITARY AND SECURITY

Military and security forces: Armed Forces Command (Commando de las Fuerzas Militares): Army (Ejercito), Navy (Armada, includes marines), Air Force (Fuerza Aerea)

Ministry of Internal Affairs: the National Police of Paraguay includes the Special Police Operations Force (Fuerza de Operaciones Policiales Especiales) (2022)

Military expenditures: 1% of GDP (2021 est.)
1% of GDP (2020 est.)
1% of GDP (2019) (approximately $590 million)
1% of GDP (2018) (approximately $590 million)
0.9% of GDP (2017) (approximately $550 million)
country comparison to the world: 132

Military and security service personnel strengths: approximately 15,000 active duty personnel (10,000 Army; 3,500 Navy; 1,500 Air Force) (2022)

Military equipment inventories and acquisitions: the Paraguayan military forces inventory is comprised of mostly older equipment from a variety of foreign suppliers, particularly Brazil and the US; since 2010, Paraguay has acquired small quantities of mostly second-hand military equipment from several countries, including Argentina, Brazil, Israel, Taiwan, and the US (2022)

Military service age and obligation: 18 years of age for compulsory (men) and voluntary (men and women) military service; conscript service obligation is 12 months for Army, 24 months for Navy; conscripts also serve in the National Police; volunteers for the Air Force must be younger than 22 years of age with a secondary school diploma (2022)
note: as of 2021, women made up about 6% of the active military

Military - note: as of 2022, the armed forces were conducting operations against the Paraguayan People's Army (Ejército del Pueblo Paraguayo, EPP), a Marxist-nationalist insurgent group operating in the rural northern part of the country along the border with Brazil; they were also assisting internal security forces in countering narco-trafficking networks

TERRORISM

Terrorist group(s): Hizballah (2022)

TRANSNATIONAL ISSUES

Disputes - international: *Paraguay-Argentina-Brazil:* unruly region at convergence of Paraguay-Argentina-Brazil borders is locus of money laundering, smuggling, arms and illegal narcotics trafficking, and fundraising for violent extremist organizations

Refugees and internally displaced persons: *refugees (country of origin):* 5,900 (Venezuela) (2022)

Illicit drugs: cannabis cultivation and the trafficking of Andean cocaine in the tri-border area shared with Argentina and Brazil facilitates money laundering, violence and other criminal activity.

PERU

INTRODUCTION

Background: Ancient Peru was the seat of several prominent Andean civilizations, most notably that of the Incas whose empire was captured by Spanish conquistadors in 1533. Peru declared its independence in 1821, and remaining Spanish forces were defeated in 1824. After a dozen years of military rule, Peru returned to democratic leadership in 1980 but experienced economic problems and the growth of a violent insurgency. President Alberto FUJIMORI's election in 1990 ushered in a decade that saw a dramatic turnaround in the economy and significant progress in curtailing guerrilla activity. Nevertheless, the president's increasing reliance on authoritarian measures and an economic slump in the late 1990s generated mounting dissatisfaction with his regime, which led to his resignation in 2000. A caretaker government oversaw a new election in the spring of 2001, which installed Alejandro TOLEDO Manrique as the new head of government - Peru's first democratically elected president of indigenous ethnicity. The presidential election of 2006 saw the return of Alan GARCIA Perez who, after a disappointing presidential term from 1985 to 1990, oversaw a robust economic rebound. Former army officer Ollanta HUMALA Tasso was elected president in June 2011, and carried on the sound, market-oriented economic policies of the three preceding administrations. Poverty and unemployment levels have fallen dramatically in the last decade, and today Peru boasts one of the best performing economies in Latin America. Pedro Pablo KUCZYNSKI Godard won a very narrow presidential runoff election in June 2016. Facing impeachment after evidence surfaced of his involvement in a vote-buying scandal, President KUCZYNSKI offered his resignation on 21 March 2018. Two days later, First Vice President Martin Alberto VIZCARRA Cornejo was sworn in as president. On 30 September 2019, President VIZCARRA invoked his constitutional authority to dissolve Peru's Congress after months of battling with the body over anticorruption reforms. New congressional elections took place on 26 January 2020 resulting in the return of an opposition-led legislature. President VIZCARRA was impeached by Congress on 9 November 2020 for a second time and removed from office after being accused of corruption and mishandling of the COVID-19 pandemic. Because of vacancies in the vice-presidential positions, constitutional succession led to the President of the Peruvian Congress, Manuel MERINO, becoming the next president of Peru. His ascension to office was not well received by the population, and large protests forced his resignation on 15 November 2020. On 17 November, Francisco SAGASTI assumed the position of President of Peru after being appointed President of the Congress the previous day. Jose Pedro CASTILLO Terrones won the second round of presidential elections on 6 June 2021 and was inaugurated on 28 July.

GEOGRAPHY

Location: Western South America, bordering the South Pacific Ocean, between Chile and Ecuador

Geographic coordinates: 10 00 S, 76 00 W

Map references: South America

Area: *total:* 1,285,216 sq km
land: 1,279,996 sq km
water: 5,220 sq km
country comparison to the world: 21

Area - comparative: almost twice the size of Texas; slightly smaller than Alaska

Land boundaries: *total:* 7,062 km
border countries (5): Bolivia 1,212 km; Brazil 2,659 km; Chile 168 km; Colombia 1,494 km; Ecuador 1,529 km

Coastline: 2,414 km

Maritime claims: *territorial sea:* 200 nm; note: the US does not recognize this claim
exclusive economic zone: 200 nm
continental shelf: 200 nm

Climate: varies from tropical in east to dry desert in west; temperate to frigid in Andes

Terrain: western coastal plain (costa), high and rugged Andes in center (sierra), eastern lowland jungle of Amazon Basin (selva)

Elevation: *highest point:* Nevado Huascaran 6,746 m
lowest point: Pacific Ocean 0 m
mean elevation: 1,555 m

Natural resources: copper, silver, gold, petroleum, timber, fish, iron ore, coal, phosphate, potash, hydropower, natural gas

Land use: *agricultural land:* 18.8% (2018 est.)
arable land: 3.1% (2018 est.)
permanent crops: 1.1% (2018 est.)
permanent pasture: 14.6% (2018 est.)
forest: 53% (2018 est.)
other: 28.2% (2018 est.)

Irrigated land: 25,800 sq km (2012)

Major lakes (area sq km): *fresh water lake(s):* Lago Titicaca (shared with Bolivia) - 8,030 sq km

Major rivers (by length in km): Amazon river source (shared with Brazil [m]) - 6,400 km
note – [s] after country name indicates river source; [m] after country name indicates river mouth

Major watersheds (area sq km): Atlantic Ocean drainage: Amazon (6,145,186 sq km)

Major aquifers: Amazon Basin

Population distribution: approximately one-third of the population resides along the desert coastal belt in the west, with a strong focus on the capital city of Lima; the Andean highlands, or sierra, which is strongly identified with the country's Amerindian population, contains roughly half of the overall population; the eastern slopes of the Andes, and adjoining rainforest, are sparsely populated

Natural hazards: earthquakes, tsunamis, flooding, landslides, mild volcanic activity
volcanism: volcanic activity in the Andes Mountains; Ubinas (5,672 m), which last erupted in 2009, is the country's most active volcano; other historically active volcanoes include El Misti, Huaynaputina, Sabancaya, and Yucamane; see note 2 under "Geography - note"

Geography - note: *note 1:* shares control of Lago Titicaca, world's highest navigable lake, with Bolivia; a remote slope of Nevado Mismi, a 5,316 m peak, is the ultimate source of the Amazon River
note 2: Peru is one of the countries along the Ring of Fire, a belt of active volcanoes and earthquake epicenters bordering the Pacific Ocean; up to 90% of the world's earthquakes and some 75% of the world's volcanoes occur within the Ring of Fire
note 3: on 19 February 1600, Mount Huaynaputina in the southern Peruvian Andes erupted in the largest volcanic explosion in South America in historical times; intermittent eruptions lasted until 5 March 1600 and pumped an estimated 16 to 32 million metric tons of particulates into the atmosphere reducing the amount of sunlight reaching the earth's surface and affecting weather worldwide; over the next two and a half years, millions died around the globe in famines from bitterly cold winters, cool summers, and the loss of crops and animals
note 4: the southern regions of Peru and the extreme northwestern part of Bolivia are considered to be the place of origin for the common potato

PEOPLE AND SOCIETY

Population: 32,275,736 (2022 est.)
country comparison to the world: 45

Nationality: *noun:* Peruvian(s)
adjective: Peruvian

Ethnic groups: Mestizo (mixed Amerindian and White) 60.2%, Amerindian 25.8%, White 5.9%, African descent 3.6%, other (includes Chinese and Japanese descent) 1.2%, unspecified 3.3% (2017 est.)

Languages: Spanish (official) 82.9%, Quechua (official) 13.6%, Aymara (official) 1.6%, Ashaninka 0.3%, other native languages (includes a large number of minor Amazonian languages) 0.8%, other (includes foreign languages and sign language) 0.2%, none 0.1%, unspecified 0.7% (2017 est.)
major-language sample(s): La Libreta Informativa del Mundo, la fuente indispensable de información básica. (Spanish)

Religions: Roman Catholic 60%, Christian 14.6% (includes Evangelical 11.1%, other 3.5%), other 0.3%, none 4%, unspecified 21.1% (2017 est.)

Demographic profile: Peru's urban and coastal communities have benefited much more from recent economic growth than rural, Afro-Peruvian, indigenous, and poor populations of the Amazon and mountain regions. The poverty rate has dropped substantially during the last decade but remains stubbornly high at about 30% (more than 55% in rural areas). After remaining almost static for about a decade, Peru's malnutrition rate began falling in 2005, when the government introduced a coordinated strategy focusing on hygiene, sanitation, and clean water. School enrollment has improved, but achievement scores reflect ongoing problems with educational quality. Many poor children temporarily or permanently drop out of school to help support their families. About a quarter to a third of Peruvian children aged 6 to 14 work, often putting in long hours at hazardous mining or construction sites.

Peru was a country of immigration in the 19th and early 20th centuries, but has become a country of emigration in the last few decades. Beginning in the 19th century, Peru brought in Asian contract laborers mainly to work on coastal plantations. Populations of Chinese and Japanese descent - among the largest in Latin America - are economically and culturally influential in Peru today. Peruvian emigration began rising in the 1980s due to an economic crisis and a violent internal conflict, but outflows have stabilized in the last few years as economic conditions have improved. Nonetheless, more than 2 million Peruvians have emigrated in the last decade, principally to the US, Spain, and Argentina.

Age structure: *0-14 years:* 25.43% (male 4,131,985/female 3,984,546)
15-24 years: 17.21% (male 2,756,024/female 2,736,394)
25-54 years: 41.03% (male 6,279,595/female 6,815,159)
55-64 years: 8.28% (male 1,266,595/female 1,375,708)
65 years and over: 8.05% (male 1,207,707/female 1,361,276) (2020 est.)

Dependency ratios: *total dependency ratio:* 50.2
youth dependency ratio: 37.1
elderly dependency ratio: 13.1
potential support ratio: 7.6 (2020 est.)

Median age: *total:* 29.1 years
male: 28.3 years
female: 29.9 years (2020 est.)
country comparison to the world: 138

Population growth rate: 0.51% (2022 est.)
country comparison to the world: 154

Birth rate: 17.21 births/1,000 population (2022 est.)
country comparison to the world: 92

Death rate: 11.32 deaths/1,000 population (2022 est.)
country comparison to the world: 19

Net migration rate: -0.75 migrant(s)/1,000 population (2022 est.)
country comparison to the world: 135

Population distribution: approximately one-third of the population resides along the desert coastal belt in the west, with a strong focus on the capital city of Lima; the Andean highlands, or sierra, which is strongly identified with the country's Amerindian population, contains roughly half of the overall population; the eastern slopes of the Andes, and adjoining rainforest, are sparsely populated

Urbanization: *urban population:* 78.7% of total population (2022)
rate of urbanization: 1.33% annual rate of change (2020-25 est.)

Major urban areas - population: 11.045 million LIMA (capital), 947,000 Arequipa, 891,000 Trujillo (2022)

Sex ratio: *at birth:* 1.05 male(s)/female
0-14 years: 1.04 male(s)/female
15-24 years: 1.01 male(s)/female
25-54 years: 0.95 male(s)/female
55-64 years: 0.9 male(s)/female
65 years and over: 0.63 male(s)/female
total population: 0.96 male(s)/female (2022 est.)

Mother's mean age at first birth: 21.9 years (2013 est.)
note: data represents median age at first birth among women 25-49

Maternal mortality ratio: 88 deaths/100,000 live births (2017 est.)
country comparison to the world: 76

Infant mortality rate: *total:* 10.8 deaths/1,000 live births
male: 11.89 deaths/1,000 live births
female: 9.65 deaths/1,000 live births (2022 est.)
country comparison to the world: 132

Life expectancy at birth: *total population:* 68.94 years
male: 65.38 years
female: 72.67 years (2022 est.)
country comparison to the world: 181

Total fertility rate: 2.2 children born/woman (2022 est.)
country comparison to the world: 88

Contraceptive prevalence rate: 76.3% (2018)

Drinking water source: *improved: urban:* 97.2% of population
rural: 82.4% of population
total: 94% of population
unimproved: urban: 2.8% of population
rural: 17.6% of population
total: 6% of population (2020 est.)

Current health expenditure: 5.2% of GDP (2019)

Physicians density: 1.37 physicians/1,000 population (2018)

Hospital bed density: 1.6 beds/1,000 population (2017)

Sanitation facility access: *improved: urban:* 93.6% of population
rural: 65.3% of population
total: 87.4% of population
unimproved: urban: 6.4% of population
rural: 34.7% of population
total: 12.6% of population (2020 est.)

HIV/AIDS - adult prevalence rate: 0.3% (2020 est.)
country comparison to the world: 90

HIV/AIDS - people living with HIV/AIDS: 91,000 (2020 est.)
country comparison to the world: 48

HIV/AIDS - deaths: (2020 est.) <1000

Major infectious diseases: *degree of risk:* very high (2020)
food or waterborne diseases: bacterial diarrhea, hepatitis A, and typhoid fever
vectorborne diseases: dengue fever, malaria, and Bartonellosis (Oroya fever)
note: widespread ongoing transmission of a respiratory illness caused by the novel coronavirus (COVID-19) is occurring throughout Peru; as of 18 August 2022, Peru has reported a total of 4,037,977 cases of COVID-19 or 12,246.73 cumulative cases of COVID-19 per 100,000 population with a total of 215,088 cumulative deaths or a rate of 652.33 cumulative deaths per 100,000 population; as of 14 August 2022, 88.19% of the population has received at least one dose of COVID-19 vaccine

Obesity - adult prevalence rate: 19.7% (2016)
country comparison to the world: 110

Alcohol consumption per capita: *total:* 5.74 liters of pure alcohol (2019 est.)
beer: 3.01 liters of pure alcohol (2019 est.)
wine: 0.46 liters of pure alcohol (2019 est.)
spirits: 2.26 liters of pure alcohol (2019 est.)
other alcohols: 0.01 liters of pure alcohol (2019 est.)
country comparison to the world: 76

Tobacco use: *total:* 8.1% (2020 est.)
male: 13.2% (2020 est.)
female: 3% (2020 est.)
country comparison to the world: 149

Children under the age of 5 years underweight: 2.4% (2019)
country comparison to the world: 105

Child marriage: *women married by age 15:* 2.5%
women married by age 18: 17.4% (2018 est.)

Education expenditures: 4.2% of GDP (2020 est.)
country comparison to the world: 96

Literacy: *definition:* age 15 and over can read and write
total population: 94.5%
male: 97%
female: 92% (2020)

School life expectancy (primary to tertiary education): *total:* 15 years
male: 15 years
female: 15 years (2017)

Unemployment, youth ages 15-24: *total:* 12.6%
male: 13%
female: 12.1% (2020 est.)

ENVIRONMENT

Environment - current issues: deforestation (some the result of illegal logging); overgrazing leading to soil erosion; desertification; air pollution in Lima; pollution of rivers and coastal waters from municipal and mining wastes; overfishing

Environment - international agreements: *party to:* Antarctic-Environmental Protection, Antarctic-Marine Living Resources, Antarctic Treaty, Biodiversity, Climate Change, Climate Change-Kyoto Protocol, Climate Change-Paris Agreement, Desertification, Endangered Species, Hazardous Wastes, Marine Dumping-London Convention, Marine Dumping-London Protocol, Nuclear Test Ban, Ozone Layer Protection, Ship Pollution, Tropical Timber 2006, Wetlands, Whaling
signed, but not ratified: none of the selected agreements

Air pollutants: *particulate matter emissions:* 24.27 micrograms per cubic meter (2016 est.)
carbon dioxide emissions: 57.41 megatons (2016 est.)
methane emissions: 30.17 megatons (2020 est.)

Climate: varies from tropical in east to dry desert in west; temperate to frigid in Andes

Land use: *agricultural land:* 18.8% (2018 est.)
arable land: 3.1% (2018 est.)
permanent crops: 1.1% (2018 est.)
permanent pasture: 14.6% (2018 est.)

forest: 53% (2018 est.)
other: 28.2% (2018 est.)

Urbanization: *urban population:* 78.7% of total population (2022)
rate of urbanization: 1.33% annual rate of change (2020-25 est.)

Revenue from forest resources: *forest revenues:* 0.12% of GDP (2018 est.)
country comparison to the world: 109

Revenue from coal: *coal revenues:* 0% of GDP (2018 est.)
country comparison to the world: 152

Waste and recycling: *municipal solid waste generated annually:* 8,356,711 tons (2014 est.)
municipal solid waste recycled annually: 334,268 tons (2012 est.)
percent of municipal solid waste recycled: 4% (2012 est.)

Major lakes (area sq km): *fresh water lake(s):* Lago Titicaca (shared with Bolivia) - 8,030 sq km

Major rivers (by length in km): Amazon river source (shared with Brazil [m]) - 6,400 km
note – [s] after country name indicates river source; [m] after country name indicates river mouth

Major watersheds (area sq km): Atlantic Ocean drainage: Amazon (6,145,186 sq km)

Major aquifers: Amazon Basin

Total water withdrawal: *municipal:* 2.797 billion cubic meters (2017 est.)
industrial: 206.6 million cubic meters (2017 est.)
agricultural: 13.1 billion cubic meters (2017 est.)

Total renewable water resources: 1.88 trillion cubic meters (2017 est.)

GOVERNMENT

Country name: *conventional long form:* Republic of Peru
conventional short form: Peru
local long form: Republica del Peru
local short form: Peru
etymology: exact meaning is obscure, but the name may derive from a native word "biru" meaning "river"

Government type: presidential republic

Capital: *name:* Lima
geographic coordinates: 12 03 S, 77 03 W
time difference: UTC-5 (same time as Washington, DC, during Standard Time)
etymology: the word "Lima" derives from the Spanish pronunciation of "Limaq," the native name for the valley in which the city was founded in 1535; "limaq" means "talker" in coastal Quechua and referred to an oracle that was situated in the valley but which was eventually destroyed by the Spanish and replaced with a church

Administrative divisions: 25 regions (regiones, singular - region) and 1 province* (provincia); Amazonas, Ancash, Apurimac, Arequipa, Ayacucho, Cajamarca, Callao, Cusco, Huancavelica, Huanuco, Ica, Junin, La Libertad, Lambayeque, Lima, Lima*, Loreto, Madre de Dios, Moquegua, Pasco, Piura, Puno, San Martin, Tacna, Tumbes, Ucayali
note: Callao, the largest port in Peru, is also referred to as a constitutional province, the only province of the Callao region

Independence: 28 July 1821 (from Spain)

National holiday: Independence Day, 28-29 July (1821)

Constitution: *history:* several previous; latest promulgated 29 December 1993, enacted 31 December 1993
amendments: proposed by Congress, by the president of the republic with the approval of the Council of Ministers or by petition of at least 0.3% of voters; passage requires absolute majority approval by the Congress membership, followed by approval in a referendum; a referendum is not required if Congress approves the amendment by greater than two-thirds majority vote in each of two successive sessions; amended many times, last in 2021

Legal system: civil law system

International law organization participation: accepts compulsory ICJ jurisdiction with reservations; accepts ICCt jurisdiction

Citizenship: *citizenship by birth:* yes
citizenship by descent only: yes
dual citizenship recognized: yes
residency requirement for naturalization: 2 years

Suffrage: 18 years of age; universal and compulsory until the age of 70

Executive branch: *chief of state:* President Jose Pedro CASTILLO Terrones (since 28 July 2021); First Vice President Dina Ercilia BOLUARTE Zegarra (since 28 July 2021); Second Vice President (vacant); note - the president is both chief of state and head of government
head of government: President Jose Pedro CASTILLO Terrones (since 28 July 2021); First Vice President Dina Ercilia BOLUARTE Zegarra (since 28 July 2021); Second Vice President (vacant)
cabinet: Council of Ministers appointed by the president
elections/appointments: president directly elected by absolute majority popular vote in 2 rounds if needed for a 5-year term (eligible for nonconsecutive terms); election last held on 11 April 2021 with a runoff on 6 June 2021 (next to be held in April 2026)
election results:
2021: Jose Pedro CASTILLO Terrones elected president in second round; percent of vote in first round - Jose Pedro CASTILLO Terrones (Free Peru) 18.9%, Keiko Sofia FUJIMORI Higuchi (Popular Force) 13.4%, Rafael LOPEZ ALIAGA Cazorla (Popular Renewal) 11.8%, Hernando DE SOTO Polar (Social Integration Party) 11.6%, Yonhy LESCANO Ancieta (Popular Action) 9.1%, Veronika MENDOZA Frisch (JP) 7.9%, Cesar ACUNA Peralta (APP) 6%, George FORSYTH Sommer (National Victory) 5.7%, Daniel Belizario URRESTI Elera (We Can Peru) 5.6%, other 10%; percent of vote second round - Jose Pedro CASTILLO Terrones (Free Peru) 50.1%, Keiko Sofia FUJIMORI Higuchi (Popular Force) 49.9%
2016: Pedro Pablo KUCZYNSKI Godard elected president in second round; percent of vote in first round - Keiko FUJIMORI Higuchi (Popular Force) 39.9%, Pedro Pablo KUCZYNSKI Godard (PPK) 21.1%, Veronika MENDOZA (Broad Front) 18.7%, Alfredo BARNECHEA (Popular Action) 7%, Alan GARCIA (APRA) 5.8%, other 7.5%; percent of vote in second round - Pedro Pablo KUCZYNSKI Godard 50.1%, Keiko FUJIMORI Higuchi 49.9%
note 1: President Martin Alberto VIZCARRA Cornejo assumed office after President Pedro Pablo KUCZYNSKI Godard resigned from office on 21 March 2018; after VIZCARRA was impeached on 9 November 2020, the constitutional line of succession led to the inauguration of the President of the Peruvian Congress, Manuel Arturo MERINO, as President of Peru on 10 November 2020; following his resignation only days later on 15 November 2020, Francisco Rafael SAGASTI Hochhausler - who had been elected by the legislature to be the new President of Congress on 16 November 2020 - was then sworn in as President of Peru on 17 November 2020 by line of succession and remained president until the inauguration of Jose Pedro CASTILLO Terrones, winner of the 2021 presidential election
note 2: Prime Minister Anibal TORRES Vasquez (since 8 February 2022) does not exercise executive power; this power rests with the president

Legislative branch: *description:* unicameral Congress of the Republic of Peru or Congreso de la Republica del Peru (130 seats; members directly elected in multi-seat constituencies by closed party-list proportional representation vote to serve single 5-year terms)
elections:
last held on 11 April 2021 (next to be held in April 2026)
election results:
percent of vote by party/coalition - NA; seats by party/coalition - Free Peru 32, Popular Force 24, AP 15, APP 15, Avanza Pais 10, Popular Renewal 9, Democratic Peru 7, We Are Peru 5, We Can Peru 5, JP 5, Purple Party 3; composition - men 78, women 52, percent of women 40%

Judicial branch: *highest court(s):* Supreme Court (consists of 16 judges and divided into civil, criminal, and constitutional-social sectors)
judge selection and term of office: justices proposed by the National Board of Justice (a 7-member independent body), nominated by the president, and confirmed by the Congress; justices can serve until mandatory retirement at age 70
subordinate courts: Court of Constitutional Guarantees; Superior Courts or Cortes Superiores; specialized civil, criminal, and mixed courts; 2 types of peace courts in which professional judges and selected members of the local communities preside

Political parties and leaders: Advance the Nation (Avanza Pais) [Aldo BORRERO Zeta]
Alliance for Progress (Alianza para el Progreso) or APP [Cesar ACUNA Peralta]
Broad Front (Frente Amplio) or FA [Marco ARANA]
Free Peru (Peru Libre) or PL [Vladimir CERRON Rojas]
Front for Hope (Frente Esperanza) [Fernando OLIVERA Vega]
National Victory (Victoria Nacional) or VN [George FORSYTH Sommer]
Popular Action (Accion Popular) or AP [Mesias GUEVARA Amasifuen]
Popular Force (Fuerza Popular) or FP [Keiko FUJIMORI Higuchi]
Popular Renewal (Renovacion Popular) or RP [Rafael LOPEZ ALIAGA]
Purple Party (Partido Morado) [Luis DURAN Rojo]
Social Integration Party (Avanza Pais - Partido de Integracion Social) [Aldo BORRERO]
Together For Peru (Juntos por el Peru) or JP [Robert SANCHEZ Palomino]
We Are Peru (Somos Peru) of SP [Patricia LI]
We Can Peru (Podemos Peru) or PP [Jose Leon LUNA Galvez]

International organization participation: APEC, BIS, CAN, CD, CELAC, EITI (compliant country),

FAO, G-24, G-77, IADB, IAEA, IBRD, ICAO, ICC (NGOs), ICCt, ICRM, IDA, IFAD, IFC, IFRCS, IHO, ILO, IMF, IMO, IMSO, Interpol, IOC, IOM, IPU, ISO, ITSO, ITU, ITUC (NGOs), LAES, LAIA, Mercosur (associate), MIGA, MINUSTAH, MONUSCO, NAM, OAS, OPANAL, OPCW, Pacific Alliance, PCA, PROSUR, SICA (observer), UN, UNAMID, UNASUR, UNCTAD, UNESCO, UNHCR, UNIDO, Union Latina, UNISFA, UNMISS, UNOCI, UN Security Council (temporary), UNWTO, UPU, WCO, WFTU (NGOs), WHO, WIPO, WMO, WTO

Diplomatic representation in the US: *chief of mission:* Ambassador Oswaldo DE RIVERO Barreto (since 17 November 2021)
chancery: 1700 Massachusetts Avenue NW, Washington, DC 20036
telephone: [1] (202) 833-9860 through 9869
FAX: [1] (202) 659-8124
email address and website:
Webadmin@embassyofperu.us
consulate(s) general: Atlanta, Boston, Chicago, Dallas, Denver, Hartford (CT), Houston, Los Angeles, Miami, New York, Paterson (NJ), San Francisco, Washington DC

Diplomatic representation from the US: *chief of mission:* Ambassador Lisa Suzanne KENNA (since 18 March 2021)
embassy: Avenida La Encalada, Cuadra 17 s/n, Surco, Lima 33
mailing address: 3230 Lima Place, Washington DC 20521-3230
telephone: [51] (1) 618-2000
FAX: [51] (1) 618-2724
email address and website:
LimaACS@state.gov
https://pe.usembassy.gov/

Flag description: three equal, vertical bands of red (hoist side), white, and red with the coat of arms centered in the white band; the coat of arms features a shield bearing a vicuna (representing fauna), a cinchona tree (the source of quinine, signifying flora), and a yellow cornucopia spilling out coins (denoting mineral wealth); red recalls blood shed for independence, white symbolizes peace

National symbol(s): vicuna (a camelid related to the llama); national colors: red, white

National anthem: *name:* "Himno Nacional del Peru" (National Anthem of Peru)
lyrics/music: Jose DE LA TORRE Ugarte/Jose Bernardo ALZEDO
note: adopted 1822; the song won a national anthem contest

National heritage: *total World Heritage Sites:* 13 (9 cultural, 2 natural, 2 mixed)
selected World Heritage Site locales: Cuzco (c); Machu Picchu (m); Chavin (c); Historic Lima (c); Huascarán National Park (n); Chan Chan (c); Manú National Park (n); Lines and Geoglyphs of Nazca (c); Rio Abiseo National Park (m); Historic Arequipa (c); Sacred City of Caral-Supe (c); Qhapaq Ñan/ Andean Road System (c)

ECONOMY

Economic overview: Peru's economy reflects its varied topography - an arid lowland coastal region, the central high sierra of the Andes, and the dense forest of the Amazon. A wide range of important mineral resources are found in the mountainous and coastal areas, and Peru's coastal waters provide excellent fishing grounds. Peru is the world's second largest producer of silver and copper.

The Peruvian economy grew by an average of 5.6% per year from 2009-13 with a stable exchange rate and low inflation. This growth was due partly to high international prices for Peru's metals and minerals exports, which account for 55% of the country's total exports. Growth slipped from 2014 to 2017, due to weaker world prices for these resources. Despite Peru's strong macroeconomic performance, dependence on minerals and metals exports and imported foodstuffs makes the economy vulnerable to fluctuations in world prices.

Peru's rapid expansion coupled with cash transfers and other programs have helped to reduce the national poverty rate by over 35 percentage points since 2004, but inequality persists and continued to pose a challenge for the Ollanta HUMALA administration, which championed a policy of social inclusion and a more equitable distribution of income. Poor infrastructure hinders the spread of growth to Peru's non-coastal areas. The HUMALA administration passed several economic stimulus packages in 2014 to bolster growth, including reforms to environmental regulations in order to spur investment in Peru's lucrative mining sector, a move that was opposed by some environmental groups. However, in 2015, mining investment fell as global commodity prices remained low and social conflicts plagued the sector.

Peru's free trade policy continued under the HUMALA administration; since 2006, Peru has signed trade deals with the US, Canada, Singapore, China, Korea, Mexico, Japan, the EU, the European Free Trade Association, Chile, Thailand, Costa Rica, Panama, Venezuela, Honduras, concluded negotiations with Guatemala and the Trans-Pacific Partnership, and begun trade talks with El Salvador, India, and Turkey. Peru also has signed a trade pact with Chile, Colombia, and Mexico, called the Pacific Alliance, that seeks integration of services, capital, investment and movement of people. Since the US-Peru Trade Promotion Agreement entered into force in February 2009, total trade between Peru and the US has doubled. President Pedro Pablo KUCZYNSKI succeeded HUMALA in July 2016 and is focusing on economic reforms and free market policies aimed at boosting investment in Peru. Mining output increased significantly in 2016-17, which helped Peru attain one of the highest GDP growth rates in Latin America, and Peru should maintain strong growth in 2018. However, economic performance was depressed by delays in infrastructure mega-projects and the start of a corruption scandal associated with a Brazilian firm. Massive flooding in early 2017 also was a drag on growth, offset somewhat by additional public spending aimed at recovery efforts.

Real GDP (purchasing power parity): $371.29 billion (2020 est.)
$417.88 billion (2019 est.)
$408.87 billion (2018 est.)
note: data are in 2017 dollars
country comparison to the world: 49

Real GDP growth rate: 2.18% (2019 est.)
3.97% (2018 est.)
2.48% (2017 est.)
country comparison to the world: 128

Real GDP per capita: $11,300 (2020 est.)
$12,900 (2019 est.)
$12,800 (2018 est.)
note: data are in 2017 dollars
country comparison to the world: 133

GDP (official exchange rate): $230.707 billion (2019 est.)

Inflation rate (consumer prices): 2.1% (2019 est.)
1.3% (2018 est.)
2.8% (2017 est.)
note: data are for metropolitan Lima, annual average
country comparison to the world: 113

Credit ratings:

Fitch rating: BBB+ (2013)

Moody's rating: A3 (2014)

Standard & Poors rating: BBB+ (2013)

GDP - composition, by sector of origin: *agriculture:* 7.6% (2017 est.)
industry: 32.7% (2017 est.)
services: 59.9% (2017 est.)

GDP - composition, by end use: *household consumption:* 64.9% (2017 est.)
government consumption: 11.7% (2017 est.)
investment in fixed capital: 21.7% (2017 est.)
investment in inventories: -0.2% (2017 est.)
exports of goods and services: 24% (2017 est.)
imports of goods and services: -22% (2017 est.)

Agricultural products: sugar cane, potatoes, rice, plantains, milk, poultry, maize, cassava, oil palm fruit, grapes

Industries: mining and refining of minerals; steel, metal fabrication; petroleum extraction and refining, natural gas and natural gas liquefaction; fishing and fish processing, cement, glass, textiles, clothing, food processing, beer, soft drinks, rubber, machinery, electrical machinery, chemicals, furniture

Industrial production growth rate: 2.7% (2017 est.)
country comparison to the world: 113

Labor force: 3.421 million (2020 est.)
note: individuals older than 14 years of age
country comparison to the world: 101

Labor force - by occupation: *agriculture:* 25.8%
industry: 17.4%
services: 56.8% (2011)

Unemployment rate: 6.58% (2019 est.)
6.73% (2018 est.)
note: data are for metropolitan Lima; widespread underemployment
country comparison to the world: 104

Unemployment, youth ages 15-24: *total:* 12.6%
male: 13%
female: 12.1% (2020 est.)
country comparison to the world: 121

Population below poverty line: 20.2% (2019 est.)

Gini Index coefficient - distribution of family income: 42.8 (2018 est.)
51 (2005)
country comparison to the world: 42

Household income or consumption by percentage share: *lowest 10%:* 1.4%
highest 10%: 36.1% (2010 est.)

Budget: *revenues:* 58.06 billion (2017 est.)
expenditures: 64.81 billion (2017 est.)

Budget surplus (+) or deficit (-): -3.1% (of GDP) (2017 est.)
country comparison to the world: 135

Public debt: 25.4% of GDP (2017 est.)
24.5% of GDP (2016 est.)

note: data cover general government debt, and includes debt instruments issued by government entities other than the treasury; the data exclude treasury debt held by foreign entities; the data include debt issued by subnational entities
country comparison to the world: 174

Taxes and other revenues: 27.1% (of GDP) (2017 est.)
country comparison to the world: 103

Fiscal year: calendar year

Current account balance: -$3.531 billion (2019 est.)
-$3.821 billion (2018 est.)
country comparison to the world: 177

Exports: $54.88 billion (2019 est.) note: data are in current year dollars
$55.84 billion (2018 est.) note: data are in current year dollars
$53.823 billion (2017 est.)
country comparison to the world: 54

Exports - partners: China 29%, United States 12%, Canada 5%, South Korea 5%, Switzerland 5% (2019)

Exports - commodities: copper, gold, refined petroleum, zinc, fishmeal, tropical fruits, lead, iron, molybdenum (2019)

Imports: $51.38 billion (2019 est.) note: data are in current year dollars
$51.41 billion (2018 est.) note: data are in current year dollars
$46.15 billion (2017 est.)
country comparison to the world: 59

Imports - partners: China 24%, United States 22%, Brazil 6% (2019)

Imports - commodities: refined petroleum, crude petroleum, cars, broadcasting equipment, delivery trucks (2019)

Reserves of foreign exchange and gold: $63.83 billion (31 December 2017 est.)
$61.81 billion (31 December 2016 est.)
country comparison to the world: 35

Debt - external: $81.333 billion (2019 est.)
$75.467 billion (2018 est.)
country comparison to the world: 60

Exchange rates: nuevo sol (PEN) per US dollar -
3.599 (2020 est.)
3.3799 (2019 est.)
3.366 (2018 est.)
3.185 (2014 est.)
2.8383 (2013 est.)

ENERGY

Electricity access: *electrification - total population:* 97% (2019)
electrification - urban areas: 99% (2019)
electrification - rural areas: 86% (2019)

Electricity: *installed generating capacity:* 15.34 million kW (2020 est.)
consumption: 49,121,370,000 kWh (2019 est.)
exports: 0 kWh (2019 est.)
imports: 60 million kWh (2019 est.)
transmission/distribution losses: 6.408 billion kWh (2019 est.)

Electricity generation sources: *fossil fuels:* 38.5% of total installed capacity (2020 est.)
solar: 1.5% of total installed capacity (2020 est.)
wind: 3.5% of total installed capacity (2020 est.)
hydroelectricity: 55.4% of total installed capacity (2020 est.)
biomass and waste: 1.1% of total installed capacity (2020 est.)

Coal: *production:* 696,000 metric tons (2020 est.)
consumption: 396,000 metric tons (2020 est.)
exports: 252,000 metric tons (2020 est.)
imports: 262,000 metric tons (2020 est.)
proven reserves: 102 million metric tons (2019 est.)

Petroleum: *total petroleum production:* 122,500 bbl/day (2021 est.)
refined petroleum consumption: 265,500 bbl/day (2019 est.)
crude oil and lease condensate exports: 6,500 bbl/day (2018 est.)
crude oil and lease condensate imports: 112,900 bbl/day (2018 est.)
crude oil estimated reserves: 858.9 million barrels (2021 est.)

Refined petroleum products - production: 166,600 bbl/day (2015 est.)
country comparison to the world: 57

Refined petroleum products - exports: 62,640 bbl/day (2015 est.)
country comparison to the world: 49

Refined petroleum products - imports: 65,400 bbl/day (2015 est.)
country comparison to the world: 71

Natural gas: *production:* 12,079,211,000 cubic meters (2020 est.)
consumption: 8,278,048,000 cubic meters (2019 est.)
exports: 5.446 billion cubic meters (2019 est.)
imports: 0 cubic meters (2021 est.)
proven reserves: 300.158 billion cubic meters (2021 est.)

Carbon dioxide emissions: 54.996 million metric tonnes of CO2 (2019 est.)
from coal and metallurgical coke: 1.171 million metric tonnes of CO2 (2019 est.)
from petroleum and other liquids: 35.119 million metric tonnes of CO2 (2019 est.)
from consumed natural gas: 18.706 million metric tonnes of CO2 (2019 est.)
country comparison to the world: 55

Energy consumption per capita: 36.465 million Btu/person (2019 est.)
country comparison to the world: 112

COMMUNICATIONS

Telephones - fixed lines: *total subscriptions:* 2.47 million (2020 est.)
subscriptions per 100 inhabitants: 7 (2020 est.)
country comparison to the world: 51

Telephones - mobile cellular: *total subscriptions:* 44 million (2020 est.)
subscriptions per 100 inhabitants: 133 (2020 est.)
country comparison to the world: 35

Telecommunication systems: *general assessment:* after suffering a sharp retraction in the number of subscriptions and revenue during 2020 due to the pandemic, Peru's telecom sector managed to stage a small recovery in the first half of 2021; it will likely be two to three years before penetration rates return to the peak levels last seen in 2018; this is especially true given the overwhelming influence of mobile on Peru's telecommunications market, which now commands almost 95% of all connections; Peru's fixed-line teledensity continued its slow dropping below 7% at the end of 2021; investment in network infrastructure is mainly focused on rolling out fiber cable for fixed broadband services in (mainly) urban areas; fixed broadband services inched higher to reach 8.4% at the end of 2020, a positive result that reflected the shift to working from home during enforced lock downs at the start of the year; yet Peru has a relatively low level of computer use, and prices for fixed broadband services are among the highest in Latin America; the overwhelmingly preferred internet access platform will remain the smartphone, with a further 8.6% growth in the number of mobile broadband subscriptions expected in 2021 (2021)
domestic: fixed-line teledensity is nearly 10 per 100 persons; mobile-cellular teledensity, spurred by competition among multiple providers, now nearly 124 telephones per 100 persons; nationwide microwave radio relay system and a domestic satellite system with 12 earth stations (2019)
international: country code - 51; landing points for the SAM-1, IGW, American Movil-Telxius, SAC and PAN-AM submarine cable systems that provide links to parts of Central and South America, the Caribbean, and US; satellite earth stations - 2 Intelsat (Atlantic Ocean) (2019)

Broadcast media: 10 major TV networks of which only one, Television Nacional de Peru, is state owned; multi-channel cable TV services are available; in excess of 5,000 radio stations including a substantial number of indigenous language stations (2021)

Internet country code: .pe

Internet users: *total:* 21,431,700 (2020 est.)
percent of population: 65% (2020 est.)
country comparison to the world: 37

Broadband - fixed subscriptions: *total:* 3.044 million (2020 est.)
subscriptions per 100 inhabitants: 9 (2020 est.)
country comparison to the world: 46

TRANSPORTATION

National air transport system: *number of registered air carriers:* 6 (2020)
inventory of registered aircraft operated by air carriers: 62
annual passenger traffic on registered air carriers: 17,758,527 (2018)
annual freight traffic on registered air carriers: 313.26 million (2018) mt-km

Civil aircraft registration country code prefix: OB

Airports: *total:* 191 (2021)
country comparison to the world: 31

Airports - with paved runways: *total:* 59
over 3,047 m: 5
2,438 to 3,047 m: 21
1,524 to 2,437 m: 16
914 to 1,523 m: 12
under 914 m: 5 (2021)

Airports - with unpaved runways: *total:* 132
2,438 to 3,047 m: 1
1,524 to 2,437 m: 19
914 to 1,523 m: 30
under 914 m: 82 (2021)

Heliports: 5 (2021)

Pipelines: 786 km extra heavy crude, 1,526 km gas, 679 km liquid petroleum gas, 1,106 km oil, 15 km refined products (2022)

Railways: *total:* 1,854.4 km (2017)

standard gauge: 1,730.4 km (2014) 1.435-m gauge (34 km electrified)
narrow gauge: 124 km (2014) 0.914-m gauge
country comparison to the world: 76

Roadways: *total:* 18,699 km (2018)
paved: 18,699 km
note: includes 27,109 km of national roads (21,434 km paved), 247,505 km of departmental roads (3,623 km paved), and 113,857 km of local roads (1,858 km paved)
country comparison to the world: 117

Waterways: 8,808 km (2011) (8,600 km of navigable tributaries on the Amazon River system and 208 km on Lago Titicaca)
country comparison to the world: 16

Merchant marine: *total:* 98
by type: general cargo 1, oil tanker 8, other 89 (2021)
country comparison to the world: 89

Ports and terminals: *major seaport(s):* Callao, Matarani, Paita
oil terminal(s): Conchan oil terminal, La Pampilla oil terminal
container port(s) (TEUs): Callao (2,313,907) (2019)
river port(s): Iquitos, Pucallpa, Yurimaguas (Amazon)

MILITARY AND SECURITY

Military and security forces: Joint Command of the Armed Forces of Peru (CCFFAA): Peruvian Army (Ejercito del Peru), Peruvian Navy (Marina de Guerra del Peru, MGP, includes naval infantry and Coast Guard), Air Force of Peru (Fuerza Aerea del Peru, FAP); Ministry of the Interior (Ministerio del Interior): Peruvian National Police (Policía Nacional del Perú, PNP) (2022)

Military expenditures: 1.1% of GDP (2021 est.)
1.2% of GDP (2020 est.)
1.2% of GDP (2019) (approximately $3.87 billion)
1.2% of GDP (2018) (approximately $3.83 billion)
1.2% of GDP (2017) (approximately $3.86 billion)
country comparison to the world: 123

Military and security service personnel strengths: information varies; approximately 95,000 active duty personnel (60,000 Army; 25,000 Navy, including about 4,000 naval infantry and 1,000 Coast Guard; 10,000 Air Force) (2022)

Military equipment inventories and acquisitions: the Peruvian military's inventory is a mix of mostly older equipment from a wide variety of suppliers, including Brazil, Europe, the former Soviet Union, and the US; since 2010, Peru has received military equipment from more than a dozen countries, led by Russia and South Korea (2022)

Military service age and obligation: 18-50 years of age for male and 18-45 years of age for female voluntary military service (12 months); no conscription (abolished in 1999) (2022)
note: as of 2019, women made up about 10% of the active duty military

Military deployments: 215 Central African Republic (MINUSCA) (May 2022)

Military - note: as of 2022, the Peruvian security forces continued to conduct operations against remnants of the Shining Path terrorist group (aka Sendero Luminoso; see Appendix T), particularly in the Apurimac, Ene, and Mantaro River Valleys (VRAEM) of eastern Peru; the military had approximately 8,000-10,000 troops in the VRAEM under a combined Special Command comprised of air, ground, naval, police, and special forces units (2022)

Maritime threats: the International Maritime Bureau reports the territorial waters of Peru are a risk for armed robbery against ships; in 2021, 18 attacks against commercial vessels were reported, a more than 50% increase over the eight attacks in 2020; all of these occurred in the main port of Callao while ships were berthed or at anchor

TERRORISM

Terrorist group(s): Shining Path (Sendero Luminoso)

TRANSNATIONAL ISSUES

Disputes - international: *Peru-Bolivia:* Peru rejects Bolivia's claim to restore maritime access through a sovereign corridor through Chile along the Peruvian border
Peru-Brazil: none identified
Peru-Chile: Bolivia continues to press for a sovereign corridor to the Pacific Ocean; any concession Chile makes to Bolivia to grant them a sovereign corridor requires approval by Peru under the terms of their treaty; in January 2018, the International Court of Justice ruled that Chile is not legally obligated to negotiate a sovereign corridor to the Pacific Ocean with Bolivia
Peru-Chile-Ecuador: Chile and Ecuador rejected Peru's November 2005 unilateral legislation to shift the axis of their joint treaty-defined maritime boundaries along the parallels of latitude to equidistance lines out to 200 nautical miles, which would give Peru 37,900 square kilometers of water
Peru-Colombia: organized illegal narcotics operations in Colombia have penetrated Peru's shared border; problems also include crossborder illegal migration, human trafficking, and contraband smuggling
Peru-Ecuador: in 1999, Tiwinza memorial park wasvcreated on lands that remains sovereign Peruvian territory, but Ecuador has the right to maintain and administer it in perpetuity

Refugees and internally displaced persons: *refugees (country of origin):* 1,286,434 (Venezuela) (economic and political crisis; includes Venezuelans who have claimed asylum, are recognized as refugees, or have received alternative legal stay) (2021)
IDPs: 60,000 (civil war from 1980-2000; most IDPs are indigenous peasants in Andean and Amazonian regions; as of 2011, no new information on the situation of these IDPs) (2021)

Illicit drugs: world's second-largest producer of cocaine, with an estimated 88,200 hectares under coca cultivation in 2020; cocaine is trafficked throughout South America for shipment to Europe, East Asia, Mexico, and the United States; major importer of precursor chemicals for cocaine production

PHILIPPINES

INTRODUCTION

Background: The Philippine Islands became a Spanish colony during the 16th century; they were ceded to the US in 1898 following the Spanish-American War. In 1935 the Philippines became a self-governing commonwealth. Manuel QUEZON was elected president and was tasked with preparing the country for independence after a 10-year transition. In 1942 the islands fell under Japanese occupation during World War II, and US forces and Filipinos fought together during 1944-45 to regain control. On 4 July 1946 the Republic of the Philippines attained its independence. A 21-year rule by Ferdinand MARCOS ended in 1986, when a "people power" movement in Manila ("EDSA 1") forced him into exile and installed Corazon AQUINO as president. Her presidency was hampered by several coup attempts that prevented a return to full political stability and economic development. Fidel RAMOS was elected president in 1992. His administration was marked by increased stability and by progress on economic reforms. In 1992, the US closed its last military bases on the islands. Joseph ESTRADA was elected president in 1998. He was succeeded by his vice-president, Gloria MACAPAGAL-ARROYO, in January 2001 after ESTRADA's stormy impeachment trial on corruption charges broke down and another "people power" movement ("EDSA 2") demanded his resignation. MACAPAGAL-ARROYO was elected to a six-year term as president in May 2004. Her presidency was marred by several corruption allegations, but the Philippine economy was one of the few to avoid contraction following the 2008 global financial crisis, expanding each year of her administration. Benigno AQUINO III was elected to a six-year term as president in May 2010 and was succeeded by Rodrigo DUTERTE in May 2016.

The Philippine Government faces threats from several groups, some of which are on the US Government's Foreign Terrorist Organization list. Manila has waged a decades-long struggle against ethnic Moro insurgencies in the southern Philippines, which led to a peace accord with the Moro National Liberation Front and a separate agreement with a break away faction, the Moro Islamic Liberation Front. The decades-long Maoist-inspired New People's Army insurgency also operates through much of the country. In 2017, Philippine armed forces battled an ISIS-East Asia siege in Marawi City, driving DUTERTE to declare martial law in the region. The Philippines faces increased tension with China over disputed territorial and maritime claims in the South China Sea.

GEOGRAPHY

Location: Southeastern Asia, archipelago between the Philippine Sea and the South China Sea, east of Vietnam

Geographic coordinates: 13 00 N, 122 00 E

Map references: Southeast Asia

Area: *total:* 300,000 sq km
land: 298,170 sq km
water: 1,830 sq km
country comparison to the world: 74

Area - comparative: slightly less than twice the size of Georgia; slightly larger than Arizona

Land boundaries: *total:* 0 km

Coastline: 36,289 km

Maritime claims: *territorial sea:* irregular polygon extending up to 100 nm from coastline as defined by 1898 treaty; since late 1970s has also claimed polygonal-shaped area in South China Sea as wide as 285 nm
exclusive economic zone: 200 nm
continental shelf: to the depth of exploitation

Climate: tropical marine; northeast monsoon (November to April); southwest monsoon (May to October)

Terrain: mostly mountains with narrow to extensive coastal lowlands

Elevation: *highest point:* Mount Apo 2,954 m
lowest point: Philippine Sea 0 m
mean elevation: 442 m

Natural resources: timber, petroleum, nickel, cobalt, silver, gold, salt, copper

Land use: *agricultural land:* 41% (2018 est.)
arable land: 18.2% (2018 est.)
permanent crops: 17.8% (2018 est.)
permanent pasture: 5% (2018 est.)
forest: 25.9% (2018 est.)
other: 33.1% (2018 est.)

Irrigated land: 16,270 sq km (2012)

Major lakes (area sq km): *salt water lake(s):* Laguna de Bay - 890 sq km

Population distribution: population concentrated where good farmlands lie; highest concentrations are northwest and south-central Luzon, the southeastern extension of Luzon, and the islands of the Visayan Sea, particularly Cebu and Negros; Manila is home to one-eighth of the entire national population

Natural hazards: astride typhoon belt, usually affected by 15 and struck by five to six cyclonic storms each year; landslides; active volcanoes; destructive earthquakes; tsunamis
volcanism: significant volcanic activity; Taal (311 m), which has shown recent unrest and may erupt in the near future, has been deemed a Decade Volcano by the International Association of Volcanology and Chemistry of the Earth's Interior, worthy of study due to its explosive history and close proximity to human populations; Mayon (2,462 m), the country's most active volcano, erupted in 2009 forcing over 33,000 to be evacuated; other historically active volcanoes include Biliran, Babuyan Claro, Bulusan, Camiguin, Camiguin de Babuyanes, Didicas, Iraya, Jolo, Kanlaon, Makaturing, Musuan, Parker, Pinatubo, and Ragang; see note 2 under "Geography -note"

Geography - note: *note 1:* for decades, the Philippine archipelago was reported as having 7,107 islands; in 2016, the national mapping authority reported that hundreds of new islands had been discovered and increased the number of islands to 7,641 - though not all of the new islands have been verified; the country is favorably located in relation to many of Southeast Asia's main water bodies: the South China Sea, Philippine Sea, Sulu Sea, Celebes Sea, and Luzon Strait
note 2: Philippines is one of the countries along the Ring of Fire, a belt of active volcanoes and earthquake epicenters bordering the Pacific Ocean; up to 90% of the world's earthquakes and some 75% of the world's volcanoes occur within the Ring of Fire
note 3: the Philippines sits astride the Pacific typhoon belt and an average of 9 typhoons make landfall on the islands each year - with about 5 of these being destructive; the country is the most exposed in the world to tropical storms

PEOPLE AND SOCIETY

Population: 114,597,229 (2022 est.)
country comparison to the world: 12

Nationality: *noun:* Filipino(s)
adjective: Philippine

Ethnic groups: Tagalog 24.4%, Bisaya/Binisaya 11.4%, Cebuano 9.9%, Ilocano 8.8%, Hiligaynon/Ilonggo 8.4%, Bikol/Bicol 6.8%, Waray 4%, other local ethnicity 26.1%, other foreign ethnicity 0.1% (2010 est.)

Languages: unspecified Filipino (official; based on Tagalog) and English (official); eight major dialects - Tagalog, Cebuano, Ilocano, Hiligaynon or Ilonggo, Bicol, Waray, Pampango, and Pangasinan
major-language sample(s): Ang World Factbook, ang mapagkukunan ng kailangang impormasyon. (Tagalog)

Religions: Roman Catholic 79.5%, Muslim 6%, Iglesia ni Cristo 2.6%, Evangelical 2.4%, National Council of Churches in the Philippines 1.1%, other 7.4%, none <0.1% (2015 est.)

Demographic profile: The Philippines is an ethnically diverse country that is in the early stages of demographic transition. Its fertility rate has dropped steadily since the 1950s. The decline was more rapid after the introduction of a national population program in the 1970s in large part due to the increased use of modern contraceptive methods, but fertility has decreased more slowly in recent years. The country's total fertility rate (TFR) – the average number of births per woman – dropped below 5 in the 1980s, below 4 in the 1990s, and below 3 in the 2010s. TFR continues to be above replacement level at 2.9 and even higher among the poor, rural residents, and the less-educated. Significant reasons for elevated TFR are the desire for more than two children, in part because children are a means of financial assistance and security for parents as they age, particularly among the poor.

The Philippines are the source of one of the world's largest emigrant populations, much of which consists of legal temporary workers known as Overseas Foreign Workers or OFWs. As of 2019, there were 2.2 million OFWs. They work in a wide array of fields, most frequently in services (such as caregivers and domestic work), skilled trades, and construction but also in professional fields, including nursing and engineering. OFWs most often migrate to Middle Eastern countries, but other popular destinations include Hong Kong, China, and Singapore, as well as employment on ships. Filipino seafarers make up 35-40% of the world's seafarers, as of 2014. Women OFWs, who work primarily in domestic services and entertainment, have outnumbered men since 1992.

Migration and remittances have been a feature of Philippine culture for decades. The government has encouraged and facilitated emigration, regulating recruitment agencies and adopting legislation to protect the rights of migrant workers. Filipinos began emigrating to the US and Hawaii early in the 20th century. In 1934, US legislation limited Filipinos to 50 visas per year except during labor shortages, causing emigration to plummet. It was not until the 1960s, when the US and other destination countries – Canada, Australia, and New Zealand – loosened their immigration policies, that Filipino emigration expanded and diversified. The government implemented an overseas employment program in the 1970s, promoting Filipino labor to Gulf countries needing more workers for their oil industries. Filipino emigration increased rapidly. The government had intended for international migration to be temporary, but a lack of jobs and poor wages domestically, the ongoing demand for workers in the Gulf countries, and new labor markets in Asia continue to spur Philippine emigration.

Age structure: *0-14 years:* 32.42% (male 18,060,976/female 17,331,781)

15-24 years: 19.16% (male 10,680,325/female 10,243,047)
25-54 years: 37.37% (male 20,777,741/female 20,027,153)
55-64 years: 6.18% (male 3,116,485/female 3,633,301)
65 years and over: 4.86% (male 2,155,840/female 3,154,166) (2020 est.)

Dependency ratios: *total dependency ratio:* 55.2
youth dependency ratio: 46.6
elderly dependency ratio: 8.6
potential support ratio: 11.7 (2020 est.)

Median age: *total:* 24.1 years
male: 23.6 years
female: 24.6 years (2020 est.)
country comparison to the world: 168

Population growth rate: 1.6% (2022 est.)
country comparison to the world: 62

Birth rate: 22.28 births/1,000 population (2022 est.)
country comparison to the world: 57

Death rate: 6.41 deaths/1,000 population (2022 est.)
country comparison to the world: 140

Net migration rate: 0.13 migrant(s)/1,000 population (2022 est.)
country comparison to the world: 80

Population distribution: population concentrated where good farmlands lie; highest concentrations are northwest and south-central Luzon, the southeastern extension of Luzon, and the islands of the Visayan Sea, particularly Cebu and Negros; Manila is home to one-eighth of the entire national population

Urbanization: *urban population:* 48% of total population (2022)
rate of urbanization: 2.04% annual rate of change (2020-25 est.)

Major urban areas - population: 14.406 million MANILA (capital), 1.908 million Davao, 1.009 million Cebu City, 931,000 Zamboanga, 925,000 Antipolo, 786,000 Cagayan de Oro City (2022)

Sex ratio: *at birth:* 1.05 male(s)/female
0-14 years: 1.04 male(s)/female
15-24 years: 1.04 male(s)/female
25-54 years: 1.03 male(s)/female
55-64 years: 0.9 male(s)/female
65 years and over: 0.46 male(s)/female
total population: 1 male(s)/female (2022 est.)

Mother's mean age at first birth: 23.5 years (2017 est.)
note: data represents median age at first birth among women 25-49

Maternal mortality ratio: 121 deaths/100,000 live births (2017 est.)
country comparison to the world: 64

Infant mortality rate: *total:* 22.23 deaths/1,000 live births
male: 24.51 deaths/1,000 live births
female: 19.84 deaths/1,000 live births (2022 est.)
country comparison to the world: 73

Life expectancy at birth: *total population:* 70.14 years
male: 66.6 years
female: 73.86 years (2022 est.)
country comparison to the world: 170

Total fertility rate: 2.78 children born/woman (2022 est.)
country comparison to the world: 58

Contraceptive prevalence rate: 54.1% (2017)

Drinking water source: *improved: urban:* 99.1% of population
rural: 95% of population
total: 97% of population
unimproved: urban: 0.9% of population
rural: 5% of population
total: 3% of population (2020 est.)

Current health expenditure: 4.1% of GDP (2019)

Physicians density: 0.77 physicians/1,000 population (2020)

Hospital bed density: 1 beds/1,000 population (2014)

Sanitation facility access: *improved: urban:* 96% of population
rural: 91% of population
total: 93.4% of population
unimproved: urban: 4% of population
rural: 9% of population
total: 6.6% of population (2020 est.)

HIV/AIDS - adult prevalence rate: 0.2% (2020 est.)
country comparison to the world: 110

HIV/AIDS - people living with HIV/AIDS: 120,000 (2020 est.)
country comparison to the world: 38

HIV/AIDS - deaths: 1,600 (2020 est.) <1,000
country comparison to the world: 50

Major infectious diseases: *degree of risk:* high (2020)
food or waterborne diseases: bacterial diarrhea, hepatitis A, and typhoid fever
vectorborne diseases: dengue fever and malaria
water contact diseases: leptospirosis

Obesity - adult prevalence rate: 6.4% (2016)
country comparison to the world: 168

Alcohol consumption per capita: *total:* 4.85 liters of pure alcohol (2019 est.)
beer: 1.47 liters of pure alcohol (2019 est.)
wine: 0.03 liters of pure alcohol (2019 est.)
spirits: 3.34 liters of pure alcohol (2019 est.)
other alcohols: 0.01 liters of pure alcohol (2019 est.)
country comparison to the world: 84

Tobacco use: *total:* 22.9% (2020 est.)
male: 39.3% (2020 est.)
female: 6.5% (2020 est.)
country comparison to the world: 67

Children under the age of 5 years underweight: 19.1% (2018)
country comparison to the world: 24

Child marriage: *women married by age 15:* 2.2%
women married by age 18: 16.5% (2017 est.)

Education expenditures: 3.2% of GDP (2019 est.)
country comparison to the world: 141

Literacy: *definition:* age 15 and over can read and write
total population: 96.3%
male: 95.7%
female: 96.9% (2019)

School life expectancy (primary to tertiary education): *total:* 13 years
male: 13 years
female: 13 years (2017)

Unemployment, youth ages 15-24: *total:* 7%
male: 6.1%
female: 8.5% (2020 est.)

People - note: one of only two predominantly Christian nations in Southeast Asia, the other being Timor-Leste

ENVIRONMENT

Environment - current issues: uncontrolled deforestation especially in watershed areas; illegal mining and logging; soil erosion; air and water pollution in major urban centers; coral reef degradation; increasing pollution of coastal mangrove swamps that are important fish breeding grounds; coastal erosion; dynamite fishing; wildlife extinction

Environment - international agreements: *party to:* Biodiversity, Climate Change, Climate Change-Kyoto Protocol, Climate Change-Paris Agreement, Comprehensive Nuclear Test Ban, Desertification, Endangered Species, Hazardous Wastes, Law of the Sea, Marine Dumping-London Convention, Marine Dumping-London Protocol, Nuclear Test Ban, Ozone Layer Protection, Ship Pollution, Tropical Timber 2006, Wetlands
signed, but not ratified: none of the selected agreements

Air pollutants: *particulate matter emissions:* 18.38 micrograms per cubic meter (2016 est.)
carbon dioxide emissions: 122.29 megatons (2016 est.)
methane emissions: 51.32 megatons (2020 est.)

Climate: tropical marine; northeast monsoon (November to April); southwest monsoon (May to October)

Land use: *agricultural land:* 41% (2018 est.)
arable land: 18.2% (2018 est.)
permanent crops: 17.8% (2018 est.)
permanent pasture: 5% (2018 est.)
forest: 25.9% (2018 est.)
other: 33.1% (2018 est.)

Urbanization: *urban population:* 48% of total population (2022)
rate of urbanization: 2.04% annual rate of change (2020-25 est.)

Revenue from forest resources: *forest revenues:* 0.18% of GDP (2018 est.)
country comparison to the world: 96

Revenue from coal: *coal revenues:* 0.07% of GDP (2018 est.)
country comparison to the world: 28

Waste and recycling: *municipal solid waste generated annually:* 14,631,923 tons (2016 est.)
municipal solid waste recycled annually: 4,096,938 tons (2014 est.)
percent of municipal solid waste recycled: 28% (2014 est.)

Major lakes (area sq km): *salt water lake(s):* Laguna de Bay - 890 sq km

Total water withdrawal: *municipal:* 8.929 billion cubic meters (2017 est.)
industrial: 15.85 billion cubic meters (2017 est.)
agricultural: 67.97 billion cubic meters (2017 est.)

Total renewable water resources: 479 billion cubic meters (2017 est.)

GOVERNMENT

Country name: *conventional long form:* Republic of the Philippines
conventional short form: Philippines
local long form: Republika ng Pilipinas
local short form: Pilipinas
etymology: named in honor of King PHILLIP II of Spain by Spanish explorer Ruy LOPEZ de

VILLALOBOS, who visited some of the islands in 1543

Government type: presidential republic

Capital: *name:* Manila
geographic coordinates: 14 36 N, 120 58 E
time difference: UTC+8 (13 hours ahead of Washington, DC, during Standard Time)
etymology: derives from the Tagalog "may-nila" meaning "where there is indigo" and refers to the presence of indigo-yielding plants growing in the area surrounding the original settlement

Administrative divisions: 81 provinces and 38 chartered cities
provinces: Abra, Agusan del Norte, Agusan del Sur, Aklan, Albay, Antique, Apayao, Aurora, Basilan, Bataan, Batanes, Batangas, Biliran, Benguet, Bohol, Bukidnon, Bulacan, Cagayan, Camarines Norte, Camarines Sur, Camiguin, Capiz, Catanduanes, Cavite, Cebu, Cotabato, Davao del Norte, Davao del Sur, Davao de Oro, Davao Occidental, Davao Oriental, Dinagat Islands, Eastern Samar, Guimaras, Ifugao, Ilocos Norte, Ilocos Sur, Iloilo, Isabela, Kalinga, Laguna, Lanao del Norte, Lanao del Sur, La Union, Leyte, Maguindanao, Marinduque, Masbate, Mindoro Occidental, Mindoro Oriental, Misamis Occidental, Misamis Oriental, Mountain, Negros Occidental, Negros Oriental, Northern Samar, Nueva Ecija, Nueva Vizcaya, Palawan, Pampanga, Pangasinan, Quezon, Quirino, Rizal, Romblon, Samar, Sarangani, Siquijor, Sorsogon, South Cotabato, Southern Leyte, Sultan Kudarat, Sulu, Surigao del Norte, Surigao del Sur, Tarlac, Tawi-Tawi, Zambales, Zamboanga del Norte, Zamboanga del Sur, Zamboanga Sibugay;
chartered cities: Angeles, Bacolod, Baguio, Butuan, Cagayan de Oro, Caloocan, Cebu, Cotabato, Dagupan, Davao, General Santos, Iligan, Iloilo, Lapu-Lapu, Las Pinas, Lucena, Makati, Malabon, Mandaluyong, Mandaue, Manila, Marikina, Muntinlupa, Naga, Navotas, Olongapo, Ormoc, Paranaque, Pasay, Pasig, Puerto Princesa, Quezon, San Juan, Santiago, Tacloban, Taguig, Valenzuela, Zamboanga

Independence: 4 July 1946 (from the US)

National holiday: Independence Day, 12 June (1898); note - 12 June 1898 was date of declaration of independence from Spain; 4 July 1946 was date of independence from the US

Constitution: *history:* several previous; latest ratified 2 February 1987, effective 11 February 1987
amendments: proposed by Congress if supported by three fourths of the membership, by a constitutional convention called by Congress, or by public petition; passage by either of the three proposal methods requires a majority vote in a national referendum; note - the constitution has not been amended since its enactment in 1987

Legal system: mixed legal system of civil, common, Islamic (sharia), and customary law

International law organization participation: accepts compulsory ICJ jurisdiction with reservations; withdrew from the ICCt in March 2019

Citizenship: *citizenship by birth:* no
citizenship by descent only: at least one parent must be a citizen of the Philippines
dual citizenship recognized: no
residency requirement for naturalization: 10 years

Suffrage: 18 years of age; universal

Executive branch: *chief of state:* President Ferdinand "BongBong" MARCOS, Jr. (since 30 June 2022); Vice President Sara DUTERTE-Carpio (since 30 June 2022); note - the president is both chief of state and head of government
head of government: President Ferdinand "BongBong" MARCOS, Jr. (since 30 June 2022); Vice President Sara DUTERTE-Carpio (since 30 June 2022)
cabinet: Cabinet appointed by the president with the consent of the Commission of Appointments, an independent body of 25 Congressional members including the Senate president (ex officio chairman), appointed by the president
elections/appointments: president and vice president directly elected on separate ballots by simple majority popular vote for a single 6-year term; election last held on 9 May 2022 (next to be held on 9 May 2028)
election results:
Ferdinand MARCOS, Jr. elected president; percent of vote - Ferdinand MARCOS, Jr. (PFP) 58.7%, Leni ROBREDO (independent) 27.9%, Manny PACQUIAO (PROMDI) 6.8%; Sara DUTERTE-Carpio elected vice president; percent of vote Sara DUTERTE-Carpio (Lakas-CMD) 61.5%, Francis PANGILINAN (LP) 17.8%, Tito SOTTO 15.8%

Legislative branch: *description:* bicameral Congress or Kongreso consists of:
Senate or Senado (24 seats; members directly elected in multi-seat constituencies by majority vote; members serve 6-year terms with one-half of the membership renewed every 3 years)
House of Representatives or Kapulungan Ng Mga Kinatawan (316 seats; 253 members directly elected in single-seat constituencies by simple majority vote and 63 representing minorities directly elected by party-list proportional representation vote; members serve 3-year terms)
elections:
Senate - elections last held on 9 May 2022 (next to be held in May 2025)
House of Representatives - elections last held on 9 May 2022 (next to be held in May 2025)
election results:
Senate - percent of vote by party - NA; seats by party - NPC 5, PDP-Laban 5, NP 4, other 5, independent 5; composition - men 17, women 7, percent of women 29%
House of Representatives - percent of vote by party - PDP-Laban 22.7%, NP 13.7%, NUP 12.6%, NPC 11.7%, Lakas-CMD 9.4%,LP 3.8%, HNP 2.5%, other 19.6% independent 4%; seats by party - PDP-Laban 66, NP, NPC 35, NUP 33, Lakas-CMD 26, LP 10, HNP 6, other 35, independent 6, party-list 63; composition - men 193, women 123, percent of women 38.9%; note - total Congress percent of women 38.2%

Judicial branch: *highest court(s):* Supreme Court (consists of a chief justice and 14 associate justices)
judge selection and term of office: justices are appointed by the president on the recommendation of the Judicial and Bar Council, a constitutionally created, 6-member body that recommends Supreme Court nominees; justices serve until age 70
subordinate courts: Court of Appeals; Sandiganbayan (special court for corruption cases of government officials); Court of Tax Appeals; regional, metropolitan, and municipal trial courts; sharia courts

Political parties and leaders: Aksyon Demokratiko [Francisco "Isko Moreno" DOMAGOSO]
Lakas ng EDSA-Christian Muslim Democrats or Lakas-CMD [Ramon "Bong" REVILLA Jr]
Liberal Party or LP [Leni ROBREDO]
Nacionalista Party or NP [Manuel "Manny" VILLAR]
National Unity Party or NUP [Ronaldo V. PUNO]
Partido Demokratiko Pilipino-Lakas ng Bayan or PDP-Laban [Aquilino PIMENTEL III]
Partido Federal ng Pilipinas or PFP [Ferdinand MARCOS, Jr.]

International organization participation: ADB, APEC, ARF, ASEAN, BIS, CD, CICA (observer), CP, EAS, FAO, G-24, G-77, IAEA, IBRD, ICAO, ICC (national committees), ICCt, ICRM, IDA, IFAD, IFC, IFRCS, IHO, ILO, IMF, IMO, IMSO, Interpol, IOC, IOM, IPU, ISO, ITSO, ITU, ITUC (NGOs), MIGA, MINUSTAH, NAM, OAS (observer), OPCW, PCA, PIF (partner), UN, UNCTAD, UNESCO, UNHCR, UNIDO, Union Latina, UNMIL, UNMOGIP, UNOCI, UNWTO, UPU, WCO, WFTU (NGOs), WHO, WIPO, WMO, WTO

Diplomatic representation in the US: *chief of mission:* Ambassador Jose Manuel del Gallego ROMUALDEZ (since 29 November 2017)
chancery: 1600 Massachusetts Avenue NW, Washington, DC 20036
telephone: [1] (202) 467-9300
FAX: [1] (202) 328-7614
email address and website:
washington.pe@dfa.gov.ph; consular@phembassy-us.org
consulate(s) general: Chicago, Honolulu, Los Angeles, New York, Saipan (Northern Mariana Islands), San Francisco, Tamuning (Guam)

Diplomatic representation from the US: *chief of mission:* Ambassador MaryKay Loss CARLSON (since 22 July 2022)
embassy: 1201 Roxas Boulevard, Manila 1000
mailing address: 8600 Manila Place, Washington DC 20521-8600
telephone: [63] (2) 5301-2000
FAX: [63] (2) 5301-2017
email address and website:
acsinfomanila@state.gov
https://ph.usembassy.gov/

Flag description: two equal horizontal bands of blue (top) and red; a white equilateral triangle is based on the hoist side; the center of the triangle displays a yellow sun with eight primary rays; each corner of the triangle contains a small, yellow, five-pointed star; blue stands for peace and justice, red symbolizes courage, the white equal-sided triangle represents equality; the rays recall the first eight provinces that sought independence from Spain, while the stars represent the three major geographical divisions of the country: Luzon, Visayas, and Mindanao; the design of the flag dates to 1897
note: in wartime the flag is flown upside down with the red band at the top

National symbol(s): three stars and sun, Philippine eagle; national colors: red, white, blue, yellow

Coat of Arms of the Philippines:

National anthem: *name:* "Lupang Hinirang" (Chosen Land)
lyrics/music: Jose PALMA (revised by Felipe PADILLA de Leon)/Julian FELIPE

note: music adopted 1898, original Spanish lyrics adopted 1899, Filipino (Tagalog) lyrics adopted 1956; although the original lyrics were written in Spanish, later English and Filipino versions were created; today, only the Filipino version is used

National heritage: *total World Heritage Sites:* 6 (3 cultural, 3 natural)
selected World Heritage Site locales: Baroque Churches of the Philippines (c); Tubbataha Reefs Natural Park (n); Rice Terraces of the Philippine Cordilleras (c); Historic Vigan (c); Puerto-Princesa Subterranean River National Park (n); Mount Hamiguitan Range Wildlife Sanctuary (n)

ECONOMY

Economic overview: The economy has been relatively resilient to global economic shocks due to less exposure to troubled international securities, lower dependence on exports, relatively resilient domestic consumption, large remittances from about 10 million overseas Filipino workers and migrants, and a rapidly expanding services industry. During 2017, the current account balance fell into the negative range, the first time since the 2008 global financial crisis, in part due to an ambitious new infrastructure spending program announced this year. However, international reserves remain at comfortable levels and the banking system is stable.

Efforts to improve tax administration and expenditures management have helped ease the Philippines' debt burden and tight fiscal situation. The Philippines received investment-grade credit ratings on its sovereign debt under the former AQUINO administration and has had little difficulty financing its budget deficits. However, weak absorptive capacity and implementation bottlenecks have prevented the government from maximizing its expenditure plans. Although it has improved, the low tax-to-GDP ratio remains a constraint to supporting increasingly higher spending levels and sustaining high and inclusive growth over the longer term.

Economic growth has accelerated, averaging over 6% per year from 2011 to 2017, compared with 4.5% under the MACAPAGAL-ARROYO government; and competitiveness rankings have improved. Although 2017 saw a new record year for net foreign direct investment inflows, FDI to the Philippines has continued to lag regional peers, in part because the Philippine constitution and other laws limit foreign investment and restrict foreign ownership in important activities/sectors - such as land ownership and public utilities.

Although the economy grew at a rapid pace under the AQUINO government, challenges to achieving more inclusive growth remain. Wealth is concentrated in the hands of the rich. The unemployment rate declined from 7.3% to 5.7% between 2010 and 2017; while there has been some improvement, underemployment remains high at around 17% to 18% of the employed population. At least 40% of the employed work in the informal sector. Poverty afflicts more than a fifth of the total population but is as high as 75% in some areas of the southern Philippines. More than 60% of the poor reside in rural areas, where the incidence of poverty (about 30%) is more severe - a challenge to raising rural farm and non-farm incomes. Continued efforts are needed to improve governance, the judicial system, the regulatory environment, the infrastructure, and the overall ease of doing business.

2016 saw the election of President Rodrigo DUTERTE, who has pledged to make inclusive growth and poverty reduction his top priority. DUTERTE believes that illegal drug use, crime and corruption are key barriers to economic development. The administration wants to reduce the poverty rate to 17% and graduate the economy to upper-middle income status by the end of President DUTERTE's term in 2022. Key themes under the government's Ten-Point Socioeconomic Agenda include continuity of macroeconomic policy, tax reform, higher investments in infrastructure and human capital development, and improving competitiveness and the overall ease of doing business. The administration sees infrastructure shortcomings as a key barrier to sustained economic growth and has pledged to spend $165 billion on infrastructure by 2022. Although the final outcome has yet to be seen, the current administration is shepherding legislation for a comprehensive tax reform program to raise revenues for its ambitious infrastructure spending plan and to promote a more equitable and efficient tax system. However, the need to finance rehabilitation and reconstruction efforts in the southern region of Mindanao following the 2017 Marawi City siege may compete with other spending on infrastructure.

Real GDP (purchasing power parity): $871.56 billion (2020 est.)
$963.83 billion (2019 est.)
$908.26 billion (2018 est.)
note: data are in 2017 dollars
country comparison to the world: 28

Real GDP growth rate: 6.04% (2019 est.)
6.34% (2018 est.)
6.94% (2017 est.)
country comparison to the world: 29

Real GDP per capita: $8,000 (2020 est.)
$8,900 (2019 est.)
$8,500 (2018 est.)
note: data are in 2017 dollars
country comparison to the world: 151

GDP (official exchange rate): $377.205 billion (2019 est.)

Inflation rate (consumer prices): 2.4% (2019 est.)
5.2% (2018 est.)
2.8% (2017 est.)
country comparison to the world: 125

Credit ratings:

Fitch rating: BBB (2017)

Moody's rating: Baa2 (2014)

Standard & Poors rating: BBB+ (2019)

GDP - composition, by sector of origin: *agriculture:* 9.6% (2017 est.)
industry: 30.6% (2017 est.)
services: 59.8% (2017 est.)

GDP - composition, by end use: *household consumption:* 73.5% (2017 est.)
government consumption: 11.3% (2017 est.)
investment in fixed capital: 25.1% (2017 est.)
investment in inventories: 0.1% (2017 est.)
exports of goods and services: 31% (2017 est.)
imports of goods and services: -40.9% (2017 est.)

Agricultural products: sugar cane, rice, coconuts, maize, bananas, vegetables, tropical fruit, plantains, pineapples, cassava

Industries: semiconductors and electronics assembly, business process outsourcing, food and beverage manufacturing, construction, electric/gas/water supply, chemical products, radio/television/communications equipment and apparatus, petroleum and fuel, textile and garments, non-metallic minerals, basic metal industries, transport equipment

Industrial production growth rate: 7.2% (2017 est.)
country comparison to the world: 30

Labor force: 41.533 million (2020 est.)
country comparison to the world: 15

Labor force - by occupation: *agriculture:* 25.4%
industry: 18.3%
services: 56.3% (2017 est.)

Unemployment rate: 5.11% (2019 est.)
5.29% (2018 est.)
country comparison to the world: 82

Unemployment, youth ages 15-24: *total:* 7%
male: 6.1%
female: 8.5% (2020 est.)
country comparison to the world: 163

Population below poverty line: 16.7% (2018 est.)

Gini Index coefficient - distribution of family income: 44.4 (2015 est.)
46 (2012 est.)
country comparison to the world: 34

Household income or consumption by percentage share: *lowest 10%:* 3.2%
highest 10%: 29.5% (2015 est.)

Budget: *revenues:* 49.07 billion (2017 est.)
expenditures: 56.02 billion (2017 est.)

Budget surplus (+) or deficit (-): -2.2% (of GDP) (2017 est.)
country comparison to the world: 109

Public debt: 39.9% of GDP (2017 est.)
39% of GDP (2016 est.)
country comparison to the world: 128

Taxes and other revenues: 15.6% (of GDP) (2017 est.)
country comparison to the world: 188

Fiscal year: calendar year

Current account balance: -$3.386 billion (2019 est.)
-$8.877 billion (2018 est.)
country comparison to the world: 176

Exports: $78.82 billion (2020 est.) note: data are in current year dollars
$94.74 billion (2019 est.) note: data are in current year dollars
$90.37 billion (2018 est.) note: data are in current year dollars
country comparison to the world: 47

Exports - partners: China 16%, United States 15%, Japan 13%, Hong Kong 12%, Singapore 7%, Germany 5% (2019)

Exports - commodities: integrated circuits, office machinery/parts, insulated wiring, semiconductors, transformers (2019)

Imports: $97.58 billion (2020 est.) note: data are in current year dollars
$131.01 billion (2019 est.) note: data are in current year dollars
$129.74 billion (2018 est.) note: data are in current year dollars
country comparison to the world: 40

Imports - partners: China 29%, Japan 8%, South Korea 7%, United States 6%, Singapore 6%, Indonesia 6%, Thailand 5%, Taiwan 5% (2019)

Imports - commodities: integrated circuits, refined petroleum, cars, crude petroleum, broadcasting equipment (2019)

Reserves of foreign exchange and gold: $81.57 billion (31 December 2017 est.)
$80.69 billion (31 December 2016 est.)
country comparison to the world: 29

Debt - external: $81.995 billion (2019 est.)
$75.192 billion (2018 est.)
country comparison to the world: 59

Exchange rates: Philippine pesos (PHP) per US dollar -
48.055 (2020 est.)
50.81 (2019 est.)
52.71 (2018 est.)
45.503 (2014 est.)
44.395 (2013 est.)

ENERGY

Electricity access: *electrification - total population:* 96% (2019)
electrification - urban areas: 100% (2019)
electrification - rural areas: 93% (2019)

Electricity: *installed generating capacity:* 27.885 million kW (2020 est.)
consumption: 90,926,990,000 kWh (2019 est.)
exports: 0 kWh (2020 est.)
imports: 0 kWh (2020 est.)
transmission/distribution losses: 9.994 billion kWh (2019 est.)

Electricity generation sources: *fossil fuels:* 77.6% of total installed capacity (2020 est.)
solar: 1.3% of total installed capacity (2020 est.)
wind: 1.1% of total installed capacity (2020 est.)
hydroelectricity: 8% of total installed capacity (2020 est.)
geothermal: 11% of total installed capacity (2020 est.)
biomass and waste: 1.1% of total installed capacity (2020 est.)

Coal: *production:* 13.752 million metric tons (2020 est.)
consumption: 32.855 million metric tons (2020 est.)
exports: 7.554 million metric tons (2020 est.)
imports: 28.358 million metric tons (2020 est.)
proven reserves: 361 million metric tons (2019 est.)

Petroleum: *total petroleum production:* 10,300 bbl/day (2021 est.)
refined petroleum consumption: 527,400 bbl/day (2019 est.)
crude oil and lease condensate exports: 12,400 bbl/day (2018 est.)
crude oil and lease condensate imports: 232,500 bbl/day (2018 est.)
crude oil estimated reserves: 138.5 million barrels (2021 est.)

Refined petroleum products - production: 215,500 bbl/day (2015 est.)
country comparison to the world: 50

Refined petroleum products - exports: 26,710 bbl/day (2015 est.)
country comparison to the world: 65

Refined petroleum products - imports: 211,400 bbl/day (2015 est.)
country comparison to the world: 33

Natural gas: *production:* 3,632,507,000 cubic meters (2019 est.)
consumption: 3,632,507,000 cubic meters (2019 est.)
exports: 0 cubic meters (2021 est.)
imports: 0 cubic meters (2021 est.)
proven reserves: 98.542 billion cubic meters (2021 est.)

Carbon dioxide emissions: 142.282 million metric tonnes of CO2 (2019 est.)
from coal and metallurgical coke: 70.82 million metric tonnes of CO2 (2019 est.)
from petroleum and other liquids: 64.418 million metric tonnes of CO2 (2019 est.)
from consumed natural gas: 7.044 million metric tonnes of CO2 (2019 est.)
country comparison to the world: 36

Energy consumption per capita: 19.261 million Btu/person (2019 est.)
country comparison to the world: 137

COMMUNICATIONS

Telephones - fixed lines: *total subscriptions:* 4,731,196 (2020 est.)
subscriptions per 100 inhabitants: 4 (2020 est.)
country comparison to the world: 32

Telephones - mobile cellular: *total subscriptions:* 149,579,406 (2020 est.)
subscriptions per 100 inhabitants: 137 (2020 est.)
country comparison to the world: 11

Telecommunication systems: *general assessment:* the Covid-19 pandemic had a relatively minor impact on the Philippine's telecom sector in 2020; subscriber numbers fell in some areas, but this was offset by strong growth in mobile data and broadband usage since a significant proportion of the population transitioned to working or studying from home; major investment programs covering LTE, 5G, and fiber broadband networks suffered slight delays due to holdups in supply chains, but activity has since ramped up in an attempt to complete the roll outs as per the original schedule; the major telecom operators had mixed financial results for the past year; overall, the number of mobile subscribers is expected to grow to 153 million by the end of 2021, with the penetration rate approaching 144%; the government remains keen, and committed, to seeing strong competition, growth, and service excellence in the telecom sector, so there is likely to be continued support (financially as well as through legislation such as enabling mobile tower sharing and number portability) to ensure that the sector remains viable for emerging players; the mobile sector will remain the Philippines' primary market for telecommunications well into the future; the unique terrain and resulting challenges associated with accessing remote parts of the archipelago means that in many areas fixed networks are neither cost-effective nor logistically viable; the bulk of telecoms investment over the coming years will continue to be in 5G and 5G-enabled LTE networks; coverage of LTE and 5G networks extends to over 95% of the population, and for the vast majority of people mobile will likely remain their only platform for telecom services (2021)
domestic: telecommunications infrastructure includes the following platforms: fixed line, mobile cellular, cable TV, over-the-air TV, radio and (very small aperture terminal) VSAT, fiber-optic cable, and satellite for redundant international connectivity; fixed-line nearly 4 per 100 and mobile-cellular nearly 155 per 100 (2019)
international: country code - 63; landing points for the NDTN, TGN-IA, AAG, PLCN, EAC-02C, DFON, SJC, APCN-2, SeaMeWe, Boracay-Palawan Submarine Cable System, Palawa-Illoilo Cable System, NDTN, SEA-US, SSSFOIP, ASE and JUPITAR submarine cables that together provide connectivity to the US, Southeast Asia, Asia, Europe, Africa, the Middle East, and Australia (2019)

Broadcast media: multiple national private TV and radio networks; multi-channel satellite and cable TV systems available; more than 400 TV stations; about 1,500 cable TV providers with more than 2 million subscribers, and some 1,400 radio stations; the Philippines adopted Japan's Integrated Service Digital Broadcast – Terrestrial standard for digital terrestrial television in November 2013 and is scheduled to complete the switch from analog to digital broadcasting by the end of 2023 (2019)

Internet country code: .ph

Internet users: *total:* 54,790,543 (2020 est.)
percent of population: 50% (2020 est.)
country comparison to the world: 18

Broadband - fixed subscriptions: *total:* 7,936,574 (2020 est.)
subscriptions per 100 inhabitants: 7 (2020 est.)
country comparison to the world: 25

TRANSPORTATION

National air transport system: *number of registered air carriers:* 13 (2020)
inventory of registered aircraft operated by air carriers: 200
annual passenger traffic on registered air carriers: 43,080,118 (2018)
annual freight traffic on registered air carriers: 835.9 million (2018) mt-km

Civil aircraft registration country code prefix: RP

Airports: *total:* 247 (2021)
country comparison to the world: 24

Airports - with paved runways: *total:* 89
over 3,047 m: 4
2,438 to 3,047 m: 8
1,524 to 2,437 m: 33
914 to 1,523 m: 34
under 914 m: 10 (2021)

Airports - with unpaved runways: *total:* 158
1,524 to 2,437 m: 3
914 to 1,523 m: 56
under 914 m: 99 (2021)

Heliports: 2 (2021)

Pipelines: 530 km gas, 138 km oil (non-operational), 185 km refined products (2017)

Railways: *total:* 77 km (2017)
standard gauge: 49 km (2017) 1.435-m gauge
narrow gauge: 28 km (2017) 1.067-m gauge
country comparison to the world: 129

Roadways: *total:* 216,387 km (2014)
paved: 61,093 km (2014)
unpaved: 155,294 km (2014)
country comparison to the world: 25

Waterways: 3,219 km (2011) (limited to vessels with draft less than 1.5 m)
country comparison to the world: 32

Merchant marine: *total:* 1,805
by type: bulk carrier 62, container ship 44, general cargo 716, oil tanker 205, other 778 (2021)
country comparison to the world: 15

Ports and terminals: *major seaport(s):* Batangas, Cagayan de Oro, Cebu, Davao, Liman, Manila
container port(s) (TEUs): Manila (5,315,500) (2019)

MILITARY AND SECURITY

Military and security forces: Armed Forces of the Philippines (AFP): Army, Navy (includes Marine Corps), Air Force (2021)
note 1: the Philippine Coast Guard is an armed and uniformed service under the Department of Transportation; it would be attached to the AFP in wartime; the Philippine National Police Force (PNP) falls under the Department of the Interior
note 2: the Philippine Government also arms and supports civilian militias; the AFP controls Civilian Armed Force Geographical Units, while the Civilian Volunteer Organizations fall under PNP command

Military expenditures: 1.1% of GDP (2021 est.)
1.1% of GDP (2020)
1.1% of GDP (2019) (approximately $6.19 billion)
1% of GDP (2018) (approximately $5.31 billion)
1.3% of GDP (2017) (approximately $6.21 billion)
country comparison to the world: 124

Military and security service personnel strengths: approximately 130,000 active duty personnel (90,000 Army; 25,000 Navy, including about 8,000 Marine Corps; 15,000 Air Force) (2022)

Military equipment inventories and acquisitions: the AFP is equipped with a mix of imported weapons systems, particularly second-hand equipment from the US; since 2014, top weapons suppliers include South Korea and the US (2022)

Military service age and obligation: 18-25 (enlisted) and 21-29 (officers) years of age for voluntary military service for men and women; no conscription (2022)
note: as of 2020, women made up about 6% of the active military; women were allowed to enter the Philippine Military Academy and train as combat soldiers in 1993

Military - note: the Armed Forces of the Philippines (AFP) were formally organized during the American colonial period as the Philippine Army; they were established by the National Defense Act of 1935 and were comprised of both Filipinos and Americans

the US and Philippines agreed to a mutual defense treaty in 1951; in 2014, the two governments signed an Enhanced Defense Cooperation Agreement (EDCA) that established new parameters for military cooperation; under the EDCA, the Philippine Government may grant US troops access to Philippine military bases on a rotational basis "for security cooperation exercises, joint and combined military training activities, and humanitarian assistance and disaster relief activities"; the Philippines has Major Non-NATO Ally (MNNA) status with the US; MNNA is a designation under US law that provides foreign partners with certain benefits in the areas of defense trade and security cooperation; while MNNA status provides military and economic privileges, it does not entail any security commitments

as of 2022, the AFP's primary air and ground operational focus was on internal security duties, particularly in the south, where several separatist Islamic insurgent and terrorist groups operated and up to 60% of the armed forces were deployed; additional combat operations were being conducted against the Communist Peoples Party/New People's Army, which was active mostly on Luzon, the Visayas, and areas of Mindanao; prior to a peace deal in 2014, the AFP fought a decades-long conflict against the Moro Islamic Liberation Front (MILF), a separatist organization based mostly on the island of Mindanao; the MILF's armed wing, the Bangsamoro Islamic Armed Forces (BIAF), had up to 40,000 fighters under arms

in addition to its typical roles of patrolling and defending the country's maritime claims, the Navy conducts interdiction operations against terrorist, insurgent, and criminal groups around the southern islands; in 2017, the Philippines began conducting joint maritime patrols with Indonesia and Malaysia to counter regional terrorist activities, particularly in the Sulu Sea; the Philippine Marine Corps assists the Army in counterinsurgency operations

the Philippines National Police (PNP) also has an active role in counterinsurgency and counter-terrorism operations alongside the AFP, particularly the Special Action Force, a PNP commando unit that specializes in urban counterterrorism operations (2022)

Maritime threats: the International Maritime Bureau reports the territorial waters of littoral states and offshore waters in the South China Sea as high risk for piracy and armed robbery against ships; an emerging threat area lies in the Celebes and Sulu Seas between the Philippines and Malaysia where 11 ships were attacked in 2021; numerous commercial vessels have been attacked and hijacked both at anchor and while underway; hijacked vessels are often disguised and cargoes stolen

TERRORISM

Terrorist group(s): Abu Sayyaf Group; Communist Party of the Philippines/New People's Army (CPP/NPA); Islamic State of Iraq and ash-Sham – East Asia (ISIS-EA) in the Philippines

TRANSNATIONAL ISSUES

Disputes - international: *Philippines-Taiwan-China-Malaysia-Vietnam:* Philippines claims sovereignty over Scarborough Reef (also claimed by China together with Taiwan) and over certain of the Spratly Islands, known locally as the Kalayaan (Freedom) Islands, also claimed by China, Malaysia, Taiwan, and Vietnam; the 2002 "Declaration on the Conduct of Parties in the South China Sea," has eased tensions in the Spratly Islands but falls short of a legally binding "code of conduct" desired by several of the disputants; in March 2005, the national oil companies of China, the Philippines, and Vietnam signed a joint accord to conduct marine seismic activities in the Spratly Islands
Philippines-Malaysia: Philippines retains a dormant claim to Malaysia's Sabah State in northern Borneo based on the Sultanate of Sulu's granting the Philippines Government power of attorney to pursue a sovereignty claim on his behalf; the disagreement resurfaced in September 2020 , when Malaysia's submission to the UN about extending its continental shelf was sharply countered by the Philippines because it included the disputed territory
Philippines-Palau: maritime delimitation negotiations continue with Palau, as of March 2022

Refugees and internally displaced persons: *IDPs:* 108,000 (government troops fighting the Moro Islamic Liberation Front, the Abu Sayyaf Group, and the New People's Army; clan feuds; armed attacks, political violence, and communal tensions in Mindanao) (2021)
stateless persons: 392 (mid-year 2021); note - stateless persons are descendants of Indonesian migrants

Illicit drugs: cannabis products, methamphetamine hydrochloride (locally known as "shabu"), and MDMA (ecstasy) are locally used; Chinese Transnational Criminal Organizations (TCOs) are the main source of methamphetamine; precursor chemicals in transit from China to Burma

PITCAIRN ISLANDS

INTRODUCTION

Background: Polynesians were the first inhabitants of the Pitcairn Islands, but the islands were uninhabited by the time they were discovered by Europeans in 1606. Pitcairn Island was rediscovered by British explorer Philip CARTERET in 1767, although he incorrectly plotted the coordinates. In 1789, Fletcher CHRISTIAN led a mutiny on the HMS Bounty and after several months of searching for Pitcairn Island, he landed on it with eight other mutineers and their Tahitian companions. They lived in isolation and evaded detection by English authorities until 1808, by which point only one man, 10 women, and 23 children remained. In 1831, with the population growing too big for the island - there were 87 people - the British attempted to move all the islanders to Tahiti, but they were soon returned to Pitcairn Island. The island became an official British colony in 1838 and in 1856, the British again determined that the population of 193 was too high and relocated all of the residents to Norfolk Island. Several families returned in 1858 and 1864, bringing the island's population to 43, and almost all of the island's current population are descendants of these returnees. In 1887, the entire population converted to the Seventh Day Adventist faith.

The UK annexed the nearby islands of Henderson, Oeno, and Ducie in 1902 and incorporated them into the Pitcairn Islands colony in 1938, although all three are uninhabited. The population peaked at 233 in 1937 as outmigration, primarily to New Zealand, has thinned the population. Only two children were born between 1986 and 2012, and in 2005, a couple

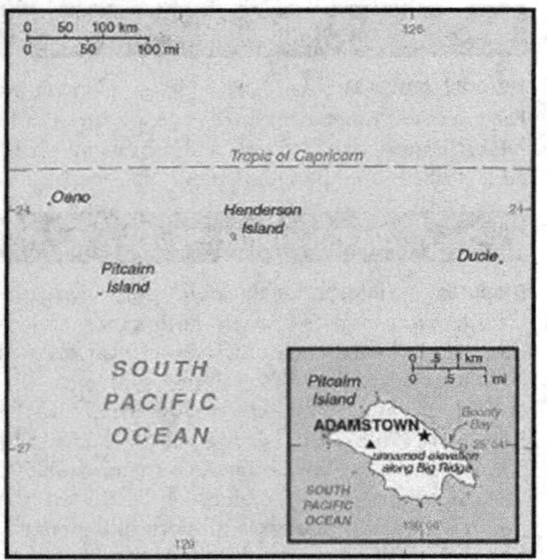

became the first new outsiders to obtain citizenship in more than a century. (The current population is below 50.) Since 2013, the Pitcairn Islands has tried to attract new migrants but has had no applicants because it requires prospective migrants to front significant sums of money and prohibits employment during a two-year trial period, at which point the local council can deny long-term resident status.

GEOGRAPHY

Location: Oceania, islands in the South Pacific Ocean, about midway between Peru and New Zealand

Geographic coordinates: 25 04 S, 130 06 W

Map references: Oceania

Area: *total:* 47 sq km
land: 47 sq km
water: 0 sq km
country comparison to the world: 233

Area - comparative: about three-tenths the size of Washington, DC

Land boundaries: *total:* 0 km

Coastline:51 km

Maritime claims: *territorial sea:* 12 nm
exclusive economic zone: 200 nm

Climate: tropical; hot and humid; modified by southeast trade winds; rainy season (November to March)

Terrain: rugged volcanic formation; rocky coastline with cliffs

Elevation: *highest point:* Palwala Valley Point on Big Ridge 347 m
lowest point: Pacific Ocean 0 m

Natural resources: miro trees (used for handicrafts), fish; note - manganese, iron, copper, gold, silver, and zinc have been discovered offshore

Land use: *agricultural land:* 0% (2011 est.)
forest: 74.5% (2018 est.)
other: 25.5% (2018 est.)

Irrigated land: 0 sq km (2012)

Population distribution: less than 50 inhabitants on Pitcairn Island, most reside near the village of Adamstown

Natural hazards: occasional tropical cyclones (especially November to March), but generally only heavy tropical storms; landslides

Geography - note: Britain's most isolated dependency; only the larger island of Pitcairn is inhabited but it has no port or natural harbor; supplies must be transported by rowed longboat from larger ships stationed offshore

PEOPLE AND SOCIETY

Population: 50 (2021 est.)
country comparison to the world: 237

Nationality: *noun:* Pitcairn Islander(s)
adjective: Pitcairn Islander

Ethnic groups: descendants of the Bounty mutineers and their Tahitian wives

Languages: English (official), Pitkern (mixture of an 18th century English dialect and a Tahitian dialect)

Religions: Seventh Day Adventist 100%

Population distribution: less than 50 inhabitants on Pitcairn Island, most reside near the village of Adamstown

Major infectious diseases: *degree of risk:* high (2020)
food or waterborne diseases: bacterial diarrhea
vectorborne diseases: malaria

ENVIRONMENT

Environment - current issues: deforestation (only a small portion of the original forest remains because of burning and clearing for settlement)

Climate: tropical; hot and humid; modified by southeast trade winds; rainy season (November to March)

Land use: *agricultural land:* 0% (2011 est.)
forest: 74.5% (2018 est.)
other: 25.5% (2018 est.)

GOVERNMENT

Country name: *conventional long form:* Pitcairn, Henderson, Ducie, and Oeno Islands
conventional short form: Pitcairn Islands
etymology: named after Midshipman Robert PITCAIRN who first sighted the island in 1767

Government type: parliamentary democracy

Dependency status: overseas territory of the UK

Capital: *name:* Adamstown
geographic coordinates: 25 04 S, 130 05 W
time difference: UTC-9 (4 hours behind Washington, DC, during Standard Time)
etymology: named after John ADAMS (1767–1829), the last survivor of the Bounty mutineers who settled on Pitcairn Island in January 1790

Administrative divisions: none (overseas territory of the UK)

Independence: none (overseas territory of the UK)

National holiday: Birthday of Queen ELIZABETH II, second Saturday in June (1926); Discovery Day (Pitcairn Day), 2 July (1767)

Constitution: *history:* several previous; latest drafted 10 February 2010, presented 17 February 2010, effective 4 March 2010

Legal system: local island by-laws

Citizenship: see United Kingdom

Suffrage: 18 years of age; universal with three years residency

Executive branch: *chief of state:* King CHARLES III (since 8 September 2022); represented by UK High Commissioner to New Zealand and Governor (nonresident) of the Pitcairn Islands Iona THOMAS (since 9 August 2022)
head of government: Mayor and Chairman of the Island Council Charlene WARREN-PEU (since 1 January 2020)
cabinet: none
elections/appointments: the monarchy is hereditary; governor and commissioner appointed by the monarch; island mayor directly elected by majority popular vote for a 3-year term; election last held on 9 November 2022 (next to be held not later than December 2025)
election results:
Simon YOUNG elected mayor and chairman of the Island Council; Island Council vote - NA; takes office 1 January 2023

Legislative branch: *description:* unicameral Island Council: 10 seats; (7 members - 5 councillors, the mayor, and the deputy mayor - elected by popular vote, and 3 ex officio non-voting members - the administrator, who serves as both the head of government and the representative of the governor of Pitcairn Islands, the governor, and the deputy governor; the councillors and the deputy mayor serve 2-year terms, the mayor serves a 3-year term, and the administrator is appointed by the governor for an indefinite term)
elections:
last held on 6 November 2019 (next scheduled election - NA)
election results:
percent of vote - NA; seats - 5 independent; composition - men 4, women 6, percent of women 60%

Judicial branch: *highest court(s):* Pitcairn Court of Appeal (consists of the court president, 2 judges, and the Supreme Court chief justice, an ex-officio member); Pitcairn Supreme Court (consists of the chief justice and 2 judges); note - appeals beyond the Pitcairn Court of Appeal are referred to the Judicial Committee of the Privy Council (in London)
judge selection and term of office: all judges of both courts appointed by the governor of the Pitcairn Islands on the instructions of the Queen of England through the Secretary of State; all judges can serve until retirement, normally at age 75
subordinate courts: Magistrate's Court

Political parties and leaders: none

International organization participation: SPC, UPU

Diplomatic representation in the US: none (overseas territory of the UK)

Diplomatic representation from the US: *embassy:* none (overseas territory of the UK)

Flag description: blue with the flag of the UK in the upper hoist-side quadrant and the Pitcairn Islander coat of arms centered on the outer half of the flag; the green, yellow, and blue of the shield represents the island rising from the ocean; the green field features a yellow anchor surmounted by a bible (both the anchor and the bible were items found on the HMS Bounty); sitting on the crest is a Pitcairn Island wheelbarrow from which springs a flowering twig of miro (a local plant)

National anthem: *name:* "We From Pitcairn Island"
lyrics/music: unknown/Frederick M. LEHMAN
note: serves as a local anthem; as an overseas territory of the UK, "God Save the King" is official (see United Kingdom)

ECONOMY

Economic overview: The inhabitants of this tiny isolated economy exist on fishing, subsistence farming, handicrafts, and postage stamps. The fertile soil of the valleys produces a wide variety of fruits and vegetables, including citrus, sugarcane, watermelons, bananas, yams, and beans. Bartering is an important part of the economy. The major sources of revenue are the sale of postage stamps to collectors and the sale of handicrafts to passing ships.

Agricultural products: honey; wide variety of fruits and vegetables; goats, chickens; fish

Industries: postage stamps, handicrafts, beekeeping, honey

Labor force: 15 (2004)
country comparison to the world: 231

Labor force - by occupation: *note:* no business community in the usual sense; some public works; subsistence farming and fishing

Budget: *revenues:* 746,000 (FY04/05)
expenditures: 1.028 million (FY04/05)

Fiscal year: 1 April - 31 March

Exports - partners: South Africa 24%, Canada 20%, Germany 13%, Czechia 8%, El Salvador 5%, Spain 5% (2019)

Exports - commodities: leather footwear, gas turbine parts, precious metal ores, clothing and apparel, beef (2019)

Imports - partners: Ecuador 43%, New Zealand 29% (2019)

Imports - commodities: crude petroleum, refined petroleum, food preparation products, plastics, iron fasteners (2019)

Exchange rates: New Zealand dollars (NZD) per US dollar -
1.416 (2017 est.)
1.4279 (2016 est.)
1.4279 (2015)
1.4279 (2014 est.)
1.2039 (2013 est.)

COMMUNICATIONS

Telecommunication systems: *general assessment:* satellite-based phone services; rural connectivity a challenge; 2G services widespread; demand for mobile broadband due to mobile services providing Internet source; the launch of the Kacific-1 satellite in 2019 will improve telecommunications in the region (2020)
domestic: local phone service with international connections via Internet (2018)
international: country code - 872; satellite earth station - 1 Inmarsat

Broadcast media: satellite TV from Fiji-based Sky Pacific offering a wide range of international channels

Internet country code: .pn

Internet users: *total:* 50 (2022 est.)
percent of population: 100% (2018 est.)
country comparison to the world: 231

Communications - note: satellite-based local phone service and broadband Internet connections available in all homes

TRANSPORTATION

Ports and terminals: *major seaport(s):* Adamstown (on Bounty Bay)

MILITARY AND SECURITY

Military - note: defense is the responsibility of the UK

TRANSNATIONAL ISSUES

Disputes - international: none identified

POLAND

INTRODUCTION

Background: Poland's history as a state began near the middle of the 10th century. By the mid-16th century, the Polish-Lithuanian Commonwealth ruled a vast tract of land in Central and Eastern Europe. During the 18th century, internal disorders weakened the nation, and in a series of agreements between 1772 and 1795, Russia, Prussia, and Austria partitioned Poland among themselves. Poland regained its independence in 1918 only to be overrun by Germany and the Soviet Union in World War II. It became a Soviet satellite state following the war. Labor turmoil in 1980 led to the formation of the independent trade union "Solidarity" that over time became a political force with over 10 million members. Free elections in 1989 and 1990 won Solidarity control of the parliament and the presidency, bringing the communist era to a close. A "shock therapy" program during the early 1990s enabled the country to transform its economy into one of the most robust in Central Europe. Poland joined NATO in 1999 and the EU in 2004.

GEOGRAPHY

Location: Central Europe, east of Germany

Geographic coordinates: 52 00 N, 20 00 E

Map references: Europe

Area: *total:* 312,685 sq km
land: 304,255 sq km
water: 8,430 sq km
country comparison to the world: 71

Area - comparative: about twice the size of Georgia; slightly smaller than New Mexico

Land boundaries: *total:* 2,865 km
border countries (6): Belarus 375 km; Czechia 699 km; Germany 467 km; Lithuania 100 km, Russia (Kaliningrad Oblast) 209 km; Slovakia 517 km; Ukraine 498 km

Coastline: 440 km

Maritime claims: *territorial sea:* 12 nm
exclusive economic zone: defined by international treaties

Climate: temperate with cold, cloudy, moderately severe winters with frequent precipitation; mild summers with frequent showers and thundershowers

Terrain: mostly flat plain; mountains along southern border

Elevation: *highest point:* Rysy 2,499 m
lowest point: near Raczki Elblaskie -2 m
mean elevation: 173 m

Natural resources: coal, sulfur, copper, natural gas, silver, lead, salt, amber, arable land

Land use: *agricultural land:* 48.2% (2018 est.)
arable land: 36.2% (2018 est.)
permanent crops: 1.3% (2018 est.)
permanent pasture: 10.7% (2018 est.)
forest: 30.6% (2018 est.)
other: 21.2% (2018 est.)

Irrigated land: 970 sq km (2012)

Major lakes (area sq km): *salt water lake(s):* Zalew Szczecinski/Stettiner Haff (shared with Germany) - 900 sq km

Major rivers (by length in km): Vistula river source and mouth (shared with Belarus and Ukraine) - 1,213 km
note - longest river in Poland

Major watersheds (area sq km): Atlantic Ocean drainage: *(Black Sea)* Danube (795,656 sq km)

Population distribution: population concentrated in the southern area around Krakow and the central area around Warsaw and Lodz, with an extension to the northern coastal city of Gdansk

Natural hazards: flooding

Geography - note: historically, an area of conflict because of flat terrain and the lack of natural barriers on the North European Plain

PEOPLE AND SOCIETY

Population: 38,093,101 (2022 est.)
country comparison to the world: 39

Nationality: *noun:* Pole(s)
adjective: Polish

Ethnic groups: Polish 96.9%, Silesian 1.1%, German 0.2%, Ukrainian 0.1%, other and unspecified 1.7% (2011 est.)
note: represents ethnicity declared first

Languages: Polish (official) 98.2%, Silesian 1.4%, other 1.1%, unspecified 1.3%; note - data represent

the language spoken at home; shares sum to more than 100% because some respondents gave more than one answer on the census; Poland ratified the European Charter for Regional or Minority Languages in 2009 recognizing Kashub as a regional language, Czech, Hebrew, Yiddish, Belarusian, Lithuanian, German, Armenian, Russian, Slovak, and Ukrainian as national minority languages, and Karaim, Lemko, Romani (Polska Roma and Bergitka Roma), and Tatar as ethnic minority languages (2011 est.)
major-language sample(s): Księga Faktów Świata, niezbędne źródło podstawowych informacji. (Polish)

Religions: Catholic 85% (includes Roman Catholic 84.8% and other Catholic 0.3%), Orthodox 1.3% (almost all are Polish Autocephalous Orthodox), Protestant 0.4% (mainly Augsburg Evangelical and Pentecostal), other 0.3% (includes Jehovah's Witness, Buddhist, Hare Krishna, Gaudiya Vaishnavism, Muslim, Jewish, Church of Jesus Christ), unspecified 12.9% (2020 est.)

Age structure: *0-14 years:* 14.83% (male 2,918,518/female 2,756,968)
15-24 years: 9.8% (male 1,928,637/female 1,823,894)
25-54 years: 43.33% (male 8,384,017/female 8,203,646)
55-64 years: 13.32% (male 2,424,638/female 2,675,351)
65 years and over: 18.72% (male 2,867,315/female 4,299,341) (2020 est.)

Dependency ratios: *total dependency ratio:* 51.4
youth dependency ratio: 23
elderly dependency ratio: 28.4
potential support ratio: 3.5 (2020 est.)

Median age: *total:* 41.9 years
male: 40.3 years
female: 43.6 years (2020 est.)
country comparison to the world: 39

Population growth rate: -0.26% (2022 est.)
country comparison to the world: 214

Birth rate: 8.5 births/1,000 population (2022 est.)
country comparison to the world: 213

Death rate: 10.71 deaths/1,000 population (2022 est.)
country comparison to the world: 26

Net migration rate: -0.33 migrant(s)/1,000 population (2022 est.)
country comparison to the world: 121

Population distribution: population concentrated in the southern area around Krakow and the central area around Warsaw and Lodz, with an extension to the northern coastal city of Gdansk

Urbanization: *urban population:* 60.1% of total population (2022)
rate of urbanization: -0.16% annual rate of change (2020-25 est.)

Major urban areas - population: 1.795 million WARSAW (capital), 770,000 Krakow (2022)

Sex ratio: *at birth:* 1.06 male(s)/female
0-14 years: 1.06 male(s)/female
15-24 years: 1.06 male(s)/female
25-54 years: 1.02 male(s)/female
55-64 years: 0.92 male(s)/female
65 years and over: 0.57 male(s)/female
total population: 0.94 male(s)/female (2022 est.)

Mother's mean age at first birth: 27.9 years (2020 est.)

Maternal mortality ratio: 2 deaths/100,000 live births (2017 est.)
country comparison to the world: 184

Infant mortality rate: *total:* 4.16 deaths/1,000 live births
male: 4.58 deaths/1,000 live births
female: 3.71 deaths/1,000 live births (2022 est.)
country comparison to the world: 186

Life expectancy at birth: *total population:* 78.76 years
male: 75.02 years
female: 82.73 years (2022 est.)
country comparison to the world: 68

Total fertility rate: 1.4 children born/woman (2022 est.)
country comparison to the world: 214

Contraceptive prevalence rate: 62.3% (2014)

Drinking water source: *improved: urban:* 99.9% of population
rural: 100% of population
total: 100% of population

Current health expenditure: 6.5% of GDP (2019)

Physicians density: 3.77 physicians/1,000 population (2020)

Hospital bed density: 6.5 beds/1,000 population (2018)

Sanitation facility access: *improved: urban:* 100% of population
rural: 100% of population
total: 100% of population

Major infectious diseases: *degree of risk:* intermediate (2016)
vectorborne diseases: tickborne encephalitis (2016)

Obesity - adult prevalence rate: 23.1% (2016)
country comparison to the world: 69

Alcohol consumption per capita: *total:* 10.96 liters of pure alcohol (2019 est.)
beer: 5.72 liters of pure alcohol (2019 est.)
wine: 0.88 liters of pure alcohol (2019 est.)
spirits: 4.36 liters of pure alcohol (2019 est.)
other alcohols: 0 liters of pure alcohol (2019 est.)
country comparison to the world: 13

Tobacco use: *total:* 24% (2020 est.)
male: 27.9% (2020 est.)
female: 20.1% (2020 est.)
country comparison to the world: 59

Children under the age of 5 years underweight: 0.7% (2010/12)
country comparison to the world: 125

Education expenditures: 4.6% of GDP (2018 est.)
country comparison to the world: 81

Literacy: *definition:* age 15 and over can read and write
total population: 99.8%
male: 99.9%
female: 99.7% (2015)

School life expectancy (primary to tertiary education): *total:* 16 years
male: 15 years
female: 17 years (2019)

Unemployment, youth ages 15-24: *total:* 10.8%
male: 10.3%
female: 11.6% (2020 est.)

ENVIRONMENT

Environment - current issues: decreased emphasis on heavy industry and increased environmental concern by post-communist governments has improved environment; air pollution remains serious because of emissions from burning low-quality coals in homes and from coal-fired power plants; the resulting acid rain causes forest damage; water pollution from industrial and municipal sources is a problem, as is disposal of hazardous wastes

Environment - international agreements: *party to:* Air Pollution, Air Pollution-Nitrogen Oxides, Air Pollution-Sulphur 94, Antarctic-Environmental Protection, Antarctic- Marine Living Resources, Antarctic Seals, Antarctic Treaty, Biodiversity, Climate Change, Climate Change-Kyoto Protocol, Climate Change-Paris Agreement, Comprehensive Nuclear Test Ban, Desertification, Endangered Species, Environmental Modification, Hazardous Wastes, Law of the Sea, Marine Dumping-London Convention, Nuclear Test Ban, Ozone Layer Protection, Ship Pollution, Tropical Timber 2006, Wetlands, Whaling
signed, but not ratified: Air Pollution-Heavy Metals, Air Pollution-Multi-effect Protocol, Air Pollution-Persistent Organic Pollutants

Air pollutants: *particulate matter emissions:* 20.54 micrograms per cubic meter (2016 est.)
carbon dioxide emissions: 299.04 megatons (2016 est.)
methane emissions: 46.62 megatons (2020 est.)

Climate: temperate with cold, cloudy, moderately severe winters with frequent precipitation; mild summers with frequent showers and thundershowers

Land use: *agricultural land:* 48.2% (2018 est.)
arable land: 36.2% (2018 est.)
permanent crops: 1.3% (2018 est.)
permanent pasture: 10.7% (2018 est.)
forest: 30.6% (2018 est.)
other: 21.2% (2018 est.)

Urbanization: *urban population:* 60.1% of total population (2022)
rate of urbanization: -0.16% annual rate of change (2020-25 est.)

Revenue from forest resources: *forest revenues:* 0.17% of GDP (2018 est.)
country comparison to the world: 98

Revenue from coal: *coal revenues:* 0.27% of GDP (2018 est.)
country comparison to the world: 19

Waste and recycling: *municipal solid waste generated annually:* 10.863 million tons (2015 est.)
municipal solid waste recycled annually: 2,866,746 tons (2015 est.)
percent of municipal solid waste recycled: 26.4% (2015 est.)

Major lakes (area sq km): *salt water lake(s):* Zalew Szczecinski/Stettiner Haff (shared with Germany) - 900 sq km

Major rivers (by length in km): Vistula river source and mouth (shared with Belarus and Ukraine) - 1,213 km
note - longest river in Poland

Major watersheds (area sq km): Atlantic Ocean drainage: *(Black Sea)* Danube (795,656 sq km)

Total water withdrawal: *municipal:* 2.028 billion cubic meters (2017 est.)
industrial: 7.035 billion cubic meters (2017 est.)
agricultural: 1.018 billion cubic meters (2017 est.)

Total renewable water resources: 60.5 billion cubic meters (2017 est.)

GOVERNMENT

Country name: *conventional long form:* Republic of Poland
conventional short form: Poland
local long form: Rzeczpospolita Polska
local short form: Polska
former: Polish People's Republic
etymology: name derives from the Polanians, a west Slavic tribe that united several surrounding Slavic groups (9th-10th centuries A.D.) and who passed on their name to the country; the name of the tribe likely comes from the Slavic "pole" (field or plain), indicating the flat nature of their country

Government type: parliamentary republic

Capital: *name:* Warsaw
geographic coordinates: 52 15 N, 21 00 E
time difference: UTC+1 (6 hours ahead of Washington, DC, during Standard Time)
daylight saving time: +1hr, begins last Sunday in March; ends last Sunday in October
etymology: the origin of the name is unknown; the Polish designation "Warszawa" was the name of a fishing village and several legends/traditions link the city's founding to a man named Wars or Warsz

Administrative divisions: 16 voivodships [provinces] (wojewodztwa, singular - wojewodztwo); Dolnoslaskie (Lower Silesia), Kujawsko-Pomorskie (Kuyavia-Pomerania), Lodzkie (Lodz), Lubelskie (Lublin), Lubuskie (Lubusz), Malopolskie (Lesser Poland), Mazowieckie (Masovia), Opolskie (Opole), Podkarpackie (Subcarpathia), Podlaskie, Pomorskie (Pomerania), Slaskie (Silesia), Swietokrzyskie (Holy Cross), Warminsko-Mazurskie (Warmia-Masuria), Wielkopolskie (Greater Poland), Zachodniopomorskie (West Pomerania)

Independence: 11 November 1918 (republic proclaimed); notable earlier dates: 14 April 966 (adoption of Christianity, traditional founding date), 1 July 1569 (Polish-Lithuanian Commonwealth created)

National holiday: Constitution Day, 3 May (1791)

Constitution: *history:* several previous; latest adopted 2 April 1997, approved by referendum 25 May 1997, effective 17 October 1997
amendments: proposed by at least one fifth of Sejm deputies, by the Senate, or by the president of the republic; passage requires at least two-thirds majority vote in the Sejm and absolute majority vote in the Senate; amendments to articles relating to sovereignty, personal freedoms, and constitutional amendment procedures also require passage by majority vote in a referendum; amended 2006, 2009

Legal system: civil law system; judicial review of legislative, administrative, and other governmental acts; constitutional law rulings of the Constitutional Tribunal are final

International law organization participation: accepts compulsory ICJ jurisdiction with reservations; accepts ICCt jurisdiction

Citizenship: *citizenship by birth:* no
citizenship by descent only: both parents must be citizens of Poland
dual citizenship recognized: no
residency requirement for naturalization: 5 years

Suffrage: 18 years of age; universal

Executive branch: *chief of state:* President Andrzej DUDA (since 6 August 2015)
head of government: Prime Minister Mateusz MORAWIECKI (since 11 December 2017); Deputy Prime Ministers Piotr GLINSKI (since 16 November 2015), Jacek SASIN (since 15 November 2019), Jaroslaw KACZYNSKI (6 October 2020) and Henryk KOWALCZYK (26 October 2021)
cabinet: Council of Ministers proposed by the prime minister, appointed by the president, and approved by the Sejm
elections/appointments: president directly elected by absolute majority popular vote in 2 rounds if needed for a 5-year term (eligible for a second term); election last held on 28 June 2020 with a second round on 12 July 2020 (next to be held in 2025); prime minister, deputy prime ministers, and Council of Ministers appointed by the president and confirmed by the Sejm
election results:
2020: Andrzej DUDA reelected president in second round; percent of vote - Andrzej DUDA (independent) 51%, Rafal TRZASKOWSKI (KO) 49%
2015: Andrzej DUDA elected president in second round; percent of vote - Andrzej DUDA (independent) 51.5%, Bronislaw KOMOROWSKI (independent) 48.5%

Legislative branch: *description:* bicameral Parliament consists of:
Senate or Senat (100 seats; members directly elected in single-seat constituencies by simple majority vote to serve 4-year terms)
Sejm (460 seats; members elected in multi-seat constituencies by party-list proportional representation vote with 5% threshold of total votes needed for parties and 8% for coalitions to gain seats; minorities exempt from threshold; members serve 4-year terms)
elections:
Senate - last held on 13 October 2019 (next to be held in October 2023)
Sejm - last held on 13 October 2019 (next to be held in October 2023)
election results:
Senate - percent of vote by party - NA; seats by party - PiS 48, KO 43, PSL 3, SLD 2, independent 4; composition (as of October 2021) - men 76, women 24, percent of women 24%
Sejm - percent of vote by party - PiS 43.6%, KO 27.4%, SLD 12.6%, PSL 8.5% Confederation 6.8%, other 1.1%; seats by party - PiS 235, KO 134, SLD 49, PSL 30, KWiN 11, MN 1; men 330, women 130, percent of women 28.3%; note -total Parliament percent of women 27.5%
note: the designation National Assembly or Zgromadzenie Narodowe is only used on those rare occasions when the 2 houses meet jointly

Judicial branch: *highest court(s):* Supreme Court or Sad Najwyzszy (consists of the first president of the Supreme Court and 120 justices organized in criminal, civil, labor and social insurance, and extraordinary appeals and public affairs and disciplinary chambers); Constitutional Tribunal (consists of 15 judges, including the court president and vice president)
judge selection and term of office: president of the Supreme Court nominated by the General Assembly of the Supreme Court and selected by the president of Poland; other judges nominated by the 25-member National Judicial Council and appointed by the president of Poland; judges serve until retirement, usually at age 65, but tenure can be extended; Constitutional Tribunal judges chosen by the Sejm for single 9-year terms
subordinate courts: administrative courts; military courts; local, regional and appellate courts subdivided into military, civil, criminal, labor, and family courts

Political parties and leaders: Civic Coalition or KO [collective leadership]
Confederation Liberty and Independence or KORWiN [Janusz KORWIN-MIKKE, Robert WINNICKI, Grzegorz BRAUN]
Law and Justice or PiS [Jaroslaw KACZYNSKI]
Polish Coalition or PSL [Wladyslaw KOSINIAK-KAMYSZ]
The Left [Wlodzimierz CZARZASTY]

International organization participation: Arctic Council (observer), Australia Group, BIS, BSEC (observer), CBSS, CD, CE, CEI, CERN, EAPC, EBRD, ECB, EIB, ESA, EU, FAO, IAEA, IBRD, ICAO, ICC (national committees), ICCt, ICRM, IDA, IEA, IFC, IFRCS, IHO, ILO, IMF, IMO, IMSO, Interpol, IOC, IOM, IPU, ISO, ITSO, ITU, ITUC (NGOs), MIGA, MONUSCO, NATO, NEA, NSG, OAS (observer), OECD, OIF (observer), OPCW, OSCE, PCA, Schengen Convention, UN, UNCTAD, UNESCO, UNHCR, UNHRC, UNIDO, UNMIL, UNMISS, UNOCI, UN Security Council (temporary), UNWTO, UPU, Wassenaar Arrangement, WCO, WFTU (NGOs), WHO, WIPO, WMO, WTO, ZC

Diplomatic representation in the US: *chief of mission:* Ambassador Marek Grzegorz MAGIEROWSKI (since 13 January 2022)
chancery: 2640 16th Street NW, Washington, DC 20009
telephone: [1] (202) 499-1700
FAX: [1] (202) 328-2152
email address and website:
washington.amb.sekretariat@msz.gov.pl
https://www.gov.pl/web/usa-en/embassy-washington
consulate(s) general: Chicago, Houston, Los Angeles, New York

Diplomatic representation from the US: *chief of mission:* Ambassador Mark BRZEZINSKI (since 19 January 2022)
embassy: Aleje Ujazdowskie 29/31, 00-540 Warsaw
mailing address: 5010 Warsaw Place, Washington, DC 20521-5010
telephone: [48] (22) 504-2000
FAX: [48] (22) 504-2088
email address and website:
acswarsaw@state.gov
https://pl.usembassy.gov/
consulate(s) general: Krakow

Flag description: two equal horizontal bands of white (top) and red; colors derive from the Polish emblem - a white eagle on a red field
note: similar to the flags of Indonesia and Monaco which are red (top) and white

National symbol(s): white crowned eagle; national colors: white, red

National anthem: *name:* "Mazurek Dabrowskiego" (Dabrowski's Mazurka)
lyrics/music: Jozef WYBICKI/traditional
note: adopted 1927; the anthem, commonly known as "Jeszcze Polska nie zginela" (Poland Has Not Yet Perished), was written in 1797; the lyrics resonate strongly with Poles because they reflect the numerous occasions in which the nation's lands have been occupied

National heritage: *total World Heritage Sites:* 17 (15 cultural, 2 natural)

selected World Heritage Site locales: Historic Krakow (c); Historic Warsaw (c); Medieval Torun (c); Wooden Tserkvas of the Carpathian Region (c); Castle of the Teutonic Order in Malbork (c); Wieliczka and Bochnia Royal Salt Mines (c); Auschwitz Birkenau Concentration Camp (c); Ancient and Primeval Beech Forests of the Carpathians (n); Białowieza Forest (n); Old City of Zamość (c)

ECONOMY

Economic overview: Poland has the sixth-largest economy in the EU and has long had a reputation as a business-friendly country with largely sound macroeconomic policies. Since 1990, Poland has pursued a policy of economic liberalization. During the 2008-09 economic slowdown Poland was the only EU country to avoid a recession, in part because of the government's loose fiscal policy combined with a commitment to rein in spending in the medium-term Poland is the largest recipient of EU development funds and their cyclical allocation can significantly impact the rate of economic growth.

The Polish economy performed well during the 2014-17 period, with the real GDP growth rate generally exceeding 3%, in part because of increases in government social spending that have helped to accelerate consumer-driven growth. However, since 2015, Poland has implemented new business restrictions and taxes on foreign-dominated economic sectors, including banking and insurance, energy, and healthcare, that have dampened investor sentiment and has increased the government's ownership of some firms. The government reduced the retirement age in 2016 and has had mixed success in introducing new taxes and boosting tax compliance to offset the increased costs of social spending programs and relieve upward pressure on the budget deficit. Some credit ratings agencies estimate that Poland during the next few years is at risk of exceeding the EU's 3%-of-GDP limit on budget deficits, possibly impacting its access to future EU funds. Poland's economy is projected to perform well in the next few years in part because of an anticipated cyclical increase in the use of its EU development funds and continued, robust household spending.

Poland faces several systemic challenges, which include addressing some of the remaining deficiencies in its road and rail infrastructure, business environment, rigid labor code, commercial court system, government red tape, and burdensome tax system, especially for entrepreneurs. Additional long-term challenges include diversifying Poland's energy mix, strengthening investments in innovation, research, and development, as well as stemming the outflow of educated young Poles to other EU member states, especially in light of a coming demographic contraction due to emigration, persistently low fertility rates, and the aging of the Solidarity-era baby boom generation.

Real GDP (purchasing power parity): $1,223,460,000,000 (2020 est.)
$1,257,440,000,000 (2019 est.)
$1,202,820,000,000 (2018 est.)
note: data are in 2017 dollars
country comparison to the world: 19

Real GDP growth rate: 4.55% (2019 est.)
5.36% (2018 est.)
4.83% (2017 est.)
country comparison to the world: 61

Real GDP per capita: $32,200 (2020 est.)
$33,100 (2019 est.)
$31,700 (2018 est.)
note: data are in 2017 dollars
country comparison to the world: 60

GDP (official exchange rate): $595.72 billion (2019 est.)

Inflation rate (consumer prices): 2.1% (2019 est.)
1.7% (2018 est.)
2% (2017 est.)
country comparison to the world: 114

Credit ratings:

Fitch rating: A- (2007)

Moody's rating: A2 (2002)

Standard & Poors rating: A- (2018)

GDP - composition, by sector of origin: *agriculture:* 2.4% (2017 est.)
industry: 40.2% (2017 est.)
services: 57.4% (2017 est.)

GDP - composition, by end use: *household consumption:* 58.6% (2017 est.)
government consumption: 17.7% (2017 est.)
investment in fixed capital: 17.7% (2017 est.)
investment in inventories: 2% (2017 est.)
exports of goods and services: 54% (2017 est.)
imports of goods and services: -49.9% (2017 est.)

Agricultural products: milk, sugar beet, wheat, potatoes, triticale, maize, barley, apples, mixed grains, rye

Industries: machine building, iron and steel, coal mining, chemicals, shipbuilding, food processing, glass, beverages, textiles

Industrial production growth rate: 7.5% (2017 est.)
country comparison to the world: 28

Labor force: 9.561 million (2020 est.)
country comparison to the world: 51

Labor force - by occupation: *agriculture:* 11.5%
industry: 30.4%
services: 57.6% (2015)

Unemployment rate: 5.43% (2019 est.)
6.08% (2018 est.)
country comparison to the world: 88

Unemployment, youth ages 15-24: *total:* 10.8%
male: 10.3%
female: 11.6% (2020 est.)
country comparison to the world: 132

Population below poverty line: 15.4% (2018 est.)

Gini Index coefficient - distribution of family income: 29.7 (2017 est.)
33.7 (2008)
country comparison to the world: 151

Household income or consumption by percentage share: *lowest 10%:* 3%
highest 10%: 23.9% (2015 est.)

Budget: *revenues:* 207.5 billion (2017 est.)
expenditures: 216.2 billion (2017 est.)

Budget surplus (+) or deficit (-): -1.7% (of GDP) (2017 est.)
country comparison to the world: 96

Public debt: 50.6% of GDP (2017 est.)
54.2% of GDP (2016 est.)
note: data cover general government debt and include debt instruments issued (or owned) by government entities other than the treasury; the data include treasury debt held by foreign entities, the data include subnational entities, as well as intragovernmental debt; intragovernmental debt consists of treasury borrowings from surpluses in the social funds, such as for retirement, medical care, and unemployment; debt instruments for the social funds are not sold at public auctions
country comparison to the world: 100

Taxes and other revenues: 39.5% (of GDP) (2017 est.)
country comparison to the world: 45

Fiscal year: calendar year

Current account balance: $2.92 billion (2019 est.)
-$7.52 billion (2018 est.)
country comparison to the world: 35

Exports: $333.54 billion (2020 est.) note: data are in current year dollars
$330.68 billion (2019 est.) note: data are in current year dollars
$324.22 billion (2018 est.) note: data are in current year dollars
country comparison to the world: 21

Exports - partners: Germany 27%, Czechia 6%, United Kingdom 6%, France 6%, Italy 5% (2019)

Exports - commodities: cars and vehicle parts, seats, furniture, computers, video displays (2019)

Imports: $292.44 billion (2020 est.) note: data are in current year dollars
$302.87 billion (2019 est.) note: data are in current year dollars
$306.43 billion (2018 est.) note: data are in current year dollars
country comparison to the world: 21

Imports - partners: Germany 25%, China 10%, Italy 5%, Netherlands 5% (2019)

Imports - commodities: cars and vehicle parts, crude petroleum, packaged medicines, broadcasting equipment, office machinery/parts (2019)

Reserves of foreign exchange and gold: $113.3 billion (31 December 2017 est.)
$114.4 billion (31 December 2016 est.)
country comparison to the world: 23

Debt - external: $351.77 billion (2019 est.)
$373.721 billion (2018 est.)
country comparison to the world: 32

Exchange rates: zlotych (PLN) per US dollar -
3.6684 (2020 est.)
3.8697 (2019 est.)
3.76615 (2018 est.)
3.7721 (2014 est.)
3.1538 (2013 est.)

ENERGY

Electricity access: *electrification - total population:* 100% (2020)

Electricity: *installed generating capacity:* 47.269 million kW (2020 est.)
consumption: 149.203 billion kWh (2020 est.)
exports: 7.357 billion kWh (2020 est.)
imports: 20.624 billion kWh (2020 est.)
transmission/distribution losses: 9.995 billion kWh (2020 est.)

Electricity generation sources: *fossil fuels:* 79.8% of total installed capacity (2020 est.)
solar: 1.4% of total installed capacity (2020 est.)
wind: 10.8% of total installed capacity (2020 est.)
hydroelectricity: 2% of total installed capacity (2020 est.)
biomass and waste: 6% of total installed capacity (2020 est.)

Coal: *production:* 108.152 million metric tons (2020 est.)
consumption: 110.674 million metric tons (2020 est.)
exports: 11.063 million metric tons (2020 est.)
imports: 13.281 million metric tons (2020 est.)
proven reserves: 26.932 billion metric tons (2019 est.)

Petroleum: *total petroleum production:* 28,400 bbl/day (2021 est.)
refined petroleum consumption: 697,700 bbl/day (2019 est.)
crude oil and lease condensate exports: 6,000 bbl/day (2018 est.)
crude oil and lease condensate imports: 542,100 bbl/day (2018 est.)

crude oil estimated reserves: 113 million barrels (2021 est.)

Refined petroleum products - production: 554,200 bbl/day (2017 est.)
country comparison to the world: 30

Refined petroleum products - exports: 104,800 bbl/day (2017 est.)
country comparison to the world: 43

Refined petroleum products - imports: 222,300 bbl/day (2017 est.)
country comparison to the world: 32

Natural gas: *production:* 5,666,815,000 cubic meters (2020 est.)
consumption: 21,463,908,000 cubic meters (2020 est.)
exports: 704.975 million cubic meters (2019 est.)
imports: 16,633,345,000 cubic meters (2020 est.)
proven reserves: 91.492 billion cubic meters (2021 est.)

Carbon dioxide emissions: 304.04 million metric tonnes of CO2 (2019 est.)
from coal and metallurgical coke: 176.938 million metric tonnes of CO2 (2019 est.)
from petroleum and other liquids: 89.944 million metric tonnes of CO2 (2019 est.)
from consumed natural gas: 37.158 million metric tonnes of CO2 (2019 est.)
country comparison to the world: 21

Energy consumption per capita: 112.831 million Btu/person (2019 est.)
country comparison to the world: 48

COMMUNICATIONS

Telephones - fixed lines: *total subscriptions:* 5,777,428 (2020 est.)
subscriptions per 100 inhabitants: 15 (2020 est.)
country comparison to the world: 24

Telephones - mobile cellular: *total subscriptions:* 49,350,724 (2020 est.)
subscriptions per 100 inhabitants: 130 (2020 est.)
country comparison to the world: 31

Telecommunication systems: *general assessment:* the liberalized telecom market has seen considerable development in the broadband and mobile sectors; the regulatory environment has encouraged market competition, partly by encouraging operators to secure spectrum and also by ensuring access to cable and fiber infrastructure; the mobile market in recent years has been characterized by the rapid extension of LTE networks and the development of mobile data services based on newly released and re-farmed spectrum; the regulator's attempts to auction spectrum in a range of bands has been delayed, with spectrum in the 5G-suitable 3.4-3.8GHz range having been suspended to later in 2021 as a result of the Covid-19 outbreak and legislative changes (2021)
domestic: several nation-wide networks provide mobile-cellular service; fixed-line roughly 15 per 100 (service lags in rural areas), mobile-cellular over 130 per 100 persons (2020)
international: country code - 48; landing points for the Baltica and the Denmark-Poland2 submarine cables connecting Poland, Denmark and Sweden; international direct dialing with automated exchanges; satellite earth station - 1 with access to Intelsat, Eutelsat, Inmarsat, and Intersputnik (2019)

Broadcast media: state-run public TV operates 2 national channels supplemented by 16 regional channels and several niche channels; privately owned entities operate several national TV networks and a number of special interest channels; many privately owned channels broadcasting locally; roughly half of all households are linked to either satellite or cable TV systems providing access to foreign television networks; state-run public radio operates 5 national networks and 17 regional radio stations; 2 privately owned national radio networks, several commercial stations broadcasting to multiple cities, and many privately owned local radio stations (2019)

Internet country code: .pl

Internet users: *total:* 31,456,228 (2020 est.)
percent of population: 83% (2020 est.)
country comparison to the world: 30

Broadband - fixed subscriptions: *total:* 8,369,218 (2020 est.)
subscriptions per 100 inhabitants: 22 (2020 est.)
country comparison to the world: 24

TRANSPORTATION

National air transport system: *number of registered air carriers:* 6 (2020)
inventory of registered aircraft operated by air carriers: 169
annual passenger traffic on registered air carriers: 9,277,538 (2018)
annual freight traffic on registered air carriers: 271.49 million (2018) mt-km

Civil aircraft registration country code prefix: SP

Airports: *total:* 126 (2021)
country comparison to the world: 46

Airports - with paved runways: *total:* 87
over 3,047 m: 5
2,438 to 3,047 m: 30
1,524 to 2,437 m: 36
914 to 1,523 m: 10
under 914 m: 6 (2021)

Airports - with unpaved runways: *total:* 39
1,524 to 2,437 m: 1
914 to 1,523 m: 17
under 914 m: 21 (2021)

Heliports: 6 (2021)

Pipelines: 14,198 km gas, 1,374 km oil, 2,483 km refined products (2018)

Railways: *total:* 19,231 km (2016)
standard gauge: 18,836 km (2016) 1.435-m gauge (11,874 km electrified)
broad gauge: 395 km (2016) 1.524-m gauge
country comparison to the world: 15

Roadways: *total:* 420,000 km (2016)
paved: 291,000 km (2016) (includes 1,492 km of expressways, 1,559 of motorways)
unpaved: 129,000 km (2016)
country comparison to the world: 18

Waterways: 3,997 km (2009) (navigable rivers and canals)
country comparison to the world: 29

Merchant marine: *total:* 143
by type: general cargo 7, oil tanker 6, other 130 (2021)
country comparison to the world: 78

Ports and terminals: *major seaport(s):* Gdansk, Gdynia, Swinoujscie
container port(s) (TEUs): Gdansk (2,073,215) (2019)

LNG terminal(s) (import): Swinoujscie
river port(s): Szczecin (River Oder)

MILITARY AND SECURITY

Military and security forces: Polish Armed Forces: Land Forces (Wojska Ladowe), Navy (Marynarka Wojenna), Air Force (Sily Powietrzne), Special Forces (Wojska Specjalne), Territorial Defense Force (Wojska Obrony Terytorialnej); Ministry of Interior and Administration: Border Guard (includes coast guard duties) (2022)
note: the Polish Armed Forces are organized into a General Staff, an Armed Forces General Command, an Armed Forces Operational Command, Territorial Defense Forces (established 2017), Military Police, and the Warsaw Garrison Command

Military expenditures: 2.4% of GDP (2022 est.)
2.3% of GDP (2021)
2.2% of GDP (2020)
2% of GDP (2019) (approximately $17.5 billion)
2% of GDP (2018) (approximately $16.8 billion)
note: in 2022, the Polish Government announced plans to increase defense spending to 3% of GDP for 2023
country comparison to the world: 45

Military and security service personnel strengths: approximately 120,000 active duty personnel (65,000 Army; 7,000 Navy; 15,000 Air Force; 3,000 Special Forces; 25,000 joint service/other; 5,000 active Territorial Defense Forces); approximately 25,000 other Territorial Defense Forces (reserves) (2022)
note: in June 2019, the Polish Government approved a plan to increase the size of the military over a period of 10 years to over 200,000 troops, including doubling the size of the Territorial Defense Forces; in 2021, it announced additional plans to increase the size of the military to over 300,000 personnel

Military equipment inventories and acquisitions: the inventory of the Polish Armed Forces consists of a mix of Soviet-era and more modern Western weapons systems; since 2010, the leading suppliers of armaments have included Finland, Germany, Italy, and the US (2021)
note: in late 2018, Poland announced a 7-year (through 2026) approximately $50 billion defense modernization plan that would include such items as 5th generation combat aircraft, unmanned aerial vehicles, rocket artillery, helicopters, submarines, frigates, and improved cyber security

Military service age and obligation: 18-28 years of age for male and female voluntary military service; conscription phased out in 2009-12; professional

soldiers serve on a permanent basis (for an unspecified period of time) or on a contract basis (for a specified period of time); initial contract period is 24 months; women serve in the military on the same terms as men (2022)
note 1: as of 2019, women made up about 7% of the military's full-time personnel
note 2: in May 2022, Poland announced a new 12-month voluntary military service program with recruits going through a 1-month basic training period with a military unit, followed by 11 months of specialized training; upon completion of service, the volunteers would be allowed to join the Territorial Defense Forces or the active reserve, and have priority to join the professional army and be given preference for employment in the public sector; the program is part of an effort to increase the size of the Polish military

Military deployments: 250 Kosovo (NATO/KFOR); up to 180 Latvia (NATO); 190 Lebanon (UNIFIL); 230 Romania (NATO) (2022)
note 1: Poland contributes about 2,500 troops to the Lithuania, Poland, and Ukraine joint military brigade (LITPOLUKRBRIG), which was established in 2014; the brigade is headquartered in Poland and is comprised of an international staff, three battalions, and specialized units; units affiliated with the multinational brigade remain within the structures of the armed forces of their respective countries until the brigade is activated for participation in an international operation
note 2: in response to Russia's 2022 invasion of Ukraine, some NATO countries, including Poland, have sent additional troops and equipment to the battlegroups deployed in NATO territory in eastern Europe

Military - note: Poland joined NATO in 1999; Czechia, Hungary, and Poland were invited to begin accession talks at NATO's Madrid Summit in 1997, and in March 1999 they became the first former members of the Warsaw Pact to join the Alliance

since 2017, Poland has hosted a US-led multi-national NATO ground force battlegroup as part of the Alliance's Enhanced Forward Presence initiative; since 2014, Poland has also hosted NATO fighter detachments at Malbork Air Base under NATO's enhanced air policing arrangements

Poland hosts a NATO-led divisional headquarters (Multinational Division Northeast; operational in 2018), which coordinates training and preparation activities of its respective subordinate battlegroups in Poland and Lithuania; Poland also hosts a corps-level headquarters (Multinational Corps Northeast) (2022)

TERRORISM

Terrorist group(s): Islamic State of Iraq and ash-Sham (ISIS)

TRANSNATIONAL ISSUES

Disputes - international: *Poland-Belarus-Ukraine*: as a member state that forms part of the EU's external border, Poland has implemented the strict Schengen border rules to restrict illegal immigration and trade along its eastern borders with Belarus and Ukraine

Refugees and internally displaced persons: *refugees (country of origin)*: 9,870 (Russia) (2019); 1,489,155 (Ukraine) (as of 8 November 2022)
stateless persons: 1,389 (mid-year 2021)

Illicit drugs: source country for amphetamines

PORTUGAL

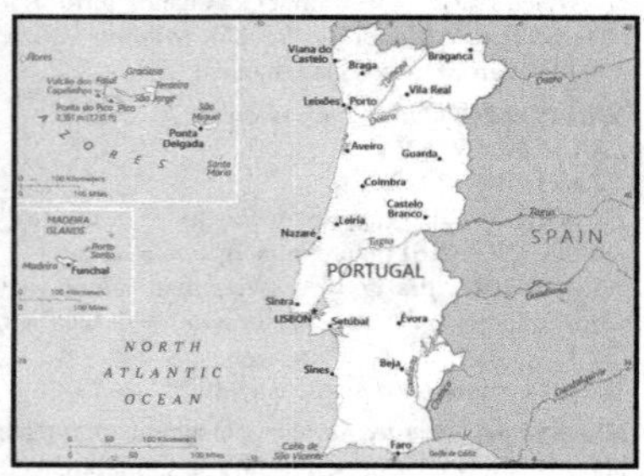

INTRODUCTION

Background: Following its heyday as a global maritime power during the 15th and 16th centuries, Portugal lost much of its wealth and status with the destruction of Lisbon in a 1755 earthquake, occupation during the Napoleonic Wars, and the independence of Brazil, its wealthiest colony, in 1822. A 1910 revolution deposed the monarchy, and for most of the next six decades, repressive governments ran the country. In 1974, a left-wing military coup installed broad democratic reforms. The following year, Portugal granted independence to all of its African colonies. Portugal is a founding member of NATO and entered the EC (now the EU) in 1986.

GEOGRAPHY

Location: Southwestern Europe, bordering the North Atlantic Ocean, west of Spain

Geographic coordinates: 39 30 N, 8 00 W

Map references: Europe

Area: *total:* 92,090 sq km
land: 91,470 sq km
water: 620 sq km
note: includes Azores and Madeira Islands
country comparison to the world: 111

Area - comparative: slightly smaller than Virginia

Land boundaries: *total:* 1,224 km
border countries (1): Spain 1,224 km

Coastline: 1,793 km

Maritime claims: *territorial sea:* 12 nm
contiguous zone: 24 nm
exclusive economic zone: 200 nm
continental shelf: 200-m depth or to the depth of exploitation

Climate: maritime temperate; cool and rainy in north, warmer and drier in south

Terrain: the west-flowing Tagus River divides the country: the north is mountainous toward the interior, while the south is characterized by rolling plains

Elevation: *highest point:* Ponta do Pico (Pico or Pico Alto) on Ilha do Pico in the Azores 2,351 m
lowest point: Atlantic Ocean 0 m
mean elevation: 372 m

Natural resources: fish, forests (cork), iron ore, copper, zinc, tin, tungsten, silver, gold, uranium, marble, clay, gypsum, salt, arable land, hydropower

Land use: *agricultural land:* 39.7% (2018 est.)
arable land: 11.9% (2018 est.)
permanent crops: 7.8% (2018 est.)
permanent pasture: 20% (2018 est.)
forest: 37.8% (2018 est.)
other: 22.5% (2018 est.)

Irrigated land: 5,400 sq km (2012)

Population distribution: concentrations are primarily along or near the Atlantic coast; both Lisbon and the second largest city, Porto, are coastal cities

Natural hazards: Azores subject to severe earthquakes
volcanism: limited volcanic activity in the Azores Islands; Fayal or Faial (1,043 m) last erupted in 1958; most volcanoes have not erupted in centuries; historically active volcanoes include Agua de Pau, Furnas, Pico, Picos Volcanic System, San Jorge, Sete Cidades, and Terceira

Geography - note: Azores and Madeira Islands occupy strategic locations along western sea approaches to Strait of Gibraltar; they are two of the four North Atlantic archipelagos that make up Macaronesia; the others are the Canary Islands (Spain) and Cabo Verde

PEOPLE AND SOCIETY

Population: 10,242,081 (2022 est.)
country comparison to the world: 91

Nationality: *noun:* Portuguese (singular and plural)
adjective: Portuguese

Ethnic groups: Portuguese 95%; citizens from Portugal's former colonies in Africa, Asia (Han Chinese), and South America (Brazilian) and other foreign born 5%

Languages: Portuguese (official), Mirandese (official, but locally used)

Religions: Roman Catholic 81%, other Christian 3.3%, other (includes Jewish, Muslim) 0.6%, none 6.8%, unspecified 8.3% (2011 est.)
note: data represent population 15 years of age and older

Age structure: *0-14 years:* 13.58% (male 716,102/female 682,582)
15-24 years: 10.94% (male 580,074/female 547,122)
25-54 years: 41.49% (male 2,109,693/female 2,164,745)
55-64 years: 13.08% (male 615,925/female 731,334)
65 years and over: 20.92% (male 860,198/female 1,294,899) (2020 est.)

Dependency ratios: *total dependency ratio:* 55.8
youth dependency ratio: 20.3
elderly dependency ratio: 35.5
potential support ratio: 2.8 (2020 est.)

Median age: *total:* 44.6 years
male: 42.7 years
female: 46.5 years (2020 est.)
country comparison to the world: 13

Population growth rate: -0.2% (2022 est.)
country comparison to the world: 210

Birth rate: 8 births/1,000 population (2022 est.)
country comparison to the world: 218

Death rate: 10.9 deaths/1,000 population (2022 est.)
country comparison to the world: 23

Net migration rate: 0.91 migrant(s)/1,000 population (2022 est.)
country comparison to the world: 66

Population distribution: concentrations are primarily along or near the Atlantic coast; both Lisbon and the second largest city, Porto, are coastal cities

Urbanization: *urban population:* 67.4% of total population (2022)
rate of urbanization: 0.44% annual rate of change (2020-25 est.)

Major urban areas - population: 2.986 million LISBON (capital), 1.320 million Porto (2022)

Sex ratio: *at birth:* 1.05 male(s)/female
0-14 years: 1.05 male(s)/female
15-24 years: 1.06 male(s)/female
25-54 years: 0.98 male(s)/female
55-64 years: 0.85 male(s)/female
65 years and over: 0.55 male(s)/female
total population: 0.9 male(s)/female (2022 est.)

Mother's mean age at first birth: 29.9 years (2020 est.)

Maternal mortality ratio: 8 deaths/100,000 live births (2017 est.)
country comparison to the world: 152

Infant mortality rate: *total:* 2.5 deaths/1,000 live births
male: 2.86 deaths/1,000 live births
female: 2.12 deaths/1,000 live births (2022 est.)
country comparison to the world: 216

Life expectancy at birth: *total population:* 81.5 years
male: 78.37 years
female: 84.79 years (2022 est.)
country comparison to the world: 39

Total fertility rate: 1.43 children born/woman (2022 est.)
country comparison to the world: 212

Contraceptive prevalence rate: 73.9% (2014)

Drinking water source: *improved: urban:* 100% of population
rural: 99.7% of population
total: 99.9% of population
unimproved: urban: 0% of population
rural: 0.3% of population
total: 0.1% of population (2020 est.)

Current health expenditure: 9.5% of GDP (2019)

Physicians density: 5.48 physicians/1,000 population (2019)

Hospital bed density: 3.5 beds/1,000 population (2018)

Sanitation facility access: *improved: urban:* 99.9% of population
rural: 100% of population
total: 99.9% of population
unimproved: urban: 0.1% of population
rural: 0% of population
total: 0.1% of population (2020 est.)

HIV/AIDS - adult prevalence rate: 0.5% (2020 est.)
country comparison to the world: 68

HIV/AIDS - people living with HIV/AIDS: 42,000 (2020 est.)
country comparison to the world: 64

HIV/AIDS - deaths: (2020 est.) <500

Obesity - adult prevalence rate: 20.8% (2016)
country comparison to the world: 95

Alcohol consumption per capita: *total:* 10.37 liters of pure alcohol (2019 est.)
beer: 2.62 liters of pure alcohol (2019 est.)
wine: 6.04 liters of pure alcohol (2019 est.)
spirits: 1.34 liters of pure alcohol (2019 est.)
other alcohols: 0.37 liters of pure alcohol (2019 est.)
country comparison to the world: 20

Tobacco use: *total:* 25.4% (2020 est.)
male: 30.5% (2020 est.)
female: 20.2% (2020 est.)
country comparison to the world: 48

Children under the age of 5 years underweight: 0.4% (2015/16)
country comparison to the world: 129

Education expenditures: 4.7% of GDP (2018 est.)
country comparison to the world: 76

Literacy: *definition:* age 15 and over can read and write
total population: 96.1%
male: 97.4%
female: 95.1% (2018)

School life expectancy (primary to tertiary education): *total:* 17 years
male: 17 years
female: 17 years (2019)

Unemployment, youth ages 15-24: *total:* 22.6%
male: 21%
female: 24.4% (2020 est.)

ENVIRONMENT

Environment - current issues: soil erosion; air pollution caused by industrial and vehicle emissions; water pollution, especially in urban centers and coastal areas

Environment - international agreements: *party to:* Air Pollution, Air Pollution-Heavy Metals, Air Pollution-Multi-effect Protocol, Antarctic-Environmental Protection, Antarctic Treaty, Biodiversity, Climate Change, Climate Change-Kyoto Protocol, Climate Change-Paris Agreement, Comprehensive Nuclear Test Ban, Desertification, Endangered Species, Hazardous Wastes, Law of the Sea, Marine Dumping-London Convention, Marine Life Conservation, Ozone Layer Protection, Ship Pollution, Tropical Timber 2006, Wetlands, Whaling
signed, but not ratified: Air Pollution-Persistent Organic Pollutants, Air Pollution-Volatile Organic Compounds, Environmental Modification, Nuclear Test Ban

Air pollutants: *particulate matter emissions:* 7.87 micrograms per cubic meter (2016 est.)
carbon dioxide emissions: 48.74 megatons (2016 est.)
methane emissions: 10.93 megatons (2020 est.)

Climate: maritime temperate; cool and rainy in north, warmer and drier in south

Land use: *agricultural land:* 39.7% (2018 est.)
arable land: 11.9% (2018 est.)
permanent crops: 7.8% (2018 est.)
permanent pasture: 20% (2018 est.)
forest: 37.8% (2018 est.)
other: 22.5% (2018 est.)

Urbanization: *urban population:* 67.4% of total population (2022)
rate of urbanization: 0.44% annual rate of change (2020-25 est.)

Revenue from forest resources: *forest revenues:* 0.13% of GDP (2018 est.)
country comparison to the world: 107

Revenue from coal: *coal revenues:* 0% of GDP (2018 est.)
country comparison to the world: 153

Waste and recycling: *municipal solid waste generated annually:* 4.71 million tons (2014 est.)
municipal solid waste recycled annually: 764,433 tons (2014 est.)
percent of municipal solid waste recycled: 16.2% (2014 est.)

Total water withdrawal: *municipal:* 914.1 million cubic meters (2017 est.)
industrial: 1.497 billion cubic meters (2017 est.)
agricultural: 8.767 billion cubic meters (2017 est.)

Total renewable water resources: 77.4 billion cubic meters (2017 est.)

GOVERNMENT

Country name: *conventional long form:* Portuguese Republic
conventional short form: Portugal
local long form: Republica Portuguesa
local short form: Portugal
etymology: name derives from the Roman designation "Portus Cale" meaning "Port of Cale"; Cale was an ancient Celtic town and port in present-day northern Portugal

Government type: semi-presidential republic

Capital: *name:* Lisbon
geographic coordinates: 38 43 N, 9 08 W
time difference: UTC 0 (5 hours ahead of Washington, DC, during Standard Time)
daylight saving time: +1hr, begins last Sunday in March; ends last Sunday in October
time zone note: Portugal has two time zones, including the Azores (UTC-1)
etymology: Lisbon is one of Europe's oldest cities (the second oldest capital city after Athens) and the origin of the name is lost in time; it may have been founded as an ancient Celtic settlement that subsequently maintained close commercial relations with the Phoenicians (beginning about 1200 B.C.); the name of the settlement may have been derived from the pre-Roman appellation for the Tagus River that runs through the city, Lisso or Lucio; the Romans named the city "Olisippo" when they took it from the Carthaginians in 205 B.C.; under the Visigoths the city name became "Ulixbona," under the Arabs it was "al-Ushbuna"; the medieval version of "Lissabona" became today's Lisboa

Administrative divisions: 18 districts (distritos, singular - distrito) and 2 autonomous regions* (regioes autonomas, singular - regiao autonoma); Aveiro, Acores (Azores)*, Beja, Braga, Braganca, Castelo

Branco, Coimbra, Evora, Faro, Guarda, Leiria, Lisboa (Lisbon), Madeira*, Portalegre, Porto, Santarem, Setubal, Viana do Castelo, Vila Real, Viseu

Independence: 1143 (Kingdom of Portugal recognized); 1 December 1640 (independence reestablished following 60 years of Spanish rule); 5 October 1910 (republic proclaimed)

National holiday: Portugal Day (Dia de Portugal), 10 June (1580); note - also called Camoes Day, the day that revered national poet Luis DE CAMOES (1524-80) died

Constitution: *history:* several previous; latest adopted 2 April 1976, effective 25 April 1976
amendments: proposed by the Assembly of the Republic; adoption requires two-thirds majority vote of Assembly members; amended several times, last in 2005

Legal system: civil law system; Constitutional Court review of legislative acts

International law organization participation: accepts compulsory ICJ jurisdiction with reservations; accepts ICCt jurisdiction

Citizenship: *citizenship by birth:* no
citizenship by descent only: at least one parent must be a citizen of Portugal
dual citizenship recognized: yes
residency requirement for naturalization: 10 years; 6 years if from a Portuguese-speaking country

Suffrage: 18 years of age; universal Executive branch
chief of state: President Marcelo REBELO DE SOUSA (since 9 March 2016)
head of government: Prime Minister Antonio Luis Santos da COSTA (since 24 November 2015)
cabinet: Council of Ministers appointed by the president on the recommendation of the prime minister
elections/appointments: president directly elected by absolute majority popular vote in 2 rounds if needed for a 5-year term (eligible for a second term); election last held on 24 January 2021 (next to be held in January 2026); following legislative elections the leader of the majority party or majority coalition is usually appointed prime minister by the president
election results:
2021: Marcelo REBELO DE SOUSA reelected president in the first round; percent of vote - Marcelo REBELO DE SOUSA (PSD) 60.7%, Ana GOMES (ran as an independent but is a member of PS) 13%, Andre VENTURA (CH) 11.9%, João FERREIRA (PCP-PEV) 4.32%, Marisa MATIAS (BE) 3.95%, other 6.16%
2016: Marcelo REBELO DE SOUSA elected president; percent of vote - Marcelo REBELO DE SOUSA (PSD) 52%, António SAMPAIO DA NOVOA (independent) 22.9%, Marisa MATIAS (BE) 10.1%, Maria DE BELEM ROSEIRA (PS) 4.2%
note: there is also a Council of State that acts as a consultative body to the president

Legislative branch: *description:* unicameral Assembly of the Republic or Assembleia da Republica (230 seats; 226 members directly elected in multi-seat constituencies by closed-list proportional representation vote and 4 members - 2 each in 2 constituencies representing Portuguese living abroad - directly elected by proportional representation vote; members serve 4-year terms)
elections:
last held on 30 January 2022 (next to be held in January 2026); note - early elections were called after parliament was dissolved on 3 November 2021 because of the 27 October 2021 rejection of the government's budget
election results:
percent of vote by party - PS 42.5%, PSD 28.4%, Enough 7.4%, IL 5%, BE 4.5%, CDU 4.4%, other 7.8%; seats by party - PS 120, PSD 72, Enough 12, IL 8, CDU 6, BE 5, other 3; composition - men NA, women NA, percent of women NA%

Judicial branch: *highest court(s):* Supreme Court or Supremo Tribunal de Justica (consists of 12 justices); Constitutional Court or Tribunal Constitucional (consists of 13 judges)
judge selection and term of office: Supreme Court justices nominated by the president and appointed by the Assembly of the Republic; judges can serve for life; Constitutional Court judges - 10 elected by the Assembly and 3 elected by the other Constitutional Court judges; judges elected for 6-year nonrenewable terms
subordinate courts: Supreme Administrative Court (Supremo Tribunal Administrativo); Audit Court (Tribunal de Contas); appellate, district, and municipal courts

Political parties and leaders: Democratic Alliance (2022 electoral alliance in the Azores, includes PSD, CDS-PP, PPM)
Democratic and Social Center/People's Party (Partido do Centro Democratico Social-Partido Popular) or CDS-PP [Nuno MELO]
Ecologist Party "The Greens" or "Os Verdes" (Partido Ecologista-Os Verdes) or PEV [Heloisa APOLONIA]
Enough (Chega) [Andre VENTURA]
Liberal Initiative (Iniciativa Liberal) or IL [Joao COTRIM DE FIGUEIREDO]
Madeira First (2022 electoral alliance in Madeira, includes PSD, CDS-PP)
People-Animals-Nature Party (Pessoas-Animais-Natureza) or PAN [Ines SOUSA REAL]
People's Monarchist Party or PPM [Gonçalo DA CAMARA PEREIRA]
Portuguese Communist Party (Partido Comunista Portugues) or PCP [Jeronimo DE SOUSA]
Social Democratic Party (Partido Social Democrata) or PSD [Luis MONTENEGRO] (formerly the Partido Popular Democratico or PPD)
Socialist Party (Partido Socialista) or PS [Antonio COSTA]
The Left Bloc (Bloco de Esquerda) or BE or O Bloco [Catarina MARTINS]
Unitary Democratic Coalition (Coligacao Democratica Unitaria) or CDU [Jeronimo DE SOUSA] (includes PCP and PEV)

International organization participation: ADB (nonregional member), AfDB (nonregional member), Australia Group, BIS, CD, CE, CERN, CPLP, EAPC, EBRD, ECB, EIB, EMU, ESA, EU, FAO, FATF, IADB, IAEA, IBRD, ICAO, ICC (national committees), ICCt, ICRM, IDA, IEA, IFAD, IFC, IFRCS, IHO, ILO, IMF, IMO, IMSO, Interpol, IOC, IOM, IPU, ISO, ITSO, ITU, ITUC (NGOs), LAIA (observer), MIGA, MINUSMA, NATO, NEA, NSG, OAS (observer), OECD, OPCW, OSCE, Pacific Alliance (observer), Paris Club (associate), PCA, Schengen Convention, SELEC (observer), UN, UNCTAD, UNESCO, UNHCR, UNIDO, Union Latina, UNWTO, UPU, Wassenaar Arrangement, WCO, WFTU (NGOs), WHO, WIPO, WMO, WTO, ZC

Diplomatic representation in the US: *chief of mission:* Ambassador Francisco Antonio Duarte LOPES (since 7 June 2022)
chancery: 2012 Massachusetts Avenue NW, Washington, DC 20036
telephone: [1] (202) 350-5400; [1] (202) 332-3007
FAX: [1] (202) 462-3726; [1] (202) 387-2768
email address and website:
info.washington@mne.pt; sconsular.washington@mne.pt
https://washingtondc.embaixadaportugal.mne.gov.pt/en/
consulate(s) general: Boston, Newark (NJ), New York, San Francisco
consulate(s): New Bedford (MA), Providence (RI)

Diplomatic representation from the US: *chief of mission:* Ambassador Randi Charno LEVINE (since 22 April 2022)
embassy: Avenida das Forcas Armadas, 1600-081 Lisboa
mailing address: 5320 Lisbon Place, Washington DC 20521-5320
telephone: [351] (21) 727-3300
FAX: [351] (21) 726-9109
email address and website:
conslisbon@state.gov
https://pt.usembassy.gov/
consulate(s): Ponta Delgada (Azores)

Flag description: two vertical bands of green (hoist side, two-fifths) and red (three-fifths) with the national coat of arms (armillary sphere and Portuguese shield) centered on the dividing line; explanations for the color meanings are ambiguous, but a popular interpretation has green symbolizing hope and red the blood of those defending the nation

National symbol(s): armillary sphere (a spherical astrolabe modeling objects in the sky and representing the Republic); national colors: red, green

National anthem: *name:* "A Portuguesa" (The Song of the Portuguese)
lyrics/music: Henrique LOPES DE MENDOCA/ Alfredo KEIL
note: adopted 1910; "A Portuguesa" was originally written to protest the Portuguese monarchy's acquiescence to the 1890 British ultimatum forcing Portugal to give up areas of Africa; the lyrics refer to the "insult" that resulted from the event

National heritage: *total World Heritage Sites:* 17 (16 cultural, 1 natural)
selected World Heritage Site locales: Historic Évora (c); Central Zone of the Town of Angra do Heroismo in the Azores (c); Cultural Landscape of Sintra (c); Laurisilva of Madeira (n); Historic Guimarães (c); Monastery of the Hieronymites and Tower of Belém in Lisbon (c); Convent of Christ in Tomar (c); Prehistoric Rock Art Sites in the Côa Valley and Siega Verde (c); University of Coimbra – Alta and Sofia (c); Sanctuary of Bom Jesus do Monte in Braga (c)

ECONOMY

Economic overview: Portugal has become a diversified and increasingly service-based economy since joining the European Community - the EU's predecessor - in 1986. Over the following two decades, successive governments privatized many state-controlled firms and liberalized key areas of the economy, including the financial and telecommunications sectors. The country joined the Economic and Monetary Union in 1999 and began circulating the euro on 1 January 2002 along with 11 other EU members.

The economy grew by more than the EU average for much of the 1990s, but the rate of growth slowed in 2001-08. After the global financial crisis in 2008, Portugal's economy contracted in 2009 and fell into recession from 2011 to 2013, as the government implemented spending cuts and tax increases to comply with conditions of an EU-IMF financial rescue package, signed in May 2011. Portugal successfully exited its EU-IMF program in May 2014, and its economic recovery gained traction in 2015 because of strong exports and a rebound in private consumption. GDP growth accelerated in 2016, and probably reached 2.5 % in 2017. Unemployment remained high, at 9.7% in 2017, but has improved steadily since peaking at 18% in 2013.

The center-left minority Socialist government has unwound some unpopular austerity measures while managing to remain within most EU fiscal targets. The budget deficit fell from 11.2% of GDP in 2010 to 1.8% in 2017, the country's lowest since democracy was restored in 1974, and surpassing the EU and IMF projections of 3%. Portugal exited the EU's excessive deficit procedure in mid-2017.

Real GDP (purchasing power parity): $331.64 billion (2020 est.)
$358.78 billion (2019 est.)
$350.07 billion (2018 est.)
note: data are in 2017 dollars
country comparison to the world: 52

Real GDP growth rate: 2.24% (2019 est.)
2.85% (2018 est.)
3.51% (2017 est.)
country comparison to the world: 125

Real GDP per capita: $32,200 (2020 est.)
$34,900 (2019 est.)
$34,000 (2018 est.)
note: data are in 2017 dollars
country comparison to the world: 61

GDP (official exchange rate): $237.698 billion (2019 est.)

Inflation rate (consumer prices): 0.3% (2019 est.)
0.9% (2018 est.)
1.3% (2017 est.)
country comparison to the world: 37

Credit ratings:

Fitch rating: BBB (2007)

Moody's rating: Baa3 (2018)

Standard & Poors rating: BBB (2019)

GDP - composition, by sector of origin: *agriculture:* 2.2% (2017 est.)
industry: 22.1% (2017 est.)
services: 75.7% (2017 est.)

GDP - composition, by end use: *household consumption:* 65.1% (2017 est.)
government consumption: 17.6% (2017 est.)
investment in fixed capital: 16.2% (2017 est.)
investment in inventories: 0.1% (2017 est.)
exports of goods and services: 43.1% (2017 est.)
imports of goods and services: -42.1% (2017 est.)

Agricultural products: milk, tomatoes, olives, grapes, maize, potatoes, pork, apples, oranges, poultry

Industries: textiles, clothing, footwear, wood and cork, paper and pulp, chemicals, fuels and lubricants, automobiles and auto parts, base metals, minerals, porcelain and ceramics, glassware, technology, telecommunications; dairy products, wine, other foodstuffs; ship construction and refurbishment; tourism, plastics, financial services, optics

Industrial production growth rate: 3.5% (2017 est.)
country comparison to the world: 89

Labor force: 4.717 million (2020 est.)
country comparison to the world: 82

Labor force - by occupation: *agriculture:* 8.6%
industry: 23.9%
services: 67.5% (2014 est.)

Unemployment rate: 6.55% (2019 est.)
7.05% (2018 est.)
country comparison to the world: 103

Unemployment, youth ages 15-24: *total:* 22.6%
male: 21%
female: 24.4% (2020 est.)
country comparison to the world: 62

Population below poverty line: 17.2% (2018 est.)

Gini Index coefficient - distribution of family income: 33.8 (2017 est.)
34 (2014 est.)
country comparison to the world: 120

Household income or consumption by percentage share: *lowest 10%:* 2.6%
highest 10%: 25.9% (2015 est.)

Budget: *revenues:* 93.55 billion (2017 est.)
expenditures: 100 billion (2017 est.)

Budget surplus (+) or deficit (-): -3% (of GDP) (2017 est.)
country comparison to the world: 134

Public debt: 125.7% of GDP (2017 est.)
129.9% of GDP (2016 est.)
note: data cover general government debt and include debt instruments issued (or owned) by government entities other than the treasury; the data include treasury debt held by foreign entities; the data include debt issued by subnational entities, as well as intragovernmental debt; intragovernmental debt consists of treasury borrowings from surpluses in the social funds, such as for retirement, medical care, and unemployment; debt instruments for the social funds are not sold at public auctions
country comparison to the world: 9

Taxes and other revenues: 42.9% (of GDP) (2017 est.)
country comparison to the world: 29

Fiscal year: calendar year

Current account balance: -$203 million (2019 est.)
$988 million (2018 est.)
country comparison to the world: 100

Exports: $85.28 billion (2020 est.) note: data are in current year dollars
$104.77 billion (2019 est.) note: data are in current year dollars
$105.76 billion (2018 est.) note: data are in current year dollars
country comparison to the world: 44

Exports - partners: Spain 23%, France 13%, Germany 12%, United Kingdom 6%, United States 5% (2019)

Exports - commodities: cars and vehicle parts, refined petroleum, leather footwear, paper products, tires (2019)

Imports: $89.31 billion (2020 est.) note: data are in current year dollars
$103.05 billion (2019 est.) note: data are in current year dollars
$103.59 billion (2018 est.) note: data are in current year dollars
country comparison to the world: 43

Imports - partners: Spain 29%, Germany 13%, France 9%, Italy 5%, Netherlands 5% (2019)

Imports - commodities: cars and vehicle parts, crude petroleum, aircraft, packaged medicines, refined petroleum, natural gas (2019)

Reserves of foreign exchange and gold: $26.11 billion (31 December 2017 est.)
$19.4 billion (31 December 2015 est.)
country comparison to the world: 55

Debt - external: $462.431 billion (2019 est.)
$483.206 billion (2018 est.)
country comparison to the world: 27

Exchange rates: euros (EUR) per US dollar -
0.82771 (2020 est.)
0.90338 (2019 est.)
0.87789 (2018 est.)
0.7525 (2014 est.)
0.7634 (2013 est.)

ENERGY

Electricity access: *electrification - total population:* 100% (2020)

Electricity: *installed generating capacity:* 22.364 million kW (2020 est.)
consumption: 48.409 billion kWh (2020 est.)
exports: 6.097 billion kWh (2020 est.)
imports: 7.553 billion kWh (2020 est.)
transmission/distribution losses: 5.269 billion kWh (2020 est.)

Electricity generation sources: *fossil fuels:* 39% of total installed capacity (2020 est.)
solar: 3.2% of total installed capacity (2020 est.)
wind: 23.3% of total installed capacity (2020 est.)
hydroelectricity: 26.5% of total installed capacity (2020 est.)
geothermal: 0.4% of total installed capacity (2020 est.)
biomass and waste: 7.7% of total installed capacity (2020 est.)

Coal: *production:* 0 metric tons (2020 est.)
consumption: 957,000 metric tons (2020 est.)
exports: 1,000 metric tons (2020 est.)
imports: 238,000 metric tons (2020 est.)
proven reserves: 36 million metric tons (2019 est.)

Petroleum: *total petroleum production:* 8,000 bbl/day (2021 est.)
refined petroleum consumption: 249,100 bbl/day (2019 est.)
crude oil and lease condensate exports: 0 bbl/day (2018 est.)
crude oil and lease condensate imports: 255,400 bbl/day (2018 est.)
crude oil estimated reserves: 0 barrels (2021 est.)

Refined petroleum products - production: 323,000 bbl/day (2017 est.)
country comparison to the world: 39

Refined petroleum products - exports: 143,500 bbl/day (2017 est.)
country comparison to the world: 36

Refined petroleum products - imports: 78,700 bbl/day (2017 est.)
country comparison to the world: 64

Natural gas: *production:* 0 cubic meters (2021 est.)
consumption: 5,935,938,000 cubic meters (2020 est.)
exports: 0 cubic meters (2021 est.)
imports: 6,091,114,000 cubic meters (2020 est.)
proven reserves: 0 cubic meters (2021 est.)

Carbon dioxide emissions: 50.37 million metric tonnes of CO2 (2019 est.)
from coal and metallurgical coke: 4.882 million metric tonnes of CO2 (2019 est.)
from petroleum and other liquids: 33.429 million metric tonnes of CO2 (2019 est.)
from consumed natural gas: 12.059 million metric tonnes of CO2 (2019 est.)
country comparison to the world: 57

Energy consumption per capita: 101.734 million Btu/person (2019 est.)
country comparison to the world: 57

COMMUNICATIONS

Telephones - fixed lines: *total subscriptions:* 5,212,507 (2020 est.)
subscriptions per 100 inhabitants: 51 (2020 est.)
country comparison to the world: 27

Telephones - mobile cellular: *total subscriptions:* 11,854,999 (2020 est.)
subscriptions per 100 inhabitants: 116 (2020 est.)
country comparison to the world: 78

Telecommunication systems: *general assessment:* Portugal has a medium-sized telecom market with a strong mobile sector and a growing broadband customer base; before the pandemic, the country had seen improving economic growth, following several years of austerity measures; revenue among some operators remains under pressure, though investments in network upgrades are continuing in an effort to attract customers to high-end services; Portugal's broadband services have grown steadily in recent years, largely the result of joint efforts between the regulator and the key market operators which have invested in significant infrastructure upgrades; these operators are focused on fiber-based services, resulting in a migration of subscribers from digital subscriber line DSL infrastructure; the government has also supported open-access wholesale networks; the mobile virtual network operator (MVNO) market remains largely undeveloped, partly because network operators have their own low-cost brands; collectively, MVNOs have about 2.9% share of the market; population coverage by 3G infrastructure is universal, and most investment in the sector is being directed to LTE and 5G technologies; the MNOs have trialed 5G and are looking to launch commercial services (2021)
domestic: integrated network of coaxial cables, open-wire, microwave radio relay, and domestic satellite earth stations; fixed-line roughly 51 per 100 persons and mobile-cellular 116 per 100 persons (2020)
international: country code - 351; landing points for the Ella Link, BUGIO, EIG, SAT-3/WASC, SeaMeWe-3, Equino, MainOne, Tat TGN-Western Europe, WACS, ACE, Atlantis2 and Columbus-III submarine cables provide connectivity to Europe, Africa, the Middle East, Asia, Southeast Asia, Australia, South America and the US; satellite earth stations - 3 Intelsat (2 Atlantic Ocean and 1 Indian Ocean), NA Eutelsat; tropospheric scatter to Azores (2019)

Broadcast media: Radio e Televisao de Portugal, the publicly owned TV broadcaster, operates 4 domestic channels and external service channels to Africa; overall, roughly 40 domestic TV stations; viewers have widespread access to international broadcasters with more than half of all households connected to multi-channel cable or satellite TV systems; publicly owned radio operates 3 national networks and provides regional and external services; several privately owned national radio stations and some 300 regional and local commercial radio stations

Internet country code: pt

Internet users: *total:* 8,031,723 (2020 est.)
percent of population: 78% (2020 est.)
country comparison to the world: 70

Broadband - fixed subscriptions: *total:* 4,160,795 (2020 est.)
subscriptions per 100 inhabitants: 41 (2020 est.)
country comparison to the world: 37

TRANSPORTATION

National air transport system: *number of registered air carriers:* 10 (2020)
inventory of registered aircraft operated by air carriers: 168
annual passenger traffic on registered air carriers: 17,367,956 (2018)
annual freight traffic on registered air carriers: 454.21 million (2018) mt-km

Civil aircraft registration country code prefix: CR, CS

Airports: *total:* 64 (2021)
country comparison to the world: 77

Airports - with paved runways: *total:* 43
over 3,047 m: 5
2,438 to 3,047 m: 7
1,524 to 2,437 m: 8
914 to 1,523 m: 15
under 914 m: 8 (2021)

Airports - with unpaved runways: *total:* 21
914 to 1,523 m: 1
under 914 m: 20 (2021)

Pipelines: 1,344 km gas, 11 km oil, 188 km refined products (2013)

Railways: *total:* 3,075.1 km (2014)
narrow gauge: 108.1 km (2014) 1.000-m gauge
broad gauge: 2,439 km (2014) 1.668-m gauge (1,633.4 km electrified)
other: 528 km (2014) (gauge unspecified)
country comparison to the world: 60

Roadways: *total:* 82,900 km (2008)
paved: 71,294 km (2008) (includes 2,613 km of expressways)
unpaved: 11,606 km (2008)
country comparison to the world: 59

Waterways: 210 km (2011) (on Douro River from Porto)
country comparison to the world: 105

Merchant marine: *total:* 726
by type: bulk carrier 86, container ship 267, general cargo 137, oil tanker 27, other 209 (2021)
country comparison to the world: 32

Ports and terminals: *major seaport(s):* Leixoes, Lisbon, Setubal, Sines
container port(s) (TEUs): Sines (1,420,000) (2019)

LNG terminal(s) (import): Sines

MILITARY AND SECURITY

Military and security forces: Portuguese Armed Forces: Portuguese Army (Exercito Portuguesa), Portuguese Navy (Marinha Portuguesa; includes Marine Corps), Portuguese Air Force (Forca Aerea Portuguesa, FAP); National Republican Guard (Guarda Nacional Republicana, GNR) (2022)
note: the GNR is a national gendarmerie force comprised of military personnel with law enforcement, internal security, civil defense, disaster response, and coast guard duties; it is responsible to the Ministry of Internal Administration and to the Ministry of National Defense; in the event of war or crisis, it may be placed under the Chief of the General Staff of the Armed Forces; the GNR has law enforcement jurisdiction in rural areas, while the Public Security Police (also under the Ministry of Internal Administration) has jurisdiction in cities

Military expenditures: 1.5% of GDP (2022 est.)
1.6% of GDP (2021)
1.4% of GDP (2020)
1.4% of GDP (2019) (approximately $4.31 billion)
1.3% of GDP (2018) (approximately $4.06 billion)
country comparison to the world: 93

Military and security service personnel strengths: approximately 27,000 active duty personnel (14,000 Army; 7,000 Navy, including about 1,000 marines; 6,000 Air Force); 24,500 National Republican Guard (military personnel) (2022)

Military equipment inventories and acquisitions: the military's inventory includes mostly European- and US-origin weapons systems along with a smaller mix of domestically-produced equipment; since 2010, Germany and the US have been the leading suppliers of armaments to Portugal; Portugal's defense industry is primarily focused on shipbuilding (2021)

Military service age and obligation: 18-30 years of age for voluntary or contract military service; no compulsory military service (abolished 2004), but conscription possible if insufficient volunteers available; women serve in the armed forces, but are prohibited from serving in some combatant specialties; contract service lasts for an initial period from two to six years, and can be extended to a maximum of 20 years of service; initial voluntary military service lasts 12 months; reserve obligation to age 35 (2022)
note: as of 2019, women made up about 12% of the military's full-time personnel

Military deployments: 200 Central African Republic (MINUSCA/EUTM); up to 150 Lithuania (NATO); approximately 170 Romania (2022)
note 1: in 2021, Portugal deployed about 80 troops to Mozambique to assist with the EU training mission
note 2: in response to Russia's 2022 invasion of Ukraine, some NATO countries, including Portugal, have sent additional troops to the battlegroups deployed in NATO territory in eastern Europe
note 3: Portugal also participates in several NATO maritime and air policing operations, as well as some EU international missions

Military - note: Portugal is a member of NATO and was one of the original 12 countries to sign the North Atlantic Treaty (also known as the Washington Treaty) in 1949

TERRORISM

Terrorist group(s): Islamic State of Iraq and ash-Sham (ISIS)

TRANSNATIONAL ISSUES

Disputes - international: *Portugal-Spain:* Portugal does not recognize Spanish sovereignty over the territory of Olivenza based on a difference of interpretation of the 1815 Congress of Vienna and the 1801 Treaty of Badajoz

Refugees and internally displaced persons: *refugees (country of origin):* 52,970 (Ukraine) (as of 3 October 2022)
stateless persons: 45 (mid-year 2021)

Illicit drugs: a European gateway for Southwest Asian heroin; transshipment point for hashish from North Africa to Europe; consumer of Southwest Asian heroin

PUERTO RICO

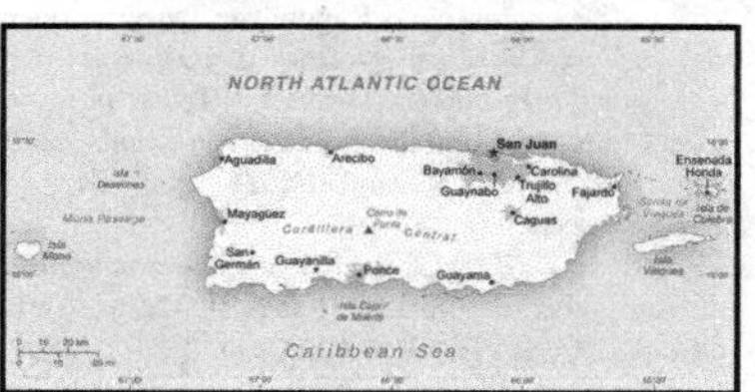

INTRODUCTION

Background: Populated for centuries by aboriginal peoples, the island was claimed by the Spanish Crown in 1493 following Christopher COLUMBUS' second voyage to the Americas. In 1898, after 400 years of colonial rule that saw the indigenous population nearly exterminated and African slave labor introduced, Puerto Rico was ceded to the US as a result of the Spanish-American War. Puerto Ricans were granted US citizenship in 1917. Popularly elected governors have served since 1948. In 1952, a constitution was enacted providing for internal self-government. In plebiscites held in 1967, 1993, and 1998, voters chose not to alter the existing political status with the US, but the results of a 2012 vote left open the possibility of American statehood. Economic recession on the island has led to a net population loss since about 2005, as large numbers of residents moved to the US mainland. The trend has accelerated since 2010; in 2014, Puerto Rico experienced a net population loss to the mainland of 64,000, more than double the net loss of 26,000 in 2010. Hurricane Maria struck the island on 20 September 2017 causing catastrophic damage, including destruction of the electrical grid that had been crippled by Hurricane Irma just two weeks before. It was the worst storm to hit the island in eight decades, and damage is estimated in the tens of billions of dollars. A referendum held in late 2020 showed a narrow preference for American statehood.

GEOGRAPHY

Location: Caribbean, island between the Caribbean Sea and the North Atlantic Ocean, east of the Dominican Republic

Geographic coordinates: 18 15 N, 66 30 W

Map references: Central America and the Caribbean

Area: *total:* 9,104 sq km
land: 8,959 sq km
water: 145 sq km
country comparison to the world: 170

Area - comparative: slightly less than three times the size of Rhode Island Land boundaries
total: 0 km

Coastline: 501 km

Maritime claims: *territorial sea:* 12 nm
exclusive economic zone: 200 nm

Climate: tropical marine, mild; little seasonal temperature variation

Terrain: mostly mountains with coastal plain in north; precipitous mountains to the sea on west coast; sandy beaches along most coastal areas

Elevation: *highest point:* Cerro de Punta 1,338 m
lowest point: Caribbean Sea 0 m
mean elevation: 261 m

Natural resources: some copper and nickel; potential for onshore and offshore oil

Land use: *agricultural land:* 22% (2018 est.)
arable land: 6.6% (2018 est.)
permanent crops: 5.6% (2018 est.)
permanent pasture: 9.8% (2018 est.)
forest: 63.2% (2018 est.)
other: 14.8% (2018 est.)

Irrigated land: 220 sq km (2012)

Population distribution: population clusters tend to be found along the coast, the largest of these is found in and around San Juan; an exception to this is a sizeable population located in the interior of the island immediately south of the capital around Caguas; most of the interior, particularly in the western half of the island, is dominated by the Cordillera Central mountains, where population density is low

Natural hazards: periodic droughts; hurricanes

Geography - note: important location along the Mona Passage - a key shipping lane to the Panama Canal; San Juan is one of the biggest and best natural harbors in the Caribbean; many small rivers and high central mountains ensure land is well watered; south coast relatively dry; fertile coastal plain belt in north

PEOPLE AND SOCIETY

Population: 3,098,423 (2022 est.)
country comparison to the world: 135

Nationality: *noun:* Puerto Rican(s) (US citizens)
adjective: Puerto Rican

Ethnic groups: White 75.8%, Black/African American 12.4%, other 8.5% (includes American Indian, Alaskan Native, Native Hawaiian, other Pacific Islander, and others), mixed 3.3% (2010 est.)
note: 99% of the population is Latino

Languages: Spanish, English
major-language sample(s): La Libreta Informativa del Mundo, la fuente indispensable de información básica. (Spanish)

Religions: Roman Catholic 56%, Protestant 33% (largely Pentecostal), other 2%, atheist 1%, none 7% (2014 est.)

Age structure: *0-14 years:* 14.22% (male 231,406/female 222,061)
15-24 years: 12.78% (male 207,169/female 200,373)
25-54 years: 37.73% (male 573,114/female 630,276)
55-64 years: 13.5% (male 197,438/female 232,931)
65 years and over: 21.77% (male 297,749/female 396,551) (2020 est.)

Dependency ratios: *total dependency ratio:* 57.7
youth dependency ratio: 24.8
elderly dependency ratio: 32.8
potential support ratio: 3 (2020 est.)

Median age: *total:* 43.6 years
male: 41.6 years
female: 45.3 years (2020 est.)
country comparison to the world: 25

Population growth rate: -1.38% (2022 est.)
country comparison to the world: 235

Birth rate: 7.87 births/1,000 population (2022 est.)
country comparison to the world: 219

Death rate: 9.76 deaths/1,000 population (2022 est.)
country comparison to the world: 39

Net migration rate: -11.9 migrant(s)/1,000 population (2022 est.)
country comparison to the world: 225

Population distribution: population clusters tend to be found along the coast, the largest of these is found in and around San Juan; an exception to this is a sizeable population located in the interior of the island immediately south of the capital around Caguas; most of the interior, particularly in the western half of the island, is dominated by the Cordillera Central mountains, where population density is low

Urbanization: *urban population:* 93.6% of total population (2022)
rate of urbanization: -0.12% annual rate of change (2020-25 est.)

Major urban areas - population: 2.443 million SAN JUAN (capital) (2022)

Sex ratio: *at birth:* 1.06 male(s)/female
0-14 years: 1.04 male(s)/female
15-24 years: 1.04 male(s)/female
25-54 years: 0.91 male(s)/female
55-64 years: 0.85 male(s)/female
65 years and over: 0.64 male(s)/female
total population: 0.89 male(s)/female (2022 est.)

Maternal mortality ratio: 21 deaths/100,000 live births (2017 est.)
country comparison to the world: 123

Infant mortality rate: *total:* 6.04 deaths/1,000 live births
male: 6.61 deaths/1,000 live births
female: 5.43 deaths/1,000 live births (2022 est.)
country comparison to the world: 170

Life expectancy at birth: *total population:* 81.68 years
male: 78.47 years
female: 85.08 years (2022 est.)
country comparison to the world: 35

Total fertility rate: 1.24 children born/woman (2022 est.)

country comparison to the world: 221

Drinking water source: *improved: total:* 100% of population
unimproved: total: 0% of population (2020 est.)

Physicians density: 3.06 physicians/1,000 population (2018)

Sanitation facility access: *improved: total:* 100% of population
unimproved: total: 0% of population (2020 est.)

Education expenditures: 6.1% of GDP (2014 est.)
country comparison to the world: 33

Literacy: *definition:* age 15 and over can read and write
total population: 92.4%
male: 92.4%
female: 92.4% (2017)

School life expectancy (primary to tertiary education): *total:* 16 years
male: 15 years
female: 18 years (2018)

Unemployment, youth ages 15-24: *total:* 26.6%
male: 28.9%
female: 23.1% (2012 est.)

ENVIRONMENT

Environment - current issues: soil erosion; occasional droughts cause water shortages; industrial pollution

Climate: tropical marine, mild; little seasonal temperature variation Land use
agricultural land: 22% (2018 est.)
arable land: 6.6% (2018 est.)
permanent crops: 5.6% (2018 est.)
permanent pasture: 9.8% (2018 est.)
forest: 63.2% (2018 est.)
other: 14.8% (2018 est.)

Urbanization: *urban population:* 93.6% of total population (2022)
rate of urbanization: -0.12% annual rate of change (2020-25 est.)

Revenue from forest resources: *forest revenues:* 0% of GDP (2018 est.)
country comparison to the world: 192

Revenue from coal: *coal revenues:* 0% of GDP (2018 est.)
country comparison to the world: 154

Waste and recycling: *municipal solid waste generated annually:* 4,170,953 tons (2015 est.)
municipal solid waste recycled annually: 583,933 tons (2013 est.)
percent of municipal solid waste recycled: 14% (2013 est.)

Total water withdrawal: *municipal:* 796 million cubic meters (2017 est.)
industrial: 2.365 billion cubic meters (2017 est.)
agricultural: 113.5 million cubic meters (2017 est.)

Total renewable water resources: 7.1 billion cubic meters (2017 est.)

GOVERNMENT

Country name: *conventional long form:* Commonwealth of Puerto Rico
conventional short form: Puerto Rico
abbreviation: PR
etymology: Christopher COLUMBUS named the island San Juan Bautista (Saint John the Baptist) and the capital city and main port Cuidad de Puerto Rico (Rich Port City); over time, however, the names were shortened and transposed and the island came to be called Puerto Rico and its capital San Juan

Government type: unincorporated organized territory of the US with local self-government; republican form of territorial government with separate executive, legislative, and judicial branches; note - reference Puerto Rican Federal Relations Act, 2 March 1917, as amended by Public Law 600, 3 July 1950

Dependency status: unincorporated organized territory of the US with commonwealth status; policy relations between Puerto Rico and the US conducted under the jurisdiction of the Office of the President

Capital: *name:* San Juan
geographic coordinates: 18 28 N, 66 07 W
time difference: UTC-4 (1 hour ahead of Washington, DC, during Standard Time)
etymology: the name dates to 1521 and the founding of the city under the name "Ciudad de San Juan Bautista de Puerto Rico" (City of Saint John the Baptist of Puerto Rico)

Administrative divisions: none (territory of the US); there are no first-order administrative divisions as defined by the US Government, but there are 78 municipalities (municipios, singular - municipio) at the second order; Adjuntas, Aguada, Aguadilla, Aguas Buenas, Aibonito, Anasco, Arecibo, Arroyo, Barceloneta, Barranquitas, Bayamon, Cabo Rojo, Caguas, Camuy, Canovanas, Carolina, Catano, Cayey, Ceiba, Ciales, Cidra, Coamo, Comerio, Corozal, Culebra, Dorado, Fajardo, Florida, Guanica, Guayama, Guayanilla, Guaynabo, Gurabo, Hatillo, Hormigueros, Humacao, Isabela, Jayuya, Juana Diaz, Juncos, Lajas, Lares, Las Marias, Las Piedras, Loiza, Luquillo, Manati, Maricao, Maunabo, Mayaguez, Moca, Morovis, Naguabo, Naranjito, Orocovis, Patillas, Penuelas, Ponce, Quebradillas, Rincon, Rio Grande, Sabana Grande, Salinas, San German, San Juan, San Lorenzo, San Sebastian, Santa Isabel, Toa Alta, Toa Baja, Trujillo Alto, Utuado, Vega Alta, Vega Baja, Vieques, Villalba, Yabucoa, Yauco

Independence: none (territory of the US with commonwealth status)

National holiday: US Independence Day, 4 July (1776); Puerto Rico Constitution Day, 25 July (1952)

Constitution: *history:* previous 1900 (Organic Act, or Foraker Act); latest ratified by referendum 3 March 1952, approved 3 July 1952, effective 25 July 1952
amendments: proposed by a concurrent resolution of at least two-thirds majority by the total Legislative Assembly membership; approval requires at least two-thirds majority vote by the membership of both houses and approval by a majority of voters in a special referendum; if passed by at least three-fourths Assembly vote, the referendum can be held concurrently with the next general election; constitutional articles such as the republican form of government or the bill of rights cannot be amended; amended 1952

Legal system: civil law system based on the Spanish civil code and within the framework of the US federal system

Citizenship: see United States

Suffrage: 18 years of age; universal; note - island residents are US citizens but do not vote in US presidential elections

Executive branch: *chief of state:* President Joseph R. BIDEN Jr. (since 20 January 2021); Vice President Kamala D. HARRIS (since 20 January 2021)
head of government: Governor Pedro PIERLUISI (since 2 January 2021)
cabinet: Cabinet appointed by governor with the consent of the Legislative Assembly
elections/appointments: president and vice president indirectly elected on the same ballot by an Electoral College of 'electors' chosen from each state; president and vice president serve a 4-year term (eligible for a second term); under the US Constitution, residents of Puerto Rico do not vote in elections for US president and vice president; however, they may vote in Democratic and Republican party presidential primary elections; governor directly elected by simple majority popular vote for a 4-year term (no term limits); election last held on 3 November 2020 (next to be held in November 2024)
election results:
2020: Pedro PIERLUISI elected governor; percent of vote - Pedro PIERLUISI (PNP) 32.9%, Carlos DELGADO (PPD) 31.6%, Alexandra LUGARO (independent) 14.2%, Juan DALMAU (PIP) 13.7%, other 7.6%
2016: Ricardo ROSSELLO elected governor; percent of vote - Ricardo ROSSELLO (PNP) 41.8%, David BERNIER (PPD) 38.9%, Alexandra LUGARO (independent) 11.1%, Manuel CIDRE (independent) 5.7%

Legislative branch: *description:*
bicameral Legislative Assembly or Asamblea Legislativa consists of:
Senate or Senado (30 seats statutory, 27 current; 16 members directly elected in 8 2-seat constituencies by simple majority vote and 11 at-large members directly elected by simple majority vote to serve 4-year terms)
House of Representatives or Camara de Representantes (51 seats; members directly elected in single-seat constituencies by simple majority vote to serve 4-year terms)
elections:
Senate - last held on 3 November 2020 (next to be held on 5 November 2024)
House of Representatives - last held on 3 November 2020 (next to be held on 5 November 2024)
election results:
Senate - percent of vote by party - NA; seats by party - PPD 12, NP 10, MVC 2, PD 1, PIP 1, independent 1; composition - men 17, women 10; percent of women 37%
House of Representatives - percent of vote by party - NA; seats by party - PPD 26, PNP 21, MVC 2, PIP 1, PD 1; composition - men 41, women 10, percent of women 19.6%; note - total Legislative Assembly percent of women 25.6%
note: Puerto Rico directly elects 1 member by simple majority vote to serve a 4-year term as a commissioner to the US House of Representatives; the commissioner can vote when serving on a committee and when the House meets as the Committee of the Whole House but not when legislation is submitted for a 'full floor' House vote; election of commissioner last held on 6 November 2018 (next to be held in November 2022)

Judicial branch: *highest court(s):* Supreme Court (consists of the chief justice and 8 associate justices)
judge selection and term of office: justices appointed by the governor and confirmed by majority Senate vote; judges serve until compulsory retirement at age 70
subordinate courts: Court of Appeals; First Instance Court comprised of superior and municipal courts

Political parties and leaders: Citizens' Victory Movement (Movimiento Victoria Ciudadana) or MVC [Manuel NATAL Albelo]
Democratic Party of Puerto Rico [Charlie RODRIGUEZ]
New Progressive Party or PNP [Pedro PIERLUISI Urrutia] (pro-US statehood)
Popular Democratic Party or PPD [Jose Luis DALMAU] (pro-commonwealth)
Project Dignity (Projecto Dignidad) or PD [Cesar VASQUEZ Muniz]
Puerto Rican Independence Party or PIP [Ruben BERRIOS Martinez] (pro-independence)
Republican Party of Puerto Rico [Jenniffer GONZALEZ]

International organization participation: AOSIS (observer), Caricom (observer), Interpol (subbureau), IOC, UNWTO (associate), UPU, WFTU (NGOs)

Diplomatic representation in the US: none (territory of the US)

Diplomatic representation from the US: *embassy:* none (territory of the US with commonwealth status)

Flag description: five equal horizontal bands of red (top, center, and bottom) alternating with white; a blue isosceles triangle based on the hoist side bears a large, white, five-pointed star in the center; the white star symbolizes Puerto Rico; the three sides of the triangle signify the executive, legislative and judicial parts of the government; blue stands for the sky and the coastal waters; red symbolizes the blood shed by warriors, while white represents liberty, victory, and peace
note: design initially influenced by the US flag, but similar to the Cuban flag, with the colors of the bands and triangle reversed

National symbol(s): Puerto Rican spindalis (bird), coqui (frog); national colors: red, white, blue

National anthem: *name:* "La Borinquena" (The Puerto Rican)
lyrics/music: Manuel Fernandez JUNCOS/Felix Astol ARTES
note: music adopted 1952, lyrics adopted 1977; the local anthem's name is a reference to the indigenous name of the island, Borinquen; the music was originally composed as a dance in 1867 and gained popularity in the early 20th century; there is some evidence that the music was written by Francisco RAMIREZ; as a commonwealth of the US, "The Star-Spangled Banner" is official (see United States)

National heritage: *total World Heritage Sites:* 1 (cultural); note - excerpted from the US entry
selected World Heritage Site locales: La Fortaleza and San Juan National Historic Site

ECONOMY

Economic overview: Puerto Rico had one of the most dynamic economies in the Caribbean region until 2006; however, growth has been negative for each of the last 11 years. The downturn coincided with the phaseout of tax preferences that had led US firms to invest heavily in the Commonwealth since the 1950s, and a steep rise in the price of oil, which generates most of the island's electricity.

Diminished job opportunities prompted a sharp rise in outmigration, as many Puerto Ricans sought jobs on the US mainland. Unemployment reached 16% in 2011, but declined to 11.5% in December 2017. US minimum wage laws apply in Puerto Rico, hampering job expansion. Per capita income is about two-thirds that of the US mainland.

The industrial sector greatly exceeds agriculture as the locus of economic activity and income. Tourism has traditionally been an important source of income with estimated arrivals of more than 3.6 million tourists in 2008. Puerto Rico's merchandise trade surplus is exceptionally strong, with exports nearly 50% greater than imports, and its current account surplus about 10% of GDP.

Closing the budget deficit while restoring economic growth and employment remain the central concerns of the government. The gap between revenues and expenditures amounted to 0.6% of GDP in 2016, although analysts believe that not all expenditures have been accounted for in the budget and a better accounting of costs would yield an overall deficit of roughly 5% of GDP. Public debt remained steady at 92.5% of GDP in 2017, about $17,000 per person, or nearly three times the per capita debt of the State of Connecticut, the highest in the US. Much of that debt was issued by state-run schools and public corporations, including water and electric utilities. In June 2015, Governor Alejandro GARCIA Padilla announced that the island could not pay back at least $73 billion in debt and that it would seek a deal with its creditors.

Hurricane Maria hit Puerto Rico square on in September 2017, causing electrical power outages to 90% of the territory, as well as extensive loss of housing and infrastructure and contamination of potable water. Despite massive efforts, more than 40% of the territory remained without electricity as of yearend 2017. As a result of the destruction, many Puerto Ricans have emigrated to the US mainland.

Real GDP (purchasing power parity): $106.82 billion (2020 est.)
$111.16 billion (2019 est.)
$109.53 billion (2018 est.)
note: data are in 2017 dollars
country comparison to the world: 86

Real GDP growth rate: -2.4% (2017 est.)
-1.3% (2016 est.)
-1% (2015 est.)
country comparison to the world: 206

Real GDP per capita: $33,400 (2020 est.)
$34,800 (2019 est.)
$34,300 (2018 est.)
note: data are in 2017 dollars
country comparison to the world: 59

GDP (official exchange rate): $104.2 billion (2017 est.)

Inflation rate (consumer prices): 1.8% (2017 est.)
-0.3% (2016 est.)
country comparison to the world: 101

Credit ratings:

Standard & Poors rating: D (2015)

GDP - composition, by sector of origin: *agriculture:* 0.8% (2017 est.)
industry: 50.1% (2017 est.)
services: 49.1% (2017 est.)

GDP - composition, by end use: *household consumption:* 87.7% (2017 est.)
government consumption: 12.2% (2017 est.)
investment in fixed capital: 11.7% (2017 est.)
investment in inventories: 0.5% (2017 est.)
exports of goods and services: 117.8% (2017 est.)
imports of goods and services: -129.8% (2017 est.)

Agricultural products: milk, plantains, bananas, poultry, tomatoes, mangoes/guavas, eggs, oranges, gourds, papayas

Industries: pharmaceuticals, electronics, apparel, food products, tourism

Industrial production growth rate: -2.1% (2017 est.)
country comparison to the world: 184

Labor force: 1.139 million (December 2014 est.)
country comparison to the world: 136

Labor force - by occupation: *agriculture:* 2.1%
industry: 19%
services: 79% (2005 est.)

Unemployment rate: 10.8% (2017 est.)
11.8% (2016 est.)
country comparison to the world: 154

Unemployment, youth ages 15-24: *total:* 26.6%
male: 28.9%
female: 23.1% (2012 est.)
country comparison to the world: 46

Budget: *revenues:* 9.268 billion (2017 est.)
expenditures: 9.974 billion (2017 est.)

Budget surplus (+) or deficit (-): -0.7% (of GDP) (2017 est.)
country comparison to the world: 68

Public debt: 51.6% of GDP (2017 est.)
50.1% of GDP (2016 est.)
country comparison to the world: 97

Taxes and other revenues: 8.9% (of GDP) (2017 est.)
country comparison to the world: 217

Fiscal year: 1 July - 30 June

Current account balance: $0 (2017 est.)
$0 (2016 est.)
country comparison to the world: 65

Exports: $73.17 billion (2017 est.)
$73.2 billion (2016 est.)
country comparison to the world: 48

Exports - partners: Italy 15%, Netherlands 15%, Belgium 9%, Japan 8%, Germany 8%, Austria 8%, Spain 7%, China 5% (2019)

Exports - commodities: packaged medicines, medical cultures/vaccines, hormones, orthopedic and medical appliances, sulfur compounds (2019)

Imports: $49.01 billion (2017 est.)
$48.86 billion (2016 est.)
country comparison to the world: 61

Imports - partners: Ireland 38%, Singapore 9%, Switzerland 8%, South Korea 5% (2019)

Imports - commodities: nitrogen compounds, sulfur compounds, refined petroleum, medical cultures/vaccines, cars (2019)

Debt - external: $56.82 billion (31 December 2010 est.)
$52.98 billion (31 December 2009 est.)
country comparison to the world: 62

Exchange rates: the US dollar is used

ENERGY

Electricity access: *electrification - total population:* 100% (2020)

Electricity: *installed generating capacity:* 6.18 million kW (2020 est.)
consumption: 15,203,140,000 kWh (2019 est.)
exports: 0 kWh (2020 est.)
imports: 0 kWh (2020 est.)

transmission/distribution losses: 2.5 billion kWh (2019 est.)

Electricity generation sources: *fossil fuels:* 94.8% of total installed capacity (2020 est.)
solar: 1.4% of total installed capacity (2020 est.)
wind: 3.4% of total installed capacity (2020 est.)
hydroelectricity: 0.3% of total installed capacity (2020 est.)
biomass and waste: 0.1% of total installed capacity (2020 est.)

Coal: *production:* 0 metric tons (2020 est.)
consumption: 1.361 million metric tons (2020 est.)
exports: 0 metric tons (2020 est.)
imports: 1.502 million metric tons (2020 est.)
proven reserves: 0 metric tons (2019 est.)

Petroleum: *total petroleum production:* 0 bbl/day (2021 est.)
refined petroleum consumption: 79,000 bbl/day (2019 est.)

Refined petroleum products - exports: 18,420 bbl/day (2015 est.)
country comparison to the world: 70

Refined petroleum products - imports: 127,100 bbl/day (2015 est.)
country comparison to the world: 46

Natural gas: *production:* 0 cubic meters (2021 est.)
consumption: 1,366,512,000 cubic meters (2020 est.)
exports: 0 cubic meters (2021 est.)
imports: 1,366,512,000 cubic meters (2020 est.)
proven reserves: 0 cubic meters (2021 est.)

Carbon dioxide emissions: 18.999 million metric tonnes of CO2 (2019 est.)
from coal and metallurgical coke: 3.774 million metric tonnes of CO2 (2019 est.)
from petroleum and other liquids: 11.407 million metric tonnes of CO2 (2019 est.)
from consumed natural gas: 3.818 million metric tonnes of CO2 (2019 est.)
country comparison to the world: 86

Energy consumption per capita: 94.379 million Btu/person (2019 est.)
country comparison to the world: 63

COMMUNICATIONS

Telephones - fixed lines: *total subscriptions:* 711,512 (2020 est.)
subscriptions per 100 inhabitants: 25 (2020 est.)
country comparison to the world: 82

Telephones - mobile cellular: *total subscriptions:* 3,483,570 (2020 est.)
subscriptions per 100 inhabitants: 122 (2020 est.)
country comparison to the world: 136

Telecommunication systems: *general assessment:* Puerto Rico has a small telecom market which in recent years has been deeply affected by a combination of economic mismanagement and natural disasters, including two hurricanes which landed in late 2017 and an earthquake which struck in January 2020; these disasters caused considerable destruction of telecom infrastructure, which in turn led to a marked decline in the number of subscribers for all services; compounding these difficulties have been a long-term economic downturn which encouraged many people not to resume telecom services after these were restored; after some delay, the FCC in late 2019 issued an order relating to the release of funds to help rebuild telecom infrastructure; although Puerto Rico is a US territory it lags well behind the mainland US states in terms of fixed-line and broadband services; this is partly due to high unemployment rates (and consequently low disposable income) and poor telecoms investment in a market; the mobile market has been impacted by several mergers and acquisitions over the last few years; the activities of large multinational telcos continue to impact the Puerto Rican market; operators have secured spectrum in the 600MHz and 3.5GHz bands, thus enabling them to expand the reach of LTE services and launch services based on 5G; the growing number of submarine cables landing in Puerto Rico is helping to drive down the cost of telecom services, creating a demand for streaming content from abroad; the uptake of cloud-based applications for both business and individuals is also creating a heightened demand for affordable services (2021)
domestic: digital telephone system; mobile-cellular services; fixed-line nearly 25 per 100 and mobile-cellular nearly 122 per 100 persons (2020)
international: country code - 1-787, 939; landing points for the GTMO-PR, AMX-1, BRUSA, GCN, PCCS, SAm-1, Southern Caribbean Fiber, Americas-II, Antillas, ARCOS, SMPR-1, and Taino-Carib submarine cables providing connectivity to the mainland US, Caribbean, Central and South America; satellite earth station - 1 Intelsat (2019)

Broadcast media: more than 30 TV stations operating; cable TV subscription services are available; roughly 125 radio stations

Internet country code: .pr

Internet users: *total:* 2,559,600 (2020 est.)
percent of population: 78% (2020 est.)
country comparison to the world: 121

Broadband - fixed subscriptions: *total:* 671,284 (2020 est.)
subscriptions per 100 inhabitants: 24 (2020 est.)
country comparison to the world: 83

TRANSPORTATION

Airports: *total:* 29 (2021)
country comparison to the world: 118

Airports - with paved runways: *total:* 17
over 3,047 m: 2
2,438 to 3,047 m: 1
1,524 to 2,437 m: 2
914 to 1,523 m: 7
under 914 m: 5 (2021)

Airports - with unpaved runways: *total:* 12
1,524 to 2,437 m: 1
914 to 1,523 m: 1
under 914 m: 10 (2021)

Roadways: *total:* 26,862 km (2012) (includes 454 km of expressways)
country comparison to the world: 101

Ports and terminals: *major seaport(s):* Ensenada Honda, Mayaguez, Playa de Guayanilla, Playa de Ponce, San Juan
container port(s) (TEUs): San Juan (2,142,662) (2019)

LNG terminal(s) (import): Guayanilla Bay

MILITARY AND SECURITY

Military and security forces: no regular indigenous military forces; US National Guard (Army and Air), State Guard, Police Force

Military - note: defense is the responsibility of the US

TRANSNATIONAL ISSUES

Disputes - international: illegal migrants from the Dominican Republic cross the Mona Passage to Puerto Rico each year looking for work

QATAR

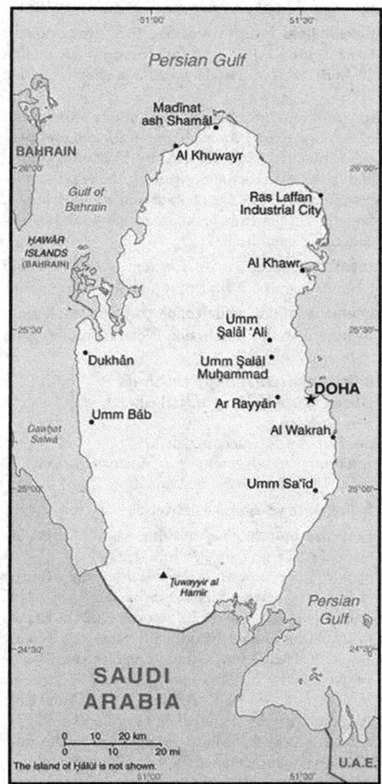

INTRODUCTION

Background: Ruled by the Al Thani family since the mid-1800s, Qatar within the last 60 years transformed itself from a poor British protectorate noted mainly for pearling into an independent state with significant oil and natural gas revenues. Former Amir HAMAD bin Khalifa Al Thani, who overthrew his father in a bloodless coup in 1995, ushered in wide-sweeping political and media reforms, unprecedented economic investment, and a growing Qatari regional leadership role, in part through the creation of the pan-Arab satellite news network Al-Jazeera and Qatar's mediation of some regional conflicts. In the 2000s, Qatar resolved its longstanding border disputes with both Bahrain and Saudi Arabia and by 2007 had attained the highest per capita income in the world. Qatar did not experience domestic unrest or violence like that seen in other Near Eastern and North African countries in 2011, due in part to its immense wealth and patronage network. In mid-2013, HAMAD peacefully abdicated, transferring power to his son, the current Amir TAMIM bin Hamad. TAMIM is popular with the Qatari public, for his role in shepherding the country through an economic embargo by some other regional countries, for his efforts to improve the country's healthcare and education systems, and for his expansion of the country's infrastructure in anticipation of Doha's hosting of the 2022 FIFA Men's World Cup.

Following the outbreak of regional unrest in 2011, Doha prided itself on its support for many popular revolutions, particularly in Libya and Syria. This stance was to the detriment of Qatar's relations with Bahrain, Egypt, Saudi Arabia, and the United Arab Emirates (UAE), which temporarily recalled their respective ambassadors from Doha in March 2014. TAMIM later oversaw a warming of Qatar's relations with Bahrain, Egypt, Saudi Arabia, and the UAE in November 2014 following Kuwaiti mediation and signing of the Riyadh Agreement. This reconciliation, however, was short-lived. In June 2017, Bahrain, Egypt, Saudi Arabia, and the UAE (the "Quartet") cut diplomatic and economic ties with Qatar in response to alleged violations of the agreement, among other complaints. They restored ties in January 2021 after signing a declaration at the Gulf Cooperation Council Summit in Al Ula, Saudi Arabia.

GEOGRAPHY

Location: Middle East, peninsula bordering the Persian Gulf and Saudi Arabia

Geographic coordinates: 25 30 N, 51 15 E

Map references: Middle East

Area: *total:* 11,586 sq km
land: 11,586 sq km
water: 0 sq km
country comparison to the world: 164

Area - comparative: almost twice the size of Delaware; slightly smaller than Connecticut

Land boundaries: *total:* 87 km
border countries (1): Saudi Arabia 87 km

Coastline: 563 km

Maritime claims: *territorial sea:* 12 nm
contiguous zone: 24 nm
exclusive economic zone: as determined by bilateral agreements or the median line

Climate: arid; mild, pleasant winters; very hot, humid summers

Terrain: mostly flat and barren desert

Elevation: *highest point:* Tuwayyir al Hamir 103 m
lowest point: Persian Gulf 0 m
mean elevation: 28 m

Natural resources: petroleum, fish, natural gas

Land use: *agricultural land:* 5.6% (2018 est.)
arable land: 1.1% (2018 est.)
permanent crops: 0.2% (2018 est.)
permanent pasture: 4.3% (2018 est.)
forest: 0% (2018 est.)
other: 94.4% (2018 est.)

Irrigated land: 130 sq km (2012)

Major aquifers: Arabian Aquifer System

Population distribution: most of the population is clustered in or around the capital of Doha on the eastern side of the peninsula

Natural hazards: haze, dust storms, sandstorms common

Geography - note: the peninsula occupies a strategic location in the central Persian Gulf near major petroleum deposits

PEOPLE AND SOCIETY

Population: 2,508,182 (2022 est.)
country comparison to the world: 143

Nationality: *noun:* Qatari(s)
adjective: Qatari

Ethnic groups: non-Qatari 88.4%, Qatari 11.6% (2015 est.)

Languages: Arabic (official), English commonly used as a second language
major-language sample(s):
كتاب حقائق العالم، المصدر الذي لا يمكن الاستغناء عنه للمعلومات الأساسية
(Arabic)

Religions: Muslim 65.2%, Christian 13.7%, Hindu 15.9%, Buddhist 3.8%, folk religion <0.1%, Jewish <0.1%, other <1%, unaffiliated <1% (2020 est.)

Age structure: *0-14 years:* 12.84% (male 158,702/female 155,211)
15-24 years: 11.78% (male 203,703/female 84,323)
25-54 years: 70.66% (male 1,439,364/female 287,575)
55-64 years: 3.53% (male 66,561/female 19,600)
65 years and over: 1.19% (male 19,067/female 10,068) (2020 est.)

Dependency ratios: *total dependency ratio:* 18.1
youth dependency ratio: 16.1
elderly dependency ratio: 2
potential support ratio: 50.1 (2020 est.)

Median age: *total:* 33.7 years
male: 35 years
female: 28.2 years (2020 est.)
country comparison to the world: 96

Population growth rate: 1.04% (2022 est.)
country comparison to the world: 92

Birth rate: 9.33 births/1,000 population (2022 est.)
country comparison to the world: 196

Death rate: 1.42 deaths/1,000 population (2022 est.)
country comparison to the world: 229

Net migration rate: 2.45 migrant(s)/1,000 population (2022 est.)
country comparison to the world: 45

Population distribution: most of the population is clustered in or around the capital of Doha on the eastern side of the peninsula

Urbanization: *urban population:* 99.3% of total population (2022)
rate of urbanization: 1.66% annual rate of change (2020-25 est.)

Major urban areas - population: Ar-Rayyan 779,000, 652,000 DOHA (capital) (2022)

Sex ratio: *at birth:* 1.02 male(s)/female
0-14 years: 1.02 male(s)/female
15-24 years: 2.26 male(s)/female
25-54 years: 5.45 male(s)/female
55-64 years: 3.42 male(s)/female
65 years and over: 1.13 male(s)/female
total population: 3.36 male(s)/female (2022 est.)

Maternal mortality ratio: 9 deaths/100,000 live births (2017 est.)
country comparison to the world: 149

Infant mortality rate: *total:* 6.62 deaths/1,000 live births
male: 7.25 deaths/1,000 live births

female: 5.96 deaths/1,000 live births (2022 est.)
country comparison to the world: 163

Life expectancy at birth: *total population:* 79.81 years
male: 77.7 years
female: 81.96 years (2022 est.)
country comparison to the world: 53

Total fertility rate: 1.9 children born/woman (2022 est.)
country comparison to the world: 130

Contraceptive prevalence rate: 37.5% (2012)

Drinking water source: *improved: total:* 99.6% of population
unimproved: total: 0.4% of population (2020 est.)

Current health expenditure: 2.9% of GDP (2019)

Physicians density: 2.49 physicians/1,000 population (2018)

Hospital bed density: 1.3 beds/1,000 population (2017)

Sanitation facility access: *improved: total:* 100% of population
unimproved: total: 0% of population (2020 est.)

HIV/AIDS - adult prevalence rate: (2020 est.) <.1%

HIV/AIDS - people living with HIV/AIDS: (2020 est.) <200

HIV/AIDS - deaths: (2020 est.) <100

Obesity - adult prevalence rate: 35.1% (2016)
country comparison to the world: 15

Alcohol consumption per capita: *total:* 0.96 liters of pure alcohol (2019 est.)
beer: 0.29 liters of pure alcohol (2019 est.)
wine: 0.07 liters of pure alcohol (2019 est.)
spirits: 0.59 liters of pure alcohol (2019 est.)
other alcohols: 0.01 liters of pure alcohol (2019 est.)
country comparison to the world: 151

Tobacco use: *total:* 11.8% (2020 est.)
male: 21.7% (2020 est.)
female: 1.9% (2020 est.)
country comparison to the world: 124

Education expenditures: 3.2% of GDP (2020 est.)
country comparison to the world: 142

Literacy: *definition:* age 15 and over can read and write
total population: 93.5%
male: 92.4%
female: 94.7% (2017)

School life expectancy (primary to tertiary education): *total:* 13 years
male: 12 years
female: 15 years (2020)

Unemployment, youth ages 15-24: *total:* 0.4%
male: 0.2%
female: 1.5% (2018 est.)

ENVIRONMENT

Environment - current issues: air, land, and water pollution are significant environmental issues; limited natural freshwater resources are increasing dependence on large-scale desalination facilities; other issues include conservation of oil supplies and preservation of the natural wildlife heritage

Environment - international agreements: *party to:* Biodiversity, Climate Change, Climate Change-Kyoto Protocol, Comprehensive Nuclear Test Ban, Desertification, Endangered Species, Hazardous Wastes, Law of the Sea, Ozone Layer Protection, Ship Pollution
signed, but not ratified: none of the selected agreements

Air pollutants: *particulate matter emissions:* 90.35 micrograms per cubic meter (2016 est.)
carbon dioxide emissions: 103.26 megatons (2016 est.)
methane emissions: 8.34 megatons (2020 est.)

Climate: arid; mild, pleasant winters; very hot, humid summers

Land use: *agricultural land:* 5.6% (2018 est.)
arable land: 1.1% (2018 est.)
permanent crops: 0.2% (2018 est.)
permanent pasture: 4.3% (2018 est.)
forest: 0% (2018 est.)
other: 94.4% (2018 est.)

Urbanization: *urban population:* 99.3% of total population (2022)
rate of urbanization: 1.66% annual rate of change (2020-25 est.)

Revenue from forest resources: *forest revenues:* 0% of GDP (2018 est.)
country comparison to the world: 193

Revenue from coal: *coal revenues:* 0% of GDP (2018 est.)
country comparison to the world: 155

Waste and recycling: *municipal solid waste generated annually:* 1,000,990 tons (2012 est.)
municipal solid waste recycled annually: 30,030 tons (2014 est.)
percent of municipal solid waste recycled: 3% (2014 est.)

Major aquifers: Arabian Aquifer System

Total water withdrawal: *municipal:* 477.2 million cubic meters (2017 est.)
industrial: 143.7 million cubic meters (2017 est.)
agricultural: 291.7 million cubic meters (2017 est.)

Total renewable water resources: 58 million cubic meters (2017 est.)

GOVERNMENT

Country name: *conventional long form:* State of Qatar
conventional short form: Qatar
local long form: Dawlat Qatar
local short form: Qatar
etymology: the origin of the name is uncertain, but it dates back at least 2,000 years since a term "Catharrei" was used to describe the inhabitants of the peninsula by Pliny the Elder (1st century A.D.), and a "Catara" peninsula is depicted on a map by Ptolemy (2nd century A.D.)
note: closest approximation of the native pronunciation is gat-tar or cot-tar

Government type: absolute monarchy

Capital: *name:* Doha
geographic coordinates: 25 17 N, 51 32 E
time difference: UTC+3 (8 hours ahead of Washington, DC, during Standard Time)
etymology: derives from the Arabic term "dohat," meaning "roundness," and refers to the small rounded bays along the area's coastline

Administrative divisions: 8 municipalities (baladiyat, singular - baladiyah); Ad Dawhah, Al Khawr wa adh Dhakhirah, Al Wakrah, Ar Rayyan, Ash Shamal, Ash Shihaniyah, Az Za'ayin, Umm Salal

Independence: 3 September 1971 (from the UK)

National holiday: National Day, 18 December (1878), anniversary of Al Thani family accession to the throne; Independence Day, 3 September (1971)

Constitution: *history:* previous 1972 (provisional); latest drafted 2 July 2002, approved by referendum 29 April 2003, endorsed 8 June 2004, effective 9 June 2005
amendments: proposed by the Amir or by one third of Advisory Council members; passage requires two-thirds majority vote of Advisory Council members and approval and promulgation by the emir; articles pertaining to the rule of state and its inheritance, functions of the emir, and citizen rights and liberties cannot be amended

Legal system: mixed legal system of civil law and Islamic (sharia) law (in family and personal matters)

International law organization participation: has not submitted an ICJ jurisdiction declaration; non-party state to the ICCt

Citizenship: *citizenship by birth:* no
citizenship by descent only: the father must be a citizen of Qatar
dual citizenship recognized: no
residency requirement for naturalization: 20 years; 15 years if an Arab national

Suffrage: 18 years of age; universal

Executive branch: *chief of state:* Amir TAMIM bin Hamad Al Thani (since 25 June 2013)
head of government: Prime Minister and Minister of Interior Sheikh KHALID bin Khalifa bin Abdul Aziz Al Thani (since 28 January 2020); Deputy Prime Minister and Minister of State for Defense Affairs KHALID bin Mohamed AL Attiyah (since 14 November 2017); Deputy Prime Minister and Minister of Foreign Affairs MOHAMED bin Abdulrahman Al Thani (since 14 November 2017)
cabinet: Council of Ministers appointed by the amir
elections/appointments: the monarchy is hereditary; prime minister and deputy prime minister appointed by the amir

Legislative branch: *description:* unicameral Advisory Council or Majlis al-Shura (45 seats; 30 members directly elected by popular vote for 4-year re-electable terms; 15 members appointed by the monarch to serve until resignation or until relieved; note -legislative drafting authority rests with the Council of Ministers and is reviewed by the Advisory Council
elections:
first election held for 30 elected members on 2 October 2021 (next to be held in 2025); date of appointed members - 14 October 2021 (next appointments - NA)
election results:
30 nonpartisan members elected; composition - men 30, women 0 15 appointed members; composition men 13, women 2, percent of women 13.3%

Judicial branch: *highest court(s):* Supreme Court or Court of Cassation (consists of the court president and several judges); Supreme Constitutional Court (consists of the chief justice and 6 members)
judge selection and term of office: Supreme Court judges nominated by the Supreme Judiciary Council, a 9-member independent body consisting of judiciary heads appointed by the Amir; judges appointed for 3-year renewable terms; Supreme Constitutional Court members nominated by the Supreme Judiciary

Council and appointed by the monarch; term of appointment NA
subordinate courts: Courts of Appeal; Administrative Court; Courts of First Instance; sharia courts; Courts of Justice; Qatar International Court and Dispute Resolution Center, established in 2009, provides dispute resolution services for institutions and bodies in Qatar, as well as internationally

Political parties and leaders: political parties are banned

International organization participation: ABEDA, AFESD, AMF, CAEU, CD, CICA (observer), EITI (implementing country), FAO, G-77, GCC, IAEA, IBRD, ICAO, ICC (national committees), ICRM, IDA, IDB, IFAD, IFC, IFRCS, IHO, ILO, IMF, IMO, IMSO, Interpol, IOC, IOM (observer), IPU, ISO, ITSO, ITU, LAS, MIGA, NAM, OAPEC, OAS (observer), OIC, OIF, OPCW, OPEC, PCA, UN, UNCTAD, UNESCO, UNHRC, UNIDO, UNIFIL, UNWTO, UPU, WCO, WHO, WIPO, WMO, WTO

Diplomatic representation in the US: *chief of mission:* Ambassador MISHAL bin Hamad bin Muhammad Al Thani (since 24 April 2017)
chancery: 2555 M Street NW, Washington, DC 20037
telephone: [1] (202) 274-1600
FAX: [1] (202) 237-0682
email address and website:
info.dc@mofa.gov.qa
https://washington.embassy.qa/en
consulate(s) general: Houston, Los Angeles

Diplomatic representation from the US: *chief of mission:* Ambassador (vacant); Charge d'Affaires Evyenia SIDEREAS
embassy: 22 February Street, Al Luqta District, P.O. Box 2399, Doha
mailing address: 6130 Doha Place, Washington DC 20521-6130
telephone: [974] 4496-6000
FAX: [974] 4488-4298
email address and website:
PasDoha@state.gov
https://qa.usembassy.gov/

Flag description: maroon with a broad white serrated band (nine white points) on the hoist side; maroon represents the blood shed in Qatari wars, white stands for peace; the nine-pointed serrated edge signifies Qatar as the ninth member of the "reconciled emirates" in the wake of the Qatari-British treaty of 1916
note: the other eight emirates are the seven that compose the UAE and Bahrain; according to some sources, the dominant color was formerly red, but this darkened to maroon upon exposure to the sun and the new shade was eventually adopted

National symbol(s): a maroon field surmounted by a white serrated band with nine white points; national colors: maroon, white

National anthem: *name:* "Al-Salam Al-Amiri" (The Amiri Salute)
lyrics/music: Sheikh MUBARAK bin Saif al-Thani/ Abdul Aziz Nasser OBAIDAN
note: adopted 1996; anthem first performed that year at a meeting of the Gulf Cooperative Council hosted by Qatar

National heritage: *total World Heritage Sites:* 1 (cultural)
selected World Heritage Site locales: Al Zubarah Archaeological Site

ECONOMY

Economic overview: Qatar's oil and natural gas resources are the country's main economic engine and government revenue source, driving Qatar's high economic growth and per capita income levels, robust state spending on public entitlements, and booming construction spending, particularly as Qatar prepares to host the World Cup in 2022. Although the government has maintained high capital spending levels for ongoing infrastructure projects, low oil and natural gas prices in recent years have led the Qatari Government to tighten some spending to help stem its budget deficit.

Qatar's reliance on oil and natural gas is likely to persist for the foreseeable future. Proved natural gas reserves exceed 25 trillion cubic meters - 13% of the world total and, among countries, third largest in the world. Proved oil reserves exceed 25 billion barrels, allowing production to continue at current levels for about 56 years. Despite the dominance of oil and natural gas, Qatar has made significant gains in strengthening non-oil sectors, such as manufacturing, construction, and financial services, leading non-oil GDP to steadily rise in recent years to just over half the total.

Following trade restriction imposed by Saudi Arabia, the UAE, Bahrain, and Egypt in 2017, Qatar established new trade routes with other countries to maintain access to imports.

Real GDP (purchasing power parity): $245.66 billion (2020 est.)
$255.01 billion (2019 est.)
$253.05 billion (2018 est.)
note: data are in 2017 dollars
country comparison to the world: 62

Real GDP growth rate: 1.6% (2017 est.)
2.1% (2016 est.)
3.7% (2015 est.)
country comparison to the world: 152

Real GDP per capita: $85,300 (2020 est.)
$90,000 (2019 est.)
$91,000 (2018 est.)
note: data are in 2017 dollars
country comparison to the world: 6

GDP (official exchange rate): $191.29 billion (2018 est.)

Inflation rate (consumer prices): -0.6% (2019 est.)
0.2% (2018 est.)
0.3% (2017 est.)
country comparison to the world: 11

Credit ratings:

Fitch rating: AA- (2017)

Moody's rating: Aa3 (2017)

Standard & Poors rating: AA- (2017)

GDP - composition, by sector of origin: *agriculture:* 0.2% (2017 est.)
industry: 50.3% (2017 est.)
services: 49.5% (2017 est.)

GDP - composition, by end use: *household consumption:* 24.6% (2017 est.)
government consumption: 17% (2017 est.)
investment in fixed capital: 43.1% (2017 est.)
investment in inventories: 1.5% (2017 est.)
exports of goods and services: 51% (2017 est.)
imports of goods and services: -37.3% (2017 est.)

Agricultural products: tomatoes, dates, camel milk, sheep milk, goat milk, pumpkins/gourds, mutton, poultry, milk, eggplants

Industries: liquefied natural gas, crude oil production and refining, ammonia, fertilizer, petrochemicals, steel reinforcing bars, cement, commercial ship repair

Industrial production growth rate: 3% (2017 est.)
country comparison to the world: 105

Labor force: 1.953 million (2017 est.)
country comparison to the world: 122

Unemployment rate: 8.9% (2017 est.)
11.1% (2016 est.)
country comparison to the world: 136

Unemployment, youth ages 15-24: *total:* 0.4%
male: 0.2%
female: 1.5% (2018 est.)
country comparison to the world: 184

Gini Index coefficient - distribution of family income: 41.1 (2007)
country comparison to the world: 53

Household income or consumption by percentage share: *lowest 10%:* 1.3%
highest 10%: 35.9% (2007)

Budget: *revenues:* 44.1 billion (2017 est.)
expenditures: 53.82 billion (2017 est.)

Budget surplus (+) or deficit (-): -5.8% (of GDP) (2017 est.)
country comparison to the world: 179

Public debt: 53.8% of GDP (2017 est.)
46.7% of GDP (2016 est.)
country comparison to the world: 88

Taxes and other revenues: 26.4% (of GDP) (2017 est.)
country comparison to the world: 112

Fiscal year: 1 April - 31 March

Current account balance: $6.426 billion (2017 est.)
-$8.27 billion (2016 est.)
country comparison to the world: 29

Exports: $70.93 billion (2020 est.) note: data are in current year dollars
$92.05 billion (2019 est.) note: data are in current year dollars
$102.56 billion (2018 est.) note: data are in current year dollars
country comparison to the world: 50

Exports - partners: Japan 17%, South Korea 16%, India 14%, China 13%, Singapore 7% (2019)

Exports - commodities: natural gas, crude petroleum, refined petroleum, ethylene polymers, fertilizers (2019)

Imports: $59.06 billion (2020 est.) note: data are in current year dollars
$66.77 billion (2019 est.) note: data are in current year dollars
$65.81 billion (2018 est.) note: data are in current year dollars
country comparison to the world: 53

Imports - partners: United States 15%, France 13%, United Kingdom 9%, China 9%, Germany 5%, Italy 5% (2019)

Imports - commodities: aircraft, gas turbines, cars, jewelry, iron piping (2019)

Reserves of foreign exchange and gold: $15.01 billion (31 December 2017 est.)
$31.89 billion (31 December 2016 est.)
country comparison to the world: 68

Debt - external: $167.8 billion (31 December 2017 est.)
$157.9 billion (31 December 2016 est.)
country comparison to the world: 45

Exchange rates: Qatari rials (QAR) per US dollar -
3.641 (2020 est.)
3.641 (2019 est.)
3.641 (2018 est.)
3.64 (2014 est.)
3.64 (2013 est.)

ENERGY

Electricity access: *electrification - total population:* 100% (2020)

Electricity: *installed generating capacity:* 10.633 million kW (2020 est.)
consumption: 44,116,984,000 kWh (2019 est.)
exports: 0 kWh (2019 est.)
imports: 0 kWh (2019 est.)
transmission/distribution losses: 2.772 billion kWh (2019 est.)

Electricity generation sources: *fossil fuels:* 100% of total installed capacity (2020 est.)

Petroleum: *total petroleum production:* 1,815,100 bbl/day (2021 est.)
refined petroleum consumption: 293,800 bbl/day (2019 est.)
crude oil and lease condensate exports: 1,264,400 bbl/day (2018 est.)
crude oil and lease condensate imports: 0 bbl/day (2018 est.)
crude oil estimated reserves: 25.244 billion barrels (2021 est.)

Refined petroleum products - production: 273,800 bbl/day (2015 est.)
country comparison to the world: 46

Refined petroleum products - exports: 485,000 bbl/day (2015 est.)
country comparison to the world: 18

Refined petroleum products - imports: 12,300 bbl/day (2015 est.)
country comparison to the world: 143

Natural gas: *production:* 167,460,996,000 cubic meters (2019 est.)
consumption: 37,701,809,000 cubic meters (2019 est.)
exports: 126,749,621,000 cubic meters (2019 est.)
imports: 0 cubic meters (2021 est.)
proven reserves: 23,860,500,000,000 cubic meters (2021 est.)

Carbon dioxide emissions: 111.922 million metric tonnes of CO_2 (2019 est.)
from petroleum and other liquids: 33.44 million metric tonnes of CO_2 (2019 est.)
from consumed natural gas: 78.482 million metric tonnes of CO_2 (2019 est.)
country comparison to the world: 38

Energy consumption per capita: 723.582 million Btu/person (2019 est.)
country comparison to the world: 1

COMMUNICATIONS

Telephones - fixed lines: *total subscriptions:* 454,701 (2020 est.)
subscriptions per 100 inhabitants: 16 (2020 est.)
country comparison to the world: 97

Telephones - mobile cellular: *total subscriptions:* 3,798,514 (2020 est.)
subscriptions per 100 inhabitants: 132 (2020 est.)
country comparison to the world: 132

Telecommunication systems: *general assessment:* Qatar had developed a mature telecom sector which has been able to absorb the additional data demands made on it during the pandemic; mobile services based on LTE are universally available to migrate to 5G; in combination with a strong fiber rollout, the country is aiming to provide gigabit services nationally; 5G services are largely based on 3.5GHz spectrum made available following an auction in early 2019 (2022)
domestic: fixed-line nearly 16 per 100 and mobile-cellular telephone subscribership nearly 132 telephones per 100 persons (2020)
international: country code - 974; landing points for the Qatar-UAE Submarine Cable System, AAE-1, FOG, GBICS/East North Africa MENA and the FALCON submarine cable network that provides links to Asia, Africa, the Middle East, Europe and Southeast Asia; tropospheric scatter to Bahrain; microwave radio relay to Saudi Arabia and the UAE; satellite earth stations - 2 Intelsat (1 Atlantic Ocean and 1 Indian Ocean) and 1 Arabsat; retains full ownership of two commercial satellites, Es'hailSat 1 and 2 (2019)

Broadcast media: TV and radio broadcast licensing and access to local media markets are state controlled; home of the satellite TV channel Al-Jazeera, which was originally owned and financed by the Qatari government but has evolved to independent corporate status; Al-Jazeera claims editorial independence in broadcasting; local radio transmissions include state, private, and international broadcasters on FM frequencies in Doha; in August 2013, Qatar's satellite company Es'hailSat launched its first communications satellite Es'hail 1 (manufactured in the US), which entered commercial service in December 2013 to provide improved television broadcasting capability and expand availability of voice and Internet; Es'hailSat launched its second commercial satellite in 2018 with aid of SpaceX (2019)

Internet country code: .qa

Internet users: *total:* 2,881,060 (2020 est.)
percent of population: 100% (2020 est.)
country comparison to the world: 116

Broadband - fixed subscriptions: *total:* 296,126 (2020 est.)
subscriptions per 100 inhabitants: 10 (2020 est.)
country comparison to the world: 107

TRANSPORTATION

National air transport system: *number of registered air carriers:* 3 (2020)
inventory of registered aircraft operated by air carriers: 251
annual passenger traffic on registered air carriers: 29,178,923 (2018)
annual freight traffic on registered air carriers: 12,666,710,000 (2018) mt-km

Civil aircraft registration country code prefix: A7

Airports: *total:* 6 (2021)
country comparison to the world: 175

Airports - with paved runways: *total:* 4
over 3,047 m: 3
1,524 to 2,437 m: 1 (2021)

Airports - with unpaved runways: *total:* 2
914 to 1,523 m: 1
under 914 m: 1 (2021)

Heliports: 1 (2021)

Pipelines: 288 km condensate, 221 km condensate/gas, 2,383 km gas, 90 km liquid petroleum gas, 745 km oil, 103 km refined products (2013)

Roadways: *total:* 7,039 km (2016)
country comparison to the world: 142

Merchant marine: *total:* 129
by type: bulk carrier 9, container ship 4, general cargo 4, oil tanker 5, other 107 (2021)
country comparison to the world: 79

Ports and terminals: *major seaport(s):* Doha, Musay'id, Ra's Laffan

LNG terminal(s) (export): Ras Laffan

MILITARY AND SECURITY

Military and security forces: Qatar Armed Forces: Qatari Amiri Land Force (QALF, includes Emiri Guard), Qatari Amiri Navy (QAN, includes Coast Guard), Qatari Amiri Air Force (QAAF); Internal Security Forces: Mobile Gendarmerie (2022)

Military expenditures: 4% of GDP (2021 est.)
4% of GDP (2020 est.)
3.4% of GDP (2019 est.) (approximately $8.44 billion)
3.3% of GDP (2018 est.) (approximately $8.23 billion)
3.4% of GDP (2017 est.) (approximately $8.22 billion)
country comparison to the world: 17

Military and security service personnel strengths: information varies; approximately 15,000 active duty personnel (10,000 Land Force, including Emiri Guard; 3,000 Navy; 2,000 Air Force) (2022)

Military equipment inventories and acquisitions: the Qatari military's inventory includes a broad mix of older and modern weapons systems, mostly from the US and Europe; in the 2010s, Qatar embarked on an extensive military expansion and modernization program with large air, ground, and naval equipment purchases; since 2010, France and the US have been the top suppliers (2022)

Military service age and obligation: conscription for men aged 18-35 introduced in 2013; compulsory service times range from 4-12 months, depending on educational and professional circumstances; since 2018, women have been permitted to serve as volunteers in the armed forces, including as uniformed officers and pilots (2022)
note 1: as of 2020, the military incorporated about 2,000 conscripts annually
note 2: Qatar recruits foreign contract soldiers to overcome manpower limitations; as of 2020, it was estimated that as much as 85% of the military was comprised of foreigners

Military - note: Qatar hosts the regional headquarters for the US Central Command (CENTCOM; established 1983) and more than 8,000 US military forces at various military facilities, including the large Al Udeid Air Base; Qatar also hosts as many as 5,000 Turkish military forces at two bases established in 2014 and 2019

Qatar has Major Non-NATO Ally (MNNA) status with the US; MNNA is a designation under US law that provides foreign partners with certain benefits in the areas of defense trade and security cooperation; while MNNA status provides military and economic privileges, it does not entail any security commitments (2022)

TRANSNATIONAL ISSUES

Disputes - international: none identified

Refugees and internally displaced persons: *stateless persons:* 1,200 (mid-year 2021)

ROMANIA

INTRODUCTION

Background: The principalities of Wallachia and Moldavia - for centuries under the suzerainty of the Turkish Ottoman Empire - secured their autonomy in 1856; they were de facto linked in 1859 and formally united in 1862 under the new name of Romania. The country gained recognition of its independence in 1878. It joined the Allied Powers in World War I and acquired new territories - most notably Transylvania - following the conflict. In 1940, Romania allied with the Axis powers and participated in the 1941 German invasion of the USSR. Three years later, overrun by the Soviets, Romania signed an armistice. The post-war Soviet occupation led to the formation of a communist "people's republic" in 1947 and the abdication of the king. The decades-long rule of dictator Nicolae CEAUSESCU, who took power in 1965, and his Securitate police state became increasingly oppressive and draconian through the 1980s. CEAUSESCU was overthrown and executed in late 1989. Former communists dominated the government until 1996 when they were swept from power. Romania joined NATO in 2004 and the EU in 2007.

GEOGRAPHY

Location: Southeastern Europe, bordering the Black Sea, between Bulgaria and Ukraine

Geographic coordinates: 46 00 N, 25 00 E

Map references: Europe

Area: *total:* 238,391 sq km
land: 229,891 sq km
water: 8,500 sq km
country comparison to the world: 83

Area - comparative: twice the size of Pennsylvania; slightly smaller than Oregon

Land boundaries: *total:* 2,844 km
border countries (5): Bulgaria 605 km; Hungary 424 km; Moldova 683 km; Serbia 531 km; Ukraine 601 km

Coastline: 225 km

Maritime claims: *territorial sea:* 12 nm
contiguous zone: 24 nm
exclusive economic zone: 200 nm
continental shelf: 200-m depth or to the depth of exploitation

Climate: temperate; cold, cloudy winters with frequent snow and fog; sunny summers with frequent showers and thunderstorms

Terrain: central Transylvanian Basin is separated from the Moldavian Plateau on the east by the Eastern Carpathian Mountains and separated from the Walachian Plain on the south by the Transylvanian Alps

Elevation: *highest point:* Moldoveanu 2,544 m
lowest point: Black Sea 0 m
mean elevation: 414 m

Natural resources: petroleum (reserves declining), timber, natural gas, coal, iron ore, salt, arable land, hydropower

Land use: *agricultural land:* 60.7% (2018 est.)
arable land: 39.1% (2018 est.)
permanent crops: 1.9% (2018 est.)
permanent pasture: 19.7% (2018 est.)
forest: 28.7% (2018 est.)
other: 10.6% (2018 est.)

Irrigated land: 31,490 sq km (2012)

Major rivers (by length in km): Danube river mouth (shared with Germany [s], Austria, Slovakia, Czechia, Hungary, Croatia, Serbia, Bulgaria, Moldova, and Ukraine) - 2,888 km
note – [s] after country name indicates river source; [m] after country name indicates river mouth

Major watersheds (area sq km): Atlantic Ocean drainage: *(Black Sea)* Danube (795,656 sq km)

Population distribution: urbanization is not particularly high, and a fairly even population distribution can be found throughout most of the country, with urban areas attracting larger and denser populations; Hungarians, the country's largest minority, have a particularly strong presence in eastern Transylvania

Natural hazards: earthquakes, most severe in south and southwest; geologic structure and climate promote landslides

Geography - note: controls the most easily traversable land route between the Balkans, Moldova, and Ukraine; the Carpathian Mountains dominate the center of the country, while the Danube River forms much of the southern boundary with Serbia and Bulgaria

PEOPLE AND SOCIETY

Population: 18,519,899 (2022 est.)
country comparison to the world: 65

Nationality: *noun:* Romanian(s)
adjective: Romanian

Ethnic groups: Romanian 83.4%, Hungarian 6.1%, Romani 3.1%, Ukrainian 0.3%, German 0.2%, other 0.7%, unspecified 6.1% (2011 est.)
note: Romani populations are usually underestimated in official statistics and may represent 5–11% of Romania's population

Languages: Romanian (official) 85.4%, Hungarian 6.3%, Romani 1.2%, other 1%, unspecified 6.1% (2011 est.)
major-language sample(s): Cartea informativa a lumii, sursa indispensabila pentru informatii de baza. (Romanian)

Religions: Eastern Orthodox (including all sub-denominations) 81.9%, Protestant (various denominations including Reformed and Pentecostal) 6.4%, Roman Catholic 4.3%, other (includes Muslim) 0.9%, none or atheist 0.2%, unspecified 6.3% (2011 est.)

Age structure: *0-14 years:* 14.12% (male 1,545,196/female 1,463,700)
15-24 years: 10.31% (male 1,126,997/female 1,068,817)
25-54 years: 46.26% (male 4,993,886/female 4,860,408)
55-64 years: 11.73% (male 1,176,814/female 1,322,048)
65 years and over: 17.58% (male 1,516,472/female 2,228,555) (2020 est.)

Dependency ratios: *total dependency ratio:* 53.3
youth dependency ratio: 23.8
elderly dependency ratio: 29.5
potential support ratio: 3.4 (2020 est.)

Median age: *total:* 42.5 years
male: 41 years
female: 44 years (2020 est.)
country comparison to the world: 34

Population growth rate: -1.09% (2022 est.)
country comparison to the world: 231

Birth rate: 8.76 births/1,000 population (2022 est.)
country comparison to the world: 207

Death rate: 15.26 deaths/1,000 population (2022 est.)
country comparison to the world: 2

Net migration rate: -4.36 migrant(s)/1,000 population (2022 est.)
country comparison to the world: 195

Population distribution: urbanization is not particularly high, and a fairly even population distribution can be found throughout most of the country, with urban areas attracting larger and denser populations; Hungarians, the country's largest minority, have a particularly strong presence in eastern Transylvania

Urbanization: *urban population:* 54.5% of total population (2022)
rate of urbanization: -0.15% annual rate of change (2020-25 est.)

Major urban areas - population: 1.785 million BUCHAREST (capital) (2022)

Sex ratio: *at birth:* 1.06 male(s)/female
0-14 years: 1.06 male(s)/female
15-24 years: 1.04 male(s)/female
25-54 years: 1 male(s)/female
55-64 years: 0.96 male(s)/female
65 years and over: 0.75 male(s)/female
total population: 0.94 male(s)/female (2022 est.)

Mother's mean age at first birth: 27.1 years (2020 est.)

Maternal mortality ratio: 19 deaths/100,000 live births (2017 est.)

country comparison to the world: 127

Infant mortality rate: *total:* 5.84 deaths/1,000 live births
male: 6.07 deaths/1,000 live births
female: 5.59 deaths/1,000 live births (2022 est.)
country comparison to the world: 172

Life expectancy at birth: *total population:* 75.75 years
male: 72.3 years
female: 79.4 years (2022 est.)
country comparison to the world: 117

Total fertility rate: 1.63 children born/woman (2022 est.)
country comparison to the world: 179

Drinking water source: *improved: urban:* 100% of population
rural: 100% of population
total: 100% of population

Current health expenditure: 5.7% of GDP (2019)

Physicians density: 2.98 physicians/1,000 population (2017)

Hospital bed density: 6.9 beds/1,000 population (2017)

Sanitation facility access: *improved: urban:* 96.9% of population
rural: 76% of population
total: 87.3% of population
unimproved: urban: 3.1% of population
rural: 24% of population
total: 12.7% of population (2020 est.)

HIV/AIDS - adult prevalence rate: 0.1% (2020 est.)
country comparison to the world: 132

HIV/AIDS - people living with HIV/AIDS: 19,000 (2020 est.)
note: estimate does not include children
country comparison to the world: 85

HIV/AIDS - deaths: (2020 est.) <500
note: estimate does not include children

Obesity - adult prevalence rate: 22.5% (2016)
country comparison to the world: 75

Alcohol consumption per capita: *total:* 10.96 liters of pure alcohol (2019 est.)
beer: 5.33 liters of pure alcohol (2019 est.)
wine: 3.38 liters of pure alcohol (2019 est.)
spirits: 2.25 liters of pure alcohol (2019 est.)
other alcohols: 0 liters of pure alcohol (2019 est.)
country comparison to the world: 14

Tobacco use: *total:* 28% (2020 est.)
male: 35.9% (2020 est.)
female: 20% (2020 est.)
country comparison to the world: 37

Education expenditures: 3.3% of GDP (2018 est.)
country comparison to the world: 137

Literacy: *definition:* age 15 and over can read and write
total population: 98.8%
male: 99.1%
female: 98.6% (2018)

School life expectancy (primary to tertiary education): *total:* 14 years
male: 14 years
female: 15 years (2019)

Unemployment, youth ages 15-24: *total:* 17.3%
male: 17.9%
female: 16.5% (2020 est.)

ENVIRONMENT

Environment - current issues: soil erosion, degradation, and desertification; water pollution; air pollution in south from industrial effluents; contamination of Danube delta wetlands

Environment - international agreements: *party to:* Air Pollution, Air Pollution-Heavy Metals, Air Pollution-Multi-effect Protocol, Air Pollution-Persistent Organic Pollutants, Antarctic-Environmental Protection, Antarctic Treaty, Biodiversity, Climate Change, Climate Change-Kyoto Protocol, Climate Change-Paris Agreement, Comprehensive Nuclear Test Ban, Desertification, Endangered Species, Environmental Modification, Hazardous Wastes, Law of the Sea, Nuclear Test Ban, Ozone Layer Protection, Ship Pollution, Tropical Timber 2006, Wetlands, Whaling
signed, but not ratified: none of the selected agreements

Air pollutants: *particulate matter emissions:* 14.29 micrograms per cubic meter (2016 est.)
carbon dioxide emissions: 69.26 megatons (2016 est.)
methane emissions: 27.62 megatons (2020 est.)

Climate: temperate; cold, cloudy winters with frequent snow and fog; sunny summers with frequent showers and thunderstorms

Land use: *agricultural land:* 60.7% (2018 est.)
arable land: 39.1% (2018 est.)
permanent crops: 1.9% (2018 est.)
permanent pasture: 19.7% (2018 est.)
forest: 28.7% (2018 est.)
other: 10.6% (2018 est.)

Urbanization: *urban population:* 54.5% of total population (2022)
rate of urbanization: -0.15% annual rate of change (2020-25 est.)

Revenue from forest resources: *forest revenues:* 0.16% of GDP (2018 est.)
country comparison to the world: 99

Revenue from coal: *coal revenues:* 0.03% of GDP (2018 est.)
country comparison to the world: 39

Waste and recycling: *municipal solid waste generated annually:* 4.895 million tons (2015 est.)
municipal solid waste recycled annually: 277,547 tons (2015 est.)
percent of municipal solid waste recycled: 5.7% (2015 est.)

Major rivers (by length in km): Danube river mouth (shared with Germany [s], Austria, Slovakia, Czechia, Hungary, Croatia, Serbia, Bulgaria, Moldova, and Ukraine) - 2,888 km
note – [s] after country name indicates river source; [m] after country name indicates river mouth

Major watersheds (area sq km): Atlantic Ocean drainage: *(Black Sea)* Danube (795,656 sq km)

Total water withdrawal: *municipal:* 1.048 billion cubic meters (2017 est.)
industrial: 4.234 billion cubic meters (2017 est.)
agricultural: 1.491 billion cubic meters (2017 est.)

Total renewable water resources: 212.01 billion cubic meters (2017 est.)

GOVERNMENT

Country name: *conventional long form:* none
conventional short form: Romania
local long form: none
local short form: Romania
former: Kingdom of Romania, Romanian People's Republic, Socialist Republic of Romania
etymology: the name derives from the Latin "Romanus" meaning "citizen of Rome" and was used to stress the common ancient heritage of Romania's three main regions - Moldavia, Transylvania, and Wallachia - during their gradual unification between the mid-19th century and early 20th century

Government type: semi-presidential republic

Capital: *name:* Bucharest
geographic coordinates: 44 26 N, 26 06 E
time difference: UTC+2 (7 hours ahead of Washington, DC, during Standard Time)
daylight saving time: +1hr, begins last Sunday in March; ends last Sunday in October
etymology: related to the Romanian word "bucura" that is believed to be of Dacian origin and whose meaning is "to be glad (happy)"; Bucharest's meaning is thus akin to "city of joy"

Administrative divisions: 41 counties (judete, singular - judet) and 1 municipality* (municipiu); Alba, Arad, Arges, Bacau, Bihor, Bistrita-Nasaud, Botosani, Braila, Brasov, Bucuresti (Bucharest)*, Buzau, Calarasi, Caras-Severin, Cluj, Constanta, Covasna, Dambovita, Dolj, Galati, Gorj, Giurgiu, Harghita, Hunedoara, Ialomita, Iasi, Ilfov, Maramures, Mehedinti, Mures, Neamt, Olt, Prahova, Salaj, Satu Mare, Sibiu, Suceava, Teleorman, Timis, Tulcea, Vaslui, Valcea, Vrancea

Independence: 9 May 1877 (independence proclaimed from the Ottoman Empire; 13 July 1878 (independence recognized by the Treaty of Berlin); 26 March 1881 (kingdom proclaimed); 30 December 1947 (republic proclaimed)

National holiday: Unification Day (unification of Romania and Transylvania), 1 December (1918)

Constitution: *history:* several previous; latest adopted 21 November 1991, approved by referendum and effective 8 December 1991
amendments: initiated by the president of Romania through a proposal by the government, by at least one fourth of deputies or senators in Parliament, or by petition of eligible voters representing at least half of Romania's counties; passage requires at least two-thirds majority vote by both chambers or – if mediation is required - by three-fourths majority vote in a joint session, followed by approval in a referendum; articles, including those on national sovereignty, form of government, political pluralism, and fundamental rights and freedoms cannot be amended; amended 2003

Legal system: civil law system

International law organization participation: accepts compulsory ICJ jurisdiction with reservations; accepts ICCt jurisdiction

Citizenship: *citizenship by birth:* no
citizenship by descent only: at least one parent must be a citizen of Romania
dual citizenship recognized: yes
residency requirement for naturalization: 5 years

Suffrage: 18 years of age; universal

Executive branch: *chief of state:* President Klaus Werner IOHANNIS (since 21 December 2014)
head of government: Prime Minister Nicolae CIUCA (since 25 November 2021); Deputy Prime Ministers Sorin GRINDEANU (since 25 November 2021) and Kelemen HUNOR (since 23 December 2020)
cabinet: Council of Ministers appointed by the prime minister
elections/appointments: president directly elected by absolute majority popular vote in 2 rounds if needed for a 5-year term (eligible for a second term); election last held on 10 November 2019 with a runoff on 24 November 2019 (next to be held in November 2024); prime minister appointed by the president with consent of Parliament
election results:
2019: Klaus IOHANNIS reelected president in second round; percent of vote - Klaus IOHANNIS (PNL) 66.1%, Viorica DANCILA (PSD) 33.9%; Nicolae CIUCA approved as prime minister with 318 votes
2014: Klaus IOHANNIS elected president in the second round; percent of vote - Klaus IOHANNIS (PNL) 54.4%, Victor PONTA (PSD) 45.6%

Legislative branch: *description:* bicameral Parliament or Parlament consists of:
Senate or Senat (136 seats; members directly elected in single- and multi-seat constituencies - including 2 seats for diaspora - by party-list, proportional representation vote; members serve 4-year terms)

Chamber of Deputies or Camera Deputatilor (330 seats; members directly elected in single- and multi-seat constituencies - including 4 seats for diaspora - by party-list, proportional representation vote; members serve 4-year terms)
elections:
Senate - last held on 6 December 2020 (next to be held in 2024)
Chamber of Deputies - last held on 6 December 2020 (next to be held in 2024)
election results:
Senate - percent of vote by party - PSD 29.3%, PNL 25.6%, 2020 USR-PLUS Alliance 15.9%, AUR 9.2%, UDMR 5.9%, other 14.1%; seats by party - PSD 47, PNL 41, 2020 USR-PLUS Alliance 25, AUR 14, UDMR 9; composition - men 111, women 25, percent of women 18.4%

Chamber of Deputies - percent of vote by party - PSD 28.9%, PNL 25.2%, 2020 USR-PLUS Alliance 15.4%, AUR 9.1%, UDMR 5.7%, other 15.7%; seats by party - PSD 110, PNL 93, 2020 USR-PLUS Alliance 55, AUR 33, UDMR 21, other 18; composition - men 267, women 63, percent of women 19.1%; note - total Parliament percent of women 18.9%

Judicial branch: *highest court(s):* High Court of Cassation and Justice (consists of 111 judges organized into civil, penal, commercial, contentious administrative and fiscal business, and joint sections); Supreme Constitutional Court (consists of 9 members)
judge selection and term of office: High Court of Cassation and Justice judges appointed by the president upon nomination by the Superior Council of Magistracy, a 19-member body of judges, prosecutors, and law specialists; judges appointed for 6-year renewable terms; Constitutional Court members - 6 elected by Parliament and 3 appointed by the president; members serve 9-year, nonrenewable terms
subordinate courts: Courts of Appeal; regional tribunals; first instance courts; military and arbitration courts

Political parties and leaders: 2020 USR-PLUS Alliance [Dan BARNA and Dacian CIOLOS] (dissolved 16 April 2021)
Alliance for the Fatherland or APP [Codrin STEFANESCU]
Alliance for the Unity of Romanians or AUR [George SIMION]
Christian-Democratic National Peasants' Party or PNT-CD [Aurelian PAVELESCU]
Civic Hungarian Party [Zsolt BIRO]
Democratic Union of Hungarians in Romania or UDMR [Hunor KELEMEN]
Ecologist Party of Romania or PER [Danut POP]
Force of the Right or FD [Ludovic ORBAN]
Greater Romania Party or PRM [Victor IOVICI]
Green Party [Marius LAZAR and Lavinia COSMA]
National Liberal Party or PNL [Nicolae CIUCA]
Party of Liberty, Unity, and Solidarity or PLUS [Dacian CIOLOS] (dissolved 16 April 2021)
Popular Movement Party or PMP [Eugen TOMAC]
PRO Romania or PRO [Victor PONTA]
Romanian Nationhood Party or PNR [Ninel PEIA]
Save Romania Union Party or USR [Catalin DRULA]
Social Democratic Party or PSD [Marcel CIOLACU]
Social Liberal Humanist Party or PUSL [Daniel IONASCU] (formerly Humanist Power Party (Social-Liberal) or PPU-SL)
United Romania Party or PRU [Robert BUGA]

International organization participation: Australia Group, BIS, BSEC, CBSS (observer), CD, CE, CEI, EAPC, EBRD, ECB, EIB, ESA, EU, FAO, G-9, IAEA, IBRD, ICAO, ICC (national committees), ICCt, ICRM, IDA, IFAD, IFC, IFRCS, IHO, ILO, IMF, IMO, IMSO, Interpol, IOC, IOM, IPU, ISO, ITSO, ITU, ITUC (NGOs), LAIA (observer), MIGA, MONUSCO, NATO, NSG, OAS (observer), OIF, OPCW, OSCE, PCA, SELEC, UN, UNCTAD, UNESCO, UNHCR, UNIDO, Union Latina, UNMIL, UNMISS, UNOCI, UNWTO, UPU, Wassenaar Arrangement, WCO, WFTU (NGOs), WHO, WIPO, WMO, WTO, ZC

Diplomatic representation in the US: *chief of mission:* Ambassador Andrei MURARU (since 15 September 2021)
chancery: 1607 23rd Street NW, Washington, DC 20008
telephone: [1] (202) 332-4829; [1] (202) 332-4846
FAX: [1] (202) 232-4748
email address and website:
washington@mae.ro (chancery)
contact@informatiiconsulare.ro (consular section)
https://washington.mae.ro/en
consulate(s) general: Chicago, Los Angeles, Miami, New York

Diplomatic representation from the US: *chief of mission:* Ambassador (vacant); Charge d'Affaires David MUNIZ (since 20 January 2021)
embassy: 4-6, Dr. Liviu Librescu Blvd., District 1, Bucharest, 015118
mailing address: 5260 Bucharest Place, Washington, DC 20521-5260
telephone: [40] (21) 200-3300
FAX: [40] (21) 200-3442
email address and website:
ACSBucharest@state.gov
https://ro.usembassy.gov/

Flag description: three equal vertical bands of cobalt blue (hoist side), chrome yellow, and vermilion red; modeled after the flag of France, the colors are those of the principalities of Walachia (red and yellow) and Moldavia (red and blue), which united in 1862 to form Romania; the national coat of arms that used to be centered in the yellow band has been removed
note: now similar to the flag of Chad, whose blue band is darker; also resembles the flags of Andorra and Moldova

National symbol(s): golden eagle; national colors: blue, yellow, red

National anthem: *name:* "Desteapta-te romane!" (Wake up, Romanian!)
lyrics/music: Andrei MURESIANU/Anton PANN
note: adopted 1990; the anthem was written during the 1848 Revolution

National heritage: *total World Heritage Sites:* 9 (7 cultural, 2 natural)
selected World Heritage Site locales: Danube Delta (n); Churches of Moldavia (c); Monastery of Horezu (c); Villages with Fortified Churches in Transylvania (c); Dacian Fortresses of the Orastie Mountains (c); Historic Center of Sighişoara (c); Wooden Churches of Maramureş (c); Ancient and Primeval Beech Forests of the Carpathians (n); Roşia Montană Mining Landscape (c)

ECONOMY

Economic overview: Romania, which joined the EU on 1 January 2007, began the transition from communism in 1989 with a largely obsolete industrial base and a pattern of output unsuited to the country's needs. Romania's macroeconomic gains have only recently started to spur creation of a middle class and to address Romania's widespread poverty. Corruption and red tape continue to permeate the business environment.

In the aftermath of the global financial crisis, Romania signed a $26 billion emergency assistance package from the IMF, the EU, and other international lenders, but GDP contracted until 2011. In March 2011, Romania and the IMF/EU/World Bank signed a 24-month precautionary standby agreement, worth $6.6 billion, to promote fiscal discipline, encourage progress on structural reforms, and strengthen financial sector stability; no funds were drawn. In September 2013, Romanian authorities and the IMF/EU agreed to a follow-on standby agreement, worth $5.4 billion, to continue with reforms. This agreement expired in September 2015, and no funds were drawn. Progress on structural reforms has been uneven, and the economy still is vulnerable to external shocks.

Economic growth rebounded in the 2013-17 period, driven by strong industrial exports, excellent agricultural harvests, and, more recently, expansionary fiscal policies in 2016-2017 that nearly quadrupled Bucharest's annual fiscal deficit, from +0.8% of GDP in 2015 to -3% of GDP in 2016 and an estimated -3.4% in 2017. Industry outperformed other sectors of the economy in 2017. Exports remained an engine of economic growth, led by trade with the EU, which accounts for roughly 70% of Romania trade. Domestic demand was the major driver, due to tax cuts and large wage increases that began last year and are set to continue in 2018.

An aging population, emigration of skilled labor, significant tax evasion, insufficient health care, and an aggressive loosening of the fiscal package compromise Romania's long-term growth and economic stability and are the economy's top vulnerabilities.

Real GDP (purchasing power parity): $556.07 billion (2020 est.)
$578.39 billion (2019 est.)
$555.47 billion (2018 est.)
note: data are in 2017 dollars
country comparison to the world: 37

Real GDP growth rate: 4.2% (2019 est.)
4.54% (2018 est.)
7.11% (2017 est.)
country comparison to the world: 71

Real GDP per capita: $28,800 (2020 est.)
$29,900 (2019 est.)
$28,500 (2018 est.)
note: data are in 2017 dollars
country comparison to the world: 67

GDP (official exchange rate): $249.543 billion (2019 est.)

Inflation rate (consumer prices): 3.8% (2019 est.)
4.6% (2018 est.)
1.3% (2017 est.)
country comparison to the world: 162

Credit ratings:

Fitch rating: BBB- (2011)

Moody's rating: Baa3 (2006)

Standard & Poors rating: BBB- (2014)

GDP - composition, by sector of origin: *agriculture:* 4.2% (2017 est.)
industry: 33.2% (2017 est.)
services: 62.6% (2017 est.)

GDP - composition, by end use: *household consumption:* 70% (2017 est.)
government consumption: 7.7% (2017 est.)
investment in fixed capital: 22.6% (2017 est.)
investment in inventories: 1.9% (2017 est.)
exports of goods and services: 41.4% (2017 est.)
imports of goods and services: -43.6% (2017 est.)

Agricultural products: maize, wheat, milk, sunflower seed, potatoes, barley, grapes, sugar beet, rapeseed, plums/sloes

Industries: electric machinery and equipment, auto assembly, textiles and footwear, light machinery, metallurgy, chemicals, food processing, petroleum refining, mining, timber, construction materials

Industrial production growth rate: 5.5% (2017 est.)
country comparison to the world: 50

Labor force: 4.889 million (2020 est.)
country comparison to the world: 80

Labor force - by occupation: *agriculture:* 28.3%
industry: 28.9%
services: 42.8% (2014)

Unemployment rate: 3.06% (2019 est.)
3.56% (2018 est.)
country comparison to the world: 41

Unemployment, youth ages 15-24: *total:* 17.3%
male: 17.9%
female: 16.5% (2020 est.)
country comparison to the world: 94

Population below poverty line: 23.8% (2018 est.)

Gini Index coefficient - distribution of family income: 36 (2017 est.)
28.2 (2010)
country comparison to the world: 95

Household income or consumption by percentage share: *lowest 10%:* 15.3%
highest 10%: 7.6% (2014 est.)

Budget: *revenues:* 62.14 billion (2017 est.)
expenditures: 68.13 billion (2017 est.)

Budget surplus (+) or deficit (-): -2.8% (of GDP) (2017 est.)
country comparison to the world: 125

Public debt: 36.8% of GDP (2017 est.)
38.8% of GDP (2016 est.)
note: defined by the EU's Maastricht Treaty as consolidated general government gross debt at nominal value, outstanding at the end of the year in the following categories of government liabilities: currency and deposits, securities other than shares excluding financial derivatives, and loans; general government sector comprises the subsectors: central government, state government, local government, and social security funds
country comparison to the world: 145

Taxes and other revenues: 29.3% (of GDP) (2017 est.)
country comparison to the world: 84

Fiscal year: calendar year

Current account balance: -$11.389 billion (2019 est.)
-$10.78 billion (2018 est.)
country comparison to the world: 194

Exports: $93.01 billion (2020 est.) note: data are in current year dollars
$100.9 billion (2019 est.) note: data are in current year dollars
$101.11 billion (2018 est.) note: data are in current year dollars
country comparison to the world: 41

Exports - partners: Germany 22%, Italy 10%, France 7% (2019)

Exports - commodities: cars and vehicle parts, insulated wiring, refined petroleum, electrical control boards, seats (2019)

Imports: $104.16 billion (2020 est.) note: data are in current year dollars
$111.18 billion (2019 est.) note: data are in current year dollars
$109.26 billion (2018 est.) note: data are in current year dollars
country comparison to the world: 39

Imports - partners: Germany 19%, Italy 9%, Hungary 7%, Poland 6%, China 5%, France 5% (2019)

Imports - commodities: cars and vehicle parts, crude petroleum, packaged medicines, insulated wiring, broadcasting equipment (2019)

Reserves of foreign exchange and gold: $44.43 billion (31 December 2017 est.)
$40 billion (31 December 2016 est.)
country comparison to the world: 43

Debt - external: $117.829 billion (2019 est.)
$115.803 billion (2018 est.)
country comparison to the world: 50

Exchange rates: lei (RON) per US dollar -
4.02835 (2020 est.)
4.31655 (2019 est.)
4.0782 (2018 est.)
4.0057 (2014 est.)
3.3492 (2013 est.)

ENERGY

Electricity access: *electrification - total population:* 100% (2020)

Electricity: *installed generating capacity:* 20.528 million kW (2020 est.)
consumption: 50,039,421,000 kWh (2019 est.)
exports: 5.459 billion kWh (2020 est.)
imports: 8.252 billion kWh (2020 est.)
transmission/distribution losses: 6.501 billion kWh (2019 est.)

Electricity generation sources: *fossil fuels:* 32.1% of total installed capacity (2020 est.)
nuclear: 20.4% of total installed capacity (2020 est.)
solar: 3.4% of total installed capacity (2020 est.)
wind: 13.4% of total installed capacity (2020 est.)
hydroelectricity: 29.9% of total installed capacity (2020 est.)
biomass and waste: 0.9% of total installed capacity (2020 est.)

Coal: *production:* 15.002 million metric tons (2020 est.)
consumption: 16.412 million metric tons (2020 est.)
exports: 2,000 metric tons (2020 est.)
imports: 1.384 million metric tons (2020 est.)
proven reserves: 291 million metric tons (2019 est.)

Petroleum: *total petroleum production:* 74,000 bbl/day (2021 est.)
refined petroleum consumption: 222,200 bbl/day (2019 est.)
crude oil and lease condensate exports: 1,400 bbl/day (2018 est.)
crude oil and lease condensate imports: 161,600 bbl/day (2018 est.)
crude oil estimated reserves: 600 million barrels (2021 est.)

Refined petroleum products - production: 232,600 bbl/day (2015 est.)
country comparison to the world: 47

Refined petroleum products - exports: 103,000 bbl/day (2015 est.)
country comparison to the world: 44

Refined petroleum products - imports: 49,420 bbl/day (2015 est.)
country comparison to the world: 81

Natural gas: *production:* 10,367,941,000 cubic meters (2019 est.)
consumption: 11,087,528,000 cubic meters (2019 est.)
exports: 11.185 million cubic meters (2019 est.)
imports: 2,800,985,000 cubic meters (2019 est.)
proven reserves: 105.48 billion cubic meters (2021 est.)

Carbon dioxide emissions: 68.746 million metric tonnes of CO2 (2019 est.)
from coal and metallurgical coke: 20.891 million metric tonnes of CO2 (2019 est.)
from petroleum and other liquids: 27.268 million metric tonnes of CO2 (2019 est.)
from consumed natural gas: 20.588 million metric tonnes of CO2 (2019 est.)
country comparison to the world: 51

Energy consumption per capita: 71.736 million Btu/person (2019 est.)
country comparison to the world: 84

COMMUNICATIONS

Telephones - fixed lines: *total subscriptions:* 3.025 million (2020 est.)
subscriptions per 100 inhabitants: 16 (2020 est.)
country comparison to the world: 43

Telephones - mobile cellular: *total subscriptions:* 22.592 million (2020 est.)
subscriptions per 100 inhabitants: 117 (2020 est.)
country comparison to the world: 54

Telecommunication systems: *general assessment:* Romania's telecom market has undergone several significant changes in recent years; the mobile market is served by network operators that have extensive LTE networks in place, while services based on 5G have been offered under their existing spectrum concessions since 2019; the delayed multi-spectrum auction, expected to be completed later in 2021, will enable the operators to expand 5G network capacity and enable consumers to make far greater use of the technology's potential; in line with legislation passed in July 2021 the MNOs will have to replace equipment provided by vendors deemed to be a security risk (2021)
domestic: fixed-line teledensity is about 16 telephones per 100 persons; mobile market served by four mobile network operators; mobile-cellular teledensity over 117 telephones per 100 persons (2020)
international: country code - 40; landing point for the Diamond Link Global submarine cable linking Romania with Georgia; satellite earth stations - 10; digital, international, direct-dial exchanges operate in Bucharest (2019)

Broadcast media: a mixture of public and private TV stations; there are 7 public TV stations (2 national, 5 regional) using terrestrial broadcasting and 187 private TV stations (out of which 171 offer local coverage) using terrestrial broadcasting, plus 11 public TV stations using satellite broadcasting and 86 private TV stations using satellite broadcasting; state-owned public radio broadcaster operates 4 national networks and regional and local stations, having in total 20 public radio stations by terrestrial broadcasting plus 4 public radio stations by satellite broadcasting; there are 502 operational private radio stations using terrestrial broadcasting and 26 private radio stations using satellite broadcasting

Internet country code: .ro

Internet users: *total:* 15,020,866 (2020 est.)
percent of population: 78% (2020 est.)
country comparison to the world: 47

Broadband - fixed subscriptions: *total:* 5,684,782 (2020 est.)
subscriptions per 100 inhabitants: 30 (2020 est.)
country comparison to the world: 32

TRANSPORTATION

National air transport system: *number of registered air carriers:* 8 (2020)
inventory of registered aircraft operated by air carriers: 60
annual passenger traffic on registered air carriers: 4,908,235 (2018)
annual freight traffic on registered air carriers: 2.71 million (2018) mt-km

Civil aircraft registration country code prefix: YR

Airports: *total:* 45 (2021)
country comparison to the world: 95

Airports - with paved runways: *total:* 26
over 3,047 m: 4
2,438 to 3,047 m: 10
1,524 to 2,437 m: 11
under 914 m: 1 (2021)

Airports - with unpaved runways: *total:* 19
914 to 1,523 m: 5
under 914 m: 14 (2021)

Heliports: 2 (2021)

Pipelines: 3,726 km gas, 2,451 km oil (2013)

Railways: *total:* 11,268 km (2014)
standard gauge: 10,781 km (2014) 1.435-m gauge (3,292 km electrified)
narrow gauge: 427 km (2014) 0.760-m gauge
broad gauge: 60 km (2014) 1.524-m gauge
country comparison to the world: 23

Roadways: *total:* 84,185 km (2012)
paved: 49,873 km (2012) (includes 337 km of expressways)
unpaved: 34,312 km (2012)
country comparison to the world: 57

Waterways: 1,731 km (2010) (includes 1,075 km on the Danube River, 524 km on secondary branches, and 132 km on canals)
country comparison to the world: 47

Merchant marine: *total:* 121
by type: general cargo 11, oil tanker 6, other 104 (2021)
country comparison to the world: 81

Ports and terminals: *major seaport(s):* Constanta, Midia
river port(s): Braila, Galati (Galatz), Mancanului (Giurgiu), Tulcea (Danube River)

MILITARY AND SECURITY

Military and security forces: Romanian Armed Forces: Land Forces, Naval Forces, Air Force; Ministry of Internal Affairs: Romanian Gendarmerie, Romanian Police, Romanian Border Police (2022)

Military expenditures: 2% of GDP (2022 est.)
2% of GDP (2021)
2% of GDP (2020)
1.8% of GDP (2019) (approximately $7.47 billion)
1.8% of GDP (2018) (approximately $6.9 billion)
country comparison to the world: 62

Military and security service personnel strengths: approximately 75,000 active duty personnel (58,000 Land Forces; 7,000 Naval Forces; 10,000 Air Force) (2022)

Military equipment inventories and acquisitions: the inventory of the Romanian Armed Forces is comprised mostly of Soviet-era and older domestically-produced weapons systems; there is also a smaller mix of Western-origin equipment received in more recent years from European countries and the US (2021)

Military service age and obligation: 18 years of age for voluntary service for men and women; all military inductees contract for an initial 5-year term of service, with subsequent successive 3-year terms until age 36; conscription ended in 2006 (2021)

Military deployments: up to 120 Poland (NATO) (2022)

Military - note: Romania became a member of NATO in 2004
Romania hosts a NATO multinational divisional headquarters (Multinational Division Southeast; became operational in 2017) and a French-led ground force battlegroup as part of NATO's tailored forward presence in the southeastern part of the Alliance; NATO reinforced the battlegroup with additional troops in response to Russia's 2022 invasion of Ukraine; Romania conducts its own air policing mission, but because of Russian aggression in the Black Sea region, NATO allies have sent detachments of fighters to augment the Romanian Air Force since 2014 (2022)

TERRORISM

Terrorist group(s): Islamic State of Iraq and ash-Sham (ISIS)

TRANSNATIONAL ISSUES

Disputes - international: *Romania-Bulgaria:* none identified
Romania-Hungary: none identified
Romania-Moldova: none identified
Romania-Serbia: none identified
Romania-Ukraine: the International Court of Justice ruled largely in favor of Romania in its dispute submitted in 2004 over Ukrainian-administered Zmiyinyy/Serpilor (Snake) Island and Black Sea maritime boundary delimitation; in 2007, Romania opposed Ukraine's construction of a navigation canal from the Danube border through Ukraine to the Black Sea, arguing that it runs through a unique ecological area, the Danube Delta

Refugees and internally displaced persons: *refugees (country of origin):* 88,831 (Ukraine) (as of 6 November 2022)
stateless persons: 314 (mid-year 2021)
note: 11,847 estimated refugee and migrant arrivals (January 2015-November 2022)

Trafficking in persons: *current situation:* human traffickers exploit domestic and foreign victims in Romania and Romanians abroad; Romania remains a primary source country for sex and labor trafficking victims in Europe; Romanian men, women, and children are subjected to forced labor in agriculture, construction, hotels, manufacturing, domestic service, commercial sex, and forced begging and theft; Romania is a destination country for a limited number of foreign trafficking victims, including migrants from Africa, Europe, and South and Southeast Asia, exploited in the construction, hotel, and food-processing industries
tier rating: Tier 2 Watch List — Romania does not fully meet the minimum standards for the elimination of trafficking but is making significant efforts to do so; the government identified more trafficking victims during the reporting period, participated in more international investigations, and conducted awareness campaigns; however, authorities investigated, prosecuted, and convicted fewer traffickers; officials complicit in trafficking crimes, especially with minors in government-run homes or placement centers, were not prosecuted; government funding of services for child trafficking victims remained inadequate (2020)

Illicit drugs: a source country for cannabis

RUSSIA

INTRODUCTION

Background: Founded in the 12th century, the Principality of Muscovy was able to emerge from over 200 years of Mongol domination (13th-15th centuries) and to gradually conquer and absorb surrounding principalities. In the early 17th century, a new ROMANOV Dynasty continued this policy of expansion across Siberia to the Pacific. Under PETER I (ruled 1682-1725), hegemony was extended to the Baltic Sea and the country was renamed the Russian Empire. During the 19th century, more territorial acquisitions were made in Europe and Asia. Defeat in the Russo-Japanese War of 1904-05 contributed to the Revolution of 1905, which resulted in the formation of a parliament and other reforms. Devastating defeats and food shortages in World War I led to widespread rioting in the major cities of the Russian Empire and to the overthrow in 1917 of the ROMANOV Dynasty. The communists under Vladimir LENIN seized power soon after and formed the USSR. The brutal rule of Iosif STALIN (1928-53) strengthened communist rule and Russian dominance of the Soviet Union at a cost of tens of millions of lives. After defeating Germany in World War II as part of an alliance with the US (1939-1945), the USSR expanded its territory and influence in Eastern Europe and emerged as a global power. The USSR was the principal adversary of the US during the Cold War (1947-1991). The Soviet economy and society stagnated in the decades following Stalin's rule, until General Secretary Mikhail GORBACHEV (1985-91) introduced glasnost (openness) and perestroika (restructuring) in an attempt to modernize communism, but his initiatives inadvertently released forces that by December 1991 led to the dissolution of the USSR into Russia and 14 other independent states.

Following economic and political turmoil during President Boris YELTSIN's term (1991-99), Russia shifted toward a centralized authoritarian state under President Vladimir PUTIN (2000-2008, 2012-present) in which the regime seeks to legitimize its rule through managed elections, populist appeals, a foreign policy focused on enhancing the country's geopolitical influence, and commodity-based economic growth. Russia faces a largely subdued rebel movement in Chechnya and some other surrounding regions, although violence still occurs throughout the North Caucasus.

GEOGRAPHY

Location: North Asia bordering the Arctic Ocean, extending from Eastern Europe (the portion west of the Urals) to the North Pacific Ocean

Geographic coordinates: 60 00 N, 100 00 E

Map references: Asia

Area: *total:* 17,098,242 sq km
land: 16,377,742 sq km
water: 720,500 sq km
country comparison to the world: 1

Area - comparative: approximately 1.8 times the size of the US

Land boundaries: *total:* 22,407 km
border countries (14): Azerbaijan 338 km; Belarus 1,312 km; China (southeast) 4,133 km and China (south) 46 km; Estonia 324 km; Finland 1,309 km; Georgia 894 km; Kazakhstan 7,644 km; North Korea 18 km; Latvia 332 km; Lithuania (Kaliningrad Oblast) 261 km; Mongolia 3,452 km; Norway 191 km; Poland (Kaliningrad Oblast) 209 km; Ukraine 1,944 km

Coastline: 37,653 km

Maritime claims: *territorial sea:* 12 nm
contiguous zone: 24 nm
exclusive economic zone: 200 nm
continental shelf: 200-m depth or to the depth of exploitation

Climate: ranges from steppes in the south through humid continental in much of European Russia; subarctic in Siberia to tundra climate in the polar north; winters vary from cool along Black Sea coast to frigid in Siberia; summers vary from warm in the steppes to cool along Arctic coast

Terrain: broad plain with low hills west of Urals; vast coniferous forest and tundra in Siberia; uplands and mountains along southern border regions

Elevation: *highest point:* Gora El'brus (highest point in Europe) 5,642 m
lowest point: Caspian Sea -28 m
mean elevation: 600 m

Natural resources: wide natural resource base including major deposits of oil, natural gas, coal, and many strategic minerals, bauxite, reserves of rare earth elements, timber, note, formidable obstacles of climate, terrain, and distance hinder exploitation of natural resources

Land use: *agricultural land:* 13.1% (2018 est.)
arable land: 7.3% (2018 est.)
permanent crops: 0.1% (2018 est.)
permanent pasture: 5.7% (2018 est.)
forest: 49.4% (2018 est.)
other: 37.5% (2018 est.)

Irrigated land: 43,000 sq km (2012)

Major lakes (area sq km): *fresh water lake(s):* Lake Baikal - 31,500 sq km; Lake Ladoga - 18,130 sq km; Lake Onega - 9,720 sq km; Lake Khanka (shared with China) - 5,010 sq km; Lake Peipus - 4,300 sq km; Ozero Vygozero - 1,250 sq km; Ozero Beloye - 1,120 sq km
salt water lake(s): Caspian Sea (shared with Iran, Azerbaijan, Turkmenistan, and Kazakhstan) - 374,000 sq km; Ozero Malyye Chany - 2,500 sq km; Curonian Lagoon (shared with Lithuania) - 1,620 sq km note - the Caspian Sea is the World's largest lake

Major rivers (by length in km): Yenisey-Angara - 5,539 km; Ob-Irtysh - 5,410 km; Amur river mouth (shared with China [s] and Mongolia) - 4,444 km; Lena - 4,400 km; Volga - 3,645 km; Kolyma - 2,513 km; Ural river source (shared with Kazakhstan [m]) - 2,428 km; Dnieper river source (shared with Belarus and Ukraine [m]) - 2,287 km; Don - 1,870 km; Pechora - 1,809 km
note – [s] after country name indicates river source; [m] after country name indicates river mouth

Major watersheds (area sq km): Arctic Ocean drainage: Kolyma (679,934 sq km), Lena (2,306,743 sq km), Ob (2,972,493 sq km), Pechora (289,532 sq km), Yenisei (2,554,388 sq km)
Atlantic Ocean drainage: *(Black Sea)* Don (458,694 sq km), Dnieper (533,966 sq km)
Pacific Ocean drainage: Amur (1,929,955 sq km)
Internal *(endorheic basin)* drainage: *(Caspian Sea basin)* Volga (1,410,951 sq km)

Major aquifers: Angara-Lena Basin, Pechora Basin, North Caucasus Basin, East European Aquifer System, West Siberian Basin, Tunguss Basin, Yakut Basin

Population distribution: population is heavily concentrated in the westernmost fifth of the country extending from the Baltic Sea, south to the Caspian Sea, and eastward parallel to the Kazakh border; elsewhere, sizeable pockets are isolated and generally found in the south

Natural hazards: permafrost over much of Siberia is a major impediment to development; volcanic activity in the Kuril Islands; volcanoes and earthquakes on the Kamchatka Peninsula; spring floods and summer/autumn forest fires throughout Siberia and parts of European Russia
volcanism: significant volcanic activity on the Kamchatka Peninsula and Kuril Islands; the peninsula alone is home to some 29 historically active volcanoes, with dozens more in the Kuril Islands; Kliuchevskoi (4,835 m), which erupted in 2007 and 2010, is Kamchatka's most active volcano; Avachinsky and Koryaksky volcanoes, which pose a threat to the city of Petropavlovsk-Kamchatsky, have been deemed Decade Volcanoes by the International Association of Volcanology and Chemistry of the Earth's Interior, worthy of study due to their explosive history and close proximity to human populations; other notable historically active volcanoes include Bezymianny, Chikurachki, Ebeko, Gorely, Grozny, Karymsky, Ketoi, Kronotsky, Ksudach, Medvezhia, Mutnovsky, Sarychev Peak, Shiveluch, Tiatia, Tolbachik, and Zheltovsky; see note 2 under "Geography - note"

Geography - note: *note 1:* largest country in the world in terms of area but unfavorably located in relation to major sea lanes of the world; despite its size, much of the country lacks proper soils and climates (either too cold or too dry) for agriculture
note 2: Russia's far east, particularly the Kamchatka Peninsula, lies along the Ring of Fire, a belt of active volcanoes and earthquake epicenters bordering the Pacific Ocean; up to 90% of the world's earthquakes and some 75% of the world's volcanoes occur within the Ring of Fire
note 3: Mount El'brus is Europe's tallest peak; Lake Baikal, the deepest lake in the world, is estimated to hold one fifth of the world's fresh surface water
note 4: Kaliningrad oblast is an exclave annexed from Germany following World War II (it was formerly part of East Prussia); its capital city of Kaliningrad

- formerly Koenigsberg - is the only Baltic port in Russia that remains ice free in the winter

PEOPLE AND SOCIETY

Population: 142,021,981 (2022 est.)
country comparison to the world: 9

Nationality: *noun:* Russian(s)
adjective: Russian

Ethnic groups: Russian 77.7%, Tatar 3.7%, Ukrainian 1.4%, Bashkir 1.1%, Chuvash 1%, Chechen 1%, other 10.2%, unspecified 3.9% (2010 est.)
note: nearly 200 national and/or ethnic groups are represented in Russia's 2010 census

Languages: Russian (official) 85.7%, Tatar 3.2%, Chechen 1%, other 10.1%; note - data represent native language spoken (2010 est.)
major-language sample(s):
Книга фактов о мире – незаменимый источник базовой информации. (Russian)

Religions: Russian Orthodox 15-20%, Muslim 10-15%, other Christian 2% (2006 est.)
note: estimates are of practicing worshipers; Russia has large populations of non-practicing believers and non-believers, a legacy of over seven decades of official atheism under Soviet rule; Russia officially recognizes Orthodox Christianity, Islam, Judaism, and Buddhism as the country's traditional religions

Age structure: *0-14 years:* 17.24% (male 12,551,611/female 11,881,297)
15-24 years: 9.54% (male 6,920,070/female 6,602,776)
25-54 years: 43.38% (male 30,240,260/female 31,245,104)
55-64 years: 14.31% (male 8,808,330/female 11,467,697)
65 years and over: 15.53% (male 7,033,381/female 14,971,679) (2020 est.)

Dependency ratios: *total dependency ratio:* 51.2
youth dependency ratio: 27.8
elderly dependency ratio: 23.5
potential support ratio: 4.3 (2020 est.)

Median age: *total:* 40.3 years
male: 37.5 years
female: 43.2 years (2020 est.)
country comparison to the world: 52

Population growth rate: -0.22% (2022 est.)
country comparison to the world: 213

Birth rate: 9.45 births/1,000 population (2022 est.)
country comparison to the world: 194

Death rate: 13.36 deaths/1,000 population (2022 est.)
country comparison to the world: 7

Net migration rate: 1.7 migrant(s)/1,000 population (2022 est.)
country comparison to the world: 56

Population distribution: population is heavily concentrated in the westernmost fifth of the country extending from the Baltic Sea, south to the Caspian Sea, and eastward parallel to the Kazakh border; elsewhere, sizeable pockets are isolated and generally found in the south

Urbanization: *urban population:* 75.1% of total population (2022)
rate of urbanization: 0.11% annual rate of change (2020-25 est.)

Major urban areas - population: 12.641 million MOSCOW (capital), 5.536 million Saint Petersburg, 1.686 million Novosibirsk, 1.521 million Yekaterinburg, 1.286 million Kazan, 1.253 million Nizhniy Novgorod (2022)

Sex ratio: *at birth:* 1.06 male(s)/female
0-14 years: 1.06 male(s)/female
15-24 years: 1.05 male(s)/female
25-54 years: 0.97 male(s)/female
55-64 years: 0.78 male(s)/female
65 years and over: 0.36 male(s)/female
total population: 0.86 male(s)/female (2022 est.)

Mother's mean age at first birth: 25.2 years (2013 est.)

Maternal mortality ratio: 17 deaths/100,000 live births (2017 est.)
country comparison to the world: 130

Infant mortality rate: *total:* 6.42 deaths/1,000 live births
male: 7.28 deaths/1,000 live births
female: 5.49 deaths/1,000 live births (2022 est.)
country comparison to the world: 168

Life expectancy at birth: *total population:* 72.44 years
male: 66.92 years
female: 78.3 years (2022 est.)
country comparison to the world: 156

Total fertility rate: 1.6 children born/woman (2022 est.)
country comparison to the world: 184

Contraceptive prevalence rate: 68% (2011)
note: percent of women aged 15-44

Drinking water source: *improved: urban:* 99.1% of population
rural: 93.1% of population
total: 97.6% of population
unimproved: urban: 0.9% of population
rural: 6.9% of population
total: 2.4% of population (2020 est.)

Current health expenditure: 5.7% of GDP (2019)

Physicians density: 3.82 physicians/1,000 population (2020)

Hospital bed density: 7.1 beds/1,000 population (2018)

Sanitation facility access: *improved: urban:* 95.2% of population
rural: 72.3% of population
total: 89.4% of population
unimproved: urban: 4.8% of population
rural: 27.7% of population
total: 10.6% of population (2020 est.)

HIV/AIDS - adult prevalence rate: 1.2% (2017 est.)
country comparison to the world: 36

HIV/AIDS - people living with HIV/AIDS: 1 million (2017 est.)
country comparison to the world: 10

Major infectious diseases: *degree of risk:* intermediate (2020)
food or waterborne diseases: bacterial diarrhea
vectorborne diseases: Crimean-Congo hemorrhagic fever, tickborne encephalitis
note: widespread ongoing transmission of a respiratory illness caused by the novel coronavirus (COVID-19) is occurring throughout the Russia; as of 18 August 2022, Russia has reported a total of 19,000,055 cases of COVID-19 or 13,019.58 cumulative cases of COVID-19 per 100,000 population with a total of 383,362 cumulative deaths or a rate of 262.69 cumulative deaths per 100,000 population; as of 14 August 2022, 57.13% of the population has received at least one dose of COVID-19 vaccine

Obesity - adult prevalence rate: 23.1% (2016)
country comparison to the world: 70

Alcohol consumption per capita: *total:* 7.29 liters of pure alcohol (2019 est.)
beer: 3.04 liters of pure alcohol (2019 est.)
wine: 0.97 liters of pure alcohol (2019 est.)
spirits: 3.16 liters of pure alcohol (2019 est.)
other alcohols: 0.12 liters of pure alcohol (2019 est.)
country comparison to the world: 56

Tobacco use: *total:* 26.8% (2020 est.)
male: 40.8% (2020 est.)
female: 12.8% (2020 est.)
country comparison to the world: 41

Education expenditures: 4.7% of GDP (2018 est.)
country comparison to the world: 77

Literacy: *definition:* age 15 and over can read and write
total population: 99.7%
male: 99.7%
female: 99.7% (2018)

School life expectancy (primary to tertiary education): *total:* 16 years
male: 16 years
female: 16 years (2019)

Unemployment, youth ages 15-24: *total:* 17%
male: 16%
female: 18.2% (2020 est.)

ENVIRONMENT

Environment - current issues: air pollution from heavy industry, emissions of coal-fired electric plants, and transportation in major cities; industrial, municipal, and agricultural pollution of inland waterways and seacoasts; deforestation; soil erosion; soil contamination from improper application of agricultural chemicals; nuclear waste disposal; scattered areas of sometimes intense radioactive contamination; groundwater contamination from toxic waste; urban solid waste management; abandoned stocks of obsolete pesticides

Environment - international agreements: *party to:* Air Pollution, Air Pollution-Nitrogen Oxides, Air Pollution-Sulphur 85, Antarctic-Environmental Protection, Antarctic-Marine Living Resources, Antarctic Seals, Antarctic Treaty, Biodiversity, Climate Change, Climate Change-Kyoto Protocol, Climate Change-Paris Agreement, Comprehensive Nuclear Test Ban, Desertification, Endangered Species, Environmental Modification, Hazardous Wastes, Law of the Sea, Marine Dumping-London Convention, Nuclear Test Ban, Ozone Layer Protection, Ship Pollution, Wetlands, Whaling
signed, but not ratified: Air Pollution-Sulfur 94

Air pollutants: *particulate matter emissions:* 13.75 micrograms per cubic meter (2016 est.)
carbon dioxide emissions: 1,732.03 megatons (2016 est.)
methane emissions: 851.52 megatons (2020 est.)

Climate: ranges from steppes in the south through humid continental in much of European Russia; subarctic in Siberia to tundra climate in the polar north; winters vary from cool along Black Sea coast to frigid in Siberia; summers vary from warm in the steppes to cool along Arctic coast

Land use: *agricultural land:* 13.1% (2018 est.)

arable land: 7.3% (2018 est.)
permanent crops: 0.1% (2018 est.)
permanent pasture: 5.7% (2018 est.)
forest: 49.4% (2018 est.)
other: 37.5% (2018 est.)

Urbanization: *urban population:* 75.1% of total population (2022)
rate of urbanization: 0.11% annual rate of change (2020-25 est.)

Revenue from forest resources: *forest revenues:* 0.29% of GDP (2018 est.)
country comparison to the world: 81

Revenue from coal: *coal revenues:* 0.53% of GDP (2018 est.)
country comparison to the world: 11

Waste and recycling: *municipal solid waste generated annually:* 60 million tons (2012 est.)
municipal solid waste recycled annually: 2.7 million tons (2012 est.)
percent of municipal solid waste recycled: 4.5% (2012 est.)

Major lakes (area sq km): *fresh water lake(s):* Lake Baikal - 31,500 sq km; Lake Ladoga - 18,130 sq km; Lake Onega - 9,720 sq km; Lake Khanka (shared with China) - 5,010 sq km; Lake Peipus - 4,300 sq km; Ozero Vygozero - 1,250 sq km; Ozero Beloye - 1,120 sq km
salt water lake(s): Caspian Sea (shared with Iran, Azerbaijan, Turkmenistan, and Kazakhstan) - 374,000 sq km; Ozero Malyye Chany - 2,500 sq km; Curonian Lagoon (shared with Lithuania) - 1,620 sq km note - the Caspian Sea is the World's largest lake

Major rivers (by length in km): Yenisey-Angara - 5,539 km; Ob-Irtysh - 5,410 km; Amur river mouth (shared with China [s] and Mongolia) - 4,444 km; Lena - 4,400 km; Volga - 3,645 km; Kolyma - 2,513 km; Ural river source (shared with Kazakhstan [m]) - 2,428 km; Dnieper river source (shared with Belarus and Ukraine [m]) - 2,287 km; Don - 1,870 km; Pechora - 1,809 km
note – [s] after country name indicates river source; [m] after country name indicates river mouth

Major watersheds (area sq km): Arctic Ocean drainage: Kolyma (679,934 sq km), Lena (2,306,743 sq km), Ob (2,972,493 sq km), Pechora (289,532 sq km), Yenisei (2,554,388 sq km)
Atlantic Ocean drainage: *(Black Sea)* Don (458,694 sq km), Dnieper (533,966 sq km)
Pacific Ocean drainage: Amur (1,929,955 sq km)
Internal *(endorheic basin)* drainage: *(Caspian Sea basin)* Volga (1,410,951 sq km)

Major aquifers: Angara-Lena Basin, Pechora Basin, North Caucasus Basin, East European Aquifer System, West Siberian Basin, Tunguss Basin, Yakut Basin

Total water withdrawal: *municipal:* 17.71 billion cubic meters (2017 est.)
industrial: 28.04 billion cubic meters (2017 est.)
agricultural: 18.66 billion cubic meters (2017 est.)

Total renewable water resources: 4.525 trillion cubic meters (2017 est.)

GOVERNMENT

Country name: *conventional long form:* Russian Federation
conventional short form: Russia
local long form: Rossiyskaya Federatsiya
local short form: Rossiya
former: Russian Empire, Russian Soviet Federative Socialist Republic
etymology: Russian lands were generally referred to as Muscovy until PETER I officially declared the Russian Empire in 1721; the new name sought to invoke the patrimony of the medieval eastern European Rus state centered on Kyiv in present-day Ukraine; the Rus were a Varangian (eastern Viking) elite that imposed their rule and eventually their name on their Slavic subjects

Government type: semi-presidential federation

Capital: *name:* Moscow
geographic coordinates: 55 45 N, 37 36 E
time difference: UTC+3 (8 hours ahead of Washington, DC, during Standard Time)
daylight saving time: does not observe daylight savings time (DST)
time zone note: Russia has 11 time zones, the largest number of contiguous time zones of any country in the world; in 2014, two time zones were added and DST dropped
etymology: named after the Moskva River; the origin of the river's name is obscure but may derive from the appellation "Mustajoki" given to the river by the Finno-Ugric people who originally inhabited the area and whose meaning may have been "dark" or "turbid"

Administrative divisions: 46 provinces (oblasti, singular - oblast), 21 republics (respubliki, singular - respublika), 4 autonomous okrugs (avtonomnyye okrugi, singular - avtonomnyy okrug), 9 krays (kraya, singular - kray), 2 federal cities (goroda, singular - gorod), and 1 autonomous oblast (avtonomnaya oblast')
oblasts: Amur (Blagoveshchensk), Arkhangelsk, Astrakhan, Belgorod, Bryansk, Chelyabinsk, Irkutsk, Ivanovo, Kaliningrad, Kaluga, Kemerovo, Kirov, Kostroma, Kurgan, Kursk, Leningrad, Lipetsk, Magadan, Moscow, Murmansk, Nizhniy Novgorod, Novgorod, Novosibirsk, Omsk, Orenburg, Orel, Penza, Pskov, Rostov, Ryazan, Sakhalin (Yuzhno-Sakhalinsk), Samara, Saratov, Smolensk, Sverdlovsk (Yekaterinburg), Tambov, Tomsk, Tula, Tver, Tyumen, Ulyanovsk, Vladimir, Volgograd, Vologda, Voronezh, Yaroslavl
republics: Adygeya (Maykop), Altay (Gorno-Altaysk), Bashkortostan (Ufa), Buryatiya (Ulan-Ude), Chechnya (Groznyy), Chuvashiya (Cheboksary), Dagestan (Makhachkala), Ingushetiya (Magas), Kabardino-Balkariya (Nal'chik), Kalmykiya (Elista), Karachayevo-Cherkesiya (Cherkessk), Kareliya (Petrozavodsk), Khakasiya (Abakan), Komi (Syktyvkar), Mariy-El (Yoshkar-Ola), Mordoviya (Saransk), North Ossetia (Vladikavkaz), Sakha [Yakutiya] (Yakutsk), Tatarstan (Kazan), Tyva (Kyzyl), Udmurtiya (Izhevsk)
autonomous okrugs: Chukotka (Anadyr'), Khanty-Mansi-Yugra (Khanty-Mansiysk), Nenets (Nar'yan-Mar), Yamalo-Nenets (Salekhard)
krays: Altay (Barnaul), Kamchatka (Petropavlovsk-Kamchatskiy), Khabarovsk, Krasnodar, Krasnoyarsk, Perm, Primorskiy [Maritime] (Vladivostok), Stavropol, Zabaykalsk [Transbaikal] (Chita)
federal cities: Moscow [Moskva], Saint Petersburg [Sankt-Peterburg]
autonomous oblast: Yevreyskaya [Jewish] (Birobidzhan)
note 1: administrative divisions have the same names as their administrative centers (exceptions have the administrative center name following in parentheses)
note 2: the United States does not recognize Russia's annexation of Ukraine's Autonomous Republic of Crimea and the municipality of Sevastopol, nor their redesignation as the "Republic of Crimea" and the "Federal City of Sevastopol"

Independence: 25 December 1991 (from the Soviet Union; Russian SFSR renamed Russian Federation); notable earlier dates: 1157 (Principality of Vladimir-Suzdal created); 16 January 1547 (Tsardom of Muscovy established); 22 October 1721 (Russian Empire proclaimed); 30 December 1922 (Soviet Union established)

National holiday: Russia Day, 12 June (1990); note - commemorates the adoption of the Declaration of State Sovereignty of the Russian Soviet Federative Socialist Republic (RSFSR)

Constitution: *history:* several previous (during Russian Empire and Soviet era); latest drafted 12 July 1993, adopted by referendum 12 December 1993, effective 25 December 1993
amendments: proposed by the president of the Russian Federation, by either house of the Federal Assembly, by the government of the Russian Federation, or by legislative (representative) bodies of the Federation's constituent entities; proposals to amend the government's constitutional system, human and civil rights and freedoms, and procedures for amending or drafting a new constitution require formation of a Constitutional Assembly; passage of such amendments requires two-thirds majority vote of its total membership; passage in a referendum requires participation of an absolute majority of eligible voters and an absolute majority of valid votes; approval of proposed amendments to the government structure, authorities, and procedures requires approval by the legislative bodies of at least two thirds of the Russian Federation's constituent entities; amended several times, last in 2020

Legal system: civil law system; judicial review of legislative acts

International law organization participation: has not submitted an ICJ jurisdiction declaration; non-party state to the ICCt

Citizenship: *citizenship by birth:* no
citizenship by descent only: at least one parent must be a citizen of Russia
dual citizenship recognized: yes
residency requirement for naturalization: 3-5 years

Suffrage: 18 years of age; universal

Executive branch: *chief of state:* President Vladimir Vladimirovich PUTIN (since 7 May 2012)
head of government: Premier Mikhail MISHUSTIN (since 16 January 2020); First Deputy Premier Andrey Removich BELOUSOV (since 21 January 2020); Deputy Premiers Yuriy TRUTNEV (since 31 August 2013), Yuriy Ivanovich BORISOV, Tatiana Alekseyevna GOLIKOVA (since 18 May 2018), Dmitriy Yuriyevich GRIGORENKO, Viktoriya Valeriyevna ABRAMCHENKO, Aleksey Logvinovich OVERCHUK, Marat Shakirzyanovich KHUSNULLIN, Dmitriy Nikolayevich CHERNYSHENKO (since 21 January 2020), Aleksandr NOVAK (since 10 November 2020)
cabinet: the "Government" is composed of the premier, his deputies, and ministers, all appointed by the president; the premier is also confirmed by the Duma
elections/appointments: president directly elected by absolute majority popular vote in 2 rounds if

needed for a 6-year term (2020 constitutional amendments allow a second consecutive term); election last held on 18 March 2018 (next to be held in March 2024); note - for the 2024 presidential election, previous presidential terms are discounted; there is no vice president; premier appointed by the president with the approval of the Duma
election results:
2018: Vladimir PUTIN reelected president; percent of vote - Vladimir PUTIN (independent) 77.5%, Pavel GRUDININ (CPRF) 11.9%, Vladimir ZHIRINOVSKIY (LDPR) 5.7%, other 4.9%; Mikhail MISHUSTIN (independent) approved as premier by Duma; vote - 383 to 0
2012: Vladimir PUTIN elected president; percent of vote - Vladimir PUTIN (United Russia) 63.6%, Gennadiy ZYUGANOV (CPRF) 17.2%, Mikhail PROKHOROV (CP) 8%, Vladimir ZHIRINOVSKIY (LDPR) 6.2%, Sergey MIRONOV (A Just Russia) 3.9%, other 1.1%; Dmitriy MEDVEDEV (United Russia) approved as premier by Duma; vote - 299 to 144
note: there is also a Presidential Administration that provides staff and policy support to the president, drafts presidential decrees, and coordinates policy among government agencies; a Security Council also reports directly to the president

Legislative branch: *description:* bicameral Federal Assembly or Federalnoye Sobraniye consists of:
Federation Council or Sovet Federatsii (170 seats; 2 members in each of the 83 federal administrative units (see note below) - oblasts, krays, republics, autonomous okrugs and oblasts, and federal cities of Moscow and Saint Petersburg -appointed by the top executive and legislative officials; members serve 4-year terms)

State Duma or Gosudarstvennaya Duma (450 seats (see note below); as of February 2014, the electoral system reverted to a mixed electoral system for the 2016 election, in which one-half of the members are directly elected by simple majority vote and one-half directly elected by proportional representation vote; members serve 5-year terms)
elections:
State Duma - last held 17 - 19 September 2021 (next to be held in September 2026)
election results:
Federation Council (members appointed); composition (as of October 2021) - men 132, women 37, percent of women 21.8%

State Duma - United Russia 50.9%, CPRF 19.3%, LDPR 7.7%, A Just Russia 7.6%, New People 5.3% other minor parties and Independents 9.2%; seats by party - United Russia 324, CPRF 57, LDPR 21, A Just Russia 27, New People 13; Rodina 1, CP 1, Party of Growth 1, independent 5; composition - men 377, women 73, percent of women 16.2%; note - total Federal Assembly percent of women 17.7%
note l: the State Duma now includes 3 representatives from the "Republic of Crimea," while the Federation Council includes 2 each from the "Republic of Crimea" and the "Federal City of Sevastopol," both regions that Russia occupied and attempted to annex from Ukraine and that the US does not recognize as part of Russia

Judicial branch: *highest court(s):* Supreme Court of the Russian Federation (consists of 170 members organized into the Judicial Panel for Civil Affairs, the Judicial Panel for Criminal Affairs, and the Military Panel); Constitutional Court (consists of 11 members, including the chairperson and deputy); note - in February 2014, Russia's Higher Court of Arbitration was abolished and its former authorities transferred to the Supreme Court, which in addition is the country's highest judicial authority for appeals, civil, criminal, administrative, and military cases, and the disciplinary judicial board, which has jurisdiction over economic disputes
judge selection and term of office: all members of Russia's 3 highest courts nominated by the president and appointed by the Federation Council (the upper house of the legislature); members of all 3 courts appointed for life
subordinate courts: regional (kray) and provincial (oblast) courts; Moscow and St. Petersburg city courts; autonomous province and district courts; note - the 21 Russian Republics have court systems specified by their own constitutions

Political parties and leaders: A Just Russia or SRZP [Sergey MIRONOV]
Civic Platform or CP [Rifat SHAYKHUTDINOV]
Communist Party of the Russian Federation or CPRF [Gennadiy ZYUGANOV]
Liberal Democratic Party of Russia or LDPR [Leonid SLUTSKY]
New People [Alexey NECHAYEV]
Party of Growth [Boris TITOV]
Rodina [Aleksei ZHURAVLYOV]
United Russia [Dmitriy MEDVEDEV]
note: 31 political parties are registered with Russia's Ministry of Justice (as of September 2021); 14 participated in the 2021 election, but only 8 parties maintain representation in Russia's national legislature

International organization participation: APEC, Arctic Council, ARF, ASEAN (dialogue partner), BIS, BRICS, BSEC, CBSS, CD, CE, CERN (observer), CICA, CIS, CSTO, EAEC, EAEU, EAPC, EAS, EBRD, FAO, FATF, G-20, GCTU, IAEA, IBRD, ICAO, ICC (national committees), ICRM, IDA, IFAD, IFC, IFRCS, IHO, ILO, IMF, IMO, IMSO, Interpol, IOC, IOM (observer), IPU, ISO, ITSO, ITU, ITUC (NGOs), LAIA (observer), MIGA, MINURSO, MONUSCO, NEA, NSG, OAS (observer), OIC (observer), OPCW, OSCE, Paris Club, PCA, PFP, SCO, UN, UNCTAD, UNESCO, UNHCR, UNIDO, UNISFA, UNMIL, UNMISS, UNOCI, UN Security Council (permanent), UNTSO, UNWTO, UPU, Wassenaar Arrangement, WCO, WFTU (NGOs), WHO, WIPO, WMO, WTO, ZC

Diplomatic representation in the US: *chief of mission:* Ambassador Anatoliy Ivanovich ANTONOV (since 8 September 2017)
chancery: 2650 Wisconsin Avenue NW, Washington, DC 20007
telephone: [1] (202) 298-5700
FAX: [1] (202) 298-5735
email address and website:
rusembusa@mid.ru
https://washington.mid.ru/en/
consulate(s) general: Houston, New York

Diplomatic representation from the US: *chief of mission:* Ambassador (vacant); Charge d'Affaires Elizabeth ROOD (since 5 September 2022)
embassy: 55,75566° N, 37,58028° E
mailing address: 5430 Moscow Place, Washington DC 20521-5430
telephone: [7] (495) 728-5000
FAX: [7] (495) 728-5090
email address and website:
MoscowACS@state.gov
https://ru.usembassy.gov/
consulate(s) general: Vladivostok (suspended status), Yekaterinburg (suspended status)

Flag description: three equal horizontal bands of white (top), blue, and red
note: the Russian flag was created when Russia built its first naval vessels, and was used mostly as a naval ensign until the nineteenth century; the colors may have been based on those of the Dutch flag; despite many popular interpretations, there is no official meaning assigned to the colors of the Russian flag; the flag inspired several other Slavic countries to adopt horizontal tricolors of the same colors but in different arrangements, and so red, blue, and white became the Pan-Slav colors

National symbol(s): bear, double-headed eagle; national colors: white, blue, red

Coat of Arms of Russia:

National anthem: *name:* "Gimn Rossiyskoy Federatsii" (National Anthem of the Russian Federation)
lyrics/music: Sergey Vladimirovich MIKHALKOV/ Aleksandr Vasilyevich ALEKSANDROV
note: in 2000, Russia adopted the tune of the anthem of the former Soviet Union (composed in 1939); the lyrics, also adopted in 2000, were written by the same person who authored the Soviet lyrics in 1943

National heritage: *total World Heritage Sites:* 30 (19 cultural, 11 natural)
selected World Heritage Site locales: Kremlin and Red Square, Moscow (c); Historic Saint Petersburg (c); Novodevichy Convent (c); Historic Monuments of Novgorod (c); Trinity Sergius Lavra in Sergiev Posad (c); Volcanoes of Kamchatka (n); Lake Baikal (n); Central Sikhote-Alin (n); Historic Derbent (c); Kazan Kremlin (c)

ECONOMY

Economic overview: Russia has undergone significant changes since the collapse of the Soviet Union, moving from a centrally planned economy towards a more market-based system. Both economic growth and reform have stalled in recent years, however, and Russia remains a predominantly statist economy with a high concentration of wealth in officials' hands. Economic reforms in the 1990s privatized most industry, with notable exceptions in the energy, transportation, banking, and defense-related sectors. The protection of property rights is still weak, and the state continues to interfere in the free operation of the private sector.

Russia is one of the world's leading producers of oil and natural gas, and is also a top exporter of metals such as steel and primary aluminum. Russia is heavily dependent on the movement of world commodity prices as reliance on commodity exports makes it vulnerable to boom and bust cycles that follow the volatile swings in global prices. The economy, which had averaged 7% growth during the 1998-2008 period as oil prices rose rapidly, has seen diminishing growth rates since then due to the exhaustion of Russia's commodity-based growth model.

A combination of falling oil prices, international sanctions, and structural limitations pushed Russia into a deep recession in 2015, with GDP falling by close to 2.8%. The downturn continued through 2016, with GDP contracting another 0.2%, but was reversed in 2017 as world demand picked up. Government support for import substitution has increased recently in an effort to diversify the economy away from extractive industries.

Real GDP (purchasing power parity): $3,875,690,000,000 (2020 est.)
$3,993,550,000,000 (2019 est.)
$3,913,980,000,000 (2018 est.)
note: data are in 2017 dollars
country comparison to the world: 6

Real GDP growth rate: 1.34% (2019 est.)
2.54% (2018 est.)
1.83% (2017 est.)
country comparison to the world: 160

Real GDP per capita: $26,500 (2020 est.)
$27,200 (2019 est.)
$26,700 (2018 est.)
note: data are in 2017 dollars
country comparison to the world: 72

GDP (official exchange rate): $1,702,361,000,000 (2019 est.)

Inflation rate (consumer prices): 4.4% (2019 est.)
2.8% (2018 est.)
3.7% (2017 est.)
country comparison to the world: 175

Credit ratings:

Fitch rating: BBB (2019)

Moody's rating: Baa3 (2019)

Standard & Poors rating: BBB- (2018)

GDP - composition, by sector of origin: *agriculture:* 4.7% (2017 est.)
industry: 32.4% (2017 est.)
services: 62.3% (2017 est.)

GDP - composition, by end use: *household consumption:* 52.4% (2017 est.)
government consumption: 18% (2017 est.)
investment in fixed capital: 21.6% (2017 est.)
investment in inventories: 2.3% (2017 est.)
exports of goods and services: 26.2% (2017 est.)
imports of goods and services: -20.6% (2017 est.)

Agricultural products: wheat, sugar beet, milk, potatoes, barley, sunflower seed, maize, poultry, oats, soybeans

Industries: complete range of mining and extractive industries producing coal, oil, gas, chemicals, and metals; all forms of machine building from rolling mills to high-performance aircraft and space vehicles; defense industries (including radar, missile production, advanced electronic components), shipbuilding; road and rail transportation equipment; communications equipment; agricultural machinery, tractors, and construction equipment; electric power generating and transmitting equipment; medical and scientific instruments; consumer durables, textiles, foodstuffs, handicrafts

Industrial production growth rate: -1% (2017 est.)
country comparison to the world: 177

Labor force: 69.923 million (2020 est.)
country comparison to the world: 6

Labor force - by occupation: *agriculture:* 9.4%
industry: 27.6%
services: 63% (2016 est.)

Unemployment rate: 4.6% (2019 est.)
4.8% (2018 est.)
country comparison to the world: 70

Unemployment, youth ages 15-24: *total:* 17%
male: 16%
female: 18.2% (2020 est.)
country comparison to the world: 96

Population below poverty line: 12.6% (2018 est.)

Gini Index coefficient - distribution of family income: 37.5 (2018 est.)
41.9 (2013)
country comparison to the world: 79

Household income or consumption by percentage share: *lowest 10%:* 2.3%
highest 10%: 32.2% (2012 est.)

Budget: *revenues:* 258.6 billion (2017 est.)
expenditures: 281.4 billion (2017 est.)

Budget surplus (+) or deficit (-): -1.4% (of GDP) (2017 est.)
country comparison to the world: 88

Public debt: 15.5% of GDP (2017 est.)
16.1% of GDP (2016 est.)
note: data cover general government debt and include debt instruments issued (or owned) by government entities other than the treasury; the data include treasury debt held by foreign entities; the data include debt issued by subnational entities, as well as intragovernmental debt; intragovernmental debt consists of treasury borrowings from surpluses in the social funds, such as for retirement, medical care, and unemployment, debt instruments for the social funds are not sold at public auctions
country comparison to the world: 194

Taxes and other revenues: 16.4% (of GDP) (2017 est.)
country comparison to the world: 181

Fiscal year: calendar year

Current account balance: $65.311 billion (2019 est.)
$115.68 billion (2018 est.)
country comparison to the world: 6

Exports: $379.12 billion (2020 est.) note: data are in current year dollars
$481.76 billion (2019 est.) note: data are in current year dollars
$508.56 billion (2018 est.) note: data are in current year dollars
country comparison to the world: 20

Exports - partners: China 14%, Netherlands 10%, Belarus 5%, Germany 5% (2019)

Exports - commodities: crude petroleum, refined petroleum, natural gas, coal, wheat, iron (2019)

Imports: $304.68 billion (2020 est.) note: data are in current year dollars
$353.25 billion (2019 est.) note: data are in current year dollars
$343.58 billion (2018 est.) note: data are in current year dollars
country comparison to the world: 20

Imports - partners: China 20%, Germany 13%, Belarus 6% (2019)

Imports - commodities: cars and vehicle parts, packaged medicines, broadcasting equipment, aircraft, computers (2019)

Reserves of foreign exchange and gold: $432.7 billion (31 December 2017 est.)
$377.7 billion (31 December 2016 est.)
country comparison to the world: 6

Debt - external: $479.844 billion (2019 est.)
$484.355 billion (2018 est.)
country comparison to the world: 26

Exchange rates: Russian rubles (RUB) per US dollar -
73.7569 (2020 est.)
63.66754 (2019 est.)
66.2 (2018 est.)
60.938 (2014 est.)
38.378 (2013 est.)

ENERGY

Electricity access: *electrification - total population:* 100% (2020)

Electricity: *installed generating capacity:* 276.463 million kW (2020 est.)
consumption: 942,895,420,000 kWh (2019 est.)
exports: 12.116 billion kWh (2020 est.)
imports: 1.377 billion kWh (2020 est.)
transmission/distribution losses: 99.077 billion kWh (2019 est.)

Electricity generation sources: *fossil fuels:* 59.4% of total installed capacity (2020 est.)
nuclear: 21% of total installed capacity (2020 est.)
solar: 0.2% of total installed capacity (2020 est.)
hydroelectricity: 19.1% of total installed capacity (2020 est.)
biomass and waste: 0.3% of total installed capacity (2020 est.)

Coal: *production:* 447.332 million metric tons (2020 est.)
consumption: 266.038 million metric tons (2020 est.)
exports: 224.324 million metric tons (2020 est.)
imports: 24.027 million metric tons (2020 est.)
proven reserves: 162.166 billion metric tons (2019 est.)

Petroleum: *total petroleum production:* 10,749,500 bbl/day (2021 est.)
refined petroleum consumption: 3.699 million bbl/day (2019 est.)
crude oil and lease condensate exports: 5.196 million bbl/day (2018 est.)
crude oil and lease condensate imports: 14,200 bbl/day (2018 est.)
crude oil estimated reserves: 80 billion barrels (2021 est.)

Refined petroleum products - production: 6.076 million bbl/day (2015 est.)
country comparison to the world: 3

Refined petroleum products - exports: 2.671 million bbl/day (2015 est.)
country comparison to the world: 2

Refined petroleum products - imports: 41,920 bbl/day (2015 est.)
country comparison to the world: 88

Natural gas: *production:* 701,544,189,000 cubic meters (2021 est.)
consumption: 460,612,169,000 cubic meters (2020 est.)
exports: 250,854,510,000 cubic meters (2021 est.)
imports: 16,112,146,000 cubic meters (2019 est.)
proven reserves: 47,805,215,000,000 cubic meters (2021 est.)

Carbon dioxide emissions: 1,848,070,000 metric tonnes of CO2 (2019 est.)
from coal and metallurgical coke: 456.033 million metric tonnes of CO2 (2019 est.)
from petroleum and other liquids: 470.289 million metric tonnes of CO2 (2019 est.)
from consumed natural gas: 921.748 million metric tonnes of CO2 (2019 est.)
country comparison to the world: 4

Energy consumption per capita: 227.898 million Btu/person (2019 est.)
country comparison to the world: 18

COMMUNICATIONS

Telephones - fixed lines: *total subscriptions:* 25,892,405 (2020 est.)
subscriptions per 100 inhabitants: 18 (2020 est.)
country comparison to the world: 9

Telephones - mobile cellular: *total subscriptions:* 238,733,217 (2020 est.)
subscriptions per 100 inhabitants: 164 (2020 est.)
country comparison to the world: 5

Telecommunication systems: *general assessment:* the telecom market is the largest in Europe, supported by a population approaching 147 million; the overall market is dominated by the western regions, particularly Moscow and St Petersburg which are the main cities and economic centers; all sectors of the market have been liberalized, with competition most prevalent in the two largest regional markets; the fiber broadband sector has shown considerable growth, supported by the government's program to extend the reach of broadband to outlying regions; the development of 5G services has been stymied by the lack of spectrum; although MNOs have licenses to use 700MHz spectrum for 5G, this spectrum will not be released until at least August 2023; progress is being made by MNOs to develop a joint strategy to deploy 5G using shared network and spectrum assets; mobile penetration is high, though this is partly due to the popularity of multiple SIM card use; there is pressure on operator revenue from the poor economic climate, lower pricing resulting from intense competition, regulatory measures introduced in 2018 which saw the end of roaming charges, and the effects of the Covid-19 pandemic (2022)
domestic: cross-country digital trunk lines run from Saint Petersburg to Khabarovsk, and from Moscow to Novorossiysk; the telephone systems in 60 regional capitals have modern digital infrastructures; cellular services, both analog and digital, are available in many areas; in rural areas, telephone services are still outdated, inadequate, and low-density; nearly 19 per 100 for fixed-line and mobile-cellular a bit over 164 per 100 persons (2020)
international: country code - 7; landing points for the Far East Submarine Cable System, HSCS, Sakhalin-Kuril Island Cable, RSCN, BCS North-Phase 2, Kerch Strait Cable and the Georgia-Russian submarine cable system connecting Russia, Japan, Finland, Georgia and Ukraine; satellite earth stations provide access to Intelsat, Intersputnik, Eutelsat, Inmarsat, and Orbita systems (2019)

Broadcast media: 13 national TV stations with the federal government owning 1 and holding a controlling interest in a second; state-owned Gazprom maintains a controlling interest in 2 of the national channels; government-affiliated Bank Rossiya owns controlling interest in a fourth and fifth, while a sixth national channel is owned by the Moscow city administration; the Russian Orthodox Church and the Russian military, respectively, own 2 additional national channels; roughly 3,300 national, regional, and local TV stations with over two-thirds completely or partially controlled by the federal or local governments; satellite TV services are available; 2 state-run national radio networks with a third majority-owned by Gazprom; roughly 2,400 public and commercial radio stations

Internet country code: .ru; note - Russia also has responsibility for a legacy domain ".su" that was allocated to the Soviet Union and is being phased out

Internet users: *total:* 122,488,468 (2020 est.)
percent of population: 85% (2020 est.)
country comparison to the world: 6

Broadband - fixed subscriptions: *total:* 33,893,305 (2020 est.)
subscriptions per 100 inhabitants: 23 (2020 est.)
country comparison to the world: 6

TRANSPORTATION

National air transport system: *number of registered air carriers:* 32 (2020)
inventory of registered aircraft operated by air carriers: 958
annual passenger traffic on registered air carriers: 99,327,311 (2018)
annual freight traffic on registered air carriers: 6,810,610,000 (2018) mt-km

Civil aircraft registration country code prefix: RA

Airports: *total:* 1,218 (2021)
country comparison to the world: 5

Airports - with paved runways: *total:* 594
over 3,047 m: 54
2,438 to 3,047 m: 197
1,524 to 2,437 m: 123
914 to 1,523 m: 95
*under 914 m:*125 (2021)

Airports - with unpaved runways: *total:* 624
over 3,047 m: 4
2,438 to 3,047 m: 13
1,524 to 2,437 m: 69
914 to 1,523 m: 81
*under 914 m:*457 (2021)

Heliports: 49 (2021)

Pipelines: 177,700 km gas, 54,800 km oil, 19,300 km refined products (2017)

Railways: *total:* 87,157 km (2014)
narrow gauge: 957 km (2014) 1.067-m gauge (on Sakhalin Island)
broad gauge: 86,200 km (2014) 1.520-m gauge (40,300 km electrified)
note: an additional 30,000 km of non-common carrier lines serve industries
country comparison to the world: 3

Roadways: *total:* 1,283,387 km (2012)
paved: 927,721 km (2012) (includes 39,143 km of expressways)
unpaved: 355,666 km (2012)
country comparison to the world: 5

Waterways: 102,000 km (2009) (including 48,000 km with guaranteed depth; the 72,000-km system in European Russia links Baltic Sea, White Sea, Caspian Sea, Sea of Azov, and Black Sea)
country comparison to the world: 1

Merchant marine: *total:* 2,873
by type: bulk carrier 13, container ship 17, general cargo 946, oil tanker 406, other 1,491 (2021)
country comparison to the world: 9

Ports and terminals: *major seaport(s):*
Arctic Ocean: Arkhangelsk, Murmansk
Baltic Sea: Kaliningrad, Primorsk, Saint Petersburg
Black Sea: Novorossiysk
Pacific Ocean: Nakhodka, Vladivostok, Vostochnyy
oil terminal(s): Kavkaz oil terminal, Primorsk
container port(s) (TEUs): Saint Petersburg (2,221,724) (2019)
river port(s): Astrakhan, Kazan (Volga River); Rostov-on-Don (Don River); Saint Petersburg (Neva River)

LNG terminal(s) (export): Sabetta, Sakhalin Island

MILITARY AND SECURITY

Military and security forces: Armed Forces of the Russian Federation: Ground Troops (Sukhoputnyye Voyskia, SV), Navy (Voyenno-Morskoy Flot, VMF), Aerospace Forces (Vozdushno-Kosmicheskiye Sily, VKS); Airborne Troops (Vozdushno-Desantnyye Voyska, VDV), and Missile Troops of Strategic Purpose (Raketnyye Voyska Strategicheskogo Naznacheniya, RVSN) referred to commonly as Strategic Rocket Forces, are independent "combat arms," not subordinate to any of the three branches

Federal National Guard Troops Service of the Russian Federation (National Guard (FSVNG), Russian Guard, or Rosgvardiya): created in 2016 as an independent agency for internal/regime security, combating terrorism and narcotics trafficking, protecting important state facilities and government personnel, and supporting border security; forces under the National Guard include the Special Purpose Mobile Units (OMON), Special Rapid Response Detachment (SOBR), and Interior Troops (VV); these troops were originally under the command of the Interior Ministry (MVD); also nominally under the National Guard's command are the forces of Chechen Republic head Ramzan KADYROV

Federal Security Services (FSB): Federal Border Guard Service (includes land and maritime forces) (2022)
note: the Air Force and Aerospace Defense Forces were merged into the VKS in 2015; VKS responsibilities also include launching military and dual-use satellites, maintaining military satellites, and monitoring and defending against space threats

Military expenditures: 4% of GDP (2021 est.)
4% of GDP (2020 est.)
3.8% of GDP (2019 est.) (approximately $104 billion)
3.7% of GDP (2018 est.) (approximately $100 billion)
4.2% of GDP (2017 est.) (approximately $104 billion)
country comparison to the world: 18

Military and security service personnel strengths: prior to Russia's invasion of Ukraine in February 2022, approximately 850,000 active-duty troops (300,000 Ground Troops; 40,000 Airborne Troops; 150,000 Navy; 160,000 Aerospace Forces; 70,000 Strategic Rocket Forces; approximately 20,000 special operations forces; approximately 100,000 other uniformed personnel (command and control, cyber, support, logistics, security, etc.); estimated 200-250,000 Federal National Guard Troops (Feb 2022)
note: in September 2022, the Russian Government called up 300,000 reservists to active military duty to support the war in Ukraine, and in August 2022 ordered the military to increase the total number of armed forces personnel by 137,000

Military equipment inventories and acquisitions: the Russian Federation's military and paramilitary services are equipped with domestically produced weapons systems, although since 2010 Russia has imported limited amounts of military hardware from several countries, including Czechia, France, Iran, Israel, Italy, Turkey, and Ukraine; the Russian defense industry is capable of designing, developing, and producing a full range of advanced air, land, missile, and naval systems; Russia is the world's second largest exporter of military hardware (2022)

Military service age and obligation: 18-27 years of age for compulsory service for men; 18-40 for voluntary/contractual service; women and non-Russian citizens (18-30) may volunteer; men are registered for the draft at 17 years of age; 12-month service obligation (Russia offers the option of serving on a 24-month contract instead of completing a 12-month conscription period); reserve obligation for non-officers to age 50; enrollment in military schools from the age of 16 (2022)
note 1: in May 2022, Russia's parliament approved a law removing the upper age limit for contractual service in the military; in November 2022, President Vladimir PUTIN signed a decree allowing dual-national Russians and those with permanent residency status in foreign countries to be drafted into the army for military service
note 2: the Russian military takes on about 260,000 conscripts each year in two semi-annual drafts (Spring and Fall); as of 2021, conscripts comprised an estimated 30% of the Russian military's active duty personnel and most reserve personnel were former conscripts; in April of 2019, the Russian Government pledged its intent to end conscription as part of a decade-long effort to shift from a large, conscript-based military to a smaller, more professional force; an existing law allows for a 21-month alternative civil service for conscripts in hospitals, nursing homes and other facilities for those who view military duty as incompatible with their beliefs, but military conscription offices reportedly often broadly ignore requests for such service
note 3: as of 2020, women made up about 5% of the active-duty military
note 4: since 2015, foreigners 18-30 with a good command of Russian have been allowed to join the military on 5-year contracts and become eligible for Russian citizenship after serving 3 years; in October 2022, the Interior Ministry opened up recruitment centers for foreigners to sign a 1-year service contract with the armed forces, other troops, or military formations participating in the invasion of Ukraine with the promise of simplifying the process of obtaining Russian citizenship

Military deployments: information varies; approximately 3,000 Armenia; approximately 2,000 Armenia/Azerbaijan (peacekeepers for Nagorno-Karabakh); estimated 3,000-5,000 Belarus; approximately 7,000-10,000 Georgia; approximately 500 Kyrgyzstan; approximately 1,500 Moldova (Transnistria); estimated 2,000-5,000 Syria; approximately 5,000 Tajikistan (February 2022)
note 1: in February 2022, Russia invaded Ukraine with an estimated 150,000 troops; prior to the invasion, it maintained an estimated 30,000 troops in areas of Ukraine occupied since 2014
note 2: prior to the invasion of Ukraine, Russia was assessed to have about 3,000-5,000 private military contractors conducting military and security operations in Africa, including in the Central African Republic, Libya, Mali, and Sudan

Military - note: as of 2022, Russian military forces continued to conduct active combat operations in Syria; Russia intervened in the Syrian civil war at the request of the ASAD government in September 2015; Russian assistance included air support, special operations forces, military advisors, private military contractors, training, arms, and equipment

Russia is the leading member of the Collective Security Treaty Organization (CSTO) and contributes approximately 8,000 troops to CSTO's rapid reaction force (2022)

TERRORISM

Terrorist group(s): Islamic State of Iraq and ash-Sham (ISIS)

TRANSNATIONAL ISSUES

Disputes - international: Russia remains concerned about the smuggling of poppy derivatives from Afghanistan through Central Asian countries
Russia-China: Russia and China have demarcated the once disputed islands at the Amur and Ussuri confluence and in the Argun River in accordance with the 2004 Agreement, ending their centuries-long border disputes
Russia-Denmark-Norway: Denmark (Greenland) and Norway have made submissions to the Commission on the Limits of the Continental Shelf (CLCS), and Russia is collecting additional data to augment its 2001 CLCS submission
Russia and Estonia: Russia and Estonia signed a technical border agreement in May 2005, but Russia recalled its signature in June 2005 after the Estonian parliament added to its domestic ratification act a historical preamble referencing the Soviet occupation and Estonia's pre-war borders under the 1920 Treaty of Tartu; Russia contends that the preamble allows Estonia to make territorial claims on Russia in the future, while Estonian officials deny that the preamble has any legal impact on the treaty text; negotiations were reopened in 2012, and a treaty was signed in 2014 without the disputed preamble, but neither country has ratified it as of 2020
Russia-Finland: various groups in Finland advocate restoration of Karelia (Kareliya) and other areas ceded to the Soviet Union following World War II but the Finnish Government asserts no territorial demands
Russia-Georgia: Russia's military support and subsequent recognition of Abkhazia and South Ossetia independence in 2008 continue to sour relations with Georgia; in 2011, Russia began to put up fences and barbed wire to fortify South Ossetia, physically dividing villages in the process; Russia continues to move the South Ossetia border fences further into Georgian territory
Russia-Japan: the sovereignty dispute over the islands of Etorofu, Kunashiri, Shikotan, and the Habomai group, known in Japan as the "Northern Territories" and in Russia as the "Southern Kurils," occupied by the Soviet Union in 1945, now administered by Russia, and claimed by Japan, remains the primary sticking point to signing a peace treaty formally ending World War II hostilities
Russia-Kazakhstan: Russia boundary delimitation was ratified on November 2005; field demarcation commenced in 2007 and was expected to be completed by 2013
Russia-Lithuania: Russia and Lithuania committed to demarcating their boundary in 2006 in accordance with the land and maritime treaty ratified by Russia in May 2003 and by Lithuania in 1999; border demarcation was completed in 2018; Lithuania operates a simplified transit regime for Russian nationals traveling from the Kaliningrad coastal exclave into Russia, while still conforming, as an EU member state with an EU external border, where strict Schengen border rules apply
Russia-North Korea: none identified
Russia-Norway: Russia and Norway signed a comprehensive maritime boundary agreement in 2010, opening the disputed territory for oil and natural gas exploration; a visa-free travel agreement for persons living near the border went into effect in May 2012
Russia-Ukraine: Russia remains involved in the conflict in eastern Ukraine while also occupying Ukraine's territory of Crimea; preparations for the demarcation delimitation of land boundary with Ukraine have commenced; the dispute over the boundary between Russia and Ukraine through the Kerch Strait and Sea of Azov is suspended due to the occupation of Crimea by Russia
Russia-US: Russian Duma has not yet ratified 1990 Bering Sea Maritime Boundary Agreement with the US; the southwesterly "Western Limit" places about 70% of the Bering Sea under U.S. maritime jurisdiction
Russia-various: Azerbaijan, Kazakhstan, and Russia ratified Caspian seabed delimitation treaties based on equidistance, while Iran continues to insist on a one-fifth slice of the sea

Refugees and internally displaced persons: *refugees (country of origin):* 2,852,395 (Ukraine) (as of 3 October 2022)
stateless persons: 56,960 (mid-year 2021); note - Russia's stateless population consists of Roma, Meskhetian Turks, and ex-Soviet citizens from the former republics; between 2003 and 2010 more than 600,000 stateless people were naturalized; most Meskhetian Turks, followers of Islam with origins in Georgia, fled or were evacuated from Uzbekistan after a 1989 pogrom and have lived in Russia for more than the required five-year residency period; they continue to be denied registration for citizenship and basic rights by local Krasnodar Krai authorities on the grounds that they are temporary illegal migrants

Trafficking in persons: *current situation:* Russia is a source, transit, and destination country for men, women, and children who are subjected to forced labor and sex trafficking, although labor trafficking is the predominant problem; people from Russia and other countries in Europe, Central Asia, Southeast Asia and Asia, including Vietnam and North Korea, are subjected to conditions of forced labor in Russia's construction, manufacturing, agriculture, repair shop, and domestic services industries, as well as forced begging and narcotics cultivation; North Koreans contracted under bilateral government arrangements to work in the timber industry in the Russian Far East reportedly are subjected to forced labor; Russian women and children were reported to be victims of sex trafficking in Russia, Northeast Asia, Europe, Central Asia, and the Middle East, while women from European, African, and Central Asian countries were reportedly forced into prostitution in Russia
tier rating: Tier 3 — Russia does not fully meet the minimum standards for the elimination of trafficking, is not making significant efforts to do, and remains in Tier 3; the government took some steps to address trafficking by convicting some traffickers, facilitating the return of Russian children from Iraq and Syria, and identifying some victims, including foreign nationals; however, there was a government policy of forced labor, the number of victims identified was negligible, and authorities penalized potential victims without screening for signs of trafficking; the government offered no funding or programs for trafficking victims' rehabilitation, prosecutions remained low

compared with the scope of Russia's trafficking problem, no national anti-trafficking strategy has been drafted, and government agencies have not been assigned roles or responsibilities (2020)

Illicit drugs: a destination country for Afghan opium and heroin; a transit country for cocaine from South America, especially Ecuador to Europe, Belgium and Netherlands; synthetic drugs are produced in clandestine drug laboratories throughout the country; cannabis cultivated in Russian Far East and the North Caucasus; the majority of hashish is smuggled in from Northern Africa

RWANDA

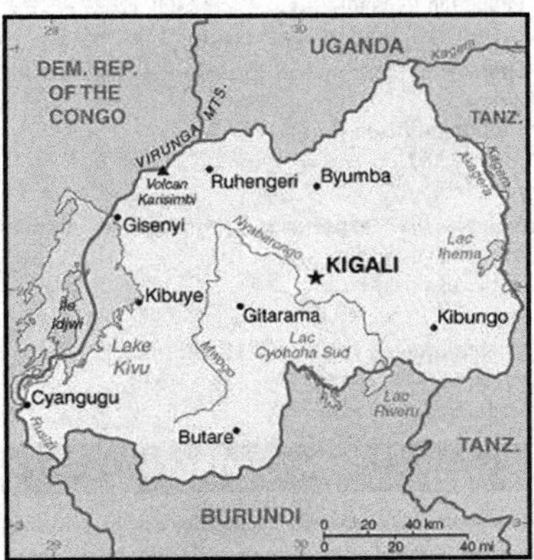

INTRODUCTION

Background: Rwanda - a small and centralized country dominated by rugged hills and fertile volcanic soil - has exerted disproportionate influence over the African Great Lakes region for centuries. A Rwandan kingdom increasingly dominated the region from the mid-18th century onward, with the Tutsi monarchs gradually extending the power of the royal court into peripheral areas and expanding their borders through military conquest. While the current ethnic labels Hutu and Tutsi predate colonial rule, their flexibility and importance have varied significantly over time. The majority Hutu and minority Tutsi have long shared a common language and culture, and intermarriage was not rare. The Rwandan royal court centered on the Tutsi king *(mwami)*, who relied on an extensive hierarchy of political, cultural, and economic relationships that intertwined Rwanda's ethnic and social groups. Social categories became more rigid during the reign of RWABUGIRI (1860-1895), who focused on aggressive expansion and solidifying Rwanda's bureaucratic structures. German colonial rule began in 1898, but Belgian forces captured Rwanda in 1916 during World War I. Both European nations quickly realized the benefits of ruling through the already centralized Rwandan kingdom. Colonial rule reinforced existing trends toward autocratic and exclusionary rule, leading to the elimination of traditional positions of authority for Hutus and a calcification of ethnic identities. Belgian administrators significantly increased requirements for communal labor and instituted harsh taxes, increasing frustration and inequality. Changing political attitudes in Belgium contributed to colonial and Catholic officials shifting their support from Tutsi to Hutu leaders in the years leading up to independence.

Newly mobilized political parties and simmering resentment of minority rule exploded in 1959, three years before independence from Belgium, when Hutus overthrew the Tutsi king. Thousands of Tutsis were killed over the next several years, and some 150,000 were driven into exile in neighboring countries. Army Chief of Staff Juvenal HABYARIMANA seized power in a coup in 1973 and ruled Rwanda as a single-party state for two decades. HABYARIMANA increasingly discriminated against Tutsi and extremist Hutu factions that gained prominence after multiple parties were introduced in the early 1990s. The children of Tutsi exiles later formed a rebel group, the Rwandan Patriotic Front (RPF) and began a civil war in 1990. The civil war exacerbated ethnic tensions and culminated in the shooting down of HABYARIMANA's private jet in April 1994. The event sparked a state-orchestrated genocide in which Rwandans killed approximately 800,000 of their fellow citizens, including approximately three-quarters of the Tutsi population. The genocide ended later that same year when the predominantly Tutsi RPF, operating out of Uganda and northern Rwanda, defeated the national army and Hutu militias and established an RPF-led government of national unity. Rwanda held its first local elections in 1999 and its first post-genocide presidential and legislative elections in 2003, formalizing President Paul KAGAME's de facto role as head of government. KAGAME won reelection in 2010, and again in 2017 after changing the constitution to allow him to run for a third term.

GEOGRAPHY

Location: Central Africa, east of the Democratic Republic of the Congo, north of Burundi

Geographic coordinates: 2 00 S, 30 00 E

Map references: Africa

Area: *total:* 26,338 sq km
land: 24,668 sq km
water: 1,670 sq km
country comparison to the world: 148

Area - comparative: slightly smaller than Maryland

Land boundaries: *total:* 930 km
border countries (4): Burundi 315 km; Democratic Republic of the Congo 221 km; Tanzania 222 km; Uganda 172 km

Coastline: 0 km (landlocked)

Maritime claims: none (landlocked)

Climate: temperate; two rainy seasons (February to April, November to January); mild in mountains with frost and snow possible

Terrain: mostly grassy uplands and hills; relief is mountainous with altitude declining from west to east

Elevation: *highest point:* Volcan Karisimbi 4,519 m
lowest point: Rusizi River 950 m
mean elevation: 1,598 m

Natural resources: gold, cassiterite (tin ore), wolframite (tungsten ore), methane, hydropower, arable land

Land use: *agricultural land:* 74.5% (2018 est.)
arable land: 47% (2018 est.)
permanent crops: 10.1% (2018 est.)
permanent pasture: 17.4% (2018 est.)
forest: 18% (2018 est.)
other: 7.5% (2018 est.)

Irrigated land: 96 sq km (2012)

Major lakes (area sq km): *fresh water lake(s):* Lake Kivu (shared with Democratic Republic of Congo) - 2,220 sq km

Major rivers (by length in km): Nile river source (shared with Tanzania, Uganda, South Sudan, Sudan, and Egypt [m]) - 6,650 km
note – [s] after country name indicates river source; [m] after country name indicates river mouth

Major watersheds (area sq km): Atlantic Ocean drainage: Congo (3,730,881 sq km), *(Mediterranean Sea)* Nile (3,254,853 sq km)

Population distribution: one of Africa's most densely populated countries; large concentrations tend to be in the central regions and along the shore of Lake Kivu in the west as shown in this population distribution map

Natural hazards: periodic droughts; the volcanic Virunga Mountains are in the northwest along the border with Democratic Republic of the Congo
volcanism: Visoke (3,711 m), located on the border with the Democratic Republic of the Congo, is the country's only historically active volcano

Geography - note: landlocked; most of the country is intensively cultivated and rugged with the population predominantly rural

PEOPLE AND SOCIETY

Population: 13,173,730 (2022 est.)
note: estimates for this country explicitly taken into account the impact of the HIV/AIDS epidemic
country comparison to the world: 76

Nationality: *noun:* Rwandan(s)
adjective: Rwandan

Ethnic groups: Hutu, Tutsi, Twa (Pygmy)

Languages: Kinyarwanda (official, universal Bantu vernacular) 93.2%, French (official) <0.1, English (official) <0.1, Swahili/Kiswahili (official, used in commercial centers) <0.1, more than one language, other 6.3%, unspecified 0.3% (2002 est.)
major-language sample(s): Inkoranya nzimbuzi y'isi, isoko fatizo y'amakuru y'ibanze. (Kinyarwanda)

Religions: Protestant 57.7% (includes Adventist 12.6%), Roman Catholic 38.2%, Muslim 2.1%, other 1% (includes traditional, Jehovah's Witness), none 1.1% (2019-20 est.)

Demographic profile: Rwanda's fertility rate declined sharply during the last decade, as a result of the government's commitment to family planning, the increased use of contraceptives, and a downward trend in ideal family size. Increases in educational attainment, particularly among girls, and exposure to social media also contributed to the reduction in the birth rate. The average number of births per woman decreased from a 5.6 in 2005 to 4.5 in 2016. Despite these significant strides in reducing fertility, Rwanda's birth rate remains very high and will continue to for an extended period of time because of its large population entering reproductive age. Because Rwanda is one of the most densely populated countries in Africa, its persistent high population growth and increasingly small agricultural landholdings will put additional strain on families' ability to raise foodstuffs and access potable water. These conditions will also hinder the government's efforts to reduce poverty and prevent environmental degradation.

The UNHCR recommended that effective 30 June 2013 countries invoke a cessation of refugee status for those Rwandans who fled their homeland between 1959 and 1998, including the 1994 genocide, on the grounds that the conditions that drove them to seek protection abroad no longer exist. The UNHCR's decision is controversial because many Rwandan refugees still fear persecution if they return home, concerns that are supported by the number of Rwandans granted asylum since 1998 and by the number exempted from the cessation. Rwandan refugees can still seek an exemption or local integration, but host countries are anxious to send the refugees back to Rwanda and are likely to avoid options that enable them to stay. Conversely, Rwanda itself hosts almost 160,000 refugees as of 2017; virtually all of them fleeing conflict in neighboring Burundi and the Democratic Republic of the Congo.

Age structure: *0-14 years:* 39.95% (male 2,564,893/female 2,513,993)
15-24 years: 20.1% (male 1,280,948/female 1,273,853)
25-54 years: 33.06% (male 2,001,629/female 2,201,132)
55-64 years: 4.24% (male 241,462/female 298,163)
65 years and over: 2.65% (male 134,648/female 201,710) (2020 est.)

Dependency ratios: *total dependency ratio:* 74.2
youth dependency ratio: 68.8
elderly dependency ratio: 5.4
potential support ratio: 18.4 (2020 est.)

Median age: *total:* 19.7 years
male: 18.9 years
female: 20.4 years (2020 est.)
country comparison to the world: 199

Population growth rate: 1.74% (2022 est.)
country comparison to the world: 53

Birth rate: 26.44 births/1,000 population (2022 est.)
country comparison to the world: 42

Death rate: 5.86 deaths/1,000 population (2022 est.)
country comparison to the world: 166

Net migration rate: -3.21 migrant(s)/1,000 population (2022 est.)
country comparison to the world: 182

Population distribution: one of Africa's most densely populated countries; large concentrations tend to be in the central regions and along the shore of Lake Kivu in the west as shown in this population distribution map

Urbanization: *urban population:* 17.7% of total population (2022)
rate of urbanization: 3.07% annual rate of change (2020-25 est.)

Major urban areas - population: 1.208 million KIGALI (capital) (2022)

Sex ratio: *at birth:* 1.03 male(s)/female
0-14 years: 1.02 male(s)/female
15-24 years: 1.01 male(s)/female
25-54 years: 0.9 male(s)/female
55-64 years: 0.82 male(s)/female
65 years and over: 0.54 male(s)/female
total population: 0.96 male(s)/female (2022 est.)

Mother's mean age at first birth: 23 years (2019/20 est.)
note: data represents median age at first birth among women 25-49

Maternal mortality ratio: 248 deaths/100,000 live births (2017 est.)
country comparison to the world: 44

Infant mortality rate: *total:* 26.39 deaths/1,000 live births
male: 28.9 deaths/1,000 live births
female: 23.81 deaths/1,000 live births (2022 est.)
country comparison to the world: 62

Life expectancy at birth: *total population:* 65.85 years
male: 63.89 years
female: 67.86 years (2022 est.)
country comparison to the world: 199

Total fertility rate: 3.33 children born/woman (2022 est.)
country comparison to the world: 42

Contraceptive prevalence rate: 53.2% (2014/15)

Drinking water source: *improved: urban:* 92.3% of population
rural: 80.7% of population
total: 82.7% of population
unimproved: urban: 7.7% of population
rural: 19.3% of population
total: 17.3% of population (2020 est.)

Current health expenditure: 6.4% of GDP (2019)

Physicians density: 0.12 physicians/1,000 population (2019)

Sanitation facility access: *improved: urban:* 89.1% of population
rural: 83.2% of population
total: 84.2% of population
unimproved: urban: 10.9% of population
rural: 16.8% of population
total: 15.8% of population (2020 est.)

HIV/AIDS - adult prevalence rate: 2.5% (2020 est.)
country comparison to the world: 19

HIV/AIDS - people living with HIV/AIDS: 220,000 (2020 est.)
country comparison to the world: 27

HIV/AIDS - deaths: 2,500 (2020 est.)
country comparison to the world: 40

Major infectious diseases: *degree of risk:* very high (2020)
food or waterborne diseases: bacterial diarrhea, hepatitis A, and typhoid fever
vectorborne diseases: malaria and dengue fever
animal contact diseases: rabies

Obesity - adult prevalence rate: 5.8% (2016)
country comparison to the world: 174

Alcohol consumption per capita: *total:* 6.35 liters of pure alcohol (2019 est.)
beer: 0.23 liters of pure alcohol (2019 est.)
wine: 0.03 liters of pure alcohol (2019 est.)
spirits: 0.09 liters of pure alcohol (2019 est.)
other alcohols: 6 liters of pure alcohol (2019 est.)
country comparison to the world: 65

Tobacco use: *total:* 13.7% (2020 est.)
male: 20.1% (2020 est.)
female: 7.2% (2020 est.)
country comparison to the world: 112

Children under the age of 5 years underweight: 7.7% (2019/20)
country comparison to the world: 64

Education expenditures: 3.4% of GDP (2020 est.)
country comparison to the world: 133

Literacy: *definition:* age 15 and over can read and write
total population: 73.2%
male: 77.6%
female: 69.4% (2018)

School life expectancy (primary to tertiary education): *total:* 11 years
male: 11 years
female: 11 years (2019)

Unemployment, youth ages 15-24: *total:* 20.5%
male: 18.8%
female: 22.4% (2019 est.)

ENVIRONMENT

Environment - current issues: deforestation results from uncontrolled cutting of trees for fuel; overgrazing; land degradation; soil erosion; a decline in soil fertility (soil exhaustion); wetland degradation and loss of biodiversity; widespread poaching

Environment - international agreements: *party to:* Biodiversity, Climate Change, Climate Change-Kyoto Protocol, Comprehensive Nuclear Test Ban, Desertification, Endangered Species, Hazardous Wastes, Nuclear Test Ban, Ozone Layer Protection, Wetlands
signed, but not ratified: Law of the Sea

Air pollutants: *particulate matter emissions:* 40.75 micrograms per cubic meter (2016 est.)
carbon dioxide emissions: 1.11 megatons (2016 est.)
methane emissions: 2.92 megatons (2020 est.)

Climate: temperate; two rainy seasons (February to April, November to January); mild in mountains with frost and snow possible

Land use: *agricultural land:* 74.5% (2018 est.)
arable land: 47% (2018 est.)
permanent crops: 10.1% (2018 est.)
permanent pasture: 17.4% (2018 est.)
forest: 18% (2018 est.)
other: 7.5% (2018 est.)

Urbanization: *urban population:* 17.7% of total population (2022)
rate of urbanization: 3.07% annual rate of change (2020-25 est.)

Revenue from forest resources: *forest revenues:* 3.75% of GDP (2018 est.)
country comparison to the world: 20

Revenue from coal: *coal revenues:* 0% of GDP (2018 est.)
country comparison to the world: 156

Waste and recycling: *municipal solid waste generated annually:* 4,384,969 tons (2016 est.)

Major lakes (area sq km): *fresh water lake(s):* Lake Kivu (shared with Democratic Republic of Congo) - 2,220 sq km

Major rivers (by length in km): Nile river source (shared with Tanzania, Uganda, South Sudan, Sudan, and Egypt [m]) - 6,650 km
note – [s] after country name indicates river source; [m] after country name indicates river mouth

Major watersheds (area sq km): Atlantic Ocean drainage: Congo (3,730,881 sq km), *(Mediterranean Sea)* Nile (3,254,853 sq km)

Total water withdrawal: *municipal:* 61.4 million cubic meters (2017 est.)
industrial: 20.5 million cubic meters (2017 est.)
agricultural: 102 million cubic meters (2017 est.)

Total renewable water resources: 13.3 billion cubic meters (2017 est.)

GOVERNMENT

Country name: *conventional long form:* Republic of Rwanda
conventional short form: Rwanda
local long form: Republika y'u Rwanda
local short form: Rwanda
former: Ruanda, German East Africa
etymology: the name translates as "domain" in the native Kinyarwanda language

Government type: presidential republic

Capital: *name:* Kigali
geographic coordinates: 1 57 S, 30 03 E
time difference: UTC+2 (7 hours ahead of Washington, DC, during Standard Time)
etymology: the city takes its name from nearby Mount Kigali; the name "Kigali" is composed of the Bantu prefix *ki* and the Rwandan *gali* meaning "broad" and likely refers to the broad, sprawling hill that has been dignified with the title of "mount"

Administrative divisions: 4 provinces (in French - provinces, singular - province; in Kinyarwanda - intara for singular and plural) and 1 city* (in French - ville; in Kinyarwanda - umujyi); Est (Eastern), Kigali*, Nord (Northern), Ouest (Western), Sud (Southern)

Independence: 1 July 1962 (from Belgium-administered UN trusteeship)

National holiday: Independence Day, 1 July (1962)

Constitution: *history:* several previous; latest adopted by referendum 26 May 2003, effective 4 June 2003
amendments: proposed by the president of the republic (with Council of Ministers approval) or by two-thirds majority vote of both houses of Parliament; passage requires at least three-quarters majority vote in both houses; changes to constitutional articles on national sovereignty, the presidential term, the form and system of government, and political pluralism also require approval in a referendum; amended several times, last in 2015

Legal system: mixed legal system of civil law, based on German and Belgian models, and customary law; judicial review of legislative acts in the Supreme Court

International law organization participation: has not submitted an ICJ jurisdiction declaration; non-party state to the ICCt

Citizenship: *citizenship by birth:* no
citizenship by descent only: the father must be a citizen of Rwanda; if the father is stateless or unknown, the mother must be a citizen
dual citizenship recognized: no
residency requirement for naturalization: 10 years

Suffrage: 18 years of age; universal

Executive branch: *chief of state:* President Paul KAGAME (since 22 April 2000)
head of government: Prime Minister Edouard NGIRENTE (since 30 August 2017)
cabinet: Council of Ministers appointed by the president
elections/appointments: president directly elected by simple majority vote for a 5-year term (eligible for a second term); note - a constitutional amendment approved in December 2016 reduced the presidential term from 7 to 5 years but included an exception that allowed President KAGAME to serve another 7-year term in 2017, potentially followed by two additional 5-year terms; election last held on 4 August 2017 (next to be held in August 2024); prime minister appointed by the president
election results:
Paul KAGAME reelected president; Paul KAGAME (RPF) 98.8%, Philippe MPAYIMANA (independent) 0.7%, Frank HABINEZA (DGPR)0.5%

Legislative branch: *description:* bicameral Parliament consists of:
Senate or Senat (26 seats; 12 members indirectly elected by local councils, 8 appointed by the president, 4 appointed by the Political Organizations Forum - a body of registered political parties, and 2 selected by institutions of higher learning; members serve 8-year terms)
Chamber of Deputies or Chambre des Deputes (80 seats; 53 members directly elected by proportional representation vote, 24 women selected by special interest groups, and 3 selected by youth and disability organizations; members serve 5-year terms)
elections:
Senate - last held on 16-18 September 2019 (next to be held in 2027)
Chamber of Deputies - last held on 3 September 2018 (next to be held in September 2023)
election results:
Senate - percent of vote by party - NA; seats by party - NA; composition - men 17, women 9, percent of women 34.6%
Chamber of Deputies - percent of vote by party - NA; seats by party - Rwandan Patriotic Front Coalition 40, PSD 5, PL 4, other 4 indirectly elected 27; composition - men 31, women 49, percent of women 54.7%; note - total Parliament percent of women 54.7%

Judicial branch: *highest court(s):* Supreme Court (consists of the chief and deputy chief justices and 15 judges; normally organized into 3-judge panels); High Court (consists of the court president, vice president, and a minimum of 24 judges and organized into 5 chambers)
judge selection and term of office: Supreme Court judges nominated by the president after consultation with the Cabinet and the Superior Council of the Judiciary (SCJ), a 27-member body of judges, other judicial officials, and legal professionals) and approved by the Senate; chief and deputy chief justices appointed for 8-year nonrenewable terms; tenure of judges NA; High Court president and vice president appointed by the president of the republic upon approval by the Senate; judges appointed by the Supreme Court chief justice upon approval of the SCJ; judge tenure NA
subordinate courts: High Court of the Republic; commercial courts including the High Commercial Court; intermediate courts; primary courts; and military specialized courts

Political parties and leaders: Democratic Green Party of Rwanda or DGPR [Frank HABINEZA]
Liberal Party or PL [Donatille MUKABALISA]
Party for Progress and Concord or PPC [Dr. Alivera MUKABARAMBA]
Rwandan Patriotic Front or RPF [Paul KAGAME]
Rwandan Patriotic Front Coalition (includes RPF, PPC) [Paul KAGAME]
Social Democratic Party or PSD [Vincent BIRUTA]
Social Party Imberakuri or PS-Imberakuri [Christine MUKABUNANI]

International organization participation: ACP, AfDB, AU, C, CEPGL, COMESA, EAC, EADB, FAO, G-77, IAEA, IBRD, ICAO, ICRM, IDA, IFAD, IFC, IFRCS, ILO, IMF, Interpol, IOC, IOM, IPU, ISO, ITSO, ITU, ITUC (NGOs), MIGA, MINUSMA, NAM, OIF, OPCW, PCA, UN, UNAMID, UNCTAD, UNESCO, UNHCR, UNIDO, UNISFA, UNMISS, UNWTO, UPU, WCO, WHO, WIPO, WMO, WTO

Diplomatic representation in the US: *chief of mission:* Ambassador Mathilde MUKANTABANA (since 18 July 2013)
chancery: 1714 New Hampshire Avenue NW, Washington, DC 20009
telephone: [1] (202) 232-2882
FAX: [1] (202) 232-4544
email address and website:
info@rwandaembassy.org
https://rwandaembassy.org/

Diplomatic representation from the US: *chief of mission:* Ambassador (vacant); Charge d'Affaires Deb MacLEAN (since February 2022)
embassy: 2657 Avenue de la Gendarmerie (Kaciyiru), P. O. Box 28 Kigali
mailing address: 2210 Kigali Place, Washington DC 20521-2210
telephone: [250] 252 596-400
FAX: [250] 252 580-325
email address and website:
consularkigali@state.gov
https://rw.usembassy.gov/

Flag description: three horizontal bands of sky blue (top, double width), yellow, and green, with a golden sun with 24 rays near the fly end of the blue band; blue represents happiness and peace, yellow economic development and mineral wealth, green hope of prosperity and natural resources; the sun symbolizes unity, as well as enlightenment and transparency from ignorance

National symbol(s): traditional woven basket with peaked lid; national colors: blue, yellow, green

National anthem: *name:* "Rwanda nziza" (Rwanda, Our Beautiful Country)
lyrics/music: Faustin MURIGO/Jean-Bosco HASHAKAIMANA
note: adopted 2001

ECONOMY

Economic overview: Rwanda is a rural, agrarian country with agriculture accounting for about 63% of export earnings, and with some mineral and agro-processing. Population density is high but, with the exception of the capital Kigali, is not concentrated in large cities – its 12 million people are spread out on a small amount of land (smaller than the state of Maryland). Tourism, minerals, coffee, and tea are Rwanda's main sources of foreign exchange. Despite Rwanda's fertile ecosystem, food production often does not keep pace with demand, requiring food imports. Energy shortages, instability in neighboring states, and lack of adequate transportation linkages to other countries continue to handicap private sector growth.

The 1994 genocide decimated Rwanda's fragile economic base, severely impoverished the population, particularly women, and temporarily stalled the country's ability to attract private and external investment. However, Rwanda has made substantial progress in stabilizing and rehabilitating its economy well beyond pre-1994 levels. GDP has rebounded with an average annual growth of 6%-8% since 2003 and inflation has been reduced to single digits. In 2015, 39% of the population lived below the poverty line, according to government statistics, compared to 57% in 2006.

The government has embraced an expansionary fiscal policy to reduce poverty by improving education, infrastructure, and foreign and domestic investment. Rwanda consistently ranks well for ease of doing business and transparency.

The Rwandan Government is seeking to become a regional leader in information and communication technologies and aims to reach middle-income status by 2020 by leveraging the service industry. In 2012, Rwanda completed the first modern Special Economic Zone (SEZ) in Kigali. The SEZ seeks to attract investment in all sectors, but specifically in agribusiness, information and communications, trade and logistics, mining, and construction. In 2016, the government launched an online system to give investors information about public land and its suitability for agricultural development.

Real GDP (purchasing power parity): $27.18 billion (2020 est.)
$28.13 billion (2019 est.)
$25.7 billion (2018 est.)
note: data are in 2017 dollars
country comparison to the world: 141

Real GDP growth rate: 6.1% (2017 est.)
6% (2016 est.)
8.9% (2015 est.)
country comparison to the world: 28

Real GDP per capita: $2,100 (2020 est.)
$2,200 (2019 est.)
$2,100 (2018 est.)
note: data are in 2017 dollars
country comparison to the world: 212

GDP (official exchange rate): $9.136 billion (2017 est.)

Inflation rate (consumer prices): 3.3% (2019 est.)
-0.3% (2018 est.)
8.4% (2017 est.)
country comparison to the world: 150

Credit ratings:

Fitch rating: B+ (2014)

Moody's rating: B2 (2016)

Standard & Poors rating: B+ (2019)

GDP - composition, by sector of origin: *agriculture:* 30.9% (2017 est.)
industry: 17.6% (2017 est.)
services: 51.5% (2017 est.)

GDP - composition, by end use: *household consumption:* 75.9% (2017 est.)
government consumption: 15.2% (2017 est.)
investment in fixed capital: 22.9% (2017 est.)
investment in inventories: 0.5% (2017 est.)
exports of goods and services: 18.2% (2017 est.)
imports of goods and services: -32.8% (2017 est.)

Agricultural products: bananas, sweet potatoes, cassava, potatoes, plantains, beans, maize, gourds, milk, taro

Industries: cement, agricultural products, small-scale beverages, soap, furniture, shoes, plastic goods, textiles, cigarettes

Industrial production growth rate: 4.2% (2017 est.)
country comparison to the world: 72

Labor force: 6.227 million (2017 est.)
country comparison to the world: 70

Labor force - by occupation: *agriculture:* 75.3%
industry: 6.7%
services: 18% (2012 est.)

Unemployment rate: 2.7% (2014 est.)
country comparison to the world: 32

Unemployment, youth ages 15-24: *total:* 20.5%
male: 18.8%
female: 22.4% (2019 est.)
country comparison to the world: 75

Population below poverty line: 38.2% (2016 est.)

Gini Index coefficient - distribution of family income: 43.7 (2016 est.)
51.3 (2010 est.)
country comparison to the world: 37

Household income or consumption by percentage share: *lowest 10%:* 2.1%
highest 10%: 43.2% (2011 est.)

Budget: *revenues:* 1.943 billion (2017 est.)
expenditures: 2.337 billion (2017 est.)

Budget surplus (+) or deficit (-): -4.3% (of GDP) (2017 est.)
country comparison to the world: 162

Public debt: 40.5% of GDP (2017 est.)
37.3% of GDP (2016 est.)
country comparison to the world: 125

Taxes and other revenues: 21.3% (of GDP) (2017 est.)
country comparison to the world: 142

Fiscal year: calendar year

Current account balance: -$622 million (2017 est.)
-$1.336 billion (2016 est.)
country comparison to the world: 128

Exports: $2.25 billion (2019 est.) note: data are in current year dollars
$2.04 billion (2018 est.) note: data are in current year dollars
country comparison to the world: 150

Exports - partners: United Arab Emirates 35%, Democratic Republic of the Congo 28%, Uganda 5% (2019)

Exports - commodities: gold, refined petroleum, coffee, tea, tin (2019)

Imports: $3.74 billion (2019 est.) note: data are in current year dollars
$3.34 billion (2018 est.) note: data are in current year dollars
country comparison to the world: 151

Imports - partners: China 17%, Kenya 10%, Tanzania 9%, United Arab Emirates 9%, India 7%, Saudi Arabia 5% (2019)

Imports - commodities: refined petroleum, gold, raw sugar, packaged medicines, broadcasting equipment (2019)

Reserves of foreign exchange and gold: $997.6 million (31 December 2017 est.)
$1.104 billion (31 December 2016 est.)
country comparison to the world: 132

Debt - external: $3.258 billion (31 December 2017 est.)
$2.611 billion (31 December 2016 est.)
country comparison to the world: 141

Exchange rates: Rwandan francs (RWF) per US dollar -
839.1 (2017 est.)
787.25 (2016 est.)
787.25 (2015 est.)
720.54 (2014 est.)
680.95 (2013 est.)

ENERGY

Electricity access: *electrification - total population:* 53% (2019)
electrification - urban areas: 76% (2019)
electrification - rural areas: 48% (2019)

Electricity: *installed generating capacity:* 265,000 kW (2020 est.)
consumption: 1,007,300,000 kWh (2019 est.)
exports: 4.5 million kWh (2019 est.)
imports: 93.96 million kWh (2019 est.)
transmission/distribution losses: 142 million kWh (2019 est.)

Electricity generation sources: *fossil fuels:* 39% of total installed capacity (2020 est.)
solar: 6.5% of total installed capacity (2020 est.)
hydroelectricity: 53.9% of total installed capacity (2020 est.)
biomass and waste: 0.6% of total installed capacity (2020 est.)

Petroleum: *total petroleum production:* 0 bbl/day (2021 est.)
refined petroleum consumption: 8,300 bbl/day (2019 est.)

Refined petroleum products - imports: 6,628 bbl/day (2015 est.)
country comparison to the world: 162

Natural gas: *proven reserves:* 56.634 billion cubic meters (2021 est.)

Carbon dioxide emissions: 1.189 million metric tonnes of CO_2 (2019 est.)
from petroleum and other liquids: 1.189 million metric tonnes of CO_2 (2019 est.)
country comparison to the world: 170

Energy consumption per capita: 1.704 million Btu/person (2019 est.)
country comparison to the world: 189

COMMUNICATIONS

Telephones - fixed lines: *total subscriptions:* 11,671 (2020 est.)
country comparison to the world: 188

Telephones - mobile cellular: *total subscriptions:* 10,614,408 (2020 est.)
subscriptions per 100 inhabitants: 82 (2020 est.)

country comparison to the world: 86

Telecommunication systems: *general assessment:* Rwanda was slow to liberalize the mobile sector; there was effective competition among three operators; the fixed broadband sector has suffered from limited fixed-line infrastructure and high prices; operators are rolling out national backbone networks which also allow them to connect to the international submarine cables on Africa's east coast; these cables gave the entire region greater internet bandwidth and ended the dependency on satellites; while the country also has a new cable link with Tanzania, and via Tanzania's national broadband backbone it has gained connectivity to the networks of several other countries in the region; the number of subscribers on LTE infrastructure has increased sharply, helped by national LTE coverage achieved in mid-2018; mobile remains the dominant platform for voice and data services; the regulator noted that the number of mobile subscribers increased 2.7% in 2021, year-on-year; there was a slight fall in the beginning of 2022 (2022)
domestic: the capital, Kigali, is connected to provincial centers by microwave radio relay, and recently by cellular telephone service; much of the network depends on wire and HF radiotelephone; fixed-line less than 1 per 100 and mobile-cellular telephone density has increased to nearly 82 telephones per 100 persons (2020)
international: country code - 250; international connections employ microwave radio relay to neighboring countries and satellite communications to more distant countries; satellite earth stations - 1 Intelsat (Indian Ocean) in Kigali (includes telex and telefax service); international submarine fiber-optic cables on the African east coast has brought international bandwidth and lessened the dependency on satellites

Broadcast media: 13 TV stations; 35 radio stations registered, including international broadcasters, government owns most popular TV and radio stations; regional satellite-based TV services available

Internet country code: .rw

Internet users: *total:* 3,497,096 (2020 est.)
percent of population: 27% (2020 est.)
country comparison to the world: 108

Broadband - fixed subscriptions: *total:* 17,685 (2020 est.)
subscriptions per 100 inhabitants: 0.1 (2020 est.)
country comparison to the world: 171

TRANSPORTATION

National air transport system: *number of registered air carriers:* 1 (2020)
inventory of registered aircraft operated by air carriers: 12
annual passenger traffic on registered air carriers: 1,073,528 (2018)

Civil aircraft registration country code prefix: 9XR

Airports: *total:* 7 (2021)
country comparison to the world: 171

Airports - with paved runways: *total:* 4
over 3,047 m: 1
914 to 1,523 m: 2
under 914 m: 1 (2021)

Airports - with unpaved runways: *total:* 3
914 to 1,523 m: 2
under 914 m: 1 (2021)

Roadways: *total:* 4,700 km (2012)
paved: 1,207 km (2012)
unpaved: 3,493 km (2012)
country comparison to the world: 148

Waterways: 90 km (2022) (Lake Kivu navigable by shallow-draft barges and native craft)
country comparison to the world: 112

Ports and terminals: *lake port(s):* Cyangugu, Gisenyi, Kibuye (Lake Kivu)

MILITARY AND SECURITY

Military and security forces: Rwanda Defense Force (RDF; Ingabo z'u Rwanda): Rwanda Army (Rwanda Land Force), Rwanda Air Force (Force Aerienne Rwandaise, FAR), Rwanda Reserve Force, Special Units (2022)

Military expenditures: 1.4% of GDP (2021 est.)
1.3% of GDP (2020 est.)
1.2% of GDP (2019 est.) (approximately $220 million)
1.2% of GDP (2018 est.) (approximately $200 million)
1.2% of GDP (2017 est.) (approximately $190 million)
country comparison to the world: 101

Military and security service personnel strengths: approximately 33,000 active RDF personnel (32,000 Army; 1,000 Air Force) (2022)

Military equipment inventories and acquisitions: the RDF's inventory includes mostly Russian, Soviet-era, and older Western - largely French and South African -equipment; since 2010, Russia has been the top supplier (2021)

Military service age and obligation: 18 years of age for men and women for voluntary military service; no conscription; Rwandan citizenship is required; enlistment is either as contract (5-years, renewable twice) or career (2021)

Military deployments: 2,450 (plus about 500 police) Central African Republic (approximately 1,700 for MINUSCA; an additional 750 troops sent separately under a bilateral agreement with CAR in August, 2021); up to 2,000 Mozambique (deployed mid-2021 under a bi-lateral agreement to assist with combating insurgency; includes both military and police forces); 2,600 (plus about 400 police) South Sudan (UNMISS) (2022)

Military - note: since 2021, Rwanda has deployed troops to the border with the Democratic Republic of the Congo (DRC) to combat the rebel Democratic Forces for the Liberation of Rwanda (FDLR); it has also been accused by the DRC Government of providing material support to the March 23 Movement (M23, aka Congolese Revolutionary Army) rebel group, which as of 2022 was fighting with DRC troops and UN peacekeeping forces

the Rwandan Armed Forces (FAR) were established following independence in 1962; after the 1990-1994 civil war and genocide, the victorious Tutsi-dominated Rwandan Patriotic Front's military wing, the Rwandan Patriotic Army (RPA), became the country's military force; the RPA participated in the First (1996-1997) and Second (1998-2003) Congolese Wars; the RPA was renamed the Rwanda Defense Force (RDF) in 2003, by which time it had assumed a more national character with the inclusion of many former Hutu officers as well as newly recruited soldiers

the RDF is widely regarded as one of Africa's best trained and most capable and professional military forces; as of 2022, over 7,000 RDF and police personnel were deployed on missions in Africa (2022)

TRANSNATIONAL ISSUES

Disputes - international: *Rwanda-Burundi:* Burundi's Ngozi province and Rwanda's Butare province dispute the two-kilometer-square hilly farmed area of Sabanerwa in the Rukurazi Valley where the Akanyaru/Kanyaru River shifted its course southward after heavy rains in 1965 around Kibinga Hill in Rwanda's Butare Province
Rwanda-Democratic Republic of Congo (DRC): the 2005 DRC and Rwanda border verification mechanism to stem rebel actions on both sides of the border remains in place
Rwanda-Uganda: a joint technical committee established in 2007 to demarcate sections of the border

Refugees and internally displaced persons: *refugees (country of origin):* 76,465 (Democratic Republic of the Congo) 48,369 (Burundi) (2022)
stateless persons: 9,500 (mid-year 2021)

SAINT BARTHELEMY

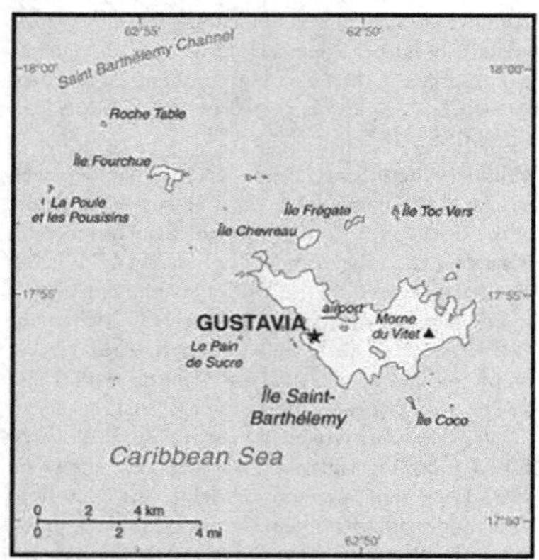

INTRODUCTION

Background: Discovered in 1493 by Christopher COLUMBUS who named it for his brother Bartolomeo, Saint Barthelemy was first settled by the French in 1648. In 1784, the French sold the island to Sweden, which renamed the largest town Gustavia, after the Swedish King GUSTAV III, and made it a free port; the island prospered as a trade and supply center during the colonial wars of the 18th century. France repurchased the island in 1877 and took control the following year. It was placed under the administration of Guadeloupe. Saint Barthelemy retained its free port status along with various Swedish appellations such as Swedish street and town names, and the three-crown symbol on the coat of arms. In 2003, the islanders voted to secede from Guadeloupe, and in 2007, the island became a French overseas collectivity. In 2012, it became an overseas territory of the EU, allowing it to exert local control over the permanent and temporary immigration of foreign workers including non-French European citizens. Hurricane Irma hit the island in September 2017 causing extensive damage, but Saint Barthelemy recovered by early 2018.

GEOGRAPHY

Location: Caribbean, island between the Caribbean Sea and the North Atlantic Ocean; located in the Leeward Islands (northern) group; Saint Barthelemy lies east of the US Virgin Islands

Geographic coordinates: 17 90 N, 62 85 W

Map references: Central America and the Caribbean

Area: *total:* 25 sq km
land: 25 sq km
water: negligible
country comparison to the world: 238

Area - comparative: less than one-eighth the size of Washington, DC

Land boundaries: *total:* 0 km

Climate: tropical, with practically no variation in temperature; has two seasons (dry and humid)

Terrain: hilly, almost completely surrounded by shallow-water reefs, with plentiful beaches

Elevation: *highest point:* Morne du Vitet 286 m
lowest point: Caribbean Ocean 0 m

Natural resources: few natural resources; beaches foster tourism

Population distribution: most of the populace concentrated in and around the capital of Gustavia, but scattered settlements exist around the island periphery

Geography - note: a 1,200-hectare marine nature reserve, the Reserve Naturelle, is made up of five zones around the island that form a network to protect the island's coral reefs, seagrass, and endangered marine species

PEOPLE AND SOCIETY

Population: 7,103 (2022 est.)
country comparison to the world: 225

Ethnic groups: French, Portuguese, Caribbean, Afro-Caribbean

Languages: French (primary), English
major-language sample(s):
The World Factbook, une source indispensable d'informations de base. (French)

Religions: Roman Catholic, Protestant, Jehovah's Witnesses

Age structure: *0-14 years:* 14.36% (male 524/female 496)
15-24 years: 7.29% (male 272/female 246)
25-54 years: 41.86% (male 1,618/female 1,363)
55-64 years: 16.43% (male 632/female 535)
65 years and over: 21.17% (male 753/female 751) (2022 est.)

Median age: *total:* 45.6 years
male: 45.5 years
female: 45.8 years (2020 est.)
country comparison to the world: 8

Population growth rate: -0.16% (2022 est.)
country comparison to the world: 208

Birth rate: 9.29 births/1,000 population (2022 est.)
country comparison to the world: 197

Death rate: 9.01 deaths/1,000 population (2022 est.)
country comparison to the world: 60

Net migration rate: -1.83 migrant(s)/1,000 population (2022 est.)
country comparison to the world: 168

Population distribution: most of the populace concentrated in and around the capital of Gustavia, but scattered settlements exist around the island periphery

Sex ratio: *at birth:* 1.06 male(s)/female
0-14 years: 1.06 male(s)/female
15-24 years: 1.09 male(s)/female
25-54 years: 1.19 male(s)/female
55-64 years: 1.18 male(s)/female
65 years and over: 0.85 male(s)/female
total population: 1.12 male(s)/female (2022 est.)

Infant mortality rate: *total:* 6.71 deaths/1,000 live births
male: 7.85 deaths/1,000 live births
female: 5.53 deaths/1,000 live births (2022 est.)
country comparison to the world: 161

Life expectancy at birth: *total population:* 80.58 years
male: 77.48 years
female: 83.81 years (2022 est.)
country comparison to the world: 47

Total fertility rate: 1.64 children born/woman (2022 est.)
country comparison to the world: 176

Drinking water source: *improved: total:* 100% of population
unimproved: total: 0% of population (2020)

Sanitation facility access: *improved: urban:* 100% of population
total: 100% of population

ENVIRONMENT

Environment - current issues: land-based pollution; urbanization; with no natural rivers or streams, fresh water is in short supply, especially in summer, and is provided by the desalination of sea water, the collection of rain water, or imported via water tanker; overfishing

Climate: tropical, with practically no variation in temperature; has two seasons (dry and humid)

GOVERNMENT

Country name: *conventional long form:* Overseas Collectivity of Saint Barthelemy
conventional short form: Saint Barthelemy
local long form: Collectivite d'outre mer de Saint-Barthelemy
local short form: Saint-Barthelemy
abbreviation: Saint-Barth (French)/ St. Barts or St. Barths (English)
etymology: explorer Christopher COLUMBUS named the island in honor of his brother Bartolomeo's namesake saint in 1493

Government type: parliamentary democracy (Territorial Council); overseas collectivity of France

Dependency status: overseas collectivity of France

Capital: *name:* Gustavia
geographic coordinates: 17 53 N, 62 51 W
time difference: UTC-4 (1 hour ahead of Washington, DC, during Standard Time)
etymology: named in honor of King Gustav III (1746-1792) of Sweden during whose reign the island was obtained from France in 1784; the name was retained when in 1878 the island was sold back to France

Independence: none (overseas collectivity of France)

National holiday: Fete de la Federation, 14 July (1790); note - local holiday is St. Barthelemy Day, 24 August (1572)

Constitution: *history:* 4 October 1958 (French Constitution)
amendments: amendment procedures of France's constitution apply

Legal system: French civil law

Citizenship: see France

Suffrage: 18 years of age, universal

Executive branch: *chief of state:* President Emmanuel MACRON (since 14 May 2017), represented by Prefect Vincent BERTON (since 28 March 2022)

head of government: President of Territorial Council Xavier LEDEE (since 3 April 2022)
cabinet: Executive Council elected by the Territorial Council; note - there is also an advisory, economic, social, and cultural council
elections/appointments: French president directly elected by absolute majority popular vote in 2 rounds if needed for a 5-year term (eligible for a second term); prefect appointed by the French president on the advice of French Ministry of Interior; president of Territorial Council indirectly elected by its members for a 5-year term; election last held on 27 March 2022 (next to be held in 2027)
election results:
2022: Xavier LEDEE (Saint Barth United) elected president; Territorial Council vote - 13 votes for, 6 blank votes
2017: Bruno MAGRAS (Saint Barth First) elected president; Territorial Council vote - 14 out of 19 votes

Legislative branch: *description:* unicameral Territorial Council (19 seats; members elected by absolute majority vote in the first round vote and proportional representation vote in the second round; members serve 5-year terms); Saint Barthelemy indirectly elects 1 senator to the French Senate by an electoral college for a 6-year term and directly elects 1 deputy (shared with Saint Martin) to the French National Assembly
elections:
Territorial Council - first round held on 20 March 2022 (next to be held in 2027); second round held on 27 March 2022
French Senate - election last held 24 September 2017 (next to be held in September 2020)
French National Assembly - election last held on 11 and 18 June 2017 (next to be held by June 2022)
election results:
Territorial Council - percent of vote by party (first round) - SBA 46.2%, Saint Barth Action Equilibre 27.1%, Unis pour Saint Barthelemy 26.8%; percent of vote by party (second round) - Saint Barth Action Equilibre and Unis pour Saint Barthelemy 50.9%, SBA 49.2%, seats by party - Saint Barth Action Equilibre and Unis pour Saint Barthelemy 13, SBA 6; composition - men NA, women NA, percent of women NA%
French Senate - percent of vote by party NA; seats by party UMP 1
French National Assembly - percent of vote by party NA; seats by party UMP 1

Political parties and leaders: All for Saint Barth (Tous pour Saint-Barth) [Bettina COINTRE]
Saint Barth Action Equilibre [Marie-Hélène BERNIER]
Saint Barth First! (Saint-Barth d'Abord!) or SBA [Romaric MAGRAS] (affiliated with France's Republican party, Les Republicans)
Saint Barth United (Unis pour Saint-Barthelemy) [Xavier LEDEE]

International organization participation: UPU

Diplomatic representation in the US: none (overseas collectivity of France)

Diplomatic representation from the US: *embassy:* none (overseas collectivity of France)

Flag description: the flag of France is used

National symbol(s): pelican

National anthem: *name:* "L'Hymne a St. Barthelemy" (Hymn to St. Barthelemy)
lyrics/music: Isabelle Massart DERAVIN/Michael VALENTI
note: local anthem in use since 1999; as a collectivity of France, "La Marseillaise" is official (see France)

ECONOMY

Economic overview: The economy of Saint Barthelemy is based upon high-end tourism and duty-free luxury commerce, serving visitors primarily from North America. The luxury hotels and villas host 70,000 visitors each year with another 130,000 arriving by boat. The relative isolation and high cost of living inhibits mass tourism. The construction and public sectors also enjoy significant investment in support of tourism. With limited fresh water resources, all food must be imported, as must all energy resources and most manufactured goods. The tourism sector creates a strong employment demand and attracts labor from Brazil and Portugal. The country's currency is the euro.

Exports - partners: France 60%, Germany 27% (2019)

Exports - commodities: beauty products, broadcasting equipment, sunflower seed oil, plastics, cars (2019)

Imports - partners: France 78%, Switzerland 7%, Italy 7% (2019)

Imports - commodities: furniture, wine, refined petroleum, jewelry, food preparation materials (2019)

Exchange rates: 0.885 (2017 est.)
0.903 (2016 est.)
0.9214 (2015 est.)
0.885 (2014 est.)

ENERGY

Electricity access: *electrification - total population:* 100% (2020)

COMMUNICATIONS

Telecommunication systems: *general assessment:* fully integrated access; 4G and LTE services (2019)
domestic: direct dial capability with both fixed and wireless systems, 3 FM channels, no broadcasting (2018)
international: country code - 590; landing points for the SSCS and the Southern Caribbean Fiber submarine cables providing voice and data connectivity to numerous Caribbean Islands (2019)

Broadcast media: 2 local TV broadcasters; 5 FM radio channels (2021)

Internet country code: .bl; note - .gp, the Internet country code for Guadeloupe, and .fr, the Internet country code for France, might also be encountered

Internet users: *total:* 7,128 (2020 est.)
percent of population: 72% (2020 est.)
country comparison to the world: 218

TRANSPORTATION

Airports: *total:* 1 (2021)
country comparison to the world: 233

Airports - with paved runways: *total:* 1
under 914 m: 1 (2021)

Roadways: *total:* 40 km
country comparison to the world: 217

Ports and terminals: *major seaport(s):* Gustavia

Transportation - note: nearest airport for international flights is Princess Juliana International Airport (SXM) located on Sint Maarten

MILITARY AND SECURITY

Military - note: defense is the responsibility of France

TRANSNATIONAL ISSUES

Disputes - international: none identified

SAINT HELENA, ASCENSION, AND TRISTAN DA CUNHA

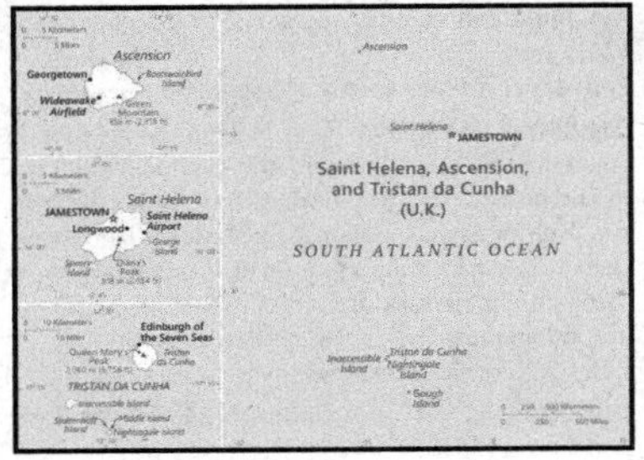

INTRODUCTION

Background: Saint Helena is a British Overseas Territory consisting of Saint Helena and Ascension Islands, and the island group of Tristan da Cunha.

Saint Helena: Uninhabited when first discovered by the Portuguese in 1502, Saint Helena was garrisoned by the British during the 17th century. It acquired fame as the place of Napoleon BONAPARTE's exile from 1815 until his death in 1821, but its importance as a port of call declined after the opening of the Suez Canal in 1869. During the Anglo-Boer War in South Africa, several thousand Boer prisoners were confined on the island between 1900 and 1903.

Saint Helena is one of the most remote populated places in the world. The British Government committed to building an airport on Saint Helena in 2005. After more than a decade of delays and construction, a commercial air service to South Africa via Namibia was inaugurated in October of 2017. The weekly service to Saint Helena from Johannesburg via Windhoek in Namibia takes just over six hours (including the refueling stop in Windhoek) and replaces the mail ship that had made a five-day journey to the island every three weeks.

Ascension Island: This barren and uninhabited island was discovered and named by the Portuguese in 1503. The British garrisoned the island in 1815 to prevent a rescue of NAPOLEON from Saint Helena. It served as a provisioning station for the Royal Navy's West Africa Squadron on anti-slavery patrol. The island remained under Admiralty control until 1922, when it became a dependency of Saint Helena. During World War II, the UK permitted the US to construct an airfield on Ascension in support of transatlantic flights to Africa and anti-submarine operations in the South Atlantic. In the 1960s the island became an important space tracking station for the US. In 1982, Ascension was an essential staging area for British forces during the Falklands War. It remains a critical refueling point in the air-bridge from the UK to the South Atlantic.

The island hosts one of four dedicated ground antennas that assist in the operation of the Global Positioning System (GPS) navigation system (the others are on Diego Garcia (British Indian Ocean Territory), Kwajalein (Marshall Islands), and at Cape Canaveral, Florida (US)). NASA and the US Air Force also operate a Meter-Class Autonomous Telescope (MCAT) on Ascension as part of the deep space surveillance system for tracking orbital debris, which can be a hazard to spacecraft and astronauts.

Tristan da Cunha: The island group consists of Tristan da Cunha, Nightingale, Inaccessible, and Gough Islands. Tristan da Cunha, named after its Portuguese discoverer (1506), was garrisoned by the British in 1816 to prevent any attempt to rescue NAPOLEON from Saint Helena. Gough and Inaccessible Islands have been designated World Heritage Sites. South Africa leases a site for a meteorological station on Gough Island.

GEOGRAPHY

Location: islands in the South Atlantic Ocean, about midway between South America and Africa; Ascension Island lies 1,300 km (800 mi) northwest of Saint Helena; Tristan da Cunha lies 4,300 km (2,700 mi) southwest of Saint Helena

Geographic coordinates: Saint Helena: 15 57 S, 5 42 W;

Ascension Island: 7 57 S, 14 22 W;

Tristan da Cunha island group: 37 15 S, 12 30 W

Map references: Africa

Area: *total:* 394 sq km
land: 122 sq km Saint Helena Island
water: 0 sq km
88 sq km Ascension Island, 184 sq km Tristan da Cunha island group (includes Tristan (98 sq km), Inaccessible, Nightingale, and Gough islands)
country comparison to the world: 203

Area - comparative: slightly more than twice the size of Washington, DC

Land boundaries: *total:* 0 km

Coastline: Saint Helena: 60 km

Ascension Island: NA

Tristan da Cunha (island only): 34 km

Maritime claims: *territorial sea:* 12 nm
exclusive fishing zone: 200 nm

Climate: Saint Helena: tropical marine; mild, tempered by trade winds;

Ascension Island: tropical marine; mild, semi-arid;

Tristan da Cunha: temperate marine; mild, tempered by trade winds (tends to be cooler than Saint Helena)

Terrain: the islands of this group are of volcanic origin associated with the Atlantic Mid-Ocean Ridge

Saint Helena: rugged, volcanic; small scattered plateaus and plains;

Ascension: surface covered by lava flows and cinder cones of 44 dormant volcanoes; terrain rises to the east;

Tristan da Cunha: sheer cliffs line the coastline of the nearly circular island; the flanks of the central volcanic peak are deeply dissected; narrow coastal plain lies between The Peak and the coastal cliffs

Elevation: *highest point:* Queen Mary's Peak on Tristan da Cunha 2,060 m; Green Mountain on Ascension Island 859 m; Diana's Peak on Saint Helena Island 818 m
lowest point: Atlantic Ocean 0 m

Natural resources: fish, lobster

Land use: *agricultural land:* 30.8% (2018 est.)
arable land: 10.3% (2018 est.)
permanent crops: 0% (2018 est.)
permanent pasture: 20.5% (2018 est.)
forest: 5.1% (2018 est.)
other: 64.1% (2018 est.)

Irrigated land: 0 sq km (2012)

Population distribution: Saint Helena - population is concentrated in and around the capital Jamestown in the northwest, with another significant cluster in the interior Longwood area; Ascension - largest settlement, and location of most of the population, is Georgetown; Tristan da Cunha - most of the nearly 300 inhabitants live in the northern coastal town of Edinburgh of the Seven Seas

Natural hazards: active volcanism on Tristan da Cunha
volcanism: the island volcanoes of Tristan da Cunha (2,060 m) and Nightingale Island (365 m) experience volcanic activity; Tristan da Cunha erupted in 1962 and Nightingale in 2004

Geography - note: Saint Helena harbors at least 40 species of plants unknown elsewhere in the world; Ascension is a breeding ground for sea turtles and sooty terns; Queen Mary's Peak on Tristan da Cunha is the highest island mountain in the South Atlantic and a prominent landmark on the sea lanes around southern Africa

PEOPLE AND SOCIETY

Population: 7,925 (2022 est.)
note: Saint Helena's Statistical Office estimated the resident population to be 4,439 in 2021; only Saint Helena, Ascension, and Tristan da Cunha islands are inhabited, none of the other nearby islands/islets are inhabited
country comparison to the world: 224

Nationality: *noun:* Saint Helenian(s)
adjective: Saint Helenian
note: referred to locally as "Saints"

Ethnic groups: African descent 50%, White 25%, Chinese 25%

Languages: English

Religions: Protestant 75.9% (includes Anglican 68.9, Baptist 2.1%, Seventh Day Adventist 1.8%, Salvation Army 1.7%, New Apostolic 1.4%), Jehovah's Witness 4.1%, Roman Catholic 1.2%, other 2.5% (includes Baha'i), unspecified 0.8%, none 6.1%, no response 9.4% (2016 est.)
note: data represent Saint Helena only

Demographic profile: The vast majority of the population of Saint Helena, Ascension, and Tristan da Cunha live on Saint Helena. Ascension has no indigenous or permanent residents and is inhabited only by persons contracted to work on the island (mainly with the UK and US military or in the space and communications industries) or their dependents, while Tristan da Cunha – the main island in a small archipelago – has fewer than 300 residents. The population of Saint Helena consists of the descendants of 17th century British sailors and settlers from the East India Company, African slaves, and indentured servants and laborers from India, Indonesia, and China. Most of the population of Ascension are Saint Helenians, Britons, and Americans, while that of Tristan da Cunha descends from shipwrecked sailors and Saint Helenians.

Change in Saint Helena's population size is driven by net outward migration. Since the 1980s, Saint Helena's population steadily has shrunk and aged as the birth rate has decreased and many working-age residents left for better opportunities elsewhere. The restoration of British citizenship in 2002 accelerated family emigration; from 1998 to 2008 alone, population declined by about 20%.

In the 2010s, the population experienced some temporary growth, as foreigners and returning Saint Helenians, came to build an international airport, but numbers faded as the project reached completion and workers departed. With the airport fully operational, increased access to the remote island has the potential to boost tourism and fishing, provide more jobs for Saint Helenians domestically, and could encourage some ex-patriots to return home. In the meantime, however, Saint Helena, Ascension, and Tristan da Cunha have to contend with the needs of an aging population. The elderly population of the islands has risen from an estimated 9.4% in 1998 to 18% in 2022.

Age structure: *0-14 years:* 14.66% (male 592/female 570)
15-24 years: 11.7% (male 472/female 455)
25-54 years: 42.59% (male 1,679/female 1,692)
55-64 years: 13.53% (male 523/female 549)
65 years and over: 18.06% (male 730/female 701) (2022 est.)

Median age: *total:* 43.2 years
male: 43.2 years
female: 43.3 years (2020 est.)
country comparison to the world: 30

Population growth rate: 0.13% (2022 est.)
country comparison to the world: 185

Birth rate: 9.34 births/1,000 population (2022 est.)
country comparison to the world: 195

Death rate: 8.08 deaths/1,000 population (2022 est.)
country comparison to the world: 86

Net migration rate: 0 migrant(s)/1,000 population (2022 est.)
country comparison to the world: 96

Population distribution: Saint Helena - population is concentrated in and around the capital Jamestown in the northwest, with another significant cluster in the interior Longwood area; Ascension - largest settlement, and location of most of the population, is Georgetown; Tristan da Cunha - most of the nearly 300 inhabitants live in the northern coastal town of Edinburgh of the Seven Seas

Urbanization: *urban population:* 40.4% of total population (2022)

rate of urbanization: 0.98% annual rate of change (2020-25 est.)

Major urban areas - population: 1,000 JAMESTOWN (capital) (2018)

Sex ratio: *at birth:* 1.06 male(s)/female
0-14 years: 1.04 male(s)/female
15-24 years: 1.04 male(s)/female
25-54 years: 1 male(s)/female
55-64 years: 0.96 male(s)/female
65 years and over: 0.81 male(s)/female
total population: 1.01 male(s)/female (2022 est.)

Infant mortality rate: *total:* 19.19 deaths/1,000 live births
male: 23.05 deaths/1,000 live births
female: 15.13 deaths/1,000 live births (2022 est.)
country comparison to the world: 86

Life expectancy at birth: *total population:* 80.48 years
male: 77.58 years
female: 83.51 years (2022 est.)
country comparison to the world: 49

Total fertility rate: 1.6 children born/woman (2022 est.)
country comparison to the world: 185

Drinking water source: *improved: total:* 99.1% of population
unimproved: total: 0.9% of population (2020)

Sanitation facility access: *improved: total:* 100% of population
unimproved: total: 0% of population (2020)

ENVIRONMENT

Environment - current issues: development threatens unique biota on Saint Helena

Climate: Saint Helena: tropical marine; mild, tempered by trade winds;

Ascension Island: tropical marine; mild, semi-arid;

Tristan da Cunha: temperate marine; mild, tempered by trade winds (tends to be cooler than Saint Helena)

Land use: *agricultural land:* 30.8% (2018 est.)
arable land: 10.3% (2018 est.)
permanent crops: 0% (2018 est.)
permanent pasture: 20.5% (2018 est.)
forest: 5.1% (2018 est.)
other: 64.1% (2018 est.)

Urbanization: *urban population:* 40.4% of total population (2022)
rate of urbanization: 0.98% annual rate of change (2020-25 est.)

GOVERNMENT

Country name: *conventional long form:* Saint Helena, Ascension, and Tristan da Cunha
conventional short form: none
etymology: Saint Helena was discovered in 1502 by Galician navigator Joao da NOVA, sailing in the service of the Kingdom of Portugal, who named it "Santa Helena"; Ascension was named in 1503 by Portuguese navigator Afonso de ALBUQUERQUE who sighted the island on the Feast Day of the Ascension; Tristan da Cunha was discovered in 1506 by Portuguese explorer Tristao da CUNHA who christened the main island after himself (the name was subsequently anglicized)

Government type: parliamentary democracy

Dependency status: overseas territory of the UK

Capital: *name:* Jamestown
geographic coordinates: 15 56 S, 5 43 W
time difference: UTC 0 (5 hours ahead of Washington, DC, during Standard Time)
etymology: founded in 1659 and named after James, Duke of York, who would become King JAMES II of England (r. 1785-1788)

Administrative divisions: 3 administrative areas; Ascension, Saint Helena, Tristan da Cunha

Independence: none (overseas territory of the UK)

National holiday: Official birthday of King Charles III, April or June as designated by the governor

Constitution: *history:* several previous; latest effective 1 September 2009 (St Helena, Ascension and Tristan da Cunha Constitution Order 2009)

Legal system: English common law and local statutes

Citizenship: see United Kingdom

Suffrage: 18 years of age

Executive branch: *chief of state:* King CHARLES III (since 8 September 2022)
head of government: Governor Nigel PHILLIPS (since 13 August 2022)
cabinet: Executive Council consists of the governor, 3 ex-officio officers, and 5 elected members of the Legislative Council
elections/appointments: none; the monarchy is hereditary; governor appointed by the monarch
note: the constitution order provides for an administrator for Ascension and Tristan da Cunha appointed by the governor

Legislative branch: *description:* unicameral Legislative Council (17 seats including the speaker and deputy speaker; 12 members directly elected in a single countrywide constituency by simple majority vote and 3 ex-officio members - the chief secretary, financial secretary, and attorney general; members serve 4-year terms)
elections:
last held on 13 October 2021 (next to be held in 2025)
election results:
percent of vote - NA; seats by party - independent 12; composition - men 14, women 3, percent women 17.6%
note: the Constitution Order provides for separate Island Councils for both Ascension and Tristan da Cunha

Judicial branch: *highest court(s):* Court of Appeal (consists of the court president and 2 justices); Supreme Court (consists of the chief justice - a nonresident - and NA judges); note - appeals beyond the Court of Appeal are heard by the Judicial Committee of the Privy Council (in London)
judge selection and term of office: Court of Appeal and Supreme Court justices appointed by the governor acting upon the instructions from a secretary of state acting on behalf of King CHARLES III; justices of both courts serve until retirement at age 70, but terms can be extended
subordinate courts: Magistrates' Court; Small Claims Court; Juvenile Court

Political parties and leaders: none

International organization participation: UPU

Diplomatic representation in the US: none (overseas territory of the UK)

Diplomatic representation from the US: *embassy:* none (overseas territory of the UK)

Flag description: blue with the flag of the UK in the upper hoist-side quadrant and the Saint Helenian shield centered on the outer half of the flag; the upper third of the shield depicts a white plover (wire bird) on a yellow field; the remainder of the shield depicts a rocky coastline on the left, offshore is a three-masted sailing ship with sails furled but flying an English flag

National symbol(s): Saint Helena plover (bird)

Coat of Arms of Saint Helena:

National anthem: *note:* as an overseas territory of the UK, "God Save the King" is official (see United Kingdom)

ECONOMY

Economic overview: The economy depends largely on financial assistance from the UK, which amounted to about $27 million in FY06/07 or more than twice the level of annual budgetary revenues. The local population earns income from fishing, raising livestock, and sales of handicrafts. Because there are few jobs, 25% of the work force has left to seek employment on Ascension Island, on the Falklands, and in the UK.

Real GDP (purchasing power parity): $31.1 million (2009 est.)
country comparison to the world: 226

Real GDP per capita: $7,800 (FY09/10 est.)
country comparison to the world: 154

Inflation rate (consumer prices): 4% (2012 est.)
country comparison to the world: 165

Agricultural products: coffee, corn, potatoes, vegetables; fish, lobster; livestock; timber

Industries: construction, crafts (furniture, lacework, fancy woodwork), fishing, collectible postage stamps

Labor force: 2,486 (1998 est.)
country comparison to the world: 225

Labor force - by occupation: *agriculture:* 6%
industry: 48%
services: 46% (1987 est.)

Unemployment rate: 14% (1998 est.)
country comparison to the world: 171

Budget: *revenues:* 8.427 million (FY06/07 est.)
expenditures: 20.7 million (FY06/07 est.)
note: revenue data reflect only locally raised revenues; the budget deficit is resolved by grant aid from the UK

Fiscal year: 1 April - 31 March

Exports: $19 million (2004 est.)
country comparison to the world: 217

Exports - partners: United States 47%, Japan 12%, South Korea 10%, France 9%, Australia 5% (2019)

Exports - commodities: crustaceans, fish, integrated circuits, air conditioners, clothing and apparel (2019)

Imports: $20.53 million (2010 est.)
country comparison to the world: 223

Imports - partners: United Kingdom 65%, South Africa 21% (2019)

Imports - commodities: refined petroleum, cranes, communion wafers, iron sheeting, cars and vehicle parts (2019)

Exchange rates: Saint Helenian pounds (SHP) per US dollar -
0.7836 (2017 est.)
0.6542 (2016 est.)

0.6542 (2015)
0.607 (2014 est.)
0.6391 (2013 est.)

ENERGY

Electricity: *installed generating capacity:* 8,000 kW (2020 est.)
consumption: 6.809 million kWh (2019 est.)
exports: 0 kWh (2020 est.)
imports: 0 kWh (2020 est.)
transmission/distribution losses: 1.688 million kWh (2019 est.)

Electricity generation sources: *fossil fuels:* 100% of total installed capacity (2020 est.)

Petroleum: *total petroleum production:* 0 bbl/day (2021 est.)
refined petroleum consumption: 100 bbl/day (2019 est.)

Refined petroleum products - imports: 65 bbl/day (2015 est.)
country comparison to the world: 209

Carbon dioxide emissions: 13,000 metric tonnes of CO2 (2019 est.)
from petroleum and other liquids: 13,000 metric tonnes of CO2 (2019 est.)
country comparison to the world: 215

Energy consumption per capita: 0 Btu/person (2019 est.)
country comparison to the world: 208

COMMUNICATIONS

Telephones - fixed lines: *total subscriptions:* 3,000 (2018 est.)
subscriptions per 100 inhabitants: 50 (2018 est.)
country comparison to the world: 210

Telephones - mobile cellular: *total subscriptions:* 4,000 (2018 est.)
subscriptions per 100 inhabitants: 67 (2019 est.)
country comparison to the world: 222

Telecommunication systems: *general assessment:* capability to communicate worldwide; ADSL-broadband service; LTE coverage of 95% of population, includes voice calls, text messages, mobile data as well as inbound and outbound roaming; Wi-Fi hotspots in Jamestown, 1 ISP, many services are not offered locally but made available for visitors; some sun outages due to the reliance of international telephone and Internet communication relying on single satellite link (2020)
domestic: automatic digital network; fixed-line roughly 50 per 100 and mobile-cellular nearly 67 per 100 persons (2019)
international: country code (Saint Helena) - 290, (Ascension Island) - 247; landing point for the SaEx1 submarine cable providing connectivity to South Africa, Brazil, Virginia Beach (US) and islands in Saint Helena, Ascension and Tristan de Cunha; international direct dialing; satellite voice and data communications; satellite earth stations - 5 (Ascension Island - 4, Saint Helena - 1) (2019)

Broadcast media: Saint Helena has no local TV station; 2 local radio stations, one of which is relayed to Ascension Island; satellite TV stations rebroadcast terrestrially; Ascension Island has no local TV station but has 1 local radio station and receives relays of broadcasts from 1 radio station on Saint Helena; broadcasts from the British Forces Broadcasting Service (BFBS) are available, as well as TV services for the US military; Tristan da Cunha has 1 local radio station and receives BFBS TV and radio broadcasts

Internet country code: .sh; note - Ascension Island assigned .ac

Internet users: *total:* 2,302 (2019 est.)
percent of population: 38% (2019 est.)
country comparison to the world: 225

Broadband - fixed subscriptions: *total:* 1,000 (2018 est.)
subscriptions per 100 inhabitants: 17 (2020 est.)
country comparison to the world: 207

Communications - note: Ascension Island hosts one of four dedicated ground antennas that assist in the operation of the Global Positioning System (GPS) navigation system (the others are on Diego Garcia (British Indian Ocean Territory), Kwajalein (Marshall Islands), and at Cape Canaveral, Florida (US)); South Africa maintains a meteorological station on Gough Island in the Tristan da Cunha archipelago

TRANSPORTATION

Civil aircraft registration country code prefix: VQ-H

Airports: *total:* 2 (2021)
country comparison to the world: 201

Airports - with paved runways: *total:* 2
over 3,047 m: 1 Ascension Island - Wideawake Field (ASI)
1,524 to 2,437 m: 1 (2021) Saint Helena (HLE);
note: weekly commercial air service to South Africa via Namibia commenced on 14 October 2017

Roadways: *total:* 198 km (2002) (Saint Helena 138 km, Ascension 40 km, Tristan da Cunha 20 km)
paved: 168 km (2002) (Saint Helena 118 km, Ascension 40 km, Tristan da Cunha 10 km)
unpaved: 30 km (2002) (Saint Helena 20 km, Tristan da Cunha 10 km)
country comparison to the world: 208

Ports and terminals: *major seaport(s):* Saint Helena

Saint Helena: Jamestown

Ascension Island: Georgetown

Tristan da Cunha: Calshot Harbor (Edinburgh)

Transportation - note: the new airport on Saint Helena opened for limited operations in July 2016, and the first commercial flight took place on 14 October 2017, marking the start of weekly air service between Saint Helena and South Africa via Namibia; the military airport on Ascension Island is closed to civilian traffic; there is no air connection to Tristan da Cunha and very limited sea connections making it one of the most isolated communities on the planet

MILITARY AND SECURITY

Military - note: defense is the responsibility of the UK

TRANSNATIONAL ISSUES

Disputes - international: none identified

SAINT KITTS AND NEVIS

INTRODUCTION

Background: Carib Indians occupied the islands of the West Indies for hundreds of years before the British and French began settlement in 1623. During the course of the 17th century, Saint Kitts became the premier base for English and French expansion into the Caribbean. The French ceded the territory to the UK in 1713. At the turn of the 18th century, Saint Kitts was the richest British Crown Colony per capita in the Caribbean, a result of the sugar trade. Although small in size and separated by only 3 km (2 mi) of water, Saint Kitts and Nevis were viewed and governed as different states until the late-19th century, when the British forcibly unified them along with the island of Anguilla. In 1967, the island territory of Saint Christopher-Nevis-Anguilla became an associated state of the UK with full internal autonomy. The island of Anguilla rebelled and was allowed to secede in 1971. The remaining islands achieved independence in 1983 as Saint Kitts and Nevis. In 1998, a referendum on Nevis to separate from Saint Kitts fell short of the two-thirds majority vote needed.

GEOGRAPHY

Location: Caribbean, islands in the Caribbean Sea, about one-third of the way from Puerto Rico to Trinidad and Tobago

Geographic coordinates: 17 20 N, 62 45 W

Map references: Central America and the Caribbean

Area: *total:* 261 sq km (Saint Kitts 168 sq km; Nevis 93 sq km)
land: 261 sq km
water: 0 sq km
country comparison to the world: 211

Area - comparative: 1.5 times the size of Washington, DC

Land boundaries: *total:* 0 km

Coastline: 135 km

Maritime claims: *territorial sea:* 12 nm
contiguous zone: 24 nm
exclusive economic zone: 200 nm
continental shelf: 200 nm or to the edge of the continental margin

Climate: tropical, tempered by constant sea breezes; little seasonal temperature variation; rainy season (May to November)

Terrain: volcanic with mountainous interiors

Elevation: *highest point:* Mount Liamuiga 1,156 m
lowest point: Caribbean Sea 0 m

Natural resources: arable land

Land use: *agricultural land:* 23.1% (2018 est.)

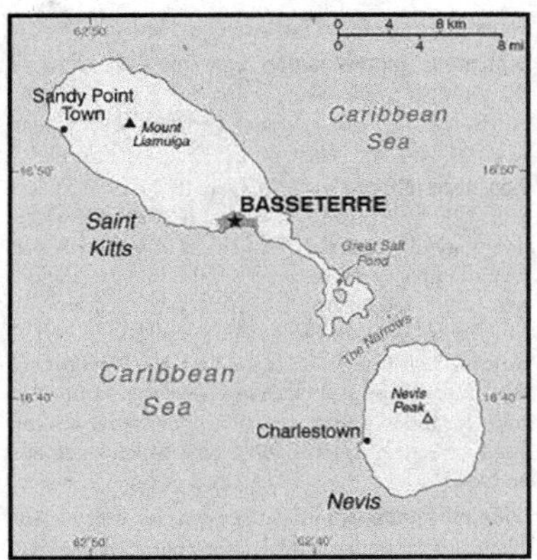

arable land: 19.2% (2018 est.)
permanent crops: 0.4% (2018 est.)
permanent pasture: 3.5% (2018 est.)
forest: 42.3% (2018 est.)
other: 34.6% (2018 est.)

Irrigated land: 8 sq km (2012)

Population distribution: population clusters are found in the small towns located on the periphery of both islands

Natural hazards: hurricanes (July to October)
volcanism: Mount Liamuiga (1,156 m) on Saint Kitts, and Nevis Peak (985 m) on Nevis, are both volcanoes that are part of the volcanic island arc of the Lesser Antilles, which extends from Saba in the north to Grenada in the south

Geography - note: smallest country in the Western Hemisphere both in terms of area and population; with coastlines in the shape of a baseball bat and ball, the two volcanic islands are separated by a 3-km-wide channel called The Narrows; on the southern tip of long, baseball bat-shaped Saint Kitts lies the Great Salt Pond; Nevis Peak sits in the center of its almost circular namesake island and its ball shape complements that of its sister island

PEOPLE AND SOCIETY

Population: 54,488 (2022 est.)
country comparison to the world: 207

Nationality: *noun:* Kittitian(s), Nevisian(s)
adjective: Kittitian, Nevisian

Ethnic groups: African descent 92.5%, mixed 3%, White 2.1%, East Indian 1.5%, other 0.6%, unspecified 0.3% (2001 est.)

Languages: English (official)

Religions: Protestant 75.6% (includes Anglican 16.6%, Methodist 15.8%, Pentecostal 10.8%, Church of God 7.4%, Baptist 5.4%, Seventh Day Adventist 5.4%, Wesleyan Holiness 5.3%, Moravian 4.8%, Evangelical 2.1%, Brethren 1.7%, Presbyterian 0.3%), Roman Catholic 5.9%, Hindu 1.8%, Jehovah's Witness 1.4%, Rastafarian 1.3%, other 5%, none 8.8%, unspecified 0.1% (2011 est.)

Age structure: *0-14 years:* 19.87% (male 5,357/female 5,336)
15-24 years: 13.46% (male 3,504/female 3,741)
25-54 years: 43.64% (male 12,010/female 11,477)
55-64 years: 13.03% (male 3,527/female 3,485)
65 years and over: 10% (male 2,540/female 2,844) (2020 est.)

Median age: *total:* 36.5 years
male: 36.7 years
female: 36.3 years (2020 est.)
country comparison to the world: 79

Population growth rate: 0.61% (2022 est.)
country comparison to the world: 142

Birth rate: 12.24 births/1,000 population (2022 est.)
country comparison to the world: 154

Death rate: 7.27 deaths/1,000 population (2022 est.)
country comparison to the world: 112

Net migration rate: 1.16 migrant(s)/1,000 population (2022 est.)
country comparison to the world: 63

Population distribution: population clusters are found in the small towns located on the periphery of both islands

Urbanization: *urban population:* 31% of total population (2022)
rate of urbanization: 1.06% annual rate of change (2020-25 est.)

Major urban areas - population: 14,000 BASSETERRE (capital) (2018)

Sex ratio: *at birth:* 1.02 male(s)/female
0-14 years: 1.01 male(s)/female
15-24 years: 0.95 male(s)/female
25-54 years: 1.04 male(s)/female
55-64 years: 1.03 male(s)/female
65 years and over: 0.75 male(s)/female
total population: 1 male(s)/female (2022 est.)

Infant mortality rate: *total:* 8.35 deaths/1,000 live births
male: 5.69 deaths/1,000 live births
female: 11.06 deaths/1,000 live births (2022 est.)
country comparison to the world: 146

Life expectancy at birth: *total population:* 77.08 years
male: 74.63 years
female: 79.58 years (2022 est.)
country comparison to the world: 95

Total fertility rate: 1.76 children born/woman (2022 est.)
country comparison to the world: 152

Drinking water source: *improved: urban:* 98.3% of population
rural: 98.3% of population
total: 98.3% of population
unimproved: urban: 1.7% of population
rural: 1.7% of population
total: 1.7% of population (2015 est.)

Current health expenditure: 5.4% of GDP (2019)

Physicians density: 2.77 physicians/1,000 population (2018)

Hospital bed density: 4.8 beds/1,000 population (2012)

Sanitation facility access: *improved: urban:* 87.3% of population
rural: 87.3% of population
total: 87.3% of population
unimproved: urban: 12.7% of population
rural: 12.7% of population
total: 12.7% of population (2017 est.)

HIV/AIDS - adult prevalence rate: 0.5% (2018 est.)
country comparison to the world: 69

HIV/AIDS - people living with HIV/AIDS: (2018) <200

HIV/AIDS - deaths: (2018) <100

Obesity - adult prevalence rate: 22.9% (2016)
country comparison to the world: 71

Alcohol consumption per capita: *total:* 8.84 liters of pure alcohol (2019 est.)
beer: 3.73 liters of pure alcohol (2019 est.)
wine: 1.02 liters of pure alcohol (2019 est.)
spirits: 3.89 liters of pure alcohol (2019 est.)
other alcohols: 0.21 liters of pure alcohol (2019 est.)
country comparison to the world: 36

Education expenditures: 2.6% of GDP (2015 est.)
country comparison to the world: 166

School life expectancy (primary to tertiary education): *total:* 17 years
male: 16 years
female: 19 years (2015)

ENVIRONMENT

Environment - current issues: deforestation; soil erosion and silting affects marine life on coral reefs; water pollution from uncontrolled dumping of sewage

Environment - international agreements: *party to:* Biodiversity, Climate Change, Climate Change-Kyoto Protocol, Climate Change-Paris Agreement, Comprehensive Nuclear Test Ban, Desertification, Endangered Species, Hazardous Wastes, Law of the Sea, Marine Dumping-London Protocol, Ozone Layer Protection, Ship Pollution, Whaling
signed, but not ratified: none of the selected agreements

Air pollutants: *particulate matter emissions:* 12.31 micrograms per cubic meter (2016 est.)
carbon dioxide emissions: 0.24 megatons (2016 est.)
methane emissions: 0.1 megatons (2020 est.)

Climate: tropical, tempered by constant sea breezes; little seasonal temperature variation; rainy season (May to November)

Land use: *agricultural land:* 23.1% (2018 est.)
arable land: 19.2% (2018 est.)
permanent crops: 0.4% (2018 est.)
permanent pasture: 3.5% (2018 est.)
forest: 42.3% (2018 est.)
other: 34.6% (2018 est.)

Urbanization: *urban population:* 31% of total population (2022)
rate of urbanization: 1.06% annual rate of change (2020-25 est.)

Revenue from forest resources: *forest revenues:* 0% of GDP (2018 est.)
country comparison to the world: 194

Revenue from coal: *coal revenues:* 0% of GDP (2018 est.)
country comparison to the world: 157

Waste and recycling: *municipal solid waste generated annually:* 32,892 tons (2015 est.)

Total water withdrawal: *municipal:* 15.4 million cubic meters (2017 est.)
industrial: 0 cubic meters (2017 est.)
agricultural: 200,000 cubic meters (2017 est.)

Total renewable water resources: 24 million cubic meters (2017 est.)

GOVERNMENT

Country name: *conventional long form:* Federation of Saint Kitts and Nevis
conventional short form: Saint Kitts and Nevis

former: Federation of Saint Christopher and Nevis
etymology: Saint Kitts was, and still is, referred to as Saint Christopher and this name was well established by the 17th century (although who first applied the name is unclear); in the 17th century a common nickname for Christopher was Kit or Kitt, so the island began to be referred to as "Saint Kitt's Island" or just "Saint Kitts"; Nevis is derived from the original Spanish name "Nuestra Senora de las Nieves" (Our Lady of the Snows) and refers to the white halo of clouds that generally wreathes Nevis Peak
note: Nevis is pronounced nee-vis

Government type: federal parliamentary democracy under a constitutional monarchy; a Commonwealth realm

Capital: *name:* Basseterre
geographic coordinates: 17 18 N, 62 43 W
time difference: UTC-4 (1 hour ahead of Washington, DC, during Standard Time)
etymology: the French name translates as "low land" in English; the reference is to the city's low-lying location within a valley, as well as to the fact that the city is on the leeward (downwind) part of the island, and is thus a safe anchorage

Administrative divisions: 14 parishes; Christ Church Nichola Town, Saint Anne Sandy Point, Saint George Basseterre, Saint George Gingerland, Saint James Windward, Saint John Capesterre, Saint John Figtree, Saint Mary Cayon, Saint Paul Capesterre, Saint Paul Charlestown, Saint Peter Basseterre, Saint Thomas Lowland, Saint Thomas Middle Island, Trinity Palmetto Point

Independence: 19 September 1983 (from the UK)

National holiday: Independence Day, 19 September (1983)

Constitution: *history:* several previous (preindependence); latest presented 22 June 1983, effective 23 June 1983
amendments: proposed by the National Assembly; passage requires approval by at least two-thirds majority vote of the total Assembly membership and assent of the governor general; amendments to constitutional provisions such as the sovereignty of the federation, fundamental rights and freedoms, the judiciary, and the Nevis Island Assembly also require approval in a referendum by at least two thirds of the votes cast in Saint Kitts and in Nevis

Legal system: English common law

International law organization participation: has not submitted an ICJ jurisdiction declaration; accepts ICCt jurisdiction

Citizenship: *citizenship by birth:* yes
citizenship by descent only: yes
dual citizenship recognized: yes
residency requirement for naturalization: 14 years

Suffrage: 18 years of age; universal

Executive branch: *chief of state:* King CHARLES III (since 8 September 2022); represented by Governor General Samuel W.T. SEATON (since 2 September 2015); note - SEATON was Acting Governor General from 20 May to 2 September 2015
head of government: Prime Minister Dr. Terrance DREW (since 6 August 2022); Deputy Prime Minister Dr. Geoffrey HANLEY (since 13 August 2022)
cabinet: Cabinet appointed by governor general in consultation with prime minister
elections/appointments: the monarchy is hereditary; governor general appointed by the monarch; following legislative elections, the leader of the majority party or majority coalition usually appointed prime minister by governor general; deputy prime minister appointed by governor general

Legislative branch: *description:* unicameral National Assembly (14 or 15 seats, depending on inclusion of attorney general; 11 members directly elected in single-seat constituencies by simple majority vote and 3 appointed by the governor general - 2 on the advice of the prime minister and the third on the advice of the opposition leader; members serve 5-year terms)
elections:
last held on 5 August 2022 (next to be held on 2027)
election results:
percent of vote by party - SKNLP 44.4%, PLP 16.1%, PAM 16.2%, CCM 12.7%, other 10.6%; seats by party - SKNLP 6, CCM 3, PLP 1, CCM 1

Judicial branch: *highest court(s):* the Eastern Caribbean Supreme Court (ECSC) is the superior court of the Organization of Eastern Caribbean States; the ECSC - headquartered on St. Lucia - consists of the Court of Appeal - headed by the chief justice and 4 judges - and the High Court with 18 judges; the Court of Appeal is itinerant, traveling to member states on a schedule to hear appeals from the High Court and subordinate courts; High Court judges reside in the member states, with 2 assigned to Saint Kitts and Nevis; note - the ECSC in 2003 replaced the Judicial Committee of the Privy Council (in London) as the final court of appeal on Saint Kitts and Nevis; Saint Kitts and Nevis is also a member of the Caribbean Court of Justice
judge selection and term of office: chief justice of Eastern Caribbean Supreme Court appointed by His Majesty, King Charles III; other justices and judges appointed by the Judicial and Legal Services Commission, an independent body of judicial officials; Court of Appeal justices appointed for life with mandatory retirement at age 65; High Court judges appointed for life with mandatory retirement at age 62
subordinate courts: magistrates' courts

Political parties and leaders: Concerned Citizens Movement or CCM [Mark BRANTLEY]
Nevis Reformation Party or NRP [Dr. Janice DANIEL-HODGE]
People's Action Movement or PAM [Shawn K. RICHARDS]
People's Labour Party or PLP [Dr. Timothy HARRIS]
Saint Kitts and Nevis Labor Party or SKNLP [Dr. Terrance DREW]

International organization participation: ACP, AOSIS, C, Caricom, CDB, CELAC, FAO, G-77, IBRD, ICAO, ICCt, ICRM, IDA, IFAD, IFC, IFRCS, ILO, IMF, IMO, Interpol, IOC, ITU, MIGA, OAS, OECS, OPANAL, OPCW, Petrocaribe, UN, UNCTAD, UNESCO, UNIDO, UPU, WHO, WIPO, WTO

Diplomatic representation in the US: *chief of mission:* Ambassador (vacant); Charge d'Affaires Shanelle Natasha SIMMONDS (since 26 August 2022)
chancery: 1203 19th St. NW, 5th Floor, Washington, DC 20036
telephone: [1] (202) 686-2636
FAX: [1] (202) 686-5740
email address and website: info@embskn.com
consulate(s) general: Los Angeles, New York

Diplomatic representation from the US: *embassy:* the US does not have an embassy in Saint Kitts and Nevis; the US Ambassador to Barbados is accredited to Saint Kitts and Nevis

Flag description: divided diagonally from the lower hoist side by a broad black band bearing two white, five-pointed stars; the black band is edged in yellow; the upper triangle is green, the lower triangle is red; green signifies the island's fertility, red symbolizes the struggles of the people from slavery, yellow denotes year-round sunshine, and black represents the African heritage of the people; the white stars stand for the islands of Saint Kitts and Nevis, but can also express hope and liberty, or independence and optimism

National symbol(s): brown pelican, royal poinciana (flamboyant) tree; national colors: green, yellow, red, black, white

National anthem: *name:* "Oh Land of Beauty!"
lyrics/music: Kenrick Anderson GEORGES
note: adopted 1983

National heritage: *total World Heritage Sites:* 1 (cultural)
selected World Heritage Site locales: Brimstone Hill Fortress National Park

ECONOMY

Economic overview: The economy of Saint Kitts and Nevis depends on tourism; since the 1970s, tourism has replaced sugar as the economy's traditional mainstay. Roughly 200,000 tourists visited the islands in 2009, but reduced tourism arrivals and foreign investment led to an economic contraction in the 2009-2013 period, and the economy returned to growth only in 2014. Like other tourist destinations in the Caribbean, Saint Kitts and Nevis is vulnerable to damage from natural disasters and shifts in tourism demand.

Following the 2005 harvest, the government closed the sugar industry after several decades of losses. To compensate for lost jobs, the government has embarked on a program to diversify the agricultural sector and to stimulate other sectors of the economy, such as export-oriented manufacturing and offshore banking. The government has made notable progress in reducing its public debt, from 154% of GDP in 2011 to 83% in 2013, although it still faces one of the highest levels in the world, largely attributable to public enterprise losses. Saint Kitts and Nevis is among other countries in the Caribbean that supplement their economic activity through economic citizenship programs, whereby foreigners can obtain citizenship from Saint Kitts and Nevis by investing there.

Real GDP (purchasing power parity): $1.24 billion (2020 est.)
$1.39 billion (2019 est.)
$1.36 billion (2018 est.)
note: data are in 2017 dollars
country comparison to the world: 205

Real GDP growth rate: 2.1% (2017 est.)
2.9% (2016 est.)
2.7% (2015 est.)
country comparison to the world: 131

Real GDP per capita: $23,300 (2020 est.)
$26,200 (2019 est.)
$25,900 (2018 est.)

note: data are in 2017 dollars
country comparison to the world: 82

GDP (official exchange rate): $964 million (2017 est.)

Inflation rate (consumer prices): 0% (2017 est.)
-0.3% (2016 est.)
country comparison to the world: 22

GDP - composition, by sector of origin: *agriculture:* 1.1% (2017 est.)
industry: 30% (2017 est.)
services: 68.9% (2017 est.)

GDP - composition, by end use: *household consumption:* 41.4% (2017 est.)
government consumption: 25.9% (2017 est.)
investment in fixed capital: 30.8% (2017 est.)
investment in inventories: 0% (2017 est.)
exports of goods and services: 62.5% (2017 est.)
imports of goods and services: -60.4% (2017 est.)

Agricultural products: coconuts, tropical fruit, roots/tubers, vegetables, sweet potatoes, pulses, watermelons, carrots/turnips, eggs, tomatoes

Industries: tourism, cotton, salt, copra, clothing, footwear, beverages

Industrial production growth rate: 5% (2017 est.)
country comparison to the world: 56

Labor force: 18,170 (June 1995 est.)
country comparison to the world: 211

Unemployment rate: 4.5% (1997)
country comparison to the world: 69

Budget: *revenues:* 307 million (2017 est.)
expenditures: 291.1 million (2017 est.)

Budget surplus (+) or deficit (-): 1.7% (of GDP) (2017 est.)
country comparison to the world: 18

Public debt: 62.9% of GDP (2017 est.)
61.5% of GDP (2016 est.)
country comparison to the world: 68

Taxes and other revenues: 31.9% (of GDP) (2017 est.)
country comparison to the world: 70

Fiscal year: calendar year

Current account balance: -$97 million (2017 est.)
-$102 million (2016 est.)
country comparison to the world: 86

Exports: $610 million (2018 est.) note: data are in current year dollars
$53.9 million (2016 est.)
country comparison to the world: 188

Exports - partners: United States 69%, Germany 8%, Italy 5% (2019)

Exports - commodities: low-voltage protection equipment, broadcasting equipment, measuring instruments, electric motor parts, electrical transformers (2019)

Imports: $590 million (2018 est.) note: data are in current year dollars
$307.9 million (2016 est.)
country comparison to the world: 199

Imports - partners: United States 59%, Peru 6%, Germany 5% (2019)

Imports - commodities: refined petroleum, jewelry, ships, cars, poultry meats, cement (2019)

Reserves of foreign exchange and gold: $365.1 million (31 December 2017 est.)
$320.5 million (31 December 2016 est.)
country comparison to the world: 162

Debt - external: $201.8 million (31 December 2017 est.)
$187.9 million (31 December 2016 est.)
country comparison to the world: 187

Exchange rates: East Caribbean dollars (XCD) per US dollar -
2.7 (2017 est.)
2.7 (2016 est.)
2.7 (2015 est.)
2.7 (2014 est.)
2.7 (2013 est.)

ENERGY

Electricity access: *electrification - total population:* 100% (2020)

Electricity: *installed generating capacity:* 71,000 kW (2020 est.)
consumption: 175.34 million kWh (2019 est.)
exports: 0 kWh (2020 est.)
imports: 0 kWh (2020 est.)
transmission/distribution losses: 40 million kWh (2019 est.)

Electricity generation sources: *fossil fuels:* 96.3% of total installed capacity (2020 est.)
wind: 3.7% of total installed capacity (2020 est.)

Petroleum: *total petroleum production:* 0 bbl/day (2021 est.)
refined petroleum consumption: 1,800 bbl/day (2019 est.)

Refined petroleum products - imports: 1,743 bbl/day (2015 est.)
country comparison to the world: 192

Carbon dioxide emissions: 268,000 metric tonnes of CO_2 (2019 est.)
from petroleum and other liquids: 268,000 metric tonnes of CO_2 (2019 est.)
country comparison to the world: 199

Energy consumption per capita: 71.96 million Btu/person (2019 est.)
country comparison to the world: 82

COMMUNICATIONS

Telephones - fixed lines: *total subscriptions:* 15,000 (2020 est.)
subscriptions per 100 inhabitants: 28 (2020 est.)
country comparison to the world: 183

Telephones - mobile cellular: *total subscriptions:* 78,000 (2020 est.)
subscriptions per 100 inhabitants: 147 (2020 est.)
country comparison to the world: 195

Telecommunication systems: *general assessment:* good interisland and international connections; broadband access; expanded FttP (Fiber to the Home) and LTE markets; regulatory development; telecom sector contributes greatly to the overall GDP; telecom sector is a growth area (2020)
domestic: interisland links via ECFS; fixed-line teledensity about 33 per 100 persons; mobile-cellular teledensity is roughly 148 per 100 persons (2019)
international: country code - 1-869; landing points for the ECFS, Southern Caribbean Fiber and the SSCS submarine cables providing connectivity for numerous Caribbean Islands (2019)

Broadcast media: the government operates a national TV network that broadcasts on 2 channels; cable subscription services provide access to local and international channels; the government operates a national radio network; a mix of government-owned and privately owned broadcasters operate roughly 15 radio stations (2019)

Internet country code: .kn

Internet users: *total:* 42,796 (2019 est.)
percent of population: 81% (2019 est.)
country comparison to the world: 201

Broadband - fixed subscriptions: *total:* 30,000 (2020 est.)
subscriptions per 100 inhabitants: 56 (2020 est.)
country comparison to the world: 154

TRANSPORTATION

Civil aircraft registration country code prefix: V4

Airports: *total:* 2 (2021)
country comparison to the world: 202

Airports - with paved runways: *total:* 2
1,524 to 2,437 m: 1
914 to 1,523 m: 1 (2021)

Railways: *total:* 50 km (2008)
narrow gauge: 50 km (2008) 0.762-m gauge on Saint Kitts for tourists
country comparison to the world: 132

Roadways: *total:* 383 km (2002)
paved: 163 km (2002)
unpaved: 220 km (2002)
country comparison to the world: 200

Merchant marine: *total:* 244
by type: bulk carrier 6, container ship 7, general cargo 45, oil tanker 53, other 133 (2021)
country comparison to the world: 62

Ports and terminals: *major seaport(s):* Basseterre, Charlestown

MILITARY AND SECURITY

Military and security forces: Ministry of National Security: St. Kitts and Nevis Defense Force (SKNDF), St. Kitts and Nevis Coast Guard, the Royal St. Christopher and Nevis Police Force (includes a paramilitary Special Services Unit) (2022)

Military and security service personnel strengths: the SKNDF has approximately 400 personnel (2022)

Military equipment inventories and acquisitions: the SKNDF is lightly armed with equipment from Belgium, the UK, and the US (2021)

Military service age and obligation: 18 years of age for voluntary military service (under 18 with written parental permission); no conscription (2022)

Military - note: St. Kitts joined the Caribbean Regional Security System (RSS) in 1984; RSS signatories (Antigua and Barbuda, Barbados, Dominica, Grenada, Saint Lucia, and Saint Vincent and the Grenadines) agreed to prepare contingency plans and assist one another, on request, in national emergencies, prevention of smuggling, search and rescue, immigration control, fishery protection, customs and excise control, maritime policing duties, protection of off-shore installations, pollution control, national and other disasters, and threats to national security

SKNDF's missions included defense of the country's territorial integrity and sovereignty, protecting natural resources, interdicting narcotics trafficking, and providing humanitarian relief as needed (2022)

TRANSNATIONAL ISSUES

Disputes - international: *Saint Kitts and Nevis-Venezuela:* joins other Caribbean states to counter Venezuela's claim that Aves Island sustains human habitation, a criterion under UN Convention on the Law of the Sea, which permits Venezuela to extend its EEZ/continental shelf over a large portion of the eastern Caribbean Sea

Illicit drugs: a transit point for cocaine and marijuana destined for North America, Europe, and elsewhere in the Caribbean

SAINT LUCIA

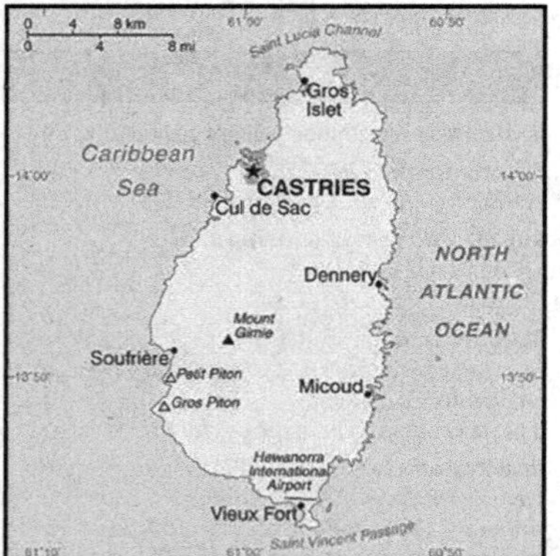

INTRODUCTION

Background: The island, with its fine natural harbor at Castries and burgeoning sugar industry, was contested by England and France throughout the 17th and early 18th centuries (changing possession 14 times); it was finally ceded to the UK in 1814 and became part of the British Windward Islands colony. Even after the abolition of slavery on its plantations in 1834, Saint Lucia remained an agricultural island, dedicated to producing tropical commodity crops. In the mid-20th century, Saint Lucia joined the West Indies Federation (1958–1962) and in 1967 became one of the six members of the West Indies Associated States, with internal self-government. In 1979, Saint Lucia gained full independence.

GEOGRAPHY

Location: Caribbean, island between the Caribbean Sea and North Atlantic Ocean, north of Trinidad and Tobago

Geographic coordinates: 13 53 N, 60 58 W

Map references: Central America and the Caribbean

Area: *total:* 616 sq km
land: 606 sq km
water: 10 sq km
country comparison to the world: 192

Area - comparative: three and a half times the size of Washington, DC

Land boundaries: *total:* 0 km

Coastline: 158 km

Maritime claims: *territorial sea:* 12 nm
contiguous zone: 24 nm
exclusive economic zone: 200 nm
continental shelf: 200 nm or to the edge of the continental margin

Climate: tropical, moderated by northeast trade winds; dry season January to April, rainy season May to August

Terrain: volcanic and mountainous with broad, fertile valleys

Elevation: *highest point:* Mount Gimie 948 m
lowest point: Caribbean Sea 0 m

Natural resources: forests, sandy beaches, minerals (pumice), mineral springs, geothermal potential

Land use: *agricultural land:* 17.4% (2018 est.)
arable land: 4.9% (2018 est.)
permanent crops: 11.5% (2018 est.)
permanent pasture: 1% (2018 est.)
forest: 77% (2018 est.)
other: 5.6% (2018 est.)

Irrigated land: 30 sq km (2012)

Population distribution: most of the population is found on the periphery of the island, with a larger concentration in the north around the capital of Castries

Natural hazards: hurricanes
volcanism: Mount Gimie (948 m), also known as Qualibou, is a caldera on the west of the island; the iconic twin pyramidal peaks of Gros Piton (771 m) and Petit Piton (743 m) are lava dome remnants associated with the Soufriere volcano; there have been no historical magmatic eruptions, but a minor steam eruption in 1766 spread a thin layer of ash over a wide area; Saint Lucia is part of the volcanic island arc of the Lesser Antilles that extends from Saba in the north to Grenada in the south

Geography - note: the twin Pitons (Gros Piton and Petit Piton), striking cone-shaped peaks south of Soufriere, are one of the scenic natural highlights of the Caribbean

PEOPLE AND SOCIETY

Population: 167,122 (2022 est.)
country comparison to the world: 186

Nationality: *noun:* Saint Lucian(s)
adjective: Saint Lucian

Ethnic groups: Black/African descent 85.3%, mixed 10.9%, East Indian 2.2%, other 1.6%, unspecified 0.1% (2010 est.)

Languages: English (official), Saint Lucian Creole

Religions: Roman Catholic 61.5%, Protestant 25.5% (includes Seventh Day Adventist 10.4%, Pentecostal 8.9%, Baptist 2.2%, Anglican 1.6%, Church of God 1.5%, other Protestant 0.9%), other Christian 3.4% (includes Evangelical 2.3% and Jehovah's Witness 1.1%), Rastafarian 1.9%, other 0.4%, none 5.9%, unspecified 1.4% (2010 est.)

Age structure: *0-14 years:* 19.24% (male 16,484/female 15,546)
15-24 years: 13.6% (male 11,475/female 11,165)
25-54 years: 42.83% (male 34,436/female 36,868)
55-64 years: 11.23% (male 8,624/female 10,075)
65 years and over: 13.1% (male 9,894/female 11,920) (2020 est.)

Dependency ratios: *total dependency ratio:* 39.4
youth dependency ratio: 25
elderly dependency ratio: 14.4
potential support ratio: 7 (2020 est.)

Median age: *total:* 36.9 years
male: 35.7 years
female: 38 years (2020 est.)
country comparison to the world: 75

Population growth rate: 0.29% (2022 est.)
country comparison to the world: 170

Birth rate: 12.02 births/1,000 population (2022 est.)
country comparison to the world: 155

Death rate: 8.07 deaths/1,000 population (2022 est.)
country comparison to the world: 87

Net migration rate: -1.09 migrant(s)/1,000 population (2022 est.)
country comparison to the world: 149

Population distribution: most of the population is found on the periphery of the island, with a larger concentration in the north around the capital of Castries

Urbanization: *urban population:* 19% of total population (2022)
rate of urbanization: 0.98% annual rate of change (2020-25 est.)

Major urban areas - population: 22,000 CASTRIES (capital) (2018)

Sex ratio: *at birth:* 1.06 male(s)/female
0-14 years: 1.06 male(s)/female
15-24 years: 1.04 male(s)/female
25-54 years: 0.94 male(s)/female
55-64 years: 0.86 male(s)/female
65 years and over: 0.75 male(s)/female
total population: 0.94 male(s)/female (2022 est.)

Maternal mortality ratio: 117 deaths/100,000 live births (2017 est.)
country comparison to the world: 67

Infant mortality rate: *total:* 11.99 deaths/1,000 live births
male: 11.23 deaths/1,000 live births
female: 12.78 deaths/1,000 live births (2022 est.)
country comparison to the world: 119

Life expectancy at birth: *total population:* 78.95 years
male: 76.21 years
female: 81.84 years (2022 est.)
country comparison to the world: 65

Total fertility rate: 1.72 children born/woman (2022 est.)
country comparison to the world: 162

Contraceptive prevalence rate: 55.5% (2011/12)

Drinking water source: *improved: urban:* 99.4% of population
rural: 98.5% of population
total: 98.7% of population
unimproved: urban: 0.6% of population
rural: 1.5% of population
total: 1.3% of population (2020 est.)

Current health expenditure: 4.3% of GDP (2019)

Physicians density: 0.64 physicians/1,000 population (2017)

Hospital bed density: 1.3 beds/1,000 population (2017)

Sanitation facility access: *improved: urban:* 97.6% of population
rural: 92.9% of population
total: 93.8% of population
unimproved: urban: 2.4% of population
rural: 7.1% of population
total: 6.2% of population (2020 est.)

HIV/AIDS - adult prevalence rate: 0.6% (2018 est.)
country comparison to the world: 61

HIV/AIDS - people living with HIV/AIDS: (2018) <1,000

HIV/AIDS - deaths: (2018) <100

Obesity - adult prevalence rate: 19.7% (2016)
country comparison to the world: 111

Alcohol consumption per capita: *total:* 9.3 liters of pure alcohol (2019 est.)
beer: 3.21 liters of pure alcohol (2019 est.)
wine: 0.4 liters of pure alcohol (2019 est.)
spirits: 5.1 liters of pure alcohol (2019 est.)
other alcohols: 0.6 liters of pure alcohol (2019 est.)
country comparison to the world: 31

Children under the age of 5 years underweight: 2.8% (2012)
country comparison to the world: 99

Education expenditures: 3.6% of GDP (2020 est.)
country comparison to the world: 119

School life expectancy (primary to tertiary education): *total:* 13 years
male: 12 years
female: 13 years (2020)

Unemployment, youth ages 15-24: *total:* 37.2%
male: 39.6%
female: 34.3% (2019 est.)

ENVIRONMENT

Environment - current issues: deforestation; soil erosion, particularly in the northern region

Environment - international agreements: *party to:* Biodiversity, Climate Change, Climate Change-Kyoto Protocol, Climate Change-Paris Agreement, Comprehensive Nuclear Test Ban, Desertification, Endangered Species, Environmental Modification, Hazardous Wastes, Law of the Sea, Marine Dumping-London Convention, Ozone Layer Protection, Ship Pollution, Wetlands, Whaling
signed, but not ratified: none of the selected agreements

Air pollutants: *particulate matter emissions:* 21.22 micrograms per cubic meter (2016 est.)
carbon dioxide emissions: 0.41 megatons (2016 est.)
methane emissions: 0.27 megatons (2020 est.)

Climate: tropical, moderated by northeast trade winds; dry season January to April, rainy season May to August

Land use: *agricultural land:* 17.4% (2018 est.)
arable land: 4.9% (2018 est.)
permanent crops: 11.5% (2018 est.)
permanent pasture: 1% (2018 est.)
forest: 77% (2018 est.)
other: 5.6% (2018 est.)

Urbanization: *urban population:* 19% of total population (2022)
rate of urbanization: 0.98% annual rate of change (2020-25 est.)

Revenue from forest resources: *forest revenues:* 0.01% of GDP (2018 est.)
country comparison to the world: 156

Revenue from coal: *coal revenues:* 0% of GDP (2018 est.)
country comparison to the world: 158

Waste and recycling: *municipal solid waste generated annually:* 77,616 tons (2015 est.)

Total water withdrawal: *municipal:* 12.5 million cubic meters (2017 est.)
industrial: 0 cubic meters (2017 est.)
agricultural: 30.4 million cubic meters (2017 est.)

Total renewable water resources: 300 million cubic meters (2017 est.)

GOVERNMENT

Country name: *conventional long form:* none
conventional short form: Saint Lucia
etymology: named after Saint LUCY of Syracuse by French sailors who were shipwrecked on the island on 13 December 1502, the saint's feast day; Saint Lucia is the only country named specifically after a woman
note: pronounced saynt-looshuh

Government type: parliamentary democracy under a constitutional monarchy; a Commonwealth realm

Capital: *name:* Castries
geographic coordinates: 14 00 N, 61 00 W
time difference: UTC-4 (1 hour ahead of Washington, DC, during Standard Time)
etymology: in 1785, the village of Carenage was renamed Castries, after Charles Eugene Gabriel de La Croix de CASTRIES (1727-1801), who was then the French Minister of the Navy and Colonies

Administrative divisions: 10 districts; Anse-la-Raye, Canaries, Castries, Choiseul, Dennery, Gros-Islet, Laborie, Micoud, Soufriere, Vieux-Fort

Independence: 22 February 1979 (from the UK)

National holiday: Independence Day, 22 February (1979)

Constitution: *history:* previous 1958, 1960 (preindependence); latest presented 20 December 1978, effective 22 February 1979
amendments: proposed by Parliament; passage requires at least two-thirds majority vote by the House of Assembly membership in the final reading and assent of the governor general; passage of amendments to various constitutional sections, such as those on fundamental rights and freedoms, government finances, the judiciary, and procedures for amending the constitution, require at least three-quarters majority vote by the House and assent of the governor general; passage of amendments approved by the House but rejected by the Senate require a majority of votes cast in a referendum; amended several times, last in 2008

Legal system: English common law

International law organization participation: has not submitted an ICJ jurisdiction declaration; accepts ICCt jurisdiction

Citizenship: *citizenship by birth:* yes
citizenship by descent only: at least one parent must be a citizen of Saint Lucia
dual citizenship recognized: yes
residency requirement for naturalization: 8 years

Suffrage: 18 years of age; universal

Executive branch: *chief of state:* King CHARLES III (since 8 September 2022); represented by Acting Governor General Errol CHARLES (since 11 November 2021)
head of government: Prime Minister Philip J. PIERRE (since 28 July 2021)
cabinet: Cabinet appointed by the governor general on the advice of the prime minister
elections/appointments: the monarchy is hereditary; governor general appointed by the monarch; following legislative elections, the leader of the majority party or majority coalition usually appointed prime minister by governor general; deputy prime minister appointed by governor general

Legislative branch: *description:* bicameral Houses of Parliament consists of:
Senate (11 seats; all members appointed by the governor general; 6 on the advice of the prime minister, 3 on the advice of the leader of the opposition, and 2 upon consultation with religious, economic, and social groups; members serve 5-year terms)
House of Assembly (18 seats; 17 members directly elected in single-seat constituencies by simple majority vote and the speaker, designated from outside the Parliament; members serve 5-year terms)
elections:
Senate - last appointments on 17 August 2021 (next in 2026)
House of Assembly - last held on 26 July 2021 (next to be held in 2026)
election results:
Senate - percent of vote by party - NA; seats by party - NA; composition - men 6, women 5, percent of women 45.5%
House of Assembly - percent of vote by party - SLP 50.1%, UWP 42.9%, other o.3%, independent 6.6%; seats by party - SLP 13, UWP 2, independent 2; composition (including the speaker) - men 16, women 2, percent of women 11.1%; note - total Parliament percent of women 24.1%

Judicial branch: *highest court(s):* the Eastern Caribbean Supreme Court (ECSC) is the superior court of the Organization of Eastern Caribbean States; the ECSC - headquartered on St. Lucia - consists of the Court of Appeal - headed by the chief justice and 4 judges - and the High Court with 18 judges; the Court of Appeal is itinerant, traveling to member states on a schedule to hear appeals from the High Court and subordinate courts; High Court judges reside in the member states with 4 on Saint Lucia; Saint Lucia is a member of the Caribbean Court of Justice
judge selection and term of office: chief justice of Eastern Caribbean Supreme Court appointed by Her Majesty, Queen ELIZABETH II; other justices and judges appointed by the Judicial and Legal Services Commission, an independent body of judicial officials; Court of Appeal justices appointed for life with mandatory retirement at age 65; High Court judges appointed for life with mandatory retirement at age 62
subordinate courts: magistrate's court

Political parties and leaders: Saint Lucia Labor Party or SLP [Philip J. PIERRE]
United Workers Party or UWP [Allen M. CHASTANET]

International organization participation: ACP, AOSIS, C, Caricom, CD, CDB, CELAC, FAO, G-77, IBRD, ICAO, ICCt, ICRM, IDA, IFAD, IFC, IFRCS, ILO, IMF, IMO, Interpol, IOC, ISO, ITU, ITUC (NGOs), MIGA, NAM, OAS, OECS, OIF, OPANAL, OPCW, Petrocaribe, UN, UNCTAD, UNESCO, UNIDO, UPU, WCO, WFTU (NGOs), WHO, WIPO, WMO, WTO

Diplomatic representation in the US: *chief of mission:* Ambassador Elizabeth DARIUS-CLARKE (since 7 June 2022)
chancery: 1629 K Street NW, Suite 1250, Washington, DC 20006
telephone: [1] (202) 364-6792
FAX: [1] (202) 364-6723
email address and website:
embassydc@gosl.gov.lc
https://www.embassyofstlucia.org/
consulate(s) general: New York

Diplomatic representation from the US: *embassy:* the US does not have an embassy in Saint Lucia; the US Ambassador to Barbados is accredited to Saint Lucia

Flag description: cerulean blue with a gold isosceles triangle below a black arrowhead; the upper edges of the arrowhead have a white border; the blue color represents the sky and sea, gold stands for sunshine and prosperity, and white and black the racial composition of the island (with the latter being dominant); the two major triangles invoke the twin Pitons (Gros Piton and Petit Piton), cone-shaped volcanic plugs that are a symbol of the island

National symbol(s): twin pitons (volcanic peaks), Saint Lucia parrot; national colors: cerulean blue, gold, black, white

National anthem: *name:* "Sons and Daughters of St. Lucia"
lyrics/music: Charles JESSE/Leton Felix THOMAS
note: adopted 1967

National heritage: *total World Heritage Sites:* 1 (natural)
selected World Heritage Site locales: Pitons Management Area

ECONOMY

Economic overview: The island nation has been able to attract foreign business and investment, especially in its offshore banking and tourism industries. Tourism is Saint Lucia's main source of jobs and income - accounting for 65% of GDP - and the island's main source of foreign exchange earnings. The manufacturing sector is the most diverse in the Eastern Caribbean area. Crops such as bananas, mangos, and avocados continue to be grown for export, but St. Lucia's once solid banana industry has been devastated by strong competition.

Saint Lucia is vulnerable to a variety of external shocks, including volatile tourism receipts, natural disasters, and dependence on foreign oil. Furthermore, high public debt - 77% of GDP in 2012 - and high debt servicing obligations constrain the CHASTANET administration's ability to respond to adverse external shocks.

St. Lucia has experienced anemic growth since the onset of the global financial crisis in 2008, largely because of a slowdown in tourism - airlines cut back on their routes to St. Lucia in 2012. Also, St. Lucia introduced a value added tax in 2012 of 15%, becoming the last country in the Eastern Caribbean to do so. In 2013, the government introduced a National Competitiveness and Productivity Council to address St. Lucia's high public wages and lack of productivity.

Real GDP (purchasing power parity): $2.25 billion (2020 est.)
$2.82 billion (2019 est.)
$2.78 billion (2018 est.)
note: data are in 2017 dollars
country comparison to the world: 194

Real GDP growth rate: 3% (2017 est.)
3.4% (2016 est.)
-0.9% (2015 est.)
country comparison to the world: 99

Real GDP per capita: $12,300 (2020 est.)
$15,400 (2019 est.)
$15,300 (2018 est.)
note: data are in 2017 dollars
country comparison to the world: 125

GDP (official exchange rate): $1.686 billion (2017 est.)

Inflation rate (consumer prices): 0.1% (2017 est.)
-3.1% (2016 est.)
country comparison to the world: 24

GDP - composition, by sector of origin: *agriculture:* 2.9% (2017 est.)
industry: 14.2% (2017 est.)
services: 82.8% (2017 est.)

GDP - composition, by end use: *household consumption:* 66.1% (2017 est.)
government consumption: 11.2% (2017 est.)
investment in fixed capital: 16.9% (2017 est.)
investment in inventories: 0.1% (2017 est.)
exports of goods and services: 62.7% (2017 est.)
imports of goods and services: -56.9% (2017 est.)

Agricultural products: bananas, coconuts, fruit, tropical fruit, plantains, roots/tubers, cassava, poultry, vegetables, mangoes/guavas

Industries: tourism; clothing, assembly of electronic components, beverages, corrugated cardboard boxes, lime processing, coconut processing

Industrial production growth rate: 6% (2017 est.)
country comparison to the world: 42

Labor force: 79,700 (2012 est.)
country comparison to the world: 182

Labor force - by occupation: *agriculture:* 21.7%
industry: 24.7%
services: 53.6% (2002 est.)

Unemployment rate: 20% (2003 est.)
country comparison to the world: 190

Unemployment, youth ages 15-24: *total:* 37.2%
male: 39.6%
female: 34.3% (2019 est.)
country comparison to the world: 20

Population below poverty line: 25% (2016 est.)

Gini Index coefficient - distribution of family income: 51.2 (2016 est.)
country comparison to the world: 12

Budget: *revenues:* 398.2 million (2017 est.)
expenditures: 392.8 million (2017 est.)

Budget surplus (+) or deficit (-): 0.3% (of GDP) (2017 est.)
country comparison to the world: 41

Public debt: 70.7% of GDP (2017 est.)
69.2% of GDP (2016 est.)
country comparison to the world: 50

Taxes and other revenues: 23.6% (of GDP) (2017 est.)
country comparison to the world: 125

Fiscal year: 1 April - 31 March

Current account balance: $21 million (2017 est.)
-$31 million (2016 est.)
country comparison to the world: 60

Exports: $1.22 billion (2018 est.) note: data are in current year dollars
$188.2 million (2016 est.)
country comparison to the world: 171

Exports - partners: United States 29%, Uruguay 16%, Barbados 8%, Trinidad and Tobago 5.5%, United Kingdom 6%, Dominica 6%, Guyana 5%, France 5% (2019)

Exports - commodities: crude petroleum, beer, jewelry, bananas, refined petroleum, rum (2019)

Imports: $1 billion (2018 est.) note: data are in current year dollars
$575.9 million (2016 est.)
country comparison to the world: 189

Imports - partners: Colombia 46%, United States 30%, Trinidad and Tobago 5% (2019)

Imports - commodities: crude petroleum, refined petroleum, cars, poultry meats, natural gas (2019)

Reserves of foreign exchange and gold: $321.8 million (31 December 2017 est.)
$320.7 million (31 December 2016 est.)
country comparison to the world: 166

Debt - external: $570.6 million (31 December 2017 est.)
$529 million (31 December 2015 est.)
country comparison to the world: 176

Exchange rates: East Caribbean dollars (XCD) per US dollar -
2.7 (2017 est.)
2.7 (2016 est.)
2.7 (2015 est.)
2.7 (2014 est.)
2.7 (2013 est.)

ENERGY

Electricity access: *electrification - total population:* 99.5% (2018)
electrification - urban areas: 97.5% (2018)
electrification - rural areas: 99.9% (2018)

Electricity: *installed generating capacity:* 92,000 kW (2020 est.)
consumption: 322.506 million kWh (2019 est.)
exports: 0 kWh (2020 est.)
imports: 0 kWh (2020 est.)
transmission/distribution losses: 27.568 million kWh (2019 est.)

Electricity generation sources: *fossil fuels:* 99.1% of total installed capacity (2020 est.)
solar: 1% of total installed capacity (2020 est.)

Petroleum: *total petroleum production:* 0 bbl/day (2021 est.)
refined petroleum consumption: 4,500 bbl/day (2019 est.)

Refined petroleum products - imports: 3,113 bbl/day (2015 est.)
country comparison to the world: 184

Carbon dioxide emissions: 659,000 metric tonnes of CO2 (2019 est.)
from petroleum and other liquids: 659,000 metric tonnes of CO2 (2019 est.)
country comparison to the world: 184

Energy consumption per capita: 50.872 million Btu/person (2019 est.)
country comparison to the world: 100

COMMUNICATIONS

Telephones - fixed lines: *total subscriptions:* 38,000 (2020 est.)
subscriptions per 100 inhabitants: 21 (2020 est.)
country comparison to the world: 165

Telephones - mobile cellular: *total subscriptions:* 203,000 (2020 est.)
subscriptions per 100 inhabitants: 111 (2020 est.)
country comparison to the world: 183

Telecommunication systems: *general assessment:* an adequate system that is automatically switched; good interisland and international connections; broadband access; expanded FttP (Fiber to the Home) and LTE markets; regulatory development; telecom sector contributes to the overall GDP; telecom sector is a growth area (2020)
domestic: fixed-line teledensity is 20 per 100 persons and mobile-cellular teledensity is roughly 102 per 100 persons (2019)
international: country code - 1-758; landing points for the ECFS and Southern Caribbean Fiber submarine cables providing connectivity to numerous Caribbean islands; direct microwave radio relay link with Martinique and Saint Vincent and the Grenadines; tropospheric scatter to Barbados (2019)

Broadcast media: 3 privately owned TV stations; 1 public TV station operating on a cable network; multi-channel cable TV service available; a mix of state-owned and privately owned broadcasters operate nearly 25 radio stations including repeater transmission stations (2019)

Internet country code: .lc

Internet users: *total:* 97,323 (2020 est.)
percent of population: 53% (2020 est.)
country comparison to the world: 181

Broadband - fixed subscriptions: *total:* 33,000 (2020 est.)
subscriptions per 100 inhabitants: 18 (2020 est.)
country comparison to the world: 149

TRANSPORTATION

Civil aircraft registration country code prefix: J6

Airports: *total:* 2 (2021)
country comparison to the world: 203

Airports - with paved runways: *total:* 2
2,438 to 3,047 m: 1
1,524 to 2,437 m: 1 (2021)

Roadways: *total:* 1,210 km (2011)
paved: 847 km (2011)
unpaved: 363 km (2011)
country comparison to the world: 179

Ports and terminals: *major seaport(s):* Castries, Cul-de-Sac, Vieux-Fort

MILITARY AND SECURITY

Military and security forces: no regular military forces; Royal Saint Lucia Police Force (includes Special Service Unit, Marine Unit) (2022)

Military - note: Saint Lucia has been a member of the Caribbean Regional Security System (RSS) since its creation in 1982; RSS signatories (Antigua and Barbuda, Barbados, Dominica, Grenada, Saint Kitts, and Saint Vincent and the Grenadines) agreed to prepare contingency plans and assist one another, on request, in national emergencies, prevention of smuggling, search and rescue, immigration control, fishery protection, customs and excise control, maritime policing duties, protection of off-shore installations, pollution control, national and other disasters, and threats to national security (2022)

TRANSNATIONAL ISSUES

Disputes - international: *Saint Lucia-Venezuela:* joins other Caribbean states to counter Venezuela's claim that Aves Island sustains human habitation, a criterion under UN Convention on the Law of the Sea, which permits Venezuela to extend its EEZ/continental shelf over a large portion of the eastern Caribbean Sea

Illicit drugs: a transit point for cocaine and marijuana destined for North America, Europe, and elsewhere in the Caribbean

SAINT MARTIN

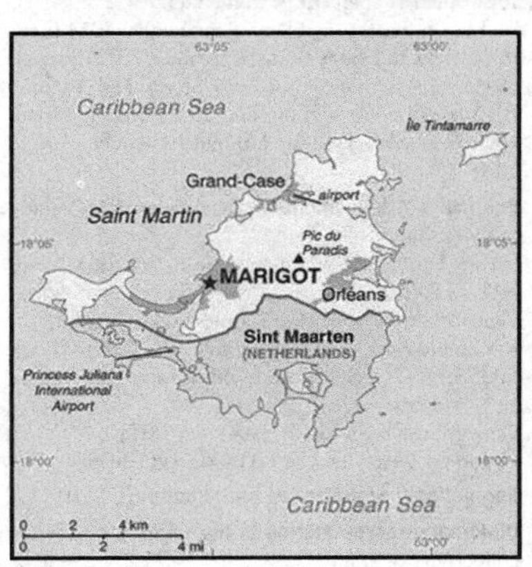

INTRODUCTION

Background: Although sighted by Christopher COLUMBUS in 1493 and claimed for Spain, it was the Dutch who occupied the island in 1631 to exploit its salt deposits. The Spanish retook the island in 1633 but continued to be harassed by the Dutch. The Spanish finally relinquished Saint Martin to the French and Dutch, who divided it between themselves in 1648. Friction between the two sides caused the border to frequently fluctuate over the next two centuries, with the French eventually holding the greater portion of the island (about 61%). The cultivation of sugarcane introduced African slavery to the island in the late 18th century; the practice was not abolished until 1848. The island became a free port in 1939; the tourism industry was dramatically expanded during the 1970s and 1980s. In 2003, the populace of Saint Martin voted to secede from Guadeloupe and in 2007, the northern portion of the island became a French overseas collectivity. In 2010, the southern Dutch portion of the island became the independent nation of Sint Maarten within the Kingdom of the Netherlands. On 6 September 2017, Hurricane Irma passed over the island of Saint Martin causing extensive damage to roads, communications, electrical power, and housing; the UN estimated that 90% of the buildings were damaged or destroyed.

GEOGRAPHY

Location: Caribbean, located in the Leeward Islands (northern) group; French part of the island of Saint Martin in the Caribbean Sea; Saint Martin lies east of the US Virgin Islands

Geographic coordinates: 18 05 N, 63 57 W

Map references: Central America and the Caribbean

Area: *total:* 50 sq km
land: 50 sq km
water: negligible
country comparison to the world: 231

Area - comparative: more than one-third the size of Washington, DC

Land boundaries: *total:* 16 km
border countries (1): Sint Maarten 16 km

Coastline: 58.9 km (for entire island)

Climate: temperature averages 27-29 degrees Celsius all year long; low humidity, gentle trade winds, brief, intense rain showers; hurricane season stretches from July to November

Elevation: *highest point:* Pic du Paradis 424 m
lowest point: Caribbean Ocean 0 m

Natural resources: salt

Population distribution: most of the population is found along the coast, with a largest concentrations around the capital Marigot, Orleans, and Grand-Case

Natural hazards: subject to hurricanes from July to November

Geography - note: *note 1:* the southern border is shared with Sint Maarten, a country within the Kingdom of the Netherlands; together, these two entities make up the smallest landmass in the world shared by two self-governing states
note 2: Simpson Bay Lagoon (aka as Simson Bay Lagoon or The Great Pond) is one of the

largest inland lagoons in the West Indies; the border between the French and Dutch halves of the island of Saint Martin runs across the center of the lagoon, which is shared by both of the island's entities

PEOPLE AND SOCIETY

Population: 32,792 (2022 est.)
country comparison to the world: 215

Ethnic groups: Creole (Mulatto), Black, Guadeloupe Mestizo (French-East Asian), White, East Indian, other

Languages: French (official), Dutch, English, Guadeloupian Creole, Haitian Creole, Italian, Martiniquan Creole, Papiamento (dialect of Netherlands Antilles), Spanish
major-language sample(s):
The World Factbook, une source indispensable d'informations de base. (French)

Religions: Roman Catholic, Jehovah's Witness, Protestant, Hindu

Age structure: *0-14 years:* 25.63% (male 4,148/female 4,197)
15-24 years: 10.28% (male 1,647/female 1,701)
25-54 years: 46.2% (male 7,201/female 7,841)
55-64 years: 8.71% (male 1,328/female 1,508)
65 years and over: 9.17% (male 1,305/female 1,680) (2020 est.)

Median age: *total:* 33.3 years
male: 32.5 years
female: 34.1 years (2020 est.)
country comparison to the world: 100

Population growth rate: 0.33% (2022 est.)
country comparison to the world: 164

Birth rate: 14.09 births/1,000 population (2022 est.)
country comparison to the world: 126

Death rate: 4.64 deaths/1,000 population (2022 est.)
country comparison to the world: 205

Net migration rate: -6.13 migrant(s)/1,000 population (2022 est.)
country comparison to the world: 209

Population distribution: most of the population is found along the coast, with a largest concentrations around the capital Marigot, Orleans, and Grand-Case

Sex ratio: *at birth:* 1.04 male(s)/female
0-14 years: 0.99 male(s)/female
15-24 years: 0.97 male(s)/female
25-54 years: 0.91 male(s)/female
55-64 years: 0.89 male(s)/female
65 years and over: 0.61 male(s)/female
total population: 0.92 male(s)/female (2022 est.)

Infant mortality rate: *total:* 6.71 deaths/1,000 live births
male: 7.85 deaths/1,000 live births
female: 5.53 deaths/1,000 live births (2022 est.)
country comparison to the world: 162

Life expectancy at birth: *total population:* 80.58 years
male: 77.48 years
female: 83.81 years (2022 est.)
country comparison to the world: 48

Total fertility rate: 1.8 children born/woman (2022 est.)
country comparison to the world: 146

Drinking water source: *improved: urban:* 100% of population
total: 100% of population

Sanitation facility access: *improved: urban:* 100% of population
total: 100% of population

ENVIRONMENT

Environment - current issues: excessive population pressure (increasing settlement); waste management; salinity intrusions into the mainland of the island; fresh water supply is dependent on desalination of sea water; over-exploitation of marine resources (reef fisheries, coral and shell); indiscriminate anchoring of boats damages coral reefs, causing underwater pollution and sedimentation

Climate: temperature averages 27-29 degrees Celsius all year long; low humidity, gentle trade winds, brief, intense rain showers; hurricane season stretches from July to November

Waste and recycling: *municipal solid waste generated annually:* 15,480 tons (2012 est.)

GOVERNMENT

Country name: *conventional long form:* Overseas Collectivity of Saint Martin
conventional short form: Saint Martin
local long form: Collectivite d'outre mer de Saint-Martin
local short form: Saint-Martin
etymology: explorer Christopher COLUMBUS named the island after Saint MARTIN of Tours because the 11 November 1493 day of discovery was the saint's feast day

Government type: parliamentary democracy (Territorial Council); overseas collectivity of France

Dependency status: overseas collectivity of France
note: the only French overseas collectivity that is part of the EU

Capital: *name:* Marigot
geographic coordinates: 18 04 N, 63 05 W
time difference: UTC-4 (1 hour ahead of Washington, DC, during Standard Time)
etymology: marigot is a French term referring to a body of water, a watercourse, a side-stream, or a tributary rivulet; the name likely refers to a stream at the site of the city's original founding

Independence: none (overseas collectivity of France)

National holiday: Fete de la Federation, 14 July (1790); note - local holiday is Schoelcher Day (Slavery Abolition Day) 12 July (1848), as well as St. Martin's Day, 11 November (1985), which commemorates the discovery of the island by COLUMBUS on Saint Martin's Day, 11 November 1493; the latter holiday celebrated on both halves of the island

Constitution: *history:* 4 October 1958 (French Constitution)
amendments: amendment procedures of France's constitution apply

Legal system: French civil law

Citizenship: see France

Suffrage: 18 years of age, universal

Executive branch: *chief of state:* President Emmanuel MACRON (since 14 May 2017); represented by Prefect Vincent BERTON (since 28 March 2022)
head of government: President of Territorial Council Louis MUSSINGTON (since 3 April 2022); First Vice President Alain RICHARDSON (since 3 April 2022)
cabinet: Executive Council; note - there is also an advisory economic, social, and cultural council
elections/appointments: French president directly elected by absolute majority popular vote in 2 rounds if needed for a 5-year term (eligible for a second term); prefect appointed by French president on the advice of French Ministry of Interior; president of Territorial Council elected by its members for a 5-year term; election last held on 3 April 2022 (next to be held in 2027)
election results:
2022: Louis MUSSINGTON (RSM) elected president; Territorial Council vote - 23 out of 23 votes
2017: Daniel Gibbs elected president: Territorial Council vote - 18 out of 23 votes

Legislative branch: *description:* unicameral Territorial Council (23 seats; members directly elected by absolute majority vote in 2 rounds if needed to serve 5-year terms); Saint Martin elects 1 member to the French Senate and 1 member (shared with Saint Barthelemy) to the French National Assembly
elections:
Territorial Council - first round held on 20 March 2022 (next to be held in March 2027) and second round held on 27 March 2022
election results:
Territorial Council - percent of vote by party (first round) - RSM 25.4%, UD 24.7%, HOPE 17.5%, Saint Martin with You 13.8%, Alternative 11.2%, Future Saint Martin 7.5%; percent of vote by party (second rate) - RSM and Alternative 49.1%, UD 33.3%, HOPE, Saint Martin with You, and Future Saint Martin 17.6%; seats by party - RSM and Alternative 15, UD 5, HOPE, Saint Martin with You, and Future Saint Martin 3; composition - men 13, women 10, percent of women 43.5%

French Senate - held on 28 September 2014 (next to be held not later than September 2020) French National Assembly - last held on 11 and 18 June 2017 (next to be held by June 2022) French Senate - 1 seat: UMP 1 French National Assembly - 1 seat: UMP 1

Political parties and leaders: Alternative [Valerie DAMASEAU]
Future Saint Martin (Avenir Saint Martin) [Yawo NYUIADZI]
Generation Hope or HOPE [Jules CHARVILLE]
Rassemblement Saint-Martinois or RSM [Louis MUSSINGTON] (formerly Movement for Justice and Prosperity or MJP)
Saint Martin with You [James HAMLET]
Union for Democracy or UD [Daniel GIBBS]

International organization participation: UPU

Diplomatic representation in the US: none (overseas collectivity of France)

Diplomatic representation from the US: *embassy:* none (overseas collectivity of France)

Flag description: the flag of France is used

National symbol(s): brown pelican

National anthem: *name:* "O Sweet Saint Martin's Land"
lyrics/music: Gerard KEMPS
note: the song, written in 1958, is used as an unofficial anthem for the entire island (both French and Dutch sides); as a collectivity of France, in addition to the local anthem, "La Marseillaise"

remains official on the French side (see France); as a constituent part of the Kingdom of the Netherlands, in addition to the local anthem, "Het Wilhelmus" remains official on the Dutch side (see Netherlands)

ECONOMY

Economic overview: The economy of Saint Martin centers on tourism with 85% of the labor force engaged in this sector. Over one million visitors come to the island each year with most arriving through the Princess Juliana International Airport in Sint Maarten. The financial sector is also important to Saint Martin's economy as it facilitates financial mediation for its thriving tourism sector. No significant agriculture and limited local fishing means that almost all food must be imported. Energy resources and manufactured goods are also imported, primarily from Mexico and the US. Saint Martin is reported to have one of the highest per capita income in the Caribbean. As with the rest of the Caribbean, Saint Martin's financial sector is having to deal with losing correspondent banking relationships.

In September 2017, Hurricane Irma destroyed 95% of the French side of Saint Martin. Along the coastline of Marigot, the nerve center of the economy, the storm wiped out restaurants, shops, banks and open-air markets impacting more than 36,000 inhabitants.

Real GDP (purchasing power parity): $561.5 million (2005 est.)
country comparison to the world: 212

Real GDP per capita: $19,300 (2005 est.)
country comparison to the world: 89

GDP (official exchange rate): $561.5 million (2005 est.)

GDP - composition, by sector of origin: *agriculture:* 1% (2000)
industry: 15% (2000)
services: 84% (2000)

Industries: tourism, light industry and manufacturing, heavy industry

Labor force: 17,300 (2008 est.)
country comparison to the world: 213

Labor force - by occupation: 85 directly or indirectly employed in tourist industry

Exports - partners: United States 35%, Netherlands 26%, Antigua and Barbuda 21%, France 10% (2019)

Exports - commodities: gold, special use vessels, furniture, scrap aluminum, rum (2019)

Imports - partners: United States 76%, Netherlands 7%, France 7% (2019)

Imports - commodities: jewelry, diamonds, pearls, recreational boats, cars (2019)

Exchange rates: euros (EUR) per US dollar -
0.885 (2017 est.)
0.903 (2016 est.)
0.9214 (2015 est.)
0.885 (2014 est.)
0.7634 (2013 est.)

ENERGY

Electricity access: *electrification - total population:* 100% (2020)

COMMUNICATIONS

Telephones - mobile cellular: *total subscriptions:* 68,840 (2017 est.)
subscriptions per 100 inhabitants: 196 (2019 est.)
country comparison to the world: 198

Telecommunication systems: *general assessment:* fully integrated access; good interisland and international connections; broadband access; expanded FttP (Fiber to the Home) and LTE markets; regulatory development; telecom sector contributes greatly to the overall GDP; telecom sector is a growth area (2020)
domestic: direct dial capability with both fixed and wireless systems (2018)
international: country code - 590; landing points for the SMPR-1, Southern Caribbean Fiber and the SSCS submarine cables providing connectivity to numerous Caribbean islands (2019)

Broadcast media: 1 local TV station; access to about 20 radio stations, including RFO Guadeloupe radio broadcasts via repeater

Internet country code: .mf; note - .gp, the Internet country code for Guadeloupe, and .fr, the Internet country code for France, might also be encountered

Internet users: *total:* 19,300 (March 2022 est.)
percent of population: 48.5% (March 2022 est.)
country comparison to the world: 212

TRANSPORTATION

Airports: *total:* 1 (2021)
country comparison to the world: 234

Airports - with paved runways: *total:* 1
914 to 1,523 m: 1 (2021)

Transportation - note: nearest airport for international flights is Princess Juliana International Airport (SXM) located on Sint Maarten

MILITARY AND SECURITY

Military and security forces: no armed forces; Saint Martin Police Force (Korps Politie Sint Marteen)

Military - note: defense is the responsibility of France

TRANSNATIONAL ISSUES

Disputes - international: none identified

Illicit drugs: transshipment point for cocaine, heroin, and marijuana destined for Puerto Rico and the U.S. Virgin Islands as well as Europe

SAINT PIERRE AND MIQUELON

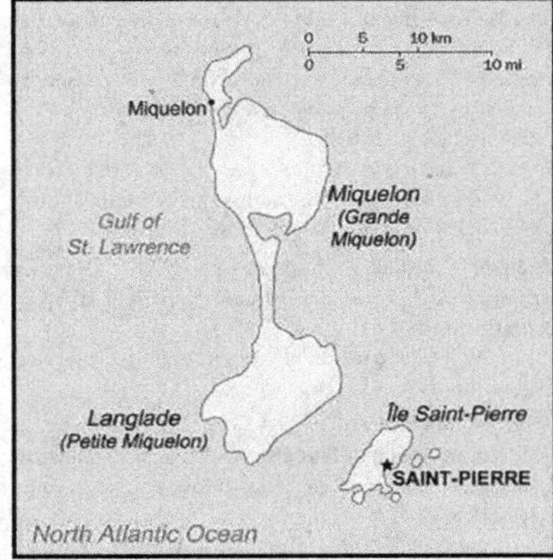

INTRODUCTION

Background: First settled by the French in the early 17th century, the islands represent the sole remaining vestige of France's once vast North American possessions. They attained the status of an overseas collectivity in 2003.

GEOGRAPHY

Location: Northern North America, islands in the North Atlantic Ocean, south of Newfoundland (Canada)

Geographic coordinates: 46 50 N, 56 20 W

Map references: North America

Area: *total:* 242 sq km
land: 242 sq km
water: 0 sq km
note: includes eight small islands in the Saint Pierre and the Miquelon groups
country comparison to the world: 213

Area - comparative: one and half times the size of Washington, DC

Land boundaries: *total:* 0 km

Coastline: 120 km

Maritime claims: *territorial sea:* 12 nm
exclusive economic zone: 200 nm

Climate: cold and wet, with considerable mist and fog; spring and autumn are often windy

Terrain: mostly barren rock

Elevation: *highest point:* Morne de la Grande Montagne 240 m
lowest point: Atlantic Ocean 0 m

Natural resources: fish, deepwater ports

Land use: *agricultural land:* 8.7% (2018 est.)
arable land: 8.7% (2018 est.)
permanent crops: 0% (2018 est.)
permanent pasture: 0% (2018 est.)
forest: 12.5% (2018 est.)
other: 78.8% (2018 est.)

Irrigated land: 0 sq km (2012)

Population distribution: most of the population is found on Saint Pierre Island; a small settlement is located on the north end of Miquelon Island

Natural hazards: persistent fog throughout the year can be a maritime hazard

Geography - note: vegetation scanty; the islands are actually part of the northern Appalachians along with Newfoundland

PEOPLE AND SOCIETY

Population: 5,257 (2022 est.)
country comparison to the world: 227

Nationality: *noun:* Frenchman(men), Frenchwoman(women)
adjective: French

Ethnic groups: Basques and Bretons (French fishermen)

Languages: French (official)
major-language sample(s):
The World Factbook, une source indispensable d'informations de base. (French)

Religions: Roman Catholic 99%, other 1%

Age structure: *0-14 years:* 13.68% (male 370/female 349)
15-24 years: 8.71% (male 240/female 218)
25-54 years: 40% (male 1,039/female 1,100)
55-64 years: 15.52% (male 419/female 397)
65 years and over: 24.1% (male 556/female 711) (2022 est.)

Median age: *total:* 48.5 years
male: 47.9 years
female: 49 years (2020 est.)
country comparison to the world: 3

Population growth rate: -1.2% (2022 est.)
country comparison to the world: 234

Birth rate: 6.47 births/1,000 population (2022 est.)
country comparison to the world: 228

Death rate: 11.22 deaths/1,000 population (2022 est.)
country comparison to the world: 21

Net migration rate: -7.23 migrant(s)/1,000 population (2022 est.)
country comparison to the world: 215

Population distribution: most of the population is found on Saint Pierre Island; a small settlement is located on the north end of Miquelon Island

Urbanization: *urban population:* 90% of total population (2022)
rate of urbanization: 0.75% annual rate of change (2020-25 est.)

Major urban areas - population: 6,000 SAINT-PIERRE (capital) (2018)

Sex ratio: *at birth:* 1.06 male(s)/female
0-14 years: 1.06 male(s)/female
15-24 years: 1.11 male(s)/female
25-54 years: 0.93 male(s)/female
55-64 years: 1.05 male(s)/female
65 years and over: 0.62 male(s)/female
total population: 0.94 male(s)/female (2022 est.)

Infant mortality rate: *total:* 8.16 deaths/1,000 live births
male: 10.12 deaths/1,000 live births
female: 6.09 deaths/1,000 live births (2022 est.)
country comparison to the world: 149

Life expectancy at birth: *total population:* 81.41 years
male: 79.05 years
female: 83.9 years (2022 est.)
country comparison to the world: 41

Total fertility rate: 1.59 children born/woman (2022 est.)
country comparison to the world: 188

Drinking water source: *improved: total:* 91.4% of population
unimproved: total: 8.6% of population (2017 est.)

Sanitation facility access: *improved: total:* 100% of population
unimproved: total: 0% of population (2020)

ENVIRONMENT

Environment - current issues: overfishing; recent test drilling for oil in waters around Saint Pierre and Miquelon may bring future development that would impact the environment

Climate: cold and wet, with considerable mist and fog; spring and autumn are often windy

Land use: *agricultural land:* 8.7% (2018 est.)
arable land: 8.7% (2018 est.)
permanent crops: 0% (2018 est.)
permanent pasture: 0% (2018 est.)
forest: 12.5% (2018 est.)
other: 78.8% (2018 est.)

Urbanization: *urban population:* 90% of total population (2022)
rate of urbanization: 0.75% annual rate of change (2020-25 est.)

GOVERNMENT

Country name: *conventional long form:* Territorial Collectivity of Saint Pierre and Miquelon
conventional short form: Saint Pierre and Miquelon
local long form: Departement de Saint-Pierre et Miquelon
local short form: Saint-Pierre et Miquelon
etymology: Saint-Pierre is named after Saint PETER, the patron saint of fishermen; Miquelon may be a corruption of the Basque name Mikelon

Government type: parliamentary democracy (Territorial Council); overseas collectivity of France

Dependency status: overseas collectivity of France

Capital: *name:* Saint-Pierre
geographic coordinates: 46 46 N, 56 11 W
time difference: UTC-3 (2 hours ahead of Washington, DC, during Standard Time)
daylight saving time: +1hr, begins second Sunday in March; ends first Sunday in November
etymology: named after Saint Peter, the patron saint of fisherman

Administrative divisions: none (territorial overseas collectivity of France); note - there are no first-order administrative divisions as defined by the US Government, but there are 2 communes at the second order - Saint Pierre, Miquelon

Independence: none (overseas collectivity collectivity of France; has been under French control since 1763)

National holiday: Fete de la Federation, 14 July (1790)

Constitution: *history:* 4 October 1958 (French Constitution)
amendments: amendment procedures of France's constitution apply

Legal system: French civil law

Citizenship: see France

Suffrage: 18 years of age; universal

Executive branch: *chief of state:* President Emmanuel MACRON (since 14 May 2017); represented by Prefect Christian POUGET (since 6 January 2021)
head of government: President of Territorial Council Bernard BRIAND (since 13 October 2020)
cabinet: Le Cabinet du Prefet
elections/appointments: French president directly elected by absolute majority popular vote in 2 rounds if needed for a 5-year term (eligible for a second term); election last held on 10 April and 24 April 2022 (next to be held in 2027); prefect appointed by French president on the advice of French Ministry of Interior; Territorial Council president elected by Territorial Council councillors by absolute majority vote; term NA; election last held on 13 October 2020; next election NA
election results:
2020: Bernard BRIAND elected President of Territorial Council; Territorial Council vote - 17 for, 2 abstentions
2017: Stephane LENORMAND elected President of Territorial Council

Legislative branch: *description:* unicameral Territorial Council or Conseil Territorial (19 seats - Saint Pierre 15, Miquelon 4; members directly elected in single-seat constituencies by absolute majority vote in 2 rounds if needed to serve 6-year terms); Saint Pierre and Miquelon indirectly elects 1 senator to the French Senate by an electoral college to serve a 6-year term and directly elects 1 deputy to the French National Assembly by absolute majority vote to serve a 5-year term
elections:
Territorial Council - first round held on 20 March 2022 (next to be held in March 2028); second round held on 27 March 2022
French Senate - last held on 24 September 2017 (next to be held no later than September 2023)
French National Assembly - last held on 11 and 18 June 2017 (next to be held by June 2022)
election results:
Territorial Council - percent of vote by party (first round) - AD 45.9%, Focus on the Future 37%, Together to Build 17.1%; percent of vote by party (second round) - AD 51.8%, Focus on the Future 38.1%, Together to Build 10.1%, seats by party - AD 15, Focus on the Future 4; composition - men NA, women NA, percent of women NA% French Senate - percent of vote by party - NA; seats by party - PS 1 (affiliated with UMP)
French National Assembly - percent of vote by party - NA; seats by party - Ensemble pour l'Avenir 1 (affiliated with PRG); the Republicans (LR) 1

Judicial branch: *highest court(s):* Superior Tribunal of Appeals or Tribunal Superieur d'Appel (composition NA)
judge selection and term of office: judge selection and tenure NA
subordinate courts: NA

Political parties and leaders: Archipelago Tomorrow (Archipel Domain) or AD (affiliated with The Republicans)
Focus on the Future (Cap sur l'Avenir) [Annick GIRARDIN] (affiliated with Left Radical Party)
Together to Build (Ensemble pour Construire) [Karine CLAIREAUX]

International organization participation: UPU, WFTU (NGOs)

Diplomatic representation in the US: none (territorial overseas collectivity of France)

Diplomatic representation from the US: *embassy:* none (territorial overseas collectivity of France)

Flag description: a yellow three-masted sailing ship facing the hoist side rides on a blue background with scattered, white, wavy lines under the ship; a continuous black-over-white wavy line divides the ship from the white wavy lines; on the hoist side, a vertical band is divided into three parts: the top part (called ikkurina) is red with a green diagonal cross extending to the corners overlaid by a white cross dividing the rectangle into four sections; the middle part has a white background with an ermine pattern; the third part has a red background with two stylized yellow lions outlined in black, one above the other; these three heraldic arms represent settlement by colonists from the Basque Country (top), Brittany, and Normandy; the blue on the main portion of the flag symbolizes the Atlantic Ocean and the stylized ship represents the Grande Hermine in which Jacques Cartier "discovered" the islands in 1536
note: the flag of France used for official occasions

National symbol(s): 16th-century sailing ship

National anthem: *note:* as a collectivity of France, "La Marseillaise" is official (see France)

ECONOMY

Economic overview: The inhabitants have traditionally earned their livelihood by fishing and by servicing fishing fleets operating off the coast of Newfoundland. The economy has been declining, however, because of disputes with Canada over fishing quotas and a steady decline in the number of ships stopping at Saint Pierre. The services sector accounted for 86% of GDP in 2010, the last year data is available for. Government employment accounts for than 46% of the GDP, and 78% of the population is working age.

The government hopes an expansion of tourism will boost economic prospects. Fish farming, crab fishing, and agriculture are being developed to diversify the local economy. Recent test drilling for oil may pave the way for development of the energy sector. Trade is the second largest sector in terms of value added created, where it contributes significantly to economic activity. The extractive industries and energy sector is the third largest sector of activity in the archipelago, attributable in part to the construction of a new thermal power plant in 2015.

Real GDP (purchasing power parity): $261.3 million (2015 est.)
$215.3 million (2006 est.)
note: supplemented by annual payments from France of about $60 million
country comparison to the world: 218

Real GDP per capita: $46,200 (2006 est.)
$34,900 (2005)
country comparison to the world: 33

GDP (official exchange rate): $261.3 million (2015 est.)

Inflation rate (consumer prices): 1.5% (2015)
4.5% (2010)
country comparison to the world: 89

GDP - composition, by sector of origin: *agriculture:* 2% (2006 est.)
industry: 15% (2006 est.)
services: 83% (2006 est.)

Agricultural products: vegetables; poultry, cattle, sheep, pigs; fish

Industries: fish processing and supply base for fishing fleets; tourism

Labor force: 4,429 (2015)
country comparison to the world: 223

Labor force - by occupation: *agriculture:* 18%
industry: 41%
services: 41% (1996 est.)

Unemployment rate: 8.7% (2015 est.)
9.9% (2008 est.)
country comparison to the world: 133

Budget: *revenues:* 70 million (1996 est.)
expenditures: 60 million (1996 est.)

Budget surplus (+) or deficit (-): 3.8% (of GDP) (1996 est.)
country comparison to the world: 10

Taxes and other revenues: 26.8% (of GDP) (1996 est.)
country comparison to the world: 104

Fiscal year: calendar year

Exports: $6.641 million (2010 est.)
$5.5 million (2005 est.)
country comparison to the world: 220

Exports - partners: Canada 79%, France 8%, Belgium 6% (2019)

Exports - commodities: crustaceans, fish, medical instruments, electrical parts, pasta (2019)

Imports: $95.35 million (2010 est.)
$68.2 million (2005 est.)
country comparison to the world: 217

Imports - partners: France 69%, Canada 22% (2019)

Imports - commodities: food preparation, packaged medicines, low-voltage protection equipment, cars, computers, iron structures (2019)

Exchange rates: euros (EUR) per US dollar -
0.885 (2017 est.)
0.903 (2016 est.)
0.9214 (2015 est.)
0.885 (2014 est.)
0.7634 (2013 est.)

ENERGY

Electricity: *installed generating capacity:* 26,000 kW (2020 est.)
consumption: 47.267 million kWh (2019 est.)
exports: 0 kWh (2020 est.)
imports: 0 kWh (2020 est.)
transmission/distribution losses: 1.733 million kWh (2019 est.)

Electricity generation sources: *fossil fuels:* 100% of total installed capacity (2020 est.)

Petroleum: *total petroleum production:* 0 bbl/day (2021 est.)
refined petroleum consumption: 600 bbl/day (2019 est.)

Refined petroleum products - imports: 650 bbl/day (2015 est.)
country comparison to the world: 203

Carbon dioxide emissions: 84,000 metric tonnes of CO2 (2019 est.)
from petroleum and other liquids: 84,000 metric tonnes of CO2 (2019 est.)
country comparison to the world: 209

Energy consumption per capita: 0 Btu/person (2019 est.)
country comparison to the world: 209

COMMUNICATIONS

Telephones - fixed lines: *total subscriptions:* 4,800 (2015 est.)
subscriptions per 100 inhabitants: 76 (2015 est.)
country comparison to the world: 205

Telecommunication systems: *general assessment:* adequate (2019)
domestic: fixed-line teledensity 76 per 100 persons (2019)
international: country code - 508; landing point for the St Pierre and Miquelon Cable connecting Saint Pierre & Miquelon and Canada; radiotelephone communication with most countries in the world; satellite earth station - 1 in French domestic satellite system (2019)

Broadcast media: 8 TV stations, all part of the French Overseas Network, and local cable provided by SPM Telecom; 3 of 4 radio stations on St. Pierre and on Miquelon are part of the French Overseas Network (2021)

Internet country code: .pm

Internet users: *total:* 4,500 (2016 est.)
percent of population: 79.5% (2016 est.)
country comparison to the world: 221

TRANSPORTATION

Airports: *total:* 2 (2021)
country comparison to the world: 204

Airports - with paved runways: *total:* 2
1,524 to 2,437 m: 1
914 to 1,523 m: 1 (2021)

Roadways: *total:* 117 km (2009)
paved: 80 km (2009)
unpaved: 37 km (2009)
country comparison to the world: 213

Ports and terminals: *major seaport(s):* Saint-Pierre

MILITARY AND SECURITY

Military - note: defense is the responsibility of France

TRANSNATIONAL ISSUES

Disputes - international: none identified

SAINT VINCENT AND THE GRENADINES

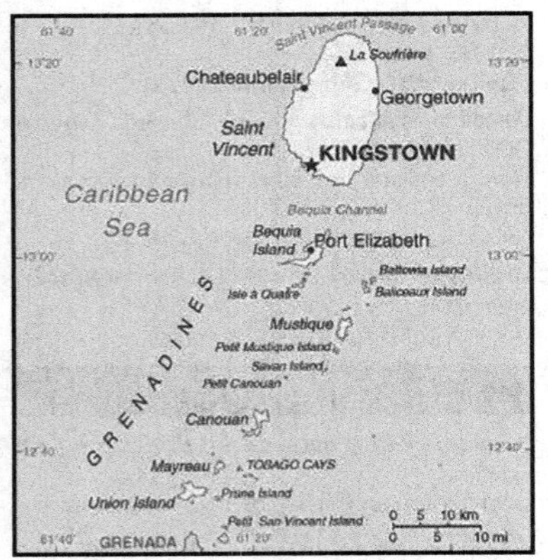

INTRODUCTION

Background: Resistance by native Caribs prevented colonization on Saint Vincent until 1719. Disputed by France and the UK for most of the 18th century, the island was ceded to the latter in 1783. The British prized Saint Vincent due to its fertile soil, which allowed for thriving slave-run plantations of sugar, coffee, indigo, tobacco, cotton, and cocoa. In 1834, the British abolished slavery. Immigration of indentured servants eased the ensuing labor shortage, as did subsequent Portuguese immigrants from Madeira and East Indian laborers. Conditions remained harsh for both former slaves and immigrant agricultural workers, however, as depressed world sugar prices kept the economy stagnant until the early 1900s. The economy then went into a period of decline with many landowners abandoning their estates and leaving the land to be cultivated by liberated slaves. Between 1960 and 1962, Saint Vincent and the Grenadines was a separate administrative unit of the Federation of the West Indies. Autonomy was granted in 1969 and independence in 1979. In April 2021, the explosive eruption of the La Soufrière volcano in the north of Saint Vincent destroyed much of Saint Vincent's most productive agricultural lands. Unlike most of its tourism-dependent neighbors, the Vincentian economy is primarily agricultural. The US provided $4.7 million in humanitarian support after the eruption.

GEOGRAPHY

Location: Caribbean, islands between the Caribbean Sea and North Atlantic Ocean, north of Trinidad and Tobago

Geographic coordinates: 13 15 N, 61 12 W

Map references: Central America and the Caribbean

Area: *total:* 389 sq km (Saint Vincent 344 sq km)
land: 389 sq km
water: 0 sq km
country comparison to the world: 204

Area - comparative: twice the size of Washington, DC

Land boundaries: *total:* 0 km

Coastline: 84 km

Maritime claims: *territorial sea:* 12 nm
contiguous zone: 24 nm
exclusive economic zone: 200 nm
continental shelf: 200 nm

Climate: tropical; little seasonal temperature variation; rainy season (May to November)

Terrain: volcanic, mountainous

Elevation: *highest point:* La Soufriere 1,234 m
lowest point: Caribbean Sea 0 m

Natural resources: hydropower, arable land

Land use: *agricultural land:* 25.6% (2018 est.)
arable land: 12.8% (2018 est.)
permanent crops: 7.7% (2018 est.)
permanent pasture: 5.1% (2018 est.)
forest: 68.7% (2018 est.)
other: 5.7% (2018 est.)

Irrigated land: 10 sq km (2012)

Population distribution: most of the population is concentrated in and around the capital of Kingstown

Natural hazards: hurricanes; La Soufriere volcano on the island of Saint Vincent is a constant threat
volcanism: La Soufriere (1,234 m) on the island of Saint Vincent last erupted in 1979; the island of Saint Vincent is part of the volcanic island arc of the Lesser Antilles that extends from Saba in the north to Grenada in the south

Geography - note: the administration of the islands of the Grenadines group is divided between Saint Vincent and the Grenadines and Grenada; Saint Vincent and the Grenadines is comprised of 32 islands and cays

PEOPLE AND SOCIETY

Population: 100,969 (2022 est.)
country comparison to the world: 195

Nationality: *noun:* Saint Vincentian(s) or Vincentian(s)
adjective: Saint Vincentian or Vincentian

Ethnic groups: African descent 71.2%, mixed 23%, Indigenous 3%, East Indian/Indian 1.1%, European 1.5%, other 0.2% (2012 est.)

Languages: English, Vincentian Creole English, French patois

Religions: Protestant 75% (Pentecostal 27.6%, Anglican 13.9%, Seventh Day Adventist 11.6%, Baptist 8.9%, Methodist 8.7%, Evangelical 3.8%, Salvation Army 0.3%, Presbyterian/Congregational 0.3%), Roman Catholic 6.3%, Rastafarian 1.1%, Jehovah's Witness 0.8%, other 4.7%, none 7.5%, unspecified 4.7% (2012 est.)

Age structure: *0-14 years:* 20.15% (male 10,309/female 10,121)
15-24 years: 14.83% (male 7,582/female 7,451)
25-54 years: 42.63% (male 22,395/female 20,824)
55-64 years: 11.68% (male 6,136/female 5,703)
65 years and over: 10.72% (male 5,167/female 5,702) (2020 est.)

Dependency ratios: *total dependency ratio:* 46.7
youth dependency ratio: 32.1
elderly dependency ratio: 14.5
potential support ratio: 6.9 (2020 est.)

Median age: *total:* 35.3 years
male: 35.4 years
female: 35.1 years (2020 est.)
country comparison to the world: 86

Population growth rate: -0.17% (2022 est.)
country comparison to the world: 209

Birth rate: 12.27 births/1,000 population (2022 est.)
country comparison to the world: 152

Death rate: 7.49 deaths/1,000 population (2022 est.)
country comparison to the world: 107

Net migration rate: -6.47 migrant(s)/1,000 population (2022 est.)
country comparison to the world: 213

Population distribution: most of the population is concentrated in and around the capital of Kingstown

Urbanization: *urban population:* 53.9% of total population (2022)
rate of urbanization: 0.94% annual rate of change (2020-25 est.)

Major urban areas - population: 27,000 KINGSTOWN (capital) (2018)

Sex ratio: *at birth:* 1.03 male(s)/female
0-14 years: 1.02 male(s)/female
15-24 years: 1.02 male(s)/female
25-54 years: 1.07 male(s)/female
55-64 years: 1.08 male(s)/female
65 years and over: 0.73 male(s)/female
total population: 1.04 male(s)/female (2022 est.)

Maternal mortality ratio: 98 deaths/100,000 live births (2017 est.)
country comparison to the world: 70

Infant mortality rate: *total:* 12.87 deaths/1,000 live births
male: 14.56 deaths/1,000 live births
female: 11.13 deaths/1,000 live births (2022 est.)
country comparison to the world: 110

Life expectancy at birth: *total population:* 76.68 years
male: 74.63 years
female: 78.79 years (2022 est.)
country comparison to the world: 101

Total fertility rate: 1.75 children born/woman (2022 est.)
country comparison to the world: 156

Drinking water source: *improved: total:* 95.1% of population
unimproved: total: 4.9% of population (2017 est.)

Current health expenditure: 4.8% of GDP (2019)

Physicians density: 0.66 physicians/1,000 population (2012)

Hospital bed density: 4.3 beds/1,000 population (2016)

Sanitation facility access: *improved: total:* 90.2% of population
unimproved: total: 9.8% of population (2017 est.)

HIV/AIDS - adult prevalence rate: 1.5% (2018 est.)
country comparison to the world: 28

HIV/AIDS - people living with HIV/AIDS: 1,200 (2018)
country comparison to the world: 142

HIV/AIDS - deaths: (2018) <100

Obesity - adult prevalence rate: 23.7% (2016)
country comparison to the world: 64

Alcohol consumption per capita: *total:* 7.48 liters of pure alcohol (2019 est.)
beer: 2.52 liters of pure alcohol (2019 est.)
wine: 0.24 liters of pure alcohol (2019 est.)
spirits: 4.48 liters of pure alcohol (2019 est.)
other alcohols: 0.23 liters of pure alcohol (2019 est.)
country comparison to the world: 52

Education expenditures: 5.7% of GDP (2018 est.)
country comparison to the world: 38

School life expectancy (primary to tertiary education): *total:* 14 years
male: 14 years
female: 15 years (2015)

ENVIRONMENT

Environment - current issues: pollution of coastal waters and shorelines from discharges by pleasure yachts and other effluents; in some areas, pollution is severe enough to make swimming prohibitive; poor land use planning; deforestation; watershed management and squatter settlement control

Environment - international agreements: *party to:* Biodiversity, Climate Change, Climate Change-Kyoto Protocol, Climate Change-Paris Agreement, Comprehensive Nuclear Test Ban, Desertification, Endangered Species, Environmental Modification, Hazardous Wastes, Law of the Sea, Marine Dumping-London Convention, Ozone Layer Protection, Ship Pollution, Whaling
signed, but not ratified: none of the selected agreements

Air pollutants: *particulate matter emissions:* 21.2 micrograms per cubic meter (2016 est.)
carbon dioxide emissions: 0.22 megatons (2016 est.)
methane emissions: 0.09 megatons (2020 est.)

Climate: tropical; little seasonal temperature variation; rainy season (May to November)

Land use: *agricultural land:* 25.6% (2018 est.)
arable land: 12.8% (2018 est.)
permanent crops: 7.7% (2018 est.)
permanent pasture: 5.1% (2018 est.)
forest: 68.7% (2018 est.)
other: 5.7% (2018 est.)

Urbanization: *urban population:* 53.9% of total population (2022)
rate of urbanization: 0.94% annual rate of change (2020-25 est.)

Revenue from forest resources: *forest revenues:* 0.02% of GDP (2018 est.)
country comparison to the world: 144

Revenue from coal: *coal revenues:* 0% of GDP (2018 est.)
country comparison to the world: 159

Waste and recycling: *municipal solid waste generated annually:* 31,561 tons (2015 est.)

Total water withdrawal: *municipal:* 8.5 million cubic meters (2017 est.)
industrial: 2,000 cubic meters (2017 est.)
agricultural: 0 cubic meters (2017 est.)

Total renewable water resources: 100 million cubic meters (2017 est.)

GOVERNMENT

Country name: *conventional long form:* none
conventional short form: Saint Vincent and the Grenadines
etymology: Saint Vincent was named by explorer Christopher COLUMBUS after Saint VINCENT of Saragossa because the 22 January 1498 day of discovery was the saint's feast day

Government type: parliamentary democracy under a constitutional monarchy; a Commonwealth realm

Capital: *name:* Kingstown
geographic coordinates: 13 08 N, 61 13 W
time difference: UTC-4 (1 hour ahead of Washington, DC, during Standard Time)
etymology: an earlier French settlement was renamed Kingstown by the British in 1763 when they assumed control of the island; the king referred to in the name is GEORGE III (r. 1760-1820)

Administrative divisions: 6 parishes; Charlotte, Grenadines, Saint Andrew, Saint David, Saint George, Saint Patrick

Independence: 27 October 1979 (from the UK)

National holiday: Independence Day, 27 October (1979)

Constitution: *history:* previous 1969, 1975; latest drafted 26 July 1979, effective 27 October 1979 (The Saint Vincent Constitution Order 1979)
amendments: proposed by the House of Assembly; passage requires at least two-thirds majority vote of the Assembly membership and assent of the governor general; passage of amendments to constitutional sections on fundamental rights and freedoms, citizen protections, various government functions and authorities, and constitutional amendment procedures requires approval by the Assembly membership, approval in a referendum of at least two thirds of the votes cast, and assent of the governor general

Legal system: English common law

International law organization participation: has not submitted an ICJ jurisdiction declaration; accepts ICCt jurisdiction

Citizenship: *citizenship by birth:* yes
citizenship by descent only: at least one parent must be a citizen of Saint Vincent and the Grenadines
dual citizenship recognized: yes
residency requirement for naturalization: 7 years

Suffrage: 18 years of age; universal

Executive branch: *chief of state:* King CHARLES III (since 8 September 2022); represented by Governor General Susan DOUGAN (since 1 August 2019)
head of government: Prime Minister Ralph E. GONSALVES (since 29 March 2001)
cabinet: Cabinet appointed by the governor general on the advice of the prime minister
elections/appointments: the monarchy is hereditary; governor general appointed by the monarch; following legislative elections, the leader of the majority party usually appointed prime minister by the governor general; deputy prime minister appointed by the governor general on the advice of the prime minister

Legislative branch: *description:* unicameral House of Assembly (23 seats; 15 representatives directly elected in single-seat constituencies by simple majority vote, 6 senators appointed by the governor general, and 2 ex officio members - the speaker of the house and the attorney general; members serve 5-year terms)
elections:
last held on 5 November 2020 (next to be held in 2025)
election results:
percent of vote by party - ULP 49.58%, NDP 50.34%, other 0.8%; seats by party - ULP 9, NDP 6

Judicial branch: *highest court(s):* the Eastern Caribbean Supreme Court (ECSC) is the superior court of the Organization of Eastern Caribbean States; the ECSC - headquartered on St. Lucia - consists of the Court of Appeal - headed by the chief justice and 4 judges - and the High Court with 18 judges; the Court of Appeal is itinerant, traveling to member states on a schedule to hear appeals from the High Court and subordinate courts; High Court judges reside in the member states, with 2 assigned to Saint Vincent and the Grenadines; note - Saint Vincent and the Grenadines is also a member of the Caribbean Court of Justice
judge selection and term of office: chief justice of Eastern Caribbean Supreme Court appointed by Her Majesty, Queen ELIZABETH II; other justices and judges appointed by the Judicial and Legal Services Commission, an independent body of judicial officials; Court of Appeal justices appointed for life with mandatory retirement at age 65; High Court judges appointed for life with mandatory retirement at age 62
subordinate courts: magistrates' courts

Political parties and leaders: New Democratic Party or NDP [Dr. Godwin L. FRIDAY]
SVG Green Party or SVGP [Ivan O'NEAL]
Unity Labor Party or ULP [Dr. Ralph GONSALVES] (formed in 1994 by the coalition of Saint Vincent Labor Party or SVLP and the Movement for National Unity or MNU)

International organization participation: ACP, AOSIS, C, Caricom, CDB, CELAC, FAO, G-77, IBRD, ICAO, ICCt, ICRM, IDA, IFAD, IFRCS, ILO, IMF, IMO, Interpol, IOC, IOM, ISO (subscriber), ITU, MIGA, NAM, OAS, OECS, OPANAL, OPCW, Petrocaribe, UN, UNCTAD, UNESCO, UNIDO, UPU, WFTU (NGOs), WHO, WIPO, WTO

Diplomatic representation in the US: *chief of mission:* Ambassador Lou-Anne Gaylene GILCHRIST (since 18 January 2017)
chancery: 1627 K Street, NW, Suite 1202, Washington, DC 20006
telephone: [1] (202) 364-6730
FAX: [1] (202) 364-6730
email address and website:
mail@embsvg.com
http://wa.embassy.gov.vc/washington/
consulate(s) general: New York

Diplomatic representation from the US: *embassy:* the US does not have an embassy in Saint Vincent and the Grenadines; the US Ambassador to Barbados is accredited to Saint Vincent and the Grenadines

Flag description: three vertical bands of blue (hoist side), gold (double width), and green; the gold band bears three green diamonds arranged in a V pattern, which stands for Vincent; the diamonds recall the islands as "the Gems of the Antilles" and are set slightly lowered in the gold band to reflect the nation's position in the Antilles; blue conveys the colors of a tropical sky and crystal waters, yellow signifies the golden Grenadine sands, and green represents lush vegetation

National symbol(s): Saint Vincent parrot; national colors: blue, gold, green

National anthem: *name:* "St. Vincent! Land So Beautiful!"
lyrics/music: Phyllis Joyce MCCLEAN PUNNETT/ Joel Bertram MIGUEL
note: adopted 1967

ECONOMY

Economic overview: Success of the economy hinges upon seasonal variations in agriculture, tourism, and construction activity, as well as remittances. Much of the workforce is employed in banana production and tourism. Saint Vincent and the Grenadines is home to a small offshore banking sector and continues to fully adopt international regulatory standards.

This lower-middle-income country remains vulnerable to natural and external shocks. The economy has shown some signs of recovery due to increased tourist arrivals, falling oil prices and renewed growth in the construction sector. The much anticipated international airport opened in early 2017 with hopes for increased airlift and tourism activity. The government's ability to invest in social programs and respond to external shocks is constrained by its high public debt burden, which was 67% of GDP at the end of 2013.

Real GDP (purchasing power parity): $1.34 billion (2020 est.)
$1.38 billion (2019 est.)
$1.37 billion (2018 est.)
note: data are in 2017 dollars
country comparison to the world: 202

Real GDP growth rate: 0.7% (2017 est.)
0.8% (2016 est.)
0.8% (2015 est.)
country comparison to the world: 181

Real GDP per capita: $12,100 (2020 est.)
$12,500 (2019 est.)
$12,500 (2018 est.)
note: data are in 2017 dollars
country comparison to the world: 127

GDP (official exchange rate): $785 million (2017 est.)

Inflation rate (consumer prices): 2.2% (2017 est.)
-0.2% (2016 est.)
country comparison to the world: 120

Credit ratings: Moody's rating: B3 (2014)

GDP - composition, by sector of origin: *agriculture:* 7.1% (2017 est.)
industry: 17.4% (2017 est.)
services: 75.5% (2017 est.)

GDP - composition, by end use: *household consumption:* 87.3% (2017 est.)
government consumption: 16.6% (2017 est.)
investment in fixed capital: 10.8% (2017 est.)
investment in inventories: -0.2% (2017 est.)
exports of goods and services: 37.1% (2017 est.)
imports of goods and services: -51.7% (2017 est.)

Agricultural products: bananas, sugar cane, roots/ tubers, plantains, vegetables, fruit, coconuts, sweet potatoes, yams, mangoes/guavas

Industries: tourism; food processing, cement, furniture, clothing, starch

Industrial production growth rate: 2.5% (2017 est.)
country comparison to the world: 118

Labor force: 57,520 (2007 est.)
country comparison to the world: 187

Labor force - by occupation: *agriculture:* 26%
industry: 17%
services: 57% (1980 est.)

Unemployment rate: 18.8% (2008 est.)
country comparison to the world: 185

Budget: *revenues:* 225.2 million (2017 est.)
expenditures: 230 million (2017 est.)

Budget surplus (+) or deficit (-): -0.6% (of GDP) (2017 est.)
country comparison to the world: 66

Public debt: 73.8% of GDP (2017 est.)
82.8% of GDP (2016 est.)
country comparison to the world: 42

Taxes and other revenues: 28.7% (of GDP) (2017 est.)
country comparison to the world: 93

Fiscal year: calendar year

Current account balance: -$116 million (2017 est.)
-$122 million (2016 est.)
country comparison to the world: 90

Exports: $320 million (2018 est.) note: data are in current year dollars
$47.3 million (2016 est.)
country comparison to the world: 198

Exports - partners: Jordan 39%, Singapore 14% (2019)

Exports - commodities: natural gas, drilling platforms and ships, recreational boats, collector's items, eddoes and dasheen (taro), arrowroot starch (2019)

Imports: $450 million (2018 est.) note: data are in current year dollars
$294.6 million (2016 est.)
country comparison to the world: 204

Imports - partners: United States 30%, Trinidad and Tobago 12%, China 8%, United Kingdom 6% (2019)

Imports - commodities: refined petroleum, ships, poultry meats, tug boats, recreational boats (2019)

Reserves of foreign exchange and gold: $182.1 million (31 December 2017 est.)
$192.3 million (31 December 2016 est.)
country comparison to the world: 178

Debt - external: $362.2 million (31 December 2017 est.)
$330.8 million (31 December 2016 est.)
country comparison to the world: 182

Exchange rates: East Caribbean dollars (XCD) per US dollar -
2.7 (2017 est.)
2.7 (2016 est.)
2.7 (2015 est.)
2.7 (2014 est.)
2.7 (2013 est.)

ENERGY

Electricity access: *electrification - total population:* 100% (2020)

Electricity: *installed generating capacity:* 49,000 kW (2020 est.)
consumption: 133.917 million kWh (2019 est.)
exports: 0 kWh (2020 est.)
imports: 0 kWh (2020 est.)
transmission/distribution losses: 11.083 million kWh (2019 est.)

Electricity generation sources: *fossil fuels:* 73.5% of total installed capacity (2020 est.)
solar: 0.7% of total installed capacity (2020 est.)
hydroelectricity: 25.8% of total installed capacity (2020 est.)

Petroleum: *total petroleum production:* 0 bbl/day (2021 est.)
refined petroleum consumption: 1,500 bbl/day (2019 est.)

Refined petroleum products - imports: 1,621 bbl/day (2015 est.)
country comparison to the world: 193

Carbon dioxide emissions: 202,000 metric tonnes of CO2 (2019 est.)
from petroleum and other liquids: 202,000 metric tonnes of CO2 (2019 est.)
country comparison to the world: 202

Energy consumption per capita: 27.821 million Btu/ person (2019 est.)
country comparison to the world: 123

COMMUNICATIONS

Telephones - fixed lines: *total subscriptions:* 12,483 (2020 est.)
subscriptions per 100 inhabitants: 11 (2020 est.)
country comparison to the world: 186

Telephones - mobile cellular: *total subscriptions:* 97,059 (2020 est.)
subscriptions per 100 inhabitants: 87 (2020 est.)
country comparison to the world: 192

Telecommunication systems: *general assessment:* adequate island-wide, fully automatic telephone system; broadband access; expanded FttP (Fiber to the Home) markets; LTE launches; regulatory development; telecom sector contributes greatly to the overall GDP; telecom sector is a growth area (2020)
domestic: fixed-line teledensity exceeds 11 per 100 persons and mobile-cellular teledensity is about 87 per 100 persons (2020)
international: country code - 1-784; landing points for the ECFS, CARCIP and Southern Caribbean Fiber submarine cables providing connectivity to US and Caribbean Islands; connectivity also provided by VHF/UHF radiotelephone from Saint Vincent to Barbados; SHF radiotelephone to Grenada and Saint Lucia; access to Intelsat earth station in Martinique through Saint Lucia (2019)

Broadcast media: St. Vincent and the Grenadines Broadcasting Corporation operates 1 TV station and 5 repeater stations that provide near total coverage to the multi-island state; multi-channel cable TV service available; a partially government-funded national radio service broadcasts on 1 station and has 2 repeater stations; about a dozen privately owned radio stations and repeater stations

Internet country code: .vc

Internet users: *total:* 24,408 (2020 est.)
percent of population: 22% (2020 est.)
country comparison to the world: 208

Broadband - fixed subscriptions: *total:* 24,733 (2020 est.)
subscriptions per 100 inhabitants: 22 (2020 est.)
country comparison to the world: 161

TRANSPORTATION

National air transport system: *number of registered air carriers:* 2 (2020)
inventory of registered aircraft operated by air carriers: 11

Civil aircraft registration country code prefix: J8

Airports: *total:* 6 (2021)
country comparison to the world: 176

Airports - with paved runways: *total:* 5
1,524 to 2,437 m: 1
914 to 1,523 m: 3
under 914 m: 1 (2021)

Airports - with unpaved runways: *total:* 1
under 914 m: 1 (2021)

Merchant marine: *total:* 792
by type: bulk carrier 27, container ship 17, general cargo 155, oil tanker 16, other 577 (2021)
country comparison to the world: 30

Ports and terminals: *major seaport(s):* Kingstown

MILITARY AND SECURITY

Military and security forces: no regular military forces; Royal Saint Vincent and the Grenadines Police Force (RSVPF; includes the Coast Guard, Special Services Unit, Rapid Response Unit, Drug Squad, and Anti-Trafficking Unit) (2022)
note: the RSVPF reports to the minister of national security, a portfolio held by the prime minister

Military - note: the country has been a member of the Caribbean Regional Security System (RSS) since its creation in 1982; RSS signatories (Antigua and Barbuda, Barbados, Dominica, Grenada, Saint Kitts, and Saint Lucia) agreed to prepare contingency plans and assist one another, on request, in national emergencies, prevention of smuggling, search and rescue, immigration control, fishery protection, customs and excise control, maritime policing duties, protection of off-shore installations, pollution control, national and other disasters, and threats to national security (2022)

TRANSNATIONAL ISSUES

Disputes - international: *Saint Vincent and the Grenadines-Venezuela:* joins other Caribbean states to counter Venezuela's claim that Aves Island sustains human habitation, a criterion under UN Convention on the Law of the Sea, which permits Venezuela to extend its EEZ/continental shelf over a large portion of the eastern Caribbean Sea

Illicit drugs: a transit point for cocaine and marijuana destined for North America, Europe, and elsewhere in the Caribbean

SAMOA

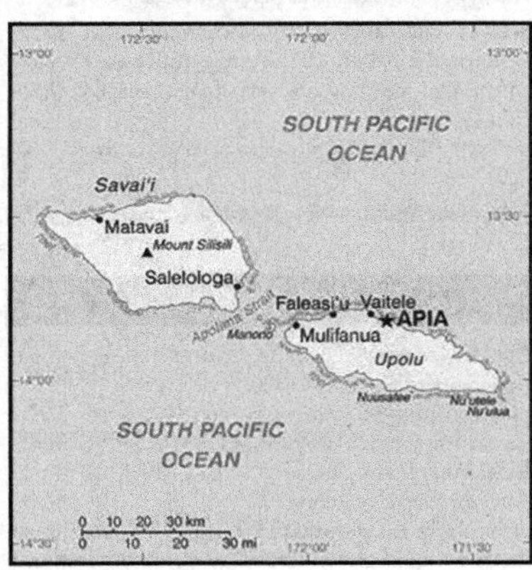

INTRODUCTION

Background: The first Austronesian settlers arrived in Samoa around 1000 B.C., and early Samoans traded and intermarried with Fijian and Tongan nobility. The fa'amatai system of titles and nobility developed, which dominates Samoan politics to this day; all but two seats in the legislature are reserved for matai, or heads of families. Dutch explorer Jacob ROGGEVEEN was the first European to spot the islands in 1722. Christian missionaries arrived in the 1830s, converting most of the population. In the 1850s, Apia became a center for Pacific trading and hosted an American commercial agent and British and German consuls. In 1892, American traders convinced the Samoan king to align his country's date with the US, moving to the east of the International Date Line.

Following the death of the Samoan king in 1841, rival families competed for his titles, devolving into civil war in 1886 with factions getting support from either Germany, the UK, or the US. All three countries sent warships to Apia in 1889, presaging a larger war, but a cyclone destroyed the ships and Malietoa LAUPEPA was installed as king. Upon LAUPEPA's death in 1898, a second civil war over succession broke out. The war ended in 1899 and the Western powers abolished the monarchy, giving the western Samoan islands to Germany and the eastern Samoan islands to the US. The UK abandoned claims in Samoa and received former German territory in the Solomon Islands.

The Mau, a non-violent popular movement to advocate for Samoan independence, formed in 1908. New Zealand annexed Samoa in 1914 after the outbreak of World War I. Opposition to New Zealand's rule quickly grew. In 1918, a New Zealand ship introduced the Spanish flu, infecting 90% of the population and killing more than 20%. In 1929, New Zealand police shot into a crowd of peaceful protestors, killing 11, in an event known as Black Sunday. In 1962, Samoa became the first Polynesian nation to reestablish its independence as Western Samoa but dropped the "Western" from its name in 1997. The Human Rights Protection Party has dominated politics since 1982, especially under Prime Minister Sailele TUILAEPA, who has been in power since 1998.

In the late 2000s, Samoa began making efforts to align more closely with Australia and New Zealand. In 2009, Samoa changed its driving orientation to the left side of the road, in line with other Commonwealth countries. In 2011, Samoa jumped forward one day - skipping December 30 - by moving to the west side of the International Date Line so that it was one hour ahead of New Zealand and three hours ahead of the east coast of Australia, rather than 23 and 21 hours behind, respectively.

GEOGRAPHY

Location: Oceania, group of islands in the South Pacific Ocean, about halfway between Hawaii and New Zealand

Geographic coordinates: 13 35 S, 172 20 W

Map references: Oceania

Area: *total:* 2,831 sq km
land: 2,821 sq km
water: 10 sq km
country comparison to the world: 177

Area - comparative: slightly smaller than Rhode Island

Land boundaries: *total:* 0 km

Coastline: 403 km

Maritime claims: *territorial sea:* 12 nm
contiguous zone: 24 nm
exclusive economic zone: 200 nm

Climate: tropical; rainy season (November to April), dry season (May to October)

Terrain: two main islands (Savaii, Upolu) and several smaller islands and uninhabited islets; narrow coastal plain with volcanic, rugged mountains in interior

Elevation: *highest point:* Mount Silisili 1,857 m
lowest point: Pacific Ocean 0 m

Natural resources: hardwood forests, fish, hydropower

Land use: *agricultural land:* 12.4% (2018 est.)
arable land: 2.8% (2018 est.)
permanent crops: 7.8% (2018 est.)
permanent pasture: 1.8% (2018 est.)
forest: 60.4% (2018 est.)
other: 27.2% (2018 est.)

Irrigated land: 0 sq km (2012)

Population distribution: about three-quarters of the population lives on the island of Upolu

Natural hazards: occasional cyclones; active volcanism
volcanism: Savai'I Island (1,858 m), which last erupted in 1911, is historically active

Geography - note: occupies an almost central position within Polynesia

PEOPLE AND SOCIETY

Population: 206,179 (2022 est.)
country comparison to the world: 184

Nationality: *noun:* Samoan(s)
adjective: Samoan

Ethnic groups: Samoan 96%, Samoan/New Zealander 2%, other 1.9% (2011 est.)
note: data represent the population by country of citizenship

Languages: Samoan (Polynesian) (official) 91.1%, Samoan/English 6.7%, English (official) 0.5%, other 0.2%, unspecified 1.6% (2006 est.)

Religions: Protestant 54.9% (Congregationalist 29%, Methodist 12.4%, Assembly of God 6.8%, Seventh Day Adventist 4.4%, other Protestant 2.3%), Roman Catholic 18.8%, Church of Jesus Christ 16.9%, Worship Centre 2.8%, other Christian 3.6%, other 2.9% (includes Baha'i, Muslim), none 0.2% (2016 est.)

Age structure: *0-14 years:* 29.31% (male 30,825/female 28,900)
15-24 years: 19.61% (male 20,519/female 19,439)
25-54 years: 37.4% (male 39,011/female 37,200)
55-64 years: 7.5% (male 7,780/female 7,505)
65 years and over: 6.18% (male 5,513/female 7,082) (2020 est.)

Dependency ratios: *total dependency ratio:* 73.3
youth dependency ratio: 64.5
elderly dependency ratio: 8.8
potential support ratio: 11.4 (2020 est.)

Median age: *total:* 25.6 years
male: 25.3 years
female: 26 years (2020 est.)
country comparison to the world: 159

Population growth rate: 0.63% (2022 est.)
country comparison to the world: 141

Birth rate: 19.21 births/1,000 population (2022 est.)
country comparison to the world: 74

Death rate: 5.37 deaths/1,000 population (2022 est.)
country comparison to the world: 187

Net migration rate: -7.51 migrant(s)/1,000 population (2022 est.)
country comparison to the world: 218

Population distribution: about three-quarters of the population lives on the island of Upolu

Urbanization: *urban population:* 17.6% of total population (2022)
rate of urbanization: -0.03% annual rate of change (2020-25 est.)

Major urban areas - population: 36,000 APIA (capital) (2018)

Sex ratio: *at birth:* 1.05 male(s)/female
0-14 years: 1.07 male(s)/female
15-24 years: 1.06 male(s)/female
25-54 years: 1.05 male(s)/female
55-64 years: 1.05 male(s)/female
65 years and over: 0.61 male(s)/female
total population: 1.03 male(s)/female (2022 est.)

Maternal mortality ratio: 43 deaths/100,000 live births (2017 est.)
country comparison to the world: 98

Infant mortality rate: *total:* 18 deaths/1,000 live births
male: 21.76 deaths/1,000 live births
female: 14.05 deaths/1,000 live births (2022 est.)
country comparison to the world: 91

Life expectancy at birth: *total population:* 75.19 years
male: 72.28 years
female: 78.25 years (2022 est.)
country comparison to the world: 127

Total fertility rate: 2.42 children born/woman (2022 est.)
country comparison to the world: 73

Contraceptive prevalence rate: 16.6% (2019/20)

Drinking water source: *improved: urban:* 100% of population
rural: 98% of population
total: 98.4% of population
unimproved: urban: 0% of population
rural: 2% of population
total: 1.6% of population (2020 est.)

Current health expenditure: 6.4% of GDP (2019)

Physicians density: 0.6 physicians/1,000 population (2020)

Sanitation facility access: *improved: urban:* 99.5% of population
rural: 99.5% of population
total: 99.5% of population
unimproved: urban: 0.5% of population
rural: 0.5% of population
total: 0.5% of population (2020 est.)

Major infectious diseases: *degree of risk:* high (2020)
food or waterborne diseases: bacterial diarrhea
vectorborne diseases: malaria

Obesity - adult prevalence rate: 47.3% (2016)
country comparison to the world: 8

Alcohol consumption per capita: *total:* 2.18 liters of pure alcohol (2019 est.)
beer: 2.01 liters of pure alcohol (2019 est.)
wine: 0 liters of pure alcohol (2019 est.)
spirits: 0.17 liters of pure alcohol (2019 est.)
other alcohols: 0 liters of pure alcohol (2019 est.)
country comparison to the world: 127

Tobacco use: *total:* 25.3% (2020 est.)
male: 36.1% (2020 est.)
female: 14.5% (2020 est.)
country comparison to the world: 49

Children under the age of 5 years underweight: 3.4% (2019/20)
country comparison to the world: 92

Child marriage: *women married by age 15:* 0.9%
women married by age 18: 7.4%
men married by age 18: 2% (2020 est.)

Education expenditures: 4.8% of GDP (2020 est.)
country comparison to the world: 73

Literacy: *definition:* age 15 and over can read and write
total population: 99.1%
male: 99%
female: 99.2% (2018)

Unemployment, youth ages 15-24: *total:* 31.9%
male: 24.6%
female: 43.4% (2017 est.)

ENVIRONMENT

Environment - current issues: soil erosion, deforestation, invasive species, overfishing

Environment - international agreements: *party to:* Biodiversity, Climate Change, Climate Change-Kyoto Protocol, Climate Change-Paris Agreement, Comprehensive Nuclear Test Ban, Desertification, Endangered Species, Hazardous Wastes, Law of the Sea, Nuclear Test Ban, Ozone Layer Protection, Ship Pollution, Wetlands
signed, but not ratified: none of the selected agreements

Air pollutants: *particulate matter emissions:* 10.56 micrograms per cubic meter (2016 est.)
carbon dioxide emissions: 0.25 megatons (2016 est.)
methane emissions: 0.27 megatons (2020 est.)

Climate: tropical; rainy season (November to April), dry season (May to October)

Land use: *agricultural land:* 12.4% (2018 est.)
arable land: 2.8% (2018 est.)
permanent crops: 7.8% (2018 est.)
permanent pasture: 1.8% (2018 est.)
forest: 60.4% (2018 est.)
other: 27.2% (2018 est.)

Urbanization: *urban population:* 17.6% of total population (2022)
rate of urbanization: -0.03% annual rate of change (2020-25 est.)

Revenue from forest resources: *forest revenues:* 0.27% of GDP (2018 est.)
country comparison to the world: 84

Revenue from coal: *coal revenues:* 0% of GDP (2018 est.)
country comparison to the world: 160

Waste and recycling: *municipal solid waste generated annually:* 27,399 tons (2011 est.)
municipal solid waste recycled annually: 9,864 tons (2013 est.)
percent of municipal solid waste recycled: 36% (2013 est.)

Total renewable water resources: 0 cubic meters (2017 est.)

GOVERNMENT

Country name: *conventional long form:* Independent State of Samoa
conventional short form: Samoa
local long form: Malo Sa'oloto Tuto'atasi o Samoa
local short form: Samoa
former: Western Samoa
etymology: the meaning of Samoa is disputed; some modern explanations are that the "sa" connotes "sacred" and "moa" indicates "center," so the name can mean "Holy Center"; alternatively, some assertions state that it can mean "place of the sacred moa bird" of Polynesian mythology; the name, however, may go back to Proto-Polynesian (PPn) times (before 1000 B.C.); a plausible PPn reconstruction has the first syllable as "sa'a" meaning "tribe or people" and "moa" meaning "deep sea or ocean" to convey the meaning "people of the deep sea"

Government type: parliamentary republic

Capital: *name:* Apia
geographic coordinates: 13 49 S, 171 46 W
time difference: UTC+13 (18 hours ahead of Washington, DC, during Standard Time)
etymology: name derives from the native village around which the capital was constructed in the 1850s; the village still exists within the larger modern capital

Administrative divisions: 11 districts; A'ana, Aiga-i-le-Tai, Atua, Fa'asaleleaga, Gaga'emauga, Gagaifomauga, Palauli, Satupa'itea, Tuamasaga, Va'a-o-Fonoti, Vaisigano

Independence: 1 January 1962 (from New Zealand-administered UN trusteeship)

National holiday: Independence Day Celebration, 1 June (1962); note - 1 January 1962 is the date of independence from the New Zealand-administered UN trusteeship, but it is observed in June

Constitution: *history:* several previous (preindependence); latest 1 January 1962
amendments: proposed as an act by the Legislative Assembly; passage requires at least two-thirds majority vote by the Assembly membership in the third reading - provided at least 90 days have elapsed since the second reading, and assent of the chief of state; passage of amendments affecting constitutional articles on customary land or constitutional amendment procedures also requires at least two-thirds majority approval in a referendum; amended several times, last in 2020

Legal system: mixed legal system of English common law and customary law; judicial review of legislative acts with respect to fundamental rights of the citizen

International law organization participation: has not submitted an ICJ jurisdiction declaration; accepts ICCt jurisdiction

Citizenship: *citizenship by birth:* no
citizenship by descent only: at least one parent must be a citizen of Samoa
dual citizenship recognized: no
residency requirement for naturalization: 5 years

Suffrage: 21 years of age; universal

Executive branch: *chief of state:* TUIMALEALI'IFANO Va'aletoa Sualauvi II (since 21 July 2017)
head of government: Prime Minister FIAME Naomi Mata'afa (since 24 May 2021)
cabinet: Cabinet appointed by the chief of state on the prime minister's advice
elections/appointments: chief of state indirectly elected by the Legislative Assembly to serve a 5-year term (2-term limit); election last held on 23 August 2022 (next to be held in 2027); following legislative elections, the leader of the majority party is usually appointed prime minister by the chief of state, approved by the Legislative Assembly
election results:
TUIMALEALI'IFANO Va'aletoa Sualauvi unanimously reelected by the Legislative Assembly on 23 August 2022

Legislative branch: *description:* unicameral Legislative Assembly or Fono (53 seats for 2021-2026 term); members from 51 single-seat constituencies directly elected by simple majority vote, with a minimum 10% representation of women in the Assembly required; members serve 5-year terms)
elections:
election last held on 9 April 2021 (next election to be held in 2026)
election results:
percent of vote by party - HRPP 55%, FAST 37%, TSP 3%, independents 5%; seats by party – FAST 30, HRPP 22, independents 1; composition - men 47, women 6, percent of women 11.3%
note: on 29 November 2021, the Election Commissioner added two women seats to parliament, bringing the HRPP's total from 20 to 22 seats

Judicial branch: *highest court(s):* Court of Appeal (consists of the chief justice and 2 Supreme Court judges and meets once or twice a year); Supreme Court (consists of the chief justice and several judges)
judge selection and term of office: chief justice appointed by the chief of state upon the advice of the prime minister; other Supreme Court judges appointed by the Judicial Service Commission, a 3-member body chaired by the chief justice and includes the attorney general and an appointee of the Minister of Justice; judges normally serve until retirement at age 68
subordinate courts: District Court; Magistrates' Courts; Land and Titles Courts; village fono or village chief councils

Political parties and leaders: Fa'atuatua i le Atua Samoa ua Tasi or FAST [FIAME Naomi Mata'afa]
Human Rights Protection Party or HRPP [TUILA'EPA Sailele Malielegaoi]
Tautua Samoa Party or TSP [Afualo Wood Uti SALELE]

International organization participation: ACP, ADB, AOSIS, C, FAO, G-77, IBRD, ICAO, ICCt, ICRM, IDA, IFAD, IFC, IFRCS, ILO, IMF, IMO, Interpol, IOC, IPU, ITU, ITUC (NGOs), MIGA, OPCW, PIF, Sparteca, SPC, UN, UNCTAD, UNESCO, UNIDO, UPU, WCO, WHO, WIPO, WMO, WTO

Diplomatic representation in the US: *chief of mission:* Ambassador Pa'olelei LUTERU (since 7 July 2021)
chancery: 685 Third Avenue, 44th Street, 11th Floor, Suite 1102, New York, NY 10017
telephone: [1] (212) 599-6196
FAX: [1] (212) 599-0797
email address and website:
samoanymission@outlook.com
https://www.un.int/samoa/samoa/embassy-independent-state-samoa-united-states-america
consulate(s) general: Pago Pago (American Samoa)

Diplomatic representation from the US: *chief of mission:* the US Ambassador to New Zealand is accredited to Samoa
embassy: 5th Floor, Accident Corporation Building, Matafele Apia
mailing address: 4400 Apia Place, Washington DC 20521-4400
telephone: [685] 21-436
FAX: [685] 22-030
email address and website:
ApiaConsular@state.gov
https://ws.usembassy.gov/

Flag description: red with a blue rectangle in the upper hoist-side quadrant bearing five white, five-pointed stars representing the Southern Cross constellation; red stands for courage, blue represents freedom, and white signifies purity
note: similar to the flag of Taiwan

National symbol(s): Southern Cross constellation (five, five-pointed stars); national colors: red, white, blue

National anthem: *name:* "O le Fu'a o le Sa'olotoga o Samoa" (The Banner of Freedom)
lyrics/music: Sauni Liga KURESA
note: adopted 1962; also known as "Samoa Tula'i" (Samoa Arise)

ECONOMY

Economic overview: The economy of Samoa has traditionally been dependent on development aid, family remittances from overseas, tourism, agriculture, and fishing. It has a nominal GDP of $844 million. Agriculture, including fishing, furnishes 90% of exports, featuring fish, coconut oil, nonu products, and taro. The manufacturing sector mainly processes agricultural products. Industry accounts for nearly 22% of GDP while employing less than 6% of the work force. The service sector accounts for nearly two-thirds of GDP and employs approximately 50% of the labor force. Tourism is an expanding sector accounting for 25% of GDP; 132,000 tourists visited the islands in 2013.

The country is vulnerable to devastating storms. In September 2009, an earthquake and the resulting tsunami severely damaged Samoa and nearby American Samoa, disrupting transportation and power generation, and resulting in about 200 deaths. In December 2012, extensive flooding and wind damage from Tropical Cyclone Evan killed four people, displaced over 6,000, and damaged or destroyed an estimated 1,500 homes on Samoa's Upolu Island.

The Samoan Government has called for deregulation of the country's financial sector, encouragement of investment, and continued fiscal discipline, while at the same time protecting the environment. Foreign reserves are relatively healthy and inflation is low, but external debt is approximately 45% of GDP. Samoa became the 155th member of the WTO in May 2012, and graduated from least developed country status in January 2014.

Real GDP (purchasing power parity): $1.25 billion (2020 est.)
$1.28 billion (2019 est.)
$1.24 billion (2018 est.)
note: data are in 2017 dollars
country comparison to the world: 203

Real GDP growth rate: 2.5% (2017 est.)
7.1% (2016 est.)
1.6% (2015 est.)
country comparison to the world: 113

Real GDP per capita: $6,300 (2020 est.)
$6,500 (2019 est.)
$6,300 (2018 est.)
note: data are in 2017 dollars
country comparison to the world: 159

GDP (official exchange rate): $841 million (2017 est.)

Inflation rate (consumer prices): 1.3% (2017 est.)
0.1% (2016 est.)
country comparison to the world: 77

GDP - composition, by sector of origin: *agriculture:* 10.4% (2017 est.)
industry: 23.6% (2017 est.)
services: 66% (2017 est.)

GDP - composition, by end use: *exports of goods and services:* 27.2% (2015 est.)
imports of goods and services: -50.5% (2015 est.)

Agricultural products: coconuts, taro, bananas, yams, tropical fruit, pineapples, mangoes/guavas, papayas, roots/tubers nes, pork

Industries: food processing, building materials, auto parts

Industrial production growth rate: -1.8% (2017 est.)
country comparison to the world: 180

Labor force: 50,700 (2016 est.)
country comparison to the world: 192

Labor force - by occupation: *agriculture:* 65%
industry: 6%
services: 29% (2015 est.)

Unemployment rate: 5.2% (2017 est.)
5.5% (2016 est.)
country comparison to the world: 84

Unemployment, youth ages 15-24: *total:* 31.9%
male: 24.6%
female: 43.4% (2017 est.)
country comparison to the world: 31

Population below poverty line: 20.3% (2013 est.)

Gini Index coefficient - distribution of family income: 38.7 (2013 est.)
country comparison to the world: 70

Budget: *revenues:* 237.3 million (2017 est.)
expenditures: 276.8 million (2017 est.)

Budget surplus (+) or deficit (-): -4.7% (of GDP) (2017 est.)
country comparison to the world: 166

Public debt: 49.1% of GDP (2017 est.)
52.6% of GDP (2016 est.)
country comparison to the world: 103

Taxes and other revenues: 28.2% (of GDP) (2017 est.)
country comparison to the world: 95

Fiscal year: June 1 - May 31

Current account balance: -$19 million (2017 est.)
-$37 million (2016 est.)
country comparison to the world: 72

Exports: $310 million (2018 est.) note: data are in current year dollars
country comparison to the world: 199

Exports - partners: American Samoa 21%, United States 13%, New Zealand 12%, Australia 10%, Tokelau 6%, Taiwan 5% (2019)

Exports - commodities: refined petroleum, fish, fruit juice, coconut oil, beer (2019)

Imports: $430 million (2018 est.) note: data are in current year dollars
$312.6 million (2016 est.)
country comparison to the world: 206

Imports - partners: New Zealand 22%, China 16%, Singapore 13%, United States 10%, Australia 9%, South Korea 8%, Fiji 5% (2019)

Imports - commodities: refined petroleum, iron products, poultry meats, cars, insulated wiring (2019)

Reserves of foreign exchange and gold: $133 million (31 December 2017 est.)
$122.5 million (31 December 2015 est.)
country comparison to the world: 180

Debt - external: $447.2 million (31 December 2013 est.)
country comparison to the world: 179

Exchange rates: tala (SAT) per US dollar -
2.54712 (2020 est.)
2.65534 (2019 est.)
2.57069 (2018 est.)
2.5609 (2014 est.)
2.3318 (2013 est.)

ENERGY

Electricity access: *electrification - total population:* 100% (2020)

Electricity: *installed generating capacity:* 50,000 kW (2020 est.)
consumption: 120.13 million kWh (2019 est.)
exports: 0 kWh (2020 est.)
imports: 0 kWh (2020 est.)
transmission/distribution losses: 15 million kWh (2019 est.)

Electricity generation sources: *fossil fuels:* 72.7% of total installed capacity (2020 est.)
wind: 0.1% of total installed capacity (2020 est.)
hydroelectricity: 27.2% of total installed capacity (2020 est.)

Petroleum: *total petroleum production:* 0 bbl/day (2021 est.)
refined petroleum consumption: 2,500 bbl/day (2019 est.)

Refined petroleum products - imports: 2,363 bbl/day (2015 est.)
country comparison to the world: 187

Carbon dioxide emissions: 355,000 metric tonnes of CO_2 (2019 est.)
from petroleum and other liquids: 355,000 metric tonnes of CO_2 (2019 est.)
country comparison to the world: 192

Energy consumption per capita: 27.111 million Btu/person (2019 est.)
country comparison to the world: 125

COMMUNICATIONS

Telephones - fixed lines: *total subscriptions:* 6,000 (2020 est.)
subscriptions per 100 inhabitants: 3 (2020 est.)
country comparison to the world: 203

Telephones - mobile cellular: *total subscriptions:* 69,000 (2020 est.)
subscriptions per 100 inhabitants: 35 (2020 est.)
country comparison to the world: 197

Telecommunication systems: *general assessment:* Samoa was one of the first Pacific Island countries to establish a regulatory infrastructure and to liberalize its telecom market; the advent of competition in the mobile market saw prices fall by around 50% and network coverage increase to more than 90% of the population; Samoa also boasts one of the highest rates of mobile phone coverage in the Pacific region; the growth of fixed-line internet has been impeded by factors including the high costs for bandwidth, under investment in fixed-line infrastructure; Samoa's telecoms sector has been inhibited by a lack of international connectivity; Samoa has had access to the Samoa-America-Samoa (SAS) cable laid in 2009, this cable has insufficient capacity to meet the country's future bandwidth needs; this issue was addressed with two new submarine cables that became available in 2018 and 2019; combined with the Samoa National Broadband Highway (SNBH), have improved internet data rates and reliability, and have helped to reduce the high costs previously associated with internet access in Samoa; in April 2022, the Samoan government announced its decision to take over control of the Samoa Submarine Cable Company, looking to the cable to generate additional revenue for the state (2022)
domestic: fixed-line roughly 4 per 100 and mobile-cellular teledensity nearly 64 telephones per 100 persons (2019)
international: country code - 685; landing points for the Tui-Samo, Manatua, SAS, and Southern Cross NEXT submarine cables providing connectivity to Samoa, Fiji, Wallis & Futuna, Cook Islands, Niue, French Polynesia, American Samoa, Australia, New Zealand, Kiribati, Los Angeles (US), and Tokelau; satellite earth station - 1 Intelsat (Pacific Ocean) (2019)

Broadcast media: state-owned TV station privatized in 2008; 4 privately owned television broadcast stations; about a half-dozen privately owned radio stations and one state-owned radio station; TV and radio broadcasts of several stations from American Samoa are available (2019)

Internet country code: .ws

Internet users: *total:* 67,012 (2019 est.)
percent of population: 34% (2019 est.)
country comparison to the world: 190

Broadband - fixed subscriptions: *total:* 1,692 (2020 est.)
subscriptions per 100 inhabitants: 1 (2020 est.)
country comparison to the world: 199

TRANSPORTATION

National air transport system: *number of registered air carriers:* 1 (2020)
inventory of registered aircraft operated by air carriers: 4
annual passenger traffic on registered air carriers: 137,770 (2018)

Civil aircraft registration country code prefix: 5W

Airports: *total:* 4 (2021)
country comparison to the world: 187

Airports - with paved runways: *total:* 1
2,438 to 3,047 m: 1 (2021)

Airports - with unpaved runways: *total:* 3
under 914 m: 3 (2021)

Roadways: *total:* 1,150 km (2018)
country comparison to the world: 181

Merchant marine: *total:* 12
by type: general cargo 3, oil tanker 3, other 6 (2021)
country comparison to the world: 152

Ports and terminals: *major seaport(s):* Apia

MILITARY AND SECURITY

Military and security forces: no regular military forces; Samoa Police Force (Ministry of Police, Prisons, and Correction Services) (2022)

Military - note: informal defense ties exist with NZ, which is required to consider any Samoan request for assistance under the 1962 Treaty of Friendship

Samoa has a "shiprider" agreement with the US, which allows local maritime law enforcement officers to embark on US Coast Guard (USCG) and US Navy (USN) vessels, including to board and search vessels suspected of violating laws or regulations within Somoa's designated exclusive economic zone (EEZ) or on the high seas; "shiprider" agreements also enable USCG personnel and USN vessels with embarked USCG law enforcement personnel to work with host nations to protect critical regional resources (2022)

TRANSNATIONAL ISSUES

Disputes - international: none identified

SAN MARINO

INTRODUCTION

Background: Geographically the third-smallest state in Europe (after the Holy See and Monaco), San Marino also claims to be the world's oldest republic. According to tradition, it was founded by a Christian stonemason named MARINUS in A.D. 301. San Marino's foreign policy is aligned with that of the EU, although it is not a member; social and political trends in the republic track closely with those of its larger neighbor, Italy.

GEOGRAPHY

Location: Southern Europe, an enclave in central Italy

Geographic coordinates: 43 46 N, 12 25 E

Map references: Europe

Area: *total:* 61 sq km
land: 61 sq km
water: 0 sq km
country comparison to the world: 228

Area - comparative: about one-third the size of Washington, DC

Land boundaries: *total:* 37 km
border countries (1): Italy 37 km

Coastline: 0 km (landlocked)

Maritime claims: none (landlocked)

Climate: Mediterranean; mild to cool winters; warm, sunny summers

Terrain: rugged mountains

Elevation: *highest point:* Monte Titano 739 m
lowest point: Torrente Ausa 55 m

Natural resources: building stone

Land use: *agricultural land:* 16.7% (2018 est.)
arable land: 16.7% (2018 est.)
permanent crops: 0% (2018 est.)
permanent pasture: 0% (2018 est.)
forest: 0% (2018 est.)
other: 83.3% (2018 est.)

Irrigated land: 0 sq km (2012)

Natural hazards: occasional earthquakes

Geography - note: landlocked; an enclave of (completely surrounded by) Italy; smallest independent state in Europe after the Holy See and Monaco; dominated by the Apennine Mountains

PEOPLE AND SOCIETY

Population: 34,682 (2022 est.)
country comparison to the world: 214

Nationality: *noun:* Sammarinese (singular and plural)
adjective: Sammarinese

Ethnic groups: Sammarinese, Italian

Languages: Italian
major-language sample(s):
L'Almanacco dei fatti del mondo, l'indispensabile fonte per le informazioni di base. (Italian)

Religions: Roman Catholic

Age structure: *0-14 years:* 14.73% (male 2,662/female 2,379)
15-24 years: 11.64% (male 2,091/female 1,894)
25-54 years: 39.12% (male 6,310/female 7,081)
55-64 years: 14.28% (male 2,367/female 2,520)
65 years and over: 20.24% (male 3,123/female 3,805) (2020 est.)

Median age: *total:* 45.2 years
male: 43.9 years
female: 46.3 years (2020 est.)
country comparison to the world: 10

Population growth rate: 0.61% (2022 est.)
country comparison to the world: 143

Birth rate: 8.85 births/1,000 population (2022 est.)
country comparison to the world: 206

Death rate: 8.82 deaths/1,000 population (2022 est.)
country comparison to the world: 65

Net migration rate: 6.11 migrant(s)/1,000 population (2022 est.)
country comparison to the world: 15

Urbanization: *urban population:* 97.7% of total population (2022)
rate of urbanization: 0.41% annual rate of change (2020-25 est.)

Major urban areas - population: 4,000 SAN MARINO (2018)

Sex ratio: *at birth:* 1.09 male(s)/female
0-14 years: 1.1 male(s)/female
15-24 years: 1.13 male(s)/female
25-54 years: 0.9 male(s)/female
55-64 years: 0.92 male(s)/female
65 years and over: 0.7 male(s)/female
total population: 0.93 male(s)/female (2022 est.)

Mother's mean age at first birth: 31.9 years (2019)

Infant mortality rate: *total:* 6.51 deaths/1,000 live births
male: 7.72 deaths/1,000 live births
female: 5.19 deaths/1,000 live births (2022 est.)
country comparison to the world: 166

Life expectancy at birth: *total population:* 83.86 years
male: 81.3 years
female: 86.65 years (2022 est.)
country comparison to the world: 5

Total fertility rate: 1.53 children born/woman (2022 est.)
country comparison to the world: 198

Drinking water source: *improved: total:* 100% of population
unimproved: total: 0% of population (2020)

Current health expenditure: 6.4% of GDP (2019)

Physicians density: 6.11 physicians/1,000 population (2014)

Hospital bed density: 3.8 beds/1,000 population (2012)

Sanitation facility access: *improved: total:* 100% of population
unimproved: total: 0% of population (2020)

Education expenditures: 3.4% of GDP (2019 est.)
country comparison to the world: 134

Literacy: *total population:* 99.9%
male: 99.9%
female: 99.9% (2018)

School life expectancy (primary to tertiary education): *total:* 12 years
male: 13 years
female: 12 years (2020)

Unemployment, youth ages 15-24: *total:* 27.4%
male: 21.4%
female: 36% (2016 est.)

ENVIRONMENT

Environment - current issues: air pollution; urbanization decreasing rural farmlands; water shortage

Environment - international agreements: *party to:* Biodiversity, Climate Change, Climate Change-Kyoto Protocol, Climate Change-Paris Agreement, Comprehensive Nuclear Test Ban, Desertification, Endangered Species, Nuclear Test Ban, Ozone Layer Protection, Whaling
signed, but not ratified: Air Pollution

Air pollutants: *particulate matter emissions:* 13.45 micrograms per cubic meter (2016 est.)
methane emissions: 0.02 megatons (2020 est.)

Climate: Mediterranean; mild to cool winters; warm, sunny summers

Land use: *agricultural land:* 16.7% (2018 est.)
arable land: 16.7% (2018 est.)
permanent crops: 0% (2018 est.)
permanent pasture: 0% (2018 est.)
forest: 0% (2018 est.)
other: 83.3% (2018 est.)

Urbanization: *urban population:* 97.7% of total population (2022)
rate of urbanization: 0.41% annual rate of change (2020-25 est.)

Revenue from forest resources: *forest revenues:* 0% of GDP (2018 est.)
country comparison to the world: 195

Waste and recycling: *municipal solid waste generated annually:* 17,175 tons (2016 est.)
municipal solid waste recycled annually: 7,737 tons (2016 est.)
percent of municipal solid waste recycled: 45.1% (2016 est.)

GOVERNMENT

Country name: *conventional long form:* Republic of San Marino

conventional short form: San Marino
local long form: Repubblica di San Marino
local short form: San Marino
etymology: named after Saint MARINUS, who in A.D. 301 founded the monastic settlement around which the city and later the state of San Marino coalesced

Government type: parliamentary republic

Capital: *name:* San Marino (city)
geographic coordinates: 43 56 N, 12 25 E
time difference: UTC+1 (6 hours ahead of Washington, DC, during Standard Time)
daylight saving time: +1hr, begins last Sunday in March; ends last Sunday in October
etymology: named after Saint MARINUS, who in A.D. 301 founded a monastic settlement around which the city and later the state of San Marino coalesced

Administrative divisions: 9 municipalities (castelli, singular - castello); Acquaviva, Borgo Maggiore, Chiesanuova, Domagnano, Faetano, Fiorentino, Montegiardino, San Marino Citta, Serravalle

Independence: 3 September 301 (traditional founding date)

National holiday: Founding of the Republic (or Feast of Saint Marinus), 3 September (A.D. 301)

Constitution: *history:* San Marino's principal legislative instruments consist of old customs (antiche consuetudini), the Statutory Laws of San Marino (Leges Statutae Sancti Marini), old statutes (antichi statute) from the1600s, Brief Notes on the Constitutional Order and Institutional Organs of the Republic of San Marino (Brevi Cenni sull'Ordinamento Costituzionale e gli Organi Istituzionali della Repubblica di San Marino) and successive legislation, chief among them is the Declaration of the Rights of Citizens and Fundamental Principles of the San Marino Legal Order (Dichiarazione dei Diritti dei Cittadini e dei Principi Fondamentali dell'Ordinamento Sammarinese), approved 8 July 1974
amendments: proposed by the Great and General Council; passage requires two-thirds majority Council vote; Council passage by absolute majority vote also requires passage in a referendum; Declaration of Civil Rights amended several times, last in 2019

Legal system: civil law system with Italian civil law influences

International law organization participation: has not submitted an ICJ jurisdiction declaration; accepts ICCt jurisdiction

Citizenship: *citizenship by birth:* no
citizenship by descent only: at least one parent must be a citizen of San Marino
dual citizenship recognized: no
residency requirement for naturalization: 30 years

Suffrage: 18 years of age; universal

Executive branch: *chief of state:* co-chiefs of state Captain Regent Oscar MONA and Captain Regent Paolo RONDELLI (for the period 1 April 2022 - 1 October 2022)
head of government: Secretary of State for Foreign and Political Affairs Luca BECCARI (since 8 January 2020)
cabinet: Congress of State elected by the Grand and General Council
elections/appointments: co-chiefs of state (captains regent) indirectly elected by the Grand and General Council for a single 6-month term; election last held in September 2021 (next to be held in March 2022); secretary of state for foreign and political affairs indirectly elected by the Grand and General Council for a single 5-year term; election last held on 28 December 2019 (next to be held by November 2024)
election results:
Oscar MINA (PDCS) and Paolo RONDELLI (RETE) elected captains regent; percent of Grand and General Council vote - NA; Luca BECCARI (PDCS) elected secretary of state for foreign and political affairs; percent of Grand and General Council vote - NA
note: the captains regent preside over meetings of the Grand and General Council and its cabinet (Congress of State), which has 7 other members who are selected by the Grand and General Council; assisting the captains regent are 7 secretaries of state; the secretary of state for Foreign Affairs has some prime ministerial roles

Legislative branch: *description:* unicameral Grand and General Council or Consiglio Grande e Generale (60 seats; members directly elected in single- and multi-seat constituencies by list proportional representation vote in 2 rounds if needed; members serve 5-year terms)
elections:
last held on 8 December 2019 (next to be held by 31 December 2024)
election results:
percent of vote by coalition/party - PDCS 35%, Tomorrow in Movement coalition 25% (RETE Movement 18.3%, Domani - Motus Liberi 6.7%), Free San Marino 16.7%, We for the Republic 13.3%, Future Republic 10%; seats by coalition/party - PDCS 21, Tomorrow in Movement coalition 15 (RETE Movement 11, Domani - Motus Liberi 4), Free San Marino 10, We for the Republic 8, Future Republic 6; composition (as of October 2021) - men 40, women 20, percent of women 33.3%

Judicial branch: *highest court(s):* Council of Twelve or Consiglio dei XII (consists of 12 members); note - the College of Guarantors for the Constitutionality and General Norms functions as San Marino's constitutional court
judge selection and term of office: judges elected by the Grand and General Council from among its own to serve 5-year terms
subordinate courts: first instance and first appeal criminal, administrative, and civil courts; Court for the Trust and Trustee Relations; justices of the peace or conciliatory judges

Political parties and leaders: Domani - Modus Liberi or DML [Lorenzo Forcellini REFFI]
Free San Marino (Libera San Marino) or Libera [Luca BOSCHI]
Future Republic or RF [Mario VENTURINI]
I Elect for a New Republic
Party of Socialists and Democrats or PSD [Paride ANDREOLI]
RETE Movement [Gloria ARCANGELONI]
Sammarinese Christian Democratic Party or PDCS [Marco GATTI]
Socialist Party or PS [Alessandro BEVITORI]
Tomorrow in Movement coalition (includes RETE Movement, DML)
We for the Republic [Denise BRONZETTI]

International organization participation: CE, FAO, IAEA, IBRD, ICAO, ICC (NGOs), ICCt, ICRM, IDA, IFRCS, ILO, IMF, IMO, Interpol, IOC, IOM (observer), IPU, ITU, ITUC (NGOs), LAIA (observer), OPCW, OSCE, Schengen Convention (de facto member), UN, UNCTAD, UNESCO, Union Latina, UNWTO, UPU, WHO, WIPO

Diplomatic representation in the US: *chief of mission:* Ambassador Damiano BELEFFI (since 21 July 2017)
chancery: 327 E 50th Street, New York, NY 10022; Embassy address: 1711 North Street NW (2nd Floor), Washington, DC 22036
telephone: [1] (212) 751-1234
[1] (202) 223-2418
[1] (202) 751-1436
FAX: [1] (212) 751-1436
email address and website:
sanmarinoun@gmail.com

Diplomatic representation from the US: *embassy:* the United States does not have an Embassy in San Marino; the US Ambassador to Italy is accredited to San Marino, and the US Consulate General in Florence maintains day-to-day ties

Flag description: two equal horizontal bands of white (top) and light blue with the national coat of arms superimposed in the center; the main colors derive from the shield of the coat of arms, which features three white towers on three peaks on a blue field; the towers represent three castles built on San Marino's highest feature, Mount Titano: Guaita, Cesta, and Montale; the coat of arms is flanked by a wreath, below a crown and above a scroll bearing the word LIBERTAS (Liberty); the white and blue colors are also said to stand for peace and liberty respectively

National symbol(s): three peaks each displaying a tower; national colors: white, blue

National anthem: *name:* "Inno Nazionale della Repubblica" (National Anthem of the Republic)
lyrics/music: no lyrics/Federico CONSOLO
note: adopted 1894; the music for the lyric-less anthem is based on a 10th century chorale piece

National heritage: *total World Heritage Sites:* 1 (cultural)
selected World Heritage Site locales: San Marino Historic Center and Mount Titano

ECONOMY

Economic overview: San Marino's economy relies heavily on tourism, banking, and the manufacture and export of ceramics, clothing, fabrics, furniture, paints, spirits, tiles, and wine. The manufacturing and financial sectors account for more than half of San Marino's GDP. The per capita level of output and standard of living are comparable to those of the most prosperous regions of Italy.

San Marino's economy contracted considerably in the years since 2008, largely due to weakened demand from Italy - which accounts for nearly 90% of its export market - and financial sector consolidation. Difficulties in the banking sector, the global economic downturn, and the sizable decline in tax revenues all contributed to negative real GDP growth. The government adopted measures to counter the downturn, including subsidized credit to businesses and is seeking to shift its growth model away from a reliance on bank and tax secrecy. San Marino does not issue public debt securities; when necessary, it finances deficits by drawing down central bank deposits.

The economy benefits from foreign investment due to its relatively low corporate taxes and low taxes on interest earnings. The income tax rate is also very low, about one-third the average EU level. San Marino continues to work towards harmonizing its fiscal laws with EU and international standards. In September 2009, the OECD removed San Marino from its list of tax havens that have yet to fully adopt global tax standards, and in 2010 San Marino signed Tax Information Exchange Agreements with most major countries. In 2013, the San Marino Government signed a Double Taxation Agreement with Italy, but a referendum on EU membership failed to reach the quorum needed to bring it to a vote.

Real GDP (purchasing power parity): $2.06 billion (2019 est.)
$2.01 billion (2018 est.)
$1.982 billion (2017 est.)
note: data are in 2017 dollars
country comparison to the world: 195

Real GDP growth rate: 1.9% (2017 est.)
2.2% (2016 est.)
0.6% (2015 est.)
country comparison to the world: 142

Real GDP per capita: $60,800 (2019 est.) note: data are in 2017 dollars
$59,600 (2018 est.) note: data are in 2017 dollars
$58,867 (2017 est.)
country comparison to the world: 16

GDP (official exchange rate): $1.643 billion (2017 est.)

Inflation rate (consumer prices): 1% (2017 est.)
0.6% (2016 est.)
country comparison to the world: 66

Credit ratings:

Fitch rating: BB+ (2020)

GDP - composition, by sector of origin: *agriculture:* 0.1% (2009)
industry: 39.2% (2009)
services: 60.7% (2009)

GDP - composition, by end use: *exports of goods and services:* 176.6% (2011)
imports of goods and services: -153.3% (2011)

Agricultural products: wheat, grapes, corn, olives; cattle, pigs, horses, beef, cheese, hides

Industries: tourism, banking, textiles, electronics, ceramics, cement, wine

Industrial production growth rate: -1.1% (2012 est.)
country comparison to the world: 178

Labor force: 21,960 (September 2013 est.)
country comparison to the world: 210

Labor force - by occupation: *agriculture:* 0.2%
industry: 33.5%
services: 66.3% (September 2013 est.)

Unemployment rate: 8.1% (2017 est.)
8.6% (2016 est.)
country comparison to the world: 128

Unemployment, youth ages 15-24: *total:* 27.4%
male: 21.4%
female: 36% (2016 est.)
country comparison to the world: 40

Budget: *revenues:* 667.7 million (2011 est.)
expenditures: 715.3 million (2011 est.)

Budget surplus (+) or deficit (-): -2.9% (of GDP) (2011 est.)
country comparison to the world: 129

Public debt: 24.1% of GDP (2017 est.)
22.5% of GDP (2016 est.)
country comparison to the world: 180

Taxes and other revenues: 40.6% (of GDP) (2011 est.)
country comparison to the world: 36

Fiscal year: calendar year

Current account balance: $0 (2017 est.)
$0 (2016 est.)
country comparison to the world: 66

Exports: $3.827 billion (2011 est.)
$2.576 billion (2010 est.)
country comparison to the world: 135

Exports - partners: Romania 10%, France 9%, United States 8%, Germany 8%, Poland 6%, Brazil 6%, Russia 6%, Austria 6% (2019)

Exports - commodities: industrial washing/bottling machinery, packaged medicines, woodworking machinery, foodstuffs, aircraft (2019)

Imports: $2.551 billion (2011 est.)
$2.132 billion (2010 est.)
country comparison to the world: 163

Imports - partners: Germany 21%, Italy 13%, Poland 10%, France 7%, Spain 7%, Belgium 6%, Romania 6% (2019)

Imports - commodities: electricity, cars, aluminum, footwear, natural gas, iron piping (2019)

Reserves of foreign exchange and gold: $392 million (2014 est.)
$539.3 million (2013 est.)
country comparison to the world: 161

Exchange rates: euros (EUR) per US dollar -
0.885 (2017 est.)
0.903 (2016 est.)
0.9214 (2015 est.)
0.885 (2014 est.)
0.7634 (2013 est.)

ENERGY

Electricity access: *electrification - total population:* 100% (2020)

COMMUNICATIONS

Telephones - fixed lines: *total subscriptions:* 16,000 (2020 est.)
subscriptions per 100 inhabitants: 47 (2020 est.)
country comparison to the world: 181

Telephones - mobile cellular: *total subscriptions:* 39,000 (2020 est.)
subscriptions per 100 inhabitants: 115 (2020 est.)
country comparison to the world: 208

Telecommunication systems: *general assessment:* automatic telephone system completely integrated into Italian system (2018)
domestic: fixed-line a little over 47 per 100 and mobile-cellular teledensity roughly 114 telephones per 100 persons (2019)
international: country code - 378; connected to Italian international network

Broadcast media: state-owned public broadcaster operates 1 TV station and 3 radio stations; receives radio and TV broadcasts from Italy (2019)

Internet country code: .sm

Internet users: *total:* 20,318 (2019 est.)
percent of population: 60% (2019 est.)
country comparison to the world: 211

Broadband - fixed subscriptions: *total:* 11,000 (2020 est.)
subscriptions per 100 inhabitants: 32 (2020 est.)
country comparison to the world: 179

TRANSPORTATION

Civil aircraft registration country code prefix: T7

Roadways: *total:* 292 km (2006)
paved: 292 km (2006)
country comparison to the world: 203

MILITARY AND SECURITY

Military and security forces: Military Corps (National Guard): Guard of the Rock (or Fortress Guard), Uniformed Militia, Guard of the Great and General Council, Corps of the Gendarmerie; Ministry of Internal Affairs: Civil Police Corps (2022)
note: the captains regent oversee the Gendarmerie and National Guard when they are performing duties related to public order and security; the Ministry of Foreign Affairs exercises control over such administrative functions as personnel and equipment, and the courts exercise control over the Gendarmerie when it acts as judicial police

Military service age and obligation: 18 is the legal minimum age for voluntary military service; no conscription; government has the authority to call up all San Marino citizens from 16-60 years of age to serve in the military (2022)

Military - note: defense is the responsibility of Italy

TRANSNATIONAL ISSUES

Disputes - international: none identified

SAO TOME AND PRINCIPE

INTRODUCTION

Background: Portugal discovered and colonized the uninhabited islands in the late 15th century, setting up a sugar-based economy that gave way to coffee and cocoa in the 19th century - all grown with African plantation slave labor, a form of which lingered into the 20th century. While independence was achieved in 1975, democratic reforms were not instituted until the late 1980s. The country held its first free elections in 1991, but frequent internal wrangling between the various political parties precipitated repeated changes in leadership and four failed, non-violent coup attempts in 1995, 1998, 2003, and 2009. In 2012, three opposition parties combined in a no confidence vote to bring down the majority government of former Prime Minister Patrice TROVOADA, but in 2014, legislative elections returned him to the

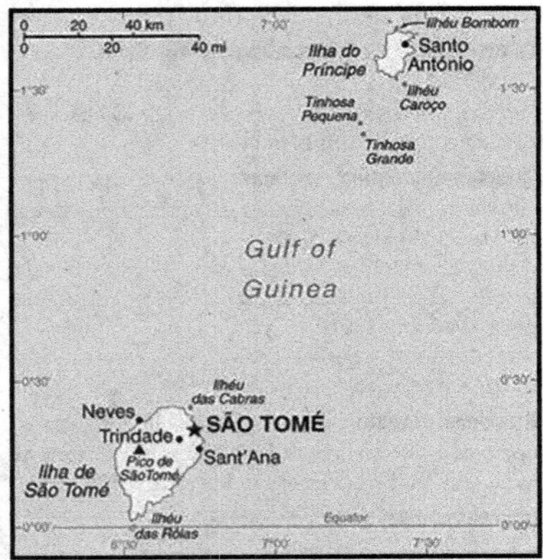

office. President Evaristo CARVALHO, of the same political party as Prime Minister TROVOADA, was elected in September 2016, marking a rare instance in which the positions of president and prime minister were held by the same party. Prime Minister TROVOADA resigned at the end of 2018 and was replaced by Jorge BOM JESUS. Carlos Vila NOVA was elected president in early September 2021 and was inaugurated 2 October 2021. New oil discoveries in the Gulf of Guinea may attract increased attention to the small island nation.

GEOGRAPHY

Location: Central Africa, islands in the Gulf of Guinea, just north of the Equator, west of Gabon

Geographic coordinates: 1 00 N, 7 00 E

Map references: Africa

Area: *total:* 964 sq km
land: 964 sq km
water: 0 sq km
country comparison to the world: 184

Area - comparative: more than five times the size of Washington, DC

Land boundaries: *total:* 0 km

Coastline: 209 km

Maritime claims: *territorial sea:* 12 nm
exclusive economic zone: 200 nm
measured from claimed archipelagic baselines

Climate: tropical; hot, humid; one rainy season (October to May)

Terrain: volcanic, mountainous

Elevation: *highest point:* Pico de Sao Tome 2,024 m
lowest point: Atlantic Ocean 0 m

Natural resources: fish, hydropower

Land use: *agricultural land:* 50.7% (2018 est.)
arable land: 9.1% (2018 est.)
permanent crops: 40.6% (2018 est.)
permanent pasture: 1% (2018 est.)
forest: 28.1% (2018 est.)
other: 21.2% (2018 est.)

Irrigated land: 100 sq km (2012)

Population distribution: Sao Tome, the capital city, has roughly a quarter of the nation's population; Santo Antonio is the largest town on Principe; the northern areas of both islands have the highest population densities as shown in this population distribution map

Natural hazards: flooding

Geography - note: the second-smallest African country (after the Seychelles); the two main islands form part of a chain of extinct volcanoes and both are mountainous

PEOPLE AND SOCIETY

Population: 217,164 (2022 est.)
country comparison to the world: 183

Nationality: *noun:* Sao Tomean(s)
adjective: Sao Tomean

Ethnic groups: Mestico, Angolares (descendants of Angolan slaves), Forros (descendants of freed slaves), Servicais (contract laborers from Angola, Mozambique, and Cabo Verde), Tongas (children of servicais born on the islands), Europeans (primarily Portuguese), Asians (mostly Chinese)

Languages: Portuguese 98.4% (official), Forro 36.2%, Cabo Verdian 8.5%, French 6.8%, Angolar 6.6%, English 4.9%, Lunguie 1%, other (including sign language) 2.4%; note - shares sum to more than 100% because some respondents gave more than one answer on the census; other Portuguese-based Creoles are also spoken (2012 est.)

Religions: Catholic 55.7%, Adventist 4.1%, Assembly of God 3.4%, New Apostolic 2.9%, Mana 2.3%, Universal Kingdom of God 2%, Jehovah's Witness 1.2%, other 6.2%, none 21.2%, unspecified 1% (2012 est.)

Demographic profile: Sao Tome and Principe's youthful age structure – more than 60% of the population is under the age of 25 – and high fertility rate ensure future population growth. Although Sao Tome has a net negative international migration rate, emigration is not a sufficient safety valve to reduce already high levels of unemployment and poverty. While literacy and primary school attendance have improved in recent years, Sao Tome still struggles to improve its educational quality and to increase its secondary school completion rate. Despite some improvements in education and access to healthcare, Sao Tome and Principe has much to do to decrease its high poverty rate, create jobs, and increase its economic growth.

The population of Sao Tome and Principe descends primarily from the islands' colonial Portuguese settlers, who first arrived in the late 15th century, and the much larger number of African slaves brought in for sugar production and the slave trade. For about 100 years after the abolition of slavery in 1876, the population was further shaped by the widespread use of imported unskilled contract laborers from Portugal's other African colonies, who worked on coffee and cocoa plantations. In the first decades after abolition, most workers were brought from Angola under a system similar to slavery. While Angolan laborers were technically free, they were forced or coerced into long contracts that were automatically renewed and extended to their children. Other contract workers from Mozambique and famine-stricken Cape Verde first arrived in the early 20th century under short-term contracts and had the option of repatriation, although some chose to remain in Sao Tome and Principe.

Today's Sao Tomean population consists of mesticos (creole descendants of the European immigrants and African slaves that first inhabited the islands), forros (descendants of freed African slaves), angolares (descendants of runaway African slaves that formed a community in the south of Sao Tome Island and today are fishermen), servicais (contract laborers from Angola, Mozambique, and Cape Verde), tongas (locally born children of contract laborers), and lesser numbers of Europeans and Asians.

Age structure: *0-14 years:* 39.77% (male 42,690/female 41,277)
15-24 years: 21.59% (male 23,088/female 22,487)
25-54 years: 31.61% (male 32,900/female 33,834)
55-64 years: 4.17% (male 4,095/female 4,700)
65 years and over: 2.87% (male 2,631/female 3,420) (2020 est.)

Dependency ratios: *total dependency ratio:* 81
youth dependency ratio: 75.6
elderly dependency ratio: 5.4
potential support ratio: 18.4 (2020 est.)

Median age: *total:* 19.3 years
male: 18.9 years
female: 19.7 years (2020 est.)
country comparison to the world: 204

Population growth rate: 1.48% (2022 est.)
country comparison to the world: 65

Birth rate: 28.19 births/1,000 population (2022 est.)
country comparison to the world: 36

Death rate: 6.2 deaths/1,000 population (2022 est.)
country comparison to the world: 149

Net migration rate: -7.19 migrant(s)/1,000 population (2022 est.)
country comparison to the world: 214

Population distribution: Sao Tome, the capital city, has roughly a quarter of the nation's population; Santo Antonio is the largest town on Principe; the northern areas of both islands have the highest population densities as shown in this population distribution map

Urbanization: *urban population:* 75.8% of total population (2022)
rate of urbanization: 2.96% annual rate of change (2020-25 est.)

Major urban areas - population: 80,000 SAO TOME (capital) (2018)

Sex ratio: *at birth:* 1.03 male(s)/female
0-14 years: 1.03 male(s)/female
15-24 years: 1.03 male(s)/female
25-54 years: 0.97 male(s)/female
55-64 years: 0.88 male(s)/female
65 years and over: 0.7 male(s)/female
total population: 1 male(s)/female (2022 est.)

Mother's mean age at first birth: 19.4 years (2008/09 est.)
note: data represents median age at first birth among women 25-29

Maternal mortality ratio: 130 deaths/100,000 live births (2017 est.)
country comparison to the world: 62

Infant mortality rate: *total:* 44.38 deaths/1,000 live births
male: 47.82 deaths/1,000 live births
female: 40.84 deaths/1,000 live births (2022 est.)
country comparison to the world: 28

Life expectancy at birth: *total population:* 67.06 years
male: 65.44 years
female: 68.72 years (2022 est.)
country comparison to the world: 194

Total fertility rate: 3.56 children born/woman (2022 est.)
country comparison to the world: 36

Contraceptive prevalence rate: 49.7% (2019)

Drinking water source: *improved: urban:* 100% of population

rural: 94% of population
total: 98.5% of population
unimproved: urban: 0% of population
rural: 6% of population
total: 1.5% of population (2020 est.)

Current health expenditure: 5.5% of GDP (2019)

Physicians density: 0.49 physicians/1,000 population (2019)

Hospital bed density: 2.9 beds/1,000 population (2011)

Sanitation facility access: *improved: urban:* 57.1% of population
rural: 42.8% of population
total: 53.4% of population
unimproved: urban: 42.9% of population
rural: 57.2% of population
total: 46.6% of population (2020 est.)

HIV/AIDS - adult prevalence rate: 0.3% (2020 est.)
country comparison to the world: 91

HIV/AIDS - people living with HIV/AIDS: (2020) <1,000

HIV/AIDS - deaths: (2020) <100

Major infectious diseases: *degree of risk:* high (2020)
food or waterborne diseases: bacterial diarrhea, hepatitis A, and typhoid fever
vectorborne diseases: malaria and dengue fever
water contact diseases: schistosomiasis

Obesity - adult prevalence rate: 12.4% (2016)
country comparison to the world: 133

Alcohol consumption per capita: *total:* 4.23 liters of pure alcohol (2019 est.)
beer: 0.42 liters of pure alcohol (2019 est.)
wine: 3.58 liters of pure alcohol (2019 est.)
spirits: 0.23 liters of pure alcohol (2019 est.)
other alcohols: 0 liters of pure alcohol (2019 est.)
country comparison to the world: 92

Tobacco use: *total:* 5.7% (2020 est.)
male: 10.1% (2020 est.)
female: 1.3% (2020 est.)
country comparison to the world: 159

Children under the age of 5 years underweight: 5.4% (2019)
country comparison to the world: 75

Child marriage: *women married by age 15:* 5.4%
women married by age 18: 28%
men married by age 18: 3.1% (2019 est.)

Education expenditures: 5.9% of GDP (2019 est.)
country comparison to the world: 35

Literacy: *definition:* age 15 and over can read and write
total population: 92.8%
male: 96.2%
female: 89.5% (2018)

School life expectancy (primary to tertiary education): *total:* 12 years
male: 12 years
female: 13 years (2015)

Unemployment, youth ages 15-24: *total:* 20.8%

ENVIRONMENT

Environment - current issues: deforestation and illegal logging; soil erosion and exhaustion; inadequate sewage treatment in cities; biodiversity preservation

Environment - international agreements: *party to:* Biodiversity, Climate Change, Climate Change-Kyoto Protocol, Climate Change-Paris Agreement, Desertification, Endangered Species, Environmental Modification, Hazardous Wastes, Law of the Sea, Ozone Layer Protection, Ship Pollution, Wetlands, Whaling
signed, but not ratified: Comprehensive Nuclear Test Ban

Air pollutants: *particulate matter emissions:* 25.66 micrograms per cubic meter (2016 est.)
carbon dioxide emissions: 0.12 megatons (2016 est.)
methane emissions: 0.04 megatons (2020 est.)

Climate: tropical; hot, humid; one rainy season (October to May)

Land use: *agricultural land:* 50.7% (2018 est.)
arable land: 9.1% (2018 est.)
permanent crops: 40.6% (2018 est.)
permanent pasture: 1% (2018 est.)
forest: 28.1% (2018 est.)
other: 21.2% (2018 est.)

Urbanization: *urban population:* 75.8% of total population (2022)
rate of urbanization: 2.96% annual rate of change (2020-25 est.)

Revenue from forest resources: *forest revenues:* 1.9% of GDP (2018 est.)
country comparison to the world: 36

Revenue from coal: *coal revenues:* 0% of GDP (2018 est.)
country comparison to the world: 161

Waste and recycling: *municipal solid waste generated annually:* 25,587 tons (2014 est.)

Total water withdrawal: *municipal:* 14.7 million cubic meters (2017 est.)
industrial: 600,000 cubic meters (2017 est.)
agricultural: 25.6 million cubic meters (2017 est.)

Total renewable water resources: 2.18 billion cubic meters (2017 est.)

GOVERNMENT

Country name: *conventional long form:* Democratic Republic of Sao Tome and Principe
conventional short form: Sao Tome and Principe
local long form: Republica Democratica de Sao Tome e Principe
local short form: Sao Tome e Principe
etymology: Sao Tome was named after Saint THOMAS the Apostle by the Portuguese who discovered the island on 21 December 1470 (or 1471), the saint's feast day; Principe is a shortening of the original Portuguese name of "Ilha do Principe" (Isle of the Prince) referring to the Prince of Portugal to whom duties on the island's sugar crop were paid

Government type: semi-presidential republic

Capital: *name:* Sao Tome
geographic coordinates: 0 20 N, 6 44 E
time difference: UTC 0 (5 hours ahead of Washington, DC, during Standard Time)
etymology: named after Saint Thomas the Apostle

Administrative divisions: 6 districts (distritos, singular - distrito), 1 autonomous region* (regiao autonoma); Agua Grande, Cantagalo, Caue, Lemba, Lobata, Me-Zochi, Principe*

Independence: 12 July 1975 (from Portugal)

National holiday: Independence Day, 12 July (1975)

Constitution: *history:* approved 5 November 1975
amendments: proposed by the National Assembly; passage requires two-thirds majority vote by the Assembly; the Assembly can propose to the president of the republic that an amendment be submitted to a referendum; revised several times, last in 2006

Legal system: mixed legal system of civil law based on the Portuguese model and customary law

International law organization participation: has not submitted an ICJ jurisdiction declaration; non-party state to the ICCt

Citizenship: *citizenship by birth:* no
citizenship by descent only: at least one parent must be a citizen of Sao Tome and Principe
dual citizenship recognized: no
residency requirement for naturalization: 5 years

Suffrage: 18 years of age; universal

Executive branch: *chief of state:* President Carlos Manuel VILA NOVA (since 2 October 2021)
head of government: Prime Minister Patrice TROVOADA (since 11 November 2022)
cabinet: Council of Ministers proposed by the prime minister, appointed by the president
elections/appointments: president directly elected by absolute majority popular vote in 2 rounds if needed for a 5-year term (eligible for a second term); election last held on 18 July 2021 and runoff on 5 September 2021 (next to be held in 2026); prime minister chosen by the National Assembly and approved by the president
election results:
2021: Carlos Manuel VILA NOVA elected president in the second round; percent of vote in the first round - Carlos Manuel VILA NOVA (IDA) 39.5%; Guilherme POSSER DA COSTA (MLSTP-PSD) 20.8%; Delfim NEVES (PCD-GR) 16.9%; Abel BOM JESUS (independent) 3.6%; Maria DAS NEVES (independent) 3.3%; other 15.9%; percent of the vote in the second round - Carlos Manuel VILA NOVA (IDA) 57.5%, Guilherme POSSER DA COSTA (MLSTP-PSD) 42.5%; note - VILA NOVA is scheduled to take office 29 September 2021
2016: Evaristo CARVALHO elected president; percent of vote - Evaristo CARVALHO (ADI) 49.8%, Manuel Pinto DA COSTA (independent) 24.8%, Maria DAS NEVES (MLSTP-PSD) 24.1%; note - first round results for CARVALHO were revised downward from just over 50%, prompting the 7 August runoff; however, on 1 August 2016 DA COSTA withdrew from the runoff, citing voting irregularities, and CARVALHO was declared the winner

Legislative branch: *description:* unicameral National Assembly or Assembleia Nacional (55 seats; members directly elected in multi-seat constituencies by closed party-list proportional representation vote to serve 4-year terms)
elections:
last held on 25 September 2022 (next to be held 30 September 2026)
election results:
percent of vote by party - ADI 46.81%, MLSTP/PSD 32.70%, MCI-PS -PUN 6.56%, BASTA Movement-8.8%, other 5.14%; seats by party - ADI 30, MLSTP-PSD 18, MCI-PS -PUN 5, BASTA Movement 2; composition - men 47, women 8, percent of women 14.5%

Judicial branch: *highest court(s):* Supreme Court or Supremo Tribunal Justica (consists of 5 judges); Constitutional Court or Tribunal Constitucional (consists of 5 judges, 3 of whom are from the Supreme Court)

judge selection and term of office: Supreme Court judges appointed by the National Assembly; judge tenure NA; Constitutional Court judges nominated by the president and elected by the National Assembly for 5-year terms
subordinate courts: Court of First Instance; Audit Court

Political parties and leaders: Union of Democrats for Citizenship and Development and Force for Democratic Change Movement or MDFM–UDD [Carlos Filomeno Agostinho DAS NEVES]
Independent Democratic Action or ADI [Patrice TROVADA]
Movement for the Liberation of Sao Tome and Principe-Social Democratic Party or MLSTP-PSD [Jorge Lopes Bom JESUS]
Party for Democratic Convergence-Reflection Group or PCD-GR [Leonel Mario D'ALVA]
Movement of Independent Citizens of São Tomé and Príncipe [António Monteiro]
other small parties

International organization participation: ACP, AfDB, AOSIS, AU, CD, CEMAC, CPLP, EITI (candidate country), FAO, G-77, IBRD, ICAO, ICRM, IDA, IFAD, IFC, IFRCS, ILO, IMF, IMO, Interpol, IOC, IOM (observer), IPU, ITU, ITUC (NGOs), MIGA, NAM, OIF, OPCW, PCA, UN, UNCTAD, UNESCO, UNIDO, Union Latina, UNWTO, UPU, WCO, WHO, WIPO, WMO, WTO (observer)

Diplomatic representation in the US: *chief of mission:* Ambassador Carlos Filomeno Azevedo Agostinho das NEVES (since 3 December 2013)
chancery: 675 Third Avenue, Suite 1807, New York, NY 10017
telephone: [1] (212) 651-8116
FAX: [1] (212) 651-8117
email address and website:
rdstppmun@gmail.com

Diplomatic representation from the US: *embassy:* the US does not have an embassy in Sao Tome and Principe; the US Ambassador to Gabon is accredited to Sao Tome and Principe
mailing address: 2290 Sao Tome Place, Washington DC 20521-2290

Flag description: three horizontal bands of green (top), yellow (double width), and green with two black five-pointed stars placed side by side in the center of the yellow band and a red isosceles triangle based on the hoist side; green stands for the country's rich vegetation, red recalls the struggle for independence, and yellow represents cocoa, one of the country's main agricultural products; the two stars symbolize the two main islands
note: uses the popular Pan-African colors of Ethiopia

National symbol(s): palm tree; national colors: green, yellow, red, black

National anthem: *name:* "Independencia total" (Total Independence)
lyrics/music: Alda Neves DA GRACA do Espirito Santo/Manuel dos Santos Barreto de Sousa e ALMEIDA
note: adopted 1975

ECONOMY

Economic overview: The economy of São Tomé and Príncipe is small, based mainly on agricultural production, and, since independence in 1975, increasingly dependent on the export of cocoa beans. Cocoa production has substantially declined in recent years because of drought and mismanagement. Sao Tome depends heavily on imports of food, fuels, most manufactured goods, and consumer goods, and changes in commodity prices affect the country's inflation rate. Maintaining control of inflation, fiscal discipline, and increasing flows of foreign direct investment into the nascent oil sector are major economic problems facing the country. In recent years the government has attempted to reduce price controls and subsidies. In 2017, several business-related laws were enacted that aim to improve the business climate.

São Tomé and Príncipe has had difficulty servicing its external debt and has relied heavily on concessional aid and debt rescheduling. In April 2011, the country completed a Threshold Country Program with The Millennium Challenge Corporation to help increase tax revenues, reform customs, and improve the business environment. In 2016, Sao Tome and Portugal signed a five-year cooperation agreement worth approximately $64 million, some of which will be provided as loans. In 2017, China and São Tomé signed a mutual cooperation agreement in areas such as infrastructure, health, and agriculture worth approximately $146 million over five years.

Considerable potential exists for development of tourism, and the government has taken steps to expand tourist facilities in recent years. Potential also exists for the development of petroleum resources in São Tomé and Príncipe's territorial waters in the oil-rich Gulf of Guinea, some of which are being jointly developed in a 60-40 split with Nigeria, but production is at least several years off.

Volatile aid and investment inflows have limited growth, and poverty remains high. Restricteded capacity at the main port increases the periodic risk of shortages of consumer goods. Contract enforcement in the country's judicial system is difficult. The IMF in late 2016 expressed concern about vulnerabilities in the country's banking sector, although the country plans some austerity measures in line with IMF recommendations under their three year extended credit facility. Deforestation, coastal erosion, poor waste management, and misuse of natural resources also are challenging issues.

Real GDP (purchasing power parity): $890 million (2020 est.)
$860 million (2019 est.)
$840 million (2018 est.)
note: data are in 2017 dollars
country comparison to the world: 206

Real GDP growth rate: 3.9% (2017 est.)
4.2% (2016 est.)
3.8% (2015 est.)
country comparison to the world: 76

Real GDP per capita: $4,100 (2020 est.)
$4,000 (2019 est.)
$4,000 (2018 est.)
note: data are in 2017 dollars
country comparison to the world: 183

GDP (official exchange rate): $0 (2018 est.)

Inflation rate (consumer prices): 7.8% (2018 est.)
5.6% (2017 est.)
5.7% (2017 est.)
country comparison to the world: 197

GDP - composition, by sector of origin: *agriculture:* 11.8% (2017 est.)
industry: 14.8% (2017 est.)
services: 73.4% (2017 est.)

GDP - composition, by end use: *household consumption:* 81.4% (2017 est.)
government consumption: 17.6% (2017 est.)
investment in fixed capital: 33.4% (2017 est.)
investment in inventories: 0% (2017 est.)
exports of goods and services: 7.9% (2017 est.)
imports of goods and services: -40.4% (2017 est.)

Agricultural products: plantains, oil palm fruit, coconuts, taro, bananas, fruit, cocoa, yams, cassava, maize

Industries: light construction, textiles, soap, beer, fish processing, timber

Industrial production growth rate: 5% (2017 est.)
country comparison to the world: 57

Labor force: 72,600 (2017 est.)
country comparison to the world: 185

Labor force - by occupation: *agriculture:* 26.1%
industry: 21.4%
services: 52.5% (2014 est.)

Unemployment rate: 12.2% (2017 est.)
12.6% (2016 est.)
country comparison to the world: 167

Unemployment, youth ages 15-24: *total:* 20.8%
country comparison to the world: 72

Population below poverty line: 66.7% (2017 est.)

Gini Index coefficient - distribution of family income: 56.3 (2017 est.)
32.1 (2000 est.)
country comparison to the world: 4

Budget: *revenues:* 103 million (2017 est.)
expenditures: 112.4 million (2017 est.)

Budget surplus (+) or deficit (-): -2.4% (of GDP) (2017 est.)
country comparison to the world: 113

Public debt: 88.4% of GDP (2017 est.)
93.1% of GDP (2016 est.)
country comparison to the world: 27

Taxes and other revenues: 26.2% (of GDP) (2017 est.)
country comparison to the world: 114

Fiscal year: calendar year

Current account balance: -$32 million (2017 est.)
-$23 million (2016 est.)
country comparison to the world: 76

Exports: $50 million (2020 est.) note: data are in current year dollars
$70 million (2019 est.) note: data are in current year dollars
$100 million (2018 est.) note: data are in current year dollars
country comparison to the world: 213

Exports - partners: Singapore 30%, Switzerland 24%, France 11%, Poland 7%, Belgium 7%, United States 5% (2019)

Exports - commodities: gas turbines, cocoa beans, aircraft parts, iron products, chocolate (2019)

Imports: $160 million (2020 est.) note: data are in current year dollars
$190 million (2019 est.) note: data are in current year dollars
$200 million (2018 est.) note: data are in current year dollars
country comparison to the world: 215

Imports - partners: Portugal 41%, Angola 17%, China 8% (2019)

Imports - commodities: refined petroleum, cars, rice, flavored water, postage stamps (2019)

Reserves of foreign exchange and gold: $58.95 million (31 December 2017 est.)
$61.5 million (31 December 2016 est.)
country comparison to the world: 185

Debt - external: $292.9 million (31 December 2017 est.)
$308.5 million (31 December 2016 est.)
country comparison to the world: 184

Exchange rates: dobras (STD) per US dollar -
22,689 (2017 est.)
21,797 (2016 est.)
22,149 (2015 est.)
22,091 (2014 est.)
18,466 (2013 est.)

ENERGY

Electricity access: *electrification - total population:* 71% (2019)
electrification - urban areas: 87% (2019)
electrification - rural areas: 25% (2019)

Electricity: *installed generating capacity:* 28,000 kW (2020 est.)
consumption: 78 million kWh (2019 est.)
exports: 0 kWh (2020 est.)
imports: 0 kWh (2020 est.)
transmission/distribution losses: 11.9 million kWh (2019 est.)

Electricity generation sources: *fossil fuels:* 89.5% of total installed capacity (2020 est.)
hydroelectricity: 10.5% of total installed capacity (2020 est.)

Petroleum: *total petroleum production:* 0 bbl/day (2021 est.)
refined petroleum consumption: 1,200 bbl/day (2019 est.)

Refined petroleum products - imports: 1,027 bbl/day (2015 est.)
country comparison to the world: 201

Carbon dioxide emissions: 173,000 metric tonnes of CO_2 (2019 est.)
from petroleum and other liquids: 173,000 metric tonnes of CO_2 (2019 est.)
country comparison to the world: 206

Energy consumption per capita: 11.636 million Btu/person (2019 est.)
country comparison to the world: 148

COMMUNICATIONS

Telephones - fixed lines: *total subscriptions:* 2,790 (2020 est.)
subscriptions per 100 inhabitants: 1 (2020 est.)
country comparison to the world: 211

Telephones - mobile cellular: *total subscriptions:* 174,203 (2020 est.)
subscriptions per 100 inhabitants: 79 (2020 est.)
country comparison to the world: 187

Telecommunication systems: *general assessment:* local telephone network of adequate quality with most lines connected to digital switches; mobile cellular superior choice to landland; dial-up quality low; broadband expensive (2018)
domestic: fixed-line roughly 1 per 100 and mobile-cellular teledensity roughly 79 telephones per 100 persons (2020)
international: country code - 239; landing points for the Ultramar GE and ACE submarine cables from South Africa to over 20 West African countries and Europe; satellite earth station - 1 Intelsat (Atlantic Ocean) (2019)

Broadcast media: 1 government-owned TV station; 1 government-owned radio station; 3 independent local radio stations authorized in 2005 with 2 operating at the end of 2006; transmissions of multiple international broadcasters are available

Internet country code: .st

Internet users: *total:* 72,323 (2020 est.)
percent of population: 33% (2020 est.)
country comparison to the world: 186

Broadband - fixed subscriptions: *total:* 2,512 (2020 est.)
subscriptions per 100 inhabitants: 1 (2020 est.)
country comparison to the world: 197

TRANSPORTATION

National air transport system: *number of registered air carriers:* 1 (2020)
inventory of registered aircraft operated by air carriers: 1

Civil aircraft registration country code prefix: S9

Airports: *total:* 2 (2021)
country comparison to the world: 205

Airports - with paved runways: *total:* 2
1,524 to 2,437 m: 1
914 to 1,523 m: 1 (2021)

Roadways: *total:* 1,300 km (2018)
paved: 230 km (2018)
unpaved: 1,070 km (2018)
country comparison to the world: 177

Merchant marine: *total:* 22
by type: general cargo 13, oil tanker 2, other 7 (2021)
country comparison to the world: 146

Ports and terminals: *major seaport(s):* Sao Tome

MILITARY AND SECURITY

Military and security forces: Armed Forces of Sao Tome and Principe (Forcas Armadas de Sao Tome e Principe, FASTP): Army, Coast Guard of Sao Tome e Principe (Guarda Costeira de Sao Tome e Principe, GCSTP), Presidential Guard, National Guard (2022)
note: the Army and Coast Guard are responsible for external security while the public security police and judicial police maintain internal security; both the public security police and the military report to the Ministry of Defense and Internal Affairs; the judicial police report to the Ministry of Justice, Public Administration, and Human Rights

Military expenditures: Not available

Military and security service personnel strengths: the FASTP has approximately 500 personnel (2022)

Military equipment inventories and acquisitions: the FASTP has a limited inventory of light weapons (2021)

Military service age and obligation: 18 is the legal minimum age for compulsory military service; 17 is the legal minimum age for voluntary service (2021)

Military - note: the FASTP is one of the smallest militaries in Africa and consists of only a few companies of ground troops and a few small patrol boats (2022)

Maritime threats: the International Maritime Bureau reports the territorial and offshore waters in the Niger Delta and Gulf of Guinea remain a very high risk for piracy and armed robbery of ships; in 2021, there were 34 reported incidents of piracy and armed robbery at sea in the Gulf of Guinea region; although a significant decrease from the total number of 81 incidents in 2020, it included the one hijacking and three of five ships fired upon worldwide; while boarding and attempted boarding to steal valuables from ships and crews are the most common types of incidents, almost a third of all incidents involve a hijacking and/or kidnapping; in 2021, 57 crew members were kidnapped in seven separate incidents in the Gulf of Guinea, representing 100% of kidnappings worldwide; Nigerian pirates in particular are well armed and very aggressive, operating as far as 200 nm offshore; the Maritime Administration of the US Department of Transportation has issued a Maritime Advisory (2022-001 - Gulf of Guinea-Piracy/Armed Robbery/Kidnapping for Ransom) effective 4 January 2022, which states in part, "Piracy, armed robbery, and kidnapping for ransom continue to serve as significant threats to US-flagged vessels transiting or operating in the Gulf of Guinea"

TRANSNATIONAL ISSUES

Disputes - international: none identified

SAUDI ARABIA

INTRODUCTION

Background: Saudi Arabia is the birthplace of Islam and home to Islam's two holiest shrines in Mecca and Medina. The king's official title is the Custodian of the Two Holy Mosques. The modern Saudi state was founded in 1932 by ABD AL-AZIZ bin Abd al-Rahman AL SAUD (Ibn Saud) after a 30-year campaign to unify most of the Arabian Peninsula. One of his male descendants rules the country today, as required by the country's 1992 Basic Law. Following Iraq's invasion of Kuwait in 1990, Saudi Arabia accepted the Kuwaiti royal family and 400,000 refugees while allowing Western and Arab troops to deploy on its soil for the liberation of Kuwait the following year. The continuing presence of foreign troops on Saudi soil after the liberation of Kuwait became a source of tension between the royal family and the public until all operational US troops left the country in 2003. Major terrorist attacks in May and November 2003 spurred a strong ongoing

campaign against domestic terrorism and extremism. US troops returned to the Kingdom in October 2019 after attacks on Saudi oil infrastructure.

From 2005 to 2015, King ABDALLAH bin Abd al-Aziz Al Saud incrementally modernized the Kingdom. Driven by personal ideology and political pragmatism, he introduced a series of social and economic initiatives, including expanding employment and social opportunities for women, attracting foreign investment, increasing the role of the private sector in the economy, and discouraging businesses from hiring foreign workers. These reforms have accelerated under King SALMAN bin Abd al-Aziz, who ascended to the throne in 2015, and has since lifted the Kingdom's ban on women driving, implemented education reforms, funded green initiatives, and allowed cinemas to operate for the first time in decades. Saudi Arabia saw some protests during the 2011 Arab Spring but not the level of bloodshed seen in protests elsewhere in the region. Shia Muslims in the Eastern Province protested primarily against the detention of political prisoners, endemic discrimination, and Bahraini and Saudi Government actions in Bahrain. Riyadh took a cautious but firm approach by arresting some protesters but releasing most of them quickly and by using its state-sponsored clerics to counter political and Islamist activism.

The government held its first-ever elections in 2005 and 2011, when Saudis went to the polls to elect municipal councilors. In December 2015, women were allowed to vote and stand as candidates for the first time in municipal council elections, with 19 women winning seats. After King SALMAN ascended to the throne in 2015, he placed the first next-generation prince, MUHAMMAD BIN NAYIF bin Abd al-Aziz Al Saud, in the line of succession as Crown Prince. He designated his son, MUHAMMAD BIN SALMAN bin Abd al-Aziz Al Saud, as the Deputy Crown Prince. In March 2015, Saudi Arabia led a coalition of 10 countries in a military campaign to restore the legitimate government of Yemen, which had been ousted by Huthi forces allied with former president ALI ABDULLAH al-Salih. The war in Yemen has drawn international criticism for civilian casualties and its effect on the country's dire humanitarian situation. In December 2015, then Deputy Crown Prince MUHAMMAD BIN SALMAN announced Saudi Arabia would lead a 34-nation Islamic Coalition to fight terrorism (it has since grown to 41 nations). In May 2017, Saudi Arabia inaugurated the Global Center for Combatting Extremist Ideology (also known as "Etidal") as part of its ongoing efforts to counter violent extremism. In June 2017, King SALMAN elevated MUHAMMAD BIN SALMAN to Crown Prince. Since then, he has jockeyed for influence with neighboring countries in a bid to be the region's main power broker.

The country remains a leading producer of oil and natural gas and holds about 17% of the world's proven oil reserves as of 2020. The government continues to pursue economic reform and diversification, particularly since Saudi Arabia's accession to the WTO in 2005, and promotes foreign investment in the Kingdom. In April 2016, the Saudi Government announced a broad set of socio-economic reforms, known as Vision 2030. Low global oil prices throughout 2015 and 2016 significantly lowered Saudi Arabia's governmental revenue. In response, the government cut subsidies on water, electricity, and gasoline; reduced government employee compensation packages; and announced limited new land taxes. In coordination with OPEC and some key non-OPEC countries, Saudi Arabia agreed to cut oil output in early 2017 to regulate supply and help elevate global prices. In early 2020, this agreement by the so-called OPEC+ coalition collapsed. Saudi Arabia launched a price war by flooding the market with low-priced oil before returning to the negotiating table to agree to OPEC+'s largest and longest-lasting output cut. This cut helped to buoy prices that had collapsed as a result of the price war and the effect of the COVID-19 pandemic.

GEOGRAPHY

Location: Middle East, bordering the Persian Gulf and the Red Sea, north of Yemen

Geographic coordinates: 25 00 N, 45 00 E

Map references: Middle East

Area: *total:* 2,149,690 sq km
land: 2,149,690 sq km
water: 0 sq km
country comparison to the world: 14

Area - comparative: slightly more than one-fifth the size of the US

Land boundaries: *total:* 4,272 km
border countries (7): Iraq 811 km; Jordan 731 km; Kuwait 221 km; Oman 658 km; Qatar 87 km; UAE 457 km; Yemen 1,307 km

Coastline: 2,640 km

Maritime claims: *territorial sea:* 12 nm
contiguous zone: 18 nm
continental shelf: not specified

Climate: harsh, dry desert with great temperature extremes

Terrain: mostly sandy desert

Elevation: *highest point:* As Sarawat range, 3,000 m
lowest point: Persian Gulf 0 m
mean elevation: 665 m

Natural resources: petroleum, natural gas, iron ore, gold, copper

Land use: *agricultural land:* 80.7% (2018 est.)
arable land: 1.5% (2018 est.)
permanent crops: 0.1% (2018 est.)
permanent pasture: 79.1% (2018 est.)
forest: 0.5% (2018 est.)
other: 18.8% (2018 est.)

Irrigated land: 16,200 sq km (2012)

Major watersheds (area sq km): Indian Ocean drainage: *(Persian Gulf)* Tigris and Euphrates (918,044 sq km)

Major aquifers: Arabian Aquifer System

Population distribution: historically a population that was mostly nomadic or semi-nomadic, the Saudi population has become more settled since petroleum was discovered in the 1930s; most of the economic activities - and with it the country's population - is concentrated in a wide area across the middle of the peninsula, from Ad Dammam in the east, through Riyadh in the interior, to Mecca-Medina in the west near the Red Sea

Natural hazards: frequent sand and dust storms
volcanism: despite many volcanic formations, there has been little activity in the past few centuries; volcanoes include Harrat Rahat, Harrat Khaybar, Harrat Lunayyir, and Jabal Yar

Geography - note: Saudi Arabia is the largest country in the world without a river; extensive coastlines on the Persian Gulf and Red Sea allow for considerable shipping (especially of crude oil) through the Persian Gulf and Suez Canal

PEOPLE AND SOCIETY

Population: 35,354,380 (2022 est.)
note: immigrants make up 38.3% of the total population, according to UN data (2019)
country comparison to the world: 41

Nationality: *noun:* Saudi(s)
adjective: Saudi or Saudi Arabian

Ethnic groups: Arab 90%, Afro-Asian 10%

Languages: Arabic (official)
major-language sample(s):
كتاب حقائق العالم، المصدر الذي لا يمكن الاستغناء عنه للمعلومات الأساسية
(Arabic)

Religions: Muslim (official; citizens are 85-90% Sunni and 10-12% Shia), other (includes Eastern Orthodox, Protestant, Roman Catholic, Jewish, Hindu, Buddhist, and Sikh) (2020 est.)
note: despite having a large expatriate community of various faiths (more than 30% of the population), most forms of public religious expression inconsistent with the government-sanctioned interpretation of Sunni Islam are restricted; non- Muslims are not allowed to have Saudi citizenship and non-Muslim places of worship are not permitted (2013)

Age structure: *0-14 years:* 24.84% (male 4,327,830/female 4,159,242)
15-24 years: 15.38% (male 2,741,371/female 2,515,188)
25-54 years: 50.2% (male 10,350,028/female 6,804,479)
55-64 years: 5.95% (male 1,254,921/female 778,467)
65 years and over: 3.63% (male 657,395/female 584,577) (2020 est.)

Dependency ratios: *total dependency ratio:* 39.3
youth dependency ratio: 34.4
elderly dependency ratio: 4.9
potential support ratio: 20.5 (2020 est.)

Median age: *total:* 30.8 years
male: 33 years
female: 27.9 years (2020 est.)
country comparison to the world: 119

Population growth rate: 1.63% (2022 est.)
country comparison to the world: 60

Birth rate: 14.22 births/1,000 population (2022 est.)

country comparison to the world: 123

Death rate: 3.42 deaths/1,000 population (2022 est.)
country comparison to the world: 222

Net migration rate: 5.52 migrant(s)/1,000 population (2022 est.)
country comparison to the world: 19

Population distribution: historically a population that was mostly nomadic or semi-nomadic, the Saudi population has become more settled since petroleum was discovered in the 1930s; most of the economic activities - and with it the country's population - is concentrated in a wide area across the middle of the peninsula, from Ad Dammam in the east, through Riyadh in the interior, to Mecca-Medina in the west near the Red Sea

Urbanization: *urban population:* 84.7% of total population (2022)
rate of urbanization: 1.69% annual rate of change (2020-25 est.)

Major urban areas - population: 7.538 million RIYADH (capital), 4.781 million Jeddah, 2.115 million Mecca, 1.545 million Medina, 1.305 million Ad Dammam, 860,000 million Hufuf-Mubarraz (2022)

Sex ratio: *at birth:* 1.05 male(s)/female
0-14 years: 1.04 male(s)/female
15-24 years: 1.08 male(s)/female
25-54 years: 1.54 male(s)/female
55-64 years: 1.62 male(s)/female
65 years and over: 0.94 male(s)/female
total population: 1.3 male(s)/female (2022 est.)

Maternal mortality ratio: 17 deaths/100,000 live births (2017 est.)
country comparison to the world: 131

Infant mortality rate: *total:* 12.27 deaths/1,000 live births
male: 13.51 deaths/1,000 live births
female: 10.97 deaths/1,000 live births (2022 est.)
country comparison to the world: 114

Life expectancy at birth: *total population:* 76.65 years
male: 75.07 years
female: 78.32 years (2022 est.)
country comparison to the world: 102

Total fertility rate: 1.92 children born/woman (2022 est.)
country comparison to the world: 121

Contraceptive prevalence rate: 24.6% (2016)

Drinking water source: *improved: total:* 100% of population
unimproved: total: 0% of population (2020 est.)

Current health expenditure: 5.7% of GDP (2019)

Physicians density: 2.74 physicians/1,000 population (2020)

Hospital bed density: 2.2 beds/1,000 population (2017)

Sanitation facility access: *improved: total:* 100% of population
unimproved: total: 0% of population (2020 est.)

HIV/AIDS - adult prevalence rate: (2020 est.) <.1%

HIV/AIDS - people living with HIV/AIDS: 12,000 (2020 est.)
country comparison to the world: 99

HIV/AIDS - deaths: (2020 est.) <200

Obesity - adult prevalence rate: 35.4% (2016)
country comparison to the world: 14

Alcohol consumption per capita: *total:* 0 liters of pure alcohol (2019 est.)
beer: 0 liters of pure alcohol (2019 est.)
wine: 0 liters of pure alcohol (2019 est.)
spirits: 0 liters of pure alcohol (2019 est.)
other alcohols: 0 liters of pure alcohol (2019 est.)
country comparison to the world: 188

Tobacco use: *total:* 14.3% (2020 est.)
male: 26.5% (2020 est.)
female: 2% (2020 est.)
country comparison to the world: 110

Literacy: *definition:* age 15 and over can read and write
total population: 97.6%
male: 98.6%
female: 96% (2020)

School life expectancy (primary to tertiary education): *total:* 16 years
male: 16 years
female: 16 years (2020)

Unemployment, youth ages 15-24: *total:* 27.2%
male: 21.5%
female: 43.8% (2020 est.)

ENVIRONMENT

Environment - current issues: desertification; depletion of underground water resources; the lack of perennial rivers or permanent water bodies has prompted the development of extensive seawater desalination facilities; coastal pollution from oil spills; air pollution; waste management

Environment - international agreements: *party to:* Biodiversity, Climate Change, Climate Change-Kyoto Protocol, Climate Change-Paris Agreement, Desertification, Endangered Species, Hazardous Wastes, Law of the Sea, Marine Dumping-London Protocol, Ozone Layer Protection, Ship Pollution
signed, but not ratified: none of the selected agreements

Air pollutants: *particulate matter emissions:* 78.38 micrograms per cubic meter (2016 est.)
carbon dioxide emissions: 563.45 megatons (2016 est.)
methane emissions: 45.47 megatons (2020 est.)

Climate: harsh, dry desert with great temperature extremes

Land use: *agricultural land:* 80.7% (2018 est.)
arable land: 1.5% (2018 est.)
permanent crops: 0.1% (2018 est.)
permanent pasture: 79.1% (2018 est.)
forest: 0.5% (2018 est.)
other: 18.8% (2018 est.)

Urbanization: *urban population:* 84.7% of total population (2022)
rate of urbanization: 1.69% annual rate of change (2020-25 est.)

Revenue from forest resources: *forest revenues:* 0% of GDP (2018 est.)
country comparison to the world: 196

Revenue from coal: *coal revenues:* 0% of GDP (2018 est.)
country comparison to the world: 162

Waste and recycling: *municipal solid waste generated annually:* 16,125,701 tons (2015 est.)
municipal solid waste recycled annually: 2,418,855 tons (2015 est.)
percent of municipal solid waste recycled: 15% (2015 est.)

Major watersheds (area sq km): Indian Ocean drainage: *(Persian Gulf)* Tigris and Euphrates (918,044 sq km)

Major aquifers: Arabian Aquifer System

Total water withdrawal: *municipal:* 3.15 billion cubic meters (2017 est.)
industrial: 1 billion cubic meters (2017 est.)
agricultural: 19.2 billion cubic meters (2017 est.)

Total renewable water resources: 2.4 billion cubic meters (2017 est.)

GOVERNMENT

Country name: *conventional long form:* Kingdom of Saudi Arabia
conventional short form: Saudi Arabia
local long form: Al Mamlakah al Arabiyah as Suudiyah
local short form: Al Arabiyah as Suudiyah
etymology: named after the ruling dynasty of the country, the House of Saud; the name "Arabia" can be traced back many centuries B.C., the ancient Egyptians referred to the region as "Ar Rabi"

Government type: absolute monarchy

Capital: *name:* Riyadh
geographic coordinates: 24 39 N, 46 42 E
time difference: UTC+3 (8 hours ahead of Washington, DC, during Standard Time)
etymology: the name derives from the Arabic word "riyadh," meaning "gardens," and refers to various oasis towns in the area that merged to form the city

Administrative divisions: 13 regions (manatiq, singular - mintaqah); Al Bahah, Al Hudud ash Shamaliyah (Northern Border), Al Jawf, Al Madinah al Munawwarah (Medina), Al Qasim, Ar Riyad (Riyadh), Ash Sharqiyah (Eastern), 'Asir, Ha'il, Jazan, Makkah al Mukarramah (Mecca), Najran, Tabuk

Independence: 23 September 1932 (unification of the kingdom)

National holiday: Saudi National Day (Unification of the Kingdom), 23 September (1932)

Constitution: *history:* 1 March 1992 - Basic Law of Government, issued by royal decree, serves as the constitutional framework and is based on the Qur'an and the life and traditions of the Prophet Muhammad
amendments: proposed by the king directly or proposed to the king by the Consultative Assembly or by the Council of Ministers; passage by the king through royal decree; Basic Law amended many times, last in 2017

Legal system: Islamic (sharia) legal system with some elements of Egyptian, French, and customary law; note - several secular codes have been introduced; commercial disputes handled by special committees

International law organization participation: has not submitted an ICJ jurisdiction declaration; non-party state to the ICCt

Citizenship: *citizenship by birth:* no
citizenship by descent only: the father must be a citizen of Saudi Arabia; a child born out of wedlock in Saudi Arabia to a Saudi mother and unknown father
dual citizenship recognized: no
residency requirement for naturalization: 5 years

Suffrage: 18 years of age; restricted to males; universal for municipal elections

Executive branch: *chief of state:* King SALMAN bin Abd al-Aziz Al Saud (since 23 January 2015); Crown Prince MUHAMMAD BIN SALMAN bin Abd al-Aziz Al Saud (born 31 August 1985)
head of government: King and Prime Minister SALMAN bin Abd al-Aziz Al Saud (since 23 January 2015); Crown Prince MUHAMMAD BIN SALMAN bin Abd al-Aziz Al Saud (born 31 August 1985)
cabinet: Council of Ministers appointed by the monarch every 4 years and includes many royal family members
elections/appointments: none; the monarchy is hereditary; an Allegiance Council created by royal decree in October 2006 established a committee of Saudi princes for a voice in selecting future Saudi kings

Legislative branch: *description:* unicameral Consultative Council or Majlis al-Shura (150 seats plus a speaker; members appointed by the monarch to serve 4-year terms); note - in early 2013, the monarch granted women 30 seats on the Council
note: composition as of 2021 - men 121, women 30, percent of women 19.9%

Judicial branch: *highest court(s):* High Court (consists of the court chief and organized into circuits with 3-judge panels, except for the criminal circuit, which has a 5-judge panel for cases involving major punishments)
judge selection and term of office: High Court chief and chiefs of the High Court Circuits appointed by royal decree upon the recommendation of the Supreme Judiciary Council, a 10-member body of high-level judges and other judicial heads; new judges and assistant judges serve 1- and 2-year probations, respectively, before permanent assignment
subordinate courts: Court of Appeals; Specialized Criminal Court, first-degree courts composed of general, criminal, personal status, and commercial courts; Labor Court; a hierarchy of administrative courts

Political parties and leaders: none

International organization participation: ABEDA, AfDB (nonregional member), AFESD, AMF, BIS, CAEU, CP, FAO, G-20, G-77, GCC, IAEA, IBRD, ICAO, ICC (national committees), ICRM, IDA, IDB, IFAD, IFC, IFRCS, IHO, ILO, IMF, IMO, IMSO, Interpol, IOC, IOM (observer), IPU, ISO, ITSO, ITU, LAS, MIGA, NAM, OAPEC, OAS (observer), OIC, OPCW, OPEC, PCA, UN, UNCTAD, UNESCO, UNIDO, UNRWA, UNWTO, UPU, WCO, WFTU (NGOs), WHO, WIPO, WMO, WTO

Diplomatic representation in the US: *chief of mission:* Ambassador Princess RIMA bint Bandar bin Abd al-Aziz Al Saud (since 8 July 2019)
chancery: 601 New Hampshire Avenue NW, Washington, DC 20037
telephone: [1] (202) 342-3800
FAX: [1] (202) 295-3625
email address and website:
info@saudiembassy.net
https://www.saudiembassy.net/
consulate(s) general: Houston, Los Angeles, New York

Diplomatic representation from the US: *chief of mission:* Ambassador (vacant); Charge d'Affaires Martina STRONG (since February 2021)
embassy: Riyadh 11564
mailing address: 6300 Riyadh Place, Washington DC 20521-6300
telephone: [966] (11) 835-4000
FAX: [966] (11) 488-7360
email address and website:
RiyadhACS@state.gov
https://sa.usembassy.gov/
consulate(s) general: Dhahran, Jeddah

Flag description: green, a traditional color in Islamic flags, with the Shahada or Muslim creed in large white Arabic script (translated as "There is no god but God; Muhammad is the Messenger of God") above a white horizontal saber (the tip points to the hoist side); design dates to the early twentieth century and is closely associated with the Al Saud family, which established the kingdom in 1932; the flag is manufactured with differing obverse and reverse sides so that the Shahada reads - and the sword points - correctly from right to left on both sides
note: the only national flag to display an inscription as its principal design; one of only three national flags that differ on their obverse and reverse sides - the others are Moldova and Paraguay

National symbol(s): palm tree surmounting two crossed swords; national colors: green, white

National anthem: *name:* "Aash Al Maleek" (Long Live Our Beloved King)
lyrics/music: Ibrahim KHAFAJI/Abdul Rahman al-KHATEEB
note: music adopted 1947, lyrics adopted 1984

National heritage: *total World Heritage Sites:* 6 (all cultural)
selected World Heritage Site locales: Hegra Archaeological Site (al-Hijr / Madā ʾin Ṣāliḥ); At-Turaif District in ad- Dir'iyah; Historic Jeddah, the Gate to Makkah; Rock Art in the Hail Region; Al-Ahsa Oasis; Ḥimā Cultural Area

ECONOMY

Economic overview: Saudi Arabia has an oil-based economy with strong government controls over major economic activities. It possesses about 16% of the world's proven petroleum reserves, ranks as the largest exporter of petroleum, and plays a leading role in OPEC. The petroleum sector accounts for roughly 87% of budget revenues, 42% of GDP, and 90% of export earnings.

Saudi Arabia is encouraging the growth of the private sector in order to diversify its economy and to employ more Saudi nationals. Approximately 6 million foreign workers play an important role in the Saudi economy, particularly in the oil and service sectors; at the same time, however, Riyadh is struggling to reduce unemployment among its own nationals. Saudi officials are particularly focused on employing its large youth population.

In 2017, the Kingdom incurred a budget deficit estimated at 8.3% of GDP, which was financed by bond sales and drawing down reserves. Although the Kingdom can finance high deficits for several years by drawing down its considerable foreign assets or by borrowing, it has cut capital spending and reduced subsidies on electricity, water, and petroleum products and recently introduced a value-added tax of 5%. In January 2016, Crown Prince and Deputy Prime Minister MUHAMMAD BIN SALMAN announced that Saudi Arabia intends to list shares of its state-owned petroleum company, ARAMCO - another move to increase revenue and outside investment. The government has also looked at privatization and diversification of the economy more closely in the wake of a diminished oil market. Historically, Saudi Arabia has focused diversification efforts on power generation, telecommunications, natural gas exploration, and petrochemical sectors. More recently, the government has approached investors about expanding the role of the private sector in the health care, education and tourism industries. While Saudi Arabia has emphasized their goals of diversification for some time, current low oil prices may force the government to make more drastic changes ahead of their long-run timeline.

Real GDP (purchasing power parity): $1,543,240,000,000 (2020 est.)
$1,609,320,000,000 (2019 est.)
$1,604,010,000,000 (2018 est.)
note: data are in 2017 dollars
country comparison to the world: 17

Real GDP growth rate: -0.9% (2017 est.)
1.7% (2016 est.)
4.1% (2015 est.)
country comparison to the world: 198

Real GDP per capita: $44,300 (2020 est.)
$47,000 (2019 est.)
$47,600 (2018 est.)
note: data are in 2017 dollars
country comparison to the world: 35

GDP (official exchange rate): $792.849 billion (2019 est.)

Inflation rate (consumer prices): -2% (2019 est.)
-4.5% (2018 est.)
-0.8% (2017 est.)
country comparison to the world: 3

Credit ratings:

Fitch rating: A (2019)

Moody's rating: A1 (2016)

Standard & Poors rating: A- (2016)

GDP - composition, by sector of origin: *agriculture:* 2.6% (2017 est.)
industry: 44.2% (2017 est.)
services: 53.2% (2017 est.)

GDP - composition, by end use: *household consumption:* 41.3% (2017 est.)
government consumption: 24.5% (2017 est.)
investment in fixed capital: 23.2% (2017 est.)
investment in inventories: 4.7% (2017 est.)
exports of goods and services: 34.8% (2017 est.)
imports of goods and services: -28.6% (2017 est.)

Agricultural products: milk, dates, poultry, fruit, watermelons, barley, wheat, potatoes, eggs, tomatoes

Industries: crude oil production, petroleum refining, basic petrochemicals, ammonia, industrial gases, sodium hydroxide (caustic soda), cement, fertilizer, plastics, metals, commercial ship repair, commercial aircraft repair, construction

Industrial production growth rate: -2.4% (2017 est.)
country comparison to the world: 186

Labor force: 13.8 million (2017 est.)
note: comprised of 3.1 million Saudis and 10.7 million non-Saudis
country comparison to the world: 39

Labor force - by occupation: *agriculture:* 6.7%
industry: 21.4%
services: 71.9% (2005 est.)

Unemployment rate: 6% (2017 est.)
5.6% (2016 est.)
note: data are for total population; unemployment among Saudi nationals is more than double
country comparison to the world: 98

Unemployment, youth ages 15-24: *total:* 27.2%
male: 21.5%
female: 43.8% (2020 est.)
country comparison to the world: 41

Gini Index coefficient - distribution of family income: 45.9 (2013 est.)
country comparison to the world: 26

Budget: *revenues:* 181 billion (2017 est.)
expenditures: 241.8 billion (2017 est.)

Budget surplus (+) or deficit (-): -8.9% (of GDP) (2017 est.)
country comparison to the world: 204

Public debt: 17.2% of GDP (2017 est.)
13.1% of GDP (2016 est.)
country comparison to the world: 193

Taxes and other revenues: 26.4% (of GDP) (2017 est.)
country comparison to the world: 113

Fiscal year: calendar year

Current account balance: $15.23 billion (2017 est.)
-$23.87 billion (2016 est.)
country comparison to the world: 20

Exports: $184.11 billion (2020 est.) note: data are in current year dollars
$285.86 billion (2019 est.) note: data are in current year dollars
$314.92 billion (2018 est.) note: data are in current year dollars
country comparison to the world: 32

Exports - partners: China 20%, India 11%, Japan 11%, South Korea 9%, United States 5% (2019)

Exports - commodities: crude petroleum, refined petroleum, polymers, industrial alcohols, natural gas (2019)

Imports: $179.8 billion (2020 est.) note: data are in current year dollars
$218.94 billion (2019 est.) note: data are in current year dollars
$209.59 billion (2018 est.) note: data are in current year dollars
country comparison to the world: 31

Imports - partners: China 18%, United Arab Emirates 12%, United States 9%, Germany 5% (2019)

Imports - commodities: cars, broadcasting equipment, refined petroleum, packaged medicines, telephones (2019)

Reserves of foreign exchange and gold: $496.4 billion (31 December 2017 est.)
$535.8 billion (31 December 2016 est.)
country comparison to the world: 4

Debt - external: $205.1 billion (31 December 2017 est.)
$189.3 billion (31 December 2016 est.)
country comparison to the world: 38

Exchange rates: Saudi riyals (SAR) per US dollar -
3.7514 (2020 est.)
3.75 (2019 est.)
3.7518 (2018 est.)
3.75 (2014 est.)
3.75 (2013 est.)

ENERGY

Electricity access: *electrification - total population:* 100% (2020)

Electricity: *installed generating capacity:* 76.785 million kW (2020 est.)
consumption: 331,381,500,000 kWh (2019 est.)
exports: 0 kWh (2020 est.)
imports: 0 kWh (2020 est.)
transmission/distribution losses: 31.055 billion kWh (2019 est.)

Electricity generation sources: *fossil fuels:* 99.9% of total installed capacity (2020 est.)
solar: 0.2% of total installed capacity (2020 est.)

Coal: *production:* 0 metric tons (2020 est.)
consumption: 73,000 metric tons (2020 est.)
exports: 0 metric tons (2020 est.)
imports: 73,000 metric tons (2020 est.)
proven reserves: 0 metric tons (2019 est.)

Petroleum: *total petroleum production:* 10,815,700 bbl/day (2021 est.)
refined petroleum consumption: 3,182,300 bbl/day (2019 est.)
crude oil and lease condensate exports: 7,340,800 bbl/day (2018 est.)
crude oil and lease condensate imports: 0 bbl/day (2018 est.)
crude oil estimated reserves: 258.6 billion barrels (2021 est.)

Refined petroleum products - production: 2.476 million bbl/day (2015 est.)
country comparison to the world: 8

Refined petroleum products - exports: 1.784 million bbl/day (2015 est.)
country comparison to the world: 5

Refined petroleum products - imports: 609,600 bbl/day (2015 est.)
country comparison to the world: 13

Natural gas: *production:* 113,776,648,000 cubic meters (2020 est.)
consumption: 113,776,648,000 cubic meters (2020 est.)
exports: 0 cubic meters (2021 est.)
imports: 0 cubic meters (2021 est.)
proven reserves: 9,422,812,000,000 cubic meters (2021 est.)

Carbon dioxide emissions: 579.925 million metric tonnes of CO2 (2019 est.)
from coal and metallurgical coke: 300,000 metric tonnes of CO2 (2019 est.)
from petroleum and other liquids: 358.414 million metric tonnes of CO2 (2019 est.)
from consumed natural gas: 221.211 million metric tonnes of CO2 (2019 est.)
country comparison to the world: 10

Energy consumption per capita: 296.949 million Btu/person (2019 est.)
country comparison to the world: 12

COMMUNICATIONS

Telephones - fixed lines: *total subscriptions:* 5,749,058 (2020 est.)
subscriptions per 100 inhabitants: 17 (2020 est.)
country comparison to the world: 25

Telephones - mobile cellular: *total subscriptions:* 43,215,439 (2020 est.)
subscriptions per 100 inhabitants: 124 (2020 est.)
country comparison to the world: 37

Telecommunication systems: *general assessment:* Saudi Arabia's telecom and ICT sectors continue to benefit from the range of programs aimed at diversifying the economy away from a dependence on oil, and establishing a wider digital transformation over the next decade; an essential element of this has been the widening reach of 5G networks, which by mid-2021 reached about half of the population and the majority of cities; the MNOs have focused investment on upgrading LTE infrastructure and further developing 5G; this in part is aimed at generating additional revenue from mobile data services, and also to their contribution to the Vision 2030 program; the ongoing pandemic has resulted in more people working and schooling from home during periods of restricted travel; this has stimulated growth in mobile data traffic, while the government has encouraged non-cash transactions and so helped develop the vast e-commerce market; while Saudi Arabia's fixed broadband penetration remains relatively low, there has been a concentration of fiber infrastructure and the Kingdom has developed one of the fastest services in the region (2022)
domestic: fixed-line over 16 per 100 and mobile-cellular subscribership has been increasing rapidly to roughly 124 per 100 persons (2020)
international: country code - 966; landing points for the SeaMeWe-3, -4, -5, AAE-1, EIG, FALCON, FEA, IMEWE, MENA/Gulf Bridge International, SEACOM, SAS-1, -2, GBICS/MENA, and the Tata TGN-Gulf submarine cables providing connectivity to Europe, Africa, the Middle East, Asia, Southeast Asia and Australia; microwave radio relay to Bahrain, Jordan, Kuwait, Qatar, UAE, Yemen, and Sudan; coaxial cable to Kuwait and Jordan; satellite earth stations - 5 Intelsat (3 Atlantic Ocean and 2 Indian Ocean), 1 Arabsat, and 1 Inmarsat (Indian Ocean region) (2019)

Broadcast media: broadcast media are state-controlled; state-run TV operates 4 networks; Saudi Arabia is a major market for pan-Arab satellite TV broadcasters; state-run radio operates several networks; multiple international broadcasters are available

Internet country code: .sa

Internet users: *total:* 34,117,590 (2020 est.)
percent of population: 98% (2020 est.)
country comparison to the world: 29

Broadband - fixed subscriptions: *total:* 7,890,261 (2020 est.)
subscriptions per 100 inhabitants: 23 (2020 est.)
country comparison to the world: 26

Communications - note: the innovative King Abdulaziz Center for World Culture (informally known as Ithra, meaning "enrichment") opened on 1 December 2017 in Dhahran, Eastern Region; its facilities include a grand library, several museums, an archive, an Idea Lab, a theater, a cinema, and an Energy Exhibit, all which are meant to provide visitors an immersive and transformative experience

TRANSPORTATION

National air transport system: *number of registered air carriers:* 12 (2020)
inventory of registered aircraft operated by air carriers: 230
annual passenger traffic on registered air carriers: 39,141,660 (2018)

annual freight traffic on registered air carriers: 1,085,470,000 (2018) mt-km

Civil aircraft registration country code prefix: HZ

Airports: *total:* 214 (2021)
country comparison to the world: 27

Airports - with paved runways: *total:* 82
over 3,047 m: 33
2,438 to 3,047 m: 16
1,524 to 2,437 m: 27
914 to 1,523 m: 2
under 914 m: 4 (2021)

Airports - with unpaved runways: *total:* 132
2,438 to 3,047 m: 7
1,524 to 2,437 m: 72
914 to 1,523 m: 37
under 914 m: 16 (2021)

Heliports: 10 (2021)

Pipelines: 209 km condensate, 2,940 km gas, 1,183 km liquid petroleum gas, 5,117 km oil, 1,151 km refined products (2013)

Railways: *total:* 5,410 km (2016)
standard gauge: 5,410 km (2016) 1.435-m gauge (with branch lines and sidings)
country comparison to the world: 35

Roadways: *total:* 221,372 km (2006)
paved: 47,529 km (2006) (includes 3,891 km of expressways)
unpaved: 173,843 km (2006)
country comparison to the world: 24

Merchant marine: *total:* 392
by type: bulk carrier 5, container ship 1, general cargo 21, oil tanker 58, other 307 (2021)
country comparison to the world: 49

Ports and terminals: *major seaport(s):* Ad Dammam, Al Jubayl, Jeddah, King Abdulla, Yanbu'
container port(s) (TEUs): Ad Dammam (1,822,642), Jeddah (4,433,991), King Abdulla (2,020,683) (2019)

MILITARY AND SECURITY

Military and security forces: Ministry of Defense: Royal Saudi Land Forces, Royal Saudi Naval Forces (includes marines, special forces, naval aviation), Royal Saudi Air Force, Royal Saudi Air Defense Forces, Royal Saudi Strategic Missiles Force; Ministry of the National Guard (SANG); Ministry of Interior: police, Border Guard, Facilities Security Force; State Security Presidency: General Directorate of Investigation (Mabahith), Special Security Forces, Special Emergency Forces (2022)
note: SANG (also known as the White Army) is a land force separate from the Ministry of Defense that is responsible for internal security, protecting the royal family, and external defense

Military expenditures: 6% of GDP (2021 est.)
7.8% of GDP (2020 est.)
8.8% of GDP (2019 est.) (approximately $92.2 billion)
10% of GDP (2018 est.) (approximately $103 billion)
11.1% of GDP (2017 est.) (approximately $111 billion)
country comparison to the world: 5

Military and security service personnel strengths: the Saudi military forces have about 225,000 total active troops; approximately 125,000 under the Ministry of Defense (75,000 Land Forces; 15,000 Naval Forces, including about 3,000 marines; 35,000 Air Force/Air Defense/Strategic Missile Forces) and approximately 100,000 in the Saudi Arabia National Guard (SANG) (2022)
note: SANG also has an irregular force (Fowj), primarily Bedouin tribal volunteers, with a total strength of approximately 25,000

Military equipment inventories and acquisitions: the inventory of the Saudi military forces, including the SANG, includes a mix of mostly modern weapons systems from the US and Europe; since 2010, the US has been the leading supplier of armaments; as of 2020-21, Saudi Arabia was the world's largest arms importer (2022)
note: as of 2022, the Saudi Navy was in the midst of a multi-year and multi-billion dollar expansion and modernization program to purchase new frigates, corvettes, and other naval craft; in 2022, it received two of an expected five corvettes as part of a joint construction effort with Spain; in 2018, it signed a contract to acquire four US-built multi-purpose littoral mission ships, which will be comparable to frigates in capabilities

Military service age and obligation: men (17-40) and women (21-40) may volunteer for military service; no conscription (2022)
note 1: in 2021, women were allowed to serve in the Army, Air Defense, Navy, Strategic Missile Force, medical services, and internal security forces up to the rank of non-commissioned officer
note 2: the National Guard is restricted to citizens, but the regular Saudi military has hired foreigners on contract for operations associated with its intervention in Yemen

Military deployments: estimated 2,500-5,000 Yemen (varies depending on operations) (2022)

Military - note: in 2015, a Saudi-led coalition of Arab states intervened militarily in Yemen in support of the Republic of Yemen Government against the separatist Huthis; Saudi Arabia also has raised and equipped paramilitary/militia security forces in Yemen--based largely on tribal or regional affiliation--to deploy along the Saudi-Yemen border, especially the areas bordering the governorates of Saada and Al-Jawf (2022)

TERRORISM

Terrorist group(s): Islamic State of Iraq and ash-Sham (ISIS); al-Qa'ida; al-Qa'ida in the Arabian Peninsula (AQAP)

TRANSNATIONAL ISSUES

Disputes - international: *Saudi Arabia-Bahrain:* none identified
Saudi Arabia-Iraq: Saudi Arabia has been building a fence along its border with Iraq to keep out militants and smugglers
Saudi Arabia-Jordan: Jordan and Saudi Arabia signed an agreement to demarcate their maritime borders in 2007
Saudi Arabia-Kuwait: Kuwait and Saudi Arabia continue discussions on a maritime boundary with Iran; in December 2019, Saudi Arabia and Kuwait signed an agreement to demarcate land in a neutral zone and to restart oil production in shared fields, which had been suspended since 2014 because of disagreements
Saudi Arabia-Oman: none identified
Saudi Arabia-Qatar: none identified
Saudi Arabia-UAE: Saudi Arabia and UAE have disputed the Shaybah oilfield, which Saudi Arabia controls
Saudi Arabia-Yemen: the two countries signed the Treaty of Jeddah in 2000, which specified the coordinates of their land and maritime border and made provisions for grazing, the placement of armed forces, and future resource exploitation; in 2010, Saudi Arabia reinforced its concrete-filled security barrier along sections of the now fully demarcated border with Yemen to stem illegal crossborder activities

Refugees and internally displaced persons: *stateless persons:* 70,000 (mid-year 2021); note - thousands of biduns (stateless Arabs) are descendants of nomadic tribes who were not officially registered when national borders were established, while others migrated to Saudi Arabia in search of jobs; some have temporary identification cards that must be renewed every five years, but their rights remain restricted; most Palestinians have only legal resident status; some naturalized Yemenis were made stateless after being stripped of their passports when Yemen backed Iraq in its invasion of Kuwait in 1990; Saudi women cannot pass their citizenship on to their children, so if they marry a non-national, their children risk statelessness

Trafficking in persons: *current situation:* Saudi Arabia is a destination country for men and women subjected to forced labor and, to a lesser extent, forced prostitution; men and women primarily from South and Southeast Asia and Africa voluntarily travel to Saudi Arabia to work in domestic service, construction, agriculture or other low-skilled jobs, but some subsequently face conditions indicative of involuntary servitude (many are forced to work months or years beyond their contract term because employers withhold passports and required exit visas); women, primarily from Asian and African countries, are reported to be forced into prostitution in Saudi Arabia
tier rating:
Tier 2 Watch List — Saudi Arabia does not fully meet the minimum standards for the elimination of trafficking, but is making significant efforts to do so and was upgraded to Tier 2 Watch List;

the government enacted the country's first-ever national referral mechanism (NRM) and increased the number of prosecutions and convictions under the anti-trafficking law; victims are identified and referred for care; the government convicted and sentenced two Saudi officials complicit in trafficking crimes; however, the government continued to fine, jail, and/or deport migrant workers for prostitution or immigration violations who may have been trafficking victims; authorities regularly misclassified potential trafficking crimes as labor law violations rather than as criminal offenses (2020)

Illicit drugs: regularly sentences drug traffickers to the death penalty, although a moratorium on executions for drug offences has been in place since at least 2020; improving anti-money-laundering legislation and enforcement

SENEGAL

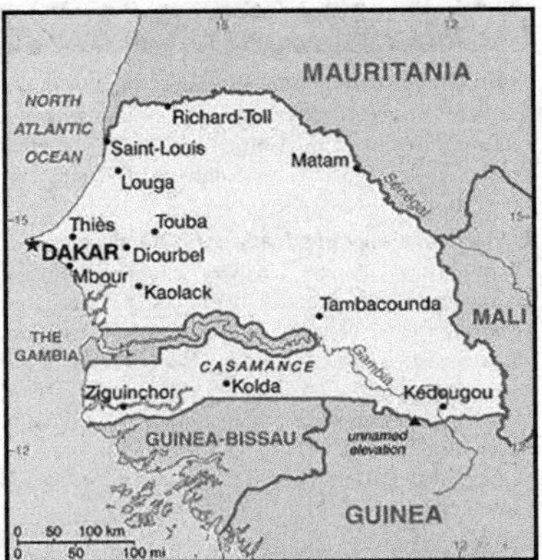

INTRODUCTION

Background: Senegal is one of the few countries in the world with evidence of continuous human life from the Paleolithic era to present. Between the 14th and 16th centuries, the Jolof Empire ruled most of Senegal. Starting in the 15th century, Portugal, the Netherlands, France, and Great Britain traded along the Senegalese coast. Senegal's location on the western tip of Africa made it a favorable base for the European slave trade. European powers used the Senegalese island of Goree as a base to purchase slaves from the warring chiefdoms on the mainland, and at the height of the slave trade in Senegal, over one-third of the Senegalese population was enslaved. In 1815, France abolished slavery and began expanding inland. During the second half of the 19th century, France took possession of Senegal as a French colony. In 1959, the French colonies of Senegal and French Sudan were merged and granted independence in 1960 as the Mali Federation. The union broke up after only a few months. In 1982, Senegal joined with The Gambia to form the nominal confederation of Senegambia. The envisaged integration of the two countries was never implemented, and the union dissolved in 1989.

Since the 1980s, the Movement of Democratic Forces in the Casamance - a separatist movement based in southern Senegal - has led a low-level insurgency. Several attempts at reaching a comprehensive peace agreement have failed. Since 2012, despite sporadic incidents of violence, an unofficial ceasefire has remained largely in effect. Senegal is one of the most stable democracies in Africa and has a long history of participating in international peacekeeping and regional mediation. The Socialist Party of Senegal ruled for 40 years until Abdoulaye WADE was elected president in 2000 and re-elected in 2007. WADE amended Senegal's constitution over a dozen times to increase executive power and weaken the opposition. In 2012, WADE's decision to run for a third presidential term sparked public backlash that led to his defeat to current President Macky SALL. A 2016 constitutional referendum limited future presidents to two consecutive five-year terms. The change, however, does not apply to SALL's first term. In February 2019, SALL won his bid for reelection; his second term will end in 2024.

GEOGRAPHY

Location: Western Africa, bordering the North Atlantic Ocean, between Guinea-Bissau and Mauritania

Geographic coordinates: 14 00 N, 14 00 W

Map references: Africa

Area: *total:* 196,722 sq km
land: 192,530 sq km
water: 4,192 sq km
country comparison to the world: 88

Area - comparative: slightly smaller than South Dakota; slightly larger than twice the size of Indiana

Land boundaries: *total:* 2,684 km
border countries (5): The Gambia 749 km; Guinea 363 km; Guinea-Bissau 341 km; Mali 489 km; Mauritania 742 km

Coastline: 531 km

Maritime claims: *territorial sea:* 12 nm
contiguous zone: 24 nm
exclusive economic zone: 200 nm
continental shelf: 200 nm or to the edge of the continental margin

Climate: tropical; hot, humid; rainy season (May to November) has strong southeast winds; dry season (December to April) dominated by hot, dry, harmattan wind

Terrain: generally low, rolling, plains rising to foothills in southeast

Elevation: *highest point:* unnamed elevation 2.8 km southeast of Nepen Diaka 648 m
lowest point: Atlantic Ocean 0 m
mean elevation: 69 m

Natural resources: fish, phosphates, iron ore

Land use: *agricultural land:* 46.8% (2018 est.)
arable land: 17.4% (2018 est.)
permanent crops: 0.3% (2018 est.)
permanent pasture: 29.1% (2018 est.)
forest: 43.8% (2018 est.)
other: 9.4% (2018 est.)

Irrigated land: 1,200 sq km (2012)

Major rivers (by length in km): Senegal (shared with Guinea [s], Mali, and Mauritania [m]) - 1,641 km; Gambia (shared with Guinea [s] and The Gambia [m]) - 1,094 km
note – [s] after country name indicates river source; [m] after country name indicates river mouth

Major watersheds (area sq km): Atlantic Ocean drainage: Senegal (456,397 sq km)

Major aquifers: Senegalo-Mauritanian Basin

Population distribution: the population is concentrated in the west, with Dakar anchoring a well-defined core area; approximately 70% of the population is rural as shown in this population distribution map

Natural hazards: lowlands seasonally flooded; periodic droughts

Geography - note: westernmost country on the African continent; The Gambia is almost an enclave within Senegal

PEOPLE AND SOCIETY

Population: 17,923,036 (2022 est.)
country comparison to the world: 68

Nationality: *noun:* Senegalese (singular and plural)
adjective: Senegalese

Ethnic groups: Wolof 39.7%, Pular 27.5%, Serer 16%, Mandinka 4.9%, Jola 4.2%, Soninke 2.4%, other 5.4% (includes Europeans and persons of Lebanese descent) (2019 est.)

Languages: French (official), Wolof, Pular, Jola, Mandinka, Serer, Soninke

Religions: Muslim 97.2% (most adhere to one of the four main Sufi brotherhoods), Christian 2.7% (mostly Roman Catholic) (2019 est.)

Demographic profile: Senegal has a large and growing youth population but has not been successful in developing its potential human capital. Senegal's high total fertility rate of almost 4.5 children per woman continues to bolster the country's large youth cohort – more than 60% of the population is under the age of 25. Fertility remains high because of the continued desire for large families, the low use of family planning, and early childbearing. Because of the country's high illiteracy rate (more than 40%), high unemployment (even among university graduates), and widespread poverty, Senegalese youths face dim prospects; women are especially disadvantaged.

Senegal historically was a destination country for economic migrants, but in recent years West African migrants more often use Senegal as a transit point to North Africa – and sometimes illegally onward to Europe. The country also has been host to several thousand black Mauritanian refugees since they were expelled from their homeland during its 1989 border conflict with Senegal. The country's economic crisis in the 1970s stimulated emigration; departures accelerated in the 1990s. Destinations shifted from neighboring countries, which were experiencing economic decline, civil wars, and increasing xenophobia, to Libya and Mauritania because of their booming oil industries and to developed countries (most notably former colonial ruler France, as well as Italy and Spain). The latter became attractive in the 1990s because of job opportunities and their periodic regularization programs (legalizing the status of illegal migrants).

Additionally, about 16,000 Senegalese refugees still remain in The Gambia and Guinea-Bissau as a result of more than 30 years of fighting between government forces and rebel separatists in southern Senegal's Casamance region.

Age structure: *0-14 years:* 40.38% (male 3,194,454/female 3,160,111)
15-24 years: 20.35% (male 1,596,896/female 1,606,084)
25-54 years: 31.95% (male 2,327,424/female 2,700,698)
55-64 years: 4.21% (male 283,480/female 378,932)
65 years and over: 3.1% (male 212,332/female 275,957) (2020 est.)

Dependency ratios: *total dependency ratio:* 84.2
youth dependency ratio: 78.4
elderly dependency ratio: 5.7
potential support ratio: 17.5 (2020 est.)

Median age: *total:* 19.4 years
male: 18.5 years
female: 20.3 years (2020 est.)
country comparison to the world: 203

Population growth rate: 2.57% (2022 est.)
country comparison to the world: 17

Birth rate: 31.51 births/1,000 population (2022 est.)
country comparison to the world: 27

Death rate: 5.08 deaths/1,000 population (2022 est.)
country comparison to the world: 193

Net migration rate: -0.71 migrant(s)/1,000 population (2022 est.)
country comparison to the world: 133

Population distribution: the population is concentrated in the west, with Dakar anchoring a well-defined core area; approximately 70% of the population is rural as shown in this population distribution map

Urbanization: *urban population:* 49.1% of total population (2022)
rate of urbanization: 3.59% annual rate of change (2020-25 est.)

Major urban areas - population: 3.326 million DAKAR (capital) (2022)

Sex ratio: *at birth:* 1.05 male(s)/female
0-14 years: 1.04 male(s)/female
15-24 years: 1.02 male(s)/female
25-54 years: 0.88 male(s)/female
55-64 years: 0.76 male(s)/female
65 years and over: 0.74 male(s)/female
total population: 0.97 male(s)/female (2022 est.)

Mother's mean age at first birth: 21.9 years (2019 est.)
note: data represents median age at first birth among women 25-49

Maternal mortality ratio: 315 deaths/100,000 live births (2017 est.)
country comparison to the world: 35

Infant mortality rate: *total:* 32.44 deaths/1,000 live births
male: 35.78 deaths/1,000 live births
female: 28.93 deaths/1,000 live births (2022 est.)
country comparison to the world: 47

Life expectancy at birth: *total population:* 69.96 years
male: 68.23 years
female: 71.77 years (2022 est.)
country comparison to the world: 171

Total fertility rate: 4.27 children born/woman (2022 est.)
country comparison to the world: 23

Contraceptive prevalence rate: 26.9% (2019)

Drinking water source: *improved: urban:* 95.9% of population
rural: 79.3% of population
total: 87.3% of population
unimproved: urban: 4.1% of population
rural: 20.7% of population
total: 12.7% of population (2020 est.)

Current health expenditure: 4.1% of GDP (2019)

Physicians density: 0.09 physicians/1,000 population (2019)

Sanitation facility access: *improved: urban:* 94.1% of population
rural: 55.5% of population
total: 74.1% of population
unimproved: urban: 5.9% of population
rural: 44.5% of population
total: 25.9% of population (2020 est.)

HIV/AIDS - adult prevalence rate: 0.3% (2020 est.)
country comparison to the world: 92

HIV/AIDS - people living with HIV/AIDS: 39,000 (2020 est.)
country comparison to the world: 65

HIV/AIDS - deaths: 1,100 (2020 est.)
country comparison to the world: 57

Major infectious diseases: *degree of risk:* very high (2020)
food or waterborne diseases: bacterial and protozoal diarrhea, hepatitis A, and typhoid fever
vectorborne diseases: malaria and dengue fever
water contact diseases: schistosomiasis
animal contact diseases: rabies
respiratory diseases: meningococcal meningitis
note: on 21 March 2022, the US Centers for Disease Control and Prevention (CDC) issued a Travel Alert for polio in Africa; Senegal is currently considered a high risk to travelers for circulating vaccine-derived polioviruses (cVDPV); vaccine-derived poliovirus (VDPV) is a strain of the weakened poliovirus that was initially included in oral polio vaccine (OPV) and *that has changed over time and behaves more like the wild or naturally occurring virus*; this means it can be spread more easily to people who are unvaccinated against polio and who come in contact with the stool or respiratory secretions, such as from a sneeze, of an "infected" person who received oral polio vaccine; the CDC recommends that before any international travel, anyone unvaccinated, incompletely vaccinated, or with an unknown polio vaccination status should complete the routine polio vaccine series; before travel to any high-risk destination, the CDC recommends that adults who previously completed the full, routine polio vaccine series receive a single, lifetime booster dose of polio vaccine

Obesity - adult prevalence rate: 8.8% (2016)
country comparison to the world: 146

Alcohol consumption per capita: *total:* 0.25 liters of pure alcohol (2019 est.)
beer: 0.21 liters of pure alcohol (2019 est.)
wine: 0.02 liters of pure alcohol (2019 est.)
spirits: 0.02 liters of pure alcohol (2019 est.)
other alcohols: 0 liters of pure alcohol (2019 est.)
country comparison to the world: 171

Tobacco use: *total:* 6.9% (2020 est.)
male: 13.1% (2020 est.)
female: 0.7% (2020 est.)
country comparison to the world: 157

Children under the age of 5 years underweight: 14.4% (2019)
country comparison to the world: 39

Child marriage: *women married by age 15:* 8.8%
women married by age 18: 30.5%
men married by age 18: 0.7% (2019 est.)

Education expenditures: 5.3% of GDP (2019 est.)
country comparison to the world: 51

Literacy: *definition:* age 15 and over can read and write
total population: 51.9%
male: 64.8%
female: 39.8% (2017)

School life expectancy (primary to tertiary education): *total:* 9 years
male: 8 years
female: 9 years (2020)

Unemployment, youth ages 15-24: *total:* 4.1%
male: 2.9%
female: 6.7% (2019 est.)

ENVIRONMENT

Environment - current issues: deforestation; overgrazing; soil erosion; desertification; periodic droughts; seasonal flooding; overfishing; weak environmental protective laws; wildlife populations threatened by poaching

Environment - international agreements: *party to:* Biodiversity, Climate Change, Climate Change-Kyoto Protocol, Climate Change-Paris Agreement, Comprehensive Nuclear Test Ban, Desertification, Endangered Species, Hazardous Wastes, Law of the Sea, Marine Life Conservation, Nuclear Test Ban, Ozone Layer Protection, Ship Pollution, Wetlands, Whaling
signed, but not ratified: none of the selected agreements

Air pollutants: *particulate matter emissions:* 37.52 micrograms per cubic meter (2016 est.)
carbon dioxide emissions: 10.9 megatons (2016 est.)
methane emissions: 11.74 megatons (2020 est.)

Climate: tropical; hot, humid; rainy season (May to November) has strong southeast winds; dry season (December to April) dominated by hot, dry, harmattan wind

Land use: *agricultural land:* 46.8% (2018 est.)
arable land: 17.4% (2018 est.)
permanent crops: 0.3% (2018 est.)
permanent pasture: 29.1% (2018 est.)
forest: 43.8% (2018 est.)
other: 9.4% (2018 est.)

Urbanization: *urban population:* 49.1% of total population (2022)
rate of urbanization: 3.59% annual rate of change (2020-25 est.)

Revenue from forest resources: *forest revenues:* 1.46% of GDP (2018 est.)
country comparison to the world: 45

Revenue from coal: *coal revenues:* 0% of GDP (2018 est.)
country comparison to the world: 163

Food insecurity: *severe localized food insecurity: due to localized shortfalls in cereal production and reduced incomes* - according to the latest analysis, about 881,000 people are estimated to be in need of humanitarian assistance between June and August 2022, mostly on account of localized shortfalls in cereal production in 2021 and reduced incomes owing to the impact of the COVID-19 pandemic (2022)

Waste and recycling: *municipal solid waste generated annually:* 2,454,059 tons (2016 est.)

Major rivers (by length in km): Senegal (shared with Guinea [s], Mali, and Mauritania [m]) - 1,641 km; Gambia (shared with Guinea [s] and The Gambia [m]) - 1,094 km
note – [s] after country name indicates river source; [m] after country name indicates river mouth

Major watersheds (area sq km): Atlantic Ocean drainage: Senegal (456,397 sq km)

Major aquifers: Senegalo-Mauritanian Basin

Total water withdrawal: *municipal:* 98 million cubic meters (2017 est.)
industrial: 58 million cubic meters (2017 est.)

agricultural: 2.065 billion cubic meters (2017 est.)

Total renewable water resources: 38.97 billion cubic meters (2017 est.)

GOVERNMENT

Country name: *conventional long form:* Republic of Senegal
conventional short form: Senegal
local long form: Republique du Senegal
local short form: Senegal
former: Senegambia (along with The Gambia), Mali Federation
etymology: named for the Senegal River that forms the northern border of the country; many theories exist for the origin of the river name; perhaps the most widely cited derives the name from "Azenegue," the Portuguese appellation for the Berber Zenaga people who lived north of the river

Government type: presidential republic

Capital: *name:* Dakar
geographic coordinates: 14 44 N, 17 38 W
time difference: UTC 0 (5 hours ahead of Washington, DC, during Standard Time)
etymology: the Atlantic coast trading settlement of Ndakaaru came to be called "Dakar" by French colonialists

Administrative divisions: 14 regions (regions, singular - region); Dakar, Diourbel, Fatick, Kaffrine, Kaolack, Kedougou, Kolda, Louga, Matam, Saint-Louis, Sedhiou, Tambacounda, Thies, Ziguinchor

Independence: 4 April 1960 (from France); note - complete independence achieved upon dissolution of federation with Mali on 20 August 1960

National holiday: Independence Day, 4 April (1960)

Constitution: *history:* previous 1959 (preindependence), 1963; latest adopted by referendum 7 January 2001, promulgated 22 January 2001
amendments: proposed by the president of the republic or by the National Assembly; passage requires Assembly approval and approval in a referendum; the president can bypass a referendum and submit an amendment directly to the Assembly, which requires at least three-fifths majority vote; the republican form of government is not amendable; amended several times, last in 2019

Legal system: civil law system based on French law; judicial review of legislative acts in Constitutional Court

International law organization participation: accepts compulsory ICJ jurisdiction with reservations; accepts ICCt jurisdiction

Citizenship: *citizenship by birth:* no
citizenship by descent only: at least one parent must be a citizen of Senegal
dual citizenship recognized: no, but Senegalese citizens do not automatically lose their citizenship if they acquire citizenship in another state
residency requirement for naturalization: 5 years

Suffrage: 18 years of age; universal

Executive branch: *chief of state:* President Macky SALL (since 2 April 2012)
head of government: Prime Minister Amadou BA (since 17 September 2022)
cabinet: Council of Ministers appointed by the president
elections/appointments: president directly elected by absolute majority popular vote in 2 rounds if needed for a single renewable 5-year term; election last held on 24 February 2019 (next to be held in February 2024)
election results:
Macky SALL elected president in first round; percent of vote - Macky SALL (APR) 58.3%, Idrissa SECK (Rewmi) 20.5%, Ousmane SONKO (PASTEF) 15.7%, other 5.5% (2019)

Legislative branch: *description:* unicameral National Assembly or *Assemblée* Nationale (165 seats; 112 members including 15 representing Senegalese diaspora directly elected by plurality vote in single- and multi-seat constituencies and 53 members directly elected by proportional representation vote in a single nationwide constituency; member term is 5-years)
elections:
National Assembly - last held on 31 July 2022 (next to be held in July 2027) (2022)
election results:
National Assembly results - percent of vote by party/coalition - BBY 46.6%, YAW 32.9%, WS 14.5%, other 6%; seats by party/coalition - BBY 82, YAW 56, WS 24, other 3; composition - men 95, women 70, percent of women 42.4% (2022)

Judicial branch: *highest court(s):* Supreme Court or Cour Supreme (consists of the court president and 12 judges and organized into civil and commercial, criminal, administrative, and social chambers); Constitutional Council or Conseil Constitutionel (consists of 7 members, including the court president, vice president, and 5 judges)
judge selection and term of office: Supreme Court judges appointed by the president of the republic upon recommendation of the Superior Council of the Magistrates, a body chaired by the president and minister of justice; judge tenure varies, with mandatory retirement either at 65 or 68 years; Constitutional Council members appointed - 5 by the president and 2 by the National Assembly speaker; judges serve 6-year terms, with renewal of 2 members every 2 years
subordinate courts: High Court of Justice (for crimes of high treason by the president); Courts of Appeal; Court of Auditors; assize courts; regional and district courts; Labor Court

Political parties and leaders: Alliance for Citizenship and Work or ACT [Abdoul MBAYE]
Alliance for the Republic-Yakaar or APR [Macky SALL]
Alliance of Forces of Progress or AFP [Moustapha NIASSE]
And-Jef/African Party for Democracy and Socialism or AJ/PADS [Landing SAVANE]
Benno Bokk Yakaar or BBY (United in Hope) [Mahammed DIONNE] (coalition includes AFP, APR, BGC, LD-MPT, PIT, PS, and UNP)
Bokk Gis Gis coalition [Pape DIOP]
Citizen Movement for National Reform or MCRN-Bes Du Nakk [Mansour Sy DJAMIL]
Dare the Future movement [Aissata Tall SALL]
Democratic League-Labor Party Movement or LD-MPT [Mamadou NDOYE]
Democratic Renaissance Congress [NA]
Front for Socialism and Democracy/Benno Jubel or FSD/BJ [Cheikh Abdoulaye Bamba DIEYE]
Gainde Centrist Bloc or BCG [Jean-Paul DIAS Mendes]
General Alliance for the Interests of the Republic or AGIR [Thierno BOCOUM]
Grand Party or GP [Malick GAKOU]
Independence and Labor Party or PIT [Maguette THIAM]
Jotna Coalition [Dr Abdoulaye Niane]
Liberate the People (Yewwi Askan Wi) or YAW [Barthelemy DIAS, Ousmane SONKO, Khalifa SALL]
Madicke 2019 coalition [Madicke NIANG]
National Union for the People or UNP [Abdoul MBAYE]
Only Senegal Movement [Pierre Goudiaby ATEPA]
Party for Truth and Development or PVD [Cheikh Ahmadou Kara MBAKE]
Party of Unity and Rally or PUR [Cheikh Mouhamadou Moustapha SY]
Patriotic Convergence Kaddu Askan Wi or CP-Kaddu Askan Wi [Abdoulaye BALDE]
Patriots of Senegal for Ethics, Work and Fraternity or PASTEF [Ousmane SONKO]
Rewmi Party [Idrissa SECK]
Save Senegal (Wallu Senegal Grand Coalition) or WS [Abdoulaye WADE] (coalition includes PDS, Jotna Coalition, Democratic Renaissance Congress)
Senegalese Democratic Party or PDS [Abdoulaye WADE]
Socialist Party or PS [Ousmane Tanor DIENG]
Tekki Movement [Mamadou Lamine DIALLO]

International organization participation: ACP, AfDB, AU, CD, CPLP (associate), ECOWAS, EITI (candidate country), FAO, FZ, G-15, G-77, IAEA, IBRD, ICAO, ICC (national committees), ICCt, ICRM, IDA, IDB, IFAD, IFC, IFRCS, ILO, IMF, IMO, IMSO, Interpol, IOC, IOM, IPU, ISO, ITSO, ITU, ITUC (NGOs), MIGA, MINUSMA, MONUSCO, NAM, OIC, OIF, OPCW, PCA, UN, UNAMID, UNCTAD, UNESCO, UNHCR, UNHRC, UNIDO, UNMIL, UNMISS, UNOCI, UNWTO, UPU, WADB (regional), WAEMU, WCO, WFTU (NGOs), WHO, WIPO, WMO, WTO

Diplomatic representation in the US: *chief of mission:* Ambassador Mansour Elimane KANE (since 6 January 2020)
chancery: 2215 M Street NW, Washington, DC 20007
telephone: [1] (202) 234-0540
FAX: [1] (202) 629-2961
email address and website:
contact@ambasenegal-us.org
http://www.ambasenegal-us.org/index.php
consulate(s) general: Houston, New York

Diplomatic representation from the US: *chief of mission:* Ambassador Michael RAYNOR (since February 2022); note - also accredited to Guinea-Bissau
embassy: Route des Almadies, Dakar
mailing address: 2130 Dakar Place, Washington DC 20521-2130
telephone: [221] 33-879-4000
email address and website:
DakarACS@state.gov
https://sn.usembassy.gov/

Flag description: three equal vertical bands of green (hoist side), yellow, and red with a small green five-pointed star centered in the yellow band; green represents Islam, progress, and hope; yellow signifies natural wealth and progress; red symbolizes sacrifice and determination; the star denotes unity and hope
note: uses the popular Pan-African colors of Ethiopia; the colors from left to right are the same as those of neighboring Mali and the reverse of those on the flag of neighboring Guinea

National symbol(s): lion; national colors: green, yellow, red

National anthem: *name:* "Pincez Tous vos Koras, Frappez les Balafons" (Pluck Your Koras, Strike the Balafons)
lyrics/music: Leopold Sedar SENGHOR/Herbert PEPPER
note: adopted 1960; lyrics written by Leopold Sedar SENGHOR, Senegal's first president; the anthem sometimes played incorporating the Koras (harp-like stringed instruments) and Balafons (types of xylophones) mentioned in the title

National heritage: *total World Heritage Sites:* 7 (5 cultural, 2 natural)
selected World Heritage Site locales: Island of Gorée (c); Niokolo-Koba National Park (n); Djoudj National Bird Sanctuary (n); Island of Saint-Louis (c); Stone Circles of Senegambia (c); Saloum Delta (c); Bassari Country: Bassari, Fula, and Bedik Cultural Landscapes (c)

ECONOMY

Economic overview: Senegal's economy is driven by mining, construction, tourism, fisheries and agriculture, which are the primary sources of employment in rural areas. The country's key export industries include phosphate mining, fertilizer production, agricultural products and commercial fishing and Senegal is also working on oil exploration projects. It relies heavily on donor assistance, remittances and foreign direct investment. Senegal reached a growth rate of 7% in 2017, due in part to strong performance in agriculture despite erratic rainfall.

President Macky SALL, who was elected in March 2012 under a reformist policy agenda, inherited an economy with high energy costs, a challenging business environment, and a culture of overspending. President SALL unveiled an ambitious economic plan, the Emerging Senegal Plan (ESP), which aims to implement priority economic reforms and investment projects to increase economic growth while preserving macroeconomic stability and debt sustainability. Bureaucratic bottlenecks and a challenging business climate are among the perennial challenges that may slow the implementation of this plan.

Senegal receives technical support from the IMF under a Policy Support Instrument (PSI) to assist with implementation of the ESP. The PSI implementation continues to be satisfactory as concluded by the IMF's fifth review in December 2017. Financial markets have signaled confidence in Senegal through successful Eurobond issuances in 2014, 2017, and 2018.

The government is focusing on 19 projects under the ESP to continue The government's goal under the ESP is structural transformation of the economy. Key projects include the Thiès-Touba Highway, the new international airport opened in December 2017, and upgrades to energy infrastructure. The cost of electricity is a chief constraint for Senegal's development. Electricity prices in Senegal are among the highest in the world. Power Africa, a US presidential initiative led by USAID, supports Senegal's plans to improve reliability and increase generating capacity.

Real GDP (purchasing power parity): $55.26 billion (2020 est.)
$54.78 billion (2019 est.)
$52.47 billion (2018 est.)
note: data are in 2017 dollars
country comparison to the world: 108

Real GDP growth rate: 7.2% (2017 est.)
6.2% (2016 est.)
6.4% (2015 est.)
country comparison to the world: 15

Real GDP per capita: $3,300 (2020 est.)
$3,400 (2019 est.)
$3,300 (2018 est.)
note: data are in 2017 dollars
country comparison to the world: 193

GDP (official exchange rate): $23.576 billion (2019 est.)

Inflation rate (consumer prices): -0.8% (2019 est.)
0.4% (2018 est.)
1.3% (2017 est.)
country comparison to the world: 9

Credit ratings: Moody's rating: Ba3 (2017)

Standard & Poors rating: B+ (2000)

GDP - composition, by sector of origin: *agriculture:* 16.9% (2017 est.)
industry: 24.3% (2017 est.)
services: 58.8% (2017 est.)

GDP - composition, by end use: *household consumption:* 71.9% (2017 est.)
government consumption: 15.2% (2017 est.)
investment in fixed capital: 25.1% (2017 est.)
investment in inventories: 3.4% (2017 est.)
exports of goods and services: 27% (2017 est.)
imports of goods and services: -42.8% (2017 est.)

Agricultural products: groundnuts, watermelons, rice, sugar cane, cassava, millet, maize, onions, sorghum, vegetables

Industries: agricultural and fish processing, phosphate mining, fertilizer production, petroleum refining, zircon, and gold mining, construction materials, ship construction and repair

Industrial production growth rate: 7.7% (2017 est.)
country comparison to the world: 26

Labor force: 6.966 million (2017 est.)
country comparison to the world: 65

Labor force - by occupation: *agriculture:* 77.5%
industry: 22.5%
industry and services: 22.5% (2007 est.)

Unemployment rate: 48% (2007 est.)
country comparison to the world: 217

Unemployment, youth ages 15-24: *total:* 4.1%
male: 2.9%
female: 6.7% (2019 est.)
country comparison to the world: 171

Population below poverty line: 46.7% (2011 est.)

Gini Index coefficient - distribution of family income: 40.3 (2011 est.)
country comparison to the world: 61

Household income or consumption by percentage share: *lowest 10%:* 2.5%
highest 10%: 31.1% (2011)

Budget: *revenues:* 4.139 billion (2017 est.)
expenditures: 4.9 billion (2017 est.)

Budget surplus (+) or deficit (-): -3.6% (of GDP) (2017 est.)
country comparison to the world: 151

Public debt: 48.3% of GDP (2017 est.)
47.8% of GDP (2016 est.)
country comparison to the world: 108

Taxes and other revenues: 19.6% (of GDP) (2017 est.)
country comparison to the world: 155

Fiscal year: calendar year

Current account balance: -$1.547 billion (2017 est.)
-$769 million (2016 est.)
country comparison to the world: 160

Exports: $5.29 billion (2018 est.) note: data are in current year dollars
$2.498 billion (2016 est.)
country comparison to the world: 123

Exports - partners: Mali 22%, Switzerland 14%, India 9%, China 7% (2019)

Exports - commodities: gold, refined petroleum, phosphoric acid, fish, ground nuts (2019)

Imports: $8.96 billion (2018 est.) note: data are in current year dollars
$4.966 billion (2016 est.)
country comparison to the world: 111

Imports - partners: China 17%, France 11%, Belgium 7%, Russia 7%, Netherlands 7% (2019)

Imports - commodities: refined petroleum, crude petroleum, rice, cars, malt extract, clothing and apparel (2019)

Reserves of foreign exchange and gold: $1.827 billion (31 December 2017 est.)
$116.9 million (31 December 2016 est.)
country comparison to the world: 122

Debt - external: $8.571 billion (31 December 2017 est.)
$6.327 billion (31 December 2016 est.)
country comparison to the world: 119

Exchange rates: Communaute Financiere Africaine francs (XOF) per US dollar -
617.4 (2017 est.)
593.01 (2016 est.)
593.01 (2015 est.)
591.45 (2014 est.)
494.42 (2013 est.)

ENERGY

Electricity access: *electrification - total population:* 71% (2019)
electrification - urban areas: 94% (2019)
electrification - rural areas: 50% (2019)

Electricity: *installed generating capacity:* 1.312 million kW (2020 est.)
consumption: 4,735,980,000 kWh (2019 est.)
exports: 0 kWh (2019 est.)
imports: 324 million kWh (2019 est.)
transmission/distribution losses: 764 million kWh (2019 est.)

Electricity generation sources: *fossil fuels:* 84.8% of total installed capacity (2020 est.)
solar: 6% of total installed capacity (2020 est.)
wind: 0.5% of total installed capacity (2020 est.)
hydroelectricity: 6.3% of total installed capacity (2020 est.)
biomass and waste: 2.4% of total installed capacity (2020 est.)

Coal: *production:* 0 metric tons (2020 est.)
consumption: 894,000 metric tons (2020 est.)
exports: 0 metric tons (2020 est.)
imports: 894,000 metric tons (2020 est.)
proven reserves: 0 metric tons (2019 est.)

Petroleum: *total petroleum production:* 0 bbl/day (2021 est.)
refined petroleum consumption: 57,500 bbl/day (2019 est.)
crude oil and lease condensate exports: 0 bbl/day (2018 est.)

crude oil and lease condensate imports: 20,500 bbl/day (2018 est.)
crude oil estimated reserves: 0 barrels (2021 est.)

Refined petroleum products - production: 17,590 bbl/day (2015 est.)
country comparison to the world: 90

Refined petroleum products - exports: 4,063 bbl/day (2015 est.)
country comparison to the world: 94

Refined petroleum products - imports: 32,050 bbl/day (2015 est.)
country comparison to the world: 98

Natural gas: *production:* 60.003 million cubic meters (2019 est.)
consumption: 60.003 million cubic meters (2019 est.)

Carbon dioxide emissions: 10.696 million metric tonnes of CO2 (2019 est.)
from coal and metallurgical coke: 1.955 million metric tonnes of CO2 (2019 est.)
from petroleum and other liquids: 8.64 million metric tonnes of CO2 (2019 est.)
from consumed natural gas: 101,000 metric tonnes of CO2 (2019 est.)
country comparison to the world: 103

Energy consumption per capita: 9.221 million Btu/person (2019 est.)
country comparison to the world: 157

COMMUNICATIONS

Telephones - fixed lines: *total subscriptions:* 228,774 (2020 est.)
subscriptions per 100 inhabitants: 1 (2020 est.)
country comparison to the world: 118

Telephones - mobile cellular: *total subscriptions:* 19,078,948 (2020 est.)
subscriptions per 100 inhabitants: 114 (2020 est.)
country comparison to the world: 63

Telecommunication systems: *general assessment:* Senegal's telecom market continues to show steady growth in all sectors; this has been supported by the particular demands made on consumers during the pandemic, which resulted in a particularly strong increase in the number of subscribers; the mobile subscriber base increased 6.7% in 2020, year-on-year, and by 4.1% in 2021, while the number of fixed broadband subscribers increased 17.5% year-on-year in 2021; mobile internet platforms account for the vast majority of all internet accesses; quality of service issues continue to plague the market, with the regulator periodically issuing fines to the market players (2022)
domestic: generally reliable urban system with a fiber-optic network; about two-thirds of all fixed-line connections are in Dakar; mobile-cellular service is steadily displacing fixed-line service, even in urban areas; fixed-line roughly 1 per 100 and mobile-cellular 114 per 100 persons (2020)
international: country code - 221; landing points for the ACE, Atlantis-2, MainOne and SAT-3/WASC submarine cables providing connectivity from South Africa, numerous western African countries, Europe and South America; satellite earth station - 1 Intelsat (Atlantic Ocean) (2019)

Broadcast media: state-run Radiodiffusion Television Senegalaise (RTS) broadcasts TV programs from five cities in Senegal; in most regions of the country, viewers can receive TV programming from at least 7 private broadcasters; a wide range of independent TV programming is available via satellite; RTS operates a national radio network and a number of regional FM stations; at least 7 community radio stations and 18 private-broadcast radio stations are available; transmissions of at least 5 international broadcasters are accessible on FM in Dakar (2019)

Internet country code: .sn

Internet users: *total:* 7,199,890 (2020 est.)
percent of population: 43% (2020 est.)
country comparison to the world: 75

Broadband - fixed subscriptions: *total:* 153,813 (2020 est.)
subscriptions per 100 inhabitants: 1 (2020 est.)
country comparison to the world: 122

TRANSPORTATION

National air transport system: *number of registered air carriers:* 2 (2020)
inventory of registered aircraft operated by air carriers: 11
annual passenger traffic on registered air carriers: 21,038 (2018)
annual freight traffic on registered air carriers: 40,000 (2018) mt-km

Civil aircraft registration country code prefix: 6V

Airports: *total:* 20 (2021)
country comparison to the world: 135

Airports - with paved runways: *total:* 9
over 3,047 m: 2
1,524 to 2,437 m: 6
914 to 1,523 m: 1 (2021)

Airports - with unpaved runways: *total:* 11
1,524 to 2,437 m: 7
914 to 1,523 m: 3
under 914 m: 1 (2021)

Pipelines: 43 km gas, 8 km refined products (2017)

Railways: *total:* 906 km (2017) (713 km operational in 2017)
narrow gauge: 906 km (2017) 1.000-m gauge
country comparison to the world: 94

Roadways: *total:* 16,665 km (2017)
paved: 6,126 km (2017) (includes 241 km of expressways)
unpaved: 10,539 km (2017)
country comparison to the world: 119

Waterways: 1,000 km (2012) (primarily on the Senegal, Saloum, and Casamance Rivers)
country comparison to the world: 68

Merchant marine: *total:* 35
by type: general cargo 5, oil tanker 1, other 29 (2021)
country comparison to the world: 129

Ports and terminals: *major seaport(s):* Dakar

MILITARY AND SECURITY

Military and security forces: Senegalese Armed Forces (les Forces Armées Sénégalaises, FAS): Army, Senegalese National Navy (Marine Senegalaise, MNS), Senegalese Air Force (l'Armee de l'Air du Senegal), National Gendarmerie (includes Territorial and Mobile components); Ministry of Interior: National Police (2022)
note: the National Police operates in major cities, while the Gendarmerie primarily operates outside urban areas

Military expenditures: 1.7% of GDP (2021 est.)
1.5% of GDP (2020)
1.5% of GDP (2019 est.) (approximately $490 million)
1.6% of GDP (2018) (approximately $490 million)
1.5% of GDP (2017) (approximately $430 million)
country comparison to the world: 83

Military and security service personnel strengths: approximately 19,000 active personnel (12,000 Army; 1,000 Navy/Coast Guard; 1,000 Air Force; 5,000 National Gendarmerie) (2022)

Military equipment inventories and acquisitions: the FAS inventory includes mostly older or second-hand equipment from a variety of countries, including France, South Africa, and Russia/former Soviet Union; in recent years, the FAS has undertaken a modernization program; since 2010, it has received small amounts of newer equipment from more than 10 countries, with France as the leading supplier (2022)

Military service age and obligation: 18 years of age for voluntary military service for men and women; 20 years of age for selective conscript service; 2-year service obligation; women have been accepted into military service since 2008 (2022)

Military deployments: 750 Gambia (ECOMIG); 970 Mali (MINUSMA); note - Senegal also has about 1,100 police deployed on various UN peacekeeping missions (2022)

Military - note: Senegalese security forces continue to be engaged in a low-level counterinsurgency campaign in the southern Casamance region against various factions of the separatist Movement of Democratic Forces of the Casamance (MDFC); while violent incidents have decreased since a tacit cease-fire was reached in 2012, the insurgency, which began in 1982, continued as of mid-2022 and remained one of longest running low-level conflicts in the world, claiming more than 5,000 lives and leaving another 60,000 displaced (2022)
note: in August 2022, a representative of the Senegalese Government and a leader of the MFDC signed an agreement in which the MFDC pledged to lay down its arms and work towards a permanent peace

TERRORISM

Terrorist group(s): Jama'at Nusrat al-Islam wal-Muslimin (JNIM)

TRANSNATIONAL ISSUES

Disputes - international: *Senegal-Guinea-Bissau:* rebels from the Movement of Democratic Forces in the Casamance find refuge in Guinea-Bissau

Refugees and internally displaced persons: *refugees (country of origin):* 11,489 (Mauritania) (2022)

IDPs: 8,400 (2021)

Trafficking in persons: *current situation:* Senegal is a source, transit, and destination country for children and women who are subjected to forced begging, forced labor, and sex trafficking; traffickers subject Senegalese children to forced labor in domestic service, mining, and prostitution; some Senegalese boys from Quranic schools and boys from The Gambia, Mali, Guinea-Bissau, and Guinea are forced to beg; Senegalese women and girls are forced into domestic servitude in neighboring countries, Europe, and the Middle East, while others are sexually exploited in Senegal; women and girls from other West African countries are subjected to domestic

servitude and sexual exploitation in Senegal; Ukrainian and Chinese women are exploited for sex trafficking in bars and nightclubs; North Korean workers are forced to work in construction
tier rating: Tier 2 Watch List — Senegal does not fully meet the minimum standards for the elimination of trafficking but is making significant efforts to do so; efforts include establishing an anti-trafficking database; planning the third phase of its program to remove vulnerable children, including trafficking victims, from the streets of major cities; launching an emergency campaign to place vulnerable children and forced begging victims in shelters due to COVID 19 pandemic; however, the government rarely proactively investigated or prosecuted traffickers exploiting children in forced begging; authorities did not take action against officials who refused to investigate such cases; officials only applied adequate prison terms in accordance with the 2005 anti-trafficking law to two convicted traffickers; authorities did not identify any adult trafficking victims; government officials continued to have a limited knowledge of trafficking; Senegal was downgraded to Tier 2 Watch List (2020)

Illicit drugs: major transit point on the cocaine route from South America to Europe; the third-largest cannabis-producing country in West Africa

SERBIA

INTRODUCTION

Background: The Kingdom of Serbs, Croats, and Slovenes was formed in 1918; its name was changed to Yugoslavia in 1929. Communist Partisans resisted the Axis occupation and division of Yugoslavia from 1941 to 1945 and fought nationalist opponents and collaborators as well. The military and political movement headed by Josip Broz "TITO" (Partisans) took full control of Yugoslavia when their domestic rivals and the occupiers were defeated in 1945. Although communists, TITO and his successors (Tito died in 1980) managed to steer their own path between the Warsaw Pact nations and the West for the next four and a half decades. In 1989, Slobodan MILOSEVIC became president of the Republic of Serbia and his ultranationalist calls for Serbian domination led to the violent breakup of Yugoslavia along ethnic lines. In 1991, Croatia, Slovenia, and Macedonia declared independence, followed by Bosnia in 1992. The remaining republics of Serbia and Montenegro declared a new Federal Republic of Yugoslavia (FRY) in April 1992 and under MILOSEVIC's leadership, Serbia led various military campaigns to unite ethnic Serbs in neighboring republics into a "Greater Serbia." These actions ultimately failed and, after international intervention, led to the signing of the Dayton Peace Accords in 1995.

MILOSEVIC retained control over Serbia and eventually became president of the FRY in 1997. In 1998, an ethnic Albanian insurgency in the formerly autonomous Serbian province of Kosovo provoked a Serbian counterinsurgency campaign that resulted in massacres and massive expulsions of ethnic Albanians living in Kosovo. The MILOSEVIC government's rejection of a proposed international settlement led to NATO's bombing of Serbia in the spring of 1999. Serbian military and police forces withdrew from Kosovo in June 1999, and the UN Security Council authorized an interim UN administration and a NATO-led security force in Kosovo. FRY elections in late 2000 led to the ouster of MILOSEVIC and the installation of democratic government. In 2003, the FRY became the State Union of Serbia and Montenegro, a loose federation of the two republics. Widespread violence predominantly targeting ethnic Serbs in Kosovo in March 2004 led to more intense calls to address Kosovo's status, and the UN began facilitating status talks in 2006. In June 2006, Montenegro seceded from the federation and declared itself an independent nation. Serbia subsequently gave notice that it was the successor state to the union of Serbia and Montenegro.

In February 2008, after nearly two years of inconclusive negotiations, Kosovo declared itself independent of Serbia - an action Serbia refuses to recognize. At Serbia's request, the UN General Assembly (UNGA) in October 2008 sought an advisory opinion from the International Court of Justice (ICJ) on whether Kosovo's unilateral declaration of independence was in accordance with international law. In a ruling considered unfavorable to Serbia, the ICJ issued an advisory opinion in July 2010 stating that international law did not prohibit declarations of independence. In late 2010, Serbia agreed to an EU-drafted UNGA Resolution acknowledging the ICJ's decision and calling for a new round of talks between Serbia and Kosovo, this time on practical issues rather than Kosovo's status. Serbia and Kosovo signed the first agreement of principles governing the normalization of relations between the two countries in April 2013 and are in the process of implementing its provisions. In 2015, Serbia and Kosovo reached four additional agreements within the EU-led Brussels Dialogue framework. These included agreements on the Community of Serb-Majority Municipalities; telecommunications; energy production and distribution; and freedom of movement. President Aleksandar VUCIC has promoted an ambitious goal of Serbia joining the EU by 2025. Under his leadership as prime minister, in 2014 Serbia opened formal negotiations for accession.

GEOGRAPHY

Location: Southeastern Europe, between Macedonia and Hungary

Geographic coordinates: 44 00 N, 21 00 E

Map references: Europe

Area: *total:* 77,474 sq km
land: 77,474 sq km
water: 0 sq km
country comparison to the world: 117

Area - comparative: slightly smaller than South Carolina

Land boundaries: *total:* 2,322 km
border countries (8): Bosnia and Herzegovina 345 km; Bulgaria 344 km; Croatia 314 km; Hungary 164 km; Kosovo 366 km; North Macedonia 101 km; Montenegro 157 km; Romania 531 km

Coastline: 0 km (landlocked)

Maritime claims: none (landlocked)

Climate: in the north, continental climate (cold winters and hot, humid summers with well-distributed rainfall); in other parts, continental and Mediterranean climate (relatively cold winters with heavy snowfall and hot, dry summers and autumns)

Terrain: extremely varied; to the north, rich fertile plains; to the east, limestone ranges and basins; to the southeast, ancient mountains and hills

Elevation: *highest point:* Midzor 2,169 m
lowest point: Danube and Timok Rivers 35 m
mean elevation: 442 m

Natural resources: oil, gas, coal, iron ore, copper, zinc, antimony, chromite, gold, silver, magnesium, pyrite, limestone, marble, salt, arable land

Land use: *agricultural land:* 57.9% (2018 est.)
arable land: 37.7% (2018 est.)
permanent crops: 3.4% (2018 est.)
permanent pasture: 16.8% (2018 est.)
forest: 31.6% (2018 est.)
other: 10.5% (2018 est.)

Irrigated land: 950 sq km (2012)

Major rivers (by length in km): Danube (shared with Germany [s], Austria, Slovakia, Czechia, Hungary, Croatia, Bulgaria, Ukraine, Moldova, and Romania [m]) - 2,888 km
note – [s] after country name indicates river source; [m] after country name indicates river mouth

Major watersheds (area sq km): Atlantic Ocean drainage: *(Black Sea)* Danube (795,656 sq km)

Population distribution: a fairly even distribution throughout most of the country, with urban areas attracting larger and denser populations

Natural hazards: destructive earthquakes

Geography - note: landlocked; controls one of the major land routes from Western Europe to Turkey and the Near East

PEOPLE AND SOCIETY

Population: 6,739,471 (2022 est.)
note: does not include the population of Kosovo
country comparison to the world: 108

Nationality: *noun:* Serb(s)
adjective: Serbian

Ethnic groups: Serb 83.3%, Hungarian 3.5%, Romani 2.1%, Bosniak 2%, other 5.7%, undeclared or unknown 3.4% (2011 est.)
note: most ethnic Albanians boycotted the 2011 census; Romani populations are usually underestimated in official statistics and may represent 5–11% of Serbia's population

Languages: Serbian (official) 88.1%, Hungarian 3.4%, Bosnian 1.9%, Romani 1.4%, other 3.4%, undeclared or unknown 1.8%; note - Serbian, Hungarian, Slovak, Romanian, Croatian, and Ruthenian (Rusyn) are official in the Autonomous Province of Vojvodina; most ethnic Albanians boycotted the 2011 census (2011 est.)
major-language sample(s):
Knjiga svetskih činjenica, neophodan izvor osnovnih informacija. (Serbian)

Religions: Orthodox 84.6%, Catholic 5%, Muslim 3.1%, Protestant 1%, atheist 1.1%, other 0.8% (includes agnostics, other Christians, Eastern, Jewish), undeclared or unknown 4.5% (2011 est.)
note: most ethnic Albanians boycotted the 2011 census

Age structure: *0-14 years:* 14.07% (male 508,242/female 478,247)
15-24 years: 11.04% (male 399,435/female 374,718)
25-54 years: 41.19% (male 1,459,413/female 1,429,176)
55-64 years: 13.7% (male 464,881/female 495,663)
65 years and over: 20% (male 585,705/female 816,685) (2020 est.)

Dependency ratios: *total dependency ratio:* 52.5
youth dependency ratio: 23.4
elderly dependency ratio: 29.1
potential support ratio: 3.4 (2020 est.)
note: data include Kosovo

Median age: *total:* 43.4 years
male: 41.7 years
female: 45 years (2020 est.)
country comparison to the world: 26

Population growth rate: -0.75% (2022 est.)
country comparison to the world: 229

Birth rate: 8.92 births/1,000 population (2022 est.)
country comparison to the world: 205

Death rate: 16.39 deaths/1,000 population (2022 est.)
country comparison to the world: 1

Net migration rate: 0 migrant(s)/1,000 population (2022 est.)
country comparison to the world: 97

Population distribution: a fairly even distribution throughout most of the country, with urban areas attracting larger and denser populations

Urbanization: *urban population:* 56.9% of total population (2022)
rate of urbanization: 0.04% annual rate of change (2020-25 est.)
note: data include Kosovo

Major urban areas - population: 1.405 million BELGRADE (capital) (2022)

Sex ratio: *at birth:* 1.06 male(s)/female
0-14 years: 1.06 male(s)/female
15-24 years: 1.05 male(s)/female
25-54 years: 1.02 male(s)/female
55-64 years: 0.95 male(s)/female
65 years and over: 0.55 male(s)/female
total population: 0.95 male(s)/female (2022 est.)

Mother's mean age at first birth: 28.2 years (2020 est.)
note: data does not cover Kosovo or Metohija

Maternal mortality ratio: 12 deaths/100,000 live births (2017 est.)
country comparison to the world: 141

Infant mortality rate: *total:* 4.81 deaths/1,000 live births
male: 5.43 deaths/1,000 live births
female: 4.16 deaths/1,000 live births (2022 est.)
country comparison to the world: 179

Life expectancy at birth: *total population:* 74.17 years
male: 71.5 years
female: 77 years (2022 est.)
country comparison to the world: 141

Total fertility rate: 1.46 children born/woman (2022 est.)
country comparison to the world: 207

Contraceptive prevalence rate: 62.3% (2019)

Drinking water source: *improved: urban:* 99.7% of population
rural: 99.4% of population
total: 99.5% of population
unimproved: urban: 0.3% of population
rural: 0.6% of population
total: 0.5% of population (2020 est.)

Current health expenditure: 8.7% of GDP (2019)

Physicians density: 3.11 physicians/1,000 population (2016)

Hospital bed density: 5.6 beds/1,000 population (2017)

Sanitation facility access: *improved: urban:* 99.6% of population
rural: 95.7% of population
total: 97.9% of population
unimproved: urban: 0.4% of population
rural: 4.3% of population
total: 2.1% of population (2020 est.)

HIV/AIDS - adult prevalence rate: (2020 est.) <.1%

HIV/AIDS - people living with HIV/AIDS: 3,300 (2020 est.)
note: estimate does not include children
country comparison to the world: 132

HIV/AIDS - deaths: (2020 est.) <100
note: estimate does not include children

Major infectious diseases: *degree of risk:* intermediate (2020)
food or waterborne diseases: bacterial diarrhea

Obesity - adult prevalence rate: 21.5% (2016)
country comparison to the world: 88

Alcohol consumption per capita: *total:* 7.45 liters of pure alcohol (2019 est.)
beer: 3.24 liters of pure alcohol (2019 est.)
wine: 1.62 liters of pure alcohol (2019 est.)
spirits: 2.37 liters of pure alcohol (2019 est.)
other alcohols: 0.22 liters of pure alcohol (2019 est.)
country comparison to the world: 55

Tobacco use: *total:* 39.8% (2020 est.)
male: 40.5% (2020 est.)
female: 39.1% (2020 est.)
country comparison to the world: 4

Children under the age of 5 years underweight: 1% (2019)
country comparison to the world: 122

Child marriage: *women married by age 15:* 1.2%
women married by age 18: 5.5% (2019 est.)

Education expenditures: 3.6% of GDP (2019 est.)
country comparison to the world: 120

Literacy: *definition:* age 15 and over can read and write
total population: 99.5%
male: 99.9%
female: 99.1% (2019)

School life expectancy (primary to tertiary education): *total:* 14 years
male: 14 years
female: 15 years (2020)

Unemployment, youth ages 15-24: *total:* 26.7%
male: 25%
female: 29.5% (2020 est.)

ENVIRONMENT

Environment - current issues: air pollution around Belgrade and other industrial cities; water pollution from industrial wastes dumped into the Sava which flows into the Danube; inadequate management of domestic, industrial, and hazardous waste

Environment - international agreements: *party to:* Air Pollution, Air Pollution-Heavy Metals, Air Pollution-Persistent Organic Pollutants, Biodiversity, Climate Change, Climate Change-Kyoto Protocol, Climate Change-Paris Agreement, Comprehensive Nuclear Test Ban, Desertification, Endangered Species, Hazardous Wastes, Law of the Sea, Marine Dumping-London Convention, Marine Life Conservation, Nuclear Test Ban, Ozone Layer Protection, Ship Pollution, Wetlands
signed, but not ratified: none of the selected agreements

Air pollutants: *particulate matter emissions:* 24.27 micrograms per cubic meter (2016 est.)
carbon dioxide emissions: 45.22 megatons (2016 est.)
methane emissions: 11.96 megatons (2020 est.)

Climate: in the north, continental climate (cold winters and hot, humid summers with well-distributed rainfall); in other parts, continental and Mediterranean climate (relatively cold winters with heavy snowfall and hot, dry summers and autumns)

Land use: *agricultural land:* 57.9% (2018 est.)
arable land: 37.7% (2018 est.)
permanent crops: 3.4% (2018 est.)
permanent pasture: 16.8% (2018 est.)
forest: 31.6% (2018 est.)
other: 10.5% (2018 est.)

Urbanization: *urban population:* 56.9% of total population (2022)
rate of urbanization: 0.04% annual rate of change (2020-25 est.)
note: data include Kosovo

Revenue from forest resources: *forest revenues:* 0.38% of GDP (2018 est.)
country comparison to the world: 73

Revenue from coal: *coal revenues:* 0.25% of GDP (2018 est.)
country comparison to the world: 20

Waste and recycling: *municipal solid waste generated annually:* 1.84 million tons (2015 est.)
municipal solid waste recycled annually: 13,984 tons (2015 est.)
percent of municipal solid waste recycled: 0.8% (2015 est.)

Major rivers (by length in km): Danube (shared with Germany [s], Austria, Slovakia, Czechia, Hungary, Croatia, Bulgaria, Ukraine, Moldova, and Romania [m]) - 2,888 km
note – [s] after country name indicates river source; [m] after country name indicates river mouth

Major watersheds (area sq km): Atlantic Ocean drainage: *(Black Sea)* Danube (795,656 sq km)

Total water withdrawal: *municipal:* 659.5 million cubic meters (2017 est.)
industrial: 4.057 billion cubic meters (2017 est.)
agricultural: 660.8 million cubic meters (2017 est.)

Total renewable water resources: 162.2 billion cubic meters (2017 est.) (note - includes Kosovo)

GOVERNMENT

Country name: *conventional long form:* Republic of Serbia
conventional short form: Serbia
local long form: Republika Srbija
local short form: Srbija
former: People's Republic of Serbia, Socialist Republic of Serbia
etymology: the origin of the name is uncertain, but seems to be related to the name of the West Slavic Sorbs who reside in the Lusatian region in present-day eastern Germany; by tradition, the Serbs migrated from that region to the Balkans in about the 6th century A.D.

Government type: parliamentary republic

Capital: *name:* Belgrade (Beograd)
geographic coordinates: 44 50 N, 20 30 E
time difference: UTC+1 (6 hours ahead of Washington, DC, during Standard Time)
daylight saving time: +1hr, begins last Sunday in March; ends last Sunday in October
etymology: the Serbian "Beograd" means "white fortress" or "white city" and dates back to the 9th century; the name derives from the white fortress wall that once enclosed the city

Administrative divisions: 117 municipalities (opstine, singular - opstina) and 28 cities (gradovi, singular - grad)
municipalities: Ada*, Aleksandrovac, Aleksinac, Alibunar*, Apatin*, Arandelovac, Arilje, Babusnica, Bac*, Backa Palanka*, Backa Topola*, Backi Petrovac*, Bajina Basta, Batocina, Becej*, Bela Crkva*, Bela Palanka, Beocin*, Blace, Bogatic, Bojnik, Boljevac, Bosilegrad, Brus, Bujanovac, Cajetina, Cicevac, Coka*, Crna Trava, Cuprija, Despotovac, Dimitrov, Doljevac, Gadzin Han, Golubac, Gornji Milanovac, Indija*, Irig*, Ivanjica, Kanjiza*, Kladovo, Knic, Knjazevac, Koceljeva, Kosjeric, Kovacica*, Kovin*, Krupanj, Kucevo, Kula*, Kursumlija, Lajkovac, Lapovo, Lebane, Ljig, Ljubovija, Lucani, Majdanpek, Mali Idos*, Mali Zvornik, Malo Crnice, Medveda, Merosina, Mionica, Negotin, Nova Crnja*, Nova Varos, Novi Becej*, Novi Knezevac*, Odzaci*, Opovo*, Osecina, Paracin, Pecinci*, Petrovac na Mlavi, Plandiste*, Pozega, Presevo, Priboj, Prijepolje, Raca, Raska, Razanj, Rekovac, Ruma*, Secanj*, Senta*, Sid*, Sjenica, Smederevska Palanka, Sokobanja, Srbobran*, Sremski Karlovci*, Stara Pazova*, Surdulica, Svilajnac, Svrljig, Temerin*, Titel*, Topola, Trgoviste, Trstenik, Tutin, Ub, Varvarin, Velika Plana, Veliko Gradiste, Vladicin Han, Vladimirci, Vlasotince, Vrbas*, Vrnjacka Banja, Zabalj*, Zabari, Zagubica, Zitiste*, Zitorada
cities: Beograd (Belgrade), Bor, Cacak, Jagodina, Kikinda*, Kragujevac, Kraljevo, Krusevac, Leskovac, Loznica, Nis, Novi Pazar, Novi Sad*, Pancevo*, Pirot, Pozarevac, Prokuplje, Sabac, Smederevo, Sombor*, Sremska Mitrovica*, Subotica*, Uzice, Valjevo, Vranje, Vrsac*, Zajecar, Zrenjanin*
note: the northern 37 municipalities and 8 cities - about 28% of Serbia's area - compose the Autonomous Province of Vojvodina and are indicated with *

Independence: 5 June 2006 (from the State Union of Serbia and Montenegro); notable earlier dates: 1217 (Serbian Kingdom established); 16 April 1346 (Serbian Empire established); 13 July 1878 (Congress of Berlin recognizes Serbian independence); 1 December 1918 (Kingdom of Serbs, Croats, and Slovenes (Yugoslavia) established)

National holiday: Statehood Day, 15 February (1835), the day the first constitution of the country was adopted

Constitution: *history:* many previous; latest adopted 30 September 2006, approved by referendum 28-29 October 2006, effective 8 November 2006
amendments: proposed by at least one third of deputies in the National Assembly, by the president of the republic, by the government, or by petition of at least 150,000 voters; passage of proposals and draft amendments each requires at least two-thirds majority vote in the Assembly; amendments to constitutional articles including the preamble, constitutional principles, and human and minority rights and freedoms also require passage by simple majority vote in a referendum

Legal system: civil law system

International law organization participation: has not submitted an ICJ jurisdiction declaration; accepts ICCt jurisdiction

Citizenship: *citizenship by birth:* no
citizenship by descent only: at least one parent must be a citizen of Serbia
dual citizenship recognized: yes
residency requirement for naturalization: 3 years

Suffrage: 18 years of age, 16 if employed; universal

Executive branch: *chief of state:* President Aleksandar VUCIC (since 31 May 2017)
head of government: Prime Minister Ana BRNABIC (since 29 June 2017)
cabinet: Cabinet elected by the National Assembly
elections/appointments: president directly elected by absolute majority popular vote in 2 rounds if needed for a 5-year term (eligible for a second term); election last held on 3 April 2022 (next to be held in April 2027); prime minister elected by the National Assembly; note - in October 2020 President VUCIC called for early elections
election results:
2022: Aleksandar VUCIC reelected in the first round; percent of vote - Aleksandar VUSIC (SNS) 60%, Zdravko PONOS (US) 18.9%, Milos JOVANOVIC (NADA) 6.1%, Bosko OBRADOVIC (Dveri-POKS) 4.5%, Milica DURDEVIC STAMENDOVSKI (SSZ) 4.3%, other 6.2%
2017: Aleksandar VUCIC elected president in the first round; percent of vote - Aleksandar VUCIC (SNS) 55.1%, Sasa JANKOVIC (independent) 16.4%, Luka MAKSIMOVIC (independent) 9.4%, Vuk JEREMIC (independent) 5.7%, Vojislav SESELJ (SRS) 4.5%, Bosko OBRADOVIC (Dveri) 2.3%, other 5.0%, invalid/blank 1.6%; Prime Minister Ana BRNABIC reelected by the National Assembly on 5 October 2020

Legislative branch: *description:* unicameral National Assembly or Narodna Skupstina (250 seats; members directly elected by party list proportional representation vote in a single nationwide constituency to serve 4-year terms)
elections:
last held on 3 April 2022 (next to be held in April 2026)
election results:
percent of vote by party/coalition - Together We Can Do Everything 44.2%, UZPS 14.1%, Ivica Dacic - Prime Minister 11.8%, NADA 5.6%, We Must 4.9%, Dveri-POKS 3.9%, SSZ 3.8%, other 11.7%; seats by party/coalition - Together We Can Do Everything 120, UZPS 38, Ivica Dacic - Prime Minister 31, NADA 15, We Must 13, Dveri-POKS 10, SSZ 10, SVM 6, SPP 3, other 4; composition - men 150, women 100, percent of women 40%

Judicial branch: *highest court(s):* Supreme Court of Cassation (consists of 36 judges, including the court president); Constitutional Court (consists of 15 judges, including the court president and vice president)
judge selection and term of office: Supreme Court justices proposed by the High Judicial Council (HJC), an 11- member independent body consisting of 8 judges elected by the National Assembly and 3 ex-officio members; justices appointed by the National Assembly; Constitutional Court judges elected - 5 each by the National Assembly, the president, and the Supreme Court of Cassation; initial appointment of Supreme Court judges by the HJC is 3 years and beyond that period tenure is permanent; Constitutional Court judges elected for 9-year terms
subordinate courts: basic courts, higher courts, appellate courts; courts of special jurisdiction include the Administrative Court, commercial courts, and misdemeanor courts

Political parties and leaders: Albanian Democratic Alternative (coalition of ethnic Albanian parties) [Shaip KAMBERI]
Alliance of Vojvodina Hungarians or SVM or VMSZ [Istvan PASZTOR]
Better Serbia or BS [Dragan JOVANOVIC]
Democratic Party or DS [Zoran LUTOVAC]
Dveri [Bosko OBRADOVIC]
Greens of Serbia or ZS [Ivan KARIC]
Ivica Dacic - Prime Minister of Serbia [Ivica DACIC] (coalition includes SPS, JS, ZS)
Justice and Reconciliation Party or SPP [Usame ZUKORLIC] (formerly Bosniak Democratic Union of Sandzak or BDZS)
Movement for the Restoration of the Kingdom of Serbia or POKS [Vojislav MIHAILOVIC]
Movement of Free Citizens or PSG [Pavle GRBOVIC]
Movement of Socialists or PS [Aleksandar VULIN]
National Democratic Alternative or NADA [Milos JOVANOVIC and Vojislav MIHAILOVIC] (coalition includes DSS and POKS)

New Democratic Party of Serbia or NDSS or New DSS [Milos JOVANOVIC] (formerly Democratic Party of Serbia or DSS)
Party of Democratic Action of the Sandzak or SDA [Sulejman UGLJANIN]
Party of Freedom and Justice or SSP [Dragan DILAS]
Party of United Pensioners, Farmers, and Proletarians of Serbia – Solidarity and Justice or PUPS - Solidarity and Justice [Milan KRKOBABIC] (formerly Party of United Pensioners of Serbia or PUPS)
People's Party or NS or Narodna [Vuk JEREMIC]
People's Peasant Party or NSS [Marijan RISTICEVIC]
Serbian Party Oathkeepers or SSZ [Stefan STAMENKOVSKI]
Serbian People's Party or SNP [Nenad POPOVIC]
Serbian Progressive Party or SNS [Aleksandar VUCIC]
Serbian Renewal Movement or SPO [Vuk DRASKOVIC]
Social Democratic Party of Serbia or SDPS [Rasim LJAJIC]
Socialist Party of Serbia or SPS [Ivica DACIC]
Strength of Serbia or PSS [Bogoljub KARIC]
Together for Serbia or ZZS [Nebojsa ZELENOVIC]
Together We Can Do Everything [Milenko JOVANOV] (includes SNS, SDPS, PUPS, PSS, SNP, SPO, PS, NSS, USS, BS)
United for the Victory of Serbia or UZPS (includes NS, SSP, DS, PSG) (dissolved April 2022)
United Peasant Party or USS [Milija MILETIC]
United Serbia or JS [Dragan MARKOVIC]
We Must or Moramo [Nebojsa ZELENOVIC, Dobrica VESELINOVIC, Aleksandar JOVANOVIC CUTA, Biljana STOJKOVIC, Radomir LAZOVIC, Biljana DORDEVIC]
note: Serbia has more than 110 registered political parties and citizens' associations

International organization participation: BIS, BSEC, CD, CE, CEI, EAPC, EBRD, EU (candidate country), FAO, G-9, IAEA, IBRD, ICAO, ICC (national committees), ICCt, ICRM, IDA, IFC, IFRCS, IHO, ILO, IMF, IMO, IMSO, Interpol, IOC, IOM, IPU, ISO, ITSO, ITU, ITUC (NGOs), MIGA, MONUSCO, NAM (observer), NSG, OAS (observer), OIF (observer), OPCW, OSCE, PCA, PFP, SELEC, UN, UNCTAD, UNESCO, UNFICYP, UNHCR, UNIDO, UNIFIL, UNMIL, UNOCI, UNTSO, UNWTO, UPU, WCO, WHO, WIPO, WMO, WTO (observer)

Diplomatic representation in the US: *chief of mission:* Ambassador Marko DJURIC (since 18 January 2021)
chancery: 2233 Wisconsin Ave NW, Suite 410, Washington, DC 20007
telephone: [1] (202) 332-0333
FAX: [1] (202) 332-3933
email address and website:
info@serbiaembusa.org
http://www.washington.mfa.gov.rs/
consulate(s) general: Chicago, New York

Diplomatic representation from the US: *chief of mission:* Ambassador Christopher R. HILL (since 1 April 2022)
embassy: 92 Bulevar kneza Aleksandra Karadjordjevica, 11040 Belgrade
mailing address: 5070 Belgrade Place, Washington, DC 20521-5070
telephone: [381] (11) 706-4000
FAX: [381] (11) 706-4481
email address and website:
belgradeacs@state.gov
https://rs.usembassy.gov/

Flag description: three equal horizontal stripes of red (top), blue, and white - the Pan-Slav colors representing freedom and revolutionary ideals; charged with the coat of arms of Serbia shifted slightly to the hoist side; the principal field of the coat of arms represents the Serbian state and displays a white two-headed eagle on a red shield; a smaller red shield on the eagle represents the Serbian nation, and is divided into four quarters by a white cross; interpretations vary as to the meaning and origin of the white, curved symbols resembling firesteels (fire strikers) or Cyrillic "C's" in each quarter; a royal crown surmounts the coat of arms
note: the Pan-Slav colors were inspired by the 19th-century flag of Russia

National symbol(s): white double-headed eagle; national colors: red, blue, white

National anthem: *name:* "Boze pravde" (God of Justice)
lyrics/music: Jovan DORDEVIC/Davorin JENKO
note: adopted 1904; song originally written as part of a play in 1872 and has been used as an anthem by the Serbian people throughout the 20th and 21st centuries

National heritage: *total World Heritage Sites:* 4 (all cultural)
selected World Heritage Site locales: Stari Ras and Sopoćani; Studenica Monastery; Gamzigrad-Romuliana, Palace of Galerius; Stećci Medieval Tombstone Graveyards

ECONOMY

Economic overview: Serbia has a transitional economy largely dominated by market forces, but the state sector remains significant in certain areas. The economy relies on manufacturing and exports, driven largely by foreign investment. MILOSEVIC-era mismanagement of the economy, an extended period of international economic sanctions, civil war, and the damage to Yugoslavia's infrastructure and industry during the NATO airstrikes in 1999 left the economy worse off than it was in 1990. In 2015, Serbia's GDP was 27.5% below where it was in 1989.

After former Federal Yugoslav President MILOSEVIC was ousted in September 2000, the Democratic Opposition of Serbia (DOS) coalition government implemented stabilization measures and embarked on a market reform program. Serbia renewed its membership in the IMF in December 2000 and rejoined the World Bank and the European Bank for Reconstruction and Development. Serbia has made progress in trade liberalization and enterprise restructuring and privatization, but many large enterprises - including the power utilities, telecommunications company, natural gas company, and others - remain state-owned. Serbia has made some progress towards EU membership, gaining candidate status in March 2012. In January 2014, Serbia's EU accession talks officially opened and, as of December 2017, Serbia had opened 12 negotiating chapters including one on foreign trade. Serbia's negotiations with the WTO are advanced, with the country's complete ban on the trade and cultivation of agricultural biotechnology products representing the primary remaining obstacle to accession. Serbia maintains a three-year Stand-by Arrangement with the IMF worth approximately $1.3 billion that is scheduled to end in February 2018. The government has shown progress implementing economic reforms, such as fiscal consolidation, privatization, and reducing public spending.

Unemployment in Serbia, while relatively low (16% in 2017) compared with its Balkan neighbors, remains significantly above the European average. Serbia is slowly implementing structural economic reforms needed to ensure the country's long-term prosperity. Serbia reduced its budget deficit to 1.7% of GDP and its public debt to 71% of GDP in 2017. Public debt had more than doubled between 2008 and 2015. Serbia's concerns about inflation and exchange-rate stability preclude the use of expansionary monetary policy.

Major economic challenges ahead include: stagnant household incomes; the need for private sector job creation; structural reforms of state-owned companies; strategic public sector reforms; and the need for new foreign direct investment. Other serious longer-term challenges include an inefficient judicial system, high levels of corruption, and an aging population. Factors favorable to Serbia's economic growth include the economic reforms it is undergoing as part of its EU accession process and IMF agreement, its strategic location, a relatively inexpensive and skilled labor force, and free trade agreements with the EU, Russia, Turkey, and countries that are members of the Central European Free Trade Agreement.

Real GDP (purchasing power parity): $125.8 billion (2020 est.)
$127.04 billion (2019 est.)
$121.87 billion (2018 est.)
note: data are in 2017 dollars
country comparison to the world: 81

Real GDP growth rate: 4.18% (2019 est.)
4.4% (2018 est.)
2.05% (2017 est.)
country comparison to the world: 72

Real GDP per capita: $18,200 (2020 est.)
$18,300 (2019 est.)
$17,500 (2018 est.)
note: data are in 2017 dollars
country comparison to the world: 93

GDP (official exchange rate): $51.449 billion (2019 est.)

Inflation rate (consumer prices): -0.1% (2019 est.)
-1.1% (2018 est.)
2% (2017 est.)
country comparison to the world: 18

Credit ratings:

Fitch rating: BB+ (2019)

Moody's rating: Ba3 (2017)

Standard & Poors rating: BB+ (2019)

GDP - composition, by sector of origin: *agriculture:* 9.8% (2017 est.)
industry: 41.1% (2017 est.)
services: 49.1% (2017 est.)

GDP - composition, by end use: *household consumption:* 78.2% (2017 est.)
government consumption: 10.1% (2017 est.)
investment in fixed capital: 18.5% (2017 est.)
investment in inventories: 2% (2017 est.)
exports of goods and services: 52.5% (2017 est.)
imports of goods and services: -61.3% (2017 est.)

Agricultural products: maize, wheat, sugar beet, milk, sunflower seed, potatoes, soybeans, plums/sloes, apples, barley

Industries: automobiles, base metals, furniture, food processing, machinery, chemicals, sugar, tires, clothes, pharmaceuticals

Industrial production growth rate: 3.9% (2017 est.)
country comparison to the world: 78

Labor force: 3 million (2020 est.)
country comparison to the world: 104

Labor force - by occupation: *agriculture:* 19.4%
industry: 24.5%
services: 56.1% (2017 est.)

Unemployment rate: 14.1% (2017 est.)
15.9% (2016 est.)
country comparison to the world: 172

Unemployment, youth ages 15-24: *total:* 26.7%
male: 25%
female: 29.5% (2020 est.)
country comparison to the world: 44

Population below poverty line: 23.2% (2018 est.)

Gini Index coefficient - distribution of family income: 36.2 (2017 est.)
28.2 (2008 est.)
country comparison to the world: 93

Household income or consumption by percentage share: *lowest 10%:* 2.2%
highest 10%: 23.8% (2011)

Budget: *revenues:* 17.69 billion (2017 est.)
expenditures: 17.59 billion (2017 est.)
note: data include both central government and local goverment budgets

Budget surplus (+) or deficit (-): 0.2% (of GDP) (2017 est.)
country comparison to the world: 43

Public debt: 62.5% of GDP (2017 est.)
73.1% of GDP (2016 est.)
country comparison to the world: 71

Taxes and other revenues: 42.7% (of GDP) (2017 est.)
country comparison to the world: 30

Current account balance: -$2.354 billion (2017 est.)
-$1.189 billion (2016 est.)
country comparison to the world: 170

Exports: $25.42 billion (2020 est.) note: data are in current year dollars
$26.13 billion (2019 est.) note: data are in current year dollars
$24.97 billion (2018 est.) note: data are in current year dollars
country comparison to the world: 74

Exports - partners: Germany 12%, Italy 10%, Bosnia and Herzegovina 7%, Romania 6%, Russia 5% (2019)

Exports - commodities: insulated wiring, tires, corn, cars, iron products, copper (2019)

Imports: $30.15 billion (2020 est.) note: data are in current year dollars
$31.29 billion (2019 est.) note: data are in current year dollars
$29.78 billion (2018 est.) note: data are in current year dollars
country comparison to the world: 71

Imports - partners: Germany 13%, Russia 9%, Italy 8%, Hungary 6%, China 5%, Turkey 5% (2019)

Imports - commodities: crude petroleum, cars, packaged medicines, natural gas, refined petroleum (2019)

Reserves of foreign exchange and gold: $11.91 billion (31 December 2017 est.)
$10.76 billion (31 December 2016 est.)
country comparison to the world: 70

Debt - external: $30.927 billion (2019 est.)
$30.618 billion (2018 est.)
country comparison to the world: 82

Exchange rates: Serbian dinars (RSD) per US dollar -
112.4 (2017 est.)
111.278 (2016 est.)
111.278 (2015 est.)
108.811 (2014 est.)
88.405 (2013 est.)

ENERGY

Electricity access: *electrification - total population:* 100% (2020)

Electricity: *installed generating capacity:* 8.986 million kW (2020 est.)
consumption: 29,933,262,000 kWh (2019 est.)
exports: 5.943 billion kWh (2020 est.)
imports: 5.002 billion kWh (2020 est.)
transmission/distribution losses: 4.332 billion kWh (2019 est.)

Electricity generation sources: *fossil fuels:* 69.2% of total installed capacity (2020 est.)
wind: 2.9% of total installed capacity (2020 est.)
hydroelectricity: 27.3% of total installed capacity (2020 est.)
biomass and waste: 0.5% of total installed capacity (2020 est.)

Coal: *production:* 39.673 million metric tons (2020 est.)
consumption: 40.83 million metric tons (2020 est.)
exports: 72,000 metric tons (2020 est.)
imports: 987,000 metric tons (2020 est.)
proven reserves: 7.514 billion metric tons (2019 est.)

Petroleum: *total petroleum production:* 15,200 bbl/day (2021 est.)
refined petroleum consumption: 79,200 bbl/day (2019 est.)
crude oil and lease condensate exports: 200 bbl/day (2018 est.)
crude oil and lease condensate imports: 53,800 bbl/day (2018 est.)
crude oil estimated reserves: 77.5 million barrels (2021 est.)

Refined petroleum products - production: 74,350 bbl/day (2015 est.)
country comparison to the world: 71

Refined petroleum products - exports: 15,750 bbl/day (2015 est.)
country comparison to the world: 73

Refined petroleum products - imports: 18,720 bbl/day (2015 est.)
country comparison to the world: 126

Natural gas: *production:* 455.787 million cubic meters (2019 est.)
consumption: 2,619,191,000 cubic meters (2019 est.)
exports: 0 cubic meters (2021 est.)
imports: 1,980,647,000 cubic meters (2019 est.)
proven reserves: 48.139 billion cubic meters (2021 est.)

Carbon dioxide emissions: 47.735 million metric tonnes of CO2 (2019 est.)
from coal and metallurgical coke: 32.686 million metric tonnes of CO2 (2019 est.)
from petroleum and other liquids: 10.17 million metric tonnes of CO2 (2019 est.)
from consumed natural gas: 4.878 million metric tonnes of CO2 (2019 est.)
country comparison to the world: 60

Energy consumption per capita: 98.195 million Btu/person (2019 est.)
country comparison to the world: 62

COMMUNICATIONS

Telephones - fixed lines: *total subscriptions:* 2,572,254 (2020 est.)
subscriptions per 100 inhabitants: 37 (2020 est.)
country comparison to the world: 49

Telephones - mobile cellular: *total subscriptions:* 8,260,758 (2020 est.)
subscriptions per 100 inhabitants: 120 (2020 est.)
country comparison to the world: 97

Telecommunication systems: *general assessment:* Serbia's telecom industry has been liberalized in line with the principles of the EU's regulatory framework for communications, focused on encouraging competition in telecom products and services, and ensuring universal access; considerable network investment has been undertaken in Serbia by incumbent and alternative operators in recent years, despite economic difficulties; this has helped to stimulate internet usage, which has also been bolstered by improved affordability as prices are reduced through competition; the pandemic has stimulated consumer take up of services, particularly mobile data; the government's various initiatives to improve rural broadband availability have also been supported by European development loans; Serbia's high mobile services, partly the result of multiple SIM card use, has weighed on revenue growth in recent years, placing further pressure on operators to develop business models which encourage consumer use of mobile data services also in response to the continued substitution of fixed-line for mobile voice calls; the regulator has yet to auction 5G-suitable frequencies, though operators are already investing in their networks in preparation for this next growth frontier; during 2021 the regulator resumed the process towards a 5G spectrum auction, which had been delayed owing to the onset of the covid-19 pandemic (2022)
domestic: fixed-line over 37 per 100 and mobile-cellular over 120 per 100 persons (2020)
international: country code - 381

Internet country code: .rs

Internet users: *total:* 5,381,318 (2020 est.)
percent of population: 78% (2020 est.)
country comparison to the world: 85

Broadband - fixed subscriptions: *total:* 1,730,496 (2020 est.)
subscriptions per 100 inhabitants: 25 (2020 est.)
country comparison to the world: 62

TRANSPORTATION

National air transport system: *number of registered air carriers:* 4 (2020)
inventory of registered aircraft operated by air carriers: 43
annual passenger traffic on registered air carriers: 2,262,703 (2018)
annual freight traffic on registered air carriers: 17.71 million (2018) mt-km

Civil aircraft registration country code prefix: YU

Airports: *total:* 26 (2021)

country comparison to the world: 125

Airports - with paved runways: *total:* 10
over 3,047 m: 2
2,438 to 3,047 m: 3
1,524 to 2,437 m: 3
914 to 1,523 m: 2 (2021)

Airports - with unpaved runways: *total:* 16
1,524 to 2,437 m: 1
914 to 1,523 m: 10
under 914 m: 5 (2021)

Heliports: 2 (2021)

Pipelines: 1,936 km gas, 413 km oil

Railways: *total:* 3,809 km (2015)
standard gauge: 3,809 km (2015) 1.435-m gauge (3,526 km one-track lines and 283 km double-track lines) out of which 1,279 km electrified (1,000 km one-track lines and 279 km double-track lines)
country comparison to the world: 53

Roadways: *total:* 44,248 km (2016)
paved: 28,000 km (2016) (16,162 km state roads, out of which 741 km highways)
unpaved: 16,248 km (2016)
country comparison to the world: 85

Waterways: 587 km (2009) (primarily on the Danube and Sava Rivers)
country comparison to the world: 87

Ports and terminals: *river port(s):* Belgrade (Danube)

MILITARY AND SECURITY

Military and security forces: Serbian Armed Forces (Vojska Srbije, VS): Land Forces (includes Riverine Component, consisting of a naval flotilla on the Danube), Air and Air Defense Forces, Serbian Guard; Police Directorate of the Serbian Ministry of Interior: Gendarmerie (2022)
note: the Serbian Guard is a brigade-sized unit that is directly subordinate to the Serbian Armed Forces Chief of General Staff; its duties include safeguarding key defense facilities and rendering military honors to top foreign, state, and military officials

Military expenditures: 1.9% of GDP (2021 est.)
2% of GDP (2020 est.)
2.2% of GDP (2019) (approximately $1.83 billion)
1.6% of GDP (2018) (approximately $1.43 billion)
1.8% of GDP (2017) (approximately $1.47 billion)
country comparison to the world: 66

Military and security service personnel strengths: approximately 25,000 active duty troops (15,000 Land Forces; 5,000 Air/Air Defense; 5,000 other); approximately 3,000 Gendarmerie (2022)

Military equipment inventories and acquisitions: the military's inventory consists of Russian and Soviet-era weapons systems; since 2010, Russia has been the largest suppliers of arms to Serbia; China has also provided a growing amount of arms (2022)

Military service age and obligation: 18 years of age for voluntary military service for men and women; conscription abolished January 2011 (2021)
note: as of 2019, women made up about 6% of the military's full-time personnel

Military deployments: 175 Lebanon (UNIFIL) (May 2022)

Military - note: the Serbian Armed Forces were established in June 2006; the Serbian military traces its origins to the First (1804-1813) and Second (1815-1817) Uprisings against the Ottoman Empire

Serbia does not aspire to join NATO, but has cooperated with the Alliance since 2006 when it joined the Partnership for Peace program; Serbia maintains security ties with Russia (2022)

TRANSNATIONAL ISSUES

Disputes - international: *Serbia-Bosnia and Herzegovina:* Serbia delimited about half of the boundary with Bosnia and Herzegovina, but sections along the Drina River remain in dispute
Serbia-Bulgaria: none identified
Serbia-Croatia: Serbia and Croatia dispute their border along the Danube; Serbia claims the border is the median between the current Danube shorelines, with the land to the eastern side of the median belonging to Serbia; Croatia contends that the boundary is demarcated according to historic maps, despite the river having meandered since then
Serbia-Hungary: none identified
Serbia-Kosovo: Serbia with several other states protested the US and other states' recognition of Kosovo's declaration of its status as a sovereign and independent state in February 2008; ethnic Serbian municipalities along Kosovo's northern border challenge final status of Kosovo-Serbia boundary; since 1999, NATO-led Kosovo Force peacekeepers under UN Interim Administration Mission in Kosovo (UNMIK) authority have continued to keep the peace within Kosovo between the ethnic Albanian majority and the Serb minority; in October 2021, NATO-led KFOR increased patrols along the border with Serbia to deescalate hostilities caused by a dispute over license plates
Serbia-Montenegro: the former republic boundary serves as the boundary until a line is formally delimited and demarcated
Serbia-North Macedonia: none identified
Serbia-Romania: none identified

Refugees and internally displaced persons: *refugees (country of origin):* 17,336 (Croatia), 7,997 (Bosnia and Herzegovina) (mid-year 2021); 22,019 (Ukraine) (includes Ukrainian refugees in Kosovo; as of 8 November 2022)

IDPs: 196,995 (most are Kosovar Serbs, some are Roma, Ashkalis, and Egyptian (RAE); some RAE IDPs are unregistered) (2021)
stateless persons: 2,113 (includes stateless persons in Kosovo) (mid-year 2021)
note: 915,658 estimated refugee and migrant arrivals (January 2015-November 2022); Serbia is predominantly a transit country and hosts an estimated 6,313 migrants and asylum seekers as of June 2022

Illicit drugs: drug trafficking groups are major players in the procurement and transportation of large quantities of cocaine destined for European markets

SEYCHELLES

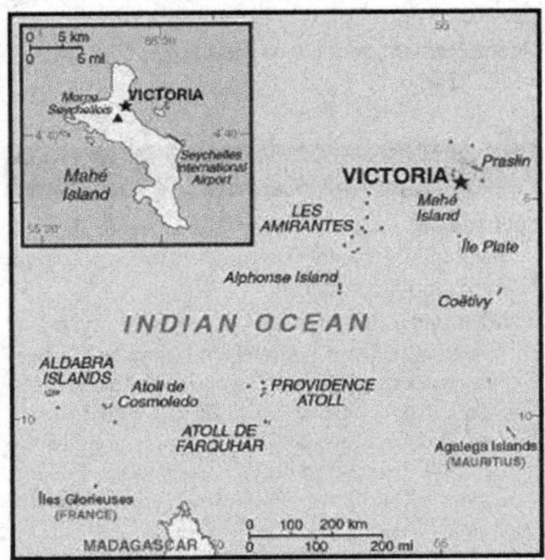

INTRODUCTION

Background: Seychelles was uninhabited prior to being discovered by Europeans early in the 16th century. A lengthy struggle between France and Great Britain for the islands ended in 1814, when they were ceded to the latter. During colonial rule, a plantation-based economy developed that relied on imported labor, primarily from European colonies in Africa. Independence came in 1976. Following a coup d'etat in 1977, the country was a socialist one-party state until adopting a new constitution and holding free elections in 1993. President France-Albert RENE, who had served since 1977, was reelected in 2001, but stepped down in 2004. Vice President James Alix MICHEL took over the presidency and in 2006 was elected to a new five-year term; he was reelected in 2011 and again in 2015. In 2016, James MICHEL resigned and handed over the presidency to his vice-president, Danny FAURE. In 2020, Wavel RAMKALAWAN was elected president, the first time an opposition candidate has won the presidency since independence.

GEOGRAPHY

Location: archipelago in the Indian Ocean, northeast of Madagascar

Geographic coordinates: 4 35 S, 55 40 E

Map references: Africa

Area: *total:* 455 sq km
land: 455 sq km
water: 0 sq km
country comparison to the world: 198

Area - comparative: 2.5 times the size of Washington, DC

Land boundaries: *total:* 0 km

Coastline: 491 km

Maritime claims: *territorial sea:* 12 nm
contiguous zone: 24 nm

exclusive economic zone: 200 nm
continental shelf: 200 nm or to the edge of the continental margin

Climate: tropical marine; humid; cooler season during southeast monsoon (late May to September); warmer season during northwest monsoon (March to May)

Terrain: Mahe Group is volcanic with a narrow coastal strip and rocky, hilly interior; others are relatively flat coral atolls, or elevated reefs; sits atop the submarine Mascarene Plateau

Elevation: *highest point:* Morne Seychellois 905 m
lowest point: Indian Ocean 0 m

Natural resources: fish, coconuts (copra), cinnamon trees

Land use: *agricultural land:* 6.5% (2018 est.)
arable land: 2.2% (2018 est.)
permanent crops: 4.3% (2018 est.)
permanent pasture: 0% (2018 est.)
forest: 88.5% (2018 est.)
other: 5% (2018 est.)

Irrigated land: 3 sq km (2012)

Population distribution: more than three-quarters of the population lives on the main island of Mahe; Praslin contains less than 10%; a smaller percent on La Digue and the outer islands as shown in this population distribution map

Natural hazards: lies outside the cyclone belt, so severe storms are rare; occasional short droughts

Geography - note: the smallest African country in terms of both area and population; the constitution of the Republic of Seychelles lists 155 islands: 42 granitic and 113 coralline; by far the largest island is Mahe, which is home to about 90% of the population and the site of the capital city of Victoria

PEOPLE AND SOCIETY

Population: 97,017 (2022 est.)
country comparison to the world: 197

Nationality: *noun:* Seychellois (singular and plural)
adjective: Seychellois

Ethnic groups: predominantly Creole (mainly of East African and Malagasy heritage); also French, Indian, Chinese, and Arab populations

Languages: Seychellois Creole (official) 89.1%, English (official) 5.1%, French (official) 0.7%, other 3.8%, unspecified 1.4% (2010 est.)

Religions: Roman Catholic 76.2%, Protestant 10.5% (Anglican 6.1%, Pentecostal Assembly 1.5%, Seventh Day Adventist 1.2%, other Protestant 1.7%), other Christian 2.4%, Hindu 2.4%, Muslim 1.6%, other non-Christian 1.1%, unspecified 4.8%, none 0.9% (2010 est.)

Demographic profile: Seychelles has no indigenous population and was first permanently settled by a small group of French planters, African slaves, and South Indians in 1770. Seychelles' modern population is composed of the descendants of French and later British settlers, Africans, and Indian, Chinese, and Middle Eastern traders and is concentrated on three of its 155 islands – the vast majority on Mahe and lesser numbers on Praslin and La Digue. Seychelles' population grew rapidly during the second half of the 20th century, largely due to natural increase, but the pace has slowed because of fertility decline. The total fertility rate dropped sharply from 4.0 children per woman in 1980 to 1.9 in 2015, mainly as a result of a family planning program, free education and health care, and increased female labor force participation. Life expectancy has increased steadily, but women on average live 9 years longer than men, a difference that is higher than that typical of developed countries.

The combination of reduced fertility and increased longevity has resulted in an aging population, which will put pressure on the government's provision of pensions and health care. Seychelles' sustained investment in social welfare services, such as free primary health care and education up to the post-secondary level, have enabled the country to achieve a high human development index score – among the highest in Africa. Despite some of its health and education indicators being nearly on par with Western countries, Seychelles has a high level of income inequality.

An increasing number of migrant workers – mainly young men – have been coming to Seychelles in recent years to work in the construction and tourism industries. As of 2011, foreign workers made up nearly a quarter of the workforce. Indians are the largest non-Seychellois population – representing half of the country's foreigners – followed by Malagasy.

Age structure: *0-14 years:* 18.85% (male 9,297/female 8,798)
15-24 years: 12.39% (male 6,283/female 5,607)
25-54 years: 49.03% (male 25,209/female 21,851)
55-64 years: 11.46% (male 5,545/female 5,455)
65 years and over: 8.27% (male 3,272/female 4,664) (2020 est.)

Dependency ratios: *total dependency ratio:* 46.7
youth dependency ratio: 34.9
elderly dependency ratio: 11.8
potential support ratio: 8.5 (2020 est.)

Median age: *total:* 36.8 years
male: 36.3 years
female: 37.4 years (2020 est.)
country comparison to the world: 76

Population growth rate: 0.64% (2022 est.)
country comparison to the world: 139

Birth rate: 12.37 births/1,000 population (2022 est.)
country comparison to the world: 148

Death rate: 6.88 deaths/1,000 population (2022 est.)
country comparison to the world: 123

Net migration rate: 0.86 migrant(s)/1,000 population (2022 est.)
country comparison to the world: 67

Population distribution: more than three-quarters of the population lives on the main island of Mahe; Praslin contains less than 10%; a smaller percent on La Digue and the outer islands as shown in this population distribution map

Urbanization: *urban population:* 58.4% of total population (2022)
rate of urbanization: 0.99% annual rate of change (2020-25 est.)

Major urban areas - population: 28,000 VICTORIA (capital) (2018)

Sex ratio: *at birth:* 1.03 male(s)/female
0-14 years: 1.06 male(s)/female
15-24 years: 1.13 male(s)/female
25-54 years: 1.17 male(s)/female
55-64 years: 0.99 male(s)/female
65 years and over: 0.47 male(s)/female
total population: 1.08 male(s)/female (2022 est.)

Infant mortality rate: *total:* 10.6 deaths/1,000 live births
male: 13.35 deaths/1,000 live births
female: 7.76 deaths/1,000 live births (2022 est.)
country comparison to the world: 133

Life expectancy at birth: *total population:* 76.1 years
male: 71.67 years
female: 80.66 years (2022 est.)
country comparison to the world: 109

Total fertility rate: 1.82 children born/woman (2022 est.)
country comparison to the world: 141

Drinking water source: *improved: total:* 96.2% of population
unimproved: total: 3.8% of population (2017 est.)

Current health expenditure: 5.2% of GDP (2019)

Physicians density: 2.25 physicians/1,000 population (2019)

Hospital bed density: 3.6 beds/1,000 population (2011)

Sanitation facility access: *improved: total:* 100% of population
unimproved: total: 0% of population (2020 est.)

HIV/AIDS - adult prevalence rate: Obesity - adult prevalence rate: 14% (2016)
country comparison to the world: 130

Alcohol consumption per capita: *total:* 9.48 liters of pure alcohol (2019 est.)
beer: 4.11 liters of pure alcohol (2019 est.)
wine: 0.49 liters of pure alcohol (2019 est.)
spirits: 4.62 liters of pure alcohol (2019 est.)
other alcohols: 0.25 liters of pure alcohol (2019 est.)
country comparison to the world: 29

Tobacco use: *total:* 20.2% (2020 est.)
male: 34% (2020 est.)
female: 6.4% (2020 est.)
country comparison to the world: 88

Children under the age of 5 years underweight: 3.6% (2012)
country comparison to the world: 89

Education expenditures: 3.9% of GDP (2019 est.)
country comparison to the world: 110

Literacy: *definition:* age 15 and over can read and write
total population: 95.9%
male: 95.4%
female: 96.4% (2018)

School life expectancy (primary to tertiary education): *total:* 14 years
male: 13 years
female: 15 years (2020)

Unemployment, youth ages 15-24: *total:* 16.4%
male: 17.4%
female: 15.5% (2020 est.)

ENVIRONMENT

Environment - current issues: water supply depends on catchments to collect rainwater; water pollution; biodiversity maintainance

Environment - international agreements: *party to:* Biodiversity, Climate Change, Climate Change-Kyoto Protocol, Climate Change-Paris Agreement, Comprehensive Nuclear Test Ban, Desertification, Endangered Species, Hazardous Wastes, Law of the Sea, Marine Dumping-London Convention, Nuclear Test Ban, Ozone Layer Protection, Ship Pollution, Wetlands
signed, but not ratified: none of the selected agreements

Air pollutants: *particulate matter emissions:* 18.72 micrograms per cubic meter (2016 est.)
carbon dioxide emissions: 0.61 megatons (2016 est.)
methane emissions: 0.1 megatons (2020 est.)

Climate: tropical marine; humid; cooler season during southeast monsoon (late May to September); warmer season during northwest monsoon (March to May)

Land use: *agricultural land:* 6.5% (2018 est.)
arable land: 2.2% (2018 est.)
permanent crops: 4.3% (2018 est.)
permanent pasture: 0% (2018 est.)
forest: 88.5% (2018 est.)
other: 5% (2018 est.)

Urbanization: *urban population:* 58.4% of total population (2022)
rate of urbanization: 0.99% annual rate of change (2020-25 est.)

Revenue from forest resources: *forest revenues:* 0.09% of GDP (2018 est.)
country comparison to the world: 116

Revenue from coal: *coal revenues:* 0% of GDP (2018 est.)
country comparison to the world: 164

Waste and recycling: *municipal solid waste generated annually:* 48,000 tons (2012 est.)

Total water withdrawal: *municipal:* 9 million cubic meters (2017 est.)
industrial: 3.8 million cubic meters (2017 est.)
agricultural: 900,000 cubic meters (2017 est.)

Total renewable water resources: 0 cubic meters (2017 est.)

GOVERNMENT

Country name: *conventional long form:* Republic of Seychelles
conventional short form: Seychelles
local long form: Republic of Seychelles
local short form: Seychelles
etymology: named by French Captain Corneille Nicholas MORPHEY after Jean Moreau de SECHELLES, the finance minister of France, in 1756

Government type: presidential republic

Capital: *name:* Victoria
geographic coordinates: 4 37 S, 55 27 E
time difference: UTC+4 (9 hours ahead of Washington, DC, during Standard Time)
etymology: founded as L'etablissement in 1778 by French colonists, the town was renamed in 1841 by the British after Queen VICTORIA (1819-1901); "victoria" is the Latin word for "victory"

Administrative divisions: 27 administrative districts; Anse aux Pins, Anse Boileau, Anse Etoile, Anse Royale, Au Cap, Baie Lazare, Baie Sainte Anne, Beau Vallon, Bel Air, Bel Ombre, Cascade, Glacis, Grand Anse Mahe, Grand Anse Praslin, Ile Perseverance I, Ile Perseverance II, La Digue, La Riviere Anglaise, Les Mamelles, Mont Buxton, Mont Fleuri, Plaisance, Pointe Larue, Port Glaud, Roche Caiman, Saint Louis, Takamaka

Independence: 29 June 1976 (from the UK)

National holiday: Constitution Day, 18 June (1993); Independence Day (National Day), 29 June (1976)

Constitution: *history:* previous 1970, 1979; latest drafted May 1993, approved by referendum 18 June 1993, effective 23 June 1993
amendments: proposed by the National Assembly; passage requires at least two-thirds majority vote by the National Assembly; passage of amendments affecting the country's sovereignty, symbols and languages, the supremacy of the constitution, fundamental rights and freedoms, amendment procedures, and dissolution of the Assembly also requires approval by at least 60% of voters in a referendum; amended several times, last in 2018

Legal system: mixed legal system of English common law, French civil law, and customary law

International law organization participation: has not submitted an ICJ jurisdiction declaration; accepts ICCt jurisdiction

Citizenship: *citizenship by birth:* no
citizenship by descent only: at least one parent must be a citizen of the Seychelles
dual citizenship recognized: no
residency requirement for naturalization: 5 years

Suffrage: 18 years of age; universal

Executive branch: *chief of state:* President Wavel RAMKALAWAN (since 26 October 2020); Vice President Ahmed AFIF (since 27 October 2020); the president is both chief of state and head of government
head of government: President Wavel RAMKALAWAN (since 26 October 2020); Vice President Ahmed AFIF (since 27 October 2020)
cabinet: Council of Ministers appointed by the president
elections/appointments: president directly elected by absolute majority popular vote in 2 rounds if needed for a 5-year term (eligible for 1 additional term); election last held on 22-24 October 2020 (originally scheduled for December 2020 but moved up to coincide with the 22-24 October National Assembly election in order to cut election costs)
election results:
2020: Wavel RAMKALAWAN elected president; Wavel RAMKALAWAN (LDS) 54.9%, Danny FAURE (US) 43.5%, other 1.6%
2015: President James Alix MICHEL reelected president in second round; percent of vote first round - James Alix MICHEL (PL) 47.8%, Wavel RAMKALAWAN (SNP) 35.3%, other 16.9%; percent of vote second round - James Alix MICHEL (PL) 50.2%, Wavel RAMKALAWAN (SNP) 49.8%

Legislative branch: *description:* unicameral National Assembly or Assemblee Nationale (35 seats in the 2020 -25 term; 26 members directly elected in single-seat constituencies by simple majority vote and up to 9 members elected by proportional representation vote; members serve 5-year terms)
elections:
last held on 22-24 Oct 2020 (next to be held October 2025); note - the election was originally scheduled for 2021 but was moved up a year and will be held alongside the presidential election in order to cut election costs
election results:
percent of vote by party - LDS 54.8%, US 42.3% , other 2.9%; seats by party - LDS 25, US10; composition - men 27, women 8, percent of women 22.9%

Judicial branch: *highest court(s):* Seychelles Court of Appeal (consists of the court president and 4 justices); Supreme Court of Seychelles (consists of the chief justice and 9 puisne judges); Constitutional Court (consists of 3 Supreme Court judges)
judge selection and term of office: all judges appointed by the president of the republic upon the recommendation of the Constitutional Appointments Authority, a 3-member body, with 1 member appointed by the president of the republic, 1 by the opposition leader in the National Assembly, and 1 by the other 2 appointees; judges serve until retirement at age 70
subordinate courts: Magistrates' Courts of Seychelles; Family Tribunal for issues such as domestic violence, child custody, and maintenance; Employment Tribunal for labor-related disputes

Political parties and leaders: Seychelles Party for Social Justice and Democracy or SPSJD [Vesna RAKIC]
Seychellois Democratic Alliance or LDS (Linyon Demokratik Seselwa/Union Démocratique Seychelloise) (coalition includes SNP and SPSJD) [Roger MANCIENNE]
Seychelles National Party or SNP [Wavel RAMKALAWAN] United Seychelles or US [Patrick HERMINIE]
note: only parties with seats in the National Assembly listed

International organization participation: ACP, AfDB, AOSIS, AU, C, CD, COMESA, EITI (candidate country), FAO, G-77, IAEA, IBRD, ICAO, ICC (NGOs), ICCt, ICRM, IDA, IFAD, IFC, IFRCS, ILO, IMF, IMO, InOC, Interpol, IOC, IOM, IPU, ISO (correspondent), ITU, MIGA, NAM, OIF, OPCW, SADC, UN, UNCTAD, UNESCO, UNIDO, UNWTO, UPU, WCO, WHO, WIPO, WMO, WTO

Diplomatic representation in the US: *chief of mission:* Ambassador Ian MADELEINE (since 1 December 2021)
chancery: 685 Third Avenue, Suite 1107, 11th Floor, New York, NY 10017
telephone: [1] (212) 972-1785
FAX: [1] (212) 972-1786
email address and website:
seychelles@un.int
consulate(s) general: New York

Diplomatic representation from the US: *embassy:* the US does not have an embassy in Seychelles; the US Ambassador to Mauritius is accredited to Seychelles

Flag description: five oblique bands of blue (hoist side), yellow, red, white, and green (bottom) radiating from the bottom of the hoist side; the oblique bands are meant to symbolize a dynamic new country moving into the future; blue represents sky and sea, yellow the sun giving light and life, red the peoples' determination to work for the future in unity and love, white social justice and harmony, and green the land and natural environment

National symbol(s): coco de mer (sea coconut); national colors: blue, yellow, red, white, green

National anthem: *name:* "Koste Seselwa" (Seychellois Unite)
lyrics/music: David Francois Marc ANDRE and George Charles Robert PAYET
note: adopted 1996

National heritage: *total World Heritage Sites:* 2 (both natural)
selected World Heritage Site locales: Aldabra Atoll; Vallée de Mai Nature Reserve

ECONOMY

Economic overview: Since independence in 1976, per capita output in this Indian Ocean archipelago has expanded to roughly seven times the pre-independence, near-subsistence level, moving the island into the high income group of countries. Growth has been led by the tourism sector, which directly employs about 26% of the labor force and directly and indirectly accounts for more than 55% of GDP, and by tuna fishing. In recent years, the government has encouraged foreign investment to upgrade hotels and tourism industry services. At the same time, the government has moved to reduce the dependence on tourism by promoting the development of the offshore financial, information, and communication sectors and renewable energy.

In 2008, having depleted its foreign exchange reserves, Seychelles defaulted on interest payments due on a $230 million Eurobond, requested assistance from the IMF, and immediately enacted a number of significant structural reforms, including liberalization of the exchange rate, reform of the public sector to include layoffs, and the sale of some state assets. In December 2013, the IMF declared that Seychelles had successfully transitioned to a market-based economy with full employment and a fiscal surplus. However, state-owned enterprises still play a prominent role in the economy. Effective 1 January 2017, Seychelles was no longer eligible for trade benefits under the US African Growth and Opportunities Act after having gained developed country status. Seychelles grew at 5% in 2017 because of a strong tourism sector and low commodity prices. The Seychellois Government met the IMF's performance criteria for 2017 but recognizes a need to make additional progress to reduce high income inequality, represented by a Gini coefficient of 46.8.

As a very small open economy dependent on tourism, Seychelles remains vulnerable to developments such as economic downturns in countries that supply tourists, natural disasters, and changes in local climatic conditions and ocean temperature. One of the main challenges facing the government is implementing strategies that will increase Seychelles' long-term resilience to climate change without weakening economic growth.

Real GDP (purchasing power parity): $2.4 billion (2020 est.)
$2.69 billion (2019 est.)
$2.65 billion (2018 est.)
note: data are in 2017 dollars
country comparison to the world: 193

Real GDP growth rate: 5.3% (2017 est.)
4.5% (2016 est.)
4.9% (2015 est.)
country comparison to the world: 39

Real GDP per capita: $24,400 (2020 est.)
$27,500 (2019 est.)
$27,300 (2018 est.)
note: data are in 2017 dollars
country comparison to the world: 79

GDP (official exchange rate): $1.748 billion (2019 est.)

Inflation rate (consumer prices): 1.8% (2019 est.)
3.7% (2018 est.)
2.8% (2017 est.)
country comparison to the world: 102

Credit ratings:

Fitch rating: B+ (2020)

GDP - composition, by sector of origin: *agriculture:* 2.5% (2017 est.)
industry: 13.8% (2017 est.)
services: 83.7% (2017 est.)

GDP - composition, by end use: *household consumption:* 52.7% (2017 est.)
government consumption: 34.4% (2017 est.)
investment in fixed capital: 26.7% (2017 est.)
investment in inventories: 0% (2017 est.)
exports of goods and services: 79.4% (2017 est.)
imports of goods and services: -93.2% (2017 est.)

Agricultural products: coconuts, vegetables, bananas, fruit, eggs, poultry, tomatoes, pork, tropical fruit, cassava

Industries: fishing, tourism, beverages

Industrial production growth rate: 2.3% (2017 est.)
country comparison to the world: 121

Labor force: 51,000 (2018 est.)
country comparison to the world: 191

Labor force - by occupation: *agriculture:* 3%
industry: 23%
services: 74% (2006)

Unemployment rate: 3% (2017 est.)
2.7% (2016 est.)
country comparison to the world: 39

Unemployment, youth ages 15-24: *total:* 16.4%
male: 17.4%
female: 15.5% (2020 est.)
country comparison to the world: 98

Population below poverty line: 25.3% (2018 est.)

Gini Index coefficient - distribution of family income: 46.8 (2013 est.)
country comparison to the world: 21

Household income or consumption by percentage share: *lowest 10%:* 4.7%
highest 10%: 15.4% (2007)

Budget: *revenues:* 593.4 million (2017 est.)
expenditures: 600.7 million (2017 est.)

Budget surplus (+) or deficit (-): -0.5% (of GDP) (2017 est.)
country comparison to the world: 63

Public debt: 63.6% of GDP (2017 est.)
69.1% of GDP (2016 est.)
country comparison to the world: 66

Taxes and other revenues: 39.6% (of GDP) (2017 est.)
country comparison to the world: 44

Fiscal year: calendar year

Current account balance: -$307 million (2017 est.)
-$286 million (2016 est.)
country comparison to the world: 110

Exports: $1.09 billion (2020 est.) note: data are in current year dollars
$1.61 billion (2019 est.) note: data are in current year dollars
$1.68 billion (2018 est.) note: data are in current year dollars
country comparison to the world: 176

Exports - partners: United Arab Emirates 17%, United Kingdom 13%, France 12%, British Virgin Islands 11%, Zambia 9%, Mauritius 5%, Japan 5% (2019)

Exports - commodities: refined petroleum, fish, recreational boats, cigarettes, animal meal (2019)

Imports: $1.35 billion (2020 est.) note: data are in current year dollars
$1.79 billion (2019 est.) note: data are in current year dollars
$1.86 billion (2018 est.) note: data are in current year dollars
country comparison to the world: 181

Imports - partners: United Arab Emirates 21%, Qatar 13%, British Virgin Islands 7%, Germany 6%, France 6%, China 5%, Spain 5%, South Africa 5% (2019)

Imports - commodities: recreational boats, refined petroleum, fish, aircraft, cars (2019)

Reserves of foreign exchange and gold: $545.2 million (31 December 2017 est.)
$523.5 million (31 December 2016 est.)
country comparison to the world: 149

Debt - external: $4.802 billion (2019 est.)
$4.613 billion (2018 est.)
country comparison to the world: 135

Exchange rates: Seychelles rupees (SCR) per US dollar -
13.64 (2017 est.)
13.319 (2016 est.)
13.319 (2015 est.)
13.314 (2014 est.)
12.747 (2013 est.)

ENERGY

Electricity access: *electrification - total population:* 100% (2020)

Electricity: *installed generating capacity:* 157,000 kW (2020 est.)
consumption: 463.894 million kWh (2019 est.)
exports: 0 kWh (2020 est.)
imports: 0 kWh (2020 est.)
transmission/distribution losses: 30 million kWh (2019 est.)

Electricity generation sources: *fossil fuels:* 99.1% of total installed capacity (2020 est.)
solar: 0.9% of total installed capacity (2020 est.)

Petroleum: *total petroleum production:* 0 bbl/day (2021 est.)
refined petroleum consumption: 7,500 bbl/day (2019 est.)

Refined petroleum products - imports: 7,225 bbl/day (2015 est.)
country comparison to the world: 155

Carbon dioxide emissions: 1.156 million metric tonnes of CO_2 (2019 est.)
from petroleum and other liquids: 1.156 million metric tonnes of CO_2 (2019 est.)
country comparison to the world: 171

Energy consumption per capita: 163.06 million Btu/person (2019 est.)
country comparison to the world: 29

COMMUNICATIONS

Telephones - fixed lines: *total subscriptions:* 18,882 (2020 est.)
subscriptions per 100 inhabitants: 19 (2020 est.)
country comparison to the world: 176

Telephones - mobile cellular: *total subscriptions:* 183,498 (2020)
subscriptions per 100 inhabitants: 187 (2020)
country comparison to the world: 185

Telecommunication systems: *general assessment:* effective system; direct international calls to over 100 countries; radiotelephone communications between islands in the archipelago; 3 ISPs; use of Internet cafes' for access to Internet; 4G services and 5G pending (2020)
domestic: fixed-line a little over 19 per 100 and mobile-cellular teledensity is nearly 187 telephones per 100 persons (2020)

international: country code - 248; landing points for the PEACE and the SEAS submarine cables providing connectivity to Europe, the Middle East, Africa and Asia; direct radiotelephone communications with adjacent island countries and African coastal countries; satellite earth station - 1 Intelsat (Indian Ocean) (2019)

Broadcast media: the national broadcaster, Seychelles Broadcasting Corporation (SBC), which is funded by taxpayer money, operates the only terrestrial TV station, which provides local programming and airs broadcasts from international services; a privately owned Internet Protocol Television (IPTV) channel also provides local programming multi-channel cable and satellite TV are available through 2 providers; the national broadcaster operates 1 AM and 1 FM radio station; there are 2 privately operated radio stations; transmissions of 2 international broadcasters are accessible in Victoria
(2019)

Internet country code: .sc

Internet users: *total:* 77,785 (2020 est.)
percent of population: 79% (2020 est.)
country comparison to the world: 184

Broadband - fixed subscriptions: *total:* 34,966 (2020 est.)
subscriptions per 100 inhabitants: 36 (2020 est.)
country comparison to the world: 148

TRANSPORTATION

National air transport system: *number of registered air carriers:* 1 (2020)
inventory of registered aircraft operated by air carriers: 7
annual passenger traffic on registered air carriers: 455,201 (2018)
annual freight traffic on registered air carriers: 7.79 million (2018) mt-km

Civil aircraft registration country code prefix: S7

Airports: *total:* 14 (2021)
country comparison to the world: 150

Airports - with paved runways: *total:* 7
2,438 to 3,047 m: 1
914 to 1,523 m: 5
under 914 m: 1 (2021)

Airports - with unpaved runways: *total:* 7
914 to 1,523 m: 2
under 914 m: 5 (2021)

Heliports: 1 (2021)

Roadways: *total:* 526 km (2015)
paved: 514 km (2015)
unpaved: 12 km (2015)
country comparison to the world: 196

Merchant marine: *total:* 27
by type: general cargo 5, oil tanker 6, other 16 (2021)
country comparison to the world: 138

Ports and terminals: *major seaport(s):* Victoria

MILITARY AND SECURITY

Military and security forces: Seychelles Defense Forces (SDF): Army (includes infantry, special forces, and a presidential security unit), Coast Guard, and Air Force; Ministry of Internal Affairs: Seychelles Police Force (includes unarmed police and an armed paramilitary Police Special Support Wing, the Anti-Narcotics Bureau, and the Marine Police Unit) (2022)
note: the military reports to the president, who acts as minister of defense

Military expenditures: 1.5% of GDP (2021 est.)
1.6% of GDP (2020 est.)
1.3% of GDP (2019 est.)
1.4% of GDP (2018 est.)
1.5% of GDP (2017 est.)
country comparison to the world: 94

Military and security service personnel strengths: approximately 500 personnel (2022)

Military equipment inventories and acquisitions: the SDF's inventory primarily consists of Soviet-era equipment delivered in the 1970s and 1980s; since 2010, the SDF has received limited amounts of more modern equipment, mostly donations of patrol boats and aircraft, from several suppliers led by China and India (2022)

Military service age and obligation: 18-28 (18-25 for officers) years of age for voluntary military service for men and women; 6-year initial commitment; no conscription (2022)

Military - note: formed in 1977, the SDF's primary responsibility is maritime security, particularly countering illegal fishing, piracy, and drug smuggling (2022)

TRANSNATIONAL ISSUES

Disputes - international: *Seychelles-UK:* Mauritius and Seychelles claim the Chagos Islands (UK-administered British Indian Ocean Territory)

Trafficking in persons: *current situation:* Seychelles is a source and destination country for children and women subjected to sex trafficking; Seychellois girls and, to a lesser extent boys, are forced into prostitution in nightclubs, bars, guest houses, hotels, brothels, private homes, and on the streets by peers, family members, and pimps; foreign tourists, sailors, and migrant workers contribute to the demand for commercial sex acts in Seychelles; some of the large population of foreign migrant workers reportedly experience the underpayment of wages and substandard housing
tier rating: Tier 2 Watch List — Seychelles does not fully meet the minimum standards for the elimination of trafficking but is making significant efforts to do so; the government allocated an operational and programmatic budget to the National Coordinating Committee on Trafficking in Persons, signed a bilateral agreement outlining procedures for employment and repatriation in Seychelles of migrant workers from Bangladesh and established a hotline to report forced labor concerns; however, no victims of trafficking were identified; efforts to address sex trafficking remained inadequate, its standard operating procedures for victim identification and referral to care services were not implemented; there are no shelters or care facilities for trafficking victims; investigations, prosecutions, and convictions of traffickers decreased; Seychelles did not establish a secretariat to support the Coordinating Committee, hindering the committee's ability to direct anti-trafficking efforts across government and drive national policy; Seychelles was downgraded to Tier 2 Watch List (2020)

SIERRA LEONE

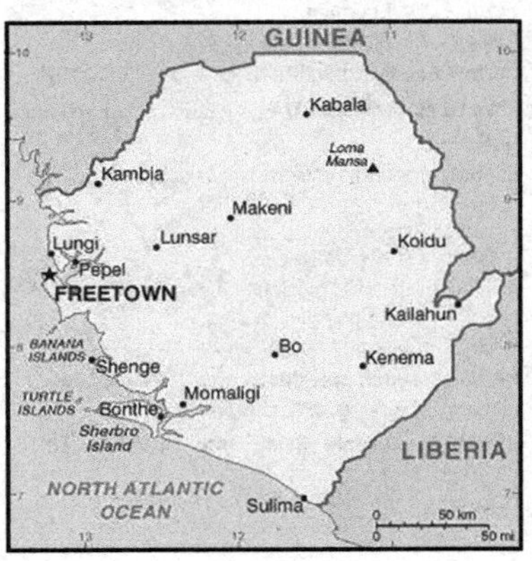

INTRODUCTION

Background: Continuously populated for at least 2,500 years, the dense jungle in the area of Sierra Leone allowed the region to remain relatively protected from invaders from empires in West Africa. Traders introduced Sierra Leone to Islam, which occupies a central role in Sierra Leonean culture and history. In the 17th century, the British set up a trading post near present-day Freetown. The trade originally involved timber and ivory but later expanded to enslaved people. In 1787, following the American Revolution, Sierra Leone became a destination for Black British loyalists from the new United States. After the abolition of the slave trade in 1807, British ships delivered thousands of liberated Africans to Sierra Leone. During the 19th century, the colony gradually expanded inland.

In 1961, Sierra Leone became independent of the UK. While Sierra Leone held free and fair elections in 1962 and 1967, Siaka STEVENS - Sierra Leone's second prime minister - quickly reverted to authoritarian tendencies, outlawing most political parties and ruling from 1967 to 1985. In 1991, Sierra Leonean soldiers launched a civil war against STEVENS' ruling party. The war caused tens of thousands of deaths and displaced more than 2 million people (about one third of the population). In 1998, a Nigerian-led West African coalition military force intervened, installing Tejan KABBAH - who was originally elected in 1996 - as prime minister. In 2002, KABBAH officially announced the end of the war. Since 1998, Sierra Leone has conducted uninterrupted democratic elections, dominated by the two main political parties. In 2018, Julius Maada BIO of the Sierra Leone People's Party won the presidential election that saw a high voter turnout despite some allegations of voter intimidation. The next presidential election is scheduled for March 2023.

GEOGRAPHY

Location: Western Africa, bordering the North Atlantic Ocean, between Guinea and Liberia

Geographic coordinates: 8 30 N, 11 30 W

Map references: Africa

Area: *total:* 71,740 sq km
land: 71,620 sq km
water: 120 sq km
country comparison to the world: 119

Area - comparative: slightly smaller than South Carolina

Land boundaries: *total:* 1,093 km
border countries (2): Guinea 794 km; Liberia 299 km

Coastline: 402 km

Maritime claims: *territorial sea:* 12 nm
contiguous zone: 24 nm
exclusive economic zone: 200 nm
continental shelf: 200 nm

Climate: tropical; hot, humid; summer rainy season (May to December); winter dry season (December to April)

Terrain: coastal belt of mangrove swamps, wooded hill country, upland plateau, mountains in east

Elevation: *highest point:* Loma Mansa (Bintimani) 1,948 m
lowest point: Atlantic Ocean 0 m
mean elevation: 279 m

Natural resources: diamonds, titanium ore, bauxite, iron ore, gold, chromite

Land use: *agricultural land:* 56.2% (2018 est.)
arable land: 23.4% (2018 est.)
permanent crops: 2.3% (2018 est.)
permanent pasture: 30.5% (2018 est.)
forest: 37.5% (2018 est.)
other: 6.3% (2018 est.)

Irrigated land: 300 sq km (2012)

Major watersheds (area sq km): Atlantic Ocean drainage: Niger (2,261,741 sq km)

Population distribution: population clusters are found in the lower elevations of the south and west; the northern third of the country is less populated as shown on this population distribution map

Natural hazards: dry, sand-laden harmattan winds blow from the Sahara (December to February); sandstorms, dust storms

Geography - note: rainfall along the coast can reach 495 cm (195 inches) a year, making it one of the wettest places along coastal, western Africa

PEOPLE AND SOCIETY

Population: 8,692,606 (2022 est.)
country comparison to the world: 100

Nationality: *noun:* Sierra Leonean(s)
adjective: Sierra Leonean

Ethnic groups: Temne 35.4%, Mende 30.8%, Limba 8.8%, Kono 4.3%, Korankoh 4%, Fullah 3.8%, Mandingo 2.8%, Loko 2%, Sherbro 1.9%, Creole 1.2% (descendants of freed Jamaican slaves who were settled in the Freetown area in the late-18th century; also known as Krio), other 5% (2019 est.)

Languages: English (official, regular use limited to literate minority), Mende (principal vernacular in the south), Temne (principal vernacular in the north), Krio (English-based Creole, spoken by the descendants of freed Jamaican slaves who were settled in the Freetown area, a lingua franca and a first language for 10% of the population but understood by 95%)

Religions: Muslim 77.1%, Christian 22.9% (2019 est.)

Demographic profile: Sierra Leone's youthful and growing population is driven by its high total fertility rate (TFR) of almost 5 children per woman, which has declined little over the last two decades. Its elevated TFR is sustained by the continued desire for large families, the low level of contraceptive use, and the early start of childbearing. Despite its high TFR, Sierra Leone's population growth is somewhat tempered by high infant, child, and maternal mortality rates that are among the world's highest and are a result of poverty, a lack of potable water and sanitation, poor nutrition, limited access to quality health care services, and the prevalence of female genital cutting.

Sierra Leone's large youth cohort – about 60% of the population is under the age of 25 – continues to struggle with high levels of unemployment, which was one of the major causes of the country's 1991-2002 civil war and remains a threat to stability today. Its estimated 60% youth unemployment rate is attributed to high levels of illiteracy and unskilled labor, a lack of private sector jobs, and low pay.

Sierra Leone has been a source of and destination for refugees. Sierra Leone's civil war internally displaced as many as 2 million people, or almost half the population, and forced almost another half million to seek refuge in neighboring countries (370,000 Sierra Leoneans fled to Guinea and 120,000 to Liberia). The UNHCR has helped almost 180,000 Sierra Leoneans to return home, while more than 90,000 others have repatriated on their own. Of the more than 65,000 Liberians who took refuge in Sierra Leone during their country's civil war (1989-2003), about 50,000 have been voluntarily repatriated by the UNHCR and others have returned home independently. As of 2015, less than 1,000 Liberians still reside in Sierra Leone.

Age structure: *0-14 years:* 41.38% (male 1,369,942/female 1,371,537)
15-24 years: 18.83% (male 610,396/female 636,880)
25-54 years: 32.21% (male 1,020,741/female 1,112,946)
55-64 years: 3.89% (male 121,733/female 135,664)
65 years and over: 3.7% (male 100,712/female 144,382) (2020 est.)

Dependency ratios: *total dependency ratio:* 76.3
youth dependency ratio: 71.1
elderly dependency ratio: 5.2
potential support ratio: 19.4 (2020 est.)

Median age: *total:* 19.1 years
male: 18.5 years
female: 19.7 years (2020 est.)
country comparison to the world: 206

Population growth rate: 2.49% (2022 est.)
country comparison to the world: 23

Birth rate: 32.2 births/1,000 population (2022 est.)
country comparison to the world: 24

Death rate: 9.32 deaths/1,000 population (2022 est.)
country comparison to the world: 50

Net migration rate: 2.03 migrant(s)/1,000 population (2022 est.)
country comparison to the world: 50

Population distribution: population clusters are found in the lower elevations of the south and west; the northern third of the country is less populated as shown on this population distribution map

Urbanization: *urban population:* 43.8% of total population (2022)
rate of urbanization: 3.02% annual rate of change (2020-25 est.)

Major urban areas - population: 1.272 million FREETOWN (capital) (2022)

Sex ratio: *at birth:* 1.03 male(s)/female
0-14 years: 1.02 male(s)/female
15-24 years: 0.97 male(s)/female
25-54 years: 0.97 male(s)/female
55-64 years: 1.25 male(s)/female
65 years and over: 0.83 male(s)/female
total population: 0.98 male(s)/female (2022 est.)

Mother's mean age at first birth: 19.6 years (2019 est.)
note: data represents median age at first birth among women 20-49

Maternal mortality ratio: 1,120 deaths/100,000 live births (2017 est.)
country comparison to the world: 3

Infant mortality rate: *total:* 73.42 deaths/1,000 live births
male: 78.45 deaths/1,000 live births
female: 68.23 deaths/1,000 live births (2022 est.)
country comparison to the world: 5

Life expectancy at birth: *total population:* 58.76 years
male: 57.16 years
female: 60.41 years (2022 est.)
country comparison to the world: 223

Total fertility rate: 3.8 children born/woman (2022 est.)
country comparison to the world: 31

Contraceptive prevalence rate: 21.2% (2019)

Drinking water source: *improved: urban:* 92.5% of population
rural: 58% of population
total: 72.8% of population
unimproved: urban: 7.5% of population
rural: 42% of population
total: 27.2% of population (2020 est.)

Current health expenditure: 8.8% of GDP (2019)

Physicians density: 0.07 physicians/1,000 population (2018)

Sanitation facility access: *improved: urban:* 79.5% of population
rural: 35.5% of population
total: 54.4% of population
unimproved: urban: 20.5% of population
rural: 64.5% of population
total: 45.6% of population (2020 est.)

HIV/AIDS - adult prevalence rate: 1.5% (2020 est.)
country comparison to the world: 29

HIV/AIDS - people living with HIV/AIDS: 80,000 (2020 est.)
country comparison to the world: 51

HIV/AIDS - deaths: 3,200 (2020 est.)
country comparison to the world: 34

Major infectious diseases: *degree of risk:* very high (2020)
food or waterborne diseases: bacterial and protozoal diarrhea, hepatitis A, and typhoid fever
vectorborne diseases: malaria and dengue fever
water contact diseases: schistosomiasis
animal contact diseases: rabies
aerosolized dust or soil contact diseases: Lassa fever
note: on 21 March 2022, the US Centers for Disease Control and Prevention (CDC) issued a Travel Alert for polio in Africa; Sierra Leone is currently considered a high risk to travelers for circulating vaccine-derived polioviruses (cVDPV); vaccine-derived poliovirus (VDPV) is a strain of the weakened poliovirus that was initially included in oral polio vaccine (OPV) and *that has changed over time and behaves more like the wild or naturally occurring virus*; this means it can be spread more easily to people who are unvaccinated against polio and who come in contact with the stool or respiratory secretions, such as from a sneeze, of an "infected" person who received oral polio vaccine; the CDC recommends that before any international travel, anyone unvaccinated, incompletely vaccinated, or with an unknown polio vaccination status should complete the routine polio vaccine series; before travel to any high-risk destination, the CDC recommends that adults who previously completed the full, routine polio vaccine series receive a single, lifetime booster dose of polio vaccine

Obesity - adult prevalence rate: 8.7% (2016)
country comparison to the world: 147

Alcohol consumption per capita: *total:* 3.22 liters of pure alcohol (2019 est.)
beer: 0.17 liters of pure alcohol (2019 est.)
wine: 0.01 liters of pure alcohol (2019 est.)
spirits: 0.15 liters of pure alcohol (2019 est.)
other alcohols: 2.9 liters of pure alcohol (2019 est.)
country comparison to the world: 107

Tobacco use: *total:* 13.5% (2020 est.)
male: 20.5% (2020 est.)
female: 6.4% (2020 est.)
country comparison to the world: 115

Children under the age of 5 years underweight: 13.5% (2019)
country comparison to the world: 41

Child marriage: *women married by age 15:* 8.6%
women married by age 18: 29.6%
men married by age 18: 4.1% (2019 est.)

Education expenditures: 9.3% of GDP (2020 est.)
country comparison to the world: 7

Literacy: *definition:* age 15 and over can read and write English, Mende, Temne, or Arabic
total population: 43.2%
male: 51.6%
female: 39.8% (2018)

Unemployment, youth ages 15-24: *total:* 9.4%
male: 14.8%
female: 6.1% (2014 est.)

ENVIRONMENT

Environment - current issues: rapid population growth pressuring the environment; overharvesting of timber, expansion of cattle grazing, and slash-and-burn agriculture have resulted in deforestation, soil exhaustion, and flooding; loss of biodiversity; air pollution; water pollution; overfishing

Environment - international agreements: *party to:* Biodiversity, Climate Change, Climate Change-Kyoto Protocol, Climate Change-Paris Agreement, Comprehensive Nuclear Test Ban, Desertification, Endangered Species, Hazardous Wastes, Law of the Sea, Marine Dumping-London Convention, Marine Dumping-London Protocol, Marine Life Conservation, Nuclear Test Ban, Ozone Layer Protection, Ship Pollution, Wetlands
signed, but not ratified: Environmental Modification

Air pollutants: *particulate matter emissions:* 20.63 micrograms per cubic meter (2016 est.)
carbon dioxide emissions: 1.09 megatons (2016 est.)
methane emissions: 3.16 megatons (2020 est.)

Climate: tropical; hot, humid; summer rainy season (May to December); winter dry season (December to April)

Land use: *agricultural land:* 56.2% (2018 est.)
arable land: 23.4% (2018 est.)
permanent crops: 2.3% (2018 est.)
permanent pasture: 30.5% (2018 est.)
forest: 37.5% (2018 est.)
other: 6.3% (2018 est.)

Urbanization: *urban population:* 43.8% of total population (2022)
rate of urbanization: 3.02% annual rate of change (2020-25 est.)

Revenue from forest resources: *forest revenues:* 6.92% of GDP (2018 est.)
country comparison to the world: 8

Revenue from coal: *coal revenues:* 0% of GDP (2018 est.)
country comparison to the world: 165

Food insecurity: *severe localized food insecurity: due to high food prices and reduced incomes* - about 1.6 million people are estimated to be severely food insecure between June and August 2022 on account of high food prices and low purchasing power, resulting in acute constraints on households' economic access to food (2022)

Waste and recycling: *municipal solid waste generated annually:* 610,222 tons (2004 est.)

Major watersheds (area sq km): Atlantic Ocean drainage: Niger (2,261,741 sq km)

Total water withdrawal: *municipal:* 111 million cubic meters (2017 est.)
industrial: 55.5 million cubic meters (2017 est.)
agricultural: 45.7 million cubic meters (2017 est.)

Total renewable water resources: 160 billion cubic meters (2017 est.)

GOVERNMENT

Country name: *conventional long form:* Republic of Sierra Leone
conventional short form: Sierra Leone
local long form: Republic of Sierra Leone
local short form: Sierra Leone
etymology: the Portuguese explorer Pedro de SINTRA named the country "Serra Leoa" (Lion Mountains) for the impressive mountains he saw while sailing the West African coast in 1462

Government type: presidential republic

Capital: *name:* Freetown
geographic coordinates: 8 29 N, 13 14 W
time difference: UTC 0 (5 hours ahead of Washington, DC, during Standard Time)
etymology: name derived from the fact that the original settlement served as a haven for free-born and freed African Americans, as well as for liberated Africans rescued from slave ships

Administrative divisions: 4 provinces and 1 area*; Eastern, Northern, North Western, Southern, Western*

Independence: 27 April 1961 (from the UK)

National holiday: Independence Day, 27 April (1961)

Constitution: *history:* several previous; latest effective 1 October 1991
amendments: proposed by Parliament; passage of amendments requires at least two-thirds majority vote of Parliament in two successive readings and assent of the president of the republic; passage of amendments affecting fundamental rights and freedoms and many other constitutional sections also requires approval in a referendum with participation of at least one half of qualified voters and at least two thirds of votes cast; amended several times, last in 2016

Legal system: mixed legal system of English common law and customary law

International law organization participation: has not submitted an ICJ jurisdiction declaration; accepts ICCt jurisdiction

Citizenship: *citizenship by birth:* no
citizenship by descent only: at least one parent or grandparent must be a citizen of Sierra Leone
dual citizenship recognized: yes
residency requirement for naturalization: 5 years

Suffrage: 18 years of age; universal

Executive branch: *chief of state:* President Julius Maada BIO (since 4 April 2018); Vice President Mohamed Juldeh JALLOH (since 4 April 2018) ; note - the president is both chief of state, head of government, and minister of defense
head of government: President Julius Maada BIO (since 4 April 2018); Vice President Mohamed Juldeh JALLOH (since 4 April 2018)
cabinet: Ministers of State appointed by the president, approved by Parliament; the cabinet is responsible to the president
elections/appointments: president directly elected by absolute majority popular vote in 2 rounds if needed for a 5-year term (eligible for a second term); election last held on 4 April 2018 (next to be in 2023) (2018)
election results:
Julius Maada BIO elected president in second round; percent of vote - Julius Maada BIO (SLPP) 51.8%, Samura KAMARA (APC) 48.2%

Legislative branch: *description:* unicameral Parliament (146 seats; 132 members directly elected in single-seat constituencies by simple majority vote and 14 seats filled in separate elections by non-partisan members of Parliament called "paramount chiefs;" members serve 5-year terms)
elections:
last held on 7 March 2018 (next to be held in March 2023)
election results:
percent of vote by party - n/a; seats by party - APC 68, SLPP 49, C4C 8, other 7; composition - men 128, women 18, percent of women 12.3%

Judicial branch: *highest court(s):* Superior Court of Judicature (consists of the Supreme Court - at the apex - with the chief justice and 4 other judges, the Court of Appeal with the chief justice and 7 other judges, and the High Court of Justice with the chief justice and 9 other judges); note – the Judicature has jurisdiction in all civil, criminal, and constitutional matters
judge selection and term of office: Supreme Court chief justice and other judges of the Judicature appointed by the president on the advice of the Judicial and Legal Service Commission, a 7-member independent body of judges, presidential appointees, and the Commission chairman, and are subject to approval by Parliament; all Judicature judges serve until retirement at age 65
subordinate courts: magistrates' courts; District Appeals Court; local courts

Political parties and leaders: All People's Congress or APC [Ernest Bai KOROMA]
Coalition for Change or C4C [Tamba R. SANDY]
National Grand Coalition or NGC [Dr. Dennis BRIGHT]
Sierra Leone People's Party or SLPP [Dr. Prince HARDING]
numerous other parties

International organization participation: ACP, AfDB, ATMIS, AU, C, ECOWAS, EITI (compliant country), FAO, G-77, IAEA, IBRD, ICAO, ICCt, ICRM, IDA, IDB, IFAD, IFC, IFRCS, IHO (pending member), ILO, IMF, IMO, Interpol, IOC, IOM, IPU, ISO (correspondent), ITU, ITUC (NGOs), MIGA, MINUSMA, NAM, OIC, OPCW, UN, UNAMID, UNCTAD, UNESCO, UNIDO, UNIFIL, UNISFA, UNSOM, UNWTO, UPU, WCO, WFTU (NGOs), WHO, WIPO, WMO, WTO

Diplomatic representation in the US: *chief of mission:* Ambassador Sidique Abou-Bakarr WAI (since 8 April 2019)
chancery: 1701 19th Street NW, Washington, DC 20009-1605
telephone: [1] (202) 939-9261
FAX: [1] (202) 483-1793
email address and website:
info@embassyofsierraleone.net
https://embassyofsierraleone.net/

Diplomatic representation from the US: *chief of mission:* Ambassador David REIMER (since 24 March 2021)
embassy: Southridge-Hill Station, Freetown
mailing address: 2160 Freetown Place, Washington DC 20521-2160
telephone: [232] 99 105 000
email address and website:
consularfreetown@state.gov
https://sl.usembassy.gov/

Flag description: three equal horizontal bands of light green (top), white, and light blue; green symbolizes agriculture, mountains, and natural resources, white represents unity and justice, and blue the sea and the natural harbor in Freetown

National symbol(s): lion; national colors: green, white, blue

National anthem: *name:* "High We Exalt Thee, Realm of the Free"
lyrics/music: Clifford Nelson FYLE/John Joseph AKA
note: adopted 1961

ECONOMY

Economic overview: Sierra Leone is extremely poor and nearly half of the working-age population engages in subsistence agriculture. The country possesses substantial mineral, agricultural, and fishery resources, but it is still recovering from a civil war that destroyed most institutions before ending in the early 2000s.

In recent years, economic growth has been driven by mining - particularly iron ore. The country's principal exports are iron ore, diamonds, and rutile, and the economy is vulnerable to fluctuations in international prices. Until 2014, the government had relied on external assistance to support its budget, but it was gradually becoming more independent. The Ebola outbreak of 2014 and 2015, combined with falling global commodities prices, caused a significant contraction of economic activity in all areas. While the World Health Organization declared an end to the Ebola outbreak in Sierra Leone in November 2015, low commodity prices in 2015-2016 contributed to the country's biggest fiscal shortfall since 2001. In 2017, increased iron ore exports, together with the end of the Ebola epidemic, supported a resumption of economic growth.

Continued economic growth will depend on rising commodities prices and increased efforts to diversify the sources of growth. Non-mining activities will remain constrained by inadequate infrastructure, such as power and roads, even though power sector projects may provide some additional electricity capacity in the near term. Pervasive corruption and undeveloped human capital will continue to deter foreign investors. Sustained international donor support in the near future will partially offset these fiscal constraints.

Real GDP (purchasing power parity): $13.15 billion (2020 est.)
$13.44 billion (2019 est.)
$12.72 billion (2018 est.)
note: data are in 2017 dollars
country comparison to the world: 157

Real GDP growth rate: 3.7% (2017 est.)
6.3% (2016 est.)
-20.5% (2015 est.)
country comparison to the world: 80

Real GDP per capita: $1,600 (2020 est.)
$1,700 (2019 est.)
$1,700 (2018 est.)
note: data are in 2017 dollars
country comparison to the world: 218

GDP (official exchange rate): $4.132 billion (2020 est.)

Inflation rate (consumer prices): 14.8% (2019 est.)
16% (2018 est.)
18.2% (2017 est.)
country comparison to the world: 214

GDP - composition, by sector of origin: *agriculture:* 60.7% (2017 est.)
industry: 6.5% (2017 est.)
services: 32.9% (2017 est.)

GDP - composition, by end use: *household consumption:* 97.9% (2017 est.)
government consumption: 12.1% (2017 est.)
investment in fixed capital: 18.1% (2017 est.)
investment in inventories: 0.4% (2017 est.)
exports of goods and services: 26.8% (2017 est.)
imports of goods and services: -55.3% (2017 est.)

Agricultural products: cassava, rice, vegetables, oil palm fruit, sweet potatoes, milk, citrus fruit, groundnuts, fruit, pulses nes

Industries: diamond mining; iron ore, rutile and bauxite mining; small-scale manufacturing (beverages, textiles, footwear)

Industrial production growth rate: 15.5% (2017 est.)
country comparison to the world: 3

Labor force: 132,000 (2013 est.)
country comparison to the world: 177

Labor force - by occupation: *agriculture:* 61.1%
industry: 5.5%
services: 33.4% (2014 est.)

Unemployment rate: 15% (2017 est.)
17.2% (2016 est.)
country comparison to the world: 175

Unemployment, youth ages 15-24: *total:* 9.4%
male: 14.8%
female: 6.1% (2014 est.)
country comparison to the world: 143

Population below poverty line: 56.8% (2018 est.)

Gini Index coefficient - distribution of family income: 35.7 (2018 est.)
62.9 (1989)
country comparison to the world: 99

Household income or consumption by percentage share: *lowest 10%:* 2.6%
highest 10%: 33.6% (2003)

Budget: *revenues:* 562 million (2017 est.)
expenditures: 846.4 million (2017 est.)

Budget surplus (+) or deficit (-): -7.9% (of GDP) (2017 est.)
country comparison to the world: 199

Public debt: 63.9% of GDP (2017 est.)
54.9% of GDP (2016 est.)
country comparison to the world: 64

Taxes and other revenues: 15.6% (of GDP) (2017 est.)
country comparison to the world: 189

Fiscal year: calendar year

Current account balance: -$407 million (2017 est.)
-$88 million (2016 est.)
country comparison to the world: 117

Exports: $740 million (2019 est.) note: data are in current year dollars
$720 million (2018 est.) note: data are in current year dollars
country comparison to the world: 184

Exports - partners: Belgium 26%, China 25%, Romania 9%, United Arab Emirates 6%, Germany 5%, Netherlands 5% (2019)

Exports - commodities: titanium, lumber, diamonds, aluminum, cocoa beans (2019)

Imports: $1.82 billion (2019 est.) note: data are in current year dollars
$2.072 billion (2018 est.)
$1.59 billion (2018 est.) note: data are in current year dollars
country comparison to the world: 176

Imports - partners: China 27%, India 11%, United States 6%, Ghana 5%, Turkey 5% (2019)

Imports - commodities: rice, plastics, packaged medicines, sauces/seasonings, cars (2019)

Reserves of foreign exchange and gold: $478 million (31 December 2017 est.)
$497.2 million (31 December 2016 est.)
country comparison to the world: 152

Debt - external: $1.615 billion (31 December 2017 est.)
$1.503 billion (31 December 2016 est.)
country comparison to the world: 159

Exchange rates: leones (SLL) per US dollar -
7,396.3 (2017 est.)
6,289.9 (2016 est.)
6,289.9 (2015 est.)
5,080.8 (2014 est.)
4,524.2 (2013 est.)

ENERGY

Electricity access: *electrification - total population:* 26% (2019)
electrification - urban areas: 52% (2019)
electrification - rural areas: 6% (2019)

Electricity: *installed generating capacity:* 180,000 kW (2020 est.)
consumption: 130.708 million kWh (2019 est.)
exports: 0 kWh (2019 est.)
imports: 0 kWh (2020 est.)
transmission/distribution losses: 77 million kWh (2019 est.)

Electricity generation sources: *fossil fuels:* 8.2% of total installed capacity (2020 est.)
solar: 2.9% of total installed capacity (2020 est.)
hydroelectricity: 87% of total installed capacity (2020 est.)
biomass and waste: 1.9% of total installed capacity (2020 est.)

Petroleum: *total petroleum production:* 0 bbl/day (2021 est.)
refined petroleum consumption: 5,900 bbl/day (2019 est.)

Refined petroleum products - imports: 6,439 bbl/day (2015 est.)
country comparison to the world: 164

Carbon dioxide emissions: 899,000 metric tonnes of CO_2 (2019 est.)
from petroleum and other liquids: 899,000 metric tonnes of CO_2 (2019 est.)
country comparison to the world: 175

Energy consumption per capita: 1.803 million Btu/person (2019 est.)
country comparison to the world: 188

COMMUNICATIONS

Telephones - fixed lines: *total subscriptions:* 189 (2020 est.)
country comparison to the world: 220

Telephones - mobile cellular: *total subscriptions:* 6,884,201 (2020 est.)
subscriptions per 100 inhabitants: 86 (2020 est.)
country comparison to the world: 108

Telecommunication systems: *general assessment:* the telecom sector has only gradually recovered from the destruction caused during the war years, and only since 2019 has there been an effective terrestrial fiber backbone infrastructure, while the cable link to neighboring Guinea was not completed until February 2020; there is considerable available capacity from the ACE submarine cable and the national fiber network, but this is used inefficiently and so the price of internet connectivity remains one of the highest in the region; the theft of equipment and cabling, compounded by neglect, mismanagement, and under investment, means that telcos continue to operate in difficult conditions; the telecom regulator has made efforts to improve the market, including the liberalization of the international gateway and regular checks on QoS; the regulator reduced the price floor for mobile voice calls in early 2020, though consumers objected to the MNOs withdrawing a number of cheap packages as a response; the mobile sector has been the main driver of overall telecom revenue (2022)
domestic: fixed-line 0 per 100 and mobile-cellular just over 86 per 100 (2020)
international: country code - 232; landing point for the ACE submarine cable linking to South Africa, over 20 western African countries and Europe; satellite earth station - 1 Intelsat (Atlantic Ocean) (2019)

Broadcast media: 1 government-owned TV station; 3 private TV stations; a pay-TV service began operations in late 2007; 1 government-owned national radio station; about two-dozen private radio stations primarily clustered in major cities; transmissions of several international broadcasters are available
(2019)

Internet country code: .sl

Internet users: *total:* 1,435,857 (2020 est.)
percent of population: 18% (2020 est.)
country comparison to the world: 138

TRANSPORTATION

National air transport system: *annual passenger traffic on registered air carriers:* 50,193 (2015)
annual freight traffic on registered air carriers: 0 (2015) mt-km

Civil aircraft registration country code prefix: 9L

Airports: *total:* 8 (2021)
country comparison to the world: 161

Airports - with paved runways: *total:* 1
over 3,047 m: 1 (2021)

Airports - with unpaved runways: *total:* 7
914 to 1,523 m: 7 (2021)

Heliports: 2 (2021)

Roadways: *total:* 11,701 km (2015)
paved: 1,051 km (2015)
unpaved: 10,650 km (2015)
urban: 3,000 km (2015)
non-urban: 8,700 km (2015)
country comparison to the world: 133

Waterways: 800 km (2011) (600 km navigable year-round)
country comparison to the world: 79

Merchant marine: *total:* 591
by type: bulk carrier 30, container ship 9, general cargo 319, oil tanker 108, other 125 (2021)
country comparison to the world: 39

Ports and terminals: *major seaport(s):* Freetown, Pepel, Sherbro Islands

MILITARY AND SECURITY

Military and security forces: Republic of Sierra Leone Armed Forces (RSLAF): operates under a Joint Force Command with Land Forces, Maritime Forces, and an Air Wing; Ministry of Internal Affairs: Sierre Leone Police (2022)

Military expenditures: 0.3% of GDP (2021 est.)
0.3% of GDP (2020 est.)
0.3% of GDP (2019 est.) (approximately $35 million)
0.3% of GDP (2018 est.) (approximately $45 million)
0.3% of GDP (2017 est.) (approximately $40 million)
country comparison to the world: 165

Military and security service personnel strengths: approximately 9,000 personnel, mostly ground forces (2022)

Military equipment inventories and acquisitions: the RSLAF has a small inventory that includes a mix of Soviet-origin and other older foreign-supplied equipment; it has received limited amounts of mostly donations and second-hand equipment since 2010 (2022)

Military service age and obligation: 18-29 for voluntary military service; women are eligible to serve; no conscription (2022)

Military - note: after the end of the civil war in 2002, the military was reduced in size and restructured with British military assistance; the RSLAF's origins lie in the Sierra Leone Battalion of the Royal West African Frontier Force (RWAFF), a multi-regiment force formed by the British colonial office in 1900 to garrison the West African colonies of Gold Coast (Ghana), Nigeria (Lagos and the protectorates of Northern and Southern Nigeria), Sierra Leone, and Gambia; the RWAFF fought in both World Wars (2022)

TRANSNATIONAL ISSUES

Disputes - international: *Sierra Leone-Guinea:* Sierra Leone opposed Guinean troops' continued occupation of Yenga, a small village on the Makona River that serves as a border with Guinea; Guinea's forces came to Yenga in the mid-1990s to help the Sierra Leonean military to suppress rebels and to secure their common border but remained there even after both countries signed a 2005 agreement acknowledging that Yenga belonged to Sierra Leone; in 2012, the two sides signed a declaration to demilitarize the area; in 2019, Sierra Leone's Minister of Foreign Affairs and International Cooperation stated that the dispute over Yenga had been resolved; however, at a 2021 ECOWAS meeting, Sierra Leone's President BIO called on the bloc to help resolve an incursion of Guinean troops in Yenga
Sierra Leone-Liberia: none identified

Refugees and internally displaced persons: IDPs: 5,500 (displacement caused by post-electoral violence in 2018 and clashes in the Pujehun region in 2019) (2021)

SINGAPORE

INTRODUCTION

Background: A Malay trading port known as Temasek existed on the island of Singapore by the 14th century. The settlement changed hands several times in the ensuing centuries and was eventually burned in the 17th century and fell into obscurity. The British founded modern Singapore as a trading colony on the site in 1819. It joined the Malaysian Federation in 1963 but was ousted two years later and became independent. Singapore subsequently became one of the world's most prosperous countries with strong international trading links (its port is one of the world's busiest in terms of tonnage handled) and with per capita GDP equal to that of the leading nations of Western Europe.

GEOGRAPHY

Location: Southeastern Asia, islands between Malaysia and Indonesia

Geographic coordinates: 1 22 N, 103 48 E

Map references: Southeast Asia

Area: *total:* 719 sq km
land: 709.2 sq km
water: 10 sq km
country comparison to the world: 190

Area - comparative: slightly more than 3.5 times the size of Washington, DC

Land boundaries: *total:* 0 km

Coastline: 193 km

Maritime claims: *territorial sea:* 3 nm
exclusive fishing zone: within and beyond territorial sea, as defined in treaties and practice

Climate: tropical; hot, humid, rainy; two distinct monsoon seasons - northeastern monsoon (December to March) and southwestern monsoon (June to September); inter-monsoon - frequent afternoon and early evening thunderstorms

Terrain: lowlying, gently undulating central plateau

Elevation: *highest point:* Bukit Timah 166 m
lowest point: Singapore Strait 0 m

Natural resources: fish, deepwater ports

Land use: *agricultural land:* 1% (2018 est.)
arable land: 0.9% (2018 est.)
permanent crops: 0.1% (2018 est.)
permanent pasture: 0% (2018 est.)
forest: 3.3% (2018 est.)
other: 95.7% (2018 est.)

Irrigated land: 0 sq km (2012)

Population distribution: most of the urbanization is along the southern coast, with relatively dense population clusters found in the central areas

Natural hazards: flash floods

Geography - note: focal point for Southeast Asian sea routes; consists of about 60 islands, by far the largest of which is Pulau Ujong; land reclamation has removed many former islands and created a number of new ones

PEOPLE AND SOCIETY

Population: 5,921,231 (2022 est.)
country comparison to the world: 113

Nationality: *noun:* Singaporean(s)
adjective: Singapore

Ethnic groups: Chinese 74.2%, Malay 13.7%, Indian 8.9%, other 3.2% (2021 est.)
note: data represent population by self-identification; the population is divided into four categories: Chinese, Malay (includes indigenous Malays and Indonesians), Indian (includes Indian, Pakistani, Bangladeshi, or Sri Lankan), and other ethnic groups (includes Eurasians, Caucasians, Japanese, Filipino, Vietnamese)

Languages: English (official) 48.3%, Mandarin (official) 29.9%, other Chinese dialects (includes Hokkien, Cantonese, Teochew, Hakka) 8.7%, Malay (official) 9.2%, Tamil (official) 2.5%, other 1.4%; note - data represent language most frequently spoken at home (2020 est.)
major-language sample(s):
The World Factbook, the indispensable source for basic information. (English)
世界概況 一 不可缺少的基本消息來源 (Mandarin)

Religions: Buddhist 31.1%, Christian 18.9%, Muslim 15.6%, Taoist 8.8%, Hindu 5%, other 0.6%, none 20% (2020 est.)

Demographic profile: Singapore has one of the lowest total fertility rates (TFR) in the world – an average of 1.15 children born per woman – and a rapidly aging population. Women's expanded educations, widened aspirations, and a desire to establish careers has contributed to delayed marriage and smaller families. Most married couples have only one or two children in order to invest more in each child, including the high costs of education. In addition, more and more Singaporeans, particularly women, are staying single. Factors contributing to this trend are a focus on careers, long working hours, the high cost of living, and long waits for public housing. With fertility at such a low rate and rising life expectancy, the proportion of the population aged 65 or over is growing and the youth population is shrinking. Singapore is projected to experience one of the largest percentage point increases in the elderly share of the population at 21% between 2019 and 2050, according to the UN. The working-age population (aged 15-64) will gradually decrease, leaving fewer workers to economically support the elderly population.

Migration has played a key role in Singapore's development. As Singapore's economy expanded during the 19th century, more and more Chinese, Indian, and Malay labor immigrants arrived. Most of Singapore's pre-World War II population growth was a result of immigration. During World War II, immigration came to a halt when the Japanese occupied the island but revived in the postwar years. Policy was restrictive during the 1950s and 1960s, aiming to protect jobs for residents by reducing the intake of low-skilled foreign workers and focusing instead on attracting professionals from abroad with specialist skills. Consequently, the nonresident share of Singapore's population plummeted to less than 3%.

As the country industrialized, however, it loosened restrictions on the immigration of manual workers. From the 1980s through the 2000s, the foreign population continued to grow as a result of policies aimed at attracting foreign workers of all skill levels. More recently, the government has instituted immigration policies that target highly skilled workers. Skilled workers are encouraged to stay and are given the opportunity to become permanent residents or citizens. The country, however, imposes restrictions on unskilled and low-skilled workers to ensure they do not establish roots, including prohibiting them from bringing their families and requiring employers to pay a monthly foreign worker levy and security bond. The country has also become increasingly attractive to international students. The growth of the foreign-born population has continued to be rapid; as of 2015, the foreign-born composed 46% of the total population. At the same time, growing numbers of Singaporeans are emigrating for education and work experience in highly skilled sectors such finance, information technology, and medicine. Increasingly, the moves abroad are permanent.

Age structure: *0-14 years:* 12.8% (male 406,983/female 387,665)
15-24 years: 15.01% (male 457,190/female 474,676)
25-54 years: 50.73% (male 1,531,088/female 1,618,844)
55-64 years: 10.58% (male 328,024/female 328,808)
65 years and over: 10.89% (male 310,123/female 366,259) (2020 est.)

Dependency ratios: *total dependency ratio:* 34.5
youth dependency ratio: 16.5
elderly dependency ratio: 18
potential support ratio: 5.6 (2020 est.)

Median age: *total:* 35.6 years
male: 35.4 years
female: 35.7 years (2020 est.)
country comparison to the world: 82

Population growth rate: 0.92% (2022 est.)
country comparison to the world: 105

Birth rate: 9.05 births/1,000 population (2022 est.)
country comparison to the world: 202

Death rate: 4.04 deaths/1,000 population (2022 est.)
country comparison to the world: 213

Net migration rate: 4.22 migrant(s)/1,000 population (2022 est.)
country comparison to the world: 28

Population distribution: most of the urbanization is along the southern coast, with relatively dense population clusters found in the central areas

Urbanization: *urban population:* 100% of total population (2022)
rate of urbanization: 0.74% annual rate of change (2020-25 est.)

Major urban areas - population: 3.040 million SINGAPORE (capital) (2022)

Sex ratio: *at birth:* 1.05 male(s)/female
0-14 years: 1.07 male(s)/female
15-24 years: 1.11 male(s)/female
25-54 years: 1 male(s)/female
55-64 years: 0.97 male(s)/female
65 years and over: 0.75 male(s)/female
total population: 1 male(s)/female (2022 est.)

Mother's mean age at first birth: 30.5 years (2015 est.)
note: data represents median age

Maternal mortality ratio: 8 deaths/100,000 live births (2017 est.)
country comparison to the world: 153

Infant mortality rate: *total:* 1.55 deaths/1,000 live births
male: 1.71 deaths/1,000 live births
female: 1.38 deaths/1,000 live births (2022 est.)
country comparison to the world: 226

Life expectancy at birth: *total population:* 86.35 years
male: 83.65 years
female: 89.2 years (2022 est.)
country comparison to the world: 2

Total fertility rate: 1.16 children born/woman (2022 est.)
country comparison to the world: 225

Drinking water source: *improved: total:* 100% of population
unimproved: total: 0% of population (2020 est.)

Current health expenditure: 4.1% of GDP (2019)

Physicians density: 2.46 physicians/1,000 population (2019)

Hospital bed density: 2.5 beds/1,000 population (2017)

Sanitation facility access: *improved: total:* 100% of population
unimproved: total: 0% of population (2020 est.)

HIV/AIDS - adult prevalence rate: 0.2% (2020 est.)
country comparison to the world: 111

HIV/AIDS - people living with HIV/AIDS: 8,000 (2020 est.)
note: estimate does not include children
country comparison to the world: 112

HIV/AIDS - deaths: (2020 est.) <100
note: estimate does not include children

Obesity - adult prevalence rate: 6.1% (2016)
country comparison to the world: 171

Alcohol consumption per capita: *total:* 1.81 liters of pure alcohol (2019 est.)
beer: 1.26 liters of pure alcohol (2019 est.)
wine: 0.27 liters of pure alcohol (2019 est.)
spirits: 0.24 liters of pure alcohol (2019 est.)
other alcohols: 0.04 liters of pure alcohol (2019 est.)
country comparison to the world: 132

Tobacco use: *total:* 16.5% (2020 est.)
male: 28% (2020 est.)
female: 5% (2020 est.)
country comparison to the world: 99

Education expenditures: 2.5% of GDP (2020 est.)
country comparison to the world: 170

Literacy: *definition:* age 15 and over can read and write
total population: 97.5%
male: 98.9%
female: 96.1% (2019)

School life expectancy (primary to tertiary education): *total:* 17 years
male: 16 years
female: 17 years (2019)

Unemployment, youth ages 15-24: *total:* 10.6%
male: 8.1%
female: 13.5% (2020 est.)

ENVIRONMENT

Environment - current issues: water pollution; industrial pollution; limited natural freshwater resources; limited land availability presents waste disposal problems; air pollution; deforestation; seasonal smoke/haze resulting from forest fires in Indonesia

Environment - international agreements: *party to:* Biodiversity, Climate Change, Climate Change-Kyoto Protocol, Climate Change-Paris Agreement, Comprehensive Nuclear Test Ban, Desertification, Endangered Species, Hazardous Wastes, Law of the Sea, Nuclear Test Ban, Ozone Layer Protection, Ship Pollution
signed, but not ratified: none of the selected agreements

Air pollutants: *particulate matter emissions:* 18.26 micrograms per cubic meter (2016 est.)
carbon dioxide emissions: 37.54 megatons (2016 est.)
methane emissions: 4.4 megatons (2020 est.)

Climate: tropical; hot, humid, rainy; two distinct monsoon seasons - northeastern monsoon (December to March) and southwestern monsoon (June to September); inter-monsoon - frequent afternoon and early evening thunderstorms

Land use: *agricultural land:* 1% (2018 est.)
arable land: 0.9% (2018 est.)
permanent crops: 0.1% (2018 est.)
permanent pasture: 0% (2018 est.)
forest: 3.3% (2018 est.)
other: 95.7% (2018 est.)

Urbanization: *urban population:* 100% of total population (2022)
rate of urbanization: 0.74% annual rate of change (2020-25 est.)

Revenue from forest resources: *forest revenues:* 0% of GDP (2018 est.)
country comparison to the world: 197

Revenue from coal: *coal revenues:* 0% of GDP (2018 est.)
country comparison to the world: 166

Waste and recycling: *municipal solid waste generated annually:* 7,704,300 tons (2017 est.)
municipal solid waste recycled annually: 4,699,623 tons (2015 est.)
percent of municipal solid waste recycled: 61% (2015 est.)

Total water withdrawal: *municipal:* 296.73 million cubic meters (2017 est.)
industrial: 336.294 million cubic meters (2017 est.)
agricultural: 26.376 million cubic meters (2017 est.)

Total renewable water resources: 600 million cubic meters (2017 est.)

GOVERNMENT

Country name: *conventional long form:* Republic of Singapore
conventional short form: Singapore
local long form: Republic of Singapore
local short form: Singapore
etymology: name derives from the Sanskrit words "simha" (lion) and "pura" (city) to describe the city-state's leonine symbol

Government type: parliamentary republic

Capital: *name:* Singapore
geographic coordinates: 1 17 N, 103 51 E
time difference: UTC+8 (13 hours ahead of Washington, DC, during Standard Time)
etymology: name derives from the Sanskrit words *simha* (lion) and *pura* (city), thus creating the city's epithet "lion city"

Administrative divisions: no first order administrative divisions; there are five community development councils: Central Singapore Development Council, North East Development Council, North West Development Council, South East Development Council, South West Development Council (2019)

Independence: 9 August 1965 (from Malaysian Federation)

National holiday: National Day, 9 August (1965)

Constitution: *history:* several previous; latest adopted 22 December 1965
amendments: proposed by Parliament; passage requires two-thirds majority vote in the second and third readings by the elected Parliament membership and assent of the president of the republic; passage of amendments affecting sovereignty or control of the Police Force or the Armed Forces requires at least two-thirds majority vote in a referendum; amended many times, last in 2020

Legal system: English common law

International law organization participation: has not submitted an ICJ jurisdiction declaration; non-party state to the ICCt

Citizenship: *citizenship by birth:* no
citizenship by descent only: at least one parent must be a citizen of Singapore
dual citizenship recognized: no
residency requirement for naturalization: 10 years

Suffrage: 21 years of age; universal and compulsory

Executive branch: *chief of state:* President HALIMAH Yacob (since 14 September 2017)
head of government: Prime Minister LEE Hsien Loong (since 12 August 2004)
cabinet: Cabinet appointed by the president on the advice of the prime minister; Cabinet responsible to Parliament
elections/appointments: president directly elected by simple majority popular vote for a fixed term of 6 years (there are no term limits); election last held on 13 September 2017 (next to be held in 2023); following legislative elections, leader of majority party or majority coalition appointed prime minister by president; deputy prime ministers appointed by the president
election results:
2017: HALIMAH Yacob was declared president on 13 September 2017, being the only eligible candidate

2011: Tony TAN Keng Yam elected president; percent of vote - Tony TAN Keng Yam (independent) 35.2%, TAN Cheng Bock (independent) 34.9%, TAN Jee Say (independent) 25%, TAN Kin Lian (independent) 4.9%

Legislative branch: *description:* unicameral Parliament (104 seats statutory, 103 current term; 93 members directly elected by simple majority popular vote, up to 9 nominated by a parliamentary selection committee and appointed by the president, and up to 12 non-constituency members from opposition parties to ensure political diversity; members serve 5-year terms); note - the number of nominated members increased to 12 for the 2020 election for the first time (2021)
elections:
last held on 10 July 2020 (next must be held by 2025)
election results:
percent of vote by party - PAP 89.2%, WP 10.6%, other 0.2%; seats by party - PAP 83, WP 10; composition of total Parliament - men 73, women 30, percent of women 29.1%

Judicial branch: *highest court(s):* Supreme Court (although the number of judges varies - as of April 2019, the court totaled 20 judges, 7 judicial commissioners, 4 judges of appeal, and 16 international judges); the court is organized into an upper tier Appeal Court and a lower tier High Court
judge selection and term of office: judges appointed by the president from candidates recommended by the prime minister after consultation with the chief justice; judges usually serve until retirement at age 65, but terms can be extended
subordinate courts: district, magistrates', juvenile, family, community, and coroners' courts; small claims tribunals; employment claims tribunals

Political parties and leaders: Democratic Progressive Party or DPP [Mohamad Hamim BIN ALIYA]
National Solidarity Party or NSP [Spencer NG]
People's Action Party or PAP [LEE Hsien Loong]
People's Power Party or PPP [Goh Meng SENG]
People's Voice or PV [Lim TEAN]
Progress Singapore Party or PSP [Francis YUEN]
Red Dot United or RDU [Ravi PHILEMON]
Reform Party or RP [Kenneth JEYARETNAM]
Singapore Democratic Alliance or SDA [Desmond LIM]
Singapore Democratic Party or SDP [Dr. CHEE Soon Juan]
Singapore Malay National Organisation or PKMS [Muhammad Hairullah AHMAD]
Singapore People's Party or SPP [Steve CHIA]
Singapore United Party or SUP [Andy ZHU]
Workers' Party or WP [Pritam SINGH]
note: the PAP has won every general election since the end of the British colonial era in 1959

International organization participation: ADB, AOSIS, APEC, Arctic Council (observer), ARF, ASEAN, BIS, C, CP, EAS, FAO, FATF, G-77, IAEA, IBRD, ICAO, ICC (national committees), ICCt, ICRM, IDA, IFC, IFRCS, IHO, ILO, IMF, IMO, IMSO, Interpol, IOC, IPU, ISO, ITSO, ITU, ITUC (NGOs), MIGA, NAM, OPCW, Pacific Alliance (observer), PCA, UN, UNCTAD, UNESCO, UNHCR, UPU, WCO, WHO, WIPO, WMO, WTO

Diplomatic representation in the US: *chief of mission:* Ambassador Ashok KUMAR Mirpuri (since 30 July 2012)
chancery: 3501 International Place NW, Washington, DC 20008
telephone: [1] (202) 537-3100
FAX: [1] (202) 537-0876
email address and website:
singemb_was@mfa.sg
https://www.mfa.gov.sg/washington/
consulate(s) general: San Francisco
consulate(s): New York

Diplomatic representation from the US: *chief of mission:* Ambassador Jonathan KAPLAN (since December 2021)
embassy: 27 Napier Road, Singapore 258508
mailing address: 4280 Singapore Place, Washington DC 20521-4280
telephone: [65] 6476-9100
FAX: [65] 6476-9340
email address and website:
singaporeusembassy@state.gov
https://sg.usembassy.gov/

Flag description: two equal horizontal bands of red (top) and white; near the hoist side of the red band, there is a vertical, white crescent (closed portion is toward the hoist side) partially enclosing five white five-pointed stars arranged in a circle; red denotes brotherhood and equality; white signifies purity and virtue; the waxing crescent moon symbolizes a young nation on the ascendancy; the five stars represent the nation's ideals of democracy, peace, progress, justice, and equality

National symbol(s): lion, merlion (mythical half lion-half fish creature), orchid; national colors: red, white

National anthem: *name:* "Majulah Singapura" (Onward Singapore)
lyrics/music: ZUBIR Said
note: adopted 1965; first performed in 1958 at the Victoria Theatre, the anthem is sung only in Malay

National heritage: *total World Heritage Sites:* 1 (cultural)
selected World Heritage Site locales: Singapore Botanic Gardens

ECONOMY

Economic overview: Singapore has a highly developed and successful free-market economy. It enjoys an open and corruption-free environment, stable prices, and a per capita GDP higher than that of most developed countries. Unemployment is very low. The economy depends heavily on exports, particularly of electronics, petroleum products, chemicals, medical and optical devices, pharmaceuticals, and on Singapore's vibrant transportation, business, and financial services sectors.

The economy contracted 0.6% in 2009 as a result of the global financial crisis, but has continued to grow since 2010. Growth from 2012-2017 was slower than during the previous decade, a result of slowing structural growth - as Singapore reached high-income levels - and soft global demand for exports. Growth recovered to 3.6% in 2017 with a strengthening global economy.

The government is attempting to restructure Singapore's economy to reduce its dependence on foreign labor, raise productivity growth, and increase wages amid slowing labor force growth and an aging population. Singapore has attracted major investments in advanced manufacturing, pharmaceuticals, and medical technology production and will continue efforts to strengthen its position as Southeast Asia's leading financial and technology hub. Singapore is a signatory of the Comprehensive and Progressive Agreement for Trans-Pacific Partnership (CPTPP), and a party to the Regional Comprehensive Economic Partnership (RCEP) negotiations with nine other ASEAN members plus Australia, China, India, Japan, South Korea, and New Zealand. In 2015, Singapore formed, with the other ASEAN members, the ASEAN Economic Community.

Real GDP (purchasing power parity): $531.04 billion (2020 est.)
$561.3 billion (2019 est.)
$553.85 billion (2018 est.)
note: data are in 2017 dollars
country comparison to the world: 38

Real GDP growth rate: 0.73% (2019 est.)
3.48% (2018 est.)
4.34% (2017 est.)
country comparison to the world: 179

Real GDP per capita: $93,400 (2020 est.)
$98,400 (2019 est.)
$98,200 (2018 est.)
note: data are in 2017 dollars
country comparison to the world: 4

GDP (official exchange rate): $372.088 billion (2019 est.)

Inflation rate (consumer prices): 0.5% (2019 est.)
0.4% (2018 est.)
0.5% (2017 est.)
country comparison to the world: 43

Credit ratings:

Fitch rating: AAA (2003)

Moody's rating: Aaa (2002)

Standard & Poors rating: AAA (1995)

GDP - composition, by sector of origin: *agriculture:* 0% (2017 est.)
industry: 24.8% (2017 est.)
services: 75.2% (2017 est.)

GDP - composition, by end use: *household consumption:* 35.6% (2017 est.)
government consumption: 10.9% (2017 est.)
investment in fixed capital: 24.8% (2017 est.)
investment in inventories: 2.8% (2017 est.)
exports of goods and services: 173.3% (2017 est.)
imports of goods and services: -149.1% (2017 est.)

Agricultural products: poultry, eggs, vegetables, pork, duck meat, spinach, pig offals, bird eggs, pig fat, cabbages

Industries: electronics, chemicals, financial services, oil drilling equipment, petroleum refining, biomedical products, scientific instruments, telecommunication equipment, processed food and beverages, ship repair, offshore platform construction, entrepot trade

Industrial production growth rate: 5.7% (2017 est.)
country comparison to the world: 46

Labor force: 3.778 million (2019 est.)
note: excludes non-residents
country comparison to the world: 92

Labor force - by occupation: *agriculture:* 0.7%
industry: 25.6%
services: 73.7% (2017)
note: excludes non-residents

Unemployment rate: 2.25% (2019 est.)
2.1% (2018 est.)
country comparison to the world: 23

Unemployment, youth ages 15-24: *total:* 10.6%
male: 8.1%
female: 13.5% (2020 est.)

country comparison to the world: 135

Gini Index coefficient - distribution of family income: 45.9 (2017)
45.8 (2016)
country comparison to the world: 27

Household income or consumption by percentage share: *lowest 10%:* 1.6%
highest 10%: 27.5% (2017)

Budget: *revenues:* 50.85 billion (2017 est.)
expenditures: 51.87 billion (2017 est.)
note: expenditures include both operational and development expenditures

Budget surplus (+) or deficit (-): -0.3% (of GDP) (2017 est.)
country comparison to the world: 55

Public debt: 111.1% of GDP (2017 est.)
106.8% of GDP (2016 est.)
note: Singapore's public debt consists largely of Singapore Government Securities (SGS) issued to assist the Central Provident Fund (CPF), which administers Singapore's defined contribution pension fund; special issues of SGS are held by the CPF, and are non-tradable; the government has not borrowed to finance deficit expenditures since the 1980s; Singapore has no external public debt
country comparison to the world: 11

Taxes and other revenues: 15.7% (of GDP) (2017 est.)
country comparison to the world: 187

Fiscal year: 1 April - 31 March

Current account balance: $63.109 billion (2019 est.)
$64.042 billion (2018 est.)
country comparison to the world: 8

Exports: $599.2 billion (2020 est.) note: data are in current year dollars
$658.54 billion (2019 est.) note: data are in current year dollars
$665.7 billion (2018 est.) note: data are in current year dollars
country comparison to the world: 10

Exports - partners: China 15%, Hong Kong 13%, Malaysia 9%, United States 8%, Indonesia 7%, India 5% (2019)

Exports - commodities: integrated circuits, refined petroleum, gold, gas turbines, packaged medicines (2019)

Imports: $490.68 billion (2020 est.) note: data are in current year dollars
$552.71 billion (2019 est.) note: data are in current year dollars
$557.49 billion (2018 est.) note: data are in current year dollars
country comparison to the world: 12

Imports - partners: China 16%, Malaysia 11%, United States 9%, Taiwan 7%, Japan 5%, Indonesia 5% (2019)

Imports - commodities: integrated circuits, refined petroleum, crude petroleum, gold, gas turbines (2019)

Reserves of foreign exchange and gold: $279.9 billion (31 December 2017 est.)
$271.8 billion (31 December 2016 est.)
country comparison to the world: 11

Debt - external: $1,557,646,000,000 (2019 est.)
$1,528,177,000,000 (2018 est.)
country comparison to the world: 16

Exchange rates: Singapore dollars (SGD) per US dollar -
1.33685 (2020 est.)
1.35945 (2019 est.)
1.3699 (2018 est.)
1.3748 (2014 est.)
1.2671 (2013 est.)

ENERGY

Electricity access: *electrification - total population:* 100% (2020)

Electricity: *installed generating capacity:* 12.24 million kW (2020 est.)
consumption: 50,742,380,000 kWh (2019 est.)
exports: 0 kWh (2019 est.)
imports: 0 kWh (2020 est.)
transmission/distribution losses: 571 million kWh (2019 est.)

Electricity generation sources: *fossil fuels:* 96.5% of total installed capacity (2020 est.)
solar: 1.2% of total installed capacity (2020 est.)
biomass and waste: 2.3% of total installed capacity (2020 est.)

Coal: *production:* 0 metric tons (2020 est.)
consumption: 423,000 metric tons (2020 est.)
exports: 1,000 metric tons (2020 est.)
imports: 424,000 metric tons (2020 est.)
proven reserves: 0 metric tons (2019 est.)

Petroleum: *total petroleum production:* 0 bbl/day (2021 est.)
refined petroleum consumption: 1.448 million bbl/day (2019 est.)
crude oil and lease condensate exports: 13,000 bbl/day (2018 est.)
crude oil and lease condensate imports: 1,121,200 bbl/day (2018 est.)
crude oil estimated reserves: 0 barrels (2021 est.)

Refined petroleum products - production: 755,000 bbl/day (2015 est.)
country comparison to the world: 24

Refined petroleum products - exports: 1.82 million bbl/day (2015 est.)
country comparison to the world: 4

Refined petroleum products - imports: 2.335 million bbl/day (2015 est.)
country comparison to the world: 1

Natural gas: *production:* 0 cubic meters (2021 est.)
consumption: 13,396,282,000 cubic meters (2019 est.)
exports: 550.818 million cubic meters (2020 est.)
imports: 14,727,709,000 cubic meters (2020 est.)
proven reserves: 0 cubic meters (2021 est.)

Carbon dioxide emissions: 238.983 million metric tonnes of CO_2 (2019 est.)
from coal and metallurgical coke: 1.588 million metric tonnes of CO_2 (2019 est.)
from petroleum and other liquids: 211.115 million metric tonnes of CO_2 (2019 est.)
from consumed natural gas: 26.28 million metric tonnes of CO_2 (2019 est.)
country comparison to the world: 28

Energy consumption per capita: 639.951 million Btu/person (2019 est.)
country comparison to the world: 2

COMMUNICATIONS

Telephones - fixed lines: *total subscriptions:* 1.891 million (2020 est.)
subscriptions per 100 inhabitants: 32 (2020 est.)
country comparison to the world: 57

Telephones - mobile cellular: *total subscriptions:* 9,034,300 (2019)
subscriptions per 100 inhabitants: 156 (2019)
country comparison to the world: 93

Telecommunication systems: *general assessment:* a wealthy city-state, Singapore has a highly developed ICT infrastructure; government supported near universal home broadband penetration and free public access to wireless network; the government's telecommunication regulator, Infocomm Media Development Authority (IMDA), issued awards in mid-2020 to telecom operators with the goal of having at least 50% of the city-state covered with a standalone 5G network by the end of 2022; government actively promoting Smart Nation initiative supporting digital innovation; government oversees service providers and controls Internet content; well served by submarine cable and satellite connections (2021)
domestic: excellent domestic facilities; fixed-line roughly 32 per 100 and mobile-cellular 144 per 100 teledensity; multiple providers of high-speed Internet connectivity (2020)
international: country code - 65; landing points for INDIGO-West, SeaMeWe -3,-4,-5, SIGMAR, SJC, i2icn, PGASCOM, BSCS, IGG, B3JS, SAEx2, APCN-2, APG, ASC, SEAX-1, ASE, EAC-C2C, Matrix Cable System and SJC2 submarine cables providing links throughout Asia, Southeast Asia, Africa, Australia, the Middle East, and Europe; satellite earth stations - 3, Bukit Timah, Seletar, and Sentosa; supplemented by VSAT coverage (2019)

Broadcast media: state controls broadcast media; 6 domestic TV stations operated by MediaCorp which is wholly owned by a state investment company; broadcasts from Malaysian and Indonesian stations available; satellite dishes banned; multi-channel cable TV services available; a total of 19 domestic radio stations broadcasting, with MediaCorp operating 11, Singapore Press Holdings, also government-linked, another 5, 2 controlled by the Singapore Armed Forces Reservists Association and one owned by BBC Radio; Malaysian and Indonesian radio stations are available as is BBC; a number of Internet service radio stations are also available (2019)

Internet country code: .sg

Internet users: *total:* 5,230,942 (2020 est.)
percent of population: 92% (2020 est.)
country comparison to the world: 87

Broadband - fixed subscriptions: *total:* 1,509,700 (2020 est.)
subscriptions per 100 inhabitants: 26 (2020 est.)
country comparison to the world: 66

TRANSPORTATION

National air transport system: *number of registered air carriers:* 4 (2020)
inventory of registered aircraft operated by air carriers: 230
annual passenger traffic on registered air carriers: 40,401,515 (2018)
annual freight traffic on registered air carriers: 5,194,900,000 (2018) mt-km

Civil aircraft registration country code prefix: 9V

Airports: *total:* 9 (2021)
country comparison to the world: 158

Airports - with paved runways: *total:* 9
over 3,047 m: 2
2,438 to 3,047 m: 2
1,524 to 2,437 m: 3

914 to 1,523 m:: *under 914 m:* 1 (2021)

Pipelines: 3,220 km domestic gas (2014), 1,122 km cross-border pipelines (2017), 8 km refined products (2013) (2013)

Roadways: *total:* 3,500 km (2017)
paved: 3,500 km (2017) (includes 164 km of expressways)
country comparison to the world: 158

Merchant marine: *total:* 3,321
by type: bulk carrier 576, container ship 514, general cargo 113, oil tanker 699, other 1,419 (2021)
country comparison to the world: 8

Ports and terminals: *major seaport(s):* Singapore
container port(s) (TEUs): Singapore (37,195,636) (2019)

LNG terminal(s) (import): Singapore

MILITARY AND SECURITY

Military and security forces: Singapore Armed Forces (SAF; aka Singapore Defense Force): Singapore Army, Republic of Singapore Navy, Republic of Singapore Air Force (includes air defense); Ministry of Home Affairs: Singapore Police Force (includes Police Coast Guard and the Gurkha Contingent) (2022)
note 1: the Gurkha Contingent of the Singapore Police Force (GCSPF) is a paramilitary unit for riot control and acts as a rapid reaction force
note 2: in 2022, the SAF announced that it would form a Digital and Intelligence Service (DIS) by the end of the year
note 3: in 2009, Singapore established a multi-agency national Maritime Security Task Force (MSTF) to work with law enforcement and maritime agencies to guard Singapore's waters, including conducting daily patrols, as well as boarding and escort operations in the Singapore Strait; the MSTF is subordinate to the Singapore Navy

Military expenditures: 3.2% of GDP (2021 est.)
3% of GDP (2020)
2.9% of GDP (2019) (approximately $15 billion)
2.9% of GDP (2018) (approximately $14.8 billion)
3% of GDP (2017) (approximately $14.8 billion)
country comparison to the world: 29

Military and security service personnel strengths: information varies; approximately 60,000 active duty troops (45,000 Army; 7,000 Navy; 8,000 Air Force) (2022)

Military equipment inventories and acquisitions: the SAF has a diverse and largely modern mix of domestically-produced and imported weapons; since 2010, the US has been the chief supplier of arms; other significant suppliers include France, Germany, Israel, and Sweden; Singapore has the most developed arms industry in Southeast Asia and is also its largest importer of weapons (2021)

Military service age and obligation: 18-21 years of age for compulsory military service for men; 16.5 years of age for voluntary enlistment (with parental consent); 24-month conscript service obligation, with a reserve obligation to age 40 (enlisted) or age 50 (officers); women are not conscripted, but they are allowed to volunteer for all services and branches, including combat arms (2022)
note 1: under the Enlistment Act, all male Singaporean citizens and permanent residents, unless exempted, are required to enter National Service (NS) upon attaining the age of 18; most NS conscripts serve in the Armed Forces, but some go into the Police Force or Civil Defense Force; as of 2020, conscripts comprised over half of the defense establishment
note 2: as of 2017, women made up about 7% of the active force
note 3: members of the Gurkha Contingent (GC) of the Singapore Police Force are mostly recruited from a small number of hill tribes in Nepal; the GC was formed in 1949 originally from selected ex-British Army Gurkhas

Military deployments: maintains permanent training detachments of military personnel in Australia, France, and the US (2022)

Military - note: Singapore is a member of the Five Powers Defense Arrangements (FPDA), a series of mutual assistance agreements reached in 1971 embracing Australia, Malaysia, New Zealand, Singapore, and the UK; the FPDA commits the members to consult with one another in the event or threat of an armed attack on any of the members and to mutually decide what measures should be taken, jointly or separately; there is no specific obligation to intervene militarily

the SAF's roots go back to 1854 when the Singapore Volunteer Rifle Corps was formed under colonial rule; the first battalion of regular soldiers, the First Singapore Infantry Regiment, was organized in 1957; the modern SAF was established in 1965; as of 2022, the SAF was widely viewed as the best equipped military in southeast Asia; the Army was largely based on conscripts and reservists with a small cadre of professional soldiers, while the Air Force and Navy were primarily comprised of well-trained professionals (2022)

Maritime threats: the International Maritime Bureau reports the territorial and offshore waters in the South China Sea as high risk for piracy and armed robbery against ships; numerous commercial vessels have been attacked and hijacked both at anchor and while underway; hijacked vessels are often disguised and cargo diverted to ports in East Asia; crews have been murdered or cast adrift; the Singapore Straits saw 35 attacks against commercial vessels in 2021, a 50% increase over 2020 and the highest number of incidents reported since 1992; vessels were boarded in 33 of the 35 incidents, one crew was injured, another assaulted and two threatened during these incidents

TRANSNATIONAL ISSUES

Disputes - international: piracy remains a problem in the Malacca Strait
Singapore-Indonesia: Indonesia and Singapore continue to work on finalization of their 1973 maritime boundary agreement by defining unresolved areas north of Indonesia's Batam Island; subsequent treaties were signed in 2009 (ratified in 2010) and 2014 (ratified in 2017) settling the two countries' boundaries in the Singapore Strait
Singapore-Malaysia: disputes with Malaysia over territorial waters, airspace, the price of fresh water delivered to Singapore from Malaysia, Singapore's extensive land reclamation works, bridge construction, and maritime boundaries in the Johor and Singapore Straits; in 2008, the International Court of Justice awarded sovereignty of Pedra Branca (Pulau Batu Puteh/Horsburgh Island) to Singapore, and Middle Rocks to Malaysia, but did not rule on maritime regimes, boundaries, or disposition of South Ledge, which is only visible at low tide

Refugees and internally displaced persons: *stateless persons:* 1,109 (mid-year 2021)

Illicit drugs: drug abuse limited because of aggressive law enforcement efforts, including carrying out death sentences; as a transportation and financial services hub, Singapore is vulnerable, despite strict laws and enforcement, as a venue for money laundering

SINT MAARTEN

INTRODUCTION

Background: Although sighted by Christopher COLUMBUS in 1493 and claimed for Spain, it was the Dutch who occupied the island in 1631 and began exploiting its salt deposits. The Spanish retook the island in 1633, but the Dutch continued to assert their claims. The Spanish finally relinquished the island of Saint Martin to the French and Dutch, who divided it between themselves in 1648. The establishment of cotton, tobacco, and sugar plantations dramatically expanded African slavery on the island in the 18th and 19th centuries; the practice was not abolished in the Dutch half until 1863. The island's economy declined until 1939 when it became a free port; the tourism industry was dramatically expanded beginning in the 1950s. In 1954, Sint Maarten and several other Dutch Caribbean possessions became part of the Kingdom of the Netherlands as the Netherlands Antilles. In a 2000 referendum, the citizens of Sint Maarten voted to become a self-governing country within the Kingdom of the Netherlands, effective October 2010. On 6 September 2017, Hurricane Irma hit Saint Martin/Sint Maarten, causing extensive damage to roads, communications, electrical power, and housing. The UN estimated the storm destroyed or damaged 90% of the buildings, and Princess Juliana International Airport was heavily damaged and closed to commercial air traffic for five weeks.

GEOGRAPHY

Location: Caribbean, located in the Leeward Islands (northern) group; Dutch part of the island of Saint

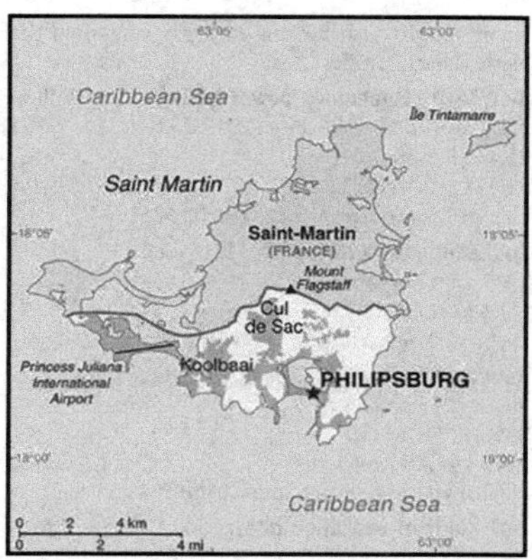

Martin in the Caribbean Sea; Sint Maarten lies east of the US Virgin Islands

Geographic coordinates: 18 4 N, 63 4 W

Map references: Central America and the Caribbean

Area: *total:* 34 sq km
land: 34 sq km
water: 0 sq km
note: Dutch part of the island of Saint Martin
country comparison to the world: 235

Area - comparative: one-fifth the size of Washington, DC

Land boundaries: *total:* 16 km
border countries (1): Saint Martin (France) 16 km

Coastline: 58.9 km (for entire island)

Maritime claims: *territorial sea:* 12 nm
exclusive economic zone: 200 nm

Climate: tropical marine climate, ameliorated by northeast trade winds, results in moderate temperatures; average rainfall of 150 cm/year; hurricane season stretches from July to November

Terrain: low, hilly terrain, volcanic origin

Elevation: *highest point:* Mount Flagstaff 383 m
lowest point: Caribbean Sea 0 m

Natural resources: fish, salt

Population distribution: most populous areas are Lower Prince's Quarter (north of Philipsburg), followed closely by Cul de Sac

Natural hazards: subject to hurricanes from July to November

Geography - note: *note 1:* the northern border is shared with the French overseas collectivity of Saint Martin; together, these two entities make up the smallest landmass in the world shared by two self-governing states
note 2: Simpson Bay Lagoon (aka as Simson Bay Lagoon or The Great Pond) is one of the largest inland lagoons in the West Indies; the border between the French and Dutch halves of the island of Saint Martin runs across the center of the lagoon, which is shared by both of the island's entities

PEOPLE AND SOCIETY

Population: 45,126 (2022 est.)
country comparison to the world: 211

Ethnic groups: Saint Maarten 29.9%, Dominican Republic 10.2%, Haiti 7.8%, Jamaica 6.6%, Saint Martin 5.9%, Guyana 5%, Dominica 4.4%, Curacao 4.1%, Aruba 3.4%, Saint Kitts and Nevis 2.8%, India 2.6%, Netherlands 2.2%, US 1.6%, Suriname 1.4%, Saint Lucia 1.3%, Anguilla 1.1%, other 8%, unspecified 1.7% (2011 est.)
note: data represent population by country of birth

Languages: English (official) 67.5%, Spanish 12.9%, Creole 8.2%, Dutch (official) 4.2%, Papiamento (a Spanish-Portuguese-Dutch-English dialect) 2.2%, French 1.5%, other 3.5% (2001 est.)

Religions: Protestant 41.9% (Pentecostal 14.7%, Methodist 10.0%, Seventh Day Adventist 6.6%, Baptist 4.7%, Anglican 3.1%, other Protestant 2.8%), Roman Catholic 33.1%, Hindu 5.2%, Christian 4.1%, Jehovah's Witness 1.7%, Evangelical 1.4%, Muslim/Jewish 1.1%, other 1.3% (includes Buddhist, Sikh, Rastafarian), none 7.9%, no response 2.4% (2011 est.)

Age structure: *0-14 years:* 18.64% (male 4,242/female 3,932)
15-24 years: 13.26% (male 2,967/female 2,849)
25-54 years: 39.08% (male 8,417/female 8,717)
55-64 years: 17.47% (male 3,638/female 4,020)
65 years and over: 11.55% (male 2,385/female 2,680) (2020 est.)

Dependency ratios: *total dependency ratio:* NA
youth dependency ratio: NA
elderly dependency ratio: NA
potential support ratio: NA

Median age: *total:* 41.1 years
male: 39.6 years
female: 42.7 years (2020 est.)
country comparison to the world: 46

Population growth rate: 1.23% (2022 est.)
country comparison to the world: 75

Birth rate: 12.56 births/1,000 population (2022 est.)
country comparison to the world: 144

Death rate: 6.07 deaths/1,000 population (2022 est.)
country comparison to the world: 155

Net migration rate: 5.83 migrant(s)/1,000 population (2022 est.)
country comparison to the world: 18

Population distribution: most populous areas are Lower Prince's Quarter (north of Philipsburg), followed closely by Cul de Sac

Urbanization: *urban population:* 100% of total population (2022)
rate of urbanization: 1.16% annual rate of change (2020-25 est. est.)

Major urban areas - population: 1,327 PHILIPSBURG (capital) (2011)

Sex ratio: *at birth:* 1.05 male(s)/female
0-14 years: 1.07 male(s)/female
15-24 years: 1.08 male(s)/female
25-54 years: 0.98 male(s)/female
55-64 years: 0.92 male(s)/female
65 years and over: 0.69 male(s)/female
total population: 0.98 male(s)/female (2022 est.)

Infant mortality rate: *total:* 7.98 deaths/1,000 live births
male: 8.8 deaths/1,000 live births
female: 7.12 deaths/1,000 live births (2022 est.)
country comparison to the world: 151

Life expectancy at birth: *total population:* 79.26 years
male: 76.91 years
female: 81.73 years (2022 est.)
country comparison to the world: 63

Total fertility rate: 1.99 children born/woman (2022 est.)
country comparison to the world: 110

Contraceptive prevalence rate: NA

Drinking water source: *improved: total:* 95.1% of population
unimproved: total: 4.9% of population (2017)

Current health expenditure: NA

Physicians density: NA

Sanitation facility access: *improved: urban:* NA
rural: NA
total: 98.8% of population
unimproved: urban: NA
rural: NA
total: 1.2% of population (2017)

HIV/AIDS - adult prevalence rate: NA

HIV/AIDS - people living with HIV/AIDS: NA

HIV/AIDS - deaths: NA

Children under the age of 5 years underweight: NA

Education expenditures: NA

Literacy: *total population:* NA
male: NA
female: NA

School life expectancy (primary to tertiary education): *total:* 12 years
male: 12 years
female: 12 years (2014)

ENVIRONMENT

Environment - current issues: scarcity of potable water (increasing percentage provided by desalination); inadequate solid waste management; pollution from construction, chemical runoff, and sewage harms reefs

Climate: tropical marine climate, ameliorated by northeast trade winds, results in moderate temperatures; average rainfall of 150 cm/year; hurricane season stretches from July to November

Urbanization: *urban population:* 100% of total population (2022)
rate of urbanization: 1.16% annual rate of change (2020-25 est. est.)

GOVERNMENT

Country name: *conventional long form:* Country of Sint Maarten
conventional short form: Sint Maarten
local long form: Land Sint Maarten (Dutch)/Country of Sint Maarten (English)
local short form: Sint Maarten (Dutch and English)
former: Netherlands Antilles; Curacao and Dependencies
etymology: explorer Christopher COLUMBUS named the island after Saint MARTIN of Tours because the 11 November 1493 day of discovery was the saint's feast day

Government type: parliamentary democracy under a constitutional monarchy

Dependency status: constituent country within the Kingdom of the Netherlands; full autonomy in internal affairs granted in 2010; Dutch Government responsible for defense and foreign affairs

Capital: *name:* Philipsburg
geographic coordinates: 18 1 N, 63 2 W
time difference: UTC-4 (1 hour ahead of Washington, DC, during Standard Time)

etymology: founded and named in 1763 by John PHILIPS, a Scottish captain in the Dutch navy

Administrative divisions: none (part of the Kingdom of the Netherlands)
note: Sint Maarten is one of four constituent countries of the Kingdom of the Netherlands; the other three are the Netherlands, Aruba, and Curacao

Independence: none (part of the Kingdom of the Netherlands)

National holiday: King's Day (birthday of King WILLEM-ALEXANDER), 27 April (1967); note - King's or Queen's Day are observed on the ruling monarch's birthday; celebrated on 26 April if 27 April is a Sunday; local holiday Sint Maarten's Day, 11 November (1985), commemorates the discovery of the island by COLUMBUS on Saint Martin's Day, 11 November 1493; celebrated on both halves of the island

Constitution: *history:* previous 1947, 1955; latest adopted 21 July 2010, entered into force 10 October 2010 (regulates governance of Sint Maarten but is subordinate to the Charter for the Kingdom of the Netherlands)
amendments: proposals initiated by the Government or by Parliament; passage requires at least a two-thirds majority of the Parliament membership; passage of amendments relating to fundamental rights, authorities of the governor and of Parliament must include the "views" of the Kingdom of the Netherlands Government prior to ratification by Parliament

Legal system: based on Dutch civil law system with some English common law influence

Citizenship: see the Netherlands

Suffrage: 18 years of age; universal

Executive branch: *chief of state:* King WILLEM-ALEXANDER of the Netherlands (since 30 April 2013); represented by Governor General Eugene HOLIDAY (since 10 October 2010)
head of government: Prime Minister Silveria JACOBS (since 28 March 2020)
cabinet: Cabinet nominated by the prime minister and appointed by the governor-general
elections/appointments: the monarch is hereditary; governor general appointed by the monarch for a 6-year term; following parliamentary elections, the leader of the majority party usually elected prime minister by Parliament
election results:
last held 9 January 2020 (next to be held in 2024)
note - on 16 January 2020, Governor Eugene HOLIDAY appoints Silveria JACOBS as *formateur* of a new government

Legislative branch: *description:* unicameral Parliament of Sint Maarten (15 seats; members directly elected by proportional representation vote to serve 4-year terms)
elections:
last held 9 January 2020 (next to be held in 2024)
election results:
percent of vote by party - NA 35.2%, UP 24.2%, US Party 13.2%, PFP 10.6%, UD 8.7%, other 8.1%; seats by party - NA 6, UP 4, PFP 2, US Party 2, UD 1

Judicial branch: *highest court(s):* Joint Court of Justice of Aruba, Curacao, Sint Maarten, and of Bonaire, Sint Eustatius and Saba or "Joint Court of Justice" (consists of the presiding judge, other members, and their substitutes); final appeals heard by the Supreme Court (in The Hague, Netherlands); note - prior to 2010, the Joint Court of Justice was the Common Court of Justice of the Netherlands Antilles and Aruba
judge selection and term of office: Joint Court judges appointed by the monarch serve for life
subordinate courts: Courts in First Instance

Political parties and leaders: National Alliance or NA [Silveria JACOBS]
Party for Progress or PFP [Melissa GUMBS]
Sint Maarten Christian Party or SMCP [Garcia ARRINDELL]
United Democrats Party or UD [Sarah WESCOT-WILLIAMS]
United People's Party or UP [Theodore HEYLIGER]
United Sint Maarten Party or US Party [Frans RICHARDSON]

International organization participation: Caricom (observer), ILO, Interpol, UNESCO (associate), UPU, WMO

Diplomatic representation in the US: none (represented by the Kingdom of the Netherlands)

Diplomatic representation from the US: *embassy:* the US does not have an embassy in Sint Maarten; the Consul General to Curacao is accredited to Sint Maarten

Flag description: two equal horizontal bands of red (top) and blue with a white isosceles triangle based on the hoist side; the center of the triangle displays the Sint Maarten coat of arms; the arms consist of an orange-bordered blue shield prominently displaying the white court house in Philipsburg, as well as a bouquet of yellow sage (the national flower) in the upper left, and the silhouette of a Dutch-French friendship monument in the upper right; the shield is surmounted by a yellow rising sun in front of which is a brown pelican in flight; a yellow scroll below the shield bears the motto: SEMPER PROGREDIENS (Always Progressing); the three main colors are identical to those on the Dutch flag
note: the flag somewhat resembles that of the Philippines but with the main red and blue bands reversed; the banner more closely evokes the wartime Philippine flag

National symbol(s): brown pelican, yellow sage (flower); national colors: red, white, blue

National anthem: *name:* O Sweet Saint Martin's Land
lyrics/music: Gerard KEMPS
note: the song, written in 1958, is used as an unofficial anthem for the entire island (both French and Dutch sides); as a collectivity of France, in addition to the local anthem, "La Marseillaise" is official on the French side (see France); as a constituent part of the Kingdom of the Netherlands, in addition to the local anthem, "Het Wilhelmus" is official on the Dutch side (see Netherlands)

ECONOMY

Economic overview: The economy of Sint Maarten centers around tourism with nearly four-fifths of the labor force engaged in this sector. Nearly 1.8 million visitors came to the island by cruise ship and roughly 500,000 visitors arrived through Princess Juliana International Airport in 2013. Cruise ships and yachts also call on Sint Maarten's numerous ports and harbors. Limited agriculture and local fishing means that almost all food must be imported. Energy resources and manufactured goods are also imported. Sint Maarten had the highest per capita income among the five islands that formerly comprised the Netherlands Antilles.

Real GDP (purchasing power parity): $1.44 billion (2018 est.) note: data are in 2017 dollars
$1.436 billion (2018 est.)
$1.538 billion (2017 est.)
country comparison to the world: 201

Real GDP growth rate: 3.6% (2014 est.)
4.1% (2013 est.)
1.9% (2012 est.)
country comparison to the world: 83

Real GDP per capita: $35,300 (2018 est.) note: data are in 2017 dollars
$35,342 (2018 est.)
$37,914 (2017 est.)
country comparison to the world: 56

GDP (official exchange rate): $304.1 million (2014 est.)

Inflation rate (consumer prices): 4% (2012 est.)
0.7% (2009 est.)
country comparison to the world: 166

GDP - composition, by sector of origin: *agriculture:* 0.4% (2008 est.)
industry: 18.3% (2008 est.)
services: 81.3% (2008 est.)

Agricultural products: sugar

Industries: tourism, light industry

Labor force: 23,200 (2008 est.)
country comparison to the world: 209

Labor force - by occupation: *agriculture:* 1.1%
industry: 15.2%
services: 83.7% (2008 est.)

Unemployment rate: 12% (2012 est.)
10.6% (2008 est.)
country comparison to the world: 166

Exports: $1.09 billion (2019 est.) note: data are in current year dollars
$800 million (2018 est.) note: data are in current year dollars
country comparison to the world: 177

Exports - commodities: sugar

Imports: $1.23 billion (2019 est.) note: data are in current year dollars
$1.22 billion (2018 est.) note: data are in current year dollars
country comparison to the world: 184

Exchange rates: Netherlands Antillean guilders (ANG) per US dollar -
1.79 (2017 est.)
1.79 (2016 est.)
1.79 (2015 est.)
1.79 (2014 est.)
1.79 (2013 est.)

ENERGY

Electricity access: *electrification - total population:* 100% (2020)

Refined petroleum products - production: 0 bbl/day (2015 est.)
country comparison to the world: 201

Refined petroleum products - exports: 0 bbl/day (2015 est.)
country comparison to the world: 202

Refined petroleum products - imports: 10,440 bbl/day (2015 est.)
country comparison to the world: 148

COMMUNICATIONS

Telephones - mobile cellular: *total subscriptions:* 68,840 (2017)
subscriptions per 100 inhabitants: 195.94 (2019)
country comparison to the world: 199

Telecommunication systems: *general assessment:* generally adequate facilities; growth sectors include mobile telephone and data segments; effective competition; LTE expansion; tourism and telecom sector contribute greatly to the GDP (2018)
domestic: extensive interisland microwave radio relay links; 196 per 100 mobile-cellular teledensity (2019)
international: country code - 1-721; landing points for SMPR-1 and the ECFS submarine cables providing connectivity to the Caribbean; satellite earth stations - 2 Intelsat (Atlantic Ocean) (2019)

Internet country code: .sx; note - IANA has designated .sx for Sint Maarten, but has not yet assigned it to a sponsoring organization

Internet users: *total:* 39,100 (March 2022)
percent of population: 89.5% (March 2022)
country comparison to the world: 204

TRANSPORTATION

Airports: *total:* 1 (2021)
country comparison to the world: 235

Airports - with paved runways: *total:* 1
1,524 to 2,437 m: 1 (2021)
note: Princess Juliana International Airport (SXM) was severely damaged on 6 September 2017 by hurricane Irma, but resumed commercial operations on 10 October 2017

Roadways: *total:* 53 km
country comparison to the world: 216

Ports and terminals: *major seaport(s):* Philipsburg
oil terminal(s): Coles Bay oil terminal

MILITARY AND SECURITY

Military and security forces: no regular military forces; Police Department for local law enforcement, supported by the Royal Netherlands Marechaussee (Gendarmerie), the Dutch Caribbean Police Force (Korps Politie Caribisch Nederland, KPCN), and the Dutch Caribbean Coast Guard (DCCG or Kustwacht Caribisch Gebied (KWCARIB)) (2022)

Military - note: defense is the responsibility of the Kingdom of the Netherlands

TRANSNATIONAL ISSUES

Disputes - international: non identified

SLOVAKIA

INTRODUCTION

Background: Slovakia traces its roots to the 9th century state of Great Moravia. Subsequently, the Slovaks became part of the Hungarian Kingdom, where they remained for the next 1,000 years. After the formation of the dual Austro-Hungarian monarchy in 1867, backlash to language and education policies favoring the use of Hungarian (Magyarization) encouraged the strengthening of Slovak nationalism and a cultivation of cultural ties with the closely related Czechs, who fell administratively under the Austrian half of the empire. After the dissolution of the Austro-Hungarian Empire at the close of World War I, the Slovaks joined the Czechs to form Czechoslovakia. The new state was envisioned as a nation with Czech and Slovak branches. During the interwar period, Slovak nationalist leaders pushed for autonomy within Czechoslovakia, and in 1939 Slovakia became an independent state created by and allied with Nazi Germany. Following World War II, Czechoslovakia was reconstituted and came under communist rule within Soviet-dominated Eastern Europe. In 1968, an invasion by Warsaw Pact troops ended the efforts of Czechoslovakia's leaders to liberalize communist rule and create "socialism with a human face," ushering in a period of repression known as "normalization." The peaceful "Velvet Revolution" swept the Communist Party from power at the end of 1989 and inaugurated a return to democratic rule and a market economy. On 1 January 1993, Czechoslovakia underwent a nonviolent "velvet divorce" into its two national components, Slovakia and the Czech Republic. Slovakia joined both NATO and the EU in the spring of 2004 and the euro zone on 1 January 2009.

GEOGRAPHY

Location: Central Europe, south of Poland

Geographic coordinates: 48 40 N, 19 30 E

Map references: Europe

Area: *total:* 49,035 sq km
land: 48,105 sq km
water: 930 sq km
country comparison to the world: 130

Area - comparative: about one and a half times the size of Maryland; about twice the size of New Hampshire

Land boundaries: *total:* 1,587 km
border countries (5): Austria 105 km; Czechia 241 km; Hungary 627 km; Poland 517 km; Ukraine 97 km

Coastline: 0 km (landlocked)

Maritime claims: none (landlocked)

Climate: temperate; cool summers; cold, cloudy, humid winters

Terrain: rugged mountains in the central and northern part and lowlands in the south

Elevation: *highest point:* Gerlachovsky Stit 2,655 m
lowest point: Bodrok River 94 m
mean elevation: 458 m

Natural resources: lignite, small amounts of iron ore, copper and manganese ore; salt; arable land

Land use: *agricultural land:* 40.1% (2018 est.)
arable land: 28.9% (2018 est.)
permanent crops: 0.4% (2018 est.)
permanent pasture: 10.8% (2018 est.)
forest: 40.2% (2018 est.)
other: 19.7% (2018 est.)

Irrigated land: 869 sq km (2012)

Major rivers (by length in km): Danube (shared with Germany [s], Austria, Hungary, Croatia, Serbia, Bulgaria, Ukraine, Moldova, and Romania [m]) - 2,888 km

note – [s] after country name indicates river source; [m] after country name indicates river mouth

Major watersheds (area sq km): Atlantic Ocean drainage: *(Black Sea)* Danube (795,656 sq km)

Population distribution: a fairly even distribution throughout most of the country; slightly larger concentration in the west in proximity to the Czech border

Natural hazards: flooding

Geography - note: landlocked; most of the country is rugged and mountainous; the Tatra Mountains in the north are interspersed with many scenic lakes and valleys

PEOPLE AND SOCIETY

Population: 5,431,252 (2022 est.)
country comparison to the world: 120

Nationality: *noun:* Slovak(s)
adjective: Slovak

Ethnic groups: Slovak 83.8%, Hungarian 7.8%, Romani 1.2%, other 1.8% (includes Czech, Ruthenian, Ukrainian, Russian, German, Polish), unspecified 5.4% (2021 est.)
note: data represent population by nationality; Romani populations are usually underestimated in official statistics and may represent 7–11% of Slovakia's population

Languages: Slovak (official) 81.8%, Hungarian 8.5%, Roma 1.8%, other 2.2%, unspecified 5.7% (2021 est.)
major-language sample(s):
Svetova Kniha Faktov, nenahraditelny zdroj zakladnej informacie. (Slovak)

Religions: Roman Catholic 55.8%, Evangelical Church of the Augsburg Confession 5.3%, Greek Catholic 4%, Reformed Christian 1.6%, other 3%, none 23.8%, unspecified 6.5% (2021 est.)

Age structure: *0-14 years:* 15.13% (male 423,180/female 400,128)
15-24 years: 10.06% (male 280,284/female 266,838)
25-54 years: 44.61% (male 1,228,462/female 1,198,747)

55-64 years: 13.15% (male 342,124/female 373,452)
65 years and over: 17.05% (male 366,267/female 561,120) (2020 est.)

Dependency ratios: *total dependency ratio:* 47.6
youth dependency ratio: 23
elderly dependency ratio: 24.6
potential support ratio: 4.1 (2020 est.)

Median age: *total:* 41.8 years
male: 40.1 years
female: 43.6 years (2020 est.)
country comparison to the world: 41

Population growth rate: -0.1% (2022 est.)
country comparison to the world: 204

Birth rate: 8.94 births/1,000 population (2022 est.)
country comparison to the world: 204

Death rate: 10.13 deaths/1,000 population (2022 est.)
country comparison to the world: 36

Net migration rate: 0.2 migrant(s)/1,000 population (2022 est.)
country comparison to the world: 78

Population distribution: a fairly even distribution throughout most of the country; slightly larger concentration in the west in proximity to the Czech border

Urbanization: *urban population:* 53.9% of total population (2022)
rate of urbanization: 0.17% annual rate of change (2020-25 est.)

Major urban areas - population: 439,000 BRATISLAVA (capital) (2022)

Sex ratio: *at birth:* 1.07 male(s)/female
0-14 years: 1.06 male(s)/female
15-24 years: 1.04 male(s)/female
25-54 years: 1.03 male(s)/female
55-64 years: 0.92 male(s)/female
65 years and over: 0.53 male(s)/female
total population: 0.94 male(s)/female (2022 est.)

Mother's mean age at first birth: 27.2 years (2020 est.)

Maternal mortality ratio: 5 deaths/100,000 live births (2017 est.)
country comparison to the world: 170

Infant mortality rate: *total:* 4.82 deaths/1,000 live births
male: 5.48 deaths/1,000 live births
female: 4.12 deaths/1,000 live births (2022 est.)
country comparison to the world: 178

Life expectancy at birth: *total population:* 78.31 years
male: 74.83 years
female: 82.04 years (2022 est.)
country comparison to the world: 75

Total fertility rate: 1.46 children born/woman (2022 est.)
country comparison to the world: 208

Drinking water source: *improved: urban:* 100% of population
rural: 100% of population
total: 100% of population

Current health expenditure: 7% of GDP (2019)

Physicians density: 3.57 physicians/1,000 population (2019)

Hospital bed density: 5.7 beds/1,000 population (2018)

Sanitation facility access: *improved: urban:* 99.9% of population
rural: 100% of population
total: 100% of population
unimproved: urban: 0.1% of population
rural: 0% of population
total: 0% of population (2020 est.)

HIV/AIDS - adult prevalence rate: (2018 est.) <.1%

HIV/AIDS - people living with HIV/AIDS: 1,200 (2018 est.)
country comparison to the world: 143

HIV/AIDS - deaths: (2018 est.) <100

Obesity - adult prevalence rate: 20.5% (2016)
country comparison to the world: 98

Alcohol consumption per capita: *total:* 10.3 liters of pure alcohol (2019 est.)
beer: 4.14 liters of pure alcohol (2019 est.)
wine: 2.01 liters of pure alcohol (2019 est.)
spirits: 4.14 liters of pure alcohol (2019 est.)
other alcohols: 0 liters of pure alcohol (2019 est.)
country comparison to the world: 21

Tobacco use: *total:* 31.5% (2020 est.)
male: 37.4% (2020 est.)
female: 25.6% (2020 est.)
country comparison to the world: 25

Education expenditures: 4% of GDP (2018 est.)
country comparison to the world: 104

School life expectancy (primary to tertiary education): *total:* 15 years
male: 14 years
female: 15 years (2019)

Unemployment, youth ages 15-24: *total:* 19.4%
male: 18.3%
female: 21.2% (2020 est.)

ENVIRONMENT

Environment - current issues: air pollution and acid rain present human health risks and damage forests; land erosion caused by agricultural and mining practices; water pollution

Environment - international agreements: *party to:* Air Pollution, Air Pollution-Heavy Metals, Air Pollution-Multi-effect Protocol, Air Pollution-Nitrogen Oxides, Air Pollution-Persistent Organic Pollutants, Air Pollution-Sulphur 85, Air Pollution-Sulphur 94, Air Pollution-Volatile Organic Compounds, Antarctic Treaty, Biodiversity, Climate Change, Climate Change-Kyoto Protocol, Climate Change-Paris Agreement, Comprehensive Nuclear Test Ban, Desertification, Endangered Species, Environmental Modification, Hazardous Wastes, Law of the Sea, Nuclear Test Ban, Ozone Layer Protection, Ship Pollution, Tropical Timber 2006, Wetlands, Whaling
signed, but not ratified: Antarctic-Environmental Protection

Air pollutants: *particulate matter emissions:* 17.54 micrograms per cubic meter (2016 est.)
carbon dioxide emissions: 32.42 megatons (2016 est.)
methane emissions: 4.43 megatons (2020 est.)

Climate: temperate; cool summers; cold, cloudy, humid winters

Land use: *agricultural land:* 40.1% (2018 est.)
arable land: 28.9% (2018 est.)
permanent crops: 0.4% (2018 est.)
permanent pasture: 10.8% (2018 est.)
forest: 40.2% (2018 est.)
other: 19.7% (2018 est.)

Urbanization: *urban population:* 53.9% of total population (2022)
rate of urbanization: 0.17% annual rate of change (2020-25 est.)

Revenue from forest resources: *forest revenues:* 0.22% of GDP (2018 est.)
country comparison to the world: 90

Revenue from coal: *coal revenues:* 0.01% of GDP (2018 est.)
country comparison to the world: 52

Waste and recycling: *municipal solid waste generated annually:* 1.784 million tons (2015 est.)
municipal solid waste recycled annually: 135,941 tons (2015 est.)
percent of municipal solid waste recycled: 7.6% (2015 est.)

Major rivers (by length in km): Danube (shared with Germany [s], Austria, Hungary, Croatia, Serbia, Bulgaria, Ukraine, Moldova, and Romania [m]) - 2,888 km
note – [s] after country name indicates river source; [m] after country name indicates river mouth

Major watersheds (area sq km): Atlantic Ocean drainage: *(Black Sea)* Danube (795,656 sq km)

Total water withdrawal: *municipal:* 293.5 million cubic meters (2017 est.)
industrial: 231.2 million cubic meters (2017 est.)
agricultural: 31.6 million cubic meters (2017 est.)

Total renewable water resources: 50.1 billion cubic meters (2017 est.)

GOVERNMENT

Country name: *conventional long form:* Slovak Republic
conventional short form: Slovakia
local long form: Slovenska republika
local short form: Slovensko
etymology: may derive from the medieval Latin word "Slavus" (Slav), which had the local form "Sloven", used since the 13th century to refer to the territory of Slovakia and its inhabitants

Government type: parliamentary republic

Capital: *name:* Bratislava
geographic coordinates: 48 09 N, 17 07 E
time difference: UTC+1 (6 hours ahead of Washington, DC, during Standard Time)
daylight saving time: +1hr, begins last Sunday in March; ends last Sunday in October
etymology: the name was adopted in 1919 after Czechoslovakia gained its independence and may derive from later transliterations of the 9th century military commander, Braslav, or the 11th century Bohemian Duke BRETISLAV I; alternatively, the name may derive from the Slovak words *brat* (brother) and *slava* (glory)

Administrative divisions: 8 regions (kraje, singular - kraj); Banska Bystrica, Bratislava, Kosice, Nitra, Presov, Trencin, Trnava, Zilina

Independence: 1 January 1993 (Czechoslovakia split into the Czech Republic and Slovakia)

National holiday: Constitution Day, 1 September (1992)

Constitution: *history:* several previous (preindependence); latest passed by the National Council 1 September 1992, signed 3 September 1992, effective 1 October 1992

amendments: proposed by the National Council; passage requires at least three-fifths majority vote of Council members; amended many times, last in 2020

Legal system: civil law system based on Austro-Hungarian codes; note - legal code modified to comply with the obligations of Organization on Security and Cooperation in Europe

International law organization participation: accepts compulsory ICJ jurisdiction with reservations; accepts ICCt jurisdiction

Citizenship: *citizenship by birth:* no
citizenship by descent only: at least one parent must be a citizen of Slovakia
dual citizenship recognized: no
residency requirement for naturalization: 5 years

Suffrage: 18 years of age; universal

Executive branch: *chief of state:* President Zuzana CAPUTOVA (since 15 June 2019)
head of government: Prime Minister Eduard HEGER (since 1 April 2021); Deputy Prime Ministers Stefan HOLY, Veronika REMISOVA, Richard SULIK (all since 21 March 2020)
cabinet: Cabinet appointed by the president on the recommendation of the prime minister
elections/appointments: president directly elected by absolute majority popular vote in 2 rounds if needed for a 5-year term (eligible for a second term); election last held on 16 March and 30 March 2019 (next to be held March 2024); following National Council elections (every 4 years), the president designates a prime minister candidate, usually the leader of the party or coalition that wins the most votes, who must win a vote of confidence in the National Council
election results:
2019: Zuzana CAPUTOVA reelected president in second round; percent of vote - Zuzana CAPUTOVA (PS) 58.4%, Maros SEFCOVIC (independent) 41.6%
2014: Andrej KISKA elected president in second round; percent of vote - Andrej KISKA (independent) 59.4%, Robert FICO (Smer-SD) 40.6%

Legislative branch: *description:* unicameral National Council or Narodna Rada (150 seats; members directly elected in a single- and multi-seat constituencies by closed, party-list proportional representation vote; members serve 4-year terms)
elections:
last held on 29 February 2020 (next to be held in February 2024)
election results:
percent of vote by party - OLaNO-NOVA 25%, Smer-SD 18.3%, Sme-Rodina 8.2%, LSNS 8%, SaS 6.2%, Za Ludi 5.8%, other 28.5%; seats by party - OLaNO-NOVA 53, Smer-SD 38, Sme-Rodina 17, LSNS 17, SaS 13, Za Ludi 12; composition (as of mid-2022) - men 118, women 32, percent of women 21.3%

Judicial branch: *highest court(s):* Supreme Court of the Slovak Republic (consists of the court president, vice president, and approximately 80 judges organized into criminal, civil, commercial, and administrative divisions with 3- and 5-judge panels); Constitutional Court of the Slovak Republic (consists of 13 judges organized into 3-judge panels)
judge selection and term of office: Supreme Court judge candidates nominated by the Judicial Council of the Slovak Republic, an 18-member self-governing body that includes the Supreme Court chief justice and presidential, governmental, parliamentary, and judiciary appointees; judges appointed by the president serve for life subject to removal by the president at age 65; Constitutional Court judges nominated by the National Council of the Republic and appointed by the president; judges serve 12-year terms
subordinate courts: regional and district civil courts; Special Criminal Court; Higher Military Court; military district courts; Court of Audit;

Political parties and leaders: Alliance-Szovetseg or A-S [Krisztian FORRO]
Direction-Social Democracy or Smer-SD [Robert FICO]
For the People or Za Ludi [Veronika REMISOVA]
Freedom and Solidarity or SaS [Richard SULIK]
Kotleba-People's Party Our Slovakia or LSNS [Marian KOTLEBA]
Ordinary People and Independent Personalities - New Majority or OLaNO-NOVA [Igor MATOVIC]
Slovak National Party or SNS [Andrej DANKO]
Voice - Social Democracy or Hlas-SD [Petr PELLIGRINI]
We Are Family or Sme-Rodina [Boris KOLLAR] (formerly Party of Citizens of Slovakia)

International organization participation: Australia Group, BIS, BSEC (observer), CBSS (observer), CD, CE, CEI, CERN, EAPC, EBRD, ECB, EIB, EMU, EU, FAO, IAEA, IBRD, ICAO, ICC (national committees), ICRM, IDA, IEA, IFC, IFRCS, ILO, IMF, IMO, IMSO, Interpol, IOC, IOM, IPU, ISO, ITU, ITUC (NGOs), MIGA, NATO, NEA, NSG, OAS (observer), OECD, OIF (observer), OPCW, OSCE, PCA, Schengen Convention, SELEC (observer), UN, UNCTAD, UNESCO, UNFICYP, UNIDO, UNTSO, UNWTO, UPU, Wassenaar Arrangement, WCO, WFTU (NGOs), WHO, WIPO, WMO, WTO, ZC

Diplomatic representation in the US: *chief of mission:* Ambassador Radovan JAVORCIK (since 18 January 2021)
chancery: 3523 International Court NW, Washington, DC 20008
telephone: [1] (202) 237-1054
FAX: [1] (202) 237-6438
email address and website:
emb.washington@mzv.sk
https://www.mzv.sk/web/washington-en
consulate(s) general: Los Angeles, New York

Diplomatic representation from the US: *chief of mission:* Ambassador (vacant); Charge d'Affaires Nicholas NAMBA (since May 2022)
embassy: P.O. Box 309, 814 99 Bratislava
mailing address: 5840 Bratislava Place, Washington DC 20521-5840
telephone: [421] (2) 5443-3338
FAX: [421] (2) 5441-8861
email address and website:
consulbratislava@state.gov
https://sk.usembassy.gov/

Flag description: three equal horizontal bands of white (top), blue, and red derive from the Pan-Slav colors; the Slovakian coat of arms (consisting of a red shield bordered in white and bearing a white double-barred cross of St. Cyril and St. Methodius surmounting three blue hills) is centered over the bands but offset slightly to the hoist side
note: the Pan-Slav colors were inspired by the 19th-century flag of Russia

National symbol(s): double-barred cross (Cross of St. Cyril and St. Methodius) surmounting three peaks; national colors: white, blue, red

National anthem: *name:* "Nad Tatrou sa blyska" (Lightning Over the Tatras)
lyrics/music: Janko MATUSKA/traditional
note: adopted 1993, in use since 1844; music based on the Slovak folk song "Kopala studienku" (She was digging a well)

National heritage: *total World Heritage Sites:* 8 (6 cultural, 2 natural)
selected World Heritage Site locales: Historic Town of Banská Štiavnica (c); Levoča, Spišský Hrad, and the Associated Cultural Monuments (c); Vlkolínec (c); Caves of Aggtelek Karst and Slovak Karst (n); Bardejov Town (c); Ancient and Primeval Beech Forests of the Carpathians (n); Wooden Churches of the Slovak Carpathians (c); Frontiers of the Roman Empire - The Danube Limes (Western Segment) (c)

ECONOMY

Economic overview: Slovakia's economy suffered from a slow start in the first years after its separation from the Czech Republic in 1993, due to the country's authoritarian leadership and high levels of corruption, but economic reforms implemented after 1998 have placed Slovakia on a path of strong growth. With a population of 5.4 million, the Slovak Republic has a small, open economy driven mainly by automobile and electronics exports, which account for more than 80% of GDP. Slovakia joined the EU in 2004 and the euro zone in 2009. The country's banking sector is sound and predominantly foreign owned.

Slovakia has been a regional FDI champion for several years, attractive due to a relatively low-cost yet skilled labor force, and a favorable geographic location in the heart of Central Europe. Exports and investment have been key drivers of Slovakia's robust growth in recent years. The unemployment rate fell to historical lows in 2017, and rising wages fueled increased consumption, which played a more prominent role in 2017 GDP growth. A favorable outlook for the Eurozone suggests continued strong growth prospects for Slovakia during the next few years, although inflation is also expected to pick up.

Among the most pressing domestic issues potentially threatening the attractiveness of the Slovak market are shortages in the qualified labor force, persistent corruption issues, and an inadequate judiciary, as well as a slow transition to an innovation-based economy. The energy sector in particular is characterized by unpredictable regulatory oversight and high costs, in part driven by government interference in regulated tariffs. Moreover, the government's attempts to maintain low household energy prices could harm the profitability of domestic energy firms while undercutting energy efficiency initiatives.

Real GDP (purchasing power parity): $165.57 billion (2020 est.)
$173.83 billion (2019 est.)
$169.57 billion (2018 est.)
note: data are in 2017 dollars
country comparison to the world: 72

Real GDP growth rate: 2.4% (2019 est.)
3.9% (2018 est.)
3.04% (2017 est.)
country comparison to the world: 116

Real GDP per capita: $30,300 (2020 est.)

$31,900 (2019 est.)
$31,100 (2018 est.)
note: data are in 2017 dollars
country comparison to the world: 65

GDP (official exchange rate): $105.388 billion (2019 est.)

Inflation rate (consumer prices): 2.6% (2019 est.)
2.5% (2018 est.)
1.3% (2017 est.)
country comparison to the world: 132

Credit ratings:

Fitch rating: A (2020)

Moody's rating: A2 (2012)

Standard & Poors rating: A+ (2015)

GDP - composition, by sector of origin: *agriculture:* 3.8% (2017 est.)
industry: 35% (2017 est.)
services: 61.2% (2017 est.)

GDP - composition, by end use: *household consumption:* 54.7% (2017 est.)
government consumption: 19.2% (2017 est.)
investment in fixed capital: 21.2% (2017 est.)
investment in inventories: 1.2% (2017 est.)
exports of goods and services: 96.3% (2017 est.)
imports of goods and services: -92.9% (2017 est.)

Agricultural products: wheat, maize, sugar beet, milk, barley, rapeseed, potatoes, sunflower seed, soybeans, pork

Industries: automobiles; metal and metal products; electricity, gas, coke, oil, nuclear fuel; chemicals, synthetic fibers, wood and paper products; machinery; earthenware and ceramics; textiles; electrical and optical apparatus; rubber products; food and beverages; pharmaceutical

Industrial production growth rate: 2.7% (2017 est.)
country comparison to the world: 114

Labor force: 2.511 million (2020 est.)
country comparison to the world: 114

Labor force - by occupation: *agriculture:* 3.9%
industry: 22.7%
services: 73.4% (2015)

Unemployment rate: 5% (2019 est.)
5.42% (2018 est.)
country comparison to the world: 78

Unemployment, youth ages 15-24: *total:* 19.4%
male: 18.3%
female: 21.2% (2020 est.)
country comparison to the world: 81

Population below poverty line: 11.9% (2018 est.)

Gini Index coefficient - distribution of family income: 25.2 (2016 est.)
26.1 (2014)
country comparison to the world: 170

Household income or consumption by percentage share: *lowest 10%:* 3.3%
highest 10%: 19.3% (2015 est.)

Budget: *revenues:* 37.79 billion (2017 est.)
expenditures: 38.79 billion (2017 est.)

Budget surplus (+) or deficit (-): -1% (of GDP) (2017 est.)
country comparison to the world: 81

Public debt: 50.9% of GDP (2017 est.)
51.8% of GDP (2016 est.)
note: data cover general Government Gross Debt and include debt instruments issued (or owned) by Government entities, including sub-sectors of central, state, local government, and social security funds
country comparison to the world: 98

Taxes and other revenues: 39.4% (of GDP) (2017 est.)
country comparison to the world: 47

Fiscal year: calendar year

Current account balance: -$3.026 billion (2019 est.)
-$2.635 billion (2018 est.)
country comparison to the world: 173

Exports: $89.92 billion (2020 est.) note: data are in current year dollars
$97.04 billion (2019 est.) note: data are in current year dollars
$100.76 billion (2018 est.) note: data are in current year dollars
country comparison to the world: 43

Exports - partners: Germany 22%, Czechia 11%, Poland 7%, France 7%, Hungary 6%, Austria 5%, United Kingdom 5% (2019)

Exports - commodities: cars and vehicle parts, video displays, broadcasting equipment, tires, refined petroleum (2019)

Imports: $87.95 billion (2020 est.) note: data are in current year dollars
$96.75 billion (2019 est.) note: data are in current year dollars
$99.92 billion (2018 est.) note: data are in current year dollars
country comparison to the world: 44

Imports - partners: Germany 18%, Czechia 18%, Poland 8%, Hungary 7%, Russia 5% (2019)

Imports - commodities: cars and vehicle parts, broadcasting equipment, crude petroleum, natural gas, insulated wiring (2019)

Reserves of foreign exchange and gold: $3.622 billion (31 December 2017 est.)
$2.892 billion (31 December 2016 est.)
country comparison to the world: 102

Debt - external: $115.853 billion (2019 est.)
$114.224 billion (2018 est.)
country comparison to the world: 52

Exchange rates: euros (EUR) per US dollar -
0.82771 (2020 est.)
0.90338 (2019 est.)
0.87789 (2018 est.)
0.885 (2014 est.)
0.7634 (2013 est.)

ENERGY

Electricity access: *electrification - total population:* 100% (2020)

Electricity: *installed generating capacity:* 7.868 million kW (2020 est.)
consumption: 26.503 billion kWh (2020 est.)
exports: 12.97 billion kWh (2020 est.)
imports: 13.288 billion kWh (2020 est.)
transmission/distribution losses: 1.589 billion kWh (2020 est.)

Electricity generation sources: *fossil fuels:* 19.7% of total installed capacity (2020 est.)
nuclear: 55.4% of total installed capacity (2020 est.)
solar: 2.4% of total installed capacity (2020 est.)
hydroelectricity: 16.8% of total installed capacity (2020 est.)
tide and wave: 0.2% of total installed capacity (2020 est.)
biomass and waste: 5.6% of total installed capacity (2020 est.)

Coal: *production:* 2.148 million metric tons (2020 est.)
consumption: 5.371 million metric tons (2020 est.)
exports: 1,000 metric tons (2020 est.)
imports: 3.111 million metric tons (2020 est.)
proven reserves: 135 million metric tons (2019 est.)

Petroleum: *total petroleum production:* 3,800 bbl/day (2021 est.)
refined petroleum consumption: 85,200 bbl/day (2019 est.)
crude oil and lease condensate exports: 100 bbl/day (2018 est.)
crude oil and lease condensate imports: 109,800 bbl/day (2018 est.)
crude oil estimated reserves: 9 million barrels (2021 est.)

Refined petroleum products - production: 131,300 bbl/day (2017 est.)
country comparison to the world: 64

Refined petroleum products - exports: 81,100 bbl/day (2017 est.)
country comparison to the world: 46

Refined petroleum products - imports: 38,340 bbl/day (2017 est.)
country comparison to the world: 91

Natural gas: *production:* 62.495 million cubic meters (2020 est.)
consumption: 4,928,199,000 cubic meters (2020 est.)
exports: 0 cubic meters (2020 est.)
imports: 4,361,410,000 cubic meters (2020 est.)
proven reserves: 14.158 billion cubic meters (2021 est.)

Carbon dioxide emissions: 32.506 million metric tonnes of CO_2 (2019 est.)
from coal and metallurgical coke: 11.521 million metric tonnes of CO_2 (2019 est.)
from petroleum and other liquids: 11.747 million metric tonnes of CO_2 (2019 est.)
from consumed natural gas: 9.238 million metric tonnes of CO_2 (2019 est.)
country comparison to the world: 74

Energy consumption per capita: 129.665 million Btu/person (2019 est.)
country comparison to the world: 42

COMMUNICATIONS

Telephones - fixed lines: *total subscriptions:* 648,462 (2020 est.)
subscriptions per 100 inhabitants: 12 (2020 est.)
country comparison to the world: 86

Telephones - mobile cellular: *total subscriptions:* 7,399,530 (2019)
subscriptions per 100 inhabitants: 135.6 (2019)
country comparison to the world: 101

Telecommunication systems: *general assessment:* the broadband market has shown steady growth in recent years; DSL remains the principal technology though in early 2020 it was eclipsed by the fast-developing fiber sector, which has been supported by sympathetic regulatory measures and considerable investment among operators; the cable sector is a distant third in terms of subscribers, though cable is particularly strong in urban areas; Slovakia's mobile market is served by four MNOs; mobile broadband access and content services are developing rapidly in

line with operators having upgraded their networks; the regulator prepared the groundwork for 5G services in line with European Union requirements, with concessions in the 3.5GHz range followed by those in the 700MHz, 900MHz and 1800MHz bands; commercial services by the first quarter of 2021 were limited, licensees have invested in 5G infrastructure and also have considerable coverage obligations (2021)
domestic: four companies have a license to operate cellular networks and provide nationwide cellular services; a few other companies provide services but do not have their own networks; fixed-line roughly 11 per 100 and mobile-cellular over 133 per 100 teledensity (2020)
international: country code - 421; 3 international exchanges (1 in Bratislava and 2 in Banska Bystrica) are available; Slovakia is participating in several international telecommunications projects that will increase the availability of external services; connects to DREAM cable (2017)

Broadcast media: state-owned public broadcaster, Radio and Television of Slovakia (RTVS), operates 2 national TV stations and multiple national and regional radio networks; roughly 50 privately owned TV stations operating nationally, regionally, and locally; about 40% of households are connected to multi-channel cable or satellite TV; 32 privately owned radio stations

Internet country code: .sk

Internet users: *total:* 4,917,528 (July 2022 est.)
percent of population: 90% (July 2022 est.)
country comparison to the world: 91

Broadband - fixed subscriptions: *total:* 1,701,561 (2020 est.)
subscriptions per 100 inhabitants: 31 (2020 est.)
country comparison to the world: 63

TRANSPORTATION

National air transport system: *number of registered air carriers:* 4 (2020)
inventory of registered aircraft operated by air carriers: 45

Civil aircraft registration country code prefix: OM

Airports: *total:* 35 (2021)
country comparison to the world: 110

Airports - with paved runways: *total:* 19
over 3,047 m: 2
2,438 to 3,047 m: 2
1,524 to 2,437 m: 3
914 to 1,523 m: 3
under 914 m: 9 (2021)

Airports - with unpaved runways: *total:* 15
914 to 1,523 m: 10
under 914 m: 5 (2021)

Heliports: 1 (2021)

Pipelines: 2,270 km gas transmission pipelines, 6,278 km high-pressure gas distribution pipelines, 27,023 km mid- and low-pressure gas distribution pipelines (2016), 510 km oil (2015) (2016)

Railways: *total:* 3,580 km (2016)
standard gauge: 3,435 km (2016) 1.435-m gauge (1,587 km electrified)
narrow gauge: 46 km (2016) 1.000-m or 0.750-m gauge
broad gauge: 99 km (2016) 1.520-m gauge
country comparison to the world: 56

Roadways: *total:* 56,926 km (2016) (includes local roads, national roads, and 464 km of highways)
country comparison to the world: 80

Waterways: 172 km (2012) (on Danube River)
country comparison to the world: 109

Ports and terminals: *river port(s):* Bratislava, Komarno (Danube)

MILITARY AND SECURITY

Military and security forces: Armed Forces of the Slovak Republic (Ozbrojene Sily Slovenskej Republiky): Land Forces (Slovenské Pozemné Sily), Air Forces (Slovenské Vzdušné Sily), Special Operations Forces (Sily Pre Speciálne Operácie) (2022)

Military expenditures: 2% of GDP (2022 est.)
1.7% of GDP (2021)
2% of GDP (2020)
1.7% of GDP (2019) (approximately $2.34 billion)
1.2% of GDP (2018) (approximately $1.72 billion)
country comparison to the world: 63

Military and security service personnel strengths: approximately 14,000 active duty personnel (8,000 Land Forces; 4,000 Air Forces; 2,000 other, including staff, special operations, and support forces) (2022)

Military equipment inventories and acquisitions: the military's inventory consists mostly of Soviet-era platforms; since 2010, it has imported limited quantities of equipment, particularly from Italy and the US (2021)

Military service age and obligation: 18-30 years of age for voluntary military service for men and women; conscription in peacetime suspended in 2004 (2021)
note: as of 2019, women made up around 12% of the military's full-time personnel

Military deployments: 240 Cyprus (UNFICYP); up to 150 Latvia (NATO) (2022)
note: in response to Russia's 2022 invasion of Ukraine, some NATO countries, including Slovakia, have sent additional troops and equipment to the battlegroups deployed in NATO territory in eastern Europe

Military - note: Slovakia became a member of NATO in 2004

in 2022, Slovakia agreed to host a NATO ground force battlegroup comprised of troops from Czechia, Germany, the Netherlands, Poland, Slovakia, Slovenia, and the US; Czechia and Poland also provide the NATO air policing mission for Slovakia

TRANSNATIONAL ISSUES

Disputes - international: *Slovakia-Austria:* none identified
Slovakia-Czechia: none identified
Slovakia-Hungary: initiated by the 1977 Budapest Treaty, Hungary and formerly Czechoslovakia agreed to a hydroelectric dam project on the Danube with dams to be constructed at Gabcikovo (Slovakia) and Nagymaros (Hungary) to prevent floods, improve river navigability, and to generate electricity; when Hungary suspended work on the project until its environmental impact could be assessed, Slovakia continued working on it and adopted a pared down strategy to divert the Danube so that all construction was within Czechoslovakian territory; Hungary terminated the project on environmental and economic grounds in 1989, and in 1992 both countries took the matter to the International Court of Justice (ICJ); the ICJ found largely in favor of then Slovakia, finding Hungary had breached their agreement; however, then Czechoslovakia should not have begun the alternative plan before the ICJ ruled on the case; in 2017, Hungary and Slovakia agreed to discontinue the ICJ proceedings
Slovakia-Poland: none identified
Slovakia-Ukraine: tens of thousands of Ukrainian refugees are crossing the border to Slovakia to escape the Russian invasion in their country

Refugees and internally displaced persons: *refugees (country of origin):* 100,041 (Ukraine) (as of 8 November 2022)
stateless persons: 1,532 (mid-year 2021)

Illicit drugs: transshipment point for Southwest Asian heroin bound for Western Europe; producer of synthetic drugs for regional market; consumer of MDMA (ecstasy)

SLOVENIA

INTRODUCTION

Background: The Slovene lands were part of the Austro-Hungarian Empire until the latter's dissolution at the end of World War I. In 1918, the Slovenes joined the Serbs and Croats in forming a new multinational state, which was named Yugoslavia in 1929. After World War II, Slovenia was one of the republics in the restored Yugoslavia, which, though communist, soon distanced itself from the Soviet Union and spearheaded the Non-Aligned Movement. Dissatisfied with the exercise of power by the majority Serbs, the Slovenes succeeded in establishing their independence in 1991 after a short 10-day war. Historical ties to Western Europe, a growing economy, and a stable democracy have assisted in Slovenia's postcommunist transition. Slovenia acceded to both NATO and the EU in the spring of 2004; it joined the euro zone and the Schengen Area in 2007.

GEOGRAPHY

Location: south Central Europe, Julian Alps between Austria and Croatia

Geographic coordinates: 46 07 N, 14 49 E

Map references: Europe

Area: *total:* 20,273 sq km
land: 20,151 sq km
water: 122 sq km

country comparison to the world: 154

Area - comparative: slightly smaller than New Jersey

Land boundaries: *total:* 1,211 km
border countries (4): Austria 299 km; Croatia 600 km; Hungary 94 km; Italy 218 km

Coastline: 46.6 km

Maritime claims: *territorial sea:* 12 nm

Climate: Mediterranean climate on the coast, continental climate with mild to hot summers and cold winters in the plateaus and valleys to the east

Terrain: a short southwestern coastal strip of Karst topography on the Adriatic; an alpine mountain region lies adjacent to Italy and Austria in the north; mixed mountains and valleys with numerous rivers to the east

Elevation: *highest point:* Triglav 2,864 m
lowest point: Adriatic Sea 0 m
mean elevation: 492 m

Natural resources: lignite, lead, zinc, building stone, hydropower, forests

Land use: *agricultural land:* 22.8% (2018 est.)
arable land: 8.4% (2018 est.)
permanent crops: 1.3% (2018 est.)
permanent pasture: 13.1% (2018 est.)
forest: 62.3% (2018 est.)
other: 14.9% (2018 est.)

Irrigated land: 60 sq km (2012)

Major watersheds (area sq km): Atlantic Ocean drainage: *(Black Sea)* Danube (795,656 sq km)

Population distribution: a fairly even distribution throughout most of the country, with urban areas attracting larger and denser populations; pockets in the mountainous northwest exhibit less density than elsewhere

Natural hazards: flooding; earthquakes

Geography - note: despite its small size, this eastern Alpine country controls some of Europe's major transit routes

PEOPLE AND SOCIETY

Population: 2,101,208 (2022 est.)
country comparison to the world: 149

Nationality: *noun:* Slovene(s)
adjective: Slovenian

Ethnic groups: Slovene 83.1%, Serb 2%, Croat 1.8%, Bosniak 1.1%, other or unspecified 12% (2002 est.)

Languages: Slovene (official) 87.7%, Croatian 2.8%, Serbo-Croatian 1.8%, Bosnian 1.6%, Serbian 1.6%, Hungarian 0.4% (official, only in municipalities where Hungarian national communities reside), Italian 0.2% (official, only in municipalities where Italian national communities reside), other or unspecified 3.9% (2002 est.)
major-language sample(s):
Svetovni informativni zvezek - neobhoden vir osnovnih informacij. (Slovene)

Religions: Catholic 57.8%, Muslim 2.4%, Orthodox 2.3%, other Christian 1%, unaffiliated 3.5%, no response or unspecified 22.8%, none 10.1% (2002 est.)

Age structure: *0-14 years:* 14.84% (male 160,134/female 151,960)
15-24 years: 9.01% (male 98,205/female 91,318)
25-54 years: 40.73% (male 449,930/female 406,395)
55-64 years: 14.19% (male 148,785/female 149,635)
65 years and over: 21.23% (male 192,420/female 253,896) (2020 est.)

Dependency ratios: *total dependency ratio:* 55.9
youth dependency ratio: 23.6
elderly dependency ratio: 32.3
potential support ratio: 3.1 (2020 est.)

Median age: *total:* 44.9 years
male: 43.4 years
female: 46.6 years (2020 est.)
country comparison to the world: 11

Population growth rate: -0.06% (2022 est.)
country comparison to the world: 202

Birth rate: 8.3 births/1,000 population (2022 est.)
country comparison to the world: 215

Death rate: 10.4 deaths/1,000 population (2022 est.)
country comparison to the world: 28

Net migration rate: 1.54 migrant(s)/1,000 population (2022 est.)
country comparison to the world: 58

Population distribution: a fairly even distribution throughout most of the country, with urban areas attracting larger and denser populations; pockets in the mountainous northwest exhibit less density than elsewhere

Urbanization: *urban population:* 55.8% of total population (2022)
rate of urbanization: 0.54% annual rate of change (2020-25 est.)

Major urban areas - population: 286,000 LJUBLJANA (capital) (2018)

Sex ratio: *at birth:* 1.04 male(s)/female
0-14 years: 1.05 male(s)/female
15-24 years: 1.08 male(s)/female
25-54 years: 1.12 male(s)/female
55-64 years: 0.99 male(s)/female
65 years and over: 0.61 male(s)/female
total population: 1 male(s)/female (2022 est.)

Mother's mean age at first birth: 29 years (2020 est.)

Maternal mortality ratio: 7 deaths/100,000 live births (2017 est.)
country comparison to the world: 156

Infant mortality rate: *total:* 1.52 deaths/1,000 live births
male: 1.63 deaths/1,000 live births
female: 1.41 deaths/1,000 live births (2022 est.)
country comparison to the world: 227

Life expectancy at birth: *total population:* 81.82 years
male: 78.96 years
female: 84.79 years (2022 est.)
country comparison to the world: 33

Total fertility rate: 1.6 children born/woman (2022 est.)
country comparison to the world: 186

Drinking water source: *improved: total:* 99.5% of population
unimproved: total: 0.5% of population (2020 est.)

Current health expenditure: 8.5% of GDP (2019)

Physicians density: 3.28 physicians/1,000 population (2019)

Hospital bed density: 4.4 beds/1,000 population (2018)

Sanitation facility access: *improved: total:* 99% of population
unimproved: total: 1% of population (2020 est.)

HIV/AIDS - adult prevalence rate: (2020 est.) <.1%

HIV/AIDS - people living with HIV/AIDS: (2020 est.) <1,000
note: estimate does not include children

HIV/AIDS - deaths: (2018 est.) <100

Obesity - adult prevalence rate: 20.2% (2016)
country comparison to the world: 104

Alcohol consumption per capita: *total:* 11.05 liters of pure alcohol (2019 est.)
beer: 4.54 liters of pure alcohol (2019 est.)
wine: 5.26 liters of pure alcohol (2019 est.)
spirits: 1.26 liters of pure alcohol (2019 est.)
other alcohols: 0 liters of pure alcohol (2019 est.)
country comparison to the world: 10

Tobacco use: *total:* 22% (2020 est.)
male: 24.4% (2020 est.)
female: 19.6% (2020 est.)
country comparison to the world: 73

Education expenditures: 4.9% of GDP (2018 est.)
country comparison to the world: 70

Literacy: *definition:* NA
total population: 99.7%
male: 99.7%
female: 99.7% (2015)

School life expectancy (primary to tertiary education): *total:* 18 years
male: 17 years
female: 18 years (2019)

Unemployment, youth ages 15-24: *total:* 14.2%
male: 12.7%
female: 16.2% (2020 est.)

ENVIRONMENT

Environment - current issues: air pollution from road traffic, domestic heating (wood burning), power generation, and industry; water pollution; biodiversity protection

Environment - international agreements: *party to:* Air Pollution, Air Pollution-Heavy Metals, Air Pollution-Multi-effect Protocol, Air Pollution-Nitrogen Oxides, Air Pollution-Persistent Organic Pollutants, Air Pollution-Sulphur 94, Antarctic Treaty, Biodiversity, Climate Change, Climate Change-Kyoto Protocol, Climate Change-Paris Agreement, Comprehensive Nuclear Test Ban, Desertification, Endangered Species, Environmental Modification, Hazardous Wastes, Law of the Sea, Marine Dumping-London Convention, Marine Dumping-London Protocol, Nuclear Test Ban, Ozone

Layer Protection, Ship Pollution, Tropical Timber 2006, Wetlands, Whaling
signed, but not ratified: none of the selected agreements

Air pollutants: *particulate matter emissions:* 15.81 micrograms per cubic meter (2016 est.)
carbon dioxide emissions: 12.63 megatons (2016 est.)
methane emissions: 2.1 megatons (2020 est.)

Climate: Mediterranean climate on the coast, continental climate with mild to hot summers and cold winters in the plateaus and valleys to the east

Land use: *agricultural land:* 22.8% (2018 est.)
arable land: 8.4% (2018 est.)
permanent crops: 1.3% (2018 est.)
permanent pasture: 13.1% (2018 est.)
forest: 62.3% (2018 est.)
other: 14.9% (2018 est.)

Urbanization: *urban population:* 55.8% of total population (2022)
rate of urbanization: 0.54% annual rate of change (2020-25 est.)

Revenue from forest resources: *forest revenues:* 0.2% of GDP (2018 est.)
country comparison to the world: 94

Revenue from coal: *coal revenues:* 0.03% of GDP (2018 est.)
country comparison to the world: 40

Waste and recycling: *municipal solid waste generated annually:* 926,000 tons (2015 est.)
municipal solid waste recycled annually: 430,034 tons (2015 est.)
percent of municipal solid waste recycled: 46.4% (2015 est.)

Major watersheds (area sq km): Atlantic Ocean drainage: *(Black Sea)* Danube (795,656 sq km)

Total water withdrawal: *municipal:* 169.5 million cubic meters (2017 est.)
industrial: 758 million cubic meters (2017 est.)
agricultural: 3.9 million cubic meters (2017 est.)

Total renewable water resources: 31.87 billion cubic meters (2017 est.)

GOVERNMENT

Country name: *conventional long form:* Republic of Slovenia
conventional short form: Slovenia
local long form: Republika Slovenija
local short form: Slovenija
former: People's Republic of Slovenia, Socialist Republic of Slovenia
etymology: the country's name means "Land of the Slavs" in Slovene

Government type: parliamentary republic

Capital: *name:* Ljubljana
geographic coordinates: 46 03 N, 14 31 E
time difference: UTC+1 (6 hours ahead of Washington, DC, during Standard Time)
daylight saving time: +1hr, begins last Sunday in March; ends last Sunday in October
etymology: likely related to the Slavic root "ljub", meaning "to like" or "to love"; by tradition, the name is related to the Slovene word "ljubljena" meaning "beloved"

Administrative divisions: 200 municipalities (obcine, singular - obcina) and 12 urban municipalities (mestne obcine, singular - mestna obcina)
municipalities: Ajdovscina, Ankaran, Apace, Beltinci, Benedikt, Bistrica ob Sotli, Bled, Bloke, Bohinj, Borovnica, Bovec, Braslovce, Brda, Brezice, Brezovica, Cankova, Cerklje na Gorenjskem, Cerknica, Cerkno, Cerkvenjak, Cirkulane, Crensovci, Crna na Koroskem, Crnomelj, Destrnik, Divaca, Dobje, Dobrepolje, Dobrna, Dobrova-Polhov Gradec, Dobrovnik/Dobronak, Dolenjske Toplice, Dol pri Ljubljani, Domzale, Dornava, Dravograd, Duplek, Gorenja Vas-Poljane, Gorisnica, Gorje, Gornja Radgona, Gornji Grad, Gornji Petrovci, Grad, Grosuplje, Hajdina, Hoce-Slivnica, Hodos, Horjul, Hrastnik, Hrpelje-Kozina, Idrija, Ig, Ilirska Bistrica, Ivancna Gorica, Izola/Isola, Jesenice, Jezersko, Jursinci, Kamnik, Kanal ob Soci, Kidricevo, Kobarid, Kobilje, Kocevje, Komen, Komenda, Kosanjevica na Krki, Kostel, Kozje, Kranjska Gora, Krizevci, Kungota, Kuzma, Lasko, Lenart, Lendava/Lendva, Litija, Ljubno, Ljutomer, Log- Dragomer, Logatec, Loska Dolina, Loski Potok, Lovrenc na Pohorju, Luce, Lukovica, Majsperk, Makole, Markovci, Medvode, Menges, Metlika, Mezica, Miklavz na Dravskem Polju, Miren-Kostanjevica, Mirna, Mirna Pec, Mislinja, Mokronog-Trebelno, Moravce, Moravske Toplice, Mozirje, Muta, Naklo, Nazarje, Odranci, Oplotnica, Ormoz, Osilnica, Pesnica, Piran/Pirano, Pivka, Podcetrtek, Podlehnik, Podvelka, Poljcane, Polzela, Postojna, Prebold, Preddvor, Prevalje, Puconci, Race-Fram, Radece, Radenci, Radlje ob Dravi, Radovljica, Ravne na Koroskem, Razkrizje, Recica ob Savinji, Rence-Vogrsko, Ribnica, Ribnica na Pohorju, Rogaska Slatina, Rogasovci, Rogatec, Ruse, Salovci, Selnica ob Dravi, Semic, Sempeter-Vrtojba, Sencur, Sentilj, Sentjernej, Sentjur, Sentrupert, Sevnica, Sezana, Skocjan, Skofja Loka, Skofljica, Slovenska Bistrica, Slovenske Konjice, Smarje pri Jelsah, Smarjeske Toplice, Smartno ob Paki, Smartno pri Litiji, Sodrazica, Solcava, Sostanj, Sredisce ob Dravi, Starse, Store, Straza, Sveta Ana, Sveta Trojica v Slovenskih Goricah, Sveti Andraz v Slovenskih Goricah, Sveti Jurij ob Scavnici, Sveti Jurij v Slovenskih Goricah, Sveti Tomaz, Tabor, Tisina, Tolmin, Trbovlje, Trebnje, Trnovska Vas, Trzic, Trzin, Turnisce, Velika Polana, Velike Lasce, Verzej, Videm, Vipava, Vitanje, Vodice, Vojnik, Vransko, Vrhnika, Vuzenica, Zagorje ob Savi, Zalec, Zavrc, Zelezniki, Zetale, Ziri, Zirovnica, Zrece, Zuzemberk
urban municipalities: Celje, Koper, Kranj, Krsko, Ljubljana, Maribor, Murska Sobota, Nova Gorica, Novo Mesto, Ptuj, Slovenj Gradec, Velenje

Independence: 25 June 1991 (from Yugoslavia)

National holiday: Independence Day/Statehood Day, 25 June (1991)

Constitution: *history:* previous 1974 (preindependence); latest passed by Parliament 23 December 1991
amendments: proposed by at least 20 National Assembly members, by the government, or by petition of at least 30,000 voters; passage requires at least two-thirds majority vote by the Assembly; referendum required if agreed upon by at least 30 Assembly members; passage in a referendum requires participation of a majority of eligible voters and a simple majority of votes cast; amended several times, last in 2016

Legal system: civil law system

International law organization participation: has not submitted an ICJ jurisdiction declaration; accepts ICCt jurisdiction

Citizenship: *citizenship by birth:* no
citizenship by descent only: at least one parent must be a citizen of Slovenia; both parents if the child is born outside of Slovenia
dual citizenship recognized: yes, for select cases
residency requirement for naturalization: 10 years, the last 5 of which have been continuous

Suffrage: 18 years of age, 16 if employed; universal

Executive branch: *chief of state:* President Borut PAHOR (since 22 December 2012)
head of government: Prime Minister Robert GOLOB (since 25 May 2022)
cabinet: Council of Ministers nominated by the prime minister, elected by the National Assembly
elections/appointments: president directly elected by absolute majority popular vote in 2 rounds if needed for a 5-year term (eligible for a second consecutive term); election last held on 23 October with a runoff on 13 November 2022 (next election to be held in 2027); following National Assembly elections, the leader of the majority party or majority coalition usually nominated prime minister by the president and elected by the National Assembly
election results:
2022: Natasa PIRC MUSAR elected in second round: percent of vote in first round - Natasa PIRC MUSAR (independent) 26.9%, Anze LOGAR (SDS) 34%, Milan BRGLEZ (SD) 15.5%, Vladimir PREBILIC (independent) 10.6%, Sabina SENCAR (Resni.ca) 5.9%, Janez CIGLER KRALJ (NSi) 4.4%, Miha KORDIS (The Left) 2.8%; percent of vote in second round - Natasa PIRC MUSAR 53.9%, Anze LOGAR 46.1%
2017: Borut PAHOR is reelected president in second round; percent of vote in first round - Borut PAHOR (independent) 47.1%, Marjan SAREC (Marjan Sarec List) 25%, Romana TOMC (SDS) 13.7%, Ljudmila NOVAK (NSi) 7.2%, other 7%; percent of vote in second round - Borut PAHOR 52.9%, Marjan SAREC 47.1%; Robert GOLOB (GS) elected prime minister on 25 May 2022, National Assembly vote - 54-30
2012: Borut PAHOR elected president; percent of vote in second round - Borut PAHOR (SD) 67.4%, Danilo TURK (independent) 32.6%; note - a snap election was held on 13 July 2014 following the resignation of Prime Minister Alenka BRATUSEK on 5 May 2014; Miro CERAR (SMC) elected prime minister; National Assembly vote - 57 to 11

Legislative branch: *description:* bicameral Parliament consists of:
National Council (State Council)or Drzavni Svet (40 seats; members indirectly elected by an electoral college to serve 5-year terms); note - the Council is primarily an advisory body with limited legislative powers
National Assembly or Drzavni Zbor (90 seats; 88 members directly elected in single-seat constituencies by proportional representation vote and 2 directly elected in special constituencies for Italian and Hungarian minorities by simple majority vote; members serve 4-year terms)
elections:
National Council - last held on 22 November 2017 (next to be held on 23 October 2022) National Assembly - last held on 24 April 2022 (next to be held in 2026)
election results:

National Council - percent of vote by party - NA; seats by party - NA; composition - men 36, women 4, percent of women 10%
National Assembly - percent of vote by party - GS 34.5%, SDS 23.5%, NSi 6.9%, SD 6.7%, Levica 4.4%, other 24%; seats by party - GS 41, SDS 27, NSi 8, SD 7, Levica 5; composition - men 54, women 36, percent of women 40%; note - total Parliament percent of women 30.8%

Judicial branch: *highest court(s):* Supreme Court (consists of the court president and 37 judges organized into civil, criminal, commercial, labor and social security, administrative, and registry departments); Constitutional Court (consists of the court president, vice president, and 7 judges)
judge selection and term of office: Supreme Court president and vice president appointed by the National Assembly upon the proposal of the Minister of Justice based on the opinions of the Judicial Council, an 11-member independent body elected by the National Assembly from proposals submitted by the president, attorneys, law universities, and sitting judges; other Supreme Court judges elected by the National Assembly from candidates proposed by the Judicial Council; Supreme Court judges serve for life; Constitutional Court judges appointed by the National Assembly from nominations by the president of the republic; Constitutional Court president selected from among its own membership for a 3-year term; other judges elected for single 9-year terms
subordinate courts: county, district, regional, and high courts; specialized labor-related and social courts; Court of Audit; Administrative Court

Political parties and leaders: Democratic Party of Pensioners of Slovenia or DeSUS [Ljubo JASNIC]
Freedom Movement or GS [Robert GOLOB] (formerly Greens Actions Party or Z.DEJ)
List of Marjan Sarec or LMS [Marjan SAREC]
New Slovenia - Christian Democrats or NSi [Matej TONIN]
Party of Alenka Bratusek or SAB [Alenka BRATUSEK] (formerly Alliance of Social Liberal Democrats or ZSD and before that Alliance of Alenka Bratusek or ZaAB)
Resni.ca [Zoran STEVANOVICH]
Slovenian Democratic Party or SDS [Janez JANSA] (formerly the Social Democratic Party of Slovenia or SDSS)
Slovenian National Party or SNS [Zmago JELINCIC Plemeniti]
Social Democrats or SD [Tanja FAJON]
The Left or Levica [Luka MESEC] (successor to United Left or ZL)

International organization participation: Australia Group, BIS, CD, CE, CEI, EAPC, EBRD, ECB, EIB, EMU, ESA (cooperating state), EU, FAO, IADB, IAEA, IBRD, ICAO, ICC (national committees), ICCt, ICRM, IDA, IFC, IFRCS, IHO, ILO, IMF, IMO, Interpol, IOC, IOM, IPU, ISO, ITU, MIGA, NATO, NEA, NSG, OAS (observer), OECD, OIF (observer), OPCW, OSCE, PCA, Schengen Convention, SELEC, UN, UNCTAD, UNESCO, UNHCR, UNIDO, UNIFIL, UNTSO, UNWTO, UPU, Wassenaar Arrangement, WCO, WHO, WIPO, WMO, WTO, ZC

Diplomatic representation in the US: *chief of mission:* Ambassador Tone KAJZER (since 23 December 2020)
chancery: 2410 California Street NW, Washington, DC 20008
telephone: [1] (202) 386-6601
FAX: [1] (202) 386-6633
email address and website:
vwa@gov.si
http://www.washington.embassy.si/index.php?id=51&L=1
consulate(s) general: Cleveland (OH)

Diplomatic representation from the US: *chief of mission:* Ambassador Jamie L. HARPOOTLIAN (since 17 February 2022)
embassy: Presernova 31, 1000 Ljubljana
mailing address: 7140 Ljubljana Place, Washington, DC 20521-7140
telephone: [386] (1) 200-5500
FAX: [386] (1) 200-5555
email address and website:
LjubljanaACS@state.gov
https://si.usembassy.gov/

Flag description: three equal horizontal bands of white (top), blue, and red, derive from the medieval coat of arms of the Duchy of Carniola; the Slovenian seal (a shield with the image of Triglav, Slovenia's highest peak, in white against a blue background at the center; beneath it are two wavy blue lines depicting seas and rivers, and above it are three six-pointed stars arranged in an inverted triangle, which are taken from the coat of arms of the Counts of Celje, the prominent Slovene dynastic house of the late 14th and early 15th centuries) appears in the upper hoist side of the flag centered on the white and blue bands

National symbol(s): Mount Triglav; national colors: white, blue, red

National anthem: *name:* "Zdravljica" (A Toast)
lyrics/music: France PRESEREN/Stanko PREMRL
note: adopted in 1989 while still part of Yugoslavia; originally written in 1848; the full poem, whose seventh verse is used as the anthem, speaks of pan-Slavic nationalism

National heritage: *total World Heritage Sites:* 5 (3 cultural, 2 natural)
selected World Heritage Site locales: Škocjan Caves (n); Ancient and Primeval Beech Forests of the Carpathians and Other Regions of Europe (n); Prehistoric Pile Dwellings around the Alps (c); Heritage of Mercury: Almadén and Idrija (c); The works of Jože Plečnik in Ljubljana (c)

ECONOMY

Economic overview: With excellent infrastructure, a well-educated work force, and a strategic location between the Balkans and Western Europe, Slovenia has one of the highest per capita GDPs in Central Europe, despite having suffered a protracted recession in the 2008-09 period in the wake of the global financial crisis. Slovenia became the first 2004 EU entrant to adopt the euro (on 1 January 2007) and has experienced a stable political and economic transition.

In March 2004, Slovenia became the first transition country to graduate from borrower status to donor partner at the World Bank. In 2007, Slovenia was invited to begin the process for joining the OECD; it became a member in 2012. From 2014 to 2016, export-led growth, fueled by demand in larger European markets, pushed annual GDP growth above 2.3%. Growth reached 5.0% in 2017 and is projected to near or reach 5% in 2018. What used to be stubbornly high unemployment fell below 5.5% in early 2018, driven by strong exports and increasing consumption that boosted labor demand. Continued fiscal consolidation through increased tax collection and social security contributions will likely result in a balanced government budget in 2019.

Prime Minister CERAR's government took office in September 2014, pledging to press ahead with commitments to privatize a select group of state-run companies, rationalize public spending, and further stabilize the banking sector. Efforts to privatize Slovenia's largely state-owned banking sector have largely stalled, however, amid concerns about an ongoing dispute over Yugoslav-era foreign currency deposits.

Real GDP (purchasing power parity): $76.75 billion (2020 est.)
$81.25 billion (2019 est.)
$78.74 billion (2018 est.)
note: data are in 2017 dollars
country comparison to the world: 98

Real GDP growth rate: 2.4% (2019 est.)
4.24% (2018 est.)
5.14% (2017 est.)
country comparison to the world: 117

Real GDP per capita: $36,500 (2020 est.)
$38,900 (2019 est.)
$38,000 (2018 est.)
note: data are in 2017 dollars
country comparison to the world: 52

GDP (official exchange rate): $54.16 billion (2019 est.)

Inflation rate (consumer prices): 1.6% (2019 est.)
1.7% (2018 est.)
1.4% (2017 est.)
country comparison to the world: 94

Credit ratings:

Fitch rating: A (2019)

Moody's rating: A3 (2020)

Standard & Poors rating: AA- (2019)

GDP - composition, by sector of origin: *agriculture:* 1.8% (2017 est.)
industry: 32.2% (2017 est.)
services: 65.9% (2017 est.)

GDP - composition, by end use: *household consumption:* 52.6% (2017 est.)
government consumption: 18.2% (2017 est.)
investment in fixed capital: 18.4% (2017 est.)
investment in inventories: 1.1% (2017 est.)
exports of goods and services: 82.3% (2017 est.)
imports of goods and services: -72.6% (2017 est.)

Agricultural products: milk, maize, wheat, grapes, barley, potatoes, poultry, apples, beef, pork

Industries: ferrous metallurgy and aluminum products, lead and zinc smelting; electronics (including military electronics), trucks, automobiles, electric power equipment, wood products, textiles, chemicals, machine tools

Industrial production growth rate: 8.6% (2017 est.)
country comparison to the world: 22

Labor force: 885,000 (2020 est.)
country comparison to the world: 143

Labor force - by occupation: *agriculture:* 5.5%
industry: 31.2%
services: 63.3% (2017 est.)

Unemployment rate: 7.64% (2019 est.)
8.25% (2018 est.)

country comparison to the world: 119

Unemployment, youth ages 15-24: *total:* 14.2%
male: 12.7%
female: 16.2% (2020 est.)
country comparison to the world: 114

Population below poverty line: 12% (2018 est.)

Gini Index coefficient - distribution of family income: 24.2 (2017 est.)
24.5 (2015)
country comparison to the world: 172

Household income or consumption by percentage share: *lowest 10%:* 3.8%
highest 10%: 20.1% (2016)

Budget: *revenues:* 21.07 billion (2017 est.)
expenditures: 21.06 billion (2017 est.)

Budget surplus (+) or deficit (-): 0% (of GDP) (2017 est.)
country comparison to the world: 46

Public debt: 73.6% of GDP (2017 est.)
78.6% of GDP (2016 est.)
note: defined by the EU's Maastricht Treaty as consolidated general government gross debt at nominal value, outstanding at the end of the year in the following categories of government liabilities: currency and deposits, securities other than shares excluding financial derivatives, and loans; general government sector comprises the central, state, local government, and social security funds
country comparison to the world: 44

Taxes and other revenues: 43.1% (of GDP) (2017 est.)
country comparison to the world: 28

Fiscal year: calendar year

Current account balance: $3.05 billion (2019 est.)
$3.17 billion (2018 est.)
country comparison to the world: 34

Exports: $41.73 billion (2020 est.) note: data are in current year dollars
$45.41 billion (2019 est.) note: data are in current year dollars
$45.93 billion (2018 est.) note: data are in current year dollars
country comparison to the world: 60

Exports - partners: Germany 18%, Italy 11%, Croatia 8%, Austria 7%, France 5%, Switzerland 5% (2019)

Exports - commodities: packaged medicines, cars and vehicle parts, refined petroleum, electrical lighting/signaling equipment, electricity (2019)

Imports: $36.6 billion (2020 est.) note: data are in current year dollars
$40.8 billion (2019 est.) note: data are in current year dollars
$41.32 billion (2018 est.) note: data are in current year dollars
country comparison to the world: 66

Imports - partners: Germany 14%, Italy 12%, Austria 8%, Switzerland 8%, China 7% (2019)

Imports - commodities: packaged medicines, cars and vehicle parts, refined petroleum, delivery trucks, electricity (2019)

Reserves of foreign exchange and gold: $889.9 million (31 December 2017 est.)
$853 million (31 December 2016 est.)
country comparison to the world: 135

Debt - external: $48.656 billion (2019 est.)
$50.004 billion (2018 est.)
country comparison to the world: 69

Exchange rates: euros (EUR) per US dollar -
0.82771 (2020 est.)
0.90338 (2019 est.)
0.87789 (2018 est.)
0.885 (2014 est.)
0.7634 (2013 est.)

ENERGY

Electricity access: *electrification - total population:* 100% (2020)

Electricity: *installed generating capacity:* 4.062 million kW (2020 est.)
consumption: 13.447 billion kWh (2020 est.)
exports: 9.123 billion kWh (2020 est.)
imports: 7.12 billion kWh (2020 est.)
transmission/distribution losses: 848 million kWh (2020 est.)

Electricity generation sources: *fossil fuels:* 27.2% of total installed capacity (2020 est.)
nuclear: 36.8% of total installed capacity (2020 est.)
solar: 2.2% of total installed capacity (2020 est.)
hydroelectricity: 32% of total installed capacity (2020 est.)
biomass and waste: 1.7% of total installed capacity (2020 est.)

Coal: *production:* 3.175 million metric tons (2020 est.)
consumption: 3.502 million metric tons (2020 est.)
exports: 3,000 metric tons (2020 est.)
imports: 335,000 metric tons (2020 est.)
proven reserves: 371 million metric tons (2019 est.)

Petroleum: *total petroleum production:* 0 bbl/day (2021 est.)
refined petroleum consumption: 54,900 bbl/day (2019 est.)

Refined petroleum products - exports: 29,350 bbl/day (2017 est.)
country comparison to the world: 63

Refined petroleum products - imports: 93,060 bbl/day (2017 est.)
country comparison to the world: 56

Natural gas: *production:* 4.899 million cubic meters (2020 est.)
consumption: 904.439 million cubic meters (2020 est.)
exports: 0 cubic meters (2020 est.)
imports: 903.108 million cubic meters (2020 est.)
proven reserves: 0 cubic meters (2021 est.)

Carbon dioxide emissions: 13.553 million metric tonnes of CO_2 (2019 est.)
from coal and metallurgical coke: 4.08 million metric tonnes of CO_2 (2019 est.)
from petroleum and other liquids: 7.967 million metric tonnes of CO_2 (2019 est.)
from consumed natural gas: 1.506 million metric tonnes of CO_2 (2019 est.)
country comparison to the world: 99

Energy consumption per capita: 134.836 million Btu/person (2019 est.)
country comparison to the world: 39

COMMUNICATIONS

Telephones - fixed lines: *total subscriptions:* 704,909 (2020 est.)
subscriptions per 100 inhabitants: 34 (2020 est.)
country comparison to the world: 84

Telephones - mobile cellular: *total subscriptions:* 2,511,980 (2019)
subscriptions per 100 inhabitants: 120.85 (2019)
country comparison to the world: 145

Telecommunication systems: *general assessment:* Slovenia's telecom sector is dominated by four operators; the mobile market has four MNOs and a small number of MVNOs, operating in a country with a potential market of just over two million people; the regulator in recent years has addressed the need for mobile operators to have more spectrum, so enabling them to improve the quality and range of services; a multi-spectrum auction was concluded in mid-2021, aimed at supporting 5G services; the broadband market continues to be dominated by a small number of players; DSL lost its dominance some years ago, being taken over by fiber as subscribers are migrated to new fiber-based networks; fiber accounted for almost half of all fixed broadband connections by March 2022 (2022)
domestic: fixed-line nearly 34 per 100 and mobile-cellular over 122 per 100 teledensity (2020)
international: country code - 386 (2016)

Broadcast media: public TV broadcaster, Radiotelevizija Slovenija (RTV), operates a system of national and regional TV stations; 35 domestic commercial TV stations operating nationally, regionally, and locally; about 60% of households are connected to multi-channel cable TV; public radio broadcaster operates 3 national and 4 regional stations; more than 75 regional and local commercial and non-commercial radio stations

Internet country code: .si

Internet users: *total:* 1,829,105 (2020 est.)
percent of population: 87% (2020 est.)
country comparison to the world: 130

Broadband - fixed subscriptions: *total:* 651,604 (2020 est.)
subscriptions per 100 inhabitants: 31 (2020 est.)
country comparison to the world: 84

TRANSPORTATION

National air transport system: *number of registered air carriers:* 2 (2020)
inventory of registered aircraft operated by air carriers: 21
annual passenger traffic on registered air carriers: 1,094,762 (2018)
annual freight traffic on registered air carriers: 540,000 (2018) mt-km

Civil aircraft registration country code prefix: S5

Airports: *total:* 16 (2021)
country comparison to the world: 144

Airports - with paved runways: *total:* 9
over 3,047 m: 1
2,438 to 3,047 m: 2
914 to 1,523 m: 3
under 914 m: 3 (2021)

Airports - with unpaved runways: *total:* 7
914 to 1,523 m: 4
under 914 m: 3 (2021)

Pipelines: 1,155 km gas, 5 km oil (2018)

Railways: *total:* 1,229 km (2014)
standard gauge: 1,229 km (2014) 1.435-m gauge (503 km electrified)
country comparison to the world: 86

Roadways: *total:* 38,985 km (2012)

paved: 38,985 km (2012) (includes 769 km of expressways)
country comparison to the world: 90

Waterways: 710 km (2022) (some transport on the Drava River)
country comparison to the world: 81

Merchant marine: *total:* 9
by type: other 9 (2021)
country comparison to the world: 159

Ports and terminals: *major seaport(s):* Koper

MILITARY AND SECURITY

Military and security forces: Slovenian Armed Forces (Slovenska Vojska, SV): structured as a combined force with air, land, maritime, special operations, combat support, and combat service support elements (2022)

Military expenditures: 1.2% of GDP (2022 est.)
1.2% of GDP (2021)
1% of GDP (2020)
1.1% of GDP (2019) (approximately $800 million)
1% of GDP (2018) (approximately $750 million)
country comparison to the world: 117

Military and security service personnel strengths: approximately 6,000 active duty troops (2022)

Military equipment inventories and acquisitions: the military's inventory is a mix of Soviet-era and smaller quantities of more modern Russian and Western equipment; since 2010, it has received limited amounts of military equipment from several countries led by France and Russia (2021)

Military service age and obligation: 18-25 years of age for voluntary military service for men and women; conscription abolished in 2003 (2021)
note: as of 2019, women comprised about 15% of the military's full-time personnel

Military deployments: 200 Kosovo (NATO); 100 Slovakia (NATO) (2022)
note: in response to Russia's 2022 invasion of Ukraine, some NATO countries, including Slovenia, have sent additional troops and equipment to the battlegroups deployed in NATO territory in eastern Europe

Military - note: Slovenia became a member of NATO in 2004; Hungary and Italy provide NATO's air policing mission for Slovenia's airspace (2022)

TRANSNATIONAL ISSUES

Disputes - international: *Slovenia-Austria:* none identified
Slovenia-Croatia: since the breakup of Yugoslavia in the early 1990s, Croatia and Slovenia have each claimed sovereignty over Piran Bay and four villages, and Slovenia has objected to Croatia's claim of an exclusive economic zone in the Adriatic Sea; in 2009, however Croatia and Slovenia signed a binding international arbitration agreement to define their disputed land and maritime borders, which led Slovenia to lift its objections to Croatia joining the EU; in June 2017, the Permanent Court of Arbitration issued a ruling on the border, but Croatia had withdrawn from the proceedings in 2015 and refused to implement it; as a member state that forms part of the EU's external border, Slovenia has implemented the strict Schengen border rules to curb illegal migration and commerce through southeastern Europe while encouraging close cross-border ties with Croatia; Slovenia continues to impose a hard border Schengen regime with Croatia, which joined the EU in 2013 but has not yet fulfilled Schengen requirements
Slovenia-Hungary: none identified
Slovenia-Italy: none identified

Refugees and internally displaced persons: *refugees (country of origin):* 8,439 (Ukraine) (as of 8 November 2022)
stateless persons: 10 (2020)
note: 551,887 estimated refugee and migrant arrivals (January 2015-September 2022)

Illicit drugs: minor transit point for cocaine and Southwest Asian heroin bound for Western Europe, and for precursor chemicals

SOLOMON ISLANDS

INTRODUCTION

Background: Settlers from Papua arrived on Solomon Islands around 30,000 years ago. About 6,000 years ago, Austronesian settlers came to Solomon Islands and the two groups mixed extensively. Despite significant inter-island trade, no attempts were made to unite the islands into a single political entity. In 1568, Spanish explorer Alvaro de MENDANA became the first European to spot the islands. After a failed Spanish attempt at creating a permanent European settlement on the islands in the late 1500s, Solomon Islands remained free of European contact until 1767 when British explorer Philip CARTERET sailed by the islands. The islands were regularly visited by European explorers and American and British whaling ships into the 1800s, followed by missionaries in the 1850s.

Germany declared a protectorate over the northern Solomon Islands in 1885, and the UK established a protectorate over the southern islands in 1893. In 1899, Germany transferred its Solomon Islands to the UK in exchange for the UK relinquishing all claims in Samoa. The UK tried to encourage plantation farming, but few Europeans were willing to go to Solomon Islands and the UK left most services - such as education and medical services - to missionaries. In 1942, Japan invaded Solomon Islands and significant battles against Allied forces during the Guadalcanal Campaign proved a turning point in the Pacific war. World War II destroyed large parts of Solomon Islands and a nationalism movement emerged near the end of the war. By 1960, the British relented to allow for some local autonomy. The islands were granted self-government in 1976 and independence two years later under Prime Minister Sir Peter KENILOREA.

In 1999, longstanding ethnic tensions between ethnic Guale in Honiara and ethnic Malaitans in Honiara's suburbs erupted in civil war, leading thousands of Malaitans to take refuge in Honiara and Guale to flee the city. In 2000, newly-elected Prime Minister Manasseh SOGAVARE focused on peace agreements and distributing resources equally among groups, but his actions bankrupted the government in 2001 and led to SOGAVARE's ouster. In 2003, Solomon Islands requested international assistance to reestablish law and order. The Australian-led Regional Assistance Mission to the Solomon Islands, which ended in 2017, was generally effective in improving the security situation. In 2006, riots broke out in Honiara and the city's Chinatown burned over allegations that the prime minister took money from China. SOGAVARE was reelected prime minister for a fourth time following elections in 2019 and that same year announced Solomon Islands would switch diplomatic recognition from Taiwan to China. In late November 2021, protestors, mostly from the island of Malaita, calling for SOGAVARE's removal and more development in Malaita, sparked rioting in Honiara.

GEOGRAPHY

Location: Oceania, group of islands in the South Pacific Ocean, east of Papua New Guinea

Geographic coordinates: 8 00 S, 159 00 E

Map references: Oceania

Area: *total:* 28,896 sq km
land: 27,986 sq km
water: 910 sq km
country comparison to the world: 143

Area - comparative: slightly smaller than Maryland

Land boundaries: *total:* 0 km

Coastline: 5,313 km

Maritime claims: *territorial sea:* 12 nm
exclusive economic zone: 200 nm
continental shelf: 200 nm
measured from claimed archipelagic baselines

Climate: tropical monsoon; few temperature and weather extremes

Terrain: mostly rugged mountains with some low coral atolls

Elevation: *highest point:* Mount Popomanaseu 2,335 m
lowest point: Pacific Ocean 0 m

Natural resources: fish, forests, gold, bauxite, phosphates, lead, zinc, nickel

Land use: *agricultural land:* 3.9% (2018 est.)
arable land: 0.7% (2018 est.)
permanent crops: 2.9% (2018 est.)

permanent pasture: 0.3% (2018 est.)
forest: 78.9% (2018 est.)
other: 17.2% (2018 est.)

Irrigated land: 0 sq km (2012)

Population distribution: most of the population lives along the coastal regions; about one in five live in urban areas, and of these some two-thirds reside in Honiara, the largest town and chief port

Natural hazards: tropical cyclones, but rarely destructive; geologically active region with frequent earthquakes, tremors, and volcanic activity; tsunamis
volcanism: Tinakula (851 m) has frequent eruption activity, while an eruption of Savo (485 m) could affect the capital Honiara on nearby Guadalcanal

Geography - note: strategic location on sea routes between the South Pacific Ocean, the Solomon Sea, and the Coral Sea; Rennell Island, the southernmost in the Solomon Islands chain, is one of the world's largest raised coral atolls; the island's Lake Tegano, formerly a lagoon on the atoll, is the largest lake in the insular Pacific (15,500 hectares)

PEOPLE AND SOCIETY

Population: 702,694 (2022 est.)
country comparison to the world: 167

Nationality: *noun:* Solomon Islander(s)
adjective: Solomon Islander

Ethnic groups: Melanesian 95.3%, Polynesian 3.1%, Micronesian 1.2%, other 0.3% (2009 est.)

Languages: Melanesian pidgin (in much of the country is lingua franca), English (official but spoken by only 1%-2% of the population), 120 indigenous languages

Religions: Protestant 73.4% (Church of Melanesia 31.9%, South Sea Evangelical 17.1%, Seventh Day Adventist 11.7%, United Church 10.1%, Christian Fellowship Church 2.5%), Roman Catholic 19.6%, other Christian 2.9%, other 4%, unspecified 0.1% (2009 est.)

Age structure: *0-14 years:* 32.99% (male 116,397/female 109,604)
15-24 years: 19.82% (male 69,914/female 65,874)
25-54 years: 37.64% (male 131,201/female 126,681)
55-64 years: 5.04% (male 17,844/female 16,704)
65 years and over: 4.51% (male 14,461/female 16,417) (2020 est.)

Dependency ratios: *total dependency ratio:* 77.6
youth dependency ratio: 71.1
elderly dependency ratio: 6.5
potential support ratio: 15.3 (2020 est.)

Median age: *total:* 23.5 years
male: 23.2 years
female: 23.7 years (2020 est.)
country comparison to the world: 176

Population growth rate: 1.72% (2022 est.)
country comparison to the world: 54

Birth rate: 22.71 births/1,000 population (2022 est.)
country comparison to the world: 52

Death rate: 3.96 deaths/1,000 population (2022 est.)
country comparison to the world: 215

Net migration rate: -1.55 migrant(s)/1,000 population (2022 est.)
country comparison to the world: 158

Population distribution: most of the population lives along the coastal regions; about one in five live in urban areas, and of these some two-thirds reside in Honiara, the largest town and chief port

Urbanization: *urban population:* 25.6% of total population (2022)
rate of urbanization: 3.57% annual rate of change (2020-25 est.)

Major urban areas - population: 82,000 HONIARA (capital) (2018)

Sex ratio: *at birth:* 1.05 male(s)/female
0-14 years: 1.06 male(s)/female
15-24 years: 1.06 male(s)/female
25-54 years: 1.04 male(s)/female
55-64 years: 1.08 male(s)/female
65 years and over: 0.74 male(s)/female
total population: 1.04 male(s)/female (2022 est.)

Mother's mean age at first birth: 22.6 years (2015 est.)
note: data represents median age at first birth among women 25-29

Maternal mortality ratio: 104 deaths/100,000 live births (2017 est.)
country comparison to the world: 69

Infant mortality rate: *total:* 20.02 deaths/1,000 live births
male: 23.89 deaths/1,000 live births
female: 15.96 deaths/1,000 live births (2022 est.)
country comparison to the world: 80

Life expectancy at birth: *total population:* 76.7 years
male: 74.05 years
female: 79.49 years (2022 est.)
country comparison to the world: 100

Total fertility rate: 2.87 children born/woman (2022 est.)
country comparison to the world: 53

Contraceptive prevalence rate: 29.3% (2015)

Drinking water source: *improved: urban:* 95% of population
rural: 65.9% of population
total: 73.1% of population
unimproved: urban: 5% of population
rural: 34.1% of population
total: 26.9% of population (2020 est.)

Current health expenditure: 4.8% of GDP (2019)

Physicians density: 0.19 physicians/1,000 population (2016)

Hospital bed density: 1.4 beds/1,000 population (2012)

Sanitation facility access: *improved: urban:* 95.6% of population
rural: 22.6% of population
total: 40.6% of population
unimproved: urban: 4.4% of population
rural: 77.4% of population
total: 59.4% of population (2020 est.)

Major infectious diseases: *degree of risk:* high (2020)
food or waterborne diseases: bacterial diarrhea
vectorborne diseases: malaria

Obesity - adult prevalence rate: 22.5% (2016)
country comparison to the world: 76

Alcohol consumption per capita: *total:* 1.19 liters of pure alcohol (2019 est.)
beer: 1.1 liters of pure alcohol (2019 est.)
wine: 0.06 liters of pure alcohol (2019 est.)
spirits: 0.02 liters of pure alcohol (2019 est.)
other alcohols: 0 liters of pure alcohol (2019 est.)
country comparison to the world: 146

Tobacco use: *total:* 36.5% (2020 est.)
male: 53.8% (2020 est.)
female: 19.2% (2020 est.)
country comparison to the world: 12

Children under the age of 5 years underweight: 16.2% (2015)
country comparison to the world: 34

Education expenditures: 10.1% of GDP (2015 est.)
country comparison to the world: 3

Unemployment, youth ages 15-24: *total:* 1.3%
male: 1%
female: 1.6% (2013)

ENVIRONMENT

Environment - current issues: deforestation; soil erosion; many of the surrounding coral reefs are dead or dying, exhibiting the effects of climate change and rising sea levels

Environment - international agreements: *party to:* Biodiversity, Climate Change, Climate Change-Kyoto Protocol, Climate Change-Paris Agreement, Desertification, Endangered Species, Environmental Modification, Law of the Sea, Marine Dumping-London Convention, Marine Life Conservation, Ozone Layer Protection, Ship Pollution, Whaling
signed, but not ratified: Comprehensive Nuclear Test Ban

Air pollutants: *particulate matter emissions:* 10.67 micrograms per cubic meter (2016 est.)
carbon dioxide emissions: 0.17 megatons (2016 est.)
methane emissions: 0.43 megatons (2020 est.)

Climate: tropical monsoon; few temperature and weather extremes

Land use: *agricultural land:* 3.9% (2018 est.)
arable land: 0.7% (2018 est.)
permanent crops: 2.9% (2018 est.)
permanent pasture: 0.3% (2018 est.)
forest: 78.9% (2018 est.)
other: 17.2% (2018 est.)

Urbanization: *urban population:* 25.6% of total population (2022)
rate of urbanization: 3.57% annual rate of change (2020-25 est.)

Revenue from forest resources: *forest revenues:* 20.27% of GDP (2018 est.)
country comparison to the world: 1

Revenue from coal: *coal revenues:* 0% of GDP (2018 est.)
country comparison to the world: 167

Waste and recycling: *municipal solid waste generated annually:* 179,972 tons (2013 est.)

Total renewable water resources: 44.7 billion cubic meters (2017 est.)

GOVERNMENT

Country name: *conventional long form:* none
conventional short form: Solomon Islands
local long form: none
local short form: Solomon Islands
former: British Solomon Islands
etymology: Spanish explorer Alvaro de MENDANA named the isles in 1568 after the wealthy biblical King SOLOMON in the mistaken belief that the islands contained great riches

Government type: parliamentary democracy under a constitutional monarchy; a Commonwealth realm

Capital: *name:* Honiara
geographic coordinates: 9 26 S, 159 57 E
time difference: UTC+11 (16 hours ahead of Washington, DC, during Standard Time)
etymology: the name derives from "nagho ni ara," which in one of the Guadalcanal languages roughly translates as "facing the eastern wind"

Administrative divisions: 9 provinces and 1 city*; Central, Choiseul, Guadalcanal, Honiara*, Isabel, Makira and Ulawa, Malaita, Rennell and Bellona, Temotu, Western

Independence: 7 July 1978 (from the UK)

National holiday: Independence Day, 7 July (1978)

Constitution: *history:* adopted 31 May 1978, effective 7 July 1978; note - in late 2017, provincial leaders agreed to adopt a new federal constitution, with passage expected in 2018, but it has been postponed indefinitely
amendments: proposed by the National Parliament; passage of constitutional sections, including those on fundamental rights and freedoms, the legal system, Parliament, alteration of the constitution and the ombudsman, requires three-fourths majority vote by Parliament and assent of the governor general; passage of other amendments requires two-thirds majority vote and assent of the governor general; amended several times, last in 2018; note - a new constitution was drafted in mid-2009 and the latest version drafted in 2013

Legal system: mixed legal system of English common law and customary law

International law organization participation: has not submitted an ICJ jurisdiction declaration; non-party state to the ICCt

Citizenship: *citizenship by birth:* no
citizenship by descent only: at least one parent must be a citizen of the Solomon Islands
dual citizenship recognized: no
residency requirement for naturalization: 7 years

Suffrage: 21 years of age; universal

Executive branch: *chief of state:* King CHARLES III (since 8 September 2022); represented by Governor General David VUNAGI (since 8 July 2019)
head of government: Prime Minister Manasseh SOGAVARE (since 24 April 2019)
cabinet: Cabinet appointed by the governor general on the advice of the prime minister
elections/appointments: the monarchy is hereditary; governor general appointed by the monarch on the advice of the National Parliament for up to 5 years (eligible for a second term); following legislative elections, the leader of the majority party or majority coalition usually elected prime minister by the National Parliament; deputy prime minister appointed by the governor general on the advice of the prime minister from among members of the National Parliament
election results:
Manasseh SOGAVARE elected prime minister on 24 April 2019

Legislative branch: *description:* unicameral National Parliament (50 seats; members directly elected in single-seat constituencies by simple majority vote to serve 4-year terms)
elections:
last held on 3 April 2019 (next to be held in April 2023)
election results:
percent of vote by party - UDP 10.7%, DAP 7.8%, PAP 4.4%, independent 56.3%, other 20.8%; seats by party - DAP 7, UDP 5, PAP 3, KPSI 1, SIPFP 1, SIPRA 1, independent 32; composition - men 46, women 4, percent of women 8%

Judicial branch: *highest court(s):* Court of Appeal (consists of the court president and ex officio members including the High Court chief justice and its puisne judges); High Court (consists of the chief justice and puisne judges, as prescribed by the National Parliament)
judge selection and term of office: Court of Appeal and High Court president, chief justices, and puisne judges appointed by the governor general upon recommendation of the Judicial and Legal Service Commission, chaired by the chief justice and includes 5 members, mostly judicial officials and legal professionals; all judges serve until retirement at age 60
subordinate courts: Magistrates' Courts; Customary Land Appeal Court; local courts

Political parties and leaders: Democratic Alliance Party or DAP [Steve ABANA]
Kadere Party of Solomon Islands or KPSI [Peter BOYERS]
People's Alliance Party or PAP [Sir Nathaniel WAENA]
Solomon Islands Party for Rural Advancement or SIPRA [Manasseh MAELANGA]
Solomon Islands People First Party or SIPFP [Dr. Jimmie RODGERS]
United Democratic Party or UDP [Sir Thomas Ko CHAN]
note: in general, Solomon Islands politics is characterized by fluid coalitions

International organization participation: ACP, ADB, AOSIS, C, EITI (candidate country), ESCAP, FAO, G-77, IBRD, ICAO, ICRM, IDA, IFAD, IFC, IFRCS, ILO, IMF, IMO, IOC, ITU, MIGA, OPCW, PIF, Sparteca, SPC, UN, UNCTAD, UNESCO, UPU, WFTU, WHO, WMO, WTO

Diplomatic representation in the US: *chief of mission:* Ambassador Jane Mugafalu Kabui WAETARA (since 16 September 2022)
chancery: 685 Third Avenue, 11th Floor, Suite 1102, New York, NY 10017
telephone: [1] (212) 599-6192; [1] (212) 599-6193
FAX: [1] (212) 661-8925
email address and website:
simun@solomons.com

Diplomatic representation from the US: *embassy:* the US does not have an embassy in the Solomon Islands; the US Ambassador to Papua New Guinea is accredited to the Solomon Islands

Flag description: divided diagonally by a thin yellow stripe from the lower hoist-side corner; the upper triangle (hoist side) is blue with five white five-pointed stars arranged in an X pattern; the lower triangle is green; blue represents the ocean, green the land, and yellow sunshine; the five stars stand for the five main island groups of the Solomon Islands

National symbol(s): *national colors:* blue, yellow, green, white

National anthem: *name:* "God Save Our Solomon Islands"
lyrics/music: Panapasa BALEKANA and Matila BALEKANA/Panapasa BALEKANA
note: adopted 1978

National heritage: *total World Heritage Sites:* 1 (natural)
selected World Heritage Site locales: East Rennell

ECONOMY

Economic overview: The bulk of the population depends on agriculture, fishing, and forestry for at least part of its livelihood. Most manufactured goods and petroleum products must be imported. The islands are rich in undeveloped mineral resources such as lead, zinc, nickel, and gold. Prior to the arrival of The Regional Assistance Mission to the Solomon Islands (RAMSI), severe ethnic violence, the closure of key businesses, and an empty government treasury culminated in economic collapse. RAMSI's efforts, which concluded in Jun 2017, to restore law and order and economic stability have led to modest growth as the economy rebuilds.

Real GDP (purchasing power parity): $1.71 billion (2020 est.)
$1.78 billion (2019 est.)
$1.76 billion (2018 est.)
note: data are in 2017 dollars
country comparison to the world: 199

Real GDP growth rate: 3.5% (2017 est.)
3.5% (2016 est.)
2.5% (2015 est.)
country comparison to the world: 86

Real GDP per capita: $2,500 (2020 est.)
$2,700 (2019 est.)
$2,700 (2018 est.)
note: data are in 2017 dollars
country comparison to the world: 203

GDP (official exchange rate): $1.298 billion (2017 est.)

Inflation rate (consumer prices): 0.5% (2017 est.)
0.5% (2016 est.)
country comparison to the world: 44

Credit ratings: Moody's rating: B3 (2015)

GDP - composition, by sector of origin: *agriculture:* 34.3% (2017 est.)
industry: 7.6% (2017 est.)
services: 58.1% (2017 est.)

GDP - composition, by end use: *exports of goods and services:* 25.8% (2011 est.)
imports of goods and services: -49.6% (2011 est.)

Agricultural products: oil palm fruit, sweet potatoes, coconuts, taro, yams, fruit, pulses, vegetables, cocoa, cassava

Industries: fish (tuna), mining, timber

Industrial production growth rate: 3.6% (2017 est.)
country comparison to the world: 83

Labor force: 202,500 (2007 est.)
country comparison to the world: 169

Labor force - by occupation: *agriculture:* 75%
industry: 5%
services: 20% (2000 est.)

Unemployment, youth ages 15-24: *total:* 1.3%
male: 1%
female: 1.6% (2013)
country comparison to the world: 183

Population below poverty line: 12.7% (2012 est.)

Gini Index coefficient - distribution of family income: 37.1 (2013 est.)
country comparison to the world: 82

Budget: *revenues:* 532.5 million (2017 est.)
expenditures: 570.5 million (2017 est.)

Budget surplus (+) or deficit (-): -2.9% (of GDP) (2017 est.)
country comparison to the world: 130

Public debt: 9.4% of GDP (2017 est.)
7.9% of GDP (2016 est.)
country comparison to the world: 198

Taxes and other revenues: 41% (of GDP) (2017 est.)
country comparison to the world: 33

Fiscal year: calendar year

Current account balance: -$54 million (2017 est.)
-$49 million (2016 est.)
country comparison to the world: 82

Exports: $430 million (2020 est.) note: data are in current year dollars
$590 million (2019 est.) note: data are in current year dollars
$680 million (2018 est.) note: data are in current year dollars
country comparison to the world: 191

Exports - partners: China 65%, Italy 9%, India 6% (2019)

Exports - commodities: lumber, fish, aluminum, palm oil, cocoa beans (2019)

Imports: $560 million (2020 est.) note: data are in current year dollars
$750 million (2019 est.) note: data are in current year dollars
$750 million (2018 est.) note: data are in current year dollars
country comparison to the world: 200

Imports - partners: China 24%, Australia 13%, South Korea 12%, Singapore 12%, Malaysia 10% (2019)

Imports - commodities: refined petroleum, fish, insulated wiring, broadcasting equipment, excavation machinery (2019)

Reserves of foreign exchange and gold: $0 (31 December 2017 est.)
$421 million (31 December 2016 est.)
country comparison to the world: 194

Debt - external: $757 million (31 December 2017 est.)
$643 million (31 December 2016 est.)
country comparison to the world: 172

Exchange rates: Solomon Islands dollars (SBD) per US dollar -
8.06126 (2020 est.)
8.10373 (2019 est.)
8.01282 (2018 est.)
7.9147 (2014 est.)
7.3754 (2013 est.)

ENERGY

Electricity access: *electrification - total population:* 66.7% (2018)
electrification - urban areas: 76.7% (2018)
electrification - rural areas: 63.5% (2018)

Electricity: *installed generating capacity:* 40,000 kW (2020 est.)
consumption: 93.527 million kWh (2019 est.)
exports: 0 kWh (2020 est.)
imports: 0 kWh (2020 est.)
transmission/distribution losses: 14 million kWh (2019 est.)

Electricity generation sources: *fossil fuels:* 94.8% of total installed capacity (2020 est.)
solar: 2.7% of total installed capacity (2020 est.)
biomass and waste: 2.6% of total installed capacity (2020 est.)

Petroleum: *total petroleum production:* 0 bbl/day (2021 est.)
refined petroleum consumption: 2,200 bbl/day (2019 est.)

Refined petroleum products - imports: 1,577 bbl/day (2015 est.)
country comparison to the world: 194

Carbon dioxide emissions: 333,000 metric tonnes of CO2 (2019 est.)
from petroleum and other liquids: 333,000 metric tonnes of CO2 (2019 est.)
country comparison to the world: 194

Energy consumption per capita: 6.955 million Btu/person (2019 est.)
country comparison to the world: 165

COMMUNICATIONS

Telephones - fixed lines: *total subscriptions:* 7,000 (2020 est.)
subscriptions per 100 inhabitants: 1 (2020 est.)
country comparison to the world: 196

Telephones - mobile cellular: *total subscriptions:* 478,116 (2019)
subscriptions per 100 inhabitants: 71 (2019)
country comparison to the world: 174

Telecommunication systems: *general assessment:* mobile services have continually expanded in the Solomon Islands; 3G services became available in 2010, leading to an increase in mobile broadband uptake; Solomon Islands currently host three ISPs; fixed broadband services are largely limited to government, corporations, and educational organizations in the Solomon Islands; telecommunication infrastructure in the Solomon Islands requires significant investment due to the geographical make-up of the islands; this presents a great challenge to rural connectivity in the country; although various international organizations such as the World Bank and the Asian Development Bank have taken a special interest in having communication services improved in both the Solomon Islands and the Pacific region in general, internet and broadband penetration remain low; the provision of broadband infrastructure, particularly to rural areas, is also hindered by land disputes; internet services have, improved with the build-out of the Coral Sea Cable System linking Papua New Guinea to the Solomon Islands, as also with a connecting cable to a landing station at Sydney; the Australian government provided most of the funding for the Coral Sea Cable System, with contributions and support from the Solomon Islands and Papua New Guinea governments; the launch of the Kacific-1 satellite in late 2019 also improved broadband satellite capacity for the region, though for telcos in Solomon Islands satellite services are now largely used as backup for international traffic; in recent years, the country has stabilized both politically and economically and this, along with improvements to mobile infrastructure, has led to a rise in mobile services and the slow uptake of broadband services; while the first LTE services were launched in late 2017 in the capital Honiara, the main platform for mobile voice and data services remains 3G, while in outlying areas GSM is still an important technology for the provision of services (2022)
domestic: fixed-line is just over 1 per 100 persons and mobile-cellular telephone density is about 71 per 100 persons; domestic cable system to extend to key major islands (2019)
international: country code - 677; landing points for the CSCS and ICNS2 submarine cables providing connectivity from Solomon Islands, to PNG, Vanuatu and Australia; satellite earth station - 1 Intelsat (Pacific Ocean) (2019)

Broadcast media: Solomon Islands Broadcasting Corporation (SIBC) does not broadcast television; multi-channel pay-TV is available; SIBC operates 2 national radio stations and 2 provincial stations; there are 2 local commercial radio stations; Radio Australia is available via satellite feed (since 2009) (2019)

Internet country code: .sb

Internet users: *total:* 80,379 (2019 est.)
percent of population: 12% (2019 est.)
country comparison to the world: 182

Broadband - fixed subscriptions: *total:* 1,000 (2020 est.)
subscriptions per 100 inhabitants: 0.2 (2020 est.)
country comparison to the world: 208

TRANSPORTATION

National air transport system: *number of registered air carriers:* 1 (2020)
inventory of registered aircraft operated by air carriers: 6
annual passenger traffic on registered air carriers: 427,806 (2018)
annual freight traffic on registered air carriers: 3.84 million (2018) mt-km

Civil aircraft registration country code prefix: H4

Airports: *total:* 36 (2021)
country comparison to the world: 109

Airports - with paved runways: *total:* 1
1,524 to 2,437 m: 1 (2021)

Airports - with unpaved runways: *total:* 35
1,524 to 2,437 m: 1
914 to 1,523 m: 10
under 914 m: 24 (2021)

Heliports: 3 (2021)

Roadways: *total:* 1,390 km (2011)
paved: 34 km (2011)
unpaved: 1,356 km (2011)
note: includes 920 km of private plantation roads
country comparison to the world: 175

Merchant marine: *total:* 24
by type: general cargo 8, oil tanker 1, other 15 (2021)
country comparison to the world: 144

Ports and terminals: *major seaport(s):* Honiara, Malloco Bay, Viru Harbor, Tulagi

MILITARY AND SECURITY

Military and security forces: no regular military forces; the Royal Solomon Islands Police Force is responsible for internal and external security and reports to the Ministry of Police, National Security, and Correctional Services (2022)

Military equipment inventories and acquisitions: China and Australia have provided equipment to the Solomons Islands Police Force; the maritime branch operates patrol boats provided by Australia (2022)

Military - note: Australia and New Zealand provide material and training assistance to the Royal Solomon Islands Police Force (2022)

TRANSNATIONAL ISSUES

Disputes - international: from 2003 to 2017, at the request of the Solomon Islands Governor-General, the Regional Assistance Mission to Solomon Islands (RAMSI), consisting of police, military, and civilian advisors drawn from 15 countries, assisted in reestablishing and maintaining civil and political order while reinforcing regional stability and security

SOMALIA

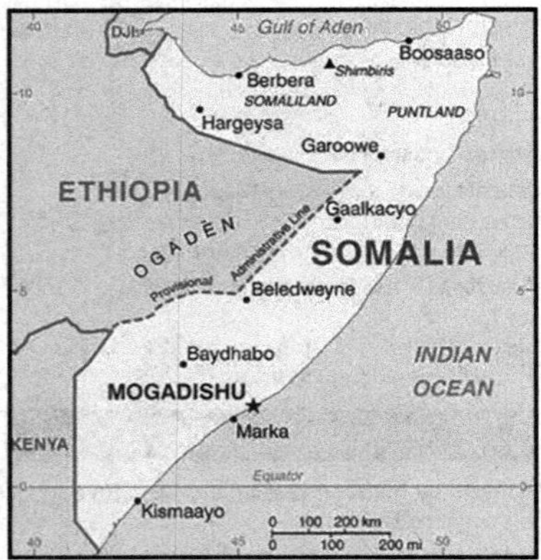

INTRODUCTION

Background: Ancient Egypt trade expeditions along the northeastern coast of Africa - including today's Eritrea, Djibouti, and Somalia - occurred at various times between the 25th and 12th centuries B.C. Between A.D. 800 and 1100, immigrant Muslim Arabs and Persians set up coastal trading posts along the Gulf of Aden and the Indian Ocean, solidifying Somalia's close trading relationship with the Arab Peninsula. In the late 19th century, Britain and Italy established colonies in the Somali Peninsula, where they remained until 1960, when British Somaliland gained independence and joined with Italian Somaliland to form the Republic of Somalia. The country functioned as a parliamentary democracy until 1969, when General Mohamed SIAD Barre took control in a coup, beginning a 22-year authoritarian socialist dictatorship. In an effort to centralize power, SIAD called for the eradication of the clan, the key cultural and social organizing principle in Somali society. Resistance to SIAD's socialist leadership, which was causing a rapid deterioration of the country, prompted allied clan militias to overthrow SIAD in early 1991, resulting in state collapse. Subsequent fighting between rival clans for resources and territory overwhelmed the country, resulting in a manmade famine and prompting international intervention. Beginning in 1993, the UN spearheaded a humanitarian mission supported by international forces, but the international community largely withdrew by 1995 following an incident that became known as Black Hawk Down in which two American Sikorsky UH-60 Black Hawk helicopters were shot down in Mogadishu. The fighting and subsequent siege and rescue resulted in 21 deaths and 82 wounded among the international forces.

International peace conferences in the 2000s resulted in a number of transitional governments that operated outside of Somalia. Left largely to themselves, Somalis in the country established alternative governance structures; some areas formed their own administrations, such as Somaliland and Puntland, while others developed localized institutions. Many local populations turned to using sharia courts, an Islamic judicial system that implements religious law. Several of these courts came together in 2006 to form the Islamic Courts Union (ICU). The ICU established order in many areas of central and southern Somalia, including Mogadishu, but was forced out when Ethiopia intervened militarily in December 2006 on behalf of the Somali Transitional Federal Government (TFG). While the TFG settled in the capital, the ICU fled to rural areas or from Somalia altogether, reemerging less than a year later as the Islamic insurgent and terrorist movement al-Shabaab, which is still active today. In January 2007, the African Union (AU) established the AU Mission in Somalia peacekeeping force, which allowed Ethiopia to withdraw its forces, took over security responsibility for the country, and gave the TFG space to develop Somalia's new government. By 2012, Somali powerbrokers agreed on a provisional constitution with a loose federal structure and established a central government in Mogadishu termed the Somali Federal Government (SFG). Since then, several interim regional administrations have been established and there have been two presidential elections. However, significant and fundamental governance and security problems remain for the SFG since al-Shabaab controls large portions of the country.

GEOGRAPHY

Location: Eastern Africa, bordering the Gulf of Aden and the Indian Ocean, east of Ethiopia

Geographic coordinates: 10 00 N, 49 00 E

Map references: Africa

Area: *total:* 637,657 sq km
land: 627,337 sq km
water: 10,320 sq km
country comparison to the world: 46

Area - comparative: almost five times the size of Alabama; slightly smaller than Texas

Land boundaries: *total:* 2,385 km
border countries (3): Djibouti 61 km; Ethiopia 1,640 km; Kenya 684 km

Coastline: 3,025 km

Maritime claims: *territorial sea:* 200 nm; note: the US does not recognize this claim
exclusive economic zone: 200 nm

Climate: principally desert; northeast monsoon (December to February), moderate temperatures in north and hot in south; southwest monsoon (May to October), torrid in the north and hot in the south, irregular rainfall, hot and humid periods (tangambili) between monsoons

Terrain: mostly flat to undulating plateau rising to hills in north

Elevation: *highest point:* Mount Shimbiris 2,460 m
lowest point: Indian Ocean 0 m
mean elevation: 410 m

Natural resources: uranium and largely unexploited reserves of iron ore, tin, gypsum, bauxite, copper, salt, natural gas, likely oil reserves

Land use: *agricultural land:* 70.3% (2018 est.)
arable land: 1.8% (2018 est.)
permanent crops: 0% (2018 est.)
permanent pasture: 68.5% (2018 est.)
forest: 10.6% (2018 est.)
other: 19.1% (2018 est.)

Irrigated land: 2,000 sq km (2012)

Major aquifers: Ogaden-Juba Basin

Population distribution: distribution varies greatly throughout the country; least densely populated areas are in the northeast and central regions, as well as areas along the Kenyan border; most populated areas are in and around the cities of Mogadishu, Marka, Boorama, Hargeysa, and Baidoa as shown on this population distribution map

Natural hazards: recurring droughts; frequent dust storms over eastern plains in summer; floods during rainy season

Geography - note: strategic location on Horn of Africa along southern approaches to Bab el Mandeb and route through Red Sea and Suez Canal

PEOPLE AND SOCIETY

Population: 12,386,248 (2022 est.)
note: this estimate was derived from an official census taken in 1975 by the Somali Government; population counting in Somalia is complicated by the large number of nomads and by refugee movements in response to famine and clan warfare
country comparison to the world: 78

Nationality: *noun:* Somali(s)
adjective: Somali

Ethnic groups: Somali 85%, Bantu and other non-Somali 15% (including 30,000 Arabs)

Languages: Somali (official, according to the 2012 Transitional Federal Charter), Arabic (official, according to the 2012 Transitional Federal Charter), Italian, English
major-language sample(s):
Buugga Xaqiiqda Aduunka, waa laga maarmaanka macluumaadka assasiga. (Somali)

Religions: Sunni Muslim (Islam) (official, according to the 2012 Transitional Federal Charter)

Demographic profile: Somalia scores very low for most humanitarian indicators, suffering from poor governance, protracted internal conflict, underdevelopment, economic decline, poverty, social and gender inequality, and environmental degradation.

Despite civil war and famine raising its mortality rate, Somalia's high fertility rate and large proportion of people of reproductive age maintain rapid population growth, with each generation being larger than the prior one. More than 60% of Somalia's population is younger than 25, and the fertility rate is among the world's highest at almost 6 children per woman – a rate that has decreased little since the 1970s.

A lack of educational and job opportunities is a major source of tension for Somalia's large youth cohort, making them vulnerable to recruitment by extremist and pirate groups. Somalia has one of the world's lowest primary school enrollment rates – just over 40% of children are in school – and one of world's highest youth unemployment rates. Life expectancy is low as a result of high infant and maternal mortality rates, the spread of preventable diseases, poor sanitation, chronic malnutrition, and inadequate health services.

During the two decades of conflict that followed the fall of the SIAD regime in 1991, hundreds of thousands of Somalis fled their homes. Today Somalia is the world's fourth highest source country for refugees, after Ukraine, Syria and Afghanistan. Insecurity, drought, floods, food shortages, and a lack of economic opportunities are the driving factors.

As of 2022, more than 660,000 Somali refugees were hosted in the region, mainly in Kenya, Yemen, Egypt, Ethiopia, Djibouti, and Uganda, while nearly 3 million Somalis were internally displaced. Since the implementation of a tripartite voluntary repatriation agreement among Kenya, Somalia, and the UNHCR in 2013, many Somali refugees have returned home, some 80,000 between 2014 and 2022. The Kenyan Government in March 2021 ordered the closure of its two largest refugee camps, Dadaab and Kakuma, which then hosted more than 410,000 mainly Somali refugees. However, the UN refugee agency presented a road map, including voluntary repatriation, relocation to third countries, and alternative stay options that persuaded the Kenyan Government to delay the closures. The plan was supposed to lead to both camps being closed by 30 June 2022. Yet, as of May 2022, few Somali refugees had decided to return home because of security concerns and the lack of job prospects, instead waiting in the camps unsure of what the future held for them. Other Somali asylum seekers brave the dangers of crossing the Gulf of Aden to reach Yemen – despite its internal conflict – with aspirations to move onward to Saudi Arabia and other locations.

Age structure: *0-14 years:* 42.38% (male 2,488,604/female 2,493,527)
15-24 years: 19.81% (male 1,167,807/female 1,161,040)
25-54 years: 30.93% (male 1,881,094/female 1,755,166)
55-64 years: 4.61% (male 278,132/female 264,325)
65 years and over: 2.27% (male 106,187/female 161,242) (2020 est.)

Dependency ratios: *total dependency ratio:* 96.3
youth dependency ratio: 90.6
elderly dependency ratio: 5.7
potential support ratio: 17.6 (2020 est.)

Median age: *total:* 18.5 years
male: 18.7 years
female: 18.3 years (2020 est.)
country comparison to the world: 210

Population growth rate: 2.42% (2022 est.)
country comparison to the world: 27

Birth rate: 37.98 births/1,000 population (2022 est.)
country comparison to the world: 8

Death rate: 11.62 deaths/1,000 population (2022 est.)
country comparison to the world: 17

Net migration rate: -2.18 migrant(s)/1,000 population (2022 est.)
country comparison to the world: 171

Population distribution: distribution varies greatly throughout the country; least densely populated areas are in the northeast and central regions, as well as areas along the Kenyan border; most populated areas are in and around the cities of Mogadishu, Marka, Boorama, Hargeysa, and Baidoa as shown on this population distribution map

Urbanization: *urban population:* 47.3% of total population (2022)
rate of urbanization: 4.2% annual rate of change (2020-25 est.)

Major urban areas - population: 2.497 million MOGADISHU (capital), 1.079 million Hargeysa (2022)

Sex ratio: *at birth:* 1.03 male(s)/female
0-14 years: 1 male(s)/female
15-24 years: 1 male(s)/female
25-54 years: 1.08 male(s)/female
55-64 years: 1.08 male(s)/female
65 years and over: 0.56 male(s)/female
total population: 1.01 male(s)/female (2022 est.)

Maternal mortality ratio: 829 deaths/100,000 live births (2017 est.)
country comparison to the world: 6

Infant mortality rate: *total:* 86.53 deaths/1,000 live births
male: 96.18 deaths/1,000 live births
female: 76.59 deaths/1,000 live births (2022 est.)
country comparison to the world: 2

Life expectancy at birth: *total population:* 55.72 years
male: 53.39 years
female: 58.12 years (2022 est.)
country comparison to the world: 225

Total fertility rate: 5.31 children born/woman (2022 est.)
country comparison to the world: 9

Contraceptive prevalence rate: 6.9% (2018/19)

Drinking water source: *improved: urban:* 96.4% of population
rural: 73.7% of population
total: 84.2% of population
unimproved: urban: 3.6% of population
rural: 26.3% of population
total: 15.8% of population (2020 est.)

Physicians density: 0.02 physicians/1,000 population (2014)

Hospital bed density: 0.9 beds/1,000 population (2017)

Sanitation facility access: *improved: urban:* 82.4% of population
rural: 33.8% of population
total: 56.2% of population
unimproved: urban: 17.6% of population
rural: 66.2% of population
total: 43.8% of population (2020 est.)

HIV/AIDS - adult prevalence rate: (2020 est.) <.1%

HIV/AIDS - people living with HIV/AIDS: 8,700 (2020 est.)
country comparison to the world: 110

HIV/AIDS - deaths: (2020 est.) <500

Major infectious diseases: *degree of risk:* very high (2020)
food or waterborne diseases: bacterial and protozoal diarrhea, hepatitis A and E, and typhoid fever
vectorborne diseases: dengue fever, malaria, and Rift Valley fever
water contact diseases: schistosomiasis
animal contact diseases: rabies
note: on 21 March 2022, the US Centers for Disease Control and Prevention (CDC) issued a Travel Alert for polio in Africa; Somalia is currently considered a high risk to travelers for circulating vaccine-derived polioviruses (cVDPV); vaccine-derived poliovirus (VDPV) is a strain of the weakened poliovirus that was initially included in oral polio vaccine (OPV) and *that has changed over time and behaves more like the wild or naturally occurring virus*; this means it can be spread more easily to people who are unvaccinated against polio and who come in contact with the stool or respiratory secretions, such as from a sneeze, of an "infected" person who received oral polio vaccine; the CDC recommends that before any international travel, anyone unvaccinated, incompletely vaccinated, or with an unknown polio vaccination status should complete the routine polio vaccine series; before travel to any high-risk destination, the CDC recommends that adults who previously completed the full, routine polio vaccine series receive a single, lifetime booster dose of polio vaccine

Obesity - adult prevalence rate: 8.3% (2016)
country comparison to the world: 153

Alcohol consumption per capita: *total:* 0 liters of pure alcohol (2019 est.)
beer: 0 liters of pure alcohol (2019 est.)
wine: 0 liters of pure alcohol (2019 est.)
spirits: 0 liters of pure alcohol (2019 est.)
other alcohols: 0 liters of pure alcohol (2019 est.)
country comparison to the world: 189

Children under the age of 5 years underweight: 23% (2009)
country comparison to the world: 15

Child marriage: *women married by age 15:* 16.8%
women married by age 18: 35.5%
men married by age 18: 5.6% (2020 est.)

ENVIRONMENT

Environment - current issues: water scarcity; contaminated water contributes to human health problems; improper waste disposal; deforestation; land degradation; overgrazing; soil erosion; desertification

Environment - international agreements: *party to:* Biodiversity, Climate Change, Climate Change-Kyoto Protocol, Climate Change-Paris Agreement, Desertification, Endangered Species, Hazardous Wastes, Law of the Sea, Ozone Layer Protection
signed, but not ratified: Nuclear Test Ban

Air pollutants: *particulate matter emissions:* 29.51 micrograms per cubic meter (2016 est.)
carbon dioxide emissions: 0.65 megatons (2016 est.)
methane emissions: 20.13 megatons (2020 est.)

Climate: principally desert; northeast monsoon (December to February), moderate temperatures in north and hot in south; southwest monsoon (May to October), torrid in the north and hot in the south, irregular rainfall, hot and humid periods (tangambili) between monsoons

Land use: *agricultural land:* 70.3% (2018 est.)
arable land: 1.8% (2018 est.)
permanent crops: 0% (2018 est.)

permanent pasture: 68.5% (2018 est.)
forest: 10.6% (2018 est.)
other: 19.1% (2018 est.)

Urbanization: *urban population:* 47.3% of total population (2022)
rate of urbanization: 4.2% annual rate of change (2020-25 est.)

Food insecurity: *exceptional shortfall in aggregate food production/supplies: due to drought conditions and internal conflict* - about 5.2 million people were estimated to face severe food insecurity in May 2022, as a result of consecutive poor rainy seasons since late 2020, which severely affected crop and livestock production, and due to worsening civil conflict since early 2021; if humanitarian assistance is not adequately scaled up, the number of food insecure is projected to increase to 7.11 million (45% of the total population) between June and September 2022 (2022)

Waste and recycling: *municipal solid waste generated annually:* 2,326,099 tons (2016 est.)

Major aquifers: Ogaden-Juba Basin

Total water withdrawal: *municipal:* 15 million cubic meters (2017 est.)
industrial: 2 million cubic meters (2017 est.)
agricultural: 3.281 billion cubic meters (2017 est.)

Total renewable water resources: 14.7 billion cubic meters (2017 est.)

GOVERNMENT

Country name: *conventional long form:* Federal Republic of Somalia
conventional short form: Somalia
local long form: Jamhuuriyadda Federaalka Soomaaliya (Somali)/ Jumhuriyat as Sumal al Fidiraliyah (Arabic)
local short form: Soomaaliya (Somali)/ As Sumal (Arabic)
former: British Somaliland, Italian Somaliland, Somali Republic, Somali Democratic Republic
etymology: "Land of the Somali" (ethnic group)

Government type: federal parliamentary republic

Capital: *name:* Mogadishu
geographic coordinates: 2 04 N, 45 20 E
time difference: UTC+3 (8 hours ahead of Washington, DC, during Standard Time)
etymology: several theories attempt to explain the city's name; one of the more plausible is that it derives from "maq'ad-i-shah" meaning "the seat of the shah," reflecting the city's links with Persia

Administrative divisions: 18 regions (plural - gobollo, singular - gobol); Awdal, Bakool, Banaadir, Bari, Bay, Galguduud, Gedo, Hiiraan, Jubbada Dhexe (Middle Jubba), Jubbada Hoose (Lower Jubba), Mudug, Nugaal, Sanaag, Shabeellaha Dhexe (Middle Shabeelle), Shabeellaha Hoose (Lower Shabeelle), Sool, Togdheer, Woqooyi Galbeed

Independence: 1 July 1960 (from a merger of British Somaliland, which became independent from the UK on 26 June 1960, and Italian Somaliland, which became independent from the Italian-administered UN trusteeship on 1 July 1960 to form the Somali Republic)

National holiday: Foundation of the Somali Republic, 1 July (1960); note - 26 June (1960) in Somaliland

Constitution: *history:* previous 1961, 1979; latest drafted 12 June 2012, adopted 1 August 2012 (provisional)
amendments: proposed by the federal government, by members of the state governments, the Federal Parliament, or by public petition; proposals require review by a joint committee of Parliament with inclusion of public comments and state legislatures' comments; passage requires at least two-thirds majority vote in both houses of Parliament and approval by a majority of votes cast in a referendum; constitutional clauses on Islamic principles, the federal system, human rights and freedoms, powers and authorities of the government branches, and inclusion of women in national institutions cannot be amended; note - in late December 2020, the president signed a decree blocking the approval of amendments

Legal system: mixed legal system of civil law, Islamic (sharia) law, and customary law (referred to as Xeer)

International law organization participation: accepts compulsory ICJ jurisdiction with reservations; non-party state to the ICCt

Citizenship: *citizenship by birth:* no
citizenship by descent only: the father must be a citizen of Somalia
dual citizenship recognized: no
residency requirement for naturalization: 7 years

Suffrage: 18 years of age; universal

Executive branch: *chief of state:* President HASSAN SHEIKH Mohamud (since 23 May 2022)
head of government: Prime Minister Hamza Abdi BARRE (since 25 June 2022)
cabinet: Cabinet appointed by the prime minister, approved by the House of the People
elections/appointments: president indirectly elected by the Federal Parliament by two-thirds majority vote in 2 rounds if needed for a single 4-year term; election last held on 15 May 2022 (next to be held in 2026); prime minister appointed by the president, approved by the House of the People; note - elections were originally scheduled for 10 October 2021 but did not take place; on 13 April 2022, the election of the House of the People representatives was completed and the presidential election date was set for 15 May 2022
election results:
2022: HASSAN SHEIKH Mohamud elected president in third round - Federal Parliament vote in the first round - Said ABDULLAHI DENI (Kaah) 20.2%, Mohamed ABDULLAHI Mohamed "Farmaajo" (TPP) 18.3%, HASSAN SHEIKH Mohamud (PDP) 16.2%, Hassan Ali KHAYRE (Independent) 14.6%, other 30.7%; Federal Parliament vote in the second round - HASSAN SHEIKH Mohamud (PDP) 34.1%, Mohamed ABDULLAHI Mohamed "Farmaajo" (TPP) 25.7%, Said ABDULLAHI DENI (Kaah) 21%, Hassan Ali KHAYRE (Independent) 19.2%; Federal Parliament vote in the third round - HASSAN SHEIKH Mohamud (PDP) 66%, Mohamed ABDULLAHI Mohamed "Farmaajo" (TPP) 34%
2017: Mohamed ABDULLAHI Mohamed "Farmaajo" elected president in second round; Federal Parliament vote in the first round - HASSAN SHEIKH Mohamud (PDP) 88, Mohamed ABDULLAHI Mohamed "Farmaajo" (TPP) 72, Sheikh SHARIF Sheikh Ahmed (ARS) 49, other 37; Federal Parliament vote in the second round - Mohamed ABDULLAHI Mohamed "Farmaajo" (TPP) 184, HASSAN SHEIKH Mohamud (PDP) 97, Sheikh SHARIF Sheikh Ahmed (ARS) 45

Legislative branch: *description:* bicameral Federal Parliament to consist of:
Senate (54 seats; senators indirectly elected by state assemblies to serve 4-year terms)
House of the People (275 seats; members indirectly elected by electoral colleges, each consisting of 51 delegates selected by the 136 Traditional Elders in consultation with sub-clan elders; members serve 4-year terms)
elections:
Senate - first held on 10 October 2016; last held 27 July - 13 November 2021 (next to be held in 2024)
House of the People - first held 23 October - 10 November 2016 (next scheduled for September - October 2021 but postponed to November 2021 and then extended numerous times until April 2022; next to be held in 2024)
election results:
Senate - percent of vote by party - NA; seats by party - NA; composition - men 40, women 14, percent of women 25.9%
House of the People - percent of vote by party - NA; seats by party - NA; composition - men 225, women 50, percent of women 22.2%; note - total Parliament percent of women 19.5%
note 1: the inaugural House of the People was appointed in September 2012 by clan elders; in 2016 and 2017, the Federal Parliament became bicameral with indirect elections scheduled for 10 October 2016 for the Upper House - renamed 'Senate' and 23 October to 10 November 2016 for the House of the People; while the elections were delayed, they were eventually held in most regions despite voting irregularities; on 27 December 2016, 41 Upper House senators and 242 House of the People Members of Parliament (MP) were sworn in
note 2: despite the formation of political parties in 2020, the 2021 parliamentary elections maintained a primarily clan-based system of appointments; seats in the legislature were apportioned to Somali member states and not by party representation

Judicial branch: *highest court(s):* the provisional constitution stipulates the establishment of the Constitutional Court (consists of 5 judges, including the chief judge and deputy chief judge); note - under the terms of the 2004 Transitional National Charter, a Supreme Court based in Mogadishu and the Appeal Court were established; yet most regions have reverted to local forms of conflict resolution, either secular, traditional Somali customary law, or Islamic law
judge selection and term of office: judges appointed by the president upon proposal of the Judicial Service Commission, a 9-member judicial and administrative body; judge tenure NA
subordinate courts: federal courts; federal member state-level courts; military courts; sharia courts

Political parties and leaders: *select National Independent Electoral Commission (NIEC) approved parties (as of 2020):*
Cosmopolitan Democratic Party [Yarow Sharef ADEN]
Green Party [Ahmed HAJI]
Himilo Qaran Party [Sharif SHEIKH AHMED]
Ilays Party [Abdulkadir OSOBLE]
Justice and Reconciliation Party
National Progressive Party
Peace and Unity Party [Asha ABDALLA]
Qaransoor Party [Abdijabaar SHEIKH AHMED]
Qiimo Qaran Party
Security and Justice Party
Social Justice Party [Mohamed NUR, chairman]

Somali Labour Party[Ali Mohamed APOLLO, chairman]
Somali Republic Party [Abdinur Ahmed DARMAN, chairman]
Somali Social Unity Party or SSUP [Yaasiin Maaxi MACALIN]
Union for Peace and Development Party or PDP [HASSAN SHEIKH Mohamud]
Wadajir Party [Abdirahman Abdishakur WARSAME]
note: in 2017 an independent electoral commission (the NIEC) was inaugurated with a mandate to oversee the process of registration of political parties in the country; as of 2021, the NIEC had registered a total of 110 parties

International organization participation: ACP, AfDB, AFESD, AMF, AU, CAEU (candidate), FAO, G-77, IBRD, ICAO, ICRM, IDA, IDB, IFAD, IFC, IFRCS, IGAD, ILO, IMF, IMO, Interpol, IOC, IOM, IPU, ITSO, ITU, LAS, NAM, OIC, OPCW, OPCW (signatory), UN, UNCTAD, UNESCO, UNHCR, UNHRC, UNIDO, UPU, WFTU (NGOs), WHO, WIPO, WMO

Diplomatic representation in the US: *chief of mission:* Ambassador Ali Sharif AHMED (since 16 September 2019)
chancery: 1609 22nd Street NW, Washington, DC 20008
telephone: [1] (202) 853-9164
email address and website:
info@somaliembassydc.net
https://somaliembassydc.net/

Diplomatic representation from the US: *chief of mission:* Ambassador Larry E. ANDRE, Jr. (since 9 February 2022)
embassy: Mogadishu, (reopened October 2019 on the grounds of the Mogadishu Airport)
mailing address: P.O. Box 606 Village Market 00621 Nairobi, Kenya
telephone: [254] 20 363-6451
email address and website:
Kenya_ACS@state.gov
https://so.usembassy.gov/

Flag description: light blue with a large white five-pointed star in the center; the blue field was originally influenced by the flag of the UN but today is said to denote the sky and the neighboring Indian Ocean; the five points of the star represent the five regions in the horn of Africa that are inhabited by Somali people: the former British Somaliland and Italian Somaliland (which together make up Somalia), Djibouti, Ogaden (Ethiopia), and the North East Province (Kenya)

National symbol(s): leopard; national colors: blue, white

National anthem: *name:* "Qolobaa Calankeed" (Every Nation Has its own Flag)
lyrics/music: lyrics/music: Abdullahi QARSHE
note: adopted 2012; written in 1959

Government - note: regional and local governing bodies continue to exist and control various areas of the country, including the self-declared Republic of Somaliland in northwestern Somalia

ECONOMY

Economic overview: Despite the lack of effective national governance, Somalia maintains an informal economy largely based on livestock, remittance/money transfer companies, and telecommunications. Somalia's government lacks the ability to collect domestic revenue and external debt – mostly in arrears – was estimated at about 77% of GDP in 2017.

Agriculture is the most important sector, with livestock normally accounting for about 40% of GDP and more than 50% of export earnings. Nomads and semi-pastoralists, who are dependent upon livestock for their livelihood, make up a large portion of the population. Economic activity is estimated to have increased by 2.4% in 2017 because of growth in the agriculture, construction and telecommunications sector. Somalia's small industrial sector, based on the processing of agricultural products, has largely been looted and the machinery sold as scrap metal.

In recent years, Somalia's capital city, Mogadishu, has witnessed the development of the city's first gas stations, supermarkets, and airline flights to Turkey since the collapse of central authority in 1991. Mogadishu's main market offers a variety of goods from food to electronic gadgets. Hotels continue to operate and are supported with private-security militias. Formalized economic growth has yet to expand outside of Mogadishu and a few regional capitals, and within the city, security concerns dominate business.

Telecommunication firms provide wireless services in most major cities and offer the lowest international call rates on the continent. In the absence of a formal banking sector, money transfer/remittance services have sprouted throughout the country, handling up to $1.6 billion in remittances annually, although international concerns over the money transfers into Somalia continues to threaten these services' ability to operate in Western nations. In 2017, Somalia elected a new president and collected a record amount of foreign aid and investment, a positive sign for economic recovery.

Real GDP (purchasing power parity): $13.19 billion (2020 est.)
$13.39 billion (2019 est.)
$13.01 billion (2018 est.)
note: data are in 2017 US dollars
country comparison to the world: 156

Real GDP growth rate: 2.3% (2017 est.)
4.4% (2016 est.)
3.9% (2015 est.)
country comparison to the world: 121

Real GDP per capita: $800 (2020 est.)
$900 (2019 est.)
$900 (2018 est.)
note: data are in 2017 dollars
country comparison to the world: 228

GDP (official exchange rate): $7.052 billion (2017 est.)

Inflation rate (consumer prices): 1.5% (2017 est.)
-71.1% (2016 est.)
country comparison to the world: 90

GDP - composition, by sector of origin: *agriculture:* 60.2% (2013 est.)
industry: 7.4% (2013 est.)
services: 32.5% (2013 est.)

GDP - composition, by end use: *household consumption:* 72.6% (2015 est.)
government consumption: 8.7% (2015 est.)
investment in fixed capital: 20% (2015 est.)
investment in inventories: 0.8% (2016 est.)
exports of goods and services: 0.3% (2015 est.)
imports of goods and services: -1.6% (2015 est.)

Agricultural products: camel milk, milk, sheep milk, goat milk, sugar cane, fruit, sorghum, cassava, vegetables, maize

Industries: light industries, including sugar refining, textiles, wireless communication

Industrial production growth rate: 3.5% (2014 est.)
country comparison to the world: 90

Labor force: 4.154 million (2016 est.)
country comparison to the world: 87

Labor force - by occupation: *agriculture:* 71%
industry: 29%
industry and services: 29% (1975)

Budget: *revenues:* 145.3 million (2014 est.)
expenditures: 151.1 million (2014 est.)

Budget surplus (+) or deficit (-): -0.1% (of GDP) (2014 est.)
country comparison to the world: 49

Public debt: 76.7% of GDP (2017 est.)
93% of GDP (2014 est.)
country comparison to the world: 39

Taxes and other revenues: 2.1% (of GDP) (2014 est.)
country comparison to the world: 221

Current account balance: -$464 million (2017 est.)
-$427 million (2016 est.)
country comparison to the world: 119

Exports: $819 million (2014 est.)
$779 million (2013 est.)
country comparison to the world: 182

Exports - partners: United Arab Emirates 47%, Saudi Arabia 19%, India 5%, Japan 5% (2019)

Exports - commodities: gold, sheep, goats, sesame seeds, insect resins, cattle (2019)

Imports: $94.43 billion (2018 est.)
$80.07 billion (2017 est.)
country comparison to the world: 42

Imports - partners: United Arab Emirates 32%, China 20%, India 17%, Turkey 7% (2019)

Imports - commodities: cigarettes, raw sugar, rice, broadcasting equipment, textiles (2019)

Reserves of foreign exchange and gold: $30.45 million (2014 est.)
country comparison to the world: 189

Debt - external: $5.3 billion (31 December 2014 est.)
country comparison to the world: 131

Exchange rates: Somali shillings (SOS) per US dollar -
23,960 (2016 est.)

ENERGY

Electricity access: *electrification - total population:* 18% (2019)
electrification - urban areas: 34% (2019)
electrification - rural areas: 4% (2019)

Electricity: *installed generating capacity:* 91,000 kW (2020 est.)
consumption: 311.2 million kWh (2019 est.)
exports: 0 kWh (2019 est.)
imports: 0 kWh (2019 est.)
transmission/distribution losses: 35 million kWh (2019 est.)

Electricity generation sources: *fossil fuels:* 95.3% of total installed capacity (2020 est.)
solar: 3% of total installed capacity (2020 est.)

wind: 1.7% of total installed capacity (2020 est.)

Petroleum: *total petroleum production:* 0 bbl/day (2021 est.)
refined petroleum consumption: 5,900 bbl/day (2019 est.)

Refined petroleum products - imports: 5,590 bbl/day (2015 est.)
country comparison to the world: 167

Natural gas: *proven reserves:* 5.663 billion cubic meters (2021 est.)

Carbon dioxide emissions: 882,000 metric tonnes of CO2 (2019 est.)
from petroleum and other liquids: 882,000 metric tonnes of CO2 (2019 est.)
country comparison to the world: 176

Energy consumption per capita: 802,000 Btu/person (2019 est.)
country comparison to the world: 195

COMMUNICATIONS

Telephones - fixed lines: *total subscriptions:* 91,000 (2020 est.)
subscriptions per 100 inhabitants: 1 (2020 est.)
country comparison to the world: 140

Telephones - mobile cellular: *total subscriptions:* 7.119 million (2018)
subscriptions per 100 inhabitants: 48.8 (2019)
country comparison to the world: 105

Telecommunication systems: *general assessment:* Somalia's economic difficulties in recent years have made it difficult for telcos and the government to sustain investment in infrastructure; the government has also had to contend with militant groups which continue on occasion to force the closure of internet services in many areas of the country; in recent years, though, the government has addressed the lack of guidance which had prevailed since 1991, when a dictatorial regime was overthrown; the National Communications Law was passed in October 2017, aimed at setting a legal and regulatory framework for the telecoms sector, while provision was made in the following year to set up a regulatory authority to oversee the telecom sector; more recently, three types of licenses were mandated to provide clarity to operators, and to bring the market closer into line with international standards; all operators were given until August 2020 to secure one of the three license types; given the poor condition of fixed-line infrastructure, operators have concentrated on mobile connectivity; their investment plans have involved the development of LTE services to provide mobile data and broadband services; the telecom market has flourished; tariffs are among the lowest in Africa, and new cable systems coming on stream in the next few years, as well as planned investments from local operators to bolster the country's national fiber backbone, will lead to downward pressure on retail pricing; on the consumer side, spending on telecoms services and devices are under pressure from the financial effect of large-scale job losses and the consequent restriction on disposable incomes as the remnants of the impact of the Covid-19 pandemic remain and as global events, such as the Russian invasion of Ukraine, continue to play out; the market is continuing a positive growth trajectory, supported by a slow economic rebound in the country (2022)
domestic: seven networks compete for customers in the mobile sector; some of these mobile-service providers offer fixed-lines and Internet services; fixed-line is 0 per 100 and mobile-cellular roughly 51 per 100 (2019)
international: country code - 252; landing points for the G2A, DARE1, PEACE, and EASSy fiber-optic submarine cable system linking East Africa, Indian Ocean Islands, the Middle East, North Africa and Europe (2019)

Broadcast media: 2 private TV stations rebroadcast Al-Jazeera and CNN; Somaliland has 1 government-operated TV station and Puntland has 1 private TV station; the transitional government operates Radio Mogadishu; 1 SW and roughly 10 private FM radio stations broadcast in Mogadishu; several radio stations operate in central and southern regions; Somaliland has 1 government-operated radio station; Puntland has roughly a half-dozen private radio stations; transmissions of at least 2 international broadcasters are available (2019)

Internet country code: .so

Internet users: *total:* 308,858 (2019 est.)
percent of population: 2% (2019 est.)
country comparison to the world: 171

Broadband - fixed subscriptions: *total:* 119,000 (2020 est.)
subscriptions per 100 inhabitants: 1 (2020 est.)
country comparison to the world: 127

TRANSPORTATION

National air transport system: *number of registered air carriers:* 6 (2020)
inventory of registered aircraft operated by air carriers: 7
annual passenger traffic on registered air carriers: 4,486 (2018)

Civil aircraft registration country code prefix: 6O

Airports: *total:* 52 (2021)
country comparison to the world: 89

Airports - with paved runways: *total:* 8
over 3,047 m: 5
2,438 to 3,047 m: 1
1,524 to 2,437 m: 2 (2021)

Airports - with unpaved runways: *total:* 44
2,438 to 3,047 m: 5
1,524 to 2,437 m: 16
914 to 1,523 m: 22
under 914 m: 1 (2021)

Roadways: *total:* 15,000 km (2018)
country comparison to the world: 124

Merchant marine: *total:* 4
by type: general cargo 1, other 3 (2021)
country comparison to the world: 169

Ports and terminals: *major seaport(s):* Berbera, Kismaayo

MILITARY AND SECURITY

Military and security forces: Ministry of Defense: Somali National Army (SNA); Ministry of Internal Security: Somali National Police (SNP, includes a maritime unit and a Turkish-trained commando unit known as Harmacad, or Cheetah); National Security and Intelligence Agency (includes a commando/counterterrorism unit) (2022)
note 1: Somalia has numerous militia and regional forces operating throughout the country; these forces include ones that are clan- and warlord-based, semi-official paramilitary and special police forces (aka darwish), and externally-sponsored militias; the SNA is attempting to incorporate some of these militia units
note 2: Somaliland has army and naval forces under the Somaliland Ministry of Defense and Armed Forces

Military expenditures: 5.6% of GDP (2019 est.) (approximately $120 million)
6% of GDP (2018 est.) (approximately $120 million)
5.9% of GDP (2017 est.) (approximately $110 million)
6% of GDP (2016 est.) (approximately $110 million)
5.9% of GDP (2015 est.) (approximately $110 million)
country comparison to the world: 7

Military and security service personnel strengths: estimates vary widely due to inconsistent data and ongoing efforts to integrate various militias; up to 20,000 active-duty SNA personnel (2022)
note 1: in 2017, the Somali Government announced a plan for the SNA to eventually number about 18,000 troops; the same plan called for 32,000 federal and regional police
note 2: as of 2021, there were estimates of up to 50,000 militia forces operating in the country

Military equipment inventories and acquisitions: the SNA is lightly armed with an inventory that includes a variety of older, second-hand equipment largely from Italy, Russia, South Africa, and the UK; since 2015, it has received small quantities of second-hand equipment as aid/donations from a variety of countries (2022)
note: the UN Security Council imposed an arms embargo on Somalia in 1992 because of civil war and factional violence; the embargo was partially lifted in 2013 to help Somalia's security forces develop and fight Islamist militants; the remaining sanctions, which require requests for certain weapons to be approved, are renewed annually

Military service age and obligation: 18 is the legal minimum age for compulsory and voluntary military service; conscription is authorized but not currently utilized; women may volunteer (2021)
note: in 2019, the Federal Government of Somalia renewed its commitment to end the recruitment and use of child soldiers by signing a roadmap detailing measures and practical actions to prevent violations against children, release children associated with armed forces, and reintegrate them into communities; the signing followed a similar accord committed to ending the use of child soldiers signed by both the Somali Transitional Government and the UN in 2012

Military - note: as of 2022, the Somali National Army (SNA) and supporting security and militia forces were actively conducting operations against the al-Shabaab terrorist group (see Appendix T); al-Shabaab controlled large parts of southern and central Somalia

as of 2022, a significant portion of the SNA was comprised of militia forces that were assessed to lack the discipline, structure, weapons, and overall capabilities for effective military operations; of the SNA's approximately 13 brigades, the most effective were assessed to be the US-trained Danab ("Lightning") Advanced Infantry Brigade and those of the Turkish-trained Gorgor ("Eagle") Special Division; as of 2022, the Danab Brigade numbered about 1,500 troops with an eventual projected strength of 3,000, while the Gorgor Division was estimated to up to 5,000 trained troops; the Somali Government also sent some 5,000 recruits to Eritrea for military training; the troops returned in 2022

the African Union Mission in Somalia (AMISOM) operated in the country with the approval of the UN from 2007-2022; its peacekeeping mission included assisting Somali forces in providing security for a stable political process, enabling the gradual handing over of security responsibilities from AMISOM to the Somali security forces, and reducing the threat posed by al-Shabaab and other armed opposition groups; in April 2022, AMISOM was reconfigured and replaced with the AU Transition Mission in Somalia (ATMIS); the ATMIS mission is to support the Somalia Federal Government (FGS) in implementing the security objectives of the FGS's security transition plan, a comprehensive strategy developed by the FGS and its international partners in 2018 and updated in 2021 to gradually transfer security responsibilities from ATMIS to Somali security forces; ATMIS is projected to gradually reduce staffing from its 2022 level of about 20,000 personnel (civilians, military, and police) to zero by the end of 2024

UN Assistance Mission in Somalia (UNSOM; established 2013) is mandated by the Security Council to work with the FGS to support national reconciliation, provide advice on peace-building and state-building, monitor the human rights situation, and help coordinate the efforts of the international community; the UN Support Office in Somalia (UNSOS; established 2015) is responsible for providing logistical field support to ATMIS, UNSOM, and the Somali security forces on joint operations with ATMIS

the European Union Training Mission in Somalia (EUTM-S) has operated in the country since 2010; the EUTM provides advice and training to the Somali military; the US, UK, and Turkey maintain separate military training missions in Somalia (the US has also supported the SNA with air strikes); the UAE maintains a military presence in Somaliland (2022)

Maritime threats: the International Maritime Bureau's (IMB) Piracy Reporting Center (PRC) received one incident of piracy and armed robbery in 2021 for the Horn of Africa; while there were no recorded incidents, the IMB PRC warns that Somalia pirates continue to possess the capacity to carry out attacks in the Somali basin and wider Indian Ocean; in particular, the report warns that, "Masters and crew must remain vigilant and cautious when transiting these waters."; the presence of several naval task forces in the Gulf of Aden and additional anti-piracy measures on the part of ship operators, including the use of on-board armed security teams, contributed to the drop in incidents; the EU naval mission, Operation ATALANTA, continues its operations in the Gulf of Aden and Indian Ocean through 2022; naval units from China, India, Japan, Pakistan, South Korea, the US, and other countries also operate in conjunction with EU forces; China has established a logistical base in Djibouti to support its deployed naval units in the Horn of Africa

TERRORISM

Terrorist group(s): al-Shabaab; Islamic State of Iraq and ash-Sham – Somalia

TRANSNATIONAL ISSUES

Disputes - international: *Somalia-Djibouti:* none identified
Somalia-Ethiopia: Ethiopian forces invaded southern Somalia and routed Islamist Courts from Mogadishu in January 2007; the border between the Ogaden region of eastern Ethiopia, which is inhabited by ethnic Somalis, and Somalia is only partially demarcated under colonial rule and has been the source of tension for decades
Somalia-Kenya: Kenya works hard to prevent the clan and militia fighting in Somalia from spreading south across the border, which has long been open to nomadic pastoralists; in 2015, the Kenyan Government began building a wall along the border to prevent the crossborder movement of militant groups; the boundary separates ethnic Somalis; in October 2021, the Somalia-Kenya Indian Ocean boundary dispute was decided by the International Court of Justice; the ruling adjusted the boundary slightly north of Somalia's claim giving Somalia the majority of the contested maritime territory, which is believed to contain rich oil and natural gas deposits; while the decision is legally binding, it has no enforcement mechanism, and Kenya has said it will not abide by it

Refugees and internally displaced persons: *refugees (country of origin):* 9,208 (Yemen) (2022)

IDPs: 2.968 million (civil war since 1988, clan-based competition for resources; famine; insecurity because of fighting between al-Shabaab and the Transitional Federal Government's allied forces) (2022)

SOUTH AFRICA

INTRODUCTION

Background: Some of the earliest human remains in the fossil record are found in South Africa. By about A.D. 500, Bantu speaking groups began settling into what is now northeastern South Africa displacing Khoisan speaking groups to the southwest. Dutch traders landed at the southern tip of present-day South Africa in 1652 and established a stopover point on the spice route between the Netherlands and the Far East, founding the city of Cape Town. After the British seized the Cape of Good Hope area in 1806, many of the settlers of Dutch descent (Afrikaners, also called "Boers" (farmers) at the time) trekked north to found their own republics, Transvaal and Orange Free State. In the 1820s, several decades of wars began as the Zulus expanded their territory, moving out of what is today southeastern South Africa and clashing with other indigenous peoples and with expanding European settlements. The discovery of diamonds (1867) and gold (1886) spurred wealth and immigration from Europe.

The Anglo-Zulu War (1879) resulted in the incorporation of the Zulu kingdom's territory into the British Empire. Subsequently, the Afrikaner republics were incorporated into the British Empire after their defeat in the Second South African War (1899-1902). However, the British and the Afrikaners ruled together beginning in 1910 under the Union of South Africa, which became a republic in 1961 after a Whites-only referendum. In 1948, the National Party was voted into power and instituted a policy of apartheid – billed as "separate development" of the races - which favored the White minority at the expense of the Black majority and other non-White groups. The African National Congress (ANC) led the opposition to apartheid and many top ANC leaders, such as Nelson MANDELA, spent decades in South Africa's prisons. Internal protests and insurgency, as well as boycotts by some Western nations and institutions, led to the regime's eventual willingness to negotiate a peaceful transition to majority rule.

The first multi-racial elections in 1994 following the end of apartheid ushered in majority rule under an ANC-led government. South Africa has since struggled to address apartheid-era imbalances in wealth, housing, education, and health care. Jacob ZUMA became president in 2009 and was reelected in 2014, but resigned in February 2018 after numerous corruption scandals and gains by opposition parties in municipal elections in 2016. His successor, Cyril RAMAPHOSA, has made some progress in reigning in corruption, though many challenges persist. In May 2019 national elections, the country's sixth since the end of apartheid, the ANC won a majority of parliamentary seats, delivering RAMAPHOSA a five-year term.

GEOGRAPHY

Location: Southern Africa, at the southern tip of the continent of Africa

Geographic coordinates: 29 00 S, 24 00 E

Map references: Africa

Area: *total:* 1,219,090 sq km
land: 1,214,470 sq km
water: 4,620 sq km

note: includes Prince Edward Islands (Marion Island and Prince Edward Island)
country comparison to the world: 26

Area - comparative: slightly less than twice the size of Texas

Land boundaries: *total:* 5,244 km
border countries (6): Botswana 1,969 km; Lesotho 1,106 km; Mozambique 496 km; Namibia 1,005 km; Eswatini 438 km; Zimbabwe 230 km

Coastline: 2,798 km

Maritime claims: *territorial sea:* 12 nm
contiguous zone: 24 nm
exclusive economic zone: 200 nm
continental shelf: 200 nm or to edge of the continental margin

Climate: mostly semiarid; subtropical along east coast; sunny days, cool nights

Terrain: vast interior plateau rimmed by rugged hills and narrow coastal plain

Elevation: *highest point:* Ntheledi (Mafadi) 3,450 m
lowest point: Atlantic Ocean 0 m
mean elevation: 1,034 m

Natural resources: gold, chromium, antimony, coal, iron ore, manganese, nickel, phosphates, tin, rare earth elements, uranium, gem diamonds, platinum, copper, vanadium, salt, natural gas

Land use: *agricultural land:* 79.4% (2018 est.)
arable land: 9.9% (2018 est.)
permanent crops: 0.3% (2018 est.)
permanent pasture: 69.2% (2018 est.)
forest: 7.6% (2018 est.)
other: 13% (2018 est.)

Irrigated land: 16,700 sq km (2012)

Major rivers (by length in km): Orange (shared with Lesotho [s], and Namibia [m]) - 2,092 km; Limpopo river source (shared with Botswana, Zimbabwe, and Mozambique [m]) - 1,800 km; Vaal [s] - 1,210 km
note – [s] after country name indicates river source; [m] after country name indicates river mouth

Major watersheds (area sq km): Atlantic Ocean drainage: Orange (941,351 sq km)

Major aquifers: Karoo Basin, Lower Kalahari-Stampriet Basin

Population distribution: the population concentrated along the southern and southeastern coast, and inland around Pretoria; the eastern half of the country is more densly populated than the west as shown in this population distribution map

Natural hazards: prolonged droughts
volcanism: the volcano forming Marion Island in the Prince Edward Islands, which last erupted in 2004, is South Africa's only active volcano

Geography - note: South Africa completely surrounds Lesotho and almost completely surrounds Eswatini

PEOPLE AND SOCIETY

Population: 57,516,665 (2022 est.)
note: estimates for this country explicitly taken into account the impact of the HIV/AIDS epidemic
country comparison to the world: 26

Nationality: *noun:* South African(s)
adjective: South African

Ethnic groups: Black African 80.9%, Colored 8.8%, White 7.8%, Indian/Asian 2.6% (2021 est.)
note: colored is a term used in South Africa, including on the national census, for persons of mixed race ancestry who developed a distinct cultural identity over several hundred years

Languages: isiZulu (official) 25.3%, isiXhosa (official) 14.8%, Afrikaans (official) 12.2%, Sepedi (official) 10.1%, Setswana (official) 9.1%, English (official) 8.1%, Sesotho (official) 7.9%, Xitsonga (official) 3.6%, siSwati (official) 2.8%, Tshivenda (official) 2.5%, isiNdebele (official) 1.6%, other (includes Khoi, Nama, and San languages) 2%; note - data represent language spoken most often at home (2018 est.)
major-language sample(s):
Die Wereld Feite Boek, n' onontbeerlike bron vir basiese informasie. (Afrikaans)

Religions: Christian 86%, ancestral, tribal, animist, or other traditional African religions 5.4%, Muslim 1.9%, other 1.5%, nothing in particular 5.2% (2015 est.)

Demographic profile: South Africa's youthful population is gradually aging, as the country's total fertility rate (TFR) has declined dramatically from about 6 children per woman in the 1960s to roughly 2.2 in 2014. This pattern is similar to fertility trends in South Asia, the Middle East, and North Africa, and sets South Africa apart from the rest of Sub-Saharan Africa, where the average TFR remains higher than other regions of the world. Today, South Africa's decreasing number of reproductive age women is having fewer children, as women increase their educational attainment, workforce participation, and use of family planning methods; delay marriage; and opt for smaller families.

As the proportion of working-age South Africans has grown relative to children and the elderly, South Africa has been unable to achieve a demographic dividend because persistent high unemployment and the prevalence of HIV/AIDs have created a larger-than-normal dependent population. HIV/AIDS was also responsible for South Africa's average life expectancy plunging to less than 43 years in 2008; it has rebounded to 63 years as of 2017. HIV/AIDS continues to be a serious public health threat, although awareness- raising campaigns and the wider availability of anti-retroviral drugs is stabilizing the number of new cases, enabling infected individuals to live longer, healthier lives, and reducing mother-child transmissions.

Migration to South Africa began in the second half of the 17th century when traders from the Dutch East India Company settled in the Cape and started using slaves from South and southeast Asia (mainly from India but also from present-day Indonesia, Bangladesh, Sri Lanka, and Malaysia) and southeast Africa (Madagascar and Mozambique) as farm laborers and, to a lesser extent, as domestic servants. The Indian subcontinent remained the Cape Colony's main source of slaves in the early 18th century, while slaves were increasingly obtained from southeast Africa in the latter part of the 18th century and into the 19th century under British rule.

After slavery was completely abolished in the British Empire in 1838, South Africa's colonists turned to temporary African migrants and indentured labor through agreements with India and later China, countries that were anxious to export workers to alleviate domestic poverty and overpopulation. Of the more than 150,000 indentured Indian laborers hired to work in Natal's sugar plantations between 1860 and 1911, most exercised the right as British subjects to remain permanently (a small number of Indian immigrants came freely as merchants). Because of growing resentment toward Indian workers, the 63,000 indentured Chinese workers who mined gold in Transvaal between 1904 and 1911 were under more restrictive contracts and generally were forced to return to their homeland.

In the late 19th century and nearly the entire 20th century, South Africa's then British colonies' and Dutch states' enforced selective immigration policies that welcomed "assimilable" white Europeans as permanent residents but excluded or restricted other immigrants. Following the Union of South Africa's passage of a law in 1913 prohibiting Asian and other non-white immigrants and its elimination of the indenture system in 1917, temporary African contract laborers from neighboring countries became the dominant source of labor in the burgeoning mining industries. Others worked in agriculture and smaller numbers in manufacturing, domestic service, transportation, and construction. Throughout the 20th century, at least 40% of South Africa's miners were foreigners; the numbers peaked at over 80% in the late 1960s. Mozambique, Lesotho, Botswana, and Eswatini were the primary sources of miners, and Malawi and Zimbabwe were periodic suppliers.

Under apartheid, a "two gates" migration policy focused on policing and deporting illegal migrants rather than on managing migration to meet South Africa's development needs. The exclusionary 1991 Aliens Control Act limited labor recruitment to the highly skilled as defined by the ruling white minority, while bilateral labor agreements provided exemptions that enabled the influential mining industry and, to a lesser extent, commercial farms, to hire temporary, low-paid workers from neighboring states. Illegal African migrants were often tacitly allowed to work for low pay in other sectors but were always under threat of deportation.

The abolishment of apartheid in 1994 led to the development of a new inclusive national identity and the strengthening of the country's restrictive immigration policy. Despite South Africa's protectionist approach to immigration, the downsizing and closing of mines, and rising unemployment, migrants from across the continent believed that the country held work opportunities. Fewer African labor migrants were issued temporary work permits and, instead, increasingly entered South Africa with visitors' permits or came illegally, which drove growth in cross-border trade and the informal job market. A new wave of Asian immigrants has also arrived over the last two decades, many operating small retail businesses.

In the post-apartheid period, increasing numbers of highly skilled white workers emigrated, citing dissatisfaction with the political situation, crime, poor services, and a reduced quality of life. The 2002 Immigration Act and later amendments were intended to facilitate the temporary migration of skilled foreign labor to fill labor shortages, but instead the legislation continues to create regulatory obstacles. Although the education system has improved and brain drain has slowed in the wake of the 2008 global financial crisis, South Africa continues to face skills shortages in several key sectors, such as health care and technology.

South Africa's stability and economic growth has acted as a magnet for refugees and asylum seekers from nearby countries, despite the prevalence of discrimination and xenophobic violence. Refugees have included an estimated 350,000 Mozambicans during its 1980s civil war and, more recently, several thousand Somalis, Congolese, and Ethiopians. Nearly all of the tens of thousands of Zimbabweans who have applied for asylum in South Africa have been categorized as economic migrants and denied refuge.

Age structure: *0-14 years:* 27.94% (male 7,894,742/female 7,883,266)
15-24 years: 16.8% (male 4,680,587/female 4,804,337)
25-54 years: 42.37% (male 12,099,441/female 11,825,193)
55-64 years: 6.8% (male 1,782,902/female 2,056,988)
65 years and over: 6.09% (male 1,443,956/female 1,992,205) (2020 est.)

Dependency ratios: *total dependency ratio:* 52.2
youth dependency ratio: 43.8
elderly dependency ratio: 8.4
potential support ratio: 11.9 (2020 est.)

Median age: *total:* 28 years
male: 27.9 years
female: 28.1 years (2020 est.)
country comparison to the world: 142

Population growth rate: 0.93% (2022 est.)
country comparison to the world: 103

Birth rate: 18.56 births/1,000 population (2022 est.)
country comparison to the world: 77

Death rate: 9.26 deaths/1,000 population (2022 est.)
country comparison to the world: 52

Net migration rate: 0 migrant(s)/1,000 population (2022 est.)
country comparison to the world: 98

Population distribution: the population concentrated along the southern and southeastern coast, and inland around Pretoria; the eastern half of the country is more densly populated than the west as shown in this population distribution map

Urbanization: *urban population:* 68.3% of total population (2022)
rate of urbanization: 1.72% annual rate of change (2020-25 est.)

Major urban areas - population: 10.110 million Johannesburg (includes Ekurhuleni), 4.801 million Cape Town (legislative capital), 3.199 million Durban, 2.74 million PRETORIA (administrative capital), 1.281 million Port Elizabeth, 909,000 West Rand (2022)

Sex ratio: *at birth:* 1.02 male(s)/female
0-14 years: 1 male(s)/female
15-24 years: 0.98 male(s)/female
25-54 years: 1.02 male(s)/female
55-64 years: 0.87 male(s)/female
65 years and over: 0.58 male(s)/female
total population: 0.98 male(s)/female (2022 est.)

Maternal mortality ratio: 119 deaths/100,000 live births (2017 est.)
country comparison to the world: 66

Infant mortality rate: *total:* 25.87 deaths/1,000 live births
male: 28.86 deaths/1,000 live births
female: 22.82 deaths/1,000 live births (2022 est.)
country comparison to the world: 64

Life expectancy at birth: *total population:* 65.32 years
male: 63.99 years
female: 66.68 years (2022 est.)
country comparison to the world: 202

Total fertility rate: 2.18 children born/woman (2022 est.)
country comparison to the world: 90

Contraceptive prevalence rate: 54.6% (2016)

Drinking water source: *improved: urban:* 99.7% of population
rural: 90.3% of population
total: 96.7% of population
unimproved: urban: 0.3% of population
rural: 9.7% of population
total: 3.3% of population (2020 est.)

Current health expenditure: 9.1% of GDP (2019)

Physicians density: 0.79 physicians/1,000 population (2019)

Sanitation facility access: *improved: urban:* 96.6% of population
rural: 86.4% of population
total: 93.2% of population
unimproved: urban: 3.4% of population
rural: 13.6% of population
total: 6.8% of population (2020 est.)

HIV/AIDS - adult prevalence rate: 19.1% (2020 est.)
country comparison to the world: 4

HIV/AIDS - people living with HIV/AIDS: 7.8 million (2020 est.)
country comparison to the world: 1

HIV/AIDS - deaths: 83,000 (2020 est.)
country comparison to the world: 1

Major infectious diseases: *degree of risk:* intermediate (2020)
food or waterborne diseases: bacterial diarrhea, hepatitis A, and typhoid fever
water contact diseases: schistosomiasis
note: widespread ongoing transmission of a respiratory illness caused by the novel coronavirus (COVID-19) is occurring throughout South Africa; as of 18 August 2022, South Africa has reported a total of 4,008,988 cases of COVID-19 or 6,759.52 cumulative cases of COVID-19 per 100,000 population with a total of 101,982 cumulative deaths or a rate of 171.95 cumulative deaths per 100,000 population; as of 17 August 2022, 37.4% of the population has received at least one dose of COVID-19 vaccine

Obesity - adult prevalence rate: 28.3% (2016)
country comparison to the world: 31

Alcohol consumption per capita: *total:* 7.21 liters of pure alcohol (2019 est.)
beer: 3.99 liters of pure alcohol (2019 est.)
wine: 1.21 liters of pure alcohol (2019 est.)
spirits: 1.31 liters of pure alcohol (2019 est.)
other alcohols: 0.7 liters of pure alcohol (2019 est.)
country comparison to the world: 58

Tobacco use: *total:* 20.3% (2020 est.)
male: 34% (2020 est.)
female: 6.5% (2020 est.)
country comparison to the world: 84

Children under the age of 5 years underweight: 5.5% (2017)
country comparison to the world: 74

Child marriage: *women married by age 15:* 0.9%
women married by age 18: 3.6%
men married by age 18: 0.6% (2016 est.)

Education expenditures: 6.8% of GDP (2020 est.)
country comparison to the world: 22

Literacy: *definition:* age 15 and over can read and write
total population: 95%
male: 95.5%
female: 94.5% (2019)

School life expectancy (primary to tertiary education): *total:* 14 years
male: 13 years
female: 14 years (2019)

Unemployment, youth ages 15-24: *total:* 59.4%
male: 55.4%
female: 64.1% (2020 est.)

ENVIRONMENT

Environment - current issues: lack of important arterial rivers or lakes requires extensive water conservation and control measures; growth in water usage outpacing supply; pollution of rivers from agricultural runoff and urban discharge; air pollution resulting in acid rain; deforestation; soil erosion; land degradation; desertification; solid waste pollution; disruption of fragile ecosystem has resulted in significant floral extinctions

Environment - international agreements: *party to:* Antarctic-Environmental Protection, Antarctic-Marine Living Resources, Antarctic Seals, Antarctic Treaty, Biodiversity, Climate Change, Climate Change-Kyoto Protocol, Climate Change-Paris Agreement, Comprehensive Nuclear Test Ban, Desertification, Endangered Species, Hazardous Wastes, Law of the Sea, Marine Dumping-London Convention, Marine Dumping-London Protocol, Marine Life Conservation, Nuclear Test Ban, Ozone Layer Protection, Ship Pollution, Wetlands, Whaling
signed, but not ratified: none of the selected agreements

Air pollutants: *particulate matter emissions:* 23.58 micrograms per cubic meter (2016 est.)
carbon dioxide emissions: 476.64 megatons (2016 est.)
methane emissions: 55.89 megatons (2020 est.)

Climate: mostly semiarid; subtropical along east coast; sunny days, cool nights

Land use: *agricultural land:* 79.4% (2018 est.)
arable land: 9.9% (2018 est.)
permanent crops: 0.3% (2018 est.)
permanent pasture: 69.2% (2018 est.)
forest: 7.6% (2018 est.)
other: 13% (2018 est.)

Urbanization: *urban population:* 68.3% of total population (2022)
rate of urbanization: 1.72% annual rate of change (2020-25 est.)

Revenue from coal: *coal revenues:* 2.4% of GDP (2018 est.)
country comparison to the world: 3

Waste and recycling: *municipal solid waste generated annually:* 18,457,232 tons (2011 est.)
municipal solid waste recycled annually: 5,168,025 tons (2011 est.)
percent of municipal solid waste recycled: 28% (2011 est.)

Major rivers (by length in km): Orange (shared with Lesotho [s], and Namibia [m]) - 2,092 km; Limpopo river source (shared with Botswana, Zimbabwe, and Mozambique [m]) - 1,800 km; Vaal [s] - 1,210 km
note – [s] after country name indicates river source; [m] after country name indicates river mouth

Major watersheds (area sq km): Atlantic Ocean drainage: Orange (941,351 sq km)

Major aquifers: Karoo Basin, Lower Kalahari-Stampriet Basin

Total water withdrawal: *municipal:* 3.89 billion cubic meters (2017 est.)
industrial: 4.1 billion cubic meters (2017 est.)
agricultural: 11.39 billion cubic meters (2017 est.)

Total renewable water resources: 51.35 billion cubic meters (2017 est.)

GOVERNMENT

Country name: *conventional long form:* Republic of South Africa
conventional short form: South Africa
former: Union of South Africa
abbreviation: RSA
etymology: self-descriptive name from the country's location on the continent; "Africa" is derived from the Roman designation of the area corresponding to present-day Tunisia "Africa terra," which meant "Land of the Afri" (the tribe resident in that area), but which eventually came to mean the entire continent

Government type: parliamentary republic

Capital: *name:* Pretoria (administrative capital); Cape Town (legislative capital); Bloemfontein (judicial capital)
geographic coordinates: 25 42 S, 28 13 E
time difference: UTC+2 (7 hours ahead of Washington, DC, during Standard Time)
etymology: Pretoria is named in honor of Andries PRETORIUS, the father of voortrekker (pioneer) leader Marthinus PRETORIUS; Cape Town reflects its location on the Cape of Good Hope; Bloemfontein is a combination of the Dutch words *bloem* (flower) and *fontein* (fountain) meaning "fountain of flowers"

Administrative divisions: 9 provinces; Eastern Cape, Free State, Gauteng, KwaZulu-Natal, Limpopo, Mpumalanga, Northern Cape, North West, Western Cape

Independence: 31 May 1910 (Union of South Africa formed from four British colonies: Cape Colony, Natal, Transvaal, and Orange Free State); 22 August 1934 (Status of the Union Act); 31 May 1961 (republic declared); 27 April 1994 (majority rule)

National holiday: Freedom Day, 27 April (1994)

Constitution: *history:* several previous; latest drafted 8 May 1996, approved by the Constitutional Court 4 December 1996, effective 4 February 1997
amendments: proposed by the National Assembly of Parliament; passage of amendments affecting constitutional sections on human rights and freedoms, non-racism and non-sexism, supremacy of the constitution, suffrage, the multiparty system of democratic government, and amendment procedures requires at least 75% majority vote of the Assembly, approval by at least six of the nine provinces represented in the National Council of Provinces, and assent of the president of the republic; passage of amendments affecting the Bill of Rights, and those related to provincial boundaries, powers, and authorities requires at least two-thirds majority vote of the Assembly, approval by at least six of the nine provinces represented in the National Council, and assent of the president; amended many times, last in 2020

Legal system: mixed legal system of Roman-Dutch civil law, English common law, and customary law

International law organization participation: has not submitted an ICJ jurisdiction declaration; accepts ICCt jurisdiction

Citizenship: *citizenship by birth:* no
citizenship by descent only: at least one parent must be a citizen of South Africa
dual citizenship recognized: yes, but requires prior permission of the government
residency requirement for naturalization: 5 year

Suffrage: 18 years of age; universal

Executive branch: *chief of state:* President Matamela Cyril RAMAPHOSA (since 15 February 2018); Deputy President David MABUZA (26 February 2018); note - the president is both chief of state and head of government; note- Jacob ZUMA resigned on 14 February 2018
head of government: President Matamela Cyril RAMAPHOSA (since 15 February 2018); deputy president David MABUZA (26 February 2018
cabinet: Cabinet appointed by the president
elections/appointments: president indirectly elected by the National Assembly for a 5-year term (eligible for a second term); election last held on 22 May 2019 (next to be held in May 2024) (2019)
election results:
Matamela Cyril RAMAPHOSA (ANC) elected president by the National Assembly unopposed

Legislative branch: *description:* bicameral Parliament consists of:
National Council of Provinces (90 seats; nine 10-member delegations, each with 6 permanent delegates and 4 special delegates, appointed by each of the 9 provincial legislatures to serve 5-year terms; note - the Council has special powers to protect regional interests, including safeguarding cultural and linguistic traditions among ethnic minorities)
National Assembly (400 seats; half the members directly elected in multi-seat constituencies and half in a single nationwide constituency, both by proportional representation popular vote; members serve 5-year terms)
elections:
National Council of Provinces and National Assembly - last held on 8 May 2019 (next to be held in 2024)
election results:
National Council of Provinces - percent of vote by party - NA; seats by party - ANC 29, DA 13, EFF 9, FF+ 2, IFP 1; composition of permanent members - men 34, women 20, percent of women 37%; note - 36 appointed members not filled
National Assembly - percent of vote by party - ANC 57.5%, DA 20.8%, EFF 10.8%, IFP 3.8%, FF+ 2.4%, other 4.7%; seats by party - ANC 230, DA 84, EFF 44, IFP 14, FF+ 10, other 18; composition as of mid-2022 (396 current seats) - men 212, women 184, percent of women 46.5%; note overall Parliament percent of women 45.3%

Judicial branch: *highest court(s):* Supreme Court of Appeals (consists of the court president, deputy president, and 21 judges); Constitutional Court (consists of the chief and deputy chief justices and 9 judges)
judge selection and term of office: Supreme Court of Appeals president and vice president appointed by the national president after consultation with the Judicial Services Commission (JSC), a 23-member body chaired by the chief justice and includes other judges and judicial executives, members of parliament, practicing lawyers and advocates, a teacher of law, and several members designated by the president of South Africa; other Supreme Court judges appointed by the national president on the advice of the JSC and hold office until discharged from active service by an Act of Parliament; Constitutional Court chief and deputy chief justices appointed by the president of South Africa after consultation with the JSC and with heads of the National Assembly; other Constitutional Court judges appointed by the national president after consultation with the chief justice and leaders of the National Assembly; Constitutional Court judges serve 12-year nonrenewable terms or until age 70
subordinate courts: High Courts; Magistrates' Courts; labor courts; land claims courts

Political parties and leaders: African Christian Democratic Party or ACDP [Kenneth MESHOE]
African Independent Congress or AIC [Mandla GALO]
African National Congress or ANC [Cyril RAMAPHOSA]
African People's Convention or APC [Themba GODI]
Agang SA [Andries TLOUAMMA]
Congress of the People or COPE [Mosiuoa LEKOTA]
Democratic Alliance or DA [John STEENHUISEN]
Economic Freedom Fighters or EFF [Julius Sello MALEMA]
Freedom Front Plus or FF+ [Pieter GROENEWALD]
GOOD [Patricia de LILLE]
Inkatha Freedom Party or IFP [Velenkosini HLABISA]
National Freedom Party or NFP [vacant]
Pan-Africanist Congress of Azania or PAC [Mzwanele NYHONTSO]
United Christian Democratic Party or UCDP [Modiri Desmond SEHUME]
United Democratic Movement or UDM [Bantu HOLOMISA]

International organization participation: ACP, AfDB, AU, BIS, BRICS, C, CD, FAO, FATF, G-20, G-24, G-5, G-77, IAEA, IBRD, ICAO, ICC (national committees), ICCt, ICRM, IDA, IFAD, IFC, IFRCS, IHO, ILO, IMF, IMO, IMSO, Interpol, IOC, IOM, IPU, ISO, ITSO, ITU, ITUC (NGOs), MIGA, MONUSCO, NAM, NSG, OECD (enhanced engagement), OPCW, Paris Club (associate), PCA, SACU, SADC, UN, UNAMID, UNCTAD, UNESCO, UNHCR, UNIDO, UNISFA, UNITAR, UNWTO, UPU, Wassenaar Arrangement, WCO, WFTU (NGOs), WHO, WIPO, WMO, WTO, ZC

Diplomatic representation in the US: *chief of mission:* Ambassador Nomaindiya MFEKETO (since 8 April 2020)
chancery: 3051 Massachusetts Avenue NW, Washington, DC 20008
telephone: [1] (202) 232-4400
FAX: [1] (202) 265-1607; [1] (202) 387-9854
email address and website:
https://www.saembassy.org/
consulate(s) general: Chicago, Los Angeles, New York

Diplomatic representation from the US: *chief of mission:* Ambassador Reuben E. BRIGETY II (since 11 August 2022)
embassy: 877 Pretorius Street, Arcadia, Pretoria
mailing address: 9300 Pretoria Place, Washington DC 20521-9300
telephone: [27] (12) 431-4000
FAX: [27] (12) 342-2299

email address and website:
ACSJohannesburg@state.gov
https://za.usembassy.gov/
consulate(s) general: Cape Town, Durban, Johannesburg

Flag description: two equal width horizontal bands of red (top) and blue separated by a central green band that splits into a horizontal Y, the arms of which end at the corners of the hoist side; the Y embraces a black isosceles triangle from which the arms are separated by narrow yellow bands; the red and blue bands are separated from the green band and its arms by narrow white stripes; the flag colors do not have any official symbolism, but the Y stands for the "convergence of diverse elements within South African society, taking the road ahead in unity"; black, yellow, and green are found on the flag of the African National Congress, while red, white, and blue are the colors in the flags of the Netherlands and the UK, whose settlers ruled South Africa during the colonial era
note: the South African flag is one of only two national flags to display six colors as part of its primary design, the other is South Sudan's

National symbol(s): springbok (antelope), king protea flower; national colors: red, green, blue, yellow, black, white

National anthem: *name:* "National Anthem of South Africa"
lyrics/music: Enoch SONTONGA and Cornelius Jacob LANGENHOVEN/Enoch SONTONGA and Marthinus LOURENS de Villiers
note: adopted 1994; a combination of "N'kosi Sikelel' iAfrica" (God Bless Africa) and "Die Stem van Suid Afrika" (The Call of South Africa), which were respectively the anthems of the non-white and white communities under apartheid; official lyrics contain a mixture of Xhosa, Zulu, Sesotho, Afrikaans, and English (i.e., the five most widely spoken of South Africa's 11 official languages); music incorporates the melody used in the Tanzanian and Zambian anthems

National heritage: *total World Heritage Sites:* 10 (5 cultural, 4 natural, 1 mixed)
selected World Heritage Site locales: Fossil Hominid Sites of South Africa (c); iSimangaliso Wetland Park (n); Robben Island (c); Maloti-Drakensberg Park (m); Mapungubwe Cultural Landscape (c); Cape Floral Region Protected Areas (n); Vredefort Dome (n); Richtersveld Cultural and Botanical Landscape (c); Khomani Cultural Landscape (c); Barberton Makhonjwa Mountains (n)

ECONOMY

Economic overview: South Africa is a middle-income emerging market with an abundant supply of natural resources; well-developed financial, legal, communications, energy, and transport sectors; and a stock exchange that is Africa's largest and among the top 20 in the world.

Economic growth has decelerated in recent years, slowing to an estimated 0.7% in 2017. Unemployment, poverty, and inequality - among the highest in the world - remain a challenge. Official unemployment is roughly 27% of the workforce, and runs significantly higher among black youth. Even though the country's modern infrastructure supports a relatively efficient distribution of goods to major urban centers throughout the region, unstable electricity supplies retard growth. Eskom, the state-run power company, is building three new power stations and is installing new power demand management programs to improve power grid reliability but has been plagued with accusations of mismanagement and corruption and faces an increasingly high debt burden.

South Africa's economic policy has focused on controlling inflation while empowering a broader economic base; however, the country faces structural constraints that also limit economic growth, such as skills shortages, declining global competitiveness, and frequent work stoppages due to strike action. The government faces growing pressure from urban constituencies to improve the delivery of basic services to low-income areas, to increase job growth, and to provide university level-education at affordable prices. Political infighting among South Africa's ruling party and the volatility of the rand risks economic growth. International investors are concerned about the country's long-term economic stability; in late 2016, most major international credit ratings agencies downgraded South Africa's international debt to junk bond status.

Real GDP (purchasing power parity): $680.04 billion (2020 est.)
$730.91 billion (2019 est.)
$729.8 billion (2018 est.)
note: data are in 2017 dollars
country comparison to the world: 33

Real GDP growth rate: 0.06% (2019 est.)
0.7% (2018 est.)
1.4% (2017 est.)
country comparison to the world: 190

Real GDP per capita: $11,500 (2020 est.)
$12,500 (2019 est.)
$12,600 (2018 est.)
note: data are in 2017 dollars
country comparison to the world: 131

GDP (official exchange rate): $350.032 billion (2019 est.)

Inflation rate (consumer prices): 4.1% (2019 est.)
4.6% (2018 est.)
5.2% (2017 est.)
country comparison to the world: 170

Credit ratings:

Fitch rating: BB- (2020)

Moody's rating: Ba2 (2020)

Standard & Poors rating: BB- (2020)

GDP - composition, by sector of origin: *agriculture:* 2.8% (2017 est.)
industry: 29.7% (2017 est.)
services: 67.5% (2017 est.)

GDP - composition, by end use: *household consumption:* 59.4% (2017 est.)
government consumption: 20.9% (2017 est.)
investment in fixed capital: 18.7% (2017 est.)
investment in inventories: -0.1% (2017 est.)
exports of goods and services: 29.8% (2017 est.)
imports of goods and services: -28.4% (2017 est.)

Agricultural products: sugar cane, maize, milk, potatoes, grapes, poultry, oranges, wheat, soybeans, beef

Industries: mining (world's largest producer of platinum, gold, chromium), automobile assembly, metalworking, machinery, textiles, iron and steel, chemicals, fertilizer, foodstuffs, commercial ship repair

Industrial production growth rate: 1.2% (2017 est.)
country comparison to the world: 151

Labor force: 14.687 million (2020 est.)
country comparison to the world: 36

Labor force - by occupation: *agriculture:* 4.6%
industry: 23.5%
services: 71.9% (2014 est.)

Unemployment rate: 28.53% (2019 est.)
27.09% (2018 est.)
country comparison to the world: 205

Unemployment, youth ages 15-24: *total:* 59.4%
male: 55.4%
female: 64.1% (2020 est.)
country comparison to the world: 2

Population below poverty line: 55.5% (2014 est.)

Gini Index coefficient - distribution of family income: 63 (2014 est.)
63.4 (2011 est.)
country comparison to the world: 1

Household income or consumption by percentage share: *lowest 10%:* 1.2%
highest 10%: 51.3% (2011 est.)

Budget: *revenues:* 92.86 billion (2017 est.)
expenditures: 108.3 billion (2017 est.)

Budget surplus (+) or deficit (-): -4.4% (of GDP) (2017 est.)
country comparison to the world: 163

Public debt: 53% of GDP (2017 est.)
51.6% of GDP (2016 est.)
country comparison to the world: 92

Taxes and other revenues: 26.6% (of GDP) (2017 est.)
country comparison to the world: 107

Fiscal year: 1 April - 31 March

Current account balance: -$10.626 billion (2019 est.)
-$13.31 billion (2018 est.)
country comparison to the world: 191

Exports: $93.01 billion (2020 est.) note: data are in current year dollars
$104.85 billion (2019 est.) note: data are in current year dollars
$110.07 billion (2018 est.) note: data are in current year dollars
country comparison to the world: 42

Exports - partners: China 15%, United Kingdom 8%, Germany 7%, United States 6%, India 6% (2019)

Exports - commodities: gold, platinum, cars, iron products, coal, manganese, diamonds (2019)

Imports: $77.86 billion (2020 est.) note: data are in current year dollars
$103.12 billion (2019 est.) note: data are in current year dollars
$108.91 billion (2018 est.) note: data are in current year dollars
country comparison to the world: 45

Imports - partners: China 18%, Germany 11%, United States 6%, India 5% (2019)

Imports - commodities: crude petroleum, refined petroleum, cars and vehicle parts, gold, broadcasting equipment (2019)

Reserves of foreign exchange and gold: $50.72 billion (31 December 2017 est.)
$47.23 billion (31 December 2016 est.)
country comparison to the world: 39

Debt - external: $179.871 billion (2019 est.)
$173.714 billion (2018 est.)
country comparison to the world: 43

Exchange rates: rand (ZAR) per US dollar -
14.9575 (2020 est.)

14.64 (2019 est.)
14.05125 (2018 est.)
12.7581 (2014 est.)
10.8469 (2013 est.)

ENERGY

Electricity access: *electrification - total population:* 94% (2019)
electrification - urban areas: 95% (2019)
electrification - rural areas: 92% (2019)

Electricity: *installed generating capacity:* 62.728 million kW (2020 est.)
consumption: 202,285,870,000 kWh (2019 est.)
exports: 14.482 billion kWh (2019 est.)
imports: 7.823 billion kWh (2019 est.)
transmission/distribution losses: 22.904 billion kWh (2019 est.)

Electricity generation sources: *fossil fuels:* 87.9% of total installed capacity (2020 est.)
nuclear: 5.2% of total installed capacity (2020 est.)
solar: 1.6% of total installed capacity (2020 est.)
wind: 2.6% of total installed capacity (2020 est.)
hydroelectricity: 2.5% of total installed capacity (2020 est.)
biomass and waste: 0.2% of total installed capacity (2020 est.)

Coal: *production:* 248.388 million metric tons (2020 est.)
consumption: 170.308 million metric tons (2020 est.)
exports: 74.965 million metric tons (2020 est.)
imports: 2.054 million metric tons (2020 est.)
proven reserves: 9.893 billion metric tons (2019 est.)

Petroleum: *total petroleum production:* 97,900 bbl/day (2021 est.)
refined petroleum consumption: 622,500 bbl/day (2019 est.)
crude oil and lease condensate exports: 9,000 bbl/day (2018 est.)
crude oil and lease condensate imports: 397,700 bbl/day (2018 est.)
crude oil estimated reserves: 15 million barrels (2021 est.)

Refined petroleum products - production: 487,100 bbl/day (2015 est.)
country comparison to the world: 33

Refined petroleum products - exports: 105,600 bbl/day (2015 est.)
country comparison to the world: 42

Refined petroleum products - imports: 195,200 bbl/day (2015 est.)
country comparison to the world: 34

Natural gas: *production:* 1,229,544,000 cubic meters (2019 est.)
consumption: 4,771,551,000 cubic meters (2019 est.)
exports: 0 cubic meters (2021 est.)
imports: 3,542,007,000 cubic meters (2019 est.)
proven reserves: 0 cubic meters (2021 est.)

Carbon dioxide emissions: 470.358 million metric tonnes of CO_2 (2019 est.)
from coal and metallurgical coke: 387.835 million metric tonnes of CO_2 (2019 est.)
from petroleum and other liquids: 73.163 million metric tonnes of CO_2 (2019 est.)
from consumed natural gas: 9.361 million metric tonnes of CO_2 (2019 est.)
country comparison to the world: 12

Energy consumption per capita: 98.474 million Btu/person (2019 est.)
country comparison to the world: 61

COMMUNICATIONS

Telephones - fixed lines: *total subscriptions:* 2,098,802 (2020 est.)
subscriptions per 100 inhabitants: 4 (2020 est.)
country comparison to the world: 55

Telephones - mobile cellular: *total subscriptions:* 96,972,500 (2019)
subscriptions per 100 inhabitants: 165.6 (2019)
country comparison to the world: 17

Telecommunication systems: *general assessment:* South Africa's telecom sector boasts one of the most advanced infrastructures on the continent; the focus in recent years has been on back haul capacity and on fiber and LTE networks to extend and improve internet service connectivity; with the ongoing migration to fiber, the incumbent telco expects to close down its copper network in 2024; the mobile sector has developed strongly in recent years, partly due to the poor availability and level of service of fixed-line networks, which meant that many people had no alternative to mobile networks for voice and data services; the multi-spectrum auction was delayed several times due to legal wrangling, and was finally held in March 2022; the delay caused difficulties for network operators, which were forced to reform spectrum for 3G and LTE use, and provide 5G services on temporary licenses; six qualified bidders acquired spectrum, netting the regulator ZAR14.4 billion in revenues; the market is shrugging off the impact of the pandemic, which had a significant impact on production and supply chains globally, and saw a slowdown in some network expansions, particularly around 5G; on the consumer side, spending on telecoms services and devices remains slightly under pressure amid ongoing macroeconomic challenges facing the country; the crucial nature of telecom services, both for general communication as well as a tool for homeworking, will offset such pressures; in many markets the net effect should be a steady though reduced increase in subscriber growth (2022)
domestic: fixed-line over 3 per 100 persons and mobile-cellular nearly 162 telephones per 100 persons; consists of carrier-equipped open-wire lines, coaxial cables, microwave radio relay links, fiber-optic cable, radiotelephone communication stations, and wireless local loops; key centers are Bloemfontein, Cape Town, Durban, Johannesburg, Port Elizabeth, and Pretoria (2020)
international: country code - 27; landing points for the WACS, ACE, SAFE, SAT-3, Equiano, SABR, SAEx1, SAEx2, IOX Cable System, METISS, EASSy, and SEACOM/ Tata TGN-Eurasia fiber-optic submarine cable systems connecting South Africa, East Africa, West Africa, Europe, Southeast Asia, Asia, South America, Indian Ocean Islands, and the US; satellite earth stations - 3 Intelsat (1 Indian Ocean and 2 Atlantic Ocean) (2019)

Broadcast media: the South African Broadcasting Corporation (SABC) operates 4 TV stations, 3 are free-to-air and 1 is pay TV; e.tv, a private station, is accessible to more than half the population; multiple subscription TV services provide a mix of local and international channels; well-developed mix of public and private radio stations at the national, regional, and local levels; the SABC radio network, state-owned and controlled but nominally independent, operates 18 stations, one for each of the 11 official languages, 4 community stations, and 3 commercial stations; more than 100 community-based stations extend coverage to rural areas

Internet country code: za

Internet users: *total:* 41,516,083 (2020 est.)
percent of population: 70% (2020 est.)
country comparison to the world: 23

Broadband - fixed subscriptions: *total:* 1,303,057 (2020 est.)
subscriptions per 100 inhabitants: 2 (2020 est.)
country comparison to the world: 68

TRANSPORTATION

National air transport system: *number of registered air carriers:* 17 (2020)
inventory of registered aircraft operated by air carriers: 243
annual passenger traffic on registered air carriers: 23,921,748 (2018)
annual freight traffic on registered air carriers: 716.25 million (2018) mt-km

Civil aircraft registration country code prefix: ZS

Airports: *total:* 407 (2021)
country comparison to the world: 20

Airports - with paved runways: *total:* 130
over 3,047 m: 11
2,438 to 3,047 m: 6
1,524 to 2,437 m: 46
914 to 1,523 m: 60
under 914 m: 7 (2021)

Airports - with unpaved runways: *total:* 277
2,438 to 3,047 m: 1
1,524 to 2,437 m: 19
914 to 1,523 m: 178
under 914 m: 79 (2021)

Pipelines: 94 km condensate, 1,293 km gas, 992 km oil, 1,460 km refined products (2013)

Railways: *total:* 20,986 km (2014)
standard gauge: 80 km (2014) 1.435-m gauge (80 km electrified)
narrow gauge: 19,756 km (2014) 1.065-m gauge (8,271 km electrified)
other: (2014) 1,150 km (passenger rail, gauge unspecified, 1,115.5 km electrified)
country comparison to the world: 14

Roadways: *total:* 750,000 km (2016)
paved: 158,124 km (2016)
unpaved: 591,876 km (2016)
country comparison to the world: 10

Merchant marine: *total:* 105
by type: bulk carrier 2, general cargo 1, oil tanker 7, other 95 (2021)
country comparison to the world: 86

Ports and terminals: *major seaport(s):* Cape Town, Durban, Port Elizabeth, Richards Bay, Saldanha Bay
container port(s) (TEUs): Durban (2,769,869) (2019)

LNG terminal(s) (import): Mossel Bay

MILITARY AND SECURITY

Military and security forces: South African National Defense Force (SANDF): South African Army (includes Reserve Force), South African Navy

(SAN), South African Air Force (SAAF), South African Military Health Services; Ministry of Police: South African Police Service (2022)
note: the South African Police Service includes a Special Task Force for counterterrorism, counterinsurgency, and hostage rescue operations

Military expenditures: 0.8% of GDP (2021 est.)
1.1% of GDP (2020)
1% of GDP (2019) (approximately $4.84 billion)
1% of GDP (2018) (approximately $4.86 billion)
1% of GDP (2017) (approximately $5.04 billion)
country comparison to the world: 146

Military and security service personnel strengths: approximately 75,000 active duty personnel (40,000 Army; 7,000 Navy; 10,000 Air Force; 8,000 Military Health Service; 10,000 other, including administrative, logistics, military police); 180,000 South African Police Service (2022)

Military equipment inventories and acquisitions: the SANDF's inventory consists of a mix of domestically-produced and foreign-supplied equipment; South Africa's domestic defense industry produced most of the Army's major weapons systems (some were jointly-produced with foreign companies), while the Air Force and Navy inventories include a mix of European-, Israeli-, and US-origin weapons systems; since 2010, Sweden has been the largest supplier of weapons to the SANDF (2021)

Military service age and obligation: 18-22 (18-26 for college graduates) years of age for voluntary military service for men and women; 2-year service obligation (2022)
note: in 2019, women comprised about 30% of the military

Military deployments: 1,150 Democratic Republic of the Congo (MONUSCO); up to 1,500 Mozambique (part of a Southern African Development Community force to help quell an insurgency) (2022)

Military - note: the SANDF was created in 1994 to replace the South African Defense Force (SADF); the SANDF was opened to all South Africans who met military requirements, while the SADF was a mostly white force (only whites were subject to conscription) with non-whites only allowed to join in a voluntary capacity; the SANDF also absorbed members of the guerrilla and militia forces of the various anti-apartheid opposition groups, including the African National Congress, the Pan Africanist Congress, and the Inkatha Freedom Party, as well as the security forces of the formerly independent Bantustan homelands; the SANDF is one of Africa's most capable militaries; over the past decade, however, its operational readiness and modernization programs have been hampered by funding shortfalls; it participates regularly in African and UN peacekeeping missions and has the ability to independently deploy throughout Africa (2022)

TERRORISM

Terrorist group(s): Islamic State of Iraq and ash-Sham (ISIS)

TRANSNATIONAL ISSUES

Disputes - international: *South Africa-Botswana:* none identified
South Africa-Eswatini: Eswatini seeks to reclaim land it says was stolen by South Africa
South Africa-Lesotho: crossborder livestock thieving, smuggling of drugs and arms, and illegal migration are problematic
South Africa-Mozambique: animal poachers cross the South Africa-Mozambique border to hunt wildlife in South Africa's Kruger National Park; border fences were removed in some areas to allow animals to roam between nature reserves in the two countries; improved patrols, technology, and crossborder cooperation are reducing the problem
South Africa-Namibia: the governments of South Africa and Namibia have not signed or ratified the text of the 1994 Surveyor's General agreement placing the boundary in the middle of the Orange River; the location of the border could affect diamond mining rights; South Africa has always claimed that the northern bank of the Orange River is the border between the two countries, while Namibia's constitution states that the border lies in the middle of the Orange River
South Africa-various: South Africa has placed military units to assist police operations along the border of Lesotho, Zimbabwe, and Mozambique to control smuggling, poaching, and illegal migration
South Africa-Zimbabwe: Zimbabweans migrate illegally into South Africa in search of work or smuggle goods to sell at a profit back home

Refugees and internally displaced persons: *refugees (country of origin):* 23,054 (Somalia), 15,629 (Ethiopia) (mid-year 2021); 56,080 (Democratic Republic of the Congo) (refugees and asylum seekers) (2022)

IDPs: 5,000 (2020)

Illicit drugs: leading regional importer of chemicals used in the production of illicit drugs especially synthetic drugs

SOUTH GEORGIA AND SOUTH SANDWICH ISLANDS

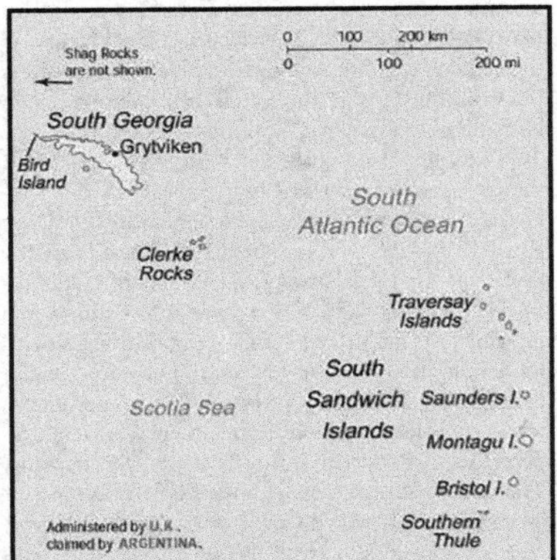

INTRODUCTION

Background: The islands, with large bird and seal populations, lie approximately 1,000 km east of the Falkland Islands and have been under British administration since 1908 - except for a brief period in 1982 when Argentina occupied them. Grytviken, on South Georgia, was a 19th and early 20th century whaling station. Famed explorer Ernest SHACKLETON stopped there in 1914 en route to his ill-fated attempt to cross Antarctica on foot. He returned some 20 months later with a few companions in a small boat and arranged a successful rescue for the rest of his crew, stranded off the Antarctic Peninsula. He died in 1922 on a subsequent expedition and is buried in Grytviken. Today, the station houses scientists from the British Antarctic Survey. Recognizing the importance of preserving the marine stocks in adjacent waters, the UK, in 1993, extended the exclusive fishing zone from 12 nm to 200 nm around each island.

GEOGRAPHY

Location: Southern South America, islands in the South Atlantic Ocean, east of the tip of South America

Geographic coordinates: 54 30 S, 37 00 W

Map references: Antarctic Region

Area: *total:* 3,903 sq km
land: 3,903 sq km
water: 0 sq km
note: includes Shag Rocks, Black Rock, Clerke Rocks, South Georgia Island, Bird Island, and the South Sandwich Islands, which consist of 11 islands
country comparison to the world: 176

Area - comparative: slightly larger than Rhode Island

Land boundaries: *total:* 0 km

Maritime claims: *territorial sea:* 12 nm
exclusive fishing zone: 200 nm

Climate: variable, with mostly westerly winds throughout the year interspersed with periods of calm; nearly all precipitation falls as snow

Terrain: most of the islands are rugged and mountainous rising steeply from the sea; South Georgia is largely barren with steep, glacier-covered mountains; the South Sandwich Islands are of volcanic origin with some active volcanoes

Elevation: *highest point:* Mount Paget (South Georgia) 2,934 m
lowest point: Atlantic Ocean 0 m

Natural resources: fish

Land use: *other:* 100% (2018 est.)

Irrigated land: 0 sq km (2011)

Natural hazards: the South Sandwich Islands have prevailing weather conditions that generally make them difficult to approach by ship; they are also subject to active volcanism

Geography - note: the north coast of South Georgia has several large bays, which provide good anchorage

PEOPLE AND SOCIETY

Population: (July 2021 est.) no indigenous inhabitants
note: the small military garrison on South Georgia withdrew in March 2001, replaced by a permanent group of scientists of the British Antarctic Survey, which also has a biological station on Bird Island; the South Sandwich Islands are uninhabited

Net migration rate: 5.9 migrant(s)/1,000 population
country comparison to the world: 16

ENVIRONMENT

Environment - current issues: reindeer - introduced to the islands in the 20th century - devastated the native flora and bird species; some reindeer were translocated to the Falkland Islands in 2001, the rest were exterminated (2013-14); a parallel effort (2010-15) eradicated rats and mice that came to the islands as stowaways on ships as early as the late 18th century

Climate: variable, with mostly westerly winds throughout the year interspersed with periods of calm; nearly all precipitation falls as snow

Land use: *other:* 100% (2018 est.)

GOVERNMENT

Country name: *conventional long form:* South Georgia and the South Sandwich Islands
conventional short form: South Georgia and South Sandwich Islands
abbreviation: SGSSI
etymology: South Georgia was named "the Isle of Georgia" in 1775 by Captain James COOK in honor of British King GEORGE III; the explorer also discovered the Sandwich Islands Group that year, which he named "Sandwich Land" after John MONTAGU, the Earl of Sandwich and First Lord of the Admiralty; the word "South" was later added to distinguish these islands from the other Sandwich Islands, now known as the Hawaiian Islands

Dependency status: overseas territory of the UK, also claimed by Argentina; administered from the Falkland Islands by a commissioner, who is concurrently governor of the Falkland Islands, representing King CHARLES III

Legal system: the laws of the UK, where applicable, apply

International organization participation: UPU

Diplomatic representation in the US: none (overseas territory of the UK, also claimed by Argentina)

Diplomatic representation from the US: none (overseas territory of the UK, also claimed by Argentina)

Flag description: blue with the flag of the UK in the upper hoist-side quadrant and the South Georgia and South Sandwich Islands coat of arms centered on the outer half of the flag; the coat of arms features a shield with a golden lion rampant, holding a torch; the shield is supported by a fur seal on the left and a Macaroni penguin on the right; a reindeer appears above the crest, and below the shield on a scroll is the motto LEO TERRAM PROPRIAM PROTEGAT (Let the Lion Protect its Own Land); the lion with the torch represents the UK and discovery; the background of the shield, blue and white estoiles, are found in the coat of arms of James Cook, discoverer of the islands; all the outer supporting animals represented are native to the islands

ECONOMY

Economic overview: Some fishing takes place in adjacent waters. Harvesting finfish and krill are potential sources of income. The islands receive income from postage stamps produced in the UK, the sale of fishing licenses, and harbor and landing fees from tourist vessels. Tourism from specialized cruise ships is increasing rapidly.

TRANSPORTATION

Ports and terminals: *major seaport(s):* Grytviken

MILITARY AND SECURITY

Military - note: defense is the responsibility of the UK

TRANSNATIONAL ISSUES

Disputes - international: *South Georgia and South Sandwich Islands (UK)-Argentina:* Argentina, which claims the islands in its constitution and briefly occupied them by force in 1982, agreed in 1995 to no longer seek settlement by force

SOUTH SUDAN

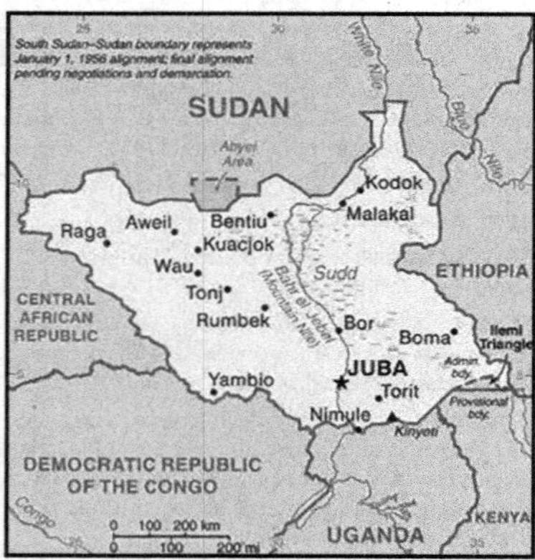

INTRODUCTION

Background: South Sudan, which gained independence from Sudan on 9 July 2011, is the world's newest country. Home to a diverse array of mainly Nilotic ethnolinguistic groups that settled in the territory in the 15th through 19th centuries, South Sudanese society is heavily dependent on seasonal fluctuations in precipitation and seasonal migration. The land comprising modern-day South Sudan was conquered first by Egypt and later ruled jointly by Egyptian-British colonial administrators in the late 19th century. Christian missionaries propagated the spread of English and Christianity, rather than Arabic and Islam, leading to significant cultural differences between the northern and southern parts of Sudan. When Sudan gained its independence in 1956, the Southern region received assurances that it would participate fully in the political system. However, the Arab government in Khartoum reneged on its promises, prompting two periods of civil war (1955-1972 and 1983-2005) in which as many as 2.5 million people died - mostly civilians - due largely to starvation and drought. The Second Sudanese civil war was one of the deadliest since WWII and left Southern Sudanese society devastated by humanitarian crises and economic deterioration. Peace talks resulted in a US-backed Comprehensive Peace Agreement, signed in January 2005, which granted the South a six-year period of autonomy followed by a referendum on final status. The result of this referendum, held in January 2011, was a vote of 98% in favor of secession.

Since independence, South Sudan has struggled to form a viable governing system and has been plagued by widespread corruption, political conflict, and communal violence. In December 2013, conflict erupted between forces loyal to President Salva KIIR, a Dinka, and forces loyal to Vice President Riek MACHAR, a Nuer. The conflict quickly spread throughout the country and unfolded along ethnic lines, killing tens of thousands and creating a dire humanitarian crisis, with millions of South Sudanese displaced and food insecure. KIIR and MACHAR signed a peace agreement in August 2015 that created a Transitional Government of National Unity in April 2016. However, in July 2016, renewed fighting broke out in Juba between KIIR and MACHAR's forces, plunging the country back into conflict and drawing in additional armed opposition groups, including those in the southern Equatoria region that had largely stayed out of the first round of civil war. A "revitalized" peace agreement was signed in September 2018, which mostly ended the fighting. The government and most armed opposition groups agreed that they would form a unified national army, create a transitional government by May 2019, and prepare for elections in December 2022. Subsequent extensions pushed elections to late 2023, and the transitional government was formed in February 2020, when MACHAR returned to Juba as first vice president. Since 2020, implementation of the peace agreement has been stalled as the parties wrangle over power-sharing arrangements, contributing to an uptick in communal violence and the country's worst food security crisis since independence, with 7 of 11 million South Sudanese citizens in need of humanitarian assistance.

GEOGRAPHY

Location: East-Central Africa; south of Sudan, north of Uganda and Kenya, west of Ethiopia

Geographic coordinates: 8 00 N, 30 00 E

Map references: Africa

Area: *total:* 644,329 sq km
land: NA
water: NA
country comparison to the world: 44

Area - comparative: more than four times the size of Georgia; slightly smaller than Texas

Land boundaries: *total:* 6,018 km
border countries (6): Central African Republic 1,055 km; Democratic Republic of the Congo 714 km; Ethiopia 1,299 km; Kenya 317 km; Sudan 2,158 km; Uganda 475 km
note: South Sudan-Sudan boundary represents 1 January 1956 alignment; final alignment pending negotiations and demarcation; final sovereignty status of Abyei Area pending negotiations between South Sudan and Sudan

Coastline: 0 km (landlocked)

Maritime claims: none (landlocked)

Climate: hot with seasonal rainfall influenced by the annual shift of the Inter-Tropical Convergence Zone; rainfall heaviest in upland areas of the south and diminishes to the north

Terrain: plains in the north and center rise to southern highlands along the border with Uganda and Kenya; the White Nile, flowing north out of the uplands of Central Africa, is the major geographic feature of the country; The Sudd (a name derived from floating vegetation that hinders navigation) is a large swampy area of more than 100,000 sq km fed by the waters of the White Nile that dominates the center of the country

Elevation: *highest point:* Kinyeti 3,187 m
lowest point: White Nile 381 m

Natural resources: hydropower, fertile agricultural land, gold, diamonds, petroleum, hardwoods, limestone, iron ore, copper, chromium ore, zinc, tungsten, mica, silver

Land use: *agricultural land:* 45% (2018)
arable land: 4.4% (2018)
permanent pasture: 40.7% (2018)
forest: 11.3% (2018)
other: 43.5% (2018)

Irrigated land: 1,000 sq km (2012)

Major rivers (by length in km): Nile (shared with Rwanda [s], Tanzania, Uganda, Sudan, and Egypt [m]) - 6,650 km
note – [s] after country name indicates river source; [m] after country name indicates river mouth

Major watersheds (area sq km): Atlantic Ocean drainage: Congo (3,730,881 sq km), *(Mediterranean Sea)* Nile (3,254,853 sq km)

Population distribution: clusters found in urban areas, particularly in the western interior and around the White Nile as shown in this population distribution map

Geography - note: landlocked; The Sudd is a vast swamp in the north central region of South Sudan, formed by the White Nile, its size is variable but can reach some 15% of the country's total area during the rainy season; it is one of the world's largest wetlands

PEOPLE AND SOCIETY

Population: 11,544,905 (2022 est.)
country comparison to the world: 82

Nationality: *noun:* South Sudanese (singular and plural)
adjective: South Sudanese

Ethnic groups: Dinka (Jieng) approximately 35-40%, Nuer (Naath) approximately 15%, Shilluk (Chollo), Azande, Bari, Kakwa, Kuku, Murle, Mandari, Didinga, Ndogo, Bviri, Lndi, Anuak, Bongo, Lango, Dungotona, Acholi, Baka, Fertit (2011 est.)
note: Figures are estimations due to population changes during South Sudan's civil war and the lack of updated demographic studies

Languages: English (official), Arabic (includes Juba and Sudanese variants), ethnic languages include Dinka, Nuer, Bari, Zande, Shilluk
major-language sample(s):
The World Factbook, the indispensable source for basic information. (English)
كتاب حقائق العالم، المصدر الذي لا يمكن الاستغناء عنه للمعلومات الأساسية
(Arabic)

Religions: Christian 60.5%, folk religion 32.9%, Muslim 6.2%, other <1%, unaffiliated <1% (2020 est.)

Demographic profile: South Sudan, independent from Sudan since July 2011 after decades of civil war, is one of the world's poorest countries and ranks among the lowest in many socioeconomic categories. Problems are exacerbated by ongoing tensions with Sudan over oil revenues and land borders, fighting between government forces and rebel groups, and inter-communal violence. Most of the population lives off of farming, while smaller numbers rely on animal husbandry; more than 80% of the populace lives in rural areas. The maternal mortality rate is among the world's highest for a variety of reasons, including a shortage of health care workers, facilities, and supplies; poor roads and a lack of transport; and cultural beliefs that prevent women from seeking obstetric care. Most women marry and start having children early, giving birth at home with the assistance of traditional birth attendants, who are unable to handle complications.

Educational attainment is extremely poor due to the lack of schools, qualified teachers, and materials. Less than a third of the population is literate (the rate is even lower among women), and half live below the poverty line. Teachers and students are also struggling with the switch from Arabic to English as the language of instruction. Many adults missed out on schooling because of warfare and displacement.

Almost 2 million South Sudanese have sought refuge in neighboring countries since the current conflict began in December 2013. Another 1.96 million South Sudanese are internally displaced as of August 2017. Despite South Sudan's instability and lack of infrastructure and social services, more than 240,000 people have fled to South Sudan to escape fighting in Sudan.

Age structure: *0-14 years:* 41.58% (male 2,238,534/female 2,152,685)
15-24 years: 21.28% (male 1,153,108/female 1,094,568)
25-54 years: 30.67% (male 1,662,409/female 1,577,062)
55-64 years: 3.93% (male 228,875/female 186,571)
65 years and over: 2.53% (male 153,502/female 113,930) (2020 est.)

Dependency ratios: *total dependency ratio:* 80.8
youth dependency ratio: 74.7
elderly dependency ratio: 6.1
potential support ratio: 16.5 (2020 est.)

Median age: *total:* 18.6 years
male: 18.9 years
female: 18.3 years (2020 est.)
country comparison to the world: 208

Population growth rate: 4.91% (2022 est.)
country comparison to the world: 2

Birth rate: 37.69 births/1,000 population (2022 est.)
country comparison to the world: 9

Death rate: 9.52 deaths/1,000 population (2022 est.)
country comparison to the world: 46

Net migration rate: 20.97 migrant(s)/1,000 population (2022 est.)
country comparison to the world: 2

Population distribution: clusters found in urban areas, particularly in the western interior and around the White Nile as shown in this population distribution map

Urbanization: *urban population:* 20.8% of total population (2022)
rate of urbanization: 4.12% annual rate of change (2020-25 est.)

Major urban areas - population: 440,000 JUBA (capital) (2022)

Sex ratio: *at birth:* 1.05 male(s)/female
0-14 years: 1.04 male(s)/female
15-24 years: 1.03 male(s)/female
25-54 years: 1.04 male(s)/female
55-64 years: 1.19 male(s)/female
65 years and over: 1.28 male(s)/female
total population: 1.05 male(s)/female (2022 est.)

Maternal mortality ratio: 1,150 deaths/100,000 live births (2017 est.)
country comparison to the world: 1

Infant mortality rate: *total:* 63.18 deaths/1,000 live births
male: 69.06 deaths/1,000 live births
female: 57 deaths/1,000 live births (2022 est.)
country comparison to the world: 8

Life expectancy at birth: *total population:* 59.16 years
male: 57.43 years
female: 60.97 years (2022 est.)
country comparison to the world: 221

Total fertility rate: 5.32 children born/woman (2022 est.)
country comparison to the world: 8

Drinking water source: *improved: urban:* 88.7% of population
rural: 75.8% of population
total: 78.4% of population
unimproved: urban: 11.3% of population
rural: 24.2% of population
total: 21.6% of population (2020 est.)

Current health expenditure: 6% of GDP (2019)

Sanitation facility access: *improved: urban:* 60.6% of population
rural: 15.5% of population
total: 24.6% of population
unimproved: urban: 39.4% of population
rural: 84.5% of population

total: 75.4% of population (2020 est.)

HIV/AIDS - adult prevalence rate: 2.3% (2020 est.)
country comparison to the world: 20

HIV/AIDS - people living with HIV/AIDS: 180,000 (2020 est.)
country comparison to the world: 33

HIV/AIDS - deaths: 8,900 (2020 est.)
country comparison to the world: 20

Major infectious diseases: *degree of risk:* very high (2020)
food or waterborne diseases: bacterial and protozoal diarrhea, hepatitis A and E, and typhoid fever
vectorborne diseases: malaria, dengue fever, Trypanosomiasis-Gambiense (African sleeping sickness)
water contact diseases: schistosomiasis
animal contact diseases: rabies
respiratory diseases: meningococcal meningitis
note: on 21 March 2022, the US Centers for Disease Control and Prevention (CDC) issued a Travel Alert for polio in Africa; South Sudan is currently considered a high risk to travelers for circulating vaccine-derived polioviruses (cVDPV); vaccine-derived poliovirus (VDPV) is a strain of the weakened poliovirus that was initially included in oral polio vaccine (OPV) and *that has changed over time and behaves more like the wild or naturally occurring virus;* this means it can be spread more easily to people who are unvaccinated against polio and who come in contact with the stool or respiratory secretions, such as from a sneeze, of an "infected" person who received oral polio vaccine; the CDC recommends that before any international travel, anyone unvaccinated, incompletely vaccinated, or with an unknown polio vaccination status should complete the routine polio vaccine series; before travel to any high-risk destination, the CDC recommends that adults who previously completed the full, routine polio vaccine series receive a single, lifetime booster dose of polio vaccine

Obesity - adult prevalence rate: 6.6% (2014)
country comparison to the world: 165

Education expenditures: 1.5% of GDP (2016 est.)
country comparison to the world: 185

Literacy: *definition:* age 15 and over can read and write
total population: 34.5%
male: 40.3%
female: 28.9% (2018)

Unemployment, youth ages 15-24: *total:* 38.6%
male: 39.5%
female: 37.4% (2017 est.)

ENVIRONMENT

Environment - current issues: water pollution; inadequate supplies of potable water; wildlife conservation and loss of biodiversity; deforestation; soil erosion; desertification; periodic drought

Environment - international agreements: *party to:* Biodiversity, Climate Change, Climate Change-Paris Agreement, Desertification, Ozone Layer Protection, Wetlands
signed, but not ratified: none of the selected agreements

Air pollutants: *particulate matter emissions:* 41.12 micrograms per cubic meter (2016 est.)
carbon dioxide emissions: 1.73 megatons (2016 est.)
methane emissions: 7.61 megatons (2020 est.)

Climate: hot with seasonal rainfall influenced by the annual shift of the Inter-Tropical Convergence Zone; rainfall heaviest in upland areas of the south and diminishes to the north

Land use: *agricultural land:* 45% (2018)
arable land: 4.4% (2018)
permanent pasture: 40.7% (2018)
forest: 11.3% (2018)
other: 43.5% (2018)

Urbanization: *urban population:* 20.8% of total population (2022)
rate of urbanization: 4.12% annual rate of change (2020-25 est.)

Revenue from forest resources: *forest revenues:* 2.65% of GDP (2015 est.)
country comparison to the world: 25

Food insecurity: *widespread lack of access: due to economic downturn, civil insecurity, lingering impact of floods and prolonged conflict* - despite sustained humanitarian assistance, food insecurity still affects large segments of the population, driven by macroeconomic challenges that have resulted in rampant food and non-food inflation, insufficient food supplies due to a stagnant agricultural production, livelihood losses owing to consecutive years with widespread floods and the escalation of organized violence at the sub-national level since 2020; about 7.74 million people, approximately 63% of the total population, are estimated to be severely food insecure during the lean season between April and July 2022 (2022)

Waste and recycling: *municipal solid waste generated annually:* 2,680,681 tons (2013 est.)

Major rivers (by length in km): Nile (shared with Rwanda [s], Tanzania, Uganda, Sudan, and Egypt [m]) - 6,650 km
note – [s] after country name indicates river source; [m] after country name indicates river mouth

Major watersheds (area sq km): Atlantic Ocean drainage: Congo (3,730,881 sq km), *(Mediterranean Sea)* Nile (3,254,853 sq km)

Total water withdrawal: *municipal:* 193 million cubic meters (2017 est.)
industrial: 225 million cubic meters (2017 est.)
agricultural: 240 million cubic meters (2017 est.)

Total renewable water resources: 49.5 billion cubic meters (2017 est.)

GOVERNMENT

Country name: *conventional long form:* Republic of South Sudan
conventional short form: South Sudan
etymology: self-descriptive name from the country's former position within Sudan prior to independence; the name "Sudan" derives from the Arabic "bilad-as-sudan" meaning "Land of the Black [peoples]"

Government type: presidential republic

Capital: *name:* Juba
geographic coordinates: 04 51 N, 31 37 E
time difference: UTC+2 (8 hours ahead of Washington, DC, during Standard Time)
etymology: the name derives from Djouba, another name for the Bari people of South Sudan

Administrative divisions: 10 states; Central Equatoria, Eastern Equatoria, Jonglei, Lakes, Northern Bahr el Ghazal, Unity, Upper Nile, Warrap, Western Bahr el Ghazal, Western Equatoria; note - in 2015, the creation of 28 new states was announced and in 2017 four additional states; following the February 2020 peace agreement, the country was reportedly again reorganized into the 10 original states, plus 2 administrative areas, Pibor and Ruweng, and 1 special administrative status area, Abyei (which is disputed between South Sudan and Sudan); this latest administrative revision has not yet been vetted by the US Board on Geographic Names

Independence: 9 July 2011 (from Sudan)

National holiday: Independence Day, 9 July (2011)

Constitution: *history:* previous 2005 (preindependence); latest signed 7 July 2011, effective 9 July 2011 (Transitional Constitution of the Republic of South Sudan, 2011); note - new constitution pending establishment under the 2018 peace agreement
amendments: proposed by the National Legislature or by the president of the republic; passage requires submission of the proposal to the Legislature at least one month prior to consideration, approval by at least two-thirds majority vote in both houses of the Legislature, and assent of the president; amended 2013, 2015, 2018

Citizenship: *citizenship by birth:* no
citizenship by descent only: at least one parent must be a citizen of South Sudan
dual citizenship recognized: yes
residency requirement for naturalization: 10 years

Suffrage: 18 years of age; universal

Executive branch: *chief of state:* President Salva KIIR Mayardit (since 9 July 2011); Vice Presidents TABAN Deng Gai, Riek MACHAR Teny Dhurgon, James Wani IGGA, Rebecca Nyandeng Chol GARANG de Mabior, Hussein ABDELBAGI Ayii (since 22 February 2020); note - the president is both chief of state and head of government; TABAN served as First Vice President from 23 July 2016 to February 2020
head of government: President Salva KIIR Mayardit (since 9 July 2011); Vice Presidents TABAN Deng Gai, Riek MACHAR Teny Dhurgon, James Wani IGGA, Rebecca Nyandeng Chol GARANG de Mabior, Hussein ABDELBAGI Ayii (since 22 February 2020); note - TABAN served as First Vice President from 23 July 2016 to February 2020
cabinet: National Council of Ministers appointed by the president, approved by the Transitional National Legislative Assembly
elections/appointments: president directly elected by simple majority popular vote for a 4-year term (eligible for a second term); election last held on 11-15 April 2010 (next election scheduled for 2015 but postponed to 2018, then 2021, and again to 2023)
election results:
2010: Salva KIIR Mayardit elected leader of then-Southern Sudan in 2010; percent of vote - Salva KIIR Mayardit (SPLM) 93%, Lam AKOL (SPLM-DC) 7%

Legislative branch: *description:* bicameral National Legislature consists of:
Council of States, pending establishment as stipulated by the 2018 peace deal
Transitional National Legislative Assembly (TNLA), established on 4 August 2016, in accordance with the August 2015 Agreement on the Resolution of the Conflict in the Republic of South Sudan; note - originally 400 seats; the TNLA was expanded to 550

members from 400 and reestablished in May 2020 under the 2018 peace agreement
elections:
Council of States - pending establishment as stipulated by the 2018 peace deal
Transitional National Legislative Assembly - 550 members; percent of vote by party - NA; seats by party - 332 SPLM, 128 SPLM-IO, 90 other political parties; composition - NA
election results:
Council of States - percent of vote by party - NA; seats by party - SPLM 20, unknown 30; composition - men 44, women 6, percent of women 12%
National Legislative Assembly - percent of vote by party - NA; seats by party - SPLM 251, DCP 10, independent 6, unknown 133; composition - men 291, women 109, percent of women 27.3%; note - total National Legislature percent of women 25.6%

Judicial branch: *highest court(s):* Supreme Court of South Sudan - pending formation (will likely consist of a chief and deputy chief justices as well as 9 other justices)
judge selection and term of office: justices will be appointed by the president upon proposal of the pending Judicial Service Council, likely consisting of a 9-member judicial and administrative body; justice tenure to be set by the National Legislature
subordinate courts: national level - Courts of Appeal; High Courts; County Courts; state level - High Courts; County Courts; customary courts; other specialized courts and tribunals

Political parties and leaders: Democratic Change or DC
Democratic Forum or DF
Labour Party or LPSS [Federico Awi VUNI]
South Sudan Opposition Alliance or SSOA [Hussein ABDELBAGI Ayii]
Sudan African National Union or SANU [Toby MADOUT]
Sudan People's Liberation Movement or SPLM [Salva KIIR Mayardit]
Sudan People's Liberation Movement-In Opposition or SPLM-IO [Riek MACHAR Teny Dhurgon]
United Democratic Salvation Front or UDSF
United South Sudan African Party or USSAP [Louis Pasquale ALEU, Secretary]
United South Sudan Party or USSP [Paulino LUKUDU Obede]
note: only parties with seats in the Transitional National Legislative Assembly included

International organization participation: AU, FAO, G-77, IBRD, ICAO, ICRM, IDA, IFAD, IFC, IFRCS, ILO, IMF, Interpol, IOM, IPU, ITU, MIGA, UN, UNCTAD, UNESCO, UPU, WCO, WHO, WMO

Diplomatic representation in the US: *chief of mission:* Ambassador Philip Jada NATANA (since 17 September 2018)
chancery: 1015 31st Street NW, Suite 300, Washington, DC 20007
telephone: [1] (202) 600-2238
FAX: [1] (202) 644-9910
email address and website:
info.ssdembassy@gmail.com
https://www.southsudanembassyusa.org/

Diplomatic representation from the US: *chief of mission:* Ambassador (vacant); Charge d'Affaires William FLENS (since 4 June 2022)
embassy: Kololo Road adjacent to the EU's compound, Juba
mailing address: 4420 Juba Place, Washington DC 20521-4420
telephone: [211] 912-105-188
email address and website:
ACSJuba@state.gov
https://ss.usembassy.gov/

Flag description: three equal horizontal bands of black (top), red, and green; the red band is edged in white; a blue isosceles triangle based on the hoist side contains a gold, five-pointed star; black represents the people of South Sudan, red the blood shed in the struggle for freedom, green the verdant land, and blue the waters of the Nile; the gold star represents the unity of the states making up South Sudan
note: resembles the flag of Kenya; one of only two national flags to display six colors as part of its primary design, the other is South Africa's

National symbol(s): African fish eagle; national colors: red, green, blue, yellow, black, white

National anthem: *name:* "South Sudan Oyee!" (Hooray!)
lyrics/music: collective of 49 poets/Juba University students and teachers
note: adopted 2011; anthem selected in a national contest

ECONOMY

Economic overview: Industry and infrastructure in landlocked South Sudan are severely underdeveloped and poverty is widespread, following several decades of civil war with Sudan. Continued fighting within the new nation is disrupting what remains of the economy. The vast majority of the population is dependent on subsistence agriculture and humanitarian assistance. Property rights are insecure and price signals are weak, because markets are not well-organized.

South Sudan has little infrastructure – about 10,000 kilometers of roads, but just 2% of them paved. Electricity is produced mostly by costly diesel generators, and indoor plumbing and potable water are scarce, so less than 2% of the population has access to electricity. About 90% of consumed goods, capital, and services are imported from neighboring countries – mainly Uganda, Kenya and Sudan. Chinese investment plays a growing role in the infrastructure and energy sectors.

Nevertheless, South Sudan does have abundant natural resources. South Sudan holds one of the richest agricultural areas in Africa, with fertile soils and abundant water supplies. Currently the region supports 10-20 million head of cattle. At independence in 2011, South Sudan produced nearly three-fourths of former Sudan's total oil output of nearly a half million barrels per day. The Government of South Sudan relies on oil for the vast majority of its budget revenues, although oil production has fallen sharply since independence. South Sudan is one of the most oil-dependent countries in the world, with 98% of the government's annual operating budget and 80% of its gross domestic product (GDP) derived from oil. Oil is exported through a pipeline that runs to refineries and shipping facilities at Port Sudan on the Red Sea. The economy of South Sudan will remain linked to Sudan for some time, given the existing oil infrastructure. The outbreak of conflict in December 2013, combined with falling crude oil production and prices, meant that GDP fell significantly between 2014 and 2017. Since the second half of 2017 oil production has risen, and is currently about 130,000 barrels per day.

Poverty and food insecurity has risen due to displacement of people caused by the conflict. With famine spreading, 66% of the population in South Sudan is living on less than about $2 a day, up from 50.6% in 2009, according to the World Bank. About 80% of the population lives in rural areas, with agriculture, forestry and fishing providing the livelihood for a majority of the households. Much of rural sector activity is focused on low-input, low-output subsistence agriculture.

South Sudan is burdened by considerable debt because of increased military spending and high levels of government corruption. Economic mismanagement is prevalent. Civil servants, including police and the military, are not paid on time, creating incentives to engage in looting and banditry. South Sudan has received more than $11 billion in foreign aid since 2005, largely from the US, the UK, and the EU. Inflation peaked at over 800% per year in October 2016 but dropped to 118% in 2017. The government has funded its expenditures by borrowing from the central bank and foreign sources, using forward sales of oil as collateral. The central bank's decision to adopt a managed floating exchange rate regime in December 2015 triggered a 97% depreciation of the currency and spawned a growing black market.

Long-term challenges include rooting out public sector corruption, improving agricultural productivity, alleviating poverty and unemployment, improving fiscal transparency - particularly in regard to oil revenues, taming inflation, improving government revenues, and creating a rules-based business environment.

Real GDP (purchasing power parity): $20.01 billion (2017 est.)
$21.1 billion (2016 est.)
$24.52 billion (2015 est.)
note: data are in 2017 dollars
country comparison to the world: 150

Real GDP growth rate: -5.2% (2017 est.)
-13.9% (2016 est.)
-0.2% (2015 est.)
country comparison to the world: 218

Real GDP per capita: $1,600 (2017 est.)
$1,700 (2016 est.)
$2,100 (2015 est.)
note: data are in 2017 dollars
country comparison to the world: 219

GDP (official exchange rate): $3.06 billion (2017 est.)

Inflation rate (consumer prices): 187.9% (2017 est.)
379.8% (2016 est.)
country comparison to the world: 225

GDP - composition, by end use: *household consumption:* 34.9% (2011 est.)
government consumption: 17.1% (2011 est.)
investment in fixed capital: 10.4% (2011 est.)
exports of goods and services: 64.9% (2011 est.)
imports of goods and services: -27.2% (2011 est.)

Agricultural products: milk, sorghum, vegetables, cassava, goat milk, fruit, beef, sesame seed, sheep milk, mutton

Unemployment, youth ages 15-24: *total:* 38.6%
male: 39.5%
female: 37.4% (2017 est.)
country comparison to the world: 15

Population below poverty line: 76.4% (2016 est.)

Gini Index coefficient - distribution of family income: 46 (2010 est.)
country comparison to the world: 25

Budget: *revenues:* 259.6 million (FY2017/18 est.)
expenditures: 298.6 million (FY2017/18 est.)

Budget surplus (+) or deficit (-): -1.3% (of GDP) (FY2017/18 est.)
country comparison to the world: 87

Public debt: 62.7% of GDP (2017 est.)
86.6% of GDP (2016 est.)
country comparison to the world: 70

Taxes and other revenues: 8.5% (of GDP) (FY2017/18 est.)
country comparison to the world: 218

Current account balance: -$154 million (2017 est.)
$39 million (2016 est.)
country comparison to the world: 94

Exports: $3.01 billion (2019 est.) note: data are in current year dollars
$3.09 billion (2018 est.) note: data are in current year dollars
country comparison to the world: 144

Exports - partners: China 88%, United Arab Emirates 5% (2019)

Exports - commodities: crude petroleum, gold, forage crops, lumber, insect resins (2019)

Imports: $3.07 billion (2019 est.) note: data are in current year dollars
$3.57 billion (2018 est.) note: data are in current year dollars
country comparison to the world: 157

Imports - partners: United Arab Emirates 37%, Kenya 18%, China 18% (2019)

Imports - commodities: cars, delivery trucks, packaged medicines, foodstuffs, clothing and apparel (2019)

Reserves of foreign exchange and gold: $73 million (31 December 2016 est.)
country comparison to the world: 184

Exchange rates: South Sudanese pounds (SSP) per US dollar -
0.885 (2017 est.)
0.903 (2016 est.)
0.9214 (2015 est.)
0.885 (2014 est.)
0.7634 (2013 est.)

ENERGY

Electricity access: *electrification - total population:* 28.2% (2018)
electrification - urban areas: 46.8% (2018)
electrification - rural areas: 23.6% (2018)

Electricity: *installed generating capacity:* 121,000 kW (2020 est.)
consumption: 531.66 million kWh (2019 est.)
exports: 0 kWh (2019 est.)
imports: 0 kWh (2019 est.)
transmission/distribution losses: 26 million kWh (2019 est.)

Electricity generation sources: *fossil fuels:* 99.2% of total installed capacity (2020 est.)
solar: 0.8% of total installed capacity (2020 est.)

Petroleum: *total petroleum production:* 157,100 bbl/day (2021 est.)
refined petroleum consumption: 12,900 bbl/day (2019 est.)
crude oil and lease condensate exports: 126,500 bbl/day (2018 est.)

Refined petroleum products - imports: 7,160 bbl/day (2015 est.)
country comparison to the world: 157

Carbon dioxide emissions: 1.778 million metric tonnes of CO2 (2019 est.)
from petroleum and other liquids: 1.778 million metric tonnes of CO2 (2019 est.)
country comparison to the world: 161

Energy consumption per capita: 2.404 million Btu/person (2019 est.)
country comparison to the world: 185

COMMUNICATIONS

Telephones - mobile cellular: *total subscriptions:* 2,221,970 (2019)
subscriptions per 100 inhabitants: 20.09 (2019)
country comparison to the world: 146

Telecommunication systems: *general assessment:* following a referendum, oil-rich South Sudan seceded from Sudan in 2011 and became an independent nation; having been deprived of investment for decades, it inherited one of the least developed telecom markets in the world; there was once investment activity among mobile network operators who sought to expand their networks in some areas of the country; operators in the telecom sector placed themselves in survival mode and are hoping for a political settlement and a return to some degree of social stability; South Sudan has one of the lowest mobile penetration rates in Africa; growth in the sector in coming years is premised on a resolution to the political crisis and a recovery of the country's economy; the virtually untapped internet and broadband market also depends to a large extent on the country gaining access to international fiber cables and on a national backbone network being in place; sophisticated infrastructure solutions are needed to reach the 80% of the population that live outside of the main urban centers; some improvement has followed from the cable link in February 2020 which connects Juba directly to the company's submarine landing station at Mombasa; the cable was South Sudan's first direct international fiber link, and has helped drive down the price of retail internet services for residential and business customers; a second cable linking to the border with Kenya was completed in December 2021 (2022)
domestic: fixed-line less than 1 per 100 subscriptions, mobile-cellular roughly 20 per 100 persons (2019)
international: country code - 211 (2017)

Broadcast media: a single TV channel and a radio station are controlled by the government; several community and commercial FM stations are operational, mostly sponsored by outside aid donors; some foreign radio broadcasts are available
(2019)

Internet country code: .ss

Internet users: *total:* 783,561 (2020 est.)
percent of population: 7% (2020 est.)
country comparison to the world: 151

Broadband - fixed subscriptions: *total:* 200 (2019 est.)
country comparison to the world: 212

TRANSPORTATION

National air transport system: *number of registered air carriers:* 2 (2020)
inventory of registered aircraft operated by air carriers: 2
annual freight traffic on registered air carriers: 0 mt-km

Civil aircraft registration country code prefix: Z8

Airports: *total:* 89 (2021)
country comparison to the world: 63

Airports - with paved runways: *total:* 4
over 3,047 m: 1
2,438 to 3,047 m: 2
1,524 to 2,437 m: 1 (2021)

Airports - with unpaved runways: *total:* 84
2,438 to 3,047 m: 1
1,524 to 2,437 m: 12
914 to 1,523 m: 38
under 914 m: 33 (2021)

Heliports: 3 (2021)

Railways: *total:* 248 km (2018)
note: a narrow gauge, single-track railroad between Babonosa (Sudan) and Wau, the only existing rail system, was repaired in 2010 with $250 million in UN funds, but is not currently operational
country comparison to the world: 126

Roadways: *total:* 90,200 km (2019)
paved: 300 km (2019)
unpaved: 89,900 km (2019)
note: most of the road network is unpaved and much of it is in disrepair; the Juba-Nimule highway connecting Juba to the border with Uganda is the main paved road in South Sudan
country comparison to the world: 54

Waterways: see entry for Sudan

MILITARY AND SECURITY

Military and security forces: South Sudan People's Defense Force (SSPDF): Ground Force (includes Presidential Guard, aka Tiger Division), Air Force, Air Defense Forces; National (or Necessary) Unified Forces (NUF) (2022)
note 1: the NUF are being formed by retraining rebel and pro-government militia fighters into military, police, and other government security forces; in August 2022, South Sudan held the first graduation ceremony for retrained personnel
note 2: numerous irregular forces operate in the country with official knowledge, including militias operated by the National Security Service (an internal security force under the Ministry of National Security) and proxy forces

Military expenditures: 2% of GDP (2021 est.)
2% of GDP (2020 est.)
3.1% of GDP (2019 est.) (approximately $1.62 billion)
3.2% of GDP (2018 est.) (approximately $1.54 billion)
2.1% of GDP (2017 est.) (approximately $660 million)
country comparison to the world: 64

Military and security service personnel strengths: estimated 150-200,000 active personnel, mostly ground forces with small contingents of air and riverine forces (2022)
note: some active SSPDF personnel may be militia; the National/Necessary Unified Forces (NUF) will have

about 50-80,000 troops from the SSPDF and armed opposition groups when it is formed; as of August 2022, approximately 20,000 NUF had been trained

Military equipment inventories and acquisitions: the SSPDF inventory is primarily of Soviet origin; South Sudan has been under a UN arms embargo since 2018 (2022)

Military service age and obligation: 18 is the legal minimum age for compulsory and voluntary military service; conscription only for men; women may volunteer; 12-24 months service (2022)
note: in 2019, women made up less than 10% of the active military

Military - note: the South Sudan People's Defense Force (SSPDF), formerly the Sudan People's Liberation Army (SPLA), was founded as a guerrilla movement against the Sudanese Government in 1983 and participated in the Second Sudanese Civil War (1983-2005); the Juba Declaration that followed the Comprehensive Peace Agreement of 2005 unified the SPLA and the South Sudan Defense Forces (SSDF), the second-largest rebel militia remaining from the civil war, under the SPLA name; in 2017, the SPLA was renamed the South Sudan Defense Forces (SSDF) and in September 2018 was renamed again as the SSPDF

the United Nations Mission in South Sudan (UNMISS) has operated in the country since 2011 with the objectives of consolidating peace and security and helping establish conditions for the successful economic and political development of South Sudan; UNMISS had about 15,000 personnel deployed in the country as of mid-2022

United Nations Interim Security Force for Abyei (UNISFA) has operated in the disputed Abyei region along the border between Sudan and South Sudan since 2011; UNISFA's mission includes ensuring security, protecting civilians, strengthening the capacity of the Abyei Police Service, de-mining, monitoring/verifying the redeployment of armed forces from the area, and facilitating the flow of humanitarian aid; as of mid-2022, UNISFA had approximately 2,000 personnel deployed

TRANSNATIONAL ISSUES

Disputes - international: *South Sudan- Central African Republic:* periodic violent skirmishes persist among related pastoral populations along the border with the Central African Republic over water and grazing rights
South Sudan-Democratic Republic of the Congo: none identified
South Sudan-Ethiopia: the unresolved demarcation of the boundary and lack of clear limitation create substantial room for territorial conflict both locally among the border populations and between the two capitals; besides a large number of indigenous farmers, the border region supports refugees and various rebel groups opposed to the governments in Khartoum and Addis Ababa
South Sudan-Kenya: the boundary that separates Kenya and South Sudan's sovereignty is unclear in the Ilemi Triangle has been unclear since British colonial times; Kenya has administered the area since colonial times
South Sudan-Sudan: present boundary represents 1 January 1956 alignment, which clearly placed the Kafia Kingi area (adjacent to Central African Republic) within South Sudan as shown on US maps although it is mostly occupied by Sudan; final alignment pending negotiations and demarcation; the final sovereignty status of Abyei Area pending negotiations between South Sudan and Sudan; clashes continue in the oil-rich Abyei region; the United Nations interim security Force for Abyei (UNISFA) has been deployed since 2011, when South Sudan became independent, Sudan accuses South Sudan of supporting Sudanese rebel groups
South Sudan-Uganda: Lord's Resistance Army operations in western Equatorial State displace and drive out local populations and steal grain stores

Refugees and internally displaced persons: *refugees (country of origin):* 309,849 (Sudan), 19,452 (Democratic Republic of the Congo) (2022)

IDPs: 2.23 million (alleged coup attempt and ethnic conflict beginning in December 2013; information is lacking on those displaced in earlier years by: fighting in Abyei between the Sudanese Armed Forces and the Sudan People's Liberation Army (SPLA) in May 2011; clashes between the SPLA and dissident militia groups in South Sudan; inter-ethnic conflicts over resources and cattle; attacks from the Lord's Resistance Army; floods and drought) (2022)
stateless persons: 10,000 (mid-year 2021)

Trafficking in persons: *current situation:* South Sudan is a source and destination country for men, women, and children subjected to forced labor and sex trafficking; South Sudanese women and girls, particularly those who are internally displaced or from rural areas, are vulnerable to forced labor and sexual exploitation in urban centers; the rising number of street children and child laborers are also exploited for forced labor and prostitution; women and girls from Uganda, Kenya, Ethiopia, and Democratic Republic of the Congo are trafficked to South Sudan with promises of legitimate jobs and are forced into the sex trade; inter-ethnic abductions continue between some communities in South Sudan; government forces use children to fight and perpetrate violence against other children and civilians, to serve as scouts, escorts, cooks, and cleaners, and to carry heavy loads while on the move
tier rating:

Tier 3 — South Sudan does not fully meet the minimum standards for the elimination of trafficking and is not making significant efforts to do so: the government's efforts include forming and staffing an anti-trafficking inter-ministerial task force, releasing 286 child soldiers, and identifying 19 potential trafficking victims; however, the recruitment of child soldiers by security and law enforcement continues and neither was held criminally responsible; authorities did not investigate or prosecute forced labor or sex trafficking crimes and made no effort to identify and protect trafficking victims; authorities continued to arrest and imprison child sex trafficking victims without screening for indicators of trafficking (2020)

SOUTHERN OCEAN

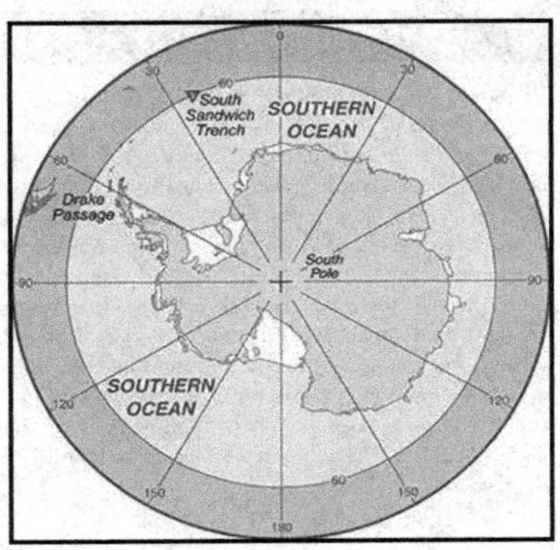

INTRODUCTION

Background: A large body of recent oceanographic research has shown that the Antarctic Circumpolar Current (ACC), an ocean current that flows from west to east around Antarctica, plays a crucial role in global ocean circulation. The region where the cold waters of the ACC meet and mingle with the warmer waters of the north defines a distinct border - the Antarctic Convergence - which fluctuates with the seasons, but which encompasses a discrete body of water and a unique ecologic region. The Convergence concentrates nutrients, which promotes marine plant life, and which, in turn, allows for a greater abundance of animal life. In 2000, the International Hydrographic Organization delimited the waters within the Convergence as a fifth world ocean - the Southern Ocean - by combining the southern portions of the Atlantic Ocean, Indian Ocean, and Pacific Ocean. The Southern Ocean extends from the coast of Antarctica north to 60 degrees south latitude, which coincides with the Antarctic Treaty region and which approximates the extent of the Antarctic Convergence. As such, the Southern Ocean is now the fourth largest of the world's five oceans (after the Pacific Ocean, Atlantic Ocean, and Indian Ocean, but larger than the Arctic Ocean). It should be noted that inclusion of the Southern Ocean does not imply recognition of this feature as one of the world's primary oceans by the US Government.

GEOGRAPHY

Location: body of water between 60 degrees south latitude and Antarctica

Geographic coordinates: 60 00 S, 90 00 E (nominally), but the Southern Ocean has the unique distinction of being a large circumpolar body of water totally encircling the continent of Antarctica; this ring of water lies between 60 degrees south latitude and the coast of Antarctica and encompasses 360 degrees of longitude

Map references: Antarctic Region

Area: *total:* 21.96 million sq km
note: includes Amundsen Sea, Bellingshausen Sea, part of the Drake Passage, Ross Sea, a small part of the Scotia Sea, Weddell Sea, and other tributary water bodies

Area - comparative: slightly more than twice the size of the US

Coastline: 17,968 km

Climate: sea temperatures vary from about 10 degrees Celsius to -2 degrees Celsius; cyclonic storms travel eastward around the continent and frequently are intense because of the temperature contrast between ice and open ocean; the ocean area from about latitude 40 south to the Antarctic Circle has the strongest average winds found anywhere on Earth; in winter the ocean freezes outward to 65 degrees south latitude in the Pacific sector and 55 degrees south latitude in the Atlantic sector, lowering surface temperatures well below 0 degrees Celsius; at some coastal points intense persistent drainage winds from the interior keep the shoreline ice-free throughout the winter

Ocean volume: *ocean volume:* 71.8 million cu km
percent of World Ocean total volume: 5.4%

Major ocean currents: the cold, clockwise-flowing Antarctic Circumpolar Current (West Wind Drift; 21,000 km long) moves perpetually eastward around the continent and is the world's largest and strongest ocean current, transporting 130 million cubic meters of water per second - 100 times the flow of all the world's rivers; it is also the only current that flows all the way around the planet and connects the Atlantic, Pacific, and Indian Oceans; the cold Antarctic Coastal Current (East Wind Drift) is the southernmost current in the world, flowing westward and parallel to the Antarctic coastline

Elevation: *highest point:* sea level
lowest point: southern end of the South Sandwich Trench -7,434 m unnamed deep
mean depth: -3,270 m

Natural resources: probable large oil and gas fields on the continental margin; manganese nodules, possible placer deposits, sand and gravel, fresh water as icebergs; squid, whales, and seals - none exploited; krill, fish

Natural hazards: huge icebergs with drafts up to several hundred meters; smaller bergs and iceberg fragments; sea ice (generally 0.5 to 1 m thick) with sometimes dynamic short-term variations and with large annual and interannual variations; deep continental shelf floored by glacial deposits varying widely over short distances; high winds and large waves much of the year; ship icing, especially May-October; most of region is remote from sources of search and rescue

Geography - note: the major chokepoint is the Drake Passage between South America and Antarctica; the Polar Front (Antarctic Convergence) is the best natural definition of the northern extent of the Southern Ocean; it is a distinct region at the middle of the Antarctic Circumpolar Current that separates the cold polar surface waters to the south from the warmer waters to the north; the Front and the Current extend entirely around Antarctica, reaching south of 60 degrees south near New Zealand and near 48 degrees south in the far South Atlantic coinciding with the path of the maximum westerly winds

ENVIRONMENT

Environment - current issues: changes to the ocean's physical, chemical, and biological systems have taken place because of climate change, ocean acidification, and commercial exploitation

Environment - international agreements: the Southern Ocean is subject to all international agreements regarding the world's oceans; in addition, it is subject to these agreements specific to the Antarctic region: International Whaling Commission (prohibits commercial whaling south of 40 degrees south [south of 60 degrees south between 50 degrees and 130 degrees west]); Convention on the Conservation of Antarctic Seals (limits sealing); Convention on the Conservation of Antarctic Marine Living Resources (regulates fishing)
note: mineral exploitation except for scientific research is banned by the Environmental Protocol to the Antarctic Treaty; additionally, many nations (including the US) prohibit mineral resource exploration and exploitation south of the fluctuating Polar Front (Antarctic Convergence), which is in the middle of the Antarctic Circumpolar Current and serves as the dividing line between the cold polar surface waters to the south and the warmer waters to the north

Marine fisheries: the Southern Ocean fishery is relatively small with a total catch of 388,901 mt in 2021; the Food and Agriculture Organization has delineated three regions in the Southern Ocean (Regions 48, 58, 88) that generally encompass the waters south of 40° to 60° South latitude; the most important producers in these regions include Norway (241,408 mt), China (47,605 mt), and South Korea (39,487 mt); Antarctic Krill made up 95.5% of the total catch in 2021, while other important species include Patagonian and Antarctic toothfish

Regional fisheries bodies: Commission on the Conservation of Antarctic Marine Living Resources

Climate: sea temperatures vary from about 10 degrees Celsius to -2 degrees Celsius; cyclonic storms travel eastward around the continent and frequently are intense because of the temperature contrast between ice and open ocean; the ocean area from about latitude 40 south to the Antarctic Circle has the strongest average winds found anywhere on Earth; in winter the ocean freezes outward to 65 degrees south latitude in the Pacific sector and 55 degrees south latitude in the Atlantic sector, lowering surface temperatures well below 0 degrees Celsius; at some coastal points intense persistent drainage winds from the interior keep the shoreline ice-free throughout the winter

GOVERNMENT

Country name: *etymology:* the International Hydrographic Organization (IHO) included the ocean and its definition as the waters south of 60 degrees south in its year 2000 revision, but this has not formally been adopted; the 2000 IHO definition, however, was circulated in a draft edition in 2002 and has acquired de facto usage by many nations and organizations, including the CIA

ECONOMY

Economic overview: Fisheries in 2013-14 landed 302,960 metric tons, of which 96% (291,370 tons-the highest reported catch since 1991) was krill and 4% (11,590 tons) Patagonian toothfish (also known as Chilean sea bass), compared to 15,330 tons in 2012-13 (estimated fishing from the area covered by the Convention of the Conservation of Antarctic Marine Living Resources, which extends slightly beyond the Southern Ocean area). International agreements were adopted in late 1999 to reduce illegal, unreported, and unregulated fishing, which in the 2000-01 season landed, by one estimate, 8,376 metric tons of Patagonian and Antarctic toothfish. A total of 73,670 tourists visited the Antarctic Treaty area in the 2019-2020 Antarctic summer, 32 percent greater than the 55,489 visitors in 2018-2019. These estimates were provided to the Antarctic Treaty by the International Association of Antarctica Tour Operators and do not include passengers on overflights. Nearly all of the tourists were passengers on commercial ships and several yachts that make trips during the summer.

TRANSPORTATION

Ports and terminals: *major seaport(s):* McMurdo, Palmer, and offshore anchorages in Antarctica
note: few ports or harbors exist on the southern side of the Southern Ocean; ice conditions limit use of most to short periods in midsummer; even then some cannot be entered without icebreaker escort; most Antarctic ports are operated by government research stations and, except in an emergency, are not open to commercial or private vessels

Transportation - note: Drake Passage offers alternative to transit through the Panama Canal

TRANSNATIONAL ISSUES

Disputes - international: *Antarctica-various:* Antarctic Treaty defers claims (see Antarctica entry), but Argentina, Australia, Chile, France, NZ, Norway, and UK assert claims (some overlapping), including the continental shelf in the Southern Ocean; several states have expressed an interest in extending those continental shelf claims under the UN Convention on the Law of the Sea to include undersea ridges; the US and most other states do not recognize the land or maritime claims of other states and have made no claims themselves (the US and Russia have reserved the right to do so); no formal claims exist in the waters in the sector between 90 degrees west and 150 degrees west

SPAIN

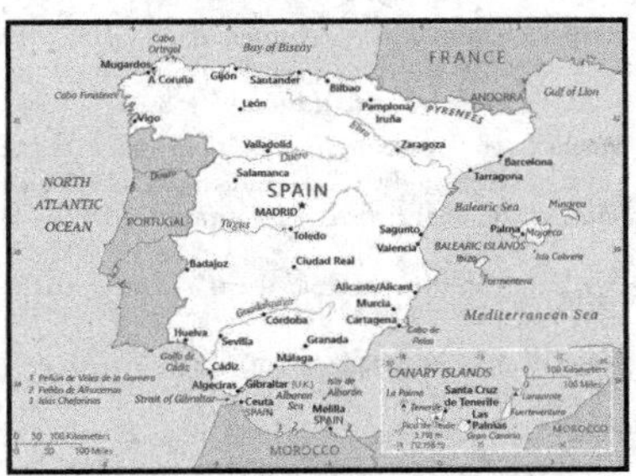

INTRODUCTION

Background: Spain's powerful world empire of the 16th and 17th centuries ultimately yielded command of the seas to England. Subsequent failure to embrace the mercantile and industrial revolutions caused the country to fall behind Britain, France, and Germany in economic and political power. Spain remained neutral in World War I and II but suffered through a devastating civil war (1936-39). A peaceful transition to democracy following the death of dictator Francisco FRANCO in 1975, and rapid economic modernization (Spain joined the EU in 1986) gave Spain a dynamic and rapidly growing economy, and made it a global champion of freedom and human rights. More recently, Spain has emerged from a severe economic recession that began in mid-2008, posting solid years of GDP growth above the EU average. Unemployment has fallen but remains high, especially among youth. Spain is the eurozone's fourth-largest economy. The country has faced increased domestic turmoil in recent years due to the independence movement in its restive Catalonia region.

GEOGRAPHY

Location: Southwestern Europe, bordering the Mediterranean Sea, North Atlantic Ocean, Bay of Biscay, and Pyrenees Mountains; southwest of France

Geographic coordinates: 40 00 N, 4 00 W

Map references: Europe

Area: *total:* 505,370 sq km
land: 498,980 sq km
water: 6,390 sq km
note: there are two autonomous cities - Ceuta and Melilla - and 17 autonomous communities including Balearic Islands and Canary Islands, and three small Spanish possessions off the coast of Morocco - Islas Chafarinas, Penon de Alhucemas, and Penon de Velez de la Gomera
country comparison to the world: 54

Area - comparative: almost five times the size of Kentucky; slightly more than twice the size of Oregon

Land boundaries: *total:* 1,952.7 km
border countries (5): Andorra 63 km; France 646 km; Gibraltar 1.2 km; Portugal 1,224 km; Morocco (Ceuta) 8 km and Morocco (Melilla) 10.5 km
note: an additional 75-meter border segment exists between Morocco and the Spanish exclave of Penon de Velez de la Gomera

Coastline: 4,964 km

Maritime claims: *territorial sea:* 12 nm
contiguous zone: 24 nm
exclusive economic zone: 200 nm (applies only to the Atlantic Ocean)

Climate: temperate; clear, hot summers in interior, more moderate and cloudy along coast; cloudy, cold winters in interior, partly cloudy and cool along coast

Terrain: large, flat to dissected plateau surrounded by rugged hills; Pyrenees Mountains in north

Elevation: *highest point:* Pico de Teide (Tenerife) on Canary Islands 3,718 m
lowest point: Atlantic Ocean 0 m
mean elevation: 660 m

Natural resources: coal, lignite, iron ore, copper, lead, zinc, uranium, tungsten, mercury, pyrites, magnesite, fluorspar, gypsum, sepiolite, kaolin, potash, hydropower, arable land

Land use: *agricultural land:* 54.1% (2018 est.)
arable land: 24.9% (2018 est.)
permanent crops: 9.1% (2018 est.)
permanent pasture: 20.1% (2018 est.)
forest: 36.8% (2018 est.)
other: 9.1% (2018 est.)

Irrigated land: 38,000 sq km (2012)

Major rivers (by length in km): Tagus river source (shared with Portugal [m]) - 1,006
note – [s] after country name indicates river source; [m] after country name indicates river mouth

Population distribution: with the notable exception of Madrid, Sevilla, and Zaragoza, the largest urban agglomerations are found along the Mediterranean and Atlantic coasts; numerous smaller cities are spread throughout the interior reflecting Spain's agrarian heritage; very dense settlement around the capital of Madrid, as well as the port city of Barcelona

Natural hazards: periodic droughts, occasional flooding
volcanism: volcanic activity in the Canary Islands, located off Africa's northwest coast; Teide (3,715 m) has been deemed a Decade Volcano by the International Association of Volcanology and Chemistry of the Earth's Interior, worthy of study due to its explosive history and close proximity to human populations; La Palma (2,426 m), which last erupted in 1971, is the most active of the Canary Islands volcanoes; Lanzarote is the only other historically active volcano

Geography - note: strategic location along approaches to Strait of Gibraltar; Spain controls a number of territories in northern Morocco including the enclaves of Ceuta and Melilla, and the islands of Penon de Velez de la Gomera, Penon de Alhucemas, and Islas Chafarinas; Spain's Canary Islands are one of four North Atlantic archipelagos that make up Macaronesia; the others are Azores (Portugal), Madeira (Portugal), and Cabo Verde

PEOPLE AND SOCIETY

Population: 47,163,418 (2022 est.)
country comparison to the world: 31

Nationality: *noun:* Spaniard(s)
adjective: Spanish

Ethnic groups: Spanish 84.8%, Moroccan 1.7%, Romanian 1.2%, other 12.3% (2021 est.)
note: data represent population by country of birth

Languages: Castilian Spanish (official nationwide) 74%, Catalan (official in Catalonia, the Balearic Islands, and the Valencian Community (where it is known as Valencian)) 17%, Galician (official in Galicia) 7%, Basque (official in the Basque Country and in the Basque-speaking area of Navarre) 2%, Aranese (official in the northwest corner of Catalonia (Vall d'Aran) along with Catalan, <5,000 speakers); note - Aragonese, Aranese Asturian, Basque, Calo, Catalan, Galician, and Valencian are recognized as regional languages under the European Charter for Regional or Minority Languages
major-language sample(s):
La Libreta Informativa del Mundo, la fuente indispensable de información básica. (Spanish)

Religions: Roman Catholic 58.2%, atheist 16.2%, agnostic 10.8%, other 2.7%, non-believer 10.5%, unspecified 1.7% (2021 est.)

Age structure: *0-14 years:* 15.02% (male 3,861,522/female 3,650,085)
15-24 years: 9.9% (male 2,557,504/female 2,392,498)
25-54 years: 43.61% (male 11,134,006/female 10,675,873)
55-64 years: 12.99% (male 3,177,080/female 3,319,823)
65 years and over: 18.49% (male 3,970,417/female 5,276,984) (2020 est.)

Dependency ratios: *total dependency ratio:* 52.4
youth dependency ratio: 21.9
elderly dependency ratio: 30.4
potential support ratio: 3.3 (2020 est.)

Median age: *total:* 43.9 years
male: 42.7 years
female: 45.1 years (2020 est.)
country comparison to the world: 19

Population growth rate: 0.13% (2022 est.)
country comparison to the world: 186

Birth rate: 7.13 births/1,000 population (2022 est.)
country comparison to the world: 222

Death rate: 10.22 deaths/1,000 population (2022 est.)
country comparison to the world: 34

Net migration rate: 4.35 migrant(s)/1,000 population (2022 est.)
country comparison to the world: 27

Population distribution: with the notable exception of Madrid, Sevilla, and Zaragoza, the largest urban agglomerations are found along the Mediterranean and Atlantic coasts; numerous smaller cities are spread throughout the interior reflecting Spain's agrarian heritage; very dense settlement around the capital of Madrid, as well as the port city of Barcelona

Urbanization: *urban population:* 81.3% of total population (2022)
rate of urbanization: 0.24% annual rate of change (2020-25 est.)
note: data include Canary Islands, Ceuta, and Melilla

Major urban areas - population: 6.714 million MADRID (capital), 5.658 million Barcelona, 837,000 Valencia (2022)

Sex ratio: *at birth:* 1.05 male(s)/female
0-14 years: 1.05 male(s)/female

15-24 years: 1.04 male(s)/female
25-54 years: 1.01 male(s)/female
55-64 years: 0.95 male(s)/female
65 years and over: 0.66 male(s)/female
total population: 0.95 male(s)/female (2022 est.)

Mother's mean age at first birth: 31.2 years (2020 est.)

Maternal mortality ratio: 4 deaths/100,000 live births (2017 est.)
country comparison to the world: 174

Infant mortality rate: *total:* 2.47 deaths/1,000 live births
male: 2.73 deaths/1,000 live births
female: 2.19 deaths/1,000 live births (2022 est.)
country comparison to the world: 217

Life expectancy at birth: *total population:* 82.55 years
male: 79.84 years
female: 85.4 years (2022 est.)
country comparison to the world: 23

Total fertility rate: 1.27 children born/woman (2022 est.)
country comparison to the world: 220

Contraceptive prevalence rate: 62.1% (2018)
note: percent of women aged 18-49

Drinking water source: *improved: urban:* 99.9% of population
rural: 100% of population
total: 99.9% of population
unimproved: urban: 0.1% of population
rural: 0% of population
total: 0.1% of population (2020 est.)

Current health expenditure: 9.1% of GDP (2019)

Physicians density: 4.44 physicians/1,000 population (2019)

Hospital bed density: 3 beds/1,000 population (2018)

Sanitation facility access: *improved: urban:* 100% of population
rural: 100% of population
total: 100% of population

HIV/AIDS - adult prevalence rate: 0.4% (2020 est.)
country comparison to the world: 78

HIV/AIDS - people living with HIV/AIDS: 150,000 (2020 est.)
note: estimate does not include children
country comparison to the world: 35

HIV/AIDS - deaths: (2020) <1,000
note: estimate does not include children

Major infectious diseases: *respiratory diseases:* Covid-19 (see note) (2020)
note: widespread ongoing transmission of a respiratory illness caused by the novel coronavirus (COVID-19) is occurring throughout Spain; as of 18 August 2022, Spain has reported a total of 13,306,301 cases of COVID-19 or 28,112.33 cumulative cases of COVID-19 per 100,000 population with a total of 111,906 cumulative deaths or a rate of 236.42 cumulative deaths per 100,000 population; as of 10 August 2022, 86.94% of the population has received at least one dose of COVID-19 vaccine; the Department of Homeland Security has issued instructions requiring US passengers who have been in Spain to travel through select airports where the US Government has implemented enhanced screening procedures

Obesity - adult prevalence rate: 23.8% (2016)
country comparison to the world: 62

Alcohol consumption per capita: *total:* 10.73 liters of pure alcohol (2019 est.)
beer: 4.67 liters of pure alcohol (2019 est.)
wine: 3.52 liters of pure alcohol (2019 est.)
spirits: 2.34 liters of pure alcohol (2019 est.)
other alcohols: 0.19 liters of pure alcohol (2019 est.)
country comparison to the world: 17

Tobacco use: *total:* 27.7% (2020 est.)
male: 28.6% (2020 est.)
female: 26.7% (2020 est.)
country comparison to the world: 39

Education expenditures: 4.2% of GDP (2018 est.)
country comparison to the world: 97

Literacy: *definition:* age 15 and over can read and write
total population: 98.6%
male: 99%
female: 98.2% (2020)

School life expectancy (primary to tertiary education): *total:* 18 years
male: 17 years
female: 18 years (2019)

Unemployment, youth ages 15-24: *total:* 38.3%
male: 37.1%
female: 39.7% (2020 est.)

ENVIRONMENT

Environment - current issues: pollution of the Mediterranean Sea from raw sewage and effluents from the offshore production of oil and gas; water quality and quantity nationwide; air pollution; deforestation; desertification

Environment - international agreements: *party to:* Air Pollution, Air Pollution-Heavy Metals, Air Pollution-Multi-effect Protocol, Air Pollution-Nitrogen Oxides, Air Pollution-Persistent Organic Pollutants, Air Pollution-Sulphur 94, Air Pollution-Volatile Organic Compounds, Antarctic-Environmental Protection, Antarctic-Marine Living Resources, Antarctic Treaty, Biodiversity, Climate Change, Climate Change-Kyoto Protocol, Climate Change-Paris Agreement, Comprehensive Nuclear Test Ban, Desertification, Endangered Species, Environmental Modification, Hazardous Wastes, Law of the Sea, Marine Dumping-London Convention, Marine Dumping-London Protocol, Marine Life Conservation, Nuclear Test Ban, Ozone Layer Protection, Ship Pollution, Tropical Timber 2006, Wetlands, Whaling
signed, but not ratified: none of the selected agreements

Air pollutants: *particulate matter emissions:* 9.48 micrograms per cubic meter (2016 est.)
carbon dioxide emissions: 244 megatons (2016 est.)
methane emissions: 36.94 megatons (2020 est.)

Climate: temperate; clear, hot summers in interior, more moderate and cloudy along coast; cloudy, cold winters in interior, partly cloudy and cool along coast

Land use: *agricultural land:* 54.1% (2018 est.)
arable land: 24.9% (2018 est.)
permanent crops: 9.1% (2018 est.)
permanent pasture: 20.1% (2018 est.)
forest: 36.8% (2018 est.)
other: 9.1% (2018 est.)

Urbanization: *urban population:* 81.3% of total population (2022)
rate of urbanization: 0.24% annual rate of change (2020-25 est.)
note: data include Canary Islands, Ceuta, and Melilla

Revenue from forest resources: *forest revenues:* 0.02% of GDP (2018 est.)
country comparison to the world: 145

Revenue from coal: *coal revenues:* 0% of GDP (2018 est.)
country comparison to the world: 168

Waste and recycling: *municipal solid waste generated annually:* 20.151 million tons (2015 est.)
municipal solid waste recycled annually: 3,393,428 tons (2015 est.)
percent of municipal solid waste recycled: 16.8% (2015 est.)

Major rivers (by length in km): Tagus river source (shared with Portugal [m]) - 1,006
note – [s] after country name indicates river source; [m] after country name indicates river mouth

Total water withdrawal: *municipal:* 4.89 billion cubic meters (2017 est.)
industrial: 5.966 billion cubic meters (2017 est.)
agricultural: 20.36 billion cubic meters (2017 est.)

Total renewable water resources: 111.5 billion cubic meters (2017 est.)

GOVERNMENT

Country name: *conventional long form:* Kingdom of Spain
conventional short form: Spain
local long form: Reino de Espana
local short form: Espana
etymology: derivation of the name "Espana" is uncertain, but may come from the Phoenician term "span," related to the word "spy," meaning "to forge metals," so, "i-spn-ya" would mean "place where metals are forged"; the ancient Phoenicians long exploited the Iberian Peninsula for its mineral wealth

Government type: parliamentary constitutional monarchy

Capital name: Madrid
geographic coordinates: 40 24 N, 3 41 W
time difference: UTC+1 (6 hours ahead of Washington, DC, during Standard Time)
daylight saving time: +1hr, begins last Sunday in March; ends last Sunday in October
time zone note: Spain has two time zones, including the Canary Islands (UTC 0)
etymology: the Romans named the original settlement "Matrice" after the river that ran through it; under Arab rule it became "Majerit," meaning "source of water"; in medieval Romance dialects (Mozarabic) it became "Matrit," which over time changed to "Madrid"

Administrative divisions: 17 autonomous communities (comunidades autonomas, singular - comunidad autonoma) and 2 autonomous cities* (ciudades autonomas, singular - ciudad autonoma); Andalucia; Aragon; Asturias; Canarias (Canary Islands); Cantabria; Castilla-La Mancha; Castilla-Leon; Cataluna (Castilian), Catalunya (Catalan), Catalonha (Aranese) [Catalonia]; Ceuta*; Comunidad Valenciana (Castilian), Comunitat Valenciana (Valencian) [Valencian Community]; Extremadura; Galicia; Illes Baleares (Balearic Islands); La Rioja; Madrid; Melilla*; Murcia; Navarra (Castilian), Nafarroa (Basque) [Navarre]; Pais Vasco (Castilian), Euskadi (Basque) [Basque Country]
note: the autonomous cities of Ceuta and Melilla plus three small islands of Islas Chafarinas, Penon

de Alhucemas, and Penon de Velez de la Gomera, administered directly by the Spanish central government, are all along the coast of Morocco and are collectively referred to as Places of Sovereignty (Plazas de Soberania)

Independence: 1492; the Iberian peninsula was characterized by a variety of independent kingdoms prior to the Muslim occupation that began in the early 8th century A.D. and lasted nearly seven centuries; the small Christian redoubts of the north began the reconquest almost immediately, culminating in the seizure of Granada in 1492; this event completed the unification of several kingdoms and is traditionally considered the forging of present-day Spain

National holiday: National Day (Hispanic Day), 12 October (1492); note - commemorates the arrival of COLUMBUS in the Americas

Constitution: *history:* previous 1812; latest approved by the General Courts 31 October 1978, passed by referendum 6 December 1978, signed by the king 27 December 1978, effective 29 December 1978
amendments: proposed by the government, by the General Courts (the Congress or the Senate), or by the self-governing communities submitted through the government; passage requires three-fifths majority vote by both houses and passage by referendum if requested by one tenth of the members of either house; proposals disapproved by both houses are submitted to a joint committee, which submits an agreed upon text for another vote; passage requires two-thirds majority vote in Congress and simple majority vote in the Senate; amended 1992, 2011

Legal system: civil law system with regional variations

International law organization participation: accepts compulsory ICJ jurisdiction with reservations; accepts ICCt jurisdiction

Citizenship: *citizenship by birth:* no
citizenship by descent only: at least one parent must be a citizen of Spain
dual citizenship recognized: only with select Latin American countries
residency requirement for naturalization: 10 years for persons with no ties to Spain

Suffrage: 18 years of age; universal

Executive branch: *chief of state:* King FELIPE VI (since 19 June 2014); Heir Apparent Princess LEONOR, Princess of Asturias (daughter of the monarch, born 31 October 2005)
head of government: President of the Government (Prime Minister-equivalent) Pedro SANCHEZ PEREZ-CASTEJON (since 2 June 2018); Vice President (and Minister of the President's Office) Maria del Carmen CALVO POYATO (since 7 June 2018)
cabinet: Council of Ministers designated by the president
elections/appointments: the monarchy is hereditary; following legislative elections, the monarch usually proposes as president the leader of the party or coalition with the largest number of seats, who is then indirectly elected by the Congress of Deputies; election last held on 10 November 2019 (next to be held November 2023); vice president and Council of Ministers appointed by the president
election results:
percent of National Assembly vote - NA
note: there is also a Council of State that is the supreme consultative organ of the government, but its recommendations are non-binding

Legislative branch: *description:* bicameral General Courts or Las Cortes Generales consists of:
Senate or Senado (265 seats; 208 members directly elected in multi-seat constituencies by simple majority vote and 57 members indirectly elected by the legislatures of the autonomous communities; members serve 4-year terms) Congress of Deputies or Congreso de los Diputados (350 seats; 348 members directly elected in 50 multi-seat constituencies by closed-list proportional representation vote, with a 3% threshold needed to gain a seat, and 2 directly elected from the North African Ceuta and Melilla enclaves by simple majority vote; members serve 4-year terms or until the government is dissolved)
elections:
Senate - last held on 10 November 2019 (next to be held no later than 30 November 2023)
Congress of Deputies - last held on 10 November 2019 (next to be held no later than 30 November 2023)
election results:
Senate - percent of vote by party - NA; seats by party - PSOE 113, PP 101, ERC 14, PNV 10, Cs 3, Junts 5, Vox 3, other 16; composition (as of mid-2022) - men 161, women 104; percent of women 39.3%
Congress of Deputies - percent of vote by party - PSOE 34.3%, PP 25.1%, Vox 14.9%, UP 9.4%, Cs 2.6%, ERC 3.7%, PNV 10, EH-Bildu 1.4, other 7.4%; seats by party - PSOE 120, PP 88, Vox 52, UP 33, Cs 9, ERC 13, PNV 6, EH-Bildu 5, other 26; composition (as mid-2022, 349 members) - men 199, women 150, percent of women 43%; note - overall General Courts percent of women 42%

Judicial branch: *highest court(s):* Supreme Court or Tribunal Supremo (consists of the court president and organized into the Civil Room, with a president and 9 judges; the Penal Room, with a president and 14 judges; the Administrative Room, with a president and 32 judges; the Social Room, with a president and 12 judges; and the Military Room, with a president and 7 judges); Constitutional Court or Tribunal Constitucional de Espana (consists of 12 judges)
judge selection and term of office: Supreme Court judges appointed by the monarch from candidates proposed by the General Council of the Judiciary Power, a 20-member governing board chaired by the monarch that includes presidential appointees, lawyers, and jurists confirmed by the National Assembly; judges can serve until age 70; Constitutional Court judges nominated by the National Assembly, executive branch, and the General Council of the Judiciary, and appointed by the monarch for 9-year terms
subordinate courts: National High Court; High Courts of Justice (in each of the autonomous communities); provincial courts; courts of first instance

Political parties and leaders: Asturias Forum or FAC [Carmen MORIYON]
Basque Country Unite (Euskal Herria Bildu) or EH Bildu [Arnaldo OTEGI] (coalition of 4 Basque pro-independence parties)
Basque Nationalist Party or PNV or EAJ [Andoni ORTUZAR]
Canarian Coalition or CC [Fernando Clavijo BATLLE] (coalition of 5 parties)
Ciudadanos Party (Citizens Party) or Cs [Ines ARRIMADAS]
Compromis - Compromise Coalition [Enric MORERA i Català]
Together for Catalonia or JuntsxCat [Laura BORRAS]
People's Party or PP [Pablo CASADO]
Republican Left of Catalonia or ERC [Oriol JUNQUERAS]
Spanish Socialist Workers Party or PSOE [Pedro SANCHEZ]
Teruel Existe or TE [Tomas GUITARTE]
Unidas Podemos (United We Can) or UP [Ione BELARRA] (formerly Podemos IU; electoral coalition formed for May 2016 election)
Union of People of Navarra or UPN [Javier ESPARZA]
Vox or VOX [Santiago ABASCAL]

International organization participation: ADB (nonregional member), AfDB (nonregional member), Arctic Council (observer), Australia Group, BCIE, BIS, CAN (observer), CBSS (observer), CD, CE, CERN, EAPC, EBRD, ECB, EIB, EITI (implementing country), EMU, ESA, EU, FAO, FATF, IADB, IAEA, IBRD, ICAO, ICC (national committees), ICCt, ICRM, IDA, IEA, IFAD, IFC, IFRCS, IHO, ILO, IMF, IMO, IMSO, Interpol, IOC, IOM, IPU, ISO, ITSO, ITU, ITUC (NGOs), LAIA (observer), MIGA, NATO, NEA, NSG, OAS (observer), OECD, OPCW, OSCE, Pacific Alliance (observer), Paris Club, PCA, PIF (partner), Schengen Convention, SELEC (observer), SICA (observer), UN, UNCTAD, UNESCO, UNHCR, UNIDO, UNIFIL, Union Latina, UNOCI, UNRWA, UNWTO, UPU, Wassenaar Arrangement, WCO, WHO, WIPO, WMO, WTO, ZC

Diplomatic representation in the US: *chief of mission:* Ambassador Santiago CABANAS Ansorena (since 17 September 2018)
chancery: 2375 Pennsylvania Avenue NW, Washington, DC 20037
telephone: [1] (202) 452-0100
FAX: [1] (202) 833-5670
email address and website:
emb.washington@maec.es
http://www.exteriores.gob.es/embajadas/washington/en/pages/inicio2.aspx
consulate(s) general: Boston, Chicago, Houston, Los Angeles, Miami, New York, San Francisco, San Juan (Puerto Rico)

Diplomatic representation from the US: *chief of mission:* Ambassador Julissa REYNOSO (since 2 February 2022); note - also accredited to Andorra
embassy: Calle de Serrano, 75, 28006 Madrid
mailing address: 8500 Madrid Place, Washington DC 20521-8500
telephone: [34] (91) 587-2200
FAX: [34] (91) 587-2303
email address and website:
askACS@state.gov
https://es.usembassy.gov/
consulate(s) general: Barcelona

Flag description: three horizontal bands of red (top), yellow (double width), and red with the national coat of arms on the hoist side of the yellow band; the coat of arms is quartered to display the emblems of the traditional kingdoms of Spain (clockwise from upper left, Castile, Leon, Navarre, and Aragon) while Granada is represented by the stylized pomegranate at the bottom of the shield; the arms are framed by two columns representing the Pillars of Hercules, which are the two promontories (Gibraltar and Ceuta) on either side of the eastern end of the Strait of Gibraltar; the red scroll across the two columns bears the imperial motto of "Plus Ultra" (further beyond) referring to Spanish lands beyond Europe; the triband arrangement with the center stripe twice the width of the outer dates to the 18th century *note:* the red and yellow colors are related to those of the oldest Spanish kingdoms: Aragon, Castile, Leon, and Navarre

National symbol(s): Pillars of Hercules; national colors: red, yellow

National anthem: *name:* "Himno Nacional Espanol" (National Anthem of Spain)
lyrics/music: no lyrics/unknown
note: officially in use between 1770 and 1931, restored in 1939; the Spanish anthem is the first anthem to be officially adopted, but it has no lyrics; in the years prior to 1931 it became known as "Marcha Real" (The Royal March); it first appeared in a 1761 military bugle call book and was replaced by "Himno de Riego" in the years between 1931 and 1939; the long version of the anthem is used for the king, while the short version is used for the prince, prime minister, and occasions such as sporting events

National heritage: *total World Heritage Sites:* 49 (43 cultural, 4 natural, 2 mixed)
selected World Heritage Site locales: Cave of Altamira and Paleolithic Cave Art of Northern Spain (c); Works of Antoni Gaudí (c); Santiago de Compostela (Old Town) (c); Historic City of Toledo (c); Archaeological Ensemble of Mérida (c); Tower of Hercules (c); Doñana National Park (n); Pyrénées - Mont Perdu (m); Alhambra, Generalife, and Albayzín in Granada (c); Old City of Salamanca (c); Teide National Park (n); Historic Walled Town of Cuenca (c); Old Town of Segovia and its Aqueduct (c); Historic Cordoba (c); El Escorial (c)

ECONOMY

Economic overview: After a prolonged recession that began in 2008 in the wake of the global financial crisis, Spain marked the fourth full year of positive economic growth in 2017, with economic activity surpassing its pre-crisis peak, largely because of increased private consumption. The financial crisis of 2008 broke 16 consecutive years of economic growth for Spain, leading to an economic contraction that lasted until late 2013. In that year, the government successfully shored up its struggling banking sector - heavily exposed to the collapse of Spain's real estate boom - with the help of an EU-funded restructuring and recapitalization program.

Until 2014, contraction in bank lending, fiscal austerity, and high unemployment constrained domestic consumption and investment. The unemployment rate rose from a low of about 8% in 2007 to more than 26% in 2013, but labor reforms prompted a modest reduction to 16.4% in 2017. High unemployment strained Spain's public finances, as spending on social benefits increased while tax revenues fell. Spain's budget deficit peaked at 11.4% of GDP in 2010, but Spain gradually reduced the deficit to about 3.3% of GDP in 2017. Public debt has increased substantially – from 60.1% of GDP in 2010 to nearly 96.7% in 2017.

Strong export growth helped bring Spain's current account into surplus in 2013 for the first time since 1986 and sustain Spain's economic growth. Increasing labor productivity and an internal devaluation resulting from moderating labor costs and lower inflation have improved Spain's export competitiveness and generated foreign investor interest in the economy, restoring FDI flows.

In 2017, the Spanish Government's minority status constrained its ability to implement controversial labor, pension, health care, tax, and education reforms. The European Commission expects the government to meet its 2017 budget deficit target and anticipates that expected economic growth in 2018 will help the government meet its deficit target. Spain's borrowing costs are dramatically lower since their peak in mid-2012, and increased economic activity has generated a modest level of inflation, at 2% in 2017.

Real GDP (purchasing power parity): $1,714,860,000,000 (2020 est.)
$1,923,330,000,000 (2019 est.)
$1,886,540,000,000 (2018 est.)
note: data are in 2017 dollars
country comparison to the world: 16

Real GDP growth rate: 1.95% (2019 est.)
2.43% (2018 est.)
2.97% (2017 est.)
country comparison to the world: 140

Real GDP per capita: $36,200 (2020 est.)
$40,800 (2019 est.)
$40,300 (2018 est.)
note: data are in 2017 dollars
country comparison to the world: 53

GDP (official exchange rate): $1,393,351,000,000 (2019 est.)

Inflation rate (consumer prices): 0.7% (2019 est.)
1.6% (2018 est.)
1.9% (2017 est.)
country comparison to the world: 55

Credit ratings:

Fitch rating: A- (2018)

Moody's rating: Baa1 (2018)

Standard & Poors rating: A (2019)

GDP - composition, by sector of origin: *agriculture:* 2.6% (2017 est.)
industry: 23.2% (2017 est.)
services: 74.2% (2017 est.)

GDP - composition, by end use: *household consumption:* 57.7% (2017 est.)
government consumption: 18.5% (2017 est.)
investment in fixed capital: 20.6% (2017 est.)
investment in inventories: 0.6% (2017 est.)
exports of goods and services: 34.1% (2017 est.)
imports of goods and services: -31.4% (2017 est.)

Agricultural products: barley, milk, wheat, olives, grapes, tomatoes, pork, maize, oranges, sugar beet

Industries: textiles and apparel (including footwear), food and beverages, metals and metal manufactures, chemicals, shipbuilding, automobiles, machine tools, tourism, clay and refractory products, footwear, pharmaceuticals, medical equipment

Industrial production growth rate: 4% (2017 est.)
country comparison to the world: 76

Labor force: 19.057 million (2020 est.)
country comparison to the world: 29

Labor force - by occupation: *agriculture:* 4.2%
industry: 24%
services: 71.7% (2009)

Unemployment rate: 14.13% (2019 est.)
15.25% (2018 est.)
country comparison to the world: 173

Unemployment, youth ages 15-24: *total:* 38.3%
male: 37.1%
female: 39.7% (2020 est.)
country comparison to the world: 17

Population below poverty line: 20.7% (2018 est.)

Gini Index coefficient - distribution of family income: 34.7 (2017 est.)
32 (2005)
country comparison to the world: 111

Household income or consumption by percentage share: *lowest 10%:* 2.5%
highest 10%: 24% (2011)

Budget: *revenues:* 498.1 billion (2017 est.)
expenditures: 539 billion (2017 est.)

Budget surplus (+) or deficit (-): -3.1% (of GDP) (2017 est.)
country comparison to the world: 136

Public debt: 98.4% of GDP (2017 est.)
99% of GDP (2016 est.)
country comparison to the world: 18

Taxes and other revenues: 37.9% (of GDP) (2017 est.)
country comparison to the world: 52

Fiscal year: calendar year

Current account balance: $29.603 billion (2019 est.)
$27.206 billion (2018 est.)
country comparison to the world: 13

Exports: $392.85 billion (2020 est.) note: data are in current year dollars
$486.15 billion (2019 est.) note: data are in current year dollars
$499.55 billion (2018 est.) note: data are in current year dollars
country comparison to the world: 18

Exports - partners: France 15%, Germany 11%, Portugal 8%, Italy 8%, United Kingdom 7%, United States 5% (2019)

Exports - commodities: cars and vehicle parts, refined petroleum, packaged medicines, delivery trucks, clothing and apparel (2019)

Imports: $373.67 billion (2020 est.) note: data are in current year dollars
$444.31 billion (2019 est.) note: data are in current year dollars
$460.98 billion (2018 est.) note: data are in current year dollars
country comparison to the world: 18

Imports - partners: Germany 13%, France 11%, China 8%, Italy 7% (2019)

Imports - commodities: crude petroleum, cars and vehicle parts, packaged medicines, natural gas, refined petroleum (2019)

Reserves of foreign exchange and gold: $69.41 billion (31 December 2017 est.)
$63.14 billion (31 December 2016 est.)
country comparison to the world: 32

Debt - external: $2,338,853,000,000 (2019 est.)
$2,366,534,000,000 (2018 est.)
country comparison to the world: 11

Exchange rates: euros (EUR) per US dollar -
0.82771 (2020 est.)
0.90338 (2019 est.)
0.87789 (2018 est.)
0.7525 (2014 est.)
0.7634 (2013 est.)

ENERGY

Electricity access: *electrification - total population:* 100% (2020)

Electricity: *installed generating capacity:* 115.837 million kW (2020 est.)
consumption: 233.267 billion kWh (2020 est.)
exports: 14.649 billion kWh (2020 est.)

imports: 17.928 billion kWh (2020 est.)
transmission/distribution losses: 23.999 billion kWh (2020 est.)

Electricity generation sources: *fossil fuels:* 32.4% of total installed capacity (2020 est.)
nuclear: 21.9% of total installed capacity (2020 est.)
solar: 8.1% of total installed capacity (2020 est.)
wind: 22.1% of total installed capacity (2020 est.)
hydroelectricity: 13.1% of total installed capacity (2020 est.)
biomass and waste: 2.6% of total installed capacity (2020 est.)

Coal: *production:* 546,000 metric tons (2020 est.)
consumption: 4.918 million metric tons (2020 est.)
exports: 2.083 million metric tons (2020 est.)
imports: 4.857 million metric tons (2020 est.)
proven reserves: 1.187 billion metric tons (2019 est.)

Petroleum: *total petroleum production:* 47,200 bbl/day (2021 est.)
refined petroleum consumption: 1.328 million bbl/day (2019 est.)
crude oil and lease condensate imports: 1,364,700 bbl/day (2018 est.)
crude oil estimated reserves: 150 million barrels (2021 est.)

Refined petroleum products - production: 1.361 million bbl/day (2017 est.)
country comparison to the world: 13

Refined petroleum products - exports: 562,400 bbl/day (2017 est.)
country comparison to the world: 16

Refined petroleum products - imports: 464,800 bbl/day (2017 est.)
country comparison to the world: 18

Natural gas: *production:* 57.993 million cubic meters (2020 est.)
consumption: 32,026,216,000 cubic meters (2020 est.)
exports: 1,185,285,000 cubic meters (2020 est.)
imports: 32,489,309,000 cubic meters (2020 est.)
proven reserves: 2.549 billion cubic meters (2021 est.)

Carbon dioxide emissions: 280.624 million metric tonnes of CO2 (2019 est.)
from coal and metallurgical coke: 16.743 million metric tonnes of CO2 (2019 est.)
from petroleum and other liquids: 191.299 million metric tonnes of CO2 (2019 est.)
from consumed natural gas: 72.582 million metric tonnes of CO2 (2019 est.)
country comparison to the world: 22

Energy consumption per capita: 122.673 million Btu/person (2019 est.)
country comparison to the world: 45

COMMUNICATIONS

Telephones - fixed lines: *total subscriptions:* 19,455,658 (2020 est.)
subscriptions per 100 inhabitants: 42 (2020 est.)
country comparison to the world: 14

Telephones - mobile cellular: *total subscriptions:* 55,354,900 (2019)
subscriptions per 100 inhabitants: 118.44 (2019)
country comparison to the world: 27

Telecommunication systems: *general assessment:* Spain's telecom sector has tracked the performance of the overall economy, which has been one of the most heavily impacted by the pandemic in all of Europe; GDP dropped by 10.8% in 2020, while telecom revenue reversed the previous five years' positive results by falling 5.3%; fixed-line services were the hardest hit, with revenue falling 13.7%; mobile voice services did not fare much better, falling 4.7%; this is despite relatively small shifts in the number of subscribers, though the harsh lockdown conditions resulted in a significant drop in usage; it had appeared that a return to growth might be possible in 2021 following lifting the state of emergency in May, but the most recent surge in cases and the continued restrictions on travel may once again put the brakes on growth until at least 2022; Spain's fixed-line broadband market managed to extend its decade-long pattern of steady growth into 2020, with a slight increase in demand caused by the need for fast internet access to support working and learning from home; while most of Spain's larger telcos delivered negative revenue and profit in 2020 (2021)
domestic: fixed-line nearly 42 per 100 and mobile-cellular 119 telephones per 100 persons (2020)
international: country code - 34; landing points for the MAREA, Tata TGN-Western Europe, Pencan-9, SAT-3/WASC, Canalink, Atlantis-2, Columbus -111, Estepona-Tetouan, FLAG Europe-Asia (FEA), Balalink, ORVAL and PENBAL-5 submarine cables providing connectivity to Europe, the Middle East, Africa, South America, Asia, Southeast Asia and the US; satellite earth stations - 2 Intelsat (1 Atlantic Ocean and 1 Indian Ocean), Eutelsat; tropospheric scatter to adjacent countries (2019)

Broadcast media: a mixture of both publicly operated and privately owned TV and radio stations; overall, hundreds of TV channels are available including national, regional, local, public, and international channels; satellite and cable TV systems available; multiple national radio networks, a large number of regional radio networks, and a larger number of local radio stations; overall, hundreds of radio stations (2019)

Internet country code: .es

Internet users: *total:* 44,047,980 (2020 est.)
percent of population: 93% (2020 est.)
country comparison to the world: 21

Broadband - fixed subscriptions: *total:* 16,188,502 (2020 est.)
subscriptions per 100 inhabitants: 35 (2020 est.)
country comparison to the world: 15

TRANSPORTATION

National air transport system: *number of registered air carriers:* 21 (2020)
inventory of registered aircraft operated by air carriers: 552
annual passenger traffic on registered air carriers: 80,672,105 (2018)
annual freight traffic on registered air carriers: 1,117,070,000 (2018) mt-km

Civil aircraft registration country code prefix: EC

Airports: *total:* 135 (2021)
country comparison to the world: 40

Airports - with paved runways: *total:* 102
over 3,047 m: 18
2,438 to 3,047 m: 16
1,524 to 2,437 m: 19
914 to 1,523 m: 26
under 914 m: 23 (2021)

Airports - with unpaved runways: *total:* 33
914 to 1,523 m: 14
under 914 m: 19 (2021)

Heliports: 13 (2021)

Pipelines: 10,481 km gas, 358 km oil, 4,378 km refined products (2017)

Railways: *total:* 15,111 km (2017) (9,699 km electrified)
standard gauge: 2,571 km (2017) 1.435-m gauge (2,571 km electrified)
narrow gauge: 1,207 km (2017) 1.000-m gauge (400 km electrified)
broad gauge: 11,333 km (2017) 1.668-m gauge (6,538 km electrified)
mixed gauge: 190 km 1.668-mm and 1.435mm gauge (190.1 km electrified); 28 km 0.914-mm gauge (28 km electrified); 4 km 0.600-mm gauge
country comparison to the world: 19

Roadways: *total:* 683,175 km (2011)
paved: 683,175 km (2011) (includes 16,205 km of expressways)
country comparison to the world: 12

Waterways: 1,000 km (2012)
country comparison to the world: 69

Merchant marine: *total:* 478
by type: bulk carrier 1, general cargo 36, oil tanker 24, other 417 (2021)
country comparison to the world: 43

Ports and terminals: *major seaport(s):*
Atlantic Ocean: Bilbao, Huelva; Las Palmas, Santa Cruz de Tenerife (in the Canary Islands)
Mediterranean Sea: Algeciras, Barcelona, Cartagena, Tarragona, Valencia
container port(s) (TEUs): Algeciras (5,125,385), Barcelona (3,324,650), Valencia (5,439,827) (2019)

LNG terminal(s) (import): Barcelona, Bilbao, Cartagena, El Musel, Huelva, Mugardos, Sagunto
river port(s): Seville (Guadalquivir River)

MILITARY AND SECURITY

Military and security forces: Spanish Armed Forces: Army (Ejercito de Tierra), Spanish Navy (Armada Espanola, AE; includes Marine Corps), Spanish Air Force (Ejercito del Aire Espanola, EdA); Civil Guard (Guardia Civil) (2022)
note: the Civil Guard is a military force with police duties (including coast guard) under both the Ministry of Defense and the Ministry of the Interior; it also responds to the needs of the Ministry of Finance

Military expenditures: 1% of GDP (2022 est.)
1% of GDP (2021)
1% of GDP (2020)
0.9% of GDP (2019) (approximately $16.8 billion)
0.9% of GDP (2018) (approximately $16.7 billion)
country comparison to the world: 133

Military and security service personnel strengths: approximately 120,000 active-duty troops (75,000 Army; 25,000 Navy, including about 5,000 marines; 20,000 Air Force); 80,000 Guardia Civil (2022)
note: a 2007 law established a maximum strength of 130,000 military personnel

Military equipment inventories and acquisitions: the inventory of the Spanish military is comprised of domestically-produced and imported Western weapons systems; France, Germany, and the US have been the leading suppliers of military hardware since 2010; Spain's defense industry manufactures land, air, and sea weapons systems and is integrated within the European defense-industrial sector (2021)

Military service age and obligation: 18-26 years of age for voluntary military service for men and women; 24-36 month initial obligation; women allowed to serve in all branches, including combat units; no conscription (abolished 2001), but the Spanish Government retains the right to mobilize citizens 19-25 years of age in a national emergency; 18-58 for the voluntary reserves (2022)
note 1: as of 2019, women comprised about 13% of the military's full-time personnel
note 2: the military recruits foreign nationals with residency in Spain from countries of its former empire, including Argentina, Costa Rica, Bolivia, Colombia, Chile, Cuba, Dominican Republic, Ecuador, El Salvador, Equatorial Guinea, Guatemala, Honduras, Mexico, Nicaragua, Panama, Paraguay, Peru, Uruguay, and Venezuela

Military deployments: approximately 200 Iraq (NATO/EU training assistance); up to 600 Latvia (NATO); 650 Lebanon (UNIFIL); approximately 500 Mali (EUTM); 150 Turkey (NATO) (2022)
note: in response to Russia's invasion of Ukraine, some NATO countries, including Spain, have sent additional troops and equipment to the battlegroups deployed in NATO territory in eastern Europe

Military - note: Spain joined NATO in 1982 but refrained from participating in the integrated military structure until 1996

the Spanish Marine Corps, established in 1537, is the oldest marine corps in the world; the Spanish Army has an infantry regiment, formed in the 13th century, that is considered the oldest still active military unit in the western world

Spain created a Spanish Legion for foreigners in 1920, but early on the Legion was primarily filled by native Spaniards due to difficulties in recruiting foreigners and most of its foreign members were from the Republic of Cuba; it was modeled after the French Foreign Legion and its purpose was to provide a corps of professional troops to fight in Spain's colonial campaigns in North Africa; in more recent years, it has been used in NATO peacekeeping deployments; today's Legion includes a mix of native Spaniards and foreigners with Spanish residency (2022)

TERRORISM

Terrorist group(s): Islamic State of Iraq and ash-Sham (ISIS); al-Qa'ida

TRANSNATIONAL ISSUES

Disputes - international: *Spain-Andorra:* none identified
Spain-France: none identified
Spain-Gibraltar (UK): in 2002, Gibraltar residents voted overwhelmingly by referendum to reject any "shared sovereignty" arrangement; the Government of Gibraltar insists on equal participation in talks between the UK and Spain; Spain does not recognize British sovereignty beyond the original fortified perimeter of the city and disapproves of UK plans to grant Gibraltar greater autonomy; after voters in the UK chose to leave the EU in a June 2016 referendum, Spain again proposed shared sovereignty of Gibraltar; UK officials rejected Spain's joint sovereignty proposal
Spain-Morocco: Morocco protests Spain's control over the coastal enclaves of Ceuta, Melilla, and the islands of Penon de Velez de la Gomera, Penon de Alhucemas, and Islas Chafarinas, and surrounding waters; both countries claim Isla Perejil (Leila Island), which remains unoccupied but was the site of a military standoff in 2002; Morocco serves as the primary embarkation area for illegal migration into mainland Spain from North Africa
Spain-Portugal: Portugal does not recognize Spanish sovereignty over the territory of Olivenza based on a difference of interpretation of the 1815 Congress of Vienna and the 1801 Treaty of Badajoz

Refugees and internally displaced persons: *refugees (country of origin):* 14,823 (Syria) (mid-year 2021); 418,200 (Venezuela) (economic and political crisis; includes Venezuelans who have claimed asylum, are recognized as refugees, or have received alternative legal stay) (2021); 151,786 (Ukraine) (as of 7 November 2022)
stateless persons: 692 (mid-year 2021)
note: 276,667 estimated refugee and migrant arrivals, including Canary Islands (January 2015-November 2022)

Illicit drugs: primary transit point in Europe for cocaine from South America and for hashish from Morocco; cocaine is shipped in raw or liquid form with mixed cargo to avoid detection; traffickers ship methamphetamine via express mail; increasing number of indoor cannabis production; illegal labs cutting, mixing, and reconstituting cocaine, and heroin and methamphetamine labs; synthetic drugs, including ketamine and MDMA (ecstasy) transit from Spain to the United States

SPRATLY ISLANDS

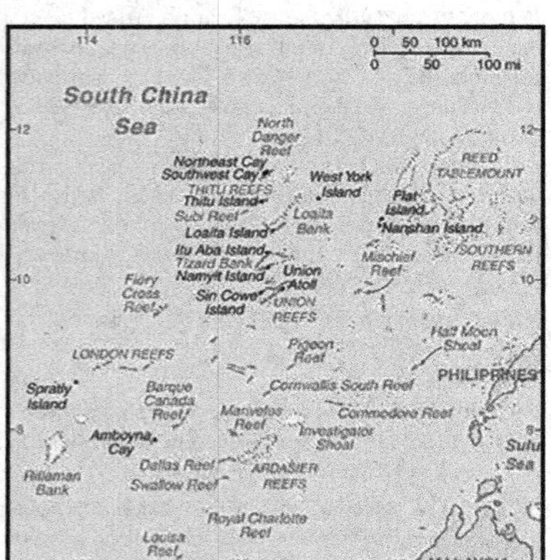

INTRODUCTION

Background: The Spratly Islands consist of more than 100 small islands or reefs surrounded by rich fishing grounds - and potentially by gas and oil deposits. They are claimed in their entirety by China, Taiwan, and Vietnam, while portions are claimed by Malaysia and the Philippines. About 45 islands are occupied by relatively small numbers of military forces from China, Malaysia, the Philippines, Taiwan, and Vietnam. Since 1985, Brunei has claimed a continental shelf that overlaps a southern reef but has not made any formal claim to the reef. Brunei claims an exclusive economic zone over this area.

GEOGRAPHY

Location: Southeastern Asia, group of reefs and islands in the South China Sea, about two-thirds of the way from southern Vietnam to the southern Philippines

Geographic coordinates: 8 38 N, 111 55 E

Map references: Southeast Asia

Area: *total:* 5 sq km less than
land: 5 sq km less than
water: 0 sq km
note: includes 100 or so islets, coral reefs, and sea mounts scattered over an area of nearly 410,000 sq km (158,000 sq mi) of the central South China Sea
country comparison to the world: 250

Area - comparative: land area is about seven times the size of the National Mall in Washington, DC

Land boundaries: *total:* 0 km

Coastline: 926 km

Climate: tropical

Terrain: small, flat islands, islets, cays, and reefs

Elevation: *highest point:* unnamed location on Southwest Cay 6 m
lowest point: South China Sea 0 m

Natural resources: fish, guano, undetermined oil and natural gas potential

Land use: *other:* 100% (2018 est.)

Natural hazards: typhoons; numerous reefs and shoals pose a serious maritime hazard

Geography - note: strategically located near several primary shipping lanes in the central South China Sea; includes numerous small islands, atolls, shoals, and coral reefs

PEOPLE AND SOCIETY

Population: (July 2021 est.) no indigenous inhabitants
note: there are scattered garrisons occupied by military personnel of several claimant states

ENVIRONMENT

Environment - current issues: China's use of dredged sand and coral to build artificial islands harms reef systems; illegal fishing practices indiscriminately harvest endangered species, including sea turtles and giant clams

Climate: tropical

Land use: *other:* 100% (2018 est.)

GOVERNMENT

Country name: *conventional long form:* none
conventional short form: Spratly Islands
etymology: named after a British whaling captain Richard SPRATLY, who sighted Spratly Island in 1843; the name of the island eventually passed to the entire archipelago

ECONOMY

Economic overview: Economic activity is limited to commercial fishing. The proximity to nearby oil- and gas-producing sedimentary basins indicate potential oil and gas deposits, but the region is largely unexplored. No reliable estimates of potential reserves are available. Commercial exploitation has yet to be developed.

TRANSPORTATION

Airports: *total:* 8 (2021)
country comparison to the world: 162

Airports - with paved runways: *total:* 6
2,438 to 3,047 m: 3
914 to 1,523 m: 2
under 914 m: 1 (2021)

Airports - with unpaved runways: *total:* 2
914 to 1,523 m: 2 (2021)

Heliports: 5 (2021)

Ports and terminals: none; offshore anchorage only

MILITARY AND SECURITY

Military - note: the Spratly Islands consist of more than 100 small islands or reefs of which about 45 are claimed and occupied by China, Malaysia, the Philippines, Taiwan, and Vietnam

China: occupies 7 outposts (Fiery Cross, Mischief, Subi, Cuarteron, Gavin, Hughes, and Johnson reefs); the outposts on Fiery Cross, Mischief, and Subi include air bases with helipads and aircraft hangers, naval port facilities, surveillance radars, air defense and anti-ship missile sites, and other military infrastructure such as communications, barracks, maintenance facilities, and ammunition and fuel bunkers

Malaysia: occupies 5 outposts in the southern portion of the archipelago, closest to the Malaysian state of Sabah (Ardasier Reef, Eric Reef, Mariveles Reef, Shallow Reef, and Investigator Shoal); all the outposts have helicopter landing pads, while Shallow Reef also has an airstrip

Philippines: occupies 9 features (Commodore Reef, Second Thomas Shoal, Flat Island, Loaita Cay, Loaita Island, Nanshan Island, Northeast Cay, Thitu Island, and West York Island); Thitu Island has the only Philippine airstrip in the Spratlys

Taiwan: maintains a coast guard outpost with an airstrip on Itu Aba Island

Vietnam: occupies about 50 outposts spread across 27 features, including facilities on 21 rocks and reefs in the Spratlys, plus 14 platforms known as "economic, scientific, and technological service stations," or Dịch vụ-Khoa (DK1), on six underwater banks to the southeast that Vietnam does not consider part of the disputed island chain, although China and Taiwan disagree; Spratly Islands outposts are on Alison Reef, Amboyna Cay, Barque Canada Reef, Central Reef, Collins Reef, Cornwallis South Reef, Discovery Great Reef, East Reef, Grierson Reef, Ladd Reef, Landsdowne Reef, Namyit Island, Pearson Reef, Petley Reef, Sand Cay, Sin Cowe Island, South Reef, Southwest Cay, Spratly Island, Tennent Reef, West Reef; Spratly Island includes an airstrip with aircraft hangers; the six underwater banks with outposts include Vanguard, Rifleman, Prince of Wales, Prince Consort, Grainger, and Alexandra; over the past few years, Vietnam has continued to make modest improvements to its outposts, including defensive positions and infrastructure (2022)

TRANSNATIONAL ISSUES

Disputes - international: *Taiwan-Brunei-China-Malaysia-Philippines-Vietnam*: all of the Spratly Islands are claimed by China (including Taiwan) and Vietnam; parts of them are claimed by Brunei, Malaysia and the Philippines; despite no public territorial claim to Louisa Reef, Brunei implicitly lays claim by including it within the natural prolongation of its continental shelf and basis for a seabed median with Vietnam; the islands are strategically located in the South China Sea and are surrounded by rich fishing groups and potential oil and natural gas deposits; claimants in November 2002 signed the "Declaration on the Conduct of Parties in the South China Sea," which eased tensions but fell short of a legally binding "code of conduct"; in March 2005, the national oil companies of China, the Philippines, and Vietnam signed a joint accord to conduct marine seismic activities in the Spratly Islands; China's island-building and military presence in the archipelago remain controversial

SRI LANKA

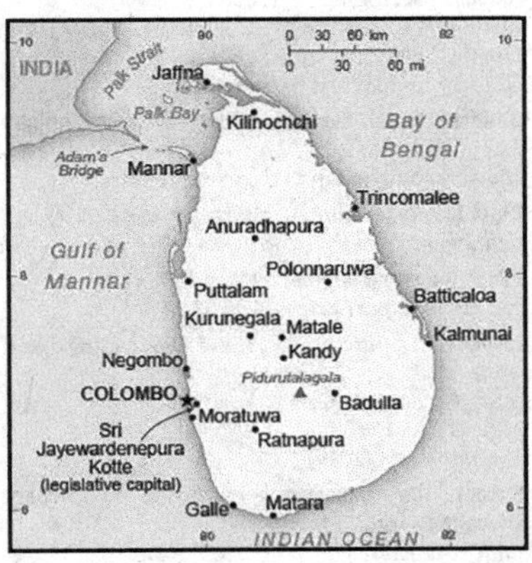

INTRODUCTION

Background: The first Sinhalese arrived in Sri Lanka late in the 6th century B.C., probably from northern India. Buddhism was introduced circa 250 B.C., and the first kingdoms developed at the cities of Anuradhapura (from circa 200 B.C. to circa A.D. 1000) and Polonnaruwa (from about 1070 to 1200). In the 14th century, a south Indian dynasty established a Tamil kingdom in northern Sri Lanka. The Portuguese controlled the coastal areas of the island in the 16th century followed by the Dutch in the 17th century. The island was ceded to the British in 1796, became a crown colony in 1802, and was formally united under British rule by 1815. As Ceylon, it became independent in 1948; its name was changed to Sri Lanka in 1972. Prevailing tensions between the Sinhalese majority and Tamil separatists erupted into war in July 1983. Fighting between the government and Liberation Tigers of Tamil Eelam (LTTE) continued for over a quarter century. Although Norway brokered peace negotiations that led to a ceasefire in 2002, the fighting slowly resumed and was again in full force by 2006. The government defeated the LTTE in May 2009.

During the post-conflict years under President Mahinda RAJAPAKSA, the government initiated infrastructure development projects, many of which were financed by loans from China. His regime faced significant allegations of human rights violations and a shrinking democratic space for civil society. In 2015, a new coalition government headed by President Maithripala SIRISENA of the Sri Lanka Freedom Party and Prime Minister Ranil WICKREMESINGHE of the United National Party came to power with pledges to advance economic, governance, anti-corruption, reconciliation, justice, and accountability reforms. However, implementation of these reforms has been uneven. In October 2018, President SIRISENA attempted to oust Prime Minister WICKREMESINGHE, swearing in former President RAJAPAKSA as the new prime minister and issuing an order to dissolve the Parliament and hold elections. This sparked a seven-week constitutional crisis that ended when the Supreme Court ruled SIRISENA's actions unconstitutional, RAJAPAKSA resigned, and WICKREMESINGHE was reinstated. In November 2019, Gotabaya RAJAPAKSA won the presidential election and appointed his brother, Mahinda, prime minister. Since Gotabaya RAJAPAKSA's election, there have been concerns about his administration's commitment to pursuing justice, human rights, and accountability reforms, as well as the risks to foreign creditors that Sri Lanka faces given its ongoing economic crisis. A combination of factors including the impact of the worldwide COVID pandemic; severe shortages of food, medicine, and fuel; and power outages have triggered increasingly violent protests in Columbo. Longtime parliamentarian and former five-time prime minister, Ranil WICKREMESINGHE replaced Mahinda RAJAPASKA as prime-minister in mid-May 2022, with a mandate to resolve the country's economic problems.

GEOGRAPHY

Location: Southern Asia, island in the Indian Ocean, south of India

Geographic coordinates: 7 00 N, 81 00 E

Map references: Asia

Area: *total:* 65,610 sq km
land: 64,630 sq km
water: 980 sq km
country comparison to the world: 122

Area - comparative: slightly larger than West Virginia

Land boundaries: *total:* 0 km

Coastline: 1,340 km

Maritime claims: *territorial sea:* 12 nm
contiguous zone: 24 nm
exclusive economic zone: 200 nm
continental shelf: 200 nm or to the edge of the continental margin

Climate: tropical monsoon; northeast monsoon (December to March); southwest monsoon (June to October)

Terrain: mostly low, flat to rolling plain; mountains in south-central interior

Elevation: *highest point:* Pidurutalagala 2,524 m
lowest point: Indian Ocean 0 m
mean elevation: 228 m

Natural resources: limestone, graphite, mineral sands, gems, phosphates, clay, hydropower, arable land

Land use: *agricultural land:* 43.5% (2018 est.)
arable land: 20.7% (2018 est.)
permanent crops: 15.8% (2018 est.)
permanent pasture: 7% (2018 est.)
forest: 29.4% (2018 est.)
other: 27.1% (2018 est.)

Irrigated land: 5,700 sq km (2012)

Population distribution: the population is primarily concentrated within a broad wet zone in the southwest, urban centers along the eastern coast, and on the Jaffna Peninsula in the north

Natural hazards: occasional cyclones and tornadoes

Geography - note: strategic location near major Indian Ocean sea lanes; Adam's Bridge is a chain of limestone shoals between the southeastern coast of India and the northwestern coast of Sri Lanka; geological evidence suggests that this 50-km long Bridge once connected India and Sri Lanka; ancient records seem to indicate that a foot passage was possible between the two land masses until the 15th century when the land bridge broke up in a cyclone

PEOPLE AND SOCIETY

Population: 23,187,516 (2022 est.)
country comparison to the world: 58

Nationality: *noun:* Sri Lankan(s)
adjective: Sri Lankan

Ethnic groups: Sinhalese 74.9%, Sri Lankan Tamil 11.2%, Sri Lankan Moors 9.2%, Indian Tamil 4.2%, other 0.5% (2012 est.)

Languages: Sinhala (official and national language) 87%, Tamil (official and national language) 28.5%, English 23.8% (2012 est.)
note: data represent main languages spoken by the population aged 10 years and older; shares sum to more than 100% because some respondents gave more than one answer on the census; English is commonly used in government and is referred to as the "link language" in the constitution

Religions: Buddhist (official) 70.2%, Hindu 12.6%, Muslim 9.7%, Roman Catholic 6.1%, other Christian 1.3%, other 0.05% (2012 est.)

Age structure: *0-14 years:* 23.11% (male 2,696,379/female 2,592,450)
15-24 years: 14.58% (male 1,700,442/female 1,636,401)
25-54 years: 41.2% (male 4,641,842/female 4,789,101)
55-64 years: 10.48% (male 1,110,481/female 1,288,056)
65 years and over: 10.63% (male 1,023,315/female 1,410,734) (2020 est.)

Dependency ratios: *total dependency ratio:* 53.7
youth dependency ratio: 36.4
elderly dependency ratio: 17.3
potential support ratio: 5.8 (2020 est.)

Median age: *total:* 33.7 years
male: 32.3 years
female: 35.1 years (2020 est.)
country comparison to the world: 97

Population growth rate: 0.61% (2022 est.)
country comparison to the world: 144

Birth rate: 13.8 births/1,000 population (2022 est.)
country comparison to the world: 131

Death rate: 6.49 deaths/1,000 population (2022 est.)
country comparison to the world: 137

Net migration rate: -1.22 migrant(s)/1,000 population (2022 est.)
country comparison to the world: 151

Population distribution: the population is primarily concentrated within a broad wet zone in the southwest, urban centers along the eastern coast, and on the Jaffna Peninsula in the north

Urbanization: *urban population:* 19% of total population (2022)
rate of urbanization: 1.22% annual rate of change (2020-25 est.)

Major urban areas - population: 103,000 Sri Jayewardenepura Kotte (legislative capital) (2018), 626,000 COLOMBO (capital) (2022)

Sex ratio: *at birth:* 1.04 male(s)/female
0-14 years: 1.04 male(s)/female
15-24 years: 1.04 male(s)/female
25-54 years: 0.97 male(s)/female
55-64 years: 0.86 male(s)/female
65 years and over: 0.61 male(s)/female
total population: 0.95 male(s)/female (2022 est.)

Mother's mean age at first birth: 25.6 years (2016 est.)
note: data represents median age at first birth among women 30-34

Maternal mortality ratio: 36 deaths/100,000 live births (2017 est.)
country comparison to the world: 106

Infant mortality rate: *total:* 8.2 deaths/1,000 live births
male: 9.18 deaths/1,000 live births
female: 7.18 deaths/1,000 live births (2022 est.)
country comparison to the world: 148

Life expectancy at birth: *total population:* 78 years
male: 74.57 years
female: 81.56 years (2022 est.)
country comparison to the world: 80

Total fertility rate: 1.98 children born/woman (2022 est.)
country comparison to the world: 113

Contraceptive prevalence rate: 64.6% (2016)

Drinking water source: *improved: urban:* 99.7% of population
rural: 91.2% of population
total: 92.8% of population
unimproved: urban: 0.3% of population
rural: 8.8% of population
total: 7.2% of population (2020 est.)

Current health expenditure: 4.1% of GDP (2019)

Physicians density: 1.23 physicians/1,000 population (2020)

Hospital bed density: 4.2 beds/1,000 population (2017)

Sanitation facility access: *improved: urban:* 96.6% of population
rural: 97.9% of population
total: 97.6% of population
unimproved: urban: 3.4% of population
rural: 2.1% of population
total: 2.4% of population (2020 est.)

HIV/AIDS - adult prevalence rate: (2020 est.) <.1%

HIV/AIDS - people living with HIV/AIDS: 3,700 (2020 est.)
country comparison to the world: 128

HIV/AIDS - deaths: (2020 est.) <200

Major infectious diseases: *degree of risk:* intermediate (2020)
vectorborne diseases: dengue fever
water contact diseases: leptospirosis
animal contact diseases: rabies

Obesity - adult prevalence rate: 5.2% (2016)
country comparison to the world: 182

Alcohol consumption per capita: *total:* 2.58 liters of pure alcohol (2019 est.)
beer: 0.22 liters of pure alcohol (2019 est.)
wine: 0.01 liters of pure alcohol (2019 est.)
spirits: 2.32 liters of pure alcohol (2019 est.)
other alcohols: 0.03 liters of pure alcohol (2019 est.)
country comparison to the world: 122

Tobacco use: *total:* 22% (2020 est.)
male: 41.4% (2020 est.)
female: 2.6% (2020 est.)
country comparison to the world: 74

Children under the age of 5 years underweight: 20.5% (2016)
country comparison to the world: 20

Child marriage: *women married by age 15:* 0.9%
women married by age 18: 9.8% (2016 est.)

Education expenditures: 2.1% of GDP (2018 est.)
country comparison to the world: 177

Literacy: *definition:* age 15 and over can read and write
total population: 92.3%
male: 93%
female: 91.6% (2019)

School life expectancy (primary to tertiary education): *total:* 14 years
male: 14 years
female: 14 years (2018)

Unemployment, youth ages 15-24: *total:* 21.1%
male: 16.6%
female: 29.4% (2018 est.)

ENVIRONMENT

Environment - current issues: deforestation; soil erosion; wildlife populations threatened by poaching and urbanization; coastal degradation from mining activities and increased pollution; coral reef destruction; freshwater resources being polluted by industrial wastes and sewage runoff; waste disposal; air pollution in Colombo

Environment - international agreements: *party to:* Biodiversity, Climate Change, Climate Change-Kyoto Protocol, Climate Change-Paris Agreement, Desertification, Endangered Species, Environmental Modification, Hazardous Wastes, Law of the Sea, Nuclear Test Ban, Ozone Layer Protection, Ship Pollution, Wetlands
signed, but not ratified: Comprehensive Nuclear Test Ban, Marine Life Conservation

Air pollutants: *particulate matter emissions:* 15.25 micrograms per cubic meter (2016 est.)
carbon dioxide emissions: 23.36 megatons (2016 est.)
methane emissions: 10.95 megatons (2020 est.)

Climate: tropical monsoon; northeast monsoon (December to March); southwest monsoon (June to October)

Land use: *agricultural land:* 43.5% (2018 est.)
arable land: 20.7% (2018 est.)
permanent crops: 15.8% (2018 est.)
permanent pasture: 7% (2018 est.)
forest: 29.4% (2018 est.)
other: 27.1% (2018 est.)

Urbanization: *urban population:* 19% of total population (2022)
rate of urbanization: 1.22% annual rate of change (2020-25 est.)

Revenue from forest resources: *forest revenues:* 0.06% of GDP (2018 est.)
country comparison to the world: 126

Revenue from coal: *coal revenues:* 0% of GDP (2018 est.)
country comparison to the world: 169

Food insecurity: *widespread lack of access: due to serious macroeconomic challenges, significant reduction in 2022 cereal output, and high food prices -* severe macroeconomic challenges, mostly reflecting dwindling foreign currency reserves after revenues from merchandise exports, remittances, and from the tourist sector declined dramatically over the last year, have had a negative impact on the country's capacity to import cereals; the 2022 cereal production sharply declined due to a government ordered reduction in the application of chemical fertilizers; unprecedentedly high food prices are constraining economic access to food for a majority of households

Waste and recycling: *municipal solid waste generated annually:* 2,631,650 tons (2016 est.)
municipal solid waste recycled annually: 336,588 tons (2016 est.)
percent of municipal solid waste recycled: 12.8% (2016 est.)

Total water withdrawal: *municipal:* 805 million cubic meters (2017 est.)
industrial: 831 million cubic meters (2017 est.)
agricultural: 11.31 billion cubic meters (2017 est.)

Total renewable water resources: 52.8 billion cubic meters (2017 est.)

GOVERNMENT

Country name: *conventional long form:* Democratic Socialist Republic of Sri Lanka
conventional short form: Sri Lanka
local long form: Shri Lanka Prajatantrika Samajavadi Janarajaya (Sinhala)/ Ilankai Jananayaka Choshalichak Kutiyarachu (Tamil)
local short form: Shri Lanka (Sinhala)/ Ilankai (Tamil)
former: Serendib, Ceylon
etymology: the name means "resplendent island" in Sanskrit

Government type: presidential republic

Capital: *name:* Colombo (commercial capital); Sri Jayewardenepura Kotte (legislative capital)
geographic coordinates: 6 55 N, 79 50 E
time difference: UTC+5.5 (10.5 hours ahead of Washington, DC, during Standard Time)
etymology: Colombo may derive from the Sinhala "kolon thota," meaning "port on the river" (referring to the Kelani River that empties into the Indian Ocean at Colombo); alternatively, the name may derive from the Sinhala "kola amba thota" meaning "harbor with mango trees"; it is also possible that the Portuguese named the city after Christopher COLUMBUS, who lived in Portugal for many years (as Cristovao COLOMBO) before discovering the Americas for the Spanish crown in 1492 - not long before the Portuguese made their way to Sri Lanka in 1505; Sri Jayewardenepura Kotte translates as "Resplendent City of Growing Victory" in Sinhala

Administrative divisions: 9 provinces; Central, Eastern, North Central, Northern, North Western, Sabaragamuwa, Southern, Uva, Western

Independence: 4 February 1948 (from the UK)

National holiday: Independence Day (National Day), 4 February (1948)

Constitution: *history:* several previous; latest adopted 16 August 1978, certified 31 August 1978
amendments: proposed by Parliament; passage requires at least two-thirds majority vote of its total membership, certification by the president of the republic or the Parliament speaker, and in some cases approval in a referendum by absolute majority of valid votes; amended many times, last in 2020

Legal system: mixed legal system of Roman-Dutch civil law, English common law, Jaffna Tamil customary law, and Muslim personal law

International law organization participation: has not submitted an ICJ jurisdiction declaration; non-party state to the ICCt

Citizenship: *citizenship by birth:* no
citizenship by descent only: at least one parent must be a citizen of Sri Lanka
dual citizenship recognized: no, except in cases where the government rules it is to the benefit of Sri Lanka
residency requirement for naturalization: 7 years

Suffrage: 18 years of age; universal

Executive branch: *chief of state:* President Ranil WICKREMESINGHE (since 20 July 2022); the president is both chief of state and head of government; prime minister (vacant)
head of government: President Ranil WICKREMESINGHE (since 20 July 2022)
cabinet: Cabinet appointed by the president in consultation with the prime minister
elections/appointments: president directly elected by preferential majority popular vote for a 5-year term (eligible for a second term); election last held on 16 November 2019 (next to be held in 2024); prime minister appointed by the president from among members of Parliament for a 5-year term)
election results:
Ranil WICKREMESINGHE elected president by Parliament on 20 July 2022; WICKREMESINGH 134 votes, Dullas ALAHAPPERUNA 82 votes
Note: amid public protests which began in March 2022, President Gotabaya RAJAPAKSE fled the country on 13 July and Ranil WICKREMESINGHE became acting president; RAJAPAKSE announced his resignation on the 14th, which was accepted by the speaker of Parliament the following day; Parliament on 20 July elected WICKREMESINGHE as president; vote - Ranil WICKREMESINGHE - 134, Dullas ALAHAPPERUMA - 82

Legislative branch: *description:* unicameral Parliament (225 seats; 196 members directly elected in multi-seat district constituencies by proportional representation vote using a preferential method in which voters select 3 candidates in order of preference; remaining 29 seats, referred to as the "national list" are allocated by each party secretary according to the island wide proportional vote the party obtains; members serve 5-year terms)
elections:
last held on 5 August 2020 (next to be held in August 2025)
election results:
percent of vote by coalition/party - SLFPA 59.1%, SJB 23.9%, JVP 3.8%, TNA 2.8%, UNP 2.2%, TNPF 0.6%, EPDP 0.5%, other 7.1%; seats by coalition/party - SLFPA 145, SJB 54, TNA 10, JVP 3, other 13; composition - men 213, women 12, percent of women 5.3%

Judicial branch: *highest court(s):* Supreme Court of the Republic (consists of the chief justice and 9 justices); note - the court has exclusive jurisdiction to review legislation
judge selection and term of office: chief justice nominated by the Constitutional Council (CC), a 9-member high-level advisory body, and appointed by the president; other justices nominated by the CC and appointed by the president on the advice of the chief justice; all justices can serve until age 65
subordinate courts: Court of Appeals; High Courts; Magistrates' Courts; municipal and primary courts

Political parties and leaders: Crusaders for Democracy or CFD [Ganeshalingam CHANDRALINGAM]
Eelam People's Democratic Party or EPDP [Douglas DEVANANDA]
Eelam People's Revolutionary Liberation Front or EPRLF [Suresh PREMACHANDRAN]
Illankai Tamil Arasu Kachchi or ITAK [Mavai SENATHIRAJAH]
Janatha Vimukthi Peramuna or JVP [Anura Kumara DISSANAYAKE]
Jathika Hela Urumaya or JHU [Karunarathna PARANAWITHANA, Ven. Hadigalle Wimalasara THERO]
National Peoples Power or JVP [Anura Kumara DISSANAYAKE]
People's Liberation Organisation of Tamil Eelam or PLOTE [D. SIDDARTHAN]
Samagi Jana Balawegaya or SJB [Sajith PREMADASA]
Sri Lanka Freedom Party or SLFP [Maithripala SIRISENA]
Sri Lanka Muslim Congress or SLMC [Rauff HAKEEM]

Sri Lanka People's Freedom Alliance or SLPFA [Mahinda RAJAPAKSA] (includes SLPFP, SLPP, and several smaller parties)
Sri Lanka Podujana Peramuna (Sri Lanka's People's Front) or SLPP [G. L. PEIRIS]
Tamil Eelam Liberation Organization or TELO [Selvam ADAIKALANATHAN]
Tamil National Alliance or TNA [Rajavarothiam SAMPANTHAN] (includes ITAK, PLOTE, TELO)
Tamil National People's Front or TNPF [Gajendrakumar PONNAMBALAM]
United National Front for Good Governance or UNFGG [Ranil WICKREMESINGHE] (coalition includes JHU, UNP)
United National Party or UNP [Ranil WICKREMESINGHE]

International organization participation: ABEDA, ADB, ARF, BIMSTEC, C, CD, CICA (observer), CP, FAO, G-11, G-15, G-24, G-77, IAEA, IBRD, ICAO, ICC (national committees), ICRM, IDA, IFAD, IFC, IFRCS, IHO, ILO, IMF, IMO, IMSO, Interpol, IOC, IOM, IPU, ISO, ITSO, ITU, ITUC (NGOs), MIGA, MINURSO, MINUSTAH, MONUSCO, NAM, OAS (observer), OPCW, PCA, SAARC, SACEP, SCO (dialogue member), UN, UNCTAD, UNESCO, UNIDO, UNIFIL, UNISFA, UNMISS, UNWTO, UPU, WCO, WFTU (NGOs), WHO, WIPO, WMO, WTO

Diplomatic representation in the US: *chief of mission:* Ambassador Mahinda SAMARASINGHE (since 1 December 2021)
chancery: 3025 Whitehaven Street NW, Washington, DC 20008
telephone: [1] (202) 483-4025 through 4028
FAX: [1] (202) 232-7181
email address and website:
slembassy@slembassyusa.org
https://slembassyusa.org/new/
consulate(s) general: Los Angeles, New York

Diplomatic representation from the US: *chief of mission:* Ambassador Julie J. CHUNG (since 17 February 2022)
embassy: 210 Galle Road, Colombo 03
mailing address: 6100 Colombo Place, Washington DC 20521-6100
telephone: [94] (11) 249-8500
FAX: [94] (11) 243-7345
email address and website:
colomboacs@state.gov
https://lk.usembassy.gov/

Flag description: yellow with two panels; the smaller hoist-side panel has two equal vertical bands of green (hoist side) and orange; the other larger panel depicts a yellow lion holding a sword on a maroon rectangular field that also displays a yellow bo leaf in each corner; the yellow field appears as a border around the entire flag and extends between the two panels; the lion represents Sinhalese ethnicity, the strength of the nation, and bravery; the sword demonstrates the sovereignty of the nation; the four bo leaves - symbolizing Buddhism and its influence on the country - stand for the four virtues of kindness, friendliness, happiness, and equanimity; orange signifies Sri Lankan Tamils, green Sri Lankan Moors, and maroon the Sinhalese majority; yellow denotes other ethnic groups; also referred to as the Lion Flag

National symbol(s): lion, water lily; national colors: maroon, yellow

National anthem: *name:* "Sri Lanka Matha" (Mother Sri Lanka)
lyrics/music: Ananda SAMARKONE
note: adopted 1951

National heritage: *total World Heritage Sites:* 8 (6 cultural, 2 natural)
selected World Heritage Site locales: Ancient City of Polonnaruwa (c); Ancient City of Sigiriya (c); Sacred City of Anuradhapura (c); Old Town of Galle and its Fortifications (c); Sacred City of Kandy (c); Sinharaja Forest Reserve (n); Rangiri Dambulla Cave Temple (c); Central Highlands of Sri Lanka (n)

ECONOMY

Economic overview: Sri Lanka's economy has historically relied upon government-guided market investments, and since 2009, several sectors have been excluded from any privatization efforts. Major infrastructure development of rural and civil war-impacted areas remains a major focus, as does small business development. Sri Lanka's longstanding high debt and large civil service have contributed to historically high budget deficits and remain a concern. Sri Lankan tourism soared since the end of conflict with the Liberation Tigers of Tamil Eelam, but the 2018 constitutional crisis, the 2019 Easter bombings, and the ongoing COVID-19 pandemic have since destabilized this key industry, leading Sri Lanka to nearly expend all foreign currency reserves. Regionally, Sri Lanka has engaged China on major infrastructure projects and currently owes $6.5 billion, which may soon be restructured.

Fiscally, Sri Lanka's focus on domestic goods—instead of export growth—further increased Sri Lanka's trade imbalance, despite its EU preferential trade status allowing tax-free garment and gem exports to the EU. From 2019 until its repeal in 2021, Sri Lanka's agricultural import ban on chemical fertilizers resulted in disastrous reductions in rice, tea, and rubber yields, increasing Sri Lanka's import dependencies for these goods. The ongoing Russo-Ukrainian War has also decreased fuel supplies and significantly increased prices. India is providing both direct fertilizer and fuel aid to offset these shortages. Power shortages plague business climates, and further stoke existing labor shortages. Additionally Sri Lanka is also considering privatizing several state-owned entities to try to spur industrial and service sectors' growth.

Monetarily, Sri Lanka remains in a dire position, further exacerbated by the 2019 tax cuts that contributed to the country's ongoing economic calamity. Already one of the highest indebted emerging markets, Sri Lanka defaulted on its current public debt payments in May 2022, and its ongoing currency crisis has crippled domestic revenues, tax collections, and economic activity, ushering in the country's worst economic crisis since independence in 1948. As a result, inflation is skyrocketing (nearing 40%), and food, fuel, and medicine shortages have led to widespread unrest and economic collapse. Sri Lanka currently seeks an immediate $3 million IMF bridge loan and $75 million in foreign currency to pay for essential goods and fuel. The World Bank, India, and the G7 countries have agreed to aid Sri Lanka in securing debt relief, but the IMF maintains that Sri Lanka must raise interest rates and taxes to secure any loan.

Current Sri Lankan priorities focus on the following goals:
—Securing a bridge loan from the IMF;
—Improving its foreign currency reserves through continued promotion of tourism and privatization of state enterprises;
—Recovering from COVID-19 pandemic-related economic disruptions and demand shocks;
—Identifying alternative fuel supply chains; and
—Restructuring preexisting infrastructure debts to China.

Real GDP (purchasing power parity): $274.8 billion (2020 est.)
$284.97 billion (2019 est.)
$278.68 billion (2018 est.)
note: data are in 2017 dollars
country comparison to the world: 56

Real GDP growth rate: 2.29% (2019 est.)
3.32% (2018 est.)
3.58% (2017 est.)
country comparison to the world: 122

Real GDP per capita: $12,500 (2020 est.)
$13,100 (2019 est.)
$12,900 (2018 est.)
note: data are in 2017 dollars
country comparison to the world: 119

GDP (official exchange rate): $84.016 billion (2019 est.)

Inflation rate (consumer prices): 4.3% (2019 est.)
4.2% (2018 est.)
6.5% (2017 est.)
country comparison to the world: 173

Credit ratings:

Fitch rating: CCC (2020)

Moody's rating: Caa1 (2020)

Standard & Poors rating: CCC+ (2020)

GDP - composition, by sector of origin: *agriculture:* 7.8% (2017 est.)
industry: 30.5% (2017 est.)
services: 61.7% (2017 est.)

GDP - composition, by end use: *household consumption:* 62% (2017 est.)
government consumption: 8.5% (2017 est.)
investment in fixed capital: 26.3% (2017 est.)
investment in inventories: 10.2% (2017 est.)
exports of goods and services: 21.9% (2017 est.)
imports of goods and services: -29.1% (2017 est.)

Agricultural products: rice, coconuts, sugar cane, plantains, milk, tea, cassava, maize, poultry, coir

Industries: processing of rubber, tea, coconuts, tobacco and other agricultural commodities; telecommunications, insurance, banking; tourism, shipping; clothing, textiles; cement, petroleum refining, information technology services, construction

Industrial production growth rate: 4.6% (2017 est.)
country comparison to the world: 64

Labor force: 8 million (2020 est.)
country comparison to the world: 60

Labor force - by occupation: *agriculture:* 27%
industry: 26%
services: 47% (31 December 2016)

Unemployment rate: 4.83% (2019 est.)
4.44% (2018 est.)
country comparison to the world: 72

Unemployment, youth ages 15-24: *total:* 21.1%
male: 16.6%
female: 29.4% (2018 est.)
country comparison to the world: 71

Population below poverty line: 4.1% (2016 est.)

Gini Index coefficient - distribution of family income: 39.8 (2016 est.)
46 (1995)
country comparison to the world: 64

Household income or consumption by percentage share: *lowest 10%:* 3%
highest 10%: 32.2% (2012 est.)

Budget: *revenues:* 12.07 billion (2017 est.)
expenditures: 16.88 billion (2017 est.)

Budget surplus (+) or deficit (-): -5.5% (of GDP) (2017 est.)
country comparison to the world: 174

Public debt: 79.1% of GDP (2017 est.)
79.6% of GDP (2016 est.)
note: covers central government debt and excludes debt instruments directly owned by government entities other than the treasury (e.g. commercial bank borrowings of a government corporation); the data includes treasury debt held by foreign entities as well as intragovernmental debt; intragovernmental debt consists of treasury borrowings from surpluses in the social funds, such as for retirement; sub-national entities are usually not permitted to sell debt instruments
country comparison to the world: 35

Taxes and other revenues: 13.8% (of GDP) (2017 est.)
country comparison to the world: 204

Fiscal year: calendar year

Current account balance: -$10 million (2019 est.)
-$17 million (2018 est.)
country comparison to the world: 69

Exports: $19.41 billion (2019 est.) note: data are in current year dollars
$20.26 billion (2018 est.) note: data are in current year dollars
$15.166 billion (2017 est.)
country comparison to the world: 83

Exports - partners: United States 24%, India 8%, United Kingdom 7%, Germany 7% (2019)

Exports - commodities: clothing and apparel, tea, used tires, rubber products, precious stones, cinnamon (2019)

Imports: $24.56 billion (2019 est.) note: data are in current year dollars
$26.84 billion (2018 est.) note: data are in current year dollars
$26.063 billion (2017 est.)
country comparison to the world: 75

Imports - partners: India 24%, China 23%, Singapore 7%, United Arab Emirates 6%, Malaysia 5% (2019)

Imports - commodities: refined petroleum, textiles, gold, cars, broadcasting equipment (2019)

Reserves of foreign exchange and gold: $7.959 billion (31 December 2017 est.)
$6.019 billion (31 December 2016 est.)
country comparison to the world: 78

Debt - external: $55.332 billion (2019 est.)
$52.567 billion (2018 est.)
country comparison to the world: 64

Exchange rates: Sri Lankan rupees (LKR) per US dollar -
185.8 (2020 est.)
181.2 (2019 est.)
178.545 (2018 est.)
135.86 (2014 est.)
130.57 (2013 est.)

ENERGY

Electricity access: *electrification - total population:* 100% (2019)

Electricity: *installed generating capacity:* 4.527 million kW (2020 est.)
consumption: 13,991,420,000 kWh (2019 est.)
exports: 0 kWh (2020 est.)
imports: 0 kWh (2020 est.)
transmission/distribution losses: 1.337 billion kWh (2019 est.)

Electricity generation sources: *fossil fuels:* 64% of total installed capacity (2020 est.)
solar: 0.7% of total installed capacity (2020 est.)
wind: 2.3% of total installed capacity (2020 est.)
hydroelectricity: 32.2% of total installed capacity (2020 est.)
biomass and waste: 0.8% of total installed capacity (2020 est.)

Coal: *production:* 0 metric tons (2020 est.)
consumption: 2.237 million metric tons (2020 est.)
exports: 0 metric tons (2020 est.)
imports: 2.586 million metric tons (2020 est.)
proven reserves: 0 metric tons (2019 est.)

Petroleum: *total petroleum production:* 0 bbl/day (2021 est.)
refined petroleum consumption: 131,100 bbl/day (2019 est.)
crude oil and lease condensate exports: 0 bbl/day (2018 est.)
crude oil and lease condensate imports: 35,300 bbl/day (2018 est.)
crude oil estimated reserves: 0 barrels (2021 est.)

Refined petroleum products - production: 34,210 bbl/day (2017 est.)
country comparison to the world: 84

Refined petroleum products - exports: 3,871 bbl/day (2015 est.)
country comparison to the world: 96

Refined petroleum products - imports: 66,280 bbl/day (2015 est.)
country comparison to the world: 70

Carbon dioxide emissions: 23.939 million metric tonnes of CO2 (2019 est.)
from coal and metallurgical coke: 5.546 million metric tonnes of CO2 (2019 est.)
from petroleum and other liquids: 18.393 million metric tonnes of CO2 (2019 est.)
country comparison to the world: 80

Energy consumption per capita: 17.268 million Btu/person (2019 est.)
country comparison to the world: 138

COMMUNICATIONS

Telephones - fixed lines: *total subscriptions:* 2,607,868 (2020 est.)
subscriptions per 100 inhabitants: 12 (2020 est.)
country comparison to the world: 48

Telephones - mobile cellular: *total subscriptions:* 30,778,600 (2019)
subscriptions per 100 inhabitants: 144 (2019)
country comparison to the world: 46

Telecommunication systems: *general assessment:* Sri Lanka's fixed-line telephony market was one of the very few in the world to experience a significant upsurge in subscriptions in 2020; while the country suffers from a relatively poor fixed-line infrastructure and a correspondingly strong mobile sector, demand for traditional phone services increased 14% in 2020; preliminary results suggest a further jump of up to 13% can also be expected in 2021; this will take Sri Lanka's fixed-line penetration to levels not seen since 2013; the most reason behind the market's reversal of fortunes is the Covid-19 crisis and Sri Lanka's ensuring lock downs; these forced much of the population back inside and reverting to 'traditional' methods of communication for both voice and data services; the fixed broadband market was equally robust, growing 20% in 2020 alone; Sri Lanka possesses a relatively low number of computers per household so the fixed broadband market's success comes off a small base; the one area of the telecommunications market that experienced a fall was the mobile segment; up until the start of the pandemic, Sri Lanka had a very high mobile penetration rate of 155%; this near-saturation level reflected the preponderance for subscribers to carry multiple SIM cards to take advantage of cheaper on-net call rates; the reduction in demand and traffic because of the pandemic led to a sharp drop in the number of active subscriptions, down to just 135% – a 17% decline in just one year; the market is expected to bounce back quickly, as soon as the country eases back on its lock down measures and reduces travel restrictions; it will also be boosted, come 2022, by the anticipated launch of commercial 5G mobile services (2021)
domestic: fixed-line roughly 11 per 100 and mobile-cellular nearly 139 per 100; national trunk network consists of digital microwave radio relay and fiber-optic links; fixed wireless local loops have been installed; competition is strong in mobile cellular systems and mobile cellular subscribership is increasing (2020)
international: country code - 94; landing points for the SeaMeWe -3,-5, Dhiraagu-SLT Submarine Cable Network, WARF Submarine Cable, Bharat Lanka Cable System and the Bay of Bengal Gateway submarine cables providing connectivity to Asia, Africa, Southeast Asia, Australia, the Middle East, and Europe; satellite earth stations - 2 Intelsat (Indian Ocean) (2019)

Broadcast media: government operates 5 TV channels and 19 radio channels; multi-channel satellite and cable TV subscription services available; 25 private TV stations and about 43 radio stations; 6 non-profit TV stations and 4 radio stations

Internet country code: .lk

Internet users: *total:* 7,671,650 (2020 est.)
percent of population: 35% (2020 est.)
country comparison to the world: 74

Broadband - fixed subscriptions: *total:* 1,781,530 (2020 est.)
subscriptions per 100 inhabitants: 8 (2020 est.)
country comparison to the world: 60

TRANSPORTATION

National air transport system: *number of registered air carriers:* 3 (2020)
inventory of registered aircraft operated by air carriers: 34
annual passenger traffic on registered air carriers: 5,882,376 (2018)
annual freight traffic on registered air carriers: 436.2 million (2018) mt-km

Civil aircraft registration country code prefix: 4R

Airports: *total:* 18 (2021)
country comparison to the world: 140

Airports - with paved runways: *total:* 11
over 3,047 m: 2

1,524 to 2,437 m: 5
914 to 1,523 m: 4 (2021)

Airports - with unpaved runways: *total:* 7
1,524 to 2,437 m: 2
914 to 1,523 m: 3
under 914 m: 2 (2021)

Heliports: 1 (2021)

Pipelines: 7 km refined products

Railways: *total:* 1,562 km (2016)
broad gauge: 1,562 km (2016) 1.676-m gauge
country comparison to the world: 82

Roadways: *total:* 114,093 km (2010)
paved: 16,977 km (2010)
unpaved: 97,116 km (2010)
country comparison to the world: 43

Waterways: 160 km (2012) (primarily on rivers in southwest)
country comparison to the world: 110

Merchant marine: *total:* 90
by type: bulk carrier 6, general cargo 13, oil tanker 11, other 60 (2021)
country comparison to the world: 97

Ports and terminals: *major seaport(s):* Colombo
container port(s) (TEUs): Colombo (7,228,337) (2019)

MILITARY AND SECURITY

Military and security forces: Sri Lanka Armed Forces: Sri Lanka Army (includes National Guard and the Volunteer Force), Sri Lanka Navy (includes Marine Corps), Sri Lanka Air Force, Sri Lanka Coast Guard; Civil Security Department (Home Guard); Ministry of Public Security: Sri Lanka National Police (2022)
note: the Sri Lanka Police includes the Special Task Force, a paramilitary unit responsible for counterterrorism and counterinsurgency operations; it coordinates internal security operations with the military

Military expenditures: 1.9% of GDP (2022 est.)
1.9% of GDP (2021 est.)
2% of GDP (2020 est.)
2% of GDP (2019 est.) (approximately $5.9 billion)
1.9% of GDP (2018 est.) (approximately $5.6 billion)
country comparison to the world: 67

Military and security service personnel strengths: approximately 240,000 total personnel (170,000 Army; 40,000 Navy; 30,000 Air Force); approximately 11,000 Special Task Force personnel (2022)

Military equipment inventories and acquisitions: the military's inventory consists mostly of Chinese and Russian-origin equipment with a smaller mix of material from countries such as India and the US; since 2010, China, India, and the US have been the leading suppliers of arms to Sri Lanka (2022)

Military service age and obligation: 18-22 years of age for voluntary military service for men and women; no conscription (2022)

Military deployments: 110 Central African Republic (MINUSCA); 125 Lebanon (UNIFIL); 240 Mali (MINUSMA) (May 2022)

Military - note: Sri Lanka traditionally has had close security ties to India; India participated in the counter-insurgency war against the Liberation Tigers of Tamil Eelam (LTTE) from 1987-1991, losing over 1,000 soldiers in the conflict; the Sri Lankan and Indian militaries continue to conduct exercises together, and India trains over 1,000 Sri Lankan soldiers per year; however, since the end of the war with LTTE, Sri Lanka has also increased military ties with China, including acquiring military equipment, hosting naval port calls, and sending personnel to China for training

since the end of the war with LTTE, the Sri Lankan military has increased its role in a range of commercial sectors including agriculture, hotels, leisure, and restaurants; this expansion has been particularly discernible in the majority Tamil-populated northern and eastern provinces where a large portion of the Army reportedly remained deployed as of 2021 (2022)

TERRORISM

Terrorist group(s): Islamic State of Iraq and ash-Sham (ISIS); Liberation Tigers of Tamil Eelam (LTTE)

TRANSNATIONAL ISSUES

Disputes - international: none identified

Refugees and internally displaced persons: IDPs: 12,000 (civil war; more than half displaced prior to 2008; many of the more than 480,000 IDPs registered as returnees have not reached durable solutions) (2021)

Trafficking in persons: *current situation:* Sri Lanka is primarily a source and, to a much lesser extent, a destination country for men, women, and children subjected to forced labor and sex trafficking; the majority of trafficking cases involve traffickers forcing Sri Lankan workers into labor overseas; men, women, and children are subjected to forced labor in the Middle East, Asia, Europe, and the United States in construction, garment manufacturing, and domestic service; authorities have identified labor trafficking victims among Sri Lankan female migrant workers who seek employment in Saudi Arabia, Kuwait, Qatar, Japan, and South Korea; traffickers force children, individuals with physical deformities, and those from socially vulnerable groups to beg or engage in criminal activity in Sri Lanka's largest cities
tier rating: Tier 2 Watch List — Sri Lanka does not fully meet the minimum standards for the elimination of trafficking but is making significant efforts to do so; efforts include convicting traffickers under its trafficking statute, identifying victims, and working on anti-trafficking training and raising awareness; however, some officials reportedly complicit in trafficking are inadequately investigated; fewer victims were identified in country and abroad; social and legal assistance for victims remained inadequate and inconsistent; the Sri Lankan Bureau of Foreign Employment did not refer potential trafficking cases to police for criminal investigation; police continued to arrest trafficking victims for prostitution, vagrancy, and immigration offenses; child sex trafficking victims remained in government detention centers (2020)

SUDAN

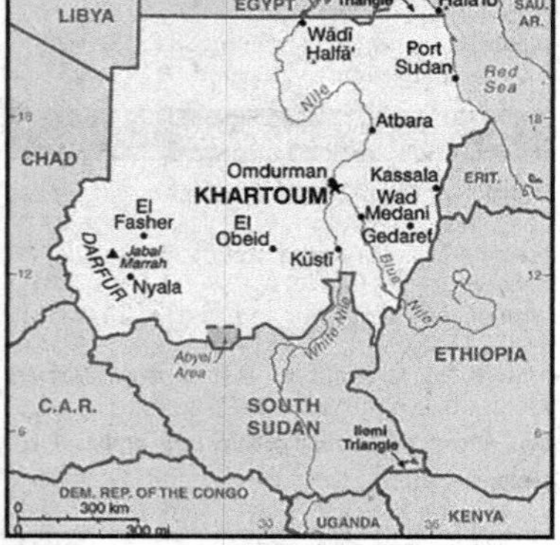

INTRODUCTION

Background: Long referred to as Nubia, modern-day Sudan was the site of the Kingdom of Kerma (ca. 2500-1500 B.C.) until it was absorbed into the New Kingdom of Egypt. By the 11th century B.C., the Kingdom of Kush gained independence from Egypt; it lasted in various forms until the middle of the 4th century A.D. After the fall of Kush, the Nubians formed three Christian kingdoms of Nobatia, Makuria, and Alodia. The latter two endured until around 1500. Between the 14th and 15th centuries much of Sudan was settled by Arab nomads, and between the 16th–19th centuries it underwent extensive Islamization. Following Egyptian occupation early in the 19th century, the British established an Anglo-Egyptian Sudan - nominally a condominium, but in effect a British colony.

Military regimes favoring Islamic-oriented governments have dominated national politics since Sudan gained independence from Anglo-Egyptian co-rule in 1956. The 30-year reign of President Omar Hassan Ahmad al-BASHIR, following months of nationwide protests, ended with the military forcing him out in April 2019. In July 2019, the country's Transitional Military Council signed an agreement with the Forces for Freedom and Change (an umbrella group of civilian actors) to form a transitional government under a Constitutional Declaration. Economist and former international civil servant Abdalla HAMDOUK al-Kinani was selected to serve as prime minister of a civilian-led transitional government, which was to have guided the country to credible democratic elections in late 2022. In October 2021, the Sudanese military organized a takeover that ousted Prime Minister HAMDOUK and his government and replaced civilian members of the Sovereign Council (Sudan's collective Head of State) with individuals selected by the military. HAMDOUK was briefly reinstated in November 2021 but resigned in January 2022.

As of March 2022, General Abd-al-Fatah al-BURHAN Abd-al-Rahman, the Chair of Sudan's Sovereign Council and Commander-in- Chief of the Sudanese Armed Forces, serves as de facto head of state and government. He presides over a Sovereign Council consisting of military leaders, former armed opposition group representatives, and civilians appointed by the military. A cabinet of acting ministers handles day-to-day administration. These acting ministers are either senior civil servants (some appointed by former Prime Minister HAMDOUK and some selected by the military) or holdover ministers from Prime Minister HAMDOUK's former cabinet who were appointed by former armed opposition groups that the military allowed to remain in their positions. The UN, the African Union, and the Intergovernmental Authority on Development are currently facilitating a Sudanese-led political process intended to enable Sudanese civilian and military stakeholders to agree on the framework for a new civilian-led transitional government.

During most of the second half of the 20th century, Sudan was embroiled in two prolonged civil wars rooted in northern economic, political, and social domination of the largely non-Muslim, non-Arab southern portion of the country. The first civil war ended in 1972, but another broke out in 1983. Peace talks gained momentum in 2002-04, and the final North/South Comprehensive Peace Agreement (CPA), signed in January 2005, granted the southern rebels autonomy for six years followed by a referendum on independence for Southern Sudan. South Sudan became independent on 9 July 2011, but Sudan and South Sudan have yet to fully implement security and economic agreements relating to the normalization of relations between the two countries.

In the 21st century, Sudan faced conflict in Darfur, Southern Kordofan, and Blue Nile starting in 2003. Together, these conflicts displaced more than 3 million people; while some repatriation has taken place, about 3.04 million IDPs remained in Sudan as of February 2022. Sudan also faces refugee influxes from neighboring countries, primarily Central African Republic, Eritrea, Ethiopia, South Sudan, and Syria.

GEOGRAPHY

Location: north-eastern Africa, bordering the Red Sea, between Egypt and Eritrea

Geographic coordinates: 15 00 N, 30 00 E

Map references: Africa

Area: *total:* 1,861,484 sq km
land: 1,731,671 sq km
water: 129,813 sq km
country comparison to the world: 17

Area - comparative: slightly less than one-fifth the size of the US

Land boundaries: *total:* 6,819 km
border countries (7): Central African Republic 174 km; Chad 1,403 km; Egypt 1,276 km; Eritrea 682 km; Ethiopia 744 km; Libya 382 km; South Sudan 2,158 km
note: Sudan-South Sudan boundary represents 1 January 1956 alignment; final alignment pending negotiations and demarcation; final sovereignty status of Abyei region pending negotiations between Sudan and South Sudan

Coastline: 853 km

Maritime claims: *territorial sea:* 12 nm
contiguous zone: 18 nm
continental shelf: 200-m depth or to the depth of exploitation

Climate: hot and dry; arid desert; rainy season varies by region (April to November)

Terrain: generally flat, featureless plain; desert dominates the north

Elevation: *highest point:* Jabal Marrah 3,042 m
lowest point: Red Sea 0 m
mean elevation: 568 m

Natural resources: petroleum; small reserves of iron ore, copper, chromium ore, zinc, tungsten, mica, silver, gold; hydropower

Land use: *agricultural land:* 100% (2018 est.)
arable land: 15.7% (2018 est.)
permanent crops: 0.2% (2018 est.)
permanent pasture: 84.2% (2018 est.)
forest: 0% (2018 est.)
other: 0% (2018 est.)

Irrigated land: 18,900 sq km (2012)

Major rivers (by length in km): Nile (shared with Rwanda [s], Tanzania, Uganda, South Sudan, and Egypt [m]) - 6,650 km; Blue Nile river mouth (shared with Ethiopia [s]) - 1,600 km
note – [s] after country name indicates river source; [m] after country name indicates river mouth

Major watersheds (area sq km): Atlantic Ocean drainage: *(Mediterranean Sea)* Nile (3,254,853 sq km) Internal *(endorheic basin)* drainage: Lake Chad (2,497,738 sq km)

Major aquifers: Nubian Aquifer System, Sudd Basin (Umm Ruwaba Aquifer)

Population distribution: with the exception of a ribbon of settlement that corresponds to the banks of the Nile, northern Sudan, which extends into the dry Sahara, is sparsely populated; more abundant vegetation and broader access to water increases population distribution in the south extending habitable range along nearly the entire border with South Sudan; sizeable areas of population are found around Khartoum, southeast between the Blue and White Nile Rivers, and througout South Darfur as shown on this population distribution map

Natural hazards: dust storms and periodic persistent droughts

Geography - note: the Nile is Sudan's primary water source; its major tributaries, the White Nile and the Blue Nile, meet at Khartoum to form the River Nile which flows northward through Egypt to the Mediterranean Sea

PEOPLE AND SOCIETY

Population: 47,958,856 (2022 est.)
country comparison to the world: 30

Nationality: *noun:* Sudanese (singular and plural)
adjective: Sudanese

Ethnic groups: Sudanese Arab (approximately 70%), Fur, Beja, Nuba, Ingessana, Uduk, Fallata, Masalit, Dajo, Gimir, Tunjur, Berti; there are over 500 ethnic groups

Languages: Arabic (official), English (official), Nubian, Ta Bedawie, Fur
major-language sample(s):
كتاب حقائق العالم، المصدر الذي لا يمكن الاستغناء عنه للمعلومات الأساسية
(Arabic)
The World Factbook, the indispensable source for basic information. (English)

Religions: Sunni Muslim, small Christian minority

Age structure: *0-14 years:* 42.01% (male 9,726,937/female 9,414,988)
15-24 years: 20.94% (male 4,852,903/female 4,687,664)
25-54 years: 29.89% (male 6,633,567/female 6,986,241)
55-64 years: 4.13% (male 956,633/female 923,688)
65 years and over: 3.03% (male 729,214/female 649,721) (2020 est.)

Dependency ratios: *total dependency ratio:* 76.9
youth dependency ratio: 70.4
elderly dependency ratio: 6.5
potential support ratio: 15.4 (2020 est.)

Median age: *total:* 18.3 years
male: 18.1 years
female: 18.5 years (2020 est.)
country comparison to the world: 211

Population growth rate: 2.55% (2022 est.)
country comparison to the world: 19

Birth rate: 33.47 births/1,000 population (2022 est.)
country comparison to the world: 20

Death rate: 6.3 deaths/1,000 population (2022 est.)
country comparison to the world: 146

Net migration rate: -1.67 migrant(s)/1,000 population (2022 est.)
country comparison to the world: 163

Population distribution: with the exception of a ribbon of settlement that corresponds to the banks of the Nile, northern Sudan, which extends into the dry Sahara, is sparsely populated; more abundant vegetation and broader access to water increases population distribution in the south extending habitable range along nearly the entire border with South Sudan; sizeable areas of population are found around Khartoum, southeast between the Blue and White Nile Rivers, and througout South Darfur as shown on this population distribution map

Urbanization: *urban population:* 36% of total population (2022)
rate of urbanization: 3.43% annual rate of change (2020-25 est.)

Major urban areas - population: 6.160 million KHARTOUM (capital), 1.012 million Nyala (2022)

Sex ratio: *at birth:* 1.05 male(s)/female
0-14 years: 1.03 male(s)/female
15-24 years: 1.03 male(s)/female
25-54 years: 0.94 male(s)/female
55-64 years: 1.01 male(s)/female
65 years and over: 1.04 male(s)/female
total population: 1.01 male(s)/female (2022 est.)

Maternal mortality ratio: 295 deaths/100,000 live births (2017 est.)
country comparison to the world: 38

Infant mortality rate: *total:* 42.27 deaths/1,000 live births
male: 47.76 deaths/1,000 live births
female: 36.5 deaths/1,000 live births (2022 est.)
country comparison to the world: 29

Life expectancy at birth: *total population:* 67.12 years
male: 64.89 years

female: 69.46 years (2022 est.)
country comparison to the world: 193

Total fertility rate: 4.6 children born/woman (2022 est.)
country comparison to the world: 17

Contraceptive prevalence rate: 12.2% (2014)

Drinking water source: *improved: urban:* 99% of population
rural: 80.7% of population
total: 87.1% of population
unimproved: urban: 1% of population
rural: 19.3% of population
total: 12.9% of population (2020 est.)

Current health expenditure: 4.6% of GDP (2019)

Physicians density: 0.26 physicians/1,000 population (2017)

Hospital bed density: 0.7 beds/1,000 population (2017)

Sanitation facility access: *improved: urban:* 72.1% of population
rural: 30.6% of population
total: 45.3% of population
unimproved: urban: 27.9% of population
rural: 69.4% of population
total: 54.7% of population (2020 est.)

HIV/AIDS - adult prevalence rate: 0.2% (2020 est.)
country comparison to the world: 112

HIV/AIDS - people living with HIV/AIDS: 49,000 (2020 est.)
country comparison to the world: 60

HIV/AIDS - deaths: 2,300 (2020 est.)
country comparison to the world: 43

Major infectious diseases: *degree of risk:* very high (2020)
food or waterborne diseases: bacterial and protozoal diarrhea, hepatitis A and E, and typhoid fever
vectorborne diseases: malaria, dengue fever, and Rift Valley fever
water contact diseases: schistosomiasis
animal contact diseases: rabies
respiratory diseases: meningococcal meningitis

Obesity - adult prevalence rate: 6.6% (2014)
country comparison to the world: 166

Alcohol consumption per capita: *total:* 1.93 liters of pure alcohol (2019 est.)
beer: 0 liters of pure alcohol (2019 est.)
wine: 0 liters of pure alcohol (2019 est.)
spirits: 0.29 liters of pure alcohol (2019 est.)
other alcohols: 1.63 liters of pure alcohol (2019 est.)
country comparison to the world: 131

Children under the age of 5 years underweight: 33% (2014)
country comparison to the world: 4

Literacy: *definition:* age 15 and over can read and write
total population: 60.7%
male: 65.4%
female: 56.1% (2018)

School life expectancy (primary to tertiary education): *total:* 8 years
male: 8 years
female: 7 years (2015)

Unemployment, youth ages 15-24: *total:* 32.6%
male: 27.4%
female: 43.5% (2011 est.)

ENVIRONMENT

Environment - current issues: water pollution; inadequate supplies of potable water; water scarcity and periodic drought; wildlife populations threatened by excessive hunting; soil erosion; desertification; deforestation; loss of biodiversity

Environment - international agreements: *party to:* Biodiversity, Climate Change, Climate Change-Kyoto Protocol, Climate Change-Paris Agreement, Comprehensive Nuclear Test Ban, Desertification, Endangered Species, Hazardous Wastes, Law of the Sea, Nuclear Test Ban, Ozone Layer Protection, Wetlands
signed, but not ratified: none of the selected agreements

Air pollutants: *particulate matter emissions:* 47.92 micrograms per cubic meter (2016 est.)
carbon dioxide emissions: 20 megatons (2016 est.)
methane emissions: 75.1 megatons (2020 est.)

Climate: hot and dry; arid desert; rainy season varies by region (April to November)

Land use: *agricultural land:* 100% (2018 est.)
arable land: 15.7% (2018 est.)
permanent crops: 0.2% (2018 est.)
permanent pasture: 84.2% (2018 est.)
forest: 0% (2018 est.)
other: 0% (2018 est.)

Urbanization: *urban population:* 36% of total population (2022)
rate of urbanization: 3.43% annual rate of change (2020-25 est.)

Revenue from forest resources: *forest revenues:* 3.01% of GDP (2018 est.)
country comparison to the world: 24

Revenue from coal: *coal revenues:* 0% of GDP (2018 est.)
country comparison to the world: 170

Food insecurity: *severe localized food insecurity: due to conflict, civil insecurity, and soaring food prices* - according to the results of the latest analysis, about 11.7 million people (24% of the analyzed population) are estimated to be severely food insecure during June to September 2022; the main drivers are macroeconomic challenges resulting in rampant food and non-food inflation, tight supplies due to a poor 2021 harvest and the escalation of intercommunal violence (2022)

Waste and recycling: *municipal solid waste generated annually:* 2,831,291 tons (2015 est.)

Major rivers (by length in km): Nile (shared with Rwanda [s], Tanzania, Uganda, South Sudan, and Egypt [m]) - 6,650 km; Blue Nile river mouth (shared with Ethiopia [s]) - 1,600 km
note – [s] after country name indicates river source; [m] after country name indicates river mouth

Major watersheds (area sq km): Atlantic Ocean drainage: *(Mediterranean Sea)* Nile (3,254,853 sq km)
Internal *(endorheic basin)* drainage: Lake Chad (2,497,738 sq km)

Major aquifers: Nubian Aquifer System, Sudd Basin (Umm Ruwaba Aquifer)

Total water withdrawal: *municipal:* 950 million cubic meters (2017 est.)
industrial: 75 million cubic meters (2017 est.)
agricultural: 25.91 billion cubic meters (2017 est.)

Total renewable water resources: 37.8 billion cubic meters (2017 est.)

GOVERNMENT

Country name: *conventional long form:* Republic of the Sudan
conventional short form: Sudan
local long form: Jumhuriyat as-Sudan
local short form: As-Sudan
former: Anglo-Egyptian Sudan, Democratic Republic of the Sudan
etymology: the name "Sudan" derives from the Arabic "bilad-as-sudan" meaning "Land of the Black [peoples]"

Government type: presidential republic

Capital: *name:* Khartoum
geographic coordinates: 15 36 N, 32 32 E
time difference: UTC+3 (8 hours ahead of Washington, DC, during Standard Time)
etymology: several explanations of the name exist; two of the more plausible are that it is derived from Arabic "al-jartum" meaning "elephant's trunk" or "hose," and likely referring to the narrow strip of land extending between the Blue and White Niles; alternatively, the name could derive from the Dinka words "khar-tuom," indicating a "place where rivers meet"

Administrative divisions: 18 states (wilayat, singular - wilayah); Blue Nile, Central Darfur, East Darfur, Gedaref, Gezira, Kassala, Khartoum, North Darfur, North Kordofan, Northern, Red Sea, River Nile, Sennar, South Darfur, South Kordofan, West Darfur, West Kordofan, White Nile
note: the peace Agreement signed in October 2020 included a provision to establish a system of governance that will likely restructure the country's current 18 provinces/states into regions

Independence: 1 January 1956 (from Egypt and the UK)

National holiday: Independence Day, 1 January (1956)

Constitution: *history:* previous 1973, 1998, 2005 (interim constitution, which was suspended in April 2019); latest initial draft completed by Transitional Military Council in May 2019; revised draft known as the "Draft Constitutional Charter for the 2019 Transitional Period," or "2019 Constitutional Declaration" was signed by the Council and opposition coalition on 4 August 2019
amendments: amended 2020 to incorporate the Juba Agreement for Peace in Sudan; the military suspended several provisions of the Constitutional Declaration in October 2021

Legal system: mixed legal system of Islamic law and English common law; note - in mid-July 2020, Sudan amended 15 provisions of its 1991 penal code

International law organization participation: accepts compulsory ICJ jurisdiction with reservations; withdrew acceptance of ICCt jurisdiction in 2008

Citizenship: *citizenship by birth:* no
citizenship by descent only: the father must be a citizen of Sudan
dual citizenship recognized: no
residency requirement for naturalization: 10 years

Suffrage: 17 years of age; universal

Executive branch: *chief of state:* Sovereign Council Chair and Commander-in-Chief of the Sudanese

Armed Forces General Abd-al-Fatah al-BURHAN Abd-al-Rahman; note – the 2019 Constitutional Declaration established a collective chief of state of the "Sovereign Council," which was chaired by al-BURHAN; on 25 October 2021, al-BURHAN dissolved the Sovereign Council but reinstated it on 11 November 2021, replacing its civilian members (previously selected by the umbrella civilian coalition the Forces for Freedom and Change) with civilians of the military's choosing; the Sovereign Council currently consists of 5 military-appointed civilians, 5 generals, and 3 representatives selected by former armed opposition groups
head of government: Sovereign Council Chair and Commander-in-Chief of the Sudanese Armed Forces General Abd-al-Fatah al-BURHAN Abd-al-Rahman; Acting Prime Minister Osman HUSSEIN (since 19 January 2022); note - former Prime Minister Abdallah HAMDOUK resigned on 2 January 2022; HAMDOUK served as prime minister from August 2019 to October 2019 before he was kidnapped; he was later freed and reinstated as prime minister on 21 November 2021
cabinet: most members of the Council of Ministers were forced from office in October 2021 by the military and subsequently resigned in November 2021; the military allowed a handful of ministers appointed by former armed opposition groups to retain their posts; at present, most of the members of the Council are senior civil servants serving in an acting minister capacity appointed either by Prime Minister HAMDOUK prior to his resignation or by the military
elections/appointments: the 2019 Constitutional Declaration originally called for elections to be held in late 2022 at the end of the transitional period; that date was pushed back to late 2023 by the Juba Peace Agreement; the methodology for future elections has not yet been defined; according to the 2019 Constitutional Declaration, civilian members of the Sovereign Council and the prime minister were to have been nominated by an umbrella coalition of civilian actors known as the Forces for Freedom and Change; this methodology was followed in selecting HAMDOUK as prime minister in August 2019; the military purports to have suspended this provision of the 2019 Constitutional Declaration in October 2021; Prime Minister HAMDOUK's restoration to office in November 2021 was the result of an agreement signed between him and Sovereign Council Chair BURHAN; military members of the Sovereign Council are selected by the leadership of the security forces; representatives of former armed groups to the Sovereign Council are selected by the signatories of the Juba Peace Agreement
election results:
NA

Legislative branch: *description:* according to the August 2019 Constitutional Declaration, which established Sudan's transitional government, the Transitional Legislative Council (TLC) was to have served as the national legislature during the transitional period until elections could be held; as of March 2022, the TLC had not been established
elections:
Council of State - last held 1 June 2015; subsequently dissolved in April 2019
National Assembly - last held on 13-15 April 2015; subsequently dissolved in April 2019
note – according to the 2019 Constitutional Declaration, elections for a new legislature are to be held in late 2023
election results:
Council of State - percent of vote by party - NA; seats by party - NA; former composition - men 35, women 19, percent of women 35.2%
National Assembly - percent of vote by party - NA; former seats by party - NCP 323, DUP 25, Democratic Unionist Party 15, other 44, independent 19; former composition - men 296 women 130, percent of women 30.5%; note - former total National Legislature percent of women 31%

Judicial branch: *highest court(s):* National Supreme Court (consists of 70 judges organized into panels of 3 judges and includes 4 circuits that operate outside the capital); Constitutional Court (consists of 9 justices including the court president); note - the Constitutional Court resides outside the national judiciary and has not been appointed since the signature of the 2019 Constitutional Declaration
judge selection and term of office: National Supreme Court and Constitutional Court judges selected by the Supreme Judicial Council, which replaced the National Judicial Service Commission upon enactment of the 2019 Constitutional Declaration
subordinate courts: Court of Appeal; other national courts; public courts; district, town, and rural courts

Political parties and leaders: Major Parties with seats in the last National Assembly election (13-15 April 2015):
Collective Leadership Umma Party
Democratic Unionist Party or DUP [Jalal al-DIGAIR]
Democratic Unionist Party–Original [Muhammad Uthman al-MIRGHANI]
Federal Umma Party [Fadl al-Sayed SHUAIB]
Freedom and Justice Party
National Freedom and Justice Party
National Congress Party or NCP [Umar Hassan Ahmad al-BASHIR]
National Umma Party or UP [Sadiq al-MAHDI]
Umma Reform and Development Party
United Umma Party
Major Parties as of April 2019:
Democratic Unionist Party [Muhammad Uthman al-MIRGHANI] Democratic Unionist Party or DUP [Babika BABIKER]
Federal Umma Party [Dr. Ahmed Babikir NAHAR]
Muslim Brotherhood or MB [Sadig Abdalla ABDELMAJID and Dr. Yousif Al-Hibir Nor-ELDAYIM]
National Congress Party or NCP [Umar Hassan Ahmad al-BASHIR]
National Umma Party or NUP [Fadlallah Baramah NASSER]
Popular Congress Party or PCP [Nawal Al-KHIDIR]
Reform Movement Now [Dr. Ghazi Salahuddin al-ATABANI]
Sudan National Front [Ali Mahmud HASANAYN]
Sudanese Communist Party or SCP [Mohammed Moktar Al-KHATEEB]
Sudanese Congress Party or SCoP [Omar El DIGAIR]
Umma Party for Reform and Development [Mubarak Al-Fadul Al-MAHDI]
Unionist Movement Party or UMP [led by DUP Chair Mohammed Osama Al-MERGHANI]
note: the National Assembly was dissolved in April 2019 to be replaced some time in 2023 with a Transitional Legislative Council with as yet undetermined party affiliations; in November 2019, the transitional government banned the National Congress Party

International organization participation: ABEDA, ACP, AfDB, AFESD, AMF, AU, CAEU, COMESA, FAO, G-77, IAEA, IBRD, ICAO, ICC (NGOs), ICRM, IDA, IDB, IFAD, IFC, IFRCS, IGAD, ILO, IMF, IMO, Interpol, IOC, IOM, IPU, ISO, ITSO, ITU, LAS, MIGA, NAM, OIC, OPCW, PCA, UN, UNCTAD, UNESCO, UNHCR, UNHRC, UNIDO, UNWTO, UPU, WCO, WFTU (NGOs), WHO, WIPO, WMO, WTO (observer)

Diplomatic representation in the US: *chief of mission:* Ambassador Mohamed Abdalla Idris MOHAMED (since 16 September 2022)
chancery: 2210 Massachusetts Avenue NW, Washington, DC 20008
telephone: [1] (202) 338-8565
FAX: [1] (202) 667-2406
email address and website:
consular@sudanembassy.org
https://www.sudanembassy.org/

Diplomatic representation from the US: *chief of mission:* Ambassador (vacant); Charge d'Affaires Lucy TAMLYN (since 3 February 2022)
embassy: P.O. Box 699, Kilo 10, Soba, Khartoum
mailing address: 2200 Khartoum Place, Washington DC 20521-2200
telephone: [249] 187-0-22000
email address and website:
ACSKhartoum@state.gov
https://sd.usembassy.gov/

Flag description: three equal horizontal bands of red (top), white, and black with a green isosceles triangle based on the hoist side; colors and design based on the Arab Revolt flag of World War I, but the meanings of the colors are expressed as follows: red signifies the struggle for freedom, white is the color of peace, light, and love, black represents the people of Sudan (in Arabic 'Sudan' means black), green is the color of Islam, agriculture, and prosperity

National symbol(s): secretary bird; national colors: red, white, black, green

National anthem: *name:* "Nahnu Djundulla Djundulwatan" (We Are the Army of God and of Our Land)
lyrics/music: Sayed Ahmad Muhammad SALIH/ Ahmad MURJAN
note: adopted 1956; originally served as the anthem of the Sudanese military

National heritage: *total World Heritage Sites:* 3 (2 cultural, 1 natural)
selected World Heritage Site locales: Gebel Barkal and the Sites of the Napatan Region (c); Archaeological Sites of the Island of Meroe (c); Sanganeb Marine National Park and Dungonab Bay – Mukkawar Island Marine National Park (n)

ECONOMY

Economic overview: Sudan has experienced protracted social conflict and the loss of three quarters of its oil production due to the secession of South Sudan. The oil sector had driven much of Sudan's GDP growth since 1999. For nearly a decade, the economy boomed on the back of rising oil production, high oil prices, and significant inflows of foreign direct investment. Since the economic shock of South Sudan's secession, Sudan has struggled to stabilize its economy and make up for the loss of foreign exchange earnings. The interruption of oil production in South Sudan in 2012 for over a year and the consequent loss of oil transit fees further exacerbated the fragile state of Sudan's economy. Ongoing conflicts in Southern Kordofan, Darfur, and the Blue Nile states, lack of basic infrastructure in large areas, and reliance by much of the population on subsistence agriculture, keep close to half of the population at or below the poverty line.

Sudan was subject to comprehensive US sanctions, which were lifted in October 2017. Sudan is attempting to develop non-oil sources of revenues, such as gold mining and agriculture, while carrying out an austerity program to reduce expenditures. The world's largest exporter of gum Arabic, Sudan produces 75-80% of the world's total output. Agriculture continues to employ 80% of the work force.

Sudan introduced a new currency, still called the Sudanese pound, following South Sudan's secession, but the value of the currency has fallen since its introduction. Khartoum formally devalued the currency in June 2012, when it passed austerity measures that included gradually repealing fuel subsidies. Sudan also faces high inflation, which reached 47% on an annual basis in November 2012 but fell to about 35% per year in 2017.

(2017)

Real GDP (purchasing power parity): $176.4 billion (2020 est.)
$179.2 billion (2019 est.)
$181.61 billion (2018 est.)
note: data are in 2017 dollars
country comparison to the world: 71

Real GDP growth rate: 1.4% (2017 est.)
3% (2016 est.)
1.3% (2015 est.)
country comparison to the world: 159

Real GDP per capita: $4,000 (2020 est.)
$4,200 (2019 est.)
$4,300 (2018 est.)
note: data are in 2017 dollars
country comparison to the world: 185

GDP (official exchange rate): $24.918 billion (2019 est.)

Inflation rate (consumer prices): 50.2% (2019 est.)
62.8% (2018 est.)
32.5% (2017 est.)
country comparison to the world: 224

GDP - composition, by sector of origin: *agriculture:* 39.6% (2017 est.)
industry: 2.6% (2017 est.)
services: 57.8% (2017 est.)

GDP - composition, by end use: *household consumption:* 77.3% (2017 est.)
government consumption: 5.8% (2017 est.)
investment in fixed capital: 18.4% (2017 est.)
investment in inventories: 0.6% (2017 est.)
exports of goods and services: 9.7% (2017 est.)
imports of goods and services: -11.8% (2017 est.)

Agricultural products: sugar cane, sorghum, milk, groundnuts, onions, sesame seed, goat milk, millet, bananas, wheat

Industries: oil, cotton ginning, textiles, cement, edible oils, sugar, soap distilling, shoes, petroleum refining, pharmaceuticals, armaments, automobile/light truck assembly, milling

Industrial production growth rate: 4.5% (2017 est.)
country comparison to the world: 66

Labor force: 11.92 million (2007 est.)
country comparison to the world: 46

Labor force - by occupation: *agriculture:* 80%
industry: 7%
services: 13% (1998 est.)

Unemployment rate: 19.6% (2017 est.)
20.6% (2016 est.)
country comparison to the world: 188

Unemployment, youth ages 15-24: *total:* 32.6%
male: 27.4%
female: 43.5% (2011 est.)
country comparison to the world: 30

Population below poverty line: 46.5% (2009 est.)

Gini Index coefficient - distribution of family income: 34.2 (2014 est.)
country comparison to the world: 117

Household income or consumption by percentage share: *lowest 10%:* 2.7%
highest 10%: 26.7% (2009 est.)

Budget: *revenues:* 8.48 billion (2017 est.)
expenditures: 13.36 billion (2017 est.)

Budget surplus (+) or deficit (-): -10.6% (of GDP) (2017 est.)
country comparison to the world: 213

Public debt: 121.6% of GDP (2017 est.)
99.5% of GDP (2016 est.)
country comparison to the world: 10

Taxes and other revenues: 18.5% (of GDP) (2017 est.)
country comparison to the world: 159

Fiscal year: calendar year

Current account balance: -$4.811 billion (2017 est.)
-$4.213 billion (2016 est.)
country comparison to the world: 183

Exports: $5.11 billion (2019 est.) note: data are in current year dollars
$5 billion (2018 est.) note: data are in current year dollars
country comparison to the world: 126

Exports - partners: United Arab Emirates 31%, China 19%, Saudi Arabia 14%, India 12%, Egypt 5% (2019)

Exports - commodities: gold, crude petroleum, sesame seeds, sheep, goats, cotton, ground nuts (2019)

Imports: $9.79 billion (2019 est.) note: data are in current year dollars
$8.24 billion (2018 est.) note: data are in current year dollars
country comparison to the world: 106

Imports - partners: China 31%, India 14%, United Arab Emirates 11%, Egypt 6% (2019)

Imports - commodities: raw sugar, wheat, packaged medicines, jewelry, tires, cars and vehicle parts (2019)

Reserves of foreign exchange and gold: $198 million (31 December 2017 est.)
$168.3 million (31 December 2016 est.)
country comparison to the world: 177

Debt - external: $56.05 billion (31 December 2017 est.)
$51.26 billion (31 December 2016 est.)
country comparison to the world: 63

Exchange rates: Sudanese pounds (SDG) per US dollar -
6.72 (2017 est.)
6.14 (2016 est.)
6.14 (2015 est.)
6.03 (2014 est.)
5.74 (2013 est.)

ENERGY

Electricity access: *electrification - total population:* 47% (2019)
electrification - urban areas: 71% (2019)
electrification - rural areas: 35% (2019)

Electricity: *installed generating capacity:* 4.354 million kW (2020 est.)
consumption: 9,682,060,000 kWh (2019 est.)
exports: 0 kWh (2019 est.)
imports: 0 kWh (2019 est.)
transmission/distribution losses: 4.599 billion kWh (2019 est.)

Electricity generation sources: *fossil fuels:* 43.5% of total installed capacity (2020 est.)
solar: 0.1% of total installed capacity (2020 est.)
hydroelectricity: 55.5% of total installed capacity (2020 est.)
biomass and waste: 0.9% of total installed capacity (2020 est.)

Petroleum: *total petroleum production:* 66,900 bbl/day (2021 est.)
refined petroleum consumption: 137,700 bbl/day (2019 est.)
crude oil and lease condensate exports: 12,900 bbl/day (2018 est.)
crude oil and lease condensate imports: 9,000 bbl/day (2018 est.)
crude oil estimated reserves: 5 billion barrels (2021 est.)

Refined petroleum products - production: 94,830 bbl/day (2015 est.)
country comparison to the world: 68

Refined petroleum products - exports: 8,541 bbl/day (2015 est.)
country comparison to the world: 85

Refined petroleum products - imports: 24,340 bbl/day (2015 est.)
country comparison to the world: 108

Natural gas: *proven reserves:* 84.95 billion cubic meters (2021 est.)

Carbon dioxide emissions: 17.319 million metric tonnes of CO_2 (2019 est.)
from petroleum and other liquids: 17.319 million metric tonnes of CO_2 (2019 est.)
country comparison to the world: 91

Energy consumption per capita: 8.047 million Btu/person (2019 est.)
country comparison to the world: 163

COMMUNICATIONS

Telephones - fixed lines: *total subscriptions:* 129,408 (2020 est.)
subscriptions per 100 inhabitants: (2020 est.) less than 1
country comparison to the world: 129

Telephones - mobile cellular: *total subscriptions:* 33,014,200 (2019)
subscriptions per 100 inhabitants: 77.11 (2019)
country comparison to the world: 44

Telecommunication systems: *general assessment:* Sudan emerged as a poorer country when South Sudan separated from it in 2011; although Sudan has about four times the population of South Sudan, the latter benefits from its control of the majority

of known oil reserves; the Sudanese economy has been affected by hyperinflation in recent years, partly the result of the loss of oil revenue but also due to domestic volatility and social unrest; the difficult economic conditions have meant that for several years telcos have reported revenue under hyper inflationary reporting standards; pressure on revenue has made it difficult for operators to invest in infrastructure upgrades, and so provide improved services to customers; despite this, the number of mobile subscribers increased 7.% in 20201, year-on-year; this level of growth is expected to have been maintained in 2022, though could slow from 2023 as the acute influences resulting the pandemic begin to wane; the country's poor fixed-line infrastructure has helped the development of mobile broadband services (2022)
domestic: consists of microwave radio relay, cable, fiber optic, radiotelephone communications, tropospheric scatter, and a domestic satellite system with 14 earth stations; teledensity fixed-line less than 1 per 100 and mobile-cellular over 80 telephones per 100 persons (2020)
international: country code - 249; landing points for the EASSy, FALCON and SAS-1,-2, fiber-optic submarine cable systems linking Africa, the Middle East, Indian Ocean Islands and Asia; satellite earth stations - 1 Intelsat (Atlantic Ocean) (2019)

Broadcast media: Following the establishment of Sudan's civilian-led transitional government in August 2019, government-owned broadcasters became increasingly independent from government and military control. Following the October 2021 military takeover, additional restrictions were imposed on these government-owned broadcasters, which now practice a heightened degree of self-censorship but still operate more independently than in the pre-2019 environment. (2022)

Internet country code: .sd

Internet users: *total:* 12,277,795 (2020 est.)
percent of population: 28% (2020 est.)
country comparison to the world: 50

Broadband - fixed subscriptions: *total:* 28,782 (2020 est.)
subscriptions per 100 inhabitants: 0.1 (2020 est.)
country comparison to the world: 156

TRANSPORTATION

National air transport system: *number of registered air carriers:* 9 (2020)
inventory of registered aircraft operated by air carriers: 42
annual passenger traffic on registered air carriers: 269,958 (2018)

Civil aircraft registration country code prefix: ST

Airports: *total:* 67 (2021)
country comparison to the world: 74

Airports - with paved runways: *total:* 17
over 3,047 m: 2
2,438 to 3,047 m: 11
1,524 to 2,437 m: 2
914 to 1,523 m: 1
under 914 m: 1 (2021)

Airports - with unpaved runways: *total:* 50
1,524 to 2,437 m: 17
914 to 1,523 m: 24
under 914 m: 9 (2021)

Heliports: 7 (2021)

Pipelines: 156 km gas, 4,070 km oil, 1,613 km refined products (2013)

Railways: *total:* 7,251 km (2014)
narrow gauge: 5,851 km (2014) 1.067-m gauge
1,400 km 0.600-m gauge for cotton plantations
country comparison to the world: 31

Roadways: *total:* 31,000 km (2019)
paved: 8,000 km (2019)
unpaved: 23,000 km (2019)
urban: 1,000 km (2019)
country comparison to the world: 97

Waterways: 4,068 km (2011) (1,723 km open year-round on White and Blue Nile Rivers)
country comparison to the world: 27

Merchant marine: *total:* 15
by type: other 15 (2021)
country comparison to the world: 150

Ports and terminals: *major seaport(s):* Port Sudan

MILITARY AND SECURITY

Military and security forces: Sudanese Armed Forces (SAF): Ground Force, Navy, Sudanese Air Force; Rapid Support Forces (RSF), Border Guards

Ministry of Interior: security police, special forces police, traffic police, Central Reserve Police (2022)
note 1: the RSF is a semi-autonomous paramilitary force formed in 2013 to fight armed rebel groups in Sudan, with Mohammed Hamdan DAGALO (aka Hemeti) as its commander (he is also a member of the Sovereign Council); it was initially placed under the National Intelligence and Security Service, then came under the direct command of former president Omar al-BASHIR, who boosted the RSF as his own personal security force; as a result, the RSF was better funded and equipped than the regular armed forces; the RSF has since recruited from all parts of Sudan beyond its original Darfuri Arab groups but remains under the personal patronage and control of DAGALO; the RSF has been accused of committing human rights abuses against civilians; it is also reportedly involved in business enterprises, such as gold mining; in late 2019, Sovereign Council Chairman and SAF Commander-in-Chief General Abd-al-Fatah al-BURHAN said the RSF would be fully integrated into the SAF, but did not give a timeline
note 2: the Central Reserve Police is a combat-trained paramilitary force that has been used against demonstrators and sanctioned by the US for human rights abuses

Military expenditures: 1% of GDP (2021 est.)
1% of GDP (2020 est.)
2.4% of GDP (2019 est.) (approximately $2.08 billion)
2% of GDP (2018 est.) (approximately $2.08 billion)
3.6% of GDP (2017 est.) (approximately $2.75 billion)
note: many defense expenditures are probably off-budget
country comparison to the world: 134

Military and security service personnel strengths: information varies widely; estimated 100-125,000 active duty armed forces personnel; approximately 30-40,000 Rapid Support Forces (2022)

Military equipment inventories and acquisitions: the SAF's inventory includes a mix of Chinese, Russian, Soviet-era, Ukrainian, and domestically-produced weapons systems; since 2010, the leading arms providers to the SAF have been Belarus, China, Russia, and Ukraine; North Korea has also provided arms; Sudan has a domestic arms industry that manufactures ammunition, small arms, and armored vehicles, largely based on older Chinese and Russian systems (2022)

Military service age and obligation: 18-33 years of age for compulsory or voluntary military service for men and women; 1-2 year service obligation (2022)
note: implementation of conscription is reportedly uneven

Military deployments: Sudan joined the Saudi-led coalition that intervened in Yemen in 2015, reportedly providing as many as 40,000 troops during the peak of the war in 2016-17, mostly from the Rapid Support Forces; by 2021, Sudan had reduced the size of the force to about a brigade (approximately 2-3,000 troops) (2022)

Military - note: the Sudanese military has been a dominant force in the ruling of the country since its independence in 1956; in addition, the Sudanese military and security forces have a large role in the country's economy, reportedly controlling over 200 commercial companies, including businesses involved in gold mining, rubber production, agriculture, and meat exports

the United Nations Interim Security Force for Abyei (UNISFA) has operated in the disputed Abyei region along the border between Sudan and South Sudan since 2011; UNISFA's mission includes ensuring security, protecting civilians, strengthening the capacity of the Abyei Police Service, de-mining, monitoring/verifying the redeployment of armed forces from the area, and facilitating the flow of humanitarian aid; UNISFA had about 2,000 personnel deployed as of mid-2022

in addition, the United Nations African Union Hybrid Operation in Darfur (UNAMID) operated in the war-torn Darfur region between 2007 and the end of its mandate in July 2021; UNAMID was a joint African Union-UN peacekeeping force with the mission of bringing stability to Darfur, including protecting civilians, facilitating humanitarian assistance, and promoting mediation efforts, while peace talks on a final settlement continued; UNAMID withdrew the last of its personnel in December 2021; note - the October 2020 peace agreement provided for the establishment of a Joint Security Keeping Forces (JSKF) comprised of 12,000 personnel tasked with securing the Darfur region in the place of UNAMID; in June 2021, Sudan's transitional government announced it would increase the size of this force to 20,000 and expand its mission scope to include the capital and other parts of the country suffering from violence; the force would include the SAF, RSF, police, intelligence, and representatives from armed groups involved in peace negotiations; in Sep 2022, the first 2,000 members of the JSKF completed training (2022)

TERRORISM

Terrorist group(s): Islamic State of Iraq and ash-Sham (ISIS); al-Qa'ida; Harakat Sawa'd Misr

TRANSNATIONAL ISSUES

Disputes - international: *Sudan-Central African Republic:* periodic violent skirmishes persist among related pastoral populations along the border with the Central African Republic over water

and grazing rights; Sudan closed its border with the Central African Republic in January 2022 due to security concerns
Sudan-Chad: Chad wants to be a helpful mediator in resolving the Darfur conflict, and in 2010 established a joint border monitoring force with Sudan, which has helped to reduce cross-border banditry and violence; however, since the August 2020 Juba Peace Agreement between the Sudanese Government and the Sudanese Revolutionary Front and the termination of the UN's peacekeeping mission, UNAMID, at the end of 2020, violence continues to break out over land and water access
Sudan-Egypt: Sudan claims, but Egypt de facto administers, security and economic development of the Halaib region north of the 22nd parallel boundary
Sudan-Eritrea: none identified
Sudan-Ethiopia: civil unrest in eastern Sudan has hampered efforts to demarcate the porous boundary with Ethiopia; clashes continue between Sudan and Ethiopia over al-Fashaga, a fertile piece of land inhabited by Ethiopian farmers for years until the Sudanese army expelled them in December 2020, claiming the land belonged to Sudan based on colonial-era maps from over 100 years ago; in February, 2022, the two countries were discussing resuming talks over the border conflict
Sudan-Libya: none identified
Sudan-South Sudan: the South Sudan-Sudan boundary represents 1 January 1956 alignment, final alignment pending negotiations and demarcation; final sovereignty status of Abyei area pending negotiations between South Sudan and Sudan; clashes continue in the oil-rich Abyei region; the United Nations Interim Security Force for Abyei (UNISFA) has been deployed since 2011, when South Sudan became independent; the United Nations Interim Security Force for Abyei (UNISFA) has condemned renewed clashes on 23 September 2022 between the Twik and Ngok Dinka communities taking place in Agok, 28 kilometres from Abyei town

Refugees and internally displaced persons: *refugees (country of origin):* 811,445 (South Sudan) (refugees and asylum seekers), 136,617 (Eritrea) (refugees and asylum seekers), 93,480 (Syria) (refugees and asylum seekers), 71,727 (Ethiopia) (refugees and asylum seekers), 24,369 (Central African Republic) (2022)

IDPs: 3.71 million (civil war 1983-2005; ongoing conflict in Darfur region; government and rebel fighting along South Sudan border; inter-tribal clashes) (2022)

Trafficking in persons: *current situation:* Sudan is a source, transit, and destination country for men, women, and children who are subjected to forced labor and sex trafficking; traffickers exploit homeless children and unaccompanied migrant children from West and Central Africa in forced labor for begging, public transportation, large markets, and in sex trafficking; business owners, informal mining operators, community members, and farmers exploit children in brick-making factories, gold mining, collecting medical waste, street vending, and agriculture; children are exposed to threats, physical and sexual abuse, and hazardous working conditions; criminal groups exploit Sudanese women and girls from rural areas in domestic work and in sex trafficking; Sudanese Armed Forces and the Rapid Support Forces, a semi-autonomous paramilitary branch of the government, have been accused of recruiting child soldiers, which they deny; Eritrean, Ethiopian, and other Africans refugees at government encampments risk exploitation
tier rating: Tier 2 Watch List — Sudan does not fully meet the minimum standards for the elimination of trafficking but is making significant efforts to do so; authorities prosecuted more suspected traffickers and launched an awareness campaign; the government streamlined its national anti-trafficking mechanism and focused resources on the National Committee to Combat Human Trafficking; a national action plan was drafted, finalized, and approved; Sudanese Armed Forces officials launched a unit for child protection efforts in conflict areas and trained more than 5,000 members of its military on child protection issues; however, the Rapid Support Forces, a semi-autonomous paramilitary branch of the government, is reported to have recruited child soldiers and government authorities have acknowledged there are child soldiers among demobilizing forces covered under the 2020 Juba Peace Agreement; the government has not developed a system to identify, demobilize, and rehabilitate victims; officials' denial of trafficking, smuggling, and kidnapping for ransom impeded anti-trafficking efforts; investigations and convictions of trafficking crimes decreased; Sudan was granted a waiver per the Trafficking Victims Protection Act from an otherwise required downgrade to Tier 3; Sudan remained on Tier 2 Watch List for the third consecutive year (2020)

SURINAME

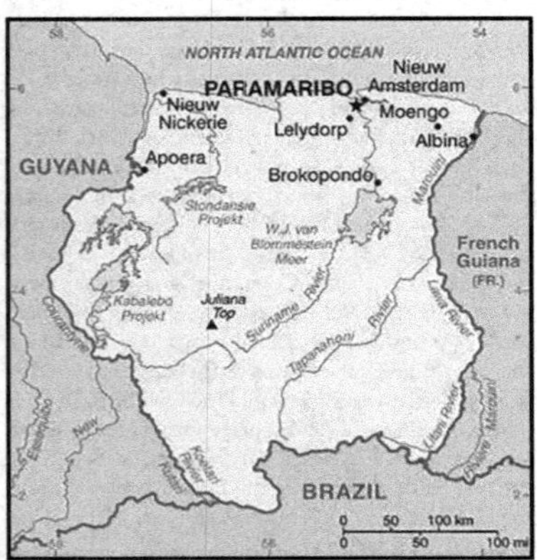

INTRODUCTION

Background: First explored by the Spaniards in the 16th century and then settled by the English in the mid-17th century, Suriname became a Dutch colony in 1667. With the abolition of African slavery in 1863, workers were brought in from India and Java. The Netherlands granted the colony independence in 1975. Five years later, the civilian government was replaced by a military regime that soon declared Suriname a socialist republic. It continued to exert control through a succession of nominally civilian administrations until 1987, when international pressure finally forced a democratic election. In 1990, the military overthrew the civilian leadership, but a democratically elected government - a four-party coalition - returned to power in 1991. The coalition expanded to eight parties in 2005 and ruled until August 2010, when voters returned former military leader Desire BOUTERSE and his opposition coalition to power. President BOUTERSE was reelected unopposed in 2015. Opposition parties campaigned hard against BOUTERSE in the lead up to the May 2020 elections and, in July 2020, a coalition led by Chandrikapersad SANTOKHI's VHP and Ronnie Brunswijk's ABOP was installed. The SANTOKHI government promised to tackle COVID-19, the economic crisis it inherited, and corruption.

GEOGRAPHY

Location: Northern South America, bordering the North Atlantic Ocean, between French Guiana and Guyana

Geographic coordinates: 4 00 N, 56 00 W

Map references: South America

Area: *total:* 163,820 sq km
land: 156,000 sq km
water: 7,820 sq km
country comparison to the world: 92

Area - comparative: slightly larger than Georgia

Land boundaries: *total:* 1,907 km
border countries (3): Brazil 515 km; French Guiana 556 km; Guyana 836 km

Coastline: 386 km

Maritime claims: *territorial sea:* 12 nm
exclusive economic zone: 200 nm

Climate: tropical; moderated by trade winds

Terrain: mostly rolling hills; narrow coastal plain with swamps

Elevation: *highest point:* Juliana Top 1,230 m
lowest point: unnamed location in the coastal plain -2 m
mean elevation: 246 m

Natural resources: timber, hydropower, fish, kaolin, shrimp, bauxite, gold, and small amounts of nickel, copper, platinum, iron ore

Land use: *agricultural land:* 0.5% (2018 est.)
arable land: 0.4% (2018 est.)
permanent crops: 0% (2018 est.)
permanent pasture: 0.1% (2018 est.)
forest: 94.6% (2018 est.)
other: 4.9% (2018 est.)

Irrigated land: 570 sq km (2012)

Major watersheds (area sq km): Atlantic Ocean drainage: Amazon (6,145,186 sq km)

Population distribution: population concentrated along the nothern coastal strip; the remainder of the country is sparsely populated

Natural hazards: flooding

Geography - note: smallest independent country on South American continent; mostly tropical rain forest; great diversity of flora and fauna that, for the most part, is increasingly threatened by new development; relatively small population, mostly along the coast

PEOPLE AND SOCIETY

Population: 632,638 (2022 est.)
country comparison to the world: 170

Nationality: *noun:* Surinamer(s)
adjective: Surinamese

Ethnic groups: Hindustani (also known locally as "East Indians"; their ancestors emigrated from northern India in the latter part of the 19th century) 27.4%, Maroon (their African ancestors were brought to the country in the 17th and 18th centuries as slaves and escaped to the interior) 21.7%, Creole (mixed White and Black) 15.7%, Javanese 13.7%, mixed 13.4%, other 7.6%, unspecified 0.6% (2012 est.)

Languages: Dutch (official), English (widely spoken), Sranang Tongo (Surinamese, sometimes called Taki-Taki, is the native language of Creoles and much of the younger population and is lingua franca among others), Caribbean Hindustani (a dialect of Hindi), Javanese
major-language sample(s):
Het Wereld Feitenboek, een omnisbare bron van informatie. (Dutch)
The World Factbook, the indispensable source for basic information. (English)

Religions: Protestant 23.6% (includes Evangelical 11.2%, Moravian 11.2%, Reformed .7%, Lutheran .5%), Hindu 22.3%, Roman Catholic 21.6%, Muslim 13.8%, other Christian 3.2%, Winti 1.8%, Jehovah's Witness 1.2%, other 1.7%, none 7.5%, unspecified 3.2% (2012 est.)

Demographic profile: Suriname is a pluralistic society consisting primarily of Creoles (persons of mixed African and European heritage), the descendants of escaped African slaves known as Maroons, and the descendants of Indian and Javanese (Indonesian) contract workers. The country overall is in full, post-industrial demographic transition, with a low fertility rate, a moderate mortality rate, and a rising life expectancy. However, the Maroon population of the rural interior lags behind because of lower educational attainment and contraceptive use, higher malnutrition, and significantly less access to electricity, potable water, sanitation, infrastructure, and health care.

Some 350,000 people of Surinamese descent live in the Netherlands, Suriname's former colonial ruler. In the 19th century, better-educated, largely Dutch-speaking Surinamese began emigrating to the Netherlands. World War II interrupted the outflow, but it resumed after the war when Dutch labor demands grew - emigrants included all segments of the Creole population. Suriname still is strongly influenced by the Netherlands because most Surinamese have relatives living there and it is the largest supplier of development aid. Other emigration destinations include French Guiana and the United States. Suriname's immigration rules are flexible, and the country is easy to enter illegally because rainforests obscure its borders. Since the mid-1980s, Brazilians have settled in Suriname's capital, Paramaribo, or eastern Suriname, where they mine gold. This immigration is likely to slowly re-orient Suriname toward its Latin American roots.

Age structure: *0-14 years:* 23.38% (male 72,642/female 69,899)
15-24 years: 17.2% (male 53,427/female 51,438)
25-54 years: 44.09% (male 136,889/female 131,868)
55-64 years: 8.78% (male 26,435/female 27,066)
65 years and over: 6.55% (male 17,437/female 22,468) (2020 est.)

Dependency ratios: *total dependency ratio:* 51.1
youth dependency ratio: 40.3
elderly dependency ratio: 10.8
potential support ratio: 9.3 (2020 est.)

Median age: *total:* 31 years
male: 30.6 years
female: 31.4 years (2020 est.)
country comparison to the world: 118

Population growth rate: 1.13% (2022 est.)
country comparison to the world: 86

Birth rate: 15.38 births/1,000 population (2022 est.)
country comparison to the world: 111

Death rate: 6.59 deaths/1,000 population (2022 est.)
country comparison to the world: 133

Net migration rate: 2.54 migrant(s)/1,000 population (2022 est.)
country comparison to the world: 44

Population distribution: population concentrated along the nothern coastal strip; the remainder of the country is sparsely populated

Urbanization: *urban population:* 66.3% of total population (2022)
rate of urbanization: 0.88% annual rate of change (2020-25 est.)

Major urban areas - population: 239,000 PARAMARIBO (capital) (2018)

Sex ratio: *at birth:* 1.07 male(s)/female
0-14 years: 1.03 male(s)/female
15-24 years: 1.05 male(s)/female
25-54 years: 1 male(s)/female
55-64 years: 0.9 male(s)/female
65 years and over: 0.55 male(s)/female
total population: 0.98 male(s)/female (2022 est.)

Maternal mortality ratio: 120 deaths/100,000 live births (2017 est.)
country comparison to the world: 65

Infant mortality rate: *total:* 30.25 deaths/1,000 live births
male: 38.27 deaths/1,000 live births
female: 21.68 deaths/1,000 live births (2022 est.)
country comparison to the world: 53

Life expectancy at birth: *total population:* 72.42 years
male: 68.81 years
female: 76.27 years (2022 est.)
country comparison to the world: 157

Total fertility rate: 1.92 children born/woman (2022 est.)
country comparison to the world: 122

Contraceptive prevalence rate: 39.1% (2018)

Drinking water source: *improved: urban:* 99.5% of population
rural: 98.2% of population
total: 99.1% of population
unimproved: urban: 0.5% of population
rural: 1.8% of population
total: 0.9% of population (2020 est.)

Current health expenditure: 9.7% of GDP (2019)

Physicians density: 0.82 physicians/1,000 population (2018)

Hospital bed density: 3 beds/1,000 population (2017)

Sanitation facility access: *improved: urban:* 98.5% of population
rural: 91.2% of population
total: 96% of population
unimproved: urban: 1.5% of population
rural: 8.8% of population
total: 4% of population (2020 est.)

HIV/AIDS - adult prevalence rate: 1.1% (2020 est.)
country comparison to the world: 41

HIV/AIDS - people living with HIV/AIDS: 5,200 (2020 est.)
country comparison to the world: 120

HIV/AIDS - deaths: (2020 est.) <200

Major infectious diseases: *degree of risk:* very high (2020)
food or waterborne diseases: bacterial and protozoal diarrhea, hepatitis A, and typhoid fever
vectorborne diseases: dengue fever and malaria

Obesity - adult prevalence rate: 26.4% (2016)
country comparison to the world: 42

Alcohol consumption per capita: *total:* 6.6 liters of pure alcohol (2019 est.)
beer: 3.4 liters of pure alcohol (2019 est.)
wine: 0.14 liters of pure alcohol (2019 est.)
spirits: 2.87 liters of pure alcohol (2019 est.)
other alcohols: 0.18 liters of pure alcohol (2019 est.)
country comparison to the world: 62

Children under the age of 5 years underweight: 6.7% (2018)
country comparison to the world: 70

Child marriage: *women married by age 15:* 8.8%
women married by age 18: 36%
men married by age 18: 19.6% (2018 est.)

Education expenditures: 7.2% of GDP (2019 est.)
country comparison to the world: 19

Literacy: *definition:* age 15 and over can read and write
total population: 94.4%
male: 96.1%
female: 92.7% (2018)

Unemployment, youth ages 15-24: *total:* 26.5%
male: 18.7%
female: 39.9% (2016 est.)

ENVIRONMENT

Environment - current issues: deforestation as timber is cut for export; pollution of inland waterways by small-scale mining activities

Environment - international agreements: *party to:* Biodiversity, Climate Change, Climate Change-Kyoto Protocol, Climate Change-Paris Agreement, Comprehensive Nuclear Test Ban, Desertification, Endangered Species, Hazardous Wastes, Law of the Sea, Marine Dumping-London Convention, Marine Dumping-London Protocol, Nuclear Test Ban, Ozone Layer Protection, Ship Pollution, Tropical Timber 2006, Wetlands, Whaling
signed, but not ratified: none of the selected agreements

Air pollutants: *particulate matter emissions:* 23.6 micrograms per cubic meter (2016 est.)
carbon dioxide emissions: 1.74 megatons (2016 est.)
methane emissions: 2.28 megatons (2020 est.)

Climate: tropical; moderated by trade winds

Land use: *agricultural land:* 0.5% (2018 est.)
arable land: 0.4% (2018 est.)
permanent crops: 0% (2018 est.)
permanent pasture: 0.1% (2018 est.)
forest: 94.6% (2018 est.)
other: 4.9% (2018 est.)

Urbanization: *urban population:* 66.3% of total population (2022)
rate of urbanization: 0.88% annual rate of change (2020-25 est.)

Revenue from forest resources: *forest revenues:* 2.36% of GDP (2018 est.)
country comparison to the world: 29

Revenue from coal: *coal revenues:* 0% of GDP (2018 est.)
country comparison to the world: 171

Waste and recycling: *municipal solid waste generated annually:* 78,620 tons (2010 est.)

Major watersheds (area sq km): Atlantic Ocean drainage: Amazon (6,145,186 sq km)

Total water withdrawal: *municipal:* 49.3 million cubic meters (2017 est.)
industrial: 135.5 million cubic meters (2017 est.)
agricultural: 431.1 million cubic meters (2017 est.)

Total renewable water resources: 99 billion cubic meters (2017 est.)

GOVERNMENT

Country name: *conventional long form:* Republic of Suriname
conventional short form: Suriname
local long form: Republiek Suriname
local short form: Suriname
former: Netherlands Guiana, Dutch Guiana
etymology: name may derive from the indigenous "Surinen" people who inhabited the area at the time of European contact

Government type: presidential republic

Capital: *name:* Paramaribo
geographic coordinates: 5 50 N, 55 10 W
time difference: UTC-3 (2 hours ahead of Washington, DC, during Standard Time)
etymology: the name may be the corruption of a Carib (Kalina) village or tribe named Parmirbo

Administrative divisions: 10 districts (distrikten, singular - distrikt); Brokopondo, Commewijne, Coronie, Marowijne, Nickerie, Para, Paramaribo, Saramacca, Sipaliwini, Wanica

Independence: 25 November 1975 (from the Netherlands)

National holiday: Independence Day, 25 November (1975)

Constitution: *history:* previous 1975; latest ratified 30 September 1987, effective 30 October 1987
amendments: proposed by the National Assembly; passage requires at least two-thirds majority vote of the total membership; amended 1992

Legal system: civil law system influenced by Dutch civil law; note - a new criminal code was enacted in 2017

International law organization participation: accepts compulsory ICJ jurisdiction with reservations; accepts ICCt jurisdiction

Citizenship: *citizenship by birth:* no
citizenship by descent only: at least one parent must be a citizen of Suriname
dual citizenship recognized: no
residency requirement for naturalization: 5 years

Suffrage: 18 years of age; universal

Executive branch: *chief of state:* President Chandrikapersad SANTOKHI (since 16 July 2020); Vice President Ronnie BRUNSWIJK (since 16 July 2020); note - the president is both chief of state and head of government
head of government: President Chandrikapersad SANTOKHI (since 16 July 2020); Vice President Ronnie BRUNSWIJK (since 16 July 2020)
cabinet: Cabinet of Ministers appointed by the president
elections/appointments: president and vice president indirectly elected by the National Assembly; president and vice president serve a 5-year term (no term limits); election last held on 13 July 2020 (next to be held in May 2025)
election results:
Chandrikapersad SANTOKHI elected president unopposed; National Assembly vote - NA

Legislative branch: *description:* unicameral National Assembly or Nationale Assemblee (51 seats; members directly elected in 10 multi-seat constituencies by party-list proportional representation vote, using the D'Hondt method, to serve 5-year terms)
elections:
last held on 25 May 2020 (next to be held in May 2025)
election results:
percent of vote by party - VHP 41.1%, NDP 29.4%, ABOP 17.6%, NPS 7.8%, other 3.9%; seats by party - VHP 21, NDP 15, ABOP 9, NPS 4, other 2; composition - men 36, women 15, percent of women 29.4%

Judicial branch: *highest court(s):* High Court of Justice of Suriname (consists of the court president, vice president, and 4 judges); note - appeals beyond the High Court are referred to the Caribbean Court of Justice; human rights violations can be appealed to the Inter-American Commission on Human Rights with judgments issued by the Inter-American Court on Human Rights
judge selection and term of office: court judges appointed by the national president in consultation with the National Assembly, the State Advisory Council, and the Order of Private Attorneys; judges serve for life
subordinate courts: cantonal courts

Political parties and leaders: Brotherhood and Unity in Politics or BEP [Ronnie ASABINA]
Democratic Alternative '91 or DA91 [Angelique DEL CASTILHO]
General Liberation and Development Party or ABOP [Ronnie BRUNSWIJK]
National Democratic Party or NDP [Desire Delano BOUTERSE]
National Party of Suriname or NPS [Gregory RUSLAND]
Party for Democracy and Development in Unity or DOE [Carl BREEVELD]
Party for National Unity and Solidarity or KTPI [Iwan GANGA]
People's Alliance (Pertjajah Luhur) or PL [Paul SOMOHARDJO]
Progressive Workers' and Farmers' Union or PALU [Jim HOK]
Progressive Reform Party or VHP [Chandrikapersad SANTOKHI]
Reform and Renewal Movement or HVB [Mike NOERSALIM]
Surinamese Labor Party or SPA [Guno CASTELEN]

International organization participation: ACP, AOSIS, Caricom, CD, CDB, CELAC, FAO, G-77, IADB, IBRD, ICAO, ICCt, ICRM, IDA, IDB, IFAD, IFC, IFRCS, IHO, ILO, IMF, IMO, Interpol, IOC, IOM, IPU, ISO (correspondent), ITU, ITUC (NGOs), LAES, MIGA, NAM, OAS, OIC, OPANAL, OPCW, PCA, Petrocaribe, UN, UNASUR, UNCTAD, UNESCO, UNIDO, UPU, WHO, WIPO, WMO, WTO

Diplomatic representation in the US: *chief of mission:* Ambassador Jan Marten Willem SCHALKWIJK (since 19 April 2022)
chancery: 4301 Connecticut Avenue NW, Suite 400, Washington, DC 20008
telephone: [1] (202) 629-4302
FAX: [1] (202) 629-4769
email address and website:
amb.vs@gov.sr
https://www.surinameembassy.org/
consulate(s) general: Miami

Diplomatic representation from the US: *chief of mission:* Ambassador Karen Lynn WILLIAMS (since 20 November 2018)
embassy: 165 Kristalstraat, Paramaribo
mailing address: 3390 Paramaribo Place, Washington DC 20521-3390
telephone: [597] 556-700
FAX: [597] 551-524
email address and website:
caparamar@state.gov
https://sr.usembassy.gov/

Flag description: five horizontal bands of green (top, double width), white, red (quadruple width), white, and green (double width); a large, yellow, five-pointed star is centered in the red band; red stands for progress and love, green symbolizes hope and fertility, white signifies peace, justice, and freedom; the star represents the unity of all ethnic groups; from its yellow light the nation draws strength to bear sacrifices patiently while working toward a golden future

National symbol(s): royal palm, faya lobi (flower); national colors: green, white, red, yellow

National anthem: *name:* "God zij met ons Suriname!" (God Be With Our Suriname)
lyrics/music: Cornelis Atses HOEKSTRA and Henry DE ZIEL/Johannes Corstianus DE PUY
note: adopted 1959; originally adapted from a Sunday school song written in 1893 and contains lyrics in both Dutch and Sranang Tongo

National heritage: *total World Heritage Sites:* 2 (1 cultural, 1 natural)
selected World Heritage Site locales: Central Suriname Nature Reserve (n); Historic Inner City of Paramaribo (c)

ECONOMY

Economic overview: Suriname's economy is dominated by the mining industry, with exports of oil and gold accounting for approximately 85% of exports and 27% of government revenues. This makes the economy highly vulnerable to mineral price volatility. The worldwide drop in international commodity prices and the cessation of alumina mining in Suriname significantly reduced government revenue and national income during the past few years. In November 2015, a major US aluminum company discontinued its mining activities in Suriname after 99 years of operation. Public sector revenues fell, together with exports, international reserves, employment, and private sector investment.

Economic growth declined annually from just under 5% in 2012 to -10.4% in 2016. In January 2011, the government devalued the currency by 20% and raised taxes to reduce the budget deficit. Suriname began instituting macro adjustments between September 2015 and 2016; these included another 20% currency devaluation in November 2015 and foreign currency interventions by the Central Bank until March 2016, after which time the Bank allowed the Surinamese dollar (SRD) to float. By December 2016, the SRD had lost 46% of its value against the dollar. Depreciation of the Surinamese dollar and increases in tariffs on electricity caused domestic prices in Suriname to rise 22.0% year-over-year by December 2017.

Suriname's economic prospects for the medium-term will depend on its commitment to responsible monetary and fiscal policies and on the introduction of structural reforms to liberalize markets and promote competition. The government's over-reliance on revenue from the extractive sector colors Suriname's economic outlook. Following two years of recession, the Fitch Credit Bureau reported a positive growth of 1.2% in 2017 and the World Bank predicted 2.2% growth in 2018. Inflation declined to 9%, down from 55% in 2016 , and increased gold production helped lift exports. Yet continued budget imbalances and a heavy debt and interest burden resulted in a debt-to-GDP ratio of 83% in September 2017. Purchasing power has fallen rapidly due to the devalued local currency. The government has announced its intention to pass legislation to introduce a new value-added tax in 2018. Without this and other measures to strengthen the country's fiscal position, the government may face liquidity pressures.

Real GDP (purchasing power parity): $9.46 billion (2020 est.)
$11.07 billion (2019 est.)
$10.95 billion (2018 est.)
note: data are in 2017 dollars
country comparison to the world: 164

Real GDP growth rate: 1.9% (2017 est.)
-5.1% (2016 est.)
-2.6% (2015 est.)
country comparison to the world: 143

Real GDP per capita: $16,100 (2020 est.)
$19,000 (2019 est.)
$19,000 (2018 est.)
note: data are in 2017 dollars
country comparison to the world: 103

GDP (official exchange rate): $3.419 billion (2017 est.)

Inflation rate (consumer prices): 22% (2017 est.)
55.5% (2016 est.)
country comparison to the world: 218

Credit ratings:

Fitch rating: C (2020)

Moody's rating: Caa3 (2020)

Standard & Poors rating: SD (2020)

GDP - composition, by sector of origin: *agriculture:* 11.6% (2017 est.)
industry: 31.1% (2017 est.)
services: 57.4% (2017 est.)

GDP - composition, by end use: *household consumption:* 27.6% (2017 est.)
government consumption: 11.7% (2017 est.)
investment in fixed capital: 52.5% (2017 est.)
investment in inventories: 26.5% (2017 est.)
exports of goods and services: 68.9% (2017 est.)
imports of goods and services: -60.6% (2017 est.)

Agricultural products: rice, sugar cane, bananas, oranges, vegetables, plantains, coconuts, poultry, cassava, eggs

Industries: gold mining, oil, lumber, food processing, fishing

Industrial production growth rate: 1% (2017 est.)
country comparison to the world: 158

Labor force: 144,000 (2014 est.)
country comparison to the world: 176

Labor force - by occupation: *agriculture:* 11.2%
industry: 19.5%
services: 69.3% (2010)

Unemployment rate: 8.9% (2017 est.)
9.7% (2016 est.)
country comparison to the world: 137

Unemployment, youth ages 15-24: *total:* 26.5%
male: 18.7%
female: 39.9% (2016 est.)
country comparison to the world: 48

Population below poverty line: 70% (2002 est.)

Budget: *revenues:* 560.7 million (2017 est.)
expenditures: 827.8 million (2017 est.)

Budget surplus (+) or deficit (-): -7.8% (of GDP) (2017 est.)
country comparison to the world: 197

Public debt: 69.3% of GDP (2017 est.)
75.8% of GDP (2016 est.)
country comparison to the world: 53

Taxes and other revenues: 16.4% (of GDP) (2017 est.)
country comparison to the world: 182

Fiscal year: calendar year

Current account balance: -$2 million (2017 est.)
-$169 million (2016 est.)
country comparison to the world: 68

Exports: $2.29 billion (2019 est.) note: data are in current year dollars
$2.24 billion (2018 est.) note: data are in current year dollars
country comparison to the world: 149

Exports - partners: Switzerland 39%, United Arab Emirates 31%, Belgium 10% (2019)

Exports - commodities: gold, lumber, refined petroleum, fish, cigarettes (2019)

Imports: $2.41 billion (2019 est.) note: data are in current year dollars
$2.07 billion (2018 est.) note: data are in current year dollars
country comparison to the world: 166

Imports - partners: United States 22%, Netherlands 14%, China 13%, Trinidad and Tobago 7%, Antigua and Barbuda 5% (2019)

Imports - commodities: refined petroleum, delivery trucks, excavation machinery, cars, construction vehicles (2019)

Reserves of foreign exchange and gold: $424.4 million (31 December 2017 est.)
$381.1 million (31 December 2016 est.)
country comparison to the world: 158

Debt - external: $1.7 billion (31 December 2017 est.)
$1.436 billion (31 December 2016 est.)
country comparison to the world: 156

Exchange rates: Surinamese dollars (SRD) per US dollar -
7.53 (2017 est.)
6.229 (2016 est.)
6.229 (2015 est.)
3.4167 (2014 est.)
3.3 (2013 est.)

ENERGY

Electricity access: *electrification - total population:* 97.4% (2018)
electrification - urban areas: 99% (2018)
electrification - rural areas: 94.3% (2018)

Electricity: *installed generating capacity:* 542,000 kW (2020 est.)
consumption: 2,938,391,000 kWh (2019 est.)
exports: 0 kWh (2019 est.)
imports: 808 million kWh (2019 est.)
transmission/distribution losses: 234 million kWh (2019 est.)

Electricity generation sources: *fossil fuels:* 40.5% of total installed capacity (2020 est.)
solar: 0.4% of total installed capacity (2020 est.)
hydroelectricity: 58.8% of total installed capacity (2020 est.)
biomass and waste: 0.3% of total installed capacity (2020 est.)

Petroleum: *total petroleum production:* 14,800 bbl/day (2021 est.)
refined petroleum consumption: 15,800 bbl/day (2019 est.)
crude oil and lease condensate exports: 0 bbl/day (2018 est.)
crude oil and lease condensate imports: 200 bbl/day (2018 est.)
crude oil estimated reserves: 89 million barrels (2021 est.)

Refined petroleum products - production: 7,571 bbl/day (2015 est.)
country comparison to the world: 101

Refined petroleum products - exports: 14,000 bbl/day (2015 est.)
country comparison to the world: 74

Refined petroleum products - imports: 10,700 bbl/day (2015 est.)
country comparison to the world: 145

Natural gas: *production:* 0 cubic meters (2020 est.)
consumption: 0 cubic meters (2020 est.)
exports: 0 cubic meters (2021 est.)
imports: 0 cubic meters (2021 est.)
proven reserves: 0 cubic meters (2021 est.)

Carbon dioxide emissions: 2.372 million metric tonnes of CO_2 (2019 est.)
from petroleum and other liquids: 2.361 million metric tonnes of CO_2 (2019 est.)
from consumed natural gas: 11,000 metric tonnes of CO_2 (2019 est.)
country comparison to the world: 156

Energy consumption per capita: 82.356 million Btu/person (2019 est.)
country comparison to the world: 71

COMMUNICATIONS

Telephones - fixed lines: *total subscriptions:* 103,240 (2020 est.)
subscriptions per 100 inhabitants: 18 (2020 est.)
country comparison to the world: 137

Telephones - mobile cellular: *total subscriptions:* 813,844 (2019)
subscriptions per 100 inhabitants: 139.99 (2019)

country comparison to the world: 165

Telecommunication systems general assessment: Suriname is the smallest nation on the South American continent, with about 580,000 inhabitants; the only Dutch-speaking nation in South America, it has close affinities with the Caribbean, and is a member of the Caribbean Community and Common Market (CARICOM); the country's fixed-line infrastructure is reasonably reliable in the more populated coastal region, though poor in the interior; fixed teledensity and broadband penetration are slightly lower than average for Latin America and the Caribbean, while mobile penetration is significantly above the regional average and much higher than would be expected given the country's relatively low GDP per capita; many Surinamese have up to three mobile lines with different providers, which has pushed up penetration figures although the number of subscribers has fallen in recent years as consumers have responded to economic pressures
(2021)
domestic: fixed-line nearly 18 per 100 and mobile-cellular teledensity over 153 telephones per 100 persons; microwave radio relay network is in place (2020)
international: country code - 597; landing point for the SG-SCS submarine cable linking South America with the Caribbean; satellite earth stations - 2 Intelsat (Atlantic Ocean) (2019)

Broadcast media: 2 state-owned TV stations; 1 state-owned radio station; multiple private radio and TV stations (2019)

Internet country code: .sr

Internet users: *total:* 410,644 (2020 est.)
percent of population: 70% (2020 est.)
country comparison to the world: 164

Broadband - fixed subscriptions: *total:* 92,270 (2020 est.)
subscriptions per 100 inhabitants: 16 (2020 est.)
country comparison to the world: 129

TRANSPORTATION

National air transport system: *number of registered air carriers:* 4 (2020)
inventory of registered aircraft operated by air carriers: 20
annual passenger traffic on registered air carriers: 272,347 (2018)
annual freight traffic on registered air carriers: 33.2 million (2018) mt-km

Civil aircraft registration country code prefix: PZ

Airports: *total:* 55 (2021)
country comparison to the world: 84

Airports - with paved runways: *total:* 6
over 3,047 m: 1
under 914 m: 5 (2021)

Airports - with unpaved runways: *total:* 49
914 to 1,523 m: 4
under 914 m: 45 (2021)

Pipelines: 50 km oil (2013)

Roadways: *total:* 4,304 km (2003)
paved: 1,119 km (2003)
unpaved: 3,185 km (2003)
country comparison to the world: 151

Waterways: 1,200 km (2011) (most navigable by ships with drafts up to 7 m)
country comparison to the world: 63

Merchant marine: *total:* 10
by type: general cargo 5, oil tanker 3, other 2 (2021)
country comparison to the world: 156

Ports and terminals: *major seaport(s):* Paramaribo, Wageningen

MILITARY AND SECURITY

Military and security forces: Suriname Army (National Leger, NL): Army, Navy, Air Force, Military Police (2022)

Military expenditures: 1.2% of GDP (2019 est.) (approximately $100 million)
1.1% of GDP (2018 est.) (approximately $95 million)
1.1% of GDP (2017 est.) (approximately $95 million)
1.2% of GDP (2016 est.) (approximately $85 million)
1.4% of GDP (2015 est.) (approximately $110 million)
country comparison to the world: 118

Military and security service personnel strengths: approximately 2,000 total personnel (2022)

Military equipment inventories and acquisitions: the Suriname Army has a limited inventory comprised of a mix of older, foreign-supplied equipment; since 2010, Suriname has received small quantities of military hardware from several countries, including the US (2022)

Military service age and obligation: 18 is the legal minimum age for voluntary military service; no conscription (2022)

Military - note: key missions for the National Leger include border control and supporting domestic security; the military police has direct responsibility for immigration control at the country's ports of entry; in addition, the military assists the police in combating crime, particularly narco-trafficking, including joint military and police patrols, as well as joint special security teams (2022)

TRANSNATIONAL ISSUES

Disputes - international: *Suriname-Brazil:* none identified
Suriname-France (French Guiana): in March 2021, Suriname and France signed an agreement to establish their border along the Maroni River and its tributary the Lawa River and to cooperate in combatting illegal gold mining; however, the area further south between the Litani and Marouini Rivers is still disputed, with Suriname claiming the border is along the Marouini to the east and France arguing it is along the Litani River to the west
Suriname-Guyana: the two countries dispute the territory between two rivers, known as the New River Triangle, with Suriname contending that the New River (also called the Upper Corentyne) to the west marks their common border, while Guyana asserts that the Kutari River to the east forms the border; each side claims that their river is the source of the Corentyne River that forms a border further north between the two countries; the Permanent Court of Arbitration settled the maritime boundary between Suriname and Guyana in 2007 in an area with potentially substantial oil reserves

Illicit drugs: a transit country for South American cocaine en route to Europe, the United States and Africa; marijuana is the primary drug consumed locally

SVALBARD

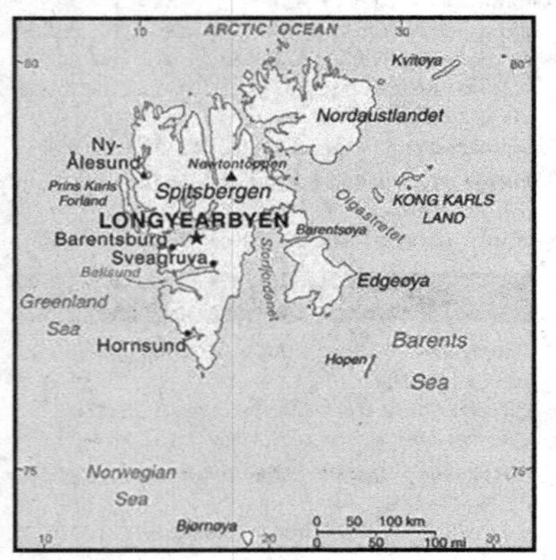

INTRODUCTION

Background: The archipelago may have been first discovered by Norse explorers in the 12th century; the islands served as an international whaling base during the 17th and 18th centuries. Norway's sovereignty was internationally recognized by treaty in 1920, and five years later it officially took over the territory. In the 20th century, coal mining started and today a Norwegian and a Russian company are still functioning. Travel between the settlements is accomplished with snowmobiles, aircraft, and boats.

GEOGRAPHY

Location: Northern Europe, islands between the Arctic Ocean, Barents Sea, Greenland Sea, and Norwegian Sea, north of Norway

Geographic coordinates: 78 00 N, 20 00 E

Map references: Arctic Region

Area: *total:* 62,045 sq km
land: 62,045 sq km
water: 0 sq km
note: includes Spitsbergen and Bjornoya (Bear Island)
country comparison to the world: 125

Area - comparative: slightly smaller than West Virginia

Land boundaries: *total:* 0 km

Coastline: 3,587 km

Maritime claims: *territorial sea:* 12 nm
contiguous zone: 24 nm
continental shelf: extends to depth of exploitation
exclusive fishing zone: 200 nm

Climate: arctic, tempered by warm North Atlantic Current; cool summers, cold winters; North Atlantic Current flows along west and north coasts of Spitsbergen, keeping water open and navigable most of the year

Terrain: rugged mountains; much of the upland areas are ice covered; west coast clear of ice about half the year; fjords along west and north coasts

Elevation: *highest point:* Newtontoppen 1,717 m
lowest point: Arctic Ocean 0 m

Natural resources: coal, iron ore, copper, zinc, phosphate, wildlife, fish

Land use: *agricultural land:* 0% (2018 est.)
other: 100% (2018 est.)

Population distribution: the small population is primarily concentrated on the island of Spitsbergen in a handful of settlements on the south side of the Isfjorden, with Longyearbyen being the largest

Natural hazards: ice floes often block the entrance to Bellsund (a transit point for coal export) on the west coast and occasionally make parts of the northeastern coast inaccessible to maritime traffic

Geography - note: northernmost part of the Kingdom of Norway; consists of nine main islands; glaciers and snowfields cover 60% of the total area; Spitsbergen Island is the site of the Svalbard Global Seed Vault, a seed repository established by the Global Crop Diversity Trust and the Norwegian Government

PEOPLE AND SOCIETY

Population: 2,926 (January 2021 est.)
country comparison to the world: 229

Ethnic groups: Norwegian 61.1%, foreign population 38.9% (consists primarily of Russians, Thais, Swedes, Filipinos, and Ukrainians) (2021 est.)
note: foreigners account for almost one third of the population of the Norwegian settlements, Longyearbyen and Ny-Alesund (where the majority of Svalbard's resident population lives), as of mid-2021

Languages: Norwegian, Russian
major-language sample(s):
Verdens Faktabok, den essensielle kilden for grunnleggende informasjon. (Norwegian)

Population growth rate: -0.03% (2019 est.)
country comparison to the world: 201

Net migration rate: -5.57 migrant(s)/1,000 population (2021 est.)
country comparison to the world: 207

Population distribution: the small population is primarily concentrated on the island of Spitsbergen in a handful of settlements on the south side of the Isfjorden, with Longyearbyen being the largest

ENVIRONMENT

Environment - current issues: ice floes are a maritime hazard; past exploitation of mammal species (whale, seal, walrus, and polar bear) severely depleted the populations, but a gradual recovery seems to be occurring

Climate: arctic, tempered by warm North Atlantic Current; cool summers, cold winters; North Atlantic Current flows along west and north coasts of Spitsbergen, keeping water open and navigable most of the year

Land use: *agricultural land:* 0% (2018 est.)
other: 100% (2018 est.)

GOVERNMENT

Country name: *conventional long form:* none
conventional short form: Svalbard (sometimes referred to as Spitsbergen, the largest island in the archipelago)
etymology: 12th century Norse accounts speak of the discovery of a "Svalbard" - literally "cold shores" - but they may have referred to Jan Mayen Island or eastern Greenland; the archipelago was traditionally known as Spitsbergen, but Norway renamed it Svalbard in the 1920s when it assumed sovereignty of the islands

Government type: non-self-governing territory of Norway

Dependency status: territory of Norway; administered by the Polar Department of the Ministry of Justice, through a governor (sysselmann) residing in Longyearbyen, Spitsbergen; by treaty (9 February 1920), sovereignty was awarded to Norway

Capital: *name:* Longyearbyen
geographic coordinates: 78 13 N, 15 38 E
time difference: UTC+1 (6 hours ahead of Washington, DC, during Standard Time)
daylight saving time: +1hr, begins last Sunday in March; ends last Sunday in October
etymology: the name in Norwegian means Longyear Town; the site was established by and named after John LONGYEAR, whose Arctic Coal Company began mining operations there in 1906

Independence: none (territory of Norway)

Legal system: the laws of Norway where applicable apply; only the laws of Norway made explicitly applicable to Svalbard have effect there; the Svalbard Act and the Svalbard Environmental Protection Act, and certain regulations, apply only to Svalbard; the Spitsbergen Treaty and the Svalbard Treaty grant certain rights to citizens and corporations of signatory nations; as of June 2017, 45 nations had ratified the Svalbard Treaty

Citizenship: see Norway

Executive branch: *chief of state:* King HARALD V of Norway (since 17 January 1991); Heir Apparent Crown Prince Haakon MAGNUS (son of the king, born 20 July 1973)
head of government: Governor Lars FAUSE (since 24 June 2021); Vice Governor Solvi ELVEDAHL (since 1 May 2020)
elections/appointments: none; the monarchy is hereditary; governor and assistant governor responsible to the Polar Department of the Ministry of Justice

Legislative branch: *description:* unicameral Longyearbyen Community Council (15 seats; members directly elected by majority vote to serve 4-year-terms); note - the Council acts very much like a Norwegian municipality, responsible for infrastructure and utilities, including power, land-use and community planning, education, and child welfare; however, healthcare services are provided by the state
elections:
last held on 7 October 2019 (next to be held in October 2023)
election results:
seats by party - Labor Party 5, Liberals 4, Conservatives 3, Progress Party 2, Green Party 1

Judicial branch: *highest court(s):* none; note - Svalbard is subordinate to Norway's Nord-Troms District Court and Halogaland Court of Appeal, both located in Tromso

Political parties and leaders: Svalbard Conservative Party [Kjetil FIGENSCHOU]
Svalbard Green Party [Pal BERG]
Svalbard Labor Party [Arild OLSEN]
Svalbard Liberal Party [Terie AUVENIK]
Svalbard Progress Party [Jorn DYBDAHL]

International organization participation: none

Flag description: the flag of Norway is used

National anthem: *note:* as a territory of Norway, "Ja, vi elsker dette landet" is official (see Norway)

ECONOMY

Economic overview: Coal mining, tourism, and international research are Svalbard's major industries. Coal mining has historically been the dominant economic activity, and the Spitzbergen Treaty of 9 February 1920 gives the 45 countries that so far have ratified the treaty equal rights to exploit mineral deposits, subject to Norwegian regulation. Although US, UK, Dutch, and Swedish coal companies have mined in the past, the only companies still engaging in this are Norwegian and Russian. Low coal prices have forced the Norwegian coal company, Store Norske Spitsbergen Kulkompani, to close one of its two mines and to considerably reduce the activity of the other. Since the 1990s, the tourism and hospitality industry has grown rapidly, and Svalbard now receives 60,000 visitors annually.

The settlements on Svalbard were established as company towns, and at their height in the 1950s, the Norwegian state-owned coal company supported nearly 1,000 jobs. Today, only about 300 people work in the mining industry.

Goods such as alcohol, tobacco, and vehicles, normally highly taxed on mainland Norway, are considerably cheaper in Svalbard in an effort by the Norwegian Government to entice more people to live on the Arctic archipelago. By law, Norway collects only enough taxes to pay for the needs of the local government; none of tax proceeds go to the central government.

Labor force: 1,590 (2013)
country comparison to the world: 227

Exchange rates: Norwegian kroner (NOK) per US dollar -
8.308 (2017 est.)
8.0646 (2016 est.)
8.0646 (2015)
8.0646 (2014 est.)
6.3021 (2013 est.)

ENERGY

Refined petroleum products - exports: 4,488 bbl/day (2012 est.)
country comparison to the world: 93

Refined petroleum products - imports: 18,600 bbl/day (2012 est.)
country comparison to the world: 127

COMMUNICATIONS

Telecommunication systems: *general assessment:* Svalbard Undersea Cable System is a twin submarine communications cable which connects Svalbard to the mainland of Norway (2022)
domestic: the Svalbard Satellite Station - connected to the mainland via the Svalbard Undersea Cable

System - is the only Arctic ground station that can see low-altitude, polar-orbiting satellites; it provides ground services to more satellites than any other facility in the world (2022)
international: country code - 47-790; the Svalbard Undersea Cable System is a twin communications cable that connects Svalbard to mainland Norway; the system is the sole telecommunications link to the archipelago (2019)

Broadcast media: the Norwegian Broadcasting Corporation (NRK) began direct TV transmission to Svalbard via satellite in 1984; Longyearbyen households have access to 3 NRK radio and 2 TV stations

Internet country code: .sj

TRANSPORTATION

Airports: *total:* 4 (2021)
country comparison to the world: 188

Airports - with paved runways: *total:* 1
2,438 to 3,047 m: 1 (2021)

Airports - with unpaved runways: *total:* 3
under 914 m: 3 (2021)

Heliports: 1 (2021)

Roadways: *total:* 40 km (2020)
country comparison to the world: 218

Ports and terminals: *major seaport(s):* Barentsburg, Longyearbyen, Ny-Alesund, Pyramiden

MILITARY AND SECURITY

Military and security forces: no regular military forces

Military - note: Svalbard is a territory of Norway, demilitarized by treaty on 9 February 1920; Norwegian military activity is limited to fisheries surveillance by the Norwegian Coast Guard (2022)

TRANSNATIONAL ISSUES

Disputes - international: *Norway-Russia:* after 40 years of on-again, off-again negotiations, the two countries signed an agreement in September 2010, defining their maritime boundaries in the Barents Sea and the Arctic Ocean; the border extends the countries' land border northward beyond the islands in the Barents Sea and into the Arctic Ocean, but the exact distance northward was not specified; because the area is considered the high seas, the passage of naval and commercial vessels will be unaffected; once their legislatures ratify the agreement, both countries will have the green light for oil and natural gas exploration in their newly defined maritime areas; Russia objects to Norway's establishment in 1977 of the Fishery Protection Zone around the Svalbard Islands, extending Norwegian sovereignty to the shelf around the archipelago; Svalbard is strategically important – as a gateway from the Berents Sea to the North Atlantic – and its waters provide rich fishing grounds

SWEDEN

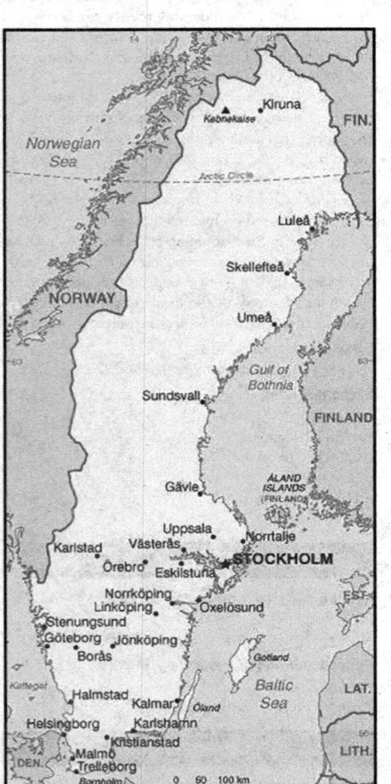

INTRODUCTION

Background: A military power during the 17th century, Sweden has not participated in any war for two centuries. An armed neutrality was preserved in both World Wars. Since then, Sweden has pursued a successful economic formula consisting of a capitalist system intermixed with substantial welfare elements. Sweden joined the EU in 1995, but the public rejected the introduction of the euro in a 2003 referendum. The share of Sweden's population born abroad increased from 11.3% in 2000 to 20% in 2021.

GEOGRAPHY

Location: Northern Europe, bordering the Baltic Sea, Gulf of Bothnia, Kattegat, and Skagerrak, between Finland and Norway

Geographic coordinates: 62 00 N, 15 00 E

Map references: Europe

Area: *total:* 450,295 sq km
land: 410,335 sq km
water: 39,960 sq km
country comparison to the world: 58

Area - comparative: almost three times the size of Georgia; slightly larger than California

Land boundaries: *total:* 2,211 km
border countries (2): Finland 545 km; Norway 1,666 km

Coastline: 3,218 km

Maritime claims: *territorial sea:* 12 nm (adjustments made to return a portion of straits to high seas)
exclusive economic zone: agreed boundaries or midlines
continental shelf: 200-m depth or to the depth of exploitation

Climate: temperate in south with cold, cloudy winters and cool, partly cloudy summers; subarctic in north

Terrain: mostly flat or gently rolling lowlands; mountains in west

Elevation: *highest point:* Kebnekaise South 2,100 m
lowest point: reclaimed bay of Lake Hammarsjon, near Kristianstad -2.4 m
mean elevation: 320 m

Natural resources: iron ore, copper, lead, zinc, gold, silver, tungsten, uranium, arsenic, feldspar, timber, hydropower

Land use: *agricultural land:* 7.5% (2018 est.)
arable land: 6.4% (2018 est.)
permanent crops: 0% (2018 est.)
permanent pasture: 1.1% (2018 est.)
forest: 68.7% (2018 est.)
other: 23.8% (2018 est.)

Irrigated land: 1,640 sq km (2012)

Major lakes (area sq km): *fresh water lake(s):* Vanern - 5,580 sq km; Vattern - 1,910 sq km; Malaren - 1,140 sq km

Population distribution: most Swedes live in the south where the climate is milder and there is better connectivity to mainland Europe; population clusters are found all along the Baltic coast in the east; the interior areas of the north remain sparsely populated

Natural hazards: ice floes in the surrounding waters, especially in the Gulf of Bothnia, can interfere with maritime traffic

Geography - note: strategic location along Danish Straits linking Baltic and North Seas; Sweden has almost 100,000 lakes, the largest of which, Vanern, is the third largest in Europe

PEOPLE AND SOCIETY

Population: 10,483,647 (2022 est.)
country comparison to the world: 89

Nationality: *noun:* Swede(s)
adjective: Swedish

Ethnic groups: Swedish 80.3%, Syrian 1.9%, Iraqi 1.4%, Finnish 1.4%, other 15%
(2020 est.)
note: data represent the population by country of birth; the indigenous Sami people are estimated to number between 20,000 and 40,000

Languages: Swedish (official)
major-language sample(s):
The World Factbook, den obestridliga källan för grundläggande information. (Swedish)

note: Finnish, Sami, Romani, Yiddish, and Meankieli are official minority languages

Religions: Church of Sweden (Lutheran) 57.6%, other (includes Roman Catholic, Orthodox, Baptist, Muslim, Jewish, and Buddhist) 8.9%, none or unspecified 33.5% (2019 est.)
note: estimates reflect registered members of faith communities eligible for state funding (not all religions are state-funded and not all people who identify with a particular religion are registered members) and the Church of Sweden

Age structure: *0-14 years:* 17.71% (male 928,413/female 878,028)
15-24 years: 10.8% (male 569,082/female 532,492)
25-54 years: 39.01% (male 2,016,991/female 1,962,617)
55-64 years: 11.9% (male 610,521/female 603,795)
65 years and over: 20.59% (male 974,410/female 1,126,142) (2020 est.)

Dependency ratios: *total dependency ratio:* 61.2
youth dependency ratio: 28.4
elderly dependency ratio: 32.8
potential support ratio: 3.1 (2020 est.)

Median age: *total:* 41.1 years
male: 40.1 years
female: 42.1 years (2020 est.)
country comparison to the world: 47

Population growth rate: 0.5% (2022 est.)
country comparison to the world: 156

Birth rate: 10.83 births/1,000 population (2022 est.)
country comparison to the world: 175

Death rate: 9.46 deaths/1,000 population (2022 est.)
country comparison to the world: 48

Net migration rate: 3.6 migrant(s)/1,000 population (2022 est.)
country comparison to the world: 33

Population distribution: most Swedes live in the south where the climate is milder and there is better connectivity to mainland Europe; population clusters are found all along the Baltic coast in the east; the interior areas of the north remain sparsely populated

Urbanization: *urban population:* 88.5% of total population (2022)
rate of urbanization: 0.89% annual rate of change (2020-25 est.)

Major urban areas - population: 1.659 million STOCKHOLM (capital) (2022)

Sex ratio: *at birth:* 1.06 male(s)/female
0-14 years: 1.06 male(s)/female
15-24 years: 1.1 male(s)/female
25-54 years: 1.04 male(s)/female
55-64 years: 1.02 male(s)/female
65 years and over: 0.69 male(s)/female
total population: 1.01 male(s)/female (2022 est.)

Mother's mean age at first birth: 29.7 years (2020 est.)

Maternal mortality ratio: 4 deaths/100,000 live births (2017 est.)
country comparison to the world: 175

Infant mortality rate: *total:* 2.3 deaths/1,000 live births
male: 2.52 deaths/1,000 live births
female: 2.06 deaths/1,000 live births (2022 est.)
country comparison to the world: 220

Life expectancy at birth: *total population:* 82.7 years
male: 80.94 years
female: 84.58 years (2022 est.)
country comparison to the world: 17

Total fertility rate: 1.67 children born/woman (2022 est.)
country comparison to the world: 173

Contraceptive prevalence rate: 70.3% (2017)
note: percent of women aged 16-49

Drinking water source: *improved: urban:* 99.8% of population
rural: 99.7% of population
total: 99.8% of population
unimproved: urban: 0.2% of population
rural: 0.3% of population
total: 0.2% of population (2020 est.)

Current health expenditure: 10.9% of GDP (2019)

Physicians density: 7.09 physicians/1,000 population (2019)

Hospital bed density: 2.1 beds/1,000 population (2018)

Sanitation facility access: *improved: urban:* 100% of population
rural: 100% of population
total: 100% of population

HIV/AIDS - adult prevalence rate: 0.2% (2016 est.)
country comparison to the world: 113

HIV/AIDS - people living with HIV/AIDS: 11,000 (2016 est.)
country comparison to the world: 101

Obesity - adult prevalence rate: 20.6% (2016)
country comparison to the world: 97

Alcohol consumption per capita: *total:* 7.1 liters of pure alcohol (2019 est.)
beer: 2.6 liters of pure alcohol (2019 est.)
wine: 3.4 liters of pure alcohol (2019 est.)
spirits: 1 liters of pure alcohol (2019 est.)
other alcohols: 0.1 liters of pure alcohol (2019 est.)
country comparison to the world: 59

Tobacco use: *total:* 24% (2020 est.)
male: 29.8% (2020 est.)
female: 18.2% (2020 est.)
country comparison to the world: 60

Education expenditures: 7.6% of GDP (2018 est.)
country comparison to the world: 15

School life expectancy (primary to tertiary education): *total:* 19 years
male: 18 years
female: 21 years (2019)

Unemployment, youth ages 15-24: *total:* 24%
male: 25%
female: 22.8% (2020 est.)

ENVIRONMENT

Environment - current issues: marine pollution (Baltic Sea and North Sea); acid rain damage to soils and lakes; air pollution; inappropriate timber harvesting practices

Environment - international agreements: *party to:* Air Pollution, Air Pollution-Heavy Metals, Air Pollution-Multi-effect Protocol, Air Pollution-Nitrogen Oxides, Air Pollution-Persistent Organic Pollutants, Air Pollution-Sulphur 85, Air Pollution-Sulphur 94, Air Pollution-Volatile Organic Compounds, Antarctic-Environmental Protection, Antarctic-Marine Living Resources, Antarctic Treaty, Biodiversity, Climate Change, Climate Change-Kyoto Protocol, Climate Change-Paris Agreement, Comprehensive Nuclear Test Ban, Desertification, Endangered Species, Environmental Modification, Hazardous Wastes, Law of the Sea, Marine Dumping- London Convention, Marine Dumping-London Protocol, Nuclear Test Ban, Ozone Layer Protection, Ship Pollution, Tropical Timber 2006, Wetlands, Whaling
signed, but not ratified: none of the selected agreements

Air pollutants: *particulate matter emissions:* 5.89 micrograms per cubic meter (2016 est.)
carbon dioxide emissions: 43.25 megatons (2016 est.)
methane emissions: 4.42 megatons (2020 est.)

Climate: temperate in south with cold, cloudy winters and cool, partly cloudy summers; subarctic in north

Land use: *agricultural land:* 7.5% (2018 est.)
arable land: 6.4% (2018 est.)
permanent crops: 0% (2018 est.)
permanent pasture: 1.1% (2018 est.)
forest: 68.7% (2018 est.)
other: 23.8% (2018 est.)

Urbanization: *urban population:* 88.5% of total population (2022)
rate of urbanization: 0.89% annual rate of change (2020-25 est.)

Revenue from forest resources: *forest revenues:* 0.21% of GDP (2018 est.)
country comparison to the world: 91

Revenue from coal: *coal revenues:* 0% of GDP (2018 est.)
country comparison to the world: 172

Waste and recycling: *municipal solid waste generated annually:* 4.377 million tons (2015 est.)
municipal solid waste recycled annually: 1,416,835 tons (2015 est.)
percent of municipal solid waste recycled: 32.4% (2015 est.)

Major lakes (area sq km): *fresh water lake(s):* Vanern - 5,580 sq km; Vattern - 1,910 sq km; Malaren - 1,140 sq km

Total water withdrawal: *municipal:* 955 million cubic meters (2017 est.)
industrial: 1.345 billion cubic meters (2017 est.)
agricultural: 75 million cubic meters (2017 est.)

Total renewable water resources: 174 billion cubic meters (2017 est.)

GOVERNMENT

Country name: *conventional long form:* Kingdom of Sweden
conventional short form: Sweden
local long form: Konungariket Sverige
local short form: Sverige
etymology: name ultimately derives from the North Germanic Svear tribe, which inhabited central Sweden and is first mentioned in the first centuries A.D.

Government type: parliamentary constitutional monarchy

Capital: *name:* Stockholm
geographic coordinates: 59 20 N, 18 03 E
time difference: UTC+1 (6 hours ahead of Washington, DC, during Standard Time)
daylight saving time: +1hr, begins last Sunday in March; ends last Sunday in October
etymology: *stock* and *holm* literally mean "log" and "islet" in Swedish, but there is no consensus as to what the words refer to

Administrative divisions: 21 counties (lan, singular and plural); Blekinge, Dalarna, Gavleborg, Gotland, Halland, Jamtland, Jonkoping, Kalmar, Kronoberg, Norrbotten, Orebro, Ostergotland, Skane, Sodermanland, Stockholm, Uppsala, Varmland, Vasterbotten, Vasternorrland, Vastmanland, Vastra Gotaland

Independence: 6 June 1523 (Gustav VASA elected king of Sweden, marking the abolishment of the Kalmar Union between Denmark, Norway, and Sweden)

National holiday: National Day, 6 June (1983); note - from 1916 to 1982 this date was celebrated as Swedish Flag Day

Constitution: *history:* Sweden has four fundamental laws which together make up the Constitution: The Instrument of Government (several previous; latest 1974); The Act of Succession (enacted 1810; changed in 1937 and 1980); The Freedom of the Press Act (many previous; latest in 1949); The Fundamental Law on Freedom of Expression (adopted 1991)
amendments: proposed by Parliament; passage requires simple majority vote in two consecutive parliamentary terms with an intervening general election; passage also requires approval by simple majority vote in a referendum if Parliament approves a motion for a referendum by one third of its members; The Instrument of Government - amended several times, last in 2018; The Act of Succession - changed in 1937, 1980; The Freedom of the Press Act - amended several times, last in 2019; The Fundamental Law on Freedom of Expression - amended several times, last in 2018

Legal system: civil law system influenced by Roman-Germanic law and customary law

International law organization participation: accepts compulsory ICJ jurisdiction with reservations; accepts ICCt jurisdiction

Citizenship: *citizenship by birth:* no
citizenship by descent only: the father must be a citizen of Sweden; in the case of a child born out of wedlock, the mother must be a citizen of Sweden and the father unknown
dual citizenship recognized: no, unless the other citizenship was acquired involuntarily
residency requirement for naturalization: 5 years

Suffrage: 18 years of age; universal

Executive branch: *chief of state:* King CARL XVI GUSTAF (since 15 September 1973); Heir Apparent Princess VICTORIA Ingrid Alice Desiree (daughter of the monarch, born 14 July 1977)
head of government: Prime Minister Ulf KRISTERSSON (since 18 October 2022); Deputy Prime Minister Ebba BUSCH (since 18 October 2022)
cabinet: Cabinet appointed by the prime minister
elections/appointments: the monarchy is hereditary; following legislative elections, the leader of the majority party or majority coalition usually becomes the prime minister

Legislative branch: *description:* unicameral Parliament or Riksdag (349 seats; 310 members directly elected in multi-seat constituencies by open party-list proportional representation vote and 39 members in "at-large" seats directly elected by open party-list proportional representation vote; members serve 4-year terms)
elections:
last held on 11 September 2022
election results:
percent of vote by party - S/SAP 30.3%, M 19.1%, SD 20.5%, C 6.7%, V 6.7%, KD 5.3%, L 4.6%, MP 5.1%, other 1.7%; seats by party - S/SAP 107, M 68, SD 73, C 24, V 24, KD 19, L 16, MP 18; composition as of mid-2022 - men 188, women 161, percent of women 46%

Judicial branch: *highest court(s):* Supreme Court of Sweden (consists of 16 justices, including the court chairman); Supreme Administrative Court (consists of 18 justices, including the court president)
judge selection and term of office: Supreme Court and Supreme Administrative Court justices nominated by the Judges Proposal Board, a 9-member nominating body consisting of high-level judges, prosecutors, and members of Parliament; justices appointed by the Government; following a probationary period, justices' appointments are permanent
subordinate courts: first instance, appellate, general, and administrative courts; specialized courts that handle cases such as land and environment, immigration, labor, markets, and patents

Political parties and leaders: Center Party (Centerpartiet) or C [Annie LOOF resigned on 15 September 2022]
Christian Democrats (Kristdemokraterna) or KD [Ebba BUSCH]
Green Party (Miljopartiet de Grona) or MP [Marta STEVENI and Per BOLUND]
Left Party (Vansterpartiet) or V [Nooshi DADGOSTAR]
Moderate Party (Moderaterna) or M [Ulf KRISTERSSON]
Sweden Democrats (Sverigedemokraterna) or SD [Jimmie AKESSON]
Swedish Social Democratic Party (Socialdemokraterna) or S/SAP [Magdalena ANDERSSON]
The Liberals (Liberalerna) or L [Johan PEHRSON]

International organization participation: ADB (nonregional member), AfDB (nonregional member), Arctic Council, Australia Group, BIS, CBSS, CD, CE, CERN, EAPC, EBRD, ECB, EIB, EITI (implementing country), EMU, ESA, EU, FAO, FATF, G-9, G-10, IADB, IAEA, IBRD, ICAO, ICC (national committees), ICCt, ICRM, IDA, IEA, IFAD, IFC, IFRCS, IGAD (partners), IHO, ILO, IMF, IMO, IMSO, Interpol, IOC, IOM, IPU, ISO, ITSO, ITU, ITUC (NGOs), MIGA, MINUSMA, MONUSCO, NC, NEA, NIB, NSG, OAS (observer), OECD, OPCW, OSCE, Paris Club, PCA, PFP, Schengen Convention, UN, UNCTAD, UNESCO, UNHCR, UNIDO, UNMISS, UNMOGIP, UNRWA, UN Security Council (temporary), UNSOM, UNTSO, UPU, Wassenaar Arrangement, WCO, WFTU (NGOs), WHO, WIPO, WMO, WTO, ZC

Diplomatic representation in the US: *chief of mission:* Ambassador Karin Ulrika OLOFSDOTTER (since 8 September 2017)
chancery: 2900 K Street NW, Washington, DC 20007
telephone: [1] (202) 467-2600
FAX: [1] (202) 467-2699
email address and website:
ambassaden.washington@gov.se
https://www.swedenabroad.se/en/embassies/usa-washington/
consulate(s) general: New York

Diplomatic representation from the US: *chief of mission:* Ambassador Erik D. RAMANATHAN (since 20 January 2022)
embassy: Dag Hammarskjolds Vag 31, SE-115 89 Stockholm
mailing address: 5750 Stockholm Place, Washington, DC 20521-5750
telephone: [46] (08) 783-53-00
FAX: [46] (08) 661-19-64
email address and website:
STKACSinfo@state.gov
https://se.usembassy.gov/

Flag description: blue with a golden yellow cross extending to the edges of the flag; the vertical part of the cross is shifted to the hoist side in the style of the Dannebrog (Danish flag); the colors reflect those of the Swedish coat of arms - three gold crowns on a blue field

National symbol(s): three crowns, lion; national colors: blue, yellow

National anthem: *name:* "Du Gamla, Du Fria" (Thou Ancient, Thou Free)
lyrics/music: Richard DYBECK/traditional
note: in use since 1844; also known as "Sang till Norden" (Song of the North), is based on a Swedish folk tune; it has never been officially adopted by the government; "Kungssangen" (The King's Song) serves as the royal anthem and is played in the presence of the royal family and during certain state ceremonies

National heritage: *total World Heritage Sites:* 15 (13 cultural, 1 natural, 1 mixed)
selected World Heritage Site locales: Royal Domain of Drottningholm (c); Laponian Area (m); High Coast/Kvarken Archipelago (n); Birka and Hovgården (c); Hanseatic Town of Visby (c); Church Town of Gammelstad, Luleå (c); Naval Port of Karlskrona (c); Rock Carvings in Tanum (c); Engelsberg Ironworks (c); Mining Area of the Great Copper Mountain in Falun (c)

ECONOMY

Economic overview: Sweden's small, open, and competitive economy has been thriving and Sweden has achieved an enviable standard of living with its combination of free-market capitalism and extensive welfare benefits. Sweden remains outside the euro zone largely out of concern that joining the European Economic and Monetary Union would diminish the country's sovereignty over its welfare system.

Timber, hydropower, and iron ore constitute the resource base of a manufacturing economy that relies heavily on foreign trade. Exports, including engines and other machines, motor vehicles, and telecommunications equipment, account for more than 44% of GDP. Sweden enjoys a current account surplus of about 5% of GDP, which is one of the highest margins in Europe.

GDP grew an estimated 3.3% in 2016 and 2017 driven largely by investment in the construction sector. Swedish economists expect economic growth to ease slightly in the coming years as this investment subsides. Global economic growth boosted exports of Swedish manufactures further, helping drive domestic economic growth in 2017. The Central Bank is keeping an eye on deflationary pressures and bank observers expect it to maintain an expansionary monetary policy in 2018. Swedish prices and wages have grown only slightly over the past few years, helping to support the country's competitiveness.

In the short and medium term, Sweden's economic challenges include providing affordable housing and successfully integrating migrants into the labor market.

Real GDP (purchasing power parity): $524.75 billion (2020 est.)
$539.96 billion (2019 est.)
$532.67 billion (2018 est.)
note: data are in 2017 dollars
country comparison to the world: 39

Real GDP growth rate: 1.29% (2019 est.)
2.06% (2018 est.)
2.82% (2017 est.)
country comparison to the world: 162

Real GDP per capita: $50,700 (2020 est.)
$52,500 (2019 est.)
$52,300 (2018 est.)
note: data are in 2017 dollars
country comparison to the world: 27

GDP (official exchange rate): $531.35 billion (2019 est.)

Inflation rate (consumer prices): 1.7% (2019 est.)
1.9% (2018 est.)
1.7% (2017 est.)
country comparison to the world: 96

Credit ratings:

Fitch rating: AAA (2004)

Moody's rating: Aaa (2002)

Standard & Poors rating: AAA (2004)

GDP - composition, by sector of origin: *agriculture:* 1.6% (2017 est.)
industry: 33% (2017 est.)
services: 65.4% (2017 est.)

GDP - composition, by end use: *household consumption:* 44.1% (2017 est.)
government consumption: 26% (2017 est.)
investment in fixed capital: 24.9% (2017 est.)
investment in inventories: 0.8% (2017 est.)
exports of goods and services: 45.3% (2017 est.)
imports of goods and services: -41.1% (2017 est.)

Agricultural products: wheat, milk, sugar beet, barley, potatoes, oats, rapeseed, pork, rye, triticale

Industries: iron and steel, precision equipment (bearings, radio and telephone parts, armaments), wood pulp and paper products, processed foods, motor vehicles

Industrial production growth rate: 4.1% (2017 est.)
country comparison to the world: 74

Labor force: 5.029 million (2020 est.)
country comparison to the world: 77

Labor force - by occupation: *agriculture:* 2%
industry: 12%
services: 86% (2014 est.)

Unemployment rate: 6.78% (2019 est.)
6.33% (2018 est.)
country comparison to the world: 108

Unemployment, youth ages 15-24: *total:* 24%
male: 25%
female: 22.8% (2020 est.)
country comparison to the world: 58

Population below poverty line: 17.1% (2018 est.)

Gini Index coefficient - distribution of family income: 28.8 (2017 est.)
25 (1992)
country comparison to the world: 156

Household income or consumption by percentage share: *lowest 10%:* 3.4%
highest 10%: 24% (2012)

Budget: *revenues:* 271.2 billion (2017 est.)
expenditures: 264.4 billion (2017 est.)

Budget surplus (+) or deficit (-): 1.3% (of GDP) (2017 est.)
country comparison to the world: 27

Public debt: 40.8% of GDP (2017 est.)
42.3% of GDP (2016 est.)
note: data cover general government debt and include debt instruments issued (or owned) by government entities other than the treasury; the data include treasury debt held by foreign entities; the data include debt issued by subnational entities, as well as intragovernmental debt; intragovernmental debt consists of treasury borrowings from surpluses in the social funds, such as for retirement, medical care, and unemployment; debt instruments for the social funds are not sold at public auctions
country comparison to the world: 124

Taxes and other revenues: 50.6% (of GDP) (2017 est.)
country comparison to the world: 16

Fiscal year: calendar year

Current account balance: $22.339 billion (2019 est.)
$13.902 billion (2018 est.)
country comparison to the world: 16

Exports: $240.08 billion (2020 est.) note: data are in current year dollars
$254.53 billion (2019 est.) note: data are in current year dollars
$254.25 billion (2018 est.) note: data are in current year dollars
country comparison to the world: 26

Exports - partners: Germany 10%, Norway 9%, United States 8%, Denmark 7%, Finland 6%, United Kingdom 5%, Netherlands 5%, China 5% (2019)

Exports - commodities: cars and vehicle parts, packaged medicines, refined petroleum, broadcasting equipment, lumber (2019)

Imports: $217.68 billion (2020 est.) note: data are in current year dollars
$232.81 billion (2019 est.) note: data are in current year dollars
$241.53 billion (2018 est.) note: data are in current year dollars
country comparison to the world: 28

Imports - partners: Germany 18%, Netherlands 9%, Denmark 7%, Norway 7%, China 6%, Finland 5%, Belgium 5%, Poland 5% (2019)

Imports - commodities: cars and vehicle parts, crude petroleum, refined petroleum, broadcasting equipment, computers (2019)

Reserves of foreign exchange and gold: $62.22 billion (31 December 2017 est.)
$59.39 billion (31 December 2016 est.)
country comparison to the world: 36

Debt - external: $911.317 billion (2019 est.)
$1,012,171,000,000 (2018 est.)
country comparison to the world: 18

Exchange rates: Swedish kronor (SEK) per US dollar -
8.49085 (2020 est.)
9.52915 (2019 est.)
9.01895 (2018 est.)
8.4335 (2014 est.)
6.8612 (2013 est.)

ENERGY

Electricity access: *electrification - total population:* 100% (2020)

Electricity: *installed generating capacity:* 43.499 million kW (2020 est.)
consumption: 124.609 billion kWh (2020 est.)
exports: 36.824 billion kWh (2020 est.)
imports: 11.827 billion kWh (2020 est.)
transmission/distribution losses: 10.434 billion kWh (2020 est.)

Electricity generation sources: *fossil fuels:* 1% of total installed capacity (2020 est.)
nuclear: 29.5% of total installed capacity (2020 est.)
solar: 0.7% of total installed capacity (2020 est.)
wind: 17.2% of total installed capacity (2020 est.)
hydroelectricity: 44.7% of total installed capacity (2020 est.)
biomass and waste: 6.9% of total installed capacity (2020 est.)

Coal: *production:* 1.07 million metric tons (2020 est.)
consumption: 3.328 million metric tons (2020 est.)
exports: 24,000 metric tons (2020 est.)
imports: 2.144 million metric tons (2020 est.)
proven reserves: 1 million metric tons (2019 est.)

Petroleum: *total petroleum production:* 10,600 bbl/day (2021 est.)
refined petroleum consumption: 295,800 bbl/day (2019 est.)
crude oil and lease condensate exports: 0 bbl/day (2018 est.)
crude oil and lease condensate imports: 403,200 bbl/day (2018 est.)
crude oil estimated reserves: 0 barrels (2021 est.)

Refined petroleum products - production: 413,200 bbl/day (2017 est.)
country comparison to the world: 36

Refined petroleum products - exports: 371,100 bbl/day (2017 est.)
country comparison to the world: 23

Refined petroleum products - imports: 229,600 bbl/day (2017 est.)
country comparison to the world: 29

Natural gas: *production:* 0 cubic meters (2021 est.)
consumption: 1,275,785,000 cubic meters (2020 est.)
exports: 34.886 million cubic meters (2020 est.)
imports: 1,310,671,000 cubic meters (2020 est.)
proven reserves: 0 cubic meters (2021 est.)

Carbon dioxide emissions: 48.144 million metric tonnes of CO2 (2019 est.)
from coal and metallurgical coke: 7.38 million metric tonnes of CO2 (2019 est.)
from petroleum and other liquids: 38.406 million metric tonnes of CO2 (2019 est.)
from consumed natural gas: 2.359 million metric tonnes of CO2 (2019 est.)
country comparison to the world: 59

Energy consumption per capita: 210.882 million Btu/person (2019 est.)
country comparison to the world: 21

COMMUNICATIONS

Telephones - fixed lines: *total subscriptions:* 1,478,610 (2020 est.)
subscriptions per 100 inhabitants: 15 (2020 est.)
country comparison to the world: 64

Telephones - mobile cellular: *total subscriptions:* 12,895,900 (2019)
subscriptions per 100 inhabitants: 128.49 (2019)
country comparison to the world: 76

Telecommunication systems: *general assessment:* Sweden's telecom market includes mature mobile and broadband sectors which have been stimulated by the progressive investment of the main telcos in developing new technologies; the country retains one of the best developed LTE infrastructures in the region, while its MNOs have benefited from the January 2021 auction of spectrum in the 3.5GHz band which will enable them to expand services nationally; the country also has one of the highest fiber broadband penetration rates in Europe; the focus of FttP is aimed at fulfilling the government's target of providing a 1Gb/s service to 98% of the population by 2025; the methodology to achieve this has rested on regulatory measures supported by public funds, as well as on the auction of spectrum in different bands; in the fixed-line broadband segment, the number of DSL subscribers is falling steadily as customers continue to migrate to fiber networks; there is also competition from HFC infrastructure, offering fiber-based broadband and investing in services based on the DOCSIS3.1 standard; this report assesses key aspects of the Swedish telecom market, providing data on fixed network services and profiling the main players; it also reviews the key regulatory issues, including interconnection, local loop unbundling, number portability, carrier preselection and NGN open access; the report also analyses the mobile market, providing data on network operators and their strategies in a highly competitive environment; in addition, the report considers the fixed and fixed-wireless broadband markets, including analyses of market dynamics and the main operators, as well as providing subscriber forecasts (2021)
domestic: fixed-line just over 16 per 100 and mobile-cellular roughly 128 per 100; coaxial and multiconductor cables carry most of the voice traffic; parallel microwave radio relay systems carry some additional telephone channels (2020)
international: country code - 46; landing points for Botina, SFL, SFS-4, Baltic Sea Submarine Cable, Eastern Light, Sweden-Latvia, BCS North-Phase1, EE-S1, LV-SE1, BCS East-West Interlink, NordBalt, Baltica, Denmark-Sweden-15,-17,-18, Scandinavian Ring -North,-South, IP-Only Denmark-Sweden, Donica North, Kattegate-1,-2, Energinet Laeso-Varberg and GC2 submarine cables providing links to other Nordic countries and Europe; satellite earth stations - 1 Intelsat (Atlantic Ocean), 1 Eutelsat, and 1 Inmarsat (Atlantic and Indian Ocean regions); note - Sweden shares the Inmarsat earth station with the other Nordic countries (Denmark, Finland, Iceland, and Norway) (2019)

Broadcast media: publicly owned TV broadcaster operates 2 terrestrial networks plus regional stations; multiple privately owned TV broadcasters operating nationally, regionally, and locally; about 50 local TV stations; widespread access to pan-Nordic and international broadcasters through multi-channel cable and satellite TV; publicly owned radio broadcaster operates 3 national stations and a network of 25 regional channels; roughly 100 privately owned local radio stations with some consolidating into near national networks; an estimated 900 community and neighborhood radio stations broadcast intermittently

Internet country code: .se

Internet users: *total:* 9,835,769 (2020 est.)
percent of population: 95% (2020 est.)
country comparison to the world: 57

Broadband - fixed subscriptions: *total:* 4,179,574 (2020 est.)
subscriptions per 100 inhabitants: 41 (2020 est.)
country comparison to the world: 36

TRANSPORTATION

National air transport system: *number of registered air carriers:* 11 (2020)
inventory of registered aircraft operated by air carriers: 316

Civil aircraft registration country code prefix: SE

Airports: *total:* 231 (2021)
country comparison to the world: 25

Airports - with paved runways: *total:* 149
over 3,047 m: 3
2,438 to 3,047 m: 12
1,524 to 2,437 m: 75
914 to 1,523 m: 22
under 914 m: 37 (2021)

Airports - with unpaved runways: *total:* 82
914 to 1,523 m: 5
under 914 m: 77 (2021)

Heliports: 2 (2021)

Pipelines: 1626 km gas (2013)

Railways: *total:* 14,127 km (2016)
standard gauge: 14,062 km (2016) 1.435-m gauge (12,322 km electrified)
narrow gauge: 65 km (2016) 0.891-m gauge (65 km electrified)
country comparison to the world: 20

Roadways: *total:* 573,134 km (2016) (includes 2,050 km of expressways)
paved: 140,100 km (2016)
unpaved: 433,034 km (2016)
note: includes 98,500 km of state roads, 433,034 km of private roads, and 41,600 km of municipal roads
country comparison to the world: 14

Waterways: 2,052 km (2010)
country comparison to the world: 42

Merchant marine: *total:* 370
by type: general cargo 49, oil tanker 22, other 299 (2021)
country comparison to the world: 50

Ports and terminals: *major seaport(s):* Brofjorden, Goteborg, Helsingborg, Karlshamn, Lulea, Malmo, Stockholm, Trelleborg, Visby

LNG terminal(s) (import): Brunnsviksholme, Lysekil

MILITARY AND SECURITY

Military and security forces: Swedish Armed Forces (Forsvarsmakten): Army, Navy, Air Force, Home Guard (2022)

Military expenditures: 1.3% of GDP (2021 est.)
1.2% of GDP (2020)
1.1% of GDP (2019) (approximately $6.78 billion)
1% of GDP (2018) (approximately $6.26 billion)
1% of GDP (2017) (approximately $6.04 billion)
country comparison to the world: 107

Military and security service personnel strengths: approximately 15,000 continuous service/full-time troops (7,000 Army; 3,000 Navy; 3,000 Air Force; 2,000 other, including staff, logistics, support, medical, cyber, intelligence, etc); approximately 21,000 Home Guard; approximately 12,000 temporary service personnel (2022)
note: Swedish Armed Forces' (SAF) personnel are divided into continuously serving (full-time) and temporary service troops (part-timers who serve periodically and have another main employer or attend school); additional personnel have signed service agreements with the SAF and mostly serve in the Home Guard; the SAF also has about 9,000 civilian employees

Military equipment inventories and acquisitions: the inventory of the SAF is comprised of domestically-produced and imported Western weapons systems; since 2010, the US is the leading supplier of military hardware to Sweden; Sweden's defense industry produces a range of air, land, and naval systems (2021)

Military service age and obligation: 18-47 years of age for male and female voluntary military service; service obligation: 7.5 months (Army), 7-15 months (Navy), 8-12 months (Air Force); after completing initial service, soldiers have a reserve commitment until age 47; compulsory military service, abolished in 2010, was reinstated in January 2018; conscription is selective, includes both men and women (age 18), and requires 9-12 months of service (2022)
note 1: Sweden conscripts about 5,500 men and women each year
note 2: as of 2021, women made up about 11% of the military's full-time personnel

Military deployments: approximately 200 Mali (MINUSMA) (2022)

Military - note: Sweden maintains a policy of military non-alignment, but cooperates with NATO and regional countries; it joined NATO's Partnership for Peace program in 1994 and has contributed to NATO-led missions, including those in Afghanistan, Iraq, and Kosovo; Sweden applied for NATO membership in May 2022

the Swedish military cooperates closely with the military forces of other Nordic countries through the Nordic Defense Cooperation (NORDEFCO), which consists of Denmark, Finland, Iceland, Norway, and Sweden; areas of cooperation include armaments, education, human resources, training and exercises, and operations; NORDEFCO was established in 2009

Sweden is a signatory of the EU's Common Security and Defense Policy and contributes to CSDP missions and operations (2022)

TERRORISM

Terrorist group(s): Islamic State of Iraq and ash-Sham (ISIS)

TRANSNATIONAL ISSUES

Disputes - international: none identified

Refugees and internally displaced persons: *refugees (country of origin):* 114,995 (Syria), 28,744 (Afghanistan), 26,911 (Eritrea), 11,574 (Somalia), 11,153 (Iraq), 7,516 (Iran) (2020); 48,087 (Ukraine) (as of 8 November 2022)
stateless persons: 50,098 (mid-year 2021); note - the majority of stateless people are from the Middle East and Somalia

SWITZERLAND

INTRODUCTION

Background: The Swiss Confederation was founded in 1291 as a defensive alliance among three cantons. In succeeding years, other localities joined the original three. The Swiss Confederation secured its independence from the Holy Roman Empire in 1499. A constitution of 1848, subsequently modified in 1874 to allow voters to introduce referenda on proposed laws, replaced the confederation with a centralized federal government. Switzerland's sovereignty and neutrality have long been honored by the major European powers, and the country was not involved in either of the two World Wars. The political and economic integration of Europe over the past half century, as well as Switzerland's role in many UN and international organizations, has strengthened Switzerland's ties with its neighbors. However, the country did not officially become a UN member until 2002. Switzerland remains active in many UN and international organizations but retains a strong commitment to neutrality.

GEOGRAPHY

Location: Central Europe, east of France, north of Italy

Geographic coordinates: 47 00 N, 8 00 E

Map references: Europe

Area: *total:* 41,277 sq km
land: 39,997 sq km
water: 1,280 sq km
country comparison to the world: 135

Area - comparative: slightly less than twice the size of New Jersey

Land boundaries: *total:* 1,770 km
border countries (5): Austria 158 km; France 525 km; Italy 698 km; Liechtenstein 41 km; Germany 348 km

Coastline: 0 km (landlocked)

Maritime claims: none (landlocked)

Climate: temperate, but varies with altitude; cold, cloudy, rainy/snowy winters; cool to warm, cloudy, humid summers with occasional showers

Terrain: mostly mountains (Alps in south, Jura in northwest) with a central plateau of rolling hills, plains, and large lakes

Elevation: *highest point:* Dufourspitze 4,634 m
lowest point: Lake Maggiore 195 m
mean elevation: 1,350 m

Natural resources: hydropower potential, timber, salt

Land use: *agricultural land:* 38.7% (2018 est.)
arable land: 10.2% (2018 est.)
permanent crops: 0.6% (2018 est.)
permanent pasture: 27.9% (2018 est.)
forest: 31.5% (2018 est.)
other: 29.8% (2018 est.)

Irrigated land: 630 sq km (2012)

Major lakes (area sq km): *fresh water lake(s):* Lake Constance (shared with Germany and Austria) - 540 sq km; Lake Geneva (shared with France) - 580 sq km

Major rivers (by length in km): Rhine river source (shared with Germany, France, and Netherlands [m]) - 1,233 km

note – [s] after country name indicates river source; [m] after country name indicates river mouth

Major watersheds (area sq km): Atlantic Ocean drainage: Rhine-Maas (198,735 sq km), *(Black Sea)* Danube (795,656 sq km), *(Adriatic Sea)* Po (76,997 sq km), *(Mediterranean Sea)* Rhone (100,543 sq km)

Population distribution: population distribution corresponds to elevation with the northern and western areas far more heavily populated; the higher Alps of the south limit settlement

Natural hazards: avalanches, landslides; flash floods

Geography - note: landlocked; crossroads of northern and southern Europe; along with southeastern France, northern Italy, and southwestern Austria, has the highest elevations in the Alps

PEOPLE AND SOCIETY

Population: 8,508,698 (2022 est.)
country comparison to the world: 101

Nationality: *noun:* Swiss (singular and plural)
adjective: Swiss

Ethnic groups: Swiss 69.2%, German 4.2%, Italian 3.2%, Portuguese 2.5%, French 2.1%, Kosovo 1.1%, Turkish 1%, other 16.7% (2020 est.)
note: data represent permanent and non-permanent resident population by country of birth

Languages: German (or Swiss German) (official) 62.1%, French (official) 22.8%, Italian (official) 8%, English 5.7%, Portuguese 3.5%, Albanian 3.3%, Serbo-Croatian 2.3%, Spanish 2.3%, Romansh (official) 0.5%, other 7.9%; note - German, French, Italian, and Romansh are all national and official languages; shares sum to more than 100% because respondents could indicate more than one main language (2019 est.)
major-language sample(s):
Das World Factbook, die unverzichtbare Quelle für grundlegende Informationen. (German)
The World Factbook, une source indispensable d'informations de base. (French)
L'Almanacco dei fatti del mondo, l'indispensabile fonte per le informazioni di base. (Italian)

Religions: Roman Catholic 34.4%, Protestant 22.5%, other Christian 5.7%, Muslim 5.4%, other 1.5%, none 29.4%, unspecified 1.1% (2020 est.)

Age structure: *0-14 years:* 15.34% (male 664,255/female 625,252)
15-24 years: 10.39% (male 446,196/female 426,708)
25-54 years: 42.05% (male 1,768,245/female 1,765,941)
55-64 years: 13.48% (male 569,717/female 563,482)
65 years and over: 18.73% (male 699,750/female 874,448) (2020 est.)

Dependency ratios: *total dependency ratio:* 51.6
youth dependency ratio: 22.7
elderly dependency ratio: 29
potential support ratio: 3.5 (2020 est.)

Median age: *total:* 42.7 years
male: 41.7 years
female: 43.7 years (2020 est.)
country comparison to the world: 33

Population growth rate: 0.65% (2022 est.)
country comparison to the world: 137

Birth rate: 10.36 births/1,000 population (2022 est.)
country comparison to the world: 183

Death rate: 8.4 deaths/1,000 population (2022 est.)
country comparison to the world: 75

Net migration rate: 4.52 migrant(s)/1,000 population (2022 est.)
country comparison to the world: 25

Population distribution: population distribution corresponds to elevation with the northern and western areas far more heavily populated; the higher Alps of the south limit settlement

Urbanization: *urban population:* 74.1% of total population (2022)
rate of urbanization: 0.79% annual rate of change (2020-25 est.)

Major urban areas - population: 1.420 million Zurich, 437,000 BERN (capital) (2022)

Sex ratio: *at birth:* 1.06 male(s)/female
0-14 years: 1.06 male(s)/female
15-24 years: 1.05 male(s)/female
25-54 years: 1 male(s)/female
55-64 years: 1.01 male(s)/female
65 years and over: 0.64 male(s)/female
total population: 0.98 male(s)/female (2022 est.)

Mother's mean age at first birth: 31.1 years (2020 est.)

Maternal mortality ratio: 5 deaths/100,000 live births (2017 est.)
country comparison to the world: 171

Infant mortality rate: *total:* 3.58 deaths/1,000 live births
male: 4.08 deaths/1,000 live births
female: 3.04 deaths/1,000 live births (2022 est.)
country comparison to the world: 194

Life expectancy at birth: *total population:* 83.23 years
male: 80.91 years
female: 85.67 years (2022 est.)
country comparison to the world: 12

Total fertility rate: 1.58 children born/woman (2022 est.)
country comparison to the world: 190

Contraceptive prevalence rate: 71.6% (2017)

Drinking water source: *improved: urban:* 100% of population
rural: 100% of population
total: 100% of population

Current health expenditure 11.3% of GDP (2019)

Physicians density: 4.38 physicians/1,000 population (2020)

Hospital bed density: 4.6 beds/1,000 population (2018)

Sanitation facility access: *improved: urban:* 100% of population
rural: 100% of population
total: 100% of population

HIV/AIDS - adult prevalence rate: 0.2% (2020 est.)
country comparison to the world: 114

HIV/AIDS - people living with HIV/AIDS: 17,000 (2020)
note: estimate does not include children
country comparison to the world: 89

HIV/AIDS - deaths: (2020) <200
note: estimate does not include children

Obesity - adult prevalence rate: 19.5% (2016)
country comparison to the world: 112

Alcohol consumption per capita: *total:* 9.41 liters of pure alcohol (2019 est.)
beer: 3.17 liters of pure alcohol (2019 est.)
wine: 4.35 liters of pure alcohol (2019 est.)
spirits: 1.76 liters of pure alcohol (2019 est.)
other alcohols: 0.12 liters of pure alcohol (2019 est.)
country comparison to the world: 30

Tobacco use: *total:* 25.5% (2020 est.)
male: 28.1% (2020 est.)
female: 22.9% (2020 est.)
country comparison to the world: 46

Education expenditures: 4.9% of GDP (2018 est.)
country comparison to the world: 71

School life expectancy (primary to tertiary education): *total:* 17 years
male: 17 years
female: 16 years (2019)

Unemployment, youth ages 15-24: *total:* 8.6%
male: 9.2%
female: 8% (2020 est.)

ENVIRONMENT

Environment - current issues: air pollution from vehicle emissions; water pollution from agricultural fertilizers; chemical contaminants and erosion damage the soil and limit productivity; loss of biodiversity

Environment - international agreements: *party to:* Air Pollution, Air Pollution-Heavy Metals, Air Pollution-Multi-effect Protocol, Air Pollution-Nitrogen Oxides, Air Pollution-Persistent Organic Pollutants, Air Pollution-Sulphur 85, Air Pollution-Sulphur 94, Air Pollution-Volatile Organic Compounds, Antarctic-Environmental Protection, Antarctic Treaty, Biodiversity, Climate Change, Climate Change-Kyoto Protocol, Climate Change-Paris Agreement, Comprehensive Nuclear Test Ban, Desertification, Endangered Species, Environmental Modification, Hazardous Wastes, Law of the Sea, Marine Dumping-London Convention, Marine Dumping- London Protocol, Marine Life Conservation, Nuclear Test Ban, Ozone Layer Protection, Ship Pollution, Tropical Timber 2006, Wetlands, Whaling
signed, but not ratified: none of the selected agreements

Air pollutants: *particulate matter emissions:* 10.21 micrograms per cubic meter (2016 est.)
carbon dioxide emissions: 34.48 megatons (2016 est.)
methane emissions: 4.98 megatons (2020 est.)

Climate: temperate, but varies with altitude; cold, cloudy, rainy/snowy winters; cool to warm, cloudy, humid summers with occasional showers

Land use: *agricultural land:* 38.7% (2018 est.)
arable land: 10.2% (2018 est.)
permanent crops: 0.6% (2018 est.)
permanent pasture: 27.9% (2018 est.)
forest: 31.5% (2018 est.)
other: 29.8% (2018 est.)

Urbanization: *urban population:* 74.1% of total population (2022)
rate of urbanization: 0.79% annual rate of change (2020-25 est.)

Revenue from forest resources: *forest revenues:* 0.01% of GDP (2018 est.)
country comparison to the world: 157

Revenue from coal: *coal revenues:* 0% of GDP (2018 est.)
country comparison to the world: 173

Waste and recycling: *municipal solid waste generated annually:* 6.056 million tons (2016 est.)
municipal solid waste recycled annually: 1,937,920 tons (2015 est.)
percent of municipal solid waste recycled: 32% (2015 est.)

Major lakes (area sq km): *fresh water lake(s):* Lake Constance (shared with Germany and Austria) - 540 sq km; Lake Geneva (shared with France) - 580 sq km

Major rivers (by length in km): Rhine river source (shared with Germany, France, and Netherlands [m]) - 1,233 km
note – [s] after country name indicates river source; [m] after country name indicates river mouth

Major watersheds (area sq km): Atlantic Ocean drainage: Rhine-Maas (198,735 sq km), *(Black Sea)* Danube (795,656 sq km), *(Adriatic Sea)* Po (76,997 sq km), *(Mediterranean Sea)* Rhone (100,543 sq km)

Total water withdrawal: *municipal:* 931 million cubic meters (2017 est.)
industrial: 642.7 million cubic meters (2017 est.)
agricultural: 160.1 million cubic meters (2017 est.)

Total renewable water resources: 53.5 billion cubic meters (2017 est.)

GOVERNMENT

Country name: *conventional long form:* Swiss Confederation
conventional short form: Switzerland
local long form: Schweizerische Eidgenossenschaft (German)/ Confederation Suisse (French)/ Confederazione Svizzera (Italian)/ Confederaziun Svizra (Romansh)
local short form: Schweiz (German)/ Suisse (French)/ Svizzera (Italian)/ Svizra (Romansh)
abbreviation: CH
etymology: name derives from the canton of Schwyz, one of the founding cantons of the Old Swiss Confederacy that formed in the 14th century

Government type: federal republic (formally a confederation)

Capital: *name:* Bern
geographic coordinates: 46 55 N, 7 28 E
time difference: UTC+1 (6 hours ahead of Washington, DC, during Standard Time)
daylight saving time: +1hr, begins last Sunday in March; ends last Sunday in October
etymology: origin of the name is uncertain, but may derive from a 2nd century B.C. Celtic place name, possibly "berna" meaning "cleft," that was subsequently adopted by a Roman settlement

Administrative divisions: 26 cantons (cantons, singular - canton in French; cantoni, singular - cantone in Italian; Kantone, singular - Kanton in German); Aargau, Appenzell Ausserrhoden, Appenzell Innerrhoden, Basel-Landschaft, Basel-Stadt, Berne/Bern, Fribourg/Freiburg, Geneve (Geneva), Glarus, Graubuenden/Grigioni/Grischun, Jura, Luzern (Lucerne), Neuchatel, Nidwalden, Obwalden, Sankt Gallen, Schaffhausen, Schwyz, Solothurn, Thurgau, Ticino, Uri, Valais/Wallis, Vaud, Zug, Zuerich
note: the canton names are in the official language(s) of the canton with the exception of Geneve and Luzern, where the conventional names (Geneva and Lucerne) have been added in parentheses; 6 of the cantons - Appenzell Ausserrhoden, Appenzell Innerrhoden, Basel-Landschaft, Basel-Stadt, Nidwalden, Obwalden - are referred to as half cantons because they elect only one member (instead of two) to the Council of States and, in popular referendums where a majority of popular votes and a majority of cantonal votes are required, these 6 cantons only have a half vote

Independence: 1 August 1291 (founding of the Swiss Confederation)

National holiday: Founding of the Swiss Confederation in 1291; note - since 1 August 1891 celebrated as Swiss National Day

Constitution: *history:* previous 1848, 1874; latest adopted by referendum 18 April 1999, effective 1 January 2000
amendments: proposed by the two houses of the Federal Assembly or by petition of at least one hundred thousand voters (called the "federal popular initiative"); passage of proposals requires majority vote in a referendum; following drafting of an amendment by the Assembly, its passage requires approval by majority vote in a referendum and approval by the majority of cantons; amended many times, last in 2018

Legal system: civil law system; judicial review of legislative acts, except for federal decrees of a general obligatory character

International law organization participation: accepts compulsory ICJ jurisdiction with reservations; accepts ICCt jurisdiction

Citizenship: *citizenship by birth:* no
citizenship by descent only: at least one parent must be a citizen of Switzerland
dual citizenship recognized: yes
residency requirement for naturalization: 12 years including at least 3 of the last 5 years prior to application

Suffrage: 18 years of age; universal

Executive branch: *chief of state:* President of the Swiss Confederation Ignazio CASSIS (since 1 January 2022); Vice President Alain BERSET (since 1 January 2022); note - the Federal Council, comprised of 7 federal councillors, constitutes the federal government of Switzerland; council members rotate the 1-year term of federal president
head of government: President of the Swiss Confederation Ignazio CASSIS (since 1 January 2022); Vice President Alain BERSET (since 1 January 2022)

cabinet: Federal Council or Bundesrat (in German), Conseil Federal (in French), Consiglio Federale (in Italian) indirectly elected by the Federal Assembly for a 4-year term
elections/appointments: president and vice president elected by the Federal Assembly from among members of the Federal Council for a 1-year, non-consecutive term; election last held on 8 December 2021 (next to be held in December 2022)
election results:
2021: Ignazio CASSIS elected president for 2022; Federal Assembly vote - Ignazio CASSIS (FDP. The Liberals) 156 of 197 votes; Alain BERSET (SP) elected vice president; Federal Assembly vote - 158 of 204
2020: Guy PARMELIN elected president for 2021; Federal Assembly vote - Guy PARMELIN (SVP) 188 of 202 votes; Ignazio CASSIS (FDP.The Liberals) elected vice president; Federal Assembly vote - 162 of 191

Legislative branch: *description:* description: bicameral Federal Assembly or Bundesversammlung (in German), Assemblée Fédérale (in French), Assemblea Federale (in Italian) consists of:
Council of States or Ständerat (in German), Conseil des États (in French), Consiglio degli Stati (in Italian) (46 seats; members in multi-seat constituencies representing cantons and single-seat constituencies representing half cantons directly elected by simple majority vote except Jura and Neuchatel cantons which use list proportional representation vote; member term governed by cantonal law)
National Council or Nationalrat (in German), Conseil National (in French), Consiglio Nazionale (in Italian) (200 seats; 195 members in cantons directly elected by proportional representation vote and 6 in half cantons directly elected by simple majority vote; members serve 4-year terms)
elections:
Council of States - last held in most cantons on 20 October 2019 (each canton determines when the next election will be held)
National Council - last held on 20 October 2019 (next to be held on 31 October 2023)
election results:
Council of States - percent of vote by party - NA; seats by party - The Center 13, FDP.The Liberals 12, SDP 9, Green Party 5, SVP 6, other 1; composition (as of mid-2022) - men 33, women 13, percent of women 28.3%
National Council - percent of vote by party - SDP 26.5%, SP 19.5%, FDP.The Liberals 15.1%, Green Party 14%, The Center 14%, GLP 7.8%, other 3.5%; seats by party - SVP 53, SP 39, FDP.The Liberals 29, Green Party 28, The Center 28, GLP 16, other 7; composition (as of mid-2022) - men 115, women 85, percent of women 42.5%; note - overall Federal Assembly percent of women 39.8%

Judicial branch: *highest court(s):* Federal Supreme Court (consists of 38 justices and 19 deputy justices organized into 7 divisions)
judge selection and term of office: judges elected by the Federal Assembly for 6-year terms; note - judges are affiliated with political parties and are elected according to linguistic and regional criteria in approximate proportion to the level of party representation in the Federal Assembly
subordinate courts: Federal Criminal Court (established in 2004); Federal Administrative Court (established in 2007); note - each of Switzerland's 26 cantons has its own courts

Political parties and leaders: Green Liberal Party (Gruenliberale Partei or GLP, Parti vert liberale or PVL, Partito Verde-Liberale or PVL, Partida Verde Liberale or PVL) [Juerg GROSSEN]
Green Party (Gruene Partei der Schweiz or Gruene, Parti Ecologiste Suisse or Les Verts, Partito Ecologista Svizzero or I Verdi, Partida Ecologica Svizra or La Verda) [Balthasar GLATTLI]
Social Democratic Party (Sozialdemokratische Partei der Schweiz or SP, Parti Socialiste Suisse or PSS, Partito Socialista Svizzero or PSS, Partida Socialdemocratica de la Svizra or PSS) [Cedric WERMUTH and Mattea MEYER]
Swiss People's Party (Schweizerische Volkspartei or SVP, Union Democratique du Centre or UDC, Unione Democratica di Centro or UDC, Uniun Democratica dal Center or UDC) [Marco CHIESA]
The Center (Die Mitte, Alleanza del Centro, Le Centre, Allianza dal Center) [Gerhard PFISTER] (merger of the Christian Democratic People's Party and the Conservative Democratic Party)
The Liberals or FDP.The Liberals (FDP.Die Liberalen, PLR.Les Liberaux-Radicaux, PLR.I Liberali, Ils Liberals) [Petra GOESSI]
other minor parties

International organization participation: ADB (nonregional member), AfDB (nonregional member), Australia Group, BIS, CD, CE, CERN, EAPC, EBRD, EFTA, EITI (implementing country), ESA, FAO, FATF, G-10, IADB, IAEA, IBRD, ICAO, ICC (national committees), ICCt, ICRM, IDA, IEA, IFAD, IFC, IFRCS, IGAD (partners), ILO, IMF, IMO, IMSO, Interpol, IOC, IOM, IPU, ISO, ITSO, ITU, ITUC (NGOs), LAIA (observer), MIGA, MINUSMA, MONUSCO, NEA, NSG, OAS (observer), OECD, OIF, OPCW, OSCE, Pacific Alliance (observer), Paris Club, PCA, PFP, Schengen Convention, UN, UNCTAD, UNESCO, UNHCR, UNIDO, UNITAR, UNMISS, UNMOGIP, UNRWA, UNTSO, UNWTO, UPU, Wassenaar Arrangement, WCO, WHO, WIPO, WMO, WTO, ZC

Diplomatic representation in the US: *chief of mission:* Ambassador Jacques Henri PITTELOUD (since 16 September 2019)
chancery: 2201 Wisconsin Avenue NW, Suite 300, Washington, DC 20007-4105
telephone: [1] (202) 745-7900
FAX: [1] (202) 387-2564
email address and website:
washington@eda.admin.ch
https://www.eda.admin.ch/washington
consulate(s) general: Atlanta, Chicago, New York, San Francisco
consulate(s): Boston

Diplomatic representation from the US: *chief of mission:* Ambassador Scott MILLER (since 11 January 2022) note - also accredited to Liechtenstein
embassy: Sulgeneckstrasse 19, CH-3007 Bern
mailing address: 5110 Bern Place, Washington DC 20521-5110
telephone: [41] (031) 357-70-11
FAX: [41] (031) 357-73-20
email address and website:
https://ch.usembassy.gov/

Flag description: red square with a bold, equilateral white cross in the center that does not extend to the edges of the flag; various medieval legends purport to describe the origin of the flag; a white cross used as identification for troops of the Swiss Confederation is first attested at the Battle of Laupen (1339)
note: in 1863, a newly formed international relief organization convening in Geneva, Switzerland sought to come up with an identifying flag or logo, they chose the inverse of the Swiss flag - a red cross on a white field - as their symbol; today that organization is known throughout the world as the International Red Cross

National symbol(s): Swiss cross (white cross on red field, arms equal length); national colors: red, white

National anthem: *name:* the Swiss anthem has four names: "Schweizerpsalm" [German] "Cantique Suisse" [French] "Salmo svizzero," [Italian] "Psalm svizzer" [Romansch] (Swiss Psalm)
lyrics/music: Leonhard WIDMER [German], Charles CHATELANAT [French], Camillo VALSANGIACOMO [Italian], and Flurin CAMATHIAS [Romansch]/Alberik ZWYSSIG
note: unofficially adopted 1961, officially 1981; the anthem has been popular in a number of Swiss cantons since its composition (in German) in 1841; translated into the other three official languages of the country (French, Italian, and Romansch), it is official in each of those languages

National heritage: *total World Heritage Sites:* 13 (9 cultural, 4 natural)
selected World Heritage Site locales: Old City of Berne (c); Swiss Alps Jungfrau-Aletsch (n); Monte San Giorgio (n); Abbey of St Gall (c); Three Castles, Defensive Wall, and Ramparts of the Market-Town of Bellinzona (c); Rhaetian Railway in the Albula/Bernina Landscapes (c); La Chaux-de-Fonds/Le Locle, Watchmaking Town Planning (c); Prehistoric Pile Dwellings around the Alps (c); Benedictine Convent of St John at Müstair (c); Lavaux, Vineyard Terraces (c)

ECONOMY

Economic overview: Switzerland, a country that espouses neutrality, is a prosperous and modern market economy with low unemployment, a highly skilled labor force, and a per capita GDP among the highest in the world. Switzerland's economy benefits from a highly developed service sector, led by financial services, and a manufacturing industry that specializes in high-technology, knowledge-based production. Its economic and political stability, transparent legal system, exceptional infrastructure, efficient capital markets, and low corporate tax rates also make Switzerland one of the world's most competitive economies.

The Swiss have brought their economic practices largely into conformity with the EU's to gain access to the Union's Single Market and enhance the country's international competitiveness. Some trade protectionism remains, however, particularly for its small agricultural sector. The fate of the Swiss economy is tightly linked to that of its neighbors in the euro zone, which purchases half of Swiss exports. The global financial crisis of 2008 and resulting economic downturn in 2009 stalled demand for Swiss exports and put Switzerland into a recession. During this period, the Swiss National Bank (SNB) implemented a zero-interest rate policy to boost the economy, as well as to prevent appreciation of the franc, and Switzerland's economy began to recover in 2010.

The sovereign debt crises unfolding in neighboring euro-zone countries, however, coupled with economic instability in Russia and other Eastern European economies drove up demand for the Swiss franc by investors seeking a safehaven currency. In January 2015, the SNB abandoned the Swiss franc's peg to the euro, roiling global currency markets and making active SNB intervention a necessary hallmark of present-day Swiss monetary policy. The independent SNB has upheld its zero interest rate policy and conducted major market interventions to prevent further appreciation of the Swiss franc, but parliamentarians have urged it to do more to weaken the currency. The franc's strength has made Swiss exports less competitive and weakened the country's growth outlook; GDP growth fell below 2% per year from 2011 through 2017.

In recent years, Switzerland has responded to increasing pressure from neighboring countries and trading partners to reform its banking secrecy laws, by agreeing to conform to OECD regulations on administrative assistance in tax matters, including tax evasion. The Swiss Government has also renegotiated its double taxation agreements with numerous countries, including the US, to incorporate OECD standards.

Real GDP (purchasing power parity): $590.71 billion (2020 est.)
$608.16 billion (2019 est.)
$601.65 billion (2018 est.)
note: data are in 2017 dollars
country comparison to the world: 35

Real GDP growth rate: 1.11% (2019 est.)
3.04% (2018 est.)
1.65% (2017 est.)
country comparison to the world: 169

Real GDP per capita: $68,400 (2020 est.)
$70,900 (2019 est.)
$70,700 (2018 est.)
note: data are in 2017 dollars
country comparison to the world: 11

GDP (official exchange rate): $731.502 billion (2019 est.)

Inflation rate (consumer prices): 0.3% (2019 est.)
0.9% (2018 est.)
0.5% (2017 est.)
country comparison to the world: 38

Credit ratings:

Fitch rating: AAA (2000)

Moody's rating: Aaa (1982)

Standard & Poors rating: AAA (1988)

GDP - composition, by sector of origin: *agriculture:* 0.7% (2017 est.)
industry: 25.6% (2017 est.)
services: 73.7% (2017 est.)

GDP - composition, by end use: *household consumption:* 53.7% (2017 est.)
government consumption: 12% (2017 est.)
investment in fixed capital: 24.5% (2017 est.)
investment in inventories: -1.4% (2017 est.)
exports of goods and services: 65.1% (2017 est.)
imports of goods and services: -54% (2017 est.)

Agricultural products: milk, sugar beet, wheat, potatoes, pork, barley, apples, maize, beef, grapes

Industries: machinery, chemicals, watches, textiles, precision instruments, tourism, banking, insurance, pharmaceuticals

Industrial production growth rate: 3.4% (2017 est.)
country comparison to the world: 92

Labor force: 5.067 million (2020 est.)
country comparison to the world: 76

Labor force - by occupation: *agriculture:* 3.3%
industry: 19.8%
services: 76.9% (2015)

Unemployment rate: 2.31% (2019 est.)
2.55% (2018 est.)
country comparison to the world: 25

Unemployment, youth ages 15-24: *total:* 8.6%
male: 9.2%
female: 8% (2020 est.)
country comparison to the world: 150

Population below poverty line: 16% (2018 est.)

Gini Index coefficient - distribution of family income: 32.7 (2017 est.)
33.1 (1992)
country comparison to the world: 136

Household income or consumption by percentage share: *lowest 10%:* 7.5%
highest 10%: 19% (2007)

Budget: *revenues:* 242.1 billion (2017 est.)
expenditures: 234.4 billion (2017 est.)
note: includes federal, cantonal, and municipal budgets

Budget surplus (+) or deficit (-): 1.1% (of GDP) (2017 est.)
country comparison to the world: 33

Public debt: 41.8% of GDP (2017 est.)
41.8% of GDP (2016 est.)
note: general government gross debt; gross debt consists of all liabilities that require payment or payments of interest and/or principal by the debtor to the creditor at a date or dates in the future; includes debt liabilities in the form of Special Drawing Rights (SDRs), currency and deposits, debt securities, loans, insurance, pensions and standardized guarantee schemes, and other accounts payable; all liabilities in the GFSM (Government Financial Systems Manual) 2001 system are debt, except for equity and investment fund shares and financial derivatives and employee stock options
country comparison to the world: 119

Taxes and other revenues: 35.7% (of GDP) (2017 est.)
country comparison to the world: 60

Fiscal year: calendar year

Current account balance: $79.937 billion (2019 est.)
$63.273 billion (2018 est.)
country comparison to the world: 5

Exports: $470.91 billion (2020 est.) note: data are in current year dollars
$478.34 billion (2019 est.) note: data are in current year dollars
$482.58 billion (2018 est.) note: data are in current year dollars
note: trade data exclude trade with Switzerland
country comparison to the world: 15

Exports - partners: Germany 16%, United States 14%, United Kingdom 8%, China 7%, France 6%, India 6%, Italy 5% (2019)

Exports - commodities: gold, packaged medicines, medical cultures/vaccines, watches, jewelry (2019)

Imports: $401.91 billion (2020 est.) note: data are in current year dollars
$394 billion (2019 est.) note: data are in current year dollars
$395.86 billion (2018 est.) note: data are in current year dollars
country comparison to the world: 17

Imports - partners: Germany 21%, Italy 8%, United States 6%, France 6%, United Kingdom 5%, United Arab Emirates 5% (2019)

Imports - commodities: gold, packaged medicines, jewelry, cars, medical cultures/vaccines (2019)

Reserves of foreign exchange and gold: $811.2 billion (31 December 2017 est.)
$679.3 billion (31 December 2016 est.)
country comparison to the world: 3

Debt - external: $1,909,446,000,000 (2019 est.)
$1,930,819,000,000 (2018 est.)
country comparison to the world: 14

Exchange rates: Swiss francs (CHF) per US dollar -
0.88995 (2020 est.)
0.98835 (2019 est.)
0.99195 (2018 est.)
0.9627 (2014 est.)
0.9152 (2013 est.)

ENERGY

Electricity access: *electrification - total population:* 100% (2020)

Electricity: *installed generating capacity:* 22.921 million kW (2020 est.)
consumption: 56,406,647,000 kWh (2020 est.)
exports: 32.549 billion kWh (2020 est.)
imports: 26.988 billion kWh (2020 est.)
transmission/distribution losses: 4.19 billion kWh (2020 est.)

Electricity generation sources: *fossil fuels:* 0.8% of total installed capacity (2020 est.)
nuclear: 34.2% of total installed capacity (2020 est.)
solar: 3.8% of total installed capacity (2020 est.)
wind: 0.2% of total installed capacity (2020 est.)
hydroelectricity: 56.3% of total installed capacity (2020 est.)
biomass and waste: 4.7% of total installed capacity (2020 est.)

Coal: *production:* 0 metric tons (2020 est.)
consumption: 150,000 metric tons (2020 est.)
exports: 0 metric tons (2020 est.)
imports: 139,000 metric tons (2020 est.)
proven reserves: 0 metric tons (2019 est.)

Petroleum: *total petroleum production:* 300 bbl/day (2021 est.)
refined petroleum consumption: 220,000 bbl/day (2019 est.)
crude oil and lease condensate exports: 0 bbl/day (2018 est.)
crude oil and lease condensate imports: 60,900 bbl/day (2018 est.)
crude oil estimated reserves: 0 barrels (2021 est.)

Refined petroleum products - production: 61,550 bbl/day (2017 est.)
country comparison to the world: 79

Refined petroleum products - exports: 7,345 bbl/day (2017 est.)
country comparison to the world: 88

Refined petroleum products - imports: 165,100 bbl/day (2017 est.)
country comparison to the world: 39

Natural gas: *production:* 0 cubic meters (2021 est.)
consumption: 3,616,169,000 cubic meters (2019 est.)

exports: 0 cubic meters (2021 est.)
imports: 3,577,884,000 cubic meters (2019 est.)
proven reserves: 0 cubic meters (2021 est.)

Carbon dioxide emissions: 38.739 million metric tonnes of CO2 (2019 est.)
from coal and metallurgical coke: 319,000 metric tonnes of CO2 (2019 est.)
from petroleum and other liquids: 31.494 million metric tonnes of CO2 (2019 est.)
from consumed natural gas: 6.926 million metric tonnes of CO2 (2019 est.)
country comparison to the world: 66

Energy consumption per capita: 137.918 million Btu/person (2019 est.)
country comparison to the world: 38

COMMUNICATIONS

Telephones - fixed lines: *total subscriptions:* 3,071,296 (2020 est.)
subscriptions per 100 inhabitants: 35 (2020 est.)
country comparison to the world: 42

Telephones - mobile cellular: *total subscriptions:* 10.829 million (2019)
subscriptions per 100 inhabitants: 126.05 (2019)
country comparison to the world: 84

Telecommunication systems: *general assessment:* Switzerland has one of the highest broadband penetration rates within Europe, with a focus on services of at least 1Gb/s; this has been supported by sympathetic regulatory measures as well as by cooperative agreements between the main telcos, and with local utilities; fast fiber is complemented by 5G services reaching about 97% of the population by early 2021; together, these networks will soon enable the telcos to provide ultra-fast broadband services nationally, ahead of most other countries in the region; the competitive mobile market is served by three network operators and a small number of MVNOs; 5G services offered by the MNOs offer data rates of up to 2Gb/s, and although various cantons have called a halt to extensions of 5G, citing health concerns, the regulator and environment ministry have put in place measures aimed at ensuring that network roll outs can continue without disruption; with the migration of subscribers to LTE and 5G networks, the MNOs have been able to begin closing down their GSM networks and repurpose physical assets and spectrum; although not a member of the EU, the country's economic integration has meant that its telecom market deregulation has followed the EU's liberalization framework, including the recent regulations on international voice roaming; this report presents an analysis of Switzerland's fixed-line telecom market, including an assessment of network infrastructure (2021)
domestic: fixed-line over 34 per 100 and mobile-cellular subscribership roughly 126 per 100 persons; extensive cable and microwave radio relay networks (2020)
international: country code - 41; satellite earth stations - 2 Intelsat (Atlantic Ocean and Indian Ocean)

Broadcast media: the publicly owned radio and TV broadcaster, Swiss Broadcasting Corporation (SRG/SSR), operates 8 national TV networks, 3 broadcasting in German, 3 in French, and 2 in Italian; private commercial TV stations broadcast regionally and locally; TV broadcasts from stations in Germany, Italy, and France are widely available via multi-channel cable and satellite TV services; SRG/SSR operates 17 radio stations that, along with private broadcasters, provide national to local coverage) (2019)

Internet country code: .ch

Internet users: *total:* 8,118,367 (2020 est.)
percent of population: 94% (2020 est.)
country comparison to the world: 69

Broadband - fixed subscriptions: *total:* 4,028,238 (2020 est.)
subscriptions per 100 inhabitants: 47 (2020 est.)
country comparison to the world: 38

TRANSPORTATION

National air transport system: *number of registered air carriers:* 6 (2020)
inventory of registered aircraft operated by air carriers: 179
annual passenger traffic on registered air carriers: 28,857,994 (2018)
annual freight traffic on registered air carriers: 1,841,310,000 (2018) mt-km

Civil aircraft registration country code prefix: HB

Airports: *total:* 63 (2021)
country comparison to the world: 78

Airports - with paved runways: *total:* 40
over 3,047 m: 3
2,438 to 3,047 m: 2
1,524 to 2,437 m: 12
914 to 1,523 m: 6
under 914 m: 17 (2021)

Airports - with unpaved runways: *total:* 23
under 914 m: 23 (2021)

Heliports: 2 (2021)

Pipelines: 1,800 km gas, 94 km oil (of which 60 are inactive), 17 km refined products (2017)

Railways: *total:* 5,466 km (2015) (includes 19 km in neighboring countries)
standard gauge: 3,836 km (2015) 1.435-m gauge (3,634 km electrified)
narrow gauge: 1,630 km (2015) 1.200-m gauge (2 km electrified) (includes 19 km in neighboring countries)
country comparison to the world: 34

Roadways: *total:* 71,557 km (2017)
paved: 71,557 km (2017) (includes 1,458 of expressways)
country comparison to the world: 66

Waterways: 1,292 km (2010) (there are 1,227 km of waterways on lakes and rivers for public transport and 65 km on the Rhine River between Basel-Rheinfelden and Schaffhausen-Bodensee for commercial goods transport)
country comparison to the world: 61

Merchant marine: *total:* 20
by type: bulk carrier 16, general cargo 1, other 3 (includes Liechtenstein) (2021)
country comparison to the world: 148

Ports and terminals: *river port(s):* Basel (Rhine)

MILITARY AND SECURITY

Military and security forces: Swiss Armed Forces: Land Forces, Swiss Air Force (Schweizer Luftwaffe) (2022)

Military expenditures: 0.7% of GDP (2021 est.)
0.8% of GDP (2020)
0.7% of GDP (2019) (approximately $5.26 billion)
0.7% of GDP (2018) (approximately $4.72 billion)
0.7% of GDP (2017) (approximately $4.67 billion)
country comparison to the world: 154

Military and security service personnel strengths: the Swiss Armed Forces maintain a full-time professional cadre of about 4,000 personnel along with approximately 18-20,000 conscripts brought in annually for 18-23 weeks of training; approximately 120,000 reserve forces (2022)

Military equipment inventories and acquisitions: the military's inventory includes a mix of domestically-produced and imported weapons systems; the US has been the leading supplier of military armaments to Switzerland since 2010; the Swiss defense industry produces a range of military land vehicles (2021)

Military service age and obligation: 18-30 years of age for compulsory military service for men; 18 years of age for voluntary military service; women may volunteer; every Swiss male has to serve at least 245 days in the armed forces; conscripts receive 18 weeks of mandatory training, followed by six 19-day intermittent recalls for training during the next 10 years (2022)
note: conscientious objectors can choose 390 days of community service instead of military service

Military deployments: up to 165 Kosovo (NATO/KFOR) (2022)

Military - note: Switzerland has long maintained a policy of military neutrality, but does periodically participate in EU, NATO, Organization for Security and Cooperation in Europe (OSCE), and UN military operations; Swiss law excludes participation in combat operations for peace enforcement, and Swiss units will only participate in operations under the mandate of the UN or OSCE; Switzerland joined NATO's Partnership for Peace program in 1996; it contributed to the NATO-led Kosovo peace-support force (KFOR) in 1999 and as of 2022, continued doing so with up to 165 personnel; Switzerland also provided a small number of staff officers to the NATO mission in Afghanistan from 2004-2007

TERRORISM

Terrorist group(s): Islamic State of Iraq and ash-Sham (ISIS)

TRANSNATIONAL ISSUES

Disputes - international: none identified

Refugees and internally displaced persons: *refugees (country of origin):* 38,219 (Eritrea), 20,043 (Syria), 14,649 (Afghanistan), 6,069 (Sri Lanka), 6,197 (Turkey) (mid-year 2021); 68,620 (Ukraine) (as of 8 November 2022)
stateless persons: 684 (mid-year 2021)

Illicit drugs: major source of precursor chemicals used in the production of illicit narcotics; a significant importer and exporter of ephedrine and pseudoephedrine

SYRIA

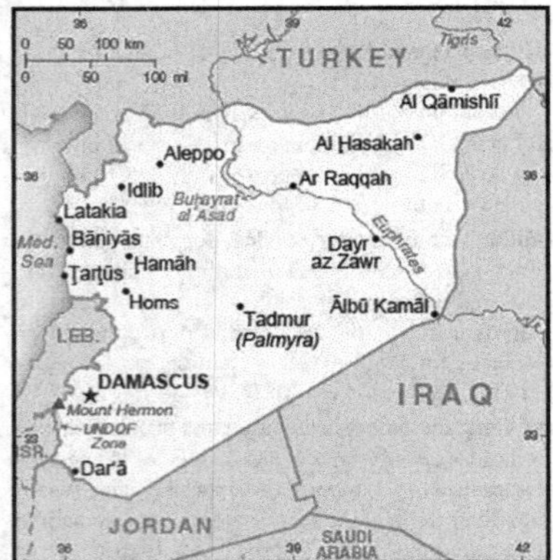

INTRODUCTION

Background: Following World War I, France acquired a mandate over the northern portion of the former Ottoman Empire province of Syria. The French administered the area as Syria until granting it independence in 1946. The new country lacked political stability and experienced a series of military coups. Syria united with Egypt in February 1958 to form the United Arab Republic. In September 1961, the two entities separated, and the Syrian Arab Republic was reestablished. In the 1967 Arab-Israeli War, Syria lost the Golan Heights region to Israel. During the 1990s, Syria and Israel held occasional, albeit unsuccessful, peace talks over its return. In November 1970, Hafiz al-ASAD, a member of the socialist Ba'ath Party and the minority Alawi sect, seized power in a bloodless coup and brought political stability to the country. Following the death of President Hafiz al-ASAD, his son, Bashar al-ASAD, was approved as president by popular referendum in July 2000. Syrian troops - stationed in Lebanon since 1976 in an ostensible peacekeeping role - were withdrawn in April 2005. During the July-August 2006 conflict between Israel and Hizballah, Syria placed its military forces on alert but did not intervene directly on behalf of its ally Hizballah. In May 2007, Bashar al-ASAD's second term as president was approved by popular referendum.

Influenced by major uprisings that began elsewhere in the region, and compounded by additional social and economic factors, antigovernment protests broke out first in the southern province of Dar'a in March 2011 with protesters calling for the repeal of the restrictive Emergency Law allowing arrests without charge, the legalization of political parties, and the removal of corrupt local officials. Demonstrations and violent unrest spread across Syria with the size and intensity of protests fluctuating. The government responded to unrest with a mix of concessions - including the repeal of the Emergency Law, new laws permitting new political parties, and liberalizing local and national elections - and with military force and detentions. The government's efforts to quell unrest and armed opposition activity led to extended clashes and eventually civil war between government forces, their allies, and oppositionists.

International pressure on the ASAD regime intensified after late 2011, as the Arab League, the EU, Turkey, and the US expanded economic sanctions against the regime and those entities that support it. In December 2012, the Syrian National Coalition, was recognized by more than 130 countries as the sole legitimate representative of the Syrian people. In September 2015, Russia launched a military intervention on behalf of the ASAD regime, and domestic and foreign government-aligned forces recaptured swaths of territory from opposition forces, and eventually the country's second largest city, Aleppo, in December 2016, shifting the conflict in the regime's favor. The regime, with this foreign support, also recaptured opposition strongholds in the Damascus suburbs and the southern province of Dar'a in 2018. The government lacks territorial control over much of the northeastern part of the country, which is dominated by the predominantly Kurdish Syrian Democratic Forces (SDF), and a smaller area dominated by Turkey. The SDF expanded its territorial hold beyond its traditional homelands, subsuming much of the northeast since 2014 as it battled the Islamic State of Iraq and Syria. Since 2016, Turkey has been engaged in northern Syria and has conducted three large-scale military operations to capture territory along Syria's northern border in the provinces of Aleppo, Ar Raqqah, and Al Hasakah. Some opposition forces organized under the Turkish-backed Syrian National Army and Turkish forces have maintained control of northwestern Syria along the Turkish border with the Afrin area of Aleppo Province since 2018. In 2019, Turkey and its opposition allies occupied formerly SDF-controlled territory between the cities of Tall Abyad to Ra's Al 'Ayn along Syria's northern border. The extremist organization Hay'at Tahrir al-Sham (formerly the Nusrah Front) in 2017 emerged as the predominate opposition force in Idlib Province, and still dominates an area also hosting additional Turkish forces. Negotiations between the government and opposition delegations at UN-sponsored Geneva conferences since 2014 and separately held discussions between Iran, Russia, and Turkey since early 2017 have failed to produce a resolution to the conflict. According to a September 2021 UN estimate, the death toll resulting from the past 10 years of civil war is more than 350,000, although the UN acknowledges that this is the minimum number of verifiable deaths and is an undercount. According to a June 2022 UN estimate, the death toll resulting from the past 10 plus years of civil war is more than 306,000. As of early 2022, approximately 6.66 million Syrians were internally displaced and 14.6 million people were in need of humanitarian assistance across the country. An additional 5.6 million Syrians were registered refugees in Turkey, Jordan, Iraq, Egypt, and North Africa. The conflict in Syria remains one of the two largest displacement crises worldwide (the other is the invasion of Ukraine).

GEOGRAPHY

Location: Middle East, bordering the Mediterranean Sea, between Lebanon and Turkey

Geographic coordinates: 35 00 N, 38 00 E

Map references Middle East

Area: *total:* 187,437 sq km
land: 185,887 sq km
water: 1,550 sq km
note: includes 1,295 sq km of Israeli-occupied territory
country comparison to the world: 89

Area - comparative: slightly more than 1.5 times the size of Pennsylvania

Land boundaries: *total:* 2,363 km
border countries (5): Iraq 599 km; Israel 83 km; Jordan 379 km; Lebanon 403 km; Turkey 899 km

Coastline: 193 km

Maritime claims territorial sea: 12 nm
contiguous zone: 24 nm

Climate: mostly desert; hot, dry, sunny summers (June to August) and mild, rainy winters (December to February) along coast; cold weather with snow or sleet periodically in Damascus

Terrain: primarily semiarid and desert plateau; narrow coastal plain; mountains in west

Elevation: *highest point:* Mount Hermon (Jabal a-Shayk) 2,814 m
lowest point: Yarmuk River -66 m
mean elevation: 514 m

Natural resources: petroleum, phosphates, chrome and manganese ores, asphalt, iron ore, rock salt, marble, gypsum, hydropower

Land use: *agricultural land:* 75.8% (2018 est.)
arable land: 25.4% (2018 est.)
permanent crops: 5.8% (2018 est.)
permanent pasture: 44.6% (2018 est.)
forest: 2.7% (2018 est.)
other: 21.5% (2018 est.)

Irrigated land: 14,280 sq km (2012)

Major rivers (by length in km): Euphrates (shared with Turkey [s], Iran, and Iraq [m]) - 3,596 km; Tigris (shared with Turkey, Iran, and Iraq [m]) - 1,950 km

note – [s] after country name indicates river source; [m] after country name indicates river mouth

Major watersheds (area sq km): Indian Ocean drainage: *(Persian Gulf)* Tigris and Euphrates (918,044 sq km)

Population distribution: significant population density along the Mediterranean coast; larger concentrations found in the major cities of Damascus, Aleppo (the country's largest city), and Hims (Homs); more than half of the population lives in the coastal plain, the province of Halab, and the Euphrates River valley
note: the ongoing civil war has altered the population distribution

Natural hazards: dust storms, sandstorms
volcanism: Syria's two historically active volcanoes, Es Safa and an unnamed volcano near the Turkish border have not erupted in centuries

Geography - note: the capital of Damascus - located at an oasis fed by the Barada River - is thought to be one of the world's oldest continuously inhabited cities; there are 42 Israeli settlements and civilian land use sites in the Israeli-controlled Golan Heights (2017)

PEOPLE AND SOCIETY

Population: 21,563,800 (2022 est.)
note: approximately 22,900 Israeli settlers live in the Golan Heights (2018)
country comparison to the world: 60

Nationality noun: Syrian(s)
adjective: Syrian

Ethnic groups: Arab ~50%, Alawite ~15%, Kurd ~10%, Levantine ~10%, other ~15% (includes Druze, Ismaili, Imami, Nusairi, Assyrian, Turkoman, Armenian)

Languages: Arabic (official), Kurdish, Armenian, Aramaic, Circassian, French, English
major-language sample(s):
كتاب حقائق العالم، المصدر الذي لا يمكن الاستغناء عنه للمعلومات الأساسية
(Arabic)

Religions: Muslim 87% (official; includes Sunni 74% and Alawi, Ismaili, and Shia 13%), Christian 10% (includes Orthodox, Uniate, and Nestorian), Druze 3%
note: the Christian population may be considerably smaller as a result of Christians fleeing the country during the ongoing civil war

Age structure: *0-14 years:* 33.47% (male 3,323,072/female 3,170,444)
15-24 years: 19.34% (male 1,872,903/female 1,879,564)
25-54 years: 37.31% (male 3,558,241/female 3,679,596)
55-64 years: 5.41% (male 516,209/female 534,189)
65 years and over: 4.46% (male 404,813/female 459,417) (2020 est.)

Dependency ratios: *total dependency ratio:* 55.4
youth dependency ratio: 47.8
elderly dependency ratio: 7.6
potential support ratio: 13.2 (2020 est.)

Median age: *total:* 23.5 years
male: 23 years
female: 24 years (2020 est.)
country comparison to the world: 177

Population growth rate: 5.91% (2022 est.)
country comparison to the world: 1

Birth rate: 22.72 births/1,000 population (2022 est.)
country comparison to the world: 51

Death rate: 4.22 deaths/1,000 population (2022 est.)
country comparison to the world: 210

Net migration rate: 40.58 migrant(s)/1,000 population (2022 est.)
country comparison to the world: 1

Population distribution: significant population density along the Mediterranean coast; larger concentrations found in the major cities of Damascus, Aleppo (the country's largest city), and Hims (Homs); more than half of the population lives in the coastal plain, the province of Halab, and the Euphrates River valley
note: the ongoing civil war has altered the population distribution

Urbanization: *urban population:* 56.8% of total population (2022)
rate of urbanization: 5.38% annual rate of change (2020-25 est.)

Major urban areas - population: 2.503 million DAMASCUS (capital), 2.098 million Aleppo, 1.398 million Hims (Homs), 964,000 Hamah (2022)

Sex ratio: *at birth:* 1.06 male(s)/female
0-14 years: 1.05 male(s)/female
15-24 years: 1.02 male(s)/female
25-54 years: 0.97 male(s)/female
55-64 years: 0.97 male(s)/female
65 years and over: 0.76 male(s)/female
total population: 1 male(s)/female (2022 est.)

Maternal mortality ratio: 31 deaths/100,000 live births (2017 est.)
country comparison to the world: 110

Infant mortality rate: *total:* 15.87 deaths/1,000 live births
male: 17.5 deaths/1,000 live births
female: 14.14 deaths/1,000 live births (2022 est.)
country comparison to the world: 96

Life expectancy at birth: *total population:* 74.28 years
male: 72.82 years
female: 75.84 years (2022 est.)
country comparison to the world: 139

Total fertility rate: 2.8 children born/woman (2022 est.)
country comparison to the world: 55

Drinking water source: *improved: urban:* 99.6% of population
rural: 100% of population
total: 99.8% of population
unimproved: urban: 0.4% of population
rural: 0.7% of population
total: 0.2% of population (2020 est.)

Physicians density: 1.29 physicians/1,000 population (2016)

Hospital bed density: 1.4 beds/1,000 population (2017)

Sanitation facility access: *improved: urban:* 99.5% of population
rural: 99.5% of population
total: 99.5% of population
unimproved: urban: 0.5% of population
rural: 0.5% of population
total: 0.5% of population (2020 est.)

HIV/AIDS - adult prevalence rate: (2020 est.) <.1%

HIV/AIDS - people living with HIV/AIDS: (2020) <1,000

HIV/AIDS - deaths: (2020) <100

Obesity - adult prevalence rate: 27.8% (2016)
country comparison to the world: 35

Alcohol consumption per capita: *total:* 0.13 liters of pure alcohol (2019 est.)
beer: 0.02 liters of pure alcohol (2019 est.)
wine: 0 liters of pure alcohol (2019 est.)
spirits: 0.11 liters of pure alcohol (2019 est.)
other alcohols: 0 liters of pure alcohol (2019 est.)
country comparison to the world: 176

Literacy: *definition:* age 15 and over can read and write
total population: 86.4%
male: 91.7%
female: 81% (2015)

School life expectancy (primary to tertiary education): *total:* 9 years
male: 9 years
female: 9 years (2013)

Unemployment, youth ages 15-24: *total:* 35.8%
male: 26.6%
female: 71.1% (2011 est.)

ENVIRONMENT

Environment - current issues: deforestation; overgrazing; soil erosion; desertification; depletion of water resources; water pollution from raw sewage and petroleum refining wastes; inadequate potable water

Environment - international agreements: *party to:* Biodiversity, Climate Change, Climate Change-Kyoto Protocol, Climate Change-Paris Agreement, Desertification, Endangered Species, Hazardous Wastes, Marine Dumping-London Convention, Nuclear Test Ban, Ozone Layer Protection, Ship Pollution, Wetlands
signed, but not ratified: Environmental Modification

Air pollutants: *particulate matter emissions:* 39.43 micrograms per cubic meter (2016 est.)
carbon dioxide emissions: 28.83 megatons (2016 est.)
methane emissions: 12.93 megatons (2020 est.)

Climate: mostly desert; hot, dry, sunny summers (June to August) and mild, rainy winters (December to February) along coast; cold weather with snow or sleet periodically in Damascus

Land use: *agricultural land:* 75.8% (2018 est.)
arable land: 25.4% (2018 est.)
permanent crops: 5.8% (2018 est.)
permanent pasture: 44.6% (2018 est.)
forest: 2.7% (2018 est.)
other: 21.5% (2018 est.)

Urbanization: *urban population:* 56.8% of total population (2022)
rate of urbanization: 5.38% annual rate of change (2020-25 est.)

Food insecurity: *exceptional shortfall in aggregate food production/supplies: due to civil conflict and economic crisis* - the latest available nationwide food security assessment estimated that about 12 million people, 60% of the overall population, were food insecure in 2021, a slight decline from 12.4 million in 2020, but 5 million more than at the end of 2019, mostly due to constrained livelihood opportunities and a rapidly worsening economy (2022)

Waste and recycling: *municipal solid waste generated annually:* 4.5 million tons (2009 est.)
municipal solid waste recycled annually: 112,500 tons (2010 est.)
percent of municipal solid waste recycled: 2.5% (2010 est.)

Major rivers (by length in km): Euphrates (shared with Turkey [s], Iran, and Iraq [m]) - 3,596 km; Tigris (shared with Turkey, Iran, and Iraq [m]) - 1,950 km
note – [s] after country name indicates river source; [m] after country name indicates river mouth

Major watersheds (area sq km): Indian Ocean drainage: *(Persian Gulf)* Tigris and Euphrates (918,044 sq km)

Total water withdrawal: *municipal:* 1.475 billion cubic meters (2017 est.)
industrial: 615.4 million cubic meters (2017 est.)
agricultural: 14.67 billion cubic meters (2017 est.)

Total renewable water resources: 16.802 billion cubic meters (2017 est.)

GOVERNMENT

Country name: *conventional long form:* Syrian Arab Republic
conventional short form: Syria
local long form: Al Jumhuriyah al Arabiyah as Suriyah
local short form: Suriyah
former: United Arab Republic (with Egypt)

etymology: name ultimately derived from the ancient Assyrians who dominated northern Mesopotamia, but whose reach also extended westward to the Levant; over time, the name came to be associated more with the western area

Government type: presidential republic; highly authoritarian regime

Capital: *name:* Damascus
geographic coordinates: 33 30 N, 36 18 E
time difference: UTC+2 (7 hours ahead of Washington, DC, during Standard Time)
daylight saving time: +1hr, begins midnight on the last Friday in March; ends at midnight on the last Friday in October
etymology: Damascus is a very old city; its earliest name, Temeseq, first appears in an Egyptian geographical list of the 15th century B.C., but the meaning is uncertain

Administrative divisions: 14 provinces (muhafazat, singular - muhafazah); Al Hasakah, Al Ladhiqiyah (Latakia), Al Qunaytirah, Ar Raqqah, As Suwayda', Dar'a, Dayr az Zawr, Dimashq (Damascus), Halab (Aleppo), Hamah, Hims (Homs), Idlib, Rif Dimashq (Damascus Countryside), Tartus

Independence: 17 April 1946 (from League of Nations mandate under French administration)

National holiday: Independence Day (Evacuation Day), 17 April (1946); note - celebrates the leaving of the last French troops and the proclamation of full independence

Constitution: *history:* several previous; latest issued 15 February 2012, passed by referendum and effective 27 February 2012; note - UN-sponsored talks, which began in late 2019 between delegates from government and opposition forces to draft a new constitution; in March 2022, the 7th round of the Syrian Constitutional Committee ended in Geneva with no results
amendments: proposed by the president of the republic or by one third of the People's Assembly members; following review by a special Assembly committee, passage requires at least three-quarters majority vote by the Assembly and approval by the president

Legal system: mixed legal system of civil and Islamic (sharia) law (for family courts)

International law organization participation: has not submitted an ICJ jurisdiction declaration; non-party state to the ICC

Citizenship: *citizenship by birth:* no
citizenship by descent only: the father must be a citizen of Syria; if the father is unknown or stateless, the mother must be a citizen of Syria
dual citizenship recognized: yes
residency requirement for naturalization: 10 years

Suffrage: 18 years of age; universal

Executive branch: *chief of state:* President Bashar al-ASAD (since 17 July 2000); Vice President Najah al-ATTAR (since 23 March 2006)
head of government: Prime Minister Hussein ARNOUS (since 30 August 2020); Deputy Prime Minister Ali Abdullah AYOUB (Lt. Gen.) (since 30 August 2020)
cabinet: Council of Ministers appointed by the president
elections/appointments: president directly elected by simple majority popular vote for a 7-year term (eligible for a second term); election last held on 26 May 2021 (next to be held in 2028); the president appoints the vice presidents, prime minister, and deputy prime ministers
election results:
2021: Bashar al-ASAD elected president; percent of vote - Bashar al-ASAD (Ba'th Party) 95.2%, Mahmoud Ahmad MAREI (Democratic Arab Socialist Union) 3.3%, Abdullah Sallum ABDULLAH (Socialist Unionist Party) 1.5%

Legislative branch: *description:* unicameral People's Assembly or Majlis al-Shaab (250 seats; members directly elected in multi-seat constituencies by simple majority preferential vote to serve 4-year terms)
elections:
last held on 19 July 2020 (next to be held in 2024)
election results:
percent of vote by party - NPF 80%, other 20%; seats by party - NPF 200, other 50; composition - men 222, women 28, percent of women 11.2%

Judicial branch: *highest court(s):* Court of Cassation (organized into civil, criminal, religious, and military divisions, each with 3 judges); Supreme Constitutional Court (consists of 7 members)
judge selection and term of office: Court of Cassation judges appointed by the Supreme Judicial Council (SJC), a judicial management body headed by the minister of justice with 7 members, including the national president; judge tenure NA; Supreme Constitutional Court judges nominated by the president and appointed by the SJC; judges serve 4-year renewable terms
subordinate courts: courts of first instance; magistrates' courts; religious and military courts; Economic Security Court; Counterterrorism Court (established June 2012)

Political parties and leaders: *legal parties/alliances:*
Arab Socialist Ba'ath Party [Bashar al-ASAD, regional secretary]
Arab Socialist Renaissance (Ba'th) Party [President Bashar al-ASAD]
Arab Socialist Union of Syria or ASU [Safwan al-QUDSI]
Democratic Arab Socialist Union [Hassan Abdul AZIM, general secretary]
National Progressive Front or NPF [Bashar al-ASAD, Suleiman QADDAH] (alliance includes Arab Socialist Renaissance (Ba'th) Party, Socialist Unionist Democratic Party)
Socialist Unionist Party [Fayiz ISMAIL]
Socialist Unionist Democratic Party [Fadlallah Nasr al-DIN]
Syrian Communist Party (two branches) [Wissal Farha BAKDASH, Yusuf Rashid FAYSAL]
Syrian Social Nationalist Party or SSNP [Ali HAIDAR]
Unionist Socialist Party [Fayez ISMAIL]

Major Kurdish parties: Kurdish Democratic Union Party or PYD [Shahoz HASAN and Aysha HISSO]
Kurdish National Council [Sa'ud MALA]
other: Syrian Democratic Party [Mustafa QALAAJI]

International organization participation: ABEDA, AFESD, AMF, CAEU, FAO, G-24, G-77, IAEA, IBRD, ICAO, ICC (national committees), ICRM, ICSID, IDA, IDB, IFAD, IFC, IFRCS, IHO, ILO, IMF, IMO, Interpol, IOC, IPU, ISO, ITSO, ITU, LAS, MIGA, NAM, OAPEC, OIC, OPCW, UN, UNCTAD, UNESCO, UNIDO, UNRWA, UNWTO, UPU, WBG, WCO, WFTU (NGOs), WHO, WIPO, WMO, WTO (observer)

Diplomatic representation in the US: *chief of mission:* Ambassador (vacant); note – embassy closed on 18 March 2014
chancery: 2215 Wyoming Avenue NW, Washington, DC 20008
telephone: [1] (202) 232-6313
FAX: [1] (202) 234-9548

Diplomatic representation from the US: *chief of mission:* Ambassador (vacant); note - on 6 February 2012, the US closed its embassy in Damascus; Czechia serves as a protecting power for US interests in Syria
mailing address: 6110 Damascus Place, Washington DC 20521-6110
email address and website:
USIS_damascus@embassy.mzv.cz
https://sy.usembassy.gov/

Flag description: three equal horizontal bands of red (top), white, and black; two small, green, five-pointed stars in a horizontal line centered in the white band; the band colors derive from the Arab Liberation flag and represent oppression (black), overcome through bloody struggle (red), to be replaced by a bright future (white); identical to the former flag of the United Arab Republic (1958-1961) where the two stars represented the constituent states of Syria and Egypt; the current design dates to 1980
note: similar to the flag of Yemen, which has a plain white band; Iraq, which has an Arabic inscription centered in the white band; and that of Egypt, which has a gold Eagle of Saladin centered in the white band

National symbol(s): hawk; national colors: red, white, black, green

National anthem: *name:* "Humat ad-Diyar" (Guardians of the Homeland)
lyrics/music: Khalil Mardam BEY/Mohammad Salim FLAYFEL and Ahmad Salim FLAYFEL
note: adopted 1936, restored 1961; between 1958 and 1961, while Syria was a member of the United Arab Republic with Egypt, the country had a different anthem

National heritage: *total World Heritage Sites:* 6 (all cultural)
selected World Heritage Site locales: Ancient City of Damascus; Ancient City of Bosra; Site of Palmyra; Ancient City of Aleppo; Crac des Chevaliers and Qal'at Salah El-Din; Ancient Villages of Northern Syria

ECONOMY

Economic overview: Syria's economy has deeply deteriorated amid the ongoing conflict that began in 2011, declining by more than 70% from 2010 to 2017. The government has struggled to fully address the effects of international sanctions, widespread infrastructure damage, diminished domestic consumption and production, reduced subsidies, and high inflation, which have caused dwindling foreign exchange reserves, rising budget and trade deficits, a decreasing value of the Syrian pound, and falling household purchasing power. In 2017, some economic indicators began to stabilize, including the exchange rate and inflation, but economic activity remains depressed and GDP almost certainly fell.

During 2017, the ongoing conflict and continued unrest and economic decline worsened the humanitarian crisis, necessitating high levels of international assistance, as more than 13 million people remain in need inside Syria, and the number of registered Syrian refugees increased from 4.8 million in 2016 to more than 5.4 million.

Prior to the turmoil, Damascus had begun liberalizing economic policies, including cutting lending interest rates, opening private banks, consolidating multiple exchange rates, raising prices on some subsidized items, and establishing the Damascus Stock Exchange, but the economy remains highly regulated. Long-run economic constraints include foreign trade barriers, declining oil production, high unemployment, rising budget deficits, increasing pressure on water supplies caused by heavy use in agriculture, industrial contaction, water pollution, and widespread infrastructure damage.

Real GDP (purchasing power parity): $50.28 billion (2015 est.)
$55.8 billion (2014 est.)
$61.9 billion (2013 est.)
note: data are in 2015 US dollars
the war-driven deterioration of the economy resulted in a disappearance of quality national level statistics in the 2012-13 period
country comparison to the world: 112

Real GDP growth rate: -36.5% (2014 est.)
-30.9% (2013 est.)
note: data are in 2015 dollars
country comparison to the world: 224

Real GDP per capita: $2,900 (2015 est.)
$3,300 (2014 est.)
$2,800 (2013 est.)
note: data are in 2015 US dollars
country comparison to the world: 197

GDP (official exchange rate): $24.6 billion (2014 est.)

Inflation rate (consumer prices): 28.1% (2017 est.)
47.3% (2016 est.)
country comparison to the world: 221

GDP - composition, by sector of origin: *agriculture:* 20% (2017 est.)
industry: 19.5% (2017 est.)
services: 60.8% (2017 est.)

GDP - composition, by end use: *household consumption:* 73.1% (2017 est.)
government consumption: 26% (2017 est.)
investment in fixed capital: 18.6% (2017 est.)
investment in inventories: 12.3% (2017 est.)
exports of goods and services: 16.1% (2017 est.)
imports of goods and services: -46.1% (2017 est.)

Agricultural products: wheat, barley, milk, olives, tomatoes, oranges, potatoes, sheep milk, lemons, limes

Industries: petroleum, textiles, food processing, beverages, tobacco, phosphate rock mining, cement, oil seeds crushing, automobile assembly

Industrial production growth rate: 4.3% (2017 est.)
country comparison to the world: 70

Labor force: 3.767 million (2017 est.)
country comparison to the world: 93

Labor force - by occupation: *agriculture:* 17%
industry: 16%
services: 67% (2008 est.)

Unemployment rate: 50% (2017 est.)
50% (2016 est.)
country comparison to the world: 218

Unemployment, youth ages 15-24: *total:* 35.8%
male: 26.6%
female: 71.1% (2011 est.)
country comparison to the world: 24

Population below poverty line: 82.5% (2014 est.)

Budget: *revenues:* 1.162 billion (2017 est.)
expenditures: 3.211 billion (2017 est.)
note: government projections for FY2016

Budget surplus (+) or deficit (-): -8.7% (of GDP) (2017 est.)
country comparison to the world: 203

Public debt: 94.8% of GDP (2017 est.)
91.3% of GDP (2016 est.)
country comparison to the world: 23

Taxes and other revenues: 4.2% (of GDP) (2017 est.)
country comparison to the world: 219

Fiscal year: calendar year

Current account balance: -$2.123 billion (2017 est.)
-$2.077 billion (2016 est.)
country comparison to the world: 168

Exports: $1.85 billion (2017 est.)
$1.705 billion (2016 est.)
country comparison to the world: 153

Exports - partners: Saudi Arabia 23%, Turkey 18%, Egypt 14%, United Arab Emirates 8%, Jordan 7%, Kuwait 5% (2019)

Exports - commodities: olive oil, cumin seeds, pistachios, tomatoes, apples, pears, spices, pitted fruits (2019)

Imports: $6.279 billion (2017 est.)
$5.496 billion (2016 est.)
country comparison to the world: 127

Imports - partners: Turkey 27%, China 22%, United Arab Emirates 14%, Egypt 5% (2019)

Imports - commodities: cigarettes, broadcasting equipment, wheat flours, sunflower oil, refined petroleum (2019)

Reserves of foreign exchange and gold: $407.3 million (31 December 2017 est.)
$504.6 million (31 December 2016 est.)
country comparison to the world: 159

Debt - external: $4.989 billion (31 December 2017 est.)
$5.085 billion (31 December 2016 est.)
country comparison to the world: 133

Exchange rates: Syrian pounds (SYP) per US dollar -
514.6 (2017 est.)
459.2 (2016 est.)
459.2 (2015 est.)
236.41 (2014 est.)
153.695 (2013 est.)

ENERGY

Electricity access: *electrification - total population:* 92% (2019)
electrification - urban areas: 100% (2019)
electrification - rural areas: 84% (2019)

Electricity: *installed generating capacity:* 10.082 million kW (2020 est.)
consumption: 13,071,080,000 kWh (2019 est.)
exports: 347 million kWh (2019 est.)
imports: 0 kWh (2019 est.)
transmission/distribution losses: 3.687 billion kWh (2019 est.)

Electricity generation sources: *fossil fuels:* 95.1% of total installed capacity (2020 est.)
hydroelectricity: 4.8% of total installed capacity (2020 est.)
biomass and waste: 0.2% of total installed capacity (2020 est.)

Coal: *production:* 0 metric tons (2020 est.)
consumption: 38,000 metric tons (2020 est.)
exports: 0 metric tons (2020 est.)
imports: 38,000 metric tons (2020 est.)
proven reserves: 0 metric tons (2019 est.)

Petroleum: *total petroleum production:* 80,800 bbl/day (2021 est.)
refined petroleum consumption: 137,900 bbl/day (2019 est.)
crude oil and lease condensate exports: 0 bbl/day (2018 est.)
crude oil and lease condensate imports: 129,100 bbl/day (2018 est.)
crude oil estimated reserves: 2.5 billion barrels (2021 est.)

Refined petroleum products - production: 111,600 bbl/day (2015 est.)
country comparison to the world: 66

Refined petroleum products - exports: 12,520 bbl/day (2015 est.)
country comparison to the world: 79

Refined petroleum products - imports: 38,080 bbl/day (2015 est.)
country comparison to the world: 92

Natural gas: *production:* 3,531,077,000 cubic meters (2019 est.)
consumption: 3,531,077,000 cubic meters (2019 est.)
exports: 0 cubic meters (2021 est.)
imports: 0 cubic meters (2020 est.)
proven reserves: 240.693 billion cubic meters (2021 est.)

Carbon dioxide emissions: 26.893 million metric tonnes of CO_2 (2019 est.)
from coal and metallurgical coke: 46,000 metric tonnes of CO_2 (2019 est.)
from petroleum and other liquids: 19.92 million metric tonnes of CO_2 (2019 est.)
from consumed natural gas: 6.927 million metric tonnes of CO_2 (2019 est.)
country comparison to the world: 76

Energy consumption per capita: 24.567 million Btu/person (2019 est.)
country comparison to the world: 130

COMMUNICATIONS

Telephones - fixed lines: *total subscriptions:* 2,857,193 (2020 est.)
subscriptions per 100 inhabitants: 16 (2020 est.)
country comparison to the world: 46

Telephones - mobile cellular: *total subscriptions:* 19,387,600 (2019)
subscriptions per 100 inhabitants: 113.58 (2019)
country comparison to the world: 62

Telecommunication systems: *general assessment:* the years of civil war and destruction to infrastructure continue to have a toll on the telecoms sector in Syria; although over the years the major mobile service providers have endeavored to restore and rebuild damaged networks, the operating environment has been difficult; following disputed demands for back taxes, MTN Group in August 2021 exited the country, after its majority stake had been transferred to judicial guardianship; this effectively meant that the mobile market became a monopoly; in February 2022 the regulator awarded a third

mobile license following a process which had been ongoing for many years; telecommunication services in Syria are highly regulated; although urban areas can make use of the network built and maintained by the government-owned incumbent, many under served remote areas in the countryside are obliged to rely on satellite communications; the domestic and international fixed-line markets in Syria remain the monopoly of the STE, despite several initiatives over the years aimed at liberalizing the market; mobile broadband penetration in Syria is still quite low, despite quite a high population coverage of 3G networks and some deployment of LTE infrastructure; this may provide potential opportunities for growth once infrastructure and economic reconstruction efforts make headway, and civil issues subside (2022)
domestic: the number of fixed-line connections increased markedly prior to the civil war in 2011 and now stands at over 16 per 100; mobile-cellular service is just over 95 per 100 persons (2020)
international: country code - 963; landing points for the Aletar, BERYTAR and UGART submarine cable connections to Egypt, Lebanon, and Cyprus; satellite earth stations - 1 Intelsat (Indian Ocean) and 1 Intersputnik (Atlantic Ocean region); coaxial cable and microwave radio relay to Iraq, Jordan, Lebanon, and Turkey; participant in Medarabtel (2019)

Broadcast media: state-run TV and radio broadcast networks; state operates 2 TV networks and 5 satellite channels; roughly two-thirds of Syrian homes have a satellite dish providing access to foreign TV broadcasts; 3 state-run radio channels; first private radio station launched in 2005; private radio broadcasters prohibited from transmitting news or political content (2018)

Internet country code: .sy

Internet users: *total:* 6,300,237 (2020 est.)
percent of population: 36% (2020 est.)
country comparison to the world: 81

Broadband - fixed subscriptions: *total:* 1,549,356 (2020 est.)
subscriptions per 100 inhabitants: 9 (2020 est.)
country comparison to the world: 64

TRANSPORTATION

National air transport system: *number of registered air carriers:* 3 (2020)
inventory of registered aircraft operated by air carriers: 11
annual passenger traffic on registered air carriers: 17,896 (2018)
annual freight traffic on registered air carriers: 30,000 (2018) mt-km

Civil aircraft registration country code prefix: YK

Airports: *total:* 90 (2021)
country comparison to the world: 62

Airports - with paved runways: *total:* 29
over 3,047 m: 5
2,438 to 3,047 m: 16
914 to 1,523 m: 3
under 914 m: 5 (2021)

Airports - with unpaved runways: *total:* 61
1,524 to 2,437 m: 1
914 to 1,523 m: 12
under 914 m: 48 (2021)

Heliports: 6 (2021)

Pipelines: 3,170 km gas, 2029 km oil (2013)

Railways: *total:* 2,052 km (2014)
standard gauge: 1,801 km (2014) 1.435-m gauge
narrow gauge: 251 km (2014) 1.050-m gauge
country comparison to the world: 74

Roadways: *total:* 69,873 km (2010)
paved: 63,060 km (2010)
unpaved: 6,813 km (2010)
country comparison to the world: 69

Waterways: 900 km (2011) (navigable but not economically significant)
country comparison to the world: 75

Merchant marine: *total:* 28
by type: bulk carrier 1, general cargo 11, other 16 (2021)
country comparison to the world: 136

Ports and terminals: *major seaport(s):* Baniyas, Latakia, Tartus

MILITARY AND SECURITY

Military and security forces: Syrian Armed Forces: Syrian Arab Army (includes Republican Guard), Syrian Naval Forces, Syrian Air Forces, Syrian Air Defense Forces, National Defense Forces (pro-government militia and auxiliary forces) (2022)
note: as of 2022, the Syrian military was supported by numerous pro-regime and pro-Iranian irregular/militia forces, the Russian armed forces, the Iran-affiliated Hizballah terrorist group, and Iran's Islamic Revolutionary Guard Corps

Military expenditures: 6.5% of GDP (2019 est.) (approximately $2.9 billion)
6.7% of GDP (2018 est.) (approximately $2.8 billion)
6.8% of GDP (2017 est.) (approximately $2.7 billion)
6.9% of GDP (2016 est.) (approximately $2.85 billion)
7.2% of GDP (2015 est.) (approximately $3.3 billion)
country comparison to the world: 4

Military and security service personnel strengths: current estimates not available; since the start of the civil war in 2011, the Syrian Armed Forces (SAF) have taken significant losses in personnel due to casualties and desertions; prior to the civil war, the SAF had approximately 300,000 active duty troops, including 200-225,000 Army, plus about 300,000 reserve forces (2022)
note: pro-government and pro-Iranian militias probably number in the tens of thousands

Military equipment inventories and acquisitions: the SAF's inventory is comprised mostly of Russian and Soviet-era equipment; since 2010, Russia has supplied nearly all of Syria's imported weapons systems, although China and Iran have also provided military equipment (2022)

Military service age and obligation: 18-42 years of age for compulsory and voluntary military service; conscript service obligation is 18 months; women are not conscripted but may volunteer to serve (2022)
note: the military is comprised largely of conscripts

Military - note: the UN Disengagement Observer Force (UNDOF) has operated in the Golan between Israel and Syria since 1974 to monitor the ceasefire following the 1973 Arab-Israeli War and supervise the areas of separation between the two countries; as of mid-2022, UNDOF consisted of about 1,000 personnel

as of 2022, multiple actors were conducting military operations in Syria in support of the ASAD government or Syrian opposition forces, as well in pursuit of their own security goals, such counterterrorism; operations have included air strikes, direct ground combat, and sponsoring proxy forces, as well as providing non-lethal military support, including advisors, technicians, arms and equipment, funding, intelligence, and training:

pro-ASAD elements operating in Syria have included **Lebanese Hizbollah, Iranian, Iranian-backed Shia militia, and Russian forces**; since early in the civil war, the ASAD government has relied on Lebanese Hizballah (see Appendix T for further information), as well as Iran and Iranian-backed irregular forces, for combat operations and to hold territory; Iran has provided military advisors and combat troops from the Iranian Revolutionary Guard Corps (including the Qods Force; see Appendix T for further information), as well as intelligence, logistical, material, technical, and financial support; it has funded, trained, equipped, and led Shia militia/paramilitary units comprised of both Syrian and non-Syrian personnel, primarily from Afghanistan, Iraq, and Pakistan; Russia intervened at the request of the ASAD government in 2015 and has since provided air support, special operations forces, military advisors, private military contractors, training, arms, and equipment; Iranian and Russian support has also included assisting Syria in combating the Islamic State of Iraq and ash-Sham (ISIS; see Appendix T) terrorist group

Turkey intervened militarily in 2016 to combat Kurdish militants and ISIS, support select Syrian opposition forces, and establish a buffer along portions of its border with Syria; as of 2022, Turkey continued to maintain a considerable military presence in northern Syria; it has armed and trained militia/proxy forces, such as the Syrian National Army, which was formed in late 2017 of Syrian Arab and Turkmen rebel factions in the Halab (Aleppo) province and northwestern Syria

the **US and some regional and European states** have at times backed Syrian opposition forces militarily and/or conducted military operations, primarily against ISIS; the US has operated in Syria since 2015 with ground forces and air strikes; as of 2022, the majority the ground forces were deployed in the Eastern Syria Security Area (ESSA, which includes parts of Hasakah and Dayr az Zawr provinces east of the Euphrates River) in support of operations by the Syrian Democratic Forces against ISIS, while the remainder were in southeast Syria around At Tanf supporting counter- ISIS operations by the Jaysh Mughawir al-Thawra (MaT, or Revolutionary Commando Army) Syrian opposition force; the US has also conducted air strikes against Syrian military targets in response to Syrian Government use of chemical weapons against opposition forces and civilians; in addition, France, Jordan, Qatar, Saudi Arabia, and the UK have provided forms of military assistance to opposition forces and/or conducted operations against ISIS, including air strikes

Israel has conducted hundreds of military air strikes in Syria against Syrian military, Hizbollah, Iranian, and/or Iranian-backed militia targets

the **Syrian Democratic Forces (SDF)** are an anti-ASAD regime coalition of forces composed primarily of Kurdish, Sunni Arab, and Syriac Christian fighters; it is dominated and led by Kurdish forces, particularly the People's Protection Units (YPG) militia; the SDF began to receive US support in 2015 and as of 2022 was the main local US partner in its counter-ISIS campaign; the SDF has internal security, counterterrorism, and commando units; Turkey views the

SDF as an extension of the Kurdistan Workers' Party (PKK), a US-designated terrorist organization (see Appendix T)

the **ISIS** terrorist group (see Appendix T) lost its last territorial stronghold to SDF forces in 2019, but continued to maintain a low-level insurgency as of 2022; in addition, the SDF held about 10,000 captured suspected ISIS fighters in detention facilities across northern Syria, including 2,000 from countries other than Iraq and Syria

as of 2022, the **Hay'at Tahrir al-Sham** (HTS; formerly known as al-Nusrah Front) terrorist organization (see Appendix T) was the dominant militant group in northwest Syria and asserted considerable influence and control over the so-called Syrian Salvation Government in the Iblib de-escalation zone (2022)

TERRORISM

Terrorist group(s): Abdallah Azzam Brigades; Ansar al-Islam; Asa'ib Ahl Al-Haq; Hizballah; Hurras al-Din; Islamic Jihad Union; Islamic Revolutionary Guard Corps (IRGC)/Qods Force; Islamic State of Iraq and ash-Sham (ISIS); Kata'ib Hizballah; Kurdistan Workers' Party (PKK); Mujahidin Shura Council in the Environs of Jerusalem; al-Nusrah Front (Hay'at Tahrir al-Sham); al-Qa'ida; Palestine Liberation Front; Popular Front for the Liberation of Palestine (PFLP); PFLP-General Command

TRANSNATIONAL ISSUES

Disputes - international: *Syria-Iraq:* none identified

Syria-Israel: Golan Heights is Israeli-controlled with UN Disengagement Observer Force (UNDOF) patrolling a buffer zone since 1974; because of ceasefire violations and increased military activity in the Golan Heights, the UN Security Council continues to extend UNDOF's mandate; since 2000, Lebanon has claimed Shab'a Farms in the Golan Heights

Syria-Jordan: the two countries signed an agreement in 2005 to settle the border dispute based on a 1931 demarcation accord; the two countries began demarcation in 2006

Syria-Lebanon: discussions on demarcating the two countries' maritime borders were held in April 2021, after Syria signed a contract with a Russian company to conduct oil and gas exploration in a disputed maritime area, but the issue was not resolved

Syria-Turkey: none identified

Refugees and internally displaced persons: *refugees (country of origin):* 568,730 (Palestinian Refugees) (2020); 12,435 (Iraq) (mid-year 2021)

IDPs: 6.662 million (ongoing civil war since 2011) (2021)

stateless persons: 160,000 (mid-year 2021); note - Syria's stateless population consists of Kurds and Palestinians; stateless persons are prevented from voting, owning land, holding certain jobs, receiving food subsidies or public healthcare, enrolling in public schools, or being legally married to Syrian citizens; in 1962, some 120,000 Syrian Kurds were stripped of their Syrian citizenship, rendering them and their descendants stateless; in 2011, the Syrian Government granted citizenship to thousands of Syrian Kurds as a means of appeasement; however, resolving the question of statelessness is not a priority given Syria's ongoing civil war

note: the ongoing civil war has resulted in almost 5.3 million registered Syrian refugees - dispersed mainly in Egypt, Iraq, Jordan, Lebanon, and Turkey - as of November 2022

Trafficking in persons: *current situation:* due to Syria's civil war, hundreds of thousands of Syrians, foreign migrant workers, and refugees have fled the country and are vulnerable to human trafficking; the lack of security and inaccessibility of the majority of the country makes it impossible to conduct a thorough analysis of the impact of the ongoing conflict on the scope and magnitude of Syria's human trafficking situation; prior to the uprising, the Syrian armed forces and opposition forces used Syrian children in combat and support roles and as human shields

tier rating: Tier 3 — Syria does not fully meet the minimum standards for the elimination of trafficking and is not making significant efforts to do so; the government does not hold any traffickers, including complicit officials, criminally accountable for trafficking; no trafficking victims were identified or received protection during the reporting period; government and pro-Syrian militias continued to forcibly recruit and use child soldiers; the government does not prevent armed opposition forces and designated terrorist organizations from recruiting children; authorities continued to arrest, detain, and severely abuse trafficking victims, including child soldiers, and punished them for unlawful acts traffickers compelled them to commit (2020)

Illicit drugs: source country for amphetamine tablets destined for Saudi Arabia, Qatar, United Arab Emirates, Libya, Sudan , and other countries in the Gulf, Mediterranean region, and Europe

TAIWAN

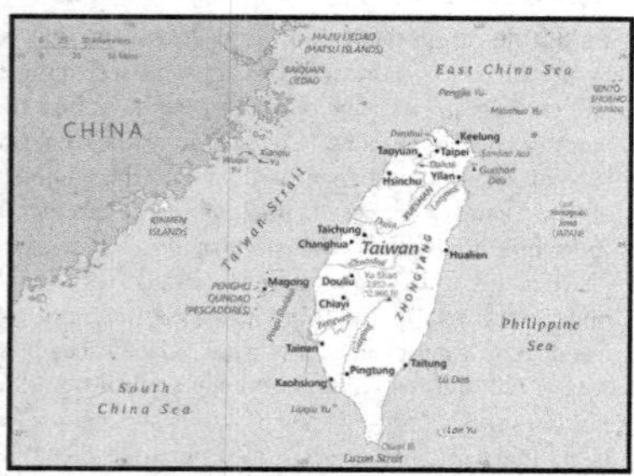

INTRODUCTION

Background: First inhabited by Austronesian people, Taiwan became home to Han immigrants beginning in the late Ming Dynasty (17th century). In 1895, military defeat forced China's Qing Dynasty to cede Taiwan to Japan, which then governed Taiwan for 50 years. Taiwan came under Chinese Nationalist (Kuomintang, KMT) control after World War II. With the communist victory in the Chinese civil war in 1949, the Nationalist-controlled Republic of China government and 2 million Nationalists fled to Taiwan and continued to claim to be the legitimate government for mainland China and Taiwan based on a 1947 constitution drawn up for all of China. Until 1987, however, the Nationalist Government ruled Taiwan under a civil war martial law declaration dating to 1948. Beginning in the 1970s, Nationalist authorities gradually began to incorporate the native population into the governing structure beyond the local level. The democratization process expanded rapidly in the 1980s, leading to the then illegal founding of the Democratic Progressive Party (DPP), Taiwan's first opposition party, in 1986 and the lifting of martial law the following year. Taiwan held legislative elections in 1992, the first in over forty years, and its first direct presidential election in 1996. In the 2000 presidential elections, Taiwan underwent its first peaceful transfer of power with the KMT loss to the DPP and afterwards experienced two additional democratic transfers of power in 2008 and 2016. Throughout this period, the island prospered, became one of East Asia's economic "Tigers," and after 2000 became a major investor in mainland China as cross-Strait ties matured. The dominant political issues continue to be economic reform and growth as well as management of sensitive relations between Taiwan and China.

GEOGRAPHY

Location: Eastern Asia, islands bordering the East China Sea, Philippine Sea, South China Sea, and Taiwan Strait, north of the Philippines, off the southeastern coast of China

Geographic coordinates: 23 30 N, 121 00 E

Map references: Southeast Asia

Area: *total:* 35,980 sq km
land: 32,260 sq km
water: 3,720 sq km
note: includes the Pescadores, Matsu, and Kinmen islands
country comparison to the world: 138

Area - comparative: slightly smaller than Maryland and Delaware combined

Land boundaries: *total:* 0 km

Coastline: 1,566.3 km

Maritime claims: *territorial sea:* 12 nm
exclusive economic zone: 200 nm

Climate: tropical; marine; rainy season during southwest monsoon (June to August); persistent and extensive cloudiness all year

Terrain: eastern two-thirds mostly rugged mountains; flat to gently rolling plains in west

Elevation: *highest point:* Yu Shan 3,952 m
lowest point: South China Sea 0 m
mean elevation: 1,150 m

Natural resources: small deposits of coal, natural gas, limestone, marble, asbestos, arable land

Land use: *agricultural land:* 22.7% (2018 est.)
arable land: 16.9% (2018 est.)
permanent crops: 5.8% (2018 est.)
other: 77.3% (2018 est.)

Irrigated land: 3,820 sq km (2012)

Population distribution: distribution exhibits a peripheral coastal settlement pattern, with the largest populations on the north and west coasts

Natural hazards: earthquakes; typhoons
volcanism: Kueishantao Island (401 m), east of Taiwan, is its only historically active volcano, although it has not erupted in centuries

Geography - note: strategic location adjacent to both the Taiwan Strait and the Luzon Strait

PEOPLE AND SOCIETY

Population: 23,580,712 (2022 est.)
country comparison to the world: 57

Nationality: *noun:* Taiwan (singular and plural)
adjective: Taiwan (or Taiwanese)
note: example - he or she is from Taiwan; they are from Taiwan

Ethnic groups: Han Chinese (including Holo, who compose approximately 70% of Taiwan's population, Hakka, and other groups originating in mainland China) more than 95%, indigenous Malayo-Polynesian peoples 2.3%
note 1: there are 16 officially recognized indigenous groups: Amis, Atayal, Bunun, Hla'alua, Kanakaravu, Kavalan, Paiwan, Puyuma, Rukai, Saisiyat, Sakizaya, Seediq, Thao, Truku, Tsou, and Yami; Amis, Paiwan, and Atayal are the largest and account for roughly 70% of the indigenous population
note 2: although not definitive, the majority of current genetic, archeological, and linguistic data support the theory that Taiwan is the ultimate source for the spread of humans across the Pacific to Polynesia; the expansion (ca. 3000 B.C. to A.D. 1200) took place via the Philippines and eastern Indonesia and reached Fiji and Tonga by about 900 B.C.; from there voyagers spread across the rest of the Pacific islands over the next two millennia

Languages: Mandarin (official), Taiwanese (Min Nan), Hakka dialects, approximately 16 indigenous languages
major-language sample(s):
世界概況 – 不可缺少的基本消息來源 (Mandarin)

Religions: Buddhist 35.3%, Taoist 33.2%, Christian 3.9%, folk religion (includes Confucian) approximately 10%, none or unspecified 18.2% (2005 est.)

Age structure: *0-14 years:* 12.42% (male 1,504,704/female 1,426,494)
15-24 years: 11.62% (male 1,403,117/female 1,339,535)
25-54 years: 45.51% (male 5,351,951/female 5,389,112)
55-64 years: 14.73% (male 1,698,555/female 1,778,529)
65 years and over: 15.72% (male 1,681,476/female 2,029,576) (2020 est.)

Dependency ratios: *total dependency ratio:* 40
youth dependency ratio: 17.8
elderly dependency ratio: 22.2
potential support ratio: 4.5 (2020 est.)

Median age: *total:* 42.3 years
male: 41.5 years
female: 43.1 years (2020 est.)
country comparison to the world: 36

Population growth rate: 0.04% (2022 est.)
country comparison to the world: 191

Birth rate: 7.39 births/1,000 population (2022 est.)
country comparison to the world: 221

Death rate: 7.89 deaths/1,000 population (2022 est.)
country comparison to the world: 98

Net migration rate: 0.85 migrant(s)/1,000 population (2022 est.)
country comparison to the world: 68

Population distribution: distribution exhibits a peripheral coastal settlement pattern, with the largest populations on the north and west coasts

Urbanization: *urban population:* 79.7% of total population (2022)
rate of urbanization: 0.65% annual rate of change (2020-25 est.)

Major urban areas - population: 4.471 million New Taipei City, 2.742 million TAIPEI (capital), 2.296 million Taoyuan, 1.547 million Kaohsiung, 1.354 million Taichung, 863,000 Tainan (2022)

Sex ratio: *at birth:* 1.06 male(s)/female
0-14 years: 1.06 male(s)/female
15-24 years: 1.06 male(s)/female
25-54 years: 1 male(s)/female
55-64 years: 0.95 male(s)/female
65 years and over: 0.73 male(s)/female
total population: 0.97 male(s)/female (2022 est.)

Infant mortality rate: *total:* 3.97 deaths/1,000 live births
male: 4.29 deaths/1,000 live births
female: 3.63 deaths/1,000 live births (2022 est.)
country comparison to the world: 190

Life expectancy at birth: *total population:* 81.16 years
male: 78.17 years
female: 84.34 years (2022 est.)
country comparison to the world: 43

Total fertility rate: 1.08 children born/woman (2022 est.)
country comparison to the world: 227

Literacy: *definition:* age 15 and over can read and write
total population: 98.5%
male: 99.7%
female: 97.3% (2014)

ENVIRONMENT

Environment - current issues: air pollution; water pollution from industrial emissions, raw sewage; contamination of drinking water supplies; trade in endangered species; low-level radioactive waste disposal

Climate: tropical; marine; rainy season during southwest monsoon (June to August); persistent and extensive cloudiness all year

Land use: *agricultural land:* 22.7% (2018 est.)
arable land: 16.9% (2018 est.)
permanent crops: 5.8% (2018 est.)
other: 77.3% (2018 est.)

Urbanization: *urban population:* 79.7% of total population (2022)
rate of urbanization: 0.65% annual rate of change (2020-25 est.)

Waste and recycling: *municipal solid waste generated annually:* 7.336 million tons (2015 est.)

Total renewable water resources: 67 cubic meters (2011)

GOVERNMENT

Country name: *conventional long form:* none
conventional short form: Taiwan
local long form: none
local short form: Taiwan
former: Formosa
etymology: "Tayowan" was the name of the coastal sandbank where the Dutch erected their colonial headquarters on the island in the 17th century; the former name "Formosa" means "beautiful" in Portuguese

Government type: semi-presidential republic

Capital: *name:* Taipei
geographic coordinates: 25 02 N, 121 31 E
time difference: UTC+8 (13 hours ahead of Washington, DC, during Standard Time)
etymology: the Chinese meaning is "Northern Taiwan," reflecting the city's position in the far north of the island

Administrative divisions: includes main island of Taiwan plus smaller islands nearby and off coast of China's Fujian Province; Taiwan is divided into 13 counties (xian, singular and plural), 3 cities (shi, singular and plural), and 6 special municipalities directly under the jurisdiction of the Executive Yuan
counties: Changhua, Chiayi, Hsinchu, Hualien, Kinmen, Lienchiang, Miaoli, Nantou, Penghu, Pingtung, Taitung, Yilan, Yunlin
cities: Chiayi, Hsinchu, Keelung
special municipalities: Kaohsiung (city), New Taipei (city), Taichung (city), Tainan (city), Taipei (city), Taoyuan (city)
note: Taiwan uses a variety of romanization systems; while a modified Wade-Giles system still dominates, the city of Taipei has adopted a Pinyin romanization for street and place names within its boundaries; other local authorities use different romanization systems

National holiday: Republic Day (National Day), 10 October (1911); note - celebrates the anniversary of the Chinese Revolution, also known as Double Ten (10-10) Day

Constitution: *history:* previous 1912, 1931; latest adopted 25 December 1946, promulgated 1 January 1947, effective 25 December 1947
amendments: proposed by at least one fourth of the Legislative Yuan membership; passage requires approval by at least three-fourths majority vote of at least three fourths of the Legislative Yuan membership and approval in a referendum by more than half of eligible voters; revised several times, last in 2005

Legal system: civil law system

International law organization participation: has not submitted an ICJ jurisdiction declaration; non-party state to the ICCt

Citizenship: *citizenship by birth:* no
citizenship by descent only: at least one parent must be a citizen of Taiwan
dual citizenship recognized: yes, except that citizens of Taiwan are not recognized as dual citizens of the People's Republic of China
residency requirement for naturalization: 5 years

Suffrage: 20 years of age; universal; note - in March 2022, the Legislative Yuan approved lowering the voting age to 18, but the change will require a constitutional amendment that must be submitted to a referendum

Executive branch: *chief of state:* President TSAI Ing-wen (since 20 May 2016); Vice President LAI Ching-te (since 20 May 2020)
head of government: Premier SU Tseng-chang (President of the Executive Yuan) (since 11 January 2019); Vice Premier SHEN Jong-chin (Vice President of the Executive Yuan) (since 19 June 2020)
cabinet: Executive Yuan - ministers appointed by president on recommendation of premier
elections/appointments: president and vice president directly elected on the same ballot by simple majority popular vote for a 4-year term (eligible for a second term); election last held on 11 January 2020 (next to be held on 11 January 2024); premier appointed by the president; vice premiers appointed by the president on the recommendation of the premier
election results:
2020: TSAI Ing-wen elected president; percent of vote - TSAI Ing-wen (DPP) 57.1%, HAN Kuo-yu (KMT) 38.6%, James SOONG (PFP) 4.2%; note - TSAI is the first woman elected president of Taiwan
2016: TSAI Ing-wen elected president; percent of vote - TSAI Ing-wen (DPP) 56.1%, Eric CHU (KMT) 31%, James SOONG (PFP) 12.8%

Legislative branch: *description:* unicameral Legislative Yuan (113 seats; 73 members directly elected in single-seat constituencies by simple majority vote, 34 directly elected in a single island-wide constituency by proportional representation vote, and 6 directly elected in multi-seat aboriginal constituencies by proportional representation vote; members serve 4-year terms)
elections:
last held on 11 January 2020 (next to be held on 11 January 2024)
election results:
percent of vote by party - Democratic Progressive Party (DPP) 34.0%, Kuomintang (KMT) 33.4%, Taiwan People's Party (TPP) 11.2%, New Power Party (NPP) 7.5%; seats by party - DPP 61, KMT 38, TPP 5, NPP 3; composition as of early 2020 - men 64, women 48, percent of women 42.5%

Judicial branch: *highest court(s):* Supreme Court (consists of the court president, vice president, and approximately 100 judges organized into 8 civil and 12 criminal divisions, each with a division chief justice and 4 associate justices); Constitutional Court (consists of the court president, vice president, and 13 justices)
judge selection and term of office: Supreme Court justices appointed by the president; Constitutional Court justices appointed by the president, with approval of the Legislative Yuan; Supreme Court justices serve for life; Constitutional Court justices appointed for 8-year terms, with half the membership renewed every 4 years
subordinate courts: high courts; district courts; hierarchy of administrative courts

Political parties and leaders: Democratic Progressive Party or DPP [TSAI Ing-wen]
Kuomintang or KMT (Nationalist Party) [Eric CHU Chi-luan]
New Power Party or NPP [CHEN Jiau-hua]
People First Party or PFP [James SOONG]
Taiwan People's Party or TPP [KO Wen-je]
Taiwan Statebuilding Party or TSP [CHEN Yi-chi]
note: the DPP and the KMT are the two major political parties; there are hundreds of registered minor parties

International organization participation: ADB (Taipei, China), APEC (Chinese Taipei), BCIE, IOC, ITUC (NGOs), SICA (observer), WTO (Taipei, China);
note - separate customs territory of Taiwan, Penghu, Kinmen, and Matsu

Diplomatic representation in the US: *chief of mission:* none; commercial and cultural relations with its citizens in the US are maintained through an unofficial instrumentality, the Taipei Economic and Cultural Representative Office in the United States (TECRO), a private nonprofit corporation that performs citizen and consular services similar to those at diplomatic posts, represented by HSIAO Bikhim (since 20 July 2020); office: 4201 Wisconsin Avenue NW, Washington, DC 20016; telephone: [1] (202) 895-1800

Taipei Economic and Cultural Offices (branch offices): Atlanta, Boston, Chicago, Denver (CO), Houston, Honolulu, Los Angeles, Miami, New York, San Francisco, Seattle

Diplomatic representation from the US: *chief of mission:* the US does not have an embassy in Taiwan; commercial and cultural relations with the people of Taiwan are maintained through an unofficial instrumentality, the American Institute in Taiwan (AIT), a private nonprofit corporation that performs citizen and consular services similar to those at diplomatic posts; it is managed by Director Sandra OUDKIRK (since July 2021)
mailing address: 4170 AIT Taipei Place, Washington DC 20521-4170
telephone: [886] 2-2162-2000
FAX: [886] 2-2162-2251
email address and website:
TaipeiACS@state.gov

https://www.ait.org.tw/
branch office(s): American Institute in Taiwan
No. 100, Jinhu Road,
Neihu District 11461, Taipei City
other offices: Kaohsiung (Branch Office)

Flag description: red field with a dark blue rectangle in the upper hoist-side corner bearing a white sun with 12 triangular rays; the blue and white design of the canton (symbolizing the sun of progress) dates to 1895; it was later adopted as the flag of the Kuomintang Party; blue signifies liberty, justice, and democracy, red stands for fraternity, sacrifice, and nationalism, and white represents equality, frankness, and the people's livelihood; the 12 rays of the sun are those of the months and the twelve traditional Chinese hours (each ray equals two hours)
note: similar to the flag of Samoa

National symbol(s): white, 12-rayed sun on blue field; national colors: blue, white, red

National anthem: *name:* "Zhonghua Minguo guoge" (National Anthem of the Republic of China)
lyrics/music: HU Han-min, TAI Chi-t'ao, and LIAO Chung-k'ai/CHENG Mao-yun
note: adopted 1930; also the song of the Kuomintang Party; it is informally known as "San Min Chu I" or "San Min Zhu Yi" (Three Principles of the People); because of political pressure from China, "Guo Qi Ge" (National Banner Song) is used at international events rather than the official anthem of Taiwan; the "National Banner Song" has gained popularity in Taiwan and is commonly used during flag raisings

ECONOMY

Economic overview: Taiwan has a dynamic capitalist economy that is driven largely by industrial manufacturing, and especially exports of electronics, machinery, and petrochemicals. This heavy dependence on exports exposes the economy to fluctuations in global demand. Taiwan's diplomatic isolation, low birth rate, rapidly aging population, and increasing competition from China and other Asia Pacific markets are other major long-term challenges.

Following the landmark Economic Cooperation Framework Agreement (ECFA) signed with China in June 2010, Taiwan in July 2013 signed a free trade deal with New Zealand - Taipei's first-ever with a country with which it does not maintain diplomatic relations - and, in November of that year, inked a trade pact with Singapore. However, follow-on components of the ECFA, including a signed agreement on trade in services and negotiations on trade in goods and dispute resolution, have stalled. In early 2014, the government bowed to public demand and proposed a new law governing the oversight of cross-Strait agreements, before any additional deals with China are implemented; the legislature has yet to vote on such legislation, leaving the future of ECFA uncertain. President TSAI since taking office in May 2016 has promoted greater economic integration with South and Southeast Asia through the New Southbound Policy initiative and has also expressed interest in Taiwan joining the Trans-Pacific Partnership as well as bilateral trade deals with partners such as the US. These overtures have likely played a role in increasing Taiwan's total exports, which rose 11% during the first half of 2017, buoyed by strong demand for semiconductors.

Taiwan's total fertility rate of just over one child per woman is among the lowest in the world, raising the prospect of future labor shortages, falling domestic demand, and declining tax revenues. Taiwan's population is aging quickly, with the number of people over 65 expected to account for nearly 20% of the island's total population by 2025.

The island runs a trade surplus with many economies, including China and the US, and its foreign reserves are the world's fifth largest, behind those of China, Japan, Saudi Arabia, and Switzerland. In 2006, China overtook the US to become Taiwan's second-largest source of imports after Japan. China is also the island's number one destination for foreign direct investment. Taiwan since 2009 has gradually loosened rules governing Chinese investment and has also secured greater market access for its investors on the mainland. In August 2012, the Taiwan Central Bank signed a memorandum of understanding (MOU) on cross-Strait currency settlement with its Chinese counterpart. The MOU allows for the direct settlement of Chinese renminbi (RMB) and the New Taiwan dollar across the Strait, which has helped Taiwan develop into a local RMB hub.

Closer economic links with the mainland bring opportunities for Taiwan's economy but also pose challenges as political differences remain unresolved and China's economic growth is slowing. President TSAI's administration has made little progress on the domestic economic issues that loomed large when she was elected, including concerns about stagnant wages, high housing prices, youth unemployment, job security, and financial security in retirement. TSAI has made more progress on boosting trade with South and Southeast Asia, which may help insulate Taiwan's economy from a fall in mainland demand should China's growth slow in 2018.

Real GDP (purchasing power parity): $1,143,277,000,000 (2019 est.)
$1,113,126,000,000 (2018 est.)
$1,083,384,000,000 (2017 est.)
note: data are in 2010 dollars
country comparison to the world: 22

Real GDP growth rate: 2.71% (2019 est.)
2.75% (2018 est.)
3.31% (2017 est.)
country comparison to the world: 104

Real GDP per capita: $24,502 (2018 est.)
$50,500 (2017 est.)
$23,865 (2017 est.)
note: data are in 2017 dollars
country comparison to the world: 76

GDP (official exchange rate): $611.391 billion (2019 est.)

Inflation rate (consumer prices): 0.5% (2019 est.)
1.3% (2018 est.)
0.6% (2017 est.)
country comparison to the world: 45

Credit ratings:

Fitch rating: AA- (2016)

Moody's rating: Aa3 (1994)

Standard & Poors rating: AA- (2002)

GDP - composition, by sector of origin: *agriculture:* 1.8% (2017 est.)
industry: 36% (2017 est.)
services: 62.1% (2017 est.)

GDP - composition, by end use: *household consumption:* 53% (2017 est.)
government consumption: 14.1% (2017 est.)
investment in fixed capital: 20.5% (2017 est.)
investment in inventories: -0.2% (2017 est.)
exports of goods and services: 65.2% (2017 est.)
imports of goods and services: -52.6% (2017 est.)

Agricultural products: rice, vegetables, pork, cabbages, poultry, sugar cane, milk, eggs, pineapples, tropical fruit

Industries: electronics, communications and information technology products, petroleum refining, chemicals, textiles, iron and steel, machinery, cement, food processing, vehicles, consumer products, pharmaceuticals

Industrial production growth rate: 3.9% (2017 est.)
country comparison to the world: 79

Labor force: 11.498 million (2020 est.)
country comparison to the world: 47

Labor force - by occupation: *agriculture:* 4.9%
industry: 35.9%
services: 59.2% (2016 est.)

Unemployment rate: 3.73% (2019 est.)
3.69% (2018 est.)
country comparison to the world: 55

Population below poverty line: 1.5% (2012 est.)

Gini Index coefficient - distribution of family income: 33.6 (2014)
32.6 (2000)
country comparison to the world: 126

Household income or consumption by percentage share: *lowest 10%:* 6.4% (2010)
highest 10%: 40.3% (2010)

Budget: *revenues:* 91.62 billion (2017 est.)
expenditures: 92.03 billion (2017 est.)

Budget surplus (+) or deficit (-): -0.1% (of GDP) (2017 est.)
country comparison to the world: 50

Public debt: 35.7% of GDP (2017 est.)
36.2% of GDP (2016 est.)
note: data for central government
country comparison to the world: 149

Taxes and other revenues: 16% (of GDP) (2017 est.)
country comparison to the world: 184

Fiscal year: calendar year

Current account balance: $65.173 billion (2019 est.)
$70.843 billion (2018 est.)
country comparison to the world: 7

Exports: $388.49 billion (2019 est.)
$383.484 billion (2018 est.)
$382.736 billion (2017 est.)
country comparison to the world: 19

Exports - partners: China 26%, United States 14%, Hong Kong 12%, Japan 7%, Singapore 7%, South Korea 5% (2019)

Exports - commodities: integrated circuits, office machinery/parts, computers, refined petroleum, liquid crystal displays (2019)

Imports: $308.744 billion (2019 est.)
$305.428 billion (2018 est.)
$303.067 billion (2017 est.)
country comparison to the world: 19

Imports - partners: China 21%, Japan 16%, United States 11%, South Korea 6% (2019)

Imports - commodities: integrated circuits, crude petroleum, photography equipment, natural gas, refined petroleum (2019)

Reserves of foreign exchange and gold: $456.7 billion (31 December 2017 est.)
$439 billion (31 December 2016 est.)
country comparison to the world: 5

Debt - external: $189.684 billion (2019 est.)
$196.276 billion (2018 est.)
country comparison to the world: 42

Exchange rates: New Taiwan dollars (TWD) per US dollar -
28.211 (2020 est.)
30.472 (2019 est.)
30.8395 (2018 est.)
31.911 (2014 est.)
30.363 (2013 est.)

ENERGY

Electricity: *installed generating capacity:* 57.738 million kW (2020 est.)
consumption: 269,570,325,000 kWh (2020 est.)
exports: 0 kWh (2020 est.)
imports: 0 kWh (2020 est.)
transmission/distribution losses: 9.484 billion kWh (2020 est.)

Electricity generation sources fossil fuels: 82.2% of total installed capacity (2020 est.)
nuclear: 11.2% of total installed capacity (2020 est.)
solar: 2.2% of total installed capacity (2020 est.)
wind: 0.9% of total installed capacity (2020 est.)
hydroelectricity: 2.2% of total installed capacity (2020 est.)
biomass and waste: 1.3% of total installed capacity (2020 est.)

Coal: *production:* 5.955 million metric tons (2020 est.)
consumption: 67.985 million metric tons (2020 est.)
exports: 118,000 metric tons (2020 est.)
imports: 63.523 million metric tons (2020 est.)
proven reserves: 1 million metric tons (2019 est.)

Petroleum: *total petroleum production:* 800 bbl/day (2021 est.)
refined petroleum consumption: 998,100 bbl/day (2019 est.)
crude oil and lease condensate exports: 0 bbl/day (2018 est.)
crude oil and lease condensate imports: 886,200 bbl/day (2018 est.)
crude oil estimated reserves: 2.4 million barrels (2021 est.)

Refined petroleum products - production: 924,000 bbl/day (2015 est.)
country comparison to the world: 21

Refined petroleum products - exports: 349,600 bbl/day (2015 est.)
country comparison to the world: 26

Refined petroleum products - imports: 418,300 bbl/day (2015 est.)
country comparison to the world: 20

Natural gas: *production:* 150.589 million cubic meters (2019 est.)
consumption: 22,002,493,000 cubic meters (2019 est.)
exports: 0 cubic meters (2021 est.)
imports: 22,172,507,000 cubic meters (2019 est.)
proven reserves: 6.23 billion cubic meters (2021 est.)

Carbon dioxide emissions: 279.206 million metric tonnes of CO2 (2019 est.)
from coal and metallurgical coke: 141.445 million metric tonnes of CO2 (2019 est.)
from petroleum and other liquids: 92.207 million metric tonnes of CO2 (2019 est.)
from consumed natural gas: 45.554 million metric tonnes of CO2 (2019 est.)
country comparison to the world: 23

Energy consumption per capita: 160.669 million Btu/person (2019 est.)
country comparison to the world: 32

COMMUNICATIONS

Telephones - fixed lines: *total subscriptions:* 12,971,900 (2019 est.)
subscriptions per 100 inhabitants: 55 (2019 est.)
country comparison to the world: 16

Telephones - mobile cellular: *total subscriptions:* 29,291,500 (2019)
subscriptions per 100 inhabitants: 123.21 (2019)
country comparison to the world: 47

Telecommunication systems: *general assessment:* Taiwan has a highly developed telecoms sector in both the fixed-line and mobile segments; in part this is due to the country's early moves to liberalize the market, allowing vigorous competition to flourish; the government has also made concerted efforts to take advantage of Taiwan's strengths in the development of high-tech, export-oriented industries to encourage and enable the rapid adoption of advanced telecom platforms, while simultaneously leveraging the same telecoms infrastructure to push even further ahead with the country's industrial development plans; Taiwan has one of the highest teledensities in the region; while fixed-line subscriber numbers are trending downwards, the rate of decline has been slowed by the major fixed-line provider investing strongly in building out a widespread fiber network to allow customers to maintain a terrestrial voice connection as part of a fixed broadband package; fiber is the dominant platform in Taiwan's fixed broadband market; cable services have retained an unusually strong following thanks to the success of cable providers in delivering competitive cable TV and telephony services as a way to get around Chunghwa Telecom's control of the last mile for its copper and fiber networks; Taiwan also has high penetration rates in its mobile and mobile broadband segments, growth in both markets is almost at a standstill because the country reached 100% penetration very early on – way back when GSM was first introduced, in mobile's case; the MNOs moved quickly to roll out 4G and 5G networks and services in rapid succession, but subscriber numbers (and market share) has barely changed; the improved quality and performance available with the new platforms will drive increased usage and ARPU; fierce competition following the launch of 4G saw the opposite happen, with price wars causing telco revenues to fall instead; it is possible that the same problem can be avoided with 5G allowing Taiwan to reach the target of 50% of subscribers on 5G by mid-2023 (2022)
domestic: fixed-line over 53 per 100 and mobile-cellular roughly 123 per 100 (2020)
international: country code - 886; landing points for the EAC-C2C, APCN-2, FASTER, SJC2, TSE-1, TPE, APG, SeaMeWe-3, FLAG North Asia Loop/REACH North Asia Loop, HKA, NCP, and PLCN submarine fiber cables provide links throughout Asia, Australia, the Middle East, Europe, Africa and the US; satellite earth stations - 2 (2019)

Broadcast media: 5 nationwide television networks operating roughly 22 TV stations; more than 300 satellite TV channels are available; about 60% of households utilize multi-channel cable TV; 99.9% of households subscribe to digital cable TV; national and regional radio networks with about 171 radio stations (2019)

Internet country code: .tw

Internet users: *total:* 21,158,750 (2019 est.)
percent of population: 89% (2019 est.)
country comparison to the world: 38

Broadband - fixed subscriptions: *total:* 5,831,470 (2019 est.)
subscriptions per 100 inhabitants: 25 (2019 est.)
country comparison to the world: 31

TRANSPORTATION

National air transport system: *number of registered air carriers:* 7 (2020)
inventory of registered aircraft operated by air carriers: 216

Civil aircraft registration country code prefix: B

Airports: *total:* 37 (2021)
country comparison to the world: 107

Airports - with paved runways: *total:* 35
over 3,047 m: 8
2,438 to 3,047 m: 7
1,524 to 2,437 m: 10
914 to 1,523 m: 8
under 914 m: 2 (2021)

Airports - with unpaved runways: *total:* 2
1,524 to 2,437 m: 1
under 914 m: 1 (2021)

Heliports: 31 (2021)

Pipelines: 25 km condensate, 2,200 km gas, 13,500 km oil (2018)

Railways: *total:* 1,613.1 km (2018)
standard gauge: 345 km (2018) 1.435-m gauge (345 km electrified)
narrow gauge: 1,118.1 km (2018) 1.067-m gauge (793.9 km electrified)
150 0.762-m gauge **note:** the 0.762-gauge track belongs to three entities: the Forestry Bureau, Taiwan Cement, and TaiPower
country comparison to the world: 81

Roadways: *total:* 43,206 km (2017)
paved: 42,793 km (2017) (includes 1,348 km of highways and 737 km of expressways)
*unpaved:*413 km (2017)
country comparison to the world: 87

Merchant marine: *total:* 429
by type: bulk carrier 37, container ship 49, general cargo 57, oil tanker 33, other 253 (2021)
country comparison to the world: 45

Ports and terminals: *major seaport(s):* Keelung (Chi-lung), Kaohsiung, Hualian, Taichung
container port(s) (TEUs): Kaohsiung (10,428,634), Taichung (1,793,966), Taipei (1,620,392) (2019)

LNG terminal(s) (import): Yung An (Kaohsiung), Taichung

MILITARY AND SECURITY

Military and security forces: Taiwan Armed Forces: Army, Navy (includes Marine Corps), Air Force; Taiwan Coast Guard Administration (a law enforcement organization with homeland security functions during peacetime and national defense missions during wartime); Ministry of Interior: National Police (2022)

Military expenditures: 2.2% of GDP (2022 est.)
2.1% of GDP (2021)
2.1% of GDP (2020)
1.8% of GDP (2019) (approximately $23.6 billion)
1.7% of GDP (2018) (approximately $21.9 billion)
country comparison to the world: 51

Military and security service personnel strengths: approximately 170,000 active duty troops (90,000 Army; 40,000 Navy, including approximately 10,000 marines; 40,000 Air Force) (2022)
note: Taiwan trains about 120,000 reservists annually, but in 2022 announced intentions to increase that figure to 260,000

Military equipment inventories and acquisitions: the Taiwan military is armed mostly with second-hand weapons and equipment provided by the US; since 2010, the US has continued to be the largest provider of arms; Taiwan also has a domestic defense industry capable of building and upgrading a range of weapons systems, including surface ships and submarines (2022)

Military service age and obligation: starting with those born in 1994, men 18-36 years of age may volunteer for military service or must complete 4 months of compulsory military training (5 weeks of basic training followed by 11 weeks of specialized training with field units); civil service can be substituted for military service in some cases; men born before December 1993 are required to complete compulsory service for 12 months (military or civil); men are subject to training recalls up to four times for periods not to exceed 20 days for 8 years after discharge; women may enlist but are restricted to noncombat roles in most cases; as part of its transition to an all-volunteer military, the last cohort of 12-month military conscripts completed their service obligations in December 2018 (2022)
note: as of 2021, women made up about 15% of the active duty military

Military - note: the US Taiwan Relations Act of April 1979 states that the US shall provide Taiwan with arms of a defensive character and shall maintain the capacity of the US to resist any resort to force or other forms of coercion that would jeopardize the security, or social or economic system, of the people of Taiwan (2022)

TRANSNATIONAL ISSUES

Disputes - international: *Taiwan-Brunei-China-Malaysia-Philippines-Vietnam:* involved in complex dispute over the Spratly Islands in the South China Sea that are thought to have large oil and natural gas reserves, as well as being located amidst prime fishing grounds and busy commercial shipping traffic; the Spratly Islands also are in a strategic position for establishing a military presence to monitor activity in the South China Sea; the 2002 "Declaration on the Conduct of Parties in the South China Sea" has eased tensions but falls short of a legally binding "code of conduct" desired by several of the disputants
Taiwan-China-Philippines: border dispute over the Scarborough Reef in the South China Sea; Scarborough Reef, like the Spratly Islands, is strategically located and is surrounded by abundant fishing grounds; it may also be ripe for oil and natural gas exploration
Taiwan-China-Vietnam: the Paracel Islands are occupied by China but claimed by Taiwan and Vietnam
Taiwan-Japan-China: in 2003, China and Taiwan became more vocal in rejecting both Japan's claims to the uninhabited islands of the Senkaku-shoto (Diaoyu Tai) and Japan's unilaterally declared exclusive economic zone in the East China Sea where all parties engage in hydrocarbon prospecting; Senkaku-shoto is situated near key shipping lanes, rich fishing grounds, and possibly significant oil and natural gas reserves

Illicit drugs: major source of precursor chemicals used in the production of illicit narcotics

TAJIKISTAN

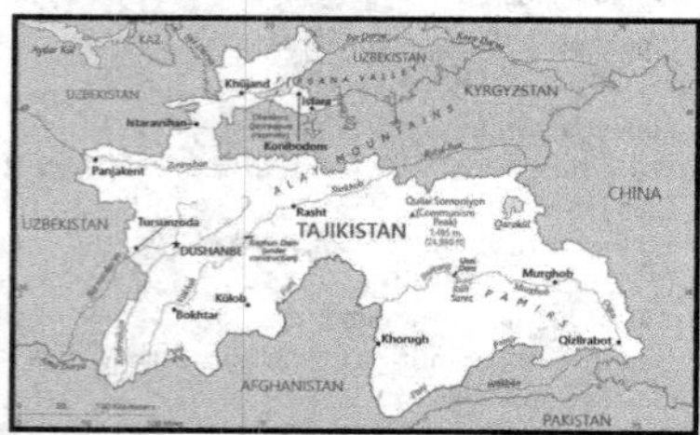

INTRODUCTION

Background: The Tajik people came under Russian imperial rule in the 1860s and 1870s, but Russia's hold on Central Asia weakened following the Revolution of 1917. At that time, bands of indigenous guerrillas (known as "basmachi") fiercely contested Bolshevik control of the area, which was not fully reestablished until 1925. Tajikistan was first created as an autonomous republic within Uzbekistan in 1924, but in 1929 the USSR designated Tajikistan a separate republic and transferred to it much of present-day Sughd Province. Ethnic Uzbeks form a substantial minority in Tajikistan, and ethnic Tajiks an even larger minority in Uzbekistan. Tajikistan became independent in 1991 following the breakup of the Soviet Union, and experienced a civil war between political, regional, and religious factions from 1992 to 1997.

Though the country holds general elections for both the presidency (once every seven years) and legislature (once every five years), observers note an electoral system rife with irregularities and abuse, with results that are neither free nor fair. President Emomali RAHMON, who came to power in 1992 during the civil war and was first elected president in 1994, used an attack planned by a disaffected deputy defense minister in 2015 to ban the last major opposition political party in Tajikistan. In December 2015, RAHMON further strengthened his position by having himself declared "Founder of Peace and National Unity, Leader of the Nation," with limitless terms and lifelong immunity through constitutional amendments ratified in a referendum. The referendum also lowered the minimum age required to run for president from 35 to 30, which made RAHMON's first-born son Rustam EMOMALI, the mayor of the capital city of Dushanbe, eligible to run for president in 2020. In April 2020, RAHMON orchestrated EMOMALI's selection as chairman of the Majlisi Milli (Tajikistan's senate), positioning EMOMALI as next in line of succession for the presidency. RAHMON opted to run in the presidential election in October 2020 and received 91% of the vote.

The country remains the poorest in the former Soviet sphere. Tajikistan became a member of the WTO in March 2013. However, its economy continues to face major challenges, including dependence on remittances from Tajikistani migrant laborers working in Russia and Kazakhstan, pervasive corruption, and the opiate trade and other destabilizing violence emanating from neighboring Afghanistan. Tajikistan has endured several domestic security incidents since 2010, including armed conflict between government forces and local strongmen in the Rasht Valley and between government forces and residents and informal leaders in Gorno-Badakhshan Autonomous Oblast. Tajikistan suffered its first ISIS-claimed attack in 2018, when assailants attacked a group of Western bicyclists with vehicles and knives, killing four.

GEOGRAPHY

Location: Central Asia, west of China, south of Kyrgyzstan

Geographic coordinates: 39 00 N, 71 00 E

Map references: Asia

Area: *total:* 144,100 sq km
land: 141,510 sq km
water: 2,590 sq km
country comparison to the world: 96

Area - comparative: slightly smaller than Wisconsin

Land boundaries: *total:* 4,130 km
border countries (4): Afghanistan 1,357 km; China 477 km; Kyrgyzstan 984 km; Uzbekistan 1,312 km

Coastline: 0 km (landlocked)

Maritime claims: none (landlocked)

Climate: mid-latitude continental, hot summers, mild winters; semiarid to polar in Pamir Mountains

Terrain: mountainous region dominated by the Alay Mountains in the north and the Pamirs in the southeast; western Fergana Valley in north, Kofirnihon and Vakhsh Valleys in southwest

Elevation: *highest point:* Qullai Somoniyon 7,495 m
lowest point: Syr Darya (Sirdaryo) 300 m
mean elevation: 3,186 m

Natural resources: hydropower, some petroleum, uranium, mercury, brown coal, lead, zinc, antimony, tungsten, silver, gold

Land use: *agricultural land:* 34.7% (2018 est.)
arable land: 6.1% (2018 est.)
permanent crops: 0.9% (2018 est.)
permanent pasture: 27.7% (2018 est.)
forest: 2.9% (2018 est.)
other: 62.4% (2018 est.)

Irrigated land: 7,420 sq km (2012)

Major rivers (by length in km): Syr Darya (shared with Kyrgyzstan [s], Uzbekistan, and Kazakhstan [m]) - 3,078 km; Amu Darya river source (shared with Turkmenistan, Afghanistan, and Uzbekistan [m]) - 2,620 km
note – [s] after country name indicates river source; [m] after country name indicates river mouth

Major watersheds (area sq km): Internal *(endorheic basin)* drainage: Tarim Basin (1,152,448 sq km), *(Aral Sea Basin)* Amu Darya (534,739 sq km), Syr Darya (782,617 sq km)

Population distribution: the country's population is concentrated at lower elevations, with perhaps as much as 90% of the people living in valleys; overall density increases from east to west

Natural hazards: earthquakes; floods

Geography - note: landlocked; highest point, Qullai Ismoili Somoni (formerly Communism Peak), was the tallest mountain in the former USSR

PEOPLE AND SOCIETY

Population: 9,119,347 (2022 est.)
country comparison to the world: 97

Nationality: *noun:* Tajikistani(s)
adjective: Tajikistani

Ethnic groups: Tajik 84.3% (includes Pamiri and Yagnobi), Uzbek 13.8%, other 2% (includes Kyrgyz, Russian, Turkmen, Tatar, Arab) (2014 est.)

Languages: Tajik (official) 84.4%, Uzbek 11.9%, Kyrgyz 0.8%, Russian 0.5%, other 2.4% (2010 est.)
major-language sample(s):

Китоби Фактҳои Ҷаҳонӣ, манбаи бебадали маълумоти асосӣ (Tajik)

note: Russian widely used in government and business

Religions: Muslim 98% (Sunni 95%, Shia 3%) other 2% (2014 est.)

Demographic profile: Tajikistan has a youthful age structure with almost 50% of the population under the age of 25. As a Soviet republic, Tajikistan had the highest fertility rate in the Soviet Union. The total fertility rate – the average number of births per woman – was highest in the mid-1970s, when it reached 6.3. In an effort to expand populations to meet economic goals, the Soviets provided resources that made large families affordable. The fertility rate decreased to 5 by the time of independence in 1991 and continued to decline thereafter. In 1996, the Tajik Government discontinued subsidies for large families and having several children became too expensive. The loss of subsidies, the 5-year civil war that followed independence, and other factors caused fertility to continue to fall steadily, but it remains above replacement level at 2.5. The availability of healthcare providers and family planning services is limited, contributing to couples having more children than they would like. As of 2017, 21% of women were using contraceptives.

Tajikistan's ethnic make-up changed with the Soviet's introduction of industrialization. Large numbers of Russian and Ukrainian immigrants arrived in the mid-1920s. Some were forced to immigrate while others came voluntarily to work in the cotton industry and in Tajikistan's Soviet Government. The Russian and Ukrainian immigrants formed urban communities, while Tajiks and Uzbeks continued to live predominantly in rural areas. In addition, thousands of Tatars and Germans were deported to Tajikistan, accused of Nazi complicity during WWII.

Tajikistan's ethnic composition was later shaped by the post-independence civil war from 1992-1997 and the economic devastation that followed. Most non-Tajik ethnic groups, including Uzbeks, Russians, Kyrgyz, and Ukrainians, fled to Russia and other former Soviet republics and many never returned, making the country overwhelming Tajik; approximately 80% of the population was Tajik by 2000.

Since the mid-1990s, labor has probably been Tajikistan's main export. Remittances accounted for 30% of GDP in 2018 and are Tajikistan's largest source of external income. Poverty, a lack of jobs, and higher wages abroad push Tajiks to emigrate. Russia – particularly Moscow – is the main destination, while a smaller number of religious Muslims, usually of Uzbek ancestry, migrate to Uzbekistan. The vast majority of labor migrants are unskilled or low-skilled young men who work primarily in construction but also agriculture, transportation, and retail. Many Tajik families are dependent on the money they send home for necessities, such as food and clothing, as well as for education and weddings rather than investment.

Age structure: *0-14 years:* 31.43% (male 1,420,271/female 1,368,445)
15-24 years: 18.13% (male 816,658/female 792,231)
25-54 years: 40.58% (male 1,789,271/female 1,811,566)
55-64 years: 6.23% (male 253,862/female 299,378)
65 years and over: 3.63% (male 132,831/female 189,156) (2020 est.)

Dependency ratios: *total dependency ratio:* 67.9
youth dependency ratio: 62.6
elderly dependency ratio: 5.3
potential support ratio: 18.7 (2020 est.)

Median age: *total:* 25.3 years
male: 24.6 years
female: 26 years (2020 est.)
country comparison to the world: 162

Population growth rate: 1.4% (2022 est.)
country comparison to the world: 69

Birth rate: 20.73 births/1,000 population (2022 est.)
country comparison to the world: 68

Death rate: 5.72 deaths/1,000 population (2022 est.)
country comparison to the world: 172

Net migration rate: -1.03 migrant(s)/1,000 population (2022 est.)
country comparison to the world: 147

Population distribution: the country's population is concentrated at lower elevations, with perhaps as much as 90% of the people living in valleys; overall density increases from east to west

Urbanization: *urban population:* 28% of total population (2022)
rate of urbanization: 2.73% annual rate of change (2020-25 est.)

Major urban areas - population: 962,000 DUSHANBE (capital) (2022)

Sex ratio: *at birth:* 1.05 male(s)/female
0-14 years: 1.04 male(s)/female
15-24 years: 1.03 male(s)/female
25-54 years: 0.98 male(s)/female
55-64 years: 0.84 male(s)/female
65 years and over: 0.48 male(s)/female
total population: 0.99 male(s)/female (2022 est.)

Mother's mean age at first birth: 23.2 years (2017 est.)

Maternal mortality ratio: 17 deaths/100,000 live births (2017 est.)
country comparison to the world: 132

Infant mortality rate: *total:* 32.33 deaths/1,000 live births
male: 37.03 deaths/1,000 live births
female: 27.39 deaths/1,000 live births (2022 est.)
country comparison to the world: 48

Life expectancy at birth: *total population:* 69.36 years
male: 66.2 years
female: 72.69 years (2022 est.)
country comparison to the world: 179

Total fertility rate: 2.45 children born/woman (2022 est.)
country comparison to the world: 70

Contraceptive prevalence rate: 29.3% (2017)

Drinking water source: *improved: urban:* 96.5% of population
rural: 79.9% of population
total: 84.4% of population
unimproved: urban: 3.5% of population
rural: 20.1% of population
total: 15.6% of population (2020 est.)

Current health expenditure: 7.1% of GDP (2019)

Physicians density: 1.72 physicians/1,000 population (2014)

Hospital bed density: 4.7 beds/1,000 population (2014)

Sanitation facility access: *improved: urban:* 98.9% of population
rural: 99.6% of population
total: 99.4% of population
unimproved: urban: 1.1% of population
rural: 0.4% of population
total: 0.6% of population (2020 est.)

HIV/AIDS - adult prevalence rate: 0.2% (2020 est.)
country comparison to the world: 115

HIV/AIDS - people living with HIV/AIDS: 14,000 (2020 est.)
country comparison to the world: 95

HIV/AIDS - deaths: (2020 est.) <500

Major infectious diseases: *degree of risk:* high (2020)
food or waterborne diseases: bacterial diarrhea, hepatitis A, and typhoid fever
vectorborne diseases: malaria
note: on 21 March 2022, the US Centers for Disease Control and Prevention (CDC) issued a Travel Alert for polio in Asia; Tajikistan is currently considered a high risk to travelers for circulating vaccine-derived polioviruses (cVDPV); vaccine-derived poliovirus (VDPV) is a strain of the weakened poliovirus that was initially included in oral polio vaccine (OPV) and *that has changed over time and behaves more like the wild or naturally occurring virus*; this means it can be spread more easily to people who are unvaccinated against polio and who come in contact with the stool or respiratory secretions, such as from a sneeze, of an "infected" person who received oral polio vaccine; the CDC recommends that before any international travel, anyone unvaccinated, incompletely vaccinated, or with an unknown polio vaccination status should complete the routine polio vaccine series; before travel to any high-risk destination, CDC recommends that adults who previously

completed the full, routine polio vaccine series receive a single, lifetime booster dose of polio vaccine

Obesity - adult prevalence rate: 14.2% (2016)
country comparison to the world: 128

Alcohol consumption per capita: *total:* 0.85 liters of pure alcohol (2019 est.)
beer: 0.38 liters of pure alcohol (2019 est.)
wine: 0.01 liters of pure alcohol (2019 est.)
spirits: 0.45 liters of pure alcohol (2019 est.)
other alcohols: 0 liters of pure alcohol (2019 est.)
country comparison to the world: 156

Children under the age of 5 years underweight: 7.6% (2017)
country comparison to the world: 66

Child marriage: *women married by age 15:* 0.1%
women married by age 18: 8.7% (2017 est.)

Education expenditures: 5.7% of GDP (2019 est.)
country comparison to the world: 39

Literacy: *definition:* age 15 and over can read and write
total population: 99.8%
male: 99.8%
female: 99.7% (2015)

School life expectancy (primary to tertiary education): *total:* 11 years
male: 12 years
female: 11 years (2013)

ENVIRONMENT

Environment - current issues: areas of high air pollution from motor vehicles and industry; water pollution from agricultural runoff and disposal of untreated industrial waste and sewage; poor management of water resources; soil erosion; increasing levels of soil salinity

Environment - international agreements: *party to:* Biodiversity, Climate Change, Climate Change-Kyoto Protocol, Climate Change-Paris Agreement, Comprehensive Nuclear Test Ban, Desertification, Endangered Species, Environmental Modification, Hazardous Wastes, Ozone Layer Protection, Ship Pollution, Wetlands
signed, but not ratified: none of the selected agreements

Air pollutants: *particulate matter emissions:* 40.05 micrograms per cubic meter (2016 est.)
carbon dioxide emissions: 5.31 megatons (2016 est.)
methane emissions: 4.87 megatons (2020 est.)

Climate: mid-latitude continental, hot summers, mild winters; semiarid to polar in Pamir Mountains

Land use: *agricultural land:* 34.7% (2018 est.)
arable land: 6.1% (2018 est.)
permanent crops: 0.9% (2018 est.)
permanent pasture: 27.7% (2018 est.)
forest: 2.9% (2018 est.)
other: 62.4% (2018 est.)

Urbanization: *urban population:* 28% of total population (2022)
rate of urbanization: 2.73% annual rate of change (2020-25 est.)

Revenue from forest resources: *forest revenues:* 1.12% of GDP (2018 est.)
country comparison to the world: 51

Revenue from coal: *coal revenues:* 0.54% of GDP (2018 est.)
country comparison to the world: 10

Waste and recycling: *municipal solid waste generated annually:* 1,787,400 tons (2013 est.)

Major rivers (by length in km): Syr Darya (shared with Kyrgyzstan [s], Uzbekistan, and Kazakhstan [m]) - 3,078 km; Amu Darya river source (shared with Turkmenistan, Afghanistan, and Uzbekistan [m]) - 2,620 km
note – [s] after country name indicates river source; [m] after country name indicates river mouth

Major watersheds (area sq km): Internal *(endorheic basin)* drainage: Tarim Basin (1,152,448 sq km), *(Aral Sea Basin)* Amu Darya (534,739 sq km), Syr Darya (782,617 sq km)

Total water withdrawal: *municipal:* 647 million cubic meters (2017 est.)
industrial: 407.8 million cubic meters (2017 est.)
agricultural: 10.44 billion cubic meters (2017 est.)

Total renewable water resources: 21.91 billion cubic meters (2017 est.)

GOVERNMENT

Country name: *conventional long form:* Republic of Tajikistan
conventional short form: Tajikistan
local long form: Jumhurii Tojikiston
local short form: Tojikiston
former: Tajik Soviet Socialist Republic
etymology: the Persian suffix "-stan" means "place of" or "country," so the word Tajikistan literally means "Land of the Tajik [people]"

Government type: presidential republic

Capital: *name:* Dushanbe
geographic coordinates: 38 33 N, 68 46 E
time difference: UTC+5 (10 hours ahead of Washington, DC, during Standard Time)
etymology: today's city was originally at the crossroads where a large bazaar occurred on Mondays, hence the name Dushanbe, which in Persian means Monday, i.e., the second day (du) after Saturday *(shambe)*

Administrative divisions: 2 provinces (viloyatho, singular - viloyat), 1 autonomous province* (viloyati mukhtor), 1 capital region** (viloyati poytakht), and 1 area referred to as Districts Under Republic Administration***; Dushanbe**, Khatlon (Bokhtar), Kuhistoni Badakhshon [Gorno-Badakhshan]* (Khorugh), Nohiyahoi Tobei Jumhuri***, Sughd (Khujand)
note: the administrative center name follows in parentheses

Independence: 9 September 1991 (from the Soviet Union)

National holiday: Independence Day (or National Day), 9 September (1991)

Constitution: *history:* several previous; latest adopted 6 November 1994
amendments: proposed by the president of the republic or by at least one third of the total membership of both houses of the Supreme Assembly; adoption of any amendment requires a referendum, which includes approval of the president or approval by at least two-thirds majority of the Assembly of Representatives; passage in a referendum requires participation of an absolute majority of eligible voters and an absolute majority of votes; constitutional articles, including Tajikistan's form of government, its territory, and its democratic nature, cannot be amended; amended 1999, 2003, 2016

Legal system: civil law system

International law organization participation: has not submitted an ICJ jurisdiction declaration; accepts ICCt jurisdiction

Citizenship: *citizenship by birth:* no
citizenship by descent only: at least one parent must be a citizen of Tajikistan
dual citizenship recognized: no
residency requirement for naturalization: 5 years or 3 years of continuous residence prior to application

Suffrage: 18 years of age; universal

Executive branch: *chief of state:* President Emomali RAHMON (since 6 November 1994; head of state and Supreme Assembly Chairman since 19 November 1992)
head of government: Prime Minister Qohir RASULZODA (since 23 November 2013)
cabinet: Council of Ministers appointed by the president, approved by the Supreme Assembly
elections/appointments: president directly elected by simple majority popular vote for a 7-year term for a maximum of two terms; however, as the "Leader of the Nation" President RAHMON can run an unlimited number of times; election last held on 11 October 2020 (next to be held in 2027); prime minister appointed by the president
election results:
2020: Emomali RAHMON reelected president; percent of vote - Emomali RAHMON (PDPT) 92.1%, Rustam LATIFZODA 3.1%, and other 4.8%
2013: Emomali RAHMOND reelected president; percent of vote 84%, Ismoil TALBAKOV 5%, other 11%

Legislative branch: *description:* bicameral Supreme Assembly or Majlisi Oli consists of:
National Assembly or Majlisi Milli (34 seats; 25 members indirectly elected by local representative assemblies or majlisi, 8 appointed by the president, and 1 reserved for each living former president; members serve 5-year terms)
Assembly of Representatives or Majlisi Namoyandagon (63 seats; 41 members directly elected in single-seat constituencies by 2-round absolute majority vote and 22 directly elected in a single nationwide constituency by closed-list proportional representation vote; members serve 5-year terms)
elections:
National Assembly - last held on 1 March 2020 (next to be held in 2025)
Assembly of Representatives - last held on 1 March 2020 (next to be held in 2025)
election results:
National Assembly - percent of vote by party - NA; seats by party - NA; composition as of mid-2202 (31 members) - men 23, women 8, percent of women 25.8%
Assembly of Representatives - percent of vote by party - PDPT 50.4%, PERT 16.6%, APT 16.5%, SPT 5.2%, DPT 5.1%, CPT 3.1%, other 3.1%; seats by party - PDPT 47, APT 7, PERT 5, CPT 2, SPT 1, DPT 1; composition as of mid 2022 -men 46, women 17, percent of women 27%; note - total Supreme Assembly percent of women 26.6%

Judicial branch: *highest court(s):* Supreme Court (consists of the chairman, deputy chairmen, and 34 judges organized into civil, family, criminal, administrative offense, and military chambers); Constitutional Court (consists of the court chairman, deputy chairman, and 5 judges); High Economic Court (consists of 16 judicial positions)

judge selection and term of office: Supreme Court, Constitutional Court, and High Economic Court judges nominated by the president and approved by the National Assembly; judges of all 3 courts appointed for 10-year renewable terms with no term limits, but the last appointment must occur before the age of 65
subordinate courts: regional and district courts; Dushanbe City Court; viloyat (province level) courts; Court of Gorno-Badakhshan Autonomous Region

Political parties and leaders: Agrarian Party of Tajikistan or APT [Rustam LATIFZODA]
Communist Party of Tajikistan or CPT [Miroj ABDULLOEV]
Democratic Party of Tajikistan or DPT [Saidjafar USMONZODA]
Party of Economic Reform of Tajikistan or PERT [Rustam RAHMATZODA]
People's Democratic Party of Tajikistan or PDPT [Emomali RAHMON]
Social Democratic Party of Tajikistan or SDPT [vacant]
Socialist Party of Tajikistan or SPT [Abduhalim GHAFFORZODA]

International organization participation: ADB, CICA, CIS, CSTO, EAEC, EAPC, EBRD, ECO, EITI (candidate country), FAO, G-77, GCTU, IAEA, IBRD, ICAO, ICC (NGOs), ICCt, ICRM, IDA, IDB, IFAD, IFC, IFRCS, ILO, IMF, Interpol, IOC, IOM, IPU, ISO (correspondent), ITSO, ITU, MIGA, NAM (observer), OIC, OPCW, OSCE, PFP, SCO, UN, UNCTAD, UNESCO, UNIDO, UNISFA, UNWTO, UPU, WCO, WFTU (NGOs), WHO, WIPO, WMO, WTO

Diplomatic representation in the US: *chief of mission:* Ambassador Farrukh HAMRALIZODA (since 17 February 2021)
chancery: 1005 New Hampshire Avenue NW, Washington, DC 20037
telephone: [1] (202) 223-6090; [1] (202) 223-2666
FAX: [1] (202) 223-6091
email address and website:
tajemus@mfa.tj; tajikistan@verizon.net
https://mfa.tj/en/washington

Diplomatic representation from the US: *chief of mission:* Ambassador John Mark POMMERSHEIM (since 15 March 2019)
embassy: 109-A Ismoili Somoni Avenue (Zarafshon district), Dushanbe 734019
mailing address: 7090 Dushanbe Place, Washington DC 20521-7090
telephone: [992] (37) 229-20-00
FAX: [992] (37) 229-20-50
email address and website:
DushanbeConsular@state.gov
https://tj.usembassy.gov/

Flag description: three horizontal stripes of red (top), a wider stripe of white, and green; a gold crown surmounted by seven gold, five-pointed stars is located in the center of the white stripe; red represents the sun, victory, and the unity of the nation, white stands for purity, cotton, and mountain snows, while green is the color of Islam and the bounty of nature; the crown symbolizes the Tajik people; the seven stars signify the Tajik magic number "seven" - a symbol of perfection and the embodiment of happiness

National symbol(s): crown surmounted by an arc of seven, five-pointed stars; snow leopard; national colors: red, white, green

National anthem: *name:* "Surudi milli" (National Anthem)
lyrics/music: Gulnazar KELDI/Sulaimon YUDAKOV
note: adopted 1991; after the fall of the Soviet Union, Tajikistan kept the music of the anthem from its time as a Soviet republic but adopted new lyrics

National heritage: *total World Heritage Sites:* 2 (1 cultural, 1 natural)
selected World Heritage Site locales: Proto-urban Site of Sarazm (c); Tajik National Park (Mountains of the Pamirs) (n)

ECONOMY

Economic overview: Tajikistan is a poor, mountainous country with an economy dominated by minerals extraction, metals processing, agriculture, and reliance on remittances from citizens working abroad. Mineral resources include silver, gold, uranium, antimony, tungsten, and coal. Industry consists mainly of small obsolete factories in food processing and light industry, substantial hydropower facilities, and a large aluminum plant - currently operating well below its capacity. The 1992-97 civil war severely damaged an already weak economic infrastructure and caused a sharp decline in industrial and agricultural production. Today, Tajikistan is the poorest among the former Soviet republics. Because less than 7% of the land area is arable and cotton is the predominant crop, Tajikistan imports approximately 70% of its food.

Since the end of the civil war, the country has pursued half-hearted reforms and privatizations in the economic sphere, but its poor business climate remains a hindrance to attracting foreign investment. Some experts estimate the value of narcotics transiting Tajikistan is equivalent to 30%-50% of GDP.

Because of a lack of employment opportunities in Tajikistan, more than one million Tajik citizens work abroad - roughly 90% in Russia - supporting families back home through remittances that in 2017 were equivalent to nearly 35% of GDP. Tajikistan's large remittances from migrant workers in Russia exposes it to monetary shocks. Tajikistan often delays devaluation of its currency for fear of inflationary pressures on food and other consumables. Recent slowdowns in the Russian and Chinese economies, low commodity prices, and currency fluctuations have hampered economic growth. The dollar value of remittances from Russia to Tajikistan dropped by almost 65% in 2015, and the government spent almost $500 million in 2016 to bail out the country's still troubled banking sector.

Tajikistan's growing public debt – currently about 50% of GDP – could result in financial difficulties. Remittances from Russia increased in 2017, however, bolstering the economy somewhat. China owns about 50% of Tajikistan's outstanding debt. Tajikistan has borrowed heavily to finance investment in the country's vast hydropower potential. In 2016, Tajikistan contracted with the Italian firm Salini Impregilo to build the Roghun dam over a 13-year period for $3.9 billion. A 2017 Eurobond has largely funded Roghun's first phase, after which sales from Roghun's output are expected to fund the rest of its construction. The government has not ruled out issuing another Eurobond to generate auxiliary funding for its second phase.

Real GDP (purchasing power parity): $34.88 billion (2020 est.)
$33.38 billion (2019 est.)
$31.08 billion (2018 est.)
note: data are in 2017 dollars
country comparison to the world: 130

Real GDP growth rate: 7.1% (2017 est.)
6.9% (2016 est.)
6% (2015 est.)
country comparison to the world: 16

Real GDP per capita: $3,700 (2020 est.)
$3,600 (2019 est.)
$3,400 (2018 est.)
note: data are in 2017 dollars
country comparison to the world: 188

GDP (official exchange rate): $2.522 billion (2019 est.)

Inflation rate (consumer prices): 7.7% (2019 est.)
3.9% (2018 est.)
7.3% (2017 est.)
country comparison to the world: 196

Credit ratings:

Moody's rating: B3 (2017)

Standard & Poors rating: B- (2017)

GDP - composition, by sector of origin: *agriculture:* 28.6% (2017 est.)
industry: 25.5% (2017 est.)
services: 45.9% (2017 est.)

GDP - composition, by end use: *household consumption:* 98.4% (2017 est.)
government consumption: 13.3% (2017 est.)
investment in fixed capital: 11.7% (2017 est.)
investment in inventories: 2.5% (2017 est.)
exports of goods and services: 10.7% (2017 est.)
imports of goods and services: -36.6% (2017 est.)

Agricultural products: milk, potatoes, wheat, watermelons, onions, tomatoes, vegetables, cotton, carrots/turnips, beef

Industries: aluminum, cement, coal, gold, silver, antimony, textile, vegetable oil

Industrial production growth rate: 1% (2017 est.)
country comparison to the world: 159

Labor force: 2.295 million (2016 est.)
country comparison to the world: 116

Labor force - by occupation: *agriculture:* 43%
industry: 10.6%
services: 46.4% (2016 est.)

Unemployment rate: 2.4% (2016 est.)
2.5% (2015 est.)
note: official rate; actual unemployment is much higher
country comparison to the world: 28

Population below poverty line: 26.3% (2019 est.)

Gini Index coefficient - distribution of family income: 34 (2015 est.)
34.7 (1998)
country comparison to the world: 118

Budget: *revenues:* 2.269 billion (2017 est.)
expenditures: 2.374 billion (2017 est.)

Budget surplus (+) or deficit (-): -1.5% (of GDP) (2017 est.)
country comparison to the world: 90

Public debt: 50.4% of GDP (2017 est.)
42% of GDP (2016 est.)
country comparison to the world: 101

Taxes and other revenues: 31.8% (of GDP) (2017 est.)
country comparison to the world: 71

Fiscal year: calendar year

Current account balance: -$35 million (2017 est.)
-$362 million (2016 est.)
country comparison to the world: 78

Exports: $1.41 billion (2020 est.) note: data are in current year dollars
$1.24 billion (2019 est.) note: data are in current year dollars
$1.12 billion (2018 est.) note: data are in current year dollars
country comparison to the world: 166

Exports - partners: Turkey 24%, Switzerland 22%, Uzbekistan 16%, Kazakhstan 12%, China 10% (2019)

Exports - commodities: gold, aluminum, cotton, zinc, antimony, lead (2019)

Imports: $3.13 billion (2020 est.) note: data are in current year dollars
$3.41 billion (2019 est.) note: data are in current year dollars
$3.22 billion (2018 est.) note: data are in current year dollars
country comparison to the world: 156

Imports - partners: China 40%, Russia 38%, Kazakhstan 19%, Uzbekistan 5% (2019)

Imports - commodities: refined petroleum, wheat, natural gas, bauxite, aircraft (2019)

Reserves of foreign exchange and gold: $1.292 billion (31 December 2017 est.)
$652.8 million (31 December 2016 est.)
country comparison to the world: 127

Debt - external: $6.47 billion (2019 est.)
$5.849 billion (2018 est.)
country comparison to the world: 128

Exchange rates: Tajikistani somoni (TJS) per US dollar -
8.764 (2017 est.)
7.8358 (2016 est.)
7.8358 (2015 est.)
6.1631 (2014 est.)
4.9348 (2013 est.)

ENERGY

Electricity access: *electrification - total population:* 100% (2020)

Electricity: *installed generating capacity:* 7.114 million kW (2020 est.)
consumption: 15,070,890,000 kWh (2019 est.)
exports: 3.175 billion kWh (2019 est.)
imports: 281 million kWh (2019 est.)
transmission/distribution losses: 2.429 billion kWh (2019 est.)

Electricity generation sources: *fossil fuels:* 8.7% of total installed capacity (2020 est.)
hydroelectricity: 91.3% of total installed capacity (2020 est.)

Coal: *production:* 2.103 million metric tons (2020 est.)
consumption: 2.16 million metric tons (2020 est.)
exports: 0 metric tons (2020 est.)
imports: 57,000 metric tons (2020 est.)
proven reserves: 375 million metric tons (2019 est.)

Petroleum: *total petroleum production:* 300 bbl/day (2021 est.)
refined petroleum consumption: 26,200 bbl/day (2019 est.)
crude oil and lease condensate exports: 0 bbl/day (2018 est.)
crude oil and lease condensate imports: 900 bbl/day (2018 est.)
crude oil estimated reserves: 12 million barrels (2021 est.)

Refined petroleum products - production: 172 bbl/day (2015 est.)
country comparison to the world: 108

Refined petroleum products - imports: 22,460 bbl/day (2015 est.)
country comparison to the world: 114

Natural gas: *production:* 18.208 million cubic meters (2019 est.)
consumption: 157.611 million cubic meters (2019 est.)
exports: 0 cubic meters (2021 est.)
imports: 139.375 million cubic meters (2019 est.)
proven reserves: 5.663 billion cubic meters (2021 est.)

Carbon dioxide emissions: 7.643 million metric tonnes of CO2 (2019 est.)
from coal and metallurgical coke: 4.362 million metric tonnes of CO2 (2019 est.)
from petroleum and other liquids: 2.971 million metric tonnes of CO2 (2019 est.)
from consumed natural gas: 309,000 metric tonnes of CO2 (2019 est.)
country comparison to the world: 121

Energy consumption per capita: 27.651 million Btu/person (2019 est.)
country comparison to the world: 124

COMMUNICATIONS

Telephones - fixed lines: *total subscriptions:* 502,000 (2020 est.)
subscriptions per 100 inhabitants: 5 (2020 est.)
country comparison to the world: 93

Telephones - mobile cellular: *total subscriptions:* 9.904 million (2019)
subscriptions per 100 inhabitants: 111.53 (2019)
country comparison to the world: 91

Telecommunication systems: *general assessment:* the nation of Tajikistan has had to struggle through a further two years of economic hardship following the onset of the Covid-19 pandemic; the strain on financial resources inevitably means a continuation of the absence of any meaningful investment or development programs for telecommunications infrastructure; the fixed line telephony and fixed broadband markets continue to languish far behind the mobile sector in terms of teledensity and penetration; with only around 6,000 fixed broadband customers (0.07% penetration), there would appear to be massive growth potential but the limited fixed line infrastructure in the country suggests there's little likelihood of that occurring any time soon; the size of Tajikistan's mobile market dwarfs the fixed line segment, with an estimated penetration rate of nearly 120%; with a number of private sector companies active in the mobile market, there been more commitment to investment in network upgrades and expansion; three MNOs have all launched commercial 5G services, initially in areas of the capital city Dushanbe; the move towards higher speed mobile services should further underpin the growth in the nascent mobile broadband market, which is still estimated to be at a relatively low penetration level of 42% (at least relative to most other Asian nations) but is predicted to be a strong compound annual growth rate of more than 8% for at least the next five years (2021)
domestic: fixed line availability has not changed significantly since 1998, while mobile cellular subscribership, aided by competition among multiple operators, has expanded; coverage now extends to all major cities and towns; fixed-line over 5 per 100 and mobile-cellular over 111 per 100 (2019)
international: country code - 992; linked by cable and microwave radio relay to other CIS republics and by leased connections to the Moscow international gateway switch; Dushanbe linked by Intelsat to international gateway switch in Ankara (Turkey); 3 satellite earth stations - 2 Intelsat and 1 Orbita

Broadcast media: state-run TV broadcasters transmit nationally on 9 TV and 10 radio stations, and regionally on 4 stations; 31 independent TV and 20 radio stations broadcast locally and regionally; many households are able to receive Russian and other foreign stations via cable and satellite (2016)

Internet country code: .tj

Internet users: *total:* 3,013,256 (July 2022 est.)
percent of population: 30.4% (July 2022 est.)
country comparison to the world: 113

Broadband - fixed subscriptions: *total:* 6,000 (2020 est.)
subscriptions per 100 inhabitants: 0.1 (2020 est.)
country comparison to the world: 184

TRANSPORTATION

National air transport system: *number of registered air carriers:* 2 (2020)
inventory of registered aircraft operated by air carriers: 6
annual passenger traffic on registered air carriers: 492,320 (2018)
annual freight traffic on registered air carriers: 2.34 million (2018) mt-km

Civil aircraft registration country code prefix: EY

Airports: *total:* 24 (2021)
country comparison to the world: 131

Airports - with paved runways: *total:* 17
over 3,047 m: 2
2,438 to 3,047 m: 4
1,524 to 2,437 m: 5
914 to 1,523 m: 3
under 914 m: 3 (2021)

Airports - with unpaved runways: *total:* 7
1,524 to 2,437 m: 1
914 to 1,523 m: 1
under 914 m: 5 (2021)

Pipelines: 549 km gas, 38 km oil (2013)

Railways: *total:* 680 km (2014)
broad gauge: 680 km (2014) 1.520-m gauge
country comparison to the world: 102

Roadways: *total:* 30,000 km (2018)
country comparison to the world: 98

Waterways: 200 km (2011) (along Vakhsh River)
country comparison to the world: 108

MILITARY AND SECURITY

Military and security forces: Armed Forces of the Republic of Tajikistan: Land Forces, Mobile Forces, Air and Air Defense Forces; National Guard; Ministry of Internal Affairs: Internal Troops (reserves for Armed Forces in wartime); State

Committee on National Security: Border Guard Forces (2022)

Military expenditures: 1.2% of GDP (2021 est.)
1% of GDP (2020 est.)
2.1% of GDP (2019 est.) (approximately $360 million)
2.1% of GDP (2018 est.) (approximately $350 million)
2.2% of GDP (2017 est.) (approximately $330 million)
country comparison to the world: 119

Military and security service personnel strengths: approximately 9,500 active duty troops (8,000 Land and Mobile Forces; 1,500 Air and Air Defense Forces) (2022)

Military equipment inventories and acquisitions: the military's inventory is comprised of older Russian and Soviet-era equipment; it has received limited quantities of weapons systems since 2010, most of which was second-hand material from Russia (2021)

Military service age and obligation: 18-27 years of age for compulsory or voluntary military service for men; 24-month conscript service obligation; in August 2021, the Tajik Government began allowing men to pay a fee in order to avoid conscription (2022)

Military - note: Tajikistan has been a member of the Collective Security Treaty Organization (CSTO) since 1994 and contributes troops to CSTO's rapid reaction force (2022)

TERRORISM

Terrorist group(s): Islamic State of Iraq and ash-Sham (ISIS)

TRANSNATIONAL ISSUES

Disputes - international: *Tajikistan-Afghanistan:* none identified
Tajikistan-China: in 2006, China and Tajikistan pledged to commence demarcation of the revised boundary agreed to in the delimitation of 2002; in 2011, Tajikistan and China ratified the 2002 border demarcation agreement whereby Tajikistan ceded approximately 1,100 square kilometers in the Pamirs to China
Tajikistan-Kyrgyzstan: disputes in Isfara Valley delay delimitation with Kyrgyzstan; in May 2021, both countries agreed to a ceasefire following recent clashes at their border
Tajikistan-Uzbekistan: talks continue with Uzbekistan to delimit border and clear minefields; as of January 2020, Uzbekistan reported that it had cleared all mines along its side of the border

Refugees and internally displaced persons: *refugees (country of origin):* 6,775 (Afghanistan) (mid-year 2021)
stateless persons: 6,141 (mid-year 2021)

Illicit drugs: Tajikistan is a major route for drug trafficking in Central Asia; opiates and cannabis travel from Afghanistan through Tajikistan to markets in Russia, Belarus, and Western and Central Europe

TANZANIA

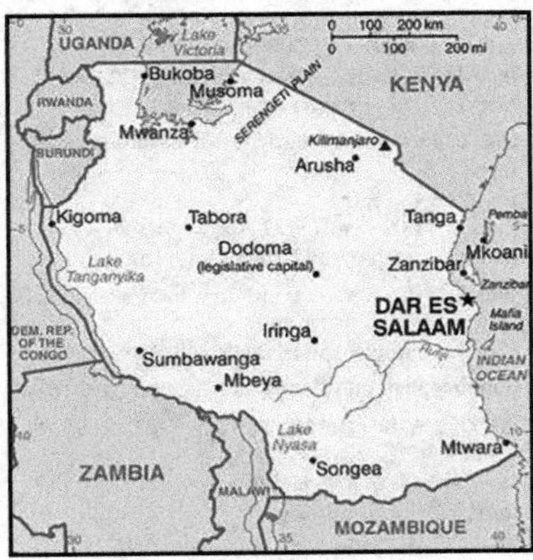

INTRODUCTION

Background: Tanzania contains some of Africa's most iconic national parks and famous paleoanthropological sites, and its diverse cultural heritage reflects the multiple ethnolinguistic groups that live in the country. Its long history of integration into trade networks spanning the Indian Ocean and the African interior led to the development of Swahili as a common language in much of east Africa and the introduction of Islam into the region. A number of independent coastal and island trading posts in what is now Tanzania came under Portuguese control after 1498 when they began to take control of much of the coast and Indian Ocean trade. By 1700, the Sultanate of Oman had become the dominant power in the region after ousting the Portuguese who were also facing a series of local uprisings. During the following hundred years, Zanzibar - an archipelago off the coast of Tanzania - became a hub of Indian Ocean trade, with Arab and Indian traders establishing and consolidating trade routes with communities in mainland Tanzania that contributed to the expansion of the slave trade. Zanzibar briefly become the capital of the Sultanate of Oman before it split into separate Omani and Zanzibar Sultanates in 1856. Beginning in the mid-1800s, European explorers, traders, and Christian missionaries became more active in the region. The Germans eventually established control over mainland Tanzania - which they called Tanganyika - and the British established control over Zanzibar. Tanganyika later came under British administration after the German defeat in World War I.

Tanganyika gained independence from Great Britain in 1961, and Zanzibar followed in 1963 as a constitutional monarchy. In Tanganyika, Julius NYERERE, a charismatic and idealistic socialist, established a one-party political system that centralized power and encouraged national self-reliance and rural development. In 1964, a popular uprising overthrew the Sultan in Zanzibar and either killed or expelled many of the Arabs and Indians who had dominated the isles for more than 200 years. Later that year, Tanganyika and Zanzibar combined to form the United Republic of Tanzania, but Zanzibar retained considerable autonomy. Their two ruling parties combined to form the Chama Cha Mapinduzi (CCM) party in 1977. NYERERE handed over power to Ali Hassan MWINYI in 1985 and remained CCM chair until 1990. Tanzania held its first multi-party elections in 1995, but CCM candidates have continued to dominate politics. Political opposition in Zanzibar has led to four contentious elections since 1995, in which the ruling party claimed victory despite international observers' claims of voting irregularities. In 2001, 35 people in Zanzibar died when soldiers fired on protestors following the 2000 election. John MAGUFULI won the 2015 presidential election, and the CCM won a two-thirds majority in Parliament. He was reelected in 2020 and the CCM increased its majority in an election that was also critiqued by observers. MAGUFULI died in March 2021 while in office and was constitutionally succeeded by his vice president, Samia Suluhu HASSAN.

GEOGRAPHY

Location: Eastern Africa, bordering the Indian Ocean, between Kenya and Mozambique

Geographic coordinates: 6 00 S, 35 00 E

Map references: Africa

Area: *total:* 947,300 sq km
land: 885,800 sq km
water: 61,500 sq km
note: includes the islands of Mafia, Pemba, and Zanzibar
country comparison to the world: 32

Area - comparative: more than six times the size of Georgia; slightly larger than twice the size of California

Land boundaries: *total:* 4,161 km
border countries (8): Burundi 589 km; Democratic Republic of the Congo 479 km; Kenya 775 km; Malawi 512 km; Mozambique 840 km; Rwanda 222 km; Uganda 391 km; Zambia 353 km

Coastline: 1,424 km

Maritime claims: *territorial sea:* 12 nm
exclusive economic zone: 200 nm

Climate: varies from tropical along coast to temperate in highlands

Terrain: plains along coast; central plateau; highlands in north, south

Elevation: *highest point:* Kilimanjaro (highest point in Africa) 5,895 m
lowest point: Indian Ocean 0 m
mean elevation: 1,018 m

Natural resources: hydropower, tin, phosphates, iron ore, coal, diamonds, gemstones (including tanzanite, found only in Tanzania), gold, natural gas, nickel

Land use: *agricultural land:* 43.7% (2018 est.)
arable land: 14.3% (2018 est.)
permanent crops: 2.3% (2018 est.)

permanent pasture: 27.1% (2018 est.)
forest: 37.3% (2018 est.)
other: 19% (2018 est.)

Irrigated land: 1,840 sq km (2012)

Major lakes (area sq km): *fresh water lake(s):* Lake Victoria (shared with Uganda and Kenya) - 62,940 sq km; Lake Tanganyika (shared with Democratic Republic of Congo, Burundi, and Zambia) - 32,000 sq km; Lake Malawi (shared with Mozambique and Malawi) - 22,490
salt water lake(s): Lake Rukwa - 5,760 sq km

Major rivers (by length in km): Nile (shared with Rwanda [s], Uganda, South Sudan, Sudan, and Egypt [m]) - 6,650 km
note – [s] after country name indicates river source; [m] after country name indicates river mouth

Major watersheds (area sq km): Atlantic Ocean drainage: Congo (3,730,881 sq km), *(Mediterranean Sea)* Nile (3,254,853 sq km)
Indian Ocean drainage: Zambezi (1,332,412 sq km)

Population distribution: the largest and most populous East African country; population distribution is extremely uneven, but greater population clusters occur in the northern half of country and along the east coast as shown in this population distribution map

Natural hazards: flooding on the central plateau during the rainy season; drought
volcanism: limited volcanic activity; Ol Doinyo Lengai (2,962 m) has emitted lava in recent years; other historically active volcanoes include Kieyo and Meru

Geography - note: Kilimanjaro is the highest point in Africa and one of only three mountain ranges on the continent that has glaciers (the others are Mount Kenya [in Kenya] and the Ruwenzori Mountains [on the Uganda-Democratic Republic of the Congo border]); Tanzania is bordered by three of the largest lakes on the continent: Lake Victoria (the world's second-largest freshwater lake) in the north, Lake Tanganyika (the world's second deepest) in the west, and Lake Nyasa (Lake Malawi) in the southwest

PEOPLE AND SOCIETY

Population: 63,852,892 (2022 est.)
note: estimates for this country explicitly taken into account the impact of the HIV/AIDS epidemic
country comparison to the world: 23

Nationality: *noun:* Tanzanian(s)
adjective: Tanzanian

Ethnic groups: mainland - African 99% (of which 95% are Bantu consisting of more than 130 tribes), other 1% (consisting of Asian, European, and Arab); Zanzibar - Arab, African, mixed Arab and African

Languages: Kiswahili or Swahili (official), Kiunguja (name for Swahili in Zanzibar), English (official, primary language of commerce, administration, and higher education), Arabic (widely spoken in Zanzibar), many local languages; note - Kiswahili (Swahili) is the mother tongue of the Bantu people living in Zanzibar and nearby coastal Tanzania; although Kiswahili is Bantu in structure and origin, its vocabulary draws on a variety of sources including Arabic and English; it has become the lingua franca of central and eastern Africa; the first language of most people is one of the local languages
major-language sample(s): The World Factbook, Chanzo cha Lazima Kuhusu Habari ya Msingi. (Kiswahili)

Religions: Christian 63.1%, Muslim 34.1%, folk religion 1.1%, Buddhist <1%, Hindu <1%, Jewish <1%, other <1%, unspecified 1.6% (2020 est.)
note: Zanzibar is almost entirely Muslim

Demographic profile: Tanzania has the largest population in East Africa and the lowest population density; almost a third of the population is urban. Tanzania's youthful population – about two-thirds of the population is under 25 – is growing rapidly because of the high total fertility rate of 4.4 children per woman, as of 2022. Progress in reducing the birth rate has stalled, sustaining the country's nearly 3% annual growth. The maternal mortality rate has improved since 2000, yet it remains very high because of early and frequent pregnancies, inadequate maternal health services, and a lack of skilled birth attendants – problems that are worse among poor and rural women. Tanzania has made strides in reducing under-5 and infant mortality rates, but a recent drop in immunization threatens to undermine gains in child health. Malaria is a leading killer of children under 5, while HIV is the main source of adult mortality

For Tanzania, most migration is internal, rural to urban movement, while some temporary labor migration from towns to plantations takes place seasonally for harvests. Tanzania was Africa's largest refugee-hosting country for decades, hosting hundreds of thousands of refugees from the Great Lakes region, primarily Burundi, over the last fifty years. However, the assisted repatriation and naturalization of tens of thousands of Burundian refugees between 2002 and 2014 dramatically reduced the refugee population. Tanzania is increasingly a transit country for illegal migrants from the Horn of Africa and the Great Lakes region who are heading to southern Africa for security reasons and/or economic opportunities. Some of these migrants choose to settle in Tanzania.

Age structure: *0-14 years:* 42.7% (male 12,632,772/female 12,369,115)
15-24 years: 20.39% (male 5,988,208/female 5,948,134)
25-54 years: 30.31% (male 8,903,629/female 8,844,180)
55-64 years: 3.52% (male 954,251/female 1,107,717)
65 years and over: 3.08% (male 747,934/female 1,056,905) (2020 est.)

Dependency ratios: *total dependency ratio:* 85.9
youth dependency ratio: 81
elderly dependency ratio: 4.9
potential support ratio: 20.4 (2020 est.)

Median age: *total:* 18.2 years
male: 17.9 years
female: 18.4 years (2020 est.)
country comparison to the world: 212

Population growth rate: 2.78% (2022 est.)
country comparison to the world: 13

Birth rate: 33.3 births/1,000 population (2022 est.)
country comparison to the world: 21

Death rate: 5.09 deaths/1,000 population (2022 est.)
country comparison to the world: 192

Net migration rate: -0.41 migrant(s)/1,000 population (2022 est.)
country comparison to the world: 123

Population distribution: the largest and most populous East African country; population distribution is extremely uneven, but greater population clusters occur in the northern half of country and along the east coast as shown in this population distribution map

Urbanization: *urban population:* 36.7% of total population (2022)
rate of urbanization: 4.89% annual rate of change (2020-25 est.)

Major urban areas - population: 262,000 Dodoma (legislative capital) (2018), 7.405 million DAR ES SALAAM (administrative capital), 1.245 million Mwanza, 766,000 Zanzibar (2022)

Sex ratio: *at birth:* 1.03 male(s)/female
0-14 years: 1.02 male(s)/female
15-24 years: 1.01 male(s)/female
25-54 years: 0.99 male(s)/female
55-64 years: 0.92 male(s)/female
65 years and over: 0.7 male(s)/female
total population: 1 male(s)/female (2022 est.)

Mother's mean age at first birth: 19.8 years (2015/16 est.)
note: data represents median age at first birth among women 20-49

Maternal mortality ratio: 524 deaths/100,000 live births (2017 est.)
country comparison to the world: 19

Infant mortality rate: *total:* 30.87 deaths/1,000 live births
male: 33.66 deaths/1,000 live births
female: 28 deaths/1,000 live births (2022 est.)
country comparison to the world: 49

Life expectancy at birth: *total population:* 70.19 years
male: 68.42 years
female: 72.02 years (2022 est.)
country comparison to the world: 169

Total fertility rate: 4.39 children born/woman (2022 est.)
country comparison to the world: 20

Contraceptive prevalence rate: 38.4% (2015/16)

Drinking water source: *improved: urban:* 95.1% of population
rural: 59.4% of population
total: 72% of population
unimproved: urban: 4.9% of population
rural: 40.6% of population
total: 28% of population (2020 est.)

Current health expenditure: 3.8% of GDP (2019)

Physicians density: 0.05 physicians/1,000 population (2018)

Hospital bed density: 0.7 beds/1,000 population

Sanitation facility access: *improved: urban:* 89.4% of population
rural: 29.2% of population
total: 50.4% of population
unimproved: urban: 10.6% of population
rural: 70.8% of population
total: 49.6% of population (2020 est.)

HIV/AIDS - adult prevalence rate: 4.7% (2020 est.)
country comparison to the world: 12

HIV/AIDS - people living with HIV/AIDS: 1.7 million (2020 est.)
country comparison to the world: 5

HIV/AIDS - deaths: 32,000 (2020 est.)
country comparison to the world: 5

Major infectious diseases: *degree of risk:* very high (2020)

food or waterborne diseases: bacterial diarrhea, hepatitis A, and typhoid fever
vectorborne diseases: malaria, dengue fever, and Rift Valley fever
water contact diseases: schistosomiasis
animal contact diseases: rabies

Obesity - adult prevalence rate: 8.4% (2016)
country comparison to the world: 151

Alcohol consumption per capita: *total:* 7.81 liters of pure alcohol (2019 est.)
beer: 0.74 liters of pure alcohol (2019 est.)
wine: 0.09 liters of pure alcohol (2019 est.)
spirits: 0.38 liters of pure alcohol (2019 est.)
other alcohols: 6.6 liters of pure alcohol (2019 est.)
country comparison to the world: 46

Tobacco use: *total:* 8.7% (2020 est.)
male: 14% (2020 est.)
female: 3.4% (2020 est.)
country comparison to the world: 141

Children under the age of 5 years underweight: 14.6% (2018)
country comparison to the world: 38

Child marriage: *women married by age 15:* 5.2%
women married by age 18: 30.5%
men married by age 18: 3.9% (2016 est.)

Education expenditures: 3.1% of GDP (2020 est.)
country comparison to the world: 146

Literacy: *definition:* age 15 and over can read and write Kiswahili (Swahili), English, or Arabic
total population: 77.9%
male: 83.2%
female: 73.1% (2015)

School life expectancy (primary to tertiary education): *total:* 9 years
male: 9 years
female: 9 years (2020)

Unemployment, youth ages 15-24: *total:* 3.9%
male: 3.1%
female: 4.6% (2014 est.)

ENVIRONMENT

Environment - current issues: water pollution; improper management of liquid waste; indoor air pollution caused by the burning of fuel wood or charcoal for cooking and heating is a large environmental health issue; soil degradation; deforestation; desertification; destruction of coral reefs threatens marine habitats; wildlife threatened by illegal hunting and trade, especially for ivory; loss of biodiversity; solid waste disposal

Environment - international agreements: *party to:* Biodiversity, Climate Change, Climate Change-Kyoto Protocol, Climate Change-Paris Agreement, Comprehensive Nuclear Test Ban, Desertification, Endangered Species, Hazardous Wastes, Law of the Sea, Marine Dumping-London Convention, Nuclear Test Ban, Ozone Layer Protection, Ship Pollution, Wetlands, Whaling
signed, but not ratified: none of the selected agreements

Air pollutants: *particulate matter emissions:* 25.59 micrograms per cubic meter (2016 est.)
carbon dioxide emissions: 11.97 megatons (2016 est.)
methane emissions: 59.08 megatons (2020 est.)

Climate: varies from tropical along coast to temperate in highlands

Land use: *agricultural land:* 43.7% (2018 est.)
arable land: 14.3% (2018 est.)
permanent crops: 2.3% (2018 est.)
permanent pasture: 27.1% (2018 est.)
forest: 37.3% (2018 est.)
other: 19% (2018 est.)

Urbanization: *urban population:* 36.7% of total population (2022)
rate of urbanization: 4.89% annual rate of change (2020-25 est.)

Revenue from forest resources: *forest revenues:* 2.19% of GDP (2018 est.)
country comparison to the world: 32

Revenue from coal: *coal revenues:* 0.02% of GDP (2018 est.)
country comparison to the world: 45

Food insecurity: *severe localized food insecurity: due to localized shortfalls in staple food production* - about 592,000 people are estimated to be in need of humanitarian assistance between May and September 2022, mainly located in northeastern regions, reflecting crop losses during the October–December "Vuli" 2021 and March–May "Masika" 2022 seasons due to poor rains; high food prices are also constraining households' economic access to food (2022)

Waste and recycling: *municipal solid waste generated annually:* 9,276,995 tons (2012 est.)

Major lakes (area sq km): *fresh water lake(s):* Lake Victoria (shared with Uganda and Kenya) - 62,940 sq km; Lake Tanganyika (shared with Democratic Republic of Congo, Burundi, and Zambia) - 32,000 sq km; Lake Malawi (shared with Mozambique and Malawi) - 22,490
salt water lake(s): Lake Rukwa - 5,760 sq km

Major rivers (by length in km): Nile (shared with Rwanda [s], Uganda, South Sudan, Sudan, and Egypt [m]) - 6,650 km
note – [s] after country name indicates river source; [m] after country name indicates river mouth

Major watersheds (area sq km): Atlantic Ocean drainage: Congo (3,730,881 sq km), *(Mediterranean Sea)* Nile (3,254,853 sq km)
Indian Ocean drainage: Zambezi (1,332,412 sq km)

Total water withdrawal: *municipal:* 527 million cubic meters (2017 est.)
industrial: 25 million cubic meters (2017 est.)
agricultural: 4.632 billion cubic meters (2017 est.)

Total renewable water resources: 96.27 billion cubic meters (2017 est.)

GOVERNMENT

Country name: *conventional long form:* United Republic of Tanzania
conventional short form: Tanzania
local long form: Jamhuri ya Muungano wa Tanzania
local short form: Tanzania
former: German East Africa, Trust Territory of Tanganyika, Republic of Tanganyika, People's Republic of Zanzibar, United Republic of Tanganyika and Zanzibar
etymology: the country's name is a combination of the first letters of Tanganyika and Zanzibar, the two states that merged to form Tanzania in 1964

Government type: presidential republic

Capital: *name:* Dar es Salaam (de facto administrative capital), Dodoma (national capital); note - Dodoma, designated the national capital in 1996, serves as the meeting place for the National Assembly and is thus the legislative capital; Dar es Salaam (the original national capital) remains the de facto capital, the country's largest city and commercial center, and the site of the executive branch offices and diplomatic representation
geographic coordinates: 6 48 S, 39 17 E
time difference: UTC+3 (8 hours ahead of Washington, DC, during Standard Time)
etymology: Dar es Salaam was the name given by Majid BIN SAID, the first sultan of Zanzibar, to the new city he founded on the Indian Ocean coast; the Arabic name is commonly translated as "abode/home of peace"; Dodoma, in the native Gogo language, means "it has sunk"; supposedly, one day during the rainy season, an elephant drowned in the area; the villagers in that place were so struck by what had occurred, that ever since the locale has been referred to as the place where "it (the elephant) sunk"

Administrative divisions: 31 regions; Arusha, Dar es Salaam, Dodoma, Geita, Iringa, Kagera, Kaskazini Pemba (Pemba North), Kaskazini Unguja (Zanzibar North), Katavi, Kigoma, Kilimanjaro, Kusini Pemba (Pemba South), Kusini Unguja (Zanzibar Central/South), Lindi, Manyara, Mara, Mbeya, Mjini Magharibi (Zanzibar Urban/West), Morogoro, Mtwara, Mwanza, Njombe, Pwani (Coast), Rukwa, Ruvuma, Shinyanga, Simiyu, Singida, Songwe, Tabora, Tanga

Independence: 26 April 1964 (Tanganyika united with Zanzibar to form the United Republic of Tanganyika and Zanzibar); 29 October 1964 (renamed United Republic of Tanzania); notable earlier dates: 9 December 1961 (Tanganyika became independent from UK-administered UN trusteeship); 10 December 1963 (Zanzibar became independent from UK)

National holiday: Union Day (Tanganyika and Zanzibar), 26 April (1964)

Constitution: *history:* several previous; latest adopted 25 April 1977; note - progress enacting a new constitution drafted in 2014 by the Constituent Assembly has stalled
amendments: proposed by the National Assembly; passage of amendments to constitutional articles including those on sovereignty of the United Republic, the authorities and powers of the government, the president, the Assembly, and the High Court requires two-thirds majority vote of the mainland Assembly membership and of the Zanzibar House of Representatives membership; House of Representatives approval of other amendments is not required; amended several times, last in 2017

Legal system: English common law; judicial review of legislative acts limited to matters of interpretation

International law organization participation: has not submitted an ICJ jurisdiction declaration; accepts ICCt jurisdiction

Citizenship: *citizenship by birth:* no
citizenship by descent only: at least one parent must be a citizen of Tanzania; if a child is born abroad, the father must be a citizen of Tanzania
dual citizenship recognized: no
residency requirement for naturalization: 5 years

Suffrage: 18 years of age; universal

Executive branch: *chief of state:* President Samia Suluhu HASSAN (since 19 March 2021); note - the president is both chief of state and head of

government; note - President John MAGUFULI died on 17 March 2021; Vice President Philip MPANGO
head of government: President Samia Suluhu HASSAN (since 19 March 2021); Vice President Philip MPANGO; Prime Minister Kassim Majaliwa MAJALIWA (since 20 November 2015) has authority over the day-to-day functions of the government, is the leader of government business in the National Assembly, and head of the Cabinet
cabinet: Cabinet appointed by the president from among members of the National Assembly
elections/appointments: president and vice president directly elected on the same ballot by simple majority popular vote for a 5-year term (eligible for a second term); election last held on 28 October 2020 (next to be held in October 2025); prime minister appointed by the president
election results:
2020: John MAGUFULI reelected president; percent of vote - John MAGUFULI (CCM) 84.4%, Tundu LISSU (CHADEMA) 13%, other 2.6%
2015: John MAGUFULI elected president; percent of vote - John MAGUFULI (CCM) 58.5%, Edward LOWASSA (CHADEMA) 40%, other 1.5%
note: Zanzibar elects a president as head of government for internal matters; elections were held on 28 October 2020; Hussein MWINYI (CCM) 76.3%, Maalim Seif SHARIF (ACT-Wazalendo) 19.9%, other 3.8%

Legislative branch: *description:* unicameral National Assembly or Parliament (Bunge) (393 seats; 264 members directly elected in singleseat constituencies by simple majority vote, 113 women indirectly elected by proportional representation vote, 5 indirectly elected by simple majority vote by the Zanzibar House of Representatives, 10 appointed by the president, and 1 seat reserved for the attorney general; members serve 5-year terms); note - in addition to enacting laws that apply to the entire United Republic of Tanzania, the National Assembly enacts laws that apply only to the mainland; Zanzibar has its own House of Representatives or Baraza La Wawakilishi (82 seats; 50 members directly elected in single-seat constituencies by simple majority vote, 20 women directly elected by proportional representation vote, 10 appointed by the Zanzibar president, 1 seat for the House speaker, and 1 ex-officio seat for the attorney general; elected members serve a 5-year term)
elections:
Tanzania National Assembly and Zanzibar House of Representatives - elections last held on 28 October 2020 (next National Assembly election to be held in October 2025; next Zanzibar election NA)
election results:
National Assembly - percent of vote by party - NA; seats by party - CCM 350, Chadema 20, ACT-Wazalendo 4, CUF 3; composition as of early 2021 (388 members) - men 245, women 143, percent of women 36.9%

Zanzibar House of Representatives - percent of vote by party - NA; seats by party - NA; composition - NA

Judicial branch: *highest court(s):* Court of Appeal of the United Republic of Tanzania (consists of the chief justice and 14 justices); High Court of the United Republic for Mainland Tanzania (consists of the principal judge and 30 judges organized into commercial, land, and labor courts); High Court of Zanzibar (consists of the chief justice and 10 justices)
judge selection and term of office: Court of Appeal and High Court justices appointed by the national president after consultation with the Judicial Service Commission for Tanzania, a judicial body of high level judges and 2 members appointed by the national president; Court of Appeal and High Court judges serve until mandatory retirement at age 60, but terms can be extended; High Court of Zanzibar judges appointed by the national president after consultation with the Judicial Commission of Zanzibar; judges can serve until mandatory retirement at age 65
subordinate courts: Resident Magistrates Courts; Kadhi courts (for Islamic family matters); district and primary courts

Political parties and leaders: Alliance for Change and Transparency (Wazalendo) or ACT-Wazalendo [Zitto KABWE]
Civic United Front (Chama Cha Wananchi) or CUF [Ibrahim Haruna LIPUMBA]
Party of Democracy and Development (Chama Cha Demokrasia na Maendeleo) or Chadema [Freeman MBOWE, Chairman]
Revolutionary Party of Tanzania (Chama Cha Mapinduzi) or CCM [Samia Suluhu HASSAN, Chairman]
note: only parties with seats in the National Assembly listed

International organization participation: ACP, AfDB, AU, C, CD, EAC, EADB, EITI, FAO, G-77, IAEA, IBRD, ICAO, ICC (NGOs), ICCt, ICRM, IDA, IFAD, IFC, IFRCS, ILO, IMF, IMO, IMSO, Interpol, IOC, IOM, IPU, ISO, ITSO, ITU, ITUC (NGOs), MIGA, MONUSCO, NAM, OPCW, SADC, UN, UNAMID, UNCTAD, UNESCO, UNHCR, UNIDO, UNIFIL, UNISFA, UNMISS, UNWTO, UPU, WCO, WFTU (NGOs), WHO, WIPO, WMO, WTO

Diplomatic representation in the US: *chief of mission:* Ambassador Elsie Sia KANZA (since August 2021)
chancery: 1232 22nd Street NW, Washington, DC 20037
telephone: [1] (202) 884-1080, [1] (202) 939-6125, [1] (202) 939-6127
FAX: [1] (202) 797-7408
email address and website:
ubalozi@tanzaniaembassy-us.org
https://tanzaniaembassy-us.org/

Diplomatic representation from the US: *chief of mission:* Ambassador Donald J. WRIGHT (since 2 April 2020)
embassy: 686 Old Bagamoyo Road, Msasani, P.O. Box 9123, Dar es Salaam
mailing address: 2140 Dar es Salaam Place, Washington, DC 20521-2140
telephone: [255] (22) 229-4000
FAX: [255] (22) 229-4721
email address and website:
DRSACS@state.gov
https://tz.usembassy.gov/

Flag description: divided diagonally by a yellow-edged black band from the lower hoist-side corner; the upper triangle (hoist side) is green and the lower triangle is blue; the banner combines colors found on the flags of Tanganyika and Zanzibar; green represents the natural vegetation of the country, gold its rich mineral deposits, black the native Swahili people, and blue the country's many lakes and rivers, as well as the Indian Ocean

National symbol(s): Uhuru (Freedom) torch, giraffe; national colors: green, yellow, blue, black

National anthem: *name:* "Mungu ibariki Afrika" (God Bless Africa)
lyrics/music: collective/Enoch Mankayi SONTONGA
note: adopted 1961; the anthem, which is also a popular song in Africa, shares the same melody with that of Zambia but has different lyrics; the melody is also incorporated into South Africa's anthem

National heritage: *total World Heritage Sites:* 7 (3 cultural, 3 natural, 1 mixed)
selected World Heritage Site locales: Ngorongoro Conservation Area (m); Ruins of Kilwa Kisiwani and Songo Mnara (c); Serengeti National Park (n); Selous Game Reserve (n); Kilimanjaro National Park (n); Stone Town of Zanzibar (c); Kondoa Rock-Art Sites (c)

ECONOMY

Economic overview: Tanzania has achieved high growth rates based on its vast natural resource wealth and tourism with GDP growth in 2009-17 averaging 6%-7% per year. Dar es Salaam used fiscal stimulus measures and easier monetary policies to lessen the impact of the global recession and in general, benefited from low oil prices. Tanzania has largely completed its transition to a market economy, though the government retains a presence in sectors such as telecommunications, banking, energy, and mining.

The economy depends on agriculture, which accounts for slightly less than one-quarter of GDP and employs about 65% of the work force, although gold production in recent years has increased to about 35% of exports. All land in Tanzania is owned by the government, which can lease land for up to 99 years. Proposed reforms to allow for land ownership, particularly foreign land ownership, remain unpopular.

The financial sector in Tanzania has expanded in recent years and foreign-owned banks account for about 48% of the banking industry's total assets. Competition among foreign commercial banks has resulted in significant improvements in the efficiency and quality of financial services, though interest rates are still relatively high, reflecting high fraud risk. Banking reforms have helped increase private-sector growth and investment.

The World Bank, the IMF, and bilateral donors have provided funds to rehabilitate Tanzania's aging infrastructure, including rail and port, which provide important trade links for inland countries. In 2013, Tanzania completed the world's largest Millennium Challenge Compact (MCC) grant, worth $698 million, but in late 2015, the MCC Board of Directors deferred a decision to renew Tanzania's eligibility because of irregularities in voting in Zanzibar and concerns over the government's use of a controversial cybercrime bill.

The new government elected in 2015 has developed an ambitious development agenda focused on creating a better business environment through improved infrastructure, access to financing, and education progress, but implementing budgets remains challenging for the government. Recent policy moves by President MAGUFULI are aimed at protecting domestic industry and have caused concern among foreign investors.

Real GDP (purchasing power parity): $152.79 billion (2020 est.)
$149.79 billion (2019 est.)

$141.59 billion (2018 est.)
note: data are in 2017 dollars
country comparison to the world: 75

Real GDP growth rate: 6.98% (2019 est.)
6.95% (2018 est.)
6.78% (2017 est.)
country comparison to the world: 17

Real GDP per capita: $2,600 (2020 est.)
$2,700 (2019 est.)
$2,600 (2018 est.)
note: data are in 2017 dollars
country comparison to the world: 202

GDP (official exchange rate): $60.633 billion (2019 est.)

Inflation rate (consumer prices): 3.4% (2019 est.)
3.5% (2018 est.)
5.3% (2017 est.)
country comparison to the world: 153

Credit ratings:

Moody's rating: B2 (2020)

GDP - composition, by sector of origin: *agriculture:* 23.4% (2017 est.)
industry: 28.6% (2017 est.)
services: 47.6% (2017 est.)

GDP - composition, by end use: *household consumption:* 62.4% (2017 est.)
government consumption: 12.5% (2017 est.)
investment in fixed capital: 36.1% (2017 est.)
investment in inventories: -8.7% (2017 est.)
exports of goods and services: 18.1% (2017 est.)
imports of goods and services: -20.5% (2017 est.)

Agricultural products: cassava, maize, sweet potatoes, sugar cane, rice, bananas, vegetables, milk, beans, sunflower seed

Industries: agricultural processing (sugar, beer, cigarettes, sisal twine); mining (diamonds, gold, and iron), salt, soda ash; cement, oil refining, shoes, apparel, wood products, fertilizer

Industrial production growth rate: 12% (2017 est.)
country comparison to the world: 8

Labor force: 24.89 million (2017 est.)
country comparison to the world: 22

Labor force - by occupation: *agriculture:* 66.9%
industry: 6.4%
services: 26.6% (2014 est.)

Unemployment rate: 10.3% (2014 est.)
country comparison to the world: 151

Unemployment, youth ages 15-24: *total:* 3.9%
male: 3.1%
female: 4.6% (2014 est.)
country comparison to the world: 173

Population below poverty line: 26.4% (2017 est.)

Gini Index coefficient - distribution of family income: 40.5 (2017 est.)
34.6 (2000)
country comparison to the world: 59

Household income or consumption by percentage share: *lowest 10%:* 2.8%
highest 10%: 29.6% (2007)

Budget: *revenues:* 7.873 billion (2017 est.)
expenditures: 8.818 billion (2017 est.)

Budget surplus (+) or deficit (-): -1.8% (of GDP) (2017 est.)
country comparison to the world: 100

Public debt: 37% of GDP (2017 est.)
38% of GDP (2016 est.)
country comparison to the world: 141

Taxes and other revenues: 15.2% (of GDP) (2017 est.)
country comparison to the world: 192

Fiscal year: 1 July - 30 June

Current account balance: -$1.313 billion (2019 est.)
-$1.898 billion (2018 est.)
country comparison to the world: 155

Exports: $9.66 billion (2019 est.) note: data are in current year dollars
$8.46 billion (2018 est.) note: data are in current year dollars
country comparison to the world: 102

Exports - partners: India 20%, United Arab Emirates 13%, China 8%, Switzerland 7%, Rwanda 6%, Kenya 5%, Vietnam 5% (2019)

Exports - commodities: gold, tobacco, cashews, sesame seeds, refined petroleum (2019)

Imports: $10.36 billion (2019 est.) note: data are in current year dollars
$10.2 billion (2018 est.) note: data are in current year dollars
country comparison to the world: 105

Imports - partners: China 34%, India 15%, United Arab Emirates 12% (2019)

Imports - commodities: refined petroleum, palm oil, packaged medicines, cars, wheat (2019)

Reserves of foreign exchange and gold: $5.301 billion (31 December 2017 est.)
$4.067 billion (31 December 2016 est.)
note: excludes gold
country comparison to the world: 94

Debt - external: $22.054 billion (2019 est.)
$20.569 billion (2018 est.)
country comparison to the world: 92

Exchange rates: Tanzanian shillings (TZS) per US dollar -
2,319 (2020 est.)
2,300 (2019 est.)
2,299.155 (2018 est.)
1,989.7 (2014 est.)
1,654 (2013 est.)

ENERGY

Electricity access: *electrification - total population:* 40% (2019)
electrification - urban areas: 71% (2019)
electrification - rural areas: 23% (2019)

Electricity: *installed generating capacity:* 1.623 million kW (2020 est.)
consumption: 6,522,440,000 kWh (2019 est.)
exports: 0 kWh (2019 est.)
imports: 113 million kWh (2019 est.)
transmission/distribution losses: 974 million kWh (2019 est.)

Electricity generation sources: *fossil fuels:* 65% of total installed capacity (2020 est.)
solar: 1.3% of total installed capacity (2020 est.)
hydroelectricity: 32.8% of total installed capacity (2020 est.)
biomass and waste: 1% of total installed capacity (2020 est.)

Coal: *production:* 712,000 metric tons (2020 est.)
consumption: 577,000 metric tons (2020 est.)
exports: 126,000 metric tons (2020 est.)
imports: 0 metric tons (2020 est.)
proven reserves: 269 million metric tons (2019 est.)

Petroleum: *total petroleum production:* 0 bbl/day (2021 est.)
refined petroleum consumption: 52,800 bbl/day (2019 est.)

Refined petroleum products - imports: 67,830 bbl/day (2015 est.)
country comparison to the world: 69

Natural gas: *production:* 1,378,773,000 cubic meters (2019 est.)
consumption: 1,378,773,000 cubic meters (2019 est.)
proven reserves: 6.513 billion cubic meters (2021 est.)

Carbon dioxide emissions: 11.491 million metric tonnes of CO2 (2019 est.)
from coal and metallurgical coke: 1.32 million metric tonnes of CO2 (2019 est.)
from petroleum and other liquids: 7.466 million metric tonnes of CO2 (2019 est.)
from consumed natural gas: 2.705 million metric tonnes of CO2 (2019 est.)
country comparison to the world: 101

Energy consumption per capita: 3.334 million Btu/person (2019 est.)
country comparison to the world: 178

COMMUNICATIONS

Telephones - fixed lines: *total subscriptions:* 72,469 (2020 est.)
country comparison to the world: 145

Telephones - mobile cellular: *total subscriptions:* 47,685,200 (2019)
subscriptions per 100 inhabitants: 82.21 (2019)
country comparison to the world: 32

Telecommunication systems: *general assessment:* Tanzania's telecom sector enjoys effective competition, particularly in the mobile segment; the government has encouraged foreign participation to promote economic growth and social development, and policy reforms have led to the country having one of the most liberal telecom sectors in Africa; the government has sought to increase broadband penetration by a range of measures, including the reduction in VAT charged on the sale of smartphones and other devices, and reductions in the cost of data; the MNOs became the leading ISPs following the launch of mobile broadband services based on 3G and LTE technologies; operators are hoping for revenue growth in the mobile data services market, given that the voice market is almost entirely prepaid; the MNOs have invested in network upgrades, which in turn has supported m-mobile data use, as well as m-money transfer services and banking services. Together, these have become a fast-developing source of revenue; the landing of the first international submarine cables in the country some years ago revolutionized the telecom market, which up to that point had entirely depended on expensive satellite connections; the government aims to complete a national fiber backbone network, having signed an agreement; in late 2021, the government announced plans to extend the national backbone network from about 8,300km to 15,000km by 2023, and to provide ongoing connectivity to more countries in the region (2022)
domestic: fixed-line telephone network inadequate with less than 1 connection per 100 persons; mobile-cellular service, aided by multiple providers, is increasing rapidly and exceeds 86 telephones per 100 persons; trunk service provided

by open-wire, microwave radio relay, tropospheric scatter, and fiber-optic cable; some links being made digital (2020)
international: country code - 255; landing points for the EASSy, SEACOM/Tata TGN-Eurasia, and SEAS fiber-optic submarine cable system linking East Africa with the Middle East; satellite earth stations - 2 Intelsat (1 Indian Ocean, 1 Atlantic Ocean) (2019)

Broadcast media: according to statistics from the Tanzania Communications Regulatory Authority (TCRA), Tanzania had 45 television stations as of 2020; 13 of those stations provided national content services (commercially broadcasting free-to-air television); there are 196 radio stations, most operating at the district level, but also including 5 independent nationally broadcasting stations and 1 state-owned national radio station; international broadcasting is available through satellite television which is becoming increasingly widespread; there are 3 major satellite TV providers (2020)

Internet country code: .tz

Internet users: *total:* 13,141,527 (2020 est.)
percent of population: 22% (2020 est.)
country comparison to the world: 48

Broadband - fixed subscriptions: *total:* 1,135,608 (2020 est.)
subscriptions per 100 inhabitants: 2 (2020 est.)
country comparison to the world: 70

TRANSPORTATION

National air transport system: *number of registered air carriers:* 11 (2020)
inventory of registered aircraft operated by air carriers: 91
annual passenger traffic on registered air carriers: 1,481,557 (2018)
annual freight traffic on registered air carriers: 390,000 (2018) mt-km

Civil aircraft registration country code prefix: 5H

Airports: *total:* 166 (2021)
country comparison to the world: 33

Airports - with paved runways: *total:* 10
over 3,047 m: 2
2,438 to 3,047 m: 2
1,524 to 2,437 m: 4
914 to 1,523 m: 2 (2021)

Airports - with unpaved runways: *total:* 156
over 3,047 m: 1
1,524 to 2,437 m: 24
914 to 1,523 m: 98
under 914 m: 33 (2021)

Pipelines: 311 km gas, 891 km oil, 8 km refined products (2013)

Railways: *total:* 4,097 km (2022)
standard gauge: 421 km (2022)
narrow gauge: 969 km (2022) 1.067 m gauge
broad gauge: 2,707 km (2022) 1.000 m guage
country comparison to the world: 47

Roadways: *total:* 145,203 km (2022)
paved: 11,201 km (2022)
unpaved: 134,002 km (2022)
country comparison to the world: 35

Waterways: 1,594 km (2022) (Lake Tanganyika 673 km, Lake Victoria 337 km, and Lake Nyasa (Lake Malawi) 584 km are the principal avenues of commerce with neighboring countries; the rivers are not navigable)
country comparison to the world: 53

Merchant marine: *total:* 314
by type: bulk carrier 4, container ship 6, general cargo 144, oil tanker 49, other 111 (2021)
country comparison to the world: 52

Ports and terminals: *major seaport(s):* Dar es Salaam, Zanzibar

MILITARY AND SECURITY

Military and security forces: Tanzania People's Defense Forces (TPDF or Jeshi la Wananchi la Tanzania, JWTZ): Land Forces, Naval Forces, Air Force, National Building Army (Jeshi la Kujenga Taifa, JKT), People's Militia (Reserves); Ministry of Home Affairs: Tanzania Police Force (2022)
note 1: the National Building Army is a paramilitary organization under the Defense Forces that provides 6 months of military and vocational training to individuals as part of their 2 years of public service; after completion of training, some graduates join the regular Defense Forces while the remainder become part of the People's (or Citizen's) Militia
note 2: the Tanzania Police Force includes the Police Field Force (aka Field Force Unit), a special police division with the responsibility for controlling unlawful demonstrations and riots

Military expenditures: 1.1% of GDP (2021 est.)
1.2% of GDP (2020 est.)
1.1% of GDP (2019 est.) (approximately $810 million)
1.2% of GDP (2018 est.) (approximately $800 million)
1% of GDP (2017 est.) (approximately $690 million)
country comparison to the world: 125

Military and security service personnel strengths: approximately 25,000 active duty personnel (21,000 Land Forces; 1,000 Naval Forces; 3,000 Air Force) (2022)

Military equipment inventories and acquisitions: the TPDF's inventory includes mostly Soviet-era and Chinese equipment; since 2010, China has been the leading supplier of arms to the TPDF (2022)

Military service age and obligation: 18-25 years of age for voluntary military service; 6-year commitment (2-year contracts afterwards); selective conscription for 2 years of public service (2022)

Military deployments: 450 Central African Republic (MINUSCA); 850 Democratic Republic of the Congo (MONUSCO); 125 Lebanon (UNIFIL) (May 2022)

Military - note: in 2021-2022, Tanzania contributed troops to the Southern African Development Community (SADC) intervention force that was assisting the Mozambique Government's fight against Islamic militants

Maritime threats: the International Maritime Bureau reports that shipping in territorial and offshore waters in the Indian Ocean remain at risk for piracy and armed robbery against ships

TERRORISM

Terrorist group(s): Islamic State of Iraq and ash-Sham - Mozambique (ISIS-M)

TRANSNATIONAL ISSUES

Disputes - international: *Tanzania-Burundi:* none identified
Tanzania-Democratic Republic of the Congo: none identified
Tanzania-Kenya: none identified
Tanzania-Malawi: dispute with Malawi over the boundary in Lake Nyasa (Lake Malawi) and the meandering Songwe River; Malawi contends that the entire lake up to the Tanzanian shoreline is its territory, while Tanzania claims the border is in the center of the lake; the conflict was reignited in 2012 when Malawi awarded a license to a British company for oil exploration in the lake
Tanzania-Mozambique: none identified
Tanzania-Rwanda: none identified
Tanzania-Uganda: none identified

Refugees and internally displaced persons: *refugees (country of origin):* 126,205 (Burundi), 80,860 (Democratic Republic of the Congo) (2022)

Trafficking in persons: *current situation:* Tanzania is a source, transit, and destination country for men, women, and children subjected to forced labor and sex trafficking; the exploitation of young girls in domestic servitude continues to be Tanzania's largest human trafficking problem; Tanzanian boys are subject to forced labor mainly on farms but also in mines, in the commercial service sector, in the sex trade, and possibly on small fishing boats; internal trafficking is more prevalent than transnational trafficking and is usually facilitated by friends, family members, or intermediaries offering education or legitimate job opportunities; trafficking victims from Burundi, Kenya, Bangladesh, Nepal, Yemen, and India are forced to work in Tanzania's agricultural, mining, and domestic service sectors or may be sex trafficked; traffickers transported Tanzanian children with physical disabilities to Kenya to work as beggars or in massage parlors; girls forced to donate a kidney to pay for supposed transportation fees to the United Arab Emirates; traffickers subject Tanzanians to forced labor, including in domestic service, and sex trafficking in other African countries, the Middle East, Europe, Asia, and the United States
tier rating: Tier 2 Watch List — Tanzania does not fully meet the minimum standards for the elimination of trafficking but is making significant efforts to do so; efforts were made to identify and refer victims for care; investigations and convictions of traffickers, training for officials, and public awareness campaigns were increased along with a National Guideline for Safe Houses; however, the government did not amend its law to remove sentencing provisions that allow fines in lieu of imprisonment; fewer prosecutions were initiated; the government did not implement the 2018-2021 national action plan; officials did not fully implement the creation of the anti-trafficking fund nor disperse funds; no formal victim identification and protection was provided (2020)

Illicit drugs: significant transit country for illicit drugs in East Africa; international drug-trafficking organizations and courier networks transit through Tanzania to smuggle heroin and methamphetamine from Southwest Asia; produces cannabis products and khat for domestic consumption and regional and international distribution; traffickers influence politicians, law enforcement, and others in positions of power with money
(2021)

THAILAND

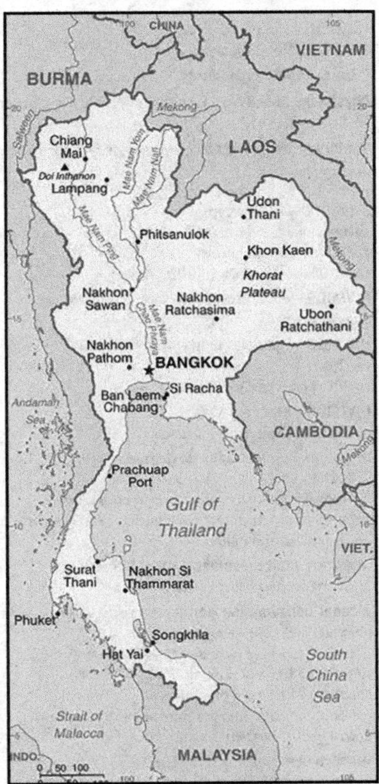

INTRODUCTION

Background: Two unified Thai kingdoms emerged in the mid-13th century. The Sukhothai, located in the south-central plains, gained its independence from the Khmer Empire to the east. By the late 13th century, Sukhothai's territory extended into present-day Burma and Laos. Sukhotai lasted until the mid-15th century. The Thai Lan Na Kingdom was established in the north with its capital at Chang Mai. Lan Na was conquered by the Burmese in the 16th century. The Ayutthaya Kingdom (14th-18th centuries) succeeded the Sukhothai and would become known as the Siamese Kingdom. During the Ayutthaya period, the Thai/Siamese peoples consolidated their hold on what is present-day central and north-central Thailand. Following a military defeat at the hands of the Burmese in 1767, the Siamese Kingdom rose to new heights under the military ruler TAKSIN, who defeated the Burmese occupiers and expanded the kingdom's territory into modern-day northern Thailand (formerly the Lan Na Kingdom), Cambodia, Laos, and the Malay Peninsula. The kingdom fought off additional Burmese invasions and raids in the late 1700s and early 1800s. In the mid-1800s, Western pressure led to Siam signing trade treaties that reduced the country's sovereignty and independence. In the 1890s and 1900s, the British and French forced the kingdom to cede Cambodian, Laotian, and Malay territories that had been under Siamese control.

A bloodless revolution in 1932 led to the establishment of a constitutional monarchy. After the Japanese invaded Thailand in 1941, the government split into a pro-Japan faction and a pro-Ally faction backed by the king. Following the war, Thailand became a US treaty ally in 1954 after sending troops to Korea and later fighting alongside the US in Vietnam. Thailand since 2005 has experienced several rounds of political turmoil including a military coup in 2006 that ousted then Prime Minister THAKSIN Chinnawat, followed by large-scale street protests by competing political factions in 2008, 2009, and 2010. THAKSIN's youngest sister, YINGLAK Chinnawat, in 2011 led the Puea Thai Party to an electoral win and assumed control of the government.

In early May 2014, after months of large-scale anti-government protests in Bangkok beginning in November 2013, YINGLAK was removed from office by the Constitutional Court and in late May 2014 the Royal Thai Army, led by Royal Thai Army Gen. PRAYUT Chan-ocha, staged a coup against the caretaker government. The military-affiliated National Council for Peace and Order (NCPO), led by PRAYUT as the appointed minister, ruled the country for more than four years, during which time the NCPO drafted a new constitution guaranteeing military sway over Thai politics in future elections by allowing the military to appoint the entire 250-member Senate and requiring a joint meeting of the House and Senate to select the prime minister, effectively giving the military a veto over the top executive. King PHUMIPHON Adunyadet passed away in October 2016 after 70 years on the throne; his only son, WACHIRALONGKON Bodinthrathepphayawarangkun (aka King RAMA X), ascended the throne in December 2016. He signed the new constitution in April 2017. A long-delayed election in March 2019, disputed and widely viewed as skewed in favor of the party aligned with the military, allowed PRAYUT to continue his premiership. The country experienced large-scale pro-democracy protests in 2020.

GEOGRAPHY

Location: Southeastern Asia, bordering the Andaman Sea and the Gulf of Thailand, southeast of Burma

Geographic coordinates: 15 00 N, 100 00 E

Map references: Southeast Asia

Area: *total:* 513,120 sq km
land: 510,890 sq km
water: 2,230 sq km
country comparison to the world: 53

Area - comparative: about three times the size of Florida; slightly more than twice the size of Wyoming

Land boundaries: *total:* 5,673 km
border countries (4): Burma 2,416 km; Cambodia 817 km; Laos 1,845 km; Malaysia 595 km

Coastline: 3,219 km

Maritime claims: *territorial sea:* 12 nm
exclusive economic zone: 200 nm
continental shelf: 200-m depth or to the depth of exploitation

Climate: tropical; rainy, warm, cloudy southwest monsoon (mid-May to September); dry, cool northeast monsoon (November to mid-March); southern isthmus always hot and humid

Terrain: central plain; Khorat Plateau in the east; mountains elsewhere

Elevation: *highest point:* Doi Inthanon 2,565 m
lowest point: Gulf of Thailand 0 m
mean elevation: 287 m

Natural resources: tin, rubber, natural gas, tungsten, tantalum, timber, lead, fish, gypsum, lignite, fluorite, arable land

Land use: *agricultural land:* 41.2% (2018 est.)
arable land: 30.8% (2018 est.)
permanent crops: 8.8% (2018 est.)
permanent pasture: 1.6% (2018 est.)
forest: 37.2% (2018 est.)
other: 21.6% (2018 est.)

Irrigated land: 64,150 sq km (2012)

Major lakes (area sq km): *salt water lake(s):* Thalesap Songkhla - 1,290 sq km

Major rivers (by length in km): Mekong (shared with China [s], Burma, Laos, Cambodia, and Vietnam [m]) - 4,350 km; Salween (shared with China [s] and Burma [m]) - 3,060 km; Mun - 1,162 km
note – [s] after country name indicates river source; [m] after country name indicates river mouth

Major watersheds (area sq km): Indian Ocean drainage: Salween (271,914 sq km)
Pacific Ocean drainage: Mekong (805,604 sq km)

Population distribution: highest population density is found in and around Bangkok; significant population clusters found througout large parts of the country, particularly north and northeast of Bangkok and in the extreme southern region of the country

Natural hazards: land subsidence in Bangkok area resulting from the depletion of the water table; droughts

Geography - note: controls only land route from Asia to Malaysia and Singapore; ideas for the construction of a canal across the Kra Isthmus that would create a bypass to the Strait of Malacca and shorten shipping times around Asia continue to be discussed

PEOPLE AND SOCIETY

Population: 69,648,117 (2022 est.)
country comparison to the world: 20

Nationality: *noun:* Thai (singular and plural)
adjective: Thai

Ethnic groups: Thai 97.5%, Burmese 1.3%, other 1.1%, unspecified <0.1% (2015 est.)
note: data represent population by nationality

Languages: Thai (official) only 90.7%, Thai and other languages 6.4%, only other languages 2.9% (includes Malay, Burmese); note -data represent population by language(s) spoken at home; English is a secondary language of the elite (2010 est.)
major-language sample(s):
สารานุกรมโลก - แหล่งข้อมูลพื้นฐานที่สำคัญ (Thai)

Religions: Buddhist 94.6%, Muslim 4.3%, Christian 1%, other <0.1%, none <0.1% (2015 est.)

Demographic profile: Thailand has experienced a substantial fertility decline since the 1960s largely due to the nationwide success of its voluntary family planning program. In just one generation, the total fertility rate (TFR) shrank from 6.5 children per woman in 1960s to below the replacement level of 2.1 in the late 1980s. Reduced fertility occurred among all segments of the Thai population, despite disparities between urban and rural areas in terms of income, education, and access to public services. The country's "reproductive revolution" gained momentum in the 1970s as a result of the government's launch of an official population policy to reduce population growth, the introduction of new forms of birth control, and the assistance of foreign non-government organizations. Contraceptive use rapidly increased as new ways were developed to deliver family planning services to Thailand's then overwhelmingly rural population. The contraceptive prevalence rate increased from just 14% in 1970 to 58% in 1981 and has remained about 80% since 2000.

Thailand's receptiveness to family planning reflects the predominant faith, Theravada Buddhism, which emphasizes individualism, personal responsibility, and independent decision-making. Thai women have more independence and a higher status than women in many other developing countries and are not usually pressured by their husbands or other family members about family planning decisions. Thailand's relatively egalitarian society also does not have the son preference found in a number of other Asian countries; most Thai ideally want one child of each sex.

Because of its low fertility rate, increasing life expectancy, and growing elderly population, Thailand has become an aging society that will face growing labor shortages. The proportion of the population under 15 years of age has shrunk dramatically, the proportion of working-age individuals has peaked and is starting to decrease, and the proportion of elderly is growing rapidly. In the short-term, Thailand will have to improve educational quality to increase the productivity of its workforce and to compete globally in skills-based industries. An increasing reliance on migrant workers will be necessary to mitigate labor shortfalls.

Thailand is a destination, transit, and source country for migrants. It has 3-4 million migrant workers as of 2017, mainly providing low-skilled labor in the construction, agriculture, manufacturing, services, and fishing and seafood processing sectors. Migrant workers from other Southeast Asian countries with lower wages – primarily Burma and, to a lesser extent, Laos and Cambodia – have been coming to Thailand for decades to work in labor-intensive industries. Many are undocumented and are vulnerable to human trafficking for forced labor, especially in the fisheries industry, or sexual exploitation. A July 2017 migrant worker law stiffening fines on undocumented workers and their employers, prompted tens of thousands of migrants to go home. Fearing a labor shortage, the Thai Government has postponed implementation of the law until January 2018 and is rapidly registering workers. Thailand has also hosted ethnic minority refugees from Burma for more than 30 years; as of 2016, approximately 105,000 mainly Karen refugees from Burma were living in nine camps along the Thailand-Burma border.

Thailand has a significant amount of internal migration, most often from rural areas to urban centers, where there are more job opportunities. Low- and semi-skilled Thais also go abroad to work, mainly in Asia and a smaller number in the Middle East and Africa, primarily to more economically developed countries where they can earn higher wages.

Age structure: *0-14 years:* 16.45% (male 5,812,803/female 5,533,772)
15-24 years: 13.02% (male 4,581,622/female 4,400,997)
25-54 years: 45.69% (male 15,643,583/female 15,875,353)
55-64 years: 13.01% (male 4,200,077/female 4,774,801)
65 years and over: 11.82% (male 3,553,273/female 4,601,119) (2020 est.)

Dependency ratios: *total dependency ratio:* 41.9
youth dependency ratio: 23.5
elderly dependency ratio: 18.4
potential support ratio: 5.4 (2020 est.)

Median age: *total:* 39 years
male: 37.8 years
female: 40.1 years (2020 est.)
country comparison to the world: 59

Population growth rate: 0.23% (2022 est.)
country comparison to the world: 178

Birth rate: 10.14 births/1,000 population (2022 est.)
country comparison to the world: 187

Death rate: 7.76 deaths/1,000 population (2022 est.)
country comparison to the world: 99

Net migration rate: -0.13 migrant(s)/1,000 population (2022 est.)
country comparison to the world: 106

Population distribution: highest population density is found in and around Bangkok; significant population clusters found througout large parts of the country, particularly north and northeast of Bangkok and in the extreme southern region of the country

Urbanization: *urban population:* 52.9% of total population (2022)
rate of urbanization: 1.43% annual rate of change (2020-25 est.)

Major urban areas - population: 10.900 million BANGKOK (capital), 1.436 Chon Buri, 1.342 million Samut Prakan, 1.198 million Chiang Mai, 992,000 Songkla, 988,000 Nothaburi (2022)

Sex ratio: *at birth:* 1.05 male(s)/female
0-14 years: 1.05 male(s)/female
15-24 years: 1.04 male(s)/female
25-54 years: 0.97 male(s)/female
55-64 years: 0.89 male(s)/female
65 years and over: 0.68 male(s)/female
total population: 0.95 male(s)/female (2022 est.)

Mother's mean age at first birth: 23.3 years (2009 est.)

Maternal mortality ratio: 37 deaths/100,000 live births (2017 est.)
country comparison to the world: 103

Infant mortality rate: *total:* 6.47 deaths/1,000 live births
male: 7.09 deaths/1,000 live births
female: 5.81 deaths/1,000 live births (2022 est.)
country comparison to the world: 167

Life expectancy at birth: *total population:* 77.66 years
male: 74.65 years
female: 80.83 years (2022 est.)
country comparison to the world: 86

Total fertility rate: 1.54 children born/woman (2022 est.)
country comparison to the world: 196

Contraceptive prevalence rate: 73% (2019)

Drinking water source: *improved: urban:* 100% of population
rural: 100% of population
total: 100% of population

Current health expenditure: 3.8% of GDP (2019)

Physicians density: 0.95 physicians/1,000 population (2020)

Sanitation facility access: *improved: urban:* 99.9% of population
rural: 100% of population
total: 100% of population
unimproved: urban: 0.1% of population
rural: 0% of population
total: 0% of population (2020 est.)

HIV/AIDS - adult prevalence rate: 1% (2020 est.)
country comparison to the world: 44

HIV/AIDS - people living with HIV/AIDS: 500,000 (2020 est.)
country comparison to the world: 17

HIV/AIDS - deaths: 12,000 (2020 est.)
country comparison to the world: 19

Major infectious diseases: *degree of risk:* very high (2020)
food or waterborne diseases: bacterial diarrhea
vectorborne diseases: dengue fever, Japanese encephalitis, and malaria

Obesity - adult prevalence rate: 10% (2016)
country comparison to the world: 140

Alcohol consumption per capita: *total:* 6.86 liters of pure alcohol (2019 est.)
beer: 1.85 liters of pure alcohol (2019 est.)
wine: 0.23 liters of pure alcohol (2019 est.)
spirits: 4.78 liters of pure alcohol (2019 est.)
other alcohols: 0 liters of pure alcohol (2019 est.)
country comparison to the world: 60

Tobacco use: *total:* 22.1% (2020 est.)
male: 41.3% (2020 est.)
female: 2.9% (2020 est.)
country comparison to the world: 71

Children under the age of 5 years underweight: 7.7% (2019)
country comparison to the world: 65

Child marriage: *women married by age 15:* 3%
women married by age 18: 20.2%
men married by age 18: 9.8% (2019 est.)

Education expenditures: 3% of GDP (2019 est.)
country comparison to the world: 151

Literacy: *definition:* age 15 and over can read and write
total population: 93.8%
male: 95.2%
female: 92.4% (2018)

School life expectancy (primary to tertiary education): *total:* 15 years
male: 15 years
female: 16 years (2016)

Unemployment, youth ages 15-24: *total:* 5.2%
male: 4.6%
female: 5.9% (2020 est.)

ENVIRONMENT

Environment - current issues: air pollution from vehicle emissions; water pollution from organic and factory wastes; water scarcity; deforestation; soil erosion; wildlife populations threatened by illegal hunting; hazardous waste disposal

Environment - international agreements: *party to:* Biodiversity, Climate Change, Climate Change-Kyoto Protocol, Climate Change-Paris Agreement, Comprehensive Nuclear Test Ban, Desertification, Endangered Species, Hazardous Wastes, Law of the Sea, Marine Life Conservation, Nuclear Test Ban, Ozone Layer Protection, Ship Pollution, Tropical Timber 2006, Wetlands
signed, but not ratified: none of the selected agreements

Air pollutants: *particulate matter emissions:* 26.23 micrograms per cubic meter (2016 est.)
carbon dioxide emissions: 283.76 megatons (2016 est.)
methane emissions: 86.98 megatons (2020 est.)

Climate: tropical; rainy, warm, cloudy southwest monsoon (mid-May to September); dry, cool northeast monsoon (November to mid-March); southern isthmus always hot and humid

Land use: *agricultural land:* 41.2% (2018 est.)
arable land: 30.8% (2018 est.)
permanent crops: 8.8% (2018 est.)
permanent pasture: 1.6% (2018 est.)
forest: 37.2% (2018 est.)
other: 21.6% (2018 est.)

Urbanization: *urban population:* 52.9% of total population (2022)
rate of urbanization: 1.43% annual rate of change (2020-25 est.)

Revenue from forest resources: *forest revenues:* 0.34% of GDP (2018 est.)
country comparison to the world: 76

Revenue from coal: *coal revenues:* 0.03% of GDP (2018 est.)
country comparison to the world: 41

Waste and recycling: *municipal solid waste generated annually:* 26,853,366 tons (2015 est.)
municipal solid waste recycled annually: 5,128,993 tons (2012 est.)
percent of municipal solid waste recycled: 19.1% (2012 est.)

Major lakes (area sq km): *salt water lake(s):* Thalesap Songkhla - 1,290 sq km

Major rivers (by length in km): Mekong (shared with China [s], Burma, Laos, Cambodia, and Vietnam [m]) - 4,350 km; Salween (shared with China [s] and Burma [m]) - 3,060 km; Mun - 1,162 km
note – [s] after country name indicates river source; [m] after country name indicates river mouth

Major watersheds (area sq km): Indian Ocean drainage: Salween (271,914 sq km)
Pacific Ocean drainage: Mekong (805,604 sq km)

Total water withdrawal: *municipal:* 2.739 billion cubic meters (2017 est.)
industrial: 2.777 billion cubic meters (2017 est.)
agricultural: 51.79 billion cubic meters (2017 est.)

Total renewable water resources: 438.61 billion cubic meters (2017 est.)

GOVERNMENT

Country name: *conventional long form:* Kingdom of Thailand
conventional short form: Thailand
local long form: Ratcha Anachak Thai
local short form: Prathet Thai
former: Siam
etymology: Land of the Tai [People]"; the meaning of "tai" is uncertain, but may originally have meant "human beings," "people," or "free people

Government type: constitutional monarchy

Capital: *name:* Bangkok
geographic coordinates: 13 45 N, 100 31 E
time difference: UTC+7 (12 hours ahead of Washington, DC, during Standard Time)
etymology: Bangkok was likely originally a colloquial name, but one that was widely adopted by foreign visitors; the name may derive from *bang ko,* where *bang* is the Thai word for "village on a stream" and *ko* means "island," both referencing the area's landscape, which was carved by rivers and canals; alternatively, the name may come from *bang makok,* where *makok* is the name of the Java plum, a plant bearing olive-like fruit; this possibility is supported by the former name of Wat Arun, a historic temple in the area, that used to be called Wat Makok;

Krung Thep Maha Nakhon, the city's Thai name, means "City of Angels, Great City" or simply "Great City of Angels" and is a shortening of the full ceremonial name: Krungthepmahanakhon Amonrattanakosin Mahintharayutthaya Mahadilokphop Noppharatratchathaniburirom Udomratchaniwetmahasathan Amonphimanawatansathit Sakkathattiyawitsanukamprasit; translated the meaning is: "City of angels, great city of immortals, magnificent city of the nine gems, seat of the king, city of royal palaces, home of gods incarnate, erected by Vishvakarman at Indra's behest"; it holds the world's record as the longest place name (169 letters); Krung Thep is used colloquially

Administrative divisions: 76 provinces (changwat, singular and plural) and 1 municipality* (maha nakhon); Amnat Charoen, Ang Thong, Bueng Kan, Buri Ram, Chachoengsao, Chai Nat, Chaiyaphum, Chanthaburi, Chiang Mai, Chiang Rai, Chon Buri, Chumphon, Kalasin, Kamphaeng Phet, Kanchanaburi, Khon Kaen, Krabi, Krung Thep* (Bangkok), Lampang, Lamphun, Loei, Lop Buri, Mae Hong Son, Maha Sarakham, Mukdahan, Nakhon Nayok, Nakhon Pathom, Nakhon Phanom, Nakhon Ratchasima, Nakhon Sawan, Nakhon Si Thammarat, Nan, Narathiwat, Nong Bua Lamphu, Nong Khai, Nonthaburi, Pathum Thani, Pattani, Phangnga, Phatthalung, Phayao, Phetchabun, Phetchaburi, Phichit, Phitsanulok, Phra Nakhon Si Ayutthaya, Phrae, Phuket, Prachin Buri, Prachuap Khiri Khan, Ranong, Ratchaburi, Rayong, Roi Et, Sa Kaeo, Sakon Nakhon, Samut Prakan, Samut Sakhon, Samut Songkhram, Saraburi, Satun, Sing Buri, Si Sa Ket, Songkhla, Sukhothai, Suphan Buri, Surat Thani, Surin, Tak, Trang, Trat, Ubon Ratchathani, Udon Thani, Uthai Thani, Uttaradit, Yala, Yasothon

Independence: 1238 (traditional founding date; never colonized)

National holiday: Birthday of King WACHIRALONGKON, 28 July (1952)

Constitution: *history:* many previous; latest drafted and presented 29 March 2016, approved by referendum 7 August 2016, signed into law by the king on 6 April 2017
amendments: amendments require a majority vote in a joint session of the House and Senate and further require at least one fifth of opposition House members and one third of the Senate vote in favor; a national referendum is additionally required for certain amendments; all amendments require signature by the king; Thailand's 2017 constitution was amended in November 2021 to increase the number of constituency members of parliament (MPs) from 350 to 400, reduce the number of party-list MPs from 150 to 100, and change the election to a two-ballot system

Legal system: civil law system with common law influences

International law organization participation: has not submitted an ICJ jurisdiction declaration; non-party state to the ICCt

Citizenship: *citizenship by birth:* no
citizenship by descent only: at least one parent must be a citizen of Thailand
dual citizenship recognized: no
residency requirement for naturalization: 5 years

Suffrage: 18 years of age; universal and compulsory

Executive branch: *chief of state:* King WACHIRALONGKON, also spelled Vajiralongkorn (since 1 December 2016)
head of government: Prime Minister PRAYUT Chan-ocha (since July 2019)
cabinet: Council of Ministers nominated by the prime minister, appointed by the king; a Privy Council advises the king
elections/appointments: the monarchy is hereditary; the House of Representatives and Senate approves a person for prime minister who must then be appointed by the King (as stated in the transitory provision of the 2017 constitution); the office of prime minister can be held for up to a total of 8 years
note: PRAYUT Chan-ocha was appointed interim prime minister in August 2014, three months after he staged the coup that removed the previously elected government of Prime Minister YINGLAK Chinnawat; on 5 June 2019 PRAYUT (independent) was approved as prime minister by the parliament

Legislative branch: *description:* bicameral National Assembly or Ratthasapha consists of:
Senate or Wuthisapha (250 seats; members appointed by the Royal Thai Army to serve 5-year terms)

House of Representatives or Saphaphuthan Ratsadon (500 seats; 375 members directly elected in single-seat constituencies by simple majority vote and 150 members elected in a single nationwide constituency by party-list proportional representation vote; members serve 4-year terms)
elections:
Senate - last held on 14 May 2019 (next to be held in 2024)
House of Representatives - last held on 24 March 2019 (next to be held in 2023)
election results:
Senate - percent of vote by party - NA; seats by party - NA; composition (248 members as of mid-2022) - men 222, women 26, percent of women 10.5%

House of Representatives - percent of vote by party in 2019 election- PPRP 23.7%, PTP 22.2%, FFP* 17.8%, DP 11.1%, PJT 10.5%, TLP 2.3%, CTP 2.2%, NEP 1.4%, PCC 1.4%, ACT 1.2%, PCP 1.2%, other 5.1%; seats by party - PTP 136, PPRP 116, FFP 81, DP 53, PJT 51, CTP 10, TLP 10, PCC 7, PCP 5, NEP 6, ACT 5, other 20; composition (489 members as of mid-2022) - men 412, women 77, percent of women 15.8%; note(s) - total National Assembly percent of women 14%; the FFP was dissolved by the Constitutional Court in February of 2020 and its representatives moved to the newly-formed Move Forward Party or to other political parties

Judicial branch: *highest court(s):* Supreme Court of Justice (consists of the court president, 6 vice

presidents, 60-70 judges, and organized into 10 divisions); Constitutional Court (consists of the court president and 8 judges); Supreme Administrative Court (number of judges determined by Judicial Commission of the Administrative Courts)
judge selection and term of office: Supreme Court judges selected by the Judicial Commission of the Courts of Justice and approved by the monarch; judge term determined by the monarch; Constitutional Court justices - 3 judges drawn from the Supreme Court, 2 judges drawn from the Administrative Court, and 4 judge candidates selected by the Selective Committee for Judges of the Constitutional Court, and confirmed by the Senate; judges appointed by the monarch serve single 9-year terms; Supreme Administrative Court judges selected by the Judicial Commission of the Administrative Courts and appointed by the monarch; judges serve for life
subordinate courts: courts of first instance and appeals courts within both the judicial and administrative systems; military courts

Political parties and leaders: Action Coalition of Thailand Party or ACT [ANEK Laothamatas]
Bhumjaithai Party (aka Phumchai Thai Party or PJT; aka Thai Pride Party) or BJT [ANUTIN Charnvirakul]
Chat Phatthana Party (National Development Party) [THEWAN Liptaphanlop]
Chat Thai Phatthana Party (Thai Nation Development Party) or CTP [VARAWUT Silpa-archa]
New Economics Party or NEP [MINGKHWAN Sangsuwan]
Move Forward Party or MFP [PHITHA Limcharoenrat] (formed in 2020 from the disbanded Future Forward Party or FPP)
Palang Pracharat Party (People's State Power Party) or PPRP [PRAWIT Wongsuwan] (a pro-military party formed in 2018 by members of the military junta's cabinet)
Prachachat Party of PCC [WAN Muhamad NOOR Matha]
Prachathipat Party (Democrat Party) or DP [JURIN Laksanawisit]
Puea Chat Party (For Nation Party) or PCP [SARUNWUT Sarunket]
Puea Thai Party (For Thais Party) or PTP [CHONLANON Sikaew]
Puea Tham Party (For Dharma Party) [NALINI Thawisin]
Seri Ruam Thai Party (Thai Liberal Party or TLP) [SERIPHISUT Temiyawet]
Thai Civilized Party or TCL [MONGKOLKIT Suksintharanon]
Thai Local Power Party or TLP [CHATCHAWAI Kong-udom]
Thai People Power Party or TLPT [NIKHOM Bunwiset]
Thai Raksa Chat Party (Thai National Preservation Party) [PRICHAPHON Phongpanit]

International organization participation: ADB, APEC, ARF, ASEAN, BIMSTEC, BIS, CD, CICA, CP, EAS, FAO, G-77, IAEA, IBRD, ICAO, ICC (national committees), ICRM, IDA, IFAD, IFC, IFRCS, IHO, ILO, IMF, IMO, IMSO, Interpol, IOC, IOM, IPU, ISO, ITSO, ITU, ITUC (NGOs), MIGA, NAM, OAS (observer), OIC (observer), OIF (observer), OPCW, OSCE (partner), PCA, PIF (partner), UN, UNAMID, UNCTAD, UNESCO, UNHCR, UNIDO, UNMOGIP, UNOCI, UNWTO, UPU, WCO, WFTU (NGOs), WHO, WIPO, WMO, WTO

Diplomatic representation in the US: *chief of mission:* Ambassador MANATSAWI Sisodaphon (since 17 February 2021)
chancery: 1024 Wisconsin Avenue NW, Suite 401, Washington, DC 20007
telephone: [1] (202) 944-3600
FAX: [1] (202) 944-3611
email address and website:
https://thaiembdc.org
consulate(s) general: Chicago, Los Angeles, New York

Diplomatic representation from the US: *chief of mission:* Ambassador Robert F. GODEC (since 7 October 2022)
embassy: 95 Wireless Road, Bangkok 10330
mailing address: 7200 Bangkok Place, Washington DC 20521-7200
telephone: [66] 2-205-4000
FAX: [66] 2-205-4103
email address and website:
acsbkk@state.gov
https://th.usembassy.gov/
consulate(s) general: Chiang Mai

Flag description: five horizontal bands of red (top), white, blue (double width), white, and red; the red color symbolizes the nation and the blood of life, white represents religion and the purity of Buddhism, and blue stands for the monarchy
note: similar to the flag of Costa Rica but with the blue and red colors reversed

National symbol(s): garuda (mythical half-man, half-bird figure), elephant; national colors: red, white, blue

National anthem: *name:* "Phleng Chat Thai" (National Anthem of Thailand)
lyrics/music: Luang SARANUPRAPAN/Phra JENDURIYANG
note: music adopted 1932, lyrics adopted 1939; by law, people are required to stand for the national anthem at 0800 and 1800 every day; the anthem is played in schools, offices, theaters, and on television and radio during this time; "Phleng Sanlasoen Phra Barami" (A Salute to the Monarch) serves as the royal anthem and is played in the presence of the royal family and during certain state ceremonies

National heritage: *total World Heritage Sites:* 6 (3 cultural, 3 natural)
selected World Heritage Site locales: Historic City of Ayutthaya (c); Historic Sukhothai and Associated Historic Towns (c); Thungyai-Huai Kha Khaeng Wildlife Sanctuaries (n); Ban Chiang Archaeological Site (c); Dong Phayayen-Khao Yai Forest Complex (n); Kaeng Krachan Forest Complex (n)

ECONOMY

Economic overview: With a relatively well-developed infrastructure, a free-enterprise economy, and generally pro-investment policies, Thailand is highly dependent on international trade, with exports accounting for about two thirds of GDP. Thailand's exports include electronics, agricultural commodities, automobiles and parts, and processed foods. The industry and service sectors produce about 90% of GDP. The agricultural sector, comprised mostly of small-scale farms, contributes only 10% of GDP but employs about one third of the labor force. Thailand has attracted an estimated 3.0-4.5 million migrant workers, mostly from neighboring countries.

Over the last few decades, Thailand has reduced poverty substantially. In 2013, the Thai Government implemented a nationwide 300 baht (roughly $10) per day minimum wage policy and deployed new tax reforms designed to lower rates on middle-income earners.

Thailand's economy is recovering from slow growth during the years since the 2014 coup. Thailand's economic fundamentals are sound, with low inflation, low unemployment, and reasonable public and external debt levels. Tourism and government spending - mostly on infrastructure and short-term stimulus measures – have helped to boost the economy, and The Bank of Thailand has been supportive, with several interest rate reductions.

Over the longer-term, household debt levels, political uncertainty, and an aging population pose risks to growth.

Real GDP (purchasing power parity): $1,206,620,000,000 (2020 est.)
$1,284,830,000,000 (2019 est.)
$1,256,360,000,000 (2018 est.)
note: data are in 2017 dollars
country comparison to the world: 21

Real GDP growth rate: 2.62% (2019 est.)
4.31% (2018 est.)
4.26% (2017 est.)
country comparison to the world: 108

Real GDP per capita: $17,300 (2020 est.)
$18,500 (2019 est.)
$18,100 (2018 est.)
note: data are in 2017 dollars
country comparison to the world: 97

GDP (official exchange rate): $543.798 billion (2019 est.)

Inflation rate (consumer prices): 0.7% (2019 est.)
1% (2018 est.)
0.6% (2017 est.)
country comparison to the world: 56

Credit ratings:

Fitch rating: BBB+ (2013)

Moody's rating: Baa1 (2003)

Standard & Poors rating: BBB+ (2004)

GDP - composition, by sector of origin: *agriculture:* 8.2% (2017 est.)
industry: 36.2% (2017 est.)
services: 55.6% (2017 est.)

GDP - composition, by end use: *household consumption:* 48.8% (2017 est.)
government consumption: 16.4% (2017 est.)
investment in fixed capital: 23.2% (2017 est.)
investment in inventories: -0.4% (2017 est.)
exports of goods and services: 68.2% (2017 est.)
imports of goods and services: -54.6% (2017 est.)

Agricultural products: sugar cane, cassava, rice, oil palm fruit, rubber, maize, tropical fruit, poultry, pineapples, mangoes/guavas

Industries: tourism, textiles and garments, agricultural processing, beverages, tobacco, cement, light manufacturing such as jewelry and electric appliances, computers and parts, integrated circuits, furniture, plastics, automobiles and automotive parts, agricultural machinery, air conditioning and refrigeration, ceramics, aluminum, chemical, environmental management, glass, granite and marble, leather, machinery and metal work, petrochemical, petroleum refining, pharmaceuticals, printing, pulp and paper, rubber, sugar, rice, fishing, cassava, world's second-largest tungsten producer and third-largest tin producer

Industrial production growth rate: 1.6% (2017 est.)
country comparison to the world: 141

Labor force: 37.546 million (2020 est.)
country comparison to the world: 16

Labor force - by occupation: *agriculture:* 31.8%
industry: 16.7%
services: 51.5% (2015 est.)

Unemployment rate: 0.99% (2019 est.)
1.06% (2018 est.)
country comparison to the world: 7

Unemployment, youth ages 15-24: *total:* 5.2%
male: 4.6%
female: 5.9% (2020 est.)
country comparison to the world: 168

Population below poverty line: 9.9% (2018 est.)

Gini Index coefficient - distribution of family income: 36.4 (2018 est.)
48.4 (2011)
country comparison to the world: 91

Household income or consumption by percentage share: *lowest 10%:* 2.8%
highest 10%: 31.5% (2009 est.)

Budget: *revenues:* 69.23 billion (2017 est.)
expenditures: 85.12 billion (2017 est.)

Budget surplus (+) or deficit (-): -3.5% (of GDP) (2017 est.)
country comparison to the world: 148

Public debt: 41.9% of GDP (2017 est.)
41.8% of GDP (2016 est.)
note: data cover general government debt and include debt instruments issued (or owned) by government entities other than the treasury; the data include treasury debt held by foreign entities; the data include debt issued by subnational entities, as well as intragovernmental debt; intragovernmental debt consists of treasury borrowings from surpluses in the social funds, such as for retirement, medical care, and unemployment; debt instruments for the social funds are sold at public auctions
country comparison to the world: 118

Taxes and other revenues: 15.2% (of GDP) (2017 est.)
country comparison to the world: 193

Fiscal year: 1 October - 30 September

Current account balance: $37.033 billion (2019 est.)
$28.423 billion (2018 est.)
country comparison to the world: 11

Exports: $258.42 billion (2020 est.) note: data are in current year dollars
$323.88 billion (2019 est.) note: data are in current year dollars
$328.58 billion (2018 est.) note: data are in current year dollars
country comparison to the world: 25

Exports - partners: United States 13%, China 12%, Japan 10%, Vietnam 5% (2019)

Exports - commodities: office machinery/parts, cars and vehicle parts, integrated circuits, delivery trucks, gold (2019)

Imports: $233.75 billion (2020 est.) note: data are in current year dollars
$272.83 billion (2019 est.) note: data are in current year dollars
$283.66 billion (2018 est.) note: data are in current year dollars
country comparison to the world: 24

Imports - partners: China 22%, Japan 14%, United States 7%, Malaysia 6% (2019)

Imports - commodities: crude petroleum, integrated circuits, natural gas, vehicle parts, gold (2019)

Reserves of foreign exchange and gold: $202.6 billion (31 December 2017 est.)
$171.9 billion (31 December 2016 est.)
country comparison to the world: 12

Debt - external: $167.89 billion (2019 est.)
$158.964 billion (2018 est.)
country comparison to the world: 44

Exchange rates: baht per US dollar -
30.03 (2020 est.)
30.29749 (2019 est.)
32.8075 (2018 est.)
34.248 (2014 est.)
32.48 (2013 est.)

ENERGY

Electricity access: *electrification - total population:* 100% (2020)

Electricity: *installed generating capacity:* 53.13 million kW (2020 est.)
consumption: 190,569,262,000 kWh (2019 est.)
exports: 2,617,583,000 kWh (2020 est.)
imports: 29,550,571,000 kWh (2020 est.)
transmission/distribution losses: 13.286 billion kWh (2019 est.)

Electricity generation sources: *fossil fuels:* 83.3% of total installed capacity (2020 est.)
solar: 2.8% of total installed capacity (2020 est.)
wind: 1.7% of total installed capacity (2020 est.)
hydroelectricity: 2.6% of total installed capacity (2020 est.)
biomass and waste: 9.6% of total installed capacity (2020 est.)

Coal: *production:* 13.251 million metric tons (2020 est.)
consumption: 35.761 million metric tons (2020 est.)
exports: 63,000 metric tons (2020 est.)
imports: 23.899 million metric tons (2020 est.)
proven reserves: 1.063 billion metric tons (2019 est.)

Petroleum: *total petroleum production:* 438,200 bbl/day (2021 est.)
refined petroleum consumption: 1,284,800 bbl/day (2019 est.)
crude oil and lease condensate exports: 28,600 bbl/day (2018 est.)
crude oil and lease condensate imports: 979,800 bbl/day (2018 est.)
crude oil estimated reserves: 252.8 million barrels (2021 est.)

Refined petroleum products - production: 1.328 million bbl/day (2015 est.)
country comparison to the world: 14

Refined petroleum products - exports: 278,300 bbl/day (2015 est.)
country comparison to the world: 29

Refined petroleum products - imports: 134,200 bbl/day (2015 est.)
country comparison to the world: 44

Natural gas: *production:* 38,420,517,000 cubic meters (2019 est.)
consumption: 54,802,466,000 cubic meters (2019 est.)
exports: 0 cubic meters (2021 est.)
imports: 14,944,842,000 cubic meters (2019 est.)
proven reserves: 138.243 billion cubic meters (2021 est.)

Carbon dioxide emissions: 305.273 million metric tonnes of CO2 (2019 est.)
from coal and metallurgical coke: 58.78 million metric tonnes of CO2 (2019 est.)
from petroleum and other liquids: 146.172 million metric tonnes of CO2 (2019 est.)
from consumed natural gas: 100.321 million metric tonnes of CO2 (2019 est.)
country comparison to the world: 20

Energy consumption per capita: 76.714 million Btu/person (2019 est.)
country comparison to the world: 79

COMMUNICATIONS

Telephones - fixed lines: *total subscriptions:* 5.003 million (2020 est.)
subscriptions per 100 inhabitants: 7 (2020 est.)
country comparison to the world: 29

Telephones - mobile cellular: *total subscriptions:* 129.614 million (2019)
subscriptions per 100 inhabitants: 186.16 (2019)
country comparison to the world: 13

Telecommunication systems: *general assessment:* Thailand's telecom sector is relatively mature and hosts a mix of public and private sector players; the mobile market is highly developed and has experienced strong growth over the last seven years; the market returned to growth in 2021 after it contracted in 2020 driven by the Covid-19 pandemic, and a steep decline in inbound tourism; it remains highly saturated, owing to overall maturity and the popularity of multiple SIM card use, which has resulted in a particularly high penetration rate; in general, the sector retains considerable potential given the impetus of 5G, the recent spectrum auctions, and continued network deployments by the country's network operators; further auctions of spectrum in the 700MHz band (being repurposed from digital TV broadcasting), and in the 3.6GHz range will further improve network capacity; in the wire line segment, the decline in fixed-line penetration is expected to continue as subscribers migrate to mobile networks for voice and data services; the emphasis among operators has been to bolster their fiber footprints in key high-value areas; the transition to fiber from DSL and cable has also been facilitated by changes to the regulatory structure that have removed some barriers to investment; this is supporting the cannibalization of older copper-based DSL lines by fiber; the returns from this investment remain a long-term prospect as consumers still favor entry-level packages; there is also strong interest from the government, as well as private vendors, in establishing Thailand as a data center hub to serve the region; the size, capacity and spread of existing data centers in the Greater Mekong Subregion (GMS) outside of Thailand is small; Thailand retains some advantages to attract investment, including improved fiber connectivity and international bandwidth; increasing submarine capacity, such as the SJC2 cable to come online later in 2022, will considerably improve Thailand's potential as a regional hub (2022)

domestic: fixed-line system provided by both a government-owned and commercial provider; wireless service expanding; fixed-line over 7 per 100 and mobile-cellular nearly 167 per 100 (2020)
international: country code - 66; landing points for the AAE-1, FEA, SeaMeWe-3,-4, APG, SJC2, TIS, MCT and AAG submarine cable systems providing links throughout Asia, Australia, Africa, Middle East, Europe, and US; satellite earth stations - 2 Intelsat (1 Indian Ocean, 1 Pacific Ocean) (2019)

Broadcast media: 26 digital TV stations in Bangkok broadcast nationally, 6 terrestrial TV stations in Bangkok broadcast nationally via relay stations - 2 of the stations are owned by the military, the other 4 are government-owned or controlled, leased to private enterprise, and all are required to broadcast government-produced news programs twice a day; multi-channel satellite and cable TV subscription services are available; radio frequencies have been allotted for more than 500 government and commercial radio stations; many small community radio stations operate with low-power transmitters (2017)

Internet country code: .th

Internet users: *total:* 54,443,983 (2020 est.)
percent of population: 78% (2020 est.)
country comparison to the world: 19

Broadband - fixed subscriptions: *total:* 11,478,265 (2020 est.)
subscriptions per 100 inhabitants: 16 (2020 est.)
country comparison to the world: 18

TRANSPORTATION

National air transport system: *number of registered air carriers:* 15 (2020)
inventory of registered aircraft operated by air carriers: 283
annual passenger traffic on registered air carriers: 76,053,042 (2018)
annual freight traffic on registered air carriers: 2,666,260,000 (2018) mt-km

Civil aircraft registration country code prefix: HS

Airports: *total:* 101 (2021)
country comparison to the world: 56

Airports - with paved runways: *total:* 63
over 3,047 m: 8
2,438 to 3,047 m: 12
1,524 to 2,437 m: 23
914 to 1,523 m: 14
under 914 m: 6 (2021)

Airports - with unpaved runways: *total:* 38
2,438 to 3,047 m: 1
1,524 to 2,437 m: 1
914 to 1,523 m: 10
under 914 m: 26 (2021)

Heliports: 7 (2021)

Pipelines: 2 km condensate, 5,900 km gas, 85 km liquid petroleum gas, 1 km oil, 1,097 km refined products (2013)

Railways: *total:* 4,127 km (2017)
standard gauge: 84 km (2017) 1.435-m gauge (84 km electrified)
narrow gauge: 4,043 km (2017) 1.000-m gauge
country comparison to the world: 46

Roadways: *total:* 180,053 km (2006) (includes 450 km of expressways)
country comparison to the world: 30

Waterways: 4,000 km (2011) (3,701 km navigable by boats with drafts up to 0.9 m)
country comparison to the world: 28

Merchant marine: *total:* 839
by type: bulk carrier 26, container ship 27, general cargo 94, oil tanker 251, other 441 (2021)
country comparison to the world: 28

Ports and terminals: *major seaport(s):* Bangkok, Laem Chabang, Map Ta Phut, Prachuap Port, Si Racha
container port(s) (TEUs): Laem Chabang (8,106,928) (2019)

LNG terminal(s) (import): Map Ta Phut

MILITARY AND SECURITY

Military and security forces: Royal Thai Armed Forces (Kongthap Thai, RTARF): Royal Thai Army (Kongthap Bok Thai, RTA), Royal Thai Navy (Kongthap Ruea Thai, RTN; includes Royal Thai Marine Corps), Royal Thai Air Force (Kongthap Akaat Thai, RTAF); Office of the Prime Minister: Royal Thai Police; Internal Security Operations Command (ISOC) (2022)
note 1: the ISOC oversees counter-insurgency operations, as well as countering terrorism, narcotics and weapons trafficking, and other internal security duties; it is primarily run by the Army
note 2: official paramilitary forces in Thailand include the Thai Rangers (Thahan Phran or "Hunter Soldiers") under the Army; the Paramilitary Marines under the Navy; the Border Patrol Police (BPP) under the Royal Thai Police; the Volunteer Defense Corps (VDC or *O So*) and National Defense Volunteers (NDV), both under the Ministry of Interior; there are also several government-backed volunteer militias created to provide village security against insurgents in the deep south or to assist the ISOC

Military expenditures: 1.3% of GDP (2021 est.)
1.4% of GDP (2020)
1.3% of GDP (2019) (approximately $14.6 billion)
1.3% of GDP (2018) (approximately $14.2 billion)
1.4% of GDP (2017) (approximately $13.8 billion)
country comparison to the world: 108

Military and security service personnel strengths: estimated 300,000 active duty personnel (200,000 Army; 70,000 Navy; 30,000 Air Force); approximately 230,000 Royal Thai Police (2022)

Military equipment inventories and acquisitions: the RTARF has a diverse array of foreign-supplied weapons systems, including a large amount of obsolescent or second-hand US equipment; since 2010, Thailand has received military equipment from nearly 20 countries, including China, South Korea, Sweden, Ukraine, and the US; as of 2022, Thailand was making efforts to increase its domestic defense production capabilities in such areas as armored vehicles, unmanned aerial systems, and military technologies (2022)

Military service age and obligation: 18 years of age for voluntary military service for men and women; 21 years of age for compulsory military service for men; men register at 18 years of age; volunteer service obligation may be as short as 6 or 12 months, depending on educational qualifications; conscript service obligation also varies by educational qualifications, but is typically 24 months (2022)
note 1: serving in the armed forces is a national duty of all Thai citizens; conscription was introduced in 1905; it includes women, however, only men over the age of 21 who have not gone through reserve training are conscripted; conscripts are chosen by lottery (on draft day, eligible draftees can request volunteer service, or they may choose to stay for the conscription lottery); approximately 75-100,000 men are drafted for military service each year and conscripts reportedly comprise as much as 50% of the armed forces
note 2: as of 2020, women comprised about 8% of active-duty military personnel

Military deployments: 280 South Sudan (UNMISS) (May 2022)

Military - note: including the most recent in 2014, the military has attempted more than 20 coups since the fall of absolute monarchy in 1932

since 2004, the military has fought against separatist insurgents in the southern provinces of Pattani, Yala, and Narathiwat, as well as parts of Songkhla; the insurgency is rooted in ethnic Malay nationalist resistance to Thai rule that followed the extension of Siamese sovereignty over the Patani Sultanate in the 18th century; the insurgency consists of several armed groups, the largest of which is the Barisan Revolusi Nasional-Koordinasi (BRN-C): since 2020, the Thai military has been negotiating with BRN, and has parallel talks with an umbrella organization, MARA Pattani, that claims to represent the insurgency groups; since 2004, violence associated with the insurgency has claimed more than 7,300 lives (as of 2022); the Thai Government has had as many as 100,000 military and paramilitary forces deployed in the south to combat the insurgency

Thailand has Major Non-NATO Ally (MNNA) status with the US; MNNA is a designation under US law that provides foreign partners with certain benefits in the areas of defense trade and security cooperation; while MNNA status provides military and economic privileges, it does not entail any security commitments (2022)

TRANSNATIONAL ISSUES

Disputes - international: *Thailand-Burma:* in 2016, Thailand expressed its interest in investing in Burma's Hatgyi Dam project on the Salween River near the Thai-Burma border; the dam has the potential to supply electricity and water during the drought season; approximately 100,000 mostly Karen refugees fleeing civil strife, political upheaval, and economic stagnation in Burma live in nine remote camps in Thailand near the border
Thailand-Cambodia: Cambodia and Thailand dispute sections of their border; in 2011, Thailand and Cambodia resorted to arms in the dispute over the location of the boundary on the precipice surmounted by Preah Vihear temple ruins, awarded to Cambodia by ICJ decision in 1962 and part of a planned UN World Heritage site; in 2013, the International Court of Justice ruled that the land with the temple was Cambodian territory but that a nearby hill belonged to Thailand
Thailand-Laos: talks continue on completion of demarcation with Laos but disputes remain over several islands in the Mekong River
Thailand-Malaysia: separatist violence in Thailand's predominantly Malay-Muslim southern provinces prompt border closures and controls with Malaysia to stem insurgent activities; disputed areas are the Bukit Jeli area at the headwaters of the Golok River and the continental shelf boundary in the Gulf of Thailand

Refugees and internally displaced persons: *refugees (country of origin):* 91,349 (Burma) (2022)
IDPs: 41,000 (2021)
stateless persons: 554,103 (mid-year 2021) (estimate represents stateless persons registered with the Thai Government; actual number may be as high as 3.5 million); note - about half of Thailand's northern hill tribe people do not have citizenship and make up the bulk of Thailand's stateless population; most lack documentation showing they or one of their parents were born in Thailand; children born to Burmese refugees are not eligible for Burmese or Thai citizenship and are stateless; most Chao Lay, maritime nomadic peoples, who travel from island to island in the Andaman Sea west of Thailand are also stateless; stateless Rohingya refugees from Burma are considered illegal migrants by Thai authorities and are detained in inhumane conditions or expelled; stateless persons are denied access to voting, property, education, employment, healthcare, and driving
note: Thai nationality was granted to more than 23,000 stateless persons between 2012 and 2016 and more than 18,000 between 2018 and 2021; in 2016, the Government of Thailand approved changes to its citizenship laws that could make 80,000 stateless persons eligible for citizenship, as part of its effort to achieve zero statelessness by 2024 (2021)

Illicit drugs: a minor producer of opium, heroin, and cannabis products; major part of the illegal drug market for the Southeast Asia region and the interconnected markets in East Asia and Oceania; transit point for illicit heroin en route to the international drug market from Burma and Laos; "Yaba," a tablet containing methamphetamine, caffeine, and other stimulants, is the most widely abused drug in Thailand

TIMOR-LESTE

INTRODUCTION

Background: Timor was actively involved in Southeast Asian trading networks for centuries, and by the 14th century exported aromatic sandalwood, slaves, honey, and wax. A number of local chiefdoms ruled the island in the early 16th century when Portuguese traders arrived, chiefly attracted by the relative abundance of sandalwood on Timor; by mid-century, the Portuguese had colonized the island. Skirmishing with the Dutch in the region eventually resulted in an 1859 treaty in which Portugal ceded the western portion of the island. Imperial Japan occupied Portuguese Timor from 1942 to 1945, but Portugal resumed colonial authority after the Japanese defeat in World War II. East Timor declared itself independent from Portugal on 28 November 1975 and was invaded and occupied by Indonesian forces nine days later. It was incorporated into Indonesia in July 1976 as the province of Timor Timur (East Timor). An unsuccessful campaign of pacification followed over the next two decades, during which an estimated 100,000 to 250,000 people died. In an August 1999 UN-supervised popular referendum, an overwhelming majority of the people of Timor-Leste voted for independence from Indonesia. However, in the next three weeks, anti-independence Timorese militias - organized and supported by the Indonesian military - commenced a large-scale, scorched-earth campaign of retribution. The militias killed approximately 1,400 Timorese and displaced nearly 500,000. Most of the country's infrastructure, including homes, irrigation systems, water supply systems, and schools, and nearly all of the country's electrical grid were destroyed. On 20 September 1999, Australian-led peacekeeping troops deployed to the country and brought the violence to an end. On 20 May 2002, Timor-Leste was internationally recognized as an independent state.

In 2006, internal tensions threatened the new nation's security when a military strike led to violence and a breakdown of law and order. At Dili's request, an Australian-led International Stabilization Force (ISF) deployed to Timor-Leste, and the UN Security Council established the UN Integrated Mission in Timor-Leste (UNMIT), which included an authorized police presence of over 1,600 personnel. The ISF and UNMIT restored stability, allowing for presidential and parliamentary elections in 2007 in a largely peaceful atmosphere. In February 2008, a rebel group staged an unsuccessful attack against the president and prime minister. The ringleader was killed in the attack, and most of the rebels surrendered in April 2008. Since the attack, the government has enjoyed one of its longest periods of post-independence stability, including successful 2012 elections for both the National Parliament and president and a successful transition of power in February 2015. In late 2012, the UN Security Council ended its peacekeeping mission in Timor-Leste and both the ISF and UNMIT departed the country.

GEOGRAPHY

Location: Southeastern Asia, northwest of Australia in the Lesser Sunda Islands at the eastern end of the Indonesian archipelago; note - Timor-Leste includes the eastern half of the island of Timor, the Oecussi (Ambeno) region on the northwest portion of the island of Timor, and the islands of Pulau Atauro and Pulau Jaco

Geographic coordinates: 8 50 S, 125 55 E

Map references: Southeast Asia

Area: *total:* 14,874 sq km
land: 14,874 sq km
water: 0 sq km
country comparison to the world: 159

Area - comparative: slightly larger than Connecticut; almost half the size of Maryland

Land boundaries: *total:* 253 km
border countries (1): Indonesia 253 km

Coastline: 706 km

Maritime claims: *territorial sea:* 12 nm
contiguous zone: 24 nm
exclusive fishing zone: 200 nm

Climate: tropical; hot, humid; distinct rainy and dry seasons

Terrain: mountainous

Elevation: *highest point:* Foho Tatamailau 2,963 m
lowest point: Timor Sea, Savu Sea, and Banda Sea 0 m

Natural resources: gold, petroleum, natural gas, manganese, marble

Land use: *agricultural land:* 25.1% (2018 est.)
arable land: 10.1% (2018 est.)
permanent crops: 4.9% (2018 est.)
permanent pasture: 10.1% (2018 est.)
forest: 49.1% (2018 est.)
other: 25.8% (2018 est.)

Irrigated land: 350 sq km (2012)

Population distribution: most of the population concentrated in the western third of the country, particularly around Dili

Natural hazards: floods and landslides are common; earthquakes; tsunamis; tropical cyclones

Geography - note: Timor comes from the Malay word for "east"; the island of Timor is part of the Malay Archipelago and is the largest and easternmost of the Lesser Sunda Islands; the district of Oecussi is an exclave separated from Timor-Leste proper by Indonesia; Timor-Leste has the unique distinction of being the only Asian country located completely in the Southern Hemisphere

PEOPLE AND SOCIETY

Population: 1,445,006 (2022 est.)
country comparison to the world: 156

Nationality: *noun:* Timorese
adjective: Timorese

Ethnic groups: Austronesian (Malayo-Polynesian) (includes Tetun, Mambai, Tokodede, Galoli, Kemak, Baikeno), Melanesian-Papuan (includes Bunak, Fataluku, Bakasai), small Chinese minority

Languages: Tetun Prasa 30.6%, Mambai 16.6%, Makasai 10.5%, Tetun Terik 6.1%, Baikenu 5.9%, Kemak 5.8%, Bunak 5.5%, Tokodede 4%, Fataluku 3.5%, Waima'a 1.8%, Galoli 1.4%, Naueti 1.4%, Idate 1.2%, Midiki 1.2%, other 4.5% (2015 est.)
note: data represent population by mother tongue; Tetun and Portuguese are official languages;

Indonesian and English are working languages; there are about 32 indigenous languages

Religions: Roman Catholic 97.6%, Protestant/ Evangelical 2%, Muslim 0.2%, other 0.2% (2015 est.)

Demographic profile: Timor-Leste's high fertility and population growth rates sustain its very youthful age structure – approximately 40% of the population is below the age of 15 and the country's median age is 20. While Timor-Leste's total fertility rate (TFR) – the average number of births per woman - decreased significantly from over 7 in the early 2000s, it remains high at 4.3 in 2021 and will probably continue to decline slowly. The low use of contraceptives and the traditional preference for large families is keeping fertility elevated. The high TFR and falling mortality rates continue to fuel a high population growth rate of nearly 2.2%, which is the highest in Southeast Asia. The country's high total dependency ratio – a measure of the ratio of dependents to the working-age population – could divert more government spending toward social programs. Timor-Leste's growing, poorly educated working-age population and insufficient job creation are ongoing problems. Some 70% of the population lives in rural areas, where most of people are dependent on the agricultural sector. Malnutrition and poverty are prevalent, with 42% of the population living under the poverty line as of 2014.

During the Indonesian occupation (1975-1999) and Timor-Leste's fight for independence, approximately 250,000 Timorese fled to western Timor and, in lesser numbers, Australia, Portugal, and other countries. Many of these emigrants later returned. Since Timor-Leste's 1999 independence referendum, economic motives and periods of conflict have been the main drivers of emigration. Bilateral labor agreements with Australia, Malaysia, and South Korea and the presence of Timorese populations abroad, are pull factors, but the high cost prevents many young Timorese from emigrating. Timorese communities are found in its former colonizers, Indonesia and Portugal, as well as the Philippines and the UK. The country has also become a destination for migrants in the surrounding region, mainly men seeking work in construction, commerce, and services in Dili.

Age structure: *0-14 years:* 39.96% (male 284,353/ female 268,562)
15-24 years: 20.32% (male 142,693/female 138,508)
25-54 years: 30.44% (male 202,331/female 218,914)
55-64 years: 5.22% (male 34,956/female 37,229)
65 years and over: 4.06% (male 27,153/female 29,024) (2020 est.)

Dependency ratios: *total dependency ratio:* 90.3
youth dependency ratio: 83.7
elderly dependency ratio: 6.6
potential support ratio: 15.2 (2020 est.)

Median age: *total:* 19.6 years
male: 18.9 years
female: 20.2 years (2020 est.)
country comparison to the world: 200

Population growth rate: 2.15% (2022 est.)
country comparison to the world: 37

Birth rate: 30.94 births/1,000 population (2022 est.)
country comparison to the world: 28

Death rate: 5.61 deaths/1,000 population (2022 est.)
country comparison to the world: 178

Net migration rate: -3.82 migrant(s)/1,000 population (2022 est.)
country comparison to the world: 189

Population distribution: most of the population concentrated in the western third of the country, particularly around Dili

Urbanization: *urban population:* 32.1% of total population (2022)
rate of urbanization: 3.31% annual rate of change (2020-25 est.)

Major urban areas - population: 281,000 DILI (capital) (2018)

Sex ratio: *at birth:* 1.07 male(s)/female
0-14 years: 1.06 male(s)/female
15-24 years: 1.03 male(s)/female
25-54 years: 0.93 male(s)/female
55-64 years: 0.9 male(s)/female
65 years and over: 0.79 male(s)/female
total population: 1 male(s)/female (2022 est.)

Mother's mean age at first birth: 23 years (2016 est.)
note: data represents median age at first birth among women 25-49

Maternal mortality ratio: 142 deaths/100,000 live births (2017 est.)
country comparison to the world: 60

Infant mortality rate: *total:* 33.69 deaths/1,000 live births
male: 36.96 deaths/1,000 live births
female: 30.2 deaths/1,000 live births (2022 est.)
country comparison to the world: 40

Life expectancy at birth: *total population:* 69.92 years
male: 68.25 years
female: 71.7 years (2022 est.)
country comparison to the world: 173

Total fertility rate: 4.21 children born/woman (2022 est.)
country comparison to the world: 26

Contraceptive prevalence rate: 26.1% (2016)

Drinking water source: *improved: urban:* 98% of population
rural: 82.5% of population
total: 87.4% of population
unimproved: urban: 2% of population
rural: 17.5% of population
total: 12.6% of population (2020 est.)

Current health expenditure: 7.2% of GDP (2019)

Physicians density: 0.76 physicians/1,000 population (2020)

Sanitation facility access: *improved: urban:* 88.7% of population
rural: 56.1% of population
total: 66.3% of population
unimproved: urban: 11.3% of population
rural: 43.9% of population
total: 33.7% of population (2020 est.)

HIV/AIDS - adult prevalence rate: 0.2% (2020 est.)
country comparison to the world: 116

HIV/AIDS - people living with HIV/AIDS: 1,200 (2020)
country comparison to the world: 144

HIV/AIDS - deaths: (2020) <100

Major infectious diseases: *degree of risk:* very high (2020)
food or waterborne diseases: bacterial diarrhea, hepatitis A, and typhoid fever
vectorborne diseases: dengue fever and malaria

Obesity - adult prevalence rate: 3.8% (2016)
country comparison to the world: 190

Alcohol consumption per capita: *total:* 0.41 liters of pure alcohol (2019 est.)
beer: 0.27 liters of pure alcohol (2019 est.)
wine: 0.09 liters of pure alcohol (2019 est.)
spirits: 0.05 liters of pure alcohol (2019 est.)
other alcohols: 0 liters of pure alcohol (2019 est.)
country comparison to the world: 166

Tobacco use: *total:* 39.2% (2020 est.)
male: 67.6% (2020 est.)
female: 10.8% (2020 est.)
country comparison to the world: 6

Children under the age of 5 years underweight: 37.5% (2013)
country comparison to the world: 2

Child marriage: *women married by age 15:* 2.6%
women married by age 18: 14.9%
men married by age 18: 1.2% (2016 est.)

Education expenditures: 6.8% of GDP (2018 est.)
country comparison to the world: 23

Literacy: *definition:* age 15 and over can read and write
total population: 68.1%
male: 71.9%
female: 64.2% (2018)

Unemployment, youth ages 15-24: *total:* 13.2%
male: 10.9%
female: 15.9% (2016 est.)

People - note: one of only two predominantly Christian nations in Southeast Asia, the other being the Philippines

ENVIRONMENT

Environment - current issues: air pollution and deterioration of air quality; greenhouse gas emissions; water quality, scarcity, and access; land and soil degradation; forest depletion; widespread use of slash and burn agriculture has led to deforestation and soil erosion; loss of biodiversity

Environment - international agreements: *party to:* Biodiversity, Climate Change, Climate Change-Kyoto Protocol, Climate Change-Paris Agreement, Desertification, Law of the Sea, Ozone Layer Protection
signed, but not ratified: Comprehensive Nuclear Test Ban

Air pollutants: *particulate matter emissions:* 17.88 micrograms per cubic meter (2016 est.)
carbon dioxide emissions: 0.5 megatons (2016 est.)
methane emissions: 4.74 megatons (2020 est.)

Climate: tropical; hot, humid; distinct rainy and dry seasons

Land use: *agricultural land:* 25.1% (2018 est.)
arable land: 10.1% (2018 est.)
permanent crops: 4.9% (2018 est.)
permanent pasture: 10.1% (2018 est.)
forest: 49.1% (2018 est.)
other: 25.8% (2018 est.)

Urbanization: *urban population:* 32.1% of total population (2022)
rate of urbanization: 3.31% annual rate of change (2020-25 est.)

Revenue from forest resources: *forest revenues:* 0.13% of GDP (2018 est.)
country comparison to the world: 108

Revenue from coal: *coal revenues:* 0% of GDP (2018 est.)
country comparison to the world: 174

Waste and recycling: *municipal solid waste generated annually:* 63,875 tons (2016 est.)

Total water withdrawal: *municipal:* 99 million cubic meters (2017 est.)
industrial: 2 million cubic meters (2017 est.)
agricultural: 1.071 billion cubic meters (2017 est.)

Total renewable water resources: 8.215 billion cubic meters (2017 est.)

GOVERNMENT

Country name: *conventional long form:* Democratic Republic of Timor-Leste
conventional short form: Timor-Leste
local long form: Republika Demokratika Timor Lorosa'e (Tetum)/ Republica Democratica de Timor-Leste (Portuguese)
local short form: Timor Lorosa'e (Tetum)/ Timor-Leste (Portuguese)
former: East Timor, Portuguese Timor
etymology: timor" derives from the Indonesian and Malay word "timur" meaning "east"; "leste" is the Portuguese word for "east", so "Timor-Leste" literally means "Eastern-East"; the local [Tetum] name "Timor Lorosa'e" translates as "East Rising Sun"
note: pronounced TEE-mor LESS-tay

Government type: semi-presidential republic

Capital: *name:* Dili
geographic coordinates: 8 35 S, 125 36 E
time difference: UTC+9 (14 hours ahead of Washington, DC, during Standard Time)

Administrative divisions: 12 municipalities (municipios, singular municipio) and 1 special adminstrative region* (regiao administrativa especial); Aileu, Ainaro, Baucau, Bobonaro (Maliana), Covalima (Suai), Dili, Ermera (Gleno), Lautem (Lospalos), Liquica, Manatuto, Manufahi (Same), Oe-Cusse Ambeno* (Pante Macassar), Viqueque
note: administrative divisions have the same names as their administrative centers (exceptions have the administrative center name following in parentheses)

Independence: 20 May 2002 (from Indonesia); note - 28 November 1975 was the date independence was proclaimed from Portugal; 20 May 2002 was the date of international recognition of Timor-Leste's independence from Indonesia

National holiday: Restoration of Independence Day, 20 May (2002); Proclamation of Independence Day, 28 November (1975)

Constitution: *history:* drafted 2001, approved 22 March 2002, entered into force 20 May 2002
amendments: proposed by Parliament and parliamentary groups; consideration of amendments requires at least four-fifths majority approval by Parliament; passage requires two-thirds majority vote by Parliament and promulgation by the president of the republic; passage of amendments to the republican form of government and the flag requires approval in a referendum

Legal system: civil law system based on the Portuguese model; note - penal and civil law codes to replace the Indonesian codes were passed by Parliament and promulgated in 2009 and 2011, respectively

International law organization participation: accepts compulsory ICJ jurisdiction with reservations; accepts ICCt jurisdiction

Citizenship: *citizenship by birth:* no
citizenship by descent only: at least one parent must be a citizen of Timor-Leste
dual citizenship recognized: no
residency requirement for naturalization: 10 years

Suffrage: 17 years of age; universal

Executive branch: *chief of state:* President José RAMOS-HORTA (since May 2022); note - the president is commander in chief of the military and is able to veto legislation, dissolve parliament, and call national elections
head of government: Prime Minister Taur Matan RUAK (since 22 June 2018)
cabinet: the governing coalition in the Parliament proposes cabinet member candidates to the prime minister, who presents these recommendations to the President of the Republic for swearing in
elections/appointments: president directly elected by absolute majority popular vote in 2 rounds if needed for a 5-year term (eligible for a second term); last election held in April 2022; following parliamentary elections, the president appoints the leader of the majority party or majority coalition as the prime minister
election results:
2022: José RAMOS-HORTA elected president in a run-off election - RAMOS-HORTA (CNRT) 62.1%, Francisco GUTERRES (FRETILIN) 37.9%
2017: Francisco GUTERRES (FRETILIN) 57.1%, António da CONCEICAO (PD) 32.46%

Legislative branch: *description:* unicameral National Parliament (65 seats; members directly elected in a single nationwide constituency by closed, party-list proportional representation vote using the D'Hondt method to serve 5-year terms)
elections:
last held on 12 May 2018 (next to be held in July 2023)
election results:
percent of vote by party - AMP - 49.6%, FRETILIN 34.2%, PD 8.1%, DDF 5.5%, other 2.6%; seats by party - AMP 34, FRETILIN 23, PD 5, DDF 3; composition - men 39, women 26, percent of women 40%

Judicial branch: *highest court(s):* Court of Appeals (consists of the court president and NA judges)
judge selection and term of office: court president appointed by the president of the republic from among the other court judges to serve a 4-year term; other court judges appointed - 1 by the Parliament and the others by the Supreme Council for the Judiciary, a body chaired by the court president and that includes mostly presidential and parliamentary appointees; other judges serve for life
subordinate courts: Court of Appeal; High Administrative, Tax, and Audit Court; district courts; magistrates' courts; military courts
note: the UN Justice System Programme, launched in 2003 and being rolled out in 4 phases through 2018, is helping strengthen the country's justice system; the Programme is aligned with the country's long-range Justice Sector Strategic Plan, which includes legal reforms

Political parties and leaders: Democratic Party or PD [Mariano Assanami SABINO Lopes]
Frenti-Mudanca (Front for National Reconstruction of Timor-Leste - Change) or FM [Jose Luis GUTERRES]
Kmanek Haburas Unidade Nasional Timor Oan or KHUNTO [Armanda BERTA DOS SANTOS]
National Congress for Timorese Reconstruction or CNRT [Kay Rala Xanana GUSMAO]
People's Liberation Party or PLP [Taur Matan RUAK]
Revolutionary Front of Independent Timor-Leste or FRETILIN [Mari ALKATIRI]
Timorese Democratic Union or UDT [Gilman SANTOS]

International organization participation: ACP, ADB, AOSIS, ARF, ASEAN (observer), CPLP, EITI (compliant country), FAO, G-77, IBRD, ICAO, ICCt, ICRM, IDA, IFAD, IFC, IFRCS, ILO, IMF, IMO, Interpol, IOC, IOM, IPU, ITU, MIGA, NAM, OPCW, PIF (observer), UN, UNCTAD, UNESCO, UNIDO, Union Latina, UNWTO, UPU, WCO, WHO, WMO

Diplomatic representation in the US: *chief of mission:* Ambassador Isilio Antonio De Fatima COELHO DA SILVA (since 6 January 2020)
chancery: 4201 Connecticut Avenue NW, Suite 504, Washington, DC 20008
telephone: [1] (202) 966-3202
FAX: [1] (202) 966-3205
email address and website:
info@timorlesteembassy.org
http://www.timorlesteembassy.org/

Diplomatic representation from the US: *chief of mission:* Ambassador (vacant), Charge d'Affaires Thomas DALEY (since August 2021)
embassy: Avenida de Portugal, Praia dos Coqueiros, Dili
mailing address: 8250 Dili Place, Washington, DC 20521-8250
telephone: (670) 332-4684, (670) 330-2400
FAX: (670) 331-3206
email address and website:
ConsDili@state.gov
https://tl.usembassy.gov/

Flag description: red with a black isosceles triangle (based on the hoist side) superimposed on a slightly longer yellow arrowhead that extends to the center of the flag; a white star - pointing to the upper hoist-side corner of the flag - is in the center of the black triangle; yellow denotes the colonialism in Timor-Leste's past, black represents the obscurantism that needs to be overcome, red stands for the national liberation struggle; the white star symbolizes peace and serves as a guiding light

National symbol(s): Mount Ramelau; national colors: red, yellow, black, white

National anthem: *name:* "Patria" (Fatherland)
lyrics/music: Fransisco Borja DA COSTA/Afonso DE ARAUJO
note: adopted 2002; the song was first used as an anthem when Timor-Leste declared its independence from Portugal in 1975; the lyricist, Francisco Borja DA COSTA, was killed in the Indonesian invasion just days after independence was declared

ECONOMY

Economic overview: Since independence in 1999, Timor-Leste has faced great challenges in rebuilding its infrastructure, strengthening the civil administration, and generating jobs for young people entering the work force. The development of offshore oil and gas resources has greatly supplemented government revenues. This technology-intensive industry, however, has done little to create jobs in part because there are no production facilities in Timor-Leste. Gas is currently piped to Australia for processing, but Timor-Leste has expressed interest in developing a domestic processing capability.

In June 2005, the National Parliament unanimously approved the creation of the Timor-Leste Petroleum Fund to serve as a repository for all petroleum revenues and to preserve the value of Timor-Leste's petroleum wealth for future generations. The Fund held assets of $16 billion, as of mid-2016. Oil accounts for over 90% of government revenues, and the drop in the price of oil in 2014-16 has led to concerns about the long-term sustainability of government spending. Timor-Leste compensated for the decline in price by exporting more oil. The Ministry of Finance maintains that the Petroleum Fund is sufficient to sustain government operations for the foreseeable future.

Annual government budget expenditures increased markedly between 2009 and 2012 but dropped significantly through 2016. Historically, the government failed to spend as much as its budget allowed. The government has focused significant resources on basic infrastructure, including electricity and roads, but limited experience in procurement and infrastructure building has hampered these projects. The underlying economic policy challenge the country faces remains how best to use oil-and-gas wealth to lift the nonoil economy onto a higher growth path and to reduce poverty.

Real GDP (purchasing power parity): $4.19 billion (2020 est.)
$4.59 billion (2019 est.)
$3.87 billion (2018 est.)
note: data are in 2017 dollars
country comparison to the world: 181

Real GDP growth rate: -4.6% (2017 est.)
5.3% (2016 est.)
4% (2015 est.)
country comparison to the world: 216

Real GDP per capita: $3,200 (2020 est.)
$3,600 (2019 est.)
$3,100 (2018 est.)
note: data are in 2017 dollars
country comparison to the world: 195

GDP (official exchange rate): $2.775 billion (2017 est.)
note: non-oil GDP

Inflation rate (consumer prices): 0.6% (2017 est.)
-1.3% (2016 est.)
country comparison to the world: 49

GDP - composition, by sector of origin: *agriculture:* 9.1% (2017 est.)
industry: 56.7% (2017 est.)
services: 34.4% (2017 est.)

GDP - composition, by end use: *household consumption:* 33% (2017 est.)
government consumption: 30% (2017 est.)
investment in fixed capital: 10.6% (2017 est.)
investment in inventories: 0% (2017 est.)
exports of goods and services: 78.4% (2017 est.)
imports of goods and services: -52% (2017 est.)

Agricultural products: rice, maize, vegetables, coffee, roots/tubers nes, other meats, cassava, pork, beans, mangoes/guavas

Industries: printing, soap manufacturing, handicrafts, woven cloth

Industrial production growth rate: 2% (2017 est.)
country comparison to the world: 133

Labor force: 286,700 (2016 est.)
country comparison to the world: 164

Labor force - by occupation: *agriculture:* 41%
industry: 13%
services: 45.1% (2013)

Unemployment rate: 4.4% (2014 est.)
3.9% (2010 est.)
country comparison to the world: 66

Unemployment, youth ages 15-24: *total:* 13.2%
male: 10.9%
female: 15.9% (2016 est.)
country comparison to the world: 117

Population below poverty line: 41.8% (2014 est.)

Gini Index coefficient - distribution of family income: 28.7 (2014 est.)
38 (2002 est.)
country comparison to the world: 158

Household income or consumption by percentage share: *lowest 10%:* 4%
highest 10%: 27% (2007)

Budget: *revenues:* 300 million (2017 est.)
expenditures: 2.4 billion (2017 est.)

Budget surplus (+) or deficit (-): -75.7% (of GDP) (2017 est.)
country comparison to the world: 222

Public debt: 3.8% of GDP (2017 est.)
3.1% of GDP (2016 est.)
country comparison to the world: 206

Taxes and other revenues: 10.8% (of GDP) (2017 est.)
country comparison to the world: 213

Fiscal year: calendar year

Current account balance: -$284 million (2017 est.)
-$544 million (2016 est.)
country comparison to the world: 106

Exports: $60 million (2020 est.) note: data are in current year dollars
$120 million (2019 est.) note: data are in current year dollars
$120 million (2018 est.) note: data are in current year dollars
country comparison to the world: 212

Exports - partners: Singapore 51%, China 20%, Japan 9%, Indonesia 6% (2019)

Exports - commodities: crude petroleum, natural gas, coffee, various vegetables, scrap iron (2019)

Imports: $850 million (2020 est.) note: data are in current year dollars
$1.04 billion (2019 est.) note: data are in current year dollars
$1.06 billion (2018 est.) note: data are in current year dollars
country comparison to the world: 194

Imports - partners: Indonesia 39%, China 27%, Singapore 10%, Malaysia 5% (2019)

Imports - commodities: refined petroleum, cars, cement, delivery trucks, motorcycles (2019)

Reserves of foreign exchange and gold: $544.4 million (31 December 2017 est.)
$437.8 million (31 December 2015 est.)
note: excludes assets of approximately $9.7 billion in the Petroleum Fund (31 December 2010)
country comparison to the world: 150

Debt - external: $311.5 million (31 December 2014 est.)
$687 million (31 December 2013 est.)
country comparison to the world: 183

Exchange rates: the US dollar is used

ENERGY

Electricity access: *electrification - total population:* 85.6% (2018)
electrification - urban areas: 100% (2018)
electrification - rural areas: 79.2% (2018)

Electricity: *installed generating capacity:* 284,000 kW (2020 est.)
consumption: -103 million kWh (2019 est.)
exports: 0 kWh (2019 est.)
imports: 0 kWh (2019 est.)
transmission/distribution losses: 103 million kWh (2019 est.)

Electricity generation sources: *fossil fuels:* 100% of total installed capacity (2020 est.)

Petroleum: *total petroleum production:* 14,000 bbl/day (2021 est.)
refined petroleum consumption: 3,500 bbl/day (2019 est.)
crude oil and lease condensate exports: 32,900 bbl/day (2018 est.)

Refined petroleum products - imports: 3,481 bbl/day (2015 est.)
country comparison to the world: 182

Natural gas: *production:* 5,104,670,000 cubic meters (2019 est.)
consumption: 0 cubic meters (2021 est.)
exports: 5,104,670,000 cubic meters (2019 est.)
imports: 0 cubic meters (2021 est.)
proven reserves: 0 cubic meters (2021 est.)

Carbon dioxide emissions: 538,000 metric tonnes of CO_2 (2019 est.)
from petroleum and other liquids: 538,000 metric tonnes of CO_2 (2019 est.)
country comparison to the world: 189

Energy consumption per capita: 5.74 million Btu/person (2019 est.)
country comparison to the world: 168

COMMUNICATIONS

Telephones - fixed lines: *total subscriptions:* 2,012 (2020 est.)
subscriptions per 100 inhabitants: (2020 est.) less than 1
country comparison to the world: 213

Telephones - mobile cellular: *total subscriptions:* 1,425,260 (2019)
subscriptions per 100 inhabitants: 110.22 (2019)
country comparison to the world: 158

Telecommunication systems: *general assessment:* Timor-Leste has been moving forward with the regeneration of its economy and rebuilding key infrastructure, including telecommunications networks, that were destroyed during the years of civil unrest; fixed-line and fixed broadband penetration in Timor-Leste remains extremely low, mainly due to the limited fixed-line infrastructure and the proliferation of mobile connectivity; in an effort to boost e-government services; the number of subscribers through to 2026 is expected to develop steadily, though from a low base; by August 2020, Timor-Leste had three telecom service providers who jointly achieved a 98% network coverage nationally; the mobile broadband market is still at an early stage of development, strong growth is predicted over the next five years; at the end of 2020, the government issued new policy guidelines to maximize the use of spectrum in Timor-Leste; it invited mobile operators to submit applications for the allocation of spectrum in the 1800MHz, 2300MHz and 2600MHz bands; in November 2020, the government approved the deployment of a submarine fiber link connecting the south of the

country to Australia via the North Western Cable System (NWCS) (2021)
domestic: system suffered significant damage during the violence associated with independence; limited fixed-line services, less than 1 per 100 and mobile-cellular services are now available in urban and most rural areas with teledensity of over 104 per 100 (2020)
international: country code - 670; international service is available; partnership with Australia telecom companies for potential deployment of a submarine fiber-optic link (NWCS); geostationary earth orbit satellite

Broadcast media: 7 TV stations (3 nationwide satellite coverage; 2 terrestrial coverage, mostly in Dili; 2 cable) and 21 radio stations (3 nationwide coverage) (2019)

Internet country code: .tl

Internet users: *total:* 382,348 (2020 est.)
percent of population: 29% (2020 est.)
country comparison to the world: 165

Broadband - fixed subscriptions: *total:* 75 (2020 est.)
subscriptions per 100 inhabitants: 0.01 (2020 est.)
country comparison to the world: 214

TRANSPORTATION

National air transport system: *number of registered air carriers:* 2 (2020)
inventory of registered aircraft operated by air carriers: 2

Civil aircraft registration country code prefix: 4W

Airports: *total:* 6 (2021)
country comparison to the world: 177

Airports - with paved runways: *total:* 2
2,438 to 3,047 m: 1
1,524 to 2,437 m: 1 (2021)

Airports - with unpaved runways: *total:* 4
914 to 1,523 m: 2
under 914 m: 2 (2021)

Heliports: 8 (2021)

Roadways: *total:* 6,040 km (2008)
paved: 2,600 km (2008)
unpaved: 3,440 km (2008)
country comparison to the world: 143

Merchant marine: *total:* 1
by type: other 1 (2021)
country comparison to the world: 186

Ports and terminals: *major seaport(s):* Dili

MILITARY AND SECURITY

Military and security forces: Timor-Leste Defense Force (Falintil-Forcas de Defesa de Timor-L'este, Falintil (F-FDTL)): Joint Headquarters with Land, Air, Naval, Service Support, and Education/Training components; Ministry of Interior: National Police (Polícia Nacional de Timor-Leste, PNTL) (2022)

Military expenditures: 1.8% of GDP (2021 est.)
1.8% of GDP (2020 est.)
1.7% of GDP (2019 est.) (approximately $45 million)
1.3% of GDP (2018 est.) (approximately $30 million)
1.6% of GDP (2017 est.) (approximately $35 million)
country comparison to the world: 74

Military and security service personnel strengths: approximately 2,000 personnel (2022)

Military equipment inventories and acquisitions: the military is lightly armed and has a limited inventory consisting of equipment donated by other countries; since 2010 it has received small amounts of material from China, South Korea, and the US (2022)

Military service age and obligation: 18 years of age for voluntary military service; compulsory service was authorized in 2020 for men and women aged 18-30 for 18 months of service, but the level of implementation is unclear (2021)

Military - note: since achieving independence, Timor-Leste has received security assistance from or has made defense cooperation arrangements with Australia, China, Indonesia, Malaysia, New Zealand, the Philippines, Portugal, the UN, and the US; some F-FDTL personnel train with the Indonesian military and the two countries maintain a joint Border Security Task Force to jointly monitor and patrol the border, particularly the Oecussi exclave area where smuggling and trafficking are prevalent (2022)

TRANSNATIONAL ISSUES

Disputes - international: *Timor-Leste-Australia:* Timor-Leste and Australia reached agreement on a treaty delimiting a permanent maritime boundary in March 2018; both countries ratified the treaty in August 2019
Timor-Leste-Indonesia: three stretches of land borders with Indonesia have yet to be delimited, two of which are in the Oecussi exclave area, and no maritime or Economic Exclusion Zone boundaries have been established between the countries; maritime boundaries with Indonesia remain unresolved; between 2005 and 2015, 500 border landmarks were placed and another 200 were proposed

Trafficking in persons: *current situation:* human traffickers exploit domestic and foreign victims in Timor-Leste, and traffickers exploit victims from Timor-Leste abroad; traffickers exploit Timorese women, girls, and occasionally young men and boys from rural areas in sex trafficking or domestic servitude; Timorese men are exploited in forced labor in agriculture, construction, and mining; families place children in bonded domestic and agricultural labor to pay debts; traffickers deceive young men and women with promises of a scholarship ,or employment opportunities in Indonesia, Malaysia, and other countries in the region only taking them to a different county, taking their passports, and forcing them into labor, including domestic servitude; sex traffickers in Timor-Leste prey on foreign women from East and Southeast Asia; traffickers also recruit Timorese women to send them to China, Indonesia, or Malaysia for commercial sex
tier rating: Tier 2 Watch List — Timor-Leste does not fully meet the minimum standards for the elimination of trafficking but is making significant efforts to do so; efforts include re-establishing funding to NGOs for victim services and integrating an anti-trafficking curriculum for officials; however, authorities decreased investigations and convictions; victim protection services were inadequate, and no government-wide standard operating procedures for victim identification were implemented; understanding of trafficking remains low among officials (2020)

Illicit drugs: NA

TOGO

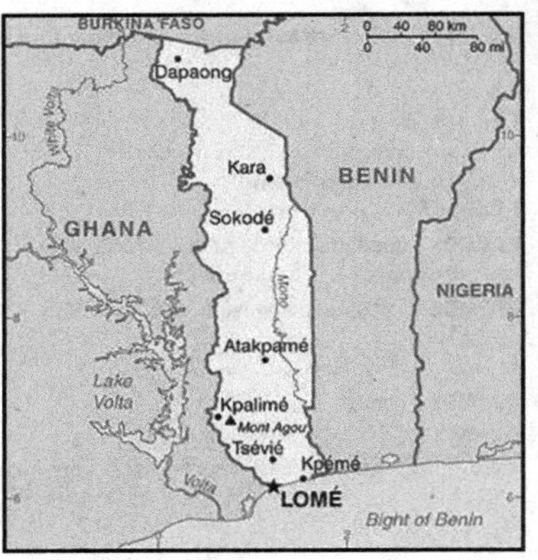

INTRODUCTION

Background: From the 11th to the 16th centuries, various ethnic groups settled the Togo region. From the 16th to the 18th centuries, the coastal region became a major trading center for enslaved people, and the surrounding region took on the name of "The Slave Coast." In 1884, Germany declared a region including present-day Togo as a protectorate called Togoland. After World War I, rule over Togo was transferred to France. French Togoland became Togo upon independence in 1960. Gen. Gnassingbe EYADEMA, installed as military ruler in 1967, ruled Togo with a heavy hand for almost four decades. Despite the facade of multi-party elections instituted in the early 1990s, the government was largely dominated by President EYADEMA, whose Rally of the Togolese People (RPT) party has been in power almost continually since 1967 and its successor, the Union for the Republic, maintains a majority of seats in today's legislature. Upon EYADEMA's death in February 2005, the military installed the president's son, Faure GNASSINGBE, and then engineered his formal election two months later. Togo held its first relatively free and fair legislative elections in October 2007. Since then, President GNASSINGBE has started the country along a gradual path to democratic reform. Togo has held multiple presidential and legislative elections, and in 2019 held its first local elections in 32 years. Despite those positive moves, political reconciliation has moved slowly, and the country experiences periodic outbursts of protests by frustrated citizens that have led to violence between security forces and protesters. Constitutional changes in 2019 to institute a runoff system in presidential elections and to establish term limits has done little to reduce the resentment many Togolese feel after more than 50 years of one-family rule. GNASSINGBE became eligible for his current fourth term and one additional fifth term under the new rules. The next presidential election will be in 2025.

GEOGRAPHY

Location: Western Africa, bordering the Bight of Benin, between Benin and Ghana

Geographic coordinates: 8 00 N, 1 10 E

Map references: Africa

Area: *total:* 56,785 sq km
land: 54,385 sq km
water: 2,400 sq km
country comparison to the world: 126

Area - comparative: slightly smaller than West Virginia

Land boundaries: *total:* 1,880 km
border countries (3): Benin 651 km; Burkina Faso 131 km; Ghana 1,098 km

Coastline: 56 km

Maritime claims: *territorial sea:* 30 nm; note: the US does not recognize this claim
exclusive economic zone: 200 nm

Climate: tropical; hot, humid in south; semiarid in north

Terrain: gently rolling savanna in north; central hills; southern plateau; low coastal plain with extensive lagoons and marshes

Elevation: *highest point:* Mont Agou 986 m
lowest point: Atlantic Ocean 0 m
mean elevation: 236 m

Natural resources: phosphates, limestone, marble, arable land

Land use: *agricultural land:* 67.4% (2018 est.)
arable land: 45.2% (2018 est.)
permanent crops: 3.8% (2018 est.)
permanent pasture: 18.4% (2018 est.)
forest: 4.9% (2018 est.)
other: 27.7% (2018 est.)

Irrigated land: 70 sq km (2012)

Major watersheds (area sq km): Atlantic Ocean drainage: Volta (410,991 sq km)

Population distribution: one of the more densely populated African nations with most of the population residing in rural communities, density is highest in the south on or near the Atlantic coast as shown in this population distribution map

Natural hazards: hot, dry harmattan wind can reduce visibility in north during winter; periodic droughts

Geography - note: the country's length allows it to stretch through six distinct geographic regions; climate varies from tropical to savanna

PEOPLE AND SOCIETY

Population: 8,492,333 (2022 est.)
note: estimates for this country explicitly taken into account the impact of the HIV/AIDS epidemic
country comparison to the world: 102

Nationality: *noun:* Togolese (singular and plural)
adjective: Togolese

Ethnic groups: Adja-Ewe/Mina 42.4%, Kabye/Tem 25.9%, Para-Gourma/Akan 17.1%, Akposso/Akebu 4.1%, Ana-Ife 3.2%, other Togolese 1.7%, foreigners 5.2%, no response 0.4% (2013-14 est.)
note: Togo has an estimated 37 ethnic groups

Languages: French (official, the language of commerce), Ewe and Mina (the two major African languages in the south), Kabye (sometimes spelled Kabiye) and Dagomba (the two major African languages in the north)

Religions: Christian 42.3%, folk religion 36.9%, Muslim 14%, Hindu <1 %, Buddhist <1 %, Jewish <1 %, other <1 %, none 6.2% (2020 est.)

Demographic profile: Togo's population is estimated to have grown to four times its size between 1960 and 2010. With nearly 60% of its populace under the age of 25 and a high annual growth rate attributed largely to high fertility, Togo's population is likely to continue to expand for the foreseeable future. Reducing fertility, boosting job creation, and improving education will be essential to reducing the country's high poverty rate. In 2008, Togo eliminated primary school enrollment fees, leading to higher enrollment but increased pressure on limited classroom space, teachers, and materials. Togo has a good chance of achieving universal primary education, but educational quality, the underrepresentation of girls, and the low rate of enrollment in secondary and tertiary schools remain concerns.

Togo is both a country of emigration and asylum. In the early 1990s, southern Togo suffered from the economic decline of the phosphate sector and ethnic and political repression at the hands of dictator Gnassingbe EYADEMA and his northern, Kabye-dominated administration. The turmoil led 300,000 to 350,000 predominantly southern Togolese to flee to Benin and Ghana, with most not returning home until relative stability was restored in 1997. In 2005, another outflow of 40,000 Togolese to Benin and Ghana occurred when violence broke out between the opposition and security forces over the disputed election of EYADEMA's son Faure GNASSINGBE to the presidency. About half of the refugees reluctantly returned home in 2006, many still fearing for their safety. Despite ethnic tensions and periods of political unrest, Togo in September 2017 was home to more than 9,600 refugees from Ghana.

Age structure: *0-14 years:* 39.73% (male 1,716,667/female 1,703,230)
15-24 years: 19.03% (male 817,093/female 820,971)
25-54 years: 33.26% (male 1,423,554/female 1,439,380)
55-64 years: 4.42% (male 179,779/female 200,392)
65 years and over: 3.57% (male 132,304/female 175,074) (2020 est.)

Dependency ratios: *total dependency ratio:* 77.1
youth dependency ratio: 72
elderly dependency ratio: 5.1
potential support ratio: 19.4 (2020 est.)

Median age: *total:* 20 years
male: 19.7 years
female: 20.3 years (2020 est.)
country comparison to the world: 196

Population growth rate: 2.48% (2022 est.)
country comparison to the world: 24

Birth rate: 31.86 births/1,000 population (2022 est.)
country comparison to the world: 25

Death rate: 5.27 deaths/1,000 population (2022 est.)
country comparison to the world: 188

Net migration rate: -1.81 migrant(s)/1,000 population (2022 est.)
country comparison to the world: 167

Population distribution: one of the more densely populated African nations with most of the population residing in rural communities, density is highest in the south on or near the Atlantic coast as shown in this population distribution map

Urbanization: *urban population:* 43.9% of total population (2022)
rate of urbanization: 3.6% annual rate of change (2020-25 est.)

Major urban areas - population: 1.926 million LOME (capital) (2022)

Sex ratio: *at birth:* 1.03 male(s)/female
0-14 years: 1.03 male(s)/female
15-24 years: 1 male(s)/female
25-54 years: 0.94 male(s)/female
55-64 years: 0.85 male(s)/female
65 years and over: 0.55 male(s)/female
total population: 0.97 male(s)/female (2022 est.)

Mother's mean age at first birth: 25 years (2017 est.)
note: data represents median age at first birth among women 25-29

Maternal mortality ratio: 396 deaths/100,000 live births (2017 est.)
country comparison to the world: 28

Infant mortality rate: *total:* 41.19 deaths/1,000 live births
male: 45.88 deaths/1,000 live births
female: 36.36 deaths/1,000 live births (2022 est.)
country comparison to the world: 31

Life expectancy at birth: *total population:* 71.36 years
male: 68.76 years
female: 74.03 years (2022 est.)
country comparison to the world: 166

Total fertility rate: 4.23 children born/woman (2022 est.)
country comparison to the world: 25

Contraceptive prevalence rate: 23.9% (2017)

Drinking water source: *improved: urban:* 93.8% of population
rural: 60.3% of population
total: 74.6% of population
unimproved: urban: 6.2% of population
rural: 39.7% of population
total: 25.4% of population (2020 est.)

Current health expenditure: 5.7% of GDP (2019)

Physicians density: 0.08 physicians/1,000 population (2020)

Hospital bed density: 0.7 beds/1,000 population (2011)

Sanitation facility access: *improved: urban:* 81.9% of population
rural: 18.3% of population
total: 45.5% of population
unimproved: urban: 18.1% of population
rural: 81.7% of population
total: 54.5% of population (2020 est.)

HIV/AIDS - adult prevalence rate: 2% (2020 est.)
country comparison to the world: 22

HIV/AIDS - people living with HIV/AIDS: 110,000 (2020 est.)
country comparison to the world: 43

HIV/AIDS - deaths: 3,000 (2020 est.)
country comparison to the world: 39

Major infectious diseases: *degree of risk:* very high (2020)

food or waterborne diseases: bacterial and protozoal diarrhea, hepatitis A, and typhoid fever
vectorborne diseases: malaria, dengue fever, and yellow fever
water contact diseases: schistosomiasis
animal contact diseases: rabies
respiratory diseases: meningococcal meningitis

Obesity - adult prevalence rate: 8.4% (2016)
country comparison to the world: 152

Alcohol consumption per capita: *total:* 1.4 liters of pure alcohol (2019 est.)
beer: 0.78 liters of pure alcohol (2019 est.)
wine: 0.09 liters of pure alcohol (2019 est.)
spirits: 0.2 liters of pure alcohol (2019 est.)
other alcohols: 0.33 liters of pure alcohol (2019 est.)
country comparison to the world: 141

Tobacco use: *total:* 6.8% (2020 est.)
male: 12.3% (2020 est.)
female: 1.2% (2020 est.)
country comparison to the world: 158

Children under the age of 5 years underweight: 15.2% (2017)
country comparison to the world: 36

Child marriage: *women married by age 15:* 6.4%
women married by age 18: 24.8%
men married by age 18: 2.6% (2017 est.)

Education expenditures: 5% of GDP (2019 est.)
country comparison to the world: 65

Literacy: *definition:* age 15 and over can read and write
total population: 66.5%
male: 80%
female: 55.1% (2019)

School life expectancy (primary to tertiary education): *total:* 13 years
male: 14 years
female: 12 years (2017)

Unemployment, youth ages 15-24: *total:* 9.5%
male: 12.3%
female: 7.4% (2017 est.)

ENVIRONMENT

Environment - current issues: deforestation attributable to slash-and-burn agriculture and the use of wood for fuel; very little rain forest still present and what remains is highly degraded; desertification; water pollution presents health hazards and hinders the fishing industry; air pollution increasing in urban areas

Environment - international agreements: *party to:* Biodiversity, Climate Change, Climate Change-Kyoto Protocol, Climate Change-Paris Agreement, Comprehensive Nuclear Test Ban, Desertification, Endangered Species, Hazardous Wastes, Law of the Sea, Nuclear Test Ban, Ozone Layer Protection, Ship Pollution, Tropical Timber 2006, Wetlands, Whaling
signed, but not ratified: none of the selected agreements

Air pollutants: *particulate matter emissions:* 32.71 micrograms per cubic meter (2016 est.)
carbon dioxide emissions: 3 megatons (2016 est.)
methane emissions: 3.06 megatons (2020 est.)

Climate: tropical; hot, humid in south; semiarid in north

Land use: *agricultural land:* 67.4% (2018 est.)
arable land: 45.2% (2018 est.)
permanent crops: 3.8% (2018 est.)
permanent pasture: 18.4% (2018 est.)
forest: 4.9% (2018 est.)
other: 27.7% (2018 est.)

Urbanization: *urban population:* 43.9% of total population (2022)
rate of urbanization: 3.6% annual rate of change (2020-25 est.)

Revenue from forest resources: *forest revenues:* 3.96% of GDP (2018 est.)
country comparison to the world: 18

Revenue from coal: *coal revenues:* 0% of GDP (2018 est.)
country comparison to the world: 175

Waste and recycling: *municipal solid waste generated annually:* 1,109,030 tons (2014 est.)
municipal solid waste recycled annually: 22,181 tons (2012 est.)
percent of municipal solid waste recycled: 2% (2012 est.)

Major watersheds (area sq km): Atlantic Ocean drainage: Volta (410,991 sq km)

Total water withdrawal: *municipal:* 140.7 million cubic meters (2017 est.)
industrial: 6.3 million cubic meters (2017 est.)
agricultural: 76 million cubic meters (2017 est.)

Total renewable water resources: 14.7 billion cubic meters (2017 est.)

GOVERNMENT

Country name: *conventional long form:* Togolese Republic
conventional short form: Togo
local long form: Republique Togolaise
local short form: none
former: French Togoland
etymology: derived from the Ewe words "to" (river) and "godo" (on the other side) to give the sense of "on the other side of the river"; originally, this designation applied to the town of Togodo (now Togoville) on the northern shore of Lake Togo, but the name was eventually extended to the entire nation

Government type: presidential republic

Capital: *name:* Lome
geographic coordinates: 6 07 N, 1 13 E
time difference: UTC 0 (5 hours ahead of Washington, DC, during Standard Time)
etymology: Lome comes from "alotime" which in the native Ewe language means "among the alo plants"; alo trees dominated the city's original founding site

Administrative divisions: 5 regions (regions, singular - region); Centrale, Kara, Maritime, Plateaux, Savanes

Independence: 27 April 1960 (from French-administered UN trusteeship)

National holiday: Independence Day, 27 April (1960)

Constitution: *history:* several previous; latest adopted 27 September 1992, effective 14 October 1992
amendments: proposed by the president of the republic or supported by at least one fifth of the National Assembly membership; passage requires four-fifths majority vote by the Assembly; a referendum is required if approved by only two-thirds majority of the Assembly or if requested by the president; constitutional articles on the republican and secular form of government cannot be amended; amended 2002, 2007, last in 2019 when the National Assembly unanimously approved a package of amendments, including setting presidential term limits of two 5-year mandates

Legal system: customary law system

International law organization participation: accepts compulsory ICJ jurisdiction with reservations; non-party state to the ICCt

Citizenship: *citizenship by birth:* no
citizenship by descent only: at least one parent must be a citizen of Togo
dual citizenship recognized: yes
residency requirement for naturalization: 5 years

Suffrage: 18 years of age; universal

Executive branch: *chief of state:* President Faure GNASSINGBE (since 4 May 2005)
head of government: Prime Minister Victoire Tomegah DOGBE (since 28 September 2020)
cabinet: Council of Ministers appointed by the president on the advice of the prime minister
elections/appointments: president directly elected by simple majority popular vote for a 5-year term (no term limits); election last held on 22 February 2020 (next to be held February 2025); prime minister appointed by the president
election results:
Faure GNASSINGBE reelected president; percent of vote - Faure GNASSINGBE (UNIR) 70.8%, Agbeyome KODJO (MPDD) 19.5%, Jean-Pierre FABRE (ANC) 4.7%, other 5% (2020)

Legislative branch: *description:* unicameral National Assembly or Assemblee Nationale (91 seats; members directly elected in multi-seat constituencies by closed, party-list proportional representation vote to serve 5-year terms)
elections:
last held on 20 December 2018 (next to be held in 2023)
election results:
percent of vote by coalition/party - NA; seats by party - UNIR 59, UFC 6, NET 3, MPDD 3, other 2, independent 18; composition - men 74, women 17, percent of women 18.7%

Judicial branch: *highest court(s):* Supreme Court or Cour Supreme (organized into criminal and administrative chambers, each with a chamber president and advisors); Constitutional Court (consists of 9 judges, including the court president)
judge selection and term of office: Supreme Court president appointed by decree of the president of the republic upon the proposal of the Supreme Council of the Magistracy, a 9-member judicial, advisory, and disciplinary body; other judicial appointments and judge tenure NA; Constitutional Court judges appointed by the National Assembly; judge tenure NA
subordinate courts: Court of Assizes (sessions court); Appeal Court; tribunals of first instance (divided into civil, commercial, and correctional chambers; Court of State Security; military tribunal

Political parties and leaders: Action Committee for Renewal or CAR [Dodji APEVON]
Alliance of Democrats for Integral Development or ADDI [Tchaboure GOGUE]
Democratic Convention of African Peoples or CDPA [Léopold GNININVI]
Democratic Forces for the Republic or FDR [Dodji APEVON]
National Alliance for Change or ANC [Jean-Pierre FABRE]
New Togolese Commitment [Gerry TAAMA]

Pan-African National Party or PNP [Tikpi ATCHADAM]
Pan-African Patriotic Convergence or CPP [Edem KODJO]
Patriotic Movement for Democracy and Development or MPDD [Agbeyome KODJO]
Socialist Pact for Renewal or PSR [Abi TCHESSA]
The Togolese Party [Nathaniel OLYMPIO]
Union of Forces for Change or UFC [N/A]
Union for the Republic or UNIR [Faure GNASSINGBE]

International organization participation: ACP, AfDB, AU, ECOWAS, EITI (compliant country), Entente, FAO, FZ, G-77, IAEA, IBRD, ICAO, ICRM, IDA, IDB, IFAD, IFC, IFRCS, ILO, IMF, IMO, Interpol, IOC, IOM, IPU, ISO (correspondent), ITSO, ITU, ITUC (NGOs), MIGA, MINURSO, MINUSMA, NAM, OIC, OIF, OPCW, PCA, UN, UNAMID, UNCTAD, UNESCO, UNHCR, UNIDO, UNMIL, UNOCI, UNWTO, UPU, WADB (regional), WAEMU, WCO, WFTU (NGOs), WHO, WIPO, WMO, WTO

Diplomatic representation in the US: *chief of mission:* Ambassador Frederic Edem HEGBE (since 24 April 2017)
chancery: 2208 Massachusetts Avenue NW, Washington, DC 20008
telephone: [1] (202) 234-4212
FAX: [1] (202) 232-3190
email address and website:
embassyoftogo@hotmail.com
https://embassyoftogousa.com/

Diplomatic representation from the US: *chief of mission:* Ambassador Elizabeth FITZSIMMONS (since 26 April 2022)
embassy: Boulevard Eyadema, B.P. 852, Lome
mailing address: 2300 Lome Place, Washington, DC 20521-2300
telephone: [228] 2261-5470
FAX: [228] 2261-5501
email address and website:
consularLome@state.gov
https://tg.usembassy.gov/

Flag description: five equal horizontal bands of green (top and bottom) alternating with yellow; a white five-pointed star on a red square is in the upper hoist-side corner; the five horizontal stripes stand for the five different regions of the country; the red square is meant to express the loyalty and patriotism of the people, green symbolizes hope, fertility, and agriculture, while yellow represents mineral wealth and faith that hard work and strength will bring prosperity; the star symbolizes life, purity, peace, dignity, and Togo's independence
note: uses the popular Pan-African colors of Ethiopia

National symbol(s): lion; national colors: green, yellow, red, white

National anthem: *name:* "Salut a toi, pays de nos aieux" (Hail to Thee, Land of Our Forefathers)
lyrics/music: Alex CASIMIR-DOSSEH
note: adopted 1960, restored 1992; this anthem was replaced by another during one-party rule between 1979 and 1992

National heritage: *total World Heritage Sites:* 1 (cultural)
selected World Heritage Site locales: Koutammakou; the Land of the Batammariba

ECONOMY

Economic overview: Togo has enjoyed a period of steady economic growth fueled by political stability and a concerted effort by the government to modernize the country's commercial infrastructure, but discontent with President Faure GNASSINGBE has led to a rapid rise in protests, creating downside risks. The country completed an ambitious large-scale infrastructure improvement program, including new principal roads, a new airport terminal, and a new seaport. The economy depends heavily on both commercial and subsistence agriculture, providing employment for around 60% of the labor force. Some basic foodstuffs must still be imported. Cocoa, coffee, and cotton and other agricultural products generate about 20% of export earnings with cotton being the most important cash crop. Togo is among the world's largest producers of phosphate and seeks to develop its carbonate phosphate reserves, which provide more than 20% of export earnings.

Supported by the World Bank and the IMF, the government's decade-long effort to implement economic reform measures, encourage foreign investment, and bring revenues in line with expenditures has moved slowly. Togo completed its IMF Extended Credit Facility in 2011 and reached a Heavily Indebted Poor Country debt relief completion point in 2010 at which 95% of the country's debt was forgiven. Togo continues to work with the IMF on structural reforms, and in January 2017, the IMF signed an Extended Credit Facility arrangement consisting of a three-year $238 million loan package. Progress depends on follow through on privatization, increased transparency in government financial operations, progress toward legislative elections, and continued support from foreign donors.

Togo's 2017 economic growth probably remained steady at 5.0%, largely driven by infusions of foreign aid, infrastructure investment in its port and mineral industry, and improvements in the business climate. Foreign direct investment inflows have slowed in recent years.

Real GDP (purchasing power parity): $17.45 billion (2020 est.)
$17.15 billion (2019 est.)
$16.26 billion (2018 est.)
note: data are in 2017 dollars
country comparison to the world: 154

Real GDP growth rate: 4.4% (2017 est.)
5.1% (2016 est.)
5.7% (2015 est.)
country comparison to the world: 63

Real GDP per capita: $2,100 (2020 est.)
$2,100 (2019 est.)
$2,100 (2018 est.)
note: data are in 2017 dollars
country comparison to the world: 213

GDP (official exchange rate): $5.232 billion (2018 est.)

Inflation rate (consumer prices): 0.6% (2019 est.)
0.9% (2018 est.)
-0.9% (2017 est.)
country comparison to the world: 50

Credit ratings:

Moody's rating: B3 (2019)

Standard & Poors rating: B (2019)

GDP - composition, by sector of origin: *agriculture:* 28.8% (2017 est.)
industry: 21.8% (2017 est.)
services: 49.8% (2017 est.)

GDP - composition, by end use: *household consumption:* 84.5% (2017 est.)
government consumption: 11.4% (2017 est.)
investment in fixed capital: 23.4% (2017 est.)
investment in inventories: -1.4% (2017 est.)
exports of goods and services: 43.1% (2017 est.)
imports of goods and services: -61% (2017 est.)

Agricultural products: cassava, maize, yams, sorghum, beans, oil palm fruit, rice, vegetables, cotton, groundnuts

Industries: phosphate mining, agricultural processing, cement, handicrafts, textiles, beverages

Industrial production growth rate: 5% (2017 est.)
country comparison to the world: 58

Labor force: 2.595 million (2007 est.)
country comparison to the world: 112

Labor force - by occupation: *agriculture:* 65%
industry: 5%
services: 30% (1998 est.)

Unemployment rate: 6.9% (2016 est.)
country comparison to the world: 111

Unemployment, youth ages 15-24: *total:* 9.5%
male: 12.3%
female: 7.4% (2017 est.)
country comparison to the world: 142

Population below poverty line: 55.1% (2015 est.)

Gini Index coefficient - distribution of family income: 43.1 (2015 est.)
country comparison to the world: 41

Household income or consumption by percentage share: *lowest 10%:* 3.3%
highest 10%: 27.1% (2006)

Budget: *revenues:* 1.023 billion (2017 est.)
expenditures: 1.203 billion (2017 est.)

Budget surplus (+) or deficit (-): -3.8% (of GDP) (2017 est.)
country comparison to the world: 154

Public debt: 75.7% of GDP (2017 est.)
81.6% of GDP (2016 est.)
country comparison to the world: 40

Taxes and other revenues: 21.5% (of GDP) (2017 est.)
country comparison to the world: 137

Fiscal year: calendar year

Current account balance: -$383 million (2017 est.)
-$416 million (2016 est.)
country comparison to the world: 114

Exports: $1.67 billion (2019 est.) note: data are in current year dollars
$1.7 billion (2018 est.) note: data are in current year dollars
country comparison to the world: 162

Exports - partners: India 16%, Benin 15%, Burkina Faso 6%, France 6%, Morocco 5% (2019)

Exports - commodities: refined petroleum, crude petroleum, electricity, calcium phosphates, cotton (2019)

Imports: $2.26 billion (2019 est.) note: data are in current year dollars
$2.33 billion (2018 est.) note: data are in current year dollars
country comparison to the world: 169

Imports - partners: China 18%, South Korea 13%, India 11%, Belgium 10%, Netherlands 8%, United States 5% (2019)

Imports - commodities: refined petroleum, motorcycles, crude petroleum, rice, broadcasting equipment (2019)

Reserves of foreign exchange and gold: $77.8 million (31 December 2017 est.)
$42.6 million (31 December 2016 est.)
country comparison to the world: 182

Debt - external: $1.442 billion (31 December 2017 est.)
$1.22 billion (31 December 2016 est.)
country comparison to the world: 161

Exchange rates: Communaute Financiere Africaine francs (XOF) per US dollar -
617.4 (2017 est.)
593.01 (2016 est.)
593.01 (2015 est.)
591.45 (2014 est.)
494.42 (2013 est.)

ENERGY

Electricity access: *electrification - total population:* 43% (2019)
electrification - urban areas: 77% (2019)
electrification - rural areas: 19% (2019)

Electricity: *installed generating capacity:* 210,000 kW (2020 est.)
consumption: 1,180,140,000 kWh (2019 est.)
exports: 118 million kWh (2019 est.)
imports: 963 million kWh (2019 est.)
transmission/distribution losses: 210 million kWh (2019 est.)

Electricity generation sources: *fossil fuels:* 82.2% of total installed capacity (2020 est.)
solar: 0.6% of total installed capacity (2020 est.)
hydroelectricity: 17.2% of total installed capacity (2020 est.)

Coal: *production:* 0 metric tons (2020 est.)
consumption: 46,000 metric tons (2020 est.)
exports: 0 metric tons (2020 est.)
imports: 46,000 metric tons (2020 est.)
proven reserves: 0 metric tons (2019 est.)

Petroleum: *total petroleum production:* 0 bbl/day (2021 est.)
refined petroleum consumption: 10,000 bbl/day (2019 est.)

Refined petroleum products - imports: 13,100 bbl/day (2015 est.)
country comparison to the world: 142

Natural gas: *production:* 0 cubic meters (2021 est.)
consumption: 0 cubic meters (2020 est.)
exports: 0 cubic meters (2021 est.)
imports: 44.797 million cubic meters (2019 est.)
proven reserves: 0 cubic meters (2021 est.)

Carbon dioxide emissions: 2.244 million metric tonnes of CO_2 (2019 est.)
from coal and metallurgical coke: 706,000 metric tonnes of CO_2 (2019 est.)
from petroleum and other liquids: 1.451 million metric tonnes of CO_2 (2019 est.)
from consumed natural gas: 87,000 metric tonnes of CO_2 (2019 est.)
country comparison to the world: 158

Energy consumption per capita: 4.113 million Btu/person (2019 est.)
country comparison to the world: 174

COMMUNICATIONS

Telephones - fixed lines: *total subscriptions:* 46,499 (2020 est.)
subscriptions per 100 inhabitants: 1 (2020 est.)
country comparison to the world: 159

Telephones - mobile cellular: *total subscriptions:* 6,239,180 (2019)
subscriptions per 100 inhabitants: 77.2 (2019)
country comparison to the world: 113

Telecommunication systems: *general assessment:* system based on a network of microwave radio relay routes supplemented by open-wire lines and a mobile-cellular system; telecoms supply 8% of GDP; 3 mobile operators; 12% of residents have access to the Internet; mobile subscribers and mobile broadband both increasing (2020)
domestic: fixed-line less than 1 per 100 and mobile-cellular nearly 79 telephones per 100 persons with mobile-cellular use predominating (2020)
international: country code - 228; landing point for the WACS submarine cable, linking countries along the west coast of Africa with each other and with Portugal; satellite earth stations - 1 Intelsat (Atlantic Ocean), 1 Symphonie (2020)

Broadcast media: 1 state-owned TV station with multiple transmission sites; five private TV stations broadcast locally; cable TV service is available; state-owned radio network with two stations (in Lome and Kara); several dozen private radio stations and a few community radio stations; transmissions of multiple international broadcasters available (2019)

Internet country code: .tg

Internet users: *total:* 1,986,897 (2020 est.)
percent of population: 24% (2020 est.)
country comparison to the world: 128

Broadband - fixed subscriptions: *total:* 52,706 (2020 est.)
subscriptions per 100 inhabitants: 0.6 (2020 est.)
country comparison to the world: 143

TRANSPORTATION

National air transport system: *number of registered air carriers:* 1 (2020)
inventory of registered aircraft operated by air carriers: 8
annual passenger traffic on registered air carriers: 566,295 (2018)
annual freight traffic on registered air carriers: 10.89 million (2018) mt-km

Civil aircraft registration country code prefix: 5V

Airports: *total:* 8 (2021)
country comparison to the world: 163

Airports - with paved runways: *total:* 2
2,438 to 3,047 m: 2 (2021)

Airports - with unpaved runways: *total:* 6
914 to 1,523 m: 4
under 914 m: 2 (2021)

Pipelines: 62 km gas

Railways: *total:* 568 km (2014)
narrow gauge: 568 km (2014) 1.000-m gauge
country comparison to the world: 111

Roadways: *total:* 9,951 km (2018)
paved: 1,794 km (2018)
unpaved: 8,157 km (2018)
urban: 1,783 km (2018)
country comparison to the world: 135

Waterways: 50 km (2011) (seasonally navigable by small craft on the Mono River depending on rainfall)
country comparison to the world: 113

Merchant marine: *total:* 411
by type: bulk carrier 1, container ship 9, general cargo 265, oil tanker 56, other 80 (2021)
country comparison to the world: 47

Ports and terminals: *major seaport(s):* Kpeme, Lome

MILITARY AND SECURITY

Military and security forces: Togolese Armed Forces (Forces Armees Togolaise, FAT): Togolese Army (l'Armee de Terre), Togolese Navy (Forces Naval Togolaises), Togolese Air Force (Armee de l'Air), National Gendarmerie (Gendarmerie Nationale Togolaise or GNT) (2022)
note: the GNT falls under the Ministry of the Armed Forces but also reports to the Ministry of Security and Civil Protection on many matters involving law enforcement and internal security

Military expenditures: 1.8% of GDP (2021 est.)
2% of GDP (2020 est.)
2.6% of GDP (2019 est.) (approximately $190 million)
1.9% of GDP (2018 est.) (approximately $140 million)
1.9% of GDP (2017 est.) (approximately $130 million)
country comparison to the world: 75

Military and security service personnel strengths: approximately 11,000 personnel (6,500 Army; 500 Air and Navy; 3,000 Gendarmerie) (2022)
note: in January 2022, the Togolese Government announced its intent to boost the size of the FAT to more than 20,000 by 2025

Military equipment inventories and acquisitions: the FAT has a small, mixed inventory of mostly older equipment from a variety of countries, including Brazil, China, France, Germany, Russia/former Soviet Union, South Africa, the UK, and the US (2022)

Military service age and obligation: 18 years of age for military service; 2-year service obligation; no conscription; women have been able to serve since 2007 (2022)

Military deployments: 730 (plus about 300 police) Mali (MINUSMA) (May 2022)

Military - note: the first Togolese Army unit was created in 1963, while the Air Force was established in 1964; the Navy was not established until 1976; since its creation, the Togolese military has a history of interfering in the country's politics with assassinations, coups, influence, and a large military crackdown in 2005 that killed hundreds; over the past decade, it has made some efforts to reform and professionalize, as well as increase its role in UN peacekeeping activities; Togolese police have also been deployed on peacekeeping operations, and Togo maintains a regional peacekeeping training center for military and police in Lome; the Navy and Air Force has increased focus on combating piracy and smuggling in the Gulf of Guinea

in June 2022, the Togolese Government declared a state of emergency in its northern border region due to the threat from Jama'at Nasr al-Islam wal Muslimin (JNIM), a coalition of al-Qa'ida-affiliated militant groups based in Mali that also operates in neighboring Burkina Faso; the declaration followed an attack on a Togolese military post in May that killed 8 soldiers and a Togolese military operation launched the same month to boost border security and prevent terrorist infiltrations (2022)

Maritime threats: the International Maritime Bureau reports the territorial and offshore waters in the Niger Delta and Gulf of Guinea remain a very high risk for piracy and armed robbery of ships; in 2021, there were 34 reported incidents of piracy and armed robbery at sea in the Gulf of Guinea region; although a significant decrease from the total number of 81 incidents in 2020, it included the one hijacking and three of five ships fired upon worldwide; while boarding and attempted boarding to steal valuables from ships and crews are the most common types of incidents, almost a third of all incidents involve a hijacking and/or kidnapping; in 2021, 57 crew members were kidnapped in seven separate incidents in the Gulf of Guinea, representing 100% of kidnappings worldwide; Nigerian pirates in particular are well armed and very aggressive, operating as far as 200 nm offshore; the Maritime Administration of the US Department of Transportation has issued a Maritime Advisory (2022-001 - Gulf of Guinea-Piracy/Armed Robbery/Kidnapping for Ransom) effective 4 January 2022, which states in part, "Piracy, armed robbery, and kidnapping for ransom continue to serve as significant threats to US-flagged vessels transiting or operating in the Gulf of Guinea"

TERRORISM

Terrorist group(s): Jama'at Nusrat al Islam wal Muslimeen (JNIM)

TRANSNATIONAL ISSUES

Disputes - international: *Togo-Benin:* in 2001, Benin claimed Togo moved boundary monuments - joint commission continues to resurvey the boundary; Benin's and Togo's Adjrala hydroelectric dam project on the Mona River, proposed in the 1990s, commenced in 2017 with funding from a Chinese bank
Togo-Burkina Faso: none identified
Togo-Ghana: none identified

Refugees and internally displaced persons: *refugees (country of origin):* 8,391 (Ghana) (2022)

Illicit drugs: transit hub for Nigerian heroin and cocaine traffickers; money laundering not a significant problem

TOKELAU

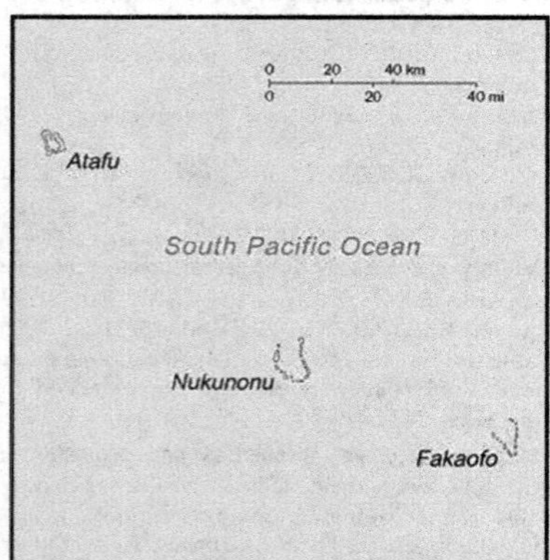

INTRODUCTION

Background: Tokelau, which comprises three atolls, was first settled by Polynesians around A.D. 1000. The three atolls operated relatively independently but had contact with one another, intermarrying and occasionally fighting wars. Fakaofo Atoll eventually subjugated the other two. British explorer John BYRON was the first European to see Atafu Atoll in 1765. British naval officer Edward EDWARDS saw Nukunonu Atoll in 1791, and ships occasionally continued to pass by Atafu and Nukunonu. In 1835, a US whaling ship became the first non-Pacific island ship to pass by Fakaofo. Catholic and Protestant missionaries arrived in 1845 and converted the population on the islands on which they landed. To this day, Nukunonu is predominantly Catholic while Atafu is mostly Protestant; Catholic and Protestant missionaries both worked in Fakaofo, and the population there is more mixed.

In 1863, Peruvian slave traders, masquerading as missionaries, kidnapped nearly all the men from Tokelau, and local governance moved to a system based on a Council of Elders, which still exists today. The atolls were repopulated when new Polynesian settlers and American and European migrants intermarried with local Tokelauan women. Tokelau became a British protectorate in 1889 and included in the Gilbert and Ellice Islands Protectorate - later a colony - in 1908. In 1925, the UK placed Tokelau under New Zealand administration. The Tokelau Islands Act of 1948 formally transferred sovereignty from the UK to New Zealand and Tokelauans were granted New Zealand citizenship. In 1979, the US relinquished its claims over Tokelau in the Treaty of Tokehega, and Tokelau relinquished its claims over Swains Island, which is part of American Samoa.

Economic opportunities in Tokelau are sparse, and about 80% of Tokelauans live in New Zealand. Tokelau held two self-governance referendums in 2006 and 2007, in which more than 60% of voters chose to go into free association with New Zealand; however, the referendums failed to achieve the two-thirds majority necessary to enact a status change. Tokelau lacks an airport and is only accessible via a day-long boat trip from Samoa, although a site for an airstrip on Nukunonu was selected in 2019. Because of its dependency on Samoa for transportation, in 2011, Tokelau followed Samoa's lead and shifted the international date line to its east, skipping December 30 and becoming one hour ahead of New Zealand rather than 23 hours behind.

GEOGRAPHY

Location: Oceania, group of three atolls in the South Pacific Ocean, about one-half of the way from Hawaii to New Zealand

Geographic coordinates: 9 00 S, 172 00 W

Map references: Oceania

Area: *total:* 12 sq km
land: 12 sq km
water: 0 sq km
country comparison to the world: 241

Area - comparative: about 17 times the size of the National Mall in Washington, DC

Land boundaries: *total:* 0 km

Coastline: 101 km

Maritime claims: *territorial sea:* 12 nm
exclusive economic zone: 200 nm

Climate: tropical; moderated by trade winds (April to November)

Terrain: low-lying coral atolls enclosing large lagoons

Elevation: *highest point:* unnamed location 5 m
lowest point: Pacific Ocean 0 m

Natural resources: Fisheries

Land use: *agricultural land:* 60% (2018 est.)
arable land: 0% (2018 est.)
permanent crops: 60% (2018 est.)
permanent pasture: 0% (2018 est.)
forest: 0% (2018 est.)
other: 40% (2018 est.)

Irrigated land: 0 sq km (2012)

Population distribution: the country's small population is fairly evenly distributed amongst the three atolls

Natural hazards: lies in Pacific cyclone belt

Geography - note: consists of three atolls (Atafu, Fakaofo, Nukunonu), each with a lagoon surrounded by a number of reef-bound islets of varying length and rising to over 3 m above sea level

PEOPLE AND SOCIETY

Population: 1,647 (2019 est.)
country comparison to the world: 233

Nationality: *noun:* Tokelauan(s)
adjective: Tokelauan

Ethnic groups: Tokelauan 64.5%, part Tokelauan/Samoan 9.7%, part Tokelauan/Tuvaluan 2.8%, Tuvaluan 7.5%, Samoan 5.8%, other Pacific Islander 3.4%, other 5.6%, unspecified 0.8% (2016 est.)

Languages: Tokelauan 88.1% (a Polynesian language), English 48.6%, Samoan 26.7%, Tuvaluan 11.2%, Kiribati 1.5%, other 2.8%, none 2.8%, unspecified 0.8% (2016 ests.)
note: shares sum to more than 100% because some respondents gave more than one answer on the census

Religions: Congregational Christian Church 50.4%, Roman Catholic 38.7%, Presbyterian 5.9%, other Christian 4.2%, unspecified 0.8% (2016 est.)

Population growth rate: -0.01% (2019 est.)
country comparison to the world: 198

Net migration rate: -3.84 migrant(s)/1,000 population (2021 est.)
country comparison to the world: 190

Population distribution: the country's small population is fairly evenly distributed amongst the three atolls

Urbanization: *urban population:* 0% of total population (2022)
rate of urbanization: 0% annual rate of change (2020-25 est.)

Drinking water source: *improved: urban:* 0% of population
rural: 99.7% of population
total: 99.7% of population
unimproved: urban: 0% of population
rural: 0.3% of population
total: 0.3% of population (2020 est.)

Sanitation facility access: *improved: total:* 100% of population
unimproved: total: 0% of population (2020 est.)

Major infectious diseases: *degree of risk:* high (2020)
food or waterborne diseases: bacterial diarrhea
vectorborne diseases: malaria

ENVIRONMENT

Environment - current issues: overexploitation of certain fish and other marine species, coastal sand, and forest resources; pollution of freshwater lenses and coastal waters from improper disposal of chemicals

Climate: tropical; moderated by trade winds (April to November)

Land use: *agricultural land:* 60% (2018 est.)
arable land: 0% (2018 est.)
permanent crops: 60% (2018 est.)
permanent pasture: 0% (2018 est.)
forest: 0% (2018 est.)
other: 40% (2018 est.)

Urbanization: *urban population:* 0% of total population (2022)
rate of urbanization: 0% annual rate of change (2020-25 est.)

Total renewable water resources: 0 cubic meters (2017 est.)

GOVERNMENT

Country name: *conventional long form:* none
conventional short form: Tokelau
former: Union Islands, Tokelau Islands
etymology: "tokelau" is a Polynesian word meaning "north wind"

Government type: parliamentary democracy under a constitutional monarchy

Dependency status: self-administering territory of New Zealand; note - Tokelau and New Zealand have agreed to a draft constitution as Tokelau moves toward free association with New Zealand; a UN-sponsored referendum on self governance in October 2007 did not meet the two-thirds majority vote necessary for changing the political status

Capital: *time difference:* UTC+13 (18 hours ahead of Washington, DC during Standard Time)
note: there is no designated, official capital for Tokelau; the location of the capital rotates among the three atolls along with the head of government or Ulu o Tokelau

Administrative divisions: none (territory of New Zealand)

Independence: none (territory of New Zealand)

National holiday: Waitangi Day (Treaty of Waitangi established British sovereignty over New Zealand), 6 February (1840)

Constitution: *history:* many previous; latest effective 1 January 1949 (Tokelau Islands Act 1948)
amendments: proposed as a resolution by the General Fono; passage requires support by each village and approval by the General Fono; amended several times, last in 2007

Legal system: common law system of New Zealand

Citizenship: see New Zealand

Suffrage: 21 years of age; universal

Executive branch: *chief of state:* King CHARLES III (since 8 September 2022); represented by Governor General of New Zealand Governor General Dame Cindy KIRO (since 21 September 2021); New Zealand is represented by Administrator Ross ARDERN (since May 2018)
head of government: (Ulu o Tokelau) Kelihiano KALOLO (since 8 March 2021); note - position rotates annually among the three Faipule (village leaders) of the atolls
cabinet: Council for the Ongoing Government of Tokelau (or Tokelau Council) functions as a cabinet; consists of 3 Faipule (village leaders) and 3 Pulenuku (village mayors)
elections/appointments: the monarchy is hereditary; governor general appointed by the monarch; administrator appointed by the Minister of Foreign Affairs and Trade in New Zealand; head of government chosen from the Council of Faipule to serve a 1-year term
note: the meeting place of the Tokelau Council rotates annually among the three atolls; this tradition has given rise to the somewhat misleading description that the capital rotates yearly between the three atolls; in actuality, it is the seat of the government councilors that rotates since Tokelau has no capital

Legislative branch: *description:* unicameral General Fono (20 seats apportioned by island - Atafu 7, Fakaofo 7, Nukunonu 6; members directly elected by simple majority vote to serve 3-year terms); note - the Tokelau Amendment Act of 1996 confers limited legislative power to the General Fono
elections:
last held on 23 January 2020 depending on island (next to be held in January 2023)
election results:
percent of vote by party - NA; seats by party - independent 20; composition - men 17, women 3, percent of women 15%

Judicial branch: *highest court(s):* Court of Appeal (in New Zealand) (consists of the court president and 8 judges sitting in 3- or 5-judge panels, depending on the case)
judge selection and term of office: judges nominated by the Judicial Selection Committee and approved by three-quarters majority of the Parliament; judges serve for life
subordinate courts: High Court (in New Zealand); Council of Elders or Taupulega

Political parties and leaders: none

International organization participation: PIF (associate member), SPC, UNESCO (associate), UPU

Diplomatic representation in the US: none (territory of New Zealand)

Diplomatic representation from the US: none (territory of New Zealand)

Flag description: a yellow stylized Tokelauan canoe on a dark blue field sails toward the manu - the Southern Cross constellation of four, white, five-pointed stars at the hoist side; the Southern Cross represents the role of Christianity in Tokelauan culture and, in conjunction with the canoe, symbolizes the country navigating into the future; the color yellow indicates happiness and peace, and the blue field represents the ocean on which the community relies

National symbol(s): tuluma (fishing tackle box); national colors: blue, yellow, white

National anthem: *name:* "Te Atua" (For the Almighty)
lyrics/music: unknown/Falani KALOLO
note: adopted 2008; in preparation for eventual self governance, Tokelau held a national contest to choose an anthem; as a territory of New Zealand, in addition to "God Defend New Zealand," "God Save the King" serves as a royal anthem (see United Kingdom); "God Save the King" normally played only when a member of the royal family or the governor-general is present; in all other cases, "God Defend New Zealand" is played (see New Zealand)

ECONOMY

Economic overview: Tokelau's small size (three villages), isolation, and lack of resources greatly restrain economic development and confine agriculture to the subsistence level. The principal sources of revenue are from sales of copra, postage stamps, souvenir coins, and handicrafts. Money is also remitted to families from relatives in New Zealand.

The people rely heavily on aid from New Zealand - about $15 million annually in FY12/13 and FY13/14 - to maintain public services. New Zealand's support amounts to 80% of Tokelau's recurrent government budget. An international trust fund, currently worth nearly $32 million, was established in 2004 by New Zealand to provide Tokelau an independent source of revenue.

Real GDP (purchasing power parity): $7,711,583 (2017 est.)
note: data are in 2017 dollars.
country comparison to the world: 228

Real GDP per capita: $6,004 (2017 est.)
$4,855 (2016 est.)
$4,292 (2015 est.)
note: data are in 2017 dollars
country comparison to the world: 164

GDP (official exchange rate): $12.658 million (2017 est.)
note: data uses New Zealand Dollar (NZD) as the currency of exchange.

Inflation rate (consumer prices): 4% (2020 est.)
2.5% (2019 est.)
11% (2017 est.)
note: Tokelau notes that its wide inflation swings are due almost entirely due to cigarette prices, a chief import.
country comparison to the world: 167

Agricultural products: coconuts, roots/tubers, tropical fruit, pork, bananas, eggs, poultry, pig offals, pig fat, fruit

Industries: small-scale enterprises for copra production, woodworking, plaited craft goods; stamps, coins; fishing

Labor force: 1,100 (2019 est.)
country comparison to the world: 228

Unemployment rate: 2% (2015 est.)
note: Underemployment may be as high as 6.6%
country comparison to the world: 21

Budget: *revenues:* 24,324,473 (2017 est.)
expenditures: 11,666,542 (2017 est.)

Fiscal year: 1 April - 31 March

Exports: $103,000 (2015 est.)
$102,826 (2002 est.)
country comparison to the world: 224

Exports - partners: Singapore 25%, France 19%, South Africa 7%, New Zealand 5%, United States 5%, Ireland 5% (2019)

Exports - commodities: oscilloscopes, house linens, fruits, nuts, recreational boats, iron products (2019)

Imports: $15,792,720 (2015 est.)
country comparison to the world: 224

Imports - partners: Samoa 35%, Ireland 17%, Philippines 14%, Malaysia 13%, South Africa 9% (2019)

Imports - commodities: oscilloscopes, integrated circuits, refined petroleum, packaged medicines, orthopedic appliances (2019)

Exchange rates: New Zealand dollars (NZD) per US dollar -
1.543 (2017 est.)

COMMUNICATIONS

Telecommunication systems: *general assessment:* modern satellite-based communications system; demand for mobile broadband increasing due to mobile services being the method of access for Internet across the region; 2G widespread with some 4G LTE service; satellite services has improved with the launch of the Kacific-1 satellite launched in 2019 (2020)
domestic: radiotelephone service between islands; fixed-line teledensity is 0 per 100 persons (2019)
international: country code - 690; landing point for the Southern Cross NEXT submarine cable linking Australia, Tokelau, Samoa, Kiribati, Fiji, New Zealand and Los Angeles, CA (USA); radiotelephone service to Samoa; government-regulated telephone service (TeleTok); satellite earth stations - 3 (2020)

Broadcast media: Sky TV access for around 30% of the population; each atoll operates a radio service that provides shipping news and weather reports (2019)

Internet country code: .tk

Internet users: *total:* 805 (2019 est.)
percent of population: 58% (2019 est.)
country comparison to the world: 228

TRANSPORTATION

Roadways: *total:* 10 km (2019)
country comparison to the world: 222

Ports and terminals: none; offshore anchorage only

MILITARY AND SECURITY

Military - note: defense is the responsibility of New Zealand

TRANSNATIONAL ISSUES

Disputes - international: *Tokelau-American Samoa (US):* Tokelau included American Samoa's Swains Island (Olosega) in its 2006 draft independence constitution; Swains Island has been administered by American Samoa since 1925; the 1980 Treaty of Tokehega delineates the maritime boundary between American Samoa and Tokelau; while not specifically mentioning Swains Island, the treaty notes in its preamble that New Zealand does not claim as part of Tokelau any island administered as part of American Samoa

TONGA

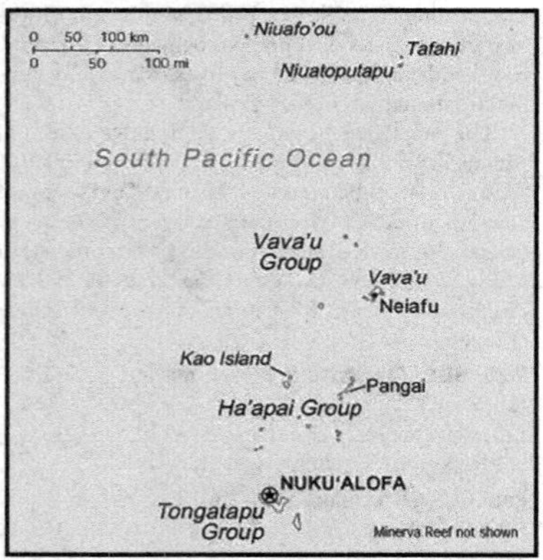

INTRODUCTION

Background: The first humans arrived in Tonga around 1000 B.C. The islands' politics were probably highly centralized under the Tu'i Tonga, or Tongan king, by A.D. 950, and by 1200, the Tu'i Tonga had expanded his influence throughout Polynesia and into Melanesia and Micronesia. The Tongan Empire began to decline in the 1300s, descending into civil wars, a military defeat to Samoa, and internal political strife that saw successive leaders assassinated. By the mid-1500s, some Tu'i Tongans were ethnic Samoan and day-to-day administration of Tonga was transferred to a new position occupied by ethnic Tongans.

Dutch sailors explored the islands in the 1600s and British Captain James COOK visited Tonga three times in the 1770s, naming them the Friendly Islands for the positive reception he thought he received, even though the Tongans he encountered were plotting ways to kill him. In 1799, Tonga fell into a new round of civil wars over succession. Wesleyan missionaries arrived in 1822, quickly converting the population. In the 1830s, a low-ranking chief from Ha'apai began to consolidate control over the islands and won the support of the missionaries by declaring that he would dedicate Tonga to God. The chief soon made alliances with leaders on most of the other islands and was crowned King George TUPOU I in 1845, establishing the only still-extant Polynesian monarchy. TUPOU I declared Tonga a constitutional monarchy in 1875 and his successor, King George TUPOU II, agreed to enter a protectorate agreement with the UK in 1900 after rival Tongan chiefs tried to overthrow him. As a protectorate, Tonga never completely lost its indigenous governance, but it did become more isolated and the social hierarchy became more stratified between a group of nobles and a large class of commoners. Today, about one third of parliamentary seats are reserved for nobles.

Queen Salote TUPOU III negotiated the end of the protectorate in 1965, which was achieved under King TUPOU IV, who in 1970 withdrew from the protectorate and joined the Commonwealth of Nations. A prodemocracy movement gained steam in the early 2000s, led by future Prime Minister 'Akilisi POHIVA, and in 2006, riots broke out in Nuku'alofa to protest the lack of progress on prodemocracy legislation. To appease the activists, in 2008, King George TUPOU V announced he was relinquishing most of his powers leading up to parliamentary elections in 2010; he died in 2012 and was succeeded by his brother 'Aho'eitu TUPOU VI. Tropical Cyclone Gita, the strongest-ever recorded storm to impact Tonga, hit the islands in February 2018 causing extensive damage.

GEOGRAPHY

Location: Oceania, archipelago in the South Pacific Ocean, about two-thirds of the way from Hawaii to New Zealand

Geographic coordinates: 20 00 S, 175 00 W

Map references: Oceania

Area: *total:* 747 sq km
land: 717 sq km
water: 30 sq km
country comparison to the world: 189

Area - comparative: four times the size of Washington, DC

Land boundaries: *total:* 0 km

Coastline: 419 km

Maritime claims: *territorial sea:* 12 nm
exclusive economic zone: 200 nm
continental shelf: 200-m depth or to the depth of exploitation

Climate: tropical; modified by trade winds; warm season (December to May), cool season (May to December)

Terrain: mostly flat islands with limestone bedrock formed from uplifted coral formation; others have limestone overlying volcanic rock

Elevation: *highest point:* Kao Volcano on Kao Island 1,046 m
lowest point: Pacific Ocean 0 m

Natural resources: arable land, fish

Land use: *agricultural land:* 43.1% (2018 est.)
arable land: 22.2% (2018 est.)
permanent crops: 15.3% (2018 est.)
permanent pasture: 5.6% (2018 est.)
forest: 12.5% (2018 est.)
other: 44.4% (2018 est.)

Irrigated land: 0 sq km (2012)

Population distribution: over two-thirds of the population lives on the island of Tongatapu; only 45 of the nation's 171 islands are occupied

Natural hazards: cyclones (October to April); earthquakes and volcanic activity on Fonuafo'ou
volcanism: moderate volcanic activity; Fonualei (180 m) has shown frequent activity in recent years, while Niuafo'ou (260 m), which last erupted in 1985, has forced evacuations; other historically active volcanoes include Late and Tofua

Geography - note: the western islands (making up the Tongan Volcanic Arch) are all of volcanic origin; the eastern islands are nonvolcanic and are composed of coral limestone and sand

PEOPLE AND SOCIETY

Population: 105,517 (2022 est.)
country comparison to the world: 191

Nationality: *noun:* Tongan(s)
adjective: Tongan

Ethnic groups: Tongan 97%, part-Tongan 0.8%, other 2.2%, unspecified <0.1% (2016 est.)

Languages: Tongan and English 76.8%, Tongan, English, and other language 10.6%, Tongan only (official) 8.7%, English only (official) 0.7%, other 1.7%, none 2.2% (2016 est.)
note: data represent persons aged 5 and older who can read and write a simple sentence in Tongan, English, or another language

Religions: Protestant 64.1% (includes Free Wesleyan Church 35%, Free Church of Tonga 11.9%, Church of Tonga 6.8%, Assembly of God 2.3%, Seventh Day Adventist 2.2%, Tokaikolo Christian Church 1.6%, other 4.3%), Church of Jesus Christ 18.6%, Roman Catholic 14.2%, other 2.4%, none 0.5%, unspecified 0.1% (2016 est.)

Age structure: *0-14 years:* 32% (male 17,250/female 16,698)
15-24 years: 19.66% (male 10,679/female 10,175)
25-54 years: 35.35% (male 18,701/female 18,802)
55-64 years: 6.17% (male 3,345/female 3,202)
65 years and over: 6.83% (male 3,249/female 3,994) (2020 est.)

Dependency ratios: *total dependency ratio:* 68.6
youth dependency ratio: 58.6
elderly dependency ratio: 10
potential support ratio: 10 (2020 est.)

Median age: *total:* 24.1 years
male: 23.6 years
female: 24.5 years (2020 est.)
country comparison to the world: 169

Population growth rate: -0.26% (2022 est.)
country comparison to the world: 215

Birth rate: 20.31 births/1,000 population (2022 est.)
country comparison to the world: 69

Death rate: 4.95 deaths/1,000 population (2022 est.)
country comparison to the world: 197

Net migration rate: -18.01 migrant(s)/1,000 population (2022 est.)
country comparison to the world: 228

Population distribution: over two-thirds of the population lives on the island of Tongatapu; only 45 of the nation's 171 islands are occupied

Urbanization: *urban population:* 23.1% of total population (2022)
rate of urbanization: 0.99% annual rate of change (2020-25 est.)

Major urban areas - population: 23,000 NUKU'ALOFA (2018)

Sex ratio: *at birth:* 1.03 male(s)/female
0-14 years: 1.03 male(s)/female
15-24 years: 1.05 male(s)/female
25-54 years: 0.99 male(s)/female
55-64 years: 1.06 male(s)/female
65 years and over: 0.7 male(s)/female
total population: 1.01 male(s)/female (2022 est.)

Mother's mean age at first birth: 24.9 years (2012 est.)
note: data represents median age at first birth among women 25-49

Maternal mortality ratio: 52 deaths/100,000 live births (2017 est.)
country comparison to the world: 94

Infant mortality rate: *total:* 12.41 deaths/1,000 live births
male: 13.43 deaths/1,000 live births
female: 11.37 deaths/1,000 live births (2022 est.)
country comparison to the world: 113

Life expectancy at birth: *total population:* 77.53 years
male: 75.89 years
female: 79.23 years (2022 est.)
country comparison to the world: 88

Total fertility rate: 2.76 children born/woman (2022 est.)
country comparison to the world: 60

Contraceptive prevalence rate: 29.3% (2019)

Drinking water source: *improved: urban:* 99.8% of population
rural: 99.6% of population
total: 99.6% of population
unimproved: urban: 0.2% of population
rural: 0.4% of population
total: 0.4% of population (2020 est.)

Current health expenditure: 5% of GDP (2019)

Physicians density: 0.95 physicians/1,000 population (2020)

Sanitation facility access: *improved: urban:* 99.4% of population
rural: 98.8% of population
total: 98.9% of population
unimproved: urban: 0.6% of population
rural: 1.2% of population
total: 1.1% of population (2020 est.)

Major infectious diseases: *degree of risk:* high (2020)
food or waterborne diseases: bacterial diarrhea
vectorborne diseases: malaria

Obesity - adult prevalence rate: 48.2% (2016)
country comparison to the world: 7

Alcohol consumption per capita: *total:* 0.31 liters of pure alcohol (2019 est.)
beer: 0.03 liters of pure alcohol (2019 est.)
wine: 0.17 liters of pure alcohol (2019 est.)
spirits: 0.11 liters of pure alcohol (2019 est.)
other alcohols: 0 liters of pure alcohol (2019 est.)
country comparison to the world: 169

Tobacco use: *total:* 31% (2020 est.)
male: 46.7% (2020 est.)
female: 15.3% (2020 est.)
country comparison to the world: 27

Children under the age of 5 years underweight: 0.8% (2019)
country comparison to the world: 124

Child marriage: *women married by age 15:* 0.4%
women married by age 18: 10.1%
men married by age 18: 2.8% (2019 est.)

Education expenditures: 8% of GDP (2019 est.)
country comparison to the world: 10

Literacy: *definition:* can read and write Tongan and/or English
total population: 99.4%
male: 99.4%
female: 99.5% (2018)

School life expectancy (primary to tertiary education): *total:* 16 years
male: 15 years
female: 17 years (2020)

Unemployment, youth ages 15-24: *total:* 8.9%
male: 5.7%
female: 13.1% (2018)

ENVIRONMENT

Environment - current issues: deforestation from land being cleared for agriculture and settlement; soil exhaustion; water pollution due to salinization, sewage, and toxic chemicals from farming activities; coral reefs and marine populations threatened

Environment - international agreements: *party to:* Biodiversity, Climate Change, Climate Change-Kyoto Protocol, Climate Change-Paris Agreement, Desertification, Endangered Species, Hazardous Wastes, Law of the Sea, Marine Dumping-London Convention, Marine Dumping-London Protocol, Marine Life Conservation, Nuclear Test Ban, Ozone Layer Protection, Ship Pollution
signed, but not ratified: none of the selected agreements

Air pollutants: *particulate matter emissions:* 10.08 micrograms per cubic meter (2016 est.)
carbon dioxide emissions: 0.13 megatons (2016 est.)
methane emissions: 0.12 megatons (2020 est.)

Climate: tropical; modified by trade winds; warm season (December to May), cool season (May to December)

Land use: *agricultural land:* 43.1% (2018 est.)
arable land: 22.2% (2018 est.)
permanent crops: 15.3% (2018 est.)
permanent pasture: 5.6% (2018 est.)
forest: 12.5% (2018 est.)
other: 44.4% (2018 est.)

Urbanization: *urban population:* 23.1% of total population (2022)
rate of urbanization: 0.99% annual rate of change (2020-25 est.)

Revenue from forest resources: *forest revenues:* 0.03% of GDP (2018 est.)
country comparison to the world: 137

Revenue from coal: *coal revenues:* 0% of GDP (2018 est.)

country comparison to the world: 176

Waste and recycling: *municipal solid waste generated annually:* 17,238 tons (2012 est.)

Total renewable water resources: 0 cubic meters (2017 est.)

GOVERNMENT

Country name: *conventional long form:* Kingdom of Tonga
conventional short form: Tonga
local long form: Pule'anga Fakatu'i 'o Tonga
local short form: Tonga
former: Friendly Islands
etymology: "tonga" means "south" in the Tongan language and refers to the country's geographic position in relation to central Polynesia

Government type: constitutional monarchy

Capital: *name:* Nuku'alofa
geographic coordinates: 21 08 S, 175 12 W
time difference: UTC+13 (18 hours ahead of Washington, DC, during Standard Time)
daylight saving time: +1hr, begins first Sunday in November; ends second Sunday in January
etymology: composed of the words *nuku*, meaning "residence or abode," and *alofa*, meaning "love," to signify "abode of love"

Administrative divisions: 5 island divisions; 'Eua, Ha'apai, Ongo Niua, Tongatapu, Vava'u

Independence: 4 June 1970 (from UK protectorate status)

National holiday: Official Birthday of King TUPOU VI, 4 July (1959); note - actual birthday of the monarch is 12 July 1959, 4 July (2015) is the day the king was crowned; Constitution Day (National Day), 4 November (1875)

Constitution: *history:* adopted 4 November 1875, revised 1988, 2016
amendments: proposed by the Legislative Assembly; passage requires approval by the Assembly in each of three readings, the unanimous approval of the Privy Council (a high-level advisory body to the monarch), the Cabinet, and assent to by the monarch; revised 1988; amended many times, last in 2013

Legal system: English common law

International law organization participation: has not submitted an ICJ jurisdiction declaration; non-party state to the ICCt

Citizenship: *citizenship by birth:* no
citizenship by descent only: the father must be a citizen of Tonga; if a child is born out of wedlock, the mother must be a citizen of Tonga
dual citizenship recognized: yes
residency requirement for naturalization: 5 years

Suffrage: 21 years of age; universal

Executive branch: *chief of state:* King TUPOU VI (since 18 March 2012); Heir Apparent Crown Prince Siaosi Manumataogo 'Alaivahamama'o 'Ahoeitu Konstantin Tuku'aho, son of the king (born 17 September 1985); note - on 18 March 2012, King George TUPOU V died and his brother, Crown Prince TUPOUTO'A Lavaka, assumed the throne as TUPOU VI
head of government: Prime Minister Siaosi SOVALENI (since 27 December 2021)
cabinet: Cabinet nominated by the prime minister and appointed by the monarch
elections/appointments: the monarchy is hereditary; prime minister and deputy prime minister indirectly elected by the Legislative Assembly and appointed by the monarch; election last held on 18 November 2021 (next to be held in November 2025)
election results:
Siaosi SOVALENI elected prime minister by the Legislative Assembly; Siaosi SOVALENI 16 votes, Aisake EKE 10
note: a Privy Council advises the monarch

Legislative branch: *description:* unicameral Legislative Assembly or Fale Alea (30 seats statutory, 27 current); 17 people's representatives directly elected in single-seat constituencies by simple majority vote, and 9 indirectly elected by hereditary leaders; members serve 4-year terms)
elections:
last held on 18 November 2021 (next to be held in November 2025)
election results:
percent of vote - NA; seats by party (elected members) - independents 11, nobles' representatives 9, Democratic Party 3, Peoples Party 3; composition - men 26, women 1, percent of women 3.7%

Judicial branch: *highest court(s):* Court of Appeal (consists of the court president and a number of judges determined by the monarch); note - appeals beyond the Court of Appeal are brought before the King in Privy Council, the monarch's advisory organ that has both judicial and legislative powers
judge selection and term of office: judge appointments and tenures made by the King in Privy Council and subject to consent of the Legislative Assembly
subordinate courts: Supreme Court; Magistrates' Courts; Land Courts

Political parties and leaders: Democratic Party of the Friendly Islands or DPFI or PTOA [Semisi SIKA]
People's Democratic Party or PDP [Tesina FUKO]
Tonga Democratic Labor Party [vacant]
Tonga Human Rights and Democracy Movement or HRDM ['Uliti UATA]
Tonga People's Party or PAK or TPPI (Paati 'a e Kakai 'o Tonga) [Pohiva TU'I'ONETOA] (split from Democratic Party of the Friendly Islands)

International organization participation: ACP, ADB, AOSIS, C, FAO, G-77, IBRD, ICAO, ICRM, IDA, IFAD, IFC, IFRCS, IHO, IMF, IMO, IMSO, Interpol, IOC, IPU, ITU, ITUC (NGOs), OPCW, PIF, Sparteca, SPC, UN, UNCTAD, UNESCO, UNIDO, UPU, WCO, WHO, WIPO, WMO, WTO

Diplomatic representation in the US: *chief of mission:* Ambassador Viliami Va'inga TONE (since 20 April 2021)
chancery: 250 East 51st Street, New York, NY 10022
telephone: [1] (917) 369-1025
FAX: [1] (917) 369-1024
email address and website:
tongaunmission@aol.com
consulate(s) general: San Francisco

Diplomatic representation from the US: *embassy:* the US does not have an embassy in Tonga; the US Ambassador to Fiji is accredited to Tonga

Flag description: red with a bold red cross on a white rectangle in the upper hoist-side corner; the cross reflects the deep-rooted Christianity in Tonga, red represents the blood of Christ and his sacrifice, and white signifies purity

National symbol(s): red cross on white field, arms equal length; national colors: red, white

Coat of arms of the Kingdom of Tonga:

National anthem: *name:* "Ko e fasi 'o e tu"i 'o e Otu Tonga" (Song of the King of the Tonga Islands)
lyrics/music: Uelingatoni Ngu TUPOUMALOHI/ Karl Gustavus SCHMITT
note: in use since 1875; more commonly known as "Fasi Fakafonua" (National Song)

ECONOMY

Economic overview: Tonga has a small, open island economy and is the last constitutional monarchy among the Pacific Island countries. It has a narrow export base in agricultural goods. Squash, vanilla beans, and yams are the main crops. Agricultural exports, including fish, make up two-thirds of total exports. Tourism is the second-largest source of hard currency earnings following remittances. Tonga had 53,800 visitors in 2015. The country must import a high proportion of its food, mainly from New Zealand.

The country remains dependent on external aid and remittances from overseas Tongans to offset its trade deficit. The government is emphasizing the development of the private sector, encouraging investment, and is committing increased funds for health care and education. Tonga's English-speaking and educated workforce offers a viable labor market, and the tropical climate provides fertile soil. Renewable energy and deep-sea mining also offer opportunities for investment.

Tonga has a reasonably sound basic infrastructure and well developed social services. But the government faces high unemployment among the young, moderate inflation, pressures for democratic reform, and rising civil service expenditures.

Real GDP (purchasing power parity): $670 million (2019 est.)
$660 million (2018 est.)
$660 million (2017 est.)
note: data are in 2017 dollars
country comparison to the world: 210

Real GDP growth rate: 2.5% (2017 est.)
4.2% (2016 est.)
3.5% (2015 est.)
country comparison to the world: 114

Real GDP per capita: $6,400 (2019 est.) note: data are in 2017 dollars
$6,400 (2018 est.) note: data are in 2017 dollars
$6,472 (2017 est.)
country comparison to the world: 158

GDP (official exchange rate): $455 million (2017 est.)

Inflation rate (consumer prices): 7.4% (2017 est.)
2.6% (2016 est.)
country comparison to the world: 195

GDP - composition, by sector of origin: *agriculture:* 19.9% (2017 est.)
industry: 20.3% (2017 est.)
services: 59.8% (2017 est.)

GDP - composition, by end use: *household consumption:* 99.4% (2017 est.)
government consumption: 21.9% (2017 est.)
investment in fixed capital: 24.1% (2017 est.)
investment in inventories: 0% (2017 est.)
exports of goods and services: 22.8% (2017 est.)
imports of goods and services: -68.5% (2017 est.)

Agricultural products: coconuts, gourds, cassava, sweet potatoes, vegetables, yams, taro, roots/tubers nes, plantains, lemons/limes

Industries: tourism, construction, fishing
Industrial production growth rate: 5% (2017 est.)
country comparison to the world: 59
Labor force: 33,800 (2011 est.)
country comparison to the world: 200
Labor force - by occupation: *agriculture:* 2,006% (2006 est.)
industry: 27.5% (2006 est.)
services: 2,006% (2006 est.)
Unemployment rate: 1.1% (2011 est.)
1.1% (2006)
country comparison to the world: 13
Unemployment, youth ages 15-24: *total:* 8.9%
male: 5.7%
female: 13.1% (2018)
country comparison to the world: 146
Population below poverty line: 22.5% (2010 est.)
Gini Index coefficient - distribution of family income: 37.6 (2015 est.)
country comparison to the world: 77
Budget: *revenues:* 181.2 million (2017 est.)
expenditures: 181.2 million (2017 est.)
Budget surplus (+) or deficit (-): 0% (of GDP) (2017 est.)
country comparison to the world: 47
Public debt: 48% of GDP (FY2017 est.)
51.8% of GDP (FY2016 est.)
country comparison to the world: 109
Taxes and other revenues: 39.8% (of GDP) (2017 est.)
country comparison to the world: 42
Fiscal year: 1 July - 30 June
Current account balance: -$53 million (2017 est.)
-$30 million (2016 est.)
country comparison to the world: 81
Exports: $90 million (2020 est.) note: data are in current year dollars
$110 million (2019 est.) note: data are in current year dollars
$100 million (2018 est.) note: data are in current year dollars
country comparison to the world: 209
Exports - partners: United States 38%, South Korea 18%, Australia 14%, New Zealand 14%, Japan 6%, (2019)
Exports - commodities: squash, fish, various fruits and nuts, antiques, coral and shells (2019)
Imports: $300 million (2020 est.) note: data are in current year dollars
$330 million (2019 est.) note: data are in current year dollars
$320 million (2018 est.) note: data are in current year dollars
country comparison to the world: 210
Imports - partners: Fiji 29%, New Zealand 23%, China 14%, United States 8%, Australia 6%, Japan 6% (2019)
Imports - commodities: refined petroleum, poultry meats, audio equipment, mutton, goat meat, broadcasting equipment (2019)
Reserves of foreign exchange and gold: $198.5 million (31 December 2017 est.)
$176.5 million (31 December 2016 est.)
country comparison to the world: 176
Debt - external: $189.9 million (31 December 2017 est.)
$198.2 million (31 December 2016 est.)
country comparison to the world: 190
Exchange rates: pa'anga (TOP) per US dollar -
2.27015 (2020 est.)
2.29095 (2019 est.)
2.22717 (2018 est.)
2.106 (2014 est.)
1.847 (2013 est.)

ENERGY

Electricity access: *electrification - total population:* 98.9% (2018)
electrification - urban areas: 98.9% (2018)
electrification - rural areas: 98.9% (2018)
Electricity: *installed generating capacity:* 26,000 kW (2020 est.)
consumption: 54.448 million kWh (2019 est.)
exports: 0 kWh (2019 est.)
imports: 0 kWh (2019 est.)
transmission/distribution losses: 5.9 million kWh (2019 est.)
Electricity generation sources fossil fuels: 100% of total installed capacity (2020 est.)
Petroleum: *total petroleum production:* 0 bbl/day (2021 est.)
refined petroleum consumption: 1,200 bbl/day (2019 est.)
Refined petroleum products - imports: 910 bbl/day (2015 est.)
country comparison to the world: 202
Carbon dioxide emissions: 171,000 metric tonnes of CO_2 (2019 est.)
from petroleum and other liquids: 171,000 metric tonnes of CO_2 (2019 est.)
country comparison to the world: 207
Energy consumption per capita: 22.841 million Btu/person (2019 est.)
country comparison to the world: 133

COMMUNICATIONS

Telephones - fixed lines: *total subscriptions:* 7,000 (2020 est.)
subscriptions per 100 inhabitants: 7 (2020 est.)
country comparison to the world: 197
Telephones - mobile cellular total subscriptions: 62,104 (2019)
subscriptions per 100 inhabitants: 59.43 (2019)
country comparison to the world: 202
Telecommunication systems: *general assessment:* high speed Internet provided by 3 MNOs, has subsequently allowed for better health care services, faster connections for education and growing e-commerce services; in 2018 new 4G LTE network; fixed-line teledensity has dropped given mobile subscriptions; mobile technology dominates given the island's geography; satellite technology is widespread and is important especially in areas away from the city; the launch in 2019 of the Kacific-1 broadband satellite has made broadband more widely available for around 89 remote communities (2020)
domestic: fixed-line 6 per 100 persons and mobile-cellular teledensity 59 telephones per 100; fully automatic switched network (2019)
international: country code - 676; landing point for the Tonga Cable and the TDCE connecting to Fiji and 3 separate Tonga islands; satellite earth station - 1 Intelsat (Pacific Ocean) (2020)
Broadcast media: 1 state-owned TV station and 3 privately owned TV stations; satellite and cable TV services are available; 1 state-owned and 5 privately owned radio stations; Radio Australia broadcasts available via satellite (2019)
Internet country code: .to
Internet users: *total:* 42,844 (2019 est.)
percent of population: 41% (2019 est.)
country comparison to the world: 200
Broadband - fixed subscriptions: *total:* 5,000 (2020 est.)
subscriptions per 100 inhabitants: 5 (2020 est.)
country comparison to the world: 189

TRANSPORTATION

National air transport system: *number of registered air carriers:* 1 (2020)
inventory of registered aircraft operated by air carriers: 1
Civil aircraft registration country code prefix: A3
Airports: *total:* 6 (2021)
country comparison to the world: 178
Airports - with paved runways: *total:* 1
2,438 to 3,047 m: 1 (2021)
Airports - with unpaved runways: *total:* 5
1,524 to 2,437 m: 1
914 to 1,523 m: 3
under 914 m: 1 (2021)
Roadways: *total:* 680 km (2011)
paved: 184 km (2011)
unpaved: 496 km (2011)
country comparison to the world: 190
Merchant marine: *total:* 32
by type: container ship 4, general cargo 13, oil tanker 1, other 14 (2021)
country comparison to the world: 132
Ports and terminals: *major seaport(s):* Nuku'alofa, Neiafu, Pangai

MILITARY AND SECURITY

Military and security forces: His Majesty's Armed Forces Tonga (aka Tonga Defense Services): Joint Force headquarters, Tonga Royal Guard, Land Force (Royal Tongan Marines), Tonga Navy, Training Wing, Air Wing, and Support Unit (2022)
Military expenditures: 2.1% of GDP (2020 est.) (approximately $10 million)
2.4% of GDP (2019 est.) (approximately $12 million)
1.5% of GDP (2018 est.) (approximately $7.1 million)
2.1% of GDP (2017 est.) (approximately $10 million)
1.7% of GDP (2016 est.) (approximately $7.6 million)
country comparison to the world: 53
Military and security service personnel strengths: approximately 650 personnel (2022)
Military equipment inventories and acquisitions: the Tonga military's inventory includes mostly light weapons and equipment from Australia, European (primarily the UK) countries, and the US (2022)
Military service age and obligation: voluntary military service for men and women 18-25 (16 with parental approval for non-combat positions); no conscription (2022)
Military - note: Tonga participated in World War I as part of the New Zealand Expeditionary Force, but the Tonga Defense Force (TDF) was not established until 1939 at the beginning of World War II; in 1943, New Zealand helped train about 2,000 Tongan troops who

saw action in the Solomon Islands; the TDF was disbanded at the end of the war, but was reactivated in 1946 as the Tonga Defense Services (TDS); in 2013, the name of the TDS was changed to His Majesty's Armed Forces of Tonga (HMAF); Tongan troops deployed to Iraq from 2004-2008 and Afghanistan to support UK forces from 2010-2014

Tonga has a "shiprider" agreement with the US, which allows local maritime law enforcement officers to embark on US Coast Guard (USCG) and US Navy (USN) vessels, including to board and search vessels suspected of violating laws or regulations within Tonga's designated exclusive economic zone (EEZ) or on the high seas; "shiprider" agreements also enable USCG personnel and USN vessels with embarked USCG law enforcement personnel to work with host nations to protect critical regional resources (2022)

TRANSNATIONAL ISSUES

Disputes - international: *Tonga-Fiji:* Fiji does not recognize Tonga's 1972 claim to the Minerva Reefs and their surrounding waters; the Minerva Reefs' 200-mile exclusive economic zone includes valuable fishing grounds

TRINIDAD AND TOBAGO

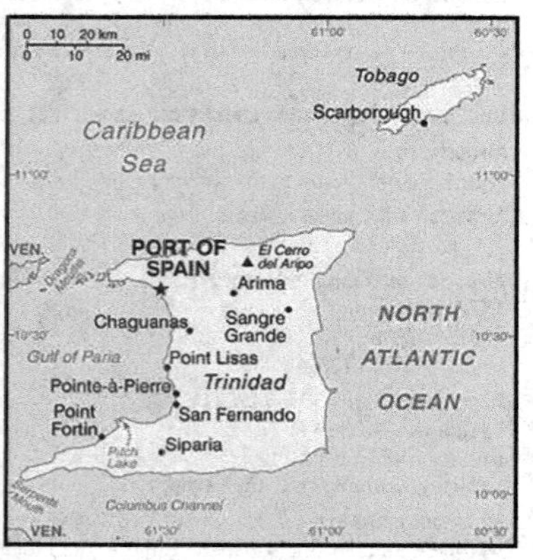

INTRODUCTION

Background: First colonized by the Spanish, the islands came under British control in the early 19th century. The islands' sugar industry was hurt by the emancipation of the slaves in 1834. Manpower was replaced with the importation of contract laborers from India between 1845 and 1917, which boosted sugar production as well as the cocoa industry. The discovery of oil on Trinidad in 1910 added another important export. Independence was attained in 1962. The country is one of the most prosperous in the Caribbean thanks largely to petroleum and natural gas production and processing. Tourism, mostly in Tobago, is targeted for expansion and is growing. The government is struggling to reverse a surge in violent crime.

GEOGRAPHY

Location: Caribbean, islands between the Caribbean Sea and the North Atlantic Ocean, northeast of Venezuela

Geographic coordinates: 11 00 N, 61 00 W

Map references: Central America and the Caribbean

Area: *total:* 5,128 sq km
land: 5,128 sq km
water: 0 sq km
country comparison to the world: 173

Area - comparative: slightly smaller than Delaware

Land boundaries: *total:* 0 km

Coastline: 362 km

Maritime claims: *territorial sea:* 12 nm
contiguous zone: 24 nm
exclusive economic zone: 200 nm
continental shelf: 200 nm or to the outer edge of the continental margin
measured from claimed archipelagic baselines

Climate: tropical; rainy season (June to December)

Terrain: mostly plains with some hills and low mountains

Elevation: *highest point:* El Cerro del Aripo 940 m
lowest point: Caribbean Sea 0 m
mean elevation: 83 m

Natural resources: petroleum, natural gas, asphalt

Land use: *agricultural land:* 10.6% (2018 est.)
arable land: 4.9% (2018 est.)
permanent crops: 4.3% (2018 est.)
permanent pasture: 1.4% (2018 est.)
forest: 44% (2018 est.)
other: 45.4% (2018 est.)

Irrigated land: 70 sq km (2012)

Population distribution: population on Trinidad is concentrated in the western half of the island, on Tobago in the southern half

Natural hazards: outside usual path of hurricanes and other tropical storms

Geography - note: Pitch Lake, on Trinidad's southwestern coast, is the world's largest natural reservoir of asphalt

PEOPLE AND SOCIETY

Population: 1,405,646 (2022 est.)
country comparison to the world: 157

Nationality: *noun:* Trinidadian(s), Tobagonian(s)
adjective: Trinidadian, Tobagonian
note: Trinbagonian is used on occasion to describe a citizen of the country without specifying the island of origin

Ethnic groups: East Indian 35.4%, African descent 34.2%, mixed - other 15.3%, mixed - African/East Indian 7.7%, other 1.3%, unspecified 6.2% (2011 est.)

Languages: English (official), Trinidadian Creole English, Tobagonian Creole English, Caribbean Hindustani (a dialect of Hindi), Trinidadian Creole French, Spanish, Chinese

Religions: Protestant 32.1% (Pentecostal/Evangelical/Full Gospel 12%, Baptist 6.9%, Anglican 5.7%, Seventh Day Adventist 4.1%, Presbyterian/Congregational 2.5%, other Protestant 0.9%), Roman Catholic 21.6%, Hindu 18.2%, Muslim 5%, Jehovah's Witness 1.5%, other 8.4%, none 2.2%, unspecified 11.1% (2011 est.)

Age structure: *0-14 years:* 19.01% (male 116,953/female 112,805)
15-24 years: 11.28% (male 70,986/female 65,389)
25-54 years: 43.77% (male 276,970/female 252,108)
55-64 years: 13.83% (male 83,650/female 83,585)
65 years and over: 12.11% (male 64,092/female 82,251) (2020 est.)

Dependency ratios: *total dependency ratio:* 46.1
youth dependency ratio: 29.3
elderly dependency ratio: 16.8
potential support ratio: 7.4 (2020 est.)

Median age: *total:* 37.8 years
male: 37.3 years
female: 38.3 years (2020 est.)
country comparison to the world: 67

Population growth rate: 0.14% (2022 est.)
country comparison to the world: 184

Birth rate: 10.79 births/1,000 population (2022 est.)
country comparison to the world: 177

Death rate: 8.38 deaths/1,000 population (2022 est.)
country comparison to the world: 77

Net migration rate: -1.01 migrant(s)/1,000 population (2022 est.)
country comparison to the world: 146

Population distribution: population on Trinidad is concentrated in the western half of the island, on Tobago in the southern half

Urbanization: *urban population:* 53.3% of total population (2022)
rate of urbanization: 0.23% annual rate of change (2020-25 est.)

Major urban areas - population: 545,000 PORT-OF-SPAIN (capital) (2022)

Sex ratio: *at birth:* 1.04 male(s)/female
0-14 years: 1.04 male(s)/female
15-24 years: 1.05 male(s)/female
25-54 years: 1.04 male(s)/female
55-64 years: 0.99 male(s)/female
65 years and over: 0.69 male(s)/female
total population: 1.01 male(s)/female (2022 est.)

Maternal mortality ratio: 67 deaths/100,000 live births (2017 est.)
country comparison to the world: 85

Infant mortality rate: *total:* 15.83 deaths/1,000 live births
male: 17.97 deaths/1,000 live births
female: 13.61 deaths/1,000 live births (2022 est.)
country comparison to the world: 97

Life expectancy at birth: *total population:* 75.94 years
male: 74.02 years
female: 77.93 years (2022 est.)
country comparison to the world: 111

Total fertility rate: 1.63 children born/woman (2022 est.)
country comparison to the world: 180

Contraceptive prevalence rate: 40.3% (2011)

Current health expenditure: 7% of GDP (2019)

Physicians density: 4.48 physicians/1,000 population (2019)

Hospital bed density: 3 beds/1,000 population (2017)

Sanitation facility access: *improved: total:* 99.9% of population
unimproved: total: 0.1% of population (2020 est.)

HIV/AIDS - adult prevalence rate: 0.7% (2020 est.)
country comparison to the world: 56

HIV/AIDS - people living with HIV/AIDS: 10,000 (2020 est.)
note: estimate does not include children
country comparison to the world: 103

HIV/AIDS - deaths: (2020 est.) <200
note: estimate does not include children

Obesity - adult prevalence rate: 18.6% (2016)
country comparison to the world: 116

Alcohol consumption per capita: *total:* 5.81 liters of pure alcohol (2019 est.)
beer: 2.92 liters of pure alcohol (2019 est.)
wine: 0.16 liters of pure alcohol (2019 est.)
spirits: 2.65 liters of pure alcohol (2019 est.)
other alcohols: 0.09 liters of pure alcohol (2019 est.)
country comparison to the world: 74

Children under the age of 5 years underweight: 4.9% (2011)
country comparison to the world: 79

Education expenditures: 3.6% of GDP (2019 est.)
country comparison to the world: 121

Literacy: *definition:* age 15 and over can read and write
total population: 99%
male: 99.2%
female: 98.7% (2015)

Unemployment, youth ages 15-24: *total:* 8.7%
male: 8.9%
female: 8.4% (2016 est.)

ENVIRONMENT

Environment - current issues: water pollution from agricultural chemicals, industrial wastes, and raw sewage; widespread pollution of waterways and coastal areas; illegal dumping; deforestation; soil erosion; fisheries and wildlife depletion

Environment - international agreements: *party to:* Biodiversity, Climate Change, Climate Change-Kyoto Protocol, Climate Change-Paris Agreement, Comprehensive Nuclear Test Ban, Desertification, Endangered Species, Hazardous Wastes, Law of the Sea, Marine Dumping-London Protocol, Marine Life Conservation, Nuclear Test Ban, Ozone Layer Protection, Ship Pollution, Tropical Timber 2006, Wetlands
signed, but not ratified: none of the selected agreements

Air pollutants: *particulate matter emissions:* 22.04 micrograms per cubic meter (2016 est.)
carbon dioxide emissions: 43.87 megatons (2016 est.)
methane emissions: 1.35 megatons (2020 est.)

Climate: tropical; rainy season (June to December)

Land use: *agricultural land:* 10.6% (2018 est.)
arable land: 4.9% (2018 est.)
permanent crops: 4.3% (2018 est.)
permanent pasture: 1.4% (2018 est.)
forest: 44% (2018 est.)
other: 45.4% (2018 est.)

Urbanization: *urban population:* 53.3% of total population (2022)
rate of urbanization: 0.23% annual rate of change (2020-25 est.)

Revenue from forest resources: *forest revenues:* 0.05% of GDP (2018 est.)
country comparison to the world: 129

Revenue from coal: *coal revenues:* 0% of GDP (2018 est.)
country comparison to the world: 177

Waste and recycling: *municipal solid waste generated annually:* 727,874 tons (2010 est.)

Total water withdrawal: *municipal:* 237.6 million cubic meters (2017 est.)
industrial: 128.9 million cubic meters (2017 est.)
agricultural: 16.7 million cubic meters (2017 est.)

Total renewable water resources: 3.84 billion cubic meters (2017 est.)

GOVERNMENT

Country name: *conventional long form:* Republic of Trinidad and Tobago
conventional short form: Trinidad and Tobago
etymology: explorer Christopher COLUMBUS named the larger island "La Isla de la Trinidad" (The Island of the Trinity) on 31 July 1498 on his third voyage; the tobacco grown and smoked by the natives of the smaller island or its elongated cigar shape may account for the "tobago" name, which is spelled "tobaco" in Spanish

Government type: parliamentary republic

Capital: *name:* Port of Spain
geographic coordinates: 10 39 N, 61 31 W
time difference: UTC-4 (1 hour ahead of Washington, DC, during Standard Time)
etymology: the name dates to the period of Spanish colonial rule (16th to late 18th centuries) when the city was referred to as "Puerto de Espana"; the name was anglicized following the British capture of Trinidad in 1797

Administrative divisions: 9 regions, 3 boroughs, 2 cities, 1 ward
regions: Couva/Tabaquite/Talparo, Diego Martin, Mayaro/Rio Claro, Penal/Debe, Princes Town, Sangre Grande, San Juan/Laventille, Siparia, Tunapuna/Piarco
borough: Arima, Chaguanas, Point Fortin
cities: Port of Spain, San Fernando
ward: Tobago

Independence: 31 August 1962 (from the UK)

National holiday: Independence Day, 31 August (1962)

Constitution: *history:* previous 1962; latest 1976
amendments: proposed by Parliament; passage of amendments affecting constitutional provisions, such as human rights and freedoms or citizenship, requires at least two-thirds majority vote by the membership of both houses and assent of the president; passage of amendments, such as the powers and authorities of the executive, legislative, and judicial branches of government, and the procedure for amending the constitution, requires at least three-quarters majority vote by the House membership, two-thirds majority vote by the Senate membership, and assent of the president; amended many times, last in 2007

Legal system: English common law; judicial review of legislative acts in the Supreme Court

International law organization participation: has not submitted an ICJ jurisdiction declaration; accepts ICCt jurisdiction

Citizenship: *citizenship by birth:* yes
citizenship by descent only: yes
dual citizenship recognized: yes
residency requirement for naturalization: 8 years

Suffrage: 18 years of age; universal

Executive branch: *chief of state:* President Paula-Mae WEEKES (since 19 March 2018)
head of government: Prime Minister Keith ROWLEY (since 9 September 2015)
cabinet: Cabinet appointed from among members of Parliament
elections/appointments: president indirectly elected by an electoral college of selected Senate and House of Representatives members for a 5-year term (eligible for a second term); election last held on 19 January 2018 (next to be held by February 2023); the president usually appoints the leader of the majority party in the House of Representatives as prime minister
election results:
Paula-Mae WEEKES (independent) elected president; ran unopposed and was elected without a vote; she is Trinidad and Tobago's first female head of state

Legislative branch: *description:* bicameral Parliament consists of:
Senate (31 seats; 16 members appointed by the ruling party, 9 by the president, and 6 by the opposition party; members serve 5-year terms;)
House of Representatives (42 seats; 41 members directly elected in single-seat constituencies by simple majority vote and the house speaker - usually designated from outside Parliament; members serve 5-year terms)
elections:
Senate - last appointments on 28 August 2020 (next appointments in August 2025)
House of Representatives - last held on 10 August 2020 (next to be held in 2025)
election results:
Senate - percent by party - NA; seats by party - NA; composition as of May 2020 - men 18, women 13, percent of women 41.9%
House of Representatives - percent by party - NA; seats by party - PNM 22, UNC 19; composition - as of May 2022 -men 31, women 11, percent of women 26.2%; note - overall Parliament percent of women 32.9%
note: Tobago has a unicameral House of Assembly (19 seats; 15 assemblymen directly elected by simple majority vote and 4 appointed councilors - 3 on the advice of the chief secretary and 1 on the advice of the minority leader; members serve 4-year terms)

Judicial branch: *highest court(s):* Supreme Court of the Judicature (consists of a chief justice for both the Court of Appeal with 12 judges and the High Court with 24 judges); note - Trinidad and Tobago can file appeals beyond its Supreme Court to the Caribbean Court of Justice, with final appeal to the Judicial Committee of the Privy Council (in London)
judge selection and term of office: Supreme Court chief justice appointed by the president after

consultation with the prime minister and the parliamentary leader of the opposition; other judges appointed by the Judicial Legal Services Commission, headed by the chief justice and 5 members with judicial experience; all judges serve for life with mandatory retirement normally at age 65
subordinate courts: Courts of Summary Criminal Jurisdiction; Petty Civil Courts; Family Court

Political parties and leaders: Congress of the People or COP [Kirt SINNETTE]
People's National Movement or PNM [Keith ROWLEY]
Progressive Democratic Patriots or PDP (Tobago) [Watson DUKE]
United National Congress or UNC [Kamla PERSAD-BISSESSAR]

International organization participation: ACP, AOSIS, C, Caricom, CDB, CELAC, EITI (compliant country), FAO, G-24, G-77, IADB, IAEA, IBRD, ICAO, ICC (NGOs), ICCt, ICRM, IDA, IFAD, IFC, IFRCS, IHO, ILO, IMF, IMO, Interpol, IOC, IOM, IPU, ISO, ITSO, ITU, ITUC (NGOs), LAES, MIGA, NAM, OAS, OPANAL, OPCW, Pacific Alliance (observer), Paris Club (associate), UN, UNCTAD, UNESCO, UNIDO, UPU, WCO, WFTU (NGOs), WHO, WIPO, WMO, WTO

Diplomatic representation in the US: *chief of mission:* Ambassador Anthony Wayne Jerome PHILLIPS-SPENCER, Brig. Gen. (Ret.) (since 27 June 2016)
chancery: 1708 Massachusetts Avenue NW, Washington, DC 20036-1975
telephone: [1] (202) 467-6490
FAX: [1] (202) 785-3130
email address and website:
embdcinfo@foreign.gov.tt
https://foreign.gov.tt/missions-consuls/tt-missions-abroad/diplomatic-missions/embassy-washington-dc-us/
consulate(s) general: Miami, New York

Diplomatic representation from the US: *chief of mission:* Ambassador (vacant); Charge d'Affaires Shante MOORE (since 20 January 2021)
embassy: 15 Queen's Park West, Port of Spain
mailing address: 3410 Port of Spain Place, Washington DC 20521-3410
telephone: (868) 622-6371
FAX: (868) 822-5905
email address and website:
acspos@state.gov
https://tt.usembassy.gov/

Flag description: red with a white-edged black diagonal band from the upper hoist side to the lower fly side; the colors represent the elements of earth, water, and fire; black stands for the wealth of the land and the dedication of the people; white symbolizes the sea surrounding the islands, the purity of the country's aspirations, and equality; red symbolizes the warmth and energy of the sun, the vitality of the land, and the courage and friendliness of its people

National symbol(s): scarlet ibis (bird of Trinidad), cocrico (bird of Tobago), Chaconia flower; national colors: red, white, black

National anthem: *name:* "Forged From the Love of Liberty"
lyrics/music: Patrick Stanislaus CASTAGNE
note: adopted 1962; song originally created to serve as an anthem for the West Indies Federation; adopted by Trinidad and Tobago following the Federation's dissolution in 1962

ECONOMY

Economic overview: Trinidad and Tobago relies on its energy sector for much of its economic activity, and has one of the highest per capita incomes in Latin America. Economic growth between 2000 and 2007 averaged slightly over 8% per year, significantly above the regional average of about 3.7% for that same period; however, GDP has slowed down since then, contracting during 2009-12, making small gains in 2013 and contracting again in 2014-17. Trinidad and Tobago is buffered by considerable foreign reserves and a sovereign wealth fund that equals about one-and-a-half times the national budget, but the country is still in a recession and the government faces the dual challenge of gas shortages and a low price environment. Large-scale energy projects in the last quarter of 2017 are helping to mitigate the gas shortages.

Energy production and downstream industrial use dominate the economy. Oil and gas typically account for about 40% of GDP and 80% of exports but less than 5% of employment. Trinidad and Tobago is home to one of the largest natural gas liquefaction facilities in the Western Hemisphere. The country produces about nine times more natural gas than crude oil on an energy equivalent basis with gas contributing about two-thirds of energy sector government revenue. The US is the country's largest trading partner, accounting for 28% of its total imports and 48% of its exports.

Economic diversification is a longstanding government talking point, and Trinidad and Tobago has much potential due to its stable, democratic government and its educated, English speaking workforce. The country is also a regional financial center with a well-regulated and stable financial system. Other sectors the Government of Trinidad and Tobago has targeted for increased investment and projected growth include tourism, agriculture, information and communications technology, and shipping. Unfortunately, a host of other factors, including low labor productivity, inefficient government bureaucracy, and corruption, have hampered economic development.

Real GDP (purchasing power parity): $33.21 billion (2020 est.)
$36.03 billion (2019 est.)
$36.48 billion (2018 est.)
note: data are in 2017 dollars
country comparison to the world: 132

Real GDP growth rate: -2.6% (2017 est.)
-6.1% (2016 est.)
1.7% (2015 est.)
country comparison to the world: 210

Real GDP per capita: $23,700 (2020 est.)
$25,800 (2019 est.)
$26,300 (2018 est.)
note: data are in 2017 dollars
country comparison to the world: 80

GDP (official exchange rate): $24.031 billion (2019 est.)

Inflation rate (consumer prices): 1.9% (2017 est.)
3.1% (2016 est.)
country comparison to the world: 108

Credit ratings:

Moody's rating: Ba1 (2017)

Standard & Poors rating: BBB- (2020)

GDP - composition, by sector of origin: *agriculture:* 0.4% (2017 est.)
industry: 47.8% (2017 est.)
services: 51.7% (2017 est.)

GDP - composition, by end use: *household consumption:* 78.9% (2017 est.)
government consumption: 16.4% (2017 est.)
investment in fixed capital: 8.2% (2017 est.)
investment in inventories: 0.6% (2017 est.)
exports of goods and services: 45.4% (2017 est.)
imports of goods and services: -48.7% (2017 est.)

Agricultural products: poultry, fruit, coconuts, citrus fruit, milk, plantains, maize, oranges, eggs, gourds

Industries: petroleum and petroleum products, liquefied natural gas, methanol, ammonia, urea, steel products, beverages, food processing, cement, cotton textiles

Industrial production growth rate: -4.3% (2017 est.)
country comparison to the world: 195

Labor force: 629,400 (2017 est.)
country comparison to the world: 152

Labor force - by occupation: *agriculture:* 3.1%
industry: 11.5%
services: 85.4% (2016 est.)

Unemployment rate: 4.9% (2017 est.)
4% (2016 est.)
country comparison to the world: 73

Unemployment, youth ages 15-24: *total:* 8.7%
male: 8.9%
female: 8.4% (2016 est.)
country comparison to the world: 148

Population below poverty line: 20% (2014 est.)

Budget: *revenues:* 5.581 billion (2017 est.)
expenditures: 7.446 billion (2017 est.)

Budget surplus (+) or deficit (-): -8.2% (of GDP) (2017 est.)
country comparison to the world: 200

Public debt: 41.8% of GDP (2017 est.)
37% of GDP (2016 est.)
country comparison to the world: 120

Taxes and other revenues: 24.5% (of GDP) (2017 est.)
country comparison to the world: 121

Fiscal year: 1 October - 30 September

Current account balance: $2.325 billion (2017 est.)
-$653 million (2016 est.)
country comparison to the world: 37

Exports: $9.57 billion (2019 est.) note: data are in current year dollars
$11.57 billion (2018 est.) note: data are in current year dollars
country comparison to the world: 103

Exports - partners: United States 33%, Guyana 9%, Spain 6%, China 6% (2019)

Exports - commodities: natural gas, industrial alcohols, crude petroleum, ammonia, iron products, refined petroleum (2019)

Imports: $7.93 billion (2019 est.) note: data are in current year dollars
$9.16 billion (2018 est.) note: data are in current year dollars
country comparison to the world: 118

Imports - partners: United States 40%, Guyana 19%, China 6% (2019)

Imports - commodities: refined petroleum, excavation machinery, shipping containers, iron, cars (2019)

Reserves of foreign exchange and gold: $8.892 billion (31 December 2017 est.)
$9.995 billion (31 December 2016 est.)
country comparison to the world: 77

Debt - external: $8.238 billion (31 December 2017 est.)
$8.746 billion (31 December 2016 est.)
country comparison to the world: 121

Exchange rates: Trinidad and Tobago dollars (TTD) per US dollar -
6.78 (2017 est.)
6.669 (2016 est.)
6.669 (2015 est.)
6.4041 (2014 est.)
6.4041 (2013 est.)

ENERGY

Electricity access: *electrification - total population:* 100% (2020)

Electricity: *installed generating capacity:* 2.123 million kW (2020 est.)
consumption: 8,213,020,000 kWh (2019 est.)
exports: 0 kWh (2019 est.)
imports: 0 kWh (2019 est.)
transmission/distribution losses: 424 million kWh (2019 est.)

Electricity generation sources: *fossil fuels:* 99.9% of total installed capacity (2020 est.)
solar: 0.1% of total installed capacity (2020 est.)

Coal: *production:* 0 metric tons (2020 est.)
consumption: 1,000 metric tons (2020 est.)
exports: 0 metric tons (2020 est.)
imports: 1,000 metric tons (2020 est.)
proven reserves: 0 metric tons (2019 est.)

Petroleum: *total petroleum production:* 81,000 bbl/day (2021 est.)
refined petroleum consumption: 35,500 bbl/day (2019 est.)
crude oil and lease condensate exports: 22,100 bbl/day (2018 est.)
crude oil and lease condensate imports: 64,700 bbl/day (2018 est.)
crude oil estimated reserves: 243 million barrels (2021 est.)

Refined petroleum products - production: 134,700 bbl/day (2015 est.)
country comparison to the world: 63

Refined petroleum products - exports: 106,100 bbl/day (2015 est.)
country comparison to the world: 40

Refined petroleum products - imports: 0 bbl/day (2015 est.)
country comparison to the world: 212

Natural gas: *production:* 30,886,691,000 cubic meters (2020 est.)
consumption: 16,247,415,000 cubic meters (2020 est.)
exports: 14,662,269,000 cubic meters (2020 est.)
imports: 0 cubic meters (2021 est.)
proven reserves: 298.063 billion cubic meters (2021 est.)

Carbon dioxide emissions: 39.652 million metric tonnes of CO2 (2019 est.)
from coal and metallurgical coke: 10,000 metric tonnes of CO2 (2019 est.)
from petroleum and other liquids: 4.631 million metric tonnes of CO2 (2019 est.)
from consumed natural gas: 35.011 million metric tonnes of CO2 (2019 est.)
country comparison to the world: 65

COMMUNICATIONS

Telephones - fixed lines: *total subscriptions:* 323,905 (2020)
subscriptions per 100 inhabitants: 23 (2020 est.)
country comparison to the world: 105

Telephones - mobile cellular: *total subscriptions:* 2,163,730 (2019)
subscriptions per 100 inhabitants: 155.11 (2019)
country comparison to the world: 147

Telecommunication systems: *general assessment:* excellent international service; good local service; broadband access; expanded FttP (Fiber to the Home) markets; LTE launch; regulatory development; major growth in mobile telephony and data segments which attacks operation investment in fiber infrastructure; moves to end roaming charges (2020)
domestic: fixed-line over 23 per 100 persons and mobile-cellular teledensity 142 per 100 persons (2020)
international: country code - 1-868; landing points for the EC Link, ECFS, Southern Caribbean Fiber, SG-SCS and Americas II submarine cable systems provide connectivity to US, parts of the Caribbean and South America; satellite earth station - 1 Intelsat (Atlantic Ocean); tropospheric scatter to Barbados and Guyana (2020)

Broadcast media: 6 free-to-air TV networks, 2 of which are state-owned; 24 subscription providers (cable and satellite); over 36 radio frequencies (2019)

Internet country code: .tt

Internet users: *total:* 1,074,126 (2019 est.)
percent of population: 77% (2019 est.)
country comparison to the world: 144

Broadband - fixed subscriptions: *total:* 376,771 (2020 est.)
subscriptions per 100 inhabitants: 27 (2020 est.)
country comparison to the world: 101

TRANSPORTATION

National air transport system: *number of registered air carriers:* 1 (2020)
inventory of registered aircraft operated by air carriers: 19
annual passenger traffic on registered air carriers: 2,525,130 (2018)
annual freight traffic on registered air carriers: 41.14 million (2018) mt-km

Civil aircraft registration country code prefix: 9Y

Airports: *total:* 4 (2021)
country comparison to the world: 189

Airports - with paved runways: *total:* 2
over 3,047 m: 1
2,438 to 3,047 m: 1 (2021)

Airports - with unpaved runways: *total:* 2
914 to 1,523 m: 1
under 914 m: 1 (2021)

Pipelines: 257 km condensate, 11 km condensate/gas, 1,567 km gas, 587 km oil (2013)

Merchant marine: *total:* 105
by type: general cargo 1, other 104 (2021)
country comparison to the world: 87

Ports and terminals: *major seaport(s):* Point Fortin, Point Lisas, Port of Spain, Scarborough
oil terminal(s): Galeota Point terminal

LNG terminal(s) (export): Port Fortin

MILITARY AND SECURITY

Military and security forces: Trinidad and Tobago Defense Force (TTDF): Army/Land Forces (Trinidad and Tobago Regiment), Coast Guard, Air Guard, Defense Force Reserves; Trinidad and Tobago Police Service (TTPS) (2022)
note: the Ministry of National Security oversees defense, immigration, and the police

Military expenditures: 1% of GDP (2020 est.)
1% of GDP (2019 est.) (approximately $350 million)
1% of GDP (2018 est.) (approximately $340 million)
1.3% of GDP (2017 est.) (approximately $420 million)
1.4% of GDP (2016 est.) (approximately $460 million)
country comparison to the world: 135

Military and security service personnel strengths: approximately 4,500 TTDF personnel (2022)

Military equipment inventories and acquisitions: the TTDF's ground force inventory includes only light weapons, while the Coast Guard and Air Guard field mostly second-hand equipment from a mix of countries, including Australia, China, the Netherlands, the UK, and the US (2022)

Military service age and obligation: 18-25 years of age for voluntary military service for men and women (some age variations between services, reserves); no conscription (2022)
note: as of 2017, women comprised about 14% of the active duty military

Military - note: the TTDF's primary responsibilities are conducting border and maritime security, providing disaster relief, and countering narcotics trafficking in support of law enforcement (2022)

TRANSNATIONAL ISSUES

Disputes - international: *Trinidad and Tobago-Barbados:* Barbados and Trinidad and Tobago abide by the April 2006 Permanent Court of Arbitration decision delimiting a maritime boundary and limiting catches of flying fish in Trinidad and Tobago's EEZ
Trinidad and Tobago-Barbados-Guyana-Venezuela: in 2005, Barbados and Trinidad and Tobago agreed to compulsory international arbitration under UN Convention on the Law of the Sea challenging whether the northern limit of Trinidad and Tobago's and Venezuela's maritime boundary extends into Barbadian waters; Guyana has expressed its intention to include itself in the arbitration, as the Trinidad and Tobago-Venezuela maritime boundary may also extend into its waters

Refugees and internally displaced persons: *refugees (country of origin):* 28,500 (Venezuela) (economic and political crisis; includes Venezuelans who have claimed asylum, are recognized as refugees, or have received alternative legal stay) (2021)

Illicit drugs: a transit point for illegal drugs destined for Europe, North America, and the rest of the Caribbean; drug trafficking organizations use proximity to Venezuela, porous borders, vulnerabilities at ports of entry, limited law enforcement capacity and resources, and law enforcement corruption to traffic illicit drugs; marijuana the only locally-produced illicit drug

TUNISIA

INTRODUCTION

Background: Tunisia has been the nexus of many different colonizations including those of the Phoenicians (as early as the 12 century B.C.), the Carthaginians, Romans, Vandals, Byzantines, various Arab and Berber kingdoms, and the Ottomans (16th to late 19th centuries). Rivalry between French and Italian interests in Tunisia culminated in a French invasion in 1881 and the creation of a protectorate. Agitation for independence in the decades following World War I was finally successful in convincing the French to recognize Tunisia as an independent state in 1956. The country's first president, Habib BOURGUIBA, established a strict one-party state. He dominated the country for 31 years, repressing Islamic fundamentalism and establishing rights for women unmatched by any other Arab nation. In November 1987, BOURGUIBA was removed from office and replaced by Zine el Abidine BEN ALI in a bloodless coup. Street protests that began in Tunis in December 2010 over high unemployment, corruption, widespread poverty, and high food prices escalated in January 2011, culminating in rioting that led to hundreds of deaths. On 14 January 2011, the same day BEN ALI dismissed the government, he fled the country, and by late January 2011, a "national unity government" was formed. Elections for the new Constituent Assembly were held in late October 2011, and in December, it elected human rights activist Moncef MARZOUKI as interim president. The Assembly began drafting a new constitution in February 2012 and, after several iterations and a months-long political crisis that stalled the transition, ratified the document in January 2014. Parliamentary and presidential elections for a permanent government were held at the end of 2014. Beji CAID ESSEBSI was elected as the first president under the country's new constitution. Following ESSEBSI's death in office in July 2019, Tunisia moved its scheduled presidential election forward two months and after two rounds of voting, Kais SAIED was sworn in as president in October 2019. Tunisia also held legislative elections on schedule in October 2019. SAIED's term, as well as that of Tunisia's 217-member parliament, expires in 2024. On 25 July 2021, SAIED seized exceptional powers allowed under Tunisia's constitution to fire the prime minister and suspend the legislature.

GEOGRAPHY

Location: Northern Africa, bordering the Mediterranean Sea, between Algeria and Libya

Geographic coordinates: 34 00 N, 9 00 E

Map references: Africa

Area: *total:* 163,610 sq km
land: 155,360 sq km
water: 8,250 sq km
country comparison to the world: 93

Area - comparative: slightly larger than Georgia

Land boundaries: *total:* 1,495 km
border countries (2): Algeria 1,034 km; Libya 461 km

Coastline: 1,148 km

Maritime claims: *territorial sea:* 12 nm
contiguous zone: 24 nm
exclusive economic zone: 12 nm

Climate: temperate in north with mild, rainy winters and hot, dry summers; desert in south

Terrain: mountains in north; hot, dry central plain; semiarid south merges into the Sahara

Elevation: *highest point:* Jebel ech Chambi 1,544 m
lowest point: Shatt al Gharsah -17 m
mean elevation: 246 m

Natural resources: petroleum, phosphates, iron ore, lead, zinc, salt

Land use: *agricultural land:* 64.8% (2018 est.)
arable land: 18.3% (2018 est.)
permanent crops: 15.4% (2018 est.)
permanent pasture: 31.1% (2018 est.)
forest: 6.6% (2018 est.)
other: 28.6% (2018 est.)

Irrigated land: 4,590 sq km (2012)

Major aquifers: North Western Sahara Aquifer System

Population distribution: the overwhelming majority of the population is located in the northern half of the country; the south remains largely underpopulated as shown in this population distribution map

Natural hazards: flooding; earthquakes; droughts

Geography - note: strategic location in central Mediterranean; Malta and Tunisia are discussing the commercial exploitation of the continental shelf between their countries, particularly for oil exploration

PEOPLE AND SOCIETY

Population: 11,896,972 (2022 est.)
country comparison to the world: 80

Nationality: *noun:* Tunisian(s)
adjective: Tunisian

Ethnic groups: Arab 98%, European 1%, Jewish and other 1%

Languages: Arabic (official, one of the languages of commerce), French (commerce), Berber (Tamazight); note - despite having no official status, French plays a major role in the country and is spoken by about two thirds of the population
major-language sample(s):
كتاب حقائق العالم، أحسن كتاب تتعلم به المعلومات الأساسية
(Arabic)

The World Factbook, une source indispensable d'informations de base. (French)

Religions: Muslim (official; Sunni) 99%, other (includes Christian, Jewish, Shia Muslim, and Baha'i) <1%

Demographic profile: The Tunisian Government took steps in the 1960s to decrease population growth and gender inequality in order to improve socioeconomic development. Through its introduction of a national family planning program (the first in Africa) and by raising the legal age of marriage, Tunisia rapidly reduced its total fertility rate from about 7 children per woman in 1960 to 2 today. Unlike many of its North African and Middle Eastern neighbors, Tunisia will soon be shifting from being a youth-bulge country to having a transitional age structure, characterized by lower fertility and mortality rates, a slower population growth rate, a rising median age, and a longer average life expectancy.

Currently, the sizable young working-age population is straining Tunisia's labor market and education and health care systems. Persistent high unemployment among Tunisia's growing workforce, particularly its increasing number of university graduates and women, was a key factor in the uprisings that led to the overthrow of the BEN ALI regime in 2011. In the near term, Tunisia's large number of jobless young, working-age adults; deficiencies in primary and secondary education; and the ongoing lack of job creation and skills mismatches could contribute to future unrest. In the longer term, a sustained low fertility rate will shrink future youth cohorts and alleviate demographic pressure on Tunisia's labor market, but employment and education hurdles will still need to be addressed.

Tunisia has a history of labor emigration. In the 1960s, workers migrated to European countries to escape poor economic conditions and to fill Europe's need for low-skilled labor in construction and manufacturing. The Tunisian Government signed bilateral labor agreements with France, Germany, Belgium, Hungary, and the Netherlands, with the expectation that Tunisian workers would eventually return home. At the same time, growing numbers of Tunisians headed to Libya, often illegally, to work in the expanding oil industry. In the mid-1970s, with European countries beginning to restrict immigration and Tunisian-Libyan tensions brewing, Tunisian economic migrants turned toward the Gulf countries. After mass expulsions from Libya in 1983, Tunisian migrants increasingly sought family reunification in Europe or moved illegally to southern Europe, while Tunisia itself developed into a transit point for Sub-Saharan migrants heading to Europe.

Following the ousting of BEN ALI in 2011, the illegal migration of unemployed Tunisian youths to Italy and onward to France soared into the tens of thousands. Thousands more Tunisian and foreign workers escaping civil war in Libya flooded into Tunisia and joined the exodus. A readmission agreement signed by Italy and Tunisia in April 2011 helped stem the outflow, leaving Tunisia and international organizations to repatriate, resettle, or accommodate some 1 million Libyans and third-country nationals.

Age structure: *0-14 years:* 25.28% (male 1,529,834/female 1,433,357)
15-24 years: 12.9% (male 766,331/female 745,888)
25-54 years: 42.85% (male 2,445,751/female 2,576,335)
55-64 years: 10.12% (male 587,481/female 598,140)
65 years and over: 8.86% (male 491,602/female 546,458) (2020 est.)

Dependency ratios: *total dependency ratio:* 49.6
youth dependency ratio: 36.3
elderly dependency ratio: 13.3
potential support ratio: 7.5 (2020 est.)

Median age: *total:* 32.7 years
male: 32 years
female: 33.3 years (2020 est.)
country comparison to the world: 107

Population growth rate: 0.69% (2022 est.)
country comparison to the world: 129

Birth rate: 14.62 births/1,000 population (2022 est.)
country comparison to the world: 119

Death rate: 6.36 deaths/1,000 population (2022 est.)
country comparison to the world: 143

Net migration rate: -1.33 migrant(s)/1,000 population (2022 est.)
country comparison to the world: 154

Population distribution: the overwhelming majority of the population is located in the northern half of the country; the south remains largely underpopulated as shown in this population distribution map

Urbanization: *urban population:* 70.2% of total population (2022)
rate of urbanization: 1.34% annual rate of change (2020-25 est.)

Major urban areas - population: 2.439 million TUNIS (capital) (2022)

Sex ratio: *at birth:* 1.06 male(s)/female
0-14 years: 1.07 male(s)/female
15-24 years: 1.03 male(s)/female
25-54 years: 0.95 male(s)/female
55-64 years: 0.96 male(s)/female
65 years and over: 0.78 male(s)/female
total population: 0.98 male(s)/female (2022 est.)

Maternal mortality ratio: 43 deaths/100,000 live births (2017 est.)
country comparison to the world: 99

Infant mortality rate: *total:* 11.87 deaths/1,000 live births
male: 13.32 deaths/1,000 live births
female: 10.32 deaths/1,000 live births (2022 est.)
country comparison to the world: 120

Life expectancy at birth: *total population:* 76.82 years
male: 75.14 years
female: 78.6 years (2022 est.)
country comparison to the world: 99

Total fertility rate: 2 children born/woman (2022 est.)
country comparison to the world: 108

Contraceptive prevalence rate: 50.7% (2018)

Drinking water source: *improved: urban:* 100% of population
rural: 97.3% of population
total: 99.2% of population
unimproved: urban: 0% of population
rural: 2.7% of population
total: 0.8% of population (2020 est.)

Current health expenditure: 7% of GDP (2019)

Physicians density: 1.3 physicians/1,000 population (2017)

Hospital bed density: 2.2 beds/1,000 population (2017)

Sanitation facility access: *improved: urban:* 98.8% of population
rural: 99.4% of population
total: 99% of population
unimproved: urban: 1.2% of population
rural: 0.6% of population
total: 1% of population (2020 est.)

HIV/AIDS - adult prevalence rate: (2020 est.) <.1%

HIV/AIDS - people living with HIV/AIDS: 4,500 (2020 est.)
country comparison to the world: 123

HIV/AIDS - deaths: (2020 est.) <200

Obesity - adult prevalence rate: 26.9% (2016)
country comparison to the world: 40

Alcohol consumption per capita: *total:* 1.51 liters of pure alcohol (2019 est.)
beer: 0.99 liters of pure alcohol (2019 est.)
wine: 0.32 liters of pure alcohol (2019 est.)
spirits: 0.17 liters of pure alcohol (2019 est.)
other alcohols: 0.03 liters of pure alcohol (2019 est.)
country comparison to the world: 139

Tobacco use: *total:* 24.6% (2020 est.)
male: 47.2% (2020 est.)
female: 2% (2020 est.)
country comparison to the world: 52

Children under the age of 5 years underweight: 1.6% (2018)
country comparison to the world: 117

Education expenditures: 7.3% of GDP (2016 est.)
country comparison to the world: 18

Literacy: *definition:* age 15 and over can read and write
total population: 81.8%
male: 89.6%
female: 74.2% (2015)

School life expectancy (primary to tertiary education): *total:* 15 years
male: 14 years
female: 16 years (2016)

Unemployment, youth ages 15-24: *total:* 34.9%
male: 33.8%
female: 37.2% (2017 est.)

ENVIRONMENT

Environment - current issues: toxic and hazardous waste disposal is ineffective and poses health risks; water pollution from raw sewage; limited natural freshwater resources; deforestation; overgrazing; soil erosion; desertification

Environment - international agreements: *party to:* Biodiversity, Climate Change, Climate Change-Kyoto Protocol, Climate Change-Paris Agreement, Comprehensive Nuclear Test Ban, Desertification, Endangered Species, Environmental Modification, Hazardous Wastes, Law of the Sea, Marine Dumping-London Convention, Nuclear Test Ban, Ozone Layer Protection, Ship Pollution, Wetlands
signed, but not ratified: Marine Life Conservation

Air pollutants: *particulate matter emissions:* 35.66 micrograms per cubic meter (2016 est.)
carbon dioxide emissions: 29.94 megatons (2016 est.)
methane emissions: 7.89 megatons (2020 est.)

Climate: temperate in north with mild, rainy winters and hot, dry summers; desert in south

Land use: *agricultural land:* 64.8% (2018 est.)
arable land: 18.3% (2018 est.)
permanent crops: 15.4% (2018 est.)
permanent pasture: 31.1% (2018 est.)
forest: 6.6% (2018 est.)
other: 28.6% (2018 est.)

Urbanization: *urban population:* 70.2% of total population (2022)
rate of urbanization: 1.34% annual rate of change (2020-25 est.)

Revenue from forest resources: *forest revenues:* 0.21% of GDP (2018 est.)
country comparison to the world: 92

Revenue from coal: *coal revenues:* 0% of GDP (2018 est.)
country comparison to the world: 178

Waste and recycling: *municipal solid waste generated annually:* 2.7 million tons (2014 est.)
municipal solid waste recycled annually: 108,000 tons (2014 est.)
percent of municipal solid waste recycled: 4% (2014 est.)

Major aquifers: North Western Sahara Aquifer System

Total water withdrawal: *municipal:* 137 million cubic meters (2017 est.)
industrial: 965 million cubic meters (2017 est.)
agricultural: 3.773 billion cubic meters (2017 est.)

Total renewable water resources: 4.615 billion cubic meters (2017 est.)

GOVERNMENT

Country name: *conventional long form:* Republic of Tunisia
conventional short form: Tunisia
local long form: Al Jumhuriyah at Tunisiyah
local short form: Tunis
etymology: the country name derives from the capital city of Tunis

Government type: parliamentary republic

Capital: *name:* Tunis
geographic coordinates: 36 48 N, 10 11 E
time difference: UTC+1 (6 hours ahead of Washington, DC, during Standard Time)

etymology: three possibilities exist for the derivation of the name; originally a Berber settlement (earliest reference 4th century B.C.), the strategic site fell to the Carthaginians (Phoenicians) and the city could be named after the Punic goddess Tanit, since many ancient cities were named after patron deities; alternatively, the Berber root word "ens," which means "to lie down" or "to pass the night," may indicate that the site was originally a camp or rest stop; finally, the name may be the same as the city of Tynes, mentioned in the writings of some ancient authors

Administrative divisions: 24 governorates (wilayat, singular - wilayah); Beja (Bajah), Ben Arous (Bin 'Arus), Bizerte (Banzart), Gabes (Qabis), Gafsa (Qafsah), Jendouba (Jundubah), Kairouan (Al Qayrawan), Kasserine (Al Qasrayn), Kebili (Qibili), Kef (Al Kaf), L'Ariana (Aryanah), Mahdia (Al Mahdiyah), Manouba (Manubah), Medenine (Madanin), Monastir (Al Munastir), Nabeul (Nabul), Sfax (Safaqis), Sidi Bouzid (Sidi Bu Zayd), Siliana (Silyanah), Sousse (Susah), Tataouine (Tatawin), Tozeur (Tawzar), Tunis, Zaghouan (Zaghwan)

Independence: 20 March 1956 (from France)

National holiday: Independence Day, 20 March (1956); Revolution and Youth Day, 14 January (2011)

Constitution: *history: history:* several previous; latest approved by Constituent Assembly 26 January 2014, signed by the president, prime minister, and Constituent Assembly speaker on 27 January 2014; note - in September 2021, President Kais SAIED issued a decree granting him certain executive, legislative, and judiciary powers, and the authority to rule by decree, but allowed continued implementation of the preamble and chapters one and two of the Constitution, which guarantee rights and freedoms; note - in a 25 July 2022 referendum, voters supported a new constitution proposed by the president
amendments: proposed by the president of the republic or by one third of the Assembly of the Representatives of the People membership; following review by the Constitutional Court, approval to proceed requires an absolute majority vote by the Assembly and final passage requires a two-thirds majority vote by the Assembly; the president can opt to submit an amendment to a referendum, which requires an absolute majority of votes cast for passage

Legal system: mixed legal system of civil law, based on the French civil code and Islamic (sharia) law; some judicial review of legislative acts in the Supreme Court in joint session

International law organization participation: has not submitted an ICJ jurisdiction declaration; accepts ICCt jurisdiction

Citizenship: *citizenship by birth:* no
citizenship by descent only: at least one parent must be a citizen of Tunisia
dual citizenship recognized: yes
residency requirement for naturalization: 5 years

Suffrage: 18 years of age; universal except for active government security forces (including the police and the military), people with mental disabilities, people who have served more than three months in prison (criminal cases only), and people given a suspended sentence of more than six months

Executive branch: *chief of state:* President Kais SAIED (elected 13 October, sworn in 23 October 2019)
head of government: Prime Minister Najla BOUDEN Romdhane (since 11 October 2021)
cabinet: selected by the prime minister and approved by the Assembly of the Representatives of the People; note - on 11 October 2021, SAIED and BOUDEN appointed a new cabinet without approval by the suspended parliament
elections/appointments: president directly elected by absolute majority popular vote in 2 rounds if needed for a 5-year term (eligible for a second term); last held on 15 September 2019 with a runoff on 13 October 2019 (next to be held in 2024); following legislative elections, the prime minister is selected by the majority party or majority coalition and appointed by the president
election results:
2019: percent vote in first round - Kais SAIED (independent) 18.4%, Nabil KAROUI (Heart of Tunisia) 15.6%, Abdelfattah MOUROU (Nahda Movement) 12.9%, Abdelkrim ZBIDI(independent) 10.7%,Youssef CHAHED (Long Live Tunisia) 7.4%, Safi SAID (independent) 7.1%, Lotfi MRAIHI (Republican People's Union) 6.6%, other 21.3%; percent of vote in second round - Kais SAIED elected president; Kais SAIED 72.7%, Nabil KAROUI 27.3%

Legislative branch: *description:* **note**: on 25 July 2021, President SAIED suspended indefinitely the Assembly, and on 30 March 2022 he dissolved the Assembly

unicameral Assembly of the Representatives of the People or Majlis Nuwwab ash-Sha'b (Assemblee des representants du peuple) (217 seats; 199 members directly elected in Tunisian multi-seat constituencies and 18 members in multi-seat constituencies living abroad by party-list proportional representation vote; members serve 5-year terms)
elections:
initial election held on 6 October 2019 (next to be held on 17 December 2022)
election results:
percent of vote by party - Ennahda 19.6%, Heart of Tunisia 14.6%, Free Destourian Party 6.6%, Democratic Current 6.4%, Dignity Coalition 5.9%, People's Movement 4.5%, TahyaTounes 4.1%, other 35.4%, independent 2.9%; seats by party - Ennahda 52, Heart of Tunisia 38, Free Destourian Party 17, Democratic Current 22, Dignity Coalition 21, People's Movement 16, Long Live Tunisia 14, other 25, independent 12; composition (as of October 2021) - men 160, women 57, percent of women 26.3%

Judicial branch: *highest court(s):* Court of Cassation (consists of the first president, chamber presidents, and magistrates and organized into 27 civil and 11 criminal chambers)
judge selection and term of office: Supreme Court judges nominated by the Supreme Judicial Council, an independent 4-part body consisting mainly of elected judges and the remainder legal specialists; judge tenure based on terms of appointment; Constitutional Court (established in the constitution but inception has been delayed; note - in mid-February 2022, President SAIED dissolved the Supreme Judicial Council and replaced it with an interim council in early March
subordinate courts: Courts of Appeal; administrative courts; Court of Audit; Housing Court; courts of first instance; lower district courts; military courts
note: the new Tunisian constitution of January 2014 called for the creation of a constitutional court by the end of 2015, but as November 2021, the court had not been appointed; the court to consist of 12 members - 4 each to be appointed by the president, the Supreme Judicial Council (an independent 4-part body consisting mainly of elected judges and the remainder are legal specialists), and the Chamber of the People's Deputies (parliament); members are to serve 9-year terms with one-third of the membership renewed every 3 years

Political parties and leaders: Afek Tounes [Fadhel ABDELKEFI]
Al Badil Al-Tounisi (The Tunisian Alternative) [Mehdi JOMAA]
Amal Party [Ridha BELHAJ]
Call for Tunisia Party (Nidaa Tounes) [Ali HAFSI]
Current of Love [Hachemi HAMDI] (formerly the Popular Petition party)
Democratic Current [Ghazi CHAOUACHI]
Democratic Patriots' Unified Party [Zied LAKHDHAR]
Dignity Coalition or Al Karama Coalition [Seifeddine MAKHLOUF]
Ennahda Movement (The Renaissance) [Rached GHANNOUCHI]
Free Destourian Party or PDL [Abir MOUSSI]
Green Tunisia Party [Abdelkader ZITOUNI]
Heart of Tunisia (Qalb Tounes) [Nabil KAROUI]
Long Live Tunisia (Tahya Tounes) [Youssef CHAHED]
Machrou Tounes (Project Tunisia) [Mohsen MARZOUK]
Movement of Socialist Democrats or MDS [Ahmed KHASKHOUSSI]
Party of the Democratic Arab Vanguard [Kheireddine SOUABNI]
People's Movement [Zouheir MAGHZAOUI]
Republican Party (Al Joumhouri) [Issam CHEBBI]
The Movement Party (Hizb Harak) [Moncef MARZOUKI]
Third Republic Party [Olfa HAMDI]
Tunisian Ba'ath Movement [Othmen Bel Haj AMOR]
Workers' Party [Hamma HAMMAMI]

International organization participation: ABEDA, AfDB, AFESD, AMF, AMU, AU, BSEC (observer), CAEU, CD, EBRD, FAO, G-11, G-77, IAEA, IBRD, ICAO, ICC (national committees), ICCt, ICRM, IDA, IDB, IFAD, IFC, IFRCS, IHO, ILO, IMF, IMO, IMSO, Interpol, IOC, IOM, IPU, ISO, ITSO, ITU, ITUC (NGOs), LAS, MIGA, MONUSCO, NAM, OAS (observer), OIC, OIF, OPCW, OSCE (partner), UN, UNCTAD, UNESCO, UNHCR, UNIDO, UNOCI, UNWTO, UPU, WCO, WFTU (NGOs), WHO, WIPO, WMO, WTO

Diplomatic representation in the US: *chief of mission:* Ambassador Hanene TAJOURI Bessassi (since 4 October 2021)
chancery: 1515 Massachusetts Avenue NW, Washington, DC 20005
telephone: [1] (202) 862-1850
FAX: [1] (202) 862-1858
email address and website:
AT.Washington@Tunisiaembassy.org
https://www.tunisianembassy.org/

Diplomatic representation from the US: *chief of mission:* Ambassador (vacant); Charge d'Affaires Natasha FRANCESCHI (since April 2022)
embassy: Les Berges du Lac, 1053 Tunis

mailing address: 6360 Tunis Place, Washington DC 20521-6360
telephone: [216] 71-107-000
FAX: [216] 71-107-090
email address and website:
tunisacs@state.gov
https://tn.usembassy.gov/

Flag description: red with a white disk in the center bearing a red crescent nearly encircling a red five-pointed star; resembles the Ottoman flag (red banner with white crescent and star) and recalls Tunisia's history as part of the Ottoman Empire; red represents the blood shed by martyrs in the struggle against oppression, white stands for peace; the crescent and star are traditional symbols of Islam
note: the flag is based on that of Turkey, itself a successor state to the Ottoman Empire

National symbol(s): encircled red crescent moon and five-pointed star; national colors: red, white

National anthem: *name:* "Humat Al Hima" (Defenders of the Homeland)
lyrics/music: Mustafa Sadik AL-RAFII and Aboul-Qacem ECHEBBI/Mohamad Abdel WAHAB
note: adopted 1957, replaced 1958, restored 1987; Mohamad Abdel WAHAB also composed the music for the anthem of the United Arab Emirates

National heritage: *total World Heritage Sites:* 8 (7 cultural, 1 natural)
selected World Heritage Site locales: Amphitheatre of El Jem (c); Archaeological Site of Carthage (c); Medina of Tunis (c); Ichkeul National Park (n); Punic Town of Kerkuane (c); Kairouan (c); Medina of Sousse (c); Dougga / Thugga (c)

ECONOMY

Economic overview: Tunisia's economy – structurally designed to favor vested interests – faced an array of challenges exposed by the 2008 global financial crisis that helped precipitate the 2011 Arab Spring revolution. After the revolution and a series of terrorist attacks, including on the country's tourism sector, barriers to economic inclusion continued to add to slow economic growth and high unemployment.

Following an ill-fated experiment with socialist economic policies in the 1960s, Tunisia focused on bolstering exports, foreign investment, and tourism, all of which have become central to the country's economy. Key exports now include textiles and apparel, food products, petroleum products, chemicals, and phosphates, with about 80% of exports bound for Tunisia's main economic partner, the EU. Tunisia's strategy, coupled with investments in education and infrastructure, fueled decades of 4-5% annual GDP growth and improved living standards. Former President Zine el Abidine BEN ALI (1987-2011) continued these policies, but as his reign wore on cronyism and corruption stymied economic performance, unemployment rose, and the informal economy grew. Tunisia's economy became less and less inclusive. These grievances contributed to the January 2011 overthrow of BEN ALI, further depressing Tunisia's economy as tourism and investment declined sharply.

Tunisia's government remains under pressure to boost economic growth quickly to mitigate chronic socio-economic challenges, especially high levels of youth unemployment, which has persisted since the 2011 revolution. Successive terrorist attacks against the tourism sector and worker strikes in the phosphate sector, which combined account for nearly 15% of GDP, slowed growth from 2015 to 2017. Tunis is seeking increased foreign investment and working with the IMF through an Extended Fund Facility agreement to fix fiscal deficiencies.

Real GDP (purchasing power parity): $114.97 billion (2020 est.)
$125.78 billion (2019 est.)
$124.48 billion (2018 est.)
note: data are in 2017 dollars
country comparison to the world: 82

Real GDP growth rate: 2% (2017 est.)
1.1% (2016 est.)
1.2% (2015 est.)
country comparison to the world: 139

Real GDP per capita: $9,700 (2020 est.)
$10,800 (2019 est.)
$10,800 (2018 est.)
note: data are in 2017 dollars
country comparison to the world: 143

GDP (official exchange rate): $38.884 billion (2019 est.)

Inflation rate (consumer prices): 6.7% (2019 est.)
7.2% (2018 est.)
5.3% (2017 est.)
country comparison to the world: 193

Credit ratings:

Fitch rating: B (2020)

Moody's rating: B2 (2018)

Standard & Poors rating: N/A (2013)

GDP - composition, by sector of origin: *agriculture:* 10.1% (2017 est.)
industry: 26.2% (2017 est.)
services: 63.8% (2017 est.)

GDP - composition, by end use: *household consumption:* 71.7% (2017 est.)
government consumption: 20.8% (2017 est.)
investment in fixed capital: 19.4% (2017 est.)
investment in inventories: 0% (2017 est.)
exports of goods and services: 43.2% (2017 est.)
imports of goods and services: -55.2% (2017 est.)

Agricultural products: wheat, milk, tomatoes, barley, olives, watermelons, green chillies/peppers, potatoes, dates, green onions/shallots

Industries: petroleum, mining (particularly phosphate, iron ore), tourism, textiles, footwear, agribusiness, beverages

Industrial production growth rate: 0.5% (2017 est.)
country comparison to the world: 166

Labor force: 4.054 million (2017 est.)
country comparison to the world: 89

Labor force - by occupation: *agriculture:* 14.8%
industry: 33.2%
services: 51.7% (2014 est.)

Unemployment rate: 15.5% (2017 est.)
15.5% (2016 est.)
country comparison to the world: 177

Unemployment, youth ages 15-24: *total:* 34.9%
male: 33.8%
female: 37.2% (2017 est.)
country comparison to the world: 27

Population below poverty line: 15.2% (2015 est.)

Gini Index coefficient - distribution of family income: 32.8 (2015 est.)
41.7 (1995 est.)
country comparison to the world: 134

Household income or consumption by percentage share: *lowest 10%:* 2.6%
highest 10%: 27% (2010 est.)

Budget: *revenues:* 9.876 billion (2017 est.)
expenditures: 12.21 billion (2017 est.)

Budget surplus (+) or deficit (-): -5.8% (of GDP) (2017 est.)
country comparison to the world: 180

Public debt: 70.3% of GDP (2017 est.)
62.3% of GDP (2016 est.)
country comparison to the world: 52

Taxes and other revenues: 24.7% (of GDP) (2017 est.)
country comparison to the world: 120

Fiscal year: calendar year

Current account balance: -$4.191 billion (2017 est.)
-$3.694 billion (2016 est.)
country comparison to the world: 180

Exports: $19.17 billion (2019 est.) note: data are in current year dollars
$19.42 billion (2018 est.) note: data are in current year dollars
country comparison to the world: 85

Exports - partners: France 29%, Italy 17%, Germany 13% (2019)

Exports - commodities: insulated wiring, clothing and apparel, crude petroleum, olive oil, vehicle parts (2019)

Imports: $23.42 billion (2019 est.) note: data are in current year dollars
$24.65 billion (2018 est.) note: data are in current year dollars
country comparison to the world: 76

Imports - partners: France 17%, Italy 16%, Germany 8%, China 8%, Algeria 7% (2019)

Imports - commodities: refined petroleum, natural gas, low-voltage protection equipment, cars, insulated wiring (2019)

Reserves of foreign exchange and gold: $5.594 billion (31 December 2017 est.)
$5.941 billion (31 December 2016 est.)
country comparison to the world: 93

Debt - external: $35.911 billion (2019 est.)
$33.79 billion (2018 est.)
country comparison to the world: 79

Exchange rates: Tunisian dinars (TND) per US dollar -
2.71795 (2020 est.)
2.8518 (2019 est.)
2.95875 (2018 est.)
1.9617 (2014 est.)
1.6976 (2013 est.)

ENERGY

Electricity access: *electrification - total population:* 100% (2020)

Electricity: *installed generating capacity:* 5.777 million kW (2020 est.)
consumption: 16,737,180,000 kWh (2019 est.)
exports: 631 million kWh (2019 est.)
imports: 472 million kWh (2019 est.)
transmission/distribution losses: 3.641 billion kWh (2019 est.)

Electricity generation sources: *fossil fuels:* 95.9% of total installed capacity (2020 est.)
nuclear: 0% of total installed capacity (2020 est.)

solar: 1.3% of total installed capacity (2020 est.)
wind: 2.6% of total installed capacity (2020 est.)
hydroelectricity: 0.3% of total installed capacity (2020 est.)

Coal: *production:* 0 metric tons (2020 est.)
consumption: 5,000 metric tons (2020 est.)
exports: 0 metric tons (2020 est.)
imports: 5,000 metric tons (2020 est.)
proven reserves: 0 metric tons (2019 est.)

Petroleum: *total petroleum production:* 42,500 bbl/day (2021 est.)
refined petroleum consumption: 107,700 bbl/day (2019 est.)
crude oil and lease condensate exports: 29,400 bbl/day (2018 est.)
crude oil and lease condensate imports: 10,200 bbl/day (2018 est.)
crude oil estimated reserves: 425 million barrels (2021 est.)

Refined petroleum products - production: 27,770 bbl/day (2015 est.)
country comparison to the world: 85

Refined petroleum products - exports: 13,660 bbl/day (2015 est.)
country comparison to the world: 75

Refined petroleum products - imports: 85,340 bbl/day (2015 est.)
country comparison to the world: 58

Natural gas: *production:* 1,025,974,000 cubic meters (2019 est.)
consumption: 5,279,951,000 cubic meters (2019 est.)
exports: 0 cubic meters (2021 est.)
imports: 4,305,994,000 cubic meters (2019 est.)
proven reserves: 65.129 billion cubic meters (2021 est.)

Carbon dioxide emissions: 23.692 million metric tonnes of CO_2 (2019 est.)
from coal and metallurgical coke: 16,000 metric tonnes of CO_2 (2019 est.)
from petroleum and other liquids: 12.982 million metric tonnes of CO_2 (2019 est.)
from consumed natural gas: 10.694 million metric tonnes of CO_2 (2019 est.)
country comparison to the world: 81

Energy consumption per capita: 35.62 million Btu/person (2019 est.)
country comparison to the world: 114

COMMUNICATIONS

Telephones - fixed lines: *total subscriptions:* 1,533,273 (2020 est.)
subscriptions per 100 inhabitants: 13 (2020 est.)
country comparison to the world: 61

Telephones - mobile cellular: *total subscriptions:* 14.771 million (2019)
subscriptions per 100 inhabitants: 126.31 (2019)
country comparison to the world: 69

Telecommunication systems: *general assessment:* Tunisia has one of the most sophisticated telecom infrastructures in North Africa; penetration rates for mobile and Internet services are among the highest in the region; government program of regulation and infrastructure projects aims to improve Internet connectivity to underserved areas; operators built extensive LTE infrastructure in 2019, and continue to discuss plans for future 5G networks and services; one operator has signed an agreement to pursue nano-satellite launches in 2023; internet censorship abolished, though concerns of government surveillance remain; legislation passed in 2017 supporting e-commerce and active e-government; importer of some integrated circuits and broadcasting equipment (including radio, television, and communications transmitters) from the PRC (2022)
domestic: in an effort to jumpstart expansion of the fixed-line network, the government awarded a concession to build and operate a VSAT network with international connectivity; rural areas are served by wireless local loops; competition between several mobile-cellular service providers has resulted in lower activation and usage charges and a surge in subscribership; fixed-line is nearly 14.1 per 100 and mobile-cellular teledensity has reached about 132 telephones per 100 persons (2022)
international: country code - 216; landing points for the SEA-ME-WE-4, Didon, HANNIBAL System and Trapani-Kelibia submarine cable systems that provides links to Europe, Africa, the Middle East, Asia and Southeast Asia; satellite earth stations - 1 Intelsat (Atlantic Ocean) and 1 Arabsat; coaxial cable and microwave radio relay to Algeria and Libya; participant in Medarabtel; 2 international gateway digital switches (2020)

Broadcast media: 2 state-owned TV stations; 10 private TV stations broadcast locally; satellite TV service is available; state-owned radio network with 2 stations; several dozen private radio stations and community radio stations; transmissions of multiple international broadcasters available (2019)

Internet country code: .tn

Internet users: *total:* 8,509,405 (2020 est.)
percent of population: 72% (2020 est.)
country comparison to the world: 63

Broadband - fixed subscriptions: *total:* 1,334,059 (2020 est.)
subscriptions per 100 inhabitants: 11 (2020 est.)
country comparison to the world: 67

TRANSPORTATION

National air transport system: *number of registered air carriers:* 7 (2020)
inventory of registered aircraft operated by air carriers: 53
annual passenger traffic on registered air carriers: 4,274,199 (2018)
annual freight traffic on registered air carriers: 13.23 million (2018) mt-km

Civil aircraft registration country code prefix: TS

Airports: *total:* 29 (2021)
country comparison to the world: 119

Airports - with paved runways: *total:* 15
over 3,047 m: 4
2,438 to 3,047 m: 6: *1,524 to 2,437 m:* 2
914 to 1,523 m: 3 (2021)

Airports - with unpaved runways: *total:* 14
1,524 to 2,437 m: 1
914 to 1,523 m: 5
under 914 m: **8** (2021)

Pipelines: 68 km condensate, 3,111 km gas, 1,381 km oil, 453 km refined products (2013)

Railways: *total:* 2,173 km (2014) (1,991 in use)
standard gauge: 471 km (2014) 1.435-m gauge
narrow gauge: 1,694 km (2014) 1.000-m gauge (65 km electrified)
dual gauge: **8** km (2014) 1.435-1.000-m gauge
country comparison to the world: 70

Roadways: *paved:* 20,000 km (2015)

Merchant marine: *total:* 71
by type: container ship 1, general cargo 8 oil tanker 1, other 61 (2021)
country comparison to the world: 102

Ports and terminals: *major seaport(s):* Bizerte, Gabes, Rades, Sfax, Skhira

MILITARY AND SECURITY

Military and security forces: Tunisian Armed Forces (Forces Armées Tunisiennes, FAT): Tunisian Army (includes Air Defense Force), Tunisian Navy, Tunisia Air Force; Ministry of Interior: National Police, National Guard (2022)
note: the National Police has primary responsibility for law enforcement in the major cities, while the National Guard (gendarmerie) oversees border security and patrols smaller towns and rural areas

Military expenditures: 3% of GDP (2021 est.)
3% of GDP (2020 est.)
3.8% of GDP (2019 est.) (approximately $2.81 billion)
3.9% of GDP (2018 est.) (approximately $2.84 billion)
4% of GDP (2017 est.) (approximately $2.81 billion)
country comparison to the world: 34

Military and security service personnel strengths: approximately 35,000 active duty personnel (25,000 Army; 5,000 Navy; 5,000 Air Force); estimated 10,000 National Guard (2022)

Military equipment inventories and acquisitions: the Tunisian military's inventory includes mostly older or second-hand US and European equipment; since 2010, the Netherlands and US have been the leading suppliers of arms to Tunisia (2022)

Military service age and obligation: 20-23 years of age for male compulsory service, 1-year service obligation; individuals engaged in higher education or vocational training programs prior to their military drafting are allowed to delay service until they have completed their programs; 18-23 years of age for voluntary service; women may volunteer (2022)
note 1: as of 2021, approximately 20-25,000 active military personnel were conscripts
note 2: women have been allowed in the service since 1975 as volunteers only, although as recently as 2018, the Tunisian Government has discussed the possibility of conscripting women; as of 2018, women constituted less than 7% of the military and served in all three services

Military deployments: 325 Central African Republic (MINUSCA); 100 Mali (MINUSMA) (May 2022)

Military - note: as of 2022, the Tunisian military's primary operational areas of focus were counterterrorism, counterinsurgency, and border security; it was conducting counterterrorism and counterinsurgency operations against al-Qa'ida in the Islamic Maghreb (AQIM) and Islamic State of ash-Sham (ISIS)-linked militants who have been fighting a low-intensity insurgency, mostly in the mountainous region along the border with Algeria, particularly the Chaambi Mountains near the city of Kasserine; the military maintained the lead role for security in this area and also routinely conducted joint operations with Algerian security forces against these groups, as well to counter smuggling and trafficking activities; the military in recent years also has increased its role in securing the southern border against militant activity, smuggling, and trafficking from war-torn Libya; since 2015, Tunisia has constructed a complex structure of berms, trenches, and water-filled moats, complemented by electronic surveillance equipment such as motion detectors, ground surveillance radars, and infrared sensors along the 220-kilometer border with Libya; in the remote southern areas of the border with Libya, buffer/exclusion zones have also been established where the military has the lead for counterterrorism efforts; outside of these border areas, the Ministry of Interior (MOI) has the lead responsibility for counter-terrorism in Tunisia, particularly for urban areas; the National Police Anti-Terrorism Brigade (BAT) and the National Guard Special Unit have the lead for MOI counterterrorism operations

Tunisia has Major Non-NATO Ally (MNNA) status with the US; MNNA is a designation under US law that provides foreign partners with certain benefits in the areas of defense trade and security cooperation; while MNNA status provides military and economic privileges, it does not entail any security commitments (2022)

TERRORISM

Terrorist group(s): Ansar al-Sharia in Tunisia; Islamic State of Iraq and ash-Sham (ISIS) network in Tunisia; al-Qa'ida in the Islamic Maghreb

TRANSNATIONAL ISSUES

Disputes - international: none identified

Illicit drugs: NA

TURKEY (TÜRKIYE)

INTRODUCTION

Background: Modern Turkey was founded in 1923 from the remnants of the defeated Ottoman Empire by national hero Mustafa KEMAL, who was later honored with the title Ataturk or "Father of the Turks." Under his leadership, the country adopted radical social, legal, and political reforms. After a period of one-party rule, an experiment with multi-party politics led to the 1950 election victory of the opposition Democrat Party and the peaceful transfer of power. Since then, Turkish political parties have multiplied, but democracy has been fractured by periods of instability and military coups (1960, 1971, 1980), which in each case eventually resulted in a return of formal political power to civilians. In 1997, the military again helped engineer the ouster - popularly dubbed a "post-modern coup" - of the then Islamic-oriented government. An unsuccessful coup attempt was made in July 2016 by a faction of the Turkish Armed Forces.

Turkey intervened militarily on Cyprus in 1974 to prevent a Greek takeover of the island and has since acted as patron state to the "Turkish Republic of Northern Cyprus," which only Turkey recognizes. A separatist insurgency begun in 1984 by the Kurdistan Workers' Party (PKK), a US-designated terrorist organization, has long dominated the attention of Turkish security forces and claimed more than 40,000 lives. In 2013, the Turkish Government and the PKK conducted negotiations aimed at ending the violence, however intense fighting resumed in 2015. Turkey joined the UN in 1945 and in 1952 it became a member of NATO. In 1963, Turkey became an associate member of the European Community; it began accession talks with the EU in 2005. Over the past decade, economic reforms, coupled with some political reforms, have contributed to a growing economy, although economic growth slowed in recent years, with occasional bouts of turmoil.

From 2015 and continuing through 2016, Turkey witnessed an uptick in terrorist violence, including major attacks in Ankara, Istanbul, and throughout the predominantly Kurdish southeastern region of Turkey. On 15 July 2016, elements of the Turkish Armed forces attempted a coup that ultimately failed following widespread popular resistance. More than 240 people were killed and over 2,000 injured when Turkish citizens took to the streets en masse to confront the coup forces. The government accused followers of the Fethullah Gulen transnational religious and social movement ("Hizmet") for allegedly instigating the failed coup and designates the movement's followers as terrorists. Since the attempted coup, Turkish Government authorities arrested, suspended, or dismissed more than 130,000 security personnel, journalists, judges, academics, and civil servants due to their alleged connection to Gulen's movement. Following the failed coup, the Turkish Government instituted a State of Emergency from July 2016 to July 2018. The Turkish Government conducted a referendum on 16 April 2017 in which voters approved constitutional amendments changing Turkey from a parliamentary to a presidential system. The amendments went into effect fully following the presidential and parliamentary elections in June 2018.

GEOGRAPHY

Location: Southeastern Europe and Southwestern Asia (that portion of Turkey west of the Bosporus is geographically part of Europe), bordering the Black Sea, between Bulgaria and Georgia, and bordering the Aegean Sea and the Mediterranean Sea, between Greece and Syria

Geographic coordinates: 39 00 N, 35 00 E

Map references: Middle East

Area: *total:* 783,562 sq km
land: 769,632 sq km
water: 13,930 sq km
country comparison to the world: 38

Area - comparative: slightly larger than Texas

Land boundaries: *total:* 2,816 km
border countries (8): Armenia 311 km; Azerbaijan 17 km; Bulgaria 223 km; Georgia 273 km; Greece 192 km; Iran 534 km; Iraq 367 km; Syria 899 km

Coastline: 7,200 km

Maritime claims: *territorial sea:* 6 nm in the Aegean Sea
exclusive economic zone: in Black Sea only: to the maritime boundary agreed upon with the former USSR
12 nm in Black Sea and in Mediterranean Sea

Climate: temperate; hot, dry summers with mild, wet winters; harsher in interior

Terrain: high central plateau (Anatolia); narrow coastal plain; several mountain ranges

Elevation: *highest point:* Mount Ararat 5,137 m
lowest point: Mediterranean Sea 0 m
mean elevation: 1,132 m

Natural resources: coal, iron ore, copper, chromium, antimony, mercury, gold, barite, borate, celestite (strontium), emery, feldspar, limestone, magnesite, marble, perlite, pumice, pyrites (sulfur), clay, arable land, hydropower

Land use: *agricultural land:* 49.7% (2018 est.)
arable land: 26.7% (2018 est.)
permanent crops: 4% (2018 est.)
permanent pasture: 19% (2018 est.)
forest: 14.9% (2018 est.)
other: 35.4% (2018 est.)

Irrigated land: 52,150 sq km (2012)

Major lakes (area sq km): *fresh water lake(s):* Lake Beysehir - 650 sq km; Lake Egridir - 520 sq km
salt water lake(s): Lake Van - 3,740 sq km; Lake Tuz - 1,640 sq km;

Major rivers (by length in km): Euphrates river source (shared with Syria, Iran, and Iraq [m]) - 3,596 km; Tigris river source (shared with Syria, Iran, and Iraq [m]) - 1,950 km
note – [s] after country name indicates river source; [m] after country name indicates river mouth

Major watersheds (area sq km): Indian Ocean drainage: *(Persian Gulf)* Tigris and Euphrates (918,044 sq km)

Population distribution: the most densely populated area is found around the Bosporus in the northwest where 20% of the population lives in Istanbul; with the exception of Ankara, urban centers remain small and scattered throughout the interior of Anatolia; an overall pattern of peripheral development exists, particularly along the Aegean Sea coast in the west, and the Tigris and Euphrates River systems in the southeast

Natural hazards: severe earthquakes, especially in northern Turkey, along an arc extending from the Sea of Marmara to Lake Van; landslides; flooding
volcanism: limited volcanic activity; its three historically active volcanoes; Ararat, Nemrut Dagi, and Tendurek Dagi have not erupted since the 19th century or earlier

Geography - note: strategic location controlling the Turkish Straits (Bosporus, Sea of Marmara,

Dardanelles) that link the Black and Aegean Seas; the 3% of Turkish territory north of the Straits lies in Europe and goes by the names of European Turkey, Eastern Thrace, or Turkish Thrace; the 97% of the country in Asia is referred to as Anatolia; Istanbul, which straddles the Bosporus, is the only metropolis in the world located on two continents; Mount Ararat, the legendary landing place of Noah's ark, is in the far eastern portion of the country

PEOPLE AND SOCIETY

Population: 83,047,706 (2022 est.)
country comparison to the world: 19

Nationality: *noun:* Turk(s)
adjective: Turkish

Ethnic groups: Turkish 70-75%, Kurdish 19%, other minorities 6-11% (2016 est.)

Languages: Turkish (official), Kurdish, other minority languages
major-language sample(s): The World Factbook, temel bilgi edinmek için vazgeçilmez bir kaynak. (Turkish)

Religions: Muslim 99.8% (mostly Sunni), other 0.2% (mostly Christians and Jews)

Age structure: *0-14 years:* 23.41% (male 9,823,553/female 9,378,767)
15-24 years: 15.67% (male 6,564,263/female 6,286,615)
25-54 years: 43.31% (male 17,987,103/female 17,536,957)
55-64 years: 9.25% (male 3,764,878/female 3,822,946)
65 years and over: 8.35% (male 3,070,258/female 3,782,174) (2020 est.)
country comparison to the world: 111

Population growth rate: 0.67% (2022 est.)
country comparison to the world: 134

Birth rate: 14.28 births/1,000 population (2022 est.)
country comparison to the world: 122

Death rate: 6.05 deaths/1,000 population (2022 est.)
country comparison to the world: 156

Net migration rate: -1.54 migrant(s)/1,000 population (2022 est.)
country comparison to the world: 157

Population distribution: the most densely populated area is found around the Bosporus in the northwest where 20% of the population lives in Istanbul; with the exception of Ankara, urban centers remain small and scattered throughout the interior of Anatolia; an overall pattern of peripheral development exists, particularly along the Aegean Sea coast in the west, and the Tigris and Euphrates River systems in the southeast

Urbanization: *urban population:* 77% of total population (2022)
rate of urbanization: 1.11% annual rate of change (2020-25 est.)

Major urban areas - population: 15.636 million Istanbul, 5.310 million ANKARA (capital), 3.056 million Izmir, 2.055 million Bursa, 1.814 million Adana, 1.773 million Gaziantep (2022)

Sex ratio: *at birth:* 1.05 male(s)/female
0-14 years: 1.05 male(s)/female
15-24 years: 1.05 male(s)/female
25-54 years: 1.03 male(s)/female
55-64 years: 0.98 male(s)/female
65 years and over: 0.61 male(s)/female
total population: 1.01 male(s)/female (2022 est.)

Mother's mean age at first birth: 26.6 years (2020 est.)

Maternal mortality ratio: 17 deaths/100,000 live births (2017 est.)
country comparison to the world: 133

Infant mortality rate: *total:* 19.35 deaths/1,000 live births
male: 21.01 deaths/1,000 live births
female: 17.61 deaths/1,000 live births (2022 est.)
country comparison to the world: 84

Life expectancy at birth: *total population:* 76.21 years
male: 73.84 years
female: 78.7 years (2022 est.)
country comparison to the world: 105

Total fertility rate: 1.93 children born/woman (2022 est.)
country comparison to the world: 119

Contraceptive prevalence rate: 69.8% (2018)

Drinking water source: *improved: urban:* 99.1% of population
rural: 98.7% of population
total: 99% of population
unimproved: urban: 0.9% of population
rural: 1.3% of population
total: 1% of population (2020 est.)

Current health expenditure: 4.3% of GDP (2019)

Physicians density: 1.93 physicians/1,000 population (2019)

Hospital bed density: 2.9 beds/1,000 population (2018)

Sanitation facility access: *improved: urban:* 99.8% of population
rural: 98.7% of population
total: 99.6% of population
unimproved: urban: 0.2% of population
rural: 1.3% of population
total: 0.4% of population (2020 est.)

Major infectious diseases: *note:* widespread ongoing transmission of a respiratory illness caused by the novel coronavirus (COVID-19) is occurring throughout Turkey; as of 18 August 2022, Turkey has reported a total of 16,528,070 cases of COVID-19 or 19,597.17 cumulative cases of COVID-19 per 100,000 population with a total of 100,058 cumulative deaths or a rate of 118.63 cumulative deaths per 100,000 population; as of 17 August 2022, 68.31% of the population has received at least one dose of COVID-19 vaccine

Obesity - adult prevalence rate: 32.1% (2016)
country comparison to the world: 17

Alcohol consumption per capita: *total:* 1.18 liters of pure alcohol (2019 est.)
beer: 0.67 liters of pure alcohol (2019 est.)
wine: 0.16 liters of pure alcohol (2019 est.)
spirits: 0.35 liters of pure alcohol (2019 est.)
other alcohols: 0 liters of pure alcohol (2019 est.)
country comparison to the world: 148

Tobacco use: *total:* 30.7% (2020 est.)
male: 42.1% (2020 est.)
female: 19.2% (2020 est.)
country comparison to the world: 29

Children under the age of 5 years underweight: 1.5% (2018/19)
country comparison to the world: 119

Child marriage: *women married by age 15:* 2%
women married by age 18: 14.7% (2018 est.)

Education expenditures: 4.3% of GDP (2018 est.)
country comparison to the world: 93

Literacy: *definition:* age 15 and over can read and write
total population: 96.7%
male: 99.1%
female: 94.4% (2019)

School life expectancy (primary to tertiary education): *total:* 18 years
male: 19 years
female: 18 years (2019)

Unemployment, youth ages 15-24: *total:* 25.1%
male: 22.5%
female: 29.9% (2020 est.)

ENVIRONMENT

Environment - current issues: water pollution from dumping of chemicals and detergents; air pollution, particularly in urban areas; deforestation; land degradation; concern for oil spills from increasing Bosporus ship traffic; conservation of biodiversity

Environment - international agreements: *party to:* Air Pollution, Antarctic-Environmental Protection, Antarctic Treaty, Biodiversity, Climate Change, Climate Change-Kyoto Protocol, Comprehensive Nuclear Test Ban, Desertification, Endangered Species, Hazardous Wastes, Nuclear Test Ban, Ozone Layer Protection, Ship Pollution, Wetlands
signed, but not ratified: Climate Change-Paris Agreement, Environmental Modification

Air pollutants: *particulate matter emissions:* 41.97 micrograms per cubic meter (2016 est.)
carbon dioxide emissions: 372.72 megatons (2016 est.)
methane emissions: 57.53 megatons (2020 est.)

Climate: temperate; hot, dry summers with mild, wet winters; harsher in interior

Land use: *agricultural land:* 49.7% (2018 est.)
arable land: 26.7% (2018 est.)
permanent crops: 4% (2018 est.)
permanent pasture: 19% (2018 est.)
forest: 14.9% (2018 est.)
other: 35.4% (2018 est.)

Urbanization: *urban population:* 77% of total population (2022)
rate of urbanization: 1.11% annual rate of change (2020-25 est.)

Revenue from forest resources: *forest revenues:* 0.08% of GDP (2018 est.)
country comparison to the world: 121

Revenue from coal: *coal revenues:* 0.05% of GDP (2018 est.)
country comparison to the world: 31

Waste and recycling: *municipal solid waste generated annually:* 31.283 million tons (2015 est.)

Major lakes (area sq km): *fresh water lake(s):* Lake Beysehir - 650 sq km; Lake Egridir - 520 sq km
salt water lake(s): Lake Van - 3,740 sq km; Lake Tuz - 1,640 sq km;

Major rivers (by length in km): Euphrates river source (shared with Syria, Iran, and Iraq [m]) - 3,596 km; Tigris river source (shared with Syria, Iran, and Iraq [m]) - 1,950 km
note – [s] after country name indicates river source; [m] after country name indicates river mouth

Major watersheds (area sq km): Indian Ocean drainage: *(Persian Gulf)* Tigris and Euphrates (918,044 sq km)

Total water withdrawal: *municipal:* 6.016 billion cubic meters (2017 est.)
industrial: 2.898 billion cubic meters (2017 est.)
agricultural: 50.05 billion cubic meters (2017 est.)

Total renewable water resources: 211.6 billion cubic meters (2017 est.)

GOVERNMENT

Country name: *conventional long form:* Republic of Turkey
conventional short form: Turkey
local long form: Turkey Cumhuriyeti
local short form: Turkey
etymology: the name means "Land of the Turks"
note: Turkiye is an approved English short-form name for Turkey

Government type: presidential republic

Capital: *name:* Ankara
geographic coordinates: 39 56 N, 32 52 E
time difference: UTC+3 (8 hours ahead of Washington, DC, during Standard Time)
etymology: Ankara has been linked with a second millennium B.C. Hittite cult center of Ankuwash, although this connection is uncertain; in classical and medieval times, the city was known as Ankyra (meaning "anchor" in Greek and reflecting the city's position as a junction for multiple trade and military routes); by about the 13th century the city began to be referred to as Angora; following the establishment of the Republic of Turkey in 1923, the city's name became Ankara

Administrative divisions: 81 provinces (iller, singular - ili); Adana, Adiyaman, Afyonkarahisar, Agri, Aksaray, Amasya, Ankara, Antalya, Ardahan, Artvin, Aydin, Balikesir, Bartin, Batman, Bayburt, Bilecik, Bingol, Bitlis, Bolu, Burdur, Bursa, Canakkale, Cankiri, Corum, Denizli, Diyarbakir, Duzce, Edirne, Elazig, Erzincan, Erzurum, Eskisehir, Gaziantep, Giresun, Gumushane, Hakkari, Hatay, Igdir, Isparta, Istanbul, Izmir (Smyrna), Kahramanmaras, Karabuk, Karaman, Kars, Kastamonu, Kayseri, Kilis, Kirikkale, Kirklareli, Kirsehir, Kocaeli, Konya, Kutahya, Malatya, Manisa, Mardin, Mersin, Mugla, Mus, Nevsehir, Nigde, Ordu, Osmaniye, Rize, Sakarya, Samsun, Sanliurfa, Siirt, Sinop, Sirnak, Sivas, Tekirdag, Tokat, Trabzon (Trebizond), Tunceli, Usak, Van, Yalova, Yozgat, Zonguldak

Independence: 29 October 1923 (republic proclaimed, succeeding the Ottoman Empire)

National holiday: Republic Day, 29 October (1923)

Constitution: *history:* several previous; latest ratified 9 November 1982
amendments: proposed by written consent of at least one third of Grand National Assembly (GNA) of Turkey (TBMM) members; adoption of draft amendments requires two debates in plenary TBMM session and three-fifths majority vote of all GNA members; the president of the republic can request TBMM reconsideration of the amendment and, if readopted by two-thirds majority TBMM vote, the president may submit the amendment to a referendum; passage by referendum requires absolute majority vote; amended several times, last in 2017

Legal system: civil law system based on various European legal systems, notably the Swiss civil code

International law organization participation: has not submitted an ICJ jurisdiction declaration; non-party state to the ICCt

Citizenship: *citizenship by birth:* no
citizenship by descent only: at least one parent must be a citizen of Turkey
dual citizenship recognized: yes, but requires prior permission from the government
residency requirement for naturalization: 5 years

Suffrage: 18 years of age; universal

Executive branch: *chief of state:* President Recep Tayyip ERDOGAN (chief of state since 28 August 2014; head of government since 9 July 2019); Vice President Fuat OKTAY (since 9 July 2018); note - the president is both chief of state and head of government
head of government: President Recep Tayyip ERDOGAN (head of government since 9 July 2019; chief of state since 28 August 2014); note - a 2017 constitutional referendum eliminated the post of prime minister after the 2018 general election
cabinet: Council of Ministers appointed by the president
elections/appointments: president directly elected by absolute majority popular vote in 2 rounds if needed for a 5-year term (eligible for a second term); election last held on 24 June 2018 (next scheduled for June 2023)
election results:
2018: Recep Tayyip ERDOGAN reelected president in the first round; Recep Tayyip ERDOGAN (AKP) 52.6%, Muharrem INCE (CHP) 30.6%, Selahattin DEMIRTAS (HDP) 8.4%, Meral AKSENER (IYI) 7.3%, other 1.1%
2013: Recep Tayyip ERDOGAN elected president in the first round; Recep Tayyip ERDOGAN (AKP) 51.8%, Ekmeleddin IHSANOGLU (independent) 38.4%, Selahattin DEMIRTAS (HDP) 9.8%

Legislative branch: *description:* unicameral Grand National Assembly of Turkey or Turkey Buyuk Millet Meclisi (600 seats - increased from 550 seats beginning with June 2018 election; members directly elected in multi-seat constituencies by closed party-list proportional representation vote to serve 5-year terms - increased from 4 to 5 years beginning with June 2018 election)
elections:
last held on 24 June 2018 (next to be held in June 2023)
election results:
percent of vote by party - People's Alliance 53.7% (AKP 42.6%, MHP 11.1%), Nation Alliance 33.9% (CHP 22.6%, IYI 10%, SP 1.3%), HDP 11.7%, other 0.7%; seats by party - People's Alliance 344 (AKP 295, MHP 49), National Alliance 189 (CHP 146, IYI 43), HDP 67; note - only parties surpassing a 10% threshold can win parliamentary seats; composition as of mid-2022 (582 members) - men 481, women 101, percent of women 17.4%

Judicial branch: *highest court(s):* Constitutional Court or Anayasa Mahkemesi (consists of the president, 2 vice presidents, and 12 judges); Court of Cassation (consists of about 390 judges and is organized into civil and penal chambers); Council of State (organized into 15 divisions - 14 judicial and 1 consultative - each with a division head and at least 5 members)
judge selection and term of office: Constitutional Court members - 3 appointed by the Grand National Assembly and 12 by the president of the republic; court president and 2 deputy court presidents appointed from among its members for 4-year terms; judges serve 12-year, nonrenewable terms with mandatory retirement at age 65; Court of Cassation judges appointed by the Board of Judges and Prosecutors, a 13-member body of judicial officials; Court of Cassation judges serve until retirement at age 65; Council of State members appointed by the Board and by the president of the republic; members serve renewable, 4-year terms
subordinate courts: regional appeals courts; basic (first instance) courts; peace courts; aggravated crime courts; specialized courts, including administrative and audit; note - a constitutional amendment in 2017 abolished military courts unless established to investigate military personnel actions during war conditions

Political parties and leaders: Democracy and Progress Party or DEVA [Ali BABACAN]
Democrat Party or DP [Gultekin UYSAL]
Democratic Regions Party or DBP [Saliha AYDENIZ, Keskin BAYINDIR]
Felicity Party (Saadet Party) or SP [Temel KARAMOLLAOGLU]
Free Cause Party or HUDA PAR [Zekeriya YAPICIOGLU]
Future Party (Gelecek Partisi) or GP [Ahmet DAVUTOGLU]
Good Party (IYI Party) [Meral AKSENER]
Grand Unity Party or BBP [Mustafa DESTICI]
Justice and Development Party or AKP [Recep Tayyip ERDOGAN]
Nation Alliance (electoral alliance includes CHP, IYI, SP, DP)
Nationalist Movement Party or MHP [Devlet BAHCELI]
Patriotic Party (Vatan Partisi) or VP [Dogu PERINCEK]
People's Alliance (electoral alliance AKP, MHP, BBP)
Peoples' Democratic Party or HDP [Pervin BULDAN, Mithat SANCAR]
Republican People's Party or CHP [Kemal KILICDAROGLU]
note: as of September 2021, 116 political parties were legally registered

International organization participation: ADB (nonregional member), Australia Group, BIS, BSEC, CBSS (observer), CD, CE, CERN (observer), CICA, CPLP (associate observer), D-8, EAPC, EBRD, ECO, EU (candidate country), FAO, FATF, G-20, IAEA, IBRD, ICAO, ICC (national committees), ICRM, IDA, IDB, IEA, IFAD, IFC, IFRCS, IHO, ILO, IMF, IMO, IMSO, Interpol, IOC, IOM, IPU, ISO, ITSO, ITU, ITUC (NGOs), MIGA, NATO, NEA, NSG, OAS (observer), OECD, OIC, OPCW, OSCE, Pacific Alliance (observer), Paris Club (associate), PCA, PIF (partner), SCO (dialogue member), SELEC, UN, UNCTAD, UNESCO, UNHCR, UNIDO, UNIFIL, UNRWA, UNWTO, UPU, Wassenaar Arrangement, WCO, WFTU (NGOs), WHO, WIPO, WMO, WTO, ZC

Diplomatic representation in the US: *chief of mission:* Ambassador Hasan MURAT MERCAN (since 20 April 2021)
chancery: 2525 Massachusetts Avenue NW, Washington, DC 20008
telephone: [1] (202) 612-6700; [1] (202) 612-6701
FAX: [1] (202) 612-6744
email address and website:

embassy.washingtondc@mfa.gov.tr
http://washington.emb.mfa.gov.tr/Mission
consulate(s) general: Boston, Chicago, Houston, Los Angeles, Miami, New York

Diplomatic representation from the US: *chief of mission:* Ambassador Jeffrey Lane FLAKE (since 26 January 2022)
embassy: 110 Ataturk Boulevard, Kavaklidere, 06100 Ankara
mailing address: 7000 Ankara Place, Washington DC 20512-7000
telephone: [90] (312) 455-5555
FAX: [90] (312) 467-0019
email address and website:
Ankara-ACS@state.gov
https://tr.usembassy.gov/
consulate(s) general: Istanbul
consulate(s): Adana

Flag description: red with a vertical white crescent moon (the closed portion is toward the hoist side) and white five-pointed star centered just outside the crescent opening; the flag colors and designs closely resemble those on the banner of the Ottoman Empire, which preceded modern-day Turkey; the crescent moon and star serve as insignia for Turkic peoples; according to one interpretation, the flag represents the reflection of the moon and a star in a pool of blood of Turkish warriors

National symbol(s): vertical crescent moon with adjacent five-pointed star; national colors: red, white

National anthem: *name:* "Istiklal Marsi" (Independence March)
lyrics/music: Mehmet Akif ERSOY/Zeki UNGOR
note: lyrics adopted 1921, music adopted 1932; the anthem's original music was adopted in 1924; a new composition was agreed upon in 1932

National heritage: *total World Heritage Sites:* 19 (17 cultural, 2 mixed)
selected World Heritage Site locales: Archaeological Site of Troy (c); Ephesus (c); Diyarbakir Fortress and Hevsel Gardens Cultural Landscape (c); Hierapolis-Pamukkale (m); Göreme National Park and the Rock Sites of Cappadocia (m); Göbekli Tepe (c); Historic Areas of Istanbul (c); Selimiye Mosque and its Social Complex (c); Neolithic Site of Çatalhöyük (c); Bursa and Cumalikizik: the Birth of the Ottoman Empire (c)

ECONOMY

Economic overview: Turkey's largely free-market economy is driven by its industry and, increasingly, service sectors, although its traditional agriculture sector still accounts for about 25% of employment. The automotive, petrochemical, and electronics industries have risen in importance and surpassed the traditional textiles and clothing sectors within Turkey's export mix. However, the recent period of political stability and economic dynamism has given way to domestic uncertainty and security concerns, which are generating financial market volatility and weighing on Turkey's economic outlook.

Current government policies emphasize populist spending measures and credit breaks, while implementation of structural economic reforms has slowed. The government is playing a more active role in some strategic sectors and has used economic institutions and regulators to target political opponents, undermining private sector confidence in the judicial system. Between July 2016 and March 2017, three credit ratings agencies downgraded Turkey's sovereign credit ratings, citing concerns about the rule of law and the pace of economic reforms.

Turkey remains highly dependent on imported oil and gas but is pursuing energy relationships with a broader set of international partners and taking steps to increase use of domestic energy sources including renewables, nuclear, and coal. The joint Turkish-Azerbaijani Trans-Anatolian Natural Gas Pipeline is moving forward to increase transport of Caspian gas to Turkey and Europe, and when completed will help diversify Turkey's sources of imported gas.

After Turkey experienced a severe financial crisis in 2001, Ankara adopted financial and fiscal reforms as part of an IMF program. The reforms strengthened the country's economic fundamentals and ushered in an era of strong growth, averaging more than 6% annually until 2008. An aggressive privatization program also reduced state involvement in basic industry, banking, transport, power generation, and communication. Global economic conditions and tighter fiscal policy caused GDP to contract in 2009, but Turkey's well-regulated financial markets and banking system helped the country weather the global financial crisis, and GDP growth rebounded to around 9% in 2010 and 2011, as exports and investment recovered following the crisis.

The growth of Turkish GDP since 2016 has revealed the persistent underlying imbalances in the Turkish economy. In particular, Turkey's large current account deficit means it must rely on external investment inflows to finance growth, leaving the economy vulnerable to destabilizing shifts in investor confidence. Other troublesome trends include rising unemployment and inflation, which increased in 2017, given the Turkish lira's continuing depreciation against the dollar. Although government debt remains low at about 30% of GDP, bank and corporate borrowing has almost tripled as a percent of GDP during the past decade, outpacing its emerging-market peers and prompting investor concerns about its long-term sustainability.

Real GDP (purchasing power parity): $2,393,960,000,000 (2020 est.)
$2,352,640,000,000 (2019 est.)
$2,331,270,000,000 (2018 est.)
note: data are in 2017 dollars
country comparison to the world: 11

Real GDP growth rate: 0.98% (2019 est.)
3.04% (2018 est.)
7.54% (2017 est.)
country comparison to the world: 173

Real GDP per capita: $28,400 (2020 est.)
$28,200 (2019 est.)
$28,300 (2018 est.)
note: data are in 2017 dollars
country comparison to the world: 68

GDP (official exchange rate): $760.028 billion (2019 est.)

Inflation rate (consumer prices): 15.4% (2019 est.)
16.2% (2018 est.)
11.1% (2017 est.)
country comparison to the world: 215

Credit ratings:
Fitch rating: BB- (2019)
Moody's rating: B2 (2020)
Standard & Poors rating: B+ (2018)

GDP - composition, by sector of origin: *agriculture:* 6.8% (2017 est.)
industry: 32.3% (2017 est.)
services: 60.7% (2017 est.)

GDP - composition, by end use: *household consumption:* 59.1% (2017 est.)
government consumption: 14.5% (2017 est.)
investment in fixed capital: 29.8% (2017 est.)
investment in inventories: 1.1% (2017 est.)
exports of goods and services: 24.9% (2017 est.)
imports of goods and services: -29.4% (2017 est.)

Agricultural products: milk, wheat, sugar beet, tomatoes, barley, maize, potatoes, grapes, watermelons, apples

Industries: textiles, food processing, automobiles, electronics, mining (coal, chromate, copper, boron), steel, petroleum, construction, lumber, paper

Industrial production growth rate: 9.1% (2017 est.)
country comparison to the world: 18

Labor force: 25.677 million (2020 est.)
note: this number is for the domestic labor force only; number does not include about 1.2 million Turks working abroad, nor refugees
country comparison to the world: 21

Labor force - by occupation: *agriculture:* 18.4%
industry: 26.6%
services: 54.9% (2016)

Unemployment rate: 13.68% (2019 est.)
11% (2018 est.)
country comparison to the world: 170

Unemployment, youth ages 15-24: *total:* 25.1%
male: 22.5%
female: 29.9% (2020 est.)
country comparison to the world: 55

Population below poverty line: 14.4% (2018 est.)

Gini Index coefficient - distribution of family income: 41.9 (2018 est.)
43.6 (2003)
country comparison to the world: 48

Household income or consumption by percentage share: *lowest 10%:* 2.1%
highest 10%: 30.3% (2008)

Budget: *revenues:* 172.8 billion (2017 est.)
expenditures: 185.8 billion (2017 est.)

Budget surplus (+) or deficit (-): -1.5% (of GDP) (2017 est.)
country comparison to the world: 91

Public debt: 28.3% of GDP (2017 est.)
28.3% of GDP (2016 est.)
country comparison to the world: 169

Taxes and other revenues: 20.3% (of GDP) (2017 est.)
country comparison to the world: 151

Fiscal year: calendar year

Current account balance: $8.561 billion (2019 est.)
-$20.745 billion (2018 est.)
country comparison to the world: 26

Exports: $203.29 billion (2020 est.) note: data are in current year dollars
$245.84 billion (2019 est.) note: data are in current year dollars
$237.54 billion (2018 est.) note: data are in current year dollars
country comparison to the world: 30

Exports - partners: Germany 9%, United Kingdom 6%, Iraq 5%, Italy 5%, United States 5% (2019)

Exports - commodities: cars and vehicle parts, refined petroleum, delivery trucks, jewelry, clothing and apparel (2019)

Imports: $232.01 billion (2020 est.) note: data are in current year dollars
$227.06 billion (2019 est.) note: data are in current year dollars
$248.09 billion (2018 est.) note: data are in current year dollars
country comparison to the world: 25

Imports - partners: Germany 11%, China 9%, Russia 9%, United States 5%, Italy 5% (2019)

Imports - commodities: gold, refined petroleum, crude petroleum, vehicle parts, scrap iron (2019)

Reserves of foreign exchange and gold: $107.7 billion (31 December 2017 est.)
$106.1 billion (31 December 2016 est.)
country comparison to the world: 24

Debt - external: $438.677 billion (2019 est.)
$454.251 billion (2018 est.)
country comparison to the world: 30

Exchange rates: Turkish liras (TRY) per US dollar -
7.81925 (2020 est.)
5.8149 (2019 est.)
5.28905 (2018 est.)
2.72 (2014 est.)
2.1885 (2013 est.)

ENERGY

Electricity access: *electrification - total population:* 100% (2020)

Electricity: *installed generating capacity:* 96.846 million kW (2020 est.)
consumption: 263.952 billion kWh (2020 est.)
exports: 2.484 billion kWh (2020 est.)
imports: 1.888 billion kWh (2020 est.)
transmission/distribution losses: 29.275 billion kWh (2020 est.)

Electricity generation sources: *fossil fuels:* 56.2% of total installed capacity (2020 est.)
solar: 3.8% of total installed capacity (2020 est.)
wind: 8.4% of total installed capacity (2020 est.)
hydroelectricity: 26.3% of total installed capacity (2020 est.)
tide and wave: 0.4% of total installed capacity (2020 est.)
geothermal: 3.4% of total installed capacity (2020 est.)
biomass and waste: 1.5% of total installed capacity (2020 est.)

Coal: *production:* 78.871 million metric tons (2020 est.)
consumption: 108.271 million metric tons (2020 est.)
exports: 54,000 metric tons (2020 est.)
imports: 40.919 million metric tons (2020 est.)
proven reserves: 11.525 billion metric tons (2019 est.)

Petroleum: *total petroleum production:* 70,300 bbl/day (2021 est.)
refined petroleum consumption: 987,300 bbl/day (2019 est.)
crude oil and lease condensate exports: 0 bbl/day (2018 est.)
crude oil and lease condensate imports: 423,500 bbl/day (2018 est.)
crude oil estimated reserves: 366 million barrels (2021 est.)

Refined petroleum products - production: 657,900 bbl/day (2017 est.)
country comparison to the world: 27

Refined petroleum products - exports: 141,600 bbl/day (2017 est.)
country comparison to the world: 37

Refined petroleum products - imports: 560,000 bbl/day (2017 est.)
country comparison to the world: 16

Natural gas: *production:* 469.464 million cubic meters (2019 est.)
consumption: 44,605,473,000 cubic meters (2019 est.)
exports: 759.372 million cubic meters (2019 est.)
imports: 45,091,248,000 cubic meters (2019 est.)
proven reserves: 3.794 billion cubic meters (2021 est.)

Carbon dioxide emissions: 391.792 million metric tonnes of CO2 (2019 est.)
from coal and metallurgical coke: 172.298 million metric tonnes of CO2 (2019 est.)
from petroleum and other liquids: 133.587 million metric tonnes of CO2 (2019 est.)
from consumed natural gas: 85.907 million metric tonnes of CO2 (2019 est.)
country comparison to the world: 17

Energy consumption per capita: 79.126 million Btu/person (2019 est.)
country comparison to the world: 76

COMMUNICATIONS

Telephones - fixed lines: *total subscriptions:* 12,448,604 (2020 est.)
subscriptions per 100 inhabitants: 15 (2020 est.)
country comparison to the world: 17

Telephones - mobile cellular: *total subscriptions:* 80,790,900 (2019)
subscriptions per 100 inhabitants: 96.84 (2019)
country comparison to the world: 20

Telecommunication systems: *general assessment:* Turkey continues to develop its capabilities within its telecom sector, becoming one of the relatively few countries able to build and develop its own communications satellites; with the successful launch of the Turksat 5A and 5B satellites in 2021, the country has vastly increased its bandwidth capacity; these satellites will be joined by the Turksat 6A in early 2023; the country's telcos have invested in fiber infrastructure; deployment of fiber-based broadband networks are well established, with fiber accounting for 26.7% of all fixed broadband connections as of early 2022; the DSL sector still dominates, accounting for about 63% of connections, but its share is steadily declining, year-on-year, while the number of fiber connections has grown strongly; improved fixed and mobile infrastructure is underpinning the country's initiatives relating to Smart City concepts, which have become a key area of focus for the emerging digital economy and the transformation to a knowledge-based economy; Turkey's National Smart Cities Strategy and Action Plan runs through to 2023 (2022)
domestic: additional digital exchanges are permitting a rapid increase in subscribers; the construction of a network of technologically advanced intercity trunk lines, using both fiber-optic cable and digital microwave radio relay, is facilitating communication between urban centers; remote areas are reached by a domestic satellite system; fixed-line nearly 15 per 100 and mobile-cellular teledensity is over 97 telephones per 100 persons (2020)
international: country code - 90; landing points for the SeaMeWe-3 & -5, MedNautilus Submarine System, Turcyos-1 & -2 submarine cables providing connectivity to Europe, Africa, the Middle East, Asia, Southeast Asia and Australia; satellite earth stations - 12 Intelsat; mobile satellite terminals - 328 in the Inmarsat and Eutelsat systems (2020)

Broadcast media: Turkish Radio and Television Corporation (TRT) operates multiple TV and radio networks and stations; multiple privately owned national television stations and 567 private regional and local television stations; multi-channel cable TV subscriptions available; 1,007 private radio broadcast stations
(2019)

Internet country code: .tr

Internet users: *total:* 65,784,472 (2020 est.)
percent of population: 78% (2020 est.)
country comparison to the world: 14

Broadband - fixed subscriptions: *total:* 16,734,853 (2020 est.)
subscriptions per 100 inhabitants: 20 (2020 est.)
country comparison to the world: 13

TRANSPORTATION

National air transport system: *number of registered air carriers:* 11 (2020)
inventory of registered aircraft operated by air carriers: 618
annual passenger traffic on registered air carriers: 115,595,495 (2018)
annual freight traffic on registered air carriers: 5,949,210,000 (2018) mt-km

Civil aircraft registration country code prefix: TC

Airports: *total:* 98 (2021)
country comparison to the world: 58

Airports - with paved runways: *total:* 91
over 3,047 m: 16
2,438 to 3,047 m: 38
1,524 to 2,437 m: 17
914 to 1,523 m: 16
under 914 m: 4 (2021)

Airports - with unpaved runways: *total:* 7
1,524 to 2,437 m: 1
914 to 1,523 m: 4
under 914 m: 2 (2021)

Heliports: 20 (2021)

Pipelines: 14,666 km gas, 3,293 km oil (2017)

Railways: *total:* 11,497 km (2018)
standard gauge: 11,497 km (2018) 1.435-m gauge (1.435 km high speed train)
country comparison to the world: 22

Roadways: *total:* 67,333 km (2018)
paved: 24,082 km (2018) (includes 2,159 km of expressways)
unpaved: 43,251 km (2018)
country comparison to the world: 71

Waterways: 1,200 km (2010)
country comparison to the world: 64

Merchant marine: *total:* 1,217
by type: bulk carrier 39, container ship 41, general cargo 317, oil tanker 126, other 694 (2021)
country comparison to the world: 23

Ports and terminals: *major seaport(s):* Aliaga, Ambarli, Diliskelesi, Eregli, Izmir, Kocaeli (Izmit), Mersin (Icel), Limani, Yarimca
container port(s) (TEUs): Ambarli (3,104,882), Mersin (Icel) (1,854,312), Izmet (1,715,193) (2019)

LNG terminal(s) (import): Aliaga, Dortyol, Ekti (Izmir), Marmara Ereglisi

MILITARY AND SECURITY

Military and security forces: Turkish Armed Forces (TSK): Turkish Land Forces (Turk Kara Kuvvetleri), Turkish Naval Forces (Turk Deniz Kuvvetleri; includes naval air and naval infantry), Turkish Air Forces (Turk Hava Kuvvetleri); Ministry of Interior: Gendarmerie of the Turkish Republic (aka Gendarmerie General Command), Turkish Coast Guard Command, National Police (2022)
note: the Gendarmerie (Jandarma) is responsible for the maintenance of the public order in areas that fall outside the jurisdiction of police forces (generally in rural areas); in wartime, the Gendarmerie and Coast Guard would be placed under the operational control of the Land Forces and Naval Forces, respectively

Military expenditures: 1.2% of GDP (2022 est.)
1.6% of GDP (2021)
1.9% of GDP (2020)
1.9% of GDP (2019) (approximately $36.3 billion)
1.8% of GDP (2018) (approximately $37.2 billion)
country comparison to the world: 120

Military and security service personnel strengths: approximately 445,000 active duty personnel (350,000 Army; 45,000 Navy; 50,000 Air Force); approximately 150,000 Gendarmerie (2022)

Military equipment inventories and acquisitions: the military's inventory is mostly comprised of a mix of domestically-produced and Western weapons systems, although in recent years, Turkey has also acquired some Chinese, Russian, and South Korean equipment; since 2010, the US has been the leading provider of armaments to Turkey; other significant suppliers included Italy, South Korea, and Spain; Turkey has a robust defense industry capable of producing a range of weapons systems for both export and internal use, including armored vehicles, naval vessels, and unmanned aerial platforms, although it is heavily dependent on Western technology; Turkey's defense industry also partners with other countries for defense production (2021)

Military service age and obligation: mandatory military service for men, age 20-41; service can be delayed if in university or in certain professions (researchers, professionals, and athletic, or those with artistic talents have the right to postpone military service until the age of 35); 6-12 months service; women may volunteer (2022)
note 1: in 2019, a new law cut the men's mandatory military service period in half, as well as making paid military service permanent; with the new system, the period of conscription was reduced from 12 months to six months for privates and non-commissioned soldiers (the service term for reserve officers chosen among university or college graduates remained 12 months); after completing six months of service, if a conscripted soldier wants to and is suitable for extending his military service, he may do so for an additional six months in return for a monthly salary; under the new law, all male Turkish citizens over the age of 20 are required to undergo a one month military training period, but they can obtain an exemption from the remaining five months of their mandatory service by paying 31,000 Turkish Liras
note 2: as of 2019, women made up about 0.3% of the military's full-time personnel

Military deployments: approximately 150 (Azerbaijan; monitoring cease-fire, clearing mines); 250 Bosnia-Herzegovina (EUFOR); approximately 30,000 Cyprus; estimated 5,000 Iraq; 300 Kosovo (NATO/KFOR); 110 Lebanon (UNIFIL); estimated 500 Libya; up to 5,000 Qatar; approximately 200 Somalia (training mission); estimated 5,000-10,000 Syria (2022)
note 1: between 2016 and 2020, Turkey conducted four significant military campaigns in northern Syria; Turkey also has deployed troops into northern Iraq on numerous occasions to combat the Kurdistan Worker's Party (PKK), including large operations involving thousands of troops in 2007, 2011, and 2018, and smaller-scale operations in 2021 and 2022; in October of 2021, Turkey's parliament extended the military's mandate to launch cross-border operations in Iraq and Syria by two more years
note 2: in 2020, Turkey deployed hundreds of Turkish troops and as many as 5,000 Syrian fighters to Libya to support the Libyan Government of National Accord

Military - note: Turkey has been a member of NATO since 1952 and hosts NATO's Land Forces Command in Izmir, as well as a NATO/US airbase at Incirlik and a NATO missile defense radar system in eastern Turkey

under a long-range (2033) strategic plan, the Turkish Armed Forces continued efforts to modernize its equipment and force structure; Land Forces sought to produce a 20-30% smaller, more highly trained force characterized by greater mobility and firepower and capable of joint and combined operations

the Turkish Navy is a regional naval power that wants to develop the capability to project power beyond Turkey's coastal waters; it is planning to launch new frigates, submarines, and a light aircraft carrier/amphibious assault ship in the next few years, adding to its current force of about 16 frigates and 12 submarines; the Navy is heavily involved in NATO, multinational, and UN operations; its roles include control of territorial waters and security for sea lines of communications

the Turkish Air Force adopted an "Aerospace and Missile Defense Concept" in 2002 and is developing an integrated missile defense system; in a controversial move that complicated its relationship with NATO and the US, it purchased the Russian S-400 air defense system for an estimated $2.5 billion in 2019; Air Force priorities include attaining a modern deployable, survivable, and sustainable force structure, and establishing a sustainable command and control system

in recent years, Turkey has taken on a greater level of international peacekeeping responsibilities, including keeping a substantial force under NATO in Afghanistan until withdrawing in 2021; Turkey also has built expeditionary military bases in Qatar, Somalia, northern Cyprus, and Sudan

the military has a substantial stake in Turkey's economy through a holding company that is involved in the automotive, energy, finance, and logistics sectors, as well as iron and steel production (2022)

TERRORISM

Terrorist group(s): Islamic State of Iraq and ash-Sham (ISIS); Islamic Movement of Uzbekistan (IMU); Islamic Revolutionary Guard Corps (IRGC)/Qods Force; Kurdistan Workers' Party (PKK); al-Qa'ida; Revolutionary People's Liberation Party/Front (DHKP/C)

TRANSNATIONAL ISSUES

Disputes - international: *Turkey-Armenia:* in 2009, Swiss mediators facilitated an accord reestablishing diplomatic ties between Armenia and Turkey, but neither side has ratified the agreement and the rapprochement effort has faltered; in early 2022, the two countries held talks twice aimed at normalizing relations, which could lead to the opening of their land border, shut since 1993; in 2000, Turkish authorities complained to UNESCO that blasting from quarries in Armenia was damaging the medieval ruins of Ani, on the other side of the Arpacay valley
Turkey-Azerbaijan: none identified
Turkey-Bulgaria: none identified
Turkey-Cyprus: status of northern Cyprus question remains
Turkey-Georgia: none identified
Turkey-Greece: complex maritime, air, and territorial disputes with Greece in the Aegean Sea, including rights to explore oil and gas reserves in the eastern Mediterranean and illegal migrants transiting from Turkey into Greece; the Aegean Maritime Boundary is complicated by the close proximity of Greek islands to the western shores of the Turkish Anatolian peninsula, representing the primary source of conflict between the two countries
Turkey-Iran: none identified
Turkey-Iraq: Turkey has expressed concern over the status of Kurds in Iraq
Turkey-Syria: Turkey completed building a wall along its border with Syria in 2018 to prevent illegal border crossings and smuggling

Refugees and internally displaced persons: *refugees (country of origin):* 3,603,724 (Syria) (2022); 145,000 (Ukraine) (as of 19 May 2022)

IDPs: 1.099 million (displaced from 1984-2005 because of fighting between the Kurdish PKK and Turkish military; most IDPs are Kurds from eastern and southeastern provinces; no information available on persons displaced by development projects) (2021)
stateless persons: 117 (2018)

Illicit drugs: transit country for heroin, opium, and cocaine trafficked to European markets; amphetamine-type stimulants (ATS) are trafficked to Middle East and Southeast Asia markets; one of the major transit routes for opiates smuggled from Afghanistan via Iran destined for Western Europe; smugglers involved in both heroin sales and transport and production and smuggling of synthetic drugs; criminal networks have interests in heroin conversion laboratories operating in Iran near the Turkish border; hashish imported or grown domestically for local consumption

TURKMENISTAN

INTRODUCTION

Background: Present-day Turkmenistan covers territory that has been at the crossroads of civilizations for centuries. The area was ruled in antiquity by various Persian empires, and was conquered by Alexander the Great, Muslim armies, the Mongols, Turkic warriors, and eventually the Russians. In medieval times, Merv (located in present-day Mary province) was one of the great cities of the Islamic world and an important stop on the Silk Road. Annexed by Russia in the late 1800s, Turkmen territories later figured prominently in the anti-Bolshevik resistance in Central Asia. In 1924, Turkmenistan became a Soviet republic; it achieved independence upon the dissolution of the USSR in 1991. President for Life Saparmyrat NYYAZOW died in December 2006, and Gurbanguly BERDIMUHAMEDOW, a deputy chairman under NYYAZOW, emerged as the country's new president. BERDIMUHAMEDOW won Turkmenistan's first multi-candidate presidential election in February 2007, and again in 2012 and in 2017 with over 97% of the vote in both instances, in elections widely regarded as undemocratic. In February 2022, BERDIMUHAMEDOW announced that he would step down from the presidency and called for an election to replace him. His son, Serdar BERDIMUHAMEDOW, won the ensuing election, held in March 2022, with 73% of the vote. Gurbanguly BERDIMUHAMEDOW, although no longer head of state, maintains an influential political position as head of the Halk Maslahaty (People's Council).

Turkmenistan has sought new export markets for its extensive hydrocarbon/natural gas reserves, which have yet to be fully exploited. As of late 2021, Turkmenistan exported the majority of its gas to China and smaller levels of gas to Russia. Turkmenistan's reliance on gas exports has made the economy vulnerable to fluctuations in the global energy market, and economic hardships since the drop in energy prices in 2014 have led many Turkmenistanis to emigrate, mostly to Turkey. Heavy restrictions placed by the government in 2020 on entry and exit into the country in response to the COVID-19 pandemic have resulted in a steep drop in emigration, however.

GEOGRAPHY

Location: Central Asia, bordering the Caspian Sea, between Iran and Kazakhstan

Geographic coordinates: 40 00 N, 60 00 E

Map references: Asia

Area: *total:* 488,100 sq km
land: 469,930 sq km
water: 18,170 sq km
country comparison to the world: 55

Area - comparative: slightly more than three times the size of Georgia; slightly larger than California

Land boundaries: *total:* 4,158 km
border countries (4): Afghanistan 804 km; Iran 1,148 km; Kazakhstan 413 km; Uzbekistan 1,793 km

Coastline: 0 km (landlocked); note - Turkmenistan borders the Caspian Sea (1,768 km)

Maritime claims: none (landlocked)

Climate: subtropical desert

Terrain: flat-to-rolling sandy desert with dunes rising to mountains in the south; low mountains along border with Iran; borders Caspian Sea in west

Elevation: *highest point:* Gora Ayribaba 3,139 m
lowest point: Vpadina Akchanaya (Sarygamysh Koli is a lake in northern Turkmenistan with a water level that fluctuates above and below the elevation of Vpadina Akchanaya, the lake has dropped as low as -110 m) -81 m
mean elevation: 230 m

Natural resources: petroleum, natural gas, sulfur, salt

Land use: *agricultural land:* 72% (2018 est.)
arable land: 4.1% (2018 est.)
permanent crops: 0.1% (2018 est.)
permanent pasture: 67.8% (2018 est.)
forest: 8.8% (2018 est.)
other: 19.2% (2018 est.)

Irrigated land: 19,950 sq km (2012)

Major lakes (area sq km): *salt water lake(s):* Caspian Sea (shared with Iran, Azerbaijan, Russia, and Kazakhstan) - 374,000 sq km

Major rivers (by length in km): Amu Darya (shared with Tajikistan [s], Afghanistan, and Uzbekistan [m]) - 2,620 km
note – [s] after country name indicates river source; [m] after country name indicates river mouth

Major watersheds (area sq km): Internal *(endorheic basin)* drainage: *(Aral Sea basin)* Amu Darya (534,739 sq km)

Population distribution: the most densely populated areas are the southern, eastern, and northeastern oases; approximately 50% of the population lives in and around the capital of Ashgabat

Natural hazards: earthquakes; mudslides; droughts; dust storms; floods

Geography - note: landlocked; the western and central low-lying desolate portions of the country make up the great Garagum (Kara-Kum) desert, which occupies over 80% of the country; eastern part is plateau

PEOPLE AND SOCIETY

Population: 5,636,011 (2022 est.)
note: some sources suggest Turkmenistan's population could be as much as 1 to 2 million people lower than available estimates because of large-scale emigration during the last 10 years
country comparison to the world: 115

Nationality: *noun:* Turkmenistani(s)
adjective: Turkmenistani

Ethnic groups: Turkmen 85%, Uzbek 5%, Russian 4%, other 6% (2003 est.)

Languages: Turkmen (official) 72%, Russian 12%, Uzbek 9%, other 7%
major-language sample(s): Dünýä Faktlar Kitaby – esasy maglumatlaryň wajyp çeşmesidir (Turkmen)

Religions: Muslim 93%, Christian 6.4%, Buddhist <1 %, folk religion <1 %, Jewish <1%, other <1 %, unspecified <1 % (2020 est.)

Demographic profile: While Turkmenistan reputedly has a population of more than 5.6 million, the figure is most likely considerably less. Getting an accurate population estimate for the country is impossible because then President Gurbanguly BERDIMUHAMEDOW withheld the results of the last two censuses. The 2012 census results reportedly show that nearly 2 million citizens have emigrated in the last decade, which prompted BERDIMUHAMEDOW to order another census. Results of this census, covering 2008-2018, also were not released to the public but purportedly are similar. Another census supposedly will be held in 2022.

Authorities have reacted to the dramatic population decline by preventing Turkmen from leaving the country, including removing citizens from international flights and refusing to provide necessary documents. Turkmenistan's rise in outmigration – mainly to Turkey, Russia, and Uzbekistan – coincided with the country's 2013-2014 economic crisis. The outflow has been sustained by poor living standards, inflation, low income, and a lack of health care. At the same time, Ashbagat is encouraging people to have more children to make up for its shrinking population.

Age structure: *0-14 years:* 25.44% (male 713,441/female 693,042)
15-24 years: 16.48% (male 458,566/female 452,469)
25-54 years: 44.14% (male 1,214,581/female 1,226,027)
55-64 years: 8.56% (male 221,935/female 251,238)
65 years and over: 5.38% (male 129,332/female 167,996) (2020 est.)

Dependency ratios: *total dependency ratio:* 55.2
youth dependency ratio: 47.8
elderly dependency ratio: 7.4
potential support ratio: 13.5 (2020 est.)

Median age: *total:* 29.2 years
male: 28.7 years
female: 29.7 years (2020 est.)
country comparison to the world: 135

Population growth rate: 0.99% (2022 est.)
country comparison to the world: 96

Birth rate: 17.51 births/1,000 population (2022 est.)
country comparison to the world: 88

Death rate: 5.95 deaths/1,000 population (2022 est.)
country comparison to the world: 162

Net migration rate: -1.71 migrant(s)/1,000 population (2022 est.)
country comparison to the world: 164

Population distribution: the most densely populated areas are the southern, eastern, and northeastern oases; approximately 50% of the population lives in and around the capital of Ashgabat

Urbanization: *urban population:* 53.5% of total population (2022)
rate of urbanization: 2.23% annual rate of change (2020-25 est.)

Major urban areas - population: 883,000 ASHGABAT (capital) (2022)

Sex ratio: *at birth:* 1.05 male(s)/female
0-14 years: 1.03 male(s)/female
15-24 years: 1.01 male(s)/female
25-54 years: 0.99 male(s)/female
55-64 years: 0.89 male(s)/female
65 years and over: 0.59 male(s)/female
total population: 0.98 male(s)/female (2022 est.)

Mother's mean age at first birth: 24.2 years (2019)

Maternal mortality ratio: 7 deaths/100,000 live births (2017 est.)
country comparison to the world: 157

Infant mortality rate: *total:* 37.62 deaths/1,000 live births
male: 45.76 deaths/1,000 live births
female: 29.07 deaths/1,000 live births (2022 est.)
country comparison to the world: 37

Life expectancy at birth: *total population:* 71.83 years
male: 68.8 years
female: 75 years (2022 est.)
country comparison to the world: 163

Total fertility rate: 2.03 children born/woman (2022 est.)
country comparison to the world: 103

Contraceptive prevalence rate: 49.7% (2019)

Drinking water source: *improved: urban:* 100% of population
rural: 100% of population
total: 100% of population

Current health expenditure: 6.6% of GDP (2019)

Physicians density: 2.23 physicians/1,000 population (2014)

Hospital bed density: 4 beds/1,000 population (2014)

Sanitation facility access: *improved: urban:* 99.8% of population
rural: 99.9% of population
total: 99.8% of population
unimproved: urban: 0.2% of population
rural: 0.1% of population
total: 0.2% of population (2020 est.)

Obesity - adult prevalence rate: 18.6% (2016)
country comparison to the world: 117

Alcohol consumption per capita: *total:* 2.88 liters of pure alcohol (2019 est.)
beer: 0.65 liters of pure alcohol (2019 est.)
wine: 1.25 liters of pure alcohol (2019 est.)
spirits: 0.98 liters of pure alcohol (2019 est.)
other alcohols: 0 liters of pure alcohol (2019 est.)
country comparison to the world: 117

Tobacco use: *total:* 5.5% (2020 est.)
male: 10.6% (2020 est.)
female: 0.4% (2020 est.)
country comparison to the world: 160

Children under the age of 5 years underweight: 3.1% (2019)
country comparison to the world: 93

Child marriage: *women married by age 15:* 0.2%
women married by age 18: 6.1% (2019 est.)

Education expenditures: 3.1% of GDP (2019 est.)
country comparison to the world: 147

Literacy: *definition:* age 15 and over can read and write
total population: 99.7%
male: 99.8%
female: 99.6% (2015)

School life expectancy (primary to tertiary education): *total:* 13 years
male: 13 years
female: 13 years (2020)

ENVIRONMENT

Environment - current issues: contamination of soil and groundwater with agricultural chemicals, pesticides; salination, water logging of soil due to poor irrigation methods; Caspian Sea pollution; diversion of a large share of the flow of the Amu Darya into irrigation contributes to that river's inability to replenish the Aral Sea; soil erosion; desertification

Environment - international agreements: *party to:* Biodiversity, Climate Change, Climate Change-Kyoto Protocol, Climate Change-Paris Agreement, Comprehensive Nuclear Test Ban, Desertification, Hazardous Wastes, Ozone Layer Protection, Ship Pollution, Wetlands
signed, but not ratified: none of the selected agreements

Air pollutants: *particulate matter emissions:* 19.02 micrograms per cubic meter (2016 est.)
carbon dioxide emissions: 70.63 megatons (2016 est.)
methane emissions: 52.09 megatons (2020 est.)

Climate: subtropical desert

Land use: *agricultural land:* 72% (2018 est.)
arable land: 4.1% (2018 est.)
permanent crops: 0.1% (2018 est.)
permanent pasture: 67.8% (2018 est.)
forest: 8.8% (2018 est.)
other: 19.2% (2018 est.)

Urbanization: *urban population:* 53.5% of total population (2022)
rate of urbanization: 2.23% annual rate of change (2020-25 est.)

Revenue from forest resources: *forest revenues:* 0% of GDP (2018 est.)
country comparison to the world: 198

Revenue from coal: *coal revenues:* 0% of GDP (2018 est.)
country comparison to the world: 179

Waste and recycling: *municipal solid waste generated annually:* 500,000 tons (2013 est.)

Major lakes (area sq km): *salt water lake(s):* Caspian Sea (shared with Iran, Azerbaijan, Russia, and Kazakhstan) - 374,000 sq km

Major rivers (by length in km): Amu Darya (shared with Tajikistan [s], Afghanistan, and Uzbekistan [m]) - 2,620 km

note – [s] after country name indicates river source; [m] after country name indicates river mouth

Major watersheds (area sq km): Internal *(endorheic basin)* drainage: *(Aral Sea basin)* Amu Darya (534,739 sq km)

Total water withdrawal: *municipal:* 755 million cubic meters (2017 est.)
industrial: 839 million cubic meters (2017 est.)
agricultural: 26.36 billion cubic meters (2017 est.)

Total renewable water resources: 24.765 billion cubic meters (2017 est.)

GOVERNMENT

Country name: *conventional long form:* none
conventional short form: Turkmenistan
local long form: none
local short form: Turkmenistan
former: Turkmen Soviet Socialist Republic
etymology: the suffix "-stan" means "place of" or "country," so Turkmenistan literally means the "Land of the Turkmen [people]"

Government type: presidential republic; authoritarian

Capital: *name:* Ashgabat (Ashkhabad)
geographic coordinates: 37 57 N, 58 23 E
time difference: UTC+5 (10 hours ahead of Washington, DC, during Standard Time)
etymology: derived from the Persian words *eshq* meaning "love" and *abad* meaning "inhabited place" or "city," and so loosely translates as "the city of love"

Administrative divisions: 5 provinces (welayatlar, singular - welayat) and 1 independent city*: Ahal Welayaty (Anew), Ashgabat*, Balkan Welayaty (Balkanabat), Dasoguz Welayaty, Lebap Welayaty (Turkmenabat), Mary Welayaty
note: administrative divisions have the same names as their administrative centers (exceptions have the administrative center name following in parentheses)

Independence: 27 October 1991 (from the Soviet Union)

National holiday: Independence Day, 27 October (1991)

Constitution: *history:* several previous; latest adopted 14 September 2016
amendments: proposed by the Mejlisi; passage requires two-thirds majority vote or absolute majority approval in a referendum; amended several times, last in 2020 (changed legislature to bicameral)

Legal system: civil law system with Islamic (sharia) law influences

International law organization participation: has not submitted an ICJ jurisdiction declaration; non-party state to the ICCt

Citizenship: *citizenship by birth:* no
citizenship by descent only: at least one parent must be a citizen of Turkmenistan
dual citizenship recognized: yes
residency requirement for naturalization: 7 years

Suffrage: 18 years of age; universal

Executive branch: *chief of state:* President Serdar BERDIMUHAMEDOW (since 19 March 2022); note - the president is both chief of state and head of government
head of government: President Serdar BERDIMUHAMEDOW (since 19 March 2022)
cabinet: Cabinet of Ministers appointed by the president
elections/appointments: president directly elected by absolute majority popular vote in 2 rounds if needed for a 7-year term (no term limits); election last held on 12 March 2022 (next to be held in 2029); note - on 11 February 2022, President Gurbanguly BERDIMUHAMEDOW announced his intent to retire setting up the early presidential election
election results:

2022: Serdar BERDIMUHAMEDOW elected president; percent of vote - Serdar BERDIMUHAMEDOW 73.0%, Khydyr NUNNAYEV 11.1%, Agadzhan BEKMYRADOV 7.2%, other 8.7%; note - Serdar BERDIMUHAMEDOW is the son of previous president Gurbanguly BERDIMUHAMEDOW
2017: Gurbanguly BERDIMUHAMEDOW reelected president in the first round; percent of vote - Gurbanguly BERDIMUHAMEDOW (DPT) 97.7%, other 2.3%

Legislative branch: *description:* bicameral National Council or Milli Genesi consists of:
People's Council or Halk Maslahaty (56 seats; 48 members indirectly elected by provincial councils and 8 members appointed by the president)

Assembly or Mejlisi (125 seats; members directly elected in single-seat constituencies by absolute majority vote in 2 rounds if needed to serve 5-year terms)
note: in September 2020, the Turkmenistani legislature (Milli Genesi) adopted a constitutional amendment creating an upper chamber, making the legislature bicameral; the chairperson of the Halk Maslahaty is now designated as the constitutional successor to the presidency; as of March 2022, Gurbanguly BERDIMUHAMEDOW continues to serve in this position after stepping away from the presidency
elections:
People's Council - first held on 28 March 2021 for 48 indirectly elected members (next to be held in 2026); first held on 14 April 2021 for 8 presidentially appointed members (next to be held NA)

Assembly - last held on 25 March 2018 (next to be held NA)
election results:
People's Council - percent of vote by party - NA; seats by party - DPT 3, independent 45; composition as of mid-2022 (55 members) - men 41, women 14, percent of women 25.5%

Assembly - percent of vote by party - NA; seats by party - DPT 55, APT 11, PIE 11, independent 48 (individuals nominated by citizen groups); composition as of mid-2022 (116 members) - men 86, women 30, percent of women 25.9%; note - total percent of National Council percent of women 25.7%

Judicial branch: *highest court(s):* Supreme Court of Turkmenistan (consists of the court president and 21 associate judges and organized into civil, criminal, and military chambers)
judge selection and term of office: judges appointed by the president for 5-year terms
subordinate courts: High Commercial Court; appellate courts; provincial, district, and city courts; military courts

Political parties and leaders: Agrarian Party of Turkmenistan or APT [Basim ANNAGURBANOW]
Democratic Party of Turkmenistan or DPT [Ata SERDAROW]
Party of Industrialists and Entrepreneurs or PIE [Saparmyrat OWGANOW]
note: all of these parties support President BERDIMUHAMEDOW; a law authorizing the registration of political parties went into effect in January 2012; unofficial, small opposition movements exist abroad

International organization participation: ADB, CIS (associate member, has not ratified the 1993 CIS charter although it participates in meetings and held the chairmanship of the CIS in 2012), EAPC, EBRD, ECO, FAO, G-77, IBRD, ICAO, ICRM, IDA, IDB, IFC, IFRCS, ILO, IMF, IMO, Interpol, IOC, IOM (observer), ISO (correspondent), ITU, MIGA, NAM, OIC, OPCW, OSCE, PFP, UN, UNCTAD, UNESCO, UNHCR, UNIDO, UNWTO, UPU, WCO, WFTU (NGOs), WHO, WIPO, WMO

Diplomatic representation in the US: *chief of mission:* Ambassador Meret ORAZOV (since 14 February 2001)
chancery: 2207 Massachusetts Avenue NW, Washington, DC 20008
telephone: [1] (202) 588-1500
FAX: [1] (202) 588-1500
email address and website:
turkmenembassyus@verizon.net
https://usa.tmembassy.gov.tm/en

Diplomatic representation from the US: *chief of mission:* Ambassador Matthew S. KLIMOW (since 26 June 2019)
embassy: 9 1984 Street (formerly Pushkin Street), Ashgabat 744000
mailing address: 7070 Ashgabat Place, Washington, DC 20521-7070
telephone: [993] (12) 94-00-45
FAX: [993] (12) 94-26-14
email address and website:
ConsularAshgab@state.gov
https://tm.usembassy.gov/

Flag description: green field with a vertical red stripe near the hoist side, containing five tribal guls (designs used in producing carpets) stacked above two crossed olive branches; five white, five-pointed stars and a white crescent moon appear in the upper corner of the field just to the fly side of the red stripe; the green color and crescent moon represent Islam; the five stars symbolize the regions or welayats of Turkmenistan; the guls reflect the national identity of Turkmenistan where carpetmaking has long been a part of traditional nomadic life
note: the flag of Turkmenistan is the most intricate of all national flags

National symbol(s): Akhal-Teke horse; national colors: green, white

National anthem: *name:* "Garassyz, Bitarap Turkmenistanyn" (Independent, Neutral, Turkmenistan State Anthem)
lyrics/music: collective/Veli MUKHATOV
note: adopted 1997, lyrics revised in 2008, to eliminate references to deceased President Saparmurat NYYAZOW

National heritage: *total World Heritage Sites:* 3 (all cultural)
selected World Heritage Site locales: Ancient Merv; Kunya-Urgench; Parthian Fortresses of Nisa

ECONOMY

Economic overview: Turkmenistan is largely a desert country with intensive agriculture in irrigated oases and significant natural gas and oil resources. The two largest crops are cotton, most of which is produced for export, and wheat, which is domestically consumed. Although agriculture accounts for almost 8% of GDP, it continues to employ nearly half of the country's workforce. Hydrocarbon exports, the bulk of which is natural gas going to China, make up 25% of Turkmenistan's GDP. Ashgabat has explored two initiatives to bring gas to new markets: a trans-Caspian pipeline that would carry gas to Europe and the Turkmenistan-Afghanistan-Pakistan-India gas pipeline. Both face major financing, political, and security hurdles and are unlikely to be completed soon.

Turkmenistan's autocratic governments under presidents NIYAZOW (1991-2006) and BERDIMUHAMEDOW (since 2007) have made little progress improving the business climate, privatizing state-owned industries, combatting corruption, and limiting economic development outside the energy sector. High energy prices in the mid-2000s allowed the government to undertake extensive development and social spending, including providing heavy utility subsidies.

Low energy prices since mid-2014 are hampering Turkmenistan's economic growth and reducing government revenues. The government has cut subsidies in several areas, and wage arrears have increased. In January 2014, the Central Bank of Turkmenistan devalued the manat by 19%, and downward pressure on the currency continues. There is a widening spread between the official exchange rate (3.5 TMM per US dollar) and the black market exchange rate (approximately 14 TMM per US dollar). Currency depreciation and conversion restrictions, corruption, isolationist policies, and declining spending on public services have resulted in a stagnate economy that is nearing crisis. Turkmenistan claims substantial foreign currency reserves, but non-transparent data limit international institutions' ability to verify this information.

Real GDP (purchasing power parity): $92.33 billion (2019 est.)
$86.86 billion (2018 est.)
$81.787 billion (2017 est.)
note: data are in 2017 dollars
country comparison to the world: 94

Real GDP growth rate: 6.5% (2017 est.)
6.2% (2016 est.)
6.5% (2015 est.)
country comparison to the world: 23

Real GDP per capita: $15,500 (2019 est.) note: data are in 2017 dollars
$14,800 (2018 est.) note: data are in 2017 dollars
$14,205 (2017 est.)
country comparison to the world: 106

GDP (official exchange rate): $40.819 billion (2018 est.)

Inflation rate (consumer prices): 8% (2017 est.)
3.6% (2016 est.)
country comparison to the world: 200

GDP - composition, by sector of origin: *agriculture:* 7.5% (2017 est.)
industry: 44.9% (2017 est.)
services: 47.7% (2017 est.)

GDP - composition, by end use: *household consumption:* 50% (2017 est.)
government consumption: 10% (2017 est.)
investment in fixed capital: 28.2% (2017 est.)
investment in inventories: 0% (2017 est.)
exports of goods and services: 26.2% (2017 est.)
imports of goods and services: -14.3% (2017 est.)

Agricultural products: milk, wheat, cotton, tomatoes, potatoes, watermelons, grapes, sugar beet, beef, rice

Industries: natural gas, oil, petroleum products, textiles, food processing

Industrial production growth rate: 1% (2017 est.)
country comparison to the world: 160

Labor force: 2.305 million (2013 est.)
country comparison to the world: 115

Labor force - by occupation: *agriculture:* 48.2%
industry: 14%

services: 37.8% (2004 est.)

Unemployment rate: 11% (2014 est.)
10.6% (2013)
country comparison to the world: 156

Population below poverty line: 0.2% (2012 est.)

Gini Index coefficient - distribution of family income: 40.8 (1998)
country comparison to the world: 58

Household income or consumption by percentage share: *lowest 10%:* 2.6%
highest 10%: 31.7% (1998)

Budget: *revenues:* 5.657 billion (2017 est.)
expenditures: 6.714 billion (2017 est.)

Budget surplus (+) or deficit (-): -2.8% (of GDP) (2017 est.)
country comparison to the world: 126

Public debt: 28.8% of GDP (2017 est.)
24.1% of GDP (2016 est.)
country comparison to the world: 167

Taxes and other revenues: 14.9% (of GDP) (2017 est.)
country comparison to the world: 197

Fiscal year: calendar year

Current account balance: -$4.359 billion (2017 est.)
-$7.207 billion (2016 est.)
country comparison to the world: 182

Exports: $7.458 billion (2017 est.)
$6.987 billion (2016 est.)
country comparison to the world: 111

Exports - partners: China 82% (2019)

Exports - commodities: natural gas, refined petroleum, crude petroleum, cotton fibers, fertilizers (2019)

Imports: $4.571 billion (2017 est.)
$5.215 billion (2016 est.)
country comparison to the world: 143

Imports - partners: Turkey 25%, Russia 18%, China 14%, Germany 6% (2019)

Imports - commodities: iron products, harvesting machinery, packaged medicines, broadcasting equipment, tractors (2019)

Reserves of foreign exchange and gold: $24.91 billion (31 December 2017 est.)
$25.05 billion (31 December 2016 est.)
country comparison to the world: 56

Debt - external: $539.4 million (31 December 2017 est.)
$425.3 million (31 December 2016 est.)
country comparison to the world: 177

Exchange rates: Turkmenistani manat (TMM) per US dollar -
4.125 (2017 est.)
3.5 (2016 est.)
3.5 (2015 est.)
3.5 (2014 est.)
2.85 (2013 est.)

ENERGY

Electricity access: *electrification - total population:* 100% (2020)

Electricity: *installed generating capacity:* 5.205 million kW (2020 est.)
consumption: 15,090,300,000 kWh (2019 est.)
exports: 3.2 billion kWh (2019 est.)
imports: 0 kWh (2019 est.)
transmission/distribution losses: 2.892 billion kWh (2019 est.)

Electricity generation sources: *fossil fuels:* 100% of total installed capacity (2020 est.)

Petroleum: *total petroleum production:* 235,300 bbl/day (2021 est.)
refined petroleum consumption: 153,400 bbl/day (2019 est.)
crude oil and lease condensate exports: 59,900 bbl/day (2018 est.)
crude oil and lease condensate imports: 0 bbl/day (2018 est.)
crude oil estimated reserves: 600 million barrels (2021 est.)

Refined petroleum products - production: 191,100 bbl/day (2015 est.)
country comparison to the world: 52

Refined petroleum products - exports: 53,780 bbl/day (2015 est.)
country comparison to the world: 53

Natural gas: *production:* 83,622,908,000 cubic meters (2019 est.)
consumption: 45,398,541,000 cubic meters (2019 est.)
exports: 38,224,367,000 cubic meters (2019 est.)
imports: 0 cubic meters (2021 est.)
proven reserves: 11,326,720,000,000 cubic meters (2021 est.)

Carbon dioxide emissions: 109.037 million metric tonnes of CO2 (2019 est.)
from petroleum and other liquids: 19.977 million metric tonnes of CO2 (2019 est.)
from consumed natural gas: 89.06 million metric tonnes of CO2 (2019 est.)
country comparison to the world: 39

Energy consumption per capita: 330.507 million Btu/person (2019 est.)
country comparison to the world: 9

COMMUNICATIONS

Telephones - fixed lines: *total subscriptions:* 717,000 (2020 est.)
subscriptions per 100 inhabitants: 12 (2020 est.)
country comparison to the world: 81

Telephones - mobile cellular: *total subscriptions:* 9.377 million (2018)
subscriptions per 100 inhabitants: 162.86 (2019)
country comparison to the world: 92

Telecommunication systems: *general assessment:* the nation of Turkmenistan, which rivals only North Korea for its isolationism, continues to keep its telecom sector along with the broader populace under tight control; the country inched up just one point off the bottom of the world rankings for press and internet freedom in the most recent report from Reporters Without Borders; most social networks in the country are blocked, although locals do have access to the government-developed platform released in 2019; all internet users, however, need to identify themselves before logging on, and strict censorship over what can be viewed is in force; the end result is that Turkmenistan has one of the lowest penetration rates for internet access in the world (2022)
domestic: fixed-line nearly 12 per 100 and mobile-cellular teledensity is about 163 per 100 persons; first telecommunication satellite was launched in 2015 (2019)
international: country code - 993; linked by fiber-optic cable and microwave radio relay to other CIS republics and to other countries by leased connections to the Moscow international gateway switch; an exchange in Ashgabat switches international traffic through Turkey via Intelsat; satellite earth stations - 1 Orbita and 1 Intelsat (2018)

Broadcast media: broadcast media is government controlled and censored; 7 state-owned TV and 4 state-owned radio networks; satellite dishes and programming provide an alternative to the state-run media; officials sometimes limit access to satellite TV by removing satellite dishes

Internet country code: .tm

Internet users: *total:* 1,247,940 (July 2022 est.)
percent of population: 25.3% (July 2022 est.)
country comparison to the world: 142

Broadband - fixed subscriptions: *total:* 10,000 (2020 est.)
subscriptions per 100 inhabitants: 0.2 (2020 est.)
country comparison to the world: 180

TRANSPORTATION

National air transport system: *number of registered air carriers:* 1 (2020)
inventory of registered aircraft operated by air carriers: 27
annual passenger traffic on registered air carriers: 2,457,474 (2018)
annual freight traffic on registered air carriers: 16.92 million (2018) mt-km

Civil aircraft registration country code prefix: EZ

Airports: *total:* 26 (2021)
country comparison to the world: 126

Airports - with paved runways: *total:* 21
over 3,047 m: 1
2,438 to 3,047 m: 9
1,524 to 2,437 m: 9
914 to 1,523 m: 2 (2021)

Airports - with unpaved runways: *total:* 5
1,524 to 2,437 m: 1
under 914 m: 4 (2021)

Heliports: 1 (2021)

Pipelines: 7,500 km gas, 1501 km oil (2013)

Railways: *total:* 5,113 km (2017)
broad gauge: 5,113 km (2017) 1.520-m gauge
country comparison to the world: 38

Roadways: *total:* 58,592 km (2002)
paved: 47,577 km (2002)
unpaved: 11,015 km (2002)
country comparison to the world: 77

Waterways: 1,300 km (2011) (Amu Darya River and Kara Kum Canal are important inland waterways)
country comparison to the world: 59

Merchant marine: *total:* 73
by type: general cargo 6, oil tanker 8, other 59 (2021)
country comparison to the world: 101

Ports and terminals: *major seaport(s):* Caspian Sea - Turkmenbasy

MILITARY AND SECURITY

Military and security forces: Armed Forces of Turkmenistan: Land Forces, Navy, Air and Air Defense Forces; Federal Border Guard Service; Ministry of Internal Affairs: Internal Troops, national police (2022)

Military expenditures: 1.9% of GDP (2019 est.) (approximately $1.54 billion)

1.8% of GDP (2018 est.) (approximately $1.45 billion)
1.8% of GDP (2017 est.) (approximately $1.32 billion)
1.8% of GDP (2016 est.) (approximately $1.3 billion)
1.5% of GDP (2015 est.) (approximately $1.1 billion)
country comparison to the world: 68

Military and security service personnel strengths: information varies; estimated 30,000 active duty troops (25,000 National Army; 1,000 Navy; 4,000 Air and Air Defense Forces) (2022)

Military equipment inventories and acquisitions: the inventory for Turkmenistan's military is comprised largely of older Russian and Soviet-era weapons systems; since 2010, however, it has attempted to diversify and purchased equipment from more than a dozen countries, with Turkey as the top supplier (2022)

Military service age and obligation: 18-30 years of age for compulsory male military service; 24-month conscript service obligation (30 months for the Navy); 20 years of age for voluntary service (including females); males may enroll in military schools from age 15 (2022)

Military - note: as of 2022, Turkmenistan continued to pursue a nationalist and isolationist security policy and has declined to participate in post-Soviet military groupings such as the Collective Security Treaty Organization military alliance (CSTO) and the Shanghai Cooperation Organization (SCO); however, in September 2020, it participated in a Russian-led multinational military exercise held in southern Russia's Astrakhan region alongside Russian, Chinese, Pakistani, Kazakh, Kyrgyz, Tajik, Uzbek, Mongolian, Syrian, Iranian, Egyptian, Belarusian, Turkish, Armenian, and Azerbaijani contingents

as of 2022, Turkmenistan continued efforts to improve its naval capabilities on the Caspian Sea, including expanding ship building capabilities and adding larger vessels to the Navy's inventory; in 2018, it opened its first naval shipyard and in August 2021, the Navy commissioned its largest warship, a corvette that was jointly constructed with Turkey

TRANSNATIONAL ISSUES

Disputes - international: *Turkmenistan-Azerbaijan:* in January 2021, the two countries reached a preliminary agreement on the joint exploration of an undersea hydrocarbon field containing oil and natural gas in the Caspian Sea
Turkmenistan-Iran: none identified
Turkmenistan-Kazakhstan: Kazakhstan and Turkmenistan signed a treaty on the delimitation and demarcation process in 2001; field demarcation of the boundaries with Kazakhstan commenced in 2005; Turkmenistan and Kazakhstan agreed to their border in the Caspian Sea in 2014
Turkmenistan-Kazakhstan-Uzbekistan: in 2017, the three countries signed an agreement of the junction of their borders
Turkmenistan-Uzbekistan: cotton monoculture in Uzbekistan and Turkmenistan creates water-sharing difficulties for Amu Darya river states; in 2021, the two countries reached an agreement to create a joint intergovernmental commission to oversee water management

Refugees and internally displaced persons: *stateless persons:* 4,107 (mid-year 2021)

Trafficking in persons: *current situation:* Turkmenistan is a source, and to a much lesser degree, destination country for men, women, and children who are subjected to forced labor and sex trafficking; Turkmen in search of work in other countries are forced to work in textile sweatshops, construction, and domestic service; some Turkmen women and girls are sex trafficked abroad; Turkey is the primary trafficking destination, followed by Russia, India, and other countries in the Middle East, South and Central Asia, and Europe; labor trafficking occurs within Turkmenistan, particularly in the construction industry; government officials require employees in private sector institutions, soldiers, and public sector workers to pick cotton without payment under the threat of penalty, such as dismissal, reduced work hours, or salary deductions to meet government-imposed quotas for the cotton harvest
tier rating: Tier 3 — Turkmenistan does not fully meet the minimum standards for the elimination of trafficking and is not making significant efforts to do so; the government approved the 2020-2022 national action plan, continued antitrafficking awareness campaigns, worked with international organizations on combating trafficking, provided training to its diplomatic corps on human trafficking, and identified potential trafficking victims at the international airport; however, the government used forced labor in the cotton harvest and public works projects; no officials were held accountable for their role in trafficking crimes; authorities did not prosecute or convict any traffickers; no victims were identified and offered protection or assistance programs (2020)

Illicit drugs: transit country for Afghan opiates to Turkish, Russian, and European markets, either directly from Afghanistan or through Iran; not a major producer or source country for illegal drugs or precursor chemicals

TURKS AND CAICOS ISLANDS

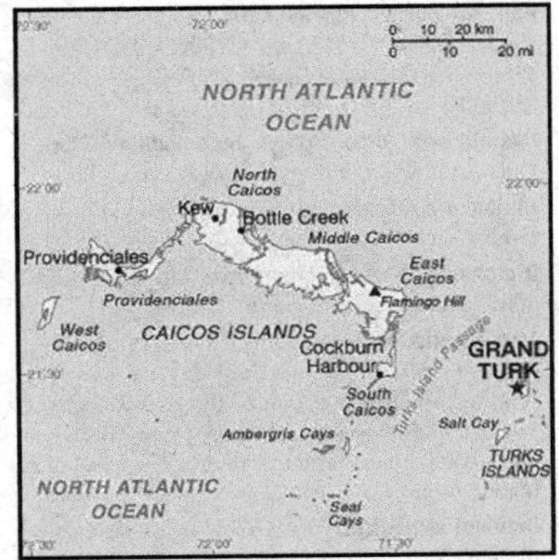

INTRODUCTION

Background: The islands were part of the UK's Jamaican colony until 1962, when they assumed the status of a separate Crown colony upon Jamaica's independence. The governor of The Bahamas oversaw affairs from 1965 to 1973. With Bahamian independence, the islands received a separate governor in 1973. Although independence was agreed upon for 1982, the policy was reversed and the islands remain a British overseas territory. Grand Turk island suffered extensive damage from Hurricane Maria on 22 September 2017 resulting in loss of power and communications, as well as damage to housing and businesses.

GEOGRAPHY

Location: two island groups in the North Atlantic Ocean, southeast of The Bahamas, north of Haiti; note - although the Turks and Caicos Islands do not border the Caribbean Sea, geopolitically they are often designated as being Caribbean

Geographic coordinates: 21 45 N, 71 35 W

Map references: Central America and the Caribbean

Area: *total:* 948 sq km
land: 948 sq km
water: 0 sq km
country comparison to the world: 185

Area - comparative: 2.5 times the size of Washington, DC

Land boundaries: *total:* 0 km

Coastline: 389 km

Maritime claims: *territorial sea:* 12 nm
exclusive fishing zone: 200 nm

Climate: tropical; marine; moderated by trade winds; sunny and relatively dry

Terrain: low, flat limestone; extensive marshes and mangrove swamps

Elevation: *highest point:* Blue Hill on Providenciales and Flamingo Hill on East Caicos 48 m
lowest point: Caribbean Sea 0 m

Natural resources: spiny lobster, conch

Land use: *agricultural land:* 1.1% (2018 est.)
arable land: 1.1% (2018 est.)
permanent crops: 0% (2018 est.)
permanent pasture: 0% (2018 est.)
forest: 36.2% (2018 est.)
other: 62.7% (2018 est.)

Irrigated land: 0 sq km (2012)

Population distribution: eight of the thirty islands are inhabited; the island of Providenciales is the most populated, but the most densely populated is Grand Turk

Natural hazards: frequent hurricanes

Geography - note: include eight large islands and numerous smaller cays, islets, and reefs; only two of the Caicos Islands and six of the Turks group are inhabited

PEOPLE AND SOCIETY

Population: 58,286 (2022 est.)
country comparison to the world: 205

Nationality: *noun:* none
adjective: none

Ethnic groups: Black 87.6%, White 7.9%, mixed 2.5%, East Indian 1.3%, other 0.7% (2006 est.)

Languages: English (official)

Religions: Protestant 72.8% (Baptist 35.8%, Church of God 11.7%, Anglican 10%, Methodist 9.3%, Seventh Day Adventist 6%), Roman Catholic 11.4%, Jehovah's Witness 1.8%, other 14% (2006 est.)

Age structure: *0-14 years:* 21.33% (male 6,077/female 5,852)
15-24 years: 13.19% (male 3,689/female 3,687)
25-54 years: 52.51% (male 14,729/female 14,637)
55-64 years: 7.81% (male 2,297/female 2,069)
65 years and over: 5.17% (male 1,364/female 1,525) (2020 est.)

Median age: *total:* 34.6 years
male: 34.9 years
female: 34.4 years (2020 est.)
country comparison to the world: 90

Population growth rate: 1.86% (2022 est.)
country comparison to the world: 47

Birth rate: 13.54 births/1,000 population (2022 est.)
country comparison to the world: 135

Death rate: 3.5 deaths/1,000 population (2022 est.)
country comparison to the world: 219

Net migration rate: 8.58 migrant(s)/1,000 population (2022 est.)
country comparison to the world: 10

Population distribution: eight of the thirty islands are inhabited; the island of Providenciales is the most populated, but the most densely populated is Grand Turk

Urbanization: *urban population:* 94% of total population (2022)
rate of urbanization: 1.46% annual rate of change (2020-25 est.)

Major urban areas - population: 5,000 GRAND TURK (capital) (2018)

Sex ratio: *at birth:* 1.05 male(s)/female
0-14 years: 1.04 male(s)/female
15-24 years: 1.01 male(s)/female
25-54 years: 1 male(s)/female
55-64 years: 1.1 male(s)/female
65 years and over: 0.74 male(s)/female
total population: 1.01 male(s)/female (2022 est.)

Infant mortality rate: *total:* 11.59 deaths/1,000 live births
male: 14.54 deaths/1,000 live births
female: 8.5 deaths/1,000 live births (2022 est.)
country comparison to the world: 124

Life expectancy at birth: *total population:* 80.82 years
male: 78.07 years
female: 83.71 years (2022 est.)
country comparison to the world: 44

Total fertility rate: 1.7 children born/woman (2022 est.)
country comparison to the world: 169

Drinking water source: *improved: total:* 94.3% of population
unimproved: total: 5.7% of population (2017)

Sanitation facility access: *improved: total:* 88% of population
unimproved: total: 12% of population (2017)

Education expenditures: 3.5% of GDP (2019 est.)
country comparison to the world: 128

School life expectancy (primary to tertiary education): *total:* 9 years

People - note: destination and transit point for illegal Haitian immigrants bound for the Bahamas and the US

ENVIRONMENT

Environment - current issues: limited natural freshwater resources, private cisterns collect rainwater

Air pollutants: *carbon dioxide emissions:* 0.22 megatons (2016 est.)

Climate: tropical; marine; moderated by trade winds; sunny and relatively dry

Land use: *agricultural land:* 1.1% (2018 est.)
arable land: 1.1% (2018 est.)
permanent crops: 0% (2018 est.)
permanent pasture: 0% (2018 est.)
forest: 36.2% (2018 est.)
other: 62.7% (2018 est.)

Urbanization: *urban population:* 94% of total population (2022)
rate of urbanization: 1.46% annual rate of change (2020-25 est.)

Revenue from forest resources: *forest revenues:* 0% of GDP (2018 est.)
country comparison to the world: 199

Revenue from coal: *coal revenues:* 0% of GDP (2018 est.)
country comparison to the world: 180

GOVERNMENT

Country name: *conventional long form:* none
conventional short form: Turks and Caicos Islands
abbreviation: TCI
etymology: the Turks Islands are named after the Turk's cap cactus (native to the islands and appearing on the flag and coat of arms), while the Caicos Islands derive from the native term "caya hico" meaning "string of islands"

Government type: parliamentary democracy

Dependency status: overseas territory of the UK

Capital: *name:* Grand Turk (Cockburn Town)
geographic coordinates: 21 28 N, 71 08 W
time difference: UTC-5 (same time as Washington, DC, during Standard Time)
etymology: named after Sir Francis COCKBURN, who served as governor of the Bahamas from 1837 to 1844

Administrative divisions: none (overseas territory of the UK)

Independence: none (overseas territory of the UK)

National holiday: Birthday of Queen ELIZABETH II, usually celebrated the Monday after the second Saturday in June

Constitution: *history:* several previous; latest signed 7 August 2012, effective 15 October 2012 (The Turks and Caicos Constitution Order 2011)
amendments: NA

Legal system: mixed legal system of English common law and civil law

Citizenship: see United Kingdom

Suffrage: 18 years of age; universal

Executive branch: *chief of state:* King CHARLES III (since 8 September 2022); represented by Governor Nigel DAKIN (since 15 July 2019)
head of government: Premier Washington MISICK (since 19 February 2021)
cabinet: Cabinet appointed by the governor from among members of the House of Assembly
elections/appointments: the monarch is hereditary; governor appointed by the monarch; following legislative elections, the leader of the majority party is appointed premier by the governor

Legislative branch: *description:* unicameral House of Assembly (21 seats; 15 members in multi-seat constituencies and a single all-islands constituency directly elected by simple majority vote, 1 member nominated by the premier and appointed by the governor, 1 nominated by the opposition party leader and appointed by the governor, and 2 from the Turks and Caicos Islands Civic Society directly appointed by the governor, and 2 ex-officio members; members serve 4-year terms)
elections:
last held on 19 February 2021 (next to be held in 2025)
election results:
percent of vote - NA; seats by party - PNP 14, PDM 1; composition as of mid-2022 (elected members) - men 12, women 3; percent of women 20%

Judicial branch: *highest court(s):* Supreme Court (consists of the chief justice and other judges, as determined by the governor); Court of Appeal (consists of the court president and 2 justices); note - appeals beyond the Supreme Court are referred to the Judicial Committee of the Privy Council (in London)
judge selection and term of office: Supreme Court and Appeals Court judges appointed by the governor in accordance with the Judicial Service Commission, a 3-member body of high-level judicial officials; Supreme Court judges serve until mandatory retirement at age 65, but terms can be extended to age 70; Appeals Court judge tenure determined by individual terms of appointment
subordinate courts: magistrates' courts

Political parties and leaders: People's Democratic Movement or PDM [Edwin ASTWOOD]
Progressive National Party or PNP [Washington MISICK]

International organization participation: Caricom (associate), CDB, Interpol (subbureau), UPU

Diplomatic representation in the US: none (overseas territory of the UK)

Diplomatic representation from the US: *embassy:* none (overseas territory of the UK)

Flag description: blue with the flag of the UK in the upper hoist-side quadrant and the colonial shield centered on the outer half of the flag; the shield is yellow and displays a conch shell, a spiny lobster, and Turk's cap cactus - three common elements of the islands' biota

National symbol(s): conch shell, Turk's cap cactus

National anthem: *name:* "This Land of Ours"
lyrics/music: Conrad HOWELL
note: serves as a local anthem; as an overseas territory of the UK, "God Save the King" is the official anthem (see United Kingdom)

ECONOMY

Economic overview: The Turks and Caicos economy is based on tourism, offshore financial services, and fishing. Most capital goods and food for domestic consumption are imported. The US is the leading source of tourists, accounting for more than three-quarters of the more than 1 million visitors that arrive annually. Three-quarters of the visitors come by ship. Major sources of government revenue also include fees from offshore financial activities and customs receipts.

Real GDP (purchasing power parity): $820 million (2020 est.)
$1.12 billion (2019 est.)
$1.06 billion (2018 est.)
note: data are in 2017 dollars
country comparison to the world: 208

Real GDP growth rate: 5.3% (2018 est.)
4.3% (2017 est.)
4.4% (2016 est.)
country comparison to the world: 40

Real GDP per capita: $21,100 (2020 est.)
$29,300 (2019 est.)
$28,200 (2018 est.)
note: data are in 2017 dollars
country comparison to the world: 85

GDP (official exchange rate): $1.02 billion (2018 est.)

Inflation rate (consumer prices): 4% (2017 est.)
0.7% (2016 est.)
country comparison to the world: 168

GDP - composition, by sector of origin: *agriculture:* 0.5% (2017 est.)
industry: 8.9% (2017 est.)
services: 90.6% (2017 est.)

GDP - composition, by end use: *household consumption:* 49% (2017 est.)
government consumption: 21.5% (2017 est.)
investment in fixed capital: 16.5% (2017 est.)
investment in inventories: -0.1% (2017 est.)
exports of goods and services: 69.5% (2017 est.)
imports of goods and services: -56.4% (2017 est.)

Agricultural products: corn, beans, cassava (manioc, tapioca), citrus fruits; fish

Industries: tourism, offshore financial services

Industrial production growth rate: 3% (2017 est.)
country comparison to the world: 106

Labor force: 4,848 (1990 est.)
country comparison to the world: 219

Labor force - by occupation: *note:* about 33% in government and 20% in agriculture and fishing; significant numbers in tourism, financial, and other services

Unemployment rate: 10% (1997 est.)
country comparison to the world: 147

Budget: *revenues:* 247.3 million (2017 est.)
expenditures: 224.3 million (2017 est.)

Fiscal year: calendar year

Exports: $830 million (2018 est.) note: data are in current year dollars
country comparison to the world: 181

Exports - partners: France 31%, United States 16%, Zambia 13%, Singapore 9%, Republic of the Congo 8% (2019)

Exports - commodities: plastic building materials, stone processing machinery, iron structures, crustaceans, integrated circuits (2019)

Imports: $540 million (2018 est.) note: data are in current year dollars
country comparison to the world: 201

Imports - partners: United States 76% (2019)

Imports - commodities: refined petroleum, cars, jewelry, furniture, soybeans (2019)

Exchange rates: the US dollar is used

ENERGY

Electricity access: *electrification - total population:* 100% (2020)

Electricity: *installed generating capacity:* 85,000 kW (2020 est.)
consumption: 231.618 million kWh (2019 est.)
exports: 0 kWh (2020 est.)
imports: 0 kWh (2020 est.)
transmission/distribution losses: 12.5 million kWh (2019 est.)

Electricity generation sources: *fossil fuels:* 100% of total installed capacity (2020 est.)

Petroleum: *total petroleum production:* 0 bbl/day (2021 est.)
refined petroleum consumption: 1,600 bbl/day (2019 est.)

Refined petroleum products - imports: 1,369 bbl/day (2015 est.)
country comparison to the world: 196

Carbon dioxide emissions: 245,000 metric tonnes of CO2 (2019 est.)
from petroleum and other liquids: 245,000 metric tonnes of CO2 (2019 est.)
country comparison to the world: 200

Energy consumption per capita: 0 Btu/person (2019 est.)
country comparison to the world: 210

COMMUNICATIONS

Telephones - fixed lines: *total subscriptions:* 4,000 (2020 est.)
subscriptions per 100 inhabitants: 10 (2020 est.)
country comparison to the world: 206

Telecommunication systems: *general assessment:* fully digital system with international direct dialing; broadband access; expanded FttP (Fiber to the Home) markets; LTE expansion points to investment and focus on data; regulatory development; telecommunication contributes to greatly to GDP (2020)
domestic: full range of services available; GSM wireless service available; fixed-line teledensity roughly 11 per 100 persons (2019)
international: country code - 1-649; landing point for the ARCOS fiber-optic telecommunications submarine cable providing connectivity to South and Central America, parts of the Caribbean, and the US; satellite earth station - 1 Intelsat (Atlantic Ocean) (2020)

Broadcast media: no local terrestrial TV stations, broadcasts from the Bahamas can be received and multi-channel cable and satellite TV services are available; government-run radio network operates alongside private broadcasters with a total of about 15 stations

Internet country code: .tc

TRANSPORTATION

National air transport system: *number of registered air carriers:* 3 (2020)
inventory of registered aircraft operated by air carriers: 22

Civil aircraft registration country code prefix: VQ-T

Airports: *total:* 8 (2021)
country comparison to the world: 164

Airports - with paved runways: *total:* 6
2,438 to 3,047 m: 1
1,524 to 2,437 m: 3
914 to 1,523 m: 1
under 914 m: 1 (2021)

Airports - with unpaved runways: *total:* 2
under 914 m: 2 (2021)

Roadways: *total:* 121 km (2003)
paved: 24 km (2003)
*unpaved:*97 km (2003)
country comparison to the world: 212

Merchant marine: *total:* 3
by type: general cargo 1, other 2 (2021)
country comparison to the world: 172

Ports and terminals: *major seaport(s):* Cockburn Harbour, Grand Turk, Providenciales

MILITARY AND SECURITY

Military - note: defense is the responsibility of the UK

TRANSNATIONAL ISSUES

Disputes - international: none identified

Illicit drugs: transshipment point for South American narcotics destined for the US and Europe

TUVALU

INTRODUCTION

Background: The islands were first populated by voyagers from either Samoa or Tonga in the first millennium A.D., and Tuvalu provided a stepping-stone for various Polynesian communities that subsequently settled in Melanesia and Micronesia. Tuvalu eventually came under Samoan and Tongan spheres of influence although proximity to Micronesia allowed some Micronesian communities to flourish in Tuvalu, in particular on Nui Atoll. In the late 1700s and early 1800s, Tuvalu was visited by a series of American, British, Dutch, and Russian ships. The islands were named the Ellice Islands in 1819. The first Christian missionaries arrived in 1861, eventually converting most of the population, and around the same time, several hundred Tuvaluans were kidnapped by people

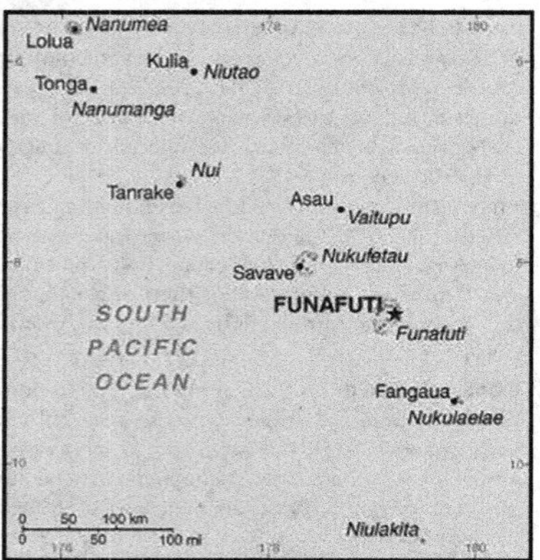

purporting to be missionaries and sent to work on plantations in Peru and Hawaii.

The UK declared a protectorate over the Ellice Islands in 1892 and merged it with the Micronesian Gilbert Islands. The Gilbert and Ellice Islands Protectorate became a colony in 1916. During World War II, the US set up military bases on a few islands, and in 1943, after Japan captured many of the northern Gilbert Islands, the UK transferred administration of the colony southward to Funafuti. After the war, Tarawa in the Gilbert Islands was once again made the colony's capital and the center of power was firmly in the Gilbert Islands, including the colony's only secondary school. Amid growing tensions with the Gilbertese, Tuvaluans voted to secede from the colony in 1974, were granted self-rule in 1975, and gained independence in 1978 as Tuvalu. In 1979, the US relinquished its claims to Tuvaluan islands in a treaty of friendship.

The Tuvalu Trust Fund was established in 1987 to provide a longterm economic future for the country. In 2000, Tuvalu negotiated a contract leasing its Internet domain name ".tv" for $50 million in royalties over a 12-year period. The contract was renewed in 2011 for a ten-year period. Tuvalu's isolation means it sees few tourists; in 2020, Funafuti International Airport had four weekly flights -three to Suva, Fiji, and one to Tarawa. Tuvalu is highly vulnerable to the effects of climate change; in 2018, sea levels in Funafuti were rising twice as fast as global averages.

GEOGRAPHY

Location: Oceania, island group consisting of nine coral atolls in the South Pacific Ocean, about half way from Hawaii to Australia

Geographic coordinates: 8 00 S, 178 00 E

Map references: Oceania

Area: *total:* 26 sq km
land: 26 sq km
water: 0 sq km
country comparison to the world: 237

Area - comparative: 0.1 times the size of Washington, DC

Land boundaries: *total:* 0 km

Coastline: 24 km

Maritime claims: *territorial sea:* 12 nm
contiguous zone: 24 nm
exclusive economic zone: 200 nm

Climate: tropical; moderated by easterly trade winds (March to November); westerly gales and heavy rain (November to March)

Terrain: low-lying and narrow coral atolls

Elevation: *highest point:* unnamed location 5 m
lowest point: Pacific Ocean 0 m
mean elevation: 2 m

Natural resources: fish, coconut (copra)

Land use: *agricultural land:* 60% (2018 est.)
arable land: 0% (2018 est.)
permanent crops: 60% (2018 est.)
permanent pasture: 0% (2018 est.)
forest: 33.3% (2018 est.)
other: 6.7% (2018 est.)

Irrigated land: 0 sq km (2012)

Population distribution: over half of the population resides on the atoll of Funafuti

Natural hazards: severe tropical storms are usually rare, but in 1997 there were three cyclones; low levels of islands make them sensitive to changes in sea level

Geography - note: one of the smallest and most remote countries on Earth; six of the nine coral atolls - Nanumea, Nui, Vaitupu, Nukufetau, Funafuti, and Nukulaelae - have lagoons open to the ocean; Nanumaya and Niutao have landlocked lagoons; Niulakita does not have a lagoon

PEOPLE AND SOCIETY

Population: 11,544 (2022 est.)
country comparison to the world: 221

Nationality: *noun:* Tuvaluan(s)
adjective: Tuvaluan

Ethnic groups: Tuvaluan 97%, Tuvaluan/I-Kiribati 1.6%, Tuvaluan/other 0.8%, other 0.6% (2017 est.)

Languages: Tuvaluan (official), English (official), Samoan, Kiribati (on the island of Nui)

Religions: Protestant 92.7% (Congregational Christian Church of Tuvalu 85.9%, Brethren 2.8%, Seventh Day Adventist 2.5%, Assemblies of God 1.5%), Baha'i 1.5%, Jehovah's Witness 1.5%, other 3.9%, none or refused 0.4% (2017 est.)

Age structure: *0-14 years:* 29.42% (male 1,711/female 1,626)
15-24 years: 16.55% (male 986/female 925)
25-54 years: 37.17% (male 2,157/female 2,059)
55-64 years: 9.25% (male 451/female 617)
65 years and over: 7.21% (male 307/female 525) (2022 est.)

Median age: *total:* 26.6 years
male: 25.6 years
female: 27.6 years (2020 est.)
country comparison to the world: 152

Population growth rate: 0.83% (2022 est.)
country comparison to the world: 111

Birth rate: 22.7 births/1,000 population (2022 est.)
country comparison to the world: 53

Death rate: 7.97 deaths/1,000 population (2022 est.)
country comparison to the world: 92

Net migration rate: -6.41 migrant(s)/1,000 population (2022 est.)
country comparison to the world: 212

Population distribution: over half of the population resides on the atoll of Funafuti

Urbanization: *urban population:* 65.5% of total population (2022)
rate of urbanization: 2.08% annual rate of change (2020-25 est.)

Major urban areas - population: 7,000 FUNAFUTI (capital) (2018)

Sex ratio: *at birth:* 1.05 male(s)/female
0-14 years: 1.05 male(s)/female
15-24 years: 1.07 male(s)/female
25-54 years: 1.02 male(s)/female
55-64 years: 0.73 male(s)/female
65 years and over: 0.53 male(s)/female
total population: 0.98 male(s)/female (2022 est.)

Infant mortality rate: *total:* 28.92 deaths/1,000 live births
male: 32.55 deaths/1,000 live births
female: 25.09 deaths/1,000 live births (2022 est.)
country comparison to the world: 56

Life expectancy at birth: *total population:* 68.38 years
male: 65.96 years
female: 70.92 years (2022 est.)
country comparison to the world: 182

Total fertility rate: 2.83 children born/woman (2022 est.)
country comparison to the world: 54

Drinking water source: *improved: urban:* 100% of population
rural: 100% of population
total: 100% of population

Current health expenditure: 24% of GDP (2019)

Physicians density: 1.19 physicians/1,000 population (2020)

Sanitation facility access: *improved: urban:* 91.8% of population
rural: 91% of population
total: 91.5% of population
unimproved: urban: 9.2% of population
rural: 9% of population
total: 8.5% of population (2017 est.)

Obesity - adult prevalence rate: 51.6% (2016)
country comparison to the world: 5

Alcohol consumption per capita: *total:* 0.93 liters of pure alcohol (2019 est.)
beer: 0.01 liters of pure alcohol (2019 est.)
wine: 0.69 liters of pure alcohol (2019 est.)
spirits: 0.22 liters of pure alcohol (2019 est.)
other alcohols: 0 liters of pure alcohol (2019 est.)
country comparison to the world: 154

Tobacco use: *total:* 35.6% (2020 est.)
male: 49.8% (2020 est.)
female: 21.3% (2020 est.)
country comparison to the world: 13

Unemployment, youth ages 15-24: *total:* 20.6%
male: 9.8%
female: 45.9% (2016)

ENVIRONMENT

Environment - current issues: water needs met by catchment systems; the use of sand as a building material has led to beachhead erosion; deforestation; damage to coral reefs from increasing ocean temperatures and acidification; rising sea levels threaten water table; in 2000, the government appealed to Australia and New Zealand to take in Tuvaluans if rising sea levels should make evacuation necessary

Environment - international agreements: *party to:* Biodiversity, Climate Change, Climate Change-Kyoto Protocol, Climate Change-Paris Agreement, Desertification, Hazardous Wastes, Law of the Sea, Ozone Layer Protection, Ship Pollution, Whaling
signed, but not ratified: Comprehensive Nuclear Test Ban

Air pollutants: *particulate matter emissions:* 11.42 micrograms per cubic meter (2016 est.)
carbon dioxide emissions: 0.01 megatons (2016 est.)
methane emissions: 0.01 megatons (2020 est.)

Climate: tropical; moderated by easterly trade winds (March to November); westerly gales and heavy rain (November to March)

Land use: *agricultural land:* 60% (2018 est.)
arable land: 0% (2018 est.)
permanent crops: 60% (2018 est.)
permanent pasture: 0% (2018 est.)
forest: 33.3% (2018 est.)
other: 6.7% (2018 est.)

Urbanization: *urban population:* 65.5% of total population (2022)
rate of urbanization: 2.08% annual rate of change (2020-25 est.)

Revenue from forest resources: *forest revenues:* 0% of GDP (2018 est.)
country comparison to the world: 200

Waste and recycling: *municipal solid waste generated annually:* 3,989 tons (2011 est.)
municipal solid waste recycled annually: 598 tons (2013 est.)
percent of municipal solid waste recycled: 15% (2013 est.)

Total renewable water resources: 0 cubic meters (2017 est.)

GOVERNMENT

Country name: *conventional long form:* none
conventional short form: Tuvalu
local long form: none
local short form: Tuvalu
former: Ellice Islands
etymology: "tuvalu" means "group of eight" or "eight standing together" referring to the country's eight traditionally inhabited islands

Government type: parliamentary democracy under a constitutional monarchy; a Commonwealth realm

Capital: *name:* Funafuti; note - the capital is an atoll of some 29 islets; administrative offices are in Vaiaku Village on Fongafale Islet
geographic coordinates: 8 31 S, 179 13 E
time difference: UTC+12 (17 hours ahead of Washington, DC, during Standard Time)
etymology: the atoll is named after a founding ancestor chief, Funa, from the island of Samoa

Administrative divisions: 7 island councils and 1 town council*; Funafuti*, Nanumaga, Nanumea, Niutao, Nui, Nukufetau, Nukulaelae, Vaitupu

Independence: 1 October 1978 (from the UK)

National holiday: Independence Day, 1 October (1978)

Constitution: *history:* previous 1978 (at independence); latest effective 1 October 1986
amendments: proposed by the House of Assembly; passage requires at least two-thirds majority vote by the Assembly membership in the final reading; amended 2007, 2010, 2013; note - in 2016, the United Nations Development Program and the Tuvaluan Government initiated a review of the country's constitution, which was ongoing as of early 2021

Legal system: mixed legal system of English common law and local customary law

International law organization participation: has not submitted an ICJ jurisdiction declaration; non-party state to the ICCt

Citizenship: *citizenship by birth:* yes
citizenship by descent only: yes; for a child born abroad, at least one parent must be a citizen of Tuvalu
dual citizenship recognized: yes
residency requirement for naturalization: na

Suffrage: 18 years of age; universal

Executive branch: *chief of state:* King CHARLES III (since 8 September 2022); represented by Governor General Tofiga Vaevalu FALANI (since 29 August 2021)
head of government: Prime Minister Kausea NATANO (since 19 September 2019)
cabinet: Cabinet appointed by the governor general on recommendation of the prime minister
elections/appointments: the monarchy is hereditary; governor general appointed by the monarch on recommendation of the prime minister; prime minister and deputy prime minister elected by and from members of House of Assembly following parliamentary elections
election results:
Kausea NATANO elected prime minister by House of Assembly; House of Assembly vote count on 19 September 2019 - 10 to 6

Legislative branch: *description:* unicameral House of Assembly or Fale I Fono (16 seats; members directly elected in single- and multiseat constituencies by simple majority vote to serve 4-year terms)
elections:
last held on 9 September 2019 (next to be held on September 2023)
election results:
percent of vote - NA; seats - independent 16 (9 members reelected)

Judicial branch: *highest court(s):* Court of Appeal (consists of the chief justice and not less than 3 appeals judges); High Court (consists of the chief justice); appeals beyond the Court of Appeal are heard by the Judicial Committee of the Privy Council (in London)
judge selection and term of office: Court of Appeal judges appointed by the governor general on the advice of the Cabinet; judge tenure based on terms of appointment; High Court chief justice appointed by the governor general on the advice of the Cabinet; chief justice serves for life; other judges appointed by the governor general on the advice of the Cabinet after consultation with chief justice; judge tenure set by terms of appointment
subordinate courts: magistrates' courts; island courts; land courts

Political parties and leaders: there are no political parties, but members of parliament usually align themselves in informal groupings

International organization participation: ACP, ADB, AOSIS, C, FAO, IBRD, IDA, IFAD, IFRCS (observer), ILO, IMF, IMO, IOC, ITU, OPCW, PIF, Sparteca, SPC, UN, UNCTAD, UNESCO, UNIDO, UPU, WHO, WIPO, WMO

Diplomatic representation in the US: *chief of mission:* Ambassador Samuelu LALONIU (since 21 July 2017)
note - also Permanent Representative to UN
telephone: [1] (212) 490-0534
FAX: [1] (212) 808-4975
email address and website: email - tuvalumission.un@gmail.com
web address - https://www.un.int/tuvalu/about
embassy: 685 Third Avenue, Suite 1104, New York, NY 10017
note - the Tuvalu Permanent Mission to the UN serves as the Embassy

Diplomatic representation from the US: *embassy:* the US does not have an embassy in Tuvalu; the US Ambassador to Fiji is accredited to Tuvalu

Flag description: light blue with the flag of the UK in the upper hoist-side quadrant; the outer half of the flag represents a map of the country with nine yellow, five-pointed stars on a blue field symbolizing the nine atolls in the ocean

National symbol(s): maneapa (native meeting house); national colors: light blue, yellow

National anthem: *name:* "Tuvalu mo te Atua" (Tuvalu for the Almighty)
lyrics/music: Afaese MANOA
note: adopted 1978; the anthem's name is also the nation's motto

ECONOMY

Economic overview: Tuvalu consists of a densely populated, scattered group of nine coral atolls with poor soil. Only eight of the atolls are inhabited. It is one of the smallest countries in the world, with its highest point at 4.6 meters above sea level. The country is isolated, almost entirely dependent on imports, particularly of food and fuel, and vulnerable to climate change and rising sea levels, which pose significant challenges to development.

The public sector dominates economic activity. Tuvalu has few natural resources, except for its fisheries. Earnings from fish exports and fishing licenses for Tuvalu's territorial waters are a significant source of government revenue. In 2013, revenue from fishing licenses doubled and totaled more than 45% of GDP.

Official aid from foreign development partners has also increased. Tuvalu has substantial assets abroad. The Tuvalu Trust Fund, an international trust fund established in 1987 by development partners, has grown to $104 million (A$141 million) in 2014 and is an important cushion for meeting shortfalls in the government's budget. While remittances are another substantial source of income, the value of remittances has declined since the 2008-09 global financial crisis, but has stabilized at nearly $4 million per year. The financial impact of climate change and the cost of climate related adaptation projects is one of many concerns for the nation.

Real GDP (purchasing power parity): $50 million (2020 est.)
$50 million (2019 est.)
$50 million (2018 est.)
note: data are in 2017 dollars
country comparison to the world: 225

Real GDP growth rate: 3.2% (2017 est.)
3% (2016 est.)
9.1% (2015 est.)

country comparison to the world: 93

Real GDP per capita: $4,400 (2020 est.)
$4,300 (2019 est.)
$3,900 (2018 est.)
note: data are in 2017 dollars
country comparison to the world: 179

GDP (official exchange rate): $40 million (2017 est.)

Inflation rate (consumer prices): 4.1% (2017 est.)
3.5% (2016 est.)
country comparison to the world: 171

GDP - composition, by sector of origin: *agriculture:* 24.5% (2012 est.)
industry: 5.6% (2012 est.)
services: 70% (2012 est.)

GDP - composition, by end use: *government consumption:* 87% (2016 est.)
investment in fixed capital: 24.3% (2016 est.)
exports of goods and services: 43.7% (2016 est.)
imports of goods and services: -66.1% (2016 est.)

Agricultural products: coconuts, vegetables, tropical fruit, bananas, roots/tubers nes, pork, poultry, eggs, pig fat, pig offals

Industries: fishing

Industrial production growth rate: -26.1% (2012 est.)
country comparison to the world: 202

Labor force: 3,615 (2004 est.)
country comparison to the world: 224

Labor force - by occupation: *note:* most people make a living through exploitation of the sea, reefs, and atolls - and through overseas remittances (mostly from workers in the phosphate industry and sailors)

Unemployment, youth ages 15-24: *total:* 20.6%
male: 9.8%
female: 45.9% (2016)
country comparison to the world: 74

Population below poverty line: 26.3% (2010 est.)

Gini Index coefficient - distribution of family income: 39.1 (2010 est.)
country comparison to the world: 67

Budget: *revenues:* 42.68 million (2013 est.)
expenditures: 32.46 million (2012 est.)
note: revenue data include Official Development Assistance from Australia

Budget surplus (+) or deficit (-): 25.6% (of GDP) (2013 est.)
country comparison to the world: 1

Public debt: 37% of GDP (2017 est.)
47.2% of GDP (2016 est.)
country comparison to the world: 142

Taxes and other revenues: 106.7% (of GDP) (2013 est.)
note: revenue data include Official Development Assistance from Australia
country comparison to the world: 1

Fiscal year: calendar year

Current account balance: $2 million (2017 est.)
$8 million (2016 est.)
country comparison to the world: 64

Exports: $10 million (2019 est.) note: data are in current year dollars
$10 million (2018 est.) note: data are in current year dollars
country comparison to the world: 218

Exports - partners: Thailand 50%, Indonesia 40% (2019)

Exports - commodities: fish, ships, coins, metal-clad products, electrical power accessories (2019)

Imports: $70 million (2019 est.) note: data are in current year dollars
$60 million (2018 est.) note: data are in current year dollars
country comparison to the world: 220

Imports - partners: China 32%, Japan 29%, Fiji 23%, New Zealand 6% (2019)

Imports - commodities: refined petroleum, fishing ships, tug boats, other ships, iron structures (2019)

Exchange rates: Tuvaluan dollars or Australian dollars (AUD) per US dollar -
1.311 (2017 est.)
1.3442 (2016 est.)

ENERGY

Electricity access: *electrification - total population:* 100% (2020)

Coal: *production:* 0 metric tons (2020 est.)
consumption: 0 metric tons (2020 est.)
exports: 0 metric tons (2020 est.)
imports: 0 metric tons (2020 est.)

Refined petroleum products - production: 0 bbl/day (2014 est.)
country comparison to the world: 211

Refined petroleum products - exports: 0 bbl/day
country comparison to the world: 212

Natural gas: *production:* 0 cubic meters (2021 est.)
consumption: 0 cubic meters (2021 est.)
exports: 0 cubic meters (2021 est.)
imports: 0 cubic meters (2021 est.)
proven reserves: 0 cubic meters (2021 est.)

Carbon dioxide emissions: 0 metric tonnes of CO2 (2019 est.)
from coal and metallurgical coke: 0 metric tonnes of CO2 (2019 est.)
from consumed natural gas: 0 metric tonnes of CO2 (2019 est.)
country comparison to the world: 218

Energy consumption per capita: 0 Btu/person (2019 est.)
country comparison to the world: 211

COMMUNICATIONS

Telephones - fixed lines: *total subscriptions:* 2,000 (2020 est.)
subscriptions per 100 inhabitants: 17 (2020 est.)
country comparison to the world: 216

Telephones - mobile cellular: *total subscriptions:* 8,000 (2018)
subscriptions per 100 inhabitants: 70.36 (2019)
country comparison to the world: 219

Telecommunication systems: *general assessment:* internal communications needs met; small global scale of over 11,000 people on 9 inhabited islands; mobile subscriber penetration about 40% and broadband about 10% penetration; govt. owned and sole provider of telecommunications services; 2G widespread; the launch in 2019 of the Kacific-1 satellite will improve the telecommunication sector for the Asia Pacific region (2020)
domestic: radiotelephone communications between islands; fixed-line teledensity over 17 per 100 and mobile-cellular over 70 per 100 (2019)
international: country code - 688; international calls can be made by satellite

Broadcast media: no TV stations; many households use satellite dishes to watch foreign TV stations; 1 government-owned radio station, Radio Tuvalu, includes relays of programming from international broadcasters (2019)

Internet country code: .tv

Internet users: *total:* 5,711 (2019 est.)
percent of population: 49% (2019 est.)
country comparison to the world: 220

Broadband - fixed subscriptions: *total:* 450 (2017 est.)
subscriptions per 100 inhabitants: 4 (2017 est.)
country comparison to the world: 211

TRANSPORTATION

Civil aircraft registration country code prefix: T2

Airports: *total:* 1 (2021)
country comparison to the world: 236

Airports - with unpaved runways: *total:* 1
1,524 to 2,437 m: 1 (2021)

Roadways: *total:* 8 km (2011)
paved: 8 km (2011)
country comparison to the world: 223

Merchant marine: *total:* 245
by type: bulk carrier 22, container ship 3, general cargo 32, oil tanker 21, other 167 (2021)
country comparison to the world: 61

Ports and terminals: *major seaport(s):* Funafuti

MILITARY AND SECURITY

Military and security forces: no regular military forces; Tuvalu Police Force (Ministry of Justice, Communications, and Foreign Affairs) (2022)

Military - note: Australia provides support to the Tuvalu Police Force, including donations of patrol boats

Tuvalu has a "shiprider" agreement with the US, which allows local maritime law enforcement officers to embark on US Coast Guard (USCG) and US Navy (USN) vessels, including to board and search vessels suspected of violating laws or regulations within Tuvalu's designated exclusive economic zone (EEZ) or on the high seas; "shiprider" agreements also enable USCG personnel and USN vessels with embarked USCG law enforcement personnel to work with host nations to protect critical regional resources (2022)

TRANSNATIONAL ISSUES

Disputes - international: none identified

UGANDA

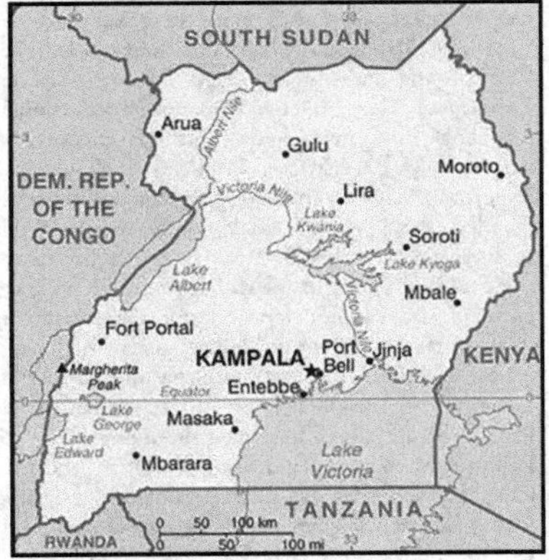

INTRODUCTION

Background: An ancient crossroads for various migrations, Uganda has as many as 65 ethnic groups that speak languages from three of Africa's four major linguistic families. As early as 1200, fertile soils and regular rainfall in the south fostered the formation of several large centralized kingdoms, including Buganda, from which the country derives its name. Muslim traders from Egypt reached northern Uganda in the 1820s, and Swahili merchants from the Indian Ocean coast arrived in the south by the 1840s. The area attracted the attention of British explorers seeking the source of the Nile River in the 1860s, and this influence expanded in subsequent decades with the arrival of Christian missionaries and trade agreements; Uganda was declared a British protectorate in 1894. Buganda and other southern kingdoms negotiated agreements with Britain to secure privileges and a level of autonomy that were rare during the colonial period in Africa. The colonial boundaries demarcating Uganda grouped together a wide range of ethnic groups with different political systems and cultures, and the disparities between how Britain governed southern and northern areas compounded these differences, complicating efforts to establish a cohesive independent country.

Uganda gained independence in 1962 with one of the more developed economies and one of the strongest education systems in Sub-Saharan Africa, but it descended within a few years into political turmoil and internal conflict that lasted more than two decades. In 1966, Prime Minister Milton OBOTE suspended the constitution and violently deposed President Edward MUTESA, who was also the king of Buganda. Idi AMIN seized power in 1971 through a military coup and led the country into economic ruin and rampant mass atrocities that killed as many as 500,000 civilians. AMIN's annexation of Tanzanian territory in 1979 provoked Tanzania to invade Uganda, depose AMIN, and install a coalition government. In the aftermath, Uganda continued to experience atrocities, looting, and political instability and had four different heads of state between 1979 and 1980. OBOTE regained the presidency in 1980 through a controversial election that sparked renewed guerrilla warfare, killing as an estimated 300,000 civilians. Gen. Tito OKELLO seized power in a coup in 1985, but his rule was short-lived, with Yoweri MUSEVENI becoming president in 1986 after his insurgency captured the capital. MUSEVENI is widely credited with restoring relative stability and economic growth to Uganda but has resisted calls to leave office. In 2017, parliament approved the removal of presidential age limits, making it possible for MUSEVENI to remain in office for life. Uganda faces numerous challenges that could affect future stability, including explosive population growth, power and infrastructure constraints, corruption, underdeveloped democratic institutions, and human rights deficits.

GEOGRAPHY

Location: East-Central Africa, west of Kenya, east of the Democratic Republic of the Congo

Geographic coordinates: 1 00 N, 32 00 E

Map references: Africa

Area: *total:* 241,038 sq km
land: 197,100 sq km
water: 43,938 sq km
country comparison to the world: 81

Area - comparative: slightly more than two times the size of Pennsylvania; slightly smaller than Oregon

Land boundaries: *total:* 2,729 km
border countries (5): Democratic Republic of the Congo 877 km; Kenya 814 km; Rwanda 172 km; South Sudan 475 km; Tanzania 391 km

Coastline: 0 km (landlocked)

Maritime claims: none (landlocked)

Climate: tropical; generally rainy with two dry seasons (December to February, June to August); semi-arid in northeast

Terrain: mostly plateau with rim of mountains

Elevation: *highest point:* Margherita Peak on Mount Stanley 5,110 m
lowest point: Albert Nile 614 m

Natural resources: copper, cobalt, hydropower, limestone, salt, arable land, gold

Land use: *agricultural land:* 71.2% (2018 est.)
arable land: 34.3% (2018 est.)
permanent crops: 11.3% (2018 est.)
permanent pasture: 25.6% (2018 est.)
forest: 14.5% (2018 est.)
other: 14.3% (2018 est.)

Irrigated land: 140 sq km (2012)

Major lakes (area sq km): *fresh water lake(s):* Lake Victoria (shared with Tanzania and Kenya) - 62,940 sq km; Lake Albert (shared with Democratic Republic of Congo) - 5,590 sq km; Lake Kyoga - 4,430 sq km; Lake Edward (shared with Democratic Republic of Congo) - 2,150 sq km

Major rivers (by length in km): Nile (shared with Rwanda [s], Tanzania, South Sudan, Sudan, and Egypt [m]) - 6,650 km
note – [s] after country name indicates river source; [m] after country name indicates river mouth

Major watersheds (area sq km): Atlantic Ocean drainage: Congo (3,730,881 sq km), *(Mediterranean Sea)* Nile (3,254,853 sq km)

Population distribution: population density is relatively high in comparison to other African nations; most of the population is concentrated in the central and southern parts of the country, particularly along the shores of Lake Victoria and Lake Albert; the northeast is least populated as shown in this population distribution map

Natural hazards: droughts; floods; earthquakes; landslides; hailstorms

Geography - note: landlocked; fertile, well-watered country with many lakes and rivers; Lake Victoria, the world's largest tropical lake and the second largest fresh water lake, is shared among three countries: Kenya, Tanzania, and Uganda

PEOPLE AND SOCIETY

Population: 46,205,893 (2022 est.)
note: estimates for this country explicitly taken into account the impact of the HIV/AIDS epidemic
country comparison to the world: 33

Nationality: *noun:* Ugandan(s)
adjective: Ugandan

Ethnic groups: Baganda 16.5%, Banyankole 9.6%, Basoga 8.8%, Bakiga 7.1%, Iteso 7%, Langi 6.3%, Bagisu 4.9%, Acholi 4.4%, Lugbara 3.3%, other 32.1% (2014 est.)

Languages: English (official language, taught in schools, used in courts of law and by most newspapers and some radio broadcasts), Ganda or Luganda (most widely used of the Niger-Congo languages and the language used most often in the capital), other Niger-Congo languages, Nilo-Saharan languages, Swahili (official), Arabic

Religions: Protestant 45.1% (Anglican 32.0%, Pentecostal/Born Again/Evangelical 11.1%, Seventh Day Adventist 1.7%, Baptist .3%), Roman Catholic 39.3%, Muslim 13.7%, other 1.6%, none 0.2% (2014 est.)

Demographic profile: Uganda has one of the youngest and most rapidly growing populations in the world; its total fertility rate is among the world's highest at close to 5.5 children per woman. Except in urban areas, actual fertility exceeds women's desired fertility by one or two children, which is indicative of the widespread unmet need for contraception, lack of government support for family planning, and a cultural preference for large families. High numbers of births, short birth intervals, and the early age of childbearing contribute to Uganda's high maternal mortality rate. Gender inequities also make fertility reduction difficult; women on average are less-educated, participate less in paid employment, and often have little say in decisions over childbearing and their own reproductive health. However, even if the birth rate were significantly reduced, Uganda's large pool of women entering reproductive age ensures rapid population growth for decades to come.

Unchecked, population increase will further strain the availability of arable land and natural resources and overwhelm the country's limited means for providing food, employment, education, health care, housing, and basic services. The country's north and northeast lag even further behind developmentally than the rest of the country as a result of long-term conflict (the Ugandan Bush War 1981-1986 and more than 20 years of fighting between the Lord's Resistance Army (LRA) and Ugandan Government forces), ongoing inter-communal violence, and periodic natural disasters.

Uganda has been both a source of refugees and migrants and a host country for refugees. In 1972, then President Idi AMIN, in his drive to return Uganda to Ugandans, expelled the South Asian population that composed a large share of the country's business people and bankers. Since the 1970s, thousands of Ugandans have emigrated, mainly to southern Africa or the West, for security reasons, to escape poverty, to search for jobs, and for access to natural resources. The emigration of Ugandan doctors and nurses due to low wages is a particular concern given the country's shortage of skilled health care workers. Africans escaping conflicts in neighboring states have found refuge in Uganda since the 1950s; the country currently struggles to host tens of thousands from the Democratic Republic of the Congo, South Sudan, and other nearby countries.

Age structure: *0-14 years:* 48.21% (male 10,548,913/female 10,304,876)
15-24 years: 20.25% (male 4,236,231/female 4,521,698)
25-54 years: 26.24% (male 5,202,570/female 6,147,304)
55-64 years: 2.91% (male 579,110/female 681,052)
65 years and over: 2.38% (male 442,159/female 589,053) (2020 est.)

Dependency ratios: *total dependency ratio:* 92.3
youth dependency ratio: 88.5
elderly dependency ratio: 3.8
potential support ratio: 26.2 (2020 est.)

Median age: *total:* 15.7 years
male: 14.9 years
female: 16.5 years (2020 est.)
country comparison to the world: 226

Population growth rate: 3.27% (2022 est.)
country comparison to the world: 8

Birth rate: 40.94 births/1,000 population (2022 est.)
country comparison to the world: 5

Death rate: 5.02 deaths/1,000 population (2022 est.)
country comparison to the world: 195

Net migration rate: -3.26 migrant(s)/1,000 population (2022 est.)
country comparison to the world: 186

Population distribution: population density is relatively high in comparison to other African nations; most of the population is concentrated in the central and southern parts of the country, particularly along the shores of Lake Victoria and Lake Albert; the northeast is least populated as shown in this population distribution map

Urbanization: *urban population:* 26.2% of total population (2022)
rate of urbanization: 5.41% annual rate of change (2020-25 est.)

Major urban areas - population: 3.652 million KAMPALA (capital) (2022)

Sex ratio: *at birth:* 1.03 male(s)/female
0-14 years: 1.03 male(s)/female
15-24 years: 0.95 male(s)/female
25-54 years: 0.86 male(s)/female
55-64 years: 0.86 male(s)/female
65 years and over: 0.71 male(s)/female
total population: 0.95 male(s)/female (2022 est.)

Mother's mean age at first birth: 19.4 years (2016 est.)
note: data represents median age at first birth among women 20-49

Maternal mortality ratio: 375 deaths/100,000 live births (2017 est.)
country comparison to the world: 30

Infant mortality rate: *total:* 30.45 deaths/1,000 live births
male: 33.88 deaths/1,000 live births
female: 26.91 deaths/1,000 live births (2022 est.)
country comparison to the world: 50

Life expectancy at birth: *total population:* 68.96 years
male: 66.71 years
female: 71.27 years (2022 est.)
country comparison to the world: 180

Total fertility rate: 5.36 children born/woman (2022 est.)
country comparison to the world: 7

Contraceptive prevalence rate: 41.8% (2018)

Drinking water source: *improved: urban:* 92.5% of population
rural: 80% of population
total: 83.1% of population
unimproved: urban: 7.5% of population
rural: 20% of population
total: 16.9% of population (2020 est.)

Current health expenditure: 3.8% of GDP (2019)

Physicians density: 0.15 physicians/1,000 population (2020)

Hospital bed density: 0.5 beds/1,000 population

Sanitation facility access: *improved: urban:* 67.3% of population
rural: 27.5% of population
total: 37.4% of population
unimproved: urban: 32.7% of population
rural: 72.5% of population
total: 62.6% of population (2020 est.)

HIV/AIDS - adult prevalence rate: 5.4% (2020 est.)
country comparison to the world: 11

HIV/AIDS - people living with HIV/AIDS: 1.4 million (2020 est.)
country comparison to the world: 8

HIV/AIDS - deaths: 22,000 (2020 est.)
country comparison to the world: 9

Major infectious diseases: *degree of risk:* very high (2020)
food or waterborne diseases: bacterial diarrhea, hepatitis A and E, and typhoid fever
vectorborne diseases: malaria, dengue fever, and Trypanosomiasis-Gambiense (African sleeping sickness)
water contact diseases: schistosomiasis
animal contact diseases: rabies
note: on 21 March 2022, the US Centers for Disease Control and Prevention (CDC) issued a Travel Alert for polio in Africa; Uganda is currently considered a high risk to travelers for circulating vaccine-derived polioviruses (cVDPV); vaccine-derived poliovirus (VDPV) is a strain of the weakened poliovirus that was initially included in oral polio vaccine (OPV) and *that has changed over time and behaves more like the wild or naturally occurring virus*; this means it can be spread more easily to people who are unvaccinated against polio and who come in contact with the stool or respiratory secretions, such as from a sneeze, of an "infected" person who received oral polio vaccine; the CDC recommends that before any international travel, anyone unvaccinated, incompletely vaccinated, or with an unknown polio vaccination status should complete the routine polio vaccine series; before travel to any high-risk destination, the CDC recommends that adults who previously completed the full, routine polio vaccine series receive a single, lifetime booster dose of polio vaccine
note: on 4 October 2022, the US Centers for Disease Control and Prevention (CDC) issued a Level Two Travel Alert (Practice Enhanced Precautions) for Ebola virus in Uganda, currently present in the following districts: Mubende, Kassandra, Kyegegwa, Kagadi, and Bunyangabu, and recommended that people avoid non-essential travel to these regions; this outbreak has been linked to the *Sudan ebolavirus* for which there are no vaccines or therapeutics approved for prevention or treatment of the *Sudan ebolavirus*; in addition, on 6 October 2022, the State Department issued a Level Three Travel Advisory to reconsider travel to Uganda and also announced the following "The Department of Homeland Security (DHS) and the CDC announced entrance screening for travelers who have been in Uganda in the last 21 days. All U.S.-bound passengers who have been in Uganda at any point in the 21 days prior to their arrival will be routed to one of the following designated airports: New York (JFK), Newark (EWR), Atlanta (ATL), Chicago (ORD), or Washington (IAD), where they will undergo enhanced screening, including a health questionnaire and temperature checks. This applies to all passengers, including U.S. citizens, lawful permanent residents, and foreign nationals (to include Diplomatic and Official visas)."

Obesity - adult prevalence rate: 5.3% (2016)
country comparison to the world: 181

Alcohol consumption per capita: *total:* 6.82 liters of pure alcohol (2019 est.)
beer: 0.85 liters of pure alcohol (2019 est.)
wine: 0.01 liters of pure alcohol (2019 est.)
spirits: 0.5 liters of pure alcohol (2019 est.)
other alcohols: 5.46 liters of pure alcohol (2019 est.)
country comparison to the world: 61

Tobacco use: *total:* 8.4% (2020 est.)
male: 13% (2020 est.)
female: 3.7% (2020 est.)
country comparison to the world: 145

Children under the age of 5 years underweight: 10.4% (2016)
country comparison to the world: 58

Child marriage: *women married by age 15:* 7.3%
women married by age 18: 34%
men married by age 18: 5.5% (2016 est.)

Education expenditures: 3% of GDP (2020 est.)
country comparison to the world: 152

Literacy: *definition:* age 15 and over can read and write
total population: 76.5%
male: 82.7%
female: 70.8% (2018)

School life expectancy (primary to tertiary education): *total:* 10 years
male: 10 years
female: 10 years (2011)

Unemployment, youth ages 15-24: *total:* 15.6%
male: 13.8%
female: 17.6% (2017 est.)

ENVIRONMENT

Environment - current issues: draining of wetlands for agricultural use; deforestation; overgrazing; soil erosion; water pollution from industrial discharge and water hyacinth infestation in Lake Victoria; widespread poaching

Environment - international agreements: *party to:* Biodiversity, Climate Change, Climate Change-Kyoto Protocol, Climate Change-Paris Agreement, Comprehensive Nuclear Test Ban, Desertification, Endangered Species, Hazardous Wastes, Law of the Sea, Marine Life Conservation, Nuclear Test Ban, Ozone Layer Protection, Ship Pollution, Wetlands
signed, but not ratified: Environmental Modification

Air pollutants: *particulate matter emissions:* 48.41 micrograms per cubic meter (2016 est.)
carbon dioxide emissions: 5.68 megatons (2016 est.)
methane emissions: 30.24 megatons (2020 est.)

Climate: tropical; generally rainy with two dry seasons (December to February, June to August); semiarid in northeast

Land use: *agricultural land:* 71.2% (2018 est.)
arable land: 34.3% (2018 est.)
permanent crops: 11.3% (2018 est.)
permanent pasture: 25.6% (2018 est.)
forest: 14.5% (2018 est.)
other: 14.3% (2018 est.)

Urbanization: *urban population:* 26.2% of total population (2022)
rate of urbanization: 5.41% annual rate of change (2020-25 est.)

Revenue from forest resources: *forest revenues:* 7.32% of GDP (2018 est.)
country comparison to the world: 7

Revenue from coal: *coal revenues:* 0% of GDP (2018 est.)
country comparison to the world: 181

Food insecurity: *severe localized food insecurity: due to weather extremes, civil insecurity, and high food prices-* in Karamoja Region, about 518,000 people, 41% of the population, are estimated to be severely food insecure between March and July 2022, as a result of consecutive poor rainy seasons that adversely affected crop and livestock production, frequent episodes of cattle rustling leading to the loss of productive assets, and high food prices (2022)

Waste and recycling: *municipal solid waste generated annually:* 7,045,050 tons (2016 est.)
municipal solid waste recycled annually: 422,703 tons (2017 est.)
percent of municipal solid waste recycled: 6% (2017 est.)

Major lakes (area sq km): *fresh water lake(s):* Lake Victoria (shared with Tanzania and Kenya) - 62,940 sq km; Lake Albert (shared with Democratic Republic of Congo) - 5,590 sq km; Lake Kyoga - 4,430 sq km; Lake Edward (shared with Democratic Republic of Congo) - 2,150 sq km

Major rivers (by length in km): Nile (shared with Rwanda [s], Tanzania, South Sudan, Sudan, and Egypt [m]) - 6,650 km
note – [s] after country name indicates river source; [m] after country name indicates river mouth

Major watersheds (area sq km): Atlantic Ocean drainage: Congo (3,730,881 sq km), *(Mediterranean Sea)* Nile (3,254,853 sq km)

Total water withdrawal: *municipal:* 328 million cubic meters (2017 est.)
industrial: 50 million cubic meters (2017 est.)
agricultural: 259 million cubic meters (2017 est.)

Total renewable water resources: 60.1 billion cubic meters (2017 est.)

GOVERNMENT

Country name: *conventional long form:* Republic of Uganda
conventional short form: Uganda
etymology: from the name "Buganda," adopted by the British as the designation for their East African colony in 1894; Buganda had been a powerful East African state during the 18th and 19th centuries

Government type: presidential republic

Capital: *name:* Kampala
geographic coordinates: 0 19 N, 32 33 E
time difference: UTC+3 (8 hours ahead of Washington, DC, during Standard Time)
etymology: the site of the original British settlement was referred to by its native name as Akasozi ke'Empala ("hill of the impala" [plural]); over time this designation was shortened to K'empala and finally Kampala

Administrative divisions: 134 districts and 1 capital city*; Abim, Adjumani, Agago, Alebtong, Amolatar, Amudat, Amuria, Amuru, Apac, Arua, Budaka, Bududa, Bugiri, Bugweri, Buhweju, Buikwe, Bukedea, Bukomansimbi, Bukwo, Bulambuli, Buliisa, Bundibugyo, Bunyangabu, Bushenyi, Busia, Butaleja, Butambala, Butebo, Buvuma, Buyende, Dokolo, Gomba, Gulu, Hoima, Ibanda, Iganga, Isingiro, Jinja, Kaabong, Kabale, Kabarole, Kaberamaido, Kagadi, Kakumiro, Kalaki, Kalangala, Kaliro, Kalungu, Kampala*, Kamuli, Kamwenge, Kanungu, Kapchorwa, Kapelebyong, Karenga, Kasese, Kasanda, Katakwi, Kayunga, Kazo, Kibaale, Kiboga, Kibuku, Kikuube, Kiruhura, Kiryandongo, Kisoro, Kitagwenda, Kitgum, Koboko, Kole, Kotido, Kumi, Kwania, Kween, Kyankwanzi, Kyegegwa, Kyenjojo, Kyotera, Lamwo, Lira, Luuka, Luwero, Lwengo, Lyantonde, Madi-Okollo, Manafwa, Maracha, Masaka, Masindi, Mayuge, Mbale, Mbarara, Mitooma, Mityana, Moroto, Moyo, Mpigi, Mubende, Mukono, Nabilatuk, Nakapiripirit, Nakaseke, Nakasongola, Namayingo, Namisindwa, Namutumba, Napak, Nebbi, Ngora, Ntoroko, Ntungamo, Nwoya, Obongi, Omoro, Otuke, Oyam, Pader, Pakwach, Pallisa, Rakai, Rubanda, Rubirizi, Rukiga, Rukungiri, Rwampara, Sembabule, Serere, Sheema, Sironko, Soroti, Tororo, Wakiso, Yumbe, Zombo

Independence: 9 October 1962 (from the UK)

National holiday: Independence Day, 9 October (1962)

Constitution: *history:* several previous; latest adopted 27 September 1995, promulgated 8 October 1995
amendments: proposed by the National Assembly; passage requires at least two-thirds majority vote of the Assembly membership in the second and third readings; proposals affecting "entrenched clauses," including the sovereignty of the people, supremacy of the constitution, human rights and freedoms, the democratic and multiparty form of government, presidential term of office, independence of the judiciary, and the institutions of traditional or cultural leaders, also requires passage by referendum, ratification by at least two-thirds majority vote of district council members in at least two thirds of Uganda's districts, and assent of the president of the republic; amended several times, last in 2017

Legal system: mixed legal system of English common law and customary law

International law organization participation: accepts compulsory ICJ jurisdiction; accepts ICCt jurisdiction

Citizenship: *citizenship by birth:* no
citizenship by descent only: at least one parent or grandparent must be a native-born citizen of Uganda
dual citizenship recognized: yes
residency requirement for naturalization: an aggregate of 20 years and continuously for the last 2 years prior to applying for citizenship

Suffrage: 18 years of age; universal

Executive branch: *chief of state:* President Yoweri Kaguta MUSEVENI (since 26 January 1986); Vice President Jessica Rose Epel ALUPO (since 21 June 2021); Prime Minister Robinah NABBANJA (since 21 June 2021); First Deputy Prime Minister Rebecca KADAGA (since 24 June 2021); Second Deputy Prime Minister Moses ALI (since 21 June 2021); note - the president is both chief of state and head of government
head of government: President Yoweri Kaguta MUSEVENI (since 26 January 1986); Vice President Jessica Rose Epel ALUPO (since 21 June 2021); Prime Minister Robinah NABBANJA (since 21 June 2021); First Deputy Prime Minister Rebecca KADAGA (since 24 June 2021); Second Deputy Prime Minister Moses ALI (since 21 June 2021)
cabinet: Cabinet appointed by the president from among elected members of the National Assembly or persons who qualify to be elected as members of the National Assembly
elections/appointments: president directly elected by absolute majority popular vote in 2 rounds if needed for a 5-year term (no term limits); election last held on 14 January 2021 (next to be held in 2026)
election results:
2021: Yoweri Kaguta MUSEVENI reelected president in the first round; percent of vote - Yoweri Kaguta MUSEVENI (NRM) 58.6%, Bobi WINE (NUP) 34.8%, Patrick Oboi AMURIAT (FDC) 3.2%, other 3.4%
2016: Yoweri Kaguta MUSEVENI reelected president in the first round; percent of vote - Yoweri Kaguta MUSEVENI (NRM) 60.6%, Kizza BESIGYE (FDC) 35.6%, other 3.8%

Legislative branch: *description:* unicameral National Assembly or Parliament (556 seats; 353 members directly elected in single-seat constituencies by simple majority vote, 146 for women directly elected in single-seat districts by simple majority vote, and 30 "representatives" reserved for special interest groups - army 10, disabled 5, youth 5, labor 5, older persons 5; 27 ex officio members appointed by the president; members serve 5-year terms)
elections:
last held on 14 January 2021 (next to be held in February 2026)
election results:
percent of vote by party - NA; seats by party - NRM 336, NUP 57, FDC 32, DP 9, UPDF 10, UPC 9, independent 76 (excludes 27 ex-officio members)

Judicial branch: *highest court(s):* Supreme Court of Uganda (consists of the chief justice and at least 6 justices)
judge selection and term of office: justices appointed by the president of the republic in consultation with the Judicial Service Commission, an 8-member independent advisory body, and approved by the National Assembly; justices serve until mandatory retirement at age 70
subordinate courts: Court of Appeal (also acts as the Constitutional Court); High Court (includes 12 High Court Circuits and 8 High Court Divisions);

Industrial Court; Chief Magistrate Grade One and Grade Two Courts throughout the country; qadhis courts; local council courts; family and children courts

Political parties and leaders: Democratic Party or DP [Norbert MAO]
Forum for Democratic Change or FDC [Patrick Oboi AMURIAT]
Justice Forum or JEEMA [Asuman BASALIRWA]
National Resistance Movement or NRM [Yoweri MUSEVENI]
National Unity Platform [Robert Kyagulanyi SSENTAMU, known as Bobi WINE]
People's Progressive Party or PPP [Jaberi Bidandi SSALI]
Uganda People's Congress or UPC [James AKENA]
note: only parties with seats in Parliament listed

International organization participation: ACP, AfDB, ATMIS, AU, C, COMESA, EAC, EADB, FAO, G-77, IAEA, IBRD, ICAO, ICC (national committees), ICCt, IDA, IDB, IFAD, IFC, IFRCS, IGAD, ILO, IMF, IMO, Interpol, IOC, IOM, IPU, ISO (correspondent), ITSO, ITU, ITUC (NGOs), MIGA, NAM, OIC, OPCW, PCA, UN, UNCTAD, UNESCO, UNHCR, UNIDO, UNISFA, UNOCI, UNSOM, UNWTO, UPU, WCO, WFTU (NGOs), WHO, WIPO, WMO, WTO

Diplomatic representation in the US: *chief of mission:* Ambassador (vacant); Charge d'Affaires Santa Mary Laker KINYERA (since 20 May 2022)
chancery: 5911 16th Street NW, Washington, DC 20011
telephone: [1] (202) 726-7100
FAX: [1] (202) 726-1727
email address and website:
washington@mofa.go.ug; info@ugandaembassysus.org; ambauganda@aol.com
https://washington.mofa.go.ug/

Diplomatic representation from the US: *chief of mission:* Ambassador Natalie E. BROWN (since 17 November 2020)
embassy: 1577 Ggaba Road, Kampala
mailing address: 2190 Kampala Place, Washington DC 20521-2190
telephone: [256] (0) 312-306-001
FAX: [256] (0) 414-259-794
email address and website:
KampalaUScitizen@state.gov
https://ug.usembassy.gov/

Flag description: six equal horizontal bands of black (top), yellow, red, black, yellow, and red; a white disk is superimposed at the center and depicts a grey crowned crane (the national symbol) facing the hoist side; black symbolizes the African people, yellow sunshine and vitality, red African brotherhood; the crane was the military badge of Ugandan soldiers under the UK

National symbol(s): grey crowned crane; national colors: black, yellow, red

National anthem: *name:* "Oh Uganda, Land of Beauty!"
lyrics/music: George Wilberforce KAKOMOA
note: adopted 1962

National heritage: *total World Heritage Sites:* 3 (1 cultural, 2 natural)
selected World Heritage Site locales: Bwindi Impenetrable National Park (n); Rwenzori Mountains National Park (n); Tombs of Buganda Kings at Kasubi (c)

ECONOMY

Economic overview: Uganda has substantial natural resources, including fertile soils, regular rainfall, substantial reserves of recoverable oil, and small deposits of copper, gold, and other minerals. Agriculture is one of the most important sectors of the economy, employing 72% of the work force. The country's export market suffered a major slump following the outbreak of conflict in South Sudan, but has recovered lately, largely due to record coffee harvests, which account for 16% of exports, and increasing gold exports, which account for 10% of exports. Uganda has a small industrial sector that is dependent on imported inputs such as refined oil and heavy equipment. Overall, productivity is hampered by a number of supply-side constraints, including insufficient infrastructure, lack of modern technology in agriculture, and corruption.

Uganda's economic growth has slowed since 2016 as government spending and public debt has grown. Uganda's budget is dominated by energy and road infrastructure spending, while Uganda relies on donor support for long-term drivers of growth, including agriculture, health, and education. The largest infrastructure projects are externally financed through concessional loans, but at inflated costs. As a result, debt servicing for these loans is expected to rise.

Oil revenues and taxes are expected to become a larger source of government funding as oil production starts in the next three to 10 years. Over the next three to five years, foreign investors are planning to invest $9 billion in production facilities projects, $4 billion in an export pipeline, as well as in a $2-3 billion refinery to produce petroleum products for the domestic and East African Community markets. Furthermore, the government is looking to build several hundred million dollars' worth of highway projects to the oil region.

Uganda faces many economic challenges. Instability in South Sudan has led to a sharp increase in Sudanese refugees and is disrupting Uganda's main export market. Additional economic risks include: poor economic management, endemic corruption, and the government's failure to invest adequately in the health, education, and economic opportunities for a burgeoning young population. Uganda has one of the lowest electrification rates in Africa - only 22% of Ugandans have access to electricity, dropping to 10% in rural areas.

Real GDP (purchasing power parity): $99.61 billion (2020 est.)
$96.84 billion (2019 est.)
$90.67 billion (2018 est.)
note: data are in 2017 dollars
country comparison to the world: 90

Real GDP growth rate: 4.8% (2017 est.)
2.3% (2016 est.)
5.7% (2015 est.)
country comparison to the world: 56

Real GDP per capita: $2,200 (2020 est.)
$2,200 (2019 est.)
$2,100 (2018 est.)
note: data are in 2017 dollars
country comparison to the world: 211

GDP (official exchange rate): $34.683 billion (2019 est.)

Inflation rate (consumer prices): 2.8% (2019 est.)
2.6% (2018 est.)
5.6% (2017 est.)
country comparison to the world: 144

Credit ratings:

Fitch rating: B+ (2015)

Moody's rating: B2 (2016)

Standard & Poors rating: B (2014)

GDP - composition, by sector of origin: *agriculture:* 28.2% (2017 est.)
industry: 21.1% (2017 est.)
services: 50.7% (2017 est.)

GDP - composition, by end use: *household consumption:* 74.3% (2017 est.)
government consumption: 8% (2017 est.)
investment in fixed capital: 23.9% (2017 est.)
investment in inventories: 0.3% (2017 est.)
exports of goods and services: 18.8% (2017 est.)
imports of goods and services: -25.1% (2017 est.)

Agricultural products: sugar cane, plantains, cassava, maize, sweet potatoes, milk, vegetables, beans, bananas, sorghum

Industries: sugar processing, brewing, tobacco, cotton textiles; cement, steel production

Industrial production growth rate: 4.4% (2017 est.)
country comparison to the world: 69

Labor force: 15.84 million (2015 est.)
country comparison to the world: 34

Labor force - by occupation: *agriculture:* 71%
industry: 7%
services: 22% (2013 est.)

Unemployment rate: 9.4% (2014 est.)
country comparison to the world: 143

Unemployment, youth ages 15-24: *total:* 15.6%
male: 13.8%
female: 17.6% (2017 est.)
country comparison to the world: 101

Population below poverty line: 21.4% (2016 est.)

Gini Index coefficient - distribution of family income: 42.8 (2016 est.)
45.7 (2002)
country comparison to the world: 43

Household income or consumption by percentage share: *lowest 10%:* 2.4%
highest 10%: 36.1% (2009 est.)

Budget: *revenues:* 3.848 billion (2017 est.)
expenditures: 4.928 billion (2017 est.)

Budget surplus (+) or deficit (-): -4.1% (of GDP) (2017 est.)
country comparison to the world: 158

Public debt: 40% of GDP (2017 est.)
37.4% of GDP (2016 est.)
country comparison to the world: 127

Taxes and other revenues: 14.5% (of GDP) (2017 est.)
country comparison to the world: 199

Fiscal year: 1 July - 30 June

Current account balance: -$1.212 billion (2017 est.)
-$707 million (2016 est.)
country comparison to the world: 151

Exports: $6.12 billion (2019 est.) note: data are in current year dollars
$5.63 billion (2018 est.) note: data are in current year dollars
$5.958 billion (2017 est.)
country comparison to the world: 119

Exports - partners: United Arab Emirates 58%, Kenya 9% (2019)

Exports - commodities: gold, coffee, milk, fish and fish products, tobacco (2019)

Imports: $9.54 billion (2019 est.) note: data are in current year dollars
$8.65 billion (2018 est.) note: data are in current year dollars
$7.44 billion (2017 est.)
country comparison to the world: 108

Imports - partners: China 19%, India 17%, Kenya 16%, United Arab Emirates 7%, Japan 5% (2019)

Imports - commodities: packaged medicines, aircraft, delivery trucks, cars, wheat (2019)

Reserves of foreign exchange and gold: $3.654 billion (31 December 2017 est.)
$3.034 billion (31 December 2016 est.)
note: excludes gold
country comparison to the world: 101

Debt - external: $13.85 billion (2019 est.)
$12.187 billion (2018 est.)
$6.241 billion (31 December 2016 est.)
country comparison to the world: 105

Exchange rates: Ugandan shillings (UGX) per US dollar -
3,680 (2020 est.)
3,685 (2019 est.)
3,735 (2018 est.)
3,234.1 (2014 est.)
2,599.8 (2013 est.)

ENERGY

Electricity access: *electrification - total population:* 29% (2019)
electrification - urban areas: 66% (2019)
electrification - rural areas: 17% (2019)

Electricity: *installed generating capacity:* 2.397 million kW (2020 est.)
consumption: 4,207,040,000 kWh (2019 est.)
exports: 299.2 million kWh (2019 est.)
imports: 104.2 million kWh (2019 est.)
transmission/distribution losses: 1.157 billion kWh (2019 est.)

Electricity generation sources: *fossil fuels:* 1.3% of total installed capacity (2020 est.)
solar: 1.6% of total installed capacity (2020 est.)
hydroelectricity: 86.4% of total installed capacity (2020 est.)
biomass and waste: 10.8% of total installed capacity (2020 est.)

Petroleum: *total petroleum production:* 0 bbl/day (2021 est.)
refined petroleum consumption: 40,900 bbl/day (2019 est.)
crude oil estimated reserves: 2.5 billion barrels (2021 est.)

Refined petroleum products - imports: 31,490 bbl/day (2015 est.)
country comparison to the world: 99

Natural gas: *proven reserves:* 14.158 billion cubic meters (2021 est.)

Carbon dioxide emissions: 5.841 million metric tonnes of CO2 (2019 est.)
from petroleum and other liquids: 5.841 million metric tonnes of CO2 (2019 est.)
country comparison to the world: 133

Energy consumption per capita: 2.943 million Btu/person (2019 est.)
country comparison to the world: 183

COMMUNICATIONS

Telephones - fixed lines: *total subscriptions:* 90,774 (2020 est.)
subscriptions per 100 inhabitants: (2020 est.) less than 1
country comparison to the world: 141

Telephones - mobile cellular: *total subscriptions:* 25,395,500 (2019)
subscriptions per 100 inhabitants: 57.37 (2019)
country comparison to the world: 49

Telecommunication systems: *general assessment:* a series of reforms within Uganda's telecom sector have provided the country with one of the most competitive markets in the region; in line with the regulator's licensing requirements by which Uganda-based companies should be broadly owned by Ugandans by mid-2022, MTN Group carried out a partial listing on the Uganda Stock Exchange in December 2021; a simplified and converged licensing regime has significantly reduced barriers to market entry and increased competition, but this has also led to price wars which have dented operator revenue; fixed-line infrastructure remains poor, with low penetration, and as a result fixed-line broadband penetration is also particularly low; consumers have largely depended on mobile infrastructure to provide voice and broadband services; there is sufficient capacity with LTE infrastructure to match data demand during the next few years; Uganda has anticipated the migration to 5G, having held trials in early 2020 though the roll out of 5G is not expected until later in 2022 (2022)
domestic: fixed-line less than 1 per 100 and mobile cellular systems teledensity about 61 per 100 persons; intercity traffic by wire, microwave radio relay, and radiotelephone communication stations (2020)
international: country code - 256; satellite earth stations - 1 Intelsat (Atlantic Ocean) and 1 Inmarsat; analog and digital links to Kenya and Tanzania

Broadcast media: public broadcaster, Uganda Broadcasting Corporation (UBC), operates radio and TV networks; 31 Free-To-Air (FTA) TV stations, 2 digital terrestrial TV stations, 3 cable TV stations, and 5 digital satellite TV stations; 258 operational FM stations

Internet country code: .ug

Internet users: *total:* 9,148,200 (2020 est.)
percent of population: 20% (2020 est.)
country comparison to the world: 60

Broadband - fixed subscriptions: *total:* 58,594 (2020 est.)
subscriptions per 100 inhabitants: 0.1 (2020 est.)
country comparison to the world: 140

TRANSPORTATION

National air transport system: *number of registered air carriers:* 6 (2020)
inventory of registered aircraft operated by air carriers: 26
annual passenger traffic on registered air carriers: 21,537 (2018)

Civil aircraft registration country code prefix: 5X

Airports: *total:* 47 (2021)
country comparison to the world: 93

Airports - with paved runways: *total:* 5
over 3,047 m: 3
1,524 to 2,437 m: 1
914 to 1,523 m: 1 (2021)

Airports - with unpaved runways: *total:* 42
over 3,047 m: 1
1,524 to 2,437 m: 8
914 to 1,523 m: 26
under 914 m: 7 (2021)

Railways: *total:* 1,244 km (2014)
narrow gauge: 1,244 km (2014) 1.000-m gauge
country comparison to the world: 85

Roadways: *total:* 20,544 km (2017) (excludes local roads)
paved: 4,257 km (2017)
unpaved: 16,287 km (2017)
country comparison to the world: 111

Waterways: 907 km (2022) (there are no long navigable stretches of river in Uganda; parts of the Albert Nile (210 km) that flow out of Lake Albert (160 km) in the northwestern part of the country are navigable; several lakes including Lake Victoria (337 km) and Lake Kyoga (199.5) have substantial traffic; Lake Albert is navigable along a 200-km stretch from its northern tip to its southern shores)
country comparison to the world: 74

Ports and terminals: *lake port(s):* Entebbe, Jinja, Port Bell (Lake Victoria)

MILITARY AND SECURITY

Military and security forces: Uganda People's Defense Force (UPDF): Land Forces, Air Forces, Marine Forces, Special Forces Command, Reserve Force (2022)
note 1: the Special Forces Command is a separate branch within the UPDF; it evolved from the former Presidential Guard Brigade and has continued to retain presidential protection duties in addition to its conventional missions, such as counterinsurgency
note 2: in 2018, President MUSEVENI created a volunteer force of Local Defense Units under the military to beef up local security in designated parts of the country

Military expenditures: 2.5% of GDP (2021 est.)
2.5% of GDP (2020 est.)
1.7% of GDP (2019) (approximately $870 million)
1.2% of GDP (2018) (approximately $640 million)
1.2% of GDP (2017) (approximately $610 million)
country comparison to the world: 43

Military and security service personnel strengths: approximately 50,000 troops, including about 1,000-1,500 air and marine personnel; approximately 20-30,000 personnel in the Local Defense Units (2022)

Military equipment inventories and acquisitions: the UPDF's inventory is mostly older Russian/Soviet-era equipment with a limited mix of more modern Russian- and Western-origin arms; since 2010, Russia has been the leading supplier of arms to the UPDF (2021)

Military service age and obligation: 18-25 years of age for voluntary military duty for men and women; 18-30 for those with degrees/diplomas in specialized fields such as medicine, engineering, chemistry, and education, or possess qualifications in some vocational skills; 9-year service obligation (2022)

Military deployments: 6,800 Somalia (6,200 ATMIS; 625 UNSOM); 250 Equatorial Guinea (training mission) (2022)

note: in December 2021, Uganda sent an undetermined number of troops into the Democratic Republic of the Congo to combat rebels from the Alliance of Democratic Front (ADF) group

Military - note: the UPDF, which is constitutionally granted seats in parliament, is widely viewed as a key constituency for MUSEVENI; it has been used by MUSEVENI and his political party to break up rallies, raid opposition offices, and surveil rival candidates

as of 2022, the UPDF was conducting operations along the border with the Democratic Republic of the Congo (including cross-border operations) against a Congo-based (and formerly based in western Uganda) Ugandan rebel group, the Allied Democratic Front (ADF), which was designated as a Foreign Terrorist Organization by the US in March 2021 as the Islamic State of Iraq and ash-Sham in the Democratic Republic of the Congo (ISIS-DRC; see Appendix T); in addition, elements of the UPDF were deployed in the northeast region of Karamoja against cattle rustlers and criminal gangs

beginning in 2012, the UPDF led regional efforts to pursue the Lord's Resistance Army (LRA), a small, violent group of Ugandan origin that conducted widespread attacks against civilians in much of Central Africa; the UPDF withdrew from the mission in 2017 after declaring that the LRA no longer posed a security threat; Uganda intervened in the South Sudan civil war in 2013-2016 and UPDF forces have clashed with South Sudanese forces along the border as recently as 2020

the military traces its history back to the formation of the Uganda Rifles in 1895 under the British colonial government; the Uganda Rifles were merged with the Central Africa Regiment and the East Africa Rifles to form the King's African Rifles (KAR) in 1902, which participated in both world wars, as well as the Mau Mau rebellion in Kenya (1952-1960); in 1962, the Ugandan battalion of the KAR was transformed into the country's first military force, the Uganda Rifles, which was subsequently renamed the Uganda Army; the Uganda People's Defense Force was established in 1995 from the former rebel National Resistance Army following the enactment of the 1995 Constitution of Uganda (2022)

TERRORISM

Terrorist group(s): al-Shabaab; Islamic State of Iraq and ash-Sham - Democratic Republic of Congo (ISIS-DRC)

TRANSNATIONAL ISSUES

Disputes - international: Uganda is subject to armed fighting among hostile ethnic groups, rebels, armed gangs, militias, and various government forces that extend across its borders

Uganda-Kenya: Kenya and Uganda have begun a joint demarcation of the boundary in 2021; Uganda and Kenya both claim Migingo Island, a tiny island in the middle of Lake Victoria, which offers good fishing

Uganda-Rwanda: a joint technical committee established in 2007 to demarcate sections of the border

Uganda-Democratic Republic of Congo(DROC): Uganda rejects the DROC claim to Margherita Peak in the Rwenzori mountains and considers it a boundary divide; there is tension and violence on Lake Albert over prospective oil reserves at the mouth of the Semliki River; Rukwanzi Island in Lake Albert is claimed by both countries

Uganda-South Sudan: Government of South Sudan protests Lord's Resistance Army operations in western Equatorial State, displacing and driving out local populations and stealing grain stores

Uganda-Sudan: none identified

Refugees and internally displaced persons: *refugees (country of origin):* 898,299 (South Sudan) (refugees and asylum seekers), 452,891 (Democratic Republic of the Congo), 61,694 (Somalia) (refugees and asylum seekers), 40,134 (Burundi), 26,821 (Eritrea), 22,290 (Rwanda), 5,316 (Ethiopia) (2022)

Trafficking in persons: *current situation:* human traffickers exploit domestic and foreign victims in Uganda, and traffickers exploit victims from Uganda abroad; young Ugandan children are exploited in forced labor in agriculture, fishing, forestry, cattle herding, mining, stone quarrying, brick making, carpentry, steel manufacturing, street vending, bars, restaurants, gold mining, and domestic service; traffickers exploit girls and boys in commercial sex; most are children from the northeastern region and are exploited in forced begging, commercial sex in brothels, or sold in markets; traffickers compel children from the Democratic Republic of Congo, Rwanda, Burundi, Kenya, Tanzania, and South Sudan into forced agricultural labor and sex trafficking in Uganda; young women most at risk for transnational trafficking seek employment as domestic workers in the Middle East and then are exploited in sex trafficking; traffickers subject Ugandans to forced labor and sex trafficking in UAE, Saudi Arabia, Oman, Qatar, Kuwait, Iraq, Iran, Egypt, Turkey, Algeria, Malaysia, Thailand, Bahrain, Jordan, China, Kenya, and India; traffickers are often relatives, friends of victims, or religious leaders who receive a fee per worker from recruiters

tier rating: Tier 2 Watch list — Uganda does not fully meet the minimum standards for the elimination of trafficking but is making significant efforts to do so; efforts include investigating allegations of complicit officials, implementing the protection and prevention provisions of the 2009 anti-trafficking act, convicting alleged traffickers, developing a plan for an anti-trafficking department within the police force; however, the government reported the lowest number of investigations in the past five years and a substantial decrease in prosecutions; authorities provided no training for law enforcement and immigration officials and identified fewer victims; the Coordination Office for Prevention of Trafficking in Persons is severely underfunded, stifling efforts to coordinate and combat trafficking; no systematic procedures to refer or assist victims have been developed, and the government provides no resources to NGOs for protective services; Uganda was downgraded to Tier 2 Watch List (2020)

UKRAINE

INTRODUCTION

Background: Ukraine was the center of the first eastern Slavic state, Kyivan Rus, which during the 10th and 11th centuries was the largest and most powerful state in Europe. Weakened by internecine quarrels and Mongol invasions, Kyivan Rus was incorporated into the Grand Duchy of Lithuania and eventually into the Polish-Lithuanian Commonwealth. The cultural and religious legacy of Kyivan Rus laid the foundation for Ukrainian nationalism through subsequent centuries. A new Ukrainian state, the Cossack Hetmanate, was established during the mid-17th century after an uprising against the Poles. Despite continuous Muscovite pressure, the Hetmanate managed to remain autonomous for well over 100 years. During the latter part of the 18th century, most Ukrainian ethnographic territory was absorbed by the Russian Empire. Following the collapse of czarist Russia in 1917, Ukraine achieved a short-lived period of independence (1917-20), but was reconquered and endured a brutal Soviet rule that engineered two forced famines (1921-22 and 1932-33) in which over 8 million died. In World War II, German and Soviet armies were responsible for 7 to 8 million more deaths. Although Ukraine achieved independence in 1991 with the dissolution of the USSR, democracy and prosperity remained elusive as the legacy of state control and endemic corruption stalled efforts at economic reform, privatization, and civil liberties.

A peaceful mass protest referred to as the "Orange Revolution" in the closing months of 2004 forced the authorities to overturn a rigged presidential election and to allow a new internationally monitored vote that swept into power a reformist slate under Viktor YUSHCHENKO. Subsequent internal squabbles in the YUSHCHENKO camp allowed his rival Viktor YANUKOVYCH to stage a comeback in parliamentary (Rada) elections, become prime minister in August 2006, and be elected president in February 2010. In October 2012, Ukraine held Rada elections, widely criticized by Western observers as flawed due to use of government resources to favor ruling party candidates, interference with media access, and harassment of opposition candidates. President YANUKOVYCH's backtracking on a trade and cooperation agreement with the EU in November 2013 - in favor of closer economic ties with Russia - and subsequent use of force against students, civil society activists, and other civilians in favor of the agreement led to a three-month protest occupation of Kyiv's central square. The government's use of violence to break up the protest camp in February 2014 led to all out pitched battles, scores of deaths, international condemnation, a failed political deal, and the president's abrupt departure for Russia. New elections in the spring allowed pro-West president Petro POROSHENKO to assume office in June 2014; he was succeeded by Volodymyr ZELENSKY in May 2019.

Shortly after YANUKOVYCH's departure in late February 2014, Russian President PUTIN ordered the invasion of Ukraine's Crimean Peninsula falsely claiming the action was to protect ethnic Russians living there. Two weeks later, a "referendum" was held regarding the integration of Crimea into the Russian Federation. The "referendum" was condemned as illegitimate by the Ukrainian Government, the EU, the US, and the UN General Assembly (UNGA). In response to Russia's illegal annexation of Crimea, 100 members of the UN passed UNGA resolution 68/262, rejecting the "referendum" as baseless and invalid and confirming the sovereignty, political independence, unity, and territorial integrity of Ukraine. In mid-2014, Russia began supplying proxies in two of Ukraine's eastern provinces with manpower, funding, and materiel driving an armed conflict with the Ukrainian Government that continues to this day. Representatives from Ukraine, Russia, and the unrecognized Russian proxy republics signed the Minsk Protocol and Memorandum in September 2014 to end the conflict. However, this agreement failed to stop the fighting or find a political solution. In a renewed attempt to alleviate ongoing clashes, leaders of Ukraine, Russia, France, and Germany negotiated a follow-on Package of Measures in February 2015 to implement the Minsk agreements. Representatives from Ukraine, Russia, the unrecognized Russian proxy republics, and the Organization for Security and Cooperation in Europe also meet regularly to facilitate implementation of the peace deal. By early 2022, more than 14,000 civilians were killed or wounded as a result of the Russian intervention in eastern Ukraine.

On 24 February 2022, Russia escalated its conflict with Ukraine by invading the country on several fronts in what has become the largest conventional military attack on a sovereign state in Europe since World War II. The invasion has received near universal international condemnation, and many countries have imposed sanctions on Russia and also supplied humanitarian and military aid to Ukraine. The invasion has also created Europe's largest refugee crisis since World War II. As of 8 November, approximately 15.11 million people had fled Ukraine, and 6.54 million people were internally displaced as of 27 October. More than 16,600 civilian casualties had been reported, as of 13 November. The invasion of Ukraine remains one of the two largest displacement crises worldwide (the other is the conflict in Syria).

GEOGRAPHY

Location: Eastern Europe, bordering the Black Sea, between Poland, Romania, and Moldova in the west and Russia in the east

Area: *total:* 603,550 sq km
land: 579,330 sq km
water: 24,220 sq km
note: approximately 43,133 sq km, or about 7.1% of Ukraine's area, is Russian occupied; the seized area includes all of Crimea and about one-third of both Luhans'k and Donets'k oblasts
country comparison to the world: 48

Area - comparative: almost four times the size of Georgia; slightly smaller than Texas
almost four times the size of Georgia; slightly smaller than Texas

Land boundaries: *total:* 5,581 km
border countries (6): Belarus 1,111 km; Hungary 128 km; Moldova 1,202 km; Poland 498 km; Romania 601 km; Russia 1,944 km, Slovakia 97 km

Maritime claims: *territorial sea:* 12 nm
exclusive economic zone: 200 nm
continental shelf: 200 m or to the depth of exploitation

Climate: temperate continental; Mediterranean only on the southern Crimean coast; precipitation disproportionately distributed, highest in west and north, lesser in east and southeast; winters vary from cool along the Black Sea to cold farther inland; warm summers across the greater part of the country, hot in the south

Terrain: mostly fertile plains (steppes) and plateaus, with mountains found only in the west (the Carpathians) or in the extreme south of the Crimean Peninsula

Elevation: *highest point:* Hora Hoverla 2,061 m
lowest point: Black Sea 0 m
mean elevation: 175 m

Natural resources: iron ore, coal, manganese, natural gas, oil, salt, sulfur, graphite, titanium, magnesium, kaolin, nickel, mercury, timber, arable land

Land use: *agricultural land:* 71.2% (2018 est.)
arable land: 56.1% (2018 est.)
permanent crops: 1.5% (2018 est.)
permanent pasture: 13.6% (2018 est.)
forest: 16.8% (2018 est.)
other: 12% (2018 est.)

Major rivers (by length in km): Danube (shared with Germany [s], Austria, Slovakia, Czechia, Hungary, Croatia, Serbia, Bulgaria, Moldova, and Romania [m]) -2,888 km; Dnieper river mouth (shared with Russia [s] and Belarus) - 2,287 km; Dniester river source and mouth (shared with Moldova) - 1,411 km; Vistula (shared with Poland [s/m] and Belarus) - 1,213 km
note – [s] after country name indicates river source; [m] after country name indicates river mouth

Population distribution: densest settlement in the eastern (Donbas) and western regions; noteable concentrations in and around major urban areas of Kyiv, Kharkiv, Donets'k, Dnipropetrovs'k, and Odesa

Geography - note: strategic position at the crossroads between Europe and Asia; second-largest country in Europe after Russia

PEOPLE AND SOCIETY

Ethnic groups: Ukrainian 77.8%, Russian 17.3%, Belarusian 0.6%, Moldovan 0.5%, Crimean Tatar 0.5%, Bulgarian 0.4%, Hungarian 0.3%, Romanian 0.3%, Polish 0.3%, Jewish 0.2%, other 1.8% (2001 est.)

Languages: Ukrainian (official) 67.5%, Russian (regional language) 29.6%, other (includes small Crimean Tatar-, Moldovan/Romanian-, and Hungarian-speaking minorities) 2.9% (2001 est.); note - in February 2018, the Constitutional Court ruled that 2012 language legislation entitling a language spoken by at least 10% of an oblast's population to be given the status of "regional language" - allowing for its use in courts, schools, and other government institutions -was unconstitutional, thus making the law invalid; Ukrainian remains the country's only official nationwide language
major-language sample(s): Світова Книга Фактів – найкраще джерело базової інформації. (Ukrainian)

Religions: Orthodox (includes the Orthodox Church of Ukraine (OCU), Ukrainian Autocephalous Orthodox Church (UAOC), and the Ukrainian Orthodox - Moscow Patriarchate (UOC-MP)), Ukrainian Greek Catholic, Roman Catholic, Protestant, Muslim, Jewish (2013 est.)
note: Ukraine's population is overwhelmingly Christian; the vast majority - up to two thirds - identify themselves as Orthodox, but many do not specify a particular branch; the OCU and the UOC-MP each represent less than a quarter of the country's population, the Ukrainian Greek Catholic Church accounts for 8-10%, and the UAOC accounts for 1-2%; Muslim and Jewish adherents each compose less than 1% of the total population

Age structure: *0-14 years:* 16.16% (male 3,658,127/female 3,438,887)
15-24 years: 9.28% (male 2,087,185/female 1,987,758)
25-54 years: 43.66% (male 9,456,905/female 9,718,758)
55-64 years: 13.87% (male 2,630,329/female 3,463,851)
65 years and over: 17.03% (male 2,523,600/female 4,957,539) (2020 est.)

Dependency ratios: *total dependency ratio:* 49.1
youth dependency ratio: 23.8
elderly dependency ratio: 25.3
potential support ratio: 4 (2020 est.)
note: data include Crimea

Population distribution: densest settlement in the eastern (Donbas) and western regions; noteable concentrations in and around major urban areas of Kyiv, Kharkiv, Donets'k, Dnipropetrovs'k, and Odesa

Major urban areas - population: 3.010 million KYIV (capital), 1.423 million Kharkiv, 1.008 million Odesa, 952,000 Dnipropetrovsk, 893,000 Donetsk (2022)

Sex ratio: *at birth:* 1.06 male(s)/female
0-14 years: 1.06 male(s)/female
15-24 years: 1.05 male(s)/female
25-54 years: 0.98 male(s)/female
55-64 years: 0.77 male(s)/female
65 years and over: 0.42 male(s)/female
total population: 0.86 male(s)/female (2022 est.)

Drinking water source: *improved: urban:* 99.4% of population
rural: 100% of population
total: 99.6% of population
unimproved: urban: 0.6% of population
rural: 0% of population
total: 0.4% of population (2020 est.)

Sanitation facility access: *improved: urban:* 100% of population
rural: 100% of population
total: 100% of population

Major infectious diseases: *note:* on 21 March 2022, the US Centers for Disease Control and Prevention (CDC) issued a Travel Alert for polio in Eastern Europe; Ukraine is currently considered a high risk to travelers for circulating vaccine-derived polioviruses (cVDPV); vaccine-derived poliovirus (VDPV) is a strain of the weakened poliovirus that was initially included in oral polio vaccine (OPV) and *that has changed over time and behaves more like the wild* *or naturally occurring virus;* this means it can be spread more easily to people who are unvaccinated against polio and who come in contact with the stool or respiratory secretions, such as from a sneeze, of an "infected" person who received oral polio vaccine; the CDC recommends that before any international travel, anyone unvaccinated, incompletely vaccinated, or with an unknown polio vaccination status should complete the routine polio vaccine series; before travel to any high-risk destination, the CDC recommends that adults who previously completed the full, routine polio vaccine series receive a single, lifetime booster dose of polio vaccine

Literacy: *definition:* age 15 and over can read and write
total population: 99.8%
male: 99.8%
female: 99.7% (2015)

ENVIRONMENT

Environment - current issues: air and water pollution; land degradation; solid waste management; biodiversity loss; deforestation; radiation contamination in the northeast from 1986 accident at Chornobyl' Nuclear Power Plant

Environment - international agreements: *party to:* Air Pollution, Air Pollution-Nitrogen Oxides, Air Pollution-Sulphur 85, Antarctic-Environmental Protection, Antarctic-Marine Living Resources, Antarctic Treaty, Biodiversity, Climate Change, Climate Change-Kyoto Protocol, Climate Change-Paris Agreement, Comprehensive Nuclear Test Ban, Desertification, Endangered Species, Environmental Modification, Hazardous Wastes, Law of the Sea, Marine Dumping-London Convention, Nuclear Test Ban, Ozone Layer Protection, Ship Pollution, Wetlands
signed, but not ratified: Air Pollution-Heavy Metals, Air Pollution-
Persistent Organic Pollutants, Air Pollution-Sulfur 94, Air Pollution-Volatile Organic Compounds

Air pollutants: *particulate matter emissions:* 18.29 micrograms per cubic meter (2016 est.)
carbon dioxide emissions: 202.25 megatons (2016 est.)
methane emissions: 63.37 megatons (2020 est.)

Climate: temperate continental; Mediterranean only on the southern Crimean coast; precipitation disproportionately distributed, highest in west and north, lesser in east and southeast; winters vary from cool along the Black Sea to cold farther inland; warm summers across the greater part of the country, hot in the south

Land use: *agricultural land:* 71.2% (2018 est.)
arable land: 56.1% (2018 est.)
permanent crops: 1.5% (2018 est.)
permanent pasture: 13.6% (2018 est.)
forest: 16.8% (2018 est.)
other: 12% (2018 est.)

Major infectious diseases: *note:* on 21 March 2022, the US Centers for Disease Control and Prevention (CDC) issued a Travel Alert for polio in Eastern Europe; Ukraine is currently considered a high risk to travelers for circulating vaccine-derived polioviruses (cVDPV); vaccine-derived poliovirus (VDPV) is a strain of the weakened poliovirus that was initially included in oral polio vaccine (OPV) and *that has changed over time and behaves more like the wild or naturally occurring virus;* this means it can be spread more easily to people who are unvaccinated against polio and who come in contact with the stool or respiratory secretions, such as from a sneeze, of an "infected" person who received oral polio vaccine; the CDC recommends that before any international travel, anyone unvaccinated, incompletely vaccinated, or with an unknown polio vaccination status should complete the routine polio vaccine series; before travel to any high-risk destination, the CDC recommends that adults who previously completed the full, routine polio vaccine series receive a single, lifetime booster dose of polio vaccine

Food insecurity: *widespread lack of access: due to conflict* - production prospects of 2022 winter crops hampered by low availability of inputs, delivery challenges, difficult physical access to fields due to the war, and eventual labor shortages; forecast for cereal exports in 2022 reduced, amid port closures, damage to infrastructure and implementation of government policies to secure sufficient domestic supplies; as of early March 2022, about 12 million people estimated to be in need of life saving assistance (2022)

Waste and recycling: *municipal solid waste generated annually:* 15,242,025 tons (2016 est.)
municipal solid waste recycled annually: 487,745 tons (2015 est.)
percent of municipal solid waste recycled: 3.2% (2015 est.)

Major rivers (by length in km): Danube (shared with Germany [s], Austria, Slovakia, Czechia, Hungary, Croatia, Serbia, Bulgaria, Moldova, and Romania [m]) -2,888 km; Dnieper river mouth (shared with Russia [s] and Belarus) - 2,287 km; Dniester river source and mouth (shared with Moldova) - 1,411 km; Vistula (shared with Poland [s/m] and Belarus) - 1,213 km
note – [s] after country name indicates river source; [m] after
country name indicates river mouth

Total water withdrawal: *municipal:* 2.397 billion cubic meters (2017 est.)
industrial: 3.577 billion cubic meters (2017 est.)
agricultural: 3.206 billion cubic meters (2017 est.)

GOVERNMENT

Country name: *conventional long form:* none
conventional short form: Ukraine
local long form: none
local short form: Ukraina
former: Ukrainian National Republic, Ukrainian State, Ukrainian Soviet Socialist Republic
etymology: name derives from the Old East Slavic word "ukraina" meaning "borderland or march (militarized border region)" and began to be used extensively in the 19th century; originally Ukrainians referred to themselves as Rusyny (Rusyns, Ruthenians, or Ruthenes), an endonym derived from the medieval Rus state (Kyivan Rus)

Capital: *name:* Kyiv (Kiev)
geographic coordinates: 50 26 N, 30 31 E
time difference: UTC+2 (7 hours ahead of Washington, DC, during Standard Time)
daylight saving time: +1hr, begins last Sunday in March; ends last Sunday in October
etymology: the name is associated with that of Kyi, who along with his brothers Shchek and Khoryv, and their sister Lybid, are the legendary founders of the medieval city of Kyiv; Kyi being the eldest brother, the city was named after him
note: pronounced KAY-yiv

Administrative divisions: 24 provinces (oblasti, singular - oblast'), 1 autonomous republic* (avtonomna respublika), and 2 municipalities** (mista, singular -misto) with oblast status; Cherkasy, Chernihiv, Chernivtsi, Crimea or Avtonomna Respublika Krym* (Simferopol), Dnipropetrovsk (Dnipro), Donetsk, Ivano-Frankivsk, Kharkiv, Kherson, Khmelnytskyi, Kirovohrad (Kropyvnytskyi), Kyiv**, Kyiv, Luhansk, Lviv, Mykolaiv, Odesa, Poltava, Rivne, Sevastopol**, Sumy, Ternopil, Vinnytsia, Volyn (Lutsk), Zakarpattia (Uzhhorod), Zaporizhzhia, Zhytomyr
note 1: administrative divisions have the same names as their administrative centers (exceptions have the administrative center name following in parentheses); plans include the eventual renaming of Dnipropetrovsk and Kirovohrad oblasts, but because these names are mentioned in the Constitution of Ukraine, the change will require a constitutional amendment
note 2: the US Government does not recognize Russia's illegal annexation of Ukraine's Autonomous Republic of Crimea and the municipality of Sevastopol, nor their redesignation as the "Republic of Crimea" and the "Federal City of Sevastopol"

Independence: 24 August 1991 (from the Soviet Union); notable earlier dates: ca. 982 (VOLODYMYR I consolidates Kyivan Rus); 1199 (Principality (later Kingdom) of Ruthenia formed); 1648 (establishment of the Cossack Hetmanate); 22 January 1918 (from Soviet Russia)

National holiday: Independence Day, 24 August (1991); note - 22 January 1918, the day Ukraine first declared its independence from Soviet Russia, and the date the short-lived Western and Greater (Eastern) Ukrainian republics united (1919), is now celebrated as Unity Day

Constitution: *history:* several previous; latest adopted and ratified 28 June 1996
amendments: proposed by the president of Ukraine or by at least one third of the Supreme Council members; adoption requires simple majority vote by the Council and at least two-thirds majority vote in its next regular session; adoption of proposals relating to general constitutional principles, elections, and amendment procedures requires two-thirds majority vote by the Council and approval in a referendum; constitutional articles on personal rights and freedoms, national independence, and territorial integrity cannot be amended; amended several times, last in 2019

Legal system: civil law system; judicial review of legislative acts

Citizenship: *citizenship by birth:* no
citizenship by descent only: at least one parent must be a citizen of Ukraine
dual citizenship recognized: no
residency requirement for naturalization: 5 years

Executive branch: *chief of state:* President Volodymyr ZELENSKYY (since 20 May 2019)
head of government: Prime Minister Denys SHMYHAL (since 4 March 2020)
cabinet: Cabinet of Ministers nominated by the prime minister, approved by the Verkhovna Rada
elections/appointments: president directly elected by absolute majority popular vote in 2 rounds if needed for a 5-year term (eligible for a second term); election last held on 31 March and 21 April 2019

(next to be held in March 2024); prime minister selected by the Verkhovna Rada
election results:
2019: Volodymyr ZELENSKYY elected president; percent of vote in the first round Volodymyr ZELENSKYY (Servant of the People) 30.2%, Petro POROSHENKO (BPP-Solidarity) 15.6%, Yuliya TYMOSHENKO (Fatherland) 13.4%, Yuriy BOYKO (Opposition Platform-For Life) 11.7%, 35 other candidates 29.1%; percent of vote in the second round Volodymyr ZELENSKYY (Servant of the People) 73.2%, Petro POROSHENKO (BPP-Solidarity) 24.5%, other 2.3%; Denys SHMYHAL (independent) elected prime minister; Verkhovna Rada vote - 291-59
2014: Petro POROSHENKO elected president in the first round; percent of vote - Petro POROSHENKO (independent) 54.5%, Yuliya TYMOSHENKO (Fatherland) 12.9%, Oleh LYASHKO (Radical Party) 8.4%, other 24.2%; Volodymyr HROYSMAN (BPP) elected prime minister; Verkhovna Rada vote - 257-50
note: there is also a National Security and Defense Council or NSDC originally created in 1992 as the National Security Council; the NSDC staff is tasked with developing national security policy on domestic and international matters and advising the president; a presidential administration helps draft presidential edicts and provides policy support to the president

Legislative branch: *description:* unicameral Supreme Council or Verkhovna Rada (450 seats; 225 members directly elected in single-seat constituencies by simple majority vote and 225 directly elected in a single nationwide constituency by closed, party-list proportional representation vote; members serve 5-year terms)
elections:
last held on 21 July 2019 (next to be held in July 2024)
election results:
percent of vote by party - Servant of the People 43.2%, Opposition Platform-For Life 13.1%, Batkivshchyna 8.2%, European Solidarity 8.1%, Voice 5.8%, other 21.6%; Servant of the People 254, Opposition Platform for Life 43, Batkivshchyna 26, European Solidarity 25, Voice 20, Opposition Bloc 6, Svoboda 1, Self Reliance 1, United Centre 1, Bila Tserkva Together 1, Independents 46; note - voting not held in Crimea and parts of two Russian-occupied eastern oblasts leaving 26 seats vacant; although this brings the total to 424 elected members (of 450 potential), article 83 of the constitution mandates that a parliamentary majority consists of 226 seats

Judicial branch: *highest court(s):* Supreme Court of Ukraine or SCU (consists of 100 judges, organized into civil, criminal, commercial and administrative chambers, and a grand chamber); Constitutional Court (consists of 18 justices); High Anti-Corruption Court (consists of 39 judges, including 12 in the Appeals Chamber)
judge selection and term of office: Supreme Court judges recommended by the High Qualification Commission of Judges (a 16-member state body responsible for judicial candidate testing and assessment and judicial administration), submitted to the High Council of Justice, a 21-member independent body of judicial officials responsible for judicial self-governance and administration, and appointed by the president; judges serve until mandatory retirement at age 65; High Anti-Corruption Court judges are selected by the same process as Supreme Court justices, with one addition – a majority of a combined High Qualification Commission of Judges and a 6-member Public Council of International Experts must vote in favor of potential judges in order to recommend their nomination to the High Council of Justice; this majority must include at least 3 members of the Public Council of International Experts; Constitutional Court justices appointed - 6 each by the president, by the Congress of Judges, and by the Verkhovna Rada; judges serve 9-year nonrenewable terms
subordinate courts: Courts of Appeal; district courts
note: specialized courts were abolished as part of Ukraine's judicial reform program; in November 2019, President ZELENSKYY signed a bill on legal reforms

Political parties and leaders: Batkivshchyna (Fatherland) [Yuliya TYMOSHENKO]
European Solidarity or YeS [Petro POROSHENKO]
Holos (Voice or Vote) [Kira RUDYK]
Opposition Bloc [Evgeny MURAYEV] (formerly known as
Opposition Bloc — Party for Peace and Development, successor of the Industrial Party of Ukraine, and resulted from a schism in the original Opposition Bloc in 2019; banned in court June 2022; ceased to exist in July 2022)
Opposition Bloc or OB (divided into Opposition Bloc - Party for Peace and Development and Opposition Platform - For Life in 2019; ceased to exist in July 2022)
Opposition Platform - For Life [Yuriy BOYKO] (resulted from a schism in the original Opposition Bloc in 2019; activities suspended by the National Security and Defense Countil in March 2022; dissolved in April 2022)
Radical Party or RPOL [Oleh LYASHKO]
Samopomich (Self Reliance) [Oksana Ivanivna SYROYID]
Servant of the People [Olena Oleksiivna SHULIAK]
Svoboda (Freedom) [Oleh TYAHNYBOK]

International organization participation: Australia Group, BSEC, CBSS (observer), CD, CE, CEI, CICA (observer), CIS (participating member, has not signed the 1993 CIS charter), EAEC (observer), EAPC, EBRD, FAO, GCTU, GUAM, IAEA, IBRD, ICAO, ICC (national committees), ICRM, IDA, IFC, IFRCS, IHO, ILO, IMF, IMO, IMSO, Interpol, IOC, IOM, IPU, ISO, ITU, ITUC (NGOs), LAIA (observer), MIGA, MONUSCO, NAM (observer), NSG, OAS (observer), OIF (observer), OPCW, OSCE, PCA, PFP, SELEC (observer), UN, UNCTAD, UNESCO, UNFICYP, UNHRC, UNIDO, UNISFA, UNMIL, UNMISS, UNOCI, UNWTO, UPU, Wassenaar Arrangement, WCO, WFTU (NGOs), WHO, WIPO, WMO, WTO, ZC

Diplomatic representation in the US: *chief of mission:* Ambassador Oksana Serhiyivna MARKAROVA (since 7 July 2021)
chancery: 3350 M Street NW, Washington, DC 20007
telephone: [1] (202) 349-2963
FAX: [1] (202) 333-0817
email address and website:
emb_us@mfa.gov.ua; consul_us@mfa.gov.ua
https://usa.mfa.gov.ua/en
consulate(s) general: Chicago, New York, San Francisco

Diplomatic representation from the US: *chief of mission:* Ambassador Bridget A. BRINK (since 18 May 2022)
embassy: 4 A. I. Igor Sikorsky Street, 04112 Kyiv
mailing address: 5850 Kyiv Place, Washington, DC 20521-5850
telephone: [380] (44) 521-5000
FAX: [380] (44) 521-5544
email address and website:
kyivacs@state.gov
https://ua.usembassy.gov/

Flag description: two equal horizontal bands of azure (top) and golden yellow; although the colors date back to medieval heraldry, in modern times they are sometimes claimed to represent grain fields under a blue sky

National anthem: *name:* "Shche ne vmerla Ukraina" (Ukraine Has Not Yet Perished)
lyrics/music: Paul CHUBYNSKYI/Mikhail VERBYTSKYI
note: music adopted 1991, lyrics adopted 2003; song first performed in 1864 at the Ukraine Theatre in Lviv; the lyrics, originally written in 1862, were revised in 2003

ECONOMY

Economic overview: After Russia, the Ukrainian Republic was the most important economic component of the former Soviet Union, producing about four times the output of the next-ranking republic. Its fertile black soil accounted for more than one fourth of Soviet agricultural output, and its farms provided substantial quantities of meat, milk, grain, and vegetables to other republics. Likewise, its diversified heavy industry supplied unique equipment such as large diameter pipes and vertical drilling apparatus, and raw materials to industrial and mining sites in other regions of the former USSR.

Shortly after independence in August 1991, the Ukrainian Government liberalized most prices and erected a legal framework for privatization, but widespread resistance to reform within the government and the legislature soon stalled reform efforts and led to some backtracking. Output by 1999 had fallen to less than 40% of the 1991 level. Outside institutions - particularly the IMF encouraged Ukraine to quicken the pace and scope of reforms to foster economic growth. Ukrainian Government officials eliminated most tax and customs privileges in a March 2005 budget law, bringing more economic activity out of Ukraine's large shadow economy. From 2000 until mid-2008, Ukraine's economy was buoyant despite political turmoil between the prime minister and president. The economy contracted nearly 15% in 2009, among the worst economic performances in the world. In April 2010, Ukraine negotiated a price discount on Russian gas imports in exchange for extending Russia's lease on its naval base in Crimea.

Ukraine's oligarch-dominated economy grew slowly from 2010 to 2013 but remained behind peers in the region and among Europe's poorest. After former President YANUKOVYCH fled the country during the Revolution of Dignity, Ukraine's economy fell into crisis because of Russia's annexation of Crimea, military conflict in the eastern part of the country, and a trade war with Russia, resulting in a 17% decline in GDP, inflation at nearly 60%, and dwindling foreign currency reserves. The international community began efforts to stabilize the Ukrainian economy, including a March 2014 IMF assistance package of $17.5 billion, of which Ukraine has received four disbursements, most recently in April 2017, bringing the total disbursed as of that date to approximately $8.4 billion. Ukraine has made progress on reforms designed to make the country prosperous, democratic, and transparent, including creation of a national anti-corruption agency, overhaul of the banking sector, establishment of a transparent VAT refund system, and increased transparency in government procurement. But more improvements are needed, including fighting corruption, developing capital markets, improving the business environment to attract foreign investment, privatizing state-owned enterprises, and land reform. The fifth tranche of the IMF program, valued at $1.9 billion, was delayed in mid-2017 due to lack of progress on outstanding reforms, including adjustment of gas tariffs to import parity levels and adoption of legislation establishing an independent anticorruption court.

Russia's occupation of Crimea in March 2014 and ongoing Russian aggression in eastern Ukraine have hurt economic growth. With the loss of a major portion of Ukraine's heavy industry in Donbas and ongoing violence, the economy contracted by 6.6% in 2014 and by 9.8% in 2015, but it returned to low growth in in 2016 and 2017, reaching 2.3% and 2.0%, respectively, as key reforms took hold. Ukraine also redirected trade activity towards the EU following the implementation of a bilateral Deep and Comprehensive Free Trade Agreement, displacing Russia as its largest trading partner. A prohibition on commercial trade with separatist-controlled territories in early 2017 has not impacted Ukraine's key industrial sectors as much as expected, largely because of favorable external conditions. Ukraine returned to international debt markets in September 2017, issuing a $3 billion sovereign bond.

Credit ratings:

Fitch rating: B (2019)

Moody's rating: B3 (2020)

Standard & Poors rating: B (2019)

GDP - composition, by end use: *household consumption:* 66.5% (2017 est.)
government consumption: 20.4% (2017 est.)
investment in fixed capital: 16% (2017 est.)
investment in inventories: 4.7% (2017 est.)
exports of goods and services: 47.9% (2017 est.)
imports of goods and services: -55.6% (2017 est.)

Agricultural products: maize, wheat, potatoes, sunflower seed, sugar beet, milk, barley, soybeans, rapeseed, tomatoes

Industries: coal, electric power, ferrous and nonferrous metals, machinery and transport equipment, chemicals, food processing

Budget: *revenues:* 29.82 billion (2017 est.)
expenditures: 31.55 billion (2017 est.)
note: this is the planned, consolidated budget

Public debt: 71% of GDP (2017 est.)
81.2% of GDP (2016 est.)
note: the total public debt of $64.5 billion consists of: domestic public debt ($23.8 billion); external public debt ($26.1 billion); and sovereign guarantees ($14.6 billion)
country comparison to the world: 49

Exports: $60.67 billion (2020 est.) note: data are in current year dollars
$63.56 billion (2019 est.) note: data are in current year dollars
$59.18 billion (2018 est.) note: data are in current year dollars
country comparison to the world: 52

Exports - commodities: corn, sunflower seed oils, iron and iron products, wheat, insulated wiring, rapeseed (2019)

Imports: $62.46 billion (2020 est.) note: data are in current year dollars
$76.07 billion (2019 est.) note: data are in current year dollars
$70.56 billion (2018 est.) note: data are in current year dollars
country comparison to the world: 51

Exchange rates: hryvnia (UAH) per US dollar -
28.10001 (2020 est.)
23.7 (2019 est.)
27.80499 (2018 est.)
21.8447 (2014 est.)
11.8867 (2013 est.)

ENERGY

Electricity: *installed generating capacity:* 56.816 million kW (2020 est.)
consumption: 124,533,790,000 kWh (2019 est.)
exports: 5.139 billion kWh (2020 est.)
imports: 2.72 billion kWh (2020 est.)
transmission/distribution losses: 16.434 billion kWh (2019 est.)

Electricity generation sources: *fossil fuels:* 37.6% of total installed capacity (2020 est.)
nuclear: 55.9% of total installed capacity (2020 est.)
solar: 1.2% of total installed capacity (2020 est.)
wind: 1.4% of total installed capacity (2020 est.)
hydroelectricity: 3.6% of total installed capacity (2020 est.)
biomass and waste: 0.3% of total installed capacity (2020 est.)

Coal: *production:* 23.908 million metric tons (2020 est.)
consumption: 41.181 million metric tons (2020 est.)
exports: 61,000 metric tons (2020 est.)
imports: 17.333 million metric tons (2020 est.)
proven reserves: 34.375 billion metric tons (2019 est.)

Petroleum: *total petroleum production:* 57,700 bbl/day (2021 est.)
refined petroleum consumption: 248,100 bbl/day (2019 est.)
crude oil and lease condensate exports: 700 bbl/day (2018 est.)
crude oil and lease condensate imports: 6,500 bbl/day (2018 est.)
crude oil estimated reserves: 395 million barrels (2021 est.)

Natural gas: *production:* 19,511,040,000 cubic meters (2019 est.)
consumption: 26,413,486,000 cubic meters (2019 est.)
exports: 0 cubic meters (2021 est.)
imports: 10,740,619,000 cubic meters (2019 est.)
proven reserves: 1,104,355,000,000 cubic meters (2021 est.)

Carbon dioxide emissions: 185.686 million metric tonnes of CO2 (2019 est.)
from coal and metallurgical coke: 105.929 million metric tonnes of CO2 (2019 est.)
from petroleum and other liquids: 30.365 million metric tonnes of CO2 (2019 est.)
from consumed natural gas: 49.392 million metric tonnes of CO2 (2019 est.)
country comparison to the world: 33

COMMUNICATIONS

Telecommunication systems: *general assessment:* the Ukraine government announced grand plans in November 2020 to enable the commercial launch of 5G mobile services by the end of 2021 (including a spectrum auction slated for October), there has been very little progress made regarding that plan; growth in the mobile sector is flat, while the market waits for the regulator and the three dominant MNOs to move towards making faster and more powerful services available for public consumption (2021)
domestic: fixed-line teledensity is nearly 8 per 100; the mobilecellular telephone system's expansion has slowed, largely due to saturation of the market that is now just over 129 mobile phones per 100 persons (2020)
international: country code - 380; landing point for the Kerch Strait Cable connecting Ukraine to Russia; 2 new domestic trunk lines are a part of the fiber-optic TAE system and 3 Ukrainian links have been installed in the fiber-optic TEL project that connects 18 countries; additional international service is provided by the Italy-Turkey-Ukraine-Russia (ITUR) fiber-optic submarine cable and by an unknown number of earth stations in the Intelsat, Inmarsat, and Intersputnik satellite systems

Broadcast media: Ukraine's media landscape is dominated by oligarch-owned news outlets, which are often politically motivated and at odds with one another and/or the government; while polls suggest most Ukrainians still receive news from traditional media sources, social media is a crucial component of information dissemination in Ukraine; almost all Ukrainian politicians and opinion leaders communicate with the public via social media and maintain at least one social media page, if not more; this allows them direct communication with audiences, and news often breaks on Facebook or Twitter before being picked up by traditional news outlets

Ukraine television serves as the principal source of news; the largest national networks are controlled by oligarchs: TRK Ukraina is owned by Rinat Akhmetov; Studio 1+1 is owned by Ihor Kolomoyskyy; Inter is owned by Dmytro Firtash and Serhiy Lyovochkin; and StarlightMedia channels (ICTV, STB, and Novyi Kanal) are owned by Victor Pinchuk; a set of 24-hour news channels also have clear political affiliations: pro-Ukrainian government Channel 5 and Pryamyi are linked to President Petro Poroshenko; 24 is owned by opposition, but not pro-Russian, politicians; UA: Suspilne is a public television station under the umbrella of the National Public Broadcasting Company of Ukraine; while it is often praised by media experts for balanced coverage, it lags in popularity; Ukrainian Radio, institutionally linked to UA: Suspilne, is one of only two national talk radio networks, with the other being the privately owned Radio NV
(2021)

Communications - note: a sorting code to expeditiously handle large volumes of mail was first set up in Ukraine (then part of the Soviet Union) in the 1930s; the sophisticated, three-part (number-letter-number) postal code system, referred to as an "index," was the world's first postal zip code; the system functioned well and was in use from 1932 to 1939 when it was abruptly discontinued

TRANSPORTATION

National air transport system: *number of registered air carriers:* 14 (2020)
inventory of registered aircraft operated by air carriers: 126
annual passenger traffic on registered air carriers: 7,854,842 (2018)
annual freight traffic on registered air carriers: 75.26 million (2018) mt-km

Pipelines: 36,720 km gas, 4,514 km oil, 4,363 km refined products (2013)

Ports and terminals: *major seaport(s):* Feodosiia, Chornomorsk, Mariupol, Mykolaiv, Odesa, Yuzhne
river port(s): Kherson, Kyiv (Dnieper River), Mykolaiv (Pivdennyy Buh River)

MILITARY AND SECURITY

Military and security forces: Armed Forces of Ukraine (AFU; Zbroyni Syly Ukrayiny or ZSU): Ground Forces (Sukhoputni Viys'ka), Naval Forces (Viys'kovo-Mors'ki Syly, VMS), Air Forces (Povitryani Syly, PS), Air Assault Forces (Desantno-shturmovi Viyska, DShV), Ukrainian Special Operations Forces (UASOF), Territorial Defense Forces (Reserves); Ministry of Internal Affairs: National Guard of Ukraine, State Border Guard Service of Ukraine (includes Maritime Border Guard) (2022)
note 1: in the event that martial law is declared, all National Guard units, with certain exceptions such as those tasked with providing for diplomatic security of embassies and consulates, would come under the command of the Ministry of Defense as auxiliary forces to the Armed Forces
note 2: the Territorial Defense Forces (TDF) were formally established in July 2021; the TDF evolved from former Territorial Defense Battalions and other volunteer militia and paramilitary units that were organized in 2014-2015 to fight Russian-backed separatists in the Donbas; in January 2022, the TDF was activated as a separate military branch; it is organized into 25 brigades of varying size representing each of the 24 oblasts, plus the city of Kyiv; the International Legion of Territorial Defense, comprised of foreigners who have volunteered for Ukrainian military service since February 2022, is under the TDF

Military and security service personnel strengths: up to 700,000 active duty personnel, including the Armed Forces, Territorial Defense Forces, National Guard, and State Border Guard (July 2022)
note 1: following the Russian invasion of Ukraine in February 2022, President ZELENSKY announced a general mobilization of the country; prior to the invasion, approximately 200,000 active Armed Forces troops (125,000 Army; 25,000 Airborne/Air Assault Forces; 2,000 Special Operations Forces; 10,000 Navy; 40,000 Air Force); approximately 50,000 National Guard; approximately 40,000 State Border Guard

Military equipment inventories and acquisitions: the Ukrainian military is equipped mostly with Russian-origin and Soviet-era weapons systems; since the Russian invasion in February 2022, it has received considerable quantities of weapons, including more modern Western systems, from European countries and the US; Ukraine has a broad defense industry capable of building, maintaining, and upgrading a variety of Soviet-era weapons systems, including armored vehicles, combat aircraft, missiles, and air defense systems (2022)

Military service age and obligation: conscription abolished in 2012, but reintroduced in 2014; 20-27 years of age for compulsory military service; prior to the Russian invasion of February 2022, conscript service obligation was 12-18 months, depending on the service (2022)
note 1: following the Russian invasion in 2022, all nonexempt men ages 18 to 60 were required to register with their local recruitment offices and undergo medical screening for possible service; the Territorial Defense Forces (TDF) accepts volunteers, 18-60 years of age; since the invasion, hundreds of thousands of Ukrainians have volunteered for the regular armed forces, the TDF, or to work in civilian defense activities **note 2:** women have been able to volunteer for military service since 1993; as of September 2022, approximately 50,000 were serving
note 3: since 2015, the Ukrainian military has allowed foreigners and stateless persons, 18-45 (in special cases up to 60), to join on 3-5-year contracts, based on qualifications; following the Russian invasion in 2022, the military began accepting medically fit foreign volunteers on a larger scale, with an emphasis on persons with combat experience; wartime volunteers serve in the International Legion of Territorial Defense of Ukraine, typically for 6 months

Military deployments: *note:* prior to the Russian invasion in 2022, Ukraine contributed about 500 troops to the Lithuania, Poland, and Ukraine joint military brigade (LITPOLUKRBRIG), which was established in 2014; the brigade is headquartered in Poland and is comprised of an international staff, three battalions, and specialized units; units affiliated with the multinational brigade remain within the structures of the armed forces of their respective countries until the brigade is activated for participation in an international operation

Military - note: Ukraine has a relationship with NATO dating back to the early 1990s when Ukraine joined the North Atlantic Cooperation Council (1991) and the Partnership for Peace program (1994); the relationship intensified in the wake of the 2014 Russia-Ukraine conflict and Russian seizure of Crimea to include NATO support for Ukrainian military capabilities development and capacity-building; NATO further increased its support to the Ukrainian military following Russia's full-scale invasion in 2022 (2022)

TRANSNATIONAL ISSUES

Disputes - international: *Ukraine-Belarus:* in 1997, Ukraine and Belarus signed a boundary delimitation treaty; the instruments of ratification were exchanged in 2013; a joint commission should be established to enable the actual demarcation to begin
Ukraine-Hungary: hundreds of thousands of Ukrainian refugees are crossing the border to Hungary to escape the Russian invasion in their country
Ukraine-Moldova: hundreds of thousands of Ukrainian refugees are crossing the border to Moldova to escape the Russian invasion in their country; Ukraine and Moldova signed an agreement officially delimiting their border in 1999, but the border has not been demarcated due to Moldova's difficulties with the break-away region of Transnistria; Moldova and Ukraine operate joint customs posts to monitor transit of people and commodities through Moldova's Transnistria Region, which remains under the auspices of an Organization for Security and Cooperation in Europe-mandated peacekeeping mission comprised of Moldovan, Transnistrian, Russian, and Ukrainian troops
Ukraine-Poland: hundreds of thousands of Ukrainian refugees are crossing the border to Poland to escape the Russian invasion in their country
Ukraine-Romania: hundreds of thousands of Ukrainian refugees are crossing the border to Romania to escape the Russian invasion in their country, the ICJ in 2009 ruled largely in favor of Romania in its dispute submitted in 2004 over Ukrainian-administered Zmiyinyy/Serpilor (Snake) Island and Black Sea maritime boundary delimitation; Romania opposes Ukraine's reopening of a navigation canal from the Danube border through Ukraine to the Black Sea
Ukraine-Russia: the dispute over the boundary between Russia and Ukraine through the Kerch Strait and Sea of Azov is suspended due to the occupation of Crimea by Russia
Ukraine-Slovakia: tens of thousands of Ukrainian refugees are crossing the border to Slovakia to escape the Russian invasion of their country

Refugees and internally displaced persons: IDPs: 1,461,700 (Russian-sponsored separatist violence in Crimea and eastern Ukraine) (2021); 6.54 million (Russian invasion), according to the UN (as of 27 October 2022); note – the more recent invasion total may reflect some double counting, since it is impossible to determine how many of the recent IDPs may also include IDPs from the earlier Russian-sponsored violence in Crimea and eastern Ukraine
stateless persons: 35,875 (mid-year 2021); note - citizens of the former USSR who were permanently resident in Ukraine were granted citizenship upon Ukraine's independence in 1991, but some missed this window of opportunity; people arriving after 1991, Crimean Tatars, ethnic Koreans, people with expired Soviet passports, and people with no documents have difficulty acquiring Ukrainian citizenship; following the fall of the Soviet Union in 1989, thousands of Crimean Tatars and their descendants deported from Ukraine under the STALIN regime returned to their homeland, some being stateless and others holding the citizenship of Uzbekistan or other former Soviet republics; a 1998 bilateral agreement between Ukraine and Uzbekistan simplified the process of renouncing Uzbek citizenship and obtaining Ukrainian citizenship

Illicit drugs: a transit country for illicit drug trafficking into the European Union due to its location amidst several important trafficking routes into western Europe, ports on the Black and Azov seas, extensive river routes, and porous northern and eastern borders; South American cocaine moves through Ukrainian seaports and airports; amphetamine and methamphetamine laboratories supply the local market

UNITED ARAB EMIRATES

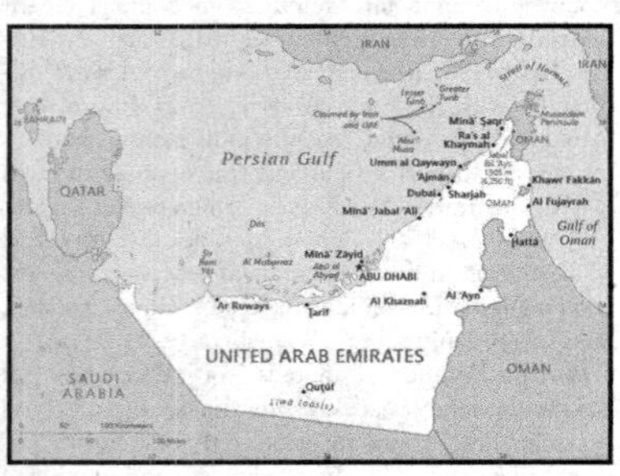

INTRODUCTION

Background: The Trucial States of the Persian Gulf coast granted the UK control of their defense and foreign affairs in 19th century treaties. In 1971, six of these states - Abu Dhabi, 'Ajman, Al Fujayrah, Ash Shariqah, Dubayy, and Umm al Qaywayn -merged to form the United Arab Emirates (UAE). They were joined in 1972 by Ra's al Khaymah. The UAE's per capita GDP is on par with those of leading West European nations. For more than three decades, oil and global finance drove the UAE's economy. In 2008-09, the confluence of falling oil prices, collapsing real estate prices, and the international banking crisis hit the UAE especially hard. The UAE did not experience the "Arab Spring" unrest seen elsewhere in the Middle East in 2010-11, partly because of the government's multi-year, $1.6-billion infrastructure investment plan for the poorer northern emirates, and its aggressive pursuit of advocates of political reform. The UAE in recent years has played a growing role in regional affairs. In addition to donating billions of dollars in economic aid to help stabilize Egypt, the UAE was one of the first countries to join the Defeat-ISIS coalition, and to participate as a key partner in a Saudi-led military campaign in Yemen. On 15 September 2020, the UAE and Bahrain signed a peace agreement (the Abraham Accords) with Israel – brokered by the US – in Washington DC. The UAE and Bahrain thus became the third and fourth Middle Eastern countries, along with Egypt and Jordan, to recognize Israel.

GEOGRAPHY

Location: Middle East, bordering the Gulf of Oman and the Persian Gulf, between Oman and Saudi Arabia

Geographic coordinates: 24 00 N, 54 00 E

Map references: Middle East

Area: *total:* 83,600 sq km
land: 83,600 sq km
water: 0 sq km
country comparison to the world: 115

Area - comparative: slightly larger than South Carolina; slightly smaller than Maine

Land boundaries: *total:* 1,066 km
border countries (2): Oman 609 km; Saudi Arabia 457 km

Coastline: 1,318 km

Maritime claims: *territorial sea:* 12 nm
contiguous zone: 24 nm
exclusive economic zone: 200 nm
continental shelf: 200 nm or to the edge of the continental margin

Climate: desert; cooler in eastern mountains

Terrain: flat, barren coastal plain merging into rolling sand dunes of vast desert; mountains in east

Elevation: *highest point:* Jabal Bil 'Ays 1,905 m
lowest point: Persian Gulf 0 m
mean elevation: 149 m

Natural resources: petroleum, natural gas

Land use: *agricultural land:* 4.6% (2018 est.)
arable land: 0.5% (2018 est.)
permanent crops: 0.5% (2018 est.)
permanent pasture: 3.6% (2018 est.)
forest: 3.8% (2018 est.)
other: 91.6% (2018 est.)

Irrigated land: 923 sq km (2012)

Population distribution: population is heavily concentrated to the northeast on the Musandam Peninsula; the three largest emirates - Abu Dhabi, Dubai, and Sharjah - are home to nearly 85% of the population

Natural hazards: frequent sand and dust storms

Geography - note: strategic location along southern approaches to Strait of Hormuz, a vital transit point for world crude oil

PEOPLE AND SOCIETY

Population: 9,915,803 (2022 est.)
note: the UN estimated the country's total population was 10,082,000 as of 2022; immigrants make up 88.1% of the total population, according to UN data (2020)
country comparison to the world: 92

Nationality: *noun:* Emirati(s)
adjective: Emirati

Ethnic groups: Emirati 11.6%, South Asian 59.4% (includes Indian 38.2%, Bangladeshi 9.5%, Pakistani 9.4%, other 2.3%), Egyptian 10.2%, Filipino 6.1%, other 12.8% (2015 est.)
note: data represent the total population; as of 2019, immigrants make up about 87.9% of the total population, according to UN data

Languages: Arabic (official), English, Hindi, Malayam, Urdu, Pashto, Tagalog, Persian
major-language sample(s):
كتاب حقائق العالم، المصدر الذي لا يمكن الاستغناء عنه للمعلومات الأساسية
(Arabic)

Religions: Muslim (official) 76%, Christian 9%, other (primarily Hindu and Buddhist, less than 5% of the population consists of Parsi, Baha'i, Druze, Sikh, Ahmadi, Ismaili, Dawoodi Bohra Muslim, and Jewish) 15% (2005 est.)
note: data represent the total population; as of 2020, immigrants make up about 88.1% of the total population, according to UN data

Age structure: *0-14 years:* 14.45% (male 745,492/female 698,330)
15-24 years: 7.94% (male 431,751/female 361,804)
25-54 years: 68.03% (male 5,204,618/female 1,592,987)
55-64 years: 7.68% (male 658,892/female 108,850)
65 years and over: 1.9% (male 146,221/female 43,138) (2020 est.)

Dependency ratios: *total dependency ratio:* 19.2
youth dependency ratio: 17.7
elderly dependency ratio: 1.5
potential support ratio: 66.4 (2020 est.)

Median age: *total:* 38.4 years
male: 40.4 years
female: 31.5 years (2020 est.)
country comparison to the world: 63

Population growth rate: 0.58% (2022 est.)
country comparison to the world: 147

Birth rate: 10.81 births/1,000 population (2022 est.)
country comparison to the world: 176

Death rate: 1.56 deaths/1,000 population (2022 est.)
country comparison to the world: 228

Net migration rate: -3.45 migrant(s)/1,000 population (2022 est.)
country comparison to the world: 187

Population distribution: population is heavily concentrated to the northeast on the Musandam Peninsula; the three largest emirates - Abu Dhabi, Dubai, and Sharjah - are home to nearly 85% of the population

Urbanization: *urban population:* 87.5% of total population (2022)
rate of urbanization: 1.5% annual rate of change (2020-25 est.)

Major urban areas - population: 2.964 million Dubai, 1.786 million Sharjah, 1.540 million ABU DHABI (capital) (2022)

Sex ratio: *at birth:* 1.06 male(s)/female
0-14 years: 1.06 male(s)/female
15-24 years: 1.2 male(s)/female
25-54 years: 3.32 male(s)/female
55-64 years: 5.41 male(s)/female
65 years and over: 1.86 male(s)/female
total population: 2.21 male(s)/female (2022 est.)

Maternal mortality ratio: 3 deaths/100,000 live births (2017 est.)
country comparison to the world: 180

Infant mortality rate: *total:* 5.14 deaths/1,000 live births
male: 5.71 deaths/1,000 live births
female: 4.53 deaths/1,000 live births (2022 est.)
country comparison to the world: 175

Life expectancy at birth: *total population:* 79.56 years
male: 78.21 years
female: 80.99 years (2022 est.)
country comparison to the world: 60

Total fertility rate: 1.64 children born/woman (2022 est.)
country comparison to the world: 177

Drinking water source: *improved: total:* 100% of population
unimproved: total: 0% of population (2020 est.)

Current health expenditure: 4.3% of GDP (2019)

Physicians density: 2.6 physicians/1,000 population (2019)

Hospital bed density: 1.4 beds/1,000 population (2017)

Sanitation facility access: Improved: *total:* 100% of population
unimproved: total: 0% of population (2020 est.)

HIV/AIDS - adult prevalence rate: 0.1% (2020)
country comparison to the world: 133

HIV/AIDS - people living with HIV/AIDS: (2020) <1,000

HIV/AIDS - deaths: 100 (2020) <100
country comparison to the world: 59

Major infectious diseases: *note:* widespread ongoing transmission of a respiratory illness caused by the novel coronavirus (COVID-19) is occurring throughout UAE; as of 18 August 2022, UAE has reported a total of 1,007,039 cases of COVID-19 or 10,181.98 cumulative cases of COVID-19 per 100,000 population with a total of 2,340 cumulative deaths or a rate of 23.65 cumulative deaths per 100,000 population

Obesity - adult prevalence rate: 31.7% (2016)
country comparison to the world: 20

Alcohol consumption per capita: *total:* 2.03 liters of pure alcohol (2019 est.)
beer: 0.21 liters of pure alcohol (2019 est.)
wine: 0.14 liters of pure alcohol (2019 est.)
spirits: 1.65 liters of pure alcohol (2019 est.)
other alcohols: 0.02 liters of pure alcohol (2019 est.)
country comparison to the world: 130

Education expenditures: 3.1% of GDP (2019 est.)
country comparison to the world: 148

Literacy: *definition:* age 15 and over can read and write
total population: 97.6%
male: 98%
female: 96.9% (2019)

School life expectancy (primary to tertiary education): *total:* 16 years
male: 15 years
female: 17 years (2020)

Unemployment, youth ages 15-24: *total:* 7.2%
male: 4.9%
female: 15% (2019 est.)

ENVIRONMENT

Environment - current issues: air pollution; rapid population growth and high energy demand contribute to water scarcity; lack of natural freshwater resources compensated by desalination plants; land degradation and desertification; waste generation, beach pollution from oil spills

Environment - international agreements: *party to:* Biodiversity, Climate Change, Climate Change-Kyoto Protocol, Climate Change-Paris Agreement, Comprehensive Nuclear Test Ban, Desertification, Endangered Species, Hazardous Wastes, Marine Dumping-London Convention, Ozone Layer Protection, Ship Pollution, Wetlands
signed, but not ratified: Law of the Sea

Air pollutants: *particulate matter emissions:* 39.44 micrograms per cubic meter (2016 est.)
carbon dioxide emissions: 206.32 megatons (2016 est.)
methane emissions: 56.55 megatons (2020 est.)

Climate: desert; cooler in eastern mountains

Land use: *agricultural land:* 4.6% (2018 est.)
arable land: 0.5% (2018 est.)
permanent crops: 0.5% (2018 est.)
permanent pasture: 3.6% (2018 est.)
forest: 3.8% (2018 est.)
other: 91.6% (2018 est.)

Urbanization: *urban population:* 87.5% of total population (2022)
rate of urbanization: 1.5% annual rate of change (2020-25 est.)

Revenue from forest resources: *forest revenues:* 0% of GDP (2018 est.)
country comparison to the world: 201

Revenue from coal: *coal revenues:* 0% of GDP (2018 est.)
country comparison to the world: 182

Waste and recycling: *municipal solid waste generated annually:* 5,413,453 tons (2015 est.)
municipal solid waste recycled annually: 1,082,691 tons (2015 est.)
percent of municipal solid waste recycled: 20% (2015 est.)

Total water withdrawal: *municipal:* 617 million cubic meters (2017 est.)
industrial: 69 million cubic meters (2017 est.)
agricultural: 3.312 billion cubic meters (2017 est.)

Total renewable water resources: 150 million cubic meters (2017 est.)

GOVERNMENT

Country name: *conventional long form:* United Arab Emirates
conventional short form: none
local long form: Al Imarat al Arabiyah al Muttahidah
local short form: none
former: Trucial Oman, Trucial States
abbreviation: UAE
etymology: self-descriptive country name; the name "Arabia" can be traced back many centuries B.C., the ancient Egyptians referred to the region as "Ar Rabi"; "emirates" derives from "amir" the Arabic word for "commander," "lord," or "prince"

Government type: federation of monarchies

Capital: *name:* Abu Dhabi
geographic coordinates: 24 28 N, 54 22 E
time difference: UTC+4 (9 hours ahead of Washington, DC, during Standard Time)
etymology: in Arabic, *abu* means "father" and *dhabi* refers to "gazelle"; the name may derive from an abundance of gazelles that used to live in the area, as well as a folk tale involving the "Father of the Gazelle," Shakhbut BIN DHIYAB AL NAHYAN, whose hunting party tracked a gazelle to a spring on the island where Abu Dhabi was founded

Administrative divisions: 7 emirates (imarat, singular - imarah); Abu Zaby (Abu Dhabi), 'Ajman, Al Fujayrah, Ash Shariqah (Sharjah), Dubayy (Dubai), Ra's al Khaymah, Umm al Qaywayn

Independence: 2 December 1971 (from the UK)

National holiday: Independence Day (National Day), 2 December (1971)

Constitution: *history:* previous 1971 (provisional); latest drafted in 1979, became permanent May 1996
amendments: proposed by the Supreme Council and submitted to the Federal National Council; passage requires at least a two-thirds majority vote of Federal National Council members present and approval of the Supreme Council president; amended 2009

Legal system: mixed legal system of Islamic (sharia) law and civil law

International law organization participation: has not submitted an ICJ jurisdiction declaration; non-party state to the ICCt

Citizenship: *citizenship by birth:* no
citizenship by descent only: the father must be a citizen of the United Arab Emirates; if the father is unknown, the mother must be a citizen
dual citizenship recognized: no
residency requirement for naturalization: 30 years

Suffrage: limited; note - rulers of the seven emirates each select a proportion of voters for the Federal National Council (FNC) that together account for about 12 percent of Emirati citizens

Executive branch: *chief of state:* President MUHAMMAD bin Zayid Al-Nuhayan (since 14 May 2022); Vice President MUHAMMAD bin Rashid Al-Maktoum (since 5 January 2006); note - MUHAMMAD bin Zayid Al-Nuhayan elected president by the Federal Supreme Council following the death of President KHALIFA bin Zayid Al-Nuhayan on 13 May 2022
head of government: Prime Minister and Vice President MUHAMMAD bin Rashid Al-Maktoum (since 5 January 2006); Deputy Prime Ministers SAIF bin Zayid Al-Nuhayan, MANSUR bin Zayid Al-Nuhayan (both since 11 May 2009), and MAKTOUM bin Mohammed Al-Maktoum (since 25 September 2021)
cabinet: Council of Ministers announced by the prime minister and approved by the president
elections/appointments: president and vice president indirectly elected by the Federal Supreme Council - composed of the rulers of the 7 emirates - for a 5-year term (no term limits); unscheduled election held on 14 May 2022, following the death of President KHALIFA bin Zayid Al-Nuhayan (next election NA); prime minister and deputy prime minister appointed by the president
election results:
MUHAMMAD bin Zayid Al-Nuhayan elected president; Federal Supreme Council vote NA
note: there is also a Federal Supreme Council (FSC) composed of the 7 emirate rulers; the FSC is the highest constitutional authority in the UAE; establishes general policies and sanctions federal legislation; meets 4 times a year; Abu Zaby (Abu Dhabi) and Dubayy (Dubai) rulers have effective veto power

Legislative branch: *description:* unicameral Federal National Council (FNC) or Majlis al-Ittihad al-Watani (40 seats; 20 members indirectly elected using single non-transferable vote by an electoral college whose members are selected by each emirate ruler proportional to its FNC membership, and 20 members appointed by the rulers of the 7 constituent states; members serve 4-year terms)
elections:
last held for indirectly elected members on 5 October 2019 (next to be held in October 2023)
election results:
all candidates ran as independents; seats by emirate - Abu Dhabi 4, Dubai 4, Sharjah 3, Ras al-Khaimah 3, Ajman 2, Fujairah 2, Umm al-Quwain 2; composition (preliminary) - 13 men, 7 women, percent of elected women 35%; note - to attain overall FNC gender parity, 13 women and 7 men will be appointed; overall FNC percent of women 50%

Judicial branch: *highest court(s):* Federal Supreme Court (consists of the court president and 4 judges; jurisdiction limited to federal cases)

judge selection and term of office: judges appointed by the federal president following approval by the Federal Supreme Council, the highest executive and legislative authority consisting of the 7 emirate rulers; judges serve until retirement age or the expiry of their appointment terms
subordinate courts: Federal Court of Cassation (determines the constitutionality of laws promulgated at the federal and emirate level; federal level courts of first instance and appeals courts); the emirates of Abu Dhabi, Dubai, and Ra's al Khaymah have parallel court systems; the other 4 emirates have incorporated their courts into the federal system; note -the Abu Dhabi Global Market Courts and the Dubai International Financial Center Courts, the country's two largest financial free zones, both adjudicate civil and commercial disputes.

Political parties and leaders: none; political parties are banned

International organization participation: ABEDA, AfDB (nonregional member), AFESD, AMF, BIS, CAEU, CICA, FAO, G-77, GCC, IAEA, IBRD, ICAO, ICC (national committees), ICRM, IDA, IDB, IFAD, IFC, IFRCS, IHO, ILO, IMF, IMO, IMSO, Interpol, IOC, IPU, ISO, ITSO, ITU, LAS, MIGA, NAM, OAPEC, OIC, OIF (observer), OPCW, OPEC, PCA, UN, UNCTAD, UNESCO, UNHRC, UNIDO, UNRWA, UNWTO, UPU, WCO, WHO, WIPO, WMO, WTO

Diplomatic representation in the US: *chief of mission:* Ambassador Yousif Mana Saeed Ahmed ALOTAIBA (since 28 July 2008)
chancery: 3522 International Court NW, Suite 400, Washington, DC 20008
telephone: [1] (202) 243-2400
FAX: [1] (202) 243-2432
email address and website:
info@uaeembassy-usa.org
https://www.uae-embassy.org/
consulate(s) general: Boston, Los Angeles, New York

Diplomatic representation from the US: *chief of mission:* Ambassador (vacant); Charge d'Affaires Sean MURPHY (since January 2021)
embassy: Embassies District, Plot 38, Sector W59-02, Street No. 4, Abu Dhabi
mailing address: 6010 Abu Dhabi Place, Washington DC 20521-6010
telephone: [971] (2) 414-2200
FAX: [971] (2) 414-2241
email address and website:
abudhabiacs@state.gov
https://ae.usembassy.gov/
consulate(s) general: Dubai

Flag description: three equal horizontal bands of green (top), white, and black with a wider vertical red band on the hoist side; the flag incorporates all four Pan-Arab colors, which in this case represent fertility (green), neutrality (white), petroleum resources (black), and unity (red); red was the traditional color incorporated into all flags of the emirates before their unification

National symbol(s): golden falcon; national colors: green, white, black, red

National anthem: *name:* "Nashid al-watani al-imarati" (National Anthem of the UAE)
lyrics/music: AREF Al Sheikh Abdullah Al Hassan/ Mohamad Abdel WAHAB
note: music adopted 1971, lyrics adopted 1996; Mohamad Abdel WAHAB also composed the music for the anthem of Tunisia

National heritage: *total World Heritage Sites:* 1 (cultural)
selected World Heritage Site locales: Cultural Sites of Al Ain (Hafit, Hili, Bidaa Bint Saud, and Oases Areas)

ECONOMY

Economic overview: The UAE has an open economy with a high per capita income and a sizable annual trade surplus. Successful efforts at economic diversification have reduced the portion of GDP from the oil and gas sector to 30%.

Since the discovery of oil in the UAE nearly 60 years ago, the country has undergone a profound transformation from an impoverished region of small desert principalities to a modern state with a high standard of living. The government has increased spending on job creation and infrastructure expansion and is opening up utilities to greater private sector involvement. The country's free trade zones -offering 100% foreign ownership and zero taxes - are helping to attract foreign investors.

The global financial crisis of 2008-09, tight international credit, and deflated asset prices constricted the economy in 2009. UAE authorities tried to blunt the crisis by increasing spending and boosting liquidity in the banking sector. The crisis hit Dubai hardest, as it was heavily exposed to depressed real estate prices. Dubai lacked sufficient cash to meet its debt obligations, prompting global concern about its solvency and ultimately a $20 billion bailout from the UAE Central Bank and Abu Dhabi Government that was refinanced in March 2014.

The UAE's dependence on oil is a significant long-term challenge, although the UAE is one of the most diversified countries in the Gulf Cooperation Council. Low oil prices have prompted the UAE to cut expenditures, including on some social programs, but the UAE has sufficient assets in its sovereign investment funds to cover its deficits. The government reduced fuel subsidies in August 2015, and introduced excise taxes (50% on sweetened carbonated beverages and 100% on energy drinks and tobacco) in October 2017. A five-percent value-added tax was introduced in January 2018. The UAE's strategic plan for the next few years focuses on economic diversification, promoting the UAE as a global trade and tourism hub, developing industry, and creating more job opportunities for nationals through improved education and increased private sector employment.

Real GDP (purchasing power parity): $655.79 billion (2019 est.)
$644.97 billion (2018 est.)
$637.384 billion (2017 est.)
note: data are in 2017 dollars
country comparison to the world: 34

Real GDP growth rate: 0.8% (2017 est.)
3% (2016 est.)
5.1% (2015 est.)
country comparison to the world: 178

Real GDP per capita: $67,100 (2019 est.) note: data are in 2017 dollars
$67,000 (2018 est.) note: data are in 2017 dollars
$67,184 (2017 est.)
country comparison to the world: 12

GDP (official exchange rate): $421.077 billion (2019 est.)

Inflation rate (consumer prices): -1.9% (2019 est.)
3% (2018 est.)
1.9% (2017 est.)
country comparison to the world: 4

Credit ratings:

Fitch rating: AA- (2020)

Moody's rating: Aa2 (2007)

Standard & Poors rating: AA (2007)

GDP - composition, by sector of origin: *agriculture:* 0.9% (2017 est.)
industry: 49.8% (2017 est.)
services: 49.2% (2017 est.)

GDP - composition, by end use: *household consumption:* 34.9% (2017 est.)
government consumption: 12.3% (2017 est.)
investment in fixed capital: 23% (2017 est.)
investment in inventories: 1.8% (2017 est.)
exports of goods and services: 100.4% (2017 est.)
imports of goods and services: -72.4% (2017 est.)

Agricultural products: dates, cucumbers, tomatoes, goat meat, eggs, milk, poultry, carrots/turnips, goat milk, sheep milk

Industries: petroleum and petrochemicals; fishing, aluminum, cement, fertilizer, commercial ship repair, construction materials, handicrafts, textiles

Industrial production growth rate: 1.8% (2017 est.)
country comparison to the world: 138

Labor force: 5.344 million (2017 est.)
note: expatriates account for about 85% of the workforce
country comparison to the world: 74

Labor force - by occupation: *agriculture:* 7%
industry: 15%
services: 78% (2000 est.)

Unemployment rate: 1.6% (2016 est.)
3.6% (2014 est.)
country comparison to the world: 15

Unemployment, youth ages 15-24: *total:* 7.2%
male: 4.9%
female: 15% (2019 est.)
country comparison to the world: 161

Population below poverty line: 19.5% (2003 est.)

Gini Index coefficient - distribution of family income: 32.5 (2014 est.)
country comparison to the world: 138

Budget: *revenues:* 110.2 billion (2017 est.)
expenditures: 111.1 billion (2017 est.)
note: the UAE federal budget does not account for emirate-level spending in Abu Dhabi and Dubai

Budget surplus (+) or deficit (-): -0.2% (of GDP) (2017 est.)
country comparison to the world: 51

Public debt: 19.7% of GDP (2017 est.)
20.2% of GDP (2016 est.)
country comparison to the world: 190

Taxes and other revenues: 28.8% (of GDP) (2017 est.)
country comparison to the world: 90

Fiscal year: calendar year

Current account balance: $26.47 billion (2017 est.)
$13.23 billion (2016 est.)
country comparison to the world: 14

Exports: $308.5 billion (2017 est.)
$298.6 billion (2016 est.)
country comparison to the world: 22

Exports - partners: India 11%, Japan 10%, Saudi Arabia 7%, Switzerland 6%, China 6%, Iraq 6% (2019)

Exports - commodities: crude petroleum, refined petroleum, gold, jewelry, broadcasting equipment (2019)

Imports: $229.2 billion (2017 est.)
$226.5 billion (2016 est.)
country comparison to the world: 26

Imports - partners: China 15%, India 12%, Untied States 7% (2019)

Imports - commodities: gold, broadcasting equipment, jewelry, refined petroleum, diamonds (2019)

Reserves of foreign exchange and gold: $95.37 billion (31 December 2017 est.)
$85.39 billion (31 December 2016 est.)
country comparison to the world: 27

Debt - external: $237.6 billion (31 December 2017 est.)
$218.7 billion (31 December 2016 est.)
country comparison to the world: 34

Exchange rates: Emirati dirhams (AED) per US dollar -
3.67315 (2020 est.)
3.67315 (2019 est.)
3.67315 (2018 est.)
3.673 (2014 est.)
3.673 (2013 est.)

ENERGY

Electricity access: *electrification - total population:* 100% (2020)

Electricity: *installed generating capacity:* 35.173 million kW (2020 est.)
consumption: 122.386 billion kWh (2019 est.)
exports: 257 million kWh (2019 est.)
imports: 245 million kWh (2019 est.)
transmission/distribution losses: 7.011 billion kWh (2019 est.)

Electricity generation sources: *fossil fuels:* 95.7% of total installed capacity (2020 est.)
nuclear: 1.3% of total installed capacity (2020 est.)
solar: 3% of total installed capacity (2020 est.)

Coal: *production:* 0 metric tons (2020 est.)
consumption: 2.563 million metric tons (2020 est.)
exports: 2,000 metric tons (2020 est.)
imports: 2.565 million metric tons (2020 est.)
proven reserves: 0 metric tons (2019 est.)

Petroleum: *total petroleum production:* 3,769,100 bbl/day (2021 est.)
refined petroleum consumption: 863,700 bbl/day (2019 est.)
crude oil and lease condensate exports: 2,427,200 bbl/day (2018 est.)
crude oil and lease condensate imports: 172,900 bbl/day (2018 est.)
crude oil estimated reserves: 97.8 billion barrels (2021 est.)

Refined petroleum products - production: 943,500 bbl/day (2017 est.)
country comparison to the world: 19

Refined petroleum products - exports: 817,700 bbl/day (2015 est.)
country comparison to the world: 10

Refined petroleum products - imports: 392,000 bbl/day (2015 est.)
country comparison to the world: 23

Natural gas: *production:* 62,889,064,000 cubic meters (2019 est.)
consumption: 73,750,936,000 cubic meters (2019 est.)
exports: 7,673,768,000 cubic meters (2019 est.)
imports: 20,041,951,000 cubic meters (2019 est.)
proven reserves: 6,090,887,000,000 cubic meters (2021 est.)

Carbon dioxide emissions: 276.236 million metric tonnes of CO2 (2019 est.)
from coal and metallurgical coke: 5.032 million metric tonnes of CO2 (2019 est.)
from petroleum and other liquids: 126.524 million metric tonnes of CO2 (2019 est.)
from consumed natural gas: 144.681 million metric tonnes of CO2 (2019 est.)
country comparison to the world: 24

Energy consumption per capita: 471.788 million Btu/person (2019 est.)
country comparison to the world: 4

COMMUNICATIONS

Telephones - fixed lines: *total subscriptions:* 2,380,866 (2020 est.)
subscriptions per 100 inhabitants: 24 (2020 est.)
country comparison to the world: 52

Telephones - mobile cellular: *total subscriptions:* 19,602,800 (2019)
subscriptions per 100 inhabitants: 200.63 (2019)
country comparison to the world: 61

Telecommunication systems: *general assessment:* the UAE has a strong mobile market; while the 5G penetration rate is the second highest globally after China; this has underpinned growth in the mobile broadband sector, and has enabled the strong development in the take-up of rich content and applications, as well as m-commerce; to help increase the capacity of 5G networks in coming years, and so keep up with data demand, the government has allowed for the GSM networks to be closed down and for spectrum and other assets to be re-purposed for 5G by the end of 2022; the fixed-broadband network in the UAE is dominated by fiber, with DSL having a minor and declining presence; this focus on a fully fiber infrastructure has also facilitated growth in e-commerce, and has supported the government's long-term aim of transitioning the economy from its dependence on oil to being knowledge-based and supported by digital services; the country stands to benefit from having signed the Abraham Accord Declaration with Israel, which aims to normalize relations between the two countries; such benefits can be seen in the agreement to enable local ISPs to access Bezeq International's submarine cable infrastructure, and so improve direct connectivity to Europe, South East Asia, and Africa; the UAE's ISPs can also access Bezeq International's data center in Tel Aviv, improving internet services (2022)
domestic: microwave radio relay, fiber-optic and coaxial cable; fixed-line roughly 24 per 100 and mobile-cellular nearly 186 per 100 (2020)
international: country code - 971; landing points for the FLAG, SEA-ME-WE-3 ,-4 & -5, Qater UAE Submarine Cable System, FALCON, FOG, Tat TGN-Gulf, OMRAN/EPEG Cable System, AAE-1, BBG, EIG, FEA, GBICS/MENA, IMEWE, Orient Express, TEAMS, TW1 and the UAE-Iran submarine cables, linking to Europe, Africa, the Middle East, Asia, Southeast Asia and Australia; satellite earth stations - 3 Intelsat (1 Atlantic Ocean and 2 Indian) (2020)

Broadcast media: except for the many organizations now operating in media free zones in Abu Dhabi and Dubai, most TV and radio stations remain government-owned; widespread use of satellite dishes provides access to pan-Arab and other international broadcasts; restrictions since June 2017 on some satellite channels and websites originating from or otherwise linked to Qatar (2018)

Internet country code: .ae

Internet users: *total:* 9,890,400 (2020 est.)
percent of population: 100% (2020 est.)
country comparison to the world: 56

Broadband - fixed subscriptions: *total:* 3,245,123 (2020 est.)
subscriptions per 100 inhabitants: 33 (2020 est.)
country comparison to the world: 45

TRANSPORTATION

National air transport system: *number of registered air carriers:* 10 (2020)
inventory of registered aircraft operated by air carriers: 497
annual passenger traffic on registered air carriers: 95,533,069 (2018)
annual freight traffic on registered air carriers: 15,962,900,000 (2018) mt-km

Civil aircraft registration country code prefix: A6

Airports: *total:* 43 (2021)
country comparison to the world: 99

Airports - with paved runways: *total:* 25
over 3,047 m: 12
2,438 to 3,047 m: 3
1,524 to 2,437 m: 5
914 to 1,523 m: 3
under 914 m: 2 (2021)

Airports - with unpaved runways: *total:* 18
over 3,047 m: 1
2,438 to 3,047 m: 1
1,524 to 2,437 m: 4
914 to 1,523 m: 6
under 914 m: 6 (2021)

Heliports: 5 (2021)

Pipelines: 533 km condensate, 3,277 km gas, 300 km liquid petroleum gas, 3287 km oil, 24 km oil/gas/water, 218 km refined products, 99 km water (2013)

Roadways: *total:* 4,080 km (2008)
paved: 4,080 km (2008) (includes 253 km of expressways)
country comparison to the world: 154

Merchant marine: *total:* 623
by type: bulk carrier 1, container ship 3, general cargo 117, oil tanker 19, other 483 (2021)
country comparison to the world: 37

Ports and terminals: *major seaport(s):* Al Fujayrah, Mina' Jabal 'Ali (Dubai), Khor Fakkan (Khawr Fakkan) (Sharjah), Mubarraz Island (Abu Dhabi), Mina' Rashid (Dubai), Mina' Saqr (Ra's al Khaymah)
container port(s) (TEUs): Dubai Port (14,111,000) (2019)

LNG terminal(s) (export): Das Island

MILITARY AND SECURITY

Military and security forces: United Arab Emirates Armed Forces: Land Forces, Navy Forces, Air Force,

Presidential Guard (includes special operations forces); Ministry of Interior: Critical Infrastructure and Coastal Patrol Agency (CICPA) (2022)
note: each emirate maintains a local police force called a general directorate, which is officially a branch of the federal Ministry of Interior; all emirate-level general directorates of police enforce their respective emirate's laws autonomously; they also enforce federal laws within their emirate in coordination with one another under the federal ministry

Military expenditures: 5.6% of GDP (2020 est.)
5.4% of GDP (2019 est.) (approximately $29 billion)
5.5% of GDP (2018 est.) (approximately $28.7 billion)
5.2% of GDP (2017 est.) (approximately $26.9 billion)
6% of GDP (2016 est.) (approximately $30 billion)
country comparison to the world: 8

Military and security service personnel strengths: approximately 65,000 active personnel (45,000 Land Forces; 3,000 Navy; 5,000 Air Force; 12,000 Presidential Guard) (2022)

Military equipment inventories and acquisitions: the military's inventory is comprised of wide variety of mostly modern imported equipment; since 2010, the UAE has acquired military equipment from more than 20 countries with France, Russia, and the US as the leading suppliers; in recent years, the UAE has tried to boost its domestic defense industry (2022)

Military service age and obligation: 18-30 years of age for compulsory military service for men (compulsory service initiated in 2014); 17 years of age for volunteers with parental approval; men can volunteer up to age 40; 24-month general service obligation, 16 months for secondary school graduates; women can volunteer to serve for 9 months regardless of education (2022)
note 1: compulsory service may be completed in the uniformed military, the Ministry of Interior, the State Security Service, or other institutions designated by the military leadership
note 2: the UAE military employs a considerable number — estimates range from a low of about 30% to as much as 70% of the force — of foreign personnel on contract; the UAE has also hired foreign mercenaries for some operations during its intervention in Yemen

Military deployments: estimates vary; reportedly a few hundred remain in Yemen; has maintained some troops at military bases in Eritrea and Somalia (Somaliland) (2022)

Military - note: the UAE hosts a multi-service French military base, which includes the French naval command for the Indian Ocean (ALINDIEN); the UAE has a defense cooperation agreement with the US and hosts about 3,500 US troops, mostly air and naval personnel

in 2015, UAE intervened militarily in Yemen as part of the Saudi-led coalition in support of the Republic of Yemen Government with an estimated 3,500 troops, as well as supporting air and naval forces; UAE withdrew its main military force from Yemen in 2019, but has retained a small military presence while working with proxies in southern Yemen, most notably the Southern Transitional Council (STC)

the UAE's military traces its origins to the establishment of the Trucial Oman Scouts in 1951, a joint UK-Abu Dhabi organization modeled after Jordan's Arab Legion, which became the Abu Dhabi Defense Force in 1965; the modern Emirati armed forces were formed in 1976 (2022)

TRANSNATIONAL ISSUES

Disputes - international: *UAE-Oman:* boundary agreement was signed and ratified with Oman in 2003 for entire border, including Oman's Musandam Peninsula and Al Madhah enclaves, but contents of the agreement and detailed maps showing the alignment have not been published
UAE-Iran: Iran and UAE dispute Tunb Islands and Abu Musa Island near the Strait of Hormuz, which Iran has occupied since 1971
UAE-Saudi Arabia: the UAE has differences with Saudi Arabia over their border and the sharing of a major oilfield there, although the issue is seldom mentioned publically

Refugees and internally displaced persons: *stateless persons:* 5 (mid-year 2021)

Illicit drugs: a transshipment point for illegal narcotics and a pass-through for drug proceeds; numerous exchange houses and general trading companies increase potential for money laundering; major source of precursor chemicals used in the production of illicit narcotics

UNITED KINGDOM

INTRODUCTION

Background: The United Kingdom has historically played a leading role in developing parliamentary democracy and in advancing literature and science. At its zenith in the 19th century, the British Empire stretched over one-fourth of the earth's surface. The first half of the 20th century saw two World Wars seriously deplete the UK's strength and the Irish Republic withdraw from the union. The second half witnessed the dismantling of the Empire and the UK rebuilding itself into a modern and prosperous European nation. As one of five permanent members of the UN Security Council and a founding member of NATO and the Commonwealth of Nations, the UK pursues a global approach to foreign policy. The Scottish Parliament, the National Assembly for Wales, and the Northern Ireland Assembly were established in 1998.

The UK was an active member of the EU after its accession in 1973, although it chose to remain outside the Economic and Monetary Union. However, motivated in part by frustration at a remote bureaucracy in Brussels and massive migration into the country, UK citizens on 23 June 2016 voted by 52 to 48 percent to leave the EU. The UK became the first country to depart the EU on 31 January 2020, after prolonged negotiations on EU-UK economic and security relationships had been hammered out.

GEOGRAPHY

Location: Western Europe, islands - including the northern one-sixth of the island of Ireland - between the North Atlantic Ocean and the North Sea; northwest of France

Geographic coordinates: 54 00 N, 2 00 W

Map references: Europe

Area: *total:* 243,610 sq km
land: 241,930 sq km
water: 1,680 sq km
note 1: the percentage area breakdown of the four UK countries is: England 53%, Scotland 32%, Wales 9%, and Northern Ireland 6%
note 2: includes Rockall and the Shetland Islands, which are part of Scotland
country comparison to the world: 80

Area - comparative: twice the size of Pennsylvania; slightly smaller than Oregon

Land boundaries: *total:* 499 km
border countries (1): Ireland 499 km

Coastline: 12,429 km

Maritime claims: *territorial sea:* 12 nm
continental shelf: as defined in continental shelf orders or in accordance with agreed upon boundaries
exclusive fishing zone: 200 nm

Climate: temperate; moderated by prevailing southwest winds over the North Atlantic Current; more than one-half of the days are overcast

Terrain: mostly rugged hills and low mountains; level to rolling plains in east and southeast

Elevation: *highest point:* Ben Nevis 1,345 m
lowest point: The Fens -4 m
mean elevation: 162 m

Natural resources: coal, petroleum, natural gas, iron ore, lead, zinc, gold, tin, limestone, salt, clay, chalk, gypsum, potash, silica sand, slate, arable land

Land use: *agricultural land:* 71% (2018 est.)
arable land: 25.1% (2018 est.)
permanent crops: 0.2% (2018 est.)
permanent pasture: 45.7% (2018 est.)
forest: 11.9% (2018 est.)
other: 17.1% (2018 est.)

Irrigated land: 950 sq km (2012)

Population distribution: the core of the population lies in and around London, with significant clusters found in central Britain around Manchester and Liverpool, in the Scottish lowlands between Edinburgh and Glasgow, southern Wales in and around Cardiff, and far eastern Northern Ireland centered on Belfast

Natural hazards: winter windstorms; floods

Geography - note: lies near vital North Atlantic sea lanes; only 35 km from France and linked by tunnel under the English Channel (the Channel Tunnel or Chunnel); because of heavily indented coastline, no location is more than 125 km from tidal waters

PEOPLE AND SOCIETY

Population: 67,791,400 (2022 est.) United Kingdom
constituent countries by percentage of total population:
England 84.3%
Scotland 8.1%
Wales 4.7%
Northern Ireland 2.8%
country comparison to the world: 22

Nationality: *noun:* Briton(s), British (collective plural)
adjective: British

Ethnic groups: White 87.2%, Black/African/Caribbean/black British 3%, Asian/Asian British: Indian 2.3%, Asian/Asian British: Pakistani 1.9%, mixed 2%, other 3.7% (2011 est.)

Languages: English
note: the following are recognized regional languages: Scots (about 30% of the population of Scotland), Scottish Gaelic (about 60,000 speakers in Scotland), Welsh (about 20% of the population of Wales), Irish (about 10% of the population of Northern Ireland), Cornish (some 2,000 to 3,000 people in Cornwall) (2012 est.)

Religions: Christian (includes Anglican, Roman Catholic, Presbyterian, Methodist) 59.5%, Muslim 4.4%, Hindu 1.3%, other 2%, unspecified 7.2%, none 25.7% (2011 est.)

Age structure: *0-14 years:* 17.63% (male 5,943,435/female 5,651,780)
15-24 years: 11.49% (male 3,860,435/female 3,692,398)
25-54 years: 39.67% (male 13,339,965/female 12,747,598)
55-64 years: 12.73% (male 4,139,378/female 4,234,701)
65 years and over: 18.48% (male 5,470,116/female 6,681,311) (2020 est.)

Dependency ratios: *total dependency ratio:* 57.1
youth dependency ratio: 27.8
elderly dependency ratio: 29.3
potential support ratio: 3.4 (2020 est.)

Median age: *total:* 40.6 years
male: 39.6 years
female: 41.7 years (2020 est.)
country comparison to the world: 50

Population growth rate: 0.53% (2022 est.)
country comparison to the world: 151

Birth rate: 10.79 births/1,000 population (2022 est.)
country comparison to the world: 178

Death rate: 9.07 deaths/1,000 population (2022 est.)
country comparison to the world: 58

Net migration rate: 3.59 migrant(s)/1,000 population (2022 est.)
country comparison to the world: 34

Population distribution: the core of the population lies in and around London, with significant clusters found in central Britain around Manchester and Liverpool, in the Scottish lowlands between Edinburgh and Glasgow, southern Wales in and around Cardiff, and far eastern Northern Ireland centered on Belfast

Urbanization: *urban population:* 84.4% of total population (2022)
rate of urbanization: 0.8% annual rate of change (2020-25 est.)

Major urban areas - population: 9.426 million LONDON (capital), 2.750 million Manchester, 2.626 million Birmingham, 1.902 million West Yorkshire, 1.681 million Glasgow, 944,000 Southampton/Portsmouth (2022)

Sex ratio: *at birth:* 1.05 male(s)/female
0-14 years: 1.05 male(s)/female
15-24 years: 1.01 male(s)/female
25-54 years: 1.03 male(s)/female
55-64 years: 0.99 male(s)/female
65 years and over: 0.73 male(s)/female
total population: 0.99 male(s)/female (2022 est.)

Mother's mean age at first birth: 29 years (2018 est.)
note: data represents England and Wales only

Maternal mortality ratio: 7 deaths/100,000 live births (2017 est.)
country comparison to the world: 158

Infant mortality rate: *total:* 3.82 deaths/1,000 live births
male: 4.27 deaths/1,000 live births
female: 3.35 deaths/1,000 live births (2022 est.)
country comparison to the world: 192

Life expectancy at birth: *total population:* 81.94 years
male: 79.95 years
female: 84.04 years (2022 est.)
country comparison to the world: 31

Total fertility rate: 1.63 children born/woman (2022 est.)
country comparison to the world: 181

Contraceptive prevalence rate: 76.1% (2010/12)
note: percent of women aged 16-49

Drinking water source: *improved: urban:* 100% of population
rural: 100% of population
total: 100% of population

Current health expenditure: 10.2% of GDP (2019)

Physicians density: 3 physicians/1,000 population (2020)

Hospital bed density: 2.5 beds/1,000 population (2019)

Sanitation facility access: *improved: urban:* 99.8% of population
rural: 99.8% of population
total: 99.8% of population
unimproved: urban: 0.2% of population
rural: 0.2% of population
total: 0.2% of population (2020 est.)

Major infectious diseases: *respiratory diseases:* Covid-19 (see note) (2020)
note: widespread ongoing transmission of a respiratory illness caused by the novel coronavirus (COVID-19) is occurring throughout the UK; as of 18 August 2022, the UK has reported a total of 23,461,239 cases of COVID-19 or 34,559.75 cumulative cases of COVID-19 per 100,000 population with a total of 187,018 cumulative deaths or a rate of 275.48 cumulative deaths per 100,000 population; as of 10 August 2022, 79.89% of the population has received at least one dose of COVID-19 vaccine; the US Department of Homeland Security has issued instructions requiring US passengers who have been in the UK to travel through select airports where the US Government has implemented enhanced screening procedures

Obesity - adult prevalence rate: 27.8% (2016)
country comparison to the world: 36

Alcohol consumption per capita: *total:* 9.8 liters of pure alcohol (2019 est.)
beer: 3.53 liters of pure alcohol (2019 est.)
wine: 3.3 liters of pure alcohol (2019 est.)
spirits: 2.35 liters of pure alcohol (2019 est.)
other alcohols: 0.61 liters of pure alcohol (2019 est.)
country comparison to the world: 24

Tobacco use: *total:* 15.4% (2020 est.)
male: 17.3% (2020 est.)
female: 13.5% (2020 est.)
country comparison to the world: 102

Child marriage: *women married by age 18:* 0.1% (2020 est.)

Education expenditures: 5.2% of GDP (2018 est.)
country comparison to the world: 55

School life expectancy (primary to tertiary education): *total:* 17 years
male: 17 years
female: 18 years (2019)

Unemployment, youth ages 15-24: *total:* 11.2%
male: 13%
female: 9.2% (2019 est.)

ENVIRONMENT

Environment - current issues: air pollution improved but remains a concern, particularly in the London region; soil pollution from pesticides and heavy metals; decline in marine and coastal habitats brought on by pressures from housing, tourism, and industry

Environment - international agreements: *party to:* Air Pollution, Air Pollution-Heavy Metals, Air Pollution-Multi-effect Protocol, Air Pollution-Nitrogen Oxides, Air Pollution-Persistent Organic Pollutants, Air Pollution-Sulphur 94, Air Pollution-Volatile Organic Compounds, Antarctic-Environmental Protection, Antarctic-Marine Living Resources, Antarctic Seals, Antarctic Treaty, Biodiversity, Climate Change, Climate Change-Kyoto Protocol, Climate Change-Paris Agreement, Comprehensive Nuclear Test Ban, Desertification, Endangered Species, Environmental Modification, Hazardous Wastes, Law of the Sea, Marine Dumping-London Convention, Marine Dumping-London Protocol, Marine Life Conservation, Nuclear Test Ban, Ozone Layer Protection, Ship Pollution, Tropical Timber 2006, Wetlands, Whaling
signed, but not ratified: none of the selected agreements

Air pollutants: *particulate matter emissions:* 10.53 micrograms per cubic meter (2016 est.)
carbon dioxide emissions: 379.02 megatons (2016 est.)
methane emissions: 49.16 megatons (2020 est.)

Climate: temperate; moderated by prevailing southwest winds over the North Atlantic Current; more than one-half of the days are overcast

Land use: *agricultural land:* 71% (2018 est.)
arable land: 25.1% (2018 est.)
permanent crops: 0.2% (2018 est.)
permanent pasture: 45.7% (2018 est.)
forest: 11.9% (2018 est.)
other: 17.1% (2018 est.)

Urbanization: *urban population:* 84.4% of total population (2022)
rate of urbanization: 0.8% annual rate of change (2020-25 est.)

Revenue from forest resources: *forest revenues:* 0.01% of GDP (2018 est.)
country comparison to the world: 158

Revenue from coal: *coal revenues:* 0% of GDP (2018 est.)
country comparison to the world: 183

Waste and recycling: *municipal solid waste generated annually:* 31.567 million tons (2014 est.)
municipal solid waste recycled annually: 8,602,008 tons (2015 est.)
percent of municipal solid waste recycled: 27.3% (2015 est.)

Total water withdrawal: *municipal:* 6.227 billion cubic meters (2017 est.)
industrial: 1.01 billion cubic meters (2017 est.)
agricultural: 1.183 billion cubic meters (2017 est.)

Total renewable water resources: 147 billion cubic meters (2017 est.)

GOVERNMENT

Country name: *conventional long form:* United Kingdom of Great Britain and Northern Ireland; note - the island of Great Britain includes England, Scotland, and Wales
conventional short form: United Kingdom
abbreviation: UK
etymology: self-descriptive country name; the designation "Great Britain," in the sense of "Larger Britain," dates back to medieval times and was used to distinguish the island from "Little Britain," or Brittany in modern France; the name Ireland derives from the Gaelic "Eriu," the matron goddess of Ireland (goddess of the land)

Government type: parliamentary constitutional monarchy; a Commonwealth realm

Capital: *name:* London
geographic coordinates: 51 30 N, 0 05 W
time difference: UTC 0 (5 hours ahead of Washington, DC, during Standard Time)
daylight saving time: +1hr, begins last Sunday in March; ends last Sunday in October
time zone note: the time statements apply to the United Kingdom proper, not to its crown dependencies or overseas territories
etymology: the name derives from the Roman settlement of Londinium, established on the current site of London around A.D. 43; the original meaning of the name is uncertain

Administrative divisions: England: 24 two-tier counties, 32 London boroughs and 1 City of London or Greater London, 36 metropolitan districts, 59 unitary authorities (including 4 single-tier counties*);
two-tier counties: Cambridgeshire, Cumbria, Derbyshire, Devon, East Sussex, Essex, Gloucestershire, Hampshire, Hertfordshire, Kent, Lancashire, Leicestershire, Lincolnshire, Norfolk, North Yorkshire, Nottinghamshire, Oxfordshire, Somerset, Staffordshire, Suffolk, Surrey, Warwickshire, West Sussex, Worcestershire

London boroughs and City of London or Greater London: Barking and Dagenham, Barnet, Bexley, Brent, Bromley, Camden, Croydon, Ealing, Enfield, Greenwich, Hackney, Hammersmith and Fulham, Haringey, Harrow, Havering, Hillingdon, Hounslow, Islington, Kensington and Chelsea, Kingston upon Thames, Lambeth, Lewisham, City of London, Merton, Newham, Redbridge, Richmond upon Thames, Southwark, Sutton, Tower Hamlets, Waltham Forest, Wandsworth, Westminster
metropolitan districts: Barnsley, Birmingham, Bolton, Bradford, Bury, Calderdale, Coventry, Doncaster, Dudley, Gateshead, Kirklees, Knowlsey, Leeds, Liverpool, Manchester, Newcastle upon Tyne, North Tyneside, Oldham, Rochdale, Rotherham, Salford, Sandwell, Sefton, Sheffield, Solihull, South Tyneside, St. Helens, Stockport, Sunderland, Tameside, Trafford, Wakefield, Walsall, Wigan, Wirral, Wolverhampton
unitary authorities: Bath and North East Somerset; Bedford; Blackburn with Darwen; Blackpool; Bournemouth, Christchurch and Poole; Bracknell Forest; Brighton and Hove; City of Bristol; Buckinghamshire; Central Bedfordshire; Cheshire East; Cheshire West and Chester; Cornwall; Darlington; Derby; Dorset; Durham County*; East Riding of Yorkshire; Halton; Hartlepool; Herefordshire*; Isle of Wight*; Isles of Scilly; City of Kingston upon Hull; Leicester; Luton; Medway; Middlesbrough; Milton Keynes; North East Lincolnshire; North Lincolnshire; North Northamptonshire; North Somerset; Northumberland*; Nottingham; Peterborough; Plymouth; Portsmouth; Reading; Redcar and Cleveland; Rutland; Shropshire; Slough; South Gloucestershire; Southampton; Southend-on-Sea; Stockton-on-Tees; Stoke-on-Trent; Swindon; Telford and Wrekin; Thurrock; Torbay; Warrington; West Berkshire; West Northamptonshire; Wiltshire; Windsor and Maidenhead; Wokingham; York

Northern Ireland: 5 borough councils, 4 district councils, 2 city councils;
borough councils: Antrim and Newtownabbey; Ards and North Down; Armagh City, Banbridge, and Craigavon; Causeway Coast and Glens; Mid and East Antrim
district councils: Derry City and Strabane; Fermanagh and Omagh; Mid Ulster; Newry, Murne, and Down
city councils: Belfast; Lisburn and Castlereagh

Scotland: 32 council areas;
council areas: Aberdeen City, Aberdeenshire, Angus, Argyll and Bute, Clackmannanshire, Dumfries and Galloway, Dundee City, East Ayrshire, East Dunbartonshire, East Lothian, East Renfrewshire, City of Edinburgh, Eilean Siar (Western Isles), Falkirk, Fife, Glasgow City, Highland, Inverclyde, Midlothian, Moray, North Ayrshire, North Lanarkshire, Orkney Islands, Perth and Kinross, Renfrewshire, Shetland Islands, South Ayrshire, South Lanarkshire, Stirling, The Scottish Borders, West Dunbartonshire, West Lothian

Wales: 22 unitary authorities;
unitary authorities: Blaenau Gwent, Bridgend, Caerphilly, Cardiff, Carmarthenshire, Ceredigion, Conwy, Denbighshire, Flintshire, Gwynedd, Isle of Anglesey, Merthyr Tydfil, Monmouthshire, Neath Port Talbot, Newport, Pembrokeshire, Powys, Rhondda Cynon Taff, Swansea, The Vale of Glamorgan, Torfaen, Wrexham

Dependent areas: Anguilla; Bermuda; British Indian Ocean Territory; British Virgin Islands; Cayman Islands; Falkland Islands; Gibraltar; Montserrat; Pitcairn Islands; Saint Helena, Ascension, and Tristan da Cunha; South Georgia and the South Sandwich Islands; Turks and Caicos Islands

Independence: *no official date of independence:* 927 (minor English kingdoms unite); 3 March 1284 (enactment of the Statute of Rhuddlan uniting England and Wales); 1536 (Act of Union formally incorporates England and Wales); 1 May 1707 (Acts of Union formally unite England, Scotland, and Wales as Great Britain); 1 January 1801 (Acts of Union formally unite Great Britain and Ireland as the United Kingdom of Great Britain and Ireland); 6 December 1921 (Anglo-Irish Treaty formalizes partition of Ireland; six counties remain part of the United Kingdom and Northern Ireland); 12 April 1927 (Royal and Parliamentary Titles Act establishes current name of the United Kingdom of Great Britain and Northern Ireland)

National holiday: the UK does not celebrate one particular national holiday

Constitution: *history:* unwritten; partly statutes, partly common law and practice
amendments: proposed as a bill for an Act of Parliament by the government, by the House of Commons, or by the House of Lords; passage requires agreement by both houses and by the monarch (Royal Assent); many previous, last in 2020 - The European Union (Withdrawal Agreement) Act 2020, European Union (Future Relationship) Act 2020

Legal system: common law system; has nonbinding judicial review of Acts of Parliament under the Human Rights Act of 1998

International law organization participation: accepts compulsory ICJ jurisdiction with reservations; accepts ICCt jurisdiction

Citizenship: *citizenship by birth:* no
citizenship by descent only: at least one parent must be a citizen of the United Kingdom
dual citizenship recognized: yes
residency requirement for naturalization: 5 years

Suffrage: 18 years of age; universal

Executive branch: *chief of state:* King CHARLES III (since 8 September 2022); Heir Apparent Prince WILLIAM (son of the king, born 21 June 1982); note - CHARLES succeeded his mother, Queen ELIZABETH II, after serving as Prince of Wales (heir apparent) for over 64 years - the longest such tenure in British history
head of government: Prime Minister Rishi SUNAK (Conservative) (since 25 October 2022)
cabinet: Cabinet appointed by the prime minister
elections/appointments: the monarchy is hereditary; following legislative elections, the leader of the majority party or majority coalition usually becomes the prime minister; election last held on 12 December 2019 (next to be held by 2 May 2024)
note: in addition to serving as the UK head of state, the British sovereign is the constitutional monarch for 14 additional Commonwealth countries (these 15 states are each referred to as a Commonwealth realm)

Legislative branch: *description:* bicameral Parliament consists of:
House of Lords (membership not fixed; as of October 2021, 787 lords were eligible to participate in the work of the House of Lords - 673 life peers, 88 hereditary peers, and 26 clergy; members are appointed by the monarch on the advice of the prime minister and non-party political members recommended by the House of Lords Appointments Commission); note - House of Lords total does not include ineligible members or members on leave of absence House of Commons (650 seats; members directly elected in single-seat constituencies by simple majority popular vote to serve 5-year terms unless the House is dissolved earlier)
elections:
House of Lords - no elections; note - in 1999, as provided by the House of Lords Act, elections were held in the House of Lords to determine the 92 hereditary peers who would remain; elections held only as vacancies in the hereditary peerage arise)
House of Commons - last held on 12 December 2019 (next to be held by 2 May 2024)
election results:
House of Lords - composition - men 554, women 222, percent of women 28.6%
House of Commons - percent of vote by party - Conservative 54.9%, Labor 30.8%, Lib Dems 2.2%, SNP 6.8%, DUP 1.2%, Sinn Fein 1.1%, Plaid Cymru .6%, other 2.5%; seats by party - Conservative 365, Labor 202, SNP 48, Lib Dems 11, DUP 8, Sinn Fein 7, Plaid Cymru 4, other 9; composition - men 425, women 225, percent of women 34.6%; total Parliament percent of women 31.3%

Judicial branch: *highest court(s):* Supreme Court (consists of 12 justices, including the court president and deputy president); note - the Supreme Court was established by the Constitutional Reform Act 2005 and implemented in 2009, replacing the Appellate Committee of the House of Lords as the highest court in the United Kingdom
judge selection and term of office: judge candidates selected by an independent committee of several judicial commissions, followed by their recommendations to the prime minister, and appointed by the monarch; justices serve for life
subordinate courts: England and Wales: Court of Appeal (civil and criminal divisions); High Court; Crown Court; County Courts; Magistrates' Courts; Scotland: Court of Sessions; Sheriff Courts; High Court of Justiciary; tribunals; Northern Ireland: Court of Appeal in Northern Ireland; High Court; county courts; magistrates' courts; specialized tribunals

Political parties and leaders: Alliance Party (Northern Ireland) [Naomi LONG]
Conservative and Unionist Party [Rishi SUNAK]
Democratic Unionist Party or DUP (Northern Ireland) [Jeffrey DONALDSON]
Green Party of England and Wales or Greens [Carla DENYER and Adrian RAMSAY]
Labor (Labour) Party [Sir Keir STARMER]
Liberal Democrats (Lib Dems) [Sir Ed DAVEY]
Party of Wales (Plaid Cymru) [Adam PRICE]
Scottish National Party or SNP [Nicola STURGEON]
Sinn Fein (Northern Ireland) [Mary Lou MCDONALD]
Social Democratic and Labor Party or SDLP (Northern Ireland) [Colum EASTWOOD]
UK Independence Party or UKIP [Neil HAMILTON]
Ulster Unionist Party or UUP (Northern Ireland) [Doug BEATTIE]

International organization participation: ADB (nonregional member), AfDB (nonregional member), Arctic Council (observer), Australia Group, BIS, C, CBSS (observer), CD, CDB, CE, CERN, EAPC, EBRD, ECB, EIB, EITI (implementing country), ESA, EU, FAO, FATF, G-5, G-7, G-8, G-10, G-20, IADB, IAEA, IBRD, ICAO, ICC (national committees), ICCt, ICRM, IDA, IEA, IFAD, IFC, IFRCS, IGAD (partners), IHO, ILO, IMF, IMO, IMSO, Interpol, IOC, IOM, IPU, ISO, ITSO, ITU, ITUC (NGOs), MIGA, MINUSMA, MONUSCO, NATO, NEA, NSG, OAS (observer), OECD, OPCW, OSCE, Pacific Alliance (observer), Paris Club, PCA, PIF (partner), SELEC (observer), SICA (observer), UN, UNCTAD, UNESCO, UNFICYP, UNHCR, UNHRC, UNMISS, UNRWA, UN Security Council (permanent), UNSOM, UPU, Wassenaar Arrangement, WCO, WHO, WIPO, WMO, WTO, ZC

Diplomatic representation in the US: *chief of mission:* Ambassador Karen Elizabeth PIERCE (since 8 April 2020)
chancery: 3100 Massachusetts Avenue NW, Washington, DC 20008
telephone: [1] (202) 588-6500
FAX: [1] (202) 588-7870
email address and website:
britishembassyenquiries@gmail.com
https://www.gov.uk/world/organisations/british-embassy-washington
consulate(s) general: Atlanta, Boston, Chicago, Denver, Houston, Los Angeles, Miami, New York, San Francisco
consulate(s): Orlando (FL), San Juan (Puerto Rico)

Diplomatic representation from the US: *chief of mission:* Ambassador (vacant); Charge d'Affaires Matthew PALMER
embassy: 33 Nine Elms Lane, London, SW11 7US
mailing address: 8400 London Place, Washington DC 20521-8400
telephone: [44] (0) 20-7499-9000
FAX: [44] (0) 20-7891-3845
email address and website:
SCSLondon@state.gov
https://uk.usembassy.gov/
consulate(s) general: Belfast, Edinburgh

Flag description: blue field with the red cross of Saint George (patron saint of England) edged in white superimposed on the diagonal red cross of Saint Patrick (patron saint of Ireland), which is superimposed on the diagonal white cross of Saint Andrew (patron saint of Scotland); properly known as the Union Flag, but commonly called the Union Jack; the design and colors (especially the Blue Ensign) have been the basis for a number of other flags including other Commonwealth countries and their constituent states or provinces, and British overseas territories

National symbol(s): lion (Britain in general); lion, Tudor rose, oak (England); lion, unicorn, thistle (Scotland); dragon, daffodil, leek (Wales); shamrock, flax (Northern Ireland); national colors: red, white, blue (Britain in general); red, white (England); blue, white (Scotland); red, white, green (Wales)

National anthem: *name:* "God Save the King"
lyrics/music: unknown
note: in use since 1745; by tradition, the song serves as both the national and royal anthem of the UK; it is known as either "God Save the Queen" or "God Save the King," depending on the gender of the reigning monarch; it also serves as the royal anthem of many Commonwealth nations

National heritage: *total World Heritage Sites:* 33 (28 cultural, 4 natural, 1 mixed); note - includes one site in Bermuda
selected World Heritage Site locales: Giant's Causeway and Causeway Coast (n); Ironbridge Gorge (c); Stonehenge, Avebury, and Associated Sites (c); Castles and Town Walls of King Edward in Gwynedd (c); Blenheim Palace (c); City of Bath (c); Tower of London (c); St Kilda (m); Maritime Greenwich (c); Old and New Towns of Edinburgh (c); Royal Botanic Gardens, Kew (c); The English Lake District (c)

ECONOMY

Economic overview: The UK, a leading trading power and financial center, is the third largest economy in Europe after Germany and France. Agriculture is intensive, highly mechanized, and efficient by European standards, producing about 60% of food needs with less than 2% of the labor force. The UK has large coal, natural gas, and oil resources, but its oil and natural gas reserves are declining; the UK has been a net importer of energy since 2005. Services, particularly banking, insurance, and business services, are key drivers of British GDP growth. Manufacturing, meanwhile, has declined in importance but still accounts for about 10% of economic output.

In 2008, the global financial crisis hit the economy particularly hard, due to the importance of its financial sector. Falling home prices, high consumer debt, and the global economic slowdown compounded the UK's economic problems, pushing the economy into recession in the latter half of 2008 and prompting the then BROWN (Labour) government to implement a number of measures to stimulate the economy and stabilize the financial markets. Facing burgeoning public deficits and debt levels, in 2010 the then CAMERON-led coalition government (between Conservatives and Liberal Democrats) initiated an austerity program, which has continued under the Conservative government. However, the deficit still remains one of the highest in the G7, standing at 3.6% of GDP as of 2017, and the UK has pledged to lower its corporation tax from 20% to 17% by 2020. The UK had a debt burden of 90.4% GDP at the end of 2017.

The UK economy has begun to slow since the referendum vote to leave the EU in June 2016. A sustained depreciation of the British pound has increased consumer and producer prices, weighing on consumer spending without spurring a meaningful increase in exports. The UK has an extensive trade relationship with other EU members through its single market membership, and economic observers have warned the exit will jeopardize its position as the central location for European financial services. The UK is slated to leave the EU at the end of January 2020.

Real GDP (purchasing power parity): $2,797,980,000,000 (2020 est.)
$3,101,640,000,000 (2019 est.)
$3,059,690,000,000 (2018 est.)
note: data are in 2017 dollars
country comparison to the world: 10

Real GDP growth rate: 1.26% (2019 est.)
1.25% (2018 est.)
1.74% (2017 est.)
country comparison to the world: 163

Real GDP per capita: $41,600 (2020 est.)
$46,400 (2019 est.)
$46,000 (2018 est.)
note: data are in 2017 dollars
country comparison to the world: 40

GDP (official exchange rate): $2,827,918,000,000 (2019 est.)

Inflation rate (consumer prices): 1.7% (2019 est.)
2.4% (2018 est.)
2.6% (2017 est.)
country comparison to the world: 97

Credit ratings:

Fitch rating: AA- (2020)

Moody's rating: Aaa (2020)

Standard & Poors rating: AA (2016)

GDP - composition, by sector of origin: *agriculture:* 0.7% (2017 est.)
industry: 20.2% (2017 est.)
services: 79.2% (2017 est.)

GDP - composition, by end use: *household consumption:* 65.8% (2017 est.)
government consumption: 18.3% (2017 est.)
investment in fixed capital: 17.2% (2017 est.)
investment in inventories: 0.2% (2017 est.)
exports of goods and services: 30.2% (2017 est.)
imports of goods and services: -31.5% (2017 est.)

Agricultural products: wheat, milk, barley, sugar beet, potatoes, rapeseed, poultry, oats, pork, beef

Industries: machine tools, electric power equipment, automation equipment, railroad equipment, shipbuilding, aircraft, motor vehicles and parts, electronics and communications equipment, metals, chemicals, coal, petroleum, paper and paper products, food processing, textiles, clothing, other consumer goods

Industrial production growth rate: 3.4% (2017 est.)
country comparison to the world: 93

Labor force: 35.412 million (2020 est.)
country comparison to the world: 17

Labor force - by occupation: *agriculture:* 1.3%
industry: 15.2%
services: 83.5% (2014 est.)

Unemployment rate: 3.17% (2019 est.)
2.51% (2018 est.)
country comparison to the world: 43

Unemployment, youth ages 15-24: *total:* 11.2%
male: 13%
female: 9.2% (2019 est.)
country comparison to the world: 129

Population below poverty line: 18.6% (2017 est.)

Gini Index coefficient - distribution of family income: 34.8 (2016 est.)
33.4 (2010)
country comparison to the world: 110

Household income or consumption by percentage share: *lowest 10%:* 1.7%
highest 10%: 31.1% (2012)

Budget: *revenues:* 1.028 trillion (2017 est.)
expenditures: 1.079 trillion (2017 est.)

Budget surplus (+) or deficit (-): -1.9% (of GDP) (2017 est.)
country comparison to the world: 102

Public debt: 87.5% of GDP (2017 est.)
87.9% of GDP (2016 est.)
note: data cover general government debt and include debt instruments issued (or owned) by government entities other than the treasury; the data include treasury debt held by foreign entities; the data include debt issued by subnational entities, as well as intragovernmental debt; intragovernmental debt consists of treasury borrowings from surpluses in the social funds, such as for retirement, medical care, and unemployment; debt instruments for the social funds are not sold at public auctions
country comparison to the world: 29

Taxes and other revenues: 39.1% (of GDP) (2017 est.)
country comparison to the world: 49

Fiscal year: 6 April - 5 April

Current account balance: -$121.921 billion (2019 est.)
-$104.927 billion (2018 est.)
country comparison to the world: 205

Exports: $741.95 billion (2020 est.) note: data are in current year dollars
$879.92 billion (2019 est.) note: data are in current year dollars
$882.65 billion (2018 est.) note: data are in current year dollars
country comparison to the world: 6

Exports - partners: United States 15%, Germany 10%, China 7%, Netherlands 7%, France 7%, Ireland 6% (2019)

Exports - commodities: cars, gas turbines, gold, crude petroleum, packaged medicines (2019)

Imports: $752.77 billion (2020 est.) note: data are in current year dollars
$914.96 billion (2019 est.) note: data are in current year dollars
$916.4 billion (2018 est.) note: data are in current year dollars
country comparison to the world: 6

Imports - partners: Germany 13%, China 10%, United States 8%, Netherlands 7%, France 6%, Belgium 5% (2019)

Imports - commodities: gold, cars, crude petroleum, refined petroleum, broadcasting equipment (2019)

Reserves of foreign exchange and gold: $150.8 billion (31 December 2017 est.)
$129.6 billion (31 December 2015 est.)
country comparison to the world: 18

Debt - external: $8,721,590,000,000 (2019 est.)
$8,696,559,000,000 (2018 est.)
country comparison to the world: 2

Exchange rates: British pounds (GBP) per US dollar -
0.7836 (2017 est.)
0.738 (2016 est.)
0.738 (2015 est.)
0.607 (2014 est.)
0.6391 (2013 est.)

ENERGY

Electricity access: *electrification - total population:* 100% (2020)

Electricity: *installed generating capacity:* 113.153 million kW (2020 est.)
consumption: 289.688 billion kWh (2020 est.)
exports: 4.481 billion kWh (2020 est.)
imports: 22.391 billion kWh (2020 est.)
transmission/distribution losses: 27.746 billion kWh (2020 est.)

Electricity generation sources: *fossil fuels:* 37.8% of total installed capacity (2020 est.)
nuclear: 15.2% of total installed capacity (2020 est.)
solar: 4.3% of total installed capacity (2020 est.)
wind: 25.2% of total installed capacity (2020 est.)
hydroelectricity: 2.6% of total installed capacity (2020 est.)
biomass and waste: 15% of total installed capacity (2020 est.)

Coal: *production:* 2.892 million metric tons (2020 est.)
consumption: 9.401 million metric tons (2020 est.)
exports: 1.309 million metric tons (2020 est.)
imports: 5.537 million metric tons (2020 est.)
proven reserves: 26 million metric tons (2019 est.)

Petroleum: *total petroleum production:* 890,400 bbl/day (2021 est.)
refined petroleum consumption: 1,578,100 bbl/day (2019 est.)
crude oil and lease condensate exports: 818,200 bbl/day (2018 est.)
crude oil and lease condensate imports: 891,700 bbl/day (2018 est.)
crude oil estimated reserves: 2.5 billion barrels (2021 est.)

Refined petroleum products - production: 1.29 million bbl/day (2017 est.)
country comparison to the world: 16

Refined petroleum products - exports: 613,800 bbl/day (2017 est.)
country comparison to the world: 14

Refined petroleum products - imports: 907,500 bbl/day (2017 est.)
country comparison to the world: 7

Natural gas: *production:* 32,482,541,000 cubic meters (2021 est.)
consumption: 75,696,895,000 cubic meters (2021 est.)
exports: 6,873,025,000 cubic meters (2021 est.)
imports: 51,050,178,000 cubic meters (2021 est.)
proven reserves: 180.661 billion cubic meters (2021 est.)

Carbon dioxide emissions: 398.084 million metric tonnes of CO_2 (2019 est.)

from coal and metallurgical coke: 23.5 million metric tonnes of CO2 (2019 est.)
from petroleum and other liquids: 216.237 million metric tonnes of CO2 (2019 est.)
from consumed natural gas: 158.346 million metric tonnes of CO2 (2019 est.)
country comparison to the world: 16

Energy consumption per capita: 119.894 million Btu/person (2019 est.)
country comparison to the world: 46

COMMUNICATIONS

Telephones - fixed lines: *total subscriptions:* 32.037 million (2020 est.)
subscriptions per 100 inhabitants: 47 (2020 est.)
country comparison to the world: 6

Telephones - mobile cellular: *total subscriptions:* 80.967 million (2019)
subscriptions per 100 inhabitants: 119.9 (2019)
country comparison to the world: 19

Telecommunication systems: *general assessment:* UK's telecom market remains one of the largest in Europe, characterized by competition, affordable pricing, and its technologically advanced systems; mobile penetration above the EU average; government to invest in infrastructure and 5G technologies with ambition for a fully-fibered nation by 2033; operators expanded the reach of 5G services in 2020; super-fast broadband available to about 95% of customers; London is developing smart city technology, in collaboration with private, tech, and academic sectors (2021)
domestic: equal mix of buried cables, microwave radio relay, and fiber-optic systems; fixed-line over 47 per 100 and mobile-cellular over 116 per 100 (2020)
international: country code - 44; Landing points for the GTT Atlantic, Scotland-Northern Ireland -1, & -2, Lanis 1,-2, &-3, Sirius North, BT-MT-1, SHEFA-2, BT Highlands and Islands Submarine Cable System, Northern Lights, FARICE-1, Celtic Norse, Tampnet Offshore FOC Network, England Cable, CC-2, E-LLan, Sirius South, ESAT -1 & -2, Rockabill, Geo-Eirgrid, UK-Netherlands-14, Circle North & South, Ulysses2, Conceto, Farland North, Pan European Crossing, Solas, Swansea-Bream, GTT Express, Tata TGN-Atlantic & -Western Europe, Apollo, EIG, Glo-1, TAT-14, Yellow, Celtic, FLAG Atlantic-1, FEA, Isle of Scilly Cable, UK-Channel Islands-8 and SeaMeWe-3 submarine cables providing links throughout Europe, Asia, Africa, the Middle East, Southeast Asia, Australia, and US; satellite earth stations - 10 Intelsat (7 Atlantic Ocean and 3 Indian Ocean), 1 Inmarsat (Atlantic Ocean region), and 1 Eutelsat; at least 8 large international switching centers (2019)

Broadcast media: public service broadcaster, British Broadcasting Corporation (BBC), is the largest broadcasting corporation in the world; BBC operates multiple TV networks with regional and local TV service; a mixed system of public and commercial TV broadcasters along with satellite and cable systems provide access to hundreds of TV stations throughout the world; BBC operates multiple national, regional, and local radio networks with multiple transmission sites; a large number of commercial radio stations, as well as satellite radio services are available (2018)

Internet country code: .uk

Internet users: *total:* 63,854,528 (2020 est.)
percent of population: 95% (2020 est.)
country comparison to the world: 15

Broadband - fixed subscriptions: *total:* 27,330,297 (2020 est.)
subscriptions per 100 inhabitants: 40 (2020 est.)
country comparison to the world: 8

Communications - note: *note 1:* the British Library claims to be the largest library in the world with well over 150 million items and in most known languages; it receives copies of all books produced in the UK or Ireland, as well as a significant proportion of overseas titles distributed in the UK; in addition to books (print and digital), holdings include: journals, manuscripts, newspapers, magazines, sound and music recordings, videos, maps, prints, patents, and drawings
note 2: on 1 May 1840, the United Kingdom led the world with the introduction of postage stamps; the Austrian Empire had examined the idea of an "adhesive tax postmark" for the prepayment of postage in 1835; while the suggestion was reviewed in detail, it was rejected for the time being; other countries (including Austria) soon followed the UK's example with their own postage stamps; by the 1860s, most countries were issuing stamps; originally, stamps had to be cut from sheets; the UK issued the first postage stamps with perforations in 1854

TRANSPORTATION

National air transport system: *number of registered air carriers:* 20 (2020)
inventory of registered aircraft operated by air carriers: 794
annual passenger traffic on registered air carriers: 165,388,610 (2018)
annual freight traffic on registered air carriers: 6,198,370,000 (2018) mt-km

Civil aircraft registration country code prefix: G

Airports: *total:* 460 (2021)
country comparison to the world: 16

Airports - with paved runways: *total:* 271
over 3,047 m: 7
2,438 to 3,047 m: 29
1,524 to 2,437 m: 89
914 to 1,523 m: 80
under 914 m: 66 (2021)

Airports - with unpaved runways: *total:* 189
1,524 to 2,437 m: 3
914 to 1,523 m: 26
*under 914 m:*160 (2021)

Heliports: 9 (2021)

Pipelines: 502 km condensate, 9 km condensate/gas, 28,603 km gas, 59 km liquid petroleum gas, 5,256 km oil, 175 km oil/gas /water, 4,919 km refined products, 255 km water (2013)

Railways: *total:* 16,837 km (2015)
standard gauge: 16,534 km (2015) 1.435-m gauge (5,357 km electrified)
broad gauge: 303 km (2015) 1.600-m gauge (in Northern Ireland)
country comparison to the world: 17

Roadways: *total:* 394,428 km (2009)
paved: 394,428 km (2009) (includes 3,519 km of expressways)
country comparison to the world: 19

Waterways: 3,200 km (2009) (620 km used for commerce)
country comparison to the world: 33

Merchant marine: *total:* 1,249
by type: bulk carrier 140, container ship 59, general cargo 109, oil tanker 84, other 857 (2021)
country comparison to the world: 21

Ports and terminals: *major seaport(s):* Dover, Felixstowe, Immingham, Liverpool, London, Southampton, Teesport (England); Forth Ports (Scotland); Milford Haven (Wales)
oil terminal(s): Fawley Marine terminal, Liverpool Bay terminal (England); Braefoot Bay terminal, Finnart oil terminal, Hound Point terminal (Scotland)
container port(s) (TEUs): Felixstowe (3,584,000), London (2,790,000), Southampton (1,924,847) (2019)

LNG terminal(s) (import): Dragon, Isle of Grain, South Hook, Teesside

Transportation - note: begun in 1988 and completed in 1994, the Channel Tunnel (nicknamed the Chunnel) is a 50.5-km (31.4-mi) rail tunnel beneath the English Channel at the Strait of Dover that runs from Folkestone, Kent, England to Coquelles, Pas-de-Calais in northern France; it is the only fixed link between the island of Great Britain and mainland Europe

MILITARY AND SECURITY

Military and security forces: United Kingdom Armed Forces (aka British Armed Forces, aka Her Majesty's Armed Forces): British Army, Royal Navy (includes Royal Marines), Royal Air Force (2022)
note: in 2021 the UK formed a joint service Space Command staffed by Army, Navy, and Air Force personnel, as well as civilians and key members of the commercial sector to manage space operations, training, and capabilities; it established a National Cyber Force comprised of military and intelligence personnel in 2020; in 2019, the UK formed the Strategic Command (formerly Joint Forces Command) to develop and manage the British military's medical services, training and education, defense intelligence, and information systems across the land, sea, air, space, and cyber domains; national-level special forces (UK Special Forces, UKSF) also fall under Strategic Command; in addition, the command manages joint overseas operations

Military expenditures: 2.1% of GDP (2022 est.)
2.5% of GDP (2021)
2.3% of GDP (2020)
2.1% of GDP (2019) (approximately $68.4 billion)
2.1% of GDP (2018) (approximately $67.8 billion)
country comparison to the world: 54

Military and security service personnel strengths: approximately 153,000 regular forces (81,000 Army; 34,000 Navy, including about 7,000 Royal Marines; 38,000 Air Force) (2022)
note: the military also has approximately 40-45,000 reserves and other personnel on active duty

Military equipment inventories and acquisitions: the inventory of the British military is comprised of a mix of domestically-produced and imported Western weapons systems; the US has been the leading supplier of armaments to the UK since 2010; the UK defense industry is capable of producing a wide variety of air, land, and sea weapons systems and is one of the world's top weapons suppliers (2021)

Military service age and obligation: some variations by service, but generally 16-36 years of age for enlisted (with parental consent under 18) and 18-29 for officers; minimum length of service 4 years;

women serve in all military services including combat roles; conscription abolished in 1963 (2022)
note 1: as of 2019, women made up about 11% of the military's full-time personnel
note 2: the British military allows Commonwealth nationals who are current UK residents and have been in the country for at least 5 years to apply; it also accepts Irish citizens
note 3: the British Army has continued the historic practice of recruiting Gurkhas from Nepal to serve in the Brigade of Gurkhas; the British began to recruit Nepalese citizens (Gurkhas) into the East India Company Army during the Anglo-Nepalese War (1814-1816); the Gurkhas subsequently were brought into the British Indian Army and by 1914, there were 10 Gurkha regiments, collectively known as the Gurkha Brigade; following the partition of India in 1947, an agreement between Nepal, India, and Great Britain allowed for the transfer of the 10 regiments from the British Indian Army to the separate British and Indian armies; four of the regiments were transferred to the British Army, where they have since served continuously as the Brigade of Gurkhas

Military deployments: approximately 1,000 Brunei; approximately 400 Canada (BATUS); approximately 2,500 Cyprus (250 for UNFICYP); approximately 1,000 Estonia (NATO); approximately 1,200 Falkland Islands; approximately 200 Germany; 570 Gibraltar; approximately 1,400 Middle East (including Bahrain, Iraq, Kuwait, Oman, Saudi Arabia, UAE); up to 350 Kenya (BATUK); approximately 350 Mali (EUTM, MINUSMA); 150 Poland (NATO) (2022)
note: in response to Russia's 2022 invasion of Ukraine, some NATO countries, including the UK, have sent additional troops and equipment to the battlegroups deployed in NATO territory in eastern Europe

Military - note: the UK is a member of NATO and was one of the original 12 countries to sign the North Atlantic Treaty (also known as the Washington Treaty) in 1949; the UK is also a member of the Five Powers Defense Arrangements (FPDA), a series of mutual assistance agreements reached in 1971 embracing Australia, Malaysia, New Zealand, Singapore, and the UK; the FPDA commits the members to consult with one another in the event or threat of an armed attack on any of the members and to mutually decide what measures should be taken, jointly or separately; there is no specific obligation to intervene militarily

in 2010, France and the UK signed a declaration on defense and security cooperation that included greater military interoperability and a Combined Joint Expeditionary Force (CJEF), a deployable, combined Anglo-French military force for use in a wide range of crisis scenarios, up to and including high intensity combat operations; the CJEF has no standing forces but would be available at short notice for UK-French bilateral, NATO, EU, UN, or other operations; combined training exercises began in 2011; as of 2020, the CJEF was assessed as having full operating capacity with the ability to rapidly deploy over 10,000 personnel capable of high intensity operations, peacekeeping, disaster relief, and humanitarian assistance

in 2014, the UK led the formation of the Joint Expeditionary Force (JEF), a pool of high-readiness military forces from Baltic and Scandinavian countries able to respond to a wide range of contingencies both in peacetime and in times of crisis or conflict; its principal geographic area of interest is the High North, North Atlantic, and Baltic Sea regions, where the JEF can complement national capabilities or NATO's deterrence posture, although it is designed to be flexible and prepared to respond to humanitarian crises further afield; the JEF consists of 10 countries (Denmark, Estonia, Finland, Iceland, Latvia, Lithuania, the Netherlands, Norway, Sweden, and the UK) and was declared operational in 2018; most of the forces in the pool are British, and the UK provides the most rapidly deployable units as well as the command and control elements

the British Armed Forces were formed in 1707 as the armed forces of the Kingdom of Great Britain when England and Scotland merged under the terms of the Treaty of Union; while the origins of the armed forces of England and Scotland stretch back to the Middle Ages, the first standing armies for England and Scotland were organized in the 1600s while the navies were formed in the 1500s; the Royal Marines were established in 1755; the Royal Air Force was created in April 1918 by the merger of the British Army's Royal Flying Corps and the Admiralty's Royal Naval Air Service (2022)

TERRORISM

Terrorist group(s): Continuity Irish Republican Army; Islamic State of Iraq and ash-Sham (ISIS); New Irish Republican Army; al-Qa'ida

TRANSNATIONAL ISSUES

Disputes - international: *UK-Argentina:* UK rejects sovereignty talks requested by Argentina, which still claims the Falkland Islands (Islas Malvinas) and South Georgia and the South Sandwich Islands
UK-Argentina-Chile: the UK's territorial claim in Antarctica (British Antarctic Territory) overlaps Argentine claim and partially overlaps Chilean claim
UK-Denmark: the UK, Iceland, and Ireland dispute Denmark's claim that the Faroe Islands' continental shelf extends beyond 200 nm; Iceland, Norway, and the Faroe Islands signed an agreement in 2019 extending the Faroe Islands' northern continental shelf area
UK (Gibraltar)-Spain: in 2002, Gibraltar residents voted overwhelmingly by referendum to reject any "shared sovereignty" arrangement between the UK and Spain; the Government of Gibraltar insisted on equal participation in talks between the two countries; Spain disapproved of UK plans to grant Gibraltar greater autonomy; London and Madrid reached a temporary agreement at the end of 2020 that allowed Gibraltar to be part of the passport-free Schengen zone; talks are expected to continue in 2022
UK-Mauritius-Seychelles: Mauritius and Seychelles claim the Chagos Archipelago (British Indian Ocean Territory); in 2001, the former inhabitants of the archipelago, evicted 1967 - 1973, were granted UK citizenship and the right of return, followed by Orders in Council in 2004 that banned rehabitation, a High Court ruling reversed the ban, a Court of Appeal refusal to hear the case, and a Law Lords' decision in 2008 denied the right of return; in addition, the UK created the world's largest marine protection area around the Chagos Islands prohibiting the extraction of any natural resources therein

Refugees and internally displaced persons: *refugees (country of origin):* 21,011 (Iran), 14,503 (Eritrea), 11,251 (Sudan), 11,412 (Syria), 9,469 (Afghanistan), 8,357 (Pakistan), 6,933 (Iraq), 5,200 (Sri Lanka) (2020); 143,100 (Ukraine) (as of 8 November 2022)
stateless persons: 3,968 (mid-year 2021)

Illicit drugs: consumer and transit country for illicit drugs; cocaine and heroin consumption rates among Europe's highest; criminal organizations engage in domestic drug trafficking and financial crimes; drug use remains linked to serious violence; major source of precursor chemicals used in the production of illicit narcotics

UNITED STATES

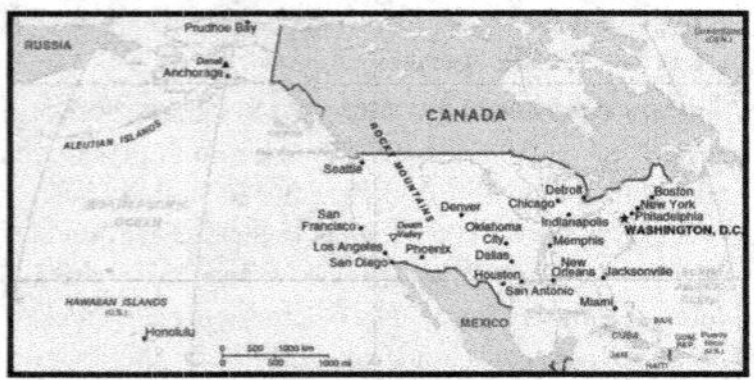

INTRODUCTION

Background: Britain's American colonies broke with the mother country in 1776 and were recognized as the new nation of the United States of America following the Treaty of Paris in 1783. During the 19th and 20th centuries, 37 new states were added to the original 13 as the nation expanded across the North American continent and acquired a number of overseas possessions. The two most traumatic experiences in the nation's history were the Civil War (1861-65), in which a northern Union of states defeated a secessionist Confederacy of 11 southern slave states, and the Great Depression of the 1930s, an economic downturn during which about a quarter of the labor force lost its jobs. Buoyed by victories in World Wars I and II and the end of the Cold War in 1991, the US remains the world's most powerful nation state. Since the end of World War II, the economy has achieved relatively steady growth, low unemployment and inflation, and rapid advances in technology.

GEOGRAPHY

Location: North America, bordering both the North Atlantic Ocean and the North Pacific Ocean, between Canada and Mexico

Geographic coordinates: 38 00 N, 97 00 W

Map references: North America

Area: *total:* 9,833,517 sq km
land: 9,147,593 sq km
water: 685,924 sq km

note: includes only the 50 states and District of Columbia, no overseas territories
country comparison to the world: 4

Area - comparative: about half the size of Russia; about three-tenths the size of Africa; about half the size of South America (or slightly larger than Brazil); slightly larger than China; more than twice the size of the European Union

Land boundaries: *total:* 12,002 km
border countries (2): Canada 8,891 km (including 2,475 km with Alaska); Mexico 3,111 km
note: US Naval Base at Guantanamo Bay, Cuba is leased by the US and is part of Cuba; the base boundary is 28.5 km

Coastline: 19,924 km

Maritime claims: *territorial sea:* 12 nm
contiguous zone: 24 nm
exclusive economic zone: 200 nm
continental shelf: not specified

Climate: mostly temperate, but tropical in Hawaii and Florida, arctic in Alaska, semiarid in the great plains west of the Mississippi River, and arid in the Great Basin of the southwest; low winter temperatures in the northwest are ameliorated occasionally in January and February by warm chinook winds from the eastern slopes of the Rocky Mountains
note: many consider Denali, the highest peak in the US, to be the world's coldest mountain because of its combination of high elevation and its subarctic location at 63 degrees north latitude; permanent snow and ice cover over 75 percent of the mountain, and enormous glaciers, up to 45 miles long and 3,700 feet thick, spider out from its base in every direction; it is home to some of the world's coldest and most violent weather, where winds of over 150 miles per hour and temperatures of -93°F have been recorded.

Terrain: vast central plain, mountains in west, hills and low mountains in east; rugged mountains and broad river valleys in Alaska; rugged, volcanic topography in Hawaii

Elevation: *highest point:* Denali 6,190 m (Mount McKinley) (highest point in North America)
lowest point: Death Valley (lowest point in North America) -86 m
mean elevation: 760 m
note: Denali is one of the most striking features on the entire planet; at 20,310 feet, it is the crowning peak of the Alaska Range and the highest mountain on North America; it towers three and one-half vertical miles above its base, making it a mile taller from base to summit than Mt. Everest; Denali's base sits at about 2,000 feet above sea level and rises over three and one-half miles to its 20,310 foot summit; Everest begins on a 14,000-foot high plain, then summits at 29,028 feet.
note: the peak of Mauna Kea (4,207 m above sea level) on the island of Hawaii rises about 10,200 m above the Pacific Ocean floor; by this measurement, it is the world's tallest mountain - higher than Mount Everest (8,850 m), which is recognized as the tallest mountain above sea level

Natural resources: coal, copper, lead, molybdenum, phosphates, rare earth elements, uranium, bauxite, gold, iron, mercury, nickel, potash, silver, tungsten, zinc, petroleum, natural gas, timber, arable land;
note 1: the US has the world's largest coal reserves with 491 billion short tons accounting for 27% of the world's total
note 2: the US is reliant on foreign imports for 100% of its needs for the following strategic resources: Arsenic, Cesium, Fluorspar, Gallium, Graphite, Indium, Manganese, Niobium, Rare Earths, Rubidium, Scandium, Tantalum, Yttrium; see Appendix H: Strategic Materials for further details

Land use: *agricultural land:* 44.5% (2018 est.)
arable land: 16.8% (2018 est.)
permanent crops: 0.3% (2018 est.)
permanent pasture: 27.4% (2018 est.)
forest: 33.3% (2018 est.)
other: 22.2% (2018 est.)

Irrigated land: 264,000 sq km (2012)

Major lakes (area sq km): *fresh water lake(s):* Michigan – 57,750 sq km; Superior* – 53,348 sq km; Huron* – 23,597 sq km; Erie* – 12,890 sq km; Ontario* – 9,220 sq km; Lake of the Woods – 4,350 sq km; Iliamna – 2,590 sq km; Okeechobee – 1,810 sq km; Belcharof – 1,190 sq km; Red – 1,170 sq km; Saint Clair – 1,113 sq km; Champlain – 1,100 sq km
note - Great Lakes* area shown as US waters
salt water lake(s): Great Salt – 4,360 sq km; Pontchartrain – 1,620 sq km; Selawik – 1,400 sq km; Salton Sea – 950 sq km

Major rivers (by length in km): Missouri - 3,768 km; Mississippi - 3,544 km; Yukon river mouth (shared with Canada [s]) - 3,190 km; Saint Lawrence (shared with Canada) - 3,058 km; Rio Grande river source (mouth shared with Mexico) - 3,057 km; Colorado river source (shared with Mexico [m]) - 2,333 km; Arkansas - 2,348 km; Columbia river mouth (shared with Canada [s]) - 2,250 km; Red - 2,188 km; Ohio - 2,102 km; Snake - 1,670 km
note – [s] after country name indicates river source; [m] after country name indicates river mouth

Major watersheds (area sq km): Atlantic Ocean drainage: *(Gulf of Mexico)* Mississippi* (3,202,185 sq km); Rio Grande (607,965 sq km); *(Gulf of Saint Lawrence)* Saint Lawrence* (1,049,636 sq km total, US only 505,000 sq km)
Pacific Ocean drainage: Yukon* (847,620 sq km, US only 23,820 sq km); Colorado (703,148 sq km); Columbia* (657,501 sq km, US only 554,501 sq km)
note - watersheds shared with Canada shown with *

Major aquifers: Northern Great Plains Aquifer, Cambrian-Ordovician Aquifer System, Californian Central Valley Aquifer System, Ogallala Aquifer (High Plains), Atlantic and Gulf Coastal Plains Aquifer

Population distribution: large urban clusters are spread throughout the eastern half of the US (particularly the Great Lakes area, northeast, east, and southeast) and the western tier states; mountainous areas, principally the Rocky Mountains and Appalachian chain, deserts in the southwest, the dense boreal forests in the extreme north, and the central prarie states are less densely populated; Alaska's population is concentrated along its southern coast - with particular emphasis on the city of Anchorage - and Hawaii's is centered on the island of Oahu

Natural hazards: tsunamis; volcanoes; earthquake activity around Pacific Basin; hurricanes along the Atlantic and Gulf of Mexico coasts; tornadoes in the Midwest and Southeast; mud slides in California; forest fires in the west; flooding; permafrost in northern Alaska, a major impediment to development
volcanism: volcanic activity in the Hawaiian Islands, Western Alaska, the Pacific Northwest, and in the Northern Mariana Islands; both Mauna Loa (4,170 m) in Hawaii and Mount Rainier (4,392 m) in Washington have been deemed Decade Volcanoes by the International Association of Volcanology and Chemistry of the Earth's Interior, worthy of study due to their explosive history and close proximity to human populations; Pavlof (2,519 m) is the most active volcano in Alaska's Aleutian Arc and poses a significant threat to air travel since the area constitutes a major flight path between North America and East Asia; St. Helens (2,549 m), famous for the devastating 1980 eruption, remains active today; numerous other historically active volcanoes exist, mostly concentrated in the Aleutian arc and Hawaii; they include: in Alaska: Aniakchak, Augustine, Chiginagak, Fourpeaked, Iliamna, Katmai, Kupreanof, Martin, Novarupta, Redoubt, Spurr, Wrangell, Trident, Ugashik-Peulik, Ukinrek Maars, Veniaminof; in Hawaii: Haleakala, Kilauea, Loihi; in the Northern Mariana Islands: Anatahan; and in the Pacific Northwest: Mount Baker, Mount Hood; see note 2 under "Geography - note"

Geography - note: *note 1:* world's third-largest country by size (after Russia and Canada) and by population (after China and India); Denali (Mt. McKinley) is the highest point (6,190 m) in North America and Death Valley the lowest point (-86 m) on the continent
note 2: the western coast of the United States and southern coast of Alaska lie along the Ring of Fire, a belt of active volcanoes and earthquake epicenters bordering the Pacific Ocean; up to 90% of the world's earthquakes and some 75% of the world's volcanoes occur within the Ring of Fire
note 3: the Aleutian Islands are a chain of volcanic islands that divide the Bering Sea (north) from the main Pacific Ocean (south); they extend about 1,800 km westward from the Alaskan Peninsula; the archipelago consists of 14 larger islands, 55 smaller islands, and hundreds of islets; there are 41 active volcanoes on the islands, which together form a large northern section of the Ring of Fire
note 4: Mammoth Cave, in west-central Kentucky, is the world's longest known cave system with more than 650 km (405 miles) of surveyed passageways, which is nearly twice as long as the second-longest cave system, the Sac Actun underwater cave in Mexico -the world's longest underwater cave system (see "Geography - note" under Mexico);
note 5: Kazumura Cave on the island of Hawaii is the world's longest and deepest lava tube cave; it has been surveyed at 66 km (41 mi) long and 1,102 m (3,614 ft) deep
note 6: Bracken Cave outside of San Antonio, Texas is the world's largest bat cave; it is the summer home to the largest colony of bats in the world; an estimated 20 million Mexican free-tailed bats roost in the cave from March to October making it the world's largest known concentration of mammals
note 7: the US is reliant on foreign imports for 100% of its needs for the following strategic resources - Arsenic, Cesium, Fluorspar, Gallium, Graphite, Indium, Manganese, Niobium, Rare Earths, Rubidium, Scandium, Tantalum, Yttrium; see Appendix H: Strategic Materials for further details
note 8: three food crops are generally acknowledged to be native to areas of what is now the United States: cranberries, pecans, and sunflowers

PEOPLE AND SOCIETY

Population: 337,341,954 (2022 est.)
note: the US Census Bureau's 2020 census results show the US population as 331,449,281 as of 1 April 2020

country comparison to the world: 3

Nationality: *noun:* American(s)
adjective: American

Ethnic groups: White 61.6%, Black or African American 12.4%, Asian 6%, Amerindian and Alaska native 1.1%, Native Hawaiian and Other Pacific Islander 0.2%, other 8.4%, two or more races 10.2% (2020 est.)
note: a separate listing for Hispanic is not included because the US Census Bureau considers Hispanic to mean persons of Spanish/Hispanic/Latino origin including those of Mexican, Cuban, Puerto Rican, Dominican Republic, Spanish, and Central or South American origin living in the US who may be of any race or ethnic group (White, Black, Asian, etc.); an estimated 18.7% of the total US population is Hispanic as of 2020

Languages: English only 78.2%, Spanish 13.4%, Chinese 1.1%, other 7.3% (2017 est.)
note: data represent the language spoken at home; the US has no official national language, but English has acquired official status in 32 of the 50 states; Hawaiian is an official language in the state of Hawaii, and 20 indigenous languages are official in Alaska

Religions: Protestant 46.5%, Roman Catholic 20.8%, Jewish 1.9%, Church of Jesus Christ 1.6%, other Christian 0.9%, Muslim 0.9%, Jehovah's Witness 0.8%, Buddhist 0.7%, Hindu 0.7%, other 1.8%, unaffiliated 22.8%, don't know/refused 0.6% (2014 est.)

Age structure: *0-14 years:* 18.46% (male 31,374,555/female 30,034,371)
15-24 years: 12.91% (male 21,931,368/female 21,006,463)
25-54 years: 38.92% (male 64,893,670/female 64,564,565)
55-64 years: 12.86% (male 20,690,736/female 22,091,808)
65 years and over: 16.85% (male 25,014,147/female 31,037,419) (2020 est.)

Dependency ratios: *total dependency ratio:* 53.9
youth dependency ratio: 28.3
elderly dependency ratio: 25.6
potential support ratio: 3.9 (2020 est.)

Median age: *total:* 38.5 years
male: 37.2 years
female: 39.8 years (2020 est.)
country comparison to the world: 61

Population growth rate: 0.69% (2022 est.)
country comparison to the world: 130

Birth rate: 12.28 births/1,000 population (2022 est.)
country comparison to the world: 151

Death rate: 8.38 deaths/1,000 population (2022 est.)
country comparison to the world: 78

Net migration rate: 3.02 migrant(s)/1,000 population (2022 est.)
country comparison to the world: 39

Population distribution: large urban clusters are spread throughout the eastern half of the US (particularly the Great Lakes area, northeast, east, and southeast) and the western tier states; mountainous areas, principally the Rocky Mountains and Appalachian chain, deserts in the southwest, the dense boreal forests in the extreme north, and the central prarie states are less densely populated; Alaska's population is concentrated along its southern coast - with particular emphasis on the city of Anchorage - and Hawaii's is centered on the island of Oahu

Urbanization: *urban population:* 83.1% of total population (2022)
rate of urbanization: 0.96% annual rate of change (2020-25 est.)

Major urban areas - population: 18.867 million New York-Newark, 12.488 million Los Angeles-Long Beach-Santa Ana, 8.901 million Chicago, 6.603 million Houston, 6.488 million Dallas-Fort Worth, 5.434 million WASHINGTON, D.C. (capital) (2022)

Sex ratio: *at birth:* 1.05 male(s)/female
0-14 years: 1.04 male(s)/female
15-24 years: 1.04 male(s)/female
25-54 years: 1.01 male(s)/female
55-64 years: 0.94 male(s)/female
65 years and over: 0.69 male(s)/female
total population: 0.97 male(s)/female (2022 est.)

Mother's mean age at first birth: 27 years (2019 est.)

Maternal mortality ratio: 19 deaths/100,000 live births (2017 est.)
country comparison to the world: 129

Infant mortality rate: *total:* 5.17 deaths/1,000 live births
male: 5.55 deaths/1,000 live births
female: 4.77 deaths/1,000 live births (2022 est.)
country comparison to the world: 174

Life expectancy at birth: *total population:* 80.59 years
male: 78.36 years
female: 82.79 years (2022 est.)
country comparison to the world: 46

Total fertility rate: 1.84 children born/woman (2022 est.)
country comparison to the world: 137

Contraceptive prevalence rate: 73.9% (2017/19)

Drinking water source: *improved: urban:* 99.9% of population
rural: 99.7% of population
total: 99.9% of population
unimproved: urban: 0.1% of population
rural: 0.3% of population
total: 0.1% of population (2020 est.)

Current health expenditure: 16.8% of GDP (2019)

Physicians density: 2.61 physicians/1,000 population (2018)

Hospital bed density: 2.9 beds/1,000 population (2017)

Sanitation facility access: *improved: urban:* 99.8% of population
rural: 98.9% of population
total: 99.7% of population
unimproved: urban: 0.2% of population
rural: 11.1% of population
total: 0.3% of population (2020 est.)

Obesity - adult prevalence rate: 36.2% (2016)
country comparison to the world: 12

Alcohol consumption per capita: *total:* 8.93 liters of pure alcohol (2019 est.)
beer: 3.97 liters of pure alcohol (2019 est.)
wine: 1.67 liters of pure alcohol (2019 est.)
spirits: 3.29 liters of pure alcohol (2019 est.)
other alcohols: 0 liters of pure alcohol (2019 est.)
country comparison to the world: 35

Tobacco use: *total:* 23% (2020 est.)
male: 28.4% (2020 est.)
female: 17.5% (2020 est.)
country comparison to the world: 66

Children under the age of 5 years underweight: 0.4% (2017/18)
country comparison to the world: 130

Education expenditures: 5% of GDP (2014 est.)
country comparison to the world: 66

School life expectancy (primary to tertiary education): *total:* 16 years
male: 16 years
female: 17 years (2019)

Unemployment, youth ages 15-24: *total:* 14.9%
male: 15%
female: 14.8% (2020 est.)

ENVIRONMENT

Environment - current issues: air pollution; large emitter of carbon dioxide from the burning of fossil fuels; water pollution from runoff of pesticides and fertilizers; declining natural freshwater resources in much of the western part of the country require careful management; deforestation; mining; desertification; species conservation; invasive species (the Hawaiian Islands are particularly vulnerable)

Environment - international agreements: *party to:* Air Pollution, Air Pollution-Heavy Metals, Air Pollution-Multi-effect Protocol, Air Pollution-Nitrogen Oxides, Antarctic-Environmental Protection, Antarctic-Marine Living Resources, Antarctic Seals, Antarctic Treaty, Climate Change, Climate Change-Paris Agreement, Desertification, Endangered Species, Environmental Modification, Marine Dumping-London Convention, Marine Life Conservation, Nuclear Test Ban, Ozone Layer Protection, Ship Pollution, Tropical Timber 2006, Wetlands, Whaling
signed, but not ratified: Air Pollution-Persistent Organic Pollutants, Air Pollution-Volatile Organic Compounds, Biodiversity, Climate Change-Kyoto Protocol, Comprehensive Nuclear Test Ban, Hazardous Wastes, Marine Dumping-London Protocol

Air pollutants: *particulate matter emissions:* 7.4 micrograms per cubic meter (2016 est.)
carbon dioxide emissions: 5,006.3 megatons (2016 est.)
methane emissions: 685.74 megatons (2020 est.)

Climate: mostly temperate, but tropical in Hawaii and Florida, arctic in Alaska, semiarid in the great plains west of the Mississippi River, and arid in the Great Basin of the southwest; low winter temperatures in the northwest are ameliorated occasionally in January and February by warm chinook winds from the eastern slopes of the Rocky Mountains
note: many consider Denali, the highest peak in the US, to be the world's coldest mountain because of its combination of high elevation and its subarctic location at 63 degrees north latitude; permanent snow and ice cover over 75 percent of the mountain, and enormous glaciers, up to 45 miles long and 3,700 feet thick, spider out from its base in every direction; it is home to some of the world's coldest and most violent weather, where winds of over 150 miles per hour and temperatures of -93°F have been recorded.

Land use: *agricultural land:* 44.5% (2018 est.)
arable land: 16.8% (2018 est.)
permanent crops: 0.3% (2018 est.)
permanent pasture: 27.4% (2018 est.)
forest: 33.3% (2018 est.)
other: 22.2% (2018 est.)

Urbanization: *urban population:* 83.1% of total population (2022)
rate of urbanization: 0.96% annual rate of change (2020-25 est.)

Revenue from forest resources: *forest revenues:* 0.04% of GDP (2018 est.)
country comparison to the world: 131

Revenue from coal: *coal revenues:* 0.2% of GDP (2018 est.)
country comparison to the world: 22

Waste and recycling: *municipal solid waste generated annually:* 258 million tons (2015 est.)
municipal solid waste recycled annually: 89.268 million tons (2014 est.)
percent of municipal solid waste recycled: 34.6% (2014 est.)

Major lakes (area sq km): *fresh water lake(s):* Michigan – 57,750 sq km; Superior* – 53,348 sq km; Huron* – 23,597 sq km; Erie* – 12,890 sq km; Ontario* – 9,220 sq km; Lake of the Woods – 4,350 sq km; Iliamna – 2,590 sq km; Okeechobee – 1,810 sq km; Belcharof – 1,190 sq km; Red – 1,170 sq km; Saint Clair – 1,113 sq km; Champlain – 1,100 sq km
note - Great Lakes* area shown as US waters
salt water lake(s): Great Salt – 4,360 sq km; Pontchartrain – 1,620 sq km; Selawik – 1,400 sq km; Salton Sea – 950 sq km

Major rivers (by length in km): Missouri - 3,768 km; Mississippi - 3,544 km; Yukon river mouth (shared with Canada [s]) - 3,190 km; Saint Lawrence (shared with Canada) - 3,058 km; Rio Grande river source (mouth shared with Mexico) - 3,057 km; Colorado river source (shared with Mexico [m]) - 2,333 km; Arkansas - 2,348 km; Columbia river mouth (shared with Canada [s]) - 2,250 km; Red - 2,188 km; Ohio - 2,102 km; Snake - 1,670 km
note – [s] after country name indicates river source; [m] after country name indicates river mouth

Major watersheds (area sq km): Atlantic Ocean drainage: *(Gulf of Mexico)* Mississippi* (3,202,185 sq km); Rio Grande (607,965 sq km); *(Gulf of Saint Lawrence)* Saint Lawrence* (1,049,636 sq km total, US only 505,000 sq km)
Pacific Ocean drainage: Yukon* (847,620 sq km, US only 23,820 sq km); Colorado (703,148 sq km); Columbia* (657,501 sq km, US only 554,501 sq km)
note - watersheds shared with Canada shown with *

Major aquifers: Northern Great Plains Aquifer, Cambrian-Ordovician Aquifer System, Californian Central Valley Aquifer System, Ogallala Aquifer (High Plains), Atlantic and Gulf Coastal Plains Aquifer

Total water withdrawal: *municipal:* 58.39 billion cubic meters (2017 est.)
industrial: 209.7 billion cubic meters (2017 est.)
agricultural: 176.2 billion cubic meters (2017 est.)

Total renewable water resources: 3.069 trillion cubic meters (2017 est.)

GOVERNMENT

Country name: *conventional long form:* United States of America
conventional short form: United States
abbreviation: US or USA
etymology: the name America is derived from that of Amerigo VESPUCCI (1454-1512) - Italian explorer, navigator, and cartographer - using the Latin form of his name, Americus, feminized to America

Government type: constitutional federal republic

Capital: *name:* Washington, DC
geographic coordinates: 38 53 N, 77 02 W
time difference: UTC-5 (during Standard Time)
daylight saving time: +1hr, begins second Sunday in March; ends first Sunday in November
time zone note: the 50 United States cover six time zones
etymology: named after George WASHINGTON (1732-1799), the first president of the United States

Administrative divisions: 50 states and 1 district*; Alabama, Alaska, Arizona, Arkansas, California, Colorado, Connecticut, Delaware, District of Columbia*, Florida, Georgia, Hawaii, Idaho, Illinois, Indiana, Iowa, Kansas, Kentucky, Louisiana, Maine, Maryland, Massachusetts, Michigan, Minnesota, Mississippi, Missouri, Montana, Nebraska, Nevada, New Hampshire, New Jersey, New Mexico, New York, North Carolina, North Dakota, Ohio, Oklahoma, Oregon, Pennsylvania, Rhode Island, South Carolina, South Dakota, Tennessee, Texas, Utah, Vermont, Virginia, Washington, West Virginia, Wisconsin, Wyoming

Dependent areas: American Samoa, Baker Island, Guam, Howland Island, Jarvis Island, Johnston Atoll, Kingman Reef, Midway Islands, Navassa Island, Northern Mariana Islands, Palmyra Atoll, Puerto Rico, Virgin Islands, Wake Island
note: from 18 July 1947 until 1 October 1994, the US administered the Trust Territory of the Pacific Islands; it entered into a political relationship with all four political entities: the Northern Mariana Islands is a commonwealth in political union with the US (effective 3 November 1986); the Republic of the Marshall Islands signed a Compact of Free Association with the US (effective 21 October 1986); the Federated States of Micronesia signed a Compact of Free Association with the US (effective 3 November 1986); Palau concluded a Compact of Free Association with the US (effective 1 October 1994)

Independence: 4 July 1776 (declared independence from Great Britain); 3 September 1783 (recognized by Great Britain)

National holiday: Independence Day, 4 July (1776)

Constitution: *history:* previous 1781 (Articles of Confederation and Perpetual Union); latest drafted July - September 1787, submitted to the Congress of the Confederation 20 September 1787, submitted for states' ratification 28 September 1787, ratification completed by nine of the 13 states 21 June 1788, effective 4 March 1789
amendments: proposed as a "joint resolution" by Congress, which requires a two-thirds majority vote in both the House of Representatives and the Senate or by a constitutional convention called for by at least two thirds of the state legislatures; passage requires ratification by three fourths of the state legislatures or passage in state-held constitutional conventions as specified by Congress; the US president has no role in the constitutional amendment process; amended many times, last in 1992

Legal system: common law system based on English common law at the federal level; state legal systems based on common law, except Louisiana, where state law is based on Napoleonic civil code; judicial review of legislative acts

International law organization participation: withdrew acceptance of compulsory ICJ jurisdiction in 2005; withdrew acceptance of ICCt jurisdiction in 2002

Citizenship: *citizenship by birth:* yes
citizenship by descent only: yes
dual citizenship recognized: no, but the US government acknowledges such situtations exist; US citizens are not encouraged to seek dual citizenship since it limits protection by the US
residency requirement for naturalization: 5 years

Suffrage: 18 years of age; universal

Executive branch: *chief of state:* President Joseph R. BIDEN, Jr. (since 20 January 2021); Vice President Kamala D. HARRIS (since 20 January 2021); note - the president is both chief of state and head of government
head of government: President Joseph R. BIDEN, Jr. (since 20 January 2021); Vice President Kamala D. HARRIS (since 20 January 2021)
cabinet: Cabinet appointed by the president, approved by the Senate
elections/appointments: president and vice president indirectly elected on the same ballot by the Electoral College of 'electors' chosen from each state; president and vice president serve a 4-year term (eligible for a second term); election last held on 3 November 2020 (next to be held on 5 November 2024)
election results:
2020: Joseph R. BIDEN, Jr. elected president; electoral vote - Joseph R. BIDEN, Jr. (Democratic Party) 306, Donald J. TRUMP (Republican Party) 232; percent of direct popular vote - Joseph R. BIDEN Jr. 51.3%, Donald J. TRUMP 46.9%, other 1.8%
2016: Donald J. TRUMP elected president; electoral vote - Donald J. TRUMP (Republican Party) 304, Hillary D. CLINTON (Democratic Party) 227, other 7; percent of direct popular vote - Hillary D. CLINTON 48.2%, Donald J. TRUMP 46.1%, other 5.7%

Legislative branch: *description:* bicameral Congress consists of:
Senate (100 seats; 2 members directly elected in each of the 50 state constituencies by simple majority vote except in Georgia and Louisiana which require an absolute majority vote with a second round if needed; members serve 6-year terms with one-third of membership renewed every 2 years)
House of Representatives (435 seats; members directly elected in single-seat constituencies by simple majority vote except in Georgia which requires an absolute majority vote with a second round if needed; members serve 2-year terms)
elections:
Senate - last held on 3 November 2020 (next to be held on 8 November 2022)
House of Representatives - last held on 3 November 2020 (next to be held on 8 November 2022)
election results:
Senate - percent of vote by party - NA; seats by party - Republican Party 50, Democratic Party 50; composition - men 76, women 24, percent of women 24%
House of Representatives - percent of vote by party - NA; seats by party - Democratic Party 221, Republican Party 211, 3 seats vacant; composition - men 312, women 120, percent of women 27.8%; note - total US Congress percent of women 27.1%
note: in addition to the regular members of the House of Representatives there are 6 non-voting

delegates elected from the District of Columbia and the US territories of American Samoa, Guam, Puerto Rico, the Northern Mariana Islands, and the Virgin Islands; these are single seat constituencies directly elected by simple majority vote to serve a 2-year term (except for the resident commissioner of Puerto Rico who serves a 4-year term); the delegate can vote when serving on a committee and when the House meets as the Committee of the Whole House, but not when legislation is submitted for a "full floor" House vote; election of delegates last held on 3 November 2020 (next to be held on 8 November 2022)

Judicial branch: *highest court(s):* US Supreme Court (consists of 9 justices - the chief justice and 8 associate justices)
judge selection and term of office: president nominates and, with the advice and consent of the Senate, appoints Supreme Court justices; justices serve for life
subordinate courts: Courts of Appeal (includes the US Court of Appeal for the Federal District and 12 regional appeals courts); 94 federal district courts in 50 states and territories
note: the US court system consists of the federal court system and the state court systems; although each court system is responsible for hearing certain types of cases, neither is completely independent of the other, and the systems often interact

Political parties and leaders: Democratic Party [Jaime HARRISON]
Green Party [collective leadership]
Libertarian Party [Angela McARDLE]
Republican Party [Ronna Romney MCDANIEL]

International organization participation: ADB (nonregional member), AfDB (nonregional member), ANZUS, APEC, Arctic Council, ARF, ASEAN (dialogue partner), Australia Group, BIS, BSEC (observer), CBSS (observer), CD, CE (observer), CERN (observer), CICA (observer), CP, EAPC, EAS, EBRD, EITI (implementing country), FAO, FATF, G-5, G-7, G-8, G-10, G-20, IADB, IAEA, IBRD, ICAO, ICC (national committees), ICRM, IDA, IEA, IFAD, IFC, IFRCS, IGAD (partners), IHO, ILO, IMF, IMO, IMSO, Interpol, IOC, IOM, ISO, ITSO, ITU, ITUC (NGOs), MIGA, MINUSMA, MINUSTAH, MONUSCO, NAFTA, NATO, NEA, NSG, OAS, OECD, OPCW, OSCE, Pacific Alliance (observer), Paris Club, PCA, PIF (partner), Quad, SAARC (observer), SELEC (observer), SICA (observer), SPC, UN, UNCTAD, UNESCO, UNHCR, UNHRC, UNITAR, UNMIL, UNMISS, UNRWA, UN Security Council (permanent), UNTSO, UPU, USMCA, Wassenaar Arrangement, WCO, WHO, WIPO, WMO, WTO, ZC

Flag description: 13 equal horizontal stripes of red (top and bottom) alternating with white; there is a blue rectangle in the upper hoist-side corner bearing 50 small, white, five-pointed stars arranged in nine offset horizontal rows of six stars (top and bottom) alternating with rows of five stars; the 50 stars represent the 50 states, the 13 stripes represent the 13 original colonies; blue stands for loyalty, devotion, truth, justice, and friendship, red symbolizes courage, zeal, and fervency, while white denotes purity and rectitude of conduct; commonly referred to by its nickname of Old Glory
note: the design and colors have been the basis for a number of other flags, including Chile, Liberia, Malaysia, and Puerto Rico

National symbol(s): bald eagle; national colors: red, white, blue

National anthem: *name:* "The Star-Spangled Banner"
lyrics/music: Francis Scott KEY/John Stafford SMITH
note: adopted 1931; during the War of 1812, after witnessing the successful American defense of Fort McHenry in Baltimore following British naval bombardment, Francis Scott KEY wrote the lyrics to what would become the national anthem; the lyrics were set to the tune of "The Anacreontic Song"; only the first verse is sung

National heritage: *total World Heritage Sites:* 24 (11 cultural, 12 natural, 1 mixed); note - includes one site in Puerto Rico
selected World Heritage Site locales: Yellowstone National Park (n); Grand Canyon National Park (n); Cahokia Mounds State Historic Site (c); Independence Hall (c); Statue of Liberty (c); Yosemite National Park (n); Papahānaumokuākea (m); Monumental Earthworks of Poverty Point (c); The 20th-Century Architecture of Frank Lloyd Wright (c); Mesa Verde National Park (c); Mammoth Cave National Park (n); Monticello (c); Olympic National Park (n)

ECONOMY

Economic overview: The US has the most technologically powerful economy in the world, with a per capita GDP of $59,500. US firms are at or near the forefront in technological advances, especially in computers, pharmaceuticals, and medical, aerospace, and military equipment; however, their advantage has narrowed since the end of World War II. Based on a comparison of GDP measured at purchasing power parity conversion rates, the US economy in 2014, having stood as the largest in the world for more than a century, slipped into second place behind China, which has more than tripled the US growth rate for each year of the past four decades.

In the US, private individuals and business firms make most of the decisions, and the federal and state governments buy needed goods and services predominantly in the private marketplace. US business firms enjoy greater flexibility than their counterparts in Western Europe and Japan in decisions to expand capital plant, to lay off surplus workers, and to develop new products. At the same time, businesses face higher barriers to enter their rivals' home markets than foreign firms face entering US markets.

Long-term problems for the US include stagnation of wages for lower-income families, inadequate investment in deteriorating infrastructure, rapidly rising medical and pension costs of an aging population, energy shortages, and sizable current account and budget deficits.

The onrush of technology has been a driving factor in the gradual development of a "two-tier" labor market in which those at the bottom lack the education and the professional/technical skills of those at the top and, more and more, fail to get comparable pay raises, health insurance coverage, and other benefits. But the globalization of trade, and especially the rise of low-wage producers such as China, has put additional downward pressure on wages and upward pressure on the return to capital. Since 1975, practically all the gains in household income have gone to the top 20% of households. Since 1996, dividends and capital gains have grown faster than wages or any other category of after-tax income.

Imported oil accounts for more than 50% of US consumption and oil has a major impact on the overall health of the economy. Crude oil prices doubled between 2001 and 2006, the year home prices peaked; higher gasoline prices ate into consumers' budgets and many individuals fell behind in their mortgage payments. Oil prices climbed another 50% between 2006 and 2008, and bank foreclosures more than doubled in the same period. Besides dampening the housing market, soaring oil prices caused a drop in the value of the dollar and a deterioration in the US merchandise trade deficit, which peaked at $840 billion in 2008. Because the US economy is energy-intensive, falling oil prices since 2013 have alleviated many of the problems the earlier increases had created.

The sub-prime mortgage crisis, falling home prices, investment bank failures, tight credit, and the global economic downturn pushed the US into a recession by mid-2008. GDP contracted until the third quarter of 2009, the deepest and longest downturn since the Great Depression. To help stabilize financial markets, the US Congress established a $700 billion Troubled Asset Relief Program in October 2008. The government used some of these funds to purchase equity in US banks and industrial corporations, much of which had been returned to the government by early 2011. In January 2009, Congress passed and former President Barack OBAMA signed a bill providing an additional $787 billion fiscal stimulus to be used over 10 years - two-thirds on additional spending and one-third on tax cuts - to create jobs and to help the economy recover. In 2010 and 2011, the federal budget deficit reached nearly 9% of GDP. In 2012, the Federal Government reduced the growth of spending and the deficit shrank to 7.6% of GDP. US revenues from taxes and other sources are lower, as a percentage of GDP, than those of most other countries.

Wars in Iraq and Afghanistan required major shifts in national resources from civilian to military purposes and contributed to the growth of the budget deficit and public debt. Through FY 2018, the direct costs of the wars will have totaled more than $1.9 trillion, according to US Government figures.

In March 2010, former President OBAMA signed into law the Patient Protection and Affordable Care Act (ACA), a health insurance reform that was designed to extend coverage to an additional 32 million Americans by 2016, through private health insurance for the general population and Medicaid for the impoverished. Total spending on healthcare - public plus private - rose from 9.0% of GDP in 1980 to 17.9% in 2010.

In July 2010, the former president signed the DODD-FRANK Wall Street Reform and Consumer Protection Act, a law designed to promote financial stability by protecting consumers from financial abuses, ending taxpayer bailouts of financial firms, dealing with troubled banks that are "too big to fail," and improving accountability and transparency in the financial system - in particular, by requiring certain financial derivatives to be traded in markets that are subject to government regulation and oversight.

The Federal Reserve Board (Fed) announced plans in December 2012 to purchase $85 billion per month of mortgage-backed and Treasury securities in an effort to hold down long-term interest rates, and to keep short-term rates near zero until unemployment dropped below 6.5% or inflation rose above 2.5%. The Fed ended its purchases during the summer of 2014, after the unemployment rate dropped to 6.2%, inflation stood at 1.7%, and public debt fell below 74% of GDP. In December 2015, the Fed raised its target for the benchmark federal funds rate by 0.25%, the first increase since the recession began. With continued low growth, the Fed opted to raise rates several times since then, and in December 2017, the target rate stood at 1.5%.

In December 2017, Congress passed and former President Donald TRUMP signed the Tax Cuts and Jobs Act, which, among its various provisions, reduces the corporate tax rate from 35% to 21%; lowers the individual tax rate for those with the highest incomes from 39.6% to 37%, and by lesser percentages for those at lower income levels; changes many deductions and credits used to calculate taxable income; and eliminates in 2019 the penalty imposed on taxpayers who do not obtain the minimum amount of health insurance required under the ACA. The new taxes took effect on 1 January 2018; the tax cut for corporations are permanent, but those for individuals are scheduled to expire after 2025. The Joint Committee on Taxation (JCT) under the Congressional Budget Office estimates that the new law will reduce tax revenues and increase the federal deficit by about $1.45 trillion over the 2018-2027 period. This amount would decline if economic growth were to exceed the JCT's estimate.

Real GDP (purchasing power parity): $19,846,720,000,000 (2020 est.)
$20,563,590,000,000 (2019 est.)
$20,128,580,000,000 (2018 est.)
note: data are in 2017 dollars
country comparison to the world: 2

Real GDP growth rate: 2.16% (2019 est.)
3% (2018 est.)
2.33% (2017 est.)
country comparison to the world: 129

Real GDP per capita: $60,200 (2020 est.)
$62,600 (2019 est.)
$61,600 (2018 est.)
note: data are in 2017 dollars
country comparison to the world: 17

GDP (official exchange rate): $21,433,228,000,000 (2019 est.)

Inflation rate (consumer prices): 1.8% (2019 est.)
2.4% (2018 est.)
2.1% (2017 est.)
country comparison to the world: 103

Credit ratings:

Fitch rating: AAA (1994)

Moody's rating: Aaa (1949)

Standard & Poors rating: AA+ (2011)

GDP - composition, by sector of origin: *agriculture:* 0.9% (2017 est.)
industry: 19.1% (2017 est.)
services: 80% (2017 est.)

GDP - composition, by end use: *household consumption:* 68.4% (2017 est.)
government consumption: 17.3% (2017 est.)
investment in fixed capital: 17.2% (2017 est.)
investment in inventories: 0.1% (2017 est.)
exports of goods and services: 12.1% (2017 est.)
imports of goods and services: -15% (2017 est.)

Agricultural products: maize, milk, soybeans, wheat, sugar cane, sugar beet, poultry, potatoes, cotton, pork

Industries: highly diversified, world leading, high-technology innovator, second-largest industrial output in the world; petroleum, steel, motor vehicles, aerospace, telecommunications, chemicals, electronics, food processing, consumer goods, lumber, mining

Industrial production growth rate: 2.3% (2017 est.)
country comparison to the world: 122

Labor force: 146.128 million (2020 est.)
note: includes unemployed
country comparison to the world: 3

Labor force - by occupation: *agriculture:* 0.7% (2009)
industry: 20.3% (2009)
services: 37.3% (2009)
industry and services: 24.2% (2009)
manufacturing: 17.6% (2009)
farming, forestry, and fishing: 0.7% (2009)
manufacturing, extraction, transportation, and crafts: 20.3% (2009)
managerial, professional, and technical: 37.3% (2009)
sales and office: 24.2% (2009)
other services: 17.6% (2009)
note: figures exclude the unemployed

Unemployment rate: 3.89% (2018 est.)
4.4% (2017 est.)
country comparison to the world: 57

Unemployment, youth ages 15-24: *total:* 14.9%
male: 15%
female: 14.8% (2020 est.)
country comparison to the world: 110

Population below poverty line: 15.1% (2010 est.)

Gini Index coefficient - distribution of family income: 41.1 (2016 est.)
40.8 (1997)
country comparison to the world: 54

Household income or consumption by percentage share: *lowest 10%:* 2%
highest 10%: 30% (2007 est.)

Budget: *revenues:* 3.315 trillion (2017 est.)
expenditures: 3.981 trillion (2017 est.)
note: revenues exclude social contributions of approximately $1.0 trillion; expenditures exclude social benefits of approximately $2.3 trillion

Budget surplus (+) or deficit (-): -3.4% (of GDP) (2017 est.)
country comparison to the world: 145

Public debt: 78.8% of GDP (2017 est.)
81.2% of GDP (2016 est.)
note: data cover only what the United States Treasury denotes as "Debt Held by the Public," which includes all debt instruments issued by the Treasury that are owned by non-US Government entities; the data include Treasury debt held by foreign entities; the data exclude debt issued by individual US states, as well as intragovernmental debt; intragovernmental debt consists of Treasury borrowings from surpluses in the trusts for Federal Social Security, Federal Employees, Hospital and Supplemental Medical Insurance (Medicare), Disability and Unemployment, and several other smaller trusts; if data for intragovernment debt were added, "gross debt" would increase by about one-third of GDP
country comparison to the world: 36

Taxes and other revenues: 17% (of GDP) (2017 est.)
note: excludes contributions for social security and other programs; if social contributions were added, taxes and other revenues would amount to approximately 22% of GDP
country comparison to the world: 172

Fiscal year: 1 October - 30 September

Current account balance: -$480.225 billion (2019 est.)
-$449.694 billion (2018 est.)
country comparison to the world: 206

Exports: $2,127,250,000,000 (2020 est.) note: data are in current year dollars
$2,528,270,000,000 (2019 est.) note: data are in current year dollars
$2,539,380,000,000 (2018 est.) note: data are in current year dollars
country comparison to the world: 2

Exports - partners: Canada 17%, Mexico 16%, China 7%, Japan 5% (2019)

Exports - commodities: refined petroleum, crude petroleum, cars and vehicle parts, integrated circuits, aircraft (2019)

Imports: $2,808,960,000,000 (2020 est.) note: data are in current year dollars
$3,105,130,000,000 (2019 est.) note: data are in current year dollars
$3,119,320,000,000 (2018 est.) note: data are in current year dollars
country comparison to the world: 1

Imports - partners: China 18%, Mexico 15%, Canada 13%, Japan 6%, Germany 5% (2019)

Imports - commodities: cars, crude petroleum, computers, broadcasting equipment, packaged medicines (2019)

Reserves of foreign exchange and gold: $123.3 billion (31 December 2017 est.)
$117.6 billion (31 December 2015 est.)
country comparison to the world: 21

Debt - external: $20,275,951,000,000 (2019 est.)
$19,452,478,000,000 (2018 est.)
note: approximately 4/5ths of US external debt is denominated in US dollars; foreign lenders have been willing to hold US dollar denominated debt instruments because they view the dollar as the world's reserve currency
country comparison to the world: 1

Exchange rates: British pounds per US dollar: 0.7836 (2017 est.), 0.738 (2016 est.), 0.738 (2015 est.), 0.607 (2014 est), 0.6391 (2013 est.)

Canadian dollars per US dollar: 1, 1.308 (2017 est.), 1.3256 (2016 est.), 1.3256 (2015 est.), 1.2788 (2014 est.), 1.0298 (2013 est.)

Chinese yuan per US dollar: 1, 6.7588 (2017 est.), 6.6445 (2016 est.), 6.2275 (2015 est.), 6.1434 (2014 est.), 6.1958 (2013 est.)
euros per US dollar: 0.885 (2017 est.), 0.903 (2016 est.), 0.9214(2015 est.), 0.885 (2014 est.), 0.7634 (2013 est.)

Japanese yen per US dollar: 111.10 (2017 est.), 108.76 (2016 est.), 108.76 (2015 est.), 121.02 (2014 est.), 97.44 (2013 est.)
note 1: the following countries and territories use the US dollar officially as their legal tender: British Virgin Islands, Ecuador, El Salvador, Marshall Islands, Micronesia, Palau, Timor Leste, Turks and Caicos, and islands of the Caribbean Netherlands (Bonaire, Sint Eustatius, and Saba)
note 2: the following countries and territories use the US dollar as official legal tender alongside local currency: Bahamas, Barbados, Belize, Costa Rica, and Panama
note 3: the following countries and territories widely accept the US dollar as a dominant currency but have yet to declare it as legal tender: Bermuda, Burma, Cambodia, Cayman Islands, Honduras, Nicaragua, and Somalia

ENERGY

Electricity access: *electrification - total population:* 100% (2020)

Electricity: *installed generating capacity:* 1,143,266,000 kW (2020 est.)
consumption: 3,897,886,551,000 kWh (2020 est.)
exports: 14,134,679,000 kWh (2020 est.)
imports: 61,448,863,000 kWh (2020 est.)
transmission/distribution losses: 198,085,480,000 kWh (2020 est.)

Electricity generation sources: *fossil fuels:* 59.9% of total installed capacity (2020 est.)
nuclear: 19.5% of total installed capacity (2020 est.)
solar: 3.2% of total installed capacity (2020 est.)
wind: 8.3% of total installed capacity (2020 est.)
hydroelectricity: 7% of total installed capacity (2020 est.)
geothermal: 0.4% of total installed capacity (2020 est.)
biomass and waste: 1.7% of total installed capacity (2020 est.)

Coal: *production:* 495.13 million metric tons (2020 est.)
consumption: 441.968 million metric tons (2020 est.)
exports: 63.276 million metric tons (2020 est.)
imports: 4.808 million metric tons (2020 est.)
proven reserves: 228.662 billion metric tons (2019 est.)

Petroleum: *total petroleum production:* 17,924,200 bbl/day (2021 est.)
refined petroleum consumption: 20,542,900 bbl/day (2019 est.)
crude oil and lease condensate exports: 2,048,100 bbl/day (2018 est.)
crude oil and lease condensate imports: 7,768,500 bbl/day (2018 est.)
crude oil estimated reserves: 47.107 billion barrels (2020 est.)

Refined petroleum products - production: 20.3 million bbl/day (2017 est.)
country comparison to the world: 1

Refined petroleum products - exports: 5.218 million bbl/day (2017 est.)
country comparison to the world: 1

Refined petroleum products - imports: 2.175 million bbl/day (2017 est.)
country comparison to the world: 2

Natural gas: *production:* 967,144,362,000 cubic meters (2021 est.)
consumption: 857,542,658,000 cubic meters (2021 est.)
exports: 188,401,779,000 cubic meters (2021 est.)
imports: 79,512,470,000 cubic meters (2021 est.)
proven reserves: 13,178,780,000,000 cubic meters (2020 est.)

Carbon dioxide emissions: 5,144,361,000 metric tonnes of CO_2 (2019 est.)
from coal and metallurgical coke: 1,077,520,000 metric tonnes of CO_2 (2019 est.)
from petroleum and other liquids: 2,382,833,000 metric tonnes of CO_2 (2019 est.)
from consumed natural gas: 1,684,008,000 metric tonnes of CO_2 (2019 est.)
country comparison to the world: 2

Energy consumption per capita: 304.414 million Btu/person (2019 est.)
country comparison to the world: 11

COMMUNICATIONS

Telephones - fixed lines: *total subscriptions:* 101.526 million (2020 est.)
subscriptions per 100 inhabitants: 31 (2020 est.)
country comparison to the world: 2

Telephones - mobile cellular: *total subscriptions:* 442.457 million (2019)
subscriptions per 100 inhabitants: 134.46 (2019)
country comparison to the world: 3

Telecommunication systems: *general assessment:* the US telecom sector adapted well to the particular demands of the pandemic, which has led to strong growth in the number of mobile, mobile broadband, and fixed broadband subscribers since 2020; the level of growth is expected to taper off from late 2022 as the demand for working and schooling from home subsides; the pandemic also encouraged the Federal government to increase its investment in broadband infrastructure; of particular note was the Infrastructure Investment and Jobs Act of November 2021, which provided $65 billion to a range of programs aimed at delivering broadband to unserved areas, providing fiber-based broadband to upgrade existing service areas, and subsidizing the cost of services to low income households; alongside these fiscal efforts have been the several spectrum auctions undertaken during the last two years, which have greatly assisted the main licensees to improve the reach and quality of their offers based on LTE and 5G; some of this spectrum, auctioned during 2021, was only made available to licensees from February 2022; the widening availability of 5G from the main providers has resulted in a dramatic increase in mobile data traffic; in tandem with the focus on 5G, operators have closed down their GSM and CDMA networks, and have either closed down 3G networks (as AT&T did in January 2022), or plan to in coming months; given the size of the US broadband market, and the growing demand for data on both fixed and mobile networks, there is continuous pressure for operators to invest in fiber networks, and to push connectivity closer to consumers; in recent years the US has seen increased activity from regional players as well as the major telcos and cablecos; although there has been considerable investment in DOCSIS4.0, some of the cablecos are looking to ditch HFC in preference for fiber broadband; the process of migrating from copper (HFC and DSL) to fiber is ongoing, but given the scale of the work involved it will take some years; some operators have investment strategies in place through to 2025, which will see the vast majority of their fixed networks being entirely on fiber; service offerings of up to 2Gb/s are becoming more widely available as the process continues (2022)
domestic: a large system of fiber-optic cable, microwave radio relay, coaxial cable, and domestic satellites carries every form of telephone traffic; a rapidly growing cellular system carries mobile telephone traffic throughout the country; fixed-line just over 31 per 100 and mobile-cellular over 134 per 100 (2020)
international: country code - 1; landing points for the Quintillion Subsea Cable Network, TERRA SW, AU-Aleutian, KKFL, AKORN, Alaska United -West, & -East & -Southeast, North Star, Lynn Canal Fiber, KetchCar 1, PC-1, SCCN, Tat TGN-Pacific & -Atlantic, Jupiter, Hawaiki, NCP, FASTER, HKA, JUS, AAG, BtoBE, Currie, Southern Cross NEXT, SxS, PLCN, Utility EAC-Pacific, SEA-US, Paniolo Cable Network, HICS, HIFN, ASH, Telstra Endeavor, Honotua, AURORA, ARCOS, AMX-1, Americas -I & -II, Columbus IIb & -III, Maya-1, MAC, GTMO-1, BICS, CFX-1, GlobeNet, Monet, SAm-1, Bahamas 2, PCCS, BRUSA, Dunant, MAREA, SAE x1, TAT 14, Apollo, Gemini Bermuda, Havfrue/AEC-2, Seabras-1, WALL-LI, NYNJ-1, FLAG Atalantic-1, Yellow, Atlantic Crossing-1, AE Connect -1, sea2shore, Challenger Bermuda-1, and GTT Atlantic submarine cable systems providing international connectivity to Europe, Africa, the Middle East, Asia, Southeast Asia, Australia, New Zealand, Pacific, & Atlantic, and Indian Ocean Islands, Central and South America, Caribbean, Canada and US; satellite earth stations - 61 Intelsat (45 Atlantic Ocean and 16 Pacific Ocean), 5 Intersputnik (Atlantic Ocean region), and 4 Inmarsat (Pacific and Atlantic Ocean regions) (2020)

Broadcast media: 4 major terrestrial TV networks with affiliate stations throughout the country, plus cable and satellite networks, independent stations, and a limited public broadcasting sector that is largely supported by private grants; overall, thousands of TV stations broadcasting; multiple national radio networks with many affiliate stations; while most stations are commercial, National Public Radio (NPR) has a network of some 900 member stations; satellite radio available; in total, over 15,000 radio stations operating (2018)

Internet country code: .us

Internet users: *total:* 301,665,983 (2020 est.)
percent of population: 91% (2020 est.)
country comparison to the world: 3

Broadband - fixed subscriptions: *total:* 121.176 million (2020 est.)
subscriptions per 100 inhabitants: 37 (2020 est.)
country comparison to the world: 2

Communications - note: *note 1:* The Library of Congress, Washington DC, USA, claims to be the largest library in the world with more than 167 million items (as of 2018); its collections are universal, not limited by subject, format, or national boundary, and include materials from all parts of the world and in over 450 languages; collections include: books, newspapers, magazines, sheet music, sound and video recordings, photographic images, artwork, architectural drawings, and copyright data
note 2: Cape Canaveral, Florida, USA, hosts one of four dedicated ground antennas that assist in the operation of the Global Positioning System (GPS) navigation system (the others are on Ascension (Saint Helena, Ascension, and Tistan da Cunha), Diego Garcia (British Indian Ocean Territory), and at Kwajalein (Marshall Islands)

TRANSPORTATION

National air transport system: *number of registered air carriers:* 99 (2020)
inventory of registered aircraft operated by air carriers: 7,249
annual passenger traffic on registered air carriers: 889.022 million (2018)
annual freight traffic on registered air carriers: 42,985,300,000 (2018) mt-km

Civil aircraft registration country code prefix: N

Airports: *total:* 13,513 (2021)
country comparison to the world: 1

Airports - with paved runways: *total:* 5,054
over 3,047 m: 189

2,438 to 3,047 m: 235
1,524 to 2,437 m: 1,478
914 to 1,523 m: 2,249
under 914 m: 903 (2021)

Airports - with unpaved runways: *total:* 8,459
over 3,047 m: 1
2,438 to 3,047 m: 6
1,524 to 2,437 m: 140
914 to 1,523 m: 1,552
under 914 m: 6,760 (2021)

Heliports: 5,287 (2021)

Pipelines: 1,984,321 km natural gas, 240,711 km petroleum products (2013)

Railways: *total:* 293,564.2 km (2014)
standard gauge: 293,564.2 km (2014) 1.435-m gauge
country comparison to the world: 1

Roadways: *total:* 6,586,610 km (2012)
paved: 4,304,715 km (2012) (includes 76,334 km of expressways)
unpaved: 2,281,895 km (2012)
country comparison to the world: 1

Waterways: 41,009 km (2012) (19,312 km used for commerce; Saint Lawrence Seaway of 3,769 km, including the Saint Lawrence River of 3,058 km, is shared with Canada)
country comparison to the world: 5

Merchant marine: *total:* 3,627
by type: bulk carrier 4, container ship 60, general cargo 103, oil tanker 69, other 3,391 (2021)
country comparison to the world: 7

Ports and terminals major seaport(s): *Atlantic Ocean:* Charleston, Hampton Roads, New York/New Jersey, Savannah
Pacific Ocean: Long Beach, Los Angeles, Oakland, Seattle/Tacoma
Gulf of Mexico: Houston
oil terminal(s): LOOP terminal, Haymark terminal
container port(s) (TEUs): Charleston (2,436,185), Hampton Roads (2,937,962), Houston (2,987,291), Long Beach (7,632,032), Los Angeles (9,337,632), New York/New Jersey (7,471,131), Oakland (2,500,431), Savannah (4,599,177), Seattle/Tacoma (3,775,303) (2019)

LNG terminal(s) (export): Calcasieu Pass (LA), Cameron (LA), Corpus Christi (TX), Cove Point (MD), Elba Island (GA), Freeport (TX), Sabine Pass (LA)
note - two additional export facilities are under construction and expected to begin commercial operations in 2023-2024

LNG terminal(s) (import): Cove Point (MD), Elba Island (GA), Everett (MA), Freeport (TX), Golden Pass (TX), Hackberry (LA), Lake Charles (LA), Neptune (offshore), Northeast Gateway (offshore), Pascagoula (MS), Sabine Pass (TX)
river port(s): Baton Rouge, Plaquemines, New Orleans (Mississippi River)
cargo ports: Baton Rouge, Corpus Christi, Hampton Roads, Houston, Long Beach, Los Angeles, New Orleans, New York, Plaquemines (LA), Tampa, Texas City
cruise departure ports (passengers): Miami, Port Everglades, Port Canaveral, Seattle, Long Beach

MILITARY AND SECURITY

Military and security forces: United States Armed Forces (aka US Military): US Army (USA), US Navy (USN; includes US Marine Corps or USMC), US Air Force (USAF), US Space Force (USSF); US Coast Guard (USCG); National Guard (Army National Guard and Air National Guard) (2022)
note 1: the US Coast Guard is administered in peacetime by the Department of Homeland Security, but in wartime reports to the Department of the Navy
note 2: the Army National Guard and the Air National Guard are reserve components of their services and operate in part under state authority; the US military also maintains reserve forces for each branch (US Army Reserve, US Navy Reserve, US Air Force Reserve, and US Coast Guard Reserve)

Military expenditures: 3.5% of GDP (2022 est.)
3.6% of GDP (2021)
3.7% of GDP (2020)
3.4% of GDP (2019) (approximately $730 billion)
3.3% of GDP (2018) (approximately $685 billion)
country comparison to the world: 25

Military and security service personnel strengths: approximately 1.39 million active duty personnel (475,000 Army; 345,000 Navy; 335,000 Air Force (includes about 8,000 Space Force); 180,000 Marine Corps; 40,000 Coast Guard); 335,000 Army National Guard; 105,000 Air National Guard (2022)

Military equipment inventories and acquisitions: the US military's inventory is comprised almost entirely of domestically-produced weapons systems (some assembled with foreign components) along with a smaller mix of imported equipment from a variety of Western countries; since 2010, Germany and the UK have been the leading suppliers of military hardware; the US defense industry is capable of designing, developing, maintaining, and producing the full spectrum of weapons systems; the US is the world's leading arms exporter (2021)

Military service age and obligation: 18 years of age (17 years of age with parental consent) for voluntary service for men and women; no conscription (currently inactive, but males aged 18-25 must register with Selective Service in case conscription is reinstated in the future); maximum enlistment age 34 (Army), 39 (Air Force), 39 (Navy), 28 (Marines), 31 (Coast Guard); 8-year service obligation, including 2-5 years active duty (Army), 2 years active duty (Navy), 4 years active duty (Air Force, Marines, Coast Guard); all military occupations and positions open to women (2022)
note: in 2020, women comprised 17.2 % of the total US military (16.9% of enlisted; 18.9% officers; highest was Air Force with women comprising 21.1% of its total personnel); a small number of American women were involved in combat during the Revolutionary (1775-1783), Mexican (1846-1848), and Civil (1861-1865) Wars, but they had to disguise themselves as men and enlist under aliases; the first official US military organization for women was the US Army Nurse Corps, established in 1901; during World War I, the US Navy and Marine Corps allowed women to enlist; nearly 350,000 women served in the US military during World War II; the 1991 Gulf War was the first war where women served with men in integrated units within a war zone; in 2015, women were allowed to serve in direct combat roles
note 2: non-citizens living permanently and legally in the US may join as enlisted personnel; must have permission to work in the US, a high school diploma, and speak, read, and write English fluently; minimum age of 17 with parental consent or 18 without; maximum age 29-39, depending on the service; under the US Nationality Act, honorable service in the military may qualify individuals to obtain expedited citizenship; under the Compact of Free Association, citizens of the Federated States of Micronesia, the Republic of Palau, and the Republic of the Marshall Islands may volunteer; under the Jay Treaty, signed in 1794 between Great Britain and the US, and corresponding legislation, Native Americans/First Nations born in Canada are entitled to freely enter the US and join the US military

Military deployments: 5,000 Africa (mostly in Djibouti, with approximately 700-1,000 in other countries of East Africa and about 700 in West Africa); 1,700 Australia; 250 Diego Garcia; 150 Canada; 650 Cuba (Guatanamo Bay); 290 Egypt (MFO); approximately 100,000 Europe (Belgium, Bulgaria, Germany, Greece, Italy, Kosovo, the Netherlands, Norway, Poland, Portugal, Romania, Spain, Turkey, UK); 150 Greenland; 6,200 Guam; 370 Honduras; 56,000 Japan; approximately 15,000 Middle East (Bahrain, Iraq, Israel, Jordan, Kuwait, Oman, Qatar, Saudi Arabia, Syria, United Arab Emirates); 125 Philippines; 28,000 South Korea; 200 Singapore; 100 Thailand (2022)
note: US military rotational policies affect deployment numbers; the US deploys ground and air units to select countries for 6-12 month rotational assignments on a continuous basis; in South Korea, for example, the US continuously rotates combat brigades (approximately 3,000 personnel) for 9 months at a time; contingencies also affect US troop deployments; in 2019-2020, the US deployed more than 15,000 additional military personnel to the Middle East for an extended period of time and in 2022, it sent more than 30,000 reinforcements to Europe in response to the Russian invasion of Ukraine; in addition, some overseas US naval bases, such as the headquarters of US Naval Forces Central Command (USNAVCENT) in Manama, Bahrain, are frequented by the crews of US ships on 6-9 month deployments; a US carrier strike group with an air wing and supporting ships typically includes over 6,000 personnel

Military - note: the US is a member of NATO and was one of the original 12 countries to sign the North Atlantic Treaty (also known as the Washington Treaty) in 1949
the US military has 11 regional- or functionally-based joint service "combatant" commands: Africa Command; Central Command, Cyber Command, European Command, Indo-Pacific Command, Northern Command, Southern Command, Space Command, Special Operations Command, Strategic Command, and Transportation Command

Congress officially created the US military in September 1789; the US Army was established in June 1775 as the Continental Army; after the declaration of independence in July 1776, the Continental Army and the militia in the service of Congress became known collectively as the Army of the United States; when Congress ordered the Continental Army to disband in 1784, it retained a small number of personnel that would form the nucleus of the 1st American Regiment for national service formed later that year; both the US Navy and the US Marines were also established in 1775, but the Navy fell into disuse after the Revolutionary War, and was reestablished by Congress in 1794; the first US military unit devoted exclusively to aviation began operations in 1913 as part of the US Army; the

Army Air Corps (AAC) was the US military service dedicated to aerial warfare between 1926 and 1941; the AAC became the US Army Air Forces in 1941 and remained as a combat arm of the Army until the establishment of the US Air Force in 1947

TERRORISM

Terrorist group(s): Hizballah; Islamic Revolutionary Guard Corps (IRGC)/Qods Force; Islamic State of Iraq and ash-Sham (ISIS); al-Qa'ida; Lashkar-e Tayyiba (LeT)

TRANSNATIONAL ISSUES

Disputes - international: *US-Antarctica:* the US has made no territorial claim in Antarctica (but has reserved the right to do so) and does not recognize the claims of any other states
US-Bahamas: the Bahamas and US have not been able to agree on a maritime boundary; the two countries have met several times to define their maritime boundary
US-Canada: Canada and the United States dispute how to divide the Beaufort Sea and the status of the Northwest Passage but continue to work cooperatively to survey the Arctic continental shelf; because of the dispute over Machias Seal Island and adjoining North Rock, the terminus of the land boundary beyond Canada's Grand Manon Island and the US state of Maine is not defined
US-Canada-Mexico: the US has intensified domestic security measures and is collaborating closely with its neighbors, Canada and Mexico, to monitor and control legal and illegal personnel, transport, and commodities across the international borders
US-Cuba: the US Naval Base at Guantanamo Bay is leased from Cuba and only mutual agreement or US abandonment of the area can terminate the lease
US-Haiti: Haiti claims US-administered Navassa Island; the dispute dates to 1857, when the US claimed the Navassa Island under the 1856 Guano Act; Haiti claims it has had ownership over Navassa Island continuously since its 1801 constitution laid claim to "adjacent lands"
US-Marshall Islands: in May 2016, the Marshall Islands filed a declaration of authority with the UN over Wake Island, which is currently a US territory, reaffirming that it considers Wake Island part of its territory; control over Wake Island would drastically increase the Marshall Islands' exclusive economic zone; the US State Department is assembling a group of experts from both countries to discuss the maritime boundary
US-Russia: 1990 Maritime Boundary Agreement in the Bering Sea still awaits Russian Duma ratification
US-Tokelau: Tokelau included American Samoa's Swains Island among the islands listed in its 2006 draft constitution; Swains Island has been administered by American Samoa since 1925; the 1980 Treaty of Tokehega delineates the maritime boundary between American Samoa and Tokelau; while not specifically mentioning Swains Island, the treaty notes in its preamble that New Zealand does not claim as part of Tokelau any island administered as part of American Samoa

Refugees and internally displaced persons: *refugees (country of origin):* the US admitted 11,411 refugees during FY2021 including: 4,891 (Democratic Republic of the Congo), 1,246 (Syria), 872 (Afghanistan), 803 (Ukraine), 772 (Burma), 513 (Sudan)
stateless persons: 47 (mid-year 2021)

Illicit drugs: world's largest consumer of cocaine (mostly from Colombia through Mexico and the Caribbean), Mexican heroin and marijuana; major consumer of MDMA (ecstasy) and Mexican methamphetamine; major consumer of fentanyl and other synthetic opioids sourced from Mexico and China, often mixed with other drugs; illicit producer of cannabis, marijuana, depressants, stimulants, hallucinogens, and methamphetamine; money-laundering center

UNITED STATES PACIFIC ISLAND WILDLIFE REFUGES

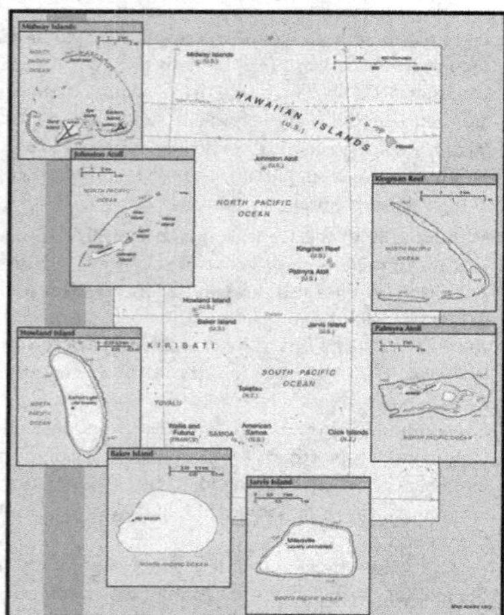

INTRODUCTION

Background: All of the following US Pacific island territories except Midway Atoll constitute the Pacific Remote Islands National Wildlife Refuge (NWR) Complex and as such are managed by the Fish and Wildlife Service of the US Department of the Interior. Midway Atoll NWR has been included in a Refuge Complex with the Hawaiian Islands NWR and also designated as part of Papahanaumokuakea Marine National Monument. These remote refuges are the most widespread collection of marine- and terrestrial-life protected areas on the planet under a single country's jurisdiction. They sustain many endemic species including corals, fish, shellfish, marine mammals, seabirds, water birds, land birds, insects, and vegetation not found elsewhere.

Baker Island: The US took possession of the island in 1857. Its guano deposits were mined by US and British companies during the second half of the 19th century. In 1935, a short-lived attempt at colonization began on this island but was disrupted by World War II and thereafter abandoned. The island was established as a NWR in 1974.

Howland Island: Discovered by the US early in the 19th century, the uninhabited atoll was officially claimed by the US in 1857. Both US and British companies mined for guano deposits until about 1890. In 1935, a short-lived attempt at colonization began on this island, similar to the effort on nearby Baker Island, but was disrupted by World War II and thereafter abandoned. The famed American aviatrix Amelia EARHART disappeared while seeking out Howland Island as a refueling stop during her 1937 round-the-world flight; Earhart Light, a day beacon near the middle of the west coast, was named in her memory. The island was established as a NWR in 1974.

Jarvis Island: First discovered by the British in 1821, the uninhabited island was annexed by the US in 1858 but abandoned in 1879 after tons of guano had been removed. The UK annexed the island in 1889 but never carried out plans for further exploitation. The US occupied and reclaimed the island in 1935. It was abandoned in 1942 during World War II. The island was established as a NWR in 1974.

Johnston Atoll: Both the US and the Kingdom of Hawaii annexed Johnston Atoll in 1858, but it was the US that mined the guano deposits until the late 1880s. Johnston and Sand Islands were designated wildlife refuges in 1926. The US Navy took over the atoll in 1934. Subsequently, the US Air Force assumed control in 1948. The site was used for high-altitude nuclear tests in the 1950s and 1960s. Until late in 2000 the atoll was maintained as a storage and disposal site for chemical weapons. Munitions destruction, cleanup, and closure of the facility were completed by May 2005. The Fish and Wildlife Service and the US Air Force are currently discussing future management options; in the interim, Johnston Atoll and the three-mile Naval Defensive Sea around it remain under the jurisdiction and administrative control of the US Air Force.

Kingman Reef: The US annexed the reef in 1922. Its sheltered lagoon served as a way station for flying boats on Hawaii-to-American Samoa flights during the late 1930s. There are no terrestrial plants on the reef, which is frequently awash, but it does support abundant and diverse marine fauna and flora. In 2001, the waters surrounding the reef out to 12 nm were designated a NWR.

Midway Islands: The US took formal possession of the islands in 1867. The laying of the transpacific cable, which passed through the islands, brought the first residents in 1903. Between 1935 and 1947, Midway was used as a refueling stop for transpacific flights. The US naval victory over a Japanese fleet off Midway in 1942 was one of the turning points of World War II. The islands continued to serve as a naval station until closed in 1993. Today the islands are a NWR and are the site of the world's largest Laysan albatross colony.

Palmyra Atoll: The Kingdom of Hawaii claimed the atoll in 1862, and the US included it among the Hawaiian Islands when it annexed the archipelago in 1898. The Hawaii Statehood Act of 1959 did not include Palmyra Atoll, which is now partly privately owned by the Nature Conservancy with the rest owned by the Federal government and managed by the US Fish and Wildlife Service. These organizations are managing the atoll as a wildlife refuge. The lagoons and surrounding waters within the 12-nm US territorial seas were transferred to the US Fish and Wildlife Service and designated a NWR in January 2001.

GEOGRAPHY

Location: Oceania

Baker Island: atoll in the North Pacific Ocean 3,390 km southwest of Honolulu, about halfway between Hawaii and Australia;

Howland Island: island in the North Pacific Ocean 3,360 km southwest of Honolulu, about halfway between Hawaii and Australia;

Jarvis Island: island in the South Pacific Ocean 2,415 km south of Honolulu, about halfway between Hawaii and Cook Islands;

Johnston Atoll: atoll in the North Pacific Ocean 1,330 km southwest of Honolulu, about one-third of the way from Hawaii to the Marshall Islands;

Kingman Reef: reef in the North Pacific Ocean 1,720 km south of Honolulu, about halfway between Hawaii and American Samoa;

Midway Islands: atoll in the North Pacific Ocean 2,335 km northwest of Honolulu near the end of the Hawaiian Archipelago, about one-third of the way from Honolulu to Tokyo;

Palmyra Atoll: atoll in the North Pacific Ocean 1,780 km south of Honolulu, about halfway between Hawaii and American Samoa

Geographic coordinates: Baker Island: 0 13 N, 176 28 W;

Howland Island: 0 48 N, 176 38 W;

Jarvis Island: 0 23 S, 160 01 W;

Johnston Atoll: 16 45 N, 169 31 W;

Kingman Reef: 6 23 N, 162 25 W;

Midway Islands: 28 12 N, 177 22 W;

Palmyra Atoll: 5 53 N, 162 05 W

Map references: Oceania

Area: *land:* 6,959.41 sq km (emergent land - 22.41 sq km; submerged - 6,937 sq km)

Baker Island: total - 129.1 sq km; emergent land - 2.1 sq km; submerged - 127 sq km

Howland Island: total - 138.6 sq km; emergent land - 2.6 sq km; submerged - 136 sq km

Jarvis Island: total - 152 sq km; emergent land - 5 sq km; submerged - 147 sq km

Johnston Atoll: total - 276.6 sq km; emergent land - 2.6 sq km; submerged - 274 sq km

Kingman Reef: total - 1,958.01 sq km; emergent land - 0.01 sq km; submerged - 1,958 sq km

Midway Islands: total - 2,355.2 sq km; emergent land - 6.2 sq km; submerged - 2,349 sq km

Palmyra Atoll: total - 1,949.9 sq km; emergent land - 3.9 sq km; submerged - 1,946 sq km

Area - comparative: Baker Island: about 2.5 times the size of the National Mall in Washington, DC;

Howland Island: about three times the size of the National Mall in Washington, DC;

Jarvis Island: about eight times the size of the National Mall in Washington, DC;

Johnston Atoll: about 4.5 times the size of the National Mall in Washington, DC;

Kingman Reef: a little more than 1.5 times the size of the National Mall in Washington, DC;

Midway Islands: about nine times the size of the National Mall in Washington, DC;

Palmyra Atoll: about 20 times the size of the National Mall in Washington, DC

Land boundaries: *total:* 0 km

Coastline: Baker Island: 4.8 km

Howland Island: 6.4 km

Jarvis Island: 8 km

Johnston Atoll: 34 km

Kingman Reef: 3 km

Midway Islands: 15 km

Palmyra Atoll: 14.5 km

Maritime claims: *territorial sea:* 12 nm
exclusive economic zone: 200 nm

Climate: Baker, Howland, and Jarvis Islands: equatorial; scant rainfall, constant wind, burning sun;

Johnston Atoll and Kingman Reef: tropical, but generally dry; consistent northeast trade winds with little seasonal temperature variation;

Midway Islands: subtropical with cool, moist winters (December to February) and warm, dry summers (May to October); moderated by prevailing easterly winds; most of the 107 cm of annual rainfall occurs during the winter;

Palmyra Atoll: equatorial, hot; located within the low pressure area of the Intertropical Convergence Zone (ITCZ) where the northeast and southeast trade winds meet, it is extremely wet with between 400-500 cm of rainfall each year

Terrain: low and nearly flat sandy coral islands with narrow fringing reefs that have developed at the top of submerged volcanic mountains, which in most cases rise steeply from the ocean floor

Elevation: *highest point:* Baker Island, unnamed location 8 m; Howland Island, unnamed location 3 m; Jarvis Island, unnamed location 7 m; Johnston Atoll, Sand Island 10 m; Kingman Reef, unnamed location 2 m; Midway Islands, unnamed location less than 13 m; Palmyra Atoll, unnamed location 3 m
lowest point: Pacific Ocean 0 m

Natural resources: terrestrial and aquatic wildlife

Land use: *other:* 100% (2018 est.)

Natural hazards: Baker, Howland, and Jarvis Islands: the narrow fringing reef surrounding the island poses a maritime hazard;

Kingman Reef: wet or awash most of the time, maximum elevation of less than 2 m makes Kingman Reef a maritime hazard;

Geography - note: Baker, Howland, and Jarvis Islands: scattered vegetation consisting of grasses, prostrate vines, and low growing shrubs; primarily a nesting, roosting, and foraging habitat for seabirds, shorebirds, and marine wildlife; closed to the public;

Johnston Atoll: Johnston Island and Sand Island are natural islands, which have been expanded by coral dredging; North Island (Akau) and East Island (Hikina) are manmade islands formed from coral dredging; the egg-shaped reef is 34 km in circumference; closed to the public;

Kingman Reef: barren coral atoll with deep interior lagoon; closed to the public;

Midway Islands: a coral atoll managed as a National Wildlife Refuge and open to the public for wildlife-related recreation in the form of wildlife observation and photography;

Palmyra Atoll: the high rainfall and resulting lush vegetation make the environment of this atoll unique among the US Pacific Island territories; supports a large undisturbed stand of Pisonia beach forest

PEOPLE AND SOCIETY

Population: no indigenous inhabitants
note: public entry is only by special-use permit from US Fish and Wildlife Service and generally restricted to scientists and educators; visited annually by US Fish and Wildlife Service

Jarvis Island: Millersville settlement on western side of island occasionally used as a weather station from 1935 until World War II, when it was abandoned; reoccupied in 1957 during the International Geophysical Year by scientists who left in 1958; currently unoccupied

Johnston Atoll: in previous years, an average of 1,100 US military and civilian contractor personnel were present; as of May 2005, all US Government personnel had left the island

Midway Islands: approximately 40 people make up the staff of US Fish and Wildlife Service and their services contractor living at the atoll

Palmyra Atoll: four to 20 Nature Conservancy, US Fish and Wildlife staff, and researchers

ENVIRONMENT

Environment - current issues: Baker Island: no natural freshwater resources; feral cats, introduced in 1937 during a short-lived colonization effort, ravaged the avian population and were eradicated in 1965

Howland Island: no natural freshwater resources; the island habitat has suffered from invasive exotic species; black rats, introduced in 1854, were eradicated by feral cats within a year of their introduction in 1937; the cats preyed on the bird population and were eliminated by 1985

Jarvis Island: no natural freshwater resources; feral cats, introduced in the 1930s during a short-lived colonization venture, were not completely removed until 1990

Johnston Atoll: no natural freshwater resources; the seven decades under US military administration (1934-2004) left the atoll environmentally degraded and required large-scale remediation efforts; a swarm of Anoplolepis (crazy) ants invaded the island in 2010 damaging native wildlife; eradication has been largely, but not completely, successful

Midway Islands: many exotic species introduced, 75% of the roughly 200 plant species on the island are non-native; plastic pollution harms wildlife, via entanglement, ingestion, and toxic contamination

Kingman Reef: none

Palmyra Atoll: black rats, believed to have been introduced to the atoll during the US military occupation of the 1940s, severely degraded the ecosystem outcompeting native species (seabirds, crabs); following a successful rat removal project in 2011, native flora and fauna have begun to recover

Climate: Baker, Howland, and Jarvis Islands: equatorial; scant rainfall, constant wind, burning sun;

Johnston Atoll and Kingman Reef: tropical, but generally dry; consistent northeast trade winds with little seasonal temperature variation;

Midway Islands: subtropical with cool, moist winters (December to February) and warm, dry summers (May to October); moderated by prevailing easterly winds; most of the 107 cm of annual rainfall occurs during the winter;

Palmyra Atoll: equatorial, hot; located within the low pressure area of the Intertropical Convergence Zone (ITCZ) where the northeast and southeast trade winds meet, it is extremely wet with between 400-500 cm of rainfall each year

Land use: *other:* 100% (2018 est.)

GOVERNMENT

Country name: *conventional long form:* none
conventional short form: Baker Island, Howland Island, Jarvis Island, Johnston Atoll, Kingman Reef, Midway Islands, Palmyra Atoll
etymology: self-descriptive name specifying the territories' affiliation and location

Dependency status: with the exception of Palmyra Atoll, the constituent islands are unincorporated, unorganized territories of the US; administered from Washington, DC, by the Fish and Wildlife Service of the US Department of the Interior as part of the National Wildlife Refuge System
note: Palmyra Atoll is partly privately owned and partly federally owned; the federally owned portion is administered from Washington, DC, by the Fish and Wildlife Service of the US Department of the Interior as an incorporated, unorganized territory of the US; the Office of Insular Affairs of the US Department of the Interior continues to administer nine excluded areas comprising certain tidal and submerged lands within the 12 nm territorial sea or within the lagoon

Legal system: the laws of the US apply where applicable

Diplomatic representation from the US: none (territories of the US)

Flag description: the flag of the US is used

ECONOMY

Economic overview: no economic activity

TRANSPORTATION

Airports: Baker Island: (2013) one abandoned World War II runway of 1,665 m covered with vegetation and unusable

Howland Island: (2013) airstrip constructed in 1937 for scheduled refueling stop on the round-the-world flight of Amelia EARHART and Fred NOONAN; the aviators left Lae, New Guinea, for Howland Island but were never seen again; the airstrip is no longer serviceable

Johnston Atoll: (2013) one closed and not maintained

Kingman Reef: (2013) lagoon was used as a halfway station between Hawaii and American Samoa by Pan American Airways for flying boats in 1937 and 1938

Midway Islands: (2013) 3 - one operational (2,377 m paved); no fuel for sale except emergencies

Palmyra Atoll: (2013) 1 - 1,846 m unpaved runway; privately owned

Airports - with paved runways: 2,438 to 3,047 m: 1 (2016) - Johnston Atoll;
note - abandoned but usable

Airports - with unpaved runways: 1,524 to 2,437 m: 1 (2016) - Palmyra Atoll

Ports and terminals: *major seaport(s):* Baker, Howland, and Jarvis Islands, and Kingman Reef

Baker, Howland, and Jarvis Islands, and Kingman Reef: none; offshore anchorage only

Johnston Atoll: Johnston Island

Midway Islands: Sand Island

Palmyra Atoll: West Lagoon

MILITARY AND SECURITY

Military - note: defense is the responsibility of the US

TRANSNATIONAL ISSUES

Disputes - international: none identified

URUGUAY

INTRODUCTION

Background: Montevideo, founded by the Spanish in 1726 as a military stronghold, soon became an important commercial center due to its natural harbor. Claimed by Argentina but annexed by Brazil in 1821, Uruguay declared its independence in 1825 and secured its freedom in 1828 after a three-year struggle. The administrations of President Jose BATLLE in the early 20th century launched widespread political, social, and economic reforms that established a statist tradition. A violent Marxist urban guerrilla movement named the Tupamaros (or Movimiento de Liberación Nacional-Tupamaros (MLN-T)), launched in the late 1960s, led Uruguay's president to cede control of the government to the military in 1973. By year-end, the rebels had been crushed, but the military continued to expand its hold over the government. Civilian rule was restored in 1985. In 2004, the left-of-center Frente Amplio Coalition won national elections that effectively ended 170 years of political control previously held by the Colorado and National (Blanco) parties. The left-of-center retained the presidency and control of both chambers of congress until 2019. Uruguay's political and labor conditions are among the freest on the continent.

GEOGRAPHY

Location: Southern South America, bordering the South Atlantic Ocean, between Argentina and Brazil

Geographic coordinates: 33 00 S, 56 00 W

Map references: South America

Area: *total:* 176,215 sq km
land: 175,015 sq km
water: 1,200 sq km
country comparison to the world: 91

Area - comparative: about the size of Virginia and West Virginia combined; slightly smaller than the state of Washington

Land boundaries: *total:* 1,591 km
border countries (2): Argentina 541 km; Brazil 1,050 km

Coastline: 660 km

Maritime claims: *territorial sea:* 12 nm
contiguous zone: 24 nm
exclusive economic zone: 200 nm
continental shelf: 200 nm or the edge of continental margin

Climate: warm temperate; freezing temperatures almost unknown

Terrain: mostly rolling plains and low hills; fertile coastal lowland

Elevation: *highest point:* Cerro Catedral 514 m
lowest point: Atlantic Ocean 0 m
mean elevation: 109 m

Natural resources: arable land, hydropower, minor minerals, fish

Land use: *agricultural land:* 87.2% (2018 est.)
arable land: 10.1% (2018 est.)
permanent crops: 0.2% (2018 est.)
permanent pasture: 76.9% (2018 est.)
forest: 10.2% (2018 est.)
other: 2.6% (2018 est.)

Irrigated land: 2,380 sq km (2012)

Major lakes (area sq km): *salt water lake(s):* Lagoa Mirim (shared with Brazil) - 2,970 sq km

Major rivers (by length in km): Rio de la Plata/Parana river mouth (shared with Brazil [s], Argentina, Paraguay) - 4,880 km; Uruguay river mouth (shared with Brazil [s] and Argentina) - 1,610 km

note – [s] after country name indicates river source; [m] after country name indicates river mouth

Major aquifers: Guarani Aquifer System

Population distribution: most of the country's population resides in the southern half of the country; approximately 80% of the populace is urban, living in towns or cities; nearly half of the population lives in and around the capital of Montevideo

Natural hazards: seasonally high winds (the pampero is a chilly and occasional violent wind that blows north from the Argentine pampas), droughts, floods; because of the absence of mountains, which act as weather barriers, all locations are particularly vulnerable to rapid changes from weather fronts

Geography - note: second-smallest South American country (after Suriname); most of the low-lying landscape (three-quarters of the country) is grassland, ideal for cattle and sheep raising

PEOPLE AND SOCIETY

Population: 3,407,213 (2022 est.)
country comparison to the world: 132

Nationality: *noun:* Uruguayan(s)
adjective: Uruguayan

Ethnic groups: White 87.7%, Black 4.6%, Indigenous 2.4%, other 0.3%, none or unspecified 5% (2011 est.)
note: data represent primary ethnic identity

Languages Spanish (official)
major-language sample(s): La Libreta Informativa del Mundo, la fuente indispensable de información básica. (Spanish)

Religions: Roman Catholic 42%, Protestant 15%, other 6%, agnostic 3%, atheist 10%, unspecified 24% (2014 est.)

Demographic profile: Uruguay rates high for most development indicators and is known for its secularism, liberal social laws, and well-developed social security, health, and educational systems. It is one of the few countries in Latin America and the Caribbean where the entire population has access to clean water. Uruguay's provision of free primary through university education has contributed to the country's high levels of literacy and educational attainment. However, the emigration of human capital has diminished the state's return on its investment in education. Remittances from the roughly 18% of Uruguayans abroad amount to less than 1 percent of national GDP. The emigration of young adults and a low birth rate are causing Uruguay's population to age rapidly.

In the 1960s, Uruguayans for the first time emigrated en masse - primarily to Argentina and Brazil - because of economic decline and the onset of more than a decade of military dictatorship. Economic crises in the early 1980s and 2002 also triggered waves of emigration, but since 2002 more than 70% of Uruguayan emigrants have selected the US and Spain as destinations because of better job prospects. Uruguay had a tiny population upon its independence in 1828 and welcomed thousands of predominantly Italian and Spanish immigrants, but the country has not experienced large influxes of new arrivals since the aftermath of World War II. More recent immigrants include Peruvians and Arabs.

Age structure: *0-14 years:* 19.51% (male 336,336/female 324,563)
15-24 years: 15.14% (male 259,904/female 252,945)
25-54 years: 39.86% (male 670,295/female 679,850)
55-64 years: 10.79% (male 172,313/female 193,045)
65 years and over: 14.71% (male 200,516/female 297,838) (2020 est.)

Dependency ratios: *total dependency ratio:* 54.9
youth dependency ratio: 31.5
elderly dependency ratio: 23.4
potential support ratio: 4.3 (2020 est.)

Median age: *total:* 35.5 years
male: 33.8 years
female: 37.3 years (2020 est.)
country comparison to the world: 85

Population growth rate: 0.27% (2022 est.)
country comparison to the world: 171

Birth rate: 12.71 births/1,000 population (2022 est.)
country comparison to the world: 142

Death rate: 9.18 deaths/1,000 population (2022 est.)
country comparison to the world: 54

Net migration rate: -0.88 migrant(s)/1,000 population (2022 est.)
country comparison to the world: 141

Population distribution: most of the country's population resides in the southern half of the country; approximately 80% of the populace is urban, living in towns or cities; nearly half of the population lives in and around the capital of Montevideo

Urbanization: *urban population:* 95.7% of total population (2022)
rate of urbanization: 0.4% annual rate of change (2020-25 est.)

Major urban areas - population: 1.767 million MONTEVIDEO (capital) (2022)

Sex ratio: *at birth:* 1.04 male(s)/female
0-14 years: 1.04 male(s)/female
15-24 years: 1.03 male(s)/female
25-54 years: 0.99 male(s)/female
55-64 years: 0.9 male(s)/female
65 years and over: 0.55 male(s)/female
total population: 0.94 male(s)/female (2022 est.)

Maternal mortality ratio: 17 deaths/100,000 live births (2017 est.)
country comparison to the world: 134

Infant mortality rate: *total:* 8.31 deaths/1,000 live births
male: 9.46 deaths/1,000 live births
female: 7.12 deaths/1,000 live births (2022 est.)
country comparison to the world: 147

Life expectancy at birth: *total population:* 78.43 years
male: 75.32 years
female: 81.64 years (2022 est.)
country comparison to the world: 71

Total fertility rate: 1.76 children born/woman (2022 est.)
country comparison to the world: 153

Contraceptive prevalence rate: 79.6% (2015)
note: percent of women aged 15-44

Drinking water source: *improved: urban:* 100% of population
rural: 100% of population
total: 100% of population

Current health expenditure: 9.4% of GDP (2019)

Physicians density: 4.94 physicians/1,000 population (2017)

Hospital bed density: 2.4 beds/1,000 population (2017)

Sanitation facility access: *improved: urban:* 99.2% of population
rural: 99.6% of population
total: 99.2% of population
unimproved: urban: 0.8% of population
rural: 0.4% of population
total: 0.8% of population (2020 est.)

HIV/AIDS - adult prevalence rate: 0.4% (2020 est.)
country comparison to the world: 79

HIV/AIDS - people living with HIV/AIDS: 12,000 (2020 est.)
country comparison to the world: 100

HIV/AIDS - deaths: (2020 est.) <200

Obesity - adult prevalence rate: 27.9% (2016)
country comparison to the world: 34

Alcohol consumption per capita: *total:* 5.42 liters of pure alcohol (2019 est.)
beer: 1.86 liters of pure alcohol (2019 est.)
wine: 2.86 liters of pure alcohol (2019 est.)
spirits: 0.71 liters of pure alcohol (2019 est.)
other alcohols: 0 liters of pure alcohol (2019 est.)
country comparison to the world: 82

Tobacco use: *total:* 21.5% (2020 est.)
male: 24.4% (2020 est.)
female: 18.5% (2020 est.)
country comparison to the world: 76

Children under the age of 5 years underweight: 1.8% (2018)
country comparison to the world: 114

Education expenditures: 4.7% of GDP (2019 est.)
country comparison to the world: 78

Literacy: *definition:* age 15 and over can read and write
total population: 98.8%
male: 98.5%
female: 99% (2019)

School life expectancy (primary to tertiary education): *total:* 19 years
male: 17 years
female: 20 years (2019)

Unemployment, youth ages 15-24: *total:* 33.5%
male: 29.4%
female: 38.8% (2020 est.)

ENVIRONMENT

Environment - current issues: water pollution from meat packing, tannery industries; heavy metal pollution; inadequate solid and hazardous waste disposal; deforestation

Environment - international agreements: *party to:* Antarctic-Environmental Protection, Antarctic-Marine Living Resources, Antarctic Treaty, Biodiversity, Climate Change, Climate Change-Kyoto Protocol, Climate Change-Paris Agreement, Comprehensive Nuclear Test Ban, Desertification, Endangered Species, Environmental Modification, Hazardous Wastes, Law of the Sea, Marine Dumping-London Protocol, Nuclear Test Ban, Ozone Layer Protection, Ship Pollution, Wetlands, Whaling
signed, but not ratified: Marine Dumping-London Convention, Marine Life Conservation

Air pollutants: *particulate matter emissions:* 8.63 micrograms per cubic meter (2016 est.)
carbon dioxide emissions: 6.77 megatons (2016 est.)
methane emissions: 25.59 megatons (2020 est.)

Climate: warm temperate; freezing temperatures almost unknown

Land use: *agricultural land:* 87.2% (2018 est.)
arable land: 10.1% (2018 est.)

permanent crops: 0.2% (2018 est.)
permanent pasture: 76.9% (2018 est.)
forest: 10.2% (2018 est.)
other: 2.6% (2018 est.)

Urbanization: *urban population:* 95.7% of total population (2022)
rate of urbanization: 0.4% annual rate of change (2020-25 est.)

Revenue from forest resources: *forest revenues:* 1.56% of GDP (2018 est.)
country comparison to the world: 41

Revenue from coal: *coal revenues:* 0% of GDP (2018 est.)
country comparison to the world: 184

Waste and recycling: *municipal solid waste generated annually:* 1,260,140 tons (2012 est.)
municipal solid waste recycled annually: 100,811 tons (2011 est.)
percent of municipal solid waste recycled: 8% (2011 est.)

Major lakes (area sq km): *salt water lake(s):* Lagoa Mirim (shared with Brazil) - 2,970 sq km

Major rivers (by length in km): Rio de la Plata/Parana river mouth (shared with Brazil [s], Argentina, Paraguay) - 4,880 km; Uruguay river mouth (shared with Brazil [s] and Argentina) - 1,610 km
note – [s] after country name indicates river source; [m] after country name indicates river mouth

Major aquifers: Guarani Aquifer System

Total water withdrawal: *municipal:* 410 million cubic meters (2017 est.)
industrial: 80 million cubic meters (2017 est.)
agricultural: 3.17 billion cubic meters (2017 est.)

Total renewable water resources: 172.2 billion cubic meters (2017 est.)

GOVERNMENT

Country name: *conventional long form:* Oriental Republic of Uruguay
conventional short form: Uruguay
local long form: Republica Oriental del Uruguay
local short form: Uruguay
former: Banda Oriental, Cisplatine Province
etymology: name derives from the Spanish pronunciation of the Guarani Indian designation of the Uruguay River, which makes up the western border of the country and whose name later came to be applied to the entire country

Government type: presidential republic

Capital: *name:* Montevideo
geographic coordinates: 34 51 S, 56 10 W
time difference: UTC-3 (2 hours ahead of Washington, DC, during Standard Time)
etymology: the name "Montevidi" was originally applied to the hill that overlooked the bay upon which the city of Montevideo was founded; the earliest meaning may have been "[the place where we] saw the hill"

Administrative divisions: 19 departments (departamentos, singular - departamento); Artigas, Canelones, Cerro Largo, Colonia, Durazno, Flores, Florida, Lavalleja, Maldonado, Montevideo, Paysandu, Rio Negro, Rivera, Rocha, Salto, San Jose, Soriano, Tacuarembo, Treinta y Tres

Independence: 25 August 1825 (from Brazil)

National holiday: Independence Day, 25 August (1825)

Constitution: *history:* several previous; latest approved by plebiscite 27 November 1966, effective 15 February 1967, reinstated in 1985 at the conclusion of military rule
amendments: initiated by public petition of at least 10% of qualified voters, proposed by agreement of at least two fifths of the General Assembly membership, or by existing "constitutional laws" sanctioned by at least two thirds of the membership in both houses of the Assembly; proposals can also be submitted by senators, representatives, or by the executive power and require the formation of and approval in a national constituent convention; final passage by either method requires approval by absolute majority of votes cast in a referendum; amended many times, last in 2004

Legal system: civil law system based on the Spanish civil code

International law organization participation: accepts compulsory ICJ jurisdiction; accepts ICCt jurisdiction

Citizenship: *citizenship by birth:* yes
citizenship by descent only: yes
dual citizenship recognized: yes
residency requirement for naturalization: 3-5 years

Suffrage: 18 years of age; universal and compulsory

Executive branch: *chief of state:* President Luis Alberto LACALLE POU (since 1 March 2020); Vice President Beatriz ARGIMON Cedeira (since 1 March 2020); the president is both chief of state and head of government
head of government: President Luis Alberto LACALLE POU (since 1 March 2020); Vice President Beatriz ARGIMON Cedeira (since 1 March 2020)
cabinet: Council of Ministers appointed by the president with approval of the General Assembly
elections/appointments: president and vice president directly elected on the same ballot by absolute majority vote in 2 rounds if needed for a 5-year term (eligible for nonconsecutive terms); election last held on 27 October 2019 with a runoff election on 24 November 2019 (next to be held in October 2024, and a runoff if needed in November 2024)
election results:
2019: Luis Alberto LACALLE POU elected president - results of the first round of presidential elections: percent of vote -Daniel MARTINEZ (FA) 40.7%, Luis Alberto LACALLE POU (Blanco) 29.7%, Ernesto TALVI (Colorado Party) 12.8%, and Guido MANINI RIOS (Open Cabildo) 11.3%, other 5.5%; results of the second round: percent of vote - Luis Alberto LACALLE POU (Blanco) 50.6%, Daniel MARTINEZ (FA) 49.4%
2014: Tabare VAZQUEZ elected president in second round; percent of vote - Tabare VAZQUEZ (Socialist Party) 56.5%, Luis Alberto LACALLE Pou (Blanco) 43.4%

Legislative branch: *description:* bicameral General Assembly or Asamblea General consists of:
Chamber of Senators or Camara de Senadores (30 seats; members directly elected in a single nationwide constituency by proportional representation vote; the vice-president serves as the presiding ex-officio member; elected members serve 5-year terms)

Chamber of Representatives or Camara de Representantes (99 seats; members directly elected in multi-seat constituencies by party-list proportional representation vote using the D'Hondt method; members serve 5-year terms)
elections:
Chamber of Senators - last held on 27 October 2019 (next to be held in October 2024)
Chamber of Representatives - last held on 27 October 2019 (next to be held in October 2024)
election results:
Chamber of Senators - percent of vote by coalition/party - NA; seats by coalition/party - Frente Amplio 13, National Party 10, Colorado Party 4, Open Cabildo 3; composition - men 21, women 9, percent of women 30%

Chamber of Representatives - percent of vote by coalition/party - NA; seats by coalition/party - Frente Amplio 42, National Party 30, Colorado Party 13, Open Cabildo 11, Independent Party 1, other 2; composition - men 75, women 24, percent of women 24.2%; note - total General Assembly percent of women 25.6%

Judicial branch: *highest court(s):* Supreme Court of Justice (consists of 5 judges)
judge selection and term of office: judges nominated by the president and appointed by two-thirds vote in joint conference of the General Assembly; judges serve 10-year terms, with reelection possible after a lapse of 5 years following the previous term
subordinate courts: Courts of Appeal; District Courts (Juzgados Letrados); Peace Courts (Juzgados de Paz); Rural Courts (Juzgados Rurales)

Political parties and leaders: Broad Front or FA (Frente Amplio) [Fernando PEREIRA] - (a broad governing coalition that comprises 34 factions including Uruguay Assembly [Danilo ASTORI], Progressive Alliance [Rodolfo NIN NOVOA], New Space [Rafael MICHELINI], Socialist Party [Gonzalo CIVILA], Vertiente Artiguista [Enrique RUBIO], Christian Democratic Party [Jorge RODRIGUEZ], For the People's Victory [Luis PUIG], Popular Participation Movement or MPP [Jose MUJICA], Big House [Constanza MOREIRA], Communist Party [Juan CASTILLO], The Federal League [Sergio LIER], Fuerza Renovadora [Mario BERGARA])
Colorado Party (including Batllistas [Julio Maria SANGUINETTI] and Ciudadanos [Adrian PENA])
Independent Party [Pablo MIERES]
National Party or Blanco (including Todos (Everyone) [Luis LACALLE POU] and National Alliance [Carlos CAMY])
Open Cabildo [Guido MANINI RIOS]
Popular Unity [Gonzalo ABELLA]

International organization participation: CAN (associate), CD, CELAC, FAO, G-77, IADB, IAEA, IBRD, ICAO, ICC (national committees), ICCt, ICRM, IDA, IFAD, IFC, IFRCS, IHO, ILO, IMF, IMO, Interpol, IOC, IOM, IPU, ISO, ITSO, ITU, LAES, LAIA, Mercosur, MIGA, MINUSTAH, MONUSCO, NAM (observer), OAS, OIF (observer), OPANAL, OPCW, Pacific Alliance (observer), PCA, SICA (observer), UN, UNASUR, UNCTAD, UNESCO, UNIDO, Union Latina, UNISFA, UNMOGIP, UNOCI, UNWTO, UPU, WCO, WFTU (NGOs), WHO, WIPO, WMO, WTO

Diplomatic representation in the US: *chief of mission:* Ambassador Andres Augusto DURAN HAREAU (since 23 December 2020)
chancery: 1913 I Street NW, Washington, DC 20006
telephone: [1] (202) 331-1313
FAX: [1] (202) 331-8142

email address and website:
urueeuu@mrree.gub.uy
consulate(s) general: Miami, New York, San Francisco

Diplomatic representation from the US: *chief of mission:* Ambassador (vacant); Charge d'Affaires Jennifer SAVAGE (since 20 January 2021)
embassy: Lauro Muller 1776, Montevideo 11200
mailing address: 3360 Montevideo Place, Washington DC 20521-3360
telephone: (+598) 1770-2000
FAX: [+598] 1770-2128
email address and website:
MontevideoACS@state.gov
https://uy.usembassy.gov/

Flag description: nine equal horizontal stripes of white (top and bottom) alternating with blue; a white square in the upper hoist-side corner with a yellow sun bearing a human face (delineated in black) known as the Sun of May with 16 rays that alternate between triangular and wavy; the stripes represent the nine original departments of Uruguay; the sun symbol evokes the legend of the sun breaking through the clouds on 25 May 1810 as independence was first declared from Spain (Uruguay subsequently won its independence from Brazil); the sun features are said to represent those of Inti, the Inca god of the sun
note: the banner was inspired by the national colors of Argentina and by the design of the US flag

National symbol(s): Sun of May (a sun-with-face symbol); national colors: blue, white, yellow

National anthem: *name:* "Himno Nacional" (National Anthem of Uruguay)
lyrics/music: Francisco Esteban ACUNA de Figueroa/Francisco Jose DEBALI
note: adopted 1848; the anthem is also known as "Orientales, la Patria o la tumba!" ("Uruguayans, the Fatherland or Death!"); it is the world's longest national anthem in terms of music (105 bars; almost five minutes); generally only the first verse and chorus are sung

National heritage: *total World Heritage Sites:* 3 (all cultural)
selected World Heritage Site locales: Historic City of Colonia del Sacramento; Fray Bentos Industrial Landscape; The work of engineer Eladio Dieste: Church of Atlántida

ECONOMY

Economic overview: Uruguay has a free market economy characterized by an export-oriented agricultural sector, a well-educated workforce, and high levels of social spending. Uruguay has sought to expand trade within the Common Market of the South (Mercosur) and with non-Mercosur members, and President VAZQUEZ has maintained his predecessor's mix of pro-market policies and a strong social safety net.

Following financial difficulties in the late 1990s and early 2000s, Uruguay's economic growth averaged 8% annually during the 2004-08 period. The 2008-09 global financial crisis put a brake on Uruguay's vigorous growth, which decelerated to 2.6% in 2009. Nevertheless, the country avoided a recession and kept growth rates positive, mainly through higher public expenditure and investment; GDP growth reached 8.9% in 2010 but slowed markedly in the 2012-16 period as a result of a renewed slowdown in the global economy and in Uruguay's main trade partners and Mercosur counterparts, Argentina and Brazil. Reforms in those countries should give Uruguay an economic boost. Growth picked up in 2017.

Real GDP (purchasing power parity): $75.06 billion (2020 est.)
$79.73 billion (2019 est.)
$79.45 billion (2018 est.)
note: data are in 2017 dollars
country comparison to the world: 99

Real GDP growth rate: 2.7% (2017 est.)
1.7% (2016 est.)
0.4% (2015 est.)
country comparison to the world: 107

Real GDP per capita: $21,600 (2020 est.)
$23,000 (2019 est.)
$23,000 (2018 est.)
note: data are in 2017 dollars
country comparison to the world: 84

GDP (official exchange rate): $56.108 billion (2019 est.)

Inflation rate (consumer prices): 7.8% (2019 est.)
7.5% (2018 est.)
6.2% (2017 est.)
country comparison to the world: 198

Credit ratings:

Fitch rating: BBB- (2013)

Moody's rating: Baa2 (2014)

Standard & Poors rating: BBB (2015)

GDP - composition, by sector of origin: *agriculture:* 6.2% (2017 est.)
industry: 24.1% (2017 est.)
services: 69.7% (2017 est.)

GDP - composition, by end use: *household consumption:* 66.8% (2017 est.)
government consumption: 14.3% (2017 est.)
investment in fixed capital: 16.7% (2017 est.)
investment in inventories: -1% (2017 est.)
exports of goods and services: 21.6% (2017 est.)
imports of goods and services: -18.4% (2017 est.)

Agricultural products: soybeans, milk, rice, maize, wheat, barley, beef, sugar cane, sorghum, oranges

Industries: food processing, electrical machinery, transportation equipment, petroleum products, textiles, chemicals, beverages

Industrial production growth rate: -3.6% (2017 est.)
country comparison to the world: 190

Labor force: 1.748 million (2017 est.)
country comparison to the world: 124

Labor force - by occupation: *agriculture:* 13%
industry: 14%
services: 73% (2010 est.)

Unemployment rate: 7.6% (2017 est.)
7.9% (2016 est.)
country comparison to the world: 118

Unemployment, youth ages 15-24: *total:* 33.5%
male: 29.4%
female: 38.8% (2020 est.)
country comparison to the world: 28

Population below poverty line: 8.8% (2019 est.)

Gini Index coefficient - distribution of family income:
39.7 (2018 est.)
41.9 (2013)
country comparison to the world: 65

Household income or consumption by percentage share: *lowest 10%:* 1.9%
highest 10%: 30.8% (2014 est.)

Budget: *revenues:* 17.66 billion (2017 est.)
expenditures: 19.72 billion (2017 est.)

Budget surplus (+) or deficit (-): -3.5% (of GDP) (2017 est.)
country comparison to the world: 149

Public debt: 65.7% of GDP (2017 est.)
61.6% of GDP (2016 est.)
note: data cover general government debt and include debt instruments issued (or owned) by government entities other than the treasury; the data include treasury debt held by foreign entities; the data include debt issued by subnational entities, as well as intragovernmental debt; intragovernmental debt consists of treasury borrowings from surpluses in the social funds, such as for retirement, medical care, and unemployment; debt instruments for the social funds are not sold at public auctions.
country comparison to the world: 58

Taxes and other revenues: 29.8% (of GDP) (2017 est.)
country comparison to the world: 79

Fiscal year: calendar year

Current account balance: $879 million (2017 est.)
$410 million (2016 est.)
country comparison to the world: 51

Exports: $13.55 billion (2020 est.) note: data are in current year dollars
$16.99 billion (2019 est.) note: data are in current year dollars
$17.04 billion (2018 est.) note: data are in current year dollars
country comparison to the world: 96

Exports - partners: China 29%, Brazil 12%, United States 5%, Netherlands 5%, Argentina 5% (2019)

Exports - commodities: sulfate wood pulp, beef, soybeans, concentrated milk, rice (2019)

Imports: $11.29 billion (2020 est.) note: data are in current year dollars
$13.31 billion (2019 est.) note: data are in current year dollars
$13.82 billion (2018 est.) note: data are in current year dollars
country comparison to the world: 100

Imports - partners: Brazil 25%, China 15%, United States 11%, Argentina 11% (2019)

Imports - commodities: crude petroleum, packaged medicines, cars, broadcasting equipment, delivery trucks (2019)

Reserves of foreign exchange and gold: $15.96 billion (31 December 2017 est.)
$13.47 billion (31 December 2016 est.)
country comparison to the world: 66

Debt - external: $43.705 billion (2019 est.)
$42.861 billion (2018 est.)
country comparison to the world: 73

Exchange rates: Uruguayan pesos (UYU) per US dollar -
42.645 (2020 est.)
37.735 (2019 est.)
32.2 (2018 est.)
27.52 (2014 est.)
23.25 (2013 est.)

ENERGY

Electricity access: *electrification - total population:* 100% (2020)

Electricity: *installed generating capacity:* 5.348 million kW (2020 est.)
consumption: 11,461,960,000 kWh (2019 est.)
exports: 1.148 billion kWh (2020 est.)
imports: 515 million kWh (2020 est.)
transmission/distribution losses: 1,329,700,000 kWh (2019 est.)

Electricity generation sources: *fossil fuels:* 2% of total installed capacity (2020 est.)
solar: 3.6% of total installed capacity (2020 est.)
wind: 42.2% of total installed capacity (2020 est.)
hydroelectricity: 30.6% of total installed capacity (2020 est.)
biomass and waste: 21.6% of total installed capacity (2020 est.)

Petroleum: *total petroleum production:* 400 bbl/day (2021 est.)
refined petroleum consumption: 50,200 bbl/day (2019 est.)
crude oil and lease condensate exports: 0 bbl/day (2018 est.)
crude oil and lease condensate imports: 41,500 bbl/day (2018 est.)
crude oil estimated reserves: 0 barrels (2021 est.)

Refined petroleum products - production: 42,220 bbl/day (2015 est.)
country comparison to the world: 81

Refined petroleum products - imports: 9,591 bbl/day (2015 est.)
country comparison to the world: 150

Natural gas: *production:* 0 cubic meters (2021 est.)
consumption: 96.872 million cubic meters (2019 est.)
exports: 0 cubic meters (2021 est.)
imports: 96.872 million cubic meters (2019 est.)
proven reserves: 0 cubic meters (2021 est.)

Carbon dioxide emissions: 6.45 million metric tonnes of CO_2 (2019 est.)
from petroleum and other liquids: 6.259 million metric tonnes of CO_2 (2019 est.)
from consumed natural gas: 190,000 metric tonnes of CO_2 (2019 est.)
country comparison to the world: 129

Energy consumption per capita: 66.909 million Btu/person (2019 est.)
country comparison to the world: 85

COMMUNICATIONS

Telephones - fixed lines: *total subscriptions:* 1,224,600 (2020 est.)
subscriptions per 100 inhabitants: 35 (2020 est.)
country comparison to the world: 70

Telephones - mobile cellular: *total subscriptions:* 4,779,790 (2019)
subscriptions per 100 inhabitants: 138.08 (2019)
country comparison to the world: 124

Telecommunication systems: *general assessment:* Uruguay has an advanced telecom market, with excellent infrastructure and one of the highest broadband penetration rates in Latin America; fixed-line teledensity is also particularly high for the region, while mobile penetration is the second highest after Panama; in terms of computer penetration, Uruguay tops all other countries in the region by a considerable margin, and this has facilitated growth in fixed-line broadband adoption; the government and telecom regulator have introduced a range of measures to help develop the deployment of fiber infrastructure, partly in a bid to encourage economic growth and stimulate e-commerce; fiber accounted for about 77% of all fixed and fixed-wireless broadband connections as of June 2020; with investment projected to reach $800 million, the state-owned incumbent Antel is expected to provide national FttP coverage by early 2022; together with the FttP network, the opening of the submarine cable system in early 2012 and August 2017 have helped boost Uruguay's internet bandwidth, and increase the data rate available to end-users; Uruguay is one of the very few Latin American countries where the local fixed-line market is neither privatized nor liberalized; other segments of the telecom market have been opened to competition, including international long-distance telephony, mobile telephony, and fixed-wireless broadband; Uruguay is also one of the few countries in the world where broadband access via cable modem does not exist; although cable networks are well equipped technologically, and digital cable TV is widely available, telecom legislation prohibits data transmission over pay TV networks; the government announced in December 2020 that it intended to introduce changes to the law to permit pay TV providers to offer internet and telephony packages over their own networks; all three operators offer mobile broadband through 3G and LTE networks; operators have achieved nationwide 3G coverage and the number of mobile broadband subscribers continues to grow; at the end of 2019, spectrum in the 5G-suitable range was auctioned, enabling operators to launch 5G services; the regulator is working on a spectrum and connectivity policy that emphasizes 5G (2021)
domestic: most modern facilities concentrated in Montevideo; nationwide microwave radio relay network; overall fixed-line roughly 34 per 100 and mobile-cellular teledensity 138 per 100 persons (2019)
international: country code - 598; landing points for the Unisor, Tannat, and Bicentenario submarine cable system providing direct connectivity to Brazil and Argentina; Bicentenario 2012 and Tannat 2017 cables helped end-users with Internet bandwidth; satellite earth stations - 2 Intelsat (Atlantic Ocean) (2020)

Broadcast media: mixture of privately owned and state-run broadcast media; more than 100 commercial radio stations and about 20 TV channels; cable TV is available; many community radio and TV stations; adopted the hybrid Japanese/Brazilian HDTV standard (ISDB-T) in December 2010 (2019)

Internet country code: .uy

Internet users: *total:* 2,987,405 (2020 est.)
percent of population: 86% (2020 est.)
country comparison to the world: 114

Broadband - fixed subscriptions: *total:* 1,063,701 (2020 est.)
subscriptions per 100 inhabitants: 31 (2020 est.)
country comparison to the world: 71

TRANSPORTATION

National air transport system: *number of registered air carriers:* 2 (2020)
inventory of registered aircraft operated by air carriers: 5

Civil aircraft registration country code prefix: CX

Airports: *total:* 133 (2021)
country comparison to the world: 42

Airports - with paved runways: *total:* 11
over 3,047 m: 1
1,524 to 2,437 m: 4
914 to 1,523 m: 4
under 914 m: 2 (2021)

Airports - with unpaved runways: *total:* 122
1,524 to 2,437 m: 3
914 to 1,523 m: 40
under 914 m: 79 (2021)

Pipelines: 257 km gas, 160 km oil (2013)

Railways: *total:* 1,673 km (2016) (operational; government claims overall length is 2,961 km)
standard gauge: 1,673 km (2016) 1.435-m gauge
country comparison to the world: 80

Roadways: *total:* 77,732 km (2010)
paved: 7,743 km (2010)
unpaved: 69,989 km (2010)
country comparison to the world: 63

Waterways: 1,600 km (2011)
country comparison to the world: 52

Merchant marine: *total:* 61
by type: container ship 1, general cargo 4, oil tanker 4, other 52 (2021)
country comparison to the world: 112

Ports and terminals: *major seaport(s):* Montevideo

MILITARY AND SECURITY

Military and security forces: Armed Forces of Uruguay (Fuerzas Armadas del Uruguay): National Army (Ejercito Nacional), National Navy (Armada Nacional, includes Coast Guard (Prefectura Nacional Naval)), Uruguayan Air Force (Fuerza Aerea); Ministry of Interior: National Police (2022)
note: the National Police includes the paramilitary National Republican Guard or Guardia Nacional Republicana

Military expenditures: 2.3% of GDP (2021 est.)
2% of GDP (2020 est.)
2.1% of GDP (2019 est.) (approximately $1.47 billion)
2.1% of GDP (2018 est.) (approximately $1.51 billion)
2% of GDP (2017 est.) (approximately $1.38 billion)
country comparison to the world: 49

Military and security service personnel strengths: approximately 22,000 active duty personnel (14,000 Army; 5,000 Navy; 3,000 Air Force) (2022)

Military equipment inventories and acquisitions: the military's inventory includes a wide variety of older or second-hand equipment; since 2010, it has imported limited amounts of military hardware from about 10 countries with Spain as the leading supplier (2022)

Military service age and obligation: 18-30 years of age (18-22 years of age for Navy) for voluntary military service for men and women; up to 40 years of age for specialists; enlistment is voluntary in peacetime, but the government has the authority to conscript in emergencies (2022)
note: as of 2017, women comprised about 19% of the active military

Military deployments: 830 Democratic Republic of the Congo (MONUSCO); 210 Golan Heights (UNDOF) (May 2022)

Military - note: the military has some domestic responsibilities, including perimeter security for a number of prisons and border security; in 2020, the military deployed more than 1,000 troops to assist the National Police in securing the land border with Brazil and the riverine border with Argentina as part of a border control law passed in 2018 (2022)

TRANSNATIONAL ISSUES

Disputes - international: *Uruguay-Argentina:* in 2010, the ICJ ruled in favor of Uruguay's operation of two paper mills on the Uruguay River, which forms the border with Argentina; the two countries formed a joint pollution monitoring regime, which ended the dispute
Uruguay-Brazil: uncontested boundary dispute between Brazil and Uruguay over Braziliera/Brasiliera Island in the Quarai/Cuareim River leaves the tripoint with Argentina in question; smuggling of firearms and narcotics continues to be an issue along the Uruguay-Brazil border

Refugees and internally displaced persons: *refugees (country of origin):* 19,000 (Venezuela) (economic and political crisis; includes Venezuelans who have claimed asylum or have received alternative legal stay) (2022)
stateless persons: 5 (mid-year 2021)

Illicit drugs: transit country for drugs mainly bound for Europe, often through sea-borne containers; limited law enforcement corruption; money laundering; weak border control along Brazilian frontier; increasing consumption of cocaine base and synthetic drugs

UZBEKISTAN

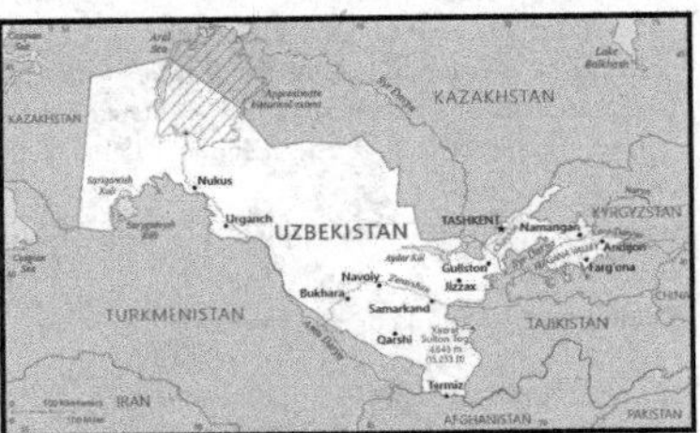

INTRODUCTION

Background: Uzbekistan is the geographic and population center of Central Asia. The country has a diverse economy and a relatively young population. Russia conquered and united the disparate territories of present-day Uzbekistan in the late 19th century. Stiff resistance to the Red Army after the Bolshevik Revolution was eventually suppressed and a socialist republic established in 1924. During the Soviet era, intensive production of "white gold" (cotton) and grain led to the overuse of agrochemicals and the depletion of water supplies, leaving the land degraded and the Aral Sea and certain rivers half-dry. Independent since the dissolution of the USSR in 1991, the country has diversified agricultural production while developing its mineral and petroleum export capacity and increasing its manufacturing base, although cotton remains a major part of its economy. Uzbekistan's first president, Islom KARIMOV, led Uzbekistan for 25 years until his death in September 2016. His successor, former Prime Minister Shavkat MIRZIYOYEV, has improved relations with Uzbekistan's neighbors and introduced wide-ranging economic, judicial, and social reforms. MIRZIYOYEV was reelected in October 2021 with 80% of the vote.

GEOGRAPHY

Location: Central Asia, north of Turkmenistan, south of Kazakhstan

Geographic coordinates: 41 00 N, 64 00 E

Map references: Asia

Area: *total:* 447,400 sq km
land: 425,400 sq km
water: 22,000 sq km
country comparison to the world: 59

Area - comparative: about four times the size of Virginia; slightly larger than California

Land boundaries: *total:* 6,893 km
border countries (5): Afghanistan 144 km; Kazakhstan 2,330 km; Kyrgyzstan 1,314 km; Tajikistan 1,312 km; Turkmenistan 1,793 km

Coastline: 0 km (doubly landlocked); note - Uzbekistan includes the southern portion of the Aral Sea with a 420 km shoreline

Maritime claims: none (doubly landlocked)

Climate: mostly mid-latitude desert, long, hot summers, mild winters; semiarid grassland in east

Terrain: mostly flat-to-rolling sandy desert with dunes; broad, flat intensely irrigated river valleys along course of Amu Darya, Syr Darya (Sirdaryo), and Zaravshan; Fergana Valley in east surrounded by mountainous Tajikistan and Kyrgyzstan; shrinking Aral Sea in west

Elevation: *highest point:* Xazrat Sulton Tog' 4,643 m
lowest point: Sariqamish Kuli -12 m

Natural resources: natural gas, petroleum, coal, gold, uranium, silver, copper, lead and zinc, tungsten, molybdenum

Land use: *agricultural land:* 62.6% (2018 est.)
arable land: 10.1% (2018 est.)
permanent crops: 0.8% (2018 est.)
permanent pasture: 51.7% (2018 est.)
forest: 7.7% (2018 est.)
other: 29.7% (2018 est.)

Irrigated land: 42,150 sq km (2012)

Major lakes (area sq km): *fresh water lake(s):* Aral Sea (shared with Kazakhstan) - largely dried up

Major rivers (by length in km): Syr Darya (shared with Kyrgyzstan [s], Tajikistan, and Kazakhstan [m]) - 3,078 km; Amu Darya river mouth (shared with Tajikistan [s], Afghanistan, and Turkmenistan) - 2,620 km
note – [s] after country name indicates river source; [m] after country name indicates river mouth

Major watersheds (area sq km): Internal *(endorheic basin)* drainage: *(Aral Sea basin)* Amu Darya (534,739 sq km), Syr Darya (782,617 sq km)

Population distribution: most of the population is concentrated in the fertile Fergana Valley in the easternmost arm of the country; the south has significant clusters of people, while the central and western deserts are sparsely populated

Natural hazards: earthquakes; floods; landslides or mudslides; avalanches; droughts

Geography - note: along with Liechtenstein, one of the only two doubly landlocked countries in the world

PEOPLE AND SOCIETY

Population: 31,104,937 (2022 est.)
country comparison to the world: 47

Nationality: *noun:* Uzbekistani
adjective: Uzbekistani

Ethnic groups: Uzbek 83.8%, Tajik 4.8%, Kazakh 2.5%, Russian 2.3%, Karakalpak 2.2%, Tatar 1.5%, other 2.9% (2017 est.)

Languages: Uzbek (official) 74.3%, Russian 14.2%, Tajik 4.4%, other 7.1%
major-language sample(s): Jahon faktlari kitobi, asosiy ma'lumotlar uchun zaruriy manba. (Uzbek)
note: in the autonomous Karakalpakstan Republic, both the Karakalpak language and Uzbek have official status

Religions: Muslim 88% (mostly Sunni), Eastern Orthodox 9%, other 3%

Age structure: *0-14 years:* 23.19% (male 3,631,693/female 3,456,750)
15-24 years: 16.63% (male 2,601,803/female 2,481,826)
25-54 years: 45.68% (male 6,955,260/female 7,006,172)
55-64 years: 8.63% (male 1,245,035/female 1,392,263)
65 years and over: 5.87% (male 768,769/female 1,025,840) (2020 est.)

Dependency ratios: *total dependency ratio:* 50.6
youth dependency ratio: 43.4
elderly dependency ratio: 7.2
potential support ratio: 13.9 (2020 est.)

Median age: *total:* 30.1 years
male: 29.4 years
female: 30.7 years (2020 est.)
country comparison to the world: 123

Population growth rate: 0.83% (2022 est.)
country comparison to the world: 112

Birth rate: 15.53 births/1,000 population (2022 est.)
country comparison to the world: 108

Death rate: 5.41 deaths/1,000 population (2022 est.)
country comparison to the world: 185

Net migration rate: -1.78 migrant(s)/1,000 population (2022 est.)
country comparison to the world: 166

Population distribution: most of the population is concentrated in the fertile Fergana Valley in the easternmost arm of the country; the south has significant clusters of people, while the central and western deserts are sparsely populated

Urbanization: *urban population:* 50.5% of total population (2022)
rate of urbanization: 1.25% annual rate of change (2020-25 est.)

Major urban areas - population: 2.574 million TASHKENT (capital) (2022)

Sex ratio: *at birth:* 1.06 male(s)/female
0-14 years: 1.05 male(s)/female
15-24 years: 1.05 male(s)/female
25-54 years: 0.99 male(s)/female
55-64 years: 0.89 male(s)/female
65 years and over: 0.63 male(s)/female
total population: 0.99 male(s)/female (2022 est.)

Mother's mean age at first birth: 23.7 years (2019 est.)

Maternal mortality ratio: 29 deaths/100,000 live births (2017 est.)
country comparison to the world: 114

Infant mortality rate: *total:* 18.98 deaths/1,000 live births
male: 22.6 deaths/1,000 live births
female: 15.14 deaths/1,000 live births (2022 est.)
country comparison to the world: 89

Life expectancy at birth: *total population:* 75.29 years
male: 72.27 years
female: 78.5 years (2022 est.)
country comparison to the world: 125

Total fertility rate: 1.73 children born/woman (2022 est.)
country comparison to the world: 160

Drinking water source: *improved: urban:* 99.6% of population
rural: 96.1% of population
total: 97.8% of population
unimproved: urban: 0.4% of population
rural: 3.9% of population
total: 2.2% of population (2020 est.)

Current health expenditure: 5.6% of GDP (2019)

Physicians density: 2.37 physicians/1,000 population (2014)

Hospital bed density: 4 beds/1,000 population (2014)

Sanitation facility access: *improved: urban:* 100% of population
rural: 100% of population
total: 100% of population

HIV/AIDS - adult prevalence rate: 0.2% (2020 est.)
country comparison to the world: 117

HIV/AIDS - people living with HIV/AIDS: 58,000 (2020 est.)
country comparison to the world: 57

HIV/AIDS - deaths: (2020 est.) <1,000

Obesity - adult prevalence rate: 16.6% (2016)
country comparison to the world: 123

Alcohol consumption per capita: *total:* 2.45 liters of pure alcohol (2019 est.)
beer: 0.18 liters of pure alcohol (2019 est.)
wine: 0.09 liters of pure alcohol (2019 est.)
spirits: 2.19 liters of pure alcohol (2019 est.)
other alcohols: 0 liters of pure alcohol (2019 est.)
country comparison to the world: 124

Tobacco use: *total:* 17.6% (2020 est.)
male: 34% (2020 est.)
female: 1.1% (2020 est.)
country comparison to the world: 96

Children under the age of 5 years underweight: 2.9% (2017)
country comparison to the world: 98

Education expenditures: 5.1% of GDP (2020 est.)
country comparison to the world: 61

Literacy: *definition:* age 15 and over can read and write
total population: 100%
male: 100%
female: 100% (2019)

School life expectancy (primary to tertiary education): *total:* 12 years
male: 13 years
female: 12 years (2019)

ENVIRONMENT

Environment - current issues: shrinkage of the Aral Sea has resulted in growing concentrations of chemical pesticides and natural salts; these substances are then blown from the increasingly exposed lake bed and contribute to desertification and respiratory health problems; water pollution from industrial wastes and the heavy use of fertilizers and pesticides is the cause of many human health disorders; increasing soil salination; soil contamination from buried nuclear processing and agricultural chemicals, including DDT

Environment - international agreements: *party to:* Biodiversity, Climate Change, Climate Change-Kyoto Protocol, Climate Change-Paris Agreement, Comprehensive Nuclear Test Ban, Desertification, Endangered Species, Environmental Modification, Hazardous Wastes, Ozone Layer Protection, Wetlands
signed, but not ratified: none of the selected agreements

Air pollutants: *particulate matter emissions:* 25.29 micrograms per cubic meter (2016 est.)
carbon dioxide emissions: 91.81 megatons (2016 est.)
methane emissions: 96.16 megatons (2020 est.)

Climate: mostly mid-latitude desert, long, hot summers, mild winters; semiarid grassland in east

Land use: *agricultural land:* 62.6% (2018 est.)
arable land: 10.1% (2018 est.)
permanent crops: 0.8% (2018 est.)
permanent pasture: 51.7% (2018 est.)
forest: 7.7% (2018 est.)
other: 29.7% (2018 est.)

Urbanization: *urban population:* 50.5% of total population (2022)
rate of urbanization: 1.25% annual rate of change (2020-25 est.)

Revenue from forest resources: *forest revenues:* 0% of GDP (2018 est.)
country comparison to the world: 202

Revenue from coal: *coal revenues:* 0.06% of GDP (2018 est.)
country comparison to the world: 30

Waste and recycling: *municipal solid waste generated annually:* 4 million tons (2016 est.)

Major lakes (area sq km): *fresh water lake(s):* Aral Sea (shared with Kazakhstan) - largely dried up

Major rivers (by length in km): Syr Darya (shared with Kyrgyzstan [s], Tajikistan, and Kazakhstan [m]) - 3,078 km; Amu Darya river mouth (shared with Tajikistan [s], Afghanistan, and Turkmenistan) - 2,620 km

note – [s] after country name indicates river source; [m] after country name indicates river mouth

Major watersheds (area sq km): Internal *(endorheic basin)* drainage: *(Aral Sea basin)* Amu Darya (534,739 sq km), Syr Darya (782,617 sq km)

Total water withdrawal: *municipal:* 2.41 billion cubic meters (2017 est.)
industrial: 2.13 billion cubic meters (2017 est.)
agricultural: 54.36 billion cubic meters (2017 est.)

Total renewable water resources: 48.87 billion cubic meters (2017 est.)

GOVERNMENT

Country name: *conventional long form:* Republic of Uzbekistan
conventional short form: Uzbekistan
local long form: O'zbekiston Respublikasi
local short form: O'zbekiston
former: Uzbek Soviet Socialist Republic
etymology: a combination of the Turkic words "uz" (self) and "bek" (master) with the Persian suffix "-stan" (country) to give the meaning "Land of the Free"

Government type: presidential republic; highly authoritarian

Capital: *name:* Tashkent (Toshkent)
geographic coordinates: 41 19 N, 69 15 E
time difference: UTC+5 (10 hours ahead of Washington, DC, during Standard Time)
etymology: *tash* means "stone" and *kent* means "city" in Turkic languages, so the name simply denotes "stone city"

Administrative divisions: 12 provinces (viloyatlar, singular - viloyat), 1 autonomous republic* (avtonom respublikasi), and 1 city** (shahar); Andijon Viloyati, Buxoro Viloyati [Bukhara Province], Farg'ona Viloyati [Fergana Province], Jizzax Viloyati, Namangan Viloyati, Navoiy Viloyati, Qashqadaryo Viloyati (Qarshi), Qoraqalpog'iston Respublikasi [Karakalpakstan Republic]* (Nukus), Samarqand Viloyati [Samarkand Province], Sirdaryo Viloyati (Guliston), Surxondaryo Viloyati (Termiz), Toshkent Shahri [Tashkent City]**, Toshkent Viloyati [Tashkent Province], Xorazm Viloyati (Urganch)
note: administrative divisions have the same names as their administrative centers (exceptions have the administrative center name following in parentheses)

Independence: 1 September 1991 (from the Soviet Union)

National holiday: Independence Day, 1 September (1991)

Constitution: *history:* several previous; latest adopted 8 December 1992
amendments: proposed by the Supreme Assembly or by referendum; passage requires two-thirds majority vote of both houses of the Assembly or passage in a referendum; amended several times, last in 2017

Legal system: civil law system; note - in early 2020, the president signed an amendment to the criminal code, criminal procedure code, and code of administrative responsibility

International law organization participation: has not submitted an ICJ jurisdiction declaration; non-party state to the ICCt

Citizenship: *citizenship by birth:* no
citizenship by descent only: at least one parent must be a citizen of Uzbekistan
dual citizenship recognized: no
residency requirement for naturalization: 5 years

Suffrage: 18 years of age; universal

Executive branch: *chief of state:* President Shavkat MIRZIYOYEV (interim president from 8 September 2016; formally elected president on 4 December 2016 to succeed longtime President Islom KARIMOV, who died on 2 September 2016
head of government: Prime Minister Abdulla ARIPOV (since 14 December 2016)
cabinet: Cabinet of Ministers appointed by the president with most requiring approval of the Senate chamber of the Supreme Assembly (Oliy Majlis)
elections/appointments: president directly elected by absolute majority popular vote in 2 rounds if needed for a 5-year term (eligible for a second term; previously a 5-year term, extended by a 2002 constitutional amendment to 7 years, and reverted to 5 years in 2011); election last held on 24 October 2021 (next to be held in 2026); prime minister nominated by majority party in legislature since 2011, but appointed along with the ministers and deputy ministers by the president
election results:
2021: Shavkat MIRZIYOYEV reelected president in first round; percent of vote - Shavkat MIRZIYOYEV (LDPU) 80.3%, Maqsuda VORISOVA (PDP) 6.7%, Alisher QODIROV (National Revival Democratic Party) 5.5%, Narzullo OBLOMURODOV (Ecological Party) 4.1%, Bahrom ABDUHALIMOV (Adolat) 3.4%
2016: Shavkat MIRZIYOYEV elected president in first round; percent of vote - Shavkat MIRZIYOYEV (LDPU) 88.6%, Hotamjon KETMONOV (PDP) 3.7%, Narimon UMAROV (Adolat) 3.5%, Sarvar OTAMURODOV (National Revival Democratic Party) 2.4%, other 1.8%

Legislative branch: *description:* bicameral Supreme Assembly or Oliy Majlis consists of:
Senate or Senat (100 seats; 84 members indirectly elected by regional governing councils and 16 appointed by the president; members serve 5-year terms)
Legislative Chamber or Qonunchilik Palatasi (150 seats; members directly elected in single-seat constituencies by absolute majority vote with a second round if needed; members serve 5-year terms)
elections:
Senate - last held 16-17 January 2020 (next to be held in 2025)
Legislative Chamber - last held on 22 December 2019 and 5 January 2020 (next to be held in December 2024)
election results:
Senate - percent of vote by party - NA; seats by party - NA; composition - men 77, women 23, percent of women 23%
Legislative Chamber - percent of vote by party - NA; seats by party - LDPU 53, National Revival Democratic Party 36, Adolat 24, PDP 22, Ecological Movement 15; composition - men 83, women, 17, percent of women 17%
note: all parties in the Supreme Assembly support President Shavkat MIRZIYOYEV

Judicial branch: *highest court(s):* Supreme Court (consists of 67 judges organized into administrative, civil, criminal, and economic sections); Constitutional Court (consists of 7 judges)
judge selection and term of office: judges of the highest courts nominated by the president and confirmed by the Senate of the Oliy Majlis; judges appointed for initial 5-year term and can be reappointed for subsequent 10-year and lifetime terms
subordinate courts: regional, district, city, and town courts

Political parties and leaders: Ecological Party of Uzbekistan (O'zbekiston Ekologik Partivasi) [Narzullo OBLOMURODOV]
Justice (Adolat) Social Democratic Party of Uzbekistan [Bahrom ABDUKHALIMOV]
Liberal Democratic Party of Uzbekistan (O'zbekiston Liberal-Demokratik Partiyasi) or LDPU [Aktam HAITOV]
National Revival Democratic Party of Uzbekistan (O'zbekiston Milliy Tiklanish Demokratik Partiyasi) [Alisher QODIROV]
People's Democratic Party of Uzbekistan (Xalq Demokratik Partiyas) or PDP [Ulugbek Ilyosovich INOYATOV] (formerly Communist Party)

International organization participation: ADB, CICA, CIS, EAEU (observer), EAPC, EBRD, ECO, EEU (observer), FAO, IAEA, IBRD, ICAO, ICC (national committees), ICCt, ICRM, IDA, IDB, IFAD, IFC, IFRCS, ILO, IMF, Interpol, IOC, ISO, ITSO, ITU, MIGA, NAM, OIC, OPCW, OSCE, PFP, SCO, UN, UNCTAD, UNESCO, UNHRC, UNIDO, UNWTO, UPU, WCO, WFTU (NGOs), WHO, WIPO, WMO, WTO (observer)

Diplomatic representation in the US: *chief of mission:* Ambassador Javlon VAHOBOV (since 29 November 2017)
chancery: 1746 Massachusetts Avenue NW, Washington, DC 20036
telephone: [1] (202) 887-5300
FAX: [1] (202) 293-6804
email address and website:
info.washington@mfa.uz
https://www.uzbekistan.org/
consulate(s) general: New York

Diplomatic representation from the US: *chief of mission:* Ambassador Daniel ROSENBLUM (since 24 May 2019)
embassy: 3 Moyqorghon, 5th Block, Yunusobod District, 100093 Tashkent
mailing address: 7110 Tashkent Place, Washington DC 20521-7110
telephone: [998] 78-120-5450
FAX: [998] 78-120-6335
email address and website:
ACSTashkent@state.gov
https://uz.usembassy.gov/

Flag description: three equal horizontal bands of blue (top), white, and green separated by red fimbriations with a vertical, white crescent moon (closed side to the hoist) and 12 white, five-pointed stars shifted to the hoist on the top band; blue is the color of the Turkic peoples and of the sky, white signifies peace and the striving for purity in thoughts and deeds, while green represents nature and is the color of Islam; the red stripes are the vital force of all living organisms that links good and pure ideas with the eternal sky and with deeds on earth; the crescent represents Islam and the 12 stars the months and constellations of the Uzbek calendar

National symbol(s): khumo (mythical bird); national colors: blue, white, red, green

National anthem: *name:* "O'zbekiston Respublikasining Davlat Madhiyasi" (National Anthem of the Republic of Uzbekistan)
lyrics/music: Abdulla ARIPOV/Mutal BURHANOV
note: adopted 1992; after the fall of the Soviet Union, Uzbekistan kept the music of the anthem from its time as a Soviet Republic but adopted new lyrics

National heritage: *total World Heritage Sites:* 5 (4 cultural, 1 natural)
selected World Heritage Site locales: Itchan Kala (c); Historic Bukhara (c); Historic Shakhrisyabz (c); Samarkand -Crossroad of Cultures (c); Western Tien Shan (n)

ECONOMY

Economic overview: Uzbekistan is a doubly landlocked country in which 51% of the population lives in urban settlements; the agriculture-rich Fergana Valley, in which Uzbekistan's eastern borders are situated, has been counted among the most densely populated parts of Central Asia. Since its independence in September 1991, the government has largely maintained its Soviet-style command economy with subsidies and tight controls on production, prices, and access to foreign currency. Despite ongoing efforts to diversify crops, Uzbek agriculture remains largely centered on cotton; Uzbekistan is the world's fifth-largest cotton exporter and seventh-largest producer. Uzbekistan's growth has been driven primarily by state-led investments, and export of natural gas, gold, and cotton provides a significant share of foreign exchange earnings.

Recently, lower global commodity prices and economic slowdowns in neighboring Russia and China have hurt Uzbekistan's trade and investment and worsened its foreign currency shortage. Aware of the need to improve the investment climate, the government is taking incremental steps to reform the business sector and address impediments to foreign investment in the country. Since the death of first President Islam KARIMOV and election of President Shavkat MIRZIYOYEV, emphasis on such initiatives and government efforts to improve the private sector have increased. In the past, Uzbek authorities accused US and other foreign companies operating in Uzbekistan of violating Uzbek laws and have frozen and seized their assets.

As a part of its economic reform efforts, the Uzbek Government is looking to expand opportunities for small and medium enterprises and prioritizes increasing foreign direct investment. In September 2017, the government devalued the official currency rate by almost 50% and announced the loosening of currency restrictions to eliminate the currency black market, increase access to hard currency, and boost investment.

Real GDP (purchasing power parity): $239.42 billion (2020 est.)
$235.54 billion (2019 est.)
$222.63 billion (2018 est.)
note: data are in 2017 dollars
country comparison to the world: 63

Real GDP growth rate: 5.3% (2017 est.)
7.8% (2016 est.)
7.9% (2015 est.)
country comparison to the world: 41

Real GDP per capita: $7,000 (2020 est.)
$7,000 (2019 est.)
$6,800 (2018 est.)
note: data are in 2017 dollars
country comparison to the world: 156

GDP (official exchange rate): $57.789 billion (2019 est.)

Inflation rate (consumer prices): 12.5% (2017 est.)

8% (2016 est.)
note: official data; based on independent analysis of consumer prices, inflation reached 22% in 2012
country comparison to the world: 212

Credit ratings:

Fitch rating: BB- (2018)

Moody's rating: B1 (2019)

Standard & Poors rating: BB- (2018)

GDP - composition, by sector of origin: *agriculture:* 17.9% (2017 est.)
industry: 33.7% (2017 est.)
services: 48.5% (2017 est.)

GDP - composition, by end use: *household consumption:* 59.5% (2017 est.)
government consumption: 16.3% (2017 est.)
investment in fixed capital: 25.3% (2017 est.)
investment in inventories: 3% (2017 est.)
exports of goods and services: 19% (2017 est.)
imports of goods and services: -20% (2017 est.)

Agricultural products: milk, wheat, potatoes, carrots/turnips, cotton, tomatoes, vegetables, grapes, onions, watermelons

Industries: textiles, food processing, machine building, metallurgy, mining, hydrocarbon extraction, chemicals

Industrial production growth rate: 4.5% (2017 est.)
country comparison to the world: 67

Labor force: 13.273 million (2018 est.)
country comparison to the world: 41

Labor force - by occupation: *agriculture:* 25.9%
industry: 13.2%
services: 60.9% (2012 est.)

Unemployment rate: 5% (2017 est.)
5.1% (2016 est.)
note: official data; another 20% are underemployed
country comparison to the world: 80

Population below poverty line: 14.1% (2013 est.)

Gini Index coefficient - distribution of family income: 36.8 (2003)
44.7 (1998)
country comparison to the world: 86

Household income or consumption by percentage share: *lowest 10%:* 2.8%
highest 10%: 29.6% (2003)

Budget: *revenues:* 15.22 billion (2017 est.)
expenditures: 15.08 billion (2017 est.)

Budget surplus (+) or deficit (-): 0.3% (of GDP) (2017 est.)
country comparison to the world: 42

Public debt: 24.3% of GDP (2017 est.)
10.5% of GDP (2016 est.)
country comparison to the world: 178

Taxes and other revenues: 31.2% (of GDP) (2017 est.)
country comparison to the world: 74

Fiscal year: calendar year

Current account balance: $1.713 billion (2017 est.)
$384 million (2016 est.)
country comparison to the world: 43

Exports: $14.52 billion (2020 est.) note: data are in current year dollars
$16.99 billion (2019 est.) note: data are in current year dollars
$14.14 billion (2018 est.) note: data are in current year dollars
country comparison to the world: 92

Exports - partners: Switzerland 19%, United Kingdom 17%, Russia 15%, China 14%, Kazakhstan 9%, Turkey 8%, Kyrgyzstan 5% (2019)

Exports - commodities: gold, natural gas, cotton fibers, copper, ethylene polymers (2019)

Imports: $22.56 billion (2020 est.) note: data are in current year dollars
$26.55 billion (2019 est.) note: data are in current year dollars
$23.44 billion (2018 est.) note: data are in current year dollars
country comparison to the world: 78

Imports - partners: China 23%, Russia 18%, South Korea 11%, Kazakhstan 9%, Turkey 6%, Germany 5% (2019)

Imports - commodities: cars and vehicle parts, packaged medicines, refined petroleum, aircraft, construction vehicles (2019)

Reserves of foreign exchange and gold: $16 billion (31 December 2017 est.)
$14 billion (31 December 2016 est.)
country comparison to the world: 65

Debt - external: $16.9 billion (31 December 2017 est.)
$16.76 billion (31 December 2016 est.)
country comparison to the world: 101

Exchange rates: Uzbekistani soum (UZS) per US dollar -
3,906.1 (2017 est.)
2,966.6 (2016 est.)
2,966.6 (2015 est.)
2,569.6 (2014 est.)
2,311.4 (2013 est.)

ENERGY

Electricity access: *electrification - total population:* 100% (2020)

Electricity: *installed generating capacity:* 16.042 million kW (2020 est.)
consumption: 57,605,687,000 kWh (2019 est.)
exports: 2.067 billion kWh (2019 est.)
imports: 3.379 billion kWh (2019 est.)
transmission/distribution losses: 3.858 billion kWh (2019 est.)

Electricity generation sources: *fossil fuels:* 88.1% of total installed capacity (2020 est.)
hydroelectricity: 11.9% of total installed capacity (2020 est.)

Coal: *production:* 3.98 million metric tons (2020 est.)
consumption: 5.668 million metric tons (2020 est.)
exports: 1,000 metric tons (2020 est.)
imports: 2.995 million metric tons (2020 est.)
proven reserves: 1.375 billion metric tons (2019 est.)

Petroleum: *total petroleum production:* 5,200 bbl/day (2021 est.)
refined petroleum consumption: 98,200 bbl/day (2019 est.)
crude oil and lease condensate exports: 0 bbl/day (2018 est.)
crude oil and lease condensate imports: 24,000 bbl/day (2018 est.)
crude oil estimated reserves: 594 million barrels (2021 est.)

Refined petroleum products - production: 61,740 bbl/day (2015 est.)
country comparison to the world: 78

Refined petroleum products - exports: 3,977 bbl/day (2015 est.)
country comparison to the world: 95

Natural gas: *production:* 46,968,227,000 cubic meters (2020 est.)
consumption: 43,882,007,000 cubic meters (2019 est.)
exports: 13,283,524,000 cubic meters (2019 est.)
imports: 0 cubic meters (2020 est.)
proven reserves: 1,840,592,000,000 cubic meters (2021 est.)

Carbon dioxide emissions: 102.965 million metric tonnes of CO_2 (2019 est.)
from coal and metallurgical coke: 7.816 million metric tonnes of CO_2 (2019 est.)
from petroleum and other liquids: 11.53 million metric tonnes of CO_2 (2019 est.)
from consumed natural gas: 83.619 million metric tonnes of CO_2 (2019 est.)
country comparison to the world: 42

Energy consumption per capita: 57.709 million Btu/person (2019 est.)
country comparison to the world: 94

COMMUNICATIONS

Telephones - fixed lines: *total subscriptions:* 3,550,069 (2020 est.)
subscriptions per 100 inhabitants: 11 (2020 est.)
country comparison to the world: 37

Telephones - mobile cellular: *total subscriptions:* 33.387 million (2022)
subscriptions per 100 inhabitants: 100 (2022)
country comparison to the world: 43

Telecommunication systems: *general assessment:* Uzbekistan's telecom markets both wireline and wireless have been playing "catch up" in terms of their development following the country's independence from the former Soviet Union; the government has formally adopted the principles of operating as a market economy, many elements of the old centrally planned economic model remain; this has had the effect of reducing the level of interest from foreign companies and investors in building out the necessary underlying infrastructure, which in turn has constrained the rate of growth in the country's telecoms sector; the last five years has seen an upswing in prospects for the sector as fiber network roll outs continue beyond the main urban centers, while the mobile market experiences some consolidation for stronger, more efficient competitors; growth is present in the fixed broadband segment with penetration projected to reach 24% by 2027 (a 5-year CAGR of 6.2%); despite the promising signs in the fixed markets, it is the mobile segment that continues to dominate Uzbekistan's telecoms sector in terms of penetration, revenue, and growth; there are four major operators providing a modicum of competition; three of the four are government owned entities; the mobile market is expected to reach 100% penetration in 2023 a 50% increase in the last five years (2022)
domestic: fixed-line nearly 11 per 100 persons and mobile-cellular teledensity nearly 100 per 100 persons; the state-owned telecommunications company, Uzbek Telecom, owner of the fixed-line telecommunications system, has used loans from the Japanese government and the China Development Bank to upgrade fixed-line services including conversion to digital exchanges; mobile-cellular services are

provided by 2 private and 3 state-owned operators with a total subscriber base of 22.8 million as of January 2018 (2020)
international: country code - 998; linked by fiber-optic cable or microwave radio relay with CIS member states and to other countries by leased connection via the Moscow international gateway switch; the country also has a link to the Trans-Asia-Europe (TAE) fiber-optic cable; Uzbekistan has supported the national fiber-optic backbone project of Afghanistan since 2008

Broadcast media: the government controls media; 17 state-owned broadcasters - 13 TV and 4 radio - provide service to virtually the entire country; about 20 privately owned TV stations, overseen by local officials, broadcast to local markets; privately owned TV stations are required to lease transmitters from the government-owned Republic TV and Radio Industry Corporation; in 2019, the Uzbek Agency for Press and Information was reorganized into the Agency of Information and Mass Communications and became part of the Uzbek Presidential Administration with recent appointment of the Uzbek President's elder daughter as it deputy director (2019)

Internet country code: .uz

Internet users: *total:* 17,161,534 (July 2022 est.)
percent of population: 50.1% (July 2022 est.)
country comparison to the world: 42

Broadband - fixed subscriptions: *total:* 4,820,009 (2020 est.)
subscriptions per 100 inhabitants: 14 (2020 est.)
country comparison to the world: 33

TRANSPORTATION

National air transport system: *number of registered air carriers:* 2 (2020)
inventory of registered aircraft operated by air carriers: 34
annual passenger traffic on registered air carriers: 3,056,558 (2018)
annual freight traffic on registered air carriers: 89.43 million (2018) mt-km

Civil aircraft registration country code prefix: UK

Airports: *total:* 53 (2021)
country comparison to the world: 88

Airports - with paved runways: *total:* 33
over 3,047 m: 6
2,438 to 3,047 m: 13
1,524 to 2,437 m: 6
914 to 1,523 m: 4
under 914 m: 4 (2021)

Airports - with unpaved runways: *total:* 20
2,438 to 3,047 m: 2
under 914 m: 18 (2021)

Pipelines: 13,700 km gas, 944 km oil (2016)

Railways: *total:* 4,642 km (2018)
broad gauge: 4,642 km (2018) 1.520-m gauge (1,684 km electrified)
country comparison to the world: 42

Roadways: *total:* 86,496 km (2000)
paved: 75,511 km (2000)
unpaved: 10,985 km (2000)
country comparison to the world: 56

Waterways: 1,100 km (2012)
country comparison to the world: 66

Ports and terminals: *river port(s):* Termiz (Amu Darya)

MILITARY AND SECURITY

Military and security forces: Armed Forces of Uzbekistan: Army, Air and Air Defense Forces; National Guard; Ministry of Internal Affairs: Internal Security Troops, Border Guards, police (2022)
note: the National Guard, also under the Ministry of Defense, ensures public order and security of diplomatic missions, radio and television broadcasting, and other state entities

Military expenditures: 2.8% of GDP (2019 est.) (approximately $3 billion)
2.9% of GDP (2018 est.) (approximately $2.88 billion)
2.7% of GDP (2017 est.) (approximately $2.65 billion)
2.5% of GDP (2016 est.) (approximately $2.49 billion)
2.5% of GDP (2015 est.) (approximately $2.4 billion)
country comparison to the world: 35

Military and security service personnel strengths: information varies; approximately 60,000 active duty troops, including 10-15,000 Air Force (2022)

Military equipment inventories and acquisitions: the Uzbek Armed Forces use mainly Soviet-era equipment; since 2010, Russia has been the leading supplier of arms, followed by China (2022)

Military service age and obligation: 18-27 years of age for compulsory military service; 12-month conscript service obligation for men (those conscripted have the option of paying for a shorter service of 1 month while remaining in the reserves until the age of 27); Uzbek citizens who have completed their service terms in the armed forces have privileges in employment and admission to higher educational institutions (2022)

Military - note: the Uzbek armed forces were established in January 1992, following the dissolution of the Soviet Union, when the newly-established Ministry for Defense Affairs assumed jurisdiction over all former Soviet ground, air, and air defense units, formations, and installations then deployed on its soil; the building hosting the headquarters for the ex-Soviet Turkestan Military District became the headquarters for the Uzbek armed forces; all former Soviet troops departed Uzbekistan by 1995; as of 2022, Uzbekistan continued to maintain bilateral defense ties with Russia based on a 2005 mutual security agreement

as of 2022, Uzbekistan was not part of the Russian-sponsored Collective Security Treaty Organization (CSTO) that is comprised of former Soviet Republics; Uzbekistan joined in the 1990s but withdrew in 1999; it returned in 2006 but left again in 2012

TERRORISM

Terrorist group(s): Islamic Jihad Union; Islamic Movement of Uzbekistan; Islamic State of Iraq and ash-Sham - Khorasan (ISIS-K)

TRANSNATIONAL ISSUES

Disputes - international: *Uzbekistan-Afghanistan:* none identified
Uzbekistan-Kazakhstan: field demarcation of the boundaries with Kazakhstan commenced in 2004; disputed territory is held by Uzbekistan but the overwhelming majority of residents are ethnic Kazakhs; the two countries agreed on draft final demarcation documents in March 2022 and plan to hold another meeting in April 2022
Uzbekistan-Kyrgyzstan: border delimitation of 130 km of border with Kyrgyzstan is hampered by serious disputes around enclaves and other areas; in 2021, border talks between Uzbek and Kyrgyz officials raised the possibility of a land swap arrangement, but a deal was not finalized
Uzbekistan-Tajikistan: none identified
Uzbekistan-Turkmenistan: prolonged drought and cotton monoculture in Uzbekistan and Turkmenistan created water-sharing difficulties for Amu Darya river states; in 2021, the two countries reached an agreement to create a joint intergovernmental commission to oversee water management

Refugees and internally displaced persons: *stateless persons:* 59,136 (mid-year 2021)

Trafficking in persons: *current situation:* Uzbekistan is a source country for men, women, and children subjected to forced labor and women and children subjected to sex trafficking; adults are victims of government-organized forced labor during Uzbekistan's annual cotton harvest; local officials in some instances force teachers, students (including children), private businesses employees, and others to work in construction and other forms of non-cotton agriculture and to clean parks, streets, and buildings; traffickers exploit Uzbek women and children in sex trafficking in the Middle East, Eurasia, and Asia, and internally in brothels, clubs, and private residences; traffickers subject Uzbek men, and to a lesser extent women, to forced labor in Kazakhstan, Russia, Moldova, Turkey, and in other Asian, Middle Eastern, and European countries in the construction, oil and gas, agricultural, retail, and food sectors
tier rating: Tier 2 Watch List — Uzbekistan does not fully comply with the minimum standards for the elimination of trafficking but is making significant efforts to do so; government efforts included addressing the use of forced adult labor during the cotton harvest by increasing pay to laborers and improving working conditions for voluntary workers and ceasing the forced use of students, teachers, and health care workers; third-party monitors were allowed access to the harvest to view changes; the government created a National Commission on Trafficking chaired by the regional governor in every area of the country; however, reports continued of corrupt officials requiring public sector employees to pick cotton or pay for a replacement worker with extorted penalties paid to them; fewer cases of traffickers were investigated and prosecuted, fewer victims of trafficking were identified, and fewer convictions carried a prison sentence; authorities conducted no investigations against corrupt officials extorting money during the cotton harvest (2020)

Illicit drugs: transit country for Afghan opium and heroin destined for Russia and the European Union; also transit country for hashish, cannabis products, New Psychoactive Substances (NPS), and synthetic drugs; cannabis and poppy are cultivated in small amounts for personal use and local sale

VANUATU

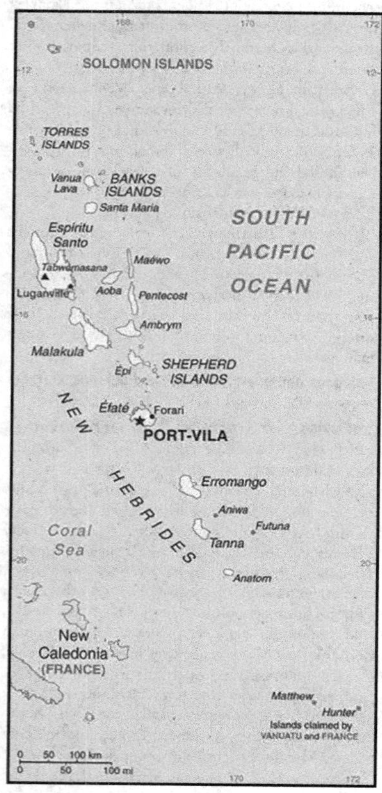

INTRODUCTION

Background: Vanuatu was first settled around 2000 B.C. by Austronesian speakers from Solomon Islands. By around 1000, localized chieftain systems began to develop on the islands. In the mid-1400s, the Kuwae Volcano erupted, causing frequent conflict and internal strife amid declining food availability, especially on Efate Island. Around 1600, Chief ROI MATA united Efate under his rule. In 1606, Portuguese explorer Pedro Fernandes de QUEIROS was the first European to see the Banks Islands and Espiritu Santo, setting up a short-lived settlement on the latter. The next European explorers arrived in the 1760s, and in 1774, British navigator James COOK named the islands the New Hebrides. The islands were frequented by whalers in the 1800s and interest in harvesting the islands' sandalwood trees caused conflict between Europeans and local Ni-Vanuatu. Catholic and Protestant missionaries arrived in the 1840s but faced difficulties converting the locals. In the 1860s, European planters in Australia, Fiji, New Caledonia, and Samoa needed labor and kidnapped almost half the adult males of the islands and forced them to work as indentured servants.

With growing and overlapping interests in the islands, France and the UK agreed that the New Hebrides would be neutral in 1878 and established a joint naval commission in 1887. In 1906, the two countries created the British-French Condominium to jointly administer the islands and they established separate laws, police forces, currencies, and education and health systems. The condominium arrangement was dysfunctional and the UK used France's defeat to Germany in World War II to assert greater control over the islands. As Japan pushed into Melanesia, the US stationed up to 50,000 soldiers in Vanuatu to prevent further advances. In 1945, US troops withdrew and sold their equipment, leading to the rise of political and religious cargo cults, such as the John Frum movement.

The France-UK condominium was reestablished after World War II. The UK was interested in moving the condominium toward independence in the 1960s, but France was hesitant and political parties agitating independence began to form, largely divided along linguistic lines. France eventually relented and elections were held in 1974 with independence granted in 1980 as Vanuatu under English-speaking Prime Minister Walter LINI. At independence, the Nagriamel Movement, with support from French-speaking landowners, declared Espiritu Santo independent, but the short-lived state was dissolved 12 weeks later. Linguistic divisions have lessened over time but highly fractious political parties have led to weak coalition governments that require support from both Anglophone and Francophone parties. Since 2008, prime ministers have been ousted through no-confidence motions or temporary procedural issues 10 times.

GEOGRAPHY

Location: Oceania, group of islands in the South Pacific Ocean, about three-quarters of the way from Hawaii to Australia

Geographic coordinates: 16 00 S, 167 00 E

Map references: Oceania

Area: *total:* 12,189 sq km
land: 12,189 sq km
water: 0 sq km
note: includes more than 80 islands, about 65 of which are inhabited
country comparison to the world: 162

Area - comparative: slightly larger than Connecticut

Land boundaries: *total:* 0 km

Coastline: 2,528 km

Maritime claims: *territorial sea:* 12 nm
contiguous zone: 24 nm
exclusive economic zone: 200 nm
continental shelf: 200 nm or to the edge of the continental margin
measured from claimed archipelagic baselines

Climate: tropical; moderated by southeast trade winds from May to October; moderate rainfall from November to April; may be affected by cyclones from December to April

Terrain: mostly mountainous islands of volcanic origin; narrow coastal plains

Elevation: *highest point:* Tabwemasana 1,877 m
lowest point: Pacific Ocean 0 m

Natural resources: manganese, hardwood forests, fish

Land use: *agricultural land:* 15.3% (2018 est.)
arable land: 1.6% (2018 est.)
permanent crops: 10.3% (2018 est.)
permanent pasture: 3.4% (2018 est.)
forest: 36.1% (2018 est.)
other: 48.6% (2018 est.)

Irrigated land: 0 sq km (2012)

Population distribution: three-quarters of the population lives in rural areas; the urban populace lives primarily in two cities, Port-Vila and Lugenville; three largest islands - Espiritu Santo, Malakula, and Efate - accomodate over half of the populace

Natural hazards: tropical cyclones (January to April); volcanic eruption on Aoba (Ambae) island began on 27 November 2005, volcanism also causes minor earthquakes; tsunamis
volcanism: significant volcanic activity with multiple eruptions in recent years; Yasur (361 m), one of the world's most active volcanoes, has experienced continuous activity in recent centuries; other historically active volcanoes include Aoba, Ambrym, Epi, Gaua, Kuwae, Lopevi, Suretamatai, and Traitor's Head

Geography - note: a Y-shaped chain of four main islands and 80 smaller islands; several of the islands have active volcanoes and there are several underwater volcanoes as well

PEOPLE AND SOCIETY

Population: 308,043 (2022 est.)
country comparison to the world: 179

Nationality: *noun:* Ni-Vanuatu (singular and plural)
adjective: Ni-Vanuatu

Ethnic groups: Melanesian 99.2%, non-Melanesian 0.8% (2016 est.)

Languages: local languages (more than 100) 63.2%, Bislama (official; creole) 33.7%, English (official) 2%, French (official) 0.6%, other 0.5% (2009 est.)

Religions: Protestant 70% (includes Presbyterian 27.9%, Anglican 15.1%, Seventh Day Adventist 12.5%, Assemblies of God 4.7%, Church of Christ 4.5%, Neil Thomas Ministry 3.1%, and Apostolic 2.2%), Roman Catholic 12.4%, customary beliefs 3.7% (including Jon Frum cargo cult), other 12.6%, none 1.1%, unspecified 0.2% (2009 est.)

Age structure: *0-14 years:* 33.65% (male 51,267/female 49,111)
15-24 years: 19.99% (male 29,594/female 30,050)
25-54 years: 36.09% (male 52,529/female 55,130)
55-64 years: 5.89% (male 8,666/female 8,904)
65 years and over: 4.39% (male 6,518/female 6,564) (2020 est.)

Dependency ratios: *total dependency ratio:* 72.5
youth dependency ratio: 66.2
elderly dependency ratio: 12.3
potential support ratio: 8.1 (2020 est.)

Median age: *total:* 23 years
male: 22.6 years
female: 23.5 years (2020 est.)
country comparison to the world: 179

Population growth rate: 1.63% (2022 est.)
country comparison to the world: 61

Birth rate: 21.57 births/1,000 population (2022 est.)
country comparison to the world: 61

Death rate: 3.98 deaths/1,000 population (2022 est.)
country comparison to the world: 214

Net migration rate: -1.3 migrant(s)/1,000 population (2022 est.)
country comparison to the world: 152

Population distribution: three-quarters of the population lives in rural areas; the urban populace lives primarily in two cities, Port-Vila and Lugenville; three largest islands - Espiritu Santo, Malakula, and Efate - accomodate over half of the populace

Urbanization: *urban population:* 25.8% of total population (2022)
rate of urbanization: 2.55% annual rate of change (2020-25 est.)

Major urban areas - population: 53,000 PORT-VILA (capital) (2018)

Sex ratio: *at birth:* 1.05 male(s)/female
0-14 years: 1.04 male(s)/female
15-24 years: 0.98 male(s)/female
25-54 years: 0.95 male(s)/female
55-64 years: 0.96 male(s)/female
65 years and over: 0.91 male(s)/female
total population: 0.99 male(s)/female (2022 est.)

Maternal mortality ratio: 72 deaths/100,000 live births (2017 est.)
country comparison to the world: 82

Infant mortality rate: *total:* 14.34 deaths/1,000 live births
male: 15.76 deaths/1,000 live births
female: 12.86 deaths/1,000 live births (2022 est.)
country comparison to the world: 105

Life expectancy at birth: *total population:* 75.14 years
male: 73.45 years
female: 76.91 years (2022 est.)
country comparison to the world: 129

Total fertility rate: 2.66 children born/woman (2022 est.)
country comparison to the world: 62

Contraceptive prevalence rate: 49% (2013)

Drinking water source: *improved: urban:* 100% of population
rural: 89.7% of population
total: 92.3% of population
unimproved: urban: 0% of population
rural: 10.3% of population
total: 7.7% of population (2020 est.)

Current health expenditure: 3.4% of GDP (2019)

Physicians density: 0.17 physicians/1,000 population (2016)

Sanitation facility access: *improved: urban:* 91.1% of population
rural: 60.4% of population
total: 68.2% of population
unimproved: urban: 8.9% of population
rural: 39.6% of population
total: 31.8% of population (2020 est.)

Major infectious diseases: *degree of risk:* high (2020)
food or waterborne diseases: bacterial diarrhea
vectorborne diseases: malaria

Obesity - adult prevalence rate: 25.2% (2016)
country comparison to the world: 52

Alcohol consumption per capita: *total:* 1.6 liters of pure alcohol (2019 est.)
beer: 0.34 liters of pure alcohol (2019 est.)
wine: 0.39 liters of pure alcohol (2019 est.)
spirits: 0.87 liters of pure alcohol (2019 est.)
other alcohols: 0 liters of pure alcohol (2019 est.)
country comparison to the world: 136

Tobacco use: *total:* 17.8% (2020 est.)
male: 33% (2020 est.)
female: 2.6% (2020 est.)
country comparison to the world: 94

Children under the age of 5 years underweight: 11.7% (2013)
country comparison to the world: 51

Education expenditures: 2.3% of GDP (2020 est.)
country comparison to the world: 174

Literacy: *definition:* age 15 and over can read and write
total population: 87.5%
male: 88.3%
female: 86.7% (2018)

Unemployment, youth ages 15-24: *total:* 18%
male: 16.1%
female: 20.1% (2019 est.)

ENVIRONMENT

Environment - current issues: population growth; water pollution, most of the population does not have access to a reliable supply of potable water; inadequate sanitation; deforestation

Environment - international agreements: *party to:* Antarctic-Marine Living Resources, Biodiversity, Climate Change, Climate Change-Kyoto Protocol, Climate Change-Paris Agreement, Comprehensive Nuclear Test Ban, Desertification, Endangered Species, Hazardous Wastes, Law of the Sea, Marine Dumping-London Convention, Marine Dumping-London Protocol, Ozone Layer Protection, Ship Pollution, Wetlands
signed, but not ratified: none of the selected agreements

Air pollutants: *particulate matter emissions:* 10.31 micrograms per cubic meter (2016 est.)
carbon dioxide emissions: 0.15 megatons (2016 est.)
methane emissions: 0.5 megatons (2020 est.)

Climate: tropical; moderated by southeast trade winds from May to October; moderate rainfall from November to April; may be affected by cyclones from December to April

Land use: *agricultural land:* 15.3% (2018 est.)
arable land: 1.6% (2018 est.)
permanent crops: 10.3% (2018 est.)
permanent pasture: 3.4% (2018 est.)
forest: 36.1% (2018 est.)
other: 48.6% (2018 est.)

Urbanization: *urban population:* 25.8% of total population (2022)
rate of urbanization: 2.55% annual rate of change (2020-25 est.)

Revenue from forest resources: *forest revenues:* 0.54% of GDP (2018 est.)
country comparison to the world: 64

Revenue from coal: *coal revenues:* 0% of GDP (2018 est.)
country comparison to the world: 185

Waste and recycling: *municipal solid waste generated annually:* 70,225 tons (2012 est.)
municipal solid waste recycled annually: 25,983 tons (2013 est.)
percent of municipal solid waste recycled: 37% (2013 est.)

Total renewable water resources: 10 billion cubic meters (2017 est.)

GOVERNMENT

Country name: *conventional long form:* Republic of Vanuatu
conventional short form: Vanuatu
local long form: Ripablik blong Vanuatu
local short form: Vanuatu
former: New Hebrides
etymology: derived from the words "vanua" (home or land) and "tu" (stand) that occur in several of the Austonesian languages spoken on the islands and which provide a meaning of "the land remains" but which also convey a sense of "independence" or "our land"

Government type: parliamentary republic

Capital: *name:* Port-Vila (on Efate)
geographic coordinates: 17 44 S, 168 19 E
time difference: UTC+11 (16 hours ahead of Washington, DC, during Standard Time)
etymology: there are two possibilities for the origin of the name: early European settlers were Portuguese and "vila" means "village or town" in Portuguese, hence "Port-Vila" would mean "Port Town"; alternatively, the site of the capital is referred to as "Efil" or "Ifira" in native languages, "Vila" is a likely corruption of these names

Administrative divisions: 6 provinces; Malampa, Penama, Sanma, Shefa, Tafea, Torba

Independence: 30 July 1980 (from France and the UK)

National holiday: Independence Day, 30 July (1980)

Constitution: *history:* draft completed August 1979, finalized by constitution conference 19 September 1979, ratified by French and British Governments 23 October 1979, effective 30 July 1980 at independence
amendments: proposed by the prime minister or by the Parliament membership; passage requires at least two-thirds majority vote by Parliament in special session with at least three fourths of the membership; passage of amendments affecting the national and official languages, or the electoral and parliamentary system also requires approval in a referendum; amended several times, last in 2013

Legal system: mixed legal system of English common law, French law, and customary law

International law organization participation: has not submitted an ICJ jurisdiction declaration; accepts ICCt jurisdiction

Citizenship: *citizenship by birth:* no
citizenship by descent only: both parents must be citizens of Vanuatu; in the case of only one parent, it must be the father who is a citizen
dual citizenship recognized: no
residency requirement for naturalization: 10 years

Suffrage: 18 years of age; universal

Executive branch: *chief of state:* President Nikenike VUROBARAVU (since 23 July 2022)
head of government: Prime Minister Ishmael KALSAKAU (since 4 November 2022)
cabinet: Council of Ministers appointed by the prime minister, responsible to Parliament

elections/appointments: president indirectly elected by an electoral college consisting of Parliament and presidents of the 6 provinces; Vanuatu president serves a 5-year term; election last held on 23 July 2022 (next to be held in 2027); following legislative elections, the leader of the majority party or majority coalition usually elected prime minister by Parliament from among its members; election for prime minister last held on 20 April 2020 (next to be held following general elections in 2024)
election results:
Nikenike VUROBARAVU elected president in the eighth round on 23 July 2022 with 48 votes; Ishmael KALSAKAU (UMP) elected prime minister on 4 November 2022 with 50 votes

Legislative branch: *description:* unicameral Parliament (52 seats; members directly elected in 8 single-seat and 9 multi-seat constituencies by single non-transferable vote to serve 4-year terms (candidates in multi-seat constituencies can be elected with only 4% of the vote)
elections:
last held on 13 October 2022 (next to be held in 2026)
election results:
percent of vote by party - NA; seats by party - UMP 7, VP 7, LPV 5, RMC 5, GJP 4, NUP 4, RDP 4, IG 3, PPP 2, VNDP 2, NAG 1, VLM 1, other 6, independent 1; composition - men 51, women 1; percent of women 2%; note - political party associations are fluid
note: the National Council of Chiefs advises on matters of culture and language

Judicial branch: *highest court(s):* Court of Appeal (consists of 2 or more judges of the Supreme Court designated by the chief justice); Supreme Court (consists of the chief justice and 6 puisne judges - 3 local and 3 expatriate)
judge selection and term of office: Supreme Court chief justice appointed by the president after consultation with the prime minister and the leader of the opposition; other judges appointed by the president on the advice of the Judicial Service Commission, a 4-member advisory body; judges serve until the age of retirement
subordinate courts: Magistrates Courts; Island Courts

Political parties and leaders: Green Confederation or GC [Moana CARCASSES Kalosil]
Iauko Group or IG [Tony NARI]
Land and Justice Party (Graon mo Jastis Pati) or GJP [Ralph REGENVANU]
Melanesian Progressive Party or MPP [Barak SOPE]
Nagriamel Movement or NAG [Frankie STEVENS]
Natatok Indigenous People's Democratic Party or (NATATOK) or NIPDP [Alfred Roland CARLOT]
National United Party or NUP [Ham LINI]
People's Progressive Party or PPP [Sato KILMAN]
People's Service Party or PSP [Don KEN]
Reunification of Movement for Change or RMC [Charlot SALWAI]
Rural Development Party or RDP [Jay NGWELE, spokesman]
Union of Moderate Parties or UMP [Alatoi Ishmael KALSAKAU]
Vanua'aku Pati (Our Land Party) or VP [Bob LOUGHMAN]
Vanuatu Democratic Party [Maxime Carlot KORMAN]
Vanuatu First or Vanuatu [Russel NARI]
Vanuatu Liberal Democratic Party or VLDP [Tapangararua WILLIE]
Vanuatu Liberal Movement or VLM [Gaetan PIKIOUNE]
Vanuatu National Development Party or VNDP [Robert Bohn SIKOL]
Vanuatu National Party or VNP [Issac HAMARILIU]
Vanuatu Republican Party or VRP [Marcellino PIPITE]

International organization participation: ACP, ADB, AOSIS, C, FAO, G-77, IBRD, ICAO, ICRM, IDA, IFC, IFRCS, ILO, IMF, IMO, IMSO, IOC, IOM, ITU, ITUC (NGOs), MIGA, NAM, OAS (observer), OIF, OPCW, PIF, Sparteca, SPC, UN, UNCTAD, UNESCO, UNIDO, UNWTO, UPU, WCO, WFTU (NGOs), WHO, WIPO, WMO, WTO

Diplomatic representation in the US: *chief of mission:* Ambassador Odo TEVI (since 8 September 2014) note - also Permanent Representative to the UN
telephone: [1] (212) 661-4303
FAX: [1] (212) 422-3427
email address and website: email - vanunmis@aol.com
web address - https://www.un.int/vanuatu/
embassy: 800 Second Avenue, Suite 400B, New York, NY 10017
note - the Vanuatu Permanent Mission to the UN serves as the embassy

Diplomatic representation from the US: *embassy:* the US does not have an embassy in Vanuatu; the US Ambassador to Papua New Guinea is accredited to Vanuatu

Flag description: two equal horizontal bands of red (top) and green with a black isosceles triangle (based on the hoist side) all separated by a black-edged yellow stripe in the shape of a horizontal Y (the two points of the Y face the hoist side and enclose the triangle); centered in the triangle is a boar's tusk encircling two crossed namele fern fronds, all in yellow; red represents the blood of boars and men, as well as unity, green the richness of the islands, and black the ni-Vanuatu people; the yellow Y-shape - which reflects the pattern of the islands in the Pacific Ocean - symbolizes the light of the Gospel spreading through the islands; the boar's tusk is a symbol of prosperity frequently worn as a pendant on the islands; the fern fronds represent peace
note: one of several flags where a prominent component of the design reflects the shape of the country; other such flags are those of Bosnia and Herzegovina, Brazil, and Eritrea

National symbol(s): boar's tusk with crossed fern fronds; national colors: red, black, green, yellow

National anthem: *name:* "Yumi, Yumi, Yumi" (We, We, We)
lyrics/music: Francois Vincent AYSSAV
note: adopted 1980; the anthem is written in Bislama, a Creole language that mixes Pidgin English and French

National heritage: *total World Heritage Sites:* 1 (cultural)
selected World Heritage Site locales: Chief Roi Mata's Domain

ECONOMY

Economic overview: This South Pacific island economy is based primarily on small-scale agriculture, which provides a living for about two thirds of the population. Fishing, offshore financial services, and tourism, with more than 330,000 visitors in 2017, are other mainstays of the economy. Tourism has struggled after Efate, the most populous and most popular island for tourists, was damaged by Tropical Cyclone Pam in 2015. Ongoing infrastructure difficulties at Port Vila's Bauerfield Airport have caused air travel disruptions, further hampering tourism numbers. Australia and New Zealand are the main source of tourists and foreign aid. A small light industry sector caters to the local market. Tax revenues come mainly from import duties. Mineral deposits are negligible; the country has no known petroleum deposits.

Economic development is hindered by dependence on relatively few commodity exports, vulnerability to natural disasters, and long distances from main markets and between constituent islands. In response to foreign concerns, the government has promised to tighten regulation of its offshore financial center.

Since 2002, the government has stepped up efforts to boost tourism through improved air connections, resort development, and cruise ship facilities. Agriculture, especially livestock farming, is a second target for growth.

Real GDP (purchasing power parity): $850 million (2020 est.)
$930 million (2019 est.)
$910 million (2018 est.)
note: data are in 2017 dollars
country comparison to the world: 207

Real GDP growth rate: 4.2% (2017 est.)
3.5% (2016 est.)
0.2% (2015 est.)
country comparison to the world: 70

Real GDP per capita: $2,800 (2020 est.)
$3,100 (2019 est.)
$3,100 (2018 est.)
note: data are in 2017 dollars
country comparison to the world: 199

GDP (official exchange rate): $870 million (2017 est.)

Inflation rate (consumer prices): 3.1% (2017 est.)
0.8% (2016 est.)
country comparison to the world: 148

GDP - composition, by sector of origin: *agriculture:* 27.3% (2017 est.)
industry: 11.8% (2017 est.)
services: 60.8% (2017 est.)

GDP - composition, by end use: *household consumption:* 59.9% (2017 est.)
government consumption: 17.4% (2017 est.)
investment in fixed capital: 28.7% (2017 est.)
investment in inventories: 0% (2017 est.)
exports of goods and services: 42.5% (2017 est.)
imports of goods and services: -48.5% (2017 est.)

Agricultural products: coconuts, roots/tubers nes, bananas, vegetables, pork, fruit, milk, beef, groundnuts, cocoa

Industries: food and fish freezing, wood processing, meat canning

Industrial production growth rate: 4.5% (2017 est.)
country comparison to the world: 68

Labor force: 115,900 (2007 est.)
country comparison to the world: 181

Labor force - by occupation: *agriculture:* 65%
industry: 5%

services: 30% (2000 est.)

Unemployment rate: 1.7% (1999 est.)
country comparison to the world: 17

Unemployment, youth ages 15-24: *total:* 18%
male: 16.1%
female: 20.1% (2019 est.)
country comparison to the world: 89

Gini Index coefficient - distribution of family income: 37.6 (2010 est.)
country comparison to the world: 78

Budget: *revenues:* 236.7 million (2017 est.)
expenditures: 244.1 million (2017 est.)

Budget surplus (+) or deficit (-): -0.9% (of GDP) (2017 est.)
country comparison to the world: 73

Public debt: 48.4% of GDP (2017 est.)
46.1% of GDP (2016 est.)
country comparison to the world: 107

Taxes and other revenues: 27.2% (of GDP) (2017 est.)
country comparison to the world: 102

Fiscal year: calendar year

Current account balance: -$13 million (2017 est.)
-$37 million (2016 est.)
country comparison to the world: 70

Exports: $380 million (2019 est.) note: data are in current year dollars
$520 million (2018 est.) note: data are in current year dollars
country comparison to the world: 196

Exports - partners: Japan 33%, Thailand 13%, Mauritania 13%, South Korea 11%, China 9%, Fiji 7% (2019)

Exports - commodities: fish and fish products, tug boats, perfume plants, mollusks, cocoa beans (2019)

Imports: $460 million (2019 est.) note: data are in current year dollars
$460 million (2018 est.) note: data are in current year dollars
country comparison to the world: 203

Imports - partners: China 29%, Australia 18%, New Zealand 11%, Fiji 11%, Taiwan 5%, Thailand 5% (2019)

Imports - commodities: refined petroleum, fishing ships, delivery trucks, poultry meats, broadcasting equipment (2019)

Reserves of foreign exchange and gold: $395.1 million (31 December 2017 est.)
$267.4 million (31 December 2016 est.)
country comparison to the world: 160

Debt - external: $200.5 million (31 December 2017 est.)
$182.5 million (31 December 2016 est.)
country comparison to the world: 188

Exchange rates: vatu (VUV) per US dollar -
111.015 (2020 est.)
117.035 (2019 est.)
113.005 (2018 est.)
108.99 (2014 est.)
97.07 (2013 est.)

ENERGY

Electricity access: *electrification - total population:* 61.8% (2018)
electrification - urban areas: 93.7% (2018)
electrification - rural areas: 51.1% (2018)

Electricity: *installed generating capacity:* 35,000 kW (2020 est.)
consumption: 62.926 million kWh (2019 est.)
exports: 0 kWh (2020 est.)
imports: 0 kWh (2020 est.)
transmission/distribution losses: 5 million kWh (2019 est.)

Electricity generation sources: *fossil fuels:* 84.5% of total installed capacity (2020 est.)
solar: 8.2% of total installed capacity (2020 est.)
wind: 7.4% of total installed capacity (2020 est.)

Petroleum: *total petroleum production:* 0 bbl/day (2021 est.)
refined petroleum consumption: 1,500 bbl/day (2019 est.)

Refined petroleum products - production: 0 bbl/day (2015 est.)
country comparison to the world: 213

Refined petroleum products - exports: 0 bbl/day (2015 est.)
country comparison to the world: 215

Refined petroleum products - imports: 1,073 bbl/day (2015 est.)
country comparison to the world: 200

Carbon dioxide emissions: 225,000 metric tonnes of CO2 (2019 est.)
from petroleum and other liquids: 225,000 metric tonnes of CO2 (2019 est.)
country comparison to the world: 201

Energy consumption per capita: 10.878 million Btu/person (2019 est.)
country comparison to the world: 153

COMMUNICATIONS

Telephones - fixed lines: *total subscriptions:* 3,472 (2020 est.)
subscriptions per 100 inhabitants: 1 (2020 est.)
country comparison to the world: 207

Telephones - mobile cellular: *total subscriptions:* 265,219 (2019)
subscriptions per 100 inhabitants: 88.44 (2019)
country comparison to the world: 180

Telecommunication systems: *general assessment:* for many years, GSM was the primary mobile technology for Vanuatu's 300,000 people; recent infrastructure projects have improved access technologies, with a transition to 3G and, to a limited degree, to LTE; Vanuatu has also benefited from the ICN1 submarine cable and the launch of the Kacific-1 satellite, both of which have considerably improved access to telecom services in recent years; Vanuatu's telecom sector is liberalized, with the two prominent mobile operators; while fixed broadband penetration remains low, the incumbent operator is slowly exchanging copper fixed-lines for fiber; a number of ongoing submarine cable developments will also assist in increasing data rates and reduce internet pricing in coming years (2021)
domestic: fixed-line teledensity a bit over 1 per 100 and mobile-cellular just over 80 per 100 (2020)
international: country code - 678; landing points for the ICN1 & ICN2 submarine cables providing connectivity to the Solomon Islands and Fiji; cables helped end-users with Internet bandwidth; satellite earth station - 1 Intelsat (Pacific Ocean) (2020)

Broadcast media: 1 state-owned TV station; multi-channel pay TV is available; state-owned Radio Vanuatu operates 2 radio stations; 2 privately owned radio broadcasters; programming from multiple international broadcasters is available

Internet country code: .vu

Internet users: *total:* 77,969 (2019 est.)
percent of population: 26% (2019 est.)
country comparison to the world: 183

Broadband - fixed subscriptions: *total:* 2,785 (2020 est.)
subscriptions per 100 inhabitants: 1 (2020 est.)
country comparison to the world: 194

TRANSPORTATION

National air transport system: *number of registered air carriers:* 1 (2020)
inventory of registered aircraft operated by air carriers: 8
annual passenger traffic on registered air carriers: 374,603 (2018)
annual freight traffic on registered air carriers: 1.66 million (2018) mt-km

Civil aircraft registration country code prefix: YJ

Airports: *total:* 31 (2021)
country comparison to the world: 113

Airports - with paved runways: *total:* 3
2,438 to 3,047 m: 1
1,524 to 2,437 m: 1
914 to 1,523 m: 1 (2021)

Airports - with unpaved runways: *total:* 28
914 to 1,523 m: 7
under 914 m: 21 (2021)

Roadways: *total:* 1,070 km (2000)
*paved:*256 km (2000)
*unpaved:*814 km (2000)
country comparison to the world: 184

Merchant marine: *total:* 306
by type: bulk carrier 18, container ship 2, general cargo 55, oil tanker 2, other 229 (2021)
country comparison to the world: 53

Ports and terminals: *major seaport(s):* Forari Bay, Luganville (Santo, Espiritu Santo), Port-Vila

MILITARY AND SECURITY

Military and security forces: no regular military forces; Ministry of Internal Affairs: Vanuatu Police Force (VPF; includes Vanuatu Mobile Force (VMF) and Police Maritime Wing (VPMW)) (2022)
note: the paramilitary Vanuatu Mobile Force also has external security responsibilities

Military - note: the separate British and French police forces were unified in 1980 under Ni-Vanuatu officers as the New Hebrides Constabulary; the force retained some British and French officers as advisors; the Constabulary was subsequently renamed the Vanuatu Police Force later in 1980

the Vanuatu Mobile Force has received training and other support from Australia, China, France, New Zealand, and the US

Vanuatu has a "shiprider" agreement with the US, which allows local maritime law enforcement officers to embark on US Coast Guard (USCG) and US Navy (USN) vessels, including to board and search vessels suspected of violating laws or regulations within Vanuatu's designated exclusive economic zone (EEZ) or on the high seas; "shiprider" agreements also enable USCG personnel and USN vessels with embarked USCG law enforcement personnel to work with host nations to protect critical regional resources (2022)

TRANSNATIONAL ISSUES

Disputes - international: *Vanuatu-France:* Matthew and Hunter Islands, two uninhabited islands east of New Caledonia, claimed by Vanuatu and France; in January 2019, a French naval mission landed officers on the islands to reinforce France's sovereignty; in November 2021, French vessels fishing near the islands raised tensions

VENEZUELA

INTRODUCTION

Background: Venezuela was one of three countries that emerged from the collapse of Gran Colombia in 1830 (the others being Ecuador and New Granada, which became Colombia). For most of the first half of the 20th century, Venezuela was ruled by military strongmen who promoted the oil industry and allowed for some social reforms. Although democratically elected governments largely held sway since 1959, the executive branch under Hugo CHAVEZ, president from 1999 to 2013, exercised increasingly authoritarian control over other branches of government. This undemocratic trend continued in 2018 when Nicolas MADURO claimed the presidency for his second term in an election boycotted by most opposition parties and widely viewed as fraudulent.

The last democratically-elected institution is the 2015 National Assembly. The president of the 2015 National Assembly, Juan GUAIDO is currently recognized by several countries - including the United States - as the interim president of Venezuela, while MADURO is recognized by most countries. In 2020, legislative elections were held for a new National Assembly, which the opposition boycotted and which were widely condemned as fraudulent. The resulting assembly is viewed by GUAIDO, most opposition parties, and many international actors as illegitimate. In November 2021, most opposition parties broke a three-year election boycott to participate in mayoral and gubernatorial elections, despite flawed conditions. As a result, the opposition more than doubled its representation at the mayoral level and retained four of 23 governorships. The 2021 regional elections marked the first time since 2006 that the EU was allowed to send an electoral observation mission to Venezuela.

The MADURO regime places strong restrictions on freedoms of expression and the press. Since CHAVEZ, the ruling party's economic policies expanded the state's role in the economy through expropriations of major enterprises, strict currency exchange and price controls that discourage private sector investment and production, and overdependence on the petroleum industry for revenues, among others. Years of economic mismanagement left Venezuela ill-prepared to weather the global drop in oil prices in 2014, sparking an economic decline that has resulted in reduced government social spending, shortages of basic goods, and high inflation. Worsened living conditions have prompted over 6 million Venezuelans to migrate, mainly settling in nearby countries. Since 2017, the US has imposed financial and sectoral sanctions on the MADURO regime. Since mid-2020, and despite MADURO regime mismanagement and faltering infrastructure, oil production has begun to rise primarily due to strengthened MADURO regime trade relations with China, Russia, Iran, and the illicit oil trade. Caracas has more recently relaxed some economic controls to mitigate the impact of its sustained economic crisis, such as allowing increased currency and liberalizing import flexibility for private citizens and companies. Other concerns include human rights abuses, rampant violent crime, political manipulation of the judicial and electoral systems, and corruption.

GEOGRAPHY

Location: Northern South America, bordering the Caribbean Sea and the North Atlantic Ocean, between Colombia and Guyana

Geographic coordinates: 8 00 N, 66 00 W

Map references: South America

Area: *total:* 912,050 sq km
land: 882,050 sq km
water: 30,000 sq km
country comparison to the world: 34

Area - comparative: almost six times the size of Georgia; slightly more than twice the size of California

Land boundaries: *total:* 5,267 km
border countries (3): Brazil 2,137 km; Colombia 2,341 km; Guyana 789 km

Coastline: 2,800 km

Maritime claims: *territorial sea:* 12 nm
contiguous zone: 15 nm
exclusive economic zone: 200 nm
continental shelf: 200-m depth or to the depth of exploitation

Climate: tropical; hot, humid; more moderate in highlands

Terrain: Andes Mountains and Maracaibo Lowlands in northwest; central plains (llanos); Guiana Highlands in southeast

Elevation: *highest point:* Pico Bolivar 4,978 m
lowest point: Caribbean Sea 0 m
mean elevation: 450 m

Natural resources: petroleum, natural gas, iron ore, gold, bauxite, other minerals, hydropower, diamonds

Land use: *agricultural land:* 24.5% (2018 est.)
arable land: 3.1% (2018 est.)
permanent crops: 0.8% (2018 est.)
permanent pasture: 20.6% (2018 est.)
forest: 52.1% (2018 est.)
other: 23.4% (2018 est.)

Irrigated land: 10,550 sq km (2012)

Major lakes (area sq km): *salt water lake(s):* Lago de Maracaibo - 13,010 sq km

Major rivers (by length in km): Rio Negro (shared with Colombia [s] and Brazil [m]) - 2,250 km; Orinoco river source and mouth (shared with Colombia) -2,101 km
note – [s] after country name indicates river source; [m] after country name indicates river mouth

Major watersheds (area sq km): Atlantic Ocean drainage: Amazon (6,145,186 sq km), Orinoco (953,675 sq km)

Population distribution: most of the population is concentrated in the northern and western highlands along an eastern spur at the northern end of the Andes, an area that includes the capital of Caracas

Natural hazards: subject to floods, rockslides, mudslides; periodic droughts

Geography - note: *note 1:* the country lies on major sea and air routes linking North and South America
note 2: Venezuela has some of the most unique geology in the world; tepuis are massive table-top mountains of the western Guiana Highlands that tend to be isolated and thus support unique endemic plant and animal species; their sheer cliffsides account for some of the most spectacular waterfalls in the world including Angel Falls, the world's highest (979 m) that drops off Auyan Tepui

PEOPLE AND SOCIETY

Population: 29,789,730 (2022 est.)
country comparison to the world: 50

Nationality: *noun:* Venezuelan(s)
adjective: Venezuelan

Ethnic groups: unspecified Spanish, Italian, Portuguese, Arab, German, African, Indigenous

Languages: Spanish (official), numerous indigenous dialects
major-language sample(s): La Libreta Informativa del Mundo, la fuente indispensable de información básica. (Spanish)

Religions: Roman Catholic 96%, Protestant 2%, other 2%

Demographic profile: Social investment in Venezuela during the CHAVEZ administration reduced poverty from nearly 50% in 1999 to about 27% in 2011, increased school enrollment, substantially decreased infant and child mortality, and improved access to potable water and sanitation through social investment. "Missions" dedicated to education, nutrition, healthcare, and sanitation were funded through petroleum revenues. The sustainability of this progress remains questionable, however, as the continuation of these social programs depends on the prosperity of Venezuela's oil industry. In the long-term, education and health care spending may increase economic growth and reduce income inequality, but rising costs and the staffing of new health care jobs with foreigners are slowing development.

While CHAVEZ was in power, more than one million predominantly middle- and upper-class Venezuelans are estimated to have emigrated. The brain drain is attributed to a repressive political system, lack of economic opportunities, steep inflation, a high crime rate, and corruption. Thousands of oil engineers emigrated to Canada, Colombia, and the United States following CHAVEZ's firing of over 20,000 employees of the state-owned petroleum company during a 2002-03 oil strike. Additionally, thousands of Venezuelans of European descent have taken up residence in their ancestral homelands. Nevertheless, Venezuela has attracted hundreds of thousands of immigrants from South America and southern Europe because of its lenient migration policy and the availability of education and health care. Venezuela also has been a fairly accommodating host to Colombian refugees, numbering about 170,000 as of year-end 2016. However, since 2014, falling oil prices have driven a major economic crisis that has pushed Venezuelans from all walks of life to migrate or to seek asylum abroad to escape severe shortages of food, water, and medicine; soaring inflation; unemployment; and violence. As of September 2022, an estimated 7.1 million Venezuelans were refugees or migrants worldwide, with almost 80% taking refuge in Latin America and the Caribbean (notably Colombia, Peru, Chile, Ecuador, Argentina, and Brazil, as well as the Dominican Republic, Aruba, and Curacao). Asylum applications increased significantly in the US and Brazil in 2016 and 2017. Several receiving countries are making efforts to increase immigration restrictions and to deport illegal Venezuelan migrants - Ecuador and Peru in August 2018 began requiring valid passports for entry, which are difficult to obtain for Venezuelans. Nevertheless, Venezuelans continue to migrate to avoid economic collapse at home.

Age structure: *0-14 years:* 25.66% (male 3,759,280/female 3,591,897)
15-24 years: 16.14% (male 2,348,073/female 2,275,912)
25-54 years: 41.26% (male 5,869,736/female 5,949,082)
55-64 years: 8.76% (male 1,203,430/female 1,305,285)
65 years and over: 8.18% (male 1,069,262/female 1,272,646) (2020 est.)

Dependency ratios: *total dependency ratio:* 54.4
youth dependency ratio: 42.1
elderly dependency ratio: 12.3
potential support ratio: 8.1 (2020 est.)

Median age: *total:* 30 years
male: 29.4 years
female: 30.7 years (2020 est.)
country comparison to the world: 124

Population growth rate: 2.43% (2022 est.)
country comparison to the world: 26

Birth rate: 17.27 births/1,000 population (2022 est.)
country comparison to the world: 91

Death rate: 6.81 deaths/1,000 population (2022 est.)
country comparison to the world: 126

Net migration rate: 13.88 migrant(s)/1,000 population (2022 est.)
country comparison to the world: 4

Population distribution: most of the population is concentrated in the northern and western highlands along an eastern spur at the northern end of the Andes, an area that includes the capital of Caracas

Urbanization: *urban population:* 88.4% of total population (2022)
rate of urbanization: 1.16% annual rate of change (2020-25 est.)

Major urban areas - population: 2.957 million CARACAS (capital), 2.333 million Maracaibo, 1.959 million Valencia, 1.241 million Barquisimeto, 1.230 million Maracay, 950,000 Ciudad Guayana (2022)

Sex ratio: *at birth:* 1.05 male(s)/female
0-14 years: 1.05 male(s)/female
15-24 years: 1.03 male(s)/female
25-54 years: 0.99 male(s)/female
55-64 years: 0.92 male(s)/female
65 years and over: 0.74 male(s)/female
total population: 0.99 male(s)/female (2022 est.)

Maternal mortality ratio: 125 deaths/100,000 live births (2017 est.)
country comparison to the world: 63

Infant mortality rate: *total:* 17.72 deaths/1,000 live births
male: 19.72 deaths/1,000 live births
female: 15.61 deaths/1,000 live births (2022 est.)
country comparison to the world: 92

Life expectancy at birth: *total population:* 73.29 years
male: 70.12 years
female: 76.62 years (2022 est.)
country comparison to the world: 147

Total fertility rate: 2.22 children born/woman (2022 est.)
country comparison to the world: 84

Contraceptive prevalence rate: 75% (2010)

Drinking water source: *improved: total:* 94.2% of population
unimproved: total: 5.8% of population (2020 est.)

Current health expenditure: 5.4% of GDP (2019)

Physicians density: 1.73 physicians/1,000 population (2017)

Hospital bed density: 0.9 beds/1,000 population (2017)

Sanitation facility access: *improved: total:* 95.8% of population
unimproved: total: 4.2% of population (2020 est.)

HIV/AIDS - adult prevalence rate: 0.5% (2020 est.)
country comparison to the world: 70

HIV/AIDS - people living with HIV/AIDS: 100,000 (2020 est.)
country comparison to the world: 44

HIV/AIDS - deaths: 4,200 (2020 est.)
country comparison to the world: 28

Major infectious diseases: *degree of risk:* high (2020)
food or waterborne diseases: bacterial diarrhea and hepatitis A
vectorborne diseases: dengue fever and malaria
note: as of 30 September 2021, the Centers for Disease Control and Prevention recommends that travelers avoid all nonessential travel to Venezuela; the country is experiencing outbreaks of infectious diseases, and adequate health care is currently not available in most of the country

Obesity - adult prevalence rate: 25.6% (2016)
country comparison to the world: 50

Alcohol consumption per capita: *total:* 2.51 liters of pure alcohol (2019 est.)
beer: 1.54 liters of pure alcohol (2019 est.)
wine: 0.01 liters of pure alcohol (2019 est.)
spirits: 0.92 liters of pure alcohol (2019 est.)
other alcohols: 0.03 liters of pure alcohol (2019 est.)
country comparison to the world: 123

Education expenditures: 1.3% of GDP (2017 est.)
country comparison to the world: 188

Literacy: *definition:* age 15 and over can read and write
total population: 97.1%
male: 97%
female: 97.2% (2016)

Unemployment, youth ages 15-24: *total:* 12.1%
male: 10.5%
female: 14.9% (2017 est.)

ENVIRONMENT

Environment - current issues: sewage pollution of Lago de Valencia; oil and urban pollution of Lago de Maracaibo; deforestation; soil degradation; urban and industrial pollution, especially along the Caribbean coast; threat to the rainforest ecosystem from irresponsible mining operations

Environment - international agreements: *party to:* Antarctic-Environmental Protection, Antarctic Treaty, Biodiversity, Climate Change, Climate Change-Kyoto Protocol, Climate Change-Paris Agreement, Comprehensive Nuclear Test Ban, Desertification, Endangered Species, Hazardous Wastes, Marine Life Conservation, Nuclear Test Ban, Ozone Layer Protection, Ship Pollution, Tropical Timber 2006, Wetlands
signed, but not ratified: none of the selected agreements

Air pollutants: *particulate matter emissions:* 15.82 micrograms per cubic meter (2016 est.)
carbon dioxide emissions: 164.18 megatons (2016 est.)
methane emissions: 68.66 megatons (2020 est.)

Climate: tropical; hot, humid; more moderate in highlands

Land use: *agricultural land:* 24.5% (2018 est.)
arable land: 3.1% (2018 est.)
permanent crops: 0.8% (2018 est.)
permanent pasture: 20.6% (2018 est.)
forest: 52.1% (2018 est.)
other: 23.4% (2018 est.)

Urbanization: *urban population:* 88.4% of total population (2022)
rate of urbanization: 1.16% annual rate of change (2020-25 est.)

Food insecurity: *widespread lack of access: due to severe economic crisis* - the national economy, highly dependent on oil production and exports, was forecast to contract in 2021 for the eighth consecutive year; with the persistent negative effects of the COVID-19 pandemic that have compounded the already severe macro-economic crisis, the access to food of the most vulnerable households is expected to deteriorate throughout 2021 and into 2022 due to widespread losses of income-generating activities and soaring food prices (2022)

Waste and recycling: *municipal solid waste generated annually:* 9,779,093 tons (2010 est.)

Major lakes (area sq km): *salt water lake(s):* Lago de Maracaibo - 13,010 sq km

Major rivers (by length in km): Rio Negro (shared with Colombia [s] and Brazil [m]) - 2,250 km; Orinoco river source and mouth (shared with Colombia) -2,101 km
note – [s] after country name indicates river source; [m] after country name indicates river mouth

Major watersheds (area sq km): Atlantic Ocean drainage: Amazon (6,145,186 sq km), Orinoco (953,675 sq km)

Total water withdrawal: *municipal:* 5.123 billion cubic meters (2017 est.)
industrial: 793.3 million cubic meters (2017 est.)
agricultural: 16.71 billion cubic meters (2017 est.)

Total renewable water resources: 1.325 trillion cubic meters (2017 est.)

GOVERNMENT

Country name: *conventional long form:* Bolivarian Republic of Venezuela
conventional short form: Venezuela
local long form: Republica Bolivariana de Venezuela
local short form: Venezuela
former: State of Venezuela, Republic of Venezuela, United States of Venezuela
etymology: native stilt-houses built on Lake Maracaibo reminded early explorers Alonso de OJEDA and Amerigo VESPUCCI in 1499 of buildings in Venice and so they named the region "Venezuola," which in Italian means "Little Venice"

Government type: federal presidential republic

Capital: *name:* Caracas
geographic coordinates: 10 29 N, 66 52 W
time difference: UTC-4 (1 hour ahead of Washington, DC, during Standard Time)
etymology: named for the native Caracas tribe that originally settled in the city's valley site near the Caribbean coast

Administrative divisions: 23 states (estados, singular - estado), 1 capital district* (distrito capital), and 1 federal dependency** (dependencia federal); Amazonas, Anzoategui, Apure, Aragua, Barinas, Bolivar, Carabobo, Cojedes, Delta Amacuro, Dependencias Federales (Federal Dependencies)**, Distrito Capital (Capital District)*, Falcon, Guarico, La Guaira, Lara, Merida, Miranda, Monagas, Nueva Esparta, Portuguesa, Sucre, Tachira, Trujillo, Yaracuy, Zulia
note: the federal dependency consists of 11 federally controlled island groups with a total of 72 individual islands

Independence: 5 July 1811 (from Spain)

National holiday: Independence Day, 5 July (1811)

Constitution: *history:* many previous; latest adopted 15 December 1999, effective 30 December 1999
amendments: proposed through agreement by at least 39% of the National Assembly membership, by the president of the republic in session with the cabinet of ministers, or by petition of at least 15% of registered voters; passage requires simple majority vote by the Assembly and simple majority approval in a referendum; amended 2009; note - in 2016, President MADURO issued a decree to hold an election to form a constituent assembly to change the constitution; the election in July 2017 approved the formation of a 545-member constituent assembly and elected its delegates, empowering them to change the constitution and dismiss government institutions and officials

Legal system: civil law system based on the Spanish civil code

International law organization participation: has not submitted an ICJ jurisdiction declaration; accepts ICCt jurisdiction

Citizenship: *citizenship by birth:* yes
citizenship by descent only: yes
dual citizenship recognized: yes
residency requirement for naturalization: 10 years; reduced to five years in the case of applicants from Spain, Portugal, Italy, or a Latin American or Caribbean country

Suffrage: 18 years of age; universal

Executive branch: *chief of state:* Notification Statement: the United States recognizes Juan GUAIDO as the Interim President of Venezuela
President Nicolas MADURO Moros (since 19 April 2013); Executive Vice President Delcy RODRIGUEZ Gomez (since 14 June 2018); note - the president is both chief of state and head of government
head of government: President Nicolas MADURO Moros (since 19 April 2013); Executive Vice President Delcy RODRIGUEZ Gomez (since 14 June 2018)
cabinet: Council of Ministers appointed by the president
elections/appointments: president directly elected by simple majority popular vote for a 6-year term (no term limits); election last held on 20 May 2018 (next election in 2024)
election results:
2018: Nicolas MADURO Moros reelected president; percent of vote - Nicolas MADURO Moros (PSUV) 68%, Henri FALCON (AP) 21%, Javier BERTUCCI 11%; note - the election was marred by serious shortcomings and electoral fraud; voter turnout was approximately 46% due largely to an opposition boycott of the election
2013: Nicolas MADURO Moros elected president; percent of vote - Nicolas MADURO Moros (PSUV) 50.6%, Henrique CAPRILES Radonski (PJ) 49.1%, other 0.3%

Legislative branch: *description:* unicameral National Assembly or Asamblea Nacional (277 seats; 3 seats reserved for indigenous peoples of Venezuela; members serve 5-year terms); note - in 2020, the National Electoral Council increased the number of seats in the National Assembly from 167 to 277 for the 6 December 2020 election
elections:
last held on 6 December 2020 (next to be held in December 2025)
election results:
percent of vote by party - GPP (pro-government) 69.32%, Democratic Alliance (opposition coalition) 17.68%, other 13%; seats by party - GPP 253, Democratic Alliance 18, indigenous peoples 3, other 3; composition - NA

Judicial branch: *highest court(s):* Supreme Tribunal of Justice (consists of 32 judges organized into constitutional, politicaladministrative, electoral, civil appeals, criminal appeals, and social divisions)
judge selection and term of office: judges proposed by the Committee of Judicial Postulation (an independent body of organizations dealing with legal issues and of the organs of citizen power) and appointed by the National Assembly; judges serve nonrenewable 12-year terms; note - in July 2017, the National Assembly named 33 judges to the court to replace a series of judges, it argued, had been illegally appointed in late 2015 by the outgoing, socialist-party-led Assembly; the Government of President MADURO and the Socialist Party-appointed judges refused to recognize these appointments, however, and many of the new judges have since been imprisoned or forced into exile
subordinate courts: Superior or Appeals Courts (Tribunales Superiores); District Tribunals (Tribunales de Distrito); Courts of First Instance (Tribunales de Primera Instancia); Parish Courts (Tribunales de Parroquia); Justices of the Peace (Justicia de Paz) Network

Political parties and leaders: A New Era or UNT [Manuel ROSALES]
Brave People's Alliance or ABP [Antonio LEDEZMA]
Cambiemos Movimiento Ciudadano or CMC [Timoteo ZAMBRANO]
Christian Democrats or COPEI [Miguel SALAZAR]
Citizens Encounter or EC [Delsa SOLORZANO]
Clear Accounts or CC [Enzo SCARENO]
Coalition of parties loyal to Nicolas MADURO - Great Patriotic Pole or GPP [Nicolas MADURO]
Coalition of opposition parties - Democratic Alliance (Alianza Democratica) (comprised of AD, EL CAMBIO, COPEI, CMC, and AP)
Come Venezuela (Vente Venezuela) or VV [Maria Corina MACHADO]
Communist Party of Venezuela or PCV [Oscar FIGUERA]
Consenso en la Zona or Conenzo [Enzo SCARANO and Leon JURADO]
Convergencia [Juan Jose CALDERA]
Democratic Action or AD [Jose Bernabe GUTIERREZ Parra]
EL CAMBIO (The Change) [Javier Alejandro BERTUCCI Carrero]
Fatherland for All (Patria para Todos) or PPT [Ilenia MEDINA]
Fuerza Vecinal or FV [leaders include mayors Gustavo DUQUE, Darwin GONZALEZ, Elias SAYEGH, Manuel FERREIRA, Josy FERNANDEZ, and Morel David RODRIGUEZ]; note - national spokesman David UZCATEGUI
Justice First (Primero Justicia) or PJ [Julio BORGES]
LAPIZ [Antonio Ecarri]
Movement to Socialism (Movimiento al Socialismo) or MAS [Segundo MELENDEZ]
Popular Will (Voluntad Popular) or VP [Leopoldo LOPEZ, Freddy SUPERLANO, and Emilio GRATERON]
Progressive Advance (Avanzada Progresista) or AP [two groups, one led by Henri FALCON and Fanny GARCIA, the other led by Luis Augusto ROMERO and Bruno GALLO]
The Radical Cause or La Causa R [Andres VELAZQUEZ]
United Socialist Party of Venezuela or PSUV [Nicolas MADURO]
Venezuela First (Primero Venezuela) or PV [Luis PARRA]

Venezuelan Progressive Movement or MPV [Simon CALZADILLA]
Venezuela Project or PV [Carlos BERRIZBEITIA]
We Are Venezuela (Somos Venezuela) or MSV [Delcy RODRIGUEZ and Vanessa MONTERO]

International organization participation: Caricom (observer), CD, CDB, CELAC, FAO, G-15, G-24, G-77, IADB, IAEA, IBRD, ICAO, ICC (national committees), ICCt (signatory), ICRM, IDA, IFAD, IFC, IFRCS, IHO, ILO, IMF, IMO, IMSO, Interpol, IOC, IOM, IPU, ITSO, ITU, ITUC (NGOs), LAES, LAIA, LAS (observer), MIGA, NAM, OAS, OPANAL, OPCW, OPEC, PCA, Petrocaribe, UN, UNASUR, UNCTAD, UNESCO, UNHCR, UNHRC, UNIDO, Union Latina, UNWTO, UPU, WCO, WFTU (NGOs), WHO, WIPO, WMO, WTO

Diplomatic representation in the US: *chief of mission:* Ambassador Carlos Alfredo VECCHIO (since 8 April 2019)
chancery: 1099 30th Street NW, Washington, DC 20007
telephone: [1] (202) 342-2214
FAX: [1] (202) 342-6820
email address and website:
despacho.embveus@mppre.gob.ve

Diplomatic representation from the US: *chief of mission:* James "Jimmy" STORY, Ambassador for the Venezuela Affairs Unit (since November 2020); note - on 11 March 2019, the Department of State announced the temporary suspension of operations of the US Embassy in Caracas and the withdrawal of diplomatic personnel; the Venezuela Affairs Unit is located at the United States Embassy in Bogota, Colombia
embassy: Venezuela Affairs Unit, Carrera 45 N. 24B-27, Bogota
previously - F St. and Suapure St.; Urb. Colinas de Valle Arriba; Caracas 1080
mailing address: 3140 Caracas Place, Washington DC 20521-3140
telephone: 1-888-407-4747
email address and website:
ACSBogota@state.gov
https://ve.usembassy.gov/

Flag description: three equal horizontal bands of yellow (top), blue, and red with the coat of arms on the hoist side of the yellow band and an arc of eight white five-pointed stars centered in the blue band; the flag retains the three equal horizontal bands and three main colors of the banner of Gran Colombia, the South American republic that broke up in 1830; yellow is interpreted as standing for the riches of the land, blue for the courage of its people, and red for the blood shed in attaining independence; the seven stars on the original flag represented the seven provinces in Venezuela that united in the war of independence; in 2006, then President Hugo CHAVEZ ordered an eighth star added to the star arc - a decision that sparked much controversy - to conform with the flag proclaimed by Simon Bolivar in 1827 and to represent the historic province of Guayana

National symbol(s): troupial (bird); national colors: yellow, blue, red

National anthem: *name:* "Gloria al bravo pueblo" (Glory to the Brave People)
lyrics/music: Vicente SALIAS/Juan Jose LANDAETA
note: adopted 1881; lyrics written in 1810, the music some years later; both SALIAS and LANDAETA were executed in 1814 during Venezuela's struggle for independence

National heritage: *total World Heritage Sites:* 3 (2 cultural, 1 natural)
selected World Heritage Site locales: Coro and its Port (c); Canaima National Park (n); Ciudad Universitaria de Caracas (c)

ECONOMY

Economic overview: Venezuela remains highly dependent on oil revenues, which account for almost all export earnings and nearly half of the government's revenue, despite a continued decline in oil production in 2017. In the absence of official statistics, foreign experts estimate that GDP contracted 12% in 2017, inflation exceeded 2000%, people faced widespread shortages of consumer goods and medicine, and the central bank's international reserves dwindled. In late 2017, Venezuela also entered selective default on some of its sovereign and state oil company, Petroleos de Venezuela, S.A., (PDVSA) bonds. Domestic production and industry continues to severely underperform and the Venezuelan Government continues to rely on imports to meet its basic food and consumer goods needs.

Falling oil prices since 2014 have aggravated Venezuela's economic crisis. Insufficient access to dollars, price controls, and rigid labor regulations have led some US and multinational firms to reduce or shut down their Venezuelan operations. Market uncertainty and PDVSA's poor cash flow have slowed investment in the petroleum sector, resulting in a decline in oil production.

Under President Nicolas MADURO, the Venezuelan Government's response to the economic crisis has been to increase state control over the economy and blame the private sector for shortages. MADURO has given authority for the production and distribution of basic goods to the military and to local socialist party member committees. The Venezuelan Government has maintained strict currency controls since 2003. The government has been unable to sustain its mechanisms for distributing dollars to the private sector, in part because it needed to withhold some foreign exchange reserves to make its foreign bond payments. As a result of price and currency controls, local industries have struggled to purchase production inputs necessary to maintain their operations or sell goods at a profit on the local market. Expansionary monetary policies and currency controls have created opportunities for arbitrage and corruption and fueled a rapid increase in black market activity.

Real GDP (purchasing power parity): $269.068 billion (2018 est.)
$381.6 billion (2017 est.)
$334.751 billion (2017 est.)
note: data are in 2017 dollars
country comparison to the world: 57

Real GDP growth rate: -19.67% (2018 est.)
-14% (2017 est.)
-15.76% (2017 est.)
country comparison to the world: 223

Real GDP per capita: $7,704 (2018 est.)
$12,500 (2017 est.)
$9,417 (2017 est.)
note: data are in 2017 dollars
country comparison to the world: 155

GDP (official exchange rate): $210.1 billion (2017 est.)

Inflation rate (consumer prices): 146,101.7% (2019 est.)
45,518.1% (2018 est.)
416.8% (2017 est.)
country comparison to the world: 227

Credit ratings:

Fitch rating: RD (2017)

Moody's rating: WR (2019)

Standard & Poors rating: SD (2017)

GDP - composition, by sector of origin: *agriculture:* 4.7% (2017 est.)
industry: 40.4% (2017 est.)
services: 54.9% (2017 est.)

GDP - composition, by end use: *household consumption:* 68.5% (2017 est.)
government consumption: 19.6% (2017 est.)
investment in fixed capital: 13.9% (2017 est.)
investment in inventories: 1.7% (2017 est.)
exports of goods and services: 7% (2017 est.)
imports of goods and services: -10.7% (2017 est.)

Agricultural products: sugar cane, maize, milk, rice, plantains, bananas, pineapples, potatoes, beef, poultry

Industries: agricultural products, livestock, raw materials, machinery and equipment, transport equipment, construction materials, medical equipment, pharmaceuticals, chemicals, iron and steel products, crude oil and petroleum products

Industrial production growth rate: -2% (2017 est.)
country comparison to the world: 183

Labor force: 14.21 million (2017 est.)
country comparison to the world: 37

Labor force - by occupation: *agriculture:* 7.3%
industry: 21.8%
services: 70.9% (4th quarter, 2011 est.)

Unemployment rate: 6.9% (2018 est.)
27.1% (2017 est.)
country comparison to the world: 112

Unemployment, youth ages 15-24: *total:* 12.1%
male: 10.5%
female: 14.9% (2017 est.)
country comparison to the world: 125

Population below poverty line: 33.1% (2015 est.)

Gini Index coefficient - distribution of family income: 39 (2011)
49.5 (1998)
country comparison to the world: 69

Household income or consumption by percentage share: *lowest 10%:* 1.7%
highest 10%: 32.7% (2006)

Budget: *revenues:* 92.8 billion (2017 est.)
expenditures: 189.7 billion (2017 est.)

Budget surplus (+) or deficit (-): -46.1% (of GDP) (2017 est.)
country comparison to the world: 220

Public debt: 38.9% of GDP (2017 est.)
31.3% of GDP (2016 est.)
note: data cover central government debt, as well as the debt of state-owned oil company PDVSA; the data include treasury debt held by foreign entities; the data include some debt issued by subnational entities, as well as intragovernmental debt; intragovernmental debt consists of treasury borrowings from surpluses in the social funds, such as for retirement, medical care, and unemployment; some debt

instruments for the social funds are sold at public auctions
country comparison to the world: 135

Taxes and other revenues: 44.2% (of GDP) (2017 est.)
country comparison to the world: 25

Fiscal year: calendar year

Current account balance: $4.277 billion (2017 est.)
-$3.87 billion (2016 est.)
country comparison to the world: 32

Exports: $83.401 billion (2018 est.)
$93.485 billion (2017 est.)
country comparison to the world: 45

Exports - partners: India 34%, China 28%, United States 12%, Spain 6% (2019)

Exports - commodities: crude petroleum, refined petroleum, industrial alcohols, gold, iron (2019)

Imports: $18.432 billion (2018 est.)
$18.376 billion (2017 est.)
country comparison to the world: 89

Imports - partners: China 28%, United States 22%, Brazil 8%, Spain 6%, Mexico 6% (2019)

Imports - commodities: refined petroleum, rice, corn, tires, soybean meal, wheat (2019)

Reserves of foreign exchange and gold: $9.661 billion (31 December 2017 est.)
$11 billion (31 December 2016 est.)
country comparison to the world: 75

Debt - external: $100.3 billion (31 December 2017 est.)
$109.8 billion (31 December 2016 est.)
country comparison to the world: 56

Exchange rates: bolivars (VEB) per US dollar -
3,345 (2017 est.)
673.76 (2016 est.)
48.07 (2015 est.)
13.72 (2014 est.)
6.284 (2013 est.)

ENERGY

Electricity access: *electrification - total population:* 99.6% (2019)
electrification - urban areas: 100% (2019)
electrification - rural areas: 99% (2019)

Electricity: *installed generating capacity:* 32.956 million kW (2020 est.)
consumption: 78,082,020,000 kWh (2019 est.)
exports: 870 million kWh (2019 est.)
imports: 0 kWh (2019 est.)
transmission/distribution losses: 26.452 billion kWh (2019 est.)

Electricity generation sources: *fossil fuels:* 30.5% of total installed capacity (2020 est.)
wind: 0.1% of total installed capacity (2020 est.)
hydroelectricity: 69.4% of total installed capacity (2020 est.)

Coal: *production:* 396,000 metric tons (2020 est.)
consumption: 33,000 metric tons (2020 est.)
exports: 685,000 metric tons (2020 est.)
imports: 1,000 metric tons (2020 est.)
proven reserves: 731 million metric tons (2019 est.)

Petroleum: *total petroleum production:* 604,800 bbl/day (2021 est.)
refined petroleum consumption: 470,600 bbl/day (2019 est.)
crude oil and lease condensate exports: 1,002,700 bbl/day (2018 est.)
crude oil and lease condensate imports: 0 bbl/day (2018 est.)
crude oil estimated reserves: 303.806 billion barrels (2021 est.)

Refined petroleum products - production: 926,300 bbl/day (2015 est.)
country comparison to the world: 20

Refined petroleum products - exports: 325,800 bbl/day (2015 est.)
country comparison to the world: 27

Refined petroleum products - imports: 20,640 bbl/day (2015 est.)
country comparison to the world: 117

Natural gas: *production:* 22,694,584,000 cubic meters (2019 est.)
consumption: 22,694,584,000 cubic meters (2019 est.)
proven reserves: 5,673,894,000,000 cubic meters (2021 est.)

Carbon dioxide emissions: 103.708 million metric tonnes of CO_2 (2019 est.)
from coal and metallurgical coke: 108,000 metric tonnes of CO_2 (2019 est.)
from petroleum and other liquids: 57.378 million metric tonnes of CO_2 (2019 est.)
from consumed natural gas: 46.222 million metric tonnes of CO_2 (2019 est.)
country comparison to the world: 41

Energy consumption per capita: 85.829 million Btu/person (2019 est.)
country comparison to the world: 67

COMMUNICATIONS

Telephones - fixed lines: *total subscriptions:* 5,251,182 (2020 est.)
subscriptions per 100 inhabitants: 18 (2020 est.)
country comparison to the world: 26

Telephones - mobile cellular: *total subscriptions:* 13,476,300 (2019)
subscriptions per 100 inhabitants: 47.26 (2019)
country comparison to the world: 73

Telecommunication systems: *general assessment:* Venezuela's fixed-line teledensity was relatively high for the region before the steady growth in the number of lines came to an end in 2015; since then, the number of lines has plummeted, and by late 2021 teledensity had fallen to about 17.3%; the cause is largely linked to the country's ongoing economic troubles, which have compelled many people to terminate fixed-line telecom services and others still to flee the country; these pressures have also distorted sector revenue and have placed into disarray operators' investment plans aimed at improving networks and expanding the reach and capabilities of new technologies and services; the fixed broadband penetration rate is lower than the regional average, while data speeds are also relatively low; there is no effective competition in the provision of DSL, and as a result the state-owned incumbent CANTV has had little incentive to improve services from its meager revenue streams; mobile penetration in Venezuela is also below the regional average; the number of mobile subscribers fell by an estimated 2.4% in 2020, year-on-year, as subscribers terminated services in a bid to reduce discretionary spending, this decline is expected to continue into 2022, with subscriber growth not returning until 2023 (2021)
domestic: two domestic satellite systems with three earth stations; recent substantial improvement in telephone service in rural areas; 3 major providers operate in the mobile market and compete with state-owned company; fixed-line over 18 per 100 and mobile-cellular telephone subscribership about 63 per 100 persons (2020)
international: country code - 58; landing points for the Venezuela Festoon, ARCOS, PAN-AM, SAC, GlobeNet, ALBA-1 and Americas II submarine cable system providing connectivity to the Caribbean, Central and South America, and US; satellite earth stations - 1 Intelsat (Atlantic Ocean) and 1 PanAmSat (2020)

Broadcast media: Venezuela has a mixture of state-run and private broadcast media that are subject to high levels of regime control, including the shuttering of opposition-leaning media outlets; 13 public service networks, 61 privately owned TV networks, a privately owned news channel with limited national coverage, and a regime-backed Pan-American channel; 3 regimerun radio networks officially control roughly 65 news stations and another 30 stations targeted at specific audiences; regime-sponsored community broadcasters include 235 radio stations and 44 TV stations; the number of private broadcast radio stations has been declining, but many still remain in operation (2021)

Internet country code: .ve

Internet users: *total:* 20,531,397 (2019 est.)
percent of population: 72% (2019 est.)
country comparison to the world: 39

Broadband - fixed subscriptions: *total:* 2,561,556 (2020 est.)
subscriptions per 100 inhabitants: 9 (2020 est.)
country comparison to the world: 52

TRANSPORTATION

National air transport system: *number of registered air carriers:* 12 (2020)
inventory of registered aircraft operated by air carriers: 75
annual passenger traffic on registered air carriers: 2,137,771 (2018)
annual freight traffic on registered air carriers: 1.55 million (2018) mt-km

Civil aircraft registration country code prefix: YV

Airports: *total:* 444 (2021)
country comparison to the world: 17

Airports - with paved runways: *total:* 127
over 3,047 m: 6
2,438 to 3,047 m: 9
1,524 to 2,437 m: 33
914 to 1,523 m: 62
under 914 m: 17 (2021)

Airports - with unpaved runways: *total:* 317
2,438 to 3,047 m: 3
1,524 to 2,437 m: 57
914 to 1,523 m: 127
*under 914 m:*130 (2021)

Heliports: 3 (2021)

Pipelines: 981 km extra heavy crude, 5941 km gas, 7,588 km oil, 1,778 km refined products (2013)

Railways: *total:* 447 km (2014)
standard gauge: 447 km (2014) 1.435-m gauge (41.4 km electrified)
country comparison to the world: 115

Roadways: *total:* 96,189 km (2014)
country comparison to the world: 49

Waterways: 7,100 km (2011) (Orinoco River (400 km) and Lake de Maracaibo navigable by oceangoing vessels)
country comparison to the world: 22

Merchant marine: *total:* 281
by type: bulk carrier 4, container ship 1, general cargo 26, oil tanker 18, other 232 (2021)
country comparison to the world: 56

Ports and terminals: *major seaport(s):* La Guaira, Maracaibo, Puerto Cabello, Punta Cardon
oil terminal(s): Jose terminal

MILITARY AND SECURITY

Military and security forces: Bolivarian National Armed Forces (Fuerza Armada Nacional Bolivariana, FANB): Bolivarian Army (Ejercito Bolivariano, EB), Bolivarian Navy (Armada Bolivariana, AB; includes marines, Coast Guard), Bolivarian Military Aviation (Aviacion Militar Bolivariana, AMB; includes a joint-service Aerospace Defense Command (Comando de Defensa Aeroespacial Integral, CODAI), Bolivarian Militia (Milicia Bolivariana), Bolivarian National Guard (Guardia Nacional Bolivaria, GNB)

Bolivarian National Police: Special Action Forces (Fuerzas de Acciones Especiales, FAES) (2022)
note 1: the Bolivarian Militia was added as a "special component" to the FANB in 2020; it is comprised of armed civilians who receive periodic training in exchange for a small stipend
note 2: the National Guard is responsible for maintaining public order, guarding the exterior of key government installations and prisons, conducting counter-narcotics operations, monitoring borders, and providing law enforcement in remote areas; it reports to both the Ministry of Defense and the Ministry of Interior, Justice, and Peace
note 3: the FAES police paramilitary unit was created by President MADURO after the 2017 anti-government protests to bolster internal security; it has been accused of multiple human rights abuses

Military expenditures: 5.2% of GDP (2019 est.) (approximately $7.5 billion)
4.4% of GDP (2018 est.) (approximately $9.9 billion)
2.9% of GDP (2017 est.) (approximately $8.5 billion)
2.2% of GDP (2016 est.) (approximately $7.7 billion)
1.8% of GDP (2015 est.) (approximately $9.3 billion)
country comparison to the world: 10

Military and security service personnel strengths: information varies; approximately 125-150,000 active personnel, including about 25-30,000 National Guard; approximately 200-225,000 Bolivarian Militia (2022)

Military equipment inventories and acquisitions: the FANB inventory is mainly of Chinese and Russian origin with a smaller mix of equipment from Western countries, including the US; since 2010, Russia has been the top supplier of military hardware to Venezuela (2022)

Military service age and obligation: 18-30 (25 for women) for voluntary service; the minimum service obligation is 24-30 months; all citizens of military service age (18-50) are obligated to register for military service and subject to military training, although "forcible recruitment" is forbidden (2022)
note: as of 2017, women made up more than 20% of the active duty military

Military - note: between 2013 and 2017, Venezuela established at least a dozen military-led firms in a variety of economic sectors, such as agriculture, banking, construction, insurance, the media, mining, oil, and tourism; as of 2020, military officers reportedly led at least 60 state-owned companies; as of 2019, 9 of 32 government ministries were controlled by the military, including the ministries of agriculture and energy

as of 2022, an estimated 1,500- 2,000 members of the terrorist organizations National Liberation Army (ELN) and Revolutionary Armed Forces of Colombia dissidents (FARC-People's Army and Segundo Marquetalia - see Appendix T) operated in Venezuela, mostly in the states of Amazonas, Apure, Bolivar, Guarico, Tachira, and Zulia; ELN was assessed to be present in 12 of Venezuela's 23 states; the groups were particularly active in Apure state where the Venezuelan military clashed several times with FARC dissidents of the 10th Front in 2020-2021 (2022)

Maritime threats: The International Maritime Bureau continues to report the territorial and offshore waters in the Caribbean Sea as at risk for piracy and armed robbery against ships; numerous vessels, including commercial shipping and pleasure craft, have been attacked and hijacked both at anchor and while underway; crews have been robbed and stores or cargoes stolen; in 2021, no attacks were reported

TERRORISM

Terrorist group(s): National Liberation Army (ELN); Revolutionary Armed Forces of Colombia-People's Army (FARC-EP); Segundo Marquetalia

TRANSNATIONAL ISSUES

Disputes - international: *Venezuela-Brazil:* none identified
Venezuela-Colombia: dispute with Colombia over maritime boundary and Venezuelan administered Los Monjes Islands near the Gulf of Venezuela; Colombian-organized illegal narcotics and paramilitary activities penetrate Venezuela's shared border region; the border between the two countries was closed from March 2020 to October 2021 due to COVID, but goods and people fleeing poverty and violence continued to be smuggled from Venezuela into Colombia, and illegal narcotics and armed men flowed into Venezuela from Colombia; since the FARC disarmed in 2016, some former members have formed armed dissident groups that operate along the border
Venezuela-Guyana: claims all of the area west of the Essequibo River in Guyana, preventing any discussion of a maritime boundary; Guyana has expressed its intention to join Barbados in asserting claims before the UN Convention on the Law of the Sea that Trinidad and Tobago's maritime boundary with Venezuela extends into their waters; in 2018, Guyana initiated proceedings against Venezuela with the International Court of Justice (ICJ); Venezuela requested a direct dialogue to settle the dispute; the ICJ ruled that it had jurisdiction to hear the case in December 2020; in September 2021, Venezuelan officials issued a statement reasserting dominion over three-quarters of Guyana, which Guyana stated was a threat to its sovereignty and territorial integrity
Venezuela-various: Venezuela claims Aves Island and thereby an economic exclusion Zone/continental shelf extending over a large portion of the eastern Caribbean Sea; Venezuela's claim to Aves Island is disputed by Dominica and several other countries because the island has rich guano deposits useful in producing fertilizer and gunpowder, as well as large fish stocks and natural gas reserves; contraband smuggling (narcotics and arms), illegal migration, trafficking in animals, plants, lumber, illegal exploitation of mineral resources

Refugees and internally displaced persons: *refugees (country of origin):* 67,935 (Colombia) (2020)
note: As of September 2022, host governments report more than 7.1 million Venezuelan refugees and migrants worldwide

Trafficking in persons: *current situation:* Venezuela is a source, transit, and destination country for men, women, and children subjected to sex trafficking and forced labor; Venezuelan women and girls are trafficked within the country for sexual exploitation, lured from the nation's interior to urban and tourist areas; women from Colombia, Peru, Haiti, China, and South Africa are also reported to have been sexually exploited in Venezuela; some Venezuelan women are transported to Caribbean islands, particularly Aruba, Curacao, and Trinidad & Tobago, where they are subjected to forced prostitution; some Venezuelan children are forced to beg on the streets or work as domestic servants, while Ecuadorian children, often from indigenous communities, are subjected to forced labor; the government provided support to FARC dissidents and the ELN, which grew through the recruitment of child soldiers and exploitation of children in sex trafficking and forced labor; Illegal armed groups lure children in vulnerable conditions and dire economic circumstances with gifts and promises of basic sustenance to later recruit them into their ranks
tier rating: Tier 3 — Venezuela does not fully meet the minimum standards for the elimination of trafficking and is not making significant efforts to do so; the government created a specialized prosecutor's office to oversee trafficking investigations and prosecutions; authorities began legal proceedings against three complicit officials in a notable case; however, the government did not assist any victims or investigate, prosecute, or convict any traffickers; little effort was made to curb the forced recruitment of Venezuelan children by Colombian armed groups operating illegally in Venezuela; authorities made little effort to screen Cuban medical professionals for trafficking indicators as the Cuban Government may have forced them to work by withholding their documentation, and coercing them to falsify medical records (2020)

Illicit drugs: a major drug transit country and trafficking route in the Western Hemisphere largely destined for the Caribbean, Central America, the United States, West Africa, and Europe for illegal drugs, predominately cocaine; government officials reportedly complicit with illegal armed narcotrafficking groups; little international drug control cooperation; significant narcotics-related money-laundering activity, increasing signs of drug-related activities by Colombian insurgents on border

VIETNAM

INTRODUCTION

Background: Ancient Vietnam was centered on the Red River Valley and was under Han Chinese rule until approximately the 10th century. The Ly Dynasty (11th-13th century) ruled the first independent Vietnamese state, which was known as Dai Viet, and established their capital at Thang Long (Hanoi). Under the Tran Dynasty (13th-15th century), Dai Viet forces led by one of Vietnam's national heroes, TRAN Hang Dao, fought off Mongol invaders in 1279. Following a brief Chinese occupation in the early 1400s, the leader of Vietnamese resistance, LE Thai To, made himself emperor and established the Le Dynasty, which lasted until the late 18th century, although not without decades of political turmoil, civil war, and division. During this period, Dai Viet expanded southward to the Central Highlands and Mekong Delta, reaching the approximate boundaries of modern-day Vietnam by the 1750s. Dai Viet suffered additional civil war and division in the latter half of the 18th century, but was reunited and renamed Vietnam under Emperor NGUYEN Phuc Anh (aka Gia Long) in 1802.

The Nguyen Dynasty would be the last Vietnamese dynasty before the conquest by France, which began in 1858 and was completed by 1884. Vietnam became part of French Indochina in 1887. It declared independence after World War II, but France continued to rule until its 1954 defeat by communist forces under Ho Chi MINH. Under the Geneva Accords of 1954, Vietnam was divided into the communist North and anti-communist South. US economic and military aid to South Vietnam grew through the 1960s in an attempt to bolster the government, but US armed forces were withdrawn following a cease-fire agreement in 1973. Two years later, North Vietnamese forces overran the South reuniting the country under communist rule. Despite the return of peace, for over a decade the country experienced little economic growth because of its diplomatic isolation, its conservative leadership policies, and the persecution and mass exodus of individuals, many of them successful South Vietnamese merchants. However, since the enactment of Vietnam's "doi moi" (renovation) policy in 1986, Vietnamese authorities have committed to increased economic liberalization and enacted structural reforms needed to modernize the economy and to produce more competitive, export-driven industries. Since implementation, the economy has seen strong growth, particularly in agricultural and industrial production, construction, exports, and foreign investment. Increased tourism has also become a key component of economic growth. Nevertheless, the Communist Party maintains tight political and social control of the country and Vietnam faces considerable challenges including rising income inequality, corruption, inadequate social welfare, and a poor human rights record.

Since withdrawing its military occupation forces from Cambodia in the late 1980s and the end of Soviet aid by 1991, Vietnam has practiced a non-aligned foreign policy that emphasizes friendly ties with all members of the international community. Relatedly, Vietnam adheres to a security doctrine called the "Four Nos" (no alliances, no siding with one country against another, no foreign bases, and no using force in international relations). Despite longstanding tensions with Beijing regarding its expansive claims that overlap with Hanoi's own claimed maritime boundaries in the South China Sea, Vietnam puts a priority on stable relations with China, given its proximity, size, and status as Vietnam's largest trading partner.

GEOGRAPHY

Location: Southeastern Asia, bordering the Gulf of Thailand, Gulf of Tonkin, and South China Sea, as well as China, Laos, and Cambodia

Geographic coordinates: 16 10 N, 107 50 E

Map references: Southeast Asia

Area: *total:* 331,210 sq km
land: 310,070 sq km
water: 21,140 sq km
country comparison to the world: 67

Area - comparative: about three times the size of Tennessee; slightly larger than New Mexico

Land boundaries: *total:* 4,616 km
border countries (3): Cambodia 1,158 km; China 1,297 km; Laos 2,161 km

Coastline: 3,444 km (excludes islands)

Maritime claims: *territorial sea:* 12 nm
contiguous zone: 24 nm
exclusive economic zone: 200 nm
continental shelf: 200 nm or to the edge of the continental margin

Climate: tropical in south; monsoonal in north with hot, rainy season (May to September) and warm, dry season (October to March)

Terrain: low, flat delta in south and north; central highlands; hilly, mountainous in far north and northwest

Elevation: *highest point:* Fan Si Pan 3,144 m
lowest point: South China Sea 0 m
mean elevation: 398 m

Natural resources: antimony, phosphates, coal, manganese, rare earth elements, bauxite, chromate, offshore oil and gas deposits, timber, hydropower, arable land

Land use: *agricultural land:* 34.8% (2018 est.)
arable land: 20.6% (2018 est.)
permanent crops: 12.1% (2018 est.)
permanent pasture: 2.1% (2018 est.)
forest: 45% (2018 est.)
other: 20.2% (2018 est.)

Irrigated land: 46,000 sq km (2012)

Major rivers (by length in km): Mekong river mouth (shared with China [s], Burma, Laos, Thailand, Cambodia) - 4,350 km; Pearl river source (shared with China [m]) - 2,200 km; Red river mouth (shared with China [s]) - 1,149 km
note – [s] after country name indicates river source; [m] after country name indicates river mouth

Major watersheds (area sq km): Pacific Ocean drainage: Mekong (805,604 sq km)

Population distribution: though it has one of the highest population densities in the world, the population is not evenly dispersed; clustering is heaviest along the South China Sea and Gulf of Tonkin, with the Mekong Delta (in the south) and the Red River Valley (in the north) having the largest concentrations of people

Natural hazards: occasional typhoons (May to January) with extensive flooding, especially in the Mekong River delta

Geography - note: *note 1:* extending 1,650 km north to south, the country is only 50 km across at its narrowest point
note 2: Son Doong in Phong Nha-Ke Bang National Park is the world's largest cave (greatest cross sectional area) and is the largest known cave passage in the world by volume; it currently measures a total of 38.5 million cu m (about 1.35 billion cu ft); it connects to Thung cave (but not yet officially); when recognized, it will add an additional 1.6 million cu m in volume; Son Doong is so massive that it contains its own jungle, underground river, and localized weather system; clouds form inside the cave and spew out from its exits and two dolines (openings (sinkhole skylights) created by collapsed ceilings that allow sunlight to stream in)

PEOPLE AND SOCIETY

Population: 103,808,319 (2022 est.)
country comparison to the world: 16

Nationality: *noun:* Vietnamese (singular and plural)
adjective: Vietnamese

Ethnic groups: Kinh (Viet) 85.3%, Tay 1.9%, Thai 1.9%, Muong 1.5%, Khmer 1.4%, Mong 1.4%, Nung 1.1%, other 5.5% (2019 est.)
note: 54 ethnic groups are recognized by the Vietnamese Government

Languages: Vietnamese (official), English (increasingly favored as a second language), some French, Chinese, and Khmer, mountain area languages (Mon-Khmer and Malayo-Polynesian)
major-language sample(s): Dữ kiện thế giới, là nguồn thông tin cơ bản không thể thiếu. (Vietnamese)

Religions: Catholic 6.1%, Buddhist 5.8%, Protestant 1%, other 0.8%, none 86.3% (2019 est.)
note: most Vietnamese are culturally Buddhist

Demographic profile: When Vietnam was reunified in 1975, the country had a youthful age structure and a high fertility rate. The population growth rate slowed dramatically during the next 25 years, as fertility declined and infant mortality and life expectancy improved. The country's adoption of a one-or-two-child policy in 1988 led to increased rates of contraception and abortion. The total fertility rate dropped rapidly from nearly 5 in 1979 to 2.1 or replacement level in 1990, and at 1.8 is below replacement level today. Fertility is higher in the more rural central highlands and northern uplands, which are inhabited primarily by poorer ethnic minorities, and is lower among the majority Kinh, ethnic Chinese, and a few other ethnic groups, particularly in urban centers. With more than two-thirds of the population of working age (15-64), Vietnam has the potential to reap a demographic dividend for approximately three decades (between 2010 and 2040). However, its ability to do so will depend on improving the quality of education and training for its workforce and creating jobs. The Vietnamese Government is also considering changes to the country's population policy because if the country's fertility rate remains below replacement level, it could lead to a worker shortage in the future.

Vietnam has experienced both internal migration and net emigration, both for humanitarian and economic reasons, for the last several decades. Internal migration – rural-rural and rural-urban, temporary and permanent – continues to be a means of coping with Vietnam's extreme weather and flooding. Although Vietnam's population is still mainly rural, increasing numbers of young men and women have been drawn to the country's urban centers where they are more likely to find steady jobs and higher pay in the growing industrial and service sectors.

The aftermath of the Vietnam War in 1975 resulted in an outpouring of approximately 1.6 million Vietnamese refugees over the next two decades. Between 1975 and 1997, programs such as the Orderly Departure Program and the Comprehensive Plan of Action resettled hundreds of thousands of Vietnamese refugees abroad, including the United States (880,000), China (260,000, mainly ethnic Chinese Hoa), Canada (160,000), Australia (155,000), and European countries (150,000).

In the 1980s, some Vietnamese students and workers began to migrate to allied communist countries, including the Soviet Union, Czechoslovakia, Bulgaria, and East Germany. The vast majority returned home following the fall of communism in Eastern Europe in the early 1990s. Since that time, Vietnamese labor migrants instead started to pursue opportunities in Asia and the Middle East. They often perform low-skilled jobs under harsh conditions for low pay and are vulnerable to forced labor, including debt bondage to the private brokers who arrange the work contracts. Despite Vietnam's current labor surplus, the country has in recent years attracted some foreign workers, mainly from China and other Asian countries.

Age structure: *0-14 years:* 22.61% (male 11,733,704/female 10,590,078)
15-24 years: 15.22% (male 7,825,859/female 7,202,716)
25-54 years: 45.7% (male 22,852,429/female 22,262,566)
55-64 years: 9.55% (male 4,412,111/female 5,016,880)
65 years and over: 6.91% (male 2,702,963/female 4,121,969) (2020 est.)

Dependency ratios: *total dependency ratio:* 45.1
youth dependency ratio: 33.6
elderly dependency ratio: 11.4
potential support ratio: 8.8 (2020 est.)

Median age: *total:* 31.9 years
male: 30.8 years
female: 33 years (2020 est.)
country comparison to the world: 112

Population growth rate: 0.97% (2022 est.)
country comparison to the world: 99

Birth rate: 15.69 births/1,000 population (2022 est.)
country comparison to the world: 105

Death rate: 5.77 deaths/1,000 population (2022 est.)
country comparison to the world: 170

Net migration rate: -0.22 migrant(s)/1,000 population (2022 est.)
country comparison to the world: 114

Population distribution: though it has one of the highest population densities in the world, the population is not evenly dispersed; clustering is heaviest along the South China Sea and Gulf of Tonkin, with the Mekong Delta (in the south) and the Red River Valley (in the north) having the largest concentrations of people

Urbanization: *urban population:* 38.8% of total population (2022)
rate of urbanization: 2.7% annual rate of change (2020-25 est.)

Major urban areas - population: 9.077 million Ho Chi Minh City, 5.067 million HANOI (capital), 1.786 million Can Tho, 1.382 million Hai Phong, 1.188 million Da Nang, 1.078 million Bien Hoa (2022)

Sex ratio: *at birth:* 1.11 male(s)/female
0-14 years: 1.12 male(s)/female
15-24 years: 1.06 male(s)/female
25-54 years: 1.02 male(s)/female
55-64 years: 0.9 male(s)/female
65 years and over: 0.5 male(s)/female
total population: 1.01 male(s)/female (2022 est.)

Maternal mortality ratio: 43 deaths/100,000 live births (2017 est.)
country comparison to the world: 100

Infant mortality rate: *total:* 14.75 deaths/1,000 live births
male: 15.09 deaths/1,000 live births
female: 14.38 deaths/1,000 live births (2022 est.)
country comparison to the world: 103

Life expectancy at birth: *total population:* 75.52 years
male: 72.95 years
female: 78.37 years (2022 est.)
country comparison to the world: 121

Total fertility rate: 2.05 children born/woman (2022 est.)
country comparison to the world: 100

Contraceptive prevalence rate: 76.5% (2018/19)

Drinking water source: *improved: urban:* 99.2% of population
rural: 95.5% of population
total: 96.9% of population
unimproved: urban: 0.8% of population
rural: 4.5% of population
total: 3.1% of population (2020 est.)

Current health expenditure: 5.3% of GDP (2019)

Physicians density: 0.83 physicians/1,000 population (2016)

Hospital bed density: 3.2 beds/1,000 population (2013)

Sanitation facility access: *improved: urban:* 98.7% of population
rural: 90% of population
total: 93.3% of population
unimproved: urban: 1.3% of population
rural: 10% of population
total: 6.7% of population (2020 est.)

HIV/AIDS - adult prevalence rate: 0.3% (2020 est.)
country comparison to the world: 93

HIV/AIDS - people living with HIV/AIDS: 250,000 (2020 est.)
country comparison to the world: 25

HIV/AIDS - deaths: 3,800 (2020 est.)
country comparison to the world: 29

Major infectious diseases: *degree of risk:* very high (2020)
food or waterborne diseases: bacterial diarrhea, hepatitis A, and typhoid fever
vectorborne diseases: dengue fever, malaria, and Japanese encephalitis

Obesity - adult prevalence rate: 2.1% (2016)
country comparison to the world: 192

Alcohol consumption per capita: *total:* 3.41 liters of pure alcohol (2019 est.)
beer: 3.18 liters of pure alcohol (2019 est.)
wine: 0.02 liters of pure alcohol (2019 est.)
spirits: 0.21 liters of pure alcohol (2019 est.)
other alcohols: 0 liters of pure alcohol (2019 est.)
country comparison to the world: 105

Tobacco use: *total:* 24.8% (2020 est.)
male: 47.4% (2020 est.)
female: 2.2% (2020 est.)
country comparison to the world: 51

Children under the age of 5 years underweight: 13.4% (2017)
country comparison to the world: 42

Education expenditures: 4.1% of GDP (2019 est.)
country comparison to the world: 101

Literacy: *definition:* age 15 and over can read and write
total population: 95.8%
male: 97%
female: 94.6% (2019)

Unemployment, youth ages 15-24: *total:* 7.6%
male: 6.6%
female: 8.9% (2020 est.)

ENVIRONMENT

Environment - current issues: logging and slash-and-burn agricultural practices contribute to deforestation and soil degradation; water pollution and overfishing threaten marine life populations; groundwater contamination limits potable water supply; air pollution; growing urban industrialization and population migration are rapidly degrading environment in Hanoi and Ho Chi Minh City

Environment - international agreements: *party to:* Biodiversity, Climate Change, Climate Change-Kyoto Protocol, Climate Change-Paris Agreement, Comprehensive Nuclear Test Ban, Desertification, Endangered Species, Environmental Modification, Hazardous Wastes, Law of the Sea, Ozone Layer Protection, Ship Pollution, Tropical Timber 2006, Wetlands
signed, but not ratified: none of the selected agreements

Air pollutants: *particulate matter emissions:* 29.66 micrograms per cubic meter (2016 est.)
carbon dioxide emissions: 192.67 megatons (2016 est.)
methane emissions: 110.4 megatons (2020 est.)

Climate: tropical in south; monsoonal in north with hot, rainy season (May to September) and warm, dry season (October to March)

Land use: *agricultural land:* 34.8% (2018 est.)
arable land: 20.6% (2018 est.)
permanent crops: 12.1% (2018 est.)
permanent pasture: 2.1% (2018 est.)
forest: 45% (2018 est.)
other: 20.2% (2018 est.)

Urbanization: *urban population:* 38.8% of total population (2022)
rate of urbanization: 2.7% annual rate of change (2020-25 est.)

Revenue from forest resources: *forest revenues:* 1.49% of GDP (2018 est.)
country comparison to the world: 43

Revenue from coal: *coal revenues:* 0.35% of GDP (2018 est.)
country comparison to the world: 16

Waste and recycling: *municipal solid waste generated annually:* 9,570,300 tons (2011 est.)
municipal solid waste recycled annually: 2,201,169 tons (2014 est.)
percent of municipal solid waste recycled: 23% (2014 est.)

Major rivers (by length in km): Mekong river mouth (shared with China [s], Burma, Laos, Thailand, Cambodia) - 4,350 km; Pearl river source (shared with China [m]) - 2,200 km; Red river mouth (shared with China [s]) - 1,149 km
note – [s] after country name indicates river source; [m] after country name indicates river mouth

Major watersheds (area sq km): Pacific Ocean drainage: Mekong (805,604 sq km)

Total water withdrawal: *municipal:* 1.206 billion cubic meters (2017 est.)
industrial: 3.074 billion cubic meters (2017 est.)
agricultural: 77.75 billion cubic meters (2017 est.)

Total renewable water resources: 884.12 billion cubic meters (2017 est.)

GOVERNMENT

Country name: *conventional long form:* Socialist Republic of Vietnam
conventional short form: Vietnam
local long form: Cong Hoa Xa Hoi Chu Nghia Viet Nam
local short form: Viet Nam
former: Democratic Republic of Vietnam (North Vietnam), Republic of Vietnam (South Vietnam)
abbreviation: SRV
etymology: "Viet nam" translates as "Viet south," where "Viet" is an ethnic self identification dating to a second century B.C. kingdom and "nam" refers to its location in relation to other Viet kingdoms

Government type: communist state

Capital: *name:* Hanoi (Ha Noi)
geographic coordinates: 21 02 N, 105 51 E
time difference: UTC+7 (12 hours ahead of Washington, DC, during Standard Time)
etymology: the city has had many names in its history going back to A.D. 1010 when it first became the capital of imperial Vietnam; in 1831, it received its current name of Ha Noi, meaning "between the rivers," which refers to its geographic location

Administrative divisions: 58 provinces (tinh, singular and plural) and 5 municipalities (thanh pho, singular and plural)
provinces: An Giang, Bac Giang, Bac Kan, Bac Lieu, Bac Ninh, Ba Ria-Vung Tau, Ben Tre, Binh Dinh, Binh Duong, Binh Phuoc, Binh Thuan, Ca Mau, Cao Bang, Dak Lak, Dak Nong, Dien Bien, Dong Nai, Dong Thap, Gia Lai, Ha Giang, Ha Nam, Ha Tinh, Hai Duong, Hau Giang, Hoa Binh, Hung Yen, Khanh Hoa, Kien Giang, Kon Tum, Lai Chau, Lam Dong, Lang Son, Lao Cai, Long An, Nam Dinh, Nghe An, Ninh Binh, Ninh Thuan, Phu Tho, Phu Yen, Quang Binh, Quang Nam, Quang Ngai, Quang Ninh, Quang Tri, Soc Trang, Son La, Tay Ninh, Thai Binh, Thai Nguyen, Thanh Hoa, Thua Thien-Hue, Tien Giang, Tra Vinh, Tuyen Quang, Vinh Long, Vinh Phuc, Yen Bai
municipalities: Can Tho, Da Nang, Ha Noi (Hanoi), Hai Phong, Ho Chi Minh City (Saigon)

Independence: 2 September 1945 (from France)

National holiday: Independence Day (National Day), 2 September (1945)

Constitution: *history:* several previous; latest adopted 28 November 2013, effective 1 January 2014
amendments: proposed by the president, by the National Assembly's Standing Committee, or by at least two thirds of the National Assembly membership; a decision to draft an amendment requires approval by at least a two-thirds majority vote of the Assembly membership, followed by the formation of a constitutional drafting committee to write a draft and collect citizens' opinions; passage requires at least two-thirds majority of the Assembly membership; the Assembly can opt to conduct a referendum

Legal system: civil law system; note - the civil code of 2005 reflects a European-style civil law

International law organization participation: has not submitted an ICJ jurisdiction declaration; non-party state to the ICCt

Citizenship: *citizenship by birth:* no
citizenship by descent only: at least one parent must be a citizen of Vietnam
dual citizenship recognized: no
residency requirement for naturalization: 5 years

Suffrage: 18 years of age; universal

Executive branch: *chief of state:* President Nguyen Xuan PHUC (since 26 July 2021)
head of government: Prime Minister Pham Minh CHINH (since 26 July 2021)
cabinet: Cabinet proposed by prime minister confirmed by the National Assembly and appointed by the president
elections/appointments: president indirectly elected by National Assembly from among its members for a single 5-year term; prime minister recommended by the president and confirmed by National Assembly; deputy prime ministers confirmed by the National Assembly and appointed by the president
election results:
2021: Nguyen Xuan PHUC (CPV) elected president; Pham Minh CHINH (CPV) confirmed as prime minister
2018: NGUYEN Phu TRONG (CPV) elected as president
2016: NGUYEN Xuan PHUC (CPV) confirmed as prime minister

Legislative branch: *description:* unicameral National Assembly or Quoc Hoi (500 seats - number following 2021 election - 499; members directly elected in multi-seat constituencies by absolute majority vote; members serve 5-year terms)
elections:
last held on 23 May 2021 (next to be held in spring 2026)
election results:
percent of vote in 2016 election by party -CPV 95.8%, non-party members 4.2%; seats by party - CPV 474, non-party CPV-approved 20, self-nominated 2; note - 494 candidates elected, 2 CPV candidates-elect were disqualified; composition - men 364, women 122, percent of women 26.6%

Judicial branch: *highest court(s):* Supreme People's Court (consists of the chief justice and 13 judges)
judge selection and term of office: chief justice elected by the National Assembly upon the recommendation of the president for a 5-year, renewable term; deputy chief justice appointed by the president from among the judges for a 5-year term; judges appointed by the president and confirmed by the National Assembly for 5-year terms
subordinate courts: High Courts (administrative, civil, criminal, economic, labor, family, juvenile); provincial courts; district courts; Military Court; note - the National Assembly Standing Committee can establish special tribunals upon the recommendation of the chief justice

Political parties and leaders: Communist Party of Vietnam or CPV [General Secretary Nguyen Phu TRONG]
note: other parties proscribed

International organization participation: ADB, APEC, ARF, ASEAN, CICA, CP, EAS, FAO, G-77, IAEA, IBRD, ICAO, ICC (NGOs), ICRM, IDA, IFAD, IFC, IFRCS, ILO, IMF, IMO, IMSO, Interpol, IOC, IOM, IPU, ISO, ITSO, ITU, MIGA, NAM, OIF, OPCW, PCA, UN, UNCTAD, UNESCO, UNIDO, UNWTO, UPU, WCO, WFTU (NGOs), WHO, WIPO, WMO, WTO

Diplomatic representation in the US: *chief of mission:* Ambassador Nguyen Quoc DUNG (since 19 April 2022)
chancery: 1233 20th Street NW, Suite 400, Washington, DC 20036

telephone: [1] (202) 861-0737
FAX: [1] (202) 861-0917
email address and website:
vanphong@vietnamembassy.us
http://vietnamembassy-usa.org/
consulate(s) general: Houston, San Francisco
consulate(s): New York

Diplomatic representation from the US: *chief of mission:* Ambassador Marc KNAPPER (since 11 February 2022)
embassy: 7 Lang Ha Street, Hanoi
mailing address: 4550 Hanoi Place, Washington, DC 20521-4550
telephone: [84] (24) 3850-5000
FAX: [84] (24) 3850-5010
email address and website:
ACShanoi@state.gov
https://vn.usembassy.gov/
consulate(s) general: Ho Chi Minh City

Flag description: red field with a large yellow five-pointed star in the center; red symbolizes revolution and blood, the five-pointed star represents the five elements of the populace - peasants, workers, intellectuals, traders, and soldiers - that unite to build socialism

National symbol(s): yellow, five-pointed star on red field; lotus blossom; national colors: red, yellow

National anthem: *name:* "Tien quan ca" (The Song of the Marching Troops)
lyrics/music: Nguyen Van CAO
note: adopted as the national anthem of the Democratic Republic of Vietnam in 1945; it became the national anthem of the unified Socialist Republic of Vietnam in 1976; although it consists of two verses, only the first is used as the official anthem

National heritage: *total World Heritage Sites:* 8 (5 cultural, 2 natural, 1 mixed)
selected World Heritage Site locales: Complex of Hué Monuments (c); Ha Long Bay (n); Hoi An Ancient Town (c); My Son Sanctuary (c); Phong Nha-Ke Bang National Park (n); Imperial Citadel of Thang Long - Hanoi (c); Citadel of the Ho Dynasty (c); Trang An Landscape Complex (m)

ECONOMY

Economic overview: Vietnam is a densely populated developing country that has been transitioning since 1986 from the rigidities of a centrally planned, highly agrarian economy to a more industrial and market based economy, and it has raised incomes substantially. Vietnam exceeded its 2017 GDP growth target of 6.7% with growth of 6.8%, primarily due to unexpected increases in domestic demand, and strong manufacturing exports.

Vietnam has a young population, stable political system, commitment to sustainable growth, relatively low inflation, stable currency, strong FDI inflows, and strong manufacturing sector. In addition, the country is committed to continuing its global economic integration. Vietnam joined the WTO in January 2007 and concluded several free trade agreements in 2015-16, including the EU-Vietnam Free Trade Agreement (which the EU has not yet ratified), the Korean Free Trade Agreement, and the Eurasian Economic Union Free Trade Agreement. In 2017, Vietnam successfully chaired the Asia-Pacific Economic Cooperation (APEC) Conference with its key priorities including inclusive growth, innovation, strengthening small and medium enterprises, food security, and climate change. Seeking to diversify its opportunities, Vietnam also signed the Comprehensive and Progressive Agreement for the Transpacific Partnership in 2018 and continued to pursue the Regional Comprehensive Economic Partnership.

To continue its trajectory of strong economic growth, the government acknowledges the need to spark a 'second wave' of reforms, including reforming state-owned-enterprises, reducing red tape, increasing business sector transparency, reducing the level of nonperforming loans in the banking sector, and increasing financial sector transparency. Vietnam's public debt to GDP ratio is nearing the government mandated ceiling of 65%.

In 2016, Vietnam cancelled its civilian nuclear energy development program, citing public concerns about safety and the high cost of the program; it faces growing pressure on energy infrastructure. Overall, the country's infrastructure fails to meet the needs of an expanding middle class. Vietnam has demonstrated a commitment to sustainable growth over the last several years, but despite the recent speed-up in economic growth the government remains cautious about the risk of external shocks.

Real GDP (purchasing power parity): $798.21 billion (2020 est.)
$775.67 billion (2019 est.)
$724.81 billion (2018 est.)
note: data are in 2017 dollars
country comparison to the world: 30

Real GDP growth rate: 6.8% (2017 est.)
7.16% (2017 est.)
6.2% (2016 est.)
country comparison to the world: 21

Real GDP per capita: $8,200 (2020 est.)
$8,000 (2019 est.)
$7,600 (2018 est.)
note: data are in 2017 dollars
country comparison to the world: 149

GDP (official exchange rate): $259.957 billion (2019 est.)

Inflation rate (consumer prices): 2.7% (2019 est.)
3.5% (2018 est.)
3.5% (2017 est.)
country comparison to the world: 137

Credit ratings:

Fitch rating: BB (2018)

Moody's rating: Ba3 (2018)

Standard & Poors rating: BB (2019)

GDP - composition, by sector of origin: *agriculture:* 15.3% (2017 est.)
industry: 33.3% (2017 est.)
services: 51.3% (2017 est.)

GDP - composition, by end use: *household consumption:* 66.9% (2017 est.)
government consumption: 6.5% (2017 est.)
investment in fixed capital: 24.2% (2017 est.)
investment in inventories: 2.8% (2017 est.)
exports of goods and services: 100% (2017 est.)
imports of goods and services: -101% (2017 est.)

Agricultural products: rice, vegetables, sugar cane, cassava, maize, pork, fruit, bananas, coffee, coconuts

Industries: food processing, garments, shoes, machine-building; mining, coal, steel; cement, chemical fertilizer, glass, tires, oil, mobile phones

Industrial production growth rate: 8% (2017 est.)
country comparison to the world: 24

Labor force: 54.659 million (2019 est.)
country comparison to the world: 11

Labor force - by occupation: *agriculture:* 40.3%
industry: 25.7%
services: 34% (2017)

Unemployment rate: 3.11% (2018 est.)
2.2% (2017 est.)
country comparison to the world: 42

Unemployment, youth ages 15-24: *total:* 7.6%
male: 6.6%
female: 8.9% (2020 est.)
country comparison to the world: 158

Population below poverty line: 6.7% (2018 est.)

Gini Index coefficient - distribution of family income:
35.7 (2018 est.)
37.6 (2008)
country comparison to the world: 100

Household income or consumption by percentage share: *lowest 10%:* 2.7%
highest 10%: 26.8% (2014)

Budget: *revenues:* 54.59 billion (2017 est.)
expenditures: 69.37 billion (2017 est.)

Budget surplus (+) or deficit (-): -6.7% (of GDP) (2017 est.)
country comparison to the world: 191

Public debt: 58.5% of GDP (2017 est.)
59.9% of GDP (2016 est.)
note: official data; data cover general government debt and include debt instruments issued (or owned) by government entities other than the treasury; the data include treasury debt held by foreign entities; the data include debt issued by subnational entities, as well as intragovernmental debt; intragovernmental debt consists of treasury borrowings from surpluses in the social funds, such as for retirement, medical care, and unemployment; debt instruments for the social funds are not sold at public auctions
country comparison to the world: 76

Taxes and other revenues: 24.8% (of GDP) (2017 est.)
country comparison to the world: 119

Fiscal year: calendar year

Current account balance: $12.478 billion (2019 est.)
$5.769 billion (2018 est.)
country comparison to the world: 22

Exports: $280.83 billion (2019 est.) note: data are in current year dollars
$258.49 billion (2018 est.) note: data are in current year dollars
$204.169 billion (2017 est.)
country comparison to the world: 24

Exports - partners: United States 23%, China 14%, Japan 8%, South Korea 7% (2019)

Exports - commodities: broadcasting equipment, telephones, integrated circuits, footwear, furniture (2019)

Imports: $261.68 billion (2019 est.) note: data are in current year dollars
$245.63 billion (2018 est.) note: data are in current year dollars
$217.684 billion (2017 est.)
country comparison to the world: 22

Imports - partners: China 35%, South Korea 18%, Japan 6% (2019)

Imports - commodities: integrated circuits, telephones, refined petroleum, textiles, semiconductors (2019)

Reserves of foreign exchange and gold: $49.5 billion (31 December 2017 est.)
$36.91 billion (31 December 2016 est.)
country comparison to the world: 40

Debt - external: $96.58 billion (31 December 2017 est.)
$84.34 billion (31 December 2016 est.)
country comparison to the world: 58

Exchange rates: dong (VND) per US dollar -
23,129 (2020 est.)
23,171.5 (2019 est.)
23,312.5 (2018 est.)
21,909 (2014 est.)
21,189 (2013 est.)

ENERGY

Electricity access: *electrification - total population:* 100% (2019)

Electricity: *installed generating capacity:* 65.283 million kW (2020 est.)
consumption: 199,846,440,000 kWh (2019 est.)
exports: 2.067 billion kWh (2019 est.)
imports: 3.316 billion kWh (2019 est.)
transmission/distribution losses: 15.479 billion kWh (2019 est.)

Electricity generation sources: *fossil fuels:* 70.7% of total installed capacity (2020 est.)
solar: 2.4% of total installed capacity (2020 est.)
wind: 0.4% of total installed capacity (2020 est.)
hydroelectricity: 25.2% of total installed capacity (2020 est.)
biomass and waste: 1.4% of total installed capacity (2020 est.)

Coal: *production:* 47.789 million metric tons (2020 est.)
consumption: 80.568 million metric tons (2020 est.)
exports: 902,000 metric tons (2020 est.)
imports: 55 million metric tons (2020 est.)
proven reserves: 3.36 billion metric tons (2019 est.)

Petroleum: *total petroleum production:* 197,700 bbl/day (2021 est.)
refined petroleum consumption: 495,500 bbl/day (2019 est.)
crude oil and lease condensate exports: 66,900 bbl/day (2018 est.)
crude oil and lease condensate imports: 103,500 bbl/day (2018 est.)
crude oil estimated reserves: 4.4 billion barrels (2021 est.)

Refined petroleum products - production: 153,800 bbl/day (2015 est.)
country comparison to the world: 58

Refined petroleum products - exports: 25,620 bbl/day (2015 est.)
country comparison to the world: 67

Refined petroleum products - imports: 282,800 bbl/day (2015 est.)
country comparison to the world: 25

Natural gas: *production:* 8,438,095,000 cubic meters (2019 est.)
consumption: 8,438,095,000 cubic meters (2019 est.)
proven reserves: 699.425 billion cubic meters (2021 est.)

Carbon dioxide emissions: 249.929 million metric tonnes of CO2 (2019 est.)
from coal and metallurgical coke: 165.775 million metric tonnes of CO2 (2019 est.)
from petroleum and other liquids: 67.775 million metric tonnes of CO2 (2019 est.)
from consumed natural gas: 16.379 million metric tonnes of CO2 (2019 est.)
country comparison to the world: 27

Energy consumption per capita: 36.392 million Btu/person (2019 est.)
country comparison to the world: 113

COMMUNICATIONS

Telephones - fixed lines: *total subscriptions:* 3,205,775 (2020 est.)
subscriptions per 100 inhabitants: 3 (2020 est.)
country comparison to the world: 40

Telephones - mobile cellular: *total subscriptions:* 136.23 million (2019)
subscriptions per 100 inhabitants: 141.23 (2019)
country comparison to the world: 12

Telecommunication systems: *general assessment:* even with Covid-19 pandemic-related mobility restrictions in place, Vietnam's economy has continued to outperform the rest of the region in 2020 and 2021; the telecom sector essentially spent most of this period in a holding pattern, focusing on maintaining service throughout the crisis while preparing for some major changes to come in the mobile market in 2022; both fixed-line telephony and mobile have experienced small drops in subscriber numbers since the start of the pandemic, but the similarities between the two markets end there; fixed-line teledensity continued its downwards trajectory towards virtual oblivion, with just 3% penetration (around 3 million subscribers) at the start of 2021; the mobile market has lost about the same number of subscribers since the end of 2019, but has been sitting on much higher penetration levels around 130% for many years; growth is expected to kick in again in 2022 following the anticipated launch of commercial 5G mobile services along with a range of government-led schemes to move consumers completely off 2G and 3G; one example is the planned redistribution of GSM/3G bandwidth to LTE; in addition to propelling Vietnam into having one of the most advanced mobile markets in the world, this should also spur on the mobile broadband segment; with a penetration level of just over 70%, mobile broadband has considerable room to grow; increasing economic prosperity coupled with the latest smartphone technology and networks should see mobile broadband underwriting the country's telecommunications sector for at least the next few years; this report includes the regulator's market data to July 2021, telcos' financial and operating data updates to June 2021, Telecom Maturity Index charts and analyses, assessment of the global impact of Covid-19 on the telecoms sector, and other recent market developments (2021)
domestic: all provincial exchanges are digitalized and connected to Hanoi, Da Nang, and Ho Chi Minh City by fiber-optic cable or microwave radio relay networks; main lines have been increased, and the use of mobile telephones is growing rapidly; fixed-line under 4 per 100 and mobile-cellular nearly 143 per 100 (2020)
international: country code - 84; landing points for the SeaMeWe-3, APG, SJC2, AAE-1, AAG and the TGN-IA submarine cable system providing connectivity to Europe, Africa, the Middle East, Asia, Southeast Asia, Australia, and the US; satellite earth stations - 2 Intersputnik (Indian Ocean region) (2020)

Broadcast media: government controls all broadcast media exercising oversight through the Ministry of Information and Communication (MIC); government-controlled national TV provider, Vietnam Television (VTV), operates a network of several channels with regional broadcasting centers; programming is relayed nationwide via a network of provincial and municipal TV stations; law limits access to satellite TV but many households are able to access foreign programming via home satellite equipment; government-controlled Voice of Vietnam, the national radio broadcaster, broadcasts on several channels and is repeated on AM, FM, and shortwave stations throughout Vietnam (2018)

Internet country code: .vn

Internet users: *total:* 68,137,008 (2020 est.)
percent of population: 70% (2020 est.)
country comparison to the world: 13

Broadband - fixed subscriptions: *total:* 16,699,249 (2020 est.)
subscriptions per 100 inhabitants: 17 (2020 est.)
country comparison to the world: 14

TRANSPORTATION

National air transport system: *number of registered air carriers:* 5 (2020)
inventory of registered aircraft operated by air carriers: 224
annual passenger traffic on registered air carriers: 47,049,671 (2018)
annual freight traffic on registered air carriers: 481.37 million (2018) mt-km

Civil aircraft registration country code prefix: VN

Airports: *total:* 45 (2021)
country comparison to the world: 96

Airports - with paved runways: *total:* 38
over 3,047 m: 10
2,438 to 3,047 m: 6
1,524 to 2,437 m: 13
914 to 1,523 m: 9 (2021)

Airports - with unpaved runways: *total:* 7
1,524 to 2,437 m: 1
914 to 1,523 m: 3
under 914 m: 3 (2021)

Heliports: 1 (2021)

Pipelines: 72 km condensate, 398 km condensate/gas, 955 km gas, 128 km oil, 33 km oil/gas/water, 206 km refined products, 13 km water (2013)

Railways: *total:* 2,600 km (2014)
standard gauge: 178 km (2014) 1.435-m gauge; 253 km mixed gauge
narrow gauge: 2,169 km (2014) 1.000-m gauge
country comparison to the world: 66

Roadways: *total:* 195,468 km (2013)
paved: 148,338 km (2013)
unpaved: 47,130 km (2013)
country comparison to the world: 28

Waterways: 47,130 km (2011) (30,831 km weight under 50 tons)
country comparison to the world: 3

Merchant marine: *total:* 1,926
by type: bulk carrier 116, container ship 41, general cargo 1,193, oil tanker 125, other 451 (2021)
country comparison to the world: 12

Ports and terminals: *major seaport(s):* Cam Pha Port, Da Nang, Haiphong, Phu My, Quy Nhon
container port(s) (TEUs): Saigon (7,220,377), Cai Mep (3,742,384), Haiphong (5,133,150) (2019)
river port(s): Ho Chi Minh (Mekong)

MILITARY AND SECURITY

Military and security forces: People's Army of Vietnam (PAVN; aka Vietnam People's Army, VPA): Ground Forces, Navy (includes naval infantry), Air Force and Air Defense, Border Defense Force, and Vietnam Coast Guard; Vietnam People's Public Security Ministry; Vietnam Civil Defense Force (2022)
note 1: the Public Security Ministry is responsible for internal security and controls the national police, a special national security investigative agency, and other internal security units, including specialized riot police regiments
note 2: the Vietnam Coast Guard was established in 1998 as the Vietnam Marine Police and renamed in 2013; Vietnam officially established a maritime self-defense force (civilian militia) in 2010 after the National Assembly passed the Law on Militia and Self-Defense Forces in 2009; the Vietnam Fisheries Resources Surveillance (VFRS), established in 2013, is responsible for patrolling, monitoring for fishing violations, and carrying out fishery inspections; it is armed, allowed to use force if necessary, and works in tandem with the Vietnam Coast Guard

Military expenditures: 2.4% of GDP (2021 est.)
2.4% of GDP (2020 est.)
2.3% of GDP (2019 est.) (approximately $11.2 billion)
2.3% of GDP (2018 est.) (approximately $10.5 billion)
2.3% of GDP (2017 est.) (approximately $9.85 billion)
country comparison to the world: 46

Military and security service personnel strengths: information is limited and varied; estimated 470,000 active duty troops (400,000 ground; 40,000 naval; 30,000 air); estimated 40,000 Border Defense Force and Coast Guard (2022)

Military equipment inventories and acquisitions: the PAVN is armed largely with weapons and equipment from Russia and the former Soviet Union; since 2010, Russia has remained the main supplier of newer PAVN military equipment, although in recent years Vietnam has purchased arms from more than a dozen other countries including Belarus, Israel, South Korea, Ukraine, and the US; Vietnam has a limited defense industry (2021)

Military service age and obligation: 18-27 years of age for compulsory and voluntary military service for men and women (in practice only men are drafted); service obligation is between 24 (Army, Air Defense) and 36 (Navy and Air Force) months (2022)

Military - note: the PAVN is the military arm of the ruling Communist Party of Vietnam (CPV) and responsible to the Central Military Commission (CMC), the highest party organ on military policy; the CMC is led by the CPV General Secretary

Vietnam has a security policy of non-alignment, commonly referred to as the 'three no's: no military alliances, no foreign bases or usage of the territory for military activities, and no siding with one country against another; however, in 2019, Vietnam noted that it would consider developing appropriate defense and security relations with other countries depending on circumstances (2022)

Maritime threats: the International Maritime Bureau reports the territorial and offshore waters in the South China Sea as high risk for piracy and armed robbery against ships; numerous commercial vessels have been attacked and hijacked both at anchor and while underway; hijacked vessels are often disguised and cargo diverted to ports in East Asia; the number of reported incidents decreased from four in 2020 to one in 2021

TRANSNATIONAL ISSUES

Disputes - international: *Vietnam-Cambodia:* Cambodia accuses Vietnam of a wide variety of illicit cross-border activities; issues include casinos built in Cambodia near the border, narcotics trafficking, trafficking of women and children, petrol smuggling, illegal logging, and illegal migration; progress on a joint development area with Cambodia is hampered by an unresolved dispute over sovereignty of offshore islands; in December 2021, leaders from the two countries agreed to fully complete the remaining border demarcation and the upgrading of border checkpoints
Vietnam-Cambodia-Laos: Cambodia and Laos protest Vietnamese squatters and armed encroachments along border; Cambodia accuses Vietnam of a wide variety of illicit cross-border activities
Vietnam-China: an estimated 300,000 Vietnamese refugees reside in China; the decade-long demarcation of the China-Vietnam land boundary was completed in 2009; small territorial exchanges were made during the demarcation; China occupies the Paracel Islands also claimed by Vietnam and Taiwan; cross border trafficking in women and children and illegal wildlife trade are problems along this border; In December 2021, China tightened its border controls over COVID concerns, restricting an important trade route for Vietnam
Vietnam-Laos: Laos opened a strategically important international border crossing with Vietnam in 2021, which will shorten the distance for goods and people transiting between Thailand and Vietnam

Refugees and internally displaced persons: *stateless persons:* 30,581 (mid-year 2021); note - Vietnam's stateless ethnic Chinese Cambodian population dates to the 1970s when thousands of Cambodians fled to Vietnam to escape the Khmer Rouge and were no longer recognized as Cambodian citizens; Vietnamese women who gave up their citizenship to marry foreign men have found themselves stateless after divorcing and returning home to Vietnam; the government addressed this problem in 2009, and Vietnamese women are beginning to reclaim their citizenship

Trafficking in persons: *current situation:* human traffickers exploit domestic and foreign victims in Vietnam, and traffickers exploit Vietnamese abroad; Vietnamese men and women who migrate abroad for work may be subject to exploitation and illegally high fees from recruiters trapping them in debt bondage; traffickers subject victims to forced labor in construction, fishing, agriculture, mining, maritime industries, logging, and manufacturing, primarily in Taiwan, Malaysia, Republic of Korea, Laos, Japan, and to a lesser extent, some parts of Europe and the UK; traffickers mislead Vietnamese women and children with fraudulent employment opportunities and sex traffick them to brothels on the borders of China, Cambodia, Laos, and elsewhere in Asia; traffickers use the Internet, gaming sites, and particularly social media to lure victims; domestic traffickers are sometimes family members or small-scale networks exploiting Vietnamese men, women, and children - including street children and children with disabilities - in forced labor as street beggars or in brick kilns and mines; child sex tourists from elsewhere in Asia and other countries exploit children; prisoners reportedly are forced to work in agriculture, manufacturing, and hazardous industries, such as cashew processing
tier rating: Tier 2 Watch List — Vietnam does not fully meet the minimum standards for the elimination of trafficking but is making significant efforts to do so; efforts include providing trafficking victims the right to legal representation in judicial proceedings, increasing the amount of shelter time for victims by one month, providing financial support, continuing large-scale awareness campaigns in vulnerable communities and to workers going overseas, and training law enforcement; however, fewer victims were identified or assisted and procedures remained slow and ineffective; provincial officials unfamiliar with anti-trafficking law impede anti-trafficking efforts; labor recruitment firms extorted illegal high fees from workers looking for overseas employment putting them at risk for forced labor; no investigations, prosecutions, or convictions of officials complicit in trafficking offenses were made (2020)

Illicit drugs: transshipment point for transnational criminal organizations (TCOs) trafficking heroin, crystal methamphetamine, and ketamine throughout East Asia and the Pacific; approximately 90% of the illicit drugs in the country originate in Laos, Burma, and Thailand

VIRGIN ISLANDS

INTRODUCTION

Background: The Danes secured control over the southern Virgin Islands of Saint Thomas, Saint John, and Saint Croix during the 17th and early 18th centuries. Sugarcane, produced by African slave labor, drove the islands' economy during the 18th and early 19th centuries. In 1917, the US purchased the Danish holdings, which had been in economic decline since the abolition of slavery in 1848. On 6 September 2017, Hurricane Irma passed over the northern Virgin Islands of Saint Thomas and Saint

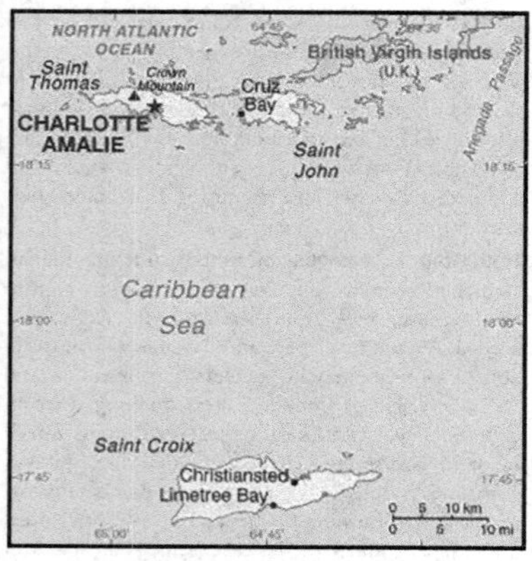

John and inflicted severe damage to structures, roads, the airport on Saint Thomas, communications, and electricity. Less than two weeks later, Hurricane Maria passed over the island of Saint Croix in the southern Virgin Islands, inflicting considerable damage with heavy winds and flooding rains.

GEOGRAPHY

Location: Caribbean, islands between the Caribbean Sea and the North Atlantic Ocean, east of Puerto Rico

Geographic coordinates: 18 20 N, 64 50 W

Map references: Central America and the Caribbean

Area: *total:* 1,910 sq km
land: 346 sq km
water: 1,564 sq km
country comparison to the world: 181

Area - comparative: twice the size of Washington, DC

Land boundaries: *total:* 0 km

Coastline: 188 km

Maritime claims: *territorial sea:* 12 nm
exclusive economic zone: 200 nm

Climate: subtropical, tempered by easterly trade winds, relatively low humidity, little seasonal temperature variation; rainy season September to November

Terrain: mostly hilly to rugged and mountainous with little flat land

Elevation: *highest point:* Crown Mountain 474 m
lowest point: Caribbean Sea 0 m

Natural resources: pleasant climate, beaches foster tourism

Land use: *agricultural land:* 11.5% (2018 est.)
arable land: 2.9% (2018 est.)
permanent crops: 2.9% (2018 est.)
permanent pasture: 5.7% (2018 est.)
forest: 57.4% (2018 est.)
other: 31.1% (2018 est.)

Irrigated land: 1 sq km (2012)

Population distribution: while overall population density throughout the islands is relatively low, concentrations appear around Charlotte Amalie on St. Thomas and Christiansted on St. Croix

Natural hazards: several hurricanes in recent years; frequent and severe droughts and floods; occasional earthquakes

Geography - note: important location along the Anegada Passage - a key shipping lane for the Panama Canal; Saint Thomas has one of the best natural deepwater harbors in the Caribbean

PEOPLE AND SOCIETY

Population: 105,413 (2022 est.)
country comparison to the world: 192

Nationality: *noun:* Virgin Islander(s) (US citizens)
adjective: Virgin Islander

Ethnic groups: Black 76%, White 15.6%, Asian 1.4%, other 4.9%, mixed 2.1% (2010 est.)
note: 17.4% self-identify as Latino

Languages: English 71.6%, Spanish or Spanish Creole 17.2%, French or French Creole 8.6%, other 2.5% (2010 est.)

Religions: Protestant 65.5%, Roman Catholic 27.1%, other Christians 2.2%, other 1.5%, none 3.7% (2010 est.)

Age structure: *0-14 years:* 19.71% (male 10,671/female 10,192)
15-24 years: 10.16% (male 5,219/female 5,535)
25-54 years: 36.07% (male 17,844/female 20,342)
55-64 years: 14.24% (male 7,222/female 7,859)
65 years and over: 19.82% (male 9,424/female 11,562) (2021 est.)

Dependency ratios: *total dependency ratio:* 66
youth dependency ratio: 32
elderly dependency ratio: 34
potential support ratio: 2.9 (2020 est.)

Median age: *total:* 41.8 years
male: 40.6 years
female: 42.8 years (2020 est.)
country comparison to the world: 42

Population growth rate: -0.45% (2022 est.)
country comparison to the world: 223

Birth rate: 11.63 births/1,000 population (2022 est.)
country comparison to the world: 161

Death rate: 8.78 deaths/1,000 population (2022 est.)
country comparison to the world: 66

Net migration rate: -7.35 migrant(s)/1,000 population (2022 est.)
country comparison to the world: 216

Population distribution: while overall population density throughout the islands is relatively low, concentrations appear around Charlotte Amalie on St. Thomas and Christiansted on St. Croix

Urbanization: *urban population:* 96.1% of total population (2022)
rate of urbanization: -0.11% annual rate of change (2020-25 est.)

Major urban areas - population: 52,000 CHARLOTTE AMALIE (capital) (2018)

Sex ratio: *at birth:* 1.06 male(s)/female
0-14 years: 1.05 male(s)/female
15-24 years: 0.94 male(s)/female
25-54 years: 0.87 male(s)/female
55-64 years: 0.93 male(s)/female
65 years and over: 0.68 male(s)/female
total population: 0.91 male(s)/female (2022 est.)

Infant mortality rate: *total:* 7.65 deaths/1,000 live births
male: 8.65 deaths/1,000 live births
female: 6.59 deaths/1,000 live births (2022 est.)
country comparison to the world: 155

Life expectancy at birth: *total population:* 80.27 years
male: 77.08 years
female: 83.65 years (2022 est.)
country comparison to the world: 51

Total fertility rate: 2 children born/woman (2022 est.)
country comparison to the world: 109

Drinking water source: *improved: total:* 98.7% of population
unimproved: total: 1.3% of population (2020 est.)

Sanitation facility access: *improved: total:* 99.4% of population
unimproved: total: 0.6% of population (2020 est.)

ENVIRONMENT

Environment - current issues: lack of natural freshwater resources; protection of coral reefs; solid waste management; coastal development; increased boating and overfishing

Climate: subtropical, tempered by easterly trade winds, relatively low humidity, little seasonal temperature variation; rainy season September to November

Land use: *agricultural land:* 11.5% (2018 est.)
arable land: 2.9% (2018 est.)
permanent crops: 2.9% (2018 est.)
permanent pasture: 5.7% (2018 est.)
forest: 57.4% (2018 est.)
other: 31.1% (2018 est.)

Urbanization: *urban population:* 96.1% of total population (2022)
rate of urbanization: -0.11% annual rate of change (2020-25 est.)

Revenue from forest resources: *forest revenues:* 0% of GDP (2017 est.)
country comparison to the world: 203

Waste and recycling: *municipal solid waste generated annually:* 146,500 tons (2012 est.)

GOVERNMENT

Country name: *conventional long form:* none
conventional short form: Virgin Islands
former: Danish West Indies
abbreviation: VI
etymology: the myriad islets, cays, and rocks surrounding the major islands reminded Christopher COLUMBUS in 1493 of Saint Ursula and her 11,000 virgin followers (Santa Ursula y las Once Mil Virgenes), which over time shortened to the Virgins (las Virgenes)

Government type: unincorporated organized territory of the US with local self-government; republican form of territorial government with separate executive, legislative, and judicial branches

Dependency status: unincorporated organized territory of the US with policy relations between the Virgin Islands and the US Federal Government under the jurisdiction of the Office of Insular Affairs, US Department of the Interior, Washington, DC

Capital: *name:* Charlotte Amalie
geographic coordinates: 18 21 N, 64 56 W
time difference: UTC-4 (1 hour ahead of Washington, DC, during Standard Time)
etymology: originally called Taphus in Danish - meaning "tap house" or "beer house" because of its many beer halls -the town received a more dignified name in 1691 when it was named Charlotte Amalie in honor of Danish King CHRISTIAN V's wife, Charlotte AMALIE of Hesse-Kassel (1650–1714)

Administrative divisions: none (territory of the US); there are no first-order administrative divisions as defined by the US Government, but there are 3 islands at the second order; Saint Croix, Saint John, Saint Thomas

Independence: none (territory of the US)

National holiday: Transfer Day (from Denmark to the US), 31 March (1917)

Constitution: *history:* 22 July 1954 - the Revised Organic Act of the Virgin Islands functions as a constitution for this US territory
amendments: amended several times, last in 2012

Legal system: US common law

Citizenship: see United States

Suffrage: 18 years of age; universal; note - island residents are US citizens but do not vote in US presidential elections

Executive branch: *chief of state:* President Joseph R. BIDEN, Jr. (since 20 January 2021); Vice President Kamala D. HARRIS (since 20 January 2021)
head of government: Governor Albert BRYAN, Jr. (since 7 January 2019), Lieutenant Governor Tregenza ROACH (since 7 January 2019)
cabinet: Territorial Cabinet appointed by the governor and confirmed by the Senate
elections/appointments: president and vice president indirectly elected on the same ballot by an Electoral College of 'electors' chosen from each state; president and vice president serve a 4-year term (eligible for a second term); under the US Constitution, residents of the Virgin Islands do not vote in elections for US president and vice president; however, they may vote in the Democratic and Republican presidential primary elections; governor and lieutenant governor directly elected on the same ballot by absolute majority vote in 2 rounds if needed for a 4-year term (eligible for a second term); election last held on 8 November 2022 (next to be held in November 2026)
election results:
Albert BRYAN, Jr. reelected governor; percent of vote - Albert BRYAN, Jr. (Democratic Party) 56%, Kurt VIALET (independent) 38%

Legislative branch: *description:* unicameral Legislature of the Virgin Islands (15 seats; senators directly elected in single- and multi-seat constituencies by simple majority popular vote to serve 2-year terms)
the Virgin Islands directly elects 1 delegate to the US House of Representatives by simple majority vote to serve a 2-year term
elections:
Legislature of the Virgin Islands last held on 6 November 2018 (next to be held in November 2020)
US House of Representatives last held on 6 November 2018 (next to be held in November 2020)
election results:
Legislature of the Virgin Islands - percent of vote by party - NA; seats by party - Democratic Party 13, independents 2; composition - men 11, women 4, percent of women 26.7%
delegate to US House of Representatives - seat by party - Democratic Party 1; composition - 1 woman
note: the Virgin Islands to the US House of Representatives can vote when serving on a committee and when the House meets as the Committee of the Whole House, but not when legislation is submitted for a "full floor" House vote

Judicial branch: *highest court(s):* Supreme Court of the Virgin Islands (consists of the chief justice and 2 associate justices); note - court established by the US Congress in 2004 and assumed appellate jurisdiction in 2007
judge selection and term of office: justices appointed by the governor and confirmed by the Virgin Islands Senate; justices serve initial 10-year terms and upon reconfirmation, during the extent of good behavior; chief justice elected to position by peers for a 3-year term
subordinate courts: Superior Court (Territorial Court renamed in 2004); US Court of Appeals for the Third Circuit (has appellate jurisdiction over the District Court of the Virgin Islands; it is a territorial court and is not associated with a US federal judicial district); District Court of the Virgin Islands

Political parties and leaders: Democratic Party [Stacey PLASKELL]
Independent Citizens' Movement or ICM [Dale BLYDEN]
Republican Party [John CANEGATA]

International organization participation: AOSIS (observer), Interpol (subbureau), IOC, UPU, WFTU (NGOs)

Diplomatic representation in the US: none (territory of the US)

Diplomatic representation from the US: none (territory of the US)

Flag description: white field with a modified US coat of arms in the center between the large blue initials V and I; the coat of arms shows a yellow eagle holding an olive branch in its right talon and three arrows in the left with a superimposed shield of seven red and six white vertical stripes below a blue panel; white is a symbol of purity, the letters stand for the Virgin Islands

National anthem: *name:* "Virgin Islands March"
lyrics/music: multiple/Alton Augustus ADAMS, Sr.
note: adopted 1963; serves as a local anthem; as a territory of the US, "The Star-Spangled Banner" is official (see United States)

ECONOMY

Economic overview: Tourism, trade, other services, and rum production are the primary economic activities of the US Virgin Islands (USVI), accounting for most of its GDP and employment. The USVI receives between 2.5 and 3 million tourists a year, mostly from visiting cruise ships. The islands are vulnerable to damage from storms, as evidenced by the destruction from two major hurricanes in 2017. Recovery and rebuilding have continued, but full recovery from these back-to-back hurricanes is years away. The USVI government estimates it will need $7.5 billion, almost twice the territory's GDP, to rebuild the territory.

The agriculture sector is small and most food is imported. In 2016, government spending (both federal and territorial together) accounted for about 27% of GDP while exports of goods and services, including spending by tourists, accounted for nearly 47%. Federal programs and grants, including rum tax cover-over totaling $482.3 million in 2016, contributed 32.2% of the territory's total revenues. The economy picked up 0.9% in 2016 and had appeared to be progressing before the 2017 hurricanes severely damaged the territory's infrastructure and the economy.

Real GDP (purchasing power parity): $3.872 billion (2016 est.)
$3.759 billion (2015 est.)
$3.622 billion (2014 est.)
note: data are in 2013 dollars
country comparison to the world: 183

Real GDP growth rate: 0.9% (2016 est.)
0.3% (2015 est.)
-1% (2014 est.)
country comparison to the world: 174

Real GDP per capita: $37,000 (2016 est.)
$35,800 (2015 est.)
$34,500 (2014 est.)
country comparison to the world: 50

GDP (official exchange rate): $5.182 billion (2016 est.)

Inflation rate (consumer prices): 1% (2016 est.)
2.6% (2015 est.)
country comparison to the world: 67

GDP - composition, by sector of origin: *agriculture:* 2% (2012 est.)
industry: 20% (2012 est.)
services: 78% (2012 est.)

GDP - composition, by end use: *household consumption:* 68.2% (2016 est.)
government consumption: 26.8% (2016 est.)
investment in fixed capital: 7.5% (2016 est.)
investment in inventories: 15% (2016 est.)
exports of goods and services: 46.7% (2016 est.)
imports of goods and services: -64.3% (2016 est.)

Agricultural products: fruit, vegetables, sorghum; Senepol cattle

Industries: tourism, watch assembly, rum distilling, construction, pharmaceuticals, electronics

Labor force: 48,550 (2016 est.)
country comparison to the world: 193

Labor force - by occupation: *agriculture:* 1%
industry: 19%
services: 80% (2003 est.)

Unemployment rate: 10.4% (2017 est.)
11% (2016 est.)
country comparison to the world: 152

Population below poverty line: 28.9% (2002 est.)

Budget: *revenues:* 1.496 billion (2016 est.)
expenditures: 1.518 billion (2016 est.)

Budget surplus (+) or deficit (-): -0.4% (of GDP) (2016 est.)
country comparison to the world: 59

Public debt: 53.3% of GDP (2016 est.)
45.9% of GDP (2014 est.)
country comparison to the world: 91

Taxes and other revenues: 28.9% (of GDP) (2016 est.)
country comparison to the world: 89

Fiscal year: 1 October - 30 September

Exports: $1.81 billion (2016 est.)
$1.537 billion (2015 est.)
country comparison to the world: 155

Exports - partners: Haiti 14%, Guadeloupe 7%, Malaysia 7%, Martinique 7%, Barbados 7%, British Virgin Islands 5% (2019)

Exports - commodities: refined petroleum, jewelry, recreational boats, watches, rum (2019)

Imports: $2.489 billion (2016 est.)
$1.549 billion (2015 est.)
country comparison to the world: 165

Imports - partners: India 18%, Algeria 14%, South Korea 9%, Argentina 9%, Sweden 7%, Brazil 5% (2019)

Imports - commodities: refined petroleum, crude petroleum, rubber piping, jewelry, beer (2019)

Exchange rates: the US dollar is used

ENERGY

Electricity access: *electrification - total population:* 100% (2020)

Electricity: *installed generating capacity:* 321,000 kW (2020 est.)
consumption: 561.24 million kWh (2019 est.)
exports: 0 kWh (2020 est.)
imports: 0 kWh (2020 est.)
transmission/distribution losses: 51 million kWh (2019 est.)

Electricity generation sources: *fossil fuels:* 98.9% of total installed capacity (2020 est.)
solar: 1.1% of total installed capacity (2020 est.)

Petroleum: *total petroleum production:* 0 bbl/day (2021 est.)
refined petroleum consumption: 16,400 bbl/day (2019 est.)

Refined petroleum products - exports: 3,285 bbl/day (2015 est.)
country comparison to the world: 97

Refined petroleum products - imports: 23,480 bbl/day (2015 est.)
country comparison to the world: 112

Carbon dioxide emissions: 2.438 million metric tonnes of CO2 (2019 est.)
from petroleum and other liquids: 2.438 million metric tonnes of CO2 (2019 est.)
country comparison to the world: 154

COMMUNICATIONS

Telephones - fixed lines: *total subscriptions:* 76,000 (2020 est.)
subscriptions per 100 inhabitants: 73 (2020 est.)
country comparison to the world: 143

Telephones - mobile cellular: *total subscriptions:* 59,121 (2018)
subscriptions per 100 inhabitants: 204.5 (2019)
country comparison to the world: 204

Telecommunication systems: *general assessment:* modern system with total digital switching, uses fiber-optic cable and microwave radio relay; good interisland and international connections; broadband access; expansion of FttP (Fiber to the Home) markets; LTE launches; regulatory development and expansion in several markets point to investment and focus on data (2020)
domestic: full range of services available; fixed-line roughly 72 per 100 persons, no recent teledensity numbers available for mobile-cellular usage, although it was approximately 75 per 100 in 2010 (2018)
international: country code - 1-340; landing points for the BSCS, St Thomas-ST Croix System, Southern Caribbean Fiber, Americas II, GCN, MAC, PAN-AM and SAC submarine cable connections to US, the Caribbean, Central and South America; satellite earth stations - NA (2020)

Broadcast media: about a dozen TV broadcast stations including 1 public TV station; multi-channel cable and satellite TV services are available; 24 radio stations

Internet country code: .vi

Internet users: *total:* 68,268 (2019 est.)
percent of population: 64% (2019 est.)
country comparison to the world: 189

TRANSPORTATION

Airports: *total:* 2 (2021)
country comparison to the world: 206

Airports - with paved runways: *total:* 2
over 3,047 m: 1
1,524 to 2,437 m: 1 (2021)

Roadways: *total:* 1,260 km (2008)
country comparison to the world: 178

Merchant marine: *total:* 1,868
by type: bulk carrier 91, container ship 39, general cargo 1,205, oil tanker 118, other 415 (2019)
country comparison to the world: 14

Ports and terminals: *major seaport(s):* Charlotte Amalie, Christiansted, Cruz Bay, Frederiksted, Limetree Bay

MILITARY AND SECURITY

Military - note: defense is the responsibility of the US

TRANSNATIONAL ISSUES

Disputes - international: none identified

WAKE ISLAND

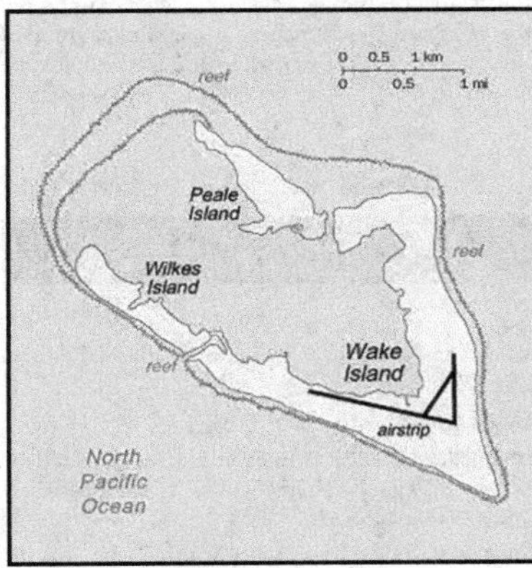

INTRODUCTION

Background: Wake Island was probably visited by Micronesian and Polynesian settlers, and oral legends tell of periodic voyages to the islands by people from the Marshall Islands. Wake Island was uninhabited when Spanish explorer Alvaro de Mendana de NEYRA became the first European to see it in 1568 and still had no human inhabitants when English captain Samuel WAKE sailed by it in 1796. The United States Exploring Expedition visited the island in 1841 and the US annexed it in 1899 to use as a cable and refueling station between its newly acquired Pacific territories of Hawaii, the Philippines, and Guam. In the 1930s, Pan American Airways built facilities on Wake Island so that it could be used as a stopover for flights from the US to China. In January 1941, the US began to install military assets on Wake Island and in early December of that year, Japan attacked Wake Island, capturing it by the end of the month after a heroic resistance. Japan held Wake Island until the end of World War II, and in 1946, commercial airlines once again used Wake Island as a refueling stop.

In 1973, the Marshall Islands claimed Wake Island based on the oral legends, although the US has not recognized these claims. In 1974, the US military took exclusive control of the island's airstrip and restricted visitors. In 1978, Bikini Islanders from the Marshall Islands, who were evacuated in the 1950s and 1960s because of US nuclear tests, considered rehoming on Wake Island, but the US military rejected that plan. Since the 1970s, the island has been important for missile defense testing. In 2009, Wake Island was included in the Pacific Remote Islands Marine National Monument.

GEOGRAPHY

Location: Oceania, atoll in the North Pacific Ocean, about two-thirds of the way from Hawaii to the Northern Mariana Islands

Geographic coordinates: 19 17 N, 166 39 E

Map references: Oceania

Area: *total:* 7 sq km
land: 6.5 sq km
water: 0 sq km
country comparison to the world: 245

Area - comparative: about 11 times the size of the National Mall in Washington, DC

Land boundaries: *total:* 0 km

Coastline: 19.3 km

Maritime claims: *territorial sea:* 12 nm
exclusive economic zone: 200 nm

Climate: tropical

Terrain: atoll of three low coral islands, Peale, Wake, and Wilkes, built up on an underwater volcano; central lagoon is former crater, islands are part of the rim

Elevation: *highest point:* unnamed location 8 m
lowest point: Pacific Ocean 0 m

Natural resources: none

Land use: *agricultural land:* 0% (2018 est.)
other: 100% (2018 est.)

Irrigated land: 0 sq km (2012)

Natural hazards: subject to occasional typhoons

Geography - note: strategic location in the North Pacific Ocean; emergency landing location for transpacific flights

PEOPLE AND SOCIETY

Population: (2018 est.) no indigenous inhabitants
note: approximately 100 military personnel and civilian contractors maintain and operate the airfield and communications facilities

ENVIRONMENT

Environment - current issues: potable water obtained through a catchment rainwater system and a desalinization plant for brackish ground water; hazardous wastes moved to an accumulation site for storage and eventual transport off site via barge

Climate: tropical

Land use: *agricultural land:* 0% (2018 est.)
other: 100% (2018 est.)

GOVERNMENT

Country name: *conventional long form:* none
conventional short form: Wake Island
etymology: although first discovered by British Captain William WAKE in 1792, the island is named after British Captain Samuel WAKE, who rediscovered the island in 1796

Dependency status: unincorporated unorganized territory of the US; administered from Washington, DC, by the Department of the Interior; activities in the atoll are currently conducted by the 11th US Air Force and managed from Pacific Air Force Support Center

Independence: none (territory of the US)

Legal system: US common law

Citizenship: see United States

Flag description: the flag of the US is used

ECONOMY

Economic overview: Economic activity is limited to providing services to military personnel and contractors located on the island. All food and manufactured goods must be imported.

ENERGY

Electricity access: *electrification - total population:* 100% (2020)

Electricity: *installed generating capacity:* 0 kW (2020 est.)
consumption: 0 kWh (2020 est.)
exports: 0 kWh (2020 est.)
imports: 0 kWh (2020 est.)
transmission/distribution losses: 0 kWh (2019 est.)

Coal: *production:* 0 metric tons (2020 est.)
consumption: 0 metric tons (2020 est.)
exports: 0 metric tons (2020 est.)
imports: 0 metric tons (2020 est.)
proven reserves: 0 metric tons (2019 est.)

Petroleum: *total petroleum production:* 0 bbl/day (2021 est.)
refined petroleum consumption: 9,500 bbl/day (2019 est.)
crude oil and lease condensate exports: 0 bbl/day (2018 est.)
crude oil and lease condensate imports: 0 bbl/day (2018 est.)
crude oil estimated reserves: 0 barrels (2021 est.)

Natural gas: *production:* 0 cubic meters (2021 est.)
consumption: 0 cubic meters (2021 est.)
exports: 0 cubic meters (2021 est.)
imports: 0 cubic meters (2021 est.)
proven reserves: 0 cubic meters (2021 est.)

Carbon dioxide emissions: 1.275 million metric tonnes of CO_2 (2019 est.)
from coal and metallurgical coke: 0 metric tonnes of CO_2 (2019 est.)
from petroleum and other liquids: 1.275 million metric tonnes of CO_2 (2019 est.)
from consumed natural gas: 0 metric tonnes of CO_2 (2019 est.)
country comparison to the world: 167

Energy consumption per capita: 0 Btu/person (2019 est.)
country comparison to the world: 212

COMMUNICATIONS

Telecommunication systems: *general assessment:* satellite communications; 2 Defense Switched Network circuits off the Overseas Telephone System (OTS); located in the Hawaii area code - 808 (2018)

Broadcast media: American Armed Forces Radio and Television Service (AFRTS) provides satellite radio/TV broadcasts (2018)

TRANSPORTATION

Airports: *total:* 1 (2021)
country comparison to the world: 237

Airports - with paved runways: *total:* 1
2,438 to 3,047 m: 1 (2021)

Ports and terminals: none; two offshore anchorages for large ships

Transportation - note: there are no commercial or civilian flights to and from Wake Island, except in direct support of island missions; emergency landing is available

MILITARY AND SECURITY

Military - note: defense is the responsibility of the US; the US Air Force is responsible for overall administration and operation of the island facilities; the launch support facility is administered by the US Missile Defense Agency (MDA)

TRANSNATIONAL ISSUES

Disputes - international: *US-Marshall Islands:* in May 2016, the Marshall Islands filed a declaration of authority with the UN over Wake Island, which is currently a US territory, reaffirming that it considers Wake Island part of its territory; control over Wake Island would drastically increase the Marshall Islands' exclusive economic zone; the US State Department is assembling a group of experts from both countries to discuss the maritime boundary

WALLIS AND FUTUNA

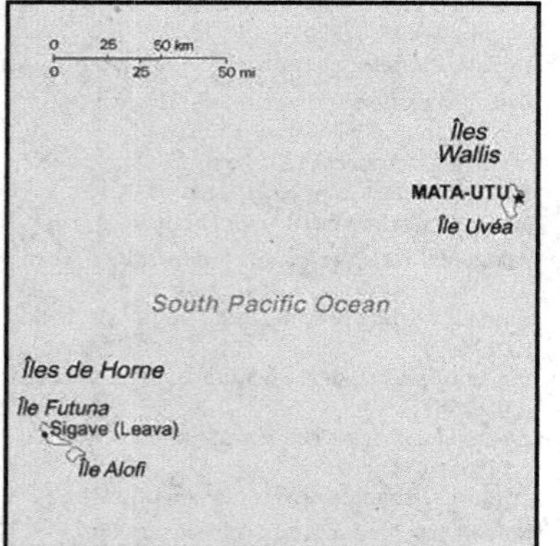

INTRODUCTION

Background: The first humans settled Wallis and Futuna around 800 B.C. The islands were a natural midpoint between Fiji and Samoa. Around A.D. 1500, Tongans invaded Wallis and a chiefdom system resembling Tonga's formal hierarchy developed on the island. Tongans attempted to settle Futuna but were repeatedly rebuffed. Samoans settled Futuna in the 1600s and a slightly less centralized chiefdom system formed. Dutch explorers were the first Europeans to see the islands in 1616, followed intermittently by other Europeans, including British explorer Samuel WALLIS in 1767. French Catholic missionaries were the first Europeans to permanently settle Wallis and Futuna in 1837. The missionaries converted most of the population of Wallis by 1842 and of Futuna by 1846. The missionaries and newly-converted King LAVELUA of Uvea on Wallis asked France for a protectorate in 1842 following a rebellion of locals. France agreed, although the protectorate status would not be ratified until 1887. In 1888, King MUSULAMU of Alo and King TAMOLE of Sigave, both on Futuna, signed a treaty establishing a French protectorate; the Wallis and Futuna protectorate was integrated into the territory of New Caledonia that same year. France renegotiated the terms of the protectorate with the territory's three kings in 1910, expanding French authority.

Wallis and Futuna was the only French colony to side with the Vichy regime during World War II until the arrival of Free French and US troops in 1942. In 1959, inhabitants of the islands voted to separate from New Caledonia and become a French overseas territory, a status it assumed in 1961. Despite the split, a significant Wallisian and Futunan community still lives in New Caledonia. In 2003, Wallis and Futuna's designation changed to that of an overseas collectivity. Wallis and Futuna became an associate member of the Pacific Islands Forum in 2018, two years after France's other Pacific territories became full members of the organization.

GEOGRAPHY

Location: Oceania, islands in the South Pacific Ocean, about two-thirds of the way from Hawaii to New Zealand

Geographic coordinates: 13 18 S, 176 12 W

Map references: Oceania

Area: *total:* 142 sq km
land: 142 sq km
water: 0 sq km
note: includes Ile Uvea (Wallis Island), Ile Futuna (Futuna Island), Ile Alofi, and 20 islets
country comparison to the world: 220

Area - comparative: 1.5 times the size of Washington, DC

Land boundaries: *total:* 0 km

Coastline: 129 km

Maritime claims: *territorial sea:* 12 nm
exclusive economic zone: 200 nm

Climate: tropical; hot, rainy season (November to April); cool, dry season (May to October); rains 250-300 cm per year (80% humidity); average temperature 26.6 degrees Celsius

Terrain: volcanic origin; low hills

Elevation: *highest point:* Mont Singavi (on Futuna) 522 m
lowest point: Pacific Ocean 0 m

Natural resources: NEGL

Land use: *agricultural land:* 42.8% (2018 est.)
arable land: 7.1% (2018 est.)
permanent crops: 35.7% (2018 est.)
permanent pasture: 0% (2018 est.)
forest: 41.9% (2018 est.)
other: 15.3% (2018 est.)

Irrigated land: 0 sq km (2012)

Natural hazards: cyclones; tsunamis

Geography - note: both island groups have fringing reefs; Wallis contains several prominent crater lakes

PEOPLE AND SOCIETY

Population: 15,891 (2022 est.)
country comparison to the world: 220

Nationality: *noun:* Wallisian(s), Futunan(s), or Wallis and Futuna Islanders
adjective: Wallisian, Futunan, or Wallis and Futuna Islander

Ethnic groups: Polynesian

Languages: Wallisian (indigenous Polynesian language) 58.9%, Futunian 30.1%, French (official) 10.8%, other 0.2% (2003 est.)

Religions: Roman Catholic 99%, other 1%

Age structure: *0-14 years:* 20.58% (male 1,702/female 1,561)
15-24 years: 14.72% (male 1,238/female 1,095)
25-54 years: 43.55% (male 3,529/female 3,376)
55-64 years: 9.99% (male 745/female 842)
65 years and over: 11.73% (male 953/female 911) (2022 est.)

Median age: *total:* 34 years
male: 33.1 years
female: 35.1 years (2020 est.)
country comparison to the world: 93

Population growth rate: 0.25% (2022 est.)
country comparison to the world: 173

Birth rate: 12.27 births/1,000 population (2022 est.)
country comparison to the world: 153

Death rate: 5.79 deaths/1,000 population (2022 est.)
country comparison to the world: 169

Net migration rate: -3.96 migrant(s)/1,000 population (2022 est.)
note: there has been steady emigration from Wallis and Futuna to New Caledonia
country comparison to the world: 192

Urbanization: *urban population:* 0% of total population (2022)
rate of urbanization: 0% annual rate of change (2020-25 est.)

Major urban areas - population: 1,000 MATA-UTU (capital) (2018)

Sex ratio: *at birth:* 1.05 male(s)/female
0-14 years: 1.09 male(s)/female
15-24 years: 1.12 male(s)/female
25-54 years: 1.07 male(s)/female
55-64 years: 0.9 male(s)/female
65 years and over: 0.91 male(s)/female
total population: 1.06 male(s)/female (2022 est.)

Infant mortality rate: *total:* 4 deaths/1,000 live births
male: 3.93 deaths/1,000 live births
female: 4.07 deaths/1,000 live births (2022 est.)
country comparison to the world: 189

Life expectancy at birth: *total population:* 80.67 years
male: 77.68 years
female: 83.81 years (2022 est.)
country comparison to the world: 45

Total fertility rate: 1.71 children born/woman (2022 est.)

country comparison to the world: 166

Drinking water source: *improved: total:* 99.1% of population
unimproved: total: 0.9% of population (2020)

Sanitation facility access: *improved: total:* 92.9% of population
unimproved: total: 7.1% of population (2020 est.)

Major infectious diseases: *degree of risk:* high (2020)
food or waterborne diseases: bacterial diarrhea
vectorborne diseases: malaria

ENVIRONMENT

Environment - current issues: deforestation (only small portions of the original forests remain) largely as a result of the continued use of wood as the main fuel source; as a consequence of cutting down the forests, the mountainous terrain of Futuna is particularly prone to erosion; there are no permanent settlements on Alofi because of the lack of natural freshwater resources; lack of soil fertility on the islands of Uvea and Futuna negatively impacts agricultural productivity

Climate: tropical; hot, rainy season (November to April); cool, dry season (May to October); rains 250-300 cm per year (80% humidity); average temperature 26.6 degrees Celsius

Land use: *agricultural land:* 42.8% (2018 est.)
arable land: 7.1% (2018 est.)
permanent crops: 35.7% (2018 est.)
permanent pasture: 0% (2018 est.)
forest: 41.9% (2018 est.)
other: 15.3% (2018 est.)

Urbanization: *urban population:* 0% of total population (2022)
rate of urbanization: 0% annual rate of change (2020-25 est.)

GOVERNMENT

Country name: *conventional long form:* Territory of the Wallis and Futuna Islands
conventional short form: Wallis and Futuna
local long form: Territoire des Iles Wallis et Futuna
local short form: Wallis et Futuna
former: Hoorn Islands is the former name of the Futuna Islands
etymology: Wallis Island is named after British Captain Samuel WALLIS, who discovered it in 1767; Futuna is derived from the native word "futu," which is the name of the fish-poison tree found on the island

Government type: parliamentary democracy (Territorial Assembly); overseas collectivity of France

Dependency status: overseas collectivity of France

Capital: *name:* Mata-Utu (on Ile Uvea)
geographic coordinates: 13 57 S, 171 56 W
time difference: UTC+12 (17 hours ahead of Washington, DC, during Standard Time)

Administrative divisions: 3 administrative precincts (circonscriptions, singular - circonscription) Alo, Sigave, Uvea

Independence: none (overseas collectivity of France)

National holiday: Bastille Day, 14 July (1789)

Constitution: *history:* 4 October 1958 (French Constitution)
amendments: French constitution amendment procedures apply

Legal system: French civil law

Citizenship: see France

Suffrage: 18 years of age; universal

Executive branch: *chief of state:* President Emmanuel MACRON (since 14 May 2017); represented by Administrator Superior Herve JONATHAN (since 11 January 2021)
head of government: President of the Territorial Assembly Munipoese MULI'AKA'AKA (since 20 March 2022)
cabinet: Council of the Territory appointed by the administrator superior on the advice of the Territorial Assembly
elections/appointments: French president elected by absolute majority popular vote in 2 rounds if needed for a 5-year term (eligible for a second term); administrator superior appointed by the French president on the advice of the French Ministry of the Interior; the presidents of the Territorial Government and the Territorial Assembly elected by assembly members
note: there are 3 traditional kings with limited powers

Legislative branch: *description:* unicameral Territorial Assembly or Assemblee Territoriale (20 seats - Wallis 13, Futuna 7; members directly elected in multi-seat constituencies by party-list proportional representation vote to serve 5-year terms)

Wallis and Futuna indirectly elects 1 senator to the French Senate by an electoral college by absolute majority vote in 2 rounds if needed for a 6-year term, and directly elects 1 deputy to the French National Assembly by absolute majority vote for a 5-year term
elections:
Territorial Assembly - last held on 20 March 2022 (next to be held in March 2027)

French Senate - last held on 24 and 27 September 2020 (next to be held by September 2023)

French National Assembly - last held on 11 June 2017 (next to be held in June 2022)
election results:
Territorial Assembly - percent of vote by party - NA; seats by party - 2 members are elected from the list Ofa mo'oni ki tou fenua and 2 members are elected from list Mauli fetokoniaki, 1 seat each from 16 other lists; composition - men NA, women NA, percent of women NA%
representation in French Senate - LR 1 (man)
representation in French National Assembly - independent 1 (man)

Judicial branch: *highest court(s):* Court of Assizes or Cour d'Assizes (consists of 1 judge; court hears primarily serious criminal cases); note - appeals beyond the Court of Assizes are heard before the Court of Appeal or Cour d'Appel (in Noumea, New Caledonia)
judge selection and term of office: NA
subordinate courts: courts of first instance; labor court; note - justice generally administered under French law by the high administrator, but the 3 traditional kings administer customary law, and there is a magistrate in Mata-Utu

Political parties and leaders: Left Radical Party or PRG [Guillaume LACROIX] (formerly Radical Socialist Party or PRS and the Left Radical Movement or MRG)
Lua Kae Tahi (Giscardians) (leader NA)
Rally for Wallis and Futuna-The Republicans (Rassemblement pour Wallis and Futuna) or RPWF-LR [Clovis LOGOLOGOFOLAU]
Socialist Party or PS
Taumu'a Lelei [Soane Muni UHILA]
Union Pour la Democratie Francaise or UDF

International organization participation: PIF (observer), SPC, UPU

Diplomatic representation in the US: none (overseas collectivity of France)

Diplomatic representation from the US: none (overseas collectivity of France)

Flag description: unofficial, local flag has a red field with four white isosceles triangles in the middle, representing the three native kings of the islands and the French administrator; the apexes of the triangles are oriented inward and at right angles to each other; the flag of France, outlined in white on two sides, is in the upper hoist quadrant
note: the design is derived from an original red banner with a white cross pattee that was introduced in the 19th century by French missionaries; the flag of France is used for official occasions

National symbol(s): red saltire (Saint Andrew's Cross) on a white square on a red field; national colors: red, white

National anthem: *note:* as a territory of France, "La Marseillaise" is official (see France)

ECONOMY

Economic overview: The economy is limited to traditional subsistence agriculture, with about 80% of labor force earnings coming from agriculture (coconuts and vegetables), livestock (mostly pigs), and fishing. However, roughly 70% of the labor force is employed in the public sector, although only about a third of the population is in salaried employment.

Revenues come from French Government subsidies, licensing of fishing rights to Japan and South Korea, import taxes, and remittances from expatriate workers in New Caledonia. France directly finances the public sector and health-care and education services. It also provides funding for key development projects in a range of areas, including infrastructure, economic development, environmental management, and health-care facilities.

A key concern for Wallis and Futuna is an aging population with consequent economic development issues. Very few people aged 18-30 live on the islands due to the limited formal employment opportunities. Improving job creation is a current priority for the territorial government.

Real GDP (purchasing power parity): $60 million (2004 est.)
country comparison to the world: 224

Real GDP per capita: $3,800 (2004 est.)
country comparison to the world: 187

GDP (official exchange rate): $195 million (2005) (2005)

Inflation rate (consumer prices): 0.9% (2015)
2.8% (2005)
country comparison to the world: 62

GDP - composition, by end use: *household consumption:* 26% (2005)
government consumption: 54% (2005)

Agricultural products: coconuts, breadfruit, yams, taro, bananas; pigs, goats; fish

Industries: copra, handicrafts, fishing, lumber

Labor force: 4,482 (2013)
country comparison to the world: 222

Labor force - by occupation: *agriculture:* 74%
industry: 3%
services: 23% (2015 est.)

Unemployment rate: 8.8% (2013 est.)
12.2% (2008 est.)
country comparison to the world: 134

Budget: *revenues:* 32.54 million (2015 est.)
expenditures: 34.18 million (2015 est.)

Budget surplus (+) or deficit (-): -0.8% (of GDP) (2015 est.)
country comparison to the world: 70

Public debt: 5.6% of GDP (2004 est.)
note: offical data; data cover general government debt and include debt instruments issued (or owned) by government entities other than the treasury; the data include treasury debt held by foreign entities; the data include debt issued by subnational entities, as well as intragovernmental debt; intragovernmental debt consists of treasury borrowings from surpluses in the social funds, such as for retirement, medical care, and unemployment; debt instruments for the social funds are not sold at public auctions
country comparison to the world: 204

Taxes and other revenues: 16.7% (of GDP) (2015 est.)
country comparison to the world: 175

Fiscal year: calendar year

Exports: $47,450 (2004 est.)
country comparison to the world: 225

Exports - partners: Singapore 47%, France 32%, Belgium 9% (2019)

Exports - commodities: integrated circuits, jewelry, cars, aircraft parts, polyacetals (2019)

Imports: $61.17 million (2004 est.)
country comparison to the world: 221

Imports - partners: France 43%, Fiji 24%, New Zealand 11%, Australia 6% (2019)

Imports - commodities: refined petroleum, beef products, poultry meats, engine parts, packaged medicines (2019)

Debt - external: $3.67 million (2004)
country comparison to the world: 201

Exchange rates: Comptoirs Francais du Pacifique francs (XPF) per US dollar -
110.2 (2015 est.)
89.8 (2014 est.)
89.85 (2013 est.)
90.56 (2012 est.)

COMMUNICATIONS

Telephones - fixed lines: *total subscriptions:* 3,132 (2018 est.)
subscriptions per 100 inhabitants: 25 (2018 est.)
country comparison to the world: 208

Telephones - mobile cellular: *total subscriptions:* 0 (2018)
subscriptions per 100 inhabitants: 0 (2019)
country comparison to the world: 224

Telecommunication systems: *general assessment:* 2G widespread; bandwidth is limited; mobile subscriber numbers are higher than fixed-line and better suited for islands; good mobile coverage in the capital cities and also reasonable coverage across more remote atolls; recent international interest in infrastructure development; increase in demand for mobile broadband as mobile services serve as primary source for Internet access; broadband satellite launched in 2019 to improve costs and capability (2020)
domestic: fixed-line teledensity 25 per 100 persons and 0 per 100 mobile subscriptions (2019)
international: country code - 681; landing point for the Tui-Samoa submarine cable network connecting Wallis & Futuna, Samoa and Fiji (2020)

Broadcast media: the publicly owned French Overseas Network (RFO), which broadcasts to France's overseas departments, collectivities, and territories, is carried on the RFO Wallis and Fortuna TV and radio stations (2019)

Internet country code: .wf

Internet users: *total:* 1,029 (2019 est.)
percent of population: 9% (2019 est.)
country comparison to the world: 227

TRANSPORTATION

Airports: *total:* 2 (2021)
country comparison to the world: 207

Airports - with paved runways: *total:* 2
1,524 to 2,437 m: 1
914 to 1,523 m: 1 (2021)

Merchant marine: *total:* 1
by type: other 1 (2021)
country comparison to the world: 187

Ports and terminals: *major seaport(s):* Leava, Mata-Utu

MILITARY AND SECURITY

Military - note: defense is the responsibility of France

TRANSNATIONAL ISSUES

Disputes - international: none identified

WEST BANK

INTRODUCTION

Background: The landlocked West Bank - the larger of the two Palestinian territories - is home to some three million Palestinians. Inhabited since at least the 15th century B.C., the West Bank has been dominated by many different peoples throughout its history; it was incorporated into the Ottoman Empire in the early 16th century. The West Bank fell to British forces during World War I, becoming part of the British Mandate of Palestine. Following the 1948 Arab-Israeli War, the West Bank was captured by Transjordan (later renamed Jordan), which annexed the West Bank in 1950; it was captured by Israel in the Six-Day War in 1967. Under a series of agreements known as the Oslo Accords signed between 1993 and 1999, Israel transferred to the newly created Palestinian Authority (PA) security and civilian responsibility for many Palestinian-populated areas of the West Bank as well as the Gaza Strip.

In addition to establishing the PA as an interim government, the Oslo Accords divided the West Bank into three areas with one fully managed by the PA, another fully administered by Israel, and a third with shared control until a permanent agreement could be reached between the Palestine Liberation Organization (PLO) and Israel. In 2000, a violent intifada or uprising began across the Palestinian territories, and in 2001 negotiations for a permanent agreement between the PLO and Israel on final status issues stalled. Subsequent attempts to re-start direct negotiations have not resulted in progress toward determining final status of the area.

The PA last held national elections in 2006, when the Islamic Resistance Movement (HAMAS) won a majority of seats in the Palestinian Legislative Council (PLC). Fatah, the dominant Palestinian political faction in the West Bank, and HAMAS failed to maintain a unity government, leading to violent clashes between their respective supporters and HAMAS's violent seizure of all PA military and governmental institutions in the Gaza Strip in June 2007. In December 2018, the Palestinian Constitutional Court dissolved the PLC. In recent years, Fatah and HAMAS have made several attempts at reconciliation, but the factions have been unable to implement agreements.

Since 1994, the PA has administered parts of the West Bank under its control, mainly the major Palestinian population centers and areas immediately surrounding them. Roughly 60% of the West Bank remains under full Israeli civil and military control, impeding movement of people and goods through the territory.

GEOGRAPHY

Location: Middle East, west of Jordan, east of Israel

Geographic coordinates: 32 00 N, 35 15 E

Map references: Middle East

Area: *total:* 5,860 sq km
land: 5,640 sq km
water: 220 sq km
note: includes West Bank, Latrun Salient, and the northwest quarter of the Dead Sea, but excludes Mt. Scopus; East Jerusalem and Jerusalem No Man's Land are also included only as a means of depicting the entire area occupied by Israel in 1967
country comparison to the world: 171

Area - comparative: slightly smaller than Delaware

Land boundaries: *total:* 478 km
border countries (2): Israel 330 km; Jordan 148 km

Coastline: 0 km (landlocked)

Maritime claims: none (landlocked)

Climate: temperate; temperature and precipitation vary with altitude, warm to hot summers, cool to mild winters

Terrain: mostly rugged, dissected upland in west, flat plains descending to Jordan River Valley to the east

Elevation: *highest point:* Khallat al Batrakh 1,020 m
lowest point: Dead Sea -431 m

Natural resources: arable land

Land use: *agricultural land:* 43.3% (2018 est.)
arable land: 7.4% (2018 est.)
permanent crops: 11% (2018 est.)
permanent pasture: 24.9% (2018 est.)
forest: 1.5% (2018 est.)
other: 55.2% (2018 est.)
note: includes Gaza Strip

Irrigated land: (2012) 240 sq km; note - includes Gaza Strip

Major lakes (area sq km): *salt water lake(s):* Dead Sea (shared with Jordan and Israel) - 1,020 sq km
note - endorheic hypersaline lake; 9.6 times saltier than the ocean; lake shore is 431 meters below sea level

Population distribution: the most populous Palestinian communities in the West Bank are located in the central ridge and western half of its territory; Jewish settlements are located throughout the West Bank, the most populous in the Seam Zone--between the 1949 Armistice Line and the separation barrier--and around Jerusalem

Natural hazards: droughts

Geography - note: landlocked; highlands are main recharge area for Israel's coastal aquifers; there are about 380 Israeli civilian sites, including about 213 settlements and 132 small outpost communities in the West Bank and 35 sites in East Jerusalem (2017)

PEOPLE AND SOCIETY

Population: 3,000,021 (2022 est.)
note: approximately 432,000 Israeli settlers live in the West Bank (2019); approximately 227,100 Israeli settlers live in East Jerusalem (2019)
country comparison to the world: 139

Ethnic groups: Palestinian Arab, Jewish, other

Languages: Arabic, Hebrew (spoken by Israeli settlers and many Palestinians), English (widely understood)
major-language sample(s):
كتاب حقائق العالم، المصدر الذي لا يمكن الاستغناء عنه للمعلومات الأساسية
(Arabic)

Religions: Muslim 80-85% (predominantly Sunni), Jewish 12-14%, Christian 1-2.5% (mainly Greek Orthodox), other, unaffiliated, unspecified <1% (2012 est.)

Age structure: *0-14 years:* 35.31% (male 525,645/female 498,458)
15-24 years: 20.75% (male 307,420/female 294,469)
25-54 years: 35.19% (male 516,758/female 503,626)
55-64 years: 5.12% (male 76,615/female 72,006)
65 years and over: 3.62% (2022 est.) (male 48,387/female 56,650) (2020 est.)

Dependency ratios: *total dependency ratio:* 71.2
youth dependency ratio: 65.7
elderly dependency ratio: 5.5
potential support ratio: 18.2 (2020 est.)
note: data represent Gaza Strip and the West Bank

Median age: *total:* 21.9 years
male: 21.7 years
female: 22.2 years (2020 est.)
country comparison to the world: 181

Population growth rate: 1.69% (2022 est.)
country comparison to the world: 55

Birth rate: 24.42 births/1,000 population (2022 est.)
country comparison to the world: 48

Death rate: 3.4 deaths/1,000 population (2022 est.)
country comparison to the world: 223

Net migration rate: -4.09 migrant(s)/1,000 population (2022 est.)
country comparison to the world: 193

Population distribution: the most populous Palestinian communities in the West Bank are located in the central ridge and western half of its territory; Jewish settlements are located throughout the West Bank, the most populous in the Seam Zone--between the 1949 Armistice Line and the separation barrier--and around Jerusalem

Urbanization: *urban population:* 77.3% of total population (2022)
rate of urbanization: 2.85% annual rate of change (2020-25 est.)
note: data represent Gaza Strip and the West Bank

Sex ratio: *at birth:* 1.06 male(s)/female
0-14 years: 1.05 male(s)/female
15-24 years: 1.04 male(s)/female
25-54 years: 1.03 male(s)/female
55-64 years: 1.06 male(s)/female
65 years and over: 0.68 male(s)/female
total population: 1.03 male(s)/female (2022 est.)

Maternal mortality ratio: 27 deaths/100,000 live births (2017 est.)
note: data represent Gaza Strip and the West Bank
country comparison to the world: 118

Infant mortality rate: *total:* 15.29 deaths/1,000 live births
male: 17.68 deaths/1,000 live births
female: 12.76 deaths/1,000 live births (2022 est.)
country comparison to the world: 98

Life expectancy at birth: *total population:* 76.38 years
male: 74.29 years
female: 78.6 years (2022 est.)
country comparison to the world: 104

Total fertility rate: 2.96 children born/woman (2022 est.)
country comparison to the world: 50

Contraceptive prevalence rate: 57.3% (2019/20)
note: includes Gaza Strip and the West Bank

Drinking water source: *improved: urban:* 98.9% of population
rural: 99% of population
total: 98.9% of population
unimproved: urban: 1.1% of population
rural: 1% of population
total: 1.1% of population (2020 est.)
note: includes Gaza Strip and the West Bank

Physicians density: 3.25 physicians/1,000 population (2020)

Hospital bed density: 1.3 beds/1,000 population (2019)

Sanitation facility access: *improved: urban:* 99.9% of population
rural: 98.6% of population
total: 99.6% of population
unimproved: urban: 0.1% of population
rural: 1.4% of population
total: 0.4% of population (2020 est.)
note: note includes Gaza Strip and the West Bank

Major infectious diseases: *note:* on 21 March 2022, the US Centers for Disease Control and Prevention (CDC) issued a Travel Alert for polio in Asia; the West Bank is currently considered a high risk to travelers for polio; the CDC recommends that before any international travel, anyone unvaccinated, incompletely vaccinated, or with an unknown polio vaccination status should complete the routine polio vaccine series; before travel to any high-risk destination, the CDC recommends that adults who previously completed the full, routine polio vaccine series receive a single, lifetime booster dose of polio vaccine

Children under the age of 5 years underweight: 2.1% (2019/20)
note: estimate is for Gaza Strip and the West Bank
country comparison to the world: 109

Child marriage: *women married by age 15:* 0.7%
women married by age 18: 13.4% (2020 est.)
note: includes both the Gaza Strip and the West Bank

Education expenditures: 5.3% of GDP (2018 est.)
note: includes Gaza Strip and the West Bank
country comparison to the world: 52

Literacy: *definition:* age 15 and over can read and write
total population: 97.5%

male: 98.8%
female: 96.2% (2020)
note: estimates are for Gaza and the West Bank

School life expectancy (primary to tertiary education): *total:* 13 years
male: 12 years
female: 14 years (2020)
note: data represent Gaza Strip and the West Bank

Unemployment, youth ages 15-24: *total:* 42.1%
male: 36.6%
female: 70% (2020 est.)
note: includes Gaza Strip

ENVIRONMENT

Environment - current issues: adequacy of freshwater supply; sewage treatment

Air pollutants: *carbon dioxide emissions:* 3.23 megatons (2016 est.)
note: data represent combined total from the Gaza Strip and the West Bank.

Climate: temperate; temperature and precipitation vary with altitude, warm to hot summers, cool to mild winters

Land use: *agricultural land:* 43.3% (2018 est.)
arable land: 7.4% (2018 est.)
permanent crops: 11% (2018 est.)
permanent pasture: 24.9% (2018 est.)
forest: 1.5% (2018 est.)
other: 55.2% (2018 est.)
note: includes Gaza Strip

Urbanization: *urban population:* 77.3% of total population (2022)
rate of urbanization: 2.85% annual rate of change (2020-25 est.)
note: data represent Gaza Strip and the West Bank

Revenue from forest resources: *forest revenues:* 0% of GDP (2018 est.)
country comparison to the world: 204

Waste and recycling: *municipal solid waste generated annually:* 1.387 million tons (2016 est.)
municipal solid waste recycled annually: 6,935 tons (2013 est.)
percent of municipal solid waste recycled: 0.5% (2013 est.)
note: data represent combined total from the Gaza Strip and the West Bank.

Major lakes (area sq km): *salt water lake(s):* Dead Sea (shared with Jordan and Israel) - 1,020 sq km
note - endorheic hypersaline lake; 9.6 times saltier than the ocean; lake shore is 431 meters below sea level

Total water withdrawal: *municipal:* 181.2 million cubic meters (2017 est.)
industrial: 32 million cubic meters (2017 est.)
agricultural: 162 million cubic meters (2017 est.)
note: data represent combined total from the Gaza Strip and the West Bank.

Total renewable water resources: 837 million cubic meters (2017 est.)
note: data represent combined total from the Gaza Strip and the West Bank.

GOVERNMENT

Country name: *conventional long form:* none
conventional short form: West Bank
etymology: name refers to the location of the region of the British Mandate of Palestine that was occupied and administered by Jordan in 1948, as it is located on the far side (west bank) of the Jordan River in relation to Jordan proper; the designation was retained following the 1967 Six-Day War and the subsequent changes in administration

ECONOMY

Economic overview: In 2017, the economic outlook in the West Bank - the larger of the two areas comprising the Palestinian Territories – remained fragile, as security concerns and political friction slowed economic growth. Unemployment in the West Bank remained high at 19.0% in the third quarter of 2017, only slightly better than 19.6% at the same point the previous year, while the labor force participation rate remained flat, year-on-year.

Longstanding Israeli restrictions on imports, exports, and movement of goods and people continue to disrupt labor and trade flows and the territory's industrial capacity, and constrain private sector development. The PA's budget benefited from an effort to improve tax collection, coupled with lower spending in 2017, but the PA for the foreseeable future will continue to rely heavily on donor aid for its budgetary needs and infrastructure development.

Real GDP (purchasing power parity): $25.91 billion (2020 est.)
$29.26 billion (2019 est.)
$28.87 billion (2018 est.)
note: data are in 2017 dollars and includes Gaza Strip
country comparison to the world: 142

Real GDP growth rate: 5.3% (2014 est.)
1% (2013 est.)
6% (2012 est.)
note: excludes Gaza Strip
country comparison to the world: 42

Real GDP per capita: $5,400 (2020 est.)
$6,200 (2019 est.)
$6,300 (2018 est.)
note: data are in 2017 dollars and includes Gaza Strip
country comparison to the world: 168

GDP (official exchange rate): $9.828 billion (2014 est.)
note: excludes Gaza Strip

Inflation rate (consumer prices): 0.2% (2017 est.)
-0.2% (2016 est.)
note: excludes Gaza Strip
country comparison to the world: 31

GDP - composition, by sector of origin: *agriculture:* 2.9% (2017 est.)
industry: 19.5% (2017 est.)
services: 77.6% (2017 est.)
note: excludes Gaza Strip

GDP - composition, by end use: *household consumption:* 91.3% (2017 est.)
government consumption: 26.7% (2017 est.)
investment in fixed capital: 23% (2017 est.)
investment in inventories: 0% (2017 est.)
exports of goods and services: 20% (2017 est.)
imports of goods and services: -61% (2017 est.)
note: excludes Gaza Strip

Agricultural products: tomatoes, cucumbers, olives, poultry, milk, potatoes, sheep milk, eggplants, gourds

Industries: small-scale manufacturing, quarrying, textiles, soap, olive-wood carvings, and mother-of-pearl souvenirs

Industrial production growth rate: 2.2% (2017 est.)
note: includes Gaza Strip
country comparison to the world: 127

Labor force: 1.24 million (2017 est.)
note: excludes Gaza Strip
country comparison to the world: 134

Labor force - by occupation: *agriculture:* 11.5%
industry: 34.4%
services: 54.1% (2013 est.)
note: excludes Gaza Strip

Unemployment rate: 27.9% (2017 est.)
27% (2016 est.)
note: excludes Gaza Strip
country comparison to the world: 201

Unemployment, youth ages 15-24: *total:* 42.1%
male: 36.6%
female: 70% (2020 est.)
note: includes Gaza Strip
country comparison to the world: 10

Population below poverty line: 18% (2011 est.)

Gini Index coefficient - distribution of family income: 33.7 (2016 est.)
38.7 (2007 est.)
note: includes Gaza Strip
country comparison to the world: 125

Household income or consumption by percentage share: *lowest 10%:* 3.2%
highest 10%: 28.2% (2009 est.)
note: includes Gaza Strip

Budget: *revenues:* 1.314 billion (2017 est.)
expenditures: 1.278 billion (2017 est.)
note: includes Palestinian Authority expenditures in the Gaza Strip

Budget surplus (+) or deficit (-): 0.4% (of GDP) (2017 est.)
country comparison to the world: 39

Public debt: 24.4% of GDP (2014 est.)
23.8% of GDP (2013 est.)
country comparison to the world: 177

Taxes and other revenues: 13.4% (of GDP) (2017 est.)
country comparison to the world: 207

Fiscal year: calendar year

Current account balance: -$1.444 billion (2017 est.)
-$1.348 billion (2016 est.)
country comparison to the world: 158

Exports: $2.65 billion (2019 est.) note: data are in current year dollars and includes Gaza Strip
$2.6 billion (2018 est.) note: data are in current year dollars and includes Gaza Strip
note: excludes Gaza Strip
country comparison to the world: 145

Exports - commodities: stone, olives, fruit, vegetables, limestone

Imports: $9.15 billion (2019 est.) note: data are in current year dollars and includes Gaza Strip
$9.02 billion (2018 est.) note: data are in current year dollars and includes Gaza Strip
note: data include the Gaza Strip
country comparison to the world: 109

Imports - commodities: food, consumer goods, construction materials, petroleum, chemicals

Reserves of foreign exchange and gold: $0 (31 December 2017 est.)
$583 million (31 December 2015 est.)
country comparison to the world: 195

Debt - external: $1.662 billion (31 March 2016 est.)
$1.467 billion (31 March 2015 est.)
note: data include the Gaza Strip
country comparison to the world: 158

Exchange rates: new Israeli shekels (ILS) per US dollar -
3.606 (2017 est.)
3.841 (2016 est.)
3.841 (2015 est.)
3.8869 (2014 est.)
3.5779 (2013 est.)

ENERGY

Electricity access: *electrification - total population:* 100% (2020)
note: data for West Bank and Gaza Strip combined

Electricity: *installed generating capacity:* 215,000 kW (2020 est.) Data represented includes both the Gaza Strip and West Bank
consumption: 5,702,816,000 kWh (2019 est.) Data represented includes both the Gaza Strip and West Bank
exports: 0 kWh (2019 est.) Data represented includes both the Gaza Strip and West Bank
imports: 5.9 billion kWh (2019 est.) Data represented includes both the Gaza Strip and West Bank
transmission/distribution losses: 847 million kWh (2019 est.) Data represented includes both the Gaza Strip and West Bank

Electricity generation sources: *fossil fuels:* 100% of total installed capacity (2020 est.) Data represented includes both the Gaza Strip and West Bank

Petroleum: *total petroleum production:* 0 bbl/day (2021 est.) Data represented includes both the Gaza Strip and West Bank
refined petroleum consumption: 24,600 bbl/day (2019 est.) Data represented includes both the Gaza Strip and West Bank

Refined petroleum products - exports: 19 bbl/day (2015 est.)
country comparison to the world: 123

Refined petroleum products - imports: 22,740 bbl/day (2015 est.)
country comparison to the world: 113

Carbon dioxide emissions: 3.341 million metric tonnes of CO2 (2019 est.) Data represented includes both the Gaza Strip and West Bank
from petroleum and other liquids: 3.341 million metric tonnes of CO2 (2019 est.) Data includes both the Gaza Strip and West Bank
country comparison to the world: 146

Energy consumption per capita: 13.604 million Btu/person (2019 est.) Data represented includes both the Gaza Strip and West Bank
country comparison to the world: 144

COMMUNICATIONS

Telephones - fixed lines: *total subscriptions:* 466,283 (2020 est.)
subscriptions per 100 inhabitants: 9 (2020 est.)
note: includes Gaza Strip
country comparison to the world: 96

Telephones - mobile cellular: *total subscriptions:* 4,274,119 (2020 est.)
subscriptions per 100 inhabitants: 84 (2020 est.)
note: includes Gaza Strip
country comparison to the world: 129

Telecommunication systems: *general assessment:* continuing political and economic instability has impeded liberalization of the telecommunications industry (2018)
domestic: Israeli has companies that are responsible for fixed-line services; two Palestinian cellular providers launched 3G mobile networks in the West Bank in January 2018 after Israel lifted its ban; fixed-line 9 per 100 and mobile-cellular subscriptions 84 per 100 (includes Gaza Strip) (2020)
international: country code 970 or 972; 1 international switch in Ramallah

Broadcast media: the Palestinian Authority operates 1 TV and 1 radio station; about 20 private TV and 40 radio stations; both Jordanian TV and satellite TV are accessible

Internet country code: .ps; note - IANA has designated .ps for the West Bank, same as Gaza Strip

Internet users: *total:* 3,602,452 (2020 est.)
percent of population: 75% (2020 est.)
note: includes the Gaza Strip
country comparison to the world: 106

Broadband - fixed subscriptions: *total:* 373,050 (2020 est.)
subscriptions per 100 inhabitants: 7 (2020 est.)
note: includes the Gaza Strip
country comparison to the world: 102

TRANSPORTATION

Airports: *total:* 2 (2021)
country comparison to the world: 208

Airports - with paved runways: *total:* 2
1,524 to 2,437 m: 1
under 914 m: 1 (2021)

Heliports: 1 (2021)

Roadways: *total:* 4,686 km (2010)
paved: 4,686 km (2010)
note: includes Gaza Strip
country comparison to the world: 149

MILITARY AND SECURITY

Military and security forces: per the Oslo Accords, the PA is not permitted a conventional military but maintains security and police forces; PA security personnel have operated almost exclusively in the West Bank since HAMAS seized power in the Gaza Strip in 2007; PA forces include National Security Forces, Presidential Guard, Civil Police, Civil Defense, Preventive Security Organization, the General Intelligence Organization, and the Military Intelligence Organization (2022)
note: the National Security Forces conduct gendarmerie-style security operations in circumstances that exceed the capabilities of the Civil Police; it is the largest branch of the PA security services and acts as the Palestinian army; the Presidential Guard protects facilities and provides dignitary protection; the Preventive Security Organization is responsible for internal intelligence gathering and investigations related to internal security cases, including political dissent

Military expenditures: not available

Military and security service personnel strengths: the PA Security Forces have approximately 30,000 active personnel (2022)

Military equipment inventories and acquisitions: the security services are armed mostly with small arms and light weapons, although since 2010, they have received small amounts of heavier equipment from Jordan (armored personnel carriers) and Russia (armored personnel carriers and transport helicopters) (2022)

Military service age and obligation: not available

TERRORISM

Terrorist group(s): Al-Aqsa Martyrs Brigade; HAMAS; Kahane Chai; Palestine Islamic Jihad; Palestine Liberation Front; Popular Front for the Liberation of Palestine

TRANSNATIONAL ISSUES

Disputes - international: *West Bank-Israel:* West Bank is Israeli-occupied with current status subject to the Israeli-Palestinian Interim Agreement - permanent status to be determined through further negotiation; in 2002, Israel began construction of a "seam line" separation barrier along parts of the Green Line and within the West Bank; as of mid-2020, plans were to continue barrier construction

Refugees and internally displaced persons: *refugees (country of origin):* 871,537 (Palestinian refugees) (2020)

IDPs: 131,000 (includes persons displaced within the Gaza strip due to the intensification of the Israeli-Palestinian conflict since June 2014 and other Palestinian IDPs in the Gaza Strip and West Bank who fled as long ago as 1967, although confirmed cumulative data do not go back beyond 2006) (2020); note - data represent Gaza Strip and West Bank

WORLD

INTRODUCTION

Background: Globally, the 20th century was marked by: (a) two devastating World Wars; (b) the Great Depression of the 1930s; (c) the end of vast colonial empires; (d) rapid advances in science and technology, from the first airplane flight at Kitty Hawk, North Carolina (US) to the landing on the moon; (e) the Cold War between the Western alliance and the Warsaw Pact nations; (f) a sharp rise in living standards in North America, Europe, and Japan; (g) increased concerns about environmental degradation including deforestation, energy and water shortages, declining biological diversity, and air pollution; (h) the onset of the AIDS epidemic; and (i) the ultimate emergence of the US as the only world superpower. The planet's population continues to explode: from 1 billion in 1820 to 2 billion in 1930, 3 billion in 1960, 4 billion in 1974, 5 billion in 1987, 6 billion in

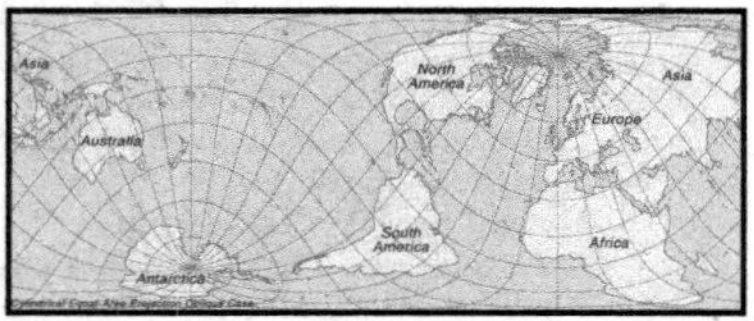

1999, and 7 billion in 2012. For the 21st century, the continued exponential growth in science and technology raises both hopes (e.g., advances in medicine and agriculture) and fears (e.g., development of even more lethal weapons of war).

GEOGRAPHY

Geographic overview: The surface of the Earth is approximately 70.9% water and 29.1% land. The former portion is divided into large bodies termed oceans. The World Factbook recognizes and describes five oceans, which are in decreasing order of size: the Pacific Ocean, Atlantic Ocean, Indian Ocean, Southern Ocean, and Arctic Ocean. Because of their immense size, the Pacific and Atlantic Oceans are generally divided at the equator into the North and South Pacific Oceans and the North and South Atlantic Oceans, thus creating seven major water bodies - the so-called "Seven Seas."

Some 97.5% of the Earth's water is saltwater. Of the 2.5% that is fresh, about two-thirds is frozen mostly locked up in the Antarctic ice sheets and mountain glaciers worldwide. If all the surface ice on earth fully melted, the sea level would rise about 70 m (230 ft).

In a 100-year period, a water molecule spends 98 years in the ocean, 20 months as ice, about two weeks in lakes and rivers, and less than a week in the atmosphere. Groundwater can take 50 years to just traverse 1 km (0.6 mi).

Earth's land portion is generally divided into several, large, discrete landmasses termed continents. Depending on the convention used, the number of continents can vary from five to seven. The most common classification recognizes seven, which are (from largest to smallest): Asia, Africa, North America, South America, Antarctica, Europe, and Australia. Asia and Europe are sometimes lumped together into a Eurasian continent resulting in six continents. Alternatively, North and South America are sometimes grouped as simply the Americas, resulting in a continent total of six (or five, if the Eurasia designation is used).

North America is commonly understood to include the island of Greenland, the isles of the Caribbean, and to extend south all the way to the Isthmus of Panama. The easternmost extent of Europe is generally defined as being the Ural Mountains and the Ural River; on the southeast the Caspian Sea; and on the south the Caucasus Mountains, the Black Sea, and the Mediterranean. Portions of five countries - Azerbaijan, Georgia, Kazakhstan, Russia, and Turkey - fall within both Europe and Asia, but in every instance the larger section is in Asia. These countries are considered part of both continents. Armenia and Cyprus, which lie completely in Western Asia, are geopolitically European countries.

Asia usually incorporates all the islands of the Philippines, Malaysia, and Indonesia. The islands of the Pacific are often lumped with Australia into a "land mass" termed Oceania or Australasia. Africa's northeast extremity is frequently delimited at the Isthmus of Suez, but for geopolitical purposes, the Egyptian Sinai Peninsula is often included as part of Africa.

Although the above groupings are the most common, different continental dispositions are recognized or taught in certain parts of the world, with some arrangements more heavily based on cultural spheres rather than physical geographic considerations.

Based on the seven-continent model, and grouping islands with adjacent continents, Africa has the most countries with 54. Europe contains 49 countries and Asia 48, but these two continents share five countries: Azerbaijan, Georgia, Kazakhstan, Russia, and Turkey. North America consists of 23 sovereign states, Oceania has 14, and South America 12.

countries by continent: Africa (54): Algeria, Angola, Benin, Botswana, Burkina Faso, Burundi, Cabo Verde, Cameroon, Central African Republic, Chad, Comoros, Democratic Republic of the Congo, Republic of the Congo, Cote d'Ivoire, Djibouti, Egypt, Equatorial Guinea, Eritrea, Eswatini, Ethiopia, Gabon, The Gambia, Ghana, Guinea, Guinea-Bissau, Kenya, Lesotho, Liberia, Libya, Madagascar, Malawi, Mali, Mauritania, Mauritius, Morocco, Mozambique, Namibia, Niger, Nigeria, Rwanda, Sao Tome and Principe, Senegal, Seychelles, Sierra Leone, Somalia, South Africa, South Sudan, Sudan, Tanzania, Togo, Tunisia, Uganda, Zambia, Zimbabwe;

Europe (49): Albania, Andorra, Austria, Azerbaijan*, Belarus, Belgium, Bosnia and Herzegovina, Bulgaria, Croatia, Czech Republic, Denmark, Estonia, Finland, France, Georgia*, Germany, Greece, Holy See (Vatican City), Hungary, Iceland, Ireland, Italy, Kazakhstan*, Kosovo, Latvia, Liechtenstein, Lithuania, Luxembourg, Malta, Moldova, Monaco, Montenegro, Netherlands, North Macedonia, Norway, Poland, Portugal, Romania, Russia*, San Marino, Serbia, Slovakia, Slovenia, Spain, Sweden, Switzerland, Turkey*, Ukraine, United Kingdom (* indicates part of the country is also in Asia);

Asia (48): Afghanistan, Armenia, Azerbaijan*, Bahrain, Bangladesh, Bhutan, Brunei, Burma, Cambodia, China, Cyprus, Georgia*, India, Indonesia, Iran, Iraq, Israel, Japan, Jordan, Kazakhstan*, North Korea, South Korea, Kuwait, Kyrgyzstan, Laos, Lebanon, Malaysia, Maldives, Mongolia, Nepal, Oman, Pakistan, Philippines, Qatar, Russia*, Saudi Arabia, Singapore, Sri Lanka, Syria, Tajikistan, Thailand, Timor-Leste, Turkey*, Turkmenistan, United Arab Emirates, Uzbekistan, Vietnam, Yemen (* indicates part of the country is also in Europe);

North America (23): Antigua and Barbuda, The Bahamas, Barbados, Belize, Canada, Costa Rica, Cuba, Dominica, Dominican Republic, El Salvador, Grenada, Guatemala, Haiti, Honduras, Jamaica, Mexico, Nicaragua, Panama, Saint Kitts and Nevis, Saint Lucia, Saint Vincent and the Grenadines, Trinidad and Tobago, United States;

Oceania (14): Australia, Fiji, Kiribati, Marshall Islands, Federated States of Micronesia, Nauru, New Zealand, Palau, Papua New Guinea, Samoa, Solomon Islands, Tonga, Tuvalu, Vanuatu;

South America (12): Argentina, Bolivia, Brazil, Chile, Colombia, Ecuador, Guyana, Paraguay, Peru, Suriname, Uruguay, Venezuela

Three of the states described above – France, Netherlands, and the United Kingdom – consist of smaller political entities that are referred to as countries. France considers French Polynesia an overseas country; the Kingdom of the Netherlands refers to all four of its constituent parts (Netherlands [proper], and the islands of Aruba, Curacao, and Sint Maarten) as countries; and the United Kingdom comprises the countries of England, Wales, Scotland, and Northern Ireland. While not recognized as sovereign states, *The World Factbook* does includes descriptive entries for the French and Dutch island "countries."

the world from space: Earth is the only planet in the Solar System to have water in its three states of matter: liquid (oceans, lakes, and rivers), solid (ice), and gas (water vapor in clouds); from a distance, Earth would be the brightest of the eight planets in the Solar System; this luminous effect would be because of the sunlight reflected by the planet's water

Earth is also the only planet in the Solar System known to be active with earthquakes and volcanoes; these events form the landscape, replenish carbon dioxide into the atmosphere, and erase impact craters caused by meteors

Earth has a slight equatorial bulge - a difference between its equatorial and polar diameters - because of the centrifugal force exerted by the rotation of the planet about its axis. The equatorial diameter is 12,756 km, but the polar diameter is 12,714 km. This results in the Earth's circumference at the equator being 40,075 km, while the polar circumference is 40,008 km.

Map references: Physical Map of the World

Area: *total:* 510.072 million sq km
land: 148.94 million sq km
water: 361.9 million sq km
note: 70.9% of the world's surface is water, 29.1% is land

Area - comparative: land area about 16 times the size of the US

Area - rankings: *top fifteen World Factbook entities ranked by size:* Pacific Ocean 155,557,000 sq km; Atlantic Ocean 76,762,000 sq km; Indian Ocean 68,556,000 sq km; Southern Ocean 20,327,000 sq km; Russia 17,098,242 sq km; Antarctica 14,200,000 sq km; Arctic Ocean 14,056,000 sq km; Canada 9,984,670 sq km; United States 9,826,675 sq km; China 9,596,960 sq km; Brazil 8,515,770 sq km; Australia 7,741,220 sq km; European Union 4,324,782 sq km; India 3,287,263 sq km; Argentina 2,780,400 sq km

top ten largest water bodies: Pacific Ocean 155,557,000 sq km; Atlantic Ocean 76,762,000 sq km; Indian Ocean 68,556,000 sq km; Southern Ocean 20,327,000 sq km; Arctic Ocean 14,056,000 sq km; Coral Sea 4,184,100 sq km; South China Sea 3,595,900 sq km; Caribbean Sea 2,834,000 sq km; Bering Sea 2,520,000 sq km; Mediterranean Sea 2,469,000 sq km

top ten largest landmasses: Asia 44,568,500 sq km; Africa 30,065,000 sq km; North America 24,473,000 sq km; South America 17,819,000 sq km; Antarctica 14,200,000 sq km; Europe 9,948,000 sq km; Australia 7,741,220 sq km; Greenland 2,166,086 sq km; New Guinea 785,753 sq km; Borneo 751,929 sq km

top ten largest islands: Greenland 2,166,086 sq km; New Guinea (Indonesia, Papua New Guinea) 785,753 sq km; Borneo (Brunei, Indonesia, Malaysia) 751,929 sq km; Madagascar 587,713 sq km; Baffin Island (Canada) 507,451 sq km; Sumatra (Indonesia) 472,784 sq km; Honshu (Japan) 227,963 sq km; Victoria Island (Canada) 217,291 sq km; Great Britain (United Kingdom) 209,331 sq km; Ellesmere Island (Canada) 196,236 sq km *top ten longest mountain ranges (land-based):* Andes (Venezuela, Colombia, Ecuador, Peru, Bolivia, Chile, Argentina) 7,000 km; Rocky Mountains (Canada, US) 4,830 km; Great Dividing Range (Australia) 3,700 km; Transantarctic Mountains (Antarctica) 3,500 km; Kunlun Mountains (China) 3,000 km; Ural Mountains (Russia, Kazakhstan) 2,640 km; Atlas Mountains (Morocco, Algeria, Tunisia) 2,500 km; Appalachian Mountains (Canada, US) 2,400 km; Himalayas (Pakistan, Afghanistan, India, China, Nepal, Bhutan) 2,300 km; Altai Mountains (Kazakhstan, Russia, Mongolia) 2,000 km; **note** - lengths are approximate; if oceans are included, the Mid-Ocean Ridge is by far the longest mountain range at 40,389 km

top ten largest forested countries (sq km and percent of land): Russia 8,149,310 (49.8%); Brazil 4,935,380 (58.9%); Canada 3,470,690 (38.2%); United States 3,103,700 (33.9%); China 2,098,640 (22.3%); Democratic Republic of the Congo 1,522,670 (67.2%); Australia 1,250,590 (16.3%); Indonesia 903,250 (49.9%); Peru 738,054 (57.7%); India 708,600 (23.8%) (2016 est.)

top ten most densely forested countries (percent of land): Suriname (98.3%), Federated States of Micronesia (91.9%), Gabon (90%), Seychelles (88.4%), Palau (87.6%), Guyana (83.9%), Laos (82.1%), Solomon Islands (77.9%), Papua New Guinea (74.1%), Finland (73.1%) (2016 est.)

top ten largest (non-polar) deserts: Sahara (Algeria, Chad, Egypt, Libya, Mali, Mauritania, Niger, Western Sahara, Sudan, Tunisia) 9,200,000 sq km; Arabian (Saudi Arabia, Iraq, Jordan, Kuwait, Oman, Qatar, United Arab Emirates, Yemen) 2,330,000 sq km; Gobi (China, Mongolia) 1,295,000 sq km; Kalahari (Botswana, Namibia, South Africa) 900,000 sq km; Patagonian (Argentina) 673,000 sq km; Syrian (Syria, Iraq, Jordan, Saudi Arabia) 500,000 sq km; Chihuahuan (Mexico) 362,000 sq km; Kara-Kum (Turkmenistan) 350,000 sq km; Great Victoria (Australia) 348,750 sq km; Great Basin (United States) 343,169 sq km; **note** - if the two polar deserts are included, they would rank first and second: Antarctic Desert 14,200,000 sq km and Arctic Desert 13,900,000 sq km

ten smallest independent countries: Holy See (Vatican City) 0.44 sq km; Monaco 2 sq km; Nauru 21 sq km; Tuvalu 26 sq km; San Marino 61 sq km; Liechtenstein 160 sq km; Marshall Islands 181 sq km; Saint Kitts and Nevis 261 sq km; Maldives 298 sq km; Malta 316 sq km

Land boundaries: the land boundaries in *The World Factbook* total 279,035.5 km (not counting shared boundaries twice); two nations, China and Russia, each border 14 other countries

note 1: the total is actually misleading in terms of accuracy, since one cannot accurately measure every river meander along a boundary; a number rounded slightly higher - to 280,000 km - makes more sense and has been coordinated with and approved by the US State Department

note 2: 46 nations and other areas are landlocked, these include: Afghanistan, Andorra, Armenia, Austria, Azerbaijan, Belarus, Bhutan, Bolivia, Botswana, Burkina Faso, Burundi, Central African Republic, Chad, Czechia, Eswatini, Ethiopia, Holy See (Vatican City), Hungary, Kazakhstan, Kosovo, Kyrgyzstan, Laos, Lesotho, Liechtenstein, Luxembourg, Macedonia, Malawi, Mali, Moldova, Mongolia, Nepal, Niger, Paraguay, Rwanda, San Marino, Serbia, Slovakia, South Sudan, Switzerland, Tajikistan, Turkmenistan, Uganda, Uzbekistan, West Bank, Zambia, Zimbabwe; two of these, Liechtenstein and Uzbekistan, are doubly landlocked

note 3: worldwide, some one-quarter of interior (non-coastal) borders are rivers; South America with 43% leads the continents, followed by North America with 32%, Africa with 30%, Europe with 23%, and Asia with 18%; Australia has no interior national river borders

Coastline: 356,000 km

note: 95 nations and other entities are islands that border no other countries, they include: American Samoa, Anguilla, Antigua and Barbuda, Aruba, Ashmore and Cartier Islands, The Bahamas, Bahrain, Baker Island, Barbados, Bermuda, Bouvet Island, British Indian Ocean Territory, British Virgin Islands, Cabo Verde, Cayman Islands, Christmas Island, Clipperton Island, Cocos (Keeling) Islands, Comoros, Cook Islands, Coral Sea Islands, Cuba, Curacao, Cyprus, Dominica, Falkland Islands (Islas Malvinas), Faroe Islands, Fiji, French Polynesia, French Southern and Antarctic Lands, Greenland, Grenada, Guam, Guernsey, Heard Island and McDonald Islands, Howland Island, Iceland, Isle of Man, Jamaica, Jan Mayen, Japan, Jarvis Island, Jersey, Johnston Atoll, Kingman Reef, Kiribati, Madagascar, Maldives, Malta, Marshall Islands, Mauritius, Mayotte, Federated States of Micronesia, Midway Islands, Montserrat, Nauru, Navassa Island, New Caledonia, New Zealand, Niue, Norfolk Island, Northern Mariana Islands, Palau, Palmyra Atoll, Paracel Islands, Philippines, Pitcairn Islands, Puerto Rico, Saint Barthelemy, Saint Helena, Saint Kitts and Nevis, Saint Lucia, Saint Pierre and Miquelon, Saint Vincent and the Grenadines, Samoa, Sao Tome and Principe, Seychelles, Singapore, Sint Maarten, Solomon Islands, South Georgia and the South Sandwich Islands, Spratly Islands, Sri Lanka, Svalbard, Taiwan, Tokelau, Tonga, Trinidad and Tobago, Turks and Caicos Islands, Tuvalu, Vanuatu, Virgin Islands, Wake Island, Wallis and Futuna

Maritime claims: a variety of situations exist, but in general, most countries make the following claims measured from the mean low-tide baseline as described in the 1982 UN Convention on the Law of the Sea: territorial sea - 12 nm, contiguous zone - 24 nm, and exclusive economic zone - 200 nm; additional zones provide for exploitation of continental shelf resources and an exclusive fishing zone; boundary situations with neighboring states prevent many countries from extending their fishing or economic zones to a full 200 nm

Climate: a wide equatorial band of hot and humid tropical climates, bordered north and south by subtropical temperate zones that separate two large areas of cold and dry polar climates

ten driest places on earth (average annual precipitation): McMurdo Dry Valleys, Antarctica 0 mm (0 in)
Arica, Chile 0.76 mm (0.03 in)
Al Kufrah, Libya 0.86 mm (0.03 in)
Aswan, Egypt 0.86 mm (0.03 in)
Luxor, Egypt 0.86 mm (0.03 in)
Ica, Peru 2.29 mm (0.09 in)
Wadi Halfa, Sudan 2.45 mm (0.1 in)
Iquique, Chile 5.08 mm (0.2 in)
Pelican Point, Namibia 8.13 mm (0.32 in)
El Arab (Aoulef), Algeria 12.19 mm (0.48 in)

ten wettest places on earth (average annual precipitation): Mawsynram, India 11,871 mm (467.4 in)
Cherrapunji, India 11,777 mm (463.7 in)
Tutunendo, Colombia 11,770 mm (463.4 in)
Cropp River, New Zealand 11,516 mm (453.4 in)
San Antonia de Ureca, Equatorial Guinea 10,450 mm (411.4 in)
Debundsha, Cameroon 10,299 mm (405.5 in)
Big Bog, US (Hawaii) 10,272 mm (404.4 in)
Mt Waialeale, US (Hawaii) 9,763 mm (384.4 in)
Kukui, US (Hawaii) 9,293 mm (365.9 in)
Emeishan, China 8,169 mm (321.6 in)

ten coldest places on earth (lowest average monthly temperature): Verkhoyansk, Russia (Siberia) -47°C (-53°F) January
Oymyakon, Russia (Siberia) -46°C (-52°F) January
Eureka, Canada -38.4°C (-37.1°F) February
Isachsen, Canada -36°C (-32.8°F) February
Alert, Canada -34°C (-28°F) February
Kap Morris Jesup, Greenland -34°C (-29°F) March
Cornwallis Island, Canada -33.5°C (-28.3°F) February
Cambridge Bay, Canada -33.5°C (28.3°F) February
Ilirnej, Russia -33°C (-28°F) January
Resolute, Canada -33°C (-27.4°F) February

ten hottest places on earth (highest average monthly temperature): Death Valley, US (California) 39°C (101°F) July
Iranshahr, Iran 38.3°C (100.9°F) June
Ouallene, Algeria 38°C (100.4°F) July
Kuwait City, Kuwait 37.7°C (100°F) July
Medina, Saudi Arabia 36°C (97°F) July
Buckeye, US (Arizona) 34°C (93°F) July
Jazan, Saudi Arabia 33°C (91°F) June
Al Kufrah, Libya 31°C (87°F) July
Alice Springs, Australia 29°C (84°F) January
Tamanrasset, Algeria 29°C (84°F) June

Terrain: tremendous variation of terrain on each of the continents; check the World "Elevation" entry for a compilation of terrain extremes; the world's ocean floors are marked by mid-ocean ridges while the ocean surfaces form a dynamic, continuously changing environment; check the "Terrain" field and its 'major surface currents' and 'ocean zones' subfields under each of the five ocean entries (Arctic, Atlantic, Indian, Pacific, and Southern) for further information on oceanic environs

Ten Cave Superlatives: compiled from "Geography - note(s)" under various country entries where more details may be found

largest cave: Son Doong in Phong Nha-Ke Bang National Park, Vietnam is the world's largest cave (greatest cross sectional area) and is the largest known cave passage in the world by volume; it currently measures a total of 38.5 million cu m (about 1.35 billion cu ft); it connects to Thung cave (but not yet officially); when recognized, it will add an additional 1.6 million cu m in volume

largest ice cave: the Eisriesenwelt (Ice Giants World) inside the Hochkogel mountain near Werfen, Austria is the world's largest and longest ice cave system at 42 km (26 mi)

longest cave: Mammoth Cave, in west-central Kentucky, is the world's longest known cave system with more than 650 km (405 mi) of surveyed passageways

longest salt cave: the Malham Cave in Mount Sodom in Israel is the world's longest salt cave at 10 km (6 mi); its survey is not complete and its length will undoubtedly increase

longest underwater cave: the Sac Actun cave system in Mexico at 348 km (216 mi) is the longest underwater cave in the world and the second longest cave worldwide

longest lava tube cave: Kazumura Cave on the island of Hawaii is the world's longest and deepest lava tube cave; it has been surveyed at 66 km (41 mi) long and 1,102 m (3,614 ft) deep
deepest cave: Veryovkina Cave in the Caucasus country of Georgia is the world's deepest cave, plunging down 2,212 m (7,257 ft)
deepest underwater cave: the Hranice Abyss in Czechia is the world's deepest surveyed underwater cave at 404 m (1,325 ft); its survey is not complete and it could end up being some 800-1,200 m deep
largest cave chamber: the Miao Room in the Gebihe cave system at China's Ziyun Getu He Chuandong National Park encloses some 10.78 million cu m (380.7 million cu ft) of volume
largest bat cave: Bracken Cave outside of San Antonio, Texas is the world's largest bat cave; it is the summer home to the largest colony of bats in the world; an estimated 20 million Mexican free-tailed bats roost in the cave from March to October making it the world's largest known concentration of mammals

Elevation: *highest point:* Mount Everest 8,849 m
lowest point: Denman Glacier (Antarctica) more than -3,500 m (in the oceanic realm, Challenger Deep in the Mariana Trench is the lowest point, lying -10,924 m below the surface of the Pacific Ocean)
mean elevation: 840 m
top ten highest mountains (measured from sea level): Mount Everest (China-Nepal) 8,849 m; K2 (Pakistan) 8,611 m; Kanchenjunga (India-Nepal) 8,598 m; Lhotse (Nepal) 8,516 m; Makalu (China-Nepal) 8,463 m; Cho Oyu (China-Nepal) 8,201 m; Dhaulagiri (Nepal) 8,167 m; Manaslu (Nepal) 8,163 m; Nanga Parbat (Pakistan) 8,125 m; Anapurna (Nepal) 8,091 m; **note -** Mauna Kea (United States) is the world's tallest mountain as measured from base to summit; the peak of this volcanic colossus lies on the island of Hawaii, but its base begins more than 70 km offshore and at a depth of about 6,000 m; total height estimates range from 9,966 m to 10,203 m
top ten highest island peaks: Puncak Jaya (New Guinea) 4,884 m (Indonesia)*; Mauna Kea (Hawaii) 4,207 m (United States); Gunung Kinabalu (Borneo) 4,095 m (Malaysia)*; Yu Shan (Taiwan) 3,952 (Taiwan)*; Mount Kerinci (Sumatra) 3,805 m (Indonesia); Mount Erebus (Ross Island) 3,794 (Antarctica); Mount Fuji (Honshu) 3,776 m (Japan)*; Mount Rinjani (Lombok) 3,726 m (Indonesia); Aoraki-Mount Cook (South Island) 3,724 m (New Zealand)*; Pico de Teide (Tenerife) 3,718 m (Spain)*; **note -** * indicates the highest peak for that Factbook entry
highest point on each continent: Asia - Mount Everest (China-Nepal) 8,849 m; South America - Cerro Aconcagua (Argentina) 6,960 m; North America - Denali (Mount McKinley) (United States) 6,190 m; Africa - Kilimanjaro (Tanzania) 5,895 m; Europe - El'brus (Russia) 5,633 m; Antarctica - Vinson Massif 4,897 m; Australia - Mount Kosciuszko 2,229 m
highest capital on each continent: South America - La Paz (Bolivia) 3,640 m; Africa - Addis Ababa (Ethiopia) 2,355 m; Asia - Thimphu (Bhutan) 2,334 m; North America - Mexico City (Mexico) 2,240 m; Europe - Andorra la Vella (Andorra) 1,023 m; Australia - Canberra (Australia) 605 m
lowest point on each continent: Antarctica - Denman Glacier more than -3,500 m; Asia - Dead Sea (Israel-Jordan) -431 m; Africa - Lac Assal (Djibouti) -155 m; South America - Laguna del Carbon (Argentina) -105 m; North America -Death Valley (United States) -86 m; Europe - Caspian Sea (Azerbaijan-Kazakhstan-Russia) -28 m; Australia - Lake Eyre -15
lowest capital on each continent: Asia - Baku (Azerbaijan) -28 m; Europe - Amsterdam (Netherlands) -2 m; Africa -Banjul (Gambia); Bissau (Guinea-Bissau), Conakry (Guinea), Djibouti (Djibouti), Libreville (Gabon), Male (Maldives), Monrovia (Liberia), Tunis (Tunisia), Victoria (Seychelles) 0 m; North America - Basseterre (Saint Kitts and Nevis), Kingstown (Saint Vincent and the Grenadines), Panama City (Panama), Port of Spain (Trinidad and Tobago), Roseau (Dominica), Saint John's (Antigua and Barbuda), Santo Domingo (Dominican Republic) 0 m; South America -Georgetown (Guyana) 0 m; Australia - Canberra (Australia) 605 m

Natural resources: the rapid depletion of nonrenewable mineral resources, the depletion of forest areas and wetlands, the extinction of animal and plant species, and the deterioration in air and water quality pose serious long-term problems

Irrigated land: 3,242,917 sq km (2012 est.)

Major lakes (area sq km): *top ten largest natural lakes:* Caspian Sea (Azerbaijan, Iran, Kazakhstan, Russia, Turkmenistan) 374,000 sq km; Lake Superior (Canada, United States) 82,100 sq km; Lake Victoria (Kenya, Tanzania, Uganda) 62,940 sq km; Lake Huron (Canada, United States) 59,600 sq km; Lake Michigan (United States) 57,750 sq km; Lake Tanganyika (Burundi, Democratic Republic of the Congo, Tanzania, Zambia) 32,000 sq km; Great Bear Lake (Canada) 31,328 sq km; Lake Baikal (Russia) 31,500 sq km; Lake Malawi (Malawi, Mozambique, Tanzania) 22,490 sq km; Great Slave Lake (Canada) 28,568 sq km
note 1: the areas of the lakes are subject to seasonal variation; only the Caspian Sea is saline, the rest are fresh water
note 2: Lakes Huron and Michigan are technically a single lake because the flow of water between the Straits of Mackinac that connects the two lakes keeps their water levels at near-equilibrium; combined, Lake Huron-Michigan is the largest freshwater lake by surface area in the world

Major rivers (by length in km): *top ten longest rivers:* Nile (Africa) 6,650 km; Amazon (South America) 6,436 km; Yangtze (Asia) 6,300 km; Mississippi-Missouri (North America) 6,275 km; Yenisey-Angara (Asia) 5,539 km; Huang He/Yellow (Asia) 5,464 km; Ob-Irtysh (Asia) 5,410 km; Congo (Africa) 4,700 km; Amur (Asia) 4,444 km; Lena (Asia) 4,400 km
note: there are 20 countries without rivers: 3 in Africa (Comoros, Djibouti, Libya), 1 in the Americas (Bahamas), 8 in Asia (Bahrain, Kuwait, Maldives, Oman, Qatar, Saudi Arabia, United Arab Emirates, Yemen), 3 in Europe (Malta, Monaco, Holy See), 5 in Oceania (Kiribati, Marshall Islands, Nauru, Tonga, Tuvalu); these countries also do not have natural lakes

Major watersheds (area sq km): *summary statement:* a watershed is a drainage basin on an area of land where precipitation collects and drains off into a common outlet, such as into a river, bay, or other body of water; oceans ultimately take in the drainage from 83% of all land area; the remaining 17% of the land drains into internal (endorheic) basins, e.g., the Caspian Sea; *The World Factbook* lists 51 different watersheds across 102 countries; of these, 18 are in Asia, 9 in Europe, 9 in Africa, 8 in North and Central America, 5 in South America, and 2 in Australia; all watersheds with an area of at least 500,000 sq km have been included along with a number of smaller, regionally significant watersheds; together, these watersheds represent the surface hydrology water flows that are the World's primary sources of fresh water for individual consumption, industry, and agriculture

Major aquifers: *summary statement:* aquifers are underground layers of water-bearing permeable rock formations; they include alluvial formations such as unconsolidated sand and gravel aquifers, sedimentary rock formations of sandstone and karst (carbonate rocks such as limestone) aquifers, as well as volcanic aquifers, and basement aquifers (igneous and metamorphic rocks that underlie sedimentary and volcanic rock sequences); groundwater from aquifers can be extracted using a water well; *The World Factbook* lists 37 major aquifers across 52 countries; of these, 13 are in Africa, 10 in Asia, 5 in North America, 3 in South America, 4 in Europe, and 2 in Australia; although aquifers can vary in size, the major aquifers listed in *The Factbook* contain the bulk of the stored volume of groundwater; the fresh water held in these aquifers represents more than 30% of the World's fresh water; in the US, groundwater is primarily used for irrigation and globally, 70% of groundwater withdrawn is used for agriculture; groundwater also supplies almost half of all drinking water worldwide

Population distribution: six of the world's seven continents are widely and permanently inhabited; Asia is easily the most populous continent with about 60% of the world's population (China and India together account for over 35%); Africa comes in second with over 15% of the earth's populace, Europe has about 10%, North America 8%, South America almost 6%, and Oceania less than 1%; the harsh conditions on Antarctica prevent any permanent habitation

Natural hazards: large areas subject to severe weather (tropical cyclones); natural disasters (earthquakes, landslides, tsunamis, volcanic eruptions)
volcanism: volcanism is a fundamental driver and consequence of plate tectonics, the physical process reshaping the Earth's lithosphere; the world is home to more than 1,500 potentially active volcanoes, with over 500 of these having erupted in historical times; an estimated 500 million people live near these volcanoes; associated dangers include lava flows, lahars (mudflows), pyroclastic flows, ash clouds, ash fall, ballistic projectiles, gas emissions, landslides, earthquakes, and tsunamis; in the 1990s, the International Association of Volcanology and Chemistry of the Earth's Interior, created a list of 16 Decade Volcanoes worthy of special study because of their great potential for destruction: Avachinsky-Koryaksky (Russia), Colima (Mexico), Etna (Italy), Galeras (Colombia), Mauna Loa (United States), Merapi (Indonesia), Nyiragongo (Democratic Republic of the Congo), Rainier (United States), Sakurajima (Japan), Santa Maria (Guatemala), Santorini (Greece), Taal (Philippines), Teide (Spain), Ulawun (Papua New Guinea), Unzen (Japan), Vesuvius (Italy); see second note under "Geography - note"

Geography - note: *note 1:* the world is now thought to be about 4.55 billion years old, just about one-third of the 13.8-billion-year age estimated for the universe; the earliest widely accepted date for life appearing

on earth is 3.48 billion years ago, but this date is conservative and may get pushed back further
note 2: although earthquakes can strike anywhere at any time, the vast majority occur in three large zones of the earth; the world's greatest earthquake belt, the Circum-Pacific Belt (popularly referred to as the Ring of Fire), is the zone of active volcanoes and earthquake epicenters bordering the Pacific Ocean; about 90% of the world's earthquakes (81% of the largest earthquakes) and some 75% of the world's volcanoes occur within the Ring of Fire; the belt extends northward from Chile, along the South American coast, through Central America, Mexico, the western US, southern Alaska and the Aleutian Islands, to Japan, the Philippines, Papua New Guinea, island groups in the southwestern Pacific, and New Zealand

the second prominent belt, the Alpide, extends from Java to Sumatra, northward along the mountains of Burma, then eastward through the Himalayas, the Mediterranean, and out into the Atlantic Ocean; it accounts for about 17% of the world's largest earthquakes; the third important belt follows the long Mid-Atlantic Ridge
note 3: information on the origin sites for many of the world's major food crops may be found in the "Geography - note" for the following countries: Argentina, Bolivia, Brazil, China, Ecuador, Ethiopia, Indonesia, Mexico, Papua New Guinea, Paraguay, Peru, and the United States

PEOPLE AND SOCIETY

Population: 7,905,336,896 (July 2022 est.)
top ten most populous countries (in millions): China 1410.54; India 1389.37; United States 337.34; Indonesia 277.33; Pakistan 242.92; Nigeria 225.08; Brazil 217.24; Bangladesh 165.65; Russia 142.02; Mexico 129.15
ten least populous countries: Holy See (Vatican City) 1,000; Saint Pierre and Miquelon 5,257; Montserrat 5,414; Saint Barthelemy 7,103; Saint Helena, Ascension, and Tristan de Cunha 7,925; Cook Islands 8,128; Nauru 9,811; Tuvalu 11,544; Wallis and Futuna 15,891; Anguilla 18,741
ten most densely populated countries (population per sq km): Macau 22,689; Monaco 15,700; Singapore 8,351.5; Hong Kong 6,781.5; Gaza Strip 5,548.1; Gibraltar 4,224.7; Bahrain 2,027; Malta 1,468.9; Bermuda 1,339.6; Maldives 1,327.2
ten least densely populated countries (population per sq km): Greenland .026; Falkland Islands .26; Mongolia 2.1; Namibia 3.3; Australia 3.4; Iceland 3.6; Guyana 4; Mauritania 4; Suriname 4.1; Libya 4.1

Languages: *most-spoken language:* English 16.5%, Mandarin Chinese 14.6%, Hindi 8.3%, Spanish 7%, French 3.6%, Arabic 3.6%, Bengali 3.4%, Russian 3.4%, Portuguese 3.3%, Indonesian 2.6% (2020 est.)
most-spoken first language: Mandarin Chinese 12.3%, Spanish 6%, English 5.1%, Arabic 5.1%, Hindi 3.5%, Bengali 3.3%, Portuguese 3%, Russian 2.1%, Japanese 1.7%, Punjabi, Western 1.3%, Javanese 1.1% (2018 est.)
note 1: the six UN languages - Arabic, Chinese (Mandarin), English, French, Russian, and Spanish (Castilian) - are the mother tongue or second language of about 45% of the world's population, and are the official languages in more than half the states in the world; some 400 languages have more than a million first-language speakers (2018)
note 2: all told, there are estimated to be just over 7,151 languages spoken in the world (2022); approximately 80% of these languages are spoken by less than 100,000 people; about 150 languages are spoken by fewer than 10 people; communities that are isolated from each other in mountainous regions often develop multiple languages; Papua New Guinea, for example, boasts about 840 separate languages (2018)
note 3: approximately 2,300 languages are spoken in Asia, 2,140, in Africa, 1,310 in the Pacific, 1,060 in the Americas, and 290 in Europe (2020)

Religions: Christian 31.1%, Muslim 24.9%, Hindu 15.2%, Buddhist 6.6%, folk religions 5.6%, Jewish <1%, other <1%, unaffiliated 15.6% (2020 est.)

Age structure: *0-14 years:* 25.18% (male 1,010,373,278/female 946,624,579)
15-24 years: 15.29% (male 614,046,344/female 574,513,854)
25-54 years: 40.6% (male 1,597,805,095/female 1,557,807,873)
55-64 years: 9.23% (male 351,094,945/female 366,240,730)
65 years and over: 9.69% male 337,244,947/female 415,884,753) (2021 est.)

Dependency ratios: *total dependency ratio:* 53.3
youth dependency ratio: 39
elderly dependency ratio: 14.3
potential support ratio: 7 (2020 est.)

Median age: *total:* 31 years
male: 30.3 years
female: 31.8 years (2020 est.)

Population growth rate: 1.03% (2021 est.)
note: this rate results in about 154 net additions to the worldwide population every minute or 2.6 people every second

Birth rate: 18.1 births/1,000 population (2020 est.)
note: this rate results in about 259 worldwide births per minute or 4.3 births every second

Death rate: 7.7 deaths/1,000 population (2020 est.)
note: this rate results in about 108 worldwide deaths per minute or 1.8 deaths every second

Population distribution: six of the world's seven continents are widely and permanently inhabited; Asia is easily the most populous continent with about 60% of the world's population (China and India together account for over 35%); Africa comes in second with over 15% of the earth's populace, Europe has about 10%, North America 8%, South America almost 6%, and Oceania less than 1%; the harsh conditions on Antarctica prevent any permanent habitation

Urbanization: *urban population:* 57% of total population (2022)
rate of urbanization: 1.73% annual rate of change (2020-25 est.)

Major urban areas - population: *ten largest urban agglomerations:* Tokyo (Japan) - 37,393,000; New Delhi (India) - 30,291,000; Shanghai (China) -27,058,000; Sao Paulo (Brazil) - 22,043,000; Mexico City (Mexico) - 21,782,000; Dhaka (Bangladesh) - 21,006,000; Cairo (Egypt) - 20,901,000; Beijing (China) - 20,463,000; Mumbai (India) - 20,411,000; Osaka (Japan) - 19,165,000 (2020)
ten largest urban agglomerations, by continent:
Africa - Cairo (Egypt) - 20,901,000; Lagos (Nigeria) - 134,368,000; Kinshasha (DRC) - 14,342,000; Luanda (Angola) -8,330,000; Dar Es Salaam (Tanzania) - 6,702,000; Khartoum (Sudan) - 5,829,000; Johannesburg (South Africa) -5,783,000; Alexandria (Egypt) - 5,281,000; Abidjan (Cote d'Ivoire) - 5,203,000; Addis Ababa (Ethiopia) - 4,794,000
Asia - Tokyo (Japan) - 37,393,000; New Delhi (India) - 30,291,000; Shanghai (China) - 27,058,000; Dhaka (Bangladesh) - 21,006,000; Beijing (China) - 20,463,000; Mumbai (India) - 20,411,000; Osaka (Japan) - 19,165,000; Karachi (Pakistan) - 16,094,000; Chongqing (China) - 15,872,000; Istanbul (Turkey) - 15,190,000
Europe - Moscow (Russia) - 12,538,000; Paris (France) - 11,017,000; London (United Kingdom) - 9,304,000; Madrid (Spain) - 6,618,000; Barcelona (Spain) - 5,586,000, Saint Petersburg (Russia) - 5,468,000; Rome (Italy) - 4,257,000; Berlin (Germany) - 3,562,000; Athens (Greece) - 3,153,000; Milan (Italy) - 3,140,000
North America - Mexico City (Mexico) - 21,782,000; New York-Newark (United States) - 18,804,000; Los Angeles-Long Beach-Santa Ana (United States) - 12,447,000; Chicago (United States) - 8,865,000; Houston (United States) -6,371,000; Dallas-Fort Worth (United States) - 6,301,000; Toronto (Canada) - 6,197,000; Miami (United States) -6,122,000; Atlanta (United States) - 5,803,000; Philadelphia (United States) - 5,717,000
Oceania - Melbourne (Australia) - 4,968,000, Sydney (Australia) - 4,926,000; Brisbane (Australia) - 2,406,000; Perth (Australia) - 2,042,000; Auckland (New Zealand) - 1,607,000; Adelaide (Australia) - 1,336,000; Gold Coast-Tweed Head (Australia) - 699,000; Canberra (Australia) - 457,000; Newcastle-Maitland (Australia) - 450,000; Wellington (New Zealand) - 415,000
South America - Sao Paulo (Brazil) - 22,043,000; Buenos Aires (Argentina) - 15,154,000; Rio de Janeiro (Brazil) -13,458,000; Bogota (Colombia) - 10,978,000; Lima (Peru) - 10,719,000; Santiago (Chile) - 6,767,000; Belo Horizonte (Brazil) - 6,084,000; Brasilia (Brazil) - 4,646,000; Porto Alegre (Brazil) - 4,137,000; Recife (Brazil) - 4,127,000 (2020)

Sex ratio: *at birth:* 1.07 male(s)/female
0-14 years: 1.07 male(s)/female
15-24 years: 1.07 male(s)/female
25-54 years: 1.03 male(s)/female
55-64 years: 0.96 male(s)/female
65 years and over: 0.81 male(s)/female
total population: 1.01 male(s)/female (2020 est.)

Maternal mortality ratio: 211 deaths/100,000 live births (2017 est.)

Infant mortality rate: *total:* 30.8 deaths/1,000 live births
male: 32.8 deaths/1,000 live births
female: 28.6 deaths/1,000 live births (2020 est.)

Life expectancy at birth: *total population:* 70.5 years
male: 68.4 years
female: 72.6 years (2020 est.)

Total fertility rate: 2.42 children born/woman (2020 est.)

Drinking water source: *improved: urban:* 96.5% of population
rural: 84.7% of population
total: 91.1% of population
unimproved: urban: 3.5% of population
rural: 15.3% of population
total: 8.9% of population (2015 est.)

Current health expenditure: 10% of GDP (2016)

Sanitation facility access: *improved: urban:* 82.3% of population
rural: 50.5% of population
total: 67.7% of population
unimproved: urban: 17.7% of population
rural: 49.5% of population
total: 32.3% of population (2015 est.)

HIV/AIDS - adult prevalence rate: 0.7% (2020 est.)

HIV/AIDS - people living with HIV/AIDS: 37.7 million (2020 est.)

HIV/AIDS - deaths: 680,000 (2020 est.)

Major infectious diseases: *note:* widespread ongoing transmission of a respiratory illness caused by the novel coronavirus (COVID-19) is occurring globally; older adults and people of any age with serious chronic medical conditions are at increased risk for severe disease; some health care systems are becoming overwhelmed and there may be limited access to adequate medical care in affected areas; many countries are implementing travel restrictions and mandatory quarantines, closing borders, and prohibiting non-citizens from entry with little advance notice; US residents may have difficulty returning to the United States; as of 18 August 2022, 590,659,276 confirmed cases of COVID-19 and 6,440,163 deaths have been reported to the World Health Organization; as of 17 August 2022, 67.41% of the World population has received at least one dose of COVID-19 vaccine

Literacy: *definition:* age 15 and over can read and write
total population: 86.7%
male: 90.1%
female: 83.3% (2020)
note: more than three quarters of the world's 750 million illiterate adults are found in South Asia and sub-Saharan Africa; of all the illiterate adults in the world, almost two thirds are women (2016)

School life expectancy (primary to tertiary education): *total:* 13 years
male: 13 years
female: 13 years (2020)

ENVIRONMENT

Environment - current issues: large areas subject to overpopulation, industrial disasters, pollution (air, water, acid rain, toxic substances), loss of vegetation (overgrazing, deforestation, desertification), loss of biodiversity; soil degradation, soil depletion, erosion; ozone layer depletion; waste disposal; global warming becoming a greater concern

Climate: a wide equatorial band of hot and humid tropical climates, bordered north and south by subtropical temperate zones that separate two large areas of cold and dry polar climates
ten driest places on earth (average annual precipitation): McMurdo Dry Valleys, Antarctica 0 mm (0 in)
Arica, Chile 0.76 mm (0.03 in)
Al Kufrah, Libya 0.86 mm (0.03 in)
Aswan, Egypt 0.86 mm (0.03 in)
Luxor, Egypt 0.86 mm (0.03 in)
Ica, Peru 2.29 mm (0.09 in)
Wadi Halfa, Sudan 2.45 mm (0.1 in)
Iquique, Chile 5.08 mm (0.2 in)
Pelican Point, Namibia 8.13 mm (0.32 in)
El Arab (Aoulef), Algeria 12.19 mm (0.48 in)
ten wettest places on earth (average annual precipitation): Mawsynram, India 11,871 mm (467.4 in)
Cherrapunji, India 11,777 mm (463.7 in)
Tutunendo, Colombia 11,770 mm (463.4 in)
Cropp River, New Zealand 11,516 mm (453.4 in)
San Antonia de Ureca, Equatorial Guinea 10,450 mm (411.4 in)
Debundsha, Cameroon 10,299 mm (405.5 in)
Big Bog, US (Hawaii) 10,272 mm (404.4 in)
Mt Waialeale, US (Hawaii) 9,763 mm (384.4 in)
Kukui, US (Hawaii) 9,293 mm (365.9 in)
Emeishan, China 8,169 mm (321.6 in)
ten coldest places on earth (lowest average monthly temperature): Verkhoyansk, Russia (Siberia) -47°C (-53°F) January
Oymyakon, Russia (Siberia) -46°C (-52°F) January
Eureka, Canada -38.4°C (-37.1°F) February
Isachsen, Canada -36°C (-32.8°F) February
Alert, Canada -34°C (-28°F) February
Kap Morris Jesup, Greenland -34°C (-29°F) March
Cornwallis Island, Canada -33.5°C (-28.3°F) February
Cambridge Bay, Canada -33.5°C (28.3°F) February
Ilirnej, Russia -33°C (-28°F) January
Resolute, Canada -33°C (-27.4°F) February
ten hottest places on earth (highest average monthly temperature): Death Valley, US (California) 39°C (101°F) July
Iranshahr, Iran 38.3°C (100.9°F) June
Ouallene, Algeria 38°C (100.4°F) July
Kuwait City, Kuwait 37.7°C (100°F) July
Medina, Saudi Arabia 36°C (97°F) July
Buckeye, US (Arizona) 34°C (93°F) July
Jazan, Saudi Arabia 33°C (91°F) June
Al Kufrah, Libya 31°C (87°F) July
Alice Springs, Australia 29°C (84°F) January
Tamanrasset, Algeria 29°C (84°F) June

Urbanization: *urban population:* 57% of total population (2022)
rate of urbanization: 1.73% annual rate of change (2020-25 est.)

Major lakes (area sq km): *top ten largest natural lakes:* Caspian Sea (Azerbaijan, Iran, Kazakhstan, Russia, Turkmenistan) 374,000 sq km; Lake Superior (Canada, United States) 82,100 sq km; Lake Victoria (Kenya, Tanzania, Uganda) 62,940 sq km; Lake Huron (Canada, United States) 59,600 sq km; Lake Michigan (United States) 57,750 sq km; Lake Tanganyika (Burundi, Democratic Republic of the Congo, Tanzania, Zambia) 32,000 sq km; Great Bear Lake (Canada) 31,328 sq km; Lake Baikal (Russia) 31,500 sq km; Lake Malawi (Malawi, Mozambique, Tanzania) 22,490 sq km; Great Slave Lake (Canada) 28,568 sq km
note 1: the areas of the lakes are subject to seasonal variation; only the Caspian Sea is saline, the rest are fresh water
note 2: Lakes Huron and Michigan are technically a single lake because the flow of water between the Straits of Mackinac that connects the two lakes keeps their water levels at near-equilibrium; combined, Lake Huron-Michigan is the largest freshwater lake by surface area in the world

Major rivers (by length in km): *top ten longest rivers:* Nile (Africa) 6,650 km; Amazon (South America) 6,436 km; Yangtze (Asia) 6,300 km; Mississippi-Missouri (North America) 6,275 km; Yenisey-Angara (Asia) 5,539 km; Huang He/Yellow (Asia) 5,464 km; Ob-Irtysh (Asia) 5,410 km; Congo (Africa) 4,700 km; Amur (Asia) 4,444 km; Lena (Asia) 4,400 km
note: there are 20 countries without rivers: 3 in Africa (Comoros, Djibouti, Libya), 1 in the Americas (Bahamas), 8 in Asia (Bahrain, Kuwait, Maldives, Oman, Qatar, Saudi Arabia, United Arab Emirates, Yemen), 3 in Europe (Malta, Monaco, Holy See), 5 in Oceania (Kiribati, Marshall Islands, Nauru, Tonga, Tuvalu); these countries also do not have natural lakes

Major watersheds (area sq km): *summary statement:* a watershed is a drainage basin on an area of land where precipitation collects and drains off into a common outlet, such as into a river, bay, or other body of water; oceans ultimately take in the drainage from 83% of all land area; the remaining 17% of the land drains into internal (endorheic) basins, e.g., the Caspian Sea; *The World Factbook* lists 51 different watersheds across 102 countries; of these, 18 are in Asia, 9 in Europe, 9 in Africa, 8 in North and Central America, 5 in South America, and 2 in Australia; all watersheds with an area of at least 500,000 sq km have been included along with a number of smaller, regionally significant watersheds; together, these watersheds represent the surface hydrology water flows that are the World's primary sources of fresh water for individual consumption, industry, and agriculture

Major aquifers: *summary statement:* aquifers are underground layers of water-bearing permeable rock formations; they include alluvial formations such as unconsolidated sand and gravel aquifers, sedimentary rock formations of sandstone and karst (carbonate rocks such as limestone) aquifers, as well as volcanic aquifers, and basement aquifers (igneous and metamorphic rocks that underlie sedimentary and volcanic rock sequences); groundwater from aquifers can be extracted using a water well; *The World Factbook* lists 37 major aquifers across 52 countries; of these, 13 are in Africa, 10 in Asia, 5 in North America, 3 in South America, 4 in Europe, and 2 in Australia; although aquifers can vary in size, the major aquifers listed in *The Factbook* contain the bulk of the stored volume of groundwater; the fresh water held in these aquifers represents more than 30% of the World's fresh water; in the US, groundwater is primarily used for irrigation and globally, 70% of groundwater withdrawn is used for agriculture; groundwater also supplies almost half of all drinking water worldwide

Total renewable water resources: 53,789.3 cubic meters (2011)

GOVERNMENT

Country name: *note:* countries with names connected to animals include: Albania "Land of the Eagles"; Anguilla (the name means "eel"); Bhutan "Land of the Thunder Dragon"; Cameroon (the name derives from "prawns"); Cayman Islands (named after the caiman, a marine crocodile); Faroe Islands (from Old Norse meaning "sheep"); Georgia "Land of the Wolves"; Italy "Land of Young Cattle"; Kosovo "Field of Blackbirds"; Sierra Leone "Lion Mountains"; Singapore "Lion City"

Capital: *time difference:* there are 21 World entities (20 countries and 1 dependency) with multiple time zones: Australia, Brazil, Canada, Chile, Democratic Republic of Congo, Ecuador, France, Greenland (part of the Danish Kingdom), Indonesia, Kazakhstan, Kiribati, Mexico, Micronesia, Mongolia, Netherlands, New Zealand, Papua New Guinea, Portugal, Russia, Spain, United States

note 1: in some instances, the time zones pertain to portions of a country that lie overseas
note 2: in 1851, the British set their prime meridian (0° longitude) through the Royal Observatory at Greenwich, England; this meridian became the international standard in 1884 and thus the basis for the standard time zones of the world; today, GMT is officially known as Coordinated Universal Time (UTC) and is also referred to as "Zulu time"; UTC is the basis for all civil time, with the world divided into time zones expressed as positive or negative differences from UTC
note 3: each time zone is based on 15° starting from the prime meridian; in theory, there are 24 time zones based on the solar day, but there are now upward of 40 because of fractional hour offsets that adjust for various political and physical geographic realities; see the Standard Time Zones of the World map included with the World and Regional Maps
daylight saving time: some 67 countries - including most of the world's leading industrialized nations - use daylight savings time (DST) in at least a portion of the country; China, Japan, India, and Russia are major industrialized countries that do not use DST; Asia and Africa generally do not observe DST and it is generally not observed near the equator, where sunrise and sunset times do not vary enough to justify it; some countries observe DST only in certain regions; for example, only southeastern Australia observes it; in fact, only a minority of the world's population - about 20% - uses DST

Administrative divisions: 195 countries, 71 dependent areas and other entities

Dependent areas: Australia dependencies: Ashmore and Cartier Islands, Christmas Island, Cocos (Keeling) Islands, Coral Sea Islands, Heard Island and McDonald Islands, Norfolk Island
France dependencies: Clipperton Island, French Polynesia, French Southern and Antarctic Lands, New Caledonia, Saint Barthelemy, Saint Martin, Saint Pierre and Miquelon, Wallis and Futuna
New Zealand dependencies: Cook Islands, Niue, Tokelau
Norway dependencies: Bouvet Island, Jan Mayen, Svalbard
United Kingdom dependencies: Anguilla; Bermuda; British Indian Ocean Territory; British Virgin Islands; Cayman Islands; Falkland Islands; Gibraltar; Montserrat; Pitcairn Islands; Saint Helena, Ascension, and Tristan da Cunha; South Georgia and the South Sandwich Islands; Turks and Caicos Islands
United States dependencies: American Samoa, Baker Island, Guam, Howland Island, Jarvis Island, Johnston Atoll, Kingman Reef, Midway Islands, Navassa Island, Northern Mariana Islands, Palmyra Atoll, Puerto Rico, Virgin Islands, Wake Island

Legal system: the legal systems of nearly all countries are generally modeled upon elements of five main types: civil law (including French law, the Napoleonic Code, Roman law, Roman-Dutch law, and Spanish law); common law (including English and US law); customary law; mixed or pluralistic law; and religious law (including Islamic sharia law); an additional type of legal system - international law - governs the conduct of independent nations in their relationships with one another

International law organization participation: all members of the UN are parties to the statute that established the International Court of Justice (ICJ) or World Court; states parties to the Rome Statute of the International Criminal Court (ICCt) are those countries that have ratified or acceded to the Rome Statute, the treaty that established the Court; as of May 2019, a total of 122 countries have accepted jurisdiction of the ICCt (see Appendix B in an online edition of *The World Factbook* for a clarification on the differing mandates of the ICJ and ICCt)

Executive branch: *chief of state:* there are 27 countries with royal families in the world, most are in Asia (13) and Europe (10), three are in Africa, and one in Oceania; monarchies by continent are as follows: Asia (Bahrain, Bhutan, Brunei, Cambodia, Japan, Jordan, Kuwait, Malaysia, Oman, Qatar, Saudi Arabia, Thailand, United Arab Emirates); Europe (Belgium, Denmark, Liechtenstein, Luxembourg, Monaco, Netherlands, Norway, Spain, Sweden, United Kingdom); Africa (Eswatini, Lesotho, Morocco); Oceania (Tonga)
note 1: Andorra and the Holy See (Vatican) are also monarchies of a sort, but they are not ruled by royal houses; Andorra has two co-princes (the president of France and the bishop of Urgell) and the Holy See is ruled by an elected pope
note 2: the sovereign of Great Britain is also the monarch for 14 of the countries (including Australia, Canada, Jamaica, New Zealand) that make up the Commonwealth; that brings to 43 the total number of countries with some type of monarchies

Legislative branch: there are 230 political entities with legislative bodies; of these 144 are unicameral (a single "house") and 86 are bicameral (both upper and lower houses); note - while there are 195 countries in the world, 35 territories, possessions, or other special administrative units also have their own governing bodies

Flag description: while a "World" flag does not exist, the flag of the United Nations (UN) - adopted on 7 December 1946 - has been used on occasion to represent the entire planet; technically, however, it only represents the international organization itself; the flag displays the official emblem of the UN in white on a blue background; the emblem design shows a map of the world in an azimuthal equidistant projection centered on the North Pole, the image is flanked by two olive branches crossed below; blue was selected as the color to represent peace, in contrast to red usually associated with war; the map projection chosen includes all of the continents except Antarctica
note 1: the flags of 12 nations: Austria, Botswana, Georgia, Jamaica, Japan, Laos, Latvia, Micronesia, Nigeria, North Macedonia, Switzerland, and Thailand have no top or bottom and may be flown with either long edge on top without any notice being taken
note 2: the most common colors found on national flags are: red (including deep red; ~75%), white (~70%), and blue (including light blue; ~50%); these three colors are so prevalent that there are only two countries, Jamaica and Sri Lanka, that do not include one of them on their flag; the next three most popular colors are: yellow/gold and green (both ~45%) and black (~30%)
note 3: flags composed of three colors are by far the most common type and, of those, the red-white-blue combination is the most widespread

National anthem: *name:* virtually every country has a national anthem; most (but not all) anthems have lyrics, which are usually in the national or most common language of the country; states with more than one national language may offer several versions of their anthem
note: the world's oldest national anthem is the "Het Wilhelmus" (The William) of the Netherlands, which dates to the 17th century; the first national anthem to be officially adopted (1795) was "La Marseillaise" (The Song of Marseille) of France; Japan claims to have the world's shortest national anthem, entitled "Kimigayo" (The Emperor's Reign), it consists of 11 measures of music (the lyrics are also the world's oldest, dating to the 10th century or earlier); the world's longest national anthem in terms of lyrics is that of Greece, "Ymnos eis tin Eleftherian" (Hymn to Liberty) with 158 stanzas - only two of which are used; the world's longest national anthem in terms of music is that of Uruguay, "Himno Nacional" (National Anthem of Uruguay) with 105 bars (almost five minutes) - generally only the first verse and chorus are sung; both Denmark and New Zealand have two official national anthems

National heritage: *total World Heritage Sites:* 1154 (897 cultural, 218 natural, 39 mixed) (2022)

ECONOMY

Economic overview: The international financial crisis of 2008-09 led to the first downturn in global output since 1946 and presented the world with a major new challenge: determining what mix of fiscal and monetary policies to follow to restore growth and jobs, while keeping inflation and debt under control. Financial stabilization and stimulus programs that started in 2009-11, combined with lower tax revenues in 2009-10, required most countries to run large budget deficits. Treasuries issued new public debt - totaling $9.1 trillion since 2008 - to pay for the additional expenditures. To keep interest rates low, most central banks monetized that debt, injecting large sums of money into their economies - between December 2008 and December 2013 the global money supply increased by more than 35%. Governments are now faced with the difficult task of spurring current growth and employment without saddling their economies with so much debt that they sacrifice long-term growth and financial stability. When economic activity picks up, central banks will confront the difficult task of containing inflation without raising interest rates so high they snuff out further growth.

Fiscal and monetary data for 2013 are currently available for 180 countries, which together account for 98.5% of world GDP. Of the 180 countries, 82 pursued unequivocally expansionary policies, boosting government spending while also expanding their money supply relatively rapidly - faster than the world average of 3.1%; 28 followed restrictive fiscal and monetary policies, reducing government spending and holding money growth to less than the 3.1% average; and the remaining 70 followed a mix of counterbalancing fiscal and monetary policies, either reducing government spending while accelerating money growth, or boosting spending while curtailing money growth.

(For more information, see attached spreadsheet.)

In 2013, for many countries the drive for fiscal austerity that began in 2011 abated. While 5 out of 6 countries slowed spending in 2012, only 1 in 2 countries slowed spending in 2013. About 1 in 3 countries actually lowered the level of their expenditures. The global growth rate for government expenditures increased from 1.6% in 2012 to 5.1%

in 2013, after falling from a 10.1% growth rate in 2011. On the other hand, nearly 2 out of 3 central banks tightened monetary policy in 2013, decelerating the rate of growth of their money supply, compared with only 1 out of 3 in 2012. Roughly 1 of 4 central banks actually withdrew money from circulation, an increase from 1 out of 7 in 2012. Growth of the global money supply, as measured by the narrowly defined M1, slowed from 8.7% in 2009 and 10.4% in 2010 to 5.2% in 2011, 4.6% in 2012, and 3.1% in 2013. Several notable shifts occurred in 2013. By cutting government expenditures and expanding money supplies, the US and Canada moved against the trend in the rest of the world. France reversed course completely. Rather than reducing expenditures and money as it had in 2012, it expanded both. Germany reversed its fiscal policy, sharply expanding federal spending, while continuing to grow the money supply. South Korea shifted monetary policy into high gear, while maintaining a strongly expansionary fiscal policy. Japan, however, continued to pursue austere fiscal and monetary policies.

Austere economic policies have significantly affected economic performance. The global budget deficit narrowed to roughly $2.7 trillion in 2012 and $2.1 trillion in 2013, or 3.8% and 2.5% of World GDP, respectively. But growth of the world economy slipped from 5.1% in 2010 and 3.7% in 2011, to just 3.1% in 2012, and 2.9% in 2013.

Countries with expansionary fiscal and monetary policies achieved significantly higher rates of growth, higher growth of tax revenues, and greater success reducing the public debt burden than those countries that chose contractionary policies. In 2013, the 82 countries that followed a pro-growth approach achieved a median GDP growth rate of 4.7%, compared to 1.7% for the 28 countries with restrictive fiscal and monetary policies, a difference of 3 percentage points. Among the 82, China grew 7.7%, Philippines 6.8%, Malaysia 4.7%, Pakistan and Saudi Arabia 3.6%, Argentina 3.5%, South Korea 2.8%, and Russia 1.3%, while among the 28, Brazil grew 2.3%, Japan 2.0%, South Africa 2.0%, Netherlands -0.8%, Croatia -1.0%, Iran -1.5%, Portugal -1.8%, Greece -3.8%, and Cyprus -8.7%.

Faster GDP growth and lower unemployment rates translated into increased tax revenues and a less cumbersome debt burden. Revenues for the 82 expansionary countries grew at a median rate of 10.7%, whereas tax revenues fell at a median rate of 6.8% for the 28 countries that chose austere economic policies. Budget balances improved for about three-quarters of the 28, but, for most, debt grew faster than GDP, and the median level of their public debt as a share of GDP increased 9.1 percentage points, to 59.2%. On the other hand, budget balances deteriorated for most of the 82 pro-growth countries, but GDP growth outpaced increases in debt, and the median level of public debt as a share of GDP increased just 1.9%, to 39.8%.

The world recession has suppressed inflation rates - world inflation declined 1.0 percentage point in 2012 to about 4.1% and 0.2 percentage point to 3.9% in 2013. In 2013 the median inflation rate for the 82 pro-growth countries was 1.3 percentage points higher than that for the countries that followed more austere fiscal and monetary policies. Overall, the latter countries also improved their current account balances by shedding imports; as a result, current account balances deteriorated for most of the countries that pursued pro-growth policies. Slow growth of world income continued to hold import demand in check and crude oil prices fell. Consequently, the dollar value of world trade grew just 1.3% in 2013.

Beyond the current global slowdown, the world faces several long standing economic challenges. The addition of 80 million people each year to an already overcrowded globe is exacerbating the problems of pollution, waste-disposal, epidemics, water-shortages, famine, over-fishing of oceans, deforestation, desertification, and depletion of non-renewable resources. The nation-state, as a bedrock economic-political institution, is steadily losing control over international flows of people, goods, services, funds, and technology. The introduction of the euro as the common currency of much of Western Europe in January 1999, while paving the way for an integrated economic powerhouse, has created economic risks because the participating nations have varying income levels and growth rates, and hence, require a different mix of monetary and fiscal policies. Governments, especially in Western Europe, face the difficult political problem of channeling resources away from welfare programs in order to increase investment and strengthen incentives to seek employment. Because of their own internal problems and priorities, the industrialized countries are unable to devote sufficient resources to deal effectively with the poorer areas of the world, which, at least from an economic point of view, are becoming further marginalized. The terrorist attacks on the US on 11 September 2001 accentuated a growing risk to global prosperity - the diversion of resources away from capital investments to counter-terrorism programs.

Despite these vexing problems, the world economy also shows great promise. Technology has made possible further advances in a wide range of fields, from agriculture, to medicine, alternative energy, metallurgy, and transportation. Improved global communications have greatly reduced the costs of international trade, helping the world gain from the international division of labor, raise living standards, and reduce income disparities among nations. Much of the resilience of the world economy in the aftermath of the financial crisis resulted from government and central bank leaders around the globe working in concert to stem the financial onslaught, knowing well the lessons of past economic failures.

Real GDP (purchasing power parity): $127.8 trillion (2017 est.)
$123.3 trillion (2016 est.)
$119.5 trillion (2015 est.)
note: data are in 2017 dollars

Real GDP growth rate: 3.7% (2017 est.)
3.2% (2016 est.)
3.3% (2014 est.)

Real GDP per capita: $17,500 (2017 est.)
$17,000 (2016 est.)
$16,800 (2015 est.)
note: data are in 2017 dollars

GDP (official exchange rate): $80.27 trillion (2017 est.) SGWP (gross world product)

Inflation rate (consumer prices): 6.4% (2017 est.)
3.7% (2016 est.)
developed countries: 1.9% (2017 est.) 0.9% (2016 est.)
developing countries: 8.8% (2017 est.) 3.7% (2016 est.)
note: the above estimates are weighted averages; inflation in developed countries is 0% to 4% typically, in developing countries, 4% to 10% typically; national inflation rates vary widely in individual cases; inflation rates have declined for most countries for the last several years, held in check by increasing international competition from several low wage countries and by soft demand due to the world financial crisis

GDP - composition, by sector of origin: *agriculture:* 6.4% (2017 est.)
industry: 30% (2017 est.)
services: 63% (2017 est.)

GDP - composition, by end use: *household consumption:* 56.4% (2017 est.)
government consumption: 16.1% (2017 est.)
investment in fixed capital: 25.7% (2017 est.)
investment in inventories: 1.4% (2017 est.)
exports of goods and services: 28.8% (2017 est.)
imports of goods and services: -28.3% (2017 est.)

Industries: dominated by the onrush of technology, especially in computers, robotics, telecommunications, and medicines and medical equipment; most of these advances take place in OECD nations; only a small portion of non-OECD countries have succeeded in rapidly adjusting to these technological forces; the accelerated development of new technologies is complicating already grim environmental problems

Industrial production growth rate: 3.2% (2017 est.)

Labor force: 3.432 billion (2017 est.)

Labor force - by occupation: *agriculture:* 31%
industry: 23.5%
services: 45.5% (2014 est.)

Unemployment rate: 7.7% (2017 est.)
7.5% (2016 est.)
note: combined unemployment and underemployment in many non-industrialized countries; developed countries typically 4%-12% unemployment (2007 est.)

Gini Index coefficient - distribution of family income: 37.9 (2012 est.)
37.9 (2005 est.)

Household income or consumption by percentage share: *lowest 10%:* 2.6%
highest 10%: 30.2% (2008 est.)

Budget: *revenues:* 21.68 trillion (2017 est.)
expenditures: 23.81 trillion (2017 est.)

Budget surplus (+) or deficit (-): -3% (of GDP) (2016 est.)

Public debt: 67.2% of GDP (2017 est.)
67.2% of GDP (2016 est.)

Taxes and other revenues: 26.7% (of GDP) (2016 est.)

Exports: $17.31 trillion (2017 est.)
$15.82 trillion (2016 est.)

Exports - commodities: the whole range of industrial and agricultural goods and services
top ten - share of world trade: 14.8 electrical machinery, including computers; 14.4 mineral fuels, including oil, coal, gas, and refined products; 14.2 nuclear reactors, boilers, and parts; 8.9 cars, trucks, and buses; 3.5 scientific and precision instruments; 3.4 plastics; 2.7 iron and steel; 2.6 organic chemicals; 2.6 pharmaceutical products; 1.9 diamonds, pearls, and precious stones (2007 est.)

Imports: $20.01 trillion (2018 est.)
$16.02 trillion (2017 est.)

Imports - commodities: the whole range of industrial and agricultural goods and services *top ten - share of world trade:* see listing for exports

Debt - external: $76.56 trillion (31 December 2017 est.)
$75.09 trillion (31 December 2016 est.)
note: this figure is the sum total of all countries' external debt, both public and private

ENERGY

Electricity access: *electrification - total population:* 90% (2019)
electrification - urban areas: 96% (2019)
electrification - rural areas: 85% (2019)

Electricity generation sources: *fossil fuels:* 60.6% of total installed capacity (2020 est.)
nuclear: 10.3% of total installed capacity (2020 est.)
solar: 3.3% of total installed capacity (2020 est.)
wind: 6.2% of total installed capacity (2020 est.)
hydroelectricity: 17% of total installed capacity (2020 est.)
geothermal: 0.4% of total installed capacity (2020 est.)
biomass and waste: 2.4% of total installed capacity (2020 est.)

Refined petroleum products - production: 88.4 million bbl/day (2014 est.)

Refined petroleum products - exports: 29.66 million bbl/day (2014 est.)

Refined petroleum products - imports: 28.62 million bbl/day (2014 est.)

Carbon dioxide emissions: 35,551,713,000 metric tonnes of CO2 (2019 est.)
from coal and metallurgical coke: 15,587,834,000 metric tonnes of CO2 (2019 est.)
from petroleum and other liquids: 12,195,793,000 metric tonnes of CO2 (2019 est.)
from consumed natural gas: 7,768,086,000 metric tonnes of CO2 (2019 est.)

COMMUNICATIONS

Telephones - fixed lines: *total subscriptions:* 901,317,598 (2020 est.)
subscriptions per 100 inhabitants: 11 (2021 est.)

Telephones - mobile cellular: *total subscriptions:* 7.8 billion (2020 est.)
subscriptions per 100 inhabitants: 106 (2020 est.)

Telecommunication systems: *general assessment:* Information, Communications, and Technology (ICT) is tied to economic growth; business, trade, and foreign direct investment are all based on effective sources of ICT, and development of ICT flourishes with a vigorous economy, open trade, and sound regulation; some 2020 estimates point to a digital economy worth $11.5 trillion globally, equivalent to 15.5% of global GDP (with ICT growing 2.5 times faster than global GDP over the past 15 years); 2020 reports indicate about 7.7 billion global mobile broadband subscriptions, rising from 3.3 billion in five years, and over 1.1 billion fixed broadband subscribers, up from 830 million in 2015
international: economic impact - telecommunications has been and continues to be one of the world's fastest growing markets; countries and firms are transitioning from analog to digital broadcasting, increasing automation capabilities and applications, adopting more high-definition technologies, and converting to digital channels

broadcasting typically refers to transmission of information to all devices in a network without any acknowledgment by the receivers; data processing parts and accessories includes many supporting elements to broadcasting equipment, such as monitors, keyboards, printers, etc.

in terms of market size, broadcasting equipment constituted $413 billion in global trade, making it the fifth most traded commodity in 2019; similarly, data processing equipment equaled $230 billion, the eighth most traded commodity globally; the chief exporters and importers of telecommunications commodities remain largely the same: 1) China leads in both broadcasting and data processing equipment exports, $208 billion and $81.5 billion respectively and 2) the United States, conversely, receives the most of both commodities, importing $81.1 billion in broadcasting equipment and $38.3 billion in data processing equipment in 2019
infrastructure - as of 2021, 428 submarine cables have been laid worldwide with a further 36 planned; the undersea cables connect to 1,245 landing stations

Internet users: *total:* 4.9 billion (2021 est.)
percent of population: 63% (2021 est.)
top ten countries by Internet usage (in millions): 730.7 China; 374.3 India; 246.8 United States; 122.8 Brazil; 116.6 Japan; 108.8 Russia; 73.3 Mexico; 72.3 Germany; 65.5 Indonesia; 61 United Kingdom (2017)

Broadband - fixed subscriptions: *total:* 1.23 billion (2020 est.) ;the number of fixed broadband subscriptions has been higher than that of fixed telephony since 2017
subscriptions per 100 inhabitants: 17 (2021 est.)

Communications - note: data centers consist of a dedicated space within a building or a group of buildings used to house computing resources and other components, such as telecommunications and storage systems; the ongoing worldwide boom in data generation is responsible for the mushrooming of data centers; the three largest data center facilities by area as of the first half of 2022 are:
no. 1. - the China Telecom data center located in the Inner Mongolia Information Park, Hohhot, China, reportedly covers 1 million sq m (10.7 million sq ft); the largest Internet data center in the world, it has over 50% market share in the Chinese data center market, with an extensive network of over 400 data centers located in prime regions in mainland China and overseas markets
no. 2. - the China Mobile data center located in the Inner Mongolia Information Park, Hohhot, China, covers 720,000 sq m (7.7 million sq ft); it is one of the world's biggest cloud computing data centers
no. 3. - The Citadel data center owned by US-based Switch, in Tahoe Reno, Nevada, covers 670,000 sq m (7.2 million sq ft); called the world's largest technology ecosystem, the facility runs on 100% renewable (solar and wind) energy

TRANSPORTATION

Airports: *total:* 41,820 (2021)
top ten by passengers (2021): Atlanta (ATL) - 75,704,760; Dallas/Fort Worth, TX (DFW) 62,465,756; Denver, CO (DEN) 58,828,552; Chicago, IL (ORD) 54,020,399; Los Angeles, CA (LAX) 48,007,284; Charlotte, NC (CLT) 43,302,230; Orlando, FL (MCO) 40,351,068; Guangzhou (CAN) 40,259,401; Chengdu (CTU) 40,117,496; Las Vegas, NV (LAS) 39,754,366 (2021)
top ten by passengers (2020): Guangzhou (CAN) 43,767,558; Atlanta (ATL) - 42,918,685; Chengdu (CTU) 40,741,509; Dallas/Fort Worth, TX (DFW) 39,364,990; Shenzhen (SZX) 37,916,054; Beijing (PEK) - 34,513,827; Denver, CO (DEN) 33,741,129; Kunming (KMG) 32,990,805; Shanghai (PVG) 31,165,641; Xi'an (XIY) 31,073,924 (2020) note - 2020 numbers included to allow for a comparison with the effects of COVID-19 restrictions on international air travel in 2020
top ten by cargo (metric tons): Hong Kong (HKG) - 5,025,495; Memphis, TN (MEM) - 4,480,465; Shanghai (PVG) -3,982,616; Anchorage, AK (ANC) - 3,555,160; Incheon (ICN) - 3,329,292; Louisville, KY (SDF) - 3,052,269; Taipei (TPE) - 2,812,065; Los Angeles, CA (LAX) 2,691,830; Tokyo (NRT) 2,644,074; Doha, Qatar (DOH) 2,620,095 (2021)

Heliports: 6,524 (2021)

Railways: *total:* 1,148,186 km (2013)

Waterways: 2,293,412 km (2017)
top ten longest rivers: Nile (Africa) 6,693 km; Amazon (South America) 6,436 km; Mississippi-Missouri (North America) 6,238 km; Yenisey-Angara (Asia) 5,981 km; Ob-Irtysh (Asia) 5,569 km; Yangtze (Asia) 5,525 km; Yellow (Asia) 4,671 km; Amur (Asia) 4,352 km; Lena (Asia) 4,345 km; Congo (Africa) 4,344 km
note 1: rivers are not necessarily navigable along the entire length; if measured by volume, the Amazon is the largest river in the world, responsible for about 20% of the Earth's freshwater entering the ocean
note 2: there are 20 countries without rivers: 3 in Africa (Comoros, Djibouti, Libya); 1 in the Americas (Bahamas); 8 in Asia (Bahrain, Kuwait, Maldives, Oman, Qatar, Saudi Arabia, United Arab Emirates, Yemen); 3 in Europe (Malta, Monaco, Holy See), 5 in Oceania (Kiribati, Marshall Islands, Nauru, Tonga, Tuvalu); these countries also do not have natural lakes
top ten largest natural lakes (by surface area): Caspian Sea (Azerbaijan, Iran, Kazakhstan, Russia, Turkmenistan) 372,960 sq km; Lake Superior (Canada, United States) 82,414 sq km; Lake Victoria (Kenya, Tanzania, Uganda) 69,490 sq km; Lake Huron (Canada, United States) 59,596 sq km; Lake Michigan (United States) 57,441 sq km; Lake Tanganyika (Burundi, Democratic Republic of the Congo, Tanzania, Zambia) 32,890 sq km; Great Bear Lake (Canada) 31,800 sq km; Lake Baikal (Russia) 31,494 sq km; Lake Nyasa (Malawi, Mozambique, Tanzania) 30,044 sq km; Great Slave Lake (Canada) 28,400 sq km
note 1: the areas of the lakes are subject to seasonal variation; only the Caspian Sea is saline, the rest are fresh water
note 2: Lakes Huron and Michigan are technically a single lake because the flow of water between the Straits of Mackinac that connects the two lakes keeps their water levels at near-equilibrium; combined, Lake Huron-Michigan is the largest freshwater lake by surface area in the world
note 3: the deepest lake in the world (1,620 m), and also the largest freshwater lake by volume (23,600 cu km), is Lake Baikal in Russia

Merchant marine: *total:* 98,202
by type: bulk carrier 12,319, container ship 5,428, general cargo 18,993, oil tanker 11,243, other 50,219 (2021)

Ports and terminals: *top twenty container ports as measured by Twenty-Foot Equivalent Units*

(TEUs) throughput: Shanghai (China) -43,303,000; Singapore (Singapore) - 37,195,636; Ningbo (China) - 27,530,000; Shenzhen (China) - 25,770,000; Guangzhou (China) - 23,236,200; Busan (South Korea) - 21,992,001; Qingdao (China) - 21,010,000; Hong Kong (China) - 18,361,000; Tianjin (China) - 17,264,000; Rotterdam (Netherlands) - 14,810,804; Dubai (UAE) - 14,111,000; Port Kelang (Malaysia) - 13,580,717; Antwerp (Belgium) - 11,860,204; Xiamen (China) - 11,122,200; Kaohsiung (Taiwan) -10,428,634; Los Angeles (US) - 9,337,632; Hamburg (Germany) - 9,274,215; Tanjung Pelepas (Malaysia) - 9,100,000; Dalian (China) - 8,760,000; Laem Chabang (Thailand) - 8,106,928 (2019)

MILITARY AND SECURITY

Military expenditures: 2.3% of GDP (2021 est.)
2.4% of GDP (2020 est.)
2.2% of GDP (2019 est.)
2.2% of GDP (2018 est.)
2.2% of GDP (2017 est.)
note: in 2021, the world's largest defense budgets belonged to the US, China, India, the UK, and Russia; total global military expenditures were estimated at more than $2 trillion

Military and security service personnel strengths: estimated 20 million active duty military personnel worldwide (2021)
note: as of 2021, the largest militaries in the world based on personnel numbers belonged to China, India, the US, North Korea, and Russia

Military equipment inventories and acquisitions: from 2010-2020, the US was assessed to be the world's leading arms exporter, followed by Russia; India and Saudi Arabia were the top arms importers for the same period

Military deployments: as of early 2022, there were about 75,000 UN peacekeepers deployed worldwide

Maritime threats: the International Maritime Bureau (IMB) reports that 2021 saw a decrease in global pirate activities; in 2021, pirates attacked a total of 132 ships worldwide including boarding 115 ships, hijacking one ship, and firing on five; this activity is a decrease from 195 incidents in 2020 and the lowest number recorded since 1994; in 2021, the number of hostages taken was eight, and the number of seafarers kidnapped for ransom decreased to 57 compared with 135 in 2020, with all taken off West Africa

the EU naval mission, Operation ATALANTA, continues its operations in the Gulf of Aden and Indian Ocean through 2022; naval units from Japan, India, and China also operate in conjunction with EU forces; China has established a logistical base in Djibouti to support its deployed naval units in the Horn of Africa

the Horn of Africa saw one incident of pirate activity in 2021, up from no attacks in 2020; the decrease in successful pirate attacks off the Horn of Africa since the peak in 2007 was due, in part, to anti-piracy operations by international naval forces, the hardening of vessels, and the increased use of armed security teams aboard merchant ships; despite these preventative measures, the assessed risk remains high

West Africa remains a dangerous area for piracy in the world, but saw a dramatic decrease in incidents with 34 attacks in 2021 compared to 81 in 2020, including one hijacking and three of five ships fired upon; Nigerian pirates are very aggressive, operating as far as 200 nm offshore and kidnapping 57 mariners in seven incidents accounting for all crew kidnappings world-wide; attacks against ships underway in the Singapore Straits increased 50% to 35 incidents in 2021; there were nine attacks in Indonesian waters in 2021 compared to 26 in 2020, primarily to ships anchored or berthed; the majority (71%) of global attacks against shipping have occurred in the offshore waters of eight countries - Colombia, Ghana, Indonesia, Malaysia/Singapore, Nigeria, Peru, Philippines, and Sao Tome and Principe (2021)

TRANSNATIONAL ISSUES

Disputes - international: stretching over some 280,000 km, the world's 325 international land boundaries separate 195 independent states and 70 dependencies, areas of special sovereignty, and other miscellaneous entities; ethnicity, culture, race, religion, and language have divided states into separate political entities as much as history, physical terrain, political fiat, or conquest, resulting in sometimes arbitrary and imposed boundaries; most maritime states have claimed limits that include territorial seas and exclusive economic zones; overlapping limits due to adjacent or opposite coasts create the potential for 430 bilateral maritime boundaries of which 209 have agreements that include contiguous and non-contiguous segments; boundary, borderland/resource, and territorial disputes vary in intensity from managed or dormant to violent or militarized; undemarcated, indefinite, porous, and unmanaged boundaries tend to encourage illegal cross-border activities, uncontrolled migration, and confrontation; territorial disputes may evolve from historical and/or cultural claims, or they may be brought on by resource competition; ethnic and cultural clashes continue to be responsible for much of the territorial fragmentation and internal displacement of the estimated 45.7 million people and cross-border displacements of approximately 31.7 million refugees and asylum seekers around the world as of yearend 2021; approximately 429,300 refugees were repatriated during 2021; other sources of contention include access to water and mineral (especially hydrocarbon) resources, fisheries, and arable land; armed conflict prevails not so much between the uniformed armed forces of independent states as between stateless armed entities that detract from the sustenance and welfare of local populations, leaving the community of nations to cope with resultant refugees, hunger, disease, impoverishment, and environmental degradation

Refugees and internally displaced persons: the UN High Commissioner for Refugees (UNHCR) estimated that as of year-end 2021 there were 89.3 million people forcibly displaced worldwide; this includes 53.2 million IDPs, 27.1 million refugees, 4.6 million asylum seekers, and 4.4 million Venezuelans displaced abroad; the UNHCR estimates there are currently more than 4.3 million stateless persons as of year-end 2021

Trafficking in persons: *current situation:* approximately 800,000 people, mostly women and children, are trafficked annually across national borders, not including millions trafficked within their own countries; at least 80% of the victims are female and up to 50% are minors; 75% of all victims are trafficked into commercial sexual exploitation; almost two-thirds of the global victims are trafficked intra-regionally within East Asia and the Pacific (260,000 to 280,000 people) and Europe and Eurasia (170,000 to 210,000 people)

Tier 2 Watch List: (44 countries) Armenia, Aruba, Azerbaijan, Barbados, Belize, Bhutan, Bosnia and Herzegovina, Brunei, Cambodia, Cameroon, Chad, Democratic Republic of the Congo, Curacao, Dominican Republic, Equatorial Guinea, Fiji, The Gambia, Guinea, Guinea-Bissau, Hong Kong, Ireland, Jordan, Kazakhstan, Kyrgyzstan, Macau, Malaysia, Maldives, Mali, Marshall Islands, Mauritania, Nigeria, Pakistan, Romania, Saudi Arabia, Senegal, Seychelles, Sri Lanka, Sudan, Tanzania, Timor-Leste, Uganda, Uzbekistan, Vietnam, Zambia

Tier 3: (19 countries) Afghanistan, Algeria, Belarus, Burma, Burundi, China, Comoros, Cuba, Eritrea, Iran, Lesotho, Nicaragua, North Korea, Papua New Guinea, Russia, South Sudan, Syria, Turkmenistan, Venezuela (2020)

Illicit drugs: *cocaine:* worldwide coca cultivation in 2020 likely amounted to 373,000 hectares, potential pure cocaine production reached 2,100 metric tons in 2020
opiates: worldwide illicit opium poppy cultivation probably reached about 265,000 hectares in 2020, with potential opium production reaching 7,300 metric tons; Afghanistan is world's primary opium producer, accounting for 85% of the global supply; Southeast Asia was responsible for 7% of global opium; Latin America opium in 2020 was sufficient to produce about 61 metric tons of pure heroin (2015)

YEMEN

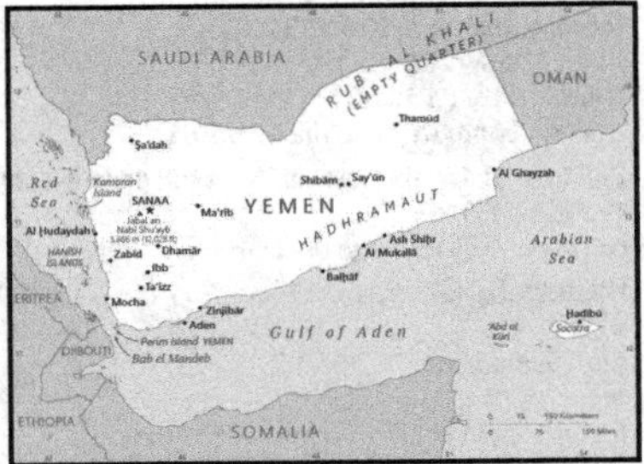

INTRODUCTION

Background: The Kingdom of Yemen (colloquially known as North Yemen) became independent from the Ottoman Empire in 1918 and in 1962 became the Yemen Arab Republic. The British, who had set up a protectorate area around the southern port of Aden in the 19th century, withdrew in 1967 from what became the People's Republic of Southern Yemen (colloquially known as South Yemen). Three years later, the southern government adopted a Marxist orientation and changed the country's name to the People's Democratic Republic of Yemen. The massive exodus of hundreds of thousands of Yemenis from the south to the north contributed to two decades of hostility between the states. The two countries were formally unified as the Republic of Yemen in 1990. A southern secessionist movement and brief civil war in 1994 was quickly subdued. In 2000, Saudi Arabia and Yemen agreed to delineate their border.

Fighting in the northwest between the government and the Huthis, a Zaydi Shia Muslim minority, continued intermittently from 2004 to 2010, and then again from 2014-present. The southern secessionist movement was revitalized in 2007.

Public rallies in Sana'a against then President Ali Abdallah SALIH - inspired by similar Arab Spring demonstrations in Tunisia and Egypt - slowly built momentum starting in late January 2011 fueled by complaints over high unemployment, poor economic conditions, and corruption. By the following month, some protests had resulted in violence, and the demonstrations had spread to other major cities. By March the opposition had hardened its demands and was unifying behind calls for SALIH's immediate ouster. In April 2011, the Gulf Cooperation Council (GCC), in an attempt to mediate the crisis in Yemen, proposed the GCC Initiative, an agreement in which the president would step down in exchange for immunity from prosecution. SALIH's refusal to sign an agreement led to further violence. The UN Security Council passed Resolution 2014 in October 2011 calling for an end to the violence and completing a power transfer deal. In November 2011, SALIH signed the GCC Initiative to step down and to transfer some of his powers to Vice President Abd Rabuh Mansur HADI. Following HADI's uncontested election victory in February 2012, SALIH formally transferred all presidential powers. In accordance with the GCC Initiative, Yemen launched a National Dialogue Conference (NDC) in March 2013 to discuss key constitutional, political, and social issues. HADI concluded the NDC in January 2014 and planned to begin implementing subsequent steps in the transition process, including constitutional drafting, a constitutional referendum, and national elections.

The Huthis, perceiving their grievances were not addressed in the NDC, joined forces with SALIH and expanded their influence in northwestern Yemen, which culminated in a major offensive against military units and rival tribes and enabled their forces to overrun the capital, Sanaa, in September 2014. In January 2015, the Huthis surrounded the presidential palace, HADI's residence, and key government facilities, prompting HADI and the cabinet to submit their resignations. HADI fled to Aden in February 2015 and rescinded his resignation. He subsequently escaped to Oman and then moved to Saudi Arabia and asked the GCC to intervene militarily in Yemen to protect the legitimate government from the Huthis. In March 2015, Saudi Arabia assembled a coalition of Arab militaries and began airstrikes against the Huthis and Huthi-affiliated forces. Ground fighting between Huthi-aligned forces and anti-Huthi groups backed by the Saudi-led coalition continued through 2016. In 2016, the UN brokered a months-long cessation of hostilities that reduced airstrikes and fighting, and initiated peace talks in Kuwait. However, the talks ended without agreement. The Huthis and SALIH's political party announced a Supreme Political Council in August 2016 and a National Salvation Government, including a prime minister and several dozen cabinet members, in November 2016, to govern in Sanaa and further challenge the legitimacy of HADI's government. However, amid rising tensions between the Huthis and SALIH, sporadic clashes erupted in mid-2017, and escalated into open fighting that ended when Huthi forces killed SALIH in early December 2017. In 2018, anti-Huthi forces made the most battlefield progress in Yemen since early 2016, most notably in Al Hudaydah Governorate. In December 2018, the Huthis and Yemeni Government participated in the first UN-brokered peace talks since 2016, agreeing to a limited cease-fire in Al Hudaydah Governorate and the establishment of a UN Mission to monitor the agreement. In April 2019, Yemen's parliament convened in Say'un for the first time since the conflict broke out in 2014. In August 2019, violence erupted between HADI's government and the pro-secessionist Southern Transition Council (STC) in southern Yemen. In November 2019, HADI's government and the STC signed a power-sharing agreement to end the fighting between them, and in December 2020, the signatories formed a new cabinet. In 2020 and 2021, fighting continued on the ground in Yemen as the Huthis gained territory, and also conducted regular UAV and missile attacks against targets in Saudi Arabia.

GEOGRAPHY

Location: Middle East, bordering the Arabian Sea, Gulf of Aden, and Red Sea, between Oman and Saudi Arabia

Geographic coordinates: 15 00 N, 48 00 E

Map references: Middle East

Area: *total:* 527,968 sq km
land: 527,968 sq km
water: 0 sq km
note: includes Perim, Socotra, the former Yemen Arab Republic (YAR or North Yemen), and the former People's Democratic Republic of Yemen (PDRY or South Yemen)
country comparison to the world: 52

Area - comparative: almost four times the size of Alabama; slightly larger than twice the size of Wyoming

Land boundaries: *total:* 1,601 km
border countries (2): Oman 294 km; Saudi Arabia 1,307 km

Coastline: 1,906 km

Maritime claims: *territorial sea:* 12 nm
contiguous zone: 24 nm
exclusive economic zone: 200 nm
continental shelf: 200 nm or to the edge of the continental margin

Climate: mostly desert; hot and humid along west coast; temperate in western mountains affected by seasonal monsoon; extraordinarily hot, dry, harsh desert in east

Terrain: narrow coastal plain backed by flat-topped hills and rugged mountains; dissected upland desert plains in center slope into the desert interior of the Arabian Peninsula

Elevation: *highest point:* Jabal an Nabi Shu'ayb 3,666 m
lowest point: Arabian Sea 0 m
mean elevation: 999 m

Natural resources: petroleum, fish, rock salt, marble; small deposits of coal, gold, lead, nickel, and copper; fertile soil in west

Land use: *agricultural land:* 44.5% (2018 est.)
arable land: 2.2% (2018 est.)
permanent crops: 0.6% (2018 est.)
permanent pasture: 41.7% (2018 est.)
forest: 1% (2018 est.)
other: 54.5% (2018 est.)

Irrigated land: 6,800 sq km (2012)

Population distribution: the vast majority of the population is found in the Asir Mountains (part of the larger Sarawat Mountain system), located in the far western region of the country

Natural hazards: sandstorms and dust storms in summer
volcanism: limited volcanic activity; Jebel at Tair (Jabal al-Tair, Jebel Teir, Jabal al-Tayr, Jazirat at-Tair) (244 m), which forms an island in the Red Sea, erupted in 2007 after awakening from dormancy; other historically active volcanoes include Harra of Arhab, Harras of Dhamar, Harra es-Sawad, and Jebel Zubair, although many of these have not erupted in over a century

Geography - note: strategic location on Bab el Mandeb, the strait linking the Red Sea and the Gulf of Aden, one of world's most active shipping lanes

PEOPLE AND SOCIETY

Population: 30,984,689 (2022 est.)
country comparison to the world: 48

Nationality: *noun:* Yemeni(s)

adjective: Yemeni

Ethnic groups: predominantly Arab; but also Afro-Arab, South Asian, European

Languages: Arabic (official); note - a distinct Socotri language is widely used on Socotra Island and Archipelago; Mahri is still fairly widely spoken in eastern Yemen
major-language sample(s):
كتاب حقائق العالم، المصدر الذي لا يمكن الاستغناء عنه للمعلومات الأساسية
(Arabic)

Religions: Muslim 99.1% (official; virtually all are citizens, an estimated 65% are Sunni and 35% are Shia), other 0.9% (includes Jewish, Baha'i, Hindu, and Christian; many are refugees or temporary foreign residents) (2020 est.)

Age structure: *0-14 years:* 39.16% (male 5,711,709 / female 5,513,526)
15-24 years: 21.26% (male 3,089,817 /female 3,005,693)
25-54 years: 32.78% (male 4,805,059 /female 4,591,811)
55-64 years: 4% (male 523,769 /female 623,100)
65 years and over: 2.8% (male 366,891 /female 435,855) (2018 est.)

Dependency ratios: *total dependency ratio:* 71.7
youth dependency ratio: 66.7
elderly dependency ratio: 5
potential support ratio: 19.9 (2020 est.)

Median age: *total:* 19.8 years (2018 est.)
male: 19.6 years
female: 19.9 years
country comparison to the world: 198

Population growth rate: 1.88% (2022 est.)
country comparison to the world: 46

Birth rate: 24.64 births/1,000 population (2022 est.)
country comparison to the world: 47

Death rate: 5.62 deaths/1,000 population (2022 est.)
country comparison to the world: 177

Net migration rate: -0.19 migrant(s)/1,000 population (2022 est.)
country comparison to the world: 112

Population distribution: the vast majority of the population is found in the Asir Mountains (part of the larger Sarawat Mountain system), located in the far western region of the country

Urbanization: *urban population:* 39.2% of total population (2022)
rate of urbanization: 3.71% annual rate of change (2015-20 est.)

Major urban areas - population: 3.182 million SANAA (capital), 1.045 million Aden (2022)

Sex ratio: *at birth:* 1.05 male(s)/female
0-14 years: 1.04 male(s)/female
15-24 years: 1.03 male(s)/female
25-54 years: 1.04 male(s)/female
55-64 years: 0.84 male(s)/female
65 years and over: 0.69 male(s)/female
total population: 1.02 male(s)/female (2022 est.)

Mother's mean age at first birth: 20.8 years (2013 est.)
note: data represents median age at first birth among women 25-49

Maternal mortality ratio: 164 deaths/100,000 live births (2017 est.)
country comparison to the world: 54

Infant mortality rate: *total:* 46.54 deaths/1,000 live births
male: 51.9 deaths/1,000 live births
female: 40.92 deaths/1,000 live births (2022 est.)
country comparison to the world: 26

Life expectancy at birth: *total population:* 67.51 years
male: 65.19 years
female: 69.94 years (2022 est.)
country comparison to the world: 189

Total fertility rate: 3.01 children born/woman (2022 est.)
country comparison to the world: 47

Contraceptive prevalence rate: 33.5% (2013)

Drinking water source: *improved: urban:* 98.5% of population
rural: 84.2% of population
total: 99.6% of population
unimproved: urban: 1.5% of population
rural: 15.8% of population
total: 10.4% of population (2020 est.)

Current health expenditure: 4.3% of GDP (2015)

Physicians density: 0.53 physicians/1,000 population (2014)

Hospital bed density: 0.7 beds/1,000 population (2017)

Sanitation facility access: *improved: urban:* 83.5% of population
rural: 44.2% of population
total: 59.1% of population
unimproved: urban: 16.5% of population
rural: 55.8% of population
total: 40.9% of population (2020 est.)

HIV/AIDS - adult prevalence rate: (2020 est.) <.1%

HIV/AIDS - people living with HIV/AIDS: 11,000 (2020 est.)
country comparison to the world: 102

HIV/AIDS - deaths: (2020 est.) <500

Major infectious diseases: *degree of risk:* high (2020)
food or waterborne diseases: bacterial diarrhea, hepatitis A, and typhoid fever
vectorborne diseases: dengue fever and malaria
water contact diseases: schistosomiasis
note: on 21 March 2022, the US Centers for Disease Control and Prevention (CDC) issued a Travel Alert for polio in Asia; Yemen is currently considered a high risk to travelers for circulating vaccine-derived polioviruses (cVDPV); vaccine-derived poliovirus (VDPV) is a strain of the weakened poliovirus that was initially included in oral polio vaccine (OPV) and *that has changed over time and behaves more like the wild or naturally occurring virus;* this means it can be spread more easily to people who are unvaccinated against polio and who come in contact with the stool or respiratory secretions, such as from a sneeze, of an "infected" person who received oral polio vaccine; the CDC recommends that before any international travel, anyone unvaccinated, incompletely vaccinated, or with an unknown polio vaccination status should complete the routine polio vaccine series; before travel to any high-risk destination, the CDC recommends that adults who previously completed the full, routine polio vaccine series receive a single, lifetime booster dose of polio vaccine

Obesity - adult prevalence rate: 17.1% (2016)
country comparison to the world: 120

Alcohol consumption per capita: *total:* 0.02 liters of pure alcohol (2019 est.)
beer: 0.02 liters of pure alcohol (2019 est.)
wine: 0 liters of pure alcohol (2019 est.)
spirits: 0 liters of pure alcohol (2019 est.)
other alcohols: 0 liters of pure alcohol (2019 est.)
country comparison to the world: 182

Tobacco use: *total:* 20.3% (2020 est.)
male: 32.5% (2020 est.)
female: 8.1% (2020 est.)
country comparison to the world: 85

Children under the age of 5 years underweight: 39.9% (2013)
country comparison to the world: 1

Literacy: *definition:* age 15 and over can read and write
total population: 70.1%
male: 85.1%
female: 55% (2015)

School life expectancy (primary to tertiary education): *total:* 9 years
male: 11 years
female: 8 years (2011)

Unemployment, youth ages 15-24: *total:* 24.5%
male: 23.5%
female: 34.6% (2014 est.)

ENVIRONMENT

Environment - current issues: limited natural freshwater resources; inadequate supplies of potable water; overgrazing; soil erosion; desertification

Environment - international agreements: *party to:* Biodiversity, Climate Change, Climate Change-Kyoto Protocol, Desertification, Endangered Species, Environmental Modification, Hazardous Wastes, Law of the Sea, Marine Dumping-London Protocol, Nuclear Test Ban, Ozone Layer Protection, Wetlands
signed, but not ratified: Climate Change-Paris Agreement, Comprehensive Nuclear Test Ban

Air pollutants: *particulate matter emissions:* 44.96 micrograms per cubic meter (2016 est.)
carbon dioxide emissions: 10.61 megatons (2016 est.)
methane emissions: 8.03 megatons (2020 est.)

Climate: mostly desert; hot and humid along west coast; temperate in western mountains affected by seasonal monsoon; extraordinarily hot, dry, harsh desert in east

Land use: *agricultural land:* 44.5% (2018 est.)
arable land: 2.2% (2018 est.)
permanent crops: 0.6% (2018 est.)
permanent pasture: 41.7% (2018 est.)
forest: 1% (2018 est.)
other: 54.5% (2018 est.)

Urbanization: *urban population:* 39.2% of total population (2022)
rate of urbanization: 3.71% annual rate of change (2015-20 est.)

Revenue from forest resources: *forest revenues:* 0.04% of GDP (2018 est.)
country comparison to the world: 132

Revenue from coal: *coal revenues:* 0% of GDP (2018 est.)
country comparison to the world: 186

Food insecurity: *widespread lack of access: due to conflict, poverty, floods, high food and fuel prices* - the number of food insecure people was projected to increase by over 1 million to 17.4 million between January and May 2022, increasing to 19 million starting from June until the end of the year; economic conditions in the country remain dire; the conflict is further hampering the already constrained livelihood activities and humanitarian access; income earning opportunities have declined due to COVID-19-related business disruptions (2022)

Waste and recycling: *municipal solid waste generated annually:* 4,836,820 tons (2011 est.)
municipal solid waste recycled annually: 386,946 tons (2016 est.)
percent of municipal solid waste recycled: 8% (2016 est.)

Total water withdrawal: *municipal:* 265 million cubic meters (2017 est.)
industrial: 65 million cubic meters (2017 est.)
agricultural: 3.235 billion cubic meters (2017 est.)

Total renewable water resources: 2.1 billion cubic meters (2017 est.)

GOVERNMENT

Country name: *conventional long form:* Republic of Yemen
conventional short form: Yemen
local long form: Al Jumhuriyah al Yamaniyah
local short form: Al Yaman
former: Yemen Arab Republic [Yemen (Sanaa) or North Yemen] and People's Democratic Republic of Yemen [Yemen (Aden) or South Yemen]
etymology: name derivation remains unclear but may come from the Arab term "yumn" (happiness) and be related to the region's classical name "Arabia Felix" (Fertile or Happy Arabia); the Romans referred to the rest of the peninsula as "Arabia Deserta" (Deserted Arabia)

Government type: in transition

Capital: *name:* Sanaa
geographic coordinates: 15 21 N, 44 12 E
time difference: UTC+3 (8 hours ahead of Washington, DC, during Standard Time)
etymology: the name is reputed to mean "well-fortified" in Sabaean, the South Arabian language that went extinct in Yemen in the 6th century A.D.

Administrative divisions: 22 governorates (muhafazat, singular - muhafazah); Abyan, 'Adan (Aden), Ad Dali', Al Bayda', Al Hudaydah, Al Jawf, Al Mahrah, Al Mahwit, Amanat al 'Asimah (Sanaa City), 'Amran, Arkhabil Suqutra (Socotra Archipelago), Dhamar, Hadramawt, Hajjah, Ibb, Lahij, Ma'rib, Raymah, Sa'dah, San'a' (Sanaa), Shabwah, Ta'izz

Independence: 22 May 1990 (Republic of Yemen was established with the merger of the Yemen Arab Republic [Yemen (Sanaa) or North Yemen] and the Marxist-dominated People's Democratic Republic of Yemen [Yemen (Aden) or South Yemen]); notable earlier dates: North Yemen became independent on 1 November 1918 (from the Ottoman Empire) and became a republic with the overthrow of the theocratic Imamate on 27 September 1962; South Yemen became independent on 30 November 1967 (from the UK)

National holiday: Unification Day, 22 May (1990)

Constitution: *history:* adopted by referendum 16 May 1991 (following unification); note - after the National Dialogue ended in January 2015, a Constitutional Drafting Committee appointed by the president worked to prepare a new draft constitution that was expected to be put to a national referendum before being adopted; however, the start of the current conflict in early 2015 interrupted the process
amendments: amended several times, last in 2009

Legal system: mixed legal system of Islamic (sharia) law, Napoleonic law, English common law, and customary law

International law organization participation: has not submitted an ICJ jurisdiction declaration; non-party state to the ICCt

Citizenship: *citizenship by birth:* no
citizenship by descent only: the father must be a citizen of Yemen; if the father is unknown, the mother must be a citizen
dual citizenship recognized: no
residency requirement for naturalization: 10 years

Suffrage: 18 years of age; universal

Executive branch: *chief of state:* Chairperson, Presidential Council Rashad Muhammad al-ALIMI, Dr. (since 19 April 2022); Vice Chairperson, Presidential Council Sultan al-ARADA (since 19 April 2022); Vice Chairperson, Presidential Council Faraj Salmin al- BAHSANI, Brig. Gen. (since 19 April 2022); Vice Chairperson, Presidential Council Abdullah Al-Alimi BA WAZIR (since 19 April 2022); Vice Chairperson, Presidential Council Uthman Hussain Faid al-MUJALI (since 19 April 2022); Vice Chairperson, Presidential Council TARIQ Muhammad Abdallah Salih, Brig. Gen. (since 19 April 2022); Vice Chairperson, Presidential Council 'Abd-al-Rahman ABU ZARA'A al-Muharrami al-Yafai, Brig. Gen. (since 19 April 2022); Vice Chairperson, Presidential Council Aydarus Qasim al-ZUBAYDI, Maj. Gen. (since 19 April 2022)
head of government: Chairperson, Presidential Council Rashad Muhammad al-ALIMI, Dr. (since 19 April 2022); Vice Chairperson, Presidential Council Sultan al-ARADA (since 19 April 2022); Vice Chairperson, Presidential Council Faraj Salmin al- BAHSANI, Brig. Gen. (since 19 April 2022); Vice Chairperson, Presidential Council Abdullah Al-Alimi BA WAZIR (since 19 April 2022); Vice Chairperson, Presidential Council Uthman Hussain Faid al-MUJALI (since 19 April 2022); Vice Chairperson, Presidential Council TARIQ Muhammad Abdallah Salih, Brig. Gen. (since 19 April 2022); Vice Chairperson, Presidential Council 'Abd-al-Rahman ABU ZARA'A al-Muharrami al-Yafai, Brig. Gen. (since 19 April 2022); Vice Chairperson, Presidential Council Aydarus Qasim al-ZUBAYDI, Maj. Gen. (since 19 April 2022)
cabinet: NA
elections/appointments: formerly, the president was directly elected by absolute majority popular vote in 2 rounds if needed for a 7-year term (eligible for a second term); election last held on 21 February 2012 (next election NA); note - a special election was held on 21 February 2012 to remove Ali Abdallah SALIH under the terms of a Gulf Cooperation Council-mediated deal during the political crisis of 2011; vice president appointed by the president; prime minister appointed by the president
election results:
2012: in a special election held on 21 February 2012, Abd Rabuh Mansur HADI (GPC) was elected as a consensus president
note: on 7 April 2022, President Abd Rabuh Mansur HADI announced the dismissal of Vice President ALI MUHSIN al-Ahmar and the formation of a Presidential Council, an eight-member body chaired by former minister Rashad AL-ALIMI; on 19 April 2022, the Council was sworn in before Parliament and began assuming the responsibilities of the president and vice president and carrying out the political, security, and military duties of the government

Legislative branch: *description:* bicameral Parliament or Majlis consists of:
Shura Council or Majlis Alshoora (111 seats; members appointed by the president; member tenure NA)
House of Representatives or Majlis al Nuwaab (301 seats; members directly elected in single-seat constituencies by simple majority vote to serve 6-year terms)
elections:
Shura Council - last appointments NA (next appointments NA)
House of Representatives - last held in April 2019 (next to be held NA)
election results:
percent of vote by party - GPC 58.0%, Islah 22.6%, YSP 3.8%, Unionist Party 1.9%, other 13.7%; seats by party - GPC 238, Islah 46, YSP 8, Nasserist Unionist Party 3, National Arab Socialist Ba'ath Party 2, independent 4

Judicial branch: *highest court(s):* Supreme Court (consists of the court president, 2 deputies, and nearly 50 judges; court organized into constitutional, civil, commercial, family, administrative, criminal, military, and appeals scrutiny divisions)
judge selection and term of office: judges appointed by the Supreme Judicial Council, which is chaired by the president of the republic and includes 10 high-ranking judicial officers; judges serve for life with mandatory retirement at age 65
subordinate courts: appeal courts; district or first instance courts; commercial courts

Political parties and leaders: General People's Congress or GPC (3 factions: pro-Hadi [Abdrabbi Mansur HADI], pro-Houthi [Sadeq Ameen Abu RAS], pro-Saleh [Ahmed SALEH]
Nasserist Unionist People's Organization [Abdulmalik al-MEKHLAFI]
National Arab Socialist Ba'ath Party [Qassem Salam SAID]
Southern Transitional Council or STC [Aidarus al-ZOUBAIDA]
Yemeni Reform Grouping or Islah [Muhammed Abdallah al-YADUMI]
Yemeni Socialist Party or YSP [Dr. Abd al-Rahman Umar al-SAQQAF]

International organization participation: AFESD, AMF, CAEU, CD, EITI (temporarily suspended), FAO, G-77, IAEA, IBRD, ICAO, ICRM, IDA, IDB, IFAD, IFC, IFRCS, ILO, IMF, IMO, IMSO, Interpol, IOC, IOM, IPU, ISO, ITSO, ITU, ITUC (NGOs), LAS, MIGA, MINURSO, MINUSMA, MONUSCO, NAM, OAS (observer), OIC, OPCW, UN, UNAMID, UNCTAD, UNESCO, UNHCR, UNIDO, UNISFA, UNMHA, UNMIL, UNMIS, UNOCI, UNVIM, UNWTO, UPU, WCO, WFTU (NGOs), WHO, WIPO, WMO, WTO

Diplomatic representation in the US: *chief of mission:* Ambassador Mohammed Al-HADHRAMI (since 2019)
chancery: 2319 Wyoming Avenue NW, Washington, DC 20008
telephone: [1] (202) 965-4760
FAX: [1] (202) 337-2017
email address and website:
Information@yemenembassy.org
https://www.yemenembassy.org/

Diplomatic representation from the US: *chief of mission:* Ambassador Steven H. FAGIN (since

1 June 2022); note - the embassy closed in March 2015; Yemen Affairs Unit currently operates out of US Embassy Riyadh
embassy: previously - Sa'awan Street, Sanaa
mailing address: 6330 Sanaa Place, Washington DC 20521-6330
telephone: US Embassy Riyadh [966] 11-488-3800
previously - [967] 1 755-2000
FAX: US Embassy Riyadh [966] 11-488-7360
email address and website:
YemenEmergencyUSC@state.gov
https://ye.usembassy.gov/

Flag description: three equal horizontal bands of red (top), white, and black; the band colors derive from the Arab Liberation flag and represent oppression (black), overcome through bloody struggle (red), to be replaced by a bright future (white)
note: similar to the flag of Syria, which has two green stars in the white band, and of Iraq, which has an Arabic inscription centered in the white band; also similar to the flag of Egypt, which has a heraldic eagle centered in the white band

National symbol(s): golden eagle; national colors: red, white, black

National anthem: *name:* "al-qumhuriyatu l-muttahida" (United Republic)
lyrics/music: Abdullah Abdulwahab NOA'MAN/ Ayyoab Tarish ABSI
note: adopted 1990; the music first served as the anthem for South Yemen before unification with North Yemen in 1990

National heritage: *total World Heritage Sites:* 4 (3 cultural, 1 natural)
selected World Heritage Site locales: Old Walled City of Shibam (c); Old City of Sana'a (c); Historic Town of Zabid (c); Socotra Archipelago (n)

ECONOMY

Economic overview: Yemen is a low-income country that faces difficult long-term challenges to stabilizing and growing its economy, and the current conflict has only exacerbated those issues. The ongoing war has halted Yemen's exports, pressured the currency's exchange rate, accelerated inflation, severely limited food and fuel imports, and caused widespread damage to infrastructure. The conflict has also created a severe humanitarian crisis - the world's largest cholera outbreak currently at nearly 1 million cases, more than 7 million people at risk of famine, and more than 80% of the population in need of humanitarian assistance.

Prior to the start of the conflict in 2014, Yemen was highly dependent on declining oil and gas resources for revenue. Oil and gas earnings accounted for roughly 25% of GDP and 65% of government revenue. The Yemeni Government regularly faced annual budget shortfalls and tried to diversify the Yemeni economy through a reform program designed to bolster non-oil sectors of the economy and foreign investment. In July 2014, the government continued reform efforts by eliminating some fuel subsidies and in August 2014, the IMF approved a three-year, $570 million Extended Credit Facility for Yemen.

However, the conflict that began in 2014 stalled these reform efforts and ongoing fighting continues to accelerate the country's economic decline. In September 2016, President HADI announced the move of the main branch of Central Bank of Yemen from Sanaa to Aden where his government could exert greater control over the central bank's dwindling resources. Regardless of which group controls the main branch, the central bank system is struggling to function. Yemen's Central Bank's foreign reserves, which stood at roughly $5.2 billion prior to the conflict, have declined to negligible amounts. The Central Bank can no longer fully support imports of critical goods or the country's exchange rate. The country also is facing a growing liquidity crisis and rising inflation. The private sector is hemorrhaging, with almost all businesses making substantial layoffs. Access to food and other critical commodities such as medical equipment is limited across the country due to security issues on the ground. The Social Welfare Fund, a cash transfer program for Yemen's neediest, is no longer operational and has not made any disbursements since late 2014.

Yemen will require significant international assistance during and after the protracted conflict to stabilize its economy. Long-term challenges include a high population growth rate, high unemployment, declining water resources, and severe food scarcity.

Real GDP (purchasing power parity): $73.63 billion (2017 est.)
$78.28 billion (2016 est.)
$90.63 billion (2015 est.)
note: data are in 2017 dollars
country comparison to the world: 100

Real GDP growth rate: -5.9% (2017 est.)
-13.6% (2016 est.)
-16.7% (2015 est.)
country comparison to the world: 219

Real GDP per capita: $2,500 (2017 est.)
$2,700 (2016 est.)
$3,200 (2015 est.)
note: data are in 2017 dollars
country comparison to the world: 204

GDP (official exchange rate): $54.356 billion (2018 est.)

Inflation rate (consumer prices): 24.7% (2017 est.)
-12.6% (2016 est.)
country comparison to the world: 219

GDP - composition, by sector of origin: *agriculture:* 20.3% (2017 est.)
industry: 11.8% (2017 est.)
services: 67.9% (2017 est.)

GDP - composition, by end use: *household consumption:* 116.6% (2017 est.)
government consumption: 17.6% (2017 est.)
investment in fixed capital: 2.2% (2017 est.)
investment in inventories: 0% (2017 est.)
exports of goods and services: 7.5% (2017 est.)
imports of goods and services: -43.9% (2017 est.)

Agricultural products: mangoes/guavas, potatoes, sorghum, onions, milk, poultry, watermelons, grapes, oranges, bananas

Industries: crude oil production and petroleum refining; small-scale production of cotton textiles, leather goods; food processing; handicrafts; aluminum products; cement; commercial ship repair; natural gas production

Industrial production growth rate: 8.9% (2017 est.)
country comparison to the world: 21

Labor force: 7.425 million (2017 est.)
country comparison to the world: 62

Labor force - by occupation: *note:* most people are employed in agriculture and herding; services, construction, industry, and commerce account for less than one-fourth of the labor force

Unemployment rate: 27% (2014 est.)
35% (2003 est.)
country comparison to the world: 199

Unemployment, youth ages 15-24: *total:* 24.5%
male: 23.5%
female: 34.6% (2014 est.)
country comparison to the world: 57

Population below poverty line: 48.6% (2014 est.)

Gini Index coefficient - distribution of family income: 36.7 (2014 est.)
37.3 (1999 est.)
country comparison to the world: 88

Household income or consumption by percentage share: *lowest 10%:* 2.6%
highest 10%: 30.3% (2008 est.)

Budget: *revenues:* 2.821 billion (2017 est.)
expenditures: 4.458 billion (2017 est.)

Budget surplus (+) or deficit (-): -5.2% (of GDP) (2017 est.)
country comparison to the world: 171

Public debt: 74.5% of GDP (2017 est.)
68.1% of GDP (2016 est.)
country comparison to the world: 41

Taxes and other revenues: 9% (of GDP) (2017 est.)
country comparison to the world: 216

Fiscal year: calendar year

Current account balance: -$1.236 billion (2017 est.)
-$1.868 billion (2016 est.)
country comparison to the world: 153

Exports: $384.5 million (2017 est.)
$940 million (2016 est.)
country comparison to the world: 195

Exports - partners: China 53%, Saudi Arabia 10%, United Arab Emirates 7%, Australia 5% (2019)

Exports - commodities: crude petroleum, gold, fish, industrial chemical liquids, scrap iron (2019)

Imports: $4.079 billion (2017 est.)
$3.117 billion (2016 est.)
country comparison to the world: 149

Imports - partners: China 25%, Turkey 10%, United Arab Emirates 9%, Saudi Arabia 8%, India 7% (2019)

Imports - commodities: wheat, refined petroleum, iron, rice, cars (2019)

Reserves of foreign exchange and gold: $245.4 million (31 December 2017 est.)
$592.6 million (31 December 2016 est.)
country comparison to the world: 170

Debt - external: $6.805 billion (2018 est.)
$7.181 billion (31 December 2016 est.)
country comparison to the world: 125

Exchange rates: Yemeni rials (YER) per US dollar -
275 (2017 est.)
214.9 (2016 est.)
214.9 (2015 est.)
228 (2014 est.)
214.89 (2013 est.)

ENERGY

Electricity access: *population without electricity:* 16 million (2019)
electrification - total population: 47% (2019)
electrification - urban areas: 72% (2019)
electrification - rural areas: 31% (2019)

Electricity: *installed generating capacity:* 1.772 million kW (2020 est.)

consumption: 2,677,920,000 kWh (2019 est.)
exports: 0 kWh (2020 est.)
imports: 0 kWh (2020 est.)
transmission/distribution losses: 753 million kWh (2019 est.)

Electricity generation sources: *fossil fuels:* 84.6% of total installed capacity (2020 est.)
solar: 15.4% of total installed capacity (2020 est.)

Coal: *production:* 0 metric tons (2020 est.)
consumption: 22,000 metric tons (2020 est.)
exports: 0 metric tons (2020 est.)
imports: 22,000 metric tons (2020 est.)
proven reserves: 0 metric tons (2019 est.)

Petroleum: *total petroleum production:* 70,100 bbl/day (2021 est.)
refined petroleum consumption: 75,700 bbl/day (2019 est.)
crude oil estimated reserves: 3 billion barrels (2021 est.)

Refined petroleum products - production: 20,180 bbl/day (2015 est.)
country comparison to the world: 89

Refined petroleum products - exports: 12,670 bbl/day (2015 est.)
country comparison to the world: 78

Refined petroleum products - imports: 75,940 bbl/day (2015 est.)
country comparison to the world: 65

Natural gas: *production:* 89.906 million cubic meters (2019 est.)
consumption: 89.906 million cubic meters (2019 est.)
proven reserves: 478.554 billion cubic meters (2021 est.)

Carbon dioxide emissions: 10.158 million metric tonnes of CO2 (2019 est.)
from coal and metallurgical coke: 79,000 metric tonnes of CO2 (2019 est.)
from petroleum and other liquids: 9.896 million metric tonnes of CO2 (2019 est.)
from consumed natural gas: 183,000 metric tonnes of CO2 (2019 est.)
country comparison to the world: 105

Energy consumption per capita: 5.453 million Btu/person (2019 est.)
country comparison to the world: 169

COMMUNICATIONS

Telephones - fixed lines: *total subscriptions:* 1.24 million (2020 est.)
subscriptions per 100 inhabitants: 4 (2020 est.)
country comparison to the world: 69

Telephones - mobile cellular: *total subscriptions:* 15,357,900 (2019)
subscriptions per 100 inhabitants: 55.18 (2019)
country comparison to the world: 68

Telecommunication systems: *general assessment:* Yemen continues to provide an exceptionally challenging market for telcos; civil unrest has caused havoc and devastation across most parts of the country, while the threat of sanctions has also made it a challenging environment in which to operate; a large proportion of the population requires humanitarian assistance, and there is little disposable income for services upon which telcos can generate revenue; essential telecom infrastructure, such as mobile towers and fiber cabling, has often been targeted, destroyed, or damaged by the opposing sides in the ongoing conflict; these difficulties have proved to be a disincentive to telcos investing in infrastructure, with the result that the country lacks basic fixed-line infrastructure, and mobile services are based on outdated GSM; this has prevented the development of a mobile broadband sector, or the evolution of mobile data services; the ownership of telecommunication services, and the scrutiny of associated revenues and taxes, have become a political issue in Yemen; until telecom infrastructure can be improved across Yemen, and until civil unrest eases, there will be little progress for the sector (2022)
domestic: the national network consists of microwave radio relay, cable, tropospheric scatter, GSM and CDMA mobilecellular telephone systems; fixed-line teledensity remains low by regional standards at roughly 4 per 100 but mobile cellular use expanding at over 55 per 100 (2019)
international: country code - 967; landing points for the FALCON, SeaMeWe-5, Aden-Djibouti, and the AAE-1 international submarine cable connecting Europe, Africa, the Middle East, Asia and Southeast Asia; satellite earth stations - 3 Intelsat (2 Indian Ocean and 1 Atlantic Ocean), 1 Intersputnik (Atlantic Ocean region), and 2 Arabsat; microwave radio relay to Saudi Arabia and Djibouti (2020)

Broadcast media: state-run TV with 2 stations; state-run radio with 2 national radio stations and 5 local stations; stations from Oman and Saudi Arabia can be accessed

Internet country code: .ye

Internet users: *total:* 7,873,719 (2019 est.)
percent of population: 27% (2019 est.)
country comparison to the world: 72

Broadband - fixed subscriptions: *total:* 391,000 (2020 est.)
subscriptions per 100 inhabitants: 1 (2020 est.)
country comparison to the world: 98

TRANSPORTATION

National air transport system: *number of registered air carriers:* 2 (2020)
inventory of registered aircraft operated by air carriers: 8
annual passenger traffic on registered air carriers: 336,310 (2018)
annual freight traffic on registered air carriers: 3.27 million (2018) mt-km

Civil aircraft registration country code prefix: 7O

Airports: *total:* 57 (2021)
country comparison to the world: 83

Airports - with paved runways: *total:* 17
over 3,047 m: 4
2,438 to 3,047 m: 9
1,524 to 2,437 m: 3
914 to 1,523 m: 1 (2021)

Airports - with unpaved runways: *total:* 40
over 3,047 m: 3
2,438 to 3,047 m: 5
1,524 to 2,437 m: 7
914 to 1,523 m: 16
under 914 m: 9 (2021)

Pipelines: 641 km gas, 22 km liquid petroleum gas, 1,370 km oil (2013)

Roadways: *total:* 71,300 km (2005)
paved: 6,200 km (2005)
unpaved: 65,100 km (2005)
country comparison to the world: 67

Merchant marine: *total:* 34
by type: general cargo 2, oil tanker 4, other 28 (2021)
country comparison to the world: 130

Ports and terminals: *major seaport(s):* Aden, Al Hudaydah, Al Mukalla

MILITARY AND SECURITY

Military and security forces: Republic of Yemen Government (ROYG) forces; Ministry of Defense: Yemeni National Army, Air Force and Air Defense, Navy and Coastal Defense Forces, Border Guard, Strategic Reserve Forces (includes Special Forces and Presidential Protection Brigades, which are under the Ministry of Defense but responsible to the president), Popular Committee Forces (government-backed tribal militia); Ministry of Interior: Special Security Forces (paramilitary; formerly known as Central Security Forces), Political Security Organization (state security), National Security Bureau (intelligence), Counterterrorism Unit

Saudi-backed forces: paramilitary/militia border security brigades based largely on tribal or regional affiliation (deployed along the Saudi-Yemen border, especially the areas bordering the governorates of Saada and Al-Jawf)

United Arab Emirates-backed forces include tribal and regionally-based militia and paramilitary forces (concentrated in the southern governates): Southern Transitional Council (STC) forces, including the Security Belt Forces, the Shabwani and Hadrami "Elite" Forces, the Support and Backup Forces (aka Logistics and Support Forces), Facilities Protection Forces, and Anti-Terrorism Forces; Republican Forces; Joint Forces

Huthi: ground, aerospace (air, missile), naval/coastal defense, presidential protection, special operations, and militia/tribal auxiliary forces (2022)
note 1: under the 2019 Riyadh Agreement, the STC forces were to be incorporated into Yemen's Ministries of Defense and Interior under the authority of the HADI government
note 2: a considerable portion--up to 70 percent by some estimates--of Yemen's military and security forces defected in whole or in part to former president SALAH and the Huthi opposition in 2011-2015

Military expenditures: prior to the start of the civil war in 2014, annual military expenditures were approximately 4-5% of Yemen's GDP

Military and security service personnel strengths: information limited and widely varied; Yemen Government: up to 300,000 estimated military, paramilitary, militia, and other security forces; UAE- and Saudi-backed forces: estimated 150-200,000 trained militia and paramilitary fighters; Huthis: up to 200,000 estimated fighters (2021)

Military equipment inventories and acquisitions: the inventory of the Yemeni Government forces consists primarily of Russian and Soviet-era equipment, although much of it has been lost in the current conflict; since the start of the civil war in 2014, it has received limited amounts of donated equipment from some Gulf States, including Saudi Arabia and UAE

Huthi forces are armed largely with weapons seized from Yemeni Government forces; they are also reported to have received military hardware from Iran (2022)

Military service age and obligation: 18 is the legal minimum age for voluntary military service; conscription abolished in 2001; 2-year service obligation (note - limited information since the start of the civil war in 2014) (2021)

Military - note: in 2015, a Saudi-led coalition of Arab states intervened militarily in Yemen in support of the Republic of Yemen Government against the separatist Huthis; as of 2022, Saudi military forces continued to conduct operations in Yemen; Saudi Arabia also has raised and equipped paramilitary/militia security forces in Yemen based largely on tribal or regional affiliation to deploy along the Saudi-Yemen border, especially the areas bordering the governorates of Saada and Al-Jawf

the United Arab Emirates (UAE) intervened in Yemen in 2015 as part of the Saudi-led coalition with about 3,500 troops, as well as supporting air and naval forces; UAE withdrew its main military force from Yemen in 2019, but has retained a smaller military presence while working with proxies in southern Yemen, most notably the Southern Transitional Council (STC); as of 2021, UAE had recruited, trained, and equipped an estimated 150-200,000 Yemeni fighters and formed them into dozens of militia and paramilitary units

Iran has provided some military and political support to the Huthis (2022)

Maritime threats: the Maritime Administration of the US Department of Transportation has issued Maritime Advisory 2022-003 (Red Sea, Gulf of Aden, Arabian Sea, and Indian Ocean-Violence Due to Regional Conflict and Piracy) effective 28 February 2022, which states in part the "Conflict in Yemen continues to pose potential risk to US flagged commercial vessels transiting the southern Red Sea, Bab al Mandeb Strait, and Gulf of Aden. Threats may come from a variety of different sources including, but not limited to, missiles, rockets, projectiles, mines, small arms, unmanned aerial vehicles, unmanned surface vessels, or waterborne improvised explosive devices. These threat vectors continue to pose a direct or collateral risk to US flagged commercial vessels operating in the region. Additionally, piracy poses a threat in the Gulf of Aden, Western Arabian Sea, and Western Indian Ocean."

TERRORISM

Terrorist group(s): Islamic Revolutionary Guard Corps (IRGC)/Qods Force; Islamic State of Iraq and ash-Sham - Yemen; al-Qa'ida in the Arabian Peninsula (AQAP)

TRANSNATIONAL ISSUES

Disputes - international: *Yemen-Oman:* none identified

Yemen-Saudia Arabia: in 2004, Saudi Arabia reinforced its concrete-filled security barrier along sections of the fully demarcated border with Yemen to stem illegal cross-border activities, including militants and arms; in 2013 and 2015, Saudi Arabia again erected fences

Refugees and internally displaced persons: *refugees (country of origin):* 69,900 (Somalia), 18,687 (Ethiopia) (2022)

IDPs: 4,288,739 (conflict in Sa'ada Governorate; clashes between al-Qa'ida in the Arabian Peninsula and government forces) (2022)

ZAMBIA

INTRODUCTION

Background: Multiple waves of Bantu-speaking groups moved into and through what is now Zambia over the past thousand years. In the 1880s, the British began securing mineral and other economic concessions from various local leaders and the territory that is now Zambia eventually came under the control of the former British South Africa Company and was incorporated as the protectorate of Northern Rhodesia in 1911. Administrative control was taken over by the UK in 1924. During the 1920s and 1930s, advances in mining spurred development and immigration.

The name was changed to Zambia upon independence in 1964. In the 1980s and 1990s, declining copper prices, economic mismanagement, and a prolonged drought hurt the economy. Elections in 1991 brought an end to one-party rule and propelled the Movement for Multiparty Democracy (MMD) into power. The subsequent vote in 1996, however, saw increasing harassment of opposition parties and abuse of state media and other resources. The election in 2001 was marked by administrative problems, with three parties filing a legal petition challenging the election of ruling party candidate Levy MWANAWASA. MWANAWASA was reelected in 2006 in an election that was deemed free and fair. Upon his death in August 2008, he was succeeded by his vice president, Rupiah BANDA, who won a special presidential byelection later that year. The MMD and BANDA lost to the Patriotic Front (PF) and Michael SATA in the 2011 general elections. SATA, however, presided over a period of haphazard economic management and attempted to silence opposition to PF policies. SATA died in October 2014 and was succeeded by his vice president, Guy SCOTT, who served as interim president until January 2015, when Edgar LUNGU won the presidential byelection and completed SATA's term. LUNGU then won a full term in August 2016 presidential elections. Hakainde HICHILEMA was elected president in August 2021.

GEOGRAPHY

Location: Southern Africa, east of Angola, south of the Democratic Republic of the Congo

Geographic coordinates: 15 00 S, 30 00 E

Map references: Africa

Area: *total:* 752,618 sq km
land: 743,398 sq km
water: 9,220 sq km
country comparison to the world: 40

Area - comparative: almost five times the size of Georgia; slightly larger than Texas

Land boundaries: *total:* 6,043.15 km
border countries (8): Angola 1,065 km; Botswana 0.15 km; Democratic Republic of the Congo 2,332 km; Malawi 847 km; Mozambique 439 km; Namibia 244 km; Tanzania 353 km; Zimbabwe 763 km

Coastline: 0 km (landlocked)

Maritime claims: none (landlocked)

Climate: tropical; modified by altitude; rainy season (October to April)

Terrain: mostly high plateau with some hills and mountains

Elevation: *highest point:* Mafinga Central 2,330 m
lowest point: Zambezi river 329 m
mean elevation: 1,138 m

Natural resources: copper, cobalt, zinc, lead, coal, emeralds, gold, silver, uranium, hydropower

Land use: *agricultural land:* 31.7% (2018 est.)
arable land: 4.8% (2018 est.)
permanent crops: 0% (2018 est.)
permanent pasture: 26.9% (2018 est.)
forest: 66.3% (2018 est.)
other: 2% (2018 est.)

Irrigated land: 1,560 sq km (2012)

Major lakes (area sq km): *fresh water lake(s):* Lake Tanganyika (shared with Democratic Republic of Congo, Tanzania, and Burundi) - 32,000 sq km; Lake Mweru (shared with Democratic Republic of Congo) - 4,350 sq km; Lake Bangweulu - 4,000-15,000 sq km seasonal variation

Major rivers (by length in km): Congo river source (shared with Angola, Republic of Congo, and Democratic Republic of Congo [m]) - 4,700 km; Zambezi river source (shared with Angola, Namibia, Botswana, Zimbabwe, and Mozambique [m]) - 2,740 km
note – [s] after country name indicates river source; [m] after country name indicates river mouth

Major watersheds (area sq km): Atlantic Ocean drainage: Congo (3,730,881 sq km)
Indian Ocean drainage: Zambezi (1,332,412 sq km)

Major aquifers: Upper Kalahari-Cuvelai-Upper Zambezi Basin

Population distribution: one of the highest levels of urbanization in Africa; high density in the central area, particularly around the cities of Lusaka, Ndola, Kitwe, and Mufulira as shown in this population distribution map

Natural hazards: periodic drought; tropical storms (November to April)

Geography - note: landlocked; the Zambezi forms a natural riverine boundary with Zimbabwe; Lake Kariba on the Zambia-Zimbabwe border forms the world's largest reservoir by volume (180 cu km; 43 cu mi)

PEOPLE AND SOCIETY

Population: 19,642,123 (2022 est.)
note: estimates for this country explicitly taken into account the impact of the HIV/AIDS epidemic
country comparison to the world: 63

Nationality: *noun:* Zambian(s)
adjective: Zambian

Ethnic groups: Bemba 21%, Tonga 13.6%, Chewa 7.4%, Lozi 5.7%, Nsenga 5.3%, Tumbuka 4.4%, Ngoni 4%, Lala 3.1%, Kaonde 2.9%, Namwanga 2.8%, Lunda (north Western) 2.6%, Mambwe 2.5%, Luvale 2.2%, Lamba 2.1%, Ushi 1.9%, Lenje 1.6%, Bisa 1.6%, Mbunda 1.2%, other 13.8%, unspecified 0.4% (2010 est.)

Languages: Bemba 33.4%, Nyanja 14.7%, Tonga 11.4%, Lozi 5.5%, Chewa 4.5%, Nsenga 2.9%, Tumbuka 2.5%, Lunda (North Western) 1.9%, Kaonde 1.8%, Lala 1.8%, Lamba 1.8%, English (official) 1.7%, Luvale 1.5%, Mambwe 1.3%, Namwanga 1.2%, Lenje 1.1%, Bisa 1%, other 9.7%, unspecified 0.2% (2010 est.)
note: Zambia is said to have over 70 languages, although many of these may be considered dialects; all of Zambia's major languages are members of the Bantu family; Chewa and Nyanja are mutually intelligible dialects

Religions: Protestant 75.3%, Roman Catholic 20.2%, other 2.7% (includes Muslim Buddhist, Hindu, and Baha'i), none 1.8% (2010 est.)

Demographic profile: Zambia's poor, youthful population consists primarily of Bantu-speaking people representing nearly 70 different ethnicities. Zambia's high fertility rate continues to drive rapid population growth, averaging almost 3 percent annually between 2000 and 2010. The country's total fertility rate has fallen by less than 1.5 children per woman during the last 30 years and still averages among the world's highest, almost 6 children per woman, largely because of the country's lack of access to family planning services, education for girls, and employment for women. Zambia also exhibits wide fertility disparities based on rural or urban location, education, and income. Poor, uneducated women from rural areas are more likely to marry young, to give birth early, and to have more children, viewing children as a sign of prestige and recognizing that not all of their children will live to adulthood. HIV/AIDS is prevalent in Zambia and contributes to its low life expectancy.

Zambian emigration is low compared to many other African countries and is comprised predominantly of the well-educated. The small amount of brain drain, however, has a major impact in Zambia because of its limited human capital and lack of educational infrastructure for developing skilled professionals in key fields. For example, Zambia has few schools for training doctors, nurses, and other health care workers. Its spending on education is low compared to other Sub-Saharan countries.

Age structure: *0-14 years:* 45.74% (male 4,005,134/female 3,964,969)
15-24 years: 20.03% (male 1,744,843/female 1,746,561)
25-54 years: 28.96% (male 2,539,697/female 2,506,724)

55-64 years: 3.01% (male 242,993/female 280,804)
65 years and over: 2.27% (male 173,582/female 221,316) (2020 est.)

Dependency ratios: *total dependency ratio:* 85.7
youth dependency ratio: 81.7
elderly dependency ratio: 4
potential support ratio: 25.3 (2020 est.)

Median age: *total:* 16.9 years
male: 16.7 years
female: 17 years (2020 est.)
country comparison to the world: 220

Population growth rate: 2.9% (2022 est.)
country comparison to the world: 12

Birth rate: 34.86 births/1,000 population (2022 est.)
country comparison to the world: 17

Death rate: 6.12 deaths/1,000 population (2022 est.)
country comparison to the world: 152

Net migration rate: 0.24 migrant(s)/1,000 population (2022 est.)
country comparison to the world: 77

Population distribution: one of the highest levels of urbanization in Africa; high density in the central area, particularly around the cities of Lusaka, Ndola, Kitwe, and Mufulira as shown in this population distribution map

Urbanization: *urban population:* 45.8% of total population (2022)
rate of urbanization: 4.15% annual rate of change (2020-25 est.)

Major urban areas - population: 3.042 million LUSAKA (capital) (2022)

Sex ratio: *at birth:* 1.03 male(s)/female
0-14 years: 1.02 male(s)/female
15-24 years: 1.01 male(s)/female
25-54 years: 1.01 male(s)/female
55-64 years: 0.9 male(s)/female
65 years and over: 0.73 male(s)/female
total population: 1 male(s)/female (2022 est.)

Mother's mean age at first birth: 19.2 years (2018 est.)
note: data represents median age at first birth among women 20-49

Maternal mortality ratio: 213 deaths/100,000 live births (2017 est.)
country comparison to the world: 46

Infant mortality rate: *total:* 37.11 deaths/1,000 live births
male: 40.57 deaths/1,000 live births
female: 33.55 deaths/1,000 live births (2022 est.)
country comparison to the world: 39

Life expectancy at birth: *total population:* 66.26 years
male: 64.52 years
female: 68.06 years (2022 est.)
country comparison to the world: 197

Total fertility rate: 4.56 children born/woman (2022 est.)
country comparison to the world: 18

Contraceptive prevalence rate: 49.6% (2018)

Drinking water source: *improved: urban:* 90.2% of population
rural: 56.6% of population
total: 71.6% of population
unimproved: urban: 9.8% of population
rural: 43.4% of population
total: 28.4% of population (2020 est.)

Current health expenditure: 5.3% of GDP (2019)

Physicians density: 1.17 physicians/1,000 population (2018)

Hospital bed density: 2 beds/1,000 population

Sanitation facility access: *improved: urban:* 76.3% of population
rural: 31.9% of population
total: 51.7% of population
unimproved: urban: 23.7% of population
rural: 68.1% of population
total: 48.3% of population (2020 est.)

HIV/AIDS - adult prevalence rate: 11.1% (2020 est.)
country comparison to the world: 8

HIV/AIDS - people living with HIV/AIDS: 1.5 million (2020 est.)
country comparison to the world: 6

HIV/AIDS - deaths: 24,000 (2020 est.)
country comparison to the world: 8

Major infectious diseases: *degree of risk:* very high (2020)
food or waterborne diseases: bacterial and protozoal diarrhea, hepatitis A, and typhoid fever
vectorborne diseases: malaria and dengue fever
water contact diseases: schistosomiasis
animal contact diseases: rabies

Obesity - adult prevalence rate: 8.1% (2016)
country comparison to the world: 155

Alcohol consumption per capita: *total:* 3.82 liters of pure alcohol (2019 est.)
beer: 1.26 liters of pure alcohol (2019 est.)
wine: 0.04 liters of pure alcohol (2019 est.)
spirits: 0.36 liters of pure alcohol (2019 est.)
other alcohols: 2.16 liters of pure alcohol (2019 est.)
country comparison to the world: 98

Tobacco use: *total:* 14.4% (2020 est.)
male: 25.1% (2020 est.)
female: 3.7% (2020 est.)
country comparison to the world: 107

Children under the age of 5 years underweight: 11.8% (2018/19)
country comparison to the world: 49

Child marriage: *women married by age 15:* 5.2%
women married by age 18: 29%
men married by age 18: 2.8% (2018 est.)

Education expenditures: 4.5% of GDP (2019)
country comparison to the world: 85

Literacy: *definition:* age 15 and over can read and write English
total population: 86.7%
male: 90.6%
female: 83.1% (2018)

Unemployment, youth ages 15-24: *total:* 30.1%
male: 32.1%
female: 27.6% (2019 est.)

ENVIRONMENT

Environment - current issues: air pollution and resulting acid rain in the mineral extraction and refining region; chemical runoff into watersheds; loss of biodiversity; poaching seriously threatens rhinoceros, elephant, antelope, and large cat populations; deforestation; soil erosion; desertification; lack of adequate water treatment presents human health risks

Environment - international agreements: *party to:* Biodiversity, Climate Change, Climate Change-Kyoto Protocol, Climate Change-Paris Agreement, Comprehensive Nuclear Test Ban, Desertification, Endangered Species, Hazardous Wastes, Law of the Sea, Nuclear Test Ban, Ozone Layer Protection, Wetlands
signed, but not ratified: none of the selected agreements

Air pollutants: *particulate matter emissions:* 24.7 micrograms per cubic meter (2016 est.)
carbon dioxide emissions: 5.14 megatons (2016 est.)
methane emissions: 14.1 megatons (2020 est.)

Climate: tropical; modified by altitude; rainy season (October to April)

Land use: *agricultural land:* 31.7% (2018 est.)
arable land: 4.8% (2018 est.)
permanent crops: 0% (2018 est.)
permanent pasture: 26.9% (2018 est.)
forest: 66.3% (2018 est.)
other: 2% (2018 est.)

Urbanization: *urban population:* 45.8% of total population (2022)
rate of urbanization: 4.15% annual rate of change (2020-25 est.)

Revenue from forest resources: *forest revenues:* 4.45% of GDP (2018 est.)
country comparison to the world: 15

Revenue from coal: *coal revenues:* 0.04% of GDP (2018 est.)
country comparison to the world: 33

Food insecurity: *severe localized food insecurity: due to reduced incomes and localized shortfalls in cereal production* - cereal production declined to a below-average level in 2022 and along with the impact of rising food prices, the number of food insecure is foreseen to increase at the end of 2022 to levels above the 1.6 million people estimated in the first quarter of 2022 (2022)

Waste and recycling: *municipal solid waste generated annually:* 2,608,268 tons (2002 est.)

Major lakes (area sq km): *fresh water lake(s):* Lake Tanganyika (shared with Democratic Republic of Congo, Tanzania, and Burundi) - 32,000 sq km; Lake Mweru (shared with Democratic Republic of Congo) - 4,350 sq km; Lake Bangweulu - 4,000-15,000 sq km seasonal variation

Major rivers (by length in km): Congo river source (shared with Angola, Republic of Congo, and Democratic Republic of Congo [m]) - 4,700 km; Zambezi river source (shared with Angola, Namibia, Botswana, Zimbabwe, and Mozambique [m]) - 2,740 km
note – [s] after country name indicates river source; [m] after country name indicates river mouth

Major watersheds (area sq km): Atlantic Ocean drainage: Congo (3,730,881 sq km)
Indian Ocean drainage: Zambezi (1,332,412 sq km)

Major aquifers: Upper Kalahari-Cuvelai-Upper Zambezi Basin

Total water withdrawal: *municipal:* 290 million cubic meters (2017 est.)
industrial: 130 million cubic meters (2017 est.)
agricultural: 1.152 billion cubic meters (2017 est.)

Total renewable water resources: 104.8 billion cubic meters (2017 est.)

GOVERNMENT

Country name: *conventional long form:* Republic of Zambia
conventional short form: Zambia

former: Northern Rhodesia
etymology: name derived from the Zambezi River, which flows through the western part of the country and forms its southern border with neighboring Zimbabwe

Government type: presidential republic

Capital: *name:* Lusaka; note - a proposal to build a new capital city in Ngabwe was announced in May 2017
geographic coordinates: 15 25 S, 28 17 E
time difference: UTC+2 (7 hours ahead of Washington, DC, during Standard Time)
etymology: named after a village called Lusaka, located at Manda Hill, near where Zambia's National Assembly building currently stands; the village was named after a headman (chief) LUSAKASA

Administrative divisions: 10 provinces; Central, Copperbelt, Eastern, Luapula, Lusaka, Muchinga, Northern, North-Western, Southern, Western

Independence: 24 October 1964 (from the UK)

National holiday: Independence Day, 24 October (1964)

Constitution: *history:* several previous; latest adopted 24 August 1991, promulgated 30 August 1991
amendments: proposed by the National Assembly; passage requires two-thirds majority vote by the Assembly in two separate readings at least 30 days apart; passage of amendments affecting fundamental rights and freedoms requires approval by at least one half of votes cast in a referendum prior to consideration and voting by the Assembly; amended 1996, 2015, 2016; note - in late 2020, an amendment which would have altered the structure of the constitution was defeated in the National Assembly

Legal system: mixed legal system of English common law and customary law

International law organization participation: has not submitted an ICJ jurisdiction declaration; accepts ICCt jurisdiction

Citizenship: *citizenship by birth:* only if at least one parent is a citizen of Zambia
citizenship by descent only: yes, if at least one parent was a citizen of Zambia
dual citizenship recognized: yes
residency requirement for naturalization: 5 years for those with an ancestor who was a citizen of Zambia, otherwise 10 years residency is required

Suffrage: 18 years of age; universal

Executive branch: *chief of state:* President Hakainde HICHILEMA (since 24 August 2021); Vice President Mutale NALUMANGO (since 24 August 2021); note - the president is both chief of state and head of government
head of government: President Hakainde HICHILEMA (since 24 August 2021); Vice President Mutale NALUMANGO (since 24 August 2021)
cabinet: Cabinet appointed by president from among members of the National Assembly
elections/appointments: president directly elected by absolute majority popular vote in 2 rounds if needed for a 5-year term (eligible for a second term); last held on 12 August 2021 (next to be held in 2026)
election results:
2021: Hakainde HICHILEMA elected president; percent of the vote - Hakainde HICHILEMA (UPND) 57.9%, Edgar LUNGU (PF) 37.3%, other 4.8%
2016: Edgar LUNGU re-elected president; percent of vote - Edgar LUNGU (PF) 50.4%, Hakainde HICHILEMA (UPND) 47.6%, other 2%

Legislative branch: *description:* unicameral National Assembly (167 seats; 156 members directly elected in single-seat constituencies by simple majority vote in 2 rounds if needed, and up to 8 appointed by the president; members serve 5-year terms); 3 exofficio members elected by National Assembly membership
elections:
last held on 12 August 2021 (next to be held in 2026)
election results:
percent of vote by party - UPND 53.9%, PF 38.1%, PNUP 0.6%, independent 7.4%; seats by party -UPND 82, PF 62, PNUP 1, independent 11; composition - men 136, women 20, percent of women 13.5%; 156 seats filled;

Judicial branch: *highest court(s):* Supreme Court (consists of the chief justice, deputy chief justice, and at least 11 judges);
Constitutional Court (consists of the court president, vice president, and 11 judges); note - the Constitutional Court began operation in June 2016
judge selection and term of office: Supreme Court and Constitutional Court judges appointed by the president of the republic upon the advice of the 9-member Judicial Service Commission, which is headed by the chief justice, and ratified by the National Assembly; judges normally serve until age 65
subordinate courts: Court of Appeal; High Court; Industrial Relations Court; subordinate courts (3 levels, based on upper limit of money involved); Small Claims Court; local courts (2 grades, based on upper limit of money involved)

Political parties and leaders: Alliance for Democracy and Development or ADD [Charles MILUPI]
Forum for Democracy and Development or FDD [Edith NAWAKWI]
Movement for Multiparty Democracy or MMD [Dr. Nevers MUMBA]
Party of National Unity and Progress or PNUP [Highvie HAMUDUDU]
Patriotic Front or PF [Edgar LUNGU]
United Party for National Development or UPND [Hakainde HICHILEMA]

International organization participation: ACP, AfDB, AU, C, COMESA, EITI (compliant country), FAO, G-77, IAEA, IBRD, ICAO, ICCt, ICRM, IDA, IFAD, IFC, IFRCS, ILO, IMF, Interpol, IOC, IOM, IPU, ISO (correspondent), ITSO, ITU, ITUC (NGOs), MIGA, MONUSCO, NAM, OPCW, PCA, SADC, UN, UNAMID, UNCTAD, UNESCO, UNHCR, UNIDO, UNISFA, UNMIL, UNMISS, UNOCI, UNWTO, UPU, WCO, WHO, WIPO, WMO, WTO

Diplomatic representation in the US: *chief of mission:* Ambassador Lazarous KAPAMBWE (since 8 April 2020)
chancery: 2200 R Street NW, Washington, DC 20008
telephone: [1] (202) 234-4009
FAX: [1] (202) 332-0826
email address and website:
info@zambiaembassy.org
https://www.zambiaembassy.org/

Diplomatic representation from the US: *chief of mission:* Ambassador (vacant); Charge d'Affaires Martin "Marty" DALE (since 2 November 2021)
embassy: Eastern end of Kabulonga Road, Ibex Hill, Lusaka
mailing address: 2310 Lusaka Place, Washington DC 20521-2310
telephone: [260] (0) 211-357-000
FAX: [260] (0) 211-357-224
email address and website:
ACSLusaka@state.gov
https://zm.usembassy.gov/

Flag description: green field with a panel of three vertical bands of red (hoist side), black, and orange below a soaring orange eagle, on the outer edge of the flag; green stands for the country's natural resources and vegetation, red symbolizes the struggle for freedom, black the people of Zambia, and orange the country's mineral wealth; the eagle represents the people's ability to rise above the nation's problems

National symbol(s): African fish eagle; national colors: green, red, black, orange

National anthem: *name:* "Lumbanyeni Zambia" (Stand and Sing of Zambia, Proud and Free)
lyrics/music: multiple/Enoch Mankayi SONTONGA
note: adopted 1964; the melody, from the popular song "God Bless Africa," is the same as that of Tanzania but with different lyrics; the melody is also incorporated into South Africa's anthem

National heritage: *total World Heritage Sites:* 1 (natural)
selected World Heritage Site locales: Mosi-oa-Tunya/Victoria Falls

ECONOMY

Economic overview: Zambia had one of the world's fastest growing economies for the ten years up to 2014, with real GDP growth averaging roughly 6.7% per annum, though growth slowed during the period 2015 to 2017, due to falling copper prices, reduced power generation, and depreciation of the kwacha. Zambia's lack of economic diversification and dependency on copper as its sole major export makes it vulnerable to fluctuations in the world commodities market and prices turned downward in 2015 due to declining demand from China; Zambia was overtaken by the Democratic Republic of Congo as Africa's largest copper producer. GDP growth picked up in 2017 as mineral prices rose.

Despite recent strong economic growth and its status as a lower middle-income country, widespread and extreme rural poverty and high unemployment levels remain significant problems, made worse by a high birth rate, a relatively high HIV/AIDS burden, by marketdistorting agricultural and energy policies, and growing government debt. Zambia raised $7 billion from international investors by issuing separate sovereign bonds in 2012, 2014, and 2015. Concurrently, it issued over $4 billion in domestic debt and agreed to Chinese-financed infrastructure projects, significantly increasing the country's public debt burden to more than 60% of GDP. The government has considered refinancing $3 billion worth of Eurobonds and significant Chinese loans to cut debt servicing costs.

Real GDP (purchasing power parity): $60.12 billion (2020 est.)
$61.99 billion (2019 est.)
$61.1 billion (2018 est.)
note: data are in 2017 dollars
country comparison to the world: 105

Real GDP growth rate: 3.4% (2017 est.)
3.8% (2016 est.)
2.9% (2015 est.)
country comparison to the world: 88

Real GDP per capita: $3,300 (2020 est.)
$3,500 (2019 est.)
$3,500 (2018 est.)
note: data are in 2017 dollars
country comparison to the world: 194

GDP (official exchange rate): $25.71 billion (2017 est.)

Inflation rate (consumer prices): 9.1% (2019 est.)
7.4% (2018 est.)
6.5% (2017 est.)
country comparison to the world: 204

Credit ratings:

Fitch rating: RD (2020)

Moody's rating: Ca (2020)

Standard & Poors rating: SD (2020)

GDP - composition, by sector of origin: *agriculture:* 7.5% (2017 est.)
industry: 35.3% (2017 est.)
services: 57% (2017 est.)

GDP - composition, by end use: *household consumption:* 52.6% (2017 est.)
government consumption: 21% (2017 est.)
investment in fixed capital: 27.1% (2017 est.)
investment in inventories: 1.2% (2017 est.)
exports of goods and services: 43% (2017 est.)
imports of goods and services: -44.9% (2017 est.)

Agricultural products: sugar cane, cassava, maize, milk, vegetables, soybeans, beef, tobacco, wheat, groundnuts

Industries: copper mining and processing, emerald mining, construction, foodstuffs, beverages, chemicals, textiles, fertilizer, horticulture

Industrial production growth rate: 4.7% (2017 est.)
country comparison to the world: 62

Labor force: 6.898 million (2017 est.)
country comparison to the world: 66

Labor force - by occupation: *agriculture:* 54.8%
industry: 9.9%
services: 35.3% (2017 est.)

Unemployment rate: 15% (2008 est.)
50% (2000 est.)
country comparison to the world: 176

Unemployment, youth ages 15-24: *total:* 30.1%
male: 32.1%
female: 27.6% (2019 est.)
country comparison to the world: 34

Population below poverty line: 54.4% (2015 est.)

Gini Index coefficient - distribution of family income: 57.1 (2015 est.)
50.8 (2004)
country comparison to the world: 3

Household income or consumption by percentage share: *lowest 10%:* 1.5%
highest 10%: 47.4% (2010)

Budget: *revenues:* 4.473 billion (2017 est.)
expenditures: 6.357 billion (2017 est.)

Budget surplus (+) or deficit (-): -7.3% (of GDP) (2017 est.)
country comparison to the world: 195

Public debt: 63.1% of GDP (2017 est.)
60.7% of GDP (2016 est.)
country comparison to the world: 67

Taxes and other revenues: 17.4% (of GDP) (2017 est.)
country comparison to the world: 169

Fiscal year: calendar year

Current account balance: -$1.006 billion (2017 est.)
-$934 million (2016 est.)
country comparison to the world: 145

Exports: $8.55 billion (2020 est.) note: data are in current year dollars
$8.26 billion (2019 est.) note: data are in current year dollars
$9.98 billion (2018 est.) note: data are in current year dollars
country comparison to the world: 105

Exports - partners: Switzerland 29%, China 16%, Namibia 12%, Democratic Republic of the Congo 9%, Singapore 5% (2019)

Exports - commodities: copper, gold, gemstones, sulfuric acid, raw sugar, tobacco (2019)

Imports: $5.92 billion (2020 est.) note: data are in current year dollars
$8.04 billion (2019 est.) note: data are in current year dollars
$10.19 billion (2018 est.) note: data are in current year dollars
country comparison to the world: 132

Imports - partners: South Africa 29%, China 14%, United Arab Emirates 12%, India 5% (2019)

Imports - commodities: refined petroleum, crude petroleum, delivery trucks, gold, fertilizers (2019)

Reserves of foreign exchange and gold: $2.082 billion (31 December 2017 est.)
$2.353 billion (31 December 2016 est.)
country comparison to the world: 121

Debt - external: $11.66 billion (31 December 2017 est.)
$9.562 billion (31 December 2016 est.)
country comparison to the world: 110

Exchange rates: Zambian kwacha (ZMK) per US dollar -
21.065 (2020 est.)
15.3736 (2019 est.)
11.855 (2018 est.)
8.6 (2014 est.)
6.2 (2013 est.)

ENERGY

Electricity access: *electrification - total population:* 37% (2019)
electrification - urban areas: 76% (2019)
electrification - rural areas: 6% (2019)

Electricity: *installed generating capacity:* 3.065 million kW (2020 est.)
consumption: 13,409,685,000 kWh (2019 est.)
exports: 976 million kWh (2019 est.)
imports: 198 million kWh (2019 est.)
transmission/distribution losses: 1,811,480,000 kWh (2019 est.)

Electricity generation sources: *fossil fuels:* 13% of total installed capacity (2020 est.)
solar: 0.9% of total installed capacity (2020 est.)
hydroelectricity: 85.5% of total installed capacity (2020 est.)
biomass and waste: 0.5% of total installed capacity (2020 est.)

Coal: *production:* 1.116 million metric tons (2020 est.)
consumption: 1.176 million metric tons (2020 est.)
exports: 39,000 metric tons (2020 est.)
imports: 99,000 metric tons (2020 est.)
proven reserves: 45 million metric tons (2019 est.)

Petroleum: *total petroleum production:* 0 bbl/day (2021 est.)
refined petroleum consumption: 25,300 bbl/day (2019 est.)
crude oil and lease condensate exports: 0 bbl/day (2018 est.)
crude oil and lease condensate imports: 12,400 bbl/day (2018 est.)
crude oil estimated reserves: 0 barrels (2021 est.)

Refined petroleum products - production: 13,120 bbl/day (2015 est.)
country comparison to the world: 98

Refined petroleum products - exports: 371 bbl/day (2015 est.)
country comparison to the world: 113

Refined petroleum products - imports: 10,150 bbl/day (2015 est.)
country comparison to the world: 149

Natural gas: *production:* 0 cubic meters (2021 est.)
consumption: 0 cubic meters (2021 est.)
exports: 0 cubic meters (2021 est.)
imports: 0 cubic meters (2021 est.)
proven reserves: 0 cubic meters (2021 est.)

Carbon dioxide emissions: 6.798 million metric tonnes of CO_2 (2019 est.)
from coal and metallurgical coke: 3.186 million metric tonnes of CO_2 (2019 est.)
from petroleum and other liquids: 3.612 million metric tonnes of CO_2 (2019 est.)
from consumed natural gas: 0 metric tonnes of CO_2 (2019 est.)
country comparison to the world: 127

Energy consumption per capita: 11.595 million Btu/person (2019 est.)
country comparison to the world: 149

COMMUNICATIONS

Telephones - fixed lines: *total subscriptions:* 71,844 (2020 est.)
subscriptions per 100 inhabitants: (2020 est.) less than 1
country comparison to the world: 146

Telephones - mobile cellular: *total subscriptions:* 17,220,600 (2019)
subscriptions per 100 inhabitants: 96.41 (2019)
country comparison to the world: 64

Telecommunication systems: *general assessment:* following elections held in August 2021, the new government immediately established a Ministry of Technology and Science to promote the use of ICT in developing economic growth and social inclusion; this focus on ICT, and on telecoms in particular, has been central to government strategies for some years; as part of the Smart Zambia initiative, investment has been made in data centers, a computer assembly plant, ICT training centers, and a Smart Education program; these efforts have been combined with the extension of broadband access and improved connectivity to international submarine cables; in turn, this has resulted in a considerable reduction in fixed-line and mobile access pricing for end-users; mobile network operators continue to invest in 3G and LTE-based services, the government contracted to upgrade the state-owned mobile infrastructure

for 5G services; delays in holding spectrum have stymied the development of 5G thus far; in mid-2021 the regulator completed a consultation of auctioning low, medium, and high band spectrum for 5G, aiming to provide sufficient spectrum to meet the anticipated increase in data traffic in coming years; fixed-line broadband services remain underdeveloped (2022)
domestic: fiber optic connections are available between most larger towns and cities with microwave radio relays serving more rural areas; 3G and LTE with FttX in limited urban areas and private Ku or Ka band VSAT terminals in remote locations; fixed-line teledensity less than 1 per 100 and mobile-cellular roughly 104 per 100 (2020)
international: country code - 260; multiple providers operate overland fiber optic routes via Zimbabwe/South Africa, Botswana/Namibia and Tanzania provide access to the major undersea cables

Broadcast media: according to the Independent Broadcast Authority, there are 137 radio stations and 47 television stations in Zambia; out of the 137 radio stations, 133 are private (categorized as either commercial or community radio stations), while 4 are public-owned; state-owned Zambia National Broadcasting Corporation (ZNBC) operates 2 television channels and 3 radio stations; ZNBC owns 75% shares in GoTV, 40% in MultiChoice, and 40% in TopStar Communications Company, all of which operate in-country
(2019)

Internet country code: .zm

Internet users: *total:* 3,676,791 (2020 est.)
percent of population: 20% (2020 est.)
country comparison to the world: 103

Broadband - fixed subscriptions: *total:* 82,317 (2020 est.)
subscriptions per 100 inhabitants: 0.5 (2020 est.)
country comparison to the world: 131

TRANSPORTATION

National air transport system: *number of registered air carriers:* 3 (2020)
inventory of registered aircraft operated by air carriers: 6
annual passenger traffic on registered air carriers: 8,904 (2018)
annual freight traffic on registered air carriers: 75.08 million (2018) mt-km

Civil aircraft registration country code prefix: 9J

Airports: *total:* 88 (2021)
country comparison to the world: 64

Airports - with paved runways: *total:* 8
over 3,047 m: 1
2,438 to 3,047 m: 3
1,524 to 2,437 m: 3
914 to 1,523 m: 1 (2021)

Airports - with unpaved runways: *total:* 80
2,438 to 3,047 m: 1
1,524 to 2,437 m: 5
914 to 1,523 m: 53
under 914 m: 21 (2021)

Pipelines: 771 km oil (2013)

Railways: *total:* 3,126 km (2014)
narrow gauge: 3,126 km (2014) 1.067-m gauge
note: includes 1,860 km of the Tanzania-Zambia Railway Authority (TAZARA)
country comparison to the world: 59

Roadways: *total:* 67,671 km (2018)
paved: 14,888 km (2018)
unpaved: 52,783 km (2018)
country comparison to the world: 70

Waterways: 2,250 km (2010) (includes Lake Tanganyika and the Zambezi and Luapula Rivers)
country comparison to the world: 40

Merchant marine: *total:* 2
by type: general cargo 1, oil tanker 1 (2021)
country comparison to the world: 178

Ports and terminals: *river port(s):* Mpulungu (Zambezi)

MILITARY AND SECURITY

Military and security forces: Zambia Defense Force (ZDF): Zambia Army, Zambia Air Force, Zambia National Service; Defense Force Medical Service; Ministry of Home Affairs and Internal Security: Zambia Police (includes a paramilitary battalion) (2022)
note: the Zambia National Service is a support organization that also does public work projects

Military expenditures: 1.3% of GDP (2021 est.)
1.3% of GDP (2020 est.)
1.3% of GDP (2019 est.) (approximately $450 million)
1.4% of GDP (2018 est.) (approximately $470 million)
1.3% of GDP (2017 est.) (approximately $420 million)
country comparison to the world: 109

Military and security service personnel strengths: approximately 17,000 active troops (15,000 Army; 2,000 Air) (2022)

Military equipment inventories and acquisitions: the ZDF's inventory is largely comprised of Chinese, Russian, and Soviet-era armaments; since 2010, China has been the leading supplier of arms to Zambia (2022)

Military service age and obligation: 18-25 years of age (16 with parental consent) for voluntary military service for men and women; no conscription; 12-year enlistment period (7 years active, 5 in the Reserves); all citizens are required to register at 16 (2022)

Military deployments: 930 Central African Republic (MINUSCA) (May 2022)

Military - note: the Zambian Defense Force (ZDF) traces its roots to the Northern Rhodesia Regiment, which was raised by the British colonial government to fight in World War II; the ZDF was established in 1964 from units of the dissolved Federation of Rhodesia and Nyasaland armed forces; it participated in a number of regional conflicts during the 1970s and 1980s; Zambia actively supported independence movements such as the Union for the Total Liberation of Angola (UNITA), the Zimbabwe African People's Union (ZAPU), the African National Congress of South Africa (ANC), and the South-West Africa People's Organization (SWAPO) (2022)

TRANSNATIONAL ISSUES

Disputes - international: *Zambia-Angola:* because the straight-line segments along the left bank (Zambian side) of the Cuando/Kwando River do not conform with the physical alignment of the unstable shoreline, Zambian residents in some areas have settled illegally on sections of shoreline that fall on the Angolan side of the boundary
Zambia-Democratic Republic of Congo(DRC): boundary commission continues discussions over Congolese-administered triangle of land on the right bank of the Lunkinda River claimed by Zambia near the DRC village of Pweto
Zambia-Tanzania: some drug smuggling may take place across the Zambia-Tanzania border; there are no known current territorial issues, as both states have continued to recognize the colonial boundaries last modified in 1937; the boundary in Lake Tanganyika remains undefined.
Zambia-Zimbabwe: in 2004, Zimbabwe dropped objections to plans between Botswana and Zambia to build a bridge over the Zambezi River, thereby de facto recognizing a short, but not clearly delimited, Botswana-Zambia boundary in the river; in May 2021, Botswana and Zambia agreed in principle to let Zimbabwe be a partner in the bridge project as it enters its lasts phase

Refugees and internally displaced persons: *refugees (country of origin):* 60,236 (Democratic Republic of the Congo) (refugees and asylum seekers), 6,948 (Burundi) (2022)

Trafficking in persons: *current situation:* human traffickers exploit domestic and foreign victims in Zambia and Zambians abroad; most trafficking occurs within Zambia's borders, with traffickers exploiting women and children from rural areas in cities in domestic servitude or forced labor in agriculture, textile production, mining, construction, small businesses, such as bakeries, and forced begging; Jerabo gangs force Zambian children into illegal mining operations, such as loading stolen copper or crushing rocks; truck drivers exploit Zambian boys and girls in sex trafficking in towns along the Zimbabwean and Tanzanian borders, and miners exploit them in Solwezi; Zambian boys are exploited for sex trafficking in Zimbabwe and women and girls in South Africa; traffickers exploit victims from Tanzania and Malawi in the Zambian timber industry
tier rating: Tier 2 Watch List — Zambia does not fully meet the minimum standards for the elimination of trafficking but is making efforts to do so; efforts included increasing law enforcement training, establishing two fast-track human trafficking courts, conducting awareness campaigns about human trafficking, slightly increasing prosecutions and convictions, and strengthening prison sentences given to traffickers; however; investigations of trafficking crimes and funding to shelters and other victim assistance programs decreased; authorities did not proactively screen for trafficking among vulnerable populations, including foreign nationals and those involved in commercial sex; authorities detained and deported potential trafficking victims involved in smuggling; the national inter-ministerial committee is weak in overseeing national anti-trafficking efforts and trends (2020)

Illicit drugs: transshipment point for moderate amounts of methaqualone, small amounts of heroin, and cocaine bound for southern Africa and possibly Europe; a poorly developed financial infrastructure coupled with a government commitment to combating money laundering make it an unattractive venue for money launderers; major consumer of cannabis

ZIMBABWE

INTRODUCTION

Background: The hunter-gatherer San people first inhabited the area that eventually became Zimbabwe. Farming communities migrated to the area around A.D. 500 during the Bantu expansion, and Shona-speaking societies began to develop in the Limpopo valley and Zimbabwean highlands around the 9th century. These societies traded with Arab merchants on the Indian Ocean coast and organized under the Kingdom of Mapungubwe in the 11th century. A series of powerful trade-oriented Shona states succeeded Mapungubwe, including the Kingdom of Zimbabwe (ca. 1220-1450), Kingdom of Mutapa (ca. 1450-1760), and the Rozwi Empire. The Rozwi Empire expelled Portuguese colonists from the Zimbabwean plateau but was eventually conquered in 1838 by the Ndebele clan of Zulu general MZILIKAZI during the era of conflict and population displacement known as the Mfecane. In the 1880s, colonists arrived with the British South Africa Company (BSAC) and obtained a written concession for mining rights from Ndebele King LOBENGULA. The king later disavowed the concession and accused the BSAC agents of deceit. The BSAC annexed Mashonaland and subsequently conquered Matabeleland by force during the First Matabele War of 1893-1894 to establish company rule over the territory. BSAC holdings south of the Zambezi River were annexed by the UK in 1923 and became the British colony of Southern Rhodesia. The 1930 Land Apportionment Act restricted Black land ownership and established structural racial inequalities that would favor the White minority for decades. A new constitution in 1961 further cemented White minority rule.

In 1965, the government under White Prime Minister Ian SMITH unilaterally declared its independence from the UK. London did not recognize Rhodesia's independence and demanded more voting rights for the Black majority in the country. International diplomacy and a liberation struggle by Black Zimbabweans finally led to biracial elections in 1979 and independence (as Zimbabwe) in 1980. Robert MUGABE, who led the uprising and became the nation's first prime minister, was the country's only ruler (as president since 1987) from independence until his forced resignation in November 2017. In the mid-1980s, the government tortured and killed thousands of civilians in a crackdown on dissent known as the Gukurahundi campaign. Economic mismanagement and chaotic land redistribution policies following independence periodically crippled the economy and resulted in widespread shortages of basic commodities. General elections in 2002, 2008, and 2013 were severely flawed and widely condemned but allowed MUGABE to remain president. In November 2017, Vice President Emmerson MNANGAGWA became president following a military intervention that forced MUGABE to resign, and MNANGAGWA cemented power by sidelining rivals Grace MUGABE (Robert MUGABE's wife) and Jonathan MOYO of the G40 faction of the ruling Zimbabwe African National Union-Patriotic Front party. In July 2018, MNANGAGWA won the presidential election after a close contest with opposition candidate Nelson CHAMISA. MNANGAGWA has resorted to the government's longstanding practice of violently disrupting protests and opposition rallies. Economic conditions remained dire under MNANGAGWA, with inflation soaring in 2019 and the country's export revenues declining dramatically in 2020 due to the COVID-19 pandemic.

GEOGRAPHY

Location: Southern Africa, between South Africa and Zambia

Geographic coordinates: 20 00 S, 30 00 E

Map references: Africa

Area: *total:* 390,757 sq km
land: 386,847 sq km
water: 3,910 sq km
country comparison to the world: 62

Area - comparative: about four times the size of Indiana; slightly larger than Montana

Land boundaries: *total:* 3,229 km
border countries (4): Botswana 834 km; Mozambique 1,402 km; South Africa 230 km; Zambia 763 km

Coastline: 0 km (landlocked)

Maritime claims: none (landlocked)

Climate: tropical; moderated by altitude; rainy season (November to March)

Terrain: mostly high plateau with higher central plateau (high veld); mountains in east

Elevation: *highest point:* Inyangani 2,592 m
lowest point: junction of the Runde and Save Rivers 162 m
mean elevation: 961 m

Natural resources: coal, chromium ore, asbestos, gold, nickel, copper, iron ore, vanadium, lithium, tin, platinum group metals

Land use: *agricultural land:* 42.5% (2018 est.)
arable land: 10.9% (2018 est.)
permanent crops: 0.3% (2018 est.)
permanent pasture: 31.3% (2018 est.)
forest: 39.5% (2018 est.)
other: 18% (2018 est.)

Irrigated land: 1,740 sq km (2012)

Major rivers (by length in km): Zambezi (shared with Zambia [s]), Angola, Namibia, Botswana, and Mozambique [m]) - 2,740 km; Limpopo (shared with South Africa [s], Botswana, and Mozambique [m]) - 1,800 km
note – [s] after country name indicates river source; [m] after country name indicates river mouth

Major watersheds (area sq km): Indian Ocean drainage: Zambezi (1,332,412 sq km)
Internal *(endorheic basin)* drainage: Okavango Basin (863,866 sq km)

Major aquifers: Upper Kalahari-Cuvelai-Upper Zambezi Basin

Population distribution: Aside from major urban agglomerations in Harare and Bulawayo, population distribution is fairly even, with slightly greater overall numbers in the eastern half as shown in this population distribution map

Natural hazards: recurring droughts; floods and severe storms are rare

Geography - note: landlocked; the Zambezi forms a natural riverine boundary with Zambia; in full flood (February-April) the massive Victoria Falls on the river forms the world's largest curtain of falling water; Lake Kariba on the Zambia-Zimbabwe border forms the world's largest reservoir by volume (180 cu km; 43 cu mi)

PEOPLE AND SOCIETY

Population: 15,121,004 (2022 est.)
note: estimates for this country explicitly taken into account the impact of the HIV/AIDS epidemic
country comparison to the world: 73

Nationality: *noun:* Zimbabwean(s)
adjective: Zimbabwean

Ethnic groups: African 99.4% (predominantly Shona; Ndebele is the second largest ethnic group), other 0.4%, unspecified 0.2% (2012 est.)

Languages: Shona (official; most widely spoken), Ndebele (official, second most widely spoken), English (official; traditionally used for official business), 13 minority languages (official; includes Chewa, Chibarwe, Kalanga, Koisan, Nambya, Ndau, Shangani, sign language, Sotho, Tonga, Tswana, Venda, and Xhosa)

Religions: Protestant 74.8% (includes Apostolic 37.5%, Pentecostal 21.8%, other 15.5%), Roman Catholic 7.3%, other Christian 5.3%, traditional 1.5%, Muslim 0.5%, other 0.1%, none 10.5% (2015 est.)

Demographic profile: Zimbabwe's progress in reproductive, maternal, and child health has stagnated in recent years. According to a 2010 Demographic and Health Survey, contraceptive use, the number of births attended by skilled practitioners, and child mortality have either stalled or somewhat deteriorated since the mid-2000s. Zimbabwe's total fertility rate has remained fairly stable at about 4 children per woman for the last two decades, although an uptick in the urban birth rate in recent years has caused a slight rise in the country's overall fertility rate. Zimbabwe's HIV prevalence rate dropped from approximately 29% to 15% since 1997 but remains among the world's highest and continues to suppress the country's life expectancy rate. The proliferation of HIV/AIDS information and prevention programs and personal experience with those suffering or dying from the disease have helped to change sexual behavior and reduce the epidemic.

Historically, the vast majority of Zimbabwe's migration has been internal – a rural-urban flow. In terms of international migration, over the last 40 years Zimbabwe has gradually shifted from being a destination country to one of emigration and, to a lesser degree, one of transit (for East African illegal migrants traveling to South Africa). As a British colony, Zimbabwe attracted significant numbers of permanent immigrants from the UK and other European countries, as well as temporary economic migrants from Malawi, Mozambique, and Zambia. Although Zimbabweans have migrated to South Africa since the beginning of the 20th century to work as miners, the first major exodus from the country occurred in the years before and after independence in 1980. The outward migration was politically and racially influenced; a large share of the white population of European origin chose to leave rather than live under a new black-majority government.

In the 1990s and 2000s, economic mismanagement and hyperinflation sparked a second, more diverse wave of emigration. This massive out migration – primarily to other southern African countries, the UK, and the US – has created a variety of challenges, including brain drain, illegal migration, and human smuggling and trafficking. Several factors have pushed highly skilled workers to go abroad, including unemployment, lower wages, a lack of resources, and few opportunities for career growth.

Age structure: *0-14 years:* 38.32% (male 2,759,155/female 2,814,462)
15-24 years: 20.16% (male 1,436,710/female 1,495,440)
25-54 years: 32.94% (male 2,456,392/female 2,334,973)
55-64 years: 4.07% (male 227,506/female 363,824)
65 years and over: 4.52% (male 261,456/female 396,396) (2020 est.)

Dependency ratios: *total dependency ratio:* 81.6
youth dependency ratio: 76.1
elderly dependency ratio: 5.5
potential support ratio: 18.3 (2020 est.)

Median age: *total:* 20.5 years
male: 20.3 years
female: 20.6 years (2020 est.)
country comparison to the world: 189

Population growth rate: 1.95% (2022 est.)
country comparison to the world: 44

Birth rate: 33.07 births/1,000 population (2022 est.)
country comparison to the world: 22

Death rate: 8.76 deaths/1,000 population (2022 est.)
country comparison to the world: 68

Net migration rate: -4.83 migrant(s)/1,000 population (2022 est.)
country comparison to the world: 200

Population distribution: Aside from major urban agglomerations in Harare and Bulawayo, population distribution is fairly even, with slightly greater overall numbers in the eastern half as shown in this population distribution map

Urbanization: *urban population:* 32.4% of total population (2022)
rate of urbanization: 2.41% annual rate of change (2020-25 est.)

Major urban areas - population: 1.558 million HARARE (capital) (2022)

Sex ratio: *at birth:* 1.03 male(s)/female
0-14 years: 0.98 male(s)/female
15-24 years: 0.96 male(s)/female
25-54 years: 1.06 male(s)/female
55-64 years: 0.62 male(s)/female
65 years and over: 0.57 male(s)/female
total population: 0.97 male(s)/female (2022 est.)

Mother's mean age at first birth: 20.3 years (2015 est.)
note: data represents median age at first birth among women 25-49

Maternal mortality ratio: 458 deaths/100,000 live births (2017 est.)
country comparison to the world: 24

Infant mortality rate: *total:* 28.53 deaths/1,000 live births
male: 32.17 deaths/1,000 live births
female: 24.77 deaths/1,000 live births (2022 est.)
country comparison to the world: 58

Life expectancy at birth: *total population:* 63.32 years
male: 61.18 years
female: 65.52 years (2022 est.)
country comparison to the world: 209

Total fertility rate: 3.89 children born/woman (2022 est.)
country comparison to the world: 30

Contraceptive prevalence rate: 66.8% (2015)

Drinking water source: *improved: urban:* 97.9% of population
rural: 66.9% of population
total: 76.9% of population
unimproved: urban: 2.1% of population
rural: 33.1% of population
total: 23.1% of population (2020 est.)

Current health expenditure: 7.7% of GDP (2019)

Physicians density: 0.2 physicians/1,000 population (2020)

Hospital bed density: 1.7 beds/1,000 population (2011)

Sanitation facility access: *improved: urban:* 96.1% of population
rural: 49% of population
total: 64.2% of population
unimproved: urban: 3.9% of population
rural: 51% of population
total: 35.8% of population (2017 est.)

HIV/AIDS - adult prevalence rate: 11.9% (2020 est.)
country comparison to the world: 5

HIV/AIDS - people living with HIV/AIDS: 1.3 million (2020 est.)
country comparison to the world: 9

HIV/AIDS - deaths: 22,000 (2020 est.)
country comparison to the world: 10

Major infectious diseases: *degree of risk:* high (2020)
food or waterborne diseases: bacterial and protozoal diarrhea, hepatitis A, and typhoid fever
vectorborne diseases: malaria and dengue fever
water contact diseases: schistosomiasis
animal contact diseases: rabies

Obesity - adult prevalence rate: 15.5% (2016)
country comparison to the world: 126

Alcohol consumption per capita: *total:* 3.11 liters of pure alcohol (2019 est.)
beer: 1.2 liters of pure alcohol (2019 est.)
wine: 0.05 liters of pure alcohol (2019 est.)
spirits: 0.39 liters of pure alcohol (2019 est.)
other alcohols: 1.47 liters of pure alcohol (2019 est.)
country comparison to the world: 110

Tobacco use: *total:* 11.7% (2020 est.)
male: 21.8% (2020 est.)
female: 1.5% (2020 est.)
country comparison to the world: 125

Children under the age of 5 years underweight: 9.7% (2019)
country comparison to the world: 59

Child marriage: *women married by age 15:* 5.4%
women married by age 18: 33.7%
men married by age 18: 1.9% (2019 est.)

Education expenditures: 3.6% of GDP (2018 est.)
country comparison to the world: 122

Literacy: *definition:* age 15 and over can read and write English
total population: 86.5%
male: 88.5%
female: 84.6% (2015)

School life expectancy (primary to tertiary education): *total:* 11 years
male: 12 years
female: 11 years (2013)

Unemployment, youth ages 15-24: *total:* 27.5%
male: 25%
female: 31.4% (2019 est.)

ENVIRONMENT

Environment - current issues: deforestation; soil erosion; land degradation; air and water pollution; the black rhinoceros herd - once the largest concentration of the species in the world - has been significantly reduced by poaching; poor mining practices have led to toxic waste and heavy metal pollution

Environment - international agreements: *party to:* Biodiversity, Climate Change, Climate Change-Kyoto Protocol, Climate Change-Paris Agreement, Comprehensive Nuclear Test Ban, Desertification, Endangered Species, Hazardous Wastes, Law of the Sea, Ozone Layer Protection, Wetlands
signed, but not ratified: none of the selected agreements

Air pollutants: *particulate matter emissions:* 19.35 micrograms per cubic meter (2016 est.)
carbon dioxide emissions: 10.98 megatons (2016 est.)
methane emissions: 12.1 megatons (2020 est.)

Climate: tropical; moderated by altitude; rainy season (November to March)

Land use: *agricultural land:* 42.5% (2018 est.)
arable land: 10.9% (2018 est.)
permanent crops: 0.3% (2018 est.)
permanent pasture: 31.3% (2018 est.)
forest: 39.5% (2018 est.)
other: 18% (2018 est.)

Urbanization: *urban population:* 32.4% of total population (2022)
rate of urbanization: 2.41% annual rate of change (2020-25 est.)

Revenue from forest resources: *forest revenues:* 1.61% of GDP (2018 est.)
country comparison to the world: 39

Revenue from coal: *coal revenues:* 0.4% of GDP (2018 est.)
country comparison to the world: 15

Food insecurity: *widespread lack of access: due to high food prices and cereal production downturn* - based on the current situation, the prevalence of food insecurity is foreseen to increase from the latest assessment that estimated 2.5 to 3 million people in need of humanitarian assistance during the peak of the lean season between February and May 2022; this most likely scenario predominantly reflects the impact of the downturn in domestic food production and rising costs of food; the forecasted slowdown in economic growth in 2022 and the lingering impacts of the COVID-19 pandemic present further downside risks to food security in 2022-2023; the decline in economic growth is seen to continue to adversely affect employment and livelihood opportunities, with negative implications for households' income and their ability to purchase foods (2022)

Waste and recycling: *municipal solid waste generated annually:* 1,449,752 tons (2015 est.)
municipal solid waste recycled annually: 231,960 tons (2005 est.)
percent of municipal solid waste recycled: 16% (2005 est.)

Major rivers (by length in km): Zambezi (shared with Zambia [s]), Angola, Namibia, Botswana, and Mozambique [m]) - 2,740 km; Limpopo (shared with South Africa [s], Botswana, and Mozambique [m]) - 1,800 km
note – [s] after country name indicates river source; [m] after country name indicates river mouth

Major watersheds (area sq km): Indian Ocean drainage: Zambezi (1,332,412 sq km)
Internal *(endorheic basin)* drainage: Okavango Basin (863,866 sq km)

Major aquifers: Upper Kalahari-Cuvelai-Upper Zambezi Basin

Total water withdrawal: *municipal:* 487.7 million cubic meters (2017 est.)
industrial: 81.4 million cubic meters (2017 est.)
agricultural: 2.77 billion cubic meters (2017 est.)

Total renewable water resources: 20 billion cubic meters (2017 est.)

GOVERNMENT

Country name: *conventional long form:* Republic of Zimbabwe
conventional short form: Zimbabwe
former: Southern Rhodesia, Rhodesia, Zimbabwe-Rhodesia
etymology: takes its name from the Kingdom of Zimbabwe (13th-15th century) and its capital of Great Zimbabwe, the largest stone structure in pre-colonial southern Africa

Government type: presidential republic

Capital: *name:* Harare
geographic coordinates: 17 49 S, 31 02 E
time difference: UTC+2 (7 hours ahead of Washington, DC, during Standard Time)
etymology: named after a village of Harare at the site of the present capital; the village name derived from a Shona chieftain, NE-HARAWA, whose name meant "he who does not sleep"

Administrative divisions: 8 provinces and 2 cities* with provincial status; Bulawayo*, Harare*, Manicaland, Mashonaland Central, Mashonaland East, Mashonaland West, Masvingo, Matabeleland North, Matabeleland South, Midlands

Independence: 18 April 1980 (from the UK)

National holiday: Independence Day, 18 April (1980)

Constitution: *history:* previous 1965 (at Rhodesian independence), 1979 (Lancaster House Agreement), 1980 (at Zimbabwean independence); latest final draft completed January 2013, approved by referendum 16 March 2013, approved by Parliament 9 May 2013, effective 22 May 2013
amendments: proposed by the Senate or by the National Assembly; passage requires two-thirds majority vote by the membership of both houses of Parliament and assent of the president of the republic; amendments to constitutional chapters on fundamental human rights and freedoms and on agricultural lands also require approval by a majority of votes cast in a referendum; amended many times, last in 2017

Legal system: mixed legal system of English common law, Roman-Dutch civil law, and customary law

International law organization participation: has not submitted an ICJ jurisdiction declaration; non-party state to the ICCt

Citizenship: *citizenship by birth:* no
citizenship by descent only: the father must be a citizen of Zimbabwe; in the case of a child born out of wedlock, the mother must be a citizen
dual citizenship recognized: no
residency requirement for naturalization: 5 years

Suffrage: 18 years of age; universal

Executive branch: *chief of state:* President Emmerson Dambudzo MNANGAGWA (since 24 November 2017); First Vice President Constantino CHIWENGA (since 28 December 2017); note - Robert Gabriel MUGABE resigned on 21 November 2017, after ruling for 37 years
head of government: President Emmerson Dambudzo MNANGAGWA (since 24 November 2017); Vice President Constantino CHIWENGA (since 28 December 2017);
cabinet: Cabinet appointed by president, responsible to National Assembly
elections/appointments: each presidential candidate nominated with a nomination paper signed by at least 10 registered voters (at least 1 candidate from each province) and directly elected by absolute majority popular vote in 2 rounds if needed for a 5-year term (no term limits); election last held on 3 July 2018 (next to be held in 2023); co-vice presidents drawn from party leadership
election results:
Emmerson MNANGAGWA reelected president in 1st round of voting; percent of vote - Emmerson MNANGAGWA (ZANU-PF) 50.8%, Nelson CHAMISA (MDC-T) 44.3%, Thokozani KHUPE (MDC-N) 0.9%, other 3%

Legislative branch: *description:* bicameral Parliament consists of:
Senate (80 seats; 60 members directly elected in multi-seat constituencies - 6 seats in each of the 10 provinces - by proportional representation vote, 16 indirectly elected by the regional governing councils, 2 reserved for the National Council Chiefs, and 2 reserved for members with disabilities; members serve 5-year terms)
National Assembly (270 seats; 210 members directly elected in single-seat constituencies by simple majority vote and 60 seats reserved for women directly elected by proportional representation vote; members serve 5-year terms)
elections:
Senate - last held for elected member on 30 July 2018 (next to be held in 2023)
National Assembly - last held on 30 July 2018 (next to be held in 2023)
election results:
Senate - percent of vote by party - NA; seats by party - ZANU-PF 34, MDC Alliance 25, Chiefs 18, people with disabilities 2, MDC-T 1; composition - men 45, women 35, percent of women 43.8%
National Assembly - percent of vote by party - NA; seats by party - ZANU-PF 179, MDC Alliance 88, MDC-T 1, NPF 1, independent 1; composition - men 185, women 25, percent of women 31.5%; note - total Parliament percent of women 34.3%

Judicial branch: *highest court(s):* Supreme Court (consists of the chief justice and 4 judges); Constitutional Court (consists of the chief and deputy chief justices and 9 judges)
judge selection and term of office: Supreme Court judges appointed by the president upon recommendation of the Judicial Service Commission, an independent body consisting of the chief justice, Public Service Commission chairman, attorney general, and 2-3 members appointed by the president; judges normally serve until age 65 but can elect to serve until age 70; Constitutional Court judge appointment NA; judges serve nonrenewable 15-year terms
subordinate courts: High Court; Labor Court; Administrative Court; regional magistrate courts; customary law courts; special courts

Political parties and leaders: Citizens Coalition for Change [Nelson CHAMISA]
Movement for Democratic Change - MDC-T [Douglas MWONZORA]
National People's Party or NPP [Conrad SANGMA] (formerly Zimbabwe People First or ZimPF)
Zimbabwe African National Union-Patriotic Front or ZANU-PF [Emmerson Dambudzo MNANGAGWA]
Zimbabwe African Peoples Union or ZAPU [Michael NKOMO]

International organization participation: ACP, AfDB, ATMIS, AU, COMESA, FAO, G-15, G-77, IAEA, IBRD, ICAO, ICRM, IDA, IFAD, IFC, IFRCS, ILO, IMF, IMO, Interpol, IOC, IOM, IPU, ISO, ITSO, ITU, ITUC (NGOs), MIGA, NAM, OPCW, PCA, SADC, UN, UNAMID, UNCTAD, UNESCO, UNIDO, UNISFA, UNMIL, UNMISS, UNOCI, UNSOM, UNWTO, UPU, WCO, WFTU (NGOs), WHO, WIPO, WMO, WTO

Diplomatic representation in the US: *chief of mission:* Ambassador Tadeous Tafirenyika CHIFAMBA (since 7 July 2021);
chancery: 1608 New Hampshire Avenue NW, Washington, DC 20009
telephone: [1] (202) 332-7100
FAX: [1] (202) 483-9326
email address and website:
general@zimembassydc.org
https://zimembassydc.org/

Diplomatic representation from the US: *chief of mission:* Ambassador (vacant); Charge d'Affaires Thomas R. HASTINGS (since August 2021)
embassy: 2 Lorraine Drive, Bluffhill, Harare
mailing address: 2180 Harare Place, Washington DC 20521-2180
telephone: [263] 867-701-1000
FAX: [263] 24-233-4320
email address and website:
consularharare@state.gov
https://zw. usembassy.gov/

Flag description: seven equal horizontal bands of green (top), yellow, red, black, red, yellow, and green with a white isosceles triangle edged in black with its base on the hoist side; a yellow Zimbabwe bird representing the long history of the country is superimposed on a red five-pointed star in the center of the triangle, which symbolizes peace; green represents agriculture, yellow mineral wealth, red the blood shed to achieve independence, and black stands for the native people

National symbol(s): Zimbabwe bird symbol, African fish eagle, flame lily; national colors: green, yellow, red, black, white

National anthem: *name:* "Kalibusiswe Ilizwe leZimbabwe" [Northern Ndebele language] "Simudzai Mureza WeZimbabwe" [Shona] (Blessed Be the Land of Zimbabwe)
lyrics/music: Solomon MUTSWAIRO/Fred Lecture CHANGUNDEGA
note: adopted 1994

National heritage: *total World Heritage Sites:* 5 (3 cultural, 2 natural)
selected World Heritage Site locales: Mana Pools National Park, Sapi, and Chewore Safari Areas (n); Great Zimbabwe National Monument (c); Khami Ruins National Monument (c); Mosi-oa-Tunya/ Victoria Falls (n); Matobo Hills (c)

ECONOMY

Economic overview: Zimbabwe's economy depends heavily on its mining and agriculture sectors. Following a contraction from 1998 to 2008, the economy recorded real growth of more than 10% per year in the period 2010-13, before falling below 3% in the period 2014-17, due to poor harvests, low diamond revenues, and decreased investment. Lower mineral prices, infrastructure and regulatory deficiencies, a poor investment climate, a large public and external debt burden, and extremely high government wage expenses impede the country's economic performance.

Until early 2009, the Reserve Bank of Zimbabwe (RBZ) routinely printed money to fund the budget deficit, causing hyperinflation. Adoption of a multi-currency basket in early 2009 - which allowed currencies such as the Botswana pula, the South Africa rand, and the US dollar to be used locally - reduced inflation below 10% per year. In January 2015, as part of the government's effort to boost trade and attract foreign investment, the RBZ announced that the Chinese renmimbi, Indian rupee, Australian dollar, and Japanese yen would be accepted as legal tender in Zimbabwe, though transactions were predominantly carried out in US dollars and South African rand until 2016, when the rand's devaluation and instability led to near-exclusive use of the US dollar. The government in November 2016 began releasing bond notes, a parallel currency legal only in Zimbabwe which the government claims will have a one-to-one exchange ratio with the US dollar, to ease cash shortages. Bond notes began trading at a discount of up to 10% in the black market by the end of 2016.

Zimbabwe's government entered a second Staff Monitored Program with the IMF in 2014 and undertook other measures to reengage with international financial institutions. Zimbabwe repaid roughly $108 million in arrears to the IMF in October 2016, but financial observers note that Zimbabwe is unlikely to gain new financing because the government has not disclosed how it plans to repay more than $1.7 billion in arrears to the World Bank and African Development Bank. International financial institutions want Zimbabwe to implement significant fiscal and structural reforms before granting new loans. Foreign and domestic investment continues to be hindered by the lack of land tenure and titling, the inability to repatriate dividends to investors overseas, and the lack of clarity regarding the government's Indigenization and Economic Empowerment Act.

Real GDP (purchasing power parity): $40.79 billion (2020 est.)
$44.34 billion (2019 est.)
$48.25 billion (2018 est.)
note: data are in 2017 dollars
country comparison to the world: 118

Real GDP growth rate: 3.7% (2017 est.)
0.7% (2016 est.)
1.4% (2015 est.)
country comparison to the world: 81

Real GDP per capita: $2,700 (2020 est.)
$3,000 (2019 est.)
$3,300 (2018 est.)
note: data are in 2017 dollars
country comparison to the world: 201

GDP (official exchange rate): $21.441 billion (2019 est.)

Inflation rate (consumer prices): 241.7% (2019 est.)
10.6% (2018 est.)
0.9% (2017 est.)
country comparison to the world: 226

GDP - composition, by sector of origin: *agriculture:* 12% (2017 est.)
industry: 22.2% (2017 est.)
services: 65.8% (2017 est.)

GDP - composition, by end use: *household consumption:* 77.6% (2017 est.)
government consumption: 24% (2017 est.)
investment in fixed capital: 12.6% (2017 est.)
investment in inventories: 0% (2017 est.)
exports of goods and services: 25.6% (2017 est.)
imports of goods and services: -39.9% (2017 est.)

Agricultural products: sugar cane, maize, milk, tobacco, cassava, vegetables, bananas, beef, cotton, oranges

Industries: mining (coal, gold, platinum, copper, nickel, tin, diamonds, clay, numerous metallic and nonmetallic ores), steel; wood products, cement, chemicals, fertilizer, clothing and footwear, foodstuffs, beverages

Industrial production growth rate: 0.3% (2017 est.)
country comparison to the world: 167

Labor force: 7.907 million (2017 est.)
country comparison to the world: 61

Labor force - by occupation: *agriculture:* 67.5%
industry: 7.3%
services: 25.2% (2017 est.)

Unemployment rate: 11.3% (2014 est.)
80% (2005 est.)
note: data include both unemployment and underemployment; true unemployment is unknown and, under current economic conditions, unknowable
country comparison to the world: 159

Unemployment, youth ages 15-24: *total:* 27.5%
male: 25%
female: 31.4% (2019 est.)
country comparison to the world: 39

Population below poverty line: 38.3% (2019 est.)

Gini Index coefficient - distribution of family income: 44.3 (2017 est.)
50.1 (2006)
country comparison to the world: 35

Household income or consumption by percentage share: *lowest 10%:* 2%
highest 10%: 40.4% (1995)

Budget: *revenues:* 3.8 billion (2017 est.)
expenditures: 5.5 billion (2017 est.)

Budget surplus (+) or deficit (-): -9.6% (of GDP) (2017 est.)
country comparison to the world: 208

Public debt: 82.3% of GDP (2017 est.)
69.9% of GDP (2016 est.)
country comparison to the world: 34

Taxes and other revenues: 21.5% (of GDP) (2017 est.)
country comparison to the world: 138

Fiscal year: calendar year

Current account balance: -$716 million (2017 est.)
-$553 million (2016 est.)
country comparison to the world: 134

Exports: $4.422 billion (2018 est.)
$6.252 billion (2017 est.)
country comparison to the world: 128

Exports - partners: United Arab Emirates 40%, South Africa 23%, Mozambique 9% (2019)

Exports - commodities: gold, tobacco, iron alloys, nickel, diamonds, jewelry (2019)

Imports: $7.215 billion (2018 est.)
$9.658 billion (2017 est.)
country comparison to the world: 124

Imports - partners: South Africa 41%, Singapore 23%, China 8% (2019)

Imports - commodities: refined petroleum, delivery trucks, packaged medicines, fertilizers, tractors (2019)

Reserves of foreign exchange and gold: $431.8 million (31 December 2017 est.)
$407.2 million (31 December 2016 est.)
country comparison to the world: 157

Debt - external: $9.357 billion (31 December 2017 est.)
$10.14 billion (31 December 2016 est.)
country comparison to the world: 115

Exchange rates: Zimbabwean dollars (ZWD) per US dollar -
82.3138 (2020 est.)
16.44579 (2019 est.)
322.355 (2018 est.)
234.25 (2010)
note: the dollar was adopted as a legal currency in 2009; since then the Zimbabwean dollar has experienced hyperinflation and is essentially worthless

ENERGY

Electricity access: *electrification - total population:* 53% (2019)
electrification - urban areas: 89% (2019)
electrification - rural areas: 36% (2019)

Electricity: *installed generating capacity:* 2.473 million kW (2020 est.)
consumption: 10,928,240,000 kWh (2019 est.)
exports: 504 million kWh (2019 est.)
imports: 1.612 billion kWh (2019 est.)
transmission/distribution losses: 1.491 billion kWh (2019 est.)

Electricity generation sources: *fossil fuels:* 32.9% of total installed capacity (2020 est.)
solar: 0.1% of total installed capacity (2020 est.)
hydroelectricity: 65.3% of total installed capacity (2020 est.)
biomass and waste: 1.7% of total installed capacity (2020 est.)

Coal: *production:* 3.888 million metric tons (2020 est.)
consumption: 3.579 million metric tons (2020 est.)
exports: 327,000 metric tons (2020 est.)
imports: 0 metric tons (2020 est.)
proven reserves: 502 million metric tons (2019 est.)

Petroleum: *total petroleum production:* 800 bbl/day (2021 est.)
refined petroleum consumption: 27,300 bbl/day (2019 est.)

Refined petroleum products - imports: 26,400 bbl/day (2015 est.)
country comparison to the world: 104

Carbon dioxide emissions: 7.902 million metric tonnes of CO_2 (2019 est.)
from coal and metallurgical coke: 3.963 million metric tonnes of CO_2 (2019 est.)

from petroleum and other liquids: 3.94 million metric tonnes of CO2 (2019 est.)
country comparison to the world: 115

Energy consumption per capita: 11.516 million Btu/person (2019 est.)
country comparison to the world: 150

COMMUNICATIONS

Telephones - fixed lines: *total subscriptions:* 252,067 (2020 est.)
subscriptions per 100 inhabitants: 2 (2020 est.)
country comparison to the world: 116

Telephones - mobile cellular: *total subscriptions:* 13,195,900 (2019)
subscriptions per 100 inhabitants: 90.1 (2019)
country comparison to the world: 74

Telecommunication systems: *general assessment:* Zimbabwe's telcos continue to be affected by the country's poor economy; this has been exacerbated by the significant economic difficulties related to the pandemic; revenue has also been under pressure from a number of recent regulatory measures and additional taxes imposed by the cash-strapped government; inflation has become so high that year-on-year revenue comparisons since 2019 have been difficult to assess meaningfully; the three MNOs continue to invest in network upgrades, partly supported by government efforts and cash released from the Universal Service Fund; as a result of these investments, LTE networks have expanded steadily, though services remain concentrated in urban areas; international bandwidth has improved since fiber links to several submarine cables were established via neighboring countries; the expansion of 3G and LTE-based mobile broadband services has meant that most of the population has access to the internet; the government has started a national broadband scheme aimed at delivering a 1Mb/s service nationally by 2030; investment in fixed broadband infrastructure has also resulted in a slow but steady growth in the number of DSL connections, and also fiber subscriptions; during 2021, most growth in the fixed broadband segment has been with fiber connections (2022)
domestic: consists of microwave radio relay links, open-wire lines, radiotelephone communication stations, fixed wireless local loop installations, fiber-optic cable, VSAT terminals, and a substantial mobile-cellular network; Internet connection is most readily available in Harare and major towns; two government owned and two private cellular providers; fixed-line teledensity at nearly 2 per 100 and mobile-cellular nearly 89 per 100 (2020)
international: country code - 263; fiber-optic connections to neighboring states provide access to international networks via undersea cable; satellite earth stations - 2 Intelsat; 5 international digital gateway exchanges

Broadcast media: government owns all local radio and TV stations; foreign shortwave broadcasts and satellite TV are available to those who can afford antennas and receivers; in rural areas, access to TV broadcasts is extremely limited; analog TV only, no digital service (2017)

Internet country code: .zw

Internet users: *total:* 4,310,249 (2020 est.)
percent of population: 29% (2020 est.)
country comparison to the world: 97

Broadband - fixed subscriptions: *total:* 203,461 (2020 est.)
subscriptions per 100 inhabitants: 1 (2020 est.)
country comparison to the world: 120

TRANSPORTATION

National air transport system: *number of registered air carriers:* 2 (2020)
inventory of registered aircraft operated by air carriers: 12
annual passenger traffic on registered air carriers: 285,539 (2018)
annual freight traffic on registered air carriers: 670,000 (2018) mt-km

Civil aircraft registration country code prefix: Z

Airports: *total:* 196 (2021)
country comparison to the world: 30

Airports - with paved runways: *total:* 17
over 3,047 m: 3
2,438 to 3,047 m: 2
1,524 to 2,437 m: 5
914 to 1,523 m: 7 (2021)

Airports - with unpaved runways: *total:* 179
1,524 to 2,437 m: 3
914 to 1,523 m: 104
under 914 m: 72 (2021)

Pipelines: 270 km refined products (2013)

Railways: *total:* 3,427 km (2014)
narrow gauge: 3,427 km (2014) 1.067-m gauge (313 km electrified)
country comparison to the world: 58

Roadways: *total:* 97,267 km (2019)
paved: 18,481 km (2019)
unpaved: 78,786 km (2019)
country comparison to the world: 48

Waterways: 223 km (2022) some navigation possible on Lake Kariba (223 km)
country comparison to the world: 104

Ports and terminals: *river port(s):* Binga, Kariba (Zambezi)

MILITARY AND SECURITY

Military and security forces: Zimbabwe Defense Forces (ZDF): Zimbabwe National Army (ZNA), Air Force of Zimbabwe (AFZ) (2022)

Military expenditures: 2.6% of GDP (2019 est.) (approximately $650 million)
1.7% of GDP (2018 est.) (approximately $510 million)
1.5% of GDP (2017 est.) (approximately $450 million)
1.8% of GDP (2016 est.) (approximately $480 million)
1.9% of GDP (2015 est.) (approximately $490 million)
country comparison to the world: 37

Military and security service personnel strengths: information varies; approximately 30,000 active duty troops, including about 4,000 Air Force personnel (2022)

Military equipment inventories and acquisitions: the ZDF inventory is comprised mostly of older Chinese- and Russian-origin equipment; since the early 2000s, Zimbabwe has been under an arms embargo from the European Union, as well as targeted sanctions from Australia, Canada, New Zealand, the UK, and the US (2021)

Military service age and obligation: 18-22 years of age for voluntary military service (18-24 for officer cadets; 18-30 for technical/specialist personnel); no conscription; women are eligible to serve (2021)

Military - note: the ZDF was formed after independence from the former Rhodesian Army and the two guerrilla forces that opposed it during the Rhodesian Civil War (aka "Bush War") of the 1970s, the Zimbabwe African National Liberation Army (ZANLA) and the Zimbabwe People's Revolutionary Army (ZIPRA); internal security is a key current responsibility, and the military continues to play an active role in the country's politics since the coup of 2017 (2022)

TRANSNATIONAL ISSUES

Disputes - international: *Zimbabwe-Mozambique:* none identified
Zimbabwe-South Africa: South Africa has placed military units to assist police operations along the border of Lesotho, Zimbabwe, and Mozambique to control smuggling, poaching, and illegal migration
Zimbabwe-Zambia: in 2004, Zimbabwe dropped objections to plans between Botswana and Zambia to build a bridge over the Zambezi River, thereby de facto recognizing a short, but not clearly delimited, Botswana-Zambia boundary in the river; in May 2021, Botswana and Zambia agreed in principle to let Zimbabwe be a partner in the bridge project as it enters its lasts phase

Refugees and internally displaced persons: *refugees (country of origin):* 11,613 (Democratic Republic of Congo) (refugees and asylum seekers), 9,871 (Mozambique) (2022)

Trafficking in persons: *current situation:* Zimbabwe is a source, transit, and destination country for men, women, and children subjected to forced labor and sex trafficking; Zimbabwean women and girls from towns bordering South Africa, Mozambique, and Zambia are subjected to forced labor, including domestic servitude, and prostitution catering to long-distance truck drivers; Zimbabwean men, women, and children experience forced labor in agriculture and domestic servitude in rural areas; family members may recruit children and other relatives from rural areas with promises of work or education in cities and towns where they end up in domestic servitude and sex trafficking; Zimbabwean women and men are lured into exploitative labor situations in South Africa and other neighboring countries
tier rating: Tier 3 - Zimbabwe does not fully comply with the minimum standards for the elimination of trafficking and is not making significant efforts to do so; the government passed an anti-trafficking law in 2014 defining trafficking in persons as a crime of transportation and failing to capture the key element of the international definition of human trafficking – the purpose of exploitation – which prevents the law from being comprehensive or consistent with the 2000 UN TIP Protocol that Zimbabwe acceded to in 2013; the government did not report on anti-trafficking law enforcement efforts during 2014, and corruption in law enforcement and the judiciary remain a concern; authorities made minimal efforts to identify and protect trafficking victims, relying on NGOs to identify and assist victims; Zimbabwe's 2014 antitrafficking law required the opening of 10 centers for trafficking victims, but none were established during the year; five existing shelters for vulnerable children and orphans may have accommodated child victims; in January 2015, an interministerial anti-trafficking committee was established, but it is unclear if the committee ever met or initiated any activities (2015)

Illicit drugs: transit point for cannabis and South Asian heroin, methaqualone, and methamphetamines en route to South Africa

APPENDIX A

ABBREVIATIONS

ABEDA	Arab Bank for Economic Development in Africa
ACP Group	African, Caribbean, and Pacific Group of States
ADB	Asian Development Bank
AfDB	African Development Bank
AFESD	Arab Fund for Economic and Social Development
AG	Australia Group
Air Pollution	Convention on Long-Range Transboundary Air Pollution
Air Pollution-Nitrogen Oxides	Protocol to the 1979 Convention on Long-Range Transboundary Air Pollution Concerning the Control of Emissions of Nitrogen Oxides or Their Transboundary Fluxes
Air Pollution-Persistent Organic Pollutants	Protocol to the 1979 Convention on Long-Range Transboundary Air Pollution on Persistent Organic Pollutants
Air Pollution-Sulphur 85	Protocol to the 1979 Convention on Long-Range Transboundary Air Pollution on the Reduction of Sulphur Emissions or Their Transboundary Fluxes by at Least 30%
Air Pollution-Sulphur 94	Protocol to the 1979 Convention on Long-Range Transboundary Air Pollution on Further Reduction of Sulphur Emissions
Air Pollution-Volatile Organic Compounds	Protocol to the 1979 Convention on Long-Range Transboundary Air Pollution Concerning the Control of Emissions of Volatile Organic Compounds or Their Transboundary Fluxes
AMF	Arab Monetary Fund
AMISOM	African Union Mission in Somalia
AMU	Arab Maghreb Union
Antarctic Marine Living Resources	Convention on the Conservation of Antarctic Marine Living Resources
Antarctic Seals	Convention for the Conservation of Antarctic Seals
Antarctic-Environmental Protocol	Protocol on Environmental Protection to the Antarctic Treaty
ANZUS	Australia-New Zealand-United States Security Treaty
AOSIS	Alliance of Small Island States
APEC	Asia-Pacific Economic Cooperation
Arabsat	Arab Satellite Communications Organization
ARF	ASEAN Regional Forum
ASEAN	Association of Southeast Asian Nations
ATMIS	African Union Transition Mission in Somalia
AU	African Union
Autodin	Automatic Digital Network
BA	Baltic Assembly
bbl/day	barrels per day
BCIE	Central American Bank for Economic Integration
BDEAC	Central African States Development Bank
Benelux	Benelux Union
BGN	United States Board on Geographic Names
BIMSTEC	Bay of Bengal Initiative for Multi-sectoral Technical and Economic Cooperation
Biodiversity	Convention on Biological Diversity
BIS	Bank for International Settlements
BRICS	(Brazil, Russia, India, China, and South Africa)
BSEC	Black Sea Economic Cooperation Zone
C	Commonwealth
c.i.f.	cost, insurance, and freight
CACM	Central American Common Market
CAEU	Council of Arab Economic Unity
CAN	Andean Community
Caricom	Caribbean Community and Common Market
CB	citizen's band mobile radio communications
CBSS	Council of the Baltic Sea States
CCC	Customs Cooperation Council
CD	Community of Democracies
CDB	Caribbean Development Bank
CE	Council of Europe
CEI	Central European Initiative
CELAC	Community of Latin America and Caribbean States

CEMA	Council for Mutual Economic Assistance
CEMAC	Economic and Monetary Community of Central Africa
CEPGL	Economic Community of the Great Lakes Countries
CERN	European Organization for Nuclear Research
CIA	Central Intelligence Agency
CICA	Conference of Interaction and Confidence-Building Measures in Asia
CIS	Commonwealth of Independent States
CITES	see Endangered Species
Climate Change	United Nations Framework Convention on Climate Change
Climate Change-Kyoto Protocol	Kyoto Protocol to the United Nations Framework Convention on Climate Change
COCOM	Coordinating Committee on Export Controls
COMESA	Common Market for Eastern and Southern Africa
Comsat	Communications Satellite Corporation
CP	Colombo Plan
CPLP	Comunidade dos Paises de Lingua Portuguesa
CSN	South American Community of Nations became UNASUL - Union of South American Nations
CSTO	Collective Security Treaty Organization
CTBTO	Preparatory Commission for the Nuclear-Test-Ban Treaty Organization
CY	calendar year
D-8	Developing Eight
DC	developed country
DDT	dichloro-diphenyl-trichloro-ethane
Desertification	United Nations Convention to Combat Desertification in Those Countries Experiencing Serious Drought and/or Desertification, Particularly in Africa
DIA	United States Defense Intelligence Agency
DSN	Defense Switched Network
DST	daylight savings time
DWT	deadweight ton
EAC	East African Community
EADB	East African Development Bank
EAEC	Eurasian Economic Community
EAPC	Euro-Atlantic Partnership Council
EAS	East Asia Summit
EBRD	European Bank for Reconstruction and Development
EC	European Community or European Commission
ECA	Economic Commission for Africa
ECB	European Central Bank
ECE	Economic Commission for Europe
ECLAC	Economic Commission for Latin America and the Caribbean
ECO	Economic Cooperation Organization
ECOMIG	ECOWAS Mission in The Gambia
ECOSOC	Economic and Social Council
ECOWAS	Economic Community of West African States
ECSC	European Coal and Steel Community
EE	Eastern Europe
EEC	European Economic Community
EEZ	exclusive economic zone
EFTA	European Free Trade Association
EIB	European Investment Bank
EITI	Extractive Industry Transparency Initiative
EMU	European Monetary Union
Endangered Species	Convention on the International Trade in Endangered Species of Wild Flora and Fauna (CITES)
Entente	Council of the Entente
Environmental Modification	Convention on the Prohibition of Military or Any Other Hostile Use of Environmental Modification Techniques
ESA	European Space Agency
ESCAP	Economic and Social Commission for Asia and the Pacific
ESCWA	Economic and Social Commission for Western Asia
est.	estimate

EU	European Union
EUFOR	European Union Force in Bosnia and Herzegovina
Euratom	European Atomic Energy Community
Eutelsat	European Telecommunications Satellite Organization
EUTM	European Union Training Mission (military force deployed to provide advice, operational training, and education to security forces in Bosnia-Herzegovina, Central African Republic, Mali, and Somalia)
Ex-Im	Export-Import Bank of the United States
f.o.b.	free on board
FAO	Food and Agriculture Organization
FATF	Financial Action Task Force
FAX	facsimile
FLS	Front Line States
FOC	flags of convenience
FSU	former Soviet Union
ft	foot
FttP	FttP: Fiber to the Home (FttP) is a pure fiber-optic cable connection running from an Internet Service Provider (ISP) directly to the user's home or business
FY	fiscal year
FZ	Franc Zone
G-10	Group of 10
G-11	Group of 11
G-15	Group of 15
G-20	Group of 20
G-24	Group of 24
G-3	Group of 3
G-5	Group of 5
G-6	Group of 6
G-7	Group of 7
G-77	Group of 77
G-8	Group of 8
G-9	Group of 9
GATT	General Agreement on Tariffs and Trade; now WTO
GCC	Gulf Cooperation Council
GCN	Global Caribbean Network
GCTU	General Confederation of Trade Unions
GDP	gross domestic product
GMT	Greenwich Mean Time
GNP	gross national product
GRT	gross register ton
GSM	global system for mobile cellular communications
GUAM	Organization for Democracy and Economic Development; acronym for member states - Georgia, Ukraine, Azerbaijan, Moldova
GWP	gross world product
Hazardous Wastes	Basel Convention on the Control of Transboundary Movements of Hazardous Wastes and Their Disposal
HF	high-frequency
HIV/AIDS	human immunodeficiency virus/acquired immune deficiency syndrome
IADB	Inter-American Development Bank
IAEA	International Atomic Energy Agency
IANA	Internet Assigned Numbers Authority
IBRD	International Bank for Reconstruction and Development (World Bank)
ICAO	International Civil Aviation Organization
ICC	International Chamber of Commerce
ICCt	International Criminal Court
ICJ	International Court of Justice (World Court)
ICRC	International Committee of the Red Cross
ICRM	International Red Cross and Red Crescent Movement
ICSID	International Center for Settlement of Investment Disputes
ICTR	International Criminal Tribunal for Rwanda
ICTY	International Criminal Tribunal for the former Yugoslavia
IDA	International Development Association

IDB	Islamic Development Bank
IDP	Internally Displaced Person
IEA	International Energy Agency
IFAD	International Fund for Agricultural Development
IFC	International Finance Corporation
IFRCS	International Federation of Red Cross and Red Crescent Societies
IGAD	Inter-Governmental Authority on Development
IHO	International Hydrographic Organization
ILO	International Labor Organization
IMF	International Monetary Fund
IMO	International Maritime Organization
IMSO	International Mobile Satellite Organization
in	inch
Inmarsat	International Maritime Satellite Organization
InOC	Indian Ocean Commission
Intelsat	International Telecommunications Satellite Organization
Interpol	International Criminal Police Organization
Intersputnik	International Organization of Space Communications
IOC	International Olympic Committee
IOM	International Organization for Migration
IPU	Inter-Parliamentary Union
ISO	International Organization for Standardization
ISP	Internet Service Provider
ITC	International Trade Center
ITSO	International Telecommunications Satellite Organization
ITU	International Telecommunication Union
ITUC	International Trade Union Confederation, the successor to ICFTU (International Confederation of Free Trade Unions) and the WCL (World Confederation of Labor)
kg	kilogram
kHz	kilohertz
km	kilometer
kW	kilowatt
kWh	kilowatt-hour
LAES	Latin American and Caribbean Economic System
LAIA	Latin American Integration Association
LAS	League of Arab States
Law of the Sea	United Nations Convention on the Law of the Sea (LOS)
LDC	less developed country
LLDC	least developed country
LNG	liquefied natural gas
London Convention	see Marine Dumping
LOS	see Law of the Sea
m	meter
Marecs	Maritime European Communications Satellite
Marine Dumping	Convention on the Prevention of Marine Pollution by Dumping Wastes and Other Matter
Marine Life Conservation	Convention on Fishing and Conservation of Living Resources of the High Seas
MARPOL	see Ship Pollution
Medarabtel	Middle East Telecommunications Project of the International Telecommunications Union
Mercosur	Southern Cone Common Market
MFO	Multinational Force & Observers--Sinai
MHz	megahertz
mi	mile
MICAH	International Civilian Support Mission in Haiti
MIGA	Multilateral Investment Guarantee Agency
MINURCAT	United Nations Mission in the Central African Republic and Chad
MINURSO	United Nations Mission for the Referendum in Western Sahara
MINUSCA	United Nations Multidimensional Integrated Stabilization Mission in the Central African Republic
MINUSMA	United Nations Multidimensional Integrated Stabilization Mission in Mali
MINUSTAH	United Nations Stabilization Mission in Haiti
mm	millimeter

MONUSCO	United Nations Organization Stabilization Mission in the Democratic Republic of the Congo
mt	metric ton
Mt.	Mount
NA	not available
NAFTA	North American Free Trade Agreement
NAM	Nonaligned Movement
NATO	North Atlantic Treaty Organization
NC	Nordic Council
NEA	Nuclear Energy Agency
NEGL	negligible
NGA	National Geospatial-Intelligence Agency
NGO	nongovernmental organization
NIB	Nordic Investment Bank
NIC	newly industrializing country
NIE	newly industrializing economy
NIS	new independent states
nm	nautical mile
NMT	Nordic Mobile Telephone
NSG	Nuclear Suppliers Group
Nuclear Test Ban	Treaty Banning Nuclear Weapons Tests in the Atmosphere, in Outer Space, and Under Water
NZ	New Zealand
OAPEC	Organization of Arab Petroleum Exporting Countries
OAS	Organization of American States
OAU	Organization of African Unity; see African Union
ODA	official development assistance
OECD	Organization for Economic Cooperation and Development
OECS	Organization of Eastern Caribbean States
OHCHR	Office of the United Nations High Commissioner for Human Rights
OIC	Organization of the Islamic Conference
OIF	International Organization of the French-speaking World
OOF	other official flows
OPANAL	Agency for the Prohibition of Nuclear Weapons in Latin America and the Caribbean
OPCW	Organization for the Prohibition of Chemical Weapons
OPEC	Organization of Petroleum Exporting Countries
OSCE	Organization for Security and Cooperation in Europe
Ozone Layer Protection	Montreal Protocol on Substances That Deplete the Ozone Layer
PCA	Permanent Court of Arbitration
PFP	Partnership for Peace
PIF	Pacific Islands Forum
PPP	purchasing power parity
Quad	Quadrilateral Security Dialogue
Ramsar	see Wetlands
RG	Rio Group
SAARC	South Asian Association for Regional Cooperation
SACEP	South Asia Co-operative Environment Program
SACU	Southern African Customs Union
SADC	Southern African Development Community
SAFE	South African Far East Cable
SCO	Shanghai Cooperation Organization
SECI	Southeast European Cooperative Initiative
SELEC	Convention of the Southeast European Law Enforcement Centers (successor to SECI)
SHF	super-high-frequency
Ship Pollution	Protocol of 1978 Relating to the International Convention for the Prevention of Pollution From Ships, 1973 (MARPOL)
SICA	Central American Integration System
Sparteca	South Pacific Regional Trade and Economic Cooperation Agreement
SPC	Secretariat of the Pacific Communities
SPF	South Pacific Forum
sq km	square kilometer
sq mi	square mile
TAT	Trans-Atlantic Telephone

TEU	Twenty-Foot Equivalent Unit, a unit of measure for containerized cargo capacity
Tropical Timber 83	International Tropical Timber Agreement, 1983
Tropical Timber 94	International Tropical Timber Agreement, 1994
UAE	United Arab Emirates
UDEAC	Central African Customs and Economic Union
UHF	ultra-high-frequency
UK	United Kingdom
UN	United Nations
UN-AIDS	Joint United Nations Program on HIV/AIDS
UN-Habitat	United Nations Center for Human Settlements
UNAMA	United Nations Assistance Mission in Afghanistan
UNAMID	African Union/United Nations Hybrid Operation in Darfur
UNASUR	Union of South American Nations
UNCLOS	United Nations Convention on the Law of the Sea, also known as LOS
UNCTAD	United Nations Conference on Trade and Development
UNDCP	United Nations Drug Control Program
UNDEF	United Nations Democracy Fund
UNDOF	United Nations Disengagement Observer Force
UNDP	United Nations Development Program
UNEP	United Nations Environment Program
UNESCO	United Nations Educational, Scientific, and Cultural Organization
UNFICYP	United Nations Peacekeeping Force in Cyprus
UNFPA	United Nations Population Fund
UNHCR	United Nations High Commissioner for Refugees
UNHRC	United Nations Human Rights Council
UNICEF	United Nations Children's Fund
UNICRI	United Nations Interregional Crime and Justice Research Institute
UNIDIR	United Nations Institute for Disarmament Research
UNIDO	United Nations Industrial Development Organization
UNIFIL	United Nations Interim Force in Lebanon
UNISFA	United Nations Interim Force for Abyei
UNITAR	United Nations Institute for Training and Research
UNMIK	United Nations Interim Administration Mission in Kosovo
UNMIL	United Nations Mission in Liberia
UNMIS	United Nations Mission in the Sudan
UNMISS	United Nations Mission in South Sudan
UNMIT	United Nations Integrated Mission in Timor-Leste
UNMOGIP	United Nations Military Observer Group in India and Pakistan
UNOCI	United Nations Operation in Cote d'Ivoire
UNODC	United Nations Office of Drugs and Crime
UNOPS	United Nations Office of Project Services
UNRISD	United Nations Research Institute for Social Development
UNRWA	United Nations Relief and Works Agency for Palestine Refugees in the Near East
UNSC	United Nations Security Council
UNSOM	United Nations Assistance Mission in Somalia
UNSSC	United Nations System Staff College
UNTSO	United Nations Truce Supervision Organization
UNU	United Nations University
UNWTO	World Tourism Organization
UPU	Universal Postal Union
US	United States
USSR	Union of Soviet Socialist Republics (Soviet Union); used for information dated before 25 December 1991
UTC	Coordinated Universal Time
UV	ultraviolet
VHF	very-high-frequency
VSAT	very small aperture terminal
WADB	West African Development Bank
WAEMU	West African Economic and Monetary Union
WCL	World Confederation of Labor
WCO	World Customs Organization

Wetlands	Convention on Wetlands of International Importance Especially As Waterfowl Habitat
WEU	Western European Union
WFP	World Food Program
WFTU	World Federation of Trade Unions
Whaling	International Convention for the Regulation of Whaling
WHO	World Health Organization
WIPO	World Intellectual Property Organization
WMO	World Meteorological Organization
WP	Warsaw Pact
WTO	World Trade Organization
ZC	Zangger Committee
°C	degree(s) Celsius, degree(s) centigrade
°F	degree(s) Fahrenheit

APPENDIX T

TERRORIST ORGANIZATIONS

This listing includes the 65-plus terrorist groups designated by the US State Department as Foreign Terrorist Organizations (FTOs), as well as an additional 10 non-designated, self-proclaimed branches and affiliates of the Islamic State of Iraq and ash-Sham (ISIS) FTO. The information provided includes details on each cited group's history, goals, leadership, organization, areas of operation, tactics, weapons, size, and sources of support.

Abdallah Azzam Brigades (AAB)

aka – AAB, Ziyad al-Jarrah Battalions of the Abdallah Azzam Brigades; Yusuf al-'Uyayri Battalions of the Abdallah Azzam Brigades; Marwan Hadid Brigades; Marwan Hadid Brigade; Abdullah Azzam Brigades in the Land of Al Sham
history – assessed as disbanded; formed around 2005 as a Sunni jihadist group with ties to al-Qa'ida; formally announced its presence in a 2009 video statement while claiming responsibility for a rocket attack against Israel; in 2013, became involved in the Syrian War where it fought against Iranian-backed forces, particularly Hizballah; has been largely dormant over the past several years and in 2019 announced that it was disbanding
goals – rid the Middle East of Western influence, disrupt Israel's economy and its efforts to establish security, and erode Shia Muslim influence in Lebanon
leadership and organization – Sirajeddin ZURAYQAT (var: Siraj al-Din Zreqat, Siraj al-Din Zuraiqat) was AAB's spiritual leader, spokesman, and commander; was divided into regionally based branches representing fighters in southern Lebanon (Ziyad al-Jarrah Battalions), the Gaza Strip (Marwan Hadid Brigade), and Syria
areas of operation – was based in Lebanon and operated chiefly in Lebanon; was also active in Gaza and Syria, but announced in November 2019 that its forces Syria were dissolving
targets, tactics, and weapons – principal targets were Shia Muslims, the Shia terrorist group Hizballah, and Israel; was responsible for several car and suicide bombing attacks against Shia Muslims in Beirut, Lebanon; claimed responsibility for numerous rocket attacks against Israel and Lebanon; members were typically armed with small arms, light machine guns, grenades, rockets, and improvised explosive devices
strength – was estimated to be down to a few dozen members prior to disbanding
financial and other support – funding support is unknown but probably received donations from sympathizers and engaged in smuggling contraband, including weapons
designation – placed on the US Department of State's list of Foreign Terrorist Organizations on 30 May 2012

Abu Sayyaf Group (ASG)

aka – al-Harakat al Islamiyya (the Islamic Movement); al-Harakat-ul al-Islamiyah; Bearer of the Sword; Father of the Executioner; Father of the Swordsman; International Harakatu'l Al-Islamia; Lucky 9; Islamic State in the Philippines; Mujahideen Commando Freedom Fighters
history – formed in 1991 when it split from the Moro Islamic Liberation Front; has carried out dozens of attacks in the Philippines; linked to al-Qa'ida in the 1990s and 2000s; in recent years, the group has focused on local violence and criminal activity, especially kidnap-for-ransom operations; some factions have declared allegiance to the Islamic State and have had a large role in the operations of ISIS-East Asia (ISIS-EA) in the Philippines, including the attack on Marawi City in 2017; ASG fighters affiliated with ISIS-EA were reportedly linked to suicide attacks in 2019 and 2020 in Jolo, Sulu province; the commander of an ASG faction, Hatib Hajan SAWADJAAN, was the acting leader of ISIS-EA until his reported death in mid-2020; continued to be active into 2022, despite considerable losses to counter-terrorism operations by Philippine security forces
goals – establish an Islamic State in the southern Philippines and ultimately across Southeast Asia
leadership and organization – leadership fragmented; loosely structured and family/clan/network-based; factions tend to coalesce around individual leaders; Sulu-based Radullan SAHIRON (aka Putol, Kahal Mohammad) reportedly became the leader in 2017; SAHIRON has not pledged allegiance to ISIS
areas of operation – the southern Philippines, especially Basilan, Jolo, and Tawi-Tawi islands and their surrounding waters, as well as Mindanao; also has been active in Malaysia
targets, tactics, and weapons – targets military and security personnel, facilities, and checkpoints; also attacks civilian targets, such as churches, markets, and ferry boats; conducted the country's deadliest terrorist attack when it bombed a ferry boat in Manila Bay in 2004, killing 116 people; known for kidnapping civilians, particularly foreigners, for ransom and has killed hostages when ransoms were not paid; tactics include car bombings, ambushes, complex assaults involving dozens of fighters, beheadings, and assassinations, as well as possible suicide bombings; has conducted acts of piracy in local waters; weapons include small arms, light and heavy machine guns, mortars, landmines, and improvised explosive devices
strength – assessed in 2022 to have less than 200 armed fighters
financial and other support – funded primarily through kidnapping-for-ransom operations and extortion; makes financial appeals on social media; may receive funding from external sources, including remittances from overseas Philippine workers and Middle East-based sympathizers; has received training and other assistance from other regional terrorist groups, such as Jemaah Islamiya; buys weapons and ammunition from corrupt local government officials or smuggles them in from nearby countries
designation – placed on the US Department of State's list of Foreign Terrorist Organizations on 8 October 1997

Al-Aqsa Martyrs Brigade (AAMB)

aka – al-Aqsa Martyrs Battalion; al-Aqsa Brigades; Martyr Yasser Arafat; Kata'ib Shuhada al-Aqsa; The Brigades; al-Aqsa Intifada Martyrs' Group; Martyrs of al-Aqsa Group
history – emerged at the outset of the second intifada in September 2000 as a loosely-organized armed wing of Yasser ARAFAT's Fatah faction in the West Bank; in 2002, some members splintered from Fatah while others remained loyal; the group carried out suicide attacks against Israeli targets between 2001-2007; most of the group's leaders have been captured or killed by Israel; following an agreement between Israel and the Palestinian Authority (PA) after the HAMAS takeover of Gaza in 2007, Israel pardoned some AAMB fighters in return for an agreement to disarm; after a trial period, those that disarmed were absorbed into PA security forces while those that refused were targeted by PA security forces; still others formed splinter groups such as the Al-Aqsa Martyrs Brigades-Nidal al-Amoudi Division and the Popular Resistance Committees in Gaza; some factions participated in operations against Israeli targets through the 2010s, including the "Stabbing Intifada" of 2015-16, as well as periodic rocket attacks in 2017-2018; claimed responsibility for an attack in 2022 by a gunman that killed 5 near Tel Aviv
goals – drive the Israeli military and Israeli settlers from the West Bank and establish a Palestinian state loyal to Fatah

leadership and organization – most of the group's original leaders have been captured or killed by Israel; typically has operated under a decentralized power structure, with each cell/faction reporting to a local leader and mostly acting independently of each other
areas of operation – Israel, Gaza, and the West Bank; has members in Palestinian refugee camps in Lebanon
targets, tactics, and weapons – primarily employed bombing and small-arms attacks against Israeli military personnel and settlers after the second intifada began in September 2000, but by 2002 had turned increasingly to attacks against civilians inside Israel, including the first female suicide bombing; since 2010, has launched numerous rocket attacks against Israeli communities; largest attack was in November 2012, when it fired more than 500 rockets into Israel during Israeli military operations in Gaza; fighters typically armed with small arms, light and heavy machine guns, grenades, mortars, improvised explosive devices, and rockets
strength – estimated in 2020 to have a few hundred members
financial and other support – Iran has provided AAMB with funds and guidance, mostly through Hizballah facilitators; has cooperated with other terrorist groups throughout its existence, including Hamas, the Popular Front for the Liberation of Palestine (PFLP), and Palestinian Islamic Jihad (PIJ)
designation –placed on the US Department of State's list of Foreign Terrorist Organizations on 27 March 2002

al-Ashtar Brigades (AAB)

aka – Saraya al-Ashtar; the military arm of the al-Wafa Islamic movement
history – is an Iranian-backed Shia militant group established in 2013 with the aim of overthrowing the ruling Sunni family in Bahrain; in 2018, formally adopted Iran's Islamic Revolutionary Guard Corps branding in its logo and flag and reaffirmed the group's loyalty to Tehran; has not claimed any attacks in recent years, but reportedly still active through 2021
goals – foment an insurgency against the ruling Sunni family of Bahrain and, ultimately, replace it with a Shia-based government; also seeks to expel US and other Western military forces from Bahrain
leadership and organization – Qassim Abdullah Ali AHMED (aka Qassim al Muamen) is the Iran-based leader of AAB; operates in cells
areas of operation – located in Bahrain; also active in Iran and Iraq
targets, tactics, and weapons – targets local security forces in Bahrain and plotted to attack oil pipelines; also has promoted violence against the British, Saudi Arabian, and US governments; methods include shootings and bombings; equipped with small arms and explosives, including improvised explosive devices
strength – not available
funding and other support – receives funding, training, and weapons support from the Iranian Revolutionary Guard Corps; also receives training from the Iraq-based Kataib Hezbollah terrorist group
designation – placed on the US Department of State's list of Foreign Terrorist Organizations on 11 July 2018

al-Mulathamun Battalion (al-Mourabitoun)

aka – al-Mulathamun Brigade; al-Muwaqqi'un bil-Dima; Those Signed in Blood Battalion (or Brigade); Signatories in Blood; Those who Sign in Blood; Witnesses in Blood; Signed-in-Blood Battalion; Masked Men Brigade; Khaled Abu al-Abbas Brigade; al-Mulathamun Masked Ones Brigade; al-Murabitoun; The "Sentinels" or "Guardians"
history – was part of al-Qa'ida in the Islamic Maghreb (AQIM) but split from AQIM in 2012 over leadership disputes; merged with the Mali-based Movement for Unity and Jihad in West Africa to form al-Murabitoun in August 2013; some members split from the group in mid-2015 and declared allegiance to the Islamic State, which acknowledged the pledge in October 2016, creating the Islamic State in the Greater Sahara; in late 2015, al-Mulathamun/al-Mourabitoun announced a re-merger with AQIM and in 2017, joined a coalition of al-Qa'ida-affiliated groups operating in the Sahel region known as Jama'at Nusrat al-Islam wal-Muslimin (JNIM); the group remained active in 2022 under the JNIM banner
goals – replace regional governments with an Islamic state
leadership and organization – unclear; Mokhtar BELMOKHTAR or Abderrahman al-SANHADJI (BELMOKHTAR has been declared killed several times since 2013); operations guided by a governing shura council but details on the sub-structure are not available
areas of operation – Algeria, Burkina Faso, Libya, Mali, and Niger
targets, tactics, and weapons – primarily targets Western interests in the Sahel but also regional military forces; known for high-profile attacks with small arms and explosives against civilian targets frequented or run by Westerners, including restaurants, hotels, mines, and energy facilities; in 2013, claimed responsibility for taking over 800 people hostage during a four-day siege at the Tiguentourine gas plant in southeastern Algeria, resulting in the deaths of 39 civilians; has claimed responsibility for suicide car bombings at military bases in Niger and Mali, including a suicide car bombing attack on a military camp in Gao, Mali, that killed at least 60 and wounded more than 100; has been involved in fighting against French military and local security forces in Mali; armed with small arms, machine guns, landmines, mortars, and improvised explosive devices
strength – not available; dated information suggests a few hundred
financial and other support – engages in kidnappings for ransom and smuggling activities; receives support through its connections to other terrorist organizations in the region; acquired weapons from Libya, battlefield captures, and seized stockpiles from local militaries
designation – placed on the US Department of State's list of Foreign Terrorist Organizations on 19 December 2013

al-Nusrah Front (ANF)/Hay'at Tahrir al-Sham (HTS)

aka – Jabhat al-Nusrah; Jabhet al-Nusrah; The Victory Front; al-Nusrah Front for the People of the Levant; al-Nusrah Front in Lebanon; Jabhat al-Nusra li-Ahl al-Sham min Mujahedi al-Sham fi Sahat al-Jihad; Support Front for the People of the Levant; Jabhat Fath al-Sham; Jabhat Fath al Sham; Jabhat Fatah al-Sham; Jabhat Fateh al-Sham; Front for the Conquest of Syria; the Front for liberation of al Sham; Front for the Conquest of Syria/the Levant; Front for the Liberation of the Levant; Conquest of the Levant Front; Fatah al-Sham Front; Fateh al-Sham Front; Hay'at Tahrir al-Sham; Hay'et Tahrir al-Sham; Hayat Tahrir al-Sham; HTS; Assembly for the Liberation of Syria; Assembly for Liberation of the Levant; Liberation of al-Sham Commission; Liberation of the Levant Organization; Tahrir al-Sham; Tahrir al-Sham Hay'at
history – formed circa late 2011 when former al-Qa'ida in Iraq (AQI) leader Abu Bakr al-BAGHDADI sent Syrian militant Abu Muhammad al-JAWLANI (var: al-GOLANI, al-JOLANI) to organize al-Qa'ida cells in Syria; split from AQI in early 2013 and became an independent entity; operated as Jabhat Fateh al-Sham briefly in 2016; in 2017, joined with four smaller Syrian Islamist factions (Harakat Nur al Din al Zenki, Liwa al Haqq, Ansar al Din, and Jaysh al Sunna) and created Hay'at Tahrir al-Sham (HTS, "Assembly for the Liberation of the Levant") as a vehicle to advance its position in Syria; since 2017, additional groups and individuals have joined; as of 2022, HTS was the dominate militant group in northwest Syria and asserted considerable influence and control over the so-called Syrian Salvation Government in the Iblib de-escalation zone where it continued to defend against attacks from Syrian Government forces and its allies and consolidate its position; maintained a tense relationship with al-Qa'ida affiliate in Syria Hurras al-Din (HAD) and refused efforts to resolve differences; has reportedly detained or killed some HAD leaders; has openly clashed with the Islamic State of Iraq and ash-Sham (ISIS) and regularly detained ISIS members seeking to use Idlib as a safehaven

goals – unify under its banner the various anti-ASAD jihadist groups operating in Syria and consolidate its control over the Idlib region; ultimately oust Syrian President Bashar al-ASAD's regime and replace it with a Sunni Islamic state
leadership and organization – led by an overall commander (al-JAWLANI) assisted by a small consultative council ("majlis-ash-shura"); has branches for political, religious, military, financial, civilian services, media, and administrative affairs; operational structure varies from clandestine cells to paramilitary/semi-conventional military units organized as battalions and brigades; claims to have 10 brigades, each with the ability to operate independently with its own infantry, armor, supply, and fire support units; reportedly operates a commando unit known as the "Red Bands" or "Band of Deaths" that is responsible for conducting raids behind regime front lines
areas of operation – headquartered in Syria's Idlib Province in the northwest, operationally active primarily in northwestern Syria after regime advances cleared opposition groups from other areas of the country
targets, tactics, and weapons – primarily attacks Syrian Government and pro-regime forces (including Iranian-backed) and other Syrian insurgent groups, including ISIS, as well as some minorities and civilians; engages in conventional and guerrilla-style attacks using small arms and other light weapons, artillery, rockets, landmines, anti-tank missiles, armored combat vehicles, and surface-to-air missiles; also known for using terrorist tactics, including assassinations and suicide attacks incorporating car bombs and explosive vests
strength – assessed in 2022 to have as many as 15,000 fighters
financial and other support – derives funding from smuggling, extortion, taxes and fines on local populations and at border crossings it controls, and donations from external Gulf-based donors; taxes imposed on local populations include income, business, and services and utilities such as access to electricity, water, and bread; also raises funds through control of the import and distribution of fuel through a front company; has conducted kidnappings-for-ransom operations in the past; maintains training camps and provides some logistical support to like-minded groups; has also reportedly received military training from private foreign contractors
designation – placed on the US Department of State's list of Foreign Terrorist Organizations on 15 May 2014; on 31 May 2018, the Department of State amended the designation of al-Nusrah Front to include Hay'at Tahrir al-Sham (HTS) and other aliases

al-Qa'ida (AQ)

aka – al-Qa'eda; al-Qaeda; Qa'idat al-Jihad (The Base for Jihad); formerly Qa'idat Ansar Allah (The Base of the Supporters of God); the Islamic Army; Islamic Salvation Foundation; The Base; The Group for the Preservation of the Holy Sites; The Islamic Army for the Liberation of the Holy Places; the World Islamic Front for Jihad Against Jews and Crusaders; the Usama Bin Ladin Network; the Usama Bin Ladin Organization; al-Jihad; the Jihad Group; Egyptian al-Jihad; Egyptian Islamic Jihad; New Jihad
history – formed under Usama BIN LADIN (UBL) circa 1988 and now one of the largest and longest-operating jihadist organizations in the world; helped finance, recruit, transport, and train fighters for the Afghan resistance against the former Soviet Union in the 1980s; in the 1990s, was based in Sudan and then Afghanistan, where it planned and staged attacks; merged with al-Jihad (Egyptian Islamic Jihad) in June 2001; developed a reputation for carrying out large-scale, mass casualty attacks against civilians; has lost dozens of mid- and senior-level operatives to counterterrorism efforts, including UBL in May 2011, which has disrupted operations but the group continues to recruit, plan, inspire, and conduct attacks; has established affiliated organizations in the Middle East, Africa, and Asia, and its contemporary strength is primarily in these affiliates; tied to the Taliban in Afghanistan and remained active there into 2022
goals – eject Western influence from the Islamic world, unite the worldwide Muslim community, overthrow governments perceived as un-Islamic, and ultimately, establish a pan-Islamic caliphate under a strict Salafi Muslim interpretation of sharia; direct, enable, and inspire individuals to conduct attacks, recruit, disseminate propaganda, and raise funds on behalf of the group around the world; destabilize local economies and governments by attacking security services, government targets, and civilian targets; maintain its traditional safe haven in Afghanistan; establish and maintain additional safehavens elsewhere
leadership and organization – not available; Egyptian Ayman al-ZAWAHIRI, who was selected to lead following UBL's death, was killed in 2022; has a leadership council ("majlis al-shura"); al-Qa'ida reportedly maintains branches for military, political, religious, financial, and media affairs; affiliates have separate emirs (leaders) and organizational structures that vary by region
areas of operation – based in Afghanistan; employs an affiliate or proxy model, which includes al-Qa'ida in the Arabian Peninsula (Yemen), al-Qa'ida in the Islamic Maghreb (North Africa and the Sahel), Hurras al-Din (Syria), al-Shabaab (Somalia), and al-Qa'ida in the Indian Subcontinent (Afghanistan, Bangladesh, India, and Pakistan); has supporters, sympathizers, and associates worldwide, including in Asia, Europe, North America, and South America; maintains a strong online presence and individuals inspired by AQ's ideology may conduct operations without direction from its central leadership; opportunistically enters (or secures the allegiance of participants in) local conflicts
targets, tactics, and weapons – considers its enemies to be Shia Muslims, US and Western interests, so-called "apostate" governments (such as Saudi Arabia) perceived to be supporting the US and the West, and the Islamic State; leader ZAWAHIRI has encouraged followers to attack European (particularly British and French), Israeli, NATO, Russian, and US targets, specifically military bases and forces; targets have included embassies, restaurants, hotels, airplanes, trains, and tourists sites; employs a combination of guerrilla warfare hit-and-run and terrorist tactics against security and military forces; known for use of suicide bombers, car bombs, explosive-laden boats, and airplanes; conducted the September 11, 2001 attacks on the US, which involved 19 operatives hijacking and crashing four US commercial jets—two into the World Trade Center in New York City, one into the Pentagon, and the last into a field in Shanksville, Pennsylvania—killing nearly 3,000 people
strength – as of 2022, it was estimated to have several hundred operatives in Afghanistan; the organization remained a focal point of inspiration for a worldwide network of affiliated groups and other sympathetic terrorist organizations, such as the Islamic Movement of Uzbekistan, Islamic Jihad Union, Lashkar i Jhangvi, Harakat ul-Mujahideen, the Haqqani Network, and Tehrik-e Taliban Pakistan
financial and other support –primarily depends on donations from like-minded supporters and from individuals, primarily in the Gulf States; uses social media platforms to solicit donations and has been channeled funds through cyberfinancing campaigns; has received some funds from kidnapping for ransom operations; historically has acquired money from Islamic charitable organizations; also recruits followers through social media
designation – placed on the US Department of State's list of Foreign Terrorist Organizations on 8 October 1999
note – has some ideological and tactical similarities with the Islamic State of Iraq and ash-Sham (ISIS) and the groups typically operate in the same conflict zones, but the relationship is mostly adversarial, and they compete for resources and recruits, and often clash militarily

al-Qa'ida in the Arabian Peninsula (AQAP)

aka – al-Qa'ida in the South Arabian Peninsula; al-Qa'ida in Yemen; al-Qa'ida of Jihad Organization in the Arabian Peninsula; al-Qa'ida Organization in the Arabian Peninsula; Tanzim Qa'idat al-Jihad fi Jazirat al-Arab; AQY; Ansar al-Shari'a; Sons of Abyan; Sons of Hadramawt; Sons of Hadramawt Committee; Civil Council of Hadramawt; National Hadramawt Council
history – formed in January 2009 when the now-deceased leader of al-Qa'ida (AQ) in Yemen, Nasir AL-WAHISHI, publicly announced that Yemeni and Saudi al-Qa'ida operatives were working together under the banner of AQAP; the announcement signaled the rebirth of an AQ franchise that previously carried out attacks in Saudi Arabia; beginning in 2014-2015, AQAP was able to take advantage of Yemen's civil war and expand operations in the country, controlling a large portion of the southern part of the Yemen by 2016"; after 2017, the group began losing territory and

fighters, as well as leaders, to internal dissensions, desertions to ISIS, and casualties from Yemeni and international military operations and fighting with ISIS and the Huthis; however, in 2022 the group continued to occupy territory, conduct attacks, and pose a significant threat in Yemen
goals – establish a caliphate and a government/society based on sharia in the Arabian Peninsula and the wider Middle East; support the broader goals of AQ's central leadership
leadership and organization – led by Khalid bin Umar BATARFI (aka Abu Miqdad al-Kindi); has a leadership council ("majlis al-shura") comprised of lieutenant commanders who are responsible for overall political direction and military operations; organized in branches or wings for military operations, political, propaganda (recruitment), and religious issues (for justifying attacks from a theological perspective while offering spiritual guidance)
areas of operation – most active in southern and central Yemen; probably has a limited presence in Saudi Arabia
targets, tactics, and weapons – chiefly targets Security Belt Forces and other groups affiliated with the United Arab Emirates and Saudi Arabia in the Shabwa and Abyan governorates, as well as the Huthis in the Bayda governorate; also targets Yemeni Government officials, oil facilities, merchant ships, and Shia Muslims; has targeted Western interests, including embassies, diplomats, business people, tourists, and airliners; has waged open warfare with Islamic State elements in Yemen since 2018; employs guerrilla-style and terrorist tactics, including ambushes, complex assaults, assassinations, snipers, bombings, and suicide attacks; equipped with small arms, machine guns, artillery, rockets, landmines, anti-tank missiles, armored combat vehicles, man-portable air defense systems (MANPADs), and improvised explosive devices, including car bombs, road side bombs, and suicide vests
strength – estimated 2-3,000 in 2022, down from as many as 6-7,000 in 2018
financial and other support – receives funding from theft, robberies, oil and gas revenue, kidnapping-for-ransom operations, and donations from like-minded supporters; for nearly a year after seizing the city of Mukallah in April 2015, had access millions of dollars from port fees and funds stolen from the central bank; many of its weapons have been seized from the Yemeni military; recruits through social media, print, and digital means
designation – placed on the US Department of State's list of Foreign Terrorist Organizations on 19 January 2010

al-Qa'ida in the Indian Subcontinent (AQIS)
aka – al-Qaeda in the Indian Subcontinent; Qaedat al-Jihad in the Indian Subcontinent, Qaedat al-Jihad, Jamaat Qaidat al-Jihad fi'shibhi al-Qarrat al-Hindiya,
history – al-Qa'ida leader Dr. Ayman al-ZAWAHIRI announced AQIS's inception in a video address in September 2014; the group claimed responsibility for a September 2014 attack on a naval dockyard in Karachi in an attempt to seize a Pakistani warship; since the assault, the group has conducted a limited number of small attacks on civilians, but has not publicly claimed any attacks since 2017, although some members fought in Afghanistan with the Taliban; suffered some losses to counter-terrorism operations in 2020-2022; in September and October 2021, the group released two propaganda videos specifically targeting India and Kashmir, and in mid-2022 threatened to conduct suicide bombings in several Indian cities; has strong ties to Lashkare Tayyiba (LeT) and a rivalry with the Islamic State's Khorasan branch
goals – establish an Islamic caliphate in the Indian subcontinent; support the broader goals of al-Qai'da's central leadership
leadership and organization – reportedly Usama MAHMOOD (alt. Osama MEHMOOD); has a shura council, which, like other AQ affiliates, probably includes subordinates and branches/wings for military, religious, propaganda, and political matters; reportedly has regional branches for Bangladesh, India, and Pakistan; Ansar al-Islam in Bangladesh has claimed to be the official wing of AQIS in Bangladesh
areas of operation – Afghanistan, Bangladesh, India, Pakistan, and possibly Burma
targets, tactics, and weapons – military and security personnel, political parties, foreigners, foreign aid workers, university professors, students, and secular bloggers; has used small arms and improvised explosive devices, as well as crude weapons such as machetes; claimed responsibility for the 2016 machete murders of two editors of a human rights magazine in Dhaka, Bangladesh
membership – estimated in 2022 to have up to 400 fighters
financial and other support – likely receives financial and material support from AQ senior leadership; also engages in kidnapping-for-ransom, extortion, and general criminal activity to raise funds
designation – placed on the US Department of State's list of Foreign Terrorist Organizations on 1 July 2016

al-Qaida in the Islamic Maghreb (AQIM)
aka – GSPC; Le Groupe Salafiste Pour la Predication et le Combat; Salafist Group for Preaching and Combat; Salafist Group for Call and Combat; Tanzim al-Qa'ida fi Bilad alMaghrib al-Islamiya
history – formed in 1998 in Algeria under Hassan HATTAB, when he split from the Armed Islamic Group; was known as the Salafist Group for Preaching and Combat (GSPC) until rebranding itself as AQIM in September 2006; has since undergone various schisms and rapprochements; in 2011, a Mauritanian-led group broke away, calling itself the Movement for Unity and Jihad in West Africa (MUJWA); in 2012, the Veiled Men Battalion split off and rebranded itself the al-Mulathamun Battalion; al-Mulathamun and MUJWA merged to form al-Mourabitoun in 2013; in late 2015, AQIM reincorporated al-Murabitoun and in 2017, the Mali Branch of AQIM and al-Murabitoun joined the Mali-based al-Qa'ida coalition Jama'at Nasr al-Islam wal-Muslimin (JNIM); continued to be active in 2022 despite heavy pressure from regional and international counterterrorism operations, particularly in using North Africa as a support zone for assisting JNIM operations in Mali and the Sahel, including operating transnational financial networks to move and share funds
goals – overthrow "apostate" African regimes and establish a regional Islamic state across all of North and West Africa; support the broader goals of al-Qai'da's central leadership
leadership and organization – Abu Obaida al-ANNABI (aka Abu Ubaydah Yusuf al-Anabi, Yazid Mubarak); has a 14-member shura council comprised of regional commanders and the heads of the political, military, judicial, and media committees; locally organized into "battalions" and "brigades," which range in size from a few dozen to several hundred fighters at any given time
areas of operation – based in northeastern Algeria, but reportedly shifting more towards the Sahel because of Algerian counterterrorism pressure; operates in northern Mali, southwest Libya, Niger, Burkina Faso, and Cote d'Ivoire
targets, tactics, and weapons – local and international military and security forces using both terrorist and guerrilla warfare tactics; employs improvised explosive devices, suicide bombers, as well as light weapons, machine guns, mortars, rockets, and landmines; also attacks "soft" civilian targets such as hotels, resorts, and restaurants that cater to Westerners and tourists with small arms, explosives, and suicide bombers; known for assassinations and kidnappings
strength – estimated in 2020 to have 500-1,000 fighters
financial and other support – engages in kidnappings-for-ransom and other criminal activities, particularly extorting drug trafficking groups and others; arms largely acquired from Libyan stockpiles, battlefield captures, or via illicit regional arms markets
designation – GSPC was designated as a Foreign Terrorist Organization on 27 March 2002; the Department of State amended the GSPC designation on 20 February 2008, after the GSPC officially joined with al-Qa'ida in September 2006 and became AQIM

al-Shabaab (AS)

aka – the Harakat Shabaab al-Mujahidin (HSM); al-Shabab; Shabaab; the Youth; Mujahidin al-Shabaab Movement; Mujahideen Youth Movement; Mujahidin Youth Movement; al-Hijra, Al Hijra, Muslim Youth Center, MYC, Pumwani Muslim Youth, Pumwani Islamist Muslim Youth Center
history – descended from Al-Ittihad Al-Islami, a Somali terrorist group whose leaders fought in Afghanistan in the 1990s and formed circa 2003; has operated as a core al-Qa'ida affiliate since 2012; was the militant wing of the former Somali Islamic Courts Council that took over parts of Somalia in 2006; since the end of 2006, has engaged in an insurgency against the transitional governments of Somalia and supporting foreign military forces and a campaign of violence against Somali civilians; responsible for numerous high-profile bombings and shootings throughout Somalia, and more than 3,000 civilian deaths since 2015; has influence in large areas of rural Somalia through coercion, control over local economies and commercial transit points; provides rudimentary government services in areas under its control, including rule of law through sharia courts, sharia-based institutions and schools, funding, services, security, and food; in 2019, was involved in more than 1,000 violent incidents in Somalia and eastern Kenya; continued to conduct widespread attacks through 2021 and 2022, particularly in central and southern Somalia and the capital Mogadishu, and was engaged in fighting with the Somali military; in July 2022, it launched an incursion into Ethiopia with several hundred fighters
goals – discredit, destabilize, and overthrow the Federal Government of Somalia; establish Islamic rule in Somalia and the border regions of Somalia-Kenya and southern Ethiopia; drive out Western influence
leadership and organization – led by Ahmad DIRIYE (aka Abu UBEYDAH/UBAIDAH, Abu Ubaidah DIREYE, Ahmad UMAR) since September 2014; structure is both hierarchical and decentralized and influenced by Somalia's many clans; DIRIYE directs a shura council made up of multiple committees and ministries, including for finance, media, and military/security operations, as well as regional commanders; military operations reportedly includes 2 sub-branches, one for external operations, and one that enforces sharia in areas under the group's control; the shura council oversees regional commanders, although regional commanders can make decisions and take actions without the approval of the emir or the council; each regional division has military and administrative wings; the group has an intelligence wing called Amiyat
areas of operation – controls a large swathe of the Lower and Middle Juba regions, as well as the Bakol, Bay, Benaadir, Gedo, and Shabelle regions; also maintains a presence in northern Somalia along the Golis Mountains and within Puntland's urban areas; has conducted attacks in Djibouti, Kenya, and Uganda; especially active in the region of Kenya adjacent to Somalia; has also mounted armed incursions into Ethiopia in 2022 and 2007 (planned attacks inside Ethiopia were reportedly disrupted in 2013 and 2014)
targets, tactics, and weapons – Somali Government officials, military units, police, and civilians, international aid workers, journalists, foreign troops (including US), and neighboring countries contributing to military stabilization operations in Somalia, particularly Kenya and Uganda; has attacked hotels, schools, military bases, police stations, shopping areas, and telecommunications towers in Kenya; has clashed with an Islamic State faction operating in northern Somalia; methods include assassinations, drive-by shootings, guerrilla style ambushes, suicide bombings, hostage taking, indiscriminate attacks on civilians, and roadside IEDs; typical attacks consist of a single or multiple suicide bombers, followed by an assault by members carrying small arms and explosives; in March 2022, for example, it conducted a complex ground assault involving multiple vehicle-mounted bombs and hundreds of militants on an international military peacekeeper base that killed more than 50 troops; in March 2019, operatives attacked a hotel in Mogadishu using a suicide bomber and small arms, killing at least 20; has placed vehicle-mounted bombs in high-density urban areas, including attacks in Mogadishu in October 2022, December 2019, and October 2017 that together killed over 700 civilians; employs insurgent-type tactics against Somali and international military forces, including ambushes, hit-and-run attacks, improvised explosive device operations, land mines, mortar attacks, and targeted killings; typically armed with small arms, light and heavy machine guns (including truck-mounted machine guns), mortars, rocket-propelled grenades, improvised explosive devices, and man-portable air defense systems
strength – estimated in 2022 to have 7,000 to 12,000 fighters
financial and other support – obtains funds primarily through extortion of businesses, taxation, and zakat (religious donations) collections from the local populations, robbery, and remittances and other money transfers from the Somali diaspora (although these funds are not always intended to support al-Shabaab members); probably receives training, arms, and bomb-making materials from other al-Qa'ida branches; operates military training camps in areas it occupies; has captured arms, ammunition, and other materiel from regional and Somali military forces; also purchases arms and ammunition through black markets
designation – placed on the US Department of State's list of Foreign Terrorist Organizations on 18 March 2008

Ansar al-Dine (AAD)

aka – Ansar Dine; Ansar al-Din; Ancar Dine; Ansar ul-Din; Ansar Eddine; Defenders of the Faith
history – created in late 2011; was among the terrorist groups (including al-Qa'ida) to take over northern Mali following the March 2012 coup that toppled the Malian government; proceeded to destroy UNESCO World Heritage sites and enforce a severe interpretation of Islam upon the civilian population living in the areas under their control; beginning in 2013, French and African military forces forced AAD and its allies out of the population centers they had seized, severely weakening AAD, although the group made a comeback in 2015 and 2016; in 2017, joined Jama'ah Nusrah al-Islam wal-Muslimin (Group for the Support of Islam and Muslims, JNIM), a coalition of al-Qa'ida-linked groups in Mali that formed the same year; continued to conduct attacks under the JNIM banner into 2022
goals – replace the Malian government with an Islamic state
leadership and organization – led by its founder Iyad Ag GHALI (aka Abu al-FADEL), who also leads JNIM; reportedly has regionally based branches
areas of operation – operates mostly in central and northern Mali
targets, tactics, and weapons – targets Malian military and security forces, French and French coalition troops, and UN Multidimensional Integrated Stabilization Mission in Mali (MINUSMA) personnel; uses a mix of guerrilla warfare hit-and-run and terrorist tactics, including ambushes, complex ground assaults involving dozens of fighters, road side bombs, rocket attacks, assassinations, kidnappings, and car and suicide bombings; fighters are armed with small arms, light and heavy machine guns, rocket-propelled grenades, landmines, mortars, rockets, trucks mounting machine guns (aka "technicals"), and explosives, including improvised explosive devices
strength – not available
financial and other support – cooperates with and has received support from al-Qa'ida since its inception; also reportedly receives funds from foreign donors and through smuggling; many of its arms were captured from the Malian Army or taken from Libyan military stockpiles; takes advantage of trans-Saharan smuggling routes to resupply from illicit markets in Libya and elsewhere in the region
designation – placed on the US Department of State's list of Foreign Terrorist Organizations on 22 March 2013

Ansar al-Islam (AAI)

aka – Ansar al-Sunna; Ansar al-Sunna Army; Devotees of Islam; Followers of Islam in Kurdistan; Helpers of Islam; Jaish Ansar al-Sunna; Jund al-Islam; Kurdish Taliban; Kurdistan Supporters of Islam; Partisans of Islam; Soldiers of God; Soldiers of Islam; Supporters of Islam in Kurdistan

history – founded in December 2001 with support from al-Qa'ida; originated in the Iraqi Kurdistan region with the merger of two Kurdish terrorist factions, Jund al-Islam and a splinter group of the Islamic Movement of Kurdistan; from 2003 to 2011, conducted attacks against a wide range of targets in Iraq, including government and security forces, as well as US and Coalition troops; in the summer of 2014, a faction of AAI pledged allegiance to ISIS and the two factions reportedly have fought each other; after 2014, most activity has been in Syria where AAI has fought against Syrian regime forces, although it claimed a bombing attack against members of a Shia militia in Iraq in late 2019; active in Syria in 2022
goals – expel Western interests from Iraq and, ultimately, establish an Iraqi state operating according to its interpretation of sharia; similar goals in Syria
leadership and organization – led by Amir Shaykh Abu Hashim Muhammad bin Abdul Rahman al-IBRAHIM; likely has a cell-based structure
areas of operation – headquartered in northern Iraq with its largest presence in Kirkuk, Tikrit, and Mosul; also active in central and western Iraq and in Syria
targets, tactics, and weapons – historically targeted Iraqi security and police forces, citizens, politicians, and Shia militia forces for assassinations, bombings, and executions; targets Syrian government forces and pro-Syrian regime militias with guerrilla-style hit-and-run assaults and terrorist attacks; equipped with small arms, light and heavy machine guns, rocket-propelled grenades, mortars, and explosives, including improvised explosive devices
strength – not available
financial and other support – receives assistance from a loose network of associates in Europe and the Middle East
designation – placed on the US Department of State's list of Foreign Terrorist Organizations on 22 March 2004

Ansar al-Shari'a groups in Libya (ASL)
aka – Ansar al-Shari'a in Benghazi; Ansar al-Sharia in Darnah; Ansar al-Shariah Brigade; Ansar al-Shari'a Brigade; Katibat Ansar al-Sharia in Benghazi; Ansar al-Shariah-Benghazi; Al-Raya Establishment for Media Production; Ansar al-Sharia; Soldiers of the Sharia; Ansar al-Shariah; Supporters of Islamic Law; Partisans of Islamic Law; Supporters of Islamic Law in Darnah, Ansar al-Sharia Brigade in Darnah; Ansar al-Sharia in Derna
history – consists of Ansar al-Shari'a in Benghazi (AAS-B) and Ansar al-Sharia in Darnah (AAS-D); AAS-B and AAS-D were formed in 2011 following the fall of the QADHAFI regime as Sunni Muslim Salafist armed groups with links to al-Qa'ida; at their peak in 2013, held territory and operated branches in Benghazi, Darnah, Sirte, Ajdabiya, and Nawfalia; promoted charitable work to gain popular support from local communities; in 2014, began fighting against the Libyan National Army (LNA) under General HIFTER and the Islamic State in Libya (ISIS-Libya) and by 2015 had lost most of their territory and suffered heavy losses; in May 2017, AAS-B announced its dissolution due to battle losses, as well as defections to ISIS-Libya; AAS-D's status in 2022 was unclear
goals – a strict implementation of sharia in Libya
leadership and organization – unknown; AAS-B's last known emir (leader) was Abu Khalid al-MADANI; the last known emir of AAS-D was founder Abu Sufian Ibrahim Ahmed Hamuda Bin QUMU who defected to ISIS in 2014; organizations are also unknown, but AAS-B reportedly had two main divisions, one dedicated to military affairs and one to charitable work
areas of operation – operated mostly in eastern Libya, particularly Benghazi and Darnah
targets, tactics, and weapons – targets Libyan political and security officials and Westerners for kidnappings, executions, bombings, and assassinations; AAS-B participated in the 2012 attacks on US diplomatic facilities in Benghazi, for example; also conducted guerrilla warfare hit-and-run and terrorist attacks against Libyan security forces, LNA militias, and other terrorist groups using small arms and light weapons, rockets, mortars, anti-tank guided missiles, anti-aircraft artillery and missiles, improvised explosive devices and suicide bombings
strength – not available
financial and other support – obtained funds from al-Qa'ida in the Islamic Maghreb, witting and unwitting Islamic charities, donations from sympathizers, and criminal activities; raided Libyan military bases for weapons and ammunition
designation – AAS-B and AAS-D were placed on the US Department of State's list of Foreign Terrorist Organizations on 13 January 2014

Ansar al-Shari'a in Tunisia (AAS-T)
aka – Al-Qayrawan Media Foundation; Supporters of Islamic Law; Ansar al-Sharia in Tunisia; Ansar al-Shari'ah; Ansar al-Shari'ah in Tunisia; Ansar al-Sharia
history – formed in April 2011 as a Sunni Salafi-jihadist militant organization linked to al-Qa'ida; combined community service, proselytization, and violence to promote its ideology and goals; in 2014, multiple AAS-T leaders swore loyalty to the Islamic State and many left the group to fight in Syria; did not claim any attacks through 2020, and its status in 2022 was unclear
goals – expand its influence in Tunisia and, ultimately, replace the Tunisian Government with one operating according to Islamic law
leadership and organization – leadership unclear; was reportedly a decentralized movement that gave considerable autonomy to local groups or cells and loosely organized into northern, central, and southern branches; included a media wing known as al-Bayariq Media (The Banners Media)
areas of operation – headquartered in Tunisia; also operated in Libya
targets, tactics, and weapons – attacked Tunisian military and security personnel with small arms and rocket-propelled grenades; also targeted Tunisian politicians, religious sites, and groups and places representing Western influence, such as tourists and tourist sites, with assassinations and bombings; organized riots and violent demonstrations against the Tunisian government; members are typically armed with small arms and other light weapons, as well as explosives, including improvised explosive devices
strength – not available
financial and other support – precise sources of financial support are not available but believed to come from Tunisian charities, private donors, and smuggling contraband
designation – placed on the US Department of State's list of Foreign Terrorist Organizations on 13 January 2014

Army of Islam (AOI)
aka – Jaysh al-Islam; Jaish al-Islam; JAI
history – formed around 2005 as a Salafi Sunni Muslim splinter from HAMAS; subscribes to Salafist ideology of global jihad blended with the traditional model of armed Palestinian resistance; traditionally focused on attacking Israel and Egypt; in September 2015, pledged allegiance to the Islamic State and declared itself part of the Islamic State's Sinai Province (IS-SP); did not claim responsibility for any attacks in 2018 or 2019, but active through 2020
goals – establish a regional Islamic emirate
leadership and organization – led by Mumtaz DUGHMUSH; group organization not available
areas of operation – headquartered in Gaza

targets, tactics, and weapons – targets the Egyptian and Israeli governments and their citizens; has attacked American, British, and New Zealand citizens; has a history of conducting rocket attacks against Israel, kidnapping civilians, and attacking Christians; conducted a bombing attack on a Coptic Christian church in Egypt in 2011 that killed 25 and wounded 100, probably has conducted joint attacks with IS-SP against Egyptian security service personnel; equipped with small arms, light and heavy machine guns, mortars, rockets, and improvised explosives devices
strength – current (2021) numbers not available, but estimated in 2018 to number in the low hundreds
financial and other support – generates funding through criminal activities conducted primarily in Gaza, including kidnappings for ransom; also receives funds from foreign sympathizers and organizations
designation – placed on the US Department of State's list of Foreign Terrorist Organizations on 19 May 2011

Asa'ib Ahl al-Haqq (AAH)
aka – Ahl al-Kahf; Band of the Righteous; Bands of Right; Islamic Shia Resistance in Iraq; Khazali Faction/Network; Khazali Special Groups Network; League of Righteousness
history – is an Iraqi Shia militia and political group that split off from Jaysh al-Mahdi in 2006; fought US military forces in Iraq from 2006 until the US withdrawal in 2011 and has continued attack planning against US and coalition interests following Operation Iraqi Freedom; following the rise of the Islamic State of Iraq and ash-Sham (ISIS) in 2013, fought alongside the Iraqi military as part of the Popular Mobilization Committee and Affiliated Forces (PMC or PMF) militia forces (aka Popular Mobilization Units or PMU) until ISIS's territorial defeat in 2017; fought in support of the ASAD regime in Syria from 2011 until at least 2017 where it claimed the loss of about 700 fighters; in 2017, AAH's affiliated political party (Al Sadiqun Bloc) was approved by the Iraqi electoral commission to run in the national election; in 2018, Al Sadiqun joined the Al Fatah Alliance (Victory), a political coalition primarily comprised of parties affiliated with Iranian-backed Shia militias; in late 2019, it participated in an assault on the US Embassy compound in Baghdad; largely follows the directives of Iran's IRGC Qods Force and has vowed revenge on the US for the death of the Iranian Qods Force commander in early 2020; continued to be active into 2022, including indirect fire attacks on US facilities in Iraq, typically using front names or proxy groups
goals – maintain a Shia-controlled government in Iraq, promote Iran's political and religious influence in Iraq, and expel the remaining US military presence
leadership and organization – led by Qays al-KHAZALI; maintains a paramilitary force inside the PMC/PMF that is divided into three brigades (the 41st, 42nd, and 43rd PMC brigades) representing geographic sectors of Iraq; reportedly models itself after Lebanese Hizballah
area(s) of operation – maintains political offices in Baghdad, Al Basrah, An Najaf, Babil, Salah ad Din, and Ninawa Governorates; militia forces reportedly dominate the area from Baghdad to Samarra; probably active in Syria in 2022
targets, tactics, and weapons – targets foreign military forces, US interests, ISIS, and Sunni Muslims; from 2006 to 2011, claimed to have conducted more than 6,000 attacks against US and Coalition forces using small arms, road side bombs, car bombs, and mortars; has carried out abductions, executions, and targeted killings of Sunni Muslims; fought as a paramilitary/irregular force in Syria and alongside the Iraqi military; armed with a variety of weapons, including small arms, machine guns, rocket-propelled grenades, mortars, rockets, artillery, armed unmanned aerial vehicles, improvised explosive devices, and armored vehicles
strength – estimated in 2021 to have approximately 10,000 fighters
financial and other support – receives funding, logistical support, training, and weapons from the Iranian Revolutionary Guard Force-Qods Force and Lebanese Hizballah; solicits donations online and through a pro-Iran television channel; also raises funds through legitimate business enterprises, as well as criminal activities, including kidnappings-for-ransom, smuggling, and taxing/extortion of economic activities in areas where the group is dominant
designation – placed on the US Department of State's list of Foreign Terrorist Organizations on 10 January 2020

Asbat al-Ansar (AAA)
aka – Band of Helpers; Band of Partisans; League of Partisans; League of the Followers; God's Partisans; Gathering of Supporters; Partisan's League; Esbat al-Ansar; Isbat al-Ansar; Osbat al-Ansar; Usbat al-Ansar; Usbat ul-Ansar
history – emerged in the early 1990s in Lebanon under the late Shaykh Hisham SHRAID, a Palestinian refugee and preacher; until the 2000s, was known for assassinating Lebanese religious leaders and government officials, as well as bombing venues it deemed un-Islamic and representing Western influence, such as nightclubs, theaters, and liquor stores; from 2005 to 2011, some members fought against US and Coalition forces in Iraq; has links to al-Qa'ida and other Sunni terrorist groups; remained active through 2021 but has not claimed responsibility for any attacks since 2018
goals – overthrow the Lebanese Government, rid Lebanon of Western influence; destroy Israel and establish an Islamic state in the Levant; oppose Christian, secular, and Shia Muslim institutes operating in the Levant
leadership and organization – not available
areas of operation – primary base of operations is the Ayn al-Hilwah Palestinian refugee camp near Sidon in southern Lebanon; has been reluctant to involve itself in operations in Lebanon in recent years, in part because of concerns of losing its safe haven in the camp
targets, tactics, and weapons – until the mid-2000s, operatives conducted small-scale bombing and shooting attacks in Lebanon against Christian, secular, and Shia Muslim figures and institutions, elements of foreign influence inside the country, and Lebanese government officials, such as judges; has also plotted against foreign diplomatic targets; weapons include small arms, rocket-propelled grenades, and improvised explosive devices
strength – estimated in 2020 to be in the low hundreds
financial resources – receives donations from sympathizers and through international Sunni extremist networks
designation – placed on the US Department of State's list of Foreign Terrorist Organizations on 27 March 2002

Boko Haram (BH)
aka – Nigerian Taliban; Jama'atu Ahlus-Sunnah Lidda'Awati Wal Jihad; Jama'atu Ahlis Sunna Lidda'awati wal-Jihad; People Committed to the Prophet's Teachings for Propagation and Jihad; Sunni Group for Preaching and Jihad
history – formed in 2002 under the late Muslim cleric Mohammed YUSUF; in 2009, launched an insurgency and campaign of terror against the Nigerian Government, its security forces, and civilians; by 2015, had captured territory roughly the size of Belgium in northeastern Nigeria; since 2015, the Nigerian military has dislodged BH from almost all of the territory it previously controlled, although the group continues to operate and conduct attacks in Nigeria, as well as in Cameroon, Chad, and Niger; in 2015, the group declared allegiance to the Islamic State in Iraq and al-Sham (ISIS) and began calling itself ISIS-West Africa; following an ISIS decision regarding a change in leadership in 2016, the group split into two factions with one group continuing its activities under the original BH leader, Abubakar bin Muhammad SHEKAU, and a new splinter group known as Wilayat Gharb Ifriqiyyah (Islamic State West Africa Province or ISWAP); continued conducting attacks and maintained a limited safehaven in northeast Nigeria into 2021; was engaged in fighting with ISWAP, as well as the Nigerian military, and suffering heavy casualties in 2021 and 2022; a high number of the group's members had reportedly defected to ISWAP or surrendered to Nigerian security forces, as well as the Multinational Joint Task Force (MNJTF), which is comprised of troops from Benin, Cameroon, Chad, Niger, and Nigeria; between 2009 and 2022, jihadist violence associated with Boko Haram and ISWAP has killed an estimated 40,000 people, mostly civilians, and displaced more than 2 million

goals – establish an Islamic state in Nigeria based on Islamic law
leadership and organization – current leadership not available; Abubakar bin Muhammad SHEKAU led BH from 2009 until his death in May 2021; BH is reportedly a fractious group with a decentralized organizational structure; had a shura council under SHEKAU that commanded the group's regionally based cells/commands; cells/commands operated with some autonomy; also under the shura were departments for logistics, propaganda, training and education, finance, weapons procurement, recruitment, and legal/religious issues
areas of operation – most active in northeastern Nigeria (Borno State); in December 2020, the group claimed the abduction of 300 schoolchildren in the northwestern Nigerian state of Katsina; also operates in northern Cameroon, southeastern Niger, and areas of Chad near Lake Chad; police have arrested suspected Boko Haram members in Chad's capital, N'Djamena
targets, tactics, and weapons – targets tourists and other foreigners (particularly businessmen), wealthy civilians, and government leaders to kidnap for ransom or kill; conducts shootings and suicide bombing attacks against government buildings, military installations, police stations, schools, markets, places of worship and entertainment, and sometimes entire villages; has kidnapped thousands of civilians, including children, many of whom are either forced or indoctrinated into fighting with the group or conducting suicide bombings; some female captives are subjected to forced labor and sexual servitude; conducts an insurgency combining guerrilla warfare and terrorist tactics against military and security forces; uses small arms, light and heavy machine guns, landmines, mortars, rockets, armored vehicles, trucks mounted with machine guns (aka "technicals"), improvised explosive devices, car bombs, and suicide bombings;
strength – unclear; estimated in late 2020 to several thousand fighters
financial and other support – largely self-financed through criminal activities such as looting, extortion, kidnapping-for-ransom, bank robberies, cattle rustling, and assassinations for hire; has seized vehicles, weapons, ammunition, and other supplies from the Nigerian and Nigerien militaries and has acquired other arms from the regional black market
designation – placed on the US Department of State's list of Foreign Terrorist Organizations on 14 November 2013

Communist Party of the Philippines/New People's Army (CPP/NPA)

aka – Communist Party of the Philippines; CPP; New People's Army; NPA; Communist Party of the Philippines-New People's Army-National Democratic Front or CPP-NPA-NDF
history – CPP formed in 1968 and followed in 1969 by the creation of its military wing, the NPA; since 1971, has waged a Maoist-based insurgency and terrorist campaign against the Philippine Government that has resulted in about 40,000 civilian and combatant deaths; from 2016 to 2019, several attempts were made to establish a cease-fire and peace deal between the CPP/NPA and the Philippine Government without success; talks typically broke down when each side accused the other of initiating attacks or violating cease-fires; in 2019 and 2020, the CPP/NPA continued attacks against security forces and civilians; the deadliest was a 2019 offensive in which CPP/NPA used improvised bombs to kill six Philippine troops on Samar Island; Philippine security forces continued to conduct operations against the group into 2022
goals – destabilize the Philippines' economy to inspire the populace to revolt; ultimately wants to overthrow the government and install a Maoist-based regime; opposes the US military and commercial presence in the Philippines
leadership and organization – Jose Maria SISON reportedly directs CPP/NPA activity from the Netherlands, where he lives in self-imposed exile; highest leadership body is its 26-member Central Committee, which reports directly to SISON; organized in "fronts," but operates in cells at the local level; overt political wing is known as the National Democratic Front
areas of operation – operates primarily in rural Luzon, Visayas, and parts of northern and eastern Mindanao but also maintains cells in Manila and other metropolitan areas
targets, tactics, and weapons – targets military and security forces, government officials and facilities, local infrastructure (including power facilities, telecommunication towers, and bridges), foreign enterprises, and businesses that refuse to pay "revolutionary taxes"; follows a Maoist-inspired protracted guerrilla warfare strategy; tactics include ambushes, bombings, assassinations, raids on military and security posts, and kidnapping security personnel; also has attacked plantations, mines, and US personnel and interests; employs small arms, light weapons, grenades, improvised explosive devices, and landmines; has employed city-based assassination squads at times
strength – estimated in 2022 to have less than 4,000 fighters (from a peak of about 25,000 armed members in the late 1980s); retains a significant amount of support from communities in rural areas
financial and other support – raises funds through theft and extortion, including extracting "revolutionary taxes" from local businesses; probably also receives donations from sympathizers in the Philippines, Europe, and elsewhere; arms and ammunition largely stolen or captured from Philippine military and security forces
designation –placed on the US Department of State's list of Foreign Terrorist Organizations on 9 August 2002

Continuity Irish Republican Army (CIRA)

aka – Continuity Army Council; Continuity IRA; Republican Sinn Fein
history – terrorist splinter group that became operational in 1986 as the clandestine armed wing of Republican Sinn Fein, following its split from Sinn Fein; "Continuity" refers to the group's belief that it is carrying on the original goal of the Irish Republican Army (IRA) of forcing the British out of Northern Ireland; rejects ceasefires, weapons decommissioning, and all peace accords, including the Belfast Agreement and the 1998 Good Friday Agreement; cooperates with the larger Real IRA (RIRA), a US-designated terrorist group; in June 2017, released a statement claiming it would disband and decommission some of its arms over the following three months, describing the conflict as a "futile war"; however, during 2019-2021 members of the group claimed several attacks
goals – disrupt the Northern Ireland peace process, remove British rule in Northern Ireland and, ultimately, unify Ireland
leadership and organization – operations are guided by its Irish Continuity Army Council
areas of operation – operates in the UK and the Republic of Ireland
targets, tactics, and weapons – targets the British military, Northern Ireland security forces, and Loyalist paramilitary groups; has carried out bombings, assassinations, hijackings, extortion operations, and robberies; on occasion, has provided advance warning to police of its attacks; members are typically equipped with small arms and explosives
strength – estimated in 2020 to have fewer than 50 members; police counterterrorism operations have reduced the group's strength considerably
financial and other support – receives donations from local and international sympathizers, but the majority of funds are obtained through criminal activity, including bank robberies, extortion, and smuggling
designation – placed on the US Department of State's list of Foreign Terrorist Organizations on 13 July 2004

HAMAS

aka – the Islamic Resistance Movement; Harakat al-Muqawama al-Islamiya; Izz al-Din al Qassam Battalions; Izz al-Din al Qassam Brigades; Izz al-Din al Qassam Forces; Students of Ayyash; Student of the Engineer; Yahya Ayyash Units; Izz al-Din al-Qassim Brigades; Izz al-Din alQassim Forces; Izz al-Din al-Qassim Battalions

history – established in 1987 at the onset of the first Palestinian uprising, or Intifada, as an outgrowth of the Palestinian branch of the Muslim Brotherhood; prior to 2005 conducted numerous attacks against Israel, including more than 50 suicide bombings; in addition to its anti-Israel stance, used a network of *Dawa* or social services that included charities, schools, clinics, youth camps, fundraising, and political activities to help build grassroots support amongst Palestinians in Gaza; won the Palestinian Legislative Council elections in 2006, giving it control of significant Palestinian Authority (PA) ministries in Gaza; expelled the PA and its dominant political faction Fatah in a violent takeover in 2007; since 2007, it has engaged in sporadic rocket attacks, border clashes, organized protests, and periodic targeted attacks against Israeli citizens, including a suicide bombing in 2016; fought significant conflicts with Israel in 2008-2009, 2012, 2014, and 2021, typically involving HAMAS rocket attacks against Israel and Israeli air and artillery counter-strikes on HAMAS targets in Gaza, as well as Israeli military ground incursions; remained the de facto ruler of Gaza and continued to have clashes with Israeli security forces in 2022
goals – maintain control of the Gaza Strip to facilitate Palestinian nationalist aims
leadership and organization – Ismail HANIYEH is the senior political leader; has a shura council as its central consultative body; has smaller shura/executive committees to supervise political activities, military operations, social services, finances, and media relations; military wing (the 'Izz al-Din al-Qassam Brigades) organized into approximately six "brigades" and various paramilitary units; Al-Aqsa TV is the group's primary media outlet
areas of operation – has controlled Gaza since 2007 and has a presence in the West Bank; also has a presence in the Palestinian refugee camps in Lebanon and key regional capitals
targets, tactics, and weapons – targets Israeli military forces and civilians, as well as Islamic State and other Salafist armed group members based in Gaza; has conducted suicide bombings (carried out a suicide attack on a bus in Jerusalem in 2016 that killed 20 people), improvised explosive attacks, shootings, and rocket launches; weapons include small arms, light and heavy machine guns, rockets (some with ranges of up to 200kms), mortars, rocket-propelled grenades, man-portable air defense systems, anti-tank missiles, unmanned aerial vehicles, and improvised explosive devices (IEDs), including balloons armed with IEDs or designed to start fires
strength – estimated in 2021 to have up to 25,000 fighters
financial and other support – receives funding, weapons, and training from Iran and procures additional weapons from the regional black market; also raises funds in Gulf countries and receives donations from Palestinian expatriates, as well as through its own charity organizations; weapons and other military support often supplied through tunnels under the border with Sinai and/or through maritime smuggling routes; trains with Palestine Islamic Jihad and other Palestinian militant groups
designation – placed on the US Department of State's list of Foreign Terrorist Organizations on 8 October 1997

Haqqani Network (HQN)
aka – Haqqani Taliban Network, Afghanistan Mujahidin
history – formed in the late 1980s during the then-Soviet Union's occupation of Afghanistan; founder, Jalaluddin HAQQANI, established a relationship with Usama BIN LADIN in the mid-1980s and joined the Taliban in 1995; helped the Taliban capture the capital, Kabul, in 1996; after the fall of the Taliban to US and allied forces in 2001, HAQQANI retreated to Pakistan where, under the leadership of his son, Sirajuddin HAQQANI (Jalaluddin HAQQANI reportedly died in 2018), continued to conduct an insurgency in Afghanistan against the Afghan Government and its security forces, Afghan civilians, and foreign military forces; insurgency continued until the collapse of the Afghan Government in August 2021; semi-autonomous component of the Afghan Taliban and a close ally of al-Qa'ida; cooperates with other regional terrorist groups, including the Islamic Movement of Uzbekistan and Lashkar e-Tayyiba; following the Taliban takeover of Afghanistan, it secured control of the de facto ministries of interior, intelligence, and immigration and largely controlled the country's internal security
goals – prior to August 2021, expel foreign military forces from Afghanistan and replace the Afghan Government with an Islamic state operating according to a strict Salafi Muslim interpretation of sharia under the Afghan Taliban
leadership and organization – operational commander is Sirajuddin HAQQANI, who leads the group through its Peshawar Shura, which features both military and political wings and consists of Haqqani family members along with veteran commanders trusted by the family; during the insurgency, it operated under Taliban command and control but maintained significant autonomy and regional influence in its area of operations in southeast Afghanistan; beginning in 2015, HAQQANI was the deputy leader of the Afghan Taliban, and as of 2022 was the de facto interior minister for the Taliban government
areas of operation – prior to August 2021, was active along the Afghanistan-Pakistan border and across much of southeastern Afghanistan, particularly in Loya Paktia; repeatedly demonstrated ability to attack Kabul; leadership historically maintained a power base around Pakistan's tribal areas and a presence in Pakistan's settled areas
targets, tactics, and weapons – employed insurgency-type tactics, including coordinated small-arms assaults coupled with the use of mortars and rockets, rocket-propelled grenades, improvised explosive devices, suicide attacks, and car/truck bombs; also targeted the Afghan Government, civilians, and foreigners with kidnappings, bombings, and suicide attacks; attacked government buildings, hotels, embassies, markets, and schools; conducted some of Afghanistan's most deadly bombings, including truck bomb attacks in Kabul in 2017 and 2018 that killed more than 250 civilians; in 2019, conducted multiple attacks in Kabul that killed 100 people and injured more than 500; equipped with small arms, light and heavy machine guns, mortars, rockets, rocket-propelled grenades, and improvised explosive devices
strength – estimated in 2022 to oversee up to 10,000 fighters; numbers likely fluctuate based on time of year and battlefield operations
financial and other support – in addition to the funding it received as part of the broader Afghan Taliban, received some assistance from donors in Pakistan and the Gulf; most funds are from taxing local commerce, extortion, smuggling, kidnapping-for-ransom, and other licit and illicit business ventures; recruits, trains, raises funds, resupplies, and plans operations in the tribal areas of Pakistan; reportedly receives weapons smuggled in from Iran and Pakistan
designation – placed on the US Department of State's list of Foreign Terrorist Organizations on 19 September 2012

Harakat Sawa'd Misr (HASM)
aka – HASM Movement; Arms of Egypt Movement; HASSAM; HASAM; Harakah Sawa'id Misr; Movement of Egypt's Arms
history – formed in 2015; the group is in part composed of alienated Muslim Brotherhood (MB) members who view violence rather than dialogue as a more effective means to overthrow the Egyptian Government and operate independent of MB; in 2016, the group claimed responsibility for the assassination of a senior Egyptian security official, as well as the attempted assassination of Egypt's former Grand Mufti; following a January 2017 shootout with Egyptian security forces in Cairo, HASM declared a jihad against the Egyptian Government; later in 2017, it claimed an ambush attack that killed more than 50 Egyptian security forces and an attack on Burma's embassy in Cairo; in January 2019, it conducted a car bomb attack targeting security forces in Giza, which it claimed killed or wounded 10 soldiers; in August of the same year, it was held responsible (but denied responsibility) for a car bomb attack on a government health institute in Cairo, killing at least 20 people and injuring dozens; continued to be active in 2022
goals – overthrow the Egyptian Government and replace it with an Islamic regime

leadership and organization – Yahya al-Sayyid Ibrahim MUSA and Alaa Ali Mohammed al-SAMAHI (both based in Turkey); organization is not available, but probably operates in small, loosely connected cells and networks
areas of operation – Egypt (some leaders in Turkey)
targets, tactics, and weapons – primarily Egyptian security officials and other government-affiliated targets; typical attacks include ambushes, shootings, and bombings, including car bombings; employs improvised explosive devices and small arms
strength – not available
financial and other support – not available
designation – placed on the US Department of State's list of Foreign Terrorist Organizations on 14 January 2021

Harakat ul-Jihad-i-Islami (HUJI)
aka – Movement of Islamic Holy War; Harkat-ul-Jihad-al Islami; Harkat-al-Jihad-ul Islami; Harkat-ul-Jehad-al-Islami; Harakat ul Jihad-e-Islami; Harakat-ul Jihad Islami
history – formed in 1980 in Afghanistan to fight against the former Soviet Union; following the Soviet withdrawal in 1989, redirected its efforts to the cause of Muslims in the Indian state of Jammu and Kashmir; also has supplied fighters to the Taliban in Afghanistan to fight Afghan, Coalition, and US forces; has experienced internal splits, and a portion of the group aligned with al-Qa'ida; largely inactive and has not publicly claimed any attacks since 2015; status unclear in 2021
goals – annexation of the state of Jammu and Kashmir into Pakistan, expulsion of foreign forces from Afghanistan, and establishment of Islamic rule in Afghanistan, India, and Pakistan
leadership and organization – leadership not available; former leader, Qari Saifullah AKHTAR, killed by Afghan security services in 2017; organization not available, although it has an affiliated branch in Bangladesh and reportedly another one in Burma
areas of operation – historically extended throughout South Asia with operations focused on Afghanistan, India, and Pakistan
targets, tactics, and weapons – targeted Pakistani military, security, and police personnel, as well as Indian security forces in the Kashmir region and Indian Government officials; also targeted Hindu and Western civilians; most significant attack was the bombing of the New Delhi High Court in 2011, which killed 11 people and injured 76; claimed the bombing was intended to force India to repeal the death sentence of a HUJI member; attacks typically involved the use of small arms, grenades, and improvised explosive devices
strength – not available
financial and other support – not available
designation – placed on the US Department of State's list of Foreign Terrorist Organizations on 6 August 2010

Harakat ul-Jihad-i-Islami/Bangladesh (HUJI-B)
aka – Harakat ul Jihad e Islami Bangladesh; Harkatul Jihad al Islam; Harkatul Jihad; Harakat ul Jihad al Islami; Harkat ul Jihad al Islami; Harkat-ul-Jehad-al-Islami; Harakat ul Jihad Islami Bangladesh; Islami Dawat-e-Kafela; IDEK
history – formed in 1992 by a group of former Bangladeshi Afghan veterans wanting to establish Islamist rule in Bangladesh; HUJI-B leaders signed the February 1998 *fatwa* sponsored by Usama BIN LADEN that declared US civilians legitimate targets; in October 2005, Bangladeshi authorities banned the group; has connections to al-Qa'ida and Pakistani terrorist groups advocating similar objectives, including HUJI and Lashkar e-Tayyiba; activities have waned in recent years, but remained active through 2021
goals – install an Islamic state in Bangladesh; draws inspiration from al-Qaida and the Afghan Taliban

leadership and organization – leadership unclear; Bangladeshi authorities executed former leader Mufti Abdul HANNAN and two of his associates in 2017 for a 2004 grenade attack on the British High Commissioner in Sylhet, Bangladesh; most of HUJI-B's other leadership have been in Bangladeshi custody for years
areas of operation – headquartered in Bangladesh and mostly active in the southeast; maintains a network of madrassas and training camps in Bangladesh; also active in India; members have reportedly fought in Burma
targets, tactics, and weapons – conducts low-level bombing attacks against Bangladeshi officials and Westerners; also targets activists, bloggers, academics, religious minorities, and political rallies; most lethal attack occurred in 2004, when operatives lobbed grenades during a political rally in Dhaka, killing 24 and injuring about 400 others; attackers typically use small arms, hand grenades, and various explosives, including petrol bombs and improvised explosive devices
strength – not available
financial and other support – garners donations from sympathetic individuals and organizations; probably also garners funds from criminal activities, including piracy, smuggling, and arms running
designation – placed on the US Department of State's list of Foreign Terrorist Organizations on 5 March 2008

Harakat ul-Mujahidin (HUM)
aka – Harakat ul-Ansar; HUA; Jamiat ul-Ansar; JUA; al-Faran; al-Hadid; al-Hadith; Harakat ul-Mujahidin; Ansar ul Ummah
history – formed in 1985 under Maulana Fazlur Rahman KHALIL in the Pakistani state of Punjab as an anti-Soviet jihadist group that splintered from Harakat ul-Jihad-i-Islami (HUJI); operated terrorist training camps in eastern Afghanistan until US air strikes destroyed them in 2001; a significant portion of the group defected to Jaysh-e-Mohammed after 2000; in 2003, began using the name Jamiat ul-Ansar; Pakistan banned the group the same year; has long been an ally of al-Qa'ida and has links to other terrorist groups in the region, including Lashkar-e-Taiba, Jaish-e-Muhammad, and Lashkar-e-Jhangvi; activities have waned in recent years; status as of late 2020 unclear; has not claimed responsibility for any attacks since 2018
goals – annex the Indian Union Territory of Jammu and Kashmir into Pakistan
leadership and organization – Dr. Badr MUNIR has led the group since 2005; organization unavailable
areas of operation – operates primarily in Afghanistan and in the Indian state of Jammu and Kashmir; also operates in Muzaffarabad in Pakistan-administered Azad Kashmir and in other cities in Pakistan
targets, tactics, and weapons – conducted numerous attacks against Indian troops, government officials, and civilians in the state of Jammu and Kashmir, as well as in India's northeastern states, especially between 2005 and 2013; also attacked Western targets, such as the 2002 suicide car bombing of a bus carrying French workers in Karachi, Pakistan, that killed 15 and wounded 20; uses various attack methods, including suicide bombings, airplane hijackings, kidnappings, and assassinations; typically used small arms, grenades, and improvised explosive devices
strength – estimated in 2020 to have only a small number of cadres active
financial and other support – receives donations from wealthy supporters in Pakistan
designation – placed on the US Department of State's list of Foreign Terrorist Organizations on 8 October 1997

Hizballah

aka – the Party of God; Hezbollah; Islamic Jihad; Islamic Jihad Organization; Revolutionary Justice Organization; Organization of the Oppressed on Earth; Islamic Jihad for the Liberation of Palestine; Organization of Right Against Wrong; Ansar Allah; Followers of the Prophet Muhammed; Lebanese Hizballah; Lebanese Hezbollah; LH; Foreign Relations Department; External Security Organization; Foreign Action Unit; Hizballah International; Special Operations Branch; External Services Organization; External Security Organization of Hezbollah

history – formed in 1982 following the Israeli invasion of Lebanon as a Shia militant group that takes its ideological inspiration from the Iranian revolution and the teachings of the late Ayatollah KHOMEINI; generally follows the religious guidance of the Iranian Supreme Leader, which since 1989 has been Ali Hoseini-KHAMENEI; closely allied with Iran and the two often work together on shared initiatives, although Hizballah also acts independently in some cases; shares a close relationship with the Syrian ASAD regime and has provided assistance – including thousands of fighters – to regime forces in the Syrian civil war; since the early 1990s, has evolved into a business and political enterprise and become a state within a state in Lebanon with strong influence in Lebanon's Shia community; actively participates in Lebanon's political system and runs social programs, such as hospitals and schools; has seats in Lebanon's parliament and has had members appointed to the Lebanese Government's ministries; military capabilities continue to expand and have the characteristics of both a paramilitary and a conventional military force; fought a month-long war with Israel in 2006 and continues to prepare for large-scale conflict with Israel; also continues to conduct direct attacks on Israel, including firing anti-tank missiles at an army base and vehicles near the border in 2019; in 2020-2022, Israel conducted multiple air strikes on Hizballah facilities in Lebanon and Syria, while Hizballah claimed responsibility for shooting down an Israel unmanned aerial vehicle (UAV) and pledged to respond to Israeli air raids; the group remained active and continued its military build up into 2022

goals – accrue military resources and political power and defend its position of strength in Lebanon; wants to expel Western influence from Lebanon and the greater Middle East, destroy the state of Israel, and establish Islamic rule in Lebanon and the Palestinian territories

leadership and organization – led by Secretary General Shaykh Sayyid Hasan NASRALLAH since 1992; NASRALLAH leads with two deputies through a 7-seat Shura Council; the Council has five subordinate specialized assemblies: the Executive, Judicial, Parliamentary, Political, and Jihad Councils; each assembly oversees several sub-entities that handle Hizballah's affairs in various sectors; for example, the Jihad/Military council reportedly has 2 wings, the Islamic Resistance (combat operations) and the Security Organ (external and internal security operations): Islamic Resistance includes up to 4 territorial commands and at least 6 infantry, rocket/artillery, amphibious/coastal defense, and commando/special forces (Unit 1800) sub-units, plus multiple Lebanese militia (or "resistance") "brigades" which serve as auxiliary forces; the Security Organ has 2 sub-branches: Islamic Jihad Organization (External Security Organization, aka Unit 910) for external operations, including the group's international terrorist operations, recruitment, fundraising, intelligence gathering, and support to Shia militias abroad; the Party Security Organ is responsible for internal security; has a youth movement called the al-Mahdi Scouts

areas of operation – headquartered in the southern suburbs of Beirut with a significant presence in the Bekaa Valley and southern Lebanon; however, operates around the world, and operatives and financiers have been arrested or detained in Africa, Asia, Europe, the Middle East, South America, and North America; deployed thousands of fighters to support the ASAD Government during the Syrian civil war; in 2018, NASRALLAH declared the group would remain in Syria indefinitely with the ASAD Government's permission and as of 2022 maintained a presence

targets, tactics, and weapons – targets include: Israeli security forces and civilians; Jews; US and Western military forces and other symbols of American/Western influence in the Middle East; entities in Syria combatting the ASAD regime, particularly Islamic State and al-Qa'ida affiliated forces; historically used a variety of guerrilla-style hit-and-run and terrorist tactics, particularly kidnappings and suicide vehicle bombings; some of its most devastating attacks involved the use of car/truck bombs, such as the 1983 attacks on the US Embassy, the US Marine barracks, and a French military base in Beirut, which killed over 300 civilians and military personnel; has conducted attacks on Israeli and Jewish targets abroad, including the 1992 bombing of the Israeli Embassy in Argentina and the 1994 suicide bombing of a Jewish community center in Argentina, which killed more than 100 and wounded more than 500 others; since the 2000s, has developed elements of a more traditional conventional military force and demonstrated considerable military capabilities in the 2006 conflict with Israel and during the Syrian civil war; forces are equipped with small arms, light and heavy machineguns, mortars, landmines, improvised explosive devises, artillery, armored combat vehicles, rockets, antiaircraft guns, ballistic missiles, anti-ship cruise missiles, armed unmanned aerial vehicles, man-portable air defense systems, and antitank guided missiles; as of 2021, the group had as many as 150,000 missiles and rockets, including some with ranges of hundreds of kilometers

strength – has tens of thousands of supporters and members worldwide; in 2021, it was estimated to have up to 45,000 fighters, divided between some 20,000 full-time and 25,000 reserve personnel; in 2021, NASRALLAH claimed the group had 100,000 trained fighters

financial and other support – receives most of its funding, training, and weapons, as well as political, diplomatic, and organizational aid, from Iran; in 2019, funding from Iran was estimated at more than $700 million per year, although economic sanctions since 2020 may have constrained Iran's ability to finance the group; Syria also furnishes training, weapons, and diplomatic and political support; has developed a network of training camps in Lebanon and runs most of its own military training; receives additional funding in the form of legal businesses, international criminal enterprises (including smuggling, narcotics trafficking, and money laundering), and donations from the Shia in Lebanon and Lebanese diaspora communities worldwide

designation – placed on the US Department of State's list of Foreign Terrorist Organizations on 8 October 1997

Hizbul Mujahideen (HM)

aka – Hizb-ul-Mujahideen; Party of Mujahideen; Party of Holy Warriors

history – formed in 1989 and is one of the largest and oldest militant separatist groups fighting against Indian rule in the state of Jammu and Kashmir; reportedly operated in Afghanistan through the mid-1990s and trained alongside the Afghan Hizb-e-Islami Gulbuddin until the Taliban takeover; made up primarily of ethnic Kashmiris and has conducted operations jointly with other Kashmiri militant groups; active in 2022

goals – supports the liberation of the territory of Jammu and Kashmir from Indian control and its accession to Pakistan, although some cadres are pro-independence

leadership and organization – led by Syed SALAHUDDIN (aka Mohammad Yusuf SHAH); reportedly organized in five regionally-based divisions; probably operates in small loosely connected networks and cells

areas of operation – headquartered in Pakistan but conducts operations primarily in India, particularly the Indian Union Territory of Jammu and Kashmir

targets, tactics, and weapons – focuses attacks on Indian security forces and politicians in the state of Jammu and Kashmir; most attacks involved small arms and grenades, although it has also utilized improvised explosive devices, including vehicle-mounted

strength – specific numbers not available, but information from 2020 suggested a cadre of up to 1,500 fighters

financial and other support – specific sources of support are not clear, but probably originate in Pakistan, as well as from local fundraising

designation – placed on the US Department of State's list of Foreign Terrorist Organizations on 17 August 2017

Hurras al-Din

aka – Tanzim Hurras al-Din; Tandhim Hurras al-Din; Hurras al-Deen; Houras al-Din; HAD; al-Qa'ida in Syria; Guardians of the Religion Organization; Sham al-Ribat

history – publicly announced itself in February 2018 as an al-Qa'ida affiliate after its members broke away from al-Nusrah Front (subsequently rebranded as Hayat Tahrir al-Sham, or HTS) because HTS publicly cut ties with al-Qa'ida; maintains allied or cooperative relationships with several extremist elements in Syria, including Jamaat Ansar al-Islam, the Turkestan Islamic Party (TIP), Sham al-Islam, and Ansar al-Tawhid; viewed as the leading force behind the "Incite the Believers" jihadist alliance in Syria, which conducts battlefield operations against Syrian Government forces in northern Syria; since 2020, has had a tense relationship HTS/al-Nusrah Front, which as of 2022 controlled Syria's northwestern province of Iblib, that has involved assassinations, open clashes, competition for recruits, and arrests of its members by HTS; as of 2022, remained active, but had been weakened by internal divisions and leadership losses and was overshadowed by HTS; rejected the March 2020 Russian-Turkish ceasefire agreement in Idlib and has attacked Turkish forces and conducted attacks in Turkish-controlled areas; in 2021, it attacked a Russian military base in eastern Raqqa province and a conducted a bombing attack against Syrian military forces in Damascus
goals – oust Syrian President Bashar al-ASAD's regime and replace it with a Sunni Islamic State; likely adheres to al-Qa'ida's chief objectives of neutralizing Israeli and US influence within the Middle East, specifically within the Levant
leadership and organization – led by Syrian jihadist Samir HIJAZI (aka Abu Hamamm al-Shami, Faruq al-Suri, Mohammed Abu Khalid al-Suri), who previously served as a top military commander in al-Nusrah Front and worked as a trainer in al-Qa'ida's camps in Afghanistan in the early 2000s; a number of veteran jihadists who defected from al-Nusrah Front or joined from other jihadist groups across the Levant serve in the group's leadership apparatus or provide support to the group's goals; has a shura council; as of 2020, was comprised of at least 16 jihadist factions; sub-structure unknown, but probably organized into cells and "battalions"
areas of operation – headquartered in Syria's Idlib Province in the northwest; also operationally active in the Syrian provinces of Latakia, Hama, and Raqqa
targets, tactics, and weapons – primarily attacks Syrian Government and pro-regime forces; has also conducted armed assaults against Turkish and Russian military forces active in Syria; potentially responsible for the kidnapping of aid workers in northwestern Syria; has encouraged violent attacks against Israeli and Western targets in its propaganda releases; has conducted assassinations and car bombings; armed largely with small arms and light weapons, including mortars, machine guns, and trucks mounting machine guns (aka "technicals")
strength – estimated in 2022 to have 1,000-3,000 fighters
financial and other support – appeals for donations under the auspices of supporting its efforts against the Syrian Government; leverages social media platforms to call for financial assistance, public support, and recruits; active in training operatives at a number of unspecified training camps in Syria
designation – placed on the US Department of State's list of Foreign Terrorist Organizations on 5 September 2019

Indian Mujahedeen (IM)
aka – Indian Mujahidin; Islamic Security Force-Indian Mujahideen (ISF-IM)
history – formed as an ultra-conservative Islamic movement circa 2004 from remnants of the radical youth organization Students Islamic Movement of India; responsible for dozens of bomb attacks throughout India since 2005 and the deaths of hundreds of civilians; maintains ties to other terrorist entities including Pakistan-based Lashkar e-Tayyiba, Jaish-e-Mohammed, and Harakat ul-Jihad Islami; outlawed in India in 2010; by 2016, was increasingly linked to the Islamic State of Iraq and ash-Sham (ISIS); that year, six IM operatives were identified in an ISIS propaganda video threatening attacks on India, and an IM cell linked to ISIS was reportedly plotting attacks on multiple targets in India; Indian authorities claimed they disrupted bombing plots by the group in 2015 and 2017 and have apprehended dozens of suspected IM operatives; did not publicly claim any attacks through 2020
goals – establish Islamic rule in India; stated goal is to carry out terrorist operations against Indians for their perceived oppression of Muslims
leadership and organization – unclear; reportedly Mohammed Riyaz BHATKA; Indian security services have captured or killed a number of alleged leaders of the group, including co-founder Yasin BHATKAL, who was arrested in 2018; organization not available but probably operates in small, loosely connected networks and cells
areas of operation – has conducted attacks throughout India since 2005; reportedly also operates in Nepal and Pakistan
targets, tactics, and weapons – known for carrying out multiple coordinated bombings in crowded areas against Indian and Western civilian and economic targets, including restaurants and commercial centers; in 2008, was responsible for 16 synchronized bomb blasts in crowded urban centers, including an attack in Delhi that killed 30 people and an attack at a local hospital in Ahmedabad that killed 38 (note - in 2022, an Indian court sentenced 38 individuals to death for the attack in Aghmedabad); in 2010, bombed a popular German bakery frequented by tourists in Pune, India, killing 17 and wounding more than 60 people; attackers typically use improvised explosive devices
strength – not available
financial and other support – probably receives funding and support from other terrorist organizations, as well as from unspecified donors in Pakistan and the Middle East
designation – placed on the US Department of State's list of Foreign Terrorist Organizations on 19 September 2011

Islamic Jihad Union (IJU)
aka – Islamic Jihad Group; IJG; Islomiy Jihod Ittihodi; al-Djihad al-Islami; Dzhamaat Modzhakhedov; Islamic Jihad Group of Uzbekistan; Jamiat al-Jihad al-Islami; Jamiyat; The Jamaat Mojahedin; The Kazakh Jama'at; The Libyan Society
history – emerged in 2002 as a splinter movement of the Islamic Movement of Uzbekistan (IMU) after internal splits over goals; originally known as the Islamic Jihad Group but was renamed Islamic Jihad Union in 2005; committed to overthrowing the government of Uzbekistan, but has been active in other areas outside Central Asia, particularly Afghanistan, but also Pakistan, Syria, and Europe; pledged allegiance to the Afghan Taliban in August 2015 and participated in Taliban attacks on the Afghan city of Kunduz, as well as Afghan military bases; was active in Afghanistan in 2022; participated in the Syrian conflict as part of a coalition of al-Qa'ida-linked terrorist groups
goals – overthrow the Uzbek government and replace it with an Islamic state; support al-Qa'ida's overall goals, including efforts to create an Islamic State in Syria
leadership and organization – Ilimbek MAMATOV; probably operates in a loose network of cells
areas of operation – most active in Afghanistan; has also been active in Syria, parts of Europe, Pakistan, Uzbekistan, and other areas of Central Asia
targets, tactics, and weapons – targets international and Afghan military and security forces in Afghanistan and Syrian regime forces using a variety of guerrilla warfare and terrorist tactics; has attacked security checkpoints, law enforcement facilities, market places, and foreign embassies in Uzbekistan, often with suicide bombers; in 2007, an IJU cell in Germany (known as the "Sauerland Cell") attempted to construct and detonate a series of car bombs to carry out a mass attack, but the militants were arrested before they could carry out the attack and were ultimately convicted; fighters are armed with small arms, light and heavy machine guns, rocket-propelled grenades, antiaircraft weapons, and various explosives including improvised explosive devices and car bombs
strength – estimated in 2021 to have 100-200 members in Afghanistan, but reportedly has strengthened since the fall of the Afghan Government in August 2021

financial and other support – specific sources of support are not available but probably receives assistance from allied terrorist groups and sympathetic donors
designation – placed on the US Department of State's list of Foreign Terrorist Organizations on 17 June 2005

Islamic Movement of Uzbekistan (IMU)
aka – Islamic Party of Uzbekistan; Islamskaia partiia Turkestana;, byvshee Islamskoe dvizhenie Uzbekistana; Islamic Movement of Turkistan
history – formed in the early 1990s as a Sunni Muslim armed group in Uzbekistan's part of the Ferghana Valley, where the Uzbek, Kyrgyz, and Tajik borders converge; moved to Pakistan after the US-led invasion of Afghanistan in 2001; operated primarily along the Afghanistan-Pakistan border and in northern Afghanistan, where it fought against international forces despite its goal of setting up an Islamic state in Uzbekistan; was allied to al-Qa'ida, the Afghan Taliban, and Tehrik-i-Taliban Pakistan, and frequently conducted joint operations with those organizations; in 2011, some fighters broke off to fight separately alongside the Taliban against the Afghan Government under the name Khatiba Imam al-Bukhari, which had fighters in both Afghanistan and Syria as of 2022; in 2015, a significant faction, including the IMU's top leadership, pledged loyalty to the Islamic State of Iraq and ash-Sham (ISIS) and began cooperating with ISIS-Khorasan (ISIS-K); numerous IMU members, including its leader, were subsequently reported to have been killed in clashes with their former Taliban allies; operational tempo has decreased in recent years, but the group was active in Afghanistan in 2022
goals – overthrow the Uzbek Government and establish an Islamic state
leadership and organization – not available; former leader Abdulaziz YULDASH killed in November 2020 in northern Afghanistan; probably structured as a network of cells
areas of operation – operates primarily along the Afghanistan-Pakistan border and in northern Afghanistan; also active in Syria, Central Asia, and Turkey
targets, tactics, and weapons – targeted military and security forces and government facilities using guerrilla warfare and terrorist tactics, including ambushes, assassinations, ground assaults, indirect fire attacks, kidnappings, and suicide bombings; in 2010 the IMU claimed responsibility for an ambush that killed 25 Tajik troops in Tajikistan; in 2014, it claimed responsibility for an attack on Karachi's international airport that resulted in the deaths of at least 39 people, as well as a 2012 attack on a Pakistani prison that freed nearly 400 prisoners (both attacks conducted jointly with the Tehrik-i-Taliban Pakistan terrorist group); also has attacked government and allied foreign military forces in Afghanistan, as well as security forces in Pakistan; typically used small arms and light weapons, mortars, rockets, and various explosives, including car bombs and suicide vests
strength – unclear; reportedly about 700 in 2021, including family members
financial and other support – receives support from a large Uzbek diaspora, allied terrorist organizations, and sympathizers from Europe, Central and South Asia, and the Middle East; also engages in narcotics trafficking and conducts kidnappings for ransom
designation – placed on the US Department of State's list of Foreign Terrorist Organizations on 25 September 2000

Islamic Revolutionary Guard Corps (IRGC)/Qods Force
aka – Islamic Revolutionary Guards, Pasdaran (Guards), Revolutionary Guards, Sepah (Corps), Sepah-e Pasdaran-e Enghelab-e Eslami; Quds ("Jerusalem") Force
history – formed in May 1979 in the immediate aftermath of Shah Mohammad Reza PAHLAVI's fall, as leftists, nationalists, and Islamists jockeyed for power; while the interim prime minister controlled the government and state institutions, such as the army, followers of Ayatollah Ruhollah KHOMEINI organized counterweights, including the IRGC, to protect the Islamic revolution; the IRGC's command structure bypassed the elected president and went directly to KHOMEINI; the Iran-Iraq War (1980–88) transformed the IRGC into more of a conventional fighting force with its own ground, air, naval, and special forces, plus control over Iran's strategic missile and rocket forces; the IRGC is highly institutionalized and a parallel military force to Iran's regular armed forces (Artesh); as of 2022, it continued to be heavily involved in internal security and have significant influence in the political and economic spheres of Iranian society, as well as Iran's foreign policy; its special operations forces are known as the Qods Force which specializes in foreign missions, providing advice, funding, guidance, material support, training, and weapons to militants in countries such as Afghanistan, Iraq, Syria, and Yemen, as well as extremist groups, including HAMAS, Hizballah, Kata'ib Hizballah, and Palestine Islamic Jihad
goals – protect Iran's Islamic revolution and the state; spread Iranian/Shia influence; provide internal security, including border control, law enforcement, and suppressing domestic opposition; influence Iran's politics, economy, and foreign policy
leadership and organization – General Hossein SALAMI is the commander of the IRGC; Brigadier General Ismail QAANI is the commander of the Qods Force; organized along the lines of a traditional conventional military force with Ground Forces, Navy (includes marines), Aerospace Force (includes the strategic missile forces), Cyber Command, Qods Force (special operations), and Basij Paramilitary Forces (aka Popular Mobilization Army); the Qods Force is reportedly divided into branches focusing on intelligence/espionage, finance, politics, sabotage, and special operations, as well as at least 8 regionally-focused directorates
areas of operation – headquartered in Tehran; active throughout Iran and the Middle East region, as well as Afghanistan, Gaza, Iraq, Lebanon, Syria, and Yemen; has a worldwide capability to commit attacks if Iranian leadership deems it appropriate; in recent years, Qods Force planning for terror attacks has been uncovered and disrupted in a number of countries worldwide, including Albania, Bahrain, Belgium, Bosnia, Bulgaria, Denmark, France, Germany, Kenya, Turkey, and the United States
targets, tactics, and weapons – targets Israel, Sunni regimes perceived as a threat (particularly Saudi Arabia), the Islamic State (ISIS), US military forces in the Middle East, Iranian dissidents; has the capability to fight conventionally and conduct a wide-range of terrorist-type attacks; also makes extensive use of proxy and partner forces such as Hizballah; provides a wide range of arms to proxy/partner forces, including small arms, rockets, and armed unmanned aerial vehicles; armed as a conventional military with typical ground, air, and naval platforms and weapons
strength – estimates vary; assessed in 2021 to be approximately 125-190,000, including the Qods Force, whose estimated size ranges from 5,000-15,000; also controls the 90,000-member Basij Paramilitary Force, which augments internal security, suppresses domestic opposition, and can increase to several hundred thousand during a major mobilization
financial and other support – receives a portion of the Iranian defense budget, by some estimates as much as 50%; IRGC-linked companies control up to 20% of Iran's economy; Qods Force also exerts control over strategic industries, commercial services, and black-market enterprises, and has engaged in large-scale illicit finance schemes and money laundering
designation – placed on the US Department of State's list of Foreign Terrorist Organizations on 15 April 2019

Islamic State of Iraq and ash-Sham (ISIS)
aka – al-Qa'ida in Iraq; al-Qa'ida Group of Jihad in Iraq; al-Qa'ida Group of Jihad in the Land of the Two Rivers; al-Qa'ida in Mesopotamia; al-Qa'ida in the Land of the Two Rivers; al-Qa'ida of Jihad in Iraq; al-Qa'ida of Jihad Organization in the Land of the Two Rivers; al-Qa'ida of the Jihad in the Land of the Two Rivers; al-Tawhid; Jam'at al-Tawhid Wa'al-Jihad; Tanzeem Qa'idat al Jihad/Bilad al Raafidaini; Tanzim Qa'idat al-Jihad fi Bilad al-Rafidayn; The Monotheism and Jihad Group; The Organization Base of Jihad/Country of the Two Rivers; The Organization Base of Jihad/Mesopotamia; The Organization of al-Jihad's Base in Iraq; The Organization of al-Jihad's Base in the Land of the Two Rivers; The

Organization of al-Jihad's Base of Operations in Iraq; The Organization of al-Jihad's Base of Operations in the Land of the Two Rivers; The Organization of Jihad's Base in the Country of the Two Rivers; al-Zarqawi Network; Islamic State of Iraq; Islamic State of Iraq and al-Sham; Islamic State of Iraq and Syria; ad-Dawla al-Islamiyya fi al-'Iraq wa-sh-Sham; Daesh; Dawla al Islamiya; Al-Furqan Establishment for Media Production; Islamic State; ISIL; ISIS; Amaq News Agency; Al Hayat Media Center; Al-Hayat Media Center; Al Hayat
history – formed in the 1990s under the name al-Tawhid wal-Jihad by Jordanian militant Abu Mus'ab al-ZARQAWI to oppose the presence of Western military forces in the Middle East and the West's support for, and the existence of, Israel; in late 2004, ZARQAWI pledged allegiance to al-Qa'ida (AQ) and the group became known as al-Qa'ida in Iraq (AQI); ZARQAWI led AQI against US and Coalition Forces in Iraq until his death in June 2006; in October 2006, renamed itself the Islamic State in Iraq; in 2013, adopted the moniker ISIS to express regional ambitions and expanded operations to Syria where it established control of a large portion of eastern Syria; in June 2014, then ISIS leader Abu Bakr al-BAGHDADI declared a worldwide Islamic caliphate with its capital in Raqqa, Syria; by 2015, held an area in Iraq and Syria with an estimated population of between 8 and 12 million, including the Iraqi city of Mosul; imposed a brutal version of Islamic law in the areas under its control and became known for brutality against perceived enemies, including the murder of large numbers of civilians, its large contingent of foreign fighters, and a substantial social media presence; by the end of 2017, had lost control of its largest population centers in both Iraq and Syria, including Mosul and Raqqa, to US and allied military forces; lost its final piece of territory in Baghuz, Syria in March 2019; has since transitioned to an insurgency, reverting to guerrilla warfare and more traditional terrorist tactics, developing sleeper cells, and assimilating into the broader population in Iraq and Syria where it continued to maintain a considerable presence and conduct operations as of 2022
goals – replace the world order with a global Islamic state based in Iraq and Syria, expand its branches and networks globally, and rule according to ISIS's strict interpretation of Islamic law; in Iraq and Syria, it seeks to reestablish itself as a viable insurgency that is capable of seizing and controlling territory
leadership and organization – Abu al-Hassan al-Hashemi al-QURASHI (likely a nom de guerre; possibly Juma Awad al-Badri) named leader in 2022 after predecessor killed; the top leader (emir) and a senior shura council determine the group's strategic direction and appoints the heads of provinces (*wilayat*); an "appointed (or delegated) committee" and up to 14 sub-bureaus or offices (*dawawin*) are reportedly charged with administrative duties, including security, finances, religious matters, recruitment, military operations, training and education, media functions, resources and plunder, etc; the group typically operates in small cells or groups of 15 or fewer in Iraq and Syria, but can organize in greater numbers for specific operations; note - when the group held territory, ISIS maintained a highly organized and large bureaucracy to run the so-called caliphate; it had 14 ministries: Judgement and Grievances, Religious Police (*Hisbah*), Preaching (*Da'wah*) and Mosques (*Masajid*), Soldiery, Public Security, Alms, Treasury, Media, Education, Health, Agriculture, Resources, Spoils (*Fay'*), Plunder (*Ghana'im*), and Services; its Soldiery ministry (military force) was organized into small operational divisions with subordinate brigades and battalions
areas of operation – core operations remain predominately in Iraq and Syria; has designated Iraq as a separate province with its own leader; operational in the rural and desert areas of central and northern Iraq, primarily within and near Sunni populations with some presence in major population areas (mostly the provinces of Anbar, Ninewa, Kirkuk, Salah ad Din, and Diyala; maintained safehavens in isolated areas such as the Hamrin Mountains of Kirkuk and the deserts of Anbar); in Syria, it continued to operate mainly in the central desert and across northern and eastern provinces, while top leaders likely remained in the western Idlib governorate; claims named external branches, networks, or *wilayat* (provinces, governorates; claimed in 2022 to have approximately 16 such *wilayats*) in more than 20 countries: Algeria, Azerbaijan, Bangladesh, the Caucasus (Russia), Central Africa (the Democratic Republic of the Congo, Mozambique), East Asia (Philippines, Indonesia), Greater Sahara (tri-border area of Burkina Faso, Mali, Niger), India, Libya, Khorasan (Afghanistan), Pakistan, Palestine (Israel), the Sahel (Mali), Sinai Peninsula (Egypt), Saudi Arabia, Somalia, Tunisia, Turkey, West Africa (northeastern Nigeria, southeastern Niger, northern Cameroon, areas of Chad around Lake Chad), and Yemen; local terrorist groups in other countries, such as Lebanon and Sudan, have pledged allegiance to ISIS; has supporters, sympathizers, and associates worldwide and has inspired or conducted attacks in Australia, Belgium, France, Germany, Iran, Maldives, Russia, Spain, Sri Lanka, Sweden, Tajikistan, Turkey, the UK, and the US; authorities in other countries, including, but not exclusive to, Austria, Brazil, Bulgaria, Canada, Greece, Israel, Italy, Jordan, Lebanon, Malaysia, and the Netherlands have arrested ISIS members or supporters or disrupted plots linked to ISIS (from 2013-2019, ISIS-affiliated groups and individuals mounted more than 3,000 attacks in some 48 countries, other than Iraq and Syria); maintains a strong online presence and continuously calls for attacks against Western countries and their interests around the world; individuals inspired by its ideology may conduct operations without direction from the ISIS's central leadership
targets, tactics, and weapons – targets governments or groups that oppose its hardline Islamist ideology, including military forces and security services, government officials, perceived Sunni rivals, Westerners, and religious and ethnic minorities; typically targets security forces in Iraq and Syria, as well as tribal and civic leaders and other symbols of government; has also targeted infrastructure in Iraq, such as electrical towers; known for indiscriminate killings, mass executions, political assassinations, torture, kidnappings, rape and sexual slavery, forced marriages and religious conversions, conscripting children, publishing videos of beheadings, and using civilians as human shields; has engaged in the systematic destruction of antiquities, places of worship, monasteries, and other elements of the cultural heritage of ancient communities; attacks places of worship, shopping centers and markets, tourist sites, hotels, concert venues, restaurants, train stations, nightclubs, government buildings, and infrastructure targets; attacks on civilians typically involve the use of small arms, vehicle bombs, explosive vests, and ramming vehicles into crowds of people; employs insurgent/guerrilla-style hit-and-run and terrorist attacks against military and security forces that include the use of ambushes, snipers, complex ground assaults, mortar and rocket attacks, road side bombs, and suicide devices; possesses a wide variety of weapons, including small arms, light and heavy machine guns, rocket-propelled grenades, mortars, rockets, man-portable air defense systems (MANPADS), anti-tank guided missiles, and a variety of improvised explosive devices, including unmanned aerial vehicles (UAVs) armed with explosives
strength – estimated in 2022 to have 6,000 to 10,000 fighters across Iraq and Syria
note: as of 2022, there were about 10,000 ISIS prisoners in Syrian Democratic Forces prisons, including approximately 2,000 foreign terrorist fighters
financial and other support – raises funds through ad hoc criminal activities, particularly kidnapping for ransom, smuggling, and extortion activities; also receives funds through private donations, crowd-sourcing, online humanitarian appeals, and investments in legitimate businesses; prior to 2019, received virtually of its funding from oil sales, taxation, and selling confiscated goods within areas it controlled in Iraq and Syria; the group currently holds no territory, which has significantly reduced its ability to generate, store, and transfer revenue, but it continues to draw on financial reserves accrued when it controlled territory (estimated in 2020 at more than $100 million); ISIS has armed itself with weapons it has captured, purchased through local arms trafficking networks, and produced on its own; also recruits members, supporters, and sympathizers online through social media platforms
designation – predecessor organization al-Qa'ida in Iraq (AQI) was placed on the US Department of State's list of Foreign Terrorist Organizations on 17 December 2004

Islamic State of Iraq and ash-Sham - East Asia (ISIS-EA) in the Philippines

aka – ISIS in the Philippines (ISIS-P); ISIL Philippines; ISIL in the Philippines; IS Philippines (ISP); Islamic State in the Philippines; Islamic State in Iraq and Syria in Southeast Asia; Dawlah Islamiyah; Dawlatul Islamiyah Waliyatul Masrik; Dawlatul Islamiyah Waliyatul Mashriq; IS East Asia Division; ISIS Branch in the Philippines; ISIS "Philippines province"

history – Islamic militants in the Philippines initially pledged allegiance to ISIS in 2014, however the group officially formed in 2016 with now-deceased leader Isnilon HAPILON as the first amir; ISIS media claimed its first attack in the Philippines against Philippine soldiers on Mindanao Island in March 2016; in May 2017, ISIS-EA and fighters from associated jihadist groups stormed and captured the city of Marawi on Mindanao; five months of subsequent fighting for the city between the militants and the Philippine military resulted in nearly 900 militants and more than 160 Philippine soldiers killed; over 300,000 residents were forced to flee the area during the fighting; in 2018, the group conducted the first ever suicide attack in the Philippines; ISIS-EA has since claimed several additional suicide and other high-profile bombings, including two suicide bombings undertaken by females within one hour of one another in August of 2020 in the capital of Sulu province; remained active in 2022 with low-level attacks and skirmishes, but was under considerable pressure from Philippine security forces
goals – create an Islamic state in the southern Philippines and across Southeast Asia adhering to ISIS's strict interpretation of sharia
leadership and organization – reportedly Jer MIMBANTAS (aka Abu Zacharia, aka Faharudin Hadji Satar); two group leaders have been killed by Philippine security forces since 2020, including Salahuddin HASSAN (October 2021) and Hatib SAWADJAAN (July 2020); ISIS-EA is comprised of a loose network of groups with varying levels of allegiance and ties to ISIS, including the Abu Sayaf Group (ASG), the Maute Group (aka Daulah Islamiyah Fi Ranao, Islamic State of Lanao, Abu Zacaria Group), Ansar al-Khilafah Philippines (AKP), and a faction of the Bangsamoro Islamic Freedom Fighters (BIFF); these groups operate autonomously and maintain their own leaders and organizational structures
areas of operation – mostly in the southern Philippines, especially the Sulu Archipelago and western and central Mindanao; probably maintains a small presence in the capital, Manila
targets, tactics, and weapons – targets Philippine security forces but increasingly targets non-Muslim civilians; has attacked government-related targets, military bases and security checkpoints, churches, internet cafés, resorts, and street festivals; employs insurgent-type tactics, including armed assaults, mortar attacks, suicide bombers, and road-side bombs; weapons include small arms, improvised explosive devices, light and heavy machine guns, rocket-propelled grenades, mortars, and hand grenades
strength – estimated in 2022 to have a few fighters
financial and other support – receives some financial assistance from ISIS-core, but mostly relies on criminal activities such as kidnappings for ransom and extortion; maintains training camps in remote areas under its control and acquires weapons through smuggling and captured or black market purchases of Philippine military arms; estimated to have a few dozen foreign fighters (mostly Indonesians and some Malaysians) who tend to assume key responsibilities such as financial and communications/media facilitators, bomb-makers, trainers, and attack planners/perpetrators; receives some media support from ISIS-core
designation – placed on the US Department of State's list of Foreign Terrorist Organizations on 28 February 2018

Islamic State of Iraq and ash-Sham - Sinai Province (ISIS-SP)
aka – Islamic State-Sinai Province (IS-SP); ISIS-Sinai Province; ISIS-Sinai; ISIL Sinai Province (ISIL-SP); The State of Sinai; Wilayat Sinai; Islamic State in the Sinai; Ansar Bayt al-Maqdes; Ansar Beit al-Maqdis; Jamaat Ansar Beit al-Maqdis; Jamaat Ansar Beit al-Maqdis fi Sinaa; Ansar Jerusalem; Supporters of Jerusalem; Supporters of the Holy Place; Allies of the Holy House
history – began as Ansar Bayt al-Maqdis (ABM), which rose to prominence in 2011 following the uprisings in Egypt; ABM was responsible for attacks against Egyptian and Israeli government and security elements and against tourists in Egypt; in November 2014, ABM officially declared allegiance to ISIS; has since conducted a bloody insurgency against Egyptian security forces under the ISIS banner and become one of the most deadly of the ISIS affiliates; the Egyptian military has deployed more than 40,000 troops to the Sinai to suppress the insurgency; the group continued to conduct attacks into 2022, although the scale of the insurgency had reportedly declined
goals – spread the Islamic caliphate by eliminating the Egyptian government, destroying Israel, and establishing an Islamic emirate in the Sinai
leadership and organization – current leader not available; reportedly has sections or branches for security, military affairs, bomb-making, and media operations
areas of operation – Egypt; operations are conducted primarily in the Sinai Peninsula, but its reach periodically extends to Cairo, the Egyptian Nile Valley, and Gaza
targets, tactics, and weapons – mainly targets Egyptian security forces, particularly checkpoints, convoys, and bases; conducts ambushes, assassinations, complex attacks involving dozens of attackers, car and suicide bombings, kidnappings, public executions, and road side bombings attacks; conducted large armed assaults on a military base in 2018 and on the Egyptian city of Sheikh Zuweid in 2014; both attacks included dozens of fighters with small arms, light and heavy machine guns, rocket-propelled grenades, mortars, car bombs, and suicide bombers; also targets Egyptian Government facilities and officials, oil pipelines and other infrastructure, tourists, religious minorities, government-allied tribes, places of worship, and airliners; two of its most deadly attacks were the 2017 assault by suicide bombers and gunmen on an Egyptian Sufi mosque that killed more than 300 and the 2015 bombing of a Russian airliner from the Egyptian resort town of Sharm el-el-Sheikh, which killed all 231 on board
strength – estimated in 2020 to have between 800 and 1,200 fighters
financial and other support – receives funding from external actors, including core ISIS, and from smuggling; weapons reportedly are smuggled in from Gaza, Sudan, and Libya
designation – placed on the US Department of State's list of Foreign Terrorist Organizations on 9 April 2014

Islamic State of Iraq and ash-Sham - West Africa (ISIS-WA)
aka – Islamic State West Africa Province (ISWAP); Islamic State of Iraq and the Levant-West Africa (ISIL-WA); Islamic State of Iraq and Syria West Africa Province; ISIS West Africa Province; ISIS-West Africa (ISIS-WA); Wilayat Gharb Ifriqiyya
history – created in 2016 when a faction of Boko Haram broke off and pledged allegiance to ISIS; the split occurred primarily because of the indiscriminate violence Boko Haram inflicted on Muslims; since its founding, has waged an insurgency against the Nigerian Government, overrunning dozens of military bases and killing hundreds of soldiers; by 2019, reportedly controlled hundreds of square miles of territory in the Lake Chad region where it governed according to a strict interpretation of Islamic law and attempted to cultivate support among local civilians by focusing on filling gaps in governance; claimed additional attacks in 2021 and 2022, including an attack that killed more than 30 Nigerian soldiers in Borno State and an assault on a Cameroonian Army base; was engaged in fighting with Boko Haram and Nigerian security forces, as well as the militaries of the Multinational Joint Task Force (Benin, Cameroon, Chad, Niger, and Nigeria) into 2022; has reportedly oustripped Boko Haram in size and capacity; between 2009 and 2022, jihadist violence associated with Boko Haram and more recently ISWAP has killed an estimated 35-40,000 people, mostly civilians, and displaced more than 2 million persons
goals – implement ISIS's strict interpretation of sharia and replace regional governments with an Islamic state
leadership and organization – leadership unclear; former leader Sani SHUWARAM reportedly killed in March 2022; organization also unclear; reportedly has a shura council and operational military commanders, but may have reorganized in 2021 into four regionally-based branches, representing Lake Chad, Tunbuna, Sambisa Forest, and Timbuktu; probably operates in small units and cells that mass for larger operations
areas of operation – Nigeria (primarily the northeast, but as of 2022 had reportedly spread to other regions of the country, including in and around the capital Abuja; greater Lake Chad region (including southeast Niger, northern Cameroon, and areas of Chad near Lake Chad)

targets, tactics, and weapons – seeks to de-legitimize the Nigerian Government by focusing its attacks on security forces, state-sponsored civilian defense groups, government targets, infrastructure, and individuals who collaborate with the government; attacks military bases and mobile columns; in 2018-2019, it overran more than 20 military bases in northeastern Nigeria, including one assault that resulted in the deaths of some 100 soldiers; in 2022, it claimed responsibility for an attack on a prison in Nigeria's capital Abuja which freed nearly 900 inmates including 60 of its members; employs ambushes, complex ground assaults, hit-and-run attacks, targeted killings, road side bombs, and kidnappings of security forces personnel; has also conducted attacks against Boko Haram and engaged in the kidnapping and murder of aid workers and Christians, as well as civilians who aid the Nigerian military; fighters typically equipped with small arms, light and heavy machine guns, vehicle mounted weapons, rocket-propelled grenades, mines, rockets, improvised explosive devices, armored vehicles (including tanks), and unmanned aerial vehicles
strength – estimated in 2022 to have between 4,000 and 5,000 active fighters
financial and other support – receives some funding from core ISIS and local sources, including kidnappings-for-ransom, taxation, and extortion practices; has captured a considerable number of vehicles, weapons, and ammunition from the Nigerian military; maintains training camps and has publicly advertised a "Caliphate Cadet School" featuring children between 8-16 years old undergoing indoctrination and military-style training
designation – placed on the US Department of State's list of Foreign Terrorist Organizations on 28 February 2018

Islamic State of Iraq and ash-Sham in Bangladesh (ISB)

aka – ISIS-Bangladesh, Caliphate in Bangladesh; Caliphate's Soldiers in Bangladesh; Soldiers of the Caliphate in Bangladesh; Khalifa's Soldiers in Bengal; Islamic State Bangladesh; Islamic State in Bangladesh; Islamic State in Bengal; Dawlatul Islam Bengal; ISIB; Abu Jandal al-Bangali; Jammat-ul Mujahadeen-Bangladesh; JMB; Neo-JMB; New JMB
history – formed in 2014 out of ISIS's desire to expand to the Indian Subcontinent; consists of individuals who defected from Jamaat-ul-Mujahideen Bangladesh and Jund at-Tawhid wal-Khilafah and pledged allegiance to ISIS; claimed responsibility for multiple small bombing attacks in 2019; active as of 2021
goals – protect Muslims in Bangladesh from perceived injustices and, ultimately, establish an Islamic caliphate in the Indian subcontinent
leadership and organization – leadership and organization not available; Muhammad Saifullah OZAKI was reportedly the leader of ISIS-Bangladesh when it was formed; probably operates in a cell-based network
areas of operation – active throughout Bangladesh but operates primarily in Dhaka
targets and tactics – primarily targets military and security personnel but also activists, bloggers, academics, religious minorities, and foreigners (particularly Westerners); has attacked restaurants, places of worship, and crowds of civilians, typically with small arms, grenades, and improvised explosives devices, including suicide bombers; most deadly attack was a 2016 armed assault on a bakery in Dhaka, where the attackers used small arms, grenades, and machetes to kill 24 people
strength – not available but estimated in 2020 to have a few hundred armed supporters; following the 2016 attack in Dhaka, Bangladeshi security forces staged nationwide raids in which they claim to have killed or captured hundreds of the group's members
financial and other support – has received some support from ISIS; other funding sources not available
designation – placed on the US Department of State's list of Foreign Terrorist Organizations on 28 February 2018

Islamic State of Iraq and ash-Sham in Libya (ISIS-L)

aka – ISIS-Libya, Islamic State-Libya; IS-Libya; Islamic State of Iraq and the Levant in Libya (ISIL-L); Wilayat Barqa; Wilayat Fezzan; Wilayat Tripolitania; Wilayat Tarablus; Wilayat al-Tarabulus; Desert Army; Jaysh al-Sahraa
history – formed in 2014 when then ISIS leader Abu Bakr al-BAGHDADI dispatched operatives from Syria to establish a branch; claimed responsibility for its first operation, a suicide attack on a hotel in Tripoli, in January 2015; from 2015 to 2016, grew to as many as 6,000 fighters, established a stronghold in Sirte, and expanded operations into Libya's oil producing region; from late 2016 to 2017, was driven from Sirte into the desert by Libyan forces, with assistance from the US military, while suffering heavy losses in personnel; since 2018, has altered its strategy to what it described as a *nikayah* (war of attrition) of guerrilla warfare and traditional terrorist tactics with small bands of fighters operating out of ungoverned spaces in Libya and conducting attacks throughout the country; claimed several small-scale attacks against local military and security services in 2020-2021 despite losses to government counterterrorism operations; although weakened, the group in 2022 retained some operational capability and was trying to reorganize and gain strength
goals – prevent the formation of a reunified Libyan state, secure control over the country's oil resources and, ultimately, establish an Islamic caliphate in Libya
leadership and organization – current leader not available; when ISIS-L held territory, its structure included three regionally-based provinces (*wilayat*) with defined state-like departments (*diwans*) and a hierarchal chain of command; reportedly operates in decentralized guerilla-style desert "brigades" and networked cells
areas of operation – unable to control any population centers, but continues to have some mobile desert camps in rural central and southern Libya; assessed to retain an undetermined number of dormant cells in some coastal cities
targets, tactics, and weapons – targets military and security forces, oil infrastructure, and entities or individuals associated with Libya's competing governments; targets include oil facilities, security checkpoints and police stations, and symbolic state targets such as Libya's electoral commission headquarters and the Ministry of Foreign Affairs; also kidnaps local notables for potential prisoner exchanges or ransom; attacks typically are hit-and-run and conducted with small arms and suicide bombers; weapons mostly include small arms, rocket-propelled grenades, mortars, light and heavy machine guns, landmines, and improvised explosive devices
strength – estimated in 2022 to have less than 50 fighters
financial and other support – ISIS core has provided ad hoc financial support; additional funding comes from smuggling and extortion, kidnappings for ransom, and external sources; has acquired weapons through captured Libyan military stockpiles and smuggling networks
designation - placed on the US Department of State's list of Foreign Terrorist Organizations on 20 May 2016

Islamic State of Iraq and ash-Sham in the Greater Sahara (ISIS-GS)

aka – ISIS in the Greater Sahara; Islamic State in the Greater Sahel; Islamic State of the Greater Sahel; ISIS in the Islamic Sahel
history – emerged in May 2015 when Adnan Abu Walid al-SAHRAWI and his followers split from the al-Qaida-affiliated group al-Murabitoun and pledged allegiance to ISIS; ISIS acknowledged the group in October 2016; has carried out attacks in the Sahel region, including one on a joint US-Nigerien military force operating near the Mali-Niger border in October 2017; since February 2018, has clashed repeatedly with French military forces and allied local militias operating under the French-sponsored counterterrorism operation known as Operation Barkhane, as well as Nigerien, Malian, and Burkinabe troops; for example, conducted attacks against Nigerien and Malian military bases in late 2019 that killed 89 and 54 soldiers, respectively; after a period of some reported cooperation, ISIS-GS has engaged in fighting in with the local al-Qa'ida-aligned coalition known as Jama'at Nusrat al-Islam wal-Muslimin (JNIM) over territory, including control of gold extraction areas and access to buyers, since 2020; fighting between the groups continued into 2022; was reportedly gaining strength in Mali and northern Benin in the latter half of 2022

goals – replace regional governments with an Islamic state; reportedly has not developed a cohesive, ideologically driven narrative but instead tries to adapt its message to what can garner the most support from local communities
leadership and organization – Abdul Bara al-SAHRAOUI (aka Abdul Bara al-Ansari, aka Abu Omarou); probably operates in small mobile cells or groups that consolidate for operations
areas of operation – mostly concentrated in the Mali-Niger border region but also operates in Burkina Faso and northern Benin
targets, tactics, and weapons – targets local military and security forces, foreign military forces (French, UN, US), ethnic groups, local government officials, humanitarian workers, and schools; since 2018, has forced the closure of an estimated 2,000 schools in the region with threats, attacks, and murders of teachers and administrators; employs insurgency-type tactics against military and security forces, including ambushes, targeted killings, hit-and-run attacks, mortar attacks, road side bombs, car and truck bombs, suicide bombers, and direct assaults; ISIS-GS fighters attacking Malian and Nigerien military bases in 2019 used assault rifles, light machine guns, motorcycles, trucks mounting machine guns, mortars, and suicide bombers
strength – estimated 400-1,000 fighters in 2022
financial and other support – specific sources not available, but probably originates from smuggling activities, local donations and taxation, kidnapping for ransom, and from other groups operating in the region
designation – placed on the US Department of State's list of Foreign Terrorist Organizations on 23 May 2018

Islamic State of Iraq and ash-Sham – Democratic Republic of the Congo (ISIS-DRC)
aka – Allied Democratic Forces (ADF); Madina Tawheed wal Mujahideen ("the City of Monotheism and Holy Warriors"); Islamic State of Iraq and ash-Sham – Central Africa (ISIS-CA); Islamic State's Central Africa Province (ISCAP); Wilayat Central Africa; Wilayah Central Africa
history – first mentioned as "ISIS-Central Africa" in an August 2018 speech by then-ISIS leader al-BAGHDADI; claimed its first attack against the Democratic Republic of the Congo (DRC) military near the border with Uganda in April 2019; has its origins in the DRC-based militant group Allied Democratic Forces (ADF), which was founded in 1995 with the stated goal of overthrowing the Ugandan Government but shifted in the late 1990s to carrying out attacks against civilians, military forces, and UN peacekeepers in the DRC; many of ADF's early members came from Uganda's Salafist movement; online posts by some ADF members in 2016 and 2017 referred to their group as Madina Tawheed wal Mujahideen ("the City of Monotheism and Holy Warriors") and displayed an ISIS-like flag; ISIS-DRC has been notorious for its brutal violence against Congolese citizens and regional military forces, with attacks killing approximately 4,000 civilians between 2014 and 2020, including about 850 in 2020; in October 2020, it launched an assault on a prison in the DRC city of Beni that resulted in the escape of about 1,300 prisoners, including nearly 250 ISIS/ADF fighters and sympathizers; continued conducting operations into 2022, including its first suicide bombing and another prison break
goals – implement ISIS's strict interpretation of sharia and establish an Islamic state in central Africa
leadership and organization – Seka Musa BALUKU, who presides over a shura/executive council of senior leaders, including a military commander; military wing reportedly has sub-commanders for intelligence, operations, training, finances, logistics, and medical services
areas of operation – DRC, primarily in the Nord Kivu and Ituri provinces; also active in Uganda
targets, tactics, and weapons – Congolese civilians and military/security forces, as well as UN personnel; methods include frequent small-scale attacks, indiscriminate killings, ambushes, assassinations, kidnappings, and suicide bombings; ADF was sanctioned in 2014 by the U.S. Department of the Treasury and the UN under the UN Security Council's DRC sanctions regime for its violence and atrocities; uses small arms, machine guns, improvised explosive devices, rocket-propelled grenades, mortars, and unmanned aerial vehicles (UAVs)
strength – assessed in 2019 to have at least 400 fighters
financial and other support – financing unclear; reportedly receives some funding from control of mines and the export of minerals; probably receives some funds from ISIS-Core; has seized weapons and ammunition from the DRC military
designation – placed on the US Department of State's list of Foreign Terrorist Organizations on 10 March 2021

Islamic State of Iraq and ash-Sham – Mozambique (ISIS-M)
aka – Ansar al-Sunna; Ahl-e-Sunnat wal Jamaa; Ahlu Sunnah Wal Jammah; Swahili Sunna; al-Shabaab in Mozambique; al-Shabab
history – based on a domestic terrorist group known as Ansar al-Sunna (aka al-Shabaab, among other names) that has conducted an insurgency against the Mozambique Government since 2017, and ISIS publicly recognized as an affiliate in June 2019; since 2017, violence associated with the group has led to the deaths of approximately 4,000 civilians, security force members, and suspected ISIS-M militants, and displaced approximately 800,000 persons in northern Mozambique (as of 2022); the group was responsible for orchestrating a series of large-scale and sophisticated attacks resulting in the capture of the port of Mocimboa da Praia, Cabo Delgado Province in August 2020, which it held for a year; in March 2021, it seized the northern Mozambican town of Palma (population 70,000), holding it for 4 days while killing dozens of civilians and security personnel; during the attack, the group targeted the local airfield, an army barracks, several banks, and a food storage warehouse; in 2021-2022, several African countries sent military troops to assist the Mozambique Government's efforts to defeat the group; these military operations have resulted in setbacks to ISIS-M, including considerable casualties and the destruction of some bases and training camps; nevertheless, the group continued to be active in 2022
goals – implement ISIS's strict interpretation of sharia and establish an Islamic state
leadership and organization – led by Abu Yasir HASSAN; organizational information limited, but reportedly has regional commands; probably operates mostly in cells and small groups, although it has shown the ability to mass fighters for large-scale attacks (an estimated 200 fighters took part in the Palma attack)
areas of operation – northern Mozambique; primarily Cabo Delgado province, an area known for rich liquid natural gas deposits; has also conducted attacks in Nampula and Niassa provinces; has conducted cross-border attacks in Tanzania
targets, tactics, and weapons – has attacked army barracks, police stations, security checkpoints, government buildings, banks, and gas stations, and captured entire villages and towns; attacks are characterized by ambushes and direct assaults on government security forces and foreign private security contractors, murders of gas industry workers and contractors, indiscriminate killings of civilians, including women and children, beheadings, kidnappings, and looting and burning out villages; in April 2020, the group killed more than 50 young men in a village for reportedly resisting recruitment; has been accused of wholesale abductions of women and girls; armed with small arms, machine guns, improvised explosives, mortars, and rocket-propelled grenades (RPG); reportedly sank a government patrol boat with an RPG in 2020; has also used motorboats to conduct raids on coastal villages
strength – unclear; possibly up to 1,200 fighters in 2022
financial and other support – unclear, although the group has targeted banks; the area's natural resources, including gas, gems, timber, and wildlife present opportunities for fund-raising; in addition, the group has taken control of food supplies in areas under its control; weapons typically captured from government security forces
designation – placed on the US Department of State's list of Foreign Terrorist Organizations on 10 March 2021

Islamic State of Iraq and ash-Sham-Khorasan Province (ISIS-K)

aka – Islamic State of Iraq and Syria-Khorasan; Islamic State in Iraq and the Levant-Khurasan (ISIL-K); Islamic State Khurasan (IS, ISK, ISISK); Islamic State of Iraq and Levant in Khorasan Province (ISKP); Islamic State's Khorasan Province; ISIL-Khorasan; Wilayat al-Khorasan; Wilayat Khurasan; ISIL's South Asia Branch; South Asian Chapter of ISIL
history – formed in January 2015 primarily from former members of Tehrik-e Taliban Pakistan, the Afghan Taliban, and the Islamic Movement of Uzbekistan; ISIS appointed former Pakistani Taliban commander Hafiz Said KHAN as leader (later killed in a US military strike); frequently fought with the Afghan Taliban over control of territory and resources; also conducted an insurgency against the Afghan Government and foreign military forces; suffered heavy losses of fighters, leaders, and territory to Afghan and US counterterrorism operations, as well as to the Taliban, but as of 2021 continued to retain the ability to orchestrate attacks, recruit, and replenish leadership positions; since the fall of the Afghan Government to the Taliban and the US/Coalition withdrawal in August 2021, has conducted dozens of attacks against the Taliban, including suicide bombings, assassinations, and ambushes on security checkpoints; in 2022, claimed a suicide bombing attack on a Shia mosque in Pakistan and a rocket attack on an Uzbek military border post
goals – establish an Islamic caliphate in Afghanistan, Pakistan, and parts of Central Asia, including Iran; eliminate Shia Muslims and defeat the Taliban
leadership and organization – Sanaullah GHAFAR (aka Shahab al-Muhaji) is the emir; operates in small cells; ISIS restructured the Khorasan Province in May 2019, when it announced the creation of separate provinces for India and Pakistan
areas of operation – mainly operates in eastern Afghanistan (particularly Kunar and Nangarhar provinces, although sleeper cells are reportedly active in other parts of the country, particularly in Kabul) and western Pakistan (note - "Khorasan" is a historical region that encompassed northeastern Iran, southern Turkmenistan, and northern Afghanistan)
targets, tactics, and weapons – targets military and security forces, Taliban members, and civilians, particularly Shia Muslims and religious minorities; known for indiscriminate attacks against civilians in both Afghanistan and Pakistan; killed an estimated 1,200 Afghan and more than 300 Pakistani civilians in armed assaults, assassinations, executions, and suicide bombings between 2016 and 2019; targets included Shia religious sites, neighborhoods, and other gathering places, diplomatic facilities in Kabul, a voter registration center, a television station, a hospital, and an election rally; in August 2020, conducted a raid on an Afghan prison that killed or wounded 80 and freed up to 400 prisoners, including ISIS-K and Taliban loyalists; in August 2021, it conducted a bombing attack on the Kabul Airport that killed 13 US military personnel and 169 Afghan civilians; in 2022, claimed responsibility for a suicide bombing attack on a Shia mosque in Pakistan that killed 63 persons; employs insurgent-type tactics, including ambushes, assassinations, hit and run attacks/raids, roadside bombings and other improvised explosive device (IEDs) operations, mortar/rocket attacks, suicide bombings, etc; typically armed with small arms, light and heavy machine guns, mortars, rockets, and various IEDs, including car bombs, road side bombs, and suicide bombers
strength – estimates in 2022 ranged between 2,000 and 4,000 fighters
financial and other support – receives periodic funding from ISIS; raises additional funds locally from commerce, taxes, and extortion practices on individuals and businesses
designation – placed on the US Department of State's list of Foreign Terrorist Organizations on 14 January 2016

Islamic State of Iraq and ash-Sham: self-proclaimed ISIS branches, networks, and provinces (non-FTO designated)

note: this appendix provides short descriptions of identified or self-proclaimed ISIS branches, networks, and provinces that have not been designated by the US State Department as Foreign Terrorist Organizations
Islamic State of Iraq and ash-Sham – Algeria: the Islamic State declared the establishment of a province in Algeria (Wilayat al-Jazair) in November 2014; includes elements of a local terrorist organization known as Jund al-Khilafa; goal is to replace the Algerian Government with an Islamic state; targets security forces, local government figures, and Western interests; largely defunct due to heavy pressure from Algerian security forces, although ISIS core claimed responsibility for a February 2020 attack on a military base near the border with Mali; historically maintained an operational and recruitment presence mostly in the northeastern part of the country
Islamic State of Iraq and ash-Sham network in Azerbaijan: ISIS declared a new network in Azerbaijan in July of 2019, although it has not claimed responsibility for any attacks; additional details of the network unavailable
Islamic State of Iraq and ash-Sham – Caucasus Province: ISIS-Caucasus Province (ISIS-CP; aka Wilayat Qawqaz) was announced in June 2015; grew out of the former al-Qa'ida-affiliated Islamic Emirate of the Caucasus, which suffered from losses to Russian counterterrorism operations, leadership disputes, and defections to ISIS; claimed responsibility for its first attack against a Russian Army barracks in September 2015; claimed at least two attacks on local security forces in 2020, including a suicide bomber who blew himself up in the North Caucasus region of Karachay-Cherkessia, injuring six police officers; Russian security services conducted multiple operations against suspect ISIS militants in 2021; operates in the North Caucasus area of the Russian Federation between the Black Sea and Caspian Sea; typically conducts attacks against local security and military forces, as well as non-Muslim civilians, with small arms, improvised explosives, and knives
Islamic State of Iraq and ash-Sham – India: the Islamic State-India (aka ISI; Islamic State-Hin; Wilayah of Hind) was announced in May 2019 when ISIS claimed it had restructured the group's Khorasan Province and created separate provinces for ISIS-affiliated elements operating in India and Pakistan; the announcement followed an attack claimed by ISIS on Indian security forces in India-administered Kashmir; ISIS-India is reportedly dominated by Kashmiri jihadists and has conducted several additional low-scale attacks targeting Indian security forces in Kashmir; estimated in 2021 to have less than 200 members, but as of 2022 was active and recruiting new members; ISIS-linked groups reportedly operating in India include Ansar-ut Tawhid fi Bilad al-Hind, Indian Mujahideen, and Junood-ul-Khilafa-Fil-Hind (aka Jundul Khilafa)
Islamic State of Iraq and ash-Sham – East Asia networks in Indonesia: comprises a loose network of ISIS affiliates, cells, and supporters throughout the country known as Jemaah Anshorut Daulau (JAD), which Aman ABDURRAHMAN (in prison) has led since 2015; goal is to replace the Indonesian Government with an Islamic state and implement ISIS's interpretation of sharia; known for attacking security forces and Christians; in 2019, a JAD member attempted to assassinate Indonesia's security minister and a local police chief; in 2018, staged simultaneous suicide bombings by families, including women and children, against three churches in Surabaya that killed more than 30 civilians; strength unknown, but maintains a clandestine operational presence across the country; local cells maintain their own structures and remain largely autonomous; JAD includes former members of the FTO-designated group Jemaah Ansharut Tauhid (JAT; aka Jemmah Ansharut Tauhid; Laskar 99), which disbanded in 2015 to join JAD (some members reportedly joined al-Qa'ida); has a relationship with the ISIS-affiliated East Indonesia Mujahideen (aka Mujahidin Indonesia Timor, or MIT), which Indonesian police linked to an assault on a village in Sulawesi in late 2020 that killed four; in 2021, Indonesian security forces disrupted planned attacks by JAD and killed the leader of MIT (Ali KALORA); other ISIS-affiliated groups in Indonesia reportedly include Muhajirin Anshar Tauhid (MAT), Firqah Abu Hamzah (FAH), Jamaah Ansharul Khilafah (JAK), and some factions of Darul Islam/Negara Islam Indonesia (DI/NII)
Islamic State of Iraq and ash-Sham - Pakistan: ISIS announced in May 2019 that it restructured the group's Khorasan Province and created separate provinces for ISIS-affiliates operating in Pakistan; operates mostly in Balochistan and northern Sindh provinces and chiefly targets non-Muslims and the local Shia population, particularly the Hazaras; claimed several attacks Baluchistan in 2020 and early 2021; ISIS has claimed

additional attacks in Pakistan, including a March 2022 suicide bombing on a Shia mosque in Peshawar that killed 64, but it is unclear if the attack was carried out by the Pakistan branch or ISIS-Khorasan

Islamic State of Iraq and ash-Sham – Somalia: announced in 2016; splinter group of al-Shabaab and reportedly founded by former al-Shabaab commander Abdulqadir MUMIN; estimated in 2022 to have less than 300 fighters; operates primarily in the remote mountains of the Bari area of the semi-autonomous Puntland region; targets Somali Government and security forces, Puntland security forces, African Union peacekeepers, and al-Shabaab elements through low-level attacks using small arms and improvised explosive devices, as well as target assassinations; continued to conduct sporadic attacks as of 2022, but also reportedly has been weakened due to counterterrorism operations and clashes with the al-Shabaab terrorist group

Islamic State of Iraq and ash-Sham network in Tunisia: a network of cells, supporters, and Islamic militant groups in Tunisia claiming allegiance to ISIS, including Jund al-Kilafah (JAK or "Soldiers of the Caliphate"); goal is to replace the Tunisian Government with an Islamic state and implement ISIS's strict interpretation of sharia; since 2015, it has conducted periodic attacks against security forces and tourist sites frequented by Westerners, such as a resort in Sousse and a museum in Tunis; attacks have included suicide bombings, improvised explosive devices mounted on motorcycles, stabbings, targeted assassinations, and bank robberies; sporadic attacks continued through 2020; claimed an attack in February 2021 that killed 4 soldiers; Tunisian security forces in 2022 claimed it had destroyed at least two terrorist cells linked to ISIS; the network is mostly active in the mountainous region along the border with Algeria, particularly the Chaambi Mountains near the city of Kasserine

Islamic State of Iraq and ash-Sham –Turkey: publicly announced in July 2019, when ISIS released a video of a group of fighters in Turkey pledging allegiance to then-ISIS leader al-BAGHDADI and declaring a new province (wilayat) in Turkey; the speaker threatened both Turkey and the US while the fighters in the video were armed with assault rifles, grenades, light machine guns, and rocket-propelled grenade launchers; ISIS has long had a presence in Turkey, which previously served as a transit point for foreign fighters traveling to Syria to join the self-declared Islamic State caliphate and participate in the civil war; prior to the declaration of a province in Turkey, the Turkish government suspected ISIS of responsibility for numerous attacks, including suicide bombings at Ataturk Airport in June 2016 and at a wedding in August 2016, as well as a shooting at a nightclub in January 2017 (the last major ISIS attack in Turkey as of 2022); since the collapse of the caliphate in early 2019, Turkey continues to be a regional transit hub for ISIS in its efforts to smuggle fighters, weapons, funding, and supplies into Syria; as of 2022, Turkish security forces continued to conduct counter-terrorism operations against ISIS and militants linked to the group

Islamic State of Iraq and ash-Sham - Yemen: publicly announced in April 2015 after a self-proclaimed ISIS affiliate calling itself "Wilayat Sana'a" claimed responsibility for a mosque bombing in Yemen that killed approximately 140 people; goal is to replace the Yemen Government and the Huthi rival government with an Islamic state and implement ISIS's strict interpretation of sharia; since 2015, has carried out hundreds of attacks against Yemeni security forces, Yemeni Government facilities and personnel, Huthi forces, Shia Muslims, and al-Qa'ida; methods include suicide bombers, car/truck bombs, road side bombs, ambushes, armed ground assaults, kidnappings, and targeted assassinations; operational primarily in south and central Yemen; reportedly has suffered heavy losses in fighting with the local al-Qa'ida affiliate (al-Qa'ida in the Arabian Pensinsula) and Huthi forces; as of 2022, group was considerably degraded in capabilities and strength

Jaish-e-Mohammed (JeM)

aka – the Army of Mohammed; Mohammed's Army; Tehrik ul-Furqaan; Khuddam-ul-Islam; Khudamul Islam; Kuddam e Islami; Jaish-i-Mohammed
history – founded in 2000 by former senior Harakat ul-Mujahideen leader Masood AZHAR upon his release from prison in India in exchange for 155 hijacked Indian Airlines passengers that JeM operatives were holding hostage; has claimed responsibility for multiple attacks in India-administered Kashmir, India, and Pakistan; after 2008, fought US and Coalition forces in Afghanistan; maintains close relations with the Taliban and al-Qa'ida in Afghanistan; outlawed in Pakistan; has conducted several attacks against Indian security forces in Jammu and Kashmir since 2018, including a suicide bombing in the city of Pulwama that killed 40 security police in February 2019; remained active in 2022
goals – annex the Indian Union Territory of Jammu and Kashmir to Pakistan
leadership and organization – led by Maulana Mohammed Masood AZHAR Alvi (aka Wali Adam Isah), with his brother and deputy, Mufti Abdul Rauf AZHAR Alvi, as well as a seven-member executive committee
areas of operation – Afghanistan (maintained training camps there as of 2022), India (stages attacks in Indian Union Territory of Jammu and Kashmir), Pakistan
targets, tactics, and weapons – attacks Indian military, security, and government officials, personnel, bases, and buildings; periodically attacks Pakistani government and security personnel; attempted to assassinate former Pakistani President Pervez MUSHARRAF in 2003; has assaulted and kidnapped Christians and foreigners; typically employs small arms, grenades, mines, improvised explosive devices, suicide bombers, and car bombs
strength – estimated in 2020 to have several hundred fighters
financial and other support – to avoid asset seizures by the Pakistani Government, JEM since 2007 has withdrawn funds from bank accounts and invested in legal businesses, such as commodity trading, real estate, and the production of consumer goods; also collects funds through donation requests, sometimes using charitable causes to solicit donations
designation – placed on the US Department of State's list of Foreign Terrorist Organizations on 26 December 2001

Jama'at Nusrat al-Islam wal-Muslimin (JNIM)

aka – Jamaat Nosrat al-Islam wal-Mouslimin; Group for the Support of Islam and Muslims; Group to Support Islam and Muslims; GSIM; GNIM; Nusrat al-Islam wal-Muslimeen
history – formed in 2017 when the Mali Branch of al-Qa'ida in the Islamic Maghreb (AQIM), al-Murabitoun, Ansar al-Dine, and the Macina Liberation Front (FLM; aka Katiba Macina or Macina Battalion/Brigade) agreed to work together as a coalition; describes itself as al-Qa'ida's official branch in Mali and has pledged allegiance to al-Qa'ida leader Ayman al-ZAWAHIRI and deceased AQIM emir Abdelmalek DROUKDEL; has conducted hundreds of attacks against local and international security troops, vowing to take "combat action against security forces, rather than attacks on the population" to preserve relations with local communities; has tried to displace the authority of local governments in the areas where it operates, including providing services through its own self-described non-profit organizations; after a period of some reported cooperation, JNIM and the Islamic State of Iraq and ash-Sham in the Greater Sahara (ISIS-GS) elements have fought each other over territory in the region; the group continued to conduct attacks against local, regional, and international security forces into 2022, despite losses in fighters and leadership personnel to counter-terrorism operations, as well as its conflict with ISIS-GS; JNIM is one of al-Qa'ida's most active affiliates
goals – unite all terrorist groups in the Sahel, eliminate Western influence in the region, force out all French and other international military forces, and establish an Islamic state centered on Mali
leadership and organization – currently led by Iyad ag GHALI (also the leader of Ansar al-Dine); has a dedicated media unit known as az-Zalaqah, but coalition members maintain their existing leadership and organizational structures; for example, the Macina Brigade has a decentralized chain of command with sub-units known as *markaz* ("centre"), each of which has a leader (*amirou markaz*), assisted by a military commander and an advisory shura council; each *markaz* exercises considerable local autonomy

areas of operation – predominantly active in Mali but also conducts operations in Niger and Burkina Faso; stronghold is in northern and central Mali, although it has conducted operations and attacks over most of the country; groups affiliated with the coalition have conducted attacks in Benin, Cote d'Ivoire, and Togo
targets, tactics, and weapons – targets French, Malian, and UN military forces; typically employs insurgent-type tactics, including hit and run attacks/raids, kidnappings, ambushes, improvised explosive devises, road-side bombings, and mortar attacks; has attacked military bases and outposts, security checkpoints, patrols, and convoys, as well as the French embassy in Burkina Faso with small arms, machine guns, rocket-propelled grenades, mortars, rockets, suicide bombers, and car bombs; also targets other symbols of the government's authority, including local leaders, civil servants, schools, teachers, and infrastructure, such as bridges, as well as foreign tourists with threats, assassinations, kidnappings, and bombings; in 2020, it murdered a European hostage held since 2016
strength – assessed in 2020 to have approximately 2,000 fighters
financial and other support – receives funding through kidnappings-for-ransom and extortion, and from smugglers who pay a tax in exchange for safe transit through JNIM-controlled trafficking routes in Mali; has attacked gold mines in areas outside government control and used the profits to recruit new members and buy weapons; equipped with arms captured from local military forces and smuggled in from Libya
designation – placed on the US Department of State's list of Foreign Terrorist Organizations on 6 September 2018

Jama'atu Ansarul Muslimina Fi Biladis-Sudan (Ansaru)
aka – Ansarul Muslimina Fi Biladis Sudan; Vanguards for the Protection of Muslims in Black Africa; JAMBS; Jama'atu Ansaril Muslimina Fi Biladis Sudan
history – formed in January 2012 as a breakaway faction of Boko Haram in the aftermath of a January 2012 Boko Haram attack in the city of Kano, Nigeria, that resulted in the deaths of at least 180 people, mostly Muslims; the Ansaru faction objected to Boko Haram's attacks on fellow Muslims and killing non-Muslims who posed no threat to Muslims; it claimed a kidnapping in 2013 and did not claim any attacks until claiming responsibility for several in 2020; the group announced its reemergence in late 2019 and was active into 2022; in January 2022, the group publicly announced that it had pledged loyalty to al-Qa'ida elements operating in the Sahel
goals – defend Muslims throughout Africa by fighting against the Nigerian Government and international interests; rid Nigeria of Western influence and establish an Islamic state in Nigeria
leadership and organization – reportedly led by Abu Usama ANSARI; previously was under Khalid al-BARNAWI until he was captured by the Nigerian Army in 2016; leads through a shura, but information on the group's organizational structure is otherwise not available; announced the creation of a new media outlet for the group in 2019 (Al Yaqut Media Center)
areas of operation – operates in the northwest and and north central regions of Nigeria, particularly Kaduna State; reportedly cooperating with some armed gangs operating in northwest Nigeria, including providing weapons; also has reportedly taken part in al-Qa'ida operations in the Sahel
targets, tactics, and weapons – targets Nigerian Government officials and security/military forces; also kidnaps and kills foreigners, especially Westerners and abducts individuals with ties to potential ransom payers; uses small arms, light weapons, and explosives to carry out coordinated attacks, including ambushes and hit-and-run assaults
strength – not available, but assessed to be considerably smaller than Boko Haram
financial and other support – unclear, although some funding probably is generated from kidnappings for ransom; the group reportedly received training and weapons from al-Qa'ida elements in Mali, as well as arms from smugglers operating in the Sahel
designation – placed on the US Department of State's list of Foreign Terrorist Organizations on 14 November 2013

Jaysh al Adl (Jundallah)
aka – Jeysh al-adl, Army of Justice; Jaish ul-Adl, Jaish al-Adl, Jaish Aladl, Jeish al-Adl; Jundullah; Jondullah; Jundollah; Jondollah; Jondallah; Army of God (God's Army); Baloch Peoples Resistance Movement (BPRM); People's Resistance Movement of Iran (PMRI); Jonbesh-i Moqavemat-i-Mardom-i Iran; Popular Resistance Movement of Iran; Soldiers of God; Fedayeen-e-Islam; Former Jundallah of Iran
history – formed in 2002 under the name Jundallah as an anti-Iranian Sunni Muslim armed group; founder and then-leader Abdulmalik RIGI was captured and executed by Iranian authorities in 2010; has engaged in numerous attacks on Iranian civilians, government officials, and security personnel; adopted the name Jaysh al Adl in 2012 and has since claimed responsibility for attacks under that name; continued to be active through 2021
goals – stated goals are to secure recognition of Balochi cultural, economic, and political rights from the Iranian government; procure greater autonomy for Balochis in Iran and Pakistan
leadership and organization – not available; reportedly has branches based on regions of Iran and Pakistan where it is active; probably organized into cells; operates a media outlet known as the Telegram Channel
areas of operation – operates primarily in the province of Sistan va Baluchestan of southeastern Iran and the Baloch areas of Afghanistan and Pakistan (outlawed in Pakistan since January 2017); note: the Sistan-Baluchestan province is home to a large community of minority Sunni Muslims who complain of discrimination in Shia-dominated Iran
targets, tactics, and weapons – primarily targets Iranian security forces but also government officials and Shia civilians; attacks include hit-and-run raids, assaults, ambushes, kidnappings, assassinations, suicide bombings, and car bombings; has conducted several ambushes of Iranian security forces near the Pakistan border in recent years; one of its recent most deadly attacks was a February 2019 suicide car bombing of a bus carrying Islamic Revolutionary Guard Corps (IRGC) personnel that killed 27; weapons include small arms, light weapons, and various improvised explosive devices such as suicide vests and car bombs
strength – limited, dated, and widely varied estimates range from a few hundred up to as many as 2,000 members
financial and other support – not available
designation – placed on the US Department of State's list of Foreign Terrorist Organizations on 4 November 2010

Jaysh Rijal al-Tariq al Naqshabandi (JRTN)
aka – Jaysh Rijal al-Tariq al-Naqshabandi; Army of the Men of the Naqshbandi Order; Armed Men of the Naqshabandi Order; Naqshbandi Army; Naqshabandi Army; Men of the Army of al-Naqshbandia Way; Jaysh Rajal al-Tariqah al-Naqshbandia; JRTN; JRN; AMNO
history – emerged in December 2006 as an Arab secular Ba'athist nationalistic armed group in response to SADDAM Husayn's execution; consisted largely of Iraqi Sunni Muslims following Naqshabandi Sufi Islam ideals; between 2006 and the 2011 withdrawal of US forces from Iraq, claimed responsibility for numerous attacks on US bases and personnel; in 2014, elements joined forces with ISIS in opposition to the Iraqi government and assisted with the taking of Mosul, but fissures later emerged between the two factions; some elements splintered off, but the majority of JRTN was subsumed by ISIS; status as of 2021 was not available; has not claimed any attacks since 2016
goals – end external influence in Iraq and, ultimately, overthrow the Iraqi Government to install a secular Ba'athist state within the internationally recognized borders of Iraq

leadership and organization – Izzat Ibrahim al-DOURI, former vice president of SADDAM Husayn's Revolutionary Council, led JRTN with former Ba'ath Party officials and military personnel under SADDAM; information on the organization not available
areas of operation – Iraq; historically had a heavy presence in Salah ad Din, Ninawa, Tikrit, Kirkuk, Mosul, and Al Hawija regions and in the north
strength – current estimates not available; most recent information (2016) indicated fewer than 5,000 members
targets, tactics, and weapons – targeted Iraqi Government military and security forces and Iraqi Kurds who belong to any of the separatist Kurdish groups; also targeted US military personnel from 2006 to 2011; used small arms, light and heavy machine guns, artillery rockets, various improvised explosive devices, including road side and vehicle-borne bombs
financial resources – received funding from former members of the SADDAM regime, major tribal figures in Iraq, and contributions from Gulf-based sympathizers
designation – placed on the US Department of State's list of Foreign Terrorist Organizations on 30 September 2015

Jemaah Islamiya (JI)
aka – Jemaa Islamiyah, Jema'a Islamiyah, Jemaa Islamiyya, Jema'a Islamiyya, Jemaa Islamiyyah, Jema'a Islamiyyah, Jemaah Islamiah, Jema'ah Islamiyah, Jemaah Islamiyyah, Jema'ah Islamiyyah, Jama'a Assalafiyah Lidda'wa Wal Jihad, Islamic Congregation, Salafi Group for Call and Holy War, Jemaah Islamia, al-Qa'ida Indonesia
history – has roots in the Darul Islam movement that emerged in Indonesia in the 1940s to resist the country's post-colonial government, which it viewed as too secular; JI's earliest efforts to organize date back to the late 1960s and early 1970 under co-founders Abu Bukar BA'ASYIR and Abdullah SUNGKAR; sent fighters to Afghanistan in the 1980s during the war with the Soviets to train; gained international notoriety in 2002 for the suicide bombing of a nightclub on the resort island of Bali that killed more than 200 people; outlawed by the Indonesian Government in 2007; since 2002 and into 2022, Indonesian authorities have killed or captured several hundred JI operatives, including several senior leaders; remains active in recruiting and cultivating support through religious boarding schools, mosques, print publications, the internet, media outlets, and charitable organizations that are fronts for the organization; trying to use political influence to press for Islamic law in Indonesia while clandestinely building a paramilitary force; has sent fighters to Iraq, the Philippines, and Syria for training and battlefield experience; affiliated with al-Qa'ida and has ties with the Abu Sayaf Group in the Philippines; Indonesian security forces captured stockpiles of weapons and ammunition and broke up a training camp in 2021; has not claimed responsibility for any attacks since 2016, but was active into 2022 and reportedly attempting to regain momentum while the Indonesian Government continued to conduct law enforcement and counter-terrorism operations against the group
goals – stated goal is to create an Islamic state comprising Malaysia, Singapore, Indonesia, and the southern Philippines
leadership and organization – current leadership not available; has a shura council, a paramilitary wing, and regional units known as *mantiqi*, which are responsible for administration and operations; each *mantiqi* is divided into smaller districts known as *wakalah*
areas of operation – operates throughout Indonesia; reportedly strongest in Java; has operated in the Philippines, Malaysia, and Singapore
targets, tactics, and weapons – targets Christians and Western interests, particularly tourist sites such as nightclubs and hotels; the majority of its victims have been civilians; attackers historically used small arms and improvised explosive devices, including car bombs and suicide vests
strength – estimated in 2022 to have approximately 6,000 members
financial and other support – fundraises through membership donations and criminal and business activities, including cultivating palm oil plantations; has received financial, ideological, and logistical support from Middle Eastern contacts and Islamic charities and organizations; collects cash remittances from Indonesians abroad; members have received weapons and explosives training in Afghanistan, Iraq, Pakistan, the Philippines, and Syria
designation – placed on the US Department of State's list of Foreign Terrorist Organizations on 23 October 2002

Kata'ib Hizballah (KH)
aka – Hizballah Brigades; Hizballah Brigades in Iraq; Hizballah Brigades-Iraq; Kata'ib Hezbollah; Khata'ib Hezbollah; Khata'ib Hizballah; Khattab Hezballah; Hizballah Brigades-Iraq of the Islamic Resistance in Iraq; Islamic Resistance in Iraq; Kata'ib Hizballah Fi al-Iraq; Katibat Abu Fathel al-A'abas; Katibat Zayd Ebin Ali; Katibut Karbalah; Brigades (or Battalions) of the Party of God
history – formed in 2007 from several predecessor networks and former members of the Badr Organization as an Iraqi Shia militia and political organization; fought against US and Coalition forces from 2007 to 2011 and earned a reputation for conducting lethal bombing and rocket attacks; sent fighters to Syria to fight alongside Lebanese Hizballah and Syrian government forces beginning in 2012; fought in Iraq against the Islamic State of Iraq and ash-Sham (ISIS) as a member of the Popular Mobilization Committee and Affiliated Forces (PMC or PMF), an umbrella group of mostly Shia militia groups; was accused of extrajudicial killings and abductions of Iraqi Sunni Muslims during this period; in 2018, its affiliated political party (Independent Popular Gathering) joined the Al Fatah (Victory) Alliance, a political coalition primarily comprised of parties affiliated with Iranian-backed Shia militias; in 2019 and early 2020, conducted several attacks against US military bases and participated in an assault on the US Embassy in Baghdad; also involved in attacking and abducting anti-government protesters in Baghdad; continued to be active in 2022; typically uses front names or proxy groups to obfuscate its involvement in attacks; has strong ties to the Iranian Revolutionary Guard Corps (IRGC) and recognizes Ayatollah KHAMENEI, the Supreme Leader of Iran, as its spiritual leader
goals – overthrow the Iraqi Government to install a government based on Shia Muslim laws and precepts; eliminate US influence in Iraq
leadership and organization – led by a shura council, with individuals reportedly selected by the IRGC; secretary general of the council is Ahmad Mohsen Faraj al-HAMIDAWI (aka Abu Hussein, Abu Zalata, Abu Zeid); shura council members are responsible for special military operations, military/paramilitary forces, funding and logistics, civil affairs, media, social/cultural affairs, and administration; KH fighters comprise three brigades of the PMC's paramilitary forces (aka Popular Mobilization Forces, PMF), the 45th, 46th, and 47th; has a political party created in 2021 called Huqooq (Rights) Movement
areas of operation – headquartered in Baghdad; also active in Ninawa, Al Anbar, Babil, and throughout Iraq's southern governorates, including Al Basrah, Maysan, Dhi Qar, and Wasit; has participated in the Syrian civil war since 2012 (remained active in Syria in 2022)
targets, tactics, and weapons – targets ISIS fighters, Sunni Muslim civilians, rival Shia factions, and US personnel and interests; employs both guerrilla-style and terrorist tactics, including hit-and-run assaults, ambushes, mortar and rocket attacks, roadside bombs, car bombs, targeted killings/assassinations, sniping, and abductions; has been accused of torturing and executing Sunni civilians, as well as looting and burning Sunni homes; fighters are equipped with small arms, machine guns, rockets (including large-caliber, up to 240mm), mortars, man-portable air defense systems (MANPADs), improvised explosive devices, rocket-propelled grenades, anti-aircraft guns, artillery, recoilless rifles, light tactical vehicles (Humvees), truck-mounted weapons (aka "technicals"), armed unmanned aerial vehicles (aka drones), and armored vehicles; reportedly has been involved in the training of Shia militants in other Gulf countries
strength – estimated in 2020 to have as many as 10,000 fighters
financial and other support – receives funding, logistical support, intelligence, training, and weapons from the IRGC-Qods Force and Lebanese Hizballah; solicits donations online and through a pro-Iran television channel; also raises funds through criminal activities, including

kidnappings-for-ransom, smuggling, and taxing/extortion of activities in areas where the group is dominant; it also has legitimate business enterprises, such as property holdings and investments
designation – placed on the US Department of State's list of Foreign Terrorist Organizations on 2 July 2009

Kurdistan Workers Party (PKK)
aka – Kongra-Gel; the Kurdistan Freedom and Democracy Congress; the Freedom and Democracy Congress of Kurdistan; KADEK; Partiya Karkeran Kurdistan; the People's Defense Force; Halu Mesru Savunma Kuvveti; Kurdistan People's Congress; People's Congress of Kurdistan; KONGRAGEL, KGK
history – founded by Abdullah OCALAN in 1978 as a Marxist-Leninist separatist organization comprised primarily of Turkish Kurds; launched a rural campaign of violence in 1984 which expanded to include urban terrorism in the early 1990s; fighting with Turkish security forces peaked in the mid-1990s with an estimated 40,000 casualties, the destruction of thousands of villages in the largely Kurdish southeast and east of Turkey, and the displacement of hundreds of thousands of Kurds; following his capture in 1999, OCALAN ordered members to refrain from violence and requested dialogue with the Turkish government; PKK foreswore violence until June 2004, when its militant wing took control, renounced the self-imposed cease-fire, and began conducting attacks from bases within Iraq; in 2009, the Turkish Government and the PKK resumed peace negotiations, but talks broke down after the PKK carried out an attack in July 2011 that left 13 Turkish soldiers dead; between 2012 and 2015, negotiations resumed but ultimately broke down owing partly to domestic political pressures and the war in Syria; since 2015, continued attacks and clashes with Turkish security forces have killed more than 3,000 PKK fighters, security forces, and civilians; the group was active into 2022
goals – advance Kurdish autonomy, political, and cultural rights in Turkey, Iran, Iraq, and Syria, and ultimately, establish an independent Kurdish state centered in southeastern Turkey
leadership and organization – OCALAN, currently serving life imprisonment in Turkey, is still the group's leader and figurehead, but day-to-day affairs and operations are run by Murat KARAYILAN and a three-man Executive Committee; the armed wing of the PKK is called the People's Defense Force
areas of operation – located primarily in northern Iraq (headquartered in the Qandil Mountains) and southeastern Turkey; affiliated groups operate in northwestern Syria, as well as in Iran
targets, tactics, and weapons – primarily attacks Turkish government personnel and security forces, including military patrols, convoys, security checkpoints, police stations, and government buildings; uses a mixture of guerrilla warfare and terrorist tactics, including armed assaults, hit-and-run attacks, kidnappings, grenade attacks, car bombs, remotely-detonated improvised explosive devices (IEDs), unmanned aerial vehicles (UAVs) mounting IEDs, and suicide bombers; weapons include small arms, machine guns, grenades, mortars, man-portable air defense systems (MANPADs), UAVs, and various improvised explosive devices
strength – estimated in 2020 to have 4,000-5,000 members
financial and other support – receives logistical and financial support from a large number of sympathizers among the Kurdish community in southeast Turkey, Syria, Iraq, and Iran, as well as the large Kurdish diaspora in Europe; additional sources of funding include criminal activity, such as narcotics smuggling and extortion
designation – placed on the US Department of State's list of Foreign Terrorist Organizations on 8 October 1997

Lashkar i Jhangvi (LJ)
aka – Lashkar-e-Jhangvi (LeJ), Lashkar-i-Jhangvi, Lashkar Jangvi, Army of Jhangvi, Lashkar e Jhangvi al-Almi, LeJ al-Alami, Usman Saifullah group
history – formed around 1996 as a terrorist offshoot of the Sunni Deobandi sectarian group Sipah-i-Sahaba Pakistan; banned by the Pakistani Goverment in August 2001 as part of an effort to rein in sectarian violence, causing many LJ members to seek refuge in Afghanistan with the Taliban, with whom the group had existing ties; after the collapse of the Taliban in Afghanistan, members became active in aiding other terrorists, providing them with safe houses, false identities, and protection in Pakistani cities; linked to al-Qa'ida and Tehrik-e Taliban Pakistan (TTP), and reportedly cooperated with the Islamic State in a 2016 attack against a police training college in Quetta, Pakistan that killed more than 60; since 2017, has lost several senior leaders to Pakistani counter-terrorism operations and has not claimed responsibility for any attacks; in mid-2020, the group reportedly pledged allegiance to TTP under the name Usman Saifullah
goals – exterminate Shia Muslims and religious minorities; rid the region of Western influence and, ultimately, establish an Islamic state under sharia in Pakistan
leadership and organization – leadership not available; crackdowns by Pakistani security forces has reportedly fractured and decentralized the organization, leading to independent cells and factions
areas of operation – based primarily in Pakistan's Punjab province, the Federally Administered Tribal Areas, Karachi, and Balochistan; has carried out attacks in both Afghanistan and Pakistan
targets, tactics, and weapons – most known for violent attacks against Shia Muslims; also targets Sufi Muslims, non-Muslims, and Westerners; has attacked buses, markets, mosques, political rallies, and other venues where Shia Muslims congregate, as well as churches and hotels; attacks on Pakistani officials and security personnel have included targeted killings (including an attempted assassination of the Pakistani prime minister in 1999), ambushes, suicide bombings, and vehicle bombings, including exploding a water tanker filled with explosives that killed or wounded more than 250 in Baluchistan, Pakistan, in 2013; operatives typically armed with small arms and light weapons, grenades, improvised explosive devices, and suicide vests
strength – assessed in 2020 to have a few hundred members
financial and other support – funding comes from donors in Pakistan and the Middle East, particularly Saudi Arabia; engages in criminal activity, including extortion
designation – placed on the US Department of State's list of Foreign Terrorist Organizations on 30 January 2003

Lashkar-e Tayyiba (LeT)
aka – Jamaat-ud-Dawa, JuD; Lashkar-i-Taiba; al Mansooreen; Al Mansoorian; Army of the Pure; Army of the Pure and Righteous; Army of the Righteous; Lashkar e-Toiba; Paasban-e-Ahle-Hadis; Paasban-e-Kashmir; Paasban-i-Ahle-Hadith; Pasban-e-Ahle-Hadith; Pasban-e-Kashmir; Jama'at al-Dawa; Jamaat ud-Daawa; Jamaat ul-Dawah; Jamaat-ul-Dawa; Jama'at-i-Dawat; Jamaiat-ud-Dawa; Jama'at-ud-Da'awah; Jama'at-ud-Da'awa; Jamaati-ud-Dawa; Idara Khidmate-Khalq; Falah-i-Insaniat Foundation; FiF; Falah-e-Insaniat Foundation; FalaheInsaniyat; Falah-i-Insaniyat; Falah Insania; Welfare of Humanity; Humanitarian Welfare Foundation; Human Welfare Foundation; Al-Anfal Trust; Tehrik-e-Hurmat-e-Rasool; TehrikeTahafuz Qibla Awwal; Al-Muhammadia Students; Al-Muhammadia Students Pakistan; AMS; Tehreek-e-Azadi-e-Kashmir; Kashmir Freedom Movement; Tehreek Azadi Jammu and Kashmir; Tehreek-e-Azadi Jammu and Kashmir; TAJK; Movement for Freedom of Kashmir; Tehrik-i-Azadi-i Kashmir; Tehreek-e-Azadi-e-Kashmir; TEK; Kashmir Freedom Movement ;Milli Muslim League; Milli Muslim League Pakistan; MML

history – formed in the late 1980s as the armed wing of Markaz ud Dawa ul-Irshad (MDI), a Pakistan-based extremist organization and charity originally formed to oppose the Soviet presence in Afghanistan; began attacking Indian troops and civilian targets in the state of Jammu and Kashmir in 1993; often operates under the guise of its charitable affiliates and other front organizations to avoid sanctions; combines with other groups like Jaish-e-Muhammad and Hizbul Mujahideen to mount anti-India attacks; linked to al-Qa'ida and has reportedly provided refuge and training to al-Qa'ida members in Pakistan; has ties to the Afghan Taliban and has sent fighters and weapons to Afghanistan; active in 2022
goals – annex the Indian Union Territory of Jammu and Kashmir to Pakistan and foment an Islamic insurgency in India; oust Western and Indian influence in Afghanistan; enhance its recruitment networks and paramilitary training in South Asia; and, ultimately, install Islamic rule throughout South Asia
leadership and organization – led by Hafiz Mohammad SAEED (currently imprisoned in Pakistan); has a robust infrastructure in Pakistan with district offices and departments (or wings) overseeing finances, charities, politics/government, foreign affairs, media and propaganda, social welfare programs, military operations (reportedly includes air and naval components), external affairs, education/students, ulema (clerics), and the building of mosques and madrassas; has zone/regional commanders; typically conducts military/terrorist operations in cells; activities are coordinated through numerous front organizations, including charities; set up a political party, the Milli Muslim League, in 2017
areas of operation – operational presence throughout Pakistan but concentrated in Azad Kashmir, Khyber-Pakhtunkhwa, and Punjab provinces, where it maintains paramilitary training camps, medical clinics, and schools; active in both the Pakistan-administered and Indian-administered Kashmir region, as well as other parts of India, including major cities such as Bangalore, Hyderabad, Mumbai, and New Delhi; also active in Afghanistan, including training camps; has global connections and a strong operational network throughout South Asia
targets, tactics, and weapons – primarily focuses on Indian military and security, government, and civilian targets; has participated in attacks against Western interests in Afghanistan and called for the killing of non-Muslims and Westerners worldwide; typical attacks include hit-and-run raids, ambushes, grenade attacks, and bombings; most notorious attack was the November 2008 operation against two luxury hotels, a Jewish center, a train station, and a café in Mumbai, India that killed 166 people and injured more than 300; attack was carried out by 10 gunmen armed with automatic weapons and grenades; operatives usually armed with assault rifles, machine guns, mortars, explosives, and grenades, including rocket-propelled grenades
strength – estimated in 2021 to have several thousand members; in 2020-2021, had an estimated 1,000 fighters in Afghanistan
financial and other support – collects donations in Pakistan and the Gulf, as well as from other donors in the Middle East and the West; raises funds in Pakistan through charities, legitimate businesses, farming, and taxation; focuses recruitment on Pakistani nationals, but also recruits internationally
designation – placed on the US Department of State's list of Foreign Terrorist Organizations on 26 December 2001

Liberation Tigers of Tamil Eelam (LTTE)
aka – Ellalan Force, Tamil Tigers
history – formed circa 1975 and began an armed campaign against the Sri Lankan government to establish a Tamil homeland in 1983; started out as a guerrilla force but developed considerable conventional military capabilities, including air, artillery, and naval; employed an integrated insurgent strategy targeting primarily Sri Lanka's key installations and senior political and military leaders; established and administered a de facto state (Tamil Eelam) with Kilinochchi as its administrative capital; provided state functions such as courts, a police force, a bank, a radio station (Voice of Tigers), a television station (National Television of Tamil Eelam), and boards for humanitarian assistance, health, and education; from 1983 until 2009, fighting between government forces and LTTE resulted in 300,000 internally displaced persons, a million Tamils leaving the country, and as many as 100,000 deaths; in early 2009, Sri Lankan forces captured the LTTE's key strongholds, including Kilinochchi, defeated the last LTTE fighting forces, killed its leader Velupillai PRABHAKARN, and declared military victory; approximately 12,000 members surrendered to Sri Lankan forces; LTTE has maintained an international network of sympathizers and financial support since its military defeat; was still active as of 2021, although the last fatality inflicted on Sri Lankan security forces was in 2014
goals – revive the movement to establish a Tamil homeland
leadership and organization – current leadership not available; previous structure included a central governing committee led by PRABHAKARAN that oversaw all LTTE activities; organization had political and military wings, as well as a women's wing; military was divided into conventionally organized brigades and regiments of infantry, artillery, air defense, anti-tank, mortars, and security forces; also included special units for naval (Sea Tigers), air (Air Tigers), and intelligence capabilities, as well as a unit of suicide bombers (Black Tigers)
areas of operation – was based in the northeastern part of Sri Lanka; since its defeat, supporters have been active in India, Malaysia, and Sri Lanka
targets, tactics, and weapons – targeted Sri Lankan Government, political, and security officials, and military forces, as well as transportation nodes and infrastructure; carried out a sustained military campaign against Sri Lankan military and security forces; employed a mix of conventional, guerrilla, and terrorist tactics, including ground assaults and numerous assassinations and suicide bombings; forces were armed with a variety of weapons, including small arms, machine guns, rocket-propelled grenades, anti-aircraft guns, anti-tank weapons, mortars, artillery, explosives, small naval craft, and light aircraft
strength – not available
financial and other support – employs charities as fronts to collect and divert funds for its activities
designation – placed on the US Department of State's list of Foreign Terrorist Organizations on 8 October 1997

National Liberation Army
aka – Ejercito de Liberacion Nacional; ELN
history – Colombian Marxist-Leninist group formed in 1964; reached its peak in the late 1990s, then suffered a marked period of decline, where it suffered from internal conflict and losses to both the Colombian security services and paramilitary forces that targeted leftist guerrilla groups; engaged in periodic negotiations with the Colombian Government throughout the 2000s and early 2010s while continuing to conduct attacks against security forces and the country's economic infrastructure; formal talks were started again in 2017 and continued into 2018; however, the government suspended the talks indefinitely following a January 2019 ELN car bomb attack on the National Police Academy in Bogota that killed 21 and wounded 68; as of 2022, continued to conduct periodic attacks and kidnappings; has expanded its presence into some areas left by the FARC following that group's peace agreement with the Colombian Government in 2016, as well as neighboring Venezuela in order to escape Colombian security forces and exploit opportunities for illicit financing and recruitment; was also engaged in periodic fighting with FARC dissidents and other criminal groups over territory and drug trafficking routes, particularly near the Colombia-Venezuela border
goals – defend Colombians who it believes to be victims of social, political, and economic injustices perpetrated by the Colombian government
leadership and organization – led by Nicolas Rodriguez BAUTISTA (aka Gabino) since 1973; at the top of the organizational structure is the Central Command ("Comando Central" or COCE, led by BAUTISTA), which oversees all ELN political, military, financial, and international operations; under the COCE is a 23-member National Directorate that serves as the link between the COCE and the seven "War Fronts" (six

regional and one urban-based front that operates in multiple large cities); each front has multiple subdivisions and subunits and operates with a significant degree of autonomy
areas of operation – operates mainly in the rural and mountainous areas of northern, northeastern, and southwestern Colombia, as well as the border regions with Venezuela; estimated to operate in at least 16 of Colombia's 32 departments, plus major cities, including Bogota; present in the Venezuelan states of Amazonas, Apure, Bolivar, Guarico, Tachira, and Zulia; maintains a narcotics trafficking presence throughout Venezuela
targets, tactics, and weapons – targets Colombia's security services and economic infrastructure, in particular oil and gas pipelines and electricity pylons; typical tactics include mortaring police stations and military bases, placing explosive devices on pipelines, electric pylons, and near roads, and engaging in sniper attacks, roadblocks, and ambushes; conducts numerous kidnappings of civilians and members of the security services; for 3 days in February 2022, orchestrated an armed strike across significant portions of Colombia (as many as 10 departments) that included violent attacks and targeted killings, blocking highways, setting off explosions, burning vehicles, hanging the ELN flag on public buildings, and patrolling streets in villages and towns in areas where the group maintains a strong presence; fighters are equipped with small arms, rocket-propelled grenades, landmines, explosives, and mortars
strength – estimated in 2021 to have up to 3,000 combatants
financial and other support – draws funding from the narcotics trade, extortion of oil and gas companies, illegal mining (expansion into Venezuela has included taking control of mines, allowing the group to use the acquisition of gold and diamond deposits to help provide funding), and kidnapping-for-ransom payments
designation – placed on the US Department of State's list of Foreign Terrorist Organizations on 8 October 1997

Palestine Islamic Jihad (PIJ)

aka – PIJ-Shaqaqi Faction; PIJ-Shallah Faction; Islamic Jihad of Palestine; Islamic Jihad in Palestine; Abu Ghunaym Squad of the Hizballah Bayt al-Maqdis; Al-Quds Squads; Al-Quds Brigades; Saraya al-Quds; Al-Awdah Brigades; Harakat al-Jihad al-Islami al-Filastin
history – formed by militant Palestinians in 1979 in Gaza; is the smaller of the two main Palestinian militant groups in Gaza, the other being the ruling HAMAS group with which it cooperates; unlike HAMAS, PIJ refuses to negotiate with Israel; since the 1980s, has conducted numerous attacks on Israel, including barrages of mortar and rocket strikes; continued active operations in 2022; it has partnered with the Hizballah terrorist group to carry out joint operations
goals – committed to the destruction of Israel and to the creation of an Islamic state in historic Palestine, an area that covers present-day Israel, Gaza, and the West Bank
leadership and organization – led by Ziyad al-NAKHALLAH and an eight-member leadership council (al-Maktab al-Am or General Bureau); has a 15-member political council, which represents PIJ members in Gaza, the West Bank, Israeli prisons, and abroad; also has an armed wing, known as the al-Quds (Jerusalem) Brigades, which has subordinate regional military commands or "brigades" that are comprised of cells and small units; in 2021-2022 reportedly had established up to 6 "brigades" representing cities in the West Bank
areas of operation – Israel, Gaza, and the West Bank; some leaders and members reside in Lebanon, Syria, and throughout the Middle East
targets, tactics, and weapons – targets Israeli civilians and military personnel with bombings, small arms attacks on military patrols, and mortar and rocket attacks; most rocket attacks have struck southern Israel, but the group has developed longer-range versions capable of reaching further into Israel, including Tel Aviv; armed with small arms and light weapons, artillery rockets, man-portable air defense systems (MANPADs), mortars, armed unmanned aerial vehicles (aka drones), antitank guided missiles, rockets, and improvised explosive devices; the group in the past targeted Israel with suicide bombings and abductions
strength – unclear; estimates in 2021 ranged from about 1,000 up to several thousand members
financial and other support – receives financial assistance, military training, and weapons primarily from Iran; Hizballah provides safe harbor to PIJ leaders and representatives in Lebanon and probably facilitates Iran's support to PIJ; trains with HAMAS; maintains a tunnel network to smuggle goods, arms, and ammunition across borders
designation – placed on the US Department of State's list of Foreign Terrorist Organizations on 8 October 1997

Palestine Liberation Front – Abu Abbas Faction

aka – PLF; PLF-Abu Abbas; Palestine Liberation Front
history – formed in the late 1970s as a splinter group from the Popular Front for the Liberation of Palestine-General Command; later split into pro-Palestine Liberation Organization (PLO), pro-Syrian, and pro-Libyan factions; pro-PLO faction was led by Muhammad ZAYDAN (aka Abu ABBAS) and was based in Baghdad, Iraq, before the US invasion in 2003; ZAYDAN died in 2004 of natural causes while in US custody in Iraq; responsible for the 1985 attack on the Italian cruise ship *Achille Lauro* and the murder of a US citizen on board; suspected of supporting terrorism against Israel by other Palestinian groups into the 1990s, but the group was largely quiet until the 2008-10 timeframe, when it claimed responsibility for several attacks on Israeli civilians and military personnel; has not publicly claimed any attacks since 2016, but as of 2021, it reportedly continued to maintain a presence in some refugee camps
goals – bolster its staging capabilities in Gaza against Israel and, ultimately, destroy the state of Israel in order to establish a secular, Marxist Palestinian state with Jerusalem as its capital
leadership and organization – led by Secretary General Dr. Wasil ABU YUSUF, a longtime member on the PLO's executive committee
areas of operation – based in Gaza, where it maintains a recruitment and paramilitary training presence in most of the refugee camps; has members in Lebanon, Syria, and the West Bank
targets, tactics, and weapons – primarily targeted Israeli military and security personnel with occasional shootings and improvised explosive device attacks; weapons include small arms, artillery rockets, and explosives, including improvised explosive devices
strength – estimated in 2018 to have between 50 and 500 members; more current estimates not available
financial and other support – not available
designation – placed on the US Department of State's list of Foreign Terrorist Organizations on 8 October 1997

Popular Front for the Liberation of Palestine (PFLP)

aka – Halhul Gang; Halhul Squad; Palestinian Popular Resistance Forces; PPRF; Red Eagle Gang; Red Eagle Group; Red Eagles; Martyr Abu-Ali Mustafa Battalion
history – formed in December 1967 as an umbrella organization for Marxist and Arab nationalist groups after Israel seized the West Bank; became the second largest faction, and the main opposition force to Fatah, within the Palestine Liberation Organization (PLO); earned a reputation for large-scale international attacks in the 1960s and 1970s, including high-profile hijackings of Israeli and Western aircraft; has been in decline since the 1980s following the collapse of the Soviet Union which had been its chief benefactor, and the emergence of non-PLO groups such as HAMAS and Palestine Islamic Jihad; since the 2000s, has focused its attacks on Israel and launched multiple joint operations with other Palestinian militant groups but its operational tempo has been low; since June 2017, only one attack has been attributed to the group; in September 2019, four members

were arrested by Israeli security services for detonating an improvised explosive device that resulted in several Israeli casualties; has not conducted any further known attacks, but remained active through 2021
goals – destroy the state of Israel and, ultimately, establish a secular, Marxist Palestinian state with Jerusalem as its capital
leadership and organization – official leader, General Secretary Ahmad SA'DAT, has been serving a 30-year prison sentence in Israel since 2006; Deputy Secretary General 'Abd-al-Rahim MALLUH (var: Abdul Rahim MALLOUH) oversees daily operations; MALLUH is also a member of the PLO's Executive Committee; has a Political Bureau and a military wing known as the Martyr Abu-Ali Mustafa Brigade
areas of operation – headquartered in Gaza; also operates in Israel, Lebanon, Syria, and the West Bank
targets, tactics, and weapons – since 2008, has claimed responsibility for numerous attacks on Israeli military forces in Gaza, as well as mortar shells and rockets fired from Gaza into Israel; members have been arrested by Israeli security forces for plotting to carry out kidnappings; in 2014, two members with axes, guns, and knives attacked a synagogue in West Jerusalem, killing five; in the early 2000s, the group assassinated the Israeli Tourism Minister and carried out at least two suicide bombings; fighters are equipped with small arms, light machine guns, artillery rockets, mortars, man-portable surface-to-air missiles, improvised weapons, and explosives, including improvised explosive devices and suicide vests
strength – not available
financial and other support – not available; historically received funds from the former Soviet Union and China; has claimed in draws support from Iran
designation – placed on the US Department of State's list of Foreign Terrorist Organizations on 8 October 1997

Popular Front for the Liberation of Palestine - General Command (PFLP-GC)

aka – PFLP-GC, Al-Jibha Sha'biya lil-Tahrir Filistin-al-Qadiya al-Ama, Ahmed Jibril Militia
history – a Marxist-Nationalist and secular group that split from the Popular Front for the Liberation of Palestine (PFLP) in 1968, claiming it wanted to concentrate more on resistance and less on politics; carried out dozens of attacks in Europe and the Middle East during the 1970s and 1980s, including bombings of two Western airliners; was also was known for cross-border terrorist attacks into Israel using unusual means, such as hot-air balloons and motorized hang gliders; since the early 1990s, has primarily focused on supporting Hizballah's attacks against Israel, training members of other Palestinian terrorist groups, and smuggling weapons; between 2012 and 2015, claimed responsibility for several rocket attacks against Israel, as well as the bombing of a bus carrying civilians; has not claimed responsibility for any attacks since 2015 but remained an active participant in the Syrian conflict through at least 2020
goals – preserve Syrian President Bashar al-ASAD's regime; destroy the state of Israel and, ultimately, establish a secular, Marxist Palestinian state
leadership and organization – Talal NAJI (elected leader in July 2021 after the death of Ahmad JIBRIL, the group's leader and founder); overall organization not available, but has a military wing known as the Jihad Jibril Brigades
areas of operation – political leadership is headquartered in Damascus and many of the group's members have fought in Syria since 2012; maintains bases in southern Lebanon and a presence in the Palestinian refugee camps in Lebanon and Syria; maintains a small presence in Gaza; claimed that it launched rockets against Israel in 2021
targets, tactics, and weapons – contemporary targets are primarily paramilitary groups combatting Syrian regime forces; previously targeted Israeli military personnel and civilians with bombings and rocket attacks; fighters are armed with small arms, light machine guns, artillery rockets; rocket-propelled grenades, and explosives, including improvised explosive devices and suicide vests
strength – assessed in 2020 to have several hundred members
financial and other support – receives funds, logistical support, military training, and weapons from Iran and Syria, as well as the designated terrorist group Hizballah; garners payments in exchange for providing training to other armed groups, including HAMAS
designation – placed on the US Department of State's list of Foreign Terrorist Organizations on 8 October 1997

Real Irish Republican Army (RIRA)

aka – Real IRA; 32 County Sovereignty Committee; 32 County Sovereignty Movement; Irish Republican Prisoners Welfare Association; Real Oglaigh Na Heireann; Óglaigh na hÉireann (ÓNH); New Irish Republican Army (New IRA or NIRA)
established – formed in 1997 as the clandestine armed wing of the 32 County Sovereignty Movement, a political pressure group dedicated to removing British forces from Northern Ireland and unifying Ireland; claims to be the true descendent of the original Irish Republican Army; many members are former Provisional Irish Republican Army who left the organization after the group renewed its ceasefire in 1997 and brought extensive experience in terrorist tactics and bomb-making to RIRA; has historically sought to disrupt the Northern Ireland peace process and did not participate in the September 2005 weapons decommissioning; despite internal rifts and calls by some jailed members, including the group's founder Michael "Mickey" McKEVITT, for a cease-fire and disbandment, RIRA has pledged to continue conducting attacks; in 2012, RIRA merged with other small dissident republican groups to form the New IRA; reportedly cooperates with the Continuity Irish Republican Army (CIRA); claimed responsibility for a bomb placed under a police officer's car in Belfast in June 2019, and Irish security forces arrested a number of New IRA members in 2020; remained active into 2022
goals – disrupt the Northern Ireland peace process, remove British rule in Northern Ireland and, ultimately, unify Ireland
leadership and organization – current leadership not available; reportedly has a command structure similar to the former Provisional IRA, with an "Army Council" consisting of a chief of staff and directors for training, operations, finance, and publicity; rank-and-file members operate in covert cells
areas of operation – United Kingdom and the Republic of Ireland
targets, tactics, and weapons – primarily targets British security forces and police officers in Northern Ireland, as well as civilians; tactics typically involve shootings and low-impact bombing attacks; weapons include small arms, mortars, and explosives, including improvised explosive devices and car bombs
strength – estimated in 2020 to have approximately 100 active members; may receive limited support from IRA hardliners and sympathizers who are dissatisfied with the IRA's ceasefire and with Sinn Fein's involvement in the peace process
financial and other support – receives funding from money laundering, smuggling, and other criminal activities; suspected of receiving funds from sympathizers in the US; has attempted to buy weapons from gun dealers in the US and the Balkans
designation – placed on the US Department of State's list of Foreign Terrorist Organizations on 16 May 2001

Revolutionary Armed Forces of Colombia – People's Army (FARC-EP)

aka – Fuerzas Armadas Revolucionarias de Colombia – Ejercito del Pueblo; FARC dissidents FARC – EP ; Revolutionary Armed Forces of Colombia dissidents FARC – EP; FARC – D/FARC – EP; Grupo Armado Organizado Residual FARC – EP; GAO-R FARC – EP; Residual Organized Armed Group FARC – EP
history – in 2016, the Revolutionary Armed Forces of Colombia (FARC) signed a peace deal in which about 13,000 fighters gave up their weapons in exchange for numerous concessions from the Colombian Government, including development programs for rural areas and the opportunity

for former guerrilla leaders to participate in local politics and avoid time in prison; however, a group of approximately 1,000 FARC "dissidents," led by Nestor Gregorio VERA Fernandez, commander of the FARC 1st Front, refused to lay down their arms; the group returned to fighting and eventually adopted the name FARC-EP; in late 2019, the Colombian Government began conducting military operations against FARC-EP, which continued into 2022; the FARC-EP in 2021 was reportedly in conflict with another FARC dissident group and US-designated Foreign Terrorist Organization (FTO), Segunda Marquetalia, over control of revenue and territory
goals – the former FARC sought to install a Marxist-Leninist regime in Colombia through a violent revolution; the group seeks to unite all FARC dissidents and leftist guerrilla groups in Colombia
leadership and organization – not available; former leader (Nestor Gregorio VERA Fernandez; aka Ivan MORDISCO) reportedly killed July 2022; reportedly organized similarly to the former FARC with regionally based commands and subordinate "fronts" or "blocs" and "mobile columns," although some information points to a more fragmented command and control structure based in large part on alliances with disparate ex-FARC members and groups, as well as criminal organizations
areas of operation – FARC-EP under VERA operates primarily in Meta, Guaviare, and Caquetá departments and has a presence in Venezuela (particularly Apure state); it also maintains alliances with ex-FARC individuals and groups in other parts of Colombia, particularly along narco-trafficking routes and areas that generate revenue; ex-FARC groups operate in many of the departments where the FARC previously operated, including along the borders with Venezuela, Brazil, and Ecuador
targets, tactics, and weapons – responsible for the vast majority of the armed attacks attributed to FARC dissident elements since 2019; FARC-EP has also been responsible for the killing of political candidates and former FARC members, the kidnapping of a political operative, and attempted assassinations of a department governor; the former FARC targeted Colombian political, military, and economic figures, as well as pro-government paramilitary groups and economic targets, such as oil pipelines; was responsible for large numbers of kidnappings-for-ransoms, including foreign citizens; combined guerrilla-style and terrorist tactics, including ambushes, complex ground assaults, grenade and mortar attacks, assassinations, kidnappings, and bombings; weapons included small arms, light and heavy machine guns, landmines, mortars, grenades, small rockets, and explosives, including improvised explosive devices
strength – unclear; possibly as many as 2,500 members in 2021; in 2021, the total number of dissidents was estimated to be about 5,000, including approximately 2,000-2,500 active and another 2,000-2,500 part-time supporters
financial and other support – generate funds through narcotics trafficking, extortion, illegal mining (typically gold), and other illicit economies; collects taxes from locals in areas it occupies
designation – placed on the US Department of State's list of Foreign Terrorist Organizations (FTO) on 30 November 2021; the designation followed the revocation of the designation of the Revolutionary Forces of Colombia (FARC) as an FTO; note – the former FARC has a political party (Comunes or "together") that holds seats in the Colombian Congress

Revolutionary People's Liberation Party/Front (DHKP/C)

aka – Dev Sol; Dev Sol Armed Revolutionary Units; Dev Sol Silahli Devrimci Birlikleri; Dev Sol SDB; Devrimci Halk Kurtulus Partisi-Cephesi; Devrimci Sol; Revolutionary Left
history – formed in Turkey originally in 1978 as Devrimci Sol, or Dev Sol, a splinter faction of Dev Genc (Revolutionary Youth); renamed in 1994 after factional infighting; "Party" refers to the group's political activities and "Front" alludes to its militant operations; advocates a Marxist-Leninist ideology and opposes the United States, NATO, and the Turkish establishment; reorganized after the death of its founder and leader Dursun KARATAS from cancer in 2008 and was reportedly in competition with the Kurdistan Workers' Party for influence in Turkey; since the late 1980s has primarily targeted Turkish security and military officials; in the 1990s began to conduct attacks against foreign—including US—interests; activities have declined in recent years, but the group remained active and continued to be targeted by Turkish security forces through 2021
goals – strives to establish a socialist state and to abolish Turkish prisons
leadership and organization – current leadership not available; Turkish authorities arrested suspected leaders Umit ILTER and Caferi Sadik EROGLU in February 2019; reportedly operates in small, clandestine cells
areas of operation – located in Turkey, primarily in Adana, Ankara, Istanbul, and Izmir; other members reside and plan operations in European countries
targets, tactics, and weapons – responsible for killing dozens of current and retired Turkish senior officials, police officers, soldiers, businessmen, and other civilians since its inception; launched rocket attacks on police and government buildings, including a rocket attack against the Istanbul police headquarters in 2017; has targeted foreign interests, especially US military and diplomatic personnel and facilities, such as a suicide bombing attack against the US Embassy in 2013; typical tactics include assassinations, hostage taking, rocket attacks, suicide bombings, remotely detonated bombs, and car bombs; weapons include small arms, hand grenades, artillery rockets, and explosives, including improvised explosive devices, suicide vests, and car bombs
strength – was estimated in 2020 to have several dozen members inside Turkey, with a support network throughout Europe
financial and other support – finances its activities chiefly through donations and extortion; raises funds primarily in Europe
designation – placed on the US Department of State's list of Foreign Terrorist Organizations on 8 October 1997

Revolutionary Struggle (RS)

aka – Epanastatikos Aghonas; EA
history – RS is a Marxist extremist group that emerged in 2003 following the arrests of members of two other Greek Marxist groups, 17 November (17N) and Revolutionary People's Struggle; first gained notoriety when it claimed responsibility for the September 2003 bombings at the Athens Courthouse during the trials of 17N members; has since conducted numerous attacks against Greek and US targets in Greece; largely inactive since the 2017 arrest of its last known leader
goals – disrupt the influence of globalization and international capitalism on Greek society and, ultimately, overthrow the Greek Government
leadership and organization – not available; former leader Panagiota ROUPA (aka Pola ROUPA) was Greece's most wanted terrorist until she was taken into Greek custody in January 2017 and later sentenced to 25 years imprisonment; organizational information not available
areas of operation – operated exclusively inside Greece, primarily in Athens
targets, tactics, and weapons – targeted Greek Government officials and buildings and officials' residences, multinational firms, domestic and foreign financial institutes, and embassies and diplomats; modeled its modus operandi on past 17N attacks, incorporating high-profile assassination attempts, armed raids, bank robberies, car bombings, and rocket attacks; used small arms and light weapons, rocket-propelled grenades, and explosives, including improvised explosive devices and car bombs
strength – not available
financial and other support – unclear, but most likely supported itself through criminal activities, including bank robberies
designation – placed on the US Department of State's list of Foreign Terrorist Organizations on 18 May 2009

Segunda Marquetalia

aka – New Marquetalia; Second Marquetalia; La Nueva Marquetalia; FARC dissidents Segunda Marquetalia; Revolutionary Armed Forces of Colombia Dissidents Segunda Marquetalia; FARC-D Segunda Marquetalia; Grupo Armado Organizado Residual Segunda Marquetalia; GAO-R Segunda Marquetalia;, Residual Organized Armed Group Segunda Marquetalia; Armed Organized Residual Group Segunda Marquetalia

history – created in August 2019 by former commanders of the Revolutionary Armed Forces of Colombia (FARC) after they abandoned the 2016 peace accord between the FARC and the Colombian Government because of frustration over perceived lack of progress in implementing the terms of the accord; attempts to carry out the key functions of the state in the areas under its control, including taxation, security, and maintaining infrastructure; as of 2021, the Colombian Government was conducting military operations against the group, and it was reportedly in conflict with US-designated Foreign Terrorist Organization (FTO) FARC-EP over control of revenue and territory; also in 2021, two senior leaders were killed in Venezuela; active in 2022

goals – the former FARC sought to install a Marxist-Leninist regime in Colombia through a violent revolution; the group seeks to unite or form alliances with armed leftist guerrilla organizations in Colombia, including ex-FARC members, the ELN (National Liberation Army), and the smaller EPL (People's Liberation Army)

leadership and organization – Luciano Marin ARANGO (aka Ivan MARQUEZ) is the founder and leader (he was the FARC's second-in-command before demobilization, commander of the Caribbean bloc, and lead negotiator during the peace talks with the Colombian Government); has a central committee (aka central command), known as the National Directorate; claims to consist of a political wing (Partido Comunista Clandestino de Colombia or Clandestine Communist Party), as well as armed guerrilla forces and both armed and unarmed militia units; similar to the former FARC, it operates in "blocs" and "fronts"

areas of operation – operates primarily in northern Colombia in former zones of control under ARANGO, including the Serranía del Perijá mountain range and the departments of La Guajira, Cesar, and Arauca, as well as in the state of Apure in Venezuela

targets, tactics, and weapons – is responsible for the killings of former FARC members and community leaders; has engaged in assassinations, hostage-taking, including the kidnapping and holding for ransom of government employees, and attempted killings of political leaders; the former FARC traditionally targeted Colombian political, military, and economic figures, as well as pro-government paramilitary groups and economic targets, such as oil pipelines; was responsible for large numbers of kidnappings-for-ransoms, including foreign citizens; combined guerrilla-style and terrorist tactics, including ambushes, complex ground assaults, grenade and mortar attacks, assassinations, kidnappings, and bombings; weapons included small arms, light and heavy machine guns, landmines, mortars, grenades, and explosives, including improvised explosive devices

strength – specific numbers not available; estimates in 2020-2021 were as high as 5,000 total dissidents, including approximately 2,000-2,500 active and another 2,000-2,500 part-time supporters

financial and other support – reportedly generates funds through narcotics trafficking, extortion, illegal mining (typically gold), and other illicit economies; collects taxes from locals in areas it occupies

designation – placed on the US Department of State's list of Foreign Terrorist Organizations on 30 November 2021; the designation followed the revocation of the designation of the Revolutionary Forces of Colombia (FARC) as an FTO; note – the former FARC has a political party (Comunes or "together") that holds seats in the Colombian Congress

Shining Path (Sendero Luminoso, SL)

aka – Ejército Guerrillero Popular (People's Guerrilla Army); EGP; Ejército Popular de Liberación (People's Liberation Army); EPL; Partido Comunista del Peru (Communist Party of Peru); PCP; Partido Comunista del Peru en el Sendero Luminoso de Jose Carlos Mariategui (Communist Party of Peru on the Shining Path of Jose Carlos Mariategui); Socorro Popular del Peru (People's Aid of Peru); SPP; Militarizado Partido Comunista del Peru; MCPC; Militarized Communist Party of Peru

history – formed in the late 1960s as a breakaway faction of the Peruvian Communist Party by former university professor Abimael GUZMAN, whose teachings provided the basis of the group's militant Maoist doctrine; was one of the most ruthless terrorist groups in the Western Hemisphere at its height in the 1980s; conducted an insurgency against the Peruvian Government and waged a campaign of violence on civilians, particularly the rural peasantry; the conflict resulted in the deaths of an estimated 70,000 Peruvians between 1980 and 2000; in September 1992, Peruvian authorities captured GUZMAN, who died in prison in 2021; following his capture, membership declined and the remnants split into two factions; by 2014, one faction had largely been eliminated, while the other continued to operate; the group continues to try to reinvent itself, organize, and proselytize, particularly amongst university students and in rural areas; in recent years has called itself Militarizado Partido Comunista del Peru (the Militarized Communist Party of Peru); remnants of the group continued to be active in 2022

goals – generate revenue by providing security to narcotics traffickers and by growing coca to produce cocaine; historically aimed to replace existing Peruvian institutions with a peasant revolutionary regime

leadership and organization – Victor Quispe PALOMINO (aka Comrade Jose); organization not available

areas of operation – Peru; most active in the Valley of the Apurimac, Ene, and Mantaro Rivers (VRAEM), which includes parts of Ayacucho, Cusco, Huancavelica, Huanuco, and Junin regions

targets, tactics, and weapons – primary targets in recent years have been Peruvian soldiers and police personnel running counter-narcotics and counter-terrorism operations against the group; also abducts and kills civilians; killed 16 civilians in an attack on a village as late as May 2021; typically uses guerrilla style hit-and-run tactics, including grenade attacks and snipers with long-range rifles; weapons include small arms and other light weapons, grenades, and other explosives, including improvised explosive devices

strength – estimated in 2022 to have less than 300 members

financial resources – primarily funded by the illicit narcotics trade

designation – placed on the US Department of State's list of Foreign Terrorist Organizations on 8 October 1997

Tehrik-e-Taliban Pakistan (TTP)

aka – Pakistani Taliban; Tehreek-e-Taliban; Tehrik-e-Taliban; Tehrik-i-Taliban Pakistan

history – formed in 2007 to oppose Pakistani military efforts in the Federally Administered Tribal Areas (FATA); previously disparate tribal militants agreed to cooperate and eventually coalesced under the leadership of now-deceased leader Baitullah MEHSUD (var. MAHSUD); emerged as one of Pakistan's deadliest terrorist organizations; responsible for assaults on a Pakistani naval base in 2011, Karachi's international airport in 2014, and a military school in Peshawar that killed 150 people, mostly students, also in 2014; entered into peace talks with the Pakistani Government in 2014, but talks collapsed that same year; beginning around 2014, the group suffered from several years of internal conflict, fragmentation, public backlash for deadly attacks targeting civilians, and members defecting to ISIS's Khorasan branch in Afghanistan; however, in 2020-2022, the group demonstrated signs of resurgence, with more than 15 jihadist groups, including Jamat-ul-Ahrar (JuA), Hizb-ul-Ahrar (HuA), and the designated FTO Lashkar I Jhangvi (LJ), pledging allegiance to TTP; JuA and HuA had split off from TTP around 2014; in addition, the group increased the number of cross-border attacks from Afghanistan into Pakistan; in March 2022, TTP announced that it was launching a spring "offensive" of attacks against Pakistani security services; TTP has ties to and draws ideological guidance from al-Qa'ida (AQ), while elements of AQ have relied

in part on TTP for safe haven in the Pashtun areas along the Afghanistan-Pakistani border; the group has conducted peace talks with the Pakistan Government accompanied by brief cease-fires in 2021 and 2022
goals – unite all the jihadist groups in Pakistan under one banner; push the Pakistani Government out of Khyber Pakhtunkwa Province (formerly known as the Federally Administered Tribal Areas) and establish strict Islamic law; ultimately, establish an Islamic caliphate over all of Pakistan
leadership and organization – led by Mufti Noor Wali MEHSUD since June 2018; has a shura council with two regional committees covering seven zones of operation; however, because TTP is a coalition of more than 15 groups, as well as tribal factions, operational levels of cooperation may vary

areas of operation – Afghanistan and Pakistan, particularly the tribal belt along the Afghanistan-Pakistan border, Kunar and Paktika Provinces in Afghanistan, and the Pakistani regions of North Waziristan, South Waziristan, and Balochistan
targets, tactics, and weapons – targets Pakistani Government officials and military, security, and police personnel, as well as pro-government tribal elders, Shia Muslims, educational figures, and Westerners; previously targeted US military personnel in Afghanistan; claimed responsibility for a failed 2010 attempt to detonate an explosive device in New York City's Times Square; suspected of involvement in the 2007 assassination of former Pakistani Prime Minister Benazir BHUTTO; has attacked an airport, buses, churches, government buildings, homes of Pakistani officials, markets, hotels, military bases and convoys, mosques, public gatherings, schools, security checkpoints, and entire neighborhoods of Shia Muslims; was heavily criticized for indiscriminate attacks on civilians, including attacks on an election campaign gathering in 2018 that killed more than 20 and an assault on a school in 2014 that killed 150, including 130 school children; however, after MEHSUD took command in 2018, the group reportedly issued new targeting guidelines restricting attacks on civilians; tactics typically have involved hit-and-run raids, small arms attacks, complex assaults, kidnappings, assassinations, suicide bombings, and grenade, mortar, and rocket attacks; weapons include small arms, light and heavy machine guns; mortars, and explosives, including remotely detonated improvised explosive devices, suicide vests, and car bombs
strength – assessed in 2022 to have between 3,000 and 5,000 fighters
financial and other support – likely raises most of its funds through kidnappings-for-ransom, extortion, and other criminal activity, including arms and narcotics trafficking
designation – placed on the US Department of State's list of Foreign Terrorist Organizations on 1 September 2010

REFERENCE MAPS

PHYSICAL MAP OF AFRICA

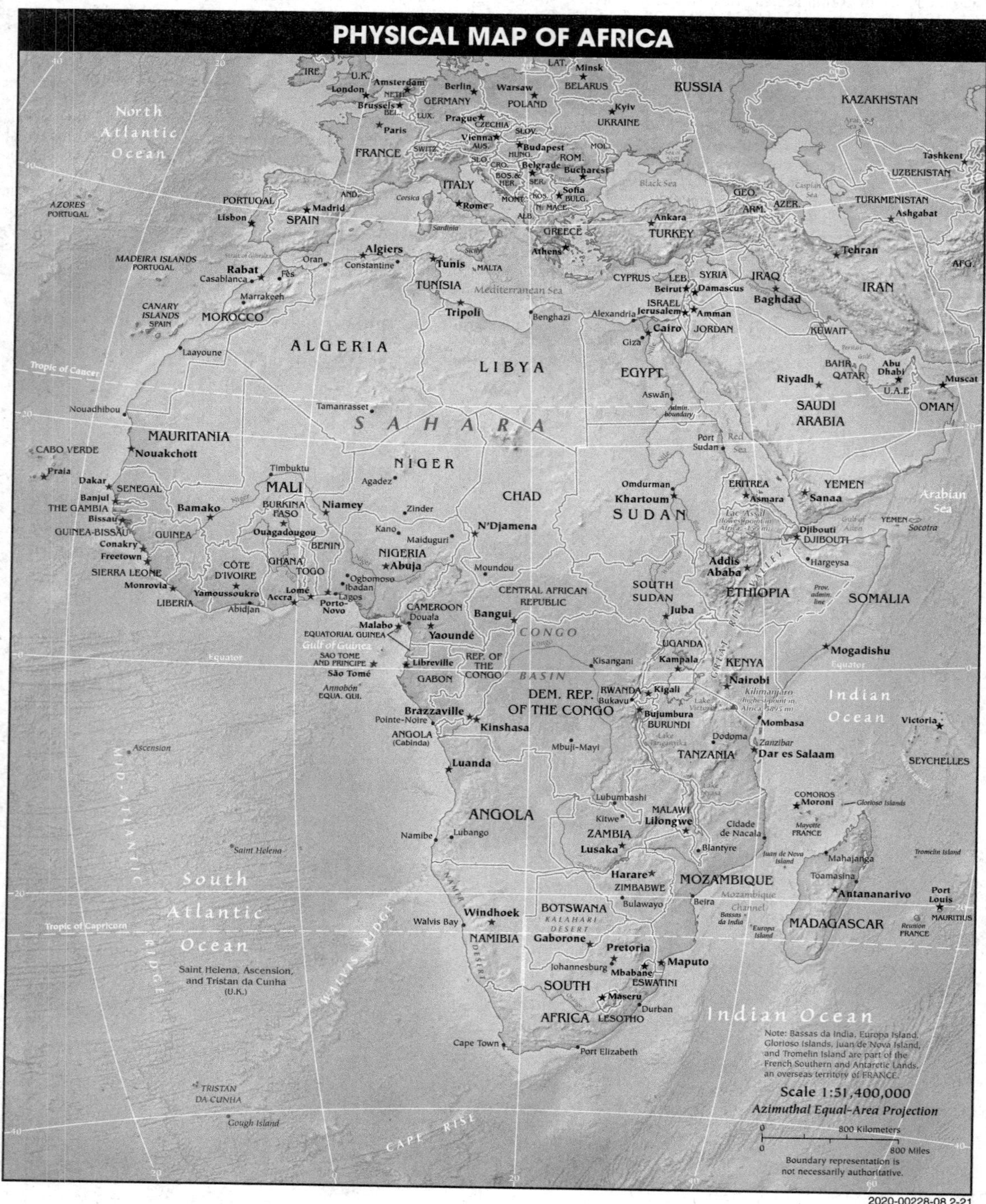

2020-00228-08 2-21

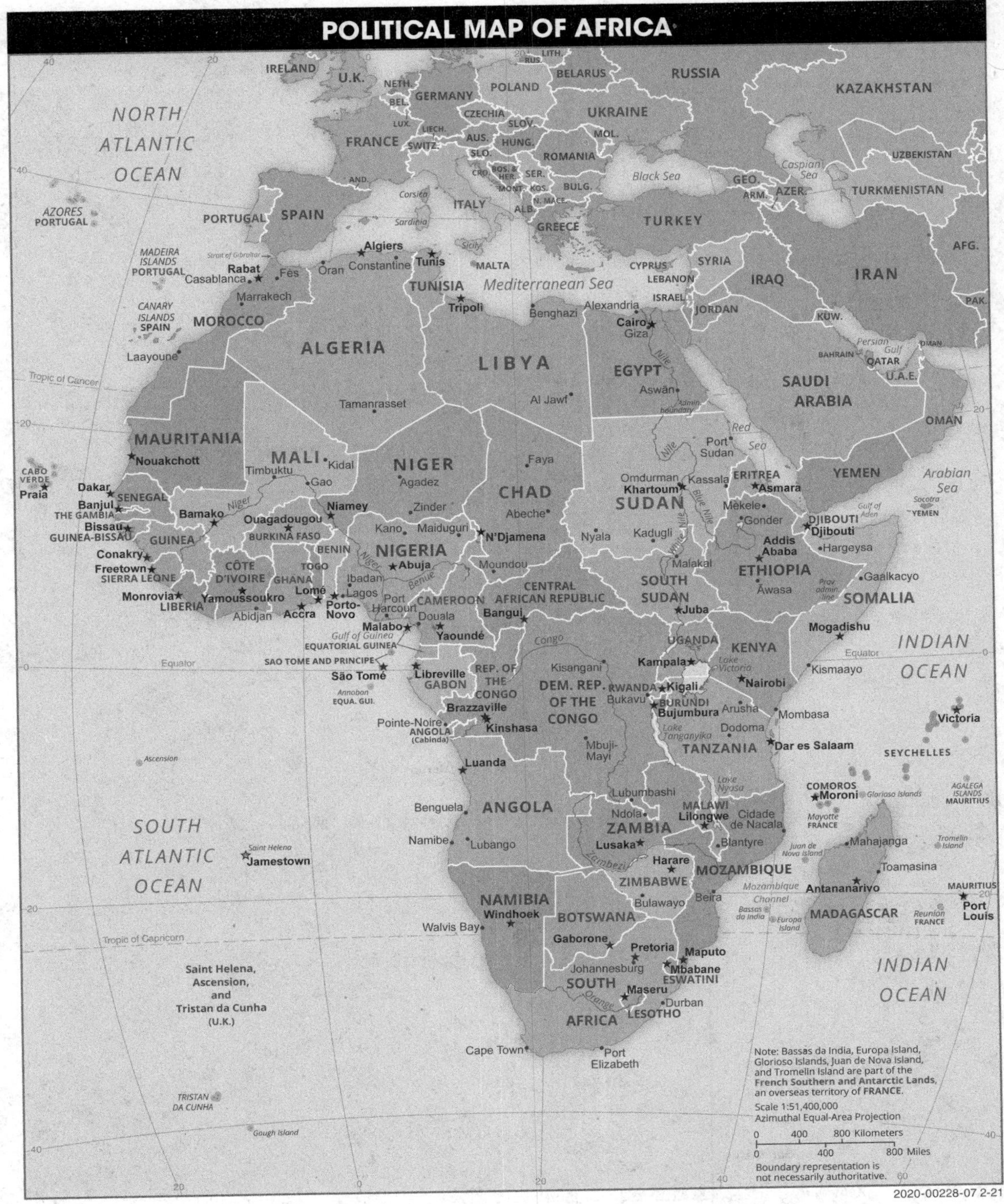
POLITICAL MAP OF AFRICA
IRELAND
U.K.
NETH.
BEL.
GERMANY
LUX.
LIECH.
SWITZ.
FRANCE
CZECHIA
AUS.
SLOV.
HUNG.
SLO.
CRO.
BOS. & HER.
SER.
MONT.
KOS.
N. MACE.
ALB.
POLAND
LITH.
RUS.
BELARUS
RUSSIA
UKRAINE
MOL.
ROMANIA
BULG.
GREECE
KAZAKHSTAN
UZBEKISTAN
TURKMENISTAN
Caspian Sea
GEO.
ARM.
AZER.
Black Sea
TURKEY
AFG.
AND.
SPAIN
PORTUGAL
Corsica
Sardinia
ITALY
Sicily
MALTA
NORTH ATLANTIC OCEAN
AZORES PORTUGAL
MADEIRA ISLANDS PORTUGAL
Strait of Gibraltar
CANARY ISLANDS SPAIN
Algiers
Tunis
Constantine
Oran
Rabat
Fès
Casablanca
Marrakech
MOROCCO
Laayoune
TUNISIA
Tripoli
Mediterranean Sea
CYPRUS
LEBANON
SYRIA
ISRAEL
JORDAN
IRAQ
IRAN
PAK.
KUW.
BAHRAIN
QATAR
U.A.E.
OMAN
Persian Gulf
SAUDI ARABIA
Benghazi
Alexandria
Cairo
Giza
ALGERIA
LIBYA
EGYPT
Nile
Aswān
Admin. boundary
Tropic of Cancer
Tamanrasset
Al Jawf
Red Sea
Port Sudan
MAURITANIA
Nouakchott
MALI
Kidal
Timbuktu
Gao
NIGER
Agadez
Faya
CHAD
CABO VERDE
Praia
Dakar
SENEGAL
Banjul
THE GAMBIA
Bissau
GUINEA-BISSAU
GUINEA
Conakry
Freetown
SIERRA LEONE
Monrovia
LIBERIA
Bamako
Niger
Ouagadougou
BURKINA FASO
Niamey
Zinder
Kano
Maiduguri
N'Djamena
Abeche
Omdurman
Khartoum
Kassala
SUDAN
ERITREA
Asmara
YEMEN
Arabian Sea
Socotra YEMEN
Gulf of Aden
Mek'ele
Gonder
DJIBOUTI
Djibouti
Hargeysa
Nyala
Kadugli
Blue Nile
White Nile
Malakal
Addis Ababa
ETHIOPIA
Gaalkacyo
CÔTE D'IVOIRE
Yamoussoukro
Abidjan
GHANA
Accra
TOGO
Lomé
BENIN
Porto-Novo
Lagos
Ibadan
NIGERIA
Abuja
Benue
Port Harcourt
Moundou
CENTRAL AFRICAN REPUBLIC
Bangui
SOUTH SUDAN
Juba
Awasa
Prov. admin. line
SOMALIA
CAMEROON
Douala
Yaoundé
Malabo
Gulf of Guinea
EQUATORIAL GUINEA
SAO TOME AND PRINCIPE
São Tomé
Annobon EQUA. GUI.
Libreville
GABON
REP. OF THE CONGO
Congo
Kisangani
DEM. REP. OF THE CONGO
UGANDA
Kampala
Lake Victoria
KENYA
Nairobi
Mogadishu
Kismaayo
INDIAN OCEAN
Equator
RWANDA
Kigali
Bukavu
BURUNDI
Bujumbura
Arusha
Mombasa
Brazzaville
Kinshasa
Pointe-Noire
ANGOLA (Cabinda)
Lake Tanganyika
Dodoma
TANZANIA
Dar es Salaam
Victoria
SEYCHELLES
Ascension
Luanda
Mbuji-Mayi
Lubumbashi
Lake Nyasa
COMOROS
Moroni
Glorioso Islands
AGALEGA ISLANDS MAURITIUS
Benguela
ANGOLA
Ndola
MALAWI
Lilongwe
Cidade de Nacala
Mayotte FRANCE
ZAMBIA
Lusaka
Blantyre
Juan de Nova Island
Mahajanga
Tromelin Island
SOUTH ATLANTIC OCEAN
Saint Helena
Jamestown
Namibe
Lubango
Zambezi
Harare
ZIMBABWE
MOZAMBIQUE
Toamasina
Antananarivo
MAURITIUS
Port Louis
Mozambique Channel
Bulawayo
Beira
NAMIBIA
Windhoek
Walvis Bay
BOTSWANA
Bassas da India
Europa Island
MADAGASCAR
Reunion FRANCE
Tropic of Capricorn
Gaborone
Pretoria
Maputo
Johannesburg
Mbabane
ESWATINI
SOUTH AFRICA
Maseru
Orange
Durban
LESOTHO
Saint Helena, Ascension, and Tristan da Cunha (U.K.)
Cape Town
Port Elizabeth
TRISTAN DA CUNHA
Gough Island
Note: Bassas da India, Europa Island, Glorioso Islands, Juan de Nova Island, and Tromelin Island are part of the French Southern and Antarctic Lands, an overseas territory of FRANCE.
Scale 1:51,400,000
Azimuthal Equal-Area Projection
0 400 800 Kilometers
0 400 800 Miles
Boundary representation is not necessarily authoritative.
2020-00228-07 2-21

PHYSICAL MAP OF ANTARCTIC REGION

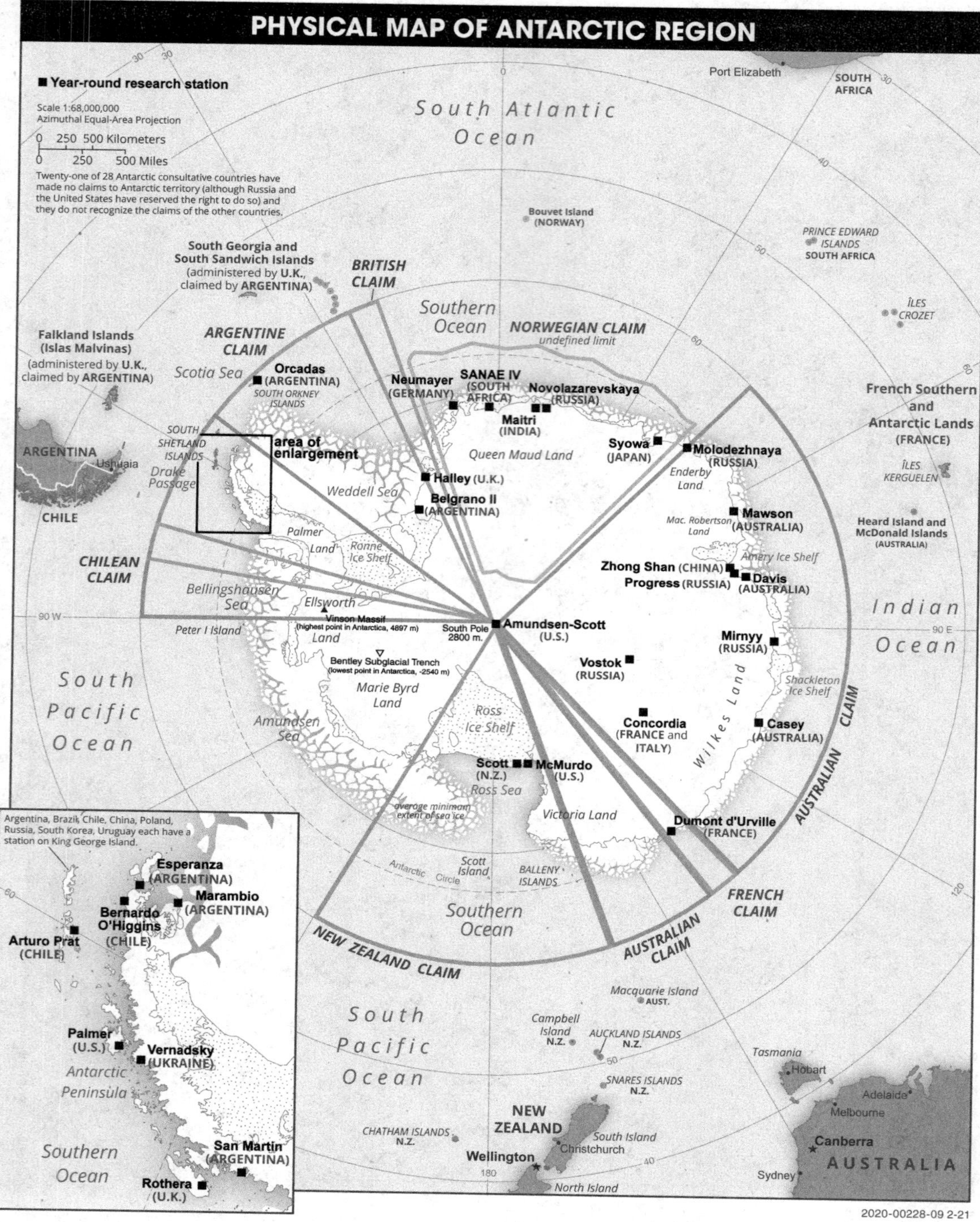

POLITICAL MAP OF ARCTIC REGION

2020-00228-03 2-21

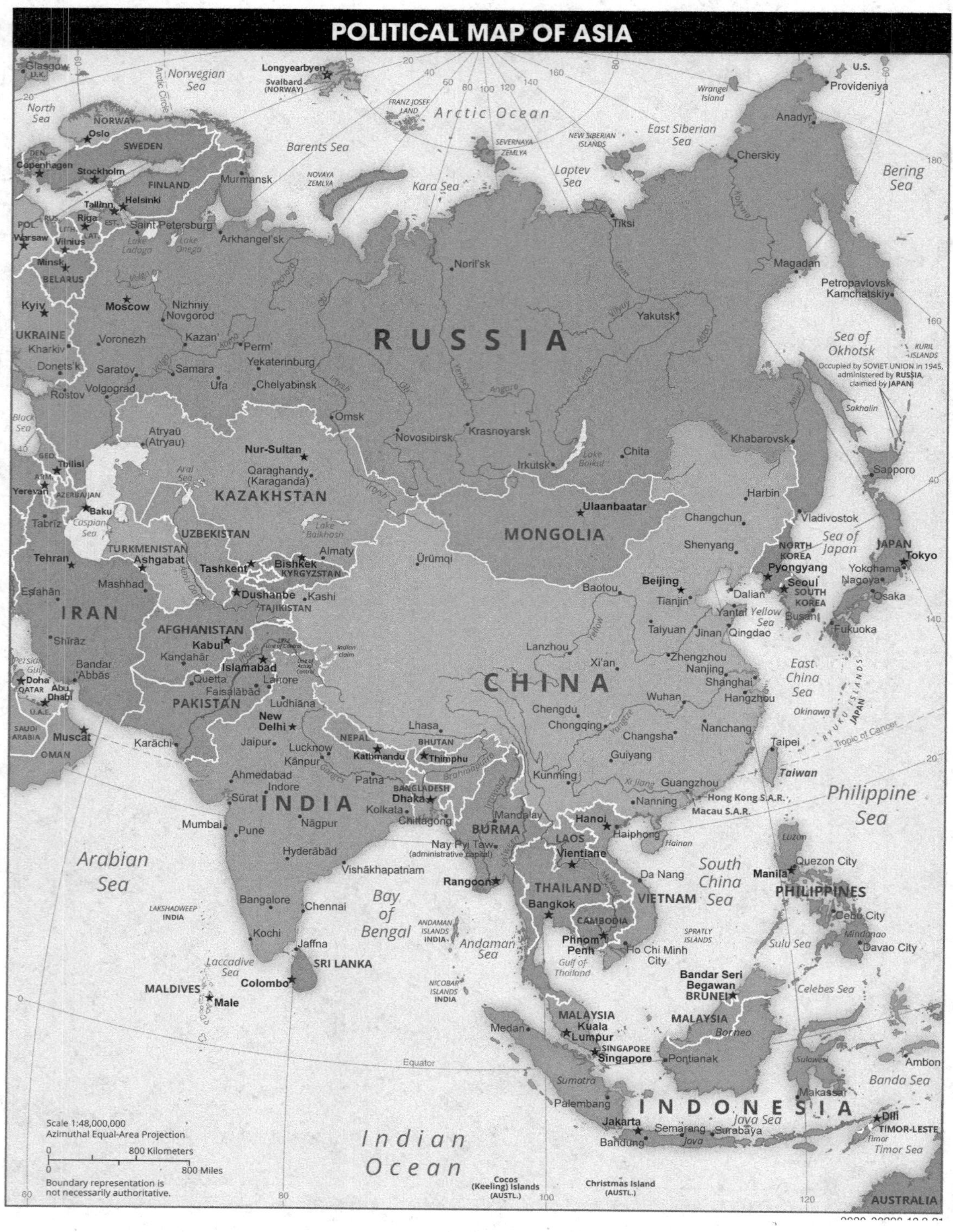
POLITICAL MAP OF ASIA
RUSSIA
CHINA
MONGOLIA
KAZAKHSTAN
INDIA
IRAN
INDONESIA
UZBEKISTAN
TURKMENISTAN
KYRGYZSTAN
TAJIKISTAN
AFGHANISTAN
PAKISTAN
NEPAL
BHUTAN
BANGLADESH
BURMA
LAOS
THAILAND
CAMBODIA
VIETNAM
MALAYSIA
BRUNEI
PHILIPPINES
SRI LANKA
MALDIVES
NORTH KOREA
SOUTH KOREA
JAPAN
TIMOR-LESTE
AUSTRALIA
NORWAY
SWEDEN
FINLAND
BELARUS
UKRAINE
OMAN
QATAR
U.A.E.
SAUDI ARABIA
Arctic Ocean
Indian Ocean
Norwegian Sea
North Sea
Barents Sea
Kara Sea
Laptev Sea
East Siberian Sea
Bering Sea
Sea of Okhotsk
Sea of Japan
Yellow Sea
East China Sea
Philippine Sea
South China Sea
Sulu Sea
Celebes Sea
Banda Sea
Java Sea
Timor Sea
Andaman Sea
Bay of Bengal
Arabian Sea
Laccadive Sea
Caspian Sea
Aral Sea
Black Sea
Lake Baikal
Lake Balkhash
Moscow
Beijing
Tokyo
New Delhi
Ulaanbaatar
Nur-Sultan
Tashkent
Bishkek
Dushanbe
Ashgabat
Kabul
Islamabad
Tehran
Kathmandu
Thimphu
Dhaka
Nay Pyi Taw (administrative capital)
Rangoon
Vientiane
Hanoi
Bangkok
Phnom Penh
Kuala Lumpur
Singapore
Bandar Seri Begawan
Manila
Jakarta
Dili
Colombo
Male
Pyongyang
Seoul
Taipei
Hong Kong S.A.R.
Macau S.A.R.
Occupied by SOVIET UNION in 1945, administered by RUSSIA, claimed by JAPAN
KURIL ISLANDS
RYUKYU ISLANDS
Tropic of Cancer
Equator
Arctic Circle
Indian claim
Line of Control
Scale 1:48,000,000
Azimuthal Equal-Area Projection
800 Kilometers
800 Miles
Boundary representation is not necessarily authoritative.
Cocos (Keeling) Islands (AUSTL.)
Christmas Island (AUSTL.)

PHYSICAL MAP OF ASIA

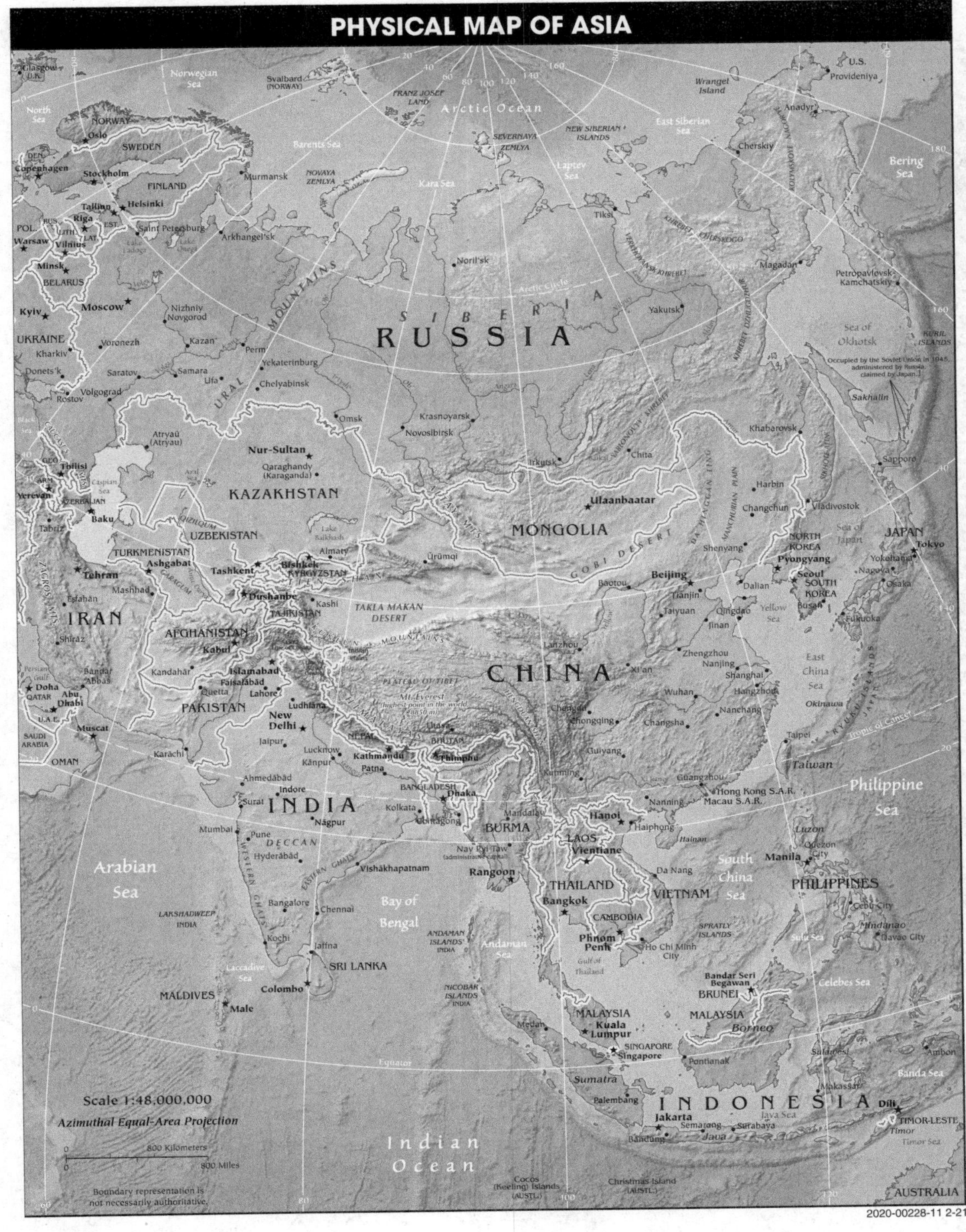

2020-00228-11 2-21

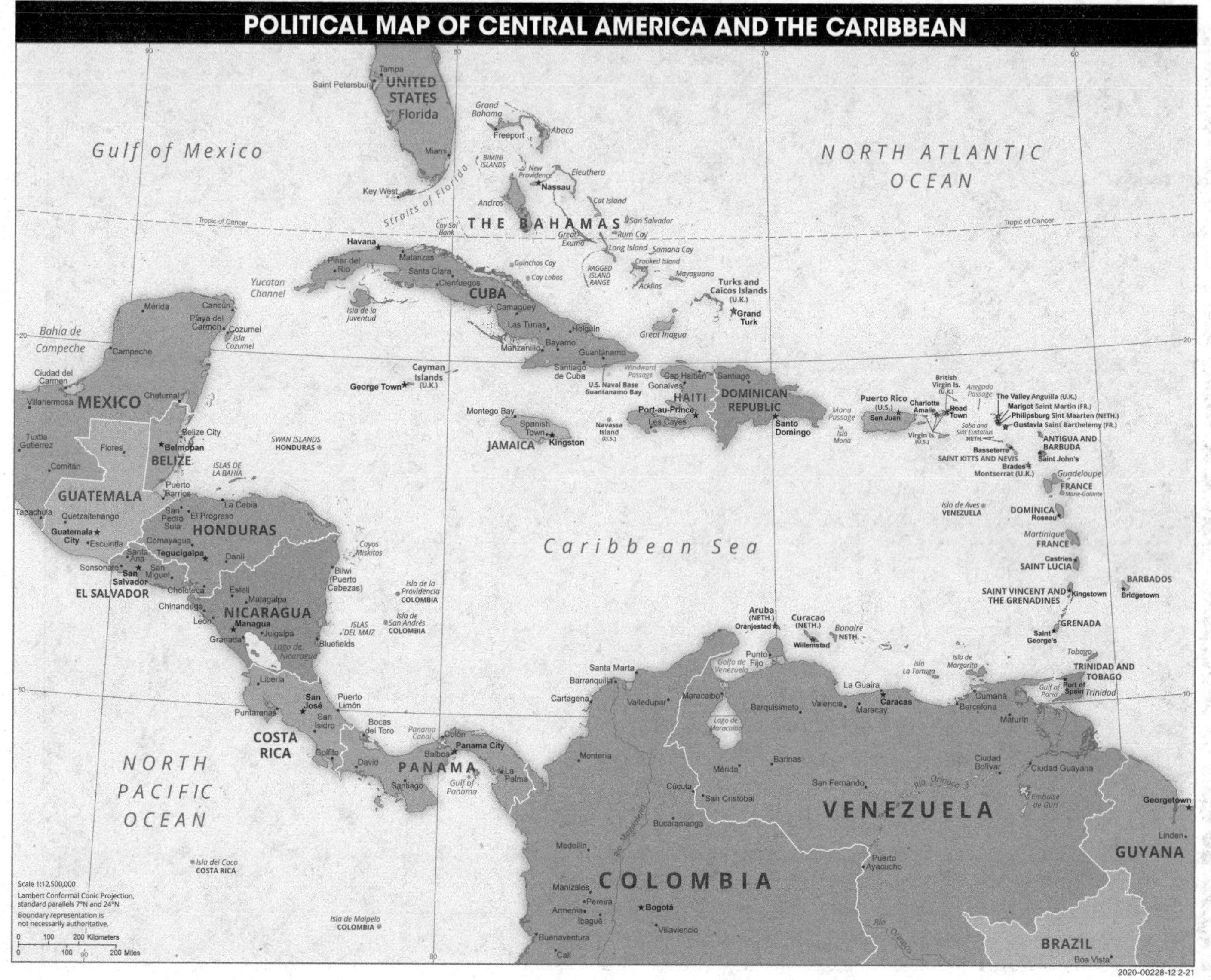
POLITICAL MAP OF CENTRAL AMERICA AND THE CARIBBEAN
NORTH ATLANTIC OCEAN
Gulf of Mexico
Caribbean Sea
NORTH PACIFIC OCEAN
Bahía de Campeche
Yucatan Channel
Straits of Florida
Tropic of Cancer
UNITED STATES
Florida
Tampa
Saint Petersburg
Miami
Key West
THE BAHAMAS
Nassau
New Providence
Freeport
Grand Bahama
Abaco
BIMINI ISLANDS
Eleuthera
Andros
Cay Sal Bank
Cat Island
San Salvador
Rum Cay
Great Exuma
Long Island
Samana Cay
Crooked Island
Mayaguana
Acklins
RAGGED ISLAND RANGE
Guinchos Cay
Cay Lobos
Great Inagua
CUBA
Havana
Matanzas
Santa Clara
Cienfuegos
Camagüey
Las Tunas
Holguín
Bayamo
Manzanillo
Santiago de Cuba
Guantánamo
Pinar del Río
Isla de la Juventud
U.S. Naval Base Guantanamo Bay
Cayman Islands (U.K.)
George Town
JAMAICA
Kingston
Spanish Town
Montego Bay
Navassa Island (U.S.)
Windward Passage
HAITI
Port-au-Prince
Cap-Haïtien
Gonaïves
Les Cayes
DOMINICAN REPUBLIC
Santo Domingo
Santiago
Turks and Caicos Islands (U.K.)
Grand Turk
Mona Passage
Isla Mona
Puerto Rico (U.S.)
San Juan
British Virgin Is. (U.K.)
Road Town
Charlotte Amalie
Virgin Is. (U.S.)
Anegada Passage
The Valley Anguilla (U.K.)
Marigot Saint Martin (FR.)
Philipsburg Sint Maarten (NETH.)
Gustavia Saint Barthelemy (FR.)
Saba and Sint Eustatius NETH.
SAINT KITTS AND NEVIS
Basseterre
ANTIGUA AND BARBUDA
Saint John's
Montserrat (U.K.)
Brades
Guadeloupe FRANCE
Marie-Galante
DOMINICA
Roseau
Martinique FRANCE
SAINT LUCIA
Castries
SAINT VINCENT AND THE GRENADINES
Kingstown
BARBADOS
Bridgetown
GRENADA
Saint George's
TRINIDAD AND TOBAGO
Port of Spain
Tobago
Trinidad
Gulf of Paria
Isla de Aves VENEZUELA
Aruba (NETH.)
Oranjestad
Curacao (NETH.)
Willemstad
Bonaire NETH.
MEXICO
Mérida
Campeche
Cancún
Playa del Carmen
Cozumel
Isla Cozumel
Chetumal
Villahermosa
Ciudad del Carmen
Tuxtla Gutiérrez
Tapachula
Comitán
BELIZE
Belmopan
Belize City
GUATEMALA
Guatemala City
Flores
Quetzaltenango
Escuintla
Puerto Barrios
HONDURAS
Tegucigalpa
San Pedro Sula
El Progreso
La Ceiba
Comayagua
Choluteca
Danlí
ISLAS DE LA BAHÍA
SWAN ISLANDS HONDURAS
EL SALVADOR
San Salvador
Santa Ana
San Miguel
Sonsonate
NICARAGUA
Managua
León
Chinandega
Estelí
Matagalpa
Granada
Juigalpa
Bluefields
Bilwi (Puerto Cabezas)
Cayos Miskitos
Lago de Nicaragua
ISLAS DEL MAIZ
COSTA RICA
San José
Puerto Limón
Liberia
Puntarenas
San Isidro
Golfito
Isla del Coco COSTA RICA
PANAMA
Panama City
Colón
Balboa
Santiago
David
Bocas del Toro
La Palma
Panama Canal
Gulf of Panama
Isla de la Providencia COLOMBIA
Isla de San Andrés COLOMBIA
Isla de Malpelo COLOMBIA
COLOMBIA
Bogotá
Barranquilla
Cartagena
Santa Marta
Valledupar
Montería
Medellín
Manizales
Pereira
Armenia
Ibagué
Cali
Buenaventura
Bucaramanga
Cúcuta
Villavicencio
Río Magdalena
VENEZUELA
Caracas
Maracaibo
Lago de Maracaibo
Golfo de Venezuela
Punto Fijo
Barquisimeto
Valencia
Maracay
La Guaira
Barinas
Mérida
San Cristóbal
San Fernando
Puerto Ayacucho
Cumaná
Barcelona
Maturín
Ciudad Bolívar
Ciudad Guayana
Embalse de Guri
Isla de Margarita
Isla La Tortuga
Río Orinoco
GUYANA
Georgetown
Linden
BRAZIL
Boa Vista
Scale 1:12,500,000
Lambert Conformal Conic Projection, standard parallels 7°N and 24°N
Boundary representation is not necessarily authoritative.
200 Kilometers
200 Miles
2020-00228-12 2-21

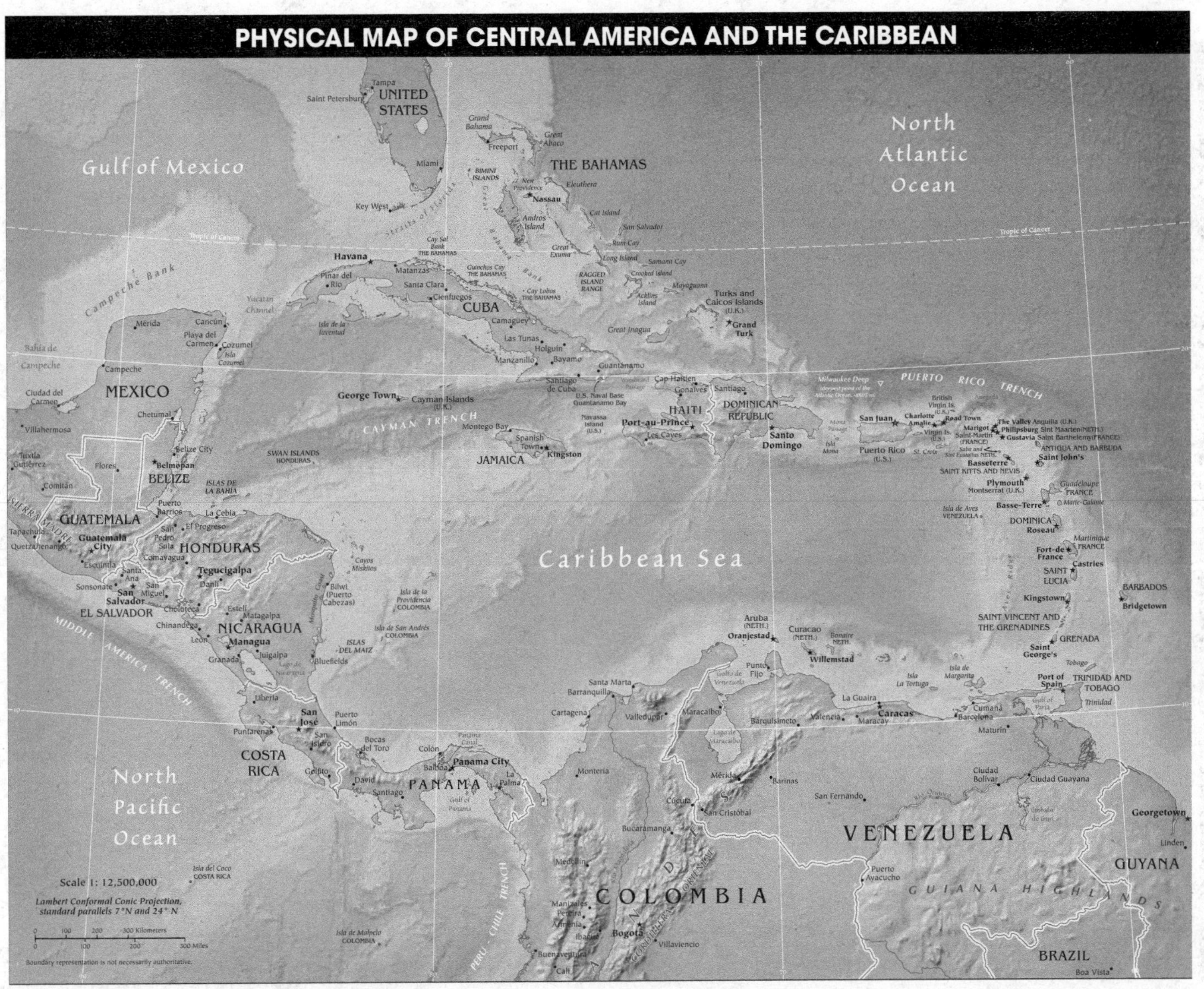
PHYSICAL MAP OF CENTRAL AMERICA AND THE CARIBBEAN
North Atlantic Ocean
Gulf of Mexico
Caribbean Sea
North Pacific Ocean
UNITED STATES
MEXICO
THE BAHAMAS
CUBA
JAMAICA
HAITI
DOMINICAN REPUBLIC
Turks and Caicos Islands (U.K.)
Puerto Rico (U.S.)
BELIZE
GUATEMALA
HONDURAS
EL SALVADOR
NICARAGUA
COSTA RICA
PANAMA
COLOMBIA
VENEZUELA
GUYANA
BRAZIL
TRINIDAD AND TOBAGO
BARBADOS
GRENADA
SAINT LUCIA
DOMINICA
SAINT VINCENT AND THE GRENADINES
SAINT KITTS AND NEVIS
ANTIGUA AND BARBUDA
Havana
Nassau
Kingston
Port-au-Prince
Santo Domingo
San Juan
Caracas
Bogotá
Panama City
San José
Managua
Tegucigalpa
San Salvador
Guatemala City
Belmopan
Georgetown
Port of Spain
Bridgetown
CAYMAN TRENCH
PUERTO RICO TRENCH
MIDDLE AMERICA TRENCH
PERU - CHILE TRENCH
GUIANA HIGHLANDS
Tropic of Cancer
Scale 1: 12,500,000
Lambert Conformal Conic Projection, standard parallels 7°N and 24°N
Boundary representation is not necessarily authoritative.

POLITICAL MAP OF EUROPE

PHYSICAL MAP OF EUROPE

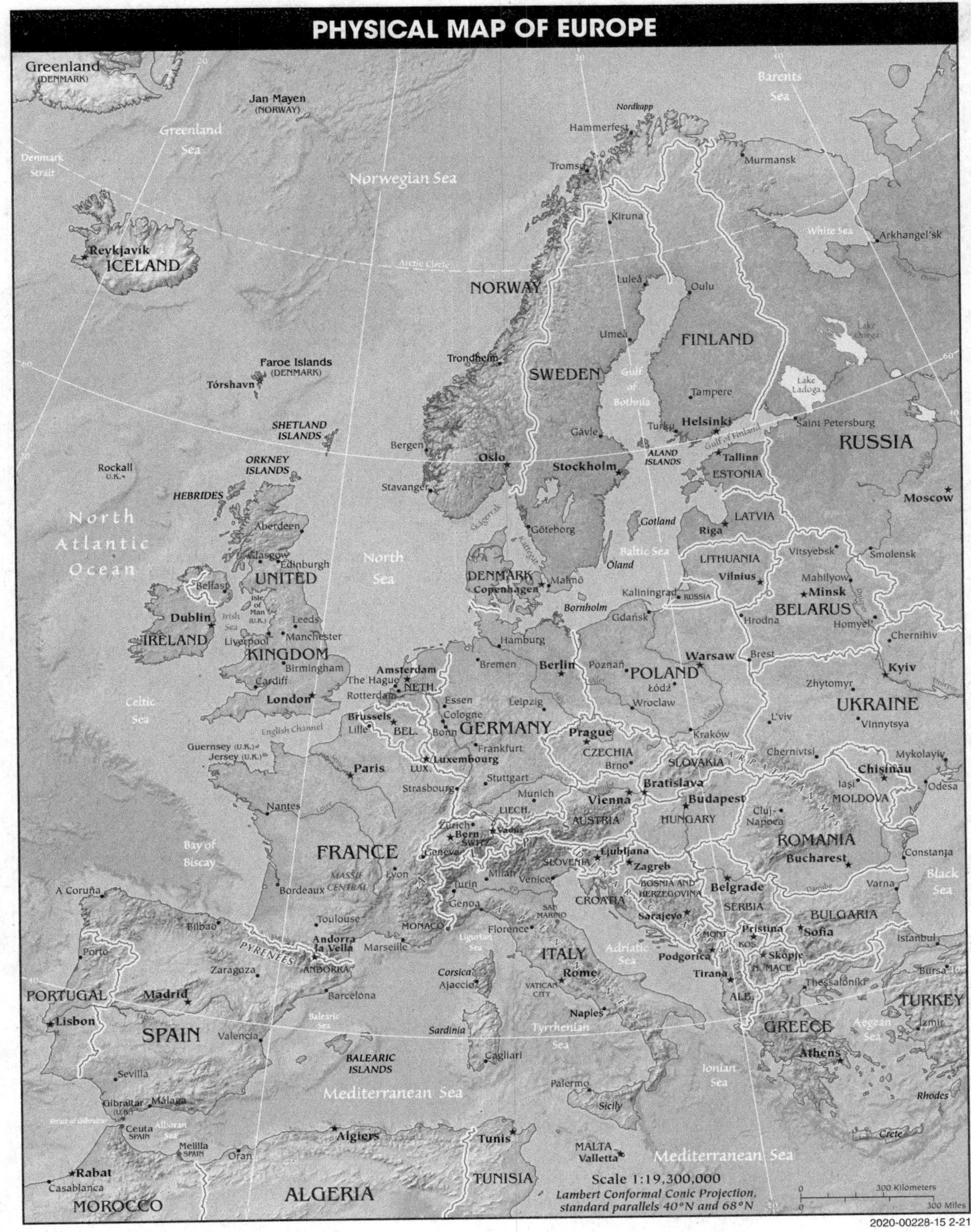

2020-00228-15 2-21

POLITICAL MAP OF MIDDLE EAST
ROMANIA
Bucharest
SER.
Sofia
BULGARIA
N. MACE.
UKR.
Sevastopol'
Constanța
Varna
Black Sea
Krasnodar
RUSSIA
Sochi
Groznyy
Sokhumi
GEORGIA
Tbilisi
Batumi
KAZAKHSTAN
Aqtau (Aktau)
UZBEKISTAN
Nukus
Dasoguz
Amu Darya
Bukhara
Caspian Sea
Thessaloniki
Istanbul
Bosporus
Bursa
Samsun
Trabzon
Aegean Sea
Dardanelles
GREECE
Athens
İzmir
Ankara
TURKEY
Erzurum
ARMENIA
Yerevan
AZERBAIJAN
Baku
Sumqayit
Türkmenbaşy
TURKMENISTAN
Turkmenabat
Balkanabat
Ashgabat
Mary
Denizli
Konya
Kayseri
Lake Van
Van
Diyarbakir
Tabrīz
Lake Urmia
Rasht
Antalya
Mersin
Adana
Gaziantep
Irákleio
Crete
Aleppo
Latakia
Dayr az Zawr
Mosul
Erbil
Zanjān
Qazvīn
Tehran
Mashhad
Nicosia
CYPRUS
SYRIA
Kirkuk
Qom
Herāt
Mediterranean Sea
LEBANON
Beirut
Homs
Damascus
Euphrates
Tigris
Kermānshāh
Arāk
Bīrjand
AFG.
ISRAEL
Tel Aviv-Yafo
Jerusalem
West Bank
Amman
Dead Sea
Ar Ramādī
Baghdad
IRAQ
Eşfahān
IRAN
Yazd
LIBYA
Alexandria
Port Said
Suez Canal
Gaza Strip
JORDAN
Ahvāz
Cairo
Giza
Suez
SINAI
Al Aqabah
An Nāşirīyah
Al Başrah
Ābādān
Kermān
Shīrāz
Zāhedān
PAK.
Gulf of Suez
Gulf of Aqaba
Tabūk
Kuwait City
KUWAIT
Bandar-e Būshehr
Asyūţ
Ḩafar al Bāţin
Ḩā'il
Bandar 'Abbās
Persian Gulf
EGYPT
Nile
Al Jubayl
Ad Dammām
Dhahran
Manama
BAHRAIN
Buraydah
Strait of Hormuz
OMAN
Luxor
Doha
QATAR
Dubai
Gulf of Oman
Abu Dhabi
Aswān
Medina
Yanbu'
Riyadh
Al 'Ayn
Şuḩār
SAUDI ARABIA
Muscat
Tropic of Cancer
U.A.E.
'Ibrī
Admin. boundary
Halā'ib
Jeddah
Mecca
OMAN
Red Sea
Port Sudan
Abhā
SUDAN
Jāzān
Şalālah
Omdurman
Khartoum
Kassala
ERITREA
Asmara
Massawa
Al Ghayzah
Sanaa
YEMEN
Arabian Sea
Al Hudaydah
Al Mukallā
White Nile
Blue Nile
El Obeid
Mekele
Assab
Ta'izz
Aden
Lake Tana
Gonder
Ed Damazin
Bab el Mandeb
Gulf of Aden
YEMEN
Socotra
DJIBOUTI
Djibouti
Desē
Boosaaso
Berbera
Malakal
SOUTH SUDAN
Addis Ababa
Dirē Dawa
Hargeysa
SOMALIA
ETHIOPIA
Āwasa
Prov. admin. line
Gaalkacyo
Scale 1:21,000,000
Lambert Conformal Conic Projection, standard parallels 12°N and 38°N
0 150 300 Kilometers
0 150 300 Miles
The United States recognized Jerusalem as Israel's capital in 2017 without taking a position on the specific boundaries of Israeli sovereignty.
The West Bank is Israeli occupied with current status subject to the Israeli-Palestinian Interim Agreement; permanent status to be determined through further negotiation.
The status of the Gaza Strip is a final status issue to be resolved through negotiations.
Boundary representation is not necessarily authoritative.
2020-00228-16 2-21

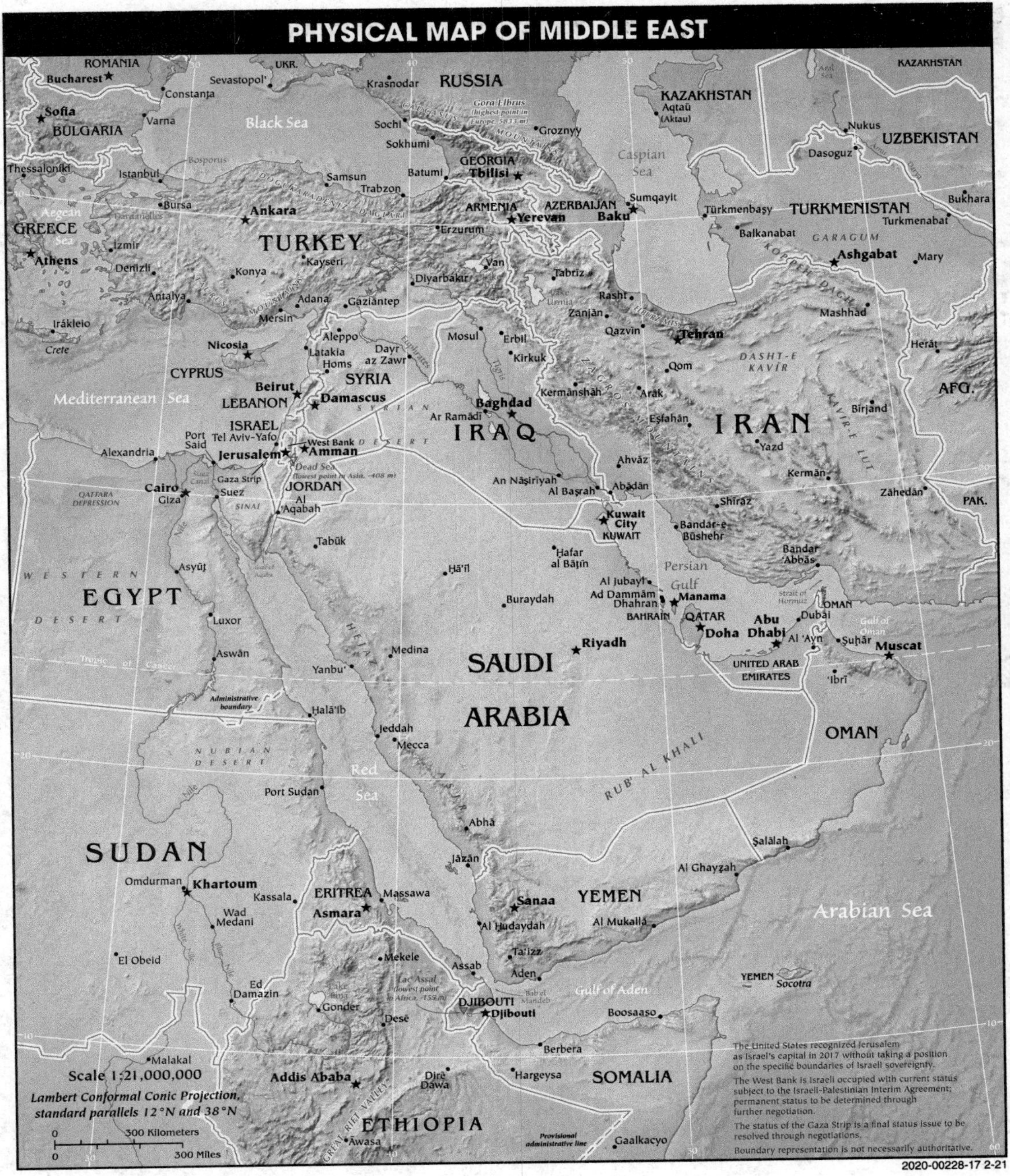
PHYSICAL MAP OF MIDDLE EAST
ROMANIA
Bucharest
UKR.
Sevastopol'
Constanța
Krasnodar
RUSSIA
KAZAKHSTAN
Aqtaū (Aktau)
Sofia
BULGARIA
Varna
Black Sea
Sochi
Sokhumi
Gora El'brus (highest point in Europe, 5633 m)
Groznyy
Nukus
UZBEKISTAN
Dasoguz
Caspian Sea
GEORGIA
Tbilisi
Thessaloniki
Istanbul
Bosporus
Samsun
Batumi
Trabzon
Sumqayit
Bukhara
Bursa
Ankara
ARMENIA
Yerevan
AZERBAIJAN
Baku
Türkmenbaşy
TURKMENISTAN
Turkmenabat
Aegean Sea
GREECE
Erzurum
Balkanabat
GARAGUM
İzmir
TURKEY
Athens
Ashgabat
Mary
Denizli
Kayseri
Van
Tabriz
Konya
Diyarbakır
Lake Urmia
Rasht
Antalya
Adana
Gaziantep
Zanjan
Mashhad
Mersin
Qazvin
Irákleio
Aleppo
Mosul
Erbil
Tehran
Crete
Nicosia
Latakia
Dayr az Zawr
Herat
Kirkuk
Homs
DASHT-E KAVĪR
CYPRUS
Qom
SYRIA
Beirut
AFG.
Mediterranean Sea
LEBANON
Damascus
Kermanshah
Arak
Birjand
Baghdad
ISRAEL
Ar Ramadi
Esfahan
IRAN
Port Said
Tel Aviv-Yafo
IRAQ
West Bank
Amman
Alexandria
Jerusalem
Yazd
Dead Sea (lowest point in Asia, -408 m)
Ahvaz
Gaza Strip
Kerman
JORDAN
An Nasiriyah
Cairo
Suez
Al Basrah
Abadan
Zahedan
QATTARA DEPRESSION
Giza
Al 'Aqabah
Shiraz
PAK.
SINAI
Kuwait City
KUWAIT
Bandar-e Bushehr
Tabūk
Hafar al Batin
Bandar 'Abbas
Asyūţ
Ha'il
Persian Gulf
Strait of Hormuz
WESTERN DESERT
EGYPT
Al Jubayl
Ad Dammam
Dhahran
Buraydah
Manama
BAHRAIN
OMAN
Dubai
Luxor
QATAR
Doha
Abu Dhabi
Gulf of Oman
Al 'Ayn
Şuḩār
Muscat
Riyadh
Medina
Aswān
Yanbu'
SAUDI ARABIA
UNITED ARAB EMIRATES
'Ibrī
Tropic of Cancer
Administrative boundary
Halā'ib
Jeddah
Mecca
OMAN
NUBIAN DESERT
Red Sea
RUB' AL KHALI
Port Sudan
Abhā
Şalālah
SUDAN
Jāzān
Al Ghayzah
Omdurman
Khartoum
Kassala
ERITREA
Massawa
Asmara
Sanaa
YEMEN
Arabian Sea
Wad Medani
Al Hudaydah
Al Mukalla
El Obeid
Mekele
Ta'izz
Assab
Aden
YEMEN
Socotra
Ed Damazin
Lac Assal (lowest point in Africa, -155 m)
Gulf of Aden
Gonder
DJIBOUTI
Djibouti
Bosaaso
Desē
Malakal
Berbera
Scale 1:21,000,000
Addis Ababa
Dirē Dawa
Hargeysa
SOMALIA
Lambert Conformal Conic Projection, standard parallels 12°N and 38°N
300 Kilometers
300 Miles
ETHIOPIA
GREAT RIFT VALLEY
Āwasa
Provisional administrative line
Gaalkacyo
The United States recognized Jerusalem as Israel's capital in 2017 without taking a position on the specific boundaries of Israeli sovereignty.
The West Bank is Israeli occupied with current status subject to the Israeli-Palestinian Interim Agreement; permanent status to be determined through further negotiation.
The status of the Gaza Strip is a final status issue to be resolved through negotiations.
Boundary representation is not necessarily authoritative.
2020-00228-17 2-21

POLITICAL MAP OF NORTH AMERICA
ARCTIC OCEAN
East Siberian Sea
RUSSIA
Cherskiy
Pevek
Anadyr
Chukchi Sea
Provideniya
Bering Strait
Nome
Bering Sea
Utqiaġvik (Barrow)
Prudhoe Bay
Beaufort Sea
UNITED STATES
Alaska
Bethel
Fairbanks
Anchorage
Valdez
Gulf of Alaska
Yukon River
Dawson
Whitehorse
Juneau
Inuvik
Mackenzie River
Great Bear Lake
Great Slave Lake
Banks Island
Victoria Island
Cambridge Bay
QUEEN ELIZABETH ISLANDS
Ellesmere Island
Alert
Resolute
Gjoa Haven
Nord
Greenland Sea
Jan Mayen (NORWAY)
Arctic Circle
Ittoqqortoormiit
ICELAND
Reykjavik
Greenland (DENMARK)
Qaanaaq (Thule)
Denmark Strait
Tasiilaq
Baffin Bay
Pond Inlet
Ilulissat
Sisimiut
Nuuk
Baffin Island
Davis Strait
Qaqortoq
Iqaluit
Labrador Sea
Rankin Inlet
CANADA
Arviat
Hudson Bay
Kuujjuaq
Happy Valley-Goose Bay
Newfoundland
St. John's
Fort Nelson
Peace River
Slave River
Lake Athabasca
Churchill
Prince George
Fort McMurray
Nelson River
Chisasibi
Gulf of St. Lawrence
St. Pierre and Miquelon (FRANCE)
Sydney
Edmonton
Saskatchewan River
Lake Winnipeg
Moosonee
Chicoutimi
Moncton
Charlottetown
Fredericton
Halifax
Saint John
Vancouver
Victoria
Calgary
Saskatoon
Regina
Québec
Seattle
Columbia River
Winnipeg
Thunder Bay
Montréal
Ottawa
Sudbury
Lake Superior
Lake Huron
Lake Ontario
Portland
Helena
Missouri River
Bismarck
Boston
Providence
Hartford
New York
Toronto
Hamilton
Buffalo
London
Lake Erie
Lake Michigan
Detroit
Minneapolis
Milwaukee
Chicago
Boise
Snake River
NORTH PACIFIC OCEAN
UNITED STATES
Cleveland
Columbus
Pittsburgh
Philadelphia
Baltimore
Washington, D.C.
San Francisco
Sacramento
Great Salt Lake
Salt Lake City
Omaha
Indianapolis
Mississippi River
Cincinnati
Bermuda (U.K.)
San Jose
Fresno
Denver
Kansas City
Arkansas River
St. Louis
Ohio River
Louisville
Virginia Beach
Las Vegas
Colorado River
Nashville
Charlotte
NORTH ATLANTIC OCEAN
Los Angeles
San Diego
Tijuana
Mexicali
Phoenix
Tucson
Albuquerque
Oklahoma City
Memphis
Atlanta
Birmingham
Dallas
Jacksonville
El Paso
Ciudad Juárez
Rio Grande
Austin
Houston
New Orleans
Orlando
Tampa
Miami
Hermosillo
Chihuahua
San Antonio
Nassau
Tur. & Cai. Is. (U.K.)
THE BAHAMAS
Gulf of California
Tropic of Cancer
Guadeloupe
Nuevo Laredo
Torreón
Culiacán
Monterrey
Matamoros
Gulf of Mexico
Havana
CUBA
HAITI
La Paz
MEXICO
San Luis Potosí
Tampico
Aguascalientes
Cancun
Navassa Island (U.S.)
Cayman Is. (U.K.)
Kingston
JAMAICA
Guadalajara
León
Querétaro
Mérida
Bahía de Campeche
ISLAS REVILLAGIGEDO MEXICO
Morelia
Mexico City
Veracruz
Toluca
Puebla
Belmopan
BELIZE
Caribbean Sea
Oaxaca
HONDURAS
Acapulco
Guatemala City
Tegucigalpa
GUATEMALA
NICARAGUA
San Salvador
Managua
EL SALVADOR
Scale 1:36,000,000
Lambert Conformal Conic Projection, standard parallels 25°N and 77°N
0 200 400 Kilometers
0 200 400 Miles
2020-00228-18 2-21

PHYSICAL MAP OF NORTH AMERICA

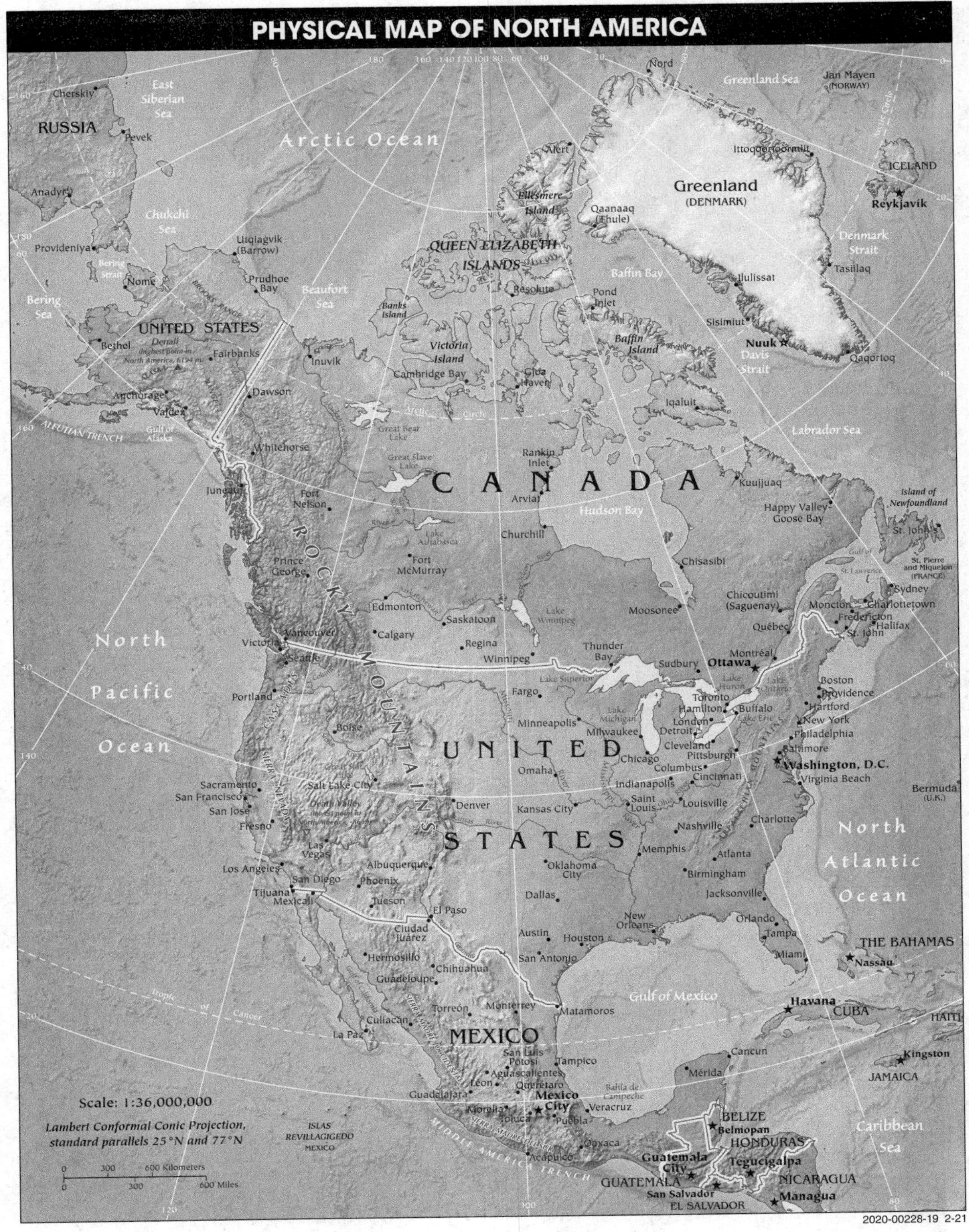

2020-00228-19 2-21

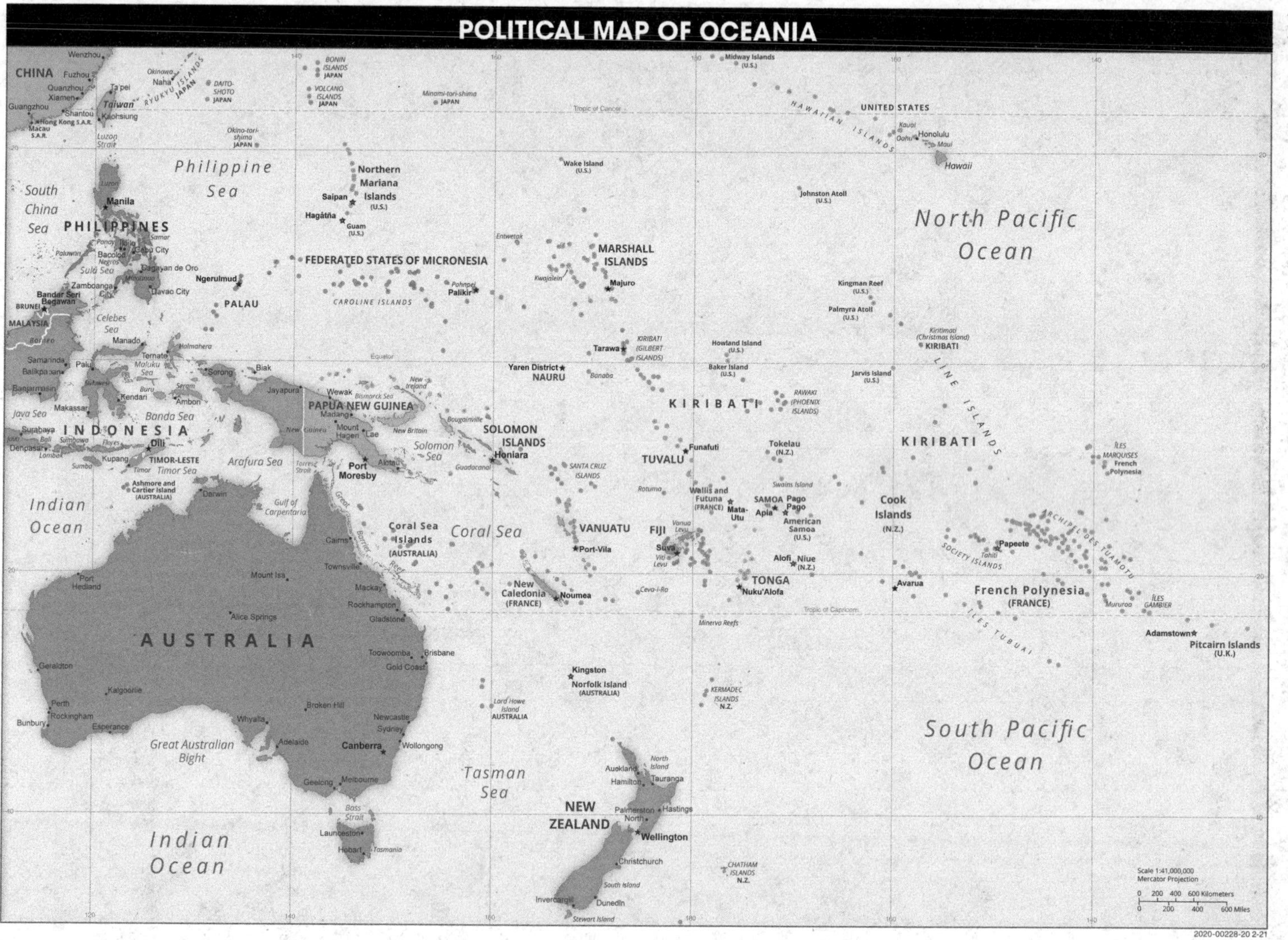
POLITICAL MAP OF OCEANIA
North Pacific Ocean
South Pacific Ocean
Indian Ocean
Philippine Sea
South China Sea
Coral Sea
Tasman Sea
Arafura Sea
Banda Sea
Solomon Sea
Celebes Sea
Timor Sea
Java Sea
Great Australian Bight
Gulf of Carpentaria
CHINA
Taiwan
PHILIPPINES
Manila
INDONESIA
MALAYSIA
BRUNEI
Bandar Seri Begawan
TIMOR-LESTE
Dili
PALAU
Ngerulmud
PAPUA NEW GUINEA
Port Moresby
AUSTRALIA
Canberra
NEW ZEALAND
Wellington
Northern Mariana Islands (U.S.)
Saipan
Hagåtña
Guam (U.S.)
FEDERATED STATES OF MICRONESIA
Palikir
CAROLINE ISLANDS
MARSHALL ISLANDS
Majuro
Wake Island (U.S.)
Yaren District
NAURU
KIRIBATI
Tarawa
SOLOMON ISLANDS
Honiara
TUVALU
Funafuti
VANUATU
Port-Vila
FIJI
Suva
New Caledonia (FRANCE)
Noumea
Wallis and Futuna (FRANCE)
Mata-Utu
SAMOA
Apia
American Samoa (U.S.)
Pago Pago
Tokelau (N.Z.)
TONGA
Nuku'Alofa
Niue (N.Z.)
Alofi
Cook Islands (N.Z.)
Avarua
French Polynesia (FRANCE)
Papeete
Pitcairn Islands (U.K.)
Adamstown
Norfolk Island (AUSTRALIA)
Kingston
Coral Sea Islands (AUSTRALIA)
Ashmore and Cartier Island (AUSTRALIA)
UNITED STATES
HAWAIIAN ISLANDS
Honolulu
Hawaii
Midway Islands (U.S.)
Johnston Atoll (U.S.)
Kingman Reef (U.S.)
Palmyra Atoll (U.S.)
Howland Island (U.S.)
Baker Island (U.S.)
Jarvis Island (U.S.)
LINE ISLANDS
Scale 1:41,000,000
Mercator Projection
2020-00228-20 2-21

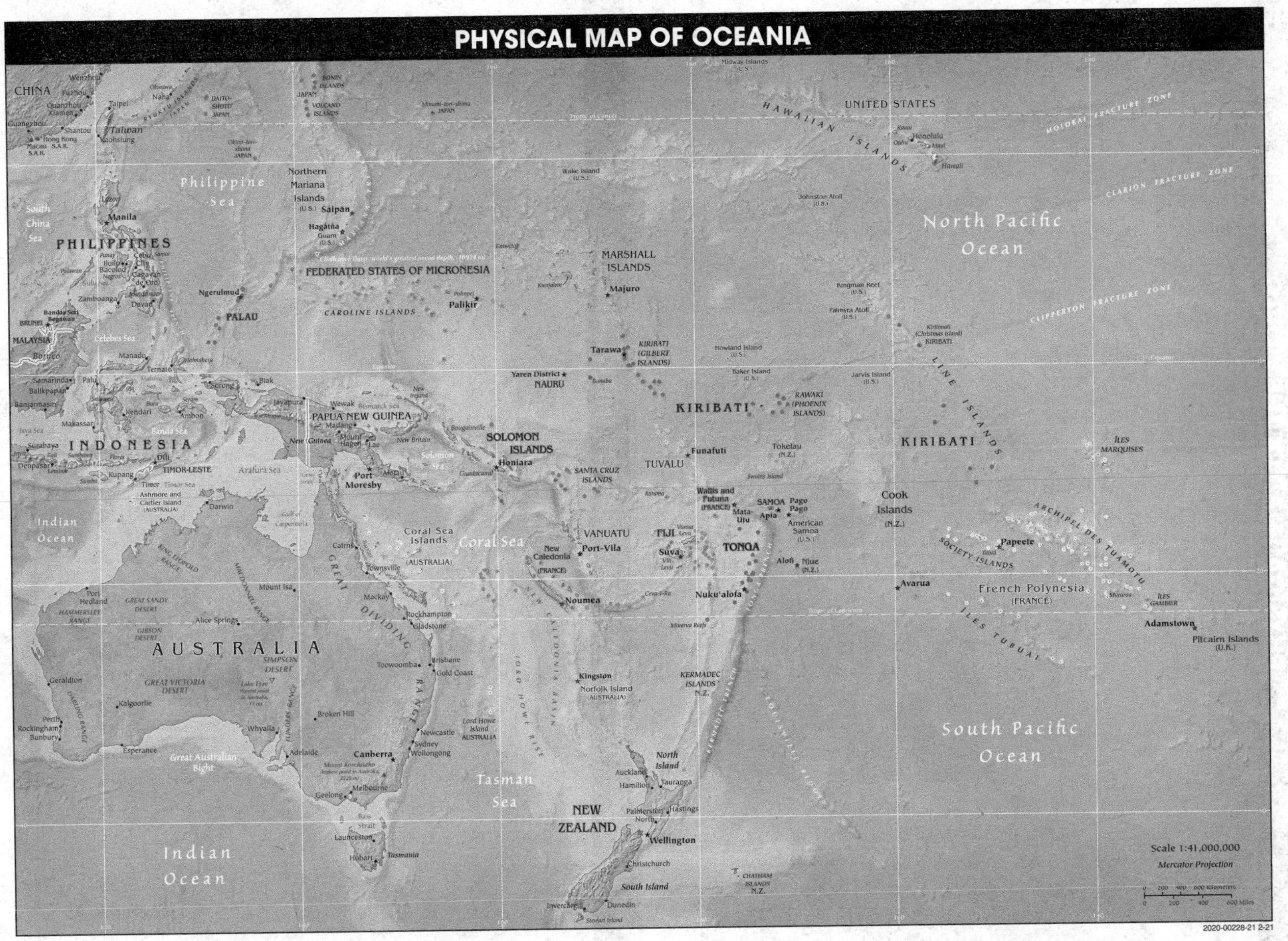
PHYSICAL MAP OF OCEANIA
CHINA
Taiwan
PHILIPPINES
Manila
Philippine Sea
South China Sea
Northern Mariana Islands (U.S.)
Saipan
Hagåtña
Guam (U.S.)
FEDERATED STATES OF MICRONESIA
CAROLINE ISLANDS
Palikir
Ngerulmud
PALAU
MARSHALL ISLANDS
Majuro
Tarawa
KIRIBATI (GILBERT ISLANDS)
Yaren District
NAURU
KIRIBATI
RAWAKI (PHOENIX ISLANDS)
UNITED STATES
HAWAIIAN ISLANDS
Honolulu
Hawaii
North Pacific Ocean
LINE ISLANDS
Kiritimati (Christmas Island) KIRIBATI
INDONESIA
TIMOR-LESTE
Dili
PAPUA NEW GUINEA
Port Moresby
SOLOMON ISLANDS
Honiara
Coral Sea
Coral Sea Islands (AUSTRALIA)
TUVALU
Funafuti
VANUATU
Port-Vila
New Caledonia (FRANCE)
Noumea
FIJI
Suva
Wallis and Futuna (FRANCE)
Mata-Utu
SAMOA
Apia
Pago Pago
American Samoa (U.S.)
Tokelau (N.Z.)
TONGA
Nuku'alofa
Alofi
Niue (N.Z.)
Cook Islands (N.Z.)
Avarua
French Polynesia (FRANCE)
Papeete
SOCIETY ISLANDS
ARCHIPEL DES TUAMOTU
ÎLES MARQUISES
ÎLES TUBUAI
Adamstown
Pitcairn Islands (U.K.)
AUSTRALIA
Darwin
Alice Springs
GREAT DIVIDING RANGE
Brisbane
Sydney
Canberra
Melbourne
Adelaide
Perth
Tasmania
Hobart
Indian Ocean
Great Australian Bight
Tasman Sea
Kingston
Norfolk Island (AUSTRALIA)
KERMADEC ISLANDS N.Z.
NEW ZEALAND
North Island
South Island
Auckland
Wellington
Christchurch
Dunedin
CHATHAM ISLANDS N.Z.
South Pacific Ocean
Scale 1:41,000,000
Mercator Projection
2020-00228-21 2-21

PHYSICAL MAP OF THE WORLD

Physical Map of the World, February 2021

AUSTRALIA — Independent state
Bermuda — Dependency or area of special sovereignty
Sicily / AZORES — Island / island group
★ — National Capital
☆ — Other Capital

POLITICAL MAP OF THE WORLD

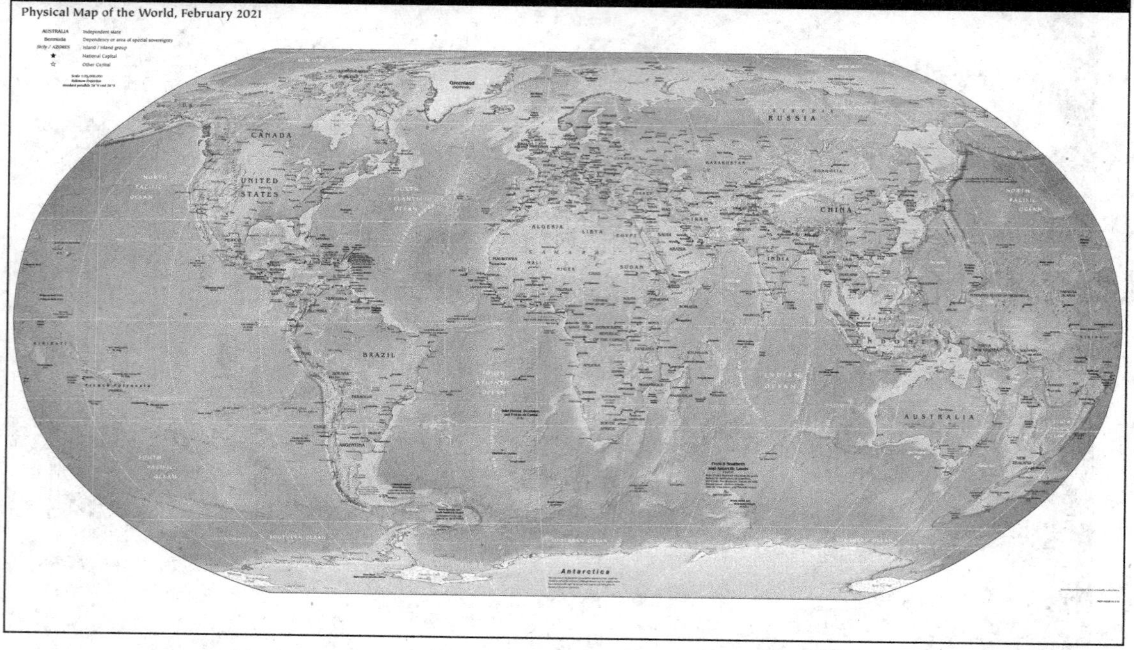

Political Map of the World, February 2021

AUSTRALIA — Independent state
Bermuda — Dependency or area of special sovereignty
Sicily / AZORES — Island / island group
★ — National capital
☆ — Other capital

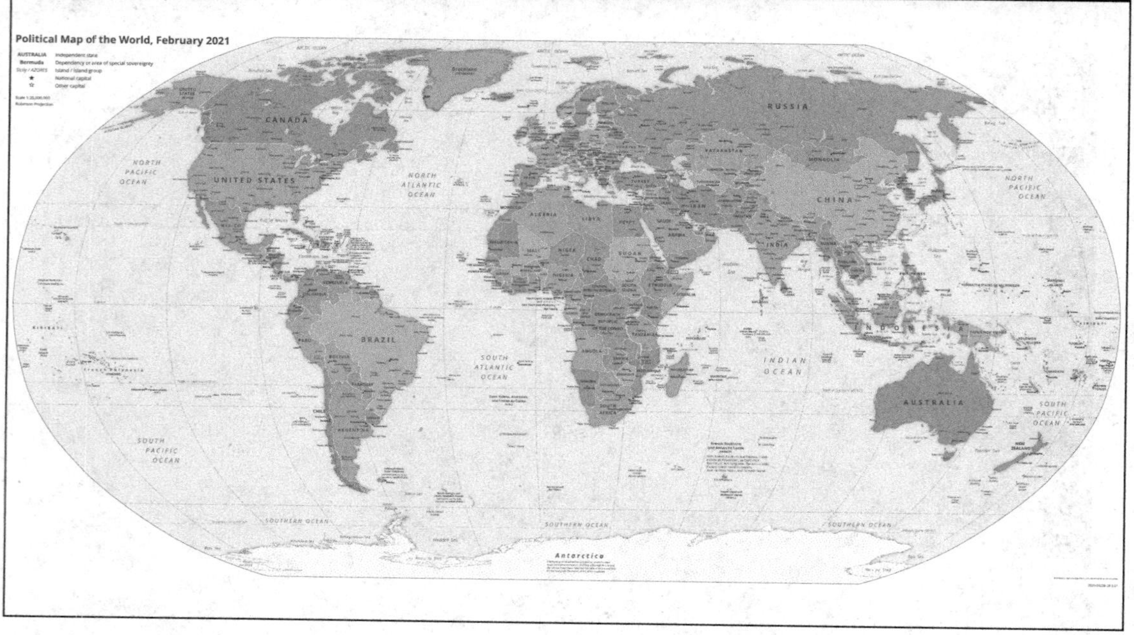

POLITICAL MAP OF SOUTH AMERICA

PHYSICAL MAP OF SOUTH AMERICA

POLITICAL MAP OF SOUTHEAST ASIA

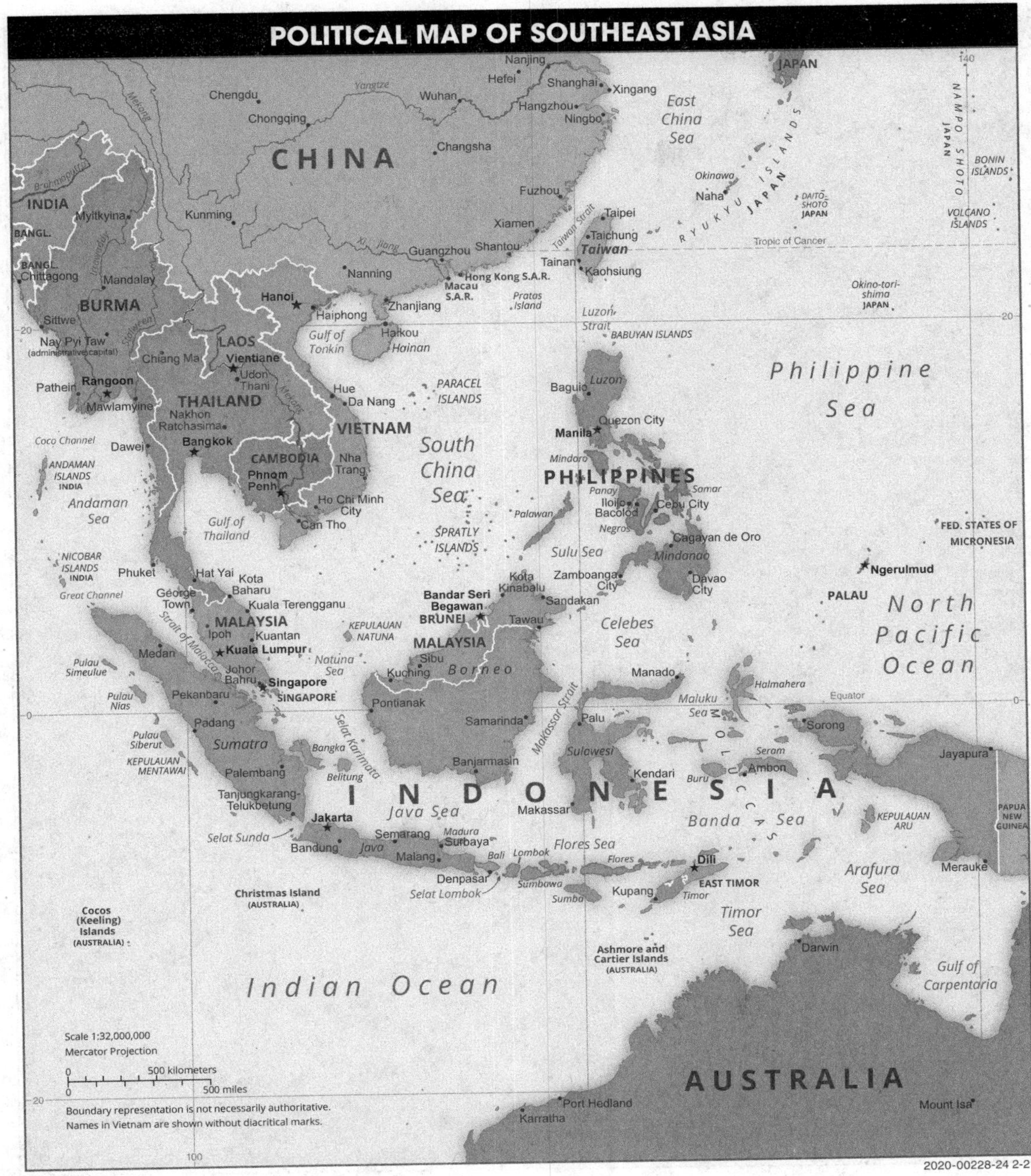

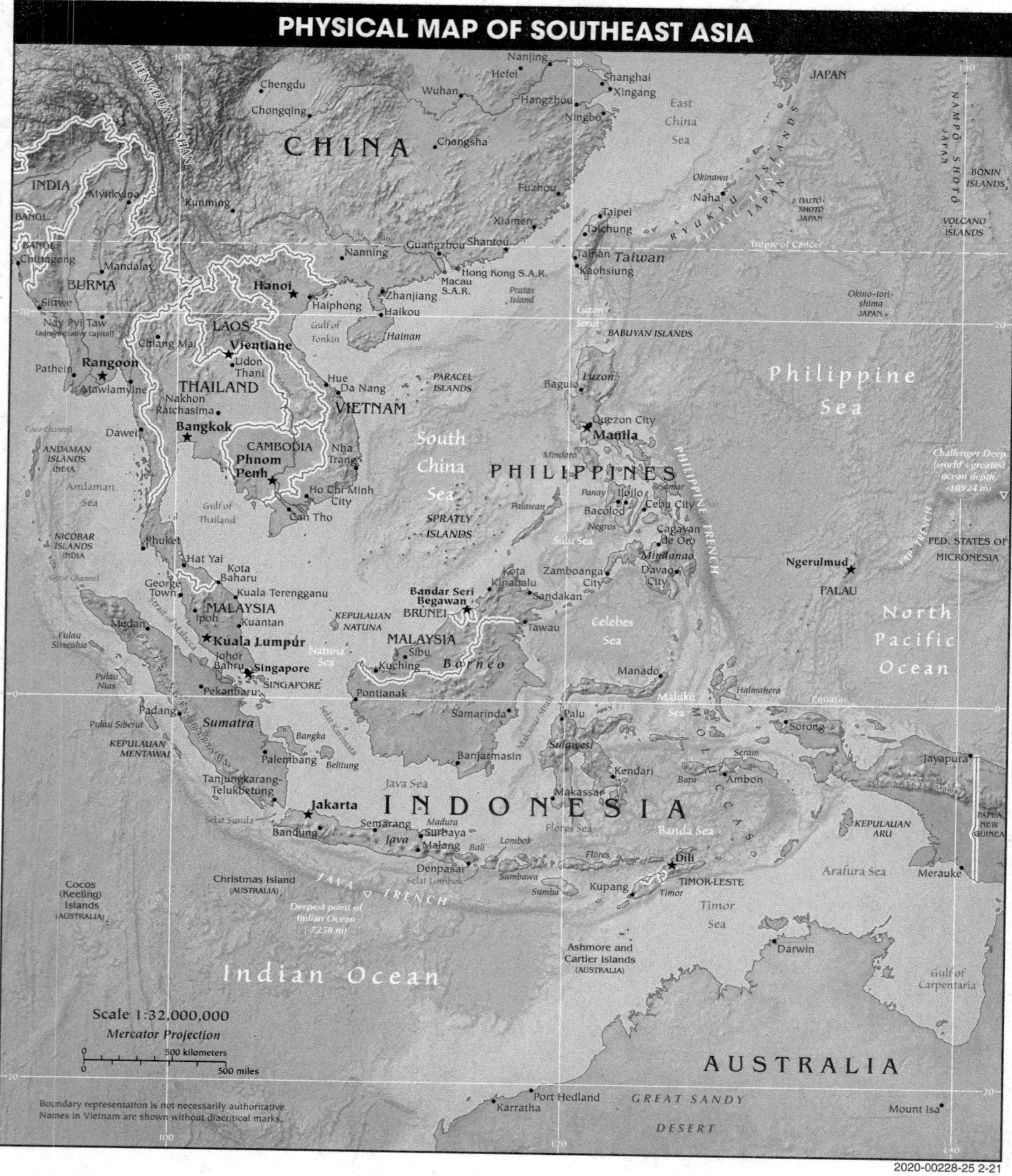
PHYSICAL MAP OF SOUTHEAST ASIA
CHINA
Chengdu
Chongqing
Wuhan
Nanjing
Hefei
Shanghai
Xingang
Hangzhou
Ningbo
East China Sea
JAPAN
Changsha
Kunming
Fuzhou
Xiamen
Guangzhou
Shantou
Nanning
Hong Kong S.A.R.
Macau S.A.R.
Zhanjiang
Haikou
Hainan
Pratas Island
Taipei
Taichung
Tainan
Taiwan
Kaohsiung
Okinawa
Naha
RYUKYU ISLANDS
RYUKYU TRENCH
NAMPŌ SHOTŌ JAPAN
BONIN ISLANDS
VOLCANO ISLANDS
Tropic of Cancer
Okino-tori-shima JAPAN
HENGDUAN SHAN
INDIA
BANGL.
Myitkyina
Chittagong
Mandalay
BURMA
Sittwe
Nay Pyi Taw (administrative capital)
Pathein
Rangoon
Mawlamyine
Dawei
Hanoi
Haiphong
Gulf of Tonkin
LAOS
Vientiane
Chiang Mai
Udon Thani
THAILAND
Nakhon Ratchasima
Bangkok
Hue
Da Nang
VIETNAM
PARACEL ISLANDS
CAMBODIA
Phnom Penh
Nha Trang
Ho Chi Minh City
Can Tho
Gulf of Thailand
ANDAMAN ISLANDS INDIA
Andaman Sea
NICOBAR ISLANDS INDIA
Phuket
Hat Yai
Kota Baharu
George Town
Kuala Terengganu
MALAYSIA
Ipoh
Kuantan
Medan
Kuala Lumpur
Johor Bahru
Singapore
SINGAPORE
Pekanbaru
Padang
Sumatra
Pulau Simeulue
Pulau Nias
Pulau Siberut
KEPULAUAN MENTAWAI
Palembang
Bangka
Belitung
Tanjungkarang-Telukbetung
Jakarta
Bandung
Semarang
Java
Madura
Surbaya
Malang
Bali
Denpasar
Lombok
Sumbawa
Sumba
Flores
Kupang
Timor
Dili
TIMOR-LESTE
Timor Sea
Java Sea
INDONESIA
Flores Sea
Banda Sea
JAVA TRENCH
Christmas Island (AUSTRALIA)
Cocos (Keeling) Islands (AUSTRALIA)
Deepest point of Indian Ocean (-7258 m)
Indian Ocean
South China Sea
SPRATLY ISLANDS
KEPULAUAN NATUNA
Natuna Sea
Bandar Seri Begawan
BRUNEI
Kota Kinabalu
Sandakan
Tawau
MALAYSIA
Sibu
Kuching
Borneo
Pontianak
Samarinda
Banjarmasin
Palu
Sulawesi
Kendari
Makassar
Manado
Celebes Sea
Halmahera
Maluku Sea
MOLUCCAS
Sorong
Seram
Buru
Ambon
Jayapura
PAPUA NEW GUINEA
KEPULAUAN ARU
Arafura Sea
Merauke
BABUYAN ISLANDS
Luzon Strait
Luzon
Baguio
Quezon City
Manila
Mindoro
PHILIPPINES
Palawan
Panay
Iloilo
Samar
Cebu City
Bacolod
Negros
Cagayan de Oro
Mindanao
Sulu Sea
Zamboanga City
Davao City
PHILIPPINE TRENCH
Philippine Sea
Challenger Deep (world's greatest ocean depth -10924 m)
Ngerulmud
PALAU
FED. STATES OF MICRONESIA
North Pacific Ocean
Equator
Darwin
Ashmore and Cartier Islands (AUSTRALIA)
Gulf of Carpentaria
AUSTRALIA
Port Hedland
Karratha
GREAT SANDY DESERT
Mount Isa
Scale 1:32,000,000
Mercator Projection
500 kilometers
500 miles
Boundary representation is not necessarily authoritative.
Names in Vietnam are shown without diacritical marks.
2020-00228-25 2-21

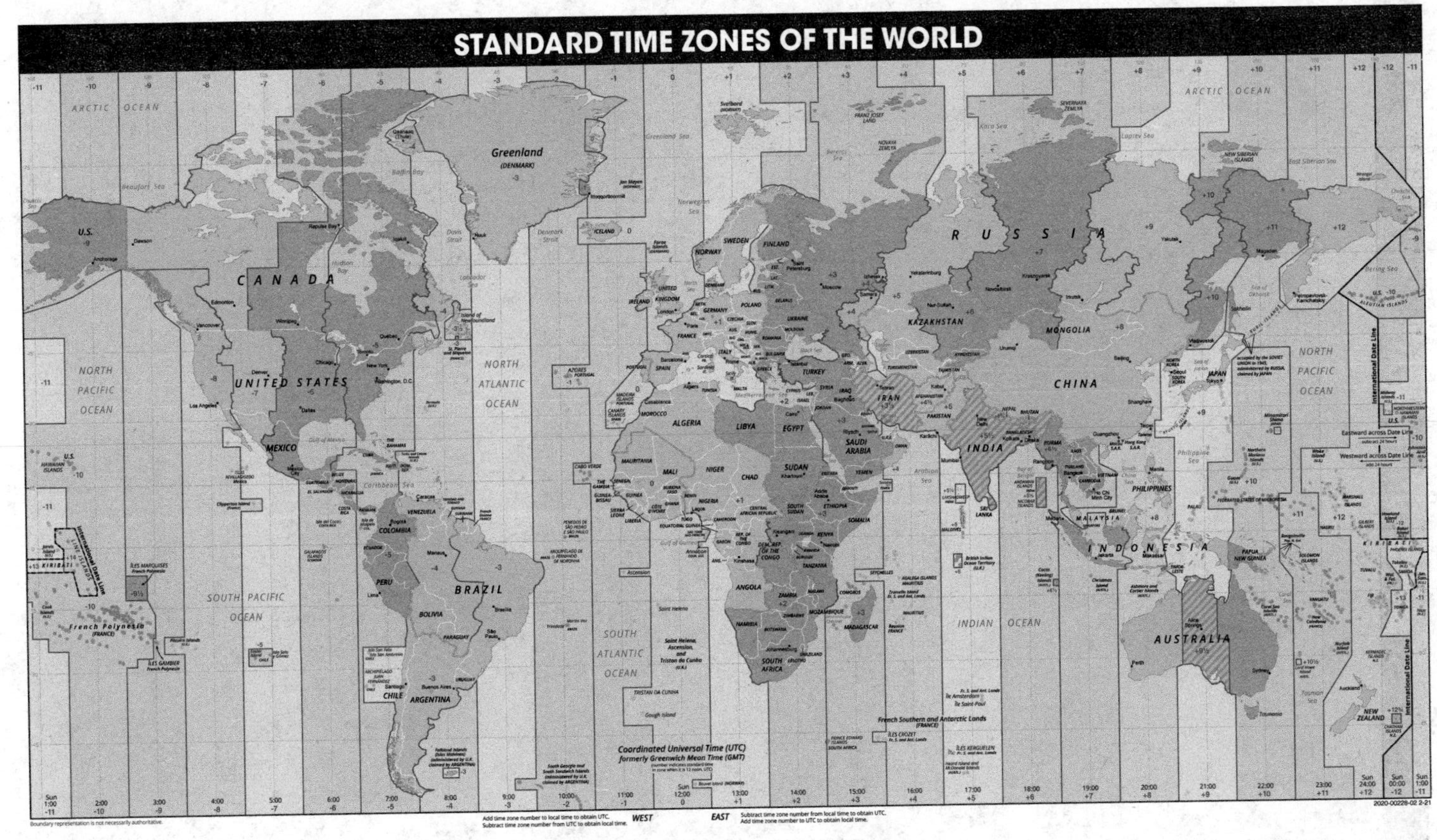
STANDARD TIME ZONES OF THE WORLD
ARCTIC OCEAN
Greenland
(DENMARK)
CANADA
UNITED STATES
MEXICO
NORTH PACIFIC OCEAN
NORTH ATLANTIC OCEAN
SOUTH PACIFIC OCEAN
SOUTH ATLANTIC OCEAN
INDIAN OCEAN
BRAZIL
PERU
COLOMBIA
VENEZUELA
BOLIVIA
ARGENTINA
CHILE
RUSSIA
KAZAKHSTAN
MONGOLIA
CHINA
INDIA
IRAN
PAKISTAN
TURKEY
SAUDI ARABIA
ALGERIA
LIBYA
EGYPT
SUDAN
MALI
NIGER
CHAD
ANGOLA
SOUTH AFRICA
ETHIOPIA
SOMALIA
MADAGASCAR
INDONESIA
PHILIPPINES
JAPAN
AUSTRALIA
NEW ZEALAND
PAPUA NEW GUINEA
French Polynesia
(FRANCE)
International Date Line
Coordinated Universal Time (UTC)
formerly Greenwich Mean Time (GMT)
WEST
EAST
Add time zone number to local time to obtain UTC.
Subtract time zone number from UTC to obtain local time.
Subtract time zone number from local time to obtain UTC.
Add time zone number to UTC to obtain local time.
Boundary representation is not necessarily authoritative.
Eastward across Date Line
Westward across Date Line
2020-00228-02 2-21

UNITED STATES

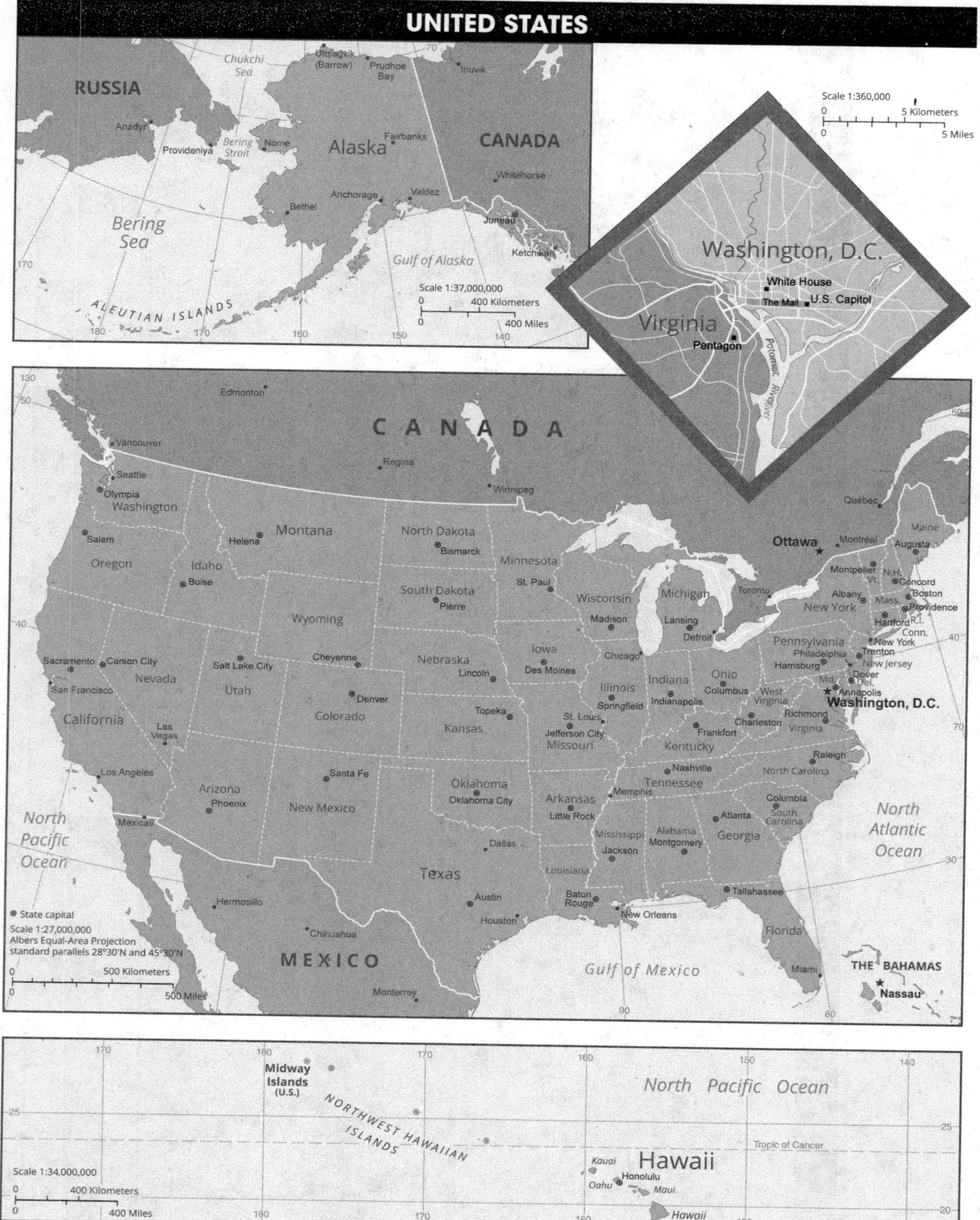

2020-00228-26 2-21

WORLD OCEANS

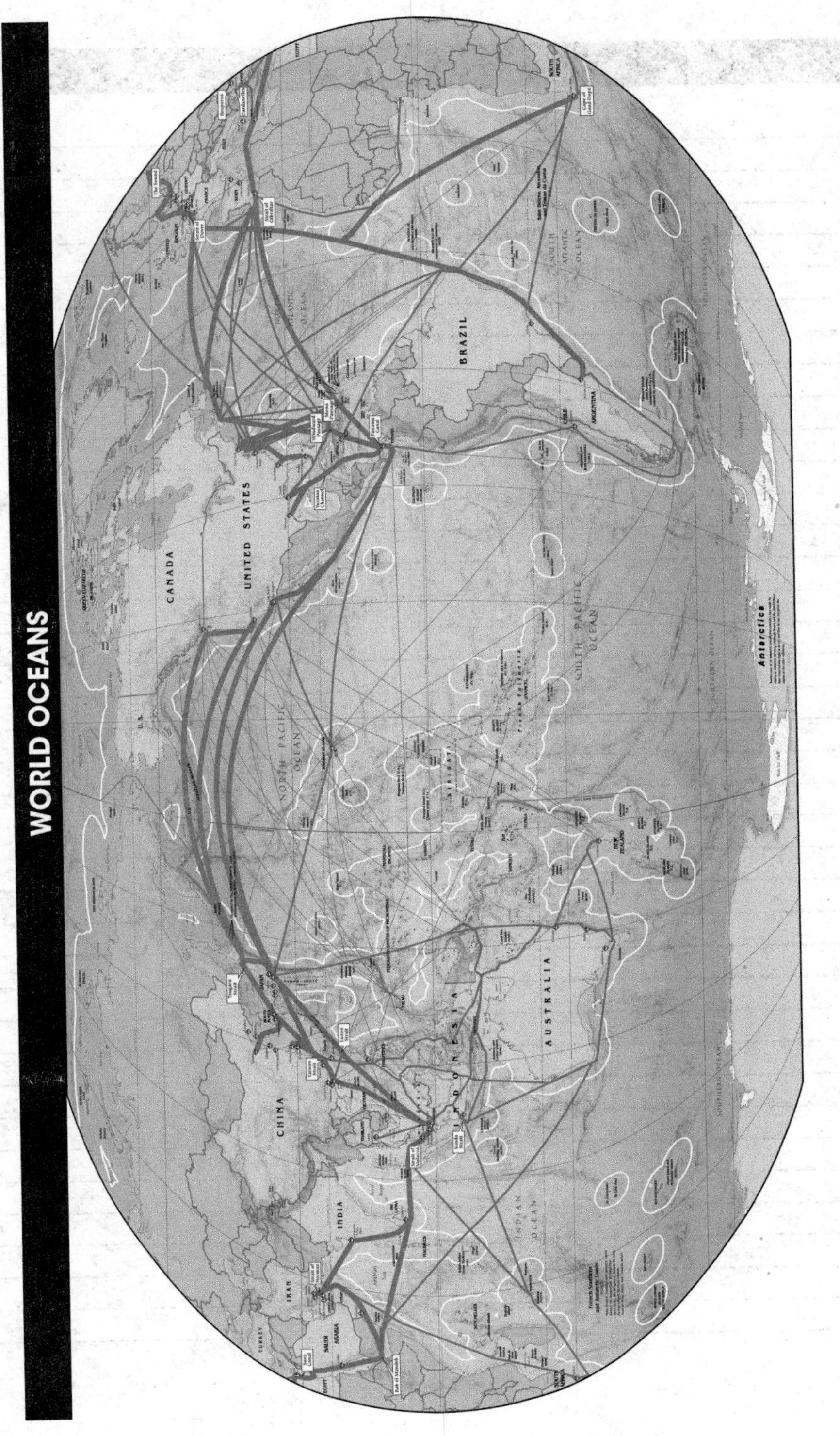

NOTES

NOTES

NOTES

NOTES

NOTES

NOTES

NOTES

NOTES

NOTES

NOTES

NOTES